Readers' Guide to
Periodical Literature
1989

READERS' GUIDE TO
PERIODICAL LITERATURE

Cumulated Volumes

READERS' GUIDE TO PERIODICAL LITERATURE

1989

An Author and Subject Index

Edited by
JEAN M. MARRA

Associate Editor
ROSEMARY STRAMMIELLO

Associate Editor for Production
CYNTHIA PITTSON

Indexers
BERNIE J. BAYLESS
BARBARA J. CARLSON
SHARON F. KATZ
JANE C. POLEWCHAK

THE H. W. WILSON COMPANY
NEW YORK   1990

International Standard Serial Number 0034-0464

Library of Congress Catalog Card Number 6-8232

PRINTED IN THE UNITED STATES OF AMERICA

ACKNOWLEDGEMENTS

In addition to the staff members whose names appear on the title page, we wish to acknowledge the contributions of Mary Jane Ballou, Ann F. Dietz, and Sylvia Sanderlin who indexed for this volume.

J.M.

PREFATORY NOTE

The *READERS' GUIDE TO PERIODICAL LITERATURE* is a cumulative author subject index to English language periodicals of general interest.

The main body of the Index consists of subject and author entries to periodical articles arranged in one alphabet. In addition there is a listing of citations to book reviews following the main body of the Index.

The Committee on Wilson Indexes of the American Library Association's Reference and Adult Services Division advises the publisher on indexing and editorial policy by means of in-depth contents studies conducted at intervals of several years.

While the responsibility for all indexing and editorial decisions rests with The H. W. Wilson Company, every effort is made by the Company to follow the recommendations of the Committee and the subscribers to a given periodical index.

Suggestions for addition or deletion of titles should be brought to the attention of The H. W. Wilson Company, 950 University Avenue, Bronx, N.Y. 10452.

This volume includes indexing for periodicals dated January 1, 1989 through December 31, 1989. It supersedes the paper issues of Readers' Guide for March 10, 1989 (Vol. 89 No. 1) through February 1990 (Vol. 89 No. 17).

SUGGESTIONS FOR THE USE OF THE
READERS' GUIDE TO PERIODICAL LITERATURE

Arrangement

Authors and subjects are arranged in one alphabet. Under authors and subjects, titles are also arranged in alphabetical order by the first word, initial articles being disregarded. Under personal names titles *by* an author precede those *about* him. Subdivisions of a subject are arranged alphabetically under the subject. Geographical subheads follow the other subdivisions in a separate alphabet.

Author Entries

Articles are indexed under the last name of the author, with the exception that author entries may be omitted for staff writers. The author's name always appears as part of the citation under the subject entry.

Ballet Reviews

Ballet reviews are indexed under the heading "Ballet reviews—Single works" with a *see* reference from the title of the work. Reviews are also indexed under the name of the choreographer.

Book Reviews

For citations to reviews of individual books, see book review section following the main body of the Index.

Cross-References

See references are made from variant forms of subject headings and personal names to the form used in READERS' GUIDE.
See also references are made from a subject to related subjects under which additional material may be found.

Dance Reviews

Modern dance reviews are indexed under the heading "Dance reviews—Single works" with a *see* reference from the title of the work. Reviews are also indexed under the name of the choreographer.

Fiction

Fiction is indexed under the author's name; titles are listed under the headings "Fiction—Single works" and "Science fiction—Single works" with a *see* reference to the author's name.

Motion Picture Reviews

Motion picture reviews are indexed under the heading "Motion picture reviews—Single works" with a *see* reference from the title of the film. Reviews are also indexed under the name of the director.

Musicals, Revues, etc.

Musicals, revues, etc. are indexed under the heading "Musicals, revues, etc.—Reviews—Single works" with a *see* reference from the title of the work.

Opera and Operetta Reviews

Opera and Operetta reviews are indexed under the composer's name with a *see* reference from the title of the opera or operetta; titles are also listed under the headings "Opera reviews—Single works" or "Operetta reviews—Single works."

Phonograph Records

Phonograph record reviews are indexed under the heading "Phonograph records." No title references are made.

Poems

Poems are indexed under the author's name; titles are listed under the headings "Poems—Single works" and "Christmas poems—Single works" with a *see* reference to the author's name.

Radio Program Reviews

Radio program reviews are indexed under the heading "Radio program reviews—Single works" with a *see* reference from the title of the program.

Short Stories

Short stories are indexed under the author's name; titles are listed under the headings "Short stories;" "Children's stories—Single works;" "Christmas stories—Single works;" and "Detective and mystery stories—Single works" with a *see* reference to the author's name.

Television Program Reviews

Television program reviews are indexed under the heading "Television program reviews—Single works" with a *see* reference from the title of the program.

Theater Reviews

Theater reviews are indexed under the dramatist's name with a *see* reference from the title of the work; titles are also listed under the heading "Theater reviews—Single works."

Videodisc and Videotape Reviews

Videodisc and Videotape reviews are indexed under the headings "Videodisc reviews—Single works" and "Videotape reviews—Single works." No title references are made.

For those unfamiliar with forms of reference used in the entries, the following explanation is given.

Sample subject entry:

> **SPACE RESEARCH**
> Back to the future [meaning of successful Discovery launch]
> M. D. Lemonick. il *Discover* 10:42-3+ Ja '89

Explanation:

> An article on the subject **SPACE RESEARCH** entitled "Back to the future," by Michael D. Lemonick, will be found, with illustrations, in the periodical *Discover*, volume 10, pages 42-43 (continued on later pages of the same issue) in the January 1989 issue. A title enhancement, "meaning of successful Discovery launch," has been added by the indexer to clarify the meaning of the title. Square brackets are used to indicate these editorial interpolations.

Sample name entry:

> **SMITH, GARY**
> Dear Mike . . . il pors *Sports Illustrated* 70:58-64+ F 27 '89
>
> *about*
>
> From the publisher. D. J. Barr. il por *Sports Illustrated* 70:1 F 27 '89

Explanation:

> An article *by* Gary Smith will be found in *Sports Illustrated*, volume 70, pages 58-64 (continued on later pages of the same issue) in the February 27, 1989 issue.
> An article *about* Gary Smith by Donald J. Barr will be found in *Sports Illustrated*, volume 70, page 1, in the February 27, 1989 issue.

ABBREVIATIONS

+	continued on later pages of same issue	Ltd	Limited
Ag	August	m	monthly
ann	annual	Mr	March
Ap	April	My	May
Assn	Association		
Aut	Autumn	N	November
Ave	Avenue	no	number
bi-m	bimonthly	O	October
bi-w	biweekly		
bibl	bibliography	p	page
bibl f	bibliographical footnotes	por	portrait
bldg	building	pt	part
Co	Company	q	quarterly
cont	continued		
Corp	Corporation	rev	revised
D	December	S	September
Dept	Department	semi-m	semimonthly
		Spr	Spring
ed	edited, edition, editor	Sr	Senior
		St	Street
F	February	Summ	Summer
f	footnotes	supp	supplement
il	illustration,-s	tr	translated, translation, translator
Inc	Incorporated		
introd	introduction, introductory		
		v	volume
Ja	January		
Je	June	w	weekly
Jl	July	Wint	Winter
Jr	Junior		
jt auth	joint author	yr	year

PERIODICALS INDEXED

All data as of latest issue received

*50 Plus. $15. m (ISSN 0163-2027) 50 Plus, 99 Garden St., Marion, OH 43302
    Name changed to New Choices for the Best Years with December 1988

A

Ad Astra. $30. m (ISSN 1041-102X) National Space Society, 922 Pennsylvania Ave., S.E., Washington, DC 20003-2140
    Continuation of: Space World

Aging. $5. q (ISSN 0002-0966) Superintendent of Documents, U.S. Government Printing Office, Washington, DC 20402

America. $28. w (except first Saturday of the year, and alternate Saturdays in Je, Jl and Ag) (ISSN 0002-7049) America Press Inc., 106 W. 56th St., New York, NY 10019

American Artist. $24. m (ISSN 0002-7375) American Artist, 1 Color Court, Marion, OH 43305

American Craft. $40. bi-m (ISSN 0194-8008) Membership Dept., American Craft Council, P.O. Box 829, Farmingdale, NY 11737

American Film. $24. m (ISSN 0361-4751) American Film, Membership Services, P.O. Box 2046, Marion, OH 43305

American Health. $14.95. m (except F, Ag) (ISSN 0730-7004) American Health: Fitness of Body and Mind, P.O. Box 3015, Harlan, IA 51537-3015

*American Heritage. $24. 8 times a yr (ISSN 0002-8738) American Heritage Subscription Dept., Forbes Building, 60 Fifth Ave., New York, NY 10011

American History Illustrated. $20. bi-m (ISSN 0002-8770) American History Illustrated, Box 8200, Harrisburg, PA 17105-8200

The American Scholar. $19. q (ISSN 0003-0937) The American Scholar, Editorial and Circulation Offices, 1811 Q St., N.W., Washington, DC 20009

The American Spectator. $30. m (ISSN 0148-8414) American Spectator, P.O. Box 10448, Arlington, VA 22210

American Visions. $18. bi-m (ISSN 0884-9390) American Visions, P.O. Box 53129, Boulder, CO 80322-3129

Americana. $14.97. bi-m (ISSN 0090-9114) Americana Subscription Office, 205 W. Center St., Marion, OH 43302

Américas. $42. bi-m (ISSN 0379-0940) Américas, Journals Div., CUA Press, 303 Administration Bldg., Catholic University of America, Washington, DC 20064

Antiques. $38. m (ISSN 0161-9284) The Magazine Antiques, Old Mill Rd., P.O. Box 1975, Marion, OH 43306

Antiques & Collecting Hobbies. $22. m (ISSN 0884-6294) Antiques & Collecting Hobbies, Circulation Dept., 1006 S. Michigan Ave., Chicago, IL 60605

Architectural Digest. $39.95. m (ISSN 0003-8520) Architectural Digest, P.O. Box 10040, Des Moines, IA 50350

Architectural Record. $42.50. m (semi-m Ap, S) (ISSN 0003-858X) Architectural Record, P.O. Box 566, Hightstown, NJ 08520

Art in America. $39.95. m (ISSN 0004-3214) Art in America, 542 Pacific Ave., Marion, OH 43306

Art News. $32.95. m (q Je-Ag) (ISSN 0004-3273) Art News, Subscription Service, P.O. Box 969, Farmingdale, NY 11737

Astronomy. $24. m (ISSN 0091-6358) Astronomy, 21027 Crossroads Circle, P.O. Box 1612, Waukesha, WI 53187

*The Atlantic. $14.95. m (ISSN 0276-9077) Atlantic Subscription Processing Center, Box 52661, Boulder, CO 80322

Audubon. $20. bi-m (ISSN 0097-7136) National Audubon Society, Membership Data Center, P.O. Box 2666, Boulder, CO 80322

Aviation Week & Space Technology. $85. w (ISSN 0005-2175) Aviation Week & Space Technology, P.O. Box 503, Hightstown, NJ 08520-9899

B

*Better Homes and Gardens. $14.97. m (ISSN 0006-0151) Better Homes and Gardens, P.O. Box 4536, Des Moines, IA 50336

Bicycling. $17.97. 10 times a yr (ISSN 0006-2073) Rodale Press, Inc., 33 E. Minor St., Emmaus, PA 18098

BioScience. $96.50. m (bi-m Jl, Ag) (ISSN 0006-3568) BioScience Circulation, AIBS, 730 11th St. N.W., Washington, DC 20001-4584

Black Enterprise. $15. m (ISSN 0006-4165) Black Enterprise, Circulation Service Center, P.O. Box 3009, Harlan, IA 51537-3009

The Bulletin of the Atomic Scientists. $30. m (except F, Ag) (ISSN 0096-3402) Bulletin of the Atomic Scientists, Circulation Dept., 6042 S. Kimbark Ave., Chicago, IL 60637

Business Week. $39.95. w (except 1 issue in Ja) (ISSN 0007-7135) Business Week, P.O. Box 430, Hightstown, NJ 08520

Byte. $29.95. m (except 2 issues in O) (ISSN 0360-5280) Byte Subscriber Service, P.O. Box 551, Hightstown, NJ 08520

C

Car and Driver. $16.98. m (ISSN 0008-6002) Car and Driver, P.O. Box 2770, Boulder, CO 80302

The Center Magazine. $25. bi-m (ISSN 0008-9125) Center Magazine, Box 4068, Santa Barbara, CA 93103
    Continued by: New Perspectives Quarterly

Change. $45. bi-m (ISSN 0009-1383) Heldref Publications, 4000 Albemarle St., N.W., Washington, DC 20016

*Changing Times. $18. m (ISSN 0009-143X) Changing Times, The Kiplinger Magazine, Editors Park, MD 20782

Channels (New York, N.Y.: 1986). $65. m (bi-m Jl/Ag) (ISSN 0895-643X) Channels, Subscription Service Dept., P.O. Box 6438, Duluth, MN 55806

Children Today. $7.50. bi-m (ISSN 0361-4336) Superintendent of Documents, U.S. Government Printing Office, Washington, DC 20402

The Christian Century. $28. w (occasional bi-w issues) (ISSN 0009-5281) Christian Century, Subscription Service Dept., 5615 W. Cermak Rd., Cicero, IL 60650

Christianity Today. $24.95. semi-m (m Ja, My, Je, Jl, Ag, D) (ISSN 0009-5753) Christianity Today Subscription Services, 465 Gundersen Dr., Carol Stream, IL 60188

Commentary. $39. m (ISSN 0010-2601) American Jewish Committee, 165 E. 56th St., New York, NY 10022

Common Cause Magazine. $20. bi-m (ISSN 0884-6537) Common Cause Membership Dept., 2030 M St., N.W., Washington, DC 20036

Commonweal. $32. bi-w (m Christmas-New Year's and Jl, Ag) (ISSN 0010-3330) Commonweal Foundation, 15 Dutch St., New York, NY 10038

Compute!. $19.94. m (ISSN 0194-357X) Compute! Publications, Inc., P.O. Box 3245, Harlan, IA 51537

Congressional Digest. $28. m (bi-m Je-Jl, Ag-S) (ISSN 0010-5899) Congressional Digest Corp., 3231 P St., N.W., Washington, DC 20007

The Conservationist. $5. bi-m (ISSN 0010-650X) Conservationist Circulation Office, P.O. Box 1500, Latham, NY 12110

Conservative Digest. $18. bi-m (ISSN 0146-0978) Conservative Digest, P.O. Box 84905, Phoenix, AZ 85071
    Ceased publication with September/October 1989

*Consumer Reports. $20. m (ISSN 0010-7174) Subscription Director, Consumer Reports, P.O. Box 53029, Boulder, CO 80322

*Consumers' Research Magazine. $24. m (ISSN 0095-2222) Circulation Dept., Consumers' Research Magazine, P.O. Box 642, Holmes, PA 19043

Country Journal. $16.95. bi-m (ISSN 0094-0526) Country Journal, P.O. Box 392, Mt. Morris, IL 61054

Scholastic Update (Teachers' edition). $20. bi-w during the school year (ISSN 0745-7065) Scholastic Update, 2931 E. McCarty St., P.O. Box 3710, Jefferson City, MO 65102-9957

Science. $120. w (except for last week in D; extra issue in Mr) (ISSN 0036-8075) American Association for the Advancement of Science, 1333 H St., N.W., Washington, DC 20005

Science News. $34.50. w (bi-w year end issue) (ISSN 0036-8423) Science News, Subscription Dept., 231 W. Center St., Marion, OH 43305

*****Scientific American.** $27. m (ISSN 0036-8733) Scientific American, P.O. Box 3187, Harlan, IA 51593-2377

Sea Frontiers. $18. bi-m (ISSN 0886-9448) International Oceanographic Foundation, 3979 Rickenbacker Causeway, Virginia Key, Miami, FL 33149

Senior Scholastic. See Scholastic Update (Teachers' edition)

*****Seventeen.** $15.95. m (ISSN 0037-301X) Seventeen Subscription Dept., Radnor, PA 19088

Sierra. $15. bi-m (ISSN 0161-7362) Sierra Club, 730 Polk St., San Francisco, CA 94109

Skiing. $11.94. 7 times a yr (S-Mr) (ISSN 0037-6264) Skiing, P.O. Box 51480, Boulder, CO 80302

Sky and Telescope. $21.95. m (ISSN 0037-6604) Sky Publishing Corp., 49 Bay State Rd., Cambridge, MA 02238-1290

Smithsonian. $20. m (ISSN 0037-7333) Smithsonian, P.O. Box 55593, Boulder, CO 80322-5593

Society. $66. bi-m (ISSN 0147-2011) Society, Box A, Rutgers–The State University, New Brunswick, NJ 08903

Southern Living. $21.95 in 17 Southern States and District of Columbia. $24 in other states. m (ISSN 0038-4305) Southern Living, Box 523, Birmingham, AL 35201

Space World. $18. m (ISSN 0038-6332) Palmer Publications, Inc., Amherst, WI 54406
Continued by: Ad Astra

Sport (New York, N.Y.). $17.94. m (ISSN 0038-7797) Sport, P.O. Box 5016, Des Moines, IA 50306

*****Sports Illustrated.** $69.66. w (except bi-w year end issue) (ISSN 0038-822X) Sports Illustrated, P.O. Box 30602, Tampa, FL 33630-0602

Stereo Review. $13.94. m (ISSN 0039-1220) Stereo Review, Circulation Dept., P.O. Box 55627, Boulder, CO 80322-5627

Successful Farming. $12. m (semi-m F, Mr) (ISSN 0039-4432) Successful Farming, Customer Service, P.O. Box 10255, Des Moines, IA 50336
Iowa edition indexed with January 1987

Sunset (Central West edition). $16 in Alaska, Ariz., Calif., Colo., Hawaii, Idaho, Mont., Nev., N.Mex., Ore., Utah, Wash., Wyo. $20 in other states. m (ISSN 0039-5404) Sunset Magazine, 80 Willow Rd., Menlo Park, CA 94025

T

Technology Review. $27. 8 times a yr (Ja, F/Mr, Ap, My/Je, Jl, Ag/S, O, N/D) (ISSN 0040-1692) Technology Review, Building W59, MIT, Cambridge, MA 02139

*****Teen.** $15.95. m (ISSN 0040-2001) Petersen Publishing Co., 8490 Sunset Blvd., Los Angeles, CA 90069

Theatre Crafts. $30. m (bi-m Je-Jl, Ag-S) (ISSN 0040-5469) Subscription Dept., Theatre Crafts, P.O. Box 470, Mt. Morris, IL 61054-0470

Time. $58.24. w (ISSN 0040-781X) Time, P.O. Box 30601, Tampa, FL 33630-0601

*****Travel Holiday.** $11. m (ISSN 0161-7184) Travel Subscription Office, Travel Bldg., Floral Park, NY 11001

TV Guide. $37.44. w (ISSN 0039-8543) TV Guide, Box 400, Radnor, PA 19088

U

U.S. Catholic. $15. m (ISSN 0041-7548) U.S. Catholic, 205 W. Monroe St., Chicago, IL 60606

*****U.S. News & World Report.** $39.75. w (except 2 issues combined in Ag and D) (ISSN 0041-5537) U.S. News & World Report, Subscription Dept., P.O. Box 55929, Boulder, CO 80323-5929

UN Chronicle. $14. q (ISSN 0251-7329) United Nations Publications, Room DC2-0853, United Nations, New York, NY 10017

*****The Unesco Courier.** $14.22 (90 French francs). m (ISSN 0041-5278) Bernan—Unipub, Periodicals Dept., 4611-F Assembly Dr., Lanham, MD 20706-4391
Formerly The Courier; name changed with June 1989

Update. See Scholastic Update (Teachers' edition)

USA Today (Periodical). $150. m (ISSN 0161-7389) The Society for the Advancement of Education, 99 W. Hawthorne Ave., Valley Stream, NY 11580

Utne Reader. $24. bi-m (ISSN 8750-0256) Utne Reader, Box 1974, Marion, OH 43305

V

Video. $12. m (ISSN 0147-8907) Video, P.O. Box 56293, Boulder, CO 80322-6293

Vital Speeches of the Day. $30. semi-m (ISSN 0042-742X) City News Publishing Co., 389 Highway 17 By-Pass, Mount Pleasant, SC 29465

Vogue. $28. m (ISSN 0042-8000) Vogue, Box 55980, Boulder, CO 80322

W

The Washington Monthly. $33. m (bi-m Jl-Ag) (ISSN 0043-0633) Washington Monthly, 1711 Connecticut Ave., N.W., Washington, DC 20009

Weatherwise. $42. bi-m (ISSN 0043-1672) Weatherwise, Circulation Office, 4000 Albemarle St., N.W., Washington, DC 20016

Wilderness. $20. q (ISSN 0736-6477) The Wilderness Society, 1400 Eye St., N.W., Washington, DC 20005

Women's Sports & Fitness. $12.97. 8 times a yr (ISSN 8750-653X) Women's Sports & Fitness, P.O. Box 472, Mt. Morris, IL 61054

Workbench. $8. bi-m (ISSN 0043-8057) Workbench Circulation Dept., 4251 Pennsylvania, Kansas City, MO 64111

Working Woman. $18. m (ISSN 0145-5761) Working Woman, P.O. Box 10132, Des Moines, IA 50340

World Health. $14. 10 times a yr (ISSN 0043-8502) World Health, WHO, Avenue Appia, 1211 Geneva 27, Switzerland

World Press Review. $24.97. m (ISSN 0195-8895) World Press Review, Box 1997, Marion, OH 43305

World Tennis. $15.94. m (ISSN 0043-910X) World Tennis Magazine, Subscription Dept., P.O. Box 420042, Palm Coast, FL 32142-0042

*****The Writer.** $23. m (ISSN 0043-9517) The Writer, Inc., 120 Boylston St., Boston, MA 02116

Readers' Guide to Periodical Literature
1989

1% FOR PEACE (PROGRAM)
A call to pig out for peace [Ben & Jerry's support] il *Newsweek* 113:45 My 8 '89

2 LIVE CREW (MUSICAL GROUP)
A rap album in the dock [obscenity case against Alexander, Ala. record store] N. Zeman. il *Newsweek* 114:72 O 16 '89

3-D ART
Making dimensional illustration. E. Rixford. il *American Artist* 53:70-2+ N '89
Exhibitions
Three-dimensional illustration comes of age. L. Montana. il *American Artist* 53:34-9 S '89

3-D CAMERAS
Testing
A born again Nimslo? [Nishika N8000] P. Kolonia. il *Popular Photography* 96:71-2 N '89

3-D COMPUTER GRAPHICS *See* Computer graphics

3-D OPTICAL STORAGE DEVICES
Multiplying computer memories into 3-D [work of Peter M. Rentzepis and Dimitri A. Parthenopoulos] I. Amato. *Science News* 136:151 S 2 '89
Three-dimensional optical storage memory. D. A. Parthenopoulos and P. M. Rentzepis. bibl f il *Science* 245:843-5 Ag 25 '89

3-D TELEVISION
Halftime spectacles [telecast in 3-D] il *Time* 133:53 Ja 23 '89

3COM CORP.
How to lose a lead [3Com Corp. let Novell gain lead in LANs] J. Pitta. il *Forbes* 144:126 Ag 7 '89

3M COMPANY *See* Minnesota Mining & Mfg. Co.

4-D *See* Hyperspace

4-H CLUBS
Costumed cows and other critters [4-H Club of Maryland sponsors costume parade at State Fair] il *National Geographic World* 167:26-9 Jl '89
Why is this woman making a wetland? [work of Florine Swanson in Iowa] J. Walter. il *Successful Farming* 87:58-9 Ag '89

7-ELEVEN STORES *See* Southland Corp.

8MM VIDEO CAMERAS *See* Video cameras

10 DOWNING STREET (LONDON, ENGLAND) *See* Number 10 Downing Street (London, England)

20 MOTT STREET RESTAURANT (NEW YORK, N.Y.) *See* New York (N.Y.)—Restaurants, nightclubs, bars, etc.

24 HOURS OF DAYTONA (RACE) *See* Automobile racing

35MM CAMERAS *See* Cameras

35MM SINGLE-LENS REFLEX CAMERAS *See* Cameras, Single-lens reflex

36 FILLETTE [film] *See* Motion picture reviews—Single works

42ND STREET (NEW YORK, N.Y.)
42nd Street: no beat of dancing feet—yet. J. S. Russell. il *Architectural Record* 177:85 Je '89

44 (NEW YORK, N.Y.: RESTAURANT) *See* New York (N.Y.)—Restaurants, nightclubs, bars, etc.

44 WALL STREET EQUITY FUND
The Marv Throneberrys of mutual funds get a hit. G. Weiss. il *Business Week* p128 Jl 17 '89
Return of 44 Wall Street. M. Schiffres. il *Changing Times* 43:22 Ja '89

44 WALL STREET FUND
The Marv Throneberrys of mutual funds get a hit. G. Weiss. il *Business Week* p128 Jl 17 '89
Return of 44 Wall Street. M. Schiffres. il *Changing Times* 43:22 Ja '89

60 MINUTES [television program] *See* Television program reviews—Single works

80 DAYS [musical] *See* Musicals, revues, etc.—Reviews—Single works

84 CHARLIE MOPIC [film] *See* Motion picture reviews—Single works

150 WOOSTER STREET (NEW YORK, N.Y.: RESTAURANT) *See* New York (N.Y.)—Restaurants, nightclubs, bars, etc.

401(K) PLAN
401(k)s: adios to those bargain loans. S. Woodley. il *Business Week* p171 O 9 '89
How you can put your rainy-day cash to work and still have it for emergencies. R. J. Klein. il *Money* 18:175-6 My '89
A loan from your 401(k). M. C. Paulson. *Changing Times* 43:96 Je '89
Making hay with a 401(k). il *Money* 18 Money Guide:62 Fall '89

Managing your company plan. il *Fortune* 120 no10 Special Issue:48 Fall '89
Rules for borrowing from retirement plans. G. W. Padwe. il *Nation's Business* 77:92 N '89
You're on your own, so learn to manage your 401(k) like a pro. D. M. Topolnicki. il *Money* 18:135-6 Jl '89

403(B) PLAN
Two academics face new choices in their retirement plans [Carmen and Robby Greenlee] H. Wheelwright. il *Money* 18:159-60 My '89

727 AIRPLANES *See* Airplanes, Jet
737 AIRPLANES *See* Airplanes, Jet
747 AIRPLANES *See* Airplanes, Jet
757 AIRPLANES *See* Airplanes, Jet
767 AIRPLANES *See* Airplanes, Jet
777 AIRPLANES *See* Airplanes, Jet

800 TELEPHONE NUMBERS *See* Toll-free telephone service

900 TELEPHONE NUMBERS
Just call up and watch. M. Burgi. il *Channels (New York, N.Y.: 1986)* 9:92 N '89
Rock's 900 lines: a hot number? J. Ressner. il *Rolling Stone* p24 Mr 23 '89
When calling back can cost plenty [scams involving 540 and 900 numbers] *U.S. News & World Report* 106:71 Ap 24 '89

1838 BOND-DEBENTURE TRADING FUND
Yield versus total return. J. Clements. il por *Forbes* 144:162-3 S 4 '89

2001: A SPACE ODYSSEY [film] *See* Motion picture reviews—Single works

10,000 MANIACS (MUSICAL GROUP)
10,000 Maniacs break loose. A. DeCurtis. il pors *Rolling Stone* p64-6+ Je 15 '89
Like 10,000 Maniacs, the band she leads, Natalie Merchant demands to be heard. J. Leland. por *Vogue* 179:82 Jl '89

A

A & D BUILDING (NEW YORK, N.Y.) *See* Architects & Designers Building (New York, N.Y.)

A-BOMBS *See* Atomic bombs

A. G. EDWARDS & SONS, INC.
The broker who wouldn't grow up [A. G. Edwards vs. Merrill Lynch] il *Business Week* p94 Mr 27 '89

A. H. ROBINS COMPANY, INC.
Day of reckoning [Dalkon Shield case] C. Breslin. il *Ms.* 17:46-52 Je '89
Fatal contraption [Dalkon Shield] M. Kort. il *Essence* 20:16+ Jl '89
How to reward the criminals [use of bankruptcy law to avoid Dalkon Shield suits] R. Shereff. *The Nation* 248:192-5 F 13 '89

A. L. WILLIAMS CORP.
The battalion that will press Primerica's sales attack. J. Friedman. il *Business Week* p91 D 4 '89
Ex-football coach Art Williams runs a winning insurance firm, but some people are crying foul. G. Stone. il pors *People Weekly* 32:161-2+ N 20 '89
The money on your life. J. B. Quinn. il *Newsweek* 113:46 My 8 '89
Tiger by the tail? H. Rudnitsky. il pors *Forbes* 144:40-1 Ag 7 '89

A. O. SMITH CORP.
The cultural revolution at A.O. Smith [teamwork] J. P. Hoerr. il *Business Week* p66+ My 29 '89

A&M RECORDS (FIRM)
Revamped A&M is L.A.'s hot studio. M. Goldberg. il *Rolling Stone* p29 F 9 '89

A&P COMPANY *See* Great Atlantic & Pacific Tea Company, Inc.

A&S *See* Abraham & Straus

A&W BRANDS INC.
Root beer gloat. E. Giltenan. il por *Forbes* 144:156+ D 11 '89

AAA *See* American Automobile Association

AAAH *See* American Association for the Advancement of the Humanities

AAAS *See* American Association for the Advancement of Science

AAFLI *See* Asian American Free Labor Institute
AAGESON, JAMES W.
City-building and the benefits of Babel. il *The Christian Century* 106:517-18 My 17 '89
AAHE *See* American Association for Higher Education
AAP *See* Association of American Publishers
AAPT *See* American Association of Physics Teachers
AARE, JUHAN
about
An interview with a leader of the Green Movement. D. Devyatkin. il *Environment* 30:13-15 D '88
AARNES, WILLIAM
Dishes [poem] *The American Scholar* 58:509-10 Aut '89
AARON, DAVID
about
Merger mystery. B. Van Voorst. il por *Time* 133:54 F 27 '89
AARON, PAUL
about
Cowboy Joe. *The New Yorker* 65:24-5 Jl 31 '89
AARONSON, ROBERT J., 1942-
Air transportation [address, May 11, 1989] *Vital Speeches of the Day* 55:592-4 Jl 15 '89
AARP *See* American Association of Retired Persons
AARP FEDERAL CREDIT UNION *See* American Association of Retired Persons. Federal Credit Union
AASHI, JALAL
The well-being of pilgrims. il map *World Health* p4-7 Jl '89
AAUP *See* American Association of University Professors; Association of American University Presses
AAUP BOOK SHOW *See* Book exhibits
ABA *See* American Bar Association; American Booksellers Association
ABALONE CULTURE
Farming sea-ears [California] T. Johnson. bibl il *Sea Frontiers* 35:232-7 Jl/Ag '89
ABALONES
Mollusk teaches ceramics to scientists [rugged shell of the red abalone; research by Mehmet Sarikaya] I. Amato. *Science News* 136:383 D 9 '89
ABANDONED CHILDREN *See* Homeless children
THE ABANDONED FIELD [film] *See* Motion picture reviews—Single works
ABAS, BRYAN
Rocky Flats: a big mistake from day one. bibl f il *The Bulletin of the Atomic Scientists* 45:18-24 D '89
ABATEMARCO, FRED
Editor's note. See issues of Personal Computing beginning November 1986 through November 1989
ABBADO, CLAUDIO
about
Abbado takes Berlin. N. Lebrecht. il por *Opera News* 54:16-17 D 23 '89
Abbado's Ravel: the piano concertos. R. Freed. il por *Stereo Review* 54:108 O '89
Claudio Abbado's Mahler Ninth. D. Hall. por *Stereo Review* 54:106 My '89
ABBATE, CAROLYN
Hiding in the shadow. il *Opera News* 53:16+ Ap 1 '89
ABBEVILLE PRESS INC.
Abbeville announces new video series on wine. il *Publishers Weekly* 236:27-8 D 1 '89
Going back to the past, using collotype art [publication of G. Catlin's North American Indian portfolio] J. P. Frank. il *Publishers Weekly* 236:62-4 Ag 4 '89
ABBEY, EDWARD, 1927-1989
Hayduke lives! [fiction] il *The Mother Earth News* 120:57-9 N/D '89
about
Obituary
Audubon il 91:14+ Jl '89. F. Graham
The Mother Earth News il por 120:56-7 N/D '89. D. Petersen
National Parks por 63:42 My/Je '89
The New York Times Book Review por 94:44-5 My 7 '89. E. Hoagland
Sierra 74:100-1 My/Je '89. P. Wild
Utne Reader il por p36-7 Jl/Ag '89. D. Foreman
ABBOT, NICHOLAS
about
A deadly struggle against the sea [cover story]; ed. by Ron Arias. J. Culver. il pors *People Weekly* 32:62-6+ Ag 21 '89
ABBOTT, JIM
about
"All I ever wanted was a shot". J. Howard. il pors *Sport (New York, N.Y.)* 80:26-9 Mr '89
Angel on the ascent. B. Anderson. il por *Sports Illustrated* 70:27 Mr 13 '89
The complete Jim Abbott. C. Leerhsen. il por *Newsweek* 113:60 Je 12 '89
Dreaming the big dreams. T. Callahan. il por *Time* 133:78 Mr 20 '89
No more doubts. il por *Sports Illustrated* 71:64-5 Jl 24 '89

One for the Angels. R. Brofman. il pors *Life* 12:118+ Je '89
ABBOTT, JUDY
"My get-along gang". il *Parents* 64:114-18 Ap '89
ABBOTT LABORATORIES
The slippery ladder at Abbott Labs [ouster of J. W. Schuler] J. F. Siler. il por *Business Week* p136-7 O 30 '89
ABBOTTS, JOHN
All the king's horses and all the king's men . . . bibl f il *The Bulletin of the Atomic Scientists* 45:49-52 Ja/F '89
ABBOUD, A. ROBERT, 1929-
about
Why Robert Abboud wants MCorp in his corral. T. Vogel. il por *Business Week* p31 Ap 10 '89
ABBOUD, JOSEPH, 1950-
about
Joseph Abboud, down to earth. E. Stern. il pors *Gentlemen's Quarterly* 59:320-5+ O '89
Past as prologue. R. La Ferla. il pors *The New York Times Magazine* p56-7 F 19 '89
ABBREVIATIONS
See also
Acronyms
Child's garden of vs. W. Safire. il *The New York Times Magazine* p16+ Je 4 '89
PRD+. S. Morgenstern. il *Home Office Computing* 7:80 Je '89
ABBY ALDRICH ROCKEFELLER FOLK ART CENTER
Abby's folk art [Treasures of American folk art] A. L. Powers. il *Americana* 16:62-5 Ja/F '89
A miniaturist of (new) Williamsburg. A. Bahar. il *Antiques & Collecting Hobbies* 94:62-5 Je '89
A pre-eminent folk art collection on tour [Treasures of American folk art] A. E. Ledes. il *Antiques* 135:46+ Ja '89
ABBY PERKINS (FICTIONAL CHARACTER)
From mouseburger to sexpot on L.A. law. B. Davidson. il pors *TV Guide* 37:8-9+ N 11-17 '89
ABC *See* American Broadcasting Companies, Inc.
ABC HOME NEWSLETTER *See* Newsletters
ABDOMINAL EXERCISES *See* Exercise
ABDUL, PAULA
about
All the right moves. D. Wild. il pors *Rolling Stone* p96-8+ N 30 '89
Music makers: lend an ear! pors *'Teen* 33:50 Je '89
Paula Abdul. por *People Weekly* 32:76-7 D 25 '89-Ja 1 '90
Paula Abdul. por *Seventeen* 48:76+ F '89
Paula Abdul's double life. N. Malkin. por *Mademoiselle* 95:94+ N '89
The sexy video divas. C. Krupp. il pors *Glamour* 87:234-5 Ag '89
ABDUL-JABBAR, KAREEM, 1947-
about
An ailing Bird, a retiring Kareem. il por *Newsweek* 113:62 My 8 '89
A fitting farewell. L. Renaud. por *Maclean's* 102:51 My 22 '89
Kareem Abdul-Jabbar: what will he do after basketball? il pors *Jet* 76:46-8+ Je 26 '89
Kareem's last hurrah. D. C. Lyons. il pors *Ebony* 44:102+ My '89
Kareem's retirement fete draws Hollywood's finest. il pors *Jet* 76:52-3+ My 15 '89
NBA Players Assn. fetes Kareem at benefit dinner. il por *Jet* 77:48-9 O 9 '89
An ominous giant's farewell. T. Callahan. il por *Time* 133:82 F 20 '89
An unhappy ending [cover story] J. McCallum. il pors *Sports Illustrated* 70:30-4 Ja 23 '89
ABDUL RAHMAN, SADIQ *See* El Mahdi, Sadiq, 1936-
ABDULLAH, ABDULLAH
about
Talking to the PLO; A personal triumph. L. Van Dusen. il por *Maclean's* 102:10-12 Ap 10 '89
ABDULLAH ABD AL-HAMID LABID *See* Labid, Abdullah Abd al-Hamid
ABDULLAH AL AHDAL *See* Al Ahdal, Abdullah
ABDULLAH IBRAHIM
about
Abdullah Ibrahim's Ekaya. F. Bouchard. il por *Down Beat* 56:58-9 D '89
ABDUS SALAM *See* Salam, Abdus, 1926-
ABDUSSALAAM, MEENAH
about
New York mother throws two children out of window. il por *Jet* 77:18 O 23 '89
ABELL, BRUCE
(jt. auth) *See* Keyworth, George A., and Abell, Bruce
ABELL CLUSTER (GALAXIES) *See* Galaxies—Clusters
ABELLEYRA, ANGÉLICA
Fernando Botero's 'obsession' [interview] il *World Press Review* 36:61 Ag '89
ABER, JOHN D., AND OTHERS
Nitrogen saturation in northern forest ecosystems. bibl f il *BioScience* 39:378-86 Je '89

ABERCROMBIE, JOHN
about
Blindfold test. B. Milkowski. il por *Down Beat* 56:43 O '89

ABERCROMBIE, JOSEPHINE
about
Architecture: Quinlan Terry: a Palladian country house in Kentucky. C. Aslet. il por *Architectural Digest* 46:282-7 O '89
An oil heiress looks for pay dirt at the track. T. Vogel. il por *Business Week* p162 My 22 '89

ABERCROMBIE, THOMAS J.
Unsettled immigrants. il *National Geographic* 176:120-9 Jl '89

ABERNATHY, RALPH D.
about
Abernathy cuts book tour because of controversy. il pors *Jet* 77:14 N 13 '89
Abernathy takes a cheap shot. J. M. Wall. por *The Christian Century* 106:971-2 N 1 '89
A bitter battle erupts over the last hours of Martin Luther King. J. S. Kunen. il pors *People Weekly* 32:40-2 O 30 '89
Eyewitness statements on King's death dispute Abernathy's accounts. il pors *Jet* 77:57-9 N 6 '89
A fight among Dr. King's faithful. il por *Newsweek* 114:31 O 23 '89
On the humanity of saints. P. Marin. il *The Nation* 249:784-6 D 25 '89
Ralph Abernathy's book denounced for 'painful distortions' about King. il pors *Jet* 77:8-10 O 30 '89
Sexual charges and Martin Luther King. F. Bruning. il *Maclean's* 102:13 N 6 '89
Tattletale memoir. por *Time* 134:42 O 23 '89

ABF *See* American Beekeeping Federation

ABIDJAN (IVORY COAST)
Streets
A colourful kaleidoscope. P. Haeringer. il *The Unesco Courier* 42:22-5 Ag '89

ABILITY
See also
Athletic ability
Creativity
Learning, Psychology of
Motor ability
Reading ability
Success

ABILITY GROUPING IN EDUCATION
The label that sticks [tracking] J. Rachlin. il *U.S. News & World Report* 107:51-2 Jl 3 '89
Tracked to fail. S. Tobias. il *Psychology Today* 23:54-8+ S '89

ABILITY TESTS *See* Aptitude tests

ABISOGUN, AKINWUNMI O., AND OTHERS
The involvement of platelet activating factor in ovulation. bibl f il *Science* 243:381-3 Ja 20 '89

ABLE, DAVID
about
When the spirit takes wing. M. Grant. il pors *People Weekly* 31:50-5 My 15 '89

ABLON, RALPH
about
It ain't glamorous, but the money sure is good. M. Roman. il *Business Week* p64-5 Ag 28 '89

ABM (ANTI-BALLISTIC MISSILE) TREATY *See* Disarmament

ABNORMALITIES
See also
Birth defects
Chromosome abnormalities
Dwarfs and dwarfism

ABOITIZ AIR TRANSPORT
Philippine carrier developing cargo network with C-130As. P. Proctor. il *Aviation Week & Space Technology* 131:79 N 13 '89

ABOLITIONISTS
Abolition revisited. J. N. Akers. il *Christianity Today* 33:13 Mr 3 '89

ABOODI, ODED
about
Even behind the scenes, the Time-Warner drama has its stars. M. Ivey; J. Friedman. il pors *Business Week* p55-6 Jl 31 '89

ABORIGINES, AUSTRALIAN *See* Australian aborigines

ABORTIFACIENTS
See also
RU 486 (Drug)
Do-it-yourself abortion is hazardous to your health. *Newsweek* 114:25 Jl 17 '89

ABORTION
See also
Abortifacients
Fetal reduction
Press and abortion
Abortion as insurrection. W. M. Hern. por *The Humanist* 49:18-20+ Mr/Ap '89
Abortion in New York [cover story] J. Kasindorf. il *New York* 22:32-8+ S 18 '89

Abortion: litmus test for NIH director. B. J. Culliton. *Science* 246:27 O 6 '89
Abortions without doctors [menstrual extraction] A. Toufexis. il *Time* 134:66 Ag 28 '89
Defying simple slogans: why 'adoption, not abortion' won't work. B. Kantrowitz. il *Newsweek* 113:36 My 1 '89
Koop finds abortion evidence "inconclusive" [Surgeon General's study on health effects does not help in prolife efforts] C. Holden. *Science* 243:730-1 F 10 '89
A setback for pro-life forces [reports by Surgeon General and the American Psychological Association find abortions pose little danger to women] D. Thompson. il *Time* 133:82 Mr 27 '89

Anecdotes, facetiae, satire, etc.
Saving my zygotes. B. Ehrenreich. il *Mother Jones* 14:10-11 D '89

History
Abortion: the usable past. L. Flanders. *The Nation* 249:175-7 Ag 7-14 '89
The abortion wars [cover story] T. Stafford. il *Christianity Today* 33:16-20 O 6 '89

Laws and regulations
See also
United States. Supreme Court—Decisions—Abortion decisions
Abortion and the rapee. W. F. Buckley. *National Review* 41:53-4 D 8 '89
Abortion debate. K. Legge. *World Press Review* 36:46 F '89
Abortion: the debate, the politics, the morality [cover story; special section] il *National Review* 41:25-31 D 22 '89
Abortion: the gathering storm [challenge to Roe v. Wade; special section] il *Ms.* 17:87-95 Ap '89
Abortion's dividing line [GOP feels impact of prochoice activists] E. Salholz. il *Newsweek* 114:31 O 23 '89
Abortive issue. F. Barnes. *The New Republic* 201:10-11 D 4 '89
After Roe. R. J. Neuhaus. il *National Review* 41:38-40 Ap 7 '89
As American as freeways. D. R. Carlin, Jr. *Commonweal* 116:392-3 Jl 14 '89
Battle of the barricades. B. Turque. il *Newsweek* 113:26 Ap 3 '89
The battle over abortion [Supreme Court confronts Roe v. Wade; cover story; special section] il *Newsweek* 113:28-32+ My 1 '89
Big movement on campus [college students push for abortion rights] P. Simpson. il *Ms.* 17:74 Je '89
Bishops, politicians and abortion [cover story] R. J. McManus. *America* 161:294-6+ N 4 '89
Black women's plight cited at pro-choice rally in D.C. il *Jet* 76:13 Ap 24 '89
Blacks agonize over abortion. J. N. Baker. il *Newsweek* 114:63 D 4 '89
A boost for abortion's foes [Michigan cases] *Newsweek* 113:26 Ap 3 '89
Bush's no-no on abortion. il *Time* 134:30 N 6 '89
Calm, cool and beleaguered [F. Wattleton; cover story] M. Szegedy-Maszak. il pors *The New York Times Magazine* p16-19+ Ag 6 '89
Can pro-choicers prevail? Feminists squabble over strategy for protecting rights. M. B. Carlson. il *Time* 134:28 Ag 14 '89
A clear majority [prochoice rally in Washington, D.C.] *The Nation* 248:579-80 My 1 '89
Day in court [Roe v. Wade] W. Dellinger. *The New Republic* 200:11-12 My 8 '89
Dear constituent: here's where I stand. J. Brandl. *Commonweal* 116:661-2 D 1 '89
The defenders of abortion win one [Florida Supreme Court decision] il *U.S. News & World Report* 107:24+ O 16 '89
Does father know best? [fathers' rights and abortion] P. Orenstein. *Vogue* 179:314+ Ap '89
Don't bury my heart [discussion of May 22, 1989 article, What can the white man . . . say to the black woman?] A. Walker. *The Nation* 249:226 S 4-11 '89
Equal rights: not for women only [fathers' rights] M. J. Weiss. il *Glamour* 87:276-7+ My '89
Father knows best [discussion of May 8, 1989 article, March to a crossroads on abortion] M. Tax. *The Nation* 249:110+ Jl 24-31 '89
Father's rights case declined by High Court. *Christianity Today* 33:53 Ja 13 '89
Fetal position [G. Bush states he would veto abortions in cases of rape or incest] Z. R. Eisenstein. *The Nation* 249:588-9 N 20 '89
The first march [prochoice march in Washington, D.C.] *National Review* 41:9-10 My 5 '89
Five political hot spots [state battles] G. J. Church. map *Time* 134:64 Jl 17 '89
The future of abortion [cover story; special section] il *Newsweek* 114:14-21+ Jl 17 '89
The great debate [challenge to Roe v. Wade] M. Webb. il *Harper's Bazaar* 122:64-5+ Jl '89
The humanist. L. L. Morain. *The Humanist* 49:2 S/O '89
If fetuses are people . . . [Missouri] W. Saletan. *The New Republic* 201:18-20 S 18-25 '89

ABORTION—Laws and regulations—*cont.*

If pro-choice is mainstream, now's the time to prove it. E. Ehrlich. il *Business Week* p64 Jl 17 '89

The importance of women. C. Kocol. *The Humanist* 49:34 N/D '89

In search of a compromise on abortion [Pennsylvania] S. V. Roberts. il *U.S. News & World Report* 107:31 N 6 '89

In the abortion battle, lower courts are important, too. T. Gest. *U.S. News & World Report* 107:30 Ag 28-S 4 '89

Is an embryo a person? C. A. Gardner. il *The Nation* 249:557-9 N 13 '89

Jane Hodgson's odyssey. *U.S. News & World Report* 107:26 D 4 '89

Letting the states set abortion policy. V. G. Rosenblum. *The Christian Century* 106:252-3 Mr 8 '89

The longer march [right to abortion march in Washington] *Commonweal* 116:259-60 My 5 '89

Loony legislation [prolife legislators' proposal to ban abortion on basis of gender selection in Pennsylvania] P. Simpson. *Ms.* 18:72 N '89

Louisiana: back to the 'dark ages'? il *Newsweek* 114:34-5 O 9 '89

March on Washington [prochoice demonstration] E. J. Bader. il *The Humanist* 49:26-8+ Jl/Ag '89

March to a crossroads on abortion [Washington, D.C.; cover story] M. Tax. *The Nation* 248:613+ My 8 '89

The morning after [consequences of overturning Roe v. Wade] B. Harvey. il *Mother Jones* 14:27-31+ My '89

New abortion fights [march on Washington to protest possible reversal of Roe v. Wade] T. Gest. il *U.S. News & World Report* 106:22-3+ Ap 24 '89

The new abortion wars [political consequences of Webster decision] M. Kondracke. *The New Republic* 201:17-19 Ag 28 '89

The new politics of abortion. M. Kinsley. il *Time* 134:96 Jl 17 '89

The new politics of abortion [anti-abortion movement] K. Gustafson. il *Utne Reader* p19+ Mr/Ap '89

Notes and comment [Mobilize for Women's Lives rally in Washington, D.C.] *The New Yorker* 65:42-3 D 4 '89

Notes and comment [Washington march to protect Roe v. Wade decision] *The New Yorker* 65:29-30 Ap 24 '89

Nothing less than perfect [F. Wattleton, president of Planned Parenthood] R. Stengel. il por *Time* 134:82-4 D 11 '89

Of many things. G. W. Hunt. *America* 160:386 Ap 29 '89

Our big choice [black women] E. Strothers. por *Essence* 20:116 Jl '89

Our bodies, our business [cover story; special section; with editorial comment by Anne Summers] il *Ms.* 18:6, 38-44+ Jl/Ag '89

Our bodies, their laws [abortion and reproductive rights] L. Villarosa. il *Essence* 20:24+ O '89

A pair of electoral tests [abortion issue in Va. and N.J.] il *Time* 134:36 O 23 '89

People's choice [prochoice march in Washington, D.C.] H. Hertzberg. *The New Republic* 200:4+ My 1 '89

Playing single-issue politics: abortion and the Massachusetts governor's race. M. Starr. il *Newsweek* 114:22 Ag 14 '89

The politics of abortion. P. Orenstein. *Vogue* 179:250-1 Je '89

The politics of abortion: New York's pro-choice mood may mean trouble for the GOP. J. Kasindorf. il *New York* 22:39 S 18 '89

The politics of abortion takes an unexpected turn [ramifications of Webster v. Reproductive Health Services] D. Baer. il *U.S. News & World Report* 107:26 Jl 31 '89

The politics of evasion. *Commonweal* 116:579-80 N 3 '89

Pols feel the heat: candidates scramble for pro-choice votes. M. Suh. il *Ms.* 18:72-3 N '89

Pro-choice: 'a sleeping giant' awakes [Washington, D.C. demonstration to oppose reversal of Roe v. Wade] E. Salholz. il *Newsweek* 113:39-40 Ap 24 '89

Pro-choice? Get lost: antiabortion views are a must at Health and Human Services. R. Lacayo. il *Time* 134:43-4 D 4 '89

Pro-choice politicking. H. Fineman. il *Newsweek* 114:34-6 O 9 '89

Prochoice forces claim momentum in Washington. il *Christianity Today* 33:59 My 12 '89

Reconcilable differences [division among women's groups over pro-choice strategies] P. Simpson. *Ms.* 18:70 O '89

Regain the body politic. *The Nation* 248:181 F 13 '89

Repro woman [interview with F. Wattleton; cover story] M. A. Gillespie. por *Ms.* 18:50-3 O '89

Save my law [Roe v. Wade plaintiff N. McCorvey at Washington, D.C. rally] G. H. Colt. il pors *Life* 12:111-12+ My '89

The shifting politics of abortion. R. Lacayo. il *Time* 134:35-6 O 23 '89

Short honeymoon? [G. Bush and abortion issue] J. Klein. il *New York* 22:16+ F 6 '89

Silent majority for choice. *The Progressive* 53:9 D '89

So much for Prince Charming [excerpt from *Dancing at the edge of the world*] U. K. Le Guin. il *Ms.* 17:101-2+ Ja/F '89

Surgeon General: abortion foe [appointee A. Novello] *Newsweek* 114:84 O 30 '89

The surging armies of abortion. R. Fly. il *Business Week* p130+ O 16 '89

Taking issue with NOW. E. Clift. il *Newsweek* 114:21-2 Ag 14 '89

Taking it to the states [prolife activists] K. A. Lawton. il *Christianity Today* 33:36-8 N 3 '89

Taking to the streets [celebrities march in support of Roe v. Wade decision in Washington, D.C.] S. Schindehette. il *People Weekly* 31:40-5 Ap 24 '89

Toward moderation of abortion law. *America* 160:75 F 4 '89

A tragedy without villains. D. R. Carlin, Jr. il *Commonweal* 116:517-18 O 6 '89

Turning back Webster [state rulings] *The Nation* 249:477 O 30 '89

Two steps back [consequences of Webster decision] B. Ehrenreich. il *Ms.* 18:24-5 O '89

The war has just begun [abortion rights] P. Simpson. il *Ms.* 18:88 S '89

The war within the states [following Supreme Court's Webster decision] J. Fowler. *National Review* 41:35-6 Ag 4 '89

What can the white man . . . say to the black woman? [address, April 8, 1989] A. Walker. il *The Nation* 248:691-2 My 22 '89

What the people said. D. Schorr. *The New Leader* 72:3 N 13 '89

Where right-to-life activists go from here [recent setbacks] il *U.S. News & World Report* 107:32 O 23 '89

Which way black America? Anti-abortion or pro-choice. P. Carr; F. Wattleton. il *Ebony* 44:134+ O '89

Who'll be hurt by new abortion restrictions? All of us [challenge to Roe v. Wade] il *Glamour* 87:184 My '89

Whose life is it? [challenge to Roe v. Wade; cover story] R. Lacayo. il *Time* 133:20-4 My 1 '89

Why I decided to march for abortion rights [interview with C. Shepherd] il por *Glamour* 87:96 Jl '89

Will the GOP trip itself as it backpedals on abortion? D. Harbrecht. il *Business Week* p47 D 4 '89

Will this be the year we lose abortion? [challenge to Roe v. Wade] L. Dusky. il *Mademoiselle* 95:214-15+ My '89

A world without Roe. M. A. Glendon. *The New Republic* 200:19-20 F 20 '89

Canada

Abortion agony [Supreme Court okays abortion sought by C. Daigle over objections of former boyfriend] B. Wallace and L. Van Dusen. il por *Maclean's* 102:12-14 Ag 21 '89

Abortion deadlock [Supreme Court refuses to rule on fetal rights] N. Underwood. il *Maclean's* 102:48 Mr 20 '89

Abortion in the courts [Quebec court upholds injunction obtained by former boyfriend preventing C. Daigle from getting abortion] B. Wallace. il por *Maclean's* 102:14-16 Ag 7 '89

Abortion on trial [cases of two women seeking abortions over objections of former boyfriends; cover story; special section; with editorial comment by Kevin Doyle] il pors *Maclean's* 102:2, 14-16+ Jl 31 '89

Bittersweet victory [Ontario court decides abortion case in favor of woman B. Dodd] G. W. Taylor. il por *Maclean's* 102:18 Jl 24 '89

Court fails to block abortion [case of C. Daigle] L. Mackey. *Christianity Today* 33:65 S 8 '89

A crusader's challenge [H. Morgentaler performs abortions at Halifax, N.S. clinic despite ban] G. Allen. il por *Maclean's* 102:14-15 N 6 '89

The final appeal [C. Daigle's fight for an abortion to go before Supreme Court] L. Van Dusen. il por *Maclean's* 102:10-11 Ag 14 '89

An inflamed debate. R. Corelli. il *Maclean's* 102:36-7 Jl 17 '89

The middle ground [Tory bill] R. Laver. il *Maclean's* 102:14-16 N 13 '89

A unanimous view [Supreme Court ruling in C. Daigle case denying partner's right to prevent an abortion] L. Van Dusen. il por *Maclean's* 102:16 N 27 '89

India

In India, they abort females. J. McGowan. por *Newsweek* 113:12 Ja 30 '89

Ireland

The 'A-word' in Ireland. D. Pedersen. il *Newsweek* 114:45 Jl 31 '89

Soviet Union

Abortion in the Soviet Union. K. Witt. *World Press Review* 36:55 Ag '89

Moral and religious aspects

See also

National Right to Life Committee

Operation Rescue

Abolition revisited. J. N. Akers. il *Christianity Today* 33:13 Mr 3 '89

Abortion and the churches [Protestants] K. L. Woodward. il *Newsweek* 114:45-6 Jl 24 '89

Abortion, Catholicism, and the Constitution. G. Gamm. por *The Humanist* 49:24-5+ Jl/Ag '89

Abortion: Catholics must change hearts as well as laws. J. L. Bernardin, Cardinal. *U.S. Catholic* 54:31-3 D '89

Abortion clinic obsolescence [RU-486] C. W. Colson. il *Christianity Today* 33:72 F 3 '89

ABORTION—Moral and religious aspects—*cont.*

Abortion: common at Christian colleges? il *Christianity Today* 33:42-3 Jl 14 '89

Abortion, lies and videotape. T. H. Stahel. *America* 161:288-9 N 4 '89; Correction. 161:313-14 N 11 '89

Abortion: right or wrong? E. Doerr. il *USA Today (Periodical)* 117:51-3 Ja '89

Abortion-rights boomerang [femicide] D. Neff. il *Christianity Today* 33:16 Mr 17 '89

Abortion: the axe at the root of human rights. J. R. Quinn. *America* 160:284-5 Ap 1 '89

Abortion: the debate, the politics, the morality [cover story; special section] il *National Review* 41:25-31 D 22 '89

The abortion wars [cover story] T. Stafford. il *Christianity Today* 33:16-20 O 6 '89

Abortion: what does 'Webster' mean? [symposium] *Commonweal* 116:425-8 Ag 11 '89

After the Webster decision. *America* 161:51 Jl 29-Ag 5 '89

After 'Webster': an uphill struggle. *America* 161:227 O 14 '89

America's holy war [Ladies Center abortion clinic in Pensacola, Fla.] P. Hamill. il por *Esquire* 112:61-4 N '89

Anti-abortion, pro-feminism? P. Erens. *Mother Jones* 14:31+ My '89

As American as freeways. D. R. Carlin, Jr. *Commonweal* 116:392-3 Jl 14 '89

Attacking the real 'Jane Roe' [N. McCorvey] S. Waldman. il por *Newsweek* 113:22 Ap 17 '89

Baby boys, to order [use of abortion if fetus is not desired sex] J. Leo. il *U.S. News & World Report* 106:59 Ja 9 '89

Barred from Communion [prochoice assemblywoman L. Killea of San Diego] *The Christian Century* 106:1193-4 D 20-27 '89

Beyond rights in abortion politics [Webster v. Reproductive Health Services] D. Heim. *The Christian Century* 106:675-6 Jl 19-26 '89

Beyond the legal right: why liberals and feminists don't like to talk about the morality of abortion [cover story] J. DeParle. *The Washington Monthly* 21:28-9+ Ap '89

Bishops, politicians and abortion [cover story] R. J. McManus. *America* 161:294-6+ N 4 '89

The Bush administration's modest plans to help pro-life backers. K. T. Walsh. *U.S. News & World Report* 106:26 Ap 24 '89

The case of the reluctant drug maker [Roussel-Uclaf will not market RU-486 outside of France] E. MacFarquhar. il *U.S. News & World Report* 106:54 Ja 23 '89

Catholic abortion rates and the abortion controversy [study by Alan Guttmacher Institute] J. R. Kelly. *America* 160:82-5 F 4 '89

Challenges facing U.S. Catholics. P. Rosenthal. *Commonweal* 116:617-18 N 17 '89

The choosing of the NIH director. D. E. Koshland, Jr. *Science* 246:981 N 24 '89

The Church strikes back [Catholic Church on the offensive against prochoice movement] J. N. Baker. il *Newsweek* 114:28 D 18 '89

Confrontation's stage is set [Supreme Court decision] K. A. Lawton. il *Christianity Today* 33:36-8 Ag 18 '89

Could this be the year? [Roe v. Wade] K. A. Lawton. il *Christianity Today* 33:36-8 Ap 7 '89

Dear constituent: here's where I stand. J. Brandl. *Commonweal* 116:661-2 D 1 '89

The debate about life. R. Laver. il *Maclean's* 102:20 Jl 31 '89

Evangels of abortion. G. Wills. bibl f il por *The New York Review of Books* 36:15+ Je 15 '89

Federal fetal transplant ban continues. *Science News* 136:310 N 11 '89

Fetal attraction [National Institutes of Health panel report recommending use of fetal tissue in medical research] R. J. Neuhaus. *National Review* 41:12-13 D 8 '89

Fetal research: the underlying issue. R. J. Levine. *Scientific American* 261:112 Ag '89

Fetal tissue transplants remain off limits. J. Palca. il *Science* 246:752 N 10 '89

Fetal tissue transplants win U.K. approval. D. Dickson. il *Science* 245:464-5 Ag 4 '89

For bread and roses [discussion of April 24, 1989 article, Minority report] C. Hitchens. *The Nation* 248:870 Je 26 '89

Fundamental rights in danger [challenge to Roe v. Wade] E. Doerr. il *The Humanist* 49:39 My/Je '89

A governor responds [discussion of October 14, 1989 article, After 'Webster': an uphill struggle] *America* 161:265 O 28 '89

How prolife protest has backfired. C. W. Colson. il *Christianity Today* 33:72 D 15 '89

Just say no: boycotts at the barricades [prochoice boycott of Domino's Pizza and prolife boycott of Maxwell House coffee] *Newsweek* 114:21 Ag 14 '89

Just who is this 'We'? [discussion of April 24, 1989 column] C. Hitchens. bibl *The Nation* 248:650+ My 15 '89

Life after Webster. D. Neff. il *Christianity Today* 33:14 Ag 18 '89

The longer march. *Commonweal* 116:259-60 My 5 '89

Minority report. C. Hitchens. *The Nation* 248:546 Ap 24 '89

A mistake in San Diego [Bishop L. T. Maher bars Assemblywoman L. Killea from receiving Communion because of pro-choice stand on abortion] *America* 161:416 D 9 '89

The moral complexity of choice. J. Leo. il *U.S. News & World Report* 107:64 D 11 '89

A new pill, a fierce battle [RU-486] S. Greenhouse. il por *The New York Times Magazine* p22-4+ F 12 '89

Of many things. G. W. Hunt. *America* 160:386 Ap 29 '89

The pill of choice? [RU-486; cover story] J. Palca. il *Science* 245:1319-23 S 22 '89

Planned Parenthood didn't plan on this: abortion foes are attacking the agency's corporate sponsors. B. Tierney. il *Business Week* p34 Jl 3 '89

The politics of evasion. *Commonweal* 116:579-80 N 3 '89

Poor women: the sacrificial lambs. C. Kocol. por *The Humanist* 49:37+ Jl/Ag '89

Presbyterians consider four views on abortion. R. Frame. *Christianity Today* 33:52-3 D 15 '89

The prolife credibility gap [alienation of black support] S. Perkins. il por *Christianity Today* 33:21-2 Ap 21 '89

"Prolife": what does it really mean? [cover story; special section] il *Christianity Today* 33:27-38 Jl 14 '89

Promises to keep [appointment of L. Sullivan as Health and Human Services Secretary disappoints prolife supporters] K. A. Lawton. il por *Christianity Today* 33:44-5 F 3 '89

Rocking the Roe boat. M. deG. Ford. *Commonweal* 116:326-8 Je 2 '89

'Roe v. Wade'—the movie. *America* 160:523-4 Je 3 '89

RU detour [abortion pill] M. Suh. il *Ms.* 17:135-6 Ja/F '89

Scanning the prolife battlefields. K. A. Lawton. *Christianity Today* 33:52-4 Je 16 '89

Short honeymoon? [G. Bush and abortion issue] J. Klein. il *New York* 22:16+ F 6 '89

Taking it to the states. K. A. Lawton. il *Christianity Today* 33:36-8 N 3 '89

Tar baby [prolife opposition to appointment of L. W. Sullivan as Health and Human Services Secretary] F. Barnes. *The New Republic* 200:12-13 F 13 '89

This is what you thought: 69% favor using fetal tissue for medical research. il *Glamour* 87:153 Je '89

Too many abortions. *Commonweal* 116:419-20 Ag 11 '89

Toward moderation of abortion law. *America* 160:75 F 4 '89

A tragedy without villains. D. R. Carlin, Jr. il *Commonweal* 116:517-18 O 6 '89

The use of aborted fetal tissue in medical research is as controversial as abortion itself. P. Orenstein. *Vogue* 179:298+ O '89

Wanted: consensus on abortion. R. V. Pierard. por *Christianity Today* 33:8 O 6 '89

What if we win? T. C. Muck. *Christianity Today* 33:13 Ap 21 '89

When does life begin? [interview with C. Grobstein] E. Hall. il pors *Psychology Today* 23:42-6 S '89

When (if) 'Roe' falls [cover story] D. A. Degnan. *Commonweal* 116:267-9 My 5 '89

When the law and medicine collide [conflict over age of fetal viability] J. Silberner. il *U.S. News & World Report* 107:23 Jl 17 '89

A winning prolife strategy. K. S. Kantzer. *Christianity Today* 33:19 D 15 '89

Winning Webster v. Reproductive Health Services: the crisis of the pro-life movement. J. R. Kelly. *America* 161:79-83 Ag 12-19 '89

You don't have to believe in God to be prolife. N. Hentoff. *U.S. Catholic* 54:28-30 Mr '89

Psychological aspects

Abortion under siege. S. Mills. il *Ms.* 18:48-51 Jl/Ag '89

Easing the anguish [support groups available to couples choosing to abort a pregnancy] M. Krance. il *American Health* 8:14 Jl/Ag '89

Is there angst after abortion? [research by Jeanne Parr Lemkau] M. Sandmaier. *Mademoiselle* 95:94+ Jl '89

Men and abortion. E. K. Goodman. il *Glamour* 87:178-9+ Jl '89

When prenatal tests bring bad news [lack of support groups available for couples choosing to abort pregnancies] M. Krance. bibl il *American Health* 8:11-12 Jl/Ag '89

Public opinion

The abortion decision: readers respond. D. Baer. il *U.S. News & World Report* 107:23-4 Ag 7 '89

Where we stand now on abortion. M. Adessa. il *Psychology Today* 23:10 O '89

Statistics

Abortion: just the facts, not the hype. D. Christiano. il *Glamour* 87:228-31 N '89

ABORTION, SPONTANEOUS *See* Miscarriage

ABORTION CLINICS

Abortion under siege. S. Mills. il *Ms.* 18:48-51 Jl/Ag '89

British Columbia

Defiance in Vancouver [protesters] P. Kopvillem. *Maclean's* 102:17 Jl 31 '89

ABORTION CLINICS—*cont.*
Canada
A network of clinics [H. Morgentaler] P. Kopvillem. il por *Maclean's* 102:19 Jl 31 '89
Florida
America's holy war [Ladies Center in Pensacola] P. Hamill. il por *Esquire* 112:61-4 N '89
Missouri
Amid a raging debate, one woman chooses abortion [D. Barber at Reproductive Health Services in St. Louis, Mo. after Supreme Court decision] D. Grogan and others. il *People Weekly* 32:89-90+ Jl 24 '89
New York (State)
Abortion in New York [cover story] J. Kasindorf. il *New York* 22:32-8+ S 18 '89
Nova Scotia
A crusader's challenge [H. Morgentaler performs abortions at Halifax clinic despite ban] G. Allen. il por *Maclean's* 102:14-15 N 6 '89
Soviet Union
Abortion in the Soviet Union. K. Witt. *World Press Review* 36:55 Ag '89
ABORTION DECISIONS *See* United States. Supreme Court—Decisions—Abortion decisions
ABORTION IN MOTION PICTURES
Abortion in film: a one-sided story. R. Rosenbaum. il *Mademoiselle* 95:104+ N '89
Video rebuts "Silent scream" [Peg Yorkin's Abortion: for survival] P. Simpson. *Ms.* 18:79 Jl/Ag '89
ABORTION IN TELEVISION
'Roe v. Wade'—the movie. *America* 160:523-4 Je 3 '89
ABOVE THE LAW [film] *See* Motion picture reviews—Single works
ABRAHAM, F. MURRAY
about
Alter ego. B. Kellow. il por *Opera News* 54:22-3 D 23 '89
ABRAHAM, GEORGE, AND ABRAHAM, KATY
Adding a homemade spice to life. il *Consumers' Research Magazine* 72:20-3 Je '89
ABRAHAM, KATY
(jt. auth) *See* Abraham, George, and Abraham, Katy
ABRAHAM, LAURIE
Should she or shouldn't she? il *Discover* 10:73 Ja '89
ABRAHAM, WILLIAM J. (WILLIAM JAMES), 1947-
Oh God, poor God: the state of contemporary theology. *The American Scholar* 58:557-63 Aut '89
ABRAHAM & STRAUS
A store is born [Manhattan branch] B. Kanner. il *New York* 22:24-5 S 18 '89
ABRAHAMS, EDWARD, 1949-
The image maker. *The New Republic* 200:41-5 Ja 30 '89
ABRAHAMS, JIM
about
All that ZAZ. I. Slifkin. il pors *Video* 13:14 S '89
ABRAHAMSON, WARREN G., AND OTHERS
Fads in ecology. bibl f il *BioScience* 39:321-5 My '89
ABRAM, MORRIS B.
CSCE Conference on the Human Dimension [statement, May 31, 1989] *Department of State Bulletin* 89:88-90 S '89
ABRAMIS, DAVID J.
Finding the fun at work. *Psychology Today* 23:36+ Mr '89
ABRAMOV, VALERY
Food irradiation—scientists' toy or everyman's joy? il *World Health* p28-9 Ap '89
ABRAMOVITZ, MELISSA
A look at animal vision. il *Sierra* 74:100-1 Mr/Ap '89
ABRAMS, DEBORAH
about
Architectural elan. P. Warner. il *Architectural Digest* 46:166-71 Ag '89
ABRAMS, ELLIOTT
Are the contras finished? *National Review* 41:30-1 Mr 10 '89
The deal in Central America. *Commentary* 87:29-32 My '89
El Salvador [discussion of May 1989 article, The deal in Central America] *Commentary* 88:8-9 S '89
ABRAMS, ISABEL S.
Chemical weapons for plants. il *Current Health 2* 15:28-9 Ap '89
ABRAMS, LEE
about
Lee Abrams: out to fill the air with heavy-metal fare. D. Foust. il por *Business Week* p107 Je 5 '89
ABRAMS, M. H. (MEYER HOWARD), 1912-
The strangeness of Wordsworth. il *The New York Review of Books* 36:45-50 D 21 '89
ABRAMS, MALCOLM, AND BERNSTEIN, HARRIET
Anticavity pills, edible pet spoons, and other future stuff [excerpt] il *Parents* 64:141-4 O '89
ABRAMS, MAXINE
The 184 best breast cancer doctors. *Good Housekeeping* 208:77-80+ Ap '89
(ed) *See* Conill, Alicia. A doctor's guide to staying well this winter
ABRAMS, MEYER HOWARD *See* Abrams, M. H. (Meyer Howard), 1912-

ABRAMS, MICHAEL
about
Architectural elan. P. Warner. il *Architectural Digest* 46:166-71 Ag '89
ABRAMS, PAMELA, AND ROSENBERG, LIZ
Pen pals: our babies' first year. il pors *Parents* 64:90-4+ N '89
ABRAMSON, E. M.
IRAs: calculating your withdrawals. il *Modern Maturity* 32:79-80 Ag/S '89
ABRUZZO NATIONAL PARK (ITALY)
The lone ranger [F. Tassi] D. Starr. il *Omni (New York, N.Y.)* 12:102+ N '89
ABSINTHE
Absinthe. W. N. Arnold. bibl il *Scientific American* 260:112-17 Je '89
Curse of the muse [V. van Gogh] B. A. MacAdam. il *Art News* 88:17 Mr '89
ABSOLUTE
The opening of the American mind [case for relativism over absolutes] A. M. Schlesinger. *The New York Times Book Review* 94:1+ Jl 23 '89
ABSORPTION (PHYSIOLOGY)
Osteoclastic bone resorption by a polarized vacuolar proton pump. H. C. Blair and others. bibl f il *Science* 245:855-7 Ag 25 '89
Reduction of intestinal carcinogen absorption by carcinogen-specific secretory immunity. L. K. Silbart and D. F. Keren. bibl f il *Science* 243:1462-4 Mr 17 '89
ABSORPTION (PLANTS)
See also
Plants—Water requirements
ABSTRACT ART *See* Art, Abstract
ABSTRACT EXPRESSIONISM
Artful survivor [H. Frankenthaler; cover story] D. Solomon. il pors *The New York Times Magazine* p30-3+ My 14 '89
ABT *See* American Ballet Theatre
ABU AHMED, HAMED
A Nobelist's inspiration [interview with N. Mahfouz] il por *World Press Review* 36:61 Ja '89
ABU DHABI (UNITED ARAB EMIRATES: EMIRATE)
See also
Bronze Age—Abu Dhabi (United Arab Emirates: Emirate)
ABU NIDAL
about
Finis for the master terrorist? D. Brand. il por *Time* 134:69 D 11 '89
ABU SALEM, FRANÇOIS
about
The story of Kufur Shamma [drama] Reviews
New York 22:45 Ag 7 '89. J. Simon
ABURDENE, PATRICIA
(jt. auth) *See* Naisbitt, John, and Aburdene, Patricia
ABUSE OF CHILDREN *See* Child abuse
ABUSE OF NURSING HOME PATIENTS *See* Nursing home patient abuse
ABUSE OF WIVES *See* Wife abuse
ABUSED WOMEN
See also
Church work with abused women
Wife abuse
Hearing and healing Hedda Nussbaum. L. L. McCloskey. *The Christian Century* 106:178-9 F 15 '89
Hedda's secret: what no one understands about abused women [with introduction by Jennifer Farbar] S. A. Feeney. por *Mademoiselle* 95:242-5+ Mr '89
Taking responsibility. C. Kocol. il *The Humanist* 49:33-4 Ja/F '89
Understanding battered women [interview with S. Schechter] M. Suh. il *Ms.* 17:62 Ap '89
Victim of love. C. Jakobson. il *Seventeen* 48:204-7+ Ap '89
THE ABYSS [film] *See* Motion picture reviews—Single works
ABYSSINIAN BAPTIST CHURCH (NEW YORK, N.Y.)
The education of Reverend Butts. E. Pooley. il pors *New York* 22:42-9 Je 26 '89
Rev. Calvin Butts installed as pastor of Abyssinian Baptist Church in New York. il pors *Jet* 77:12-13 D 11 '89
ABZYMES *See* Catalytic antibodies
ACACIAS
Tropical forest gardening: an alternative to destruction [Panama] il *The Futurist* 23:53 My/Je '89
ACADEMIC ACHIEVEMENTS *See* Student achievements
ACADEMIC DEGREES *See* Degrees, Academic
ACADEMIC FREEDOM
See also
Tennessee evolution controversy
AAUP censures Southeastern Seminary. R. L. Hester. *The Christian Century* 106:742-4 Ag 16-23 '89
Academic freedom and the Catholic University of America [implications of Curran case] F. R. McManus. *America* 160:506-9 My 27 '89
The campus: "an island of repression in a sea of freedom". C. E. Finn. *Commentary* 88:17-23 S '89
The case of Michael Levin [CCNY professor censored for article on black intelligence] D. Seligman. *National Review* 41:38-40 My 5 '89

ACADEMIC FREEDOM—cont.

Catholic oaths and academic freedom. M. B. Lukens. *The Christian Century* 106:982-4 N 1 '89

Free speech on the campus. N. Hentoff. il *The Progressive* 53:12-13 My '89

Good news from Dartmouth [administration backs student protesting teacher S. Sully's finding of racism in submitted essay] *National Review* 41:18 S 15 '89

In rejoinder: what next at Catholic U? [special section] il *Commonweal* 116:270-5+ My 5 '89

Is academic freedom bad for business? [denial of tenure to MIT professor D. Noble] K. Hart. il por *The Bulletin of the Atomic Scientists* 45:28-31+ Ap '89

The new left vigilantes. J. P. Roche. il *National Review* 41:34-5 D 8 '89

SBC seminary accused [alleged infringements of academic freedom at Southeastern Baptist Theological Seminary] *The Christian Century* 106:41 Ja 18 '89

The speech supression movement [universities] D. Seligman. il *Fortune* 119:195-6 Je 19 '89

ACADEMIC RESEARCH *See* Colleges and universities—Research

ACADEMIC TENURE *See* College teachers—Tenure

ACADEMY AWARDS

The Academy Awards: back in the envelope, please. P. Arthur. il *USA Today (Periodical)* 118:93 Jl '89

Call it Dangerous excess as loads of Oscar's ladies bust out and take the plunge. il *People Weekly* 31:136-7 Ap 17 '89

Don't believe the hype [magazine coverage of nominees] *Film Comment* 25:6 My/Je '89

The five nominees and how they grew [foreign language film Oscar nominations] H. A. Rodman. *Film Comment* 25:8+ Mr/Ap '89

His Oscars Gone with the wind, art director Lyle Wheeler fights to regain more than statuettes [attempts to halt auction of trophies] S. K. Reed. il pors *People Weekly* 31:91-2 Mr 27 '89

In darkest Hollywood. S. Elkin. il *Harper's* 279:51-61 D '89

A night for the dwarfs. il *Newsweek* 113:77 Ap 10 '89

The night the rains came [critics' predictions] R. Corliss. il *Film Comment* 25:9 Mr/Ap '89

Oscar wanna-bees. A. Thompson. il *Film Comment* 25:56+ Ja/F '89

The prize is right [O. Siegel casts the Oscar statuettes] E. Stern. il por *Gentlemen's Quarterly* 59:49+ Mr '89

What TV doesn't tell you about the Oscars [cover story] M. Beck. il *TV Guide* 37:4-7 Mr 25-31 '89

Anecdotes, facetiae, satire, etc.

Oscars on the verge of a nervous breakdown. C. Krupp and D. Denicolo. il *Glamour* 87:223 Ap '89

ACADEMY FOR THE ADVANCEMENT OF TEACHING AND MANAGEMENT

The Academy: New Jersey improves professional growth opportunities for teachers. S. Cooperman and S. Nadel. il *Phi Delta Kappan* 70:619-23 Ap '89

ACADEMY OF CIVIL AVIATION (SOVIET UNION)

Soviet Aviation Academy seeks cooperation with other nations. il *Aviation Week & Space Technology* 130:88 Je 5 '89

ACADEMY OF SCIENCES OF THE USSR

Election turmoil at Soviet Academy. D. Dickson. *Science* 243:1659 Mr 31 '89

First word. D. Goldfarb. il *Omni (New York, N.Y.)* 11:8 F '89

Marchuk admits flaws in election. D. Dickson. *Science* 243:1548 Mr 24 '89

Moscow subversive chic. T. Rothman. *Scientific American* 261:16+ Jl '89

Sakharov declines to run for Moscow seat. D. Dickson. *Science* 243:1001 F 24 '89

Sakharov elected to presidium of Soviet Academy of Sciences. W. Sweet. il *Physics Today* 42:61-4 Ja '89

Soviet Academy attacked for being undemocratic. D. Dickson. il *Science* 243:728-9 F 10 '89

Soviet scientists rebel, Sakharov and Sagdeev elected to new Congress. W. Sweet. il *Physics Today* 42:65-6 My '89

US and Soviet academies reach global ecology agreement. W. Sweet. *Physics Today* 42:101-2 F '89

ACADIA NATIONAL PARK (ME.)

Acadia. M. Pfeiff. il *Better Homes and Gardens* 67:176 Ap '89

Acadia National Park puts its best seasons forward. B. McBride. il map *Travel Holiday* 171:48-55 F '89

The pleasures of a big park on a small island. il map *U.S. News & World Report* 106:78 My 8 '89

ACADIAN HISTORICAL VILLAGE (N.B.)

Tucked away in rural Acadia. W. Scheller. il map *Travel Holiday* 171:42-8 F '89

ACADIANS

New Brunswick

Tucked away in rural Acadia. W. Scheller. il map *Travel Holiday* 171:42-8 F '89

ACADIANS IN POETRY

Longfellow's lovers [Evangeline] W. Schemmel. *Travel Holiday* 171:45 F '89

ACANTHAMOEBA KERATITIS *See* Eye—Diseases and defects

ACC *See* American Craft Council

ACC SYNTHASE *See* Synthases

ACCELERATION (MECHANICS)

See also

Automobiles—Acceleration

ACCELERATOR MASS SPECTROMETRY

Archeological use

The Holly Oak shell [discussion of December 2, 1988 article, Mammoth fraud exposed] R. Lewin. *Science* 243:151-2 Ja 13 '89

New evidence ages modern Europeans [accelerator mass spectrometry dating of Aurignacian remains; work of James L. Bischoff] B. Bower. *Science News* 136:388 D 16 '89

ACCELERATORS (ELECTRONS, ETC.)

See also

Superconducting Super Collider

Accelerator eyed for warhead tritium. M. Crawford. *Science* 243:469 Ja 27 '89

Armies of physicists struggle to discover proof of a Scot's brainchild [search for Higgs boson at CERN and Stanford] C. C. Mann. bibl (p191) il *Smithsonian* 19:106-10+ Mr '89

Catching a light ride on a plasma wave [photon accelerator; research by John M. Dawson and Scott C. Wilks] I. Peterson. *Science News* 135:358 Je 10 '89

A colossal collision course [CERN's large electron-positron collider] M. D. Lemonick. il *Time* 134:72 Jl 17 '89

European Z° factory LEPs ahead. *Science News* 136:159 S 2 '89

Heavy-ion fusion. J. Horgan. il *Scientific American* 261:30+ O '89

Japan's big gamble on synchrotrons. M. Crawford. *Science* 246:1383 D 15 '89

Junk [electromagnet at Columbia University involved in 1939 splitting of an atom] *The New Yorker* 65:28-9 My 29 '89

LEP, the world's biggest accelerator, is on the air [cover story] B. M. Schwarzschild. il *Physics Today* 42:17-20 O '89

Linear collider makes a Z [Stanford Linear Collider] *Science News* 135:245 Ap 22 '89

Michigan team to join in first experiment at Soviet accelerator [UNK accelerator] W. Sweet. *Physics Today* 42 pt1:58 Ag '89

New machine sparks rivalries at CERN [large electron-proton collider] D. Dickson. il *Science* 244:1257-60 Je 16 '89

New physics, old rivalries [SLAC vs. CERN] J. Cherfas. il *Science* 246:323-4 O 20 '89

NSAC backs Brookhaven's RHIC and suggests closings to come [Relativistic Heavy Ion Collider] I. Goodwin. *Physics Today* 42:54 O '89

NSAC delays clear decision on Canada's kaon factory. I. Goodwin. *Physics Today* 42:44 Je '89

Plasma particle accelerators. J. M. Dawson. bibl il *Scientific American* 260:54-61 Mr '89

Siberian snake. J. Horgan. *Scientific American* 261:24+ N '89

SLAC feels the thrill of the chase [Z particles] M. M. Waldrop. il *Science* 244:771-3 My 19 '89

Slacking off [creating Z particles with the CERN and Stanford accelerators] G. Taubes. il *Discover* 10:58-9 Ja '89

Smashing atom dust [Large Electron-Positron Collider] S. O'Dy. *World Press Review* 36:67 S '89

A snake-in-the-ring keeps spins aligned [Siberian snake device] R. Cowen. *Science News* 136:118 Ag 19 '89

The Stanford Linear Collider [cover story] J. R. Rees. il *Scientific American* 261:58-65 O '89

Stanford Linear Collider finally starts producing the Z⁰. B. M. Schwarzschild. il *Physics Today* 42:17-21 Jl '89

Subcommittee encourages U.S. to join Canadian kaon factory [TRIUMF cyclotron] B. M. Schwarzschild. il *Physics Today* 42:17-19 My '89

Anecdotes, facetiae, satire, etc.

How to build a Planck-mass accelerator in your solar system. A. Akahito. il *Scientific American* 260:112-15 Ap '89

Medical use

Accelerated medicine [proton therapy] G. Levoy. il *Omni (New York, N.Y.)* 11:26+ Mr '89

Chiseling away at tumors with protons [work of James M. Slater] *Science News* 135:46 Ja 21 '89

ACCENTS

See also

English language—Accents

English language in Great Britain—Accents

ACCESS (MUSICAL GROUP)

Musical events:

Selections from R. Session's Montezuma, Duo for violin and cello, and Waltz. A. Porter. *The New Yorker* 64:94-5 Ja 23 '89

ACCESS EQUIPMENT (FIRM)

A limited partnership that's frankly a gamble [options on lease residuals] L. Zinn. *Business Week* p170 O 30 '89

ACCESS SYNDICATION (FIRM)

Picking on the little guys. A. B. Block. il *Channels (New York, N.Y.: 1986)* 9:76-9 F '89

ACCESSIONS, MUSEUM *See* Art galleries and museums—Acquisitions
ACCESSORIES, DRESS *See* Dress accessories
ACCESSORIES, HOUSEHOLD *See* Household furnishings
ACCESSORY PROGRAMS *See* Computer programming
ACCESSORY TABLES (MACHINE WORK) *See* Machinery—Stands, tables, etc.
ACCIDENT INSURANCE *See* Insurance, Accident
ACCIDENT LAW
    See also
    Damages
    Liability (Law)
THE ACCIDENTAL TOURIST [film] *See* Motion picture reviews—Single works
ACCIDENTS
    See also
    Agriculture—Accidents
    Aircraft carriers—Accidents and explosions
    Amusement parks—Accidents
    Artificial satellites—Accidents
    Aviation—Accidents
    Boats and boating—Accidents
    Burns and scalds
    Communications satellites—Accidents
    Drowning
    Falls (Accidents)
    Firearms—Accidents
    First aid in illness and injury
    Hydrogen bombs—Accidents
    Ice accidents
    Lawn mowers—Accidents
    Mountaineering—Accidents
    Nuclear weapons—Accidents
    Railroads—Accidents
    Rescue work
    Shipwrecks
    Skin diving—Accidents and injuries
    Space flight—Accidents
    Space vehicles—Accidents and explosions
    Traffic accidents
    Traumatism
    Zoos—Accidents
Now, on the other hand [left-handed people more accident prone] il *U.S. News & World Report* 107:18 Ag 21 '89
When accidents happen to kids. P. E. King. *McCall's* 116:51 Jl '89
                Anecdotes, facetiae, satire, etc.
Travels on my stomach. M. G. Stoddard. il *The Saturday Evening Post* 261:58-9 Jl/Ag '89
                Prevention
    See also
    Safety education
Backyard safety guide [views of Stephen P. Teret] P. G. O'Brien. *Ladies' Home Journal* 106:24 Jl '89
The complete summer-safety guide. C. Sherman. il *Parents* 64:103-6+ Jl '89
Home safe home [special section] il *Home Mechanix* 85:33+ N '89
How to prevent home accidents [children] il *USA Today (Periodical)* 118:12 D '89
Rx for a healthy summer [views of Mark D. Windome] E. Grossman. il *Good Housekeeping* 208:71-2 Je '89
Safety first [toddler-proofing your home] J. T. Gibson. il *Parents* 64:157 Jl '89
Safety program reduces risks of home accidents. *Aging* no359:35 '89
Six-million-dollar man [cost effectiveness of accident prevention] J. Bennet. *The New Republic* 200:18 Ja 23 '89
ACCIDENTS, INDUSTRIAL *See* Industrial accidents
ACCLIMATIZATION
    See also
    Animal introduction
ACCOMMODATION, VISUAL *See* Eye—Accommodation and refraction
ACCOMPANIMENT, MUSICAL *See* Musical accompaniment
ACCOUNTABILITY (EDUCATION)
Accountability comes around again. C. Pipho. *Phi Delta Kappan* 70:662-3 My '89
Teacher professionalism and accountability. L. Darling-Hammond. *The Education Digest* 55:15-19 S '89
ACCOUNTANTS
    See also
    Women accountants
Choosing your accountant. B. A. McKee. *Nation's Business* 77:28 N '89
ACCOUNTING
    See also
    Accrual accounting
    Amortization
    Auditing
    Billing
    Cash flow
    Computer service industries—Accounting
    Computers—Accounting use
    Corporations—Accounting
    Corporations—Subsidiaries—Accounting
    Credit cards—Accounting
    Depreciation—Accounting

Finance companies—Accounting
Financial statements
Goodwill in business—Accounting
Insurance, Health—Accounting
Insurance, Life—Accounting
Leveraged buyouts—Accounting
Management accounting
Motion picture theaters—Accounting
Photographic industry—Accounting
Retirement benefits—Accounting
Small business—Accounting
Unbundled stock units—Accounting
Videotapes—Accounting use
                Standards
    See also
    Financial Accounting Standards Board
    Government Accounting Standards Board
                Study and teaching
                Aids and devices
Accounting help! [video and disk tutorials] S. Miller. il *Home Office Computing* 7:32 Mr '89
                Great Britain
Britain's goodwill games. D. Wechsler. il *Forbes* 144:65+ O 2 '89
ACCOUNTING ETHICS
    See also
    Confidential communications—Accountants
Annual reports: the SEC cracks the whip. T. Smart. il *Business Week* p74 Ap 10 '89
Cute tricks on the bottom line. G. Hector. il *Fortune* 119:193+ Ap 24 '89
Numbers game. See issues of Forbes
Still pussyfooting. S. N. Chakravarty. il *Forbes* 144:51 Ag 21 '89
ACCOUNTING FIRMS
    See also
    Arthur Andersen & Company
    Arthur Young & Company
    Ernst & Whinney
    Price Waterhouse Company
                Acquisitions and mergers
Less is more among the bean counters. *U.S. News & World Report* 107:11 Jl 17 '89
The new numbers game in accounting. D. Greising. il *Business Week* p20-1 Jl 24 '89
When one plus one equals no. 1 [Ernst & Whinney's merger with Arthur Young] J. M. Laderman. *Business Week* p92+ Je 5 '89
Why Andersen dumped Price. D. Greising. *Business Week* p47 O 9 '89
ACCOUNTING IN LITERATURE
D. Larry Crumbley: laying bare the fleshpots of accounting. T. Vogel. il por *Business Week* p91 Je 26 '89
ACCOUNTS, BANK *See* Bank accounts
ACCOUNTS, COLLECTING OF *See* Collecting of accounts
ACCOUNTS, ESCROW *See* Escrow accounts
ACCOUNTS RECEIVABLE
    See also
    Payment of accounts
Fewer companies have bad cases of strained finances. G. Koretz. il *Business Week* p26 Ja 9 '89
ACCREDITATION, THEOLOGICAL SEMINARY *See* Theological seminaries—Accreditation
ACCRUAL ACCOUNTING
Accrual, cruel world. G. W. Padwe. il *Nation's Business* 77:60 D '89
ACCULTURATION
    See also
    East and West
How Maya culture withstood colonial force [Tipu and Lamanai sites; research by Elizabeth Graham] B. Bower. *Science News* 136:373 D 9 '89
On the fringes of conquest: Maya-Spanish contact in colonial Belize [Tipu and Lamanai sites] E. Graham and others. bibl f il map *Science* 246:1254-9 D 8 '89
THE ACCUSED [film] *See* Motion picture reviews—Single works
ACCUTANE *See* Isotretinoin
ACE ARCHITECTS
Ace Architects: historical gamesmanship in San Francisco. J. Chatfield-Taylor. il *Architectural Digest* 46:84-7+ Ag '89
ACETAMINOPHEN
Analgesics can harm kidney [research by Dale P. Sandler] *Science News* 135:294 My 13 '89
ACETONITRILE
Artificial nail remover poses poisoning risk. D. Blumenthal. il *FDA Consumer* 23:22-3 Je '89
ACETYLATION
Degradation of proteins with acetylated amino termini by the ubiquitin system. A. Mayer and others. bibl f il *Science* 244:1480-3 Je 23 '89
ACETYLCHOLINE
Acetylcholine and GABA mediate opposing actions on neuronal chloride channels in crayfish. C. Pfeiffer-Linn and R. M. Glantz. bibl f il *Science* 245:1249-51 S 15 '89

ACETYLCHOLINE—cont.
Early glimmerings of heart disease [work of Joseph A. Vita]
K. Fackelmann. Science News 136:349 N 25 '89
ACETYLCHOLINE RECEPTORS See Chemoreceptors
ACETYLSALICYLIC ACID See Aspirin
ACH See Acetylcholine
ACHENBACH, JOEL
Bachelor angst. il Utne Reader p58-9 Mr/Ap '89
Cruising. il Seventeen 48:304-7+ Ag '89
ACHENBACH, JOEL, AND STAPP, MARY
Miami. il Esquire 112:209+ O '89
ACHIEVEMENT See Success
ACHIEVEMENT TESTS See Educational tests and measurements
ACHIEVEMENTS, STUDENT See Student achievements
ACHILLE LAURO SHIP HIJACKING, 1985, IN TELEVISION
'For God sakes, don't hide—they'll kill you!'. R. Townley.
il TV Guide 37:24-7 F 11-17 '89
ACID LAKES See Lakes
ACID RAIN
The acid rain report [excerpts from the National Acid
Precipitation Assessment Program's Interim assessment of
the causes and effects of acidic deposition] Congressional
Digest 68:38-9 F '89
Acid rain—one of America's worst killers. il Utne Reader
p61-2 S/O '89
Biotic impoverishment at home and abroad. D. W. Schindler.
BioScience 39:426 Jl/Ag '89
Bungle in the jungle [deforestation] C. Spencer. Omni (New
York, N.Y.) 11:48-9 S '89
Cistern water: soft—and corrosive. Science News 135:191
Mr 25 '89
Ill winds: air pollution's toll on trees and crops. J. J.
MacKenzie and M. T. El-Ashry. il map Technology Review
92:64-71 Ap '89
Letters [discussion of August 1988 article, The challenge
of acid rain] V. A. Mohnen. Scientific American 260:7
Ja '89
Matters of measure. G. Reiger. il Field & Stream 94:13-14
Je '89
Nitrogen saturation in northern forest ecosystems. J. D. Aber
and others. bibl f il BioScience 39:378-86 Je '89
Laws and regulations
The Clean Air Act [and the Acid Deposition Control Act]
il Congressional Digest 68:35-64 F '89
Clean Air reactions [Bush administration proposals]
Environment 31:2-4 Jl/Ag '89
Our dirty air [proposed new Clean Air Act; cover story]
M. McLoughlin. il map U.S. News & World Report
106:48-9+ Je 12 '89
International aspects
The acid challenge to security. J. E. Carroll. bibl f il The
Bulletin of the Atomic Scientists 45:32-4 O '89
North America
Canada and the United States in a global context [address,
September 22, 1989] D. Burney. Vital Speeches of the
Day 56:43-5 N 1 '89
A diplomatic exchange [visit of B. Mulroney to Washington]
H. Mackenzie. il por Maclean's 102:20 My 15 '89
Fighting acid rain [Bush plan; cover story; special section;
with editorial comment by Kevin Doyle] il map Maclean's
102:2, 38-46 Je 26 '89
How we're destroying the Canadian wilderness. T. H. Cole.
il map Popular Mechanics 166:40 Ag '89
Alaska
Peatlands as source of acid rain [study by Lee F. Klinger]
R. Monastersky. Science News 136:413 D 23-30 '89
Germany (West)
Air pollution and forest decline in a spruce (Picea abies)
forest. E.-D. Schulze. bibl f il map Science 244:776-83
My 19 '89
Where acids reign: do dying stands of Bavarian timber portend
the future of polluted U.S. forests? [research by Ernst-Detlef
Schulze; cover story] J. Raloff. il Science News 136:56-8
Jl 22 '89
North America
Acid deposition: unraveling a regional phenomenon. S. E.
Schwartz. bibl f il maps Science 243:753-63 F 10 '89
Southeastern States
Southeast waterways will face an acid test [research by M.
Robbins Church] J. Raloff. Science News 136:151 S 2
'89
ACIDOPHILUS MILK See Milk, Acidophilus
ACIDOSIS
Problems reported with two heart rescues [sodium bicarbonate
injections] S. Hart. Science News 136:85 Ag 5 '89
ACIDS
See also
Nucleic acids
ACIDS, FATTY
See also
Arachidonic acid
Eicosapentaenoic acid
Linoleic acid
Linolenic acid
Lipids
Myristic acid

Oils and fats, Edible
Prostaglandins
Arachidonic acid and other fatty acids directly activate
potassium channels in smooth muscle cells. R. W. Ordway
and others. bibl f il Science 244:1176-9 Je 9 '89
Eggs naturally rich in 'fish oils' [omega-3 fatty acids from
purslane] Science News 136:351 N 25 '89
It's not fish oil, but . . . [conversion of vegetable-derived
linolenic acid in the body; research by Edward A. Emken]
Science News 135:237 Ap 15 '89
Pouring it on for good health [Cheez Whiz spread found
to contain altered fatty acids which may help in cancer
prevention] il Newsweek 113:70 Mr 6 '89
ACIDS, ORGANIC
See also
Lactic acid
Tartaric acid
ACKERLEY, J. R. (JOE RANDOLPH), 1896-1967
about
Cousins once removed. P. Parker. il pors History Today
39:7-8 S '89
ACKERLEY, JOE RANDOLPH See Ackerley, J. R. (Joe
Randolph), 1896-1967
ACKERLY, JOHN
(jt. auth) See Kerr, Blake, and Ackerly, John
ACKERMAN, DIANE
O muse! You do make things difficult! il The New York
Times Book Review 94:1+ N 12 '89
Penguins. il The New Yorker 65:38-42+ Jl 10 '89
ACKERMAN, MARTIN S.
about
A raider tries to beat Asher Edelman at his own game.
G. Lewis. il pors Business Week p50 S 25 '89
ACKERMAN, STEPHEN J.
Doing more good than harm with children's medications.
il FDA Consumer 23:28-31 Mr '89
Flu shots: do you need one? il FDA Consumer 23:8-11
O '89
Real estate appraisals. il Consumers' Research Magazine
72:16-18 F '89
ACKERMANN-BLOUNT, JOAN
Be my handy man. il Gentlemen's Quarterly 59:307+ S '89
ACLU See American Civil Liberties Union
ACNE
Accutane: under attack. J. Kaplan. Vogue 179:112-13 Ja
'89
Images: beauty answers. L. F. McCarthy. Vogue 179:64 Jl
'89
A miracle goes sour [Accutane and birth defects] C. Raymond.
il Discover 10:72 Ja '89
Yes, there's help. P. A. Feuerstein. il Current Health 2
15:10-11 F '89
ACOCELLA, JOAN ROSS
Ballet archeology à la Russe. il Art in America 77:51+ D
'89
Diaghilev sits out WWI in Spain: Iberian idyll. il pors Dance
Magazine 63:45-8 Je '89
ACORN FUND, INC.
Big payoffs from small stocks [interview with R. Wanger]
J. Mendes. il por Fortune 120:35-7 Jl 17 '89
ACORNS
Diseases and pests
Life in a nutshell [inhabitants of acorns] M. W. Moffett.
il National Geographic 175:782-96 Je '89
ACOSTA, ARMANDO
about
Wherefore art thou Romeo, if Juliet is a castrated cat?
J. Stark. il por People Weekly 31:281-3 Mr 6 '89
ACOUSTIC DIRECTED-ENERGY PULSE TRAINS See Pulse
techniques (Electronics)
ACOUSTIC EMISSIONS
Acoustic emission technique tests aircraft integrity. C. Fotos.
Aviation Week & Space Technology 131:76 Ag 28 '89
When he hears, others listen [S. J. Vahaviolos] B. E. Thornbury. il por Nation's Business 77:18+ N '89
ACOUSTIC MICROSCOPES
Sounds of a cell. il Discover 10:16 Je '89
ACOUSTIC PHENOMENA IN NATURE
See also
Thunderstorms
ACOUSTICAL ENGINEERING See Audio engineering
ACOUSTICAL SOCIETY OF AMERICA
Acoustical Society elects Powell president. il por Physics
Today 42 pt1:58-9 Ag '89
ACOUSTICS See Music—Acoustics and physics; Sound
ACOUSTICS, ARCHITECTURAL
Acoustics at Anchorage [Alaska Center for the Performing
Arts] M. Holden. il Architectural Record 177:106-10 Ap
'89
The basics of concert hall acoustics. J. Borish. il High Fidelity
(New York, N.Y.) 39:40-7 Jl '89
But . . . how does it play? [Eugene McDermott Concert
Hall in Dallas] K. Ames. il Newsweek 114:64 S 25 '89
New graphics program debuts in concert hall [acoustic design
graphics program developed by Donald Greenberg and
Adam Stettner] A. S. Moffat. il Science 245:1452 S 29
'89

ACOUSTICS, UNDERWATER See Underwater acoustics

ACOVONE, JAY
Photographs and photography
The theatrical headshot. G. Bernstein. il por *Petersen's Photographic Magazine* 18:12 D '89

ACQUIRED IMMUNODEFICIENCY SYNDROME See AIDS (Disease)

ACQUISITIONS, MUSEUM See Art galleries and museums—Acquisitions

ACREMONIUM COENOPHIALUM
Trespassers will be poisoned [endophyte-infected tall fescue] K. Clay. il *Natural History* p8+ S '89

ACROCHORDUS GRANULATUS See Snakes

ACRONYMS
Anecdotes, facetiae, satire, etc.
Last word. S. Fox. il *Omni (New York, N.Y.)* 11:124 My '89

ACROPHOBIA
High anxiety [fear of riding ski lifts] J. Older. il *Skiing* 42:33-4 O '89

ACRYLIC FIBERS
If you get blisters, check your socks [acrylics more effective than cotton in preventing foot blisters; views of Kirk M. Herring] il *Prevention (Emmaus, Pa.)* 41:12+ Jl '89

ACRYLIC PAINT See Paint

ACT See American College Testing Program

ACT III COMMUNICATIONS INC.
Norman Lear, meet Adam Smith [Greater Rochester Cablevision owned by Time Warner competes with Act III Broadcasting's independent station in syndicated market] P. Newcomb. il *Forbes* 144:206+ N 27 '89

ACT-SO AWARDS
Making excellence popular [programs sponsored by V. Jarrett and C. Rowan] il pors *Ebony* 44:90+ S '89

ACT UP (ORGANIZATION)
In a rage over AIDS [ACT UP targets Cardinal J. O'Connor] E. Magnuson. il *Time* 134:33 D 25 '89
The way I live now. D. Leavitt. il *The New York Times Magazine* p28-32+ Jl 9 '89

ACTIN
A yeast actin-binding protein is encoded by *SAC6*, a gene found by suppression of an actin mutation. A. E. M. Adams and others. bibl f il *Science* 243:231-3 Ja 13 '89

ACTING
See also
Dramatization in education
Impersonation
Study and teaching
Practice made perfect [acting teachers on screen] L. Klady. *Film Comment* 25:39 N/D '89
Stella Adler. P. Brock. il pors *People Weekly* 32:66-8+ Jl 17 '89

ACTION CANADA SPORTS NETWORK See Sports Network

ACTION PHOTOGRAPHY See Photography of moving objects

ACTIONS AND DEFENSES
See also
Airlines—Suits and claims
Airplane industry—Suits and claims
Asbestos industry—Suits and claims
Banks and banking—Suits and claims
Bhopal poisonous gas disaster, India, 1984—Suits and claims
Blood banks—Suits and claims
Computer industry—Suits and claims
Computer service industries—Suits and claims
Damages
Drug industry—Suits and claims
Entertainment industry—Suits and claims
Exxon Valdez (Ship) oil spill, 1989—Suits and claims
Fear of death lawsuits
Libel and slander
Motion picture industry—Suits and claims
Prize contests—Suits and claims
Railroads—Suits and claims
Strategic lawsuits against public participation
Telephone companies—Suits and claims
Theatrical agencies and agents—Suits and claims
Torts
The lesson of the box [deficiencies of American legal system] L. Van Goethem. *Reader's Digest* 134:17-18 Ja '89
Limiting the damage from liability suits. T. Gest. *U.S. News & World Report* 106:50 My 15 '89
The Minor Suit Award returns [petty cases of education litigation] P. A. Zirkel. bibl f il *Phi Delta Kappan* 70:484-5 F '89

ACTIVE MAGNETOSPHERE PARTICLE TRACER EXPLORERS (SATELLITES) See Artificial satellites—Meteorological use

ACTIVIN
Secretion of activin by interstitial cells in the testis. W. Lee and others. bibl f il *Science* 243:396-8 Ja 20 '89

ACTIVISM, SOCIAL See Social action

ACTON, EDWARD J.
about
Acton and Dystel form partnership. il pors *Publishers Weekly* 235:16 Ap 21 '89

ACTON, LOREN
about
Space travelers rendezvous in Chicago. J. Liss. *Ad Astra* 1:41-4 D '89

ACTON AND DYSTEL INC.
Acton and Dystel form partnership. il pors *Publishers Weekly* 235:16 Ap 21 '89

ACTON CORP.
Acton in action. T. Jaffe. *Forbes* 144:164-5 Ag 7 '89

ACTORS AND ACTRESSES
See also
Acting
Black actors and actresses
Children as actors and actresses
Deaf actors and actresses
Impersonators, Female
Impersonators, Male
Motion picture actors and actresses
Television performers
Youth as actors and actresses
See also names of actors and actresses
The ladies of London. J. Kroll. il *Newsweek* 113:52-3 Ja 9 '89
Rare flair. il *Harper's Bazaar* 122:110-21 My '89
Agencies and agents
See Theatrical agencies and agents
Training
See Acting—Study and teaching

ACTORS AND ACTRESSES, HANDICAPPED
For Chris Burke, the first actor with Down syndrome to star on TV, Life goes on in a big way. K. McMurran. il pors *People Weekly* 32:61-2+ O 16 '89
"My son will always amaze me" [C. Burke, actor with Down syndrome]; ed. by Sara Nelson. M. Burke. il pors *Redbook* 174:48+ N '89
Takes guts [C. Burke, actor with Down syndrome, on TV show Life goes on; cover story] J. B. McDaniel. il pors *Life* 12:70-2+ N '89

ACTORS THEATER OF LOUISVILLE
Actors Theatre of Louisville. M. Sommers. il *Theatre Crafts* 23:34-9+ Mr '89
Some vigor and vinegar [Humana Festival] W. A. Henry. il *Time* 133:70-1 Ap 17 '89

ACTRESSES See Actors and actresses; Black actors and actresses; Motion picture actors and actresses

ACTUALIZATION, SELF See Self realization

ACUPRESSURE
See also
Reflexology

ACUPUNCTURE
Acupuncture wins the West [veterinary use] D. Kendall. il *The Mother Earth News* 117:42+ My/Je '89
In the age of aquariums, Wu Li-Hsia finds acupuncture is not a tankless job [treating fish] il por *People Weekly* 31:268 Mr 6 '89
Pet acupuncture [work of A. Schoen] R. H. Loeb. il pors *Good Housekeeping* 209:150+ N '89
Sticking it to Rover [for animals] il *FDA Consumer* 23:22 Ap '89

ACURA (AUTOMOBILE) See Automobiles, Foreign

ACUSTAR INC.
Forest Farmer: Chrysler's component parts president. C. Whitaker. il pors *Ebony* 44:90-2+ Mr '89

ACYLATION
See also
Aminoacylation

ACZEL, TAMAS
Hungary hearts. *The New Republic* 201:13-15 D 25 '89

AD ASTRA (PERIODICAL)
T plus one year. K. McMains. *Ad Astra* 1:48 D '89
"To the stars". *Ad Astra* 1:3 Ja '89

ADA (COMPUTER LANGUAGE)
Ada for supercomputers—a trend. *High Technology Business* 9:32 Ja '89
IntegrAda [Ada programming support environment] K. Nyberg and J. Udell. il *Byte* 14:213-14+ Ja '89

ADA DEFICIENCY DISORDER See Adenosine deaminase deficiency disorder

ADAGES See Maxims; Proverbs

ADAIR, WILLIAM, 1950?-
about
Gilt trip. G. Harrell. il por *House & Garden* 161:120+ S '89

ADAIR COUNTY FREE PRESS
A tapestry of prairie life [Greenfield, Iowa] H. Sidey. il *Time* 134:30-2+ O 9 '89

ADAM, JOHN
Eat hot lead, R2D2. il *The New Republic* 201:14+ Jl 17-24 '89

ADAMANTIUS See Origen

ADAMS, ALISON E. M., AND OTHERS
A yeast actin-binding protein is encoded by *SAC6*, a gene found by suppression of an actin mutation. bibl f il *Science* 243:231-3 Ja 13 '89

ADAMS, ALVIN P., JR.
Iran's threats against author [statement, March 8, 1989] *Department of State Bulletin* 89:78-80 My '89

ADAMS, ANSEL, 1902-1984
A field. il pors *Sierra* 74:20-1 Ja/F '89
ADAMS, BROCK
Scientists and politicians: can they work together? *USA Today (Periodical)* 117:32-3 My '89
Should the Congress adopt the "Textile and Apparel Trade Act of 1987"? [excerpts from address, September 15, 1988] *Congressional Digest* 68:19+ Ja '89
Should the Senate-passed Immigration Act of 1989 be approved? [excerpts from debate, July 13, 1989] *Congressional Digest* 68:252+ O '89
ADAMS, BROOKS
Contemplating the rose hip. il *Art in America* 77:164-7 D '89
The delirious palace. il *Art in America* 77:136-45 D '89
Double vision. il pors *Harper's Bazaar* 122:142-3+ Ag '89
Edward Hopper: shades of summer. il pors *Harper's Bazaar* 122:90-3+ Jl '89
The museum as studio. il *Art in America* 77:63+ O '89
Quadrilateral drift. il *Art in America* 77:188-91 My '89
A Ring for the '80s. il *Art in America* 77:222-9 Ap '89
A rue with a view. il *Harper's Bazaar* 122:116+ D '89
The San Juan master. il *Art in America* 77:51+ Ja '89
Victorian revival. il *House & Garden* 161:102-9 D '89
ADAMS, BRYAN
about
Bryan Adams likes the small-town vibe. il por *Rolling Stone* p44 Jl 13-27 '89
ADAMS, CHARLES FRANCIS, 1835-1915
about
Men who made the rules. P. Baida. il *American Heritage* 40:18+ F '89
ADAMS, CINDY
Bess Myerson: how I survived. il por *Ladies' Home Journal* 106:106-7+ Jl '89
There's Morton Downey sipping champagne from a loafer . . . Tony Danza singing harmony on 59th Street. il *TV Guide* 37:20-2 Je 17-23 '89
ADAMS, DENNIS, 1948-
about
Street scenes. E. Heartney. bibl f il *Art in America* 77:230-7+ Ap '89
ADAMS, HANK MURTA, 1956-
about
Hank Murta Adams/Dorothy Weiss Gallery. C. White. il *American Craft* 49:80-1 O/N '89
ADAMS, HENRY
Thomas Hart Benton [cover story] il pors *USA Today (Periodical)* 118:32-44 N '89
ADAMS, HENRY, 1838-1918
about
American Gothic. A. Kazin. il *The New York Review of Books* 36:45-6 N 23 '89
The seer of Lafayette Square. A. Delbanco. il *The New Republic* 201:32-8 O 16 '89
ADAMS, JAMES RING
The big fix [cover story] il *The American Spectator* 22:21-4 Mr '89
Now it's broke. *The New Republic* 201:16-18 N 13 '89
ADAMS, JILL M.
Paris/London: the chic beat. il *Seventeen* 48:172+ Ap '89
ADAMS, JIM
Picture winter. il *Petersen's Photographic Magazine* 17:16-18+ F '89
ADAMS, JOHN
about
Nixon in China [opera] Reviews
Opera News il 54:20-2 Jl '89. P. J. Smith
ADAMS, JOHN, 1735-1826
about
"An office of unprofitable dignity". J. E. Ferling. il pors *American History Illustrated* 24:12-23+ Mr '89
ADAMS, MARCIA
Apple polishing. il *The New York Times Magazine* p71-2 O 8 '89
Country kitchen. il por *McCall's* 117:120 D '89
Country kitchen. il por *McCall's* 116:104 Ag '89
Golden tomato fritters from an Amish kitchen [excerpt from Cooking from quilt country] il *Redbook* 173:36 Je '89
ADAMS, MARGO
about
Facing the music [cover story] E. M. Swift. il pors *Sports Illustrated* 70:38-40+ Mr 6 '89
ADAMS, MICHAEL
The artist and the businessman. B. E. Johnson. il *Antiques & Collecting Hobbies* 94:44-5+ O '89
ADAMS, NATHAN M.
Greece: sanctuary of international terrorism. il map *Reader's Digest* 134:199-200+ Je '89
The ship that outsailed time. il *Reader's Digest* 135:117-24+ S '89
ADAMS, NICHOLAS
about
Bailout bulls. J. Zweig. il pors *Forbes* 143:167 Ap 3 '89
ADAMS, PATRICIA
Saving forests—with debt. il *World Press Review* 36:47 O '89

ADAMS, PHOEBE
about
Phoebe Adams: Curt Marcus. L. Holst. il *Art News* 88:198 O '89
ADAMS, PHOEBE-LOU
Brief reviews. See issues of The Atlantic
ADAMS, RANDALL DALE
about
'Because I was a nobody'. D. Hill. il pors *TV Guide* 37:20-2 My 20-26 '89
Crossing a line that is not thin at all, Randall Dale Adams wins release from a Texas prison. M. Brower. il pors *People Weekly* 31:155-6 Ap 10 '89
Crossing 'The thin blue line'. M. Lasswell. il por *Rolling Stone* p30 O 19 '89
Department of amplification. M. Singer. *The New Yorker* 65:119-20 Ap 10 '89
A movie for the defense. J. N. Baker. il por *Newsweek* 113:27 Mr 13 '89
No happy ending. J. E. Gallagher. il por *Time* 133:56 Mr 6 '89
Recrossing The thin blue line. M. B. Carlson. il por *Time* 133:23 Ap 3 '89
Why did Randall Adams almost die? F. Bruning. il *Maclean's* 102:9 Mr 27 '89
ADAMS, ROBERT MCCORMICK, 1926-
Smithsonian horizons. See issues of Smithsonian beginning October 1984
ADAMS-ENDER, CLARA
about
Nurse Corps chief. D. M. Cheers. il pors *Ebony* 44:64+ Je '89
ADAMSON, GEORGE
about
Obituary
Newsweek il por 114:32 S 4 '89. C. S. Manegold
People Weekly il pors 32:46-51 S 11 '89. M. Vollers
Time il por 134:21 S 4 '89
ADAMSON, LOUISE
about
One of Atlanta's bravest. P. Yancey. il pors *Christianity Today* 33:12-13 N 17 '89
ADAMSON, ROBERT J.
Home ports. il *House & Garden* 161:60 Je '89
ADAPTATION (BIOLOGY)
Adaptive nature of skeletal design [plasticity to cope with locomotive stress] K. R. Gordon. bibl f il *BioScience* 39:784-90 D '89
A biochemical correlate of the critical period for synaptic modification in the visual cortex. S. M. Dudek and M. F. Bear. bibl f il *Science* 246:673-5 N 3 '89
Biologists disagree over bold signature of nature [species-richness gradient; views of George Stevens] R. Lewin. il *Science* 244:527-8 My 5 '89
Body's thermostat runs hot and cold. il *USA Today (Periodical)* 118:13-14 D '89
Brain changes [area in the brain responsible for sense of touch shows adaptability to injury; work of Michael Merzenich] J. Rubin. *Psychology Today* 23:26 Mr '89
Couch potatoes' half-baked future [inactivity affects muscle adaptability; research by Gary C. Sieck] il *USA Today (Periodical)* 117:13 Ap '89
The diving seal [harbor seals; research by Ronald W. Millard] S. Kleene. bibl il *Sea Frontiers* 35:370-4 N/D '89
Inescapable versus escapable shock modulates long-term potentiation in the rat hippocampus [evidence that controllability modulates plasticity] T. J. Shors and others. bibl f il *Science* 244:224-6 Ap 14 '89
The return of the mind [M. Diamond's theory that brain's plasticity allows it to keep growing into old age] S. Blakeslee. il por *American Health* 8:94-6 Mr '89
ADAPTATIONS, MOTION PICTURE *See* Motion picture adaptations
ADAPTATIONS, TELEVISION *See* Television adaptations
ADAPTATIONS, THEATRICAL *See* Theatrical adaptations
ADDICTION RESEARCH AND TREATMENT CORPORATION
Medic with a mission [B. Primm] R. E. McKinney. il pors *Ebony* 44:134 Ag '89
ADDICTIVE BEHAVIOR
Addiction chic: are we hooked on being hooked? M. Dowd. *Mademoiselle* 95:216-17+ O '89
Breaking the patterns that lead to relapse. E. Chiauzzi. il *Psychology Today* 23:18-19 D '89
No-fault psychology. C. Tavris. *Vogue* 179:116 Ja '89
Roots of addiction [cover story] D. Gelman. il *Newsweek* 113:52-7 F 20 '89
The struggle of Kitty Dukakis. A. Toufexis. il por *Time* 133:79 F 20 '89
Bibliography
On the road to recovery with Prentice Hall, Ballantine et al. J. Crichton. il *Publishers Weekly* 236:52-3 N 3 '89
ADDICTS, DRUG *See* Drug abuse
ADDITIONS, HOUSE *See* Houses, Remodeled
ADDITIVES, FOOD *See* Food additives
ADDRESS BOOKS
Address Book Plus [mailing list manager] B. Gingher. il *Compute!* 11:76-7 My '89

ADDRESS BOOKS—*cont.*
Addressing a common problem [Address Book Plus version B.00; mailing list manager] B. Krasnoff. il *Personal Computing* 13:204+ Ap '89

ADEL ROOTSTEIN INC.
Adel Rootstein knows the fanciest dummies in fashion. H. Shapiro. il pors *People Weekly* 32:123-4 S 18 '89

ADELMAN, KENNETH L.
Arms control: games Soviets play. *Reader's Digest* 134:65-9 Mr '89
Fact and fiction on the nuclear age. *National Review* 41:38-40+ F 24 '89
about
West meets East. il pors *Esquire* 111:62-5 Ja '89

ADELMANN VON ADELMANNSFELDEN, RAINER RENE
Count Dracula makes an offer [letter sent to bankrupt persons offering to buy one of their kidneys in West Germany]; tr. by Elliott Rabin. *Harper's* 278:23-4 Mr '89

ADELSHEIM, DAVID
about
The fruit of vine. M. Barrier. il por *Nation's Business* 77:14+ S '89

ADELSHEIM VINEYARD
The fruit of vine. M. Barrier. il por *Nation's Business* 77:14+ S '89

ADELSON, JOSEPH
Drugs and youth [cover story] *Commentary* 87:24-8 My '89

ADENOSINE DEAMINASE DEFICIENCY DISORDER
Therapy
ADA deficiency: a prime candidate. B. J. Culliton. il *Science* 246:751 N 10 '89

ADENOSINE MONOPHOSPHATE
Blood cells yield cystic fibrosis clues [cyclic adenosine monophosphate-regulated chloride channel in lymphocytes; research by Jennifer H. Chen and others] *Science News* 135:110 F 18 '89
A cAMP-regulated chloride channel in lymphocytes that is affected in cystic fibrosis. J. H. Chen and others. bibl f il *Science* 243:657-60 F 3 '89
Is regulation of a chloride channel in lymphocytes affected in cystic fibrosis? [discussion of February 3, 1989 article, A cAMP-regulated chloride channel in lymphocytes that is affected in cystic fibrosis] J. H. Chen and others. *Science* 246:1049-50 N 24 '89
Role of prostaglandins and cAMP in the secretory effects of cholera toxin. J. W. Peterson and L. G. Ochoa. bibl f il *Science* 245:857-9 Ag 25 '89

ADENOSINE TRIPHOSPHATASE
Osteoclastic bone resorption by a polarized vacuolar proton pump. H. C. Blair and others. bibl f il *Science* 245:855-7 Ag 25 '89

ADENOSINE TRIPHOSPHATE
Direct measurements of sliding between outer doublet microtubules in swimming sperm flagella [sea urchins] C. J. Brokaw. bibl f il *Science* 243:1593-6 Mr 24 '89
Hyperpolarizing vasodilators activate ATP-sensitive K$^+$ channels in arterial smooth muscle. N. B. Standen and others. bibl f il *Science* 245:177-80 Jl 14 '89

ADENOVIRUSES *See* Viruses

ADENYLATE CYCLASE
Adenylyl cyclase amino acid sequence: possible channel- or transporter-like structure. J. Krupinski and others. bibl f il *Science* 244:1558-64 Je 30 '89
Autonomic regulation of a chloride current in heart. R. D. Harvey and J. R. Hume. bibl f il *Science* 244:983-5 My 26 '89
G$_{olf}$: an olfactory neuron specific-G protein involved in odorant signal transduction. D. T. Jones and R. R. Reed. bibl f il *Science* 244:790-5 My 19 '89
Splice variants of the α subunit of the G protein G$_S$ activate both adenylyl cyclase and calcium channels. R. Mattera and others. bibl f il *Science* 243:804-7 F 10 '89

ADENYLYL CYCLASE *See* Adenylate cyclase

ADEPTS (ACOUSTIC DIRECTED-ENERGY PULSE TRAINS) *See* Pulse techniques (Electronics)

ADEYEMO, TOKUNBOH
about
The church in Africa [interview] il por *Christianity Today* 33:52-3 O 20 '89

ADHESION
Endothelial interleukin-8: a novel inhibitor of leukocyte-endothelial interactions. M. A. Gimbrone and others. bibl f il *Science* 246:1601-3 D 22 '89
Endothelial leukocyte adhesion molecule 1: an inducible receptor for neutrophils related to complement regulatory proteins and lectins. M. P. Bevilacqua and others. bibl f il *Science* 243:1160-5 Mr 3 '89
Fusion factor in AIDS cells identified [role of leukocyte adhesion receptor LFA-1 in syncytium formation; research by James E. K. Hildreth and Rimas J. Orentas] *Science News* 135:366 Je 10 '89
An inducible endothelial cell surface glycoprotein mediates melanoma adhesion. G. E. Rice and M. P. Bevilacqua. bibl f il *Science* 246:1303-6 D 8 '89
Involvement of a leukocyte adhesion receptor (LFA-1) in HIV-induced syncytium formation. J. E. K. Hildreth and R. J. Orentas. bibl f il *Science* 244:1075-8 Je 2 '89

Molecular mechanisms and forces involved in the adhesion and fusion of amphiphilic bilayers. C. A. Helm and others. bibl f il *Science* 246:919-22 N 17 '89
Neural cadherin: role in selective cell-cell adhesion. S. Miyatani and others. bibl f il *Science* 245:631-5 Ag 11 '89
Neutrophil Mac-1 and MEL-14 adhesion proteins inversely regulated by chemotactic factors. T. K. Kishimoto and others. bibl f il *Science* 245:1238-41 S 15 '89
New family of adhesion proteins discovered. J. L. Marx. *Science* 243:1144 Mr 3 '89
Preventing postsurgical tissue 'gluing' [use of hyaluronic coatings; work of Eugene P. Goldberg] *Science News* 136:222 S 30 '89
Topobiology [role of cell adhesion molecules in molecular embryology] G. M. Edelman. bibl il *Scientific American* 260:76-8+ My '89

ADHESIVES
See also
Loctite Corp.
Household glues. il *Consumer Reports* 54:340-4 D '89
Secrets of the superglues. A. J. Hand. il *Popular Science* 234:80-3+ F '89

ADIPOCYTES *See* Cells

ADIPSIN
Adipsin and complement factor D activity: an immune-related defect in obesity. B. S. Rosen and others. bibl f il *Science* 244:1483-7 Je 23 '89

ADIRONDACK CHAIRS *See* Chairs

ADIRONDACK FOREST PRESERVE (N.Y.)
Wilderness: New York sets a global stage. G. D. Davis. il pors *The Conservationist* 44:2-9+ N/D '89

ADIRONDACK LAKES *See* Lakes—New York (State)

ADIRONDACK MOUNTAINS (N.Y.)
See also
College of Environmental Science and Forestry. Adirondack Wildlife Program
Adventures of a reluctant Forty-sixer [hiking in the Adirondacks] L. P. Fortin. il *The Conservationist* 44:10-15 N/D '89

Social history
One hundred years in the Adirondack wilderness [North Woods Club] L. F. Wilson. il *The Conservationist* 43:40-5 My/Je '89

ADIRONDACK PARK (N.Y.)
The Adirondacks in microcosm [visitor interpretive centers] M. Storey. il *The Conservationist* 43:14-19 My/Je '89
For sale [cover story] J. H. Kunstler. il *The New York Times Magazine* p22-5+ Je 18 '89
Studying the big woods. P. Byrnes. *Wilderness* 53:6+ Wint '89
A wild island of hope. J. G. Mitchell. il *Wilderness* 53:42-51 Fall '89

ADIRONDACK WILDLIFE PROGRAM *See* College of Environmental Science and Forestry. Adirondack Wildlife Program

ADJANI, ISABELLE
about
Adjani anew. G. Howell. il pors *Vogue* 179:342-9+ D '89
Art lovers. A.-E. Moutet. il pors *Vogue* 179:498-503+ Mr '89

ADJUSTABLE RATE MORTGAGES *See* Mortgages

ADJUSTERS, INSURANCE *See* Insurance adjusters

ADJUSTMENT (PSYCHOLOGY)
See also
Maturity
Resilience (Psychology)
Security and insecurity (Psychology)

ADLER, BILL
(jt. auth) See Richardson, Peggy A., and Adler, Bill

ADLER, BILL, 1929-
What is love? il *McCall's* 116:106 F '89

ADLER, DICK, 1937-
(ed) See Brown, Edmund G., 1905-. Private mercy

ADLER, HERBERT
about
Chacun à son pocketbook. C. Brown. il pors *Forbes* 144:144-5 D 25 '89

ADLER, MORTIMER JEROME, 1902-
about
The war of the Great books. B. McArthur. il *American Heritage* 40:57-8+ F '89

ADLER, RUBEN, AND HATLEE, MICHAEL
Plasticity and differentiation of embryonic retinal cells after terminal mitosis. bibl f il *Science* 243:391-3 Ja 20 '89

ADLER, STELLA
about
Stella Adler. P. Brock. il pors *People Weekly* 32:66-8+ Jl 17 '89

ADLER, WILLIAM M.
The Bear trap. il por *Esquire* 112:204-6+ S '89

ADLER (ARTHUR A.) (FIRM) *See* Arthur A. Adler (Firm)

ADLER & SHAYKIN
Wanted: ailing companies. Call: Leonard Shaykin. P. Finch. il por *Business Week* p75+ F 27 '89

ADLER PLANETARIUM
"Seeing the universe". R. T. Fienberg. il *Sky and Telescope* 78:257 S '89

ADLON, PERCY
about
Bagdad Cafe [film] Reviews
  Video il 12:61-2 F '89. M. Coyle
ADMINISTRATIVE LAW
  See also
  Regulatory agencies
ADMINISTRATIVE REMEDIES
  See also
  Ombudsman
ADMIRALS
  See also
  Halsey, William Frederick, 1882-1959
ADMISSION TO COLLEGE *See* Colleges and universities—Admission
ADMISSION TO HIGH SCHOOL *See* High schools—Admission
ADOBE BUILDINGS
Architectural digest visits: Charles Bronson and Jill Ireland [Malibu adobe decorated by King Zimmerman] J. Ireland. il por *Architectural Digest* 46:98-103+ Jl '89
Building with mud signifies success in the Southwest. D. J. Preston. il *Smithsonian* 20:144-8+ N '89
Contemporary Southwest [Santa Fe adobe home of S. S. Lewis] R. Morris. il *Architectural Digest* 46:148-55 Ap '89
Entire cities built of mud. il *UN Chronicle* 26:45 Je '89
The Santa Fe adobe. il *Esquire* 112:80 D '89
ADOBE SYSTEMS INC.
Adobe's vision for PostScript. M. Antonoff. il *Personal Computing* 13:265-6 Ap '89
A man of characters [J. Warnock] M. Antonoff. por *Personal Computing* 13:86 Jl '89
ADOLESCENCE
  See also
  Black youth
  High school students
  Peer groups
  Problem children
  Puberty
  Young men
  Young women
  Youth
  Youth counseling
As they grow/11 through 13. J. P. Comer. See issues of Parents
As they grow/14 through 18. D. Elkind. See issues of Parents beginning January 1987
Providing a structure for adolescent development. F. A. J. Ianni. bibl f il *Phi Delta Kappan* 70:673-82 My '89
Relating. A. Wood. See issues of Seventeen
Surviving family blues [ability of teens to cope with depressed parents; research by William R. Beardslee and Dona Podorefsky] J. Folkenberg. *American Health* 8:119 Mr '89
What happens when markers of maturity disappear? D. Elkind. *The Education Digest* 54:34-6 Ja '89
Young beyond their years [postponing move into adulthood] K. L. Woodward. il *Newsweek* 114 Special Issue:54-5+ Wint '89/Spr '90
Youth of today [special issue] il *World Health* p3-29 Mr '89
ADOLESCENT DRINKING *See* Alcohol and youth
ADOLESCENT LITERATURE *See* Young adults' literature
ADOLESCENT MEDICAL CARE *See* Youth—Medical care
ADOLESCENT PSYCHIATRY
Committed youth. N. Darnton. il *Newsweek* 114:66-9+ Jl 31 '89
Research on child and adolescent mental disorders. B. A. Hamburg. *Science* 246:738 N 10 '89
ADOLESCENT RUNAWAYS *See* Runaways
ADOLESCENT SUICIDE *See* Suicide
ADOLFO, 1933-
about
Adolfo in New York. B. Morris. il por *Architectural Digest* 46:132-7 S '89
ADOLPH COORS CO.
Coors 'Inside black America' begins 5th broadcasting year. il *Jet* 75:9 Ja 30 '89
Coors may take a gulp of a rival brew [Stroh Brewery] S. D. Atchison. il *Business Week* p70 Ag 21 '89
One last call for fading beer brands [S&P launches antitrust suit against Adolph Coors Co.'s acquisition of Stroh Brewery] L. Armstrong. il *Business Week* p68 O 16 '89
The "S" factor [surprises tied to stock performance] K. L. Fisher. il *Forbes* 144:116 Ag 21 '89
ADOPT-A-STREAM FOUNDATION
Adopt-a-Stream. J. Miller. il *Harper's Bazaar* 122:64-5 Ja '89
ADOPTION AND ADOPTED CHILDREN
Adoption. P. Godwin. il pors *Better Homes and Gardens* 67:44+ My '89
The 'adoption alternative' [adoption recommended to federal workers] B. Kantrowitz. il *Newsweek* 114:84 N 20 '89
Adoption in America [study by the Child Welfare League of America] il *Children Today* 18:3-4 My/Je '89
Alabama police investigate "gift babies" [Unification Church members give infants to Mobile, Ala. families] *Christianity Today* 33:43-4 Mr 17 '89

An All-star father [baseball player T. Burke adopts special needs, Guatemalan child] R. Demak. il pors *Sports Illustrated* 71:69 Jl 24 '89
All-star pitcher Tim Burke goes home a winner with a baby boy [adopts special needs, Guatemalan child] il pors *People Weekly* 32:82-3 Ag 7 '89
Avenging years of sexual abuse, twins take their adoptive father to court [case of R. and T. Royce] C. McCall. il pors *People Weekly* 31:54-6+ Je 26 '89
The baby chase [cover story; special section] il *Time* 134:86-92+ O 9 '89
The blood-brain barrier [study of adoptees and intelligence by David W. Fulker and John C. DeFries] K. Wright. il *Scientific American* 260:27+ Mr '89
Breaking in to family life [B. Reynolds and L. Anderson with adopted son] il pors *People Weekly* 32:98-9+ N 6 '89
Charlie Smith's second chance [adoption of child from Japanese orphanage] C. Phillips. il *Reader's Digest* 135:29-30+ N '89
Court backs two-mom family [lesbians recognized as legal parents in Washington State] K. Monagle. il *Ms.* 18:69 O '89
Defying simple slogans: why 'adoption, not abortion' won't work. B. Kantrowitz. il *Newsweek* 113:36 My 1 '89
Disclosing adoption. C. Hoffman-Riem. *Society* 26:26-31 My/Je '89
From infertility to adoption. L. Grossman. il *Parents* 64:96+ Mr '89
"God made you little and special" [adoption of dwarfs Davina and Matt Wilson]; ed. by Rebecca Nappi. B. Wilson. il *Redbook* 173:84+ O '89
Little girl lost [wondering what happened to the sister given up for adoption] B. E. Hall. por *Essence* 20:12 O '89
Nobody's children [special needs adoption] R. Lacayo. il *Time* 134:91-2+ O 9 '89
'One Church, One Child' seeks homes for infants [black infants] il *Jet* 75:36 F 20 '89
Television distorts perceptions of adoption; U.S. adoption fails both childless couples and adoptable children; Older-child adoptions successful. *Society* 26:2-4 S/O '89
Thank you, Melissa [open adoption] D. Gage. il pors *Good Housekeeping* 209:84+ O '89
Travis comes home [T. Smigiel, child who survived illegal adoption by Joel Steinberg] M. Jacobbi. il pors *Good Housekeeping* 209:103+ Jl '89
The unhappy politics of interracial adoption. B. Brophy. il *U.S. News & World Report* 107:72+ N 13 '89
"We're afraid of our son" [mentally ill adoptee was abused by natural parents] B. Harlow. il pors *Ladies' Home Journal* 106:18+ Mr '89
With two houses and a big heart, Generations star Taurean Blacque becomes a single father to nine. C. Sanz. il pors *People Weekly* 32:101-2+ O 9 '89
ADRENAL GLANDS
  See also
  Chromaffin cells
      Surgery
Selective loss of hippocampal granule cells in the mature rat brain after adrenalectomy. R. Sloviter and others. bibl f il *Science* 243:535-8 Ja 27 '89
      Transplantation
Brain repair [Parkinson's disease] A. Hollister. il *Life* 12:76-80+ My '89
New trial evaluates Parkinsonian therapy. R. Lewin. *Science* 243:892 F 17 '89
Transplants offer promise [adrenal medulla transplants as treatment for Parkinson's disease] *USA Today (Periodical)* 118:11-12 O '89
ADRENALECTOMY *See* Adrenal glands—Surgery
ADRENERGIC BLOCKING AGENTS
  See also
  Propranolol
Leaner and meatier [use of beta agonists for hogs and beef] J. R. Borcherding and C. Peterson, Jr. il *Successful Farming* 87:40 D '89
ADRENERGIC RECEPTORS *See* Chemoreceptors
ADRIENNE (NEW YORK, N.Y.: RESTAURANT) *See* New York (N.Y.)—Restaurants, nightclubs, bars, etc.
ADRS *See* American depositary receipts
ADS *See* Advertising
ADSORPTION
Atomic resolution imaging of adsorbates on metal surfaces in air: iodine adsorption on pt(111) [use of scanning tunneling microscope] B. C. Schardt and others. bibl f il *Science* 243:1050-3 F 24 '89
Orthogonal self-assembled monolayers: alkanethiols on gold and alkane carboxylic acids on alumina. P. E. Laibinis and others. bibl f il *Science* 245:845-7 Ag 25 '89
Ripples in a crystalline copper bed [chemisorption process; research by Young Kuk] I. Peterson. *Science News* 135:62 Ja 28 '89
ADULT-CHILD RELATIONSHIP *See* Child-adult relationship
ADULT CHILDREN AND PARENTS *See* Parent-child relationship

ADULT COMMUNITIES *See* Retirement communities
ADULT EDUCATION
> *See also*
> Aged—Education
> Grandparent education
> Labor—Education
> Learning Alliance
> Literacy education
> Refugees—Education
> University extension
> Veterans—Education

Adult education [courses in New York City] M. W. Robbins. il *New York* 22:50-2+ Ag 14 '89
The importance of community-based art education programs for adults. M. Y. Roberts. bibl f *Design for Arts in Education* 90:43-8 Jl/Ag '89
Students come of age [midlife college students; case of R. Wallick] il por *New Choices for the Best Years* 29:16 O '89
ADULT-YOUTH RELATIONSHIP *See* Youth-adult relationship
ADULTERY
> *See also*
> WATCH (Organization)

Abernathy takes a cheap shot [revelations about M. L. King] J. M. Wall. por *The Christian Century* 106:971-2 N 1 '89
A bitter battle erupts over the last hours of Martin Luther King [R. Abernathy supports longstanding rumors about sexual indiscretions] J. S. Kunen. il pors *People Weekly* 32:40-2 O 30 '89
Can men be faithful? M. Marriott. il *Essence* 20:61-2+ N '89
Eyewitness statements on King's death dispute Abernathy's accounts. il por *Jet* 77:57-9 N 6 '89
A fight among Dr. King's faithful [revelations by R. Abernathy] il por *Newsweek* 114:31 O 23 '89
His unfaithful heart. il *Glamour* 87:161-2 S '89
"I had an affair with the teenager next door". M. D. Rosen. il *Ladies' Home Journal* 106:12+ Mr '89
Infidelity. M. Mercer. il *New Choices for the Best Years* 29:58-62 Je '89
On the humanity of saints [R. D. Abernathy's revelations about M. L. King] P. Marin. il *The Nation* 249:784-6 D 25 '89
Secrets of staying together [condensed from Private lies] F. S. Pittman. il *Reader's Digest* 134:151-4 Mr '89
Sexual charges and Martin Luther King [book by R. D. Abernathy] F. Bruning. il *Maclean's* 102:13 N 6 '89
Tattletale memoir [R. D. Abernathy's account of M. L. King's philandering] por *Time* 134:42 O 23 '89
A therapist who's been there urges sympathy for the 'other woman' [interview with J. Bitner] S. Adelson. il pors *People Weekly* 32:116+ O 30 '89
The way we are [wife punishes husband after his infidelity] L. Wyse. il *Good Housekeeping* 209:288 O '89
Would you love a married man?:
No way! J. Sullivan. *Essence* 20:82+ S '89
Why not? C. Patterson. *Essence* 20:83-4+ S '89
ADULTERY IN TELEVISION
The bittersweet truth about love triangles [Single women, married men] J. Lazar. il por *TV Guide* 37:9 O 21-27 '89
ADULTERY IN THE BIBLE
Redeemer [woman caught in adultery] P. J. Ryan. il *America* 160:207 Mr 4 '89
ADULTHOOD *See* Maturity
ADULTS AND CHILDREN *See* Child-adult relationship
ADULTS AND YOUTH *See* Youth-adult relationship
ADULYADEJ, BHUMIBOL *See* Bhumibol Adulyadej, King of Thailand
ADVANCE DISPLAY TECHNOLOGIES INC.
Severed heads and wasted resources [Fibermedia charged with stealing trade secrets from Advance Display Technologies Inc.] G. F. Gilder. il *Forbes* 143:45-6+ Je 26 '89
ADVANCED MEDIUM-RANGE AIR-TO-AIR MISSILES *See* Guided missiles—Launching from airplanes
ADVANCED PRODUCTS & TECHNOLOGIES (FIRM)
The accidental tourist [S. A. Rondel's Voice computer] M. Barrier. il por *Nation's Business* 77:78 Ap '89
Instant spoken translation [S. A. Rondel's Voice computer] W. J. Hawkins. il por *Popular Science* 234:78+ My '89
On the front lines in the trade war. S. A. Rondel. il *Nation's Business* 77:10 Je '89
ADVANCED X-RAY ASTROPHYSICS FACILITY *See* Artificial satellites—Astronomical use
ADVENT
> *See also*
> Second Advent

Cataclysms. P. J. Ryan. il *America* 161:387 N 25 '89
A child shall lead us. L. O. Sanneh. *The Christian Century* 106:1146 D 6 '89
Dreams and letting God be God. L. O. Sanneh. *The Christian Century* 106:1195 D 20-27 '89
Hope. P. J. Ryan. il *America* 161:411 D 2 '89
More than a prophet. P. J. Ryan. *America* 161:435 D 9 '89

More than a prophetess. P. J. Ryan. il *America* 161:435 D 9 '89
The spirituality of Advent. J. M. Staudenmaier. *America* 161:403 D 2 '89
Waiting on God. L. O. Sanneh. *The Christian Century* 106:1170 D 13 '89
Wrestling with Advent [film Hail Mary] J. K. Larson. *The Christian Century* 106:1166-8 D 13 '89
ADVENT CALENDARS *See* Calendars
ADVENTURE AND ADVENTURERS
> *See also*
> Voyages
> Voyages around the world

The joy of risk. J. Etra. *Harper's Bazaar* 122:162-3+ My '89
On the royal road to adventures with 'Daring Dick' [R. Halliburton] D. M. Schwartz. il pors *Smithsonian* 19:159-60+ Mr '89
ADVENTURE STORIES
> *See also*
> Detective and mystery stories
> Publishers and publishing—Adventure stories
> Western stories

ADVENTURE VACATIONS *See* Vacations
ADVENTURE VIDEO GAMES *See* Video games
THE ADVENTURES OF BARON MUNCHAUSEN [film] *See* Motion picture reviews—Single works
ADVERSE POSSESSION
This land is my land . . . or is it? D. Fanning. il *Forbes* 143:62 Ja 23 '89
ADVERTISEMENTS *See* Advertising
ADVERTISING
> *See also*
> Advocacy advertising
> Aged in advertising
> Agricultural industries—Advertising
> Airlines—Advertising
> Amusement parks—Advertising
> Astronomical equipment—Advertising
> Australia in advertising
> Automobile dealers—Advertising
> Automobile industry—Advertising
> Automobiles—Leasing and renting—Advertising
> Baldness remedies—Advertising
> Banks and banking—Advertising
> Bathroom fixtures—Advertising
> Beauty shops—Advertising
> Berlin Wall, 1961-1989, in advertising
> Blacks in advertising
> Books—Advertising
> Brewing industry—Advertising
> Brokers—Advertising
> Cable television advertising
> Cereal foods—Advertising
> Chewing gum—Advertising
> Cigarette industry—Advertising
> Clothing industry—Advertising
> Coffee industry—Advertising
> Computer industry—Advertising
> Condoms—Advertising
> Cosmetics industry—Advertising
> Cycling in advertising
> Executives in advertising
> Family corporations—Advertising
> Fast food restaurants—Advertising
> Firearms industry—Advertising
> Food in advertising
> Food industry—Advertising
> Hosiery industry—Advertising
> Infant formula industry—Advertising
> Investment trusts—Advertising
> Investments—Advertising
> Jelly, jam, etc.—Advertising
> Lawyers—Advertising
> Laxatives—Advertising
> Lesbianism in advertising
> Liquor industry—Advertising
> Men in advertising
> Minorities in advertising
> Mortgages—Advertising
> Motion picture industry—Advertising
> Music in advertising
> Nostalgia in advertising
> Nuclear industry—Advertising
> Opera in advertising
> Perfume industry—Advertising
> Physicians—Advertising
> Potatoes—Advertising
> Premiums
> Presidents in advertising
> Public relations
> Razors—Advertising
> Regional advertising
> Retail trade—Advertising
> Samples (Merchandising)
> Sex discrimination in advertising
> Sex in advertising
> Shoe industry—Advertising

ADVERTISING—See also—*cont.*
  Silver—Advertising
  Soft drink industry—Advertising
  Space colonies—Advertising
  Television advertising
  Television industry—Advertising
  Video equipment—Advertising
  Video stores—Advertising
  Women in advertising
The future of advertising [address, May 9, 1989] R. D. O'Connor. *Vital Speeches of the Day* 55:583-7 Jl 15 '89
It's a whole nuevo mundo out there [Hispanic market] E. Pomice. il *U.S. News & World Report* 106:45-6 My 15 '89
On Madison Avenue. B. Kanner. See issues of New York
Power to the consumer. C. Warden. *Consumers' Research Magazine* 72:19 Je '89
'Se habla español'. il *U.S. News & World Report* 106:15-16 Mr 6 '89
Selling it. See issues of Consumer Reports
Toll-free tech. M. Wilkins and J. Barth. il *Rolling Stone* p120 Je 15 '89
Two different animals: brand awareness & corporate image [interview with M. S. Forbes] *Forbes* 143:20 Mr 6 '89

Anecdotes, facetiae, satire, etc.
Not available in any store. R. Rosen. il *New York* 22:42-6 N 20 '89

Awards
The best of advertising [1988] il *Business Week* p127 Ja 9 '89

Anecdotes, facetiae, satire, etc.
Madison Ave.: winners and sinners of 1989. B. Kanner. il *New York* 22:25-6+ D 25 '89-Ja 1 '90

Laws and regulations
See also
  Television advertising—Laws and regulations
A comeback may be ahead for Brand X [suing over ads that name rivals made easier due to changes in trademark statute] M. Galen. il *Business Week* p35 D 4 '89
The neo-prohibitionists [address, February 8, 1989] K. Roman. *Vital Speeches of the Day* 55:441-4 My 1 '89

Moral and religious aspects
See also
  Religious advertising

Prize contests
See Prize contests

Psychological aspects
Desperately seeking "Jeepness". J. Levine. il *Forbes* 143:134+ My 15 '89
From the subliminal to the ridiculous. B. Kanner. il *New York* 22:18+ D 4 '89
Mind games [cover story] B. Kanner. il *New York* 22:34-40 My 8 '89
Psyching out consumers. A. Miller and D. Tsiantar. il *Newsweek* 113:46-7 F 27 '89
Selling feelings [Canada] P. Chisholm. il *Maclean's* 102:30-1 F 27 '89

Taxation
Taxation of advertising: a violation of free speech? W. Murray. il *USA Today (Periodical)* 117:23-4 Mr '89

Testimonials
The Age of Andre: a marketing empire is born [tennis player A. Agassi's endorsement deals] R. Wetzsteon. il pors *Sport (New York, N.Y.)* 80:88+ Je '89
Blacks again dominate top marketing Q-ratings [sports stars] il *Jet* 76:50 My 22 '89
Can world's greatest woman athlete cash in on Olympic gold? [J. Joyner-Kersee] il pors *Ebony* 44:96+ Ap '89
Celebrity scents. il *Vogue* 179:352 S '89
Coming soon to a commercial near you [endorsement potential of various athletes; views of Marty Blackman] G. Castle. il *Sport (New York, N.Y.)* 80:13 S '89
Entertainer Bill Cosby is favorite celebrity endorser. il por *Jet* 77:22 N 6 '89
Faces that can sell a thousand computers [celebrity spokespersons] G. Keizer. il *Compute!* 11:4 Mr '89
The hero as huckster [Super Bowl MVP J. Rice complains of being slighted by press] R. Fimrite. por *Sports Illustrated* 70:92 F 13 '89
It's an ad, ad, ad . . . [company logos at sports events] il *Sports Illustrated* 71:22 D 4 '89
A lot of McMoney at stake [decrease in endorsement demand for quarterback J. McMahon] G. Castle. il *Sport (New York, N.Y.)* 80:13 Ag '89
Mister spokesman [T. O'Neill] B. Kanner. il pors *New York* 22:20+ N 6 '89
Murphy does $multimillion car commercials in Japan [Eddie Murphy] por *Jet* 77:36 O 23 '89
Nonalcoholic sports [beer commercials on TV] L. Cryderman. *Christianity Today* 33:15 S 22 '89
Now pitching for Team Xerox . . . [endorsement market for athletes] E. Comte. il *Sport (New York, N.Y.)* 80:92 Je '89
One year in the life . . . [tennis equipment endorsements and prize money] D. Goldie. il por *World Tennis* 36:24+ Ap '89
Singer Tina Turner completes Chrysler ads. il pors *Jet* 76:57 S 18 '89

The smell of success [celebrity perfumes] R. Dolphin. il *Maclean's* 102:46 Mr 6 '89
The spoils of victory [F. Griffith Joyner retires from track to pursue business opportunities] K. Moore. il pors *Sports Illustrated* 70:50-3+ Ap 10 '89
Testimonials from a less suspicious era [politicians] J. Adler. il por *Newsweek* 113:20 Je 12 '89
They are hip, hot—and dead [late celebrities used in advertising] J. Hammer and K. Springen. il *Newsweek* 114:34 Jl 10 '89
Tyson pockets $150,000 for 'Lean on me' plug. por *Jet* 75:48 Mr 20 '89
Warning: sports stars may be hazardous to your health [cigarette ads; cover story] J. DeParle. il *The Washington Monthly* 21:34-44+ S '89
Who's got clout—and who's out [athletes] H. Polskin. il *TV Guide* 37:22 F 25-Mr 3 '89

Canada
Selling feelings. P. Chisholm. il *Maclean's* 102:30-1 F 27 '89

Soviet Union
Madison Avenue, Moscow style. il *U.S. News & World Report* 106:14 Ja 16 '89

ADVERTISING, CLASSIFIED
See also
  Personals
Cable closes in on the classifieds [NuCable Resources] J. Loftus. il por *Channels (New York, N.Y.: 1986)* 9:52-4 Mr '89
The truth behind get-rich-quick ads [business opportunity classifieds] E. King. il *Home Office Computing* 7:61-2 N '89
Wanted: touring companion [bicycle trip partners] S. Martin. il *Bicycling* 30:32-4+ Ag '89
War is swell? [Soldier of fortune's classifieds held accountable in murder cases] J. Zweig and P. Klebnikov. il por *Forbes* 144:223 S 18 '89

ADVERTISING, DIRECT MAIL
See also
  Advertising, Political
  Advo-System, Inc.
  Blue Chip Marketing Group
  Catalogs, Commercial
  Mailing lists
"Fax unto others as you would have them fax unto you" [junk fax] S. Harvey. il *Home Office Computing* 7:14 My '89
Junk fax. il *Changing Times* 43:58 O '89
Taking a flyer on direct mail [D. Carmel's plans for business aimed at aged] K. H. Hammonds. il por *Business Week* p41 Jl 24 '89
Tea, sympathy and direct mail [Marriott's marketing of lifecare facilities] J. Novack. il *Forbes* 144:210-11 S 18 '89
The technological fax of life [junk fax mail legislation] il *U.S. News & World Report* 106:14 Je 5 '89
Use the mail to build your business [special section] L. Arden. il *Home Office Computing* 7:49-55 Mr '89
What sort of car-rt-sort am I? [junk mail] E. Larson. il *Harper's* 279:64-9 Jl '89

ADVERTISING, GOVERNMENT *See* Government publicity

ADVERTISING, MAGAZINE
See also
  Personals
Alternative currents. *U.S. News & World Report* 106:54 F 20 '89
Punitive taxation of science and engineering. P. H. Abelson. *Science* 243:1417 Mr 17 '89

ADVERTISING, NEWSPAPER
See also
  Advertising, Classified
  Personals
As price tags shrink, so will the daily newspaper [retail ads] W. Konrad. il *Business Week* p44 Jl 3 '89
Citizen Kane meets Adam Smith [cover story] S. N. Chakravarty. il *Forbes* 143:82-5 F 20 '89
Knocking newspapers [WVEC's campaign for advertising dollar in Norfolk, Va.] A. Snyder. il *Channels (New York, N.Y.: 1986)* 9:32-3 F '89

ADVERTISING, OUTDOOR
See also
  Airships in advertising
  Billboards

ADVERTISING, POLITICAL
Down the tube [presidential campaign] A. Ferguson. *The American Spectator* 22:49 Ap '89
"Even the TV people don't understand" [Ripon College conference on 1988 presidential campaign] T. H. Stahel. *America* 161:354-5 N 18 '89
Fellow Republicans [Progressive readers receive fund raising letters from Republican Party] E. Knoll. *The Progressive* 53:4 D '89
Political quick-step [TV marketers using audience research tactics developed by political campaigns] M. Couzens. il *Channels (New York, N.Y.)* 9:26 F '89
The pollution of politics [negative ads] G. F. Will. il *Newsweek* 114:92 N 6 '89

ADVERTISING, POLITICAL—*cont.*

Reactionaries' reaction [collapse of R. Viguerie's direct mail business] A. P. Crawford. il *The Nation* 248:231+ F 20 '89

Unanswered letters [Progressive editor receives fund raising letter] E. Knoll. *The Progressive* 53:4 N '89

Chile

A clown—and an anchorman—take on a dictator [TV ads] D. Marash. il *TV Guide* 37:28 F 25-Mr 3 '89

ADVERTISING, PUBLIC SERVICE

'Cosby' kid releases safe sex campaign spots [M.-J. Warner] il por *Jet* 75:18 Mr 6 '89

Raise the halo high. D. Bollier. il *Channels (New York, N.Y.: 1986)* 9:32-4+ Ap '89

With a little help from my TV [Fox Television's health-oriented campaign called Life: be in it] M. Edelston. il *American Health* 8:38 Je '89

ADVERTISING, RELIGIOUS *See* Religious advertising

ADVERTISING AGENCIES

See also

Bronner Slosberg Associates
D'Arcy Masius Benton & Bowles, Inc.
Della Femina, McNamee WCRS
East Coast Media (Firm)
Fallon McElligott (Firm)
Foote, Cone & Belding Communications, Inc.
Franklin Spier Inc.
Goldsmith/Jeffrey (Firm)
Grey Advertising Inc.
Hill, Holliday, Connors, Cosmopulos Inc.
J. Walter Thompson Company
Kirshenbaum & Bond
Lowe Tucker Metcalf (Firm)
Messner Vetere Berger Carey Schmetter (Firm)
Ogilvy Group Inc.
Tarlow Advertising
Vitt Media International, Inc.
Young & Rubicam Inc.

Acquisitions and mergers

The LBO sails down Madison Avenue. T. Mason and others. il *Business Week* p69+ S 18 '89

International aspects

Brits buy up the ad business [WPP Group and Saatchi & Saatchi; cover story] R. Rothenberg. il por *The New York Times Magazine* p14-19+ Jl 2 '89

Confessions of an advertising man [WPP's M. Sorrell negotiates takeover of Ogilvy] R. I. Kirkland, Jr. il por *Fortune* 119:131-2 Je 5 '89

The 'fax attack' that has Ogilvy fuming [WPP Group plc bids for Ogilvy Group] W. Konrad. il por *Business Week* p36 My 15 '89

Machiavelli on Madison Avenue [WPP Group's bid for Ogilvy Group] B. Rudolph. il por *Time* 133:58 My 15 '89

The man who would be king of Madison Ave. [M. Sorrell's WPP Group bids for Ogilvy Group] L. Reibstein. il por *Newsweek* 113:52 My 15 '89

Mediums and messages [WPP buys Ogilvy] A. Walmsley. il por *Maclean's* 102:42 My 29 '89

WPP, the new giant of . . . PR? [WPP buys Ogilvy] W. Konrad. *Business Week* p32 My 29 '89

Marketing

It's raining rainmakers on Madison Avenue. W. Konrad. il *Business Week* p56+ Ag 21 '89

Great Britain

See also

Saatchi & Saatchi Company plc

Japan

See also

Dentsu Inc.

ADVERTISING AND CHILDREN

See also

Cable television advertising and children
Television advertising and children

First, this message. S. Bates. *The New Republic* 201:16+ O 16 '89

The selling of our schools [cover story] T. Moore. il *U.S. News & World Report* 107:34-6+ N 6 '89

ADVERTISING ART

See also

Poster stamps

Collectors and collecting

Advertising art [pre-1920 advertising signs] F. Donegan. bibl il *Americana* 17:62-4 S/O '89

American advertising art. C. Martignette. il *Antiques & Collecting Hobbies* 94:32-4 N '89

Collecting advertising thermometers. D. Stewart. il *Antiques & Collecting Hobbies* 94:36-8+ My '89

Old wine in new bottles [M. Shanken's collection of old advertising posters] C. Brown. il por *Forbes* 144:279-80 O 16 '89

ADVERTISING AWARDS *See* Advertising—Awards

ADVERTISING CARDS

Collectors and collecting

Nineteenth-century jewelers' trade cards. R. A. Green. il *Antiques & Collecting Hobbies* 94:64-7 N '89

ADVERTISING CHARACTERS

Man of a thousand faces [actor J. Leighton] B. Kanner. il pors *New York* 22:20-1 My 29 '89

ADVERTISING ETHICS

See also

Mail fraud

A comeback may be ahead for Brand X [suing over ads that name rivals made easier due to changes in trademark statute] M. Galen. il *Business Week* p35 D 4 '89

The era of the big blur [blurring lines between advertising and editorial content] J. Alter. il *Newsweek* 112:73+ My 22 '89

The truth behind get-rich-quick ads [business opportunity classifieds] E. King. il *Home Office Computing* 7:61-2 N '89

What role do advertisers play in deciding the news? [excerpt from Inventing reality] M. Parenti. *Utne Reader* p66 N/D '89

ADVERTISING JINGLES

See also

Phonograph records—Advertising jingles

ADVERTISING MEDIUMS

The proper place for commercials. J. Leo. il *U.S. News & World Report* 107:71 O 30 '89

Books

See Books in advertising

Computer programming

The following floppy is brought to you by . . . M. Shao. il *Business Week* p64-5 D 4 '89

Motion pictures

See also

Motion picture product placement

Hoots and howls at ads [audience resistance] G. Clarke. il *Time* 134:70 S 18 '89

Nowhere to hide. B. Kanner. il *New York* 22:24-5 Ja 23 '89

Public comfort stations

Washroom ads: 'paid-for graffiti'. il *Newsweek* 113:42 F 20 '89

Purchasing

See also

Cable television advertising—Time purchasing
Television advertising—Time purchasing

Alternative currents. *U.S. News & World Report* 106:54 F 20 '89

Recreational vehicles

See Recreational vehicles in advertising

Space vehicles

See Space vehicles in advertising

Videotapes

The following floppy is brought to you by . . . M. Shao. il *Business Week* p64-5 D 4 '89

Hoots and howls at ads [audience resistance] G. Clarke. il *Time* 134:70 S 18 '89

ADVERTISING PHOTOGRAPHY *See* Photography, Advertising

ADVERTISING PREMIUMS *See* Premiums

ADVERTISING PROPERTIES

Prop art [work of J. Canto] B. Kanner. il por *New York* 22:20+ N 27 '89

ADVERTISING RESEARCH

Desperately seeking "Jeepness". J. Levine. il *Forbes* 143:134+ My 15 '89

Mind games [cover story] B. Kanner. il *New York* 22:34-40 My 8 '89

Political quick-step [TV marketers using audience research tactics developed by political campaigns] M. Couzens. il *Channels (New York, N.Y.: 1986)* 9:26 F '89

Psyching out consumers. A. Miller and D. Tsiantar. il *Newsweek* 113:46-7 F 27 '89

Science 1, advertisers 0 [studies on efficacy of TV ads] W. F. Allman. il *U.S. News & World Report* 106:60-1 My 1 '89

ADVERTISING SIGNS *See* Billboards; Signs and signboards

ADVICE

See also

Mentors

Advice for advice-givers: don't! E. Kaye. *Mademoiselle* 95:124 Ag '89

Being an expert about expert advice. *Glamour* 87:116 N '89

Anecdotes, facetiae, satire, etc.

What my grandmother told me. K. Fury. il *Working Woman* 14:114 Ja '89

ADVICE COLUMNS *See* Newspapers—Advice columns

ADVISERS, BUSINESS *See* Business consultants

ADVISERS, ECONOMIC *See* Economists

ADVISERS, INVESTMENT *See* Investment advisers

ADVISERS, POLITICAL *See* Political consultants

ADVISORY COMMISSIONS, GOVERNMENT *See* Government commissions

ADVO-SYSTEM, INC.

A junk mailer that could deliver. G. Weiss and J. M. Laderman. *Business Week* p106 F 27 '89

ADVOCACY, POLITICAL *See* Lobbyists and lobbying

ADVOCACY ADVERTISING

The era of the big blur [blurring lines between advertising and editorial content] J. Alter. il *Newsweek* 112:73+ My 22 '89

ADVOKAT, STEVEN

Office gear on the go. il *Nation's Business* 77:56+ N '89

ADZER, LAISE
about
The Moroccan moods of Laise Adzer. I. Borger. il por *Architectural Digest* 46:168-73 S '89
AEA INVESTORS, INC.
The richest little club in the world. C. Knowlton. il *Fortune* 119:73+ Je 5 '89
AEGEAN ISLANDS
See also
Crete
Thera (Greece: Island)
Description and travel
See also
Cruising—Aegean Islands
AEGEAN ISLANDS IN ART
Caroline Huff. J. Wechsler. il por *American Artist* 53:52-7+ Je '89
AEGEAN SEA REGION
See also
Geology—Aegean Sea region
AEI MUSIC NETWORK INC.
Mike Malone and the slumbering giant. M. Beauchamp. il por *Forbes* 143:90+ F 20 '89
AEL INDUSTRIES INC.
Hughes/AEL team wins Navy contract for upgraded radar warning receiver. B. W. Henderson. il *Aviation Week & Space Technology* 131:60-1 Ag 28 '89
AENEAS (LEGENDARY CHARACTER)
Aeneas, Rome's man of destiny. J.-P. Brisson. il *The Unesco Courier* 42:22-7 S '89
AENEID
Aeneas, Rome's man of destiny. J.-P. Brisson. il *The Unesco Courier* 42:22-7 S '89
AER LINGUS
Dublin trims international, domestic competition between Irish carriers. J. Ott. *Aviation Week & Space Technology* 131:107-8 O 2 '89
AERATION OF GRAIN See Grain—Aeration
AERIAL PHOTOGRAPHY See Photography, Aerial
AERIAL RECONNAISSANCE
See also
Artificial satellites—Military use
Navy tests near real-time reconnaissance system using commercial magnetic camera. P. J. Klass. il *Aviation Week & Space Technology* 131:98-9+ O 2 '89
AERIAL SPRAYING AND DUSTING IN AGRICULTURE
See Airplanes in agriculture
AERITALIA SPA
Brazilian Air Force to accept first production AMX in August. E. H. Kolcum. il *Aviation Week & Space Technology* 130:87 Mr 20 '89
Consortium to decide on boosting ATR regional transport production. J. M. Lenorovitz. il *Aviation Week & Space Technology* 130:68 Mr 13 '89
Dornier, Aeritalia to use twin-engine design for advanced amphibian concept. il *Aviation Week & Space Technology* 130:64 Je 19 '89
European consortium nears decisions on production rate, upgraded ATR72 development. J. M. Lenorovitz. il *Aviation Week & Space Technology* 131:55-6 N 6 '89
GPA Jetprop prepares for 1990s with orders for ATRs, Dash 8s. J. M. Lenorovitz. il *Aviation Week & Space Technology* 130:90 Mr 27 '89
AERO BARS See Bicycles—Steering gear
AEROBATIC AIRPLANES See Airplanes, Aerobatic
AEROBATICS See Aviation—Stunt flying
AEROBIC RACE WALKING See Race walking
AEROBICS
See also
Boxercise
Circuit training
Interval training
Jazzercise, Inc.
Aerobic videos: ten you can trust. K. L. Clark and T. Thompson. il *Women's Sports & Fitness* 11:44-6+ S '89
Aerobics update '89 [special section] M. Madsen. il *Women's Sports & Fitness* 11:22-7 Ja/F '89
Dance fever. il *Runner's World* 24:46 D '89
Does your class make the grade? K. Williams. il por *Women's Sports & Fitness* 11:14 Mr '89
Emotional rescue [nonimpact aerobics; work of Debbie and Carlos Rosas] E. Rogers. il *American Health* 8:44 Ap '89
Fitness: getting to the heart of the matter. L. E. Koszuta. il *Current Health 2* 16:10-11 O '89
For arthritis, try fitness. il *Prevention (Emmaus, Pa.)* 41:10+ S '89
How low-impact can you go? [nonimpact aerobics] E. Rogers. il *Women's Sports & Fitness* 11:20-1 Ap '89
Low-impact, high-value exercise. L. E. Koszuta. il *Current Health 2* 15:26-7 Mr '89
Perestroika, part two [Soviets take up aerobics] M. Madsen. *Women's Sports & Fitness* 11:58-9 O '89
Soulful strut [Afrobics] M. Southgate. il *Essence* 20:13 D '89
Sweating and sharing [class in Pennington, N.J. serves as women's socializing center] J. D. Reed. il *Time* 134:12-13 Jl 10 '89

Upstairs, downstairs [Bench Blast program based on stair climbing; work of Gin Miller and Connie Williams] C. Moekle. il *American Health* 8:36 Jl/Ag '89
When the class is beneath your level [adjusting intensity level] J. Weller. il *Women's Sports & Fitness* 11:16 N/D '89
Competitions
Aerobic athletes vie for Reebok national title. il *Jet* 76:50 O 2 '89
Equipment
See also
Aerobics shoes
Psychological aspects
Working out the invisible self. A. G. Britton. il *American Health* 8:68-70+ Mr '89
AEROBICS SHOES
Aerobic impact. il *Women's Sports & Fitness* 11:41-2 Mr '89
Shoe biz. il *Women's Sports & Fitness* 11:24-5 Ja/F '89
AEROBICS TEACHERS
They just can't stop dancing [former dancer D. Nillo's fitness class at the Hollywood YMCA] E. Zimmer. il por *Dance Magazine* 63:82-3 Je '89
AEROCARS
Flying cars were a dream that never got off the ground. J. R. Chiles. il *Smithsonian* 19:144-6+ F '89
AERODIS AMERICA (FIRM)
Aerodis America designing light jet trainer, tactical aircraft. E. H. Phillips. il *Aviation Week & Space Technology* 130:39+ Je 26 '89
AERODYNAMICS
See also
Bicycles—Aerodynamics
Central Aero-Hydrodynamic Institute (Soviet Union)
Drag (Aerodynamics)
Hypersonics
Trajectories
Trucks—Aerodynamics
Vortex generators
Vortex motion
Wind tunnels
Computational aerodynamics for aircraft design [cover story] A. Jameson. bibl f il *Science* 245:361-71 Jl 28 '89
Go with the flow. il *National Geographic World* 168:26-31 Ag '89
Model student [learning about aerodynamics from balsa model airplane] P. Garrison. il *Flying* 116:82-3 Mr '89
NASA adds to understanding of high angle of attack regime [cover story] W. B. Scott. il *Aviation Week & Space Technology* 130:36-8+ My 22 '89
U.S. firm claims modified F-16 could match Su-27 'Cobra' maneuver [Eidetics International] M. A. Dornheim. il *Aviation Week & Space Technology* 131:54-5 Ag 14 '89
AEROFLOT
Aeroflot, Marriott cooperate on in-flight catering service. J. Ott. *Aviation Week & Space Technology* 130:64-5 Ja 23 '89
Aeroflot pursues leases for five A310s, signs CRS and hotel pacts. J. T. McKenna. *Aviation Week & Space Technology* 131:55 O 30 '89
Aeroflot signs letter of intent to purchase five Airbus A310-300s. *Aviation Week & Space Technology* 131:18 N 6 '89
Aeroflot takes off for joint-ventureland. R. Brady and others. il *Business Week* p48-9 O 30 '89
Leona Helmsley, can you top this? [freebies offered] il *U.S. News & World Report* 107:18 Ag 14 '89
Perestroika spurs Aeroflot to begin major changes in business operations. il *Aviation Week & Space Technology* 130:84-7 Je 5 '89
Soviets attempt to set up competitor for Aeroflot. J. T. McKenna and R. G. O'Lone. *Aviation Week & Space Technology* 131:42-3 D 11 '89
AEROJET-GENERAL CORP.
Advanced weather sensor enhances next-generation defense satellite [Special Sensor Microwave Imager Sounder] B. W. Henderson. il *Aviation Week & Space Technology* 131:47+ Ag 14 '89
Aerojet TechSystems facility to test hypersonic engines designed for NASP [National Aero-Space Plane] il *Aviation Week & Space Technology* 130:263 Je 12 '89
NASA selects Lockheed/Aerojet to build shuttle's advanced solid rocket motor. T. M. Foley. il *Aviation Week & Space Technology* 130:31-2 My 1 '89
AEROJET ORDNANCE CO.
Top Aerojet Ordnance managers dismissed; other workers laid off. *Aviation Week & Space Technology* 131:36 D 11 '89
AEROLEASING FAR EAST (FIRM)
Charter operators gain ground in Pacific, despite red tape. P. Proctor. il *Aviation Week & Space Technology* 131:87+ O 2 '89
AEROLIFT (FIRM)
Aerolift will use new Beech 1900Cs to expand domestic service, challenge Philippine Airlines. il *Aviation Week & Space Technology* 131:103 Ag 21 '89

AERONAUTIC RESEARCH *See* Aviation research
AERONAUTICA MACCHI
Brazilian Air Force to accept first production AMX in August.
E. H. Kolcum. il *Aviation Week & Space Technology*
130:87 Mr 20 '89
AERONAUTICS *See* Aviation
AERONAUTICS, MILITARY *See* Aviation, Military
AEROSMITH (MUSICAL GROUP)
Aerosmith. D. Gates. il *Newsweek* 114:64-5 O 16 '89
AEROSOLS
Aerosols, cloud microphysics, and fractional cloudiness. B.
A. Albrecht. bibl f il *Science* 245:1227-30 S 15 '89
Smallest aerosol pollutants linked to disease [research by
C. A. Pope] J. Raloff. *Science News* 135:277 My 6 '89
AEROSPACE INDUSTRIES
See also
Aerojet-General Corp.
Airplane industry
Avionics industry
Ball Aerospace (Firm)
Ball Corporation
Boeing Co.
Collective labor agreements—Aerospace industries
E-Prime Aerospace Corporation
General Dynamics Corp.
General Electric Co. Astro Space Division
Grumman Corp.
Guided missile industries
Hercules Aerospace Company
Hughes Aircraft Co.
Kaman Corp.
Lockheed Corp.
LTV Aerospace & Defense Co.
Martin Marietta Corp.
Pioneer Aerospace (Firm)
Rocketdyne (Firm)
Rockwell International Corp.
Strikes—Aerospace industries
Textron Inc.
Aerospace perspectives: Aviation week editors define the
issues [cover story; special issue; with editorial comment
by Donald E. Fink] il *Aviation Week & Space Technology*
131:7, 17-22+ D 18-25 '89
Industry observer. See issues of Aviation Week & Space
Technology

Acquisitions and mergers
International aspects
Exon-Florio an imperfect tool for protecting U.S. technology.
V. D. Cohen. por *Aviation Week & Space Technology*
131:68-9 N 6 '89
Germany (West)
Daimler accepts German constraints on its buyout of MBB.
Aviation Week & Space Technology 131:31 S 18 '89
European aerospace industry enters period of restructuring.
J. M. Lenorovitz. il *Aviation Week & Space Technology*
131:34-5 Jl 3 '89
The even-bigger shadow Daimler could cast [MBB takeover]
J. Templeman. il por *Business Week* p54-5 My 22 '89
German Cartel Office raises antitrust issues in MBB takeover
[acquisition by Daimler-Benz] *Aviation Week & Space
Technology* 130:271 Mr 20 '89
Herr Reuter takes to the skies [Daimler-Benz] P. Fuhrman.
il por *Forbes* 143:88+ Mr 20 '89
Employees
See also
International Association of Machinists and Aerospace
Workers
Boeing borrows skilled workers from Lockheed for 747-400
program. R. G. O'Lone. *Aviation Week & Space Technology*
130:66 Mr 13 '89
Reduced spending on military aircraft spurs decline in
aerospace employment. il *Aviation Week & Space
Technology* 130:78+ My 29 '89
Health and hygiene
OSHA threatens to fine Lockheed $1.5 million. *Aviation
Week & Space Technology* 130:20 Ap 3 '89
Ethical aspects
See also
Pentagon procurement scandal
Boeing pleads guilty to trafficking in classified documents,
pays $5-million fine. *Aviation Week & Space Technology*
131:38 N 20 '89
Judge fines Rockwell $5.5 million for concealing Navstar
double-billing. M. A. Dornheim. *Aviation Week & Space
Technology* 130:24-5 Mr 13 '89
Management-by-rote is the fallout from overzealous prosecu-
tion. M. A. Dornheim. il *Aviation Week & Space Technology*
131:32-3 D 18-25 '89
Northrop, five employees indicted in fraud case. *Aviation
Week & Space Technology* 130:29 Ap 17 '89
Suit claims Northrop wrongfully took $20 billion for Stealth
bomber work. B. A. Smith. *Aviation Week & Space
Technology* 131:26-7 N 13 '89
Whistleblowing on U.S. defense contractors is out of control
[case of John M. Cockerham and Associates] J. M. Cocker-
ham. por *Aviation Week & Space Technology* 130:99+
Ap 10 '89

Exhibitions
See Aviation—Exhibitions
Export-import trade
Focus on Mideast markets: Dubai Air Show [special section]
il *Aviation Week & Space Technology* 130:18-20 F 6 '89
Federal aid
U.S. aerospace leaders see little hope of improving defense
procurement. P. A. Gilmartin. il *Aviation Week & Space
Technology* 131:26-7 O 2 '89
Finance
Aerospace/defense financial report [special section] il *Aviation
Week & Space Technology* 130:48-50+ My 29 '89
Aerospace and defense. H. Banks. il *Forbes* 143:82-3 Ja
9 '89
Defense cuts will trim aerospace firms' earnings, despite
civil gains. il *Aviation Week & Space Technology* 130:80+
Mr 20 '89
Growth trends: U.S. aerospace industry [chart] il *Aviation
Week & Space Technology* 130:38-9 Mr 20 '89
Strong performances early in 1988 boosted aerospace firm's
earnings. *Aviation Week & Space Technology* 130:101 F
13 '89
International aspects
Aerospace forecast & inventory [cover story; special issue]
il *Aviation Week & Space Technology* 130:17+ Mr 20
'89
Defense companies seek joint ventures to maintain market
share. *Aviation Week & Space Technology* 130:35 Je 19
'89
Laurels 1988 [cover story; special section] il *Aviation Week
& Space Technology* 130:11-18 Ja 2 '89
Saudi-U.S. joint ventures formed under AWACS offset pro-
gram will start operations this year. *Aviation Week &
Space Technology* 130:20 F 6 '89
Management
Management-by-rote is the fallout from overzealous prosecu-
tion. M. A. Dornheim. il *Aviation Week & Space Technology*
131:32-3 D 18-25 '89
Total quality management [address, November 29, 1988]
B. P. Randolph. *Vital Speeches of the Day* 55:322-4 Mr
15 '89
Quality control
Making total quality management work: lessons from industry.
C. Leader. por *Aviation Week & Space Technology* 131:65+
O 30 '89
Total quality management will require procurement changes,
perseverance. B. A. Smith. il *Aviation Week & Space
Technology* 131:59-60 D 18-25 '89
TQM expected to boost productivity, ensure survival of
U.S. industry [total quality management] W. B. Scott.
il *Aviation Week & Space Technology* 131:64-5+ D 4 '89
Securities
Buy 'em when they're not hot. K. L. Fisher. il *Forbes* 143:338
My 29 '89
Continued defense stock downturn reflects long-term business
outlook. N. C. Kernstock. il *Aviation Week & Space
Technology* 131:81 N 13 '89
For defense stocks, peace is hell. J. Egan. il *U.S. News
& World Report* 106:67 Ja 16 '89
Heard on the Street [Wall Street defense watchers] L. Feinstein.
il *Common Cause Magazine* 15:12-15 Jl/Ag '89
Market focus. N. C. Kernstock. See issues of Aviation Week
& Space Technology beginning October 3, 1988
Wall Street upbeat on airlines, gloomy about defense stocks.
il *Aviation Week & Space Technology* 130:48-50 My 29
'89
Argentina
See also
Fabrica Argentina de Material Aerospacial
Australia
See also
Aerospace Technologies of Australia Pty. Ltd.
Hawker de Havilland Australia Pty. Ltd.
Belgium
See also
Belge de Constructions Aéronautiques SA
Brazil
See also
Avibras Industria Aeroespacial SA
Canada
See also
Bristol Aerospace Ltd.
Canadair Ltd.
Canadian firms concerned that 1992 may hinder marketing
efforts in Europe. il *Aviation Week & Space Technology*
130:139+ Je 12 '89
Canadian firms expect steady growth in aerospace market.
D. Hughes. il *Aviation Week & Space Technology* 130:98-9+
Mr 20 '89
China
See also
Beijing Institute of Aeronautical Materials
China Great Wall Industry Corporation
China aviation: at a critical crossroads [cover story; special
section; with editorial comment] D. E. Fink and P. Proctor.
il *Aviation Week & Space Technology* 131:23, 48-9+ D
11 '89

AEROSPACE INDUSTRIES—China—*cont.*
Chinese make strong pitch to sell military hardware, launch services [Dubai '89 Airshow] *Aviation Week & Space Technology* 130:19 F 6 '89
Contractors remain outside China as violence continues. M. Mecham. *Aviation Week & Space Technology* 130:31 Je 26 '89
International aerospace firms begin evacuating employees from China. P. Proctor. il *Aviation Week & Space Technology* 130:68-9 Je 12 '89
MiG-29 crash, turmoil in China mar start of show [Paris Air Show] il *Aviation Week & Space Technology* 130:60-3 Je 12 '89

Dubai (United Arab Emirates: Emirate)
Additional exhibit space, larger flight displays planned for 1991 Dubai Air Show. D. A. Brown. il *Aviation Week & Space Technology* 130:28 F 13 '89
Focus on Mideast markets: Dubai Air Show [special section] il *Aviation Week & Space Technology* 130:18-20 F 6 '89

France
See also
Aerospatiale
Matra SA
Société Européenne de Propulsion
French aerospace firms seek stronger European ties to bolster market position. il *Aviation Week & Space Technology* 130:103-4+ Je 12 '89

Germany (West)
See also
Deutsche Aerospace AG
Dornier GmbH
Intospace GmbH
Kayser-Threde GmbH
Messerschmitt-Bölkow-Blohm GmbH
Labor problems may weaken Germany's position in unified European market. il *Aviation Week & Space Technology* 130:113 Je 12 '89

Great Britain
See also
British Aerospace plc
Plessey Co. plc
Britain wary of 1992's impact on relations with U.S. firms. il *Aviation Week & Space Technology* 130:115 Je 12 '89

Israel
See also
Israel Aircraft Industries Ltd.

Italy
See also
BPD (Firm)
Southern nations will play larger role in European aerospace programs. il *Aviation Week & Space Technology* 130:116-17 Je 12 '89

Japan
Japan raises defense spending to fund missile, aircraft programs. il *Aviation Week & Space Technology* 130:88+ Mr 20 '89
Japan showcases maturing space program, manufacturing capabilities [Paris Air Show] il *Aviation Week & Space Technology* 130:66+ Je 19 '89

Korea (South)
See also
Samsung Aerospace Industries Ltd.
South Korea: nation at a crossroads [special section] J. D. Morrocco. il maps *Aviation Week & Space Technology* 130:176-7+ Je 12 '89
South Korea's new destination: the wild blue yonder. L. Nakarmi. il *Business Week* p50 S 11 '89

Persian Gulf region
Focus on Mideast markets: Dubai Air Show [special section] il *Aviation Week & Space Technology* 130:18-20 F 6 '89

Soviet Union
See also
Technopribor (Firm)
Perestroika's changes grip Soviet aerospace industry [cover story; special section; with editorial comment by Donald E. Fink] il *Aviation Week & Space Technology* 130:7, 34-5+ Je 5 '89

Spain
See also
Construcciones Aeronauticas SA
Southern nations will play larger role in European aerospace programs. il *Aviation Week & Space Technology* 130:116-17 Je 12 '89

Sweden
See also
Saab-Scania AB
Volvo AB

United States
See Aerospace industries

Western Europe
See also
Arianespace
1992: unifying Europe's markets [special section; with editorial comment by Donald E. Fink] il map *Aviation Week & Space Technology* 130:51, 78-9+ Je 12 '89
Arianespace, European companies sign production contracts for 50 Ariane 4s. J. M. Lenorovitz. *Aviation Week & Space Technology* 130:28 F 20 '89

High costs, political rows hinder Europe's combat aircraft programs. D. A. Brown. il *Aviation Week & Space Technology* 130:95-6 Mr 20 '89
Study finds Europe must boost R&D spending to remain competitive. il *Aviation Week & Space Technology* 130:79-80 Ja 30 '89

AEROSPACE TECHNOLOGIES OF AUSTRALIA PTY. LTD.
Restructured ASTA turns profit, diversifies with new ventures. P. Proctor. il *Aviation Week & Space Technology* 130:45-6 F 6 '89

AEROSPACE WORKERS *See* Aerospace industries—Employees

AEROSPACEPLANE *See* Spaceplane

AEROSPATIALE
Aerospatiale and MBB disagree on A320/A321 assembly location. J. M. Lenorovitz. il *Aviation Week & Space Technology* 131:70 O 23 '89
Aerospatiale defines Mach 2 Concorde follow-on. *Aviation Week & Space Technology* 131:56 D 4 '89
Consortium to decide on boosting ATR regional transport production. J. M. Lenorovitz. il *Aviation Week & Space Technology* 130:68 Mr 13 '89
European consortium nears decisions on production rate, upgraded ATR72 development. J. M. Lenorovitz. il *Aviation Week & Space Technology* 131:55-6 N 6 '89
GPA Jetprop prepares for 1990s with orders for ATRs, Dash 8s. J. M. Lenorovitz. il *Aviation Week & Space Technology* 130:90 Mr 27 '89

AEROSPATIALE. HELICOPTER DIVISION
Aerospatiale takes first civilian order for Super Puma Mk. 2 helicopters [Bristow Helicopter Group order] il *Aviation Week & Space Technology* 130:73 Je 26 '89
Day of the Dauphin [Aerospatiale Dauphin 2] J. M. McClellan. il *Flying* 116:76-8+ S '89

AES *See* Audio Engineering Society

AESCULUS *See* Horse chestnut

AESTHETICS
See also
Architecture—Philosophy
Basketball, Professional—Aesthetics
Grace (Aesthetics)
Kitsch
Modernism (Aesthetics)
Motion pictures—Aesthetics
Romanticism
Skiing—Aesthetics
Beauty and the aesthetics of survival. P. Delattre. il *Utne Reader* p64-7+ Jl/Ag '89
Nose by Nefertiti. K. Pryor. il *Art News* 88:15-16 F '89
The quality quandary. M. Cantwell. il *House & Garden* 161:64+ Ap '89
Taste be damned. Q. Crisp. il *House & Garden* 161:90-1 Ag '89

AFANAS'EV, VIKTOR GRIGOR'EVICH
about
Dear editor: You're fired. Signed, Mikhail Gorbachev. W. R. Doerner. il pors *Time* 134:62-3 O 30 '89
Gorbachev's one-two punch. A. Deming. il *Newsweek* 114:54-5 O 30 '89

AFANAS'EV, YURI
about
De-Stalinizing the Soviet past [interview] S. F. Cohen and K. Vanden Heuvel. *Harper's* 279:32+ O '89
Filling in the blank spots in Soviet history [interview]; tr. by Vladimir Voronin and Adam Shulman. A. Sirotkin. il *History Today* 39:12-17 F '89

AFFECTION
See also
Embracing
Intimacy
Kissing
The importance of hugging [link between absence of childhood affection and violence in Bedouin society; excerpt from The Lucifer principle] H. Bloom. il *Omni (New York, N.Y.)* 11:30+ F '89
Love me tender. C. L. Mithers. il *Ladies' Home Journal* 106:90+ Mr '89

AFFILIATED PUBLICATIONS, INC.
Boston's accidental demibillionaires. M. Fritz. il por *Forbes* 144 Special Issue:112+ O 23 '89
Life without McCaw. N. J. Perry. il *Fortune* 120:75 Ag 14 '89

AFFILIATES, TELEVISION *See* Television stations

AFFINITY CARDS
A new way to charge it—on your state [Montana sponsors an affinity card] *Newsweek* 113:20 Je 26 '89

Canada
Playing favorites. S. McKay. il *Maclean's* 102:32-3 F 27 '89

AFFIRMATIVE ACTION *See* Discrimination

AFFIRMATIVE ACTION IN EMPLOYMENT *See* Blacks—Employment; Discrimination in employment; Women—Employment

AFFLICTION *See* Suffering

AFGHAN REFUGEES *See* Refugees, Afghan

AFGHANISTAN
See also
Afghans

AFGHANISTAN—See also—*cont.*
  Jalalabad (Afghanistan)
  Kabul (Afghanistan)
  Military assistance, American—Afghanistan
  Press and politics—Afghanistan
  Relief work—Afghanistan
  United Nations—Afghanistan
  Women—Afghanistan

Foreign relations
Pakistan

Security Council considers Afghan complaint against Pakistan. il *UN Chronicle* 26:26-7 S '89
Soviet troop withdrawal from Afghanistan completed on time on 15 February 1989. il *UN Chronicle* 26:20-2 Je '89

Politics and government
See also
  Afghanistan—Russian invasion, 1979-1989

Afghan follow-through. *National Review* 41:12 My 19 '89
Afghan sitzkrieg. R. Sikorski. il *National Review* 41:37-8 Ap 21 '89
Afghanistan [following Soviet withdrawal; special section] il *World Press Review* 36:22-5 Ap '89
Afghanistan: "back to feudalism". B. R. Rubin. bibl f *Current History* 88:421-4+ D '89
Afghanistan: Soviet occupation and withdrawal. il maps *Department of State Bulletin* 89:72-90 Mr '89
Afghanistan's uncertain fate. B. R. Rubin. il *The Nation* 248:264-7+ F 27 '89
After the Soviets go. E. MacFarquhar. il map *U.S. News & World Report* 106:32-4+ F 13 '89
Annals of the freedom fighters [reporting on the mujahadeen] A. Cockburn. *The Nation* 248:803 Je 12 '89
Another chance for Afghanistan. *National Review* 41:15+ N 10 '89
A city under siege [Kabul] B. Levin. il *Maclean's* 102:28 F 27 '89
'The end could come any day'. H. Anderson. il map *Newsweek* 113:30-1 F 6 '89
An end game in Afghanistan: the rebel strategy: first Jalalabad, then Kabul. H. Anderson. il map *Newsweek* 113:38 Mr 27 '89
Fighting for Jalalabad. M. Strmecki. il *The American Spectator* 22:30-2 Je '89
The fragmentation of Afghanistan. B. R. Rubin. *Foreign Affairs* 68:150-68 Wint '89/'90
Grave concern expressed over escalating fighting in Afghanistan. il *UN Chronicle* 26:22 D '89
Inside a frightened city [Kabul] M. Liu. il *Newsweek* 113:36+ Mr 13 '89
Leaving the quagmire. H. Anderson. il map *Newsweek* 113:32-4 F 13 '89
Legacy of a bloody war. A. Wilson-Smith. il *Maclean's* 102:18-20 F 20 '89
Liberty, fraternity—disunity [relations between rival mujahedin factions] il *Time* 134:25 Jl 31 '89
Misplaced optimism [mujahedin gaining little ground] J. Elson. il *Time* 133:40-1 My 15 '89
Rebels with too many causes: who's who behind the mujahedin's quarreling factions. W. R. Doerner. il *Time* 133:39 F 27 '89
Rising fear in Kabul. A. Wilson-Smith. il *Maclean's* 102:22-3 F 13 '89
The scent of victory divides Afghan rebels. E. Girardet. il *U.S. News & World Report* 106:34 F 27 '89
Stalemate at Jalalabad. E. Ahmad. il *The Nation* 249:384-7 O 9 '89
State of emergency. M. Liu. il *Newsweek* 113:43 F 27 '89
Still-life by shellfire. R. Sikorski. il *National Review* 41:22-3 Ap 7 '89
A surprise turnaround in Afghanistan. map *Newsweek* 114:36 Jl 17 '89
Target: Kabul. D. Lorch. il pors map *The New York Times Magazine* p32-5+ F 12 '89
A U.S. victory begins to unravel [failure of mujahedin to oust Communist regime] L. Lief. il *U.S. News & World Report* 107:38 Jl 24 '89
Victors' justice: danger ahead. W. F. Buckley. *National Review* 41:54 Mr 24 '89
Waiting for the end. E. W. Desmond. il *Time* 133:38-40 F 6 '89
What will follow the pullout? S. R. Galster. il *The Nation* 248:9-10+ Ja 2 '89
When Kabul falls [letter to mujahedin commander] R. Sikorski. *National Review* 41:20 F 24 '89
Why are we in Afghanistan? R. Wright. *The New Republic* 201:23-5 S 4 '89
Without a look back: as the Soviets leave, rebels prepare to strike. J. Smolowe. il *Time* 133:42-3 F 20 '89

Religious institutions and affairs
See also
  Missions—Afghanistan
  Muslims—Afghanistan

Russian invasion, 1979-1989

Postmortem. R. D. Kaplan. il *The Atlantic* 263:26+ Ap '89
Vietnam 'vets' & the Soviet experience. B. Shephard. il *History Today* 39:10-12 Jl '89

War lord [former Allentown, Pa. youth becomes troop commander in Afghanistan] il pors *Life* 12:121-2+ My '89
When American vets meet Soviet vets [Vietnam and Afghanistan veterans] C. Thibaud. *World Press Review* 36:70 S '89
The wounds of two wars [meeting between Vietnam and Afghanistan veterans in the Soviet Union] P. P. Mahoney. il *The New York Times Magazine* p60-1+ Je 11 '89

Aerial operations

Sukhoi incorporates changes to Su-25 based on Afghan combat experience. il *Aviation Week & Space Technology* 130:31 Je 19 '89

Medical and sanitary affairs

Afghanistan after the turmoil. M. Hussein. il *World Health* p11-12 Jl '89
Legacy of an unpopular war [wounded Soviet soldiers] il *Time* 133:64-5 Ap 10 '89
Scarred and shell-shocked [Soviet soldiers] A. Wilson-Smith. il *Maclean's* 102:20 F 20 '89

Missing in action

Searching for Soviet MIAs. S. Le Vine. il *Newsweek* 114:28 Jl 10 '89

Peace and mediation

Afghanistan [following Soviet withdrawal; special section] il *World Press Review* 36:22-5 Ap '89
Afghanistan: "back to feudalism". B. R. Rubin. bibl f *Current History* 88:421-4+ D '89
Afghanistan: Soviet occupation and withdrawal. il maps *Department of State Bulletin* 89:72-90 Mr '89
Afghanistan's uncertain fate. B. R. Rubin. il *The Nation* 248:264-7+ F 27 '89
After the Soviets go. E. MacFarquhar. il map *U.S. News & World Report* 106:32-4+ F 13 '89
As Kabul teeters, Gorbachev lands on his feet. P. Galuszka and others. il *Business Week* p51 F 20 '89
Casualties of war [right wing platitudes die in Soviet Afghan pullout] H. Hertzberg. *The New Republic* 200:4+ Mr 6 '89
A city under siege [Kabul] M. Nemeth. il *Maclean's* 102:22 F 6 '89
A city under siege [Kabul] B. Levin. il *Maclean's* 102:28 F 27 '89
'The end could come any day'. H. Anderson. il map *Newsweek* 113:30-1 F 6 '89
'Faithful implementation' of Geneva agreements asked. il *UN Chronicle* 26:60-1 Mr '89
The fragmentation of Afghanistan. B. R. Rubin. *Foreign Affairs* 68:150-68 Wint '89/'90
Hard lessons from a hard land. il *U.S. News & World Report* 106:12-13 F 20 '89
Leaving the quagmire. H. Anderson. il map *Newsweek* 113:32-4 F 13 '89
Legacy of a bloody war. A. Wilson-Smith. il *Maclean's* 102:18-20 F 20 '89
Lessons of Afghanistan. R. Watson. il *Newsweek* 113:26-7 F 20 '89
Ninth anniversary of Soviet invasion of Afghanistan [statement, December 27, 1988] R. Reagan. *Department of State Bulletin* 89:89 Mr '89
President holds session with news reporters [excerpts, February 16, 1989] G. Bush. *Department of State Bulletin* 89:5-6 Ap '89
Rising fear in Kabul. A. Wilson-Smith. il *Maclean's* 102:22-3 F 13 '89
Security Council considers Afghan complaint against Pakistan. il *UN Chronicle* 26:26-7 S '89
A Soviet bluff on Afghanistan? F. Coleman. il *Newsweek* 113:38 Ja 23 '89
Soviet troop withdrawal from Afghanistan completed on time on 15 February 1989. il *UN Chronicle* 26:20-2 Je '89
Soviets withdraw from Afghanistan [statement, February 16, 1989] G. Bush. *Department of State Bulletin* 89:48 Ap '89
Target: Kabul. D. Lorch. il pors map *The New York Times Magazine* p32-5+ F 12 '89
UN calls for full implementation of Afghanistan peace accords [statement and text of resolution, November 3, 1988] V. A. Walters. *Department of State Bulletin* 89:40-1 Ja '89
Victors' justice: danger ahead. W. F. Buckley. *National Review* 41:54 Mr 24 '89
Waiting for the end. E. W. Desmond. il *Time* 133:38-40 F 6 '89
What will follow the pullout? S. R. Galster. il *The Nation* 248:9-10+ Ja 2 '89
When Kabul falls [letter to mujahedin commander] R. Sikorski. *National Review* 41:20 F 24 '89
Without a look back: as the Soviets leave, rebels prepare to strike. J. Smolowe. il *Time* 133:42-3 F 20 '89

Prisoners and prisons
See also
  International Committee for the Rescue of Soviet Prisoners of War in Afghanistan

Public opinion

Casualties of war [right wing platitudes die in Soviet Afghan pullout] H. Hertzberg. *The New Republic* 200:4+ Mr 6 '89

AFGHANISTAN—Russian invasion, 1979-1989—*cont.*
Reporters and reporting
Bizarre bazaar. P. J. O'Rourke. il *Rolling Stone* p87-8+ Ap 20 '89
Truth and consequences [CBS's alleged use of faked footage] il *Time* 134:98 O 9 '89
AFGHANS
United States
War lord [former Allentown, Pa. youth becomes troop commander in Afghanistan] il pors *Life* 12:121-2+ My '89
AFI *See* American Film Institute
AFL-CIO
As labor and Dole warm up, business is feeling a chill. S. B. Garland. il *Business Week* p35 Mr 6 '89
AFL-CIO. AMERICAN INSTITUTE FOR FREE LABOR DEVELOPMENT *See* American Institute for Free Labor Development
AFLATOXINS
Aflatoxin in corn. *FDA Consumer* 23:2-3 My '89
Corn that glows can still be safe from aflatoxin. *Successful Farming* 87:43 Ja '89
Gut-level control of aflatoxin [use of hydrated sodium calcium aluminosilicate in feeds; research by Roger B. Harvey] *Science News* 135:111 F 18 '89
A harvest of toxin [corn] C. Wood. il *Maclean's* 102:49 Mr 6 '89
Mold on corn tough on dairies hit by drought. J. R. Borcherding. *Successful Farming* 87:54 F '89
A scare in the Corn Belt. R. Givens. il *Newsweek* 113:70 Mr 6 '89
AFMS *See* Atomic force microscopes
AFONSO, JOHN CORREIA- *See* Correia-Afonso, John
AFRICA, BIRDIE *See* Ward, Michael Moses
AFRICA

   See also
   Africans
   AIDS (Disease)—Africa
   Americans—Africa
   Blacks—Africa
   Civil rights—Africa
   Dams—Africa
   East Africa
   Economic assistance—Africa
   Economic assistance, American—Africa
   Environmental policy—Africa
   Family—Africa
   Famines—Africa
   Food supply—Africa
   Foreign correspondents—Africa
   Hospitals—Africa
   Information systems—Africa
   Loans, Bank—Africa
   Music—Africa
   North Africa
   Paleontology—Africa
   Periodicals—Africa
   Public health—Africa
   Relief work—Africa
   Rivers—Africa
   Slave trade—Africa
   Southern Africa
   Sports—Africa
   United Nations—Africa
   Water resources development—Africa
   Wildlife—Africa
   Wildlife conservation—Africa
   Women—Africa
   Zambezi River
Regional report: Africa. B. Shelby. See issues of World Press Review beginning June 1986
Bibliography
Books on Africa. F. J. Parker. *America* 161:117-21 Ag 26-S 2 '89
On Africa. *Current History* 88:238+ My '89
Description and travel
Africa up close. S. Rule. il *The New York Times Magazine* p36+ Ap 30 '89
Over Africa [flying boat] R. Alleman. il *Vogue* 179:320+ Ap '89
Economic conditions
   See also
   United Nations. Programme of Action for African Economic Recovery and Development
African economic performance to dip in 1989. il *UN Chronicle* 26:77 Mr '89
Economic history
Exploitation or benefaction? [colonialism] P. Brimelow. il por *Forbes* 144:110+ N 27 '89
Economic policy
An African view of the debt [interview with J. Ki-Zerbo] H. Ziady. il por *World Press Review* 36:50 Ag '89
Can Africa finally break with the past? M. W. Karmin. il *U.S. News & World Report* 107:47 D 25 '89-Ja 1 '90
Economic restructuring in Sub-Saharan Africa. C. Lancaster. *Current History* 88:213-16+ My '89

Foreign relations
   United States
   See United States—Foreign relations—Africa
Industries
   See also
   Black business enterprises—Africa
   Motion picture industry—Africa
Politics and government
Africa, 1989 [cover story; special issue] bibl f map (inside back cover) *Current History* 88:209-50+ My '89
Africa: a continent adrift. J. A. Marcum. bibl f *Foreign Affairs* 68 Special Issue:159-79 ['89]
Drumrolls for peace are heard in Africa. *U.S. News & World Report* 107:9+ Jl 3 '89
Efforts for peace in Africa [remarks, October 4, 1988] G. P. Shultz. *Department of State Bulletin* 88:20-2 D '88
Get rid of the dictators. S. Diallo. *World Press Review* 36:64 My '89
Peace is in the air. C. C. Williams and K. Crooks. il *Black Enterprise* 20:32 O '89
The seedlings of hope: U.S. policy in Africa [address, June 11, 1989] E. J. Perkins. *Department of State Bulletin* 89:69-72 Ag '89
Religious institutions and affairs
   See also
   Christians—Africa
   Evangelical churches—Africa
Social conditions
Why Africans go hungry. il *Scholastic Update (Teachers' edition)* 121:8-10 Ja 27 '89
AFRICA AND THE UNITED STATES
   See also
   Exchanges, Literary and scientific
L'AFRICAINE [opera] *See* Meyerbeer, Giacomo, 1791-1864
AFRICAN-AMERICAN (TERM)
African-American or black: what's in a name? il *Ebony* 44:76+ Jl '89
Broad coalition seeks 'African American' name. il *Jet* 75:53 Ja 16 '89
By any other name. K. D. Thompson. il por *Black Enterprise* 19:22 Ap '89
Cambridge diarist [J. Jackson's campaign for term African-American to replace black] M. Peretz. *The New Republic* 200:43 F 6 '89
From 'black' to 'African-American'? *Newsweek* 113:28 Ja 2 '89
In search of a good name [black vs. African-American] R. Lacayo. il *Time* 133:32 Mr 6 '89
Just say Afro. S. Thernstrom. *The New Republic* 200:10+ Ja 23 '89
Loaded terms. E. K. Braxton. *Commonweal* 116:328-9 Je 2 '89
AFRICAN AMERICAN SUMMIT
Blacks discuss ways to halt race's setbacks at African American Summit. D. M. Cheers. il *Jet* 76:4-6 My 8 '89
AFRICAN ART *See* Art, African
AFRICAN DANCE *See* Dance, African
AFRICAN DEVELOPMENT BANK
Banking on African conservation [debt-for-nature swaps] *Science News* 135:62 Ja 28 '89
AFRICAN FASHION DESIGNERS *See* Fashion designers
AFRICAN HOUSE DECORATION *See* House decoration, African
AFRICAN HUNTING DOGS
Serengeti's painted wolves [cover story] J. H. Fanshawe. il *Natural History* p56-67 Mr '89
AFRICAN INDEPENDENT CHURCH (SOUTH AFRICA)
Zulu spiritual leader murdered [the Londaukosi Shembe] I. Hexham and K. O. Poewe-Hexham. *Christianity Today* 33:65 Je 16 '89
AFRICAN JEWELRY *See* Jewelry, African
AFRICAN LOCUSTS *See* Grasshoppers
AFRICAN NATIONAL CONGRESS
Black leaders: free at last. S. Reiss. il *Newsweek* 114:58 O 30 '89
Bound by blood. R. W. Wilkins. il por *Mother Jones* 14:20+ My '89
Ex-ANC leader talks about 26 years of imprisonment [W. Sisulu] il por *Jet* 77:30 N 6 '89
Freedom at last [eight activists released] M. Nemeth. il *Maclean's* 102:34-5 O 23 '89
Glasnost meets apartheid [Soviet Union disowns African National Congress] B. Crozier. *National Review* 41:22 My 5 '89
A movement but no revolution. *Time* 134:46 S 18 '89
Moving to the next stage. M. Gevisser. il *The Nation* 249:674+ D 4 '89
Pretoria outflanks the ANC [Angola deal] S. Reiss. il map *Newsweek* 113:37 Ja 23 '89
The secrets of South Africa's hit squad [D. Coetzee tells of attacks] *Newsweek* 114:56 N 27 '89
Testing the waters. B. W. Nelan. il *Time* 134:66-7+ O 30 '89
Time to talk in South Africa. S. Reiss. il *Newsweek* 114:40-1 Ag 28 '89
AFRICAN STUDENTS IN CHINA *See* Foreign students—China

AFRICAN TEXTILES See Textile fabrics
AFRICAN VIOLETS
Tracing the roots of the world's favorite houseplant. J. Lovett. il *International Wildlife* 19:34-7 Mr/Ap '89
AFRICANIZED HONEY BEES See Bees
AFRICANS
Soviet Union
Racism in the Soviet Union. B. Asoyan. *World Press Review* 36:85 O '89
AFRO-AMERICAN (BLACK) HISTORY MONTH See Black History Month
AFRO-AMERICAN STUDIES See Black studies
AFRO-AMERICANS See Blacks
AFTER SCHOOL PROGRAMS
See also
Early Adolescent Helper Program
Pick the best after-school care [latchkey children] E. Klavan. il *Parents* 64:72+ S '89
Schools that never close. C. Leslie. il *Newsweek* 113:60 My 15 '89
Starting a senior center latchkey program. *Children Today* 18:5 Jl/Ag '89
Vote to continue programs for latchkey kids in L.A. il *Jet* 77:52 O 9 '89
AFTERNOON TEAS See Teas
AGANBEGIĀN, ABEL GEZEVICH
about
The dictatorship of the consumer [interview] N. Gardels. il *New Perspectives Quarterly* 5:26-9 Wint '88/'89
The man behind Gorbachev. R. I. Kirkland. por *Fortune* 119:47 Ja 2 '89
'Waiting is death. It cannot be tolerated any longer' [interview] por *U.S. News & World Report* 107:35 S 25 '89
'We made some serious mistakes' [interview] F. Coleman. por *Newsweek* 113:30 Mr 13 '89
AGASE, ALEX
about
An open letter to Alex. R. Telander. il por *Sports Illustrated* 71:106 N 27 '89
AGASSI, ANDRE
about
The Age of Andre: a marketing empire is born. R. Wetzsteon. il pors *Sport (New York, N.Y.)* 80:88+ Je '89
Born to serve. C. Kirkpatrick. il pors *Sports Illustrated* 70:64-8+ Mr 13 '89
Call it the Loving Cup. F. Lidz. il pors *Sports Illustrated* 70:76 Ap 17 '89
The frosted flake [cover story] G. Hirshey. il pors *Gentlemen's Quarterly* 59:416-21+ S '89
I was a teenage U.S. hope. R. Wetzsteon. il pors *Sport (New York, N.Y.)* 80:60-2+ Jl '89
A lesson to be learned. B. Press. il por *World Tennis* 36:142 Ap '89
My letter to Andre. S. Flink. il por *World Tennis* 37:16+ Je '89
Special D from this Courier. C. Kirkpatrick. il pors *Sports Illustrated* 70:84+ Je 12 '89
AGAVE
Fatal attraction? [demise of long-nosed bat] K. Heacox. il *International Wildlife* 19:38-43 My/Je '89
AGE
See also
Aging
Athletes—Age
Black executives—Age
Clergy—Age
Earth—Age
Executives—Age
Fishermen—Age
Hockey players—Age
Longevity
Middle age
Physicians—Age
School age
Stars—Age
Sun—Age
Psychology
Can love conquer the age gap? [special section] il *New Choices for the Best Years* 29:60-2 Ap '89
Forever young [cover story; special section; with editorial comment by Owen J. Lipstein] il *American Health* 8:49-56+, 144 Jl/Ag '89
The generation blur. B. D. Colen. il *Health (New York, N.Y.)* 21:30-1 O '89
I won't grow up. G. Sheehan. il *Runner's World* 24:14 Ja '89
Longevity blooms with younger grooms [research by Laurel Klinger-Vartabedian] J. Davidson. *Psychology Today* 23:72 D '89
Loving an older man. A. R. Shapiro. il *Mademoiselle* 95:182-3+ O '89
Twenty-four going on forty: the new mid-life crisis comes early. R. Grant. il *Mademoiselle* 95:246-7+ S '89
Why I never trust a woman under 30. C. Brown. il *Mademoiselle* 95:188+ N '89
Anecdotes, facetiae, satire, etc.
Boadicea, my love [older women and younger men] M. Richler. il *Gentlemen's Quarterly* 59:115-16 F '89

Women on the verge [turning 30] L. Kaylin. il *Gentlemen's Quarterly* 59:178+ D '89
AGE AND EMPLOYMENT
See also
Aged—Employment
Children—Employment
Retirement
Youth—Employment
Age vs. wage: how baby boomers may cool inflation. G. Koretz. il *Business Week* p26 F 6 '89
Managing old-timers when you're the young kid on the block. *Working Woman* 14:28 My '89
AGE DETERMINATION BY RADIOACTIVITY See Radioactive dating
AGE FOR MARRIAGE See Marriage
AGE-RELATED MACULAR DEGENERATION See Macular degeneration
AGECROFT HALL (RICHMOND, VA.)
Gardens
A garden grows younger at Agecroft. il *Southern Living* 24:42 Ag '89
AGED
See also
Aging
Alcohol and the aged
Architecture and the aged
Asociacion Nacional Pro Personas Mayores
Centenarians
Drugs and the aged
Gerontology
Indians of North America—Aged
National Caucus and Center on Black Aged
National Pacific/Asian Resource Center on Aging
National Retiree Volunteer Center
Notch babies
Nursing home patients
Retirement
Smoking and the aged
United States. Administration on Aging
Experience exchange. See issues of Aging
Forget the rocking chairs. il *Business Week* p145+ S 25 '89
The geezer boom. M. Beck. il *Newsweek* 114 Special Issue:62-3+ Wint '89/Spr '90
Geroethics: a humanist issue. G. A. Larue. il por *The Humanist* 49:5-10+ Jl/Ag '89
News notes. See issues of Aging
No dancing [life of a New York City woman] *The New Yorker* 64:26-7 Ja 23 '89
Older Americans in a changing society [address, March 22, 1989] L. Crooks. *Vital Speeches of the Day* 55:556-8 Jl 1 '89
State and community news. See issues of Aging
Activities
See also
Aged—Political activities
Aged—Travel
Volunteer service
Experience exchange. See issues of Aging
Attitudes
The basics. M. E. Marty. *The Christian Century* 106:191 F 15 '89
Bibliography
Mining the golden years. J. Viorst. il *The New York Times Book Review* 94:30-1 Ap 9 '89
Publications. See issues of Aging
Care and hygiene
See also
Aged—Housing
Aged—Medical care
Dependent care (Employee benefits)
Home care services
Industry—Elderly services programs
Life care communities
Nursing homes
Rest homes
Body and mind shape-ups. S. Brewer. il *New Choices for the Best Years* 29:9 Ag '89
Caring for our parents [poll results] I. Groller. il *Parents* 64:31 My '89
Caring for your aging parents [special section] bibl il *Money* 18:136-7+ O '89
Celebrating my change of life [D. L. Siegal] R. Loth. il por *New Choices for the Best Years* 29:16+ My '89
Challenge of gravity [falls and the elderly] B. H. Dobkin. il *The New York Times Magazine* p36-7 Ag 27 '89
The good daughter. A. Gross. il *Ladies' Home Journal* 106:216-17+ N '89
Help wanted—the crisis of elder care. G. W. Weinstein. il *Ms.* 18:72-4+ O '89
Love blooms in the aisles [shopping malls used for walking] J. Pereira. il *The Saturday Evening Post* 261:54-5+ S '89
Shame deters getting help [incontinence; views of Joanne Stevenson] *USA Today (Periodical)* 118:8-9 O '89
Spry energy [81 year old W. Stack] J. Brant. il pors *Runner's World* 24:30-2 My '89
Staying well. J. Wood. See issues of Modern Maturity

AGED—Care and hygiene—*cont.*

What do we owe to the elderly? L. Smith. il *Fortune* 119:54-5+ Mr 27 '89

Who stays fit [lifelong link between personality and exercise habits; research by Paula Schnurr and others] E. Stark. *Psychology Today* 23:73 N '89

Who will care for mom and dad? P. Godwin. il *Better Homes and Gardens* 67:32+ O '89

Clubs and societies

See also

Senior centers

Crime

Pushing his luck—and his blood pressure—an aged bank robber is caught red-handed [J. Kelm in Denver, Colo.] il por *People Weekly* 31:108 Ap 17 '89

Crimes against

See also

Aged—Mistreatment

Economic conditions

See also

Retirement income

The best ways to help financially. M. T. Smith. il *Money* 18:148-50+ O '89

A certain species of helplessness [with editorial comment] R. J. Margolis. il *The New Leader* 72:2, 10-12 Ag 7-21 '89

The crunch of caring for both parents and kids. E. Schurenberg. il *Money* 18:93-4 Mr '89

A daughter seeks to stretch her ailing parents' money [Arlene Schler] L. Luciano. il *Money* 18:153+ Je '89

The economic status of the elderly. M. D. Hurd. bibl f il *Science* 244:659-64 My 12 '89

Money. A. Winter. See issues of Modern Maturity beginning October/November 1989

On coming into money. M. Hodge. il *New Choices for the Best Years* 29:56-9+ Ja '89

A question of money. M. Rowland. See issues of New Choices for the Best Years beginning January 1989

Social security should benefit only the elderly poor. G. S. Becker. il *Business Week* p20 Ja 16 '89

To make a harvest honeymoon last, first decide what's yours, mine and ours. D. M. Topolnicki. il *Money* 18:145-6 S '89

What do we owe to the elderly? L. Smith. il *Fortune* 119:54-5+ Mr 27 '89

When your parents need your help. R. R. Roha. il *Changing Times* 43:81-4 My '89

Where to get financial advice. M. Hodge and J. Blyskal. il *New Choices for the Best Years* 29:43-7 Mr '89

Women living alone. A. Quinlan. il *New Choices for the Best Years* 29:13 Ja '89

The young and the old are not enemies. W. R. Hutton. il *USA Today (Periodical)* 117:63-5 Mr '89

Education

See also

Eckerd College. Academy of Senior Professionals

Elderhostel

Grandparent education

Older students quick studies. il *Modern Maturity* 32:97 D '89/Ja '90

Still hungry for knowledge at 105, Gertrude Palmer is one for the books [named Senior Adult Student of the Year in Lemon Grove, Calif.] il pors *People Weekly* 31:116-17 Mr 20 '89

Employment

See also

Aged and business

The challenge of older workers. *Society* 26:2-3 Jl/Ag '89

Cultivating the gray [managing seniors at Days Inns] D. Machan. il pors *Forbes* 144:126+ S 4 '89

Institutional barriers to employment of older workers. D. E. Herz and P. L. Rones. bibl f *Monthly Labor Review* 112:14-21 Ap '89

Making better use of older workers. A. Ramirez. il *Fortune* 119:179-80+ Ja 30 '89

New challenges in the workplace [Workforce 2000] L. Crooks. il *Modern Maturity* 32:10-11 F/Mr '89

Older workers. *Monthly Labor Review* 112:2 F '89

Paying to work [report from National Center for Policy Analysis] J. W. Merline. il *Consumers' Research Magazine* 72:38 Ag '89

Peaking after 65: here's how [research by Lydia Bronte] J. C. Horn. *Psychology Today* 23:33-4 Jl/Ag '89

The truth about post-job jobs. A. Rock. il *Money* 18 Money Guide:73-4+ Fall '89

Working late: on the outside looking in [age discrimination] R. Hoopes. il *Modern Maturity* 32:32-5+ Je/Jl '89

Working late: the case of the myopic watchdog [EEOC's handling of age discrimination cases] R. Hoopes. il *Modern Maturity* 32:36-9+ Ap/My '89

Working late: the railroad to retirement. R. Hoopes. il *Modern Maturity* 32:34-7+ F/Mr '89

Family relationships

Caring for our parents [poll results] I. Groller. il *Parents* 64:31 My '89

Caring for your aging parents [special section] bibl il *Money* 18:136-7+ O '89

Confronting the death of a parent. M. Silver. bibl il *U.S. News & World Report* 106:74-5 My 22 '89

The crunch of caring for both parents and kids. E. Schurenberg. il *Money* 18:93-4 Mr '89

A daughter seeks to stretch her ailing parents' money [Arlene Schler] L. Luciano. il *Money* 18:153+ Je '89

Full-moon wisdom [treatment of the elderly in Hispanic and Indian cultures] R. Coles. il *New Choices for the Best Years* 29:94+ S '89

The good daughter. A. Gross. il *Ladies' Home Journal* 106:216-17+ N '89

Help wanted—the crisis of elder care. G. W. Weinstein. il *Ms.* 18:72-4+ O '89

How I spent my summer vacation [visit to mother's Kentucky home] F. Johnson. il *The New York Times Magazine* p22+ O 1 '89

My mother could no longer care for herself. il *Good Housekeeping* 209:40+ Jl '89

Parenting my parents. C. B. Gibson. il *Glamour* 87:296 Mr '89

When your parents need your help. R. R. Roha. il *Changing Times* 43:81-4 My '89

Who will care for mom and dad? P. Godwin. il *Better Homes and Gardens* 67:32+ O '89

Federal aid

See Old age assistance

Gardens and gardening

Barren ground [eighty year old's garden uprooted by son-in-law] S. O. Daniels. il *Organic Gardening* 36:5 S '89

How to think like a plant [cover story] B. Damrosch. bibl il *New Choices for the Best Years* 29:55-60 My '89

Health and hygiene

See Aged—Care and hygiene

Housing

See also

Life care communities

Nursing homes

Rest homes

Retirement communities

Beverly Hills HUD [subsidized housing for the elderly] T. Noah. *The New Republic* 201:14-16 Ag 21 '89

Cashing in on your big blue chip. W. L. Updegrave. il *Money* 18 Money Guide:83-4+ Fall '89

Colton, California, competition for affordable senior housing. il *Architectural Record* 177:64-5 O '89

Dream homes [cover story; special section] il *New Choices for the Best Years* 29:32-8 Je '89

Finding health care and housing. L. Luciano. il *Money* 18:158-60+ O '89

Homing options in the '80s—and beyond. J. Porcino. il *New Choices for the Best Years* 29:34-5 My '89

Housing options for the elderly. A. F. Shashaty. il *Good Housekeeping* 208:166 F '89

Housing: promise and problems. H. B. Deets. il *Modern Maturity* 32:11 Ag/S '89

New ways to live together. G. Rosenblum. il *New Choices for the Best Years* 29:29-35 My '89

Recruiting retirees can help turn a bust into a boomtown. S. R. Gregg. il *U.S. News & World Report* 106:46-7 Mr 6 '89

Reverse mortgages: a new cash source for older folks. M. Daly. il *Better Homes and Gardens* 67:156-7 Ap '89

Sharing a house of one's own. R. Givens. il *Newsweek* 113:74 Mr 20 '89

Watch out when you sell your home. A. Winter. *Modern Maturity* 32:14 F/Mr '89

When your aged parent moves in with you . . . [make your home safer and more comfortable] P. A. Seefeldt. il *Good Housekeeping* 209:270 S '89

Your money: should you give your house to your kids? E. Lank. *Modern Maturity* 32:20 Ag/S '89

International aspects

Youth and the elderly. A. Kalache. il *World Health* p8-9 Mr '89

Legal status, laws, etc.

The gulag of guardianship. D. M. Topolnicki. il *Money* 18:140-1+ Mr '89

Medical care

See also

Home care services

Medicaid

Medical care proxies

Medicare

. . . and be the perfect patient. A. Levin. *Modern Maturity* 32:73-4 Ag/S '89

Before the well runs dry: cutting the cost of retiree health benefits. C. A. Hanks. *USA Today (Periodical)* 117:86-8 My '89

Finding health care and housing. L. Luciano. il *Money* 18:158-60+ O '89

Health campaign reaps results [AARP's Health Care Campaign] il *Modern Maturity* 32:93 O/N '89

Health policy for the elderly. S. P. Wallace and C. L. Estes. bibl il *Society* 26:66-75 S/O '89

How to find the perfect doctor . . . W. H. Jones. bibl il *Modern Maturity* 32:72-4+ Ag/S '89

AGED—Medical care—*cont.*
Ombudsmen train young doctors [nursing home ombudsmen and Medical College of Ohio program] il *Aging* no359:24-5 '89
The prolongation of life [address, December 3, 1988] E. M. Skinner. *Vital Speeches of the Day* 55:271-3 F 15 '89
Rainy-day plan [New York State program] D. Wise. il *New York* 22:121-2+ D 4 '89
What is too old? M. S. Wilkes and M. Shuchman. il *The New York Times Magazine* p58+ Je 4 '89
Where a ride to the doctor costs $20 [West Alabama Health Services, Inc.] S. Hullett. il *Aging* no359:14-16 '89
Your health: exposing fraud isn't magic. J. Randi. *Modern Maturity* 32:22 Je/Jl '89

Mental health
See Aged—Psychology

Mistreatment
See also
Nursing home patient abuse
Elder abuse [research by Karl Pillemer and David Finkelhor] J. Folkenberg. il *American Health* 8:87 N '89
Relative downfalls behind elder abuse [research by Karl Pillemer and David Finkelhor] B. Bower. *Science News* 135:276-7 My 6 '89

Nutrition
The oldest diet ever—but it works. J. Wood. *Modern Maturity* 32:30-1 Ap/My '89
Study of meals programs. il *Aging* no359:30-1 '89
Tips for older adults [views of Ann Martin] *USA Today (Periodical)* 118:11 O '89
What can I eat these days? E. E. Rosenbaum. il *New Choices for the Best Years* 29:24-5 S '89

Occupations
Jobs that will keep you working happily ever after. T. Thompson. il *U.S. News & World Report* 107:64-6+ Ag 14 '89
A new job, a new life [cover story] G. Rosenblum. il *New Choices for the Best Years* 29:27-34 Ja '89
Shifting gears in midlife: attitude is all. R. Coles. il *New Choices for the Best Years* 29:85+ My '89
When it's time to change careers. E. McGrath. il *New Choices for the Best Years* 29:45-9 S '89

Pensions
See Pensions

Political activities
See also
Grandmothers for Peace (Organization)
Lobbyists and lobbying
Grandmother as lawbreaker [peace activist D. Eber] M. Ervin. il por *The Progressive* 53:11 Ja '89
Why the catastrophic-care fight will change generational politics. G. Borger. il *U.S. News & World Report* 107:18 O 9 '89

Psychiatric care
Depression can be conquered. L. Crooks. il *Modern Maturity* 32:10-11 O/N '89
Mobile mental health team reaches minorities [Pacific Clinics mental health center in Pasadena, Calif.] A. H. Hernandez and C. Schween. il *Aging* no359:12-13 '89

Psychology
Are we obsessed with age? [views of Mary Adams] il *USA Today (Periodical)* 117:7 Ap '89
Day by day. R. Coles. See issues of New Choices for the Best Years beginning March 1989
Feeling out 50. L. C. Pogrebin. il por *Ms.* 17:26 Je '89
Forever young: five success stories. E. E. Rosenbaum. il *New Choices for the Best Years* 29:24+ My '89
Peaking after 65: here's how [research by Lydia Bronte] J. C. Horn. *Psychology Today* 23:33-4 Jl/Ag '89
Trying on old age [experiment by college students] H. Hall. *Psychology Today* 22:67 D '88

Recreation
See also
Aged—Travel
Elderhostel
John Cristi, who sees 300 plays and concerts a year, may be the greatest show man on earth. S. Dougherty. il pors *People Weekly* 32:81+ O 2 '89
Parked in the middle of nowhere [retirees with RVs migrate to Quartzsite, Ariz. for the winter] J. Ackermann-Blount. il map *Time* 133:108-9 My 22 '89

Religious life
See also
Church work with the aged

Retirement
See Retirement

Sexual behavior
Ageless sex [research by Judy Bretschneider and Norma McCoy] P. McCarthy. *Psychology Today* 23:62 Mr '89
Sex after sixty. A. Poinsett. il *Ebony* 44:60+ Jl '89
Sex in midlife [quiz] T. H. Walz and N. S. Blum. il *New Choices for the Best Years* 29:60-2 Jl '89

Sleep
See Sleep

Social security
See Social security

Sports
See also
Fifty-Plus Runners Association
Senior Olympics
World Veterans Games
Grammy award [54 year old D. D. Allen wins Ms. Los Angeles '88 title] C. O'Connor. il por *Women's Sports & Fitness* 11:58 Je '89
Playing to win [tennis] R. M. Williams. il por *New Choices for the Best Years* 29:14+ N '89
Retirement benefits [taking up tennis later in life] A. Rich. il por *World Tennis* 37:22 O '89
Senior partners [doubles tennis players] G. M. Heldman. il *World Tennis* 36:66+ Ap '89
Seniority run rampant [senior sports deprive today's stars of their due] R. Reilly. por *Sports Illustrated* 71:80 Jl 17 '89
Speedy septuagenarians [marathon runners] M. Tymn. il *Runner's World* 24:26 N '89
That was then, this is now [senior tennis players] G. M. Heldman. il *World Tennis* 37:34-6 N '89
A wheel good time [tandem cycling; cover story] G. Lichtenstein. il *New Choices for the Best Years* 29:39-42 Ap '89
Whoa, whippersnapper! [discussion of July 17, 1989 article, Seniority run rampant] R. Reilly. il *Sports Illustrated* 71:90 Ag 14 '89
Woman of the century [H. Klein, 66 year old ultramarathoner] P. L. Potts. il pors *Runner's World* 24:34-6 Je '89

State aid
See Old age assistance

Statistics
More elderly than expected. *USA Today (Periodical)* 117:5-6 Ap '89

Suicide
See Suicide

Taxation
Are IRA's a hazard to your old age? *Newsweek* 114:42 S 18 '89
Cat scam [repeal of the Medicare Catastrophic Coverage Act] J. Weisberg. *The New Republic* 201:11-12 O 30 '89
Catastrophic follies [Medicare surcharge] P. Longman. *The New Republic* 201:16-18 Ag 21 '89
Catastrophic health benefits translate into catastrophic taxes [Medicare surcharge; cover story] P. J. Ferrara. *Consumers' Research Magazine* 72:11-14 Ap '89
Catastrophic politics [Congress repeals catastrophic health insurance] *National Review* 41:12-13 N 24 '89
Catastrophic tax bite [Medicare surcharge] J. W. Merline. il *Consumers' Research Magazine* 72:38 My '89
De-taxification [repeal of Catastrophic Health Care Act] D. Corn. *The Nation* 249:480-1 O 30 '89
The elderly duke it out [Medicare surcharge stirs senior lobby] A. Miller. il *Newsweek* 114:42-3 S 11 '89
Facing the new facts of life [older married couples] S. Weinman. il *Money* 18:178+ D '89
How to beat the bite of the new Medicare income tax surcharge. *Money* 18:17-18 Mr '89
Invitation to catastrophe [Congress votes to rescind catastrophic health insurance] *Time* 134:33 O 16 '89
IRS traps for the unwary home seller [tax exclusion on profits for those over age 55] L. Wiener. il *U.S. News & World Report* 106:80 My 22 '89
Medicare tax [municipal bond strategy as way to avoid surtax] B. Weberman. il *Forbes* 143:213 Mr 20 '89
Paying to work [report from National Center for Policy Analysis] J. W. Merline. il *Consumers' Research Magazine* 72:38 Ag '89
Repeal a bad health bill [Medicare Catastrophic Coverage Act] D. Gergen. il *U.S. News & World Report* 107:76 S 25 '89
A senior citizen rebellion has Congress retreating in disarray [Medicare tax surcharge] S. B. Garland. il *Business Week* p43 S 11 '89
Still time to save on taxes. A. Winter. il *Modern Maturity* 32:30+ D '89/Ja '90
Taking the teeth out of a new tax bite [Medicare surcharge] L. J. Nathans. *Business Week* p156 Mr 13 '89
Taxing the elderly. E. Rubenstein. *National Review* 41:29 O 13 '89
The torpedo that slammed into catastrophic health care [National Committee to Preserve Social Security] P. Dwyer. il *Business Week* p70 O 23 '89
Uncle Sam's retirement gift [tax exclusion on house sale profits] M. C. Paulson. *Changing Times* 43:104 Ja '89
A victory for the haves? [Congress votes to trim catastrophic health care due to uproar over income tax surcharge] E. Clift. il *Newsweek* 114:38 O 16 '89
Where the living is easy and taxes are low. T. Tritch. il *Money* 18 Money Guide:84 Fall '89
Why shifting investments to beat the Medicare tax can be a bad idea. M. C. Paulson. il *Changing Times* 43:120-2 Ap '89

AGED—Taxation—*cont.*

Your tax-time survival guide. M. Hodge. il *New Choices for the Best Years* 29:69-71 F '89

Travel

Cut-rate colleges, trains, planes and other top deals for travelers over 50. D. M. Topolnicki. il *Money* 18:145-6 F '89

Great short stops [weekend vacations; special section] il *New Choices for the Best Years* 29:48-55 Ja '89

Marketing to the older traveler [guidebooks] J. Crichton. il *Publishers Weekly* 235:56+ Ja 20 '89

Money savers. S. Brewer. il *New Choices for the Best Years* 29:11 Jl '89

Road tripping circa 2015. T. Blankenhorn. il *Road & Track* 40:54-6 My '89

Sans doute. *The New Yorker* 65:45-7 N 20 '89

Travelog. C. N. Barnard. See issues of Modern Maturity

Winter in the Texas tropics [retirees in the Rio Grande Valley; cover story] N. Cornell. il *New Choices for the Best Years* 29:22-6 N '89

Bibliography

Four for the road. il *New Choices for the Best Years* 29:11-12 My '89

Volunteer service

See Volunteer service

Japan

Growing old in Japan. R. L. Anders and M. Kanai-Pak. il *World Health* p8-11 D '88

Pacific region

The elderly. N. V. Nair. il *World Health* p23 N '89

United States

See Aged

Western Europe

Grappling with the graying of Europe. J. Templeman. il *Business Week* p54-6 Mr 13 '89

Is Europe worth the big price? [retirement] A. Rand. il map *New Choices for the Best Years* 29:38-40+ F '89

AGED AND ANIMALS

Who will care for my pets? A. Winter. *Modern Maturity* 32:18+ D '89/Ja '90

AGED AND BUSINESS

Retire and go to work? M. C. Paulson. il *Changing Times* 43:103 Ja '89

Turning your hobby into a business [cover story; special section] D. E. Gumpert and D. Davis. il *New Choices for the Best Years* 29:47-53 O '89

AGED AND CHILDREN *See* Child-adult relationship

AGED AND THE ENVIRONMENT

Let us protect our environment. L. Crooks. il *Modern Maturity* 32:14-15 D '89/Ja '90

Lewis & Nathan Clark: friends and brothers. B. Fuller. il pors *Sierra* 74:148-50+ Ja/F '89

AGED AND YOUTH *See* Youth-adult relationship

AGED AS ARTISTS

The Grand generation: memory, mastery, legacy. P. Jones. il *Aging* no359:44-5 '89

AGED AS CONSUMERS *See* Aged market

AGED AS MUSICIANS

Struttin' their stuff, the Dixie Belles are having a ball. il *People Weekly* 32:98-9 Jl 3 '89

AGED AUTOMOBILE DRIVERS

Age and driver fitness. E. Henry. *Changing Times* 43:100 My '89

Can a driver be too old? J. Carney. il *Time* 133:28 Ja 16 '89

Driven off the road by brain disease [research by Larry E. Tune] B. Bower. *Science News* 135:318 My 20 '89

The road to reason. M. E. Johnson. il *New Choices for the Best Years* 29:11 Mr '89

Road tripping circa 2015. T. Blankenhorn. il *Road & Track* 40:54-6 My '89

AGED IMMIGRANTS

Older immigrants find a new life [cover story; special issue; with editorial comment by Joyce T. Berry] il *Aging* no359:2-11+ '89

AGED IN ADVERTISING

Is that you on TV, Grandpa? J. Castro. il *Time* 133:53 Mr 6 '89

AGED LOBBY *See* Lobbyists and lobbying

AGED MARKET

The age wave—and how to ride it. C. Farrell. il *Business Week* p112+ O 16 '89

Discounts: yours for the asking. M. C. Paulson. *Changing Times* 43:124+ O '89

In search of older readers [over-50 book market] J. Crichton. il por *Publishers Weekly* 236:20+ Jl 7 '89

Is that you on TV, Grandpa? J. Castro. il *Time* 133:53 Mr 6 '89

Small gadgets that can change lives. F. Lunzer. bibl il *U.S. News & World Report* 106:58-60 Mr 6 '89

Taking a flyer on direct mail [D. Carmel's plans for business aimed at aged] K. H. Hammonds. il por *Business Week* p41 Jl 24 '89

U.S. companies go for the gray. W. Konrad and G. DeGeorge. il *Business Week* p64-7 Ap 3 '89

Wooing the whoopies. B. Kanner. il *New York* 22:20+ Mr 6 '89

Canada

Postponed pleasures. P. Chisholm. il *Maclean's* 102:24-5 Ja 9 '89

AGED PRISONERS

Growing old behind bars. G. Carroll. il *Newsweek* 114:70 N 20 '89

AGED REFUGEES

Older immigrants find a new life [cover story; special issue; with editorial comment by Joyce T. Berry] il *Aging* no359:2-11+ '89

Education

See also

Project LEIF

Elderly refugees and language learning. A. G. Grognet. il *Aging* no359:8-11 '89

Employment

Employment of older refugees: New York State initiatives. J. E. Bloom. il *Aging* no359:27-8 '89

N.Y. trains refugees to be counselors in service agencies. il *Aging* no359:29 '89

AGEE, JOEL

As the Wall came tumbling down. il *The New York Times Magazine* p42-3+ N 26 '89

A fury of symbols. il *Harper's* 278:49-52+ Ja '89

(tr) See Vilar, Esther. Experienced, qualified—and stupid

AGEE, WILLIAM MCREYNOLDS

about

Bill Agee gets a second chance. C. Knowlton. il por *Fortune* 119:94-6 Mr 27 '89

AGENCIES, ADVERTISING *See* Advertising agencies

AGENCIES, EMPLOYMENT *See* Employment agencies

AGENCIES, FEDERAL *See* United States—Executive departments

AGENCIES, GOVERNMENT *See* Government agencies

AGENCIES, LITERARY *See* Literary agencies and agents

AGENCIES, QUASI-GOVERNMENT *See* Quasi-government agencies

AGENCIES, REGULATORY *See* Regulatory agencies

AGENCIES, TRAVEL *See* Travel agencies and agents

AGENDA (COMPUTER PROGRAM) *See* Personal information management software

AGENT ORANGE

Agent Orange: Congress impatient for answers [Centers for Disease Control study vs. Stellman study] M. Barinaga. il *Science* 245:249-50 Jl 21 '89

AGENTS, LITERARY *See* Literary agencies and agents

AGENTS, REAL ESTATE *See* Real estate agencies and agents

AGENTS, SPORTS *See* Sports agencies and agents

AGENTS, TALENT *See* Theatrical agencies and agents

AGENZIA SPAZIALE ITALIANA

New Italian space agency awards first two development contracts. J. M. Lenorovitz. *Aviation Week & Space Technology* 130:97+ My 1 '89

New Italian space agency faces management and policy problems. J. M. Lenorovitz. *Aviation Week & Space Technology* 129:27 Mr 6 '89

AGGLUTININS

See also

Lectins

AGGRESSIVE BEHAVIOR IN ARACHNIDS *See* Arachnids—Habits and behavior

AGGRESSIVENESS (PSYCHOLOGY)

See also

Assertiveness (Psychology)

Fighting (Psychology)

Hostility (Psychology)

Passive-aggressive personality

Violence

Are men just born to be mean? B. G. Harrison. *Mademoiselle* 95:102 F '89

AGGRESSIVENESS IN CHILDREN

See also

Bullying

Rough-and-tumble play. S. Nurss. il *Parents* 64:243-4+ N '89

AGHEE, MIRA B.

The tobacco tradition in India. il *World Health* p23 Ja/F '89

AGILITY *See* Motor ability

AGING

See also

Gerontology

National Leadership Institute on Aging

Progeria

Aging bull. K. C. Cole. il *Ms.* 17:44+ Ap '89

Aging comes of age. T. Beardsley. il *Scientific American* 260:17+ My '89

The aging eye. R. M. Henig. il *The New York Times Magazine* p47-8 Mr 26 '89

Blood clotting may increase with age [research by Robert Rosenberg] J. L. Marx. *Science* 243:316 Ja 20 '89

Can you preserve a lean body? [loss is part of the aging process; study by Margaret Flynn] il *USA Today (Periodical)* 118:6 O '89

Cellular aging [evidence that mitochondrial DNA damage leads to decrease in cellular respiration; research by Anthony Linnane and others] *Discover* 10:13-14 S '89

AGING—*cont.*

Corticosteroid modulation of hippocampal potentials: increased effect with aging. D. S. Kerr and others. bibl f il *Science* 245:1505-9 S 29 '89

Daily de-aging: how to take years off your looks every morning. il *Ladies' Home Journal* 106:116-19+ Ja '89

Give your lips a lift. J. Jones. il *Redbook* 172:100-3 F '89

Growing old together: fruit flies and you [effects of catalase production on cell aging in Drosophila; research by Glenn Bewley] il *Discover* 10:8 Ap '89

Health celebrates life [cover story; special section; with editorial comment by Robert N. Butler] il *Health (New York, N.Y.)* 21:8, 53-9+ O '89

How to take better care of your hair. L. Heller. il *Redbook* 172:98-9+ Ja '89

Life after work [stretching the mind] J. Groch. il *American Health* 8:98+ Mr '89

Lives of the body. S. Tisdale. *Harper's* 279:38+ O '89

Now, where did I put my . . . [effects of aging on memory] J. Hooper. il *Health (New York, N.Y.)* 21:72-3 N '89

Older brains don't fade away [cell shrinkage; research by Robert D. Terry] S. Chollar. il *Psychology Today* 22:22 D '88

Postponing red-cell retirement. R. Weiss. il *Science News* 136:424-5 D 23-30 '89

The return of the mind [M. Diamond's theory that brain's plasticity allows it to keep growing into old age] S. Blakeslee. il por *American Health* 8:94-6 Mr '89

A ride on the age wave [views of K. Dychtwald] S. Walton. il *Health (New York, N.Y.)* 21:40+ Jl '89

The senior boom: how it will change America [views of K. Dychtwald] F. S. Chapman. il por *Fortune* 119:62 Mr 27 '89

Slow forward [antiaging strategies] P. Dranov. il *American Health* 8:62-4+ Jl/Ag '89

Slowing down the march of time. T. Prentice. *World Press Review* 36:31-2 F '89

Thirty years of fortitude [staying active to offset physical decline] J. Poppy. il *Esquire* 112:83-5 D '89

The wandering mind of youth [minds wander less as people get older; research by Alicia Grodsky and Leonard Giambra] P. Chance. *Psychology Today* 22:22 D '88

When our senses grow old . . . L. J. Brown. il *Good Housekeeping* 208:170-1 Ja '89

Nutritional aspects

Curtailing calories may lengthen life. il *FDA Consumer* 23:3-4 F '89

Wanted: 40 more years. D. Teresi. il *Health (New York, N.Y.)* 21:58-9+ O '89

Psychology

See Aged—Psychology

Research

See Gerontology

AGING ADMINISTRATION (U.S.) *See* United States. Administration on Aging

AGING AIRCRAFT TASK FORCE

Airworthiness Task Force coordinating review of world transport fleet. *Aviation Week & Space Technology* 131:67 Jl 24 '89

AGNELLI, GIOVANNI

The Europe of 1992. *Foreign Affairs* 68:61-70 Fall '89

about

Agnelli on cars, greens, and Japan. R. I. Kirkland, Jr. il pors *Fortune* 120:133+ Jl 31 '89

AGNES B. *See* B., Agnes

AGNEW, SPIRO, 1918-

English, anyone? por *Conservative Digest* 15:44-5 My/Je '89

AGNOS, ART

about

Art Agnos: scapegoat by the Bay? J. O. Hamilton. il por *Business Week* p46+ Ap 17 '89

Digging out from under. il pors *People Weekly* 32:46-51 N 6 '89

AGOR, WESTON H., 1939-

Intuition & strategic planning. il por *The Futurist* 23:20-3 N/D '89

AGRACETUS INC.

Breaking biotech barriers in botany [work of W. J. Brill] L. Therrien. il por *Business Week* Special Issue:78 Je 16 '89

AGRAFIOTIS, PETER

about

Soothing memories. M. Clark. il por *American Artist* 53:60-5+ O '89

AGRARIAN REFORM *See* Land reform

AGRE, PETER, 1949-, AND OTHERS

Cognate DNA binding specificity retained after leucine zipper exchange between GCN4 and C/EBP. bibl f il *Science* 246:922-6 N 17 '89

AGREEMENTS *See* Contracts

AGREEMENTS, COLLECTIVE LABOR *See* Collective labor agreements

AGREST & GANDELSONAS

Agrest and Gandelsonas: a sleek Manhattan remodel. P. Goldberger. il *Architectural Digest* 46:94-7+ Ap '89

Homage to Loos [duplex Manhattan apartment] M. F. Schmertz. il *Architectural Record* 177:50-7 mid-S '89

AGRESTO, JOHN

Letting great books speak to students. *The Education Digest* 54:33-4 F '89

AGRIBUSINESS *See* Agricultural industries

AGRICULTURAL ACCIDENTS *See* Agriculture—Accidents

AGRICULTURAL ADMINISTRATION

See also

Federal Crop Insurance Corporation

Land reform

Soil conservation—Laws and regulations

United States. Dept. of Agriculture

Alternatives for US agriculture [National Research Council report] il *BioScience* 39:660 O '89

The attraction is chemical [cooperation between farmers and environmentalists] J. Schwab. *The Nation* 249:416+ O 16 '89

Bush's farmer in the White House [C. Evans] G. Vincent. il por *Successful Farming* 87:34AF mid-F '89

Business. B. Helming. il *Successful Farming* 87 no4:15 Mr '89

Business. B. Helming. il *Successful Farming* 87:14 Ap '89

Business. B. Helming. il *Successful Farming* 87:11 N '89

Business. B. Helming. il *Successful Farming* 87:17 My '89

Business [reduced government cash subsidy payments] B. Helming. il *Successful Farming* 87:9 D '89

The canola caper. J. Novack. il *Forbes* 144:132 O 16 '89

Dairymen say 'Happy New Year,' to prices in 1989. J. R. Borcherding. *Successful Farming* 87:62 F '89

Ever heard of Dick Darman? It's time you did. P. Smith. *Successful Farming* 87:34 Ag '89

Expect new farm bill to shape up by mid-1990. P. Smith. *Successful Farming* 87:48 O '89

Farm futures [adaptation of 1987 address] D. Terry. il *Mother Jones* 14:6-8 O '89

Farmers have two minds on farm policy. *Successful Farming* 87:4 Je '89

A fresh crop of ideas [state programs] S. DeMarco. il *The Progressive* 53:26-31 Ja '89

Greening of the farm bill. R. L. Meyers. *BioScience* 39:599 O '89

Helping farms caught in the middle. W. Meyers. il *Successful Farming* 87:48U mid-Mr '89

His farm bill helps family farms and the environment. C. Hassebrook. *Successful Farming* 87:32G S '89

How politics shaped 1989 crop disaster bill. P. Smith. *Successful Farming* 87:32 S '89

Letters from home [tax fugitive M. Rich gets U.S. export subsidies on wheat deals with the Soviets] J. Willoughby. il por *Forbes* 143:38-9 Je 12 '89

Nature vs. nurture on the farm [Alternative agriculture report by the National Research Council] K. R. Sheets. il *U.S. News & World Report* 107:53-4 S 18 '89

PACs: farmers' $8-million muscle man. P. Smith. il *Successful Farming* 87:8-9 Ap '89

Sold on organic [cover story; with editorial comment by Stevie O. Daniels] J. Poncavage. il map *Organic Gardening* 36:5, 42-6 Je '89

Sugar lumps [U.S. sugar program] P. C. Montgomery. il *Common Cause Magazine* 15:10-11 Ja/F '89

They don't need Farm Aid concerts now. R. Reiff. il *Forbes* 143:68-71 Ap 17 '89

Three yards and a cloud of (sugar) dust [protectionist U.S. sugar policy] J. Novack. il *Forbes* 144:39-41 S 4 '89

U.S. consumers, and the Caribbean, are getting a sour deal on sugar. P. Magnusson. il *Business Week* p41 My 8 '89

Uncle Sam's farm follies [agricultural subsidies] B. Hurst. il *Reader's Digest* 134:124-6 Ja '89

Washington report. P. Smith. See issues of Successful Farming beginning April 1987 through January 1989

Wine and roses on the farm. H. Banks. il *Forbes* 143:35-6 Je 26 '89

International aspects

The agricultural swamp [subsidies] J. Bovard. il *National Review* 41:46-8 F 10 '89

Economist tells danger of totally free markets [views of Daryll Ray] *Successful Farming* 87:48E N '89

How GATT will affect the 1990 farm bill. *Successful Farming* 87:32A Je '89

Canada

Chicken wars in the Great White North [L. and P. Trottier fight Ontario marketing board over right to raise chickens] D. Francis. il *Maclean's* 102:11 Ja 9 '89

China

China prepares for a bitter harvest [effects of student crackdown] E. MacFarquhar. il *U.S. News & World Report* 107:34-5 Jl 10 '89

Developing countries

Sustaining agriculture on marginal land: a policy framework. E. B. Barbier. bibl f il *Environment* 31:12-17+ N '89

Poland

Polish farmers use food as a weapon. il *U.S. News & World Report* 107:34-5 Ag 14 '89

Puerto Rico

Puerto Rico: growth, change, progress, development. B. Wallach. il maps *Focus (New York, N.Y.: 1950)* 39:27-33 Summ '89

AGRICULTURAL ADMINISTRATION—*cont.*
Switzerland
Views from a Swiss farm. R. M. Ketchum. il *Country Journal* 16:34-8 N/D '89
United States
See Agricultural administration
Western Europe
See also
European Economic Community
AGRICULTURAL AIRPLANES *See* Airplanes in agriculture
AGRICULTURAL BANKS *See* Agricultural credit
AGRICULTURAL CHEMICALS
See also
Herbicides
Pesticides
Disposal
Illinois county holds second chemical cleanup. R. Fee. *Successful Farming* 87:26 Ja '89
Handling
Air power gets the job done. D. Mowitz. il *Successful Farming* 87:22-3 mid-Mr '89
AGRICULTURAL CHEMICALS INDUSTRY
Management
Productivity trends in agricultural chemicals. H. Brand and K. Bryant. bibl f il *Monthly Labor Review* 112:21-8 Mr '89
AGRICULTURAL COLLEGES
Curriculum
Ag schools out-of-step? C. Tevis. il *Successful Farming* 87:17 N '89
AGRICULTURAL CONSULTANTS
'I'm in the dark' [views of R. Allen] G. Johnston. il por *Successful Farming* 87:34X mid-F '89
Market advisers get a report card [crop marketing] il *Successful Farming* 87:15 mid-Mr '89
This is the year to scout for a scout. B. Freese. il *Successful Farming* 87:50AC Ja '89
AGRICULTURAL COOPERATION *See* Agriculture, Cooperative
AGRICULTURAL COOPERATIVES *See* Agriculture, Cooperative
AGRICULTURAL CREDIT
See also
Federal Agricultural Mortgage Corporation
United States. Farmers Home Administration
Ag loans showing pep in Midwest. *Successful Farming* 87:48A N '89
How to lower your interest rate. D. Allen. il *Successful Farming* 87:66Z F '89
Why you'll be borrowing more this year. *Successful Farming* 87:50C Ja '89
History
The cotton crisis. A. S. Johnson. *The New Republic* 201 [Reprint v1]:17-18 N 6 '89 [N 7 '14]
International aspects
Love 'em and leave 'em. M. Fritz. il *Forbes* 144:48 N 13 '89
AGRICULTURAL DIVERSIFICATION *See* Diversification in agriculture
AGRICULTURAL ECOLOGY
The attraction is chemical [cooperation between farmers and environmentalists] J. Schwab. *The Nation* 249:416+ O 16 '89
Back to Eden [work of W. Jackson; cover story; with editorial comment] E. Eisenberg. il por *The Atlantic* 264:6, 57-9+ N '89
Breadbasket ecology [Land Institute; work of W. Jackson] D. Hand. il map por *American Health* 8:66-8 S '89
The climatic advantages of pigging out [study by Florentin Krause] *Science News* 136:381 D 9 '89
Cultivating alternative agriculture [National Research Council report] *Science News* 136:204 S 23 '89
Farmers are learning new tricks from Mother Nature [alternative or sustainable agriculture] E. T. Smith. il *Business Week* p76+ N 6 '89
Greening of the farm bill. R. L. Meyers. *BioScience* 39:599 O '89
His farm bill helps family farms and the environment. C. Hassebrook. *Successful Farming* 87:32G S '89
Prophet of the prairie [work of W. Jackson at the Land Institute] J. R. Luoma. il pors map *Audubon* 91:54-60 N '89
Range war [National Research Council report on alternative agriculture] T. Beardsley. *Scientific American* 261:20D+ D '89
Saving the land. E. Levy. *The Nation* 249:418 O 16 '89
"Soil is not a factory" [sustainable agriculture] J. R. Luoma. il *Audubon* 91:61-3 N '89
Sustaining agriculture on marginal land: a policy framework. E. B. Barbier. bibl f il *Environment* 31:12-17+ N '89
AGRICULTURAL ECONOMICS *See* Agriculture—Economic aspects
AGRICULTURAL EDUCATION
See also
4-H clubs
AGRICULTURAL EQUIPMENT
See also
All terrain vehicles—Agricultural use

Blowers (Machinery)
Cultivators
Grain handling
Harvesting machinery
Hay handling—Equipment
Irrigation equipment
Planters (Farm machines)
Spraying equipment
Machinery. See issues of Successful Farming
Power blowers: rev 'em up to clean the farm. D. Mowitz. il *Successful Farming* 87:24-5 F '89
Lighting
More machinery accidents prompt new lighting rules. C. Finck. *Successful Farming* 87:50I Ja '89
Maintenance and repair
Deere pleased with stocking parts on farms. *Successful Farming* 87:44 Ag '89
Gadget gallery. D. Mowitz. il *Successful Farming* 87:26-9 Ap '89
A shop on the spot [farm service truck] C. Finck. il *Successful Farming* 87:28 F '89
Tool trucks. D. Mowitz. il *Successful Farming* 87:66V-66W F '89
Safety devices and measures
Industry can't make fail-safe farms. il *Successful Farming* 87:18N mid-F '89
AGRICULTURAL EQUIPMENT INDUSTRY
See also
Caterpillar Inc.
Deere & Company
J. I. Case Company
Tenneco Inc.
Finance
Big bruisers come back to the farm [tractors] K. R. Sheets. il *U.S. News & World Report* 106:51+ Je 19 '89
AGRICULTURAL ETHICS *See* Agriculture—Ethical aspects
AGRICULTURAL EXHIBITIONS
Great Britain
Royal shows & agricultural progress, 1839-1989. N. Goddard. bibl il *History Today* 39:44-51 Jl '89
AGRICULTURAL INDUSTRIES
See also
Alico Inc.
Archer-Daniels-Midland Co.
Cargill, Inc.
ConAgra, Inc.
Dekalb Corp.
Inspiration Resources Corp.
J.G. Boswell Company
Pioneer Hi-Bred International, Inc.
Advertising
The farmer's market [Memphis independent TV station WPTY attracting agriculture ad dollars] R. Katz. il map *Channels (New York, N.Y.: 1986)* 9:12+ My '89
Export-import trade
Cocaine countries try to grow straight [America's protectionist policy towards South American agricultural imports] A. Gabor. il *U.S. News & World Report* 107:57 O 23 '89
Finance
The 400 largest farms in the U.S. [with editorial comment by Loren Kruse] G. Johnston and D. Ohrtman. il *Successful Farming* 87:1, 8-15 My '89
Food processors. J. Novack. il *Forbes* 143:144+ Ja 9 '89
United States
See Agricultural industries
AGRICULTURAL LAWS AND REGULATIONS *See* Agricultural administration
AGRICULTURAL MACHINERY *See* Agricultural equipment
AGRICULTURAL MACHINERY INDUSTRY *See* Agricultural equipment industry
AGRICULTURAL MARKETING *See* Farm produce—Marketing; Produce trade
AGRICULTURAL MARKETING CONSULTANTS *See* Agricultural consultants
AGRICULTURAL MUSEUMS
See also
Farmers' Museum
Living History Farms (Des Moines, Iowa)
Malabar Farm State Park (Lucas, Ohio)
AGRICULTURAL PLANNING *See* Farm management
AGRICULTURAL POLICY *See* Agricultural administration
AGRICULTURAL PRODUCE TRADE *See* Produce trade
AGRICULTURAL PRODUCTION *See* Production, Agricultural
AGRICULTURAL PRODUCTS *See* Farm produce
AGRICULTURAL RESEARCH
See also
Field experiments (Agriculture)
Food supply—New sources
Horticultural research
Land Institute (Kan.)
Plant genetics
Rodale Research Center
Biotechnology and agriculture [address, November 3, 1989] R. McGuire. *Vital Speeches of the Day* 56:147-50 D 15 '89
Wanted: purer food. R. Rodale. il *Prevention (Emmaus, Pa.)* 41:26+ Je '89

AGRICULTURAL RESEARCH—cont.

Federal aid

Agricultural groups push research plan [USDA competitive grants program] M. Crawford. il *Science* 244:140 Ap 14 '89

NRC unveils agriculture R&D plan. M. Crawford. *Science* 246:27 O 6 '89

International aspects

Quarantine and the exchange of crop genetic resources. D. L. Plucknett and N. J. H. Smith. bibl f il *BioScience* 39:16-23 Ja '89

Strategies for agriculture. P. R. Crosson and N. J. Rosenberg. bibl il *Scientific American* 261:128-35 S '89

World food research. P. H. Abelson. *Science* 244:125 Ap 14 '89

Developing countries

Appropriate biotech. T. Kiely. il *Technology Review* 92:11-12 Ag/S '89

AGRICULTURAL SOCIETIES

See also

4-H clubs
National Pork Producers Council
Royal Agricultural Society of England

AGRICULTURAL SUBSIDIES *See* Agricultural administration

AGRICULTURAL SURPLUS PRODUCTS *See* Surplus products, Agricultural

AGRICULTURAL WASTE *See* Farm waste

AGRICULTURAL WORKERS *See* Farm labor

AGRICULTURE

See also

Airplanes in agriculture
All terrain vehicles—Agricultural use
Aquaculture
Burning of land
Computers—Agricultural use
Contour farming
Dairying
Diversification in agriculture
Dry farming
Electronics in agriculture
Farm corporations
Farm labor
Farm life
Farm management
Farmers
Food supply
Homesteads
Hydroponics
Indians of North America—Agriculture
Indians of South America—Agriculture
Irrigation
Livestock
Organic farming
Peasantry
Poultry industry
Religion and agriculture
Seeding
Seeds
Shifting cultivation
Strip cropping
Terraces (Agriculture)
Tillage
Tracked vehicles—Agricultural use
Truck farming
Urban agriculture
Viticulture

Accidents

Courage on wheels. D. Gosch. il por *The Mother Earth News* 119:38-9 S/O '89

Farm group focuses on first aid. N. Stannard. il *Successful Farming* 87:54 Ag '89

More machinery accidents prompt new lighting rules. C. Finck. *Successful Farming* 87:50I Ja '89

Too tough to die [Airedale comes to aid of J. Tarpley who was crushed by a tractor] P. O. D'Aulaire and E. D'Aulaire. il *Reader's Digest* 135:81-6 N '89

We kill too many farm kids [special section] C. Tevis and C. Finck. il *Successful Farming* 87:18A-18B+ mid-F '89

Economic aspects

See also

Agricultural administration
Agricultural credit
Agricultural industries
Farm produce—Prices
Farm rents
Farms—Size
Land reform
Land values
Organic farming—Economic aspects
Produce trade
Production, Agricultural

1988 farm profits dried up. G. Johnston. il *Successful Farming* 87:16-17 Ag '89

All that rain has been good for most farmers—and every shopper. T. Young. il *Fortune* 120:25+ S 11 '89

Business. B. Helming. il *Successful Farming* 87:9 D '89

The farm crisis is not going away. B. Ahlberg. il *Utne Reader* p89-91 Jl/Ag '89

Gene Johnston: production. G. Johnston. il *Successful Farming* 87:21 Ag '89

Inflation returns to farm country. G. Johnston. *Successful Farming* 87:50A Ja '89

Money. See issues of Successful Farming

They don't need Farm Aid concerts now. R. Reiff. il *Forbes* 143:68-71 Ap 17 '89

Tough times on Canada's farms. D. Francis. il *Maclean's* 102:11 S 4 '89

Trouble on Canada's farms. D. Francis. *World Press Review* 36:61 N '89

Wintertime—and the farmers aren't easy. K. A. Behof. il *Business Week* p24-5 Mr 6 '89

With a little bit of luck, farmers could clean up. R. Mitchell. il *Business Week* p98-9 Ja 9 '89

Environmental aspects

See Agricultural ecology

Ethical aspects

Ethical choice in food systems [address, October 26, 1989] J. C. Rennie. *Vital Speeches of the Day* 56:143-7 D 15 '89

Exhibitions

See Agricultural exhibitions

Federal aid

See Agricultural administration

History

See also

Agriculture, Prehistoric

Production [best and the worst of farming in the 1980s] G. Johnston. il *Successful Farming* 87:23 N '89

Periodicals

See also

Successful farming (Periodical)

Public relations

Agriculture and animal rights [address, July 27, 1989] R. McGuire. *Vital Speeches of the Day* 55:766-8 O 1 '89

Religious aspects

See Religion and agriculture

Research

See Agricultural research

Scholarships and fellowships

Here's help from ag scholarships. C. Tevis. il *Successful Farming* 87:48H-48I mid-Mr '89

The winners are . . . C. Tevis. il *Successful Farming* 87:56 Ag '89

Taxation

See also

Farmers—Taxation

Terminology

Down-to-earth language. R. Lederer. il *Country Journal* 16:48-9 Ja '89

Alaska

See also

Tiny Moose Farm

California

Sonoma County: fresh from the farm. C. Bates. il map *Gourmet* 49:86-91+ S '89

Testing toxins at $100 a day [testing of banned pesticides on humans] J. H. Kay. il *The Nation* 248:300-2 Mr 6 '89

Canada

See also

Agricultural administration—Canada

Tough times on Canada's farms. D. Francis. il *Maclean's* 102:11 S 4 '89

Trouble on Canada's farms. D. Francis. *World Press Review* 36:61 N '89

China

See also

Agricultural administration—China

Colorado

Lobbyist in the winter/farmer in the summer [K. Kelley] il por *Successful Farming* 87:39 Ja '89

Developing countries

See also

Agricultural administration—Developing countries

Florida

See also

Hardee Farms

Great Britain

See also

Royal Agricultural Society of England

Around and around in circles [crop field rings in southern England] S. B. Donnelly. il *Time* 134:50 S 18 '89

The thumb prints of the gods? [unexplained circular patterns of wheat] il *U.S. News & World Report* 107:13 S 11 '89

History

Nurturing nature: agriculture in history [cover story; special section] bibl f il maps *History Today* 39:26-50 Jl '89

Idaho

Immigrating dairies push into Idaho. J. R. Borcherding. il *Successful Farming* 87:22 S '89

Illinois

See also

Frank Farms, Inc.

How I made $812 in the oat bran craze. P. W. Moser. il *Fortune* 120:125+ O 9 '89

AGRICULTURE—cont.

Indiana

His own labor, custom work turns farm around. il *Successful Farming* 87:66I F '89

Successful family farm [Milligan family of Dana] M. Holmberg. il pors *Successful Farming* 87:60-2 O '89

Iowa

See also

Commercial Cattle Feeders of Iowa

Stewart's Duroc Farm

Why is this woman making a wetland? [work of Florine Swanson] J. Walter. il *Successful Farming* 87:58-9 Ag '89

Israel

Desert bloom [runoff agriculture in the Negev Desert; work of M. Evenari] D. Starr. il *Omni (New York, N.Y.)* 11:28+ Mr '89

Italy

History

The nuts of Pompeii [work of Frederick Meyer] il *Discover* 10:14 N '89

Kansas

See also

Land Institute (Kan.)

Long Island (N.Y.)

The Wickham family holds fast. S. Wick. il *Country Journal* 16:61-6 My/Je '89

Michigan

Farm wife shares drought journal of despair, hope. M. Wilcox. il *Successful Farming* 87:66AI F '89

Middle Western States

Anecdotes, facetiae, satire, etc.

Plains? Great! P. Nelson. il *Mother Jones* 14:53-4 Je '89

Nebraska

See also

Bader Family Farm

You can come home again [swine farm liquidated by R. Kahle now run by son S. Kahle] B. Freese. il pors *Successful Farming* 87:15 D '89

New Hampshire

Family farms forever! [Tuttle farm named oldest in America] J. Walter. il map *Successful Farming* 87:22-4 Ja '89

Long road home to an upland farm. M. Kumin. il *Country Journal* 16:75-9 My/Je '89

New York (State)

See also

Coach Farm

Harvest of pride [Van Vorst family] G. Norman. il pors *New Choices for the Best Years* 29:30-5 Jl '89

Successful family farm: deep roots and dairy traditions [Skellie farm] J. R. Borcherding. il *Successful Farming* 87:46-8 Ag '89

Newfoundland

The cucumber scandal [Minister C. Power resigns] C. White. *Maclean's* 102:16 Ja 23 '89

Nicaragua

Bad seeds in Nicaragua. B. Weinberg. *The Nation* 249:50+ Jl 10 '89

North Dakota

Dimples on a black desert [wetland conservation efforts hampered by farmers] T. Williams. il *Audubon* 91:36-8+ S '89

Hay growers go for quality; then set price! il *Successful Farming* 87:64G Ap '89

Ohio

An Amish drought journal. D. Kline. il *The Mother Earth News* 118:60-1 Jl/Ag '89

Oklahoma

History

The Dust Bowl [Cimarron County, Okla.; cover story] M. Parfit. bibl (p174) il *Smithsonian* 20:44-54+ Je '89

Pennsylvania

Out to pasture, in the money. J. R. Borcherding. il *Successful Farming* 87:29 My '89

Poland

See also

Agricultural administration—Poland

South America

A center of crop genetic diversity in western Amazonia. C. R. Clement. bibl f il maps *BioScience* 39:624-31 O '89

Cocaine countries try to grow straight [America's protectionist policy towards agricultural imports] A. Gabor. il *U.S. News & World Report* 107:57 O 23 '89

South Dakota

Successful family farm [Koskan family of Wood] J. Walter. il *Successful Farming* 87:46-8 D '89

Soviet Union

A blight on the fruited plain. *Business Week* p57+ Je 5 '89

Can Gorbachev feed Russia? M. Kramer. il *The New York Times Magazine* p42-3+ Ap 9 '89

Comrade Gorbachev's leap in the dark. *National Review* 41:13-14 Ap 21 '89

Farming for dollars: Gorbachev's latest gamble. P. Galuszka. il *Business Week* p44 Ag 28 '89

Gorby's farm reform a hard row to hoe. por *U.S. News & World Report* 106:9-10 Mr 27 '89

Half a loaf, on a good day. il *U.S. News & World Report* 107:36 N 20 '89

New masters of the land. il *Time* 133:53 Mr 27 '89

Soviet farm manager goes for 'profit' too. G. Vincent. il *Successful Farming* 87:50AH Ja '89

Why Russia can't feed itself. D. Satter. *Reader's Digest* 135:61-6 O '89

Switzerland

See also

Agricultural administration—Switzerland

Tanzania

Tanzania's agricultural woes [study by Sitna Mohamed] *Focus (New York, N.Y.: 1950)* 38:29-30 Wint '88

Texas

See also

Texas. Dept. of Agriculture

Farm workers don't have to be poor. T. Rosenberg. *The Washington Monthly* 21:22-4+ Ap '89

Successful family farm [sweet corn and fresh vegetable business owned by Wieck family] M. Holmberg. il *Successful Farming* 87:38-40 mid-Mr '89

History

Watermelon king remembered [R. Chatham] P. S. Prather. il por *American Visions* 4:38-9 Ag '89

Ukraine

Milking a profit from Mayak farm. il *U.S. News & World Report* 106:46-7 Ap 3 '89

Planting some new ideas [Ohioan R. Dull participates in farm exchange program] W. Sloane. il por *Time* 134:14-15 O 2 '89

Vermont

See also

Rodgers Dairy Farm

Condos where cows once grazed. K. J. Kelley. il *The Progressive* 53:28 N '89

Wisconsin

See also

Fitz-Haven Dairy

AGRICULTURE, COOPERATIVE

See also

Collective settlements

Ganados del Valle (Organization)

Neighbors are partners in his Hereford herd [D. Catey] L. F. Hoffman. por *Successful Farming* 87:44 F '89

AGRICULTURE, PREHISTORIC

Conflict enters early European farm life [research by Lawrence H. Keeley] B. Bower. *Science News* 136:165 S 9 '89

Corn and culture in central Andean prehistory. S. Johannessen and C. A. Hastorf. bibl f il *Science* 244:690-2 My 12 '89

Origins of agriculture in eastern North America. B. D. Smith. bibl f il map *Science* 246:1566-71 D 22 '89

The origins of Indo-European languages. C. Renfrew. bibl il maps *Scientific American* 261:106-14 O '89

Stone blades yield early cultivation clues [research by Romana Unger-Hamilton] B. Bower. *Science News* 135:101 F 18 '89

AGRICULTURE, URBAN See Urban agriculture

AGRICULTURE AND CLIMATE See Plants, Effect of climate on

AGRICULTURE AND STATE See Agricultural administration

AGRICULTURE DEPT. (TEX.) See Texas. Dept. of Agriculture

AGRICULTURE DEPT. (U.S.) See United States. Dept. of Agriculture

AGRUSA, LISA

about

Careers by design. il pors *Harper's Bazaar* 122:188-91+ Mr '89

AGTERBERG, FREDERIK P.

Computer programs for mineral exploration. bibl f il maps *Science* 245:76-81 Jl 7 '89

AGUALLO, THOMALINE

To love again [story] il *Good Housekeeping* 208:28+ Mr '89

AGUARUNA INDIANS

Dark side of the shaman. M. F. Brown. *Natural History* p8+ N '89

AGUIRRE, MARK

about

And the winner is . . . J. McCallum. il pors *Sports Illustrated* 70:34-6 Mr 6 '89

AGULHON, MAURICE

The once and future Revolution. il *The Courier (Unesco)* 42:17-22 Mr '89

AGUSTA SPA

A+: Agusta A109 MkII Plus [cover story] J. M. McClellan. il *Flying* 116:34-8+ F '89

AHA See American Humane Association

AHARONOV-BOHM EFFECT

Quantum interference and the Aharonov-Bohm effect. Y. Imry and R. A. Webb. bibl il *Scientific American* 260:56-62 Ap '89

AHARONOV-CASHER EFFECT

Out of its field. R. Ruthen. *Scientific American* 261:26 O '89

Quantum interference. I. Peterson. *Science News* 136:363 D 2 '89

AHDAL, ABDULLAH AL *See* Al Ahdal, Abdullah
AHEARN, C. DENNIS
Government procurement: friend or foe? *Ad Astra* 1:36 S '89
AHEARNE, JOHN F.
Fixing the nation's nuclear-weapons plants. il *Technology Review* 92:24-9 Jl '89
AHERN, PATRICK V.
The cantata of love. *America* 160:53 Ja 28 '89
AHLADAS, JOHN A.
Global warming [address, February 7, 1989] *Vital Speeches of the Day* 55:381-4 Ap 1 '89
AHLBERG, BRIAN
The farm crisis is not going away. il *Utne Reader* p89-91 Jl/Ag '89
AHLBORN, GARY
(jt. auth) *See* Jackson, Rodney, and Ahlborn, Gary
AHMAD, EQBAL
Stalemate at Jalalabad. il *The Nation* 249:384-7 O 9 '89
AHMAD HASAN DANI *See* Dani, Ahmad Hasan
AHMED, AKBAR S.
A third encounter of the close kind [cover story] il *History Today* 39:4-9 N '89
AHMED, WILLIAM
about
A man in orbit. *Time* 134:26 Jl 3 '89
AHN, JUNGHYO, 1941-
about
Soho launches Korean novelist in the U.S. il por *Publishers Weekly* 236:57-8 O 6 '89
AHOLD U.S.A., INC.
Shopping for bargains [Ahold USA] J. Zweig. il por *Forbes* 144:274 Jl 24 '89
AHRENS, HANNO, 1954-
about
Hanno Ahrens: wood spirits. D. Rubey. il por *Art News* 88:85-6 F '89
AHRENS, RÜDIGER
(jt. auth) *See* White, Edward M. (Edward Michael), 1933-, and Ahrens, Rüdiger
AI *See* Artificial intelligence
AIA *See* American Institute of Architects
AIBS *See* American Institute of Biological Sciences
AID (ARTIFICIAL INSEMINATION WITH DONOR) *See* Artificial insemination, Human
AID (AUTOMATIC IMPLANTABLE DEFIBRILLATORS) *See* Defibrillators
AIDA [opera] *See* Verdi, Giuseppe, 1813-1901
AIDS (DISEASE)
See also
ACT UP (Organization)
AIDS ARMS Network
Fetal AIDS syndrome
1989: AIDS. M. Beck. il *Newsweek* 114:57 Jl 3 '89
An AIDS-associated microbe unmasked [Mycoplasma incognita; research by Shyh-Ching Lo] A. McKenzie. *Science News* 136:356 D 2 '89
AIDS panel urges new focus [National Research Council report] G. Byrne. *Science* 243:887 F 17 '89
AIDS researchers upset by refusal to share probes on mysterious microbe [case of Shyh-Ching Lo] W. Booth. *Science* 244:416 Ap 28 '89
Are we closing in on AIDS? J. Pekkanen. *Reader's Digest* 135:79-85 D '89
Darrell Yates Rist replies [discussion of February 13, 1989 article, The deadly costs of an obsession] D. Y. Rist. *The Nation* 248:834+ Je 19 '89
The deadly costs of an obsession [concern with AIDS diverts campaign for gay rights; cover story] D. Y. Rist. il *The Nation* 248:181+ F 13 '89
Exchange [discussion of February 13, 1989 article, The deadly costs of an obsession] D. Y. Rist. *The Nation* 248:578+ My 1 '89
Fending off AIDS with deep sleep? [research by Suzan E. Norman] K. Fackelmann. *Science News* 136:13 Jl 1 '89
Gay politics and AIDS [discussion of February 13, 1989 article, The deadly costs of an obsession] D. Y. Rist. *The Nation* 248:362+ Mr 20 '89
How to block a killer's path. J. Langone. il *Time* 133:60-2 Ja 30 '89
The latest on AIDS. A. Atkins. *Better Homes and Gardens* 67:52+ Ap '89
Letters [discussion of October 1988 article, AIDS in 1988] R. C. Gallo and L. Montagnier. *Scientific American* 260:10-11 Je '89
My life stalking AIDS. R. C. Gallo. il por *Discover* 10:30-3+ O '89
The new face of AIDS. B. D. Colen. il *Health (New York, N.Y.)* 21:36+ D '89
Phoenix rising [influence of AIDS on changes in health care; cover story] L. Marsa. il *Omni (New York, N.Y.)* 12:50-4+ D '89
Plasma HIV reflects AIDS progression. K. Fackelmann. *Science News* 136:389 D 16 '89
Questions about AIDS. *Consumer Reports* 54:142 Mr '89
Remembering AIDS. *Harper's* 278:24-6 Ap '89
Talking AIDS to death. R. Shilts. por *Esquire* 111:123-6+ Mr '89

Animal models
The human mouse [infection of SCID-hu mouse by HIV; work of M. McCune; cover story; with editorial comment by Paul Hoffman] G. Montgomery. il por *Discover* 10:4, 48-55 Ag '89
Immunodeficiency and clonal growth of target cells induced by helper-free defective retrovirus. M. Huang and others. bibl f il *Science* 246:1614-17 D 22 '89
Monkey vaccine prevents AIDS-like disease [research by Ronald C. Desrosiers] K. Fackelmann. *Science News* 136:116 Ag 19 '89

Bibliography
AIDS words. G. Kolovakos. *The Nation* 248:598-602 My 1 '89

Causes
See also
HIV viruses
15 ways you can't get AIDS. A. Roblin. *Prevention (Emmaus, Pa.)* 41:49-54 Mr '89
Addicted to life [AIDS and drugs] M. B. Zuckerman. il *U.S. News & World Report* 106:84 Ap 24 '89
AIDS and IV drug use. D. Des Jarlais and S. R. Friedman. *Science* 245:578 Ag 11 '89
AIDS, blood and money [lawsuits against blood banks] J. Hammer. il *Newsweek* 113:43 Ja 23 '89
AIDS paper raises red flag at PNAS [P. H. Duesberg article in the Proceedings of the National Academy of Sciences] W. Booth. *Science* 243:733 F 10 '89
Bad blood? [AIDS and blood supply] M. Cimons. *Essence* 20:21-2 S '89
Challenging the traditional transfusion. T. L. Crenshaw. il *The Saturday Evening Post* 261:66-8 Ap '89
Global Blood Safety Initiative. D. Harris. il *World Health* p28-9 O '89
Herpesvirus may boost AIDS expression [study of T cells by Paolo Lusso and Robert C. Gallo] K. Fackelmann. *Science News* 135:55 Ja 28 '89
HIV and IV drug abuse. K. Fackelmann. il *Science News* 135:168-9+ Mr 18 '89
Justice in Milwaukee [victim J. Carroll wins suit against Blood Center of Southeast Wisconsin] H. G. Miller. il pors *The Saturday Evening Post* 261:44-8+ My/Je '89
A life in limbo [hemophiliac tests positive for AIDS] P. B. Bayer. il por *The New York Times Magazine* p48+ Ap 2 '89
Some gays reverting to risky sex. L. M. Keen. *Utne Reader* p111-12 N/D '89
A surgical patient's transfusion survival guide [intraoperative autologous transfusions] T. L. Crenshaw. il por *The Saturday Evening Post* 261:60+ Mr '89
Transfusions: it's a bloody shame [intraoperative autologous transfusion as alternative to traditional transfusion] T. L. Crenshaw. il por *The Humanist* 49:16-20+ My/Je '89

Conferences
AIDS ruckus in the Vatican. *Time* 134:58 N 27 '89
Biomedicine [Montreal conference] R. Weiss. *Science News* 135:382 Je 17 '89
Checking up on a killer [Montreal conference] J. Seligmann. il *Newsweek* 113:59-60 Je 12 '89
The emerging strategy to contain AIDS [Montreal conference] S. Findlay. il *U.S. News & World Report* 106:46 Je 19 '89
The era of bad feelings [Montreal conference] R. Shilts. il *Mother Jones* 14:32-6+ N '89
Fifth AIDS conference [Montreal] J. Benditt. *Scientific American* 261:21-3 Ag '89
Hecklers and protesters liven up a dull meeting [Montreal conference] J. L. Marx. il *Science* 244:1255 Je 16 '89
Media seminars on AIDS . . . and a Cameroon symposium. il *World Health* p30-1 Ag/S '89
Road maps to AIDS [Montreal conference] D. Burke. il *Maclean's* 102:40-1+ Je 19 '89

Costs
Who should foot the AIDS bill? A. Sachs. il *Time* 134:88 O 16 '89

Diagnosis
AIDS testing. L. F. Webb. il *Essence* 19:16+ Ja '89
AIDS testing: are you positive you're negative? L. David. il *Mademoiselle* 95:138+ N '89
High 'I do' blood-test dues [mandatory AIDS testing for marriage license applicants in Illinois] *Science News* 135:357 Je 10 '89
HIV can linger years with no antibodies [research by David T. Imagawa] R. Weiss. *Science News* 135:340 Je 3 '89
Keeping breast milk safe [testing at milk banks] H. Wolinsky. il *American Health* 8:20+ Ja/F '89
The loss of a husband and father [misdiagnosis of AIDS; case of E. Young] C. SerVaas. il por *The Saturday Evening Post* 261:94+ Jl/Ag '89
Mail-order AIDS tests: FDA confronts the implications. R. Weiss. *Science News* 135:268 Ap 29 '89
More questions than answers: a gay man takes the AIDS test. J. Green. il *Gentlemen's Quarterly* 59:152+ D '89
The mystery of 'silent' AIDS infections [deficiencies of standard test] J. Seligmann. il *Newsweek* 113:59 Je 12 '89
Notes and comment [blood test required as part of health insurance application] *The New Yorker* 65:27-8 My 22 '89

AIDS (DISEASE)—Diagnosis—cont.
Silent AIDS [deficiencies of antibody test] *Time* 133:61 Je 12 '89
Test diagnoses AIDS in newborns [work of Chin-Yih Ou] I. Wickelgren. *Science News* 135:389 Je 24 '89
Who should be tested? S. M. Halpern. *Ms.* 17:84 My '89
The worst lie of all: what they'll say for sex [lying about having had an AIDS test] L. Sanders. *Mademoiselle* 95:216 Je '89

Epidemiology
Desperately seeking sexual statistics [survey by the National Institute of Child Health and Human Development] R. Weiss. *Science News* 136:28 Jl 8 '89
Prevalence and patterns of same-gender sexual contact among men. R. E. Fay and others. bibl f il *Science* 243:338-48 Ja 20 '89
Sex survey provides data on homosexuals. B. Bower. *Science News* 135:54 Ja 28 '89
Understanding the figures. J. Chin. il *World Health* p8-9 O '89

Fund raising
AIDS benefits planned [rock music] J. Ressner. *Rolling Stone* p16 Ap 6 '89
Dionne Warwick rounds up her celeb pals to fight AIDS. il pors *People Weekly* 31:73-4 Je 26 '89
Dionne Warwick says death of her valet prompts her crusade against AIDS [cover story] C. Waldron. il pors *Jet* 75:58-61 Mr 27 '89
For a star-studded gala against children's AIDS, some politicians will even cross party lines. il *People Weekly* 32:104-5 Jl 10 '89
Hollywood helps a brave couple raise money for children dying of AIDS [P. and E. Glaser host premiere of Immediate family] il pors *People Weekly* 32:58-9 N 13 '89
Hollywood puts on the dog—and ponies up—to do battle with AIDS [Art against AIDS] il *People Weekly* 31:118-19 F 13 '89
Pocket extends an "Open Hand" in new cookbook to benefit AIDS organization. B. Levine. il *Publishers Weekly* 236:58 Ag 4 '89
Running for our lives [running across U.S. to raise public consciousness]; ed. by Gary Smith. B. N. Earle. il pors *People Weekly* 32 Special Issue:134-5+ Fall '89
Superstars shine as they raise funds to fight against AIDS [W. and C. Houston and D. Warwick; cover story] C. Waldron. il pors *Jet* 76:56-9 Jl 17 '89

Government policy
AIDS page. See issues of FDA Consumer beginning December 1988/January 1989
AIDS research gets the grants. M. Beck. il *Newsweek* 113:46-7 Mr 6 '89
Epidemics and delusions. M. B. Zuckerman. il *U.S. News & World Report* 107:92 N 13 '89
Great expectations: is the U.S. doing its best to beat AIDS? [interview with P. Parkman] D. C. McLearn. il pors *FDA Consumer* 23:36-8 F '89
The incredible shrinking AIDS epidemic. M. Fumento. il *The American Spectator* 22:21-6 My '89
Leadership and AIDS. W. Booth. *Science* 243:164 Ja 13 '89
The lost opportunity in AIDS research. D. Baltimore. il *Technology Review* 92:24-5 F/Mr '89
Notes and comment [C. E. Koop] *The New Yorker* 65:29-30 Ag 7 '89
Straight talk about AIDS [views of M. Fumento] J. Queenan. il por *Forbes* 143:41-2 Je 26 '89
Why did Forbes run Fumento's fulminations on AIDS? [discussion of June 26, 1989 article, Straight talk about AIDS] J. Queenan. *Forbes* 144:20-1 Jl 10 '89

Insurance
The impact of AIDS on benefit plans. *Nation's Business* 77:60-1 Mr '89
Now that AIDS is treatable, who'll pay the crushing cost? [AZT] N. J. Freundlich. il *Business Week* p115+ S 11 '89

International aspects
See also
World AIDS Day
AIDS: a worldwide effort will stop it! [cover story; special issue] il *World Health* p3-29 O '89
WHO seeks global data on sexual practices. W. Booth. *Science* 244:418-19 Ap 28 '89
WHO vs. AIDS [interview with H. Nakajima] J.-Y. Nau and F. Nouchi. il por *World Press Review* 36:52 Mr '89
The world's struggle against AIDS. C. G. Wagner. bibl il *The Futurist* 23:17-21 My/Je '89

Legal aspects
AIDS and discrimination. J. M. Mann. il *World Health* p14-15 Ap '89
AIDS: infected children have the right to attend school. R. J. Shoop. *USA Today (Periodical)* 117:68-70 My '89
AIDS: students in glass houses? [case of E. Martinez in Tampa, Fla.] P. A. Zirkel. bibl f il *Phi Delta Kappan* 70:646-8 Ap '89
Choreographer charges AIDS discrimination at Legs Diamond [case of M. Shawn] R. Sandla. por *Dance Magazine* 63:18 Je '89

Lovers, liars and other strangers [M. Christian's claim against R. Hudson estate] pors *Newsweek* 113:61 F 27 '89
The price of betrayal [M. Christian awarded $21.75 million in lawsuit against estate of R. Hudson] P. Chin. il pors *People Weekly* 31:180-3 Mr 6 '89

Mortality
See also
AIDS Quilt

Prevention
Circumcision may protect against the AIDS virus [results of African studies] J. L. Marx. il *Science* 245:470-1 Ag 4 '89
Condoms in the cells [Philadelphia prisons] A. Hornblum. *The Progressive* 53:12 F '89
Dating, dishonesty and AIDS [study by Susan Cochran] M. Roberts. il *Psychology Today* 22:60 D '88
Fearless flying [impact of AIDS risk on sexual behavior] M. Rafferty. il *Ms.* 17:51+ My '89
Moral propaganda [curbing spread of AIDS through needle exchange programs] K. McAuliffe. *Omni (New York, N.Y.)* 12:41 O '89
Partner tracing [Colorado program] L. M. Kase. *Vogue* 179:258+ My '89
The push for prevention. J. Seligmann. il *Newsweek* 113:71 Je 19 '89
Sex, spies and videotape [private detectives investigate for AIDS] C. Leerhsen. il *Newsweek* 114:66 O 2 '89
Teen boys get condom sense [survey] E. Stark. *Psychology Today* 23:62-3 O '89
Trading good needles for bad [D. Purchase tries to fight AIDS in Tacoma] R. Givens. il por *Newsweek* 113:49 Ja 9 '89
Yolanda Serrano [work in AIDS prevention in New York City] K. Dobie. il por *Ms.* 17:79-83 Ja/F '89

Psychological aspects
AIDS and personality. E. Smith. *Psychology Today* 23:74 Mr '89
Coming out in the age of AIDS. M. Dregni. il *Utne Reader* p19-20 S/O '89

Religious aspects
See also
Church work with AIDS patients
AIDS as metaphor [study of seven religious groups] S. J. Palmer. bibl *Society* 26:44-50 Ja/F '89
AIDS ruckus in the Vatican. *Time* 134:58 N 27 '89
Forty hours [devotions for end to AIDS at Most Holy Redeemer Catholic Church in San Francisco] T. McGrath. il *U.S. Catholic* 54:20-7 N '89
Gay community frowns on disco diva Donna Summer. por *Jet* 76:38 S 18 '89
In a rage over AIDS [ACT UP targets Cardinal J. O'Connor] E. Magnuson. il *Time* 134:33 D 25 '89
One of our own: one man's struggle with AIDS [interview with S. Cox] *Christianity Today* 33:56 F 3 '89
Religious responses to AIDS. P. Bock. il *USA Today (Periodical)* 117:66-7 My '89
Triple play [U.S. Catholic bishops' statement] *Commonweal* 116:581-2 N 3 '89
The U.S. bishops' statements on AIDS. *America* 161:391 D 2 '89

Statistics
AIDS counts. P. Wallich. il *Scientific American* 260:17-18 Ap '89
AIDS: the numbers game [overwhelmed hospitals in New York City] K. Loomis. il map *New York* 22:44-9 Mr 6 '89
The incredible shrinking AIDS epidemic. M. Fumento. il *The American Spectator* 22:21-6 My '89
Is AIDS underreported? [white Americans who have the disease] *Newsweek* 113:71 Je 19 '89
Is the AIDS epidemic slowing? J. Palca. *Science* 246:1560 D 22 '89
Monitoring the AIDS epidemic in the United States: a network approach [General Social Survey findings] E. O. Laumann and others. bibl f il *Science* 244:1186-9 Je 9 '89
Monitoring the U.S. AIDS epidemic [discussion of June 9, 1989 article, Monitoring the AIDS epidemic in the United States: a network approach] E. O. Laumann and others. *Science* 245:908-10 S 1 '89
A recount of AIDS carriers. il *Time* 134:103 O 9 '89
Straight talk about AIDS [views of M. Fumento] J. Queenan. il por *Forbes* 143:41-2 Je 26 '89
Understanding the figures. J. Chin. il *World Health* p8-9 O '89
Why did Forbes run Fumento's fulminations on AIDS? [discussion of June 26, 1989 article, Straight talk about AIDS] J. Queenan. *Forbes* 144:20-1 Jl 10 '89

Testing
See AIDS (Disease)—Diagnosis

Therapy
An abrupt reversal [making available unapproved AIDS drugs in Canada] M. Nichols. il *Maclean's* 102:49+ Mr 13 '89
Affirmative action [need for more minorities in clinical trials] J. Horgan. *Scientific American* 261:34 D '89
AIDS: bioscience attacks a killer [cover story] F. Lunzer. il *High Technology Business* 9:18-21+ F '89
AIDS drug DDI under treatment IND. il *FDA Consumer* 23:2-3 D '89/Ja '90

AIDS (DISEASE)—Therapy—*cont.*

AIDS drug shows promise [DDI; research by Robert Yarchoan] *Science News* 136:69 Jl 29 '89

AIDS drug trials enter new age. J. Palca. il *Science* 246:19-21 O 6 '89

AIDS drugs remain unavailable for kids. B. J. Culliton. *Science* 246:22 O 6 '89

AIDS drugs—coming but not here. J. L. Marx. il *Science* 244:287 Ap 21 '89

AIDS predictors [measures of a drug's efficacy] K. Fackelmann. il *Science News* 136:298-9 N 4 '89

AIDS profiteering [AZT] P. C. Montgomery. il *Common Cause Magazine* 15:9 Ja/F '89

AIDS research comes to patients' home towns [FDA program] F. E. Young. il *FDA Consumer* 23:6-7 My '89

AIDS research focuses on CD4. *High Technology Business* 9:30 Jl/Ag '89

AIDS: the high cost of hope. il *Scholastic Update (Teachers' edition)* 122:12 N 3 '89

The arsenal gets larger. M. Patlak. il *Discover* 10:22-3 Ap '89

At last, quicker access to AIDS drugs. J. Seligmann. *Newsweek* 114:76 Jl 10 '89

AZT helps in early AIDS. *Science News* 136:102 Ag 12 '89

AZT reverses AIDS dementia in children. B. J. Culliton. il *Science* 246:21-3 O 6 '89

AZT slows HIV infection. *FDA Consumer* 23:5 N '89

AZT still on trial. J. Cherfas. *Science* 246:882 N 17 '89

Blue-green algae kill HIV in culture [research by Michael R. Boyd] *Science News* 136:141 Ag 26 '89

Desperation drugs. S. Begley. il *Newsweek* 114:48-51 Ag 7 '89

Docking site decoy, antibody fragment wed [immunoadhesins; research by Daniel J. Capon] R. Weiss. *Science News* 135:86 F 11 '89

Drug combo: double whammy with a bonus [AZT and interferon for AIDS patients with Kaposi's sarcoma; research by H. Clifford Lane] *Science News* 136:141 Ag 26 '89

Drug-resistant strains of AIDS virus found [AZT-resistant] J. L. Marx. *Science* 243:1551-2 Mr 24 '89

Drug testing on trial [problems of human testing] S. Vogel. il *Discover* 10:28-9 Je '89

Drugs from the underground [FDA allows wider use of experimental drugs] D. Thompson. il *Time* 134:49 Jl 10 '89

Early AZT use slows progression to AIDS. K. Fackelmann. *Science News* 136:135 Ag 26 '89

The emerging strategy to contain AIDS [Montreal conference] S. Findlay. il *U.S. News & World Report* 106:46 Je 19 '89

FDA broadens use of unproven AIDS drug [DDI in; dextran sulfate out] D. E. Loupe. *Science News* 136:231 O 7 '89

Fighting AIDS all the way [use of AZT and dideoxyinosine] L. Josephs. il *The New York Times Magazine* p42+ O 8 '89

From China, a drug that takes aim at AIDS [GLQ223; work of Michael S. McGrath] J. O. Hamilton. il *Business Week* p29 Ap 24 '89

Gene implants [battling HIV; research by Steven L. McKnight] G. Montgomery. il *Discover* 10:24 Mr '89

Gout drug might cut AZT dosage by half [probenecid; research by David M. Kornhauser] S. Hart. *Science News* 136:167 S 9 '89

Government DDI trials on trial. J. Palca. *Science* 246:1244 D 8 '89

Great expectations: is the U.S. doing its best to beat AIDS? [interview with P. Parkman] D. C. McLearn. il pors *FDA Consumer* 23:36-8 F '89

Hardy viruses survive drug assault [studies by Kim S. Erlich and Alejo Erice] *Science News* 135:110 F 18 '89

Help on the way [FDA approval of pentamidine] *Time* 133:65 F 13 '89

HIV with reduced sensitivity to zidovudine (AZT) isolated during prolonged therapy. B. A. Larder and others. bibl f il *Science* 243:1731-4 Mr 31 '89

How much for a reprieve from AIDS? [Burroughs Wellcome lowers price of AZT] C. Gorman. il *Time* 134:81-2 O 2 '89

In vivo activity against HIV and favorable toxicity profile of 2', 3'-dideoxyinosine. R. Yarchoan and others. bibl f il *Science* 245:412-15 Jl 28 '89

Interferon-α but not AZT suppresses HIV expression in chronically infected cell lines. G. Poli and others. bibl f il *Science* 244:575-7 My 5 '89

Longer life for AIDS patients. D. Thompson. il *Time* 133:52 Je 19 '89

Lyphomed's vital signs are stabilizing [pentamidine] J. F. Siler. il *Business Week* p46 Jl 3 '89

Making do without a magic bullet. *U.S. News & World Report* 106:12 F 20 '89

A new AIDS alert [early intervention with AZT] N. Underwood. *Maclean's* 102:55 Ap 3 '89

A new AIDS drug gets the go-ahead [DDI] *Newsweek* 114:40 O 9 '89

New AIDS drug passes first clinical test [DDI] J. L. Marx. il *Science* 245:353 Jl 28 '89

New AIDS drugs take careful aim. J. Palca. il *Science* 246:1559-60 D 22 '89

A new AIDS finding [DDI] G. W. Taylor. il *Maclean's* 102:47 Ag 7 '89

A new antiviral drug: promising or problematic? [DDI] J. Palca. *Science* 246:20 O 6 '89

New hope [AZT slows onset of AIDS] il *Time* 134:56 Ag 14 '89

New information available about AIDS treatments [telephone listing of FDA-recognized clinical efficacy trials] F. E. Young. il *FDA Consumer* 23:6-7 N '89

A new reprieve for AIDS victims [AZT slows onset of disease] *U.S. News & World Report* 107:13+ Ag 28-S 4 '89

A new war on AIDS [access to experimental drugs] N. Underwood. il *Maclean's* 102:62 S 18 '89

NIH offers AZT to exposed workers. W. Booth. *Science* 243:1137 Mr 3 '89

Now that AIDS is treatable, who'll pay the crushing cost? [AZT] N. J. Freundlich. il *Business Week* p115+ S 11 '89

A possible design for 'mopping up' AIDS [Chimeric CD4] *Newsweek* 113:58 F 20 '89

Promising drug for children with AIDS [AZT; research by Pim Brouwers] *Science News* 135:88 F 11 '89

Proposal seeks wider access to AIDS drugs [views of Anthony S. Fauci] K. Fackelmann. *Science News* 136:6 Jl 1 '89

Quick release of AIDS drugs. E. Marshall. il *Science* 245:345+ Jl 28 '89

A risky lifeline for AIDS victims [Bristol-Myers distributes unproven drug] *U.S. News & World Report* 107:14 Jl 24 '89

Rx for the FDA [pressure to speed up drug approval process] J. E. Groopman. *The New Republic* 200:17-18+ F 13 '89

Shooting the messenger [antisense RNA prevents HIV virus production; research by Jack Cohen] G. Montgomery. il *Discover* 10:32 N '89

Testing, testing [FDA and new drug DDI] D. Ellen. *The New Republic* 201:14-15 Ag 28 '89

The trials of conducting AIDS drugs trials. J. L. Marx. il *Science* 244:916-18 My 26 '89

The underground test of Compound Q. D. Wyss. il *Time* 134:18+ O 9 '89

The virus strikes back [AZT-resistant strains] P. Gadsby. il *Discover* 10:20 Jl '89

Wider use of AIDS drugs advocated [AZT can delay development of AIDS] J. L. Marx. *Science* 245:811 Ag 25 '89

Wider use of pneumonia drug approved [pentamidine] il *FDA Consumer* 23:4 Ap '89

Zeroing in on AIDS [drug GLQ223] N. Underwood. *Maclean's* 102:58 My 15 '89

Vaccines and vaccination

AIDS vaccine: preliminary but promising. R. Weiss. *Science News* 135:375 Je 17 '89

Clues to stimulating AIDS immunity. R. Weiss. *Science News* 136:372 D 9 '89

A formalin-inactivated whole SIV vaccine confers protection in macaques. M. Murphey-Corb and others. bibl f il *Science* 246:1293-7 D 8 '89

Hope for AIDS vaccines. J. Cherfas. *Science* 246:23-4 O 6 '89

Monkey vaccine prevents AIDS-like disease [research by Ronald C. Desrosiers] K. Fackelmann. *Science News* 136:116 Ag 19 '89

New hope on the AIDS vaccine front. J. L. Marx. il *Science* 244:1254+ Je 16 '89

One step closer to an AIDS vaccine [inoculation of monkeys with SIV virus; work of Michael Murphey-Corb and others] *Newsweek* 114:66 D 18 '89

Progress in vaccines against AIDS. D. Bolognesi. bibl f *Science* 246:1233-4 D 8 '89

Prospects for a vaccine. J. Esparza. il *World Health* p10-11 O '89

A research tool in the war against AIDS [computers at National Institute of Allergies and Infectious Diseases] P. Honan. il por *Personal Computing* 13:182-4 O '89

A simian clue to the prevention of AIDS [vaccine combats SIV virus; research by Michael Murphey-Corb and others] il *U.S. News & World Report* 107:10-11 D 18 '89

Africa

Circumcision may protect against the AIDS virus. J. L. Marx. il *Science* 245:470-1 Ag 4 '89

Brazil

Brazilians take on AIDS epidemic. W. Steif. il *The Progressive* 53:17 My '89

Canada

An abrupt reversal [making available unapproved AIDS drugs] M. Nichols. il *Maclean's* 102:49+ Mr 13 '89

A new AIDS alert [early intervention with AZT] N. Underwood. *Maclean's* 102:55 Ap 3 '89

Haiti

On truth and fiction [factual basis for book Slave trade involving homosexual boys in Haiti] H. Gold. *The Nation* 249:759-61 D 18 '89

Philippines

The bar girls of Subic Bay: the military, women and AIDS. S. Sturdevant. il *The Nation* 248:444-6 Ap 3 '89

AIDS (DISEASE)—cont.

Soviet Union

Red scare. J. E. Groopman. il *The New Republic* 200:25-7 Ap 17 '89

Soviet describes AIDS errors. R. Weiss. *Science News* 135:382 Je 17 '89

Uganda

Giving AIDS a new face. S. I. Okware. il *World Health* p18-20 O '89

United States

See AIDS (Disease)

AIDS (DISEASE) AND ARTISTS

The artists' diagnosis. M. Horn. il *U.S. News & World Report* 106:62-3, 66+ Mr 27 '89

Days of rage [NEA rescinds funding for Witnesses: against our vanishing] K. Larson. il *New York* 22:80+ N 27 '89

Disaster at the NEA [rescinds funding for AIDS exhibit Witnesses: against our vanishing] R. Brustein. *The New Republic* 201:28-30 D 11 '89

Just say know [interview with K. Haring] D. Sheff. il por *Rolling Stone* p58-9+ Ag 10 '89

Testing the new arts rules [NEA rescinds funds and later decides to support AIDS exhibit Witnesses: against our vanishing] *Newsweek* 114:43 N 27 '89

AIDS (DISEASE) AND BLACKS

Bad blood? [AIDS and blood supply] M. Cimons. *Essence* 20:21-2 S '89

A boy's life [gay black teenager] D. L. Kirp. il *Mother Jones* 14:32-8 Jl/Ag '89

D.C. confab on AIDS and blacks slated for August. il *Jet* 76:22 Jl 10 '89

Dying AIDS victim calls for safe sex and understanding [D. Scarborough] J. Reno. il pors *Ebony* 44:148+ Mr '89

Expand outreach effort to inform blacks about AIDS risk in sex action. il *Jet* 75:17 Ja 30 '89

Joining the AIDS fight [black churches] J. N. Baker and R. Elam. il *Newsweek* 113:26-7 Ap 17 '89

AIDS (DISEASE) AND BUDDHISTS

Buddhist editor leaves amid controversy [Vajradhatu sun's coverage of allegations that American Buddhist leader, O. Tendzin, had contracted AIDS] J. Walljasper. il *Utne Reader* p36-7 Jl/Ag '89

His master's voice [Vajradhatu leader O. Tendzin contracts AIDS] *Newsweek* 113:51 Mr 6 '89

AIDS (DISEASE) AND CELEBRITIES

Friends—and her doctor—say A.I.D.S., not cancer, killed Gunsmoke's Amanda Blake. J. Stark. il pors *People Weekly* 32:68-9 N 20 '89

Rock Hudson. B. Darrach. il pors *People Weekly* 32 Special Issue:65-6 Fall '89

AIDS (DISEASE) AND CHILDREN

See also

AIDS (Disease) education

Pediatric AIDS Foundation

AIDS and young people. J. Ferguson. il *World Health* p12-13 O '89

AIDS drugs remain unavailable for kids. B. J. Culliton. *Science* 246:22 O 6 '89

AIDS: face fears with new facts. E. Karlsberg. *Teen* 33:34+ S '89

AIDS in America's schoolhouses: learning the hard lessons [cover story; with editorial comment by Pauline B. Gough] D. L. Kirp and S. Epstein. il *Phi Delta Kappan* 70:578, 584-93 Ap '89

AIDS: infected children have the right to attend school. R. J. Shoop. *USA Today (Periodical)* 117:68-70 My '89

AIDS: students in glass houses? [case of E. Martinez in Tampa, Fla.] P. A. Zirkel. bibl f il *Phi Delta Kappan* 70:646-8 Ap '89

AIDS: the youngest victims. P. Klass. il *The New York Times Magazine* p34-5+ Je 18 '89

The AIDS threat to teenagers. P. Dworkin. il *U.S. News & World Report* 107:29-30 O 23 '89

"Are you going to love me?" Children with AIDS. E. Steinbaum. il *McCall's* 116:57-9 Jl '89

AZT reverses AIDS dementia in children. B. J. Culliton. il *Science* 246:21-3 O 6 '89

A boy's life [gay black teenager] D. L. Kirp. il *Mother Jones* 14:32-8 Jl/Ag '89

Can a child catch AIDS in school? F. Roberts. il *Parents* 64:51 My '89

Princess Di visits infant AIDS victims in Harlem. il pors *Jet* 75:10 F 20 '89

Promising drug for children with AIDS [AZT; research by Pim Brouwers] *Science News* 135:88 F 11 '89

Q. Why did Judith Light smash a window in anger? A. Her emotions spilled over playing the mother of a son with AIDS [R. White story]; ed. by Jeff Kaye. J. Light. il por *TV Guide* 37:14-15 Ja 7-13 '89

Test diagnoses AIDS in newborns [work of Chin-Yih Ou] I. Wickelgren. *Science News* 135:389 Je 24 '89

"We have a problem" [child fears getting AIDS after uncle dies] J. Marks. il *Parents* 64:50+ Jl '89

AIDS (DISEASE) AND COLLEGE STUDENTS

AIDS on campus. *Glamour* 87:116 O '89

Study reveals AIDS crisis on campuses; new study is planned for black colleges. *Jet* 76:36 Je 12 '89

AIDS (DISEASE) AND EMPLOYMENT

AIDS concerns for business. I. D. Singer. il *Nation's Business* 77:75-7 Je '89

AIDS: what effect on the workplace? [views of Willis B. Goldbeck] *USA Today (Periodical)* 117:1-2 F '89

The impact of AIDS on benefit plans. *Nation's Business* 77:60-1 Mr '89

AIDS (DISEASE) AND HEALTH WORKERS

NIH offers AZT to exposed workers. W. Booth. *Science* 243:1137 Mr 3 '89

A very risky business. J. Seligmann. il *Newsweek* 114:82-3 N 20 '89

AIDS (DISEASE) AND MINORITIES

Affirmative action [need for more minorities in clinical trials] J. Horgan. *Scientific American* 261:34 D '89

AIDS (DISEASE) AND NURSES

David Kessler: home nursing for AIDS patients. D. Castellon. il por *Business Week* p117 N 6 '89

AIDS (DISEASE) AND PHYSICIANS

Coming of age with AIDS. E. Rosenthal. il *Discover* 10:34+ S '89

A very risky business. J. Seligmann. il *Newsweek* 114:82-3 N 20 '89

AIDS (DISEASE) AND PRISONERS

Condoms in the cells [Philadelphia] A. Hornblum. *The Progressive* 53:12 F '89

Learning to live with AIDS in prison. J. N. Baker. il *Newsweek* 113:27-8 F 13 '89

AIDS (DISEASE) AND SERVICEMEN

The bar girls of Subic Bay: the military, women and AIDS [Philippines] S. Sturdevant. il *The Nation* 248:444-6 Ap 3 '89

AIDS (DISEASE) AND THE HOMELESS

Thousands may die in the streets [homeless AIDS patients in New York City] S. Schulman. il *The Nation* 248:480-2 Ap 10 '89

AIDS (DISEASE) AND THE PRESS

The delayed reporting of the AIDS epidemic. E. M. Rogers and J. W. Dearing. *USA Today (Periodical)* 117:64-5 My '89

The outsider [New York native editor C. Ortleb] K. Leishman. il por *Rolling Stone* p75-6+ Mr 23 '89

AIDS (DISEASE) AND WOMEN

AIDS commissioner Belinda Mason speaks with ringing authority about the disease: she has it. L. Kramer. il pors *People Weekly* 32:147+ D 11 '89

AIDS ranked 5th leading killer of black women. *Jet* 77:36 D 4 '89

AIDS: rethinking the risk. S. M. Halpern. il *Ms.* 17:80-2+ My '89

AIDS testing. L. F. Webb. il *Essence* 19:16+ Ja '89

AIDS testing: are you positive you're negative? L. David. il *Mademoiselle* 95:138+ N '89

Alison Gertz: Woman of the Year [AIDS victim] il por *Esquire* 112:102-3 Ag '89

Alison's fight for life [victim A. Gertz] M. Jacobbi. il pors *Good Housekeeping* 209:196-7+ S '89

For women: education and mutual support [women prisoners] *Newsweek* 113:28 F 13 '89

Testimony of Dorothy L. Polikoff before the Presidential Commission on the HIV Epidemic, May 18, 1988 [AIDS patient whose husband died from tainted blood transfusion] D. Polikoff. *The Humanist* 49:18-19 My/Je '89

Women and AIDS. R. Danziger. il *World Health* p14-15 O '89

Women and AIDS: what you must know now. G. Kolata. il *Ladies' Home Journal* 106:98+ N '89

Women: the invisible victims of AIDS. P. De la Fuente. il *Utne Reader* p18-20 N/D '89

AIDS (DISEASE) AND YOUTH *See* AIDS (Disease) and children

AIDS (DISEASE) EDUCATION

Educating youth about AIDS: a model program [Girls Club of New York] W. Amer-Hirsch. bibl f il *Children Today* 18:16-19 S/O '89

Talking AIDS. C. Viedma. il *World Health* p16-17 Mr '89

Talking to your children about AIDS. J. Koch. il *Psychology Today* 23:62-3 O '89

Time to talk [teenagers should learn about AIDS in the classroom] L. Ullmann. *Seventeen* 48:112-13 S '89

Will your child get AIDS? D. Neff. *Christianity Today* 33:15 S 22 '89

Aids and devices

An AIDS game that is deadly serious [BLOCKAIDS video game] il *U.S. News & World Report* 107:17 S 18 '89

Understanding AIDS & Alcohol [computer programs] K. Sternberg. *Compute!* 11:122+ O '89

AIDS (DISEASE) IN ART

The artists' diagnosis. M. Horn. il *U.S. News & World Report* 106:62-3, 66+ Mr 27 '89

Exhibitions

David Wojnarowicz At P.P.O.W. H. Cotter. il *Art in America* 77:180 Je '89

Gilbert & George: the AIDS pictures [cover story] R. Rosenblum. il *Art in America* 77:152-5 N '89

AIDS (DISEASE) IN MASS MEDIA

Media seminars on AIDS . . . and a Cameroon symposium. il *World Health* p30-1 Ag/S '89

AIDS (DISEASE) IN TELEVISION
Q. Why did Judith Light smash a window in anger? A.
Her emotions spilled over playing the mother of a son
with AIDS [R. White story]; ed. by Jeff Kaye. J. Light.
il por *TV Guide* 37:14-15 Ja 7-13 '89

AIDS (DISEASE) LITERATURE
See also
AIDS (Disease)—Bibliography
Los Angeles-based AIDS project gives first literary awards
[Words Project for AIDS] L. See. il *Publishers Weekly*
235:38 Ap 7 '89
Now, metaphor as illness [S. Sontag's AIDS and its metaphors]
D. Gates. il por *Newsweek* 113:79 Ja 30 '89
A plague of blame and fear. L. Fleischer. *Publishers Weekly*
236:25 Jl 21 '89

AIDS (DISEASE) VIRUSES See HIV viruses

AIDS ARMS NETWORK
The network of life and death. S. Dentzer. il *U.S. News
& World Report* 106:42-4 Je 19 '89

AIDS COALITION TO UNLEASH POWER See ACT UP
(Organization)

AIDS PATIENTS
See also
AIDS ARMS Network
AIDS Quilt
Church work with AIDS patients
STEPS Theater Company
Coming of age with AIDS. E. Rosenthal. il *Discover* 10:34+
S '89
Residence on earth: living with AIDS in the '80s. E. White.
Life 12:135 Fall '89
Virus de résistance [drug resistant viruses in AIDS patients]
K. Wright. *Scientific American* 260:29+ Ap '89

Dental care
A dentist to fight cavities—and pain [M. Andriolo] A. Witchel.
il por *New York* 22:30 D 18 '89

Employment
See AIDS (Disease) and employment

Family relationships
A brother's death. B. L. Ascher. il *The New York Times
Magazine* p30+ N 19 '89
Someone you know? B. Ehrenreich. il *Ms.* 17:35-6 Mr '89
A son dies of AIDS. T. J. Cottle. il *The New Leader* 72:15-17
N 13 '89

Legal status, laws, etc.
See AIDS (Disease)—Legal aspects

Nutrition
See also
Project Open Hand

Photographs and photography
Nicholas Nixon: Museum of Modern Art; Zabriskie. R. B.
Woodward. il por *Art News* 88:132+ Ja '89

Psychology
See AIDS (Disease)—Psychological aspects

AIDS QUILT
And sew it goes [C. Jones] D. Bellm. por *Mother Jones*
14:34-5 Ja '89
The NAMES project: a catharsis of grief. J. Gentry. *The
Christian Century* 106:550-1 My 24-31 '89

AIELLO, DANNY
about
Harlem nights. C. Fleming. il por *American Film* 15:63
N '89

AIELLO, ROBERT
about
A conversation with Robert Aiello. C. Movalli. il por *American
Artist* 53:48-53+ Ja '89

AIHUI (CHINA)
Watermelon diplomacy on the border [Sino-Soviet thaw along
Amur River] J. Trimble. il map *U.S. News & World
Report* 106:33 My 15 '89

AIKEN, JOAN, 1924-
Plot and character in suspense fiction. *The Writer* 102:9-13
My '89

AIKMAN, TROY
about
A duel in the sun: quarterbacks Troy Aikman and Steve
Walsh compete to be the Cowboys' starter [cover story]
A. Murphy. il pors *Sports Illustrated* 71:30-2+ Ag 21 '89

AILES, ROGER, 1940-
How to make a good impression [condensed from You
are the message]; ed. by Jon Kraushar. il *Reader's Digest*
135:139-42 S '89
about
Roger Ailes: 'I have to take the heat'. H. Fineman and
P. McKillop. por *Newsweek* 114:34 N 6 '89
Rudy's fall from grace: can Ailes put Giuliani's campaign
back together again? J. Klein. il pors *New York* 22:40-3
Ag 21 '89
Willie Ailes. J. Klein. il por *New York* 22:38+ D 4 '89

AILEY, ALVIN
about
Obituary
Jet il pors 77:18 D 18 '89
People Weekly il por 32:166 D 18 '89
Opus McShann [dance] Reviews
Down Beat il 56:47-9 Ap '89. B. S. Comer

AILMENTS See Diseases

AINSA, FERNANDO
Literary detection and Latin American writing. il *The Courier
(Unesco)* 42:21-3 My '89

AINU (JAPANESE PEOPLE)
Samurai anthropologist [evidence that samurai were descen-
dants of the Ainu people; research by C. Loring Brace]
Discover 10:12-13 S '89

AIP See American Institute of Physics

AIR
See also
Atmosphere
Compressed air
Humidity

Analysis
See also
Air pollution—Measurement
Glacier bubbles are telling us what was in Ice Age air.
J. Weiner. bibl (p164) il *Smithsonian* 20:78-84+ My '89

AIR AMERICA
Air America's flyboys. D. Brock. il *The American Spectator*
22:37-8 D '89

AIR BAGS, AUTOMOBILE See Automobiles—Air bags

AIR BASES
See also
Guided missile bases
. . . detention [conviction of anti-nuclear activists for trespassing at Whiteman Air Force Base] J. Munves. *The Nation*
248:509 Ap 17 '89
Who will yell fire when the house is ablaze? [conviction
of anti-nuclear activist S. Komisaruk for damaging computer
at Vandenburg Air Force Base] R. E. Burns. *U.S. Catholic*
54:2 F '89

Security measures
USAF developing better camouflage to protect bases from
enemy attack. W. B. Scott. il *Aviation Week & Space
Technology* 131:85+ S 25 '89

Shutdowns
Five Air Force bases are among 86 slated for closure. *Aviation
Week & Space Technology* 130:40 Ja 2 '89
Pease AFB could become major commercial airport [Ports-
mouth, N.H.] *Aviation Week & Space Technology* 130:69
Ja 23 '89

AIR BLADDERS (FISH) See Swim bladders (Fish)

AIR BUBBLES See Bubbles

AIR BUSES See Airplanes, Jet

AIR CANADA
Government to sell 41.1 million shares of Air Canada stock,
finish privatization. N. C. Kernstock. il *Aviation Week
& Space Technology* 130:171-2 Je 19 '89

AIR CLEANERS See Air filters

AIR COMPRESSORS
TFH tool report: air power. K. Collier. il *The Family
Handyman* 39:84+ Ap '89
Working on air (I). il *Home Mechanix* 85:44-7 Ja '89
Working on air (II). M. Morris. il *Home Mechanix* 85:74-7
F '89

AIR CONDITIONING
See also
Automobiles—Air conditioning
Cool storage
Dance theaters—Air conditioning
Solar air conditioning

Anecdotes, facetiae, satire, etc.
A/C in D.C.: my struggle to stay cool. C. T. Buckley. il
Architectural Digest 46:106+ Je '89

History
Whistle up a breeze. P. Steinhart. il *Audubon* 91:24-7 Jl
'89

AIR CONDITIONING EQUIPMENT
See also
Dehumidifiers
Heat pumps
Humidifiers
Air-conditioners for mid-sized rooms. il *Consumer Reports*
54:432-6 Jl '89
Air conditioners that don't hog your windows [ductless split]
D. H. Dunn. il *Business Week* p164 Je 26 '89
Cool tips for the summer. il map *Consumers' Research
Magazine* 72:23-7 Jl '89
Mid-sized room air-conditioners. il *Consumer Reports*
54:329-32 D '89

AIR CONDITIONING EQUIPMENT INDUSTRY
See also
Fedders Corp.

AIR CUSHION VEHICLES
Don't rock the boat! B. McKeown. il *Popular Science* 234:74-5+
F '89
Flier Paul Moller is a former alien with a real flying saucer.
W. Plummer. il pors *People Weekly* 31:149-50 Je 19 '89

Testing
Air power [hovercraft] J. Skorupa. il *Popular Mechanics*
166:80-2 Je '89
License to fly [flarecraft ground effect vehicle; cover story]
T. H. Cole. il *Popular Mechanics* 166:57-9+ Jl '89

AIR DEFENSES
See also
Airplanes, Military

AIR DEFENSES—See also—*cont.*
   Guided missiles
   Guns, Anti-aircraft
   Radar defense networks
AIR EUROPE LTD.
The lofty dreams of upstart Air Europe. M. Maremont. il por *Business Week* p52+ Ap 17 '89
Two British carriers launch efforts to boost international market shares. C. A. Shifrin. *Aviation Week & Space Technology* 131:125 S 18 '89
AIR FILTERS
   See also
   Automobile engines—Filters
Air purifiers. il *Consumer Reports* 54:88-93 F '89
Air purifiers. il *Consumer Reports* 54:333-7 D '89
How to compare room air cleaners. il *Consumers' Research Magazine* 72:34-7 My '89
Passing a clean air act in your home. K. Jacobs. il *Business Week* p148 D 11 '89
AIR FLOW
   See also
   Vortex generators
AIR FORCE ASTRONAUTICS LABORATORY (U.S.)
USAF builds facility to study dynamics of lightweight space-based structures. W. B. Scott. il *Aviation Week & Space Technology* 130:51 F 20 '89
AIR FORCE LOGISTICS COMMAND (U.S.) *See* United States. Air Force Logistics Command
AIR FORCE MUSEUM (CHINA)
Air Force Museum features 131 aircraft, other weapon systems at former base. il *Aviation Week & Space Technology* 131:90-1 D 11 '89
AIR FORCE ONE (AIRPLANE) *See* Airplanes, Government
AIR FORCE PILOTS *See* Air pilots
AIR FORCE WEAPONS LABORATORY *See* United States. Air Force Weapons Laboratory
AIR FORCE WRIGHT AERONAUTICAL LABORATORIES
USAF seeks aerospace applications for innovative X-ray tomography. B. W. Henderson. il *Aviation Week & Space Technology* 131:93+ Jl 31 '89
AIR FRANCE
Air France, Lufthansa sign pact for broad cooperative policies. J. M. Lenorovitz. il *Aviation Week & Space Technology* 131:108 S 25 '89
AIR FREIGHT SERVICE
   See also
   Airborne Freight Corp.
   Airplanes, Freight
   CF AirFreight, Inc.
   Emery Air Freight Corp.
   Federal Express Corp.
   Flying Tiger Line Inc.
   Skyway Freight Systems Inc.
   Tiger International, Inc.
   United Parcel Service of America, Inc.
Tips on sending art through the mail. A. S. Bamberger. il *Antiques & Collecting Hobbies* 94:18 My '89
U.S. Postal Service expands express shipment services. P. Proctor. il *Aviation Week & Space Technology* 130:111+ My 1 '89

Acquisitions and mergers
Consolidated Freightways to acquire Emery Air Freight for $230 million. R. G. O'Lone. *Aviation Week & Space Technology* 130:119 F 20 '89
Emery's failing finances spur approval of merger [purchase by Consolidated Freightways] il *Aviation Week & Space Technology* 130:97 Ap 10 '89
Federal Express/Tigers merger would reshape cargo industry. J. T. McKenna. *Aviation Week & Space Technology* 130:106 Ja 2 '89
Fred Smith [Federal Express buys Flying Tiger] D. Foust. il por *Business Week* Special Issue:102 Ap 14 '89
Mr. Smith goes global [Federal Express merger with Tiger International; cover story] D. Foust. il pors map *Business Week* p66-8+ F 13 '89
"This global thing is not a fad" [Consolidated Freightways takeover of Emery Air Freight] M. Beauchamp. il *Forbes* 144:122+ D 11 '89

International aspects
UPS buys seven European parcel delivery firms to expand international presence. *Aviation Week & Space Technology* 130:67 Ja 23 '89

International aspects
Airlines boost international cargo services to protect market shares. J. T. McKenna. il *Aviation Week & Space Technology* 131:124-5 N 20 '89
The flying-package trade takes off [expansion of Federal Express and UPS] C. P. Work. il *U.S. News & World Report* 107:47+ O 2 '89

Routes
Western Europe
Mail war. F. Vaysse. il *World Press Review* 36:62 S '89
Philippines
   See also
   Aboitiz Air Transport
AIR GUNS
Sharpshooters. J. Bashline. il *Popular Mechanics* 166:76-8 O '89

AIR INLETS (AIRPLANES) *See* Airplane engines, Jet—Air intakes
AIR LAYERING OF PLANTS *See* Plant propagation
AIR LINE PILOTS ASSOCIATION
ALPA begins drive to win pilots' support for United buyout. *Aviation Week & Space Technology* 131:124 S 18 '89
ALPA claims Gander probe relied on some faulty, fabricated data [1985 crash] D. Hughes. *Aviation Week & Space Technology* 131:66-7 Jl 3 '89
ALPA prepares for possible sale of all or part of TWA. J. T. McKenna. *Aviation Week & Space Technology* 131:128-9 N 20 '89
ALPA to seek elimination of two-tier wage scales. *Aviation Week & Space Technology* 130:93 F 13 '89
Davis ups buyout bid for United but pilot offer still stronger. J. Ott and C. A. Shifrin. il *Aviation Week & Space Technology* 131:126-7 S 11 '89
Eastern asks court's permission to break contract with pilots. *Aviation Week & Space Technology* 130:92 Je 26 '89
Giving 'United' a new meaning [pilot buyout] J. Schwartz. il *Newsweek* 114:34 S 25 '89
Management miscalculated pilots' response to IAM strike [Eastern Air Lines strike] il *Aviation Week & Space Technology* 130:23 Mr 13 '89
Pilots' buyout of United swaps concessions for company control [with editorial comment] C. Fotos. *Aviation Week & Space Technology* 131:9, 109 S 25 '89
Pilots vote to continue Eastern strike, but many decide to cross picket lines. *Aviation Week & Space Technology* 131:59 Ag 14 '89
Pilots will press Eastern to deal or face shutdown. J. T. McKenna and E. H. Kolcum. *Aviation Week & Space Technology* 131:68-9 F 27 '89
U.S. asks United buyout group for details on debt, foreign stake. C. Fotos. *Aviation Week & Space Technology* 131:105 O 2 '89
U.S. pilot data. *Aviation Week & Space Technology* 130:92 F 13 '89
UAL sets aside buyout effort, but pilots still pursue takeover. C. Fotos. *Aviation Week & Space Technology* 131:54 O 30 '89
United: why labor needs some parachutes on board [pilots plan buyout of United Air Lines] J. E. Ellis. il *Business Week* p28 S 18 '89
Why the United buyout is no great deal for workers. R. Kuttner. il *Business Week* p26 O 9 '89
Will everybody get on board? [UAL buyout bid by executives and pilots] J. Greenwald. il *Time* 134:63 S 18 '89
AIR NATIONAL GUARD (U.S.) *See* United States. Air National Guard
AIR NAVIGATION
Aids and devices
   See also
   Artificial satellites—Navigational use
   Aviation charts
   Computers—Aviation use
   Inertial guidance systems
   Loran
   Microwave landing systems
Falcon Eye Flir, GEC helmet aid F-16 mission flexibility [cover story] W. B. Scott. il *Aviation Week & Space Technology* 130:34-6+ Ap 17 '89
Hughes developing head-up display for general aviation aircraft. il *Aviation Week & Space Technology* 131:91 Ag 21 '89
Kaiser improves helmet-mounted display to boost pilot's kill capability. B. W. Henderson. il *Aviation Week & Space Technology* 130:119+ Je 19 '89
Pilots sense attitude with peripheral vision using new Garrett display. B. D. Nordwall. il *Aviation Week & Space Technology* 130:97+ My 8 '89
Steady improvements in head-up technology [fighter pilots] il *Popular Mechanics* 166:30 O '89
AIR NEW ZEALAND
Air New Zealand bolsters operations to prepare for increased competition. P. Proctor. il *Aviation Week & Space Technology* 130:74-6 Ja 30 '89
Air New Zealand says it will sell or lease first 747-400 [contract dispute with pilots] *Aviation Week & Space Technology* 131:136 O 9 '89
Qantas, American, JAL gain shares in Air New Zealand. *Aviation Week & Space Technology* 130:108 Ja 2 '89
AIR PILOTS
   See also
   Air Line Pilots Association
   Airplanes—Piloting
   Airplanes, Business—Piloting
   Airplanes, Light—Piloting
   Airplanes, Training—Piloting
   Alcohol and air pilots
   Barr, Danny
   Celebrities as air pilots
   Children as air pilots
   Drugs and air pilots
   Helicopter pilots
   Helicopters—Piloting
   Myers, Hank
   Payne, Carl

AIR PILOTS—See also—*cont.*
  Seaplanes—Piloting
  Strikes—Air pilots
  Wade, Bob
  Women air pilots
Benefit of the doubt [role of pilot in crash of Surinam Airways DC-8 in June 1989] L. Morgan. map *Flying* 116:114-15 O '89
Flight safety advances hinge on pilot-management teamwork. C. Fotos. il *Aviation Week & Space Technology* 131:31-2 O 9 '89
High tech and human error above the clouds. il *U.S. News & World Report* 106:8-9 Ja 23 '89

Examinations

Flight reviews: getting personal. A. Laboda. il *Flying* 116:26-7 Jl '89

Health and hygiene

F-117A crash reports cite pilot fatigue, disorientation [Stealth fighter accidents in 1986 and 1987] W. B. Scott. *Aviation Week & Space Technology* 130:22-3 My 15 '89
Pressure group: it's your altitude [altitude chamber flight at Andrews Air Force Base] P. Scott. il *Flying* 116:36+ Ag '89

Legal status, laws, etc.

Busted! J. M. McClellan. il *Flying* 116:42-4+ F '89
We're here to help [FAA] W. Garvey. il *Flying* 116:8 Je '89

Licenses

Recreational certificate: it's for real. *Flying* 116:10-11 Je '89

Promotion

The numbers game [seniority system] L. Morgan. il *Flying* 116:118-19 Je '89

Psychology

Err of expectancy [failure to respond to unexpected developments] P. Garrison. il *Flying* 116:62-5 Ja '89
Infrequent fliers. P. Body. il *Flying* 116:76-8+ My '89
Mach heroics [fighter pilots vs. transport pilots] L. Morgan. il *Flying* 116:98-9 Mr '89
The next best thing [learning to fly a new airplane] L. Morgan. il *Flying* 116:128-9 Ag '89
Pilots react to the automated cockpit [NASA study of Boeing 757 pilots; cover story; special section] il *Aviation Week & Space Technology* 131:32-6 Ag 7 '89
Your career on the line. L. Morgan. il *Flying* 116:126-7 S '89

Rating

Double-barrelled rating [multiengine training] N. Moll. il *Flying* 116:58-60+ Ap '89
Keeping IFR currency in check. J. M. McClellan. il *Flying* 116:40-1 Ag '89

Retirement

FAA reaffirms rule limiting service of airline pilots over 60 years old. *Aviation Week & Space Technology* 130:110 Je 5 '89
Getting older, or getting better? L. Morgan. il *Flying* 116:132+ N '89
Still there for the axing at age 60. *Flying* 116:26 S '89

Salaries, pensions, etc.

  See also
  Collective bargaining—Airlines
ALPA to seek elimination of two-tier wage scales. *Aviation Week & Space Technology* 130:93 F 13 '89
Military services endorse use of bonus programs to retain pilots. il *Aviation Week & Space Technology* 130:54+ My 1 '89
Senate bill would increase flight pay to stem loss of military pilots. *Aviation Week & Space Technology* 130:20 Ap 10 '89
Spooked by prosperity [Dave McWilliams family] S. Seixas. il *Money* 18:124-8+ Je '89

Songs and music

Minority report [recreational songbook of the 77th Tactical Fighter Squadron] C. Hitchens. *The Nation* 248:187 F 13 '89

Statistics

On the numbers [pilots in Europe] il *Flying* 116:97 Jl '89
U.S. pilot data. *Aviation Week & Space Technology* 130:92 F 13 '89

Supply and demand

Eastern building pilot corps amid strike, bankruptcy battles. C. Fotos. il *Aviation Week & Space Technology* 131:101-2 Jl 31 '89
Hire education [Future Aviation Professionals of America] A. Laboda. il *Flying* 116:70-2 Mr '89
Pilot shortage shrinks staffs of corporate flight departments. il *Aviation Week & Space Technology* 131:71+ O 2 '89
Pilot supply may be key issue in talks on Eastern recovery. J. T. McKenna. *Aviation Week & Space Technology* 130:315 Je 12 '89
Pilot turnover prompts regional airlines to expand, improve training programs. D. Hughes. il *Aviation Week & Space Technology* 131:91+ O 16 '89
Retirement of old transports is not likely to cut demand for commercial pilots. il *Aviation Week & Space Technology* 131:86 Jl 24 '89

Senate hearing focuses on growing pilot shortage. J. Ott. il *Aviation Week & Space Technology* 131:56-7 Ag 14 '89
What is the Air Force really worried about: national security or job security? G. Easterbrook. *The Washington Monthly* 21:18-20+ S '89

Training

  See Aviation—Study and teaching

Vision

  See Vision

AIR PILOTS' HEADPHONES *See* Headphones

AIR POLLUTION
  See also
  Acid rain
  Airplanes, Supersonic—Environmental aspects
  Automobiles—Environmental aspects
  Coal industry—Environmental aspects
  Dust
  Electric plants—Environmental aspects
  Forest products industry—Environmental aspects
  Indoor air pollution
  Plants, Effect of air pollution on
  Radon pollution
  Sick building syndrome
  Smog
  Smoke
  Trees, Effect of air pollution on
  Trucks—Environmental aspects
Congress releases air-toxics survey; EPA reports air quality is improving. *Science News* 135:204 Ap 1 '89
Is breathing hazardous to your health? [EPA report on toxics] S. Begley. il *Newsweek* 113:25 Ap 3 '89
The newest health hazard: breathing. B. Carpenter. il *U.S. News & World Report* 106:50-1 Je 12 '89
Something in the air [pollution obscuring visibility in national parks and forests] L. Kahaner. il *Wilderness* 52:18-27 Wint '88
Urban air pollution: state of the science. J. H. Seinfeld. bibl f il *Science* 243:745-52 F 10 '89

Control

  See also
  Dust collectors
  Industry and the environment
Air [Environmental Quality Index] il *National Wildlife* 27:35 F/Mr '89
Air pollution: it's all legal. G. Easterbrook. il *Newsweek* 114:28-9+ Jl 24 '89
New catalysts scavenge NO_x emissions. J. Raloff. *Science News* 135:271 Ap 29 '89
Silver lining for pollution's cloud? *The Futurist* 23:49 N/D '89
Tackling smog ozone: tougher than thought [Office of Technology Assessment report] I. Wickelgren. *Science News* 136:53 Jl 22 '89

International aspects

The changing atmosphere [human activity is altering the complex mixture of gases] T. E. Graedel and P. J. Crutzen. bibl il *Scientific American* 261:58-64+ S '89
Monitoring the global environment: an assessment of urban air quality [cover story] bibl f il *Environment* 31:6-13+ O '89

Laws and regulations

  See also
  Clean Air Act
  Emission reduction credits

Measurement

Monitoring the global environment: an assessment of urban air quality [cover story] bibl f il *Environment* 31:6-13+ O '89

Amazon River Valley

What is clean air? [Amazon Boundary Layer Experiment] S. A. Motley. il *Technology Review* 92:8+ Ja '89

Arizona

Study finds source of canyon haze [Navajo Generating Station near Grand Canyon] il *National Parks* 63:10 Jl/Ag '89

California

  See also
  Los Angeles (Calif.)—Air pollution
"Moderately radical". M. Beauchamp. il por *Forbes* 143:148 My 15 '89

Canada

Canada, carbon dioxide, and the greenhouse effect. L. Hughes and S. Scott. bibl f il *Environment* 31:4-5+ N '89

China

SPM levels in China. il *Environment* 31:30 O '89

Colorado

Colorado proposes protecting vistas. *National Parks* 63:13-14 Ja/F '89

Developing countries

Air pollution. K. R. Smith. bibl f il *Environment* 30:16-20+ D '88
Air pollution [discussion of December 1988 article] K. R. Smith. il *Environment* 31:2-3 My '89

  Georgia

  See also
  Atlanta (Ga.)—Air pollution

AIR POLLUTION—*cont.*

Mexico

See also

Mexico City (Mexico)—Air pollution

New Brunswick

See also

Saint John (N.B.)—Air pollution

Oregon

Farmers playing with fire [burning of grass seed threatens air quality in Willamette Valley] J. Stiak. il *Sierra* 74:92-3 Mr/Ap '89

United States

See Air pollution

AIR PRESSURE *See* Atmospheric pressure

AIR PRODUCTS AND CHEMICALS, INC.

Keeping the cow, selling the milk [Air Products' ten year plan contrasted with Federal Reserve anxiety about tight industrial capacity] H. Banks. il por *Forbes* 143:40-1 Mr 20 '89

AIR PUMPS

Maintenance and repair

Air to spare [bicycle pumps] J. Langley. il *Bicycling* 30:146-7 Ja/F '89

AIR PURIFIERS *See* Air filters

AIR RACES *See* Airplane racing

AIR ROUTES *See* Airlines—Routes

AIR SAFETY *See* Aviation—Safety devices and measures

AIR-SEA INTERACTION *See* Ocean-atmosphere interaction

AIR SHIPS *See* Airships

AIR SHOWS *See* Aviation—Exhibitions

AIR SHUTTLE SERVICE *See* Airlines—Shuttle service; Helicopter airlines—Shuttle service

AIR-SOIL INTERACTION *See* Soil-atmosphere interaction

AIR SPACE (INTERNATIONAL LAW) *See* Airspace (International law)

AIR SPEEDS *See* Airplanes—Speed

AIR STEWARDESSES *See* Flight attendants

AIR TAXI SERVICE

See also

Helicopter airlines

Airlines ignore a crucial market: air taxis for business travelers. J. B. Taylor. por *Aviation Week & Space Technology* 130:73-4 Jl 10 '89

AIR TOOLS *See* Pneumatic tools

AIR TRAFFIC *See* Airlines—Traffic

AIR TRAFFIC CONTROL

See also

Airplanes—Collision avoidance systems

Computers—Aviation use

Radar in aviation

Air traffic control planners seek airport capacity gains. *Aviation Week & Space Technology* 129:71 Mr 6 '89

Boosting operations at underused airports can ease congestion in U.S. G. W. Hamlin. por *Aviation Week & Space Technology* 130:173-4+ Je 19 '89

Dangerous traffic. W. Stockton. il *The New York Times Magazine* p40-1+ Je 4 '89

Despite O'Hare limits, U.S. flight delays fell in 1988. *Aviation Week & Space Technology* 130:71 F 27 '89

FAA task force will study solutions to capacity crisis. J. Ott. il *Aviation Week & Space Technology* 130:119+ My 29 '89

Flight in the fast lane [VFR flying in high-density areas] P. Garrison. il *Flying* 116:68-70+ Ja '89

Industry, academic leaders foresee little short-term relief of congestion. C. Fotos. *Aviation Week & Space Technology* 130:94-5 Ap 10 '89

Mega-TCA for D.C.? [terminal control area] *Flying* 116:16 Je '89

Microburst radar may spur review of tower's role in aborting landings [Doppler radar tested at Denver] P. J. Klass. il *Aviation Week & Space Technology* 130:79+ My 1 '89

NASA shuttle commander involved in near collision with Pan Am A310 [D. M. Walker] *Aviation Week & Space Technology* 130:105 My 22 '89

Northeast ATC review cites potential threats to safety. J. T. McKenna. *Aviation Week & Space Technology* 130:66 Ap 3 '89

Preserving access key issue to business, general aviation. il *Aviation Week & Space Technology* 130:237-9 Mr 20 '89

"See and avoid," or blind faith? [collision of Piper Navajo Army U-21 near Kansas City] J. M. McClellan. *Flying* 116:30-1 Ap '89

Squeeze play [ATC turn command sends Piper Seneca into thunderstorm] P. Steeves. il *Flying* 116:128-9 S '89

International aspects

Major coordinated effort required to avoid global airport congestion. R. G. O'Lone. il *Aviation Week & Space Technology* 131:54+ N 20 '89

Japan

Lack of pilots, controllers endangers growth in Japan. *Aviation Week & Space Technology* 131:113 N 20 '89

North Atlantic region

New communication, navigation systems will increase North Atlantic capacity. D. Hughes. il *Aviation Week & Space Technology* 131:115+ N 20 '89

Pacific region

Pacific Rim carriers struggle to cope with impending traffic boom. P. Proctor. il *Aviation Week & Space Technology* 131:110-11 N 20 '89

Pacific Rim traffic growth to continue, barring capacity limits. P. Proctor. *Aviation Week & Space Technology* 131:83 O 16 '89

Western Europe

Eurocontrol agrees to set up Brussels unit to coordinate air traffic across Europe. *Aviation Week & Space Technology* 130:64 Jl 10 '89

European airlines will study forming a single ATC system. *Aviation Week & Space Technology* 130:71 F 27 '89

Europe's business aircraft operators fight for access to airspace, airports. il *Aviation Week & Space Technology* 131:91+ O 2 '89

IATA to convene European air congestion assembly. C. A. Shifrin. il *Aviation Week & Space Technology* 131:18-20 N 6 '89

Lack of centralized European ATC could hinder trade reforms in 1992. E. H. Phillips. il *Aviation Week & Space Technology* 131:73 S 4 '89

Two organizations differ in forecasts of European air traffic growth. il *Aviation Week & Space Technology* 131:108-9 Jl 31 '89

AIR TRAFFIC CONTROL, MILITARY

USAF controllers, F-15 pilots train for combat using multiship simulation. S. W. Kandebo. il *Aviation Week & Space Technology* 130:71+ Mr 27 '89

AIR TRAFFIC CONTROLLERS (PERSONS)

See also

Collective labor agreements—Air traffic controllers (Persons)

National Air Traffic Controllers Association

Training

Britain's Rediffusion Simulation offers microcomputer-based ATC trainer. C. A. Shifrin. il *Aviation Week & Space Technology* 131:83+ Ag 21 '89

AIR TRANSPORT

See also

Hunting dogs—Air transport

AIR TRANSPORT ASSOCIATION OF AMERICA

ATA president blasts U.S. government's failure to reform aviation agency [views of Robert J. Aaronson] *Aviation Week & Space Technology* 130:105 My 1 '89

ATA will establish task force to critique MLS programs [microwave landing systems] J. T. McKenna. il *Aviation Week & Space Technology* 129:68-9 Mr 6 '89

AIR TRAVEL

See also

Airlines

Blind—Travel

Computers and air travel

Fear of flying

Frequent flier programs

Handicapped—Travel

Jet lag

Partnership for Improved Air Travel

Private flying

Behind the cockpit door [pilot recalls unforgettable run from over 30 years ago] L. Morgan. il *Flying* 116:100-1 Ap '89

The empire of the sun. R. Rosenblatt. il *U.S. News & World Report* 106:8-9 Mr 20 '89

Exercising your flight rights [with editorial comment by Diane P. Marshall] B. J. Janesh. il *Travel Holiday* 171:6, 35-9 Je '89

Flying through airline loopholes [interview with G. A. Brown] J. Popkin. il por *U.S. News & World Report* 107:61 Jl 31 '89

Have goggles, will travel [M. Esch hitches rides across U.S. in vintage airplanes] G. Baxter. il por *Flying* 116:86+ My '89

It's safer, better to fly. il *Consumers' Research Magazine* 72:25-7 Mr '89

This is what you thought: 65% are now more frightened of flying [survey results] il *Glamour* 87:93 Jl '89

Who wins the air wars? [deregulation's effect on passengers] C. Friday and J. Schwartz. il *Newsweek* 114:41 S 18 '89

Your airline survival guide [cover story] J. Blyskal and M. Hodge. il *New York* 22:30-41 Ag 28 '89

History

Time travel [1930s] L. Morgan. il *Flying* 116:106-7 D '89

Physiological aspects

See Aviation—Physiological aspects

Security measures

Late alarums, failed alerts [Pan Am Flight 103] J. Smolowe. il *Time* 133:53 Mr 27 '89

Remedy for terror: fight back [interview with Y. Alexander] T. Nugent. il por *People Weekly* 32:64 D 18 '89

The sovereign share. *Aviation Week & Space Technology* 130:15 My 29 '89

Upping the ante on airline security: is forewarned forearmed? H. Gieseking. il *Travel Holiday* 172:18-20 S '89

The warnings that weren't [Pan American Flight 103] A. Platt. il *Newsweek* 113:42 Mr 27 '89

AIR TRAVEL WITH PETS See Travel with pets
AIR TURBINES
    See also
    Wind power
AIR WARFARE
    See also
    Airplanes, Military
    Close air support
    Guns, Anti-aircraft
    Tactical Air Warfare Center (U.S.)
    Topgun Aviation (Firm)
    USAF controllers, F-15 pilots train for combat using multiship simulation. S. W. Kandebo. il *Aviation Week & Space Technology* 130:71+ Mr 27 '89
    Maneuvers
    See Military maneuvers
AIRBORNE FLIGHT INFORMATION SYSTEMS See Aviation—Communication systems
AIRBORNE FREIGHT CORP.
    Small fish, big bites. il *Forbes* 143:84 Ja 9 '89
    Why Airborne may really deliver. G. G. Marcial. *Business Week* p88 Ag 21 '89
AIRBORNE LAW ENFORCEMENT ASSOCIATION
    ALEA cops turning up the heat. *Flying* 116:22 N '89
AIRBORNE WARNING AND CONTROL SYSTEM See Airplanes, Military—Radar equipment
AIRBRUSH ART
    Airbrush artistry [photographs] S. A. Rafiq. il *Petersen's Photographic Magazine* 18:90-3 D '89
    Creating imaginary places [work of J. Buckels] M. E. Stegmaier. il pors *American Artist* 53:56-9+ O '89
    Warner Friedman. E. Agar. il por *American Artist* 53:44-7+ Ja '89
AIRBUS INDUSTRIE
    Aeroflot signs letter of intent to purchase five Airbus A310-300s. *Aviation Week & Space Technology* 131:18 N 6 '89
    Aerospatiale and MBB disagree on A320/A321 assembly location. J. M. Lenorovitz. il *Aviation Week & Space Technology* 131:70 O 23 '89
    Airbus Industrie expects to launch production of A321-100 by fall. il *Aviation Week & Space Technology* 130:159 Je 19 '89
    Airbus Industrie members approve reorganization plan. *Aviation Week & Space Technology* 130:91 Mr 27 '89
    Airbus Industrie partners approve development of stretched A320. J. M. Lenorovitz. il *Aviation Week & Space Technology* 131:31-2 D 4 '89
    Airbus Industrie records 60 firm orders, options for range of aircraft. *Aviation Week & Space Technology* 130:102 My 8 '89
    Airbus nears launch authorization for stretched version of A320. *Aviation Week & Space Technology* 130:26 Ap 24 '89
    Airbus: still in the red despite subsidies. S. Toy and J. Templeman. il *Business Week* p36 My 8 '89
    Bailing out of Airbus [R. Smith] S. Toy. il *Business Week* p47 D 18 '89
    Braniff will use 50 A320s to expand service from Kansas City to coasts. il *Aviation Week & Space Technology* 130:63 Ja 9 '89
    Cathay Pacific orders 10 A330s to replace L-1011s. J. M. Lenorovitz. il *Aviation Week & Space Technology* 130:91 Ap 10 '89
    Commission approves subsidies for Airbus. *Aviation Week & Space Technology* 130:67 Mr 13 '89
    Continental orders 20 Airbus A330, A340 aircraft. *Aviation Week & Space Technology* 131:46 N 20 '89
    ILFC negotiates pact to buy 16 stretched Airbus A320s. il *Aviation Week & Space Technology* 130:111 Je 5 '89
    Lufthansa boosts firm order total for Airbus A321-100 transports. C. A. Shifrin. *Aviation Week & Space Technology* 131:58-9 Ag 14 '89
    This engine maker is finally seeing a patch of blue [International Aero Engines' Braniff deal] R. W. King. *Business Week* p39-40 Ja 23 '89
    TWA commitment strengthens Airbus' position in North American market. J. M. Lenorovitz. il *Aviation Week & Space Technology* 130:65 Ap 3 '89
    TWA orders Airbus A330s to upgrade aging fleet. C. Fotos. il *Aviation Week & Space Technology* 130:64-5 Ap 3 '89
    U.S. criticizes E.C. plan to shield MBB from fluctuations in exchange rate. M. Mecham. *Aviation Week & Space Technology* 130:91 Mr 27 '89
AIRBUSES See Airplanes, Jet
AIRCRAFT
    See also
    Airplanes
    Airships
    Balloons
    Gliders (Aviation)
    Helicopters
    Rotor aircraft
AIRCRAFT CARRIERS
    See also
    Airplanes, Military—Landing on carriers
    Lexington (Aircraft carrier)

    Carrier air wings trained for coordinated strikes [Naval Strike Warfare Center] B. M. Greeley, Jr. il *Aviation Week & Space Technology* 130:46-7 F 27 '89
    Accidents and explosions
    Five die on Lexington as student pilot crashes. *Aviation Week & Space Technology* 131:31 N 6 '89
    Electronic equipment
    French electro-optic, IR firms to bid on U.S. aircraft carrier systems. B. D. Nordwall. il *Aviation Week & Space Technology* 130:89+ My 8 '89
AIRCRAFT CARRIERS, RUSSIAN
    See also
    Tbilisi (Aircraft carrier)
AIRCRAFT INDUSTRY See Airplane industry
AIREDALE TERRIERS
    Too tough to die [Airedale comes to aid of J. Tarpley who was crushed by a tractor] P. O. D'Aulaire and E. D'Aulaire. il *Reader's Digest* 135:81-6 N '89
AIRFOILS
    See also
    Airplanes—Wings
AIRFRAME INDUSTRY See Airplane industry
AIRFRAMES
    See also
    Airplanes, Business—Frames
AIRGLOW
    Telescopes observe earth's atmosphere [research by Paul A. Bernhardt] il *Sky and Telescope* 78:129 Ag '89
AIRLIE GROUP
    The power behind Pan Am's bid for Northwest. C. Power and K. Kelly. il por *Business Week* p29 Je 12 '89
AIRLINE FLIGHT ATTENDANTS See Flight attendants
AIRLINE PASSENGER CLUBS See Airlines—Passenger service
AIRLINE PASSENGERS See Air travel
AIRLINE SCHEDULES See Airlines—Schedules
AIRLINE STOCKS See Airlines—Securities
AIRLINE TICKET BROKERS
    Flying the shadow market [frequent flier ticket brokers] J. Popkin. il *U.S. News & World Report* 107:77-80+ N 13 '89
AIRLINES
    See also
    Air Transport Association of America
    Aloha Airgroup Inc.
    Aloha Airlines, Inc.
    American Airlines, Inc.
    AMR Eagle (Firm)
    Braniff, Inc.
    Collective bargaining—Airlines
    Collective labor agreements—Airlines
    Continental Air Lines, Inc.
    Delta Air Lines, Inc.
    Eastern Air Lines, Inc.
    Hawaiian Airlines, Inc.
    Key Airlines
    MGM Grand Air Inc.
    Midwest Express
    Northwest Airlines, Inc.
    Pan American World Airways, Inc.
    Partnership for Improved Air Travel
    People Express Inc.
    Presidential Airways, Inc.
    Texas Air Corp.
    Trans World Airlines Inc.
    UAL Corporation
    United Air Lines, Inc.
    USAir, Inc.
    Airline observer. See issues of Aviation Week & Space Technology
    Your airline survival guide [cover story] J. Blyskal and M. Hodge. il *New York* 22:30-41 Ag 28 '89
    Acquisitions and mergers
    Airline buyouts: losing altitude but not grounded yet. J. E. Ellis. il *Business Week* p31 O 30 '89
    Airline takeovers: who's in play, what's at stake? [special section; with editorial comment] il *Aviation Week & Space Technology* 131:9, 18-22 Ag 14 '89
    ALPA begins drive to win pilots' support for United buyout. *Aviation Week & Space Technology* 131:124 S 18 '89
    ALPA prepares for possible sale of all or part of TWA [Air Line Pilots Assn.] J. T. McKenna. *Aviation Week & Space Technology* 131:128-9 N 20 '89
    Back to you, Frank [F. Lorenzo's deal with P. Ueberroth for Eastern Air Lines collapses] A. Bernstein and C. Power. il pors *Business Week* p24-6 Ap 24 '89
    The balloon bursts for Wall Street arbs [collapse of UAL takeover bid] J. Egan. il *U.S. News & World Report* 107:71 N 6 '89
    Bankers' concerns, challenged forecasts derailed UAL buyout. C. Fotos and N. C. Kernstock. il *Aviation Week & Space Technology* 131:17-19 O 23 '89
    The best and the brassiest [D. Trump's bid for American Airlines] C. P. Work. il pors *U.S. News & World Report* 107:52-4 O 23 '89
    Board decisions muddle rules on union role after mergers [National Mediation Board rulings] J. Ott. *Aviation Week & Space Technology* 131:68 Ag 28 '89

AIRLINES—Acquisitions and mergers—cont.

Boxed in by Trump [bid for American Airlines; special section] il por *Business Week* p54-6 O 23 '89

Can United afford to be taken over? K. Labich. il *Fortune* 120:145-6+ S 11 '89

The Cayman connection [foreign investments in Coniston Partners may endanger deal for control of UAL] S. Flack. il *Forbes* 144:42-3 D 11 '89

Concerns about leverage cool market for airline takeovers. N. C. Kernstock. il *Aviation Week & Space Technology* 131:71-4 N 20 '89

Congress would probe Pan Am-NWA merger's effect on U.S. competition. J. Ott. *Aviation Week & Space Technology* 130:72-3 My 15 '89

Court approves proposed sale of Eastern air-shuttle. J. T. McKenna. *Aviation Week & Space Technology* 130:102-3 My 22 '89

The crowded skies [bidders for Eastern Air Lines] A. Walmsley. *Maclean's* 102:32 Ap 10 '89

Davis increases bid for UAL, threatens to oust board if offer is rejected. *Aviation Week & Space Technology* 131:95 Ag 21 '89

Davis ups buyout bid for United but pilot offer still stronger. J. Ott and C. A. Shifrin. il *Aviation Week & Space Technology* 131:126-7 S 11 '89

Debt propelled [effect of takeovers on jet maintenance] J. Greenwald. il *Time* 134:52-3 S 25 '89

The designated hero [P. Ueberroth's plan to buy Eastern] J. Castro. il por *Time* 133:44-6 Ap 17 '89

A dogfight for dominance of the skies. K. R. Sheets and P. Dworkin. il *U.S. News & World Report* 107:54-5 S 11 '89

Donald Trump's buy-American plan [bid for American Airlines] il por *U.S. News & World Report* 107:23-4 O 16 '89

Eastern's merry-go-round [collapse of P. Ueberroth deal] *Newsweek* 113:62 Ap 24 '89

An ego as big as American [D. Trump bids for American Airlines] L. Reibstein. il pors *Newsweek* 114:56-7 O 16 '89

A far-out merger scheme that could just fly [Pan Am-Northwest deal] C. Power and A. Bernstein. il *Business Week* p36-7 My 22 '89

Feeding frenzy at the airlines. W. Woods. il *Fortune* 120:8 O 9 '89

A fight for the friendly skies: takeover artists go after Eastern and Northwest. L. Reibstein. il *Newsweek* 113:50 Ap 10 '89

Final integration of Piedmont into USAir completed smoothly. *Aviation Week & Space Technology* 131:58 Ag 14 '89

Giving 'United' a new meaning [pilot buyout] J. Schwartz. il *Newsweek* 114:34 S 25 '89

Going, going, gone [sale of Hawaiian Airlines] K. Hannon. il *Forbes* 144:10 S 18 '89

Hawaiian Airlines board backs $22/share buyout bid. *Aviation Week & Space Technology* 131:71 Ag 28 '89

The heat is on airline deals. S. Payne. il por *Business Week* p32 O 2 '89

Here comes Donald, duck! [D. Trump's bid for American Airlines] C. Gorman. il por *Time* 134:52+ O 16 '89

He's hungry to buy an airline [M. Davis' bid for UAL] J. Castro. il por *Time* 134:42 Ag 21 '89

House passes bill to curb airline mergers, takeovers. M. Mecham. *Aviation Week & Space Technology* 131:54 N 6 '89

House tax panel probes airline bailout threat. M. Mecham. il *Aviation Week & Space Technology* 131:52-3 O 30 '89

In hot pursuit of airlines [bid for UAL] L. Reibstein. il por *Newsweek* 114:40 Ag 21 '89

Investor group mounts new bid to buy UAL Corp., replace board. C. Fotos. *Aviation Week & Space Technology* 131:72 N 13 '89

Investors plan to revamp Hawaiian's operations. *Aviation Week & Space Technology* 131:71 S 4 '89

Is a nutsy-boltsy company out to nail Midway Airlines? [Ampco-Pittsburgh] M. Schroeder. il *Business Week* p26 Ag 21 '89

Is Icahn taxiing TWA to the auction block? T. Vogel. il *Business Week* p58 D 11 '89

Is Mesa Airlines facing a dogfight? [stake by StatesWest Airlines] G. G. Marcial. *Business Week* p130 Jl 17 '89

Judge set to rule on shuttle sale, Eastern business plan. *Aviation Week & Space Technology* 130:72 My 15 '89

Judge threatens to auction Eastern after buyout fails [bid by P. Ueberroth] J. T. McKenna and E. H. Kolcum. *Aviation Week & Space Technology* 130:60-1 Ap 17 '89

Justice Dept. vows stronger antitrust policy on mergers. M. Mecham. il *Aviation Week & Space Technology* 130:64-5 Mr 13 '89

Landing Northwest [A. Checchi] R. Grover and R. Mitchell. il por *Business Week* p24-5 Jl 3 '89

Lawmakers fear LBOs threaten fitness of U.S. airline industry. M. Mecham. *Aviation Week & Space Technology* 131:104-5+ Jl 31 '89

Lorenzo weighs selling stake in Continental. *Aviation Week & Space Technology* 131:69-70 S 4 '89

Lorenzo's magnificent airline [offers to purchase Eastern] il *U.S. News & World Report* 106:14+ Ap 10 '89

Memo to the airlines: deregulation's days are numbered. S. Payne. *Business Week* p59 N 13 '89

Northwest asks pilots to cooperate in thwarting hostile takeover. *Aviation Week & Space Technology* 130:106 My 1 '89

Northwest pilots warn that talks on new contract near breakdown. *Aviation Week & Space Technology* 131:99 Jl 24 '89

Northwest stockholders weigh options in face of various takeover offers. C. Fotos. map *Aviation Week & Space Technology* 130:103-4 My 22 '89

Now, the sky's the limit [bid for United] J. E. Ellis. il *Business Week* p24-6 Ag 21 '89

NWA rejects bids; new date set for proposals. *Aviation Week & Space Technology* 130:315 Je 12 '89

NWA seeks strategy to block Davis' $3.1-billion takeover attempt. *Aviation Week & Space Technology* 130:107 Ap 24 '89

The odd couple chasing Northwest Airlines [A. Checchi and G. L. Wilson] R. Grover. il pors *Business Week* p126 Ap 24 '89

Off we go into the hazy blue yonder. C. Power. il *Business Week* p26-7 S 18 '89

Pan Am considers entering field of Northwest bidders. C. Fotos. *Aviation Week & Space Technology* 130:70-1 My 15 '89

Pan Am Corp., Davis among Northwest bidders. C. Fotos. il *Aviation Week & Space Technology* 130:108-9 Je 5 '89

Pan Am Corp. seeks alternatives after failed Northwest bid. *Aviation Week & Space Technology* 130:91 Je 26 '89

Pan Am Corp. will sell World Services in attempt to give Plaskett more time. J. T. McKenna. il *Aviation Week & Space Technology* 130:68-9 Ja 23 '89

Pan Am intensifies efforts to bail out Airways unit. *Aviation Week & Space Technology* 131:111 D 18-25 '89

Pan Am looks Northwest. C. Friday. il *Newsweek* 112:62 My 22 '89

Pan Am needs a partner, but does anybody need Pan Am? C. Power. il por *Business Week* p92+ Ap 10 '89

Peter Ueberroth's Hawaiian adventure [Hawaiian Airlines] E. Schine. il por *Business Week* p32 S 4 '89

A pilot with a golden record [P. Ueberroth wants to purchase Eastern Airlines] il por *U.S. News & World Report* 106:14-15 Ap 17 '89

Pilots' buyout of United swaps concessions for company control [with editorial comment] C. Fotos. *Aviation Week & Space Technology* 131:9, 109 S 25 '89

Pilots union threatens to seek declaration of impasse in talks with Northwest Airlines. *Aviation Week & Space Technology* 131:97 Jl 17 '89

The power behind Pan Am's bid for Northwest [Airlie Group] C. Power and K. Kelly. il por *Business Week* p29 Je 12 '89

A promising flight plan—if no raiders show [USAir-Piedmont deal] S. Payne. il *Business Week* p81-2 Ag 14 '89

Raiders may not make the best airline pilots. C. Power. il *Business Week* p35 My 15 '89

The sky kings rule the routes. J. Castro. il *Time* 133:52-4 My 15 '89

A squeeze play at Northwest [M. Davis' bid] C. Power. il *Business Week* p30 My 1 '89

Still trying to land UAL [Coniston Partners' proxy fight] J. E. Ellis. il *Business Week* p28-9 N 20 '89

Takeover talk lifts the airline stocks. E. Schultz. il *Fortune* 120:46 Jl 31 '89

Takeover weather for the airlines. il *U.S. News & World Report* 107:16 Ag 21 '89

'This is too big a genie to put back in the bottle' [botched UAL takeover] J. E. Ellis. il por *Business Week* p43 N 6 '89

"This will be all-out war" [NWA rebuffs bid by M. Davis] J. Greenwald. il por *Time* 133:46 Ap 17 '89

Transportation Dept. considers standards for regulating LBOs. *Aviation Week & Space Technology* 131:128 S 11 '89

Trump mounts bid to buy American for $7.5 billion. *Aviation Week & Space Technology* 131:139 O 9 '89

TWA unions attempt to shape strategy for gaining leverage over airline sale. J. T. McKenna. *Aviation Week & Space Technology* 131:32-3 D 4 '89

U.S. asks United buyout group for details on debt, foreign stake. C. Fotos. *Aviation Week & Space Technology* 131:105 O 2 '89

UAL investigates alternatives to Davis' $6.19-billion takeover bid. C. Fotos. *Aviation Week & Space Technology* 131:70 Ag 28 '89

UAL sets aside buyout effort, but pilots still pursue takeover. C. Fotos. *Aviation Week & Space Technology* 131:54 O 30 '89

The Ueberroth touch [dealing for Eastern Air Lines] L. Reibstein. il por *Newsweek* 113:44-5 Ap 17 '89

Ueberroth woos unions in bid to take over Eastern, resume flight operations. J. T. McKenna and E. H. Kolcum. *Aviation Week & Space Technology* 130:89 Ap 10 '89

Union plan for Eastern takeover released at congressional hearing. il *Aviation Week & Space Technology* 130:22 Mr 13 '89

AIRLINES—Acquisitions and mergers—*cont.*

Unions, investor plead for time to negotiate pact to buy Eastern. *Aviation Week & Space Technology* 130:113 Je 5 '89

Unions, Minnesota officials vow to fight any break-up of Northwest. *Aviation Week & Space Technology* 130:90 Ap 10 '89

United: why labor needs some parachutes on board [pilots plan buyout of United Air Lines] J. E. Ellis. il *Business Week* p28 S 18 '89

United's buyers may be wearing rose-colored goggles. J. E. Ellis. il *Business Week* p36 O 16 '89

United's flight attendants authorize strike; takeover reports push stock price up. J. T. McKenna. *Aviation Week & Space Technology* 131:95 Jl 17 '89

USAir prepares to complete acquisition of Piedmont. J. Ott. il *Aviation Week & Space Technology* 131:94-5 Jl 17 '89

USAir takeover unlikely despite SEC filing [Steinhardt Partners raises stake] *Aviation Week & Space Technology* 131:102 Jl 31 '89

What could stall a run on Northwest. C. Power and R. Mitchell. il *Business Week* p30 Ap 10 '89

Where's my escape hatch? [P. Ueberroth's deal with Eastern stalls] il *Time* 133:51 Ap 24 '89

White House, Hill clash over airline takeovers [with editorial comment] M. Mecham. *Aviation Week & Space Technology* 131:7, 16-17 O 23 '89

Why Mike Milken was so eager to help Peter Ueberroth [Eastern Air Lines takeover] A. Bernstein. *Business Week* p30 My 1 '89

Why the United buyout is no great deal for workers. R. Kuttner. il *Business Week* p26 O 9 '89

Will everybody get on board? [UAL buyout bid by executives and pilots] J. Greenwald. il *Time* 134:63 S 18 '89

Wings Holdings chief pledges to keep Northwest growing [A. A. Checchi] C. Fotos. *Aviation Week & Space Technology* 130:90-1 Je 26 '89

The workingman's man at the takeover table [B. Freeman] C. Tucher. il por *Business Week* p62 S 4 '89

International aspects

American Airlines, Canadian investors weigh bids for Wardair. C. Fotos. *Aviation Week & Space Technology* 130:108-9 Ap 24 '89

Beard for hire. S. Flack. il *Forbes* 144:10 O 2 '89

Birds of a feather . . . are doing deals together. C. Power and S. Payne. il *Business Week* p32-3 S 11 '89

Front man [A. Checchi fronting for KLM in Northwest takeover] S. Flack. il *Forbes* 144:69 Jl 10 '89

International flights of fancy. K. R. Sheets. il *U.S. News & World Report* 107:53 O 23 '89

It's not even flying yet, and already there's a flap [Discovery Airways' Japanese financing] J. B. Levine and S. Payne. il *Business Week* p36-7 D 4 '89

Marketing pacts, equity agreements bring world's airlines closer together. C. A. Shifrin. il *Aviation Week & Space Technology* 131:67+ D 18-25 '89

Qantas, American, JAL gain shares in Air New Zealand. *Aviation Week & Space Technology* 130:108 Ja 2 '89

Skinner's limits on NWA buyout fail to dissuade drive for LBO controls. C. Fotos. *Aviation Week & Space Technology* 131:138-9 O 9 '89

U.S. must assess buyout bid's impact on safety at Northwest [KLM's role in Wings Holdings' bid under scrutiny] *Aviation Week & Space Technology* 130:92-3 Je 26 '89

Canada

The end of Ward's dream [Wardair sold to Pacific Western Airlines] P. Chisholm. il pors *Maclean's* 102:34-5 Ja 30 '89

PWA Corp. to lay off 1,900 airline personnel [combining Canadian Airlines International and Wardair into one airline] *Aviation Week & Space Technology* 131:45 D 11 '89

Wardair founder agrees to sell airline to PWA Corp. D. Hughes. il *Aviation Week & Space Technology* 130:72-3 Ja 30 '89

Western Europe

Belgium will sell British Airways, KLM 20% stakes in new Sabena. *Aviation Week & Space Technology* 130:95 Je 26 '89

Birds of a feather . . . are doing deals together. C. Power and S. Payne. il *Business Week* p32-3 S 11 '89

SAS, Airlines of Britain to discuss possible operational merger. *Aviation Week & Space Technology* 130:109 Ja 2 '89

Advertising

The Madman of Mad Ave prepares for takeoff [Pan Am account goes to Della Femina] W. Konrad. il por *Business Week* p124 F 20 '89

Agreements

See Airlines—Cooperation

Antitrust cases

Congress seeks remedies to concentration at hubs. J. Ott. il *Aviation Week & Space Technology* 130:100-1 My 8 '89

How 'Sam the Hammer' could nail the airlines [S. Skinner] S. Payne. il por *Business Week* p126-7 Je 26 '89

Justice Dept. vows stronger antitrust policy on mergers. M. Mecham. il *Aviation Week & Space Technology* 130:64-5 Mr 13 '89

Senate panel widens probe of airline concentration. J. Ott. il *Aviation Week & Space Technology* 130:312-13 Je 12 '89

Skinner calls USAir bid for more Philadelphia gates anticompetitive [Eastern gates] *Aviation Week & Space Technology* 130:110 Je 5 '89

Automation

Computers may turn the world into one big commodities pit [Marketel International's system will establish electronic market for air fares] R. Kuttner. il *Business Week* p17 S 11 '89

Baggage handling

See Airlines—Luggage handling

Collectibles

"Off we go into the wild blue yonder . . .". H. L. Rinker. il *Antiques & Collecting Hobbies* 94:20+ N '89

Cooperation

Air France, Lufthansa sign pact for broad cooperative policies. J. M. Lenorovitz. il *Aviation Week & Space Technology* 131:108 S 25 '89

All Nippon taps partners' fleets to expand international service. J. Ott. il *Aviation Week & Space Technology* 130:44 My 8 '89

British Airways, United Airlines will expand cooperative services. map *Aviation Week & Space Technology* 130:69 Mr 13 '89

Marketing pacts, equity agreements bring world's airlines closer together. C. A. Shifrin. il *Aviation Week & Space Technology* 131:67+ D 18-25 '89

Presidential Airways' woes show code sharing no guarantee of success. C. Fotos. *Aviation Week & Space Technology* 131:43-4 D 11 '89

SAS, Swissair agree to cooperate on traffic and travel services system. *Aviation Week & Space Technology* 131:104 O 2 '89

U.S. airlines forge marketing agreements with overseas carriers. C. Fotos. il *Aviation Week & Space Technology* 131:75+ N 20 '89

Employees

See also

Air pilots

Airplane crews

Airplane mechanics (Persons)

Flight attendants

International Association of Machinists and Aerospace Workers

Labor unions—Airline employees

Strikes—Airline employees

Salaries, pensions, etc.

Will the carrot and stick work at United? J. E. Ellis. il por *Business Week* p56-7 F 6 '89

Ethical aspects

Phoenix Airlines may get its wings clipped. D. Foust. il por *Business Week* p114 Mr 13 '89

Fares

See also

Airline ticket brokers

Frequent flier programs

Airfares: speak up for a discount. il *Consumer Reports* 54:363-6 Je '89

The airlines just don't know how to stay out of fights. J. E. Ellis. il *Business Week* p55 O 23 '89

Beating the overheated fares. B. Kobliner. il *Money* 18:64-5 F '89

Caught in Eastern's slipstream [airlines raise fares as a result of strike] il *U.S. News & World Report* 106:10+ Mr 27 '89

Computers may turn the world into one big commodities pit [Marketel International's system will establish electronic market for air fares] R. Kuttner. il *Business Week* p17 S 11 '89

Congress seeks remedies to concentration at hubs. J. Ott. il *Aviation Week & Space Technology* 130:100-1 My 8 '89

Congress will seek ways to spur hub competition. *Aviation Week & Space Technology* 130:126 F 20 '89

The costly skies [Canada] J. Daly. il *Maclean's* 102:26-7 Je 26 '89

European Aviation Conference, U.S. fail to agree on extending fare pact. il *Aviation Week & Space Technology* 131:66 Ag 14 '89

European Court ruling could ban bilateral air fare agreements. *Aviation Week & Space Technology* 130:32 Ap 17 '89

Finding bargain air fares [cover story] M. Hopkins. il *Consumers' Research Magazine* 72:10-12 Jl '89

Plane truth [case for reregulation] R. Kuttner. *The New Republic* 201:21-3 Jl 17-24 '89

Regaining altitude [fewer airlines charging higher fares in Canada] J. Daly. il *Maclean's* 102:46-8 N 6 '89

Senate panel widens probe of airline concentration. J. Ott. il *Aviation Week & Space Technology* 130:312-13 Je 12 '89

There's the hub. J. W. Merline. *Consumers' Research Magazine* 72:38 Ap '89

TWA leads U.S. carriers in cutting domestic fares. J. T. McKenna. *Aviation Week & Space Technology* 131:92-3 Ag 21 '89

AIRLINES—cont.

Federal aid
Budget squeeze forces House panel to reject more funding for Essential Air Service program. *Aviation Week & Space Technology* 130:109 Ap 24 '89

Pentagon pursues additional commitments from airlines to boost U.S. airlift capacity. *Aviation Week & Space Technology* 130:24 Ja 30 '89

States, not Washington, must develop Essential Air Services. K. B. Creedy. por *Aviation Week & Space Technology* 131:113-16 S 25 '89

Finance
Air transport. H. Banks. il *Forbes* 143:84-5 Ja 9 '89

Airline income and expense: yearly 1988. il *Aviation Week & Space Technology* 131:86 Ag 7 '89

The airlines hit cruising altitude. C. Power. il *Business Week* p88 Ja 9 '89

Airlines prosper under tight management; leasing transforms commercial transport. il *Aviation Week & Space Technology* 130:90-1+ My 29 '89

Heavy debt could put airlines at risk if traffic growth slows. C. Fotos. il *Aviation Week & Space Technology* 130:203+ Mr 20 '89

Majors post healthy profits; Eastern hobbles Texas Air. C. Fotos. *Aviation Week & Space Technology* 130:102 My 8 '89

One more reason for fear of flying [need for additional security and maintenance imperils financial outlook] C. Power. il *Business Week* p31 Ja 16 '89

Operating profits, net income rose in 1980s with market consolidation. il *Aviation Week & Space Technology* 131:85 N 20 '89

Small planes, tiny towns, big bucks [commuter lines] S. Ticer. il *Business Week* p64-5 Ag 7 '89

Strong earnings enable airlines to finance fleet expansion. il *Aviation Week & Space Technology* 131:85 Jl 24 '89

Flight attendants
See Flight attendants

Food service
Aeroflot, Marriott cooperate on in-flight catering service. J. Ott. *Aviation Week & Space Technology* 130:64-5 Ja 23 '89

Foul flying subs [tainted submarine sandwiches served by Northwest Airlines] il *FDA Consumer* 23:34-5 Jl/Ag '89

You want me to eat this? N. R. Gibbs. il *Time* 133:76+ Mr 13 '89

Freight service
See Air freight service

Interline agreements
See Airlines—Cooperation

International aspects
See also
International Air Transport Association

International air transport: the price of progress [cover story; special section] il *Aviation Week & Space Technology* 131:48-51+ N 20 '89

Laws and regulations
See Aviation—Laws and regulations

Local service
See also
America West Airlines, Inc.
Chalk's International Airlines
Express Airlines 1, Inc
Mesa Airlines, Inc.
Metro Airlines, Inc.
Midway Airlines, Inc.
Phoenix Airline Services Inc.
Piedmont Aviation, Inc.
Southwest Airlines Co.
StatesWest Airlines Inc.
WestAir Airlines

Budget squeeze forces House panel to reject more funding for Essential Air Service program. *Aviation Week & Space Technology* 130:109 Ap 24 '89

Japanese commuters diversify role by providing new intercity service. J. Ott. il *Aviation Week & Space Technology* 130:48+ My 8 '89

Regionals will focus on improving operations, adding larger aircraft. C. A. Shifrin. il *Aviation Week & Space Technology* 130:221+ Mr 20 '89

Small planes, tiny towns, big bucks [commuter lines] S. Ticer. il *Business Week* p64-5 Ag 7 '89

States, not Washington, must develop Essential Air Services. K. B. Creedy. por *Aviation Week & Space Technology* 131:113-16 S 25 '89

U.S. commuter airline growth to parallel majors in 1990s. il *Aviation Week & Space Technology* 131:83-4 N 20 '89

Luggage handling
Best bags to take on board [carry-on luggage] D. Moreau. il *Changing Times* 43:111-12+ Ap '89

FAA issues stricter baggage inspection requirements [response to bombing of Pan Am Flight 103] *Aviation Week & Space Technology* 130:29+ Ja 9 '89

Maintenance
See Airplane service stations; Airplanes, Jet—Maintenance and repair

Management
Donald Burr may be ready to take to the skies again. J. A. Byrne. il por *Business Week* p74-5 Ja 16 '89

Flight safety advances hinge on pilot-management teamwork. C. Fotos. il *Aviation Week & Space Technology* 131:31-2 O 9 '89

Marketing
See also
Frequent flier programs

Leona Helmsley, can you top this? [freebies offered by Aeroflot] il *U.S. News & World Report* 107:18 Ag 14 '89

Medical aspects
See Aviation—Medical aspects

Non-scheduled operations
See also
Aeroleasing Far East (Firm)
Australian Jet Charter (Firm)
Monarch Airlines

Smooth operators? D. M. Koma. il *Travel Holiday* 171:67-70 My '89

Southern European traffic downturn expected to continue into early 1990s. J. M. Lenorovitz. il *Aviation Week & Space Technology* 131:106-7+ N 20 '89

Passenger entertainment
See also
Videotapes on airplanes

Passenger service
British Airways seeks larger share of first-class market. C. A. Shifrin. il *Aviation Week & Space Technology* 130:106 My 8 '89

Clubhouse comfort [airline passenger clubs and hotel services for business travelers] R. J. Christmas. il *Black Enterprise* 19:72+ Mr '89

Coffee, tea, and the power of positive thinking: seminars teach Continental's workers that good service 'feels' better. C. Power. il *Business Week* p36 Jl 31 '89

MGM Grand: affluence in the air. M. C. Lehrer. il *USA Today (Periodical)* 117:34-7 Mr '89

A traveler's guide to finding refuge at the airports [passenger clubs] *Travel Holiday* 171:107 Ap '89

Passenger traffic
See Airlines—Traffic

Passengers
See Air travel

Rates
See Airlines—Fares

Regional service
See Airlines—Local service

Regulation
See Aviation—Laws and regulations

Reservation systems
Automation
American, Delta computer reservations deal may intensify global competition. C. A. Shifrin. il *Aviation Week & Space Technology* 130:94-5 F 13 '89

American, Delta lower price for shares of joint CRS venture [computer reservations system] *Aviation Week & Space Technology* 130:108 Ap 24 '89

Big eagles and sitting ducks [computerized reservation systems] T. McCarroll. il *Time* 133:54 My 15 '89

What the traffic will bear. E. Dyson. il *Forbes* 143:282 My 29 '89

Routes
Eastern Europe
Airlines likely to benefit from 'liberalization' of economies, foreign travel rules in Eastern Europe. *Aviation Week & Space Technology* 131:29 N 20 '89

European-Asiatic
All Nippon taps partners' fleets to expand international service. J. Ott. il *Aviation Week & Space Technology* 130:44 My 8 '89

Lufthansa begins 747-400 service to Pacific Rim. il *Aviation Week & Space Technology* 131:97 N 20 '89

Monarch Airlines will expand EROPS 757 service to Far East [extended range overwater operations] D. A. Brown. *Aviation Week & Space Technology* 130:71 Ja 9 '89

Two carriers begin using 747-400s in nonstop service to Europe, Asia [Singapore Airlines and Northwest Airlines] M. Mecham. *Aviation Week & Space Technology* 130:316-17 Je 12 '89

Latin America
Eastern resumes efforts to sell South American route network [to American Airlines] *Aviation Week & Space Technology* 131:83 N 27 '89

The scramble to capture Eastern's turf. map *Newsweek* 113:22-3 Mr 20 '89

South American economic outlook spurs optimism for growth air transport. E. H. Kolcum. il *Aviation Week & Space Technology* 131:100-1 N 20 '89

Southeast Asia
SIA regional airline operates MD-87 to six Southeast Asian points [Tradewinds] il *Aviation Week & Space Technology* 130:317 Je 12 '89

Transatlantic
Air service rights will be key issue for U.S. carriers in Europe. il *Aviation Week & Space Technology* 130:157+ Je 12 '89

AIRLINES—Routes—Transatlantic—*cont.*

American plans to increase international route system. il *Aviation Week & Space Technology* 131:20-1 N 6 '89

British Airways starts transatlantic service with new Boeing 747-400s. C. A. Shifrin. il *Aviation Week & Space Technology* 131:62-3+ Ag 14 '89

European Aviation Conference, U.S. fail to agree on extending fare pact. il *Aviation Week & Space Technology* 131:66 Ag 14 '89

New routes will develop to meet demand for international service. il *Aviation Week & Space Technology* 130:212-14 Mr 20 '89

U.S. airlines establish new European flights before 1992 market restructuring. J. T. McKenna. il *Aviation Week & Space Technology* 131:79+ N 20 '89

UAL plans to begin service between U.S., Europe. *Aviation Week & Space Technology* 131:96 Jl 24 '89

Transpacific

America West has the hub—now it needs the spokes. E. Schine. il *Business Week* p104 D 18 '89

International carriers vie for routes to Northeast Asia. J. Ott. il *Aviation Week & Space Technology* 130:76-7 My 8 '89

New routes will develop to meet demand for international service. il *Aviation Week & Space Technology* 130:212-14 Mr 20 '89

Pacific Rim traffic growth to continue, barring capacity limits. P. Proctor. *Aviation Week & Space Technology* 131:83 O 16 '89

Pulling out the stops [new planes designed for long-haul routes] G. Eichler. il *Esquire* 112:60 Ag '89

Surging demand prompts U.S., Japan to boost capacity 30%. J. Ott. il *Aviation Week & Space Technology* 131:20-1 N 13 '89

Two carriers begin using 747-400s in nonstop service to Europe, Asia [Singapore Airlines and Northwest Airlines] M. Mecham. *Aviation Week & Space Technology* 130:316-17 Je 12 '89

United States

Pilots accuse Northwest of mismanaging hubs. P. Proctor. *Aviation Week & Space Technology* 130:71 Ap 3 '89

The scramble to capture Eastern's turf. map *Newsweek* 113:22-3 Mr 20 '89

Western Europe

Southern European traffic downturn expected to continue into early 1990s. J. M. Lenorovitz. il *Aviation Week & Space Technology* 131:106-7+ N 20 '89

Two organizations differ in forecasts of European air traffic growth. il *Aviation Week & Space Technology* 131:108-9 Jl 31 '89

Safety devices and measures

See Aviation—Safety devices and measures

Schedules

AEA international traffic grows; departure delays reach 28.3%. il *Aviation Week & Space Technology* 131:59 D 4 '89

Despite O'Hare limits, U.S. flight delays fell in 1988. *Aviation Week & Space Technology* 130:71 F 27 '89

European airlines report delays in flight operations. J. M. Lenorovitz. *Aviation Week & Space Technology* 130:107 My 8 '89

Seating policy

Blind passengers protest exit row seating policy. C. Fotos. *Aviation Week & Space Technology* 130:94-5 Mr 27 '89

FAA seating restrictions clip the wings of handicapped and other flyers. M. Di Landro. il *Travel Holiday* 172:22-3 S '89

Lives at stake [FAA rule excluding blind passengers from seats in exit rows] *Aviation Week & Space Technology* 130:9 Ap 3 '89

Securities

The airline rally wows Wall Street. G. Weiss. il *Business Week* p119 My 1 '89

Caution: downgrade [airport bonds] B. Weberman. il *Forbes* 144:251 O 30 '89

Having it both ways. F. E. Rowe. por *Forbes* 144:312 S 4 '89

Market focus. N. C. Kernstock. See issues of Aviation Week & Space Technology beginning October 3, 1988

Off we go into the hazy blue yonder. C. Power. il *Business Week* p26-7 S 18 '89

Takeover talk lifts the airline stocks. E. Schultz. il *Fortune* 120:46 Jl 31 '89

Wall Street upbeat on airlines, gloomy about defense stocks. il *Aviation Week & Space Technology* 130:48-50 My 29 '89

Shuttle service

See also

Trump Shuttle (Firm)

Court approves proposed sale of Eastern air-shuttle. J. T. McKenna. *Aviation Week & Space Technology* 130:102-3 My 22 '89

Eastern reopens bidding for shuttle as Trump balks at $365 million price. P. Proctor and J. T. McKenna. *Aviation Week & Space Technology* 130:31 Mr 27 '89

Eastern's shuttlers vote with their seats [impact of strike] il *Newsweek* 113:46 Mr 27 '89

Judge set to rule on shuttle sale, Eastern business plan. *Aviation Week & Space Technology* 130:72 My 15 '89

Trump Shuttle begins flying Eastern's former routes in repainted aircraft. il *Aviation Week & Space Technology* 130:314 Je 12 '89

War of the shuttles [Pan Am vs Trump] S. Payne. il *Business Week* p38 F 20 '89

Smoking problem

See Smoking on airplanes

Statistics

Narrow-body aircraft direct expenses: first quarter 1988. il *Aviation Week & Space Technology* 130:70-1 Ja 23 '89

Narrow-body aircraft direct expenses: yearly 1988. il *Aviation Week & Space Technology* 131:72-3 Ag 28 '89

Wide-body aircraft operating costs: first quarter 1988. il *Aviation Week & Space Technology* 130:72-3 Ja 23 '89

Suits and claims

The 'fear of death' lawsuits [legal action after Flight 232 crash at Sioux City, Iowa] K. Springen. il *Newsweek* 114:27 Ag 7 '89

Showdown in "Sue City" [suits filed after United DC-10 crash] A. Sachs. il *Time* 134:42 Ag 7 '89

Taxation

House tax panel probes airline bailout threat. M. Mecham. il *Aviation Week & Space Technology* 131:52-3 O 30 '89

Tickets

See also

Airline ticket brokers

Traffic

AEA international traffic grows; departure delays reach 28.3%. il *Aviation Week & Space Technology* 131:59 D 4 '89

Airline traffic: first quarter 1988. il *Aviation Week & Space Technology* 130:68 Ja 16 '89

Airline traffic: first quarter 1989. il *Aviation Week & Space Technology* 131:130 N 20 '89

Airline traffic: second quarter 1988. il *Aviation Week & Space Technology* 130:70 Ja 16 '89

Airline traffic: yearly 1988. il *Aviation Week & Space Technology* 131:85 Ag 7 '89

Airlines expect traffic growth to remain strong through 1989. P. Proctor. il *Aviation Week & Space Technology* 130:74 Ja 23 '89

Airlines shuffle operations as China service loads plunge [wake of government's crackdown on pro-democracy demonstrators] il *Aviation Week & Space Technology* 130:161 Je 19 '89

American makes record jumps in June traffic and capacity. *Aviation Week & Space Technology* 131:99-100 Jl 24 '89

American's lead over U.S. majors spurred by capacity expansion. C. Fotos. *Aviation Week & Space Technology* 130:162 Je 19 '89

Heavy debt could put airlines at risk if traffic growth slows. C. Fotos. il *Aviation Week & Space Technology* 130:203+ Mr 20 '89

International air transport: the price of progress [cover story; special section] il *Aviation Week & Space Technology* 131:48-51+ N 20 '89

Northwest's traffic growth leads major carriers. C. Fotos. *Aviation Week & Space Technology* 131:129 N 20 '89

U.S. majors report mixed traffic results for September. C. Fotos. *Aviation Week & Space Technology* 131:75 O 23 '89

Vacation travel spurs record April for American Airlines. C. Fotos. *Aviation Week & Space Technology* 130:106 My 22 '89

Alaska

See also

Alaska Airlines, Inc.

Arab countries

Royal Jordanian seeks alliance of Arab carriers. M. Mecham. il *Aviation Week & Space Technology* 130:67+ Ja 9 '89

Australia

See also

Australian Jet Charter (Firm)

Qantas Airways Ltd.

Australia struggles to restore air service using military, regional and foreign aircraft [pilot resignations] *Aviation Week & Space Technology* 131:70 S 4 '89

Australian carriers expand services without union pilots. *Aviation Week & Space Technology* 131:124 S 18 '89

Foreign aircraft, crews replace flights halted by Australian pilots. *Aviation Week & Space Technology* 131:129 S 11 '89

Maintenance technician shortages constrain growth of Australia's airlines. P. Proctor. *Aviation Week & Space Technology* 131:98 Jl 17 '89

Belgium

See also

Sabena World Airlines

Canada

See also

Air Canada

Canadian Airlines International

Inter-Canadian (Firm)

Pacific Western Airlines Ltd.

Wardair Inc.

The costly skies. J. Daly. il *Maclean's* 102:26-7 Je 26 '89

Regaining altitude [fewer airlines charging higher fares] J. Daly. il *Maclean's* 102:46-8 N 6 '89

AIRLINES—*cont.*

China

CAAC continues restructuring effort; regionals pursue international routes. il *Aviation Week & Space Technology* 131:63-4 D 11 '89

Competition, new equipment improve airline service; intra-China flying still challenges passengers. il *Aviation Week & Space Technology* 131:64+ D 11 '89

U.S. permits Boeing to transfer four 757s to Chinese airlines. *Aviation Week & Space Technology* 131:96 Jl 17 '89

Czechoslovakia

See also
Czechoslovak Airlines

East Asia

Northeast Asia: pacesetter for world transport [cover story; special section] J. Ott. il *Aviation Week & Space Technology* 130:36-7+ My 8 '89

Eastern Europe

Eastern bloc nations seek Western-built transports to meet growing demand. il *Aviation Week & Space Technology* 131:102+ N 20 '89

Ethiopia

See also
Ethiopian Airlines

France

See also
Air France

Germany (West)

See also
LTU Lufttransport Unt GmbH & Co. KG
Lufthansa

Great Britain

See also
Air Europe Ltd.
Airlines of Britain Holdings plc
British Airways plc
British Midland Airways Ltd.
Monarch Airlines

Hawaii

See also
Discovery Airways Inc.

Hong Kong

See also
Cathay Pacific Airways Ltd.

Hungary

See also
Malev Hungarian Airlines

Ireland

See also
Aer Lingus
Ryanair (Firm)

Israel

See also
El Al Israel Airlines Ltd.

Japan

See also
All Nippon Airways Co. Ltd.
Japan Air Lines Co. Ltd.
Japan Air System (Firm)

Japanese commuters diversify role by providing new intercity service. J. Ott. il *Aviation Week & Space Technology* 130:48+ My 8 '89

Lack of pilots, controllers endangers growth in Japan. *Aviation Week & Space Technology* 131:113 N 20 '89

Jordan

See also
Alia-The Royal Jordanian Airline

Korea (South)

See also
Asiana Airlines
Korean Air Lines Co. Ltd.

Latin America

South American economic outlook spurs optimism for growth air transport. E. H. Kolcum. il *Aviation Week & Space Technology* 131:100-1 N 20 '89

Malaysia

See also
Malaysia Airlines

Netherlands

See also
KLM Royal Dutch Airlines

New Zealand

See also
Air New Zealand
Ansett New Zealand (Firm)

Pacific region

Pacific Rim carriers struggle to cope with impending traffic boom. P. Proctor. il *Aviation Week & Space Technology* 131:110-11 N 20 '89

Philippines

See also
Aerolift (Firm)
Philippine Airlines Inc.

Philippine air transport [special section] il map *Aviation Week & Space Technology* 131:99+ Ag 21 '89

Scandinavia

See also
SAS

Singapore

See also
Aeroleasing Far East (Firm)
Singapore Airlines Ltd.
Tradewinds (Firm)

Soviet Union

See also
Aeroflot
Aviakompaniya Sverkhdalnykh Avialiniy

Switzerland

See also
Swissair AG

Taiwan

See also
China Airlines Ltd.
Far Eastern Air Transport

Thailand

See also
Thai Airways International Ltd.

United States

See Airlines

Western Europe

See also
Association of European Airlines
Atlas (Group)

European Court ruling could ban bilateral air fare agreements. *Aviation Week & Space Technology* 130:32 Ap 17 '89

European regionals register growth despite congestion, post-1992 concerns. C. A. Shifrin. il *Aviation Week & Space Technology* 131:87+ N 20 '89

Europe's business aircraft operators fight for access to airspace, airports. il *Aviation Week & Space Technology* 131:91+ O 2 '89

Flag carrier concept may vanish in post-1992 airline competition. il *Aviation Week & Space Technology* 130:151+ Je 12 '89

Southern European traffic downturn expected to continue into early 1990s. J. M. Lenorovitz. il *Aviation Week & Space Technology* 131:106-7+ N 20 '89

AIRLINES OF BRITAIN HOLDINGS PLC

SAS, Airlines of Britain to discuss possible operational merger. *Aviation Week & Space Technology* 130:109 Ja 2 '89

AIROD SENDIRIAN BERHAD

Airod expands maintenance capability to attract commercial customers. il *Aviation Week & Space Technology* 131:63 N 6 '89

AIRPLANE ACCIDENTS *See* Aviation—Accidents

AIRPLANE BROKERS

See also
International Lease Finance Corporation

Ireland

See also
GPA Group, Ltd.
GPA Jetprop, Ltd.

AIRPLANE CARRIERS *See* Aircraft carriers

AIRPLANE CREWS

Operations: crew of Aloha Flight 243 [aircraft brought down safely after loss of upper fuselage; aerospace laureate] il *Aviation Week & Space Technology* 130:17 Ja 2 '89

Safety Board blames lax crew behavior but also faults Delta, FAA for Dallas crash [August 1988] J. Ott. *Aviation Week & Space Technology* 131:103-4 O 2 '89

Dismissal

Delta accepts responsibility for crash, dismisses flight crew [failure to set flaps and slats properly blamed for August 1988 crash at Dallas/Ft. Worth] J. T. McKenna. *Aviation Week & Space Technology* 131:76-7 Ag 7 '89

Psychology

New approaches to pilot training stress human factors, coordination. D. Hughes. il *Aviation Week & Space Technology* 131:86-7 O 16 '89

Pushed to the limit [crash of Fairchild Metro III at Raleigh-Durham International Airport] P. Garrison. *Flying* 116:26+ O '89

Teaching teamwork [Continental Air Lines course] N. Moll. il *Flying* 116:84-5 Ap '89

Training

See Aviation—Study and teaching

AIRPLANE DEALERS

See also
AMR Services Corporation

AIRPLANE ENGINES

See also
Airplane engines, Jet
Diesel engines, Aircraft
Engine Components, Inc.
Helicopter engines
Michael Zoche (Firm)
Motorlet (Firm)

Cooling

The big chill: intercooling [turbocharged airplanes] F. George. il *Flying* 116:38+ N '89

In the heat of the flight. P. Garrison. il *Flying* 116:78-80+ Je '89

Liquid-cooled engine mod for 414A. il *Flying* 116:18 F '89

Now, Voyager [liquid cooled Voyager series piston engines] J. M. McClellan. il *Flying* 116:34-5 My '89

AIRPLANE ENGINES—Cooling—*cont.*
Wolf in RAM's clothing [converted Cessna 414A with liquid-cooled engines] J. M. McClellan. il *Flying* 116:70-6 D '89

Cylinders
Bad vibrations [high EGT on Piper Cherokee Six cylinder] G. Noble. il *Flying* 116:142 Jl '89
Coatings
Engine Components uses coating to increase life of piston cylinder [Cermicrome process] E. H. Phillips. il *Aviation Week & Space Technology* 131:40-2 S 18 '89
Design
Power revolution [Dyna-Cam] F. Mackerodt. il *Popular Mechanics* 166:56-7 Je '89
Rotary engine gets airborne. F. Mackerodt. il *Popular Mechanics* 166:44-5 F '89
Rotary-mill renaissance. N. Moll. *Flying* 116:23 Ap '89
Energy usage
Don't be fuelish. J. M. McClellan. il *Flying* 116:96+ O '89
Going with the flow [fuel management] P. Garrison. il *Flying* 116:62-4+ F '89
Failure
Double-barrelled rating [multiengine training] N. Moll. il *Flying* 116:58-60+ Ap '89
Forced field [Musketeer's fuel tank runs dry] D. Kraft. il *Flying* 116:134 Ag '89
The longest minute [water in Beech Sundowner's fuel system] D. White. il *Flying* 116:120-1 O '89
Fuel
Contamination
The longest minute [water in Beech Sundowner's fuel system] D. White. il *Flying* 116:120-1 O '89
Fuel consumption
See Airplane engines—Energy usage
Fuel feeding
Forced field [Musketeer's fuel tank runs dry] D. Kraft. il *Flying* 116:134 Ag '89
Going with the flow [fuel management] P. Garrison. il *Flying* 116:62-4+ F '89
Lubrication and lubricants
See Airplanes—Lubrication and lubricants
Maintenance and repair
Blueprinters [custom overhauls] F. George. il *Flying* 116:66-8+ Ag '89
Clock-wise [overhauls] N. Moll. il *Flying* 116:48-50+ Mr '89
Noise
See Airplanes—Noise
Specifications
U.S. reciprocating engines [tables] il *Aviation Week & Space Technology* 130:189-90 Mr 20 '89
Standards
Piper's Continental-powered Malibu is beached again [emergency airworthiness directive] il *Flying* 116:18 S '89
Superchargers
The big chill: intercooling. F. George. il *Flying* 116:38+ N '89
Sabre-toothed Mooney [turbocharged Lycoming Sabre] F. George. il *Flying* 116:86-90+ Ag '89
Testing
Now, Voyager [liquid cooled Voyager series piston engines] J. M. McClellan. il *Flying* 116:34-5 My '89
AIRPLANE ENGINES, JET
See also
Allison Gas Turbine Operations
Central Institute for Aviation Motors (Moscow, Soviet Union)
Chengdu Engine Company
Garrett Corporation
General Electric Co.
International Aero Engines
Liming Engine Manufacturing Corporation
Pratt & Whitney Aircraft Group
Progress Engine Design Bureau (Soviet Union)
Rolls-Royce Ltd.
SNECMA
Soloy Conversions (Firm)
Spaceplane engines
Williams International
Zaporozhye Motorworks (Soviet Union)
Air intakes
F-16C/D high angle of attack instability overcome by flight control modifications. W. B. Scott. il *Aviation Week & Space Technology* 131:61+ N 13 '89
Blades
Defects
Investigators study blade fracture's role in 737 crash [British Midland aircraft] *Aviation Week & Space Technology* 130:31 F 20 '89
NTSB investigates fan-blade failure on Northwest Airlines DC-10 [forced to make emergency landing at Denver] E. H. Phillips. *Aviation Week & Space Technology* 131:93 Ag 21 '89
U.K., U.S. ground 737-400s in wake of CFM56-3C failures. il *Aviation Week & Space Technology* 130:160 Je 19 '89

Certification
See Airplane engines, Jet—Standards
Defects
See also
Airplane engines, Jet—Mounting—Defects
737-400 crash investigation turns to engine instruments [British Midland Airways jet] *Aviation Week & Space Technology* 130:67 Ja 23 '89
Crash of 737-400 prompts stricter CFM56 engine checks [British Midland Airways jet] D. A. Brown. il *Aviation Week & Space Technology* 130:60-1 Ja 16 '89
Design
Allison considers development of new high-performance engine. *Aviation Week & Space Technology* 131:78 Jl 17 '89
Allison engine chosen for Saab 2000; Sweden certifies Saab 340B transport. il *Aviation Week & Space Technology* 131:29 Jl 17 '89
Britain, U.S. narrow candidates for ASTOVL propulsion system [advanced short takeoff/vertical landing combat aircraft] il *Aviation Week & Space Technology* 129:25 Mr 6 '89
Czech M602 turboprop engine designed for rugged environment. U. Hradiste. il *Aviation Week & Space Technology* 130:41 Ap 3 '89
Denver to Seoul, nonstop [superfan engines] H. Banks. il *Forbes* 143:284+ My 29 '89
Douglas may offer three MD-90 versions with V2500 powerplants. C. A. Shifrin. il *Aviation Week & Space Technology* 131:56-7 Jl 3 '89
GE offers F110-GE-100 engine as alternative to Pratt & Whitney powerplant in new F-16A/Bs. *Aviation Week & Space Technology* 131:23 N 27 '89
HSCT propulsion studies focus on reducing emissions, noise [cover story] S. W. Kandebo. il *Aviation Week & Space Technology* 130:34-6 Jl 10 '89
International engine manufacturers expect to work on Japan's HSCT propulsion effort [high-speed civil transport] S. W. Kandebo. *Aviation Week & Space Technology* 131:39-40 D 11 '89
Manufacturers predict $50-billion engine market during next decade. S. W. Kandebo. il *Aviation Week & Space Technology* 130:218-20 Mr 20 '89
Navy selects GE for future F404 turbofan orders, drops Pratt as second source. *Aviation Week & Space Technology* 131:26 Ag 28 '89
New propulsion schemes give hover planes a lift. il *Popular Mechanics* 166:18 Ag '89
Pratt & Whitney to supply 60% of Air Force's fighter engines. *Aviation Week & Space Technology* 130:32 Mr 13 '89
Propulsion research center focuses on developing fuel-efficient aircraft [Central Institute for Aviation Motors in Moscow] il *Aviation Week & Space Technology* 130:40-3 Je 5 '89
Regional airlines spur development of new, derivative engine class. il *Aviation Week & Space Technology* 131:80-1 O 2 '89
Rolls assessing market interest in RB580 engine. il *Aviation Week & Space Technology* 130:24 Jl 10 '89
Rolls-Royce developing more powerful version of Pegasus engine for third-generation Harrier. *Aviation Week & Space Technology* 130:30 My 29 '89
Tupolev Bureau develops ultrahigh bypass, turbofan engine concepts for Tu-334 transport [Soviet aircraft] il *Aviation Week & Space Technology* 130:96 Je 5 '89
Turbine engines will improve CL-215's fire-fighting capability [Quebec Air Service] il *Aviation Week & Space Technology* 131:50+ Ag 21 '89
Energy usage
Denver to Seoul, nonstop [superfan engines] H. Banks. il *Forbes* 143:284+ My 29 '89
Free fall [forced landing of Air Canada Flight 143 due to fuel problems; condensation] W. Hoffer and M. Hoffer. il *Reader's Digest* 134:197-202+ Ap '89
Export-import trade
See Airplane industry—Export-import trade
Failure
After the crash, cash [General Electric offering rewards for scattered engine parts from Sioux City, Iowa plane crash] il *Newsweek* 114:32 O 23 '89
Free fall [forced landing of Air Canada Flight 143 due to fuel problems; condensation] W. Hoffer and M. Hoffer. il *Reader's Digest* 134:197-202+ Ap '89
Investigators find reconstructed tail of DC-10 riddled with damage [disintegration of engine in Iowa crash] J. Ott. il *Aviation Week & Space Technology* 131:22-3 Ag 7 '89
NTSB, GE inquiry into United DC-10 crash focuses on fan disk recovered from Iowa farm field [July 1989 crash landing] il map *Aviation Week & Space Technology* 131:84 O 16 '89
A perilous passage through volcanic ash [KLM Royal Dutch Airlines' loss of engine power near Redoubt Volcano] R. Monastersky. *Science News* 136:407 D 23-30 '89
Point of know return [1987 crash of twin-engine Caribou in Yukon river valley during attempted go-around from single-engine approach] P. Garrison. *Flying* 116:24+ D '89
Probe focuses on failure of fan disk in DC-10 crash [crash landing at Sioux City, Iowa] J. Ott. il *Aviation Week & Space Technology* 131:30-1 Jl 31 '89

AIRPLANE ENGINES, JET—Failure—*cont.*

Sioux City hearings focus on history of failed disk [United Airlines DC-10 crash in July 1989] C. Fotos. *Aviation Week & Space Technology* 131:56 N 6 '89

Stalling for time [compressor stall on 747 during takeoff in strong crosswinds] J. Kulski. il *Flying* 116:110 My '89

Fuel consumption
See Airplane engines, Jet—Energy usage

Inspection
FAA orders inspections of CF6-6 powerplants [result of Sioux City DC-10 accident in July 1989] *Aviation Week & Space Technology* 131:33 O 2 '89

NTSB says CF6-6s may require new inspection techniques [investigation of Sioux City crash in July 1989] *Aviation Week & Space Technology* 131:73 N 13 '89

Sioux City DC-10 accident may force extensive inspection of CF6 engines. M. Mecham. *Aviation Week & Space Technology* 131:28-9 Ag 28 '89

Maintenance and repair
See also
Airplane engines, Jet—Inspection

Turbine powerhouse [Soloy Conversions; cover story] N. Moll. il por *Flying* 116:44-8+ O '89

Materials
A touch of glass [ceramic engine components] P. Garrison. il *Flying* 116:94+ Je '89

Mounting
Defects

Investigation of Boeing 737 engine separation focuses on failure of rear bolt cone [Piedmont transport] J. Ott. il *Aviation Week & Space Technology* 130:71 Ja 30 '89

Noise
See Airplanes—Noise

Nozzles
2D nozzle's Stealth benefits make use on ATF more likely [advanced tactical fighter] D. F. Bond. *Aviation Week & Space Technology* 131:28-9 S 25 '89

F-15 S/MTD makes first flight with 2D exhaust nozzles. S. W. Kandebo. il *Aviation Week & Space Technology* 130:18 My 15 '89

Pratt ground tests thrust-reversing, 2D nozzle for STOL demonstrator. il *Aviation Week & Space Technology* 131:29 S 25 '89

Prices
American signs long-term CF6 pricing pact with GE. S. W. Kandebo. il *Aviation Week & Space Technology* 130:20 F 13 '89

Refueling
Air Force to retrofit KC-10s with air refueling pods [cover story] W. B. Scott. il *Aviation Week & Space Technology* 131:36-7+ N 13 '89

Specifications
International gas turbine engines [tables] il *Aviation Week & Space Technology* 130:180-1+ Mr 20 '89

Multinational gas turbine engines [tables] il *Aviation Week & Space Technology* 130:185 Mr 20 '89

U.S. gas turbine engines [tables] il *Aviation Week & Space Technology* 130:175+ Mr 20 '89

Standards
GE-powered 747-400 gets initial approval in Europe after Boeing accepts design changes. *Aviation Week & Space Technology* 130:105 My 22 '89

Testing
Assembly of second, third EJ200 test engines nears end. K. F. Mordoff. *Aviation Week & Space Technology* 130:26 Ja 30 '89

Douglas prepares to flight test PW-Allison propfan powerplant. il *Aviation Week & Space Technology* 130:35 Ja 2 '89

Experimental PW-Allison propfan begins flight testing [ultrahigh bypass engine] W. B. Scott. il *Aviation Week & Space Technology* 130:63-4 Ap 17 '89

Experimental tractor propfan flight tested on Ilyushin Il-76. il *Aviation Week & Space Technology* 130:51 Je 5 '89

Fans fantastique [reengined Falcon 20] F. George. il *Flying* 116:88-90+ O '89

GE completes proof-of-concept ground tests of engine candidate for ATF [advanced tactical fighter] il *Aviation Week & Space Technology* 130:73 Je 12 '89

Leader of the Pratts [PW305] N. Moll. *Flying* 116:105 N '89

NASA will extend propfan test assessment program. *Aviation Week & Space Technology* 130:31 F 6 '89

Pratt, General Electric to deliver ATF engines to Air Force by year-end [advanced tactical fighter] il *Aviation Week & Space Technology* 131:21 D 4 '89

Rolls-Royce completes initial testing of improved Pegasus engine for Harrier. C. A. Shifrin. il *Aviation Week & Space Technology* 131:28-9 Ag 21 '89

STOL Scout begins flight tests with Astazou 16 powerplants. W. B. Scott. il *Aviation Week & Space Technology* 130:64 F 13 '89

Thrust
2D nozzle's Stealth benefits make use on ATF more likely [advanced tactical fighter] D. F. Bond. *Aviation Week & Space Technology* 131:28-9 S 25 '89

IAE plans increased thrust version of V2500 to power A320, MD-90. *Aviation Week & Space Technology* 130:62-3 Ap 17 '89

Latest F404 procurement includes upgraded version. S. W. Kandebo. il *Aviation Week & Space Technology* 131:27 Ag 28 '89

Turning on a dime—in midair [vectored thrust engine provides enhanced maneuverability for fighter planes] W. J. Cook. il *U.S. News & World Report* 106:56-8 F 20 '89

Williams, Rolls plan to certify 1,900-lb.-thrust FJ44 in 1992 [business jet engine] S. W. Kandebo. il *Aviation Week & Space Technology* 131:47 N 6 '89

Thrust reversers
Pratt ground tests thrust-reversing, 2D nozzle for STOL demonstrator. il *Aviation Week & Space Technology* 131:29 S 25 '89

Reverse psychology [crash landing of CASA C-212 regional airliner in Detroit blamed on pilot's use of beta mode in flight] J. M. McClellan. *Flying* 116:108-9 Je '89

AIRPLANE EQUIPMENT INDUSTRY *See* Airplane industry

AIRPLANE FACTORIES

Boeing expanding facilities for standard-body transports. *Aviation Week & Space Technology* 130:93 Mr 27 '89

Automation
Automated equipment used to maintain close tolerances in B-2 production. il *Aviation Week & Space Technology* 131:125 O 9 '89

B-2s built in unique manner. *Aviation Week & Space Technology* 130:19 Ap 3 '89

Computer-controlled drill designed to meet unique B-2 fabrication needs. il *Aviation Week & Space Technology* 130:51-2 Ap 17 '89

Western Europe
Aerospatiale and MBB disagree on A320/A321 assembly location. J. M. Lenorovitz. il *Aviation Week & Space Technology* 131:70 O 23 '89

AIRPLANE FARES *See* Airlines—Fares

AIRPLANE HIJACKING

See also
Beirut airplane hijacking, 1985

Prevention
See also
Airports—Security measures

AIRPLANE INDUSTRY

See also
Aerodis America (Firm)
Airplane factories
Allison Gas Turbine Operations
American General Aviation Corporation
Avtek Corporation
Ayres Corporation
Beech Aircraft Corp.
Boeing Co.
Bromon Aircraft Company
Cessna Aircraft Company
Christen Industries
Commander Aircraft (Firm)
Eidetics International (Firm)
Engine Components, Inc.
Fairchild Aircraft Corporation
Garrett Corporation
General Aviation Manufacturers Association
General Dynamics Corp.
Grumman Corp.
Gulfstream Aerospace Corp.
Helicopter industry
Hughes Aircraft Co.
Jaffe Aircraft Corporation
Lacadre, Inc.
Lockheed Corp.
McDonnell Douglas Corp.
Mooney Aircraft Corporation
National Business Aircraft Association
Northrop Corp.
Omac, Inc.
Piper Aircraft Corp.
Pratt & Whitney Aircraft Group
RAM (Firm)
Rockwell International Corp.
Rutan Aircraft Factory
Ryder System, Inc.
Sabreliner Corporation
Scaled Composites, Inc.
Schweizer Aircraft Corp.
Skytrader Corporation
Snow Aviation International, Inc.
Soloy Conversions (Firm)
Swearingen Engineering and Technologies (Firm)
Victor Aviation Services
Vulcan Aircraft Company
Williams International

Industry observer. See issues of Aviation Week & Space Technology

Acquisitions and mergers
A beleaguered Boeing may be on Lockheed's tail. G. G. Marcial. il *Business Week* p130 Mr 13 '89

AIRPLANE INDUSTRY—Acquisitions and mergers—*cont.*

International aspects

Bombardier, GEC-Fokker team lead field of suitors for Northern Ireland's Short Brothers. *Aviation Week & Space Technology* 130:31 Mr 13 '89

Bombardier of Canada wins competition to buy Short Brothers. *Aviation Week & Space Technology* 130:63 Je 12 '89

Exhibitions

See Aviation—Exhibitions

Export-import trade

See also

Soviet Union. Aviaexport

Aeroflot signs letter of intent to purchase five Airbus A310-300s. *Aviation Week & Space Technology* 131:18 N 6 '89

Airbus Industrie records 60 firm orders, options for range of aircraft. *Aviation Week & Space Technology* 130:102 My 8 '89

All Nippon buys 20 747-400s, a record order. C. Fotos. il *Aviation Week & Space Technology* 130:69-70 F 27 '89

Allison engine chosen for Saab 2000; Sweden certifies Saab 340B transport. il *Aviation Week & Space Technology* 131:29 Jl 17 '89

American Fokker 100 order caps carrier's growth plan. J. T. McKenna. il *Aviation Week & Space Technology* 130:88-9 Mr 27 '89

AMR Eagle boosts Saab-Scania with firm order for 50 SF340Bs. C. Fotos. il *Aviation Week & Space Technology* 130:110-11 My 29 '89

AMR Eagle places 100 orders, options for Jetstream aircraft. *Aviation Week & Space Technology* 130:167 Je 19 '89

Belgium will use equipment provided under offset pact to expand industry [F-16 deal with General Dynamics] il *Aviation Week & Space Technology* 130:57 F 13 '89

Boeing sets new mark with orders totaling $31.2 billion. *Aviation Week & Space Technology* 130:27 My 29 '89

Braniff will use 50 A320s to expand service from Kansas City to coasts. il *Aviation Week & Space Technology* 130:63 Ja 9 '89

Britain accepting fraction of Boeing's offset claims [purchase of E-3A Airborne Warning and Control System aircraft] D. A. Brown. il *Aviation Week & Space Technology* 131:76-7 Jl 17 '89

British Airways starts transatlantic service with new Boeing 747-400s. C. A. Shifrin. il *Aviation Week & Space Technology* 131:62-3+ Ag 14 '89

Cathay Pacific orders 10 A330s to replace L-1011s. J. M. Lenorovitz. il *Aviation Week & Space Technology* 130:91 Ap 10 '89

China Expo attendance drops; companies eye trunkliner project. P. Proctor. il *Aviation Week & Space Technology* 131:28 O 23 '89

China uses Trinidad TB-20s to replace aging Y-5 biplanes in pilot training. il *Aviation Week & Space Technology* 131:97 Ag 21 '89

Consortium to decide on boosting ATR regional transport production. J. M. Lenorovitz. il *Aviation Week & Space Technology* 130:68 Mr 13 '89

Continental orders 20 Airbus A330, A340 aircraft. *Aviation Week & Space Technology* 131:46 N 20 '89

Czechs seek wider market for L410, L610 transports [cover story] J. M. Lenorovitz. il *Aviation Week & Space Technology* 130:36-8+ Ap 3 '89

Daewoo wins contract to assemble wing panels for Lockheed P-7A. M. A. Dornheim. *Aviation Week & Space Technology* 131:29 S 4 '89

Deficit woes prompt Jordan to postpone Tornado purchase. M. Mecham. *Aviation Week & Space Technology* 130:32-3 Ap 3 '89

Eastern bloc nations seek Western-built transports to meet growing demand. il *Aviation Week & Space Technology* 131:102+ N 20 '89

European, African, Asian carriers order 19 MD-11s. D. A. Brown. il *Aviation Week & Space Technology* 130:18-19 F 13 '89

European engine makers fear social issues may impede sales. *Aviation Week & Space Technology* 130:134 Je 19 '89

Exports of Gripen could equal sales to Sweden's Air Force. D. A. Brown. il *Aviation Week & Space Technology* 130:73-4 Ja 9 '89

Fairchild Aircraft, Spain's CASA to cooperate on C-212 marketing. *Aviation Week & Space Technology* 130:61 Je 26 '89

Fokker initiates North American service with Inter-Canadian. C. Fotos. il *Aviation Week & Space Technology* 130:98 F 13 '89

GPA Group poised to order 'well over 200' transports. D. A. Brown. il *Aviation Week & Space Technology* 130:16-17 Ap 17 '89

GPA Jetprop prepares for 1990s with orders for ATRs, Dash 8s. J. M. Lenorovitz. il *Aviation Week & Space Technology* 130:90 Mr 27 '89

ILFC negotiates pact to buy 16 stretched Airbus A320s. il *Aviation Week & Space Technology* 130:111 Je 5 '89

Korean Air, Asiana order U.S. transports valued at $1.35 billion. J. Ott. *Aviation Week & Space Technology* 130:17 Ap 17 '89

Large leasing company orders restructure aircraft acquisition [orders by GPA and others; special section] il *Aviation Week & Space Technology* 130:24-7+ Ap 24 '89

Lufthansa boosts firm order total for Airbus A321-100 transports. C. A. Shifrin. *Aviation Week & Space Technology* 131:58-9 Ag 14 '89

Northwest commuter boosts Saab sales with orders for 340B, 2000 aircraft [Express Airlines I] C. A. Shifrin. il *Aviation Week & Space Technology* 131:62 N 6 '89

Pan Am will use Jetstreams to bolster Miami operations. J. T. McKenna. *Aviation Week & Space Technology* 131:82-3 N 27 '89

Piaggio picks AMR for Avanti [North American sales and support organization] *Flying* 116:14+ Ap '89

Piaggio selects AMR Services to market P. 180 in North America [business aircraft] *Aviation Week & Space Technology* 130:27 Ja 30 '89

Powerplant manufacturers foresee little market change after 1992 liberalization [European Community unification] *Aviation Week & Space Technology* 130:172 Je 12 '89

Proposal to sell F-16s to Pakistan [statement, August 2, 1989] T. Schaffer. *Department of State Bulletin* 89:65-6 O '89

Regionals: green lights, big orders. il *Flying* 116:16 Ag '89

Snecma to deliver Atar 9K50 powerplants for use in prototypes of upgraded Kfir. il *Aviation Week & Space Technology* 131:19 O 30 '89

Sukhoi Su-26M for sale in the U.S. [Soviet aerobatic airplane] il *Flying* 116:12 O '89

Thai International to equip three Airbus A300-600Rs with PW4158 engines. P. Proctor. *Aviation Week & Space Technology* 131:76 Ag 7 '89

This engine maker is finally seeing a patch of blue [International Aero Engines' Braniff deal] R. W. King. *Business Week* p39-40 Ja 23 '89

TWA commitment strengthens Airbus' position in North American market. J. M. Lenorovitz. il *Aviation Week & Space Technology* 130:65 Ap 3 '89

TWA orders Airbus A330s to upgrade aging fleet. C. Fotos. il *Aviation Week & Space Technology* 130:64-5 Ap 3 '89

U.S. criticizes E.C. plan to shield MBB from fluctuations in exchange rate. M. Mecham. *Aviation Week & Space Technology* 130:91 Mr 27 '89

U.S. permits Boeing to transfer four 757s to Chinese airlines. *Aviation Week & Space Technology* 131:96 Jl 17 '89

U.S., West Germany may delay P-7 agreement until September [Lockheed antisubmarine warfare aircraft] J. D. Morrocco. il *Aviation Week & Space Technology* 130:62 Je 19 '89

Unit set up to finance Saudi military buys from Britain. *Aviation Week & Space Technology* 131:24 D 4 '89

West Germany's LTU expands fleet with Boeing 767-300ERs. B. A. Smith. il *Aviation Week & Space Technology* 130:92-3 Mr 27 '89

White House sends Pakistan F-16 proposal to Congress. *Aviation Week & Space Technology* 130:42 Je 19 '89

Finance

Airframe makers exploit boom by adding production capacity. il *Aviation Week & Space Technology* 130:95+ My 29 '89

Manufacturers predict $50-billion engine market during next decade. S. W. Kandebo. il *Aviation Week & Space Technology* 130:218-20 Mr 20 '89

Planemakers have it so good, it's bad [special section] il *Business Week* p34-6 My 8 '89

Preserving access key issue to business, general aviation. il *Aviation Week & Space Technology* 130:237-9 Mr 20 '89

Shakeout [fighter makers] H. Banks. il *Forbes* 143:114-15+ My 1 '89

Transport manufacturers prosper as demand far exceeds supply. R. G. O'Lone. il *Aviation Week & Space Technology* 131:63+ D 18-25 '89

International aspects

See also

International Aero Engines

Bush approves FS-X codevelopment, but Japan must accept new terms. M. Mecham. *Aviation Week & Space Technology* 130:22 Mr 27 '89

Bush wins victory on FS-X development despite Senate anger on Japanese trade. M. Mecham. *Aviation Week & Space Technology* 130:31 My 22 '89

Business flying: resurgent, but embattled [cover story; special section] il *Aviation Week & Space Technology* 131:38-9+ O 2 '89

Can the Pentagon keep shielding Japan? [FSX co-development deal] P. Magnusson. il *Business Week* p47-8 Mr 27 '89

A deal that nearly came undone [U.S. agrees to help Japan build the FSX jet] C. Gorman. il *Time* 133:70-1 Mr 27 '89

Friend or foe? [FSX deal symbolic of strain in relations between the U.S. and Japan] J. Greenwald. il *Time* 133:44-5 Ap 24 '89

The FS-X question [U.S.-Japanese codevelopment] *National Review* 41:14-16 Ap 21 '89

AIRPLANE INDUSTRY—International aspects—*cont.*

The FSX and Japan's strategy for aerospace. R. J. Samuels and B. C. Whipple. il *Technology Review* 92:42-51 O '89

FSX coproduction prohibition disapproved by president [letter to the Senate, July 31, 1989] G. Bush. *Department of State Bulletin* 89:32 O '89

General Dynamics alters marketing as Europeans focus on F-16 upgrades. il *Aviation Week & Space Technology* 130:57+ F 13 '89

Gulfstream/Soviet SST bizjet. il *Flying* 116:17 S '89

Gulfstream, Soviets expect to select basic supersonic business jet design in November. *Aviation Week & Space Technology* 131:46 O 16 '89

Japan bashing bashes the United States [agreement on FSX] C. W. Weinberger. il *Forbes* 143:31 Mr 20 '89

Japan unlikely to parlay FSX work into civilian aircraft leadership role. C. Leader. por *Aviation Week & Space Technology* 130:97+ Mr 27 '89

Japan's FS-X puzzle [U.S. government's decision to defer approval of plan to share F-16 technology with Japan] *Aviation Week & Space Technology* 130:9 F 27 '89

Korea fears U.S. technology transfer opponents could hamper its FX program. J. D. Morrocco. *Aviation Week & Space Technology* 130:23 Ap 3 '89

A 'little old agreement' on the F-16 [FSX deal between General Dynamics and Mitsubishi Heavy Industries] *Newsweek* 113:34 Ja 30 '89

Managers chosen for German/Chinese MPC-75 transport aircraft program. *Aviation Week & Space Technology* 130:101 My 8 '89

MD-82 transport assembly accelerates at Shanghai. il *Aviation Week & Space Technology* 131:68-9 D 11 '89

Pentagon, Commerce at impasse on FS-X after deal falls apart [sharing F-16 technology with Japan] M. Mecham. *Aviation Week & Space Technology* 130:28 Mr 13 '89

The plane drain: the FSX deal and other transfers of technology. H. D. Bentley. il por *Conservative Digest* 15:54-7 Jl/Ag '89

Revised FS-X pact eases trade, technology concerns [U.S./Japan fighter codevelopment] J. D. Morrocco. il *Aviation Week & Space Technology* 130:16-18 My 8 '89

Senate bolsters Commerce Dept.'s authority in reviewing cooperative arms agreements. J. D. Morrocco. *Aviation Week & Space Technology* 131:28 Ag 7 '89

Soviet/Gulfstream supersonic aircraft hinges on bilateral certification agreement. C. Fotos. *Aviation Week & Space Technology* 131:110-11 D 18-25 '89

The Soviets want to help build a capitalist status symbol [Gulfstream supersonic corporate jet] C. Hawkins and R. Brady. il *Business Week* p42 O 9 '89

Sukhoi, Gulfstream to study supersonic business jet [business aviation events at Paris Air Show] D. A. Brown. il *Aviation Week & Space Technology* 130:54+ Je 26 '89

Technology concerns delay approval of FS-X agreement [sharing F-16 technology with Japan] M. Mecham. il *Aviation Week & Space Technology* 130:16-17 F 20 '89

U.S., Japan agree to codevelop FSX aircraft [statements, April 28 and May 3, 1989] G. Bush; L. S. Eagleburger. *Department of State Bulletin* 89:48-9 Jl '89

U.S.-Soviet team plans to fly supersonic business jet by 1993 [Gulfstream Aerospace and Sukhoi Design Bureau] E. H. Kolcum. il *Aviation Week & Space Technology* 131:22-4 S 25 '89

Marketing

Airlines cite delays of up to three months in Boeing 747-400 deliveries. R. G. O'Lone. il *Aviation Week & Space Technology* 130:61 F 6 '89

Business jets may erode market for turboprop aircraft in 1990s. E. H. Phillips. il *Aviation Week & Space Technology* 131:89+ Ag 21 '89

Delays force Boeing to revise 747-400 delivery schedules. R. G. O'Lone. *Aviation Week & Space Technology* 130:73 Ja 30 '89

Douglas launches MD90 transport with Delta order. B. A. Smith. il *Aviation Week & Space Technology* 131:34-5 N 20 '89

Garrett's APU market dominance challenged by new competitors [special section] il *Aviation Week & Space Technology* 130:69+ Ap 10 '89

General aviation deliveries up for first time in decade. *Flying* 116:14 Ap '89

General aviation sales increase, but product liability fight looms. E. H. Phillips. il *Aviation Week & Space Technology* 130:31 Ja 23 '89

Huge aircraft order signals revitalization of United [Boeing transports; special section] il *Aviation Week & Space Technology* 130:34-5+ My 1 '89

MD90, 737 transport orders set stage for Delta's increased share of U.S. market. il *Aviation Week & Space Technology* 131:35+ N 20 '89

Midway triples MD-80 order; Douglas predicts more delays. *Aviation Week & Space Technology* 130:34 Ap 3 '89

Multibillion-dollar MD-11 order [American Airlines; special section] il *Aviation Week & Space Technology* 130:16-21 F 13 '89

NBAA Show: new, derivative aircraft enhance upbeat atmosphere at exhibition [special section; with editorial comment] il *Aviation Week & Space Technology* 131:19, 36-8 O 9 '89

Shipment of general aviation aircraft: first-half 1989 GAMA shipments/billings. il *Aviation Week & Space Technology* 131:59 Ag 28 '89

Strong earnings enable airlines to finance fleet expansion. il *Aviation Week & Space Technology* 131:85 Jl 24 '89

Suits and claims

Cessna pistons still on hold [liability concerns] *Flying* 116:8 Jl '89

Commander lawsuit settled. il *Flying* 116:10 Ag '89

General aviation sales increase, but product liability fight looms. E. H. Phillips. il *Aviation Week & Space Technology* 130:31 Ja 23 '89

Lawsuit against Rutans could test liability of designers, test pilots [filed by Aviation Composites Co.] *Aviation Week & Space Technology* 130:61 Ja 23 '89

Liability bill blocked [general aviation] il *Flying* 116:16 Ja '89

Piper may still be carrying excess baggage. G. DeGeorge. il por *Business Week* p76 Je 12 '89

Argentina

See also
Fabrica Argentina de Material Aerospacial

Belgium

See also
Belge de Constructions Aéronautiques SA

Brazil

See also
Embraer Empresa Brasileira de Aeronautica SA

Canada

See also
Bristol Aerospace Ltd.
Canadair Ltd.
DeHavilland Aircraft of Canada, Limited
Pratt & Whitney Aircraft of Canada Ltd.

China

See also
Chengdu Aircraft Corporation
Chengdu Engine Company
Liming Engine Manufacturing Corporation
MPC Aircraft GmbH
Nanchang Aircraft Manufacturing Company
Shanghai Aviation Industrial Corporation
Shenyang Aircraft Corporation

China aviation: at a critical crossroads [cover story; special section; with editorial comment] D. E. Fink and P. Proctor. il *Aviation Week & Space Technology* 131:23, 48-9+ D 11 '89

China Expo attendance drops; companies eye trunkliner project. P. Proctor. il *Aviation Week & Space Technology* 131:28 O 23 '89

Czechoslovakia

See also
LET National Corporation
Motorlet (Firm)

France

See also
Aerospatiale
Dassault Breguet Aviation (Avions Marcel)
SNECMA
SOCATA

Germany (West)

See also
Michael Zoche (Firm)
MPC Aircraft GmbH

Great Britain

See also
Airship Industries, Ltd.
Marshall of Cambridge (Engineering) Ltd.

Hong Kong

See also
Hong Kong Aircraft Engineering Co. Ltd.

Italy

See also
Aeritalia SpA
Aeronautica Macchi
Agusta SpA
Rinaldo Piaggio (Firm)

Japan

The FSX and Japan's strategy for aerospace. R. J. Samuels and B. C. Whipple. il *Technology Review* 92:42-51 O '89

Japan unlikely to parlay FSX work into civilian aircraft leadership role. C. Leader. por *Aviation Week & Space Technology* 130:97+ Mr 27 '89

Korea (South)

See also
Samsung Aerospace Industries Ltd.

Netherlands

See also
Fokker BV

Northern Ireland

See also
Short Brothers Ltd.

AIRPLANE INDUSTRY—cont.
Soviet Union
See also
Antonov Design Bureau (Soviet Union)
Ilyushin Design Bureau (Soviet Union)
Mikoyan Design Bureau (Soviet Union)
Progress Engine Design Bureau (Soviet Union)
Soviet Union. Aviaexport
Sukhoi Design Bureau (Soviet Union)
Tupolev Design Bureau (Soviet Union)
Voronezh Aircraft Production Association (Soviet Union)
Zaporozhye Motorworks (Soviet Union)
Age of *aerostroika* [Soviets at air shows] W. Garvey. il *Flying* 116:8 N '89
Airshow Canada [Soviet displays; special section; with editorial comment] il *Aviation Week & Space Technology* 131:11, 30-2 Ag 21 '89
Fine red whines and other delicacies of the 1989 Paris Air Show. N. Moll. il *Flying* 116:74-8+ O '89
From antiques to Antonovs [Soviet cargo plane highlight of Oshkosh '89] G. Baxter. il *Flying* 116:86-8+ N '89
Perestroika's changes grip Soviet aerospace industry [cover story; special section; with editorial comment by Donald E. Fink] il *Aviation Week & Space Technology* 130:7, 34-5+ Je 5 '89
Soviet aerospace industry [special section] il *Aviation Week & Space Technology* 130:305+ Je 12 '89
Soviet displays, kit-built aircraft highlight EAA show at Oshkosh [with editorial comment] E. H. Phillips. il *Aviation Week & Space Technology* 131:7, 24-5 Ag 7 '89
Soviets display concept aircraft models at Paris Air Show pavilion. il *Aviation Week & Space Technology* 130:63 Je 26 '89
Soviets plan high profile at 1989 Paris Air Show [with editorial comment] J. M. Lenorovitz. il map *Aviation Week & Space Technology* 130:15, 44-6+ My 1 '89
Strong Soviet presence enlivens Canadian air show. R. G. O'Lone. *Aviation Week & Space Technology* 131:33 Ag 14 '89
Spain
See also
Construcciones Aeronauticas SA
Switzerland
See also
Pilatus Aircraft
Western Europe
See also
Airbus Industrie
Eurojet Turbo GmbH
Panavia Aircraft GmbH
European airframe manufacturers expand production, broaden choices. J. M. Lenorovitz. il *Aviation Week & Space Technology* 130:225-8 Mr 20 '89
European airframe manufacturers work to improve production efficiency. il map *Aviation Week & Space Technology* 130:162-3+ Je 12 '89
European engine makers fear social issues may impede sales. *Aviation Week & Space Technology* 130:134 Je 19 '89
AIRPLANE INSPECTION See Airplanes, Jet—Inspection; Airplanes, Light—Inspection
AIRPLANE MECHANICS (PERSONS)
Supply and demand
Maintenance technician shortages constrain growth of Australia's airlines. P. Proctor. *Aviation Week & Space Technology* 131:98 Jl 17 '89
Needs work [shortage of mechanics] il *Time* 134:43 Ag 21 '89
The worrisome shortage of airline mechanics. A. Ramirez. il *Fortune* 120:14 Ag 28 '89
AIRPLANE MODEL RACING
Doolittle's disciples [recreating the Schneider Cup races of the 1920s and 1930s] M. Gianturco. il *Forbes* 144:142-4 D 25 '89
AIRPLANE MODELS
Model student [learning about aerodynamics from balsa model airplane] P. Garrison. il *Flying* 116:82-3 Mr '89
AIRPLANE OWNERSHIP See Airplanes—Private ownership
AIRPLANE PARTS
New USAF contracts speed up aerospace component redesign. B. W. Henderson. *Aviation Week & Space Technology* 131:74 Ag 21 '89
AIRPLANE PILOTS See Air pilots
AIRPLANE PROPELLERS See Airplanes—Propellers
AIRPLANE RACING
History
Rerun: 1929 Women's Air Derby [S. Dusenbury to trace route of winner L. Thaden] *Flying* 116:20 Ag '89
When prop planes ruled the skies [Schneider Cup races from 1913 to 1931] M. Gianturco. *Forbes* 144:143 D 25 '89
AIRPLANE SERVICE STATIONS
See also
AMR Services Corporation
Beech craftmasters. J. M. McClellan. *Flying* 116:26 Ap '89
Fixed-base operators enhance service to lure business from competitors. il *Aviation Week & Space Technology* 131:67+ O 2 '89

Growing aircraft maintenance needs press U.S. repair and modification capacity. il *Aviation Week & Space Technology* 131:48+ Jl 24 '89
International aspects
Congress should avoid undue meddling in U.S. aviation interests abroad [overseas repair regulations] P. Proctor. *Aviation Week & Space Technology* 131:85+ D 18-25 '89
Threatened job losses fuel congressional opposition to FAA's foreign repair rules [with editorial comment] M. Mecham. *Aviation Week & Space Technology* 131:7, 29-30 Jl 3 '89
Malaysia
See also
Airod Sendirian Berhad
AIRPLANE SIMULATORS See Flight simulators
AIRPLANE SPEED RECORDS
Propeller-driven machbuster [B. Montagne trying to break sound barrier in racer with Oldsmobile V8 engine] M. Lamm. il por *Popular Mechanics* 166:48+ Ag '89
AIRPLANE TAILS See Airplanes—Tails
AIRPLANE TRAVEL See Air travel
AIRPLANES
See also
Airplanes, Aerobatic
Airplanes, Antique
Airplanes, Business
Airplanes, Experimental
Airplanes, Freight
Airplanes, Government
Airplanes, Home-built
Airplanes, Jet
Airplanes, Light
Airplanes, Military
Airplanes, Racing
Airplanes, Remodeled
Airplanes, Short take-off and landing
Airplanes, Supersonic
Airplanes, Training
Airplanes, Used
Airplanes, Vertical take-off and landing
Autogiros
Aviation
Helicopters
Human powered aircraft
Remotely piloted vehicles
Seaplanes
Tank airplanes
Accidents
See Aviation—Accidents
Aerodynamics
See Aerodynamics
Bird collisions
See Aviation—Bird hazards
Cabins
Pressurization
See Airplanes—Pressurization
Chartering
See Airlines—Non-scheduled operations
Charts
See Aviation charts
Collision avoidance systems
Avionics manufacturers target aging aircraft for instrument, TCAS sales. il *Aviation Week & Space Technology* 131:89+ Jl 24 '89
Bendix/King gears up to meet demand for T/CAS in 1990s. E. H. Kolcum. il *Aviation Week & Space Technology* 130:109+ F 20 '89
Collision vision [traffic alert and collision avoidance system] J. M. McClellan. il *Flying* 116:54-6+ My '89
Congressional Office urges relaxing TCAS timetable [Office of Technology Assessment] P. J. Klass. *Aviation Week & Space Technology* 130:95 Mr 27 '89
Deadline for T/CAS installation may be extended to 1992 or 1993. il *Aviation Week & Space Technology* 130:109 My 22 '89
Norden develops system to warn controllers of runway incursions [Runway Incursion Management system] B. D. Nordwall. *Aviation Week & Space Technology* 130:28 My 29 '89
Studies find few problems with T/CAS in dense traffic. *Aviation Week & Space Technology* 129:71 Mr 6 '89
Design
The Airplane Factory [video game] R. G. Sheffield. il *Compute!* 11:74-5 Ag '89
Computational aerodynamics for aircraft design [cover story] A. Jameson. bibl f il *Science* 245:361-71 Jl 28 '89
Electronic equipment
See also
Air navigation—Aids and devices
Airplanes—Collision avoidance systems
Energy usage
See Airplane engines—Energy usage
Engines
See Airplane engines
Equipment
See also
Altimeters
Flight recorders

AIRPLANES—Equipment—*cont.*
FAA issues new minimum-equipment rule. il *Flying* 116:14
Mr '89

Exhibitions
See Aviation—Exhibitions

Fuel
See Airplane engines—Fuel

Fuel consumption
See Airplane engines—Energy usage

Fuselage
Burnelli's lifting fuselage. P. Garrison. il por *Flying* 116:80+
Ap '89

History
See Aviation—History

Hydraulic equipment
Fluid motions. P. Garrison. il *Flying* 116:102+ D '89

Landing
See also
Microwave landing systems
NASA, McDonnell Douglas test helmet-mounted landing
system. E. H. Phillips. il *Aviation Week & Space Technology*
130:126-7 Je 19 '89

Laws and regulations
See Aviation—Laws and regulations

Leasing and renting
See also
Commander Aircraft (Firm)
Rent control. E. Weiner. il *Flying* 116:74+ Ap '89

Lubrication and lubricants
Slick oil [Mobil AV 1] J. M. McClellan. il *Flying* 116:40
Je '89

Maintenance and repair
See also
Airplane engines—Maintenance and repair
Airplane mechanics (Persons)
Airplane service stations

Manufacture
See Airplane industry

Materials
See also
Scaled Composites, Inc.

Noise
Ear shields [pilot headphones that block noise] W. J. Hawkins.
il *Popular Science* 235:44 D '89
EEC delays action on aircraft that fail to meet noise limits.
E. H. Phillips. il *Aviation Week & Space Technology* 130:30
F 13 '89
Europe may exempt business jets from Stage 2 nonaddition
rule. il *Aviation Week & Space Technology* 131:53+ O
2 '89
FAA begins formal investigation of transport aircraft noise
[conference in Washington] P. Proctor. *Aviation Week &
Space Technology* 130:60 F 6 '89
ICAO assembly fails to agree on aircraft noise restrictions.
D. Hughes. il *Aviation Week & Space Technology* 131:82-3
O 16 '89
NATO tightens limit on training flights to ease West German
concerns. *Aviation Week & Space Technology* 131:30 O
2 '89
Restrictions on Chapter 2 aircraft could cost airlines billions
of dollars. il *Aviation Week & Space Technology* 131:61+
N 20 '89

Parts
See Airplane parts

Passenger service
See Airlines—Passenger service

Patrol work
See Airplanes in patrol work

Piloting
See also
Air navigation
Aviation—Instrument flying
Aviation—Overwater flying
Flight in the fast lane [VFR flying in high-density areas]
P. Garrison. il *Flying* 116:68-70+ Ja '89
I learned about flying from that. See issues of Flying
The shooting gallery. G. Baxter. il *Flying* 116:92+ Ap '89
Unicom. See issues of Flying beginning February 1989
Vectors. L. Morgan. See issues of Flying
VFR in IMC: taking it to the limit [flying VFR in instrument
meteorological conditions; NTSB accident statistics] J. M.
McClellan. *Flying* 116:38 S '89

Pressurization
Pressure group: it's your altitude [altitude chamber flight
at Andrews Air Force Base] P. Scott. il *Flying* 116:36+
Ag '89

Private ownership
See also
Airplanes, Used—Purchasing
In from the cold. W. Garvey. il *Flying* 116:8-9 S '89

Propellers
When push comes to shove. P. Garrison. il *Flying* 116:108-11
Jl '89

Pumps, Vacuum
See Vacuum pumps

Radar equipment
See also
Airplanes—Collision avoidance systems

Radar meteorology

Radio equipment
See also
Radiotelephone on airplanes
FCC kills crystal coms. *Flying* 116:14 N '89
Speak softly? Carry headsets and intercom [Concept Industries'
Softcomm C-40 headsets and ATC-4 intercom system for
pilots and passengers] il *Flying* 116:37 Je '89

Sales
See Airplane industry—Marketing

Specifications
Experimental/research/testbed aircraft (military/government
sponsored) [tables] il *Aviation Week & Space Technology*
130:191 Mr 20 '89
International aircraft [tables] il *Aviation Week & Space
Technology* 130:137-9+ Mr 20 '89
Multinational aircraft [tables] il *Aviation Week & Space
Technology* 130:153 Mr 20 '89
Soviet aircraft [tables] il *Aviation Week & Space Technology*
130:152-3 Mr 20 '89
Turbine-powered business aircraft [tables] il *Aviation Week
& Space Technology* 130:154-5 Mr 20 '89
U.S. business, personal, utility aircraft [tables] il *Aviation
Week & Space Technology* 130:156-7 Mr 20 '89
U.S. commercial cargo transports [tables] il *Aviation Week
& Space Technology* 130:150 Mr 20 '89
U.S. commercial passenger transports [tables] il *Aviation Week
& Space Technology* 130:150-1 Mr 20 '89
U.S. military aircraft [tables] il *Aviation Week & Space
Technology* 130:146-9 Mr 20 '89

Speed
On the mark. J. M. McClellan. il *Flying* 116:112-13 Je
'89

Records
See Airplane speed records

Spinning
Spin cycle [spin training] W. Garvey. il *Flying* 116:21-2
Jl '89

Stability and stabilizers
Balancing act. P. Garrison. il *Flying* 116:90-2 My '89

Tails
Is the T tail a tall tale? P. Garrison. il *Flying* 116:108+
S '89

Testing
See also
Tank airplanes—Testing

Vacuum pumps
See Vacuum pumps

Wings
Once upon a winglet. P. Garrison. il *Flying* 116:108+ Ag
'89

AIRPLANES, AEROBATIC
Sukhoi Su-26M for sale in the U.S. il *Flying* 116:12 O
'89

Testing
Extra! [Extra 300] N. Moll. il *Flying* 116:64-9 D '89
AIRPLANES, AMPHIBIOUS *See* Seaplanes
AIRPLANES, ANTIQUE
Have goggles, will travel [M. Esch hitches rides across U.S.
in vintage airplanes] G. Baxter. il por *Flying* 116:86+
My '89
Jenny in a barn. G. Baxter. il *Flying* 116:130+ Ag '89
AIRPLANES, BUSINESS
See also
Airplanes in business
National Business Aircraft Association

Certification
See Airplanes, Business—Standards

Cockpits
New avionics put business jet cockpits on par with advanced
transport aircraft. il *Aviation Week & Space Technology*
131:83+ O 2 '89

Defects
Commander lawsuit settled. il *Flying* 116:10 Ag '89

Design
Beech plans to boost production, introduces Model 350 Super
King Air. E. H. Phillips. il *Aviation Week & Space
Technology* 131:41-2 O 16 '89
British Aerospace launches BAe 1000 business jet. C. A.
Shifrin. il *Aviation Week & Space Technology* 131:43+
O 16 '89
Canadair to build Challenger 601-S. *Flying* 116:20 S '89
Cessna plans to boost Citation production. *Aviation Week
& Space Technology* 131:28 Jl 17 '89
Dassault launches twin-engine, transcontinental business jet
as signs of market recovery are seen [Falcon X] *Aviation
Week & Space Technology* 130:34 Je 19 '89
Dassault seeks partner for Falcon 2000 production. il *Aviation
Week & Space Technology* 131:30 O 30 '89
Drag eraser [Piaggio Avanti; cover story] J. M. McClellan.
il *Flying* 116:28-32+ Ja '89
Future Falcon jet [views of Bernard Leroldier] *Flying* 116:26
Je '89
Gulfstream/Soviet SST bizjet. il *Flying* 116:17 S '89
Gulfstream, Soviets expect to select basic supersonic business
jet design in November. *Aviation Week & Space Technology*
131:46 O 16 '89

AIRPLANES, BUSINESS—Design—*cont.*

Jaffe Group to replace Gulfstream as partner in SA-30 development. E. H. Phillips. il *Aviation Week & Space Technology* 131:37 S 11 '89

Leopard makes leap for bizjet market. N. Moll. il por *Flying* 116:20-2 Ap '89

Millennium [BAe 1000] J. M. McClellan. il *Flying* 116:102-4 N '89

NBAA means business [Atlanta convention] il *Flying* 116:8-10+ D '89

NBAA Show: new, derivative aircraft enhance upbeat atmosphere at exhibition [special section; with editorial comment] il *Aviation Week & Space Technology* 131:19, 36-8 O 9 '89

OMAC to offer two versions of Laser 300. *Aviation Week & Space Technology* 130:31 F 20 '89

Paulson to build Swearingen jet. il *Flying* 116:14 Ja '89

Piaggio Avanti, Beech Starship offer differing performance characteristics. il *Aviation Week & Space Technology* 131:75+ O 2 '89

Piaggio will select U.S. site for Avanti airframe production. E. H. Phillips. il *Aviation Week & Space Technology* 130:101 My 22 '89

Sabreliner Corp. seeks partner to resume business jet production. E. H. Phillips. *Aviation Week & Space Technology* 130:27 Mr 27 '89

Socata, Mooney proceed with TBM 700 production. J. M. Lenorovitz. il *Aviation Week & Space Technology* 130:53-4 Je 26 '89

The Soviets want to help build a capitalist status symbol [Gulfstream supersonic corporate jet] C. Hawkins and R. Brady. il *Business Week* p42 O 9 '89

The Starship chronicles. J. M. McClellan. il *Flying* 116:56-60+ Mr '89

Sukhoi, Gulfstream to study supersonic business jet [business aviation events at Paris Air Show] D. A. Brown. il *Aviation Week & Space Technology* 130:54+ Je 26 '89

Swearingen, Jaffe Group work on schedule for SA-30 business jet development. il *Aviation Week & Space Technology* 131:24 S 25 '89

A Swiss to watch [Pilatus PC-12] N. Moll. il *Flying* 116:80-4 N '89

Switzerland's Pilatus unveils PC-12 aircraft at NBAA convention. D. A. Brown. il *Aviation Week & Space Technology* 131:31 O 2 '89

U.S.-Soviet team plans to fly supersonic business jet by 1993 [Gulfstream Aerospace and Sukhoi Design Bureau] E. H. Kolcum. il *Aviation Week & Space Technology* 131:22-4 S 25 '89

Electronic equipment

Grade-A Primus [Honeywell Primus 2000] J. M. McClellan. il *Flying* 116:52-4+ O '89

HERF: a new hurdle for new aircraft. *Flying* 116:16 S '89

High-energy radiation field testing delays full certification of Starship 1. *Aviation Week & Space Technology* 131:91 Jl 17 '89

New avionics put business jet cockpits on par with advanced transport aircraft. il *Aviation Week & Space Technology* 131:83+ O 2 '89

Engines

See Airplane engines, Jet

Export-import trade

See Airplane industry—Export-import trade

Frames

Socata/Mooney TBM 700 flown with airframe modifications. il *Aviation Week & Space Technology* 131:54 Jl 3 '89

History

The stuff dreams are made of [Learjet turns 25] J. M. McClellan. il *Flying* 116:58-60+ S '89

Manufacture

See Airplane industry

Marketing

See Airplane industry—Marketing

Piloting

Falcon ferry tale [hand-flying new Falcon 50 across the Atlantic] J. M. McClellan. il *Flying* 116:46-8+ Ap '89

Purchasing

Bizjet Olympics [competition for Air Force's tanker transport training system contract] W. Garvey. il *Flying* 116:76-9 F '89

USAF releases draft request for bids on tanker-transport training system. *Aviation Week & Space Technology* 130:31 Ap 3 '89

USAF tanker-transport training to stress low and high altitude mission profiles. E. H. Phillips. il *Aviation Week & Space Technology* 130:51-2 My 1 '89

Remodeled airplanes

See Airplanes, Remodeled

Specifications

See Airplanes—Specifications

Speed

TBM: 300 knots or your money back [TBM 700] il *Flying* 116:10 Jl '89

Standards

High-energy radiation field testing delays full certification of Starship 1. *Aviation Week & Space Technology* 131:91 Jl 17 '89

Lacadre to certify Avtec 400A aircraft. E. H. Phillips. *Aviation Week & Space Technology* 131:138 N 20 '89

Optimistic data, schedule blamed for Starship certification delays. E. H. Phillips. *Aviation Week & Space Technology* 131:30 D 4 '89

Soviet/Gulfstream supersonic aircraft hinges on bilateral certification agreement. C. Fotos. *Aviation Week & Space Technology* 131:110-11 D 18-25 '89

Starship 1 begins final tests to certify pneumatic deicers. E. H. Phillips. *Aviation Week & Space Technology* 130:105 Ja 2 '89

The Starship chronicles. J. M. McClellan. il *Flying* 116:56-60+ Mr '89

Testing

Citation 5 provides larger cabin, improved performance. E. H. Phillips. il *Aviation Week & Space Technology* 130:246-7+ Je 12 '89

Gulfstream IV. F. George. il *Flying* 116:92-6+ N '89

High five [Cessna's Citation V; cover story] J. M. McClellan. il *Flying* 116:50-4+ Ag '89

Interurban turbine express [TBM 700; cover story] F. George. il *Flying* 116:42-6+ D '89

King Air 350 [cover story] F. George. il *Flying* 116:46-50+ N '89

Lear 55C: the delta difference. J. M. McClellan. il *Flying* 116:64-9 Mr '89

Star quality [Israel Aircraft Industries Astra 1125; cover story] F. George. il *Flying* 116:28-32+ Jl '89

Wings

Langley uses Learjet to study wave disturbances in laminar flow. il *Aviation Week & Space Technology* 130:270-1 Je 12 '89

AIRPLANES, COMMUTER *See* Airplanes, Jet

AIRPLANES, DRONE *See* Remotely piloted vehicles

AIRPLANES, EXPERIMENTAL

See also

Experimental Aircraft Association

Spaceplane

Experimental/research/testbed aircraft (military/government sponsored) [tables] il *Aviation Week & Space Technology* 130:191 Mr 20 '89

Design

Burt Rutan: a profile. P. Garrison. il pors *Flying* 116:48-50+ F '89

AIRPLANES, FREIGHT

See also

Air freight service

Canadair ships Airbus fuselage sections to France on Soviet An-124 transports. il *Aviation Week & Space Technology* 131:135 N 20 '89

From antiques to Antonovs [Soviet cargo plane highlight of Oshkosh '89] G. Baxter. il *Flying* 116:86-8+ N '89

Design

An-124 offered to international customers on charter basis [Soviet cargo transport] il *Aviation Week & Space Technology* 130:77 Je 5 '89

An-225 super heavylift transport can carry 80-meter external payload [Soviet transport] J. M. Lenorovitz. il *Aviation Week & Space Technology* 130:52-3 Je 19 '89

Ansett New Zealand 146QC transport begins daily passenger, cargo flights. il *Aviation Week & Space Technology* 131:62 D 4 '89

First Airshow Canada will feature Soviet An-225, MiG-29 aircraft. *Aviation Week & Space Technology* 131:25 Ag 7 '89

Landing

Point of know return [1987 crash of twin-engine Caribou in Yukon river valley during attempted go-around from single-engine approach] P. Garrison. *Flying* 116:24+ D '89

Remodeled airplanes

See Airplanes, Remodeled

Testing

Antonov An-225 takes heavyweight transport title [Soviet transport] il *Popular Mechanics* 166:13 Jl '89

Certification of super heavy-lift Antonov An-225 planned for 1990 [Soviet transport] il *Aviation Week & Space Technology* 130:72-3+ Je 5 '89

Six-engine Antonov An-225 begins flight tests. il *Aviation Week & Space Technology* 130:128 F 20 '89

AIRPLANES, GOVERNMENT

Hail to the chief's pilot [presidential pilot D. Barr] W. Garvey. il por *Flying* 116:8-9 Ag '89

USAF may transfer six C-29As, crews to FAA for flight inspection mission. *Aviation Week & Space Technology* 131:108 D 18-25 '89

Tracking

Bureau of Land Management evaluates automated flight following system [Radio Determination Satellite System] il *Aviation Week & Space Technology* 130:32-3 Je 26 '89

AIRPLANES, HOME-BUILT

Kit-built aircraft fuel renaissance in industry dominated by old designs. E. H. Phillips. il *Aviation Week & Space Technology* 131:93+ D 18-25 '89

Design

Bede ayes [designer J. Bede] G. Baxter. il por *Flying* 116:108+ D '89

AIRPLANES, HOME-BUILT—Design—cont.

Homebuilt machbuster [J. Bede's BD-10J; cover story] W. Garvey. il *Popular Mechanics* 166:68-71 D '89

Soviet displays, kit-built aircraft highlight EAA show at Oshkosh [with editorial comment] E. H. Phillips. il *Aviation Week & Space Technology* 131:7, 24-5 Ag 7 '89

History

Still flying [Pietenpol Air Camper] il *Home Mechanix* 85:4 F '89

Materials

I want my M2 [composite materials] P. Garrison. il *Flying* 116:100-2 O '89

Testing

Kit-built Wheeler Express FT developed to fill gap in 4-seat, fixed-gear market. E. H. Phillips. il *Aviation Week & Space Technology* 131:86-7+ Jl 17 '89

AIRPLANES, JET

See also
Airplanes, Business
Airplanes, Military
Airplanes, Supersonic

Accidents

See Aviation—Accidents

Auxiliary power supply

Garrett's APU market dominance challenged by new competitors [special section] il *Aviation Week & Space Technology* 130:69+ Ap 10 '89

Cabins

Lufthansa begins 747-400 service to Pacific Rim. il *Aviation Week & Space Technology* 131:97 N 20 '89

Certification

See Airplanes, Jet—Standards

Cockpits

Pilots react to the automated cockpit [NASA study of Boeing 757 pilots; cover story; special section] il *Aviation Week & Space Technology* 131:32-6 Ag 7 '89

Control

See also
Airplanes, Jet—Stability and stabilizers

Control conundrum [crash of Air New Orleans Flight 962 in May 1987] P. Garrison. *Flying* 116:26-7 Mr '89

Flying the electric skies [Airbus A320 with fly-by-wire] M. M. Waldrop. il *Science* 244:1532-4 Je 30 '89

Corrosion and anticorrosives

Airline, industry officials discuss problems of corrosion. D. A. Brown. *Aviation Week & Space Technology* 129:66 Mr 6 '89

Safety Board recommends upgrade in corrosion control research [investigation of fuselage failure on Aloha Airlines 737 in April 1988] *Aviation Week & Space Technology* 131:70-1 N 6 '89

Cost of operation

Economic impact of aging aircraft fixes remains unclear. C. Fotos. il *Aviation Week & Space Technology* 130:26-7 My 29 '89

Economics, not safety, is key issue in replacement of older transports. il *Aviation Week & Space Technology* 131:69+ Jl 24 '89

Narrow-body aircraft direct expenses: first quarter 1988. il *Aviation Week & Space Technology* 130:70-1 Ja 23 '89

Narrow-body aircraft direct expenses: yearly 1988. il *Aviation Week & Space Technology* 131:72-3 Ag 28 '89

Wide-body aircraft operating costs: first quarter 1988. il *Aviation Week & Space Technology* 130:72-3 Ja 23 '89

Costs

Bromon Aircraft suspends operations, orders suppliers to stop BR2000 work [twin-turboprop transport] *Aviation Week & Space Technology* 131:18 O 30 '89

Defects

See also
Airplane engines, Jet—Mounting—Defects

New qualms about the DC-10. J. Birnbaum. il *Time* 134:20 Ag 7 '89

Design

Airbus Industrie expects to launch production of A321-100 by fall. il *Aviation Week & Space Technology* 130:159 Je 19 '89

Airbus Industrie partners approve development of stretched A320. J. M. Lenorovitz. il *Aviation Week & Space Technology* 131:31-2 D 4 '89

Airbus nears launch authorization for stretched version of A320. *Aviation Week & Space Technology* 130:26 Ap 24 '89

Airframe makers use aging aircraft experience to refine design practices. *Aviation Week & Space Technology* 131:94-5 Jl 24 '89

Airport cramp [Boeing 7x7 or 767-X] H. Banks. il *Forbes* 144:85 Jl 24 '89

Big bird [747-400; cover story] F. Mackerodt. il *Popular Mechanics* 166:74-85 Mr '89

Boeing agrees to 747-400 design changes sought by European aviation authorities. *Aviation Week & Space Technology* 131:58 N 6 '89

Boeing borrows skilled workers from Lockheed for 747-400 program. R. G. O'Lone. *Aviation Week & Space Technology* 130:66 Mr 13 '89

Boeing seeks customers for wider-body 767-X. il *Aviation Week & Space Technology* 130:35 My 1 '89

Boeing selects design for 777 candidate. R. G. O'Lone and J. T. McKenna. il *Aviation Week & Space Technology* 131:106-7 D 18-25 '89

Boeing will produce two new 747-400 versions. R. G. O'Lone. il *Aviation Week & Space Technology* 131:102-3 O 2 '89

British Aerospace decides to proceed with Jetstream 41 development program [turboprop commuter aircraft] *Aviation Week & Space Technology* 130:111 My 29 '89

Canadair group expands operations to meet new program requirements [Airbus subcontracting and Regional Jet program] D. Hughes. il *Aviation Week & Space Technology* 130:75-7 My 15 '89

Canadair RJ: go ahead. il *Flying* 116:9 Jl '89

Commercial airframe makers take conservative approach. R. G. O'Lone. il *Aviation Week & Space Technology* 130:197-9 Mr 20 '89

Consortium to decide on boosting ATR regional transport production. J. M. Lenorovitz. il *Aviation Week & Space Technology* 130:68 Mr 13 '89

Czechs seek wider market for L410, L610 transports [cover story] J. M. Lenorovitz. il *Aviation Week & Space Technology* 130:36-8+ Ap 3 '89

Delays force Boeing to revise 747-400 delivery schedules. R. G. O'Lone. *Aviation Week & Space Technology* 130:73 Ja 30 '89

Development of Metro 5 commuter aircraft delayed [Fairchild turboprop] *Aviation Week & Space Technology* 130:39 Ap 24 '89

Douglas launches MD90 transport with Delta order. B. A. Smith. il *Aviation Week & Space Technology* 131:34-5 N 20 '89

Douglas may offer three MD-90 versions with V2500 powerplants. C. A. Shifrin. il *Aviation Week & Space Technology* 131:56-7 Jl 3 '89

Douglas receiving strong customer interest in MD90-30 version of proposed new twinjet. B. A. Smith. il *Aviation Week & Space Technology* 131:85 O 16 '89

Embraer developing stretched Brasilia for regional market. C. A. Shifrin. il *Aviation Week & Space Technology* 130:158 Je 19 '89

Embraer will launch two civil aircraft programs [commuter aircraft] C. Fotos. il *Aviation Week & Space Technology* 131:65-7 S 4 '89

European consortium nears decisions on production rate, upgraded ATR72 development. J. M. Lenorovitz. il *Aviation Week & Space Technology* 131:55-6 N 6 '89

Fairchild prepares for Metro 25 commuter production decision [twin turboprop] D. A. Brown. il *Aviation Week & Space Technology* 131:31-2 O 16 '89

GE-powered 747-400 gets initial approval in Europe after Boeing accepts design changes. *Aviation Week & Space Technology* 130:105 My 22 '89

Ilyushin Design Bureau plans three new transports for export [Soviet transports] il *Aviation Week & Space Technology* 130:65+ Je 5 '89

Lufthansa boosts firm order total for Airbus A321-100 transports. C. A. Shifrin. *Aviation Week & Space Technology* 131:58-9 Ag 14 '89

Managers chosen for German/Chinese MPC-75 transport aircraft program. *Aviation Week & Space Technology* 130:101 My 8 '89

MD-82 transport assembly accelerates at Shanghai. il *Aviation Week & Space Technology* 131:68-9 D 11 '89

Multibillion-dollar MD-11 order [American Airlines; special section] il *Aviation Week & Space Technology* 130:16-21 F 13 '89

Pulling out the stops [new planes designed for long-haul routes] G. Eichler. il *Esquire* 112:60 Ag '89

Saab completes definition work, selects contractors for Saab 2000 [regional turboprop transport] C. A. Shifrin. il *Aviation Week & Space Technology* 131:72-3 O 23 '89

Saab story [Saab 2000] il *Flying* 116:13 Mr '89

Soviet aerospace industry [special section] il *Aviation Week & Space Technology* 130:305+ Je 12 '89

Soviets display concept aircraft models at Paris Air Show pavilion. il *Aviation Week & Space Technology* 130:63 Je 26 '89

Doors

Defects

Blowout over the Pacific [cargo door failure on Honolulu-Auckland flight] R. Lacayo. il *Time* 133:28-9 Mr 6 '89

Board suggests changing cargo door latch design [United Flight 811] *Aviation Week & Space Technology* 131:29 Ag 28 '89

Close look at cargo door workings fails to reveal cause of accident [United Flight 811 accident in February 1989] il *Aviation Week & Space Technology* 130:86-7+ My 22 '89

Flight 811: a nightmare in the sky [cargo door rips open] G. Hackett. il *Newsweek* 113:26 Mr 6 '89

Home on a wing and a prayer [passengers recount details of United Airlines Flight 811 after cargo door ripped open] W. Plummer. il *People Weekly* 31:38-43 Mr 13 '89

United 747 accident [nine killed as cargo door blows out; special section] il *Aviation Week & Space Technology* 129:18-22 Mr 6 '89

AIRPLANES, JET—Doors—Defects—*cont.*
United officials tell NTSB AD procedures not followed [hearings on Flight 811 cargo door accident in February 1989] B. W. Henderson. *Aviation Week & Space Technology* 130:107 My 1 '89

Electronic equipment
See also
Air navigation—Aids and devices
Computers—Aviation use
Avionics manufacturers target aging aircraft for instrument, TCAS sales. il *Aviation Week & Space Technology* 131:89+ Jl 24 '89

Energy usage
See Airplane engines, Jet—Energy usage

Engines
See Airplane engines, Jet

Fires and fire prevention
Boeing: new dents in a sterling record [flaws in fire extinguisher systems] *Newsweek* 113:51 F 13 '89
Boeing takes steps to prevent fire extinguisher malfunctions. *Aviation Week & Space Technology* 130:71 F 27 '89
FAA probes Boeing's reporting of faulty wiring in 757 extinguisher systems. C. Fotos. *Aviation Week & Space Technology* 130:66 Ja 23 '89
Put teeth into air safety recommendations [report on British Airtours Boeing 737 fire in August 1985] *Aviation Week & Space Technology* 130:7 Ap 17 '89

Flaps
Delta accepts responsibility for crash, dismisses flight crew [failure to set flaps and slats properly blamed for August 1988 crash at Dallas/Ft. Worth] J. T. McKenna. *Aviation Week & Space Technology* 131:76-7 Ag 7 '89
Sins of omission [Detroit crash of Northwest MD-82 blamed on failure to set wing slats and flaps for takeoff] J. M. McClellan. *Flying* 116:26-7 F '89

Fuel consumption
See Airplane engines, Jet—Energy usage

Fuselage
Canadair ships Airbus fuselage sections to France on Soviet An-124 transports. il *Aviation Week & Space Technology* 131:135 N 20 '89
Modified LEBU devices could cut skin-friction drag. E. H. Phillips. il *Aviation Week & Space Technology* 131:71+ Ag 21 '89

Defects
20-inch crack spurs FAA to order 727-100 checks. J. Ott. *Aviation Week & Space Technology* 130:62-3 Jl 10 '89
Aloha 737 fuselage skin, structures undergo detailed fatigue inspections [April 1988 accident] il *Aviation Week & Space Technology* 131:129-30 S 18 '89
Aloha Airlines probe raises questions about FAA surveillance of maintenance [fuselage failure on Boeing 737 in April 1988] *Aviation Week & Space Technology* 131:77+ Ag 28 '89
Cracks in geriatric aircraft [Boeing 737s and other passenger planes] E. Marshall. il *Science* 243:595-7 F 3 '89
Device simplifies skin crack detection [Physical Research's magneto-optic imager] il *Aviation Week & Space Technology* 131:137 O 9 '89
FAA proposes checks for cracks on 727s. *Aviation Week & Space Technology* 130:63 Ja 16 '89
Investigators detail failure of Aloha 737's fuselage [April 1988 accident] il *Aviation Week & Space Technology* 131:76-8 S 4 '89
Investigators suspect faulty repair as cause of 727 fuselage failure [Eastern Air Lines jet forced to make emergency landing] il *Aviation Week & Space Technology* 130:107 Ja 2 '89
NTSB probes Aloha 737's maintenance records [fuselage failure during April 1988 flight] *Aviation Week & Space Technology* 131:131+ S 11 '89
NTSB raps Aloha, aviation system for fuselage failure [Boeing 737 in April 1988] J. Ott. il *Aviation Week & Space Technology* 130:24-6 My 29 '89
NTSB urges increase in frequency of fatigue testing of transports [investigation of fuselage failure on Aloha Airlines 737 in April 1988] *Aviation Week & Space Technology* 131:83-6 N 13 '89
Operations: crew of Aloha Flight 243 [aircraft brought down safely after loss of upper fuselage; aerospace laureate] il *Aviation Week & Space Technology* 130:17 Ja 2 '89
Safety Board analyzes how Aloha 737 fuselage failed [April 1988 accident] *Aviation Week & Space Technology* 131:145-6+ O 9 '89
Safety Board examines Aloha's maintenance of aging 737s [investigation of fuselage failure during April 1988 flight] *Aviation Week & Space Technology* 131:117+ S 25 '89
Safety Board urges FAA to revamp maintenance, inspection training [investigation of fuselage failure on Aloha Airlines 737 in April 1988] *Aviation Week & Space Technology* 131:77+ O 23 '89

Painting
Airlines urged not to paint fuselages as concerns about aging fleet rise. J. Ott. il *Aviation Week & Space Technology* 130:62-4 F 6 '89

Hydraulic equipment
Shutoff valve to isolate DC-10 tail hydraulics. *Aviation Week & Space Technology* 131:32 S 25 '89

Inspection
20-inch crack spurs FAA to order 727-100 checks. J. Ott. *Aviation Week & Space Technology* 130:62-3 Jl 10 '89
Acoustic emission technique tests aircraft integrity. C. Fotos. *Aviation Week & Space Technology* 131:76 Ag 28 '89
Aging aircraft issue presents major challenge to industry [special section] il *Aviation Week & Space Technology* 131:42-3+ Jl 24 '89
Airlines inspect cargo doors in wake of United accident. *Aviation Week & Space Technology* 129:22 Mr 6 '89
Aloha 737 fuselage skin, structures undergo detailed fatigue inspections [April 1988 accident] il *Aviation Week & Space Technology* 131:129-30 S 18 '89
Busey embarks on plan to boost FAA safety inspectors, shift duties. J. Ott. il *Aviation Week & Space Technology* 131:108-9 D 18-25 '89
Detecting threats to airplane safety. S. Garfinkel. il *Technology Review* 92:10+ F/Mr '89
Device simplifies skin crack detection [Physical Research's magneto-optic imager] il *Aviation Week & Space Technology* 131:137 O 9 '89
FAA hiring field inspectors to monitor aging aircraft. M. Mecham. *Aviation Week & Space Technology* 130:110-11 Ap 24 '89
FAA proposes checks for cracks on 727s. *Aviation Week & Space Technology* 130:63 Ja 16 '89
NTSB urges increase in frequency of fatigue testing of transports [investigation of fuselage failure on Aloha Airlines 737 in April 1988] *Aviation Week & Space Technology* 131:83-6 N 13 '89
Report urges stronger inspection procedures for aging commuter aircraft. E. H. Phillips. il *Aviation Week & Space Technology* 131:103 Jl 31 '89
Safety Board urges FAA to revamp maintenance, inspection training [investigation of fuselage failure on Aloha Airlines 737 in April 1988] *Aviation Week & Space Technology* 131:77+ O 23 '89
Update commercial transport inspections [nondestructive inspection technology] *Aviation Week & Space Technology* 130:7 Jl 10 '89

Landing
Board urges closer review of special approach procedures, pilots' skills [Trans-Colorado Airlines crash in January 1988] *Aviation Week & Space Technology* 131:111+ Jl 31 '89
Free fall [forced landing of Air Canada Flight 143 due to fuel problems; condensation] W. Hoffer and M. Hoffer. il *Reader's Digest* 134:197-202+ Ap '89
Metro 3 crashed during special approach to airport in Colorado [January 1988] *Aviation Week & Space Technology* 130:75+ Jl 10 '89
Reverse psychology [crash landing of CASA C-212 regional airliner in Detroit blamed on pilot's use of beta mode in flight] J. M. McClellan. *Flying* 116:108-9 Je '89
Safety Board cites captain's failure to monitor approach as key in crash [Trans-Colorado Airlines crash in January 1988] *Aviation Week & Space Technology* 131:103+ Jl 17 '89
Snow storm [cocaine and lack of skill blamed for crash of commuter airliner on approach to Durango, Colo.] P. Garrison. *Flying* 116:30-2 N '89

Landing gear
Defects
Accident investigators seek cause of Fokker 100 landing gear failure [KLM flight to Geneva] *Aviation Week & Space Technology* 130:64 Mr 13 '89
Airworthiness directives issued following Fokker 100 gear failure [KLM landing accident at Geneva] *Aviation Week & Space Technology* 130:267 Mr 20 '89

Leasing and renting
See also
GPA Group, Ltd.
GPA Jetprop, Ltd.
International Lease Finance Corporation
Air New Zealand says it will sell or lease first 747-400 [contract dispute with pilots] *Aviation Week & Space Technology* 131:136 O 9 '89
Airlines prosper under tight management; leasing transforms commercial transport. il *Aviation Week & Space Technology* 130:90-1+ My 29 '89
Large leasing company orders restructure aircraft acquisition [orders by GPA and others; special section] il *Aviation Week & Space Technology* 130:24-7+ Ap 24 '89
Need for international standards on aircraft maintenance is cited. J. T. McKenna. il *Aviation Week & Space Technology* 130:112-13 My 29 '89

Maintenance and repair
See also
Aging Aircraft Task Force
Airplanes, Jet—Inspection
Aging aircraft issue presents major challenge to industry [special section] il *Aviation Week & Space Technology* 131:42-3+ Jl 24 '89
Airlines evaluate boron/epoxy for repair of aircraft structures. D. Hughes. il *Aviation Week & Space Technology* 130:67+ Jl 10 '89

AIRPLANES, JET—Maintenance and repair—*cont.*

Aloha Airlines probe raises questions about FAA surveillance of maintenance [fuselage failure on Boeing 737 in April 1988] *Aviation Week & Space Technology* 131:77+ Ag 28 '89

American invests in maintenance, overhaul capabilities. C. Fotos. il *Aviation Week & Space Technology* 130:64-5 Jl 10 '89

Congress should avoid undue meddling in U.S. aviation interests abroad [overseas repair regulations] P. Proctor. *Aviation Week & Space Technology* 131:85+ D 18-25 '89

CTA develops new computer system to speed civil aircraft maintenance. B. D. Nordwall. *Aviation Week & Space Technology* 130:153+ Je 19 '89

Debt propelled [effect of takeovers on jet maintenance] J. Greenwald. il *Time* 134:52-3 S 25 '89

Economic impact of aging aircraft fixes remains unclear. C. Fotos. il *Aviation Week & Space Technology* 130:26-7 My 29 '89

FAA cites recurring failures in maintenance at Eastern. J. T. McKenna. *Aviation Week & Space Technology* 131:7, 64-5 Jl 3 '89

How safe are you in the air? A. Ramirez. il *Fortune* 119:75-6 My 22 '89

Industry proposes $800-million program for aging aircraft [with editorial comment] C. Fotos. il *Aviation Week & Space Technology* 129:9, 64-5 Mr 6 '89

Need for international standards on aircraft maintenance is cited. J. T. McKenna. il *Aviation Week & Space Technology* 130:112-13 My 29 '89

New approach to airline safety. W. E. Sheeline. il *Fortune* 119:8 Mr 27 '89

NTSB probes Aloha 737's maintenance records [fuselage failure during April 1988 flight] *Aviation Week & Space Technology* 131:131+ S 11 '89

Old planes, new rules. G. Eichler. il *Esquire* 112:86 N '89

One more reason for fear of flying [need for additional security and maintenance imperils financial outlook] C. Power. il *Business Week* p31 Ja 16 '89

Safety Board examines Aloha's maintenance of aging 737s [investigation of fuselage failure during April 1988 flight] *Aviation Week & Space Technology* 131:117+ S 25 '89

Safety Board urges FAA to revamp maintenance, inspection training [investigation of fuselage failure on Aloha Airlines 737 in April 1988] *Aviation Week & Space Technology* 131:77+ O 23 '89

Tarnished wings [airlines plan to overhaul jets] J. Greenwald. il *Time* 133:40-1 Mr 13 '89

Task force outlines fixes for aging Douglas fleet. C. Fotos. il *Aviation Week & Space Technology* 131:122-3 S 18 '89

Threatened job losses fuel congressional opposition to FAA's foreign repair rules [with editorial comment] M. Mecham. *Aviation Week & Space Technology* 131:7, 29-30 Jl 3 '89

Marketing
See Airplane industry—Marketing

Materials

Airlines evaluate boron/epoxy for repair of aircraft structures. D. Hughes. il *Aviation Week & Space Technology* 130:67+ Jl 10 '89

Composites give wing to new aircraft design. il *Popular Mechanics* 166:16 Ag '89

Soviets using composites in Il-96-300 construction. il *Aviation Week & Space Technology* 130:307 Je 12 '89

Piloting
See also
Air navigation

Propellers

Douglas prepares to flight test PW-Allison propfan powerplant. il *Aviation Week & Space Technology* 130:35 Ja 2 '89

Experimental PW-Allison propfan begins flight testing [ultrahigh bypass engine] W. B. Scott. il *Aviation Week & Space Technology* 130:63-4 Ap 17 '89

Experimental tractor propfan flight tested on Ilyushin Il-76. il *Aviation Week & Space Technology* 130:51 Je 5 '89

NASA will extend propfan test assessment program. *Aviation Week & Space Technology* 130:31 F 6 '89

Safety devices and measures
See also
Airplanes, Jet—Inspection
Airplanes, Jet—Maintenance and repair

The case for safer seats. il *Time* 134:20 Ag 7 '89

Detecting threats to airplane safety. S. Garfinkel. il *Technology Review* 92:10+ F/Mr '89

Far Eastern Air Transport of Taiwan reduces flying hours of older 737s. J. Ott. il *Aviation Week & Space Technology* 130:68 My 8 '89

Growing old gracefully: are aging aircraft safe? H. Gieseking. il *Travel Holiday* 171:75-6 Je '89

Horror in the skies [aging fleet; cover story] W. Hoffer. il *Popular Mechanics* 166:67-70+ Je '89

Keeping kids safer on planes [safety seats] B. Weinhouse. *Redbook* 174:132 N '89

The killer compliance gap. *Aviation Week & Space Technology* 129:9 Mr 6 '89

Sure, the plane is old—but is it dangerous? S. Payne. il *Business Week* p36 Mr 13 '89

Seats

The case for safer seats. il *Time* 134:20 Ag 7 '89

Keeping kids safer on planes [safety seats] B. Weinhouse. *Redbook* 174:132 N '89

Specifications
See Airplanes—Specifications

Stability and stabilizers

NTSB receives reports of 737 trim problems [investigation of crash of USAir Flight 5050 at LaGuardia Airport] *Aviation Week & Space Technology* 131:73 N 13 '89

NTSB seeks to verify reports of 737 rudder trim problems [probe of USAir Flight 5050 crash at LaGuardia Airport] *Aviation Week & Space Technology* 131:69 O 23 '89

Stalling

Frost bite [crash of Continental DC-9 at Denver in 1987] P. Garrison. *Flying* 116:122+ Jl '89

Stalling for time [compressor stall on 747 during takeoff in strong crosswinds] J. Kulski. il *Flying* 116:110 My '89

Standards

Allison engine chosen for Saab 2000; Sweden certifies Saab 340B transport. il *Aviation Week & Space Technology* 131:29 Jl 17 '89

Dornier freezes DO. 328 design; joint certification effort planned [regional turboprop transport] il *Aviation Week & Space Technology* 131:36 Jl 3 '89

Take-off

Douglas asks NTSB to reopen probe of Northwest MD-82 crash [charging that pilots disconnected warning system that could have prevented August 1987 crash in Detroit] C. Fotos. *Aviation Week & Space Technology* 130:106 My 1 '89

NASA develops system to monitor aircraft performance on takeoff. J. T. McKenna. il *Aviation Week & Space Technology* 131:43+ N 13 '89

Pushed to the limit [crash of Fairchild Metro III at Raleigh-Durham International Airport] P. Garrison. *Flying* 116:26+ O '89

Sins of omission [Detroit crash of Northwest MD-82 blamed on failure to set wing slats and flaps for takeoff] J. M. McClellan. *Flying* 116:26-7 F '89

Testing

Boeing 737-500 rolled out; first flight set for June 30. il *Aviation Week & Space Technology* 130:163 Je 19 '89

Czech regional transport designed for rugged operations [LET L610] J. M. Lenorovitz. il *Aviation Week & Space Technology* 130:96 F 13 '89

Douglas prepares initial MD-11 for first flight. il *Aviation Week & Space Technology* 131:19 O 23 '89

Flight testing of Il-96-300 transport on schedule for certification in 1990 [Soviet aircraft] il *Aviation Week & Space Technology* 131:45 Jl 3 '89

Tupolev Tu-204, Ilyushin Il-96-300 undergo pre-Paris Show flight tests [Soviet transports] il *Aviation Week & Space Technology* 130:89 Je 5 '89

Tupolev Tu-204 inspected before leaving for Paris. il *Aviation Week & Space Technology* 130:309 Je 12 '89

Used airplanes
See Airplanes, Used

Wings

NASA tests indicate heavy rainfall can reduce lift at high angles of attack. E. H. Phillips. il *Aviation Week & Space Technology* 131:64-5 Ag 28 '89

NASA will study heavy rain effects on wing aerodynamics [cover story] E. H. Phillips. il *Aviation Week & Space Technology* 130:38-9+ F 13 '89

AIRPLANES, LIGHT
See also
Airplanes, Aerobatic
Airplanes, Business
Airplanes, Home-built
Human powered aircraft

The little yellow airplane [boy's first flight in Piper Cub] J. Doub. il *Reader's Digest* 135:197-8+ O '89

Automobile combinations
See Aerocars

Certification
See Airplanes, Light—Standards

Design

Aerodis America designing light jet trainer, tactical aircraft. E. H. Phillips. il *Aviation Week & Space Technology* 130:39+ Je 26 '89

Grummans to purr again [Grumman American line] K. Connes. il *Flying* 116:11-12 Ag '89

Lawsuit against Rutans could test liability of designers, test pilots [filed by Aviation Composites Co.] *Aviation Week & Space Technology* 130:61 Ja 23 '89

Electric generators

The sun also sets [Cessna 172] D. Froseth. il *Flying* 116:138-9 N '89

Engines
See Airplane engines

Inspection

Once-over annually. J. M. McClellan. il *Flying* 116:38-40 D '89

AIRPLANES, LIGHT—cont.

Instrument flying

See Aviation—Instrument flying

Landing

Err of expectancy [failure to respond to unexpected developments] P. Garrison. il *Flying* 116:62-5 Ja '89

Forced field [Musketeer's fuel tank runs dry] D. Kraft. il *Flying* 116:134 Ag '89

Grass routes [flying across the nation landing only on dirt and turf] R. Munson. il *Flying* 116:62-3+ O '89

Grave expectations [flying an approach into low IFR weather] J. M. McClellan. il *Flying* 116:39-40 O '89

Greaser is the word. J. M. McClellan. il *Flying* 116:78-9 Ap '89

Ice lander [landing Cherokee 140 on snow-covered runway] R. Gamm. il *Flying* 116:112 D '89

Self-test pattern. J. M. McClellan. il *Flying* 116:22+ Jl '89

Wind socked [shift in wind results in rough landing] J. Emmerling. il *Flying* 116:102 Ap '89

Landing gear

Gear up [when to retract gear] J. M. McClellan. il *Flying* 116:104 F '89

Maintenance and repair

See also

Airplanes, Light—Inspection

Piloting

Anecdotes, facetiae, satire, etc.

Oh solo mio. A. Harr. il *Flying* 116:86+ D '89

Remodeled airplanes

See Airplanes, Remodeled

Specifications

See Airplanes—Specifications

Speed

All shook up [airspeed in turbulence] J. M. McClellan. il *Flying* 116:106+ N '89

Stalling

Stick to your wings technology: vortex generators [Friday International system] J. M. McClellan. il *Flying* 116:22-3 O '89

Standards

Caravan II [Cessna 406 turbine twin; cover story] J. M. McClellan. il *Flying* 116:38-42+ My '89

Orders mounting for Huskys. il *Flying* 116:16 My '89

Piper's Continental-powered Malibu is beached again [emergency airworthiness directive] il *Flying* 116:18 S '89

Recreational certificate: it's for real. *Flying* 116:10-11 Je '89

Take-off

Beat the heat [high density altitude takeoffs] J. M. McClellan. il *Flying* 116:104-6 Ag '89

Self-test pattern. J. M. McClellan. il *Flying* 116:22+ Jl '89

Takeoff minimums [low-visibility IFR takeoffs] J. M. McClellan. il *Flying* 116:106-7 S '89

Testing

Caravan II [Cessna 406 turbine twin; cover story] J. M. McClellan. il *Flying* 116:38-42+ My '89

The flying eye [Optica] N. Moll. il *Flying* 116:44-7 Mr '89

Optica Scout provides multi-mission capability. E. H. Phillips. il *Aviation Week & Space Technology* 130:44-7 Ja 2 '89

Piper Seneca III. N. Moll. il *Flying* 116:94-8 Ag '89

Piper's Malibu Mirage [cover story] J. M. McClellan. il *Flying* 116:32-6+ Ap '89

Sabre-toothed Mooney [turbocharged Lycoming Sabre] F. George. il *Flying* 116:86-90+ Ag '89

Simply irresistible [Bonanza A36; cover story] J. M. McClellan. il *Flying* 116:46-50+ S '89

Tobago from Tarbes [Aerospatiale Tobago; cover story] W. Garvey. il *Flying* 116:30-2+ Mr '89

Upgraded engine, systems increase Malibu reliability [Malibu Mirage; cover story] E. H. Phillips. il *Aviation Week & Space Technology* 130:36-9+ Mr 27 '89

Used airplanes

See Airplanes, Used

Wings

Stick to your wings technology: vortex generators [Friday International system] J. M. McClellan. il *Flying* 116:22-3 O '89

AIRPLANES, MILITARY

See also

Airplanes, Training

Remotely piloted vehicles

Space vehicles—Launching from airplanes

Spaceplane

Stealth aircraft

Irresistible force [Stealth, B-52 and B-1 bombers; cover story] T. H. Cole. il *Popular Mechanics* 166:59-62 O '89

Accidents

See Aviation—Accidents

Armaments

See also

Guided missiles—Launching from airplanes

Budget cuts, cost growth cloud F-16 plans for 1990s. D. F. Bond. *Aviation Week & Space Technology* 131:18-19 D 4 '89

Close air support move in Congress might disrupt production of F-16. D. F. Bond and J. D. Morrocco. il *Aviation Week & Space Technology* 131:22-4 N 13 '89

Congress eases F-16 production curbs; Pentagon debates CAS responsibilities [close air support] D. F. Bond. *Aviation Week & Space Technology* 131:32 N 20 '89

Defense Dept. plans CAS review; Congress seeks upgrades agreement [close air support] D. F. Bond. il *Aviation Week & Space Technology* 131:31-3 S 11 '89

Pentagon proposes testing plan to resolve CAS aircraft dispute [close air support] J. D. Morrocco. *Aviation Week & Space Technology* 130:97+ F 20 '89

Rockwell's loss on AC-130U estimated at $81 million [gunship program] *Aviation Week & Space Technology* 130:265 Mr 20 '89

TAC demonstration bolsters support for F-16 in CAS role [close air support] C. A. Shifrin. il *Aviation Week & Space Technology* 130:49-50 Ap 17 '89

USAF to accept plan on modifying F-16, A-10 for close air support. *Aviation Week & Space Technology* 130:28 Mr 13 '89

Cockpits

Changing combat aircraft cockpits reflect evolution in role of pilots. D. M. North. il *Aviation Week & Space Technology* 131:102-4 D 18-25 '89

Mikoyan Design Group upgrading MiG-29 with fly-by-wire controls, new cockpit. il *Aviation Week & Space Technology* 130:81 Je 5 '89

Simulator, flight tests validate integrated pictorial cockpit display. W. B. Scott. il *Aviation Week & Space Technology* 130:51+ Ja 9 '89

TA-4K Skyhawk with production version of digital cockpit tested in New Zealand. il *Aviation Week & Space Technology* 131:63 Ag 7 '89

Control

See also

Airplanes, Military—Stability and stabilizers

Computers—Aviation use

Air Force, NASA conduct tests to define fighter aircraft agility. W. B. Scott. il *Aviation Week & Space Technology* 130:45+ Ja 9 '89

F-16C/D high angle of attack instability overcome by flight control modifications. W. B. Scott. il *Aviation Week & Space Technology* 131:61+ N 13 '89

Speed ain't everything [Harrier] il *U.S. News & World Report* 106:58 F 20 '89

Turning on a dime—in midair [vectored thrust engine provides enhanced maneuverability] W. J. Cook. il *U.S. News & World Report* 106:56-8 F 20 '89

X-31: how they're inventing a radical new way to fly [cover story] J. L. Schefter. il *Popular Science* 234:58-64 F '89

Costs

Additional P-7A design work may cost Lockheed $300 million. il *Aviation Week & Space Technology* 131:22-3 N 27 '89

Budget cuts, cost growth cloud F-16 plans for 1990s. D. F. Bond. *Aviation Week & Space Technology* 131:18-19 D 4 '89

Budget pressures forcing USAF to ease requirements for ATF [advanced tactical fighter] J. D. Morrocco. *Aviation Week & Space Technology* 131:23+ Ag 28 '89

Close air support move in Congress might disrupt production of F-16. D. F. Bond and J. D. Morrocco. il *Aviation Week & Space Technology* 131:22-4 N 13 '89

Conferees approve substantial funding for ATF program, cut C-17 appropriations. P. A. Gilmartin. *Aviation Week & Space Technology* 131:33 N 20 '89

Congress eases F-16 production curbs; Pentagon debates CAS responsibilities [close air support] D. F. Bond. *Aviation Week & Space Technology* 131:32 N 20 '89

Heard on the Street [Wall Street defense watchers] L. Feinstein. il *Common Cause Magazine* 15:12-15 Jl/Ag '89

House appropriation action signals trouble for ATF, advanced cruise missiles. P. A. Gilmartin. *Aviation Week & Space Technology* 131:27-8 Ag 7 '89

House defense leader attacks Air Force plan to add $1.4 billion to B-1B program [L. Aspin] P. A. Gilmartin. *Aviation Week & Space Technology* 130:31 My 29 '89

House panel backs plan to cancel V-22, F-14D. P. A. Gilmartin and D. F. Bond. il *Aviation Week & Space Technology* 130:28-9 Je 26 '89

Naval aviation modernization hit hard by Pentagon cuts. *Aviation Week & Space Technology* 130:23 Ap 24 '89

No-growth budget would force cuts in USAF tactical programs. P. A. Gilmartin. il *Aviation Week & Space Technology* 130:93+ F 20 '89

Panel boosts conventional weapons spending, cuts strategic bomber funds. P. A. Gilmartin. *Aviation Week & Space Technology* 130:19-20 Jl 10 '89

Shakeout. H. Banks. il *Forbes* 143:114-15+ My 1 '89

Stop B-1B bashing. *Aviation Week & Space Technology* 130:9 Ap 3 '89

USAF will begin full-scale development of new F-16 aircraft in fiscal 1990-91. P. A. Gilmartin. il *Aviation Week & Space Technology* 130:20 Ja 16 '89

What is the Air Force really worried about: national security or job security? G. Easterbrook. *The Washington Monthly* 21:18-20+ S '89

Design

Ayres Corp. developing low-cost, multimission Vigilante aircraft. E. H. Phillips. il *Aviation Week & Space Technology* 131:52-3 S 4 '89

AIRPLANES, MILITARY—Design—*cont.*

Britain, U.S. narrow candidates for ASTOVL propulsion system [advanced short takeoff/vertical landing combat aircraft] il *Aviation Week & Space Technology* 129:25 Mr 6 '89

Defense Dept. plans CAS review; Congress seeks upgrades agreement [close air support] D. F. Bond. il *Aviation Week & Space Technology* 131:31-3 S 11 '89

Delays in Navy ATF program bolster case for F-14D. J. D. Morrocco. il *Aviation Week & Space Technology* 131:30-1 S 4 '89

U.S. firm claims modified F-16 could match Su-27 'Cobra' maneuver [Eidetics International] M. A. Dornheim. il *Aviation Week & Space Technology* 131:54-5 Ag 14 '89

USAF plans no major changes to A-12 engines, airframe. *Aviation Week & Space Technology* 131:25 Ag 14 '89

USAF to accept plan on modifying F-16, A-10 for close air support. *Aviation Week & Space Technology* 130:28 Mr 13 '89

Why not take the X-29 to Farnborough? *Aviation Week & Space Technology* 131:9 S 25 '89

Electronic equipment

See also
Air navigation—Aids and devices
Airplanes, Military—Radar equipment
Computers—Aviation use

Airborne Optical Adjunct program threatened with cancellation. P. A. Gilmartin. *Aviation Week & Space Technology* 131:24 Ag 21 '89

Boeing 720B testbed begins new phase of avionic evaluations. P. J. Klass. il *Aviation Week & Space Technology* 131:50-1 N 6 '89

Boeing modifies 720B to serve as advanced avionics testbed. B. W. Henderson. il *Aviation Week & Space Technology* 130:83-5+ Mr 27 '89

Breaking away [Ovonic Imaging Systems] R. Reiff. il por *Forbes* 144:132+ D 25 '89

Changing combat aircraft cockpits reflect evolution in role of pilots. D. M. North. il *Aviation Week & Space Technology* 131:102-4 D 18-25 '89

Coast Guard uses Hu-25 Flir, radar to detect smugglers. il *Aviation Week & Space Technology* 130:42+ Ja 30 '89

Congress permits B-1B electronic countermeasures modifications, but imposes strict controls. il *Aviation Week & Space Technology* 131:24 N 13 '89

Electronic warfare (I) [cover story; special section; with editorial comment] il *Aviation Week & Space Technology* 131:19, 44-7+ S 11 '89

Electronic warfare (II) [cover story; special section] il *Aviation Week & Space Technology* 131:18 S 18 '89

Falcon Eye Flir, GEC helmet aid F-16 mission flexibility [cover story] W. B. Scott. il *Aviation Week & Space Technology* 130:34-6+ Ap 17 '89

Flight testing of new ILS display format to begin; enhanced B-1B software could fly in December. *Aviation Week & Space Technology* 130:21 Ap 3 '89

Lockheed establishes military avionics unit in Sanders affiliate. D. Hughes. il *Aviation Week & Space Technology* 130:92-3+ Ap 24 '89

Marine OV-10Ds with Flir systems detect, track aircraft smuggling narcotics into southeast U.S. [forward-looking infrared systems] *Aviation Week & Space Technology* 130:49 Jl 10 '89

Navy chooses LCD technology for new A-12 color displays. B. D. Nordwall. il *Aviation Week & Space Technology* 131:56-7 S 4 '89

Pilots sense attitude with peripheral vision using new Garrett display. B. D. Nordwall. il *Aviation Week & Space Technology* 130:97+ My 8 '89

Royal Air Force completing tests of upgraded avionics for A-4s [New Zealand] il *Aviation Week & Space Technology* 130:51 F 6 '89

Simulator, flight tests validate integrated pictorial cockpit display. W. B. Scott. il *Aviation Week & Space Technology* 130:51+ Ja 9 '89

TA-4K Skyhawk with production version of digital cockpit tested in New Zealand. il *Aviation Week & Space Technology* 131:63 Ag 7 '89

USAF seeks less risk in ATF avionics suite development [advanced tactical fighter] B. D. Nordwall. *Aviation Week & Space Technology* 130:21 Ja 30 '89

Engines
See Airplane engines, Jet

Escape devices

Soviet K-36 ejection seat has wide operating range. il *Aviation Week & Space Technology* 130:34 Je 19 '89

USAF, Sandia developing new parachute system for F-111 crew escape module. il *Aviation Week & Space Technology* 129:54-5 Mr 6 '89

Export-import trade
See Airplane industry—Export-import trade

Fires and fire prevention

Sukhoi incorporates changes to Su-25 based on Afghan combat experience. il *Aviation Week & Space Technology* 130:31 Je 19 '89

Flaps

Forward flap lifts fighters. M. DiChristina. il *Popular Science* 235:83 Jl '89

NASA Langley expands flight envelope of F-106B equipped with vortex flaps. E. H. Phillips. il *Aviation Week & Space Technology* 130:22-3 Je 5 '89

History

See also
Enola Gay (Airplane)

Ghost story [World War II aircraft of Confederate Air Force] N. Moll. il *Flying* 116:68-72+ F '89

Landing

Flight testing of new ILS display format to begin; enhanced B-1B software could fly in December. *Aviation Week & Space Technology* 130:21 Ap 3 '89

Restricted instrument landing systems hamper B-1B crews, crash documents show [November 1988 crash at Ellsworth AFB] B. M. Greeley, Jr. *Aviation Week & Space Technology* 130:29 F 6 '89

USAF investigators report on crash that destroyed B-1B on approach [November 1988 crash at Ellsworth AFB] *Aviation Week & Space Technology* 129:72-3 Mr 6 '89

Landing gear
Defects

Emergency landing damage on B-1B limited to radome, bulkhead, engines. W. B. Scott. il *Aviation Week & Space Technology* 131:43+ O 30 '89

Landing on carriers

Five die on Lexington as student pilot crashes. *Aviation Week & Space Technology* 131:31 N 6 '89

Soviet aircraft conduct flight trials from new, large-deck carrier Tbilisi. il *Aviation Week & Space Technology* 131:113 D 18-25 '89

Maintenance and repair

B-1Bs achieving higher utilization rate as fleet reaches maturity. D. M. North. il *Aviation Week & Space Technology* 130:272-3 Je 12 '89

Bristol remanufacturing Canadian Forces F-5s. il *Aviation Week & Space Technology* 131:60+ N 27 '89

USAF expects robotic inspection facility to cut maintenance costs. B. W. Henderson. il *Aviation Week & Space Technology* 130:53-5+ Mr 13 '89

Materials

A-6E with composite wing begins flight test program. B. M. Greeley. il *Aviation Week & Space Technology* 130:28 Ap 10 '89

Computer-controlled drill designed to meet unique B-2 fabrication needs. il *Aviation Week & Space Technology* 130:51-2 Ap 17 '89

Lockheed nears completion of work on new Palmdale composite facility. il *Aviation Week & Space Technology* 130:26 My 1 '89

New tape laying machine eases preparation of thermoplastic material. il *Aviation Week & Space Technology* 131:83 S 18 '89

Westinghouse developing 'smart skin' technology. il *Aviation Week & Space Technology* 130:284 Je 12 '89

Noise

Military sonic booms shake Fort Jefferson. il *National Parks* 63:10-11 Mr/Ap '89

Radar equipment

Britain accepting fraction of Boeing's offset claims [purchase of E-3A Airborne Warning and Control System aircraft] D. A. Brown. il *Aviation Week & Space Technology* 131:76-7 Jl 17 '89

Coast Guard radar images are key to tracking oil spill [Alaska] il *Aviation Week & Space Technology* 130:18 Ap 10 '89

Coast Guard uses Hu-25 Flir, radar to detect smugglers. il *Aviation Week & Space Technology* 130:42+ Ja 30 '89

Customs integrates P-3B Orion into surveillance aircraft fleet [narcotics regulations] il *Aviation Week & Space Technology* 130:53 Ja 30 '89

Disagreement between Britain, Germany over radar could threaten EFA's future [European fighter aircraft] *Aviation Week & Space Technology* 130:21 F 20 '89

Eaton to propose $600 million modification to ALQ-161 system [B-1B] *Aviation Week & Space Technology* 130:75+ Je 26 '89

Electronic warfare (I) [cover story; special section; with editorial comment] il *Aviation Week & Space Technology* 131:19, 44-7+ S 11 '89

Grumman prepares for flight tests of advanced capability EA-6B. S. W. Kandebo. il *Aviation Week & Space Technology* 131:41+ S 25 '89

Grumman to roll out new Navy tactical electronic warfare aircraft next month [EA-6B ADVCAP] il *Aviation Week & Space Technology* 131:32 S 11 '89

Hughes/AEL team wins Navy contract for upgraded radar warning receiver. B. W. Henderson. il *Aviation Week & Space Technology* 131:60-1 Ag 28 '89

IAI develops low-cost, long-range Phalcon airborne early warning system. D. A. Brown. il *Aviation Week & Space Technology* 130:54-5 Je 19 '89

ITT Avionics emphasizes development of software, improves electronic system. B. D. Nordwall. il *Aviation Week & Space Technology* 131:83+ Jl 17 '89

Loral to produce advanced radar warning systems for USAF. *Aviation Week & Space Technology* 130:34 Ja 2 '89

Need to detect signals instantly spurs call for digital components. il *Aviation Week & Space Technology* 131:104-5 S 18 '89

AIRPLANES, MILITARY—Radar equipment—*cont.*

New type of phased-array antenna could cut cost, weight of airborne systems [Sedco Systems] il *Aviation Week & Space Technology* 131:105+ S 18 '89

Pentagon awards production contracts for ALQ-165 to ITT, Westinghouse [airborne self-protection jammer] P. J. Klass. il *Aviation Week & Space Technology* 131:59+ O 16 '89

R & D work in low observables shifts emphasis from coatings to structures. il *Aviation Week & Space Technology* 131:109+ S 18 '89

Rockwell declines AIL deal due to plan's complexity [plan to acquire AIL subsidiary of Eaton Corp. to expedite fixes to B-1B bomber's ALQ-161 system] *Aviation Week & Space Technology* 130:67 F 6 '89

Rockwell working with AIL to develop B-1B avionics fix. *Aviation Week & Space Technology* 130:101+ Ja 2 '89

Sanders develops MMIC for phased array systems [monolithic microwave integrated circuit device] *Aviation Week & Space Technology* 130:291 Je 12 '89

Stealth/counter-Stealth technologies [cover story; special section] il *Aviation Week & Space Technology* 131:38-42 D 4 '89

Tests to verify airworthiness of new ES-3A configuration. B. D. Nordwall. il *Aviation Week & Space Technology* 131:36-7+ S 25 '89

Tomcat 21 will include technologies to reduce F-14's radar signature. J. D. Morrocco. il *Aviation Week & Space Technology* 130:30-1 My 22 '89

USAF building new anechoic chamber capable of accommodating B-1, B-2. W. B. Scott. il *Aviation Week & Space Technology* 130:55+ F 27 '89

USAF says F-15E integration problems may delay initial operating capability [ALQ-135 jammer] P. A. Gilmartin. *Aviation Week & Space Technology* 130:21 My 15 '89

USAF studies linking phased array radar with fiber-optic cable. *Aviation Week & Space Technology* 130:61+ Ja 30 '89

USAF to buy used Boeing 707s for use as Joint STARS platforms [Surveillance Target Attack Radar System] P. A. Gilmartin. *Aviation Week & Space Technology* 131:25 N 13 '89

USAF will develop major radar upgrade for its E-3 AWACS fleet. D. Hughes. il *Aviation Week & Space Technology* 130:45+ Ja 23 '89

USAF will use stand-alone radar warning system to shore up B-1B's EW capabilities. *Aviation Week & Space Technology* 130:101 Ja 2 '89

Westinghouse developing 'smart skin' technology. il *Aviation Week & Space Technology* 130:284 Je 12 '89

Westinghouse mounts effort to build entire jammer on single Ga-As wafer. il *Aviation Week & Space Technology* 131:102 S 18 '89

Defects

GAO cites faulty test equipment for hampering EW system readiness [Air Force's electronic warfare systems] B. D. Nordwall. il *Aviation Week & Space Technology* 131:133+ O 9 '89

The Navy: that blip on the screen may be a blooper [Airborne Self-Protection Jammer] D. Griffiths. *Business Week* p43 O 2 '89

Remodeled airplanes
See Airplanes, Remodeled

Safety devices and measures
See also
Airplanes, Military—Escape devices

Specifications
See Airplanes—Specifications

Stability and stabilizers
B-1B stability enhancement tests verify low-level mission capability. W. B. Scott. il *Aviation Week & Space Technology* 130:34-5 Je 26 '89

Stalling
Soviets say engine stall caused crash of MiG-29 at Le Bourget [Paris Air Show] il *Aviation Week & Space Technology* 130:32-3 Je 19 '89

Tails
Defects
E-6A empennage fails during tests of change to correct earlier problem. il *Aviation Week & Space Technology* 131:33 O 9 '89

E-6A loses third of tail in dive test. *Aviation Week & Space Technology* 130:26 F 27 '89

E-6A Tacamo tail damage prompts delivery delay [submarine communications aircraft] M. A. Dornheim. il *Aviation Week & Space Technology* 130:28-9 Ap 17 '89

Testing
See also
Military maneuvers

A-6E with composite wing begins flight test program. B. M. Greeley. il *Aviation Week & Space Technology* 130:28 Ap 10 '89

Air Force, NASA conduct tests to define fighter aircraft agility. W. B. Scott. il *Aviation Week & Space Technology* 130:45+ Ja 9 '89

B-1B stability enhancement tests verify low-level mission capability. W. B. Scott. il *Aviation Week & Space Technology* 130:34-5 Je 26 '89

Bird of prey [F-16 fighter] T. H. Cole. il *Popular Mechanics* 166:70-2+ Jl '89

F-14 maintains supersonic cruise without afterburner in tests. S. W. Kandebo. *Aviation Week & Space Technology* 131:45 O 30 '89

F-15 S/MTD makes first flight with 2D exhaust nozzles. S. W. Kandebo. il *Aviation Week & Space Technology* 130:18 My 15 '89

Flight tests of Gripen to resume this year [new control logic devised to correct flaw in flight control system software] *Aviation Week & Space Technology* 130:64 Je 26 '89

GAO criticizes Defense Dept. testing of aircraft for bird strikes. *Aviation Week & Space Technology* 131:62-3 Ag 7 '89

Gripen crash delays flight test program. il *Aviation Week & Space Technology* 130:22 F 13 '89

Grumman prepares for flight tests of advanced capability EA-6B. S. W. Kandebo. il *Aviation Week & Space Technology* 131:41+ S 25 '89

Modified F-15B to demonstrate STOL, maneuver capability [cover story] S. W. Kandebo. il *Aviation Week & Space Technology* 130:44-5+ My 29 '89

NASA adds to understanding of high angle of attack regime [cover story] W. B. Scott. il *Aviation Week & Space Technology* 130:36-8+ My 22 '89

Pentagon proposes testing plan to resolve CAS aircraft dispute [close air support] J. D. Morrocco. *Aviation Week & Space Technology* 130:97+ F 20 '89

Planned Air Force electronic warfare range would be used to test B-2, ATF. il *Aviation Week & Space Technology* 131:58-9 S 11 '89

R&D unit boosts RAAF capabilities through tightly run test programs [Royal Australian Air Force] P. Proctor. il *Aviation Week & Space Technology* 130:41-2 F 6 '89

Second X-29 completes initial checks prior to high angle of attack flights. W. B. Scott. il *Aviation Week & Space Technology* 131:39 S 18 '89

Soviets let Canadian CF-18 pilot fly MiG-29 trainer at air show [pilot B. Wade at Airshow Canada] il *Aviation Week & Space Technology* 131:32 Ag 21 '89

TAC demonstration bolsters support for F-16 in CAS role [close air support] C. A. Shifrin. il *Aviation Week & Space Technology* 130:49-50 Ap 17 '89

Tests to verify airworthiness of new ES-3A configuration. B. D. Nordwall. il *Aviation Week & Space Technology* 131:36-7+ S 25 '89

Upgrades of OV-10s will extend aircraft's service life into 1990s [Marine Corps aircraft] W. B. Scott. il *Aviation Week & Space Technology* 130:40-1+ Jl 10 '89

USAF building new anechoic chamber capable of accommodating B-1, B-2. W. B. Scott. il *Aviation Week & Space Technology* 130:55+ F 27 '89

USAF, McDonnell Douglas prepare to deploy F-15E for winter testing. W. B. Scott. il *Aviation Week & Space Technology* 130:79+ Ja 2 '89

USAF says B-2's range exceeds B-1B's with varied payloads, flight profiles. D. F. Bond. *Aviation Week & Space Technology* 131:30-1 O 23 '89

USAF testing electronic warfare systems in new anechoic chamber. il *Aviation Week & Space Technology* 131:81-2 S 11 '89

Wings
A-6E with composite wing begins flight test program. B. M. Greeley. il *Aviation Week & Space Technology* 130:28 Ap 10 '89

Daewoo wins contract to assemble wing panels for Lockheed P-7A. M. A. Dornheim. *Aviation Week & Space Technology* 131:29 S 4 '89

Defects
Air Force grounds B-1B fleet following wing cycling problem. il *Aviation Week & Space Technology* 130:21-2 Ap 3 '89

USAF, contractor investigations cite two parts in B-1B wingsweep failure that damaged fuel tank. *Aviation Week & Space Technology* 130:30 Ap 17 '89

USAF, LTV probe wing cracks that grounded Air Guard A-7s. E. H. Phillips. il *Aviation Week & Space Technology* 130:29-30 My 29 '89

Wrecking
Ghost story [demolition of U.S. aircraft at end of World War II] J. Myers. il *Flying* 116:70-2+ F '89

Australia
Military preparedness in the South Pacific: Australia [cover story; special section] il map *Aviation Week & Space Technology* 130:34-5+ F 6 '89

Belgium
General Dynamics alters marketing as Europeans focus on F-16 upgrades. il *Aviation Week & Space Technology* 130:57+ F 13 '89

Brazil
Brazilian Air Force to accept first production AMX in August. E. H. Kolcum. il *Aviation Week & Space Technology* 130:87 Mr 20 '89

Embraer AMX production on schedule; second, third aircraft in final assembly. il *Aviation Week & Space Technology* 131:66 S 4 '89

AIRPLANES, MILITARY—*cont.*

Canada

Bristol remanufacturing Canadian Forces F-5s. il *Aviation Week & Space Technology* 131:60+ N 27 '89

China

Chengdu Aircraft Corp. builds export F-7M, upgraded F-7-3. il *Aviation Week & Space Technology* 131:82-3 D 11 '89

China modernizes military aircraft in atmosphere of fiscal austerity. il *Aviation Week & Space Technology* 131:55+ D 11 '89

Chinese find little interest in F-8 fighter at Paris. il *Aviation Week & Space Technology* 130:37 Je 19 '89

France

Britain, France raise concerns about cuts in combat aircraft. il *Aviation Week & Space Technology* 130:20 Je 5 '89

Dassault nears end of production on two Mirage fighter versions. il *Aviation Week & Space Technology* 131:66 N 13 '89

Germany (West)

RAF, German Air Force jets collide over Germany. K. F. Mordoff. *Aviation Week & Space Technology* 130:29 Ja 23 '89

U.S., West Germany may delay P-7 agreement until September [Lockheed antisubmarine warfare aircraft] J. D. Morrocco. il *Aviation Week & Space Technology* 130:62 Je 19 '89

Great Britain

Britain accepting fraction of Boeing's offset claims [purchase of E-3A Airborne Warning and Control System aircraft] D. A. Brown. il *Aviation Week & Space Technology* 131:76-7 Jl 17 '89

Britain, France raise concerns about cuts in combat aircraft. il *Aviation Week & Space Technology* 130:20 Je 5 '89

Britain to get airborne INF. M. Flournoy. *The Bulletin of the Atomic Scientists* 45:4 Jl/Ag '89

Britain, U.S. narrow candidates for ASTOVL propulsion system [advanced short takeoff/vertical landing combat aircraft] il *Aviation Week & Space Technology* 129:25 Mr 6 '89

RAF, German Air Force jets collide over Germany. K. F. Mordoff. *Aviation Week & Space Technology* 130:29 Ja 23 '89

Israel

IAI develops low-cost, long-range Phalcon airborne early warning system. D. A. Brown. il *Aviation Week & Space Technology* 130:54-5 Je 19 '89

Snecma to deliver Atar 9K50 powerplants for use in prototypes of upgraded Kfir. il *Aviation Week & Space Technology* 131:19 O 30 '89

Italy

Italy approves naval use of fixed-wing aircraft [short take-off/vertical landing aircraft] il *Aviation Week & Space Technology* 130:21 F 6 '89

Japan

Bush approves FS-X codevelopment, but Japan must accept new terms. M. Mecham. *Aviation Week & Space Technology* 130:22 Mr 27 '89

Bush wins victory on FS-X development despite Senate anger on Japanese trade. M. Mecham. *Aviation Week & Space Technology* 130:31 My 22 '89

Can the Pentagon keep shielding Japan? [FSX co-development deal] P. Magnusson. il *Business Week* p47-8 Mr 27 '89

A deal that nearly came undone [U.S. agrees to help Japan build the FSX jet] C. Gorman. il *Time* 133:70-1 Mr 27 '89

Friend or foe? [FSX deal symbolic of strain in relations between the U.S. and Japan] J. Greenwald. il *Time* 133:44-5 Ap 24 '89

The FS-X question [U.S.-Japanese codevelopment] *National Review* 41:14-16 Ap 21 '89

The FSX and Japan's strategy for aerospace. R. J. Samuels and B. C. Whipple. il *Technology Review* 92:42-51 O '89

FSX coproduction prohibition disapproved by president [letter to the Senate, July 31, 1989] G. Bush. *Department of State Bulletin* 89:32 O '89

Japan bashing bashes the United States [agreement on FSX] C. W. Weinberger. il *Forbes* 143:31 Mr 20 '89

Japan unlikely to parlay FSX work into civilian aircraft leadership role. C. Leader. por *Aviation Week & Space Technology* 130:97+ Mr 27 '89

Japan's FS-X puzzle [U.S. government's decision to defer approval of plan to share F-16 technology with Japan] *Aviation Week & Space Technology* 130:9 F 27 '89

A 'little old agreement' on the F-16 [FSX deal between General Dynamics and Mitsubishi Heavy Industries] *Newsweek* 113:34 Ja 30 '89

Pentagon, Commerce at impasse on FS-X after deal falls apart [sharing F-16 technology with Japan] M. Mecham. *Aviation Week & Space Technology* 130:28 Mr 13 '89

The plane drain: the FSX deal and other transfers of technology. H. D. Bentley. il por *Conservative Digest* 15:54-7 Jl/Ag '89

Revised FS-X pact eases trade, technology concerns [U.S./Japan fighter codevelopment] J. D. Morrocco. il *Aviation Week & Space Technology* 130:16-18 My 8 '89

Senate bolsters Commerce Dept.'s authority in reviewing cooperative arms agreements. J. D. Morrocco. *Aviation Week & Space Technology* 131:28 Ag 7 '89

Technology concerns delay approval of FS-X agreement [sharing F-16 technology with Japan] M. Mecham. il *Aviation Week & Space Technology* 130:16-17 F 20 '89

U.S., Japan agree to codevelop FSX aircraft [statements, April 28 and May 3, 1989] G. Bush; L. S. Eagleburger. *Department of State Bulletin* 89:48-9 Jl '89

Jordan

Deficit woes prompt Jordan to postpone Tornado purchase. M. Mecham. *Aviation Week & Space Technology* 130:32-3 Ap 3 '89

Korea (South)

Korea fears U.S. technology transfer opponents could hamper its FX program. J. D. Morrocco. *Aviation Week & Space Technology* 130:23 Ap 3 '89

South Korea: nation at a crossroads [special section] J. D. Morrocco. il maps *Aviation Week & Space Technology* 130:176-7+ Je 12 '89

Libya

Chemical reaction [U.S. fighters shoot down Libyan MiGs] E. Magnuson. il por *Time* 133:18-21 Ja 16 '89

Gunning for Gadhafi [U.S. shoots down two jets and claims Libya will soon make chemical weapons] J. Bierman. il *Maclean's* 102:18-19 Ja 16 '89

Hypocritical warfare [downing of Libyan MiGs and controversy over alleged chemical weapons plant] *The Nation* 248:73 Ja 23 '89

Libya [U.S. downing of two Libyan MiG-23s over the Mediterranean] *Business Week* p50 Ja 16 '89

Libyan planes downed [Defense Dept. statement, January 4, 1989] *Department of State Bulletin* 89:70 Mr '89

Libyan planes fall, questions rise. *America* 160:27 Ja 21 '89

Red mischief [Soviet sale of bombers] *The New Republic* 200:10-11 My 1 '89

Showdown with Libya [cover story; special section] il por *Newsweek* 113:16-25 Ja 16 '89

Soviet sale of Su-24 deepens concern about Mideast weapons proliferation. M. Mecham. il *Aviation Week & Space Technology* 130:19-20 Ap 10 '89

Text deploring downing of Libyan planes vetoed in Security Council: United States calls it 'self-defence'. il *UN Chronicle* 26:33 Je '89

U.S. F-14s down Libyan MiG-23s in dogfight over Mediterranean. B. M. Greeley, Jr. il map *Aviation Week & Space Technology* 130:20-1 Ja 9 '89

U.S. reports to United Nations on downing of Libyan planes [letter and statement, January 4-5, 1989] H. S. Okun. *Department of State Bulletin* 89:90-1 Mr '89

The U.S. vs. Libya. *World Press Review* 36:8 F '89

New Zealand

New Zealand upgrades forces to face low-intensity fighting. P. Proctor. il *Aviation Week & Space Technology* 130:47+ F 6 '89

Royal Air Force completing tests of upgraded avionics for A-4s. il *Aviation Week & Space Technology* 130:51 F 6 '89

TA-4K Skyhawk with production version of digital cockpit tested in New Zealand. il *Aviation Week & Space Technology* 131:63 Ag 7 '89

Pakistan

Proposal to sell F-16s to Pakistan [statement, August 2, 1989] T. Schaffer. *Department of State Bulletin* 89:65-6 O '89

White House sends Pakistan F-16 proposal to Congress. *Aviation Week & Space Technology* 130:42 Je 19 '89

Saudi Arabia

Unit set up to finance Saudi military buys from Britain. *Aviation Week & Space Technology* 131:24 D 4 '89

Soviet Union

See also

Spaceplane, Russian

Agile Sukhoi Su-27 leads strong Soviet presentation [Paris Air Show] il *Aviation Week & Space Technology* 130:28-30 Je 19 '89

Design of Su-25 combines simplicity, survivability [close air support aircraft] il *Aviation Week & Space Technology* 131:43 Jl 3 '89

First Airshow Canada will feature Soviet An-225, MiG-29 aircraft. *Aviation Week & Space Technology* 131:25 Ag 7 '89

Flight rules for future Paris shows unaffected by Soviet MiG-29 crash. il *Aviation Week & Space Technology* 130:36-7 Je 26 '89

MIG-making. B. Weber. il *The New York Times Magazine* p42 Jl 2 '89

Mikoyan Design Group upgrading MiG-29 with fly-by-wire controls, new cockpit. il *Aviation Week & Space Technology* 130:81 Je 5 '89

Pentagon purchases Soviet hardware on open market for operational testing. J. D. Morrocco. il *Aviation Week & Space Technology* 130:24-5 Ja 23 '89

Report from Paris [1989 Paris Air Show] F. Mackerodt. il *Popular Mechanics* 166:54 O '89

Soviet aircraft conduct flight trials from new, large-deck carrier Tbilisi. il *Aviation Week & Space Technology* 131:113 D 18-25 '89

Soviet K-36 ejection seat has wide operating range. il *Aviation Week & Space Technology* 130:34 Je 19 '89

AIRPLANES, MILITARY—Soviet Union—*cont.*

Soviet MiG-29 fighter crashes during flight demonstration [Paris Air Show] il *Aviation Week & Space Technology* 130:60-1 Je 12 '89

Soviets let Canadian CF-18 pilot fly MiG-29 trainer at air show [pilot B. Wade at Airshow Canada] il *Aviation Week & Space Technology* 131:32 Ag 21 '89

Soviets plan high profile at 1989 Paris Air Show [with editorial comment] J. M. Lenorovitz. il map *Aviation Week & Space Technology* 130:15, 44-6+ My 1 '89

Soviets say engine stall caused crash of MiG-29 at Le Bourget [Paris Air Show] il *Aviation Week & Space Technology* 130:32-3 Je 19 '89

Soviets will bring Su-25 Frogfoot to Paris; orbiter may join it. *Aviation Week & Space Technology* 130:22 Ap 17 '89

Sukhoi incorporates changes to Su-25 based on Afghan combat experience. il *Aviation Week & Space Technology* 130:31 Je 19 '89

U.S. firm claims modified F-16 could match Su-27 'Cobra' maneuver [Eidetics International] M. A. Dornheim. il *Aviation Week & Space Technology* 131:54-5 Ag 14 '89

Warsaw Pact unable to track MiG that crashed in Belgium after pilot ejected over Poland. il *Aviation Week & Space Technology* 130:28 Jl 10 '89

Western experts given close-up view of Su-27 [Paris Air Show] il *Aviation Week & Space Technology* 131:37 Jl 3 '89

Sweden

Exports of Gripen could equal sales to Sweden's Air Force. D. A. Brown. il *Aviation Week & Space Technology* 130:73-4 Ja 9 '89

Flight tests of Gripen to resume this year [new control logic devised to correct flaw in flight control system software] *Aviation Week & Space Technology* 130:64 Je 26 '89

Gripen crash delays flight test program. il *Aviation Week & Space Technology* 130:22 F 13 '89

Sweden says JAS-39 Gripen stretchout will boost program's cost by 16%. *Aviation Week & Space Technology* 131:27 O 16 '89

Sweden's first Gripen prototype destroyed in crash on landing. il *Aviation Week & Space Technology* 130:25 F 6 '89

Swedish defense planners seek more funds, cost cuts on Gripen. D. A. Brown. *Aviation Week & Space Technology* 130:25-6 Ja 30 '89

United States
See Airplanes, Military

Western Europe

Bush includes combat aircraft cuts in NATO arms proposal [Brussels summit; special section] il map *Aviation Week & Space Technology* 130:16-21 Je 5 '89

Disagreement between Britain, Germany over radar could threaten EFA's future [European fighter aircraft] *Aviation Week & Space Technology* 130:21 F 20 '89

General Dynamics alters marketing as Europeans focus on F-16 upgrades. il *Aviation Week & Space Technology* 130:57+ F 13 '89

High costs, political rows hinder Europe's combat aircraft programs. D. A. Brown. il *Aviation Week & Space Technology* 130:95-6 Mr 20 '89

NATO weighs air force modernization in light of conventional arms cuts. J. D. Morrocco. il *Aviation Week & Space Technology* 131:29-30 Jl 24 '89

Vienna talks trigger NATO air force review [cover story; special section] J. D. Morrocco. il map *Aviation Week & Space Technology* 131:34-7+ O 30 '89

AIRPLANES, MILITARY TRANSPORT
See also
United States. Civil Reserve Air Fleet

Costs

Conferees approve substantial funding for ATF program, cut C-17 appropriations. P. A. Gilmartin. *Aviation Week & Space Technology* 131:33 N 20 '89

Lockheed weighs investment risks of developing new C-130 version. E. H. Kolcum. il *Aviation Week & Space Technology* 131:45+ N 27 '89

Design

Fairchild delivers first two C-26As to Air National Guard [cover story] C. A. Shifrin. il *Aviation Week & Space Technology* 130:36-7+ Ap 24 '89

Special report: covert aircraft. il *Popular Mechanics* 166:25 Mr '89

Purchasing

USAF may transfer six C-29As, crews to FAA for flight inspection mission. *Aviation Week & Space Technology* 131:108 D 18-25 '89

Testing

AT³ demonstrates feasibility of cargo STOL with long range [advanced technology tactical transport; cover story] W. B. Scott. il *Aviation Week & Space Technology* 131:38-40+ S 4 '89

Future C-130 version may incorporate STOL features and autonomous capability. W. B. Scott. il *Aviation Week & Space Technology* 130:34-5 My 29 '89

Scaled Composites rolls out modified ATTT for DARPA tests [advanced technology tactical transport] il *Aviation Week & Space Technology* 130:30 Ap 17 '89

STOL Scout begins flight tests with Astazou 16 powerplants. W. B. Scott. il *Aviation Week & Space Technology* 130:64 F 13 '89

Western Europe

European companies restructure FIMA transport team. il *Aviation Week & Space Technology* 130:66 Je 12 '89

AIRPLANES, MODEL *See* Airplane models

AIRPLANES, PRIVATE
See also
Airplanes—Private ownership
Private flying

AIRPLANES, RACING

Propellers

Propeller-driven machbuster [B. Montagne trying to break sound barrier in racer with Oldsmobile V8 engine] M. Lamm. il por *Popular Mechanics* 166:48+ Ag '89

AIRPLANES, RECONNAISSANCE *See* Airplanes, Military

AIRPLANES, REMODELED

Bizjet Olympics [competition for Air Force's tanker transport training system contract] W. Garvey. il *Flying* 116:76-9 F '89

Blueprinters [custom overhauls] F. George. il *Flying* 116:66-8+ Ag '89

Boeing modifies 720B to serve as advanced avionics testbed. B. W. Henderson. il *Aviation Week & Space Technology* 130:83-5+ Mr 27 '89

British cargo conversion of TriStar offered to airline operators. D. A. Brown. il *Aviation Week & Space Technology* 131:63+ Ag 21 '89

Gooney squadron [DC-3s refurbished by W. Basler] G. Baxter. il por *Flying* 116:84-6 Mr '89

Liquid-cooled engine mod for 414A. il *Flying* 116:18 F '89

Piper upgrades Commanche, Globe Swift for general aviation, military markets. E. H. Phillips. il *Aviation Week & Space Technology* 130:79+ My 22 '89

Upgrades of OV-10s will extend aircraft's service life into 1990s [Marine Corps aircraft] W. B. Scott. il *Aviation Week & Space Technology* 130:40-1+ Jl 10 '89

USAF releases draft request for bids on tanker-transport training system. *Aviation Week & Space Technology* 130:31 Ap 3 '89

USAF tanker-transport training to stress low and high altitude mission profiles. E. H. Phillips. il *Aviation Week & Space Technology* 130:51-2 My 1 '89

USAF to buy used Boeing 707s for use as Joint STARS platforms [Surveillance Target Attack Radar System] P. A. Gilmartin. *Aviation Week & Space Technology* 131:25 N 13 '89

Testing

Fans fantastique [reengined Falcon 20] F. George. il *Flying* 116:88-90+ O '89

LTV begins flight tests of reengined A-7F for Air Guard mission. D. A. Brown. il *Aviation Week & Space Technology* 131:19-21 D 4 '89

Turbine powerhouse [Soloy Conversions; cover story] N. Moll. il por *Flying* 116:44-8+ O '89

Wolf in RAM's clothing [converted Cessna 414A with liquid-cooled engines] J. M. McClellan. il *Flying* 116:70-6 D '89

AIRPLANES, RESTORED
See also
Confederate Air Force
Paul E. Garber Preservation, Restoration and Storage Facility

AIRPLANES, SHORT TAKE-OFF AND LANDING
See also
Airplanes, Military
Airplanes, Military transport

Design

Snow Aviation is developing short takeoff, landing aircraft. il *Aviation Week & Space Technology* 130:115 F 20 '89

Engines
See Airplane engines, Jet

Testing

STOL Scout begins flight tests with Astazou 16 powerplants. W. B. Scott. il *Aviation Week & Space Technology* 130:64 F 13 '89

AIRPLANES, SHORT TAKE-OFF AND VERTICAL LANDING

Design

Britain, U.S. narrow candidates for ASTOVL propulsion system. il *Aviation Week & Space Technology* 129:25 Mr 6 '89

Italy approves naval use of fixed-wing aircraft. il *Aviation Week & Space Technology* 130:21 F 6 '89

New propulsion schemes give hover planes a lift. il *Popular Mechanics* 166:18 Ag '89

AIRPLANES, SUPERSONIC
See also
Airplanes, Business
Airplanes, Military

Concorde cruising speed [around the world flight] W. F. Buckley. il *National Review* 41:26-8+ My 19 '89

Full circle [Concorde flight around the world] W. F. Buckley. *National Review* 41:37-40 Je 2 '89

The market for transoceanic airliners. T. A. Heppenheimer. il *High Technology Business* 9:22-5 Ja '89

AIRPLANES, SUPERSONIC—*cont.*

Design

Aerospatiale defines Mach 2 Concorde follow-on. *Aviation Week & Space Technology* 131:56 D 4 '89

Bede ayes [designer J. Bede] G. Baxter. il por *Flying* 116:108+ D '89

Boeing upgrades high-speed civil transport study effort. R. G. O'Lone. il *Aviation Week & Space Technology* 130:108 My 22 '89

Homebuilt machbuster [J. Bede's BD-10J; cover story] W. Garvey. il *Popular Mechanics* 166:68-71 D '89

Industry, government join in HSCT research. J. Ott. *Aviation Week & Space Technology* 130:53 My 8 '89

Japan to set up R&D programs on advanced engines, heat-resistant materials for supersonic transport. *Aviation Week & Space Technology* 131:138 O 9 '89

Keep the HSCT on track. *Aviation Week & Space Technology* 131:11 S 18 '89

Lack of U.S. interest derails international HSCT consortium. J. Ott. il *Aviation Week & Space Technology* 131:28-9 S 11 '89

Engines

See Airplane engines, Jet

Environmental aspects

HSCT propulsion studies focus on reducing emissions, noise [cover story] S. W. Kandebo. il *Aviation Week & Space Technology* 130:34-6 Jl 10 '89

HSCT research focuses on environmental issues. J. Ott. il map *Aviation Week & Space Technology* 131:54-6 D 4 '89

Maintenance and repair

Growing up with Concorde: supersonic maintenance. *Flying* 116:14 D '89

Noise

See also
Sonic boom

HSCT propulsion studies focus on reducing emissions, noise [cover story] S. W. Kandebo. il *Aviation Week & Space Technology* 130:34-6 Jl 10 '89

HSCT research focuses on environmental issues. J. Ott. il map *Aviation Week & Space Technology* 131:54-6 D 4 '89

AIRPLANES, TANK *See* Tank airplanes
AIRPLANES, TOY *See* Toys
AIRPLANES, TRAINING

Defects

Navy, McDonnell Douglas agree on modifications to T-45A trainer. *Aviation Week & Space Technology* 131:21 S 25 '89

Team correcting deficiencies in Navy's T-45A trainer aircraft. E. H. Phillips. il *Aviation Week & Space Technology* 131:46-8 O 30 '89

Design

Aerodis America designing light jet trainer, tactical aircraft. E. H. Phillips. il *Aviation Week & Space Technology* 130:39+ Je 26 '89

Bizjet Olympics [competition for Air Force's tanker transport training system contract] W. Garvey. il *Flying* 116:76-9 F '89

Trainer aircraft at Le Bourget geared toward USAF/Navy buy [primary aircraft training system] C. Covault. il *Aviation Week & Space Technology* 130:67+ Je 26 '89

USAF releases draft request for bids on tanker-transport training system. *Aviation Week & Space Technology* 130:31 Ap 3 '89

USAF tanker-transport training to stress low and high altitude mission profiles. E. H. Phillips. il *Aviation Week & Space Technology* 130:51-2 My 1 '89

Electronic equipment

Flight restrictions prompt U.S. Air Force to reassess Lantirn training in Germany. J. D. Morrocco. map *Aviation Week & Space Technology* 131:26-7 O 16 '89

History

Harvard graduate [American receives Royal Canadian Air Force training on AT-6 Harvard during World War II] L. Morgan. il *Flying* 116:82+ F '89

Piloting

Toward pure energy [flying the T-38] L. Gonzales. il *Harper's* 279:72-6 Ag '89

Testing

IA-63 trainer offers smooth handling, expanded envelope [Pampa jet; cover story] B. M. Greeley, Jr. il *Aviation Week & Space Technology* 129:36-9+ Mr 6 '89

Navy to modify T-45A trainers based on operational test flights. B. A. Smith. *Aviation Week & Space Technology* 130:29 Ja 16 '89

Piper upgrades Commanche, Globe Swift for general aviation, military markets [familiarization flight in Swiftfire] E. H. Phillips. il *Aviation Week & Space Technology* 130:79+ My 22 '89

Piper's new Cadet. N. Moll. il *Flying* 116:42-6 Ja '89

Argentina

IA-63 trainer offers smooth handling, expanded envelope [Pampa jet; cover story] B. M. Greeley, Jr. il *Aviation Week & Space Technology* 129:36-9+ Mr 6 '89

China

China uses Trinidad TB-20s to replace aging Y-5 biplanes in pilot training. il *Aviation Week & Space Technology* 131:97 Ag 21 '89

Nanchang developing L-8, N-5A aircraft for international civil market. il *Aviation Week & Space Technology* 131:78+ D 11 '89

Germany (West)

Flight restrictions prompt U.S. Air Force to reassess Lantirn training in Germany. J. D. Morrocco. map *Aviation Week & Space Technology* 131:26-7 O 16 '89

Germany's burden [NATO flight training in German air space] *Aviation Week & Space Technology* 130:9 F 6 '89

NATO tightens limit on training flights to ease West German concerns. *Aviation Week & Space Technology* 131:30 O 2 '89

USAFE study likely to recommend against cutting low-level flights. K. F. Mordoff. il *Aviation Week & Space Technology* 130:95-6 Ja 2 '89

AIRPLANES, USED

Prices

Budget flight. F. Mackerodt. il *Popular Mechanics* 166:54+ Ap '89

Purchasing

Big iron [corporate chieftans buy used jets] il *Forbes* 144:324-5 N 13 '89

In from the cold. W. Garvey. il *Flying* 116:8-9 S '89

USAF to buy used Boeing 707s for use as Joint STARS platforms [Surveillance Target Attack Radar System] P. A. Gilmartin. *Aviation Week & Space Technology* 131:25 N 13 '89

Used, or abused? J. M. McClellan. il *Flying* 116:68-70+ Ap '89

AIRPLANES, VERTICAL TAKE-OFF AND LANDING

Flier Paul Moller is a former alien with a real flying saucer. W. Plummer. il pors *People Weekly* 31:149-50 Je 19 '89

Testing

Vulcan ends initial wind tunnel tests on VTOL, fan-in-wing Starfire model. E. H. Phillips. il *Aviation Week & Space Technology* 131:64+ N 13 '89

AIRPLANES IN AGRICULTURE

Crop dusters. R. Munson. il *Flying* 116:52-6+ D '89

Katy duster [pilot couple C. and C. Payne] G. Baxter. il por *Flying* 116:138-9 Jl '89

Nanchang developing L-8, N-5A aircraft for international civil market. il *Aviation Week & Space Technology* 131:78+ D 11 '89

U.S. agricultural aircraft [tables] il *Aviation Week & Space Technology* 130:161 Mr 20 '89

AIRPLANES IN ASTRONOMY

High-flying astronomers observe Supernova 1987A [Kuiper Airborne Observatory] il *Sky and Telescope* 77:353-5 Ap '89

AIRPLANES IN BUSINESS

See also
Airplanes, Business
National Business Aircraft Association

Big iron [corporate chieftans buy used jets] il *Forbes* 144:324-5 N 13 '89

Business flying: resurgent, but embattled [cover story; special section] il *Aviation Week & Space Technology* 131:38-9+ O 2 '89

Flying like the boss. G. Eichler. il *Esquire* 111:104 Mr '89

AIRPLANES IN ENVIRONMENTAL RESEARCH

See also
Project Lighthawk

AIRPLANES IN FOREST FIRE CONTROL

Airborne surveillance will give Forest Service real-time fire maps. B. D. Nordwall. il *Aviation Week & Space Technology* 130:105+ My 29 '89

Canadair's CL-215 [firefighter aircraft spurned in U.S.] A. Laboda. il *Flying* 116:58 Ja '89

Fighting fires from the air: Quebec will upgrade CL-215 waterbomber fleet [cover story; special section] D. Hughes. il *Aviation Week & Space Technology* 131:36-7+ Ag 21 '89

Yellowstone's bombers. P. Cone. il *Flying* 116:48-50+ Ja '89

AIRPLANES IN HUNTING AND FISHING

Fishing the bush on a budget [Far North Recreation] N. Strung. il *Field & Stream* 93:42+ Ap '89

AIRPLANES IN MEDICAL CARE

See also
Project Orbis

Satcom calling [air ambulance equipped with Aerosat communications system] il *Flying* 116:19 F '89

AIRPLANES IN METEOROLOGY

Arctic air primed to destroy ozone [airborne mission] R. Monastersky. *Science News* 135:116 F 25 '89

Arctic ozone is poised for a fall [airborne expedition] R. A. Kerr. il *Science* 243:1007-8 F 24 '89

House bill supports continued WC-130 use [hurricane hunter aircraft] *Aviation Week & Space Technology* 131:30 S 18 '89

Hurricane hunters. H. Brandli. il *Popular Mechanics* 166:68-70+ S '89

AIRPLANES IN METEOROLOGY—*cont.*

Into the eye of a hurricane [flying into Hurricane Frances; condensed from Jaguars ripped my flesh] T. Cahill. il *Reader's Digest* 135:81-4 S '89

Scientific mission finds potential for ozone destruction in Arctic. R. G. O'Lone. il *Aviation Week & Space Technology* 130:33 F 27 '89

U.S. scientists, aircraft study ozone depletion above Arctic. B. W. Henderson. il *Aviation Week & Space Technology* 130:45+ Ja 16 '89

AIRPLANES IN NARCOTICS REGULATION

Marine OV-10Ds with Flir systems detect, track aircraft smuggling narcotics into southeast U.S. [forward-looking infrared systems] *Aviation Week & Space Technology* 130:49 Jl 10 '89

Pentagon offers P-3As, utility helicopters for antidrug effort. M. Mecham. il *Aviation Week & Space Technology* 130:27 F 27 '89

Pilots in the line of fire [shooting down drug planes] il *Flying* 116:10-11 N '89

U.S. antidrug operations [cover story; special section; with editorial comment] M. Mecham. il map *Aviation Week & Space Technology* 130:9, 34-8+ Ja 30 '89

The 'you fly, you die' debate [shooting down drug planes] J. N. Baker. il *Newsweek* 114:26 O 2 '89

AIRPLANES IN NARCOTICS TRADE

The Federal Express connection. *Newsweek* 114:18 Ag 21 '89

Flight into danger [U.S. agents chase plane into Canada] R. Dolphin. il *Maclean's* 102:12-13 Ap 3 '89

Pilots in the line of fire [shooting down drug planes] il *Flying* 116:10-11 N '89

Shuttle to jail [two Colombian pilots sentenced for smuggling cocaine into Canada] P. Kopvillem. il *Maclean's* 102:14-15 N 27 '89

The 'you fly, you die' debate [shooting down drug planes] J. N. Baker. il *Newsweek* 114:26 O 2 '89

AIRPLANES IN OIL POLLUTION CONTROL

Alaskan oil spill flight operations [special section] il *Aviation Week & Space Technology* 130:16-18 Ap 10 '89

CH-54, C-5 aircraft play key roles in cleanup of Alaskan oil spill. il *Aviation Week & Space Technology* 130:73-4 My 1 '89

AIRPLANES IN PATROL WORK

The flying eye [Optica] N. Moll. il *Flying* 116:44-7 Mr '89

Optica Scout provides multi-mission capability. E. H. Phillips. il *Aviation Week & Space Technology* 130:44-7 Ja 2 '89

AIRPLANES IN PHOTOGRAPHY *See* Photography, Aerial

AIRPLANES IN POLICE WORK

  See also

  Airborne Law Enforcement Association

AIRPLANES IN SIGHTSEEING

Over Africa [flying boat] R. Alleman. il *Vogue* 179:320+ Ap '89

AIRPLANES IN SNOW AND ICE CLIMBING

Daredevil pilots take glacier flying to new heights [Alaska; cover story] J. Krakauer. bibl (p147) il *Smithsonian* 19:96-100+ Ja '89

AIRPORT BUILDINGS

Deregulation and design: four new airports. il *Architectural Record* 177:71 Je '89

Winged victories [with introd. by Paul M. Sachner] il *Architectural Record* 177:130-41 Je '89

AIRPORT HOTELS, MOTELS, ETC. *See* Airports—Hotels, motels, etc.

AIRPORT RADAR SERVICE AREAS *See* Radar in aviation

AIRPORT RESTAURANTS *See* Airports—Restaurants, nightclubs, bars, etc.

AIRPORTS

  See also

  Air bases

  Airplane service stations

  Wayports

Boosting operations at underused airports can ease congestion in U.S. G. W. Hamlin. por *Aviation Week & Space Technology* 130:173-4+ Je 19 '89

New airports just can't get off the ground. il *U.S. News & World Report* 106:10 My 29 '89

U.S. airport executives seek change in bilateral negotiations. C. Fotos. il *Aviation Week & Space Technology* 130:112 Ap 24 '89

Air traffic control

  See Air traffic control

Bird hazards

  See Aviation—Bird hazards

Buildings

  See Airport buildings

Federal aid

Airport '89 [H. R. Perot's Alliance Airport receives federal funding] E. Buckberg. *The New Republic* 201:12-13 Ag 21 '89

Congress will seek ways to spur hub competition. *Aviation Week & Space Technology* 130:126 F 20 '89

Congressional pledge of $500 million for Denver airport seen as key victory. *Aviation Week & Space Technology* 131:71 O 23 '89

Congressmen, industry leaders say U.S. should pay for bomb detectors. C. Fotos. *Aviation Week & Space Technology* 130:69 Ap 3 '89

FAA task force will study solutions to capacity crisis. J. Ott. il *Aviation Week & Space Technology* 130:119+ My 29 '89

House passes security bill, raising possibility of federal TNA funding [thermal neutron analysis bomb detection system] *Aviation Week & Space Technology* 131:108-9 O 2 '89

Massport drops PACE to avoid loss of U.S. aid [landing fee schedule at Logan International Airport] *Aviation Week & Space Technology* 130:109 Ja 2 '89

Proposed Denver International passes environmental test, but funding slips. M. Mecham. *Aviation Week & Space Technology* 131:94-5 Ag 21 '89

U.S., industry officials debate funding for new security gear. J. Ott. *Aviation Week & Space Technology* 130:118 F 20 '89

Fees

Boston isn't the only airport. J. M. McClellan. *Flying* 116:104 Ja '89

Court grounds Logan fees. il *Flying* 116:12 N '89

Industry, academic leaders foresee little short-term relief of congestion. C. Fotos. *Aviation Week & Space Technology* 130:94-5 Ap 10 '89

Massport drops PACE to avoid loss of U.S. aid [landing fee schedule at Logan International Airport] *Aviation Week & Space Technology* 130:109 Ja 2 '89

Massport suspends Logan's higher fees. *Flying* 116:12-13 Mr '89

Welfare for the rich. A. Etzioni. il *The New Leader* 72:13-14 My 1 '89

Finance

  See also

  Airports—Federal aid

Buyers are starting to circle the airports [new era in privatization] S. Payne and E. Schine. il *Business Week* p38 O 2 '89

Why new airports are backed up on the runway [politics and corporate self-interest stall construction] W. C. Symonds and S. Payne. il *Business Week* p36-7 My 22 '89

Fires and fire prevention

Rescue coordination, drills helped speed evacuation of survivors [United Airlines DC-10 crash at Sioux City, Iowa] D. Hughes. *Aviation Week & Space Technology* 131:31+ Jl 31 '89

Hotels, motels, etc.

First rate conventions you can afford. L. Hazelton. *Black Enterprise* 19:76-7 Mr '89

International aspects

Major coordinated effort required to avoid global airport congestion. R. G. O'Lone. il *Aviation Week & Space Technology* 131:54+ N 20 '89

Laws and regulations

  See also

  Air traffic control

Luggage handling

  See Airlines—Luggage handling

Restaurants, nightclubs, bars, etc.

Smooth take-off [B. Marder's DC3 at Santa Monica Airport] P. Viladas. il por *House & Garden* 161:42 Ap '89

Runways

Grass routes [flying across the nation landing only on dirt and turf] R. Munson. il *Flying* 116:62-3+ O '89

Safety devices and measures

  See also

  Airports—Fires and fire prevention

  Radar in aviation

Security measures

Air transport: new security measures [special section] il *Aviation Week & Space Technology* 130:60-2 Ja 9 '89

Airlines say FAA moving too fast on plan to install bomb detectors. M. Mecham. *Aviation Week & Space Technology* 131:96-7 Jl 17 '89

Antiterrorist bomb scanners installed [thermal neutron analyzer] il *Popular Mechanics* 166:16 D '89

Asian carriers have long-term commitment to security programs. J. Ott. *Aviation Week & Space Technology* 130:77 My 8 '89

Britain to implement new airport, airline security measures. *Aviation Week & Space Technology* 130:107 My 1 '89

British, Czechs push for tighter controls on plastic explosives [proposal at International Civil Aviation Organization assembly] D. Hughes. *Aviation Week & Space Technology* 131:26 S 25 '89

Close the airport security gap. *Aviation Week & Space Technology* 131:7 O 23 '89

Congressmen, industry leaders say U.S. should pay for bomb detectors. C. Fotos. *Aviation Week & Space Technology* 130:69 Ap 3 '89

A daunting new quest to secure the skies [aftermath of Pan Am Flight 103 bombing] il *U.S. News & World Report* 106:9-10 Ja 9 '89

A deceptive killer [methods of detecting plastic explosives] *Time* 133:27 Ja 9 '89

Easier detection of plastic explosives urged by Security Council. *UN Chronicle* 26:19 S '89

AIRPORTS—Security measures—*cont.*

Experts say total security program needed to counter terrorist threat. B. W. Henderson. il *Aviation Week & Space Technology* 131:67+ N 20 '89

Extra flight insurance [bomb detectors] il *High Technology Business* 9:8-9 Ap '89

FAA fights back on plastic explosives. M. M. Waldrop. il *Science* 243:165-6 Ja 13 '89

FAA issues stricter baggage inspection requirements [response to bombing of Pan Am Flight 103] *Aviation Week & Space Technology* 130:29+ Ja 9 '89

FAA orders U.S. airlines to install bomb detectors [thermal neutron analysis device] J. Ott. *Aviation Week & Space Technology* 131:68-9 S 4 '89

FAA security panel examines means of improving defense against terrorists. J. Ott. il *Aviation Week & Space Technology* 131:75+ N 13 '89

FAA seeks detectors requiring little human judgment to find explosives. C. Fotos. il *Aviation Week & Space Technology* 130:65-7 Ja 16 '89

FAA's bomb scanner: an awkward Goliath? [thermal neutron analysis device developed by Tsahi Gozani] E. Marshall. il *Science* 245:926-7 S 1 '89

France funds weapon detectors, issues new airport ID cards. J. M. Lenorovitz. il *Aviation Week & Space Technology* 130:64 Ja 16 '89

The hard road to airport security. C. A. Riley, II. il *Fortune* 119:84 My 22 '89

High-speed X-ray CT scanner could meet FAA's explosive detection requirements. B. W. Henderson. il *Aviation Week & Space Technology* 131:78-9 N 13 '89

House passes security bill, raising possibility of federal TNA funding [thermal neutron analysis bomb detection system] *Aviation Week & Space Technology* 131:108-9 O 2 '89

ICAO members urged to boost efforts against sabotage [International Civil Aviation Organization] D. Hughes. *Aviation Week & Space Technology* 130:116-17 F 20 '89

ICAO upgrades security unit as part of antiterrorist effort [views of Secretary General S. S. Sidhu] J. Ott. por *Aviation Week & Space Technology* 130:109+ My 1 '89

Increasing TNA sensitivity causes higher number of false alarms [thermal neutron analysis bomb detection device] B. W. Henderson. il *Aviation Week & Space Technology* 131:127-8 S 18 '89

Inside track [foiling airport crime] K. Best. *Travel Holiday* 171:78 Ja '89

It's a bomb all right [thermal neutron bomb detectors] J. Drummond. il *Forbes* 144:41-2 S 4 '89

Kaboom! G. Slutsker. il *Forbes* 143:120-1 F 20 '89

Lockerbie disaster: bomb destroys Pan Am 747 in blast over Scotland [special section] il map *Aviation Week & Space Technology* 130:28-32 Ja 2 '89

The next bomb [views of I. Yeffet; cover story] E. Barnes. il por *Life* 12:130-4+ Mr '89

One more reason for fear of flying [need for additional security and maintenance imperils financial outlook] C. Power. il *Business Week* p31 Ja 16 '89

Qantas security chief seeks new tools to detect terrorists [views of Ronald Armstrong] D. A. Brown. *Aviation Week & Space Technology* 130:125 F 20 '89

Reporters as stunt men [French journalists test airport security] J. Alter. il *Newsweek* 113:47+ Ja 16 '89

Security levels increased at Frankfurt, Heathrow [following Pan Am Flight 103 bombing] K. F. Mordoff. il *Aviation Week & Space Technology* 130:28-9 Ja 9 '89

Security: the 'invisible' bomb. H. Anderson. il *Newsweek* 113:20 Ja 2 '89

Thermedics begins production of portable bomb detection unit [EGIS system] D. Hughes. *Aviation Week & Space Technology* 130:164-6 Je 19 '89

TNA system at JFK detects 94-99% of explosives in first weeks of test [thermal neutron analysis system] J. T. McKenna. *Aviation Week & Space Technology* 131:143 O 9 '89

Transportation Dept. will require wider use of advanced bomb detectors. *Aviation Week & Space Technology* 130:69 Ap 17 '89

U.S., industry officials debate funding for new security gear. J. Ott. *Aviation Week & Space Technology* 130:118 F 20 '89

When terrorists strike America, who responds? M. Mecham. *Aviation Week & Space Technology* 131:81+ D 18-25 '89

X-ray backscatter equipment provides automatic screening for explosives. D. Hughes. il *Aviation Week & Space Technology* 130:65+ Ap 17 '89

Snow and ice removal

Ice lander [landing Cherokee 140 on snow-covered runway] R. Gamm. il *Flying* 116:112 D '89

Stores

Airport shopping gets an upgrade to first class. A. Dunkin. il *Business Week* p54-5 Mr 6 '89

How Europe 1992 could cost its airports $2 billion [loss of duty free business] B. Baudoin and others. il *Business Week* p55 Mr 6 '89

Soaring sales at duty-free shops. H. Weil. il *Fortune* 119:225+ Ap 24 '89

Traffic control

See Air traffic control

Transportation

Avanti [stretch of track that will connect Leonardo da Vinci Airport with Ostiense station in Rome] B. Weber. il *The New York Times Magazine* p94 S 24 '89

Alabama

See also

Huntsville (Ala.)—Airports

Belgium

See also

Brussels (Belgium)—Airports

California

See also

Los Angeles (Calif.)—Airports

Oakland (Calif.)—Airports

San Francisco (Calif.)—Airports

NTSB report says safety diminished at Coast Tracon [southern California] *Aviation Week & Space Technology* 130:42 My 29 '89

Canada

Canada, airlines develop plan to test MLS capabilities [microwave landing system] J. T. McKenna. *Aviation Week & Space Technology* 131:70-1 S 4 '89

Anecdotes, facetiae, satire, etc.

The national slogan is 'never complain'. A. Fotheringham. il *Maclean's* 102:88 N 13 '89

Colorado

See also

Denver (Colo.)—Airports

East Asia

Asian carriers have long-term commitment to security programs. J. Ott. *Aviation Week & Space Technology* 130:77 My 8 '89

Three Asian nations expand airports to relieve overburdened facilities. J. Ott. il map *Aviation Week & Space Technology* 130:70-1 My 8 '89

Florida

See also

Miami (Fla.)—Airports

Palm Beach (Fla.)—Airports

France

France funds weapon detectors, issues new airport ID cards. J. M. Lenorovitz. il *Aviation Week & Space Technology* 130:64 Ja 16 '89

Germany (West)

See also

Frankfurt am Main (Germany)—Airports

Great Britain

See also

London (England)—Airports

Britain to implement new airport, airline security measures. *Aviation Week & Space Technology* 130:107 My 1 '89

Illinois

See also

Chicago (Ill.)—Airports

Iowa

See also

Sioux City (Iowa)—Airports

Italy

See also

Rome (Italy)—Airports

Japan

See also

Osaka (Japan)—Airports

Macao

International airport to be built on Macau. map *Aviation Week & Space Technology* 131:77 Ag 7 '89

Malaysia

Malaysia developing nationwide network of modern airports. P. Proctor. *Aviation Week & Space Technology* 131:67 N 6 '89

Massachusetts

See also

Boston (Mass.)—Airports

Missouri

See also

Kansas City (Mo.)—Airports

New Hampshire

See also

Lebanon (N.H.)—Airports

Portsmouth (N.H.)—Airports

New Jersey

N.J. airports feel the pinch [privately owned airports] il *Flying* 116:19 Ja '89

New York (State)

See also

Albany County (N.Y.)—Airports

New York (N.Y.)—Airports

Pennsylvania

See also

Philadelphia (Pa.)—Airports

Pittsburgh (Pa.)—Airports

Philippines

See also

Manila (Philippines)—Airports

AIRPORTS—cont.

Texas
See also
Fort Worth (Tex.)—Airports
United States
See Airports
Utah
Glen Canyon airport expansion under fire. il *National Parks* 63:10-11 Jl/Ag '89
Washington (D.C.)
See Washington (D.C.)—Airports
Western Europe
How Europe 1992 could cost its airports $2 billion [loss of duty free business] B. Baudoin and others. il *Business Week* p55 Mr 6 '89

AIRSHIP INDUSTRIES, LTD.
First airship to be FAA certified [Skyship 600] il *Flying* 116:18 Ag '89

AIRSHIPS
See also
American Blimp (Firm)
Certification
See Airships—Standards
History
See also
Graf Zeppelin (Airship)
Shenandoah (Airship)
Standards
First airship to be FAA certified [Airship Industries' Skyship 600] il *Flying* 116:18 Ag '89

AIRSHIPS, RUSSIAN
Soviets designing large airship to carry payloads in remote sites [Thermoplane project] il *Aviation Week & Space Technology* 131:127 O 9 '89

AIRSHIPS IN ADVERTISING
Brighter-than-e'er Lightship. il *Flying* 116:20-1 N '89

AIRSHOW CANADA *See* Aviation—Exhibitions

AIRSPACE (INTERNATIONAL LAW)
See also
Iranian air disaster, 1988
Korean Air Lines Flight 007 disaster, 1983
Flight into danger [U.S. agents chase plane into Canada] R. Dolphin. il *Maclean's* 102:12-13 Ap 3 '89

AIRSPEEDS *See* Airplanes—Speed; Airplanes, Light—Speed

AIRWAYS
See also
Airlines—Routes
Traffic control
See Air traffic control

AIRWORTHINESS ASSURANCE TASK FORCE *See* Aging Aircraft Task Force

AIRWORTHINESS CERTIFICATION OF AIRPLANES *See* Airplanes, Jet—Standards

AITMATOV, CHINGIZ
The place of the skull [fiction] il por *Time* 133:120-2 Ap 10 '89

AIX-EN-PROVENCE (FRANCE)
Music
See also
Opera—France

AIX-EN-PROVENCE FESTIVAL *See* Music festivals—France

AIX-LES-BAINS (FRANCE)
A love affair with water. A. Furst. il map *New Choices for the Best Years* 29:56-61 F '89

AIX OPERATING SYSTEM *See* UNIX operating system

AIYANGAR, SRINIVASA RAMANUJAN *See* Ramanujan Aiyangar, Srinivasa, 1887-1920

AJAMI, FOUAD
A city of banditry and extortion. il *U.S. News & World Report* 106:33 Ap 10 '89
The folly of absent-minded imperialism. il *U.S. News & World Report* 106:44 Ap 10 '89
The graveyards of Jerusalem. *The New Republic* 201:24-5 S 11 '89
Inside the mind of a movement. il *U.S. News & World Report* 107:28 Ag 14 '89
Now that the millennium has ended. il por *U.S. News & World Report* 106:35 Je 19 '89
The tentative triumph of the ballot. il *U.S. News & World Report* 107:40+ D 4 '89
Trapped between prison and anarchy. il *U.S. News & World Report* 107:31 O 9 '89

AJINOMOTO CO., INC.
"We have our eyes open". A. Tanzer. il *Forbes* 144:57-8 S 4 '89

AJOOBA [film] *See* Motion picture reviews—Single works

AKAHITO, ANTONI
How to build a Planck-mass accelerator in your solar system. il *Scientific American* 260:112-15 Ap '89

AKAI ELECTRIC CO., LTD.
Au revoir, Akai! R. Long. il *High Fidelity (New York, N.Y.)* 39:17 F '89

AKASOFU, SYUN-ICHI
The dynamic aurora [cover story] bibl il *Scientific American* 260:90-7 My '89

AKBAR, NA'IM
about
Free your mind [interview] J. Nelson. por *Essence* 19:69-70+ F '89

AKERS, JOHN F., 1934-
about
Reinventing IBM [cover story] J. Dreyfuss. il por *Fortune* 120:30-5+ Ag 14 '89
A slimmer IBM may still be overweight. J. W. Verity. il por *Business Week* p107-8 D 18 '89
What's ailing IBM? More than this year's earnings. J. W. Verity. il por *Business Week* p75+ O 16 '89

AKERS, KAREN
about
Taking the stage. pors *Harper's Bazaar* 122:150-3+ Ag '89

ÅKERSTRÖM, MALIN
Snitches on snitching. bibl *Society* 26:22-6 Ja/F '89

AKHROMEYEV, SERGEI, 1923-
about
From cold war to odd couple. J. Barry. il pors *Newsweek* 114:42 Jl 31 '89
Government/military: Lord Carrington, Paul H. Nitze, Marshal Sergei Fedorovich Akhromeyev. il pors *Aviation Week & Space Technology* 130:18 Ja 2 '89
A soldier talks peace [interview] J. Kohan and K. Prager. il por *Time* 134:58-60 N 13 '89
Soviet military adviser addresses House panel. *Aviation Week & Space Technology* 131:26 Jl 31 '89

AKIHITO, EMPEROR OF JAPAN
about
Akihito: the son also rises. M. Walsh. il por *Time* 133:32 Ja 16 '89
'I can't imagine another way of life'. D. Benkoil. il por *Newsweek* 113:36 Ja 16 '89
The last of Hirohito, the last of an era. il por *U.S. News & World Report* 106:12+ Ja 16 '89
What kind of power to be? *World Press Review* 36:12 Ap '89

AKIYOSHI, TOSHIKO, 1929-
about
Blindfold test [reprint from November 1982 issue] L. Feather. il por *Down Beat* 56:96 S '89

AKSELROD, YULIA
Why my grandfather Leon Trotsky must be turning in his grave. *Commentary* 87:39-43 Ap '89

AKST, DANIEL
How Barry Minkow fooled the auditors. il pors *Forbes* 144:126-7+ O 2 '89

AL AHDAL, ABDULLAH
about
Khomeini strikes back. J. Bierman. il por *Maclean's* 102:25 Ap 10 '89
Murder in the mosque. *Newsweek* 113:41 Ap 10 '89

AL B. SURE! *See* Sure!, Al B.

AL-FAYED, MOHAMED, 1933-
about
Banned in Britain: a new chapter in the Harrods saga. M. Maremont. pors *Business Week* p36 Ap 17 '89
Brawling over Harrods. S. Lohr. il pors *The New York Times Magazine* p32-3+ O 8 '89
Tiny Rowland versus Mohamed Al-Fayed (cont.). E. F. Cone. il pors *Forbes* 143:10 My 1 '89
Tit for tat on London's High Street. J. Barnes. il pors *U.S. News & World Report* 106:63 Ja 30 '89

AL-HUSSEINI, FAISAL
about
Local hero. *The New Republic* 200:8+ F 20 '89

AL-KHATEEB, MUHAMMAD
New lifestyles, new diseases. il *World Health* p22-3 Jl '89

AL-QADDAFI, MUAMMAR *See* Qaddafi, Muammar al-, 1942-

AL-RAYYAN (FIRM)
Pyramid scheme. W. P. Barrett. il *Forbes* 143:106+ Ap 17 '89

AL-TERZI, ZEHDI LABIB *See* Terzi, Zehdi

ALABAMA
See also
Architecture, Domestic—Alabama
Blacks—Alabama
Criminal justice, Administration of—Alabama
Hunting—Alabama
Medical care—Alabama
Poor—Alabama
Tree farms—Alabama
Wildlife—Alabama
History
See also
Alabama. Dept. of Archives and History
Politics and government
The next George Wallace. D. Baer. il pors *Gentlemen's Quarterly* 59:292-7+ D '89
Race relations
Ala. Klan must take course on civil rights: settlement. il *Jet* 76:7 Ag 14 '89
Social history
The spirit of Christmas South. G. Norman. il *Southern Living* 24:84 D '89

ALABAMA. DEPT. OF ARCHIVES AND HISTORY
A new look at Alabama archives. il *Southern Living* 24:49 O '89
ALABAMA (MUSICAL GROUP)
Rodeo round-up: three big ones in the country corral. il pors *'Teen* 33:53 S '89
ALABAMA IN TELEVISION
Outcast to hero [R. Flowers Jr.] J. Wooten. il pors *TV Guide* 37:36-8 Ja 14-20 '89
ALAIA (FIRM)
Downtown chic. A. Radakovich. il por *Harper's Bazaar* 122:72 N '89
ALAKAI SWAMP (KAUAI, HAWAII)
Living on the edge [botanist M. Doyle's studies of gunnera] J. Nielsen. il pors *National Wildlife* 27:20-3 O/N '89
ALAMOSA NATIONAL WILDLIFE REFUGE (COLO.)
The numbers game puts birds at risk [avian disease] F. Graham. il map *Audubon* 91:18+ Ja '89
ALAN, RAY
An Anglo-Spanish nightmare. *The New Leader* 72:10-11 N 13 '89
ALANINE
High-resolution epitope mapping of hGH-receptor interactions by alanine-scanning mutagenesis. B. C. Cunningham and J. A. Wells. bibl f il *Science* 244:1081-5 Je 2 '89
Possible role of carbamates in neurotoxicity and neurotransmitter inactivation [discussion of August 19, 1988 article, Beta-N-methylamino-L-alanine neurotoxicity: requirement for bicarbonate as a cofactor] J. H. Weiss and D. W. Choi. *Science* 243:1615 Mr 24 '89
ALAR (CHEMICAL) *See* Daminozide
ALARMS

See also
Automobiles—Alarms
Boats and boating—Alarms
Sirens
Swimming pools—Alarms

Alarm systems that pay off in peace of mind. J. E. Davis. il *Business Week* p98-9 Ap 10 '89
Alarming developments. il *Home Mechanix* 85:48-53 N '89
Burglarproofing your home. C. Schaeffer. il *Changing Times* 43:69-72 Ja '89
High-tech home security [cover story] H. Friedman. il *Radio-Electronics* 60:33-7+ Ap '89
Home security [special section] il map *Popular Science* 235:76-80+ O '89
Install a home security system. H. Friedman and B. C. Fenton. il *Radio-Electronics* 60:42-6+ Ap '89
Programmable phasor property guard [cover story] R. E. Iannini. il *Radio-Electronics* 60:37-41+ D '89
Sounding off on security systems [interview with D. Bugbee] A. Cala. il por *Home Mechanix* 85:20-1+ N '89
Total security [house protection] J. Sanger. il *Home Mechanix* 85:42+ N '89
Wireless security system. D. Becker. il *Radio-Electronics* 60:47-52+ Ap '89
ALASKA

See also
Acid rain—Alaska
Anti-nuclear movement—Alaska
Arctic National Wildlife Refuge (Alaska)
Aviation—Alaska
Bering Strait
Bird sanctuaries—Alaska
Chugach Mountains (Alaska)
Cross country skiing—Alaska
Denali National Park and Preserve (Alaska)
Discrimination in employment—Alaska
Environmental movement—Alaska
Exxon Valdez (Ship) oil spill, 1989
Fishing—Alaska
Forests and forestry—Alaska
Girdwood (Alaska)
Health resorts, watering places, etc.—Alaska
Indians of North America—Alaska
McNeil River State Game Sanctuary (Alaska)
Mount McKinley (Alaska)
Narcotics trade—Alaska
National parks and reserves—Alaska
Petroleum—Alaska
Petroleum pipelines—Alaska
Prince William Sound (Alaska)
Redoubt Volcano (Alaska)
Russians—Alaska
Tongass National Forest (Alaska)
Wales (Alaska)
Wilderness areas—Alaska
Wildlife conservation—Alaska
Wrangell Island (Alaska)
Yukon River (Yukon and Alaska)
Yukon Territory

Boundaries
Thaw on the Bering Strait. J. Mettke. il *World Press Review* 36:58 Ja '89

Climate
Alaskan weather. D. M. Ludlum. See issues of Weatherwise
Baby, how cold can it get outside? il *U.S. News & World Report* 106:12-13 F 13 '89

Even the Eskimos froze [cold wave] J. Langone. il *Time* 133:65 F 13 '89

Description and travel

See also
Cruising—Alaska
Alaska on my mind. E. Cox. il *Ms.* 17:63-5 Je '89
Alaska: the last frontier. A. Reid-Dove. il *Black Enterprise* 20:99-100+ S '89
Ferry tales [southeast Alaska] M. Steere. il map *Travel Holiday* 172:58-67 Ag '89
Kayaking the wilderness waterways of southern Alaska. il map *Sunset (Central West edition)* 182:70+ Je '89

Industries

See also
Fisheries—Alaska
Fur industry—Alaska
Petroleum industry—Alaska
Wards Cove Packing Co.
ALASKA AIR GROUP INC.
Alaska Air prospers by focusing on niche markets, profitability. N. C. Kernstock. il map *Aviation Week & Space Technology* 131:110-11 S 25 '89
"We're vulnerable". M. Beauchamp. il por *Forbes* 143:80+ Mr 6 '89
ALASKA AIRLINES, INC.

See also
Alaska Air Group Inc.
Alaska Air prospers by focusing on niche markets, profitability. N. C. Kernstock. il map *Aviation Week & Space Technology* 131:110-11 S 25 '89
"We're vulnerable". M. Beauchamp. il por *Forbes* 143:80+ Mr 6 '89
ALASKA CENTER FOR THE PERFORMING ARTS (ANCHORAGE, ALASKA)
Acoustics at Anchorage. M. Holden. il *Architectural Record* 177:106-10 Ap '89
Alaska Center for the Performing Arts. M. LaRue. il *Theatre Crafts* 23:34+ N '89
Northern lights. M. F. Schmertz. il *Architectural Record* 177:96-105 Ap '89
ALASKA CHILKAT BALD EAGLE PRESERVE *See* Bird sanctuaries—Alaska
ALASKA GOURMET SEAFOOD (FIRM)
To market, to market [P. Schilling of Alaska Gourmet Seafood and B. Woldrop of Silver Lining Seafood] N. C. Baker. il por *Nation's Business* 77:61 Ja '89
ALASKA SISTER SCHOOLS NETWORK
Pacific Rim partnerships: Alaska's bold initiative. W. H. Parrett and A. Calkins. il *Phi Delta Kappan* 70:550-2 Mr '89
ALASKAN OIL SPILL, 1989 *See* Exxon Valdez (Ship) oil spill, 1989
ALBANESE, ENZO

about
For real haute dogs, these shoes are made for stalking. il *People Weekly* 32:102-3 Ag 14 '89
ALBANIA

See also
Albanians

Kings and rulers

See also
Zog, King of Albania, 1895-1961

Politics and government
In the shadows. A. Daniels. *National Review* 41:24-5 Jl 14 '89
ALBANIANS

United States
Muttontown's King [Knollwood mansion home to Albania's King Zog from 1951 to 1955] *The New Yorker* 65:33-4 S 11 '89

Yugoslavia
Nationalist rage [rioting in Kesovo] A. Bilski. il *Maclean's* 102:24 Ap 10 '89
Relighting the Balkan powder keg. G. Porzio. *World Press Review* 36:17-18 Je '89
Religious nationalism strains Yugoslavia. J. A. Broun. *The Christian Century* 106:885-8 O 4 '89
ALBANY (CALIF.)

Restaurants, nightclubs, bars, etc.
Spécialités de la maison:
Yujean's. C. Bates. il *Gourmet* 49:36+ Ag '89
ALBANY COUNTY (N.Y.)

Airports
Buyers are starting to circle the airports [new era in privatization] S. Payne and E. Schine. il *Business Week* p38 O 2 '89
FAA rejects two proposals to privatize Albany airport. J. Ott. *Aviation Week & Space Technology* 131:44-5 D 11 '89
ALBANY HOME FOR CHILDREN *See* Orphans and orphanages
ALBARETTO DELLA TORRE (ITALY)

Restaurants, nightclubs, bars, etc.
Hail, Cesare! [chef and restaurant owner C. Giaccone of Dei Cacciatore] J. Steingarten. il por *Vogue* 179:600-1+ S '89
ALBÁS, JOSÉ MARIA ESCRIVÁ DE BALAGUER Y *See* Escrivá de Balaguer y Albás, José Maria, 1902-1975

ALBATROSS AWARD
Bagging the Albatross [awarded to J. Reid] G. Byrne. il *Science* 243:32 Ja 6 '89
ALBATROSSES
Albatross alley [Falklands; cover story] I. J. Strange. il *Natural History* p26-33 Jl '89
March of the feathered thugs: Johnny Rook birds in the Falklands wreak havoc on an albatross colony. T. De Roy. il *International Wildlife* 19:52-9 Mr/Ap '89
Northern Hemisphere albatrosses. J. Kenyon. bibl il *Sea Frontiers* 35:342-7 N/D '89
ALBEE, EDWARD, 1928-
about
Who's afraid of Virginia Woolf? [drama] Reviews
Newsweek il 114:66 O 16 '89. J. Kroll
ALBERI, MARY
Alcuin and the 'new Athens'. il por *History Today* 39:35-41 S '89
ALBERS, DANIEL
What makes a rainy day. il *Sierra* 74:104-5 N/D '89
ALBERS, HERMANN G.
about
For Rolls-Royce owners across America, all roads lead to Zionsville, Indiana. il por *People Weekly* 31:117 Ap 17 '89
ALBERT, MARV
about
The yessss! man can play rough. L. Feldman. il por *TV Guide* 37:16-18 Jl 1-7 '89
ALBERT HOFMANN FOUNDATION
Encyclopedia psychedelia [established by LSD researchers] A. J. S. Rayl. il *Omni (New York, N.Y.)* 11:30+ Je '89
ALBERT LASKER MEDICAL RESEARCH AWARDS See
Lasker Medical Research Awards
ALBERTA
See also
Athabasca River (Alta.)
Banff National Park (Alta.)
Calgary (Alta.)
Edmonton (Alta.)
Forests and forestry—Alberta
Lake Louise (Alta.)
Paleontology—Alberta
Resorts—Alberta
Television festivals—Alberta
Water pollution—Alberta
Waterton-Glacier International Peace Park (Alta. and Mont.)
Politics and government
See also
Politics, Corruption in—Alberta
Alberta's 'loose cannon' [Calgary mayor R. Klein to run as Conservative in next provincial election] J. Howse. il por *Maclean's* 102:12 Ja 23 '89
By popular demand [S. Waters' nomination election victory part of drive to reform Senate; special section] il por *Maclean's* 102:24-5+ O 30 '89
From Alberta with ire [Reform Party] J. Howse. il *Maclean's* 102:24-5 N 13 '89
Post-election realities. P. Kopvillem. il por *Maclean's* 102:18+ Je 12 '89
A quarterback sack [D. Getty loses seat in provincial election] J. Howse. il por *Maclean's* 102:14 Ap 3 '89
Upset in the West [Reform Party candidate D. Grey wins byelection] J. Howse. il por *Maclean's* 102:12-13 Mr 27 '89
The winds of change [plans to elect a senator] J. Howse. il *Maclean's* 102:15 F 13 '89
ALBERTA BALLET COMPANY
Reviews:
Spring season in Calgary. M. Crabb. il *Dance Magazine* 63:53 Ag '89
ALBERTA-PACIFIC FOREST INDUSTRIES INC.
The forest fight [environmental concerns over proposed pulp mill on Athabasca River in Alberta] R. Corelli. il *Maclean's* 102:60 N 13 '89
How do you say 'tim-ber' in Japanese? T. Mason. il *Business Week* p52 D 4 '89
ALBERTA WILDERNESS ASSOCIATION
Drills across the border [Shell Canada's plans to drill near Waterton-Glacier International Peace Park] K. Van Tighem. il *Wilderness* 52:54-6 Wint '88
ALBERTINA (VIENNA, AUSTRIA) See Graphische Sammlung Albertina
ALBERTO-CULVER CO.
Washing the gray out at Alberto-Culver. J. F. Siler. il pors *Business Week* p138 Je 26 '89
ALBERTSON'S INC.
Food for thought. M. Beauchamp. il por *Forbes* 143:73 Ap 17 '89
One man's poison . . . [competitors take advantage of leveraged rivals] N. Alster. il *Forbes* 144:38-9 O 16 '89
ALBERTVILLE OLYMPICS, 1992 See Olympic Games—1992—Winter Olympics

ALBI (FRANCE)
Historic houses, sites, etc.
Historic houses: Henri de Toulouse-Lautrec: the painter's ancestral home in Albi. S. M. Alsop. il *Architectural Digest* 46:114-19+ Ja '89
ALBINO, JOSEPH
The Old Erie Canal State Park. il *The Conservationist* 44:2-7 Jl/Ag '89
ALBRECHT, BRUCE A.
Aerosols, cloud microphysics, and fractional cloudiness. bibl f il *Science* 245:1227-30 S 15 '89
ALBRIGHT, DAVID
Bomb potential for South America. bibl f il map *The Bulletin of the Atomic Scientists* 45:16-20 My '89
ALBRIGHT, DAVID, AND BEARD, JAMES
The tritium follies. bibl f il *The Bulletin of the Atomic Scientists* 45:42-5 N '89
ALBRIGHT, DAVID, AND ZAMORA, TOM
India, Pakistan's nuclear weapons: all the pieces in place [cover story] bibl f il map *The Bulletin of the Atomic Scientists* 45:20-6 Je '89
ALBUM COVERS, PHONOGRAPH RECORD See Phonograph record covers
ALBUMINS
See also
Serum albumin
The role of cis-acting promoter elements in tissue-specific albumin gene expression. P. Maire and others. bibl f il *Science* 244:343-6 Ap 21 '89
ALBUMS
See also
Photograph albums
ALBUQUERQUE, LUIS DE
Of caravels and cartographers . . . il *The Courier (Unesco)* 42:10-13 Ap '89
ALBUQUERQUE (N.M.)
Architecture
Organically grown [Prince House] K. D. Stein. il *Architectural Record* 177:106-13 mid-Ap '89
Economic conditions
A delicate balance built on the land. D. Pedersen. il *Newsweek* 113:49 F 6 '89
Galleries and museums
See also
Indian Pueblo Cultural Center (Albuquerque, N.M.)
Industries
New Mexico shoot-out [TV stations] R. Mahler. il *Channels (New York, N.Y.: 1986)* 9:84-5 Ja '89
ALC COMMUNICATIONS CORPORATION
The smart operator untangling the mess at ALC [J. M. Zrno] W. Zellner. il por *Business Week* p137-8 My 15 '89
ALCAYAGA, LUCILA GODOY See Mistral, Gabriela, 1889-1957
ALCESTE [opera] See Gluck, Christoph Willibald, Ritter von, 1714-1787
ALCINDOR, LEW See Abdul-Jabbar, Kareem, 1947-
ALCOA See Aluminum Co. of America
ALCOCK, JOHN, 1942-
Freedom fighters. il *Natural History* p68-74 Mr '89
ALCOHOL
See also
Drinking customs
Phosphatidylethanol
Prohibition
Physiological effects
See also
Alcohol antagonists
Blood—Alcohol content
Fetal alcohol syndrome
Can alcohol ease suffering? [study by Kenneth Woodrow and Lorne Eltherington] *USA Today (Periodical)* 117:10-11 F '89
Drugs and alcohol: a dangerous mix. il *McCall's* 116:90 Ja '89
Ethanol inhibits NMDA-activated ion current in hippocampal neurons. D. M. Lovinger and others. bibl f il *Science* 243:1721-4 Mr 31 '89
A good drink. R. A. Barnett. il *American Health* 8:66-8+ N '89
The news on booze [effect on cycling performance] E. Coleman. il *Bicycling* 30:70-1 O/N '89
Weakness for alcohol borne by muscles [research by Emanuel Rubin] I. Wickelgren. *Science News* 135:117 F 25 '89
Psychological effects
Depression and drinking [interview with E. Stutzman] B. K. Mills. il por *People Weekly* 32:118 N 27 '89
ALCOHOL AND AIR PILOTS
Have one for the runway: how Transportation Department policies add new meaning to the word "red-eye" [FAA policies] D. Nather. *The Washington Monthly* 21:12-14+ Ap '89
Party animal [Army pilot on training flight] A. Starner. il *Flying* 116:100 Mr '89
ALCOHOL AND ARTISTS
Curse of the muse [V. van Gogh and absinthe] B. A. MacAdam. il *Art News* 88:17 Mr '89

ALCOHOL AND AUTOMOBILE DRIVERS
D.W.I. [controlled experiment] C. Csere. il *Car and Driver* 34:127+ My '89

Drunk driving and statistical morality. D. E. Koshland, Jr. *Science* 244:513 My 5 '89

Miscellaneous ramblings [Volkswagen/MADD Drive for Life campaign] T. L. Bryant. il *Road & Track* 40:33-4 Ag '89

ALCOHOL AND CELEBRITIES
Celebs speak out on addiction [C. Haim, D. Barrymore and G. O'Neal] L. E. Brooks. pors *Teen* 33:30+ S '89

A fine madness [restaurateur P. Langan] P. Wilkinson. il pors *Gentlemen's Quarterly* 59:430-5+ S '89

'I thought there was something emotionally wrong with me' [J. Walton] E. Warren. por *TV Guide* 37:26 Ap 15-21 '89

'I wanted people to know I had a problem' [D. Barrymore] E. Warren. il pors *TV Guide* 37:16-18 Mr 25-31 '89

John Larroquette: "I was born an alcoholic". B. Weinhouse. il pors *Redbook* 172:30+ Ap '89

Mr. Jones goes to D.C. [B. Jones] G. Jaynes. il *Life* 12:19 My '89

The secret Drew Barrymore [cover story]; ed. by Todd Gold. D. Barrymore. il pors *People Weekly* 31:70-2+ Ja 16 '89

A skating star's long fall from grace [cover story]; ed. by Lois Armstrong. T. Babilonia. il pors *People Weekly* 31:86-8+ Ap 17 '89

ALCOHOL AND EMPLOYMENT
What all career women need to know about drinking. H. B. Braiker. il *Working Woman* 14:72-5+ Ag '89

ALCOHOL AND MOTORCYCLISTS
Down but not out [Canadian cabinet member B. Valcourt resigns after crashing his motorcycle while impaired] M. Clark. il por *Maclean's* 102:14 Ag 14 '89

ALCOHOL AND MUSICIANS
Ringo on the rebound [cover story] S. Dougherty. il pors *People Weekly* 32:66-9 Ag 28 '89

ALCOHOL AND POLITICIANS
"Dead soldiers" along the Potomac. H. Sidey. il *Time* 133:22 Mr 13 '89

Down but not out [Canadian cabinet member B. Valcourt resigns after crashing his motorcycle while impaired] M. Clark. il por *Maclean's* 102:14 Ag 14 '89

Is my SecDef drunk? [J. Tower nomination] W. F. Buckley. *National Review* 41:62 Ap 7 '89

Tippling in Washington. S. Waldman. il *Newsweek* 113:23 Mr 6 '89

Wine, women and irony [J. Tower's behavior] M. Greenfield. il *Newsweek* 113:72 F 20 '89

Wine, women, and World War III [J. Tower's nomination as Defense Secretary] D. Neff. *Christianity Today* 33:15 Ap 7 '89

ALCOHOL AND RELIGION
Diagnosing drinking [discussion of July 19-26, 1989 article, Rethinking drinking: the moral context] L. H. Steffen. il *The Christian Century* 106:987-90 N 1 '89

Rethinking drinking: the moral context [cover story] L. H. Steffen. *The Christian Century* 106:684-6 Jl 19-26 '89

ALCOHOL AND SEAMEN
Captain Hazelwood: what Exxon knew [Exxon Valdez captain] B. Amero. *Harper's* 279:22-4 Jl '89

He devastated Alaska, but Capt. Jeff Hazelwood, friends say, is an environmentalist [captain of Exxon Valdez whose negligence led to oil spill] K. Gross. il por *People Weekly* 31:48-50 Ap 24 '89

ALCOHOL AND SPORTS
Glenn Davis [baseball player's anti-alcohol stand] S. Kanfer. il por *People Weekly* 32 Special Issue:125 Fall '89

Henderson blames drunks for '88 Yankee downfall. por *Jet* 75:50 Mr 20 '89

The news on booze [effect on cycling performance] E. Coleman. il *Bicycling* 30:70-1 O/N '89

ALCOHOL AND THE AGED
A sobering story. G. Rosenblum. il *New Choices for the Best Years* 29:62-9 My '89

ALCOHOL AND WOMEN
See also
　Fetal alcohol syndrome

From Kitty Dukakis, a cry of despair [cover story] J. S. Kunen. il pors *People Weekly* 32:114-19 N 27 '89

I am an alcoholic. il *Good Housekeeping* 208:30+ F '89

The losses keep mounting [personal and political difficulties faced by K. and M. Dukakis] R. Ajemian. il pors *Time* 134:66 N 20 '89

'She clearly recognizes she has a sickness' [K. Dukakis] B. Kantrowitz and M. Starr. il por *Newsweek* 113:54-5 F 20 '89

Should she or shouldn't she? [link between alcohol and breast cancer] L. Abraham. il *Discover* 10:73 Ja '89

The struggle of Kitty Dukakis. A. Toufexis. il por *Time* 133:79 F 20 '89

The thinking girl's guide to drinking. J. Wasser. il *Mademoiselle* 95:156 S '89

'Trying to ease the pain' [K. Dukakis] B. Turque. il por *Newsweek* 114:55 N 20 '89

Twelve steps for women alcoholics. G. Unterberger. *The Christian Century* 106:1150-2 D 6 '89

"We have a problem". J. Marks. il *Parents* 64:54+ N '89

What all career women need to know about drinking. H. B. Braiker. il *Working Woman* 14:72-5+ Ag '89

What did happen to Kitty Dukakis? M. Jacobbi. il pors *Good Housekeeping* 208:52+ Je '89

ALCOHOL AND YOUTH
See also
　Alcohol education

Bottle babies. S. P. Policoff. il *Ladies' Home Journal* 106:182-3+ My '89

Drinking, drugs, & children. G. Youcha and J. S. Seixas. il *Parents* 64:142-4+ Mr '89

Miller guy life [spring break beer ads] T. Riordan. *The New Republic* 200:16-17 Mr 27 '89

An outbreak of teen alcoholism [interview with D. Miller] G. Breu. il por *People Weekly* 31:81 Ja 16 '89

Saying no nicely. il *Current Health 2* 16:14-16 S '89

ALCOHOL ANTAGONISTS
Sober-up drug counteracts intoxication [drug 4513; research by Peter J. Syapin] *USA Today (Periodical)* 117:9 Ja '89

ALCOHOL AS FUEL
Alcohol problem. P. Brand. il *The Family Handyman* 39:98 My '89

Alternative fuels [cars] J. W. Merline. il *Consumers' Research Magazine* 72:38 Ag '89

Corn hits a hot streak [ethanol] R. Fee. il *Successful Farming* 87:50AL-50AM Ja '89

Ethanol [with editorial comment by Loren Kruse] R. Fee. il *Successful Farming* 87:1, 28-9 S '89

Ethanol and diesel fuel do mix. C. Peterson, Jr. *Successful Farming* 87 no4:64F Mr '89

Fuel additives offer solution to auto pollution. *High Technology Business* 9:30 Je '89

Put a cassava in your tank [genetically altered yeast cells produce ethanol] il *Discover* 10:10 F '89

Test: ethanol works fine in small engines. G. Vincent. il *Successful Farming* 87:10-11 mid-F '89

ALCOHOL EDUCATION
Alcohol and drug education in elementary schools. D. F. Bradley. *The Education Digest* 54:61-3 Mr '89

Aids and devices
Understanding AIDS & Alcohol [computer programs] K. Sternberg. *Compute!* 11:122+ O '89

ALCOHOLIC BEVERAGES
See also
　Beer
　Cocktails
　Drinking customs
　Liqueurs
　Stout (Beverage)
　Wine
　Wine coolers

1990's fashions in drinks and food. J. F. Mariani. il *Motor Boating & Sailing* 164:26+ S '89

Amazing aperitifs! E. Fried. il *Black Enterprise* 19:213 F '89

Here's to the end of the year! The end of the decade! Lo, the end of an era! il *Esquire* 112:180-1 D '89

Something sublime, with a twist [aperitifs] W. Grimes. il *Esquire* 111:40 Je '89

Tropical drinks. il *Gourmet* 49:64-5+ Ag '89

Winter warm-ups. E. Fried. il *Black Enterprise* 19:76 Ja '89

Taxation
Laying the blame [sin taxes] B. D. Colen. il *Health (New York, N.Y.)* 21:38-9 Ag '89

Smokers may be keeping social security healthy . . . but pricier smokes and drinks may still make economic sense. G. Koretz. il *Business Week* p27 Je 5 '89

Taxing the wages of sin. P. Wallich. *Scientific American* 260:22 Je '89

ALCOHOLICS AND ALCOHOLISM
See also
　Alcohol—Physiological effects
　Alcohol—Psychological effects
　Children of alcoholics
　Computers and alcoholics

Alcohol: everyone's problem. E. E. Rosenbaum. il *New Choices for the Best Years* 29:27-31 F '89

Are we too sober about alcohol? B. G. Harrison. *Mademoiselle* 95:124 O '89

The clay moves awry . . . S. Callery. il *Commonweal* 116:519-21 O 6 '89

Confusion over alcoholism: psychiatry, medicine, and the law disagree. R. E. Vatz and L. S. Weinberg. il *USA Today (Periodical)* 118:68-70 S '89

Early alcoholism: crime, depression higher [research by Laure Buydens-Branchey] B. Bower. *Science News* 135:180 Mr 25 '89

Interview: James Schaefer. A. J. S. Rayl. il pors *Omni (New York, N.Y.)* 12:106-8+ O '89

Lookin' for science in all the wrong places [J. M. Schaefer's study of the relationship between drinking and country music] J. Stone. il *Discover* 10:96-9 Mr '89

Roots of addiction [cover story] D. Gelman. il *Newsweek* 113:52-7 F 20 '89

The usual. J. Schwartz. il *Gentlemen's Quarterly* 59:110+ D '89

ALCOHOLICS AND ALCOHOLISM—*cont.*
Genetic aspects
Blood test linked to alcoholism risk [work of Gerald C. Mueller] *Science News* 135:13 Ja 7 '89
Mysteries of the mind. il *Good Housekeeping* 208:46+ Ja '89
Rehabilitation
See Alcoholics and alcoholism—Therapy
Therapy
See also
Alcohol antagonists
Alcoholics Anonymous
Church work with alcoholics
Comedians' Drug and Alcohol Abuse Foundation
Hazelden Foundation
Breaking the patterns that lead to relapse. E. Chiauzzi. il *Psychology Today* 23:18-19 D '89
Getting clean [cover story] P. Hoban. il *New York* 22:38-45 F 20 '89
Lithium dissolves as alcoholism treatment [research by Walter Dorus] B. Bower. *Science News* 135:309 My 20 '89
Soviet Union
Soviets seek U.S. help in combating alcoholism. C. Holden. il *Science* 246:878-9 N 17 '89
Where Slava starts over again [Moscow Beginners, first Soviet Alcoholics Anonymous group] G. Garelik. il *Time* 133:10+ Ap 10 '89
ALCOHOLICS AND ALCOHOLISM IN TELEVISION
Television's drinking problem [views of George Gerbner] B. Portnow. il *American Health* 8:130+ Jl/Ag '89
ALCOHOLICS ANONYMOUS
The drunk who helped millions get sober [W. G. Wilson] M. O'Connell-Cahill. il *U.S. Catholic* 54:10-12 F '89
Getting clean [cover story] P. Hoban. il *New York* 22:38-45 F 20 '89
Twelve steps for women alcoholics. G. Unterberger. *The Christian Century* 106:1150-2 D 6 '89
Very personal computing. D. L. Gonzalez. il *Newsweek* 114:64 Ag 28 '89
Where Slava starts over again [Moscow Beginners, first Soviet group] G. Garelik. il *Time* 133:10+ Ap 10 '89
ALCOHOLISM *See* Alcoholics and alcoholism
ALCOHOLS
See also
Methanol
ALCOMBRACK, GARY
about
A pizza the action. M. Barrier. il por *Nation's Business* 77:68 My '89
ALCOR LIFE EXTENSION FOUNDATION
Reruns will keep sitcom writer Dick Clair on ice—indefinitely. J. S. Kunen. il pors *People Weekly* 32:57+ Jl 17 '89
ALCUIN, 735-804
about
Alcuin and the 'new Athens'. M. Alberi. il por *History Today* 39:35-41 S '89
ALDA, ALAN
about
Alan Alda. por *People Weekly* 31 Special Issue:55 Summ '89
ALDEBURGH FESTIVAL OF MUSIC & THE ARTS *See* Music festivals—Great Britain
ALDEN, PAULETTE BATES, 1947-
A reluctant education. il *The New York Times Magazine* p44+ D 10 '89
ALDERSON, SANDY
about
Baseball meets Harvard Law. A. P. Sanoff. il por *U.S. News & World Report* 107:48-9 Jl 31 '89
ALDISS, BRIAN WILSON, 1925-
about
A chat with Brian W. Aldiss. R. Herbert. il por *Publishers Weekly* 236:24 N 10 '89
ALDOUS, JOAN
What if inflation returns? bibl il *Society* 26:76-82 S/O '89
ALDREDGE, THEONI
about
Taking the stage. pors *Harper's Bazaar* 122:150-3+ Ag '89
ALDRICH, BARBARA
Webs [poem] *Good Housekeeping* 209:262 N '89
ALDRIDGE, JOHN W.
Hostages to fortune. *The American Scholar* 58:61-75 Wint '89
ALDRIDGE, RICHARD J. (RICHARD JOHN), AND BRIGGS, DEREK E. G.
A soft body of evidence. il *Natural History* p6+ My '89
ALDRIDGE FAMILY
about
Hostages to fortune. J. W. Aldridge. *The American Scholar* 58:61-75 Wint '89
ALDRIN, BUZZ
about
Of space and the moon man. P. Axthelm. il pors *People Weekly* 32:30-3 Jl 3 '89
ALDRIN, BUZZ, AND MCCONNELL, MALCOLM
Men from earth [condensation] il por *Reader's Digest* 135:30-8+ Jl '89

Venturing outward: 1969-2009 [excerpt from Men from earth] il por *Ad Astra* 1:55-7 Jl/Ag '89
ALDRIN, EDWIN E. *See* Aldrin, Buzz
ALERTNESS *See* Attention
ALESHIRE, JOAN
Air show [poem] *The Nation* 249:434 O 16 '89
Full flower moon [poem] *The Nation* 248:746 My 29 '89
ALESSI SPA
The domestic landscape. K. D. Stein. il *Architectural Record* 177:104-7 mid-S '89
ALEX HALEY HOUSE MUSEUM
Where "Roots" was born. il *Southern Living* 24:40 Je '89
ALEXANDER, THE GREAT, 356-323 B.C.
about
Herodotus, Alexander, and Rome. G. W. Bowersock. *The American Scholar* 58:407-14 Summ '89
ALEXANDER, BENJAMIN H.
Reflections on education and our society [address, April 16, 1989] *Vital Speeches of the Day* 55:563-5 Jl 1 '89
Why is the environmental crisis happening? [address, September 13, 1989] *Vital Speeches of the Day* 56:124-8 D 1 '89
ALEXANDER, BRYAN
Keepers of the game. il *International Wildlife* 19:34-40 S/O '89
ALEXANDER, CAROLINE
Profiles [D. Park] il por *The New Yorker* 64:57-71 Ja 30 '89
ALEXANDER, DAVID
The land of bilk and money. il *The Humanist* 49:43-4 N/D '89
ALEXANDER, EDWARD, 1936-
Israel & American Jews [discussion of September 1988 article, Where is Zion?] *Commentary* 87:8-11 F '89
Professor of terror. *Commentary* 88:49-50 Ag '89
"Professor of terror" [discussion of August 1989 article] *Commentary* 88:2-7+ D '89
ALEXANDER, HUGH
about
Baseball lives [excerpt] M. Bryan. il por *Sports Illustrated* 70:76-8 Ap 24 '89
ALEXANDER, JANET, D. 1986
about
When mental illness hits home [cover story; special section] E. E. Goode. il pors *U.S. News & World Report* 106:54-7+ Ap 24 '89
ALEXANDER, JASON
about
Alexander the great. R. D. Story. il por *New York* 22:38 F 27 '89
ALEXANDER, JULIE
about
All alone by his telephone, big talker Larry King reaches out and marries someone. W. Plummer. il pors *People Weekly* 32:115+ O 23 '89
ALEXANDER, KYLE
about
"God wouldn't mess with an angry mother!". S. Weller. il por *McCall's* 116:130+ My '89
ALEXANDER, LAMAR
about
Lamar Alexander on schools and business [interview] D. C. Bacon. il por *Nation's Business* 77:24 Ap '89
ALEXANDER, LORRAINE
Point Reyes. il *Gourmet* 49:100-7+ D '89
ALEXANDER, RATONUA
about
Whitest city in Illinois graduates only black teen from high school. il por *Jet* 76:14 Je 26 '89
ALEXANDER, ROBERT
about
Chicago couple wins $6 mil. in Illinois state lottery. il por *Jet* 76:10 S 25 '89
ALEXANDER, SADIE TANNER MOSELL, D. 1989
about
Obituary
Jet il por 77:52 N 20 '89
ALEXANDER, SHANA
about
Appeal Court reverses libel ruling against Doubleday's 'Nutcracker'. C. Reid. *Publishers Weekly* 235:22 Ja 6 '89
ALEXANDER, STANFORD J., 1928-
about
Discipline, discipline, discipline. J. H. Taylor. il por *Forbes* 144:42-3 Jl 24 '89
ALEXANDER, YONAH
about
Remedy for terror: fight back [interview] T. Nugent. il por *People Weekly* 32:64 D 18 '89
ALEXANDER CITY (ALA.)
Moral conditions
A rap album in the dock [obscenity case against record store selling The 2 Live Crew] N. Zeman. il *Newsweek* 114:72 O 16 '89

ALEXANDER-MOEGERLE, GIL
about
James Dobson sued by former employees. K. A. Lawton. il pors *Christianity Today* 33:42 F 3 '89
ALEXANDRE, 1922-
about
Alexandre has influenced hairstyles the world over for nearly fifty years. J. Burstall. il pors *Vogue* 179:285+ S '89
ALEXANDRIA (EGYPT)
Hotels, motels, etc.
High tea and hashish [Cecil Hotel] R. Shorto. il *Gentlemen's Quarterly* 59:64+ N '89
Libraries
All the books in the world. il *UN Chronicle* 26:46-7 Je '89
Bibliotheca Alexandrina. L. Soliman. il map *The Courier (Unesco)* 41:8-11 N '88
ALEXANDRIA (VA.)
Architecture
Adding up [house in Rosemont area] il *Southern Living* 24:158 Ap '89
Vintage townhouse for a young family. il *Southern Living* 24:178-9 N '89
Art
See also
Torpedo Factory Art Center (Alexandria, Va.)
Housing
Va. woman gets $120,000 in civil rights lawsuit [F. Bradley] *Jet* 77:9 N 13 '89
ALEXANDROV RED ARMY SONG AND DANCE ENSEM-BLE *See* Red Army Chorus
ALEXIS, KIM
about
Kim Alexis—pregnancy the second time around. L. MacCallum. il por *Glamour* 87:32 Jl '89
A steady grace. C. Valentino. il pors *American Health* 8:86-7 O '89
ALEXIS (ARRAY OF LOW-ENERGY X-RAY IMAGING SENSORS) *See* Artificial satellites—Astronomical use
ALEXITHYMIA
Men without passion. L. Miller. il *Psychology Today* 22:20-2 D '88
ALEXOPOULOS, HELENE
about
Helene Alexopoulos, New York City Ballet's newest ballerina, is also one of Balanchine's last protégées. D. Daniel. il por *Vogue* 179:260 N '89
ALF (FICTIONAL CHARACTER)
Could that ALF cartoon be flashing a hidden message? [subliminal messages] D. Hill and K. Sobel. il *TV Guide* 37:6-7+ Ag 12-18 '89
ALFA ROMEO (AUTOMOBILE) *See* Automobiles, Foreign; Sports cars
ALFALFA
Bovine 'balers' stack big profits [controlled grazing of alfalfa] J. Walter. il *Successful Farming* 87:32-3 mid-Mr '89
ALFONSÍN, RAÚL
about
Argentina after Villa Martelli. A. M. Shapiro. il *The New Leader* 72:11-12 Ja 9 '89
Resignation
Abdication in Argentina. J. Contreras. il por *Newsweek* 113:46-7 Je 26 '89
ALFONSO, KRISTIAN
about
'I don't want to stand there like a cheese omelet!'. B. Davidson. il pors *TV Guide* 37:31-2+ Ap 22-28 '89
ALFORD, RON
about
Staking an insurance claim [interview] M. Henkenius. il por *Home Mechanix* 85:40-3 O '89
ALFORD, STEVE
The Knight I knew [excerpt from Playing for Knight]; ed. by John Garrity. il pors *The Saturday Evening Post* 261:66-8+ N/D '89
ALFORD, THOMAS
about
A social contract? Master against servant in the Court of Requests. P. S. Seaver. il *History Today* 39:50-6 S '89
ALFRED C. KINSEY INSTITUTE FOR SEX RESEARCH
See also
Kinsey Institute for Research in Sex, Gender and Reproduction
ALFVÉN, HANNES OLOF GÖSTA, 1908-
about
Geophysical Union salutes excellent work in the field. pors *Physics Today* 42:87-91 D '89
ALGAE
See also
Brown tide
Coccolithophores
Kelp
Phytoplankton
Plankton
Prochlorophytes
Red tide
Seaweed
Stoneworts

Water bloom
Blue-green algae kill HIV in culture [research by Michael R. Boyd] *Science News* 136:141 Ag 26 '89
Caribbean coral reefs: are they becoming algal reefs? B. E. Lapointe. il *Sea Frontiers* 35:82-91 Mr/Ap '89
Land plants' algal roots [research by Charles F. Delwiche] *Science News* 136:70 Jl 29 '89
Lignin-like compounds and sporopollenin in Coleochaete, an algal model for land plant ancestry. C. F. Delwiche and others. bibl f il *Science* 245:399-401 Jl 28 '89
ALGAE, FOSSIL
Cold death questioned for early algae [Pertatataka acritarchs; research by Wen-Long Zang and Malcolm R. Walter] *Science News* 135:126 F 25 '89
ALGAL BLOOM *See* Water bloom
ALGEBRA
See also
Algorithms
The creative computer [Q1 algebra; work of B. Williams] B. Lawren. il *Omni (New York, N.Y.)* 11:28+ Je '89
Say it again in plain algebra [Susan Landau devises algorithm to denest radicals produced by computer algebra systems] B. A. Cipra. *Science* 245:1190-1 S 15 '89; Correction. 246:997 N 24 '89
ALGERIA
See also
Algerians
Birth control—Algeria
Government and the press—Algeria
Investments, Foreign—Algeria
Midwives—Algeria
Motion pictures—Algeria
Riots—Algeria
Women—Algeria
Economic policy
Algeria tries untying the knots of socialism. S. Toy. il por *Business Week* p49 Jl 31 '89
Foreign opinion
French
Letter from Europe. J. Kramer. *The New Yorker* 64:72-4+ Ja 30 '89
Foreign relations
Morocco
See also
Western Sahara conflict, 1975-
ALGERIANS
France
Letter from Europe. J. Kramer. *The New Yorker* 64:72-4+ Ja 30 '89
ALGONQUIN (NEW YORK, N.Y.: HOTEL) *See* New York (N.Y.)—Hotels, motels, etc.
ALGONQUIN ROUND TABLE
The Algonquin—nights at the Round Table. H. H. Broun. il *Architectural Digest* 46:184+ N '89
A night of the Round Table [recreation to raise money for the Writers Theatre] D. Blum. il *New York* 22:15 Ja 2 '89
ALGORITHMS
See also
Genetic algorithms
Focus on algorithms. D. Pountain. See issues of Byte beginning June 1987 through March 1988
Light reflection models for computer graphics. D. Greenberg. bibl f il *Science* 244:166-73 Ap 14 '89
A near-optimum parallel planarization algorithm. Y. Takefuji and K.-C. Lee. bibl f il *Science* 245:1221-3 S 15 '89
Say it again in plain algebra [Susan Landau devises algorithm to denest radicals produced by computer algebra systems] B. A. Cipra. *Science* 245:1190-1 S 15 '89; Correction. 246:997 N 24 '89
The shortest-network problem [Steiner problem] M. W. Bern and R. L. Graham. bibl il map *Scientific American* 260:84-9 Ja '89
ALHADEFF, VICTOR
about
Soft in the head? L. Jereski. il *Forbes* 143:54 Mr 6 '89
ALI, KHALILAH
about
Ali's ex-wife, Khalilah, has child, will marry. il por *Jet* 77:55 O 9 '89
Khalilah Ali marries in her Flossmoor mansion. il pors *Jet* 77:15 O 30 '89
ALI, MUHAMMAD, 1942-
about
Ali says former champs 'are all the greatest'. il por *Jet* 77:54 N 20 '89
Arsenio jokes with 3 champs—Ali, Tyson, Leonard—on show. il pors *Jet* 76:46-7 Ag 21 '89
A celebration of Muhammad Ali [cover story] G. Smith. il pors *Sports Illustrated* 71 Special Issue:214-18+ N 15 '89
DNA test says Ali isn't father of Houston girl. il pors *Jet* 75:52 F 20 '89
Float like a butterfly, sting like a bee . . . the man for all seasons was Muhammad Ali. D. Hiltbrand. il por *TV Guide* 37:41-2 My 6-12 '89
Great men die twice. M. Kram. il pors *Esquire* 111:210-14+ Je '89

ALI, MUHAMMAD, 1942-—about—*cont.*
Muhammad Ali: an intimate new look at a legend. H. J. Massaquoi. i pors *Ebony* 45:174-6+ N '89
My dinner with Ali. D. Miller. il pors *Sport (New York, N.Y.)* 80:70-2+ My '89

ALI, TARIQ
Cortege to hell [poem] *The Nation* 248:872-3 Je 26 '89

about
Iranian nights [drama] Reviews
Newsweek il 113:43 My 1 '89

ALIA-THE ROYAL JORDANIAN AIRLINE
Royal Jordanian seeks alliance of Arab carriers. M. Mecham. il *Aviation Week & Space Technology* 130:67+ Ja 9 '89

ALIBRANDI, JOSEPH F., 1928-
Century 21 education [address, October 11, 1988] *Vital Speeches of the Day* 55:247-50 F 1 '89

ALICE COOPER *See* Cooper, Alice

ALICE IN WONDERLAND (FICTIONAL CHARACTER)
Alice in Drugland [scenario by Dennis Thompson] il *USA Today (Periodical)* 118:18-19 O '89

ALICO INC.
The last of the citrus barons [B. H. Griffin] T. Trussell. il pors *Nation's Business* 77:46+ F '89

ALIEN ANIMALS *See* Animal introduction
ALIEN INSECTS *See* Insect introduction
ALIEN LABOR
See also
Migrant labor
Hiring foreign experts. R. M. Foley. *High Technology Business* 9:12-13 Ja '89
Opening doors for immigrants. J. C. Szabo. il *Nation's Business* 77:48-9 Ag '89
Raids, racism and the I.N.S. [on trial for harassing Mexican immigrants in California] E. Shorris. il *The Nation* 248:628-30 My 8 '89
Roll out America's red carpet for the skilled. M. J. Mandel. il *Business Week* p128 O 30 '89
Singing the green card blues [hiring a foreigner as a household employee] N. Henderson. il *Changing Times* 43:71-4 O '89
Take a number and wait [immigration amnesty program] D. Shaw. *The Washington Monthly* 21:28-30+ S '89
Why I am homeless. C. C. Bruno. il por *The Humanist* 49:10-11+ My/Je '89

Salaries, pensions, etc.
Immigrant workers fight for wages. S. Paterno. il *The Progressive* 53:13-14 Je '89

Western Europe
Scorned today, hailed tomorrow? D. Lawday. il *U.S. News & World Report* 106:51-3 Ja 30 '89

ALIEN NATION [film] *See* Motion picture reviews—Single works
ALIEN NATION [television program] *See* Television program reviews—Single works

ALIENATION (SOCIAL PSYCHOLOGY)
Literacy acquisition and alienation [whole language learning] S. Harman and C. Edelsky. *The Education Digest* 55:35-9 D '89
Student alienation and academic achievement. R. L. Calabrese. *The Education Digest* 54:7-9 My '89

ALIENS
See also
Alien labor
Citizenship
Strangers
United States. Immigration and Naturalization Service

Deportation
See Deportation

Statistics
Census and citizenship [counting of illegal aliens for purposes of congressional apportionment] *National Review* 41:14+ S 29 '89
Finding out who counts [undercounting minorities and aliens in the census] S. Rabinove. il *Commonweal* 116:360-1 Je 16 '89
Who should count in the 1990 census? C. Norman. il *Science* 243:601-2 F 3 '89

Mexico
The journey to the Rio Grande [undocumented Central Americans cross Mexico] J. Reyes Estrada. il *World Press Review* 36:30-1 Ap '89

ALIGNMENT OF AUTOMOBILE WHEELS *See* Automobiles—Wheels
ALIGNMENT OF PLANETS *See* Conjunctions (Astronomy)
ALIMONY
Isaac Hayes jailed for failing to pay alimony. il por *Jet* 75:8 Mr 13 '89

ALINE, COUNTESS OF ROMANONES
A reign in Spain: the Countess of Romanones in Extremadura and New York. il pors *Architectural Digest* 46:192-9 Ap '89

ALINSKY, SAUL
about
Saul Alinsky: homo ludens for urban democracy. R. Luecke. il por *The Christian Century* 106:1050-3 N 15 '89

ALIQUIPPA (PA.)
Religious institutions and affairs
Aliquippa's star attraction [Community of Celebration] J. Duin. il *Christianity Today* 33:14+ Ja 13 '89

ALISON ON DOMINICK STREET (NEW YORK, N.Y.: RESTAURANT) *See* New York (N.Y.)—Restaurants, nightclubs, bars, etc.

ALISTAIR MCALPINE (FIRM)
The New Curiosity Shop. P. Kinmonth. il por *House & Garden* 161:78+ Mr '89

ALKALINE PAPER *See* Paper

ALKALOIDS
Giving neurotransmitters a second wind [huperzine A; work of Alan P. Kozikowski] *Science News* 135:366 Je 10 '89

ALKON, DANIEL L.
Memory storage and neural systems. il *Scientific American* 261:42-50 Jl '89

ALL-AMERICA SELECTIONS (PLANTS) *See* Plants—All-America Selections
ALL-AMERICAN FOOTBALL PLAYERS *See* Football players
ALL-AMERICAN GIRL CONTEST
All-American Girl-talk [finalist D. Feil] il pors *'Teen* 33:92 Ag '89
All-American Girl-talk [finalist D. Owens] il pors *'Teen* 33:8 O '89
All-American Girl-talk [finalist J. Scher] il pors *'Teen* 33:12 S '89
All-American Girl-talk [finalist T. Sanborn] il pors *'Teen* 33:98 N '89
Star-spangled style! [winner P. Yi] il pors *'Teen* 33:64-8 Jl '89

ALL-AMERICAN SOAP BOX DERBY *See* Soap box derbies
ALL DOGS GO TO HEAVEN [film] *See* Motion picture reviews—Single works
ALL ENGLAND LAWN TENNIS AND CROQUET CLUB
Garden party [flowers on club grounds] il *World Tennis* 37:38-9 Jl '89
ALL GOD'S DANGERS [drama] *See* Rosengarten, Theodore
ALL IN THE FAMILY [television program] *See* Television program reviews—Single works
ALL MY CHILDREN [television program] *See* Television program reviews—Single works
ALL NIPPON AIRWAYS CO. LTD.
All Nippon buys 20 747-400s, a record order. C. Fotos. il *Aviation Week & Space Technology* 130:69-70 F 27 '89
All Nippon taps partners' fleets to expand international service. J. Ott. il *Aviation Week & Space Technology* 130:44 My 8 '89
ALL-PHILADELPHIA JAZZ ENSEMBLE
All-Philadelphia Jazz. R. Woessner. il por *Down Beat* 56:24-5 O '89
ALL-PRO BASKETBALL PLAYERS *See* Basketball players
ALL-PRO FOOTBALL PLAYERS *See* Football players
ALL SOULS' DAY
Skeletons at the feast [Mexican Feast of the Dead] J. Pérez Siller. il *The Unesco Courier* 42:19-24 D '89
ALL-STAR GAMES *See* Baseball, Professional—All-star games; Basketball, Professional—All-star games
ALL TERRAIN BICYCLES *See* Bicycles
ALL TERRAIN VEHICLES
Agricultural use
Agile aces for gentle jobs. D. Mowitz. il *Successful Farming* 87:22-3 Je '89
ATV tools tackle livestock chores. D. Mowitz. il *Successful Farming* 87:28-9 N '89
Bantamweight sprayers, heavyweight results [ATV sprayers] D. Mowitz and C. Finck. il *Successful Farming* 87:66N-66O F '89
Environmental aspects
Ethics and USGS [discussion of November 3, 1989 article, Ethics debate sends tremors through USGS] E. Marshall. *Science* 246:1548-9 D 22 '89
Ethics debate sends tremors through USGS [case of H. G. Wilshire] E. Marshall. il por *Science* 246:570-1 N 3 '89
Interior may lift Cape Cod ORV ban. il *National Parks* 63:8-9 S/O '89
An old foe with new tricks. D. Dagget. il *Sierra* 74:30-2 Ja/F '89
Safety devices and measures
All terrain vehicles: a safety success story. T. M. Scanlon. il *Consumers' Research Magazine* 72:29-31 Je '89
Shock absorbers
Shocking improvements. T. Opre. il *Outdoor Life* 184:52-4 Ag '89
Testing
Red ride on the beach [Honda Pilot] T. Van Hooydonk and J. P. Burns. il *Cycle* 40:38-42+ F '89
ALL-UNION LENIN YOUNG COMMUNIST LEAGUE
The young fight for the 'three Ds'. K. Vanden Heuvel. il *The Nation* 248:729-31 My 29 '89
ALL-WAYS BEST DAIRY
Milk and more in family farm store. J. R. Borcherding. il *Successful Farming* 87:48 Ja '89
ALL WEATHER CAMERAS *See* Cameras
ALLBERY, DEBRA
In the dream she doesn't tell him [poem] *The Nation* 248:708 My 22 '89

ALLEGHENY AIRLINES, INC. *See* USAir, Inc.
ALLEGHENY INTERNATIONAL INC.
Allegheny's battle to come back from the abyss. M. Schroeder. il *Business Week* p130+ Je 26 '89
ALLEGHENY LUDLUM CORP.
Specialty metals that are special indeed. G. L. Miles. il *Business Week* Special Issue:129 Je 16 '89
ALLEGHENY MOUNTAINS REGION
Description and travel
Ridge runners [ridge soaring in sailplanes] N. Moll. il *Flying* 116:58-62+ Ag '89
L'ALLEGRO, IL PENSEROSO ED IL MODERATO [dance]
See Dance reviews—Single works
ALLEMAN, RICHARD
Travel news. See issues of Vogue
ALLEN, BARBARA
(jt. auth) See Hogan, Barbara, and Allen, Barbara
ALLEN, BONNIE
Anne Archer. il por *Ms.* 17:76-8 Ja/F '89
Glenn Close: sitting pretty [cover story] il pors *Ms.* 18:46-50 N '89
Hot voice, cool head [cover story] il pors *Ms.* 17:42-5 Je '89
ALLEN, CHARLOTTE LOW
The mysteries of RU-486. il *The American Spectator* 22:17-20 O '89
ALLEN, DEBBIE
about
Debbie Allen and Norman Nixon tell how they mix marriage, business and parenthood [cover story] il pors *Jet* 76:56-8 Jl 31 '89
Doing it all—her way!! il pors *Ebony* 45:54+ N '89
Phylicia, Debbie and Keshia head all-star cast in TV musical, Polly [cover story] il pors *Jet* 77:58-60 N 13 '89
Raiding Cosby for her stars, Debbie Allen turns Pollyanna into a black musical, Polly. J. Park. il pors *People Weekly* 32:102-4 Ag 28 '89
ALLEN, DEBORAH
about
The sky is rising? P. Brimelow. il pors *Forbes* 144:156+ N 13 '89
ALLEN, DEE DEE
about
Grammy award. C. O'Connor. il por *Women's Sports & Fitness* 11:58 Je '89
ALLEN, EDWARD, 1948-
The beautiful ones [story] *The New Yorker* 65:48-9 D 11 '89
ALLEN, FRED, 1894-1956
about
Radio days. M. Richler. il por *Gentlemen's Quarterly* 59:122+ Je '89
ALLEN, GERI
about
Back to Africa. K. Kevorkian. il por *Mother Jones* 14:15 N '89
ALLEN, GILBERT, 1951-
Twelve words on a windy day [poem] *The American Scholar* 58:76-8 Wint '89
ALLEN, GRACIE, 1906?-1964
about
Amazing Gracie. M. G. Stoddard. il pors *The Saturday Evening Post* 261:58-9 Mr '89
ALLEN, HARRY
Hip-hop madness. il *Essence* 19:78-80+ Ap '89
ALLEN, HENRY
Henry Allen explores the history of White House entertaining, concluding that food and fashion are not the point. il *Vogue* 179:450+ N '89
ALLEN, JAMES PAUL, 1936-, AND TURNER, EUGENE, 1946-
Asians dominate recent immigration trends. il *Utne Reader* p104 Mr/Ap '89
ALLEN, JANET M., AND SEED, BRIAN
Isolation and expression of functional high-affinity Fc receptor complementary DNAs. bibl f il *Science* 243:378-81 Ja 20 '89
ALLEN, JENNIFER
Antiquing in Scotland. il pors maps *Architectural Digest* 46:166-73+ O '89
Architectural digest visits: Joan Rivers. il pors *Architectural Digest* 46:134-9+ F '89
Bob Mackie: casual comfort in Beverly Hills. il por *Architectural Digest* 46:146-51+ S '89
Phone-a-go-go. *Utne Reader* p94-5 S/O '89
ALLEN, JOSEPH P.
Commercial space: lost on the way to Mars? *Ad Astra* 1:3 D '89
ALLEN, LEAH
My year of loving dangerously: confessions of a non-condom-user. *Mademoiselle* 95:221+ Mr '89
ALLEN, MARK, 1958-
about
Big splash in Hawaii. K. Moore. il pors *Sports Illustrated* 71:62-4+ O 23 '89
Tips from the super jocks. P. Serrani. il pors *Gentlemen's Quarterly* 59:250-7 My '89

ALLEN, PAULA GUNN
America's Founding Mothers: our Native American roots [excerpt from The sacred hoop] il *Utne Reader* p108-9 Mr/Ap '89
ALLEN, PETER
about
Legs Diamond comes to Broadway: give 'em the old razzle-dazzle [cover story] K. Grubb. il pors *Dance Magazine* 63:40-4 Ja '89
ALLEN, PHYLICIA AYERS- See Rashad, Phylicia
ALLEN, RANDY
about
'I'm in the dark'. G. Johnston. il por *Successful Farming* 87:34X mid-F '89
ALLEN, ROBERT E.
Policies for a competitive America [address, February 16, 1989] *Vital Speeches of the Day* 55:413-16 Ap 15 '89
about
Bob Allen is turning AT&T into a live wire. J. J. Keller. il por *Business Week* p140-1+ N 6 '89
Bob Allen rattles the cages at AT&T [cover story] A. Kupfer. il pors *Fortune* 119:58-61+ Je 19 '89
Robert Allen. J. J. Keller. por *Business Week* Special Issue:109 Ap 14 '89
ALLEN, STEVE, 1921-
about
The gift of gab [interview] L. Konner. pors *New Choices for the Best Years* 29:11-12 S '89
ALLEN, TERRY, 1943-
about
Song and set. T. Frick. il por *Art in America* 77:67+ D '89
True grit. P. Clothier. il por *Art News* 88:102-7 Ja '89
ALLEN, THOMAS B., 1929-
Shaking gold from China's treetops. il *International Wildlife* 19:34-6 Jl/Ag '89
ALLEN, WILLIAM B.
The new racism is the old power grab [cover story] il por *Conservative Digest* 15:16-21 Jl/Ag '89
about
Off the record. Cato. *National Review* 41:64 N 24 '89
ALLEN, WOODY
about
Another woman [film] Reviews
Video 13:62+ Je '89. I. Robbins
Crimes and misdemeanors [film] Reviews
America 161:429-30 D 9 '89. R. A. Blake
The Christian Century il por 106:991 N 1 '89. J. M. Wall
Commonweal 116:706 D 15 '89. T. O'Brien
Maclean's il por 102:68 O 23 '89. B. D. Johnson
The Nation 249:575-6 N 13 '89. S. Klawans
National Review il 41:46-8 D 8 '89. J. Simon
The New Republic 201:43 N 27 '89. L. Wieseltier
The New Republic 201:22-3 N 13 '89. S. Kauffmann
New York il 22:124+ O 23 '89. D. Denby
The New Yorker 65:76-8 O 30 '89. P. Kael
Newsweek il por 114:67 O 16 '89. J. Kroll
People Weekly il por 32:13 O 16 '89. R. Novak
Rolling Stone il p35 N 2 '89. P. Travers
Time il por 134:82 O 16 '89. R. Schickel
'Crimes' story. M. Pally. il por *Film Comment* 25:11-12+ N/D '89
New York stories [film] Reviews
America 160:353 Ap 15 '89. R. A. Blake
The American Spectator il 22:37-8 My '89. B. Bawer
Commonweal il 116:212-13 Ap 7 '89. T. O'Brien
Maclean's il pors 102:62 Mr 13 '89. B. D. Johnson
The Nation 248:426-7 Mr 27 '89. S. Klawans
National Review 41:45+ Je 16 '89. J. Simon
The New Leader il 72:20-1 Mr 6 '89. J. Morrone
The New Republic 200:24-6 Mr 27 '89. S. Kauffmann
New York il 22:63-4 Mr 13 '89. D. Denby
The New Yorker 65:93-6 Mr 20 '89. P. Kael
Newsweek il 113:58 Mr 6 '89. D. Ansen
People Weekly il 31:15-16 Mr 13 '89. S. Haller
Time il 133:68 Mr 6 '89. R. Schickel
Play it again, Woody. T. A. Sancton. il por *Time* 134:76-8 O 23 '89
ALLEN-BRADLEY CO.
Computer-controlled drill designed to meet unique B-2 fabrication needs. il *Aviation Week & Space Technology* 130:51-2 Ap 17 '89
ALLEN-EDMONDS SHOE CORP.
Party crasher. R. Reiff. il por *Forbes* 143:128+ Je 12 '89
U.S. shoe firms thrive in high-quality market. J. E. Bahls. il *Nation's Business* 77:38-40 F '89
ALLENDE GOSSENS, SALVADOR, 1908-1973
about
Innocent abroad. R. Jordan. il *The Progressive* 53:46 Ag '89
ALLENDE METEORITE See Meteorites
ALLERGENS
Allergy-triggering receptor made en masse [work of Jean Pierre Kinet] R. Weiss. *Science News* 135:246 Ap 22 '89
Expression of high-affinity binding of human immunoglobulin E by transfected cells. L. Miller and others. bibl f il *Science* 244:334-7 Ap 21 '89

ALLERGIC BRONCHIAL ASTHMA See Asthma
ALLERGY
See also
Allergens
Anaphylaxis
Contact dermatitis
Environmental illness
Food allergy
Hay fever
National Institute of Allergy and Infectious Diseases (U.S.)
Poison ivy
25 breathe-easy tips from America's top allergists. M. McGrath. il *Prevention (Emmaus, Pa.)* 41:33-40 Ag '89
Allergic reactions [children] S. Carrell. il *Better Homes and Gardens* 67:32+ Mr '89
Allergy causes colitis. C. SerVaas. il *The Saturday Evening Post* 261:98+ Ja/F '89
Allergy warfare [cover story; special section] il *U.S. News & World Report* 106:68-72+ F 20 '89
Coping with summer allergies. C. Slom. *McCall's* 116:88 Ag '89
Could you have a hidden allergy? K. Keller. il *Redbook* 173:142-3+ O '89
Emotions and allergies: the Pavlov connection [research by Glenda MacQueen] B. L. Benderly. *Psychology Today* 23:17 Je '89
Help for the allergic pet. A. R. Marder. il *Prevention (Emmaus, Pa.)* 41:97-100+ N '89
Is that sniffle a cold or an allergy? *McCall's* 116:81 Ja '89
Pavlov's rats [allergic reaction produced by Pavlovian conditioning] il *Discover* 10:14 My '89
Puffy, watery eyes and a swollen, runny nose can defeat the most rigorous beauty routine. L. F. McCarthy. *Vogue* 179:386 S '89
Scent allergy alert. 1 *Essence* 20:46 D '89
Sneeze calendar [chart listing types of pollen by geographic location] il *American Health* 8:16 Jl/Ag '89
Stop sneezing and sniffling [views of Robert Bush] il *USA Today (Periodical)* 118:14 Ag '89
Wheezes, sneezes, and rashes [children] J. T. Gibson. il *Parents* 64:142 Ag '89
ALLEY, KIRSTIE
about
Kirstie Alley's animal magnetism. L. Morice. il por *Mademoiselle* 95:82 O '89
ALLEY, WILLIAM J., 1929-
about
Break up or build up? il por *Forbes* 143:102 Ja 9 '89
ALLIANCE (NEB.)
Monuments, statues, etc.
In a Nebraska wheat field stands Carhenge, attracting a bumper crop of tourists—and trouble [monument created from used automobiles by J. Reinders] M. Neill. il por *People Weekly* 32:196-7 D 11 '89
ALLIANCE CAPITAL MANAGEMENT CORP.
Trolling for prizes in 'the backwater of the fixed-income market' [views of S. G. Peabody] L. Light. il por *Business Week* p133 D 25 '89-Ja 1 '90
ALLIANCE DEFENSE CORPORATION
Alliance Defense Corp. leads MSOW competition [modular stand-off weapons system] *Aviation Week & Space Technology* 130:33 Je 19 '89
ALLIANCE FOR ENVIRONMENTAL EDUCATION
A national network for environmental education. D. A. Pemberton. *The Education Digest* 54:42-5 My '89
ALLIANCES
See also
ANZUS Council
ASEAN
North Atlantic Treaty Organization
South Asian Association for Regional Cooperation
Warsaw Treaty Organization
ALLIED CORP.
See also
Allied-Signal Inc.
ALLIED PRODUCTS CORP.
Down on the farm. T. Jaffe. *Forbes* 143:124 Ja 23 '89
Knee-deep in debt. M. Berss. il *Forbes* 144:88 N 13 '89
ALLIED-SIGNAL INC.
Step aside, Superman [Kevlar vs. Spectra Shield] A. A. Lappen. il *Forbes* 143:124+ F 6 '89
Turnaround time at Allied-Signal. il *Money* 18:10 My '89
ALLIED STORES CORP.
Campeau is up on that high wire again. C. Hawkins and S. Phillips. il por *Business Week* p108-10 My 15 '89
Walking a fine line [R. Campeau] P. Chisholm. il por *Maclean's* 102:50-1 Ja 2 '89
ALLIGATOR RIVER NATIONAL WILDLIFE REFUGE (N.C.)
Praise for a red predator [reintroduction of red wolves] N. Angier. il maps *American Health* 8:74-6+ S '89
ALLIGATORS
See also
Crocodiles
Return of a reptile [Florida] J. Gorman. il *Sports Illustrated* 70:50-2+ Mr 6 '89

ALLISON, STACY
about
What it takes to reach the summit. J. Skow. il pors *Time* 133:14-15+ Mr 6 '89
ALLISON, WICK
How to win an election. *National Review* 41:24 O 13 '89
ALLISON GAS TURBINE OPERATIONS
Allison considers development of new high-performance engine. *Aviation Week & Space Technology* 131:78 Jl 17 '89
Allison engine chosen for Saab 2000; Sweden certifies Saab 340B transport. il *Aviation Week & Space Technology* 131:29 Jl 17 '89
Allison will apply GM mass-production experience to expendable engine efforts. S. W. Kandebo. il *Aviation Week & Space Technology* 129:63 Mr 6 '89
Douglas prepares to flight test PW-Allison propfan powerplant. il *Aviation Week & Space Technology* 130:35 Ja 2 '89
ALLMAN, T. D.
The jewel of the Chao Phraya. il *Gentlemen's Quarterly* 59:160-5+ Ja '89
ALLMAN, WILLIAM F.
Alphabet medicine. il *Health (New York, N.Y.)* 21:34+ Ja '89
ALLMAN BROTHERS BAND
Allman Brothers retrospective due. P. Howard. il *Rolling Stone* p27 Je 1 '89
The Allmans' beautiful 'Dreams'. J. Guterman. il *Rolling Stone* p161-2 Jl 13-27 '89
ALLMON, CHARLES
about
The long and short of it. M. Hulbert. il *Forbes* 143:217 Mr 20 '89
"Star" funds: three hits, three misses. M. Schiffres. il pors *Changing Times* 43:59-63 My '89
ALLNET COMMUNICATION SERVICES, INC.
See also
ALC Communications Corporation
ALLOCATION OF RESOURCES See Resource allocation
ALLOSTERISM
Triggering of allostery in an enzyme by a point mutation: ornithine transcarbamoylase. L. C. Kuo and others. bibl f il *Science* 245:522-4 Ag 4 '89
ALLOWANCES, CHILDREN'S See Children's allowances
ALLOYS
See also
Quasicrystals
Spin glasses
ALLSTON, LYNETTE L.
about
Upscale undies. R. D. Manuel. il por *Essence* 19:41 F '89
ALLWASTE INC.
Bubba Nelson fights for the dirty jobs. T. Vogel. il por *Business Week* p96 My 22 '89
ALMANACS
See also
Astronomy—Almanacs
Dog days, cat nights and pogonips [editing the Old farmer's almanac] M. White. il *Reader's Digest* 135:5-6 Jl '89
Dog days, cat nights and pogonips [editing the Old farmer's almanac] M. White. il por *The New York Times Magazine* p38+ Ap 2 '89
ALMASHREK BANK
License to loot [R. Tamraz] Z. Sawaya. il por *Forbes* 143:157 Mr 6 '89
ALMODÓVAR, PEDRO
about
Matador [film] Reviews
American Film il por 15:70 N '89. P. Rainer
Pedro on the verge of a nervy breakthrough. R. Corliss. il por *Time* 133:68-9 Ja 30 '89
Why I wear what I wear: Man of La Mania. D. Appell. il por *Gentlemen's Quarterly* 59:104+ N '89
A winner from Spain. M. Bayón. il por *World Press Review* 36:60 Ap '89
Women on the verge of a nervous breakdown [film] Reviews
America 160:41+ Ja 21 '89. R. A. Blake
American Film il 15:70 D '89. P. Rainer
Maclean's il 102:50 Ja 30 '89. B. D. Johnson
ALMONDS
A family feud over organic farming pits the Anderson brothers against each other [G. and R. Anderson, growers in the San Joaquin Valley] P. Freeman. il pors *People Weekly* 32:47-8 Jl 24 '89
ALMOST GROWN [television program] See Television program reviews—Single works
ALMS AND ALMSGIVING See Charity
ALOE
Aloe: the healing plant. B. Dunham. il *Flower and Garden* 33:37 N/D '89
ALOFF, MINDY
Africa oye! il *Art in America* 77:63 Jl '89
Dance. See occasional issues of The Nation
Josephine Baker's naughty jiggle makes a comeback: Jazz Age princess. il pors *Dance Magazine* 63:32-4 Jl '89

ALOHA AIRGROUP INC.
Aloha Airgroup modernizes fleet, markets maintenance, cargo services. il *Aviation Week & Space Technology* 130:70-1 Ap 3 '89

ALOHA AIRLINES
Aloha Airgroup modernizes fleet, markets maintenance, cargo services. il *Aviation Week & Space Technology* 130:70-1 Ap 3 '89
Aloha Airlines probe raises questions about FAA surveillance of maintenance [fuselage failure on Boeing 737 in April 1988] *Aviation Week & Space Technology* 131:77+ Ag 28 '89
Aloha upgrades maintenance program, modernizes fleet. il *Aviation Week & Space Technology* 131:79+ Jl 24 '89
NTSB probes Aloha 737's maintenance records [fuselage failure during April 1988 flight] *Aviation Week & Space Technology* 131:131+ S 11 '89
NTSB raps Aloha, aviation system for fuselage failure [Boeing 737 in April 1988] J. Ott. il *Aviation Week & Space Technology* 130:24-6 My 29 '89
Safety Board examines Aloha's maintenance of aging 737s [investigation of fuselage failure during April 1988 flight] *Aviation Week & Space Technology* 131:117+ S 25 '89
Safety Board urges FAA to revamp maintenance, inspection training [investigation of fuselage failure on 737 in April 1988] *Aviation Week & Space Technology* 131:77+ O 23 '89

ALONSO, ALICIA
about
Pirouettes: placed and paced. M. Horosko. il *Dance Magazine* 63:68-9 S '89

ALOVERT, NINA
From St. Petersburg to Leningrad: Lupokhov's legacy. il pors *Dance Magazine* 63:42-6 Mr '89
Makarova returns to the Kirov: going home. il pors *Dance Magazine* 63:36-7 My '89
The new improved Kirov: an interview with Oleg Vinogradov. il por *Dance Magazine* 63:42-4 Jl '89
Two decades of Kirov danseurs: generation in shadow. il *Dance Magazine* 63:52-5 Ap '89

ALPER, JOSEPH
Cold and flu update. *McCall's* 116:81-2+ Ja '89
Expert's guide to relieving back pain. il *McCall's* 116:101-2+ Mr '89
Order on the couch. il *The Atlantic* 263:24-7+ My '89

ALPERT, ARNIE
War and peace in the White Mountains. il *The Progressive* 53:13-14 Mr '89

ALPERT, MICHAEL
Uncivil War—the military struggle. il map *History Today* 39:13-19 Mr '89

ALPERT, RICHARD *See* Ram Dass

ALPES-MARITIMES (FRANCE)
Description and travel
The Alpes-Maritimes: Riviera refuge. K. Eldredge. il *Harper's Bazaar* 122:91-2 My '89

ALPHA, KAREN
Love never forgets [story] il *Redbook* 172:84+ Ap '89

ALPHA BETA CO.
American: can it mine Lucky Stores' magic? R. Grover. il *Business Week* p141+ Ap 24 '89

ALPHA FETOPROTEIN *See* Fetoprotein
ALPHA PHI ALPHA FRATERNITY *See* College fraternities
ALPHA WAVES *See* Brain waves

ALPHABET
See also
Greek alphabet
A Christmas alphabet [excerpt] C. Wells. il *Good Housekeeping* 209:148-51 D '89
The New Talking Stickybear Alphabet. N. Rentschler. il *Compute!* 11:69-70 My '89

ALPINE (WYO.)
Restaurants, nightclubs, bars, etc.
Chrysler would prefer a bar by any other name, but Jeep Molnar would rather fight than switch [suit filed against owner of Jeep's Bar] il por *People Weekly* 31:63 Ap 3 '89

ALPS
Alpine fling. B. W. Yates. il *Car and Driver* 35:158 Jl '89
ALS *See* Amyotrophic lateral sclerosis

ALSACE (FRANCE)
Description and travel
The inns of Alsace. J. Lubarsky. il map *Travel Holiday* 171:48-54 Ja '89

ALSATIAN COOKING *See* Cooking, French
ALSDURF, JIM, AND ALSDURF, PHYLLIS E.
Battered into submission [excerpt] il *Christianity Today* 33:24-7 Je 16 '89

ALSDURF, PHYLLIS E.
(jt. auth) *See* Alsdurf, Jim, and Alsdurf, Phyllis E.

ALSON, JEFFREY A., 1956-
(jt. auth) *See* Gray, Charles L., 1946-, and Alson, Jeffrey A., 1956-

ALSON, PETER
Chan is bluffing (we think). il por *Esquire* 111:166-8+ My '89

ALSOP, JOSEPH, 1910-1989
The WASP ascendancy [cover story]; ed. by Adam Platt. il pors *The New York Review of Books* 36:48-56 N 9 '89
about
Obituary
National Review por 41:48-9 N 10 '89. E. M. Yoder, Jr.
The New Republic 201:10 S 18-25 '89. H. Fairlie
Newsweek il 114:68 S 11 '89. G. F. Will

ALSPAUGH, NANCY
about
TV pros: on the same wavelength. A. L. Ball. il pors *Working Woman* 14:140+ O '89

ALT, CAROL
about
Waiting for the call. A. Murphy. il pors *Sports Illustrated* 70 Special Issue:179-82+ F '89

ALTAVISTA (VA.)
City planning
Altavista gets a heart. il *Southern Living* 24:147 O '89

ALTBACH, PHILIP G.
Needed: an international perspective. il *Phi Delta Kappan* 71:243-5 N '89

ALTENA, MAARTEN
about
Maarten Altena. B. Shoemaker. il por *Down Beat* 56:46-7 Mr '89

ALTER, JONATHAN
Hot reporter [interview with J. Greenfield] il por *Rolling Stone* p102+ My 18 '89
I've tilted at windmills, and the windmills won. *The Washington Monthly* 21:44-5 Mr '89
(jt. auth) *See* Keisling, Phillip, and Alter, Jonathan

ALTER, ROBERT
Jewish mysticism in dispute. *Commentary* 88:53-9 S '89
What was T. S. Eliot? *Commentary* 87:31-7 Mr '89

ALTERATION OF CLOTHING *See* Tailoring
ALTERED STATES OF CONSCIOUSNESS *See* Consciousness

ALTERMAN, ERIC
Black universities: in demand and in trouble. il *The New York Times Magazine* p60-3+ N 5 '89
Ollie's true colors. *The New Republic* 200:13-14 Mr 13 '89
Playing hardball. il pors *The New York Times Magazine* p30-1+ Ap 30 '89

ALTERNATIVE FAMILY
Non-nuclear proliferation: alternative "family" arrangements grow more common across U.S. D. R. Harris. il *Utne Reader* p22-3 Mr/Ap '89
Variations on a theme. J. Seligmann. il *Newsweek* 114 Special Issue:38-40+ Wint '89/Spr '90

ALTERNATIVE LIFE STYLES *See* Counterculture
ALTERNATIVE MEDICINE *See* Holistic medicine
ALTERNATIVE MINIMUM TAX
The AMT trap in the tax code. il *Fortune* 120 no10 Special Issue:204 Fall '89
Time bomb. L. Saunders. il *Forbes* 143:64-5 F 6 '89

ALTERNATIVE OPERATOR SERVICES
See also
International Telecharge Inc.
Alternative operator services. K. K. Gracey. *Consumers' Research Magazine* 72:2 My '89
Calling from the road shouldn't be highway robbery. F. Seghers. il *Business Week* p40 Ap 3 '89
An end to phone-call gouges. P. Plawin. *Changing Times* 43:90+ F '89
Not-so-easy access: telephoning home may cost more than you think. H. Gieseking. il *Travel Holiday* 172:16-18 Ag '89
You call, they collect. G. Eichler. il *Esquire* 112:124 S '89

ALTERNATIVE PERFORMANCE CENTERS *See* Theater buildings
ALTERNATIVE PRESS
Have Mac, will publish. J. Eisendrath. *The Washington Monthly* 21:28-34+ Je '89
Recommended reading. See issues of Utne Reader
Reforming the newspaper: how to get the facts straight [news services] H. Cordes. il *Utne Reader* p34 N/D '89
Zeitgeist. J. Walljasper. See issues of Utne Reader beginning January/February 1988
Poland
Up from the underground in Poland. A. Husarska. il *The New York Times Book Review* 94:1+ O 8 '89

ALTERNATIVE PRESS AWARDS
The Alternative Press Awards. il *Utne Reader* p90-1 S/O '89
The Alternative Press Awards [nominees] il *Utne Reader* p134-5 Jl/Ag '89

ALTERNATIVE SCHOOLS *See* Experimental education
ALTERNATIVE SENTENCES (CRIMINAL JUSTICE) *See* Criminal justice, Administration of
ALTERNATORS, AIRPLANE *See* Airplanes, Light—Electric generators

ALTHORP, CHARLES EDWARD MAURICE SPENCER, VISCOUNT

about

'Champagne Charlie,' Di's dashing brother, takes a bride decked in . . . gold. M. H. J. Farrell. il pors *People Weekly* 32:42-5 O 2 '89

Lord Althorp, Di's impetuous brother, proposes to a model he met only two months ago. T. Allis. il pors *People Weekly* 32:32-3 Jl 24 '89

ALTIMETERS

AltAlert beats altitude busts. J. M. McClellan. il *Flying* 116:20 Ja '89

Altimeter man [W. Peet demonstrates efficacy of hand-held altimeter in exploring Fort Tryon Park] *The New Yorker* 65:48-50 S 25 '89

ALTITUDE

See also

High altitude

Measurement

See also

Altimeters

ALTITUDE FLYING See Aviation—Altitude flying

ALTMAN, BILLY

Restoring harmony. il *High Fidelity (New York, N.Y.)* 39:54-6 My '89

ALTMAN, KATHRYN

about

Architecture: Franklin D. Israel: Kathryn and Robert Altman's Malibu residence. P. Goldberger. il pors *Architectural Digest* 46:120-5+ Jl '89

ALTMAN, ROBERT, 1925-

about

Architecture: Franklin D. Israel: Kathryn and Robert Altman's Malibu residence. P. Goldberger. il pors *Architectural Digest* 46:120-5+ Jl '89

ALTMAN, SIDNEY

about

Catalytic RNA wins Chemistry Nobel. M. M. Waldrop. il pors *Science* 246:325 O 20 '89

Chemistry. il pors *Time* 134:73 O 23 '89

Chemistry of life. R. Corelli. il por *Maclean's* 102:58 O 23 '89

RNA researchers earn Chemistry Nobel. I. Amato. *Science News* 136:262 O 21 '89

ALTMAN (B.) & CO. See B. Altman & Co.

ALTMANN, JEANNE, AND SAMUELS, AMY

Upscale baboons. il *Natural History* p60-3 My '89

ALTROSE

Bovine stomach holds sugary surprise [L-altrose; research by Robert J. Stack] *Science News* 135:46 Ja 21 '89

ALTRUISM

See also

Assistance in emergencies

Helping behavior

Accounting for others' needs [study by E. Gil Clary] B. Fischman. *Psychology Today* 22:66 D '88

Doing good. A. Kohn. *Current (Washington, D.C.)* 309:4-6 Ja '89

ALTRUISM IN BIRDS See Birds—Habits and behavior

ALTSHULER, IGOR IZODOROVICH, AND MNAT-SAKANYAN, RUBEN ARTYOMOVICH

Excerpts from a roundtable at Moscow State University. il *Environment* 30:10-12 D '88

ALUMINA

Orthogonal self-assembled monolayers: alkanethiols on gold and alkane carboxylic acids on alumina. P. E. Laibinis and others. bibl f il *Science* 245:845-7 Ag 25 '89

ALUMINOSILICATES

Gut-level control of aflatoxin [use of hydrated sodium calcium aluminosilicate in feeds; research by Roger B. Harvey] *Science News* 135:111 F 18 '89

ALUMINUM

Prices

Has aluminum climbed off its roller coaster? M. Schroeder. il *Business Week* p106+ My 1 '89

ALUMINUM BASEBALL BATS See Baseball bats

ALUMINUM BEVERAGE CONTAINERS See Beverage containers

ALUMINUM CAN RECYCLING See Cans—Recycling

ALUMINUM CO. OF AMERICA

Has Alcoa become recession-proof? J. M. Laderman. *Business Week* p80 Jl 3 '89

ALUMINUM FOIL

Aluminum in microwaves. K. K. Gracey. il *Consumers' Research Magazine* 72:2 Ja '89

ALUMINUM INDUSTRY

See also

Aluminum Co. of America

Reynolds Metals Co.

Finance

Has aluminum climbed off its roller coaster? M. Schroeder. il *Business Week* p106+ My 1 '89

Developing countries

A first world fugitive dabbles in the third world [M. Rich] J. Zweig. por *Forbes* 144:12 N 13 '89

Germany (West)

See also

Hoogovens Aluminium GmbH

ALUMINUM OXIDES

See also

Alumina

ALUMINUM SILICATES

See also

Cordierite

ALUMNI, COLLEGE See College graduates

ALURKAR, SADANAND K., AND BHONSLE, RAJARAM V.

Probing the heliosphere from India. il map *Sky and Telescope* 78:151 Ag '89

ALVARADO, ELVIA

about

Campesina fights hunger and its causes. M. C. Turck. por *The Progressive* 53:14 My '89

ALVARADO-JUAREZ, FRANCISCO

about

Francisco Alvarado-Juarez: BACA Downtown; Studio Museum of Harlem. E. Heartney. il *Art News* 88:209 Ap '89

ALVAREZ, A. (ALFRED), 1929-

A poet and her myths. il por *The New York Review of Books* 36:34-6 S 28 '89

Sylvia Plath: an exchange [discussion of September 28, 1989 article, A poet and her myths] *The New York Review of Books* 36:68 O 26 '89

ALVAREZ, ALFRED See Alvarez, A. (Alfred), 1929-

ALVAREZ, LUIS W.

about

Obituary

Physics Today il por 42:100+ Je '89. G. Goldhaber and W. K. H. Panofsky

ALVAREZ, ROBERT, AND MAKHIJANI, ARJUN

Cleaning up after the Pentagon: the dangers of nuclear weapons waste. il *Utne Reader* p50-2 Ja/F '89

ALVAREZ DEL CASTILLO, ENRIQUE

about

Mexico's war on drugs [interview] il *New Perspectives Quarterly* 6:46-9 Summ '89

ALVES, MARCIA RODRIGUES See Rodrigues Alves, Marcia

ALVIN (SUBMARINE) See Oceanographic submersibles

ALVIN AILEY AMERICAN DANCE THEATER

Alvin Ailey's Opus McShann: City Center Theatre/New York. B. S. Comer. il *Down Beat* 56:47-9 Ap '89

Carnal knowledge [New York City performance] T. Tobias. il *New York* 22:54-5 Ja 2 '89

Reviews:

Performances in Kansas City. K. LaFave. *Dance Magazine* 63:88-90 Mr '89

ALY, ABDULMONEIM

Health education through religion. il *World Health* p27-8 Jl '89

ALZA CORP.

Drug extender. I. Chithelen. il por *Forbes* 144:95-6 Jl 10 '89

ALZHEIMER'S DISEASE

Alzheimer's disease: mystery of the mind. K. Flieger. il *FDA Consumer* 23:19 S '89

Alzheimer's disease: the search for a cure. C. Dilks. il *Nation's Business* 77:86 O '89

Alzheimer's rise [Harvard Medical School study] A. Purvis. il *Time* 134:118 N 20 '89

The brain killer [cover story; special section] il *Newsweek* 114:54-60+ D 18 '89

Driven off the road by brain disease [research by Larry E. Tune] B. Bower. *Science News* 135:318 My 20 '89

Hints of a brain toxin in Alzheimer's [research by Rachael L. Neve] R. Weiss. *Science News* 136:68 Jl 29 '89

The loss of self. M. Konner. il *The New York Times Magazine* p42-3 Je 25 '89

New alarm over Alzheimer's disease [Harvard Medical School study] *Newsweek* 114:84 N 20 '89

Scary new facts about Alzheimer's [Harvard Medical School study] *U.S. News & World Report* 107:13+ N 20 '89

A town faces Alzheimer's [Westport, Mass.] M. E. Johnson. il *New Choices for the Best Years* 29:12-13 Mr '89

Diagnosis

Alzheimer's clue [beta amyloid detected in the skin; work of Dennis J. Selkoe] *Time* 134:86 O 2 '89

Alzheimer's not restricted to brain [research by Dennis J. Selkoe] R. Weiss. *Science News* 136:197 S 23 '89

Tracing Alzheimer's telltale protein [research by Dennis J. Selkoe] *U.S. News & World Report* 107:14 O 2 '89

Genetic aspects

Amyloid β protein enhances the survival of hippocampal neurons in vitro. J. S. Whitson and others. bibl f il *Science* 243:1488-90 Mr 17 '89

Brain protein yields clues to Alzheimer's disease [β-amyloid] J. L. Marx. il *Science* 243:1664-6 Mr 31 '89

Neurotoxicity of a fragment of the amyloid precursor associated with Alzheimer's disease. B. A. Yankner and others. bibl f il *Science* 245:417-20 Jl 28 '89

A novel mRNA of the A4 amyloid precursor gene coding for a possibly secreted protein. F. De Sauvage and J.-N. Octave. bibl f il *Science* 245:651-3 Ag 11 '89

Public opinion

Myths fuel anxiety [survey results discussed by Neal E. Cutler] il *USA Today (Periodical)* 118:1-2 O '89

ALZHEIMER'S DISEASE—*cont.*
Therapy
Giving neurotransmitters a second wind [huperzine A; work of Alan P. Kozikowski] *Science News* 135:366 Je 10 '89
ALZHEIMER'S DISEASE EDUCATION
Alzheimer's: questions children ask. R. S. Scott. il *Children Today* 18:23-5 Jl/Ag '89
ALZHEIMER'S DISEASE PATIENTS
Family relationships
Coping with Alzheimer's. B. M. O'Beirne. *America* 161:156-7 S 23 '89
Just as you are. V. S. Dustin. il *Good Housekeeping* 208:66+ Mr '89
NIA/AoA conferences on caregiving and support in Alzheimer's families. il *Aging* no359:38-9 '89
Support group eases pain of Alzheimer's. C. Tevis. il *Successful Farming* 87:49 mid-Mr '89
Trapped inside her own world [I. Connolly] B. Kantrowitz. il pors *Newsweek* 114:56-8 D 18 '89
AM INTERNATIONAL, INC.
Williams bids farewell [J. O. Williams] A. Edmond, Jr. por *Black Enterprise* 19:14 Ja '89
AM RADIO BROADCASTING *See* Radio broadcasting
AMA *See* American Medical Association
AMAGANSETT (N.Y.)
Architecture
Newlyweds Ian Irving and Carolina Estrada have transformed a small house at the shore with big-impact color. J. Etra. il pors *Vogue* 179:260-1+ Ag '89
AMALGAM DENTAL FILLINGS *See* Dental materials
AMALRIC, JACQUES, AND FRACHON, ALAIN
A talk with Dr. No [Y. Shamir] il por *World Press Review* 36:27-8 Ap '89
AMANITA *See* Poisonous mushrooms
AMARILLO (TEX.)
Education
Bill Cosby makes academic deal with Texas students [Carver Elementary Academy] il pors *Jet* 77:33 N 20 '89
AMAS REPERTORY THEATRE, INC.
In the sun [founder R. LeNoire honored] *The New Yorker* 65:24-5 F 27 '89
AMATEUR ARCHEOLOGISTS *See* Archeologists, Amateur
AMATEUR ASTRONOMERS *See* Astronomers, Amateur
AMATEUR JOURNALISM *See* Journalism, Amateur
AMATEUR MOTION PICTURES *See* Motion pictures—Amateur films
AMATEUR MUSICIANS *See* Musicians, Amateur
AMATEUR RADIO *See* Ham radio
AMATEUR SCIENTISTS *See* Scientists, Amateur
AMATEUR TAPE RECORDINGS *See* Tape recordings—Amateur recordings
AMATEUR VIDEOTAPE RECORDINGS *See* Videotapes—Amateur recordings
AMATEURISM (SPORTS)
See also
International Amateur Athletic Federation
Attack the gender gap in amateur sports [lack of women on National Governing Bodies] K. M. Reith. il *Women's Sports & Fitness* 11:64 Je '89
AMAX INC.
Getting the best price [Falconbridge Ltd. favoring AMAX over Noranda in takeover battle; special section] il *Maclean's* 102:34-7 Ag 14 '89
Luck and mettle. il *Forbes* 143:110 Ja 9 '89
Shareholders say 'thanks' to these CEOs [R. L. Taylor and A. Born] D. Foust and M. Roman. il pors *Business Week* p48 My 1 '89
AMAZING RANDI *See* Randi, James
AMAZON RIVER
Amazon River discharge and climate variability: 1903 to 1985. J. E. Richey and others. bibl f il map *Science* 246:101-3 O 6 '89
Joe Kane ran the mighty Amazon and lived to tell the tale. K. McMurran. il pors *People Weekly* 32:83+ Jl 17 '89
AMAZON RIVER VALLEY
See also
Air pollution—Amazon River Valley
Botany—Amazon River Valley
The Amazon's savvy Indians [Kaiapo] M. Simons. il map *The New York Times Magazine* p36-7+ F 26 '89
A catbird's seat on Amazon destruction [monitoring of illegal agricultural burning by remote sensing satellites] F. Golden. il *Science* 246:201-2 O 13 '89
A center of crop genetic diversity in western Amazonia. C. R. Clement. bibl f il maps *BioScience* 39:624-31 O '89
Defenders of the Amazon [Brazil's rubber tappers; cover story] S. Hecht and A. Cockburn. il *The Nation* 248:695-6+ My 22 '89
Deforestation in Amazonia. P. M. Fearnside. bibl f il map *Environment* 31:16-20+ My '89
Deforestation in the Amazon [discussion of May 1989 article, Deforestation in Amazonia] P. M. Fearnside. *Environment* 31:4-5 S '89
A dubious plan for the Amazon [Brazil] M. S. Serrill. il *Time* 133:67 Ap 17 '89

Extractive reserves in Brazilian Amazonia [rubber workers' proposal to fight deforestation] P. M. Fearnside. bibl f il map *BioScience* 39:387-93 Je '89
Hegel and the Amazon Basin [environmental cost of hydroelectric dams] S. C. Florman. il *Technology Review* 92:19 O '89
The past and future Amazon. P. A. Colinvaux. bibl il maps *Scientific American* 260:102-8 My '89
Playing with fire [destruction of Brazilian rain forest; cover story] E. Linden. il map *Time* 134:76-80+ S 18 '89
Rain forest politics [discussion of May 22, 1989 article, Defenders of the Amazon] S. Hecht and A. Cockburn. *The Nation* 249:262+ S 18 '89
The scorched earth. A. DeCurtis. il *Rolling Stone* p40-9 F 23 '89
A tale of two forests. *World Press Review* 36:40+ S '89
Tom Lovejoy and the last crusade [battle to save the Brazilian rain forest] R. Migler. il pors *Gentlemen's Quarterly* 59:286-9+ O '89
Whose hands will shape the future of the Amazon's green mansions? [plight of the rubber tappers; cover story] M. Parfit. bibl (p245) il maps *Smithsonian* 20:58-68+ N '89
The world's largest lab. S. Begley. il map *Newsweek* 113:46-7 F 20 '89
AMAZONIA *See* Amazon River Valley
AMBASSADOR HOTEL (LOS ANGELES, CALIF.)
This Hollywood landmark could be gone with the wind. K. Kerwin. il *Business Week* p38 Mr 27 '89
AMBASSADORS
See also
Negroponte, John
Appointment, qualifications, etc.
Notorious ambassadors [Bush appointments] G. Hackett. il *Newsweek* 113:25-6 Je 5 '89
Picking lemons for the plums? [G. Bush's ambassadorial nominations] R. Lacayo. il *Time* 134:17 Jl 31 '89
State troopers [ambassadorial appointments] *The Nation* 248:651-2 My 15 '89
The sum of their possessions [Bush appointments] M. Waas. *Harper's* 279:66-7 S '89
AMBASZ, EMILIO
about
Holl and Ambasz, in a manner of speaking. R. Kimball. il *Architectural Record* 177:51+ Ap '89
Myth master. H. Muschamp. il *Vogue* 179:340+ Mr '89
The new faces of modernism on show. il *Architectural Record* 177:47 Mr '89
Reclaiming Eden. E. Edelman. il por *Art News* 88:73-4 F '89
AMBER
Amber reveals the past. P. Barnes-Svarney. il *Earth Science* 41:13-15 Wint '88
AMBERG, JAY
Higher (-priced) education. *The American Scholar* 58:521-32 Aut '89
AMBIGRAMS
Games. S. Morris. il *Omni (New York, N.Y.)* 11:120-1 Mr '89
AMBIGUITY
Living in an ambiguous world. G. F. Kreyche. il *USA Today (Periodical)* 118:98 N '89
AMBITION
Ambition. T. H. Kelly, Jr. il *Field & Stream* 94:54+ S '89
The roots of my ambition [inspiration of mother; condensed from The good times] R. Baker. il por *Reader's Digest* 135:115-18 N '89
AMBIVALENCE
Hot mood. K. Andersen. il *Rolling Stone* p58-60 My 18 '89
Not the best of times, not the worst. K. Andersen. il *Utne Reader* p92 S/O '89
AMBLER, MARJANE
The lands the feds forgot. il *Sierra* 74:44-6+ My/Je '89
AMBLIN ENTERTAINMENT
Fear not, Hollywood: golden boy is still golden [S. Spielberg] R. Grover. il por *Business Week* p64-5 My 29 '89
AMBOISE (FRANCE)
Historic houses, sites, etc.
See also
Clos-Lucé (Amboise, France)
AMBOSELI NATIONAL PARK (KENYA)
Upscale baboons. J. Altmann and A. Samuels. il *Natural History* p60-3 My '89
AMBROISE-RENDU, MARC
Cuba says, 'Come on down'. il *World Press Review* 36:62 My '89
AMBROTYPES
The ambrotype. il *American History Illustrated* 24:40-1 S/O '89
AMBULANCE SERVICE
See also
Washington (D.C.)—Ambulance service
AMC *See* American Motors Corp.
AMDUR, NEIL
Editor's page. See issues of World Tennis beginning June 1984

AMDURA (FIRM)
"We were shaking with rage" [F. J. A. Cilluffo wins control] A. A. Lappen. il pors *Forbes* 144:119+ O 30 '89

AMEBAS
Mystery amoeba [Entamoeba histolytica] S. Hart. il *Science News* 136:216-17+ S 30 '89

AMEBIASIS
Mystery amoeba [Entamoeba histolytica] S. Hart. il *Science News* 136:216-17+ S 30 '89

AMEBIC DYSENTERY *See* Amebiasis

AMELOGENIN
Scientists home in on tooth enamel gene [research by Eduardo C. Lau] *Science News* 135:269 Ap 29 '89

AMEN [television program] *See* Television program reviews—Single works

AMEND, PAT
Under the eye of the consultant. il *Working Woman* 14:37-8 O '89

AMENDMENTS TO THE CONSTITUTION *See* United States. Constitution—Amendments; United States. Constitution. 1st-10th amendments

AMENORRHEA *See* Menstruation—Disorders

AMER-HIRSCH, WENDY
Educating youth about AIDS: a model program. bibl f il *Children Today* 18:16-19 S/O '89

AMERICA
    See also
    Canada
    Latin America
    North America
    United States

        Antiquities
    See also
    Paleo-Indians

       Description and travel
Quest for the holy trail. D. Buck and A. Meadows. il map *Américas* 41 no1:14-19 '89

      Discovery and exploration
    See also
    Santa Maria (Ship)
The accidental conqueror [importance of animal and plant domestication in the European colonization of the New World] J. M. Diamond. il *Discover* 10:70-6 D '89
Disease and death in the New World [debate over the size of pre-Columbian populations] L. Roberts. il *Science* 246:1245-7 D 8 '89
Voyages into the unknown. il map *National Geographic World* 170:12-15 O '89
Where did Columbus land? [research by Kim Gainer indicates San Salvador more likely than Samana Cay] map *USA Today (Periodical)* 117:10 Ap '89
      Centennial celebrations, etc.
Holy Columbus! P. C. Montgomery. il *Common Cause Magazine* 15:24-7 N/D '89
The Santa Maria's excess baggage. il *U.S. News & World Report* 107:14 O 2 '89
Shipshape [replicas of the Niña, Pinta and Santa Maria] il por *Life* 12:26-30 Ap '89
The three sisters [replica of Columbus' ship Santa Maria] B. Weber. il *The New York Times Magazine* p102 My 14 '89

        Population
Disease and death in the New World [debate over the size of pre-Columbian populations] L. Roberts. il *Science* 246:1245-7 D 8 '89

AMERICA (WASHINGTON, D.C.: RESTAURANT) *See* Washington (D.C.)—Restaurants, nightclubs, bars, etc.

AMERICA IN ART
Orozco's American epic [acquisition of fresco cycle by Hood Museum of Art] C. Giuliano. il por *Art News* 88:53+ N '89

AMERICA IN SPACE NATIONAL HISTORICAL PARK (PROPOSED)
Man in space. E. Bruske. il *National Parks* 63:32-8 Ja/F '89

AMERICA WEST AIRLINES, INC.
America West has the hub—now it needs the spokes. E. Schine. il por *Business Week* p104 D 18 '89
America West is flying high again—but for how long? S. Toy. il por *Business Week* p41-2 F 6 '89
Judge set to rule on shuttle sale, Eastern business plan. *Aviation Week & Space Technology* 130:72 My 15 '89

AMERICAN ACADEMY OF RELIGION
The ivory tower comes to the Windy City [1988 meeting; cover story] R. Clapp. il *Christianity Today* 33:16-21 Ap 7 '89
Serious religious publishers ponder their problems [annual meeting] T. Unsworth. *Publishers Weekly* 235:77 Ja 6 '89

AMERICAN AIRLINES, INC.
American aims for the sky. K. Kelly and T. Mason. il por *Business Week* p54-5+ F 20 '89
American Airlines, Canadian investors weigh bids for Wardair. C. Fotos. *Aviation Week & Space Technology* 130:108-9 Ap 24 '89
American, Delta computer reservations deal may intensify global competition. C. A. Shifrin. il *Aviation Week & Space Technology* 130:94-5 F 13 '89

American, Delta lower price for shares of joint CRS venture [computer reservations system] *Aviation Week & Space Technology* 130:108 Ap 24 '89
American Fokker 100 order caps carrier's growth plan. J. T. McKenna. il *Aviation Week & Space Technology* 130:88-9 Mr 27 '89
American invests in maintenance, overhaul capabilities. C. Fotos. il *Aviation Week & Space Technology* 130:64-5 Jl 10 '89
American makes record jumps in June traffic and capacity. *Aviation Week & Space Technology* 131:99-100 Jl 24 '89
American offers to use its pilots, simulators to evaluate MLS curved approach capabilities [microwave landing system] il *Aviation Week & Space Technology* 129:69 Mr 6 '89
American plans to increase international route system. il *Aviation Week & Space Technology* 131:20-1 N 6 '89
American's lead over U.S. majors spurred by capacity expansion. C. Fotos. *Aviation Week & Space Technology* 130:162 Je 19 '89
The best and the brassiest [D. Trump's bid] C. P. Work. il pors *U.S. News & World Report* 107:52-4 O 23 '89
Boxed in by Trump [bid for American Airlines; special section] il por *Business Week* p54-6 O 23 '89
Commercial air transport: Robert L. Crandall [aerospace laureate] por *Aviation Week & Space Technology* 130:16 Ja 2 '89
Donald Trump's buy-American plan. il por *U.S. News & World Report* 107:23-4 O 16 '89
Eastern resumes efforts to sell South American route network. *Aviation Week & Space Technology* 131:83 N 27 '89
An ego as big as American [D. Trump bids for American Airlines] L. Reibstein. il pors *Newsweek* 114:56-7 O 16 '89
A future up in the air: flight attendants contest weight rules. M. Suh. il *Ms.* 18:83-4 S '89
Here comes Donald, duck! [D. Trump's bid] C. Gorman. il por *Time* 134:52+ O 16 '89
How the new no. 1 got there. R. Woodbury. il por *Time* 133:57 My 15 '89
Interview: Robert Crandall. W. Garvey. il pors *Flying* 116:86-8+ Je '89
Multibillion-dollar MD-11 order [special section] il *Aviation Week & Space Technology* 130:16-21 F 13 '89
Property? Or perk? [American Airlines charges Coupon Connection with conspiring to defraud American by buying and selling frequent flier awards] D. Fanning. il *Forbes* 143:136 Je 26 '89
Qantas, American, JAL gain shares in Air New Zealand. *Aviation Week & Space Technology* 130:108 Ja 2 '89
Trump mounts bid to buy American for $7.5 billion. *Aviation Week & Space Technology* 131:139 O 9 '89
Vacation travel spurs record April for American Airlines. C. Fotos. *Aviation Week & Space Technology* 130:106 My 22 '89

AMERICAN ANTELOPE HUNTING *See* Pronghorn hunting

AMERICAN-ARAB ANTI-DISCRIMINATION COMMITTEE
A Halloween recall [Spencer Gifts withdraws mask of sheik after Arab American protests] il *Newsweek* 114:61 N 6 '89

AMERICAN ART *See* Art, American

AMERICAN ARTISTS *See* Artists, American

AMERICAN ASSOCIATION FOR HIGHER EDUCATION
Claiming ourselves as teachers [Forum on Extraordinary Teaching] D. Gillespie. il *Change* 21:56-9 Jl/Ag '89

AMERICAN ASSOCIATION FOR THE ADVANCEMENT OF SCIENCE
AAAS presidents. R. S. Nicholson. *Science* 245:905 S 1 '89
Dr. Walter E. Massey [chairman] D. C. Lyons. il pors *Ebony* 44:62-3+ Ag '89
Inside AAAS. See occasional issues of Science beginning October 7, 1988
Progress at AAAS. P. H. Abelson. *Science* 243:149 Ja 13 '89

        Meetings
1990 AAAS annual meeting [program; cover story] il *Science* 246:1313-28 D 8 '89
AAAS meeting draws a crowd [special section] il *Science* 243:474-6 Ja 27 '89
Awards [presented at AAAS winter meeting] il *Science* 243:672-3 F 3 '89
The centennial annual meeting, starring Harry Truman and civil liberties [excerpt from Renewing a scientific society] D. L. Wolfle. il por *Science* 246:130-1 O 6 '89

AMERICAN ASSOCIATION FOR THE ADVANCEMENT OF THE HUMANITIES
Organizing the humanities. J. M. Banner, Jr. il *Change* 21:44-51 Mr/Ap '89

AMERICAN ASSOCIATION OF PHYSICS TEACHERS
AAPT top honors awarded to French and Birgeneau. pors *Physics Today* 42:126-8 Mr '89

AMERICAN ASSOCIATION OF RETIRED PERSONS
Older Americans in a changing society [address, March 22, 1989] L. Crooks. *Vital Speeches of the Day* 55:556-8 Jl 1 '89

AMERICAN ASSOCIATION OF RETIRED PERSONS—
cont.
Our opinion. H. B. Deets. See issues of Modern Maturity beginning April/May 1988
Our opinion. L. Crooks. See issues of Modern Maturity beginning June/July 1988
AMERICAN ASSOCIATION OF RETIRED PERSONS. FEDERAL CREDIT UNION
Why an AARP credit union? H. B. Deets. il *Modern Maturity* 32:11 F/Mr '89
AMERICAN ASSOCIATION OF UNIVERSITY PROFESSORS
AAUP censures Southeastern Seminary [academic freedom issues] R. L. Hester. *The Christian Century* 106:742-4 Ag 16-23 '89
AMERICAN ASTRONOMICAL SOCIETY
AAS announces 1989 Russell Lecturer; Heineman, Warner and Pierce prizes. il *Physics Today* 42 pt1:81-2 Ag '89
AMERICAN AUTHORS See Authors, American
AMERICAN AUTOMOBILE ASSOCIATION
The paperless office comes true. P. Carroll. il *Working Woman* 14:73-4+ O '89
AMERICAN BALLET THEATRE
ABT unveils plans for golden anniversary. il *Dance Magazine* 63:8 Ap '89
Amanda McKerrow takes stage: the real thing. O. Stuart. il pors *Dance Magazine* 63:40-3 Ap '89
Andris Liepa leaps to the U.S., but with *glasnost* the Bolshoi star can go home again. R. Arias. il pors *People Weekly* 31:50-2 My 29 '89
At American Ballet Theatre—Hermann, Smith, and Taras take up the slack. J. H. Mazo. il pors *Dance Magazine* 63:16-17 D '89
Baryshnikov takes on Swan Lake: something old, something new. L. Horn. il *Dance Magazine* 63:44-9 My '89
Baryshnikov's stewardship. C. Barnes. il por *Dance Magazine* 63:106 S '89
Can you forgive her? [work of T. Tharp in repertory] T. Tobias. il *New York* 22:95-6 Je 5 '89
Dancing:
Resignation of M. Baryshnikov and overview of recently completed season. A. Croce. *The New Yorker* 65:84-6 Jl 17 '89
Swan Lake. A. Croce. *The New Yorker* 65:105-7 My 29 '89
Works of Twyla Tharp. A. Croce. *The New Yorker* 65:94-5 Je 12 '89
Help wanted [additions to repertory] T. Tobias. il *New York* 22:66-7 Je 19 '89
On dance [performances at the Metropolitan Opera House] L. A. Jacobs. *The New Leader* 72:23 Je 12-26 '89
On the town [gala dinner for 50th anniversary] J. Gruen. il *Dance Magazine* 63:58-9 S '89
Reviews:
All-Tharp program during spring season. N. V. Dalva. il *Dance Magazine* 63:62 O '89
Spring season in New York City. L. Garafola. il *Dance Magazine* 63:63-5+ O '89
Starry nights for ABT and NYCB [galas] J. Gruen. il *Dance Magazine* 63:90-1 O '89
Swan song [M. Baryshnikov's production of Swan Lake] T. Tobias. il *New York* 22:70 My 29 '89
Swan's way [S. Jaffe] A. L. Ball. il pors *New York* 22:40-4 Je 5 '89
AMERICAN BALLROOM THEATER
Soft touch [performance at the Joyce Theater, New York City] T. Tobias. il *New York* 22:114+ My 15 '89
AMERICAN BANDSTAND [television program] See Television program reviews—Single works
AMERICAN BAR ASSOCIATION
Atlanta minority law firm shares resources with white firm in unique bar program [Arrington & Hollowell and Hurt, Richardson, Garner, Todd & Cadenhead] il *Jet* 76:24 O 2 '89
Darryl DePriest: lawyers' lawyer. R. Brown. il pors *Ebony* 44:27-8 Je '89
The flowering of legal ethics in America [cover story] R. F. Drinan. il *America* 161:76-8 Ag 12-19 '89
AMERICAN BARRICK RESOURCES CORP.
A place to be bullish on bullion. G. G. Marcial. *Business Week* p88 F 6 '89
AMERICAN BEEKEEPING FEDERATION
Beekeepers gather for sweet talk. F. D. Cavinder. il *The Saturday Evening Post* 261:14 Ap '89
AMERICAN BISON See Bison, American
AMERICAN BLACK ACHIEVEMENT AWARDS
Jackée and Clifton Davis host 10th annual TV show of America's best talent [cover story] il *Jet* 75:52-8 Ja 9 '89
Natalie and Flip host American Black Achievement Awards' 11th annual TV show [cover story] il *Jet* 77:58-63 D 25 '89-Ja 1 '90
Tenth anniversary: American Black Achievement Awards. il *Ebony* 44:134-6+ Ja '89
AMERICAN BLIMP (FIRM)
Brighter-than-e'er Lightship. il *Flying* 116:20-1 N '89

AMERICAN BOOKSELLERS ASSOCIATION
ABA launches group buying for store bags. J. Mutter. *Publishers Weekly* 235:18 My 19 '89
Help the homeless [J. Kozol book inspires campaign] L. Fleischer. *Publishers Weekly* 235:446 Ja 27 '89
Meetings
ABA 1989 [special section] J. Mutter and M. J. O'Brien. il *Publishers Weekly* 235:29-34+ Je 30 '89
ABA 1989: Washington [cover story; special section] il *Publishers Weekly* 235:111-37+ My 12 '89
ABA adds two sections to 1990 convention. J. Mutter and others. *Publishers Weekly* 236:11-12 O 13 '89
Audio and video: a tour of the ABA convention. J. Zinsser. il *Publishers Weekly* 236:34-6 Jl 7 '89
Random notes [censorship issue] D. Klinghoffer. *National Review* 41:44 Jl 14 '89
Washington ABA: busy, bursting at the seams. J. F. Baker. il *Publishers Weekly* 235:10 Je 16 '89
Security measures
Security [measures taken in wake of Rushdie death threat] M. J. O'Brien. il *Publishers Weekly* 235:33-4 Je 30 '89
AMERICAN BRANDS, INC.
Break up or build up? il por *Forbes* 143:102 Ja 9 '89
Smoke or fire? T. Jaffe. *Forbes* 143:172 F 6 '89
Smoke signals on BAT and American Brands. G. G. Marcial. il *Business Week* p98 S 11 '89
AMERICAN BROADCASTING COMPANIES, INC.
The ABCs of making news profits [R. Arledge; cover story] C. Capuzzi. il por *Channels (New York, N.Y.: 1986)* 9:30-5 Mr '89
The ABCs of Peter Jennings [interview] N. Atkins. por *Rolling Stone* p60-2+ My 4 '89
Stranger in a strange land [interview with television entertainment division president R. Iger] N. Koch. il pors *Channels (New York, N.Y.: 1986)* 9:78-9 S '89
Winning Diane: how ABC's Roone Arledge snatched her away from CBS [cover story] E. Klein. il pors *New York* 22:36-43 Mr 13 '89
AMERICAN BUSINESS ASSOCIATES
Business and personal services. il por *Home Office Computing* 7:44 Je '89
AMERICAN BUSINESS NETWORK
German and U.S. leaders confer on trade issues [BizNet teleconference] A. Holzinger. il *Nation's Business* 77:78-9 Ja '89
Trading views with Japan [BizNet teleconference] A. Holzinger. il *Nation's Business* 77:34+ My '89
AMERICAN BUSINESSMEN IN FOREIGN COUNTRIES See Americans—Foreign countries
AMERICAN BUSINESSWOMEN IN FOREIGN COUNTRIES See Americans—Foreign countries
AMERICAN CAN COMPANY
See also
Primerica Corp.
AMERICAN CANCER SOCIETY
Crisis time for the non-profits [address, September 10, 1988] F. W. Wylie. *Vital Speeches of the Day* 55:170-2 Ja 1 '89
Dr. Harold P. Freeman [president] D. C. Lyons. il pors *Ebony* 44:60+ Ag '89
AMERICAN CIMFLEX CORPORATION
See also
Cimflex Teknowledge Corporation
AMERICAN CITIZENSHIP See Citizenship
AMERICAN CITY BUSINESS JOURNALS, INC.
Thinking small [R. Shaw buys American City Business Journals] R. Reiff. il por *Forbes* 144:171+ D 11 '89
AMERICAN CIVIL LIBERTIES UNION
ACLU history from Oxford [work of Samuel Walker] C. Goodrich. *Publishers Weekly* 236:40 O 27 '89
Impeccable judgments or tainted policies? J. T. Leeds. il *The New York Times Magazine* p72+ S 10 '89
New members, new problems. J. Ledbetter. il *The Nation* 248:442-4 Ap 3 '89
AMERICAN COINS See Coins
AMERICAN COLLEGE OF SPORTS MEDICINE
In search of a magic bullet [annual convention] A. Burfoot. il *Runner's World* 24:73-7 O '89
AMERICAN COLLEGE TESTING PROGRAM
A better grade of entrance exam. *Newsweek* 113:47 Ja 16 '89
Fiddling with the ACTs and SATs. B. Diamond. il *Seventeen* 48:44 O '89
AMERICAN COMEDY AWARDS
Comedy Awards Show honors Arsenio Hall, salutes Dick Gregory. il por *Jet* 76:53 Je 19 '89
AMERICAN COMPOSERS See Composers, American
AMERICAN CONDUCTORS See Conductors (Music)
AMERICAN CONSERVATISM See Conservatism
AMERICAN CONSERVATORY THEATRE
Trying to get its A.C.T. together. W. A. Henry. il *Time* 133:102 F 20 '89
AMERICAN CONTINENTAL CORP.
Charlie Keating in the Show Me state [American Continental Corp.'s bankruptcy hits broker R. Ruppert] G. Morgenson. il por *Forbes* 143:12 My 29 '89

AMERICAN CONTINENTAL CORP.—*cont.*
For Charlie Keating, the best defense is a lawsuit [declares American Continental bankrupt as feds close in on Lincoln Savings & Loan] K. Kerwin. il por *Business Week* p32+ My 1 '89
Good timing, Charlie [C. Keating] H. Rudnitsky. il por *Forbes* 144:140-2+ N 27 '89

AMERICAN COOKING *See* Cooking, American

AMERICAN CORRESPONDENTS IN FOREIGN COUNTRIES *See* Foreign correspondents

AMERICAN COUNCIL FOR THE ARTS
ACA: a view from the field. M. Rhodes. See issues of Horizon (Tuscaloosa, Ala.)

AMERICAN CRAFT COUNCIL
Six join Council Board. il *American Craft* 49:8-9 F/Mr '89

AMERICAN CRAFT MUSEUM (NEW YORK, N.Y.)
Benefit nets $180,000 for Craft Museum. il *American Craft* 49:6 F/Mr '89
Janet Kardon named director of American Craft Museum. por *American Craft* 49:10 Ag/S '89

AMERICAN CRYSTALLOGRAPHIC ASSOCIATION
ACA honors excellence in research, public service and student work. *Physics Today* 42:113 N '89

AMERICAN CULTURE *See* United States—Civilization

AMERICAN DANCE *See* Dance

AMERICAN DANCE FESTIVAL
American Dance Festival. L. Lourdeaux. il *Dance Magazine* 63:74-6 D '89
Black choreographers at N.C. dance festival. il *American Visions* 4:28 Je '89

AMERICAN DECORATIVE ARTS *See* Decoration and ornament

AMERICAN DENTAL ASSOCIATION
Jaw experts out of joint [views on diagnosis and treatment of TMJ syndrome] J. Pinkham. il *American Health* 8:38 D '89

AMERICAN DEPOSITARY RECEIPTS
Benetton targets a new customer—Wall Street. J. Rossant and A. Dunkin. il *Business Week* p32-3 My 29 '89

AMERICAN DESIGNER HEIRLOOMS (FIRM)
From art director to rug designer [S. O'Connor] D. E. Gumpert and D. Davis. il por *New Choices for the Best Years* 29:48-9 O '89

AMERICAN DOCUMENT [dance] See Dance reviews—Single works

AMERICAN DRAWING *See* Drawing, American

AMERICAN DREAM (PHILOSOPHY)
The American dream [cover story; special section] M. Dovel and T. J. Miller. il *Changing Times* 43:27-39+ Mr '89
The new American dream [survey results; cover story] D. Yankelovich and J. Gurin. il *American Health* 8:63-7 Mr '89
To snare the feet of greatness [address, June 16, 1989] J. D. Griffin. *Vital Speeches of the Day* 55:735-6 S 15 '89

AMERICAN ECONOMIC ASSISTANCE *See* Economic assistance, American

AMERICAN ECONOMIC ASSOCIATION
It's dismal, all right—but is it a science? R. Kuttner. il *Business Week* p16 Ja 30 '89
Live from New York: it's the American Economic Assn. K. Pennar. il *Business Week* p24 Ja 16 '89

AMERICAN-EUROPEAN EXPRESS
Reinventing the train. J. Skow. il *Time* 134:104 N 13 '89

THE AMERICAN EXPERIENCE [television program] See Television program reviews—Single works

AMERICAN EXPLORATION CO.
Petro-vulture [M. Andrews] J. R. Hayes. il por *Forbes* 143:96+ F 20 '89

AMERICAN EXPRESS CANADA, INC.
Bankers against Tories [bids for bank status] M. Clark. il *Maclean's* 102:16 F 6 '89

AMERICAN EXPRESS CO.
American Express: service that sells [cover story] J. P. Newport, Jr. il pors *Fortune* 120:80-2+ N 20 '89
American Express slings mud—and gets splattered [smear campaign against financier E. Safra] W. Glasgall and J. Meehan. il por *Business Week* p102+ Ag 14 '89
Bank shot: Edmond Safra turns the tables on American Express. J. Taylor. il pors *New York* 22:42-7 S 18 '89
Can AmEx win the masses—and keep its class? J. Friedman and J. Meehan. il *Business Week* p134-6+ O 9 '89
A credit card is not a commodity. S. N. Chakravarty. il *Forbes* 144:128-30 O 16 '89
Is Shearson no. 1 on Amex' sell list? G. G. Marcial. *Business Week* p130 Mr 13 '89
Leave home without it [cover story] M. Lewis. il *The New Republic* 201:19-20+ S 4 '89
Membership has its follies. A. P. Tobias. il *Time* 133:45 Je 19 '89
RJR's gain could mean pain for Amex [resignation of L. Gerstner] F. A. Miller. il *Business Week* p33 Mr 27 '89

AMERICAN EXPRESS PUBLISHING CORP.
AMEX goes for the glossies [editorial director P. Fiori] A. Rothman. il por *Business Week* p66 O 23 '89

AMERICAN FAMILY CORP.
Premium pricing [Tokyo/New York arbitrage play in American Family Corp. shares] S. N. Chakravarty. *Forbes* 144:261 O 30 '89

AMERICAN FASHION DESIGNERS *See* Fashion designers

AMERICAN FEDERAL BANK FSB (DALLAS, TEX.)
So you think buying a sick thrift is just a license to print money [W. E. Gibson] K. Kelly. il pors *Business Week* p78-9 Je 19 '89

AMERICAN FEDERATION OF LABOR AND CONGRESS OF INDUSTRIAL ORGANIZATIONS *See* AFL-CIO

AMERICAN FESTIVAL BALLET
Paul Russell leads ballet in Idaho. S. English. il *Dance Magazine* 63:18 O '89

AMERICAN FICTION
See also
Western stories
The Esquire summer reader [special section] *Esquire* 112:117-24+ Jl '89
Stalking the billion-footed beast [abandonment of realistic tradition by American novelists; cover story] T. Wolfe. il *Harper's* 279:45-56 N '89
Wolfe among the pigeons [T. Wolfe criticizes American novelists for departing from realistic tradition] D. Aikman. il por *Time* 134:78 N 27 '89
The writers of wrong: a novelist carves the critics [cover story] J. McInerney. il por *Esquire* 112:104-8+ Jl '89
Study and teaching
See American literature—Study and teaching

AMERICAN FILM (PERIODICAL)
The editing room. C. Hodenfield. See issues of American Film
The more things change . . . [excerpts from articles printed in the 1980s] il *American Film* 15:80 N '89

AMERICAN FILM INSTITUTE
AFI calendar. J. P. Firstenberg. See issues of American Film
The question of the night: who wasn't at the A.F.I. party honoring Gregory Peck? [Life Achievement Award] il pors *People Weekly* 31:38-9 Mr 27 '89

AMERICAN FILM MARKET
Cannes without the glamour. L. Gubernick. il *Forbes* 143:154 Ap 3 '89

AMERICAN FILM TECHNOLOGIES INC.
The rainbow maker. C. A. Jaffe. il por *Nation's Business* 77:41+ N '89

AMERICAN FLAG
The banner yet waves. il *Reader's Digest* 135:49-50 S '89
A fiery furor over the flag. il *Life* 12:106-8+ Ag '89
Giving honor to Old Glory. H. Sidey. il *Time* 134:16 Jl 3 '89
Notes and comment. il *The New Yorker* 65:25-6 Jl 10 '89
Mutilation, defacement, etc.
See also
Flag burning
Art for whose sake? [furor over American flag on floor at School of the Art Institute of Chicago exhibition] S. Marlin. *National Review* 41:21-2 Ap 21 '89
Flag furor [S. Tyler's What is the proper way to display a U.S. flag? at School of the Art Institute of Chicago] S. Hochfield. il por *Art News* 88:43-4+ Summ '89
When is a flag desecrated? *Harper's* 279:19 D '89

AMERICAN FLAG IN ART
Exhibitions
Art for whose sake? [furor over American flag on floor at School of the Art Institute of Chicago exhibition] S. Marlin. *National Review* 41:21-2 Ap 21 '89
Flag furor [S. Tyler's What is the proper way to display a U.S. flag? at School of the Art Institute of Chicago] S. Hochfield. il por *Art News* 88:43-4+ Summ '89
Old Glory [largest illuminated manuscript in the world made by A. and G. Mungo on view at Fordham University] E. H. Gustafson. il *Antiques* 136:728+ O '89
"A time of sharpened swords" [impact of Supreme Court decisions on artists] D. Waterman. il *Art News* 88:59+ N '89

AMERICAN FOLK ART *See* Folk art

AMERICAN FOLK MUSIC *See* Folk music, American

AMERICAN FREEDOM COALITION
Rev. Moon's rising political influence. J. B. Judis. il *U.S. News & World Report* 106:27-9+ Mr 27 '89

AMERICAN FRUCTOSE CORP.
American Fructose may be making two mouths water. G. G. Marcial. il *Business Week* p166 N 27 '89

AMERICAN FURNITURE *See* Furniture, American

AMERICAN GENERAL AVIATION CORPORATION
Grummans to purr again [Grumman American line] K. Connes. il *Flying* 116:11-12 Ag '89

AMERICAN GEOGRAPHICAL SOCIETY
The American Geographical Society's continuing commitment to exploration. il *Focus (New York, N.Y.: 1950)* 39:28-9 Fall '89

AMERICAN GEOPHYSICAL UNION
Geophysical Union salutes excellent work in the field. pors *Physics Today* 42:87-91 D '89

AMERICAN GLADIATORS [television program] See Television program reviews—Single works

AMERICAN GUILD OF MUSICAL ARTISTS
Beyond the dotted line. M. Horosko. il *Dance Magazine* 63:85 Ja '89

AMERICAN HEALTH AND BEAUTY AIDS INSTITUTE
Jory Luster is elected new AHBAI chairman. por *Jet* 76:31 S 25 '89

AMERICAN HEART ASSOCIATION
A Good Heartkeeping seal of approval [labeling of approved processed foods] C. Jennings-Sauer. il *American Health* 8:16 Je '89
Healthy hearts across America [Food Festival] M. Roberts. *Psychology Today* 23:33 S '89
Heart-to-heart with new heart chief [interview with M. Weisfeldt] por *American Health* 8:14 O '89
The high price of health approval [HeartGuide seal program] C. Sugarman. il *Consumers' Research Magazine* 72:33-4 N '89

AMERICAN HERITAGE (PERIODICAL)
Letter from the editor. B. Dobell. See issues of American Heritage

AMERICAN HISTORY See United States—History

AMERICAN HOIST & DERRICK CO.
See also
Amdura (Firm)
Hoisting profits. il *Forbes* 143:127 Ja 9 '89

AMERICAN HOUSE DECORATION See House decoration, American

AMERICAN HUMANE ASSOCIATION
Speaking up for 'abused' animals, Bob Barker is hit with a lawsuit [United Activists for Animal Rights charges that American Humane Association is negligent in preventing abuse of animals in show business] L. Smith. il por *People Weekly* 32:75-6 S 18 '89

AMERICAN HUMOR See Humor, American

AMERICAN ILLUSTRATION See Illustration

AMERICAN INDIAN DANCE THEATRE
Folk movements. L. A. Jacobs. *The New Leader* 72:22-3 O 30 '89
An ongoing beat [cover story] H. Fenwick. il *Modern Maturity* 32:34-8 O/N '89
Regional diary. T. Tobias. il *New York* 22:84 O 9 '89

AMERICAN INDIANS See Indians (American)

AMERICAN INSTITUTE FOR FREE LABOR DEVELOPMENT
The AFL-CIO meddles abroad. M. Harvey. il *Utne Reader* p26+ Jl/Ag '89

AMERICAN INSTITUTE OF ARCHITECTS
Agreeing to try to agree [issue of interior designer licensing] M. F. Schmertz. *Architectural Record* 177:9 F '89
Design awards/competitions. See issues of Architectural Record
Meetings
The 1989 AIA convention in St. Louis: moving toward the 21st century. C. K. Hoyt. il *Architectural Record* 177:35+ Je '89
Making history in St. Louis [Public Day] M. F. Schmertz. *Architectural Record* 177:9 My '89

AMERICAN INSTITUTE OF BIOLOGICAL SCIENCES
1989 AIBS Distinguished Service Award to Alfred E. Harper. por *BioScience* 39:499 Jl/Ag '89
AIBS news. See occasional issues of BioScience
Annual AIBS meeting. See issues of BioScience

AMERICAN INSTITUTE OF PHYSICS
AIP awards made to Amaldi, Holton, Redington and Littmann. J. Kumagai. il *Physics Today* 42:57-8 D '89
AIP in 1988: an annual report. il *Physics Today* 42:47-58 Je '89
AIP releases report on membership of member societies. P. Janowski. *Physics Today* 42:67 Je '89
Corporate Associates meet at GM, focus on competition. W. Sweet. il *Physics Today* 42:55-7 D '89

AMERICAN INSTITUTE OF WINE AND FOOD
Food for thought [J. Child] M. Barrier. il pors *Nation's Business* 77:29+ D '89

AMERICAN INTERNATIONAL GROUP, INC.
AIG thrives on business other companies won't touch. C. Farrell. il *Business Week* p74-5 Ag 21 '89
Reading Posner the riot act. G. DeGeorge. il por *Business Week* p48 D 18 '89
Victor Posner and the case of the mystery financier [plan to sell Fischbach to an English investor] G. DeGeorge and R. A. Melcher. il por *Business Week* p34 Ag 28 '89

AMERICAN INVESTMENTS See Investments, American

AMERICAN JAZZ ORCHESTRA
The AJO tribute to Count Basie: Cooper Union/New York. M. Bourne. il *Down Beat* 56:54-5 My '89
Survival of the hippest. J. Miller. il *Newsweek* 113:60 Ja 2 '89

AMERICAN JEWISH COMMITTEE
An all-star cast turns out to toast Jane Fonda, queen of workouts, for good works [honored for work on behalf of Soviet Jewry] il pors *People Weekly* 31:49-50 Je 26 '89

AMERICAN LEADERSHIP FORUM
With a little help from her friends [mentoring program started by Oregon chapter] J. C. Johnson. il *Nation's Business* 77:28 Ja '89

AMERICAN LIBERALISM See Liberalism

AMERICAN LITERATURE
See also
Black literature

Bibliography
See also
Library of America (Firm)
Study and teaching
In pursuit of cultural literacy [challenging views of E. D. Hirsch as applied to teaching of contemporary American fiction] E. H. Schuster. il *Phi Delta Kappan* 70:539-42 Mr '89
Knowing and not knowing [serving as evaluator at American literature seminar for master teachers of high school English] B. DeMott. *Change* 21:62 S/O '89
Translations into Russian
Why you'll never have fun in Russian [translation as a form of *glasnost*] R. Lourie and A. Mikhalev. *The New York Times Book Review* 94:1+ Je 18 '89

AMERICAN LOYALISTS
Benjamin Church: Son of Liberty, Tory spy. M. G. Stoler. il pors *American History Illustrated* 24:28-35 N/D '89
The Church cryptogram: to catch a Tory spy [message intercepted by Washington's forces] M. L. Peterson. il *American History Illustrated* 24:36-43 N/D '89

AMERICAN MANUSCRIPTS See Manuscripts, American

AMERICAN MEDICAL ASSOCIATION
Does the AMA need to heal itself? J. F. Siler. il *Business Week* p50 N 13 '89
The RCT proposal and the nursing shortage [registered care technologists; address, January 5, 1989] J. H. Sammons. *Vital Speeches of the Day* 55:373-5 Ap 1 '89

AMERICAN MEDICAL ASSOCIATION JOURNAL See Journal of the American Medical Association

AMERICAN MEDICAL INTERNATIONAL, INC.
'A lot of people don't know who Mel Klein is' [bid for American Medical International] T. Vogel. il por *Business Week* p24-5 Jl 24 '89
With all these buyers, AMI must be getting better. P. Cole. *Business Week* p64-5 Je 26 '89

AMERICAN METAL CLIMAX, INC. See AMAX Inc.

AMERICAN MILITARY ASSISTANCE See Military assistance, American

AMERICAN MINORITIES See Minorities

AMERICAN MOTORS CORP.
One company's China debacle [excerpt from Beijing Jeep] J. Mann. il por *Fortune* 120:145+ N 6 '89

AMERICAN MOVIE CLASSICS (FIRM)
Cablers' antidote for syndex chaos [syndicated-exclusivity rule] R. Katz. il *Channels (New York, N.Y.: 1986)* 9:70-1 S '89

AMERICAN MUSEUM OF NATURAL HISTORY
At the American Museum. See issues of Natural History
The living museum. See issues of Natural History
Student-crushing China cows Natural History Museum [film The first emperor of China not shown] M. S. Forbes. il *Forbes* 144:20 Ag 7 '89

AMERICAN MUSEUM OF NATURAL HISTORY. HALL OF SOUTH AMERICAN PEOPLES
Hall of South American Peoples. il *Natural History* p82-4 Ja '89
Portrait of an archeologist [J. B. Bird] J. Hyslop. il pors *Natural History* p84+ F '89

AMERICAN MUSEUM OF NATURAL HISTORY. WHITNEY WING
A wing for the birds. M. LeCroy. il *Natural History* p90-1 S '89

AMERICAN MUSEUM OF THE MOVING IMAGE (NEW YORK, N.Y.)
Double feature [cover story] D. Dietsch. il *Architectural Record* 177:110-21 My '89
Media mecca. R. Gehr. il *Video* 12:15 Ja '89
Poitier's stellar career saluted in New York City. il pors *Jet* 75:62-3 Mr 20 '89
The television nation gets new monument in borough of Queens. F. Moore. il *Channels (New York, N.Y.: 1986)* 9:18 F '89

AMERICAN MUSIC See Music, American

AMERICAN MUSIC AWARDS
Dionne Warwick is not happy with Dick Clark. J. D. Stem. il pors *TV Guide* 37:6-8 Ap 8-14 '89
Houston, D.J. Jazzy Jeff & Fresh Prince, Jackson top American Music Awards. il *Jet* 75:55-6 F 20 '89
Random notes. il *Rolling Stone* p15 Mr 23 '89

AMERICAN NATIONAL RED CROSS See American Red Cross

AMERICAN NOVELISTS See Novelists, American

AMERICAN OCEANS CAMPAIGN
Ted Danson's crusade. T. Green. il por *Oceans* 22:18-20+ Mr/Ap '89

AMERICAN PAINTING See Painting, American

AMERICAN PATRIOTISM See Patriotism

AMERICAN PHYSICAL SOCIETY
APS presents a host of awards at spring meeting in Baltimore. il *Physics Today* 42:95-8 Je '89
An APS president reflects on his two-year term. V. L. Fitch. il por *Physics Today* 42:49-53 D '89
In defense of confidentiality. D. Lazarus. *Physics Today* 42:57-9 O '89
News from APS. See occasional issues of Physics Today

AMERICAN PHYSICAL SOCIETY—cont.
Meetings
APS meets in St. Louis. M. Siegel. il *Physics Today* 42:61-5 Mr '89
AMERICAN PLACE (NEW YORK, N.Y.: RESTAURANT)
See New York (N.Y.)—Restaurants, nightclubs, bars, etc.
AMERICAN POETS LAUREATE *See* Poets laureate, American
AMERICAN PORTRAITS *See* Portraits, American
AMERICAN POTTERY *See* Pottery, American
AMERICAN PROPAGANDA *See* Propaganda
AMERICAN PSYCHIATRIC ASSOCIATION
The diagnostic dilemma [revision of the Diagnostic and statistical manual of mental disorders] B. Bower. il *Science News* 135:120-2 F 25 '89
AMERICAN PUBLIC OPINION *See* Public opinion
AMERICAN QUASAR PETROLEUM CO.
See also
Wolverine Exploration Company
AMERICAN RADIO COMPANY OF THE AIR [radio program] See Radio program reviews—Single works
AMERICAN RED CROSS
Clara Barton: founder of the American Red Cross. C. Schurr. il pors *American History Illustrated* 24:50-8+ N/D '89
AMERICAN REPERTORY THEATRE
Six characters in Madrid: American Repertory Theatre tours to Europe. S. Lieberman. il *Theatre Crafts* 23:34-5+ My '89
AMERICAN RESEARCH BUREAU *See* Arbitron Ratings Company
AMERICAN REVOLUTION *See* United States—History—Revolution, 1775-1783
AMERICAN ROCKET COMPANY
Amroc retains key personnel despite cutbacks after pad fire. M. A. Dornheim. *Aviation Week & Space Technology* 131:20 O 30 '89
AMERICAN SAMOA
Description and travel
Whose nation is this anyway? P. Iyer. il map *Time* 133:12+ My 15 '89
AMERICAN SAVINGS & LOAN ASSN.
Help your country and help yourself [Robert M. Bass Group's takeover] S. C. Gwynne. il *Time* 133:72 F 20 '89
AMERICAN SCIENCE & ENGINEERING, INC.
X-ray backscatter equipment provides automatic screening for explosives. D. Hughes. il *Aviation Week & Space Technology* 130:65+ Ap 17 '89
AMERICAN SCULPTURE *See* Sculpture, American
AMERICAN SIGN LANGUAGE *See* Sign language
AMERICAN SOCIETY OF ARCHITECTURAL PERSPECTIVISTS
Design awards/competitions: architecture in perspective III [1988 competition exhibition] il *Architectural Record* 177:48-9 F '89
AMERICAN SOCIETY OF INTERIOR DESIGNERS
Agreeing to try to agree [issue of interior designer licensing] M. F. Schmertz. *Architectural Record* 177:9 F '89
AMERICAN SOCIOLOGICAL ASSOCIATION
Dr. William Julius Wilson [president] D. C. Lyons. il pors *Ebony* 44:64-6 Ag '89
AMERICAN SPECTATOR (PERIODICAL)
Anecdotes, facetiae, satire, etc.
A Danny Quayle reader [cover story] il *The American Spectator* 22:13 Je '89
Deconstructing the Danny Quayle reader [discussion of June 1989 article] il *The American Spectator* 22:26-7 Ag '89
AMERICAN STATISTICAL ASSOCIATION
Conference papers. *Monthly Labor Review* 112:29-33 O '89
AMERICAN STOCK EXCHANGE
American anomaly. T. Jaffe. il *Forbes* 144:164 Ag 7 '89
Playing for real [bridge masters M. Becker and R. Rubin become options traders] N. Hass. il pors *New York* 22:60-2+ D 11 '89
Will the Amex and Philly team up against Chicago? [merge options trading] L. J. Nathans. il *Business Week* p78 Jl 31 '89
AMERICAN STORES CO.
American: can it mine Lucky Stores' magic? R. Grover. il *Business Week* p141+ Ap 24 '89
AMERICAN STUDENTS IN GREAT BRITAIN *See* Foreign students—Great Britain
AMERICAN TELEPHONE & TELEGRAPH CO.
Almost everyone is listening in on the telephone talks. A. Bernstein and S. B. Garland. il *Business Week* p32 Ap 10 '89
AT&T: all in the family [dependent care package included in new contract] il *Newsweek* 113:45 Je 12 '89
AT&T rings up profits from new (and old) ventures. il *Money* 18:44 N '89
AT&T settlement. *Monthly Labor Review* 112:49-50 Ag '89
AT&T unchained: business may be the winner [FCC's rate cap proposal] F. Seghers. il *Business Week* p42 Mr 20 '89
Bob Allen is turning AT&T into a live wire. J. J. Keller. il por *Business Week* p140-1+ N 6 '89
Bob Allen rattles the cages at AT&T [cover story] A. Kupfer. il pors *Fortune* 119:58-61+ Je 19 '89

Don't laugh: this plan for regulating AT&T actually sounds good [price caps for long distance service] A. S. Blinder. il *Business Week* p14 Je 12 '89
How deregulation spelled opportunity [P. Higgins] J. A. Werman. il por *Working Woman* 14:56+ My '89
Is AT&T laying the cable for a hookup with NCR? G. G. Marcial. il *Business Week* p92 Ap 3 '89
One step forward, two steps back [Lorance v. AT&T Technologies; Supreme Court decision] P. Simpson. il por *Ms.* 18:96 S '89
Payday for Johnny Appleseed [UNIX] N. Alster. il *Forbes* 144:218-19 O 30 '89
Policies for a competitive America [address, February 16, 1989] R. E. Allen. *Vital Speeches of the Day* 55:413-16 Ap 15 '89
Revolt of Uncle Sam's paper pushers [AT&T and Sprint cope with replacing the federal government's aging telephone network] M. Lewyn. il *Business Week* p156 O 30 '89
Robert Allen. J. J. Keller. por *Business Week* Special Issue:109 Ap 14 '89
Was breaking up AT&T a good idea? K. Labich. il *Fortune* 119:82-7 Ja 2 '89
Who won what at AT&T? L. A. Winokur. il *The Progressive* 53:29-32 D '89
AMERICAN TENNIS PLAYERS *See* Tennis players
AMERICAN TOP 40 [radio program] See Radio program reviews—Single works
AMERICAN TOXXIC CONTROL INC.
A curiosity wrapped in a mystery. E. Paris. il por *Forbes* 143:116+ Mr 6 '89
AMERICAN TRADE CONSORTIUM
Breakthrough [agreement with the Soviet government] *The New Yorker* 65:30-1 Ap 17 '89
The deal of the decade may get done in Moscow. P. Galuszka and R. Brady. il *Business Week* p54-5 F 27 '89
Top U.S. companies move into Russia. L. Kraar. il *Fortune* 120:165-6+ Jl 31 '89
AMERICAN VACUUM SOCIETY
AVS meets in Boston. il *Physics Today* 42:61-3 O '89
AMERICAN WATERCOLOR SOCIETY
Notes from the editor . . . M. S. Doherty. il *American Artist* 53:10+ Ag '89
AMERICAN WING *See* Metropolitan Museum of Art (New York, N.Y.). American Wing
AMERICAN WOMEN'S BASEBALL ASSOCIATION
Diamonds in the rough. B. Hey. il *American Health* 8:43 Ap '89
AMERICAN YOUTH *See* Youth
AMERICANA
Antiques & Americana. G. Michael. See issues of Antiques & Collecting Hobbies beginning October 1988
Colonial collectibles. K. Lineberger. il *Harper's Bazaar* 122:92 O '89
AMERICANS
See also
Arab Americans
Californians
Cambodian Americans
Chinese Americans
Cuban Americans
Irish Americans
Italian Americans
Japanese Americans
Korean Americans
Mexican Americans
Morale, National
Portuguese Americans
Southerners
Swiss Americans
Texans
Are you an "average" person? [statistics on American life] B. Cutler. *Reader's Digest* 135:189-90+ S '89
The attitudes behind American exceptionalism. B. J. Wattenberg. il *U.S. News & World Report* 107:25 Ag 7 '89
The elusive dream of home: the longings of a nation of immigrants. P. Marin. il *Utne Reader* p106-9 Mr/Ap '89
The Esquire register 1989 [special section] il *Esquire* 112:93+ D '89
Habit forming [survey by Mel Poretz and Barry Sinrod] il *Time* 134:63 N 6 '89
The innovators [special section; cover story] il *Newsweek* 114:34-5 O 2 '89
Real Americans. *New Choices for the Best Years* 29:15 Ap '89
What's right with America? R. Reeves. il *New Choices for the Best Years* 29:64-9 Ap '89
Foreign countries
Anecdotes, facetiae, satire, etc.
It's not all absinthe and croissants. P. Margoshes. *The Writer* 102:5-6 Jl '89
Africa
Where I enter [black American woman growing up in Africa] C. McCourtie. por *Essence* 19:83-4+ Ap '89
Austria
Masters of deception [Heilbrunn family, accused of operating Indianapolis drug ring, now living in Austria] B. Shaw and D. Van Biema. il *People Weekly* 31:46-51 Je 19 '89

AMERICANS—*cont.*

Belgium

An American in Brussels [M. Morris] J. Dupont. il pors *The New York Times Magazine* p22-3+ Ja 22 '89

Canada

History

Harvard graduate [American receives Royal Canadian Air Force training on AT-6 Harvard during World War II] L. Morgan. il *Flying* 116:82+ F '89

China

Demonstrations in China [State Dept. and White House statements, May 18-June 20, 1989] *Department of State Bulletin* 89:75-7 Ag '89

International aerospace firms begin evacuating employees from China. P. Proctor. il *Aviation Week & Space Technology* 130:68-9 Je 12 '89

Not like here [New York Express break dancers touring China] *The New Yorker* 64:25-7 F 13 '89

'Science and democracy' in Tiananmen Square. W. R. Garrett. il *The Christian Century* 106:646-7 Jl 5-12 '89

True power to the people [Hebei University students join demonstrations] G. Jochnowitz. il *National Review* 41:22-3 Je 30 '89

The words of Marx, the methods of Lenin. G. Jochnowitz. *National Review* 41:31-2 Ag 4 '89

History

"Excellent! Excellent! World-honored Sakyamuni!" [L. Sickman] il por *Art News* 88:32+ F '89

Costa Rica

Bipartisan arm-twisting in Central America [letter from congressmen to O. Arias Sanchez concerning J. Hull] *Harper's* 278:24 Je '89

Costa Rica diarist: democracia. H. Hertzberg. *The New Republic* 201:46 D 4 '89

John Hull, once Oliver North's man in Costa Rica, is now accused of running guns and drugs. R. Arias. il pors *People Weekly* 31:52-4+ My 1 '89

Cuba

Our man in Havana [J. A. Michener] B. Levine. il por *Publishers Weekly* 236:50-1 Jl 14 '89

Cyprus

Going to Cyprus. J. Webb. il pors *Seventeen* 48:166+ Mr '89

East Asia

So you'll be moving to Asia. J. M. Fallows. il *Fortune* 120 no13 Special Issue:91+ Fall '89

Eastern Europe

Pushing capitalism for fun and profit. S. V. Roberts. il *U.S. News & World Report* 107:38-9 D 4 '89

Egypt

Jackson makes European-African policy journey [J. L. Jackson] il por *Jet* 76:7-8 Ag 7 '89

El Salvador

Home for the holidays—from El Salvador [church worker J. J. Casolo] por *Newsweek* 114:52 D 25 '89

Notes and comment [plight of Green Berets and American church worker J. J. Casolo] *The New Yorker* 65:42-4 D 11 '89

Ethiopia

History

The emperor wore clothes: visiting Haile Selassie in 1943. H. Courlander. *The American Scholar* 58:271-81 Spr '89

See also

United States—Armed Forces—Forces in Europe

Fiji

Cross-culture shock [long-distance editing by Atlantic Monthly Press of J. McIntyre Varawa's book on Fijian marriage] L. Fleischer. *Publishers Weekly* 235:207 F 24 '89

Joana McIntyre, 58, crosses cultures and generations to marry Fijian Malé Varawa, 28. R. Arias. il pors *People Weekly* 32:69-70+ Jl 31 '89

Foreign countries

See also

United States—Armed Forces—Forces in foreign countries

Blunders abroad. C. F. Valentine. il *Nation's Business* 77:54+ Mr '89

Homes across the sea. K. McManus. il *Changing Times* 43:98-103 Mr '89

People who meet people [meet-the-people programs bring tourists together with residents] B. Wallraff. il *The Atlantic* 263:108+ Ja '89

To go or not to go? K. Castle. il *Travel Holiday* 171:16-17+ F '89

Employment

Overseas transfers: the career move of the '90s. L. Touby. *Working Woman* 14:14+ F '89

The pause that refreshes. L. Tarshis. *Harper's Bazaar* 122:32+ Je '89

Security awareness, measures, and management [address, November 2, 1988] G. P. Shultz. *Department of State Bulletin* 89:4-5 Ja '89

Taxation

A whole new tax life. D. Carpenter. il *Money* 18:178+ N '89

France

The houses of a French summer. J. Salter. il *Esquire* 111:145-53 Ap '89

Jackson makes European-African policy journey [J. L. Jackson] il por *Jet* 76:7-8 Ag 7 '89

Provence Pilgrims [Thanksgiving dinner] P. Wells. il *The New York Times Magazine* p93-4 N 5 '89

Germany (East)

As the Wall came tumbling down. J. Agee. il *The New York Times Magazine* p42-3+ N 26 '89

Germany (West)

See also

United States. Air Force—Forces in Germany (West)
United States. Army—Forces in Germany (West)

A dancer's audition guide: building careers in Europe. V. Fell. il *Dance Magazine* 63:66-7 F '89

Iceland

President Vigdís [helps Americans free car from a snowdrift] *The New Yorker* 65:36-7 Mr 20 '89

Iran

See also

Iranian seizure of United States embassy, 1979-1981

Israel

Different strokes: eleven kids from Brooklyn try life on a kibbutz [project initiated by teacher S. Bialer] J. Taylor. il por *New York* 22:56-8+ Je 12 '89

Italy

How do you say 'slam dunk' in Italian? [basketball players] J. Rossant. il *Business Week* p48 Ag 28 '89

Sitting pretty in Rome [basketball player D. Ferry] C. Kirkpatrick. il pors *Sports Illustrated* 71:26-8+ O 9 '89

Japan

Japan lays out welcome mat for U.S. scientists. M. Sun. *Science* 243:1546-7 Mr 24 '89

The master of besaboru [baseball player W. Cromartie] R. Whiting. il por *Sports Illustrated* 71:68-9 Ag 21 '89

The new bicoastals: love on Tokyo time [couples who commute between the West Coast and Japan] J. Hammer. il *Newsweek* 113:50 F 13 '89

An open door the U.S. isn't using [few American researchers in Japan's labs] A. Borrus. il *Business Week* p59+ My 15 '89

Two teachers find a better life in Tokyo [Tim and Jane George] S. Seixas. il *Money* 18:92-5+ F '89

Western stars shine in the East. il por *U.S. News & World Report* 107:15 N 6 '89

History

See also

Japan—History—Allied occupation, 1945-1952

Korea

See also

Korean War, 1950-1953—American participation

Korea (North)

Pastors given rare glimpse of North Korea [Korean-American Southern Baptist pastors attend Easter service] D. Burton. *Christianity Today* 33:63 Je 16 '89

Korea (South)

See also

United States. Air Force—Forces in Korea (South)

Lebanon

See also

Beirut airplane hijacking, 1985
Lebanon hostage cases, 1984-

Mozambique

An American doctor in the schools of hell [child psychologist N. Boothby treats Mozambicans] B. Duffy. il pors map *U.S. News & World Report* 106:32-5 Ja 16 '89

Nicaragua

I visited Nicaragua. B. Carey. il por *The Humanist* 49:20-2+ S/O '89

History

El presidente gringo [W. Walker] R. Bruns and B. Kennedy. il por map *American History Illustrated* 23:14-21+ F '89

Norway

History

The year I met Santa [Christmas, 1951] K. St. Vincent. il pors *Good Housekeeping* 209:62+ D '89

Philippines

Exploring the dark side of paradise, an American couple takes up misery's gauntlet [work of D. and T. Palmeri] M. Green. il pors *People Weekly* 32:93-4+ N 27 '89

South Africa

South Africa: the saga continues [runners suspended for attending track meet] A. Burfoot and B. Wischnia. il *Runner's World* 24:8-9 F '89

Soviet Union

The day we blasted Moscow [American softball team challenges Soviets] R. Fimrite. il *Sports Illustrated* 70:46-8+ Je 19 '89

Here and there [dance exchanges] M. Horosko. il *Dance Magazine* 63:62 D '89

Jackson visits earthquake victims in Soviet Union. D. M. Cheers. il pors *Jet* 75:4-6+ F 20 '89

Living the history of modern Russia: Nina and Edmund Stevens in Moscow. E. Stevens. il *Architectural Digest* 46:164-7+ F '89

AMERICANS—Soviet Union—*cont.*
Michael Shannon, a California beach boy who's making waves with the Bolshoi Ballet. il por *People Weekly* 32:74 Ag 21 '89
Missile check [U.S. arms-control verification team] A. Sabirov. *World Press Review* 36:40 Mr '89
A mission to Moscow [delegation of International Committee for the Rescue of Soviet Prisoners of War in Afghanistan] M. G. Harter. *America* 160:28-9 Ja 21 '89
Mothers on a diplomatic mission [Mothers Embracing Nuclear Disarmament] V. Cadden. il *McCall's* 116:86+ Ap '89
Planting some new ideas [Ohioan R. Dull participates in farm exchange program in the Ukraine] W. Sloane. il por *Time* 134:14-15 O 2 '89
Women at work: Holly Eissler [explosion seismologist with Soviet-American joint effort to monitor compliance with Threshold Test Ban Treaty] L. Dawson-Medina. il pors *Ms.* 18:34-6 O '89
The wounds of two wars [meeting between Vietnam and Afghanistan veterans] P. P. Mahoney. il *The New York Times Magazine* p60-1+ Je 11 '89

Spain
Abigail y yo. C. Trillin. *The New Yorker* 65:83-8 Je 26 '89
On alienation and the ESL student [English teacher's year in Spain] L. Carey. il *Phi Delta Kappan* 71:74-5 S '89

Switzerland
Three Samaritans [youths assist injured woman during visit to Switzerland] B. O'Sullivan. il *Reader's Digest* 135:55-6+ O '89

History
Letter from a goddamn Alp. D. Parker. por *Esquire* 112:144-7 Ag '89

Ukraine
Ukrainian odyssey [American-Soviet International Peace Walk] V. B. Browback. il map *Modern Maturity* 32:58-9+ Ag/S '89

Vietnam
American archbishops visit Vietnam. R. Bautch. *America* 160:132-3 F 18 '89

History
See also
Vietnamese War, 1957-1975—American participation

Western Europe
Is Europe worth the big price? [retirement] A. Rand. il map *New Choices for the Best Years* 29:38-40+ F '89
It's a bird, it's a plane, it's Euroman [American businessmen] D. Lawday. il *U.S. News & World Report* 107:45 D 25 '89-Ja 1 '90

AMERICANS ABROAD *See* Americans—Foreign countries
AMERICARES FOUNDATION
With an entrepreneur's energy, Americares' Bob Macauley brings help to the world's needy. K. Hubbard. il pors *People Weekly* 31:71+ My 29 '89
AMERICAS *See* America
AMERICA'S CUP RACES
The Cup that ran amok. R. Seitz. il *The American Spectator* 22:21-3 Je '89
The Cup turneth over [judge awards 1988 Cup to New Zealand] il *Time* 133:42 Ap 10 '89
Storm clouds over San Diego. J. A. Fishman. il *Motor Boating & Sailing* 163:38+ Je '89
AMERICA'S MOST WANTED [television program] *See* Television program reviews—Single works
AMERICUS SHAREOWNER SERVICE CORPORATION
Blue-chip quality and junk-bond yields. D. P. Wiener. il *U.S. News & World Report* 107:107 N 6 '89
How to get bigger dividends or bigger price gains—from the same blue-chip stock. M. Schiffres. il *Changing Times* 43:98 F '89
Sure, stocks are flying—but 'Scores' are in orbit. L. Jereski. il *Business Week* p86 Ag 21 '89
AMERITECH COMMUNICATIONS, INC.
Good connection. C. Siler. il por *Forbes* 143:107 Mr 6 '89
AMERMAN, JOHN W.
about
Mattel is putting its dollhouse in order. P. Cole. il por *Business Week* p66-7 Ag 28 '89
AMERO, BRUCE
Captain Hazelwood: what Exxon knew. *Harper's* 279:22-4 Jl '89
AMERY, LEOPOLD CHARLES MAURICE STENNETT, 1873-1955
about
Leo Amery, the last imperialist. M. Beloff, Baron. bibl il pors *History Today* 39:13-18 Ja '89
AMES, BRUCE N.
Be most wary of nature's own pesticides. *Consumers' Research Magazine* 72:13-14 My '89
about
Is broccoli more toxic than dioxin? L. Lamb. il *Utne Reader* p11-12 Mr/Ap '89
Ode to Cheez Whiz. J. Hooper. il *Health (New York, N.Y.)* 21:44+ O '89

AMES, JONATHAN
about
Brat Pack II. A. Heard. il *The American Spectator* 22:27-9 O '89
AMES, KENNETH L.
Folk, or art? bibl f il *Antiques* 135:276-8 Ja '89
AMES DEPARTMENT STORES, INC.
How Ames is digesting its 'whale' [Zayre stores] C. Tucher. il *Business Week* p62 S 11 '89
AMES RESEARCH CENTER
Fastest supercomputer [Cray Y-MP] A. Fisher. il *Popular Science* 234:8+ F '89
Simulators aid LHX design [Army helicopter; cover story; special section] il *Aviation Week & Space Technology* 131:34-5+ N 27 '89
AMEX *See* American Stock Exchange
AMGEN INC.
Amgen is hot—and bothered. J. O. Hamilton and C. Brown. il *Business Week* p40+ Ja 23 '89
A biotech bonanza [FDA OKs erythropoietin] L. Armstrong. il *Business Week* p30 Jl 31 '89
A drug that could replace transfusions—if it ever reaches the market [Ortho vs. Amgen in battle over erythropoietin] J. O. Hamilton and J. Weber, Jr. il *Business Week* p60+ Mr 27 '89
AMI *See* American Medical International, Inc.
AMI (WORD PROCESSOR PROGRAM) *See* Word processors and processing—Programming
AMIC, IRÈNE
about
The essence of Provence. C. Carter. il por *House & Garden* 161:126-31+ Jl '89
AMIC, JEAN
about
The essence of Provence. C. Carter. il por *House & Garden* 161:126-31+ Jl '89
AMICA SPACE STATIONS *See* Space stations, European
AMIDEI, NANCY
Fighting or friendly? *Commonweal* 116:5-6 Ja 13 '89
AMIEL, BARBARA
Column. *See* occasional issues of Maclean's
Feminism hits middle age [cover story] il *National Review* 41:23-5+ N 24 '89
AMIEL, JON
about
Queen of hearts [film] Reviews
Commonweal 116:591 N 3 '89. T. O'Brien
Maclean's 102:86 N 6 '89. B. D. Johnson
The New Leader 72:21 O 2-16 '89. J. Morrone
Time 134:90 O 2 '89. R. Corliss
AMIES, HARDY
about
The reign of Hardy Amies: the Queen's couturier in London and Gloucestershire. E. Lambert. il por *Architectural Digest* 46:204-9+ S '89
AMIGA (COMPUTER) *See* Computers
AMINES
See also
Cholestyramine
Histamine
Nitrosamines
Direct Brønsted analysis of the restoration of activity to a mutant enzyme by exogenous amines. M. D. Toney and J. F. Kirsch. bibl f il *Science* 243:1485-8 Mr 17 '89
AMINO ACID SEQUENCE
See also
Homeoboxes
Adenylyl cyclase amino acid sequence: possible channel- or transporter-like structure. J. Krupinski and others. bibl f il *Science* 244:1558-64 Je 30 '89
β-adrenergic receptor kinase: primary structure delineates a multigene family. J. L. Benovic and others. bibl f il *Science* 246:235-40 O 13 '89
Lutropin-choriogonadotropin receptor: an unusual member of the G protein-coupled receptor family. K. C. McFarland and others. bibl f il *Science* 245:494-9 Ag 4 '89
Mass specs move in on protein sequencers. M. Barinaga. il *Science* 246:33 O 6 '89
Molecular characterization of the human B₂-adrenergic receptor. L. J. Emorine and others. bibl f il *Science* 245:1118-21 S 8 '89
Neural cadherin: role in selective cell-cell adhesion. S. Miyatani and others. bibl f il *Science* 245:631-5 Ag 11 '89
The neuron-specific protein PGP 9.5 is a ubiquitin carboxyl-terminal hydrolase. K. D. Wilkinson and others. bibl f il *Science* 246:670-3 N 3 '89
Structure and function of human amphiregulin: a member of the epidermal growth factor family. M. Shoyab and others. bibl f il *Science* 243:1074-6 F 24 '89
Synapsins: mosaics of shared and individual domains in a family of synaptic vesicle phosphoproteins. T. C. Südhof and others. bibl f il *Science* 245:1474-80 S 29 '89
AMINO ACIDS
See also
Alanine
Arginine

AMINO ACIDS—See also—*cont.*
Glutamic acid
Glycine
Leucine
Peptides
Tryptophan

Building new proteins with odd parts [work of A. Richard Chamberlin] I. Amato. *Science News* 136:246 O 14 '89

Effects of buried ionizable amino acids on the reduction potential of recombinant myoglobin. R. Varadarajan and others. bibl f il *Science* 243:69-72 Ja 6 '89

A general method for site-specific incorporation of unnatural amino acids into proteins. C. J. Noren and others. bibl f il *Science* 244:182-8 Ap 14 '89

The impact giveth . . . [amino acids found in Cretaceous-Tertiary boundary clay; research by Meixun Zhao and Jeffrey L. Bada] J. Horgan. *Scientific American* 261:24+ S '89

New impact evidence: amino acids from space [Cretaceous-Tertiary boundary clay; research by Meixun Zhao and Jeffrey L. Bada] *Astronomy* 17:11+ O '89

On the trail of transfer RNA identity. C. Mlot. il *BioScience* 39:756-9 D '89

Rare amino acids support impact theory [Cretaceous-Tertiary boundary clays; research by Jeffrey L. Bada] R. Monastersky. *Science News* 135:356 Je 10 '89

Role for excitatory amino acids in methamphetamine-induced nigrostriatal dopaminergic toxicity. P. K. Sonsalla and others. bibl f il *Science* 243:398-40 Ja 20 '89

The role of excitatory amino acids and NMDA receptors in traumatic brain injury. A. I. Faden and others. bibl f il *Science* 244:798-800 My 19 '89

Synthesis
BAS1 has a myb motif and activates HIS4 transcription only in combination with BAS2 [Saccharomyces] K. Tice-Baldwin and others. bibl f il *Science* 246:931-5 N 17 '89

Therapeutic use
Battling disease with the amino factor. G. Maleskey. *Prevention (Emmaus, Pa.)* 41:61-5 My '89

AMINOACYLATION
Structural basis for misaminoacylation by mutant E. coli glutaminyl-tRNA synthetase enzymes. J. J. Perona and others. bibl f il *Science* 246:1152-4 D 1 '89

AMINOBUTYRIC ACID
Acetylcholine and GABA mediate opposing actions on neuronal chloride channels in crayfish. C. Pfeiffer-Linn and R. M. Glantz. bibl f il *Science* 245:1249-51 S 15 '89

Type I and type II $GABA_A$-benzodiazepine receptors produced in transfected cells. D. B. Pritchett and others. bibl f il *Science* 245:1389-92 S 22 '89

AMINOTRANSFERASES *See* Transaminases

AL AMIR (LOS ANGELES, CALIF.: RESTAURANT) *See* Los Angeles (Calif.)—Restaurants, nightclubs, bars, etc.

AMIS, KINGSLEY, 1922-
The lobster's claw. il *National Review* 41:60-2 Je 2 '89
about
A misunderstood misanthrope. D. Lida. il por *Harper's Bazaar* 122:76+ My '89

AMIS, SUZY
about
The natural. B. Goodwin. il pors *Vogue* 179:120+ Mr '89

AMISH
The Amish answer. P. Stone. il *The Mother Earth News* 118:56-60 Jl/Ag '89

An Amish drought journal [Ohio] D. Kline. il *The Mother Earth News* 118:60-1 Jl/Ag '89

Cooking up a future [Keim Family Bakery] M. E. Johnson and S. Brewer. il *New Choices for the Best Years* 29:6 D '89

In country [Lancaster, Pa.] il map *Seventeen* 48:182-8 S '89

Lancaster County [cover story] S. Wilding. il *Gourmet* 49:112-17+ N '89

Education
What can we learn from Amish education? D. Kackel. *The Education Digest* 55:61-3 N '89

Photographs and photography
Amish odyssey [condensation] B. Coleman. il *Reader's Digest* 135:88-94 Jl '89

AMISH COOKING *See* Cooking, Amish

AMISTAD (SCHOONER)
Children of the Amistad. E. N. Lawson. il *American Visions* 4:38-41 F '89

AMMONIA
Surprising chemistry in the shower [mixture of shampoo and soap lathers releases ammonia] il *Consumer Reports* 54:610 O '89

AMMONIA FEED SUPPLEMENTS *See* Feed supplements
AMMONIA FERTILIZERS *See* Fertilizers and manures
AMMUNITION
See also
Cartridges
Projectiles

AMNESIA
The anatomy of memory loss [abnormality in the hippocampal formation of amnesia patients; research by Gary A. Press] *Science News* 136:204 S 23 '89
Causes
What really causes amnesia? il *USA Today (Periodical)* 117:13 Ap '89

AMNESTY
Take a number and wait [immigration amnesty program] D. Shaw. *The Washington Monthly* 21:28-30+ S '89

AMNESTY INTERNATIONAL
O'Sullivan's first law [opposition to death penalty shows abandonment of political neutrality] J. O'Sullivan. *National Review* 41:14 O 27 '89

Whirlwind worldwide touring: Amnesty International's Human Rights Now tour. M. Loeffler. il *Theatre Crafts* 23:50-4 My '89

AMNIOCENTESIS
In India, they abort females. J. McGowan. por *Newsweek* 113:12 Ja 30 '89

AMNIOTIC FLUID
Spina bifida: paralyzing fluid in the womb? [research by Dan S. Heffez] I. Wickelgren. *Science News* 135:342 Je 3 '89

When your water breaks. P. A. Hillard. il *Parents* 64:135-6 Ag '89

AMOCO CORPORATION
First-rate company. J. Cook. il por *Forbes* 143:84+ My 1 '89

AMOCO FABRICS & FIBERS COMPANY
Polypropylene strikes back [stain resistant carpet fiber] J. Harris. il *Forbes* 144:122 Ag 7 '89

AMOEBAS *See* Amebas
AMOEBIASIS *See* Amebiasis
AMORPHOUS SOLIDS *See* Solids
AMORTIZATION
A Banker's Secret [computer program figures amortization schedules] L. Kleinholz. il *Home Office Computing* 7:78-9 F '89

Earnings helper. D. Wechsler. il *Forbes* 143:150+ Je 12 '89

AMORY, JAN
about
Spirit! Ring in the season. M. Matousek. il pors *Harper's Bazaar* 122:154-7+ D '89

AMOS, JOHN
about
John Amos raps critics of interracial cast in Shakespeare's '12th night'. il por *Jet* 76:63 Jl 17 '89

AMOT CONTROLS CORPORATION
Cultural changes in a family firm. S. Nelton. il *Nation's Business* 77:62-3+ Ja '89

AMOXICILLIN
Corporate-funded research may be hazardous to your health [case of E. Cantekin, Univ. of Pittsburgh Medical School professor who questioned effectiveness of antibiotic amoxicillin] K. Hart. *The Bulletin of the Atomic Scientists* 45:32 Ap '89

AMP *See* Adenosine monophosphate
AMPCO-PITTSBURGH CORP.
Educating Marshall Berkman. K. Hannon. il por *Forbes* 144:72 O 30 '89

Is a nutsy-boltsy company out to nail Midway Airlines? M. Schroeder. il *Business Week* p26 Ag 21 '89

AMPÈRE, ANDRÉ MARIE, 1775-1836
about
André-Marie Ampère. L. P. Williams. il por *Scientific American* 260:90-7 Ja '89

AMPHETAMINES
See also
Crank (Drug)
Fenfluramine
Ice (Drug)
MDMA (Drug)
Methamphetamine
Methylphenidate

Factors that predict individual vulnerability to amphetamine self-administration. P. V. Piazza and others. bibl f il *Science* 245:1511-13 S 29 '89

Rats yield active clues to drug addiction [research by Pier Vincenzo Piazza] B. Bower. *Science News* 136:215 S 30 '89

AMPHIBIA
See also
Embryology—Amphibia
Frogs
Hearing—Amphibia
Salamanders

Eggs
Photographs and photography
From eggs to legs. M. Fogden. il *Natural History* p112-13 F '89

Reproduction
Marsupial frogs. E. M. del Pino. il *Scientific American* 260:110-18 My '89

AMPHIBIA, EFFECT OF TEMPERATURE ON
Temperature and sperm incorporation in polyploid salamanders. J. P. Bogart and others. bibl f il *Science* 246:1032-4 N 24 '89

AMPHIBIOUS AIRPLANES *See* Seaplanes

AMPHIBOLITES
Effect of water on the composition of partial melts of greenstone and amphibolite. J. S. Beard and G. E. Lofgren. bibl f il *Science* 244:195-7 Ap 14 '89

AMPHIPHILES
Molecular mechanisms and forces involved in the adhesion and fusion of amphiphilic bilayers. C. A. Helm and others. bibl f il *Science* 246:919-22 N 17 '89

AMPHIREGULIN
Structure and function of human amphiregulin: a member of the epidermal growth factor family. M. Shoyab and others. bibl f il *Science* 243:1074-6 F 24 '89

AMPLIFIERS
Amplifiers. il *Stereo Review* 54:78-92 F '89

Design
Active antenna. R. A. Kreuter. il *Radio-Electronics* 60:51-2+ F '89
Basic op-amps. R. Marston. il *Radio-Electronics* 60:69-72+ Mr '89
Compound op-amps. R. Marston. il *Radio-Electronics* 60:69-72+ Ja '89
High-power hi-fi audio amp for your home or car. L. K. Ross and A. Watts. il *Radio-Electronics* 60:51-5+ Mr '89
Op-amp oscillators. R. Marston. il *Radio-Electronics* 60:51-5 Jl '89
Op-amps in instrumentation. R. Marston. il *Radio-Electronics* 60:59-63 S '89
Working with op-amps. R. Marston. il *Radio-Electronics* 60:54-8 My '89

Energy usage
The importance of amplifier output current. L. Klein. il *Radio-Electronics* 60:70-1 Ap '89

Noise
How important is Slew Factor? L. Klein. il *Radio-Electronics* 60:87-8 Je '89

Specifications
Amplifier damping factor: how important is it? L. Klein. il *Radio-Electronics* 60:78-9 Ja '89

Testing
Denon AVC-2000 integrated audio/video amplifier. J. D. Hirsch. il *Stereo Review* 54:45-7 S '89
Grundig Fine Arts A-903 integrated amplifier. J. D. Hirsch. il *Stereo Review* 54:59-60 My '89
Hafler IRIS preamplifier. J. D. Hirsch. il *Stereo Review* 54:65+ D '89
Hafler XL-600 power amplifier. J. D. Hirsch. il *Stereo Review* 54:48+ Ap '89
Hafler XL-600 power amplifier. M. Riggs. il *High Fidelity (New York, N.Y.)* 39:49-50 Ja '89
JVC AX-Z911BK integrated amplifier. M. Riggs. il *High Fidelity (New York, N.Y.)* 39:35+ Mr '89
Linn LK1 preamplifier and LK280 power amplifier [cover story] J. D. Hirsch. il *Stereo Review* 54:56+ Ja '89
Luxman TP-117 tuner/preamplifier and multiroom system controller. J. D. Hirsch. il *Stereo Review* 54:64+ S '89
Marantz PM-65AV audio-video integrated amplifier. R. Long. il *High Fidelity (New York, N.Y.)* 39:28-9 Mr '89
Rockford Fosgate RF-2000 power amplifier. R. Long. il *High Fidelity (New York, N.Y.)* 39:22-3 Jl '89
Rockford Fosgate RF200 preamplifier and RF2000 power amplifier. J. D. Hirsch. il *Stereo Review* 54:50+ Je '89
Rotel RTC-850 tuner/preamplifier. R. Long. il *High Fidelity (New York, N.Y.)* 39:26-7+ Jl '89
Sony TA-E1000ESD digital preamplifier. J. D. Hirsch. il *Stereo Review* 54:90-4 O '89

Volume control
How loud is real? L. Klein. il *Radio-Electronics* 60:8-9+ Jl '89

AMPLITUDE MODULATION RADIO BROADCASTING
See Radio broadcasting

AMPTE (ACTIVE MAGNETOSPHERE PARTICLE TRACER EXPLORERS) SATELLITES *See* Artificial satellites—Meteorological use

AMPUTEES
Special pursuits: Oscar-winner Harold Russell. S. C. Soman. il por *Home Office Computing* 7:16 D '89

Rehabilitation
Helping amputees walk again [work of David Thompson] il *USA Today (Periodical)* 117:12 F '89

Sports
Injured in a climbing accident, a doctor tests his will in the mountains again [J. Donlou] D. Chu. il pors *People Weekly* 31:93-4+ Mr 20 '89

AMR CORP.
Boxed in by Trump [bid for American Airlines; special section] il por *Business Week* p54-6 O 23 '89
Trump mounts bid to buy American for $7.5 billion. *Aviation Week & Space Technology* 131:139 O 9 '89

AMR EAGLE (FIRM)
AMR Eagle boosts Saab-Scania with firm order for 50 SF340Bs. C. Fotos. il *Aviation Week & Space Technology* 130:110-11 My 29 '89
AMR Eagle places 100 orders, options for Jetstream aircraft. *Aviation Week & Space Technology* 130:167 Je 19 '89

AMR SERVICES CORPORATION
Piaggio picks AMR for Avanti [North American sales and support organization] *Flying* 116:14+ Ap '89

Piaggio selects AMR Services to market P. 180 in North America [business aircraft] *Aviation Week & Space Technology* 130:27 Ja 30 '89

AMRAAM (ADVANCED MEDIUM-RANGE AIR-TO-AIR MISSILES) *See* Guided missiles—Launching from airplanes

AMRE, INC.
How a hot-growth company got decked [acquisition of Champion Building Systems Inc.] T. Mason. il *Business Week* p34+ F 13 '89

AMREIN, M., AND OTHERS
Scanning tunneling microscopy of uncoated recA-DNA complexes. bibl f il *Science* 243:1708-11 Mr 31 '89

AMSDEN, ALICE H.
Asia's next giant. il *Technology Review* 92:46-53 My/Je '89

AMSTERDAM, SUSAN
Midlife crises in men: are women to blame? il *TV Guide* 37:18-20 Jl 22-28 '89

AMSTERDAM (NETHERLANDS)

Description
Gourmet holidays: Amsterdam. I. Keown. il *Gourmet* 49:74-9+ Ap '89

Galleries and museums
See also
Haags Gemeentemuseum (Netherlands)
Rijksmuseum (Netherlands)

AMSTERDAM NEWS (NEW YORK, N.Y.)
Procope sells interest in N.Y. Amsterdam news. por *Jet* 76:18 Jl 17 '89

AMSTRAD PLC
Cutting corners is cutting into Amstrad's bottom line. M. Maremont. il por *Business Week* p109-10 D 11 '89

AMTRAK *See* National Railroad Passenger Corp.

AMULETS AGAINST THE DRAGON FORCES [drama] *See* Zindel, Paul

AMUR RIVER (CHINA AND SOVIET UNION)
Watermelon diplomacy on the border [Sino-Soviet thaw along Amur River] J. Trimble. il map *U.S. News & World Report* 106:33 My 15 '89

AMUSEMENT PARKS
See also
Boardwalk and Baseball (Amusement park)
Disney-MGM Studios Theme Park (Fla.)
EPCOT (Fla.)
Heritage USA (S.C.)
Walt Disney World (Fla.)
WOOZ (Vacaville, Calif.)
Disney World and the four dwarfs. C. Clark. il *The Saturday Evening Post* 261:86-7 Mr '89
Theme parks—what's the attraction? K. Whittemore. il *Seventeen* 48:235-6+ Ag '89

Accidents
Scared to death! Terror and tragedy at America's amusement parks. E. Davidowitz. il por *Redbook* 173:106-7+ Jl '89

Acquisitions and mergers
Even August Busch can only handle so much beer. J. F. Siler. il por *Business Week* p182+ S 25 '89
HBJ sells theme parks to Anheuser for $1.1 billion. C. Reid. *Publishers Weekly* 236:11 O 13 '89

Advertising
Walt Disney World chooses Ebony to boost its new MGM Theme Park. il *Jet* 76:62 Je 12 '89

Environmental aspects
Gateway theme park plans dropped. J. Weinberg. *National Parks* 63:13 N/D '89

Equipment
See also
Eli Bridge Company
Ferris wheels
Roller coasters
Amusement park thrills [role of gravity in ride design] il *National Geographic World* 171:20-3 N '89

Denmark
See also
Legoland Park (Billund, Denmark)

France
See also
Big Bang Schtroumpfs

AMUSEMENT RIDES *See* Amusement parks—Equipment

AMWAY CORP.
Amway's big, happy family is all smiles—in Japan. T. Holden. il *Business Week* p47+ S 4 '89
A takeover of Avon could mean a makeover for Amway. W. Zellner. il *Business Week* p38-9 My 22 '89

AMYGDALA *See* Brain

AMYLASES
Metastatic hibernomas in transgenic mice expressing an α-amylase-SV40 T antigen hybrid gene. N. Fox and others. bibl f il *Science* 244:460-3 Ap 28 '89

AMYLOID
Alzheimer's clue [beta amyloid detected in the skin; work of Dennis J. Selkoe] *Time* 134:86 O 2 '89
Alzheimer's protein not restricted to brain [research by Dennis J. Selkoe] R. Weiss. *Science News* 136:197 S 23 '89
Amyloid β protein enhances the survival of hippocampal neurons in vitro. J. S. Whitson and others. bibl f il *Science* 243:1488-90 Mr 17 '89

AMYLOID—*cont.*
Brain protein yields clues to Alzheimer's disease. J. L. Marx. il *Science* 243:1664-6 Mr 31 '89
Hints of a brain toxin in Alzheimer's [research by Rachael L. Neve] R. Weiss. *Science News* 136:68 Jl 29 '89
Neurotoxicity of a fragment of the amyloid precursor associated with Alzheimer's disease. B. A. Yankner and others. bibl f il *Science* 245:417-20 Jl 28 '89
A novel mRNA of the A4 amyloid precursor gene coding for a possibly secreted protein. F. De Sauvage and J.-N. Octave. bibl f il *Science* 245:651-3 Ag 11 '89
Relation of the amyloid β protein precursor to heparan sulfate proteoglycans [discussion of July 8, 1988 article, Amyloid β protein precursor as possibly a heparan sulfate proteoglycan core protein] D. Schubert and others. *Science* 244:826-8 My 19 '89
Tracing Alzheimer's telltale protein [research by Dennis J. Selkoe] *U.S. News & World Report* 107:14 O 2 '89
AMYOTROPHIC LATERAL SCLEROSIS
ALS a challenge. C. SerVaas. il *The Saturday Evening Post* 261:94+ N/D '89
Lou Gehrig's medical legacy. A. Dane. il *American Health* 8:17 S '89
Stephen Hawking shoots for the stars. il por *Home Office Computing* 7:12 S '89
AN-NA'IM, ABDULLAHI AHMED
Rushdie is within Islamic tradition. il *New Perspectives Quarterly* 6:49-50 Spr '89
AN-SKI, S. *See* Ansky, S., 1863-1920
ANABAPTISTS
See also
Hutterian Brethren
ANABOLIC STEROIDS *See* Steroids
ANACOMP, INC.
Turnaround, take two. G. Morgenson. il *Forbes* 144:374 N 13 '89
ANAEROBIC TRAINING
Anaerobic threshold [cycling] S. Johnson. *Bicycling* 30:178 Mr '89
ANAHEIM STADIUM
Peanuts, popcorn . . . cinnamon rolls? E. Cohen. il *Sport (New York, N.Y.)* 80:83 My '89
ANAHID
about
Anahid. *The New Yorker* 65:23-4 Jl 31 '89
ANALGESIA AND ANALGESICS
See also
Acetaminophen
Acupuncture
Aspirin
Buprenorphine
Heroin
Ibuprofen
Placebos
99 pain stoppers [with editorial comment by Mark Bricklin] G. McVeigh. il *Prevention (Emmaus, Pa.)* 41:33-45+, 144+ O '89
Can alcohol ease suffering? [study by Kenneth Woodrow and Lorne Eltherington] *USA Today (Periodical)* 117:10-11 F '89
The dope on painkillers. P. G. Gill, Jr. il *Outdoor Life* 184:72+ N '89
Dual demons [use of painkillers to treat pain from wrist fracture] B. D. Colen. il *Health (New York, N.Y.)* 21:34-5 Jl '89
High-risk pain pills. L. Morgenroth. il *The Atlantic* 264:36+ D '89
Less pain for the littlest patients [use of painkillers for children during and after surgery] J. Carey. il *U.S. News & World Report* 106:62-3 F 27 '89
Radioactive drugs ease bone-tumor pain. I. Wickelgren. *Science News* 135:373 Je 17 '89
Suffering in silence. M. Shuchman and M. S. Wilkes. il *The New York Times Magazine* p36-7 Jl 23 '89
What can be done when the pain won't go away. E. Weck. il *FDA Consumer* 23:28-31 Jl/Ag '89
ANALGESICS *See* Analgesia and analgesics
ANALOG DEVICES, INC.
Chipping in with 18-bit DACs. D. Ranada. il *High Fidelity (New York, N.Y.)* 39:18 F '89
ANALOG-TO-DIGITAL CONVERTERS
A/D converter accuracy. D. Lancaster. il *Radio-Electronics* 60:34 Ja '89
Hardware hacker [Delta-Sigma A/D conversion] D. Lancaster. il *Radio-Electronics* 60:67-74 Je '89
ANALOGY
It's like, you know . . . [young children's abilities to use analogies to acquire information; research by Stella Vosniadou and Marlene Schommer] G. W. Bracey. il *Phi Delta Kappan* 70:560-1 Mr '89
ANALYSIS, CONFORMATIONAL *See* Conformational analysis
ANANGEL-AMERICAN SHIPHOLDINGS LTD.
Safer harbor. M. Schifrin. il *Forbes* 144:378+ N 13 '89
ANAPHYLACTIC SHOCK *See* Anaphylaxis
ANAPHYLAXIS
Anaphylaxis: an allergic reaction that can kill. M. Segal. il *FDA Consumer* 23:21-3 My '89

Backward protection. E. Rosenthal. il *The New York Times Magazine* p27-8 Jl 2 '89
When your immune system panics. E. Rosenthal. il *The Saturday Evening Post* 261:60-1 O '89
ANARCHISM
See also
Terrorism
ANAREN MICROWAVE, INC.
Need to detect signals instantly spurs call for digital components. il *Aviation Week & Space Technology* 131:104-5 S 18 '89
ANAS, DAVID
about
From real-estate broker to chocolate maker. D. E. Gumpert and D. Davis. il por *New Choices for the Best Years* 29:52-3 O '89
ANASAZI CULTURE *See* Pueblo Indians
ANASTOS, PETER
about
The gilded bat [ballet] Reviews
Dance Magazine il 63:8 N '89. E. Kendall
ANATOMY
See also
Homology (Biology)
Human body
Men—Anatomy and physiology
Women—Anatomy and physiology
Atlases
An atlas for organ country [work of F. Netter] il por *Newsweek* 114:61 O 2 '89
ANATOMY, ARTISTIC
An atlas for organ country [work of F. Netter] il por *Newsweek* 114:61 O 2 '89
ANAWALT, SASHA
The "steady strengthening" of a ballerina [cover story] il pors *Dance Magazine* 63:34-9 N '89
ANCESTOR WORSHIP
Ways of the ancestors [Madagascar] J. Mack. il *Natural History* p24+ Ap '89
ANCESTRY *See* Genealogy
ANCHORAGE
See also
Condominiums (Boat docking)
Marinas
Anchoring: a new system. S. Stapleton. il *Motor Boating & Sailing* 163:142+ Ja '89
The long rode to success [rope and anchor techniques] B. Stearns. il *Field & Stream* 94:68+ O '89
ANCHORAGE (ALASKA)
Arts
See also
Alaska Center for the Performing Arts (Anchorage, Alaska)
Description
The dog days of winter [Iditarod Trail Sled Dog Race] K. Castle. il *Travel Holiday* 171:60-1 Ja '89
ANCHORAGE (NEW YORK, N.Y.)
The Anchorage. *The New Yorker* 65:35-6 S 18 '89
ANCHORING *See* Anchorage
ANCHORS
Build a wind anchor. B. Volkart. il *Field & Stream* 93:78 F '89
Light weight aluminum anchors. B. Gladstone and others. il *Motor Boating & Sailing* 164:65 D '89
Ocean grabber. D. H. Van Liew. il *Popular Science* 234:110-11 Mr '89
ANCHORS (NEWSCASTERS) *See* Television broadcasting—News
ANCIENT ASTRONOMY *See* Astronomy, Ancient
ANCIENT GREECE *See* Greece—History
ANCIENT ROME *See* Rome
ANDALUSIA (SPAIN)
Description and travel
Andalusia's age of the Expo. H. Gordon. il *World Press Review* 36:76 N '89
ANDALUSIAN EXPRESS (TRAIN) *See* Railroads—Trains
ANDEREGG, KAREN
about
The beauty elite. il pors *Harper's Bazaar* 122:40+ Ag '89
ANDEREGG, M. L.
(jt. auth) *See* Vergason, Glenn A., and Anderegg, M. L.
ANDERS, DAVID
about
6,500 'I do's' make for one sturdy marriage for Susan Goeppinger and fellow actor David Anders. P. Freeman. il pors *People Weekly* 31:89-90 My 1 '89
ANDERS, ROBERT L., AND KANAI-PAK, MASAKO
Growing old in Japan. il *World Health* p8-11 D '88
ANDERSEN, CATHY
about
Reader of the Year. il *McCall's* 117:57-63+ O '89
ANDERSEN, CHRISTOPHER P.
Jane Fonda: "I'm stronger than ever" [cover story] il pors *Ladies' Home Journal* 106:112+ O '89
Kate the great. il pors *Ladies' Home Journal* 106:142-4+ S '89
A lunch with Lord Larry. il pors *Ladies' Home Journal* 106:122+ D '89

ANDERSEN, GABRIELE
about
Swift Swiss. M. Will-Weber. il por *Runner's World* 24:93
Ja '89
ANDERSEN, KURT, 1954-
An architectural presence in the Manhattan art world. il
por *Architectural Digest* 46:170+ N '89
Hot mood. il *Rolling Stone* p58-60 My 18 '89
Not the best of times, not the worst. il *Utne Reader* p92
S/O '89
Robert A. M. Stern: new interpretation of the shingle style
on Long Island. il por *Architectural Digest* 46:66-71+ Ag
'89
(jt. auth) See Rudnick, Paul, and Andersen, Kurt, 1954-
ANDERSEN, LARRY
about
Now some comic relief. F. Lidz. il por *Sports Illustrated*
70:89 My 1 '89
ANDERSEN, MARTIN
Dirty secrets of the 'dirty war'. *The Nation* 248:339-40+
Mr 13 '89
ANDERSEN (ARTHUR) & COMPANY See Arthur Andersen
& Company
ANDERSON, BOB, 1945-
Eight minutes to stretch [cover story] il *Women's Sports
& Fitness* 11:46-8+ N/D '89
The flex factor [cover story] il *Runner's World* 24:38-43
F '89
ANDERSON, BRUCE
At last a title for the Cowboys. il *Sports Illustrated* 70:70-1
Mr 27 '89
The Devils turned on the heat. il *Sports Illustrated* 70:72-3
F 13 '89
On top of the world. il pors *Sports Illustrated* 71:40-1 Ag
14 '89
Playing for the Peacock. il *Sports Illustrated* 71:95 Jl 24
'89
Scherr determination. il pors *Sports Illustrated* 70:71+ Ap
10 '89
Their final shots. il pors *Sports Illustrated* 71:24-5 Jl 10
'89
ANDERSON, CHRIS, 1955-
Sharpening the silence. *Commonweal* 116:230 Ap 21 '89
ANDERSON, COLLEEN
A gift of life [story] il *Redbook* 173:62+ Ag '89
ANDERSON, CRISTINA
Fair-weather friend [story] il *'Teen* 33:42+ O '89
ANDERSON, DENISE
about
For Denise Anderson, the jury forewoman, passing judgment
on Ollie North was a trial by fire. P. Chin. il pors *People
Weekly* 31:49-50 My 22 '89
ANDERSON, DIGBY C.
Tasteless Dutch tomatoes and waiters named Terry. *The
New York Times Magazine* p60+ D 3 '89
ANDERSON, DON L.
Composition of the earth. bibl f il *Science* 243:367-70 Ja
20 '89
Where on earth is the crust? bibl f il *Physics Today* 42:38-46
Mr '89
ANDERSON, GEORGE M.
Deafness and poverty in third-world countries. il *America*
160:531-4 Je 3 '89
Defending the poor: a harder task [cover story] il *America*
160:4-7 Ja 7-14 '89
Mass transit and the poor. il *America* 161:399-402 D 2
'89
ANDERSON, GLENN
about
A family feud over organic farming pits the Anderson brothers
against each other. P. Freeman. il pors *People Weekly*
32:47-8 Jl 24 '89
ANDERSON, JAMES W.
Taking oat bran to heart. il *The Saturday Evening Post*
261:18+ Jl/Ag '89
ANDERSON, JAY
Eclipse prospects for the 1990s. il maps *Astronomy* 17:71-6
F '89
ANDERSON, JOHN W.
Scrambling for biotech bucks. il *The Nation* 248:476-8 Ap
10 '89
ANDERSON, KENNY
about
On deck. il por *Sport (New York, N.Y.)* 80:16 Ap '89
ANDERSON, KEVIN
about
Anderson ascending. R. Wetzsteon. il por *New York* 22:40
S 11 '89
ANDERSON, KIM
Best tips for beating sinusitis. il *Prevention (Emmaus, Pa.)*
41:38-43 Ja '89
Just desserts. il *Runner's World* 24:40-4 S '89
Pick your pace. il *Health (New York, N.Y.)* 21:58-9 S '89
Push it. il *Runner's World* 24:40-4 Ag '89

ANDERSON, LAURIE, 1947-
about
New Music Fest marks tenth year; A double dose of Laurie
Anderson. F. Goodman. il por *Rolling Stone* p37 N 30
'89
Projecting her voice. B. Weber. il por *The New York Times
Magazine* p94 Je 4 '89
ANDERSON, LINDA
Agenda 2000. por *Essence* 20:132 D '89
ANDERSON, LISA
about
Citizens organize against neo-Nazis. A. Sochocky and C.
Siegner. il por *The Progressive* 53:15 Ag '89
ANDERSON, LONI
about
Breaking in to family life. il pors *People Weekly* 32:98-9+
N 6 '89
ANDERSON, LOUIE
Why a comedian? Louie Anderson recalls his tormented
life with father [excerpt from Dear dad] il pors *TV Guide*
37:24-7 O 14-20 '89
ANDERSON, MARCIA
about
Marcia Anderson and Jim Diebold marry for money—the
dollars their guests gave to charity. P. Freeman. il pors
People Weekly 31:139+ Je 19 '89
ANDERSON, MARIAN, 1902-
about
The first lady. M. Sweeley. il *National Review* 41:65-6 S
29 '89
A tribute to Marian Anderson. il por *Ebony* 45:182+ N
'89
ANDERSON, MICHAEL, 1920-
about
Millennium [film] Reviews
People Weekly il 32:13 S 18 '89. R. Novak
ANDERSON, NANCY
Kevin Costner. il pors *Good Housekeeping* 209:76+ Ag '89
Tom Hanks. il pors *Good Housekeeping* 208:168+ My '89
ANDERSON, OWEN
How big a setback is a temporary cutback? il *Women's
Sports & Fitness* 11:18 Ap '89
Just how good are those special insoles? il *Women's Sports
& Fitness* 11:14 Ja/F '89
A question that's gone round & round. il *Women's Sports
& Fitness* 11:58 Ja/F '89
Raising your carbo consciousness. il *Women's Sports & Fitness*
11:18 O '89
A run a day keeps the doctor away? il *Runner's World*
24:54-7 Ja '89
A vitamin exercisers need to watch closely. il *Women's
Sports & Fitness* 11:22 S '89
Will weight training improve your running? bibl il *Women's
Sports & Fitness* 11:22-3 Ap '89
ANDERSON, PHILIP WARREN, 1923-
Spin glass: real power brought to bear. il por *Physics Today*
42:9+ Jl '89
Spin glass: spin glass as cornucopia. por *Physics Today* 42:9+
S '89
ANDERSON, RAY
about
Ray Anderson: slidin' into first. J. Levenson. il pors *Down
Beat* 56:27-9 Ag '89
ANDERSON, RAY C.
about
Carpet tile king. A. A. Lappen. il por *Forbes* 143:60+ Ap
17 '89
ANDERSON, ROBERT HENRY, 1918-
A second wave of interest in team teaching. *The Education
Digest* 54:18-21 F '89
ANDERSON, ROBERT ORVILLE, 1917-
about
Pauley hits more red ink than black gold. R. Grover. il
por *Business Week* p81 S 11 '89
ANDERSON, ROBERT WOODRUFF, 1917-
Travel writing: a primer. *The Writer* 102:14-16 Je '89
**ANDERSON, ROLAND C., AND VANDERWERFF, JOYCE
E.**
In pursuit of the suburban squid. il *Sea Frontiers* 35:165-9
My/Je '89
ANDERSON, RON
about
A family feud over organic farming pits the Anderson brothers
against each other. P. Freeman. il pors *People Weekly*
32:47-8 Jl 24 '89
ANDERSON, STEVE
Editorial. See issues of Cycle beginning March 1989
ANDERSON, STUART
Gorbie's choice. *The New Republic* 200:11-12 Ap 17 '89
ANDERSON, SUSAN
Eyes on the prizes, not the people [cover story] il *The
Nation* 249:405+ O 16 '89
ANDERSON, TERRY
Kidnapping
The lost life of Terry Anderson. S. MacLeod. il pors *Time*
133:39+ Mr 20 '89

ANDERSON, W. FRENCH, 1936-
about
French Anderson's 20-year crusade. B. J. Culliton. por *Science* 246:748 N 10 '89
A genetic road map. D. Glick. il por *Newsweek* 114:46 O 2 '89
ANDERSON, WILLIAM T., 1952-
In the footsteps of the Lincolns. il map *The Saturday Evening Post* 261:64-7+ Jl/Ag '89
Mr. Lincoln's Springfield. il *American History Illustrated* 24:26-31 Mr '89
ANDERSON (M.D.) CANCER CENTER See M.D. Anderson Cancer Center
ANDERSON RANCH ARTS CENTER
The ranch artistically reconsidered [designed by Harry Teague] J. S. Russell. il *Architectural Record* 177:74-7 Ap '89
ANDERTON, CINDY
about
The amazing Andertons. L. Gourse. il pors *McCall's* 116:92+ Ja '89
ANDERTON, STEVE
about
The amazing Andertons. L. Gourse. il pors *McCall's* 116:92+ Ja '89
ANDES CLIMBS See Mountaineering
ANDRADE, JOAQUIM PEDRO DE
about
Macunaima [film] Reviews
The Unesco Courier il 42:14-17 O '89. A. Rodrigues
ANDRADE, ZILTON A.
. . . and how it was fought. il *World Health* p26-7 D '88
ANDREAS, PETER
Cocaine chemistry. *The New Republic* 201:12+ N 20 '89
Drug war zone. *The Nation* 249:704-5 D 11 '89
ANDREEVA, NINA
about
Holding back. J. Elson. il por *Time* 133:66+ Ap 10 '89
ANDREOTTI, GIULIO
about
In Andreotti's tent. B. Crozier. *National Review* 41:20 Ag 18 '89
ANDRETTI, MARIO
about
The Andretti assault. T. Mulgannon. il pors *Sport (New York, N.Y.)* 80:68-70+ Je '89
Bump and run. S. Moses. il pors *Sports Illustrated* 70:33 Ap 24 '89
Like Mario, like Michael. L. Griffin. il pors *Car and Driver* 35:145-53 S '89
On board with Mario Andretti. L. Rudeen. il pors *Motor Boating & Sailing* 163:66-9+ Ja '89
ANDRETTI, MICHAEL
about
The Andretti assault. T. Mulgannon. il pors *Sport (New York, N.Y.)* 80:68-70+ Je '89
Like Mario, like Michael. L. Griffin. il pors *Car and Driver* 35:145-53 S '89
ANDREW, PRINCE, DUKE OF YORK, 1960-
about
Discordant notes [visit to Canada] M. Nichols. il pors *Maclean's* 102:36 Jl 31 '89
Royal revenge [visits to Canada; cover story; special section; with editorial comment by Kevin Doyle] il pors *Maclean's* 102:4, 36-42+ Jl 24 '89
ANDREW W. MELLON FOUNDATION
The fine art of giving [interview with P. Mellon] S. Allis. il por *Time* 134:86-7 S 18 '89
ANDREWS, BENNY, 1930-
The first death. il *American Visions* 4:18-20 Ap '89
ANDREWS, CECILY ISABEL FAIRFIELD See West, Dame Rebecca, 1892-1983
ANDREWS, FRANCES TOWNSEND
Nickel silver. il *Antiques & Collecting Hobbies* 94:27-9 Je '89
ANDREWS, JULIE
about
Julie and Carol together again. E. Sirkin and D. Lamanna. il pors *Ladies' Home Journal* 106:62+ D '89
ANDREWS, MARK E., III
about
Petro-vulture. J. R. Hayes. il por *Forbes* 143:96+ F 20 '89
ANDREWS, TEDDY
about
Holding office is kid's stuff for 8-year-old Teddy Andrews. il pors *People Weekly* 31:91-2 My 8 '89
ANDREWS & MCMEEL
Andrews & McMeel: a hit with syndicated satire. T. Unsworth. *Publishers Weekly* 235:45 F 10 '89
Doonesbury comes home to Andrews & McMeel [G. Trudeau] por *Publishers Weekly* 235:61 Ja 13 '89
ANDREWS GROUP INC.
The incredible Perelman. T. Jaffe. il *Forbes* 143:164 My 15 '89
ANDRIOLO, MARIO, JR.
about
A dentist to fight cavities—and pain. A. Witchel. il por *New York* 22:30 D 18 '89

ANDROGENS
See also
Dehydroepiandrosterone
Testosterone
ANDROGYNY (PSYCHOLOGY)
Androgyny is going strong in the streets and salons, promoted by today's hot stars. L. Wolfe. il *Vogue* 179:45-6 Ja '89
Android's revenge [terminology] W. Safire. il *The New York Times Magazine* p8+ Ja 15 '89
Boyish good looks [menswear for women] B. Boehlert. il *Vogue* 179:78-9 F '89
A dash of haberdashery [menswear for women] il *Glamour* 87:251 Ap '89
ANDROMEDA (GALAXY) See Galaxies
ANECHOIC CHAMBERS
Shhh . . .! il *National Geographic World* 169:21-3 S '89
USAF building new anechoic chamber capable of accommodating B-1, B-2. W. B. Scott. il *Aviation Week & Space Technology* 130:55+ F 27 '89
USAF testing electronic warfare systems in new anechoic chamber. il *Aviation Week & Space Technology* 131:81-2 S 11 '89
ANEMIA
See also
Fanconi anemia
Sickle cell anemia
Anemia—a simple disorder that can cause serious problems. K. McCoy. *Seventeen* 48:156 Mr '89
Anemic and considered dangerous. B. Kaplan. il *Current Health 2* 16:10-11 N '89
Bad blood. W. T. Buckley. *Redbook* 173:104-5+ Je '89
Blood deficiency signals problems. *USA Today (Periodical)* 117:3 F '89
Body's protein does malaria's dirty work [research by Kathleen L. Miller] F. Flam. *Science News* 135:293 My 13 '89
Rust never sleeps [iron imbalances] J. Scandura. *American Health* 8:151-2 Mr '89
Therapy
Anemia drug approved [erythropoietin] *FDA Consumer* 23:2 S '89
An 'insulin' for anemia sufferers [Epogen replaces erythropoietin in kidney dialysis patients] *U.S. News & World Report* 106:13 Je 12 '89
ANEMOMETERS
Building an automated recording anemometer [computer program] A. Bernier and H. Schmies. il *Weatherwise* 42:164-6 Je '89
ANESTHESIA AND ANESTHETICS
See also
Fentanyl
Nitrous oxide
PCP
Less pain for the littlest patients [use of painkillers for children during and after surgery] J. Carey. il *U.S. News & World Report* 106:62-3 F 27 '89
Modern anesthesia: going under safely [cover story] V. Modeland. il *FDA Consumer* 23:13-17 D '89/Ja '90
ANESTHESIOLOGISTS
The unsung hero. E. Rosenthal. il *The New York Times Magazine* p53-4 Ap 30 '89
ANESTHETICS See Anesthesia and anesthetics
ANEURYSMS
The $50,000 haircut [recovery from brain aneurysm] F. Swertlow. il pors *Money* 18:84-94+ My '89
Surgery
Balloon angioplasty finds other applications. il *Popular Mechanics* 166:16 Ap '89
Brain saver [work of Julian Bailes] *Prevention (Emmaus, Pa.)* 41:20-1 N '89
Defusing a bomb in the brain [use of balloon angioplasty; work of Grant Hieshima] G. McBride. il *American Health* 8:9-10 D '89
ANGEL, HEATHER, 1941-
about
Angel of nature [interview] il *Petersen's Photographic Magazine* 18:48-51+ Ag '89
ANGEL DUST (DRUG) See PCP
ANGELA CAPONIGRO DANCE ENSEMBLE
Reviews:
Performances at Cunningham Studio, New York City. J. Lewis. il por *Dance Magazine* 63:68 O '89
ANGELICA CORP.
Finding plays without fancy footwork. G. G. Marcial. il *Business Week* p124 My 1 '89
ANGELL, ROGER
The Bay and before. *The New Yorker* 65:58-60+ D 11 '89
Greetings, friends! [poem] il *The New Yorker* 65:36 D 25 '89
No, but I saw the game. *The New Yorker* 65:41+ Jl 31 '89
State of the art. il *The New Yorker* 65:54+ My 8 '89
ANGELMAN SYNDROME
Prader lacks fader; Angelman misses mom? [research by Robert D. Nicholls] R. Weiss. *Science News* 136:324 N 18 '89
ANGELO, JOHN
Bookworks: a bookselling thoroughbred. il *Publishers Weekly* 236:24-6 D 1 '89

ANGELOU, MAYA
Oprah Winfrey. il por *Ms.* 17:88-9 Ja/F '89
They came to stay. *National Geographic* 176:208 Ag '89
ANGELS (THEATER) *See* Theater—Economic aspects
ANGELS IN ART
Angels! H. Muschamp. il *Vogue* 179:278-87 D '89
ANGER
    See also
    Indignation
    Peeves
    Temper
Angry [black women] J. Malveaux. *Essence* 20:64+ My '89
Christians can be good and angry [with readers' comments]
  R. M. Brown. *U.S. Catholic* 54:14-15 N '89
Healthy anger. R. Hyatt. il *USA Today (Periodical)* 117:75-7
  Ja '89
How to be mad at the man you're mad for. D. Heyn.
  Mademoiselle 95:108 O '89
What, me angry? M. Scarf. il *The New York Times Magazine*
  p22+ Ap 23 '89
Who, me—angry? How guys hide their ire. D. Heyn.
  Mademoiselle 95:76 Je '89
Wild with anger? Tame that tiger. E. Karlsberg. il *'Teen*
  33:24+ My '89
    Anecdotes, facetiae, satire, etc.
Kick a radio and call me in the morning. J. Skow. il
  Smithsonian 20:256 N '89
ANGER IN CHILDREN
Good ways to handle a child's anger. B. Spock. por *Redbook*
  174:28+ D '89
Understanding a child's anger. L. Salk. il *McCall's* 116:71
  F '89
"We have a problem". J. Marks. il *Parents* 64:64+ My '89
ANGIER, NATALIE
25 and taking over: the high-expectation, low-sweat generation.
  il *Mademoiselle* 95:214-15+ Ag '89
Baby chic: what's behind the new diaper rush? il *Mademoiselle*
  95:194-5+ Je '89
Fear of finance. il *Mademoiselle* 95:114-15+ Ja '89
The gene dream. il *American Health* 8:102-6+ Mr '89
A granddaughter's fear. il *The New York Times Magazine*
  p22+ My 7 '89
Life in the stress lane: diary of a wired day. il pors
  Mademoiselle 95:192-5+ F '89
Praise for a red predator. il maps *American Health* 8:74-6+
  S '89
Saving the cracids. il *The Atlantic* 264:26+ Ag '89
ANGIOGENESIS
Bloodless coup [inhibition of angiogenesis; research by Judah
  Folkman] T. Beardsley. *Scientific American* 261:18-19 Ag
  '89
Control of angiogenesis with synthetic heparin substitutes.
  J. Folkman and others. bibl f il *Science* 243:1490-3 Mr
  17 '89
Vascular endothelial growth factor is a secreted angiogenic
  mitogen. D. W. Leung and others. bibl f il *Science*
  246:1306-9 D 8 '89
ANGIOPLASTY, ARTERIAL *See* Arteries—Diseases—Therapy
ANGIOSPERMS
Directed movement of latex particles in the gynoecia of
  three species of flowering plants. L. C. Sanders and E.
  M. Lord. bibl f il *Science* 243:1606-8 Mr 24 '89
ANGIOSPERMS, FOSSIL
Angiosperm diversification and paleolatitudinal gradients in
  Cretaceous floristic diversity. P. R. Crane and S. Lidgard.
  bibl f il *Science* 246:675-8 N 3 '89
Flowering plants leave earth cold [research by Tyler Volk]
  Science News 135:188 Mr 25 '89
ANGIOTENSIN
Angiotensin II: does it have a direct obligate role in ovulation?
  [discussion of June 17, 1988 article, Blockage of ovulation
  by an angiotensin antagonist] A. Pellicer and others. il
  Science 245:870-1 Ag 25 '89
Inhibitors of angiotensin-converting enzyme prevent myoin-
  timal proliferation after vascular injury [use of cilazapril
  after balloon catheterization] J. S. Powell and others. bibl
  f il *Science* 245:186-8 Jl 14 '89
ANGIOTENSIN RECEPTORS *See* Hormone receptors
**ANGKOR WAT (SAN FRANCISCO, CALIF.:
RESTAURANT)** *See* San Francisco (Calif.)—Restaurants,
nightclubs, bars, etc.
ANGLERFISH
    See also
    Frogfish
ANGLES
The game of angles [fishing] J. Gibbs. il *Outdoor Life* 183:20+
  Mr '89
ANGLICAN CHURCH *See* Church of England
ANGLICAN COMMUNION
Anglican leaders try to preserve unity [ordination of women
  discussed at meeting in Cyprus] R. Walker. il *Christianity
  Today* 33:54-5 Je 16 '89
ANGLING *See* Fishing
ANGLO-AMERICAN INSURANCE COMPANY
Did this insurance whiz undercut and run? [C. Miro] T.
  Smart. il por *Business Week* p120+ O 23 '89

ANGLO-DUTCH WARS, 1652-1784
Cromwell's soldier-admirals. M. Baumber. bibl il pors *History
  Today* 39:42-7 O '89
ANGLUND, JOAN WALSH
Merry Christmas. il *Good Housekeeping* 209:124+ D '89
ANGOLA
    See also
    Military assistance, American—Angola
    Military assistance, Cuban—Angola
    Political prisoners—Angola
    Economic policy
After accord, Angola turns to economic development. M.
  A. Fortune. il map *Black Enterprise* 19:20 Mr '89
Suddenly, the business of Angola is business. S. Askin. il
  Business Week p45 My 1 '89
    Economic relations
      United States
    See United States—Economic relations—Angola
    Foreign relations
      South Africa
    See South Africa—Foreign relations—Angola
      United States
    See United States—Foreign relations—Angola
    Politics and government
The Angola/Namibia accords. C. W. Freeman. *Foreign Affairs*
  68:126-41 Summ '89
Angola/Namibia accords [special section] il maps *Department
  of State Bulletin* 89:10-23 F '89
The end of the affair [J. Savimbi and U.S. support for
  UNITA] B. Turque. il por *Newsweek* 114:54 O 16 '89
How macho are the Cubans? H. Hamann. il *Conservative
  Digest* 15:54-7 S/O '89
The last battle? R. Sikorski. *National Review* 41:19-20 Ag
  4 '89
Minority report [J. Savimbi] C. Hitchens. *The Nation* 248:690
  My 22 '89
The mystique of Savimbi. R. Sikorski. il por *National Review*
  41:34-7 Ag 18 '89
Namibia: the making of a new nation [tripartite agreement
  among Angola, Cuba, and South Africa; cover story; special
  section] il map *UN Chronicle* 26:34-48 Mr '89
Peace at last in Namibia? G. Lister and M. Verbaan. il
  The Nation 248:18+ Ja 2 '89
Peace in Angola? P. M. Martin. bibl f *Current History*
  88:229-32+ My '89
Peace is in the air. C. C. Williams and K. Crooks. il *Black
  Enterprise* 20:32 O '89
Pretoria outflanks the ANC. S. Reiss. il map *Newsweek*
  113:37 Ja 23 '89
Silencing the guns of Angola. il *Newsweek* 114:31 Jl 3 '89
"We have taken the first step" [President E. Dos Santos
  and J. Savimbi agree to cease-fire] B. W. Nelan. il pors
  map *Time* 134:28 Jl 3 '89
ANGSTADT, ROBERT B.
(jt. auth) See Diehl, Jack D., Jr., and Angstadt, Robert
  B.
ANGUILLA
    See also
    Resorts—Anguilla
ANGULAR MOMENTUM
Length-of-day variations caused by El Niño-Southern Oscilla-
  tion and Quasi-Biennial Oscillation. B. F. Chao. bibl f
  il *Science* 243:923-5 F 17 '89
Stratospheric winds alter day's length [research by B. Fong
  Chao] R. Monastersky. *Science News* 135:102 F 18 '89
ANGULO, GERRY
    about
Count the cash and go home early. T. Pouschine. il por
  Forbes 143:124+ My 29 '89
ANHEUSER-BUSCH, INC.
A dry beer puts new fizz in Anheuser-Busch. il *Money*
  18:42 Ag '89
Even August Busch can only handle so much beer. J. F.
  Siler. il por *Business Week* p182+ S 25 '89
Good times or bad, this brewer barrels along. P. Sellers.
  il *Fortune* 120:42+ Jl 31 '89
HBJ sells theme parks to Anheuser for $1.1 billion. C.
  Reid. *Publishers Weekly* 236:11 O 13 '89
The king of beer stocks at a commoner's price. P. Sellers.
  il *Fortune* 120:42 D 18 '89
A warning shot from the king of beers. J. F. Siler. il *Business
  Week* p124 D 18 '89
ANHYDROUS AMMONIA FERTILIZERS *See* Fertilizers and
manures
ANILOCRA
Hangers-on. L. Bunkley-Williams and E. H. Williams. il
  Natural History p40-1 Ja '89
ANIMAL BEHAVIOR *See* Animals—Habits and behavior
ANIMAL BEHAVIOR [film] *See* Motion picture reviews—
Single works
ANIMAL BITES
Pet-associated injuries: the trouble with children's best friends.
  P. M. Wishon and A. Huang. bibl il *Children Today*
  18:24-7 My/Je '89
Why bite the right of a trilobite? [research by Loren E.
  Babcock] R. Monastersky. il *Science News* 136:78 Jl 29
  '89

ANIMAL BREEDING See Breeding
ANIMAL CALLING
See also
Bird calling
Bears by invitation [black bears; cover story] M. Strandlund. il *Outdoor Life* 184:82-3+ N '89
Beyond the bugle. J. Byers. il *Outdoor Life* 184:64-5+ Ag '89
How to tickle a whitetail [antlers used as deer calls] J. Weiss. il *Outdoor Life* 184:74-5+ S '89
Hunting the hunters [predators at night with varmint calls] B. Tarrant. il *Field & Stream* 94:95-6 Jl '89
The sounds deer make. J. Trout. il *Field & Stream* 94:130 S '89
A squirrel call that works. M. Pearce. il *Outdoor Life* 184:76-7+ S '89
Words to the whitetail [cover story] P. Fiduccia. il *Outdoor Life* 184:63+ Ag '89
ANIMAL CAMOUFLAGE See Mimicry (Biology)
ANIMAL COMMUNICATION
See also
Bird communication
Insect communication
Calls in the wild [study by Christopher Boehm of chimpanzees] *Science News* 135:223 Ap 8 '89
Conversations with the dolphins [work of L. M. Herman] S. Chollar. il pors *Psychology Today* 23:52-6 Ap '89
The day of the dolphins. J. Kaplan. il *Omni (New York, N.Y.)* 11:42-4+ Je '89
Elephant talk [cover story] K. Payne. il maps *National Geographic* 176:264-77 Ag '89
The inscrutable cat; The cat's meow. L. Spiotta-DeMare. il *American Health* 8:128 S '89
Interview: Louis Herman [dolphin communication] J. Kaplan. il pors *Omni (New York, N.Y.)* 11:76-8+ Je '89
Reach out and branch someone [branch dragging by pygmy chimps; research by Ellen J. Ingmanson] B. Bower. *Science News* 135:251 Ap 22 '89
ANIMAL DEFENSES See Defense mechanisms (Biology)
ANIMAL DENTISTRY See Veterinary dentistry
ANIMAL DRUGS See Veterinary drugs
ANIMAL ECOLOGY
See also
Animal introduction
Wildlife management
ANIMAL EXPERIMENTATION
See also
Laboratory for Experimental Medicine and Surgery in Primates
Xenografts
Alternatives to animals in toxicity testing. A. M. Goldberg and J. M. Frazier. bibl il *Scientific American* 261:24-30 Ag '89
Animal research is unnecessary and dangerous to human health. S. Siegel. il *Utne Reader* p47-9 S/O '89
Animal research necessary, says report [National Research Council] *FDA Consumer* 23:4 F '89
Animal rights and animal wrongs. D. E. Koshland, Jr. *Science* 243:1253 Mr 10 '89
Can you love animals and kill them? N. C. Comfort. il *Utne Reader* p46+ S/O '89
Necessary evil? K. Barrett and R. Greene. il *Redbook* 173:160-1+ S '89
New test could spare rabbits [use of Tetrahymena] il *USA Today (Periodical)* 117:4-5 Je '89
A preemptive strike for animal research [work of New York University and others] C. Holden. il *Science* 244:415-16 Ap 28 '89
A scientist: 'I am the enemy'. R. Karpati. por *Newsweek* 114:12-13 D 18 '89
An uncaged vision of nonhuman creation [views of A. Linzey] J. M. Wall. *The Christian Century* 106:947-8 O 25 '89
Unkind to animals. P. Singer. bibl f il *The New York Review of Books* 36:36-8 F 2 '89
Laws and regulations
Cambridge to oversee animal research. C. Holden. *Science* 244:1253 Je 16 '89
Compromise in sight on animal regulations. C. Holden. il *Science* 245:124-5 Jl 14 '89
Will relief for lab animals spell pain for consumers? J. Carey. il *Business Week* p43-4 O 30 '89
Protests, demonstrations, etc.
Animal Activism 101 [scientists get advice on how to combat attacks by animal activists] M. Barinaga. il *Science* 246:756-7 N 10 '89
Universities fight animal activists. C. Holden. il *Science* 243:17-19 Ja 6 '89
ANIMAL EXTINCTION See Extinct animals
ANIMAL GENETICS
Biotech on the farm: geneticists in the pasture. G. E. Seidel. *Current (Washington, D.C.)* 316:21-6 O '89
Brave new mouse [first animal patent for cancer-prone mouse] A. Kozlov. il *Discover* 10:78 Ja '89
Europe says no to animal patents. D. Dickson. *Science* 245:25 Jl 7 '89
The farm animals of tomorrow. il *The Futurist* 23:47-8 N/D '89

Genetic engineering of livestock. V. G. Pursel and others. bibl f il *Science* 244:1281-8 Je 16 '89
Geneticists in the pasture. G. E. Seidel. il *Technology Review* 92:42-50+ Ap '89
Get nosy, cattlemen [genetic tracking] V. Ehmke. il *Successful Farming* 87:34 S '89
No patent for Harvard's mouse? [rejection by European Patent Office] D. Dickson. *Science* 243:1003 F 24 '89
Patenting genetic 'inventions'. J. E. Bahls. il *High Technology Business* 9:10 Je '89
Public responses to genetic engineering. B. Hanson and D. Nelkin. *Society* 27:76-80 N/D '89
A tiny mouse came forth [patented oncomouse] E. Corcoran. *Scientific American* 260:73 F '89
ANIMAL HOSPITALS See Veterinary hospitals
ANIMAL INTELLIGENCE
Are cats smart? P. W. Moser. il *Reader's Digest* 135:112-16 O '89
Do bees think? [work of D. R. Griffin] J. Horgan. il por *Scientific American* 260:36-8 My '89
ANIMAL INTRODUCTION
Bill calls for wolf recovery EIS [reintroduction of grey wolves to Yellowstone] il *National Parks* 63:9 S/O '89
The brawl of the wild [controversial plan to reintroduce wolves in Yellowstone] J. Skow. il *Time* 134:13-14+ N 6 '89
The far side of paradise [brown tree snakes on Guam] il *U.S. News & World Report* 106:15 F 13 '89
Praise for a red predator [reintroduction of red wolves into Alligator River National Wildlife Refuge] N. Angier. il maps *American Health* 8:74-6+ S '89
Reintroduction of captive mammals for conservation [cover story] D. G. Kleiman. bibl f il *BioScience* 39:152-61 Mr '89
Return of the mighty muskox. P. C. Lent. il *Natural History* p50-9 N '89
Return of the natives [rare species reintroduction] D. E. Brown. il *Wilderness* 52:40-52 Wint '88
Showdown at mussel beach [zebra mussel invasion of Lake Erie] G. Cowley. il *Newsweek* 114:66 N 20 '89
Starting over [reintroduction of prairie dogs in Utah] J. L. Ferrara. il *National Wildlife* 27:18-21 F/Mr '89
Translocation as a species conservation tool: status and strategy. B. Griffith and others. bibl f il *Science* 245:477-80 Ag 4 '89
ANIMAL LANGUAGE See Animal communication
ANIMAL LEARNING
Boosting memory in the blink of an eye [use of nimodipine with aging rabbits; work of Richard A. Deyo] B. Bower. *Science News* 135:86 F 11 '89
Imaging of memory-specific changes in the distribution of protein kinase C in the hippocampus [associative learning experiment] J. L. Olds and others. bibl f il *Science* 245:866-9 Ag 25 '89
Memory in a neuron [associative learning in Hermissenda; work of Daniel L. Alkon] J. Kinoshita. *Scientific American* 260:28+ Ja '89
Nimodipine facilitates associative learning in aging rabbits [could counteract memory loss in the aged] R. A. Deyo and others. bibl f il *Science* 243:809-11 F 10 '89
Rabbit punch [use of nimodipine to boost memory in aging rabbits] il *Discover* 10:12 Je '89
ANIMAL LOCOMOTION
See also
Fish locomotion
The diving seal [adaptations of harbor seals; research by Ronald W. Millard] S. Kleene. bibl il *Sea Frontiers* 35:370-4 N/D '89
Incredible diving machines [northern elephant seals; cover story] B. J. Le Boeuf. il *Natural History* p34-41 F '89
Is man the fastest animal? N. Myers. il *International Wildlife* 19:33 S/O '89
Pulmonary blood flow regulation in an aquatic snake [diving by Acrochordus granulatus] H. B. Lillywhite and J. A. Donald. bibl f il *Science* 245:293-5 Jl 21 '89
Spatial selectivity of rat hippocampal neurons: dependence on preparedness for movement. T. C. Foster and others. bibl f il *Science* 244:1580-2 Je 30 '89
Standing pterosaurs on two feet [research by Christopher S. Bennett] R. Monastersky. *Science News* 136:318 N 11 '89
Vertebrate locomotion [cover story; special section] bibl f il *BioScience* 39:764-804 D '89
Visuomotor coordination in reaching and locomotion. A. P. Georgopoulos and S. Grillner. bibl f *Science* 245:1209-10 S 15 '89
ANIMAL MODELS OF DRUG ABUSE See Drug abuse—Animal models
ANIMAL MODELS OF HUMAN DISEASES See Diseases—Animal models
ANIMAL NAMES See Zoology—Nomenclature
ANIMAL POPULATIONS
See also
Fish populations
Population genetics—Animals
Control
See also
Animals, Predatory—Control

ANIMAL POPULATIONS—Control—See also—*cont.*
  Wildlife management
ANIMAL PRINT FABRICS *See* Textile fabrics
ANIMAL PRODUCTS
  The great bear aphrodisiac caper [animal parts mixed into
  nostrums] il *U.S. News & World Report* 106:14 F 6 '89
    Export-import trade
  Changing your buying habits. M. Di Landro. il *Travel Holiday*
  171:52-4 Ap '89
  Threatened animals. D. Jenish. il *Maclean's* 102:44-5 Ag
  7 '89
ANIMAL RIGHTS MOVEMENT
    See also
    American Humane Association
    Antifur movement
    People for the Ethical Treatment of Animals
    United Activists for Animal Rights
  Agriculture and animal rights [address, July 27, 1989] R.
  McGuire. *Vital Speeches of the Day* 55:766-8 O 1 '89
  Animal Activism 101 [scientists get advice on how to combat
  attacks by animal activists] M. Barinaga. il *Science* 246:756-7
  N 10 '89
  Animal activists antagonize allies. R. Ryan. il *Utne Reader*
  p50-2 S/O '89
  Animal activists: get green! P. Greanville. il *Utne Reader*
  p52 S/O '89
  Animal rights and animal wrongs. D. E. Koshland, Jr. *Science*
  243:1253 Mr 10 '89
  Cambridge to oversee animal research. C. Holden. *Science*
  244:1253 Je 16 '89
  Ethics and animals. S. Zak. il *The Atlantic* 263:68-74 Mr
  '89
  Fight animal welfare emotion with emotionalism. *Successful
  Farming* 87:41 D '89
  In defense of the animals. M. Greenfield. il *Newsweek* 113:78
  Ap 17 '89
  Necessary evil? K. Barrett and R. Greene. il *Redbook*
  173:160-1+ S '89
  Owl connections. L. Troiano. il *American Health* 8:90+ Mr
  '89
  A preemptive strike for animal research [work of New York
  University and others] C. Holden. il *Science* 244:415-16
  Ap 28 '89
  Pressuring Perdue [H. Spira] B. Feder. il por *The New York
  Times Magazine* p32+ N 26 '89
  Save the chickens. R. E. Tyrrell. il *The American Spectator*
  22:10-11 F '89
  Save the wails. C. W. Colson. il *Christianity Today* 33:72
  Jl 14 '89
  A scientist: 'I am the enemy'. R. Karpati. por *Newsweek*
  114:12-13 D 18 '89
  An uncaged vision of nonhuman creation [views of A. Linzey]
  J. M. Wall. *The Christian Century* 106:947-8 O 25 '89
  Universities fight animal activists. C. Holden. il *Science*
  243:17-19 Ja 6 '89
  Unkind to animals. P. Singer. bibl f il *The New York Review
  of Books* 36:36-8 F 2 '89
  What's wrong with animal rights? B. G. Harrison.
  Mademoiselle 95:76 Jl '89
    International aspects
  Animal rights groups win 1, lose 2 in 1988. B. Eftink.
  Successful Farming 87:15 F '89
  Meet the meatless. R. Behar. il *Forbes* 143:43-4 Mr 20
  '89
ANIMAL SOCIETIES *See* Animals—Habits and behavior
ANIMAL SOUNDS
    See also
    Animal communication
    Birds—Song
    Phonograph records—Animal sounds
  Humpback poets [songs of whales; research by Katharine
  Payne and Linda Guinee] M. Kemp. il *Discover* 10:22
  Jl '89
  Listening in the dark [coon hounds] B. Tarrant. il *Field
  & Stream* 93:94+ Ja '89
  Rap songs from the deep [humpback whales; study by Linda
  Guinee and Katharine Payne] G. Cowley. il *Newsweek*
  113:63 Mr 20 '89
ANIMAL TEMPERATURE *See* Temperature, Animal and
  human
ANIMAL TRACKS AND TRAILS
  Messages in the snow. G. H. Harrison. il *National Wildlife*
  27:50-1 F/Mr '89
  Signs of life: tracking wildlife in the national parks. A.-M.
  Praetzel. il *National Parks* 63:39-42 Ja/F '89
  Tracks [snow] D. Spier. il *The Conservationist* 44:54-5 N/D
  '89
  What game tracks reveal [reprint from October 1958 issue]
  T. Trueblood. il *Field & Stream* 94:30+ N '89
ANIMALS
    See also
    Castration—Animals
    Children and animals
    Eye—Animals
    Frozen embryos—Animals
    Game
    Horns—Animals
    Livestock

  Pets
  Poisonous animals
  Pregnancy in animals
  Rare animals
  Vision—Animals
  Wildlife
  Zoology
    See also names of animals
    Accidents and hazards
    See also
  Automobile driving—Animal hazards
    Breeding
    See Breeding
    Civil rights
    See Animal rights movement
    Collisions with automobiles
    See Automobile driving—Animal hazards
    Coloration
    See Color of animals
    Diseases and pests
    See also
  Cancer in animals
  Diabetes in animals
  Rabies
  Veterinary medicine
    Domestication
    See Domestication
    First aid
    See First aid for animals
    Food and feeding
    See also
  Carnivores
  Grazing
  Herbivores
  Pet food
    Habits and behavior
    See also
  Animal intelligence
  Deception—Animals
  Defense mechanisms (Biology)
  Hibernation
  Mimicry (Biology)
  Parental behavior in animals
  Sexual behavior—Animals
  Territoriality (Zoology)
  Tracking and trailing
  The brotherhood of cheetahs [Serengeti National Park; cover
  story] T. Caro. il *Natural History* p50-9 Je '89
  Bucks where you least expect them [sleep habits] G. Miller.
  il *Outdoor Life* 184:92-3+ N '89
  Is peace as natural as violence? [reconciliation in primates;
  work of Frans de Waal] B. L. Benderly. *Psychology Today*
  23:70 D '89
  The joys of a big brain [social behavior of dolphins] W.
  Booth. il *Psychology Today* 23:57 Ap '89
  Ms. Monkey [female macaque's social climbing; study in
  La Forêt des Singes, France] M. F. Small. il *Natural
  History* p10+ Ja '89
  Secrets of a high society [social behavior of bottlenose
  dolphins; cover story] R. S. Wells. il por *National Wildlife*
  27:38-44 Ag/S '89
  Sleeping giants [excerpt from Polar bears; cover story] I.
  Stirling. il *Natural History* p34-9 Ja '89
  Women on the run [female dispersal in mammalian groups;
  study by Tim Clutton-Brock] il *Discover* 10:20 My '89
    Intelligence
    See Animal intelligence
    Language
    See Animal communication
    Navigation
    See Orientation
    Nomenclature
    See Zoology—Nomenclature
    Photographs and photography
  Assignment: poster [L.A. Zoo fund raising poster] B. Hurter.
  il *Petersen's Photographic Magazine* 17:24-7 Mr '89
  Top bananas. il *People Weekly* 31:162-4+ Mr 6 '89
    Protection
    See Game laws; Wildlife conservation; Wildlife sanc-
  tuaries
    Religious aspects
  An uncaged vision of nonhuman creation [views of A. Linzey]
  J. M. Wall. *The Christian Century* 106:947-8 O 25 '89
    Temperature
    See Temperature, Animal and human
    Tracks
    See Animal tracks and trails
    Training
  World's greatest showman [circus animal trainer G. Gebel-
  Williams] J. Culhane. il pors *Reader's Digest* 135:90-5
  N '89
    Transportation
  The incredible odyssey of the president's beasts [transporting
  live specimens from the Lewis and Clark Expedition to
  T. Jefferson] B. Gilbert. il por *Audubon* 91:100-2+ Ja
  '89

ANIMALS—*cont.*

Treatment

See also
Animal experimentation
Animal rights movement
Calves—Treatment
Dolphins—Treatment
Hunting—Ethical aspects
Monkeys—Treatment
Trapping

Agriculture and animal rights [address, July 27, 1989] R. McGuire. *Vital Speeches of the Day* 55:766-8 O 1 '89

Am I blue? Thoughts on animal feelings, human rights, and justice for all. A. Walker. il *Utne Reader* p98-9+ Ja/F '89

In defense of the animals. M. Greenfield. il *Newsweek* 113:78 Ap 17 '89

Anecdotes, facetiae, satire, etc.

Last word [petting zoo animals take their revenge] B. Mangino. il *Omni (New York, N.Y.)* 11:132 Ap '89

War use

See also
United States. Navy. Marine Mammal Program

ANIMALS, CAROUSEL *See* Carousel art

ANIMALS, EFFECT OF COLD ON *See* Cold—Physiological effects

ANIMALS, EFFECT OF ULTRASONIC WAVES ON

The mysterious binoculars [ultrasonic device alleged to be cause of horse throwing jockey in race at Royal Ascot] il *Sports Illustrated* 71:24 N 20 '89

ANIMALS, EXTINCT *See* Extinct animals

ANIMALS, FOSSIL *See* Paleontology

ANIMALS, GEOGRAPHICAL DISTRIBUTION OF *See* Biogeography

ANIMALS, INFANCY OF

See also
Parental behavior in animals

Defensive behaviors in infant rhesus monkeys: environmental cues and neurochemical regulation. N. H. Kalin and S. E. Shelton. bibl f il *Science* 243:1718-21 Mr 31 '89

Zoo babies [San Diego Zoo] P. Gustke. il *Good Housekeeping* 208:60 F '89

ANIMALS, MINIATURE

Pint-size pets. K. Wells. il *The Saturday Evening Post* 261:16-17+ Jl/Ag '89

ANIMALS, MYTHICAL

Monster mania. il *National Geographic World* 168:22-5 Ag '89

ANIMALS, PREDATORY

See also
Baboons
Carnivores
Coyotes
Foxes
Wolves

Calling

See Animal calling

Control

The balancing game. S. Curtis. il *Field & Stream* 94:72 Jl '89

Taming our fear of predators [cover story] P. Steinhart. il *National Wildlife* 27:4-13 F/Mr '89

ANIMALS, PREHISTORIC *See* Extinct animals

ANIMALS, STUFFED *See* Toys

ANIMALS AND AGED *See* Aged and animals

ANIMALS AND CIVILIZATION

The accidental conqueror [importance of animal and plant domestication in the European colonization of the New World] J. M. Diamond. il *Discover* 10:70-6 D '89

The ancient contract [evidence suggesting domestication of animals was a result of coevolution; cover story] S. Budiansky. il *U.S. News & World Report* 106:74-9 Mr 20 '89

Phenomena, comment and notes. M. Robinson. il *Smithsonian* 19:38+ F '89

Pushy wildlife: animals that thrive on human habitat. J. Lazell. il *National Parks* 63:18-25 S/O '89

ANIMALS AND THE HANDICAPPED *See* Handicapped and animals

ANIMALS AS ACTORS

See also
Animals in motion pictures

Speaking up for 'abused' animals, Bob Barker is hit with a lawsuit [United Activists for Animal Rights charges that American Humane Association is negligent in preventing abuse of animals in show business] L. Smith. il por *People Weekly* 32:75-6 S 18 '89

ANIMALS AS ARTISTS

See also
Chimpanzees as artists
Elephants as artists

ANIMALS AS CARRIERS OF INFECTION

See also
Cats as carriers of infection
Rats as carriers of infection

Lyme disease: not just deer ticks: mosquitoes, pets, even rabbits, can transmit the germ. J. Hamilton. il *American Health* 8:13-14 Je '89

More than you bargained for. T. Thomas. il *Field & Stream* 94:62-3+ N '89

ANIMALS IN ART

See also
Birds in art
Dinosaurs in art
Horses in art

Animals as subjects in contemporary art [wildlife] P. Van Gelder. il *American Artist* 53:44-51+ My '89

Artist in residence: Count and Countess de Claviére d'Hust on Long Island. S. Stephens. il pors *Architectural Digest* 46:156-61+ D '89

The Derby animal band [porcelain] S. Bagdade and A. Bagdade. il *Antiques & Collecting Hobbies* 94:19 My '89

Extracting art from nature [work of A. Dürer] J. Kastner. il *Natural History* p76+ S '89

Feast of beasts [pottery of B. Palissy] M. Guralnick. il *House & Garden* 161:98+ S '89

The first wildlife artists. S. Begley. il *International Wildlife* 19:22-7 Mr/Ap '89

For real haute dogs, these shoes are made for stalking [flats by E. Albanese] il *People Weekly* 32:102-3 Ag 14 '89

Hair, dust and sky [S. Combes' paintings of wildlife in Africa] H. Gibson. il por *International Wildlife* 19:52-9 S/O '89

He upped and quit [sculptor P. Tadlock] W. P. Barrett. il pors *Forbes* 144:282+ O 16 '89

Exhibitions

See also
Wildlife of the American West Art Museum (Jackson, Wyo.)

Claude and François-Xavier Lalanne at Marisa del Re [animal-shaped furniture] L. Campbell. il *Art in America* 77:166-7 F '89

ANIMALS IN CAPTIVITY *See* Zoos

ANIMALS IN LITERATURE

Bibliography

Children's books/animals. A. Cohn. il *The New York Times Book Review* 94:38-9 Ja 29 '89

ANIMALS IN MOTION PICTURES

See also
Bears in motion pictures
Cats in motion pictures
Dogs in motion pictures

Animal stars. E. D'Aulaire. il *Good Housekeeping* 208:60+ My '89

ANIMALS IN POETRY

Time out for nonsense [winners of International wildlife's animal limerick contest] il *International Wildlife* 19:42-4 S/O '89

ANIMALS IN TELEVISION

See also
Dolphins in television
Livestock in television

ANIMAS (N.M.)

Sports

Out of the blue [high school football team on longest winning streak in the country] G. Smith. il *Life* 12:82-4+ N '89

ANIMATED CARTOONS *See* Television advertising—Cartoons; Television broadcasting—Cartoons

ANIMATED FILMS *See* Motion pictures—Animated films; Videotapes—Animated films

ANIRIDIA *See* Eye—Diseases and defects

ANJARD, RONALD P.

Collecting date nails. il *Antiques & Collecting Hobbies* 94:38 Jl '89

A new collectible art form: the pau dau. il *Antiques & Collecting Hobbies* 94:69 Jl '89

Our heritage of Indian names. *Antiques & Collecting Hobbies* 94:22 Jl '89

ANKENY, DEWALT H., JR.

about

Pete's problem. J. Zweig. il por *Forbes* 143:134-5 F 20 '89

ANKER, ROY M.

Yikes! Nightmares from Hollywood [cover story] il *Christianity Today* 33:18-23 Je 16 '89

ANKLE

Wounds and injuries

A classy joint. R. McGuire. il *Women's Sports & Fitness* 11:52-5 O '89

Feet first [dancers] M. Horosko. il *Dance Magazine* 63:56-7 N '89

RICE as a side dish [rest, ice, compression, elevation] *Women's Sports & Fitness* 11:54 O '89

ANKLE EXERCISES

Saving your ankles [injury prevention] M. Ratner. il *Women's Sports & Fitness* 11:15 My '89

ANKYLOSING SPONDYLITIS

The case of the harrowing back pain [case of J. Bruckel] A. Roblin. il *Prevention (Emmaus, Pa.)* 41:102+ Je '89

ANN ARBOR (MICH.)

Education

Youth Opportunity: a private sector investment in prevention [summer work at Domino's Pizza Inc.'s Whatley Farm] C. H. Tice. il *Children Today* 18:20-3 Mr/Ap '89

ANN ARBOR (MICH.)—*cont.*

Social life and customs

Domino's [after-school job at Domino's Pizza] *The New Yorker* 65:37 Mr 27 '89

ANN ARBOR ANTIQUES MARKET *See* Antiques—Exhibitions

ANN-MARGRET, 1941-

'My love is not a burden'; ed. by Patricia Nolan. por *New Choices for the Best Years* 29:14+ Ja '89

ANN NORTON SCULPTURE GARDEN

Landscaping with sculpture. S. Guy. il *Horizon (Tuscaloosa, Ala.)* 32:29-30 Ja/F '89

ANNAN, GABRIELE

On the high wire. il *The New York Review of Books* 36:3-4 D 7 '89

ANNAN, NOEL GILROY ANNAN, BARON, 1916-

Oh what a lovely war! il *The New York Review of Books* 36:3-4+ S 28 '89

The upper class and the underworld. il *The New York Review of Books* 36:24-9 Ap 13 '89

ANNAPOLIS (MD.)

Architecture

A waterfront retreat [house on a creek] il *Southern Living* 24:128-9 My '89

ANNAPURNA CONSERVATION AREA PROJECT (NEPAL)

Annapurna: sanctuary for the Himalaya. G. A. Rowell. il map *National Geographic* 176:390-405 S '89

ANNAUD, JEAN-JACQUES

about

The bear [film] Reviews

Commonweal 116:706-7 D 15 '89. T. O'Brien

Gentlemen's Quarterly il 59:129-30+ N '89. K. Turan

Life il 12:89-91 Spr '89. T. Skari

Maclean's il por 102:94+ O 30 '89. B. D. Johnson

New York il 22:70 O 30 '89. D. Denby

The New Yorker 65:121-3 N 13 '89. P. Kael

Newsweek il 114:92 N 13 '89. D. Ansen

People Weekly il 32:87-8 N 6 '89. I. Lacher

Time il 134:97 O 30 '89. R. Schickel

Quest for fur. A. Thompson. il por *Film Comment* 25:2+ S/O '89

ANNE, PRINCESS, DAUGHTER OF ELIZABETH II, QUEEN OF GREAT BRITAIN, 1950-

about

A crisis rocks a royal marriage [cover story] J. Kaufman. il pors *People Weekly* 31:66-8+ Ap 24 '89

No fairy-tale ending. A. Phillips. il pors *Maclean's* 102:61 S 11 '89

Princess Anne. por *People Weekly* 32:57 D 25 '89-Ja 1 '90

With no hope for a happy ending, Princess Anne brings her storybook marriage to a close. M. H. J. Farrell. il pors *People Weekly* 32:114-17 S 18 '89

ANNE OF GREEN GABLES (FICTIONAL CHARACTER)

Collectibles

Anger on the Island. R. Corelli. il *Maclean's* 102:40 Jl 10 '89

ANNELIDS

See also

Nervous system—Annelids

ANNENBERG, WALTER H., 1908-

about

Strength of vision. H. Drohojowska. il *Harper's Bazaar* 122:204-7+ Ap '89

ANNENBERG SCHOOL OF COMMUNICATIONS

The Annenberg School's problem: how to spend a billion dollars. A. Snyder. il *Channels (New York, N.Y.: 1986)* 9:10 F '89

ANNIE 2: MISS HANNIGAN'S REVENGE [musical] *See* Musicals, revues, etc.—Reviews—Single works

ANNIE'S ALL-NATURAL POPCORN (FIRM)

A feud that's really popping [Smartfoods vs. Annie's All-Natural Popcorn] A. Miller. il por *Newsweek* 114:52 Jl 24 '89

ANNIVERSARIES

See also

Wedding anniversaries

10s, 20s, 50s, 100s [guide to the 1990s] J. Adler. il *Newsweek* 114:78-80 D 18 '89

ANNUAL MEETINGS, STOCKHOLDERS' *See* Stockholders' meetings

ANNUAL REPORTS, CORPORATE *See* Corporation reports

ANNUALS, COLLEGE *See* College yearbooks

ANNUALS (PLANTS)

Annuals survive winter, bloom in spring. L. A. Weathers. il *Southern Living* 24:58 N '89

Flowers through thick and thin. S. Bender. il *Southern Living* 24:106-8 My '89

Roses and annuals together. il *Sunset (Central West edition)* 182:156 F '89

ANNUITIES

See also

Certificates of annuity

Charitable gift annuities

The cold call cowboy says: "annuities beat mutual funds". P. Wang. il *Money* 18:100-2+ N '89

How these annuities can save your lifestyle. D. H. Dunn. il *Business Week* p139 D 25 '89-Ja 1 '90

How to tell if an immediate annuity makes sense for you. D. M. Topolnicki. il *Money* 18:183-4 My '89

The ins and outs of annuities. il *Money* 18 Money Guide:64 Fall '89

Membership has its follies [American Express Privileged Assets annuity] A. P. Tobias. il *Time* 133:45 Je 19 '89

Taxation

Annuities reconsidered. J. B. Quinn. il *Newsweek* 114:42 Jl 17 '89

Insurance shelters: are they worth the price? T. Segal. il *Business Week* p152-3 Ap 24 '89

The tax shelter that's still left. E. Giltenan. il *Forbes* 143:132-3 F 6 '89

ANNUNCIATION OF THE VIRGIN MARY *See* Mary, Blessed Virgin, Saint—Annunciation

ANNUNZIATA, PATRICK

about

Fashion statement. S. Stephens. il *Architectural Digest* 46:92-7 Jl '89

ANOREXIA NERVOSA

The big fat lie: when thin does you in. E. Karlsberg. il *'Teen* 33:28-9+ Jl '89

Bigger plates, smaller portions [linked to distorted perceptions of food; research by Kay Walker] P. McCarthy. il *American Health* 8:50 My '89

Eating disorders and pregnancy. P. A. Hillard. il *Parents* 64:202+ N '89

A tragic obsession. D. Jenish. il *Maclean's* 102:52+ O 9 '89

ANOS, JOANNA

We have no need [poem] *The American Scholar* 58:563 Aut '89

ANOTHER WOMAN [film] *See* Motion picture reviews—Single works

ANOXEMIA

See also

Mountain sickness

ANSEL ADAMS AWARDS

Ansel Adams Awards [winners A. Cranston and W. V. Roth] il pors *Wilderness* 52:9 Summ '89

ANSELMO, GIOVANNI

about

Giovanni Anselmo at Marian Goodman. H. Cotter. il *Art in America* 77:201 S '89

ANSETT NEW ZEALAND (FIRM)

Ansett New Zealand 146QC transport begins daily passenger, cargo flights. il *Aviation Week & Space Technology* 131:62 D 4 '89

ANSKY, S., 1863-1920

about

The dybbuk [drama] Reviews

The Nation 249:255-6 S 4-11 '89. T. M. Disch

ANSON, ELVA

Get your kids to help at home [condensed from How to get kids to help at home] il *Reader's Digest* 135:27-8+ Ag '89

ANSON, MIKE

Starting grid. See issues of Motor Trend beginning October 1986 through July 1989

ANSON, ROBERT SAM, 1945-

Apocalypse then [excerpt from War news] *The Washington Monthly* 21:14+ O '89

ANSWER CORPORATION

Computers, customers and hand-holding. E. Dyson. il *Forbes* 144:128 Ag 7 '89

ANSWERS TO QUESTIONS *See* Questions and answers

ANT FARMS

Unusual pets. S. L. Gerstenfeld. il *Parents* 64:257 O '89

ANTARCTIC EXPLORATION

See also

Byrd Antarctic Expedition

The 4,000-mile marathon [W. Steger and sled dogs prepare for expedition] L. Troiano. il por *American Health* 8:95-7 Jl/Ag '89

At last, the South Pole [W. Steger's dogsled expedition] R. Sullivan. il *Sports Illustrated* 71:14 D 18 '89

The iceman cometh [W. Steger plans to cross Antarctica by dogsled and on foot] R. Sullivan. il pors map *Sports Illustrated* 71:40-5+ Jl 31 '89

The last treasure [W. Steger and J.-L. Etienne plan to cross Antarctica by dogsled and on foot] *The New Yorker* 65:27-8 Jl 17 '89

Odyssey over ice [ski trek] A. Steacy. il *Maclean's* 102:55 F 6 '89

The price of human folly [comparison of R. F. Scott's Antarctic expedition to author's experiences in New Guinea] J. M. Diamond. il *Discover* 10:72-7 Ap '89

South Pole or bust [S. Metz's skiing expedition] B. Sims. il por *Skiing* 42:18 O '89

To the South Pole by sled [Trans-Antarctica Expedition] A. Toufexis. il map *Time* 134:73 D 25 '89

ANTARCTIC REGIONS

See also

Antarctic exploration

Astronomical observatories—Antarctic regions

Cruising—Antarctic regions

Fish—Antarctic regions

Ice—Polar regions

ANTARCTIC REGIONS—See also—*cont.*
> Mines and mineral resources—Antarctic regions
> Oil pollution—Antarctic regions
> Pollution—Antarctic regions
> Skiing—Antarctic regions
> Squid fisheries—Antarctic regions

Climate

Antarctic ozone hole unexpectedly severe. R. Monastersky. il *Science News* 136:246 O 14 '89

Depleted ring around ozone hole [research by Michael H. Proffitt] R. Monastersky. *Science News* 136:324 N 18 '89

Does the ozone hole threaten Antarctic life? [effect of ultraviolet radiation on phytoplankton] L. Roberts. il map *Science* 244:288-9 Ap 21 '89

Low-zone [influence of ozone hole] T. Beardsley. *Scientific American* 261:26+ O '89

Ozone hits bottom again. R. A. Kerr. *Science* 246:324 O 20 '89

Ozone hole hikes Antarctic ultraviolet [has not caused significant harm to phytoplankton] R. Monastersky. *Science News* 135:228 Ap 15 '89

Ozone hole peril to Antarctic life [research by John Frederick] il *USA Today (Periodical)* 117:6 Je '89

The ozone hole that didn't eat the world. R. Bailey. il *Forbes* 144:224-5 O 30 '89

Ozone hole threatens polar plankton [research by Sayed El-Sayed] *Science News* 136:284 O 28 '89

Ozone hole's reappearance linked to chlorofluorocarbons [data of Total Ozone Mapping Spectrometer on Nimbus 7 satellite] il *Aviation Week & Space Technology* 131:28 O 30 '89

Rate of formation of the ClO dimer in the polar stratosphere: implications for ozone loss. S. P. Sander and others. bibl f il *Science* 245:1095-8 S 8 '89

Ultraviolet levels under sea ice during the Antarctic spring [discussion of July 22, 1988 article, Ultraviolet radiation levels during the Antarctic spring] J. E. Frederick and H. E. Snell. *Science* 245:194-5 Jl 14 '89

Industries
> *See also*
> Tourist trade—Antarctic regions

ANTARCTIC RESEARCH

Antarctic meltdown [work of researchers tracking movement of West Antarctica Ice Sheet] M. Parfit. il *Discover* 10:38-40+ S '89

Life at the bottom of the world [Amundsen-Scott South Pole Station] il *Sky and Telescope* 77:602 Je '89

Our frail planet in cold, clear view [cover story] B. H. Lopez. il *Harper's* 278:43-9 My '89

Environmental aspects

Antarctic pollution. il *Sea Frontiers* 35:133 My/Je '89

Antarctic tourism '89 [cover story] Y. Cardozo and B. Hirsch. bibl il map *Sea Frontiers* 35:282-91 S/O '89

ANTARCTIC TREATY (1959)

'Why tempt the devil?'. C. Dickey and F. Gleizes. il *Newsweek* 114:39 O 23 '89

ANTELOPE HUNTING
> *See also*
> Pronghorn hunting

ANTELOPES
> *See also*
> Impalas

ANTENNAS (ELECTRONICS)
> *See also*
> Radio antennas
> Television antennas

ANTHOLOGIES
> *See also*
> Short story—Anthologies

ANTHONY, JOSEPH

Sweet charity. il *Mother Jones* 14:51-2+ D '89

ANTHONY, PIERS

Think of the reader. *The Writer* 102:11-13+ Ag '89

ANTHONY, SUSAN

Lust at sea. il *Ms.* 17:128-9 Ja/F '89

ANTHONY ROSE [drama] See Feiffer, Jules

ANTHRACNOSE

Dogwood's day. B. Pleasant. il *Organic Gardening* 36:34-8 Jl/Ag '89

Dogwoods fight fungus; fungus wins [research by Frank S. Santamour] *Science News* 135:110 F 18 '89

ANTHROPOLOGICAL LITERATURE

Authorship

Ethnography as art [views of C. Geertz] J. Horgan. *Scientific American* 261:28+ Jl '89

ANTHROPOLOGISTS
> *See also*
> Geertz, Clifford
> Leakey, Richard E., 1944-

ANTHROPOLOGY
> *See also*
> Acculturation
> Archeology
> Ethnobiology
> Evolution
> Forensic anthropology
> Intercultural research
> Man

Man, Prehistoric

Ethical aspects

'Dead Indians out, live Indians in' [museums return artifacts to Indian tribes] B. E. Johansen. il *The Progressive* 53:15-16 D '89

Museums [native peoples exhibits] E. Chappell. *The Nation* 249:655-60 N 27 '89

Returning bones of contention [Smithsonian agrees to return Indian remains and burial artifacts] J. Elson. il *Time* 134:61 S 25 '89

Skeletons in our museums' closets: Native Americans want their ancestors' bones back. D. J. Preston. il *Harper's* 278:66-70+ F '89

Skeletons in the attic [Indian remains in museums] C. Spotted Elk. il *Scholastic Update (Teachers' edition)* 121:25 My 26 '89

Smithsonian, Indian leaders call a truce. E. Marshall. il *Science* 245:1184-6 S 15 '89

Walter Echo-Hawk fights for his people's right to rest in peace—not in museums. M. Brower. il pors *People Weekly* 32:42-4 S 4 '89

ANTHROPOLOGY MUSEUM OF JALAPA (MEXICO)

Jalapa moves ahead. L. Cahill. il *Américas* 41 no1:7 '89

ANTI-AGING SKIN CARE COSMETICS See Cosmetics

ANTI-AGING SKIN CARE DRUGS See Skin—Care and hygiene

ANTI-AIRCRAFT GUNS See Guns, Anti-aircraft

ANTI-BALLISTIC MISSILE TREATY See Disarmament

ANTI-CATHOLICISM

Those turbulent bishops [New York times' criticism of positions taken by Catholic bishops] R. J. Neuhaus. il *National Review* 41:32-3 D 31 '89

History

The American Revolution: a war of religion? J. C. D. Clark. bibl il *History Today* 39:10-16 D '89

ANTI-COMMUNIST MOVEMENTS
> *See also*
> CAUSA (Organization)
> United States—Foreign relations—Anti-Communist measures

Anticommunism redefined. M. Greenfield. il *Newsweek* 113:72 Je 12 '89

Anecdotes, facetiae, satire, etc.

A call for a new McCarthyism. P. J. O'Rourke. il *The American Spectator* 22:14-15 Jl '89

Let's bring back McCarthyism. P. J. O'Rourke. *Utne Reader* p118-19 N/D '89

The new enemies list: no end in sight. P. J. O'Rourke. il *The American Spectator* 22:17-21 N '89

A new McCarthyism: the list continues. P. J. O'Rourke. il *The American Spectator* 22:14-16 O '89

History
> *See also*
> Blacklisting
> Congress for Cultural Freedom

Battle hymns, ancient and modern [former Nation editor F. Kirchwey] A. Cockburn. *The Nation* 249:266-7 S 18 '89

The brief life of liberal anti-communism. P. Coleman. il *National Review* 41:34-6 S 15 '89

The intellectuals & the cold war. G. Szamuely. *Commentary* 88:54-6 D '89

Owen Lattimore and the 'cold war'; Lattimore & Wicker. W. F. Buckley. *National Review* 41:54-5 Ag 18 '89

Owen Lattimore, RIP [effects on China policy brought about by McCarthyism; excerpt from column, September 1979] W. F. Buckley. *National Review* 41:18-20 Je 30 '89

Pride and perjury [firing of teacher and scientist A. Novikoff for Communist activities by the University of Vermont during McCarthy era] D. M. Oshinsky. por *The New Leader* 72:14-17 S 4 '89

Why are the liberals whitewashing? [case of O. Lattimore] W. F. Buckley. *National Review* 41:60 Jl 14 '89

Conferences

Anticommunism and mental health [Anti-communism and the U.S.: history and consequences] D. Evanier and H. Klehr. il *The American Spectator* 22:28-30 F '89

Fellow-traveling lives [Anti-communism and the U.S.: history and consequences] W. F. Buckley. *National Review* 41:70-1 Ja 27 '89

Letters [discussion of December 12, 1988 article, Campus voices right and left] J. Wiener. *The Nation* 248:146 F 6 '89

A murderous word [adaptation of address, November 1988] H. Zinn. il *The Progressive* 53:16-17 F '89

Philippines

Vigilante justice. J. Ross. *The New Republic* 201:9-21 N 27 '89

United States
> See Anti-Communist movements

ANTI-FREEZE PROTEINS

Antifreezes in fish work quite similarly [research by Arthur L. DeVries] F. Flam. *Science News* 135:102 F 18 '89

Fish on ice [research by Arthur DeVries] *Discover* 10:19 Jl '89

Insect cold-hardiness: to freeze or not to freeze. R. E. Lee, Jr. bibl f il *BioScience* 39:308-13 My '89

ANTI-FREEZE PROTEINS—*cont.*

Melting inhibition and superheating of ice by an antifreeze glycopeptide. C. A. Knight and A. L. DeVries. bibl f il *Science* 245:505-7 Ag 4 '89

ANTI-HELICOPTER WEAPONS

Non-line-of-sight missile will use platinum silicide infrared detectors. il *Aviation Week & Space Technology* 130:67+ Mr 27 '89

ANTI-INFLAMMATORY AGENTS

See also

Ibuprofen

Increasing evidence links ulcers and NSAIDs. il *Prevention (Emmaus, Pa.)* 41:16+ Je '89

ANTI-NAZI MOVEMENT

Germany
Bibliography

Facing up to the Nazis. G. A. Craig. il *The New York Review of Books* 36:10-15 F 2 '89

ANTI-NUCLEAR MOVEMENT

See also

Citizens' Association for Sound Energy
Grandmothers for Peace (Organization)
MEND (Organization)

Arms race as sitcom plot [decline of nuclear awareness among college students] P. S. Boyer. il *The Bulletin of the Atomic Scientists* 45:6-8 Je '89

Court rejects activists' bid to halt Galileo/shuttle launch [nuclear powered spacecraft] *Aviation Week & Space Technology* 131:21 O 16 '89

Daniel Ellsberg [interview; cover story] B. Blanchard and S. Watrous. il por *The Progressive* 53:17-21 S '89

. . . detention [conviction of anti-nuclear activists for trespassing at Whiteman Air Force Base] J. Munves. *The Nation* 248:509 Ap 17 '89

Grandmother as lawbreaker [peace activist D. Eber] M. Ervin. il por *The Progressive* 53:11 Ja '89

Greenpeace gets boost from R.E.M. K. Terry. *Rolling Stone* p67 Jl 13-27 '89

NASA prepares for protests over nuclear system launch on shuttle in October [Galileo mission to Jupiter] T. M. Foley. *Aviation Week & Space Technology* 130:83+ Je 26 '89

Necessary defense or technological toy? [protest against proposed Special Isotope Separation project at Idaho National Engineering Laboratory] S. Cline. *Sierra* 74:95-6 Mr/Ap '89

Prisoner of conscience [experiences while jailed for antinuclear activities; cover story] B. Urfer. il *The Progressive* 53:18-21 My '89

Public always the last to know [Energy Dept. fighting to avoid giving data on underground nuclear tests to arms control groups] W. J. Lanouette. il *The Bulletin of the Atomic Scientists* 45:11-12 O '89

Rifkin tries to stop Galileo launch [nuclear fears] M. M. Waldrop. il *Science* 246:30 O 6 '89

Rise and fall of the Washington peace industry. M. Szegedy-Maszak. il *The Bulletin of the Atomic Scientists* 45:18-23 Ja/F '89

Sam Day's example [jailed for trespassing on missile silo site during protest] E. Knoll. *The Progressive* 53:4 Je '89

Sentence for trespassing [religious pacifist J. Haines given nine months for trespassing at Rocky Flats Plant] *The Christian Century* 106:256 Mr 8 '89

"Serving justice" [activist P. Berrigan] C. Moekle. il por *American Health* 8:67 Ap '89

Showdown at Pad 39-B [nuclear powered space vehicles] R. G. Nichols. il *Ad Astra* 1:8-12+ N '89

"Stop the plutonium shuttle!" [Galileo mission to Jupiter] M. M. Waldrop. *Science* 245:1328 S 22 '89

What next for the peace movement? [cover story; special section] il *The Progressive* 53:14-22 Ja '89

Who will yell fire when the house is ablaze? [conviction of anti-nuclear activist S. Komisaruk for damaging computer at Vandenburg Air Force Base] R. E. Burns. *U.S. Catholic* 54:2 F '89

Alaska

Project Chariot: how Alaska escaped nuclear excavation [1958 plan to create a harbor by detonating thermonuclear bombs; cover story] D. O'Neill. bibl f il maps *The Bulletin of the Atomic Scientists* 45:28-37 D '89

Brazil

FAS and Brazilian physicists discuss improved nuclear safeguards. W. Sweet. *Physics Today* 42:57-8 Ap '89

Germany (West)

Can NATO survive détente? R. Mauthner. *World Press Review* 36:22-3 F '89

Japan

Classified top secret: H-bomb overboard [rolls off U.S. carrier Ticonderoga headed toward Japanese port] *Newsweek* 113:45 My 15 '89

Netherlands

Where the peace movement goes when it disappears. P. P. Everts. bibl f il *The Bulletin of the Atomic Scientists* 45:26-30 N '89

New Zealand

Black Birch observatory under fire in New Zealand. il *Sky and Telescope* 78:9-10 Jl '89

United States

See Anti-nuclear movement

Western Europe

Where the peace movement goes when it disappears. P. P. Everts. bibl f il *The Bulletin of the Atomic Scientists* 45:26-30 N '89

ANTI-SATELLITE WEAPONS

See also

Railguns

Army presses case for ground-based ASAT system over competing sea- and mixed-based alternatives. P. A. Gilmartin. *Aviation Week & Space Technology* 131:47 D 4 '89

ASATs: Star Wars on the cheap. C. A. Monfort. bibl f il *The Bulletin of the Atomic Scientists* 45:10-13 Ap '89

Defense Dept. to launch design competition for new antisatellite weapon for the 1990s. P. A. Gilmartin. *Aviation Week & Space Technology* 131:30 Jl 24 '89

Ivan's eyes. J. Horgan. il *Scientific American* 260:19+ Je '89

Navy and Army initiate ASAT programs, with test ban lifted. W. Sweet. *Physics Today* 42:59 Ap '89

Pentagon board names Army to lead revamped ASAT program. *Aviation Week & Space Technology* 130:31 Ja 16 '89

Pentagon officials expect to field ASAT system by mid or late 1990s. P. A. Gilmartin. il *Aviation Week & Space Technology* 130:266 Mr 20 '89

You can't keep a bad weapon down. J. D. Isaacs. il *The Bulletin of the Atomic Scientists* 45:3 Ap '89

Testing

U.S., Soviet scientists propose system to monitor laser ASATs. T. M. Foley. *Aviation Week & Space Technology* 130:31 My 15 '89

ANTI-SEMITISM

See also

Neo-Nazis

Anti-Semitism in Atlanta [construction of synagogue in Snellville] *The Christian Century* 106:808 S 13-20 '89

Are "JAP" jokes anti-Semitic? [views of Mimi Alperin] *USA Today (Periodical)* 117:5 Ap '89

Blacks and Jews: the uncivil war [Chicago; with editorial comment by Lee Eisenberg] T. Branch. il *Esquire* 111:25, 89-90+ My '89

JAP jokes are nothing to laugh at [Jewish American Princess jokes] L. Lamb. il *Utne Reader* p30+ My/Je '89

Lausanne group addresses anti-Semitism. il *Christianity Today* 33:56 Je 16 '89

Public Enemy number one [S. Lee's reaction to anti-Semitic remarks made by Professor Griff] M. Horowitz. il por *American Film* 14:15 S '89

History

See also

Holocaust, Jewish (1939-1945)
National socialism

Anti-Semitism and Jewish identity. M. A. Meyer. *Commentary* 88:35-40 N '89

Father Coughlin and the Jews: a broadcast remembered [justifying Kristallnacht] R. Modras. *America* 160:219-22 Mr 11 '89

Jews and geniuses [recent essays on the politics of I. Stravinsky, A. Einstein, and A. Schoenberg] R. Craft. il pors *The New York Review of Books* 36:35-7 F 16 '89

'Jews and geniuses': an exchange [discussion of February 16, 1989 article] R. Craft. il *The New York Review of Books* 36:57-8 Je 15 '89

Belgium
History

The strange case of Paul de Man. D. Donoghue. il *The New York Review of Books* 36:32-7 Je 29 '89

Eastern Europe

Freedom's ugly underside. S. Talbott. il *Time* 134:53 N 27 '89

Europe
History

Anti-Semitism [discussion of August 1988 article, Communism, anti-Semitism & the Jews] J. Z. Muller. *Commentary* 87:11-12+ Ja '89

France
History

A shifty-eyed spy who was likely the nastiest man ever [C. F. W. Esterhazy responsible for the Dreyfus Affair] R. Wernick. il pors *Smithsonian* 20:114-16+ Ag '89

Germany (West)

Courage to face the truth of the Holocaust [special section] *Society* 26:4-9 Mr/Ap '89

Jewish victims and German sensitivity [discussion of December 14, 1988 article, Jewish victims and German indifference] J. B. Miller. *The Christian Century* 106:287-8 Mr 15 '89

Italy

A disturbing echo. A. Stille. il *The Atlantic* 263:20-1+ F '89

Japan

David and Godzilla. W. M. Stern. *The New Republic* 200:17-18 F 27 '89

ANTI-SEMITISM—*cont.*
United States
See Anti-Semitism
ANTI-SEMITISM IN POETRY
Two cheers for heterogeneity [Christopher Ricks' T. S. Eliot and prejudice] M. E. Marty. *The Christian Century* 106:837 S 27 '89
ANTI-SMOKING CAMPAIGNS *See* Smoking
ANTI-SMOKING LAWS AND REGULATIONS *See* Smoking—Laws and regulations
ANTI-SUBMARINE HELICOPTERS *See* Helicopters—Military use
ANTI-SUBMARINE WARFARE
DARPA studies optical, radar techniques for spotting submarines from air, space. P. J. Klass. *Aviation Week & Space Technology* 129:27+ Mr 6 '89
Expert system puts clamp on enemy subs. *High Technology Business* 9:34 S/O '89
Quiet Soviet subs prompt concern. C. Norman. il *Science* 243:1653-4 Mr 31 '89
TRW seeks to parlay experience from space into broader ASW role. B. D. Nordwall. *Aviation Week & Space Technology* 131:65+ Ag 7 '89
U.S. Navy debates how to meet ASW needs with tighter budgets. B. D. Nordwall. il *Aviation Week & Space Technology* 130:50-1+ F 27 '89
U.S., West Germany may delay P-7 agreement until September [Lockheed antisubmarine warfare aircraft] J. D. Morrocco. il *Aviation Week & Space Technology* 130:62 Je 19 '89
ANTI-TANK WEAPONS
Costs
Anecdotes, facetiae, satire, etc.
The $5,347 rock. J. Richard. *The Washington Monthly* 21:26-7 Je '89
ANTIBACTERIAL AGENTS *See* Antibiotics
ANTIBIOTIC FEED SUPPLEMENTS
Ignoring animal rights doesn't solve problem [views of John Walton] *Successful Farming* 87:40 Ag '89
ANTIBIOTICS
See also
Amoxicillin
Bacteria—Resistance and sensitivity
Brefeldin
Cephalosporin
Chloramphenicol
Doxycycline
Gentamicin
Gramicidins
Magainins
Sulfonamides
Calicheamicin γ_1^I and DNA: molecular recognition process responsible for site-specificity. N. Zein and others. bibl f il *Science* 244:697-9 My 12 '89
The heart part [failure of dentists to treat heart patients to prevent endocarditis] C. Sears. il *American Health* 8:44 Je '89
Winter vacation alert! [heightened sensitivity to sunlight] L. Schroepfer. *American Health* 8:31 Mr '89
ANTIBODIES *See* Antigens and antibodies
ANTICHRIST
Gorby the Antichrist [excerpt from Gorbachev! Has the real Antichrist come?] R. W. Faid. *Harper's* 278:24+ Ja '89
ANTICOAGULANTS
See also
Aspirin
Eminase (Drug)
Heparin
Ticlopidine
TPA (Drug)
Clot-buster's cost-effectiveness questioned [TPA vs. streptokinase] R. Weiss. *Science News* 135:214 Ap 8 '89
When less may be more [drugs as effective as invasive methods] J. Langone. il *Time* 133:61 Mr 20 '89
ANTIDEPRESSANTS
See also
Clomipramine
Fluoxetine
Wellbutrin
ANTIEMETICS
See also
Ondansetron
ANTIETAM, BATTLE OF, 1862
The Civil War's greatest scoop [account of Battle of Antietam by New York tribune correspondent G. W. Smalley] J. Weeks. il por *American Heritage* 40:100+ Jl/Ag '89
ANTIETAM NATIONAL BATTLEFIELD (MD.)
County vote helps shield Antietam. *National Parks* 63:13 N/D '89
The terrible price of freedom. S. W. Sears. il maps *American Heritage* 40:92-9+ Ap '89
ANTIFOULING PAINT *See* Paint, Protective
ANTIFUNGAL AGENTS
See also
Ketoconazole
A chitin-binding lectin from stinging nettle rhizomes with antifungal properties. W. F. Broekaert and others. bibl f il *Science* 245:1100-2 S 8 '89

ANTIFUR MOVEMENT
Champions of synthetic fiber, angry human stars make the fur fly at a benefit for animal rights. il *People Weekly* 31:266-7 Mr 6 '89
The furor over wearing furs. J. D. Reed. il *Time* 134:72 D 18 '89
The furriers fight back. il *Newsweek* 114:82 D 18 '89
Grand illusions [fake furs] C. Bushnell. il *Health (New York, N.Y.)* 21:72-7+ S '89
Trappers and rattlers. G. Reiger. il *Field & Stream* 94:15-16 Jl '89
ANTIGENS AND ANTIBODIES
See also
Allergens
Catalytic antibodies
CD4 proteins
Complements (Immunity)
H-Y antigen
Immunoassay
Immunogenetics
Immunoglobulins
Immunologic diseases
Immunological tolerance
Major histocompatibility complex
Monoclonal antibodies
Antigen-specific helper function of cell-free T cell products bearing TCR $V_\beta 8$ determinants. R. Guy and others. bibl f il *Science* 244:1477-80 Je 23 '89
Contingent generative regulatory events in T lymphocyte activation. G. R. Crabtree. bibl f il *Science* 243:355-61 Ja 20 '89
How T cells see antigen. H. M. Grey and others. bibl il *Scientific American* 261:56-64 N '89
In vivo modulation of cytolytic activity and thy-1 expression in TCR-$\gamma\delta^+$ intraepithelial lymphocytes. L. Lefrancois and T. Goodman. bibl f il *Science* 243:1716-18 Mr 31 '89
Isolation of a cDNA clone derived from a blood-borne non-A, non-B viral hepatitis genome. Q.-L. Choo and others. bibl f il *Science* 244:359-62 Ap 21 '89
Lyme on the lam [antibodies unable to recognize Borrelia bacteria; research by Tom Schwan] il *Discover* 10:10 S '89
Metastatic hibernomas in transgenic mice expressing an α-amylase-SV40 T antigen hybrid gene. N. Fox and others. bibl f il *Science* 244:460-3 Ap 28 '89
New frontiers [cancer research in Canada] A. Steacy. il *Maclean's* 102:45-6 Jl 24 '89
The role of somatic hypermutation in the generation of antibody diversity. D. L. French and others. bibl f il *Science* 244:1152-7 Je 9 '89
ANTIGUA AND BARBUDA
Politics and government
Ancient rights [controversy over land rights and development on Barbuda] R. Coram. *The New Yorker* 64:76-86+ F 6 '89
ANTIHISTAMINES
See also
Cromolyn
ANTIHYPERTENSIVE AGENTS
See also
Propranolol
Hypertension drugs: how much is hype? N. J. Freundlich. il *Business Week* p98+ N 20 '89
Outsmarting the 'silent killer' [excerpt from Lower your blood pressure and live longer] M. Moser. *Prevention (Emmaus, Pa.)* 41:53-9 O '89
ANTIMALARIALS
See also
Artemisinin
Quinine
Blood, genes, and malaria. J. M. Diamond. il maps *Natural History* p8+ F '89
ANTIMATTER
Antimatter matters. *The Futurist* 23:56-7 My/Je '89
Penned-in positrons [first antimatter plasma] F. Flam. *Science News* 135:154 Mr 11 '89
ANTIMISSILE DEFENSE SYSTEM *See* Guided missiles—Defenses
ANTIMYCOTICS *See* Antifungal agents
ANTINUTRIENTS
Full of beans . . . and better for it [beneficial properties; research by Lilian U. Thompson] R. Green. il *Health (New York, N.Y.)* 21:58-61 D '89
ANTIOXIDANTS
See also
Vitamin E
Crab-shell derivative retards rancidity [chitosan compound, NCMC, developed by John R. Vercellotti and Allen J. St. Angelo] J. Raloff. *Science News* 136:189 S 16 '89
ANTIPAS *See* Herod Antipas, ca. 21 B.C.-39
ANTIPERSPIRANTS *See* Deodorants
ANTIPROTONS
Antiproton trapping [work of Gerald Gabrielse] T. Waters. il *Discover* 10:32-3 Jl '89
ANTIQUE AIRPLANES *See* Airplanes, Antique
ANTIQUE AUTOMOBILES *See* Automobiles, Antique
ANTIQUE CHRISTMAS DECORATIONS *See* Christmas decorations

ANTITRUST LAW—See also—*cont.*
United States. Dept. of Justice. Antitrust Division
Video games—Antitrust cases
Antitrust policy and competitiveness. T. J. DiLorenzo. bibl *Society* 27:67-71 N/D '89
Rivets and revelation [Textron's acquisition of Avdel prompts FTC antitrust case concerning blind rivets] H. Banks. *Forbes* 143:153 Je 12 '89

Canada
See also
Canada. Bureau of Competition Policy
The invasion of the frenzy-feeders. D. Francis. il *Maclean's* 102:11 Mr 20 '89

Western Europe
Joint ventures with the EC. S. Y. Chow. il *High Technology Business* 9:10 Jl/Ag '89

ANTITRYPSIN
A genetic shield to prevent emphysema? [work of Ronald G. Crystal with antitrypsin gene-carrying retrovirus] B. J. Culliton. il *Science* 246:750-1 N 10 '89
New treatment found for hereditary emphysema [research by Ronald Crystal] J. L. Marx. il *Science* 243:315-16 Ja 20 '89
Two new approaches to genetic emphysema [antitrypsin gene-carrying retrovirus; work of Ronald G. Crystal] S. Hart and A. McKenzie. *Science News* 136:233 O 7 '89

ANTITUMOR SUBSTANCES *See* Cancer inhibiting substances
ANTIVIRAL PROTEINS *See* Interferon
ANTIVIVISECTION MOVEMENT *See* Animal rights movement

ANTLE, SHARON
(jt. auth) See Edwards, Karen S., and Antle, Sharon

ANTLERS
All about antlers [deer and elk] S. Curtis. il *Field & Stream* 94:42 N '89
How to tickle a whitetail [antlers used as deer calls] J. Weiss. il *Outdoor Life* 184:74-5+ S '89
Of moose, megaloceros and miracles. D. Petersen. il map *The Mother Earth News* 116:102-7 Mr/Ap '89
Wild things [horn and antler furniture] A. De Moubray. il *House & Garden* 161:28-9 Ja '89

ANTLEY, CHRIS, 1966?-
about
The Ant gallops toward Joe D. A. Lennard. il por *Sports Illustrated* 70:16 Ap 24 '89

ANTOIAN, EDWARD
about
How to spot trends for fun and profit [interview] P. Sellers. il por *Fortune* 120:40-1 S 11 '89

ANTOINETTE PERRY AWARDS *See* Tony Awards
ANTONINI, JOSEPH
about
Attention, K Mart shoppers. P. Sellers. il por *Fortune* 119:41 Ja 2 '89

ANTONOFF, MICHAEL
Desktop publishing. See issues of Personal Computing beginning April 1989

ANTONOV DESIGN BUREAU (SOVIET UNION)
An-225 super heavylift transport can carry 80-meter external payload. J. M. Lenorovitz. il *Aviation Week & Space Technology* 130:52-3 Je 19 '89
Certification of super heavy-lift Antonov An-225 planned for 1990. il *Aviation Week & Space Technology* 130:72-3+ Je 5 '89
Six-engine Antonov An-225 begins flight tests. il *Aviation Week & Space Technology* 130:128 F 20 '89

ANTONOVA, IRINA ALEKSANDROVNA, 1922-
about
Leaps and boundaries. D. Matlock. il por *Art News* 88:69-70 Ja '89

ANTONUCCI, EMIL
Our task is to create worlds. il *Commonweal* 116:334-5 Je 2 '89

ANTS
See also
Fire ants
Biological pest control [Chinese use of carnivorous ants to protect mandarin oranges] R. K. G. Temple. il *The Courier (Unesco)* 41:24 O '88
Trap-jaw ants: set for prey. M. W. Moffett. il *National Geographic* 175:394-400 Mr '89

ANTWERP (BELGIUM)
Galleries and museums
See also
Rubenshuis (Antwerp, Belgium)

ANUSAKSATHIEN, ORANUCH
New seasons, new joys. il *World Health* p27-8 Mr '89

ANXIETY
See also
Fear
Panic disorder
Social anxiety
Stage fright
Worry
50 ways to scare your lover. W. D. Leight. *Mademoiselle* 95:84 Je '89

Breathing space [labored breathing, brought on by anxiety, cured by visiting garden] S. Safransky. il por *Organic Gardening* 36:83-4 O '89
Conquering your fears. D. Goleman. *McCall's* 117:154+ O '89
The medical side of anxiety [study by Kenneth B. Wells] *Science News* 136:381 D 9 '89
Neuroanatomical correlates of anticipatory anxiety [study of brain blood flow by positron emission tomography] E. M. Reiman and others. bibl f il *Science* 243:1071-4 F 24 '89
Overcome "information anxiety" [condensed from Information anxiety] R. S. Wurman. il *Reader's Digest* 134:127-30 My '89
PET pictures produce a palette of anxiety [research by Eric M. Reiman] B. Bower. il *Science News* 135:116-17 F 25 '89
Sleep problems send psychiatric signals [research by Daniel E. Ford and Douglas B. Kamerow] B. Bower. *Science News* 136:180 S 16 '89

ANXIETY IN CHILDREN
An early start for panic [research by James C. Ballenger] *Science News* 136:61 Jl 22 '89

ANYONS
Bosons condense and fermions 'exclude,' but anyons . . .? A. Khurana. il *Physics Today* 42:17-21 N '89

ANYTHING BUT LOVE [television program] See Television program reviews—Single works

ANZUS COUNCIL
New Zealand takes on the U.S. [interview with D. Lange] M. Gawenda. il por *Time* 133:45 My 8 '89

AOA *See* United States. Administration on Aging
AOKI, HIROYOSHI
about
Hotelier by default. H. Katayama. il por *Forbes* 144:240 O 30 '89

AOKI, ROCKY
about
Rocky's road. E. Schmuckler. il por *Forbes* 143:80+ Mr 20 '89

AOKI CORP.
Hotelier by default [H. Aoki] H. Katayama. il por *Forbes* 144:240 O 30 '89

AORTA
Abnormalities
See also
Aortic coarctation

AORTIC COARCTATION
Fixing a child's heart [use of magnetic resonance imaging] J. Stone. il *The New York Times Magazine* p37-8 Ag 13 '89

AOS *See* Alternative operator services
AOUITA, SAID
about
Much sweeta for Aouita. M. Noden. il por *Sports Illustrated* 70:32-4 F 13 '89
Smashing! M. Noden. il pors *Sports Illustrated* 71:16-19 Ag 28 '89

AOUN, MICHEL
about
Beleaguered Beirut. L. Marlowe. il *Maclean's* 102:26-7 My 8 '89
Celebrations and bombs. A. Bilski. il por *Maclean's* 102:42-3 N 20 '89
The nation that has made hell routine. L. Lief. il por *U.S. News & World Report* 106:46-7 My 1 '89

APA *See* American Psychiatric Association
APACHE BASKETS, MINIATURE *See* Indians of North America—Baskets, Miniature
APARTHEID
See also
Church and race relations—South Africa
Mass Democratic Movement (South Africa)
200 women arrested during protest in South Africa. il *Jet* 76:9 S 18 '89
AAP report hits book embargo of South Africa as 'misguided'. C. Reid. *Publishers Weekly* 236:8+ D 1 '89
Aftermath of the exodus [U.S. disinvestment] J. Jones. il *U.S. News & World Report* 106:49-50 My 1 '89
Anti-apartheid notes. il *UN Chronicle* 26:49 Mr '89
Anti-apartheid notes. il *UN Chronicle* 26:14 D '89
Anti-apartheid notes. il *UN Chronicle* 26:12 S '89
Anti-apartheid notes. il *UN Chronicle* 26:18 Je '89
Apartheid and the Canada connection [Bank of Nova Scotia's involvement in financing Minorco's bid for Consolidated Gold Fields] P. C. Newman. il *Maclean's* 102:29 F 13 '89
Ashe applauds ATP move to avoid South Africa. por *Jet* 76:48 S 18 '89
The beginning of the end of apartheid? [F. W. De Klerk's reforms] S. V. Roberts. il *U.S. News & World Report* 107:55 O 30 '89
Black leaders: free at last. S. Reiss. il *Newsweek* 114:58 O 30 '89
Botha vs. De Klerk: same song, different singer? F. D. Brown. il *Black Enterprise* 20:26 N '89
Botha's untimely stroke. M. Nemeth. il por *Maclean's* 102:28 Ja 30 '89

APARTHEID—cont.

Bound by blood. R. W. Wilkins. il por *Mother Jones* 14:20+ My '89

Brother against brother [F. W. and W. De Klerk] S. MacLeod. il pors *Time* 134:49 O 9 '89

A call for unity. S. L. Taylor. il *Essence* 20:59 My '89

Canada in a hot seat [business transactions with South Africa questioned at Commonwealth meeting] M. Nemeth. il por *Maclean's* 102:21 F 20 '89

Choices [political campaign] R. Bonner. *The New Yorker* 65:43-8+ D 25 '89

Color picture out of focus [plans for men's tennis tournaments in South Africa] M. Mathabane. il *World Tennis* 37:27+ Je '89

Covering news where networks fear to tread [South Africa now] C. Reece. il *Channels (New York, N.Y.: 1986)* 9:17 Ja '89

Cutting apartheid to the bone [fight to integrate hospitals in South Africa] il *U.S. News & World Report* 107:10 Ag 14 '89

Dark content: getting South Africa news [South Africa now TV show] E. Hedegaard. il *Mother Jones* 14:49 S '89

Decline and fall of a heroine [W. Mandela] B. W. Nelan. il por *Time* 133:36 F 27 '89

Diplomacy and dissent: black protests grow on the eve of an election. J. Bierman. il *Maclean's* 102:22+ S 11 '89

Divestment update [chart] *Black Enterprise* 19:41 Mr '89

The divisions in South Africa get even deeper. J. Kapstein. il por *Business Week* p55 S 18 '89

Do South African sanctions make sense? D. Reed. il *Reader's Digest* 134:51-6 F '89

'Eminent Persons' call for stricter sanctions against South Africa. il *UN Chronicle* 26:61 D '89

The end of an era: President Botha bids a resentful goodbye. A. Bilski. il por *Maclean's* 102:22 Ag 28 '89

Ex-ANC leader talks about 26 years of imprisonment [W. Sisulu] il por *Jet* 77:30 N 6 '89

An exceptional protest [Cape Town march] M. Nemeth. il *Maclean's* 102:34+ S 25 '89

'F.W.' brings cautious hope for reform [F. W. De Klerk] B. Schiller. *World Press Review* 36:30-1 N '89

Falling apartheid [upcoming elections favor F. W. De Klerk] M. R. Hoffenberg. *The New Republic* 201:16-17 Jl 31 '89

Family quarrel [British opposition to sanctions against South Africa at Commonwealth summit in Kuala Lumpur, Malaysia] R. Laver. il *Maclean's* 102:40-1 O 30 '89

Fighting back [W. Mandela battles accusers] J. Bierman. il por *Maclean's* 102:20 Mr 6 '89

Filling the South Africa void [South Africa now TV show] N. S. Mehta. il *Time* 133:58 Mr 6 '89

A free-market cure for apartheid ills [black businesses] J. Jones. il *U.S. News & World Report* 107:47 Ag 7 '89

Free Winnie! [W. Mandela] E. Brown. por *Essence* 20:128 Je '89

Freedom at last [eight activists released] M. Nemeth. il *Maclean's* 102:34-5 O 23 '89

Getting out the truth [South Africa now TV show] J. M. Robins. il *Channels (New York, N.Y.: 1986)* 9:52-4 N '89

Glasnost meets apartheid [Soviet Union disowns African National Congress] B. Crozier. *National Review* 41:22 My 5 '89

A glimmer of peace [meeting between N. Mandela and P. Botha] C. Erasmus. il por *Maclean's* 102:26 Jl 24 '89

The great white hope [F. W. De Klerk] B. W. Nelan. il por *Time* 134:42 S 11 '89

The group. J. Carlin. *The New Republic* 201:21-3 N 27 '89

Harry Oppenheimer's empire: going for the gold. P. Schmeisser. il por *The New York Times Magazine* p32-3+ Mr 19 '89

How far will De Klerk go? C. S. Wren. il por *The New York Times Magazine* p42-3+ N 19 '89

The illusion of reform in South Africa. D. Palos and T. Soeldner. *The Christian Century* 106:447-50 Ap 26 '89

In the teeth of the 'Great Crocodile' [P. W. Botha] S. Reiss. il pors *Newsweek* 113:39 Mr 27 '89

Just two women. J. Hey. il *The New York Times Magazine* p40+ S 10 '89

The last wave [surfers boycott South African competitions] E. Silver. il *Mother Jones* 14:12 D '89

Mandela's mess [W. Mandela] il por *World Press Review* 36:42 Ap '89

Masked by turmoil, apartheid weakens. R. Knight and J. Jones. il *U.S. News & World Report* 107:34-6 S 11 '89

Meeting of different minds [F. W. De Klerk and N. Mandela] S. MacLeod. il pors *Time* 134:28 D 25 '89

Mobil's big pullout. *Newsweek* 113:42 My 8 '89

Moving to the next stage. M. Gevisser. il *The Nation* 249:674+ D 4 '89

Mrs. Mandela's disgrace [Mandela United Football Club of young bodyguards] S. Reiss. il por *Newsweek* 113:44 F 27 '89

The mystery of Winnie Mandela. G. Bain. il *Maclean's* 102:50 Mr 20 '89

The need to break the stalemate. M. Swilling. il por *World Press Review* 36:32 N '89

"New labels on old dogma". F. D. Brown. il *Black Enterprise* 20:32 O '89

New steps in a freedom walk [F. W. De Klerk frees eight black leaders] il *U.S. News & World Report* 107:17 O 23 '89

New wave of defiance in South Africa [Mass Democratic Movement; cover story] P. Green. il *The Nation* 249:261+ S 18 '89

Peace at the mouth of the water cannon [President F. W. De Klerk's show of moderation] il por *U.S. News & World Report* 107:14 S 25 '89

Pedestal politics [controversy over W. Mandela] *The Nation* 248:325 Mr 13 '89

A pilgrim's progress [black South African marathoner M. Plaatjes] J. Brant. il pors *Runner's World* 24:66-71 D '89

The point system. A. Kopkind. *The Nation* 248:761-2 Je 5 '89

Poised for change [special section] J. Bierman. il *Maclean's* 102:18-22+ Mr 13 '89

Politics in South Africa. P. O'Meara. *Current History* 88:217-20+ My '89

President meets with South African antiapartheid activist [statement, June 30, 1989] G. Bush. il pors *Department of State Bulletin* 89:71 S '89

Pretoria outflanks the ANC [Angola deal] S. Reiss. il map *Newsweek* 113:37 Ja 23 '89

Pretoria's mixed signals. *Commonweal* 116:692-3 D 15 '89

Pretoriastroika? [policies of F. W. De Klerk] *The New Republic* 201:9 O 23 '89

Probing the hit squads [F. W. De Klerk orders investigation into rash of political murders] *Time* 134:30 D 18 '89

A race against time [tennis] R. Moore. il *World Tennis* 37:96 O '89

Real sanctions. *The Nation* 249:372 O 9 '89

Return of the Great Crocodile [P. W. Botha] B. W. Nelan. il por *Time* 133:56 Mr 27 '89

Review of U.S.-South Africa relations [address, June 6, 1989] E. J. Perkins. *Department of State Bulletin* 89:69-73 S '89

S. Africa tour furor basis for Milan Williams firing from 'Commodores' group. il por *Jet* 76:17 Ag 14 '89

Scandal in Soweto: black rights leaders disown Winnie Mandela. J. Bierman. il por *Maclean's* 102:26-7 F 27 '89

The secrets of South Africa's hit squad [D. Coetzee tells of attacks on African National Congress] *Newsweek* 114:56 N 27 '89

Showdown in Cape Town [P. W. Botha battles his party for power] M. Nemeth. por *Maclean's* 102:30 Mr 27 '89

South Africa: a step forward on Namibia, a step backward at home? A. Fine. il *Business Week* p66 Mr 13 '89

South Africa goes black. A. Sparks. *World Press Review* 36:64 Je '89

South Africa: signs of change. il *Scholastic Update (Teachers' edition)* 122:8 N 3 '89

South Africa: the saga continues [runners suspended for attending track meet] A. Burfoot and B. Wischnia. il *Runner's World* 24:8-9 F '89

South Africa: the squeeze is on. J. Kapstein. il por *Business Week* p44-5+ S 11 '89

A South African cop breaks ranks over police violence [G. Rockman reports brutality during student demonstration near Cape Town] B. Hewitt. il pors *People Weekly* 32:44-6 O 16 '89

South Africa's 'death wish' [death penalty] J. Carlin. *World Press Review* 36:57 Ag '89

South Africa's violent rage [election violence; cover story; special section; with editorial comment by Kevin Doyle] il pors *Maclean's* 102:4, 32-6+ S 18 '89

Soweto's 'Winnie problem' [controversy surrounding W. Mandela's Mandela United Football Club] S. Reiss. il por *Newsweek* 113:35 F 13 '89

Squeezed left, squeezed right [results of parliamentary elections] B. W. Nelan. il por *Time* 134:46-7 S 18 '89

Stopping apartheid on the beach. il *U.S. News & World Report* 107:14+ N 27 '89

The sudden unmaking of Winnie Mandela [controversy surrounding Mandela United Football Club] il por *U.S. News & World Report* 106:13 F 27 '89

Taking apartheid to court [Legal Resources Center] B. W. Nelan. il *Time* 134:44 Ag 14 '89

Teatime in Pretoria [N. Mandela meets with P. W. Botha] C. S. Manegold. il *Newsweek* 114:24 Jl 24 '89

Testing the waters. B. W. Nelan. il *Time* 134:66-7+ O 30 '89

The Thatcher factor [banks reschedule South African debt] R. Laver. il *Maclean's* 102:42 O 30 '89

Then there was one [release of all political prisoners except N. Mandela] S. MacLeod. il *Time* 134:49-50 O 23 '89

A thorny dispute [Britain refuses to endorse call for sanctions against South Africa at Commonwealth conference in Malaysia] R. Laver. il por *Maclean's* 102:36-7 N 6 '89

Time to talk in South Africa. S. Reiss. il *Newsweek* 114:40-1 Ag 28 '89

Two cheers for moderation. S. Reiss. il *Newsweek* 114:31 S 18 '89

An unlikely tea for two [N. Mandela meets with P. Botha] B. W. Nelan. il pors *Time* 134:29 Jl 24 '89

APARTHEID—cont.

Upstaging South Africa's elections [black protests] S. Reiss. il *Newsweek* 114:34 S 11 '89

Warrior against racism [J. Clegg] K. McKenna. il por *Scholastic Update (Teachers' edition)* 121:16 Ja 27 '89

'We're committed to reform, and we really mean business' [interview with F. W. De Klerk] S. Reiss and W. Claiborne. il por *Newsweek* 114:70 D 4 '89

Where disinvestment pinches [South African gold mines] J. Cook. il por *Forbes* 143:62+ Je 26 '89

Winnie the shrew. S. Mufson. *The New Republic* 200:14-16 Mr 13 '89

Word from South Africa [interview with Z. M. Dlamini] S. L. Taylor and E. B. Washington. il por *Essence* 20:42-4+ Jl '89

Photographs and photography

South Africa: the cordoned heart. il *Society* 26:83-7 My/Je '89

APARTHEID IN LITERATURE

Books on Africa. F. J. Parker. *America* 161:117-21 Ag 26-S 2 '89

Can South Africa change? [cover story] G. M. Fredrickson. il *The New York Review of Books* 36:48-55 O 26 '89

Time stands still. M. Gevisser. *The Nation* 249:390-3 O 9 '89

True confessions of an exiled Afrikaner [B. Breytenbach] G. Marzorati. il pors *The New York Times Magazine* p32-3+ Ag 27 '89

APARTHEID IN MOTION PICTURES

Brando says studio sold him out on 'Dry white season'. il por *Jet* 77:63 O 23 '89

Euzhan Palcy has a face the camera loves but finds the view better behind the lens [director of A dry white season] I. Lacher. il pors *People Weekly* 32:71-2 O 16 '89

Richard Attenborough [interview] C. Vieler-Porter. il pors *The Unesco Courier* 42:4-7 Ag '89

Tempest [interview with E. Palcy] M. Glicksman. il por *Film Comment* 25:64-6+ S/O '89

Tough, passionate, persuasive [E. Palcy's A dry white season] K. McKenna. il por *American Film* 14:32-7 S '89

A woman for all seasons [E. Palcy, director of A dry white season] M. Rosen. il por *Ms.* 18:18+ O '89

Women in film [E. Palcy's A dry white season] M. Southgate. il pors *Essence* 20:31-2 O '89

APARTMENT HOUSES

See also

New Orleans (La.)—Housing

New York (N.Y.)—Housing

The concierge concept [full service buildings] D. Di Costanzo. il *House & Garden* 161:156-7 F '89

Cooperative ownership

See also

Project Family Independence

Co-op quake [shaky limited partnership deals used to finance co-op conversion in New York City] C. Byron. il *New York* 22:22+ N 20 '89

APARTMENTS

See also

Loft apartments

Abloom in the city [E. Niven's New York apartment decorated by Genevieve Faure] J. Conlin. il por *House & Garden* 161:168-73+ My '89

Above it all [Manhattan triplex of F. and J. Biggs] J. Reginato. il por *House & Garden* 161:152-9+ Je '89

Adolfo in New York. B. Morris. il por *Architectural Digest* 46:132-7 S '89

Anglo-Indian impressions [A. P. Browne's Gothic revival apartment in Georgetown] S. M. Alsop. il por *Architectural Digest* 46:222-6+ Mr '89

Architectural digest visits: Cher [Manhattan apartment decorated by Ron Wilson] S. M. L. Aronson. il pors *Architectural Digest* 46:160-7+ Mr '89

Architectural digest visits: Cynthia Gregory [Manhattan apartment decorated by Miriam Weinreb] J. Gruen. il pors *Architectural Digest* 46:236-41+ N '89

Architectural digest visits: Liv Ullmann [Boston apartment decorated by Helen I. Rosenthal] D. Roberts. il por *Architectural Digest* 46:208-14+ D '89

Architectural elan [Manhattan apartment decorated by R. Scott Bromley and Robin Jacobsen for M. and D. Abrams] P. Warner. il *Architectural Digest* 46:166-71 Ag '89

Balancing act [Lipschutz/Jones apartment, New York City; Frank Lupo and Daniel Rowen, architects] D. Dietsch. il *Architectural Record* 177:120-3 Je '89

Below the surface [interiors by Bentley LaRosa Salasky] J. S. Russell. il *Architectural Record* 177:108-13 Ag '89

Born in U.S.A. [Riki Gail Zuriff's New York apartment] C. Vogel. il *The New York Times Magazine* p68-9 Ap 16 '89

Brave new worlds [downtown, New York City] M. Bethany. il *New York* 22:114-16+ D 25 '89-Ja 1 '90

Bright light in the big city [J. McInerney's Manhattan penthouse decorated by Alison Spear] C. K. Gandee. il pors *House & Garden* 161:190-5 O '89

Buenos Aires alchemy: Jean-Pierre and Rosemarie Marcie-Rivière's city apartment [decorated by Alberto Pinto] Suzy. il pors *Architectural Digest* 46:220-7 O '89

Caroline Charles: the practical charms of a very English apartment in Knightsbridge. E. Lambert. il por *Architectural Digest* 46:128-31 S '89

Carolyn Roehm: an opulent aesthetic for the designer's Manhattan residence [decorated by Vincent Fourcade] Suzy. il por *Architectural Digest* 46:112-19 S '89

Carving out a niche [W. Lehman's Manhattan residence decorated by Keith Irvine] R. Koenig. il por *House & Garden* 161:218-23 O '89

Chez Claude [C. Montana's Paris apartment] C. Petkanas. il pors *Harper's Bazaar* 122:104-9+ Je '89

Chicago vistas [penthouse decorated by Bruce Gregga] J. Neisser. il *Architectural Digest* 46:70-7 Jl '89

Classical translation [M. Goodwin's London flat] D. Hall. il por *House & Garden* 161:116-23 Mr '89

Claude Montana: an avant-garde elegance on the Left Bank. C. Aillaud. il por *Architectural Digest* 46:120-7 S '89

The collectors: neoclassical aesthetic: fashion designer Gaston Choron in Wiesbaden. D. H. Minassian. il por *Architectural Digest* 46:240-6+ Ap '89

Continental calm on high [Manhattan penthouse decorated by Mario Buatta for D. and G. Pattee] Suzy. il por *Architectural Digest* 46:220-7+ N '89

Continental impressions on Nob Hill [San Francisco apartment decorated by Val Arnold for E. Killebrew] H. Junker. il por *Architectural Digest* 46:288-94+ O '89

Cosmopolitan mise-en-scéne [Manhattan apartment of L. and A. Blanco decorated by Juan Montoya] C. McGee. il *Architectural Digest* 46:186-91 Ap '89

Creole comforts [M. Villa's New Orleans studio] N. Lemann. il por *House & Garden* 161:180-5+ S '89

Déco interpretations: Karl Springer on the Upper East Side. J. Thurman. il por *Architectural Digest* 46:228-35 N '89

Diary of a duplex: Barbara Goldsmith and Frank Perry on Park [Manhattan apartment decorated by Renny B. Saltzman] B. Goldsmith. il pors *Architectural Digest* 46:310-15 N '89

Earning his stripes [Manhattan home of J. and P. Lawrence decorated by S. Sill; cover story] J. Reginato. il pors *House & Garden* 161:224-7+ O '89

Elements of style [East Side Manhattan apartment decorated by Robert Metzger and Michael Christiano] P. Carlsen. il *Architectural Digest* 46:212-19 N '89

Eminent Victorian [New York City apartment of Christopher Ostafin] M. Bethany. il *New York* 22:48-50 F 6 '89

Empire building [J. Epstein's New York City apartment] J. J. Buck. il por *Vogue* 179:350-1+ N '89

Evolution of a classic: a Fifth Avenue signature by the late Melanie Kahane. S. Stephens. il *Architectural Digest* 46:242-9+ N '89

Fashion statement [New York apartment decorated by Samuel Botero for D. Morgan and P. Annunziata] S. Stephens. il *Architectural Digest* 46:92-7 Jl '89

A Florida composition [Miami apartment decorated by Michael De Santis for B. and M. Kaplan] C. McGee. il *Architectural Digest* 46:144-9 Jl '89

Foreigner affair [Manhattan home of M. and A. Jones] W. P. Rayner. il por *House & Garden* 161:72+ O '89

Forging ahead [converted garage apartment of A. Dubreuil in London] C. Maclean. il por *House & Garden* 161:150-5+ N '89

Framer's art [Boston apartment of R. Lussier] S. Barron. il por *House & Garden* 161:150-7+ D '89

A garden view [New York City apartment of Cynthia Gibson] il *Redbook* 173:136-9 My '89

Gentleman's quarters [T. Fallon's New York apartment] M. Cantwell. il por *House & Garden* 161:78-81+ Ja '89

George Stavropoulos: a master of classical line in Manhattan. C. R. Milbank. il pors *Architectural Digest* 46:158-61+ S '89

Grand allusions [Manhattan residence of Valentino] A. L. Talley. il por *Vogue* 179:510-17+ Mr '89

Hanae Mori: East meets West in the designer's Paris residence [decorated by Chiyoko Motono] C. Aillaud. il por *Architectural Digest* 46:152-7 S '89

The hands of time [an American's Paris apartment] I. Sischy. il *House & Garden* 161:136-41+ Jl '89

Haut Catroux [decorator of Paris apartment] C. Petkanas. il *House & Garden* 161:160-7+ Ap '89

He knows what he likes [M. Galabert's Paris apartment] P. Viladas. il pors *House & Garden* 161:26+ F '89

He's the tops [Kenneth's New York penthouse] D. Kazanjian. il pors *House & Garden* 161:120-5+ F '89

High style in Manhattan [Sutton Place apartment decorated for A. and B. Currey by Anthony Hail] J. Taylor. il *Architectural Digest* 46:134-41 D '89

Homage to Loos [duplex Manhattan apartment by Agrest and Gandelsonas] M. F. Schmertz. il *Architectural Record* 177:50-7 mid-S '89

Imperial standard [Manhattan apartment] B. Felner. il *House & Garden* 161:204-13 O '89

In her own fashion [B. de Ganay's Paris apartment] J. Burstall. il pors *House & Garden* 161:114-17 Jl '89

In memory of his wife, Joe Furey created an unusual artwork that may not survive [decoration of Brooklyn, N.Y. apartment] R. Arias. il pors *People Weekly* 32:104-5 S 4 '89

In the West Village: Peggy Pierrepont's New York apartment. S. M. Alsop. il por *Architectural Digest* 46:152-7 F '89

APARTMENTS—cont.

Interior: the good life [New York City apartments; cover story] M. Bethany. il *New York* 22:56-83 Ap 10 '89

Love nest [New York City apartment of K. Ridder and P. Pennoyer] M. Baker. il pors *New York* 22:56-9 O 2 '89

Luciano Soprani: quiet style for his Milan apartment. C. Galimberti. il pors *Architectural Digest* 46:162-7+ S '89

Maestro at the Met [New York apartment of Metropolitan Museum of Art curator E. Fahy] C. McGee. il por *House & Garden* 161:50+ S '89

Making room for art [J. and E. Spiegel's Manhattan apartment designed by Peter Shelton and Lee Mindel] J. Giovannini. il *House & Garden* 161:132-9 D '89

Manhattan country [decorated by W. Diamond] D. Sacks. il *House & Garden* 161:132-43 Ap '89

Manhattan revision: an East River penthouse with an old world look [interior by Kalef Alaton] J. Gruen. il *Architectural Digest* 46:100-7 F '89

Manhattan transformation [Park Avenue apartment decorated for L. Simone by John Saladino] J. Giovannini. il *Architectural Digest* 46:182-7+ Mr '89

Metropolitan flair: telling details for Jackie Rogers in Manhattan. C. R. Milbank. il por *Architectural Digest* 46:286-9 N '89

Metropolitan reflections: a play of surfaces in a Los Angeles penthouse [home of N. Jensen decorated by Ron Wilson] M. Webb. il *Architectural Digest* 46:270-5 My '89

Mixed company [Manhattan home of J. Holtzman] P. Viladas. il por *House & Garden* 161:66+ N '89

Nassau via New York [homes of I. and T. A. Kramer decorated by Mark Hampton] Suzy. il *Architectural Digest* 46:142-51 Mr '89

Neoclassical overtones: Georgette Mosbacher's Sutton Place pied-à-terre [decorated by Billy McMaster] Suzy. il por *Architectural Digest* 46:258-63 N '89

New York state of mind: Hannah and Alan J. Pakula's apartment in the sky. R. Fizdale and A. Gold. il pors *Architectural Digest* 46:270-3 N '89

New York story: romantic traditions fill a designer's East Side residence [M. Meehan] S. M. L. Aronson. il por *Architectural Digest* 46:112-19+ Jl '89

Nob Hill epigram: an antiquarian's San Francisco apartment [home of J. Leen] H. Junker. il por *Architectural Digest* 46:250-5 My '89

Noble Roman [F. Forquet's Rome apartment] M. Mewshaw. il por *House & Garden* 161:128-39+ My '89

On Belgrave Square: a signature space for Rose Tarlow in London [cover story] E. Lambert. il por *Architectural Digest* 46:132-41+ Mr '89

On the Rue de Rivoli [Paris apartment of M.-P. Pellé] C. K. Gandee. il por *House & Garden* 161:68-77 Jl '89

Once upon a time [twin four year old girls in Manhattan apartment] C. K. Gandee. il *House & Garden* 161:110-15+ Ag '89

A page from the past: infusing a Manhattan apartment with period flair [interior by Kevin McNamara] S. Stephens. il *Architectural Digest* 46:174-9 F '89

Pared down penthouse [Manhattan home of P. Rogers] A. Virshup. il por *House & Garden* 161:186-91 S '89

Paris on Park: Countess Eugenia de Serigny's Manhattan apartment [decorated by Juan Pablo Molyneux] J. Reginato. il por *Architectural Digest* 46:156-61 Ap '89

Patrick Kelly: exuberant style animates the American designer's Paris atelier. M. Gross. il por *Architectural Digest* 46:218-24 S '89

A penthouse with period grace [Manhattan apartment decorated by Mark Hampton] P. T. Buckley. il *Architectural Digest* 46:250-7 N '89

Petit palais [K. Lagerfeld's Paris apartment] A. L. Talley. il por *Vogue* 179:390-1 Ap '89

A reign in Spain: the Countess of Romanones in Extremadura and New York. Aline, Countess of Romanones. il pors *Architectural Digest* 46:192-9 Ap '89

A renter's guide to decorating [apartment of Beverly McGuire] il *Glamour* 87:252-4 N '89

Roman revival [A. Magistretti's apartment] J. Turner. il por *House & Garden* 161:114-19+ Ja '89

Royal lineage [J. Garcia's Paris apartment] G. Y. Dryansky. il por *House & Garden* 161:148-55+ Jl '89

Scented rooms [B. M. Ohrbach's Manhattan apartment] J. Seymore. il por *House & Garden* 161:170-5+ N '89

A skyline view [Central Park West apartment decorated by Michael de Santis] J. Simpson. il *Architectural Digest* 46:264-9 N '89

Stockholm on the Hudson [Upper East Side apartment decorated by Peter Marino] S. M. L. Aronson. il *Architectural Digest* 46:296-303 N '89

A tale of two cities: a designer's Los Angeles and San Francisco abodes [V. Arnold] I. Borger. il *Architectural Digest* 46:214-21+ My '89

Unconventional appeal [Park Avenue duplex decorated by Betty Sherrill and Ethel Smith] S. M. Alsop. il *Architectural Digest* 46:280-5 N '89

Undone in Paris [C. Pringle's apartment] E. White. il por *House & Garden* 161:24+ Ja '89

A very private collection [Manhattan apartment decorated by S. Parish] J. Richardson. il *House & Garden* 161:154-61 O '89

Vicky Tiel: American elan in a Paris apartment. S. Stephens. il por *Architectural Digest* 46:188-91 S '89

Victor Edelstein: period clarity for the couturier's London flat. E. Lambert. il por *Architectural Digest* 46:184-7+ S '89

A Victorian Paris: Beatriz Patiño's Plaine Monceau pied-à-terre [interior design by François Catroux] C. Aillaud. il *Architectural Digest* 46:100-7 Ja '89

Victoria's secret [Manhattan residence of V. Hagan] L. Snowden. il por *House & Garden* 161:188-91+ My '89

Well-read women [Manhattan homes of L. Nesbit, J. Evans, and N. Evans] D. Lida. il pors *House & Garden* 161:228-31 O '89

Where John Barrymore once hid from fans, Paul Rudnick has found the actor's ghost—and medieval inspiration [Greenwich Village apartment] P. Rudnick. il por *Vogue* 179:130-2 Jl '89

Writer's turf [D. Dunne's Manhattan penthouse] M. Cantwell. il por *House & Garden* 161:108+ O '89

Wry Manhattan: Robert Woolley's Fifth Avenue apartment. C. T. Buckley. il por *Architectural Digest* 46:322-7+ N '89

Anecdotes, facetiae, satire, etc.

Enter laughing [home of P. Jillette] Teller. il pors *Gentlemen's Quarterly* 59:236-9+ Ag '89

Leasing and renting

See also
  Landlord and tenant
  Rent laws

APARTMENTS, REMODELED

Agrest and Gandelsonas: a sleek Manhattan remodel. P. Goldberger. il *Architectural Digest* 46:94-7+ Ap '89

Parlor game [Greenwich Village duplex by Joe D'Urso] C. K. Gandee. il *House & Garden* 161:92-7 Ag '89

Revisionist history [Manhattan duplex of Diana Agrest and Mario Gandelsonas] P. Viladas. il *House & Garden* 161:162-9 N '89

Top-notch [David S. Rockwell's Manhattan apartment] C. Vogel. il *The New York Times Magazine* p74-5 My 14 '89

Vintage New Orleans: contemporary renovation in the Pontalba Buildings [architecture by Leonard Salvato with interiors by Ann Dupuy and Ann Holden] W. L. Douglas. il *Architectural Digest* 46:158-63+ F '89

APATHEIA (TERM)

Don't worry, be still. J. Garvey. il *Commonweal* 116:489-90 S 22 '89

APATITE

See also
  Hydroxyapatite

APBPA *See* Association of Professional Ball Players of America

APERITIFS *See* Alcoholic beverages

APES

See also
  Chimpanzees
  Gorillas
  Orangutans

APHELION

about

To Diana and Ivana, a nose by any other name than 'Aphelion' wouldn't smell as sweet. D. Marlow. il pors *People Weekly* 32:78-80 Jl 24 '89

APHIDS

See also
  Woolly aphids

A 48-million-year-old aphid-host plant association and complex life cycle: biogeographic evidence [aphid subtribe Melaphidina and sumac host plant] N. A. Moran. bibl f il map *Science* 245:173-5 Jl 14 '89

Alien influence [wasp larvae manipulation of potato aphid behavior; research by Jacques Brodeur and Jeremy N. McNeil] T. Beardsley. *Scientific American* 261:26 Jl '89

Dying aphids obey wasp's commands [research by Jacques Brodeur and Jeremy N. McNeil] R. Weiss. *Science News* 135:231 Ap 15 '89

Seasonal microhabitat selection by an endoparasitoid through adaptive modification of host behavior. J. Brodeur and J. N. McNeil. bibl f il *Science* 244:226-8 Ap 14 '89

Control

Plant hybrid zones as sinks for pests [aphids on hybrid cottonwoods] T. G. Whitham. bibl f il *Science* 244:1490-3 Je 23 '89

APHORISMS AND APOTHEGMS

See also
  Maxims

APHRODISIACS

Aphrodite was no lady. J. Birnbaum. il *Time* 133:92 Ap 24 '89

The great bear aphrodisiac caper [animal parts mixed into nostrums] il *U.S. News & World Report* 106:14 F 6 '89

A legal aphrodisiac? [Wellbutrin] A.-M. Stan. *New Choices for the Best Years* 29:13 Ja '89

APHRODISIAS (ANCIENT CITY)
A white marble city that an emperor chose for his own [work of K. T. Erim] D. J. Hamblin. il *Smithsonian* 19:142-8+ Mr '89

APHRODITE (GREEK DEITY) IN ART
Nothing to hide [discussion of Summer 1989 article, An outrageous anomaly] A. E. Elsen. il *Art News* 88:190 D '89

An outrageous anomaly [Getty Museum refuses to disclose source of Aphrodite sculpture] A. E. Elsen. il *Art News* 88:196 Summ '89

APKER AWARD
Kuchnir and Simon are co-winners of undergraduate Apker Award. pors *Physics Today* 42:85 D '89

APLYSIA NERVOUS SYSTEM *See* Nervous system—Mollusks

APNEA
See also
Sleep apnea

APOCALYPTIC ART
Kandinsky's Moscow. M. Werenskiold. bibl f il *Art in America* 77:96-111 Mr '89

APOCALYPTIC THOUGHT *See* Eschatology

APOLIPOPROTEINS
Heritable allele-specific differences in amounts of apoB and low-density lipoproteins in plasma. D. Gavish and others. bibl f il *Science* 244:72-6 Ap 7 '89

Lipoprotein(a)'s role in heart attacks explored [research by Richard Lawn] J. L. Marx. *Science* 243:316 Ja 20 '89

Meet apo A-I and apo B. *Prevention (Emmaus, Pa.)* 41:19-20 S '89

The mysteries of lipoprotein(a). G. Utermann. bibl f il *Science* 246:904-10 N 17 '89

APOLLO [ballet] *See* Ballet reviews—Single works

APOLLO 11 FLIGHT *See* Space flight to the moon—Apollo 11 flight

APOLLO COMPUTER, INC.
Can Apollo stop hurtling toward earth? L. Helm. il por *Business Week* p108 F 27 '89

HP: now no. 1 in workstations [deal for Apollo] J. B. Levine. il *Business Week* p30 Ap 24 '89

APOLLO PROJECT *See* Space flight to the moon

APOLLO PROJECT ASTRONAUTS *See* Astronauts

APOLLO THEATRE RECORDS
Motown deal sounds sweet [joining forces with Apollo Theatre] P. Sharif. il *Black Enterprise* 20:24 N '89

APOLLONIA
about
Apollonia arrested for marijuana; claims buy was research for movie. il por *Jet* 77:31 O 23 '89

APOLOGIES
Man at his best. J. Elliott. *Reader's Digest* 135:95-6 Jl '89

APONTE, CHRISTOPHER
about
Its director at odds with its board, Spokane Ballet seeks stability. S. English. por *Dance Magazine* 63:18 Mr '89

APONTE, WAYNE LIONEL
'Talkin' white'. por *Essence* 19:11 Ja '89

APP, TIMOTHY, 1947-
about
Timothy App at Linda Durham. K. Shields. il *Art in America* 77:184-5 Je '89

APPALACHIAN REGION
See also
National forests—Appalachian region
Wilderness areas—Appalachian region
Politics and government
Homegrown activism takes root in Appalachia. D. Davis. il *Utne Reader* p26 My/Je '89
Social conditions
Down here on the edge of things. A. Yale. il *The Nation* 249:591-2 N 20 '89

APPALACHIAN STUDIES
See also
East Tennessee State University. Center for Appalachian Studies and Services

APPAREL INDUSTRY *See* Clothing industry

APPARITIONS
See also
Jesus Christ—Apparitions and miracles

APPELBAUM, JUDITH
Hidden supersellers: backlist books whose annual sales rival frontlist topsellers. *Publishers Weekly* 235:53-5 Mr 10 '89

Hidden supersellers II: more backlist books with annual sales rivaling frontlist topsellers. il *Publishers Weekly* 236:36-7 D 22 '89

APPELBAUM, RICHARD P.
The affordability gap. *Society* 26:6-8 My/Je '89

APPELBAUM, STEPHEN
about
Stephen Appelbaum gives lawyers a hand, a leg, or any other body part for their day in court. A. Abrahams. il pors *People Weekly* 31:143-4+ My 22 '89

APPELLATE COURTS
See also
United States. Court of Appeals (District of Columbia Circuit)

APPELO, TIM
Student television learns to network. il *Rolling Stone* p107-8+ O 5 '89

APPETITE
See also
Anorexia nervosa
Bulimia
Food cravings
Hunger

Another dietary advantage to fiber [research by Allen S. Levine] *Science News* 136:412 D 23-30 '89

Overeating remedy [use of pectin] il *Prevention (Emmaus, Pa.)* 41:10 My '89

Pigging out [blocking cholecystokinin in pigs increases appetite; work of Jerome Pekas] *Discover* 10:20 My '89

Postponement of satiety by blockade of brain cholecystokinin (CCK-B) receptors. C. T. Dourish and others. bibl f il *Science* 245:1509-11 S 29 '89

Why are you hungry? D. Freedman. il *Nation's Business* 77:69 My '89

Why you can—or can't—eat another bite [role of cholecystokinin] C. Hacinli. il *Mademoiselle* 95:96+ Jl '89

APPETITE SUPPRESSING DRUGS *See* Weight reducing products

APPETIZERS
Appetizers invite a party. il *Southern Living* 24:199 Mr '89

Cheese combinations as quick appetizers. il *Sunset (Central West edition)* 182:198 My '89

Delectable dips. J. Nash. il *Essence* 20:102 My '89

Elegant 5-minute appetizers. il *Ladies' Home Journal* 106:68 Ja '89

Finger-food feasts. il *Health (New York, N.Y.)* 21:76-83 D '89

Hot canapés. il *Gourmet* 49:142 Ja '89

Last-minute appetizers [microwaving] J. Galton. il *Parents* 64:197-201 N '89

Lucky breaks [New Year's open house] R. Schrambling. il *The New York Times Magazine* p25-6 D 24 '89

Micro-way: festive first courses. il *McCall's* 117:151 N '89

The parties of winter [low calorie] R. A. Barnett. il *American Health* 8:68-70+ D '89

Party starters. il *Good Housekeeping* 208:134+ Ja '89

Pupu party. il *Sunset (Central West edition)* 183:62-4, 106 Ag '89

Quick and easy appetizers. il *McCall's* 116:69 Ja '89

Quick! Offer an appetizer. il *Southern Living* 24:116 D '89

Tempting appetizers from the frugal gourmet. il *McCall's* 116:44-6+ Ap '89

Tiny bites, mighty taste. P. Wolfert. il *Modern Maturity* 32:72-5 F/Mr '89

APPLAUSE THEATRE BOOKS
Loud Applause. L. Fleischer. *Publishers Weekly* 235:207 F 24 '89

APPLE, MAX
Peace [story] il *Harper's* 278:56-61 F '89

APPLE AWARDS *See* Mott's Apple Awards

APPLE CIDER *See* Cider

APPLE COMPUTER INC.
Allan Loren. M. Shao. il por *Business Week* Special Issue:158 Ap 14 '89

Apple Computer's risky revolution. B. O'Reilly. il por *Fortune* 119:75-6+ My 8 '89

Apple turns from revolution to evolution. M. Shao. il por *Business Week* p90+ Ja 23 '89

A battle over a user-friendly computer [Xerox sues Apple over software copyright] il *Newsweek* 114:59 D 25 '89

Double birth announcement from Apple [Macintosh portable and Mac IIci] E. P. Stevenson. il *Home Office Computing* 7:12 N '89

Innovation at Apple and IBM. R. A. Shaffer. il *Personal Computing* 13:45-6 S '89

Interview: Alan Kay. D. Sobel. il por *Omni (New York, N.Y.)* 12:80-2+ N '89

John Sculley on sabbatical. B. O'Reilly. il por *Fortune* 119:79-80 Mr 27 '89

Macinations. D. E. Crabb. See issues of Byte beginning August 1988

Macintosh special edition. il *Byte* 14 Mac Special Ed:MAC217+ Je '89

Macintosh special edition. il *Byte* 14 Mac Special Ed:MAC1-MAC2+ Mr '89

Macintosh special supplement. il *Byte* 14 Mac Special Supp:MAC185+ Ag '89

A Macintosh who's who. T. Thompson. il *Byte* 14:146-7 Je '89

Seeking Buddha in the details [J. Gassée] J. Littman. por *Personal Computing* 13:77 Jl '89

Selling look and feel. J. Pitta. il *Forbes* 144:229 O 2 '89

Suddenly, the PC juggernaut is stuck in the mud. D. A. Depke and others. il *Business Week* p45 D 25 '89-Ja 1 '90

A teacher for Apple. A. Edmond, Jr. il pors *Black Enterprise* 19:176-8 F '89

Why Apple went sour. M. Shao. il *Business Week* p30-1 F 13 '89

APPLE COMPUTER INC.—*cont.*
Why don't we do it in the courts? [Apple Corps records sues Apple Computer in trade name dispute] *Newsweek* 113:44 Mr 6 '89

Anecdotes, facetiae, satire, etc.
Mice in the kitchen. D. Gookin. *Compute!* 11:143 N '89

APPLE CORPS LTD.
Why don't we do it in the courts? [Apple Corps records sues Apple Computer in trade name dispute] *Newsweek* 113:44 Mr 6 '89

APPLE DESSERTS *See* Desserts
APPLE DUMPLINGS *See* Dumplings
APPLE FRUIT FLIES *See* Fruit flies
APPLE JUICE
Apple juice. il *Consumer Reports* 54:237-41 D '89
Apple juice: a long way from the tree. il *Consumer Reports* 54:293-4 My '89

Labeling
Bad apples: in the executive suite [Beech-Nut bogus apple juice case] il *Consumer Reports* 54:294-6 My '89

APPLE TREES
Grafting apples. J. Vara. il *Country Journal* 16:44-9 Mr/Ap '89
Picking the best apples. il *Southern Living* 24:72 Ja '89
Training "5-n-1" fruit trees [grafting] I. Merwin. il *Organic Gardening* 36:34-5 Mr '89

APPLEBY, R. SCOTT
about
Unflinching faith: what fires up the world's fundamentalists? [interview; cover story] il por *U.S. Catholic* 54:6-13 D '89

APPLEGATE, CHRISTINA
about
Christina Applegate. T. Carlson. por *TV Guide* 37:6 S 23-29 '89
Married . . . with children's Christina Applegate is no sexpot, except, um, for that poster. J. Stark. il pors *People Weekly* 32:129-30 D 4 '89

APPLEGATE, LIZ
A never-drag-again eating plan. il *Health (New York, N.Y.)* 21:52-3 F '89
Nutrition. See issues of Runner's World
(jt. auth) See Stern, Judith S., and Applegate, Liz

APPLES
See also
Apple trees
Cooking—Fruit
Apple country [Carolina mountains] K. Boling. il *Southern Living* 24:162 N '89

Contamination
The Alar debate [with reply by M. Stanton Evans] E. Groth, III. *Consumers' Research Magazine* 72:28-30 Jl '89
Alar: not gone, not forgotten [cover story] il *Consumer Reports* 54:288-92 My '89
Apples without Alar. il *Newsweek* 114:86 O 30 '89
Bad apples [daminozide] R. Coorsh. il *Consumers' Research Magazine* 72:4 Ap '89
Daminozide: now you see it . . . *Science News* 135:155 Mr 11 '89
Does everything cause cancer? [Alar in apples and other carcinogens; cover story; special section] il *Consumers' Research Magazine* 72:11-18 My '89
The EPA is looking for a few bad apples [effects of chemical Alar] *Newsweek* 113:65 F 13 '89
Risky business [Alar and cancer] T. Beardsley. *Scientific American* 260:35-6 My '89

Diseases and pests
Apples, worms, and synthetic mating hormones. il *Sunset (Central West edition)* 182:200-1 Mr '89

APPLES IN DECORATION *See* Fruits, vegetables, etc. in decoration

APPLETALK (LOCAL AREA NETWORK)
Hands-on parallel processing [hypercube system using Macs and AppleTalk] G. C. Fox and others. bibl f il *Byte* 14:287-93 O '89
LAN aid: Mac booster modules [DaynaTalk and FlashBox] T. Thompson. il *Byte* 14:219-20+ N '89
Two tin cans and some string. R. Grehan. il *Byte* 14:303-4+ O '89

APPLETON, MARC
about
Project: Marc Appleton: plans for a producer's dream estate. il por *Architectural Digest* 46:82-3 Ag '89

APPLEWORKS (COMPUTER PROGRAM)
AppleWorks gets a makeover [GS] D. Kovacs. il *Home Office Computing* 7:78+ O '89
AppleWorks GS. G. Keizer. il *Compute!* 11:69-70 Mr '89
TimeOut SpreadTools, MacroTools, and MacroTools II. V. D. O'Connor. il *Compute!* 11:64-5 Jl '89

APPLIANCES, HOUSEHOLD *See* Household appliances
APPLIANCES, PERSONAL CARE *See* Personal care appliances
APPLICATIONS FOR POSITIONS *See* Job applications
APPLIED MICROBIOLOGY INC.
This biotech baby is growing up fast. G. G. Marcial. *Business Week* p86 Ja 23 '89

APPLIED SCIENCE *See* Technology
APPLIQUÉ WORK
One-of-a-kind appliqués as Christmas cards. il *Sunset (Central West edition)* 183:134 N '89

APPOINTMENT BOOKS *See* Datebooks
APPORTIONMENT (ELECTION LAW)
See also
Gerrymander
Census and citizenship [counting of illegal aliens for purposes of congressional apportionment] *National Review* 41:14+ S 29 '89
Come to our census! [reapportionment of congressional seats after 1990 census] A. F. Lewis. *Ms.* 18:76 Jl/Ag '89

APPRAISAL, BUSINESS *See* Corporations—Valuation
APPRAISAL, REAL PROPERTY *See* Real property—Valuation
APPRAISAL OF EMPLOYEES *See* Employees—Rating
APPRAISERS
Ethical aspects
Real estate appraisals. S. J. Ackerman. il *Consumers' Research Magazine* 72:16-18 F '89

APPRECIATION OF ART *See* Art—Appreciation
APPRENTICES
International aspects
International developments in apprenticeship. M. Brodsky. il *Monthly Labor Review* 112:40-1 Jl '89
Great Britain
History
A social contract? Master against servant in the Court of Requests [case of Bristol notary W. Yeamans and his apprentice T. Alford] P. S. Seaver. il *History Today* 39:50-6 S '89

APPROACH PLATE BOOKS *See* Aviation charts
APPROACHING ZANZIBAR [drama] *See* Howe, Tina
APPROPRIATIONS COMMITTEE (HOUSE) *See* United States. Congress. House. Committee on Appropriations
L'APRÈS-MIDI D'UN FAUNE [ballet] *See* Ballet reviews—Single works
APRICOTS
Hybrids
Apricot crossed with a plum? [apriums, pluots, and plumcots] il *Sunset (Central West edition)* 182:140 Ja '89

APRIL
The April almanac. il *The Atlantic* 263:12 Ap '89
APS *See* American Physical Society
APTED, MICHAEL
about
Gorillas in the mist [film] Reviews
Video il 13:64 Je '89. S. L. Siegel

APTER, JEFF
'Worse than Robben Island'. *The Progressive* 53:15-16 Jl '89

APTITUDE TESTS
See also
General Aptitude Test Battery
Scholastic Aptitude Test
IQ and intelligence: what's wrong with testing? [excerpt from More like us] J. M. Fallows. *Current (Washington, D.C.)* 315:4-10 S '89
Might you be happier doing something else? [job aptitude tests] S. Chan. *Working Woman* 14:119+ Ap '89
The Perfect Career [computer program] H. E. H. Aycock. il *Compute!* 11:72-3 Mr '89
What can a test tell you? [job aptitude] E. McGrath. *New Choices for the Best Years* 29:49 S '89
What's wrong with testing? [excerpt from More like us] J. M. Fallows. *The Washington Monthly* 21:12-14+ My '89

APTUS (FIRM)
An executive turns puzzle maker [W. Harms] D. E. Gumpert and D. Davis. il por *New Choices for the Best Years* 29:50-1 O '89

AQUACISES *See* Water exercises
AQUACULTURE
See also
Fish culture
Field of fish [special section] D. Florio. il *Health (New York, N.Y.)* 21:71-7+, 94 My '89

AQUANAUTICS CORPORATION
Artificial gill. D. Stover. il *Popular Science* 234:121-3+ Ap '89

AQUARIUM (MUSICAL GROUP)
Glasnost rock [B. Grebenshikov] F. Rose. il pors *New York* 22:56-60+ Mr 20 '89

AQUARIUMS
See also
Maritime Center (Norwalk, Conn.)
New England Aquarium
Sea World (Orlando, Fla.)
Aquariums. See issues of Oceans beginning January/February 1987 through September/October 1989
Flashy new 'items' make a big splash in the aquarium world [home aquariums] R. Conniff. il *Smithsonian* 20:90-4+ My '89
Starting an aquarium. S. L. Gerstenfeld. il *Parents* 64:250 My '89

AQUATIC BIOLOGY
See also
Marine biology

AQUATIC BIOLOGY—See also—*cont.*
Marine fauna
AQUATIC ECOSYSTEMS *See* Marine ecology
AQUATIC PLANTS
See also
Algae
Duckweeds
Kariba weeds
Lotus
Water gardens and gardening
Water hyacinths
Water lilies
AQUATIC SPORTS
See also
Boats and boating
Diving
Rowing
Sailing
Skin diving
Surfing
Swimming
Water skiing
Come on in, the water's fine! N. R. Gibbs. il *Time* 134:80-1
Ag 14 '89
Water: a summerful of ways to enjoy it. il *Glamour* 87:146-51
Jl '89

Equipment
See also
Jet skis
Great gear. J. Wooldridge. il *Popular Mechanics* 166:104-6+
F '89

Photographs and photography
You are there! [use of remote-control, helmet-mounted camera]
R. Doyle. il *Petersen's Photographic Magazine* 18:14-16
Ag '89
AQUATIC WEED CONTROL
Waterweed invasions [kariba weed and water hyacinth] S.
C. H. Barrett. bibl il map *Scientific American* 261:90-7
O '89
AQUATIC WEEDS
Walleyes for shore. J. Weiss. il *Outdoor Life* 183:79+ Ap
'89
AQUAVIT
Don't blame me, I'm Swedish. P. Nelson. il *Esquire* 111:29
F '89
AQUEDUCTS
The Roman aqueduct of Nîmes. G. F. W. Hauck. bibl
f map *Scientific American* 260:98-100+ Mr '89
AQUINAS, THOMAS *See* Thomas, Aquinas, Saint, 1225?-1274
AQUINO, BELINDA A.
Democracy in the Philippines. bibl f *Current History* 88:181-4+
Ap '89
AQUINO, CORAZON
about
Aquino's new economic agenda. M. Feria. *World Press Review*
36:54 My '89
Cory's coup. W. S. Thompson. il *National Review* 41:18-19
D 31 '89
Democracy in peril. M. Nemeth. il *Maclean's* 102:39 D
11 '89
Democracy in the Philippines. B. A. Aquino. bibl f *Current
History* 88:181-4+ Ap '89
George Bush's thriller in Manila. il por *U.S. News & World
Report* 107:14-15 D 11 '89
A hard-fought victory. M. Nemeth. il *Maclean's* 102:26+
D 18 '89
Letter from the Philippines. S. Blaustein. *The New Yorker*
65:95-106 D 18 '89
The Philippine rebels aimed for Aquino—but hit the economy.
K. S. Barnes and D. J. Yang. por *Business Week* p68
D 18 '89
Plenty of nice people. D. Murphy. *America* 160:150-2 F
18 '89
Shoot-out in Manila. C. S. Manegold. il map por *Newsweek*
114:56-8 D 11 '89
So much for people power. C. S. Manegold. il por *Newsweek*
114:38-9 D 18 '89
Soldier power. H. G. Chua-Eoan. il map por *Time* 134:50-2
D 11 '89
There is always a next time. H. G. Chua-Eoan. il por *Time*
134:28-9 D 18 '89
Visit to the United States, 1989
No thrilla in Manila [with interview] D. J. Yang and K.
S. Barnes. il por *Business Week* p64+ N 6 '89
ARAB AMERICANS
See also
American-Arab Anti-Discrimination Committee
I am not a terrorist. E. M. Collier. il *Glamour* 87:135 Ag
'89
Political activities
Casey Kasem's flip side. B. Ohanian. il pors *Mother Jones*
14:21-3+ O '89
ARAB CIVILIZATION *See* Civilization, Arab
ARAB COUNTRIES
See also
Oman
Saudi Arabia

Foreign relations
Israel
See Jewish-Arab relations
History
See also
World War, 1914-1918—Campaigns and battles—Arab
countries
Industries
See also
Airlines—Arab countries
Israeli occupation, 1967-
See Israel-Arab Wars, 1967- —Territorial questions
Nationalism
Self-determination, Arab style. D. Pryce-Jones. *Commentary*
87:39-46 Ja '89
Politics and government
See also
Arab League
Trapped between prison and anarchy. F. Ajami. il *U.S.
News & World Report* 107:31 O 9 '89
ARAB-ISRAEL WAR, 1948-1949 *See* Israel-Arab War, 1948-
1949
ARAB-ISRAEL WARS, 1967- *See* Israel-Arab Wars, 1967-
ARAB-JEWISH RELATIONS *See* Jewish-Arab relations
ARAB LEAGUE
Beleaguered Beirut [calls another ceasefire] L. Marlowe. il
Maclean's 102:26-7 My 8 '89
A struggle for unity. M. Nemeth. il *Maclean's* 102:25 Je
5 '89
ARAB REBELLION, 1936-1939 *See* Palestine—History—Arab
rebellion, 1936-1939
ARAB TERRORISTS *See* Terrorists, Arab
ARABIA (STEAMSHIP)
Raise the Arabia! K. Lohr. il *The Saturday Evening Post*
261:48-9+ Jl/Ag '89
ARABIAN HORSES *See* Horses
ARABIC LITERATURE
Interview with Najib Mahfouz. V. Massuh. il por *The Unesco
Courier* 42:4-6 D '89
ARABIC MATHEMATICS *See* Mathematics, Arabic
ARABIDOPSIS *See* Mouse ear cress
ARABS
See also
Bedouins
Jewish-Arab relations
Palestinian Arabs
United States
See also
Arab Americans
ARABS IN MOTION PICTURES
An Orient of myth and mystery. A. Fahdel. il *The Unesco
Courier* 42:24-9 O '89
ARACHIDONIC ACID
Arachidonic acid and other fatty acids directly activate
potassium channels in smooth muscle cells. R. W. Ordway
and others. bibl f il *Science* 244:1176-9 Je 9 '89
Potassium channels in cardiac cells activated by arachidonic
acid and phospholipids. D. Kim and D. E. Clapham.
bibl f il *Science* 244:1174-6 Je 9 '89
Treatment with tin prevents the development of hypertension
in spontaneously hypertensive rats. D. Sacerdoti and others.
bibl f il *Science* 243:388-90 Ja 20 '89
ARACHNIDS
See also
Eye—Arachnids
Mites
Spiders
Habits and behavior
Games spiders play [use of game theory to predict fighting
among woodland spiders; research by Susan E. Riechert]
J. A. Miller. *BioScience* 39:225 Ap '89
Metabolism
Run, arachnids, run! [low stamina of spiders due to anaerobic
metabolism; research by Kenneth Prestwich] *Discover* 10:12+
Ag '89
ARAD, RON, 1951-
about
Man of steel. N. Shulman. il por *Harper's Bazaar* 122:130
S '89
ARADER, W. GRAHAM, III
about
'Arader is up again!' and his galleries are in full bloom.
P. Patton. il pors *Smithsonian* 20:86-92+ D '89
ARADER (W. GRAHAM III) GALLERY *See* W. Graham
Arader III Gallery
ARAFAT, YASIR, 1929-
about
Agonizing reappraisal in Israel [cover story] E. Salpeter. *The
New Leader* 72:5-6 Ja 9 '89
Arafat chic. *The New Republic* 200:8-9 Mr 6 '89
The Arafat shuffle. il *The New Republic* 200:9-10+ Ja 9-16
'89
Arafat to Israel: pardon my French. il por *Newsweek* 113:48
My 15 '89
Arafat's man in New York. D. Smith. il pors *New York*
22:40-6 Ja 23 '89
Arafat's types of ambiguity. A. Shammas. *Harper's* 278:60-1
Mr '89

ARAFAT, YASIR, 1929——about—*cont.*

Assembly renews call for Middle East peace conference. il *UN Chronicle* 26:50-4 Mr '89

At the end of his rope. A. Platt. il por *Newsweek* 114:35 S 18 '89

Beat the devil. A. Cockburn. *The Nation* 248:6-7 Ja 2 '89

Finding a response to Arafat's yes. J. B. Miller. *The Christian Century* 106:165-6 F 15 '89

How the PLO was legitimized [cover story] J. J. Kirkpatrick. *Commentary* 88:21-8 Jl '89

Indiana University to publish controversial Arafat biography. il por *Publishers Weekly* 235:43 F 17 '89

A letter to Yasir Arafat. M. Z. Rosensaft. por *Newsweek* 114:14 D 11 '89

Local hero. *The New Republic* 200:8+ F 20 '89

Masters of double-talk. il pors *Time* 134:30-1 Ag 7 '89

Middle East [statements and press conferences, November 26-December 18, 1988; special section] *Department of State Bulletin* 89:51-60 F '89

Next year in Jerusalem? [interview with Y. Arafat] J. Fuentes. il por *World Press Review* 36:29 Ap '89

Null and void. *Time* 133:45 My 15 '89

Old dogs, old tricks. *The New Republic* 200:10-12 Ja 30 '89

The Palestinians. il *World Press Review* 36:8+ Ja '89

The PLO [discussion of July 1989 article, How the PLO was legitimized] J. J. Kirkpatrick. *Commentary* 88:7-8 N '89

Saying no to Arafat. S. MacLeod. il pors *Time* 133:81-2 Ja 2 '89

Secretary's interview on "This week with David Brinkley" [interview with G. P. Shultz; transcript of program, December 4, 1988] *Department of State Bulletin* 89:7-9 F '89

Send in the pols. J. Klein. il por *New York* 22:10-11 Ja 9 '89

Setting Yasser straight. S. Weller. il pors *Ms.* 17:84 Mr '89

Should we trust Yasir Arafat? D. Reed. por *Reader's Digest* 135:143-8 S '89

A talk with Arafat [cover story] R. O. Freedman. il *The New York Review of Books* 36:8+ Ap 13 '89

Virtuoso transformations. S. Talbott. il *Time* 133:36 Ja 9 '89

What America should say to Arafat. R. N. Perle. il por *U.S. News & World Report* 106:58-9 Mr 20 '89

Why should Israel trust the PLO? B. Amiel. il *Maclean's* 102:9 Je 5 '89

ARANSAS NATIONAL WILDLIFE REFUGE (TEX.)

Barges, boats and big birds [boat traffic on the Gulf Intracoastal Waterway eroding whooping crane habitat] T. Turner. il *The Mother Earth News* 118:112 Jl/Ag '89

ARASKOG, RAND V.

How I fought off the raiders [excerpts from The ITT wars] il pors *Fortune* 119:110-12+ F 27 '89

about

Are raiders ready to take on ITT again? G. G. Marcial. il *Business Week* p130 Ap 24 '89

ARAUJO, CARLOS A. PAZ DE *See* Paz de Araujo, Carlos A.

ARBEL, AVNER, 1935-

about

Avner Arbel's crystal ball. M. Schifrin. *Forbes* 144:374 N 13 '89

Dangerously inefficient. M. Schifrin. il por *Forbes* 144:60-1 Jl 10 '89

ARBETTER, SANDRA R.

Confessions of a whiz kid. il *Current Health 2* 15:25-7 F '89

Eating cues. il *Current Health 2* 16:25-7 O '89

Eating disorders: emotional food fights [cover story] bibl il *Current Health 2* 15:4-10 Mr '89

Schizophrenia: fact vs. fantasy. il *Current Health 2* 16:23-5 S '89

The way it is: the remarried family. il *Current Health 2* 15:17-19 Mr '89

ARBITRAGE

See also

Sports arbitrage

Arb no more [Comdisco's K. Pontikes] J. Zweig. il por *Forbes* 144:348 N 13 '89

The balloon bursts for Wall Street arbs. J. Egan. il *U.S. News & World Report* 107:71 N 6 '89

Being an arb without turning pro. L. J. Nathans. *Business Week* p136 F 27 '89

How d'ya say "liquidator" in Japanese? [I. Jacobs plays Tokyo-New York arbitrage in raids on Shaklee and Avon] S. Flack. il por *Forbes* 143:39-40 Je 12 '89

Is program trading the target of a 'witch-hunt'? G. Weiss. il *Business Week* p122-3 N 13 '89

A new kind of arbitrage [discrepancy between Tokyo and New York P/Es] E. Sturza. il *Forbes* 144:128 Jl 10 '89

Premium pricing [Tokyo/New York arbitrage play in American Family Corp. shares] S. N. Chakravarty. *Forbes* 144:261 O 30 '89

Sayonara [New York-Tokyo arbitrage played by Honeywell] S. Flack. il *Forbes* 144:10 Ag 21 '89

ARBITRATION, COMMERCIAL

Battling your broker just got a bit easier [SEC rules] L. Zinn. *Business Week* p142 Je 5 '89

Wall Street's other arbs [stockholders vs. brokers in arbitration] E. Giltenan. il *Forbes* 143:196-7 Mr 20 '89

ARBITRATION, INDUSTRIAL

See also

Collective bargaining

ARBITRATION, SPORTS

A crucial inning for baseball. W. C. Symonds. il por *Business Week* p90 O 23 '89

ARBITRATION AND AWARD

Have a dispute? Try mediation. il *Modern Maturity* 32:88 Ag/S '89

A kinder claims court [alternative dispute resolution] il *Esquire* 112:128 S '89

ARBITRON RATINGS COMPANY

Denver does ScanAmerica. M. Couzens. *Channels (New York, N.Y.: 1986)* 9:24 N '89

Want a local meter? [ScanAmerica] M. Couzens. il *Channels (New York, N.Y.: 1986)* 9:26 Ja '89

ARBOR DRUGS, INC.

Arbor flowers. T. Jaffe. il *Forbes* 143:346 My 29 '89

ARBORETUMS

See also

North Carolina State University at Raleigh. Arboretum

ARBORS

Arbors and lattice. il *Sunset (Central West edition)* 182:166-7 F '89

Outer spaces. J. Truini. il *Home Mechanix* 85:44-51 Ag '89

ARBY'S INC.

Fed-up franchisees: they're mad as hell and . . . G. DeGeorge. il por *Business Week* p83+ N 13 '89

ARCADES

Tunnel visions [Paris arcades] P. S. Green. il *House & Garden* 161:164-5 Jl '89

ARCAND, DENYS

about

Jesus of Montreal [film] Reviews

Maclean's il 102:74 S 18 '89. B. D. Johnson

Maclean's il por 102:54-5 My 29 '89. B. D. Johnson

ARCATA (CALIF.)

Sanitary affairs

A swamp makes waste to be sweet again [Arcata Marsh and Wildlife Sanctuary] J. Willwerth. il *Time* 133:10+ Mr 20 '89

ARCATA GRAPHICS CO.

Arcata improves its round-backing capability. J. P. Frank. il *Publishers Weekly* 235:62 Je 2 '89

ARCATA MARSH AND WILDLIFE SANCTUARY (CALIF.)

A swamp makes waste to be sweet again. J. Willwerth. il *Time* 133:10+ Mr 20 '89

ARCHAEBACTERIA

See also

Halobacteria

ARCHAEOLOGY *See* Archeology

ARCHAEOMETRY

Authenticating ancient marble sculpture. S. V. Margolis. bibl il map *Scientific American* 260:104-10 Je '89

ARCHAEOPTERYX *See* Birds, Fossil

ARCHBISHOPS *See* Bishops

ARCHE DE LA DÉFENSE (PARIS, FRANCE)

Paris' new arch. J. Pierrard. il *World Press Review* 36:73 N '89

ARCHED BRIDGES *See* Bridges

ARCHEOLOGICAL HOAXES *See* Hoaxes

ARCHEOLOGICAL PILLAGE *See* Pillage

ARCHEOLOGISTS

See also

Chase, Arlen

Erim, Kenan T.

Executives as archeologists

Heafitz, Bruce

Korfmann, Manfred

ARCHEOLOGISTS, AMATEUR

Going digging. il *Sunset (Central West edition)* 182:74+ Ap '89

ARCHEOLOGY

See also

Anthropology

Antiquities

Art, Prehistoric

Belize—Antiquities

Bronze Age

Caracol site (Belize)

Cave drawings and paintings

Chile—Antiquities

Colorado—Antiquities

Crete—Antiquities

Czechoslovakia—Antiquities

Easter Island—Antiquities

Egypt—Antiquities

Florence (Italy)—Antiquities

Guatemala—Antiquities

Iron Age

Israel—Antiquities

Jerusalem—Antiquities

ARCHEOLOGY—See also—*cont.*
Kelheim (Germany)—Antiquities
Kentucky—Antiquities
Lincoln (England)—Antiquities
London (England)—Antiquities
Man, Prehistoric
Maui (Hawaii)—Antiquities
Mayas—Antiquities
Megalithic monuments
Montana—Antiquities
Mummies
New Mexico—Antiquities
Nîmes (France)—Roman antiquities
Paris (France)—Antiquities
Peru—Antiquities
Petroglyphs
Pompeii (Ancient city)
Roman antiquities
Rome (Italy)—Antiquities
Stele (Archeology)
Stone Age
Stone implements and weapons
Yucatan (Mexico: State)—Antiquities
Anecdotes, facetiae, satire, etc.
Last word. M. Coleman and D. Jaffe. il *Omni (New York, N.Y.)* 11:110 Ja '89
Bibliography
1988 Archaeological Book of the Year Award. A. Selkirk. il *History Today* 39:51 Ja '89
Methodology
See also
Accelerator mass spectrometry—Archeological use
Archaeometry
Polymerase chain reaction—Archeological use
Getting the lead out [comparison of modern and ancient lead levels; research by Jonathon E. Ericson] B. Bower. *Science News* 135:44 Ja 21 '89
Modern humans take a spin back in time [electron spin resonance dating of Skhul site; research by Christopher B. Stringer] B. Bower. *Science News* 135:263 Ap 29 '89
Revealing the ancient world through high technology. V. Lightfoot and D. Lightfoot. il *Technology Review* 92:54-61 My/Je '89
Philosophy
One world archaeology. P. J. Ucko. il *History Today* 39:10-12 Mr '89
ARCHEOLOGY, ASTRONOMICAL *See* Astronomy, Ancient
ARCHEOLOGY, SUBMARINE
See also
Arabia (Steamship)
Bismarck (Battleship)
Central America (Steamship)
City of Rio de Janeiro (Ship)
Kronan (Ship)
Pandora (Ship)
Titanic (Steamship)
Treasure trove
Boat resurfaces at Sea of Galilee. B. Bower. *Science News* 135:44 Ja 21 '89
Civilization under the sea. G. F. Bass. bibl il por *Modern Maturity* 32:58-64 Ap/My '89
Heyday of the horse ferry [teamboat discovered on bottom of Lake Champlain] D. G. Shomette. il map *National Geographic* 176:548-56 O '89
Is a treasure hunter's gain history's loss? B. Carpenter. il *U.S. News & World Report* 107:54-5 Ag 21 '89
ARCHER, ANNE
about
Anne Archer. B. Allen. il por *Ms.* 17:76-8 Ja/F '89
ARCHER, DAVE
about
Current affairs. A. McDonald. il por *Omni (New York, N.Y.)* 11:66-71 S '89
ARCHER-DANIELS-MIDLAND CO.
A bag battle pits Big Oil vs. Big Ag [Archer-Daniels-Midland Co.'s biodegradable trash bags threaten conventional bag manufacturers] P. Sherrid. il *U.S. News & World Report* 106:52 Ap 24 '89
ARCHER M. HUNTINGTON ART GALLERY (AUSTIN, TEX.)
Collecting the West [C. R. Smith Collection of Western American art; cover story] R. H. Saunders. il *American History Illustrated* 23:22-33 Ja '89
ARCHERY
See also
Hunting with bow and arrow
Psychological aspects
Finding 'the zone'. L. Shainberg. il pors *The New York Times Magazine* p34-6+ Ap 9 '89
Study and teaching
Practical bow practice. J. Barsness. il *Field & Stream* 94:54-5+ My '89
ARCHES
See also
Gateway Arch (Saint Louis, Mo.)
ARCHES, TRIUMPHAL AND MEMORIAL
See also
Arche de la Défense (Paris, France)

ARCHEY, WILLIAM T.
about
What to expect from EC92 [interview] por *Nation's Business* 77:24 Je '89
ARCHIBALD, NOLAN D.
about
Black & Decker cuts a neat dovetail joint. J. Weber, Jr. il por *Business Week* p52-3 Jl 31 '89
The new power in Black & Decker. J. Huey. il por *Fortune* 119:89-91+ Ja 2 '89
ARCHIBALD PRIZE
People's choice. J. Turner. il *Art News* 88:18 Mr '89
ARCHITECTS
See also
Ambasz, Emilio
American Institute of Architects
Arad, Ron, 1951-
Architectural firms
Berkus, Barry A.
Bill, Max, 1908-
Binazzi, Lapo, 1943-
Brown, Terry
Bullfinch, Charles
Calatrava, Santiago, 1951-
Cardinal, Douglas
Davis, Alexander Jackson, 1803-1892
Eisenman, Peter, 1932-
Erickson, Arthur, 1924-
Ferri, Roger C., 1949-
Fontaine, Pierre François Léonard, 1762-1853
Foster, Norman, 1935-
Freed, James Ingo, 1930-
Gaudí, Antoni, 1852-1926
Gehry, Frank
Giurgola, Romaldo, 1920-
Goff, Bruce, 1904-1982
Gough, Piers, 1946-
Grimshaw, Nicholas Thomas
Gropius, Walter, 1883-1969
Harrison, Wallace Kirkman, 1895-1981
Holl, Steven, 1947-
Isozaki, Arata
Israel, Franklin David, 1945-
Jacobsen, Hugh Newell
Jencks, Charles, 1939-
Johnson, Philip Cortelyou, 1906-
Jones, Fay, 1921-
Lapidus, Alan H.
Lautner, John
Le Corbusier, 1887-1965
Leathers, Robert
Lutyens, Sir Edwin Landseer, 1869-1944
Mackintosh, Charles Rennie, 1868-1928
Maki, Fumihiko, 1928-
May, Clifford, 1908-
McIntire, Samuel, 1757-1811
Meier, Richard, 1934-
Mendelsohn, Erich, 1887-1953
Mollino, Carlo, 1905-1973
Morgan, Sherley Warner
Ott, Carlos
Outram, John, 1934-
Palladio, Andrea, 1508-1580
Pei, I. M., 1917-
Percier, Charles, 1764-1838
Perrault, Dominique, 1953-
Platonov, Yuri
Robertson, Jaquelin Taylor
Rogers, Richard, 1933-
Rudolph, Paul, 1918-
Rybczynski, Witold
Safdie, Moshe, 1938-
Schinkel, Karl Friedrich, 1781-1841
Shaw, Howard Van Doren, 1869-1926
Simon, Mark
Skolnick, Lee H.
Soleri, Paolo, 1919-
Solomon, Daniel
Stern, Robert A. M., 1939-
Stirling, James Frazer
Tapley, Charles Reilly, 1931-
Terry, Quinlan, 1937-
Terry, Roland, 1917-
Tigerman, Stanley, 1930-
Venturi, Robert
White, Stanford, 1853-1906
Wilkes, Kevin
Women architects
Wright, Frank Lloyd, 1867-1959
Design for eating [tableware] T. Hine. il *Gentlemen's Quarterly* 59:78+ N '89
Should future architects practice as generalists, specialists, or both? H. L. Smith, Jr. il *Architectural Record* 177:39 Ag '89
Legal status, laws, etc.
Architects, engineers, and the "practice overlap". M. F. Schmertz. *Architectural Record* 177:11 Jl '89

ARCHITECTS—Legal status, laws, etc.—*cont.*
Responsibility equals market opportunity? M. F. Schmertz. *Architectural Record* 177:9 N '89
Watch out for this new "model" owner/design-professional agreement [contract proposed for public work] A. Kornblut. il por *Architectural Record* 177:29+ F '89
When liability insurance can cover your construction-cost estimate problems. A. Kornblut. por *Architectural Record* 177:31 Ap '89
Who will design buildings for human habitation? (I) [interview with M. Lunch] C. M. Sapers. pors *Architectural Record* 177:41+ Je '89
Who will design buildings for human habitation? (II) [interview with M. Lunch] C. M. Sapers. il por *Architectural Record* 177:41-2 Jl '89
The whole building industry heats up over new contracts for public work. P. Hoffmann. *Architectural Record* 177:31 S '89

Licenses and registration
See also
National Council of Architectural Registration Boards
The ability to practice as a corporation gains new impetus. C. M. Sapers. il *Architectural Record* 177:39 S '89

Training
See Architecture—Study and teaching

ARCHITECTS & DESIGNERS BUILDING (NEW YORK, N.Y.)
In passing [lobby and facade renovation] M. Gaskie. il *Architectural Record* 177:64-7 mid-S '89

ARCHITECTS' CONTRACTS *See* Building—Contracts and specifications

ARCHITECTS' OFFICES
Two partners, one floor plan [office of K. Quinn and L. Searl] L. Rosch. il por *Working Woman* 14:69 Ja '89

ARCHITECTURAL ACOUSTICS *See* Acoustics, Architectural

ARCHITECTURAL COMPETITIONS *See* Architecture—Competitions

ARCHITECTURAL CONFERENCES *See* Architecture—Conferences

ARCHITECTURAL DESIGN
See also
Architectural drawing
Designer's Saturday

ARCHITECTURAL DIGEST
Professional space, personal grace. L. Rosch. il pors *Working Woman* 14:94-5 Je '89

ARCHITECTURAL DRAWING
See also
Pattern books

Collectors and collecting
Works on paper by contemporary architects [B. Pine's collection] P. Goldberger. il por *Architectural Digest* 46:198+ N '89

Exhibitions
Art [G. Weiss organizes exhibit of proposals to link the Diomede Islands] N. Princenthal. il por *Vogue* 179:140+ Je '89
The brio of a great all-rounder [work of I. Jones] R. Hughes. il *Time* 133:125 My 22 '89
Design awards/competitions: architecture in perspective III [1988 competition exhibition of the American Society of Architectural Perspectivists] il *Architectural Record* 177:48-9 F '89
Fall into the gap [Exhibition Diomede at the Clocktower] K. Larson. il *New York* 22:99 Je 5 '89
John Hejduk at Max Profetch. E. Saxon. il *Art in America* 77:164-5 F '89

ARCHITECTURAL EDUCATION *See* Architecture—Study and teaching

ARCHITECTURAL ENGINEERING *See* Structural engineering

ARCHITECTURAL FIRMS
See also
Ace Architects
Agrest & Gandelsonas
Arquitectonica International Corporation
Art In Construction (Firm)
Bentley-LaRosa-Salasky Design
Ellerbe Becket Inc.
Fernau & Hartman Architects
Jules Fisher & Paul Marantz, Inc.
MGS Architects
Morphosis (Firm)
Murray & Associates
Osborn Engineering Company
P. Michael Marino Associates
Page-Zebrowski Architects
Perkins Geddis Eastman (Firm)
Quinn and Searl, Architects
Shope Reno Wharton Associates

Export-import trade
The market for American architectural services in Japan comes of age. A. A. Layne. il *Architectural Record* 177:33+ Mr '89

Federal aid
Brokers at HUD illustrate the architects' dilemma: just whose services are worth the most? C. Pearson. il *Architectural Record* 177:29+ S '89

Finance
Congress's initiatives seen as threats to small architectural firms and the costs of construction. P. Hoffmann. il *Architectural Record* 177:21 Ap '89

Management
Workable firm-ownership transitions through ESOPs. C. M. Sapers. por *Architectural Record* 177:37+ Ja '89

Marketing
Awards program reveals the latest techniques [Society for Marketing Professional Services] E. E. Burden. il *Architectural Record* 177:29+ Ja '89
Marketing survey produces answers—and questions? [AIA survey] C. K. Hoyt. il *Architectural Record* 177:27+ Mr '89
The myths and realities of how architectural services are sold. M. A. Cameron. il *Architectural Record* 177:40 O '89
Responsibility equals market opportunity? M. F. Schmertz. *Architectural Record* 177:9 N '89

Canada
See also
IKOY Partnership

Japan
The market for American architectural services in Japan comes of age. A. A. Layne. il *Architectural Record* 177:33+ Mr '89

ARCHITECTURAL FITTINGS *See* Building fittings

ARCHITECTURAL FORECASTING
On the home front. D. P. Wiener. il *U.S. News & World Report* 107:80 D 25 '89-Ja 1 '90

ARCHITECTURAL MODELS
See also
Origami architecture
Stadium models
Antiques: architectural models. N. F. Weber. il *Architectural Digest* 46:188-93+ Mr '89
Hometown, U.S.A. [model building design program] N. Rentschler. il *Compute!* 11:77-8 Je '89

Exhibitions
See also
Window on China (Taiwan)

ARCHITECTURAL RECORD (PERIODICAL)
In the public interest: recreational facilities [annual awards program] M. F. Schmertz. *Architectural Record* 177:9 Mr '89
In this issue [In the Public Interest Award; special issue] il *Architectural Record* 177:83-137 N '89
Record Houses 1989 [with introd. by Deborah Dietsch] il *Architectural Record* 177:41-113 mid-Ap '89
Record Interiors 1989 [cover story; special issue; with introd. by Karen D. Stein] il *Architectural Record* 177:49-125 mid-S '89

ARCHITECTURAL RENDERING *See* Architectural drawing

ARCHITECTURAL SCHOOLS
See also
University of Florida. College of Architecture

ARCHITECTURAL SOCIETIES
See also
American Institute of Architects
Build Boston (Organization)
Connecticut Society of Architects

ARCHITECTURE
See also
Airport buildings
Apartment houses
Arcades
Architects
Architectural drawing
Art and architecture
Art centers—Architecture
Art galleries and museums—Architecture
Bank buildings
Barns and stables—Architecture
Beach architecture
Building materials
Camp sites, facilities, etc.—Architecture
Carpentry
Castles
Ceilings
Centers for the performing arts
Churches (Buildings)
City halls—Architecture
City planning
Classicism in architecture
Clothing stores—Architecture
College architecture
Community centers—Architecture
Computers—Architectural use
Concert halls
Concrete construction
Copyright—Architecture
Courtyards
Desert architecture
Domes
Environmental engineering (Buildings)
Follies (Architecture)
Garden houses, shelters, etc.
Greenhouses

ARCHITECTURE—See also—cont.
  Gymnasiums
  Health facilities—Architecture
  Hillside architecture
  Hospitals—Architecture
  Hotels, motels, etc.—Architecture
  Information systems—Architectural use
  Lakeside architecture
  Landscape architecture
  Library architecture
  Lodges
  Palaces
  Pavilions
  Public buildings
  Pyramids
  Recreation centers
  Roofs and roofing
  School buildings
  Stone construction
  Theater buildings
  Walls
  Wood construction
The best of architecture [1988] il *Business Week* p129 Ja 9 '89

Archives
  See also
  Howard-Tilton Memorial Library. Southeastern Architectural Archive

Awards
  See also
  Pritzker Architecture Prize
  Southern Home Awards
  Western Home Awards
Awards program reveals the latest techniques [Society for Marketing Professional Services] E. E. Burden. il *Architectural Record* 177:29+ Ja '89
Design awards/competitions. See issues of Architectural Record
In the public interest: recreational facilities [Architectural record annual awards program] M. F. Schmertz. *Architectural Record* 177:9 Mr '89
In this issue [In the Public Interest Award; special issue] il *Architectural Record* 177:83-137 N '89
Record Houses 1989 [with introd. by Deborah Dietsch] il *Architectural Record* 177:41-113 mid-Ap '89

Bibliography
Architecture. P. Goldberger. il *The New York Times Book Review* 94:21+ D 3 '89
Bringing architecture alive for young readers. il *Sunset (Central West edition)* 183:80 D '89
Exploring space. M. Sorkin. il *House & Garden* 161:80+ S '89

Competitions
Design awards/competitions. See issues of Architectural Record

Conferences
  See also
  Designer's Saturday
Calendar. See issues of Architectural Record

Conservation and restoration
  See also
  Barns and stables—Conservation and restoration
  Churches (Buildings)—Conservation and restoration
  Concert halls—Conservation and restoration
  Historic houses, sites, etc.
  Hotels, motels, etc.—Conservation and restoration
  Houses, Restored
  Opera houses—Conservation and restoration
  Theater buildings—Conservation and restoration
  Villages, Restored

Contracts and specifications
  See Building—Contracts and specifications

Designs and plans
  See also
  Architectural drawing
  Architecture, Domestic—Designs and plans
The pitfalls in protecting your designs from the clutches of others. S. A. Glazer. il *Architectural Record* 177:37+ My '89

Exhibitions
  See also
  Architectural drawing—Exhibitions
  Architecture, Domestic—Exhibitions
  Architecture, Modern—Exhibitions
Calendar. See issues of Architectural Record

History
  See also
  Heritage education

Mutilation, defacement, etc.
Doing right by Wright. E. M. Gomez. il *Art News* 88:36+ Ja '89

Periodicals
  See also
  Architectural record (Periodical)

Philosophy
Of detritus and denial [interview with F. Gehry] W. Meis and M. B. Snell. il *New Perspectives Quarterly* 5:57-60 Wint '88/'89

Social aspects
  See also
  Architecture and the handicapped
The house that dreams are made of [interview with W. Rybczynski] A. P. Sanoff. il por *U.S. News & World Report* 107:55 Jl 3 '89

Study and teaching
  See also
  Bauhaus
  Canadian Centre for Architecture (Montreal, Québec)
Should future architects practice as generalists, specialists, or both? H. L. Smith, Jr. il *Architectural Record* 177:39 Ag '89

Austria
  See also
  Vienna (Austria)—Architecture
Over the edge [Coop Himmelblau projects; cover story] K. D. Stein. il *Architectural Record* 177:82-91 Ag '89

Bahamas
  See also
  Nassau (Bahamas)—Architecture

California
  See also
  Beverly Hills (Calif.)—Architecture
  Brentwood (Los Angeles, Calif.)—Architecture
  Coronado (Calif.)—Architecture
  Hollywood (Calif.)—Architecture
  Irvine (Calif.)—Architecture
  Julian (Calif.)—Architecture
  Los Angeles (Calif.)—Architecture
  Montara (Calif.)—Architecture
  Nevada City (Calif.)—Architecture
  Palm Springs (Calif.)—Architecture
  Redding (Calif.)—Architecture
  Rutherford (Calif.)—Architecture
  San Francisco (Calif.)—Architecture
  Santa Barbara (Calif.)—Architecture
  Santa Monica (Calif.)—Architecture
  Sherman Oaks (Calif.)—Architecture
  Stinson Beach (Calif.)—Architecture
  Temecula (Calif.)—Architecture
California architecture. J. Chase. il *Art News* 88:138-43 D '89
California design [cover story; special issue] il *Architectural Digest* 46:36+ My '89
Design awards/competitions: 1989 CCAIA Design Awards. il *Architectural Record* 177:60-3 Jl '89

Colorado
  See also
  Telluride (Colo.)—Architecture

Connecticut
  See also
  New Canaan (Conn.)—Architecture

Florida
  See also
  Cocoa Beach (Fla.)—Architecture
  Indian Creek (Fla.)—Architecture
  Miami (Fla.)—Architecture
  Quincy (Fla.)—Architecture
  Seaside (Fla.)—Architecture
  West Palm Beach (Fla.)—Architecture
Florida Association/AIA 1989 Awards for Excellence in Architecture. il *Architectural Record* 177:62-4 N '89

France
  See also
  Oppède-le-Vieux (France)—Architecture
  Paris (France)—Architecture
Building an empire [work of architects C. Percier and P. F. L. Fontaine in early nineteenth century France] O. Bernier. il *House & Garden* 161:40+ D '89

Georgia
The Georgia Association/AIA 1988 Design Awards. il *Architectural Record* 177:52-3 Mr '89

Great Britain
  See also
  London (England)—Architecture
Charles and the 'carbuncle' [modern architecture] por *Newsweek* 114:37 S 18 '89
Charles: England's designing prince [A vision of Britain documentary] M. Filler. il pors *House & Garden* 161:158-61+ Mr '89
The prince and the architects [views of Prince Charles] C. Knevett. il *Architectural Record* 177:57+ O '89
Terry: keeper of the faith [English classical architect] M. Filler. il por *House & Garden* 161:162-3+ Mr '89
A vision of Britain—architecture in crisis [excerpt] Prince Charles. il pors *Architectural Digest* 46:32-4+ O '89
The winds of Windsorism [views of Prince Charles; cover story] H. Muschamp. *The New Republic* 201:30-5 D 11 '89

Illinois
  See also
  Chicago (Ill.)—Architecture
  Glencoe (Ill.)—Architecture

Israel
Pioneering the modern movement in Palestine [E. Mendelsohn] J. Rykwert. il por *Architectural Digest* 46:82+ O '89

ARCHITECTURE—*cont.*

Mississippi

See also
Jackson (Miss.)—Architecture

New Jersey

See also
Princeton (N.J.)—Architecture

New Mexico

See also
Albuquerque (N.M.)—Architecture
Santa Fe (N.M.)—Architecture

New York (State)

See also
Amagansett (N.Y.)—Architecture
Kings Point (N.Y.)—Architecture
New York (N.Y.)—Architecture
Woodstock (N.Y.)—Architecture

North Carolina

See also
Asheville (N.C.)—Architecture
Burnsville (N.C.)—Architecture

Ontario

See also
Ontario Association of Architects

Southeast Asia

Resolutely modernist [P. Rudolph; special section] M. F. Schmertz. il *Architectural Record* 177:74-85 Ja '89

Soviet Union

Gateway to a new detente [architect Y. Platonov's visit to the U.S.] M. F. Schmertz. *Architectural Record* 177:9 Je '89

Spain

An architect's impressions of Spain. A. M. Stern. il por *Architectural Digest* 46:128+ Mr '89

Tennessee

See also
Memphis (Tenn.)—Architecture
Nashville (Tenn.)—Architecture

Thailand

See also
Bangkok (Thailand)—Architecture

Washington (State)

See also
Port Blakely (Wash.)—Architecture
Yakima (Wash.)—Architecture

ARCHITECTURE, CLASSICAL

See also
Classicism in architecture
Neoclassicism (Architecture)

ARCHITECTURE, COMPUTER *See* Computer architecture

ARCHITECTURE, DOMESTIC

See also
Apartment houses
Apartments
Architects
Baubiologie
Beach architecture
Brick houses
Bungalows
Cabins
City houses
Concrete houses
Condominiums
Cottages
Country estates
Decks, patios, terraces, etc.
Farmhouses
Garages
Guest houses
Hillside architecture
House construction
Houses
Houses, Earth sheltered
Houses, Prefabricated
Houses, Remodeled
Housing
Lakeside architecture
Lodges
Loft apartments
Log cabins, houses, etc.
Model houses
Pole houses
Pyramid houses
Ranch houses
Row houses
Solar houses
Stone houses
Suburban homes
Two family houses
Vacation houses

The house of the future [postsuburbia] J. Adler. il *Newsweek* 114 Special Issue:72-6 Wint '89/Spr '90

The house that dreams are made of [interview with W. Rybczynski] A. P. Sanoff. il por *U.S. News & World Report* 107:55 Jl 3 '89

What you want in a new home today [design by Jack Bloodgood] S. Sheetz. il *Better Homes and Gardens* 67:95-102 My '89

Designs and plans

6 summer houses for year-round living. A. W. Lees. il *Popular Science* 234:128-32+ Ap '89

10 prizewinning new houses. J. McCloskey and W. L. Nolan. il *Better Homes and Gardens* 68:59-62+ F '89

All the comforts of home. il *Southern Living* 24:88 Ag '89

The Bel Air. il *Southern Living* 24:186 N '89

Classical style of the Delta. il *Southern Living* 24:140 Je '89

Federal house—Creole style. il *Southern Living* 24:152 Mr '89

A house for Monte Sano. il *Southern Living* 24:160 S '89

In the brick tradition. il *Southern Living* 24:116 Ja '89

Innovation house. T. Jackson. il *Better Homes and Gardens* 67:67-77 Mr '89

Louisiana plantation house. il *Southern Living* 24:102 F '89

On May Woods Lane [Memphis, Tenn.] il *Southern Living* 24:132 My '89

Our Folk Victorian Cottage. il *Southern Living* 24:116 Jl '89

Our southern homeplace. il *Southern Living* 24:94 O '89

Our Virginia homestead. il *Southern Living* 24:156 Ap '89

Project: Marc Appleton: plans for a producer's dream estate. il por *Architectural Digest* 46:82-3 Ag '89

Record Houses 1989 [with introd. by Deborah Dietsch] il *Architectural Record* 177:41-113 mid-Ap '89

Saddlebrook House. il *Southern Living* 24:94 D '89

Seaside sensation [cover story] il *Home Mechanix* 86:44-8+ Ap '89

Environmental engineering

See Environmental engineering (Buildings)

Exhibitions

40 years old, it's a "classic modern" [Case Study program exhibition at the Museum of Contemporary Art, Los Angeles] il *Sunset (Central West edition)* 183:224 O '89

Morphosis at the Walker Arts Center [Three houses exhibit] D. R. Suisman. il *Architectural Record* 177:65 Jl '89

Alabama

A house for Monte Sano. il *Southern Living* 24:160 S '89

Arizona

Owner-built, an eight-year labor of love. il *Sunset (Central West edition)* 183:134 O '89

Arkansas

See also
Little Rock (Ark.)—Architecture

Bahamas

See also
Nassau (Bahamas)—Architecture

Block Island (R.I.)

Block Island light [home of E. and G. Rigby-Leather] J. Kaplan. il pors *House & Garden* 161:84-91 Je '89

California

See also
Beverly Hills (Calif.)—Architecture
Brentwood (Los Angeles, Calif.)—Architecture
Coronado (Calif.)—Architecture
Hermosa Beach (Calif.)—Architecture
Hollywood (Calif.)—Architecture
Irvine (Calif.)—Architecture
Julian (Calif.)—Architecture
Los Angeles (Calif.)—Architecture
Malibu (Calif.)—Architecture
Montara (Calif.)—Architecture
Nevada City (Calif.)—Architecture
Palm Springs (Calif.)—Architecture
Redding (Calif.)—Architecture
Rutherford (Calif.)—Architecture
San Diego (Calif.)—Architecture
San Francisco (Calif.)—Architecture
Santa Barbara (Calif.)—Architecture
Santa Monica (Calif.)—Architecture
Sherman Oaks (Calif.)—Architecture
Stinson Beach (Calif.)—Architecture
Temecula (Calif.)—Architecture

After Fallingwater: a California house inspired by Frank Lloyd Wright [home of K. Behring decorated by Steve Chase] J. Chatfield-Taylor. il *Architectural Digest* 46:214-21 Mr '89

California design [cover story; special issue] il *Architectural Digest* 46:36+ My '89

Napa renewed [home of W. C. Swanson decorated by Thomas Britt] J. Simpson. il *Architectural Digest* 46:196-203 O '89

New house, classic craft [home based on designs of C. and H. Greene] P. Harper. il *Home Mechanix* 85:66-8+ F '89

The rambling ranch idea . . . updated in the wine country. il *Sunset (Central West edition)* 183:116-17 O '89

Ranch house with a veranda that invites you to slow down [Napa Valley] il *Sunset (Central West edition)* 183:102 O '89

Spacious, bold on a very tight beach lot. il *Sunset (Central West edition)* 183:122 O '89

Stucco compound rising out of Riverside County vineyard. il *Sunset (Central West edition)* 183:130-1 O '89

ARCHITECTURE, DOMESTIC—*cont.*

Cape Cod (Mass.)

Imagining Hill House. P. Theroux. il por *Architectural Digest* 46:32+ D '89

Seaside sensation [cover story] il *Home Mechanix* 86:44-8+ Ap '89

Catskill Mountains region (N.Y.)

Wildcat mountain [Catskills summer house] L. Auchincloss. il por *Architectural Digest* 46:29+ Je '89

Colorado

See also
Aspen (Colo.)—Architecture
Telluride (Colo.)—Architecture

Connecticut

The barn collectors [S. Spillane's and R. Leech's Connecticut house contructed of reassembled barns] M. Cantwell. il pors *House & Garden* 161:126-35 F '89

Fishers Island (N.Y.)

Gothic getaway [Charlotte McKim's Victorian home designed by M. Simon] M. Filler. il *House & Garden* 161:104-9 Je '89

Florida

See also
Cocoa Beach (Fla.)—Architecture
Indian Creek (Fla.)—Architecture
Miami (Fla.)—Architecture
Quincy (Fla.)—Architecture
Seaside (Fla.)—Architecture
Tampa (Fla.)—Architecture
West Palm Beach (Fla.)—Architecture

An airy Florida cottage. L. Hallam. il *Southern Living* 24:82-3 Je '89

France

See also
Oppède-le-Vieux (France)—Architecture
Paris (France)—Architecture

Georgia

Saddlebrook House. il *Southern Living* 24:94 D '89

Teammates [design by M. Louis Goodman] C. Vogel. il *The New York Times Magazine* p76-7 Jl 9 '89

Great Britain

See also
London (England)—Architecture

Great Cranberry Island (Me.)

Woodland boundary [Ward House] M. F. Schmertz. il *Architectural Record* 177:82-7 mid-Ap '89

Hawaii

Hawaiian H. il *Sunset (Central West edition)* 182:158-9 My '89

Illinois

See also
Chicago (Ill.)—Architecture
Glencoe (Ill.)—Architecture

Japan

An American builds in Japan [Lindal Cedar house] A. R. Gould. il *Workbench* 45:12 S/O '89

Lake Tahoe region (Calif. and Nev.)

Alpine echoes above Lake Tahoe [Carole and Robert McNeil's adapted alpine chalet designed by Valerian Rybar and Jean-François Daigre] J. Taylor. il *Architectural Digest* 46:84-91 Jl '89

Contemporary traditions on Lake Tahoe [lodge remodeled by Robert V. Arrigoni and decorated by Charles Pfister] J. Chatfield-Taylor. il *Architectural Digest* 46:270-5+ O '89

Long Island (N.Y.)

House of six gables [house on the North Shore] M. Gaskie. il *Architectural Record* 177:96-9 mid-Ap '89

Robert A. M. Stern: new interpretation of the shingle style on Long Island. K. Andersen. il por *Architectural Digest* 46:66-71+ Ag '89

Louisiana

The Bel Air. il *Southern Living* 24:186 N '89

Lively cottage for the weekend [Lake Pontchartrain; cover story] L. Hallam. il *Southern Living* 24:106-7 Jl '89

Louisiana plantation house. il *Southern Living* 24:102 F '89

Martha's Vineyard (Mass.)

Carly Simon's Vineyard. J. Brackman. il pors *House & Garden* 161:182-7+ N '89

Maryland

See also
Annapolis (Md.)—Architecture

Maui (Hawaii)

Maui vacation house is a five-unit compound. il *Sunset (Central West edition)* 182:80 Ja '89

Merritt Island (Fla.)

Cool house for a hot climate [Mark and Jennifer Zegels' home utilizes passive cooling] D. Stover. il *Popular Science* 235:74-5 Ag '89

Mississippi

See also
Jackson (Miss.)—Architecture

At home in the Delta [south Louisiana style] C. Engle. il *Southern Living* 24:90-3 My '89

Classical style of the Delta. il *Southern Living* 24:140 Je '89

Vernacular on a budget [country house near Meridian] L. Hallam. il *Southern Living* 24:160+ Ap '89

New Jersey

See also
Princeton (N.J.)—Architecture

Open house: hanging out new shingles [shingle style house designed by Lee Mindel] C. Vogel. il *The New York Times Magazine* p70-1 S 24 '89

New Mexico

See also
Albuquerque (N.M.)—Architecture

New York (State)

See also
East Hampton (N.Y.)—Architecture
Kings Point (N.Y.)—Architecture
Woodstock (N.Y.)—Architecture

Alan Flusser upstate: an offbeat cabin designed with humor in New York. S. M. L. Aronson. il pors *Architectural Digest* 46:192-7+ S '89

In the Wright spirit [Hudson River house by Theodore M. Ceraldi] A. Rieselbach. il *Architectural Record* 177:42-9 mid-Ap '89

Square roots [Hudson Valley home of Mark McDonald and Ralph Cutler] C. Vogel. il *The New York Times Magazine* p64-5 F 19 '89

North Carolina

See also
Asheville (N.C.)—Architecture
Burnsville (N.C.)—Architecture

Oregon

See also
Portland (Or.)—Architecture

Pennsylvania

Village of one's own [house of Stephen and Suzanne Jacobs designed by H. N. Jacobsen] J. Giovannini. il por *House & Garden* 161:116-23 Ap '89

Pocono Mountains region (Pa.)

Cozy comfort in the mountains [home of Steve and Geryl Deixler] M. Walker. il *New Choices for the Best Years* 29:33-4 Je '89

Rhode Island

See also
Newport (R.I.)—Architecture

San Juan Islands (Wash.)

In the San Juan Islands: driftwood and sod shape a Seattle architect's residence [home of R. Terry; cover story] J. Krakauer. il *Architectural Digest* 46:188-93 Je '89

Vacation house as summer camp. il *Sunset (Central West edition)* 183:94-5 O '89

Southern States

See also
Southern Home Awards

All the comforts of home. il *Southern Living* 24:88 Ag '89

Federal house—Creole style. il *Southern Living* 24:152 Mr '89

In the brick tradition. il *Southern Living* 24:116 Ja '89

Our southern homeplace. il *Southern Living* 24:94 O '89

The Twin Gables: back to basics [1988 Idea House built in conjunction with the American Wood Council] C. Engle. il *Southern Living* 24:100-2+ Ja '89

Southwestern States

Building with mud signifies success in the Southwest [adobes] D. J. Preston. il *Smithsonian* 20:144-8+ N '89

Tennessee

See also
Memphis (Tenn.)—Architecture

Texas

See also
Austin (Tex.)—Architecture

A house made by hand [East Texas home modeled on 1840 plantation house] E. Wood. il *Southern Living* 24:72-4 Ag '89

Thailand

See also
Bangkok (Thailand)—Architecture

United States

See Architecture, Domestic

Vermont

Warm elegance in ski country [home of Doris La Porte] O. Buehl. il *New Choices for the Best Years* 29:34-6 Je '89

Virginia

See also
Alexandria (Va.)—Architecture

Our Virginia homestead. il *Southern Living* 24:156 Ap '89

Washington (D.C.)

See Washington (D.C.)—Architecture

Washington (State)

See also
Port Blakely (Wash.)—Architecture
Seattle (Wash.)—Architecture
Yakima (Wash.)—Architecture

Planned for privacy on a shallow beach lot. il *Sunset (Central West edition)* 183:124 O '89

Vacation cottage with seaside lounging in mind. il *Sunset (Central West edition)* 183:118+ O '89

ARCHITECTURE, DOMESTIC—*cont.*
Western States
See also
Western Home Awards
ARCHITECTURE, ECCLESIASTICAL *See* Churches (Buildings)
ARCHITECTURE, FANTASTIC
The Ideal Palace: Ferdinand Cheval's fantasy in the Rhône Valley. Y. Blumenfeld. il *Architectural Digest* 46:108-13+ Ja '89
The postman's palace [Le Palais Idéal conceived by F. Cheval] B. Weber. il por *The New York Times Magazine* p122 S 10 '89
ARCHITECTURE, FEDERAL
Behind the Federal facade [houses designed by C. Bullfinch] A. O. Boulton. il pors *American Heritage* 40:68-75 My/Je '89
ARCHITECTURE, GEORGIAN
The best of Georgian. A. O. Boulton. il por *American Heritage* 40:110-17 F '89
A blow to Jamaica's treasure houses [Hurricane Gilbert's effect] A. R. Williams. il *Américas* 41 no1:8-13 '89
ARCHITECTURE, GOTHIC
See also
Cathedrals
ARCHITECTURE, GOTHIC REVIVAL
The Gothic awakening. A. O. Boulton. il *American Heritage* 40:140-8 N '89
ARCHITECTURE, GREEK REVIVAL
A. J. Davis and American classicism [cover story] C. S. Laise. bibl f il por *Antiques* 136:1320-33 D '89
A young nation builds its temples to the future. R. G. Kennedy. bibl (p230) il *Smithsonian* 20:170-5 O '89
ARCHITECTURE, MODERN
See also
Bauhaus
Deconstructivist architecture
Minimal architecture
Neoclassicism (Architecture)
Postmodernism (Architecture)
Against all odds [projects by Ellerbe Becket] K. D. Stein. il *Architectural Record* 177:90-5 Ap '89
Architects' dialogue [views of H. Hollein and C. Jencks] H. Hollein. il pors *Architectural Digest* 46:72+ Ap '89
Charles and the 'carbuncle' [modern British architecture] por *Newsweek* 114:37 S 18 '89
Charles: England's designing prince [A vision of Britain documentary] M. Filler. il pors *House & Garden* 161:158-61+ Mr '89
Contemporary transformations of modern architecture. W. J. R. Curtis. il *Architectural Record* 177:108-19 Je '89
Icons of modernism or machine-age dinosaurs? J. S. Russell. il *Architectural Record* 177:142-7 Je '89
Pioneering the modern movement in Palestine [E. Mendelsohn] J. Rykwert. il por *Architectural Digest* 46:82+ O '89
The prince and the architects [views of Prince Charles] C. Knevett. il *Architectural Record* 177:57+ O '89
A vision of Britain—architecture in crisis [excerpt] Prince Charles. il pors *Architectural Digest* 46:32-4+ O '89
The winds of Windsorism [views of Prince Charles; cover story] H. Muschamp. *The New Republic* 201:30-5 D 11 '89
Exhibitions
Holl and Ambasz, in a manner of speaking. R. Kimball. il *Architectural Record* 177:51+ Ap '89
The new faces of modernism on show [Emilio Ambasz/Steven Holl: architecture] il *Architectural Record* 177:47 Mr '89
ARCHITECTURE, PUEBLO *See* Pueblo architecture
ARCHITECTURE, ROCOCO
Catherine the Great's Chinese jewel box [Chinese Palace near Leningrad] P. Lauritzen. il *Architectural Digest* 46:174-9 O '89
ARCHITECTURE, VICTORIAN
Back Bay Victorian [Boston town house decorated by Bruce Gregga for B. and F. Herman] D. Roberts. il *Architectural Digest* 46:152-9 Mr '89
The Colorado Victorian [Telluride] il *Esquire* 112:62 Ag '89
Gothic getaway [Charlotte McKim's Fishers Island home designed by M. Simon] M. Filler. il *House & Garden* 161:104-9 Je '89
Our Folk Victorian Cottage. il *Southern Living* 24:116 Jl '89
A stick style curiosity on the Jersey coast [Emlen Physick House in Cape May] V. J. Scully. il por *Architectural Digest* 46:34+ Mr '89
Two masterworks of American architecture [work of F. Furness] A. Berman. il por *Architectural Digest* 46:314+ O '89
Warm colors, personal style [restored Oxford, Miss. house] il *Southern Living* 24:172-3 N '89
ARCHITECTURE AND ART *See* Art and architecture
ARCHITECTURE AND THE AGED
When your aged parent moves in with you . . . [make your home safer and more comfortable] P. A. Seefeldt. il *Good Housekeeping* 209:270 S '89

ARCHITECTURE AND THE HANDICAPPED
See also
Wilderness on Wheels (Organization)
New handicapped bill hobbled by vagueness. P. Hoffmann. il *Architectural Record* 177:35 O '89
ARCHITECTURE IN ART
The watercolor page [paintings of architectural facades] R. E. Buchanan. il por *American Artist* 53:44-7 Mr '89
ARCHITECTURE IN MOTION PICTURES
Design for dreaming. L. Van Schaik. il *Film Comment* 25:28-30+ Mr/Ap '89
ARCHIVE FILM PRODUCTIONS INC.
Don't Bogart that footage. J. Bernard. il *Video* 13:16 Jl '89
ARCHIVES
See also
Alabama. Dept. of Archives and History
Arts—Archives
Bergman, Ingrid, 1915-1982—Archives
Motion picture collections
Rock music—Archives
Space research—Archives
United States. National Archives and Records Administration
International aspects
From the world's archives. il *The Courier (Unesco)* 42:12-13 My '89
ARCO *See* Atlantic Richfield Co.
ARCO SOLAR, INC.
ARCO Solar sale raises concerns over potential technology export. M. Crawford. *Science* 244:918 My 26 '89
In defense of confidentiality. D. Lazarus. *Physics Today* 42:57-9 O '89
ARCS (ASTRONOMY)
The baffling ring arcs of Neptune. A. Brahic and W. B. Hubbard. il *Sky and Telescope* 77:606-9 Je '89
ARCTIC ALASKA FISHERIES (FIRM)
Fishing for respect on Wall Street. B. Buell. il *Business Week* p100 My 22 '89
ARCTIC EXPLORATION
See also
Cook Expedition (1908-1909)
Peary Expeditions (1886-1909)
Black man overcomes frostbite to become youngest American to walk to the North Pole [D. Roberts] D. M. Cheers. il pors map *Jet* 76:12-14 Je 12 '89
Polar dare [H. Thayer's ski expedition to the North Pole] P. Turner. il por *Ms.* 17:55-7 Je '89
ARCTIC FOXES *See* Foxes
ARCTIC HURRICANES *See* Hurricanes
ARCTIC NATIONAL WILDLIFE REFUGE (ALASKA)
Adversaries in the Arctic. M. Hager. il map *Newsweek* 113:60 F 27 '89
Arctic National Wildlife Refuge [discussion of May 1989 article, Oil development and the Arctic National Wildlife Refuge] L. Speer. il *Environment* 31:2-4 S '89
Beating the drum for caribou [Gwich'in people bordering Arctic National Wildlife Refuge oppose oil development] M. Peale. il *Sierra* 74:32+ My/Je '89
Explore no more? E. F. Cone. il *Forbes* 143:10 My 15 '89
The future of big oil [drilling in Arctic National Wildlife Refuge after Exxon oil spill; cover story] P. Nulty. il map *Fortune* 119:46-9 My 8 '89
Impacts of petroleum development in the Arctic [discussion of November 6, 1987 article, Cumulative impacts of oil fields on northern Alaskan landscapes] D. A. Walker and others. *Science* 245:764-6 Ag 18 '89
Oil development and the Arctic National Wildlife Refuge. L. Speer. bibl f il *Environment* 31:42-3 My '89
Shadow over an ancient land [T. Gilbert, member of Gwich'in tribe opposing oil development] S. K. Reed. il pors *People Weekly* 32:48-53 S 18 '89
Summer trekking in Alaska's Arctic. il *Sunset (Central West edition)* 182:251 Je '89
A tale of two villages [natives bordering Arctic National Wildlife Refuge hold opposing viewpoints on oil development] E. Linden. il *Time* 133:62 Ap 17 '89
Tundra plunder [proposed oil exploration] *The New Republic* 200:8+ My 1 '89
ARCTIC OCEAN
The Arctic: a key to world climate. P. H. Abelson. *Science* 243:873 F 17 '89
Hydrolysis of carbon tetrachloride [discussion of November 4, 1988 article, Arctic Ocean ventilation studied with a suite of anthropogenic halocarbon tracers] M. Krysell and D. W. R. Wallace. il *Science* 246:1638-9 D 22 '89
ARCTIC PEOPLES
See also
Eskimos
ARCTIC REGIONS
See also
Alaska
Gardens and gardening—Arctic regions
North Pole
Northwest Passage
Paleontology—Arctic regions
Skiing—Arctic regions

ARCTIC REGIONS—See also—cont.
Social science research—Arctic regions
Yukon Territory
Climate
The Arctic: a key to world climate. P. H. Abelson. *Science* 243:873 F 17 '89
Arctic air primed to destroy ozone [airborne mission] R. Monastersky. *Science News* 135:116 F 25 '89
Arctic angst. T. Beardsley. il *Scientific American* 260:26-7 Ap '89
Arctic ozone is poised for a fall [airborne expedition] R. A. Kerr. il *Science* 243:1007-8 F 24 '89
Arctic storms resemble tropical hurricanes. il *Earth Science* 42:8-9 Fall '89
Depressed ozone seen in Arctic [study by Michael H. Proffitt] R. Monastersky. *Science News* 136:413 D 23-30 '89
Fate of Arctic ozone remains up in the air. R. Monastersky. *Science News* 135:37 Ja 21 '89
How much heat in the Arctic? [series of airborne experiments led by the National Oceanic and Atmospheric Administration] *Science News* 135:126 F 25 '89
The poles in peril [ozone layer] R. Dolphin. *Maclean's* 102:50 F 27 '89
Scientific mission finds potential for ozone destruction in Arctic. R. G. O'Lone. il *Aviation Week & Space Technology* 130:33 F 27 '89
U.S. scientists, aircraft study ozone depletion above Arctic. B. W. Henderson. il *Aviation Week & Space Technology* 130:45+ Ja 16 '89
Winter ozone gap detected over the Arctic [research by David J. Hofmann] R. Monastersky. *Science News* 136:54 Jl 22 '89
Defenses
See also
Soviet Union—Navy—Forces in the Arctic
International status
Hands across the Pole [co-operation between Canada and Soviet Union] B. Bergman. il map *Maclean's* 102:24-5 N 27 '89
ARCTIC RESEARCH
International aspects
Soviets encourage joint research of Arctic areas. R. G. O'Lone. *Aviation Week & Space Technology* 130:83 Ja 30 '89
ARDAGH, JOHN, 1928-
Lille gets ready for '92. il map *The New York Times Magazine* p58-60+ D 3 '89
ARDEN, HARVEY
Who owns our past? il map *National Geographic* 175:376-93 Mr '89
ARDEN (ELIZABETH) INC. See Elizabeth Arden, Inc.
ARDENT COMPUTER INC.
See also
Stardent (Firm)
Ardent's Daddy Warbucks [Kubota Ltd.] J. B. Levine. il *Business Week* p26-7 Je 12 '89
"I love the tumult" [career of A. Michels] J. Pitta. il pors *Forbes* 144:296-8 N 13 '89
ARDITTI STRING QUARTET
No frills. P. G. Davis. il *New York* 22:76 Mr 27 '89
ARDMORE, JANE
Like mother . . . like daughter [cover story] il *Good Housekeeping* 209:110-11+ Jl '89
ARDOIN, JOHN
Bernstein at seventy. *National Review* 41:62-4 Ja 27 '89
Domestic vintage. *National Review* 41:50+ Je 30 '89
Faces in the crowd. il *National Review* 41:48+ Ag 18 '89
A time for Mozart. il *National Review* 41:49-50 Ap 21 '89
ARDOLINO, EMILE
about
Chances are [film] Reviews
Maclean's il 102:59 Mr 20 '89. B. D. Johnson
Newsweek 113:83 Mr 20 '89. D. Ansen
People Weekly il 31:11 Mr 27 '89. R. Novak
ARE YOU EXPERIENCED? LTD.
The curator of solid gold [A. Douglas manages J. Hendrix archives] S. Fried. il por *Gentlemen's Quarterly* 59:78+ Ja '89
AREA STUDIES
See also
East European studies
Egyptian studies
Japanese studies
Soviet studies
ARECIBO OBSERVATORY See Astronomical observatories—Puerto Rico
AREGOOD, RICHARD
NBA stars are the best athletes in pro sports. il *TV Guide* 37:14-15 Mr 25-31 '89
AREMBEPE (BRAZIL)
Social conditions
The women of Arembepe [families] M. de A. Figueiredo and D. Prado. il *The Unesco Courier* 42:38-41 Jl '89
ARENA BRAINS [film] See Motion picture reviews—Single works
ARENA FOOTBALL
The wild indoors [Pittsburgh vs. Chicago] J. D. Miller. il *Sport (New York, N.Y.)* 80:13 N '89

ARENAS, SPORTS See Stadiums
ARENS, MOSHE
Secretary meets with Israeli foreign minister [remarks, March 13, 1989] *Department of State Bulletin* 89:63 My '89
about
Arens: Mr. Hard-liner. por *Time* 133:82 Ja 2 '89
ARENSTEIN, SETH
Blizzard from Baikonur. il *Ad Astra* 1:14-18 F '89
Marketing the Proton. il *Ad Astra* 1:31-4 D '89
AREQUIPA (PERU)
Churches (Buildings)
Out of sight, out of time [convents Santa Catalina and Santa Rosa] M. R. Day. il *Américas* 41 no2:11-15 '89
ARESON, TODD W.
(jt. auth) See Whicker, Marcia Lynn, and Areson, Todd W.
ARFONS, CRAIG
about
Final run for a speed legend. J. Skorupa. il por *Popular Mechanics* 166:26 N '89
ARGENTINA
See also
Airplanes, Training—Argentina
Ballet—Argentina
Buenos Aires (Argentina)
Civil rights—Argentina
Country estates—Argentina
Industry and state—Argentina
Jews—Argentina
Mendoza (Argentina)
Morale, National—Argentina
Nuclear energy—Argentina
Paleontology—Argentina
Privatization—Argentina
Resorts—Argentina
Terrorism—Argentina
United States—Diplomatic and consular service—Argentina
Wildlife conservation—Argentina
Army
Argentina after Villa Martelli [insurrection] A. M. Shapiro. il *The New Leader* 72:11-12 Ja 9 '89
Carlos Menem in the driver's seat. A. M. Shapiro. il *The New Leader* 72:10-11 Jl 10-24 '89
Cry, Argentina [C. S. Menem pardons military personnel convicted of civil rights violations] J. Malamud-Goti. *The Nation* 249:517-18 N 6 '89
Dirty secrets of the 'dirty war'. M. Andersen. *The Nation* 248:339-40+ Mr 13 '89
The generals don't repent. P. Lacefield. *Commonweal* 116:583-4 N 3 '89
Defenses
Bomb potential for South America. D. Albright. bibl f il map *The Bulletin of the Atomic Scientists* 45:16-20 My '89
See also
Inflation (Finance)—Argentina
Economic conditions
See also
Inflation (Finance)—Argentina
Economic policy
Argentina drifts toward disaster [cover story] A. Evans-Pritchard. il *The American Spectator* 22:19-21+ S '89
Argentina gets ready for 'surgery without anesthetic' [with interview with C. Menem] J. Ryser and R. A. Kessler. il por *Business Week* p46+ O 2 '89
Carlos Menem: a Peronist who may rule like a pragmatist. J. Ryser and R. A. Kessler. il por *Business Week* p41 Jl 3 '89
The fall and fall of Argentina. C. Gorman. il *Time* 133:47 Je 12 '89
"Get up and walk!" [C. S. Menem's recovery plan] G. D. Garcia. il por *Time* 134:39 Jl 24 '89
Should anyone cry for Argentina? [C. Menem's reforms] C. A. Robbins and J. Staubus. il por *U.S. News & World Report* 107:51+ O 30 '89
We cry for you, Argentina [C. Menem's reforms] C. A. Robbins. il *U.S. News & World Report* 107:22 Jl 24 '89
Foreign relations
Great Britain
See Great Britain—Foreign relations—Argentina
Industries
See also
Bunge & Born
Fabrica Argentina de Material Aeroespacial
Languages
See also
Spanish language in Argentina
Politics and government
See also
Elections—Argentina
Peronism
Political campaigns—Argentina
Socialism—Argentina
Abdication in Argentina [R. Alfonsin resigns] J. Contreras. il por *Newsweek* 113:46-7 Je 26 '89
Argentina after Villa Martelli [insurrection] A. M. Shapiro. il *The New Leader* 72:11-12 Ja 9 '89
The battle of La Tablada [leftist group attacks army base] J. Smolowe. il *Time* 133:45 F 6 '89

ARGENTINA—Politics and government—cont.
Carlos Menem in the driver's seat. A. M. Shapiro. il The New Leader 72:10-11 Jl 10-24 '89
Cry, Argentina [C. S. Menem pardons military personnel convicted of civil rights violations] J. Malamud-Goti. The Nation 249:517-18 N 6 '89
Dirty secrets of the 'dirty war'. M. Andersen. The Nation 248:339-40+ Mr 13 '89
The generals don't repent. P. Lacefield. Commonweal 116:583-4 N 3 '89
Menem's dangerous maneuvers. A. M. Shapiro. il The New Leader 72:12-13 N 13 '89
An ominous leftist uprising in Argentina [All for the Country rebels] il Newsweek 113:33 F 6 '89

ARGENTO, DOMINICK
about
The Aspern papers [opera] Reviews
National Review 41:50+ Je 30 '89. J. Ardoin
Opera News 53:38 F 18 '89. P. Swank

ARGININE
The anticodon contains a major element of the identity of arginine transfer RNAs. L. H. Schulman and H. Pelka. bibl f il Science 246:1595-7 D 22 '89

ARGON ISOTOPE DATING See Radioactive dating

ARGONAUTS (GREEK MYTHOLOGY)
Jason's thunderbolt salve: it works like a charm. M. Reed. il Weatherwise 42:336-8 D '89

ARGONNE NATIONAL LABORATORY
At Argonne lab, the bottle comes up empty [cold fusion] J. F. Siler. il Business Week p110 My 8 '89

ARGUE, HAZEN ROBERT
about
Questions of privilege. B. Wallace and D. Jenish. il por Maclean's 102:17 N 27 '89

ARGUMENT (PSYCHOLOGY) See Quarrels

ARGYLL (SCOTLAND)
Tropical Scotland [gardens] C. Maclean. il House & Garden 161:136-41+ F '89

ARIAAL RENDILE (AFRICAN PEOPLE) See Rendile (African people)

ARIANE (LAUNCH VEHICLE) See Space vehicles— Propulsion systems

ARIANESPACE
Ariane 4 vehicle to orbit Hughes payloads in 1990. Aviation Week & Space Technology 131:35 Jl 24 '89
Ariane planning complicated by launcher, payload delays. il Aviation Week & Space Technology 131:123 O 9 '89
Ariane to continue key role in launch service market. il Aviation Week & Space Technology 130:131 Mr 20 '89
Arianespace, European companies sign production contracts for 50 Ariane 4s. J. M. Lenorovitz. Aviation Week & Space Technology 130:28 F 20 '89
Arianespace launches JCSAT, Meteosat; nine Ariane missions planned for 1989. J. M. Lenorovitz. il Aviation Week & Space Technology 130:29-30 Mr 13 '89
Arianespace plans 1989 launches to clear backlog of payloads. J. M. Lenorovitz. il Aviation Week & Space Technology 130:28-9 Ja 30 '89
Arianespace weighs marketing satellite launches for Pegasus. Aviation Week & Space Technology 130:56 Je 19 '89
Work on Ariane 5 launch, assembly facilities proceeds at site in Kourou. il Aviation Week & Space Technology 130:175 Je 12 '89

ARIAS
See also
Compact discs—Arias
Phonograph records—Arias
The furtive tear. F. Merkling. il Opera News 53:28-9 Ap 15 '89
Too strong for fantasias [popularization of opera tunes through nineteenth century piano transcriptions] B. Ivry. il Opera News 53:20-1+ Ja 21 '89

ARIAS SANCHEZ, OSCAR
about
Bipartisan arm-twisting in Central America [letter from congressmen to O. Arias Sanchez concerning J. Hull] Harper's 278:24 Je '89

ARIDJIS, HOMERO
The death of a masterpiece. il New Perspectives Quarterly 6:40-3 Spr '89

ARIEL (SATELLITE) See Uranus (Planet)—Satellites

ARIKHA, AVIGDOR, 1929-
Giacometti's code. il pors The New York Review of Books 36:20+ My 18 '89

ARION PRESS
Novel ideas [limited editions illustrated by R. Motherwell and J. Baldessari] R. B. Woodward. il Art News 88:127 Ap '89

ARISTECH CHEMICAL CORPORATION
Eyes are on a plastics prize. G. G. Marcial. Business Week p76 Ap 17 '89

ARISTIDE, JEAN-BERTRAND
about
Exalted violence. The Nation 248:76-7 Ja 23 '89
Little priest, big general. S. Rodman. il National Review 41:24-5 S 29 '89

ARISTIDES See Epstein, Joseph

ARISTOCRACY
See also
Elite (Social sciences)
Nobility

ARISTOCRATS [drama] See Friel, Brian

ARISTOTLE, 384-322 B.C.
about
The living end. R. Makoul. il The Writer 102:7-8 F '89

ARITA, HAJIME
about
Japanese family fights to remove racially-offensive products in their country. il por Jet 76:37 S 4 '89

ARITHMETIC
See also
Floating-point arithmetic
Fractions
Study and teaching
Aids and devices
Fraction Munchers [computer program] C. S. Holzberg. il Home Office Computing 7:70 Jl '89

ARITHMETIC PROGRESSIONS See Series (Mathematics)

ARIYOSHI, RITA
Where the world's day begins. il map Travel Holiday 171:40-7 Ja '89

ARIZONA
See also
Air pollution—Arizona
Architecture, Domestic—Arizona
Botany—Arizona
Colorado River (Colo.-Mexico)
Environmental movement—Arizona
Fish—Arizona
Glen Canyon National Recreation Area (Ariz. and Utah)
Grand Canyon (Ariz.)
Grand Canyon National Park (Ariz.)
Health resorts, watering places, etc.—Arizona
Historic houses, sites, etc.—Arizona
Meteor Crater (Ariz.)
Organ Pipe Cactus National Monument (Ariz.)
Paleontology—Arizona
Petrified Forest National Park (Ariz.)
Police—Arizona
Saguaro National Monument (Ariz.)
Sonoran Desert
Sports—Arizona
Tonto National Forest (Ariz.)
Wetlands—Arizona
Wildlife—Arizona
Willcox Playa (Ariz.)
Workman Creek Falls (Ariz.)
Description and travel
See also
Automobile touring—Arizona
Industries
See also
Uranium mines and mining—Arizona
Politics and government
A 'Christian nation' in the Far West [declaration by E. Mecham supporters] U.S. News & World Report 106:14 Mr 27 '89
How hot is it? J. Toobin. The New Republic 201:12-14 Ag 7-14 '89
O'Connor fumbles 'Christian nation' case [Justice S. D. O'Connor's letter in support of Arizona Republican Party resolution] E. M. Gaffney, Jr. The Christian Century 106:373-5 Ap 12 '89
The resurrection of Evan Mecham. K. V. Smith. il por National Review 41:42-3 My 19 '89
Race relations
Arizona finally gets a M. L. King state holiday. il Jet 77:18 O 9 '89
M.L.K. Jr. bill reaches another snag in Arizona. Jet 76:38 Jl 24 '89

ARIZONA INSTRUMENT CORP.
An underground stock surfaces. G. G. Marcial. Business Week p96 Je 12 '89

ARIZONA-SONORA DESERT MUSEUM
The desert comes alive! [cover story] il map National Geographic World 170:4-9 O '89

ARIZONA STATE UNIVERSITY. UNIVERSITY ART MUSEUM
ASU Art Museum. E. Lebow. il por American Craft 49:64-9 Ag/S '89

ARKANSAS
See also
Courts—Arkansas
Fishing—Arkansas
Governors' mansions—Arkansas
Mount Magazine (Ark.)
Ouachita National Forest (Ark. and Okla.)
Public health—Arkansas
History
Looking into a shared past [K. W. Sakaris and C. O. Hervey trace roots] D. Young. il pors Southern Living 24:79+ D '89

ARKANSAS—cont.
Parks and reserves
See also
Toltec Mounds Archaeological State Park (Ark.)
ARKES, HADLEY
Moral obtuseness in America. il National Review 41:33-6 Je 16 '89
Our guest tonight is Socrates, himself a noted interviewer. National Review 41:23 Mr 10 '89
ARKIN, WILLIAM M.
Arms at sea [discussion of January 1989 article, Troubled waters] il Technology Review 92:6-7+ Ag/S '89
The buildup that wasn't. il The Bulletin of the Atomic Scientists 45:6-10 Ja/F '89
Gorbachev talks but who listens? il por The Bulletin of the Atomic Scientists 45:5-6 Mr '89
Stealth cruise sneaks into Canada. il The Bulletin of the Atomic Scientists 45:6-7 My '89
Troubled waters: the Navy's aggressive war strategy. il Technology Review 92:54-63 Ja '89
ARKIN, WILLIAM M., AND HANDLER, JOSHUA
Nuclear disasters at sea, then and now. bibl f il The Bulletin of the Atomic Scientists 45:20-4 Jl/Ag '89
ARKINS, DIANE C.
Keep antique ornaments alive. il Americana 17:55-8 N/D '89
ARKUS-DUNTOV, ZORA
about
The marque of Zora. P. Lyons. il pors Car and Driver 34:60-1+ Je '89
ARLECCHINO [opera] See Busoni, Ferruccio, 1866-1924
ARLEDGE, ROONE
about
The ABCs of making news profits [cover story] C. Capuzzi. il por Channels (New York, N.Y.: 1986) 9:30-5 Mr '89
Winning Diane: how ABC's Roone Arledge snatched her away from CBS [cover story] E. Klein. il pors New York 22:36-43 Mr 13 '89
ARLEN, HAROLD, 1905-1986
about
Brother Harold. D. Okrent. por Esquire 111:32 Ja '89
ARLEN, MICHAEL J.
Faucet sales and crush syndrome [cover story] il The Nation 248:548-50+ Ap 24 '89
ARLEN CORP.
How Arthur Cohen came back. J. D. Greenberg. il por Forbes 144:252-3 O 16 '89
ARLES (FRANCE)
Description
Gourmet holidays: a corner of Provence. D. Beal. il map Gourmet 49:44-9+ Jl '89
ARLETA (LOS ANGELES, CALIF.)
Crime
Karen Severson swore she'd find her best friend's murderer—now she stands accused of the crime [murder of M. Avila] K. Kingsbury. il pors People Weekly 32:147-8+ S 18 '89
ARLINGTON INTERNATIONAL RACECOURSE (ILL.)
A new and glorious Arlington. il Sports Illustrated 71:14 Jl 10 '89
ARLINGTON PARK (ILL.: RACETRACK)
Echoes of an equine past [horse-loving teenager at Arlington Park in the 1950s] W. Nack. il Sports Illustrated 71:84-8+ S 18 '89
ARLT, WILLIAM
about
The discreet charm of the ball cap. R. Merkin. il Gentlemen's Quarterly 59:143+ O '89
ARM
Paranthropus yields mosaic arm bone [work of Randall L. Susman and Frederick E. Grine] B. Bower. Science News 135:251 Ap 22 '89
Surgery
Armed with a miracle [San Francisco Giants pitcher D. Dravecky returns after surgery to remove tumor] il pors Sports Illustrated 71:18 Ag 21 '89
Wounds and injuries
After a courageous comeback, a star pitcher breaks his arm but keeps his faith intact; ed. by Liz McNeil. D. Dravecky. il pors People Weekly 32:69-70+ S 11 '89
Giant comeback cut short [pitcher D. Dravecky] J. Carvalho. il por Christianity Today 33:54+ O 20 '89
'It felt like I lost my arm' [baseball player D. Dravecky breaks arm during comeback from cancer surgery] il por Newsweek 114:65 Ag 28 '89
ARMACOST, MICHAEL H.
about
Tilting toward toughness at the Tokyo embassy. R. Neff. il por Business Week p47 Ag 7 '89
Under Secretary Armacost's interview on "Face the nation" [transcript of program, December 18, 1988] Department of State Bulletin 89:54-5 F '89
ARMADA, 1588 See Spanish Armada, 1588
ARMADILLOS
Rising star [work of E. Storrs and H. Burchfield] J. Watson. il pors National Wildlife 27:46-9 O/N '89
ARMAH, AYI KWEI, 1938-
Doctor Kamikaze [story] il Mother Jones 14:34-8+ O '89

ARMAMENT INDUSTRIES See Munitions
ARMAMENTS
See also
Airplanes, Military—Armaments
Disarmament
Munitions
ARMANI, GIORGIO
about
Armani takes Fifth. M. Gross. il por New York 22:20 Mr 20 '89
ARMBRISTER, TREVOR
New Jersey's battle for better schools. Reader's Digest 135:159-64 N '89
Return of Marie Balter. il por Reader's Digest 135:123-7 Jl '89
Scandal in our trade schools. Reader's Digest 134:85-90 Ja '89
When companies care. Reader's Digest 134:25-6+ Ap '89
ARMBRUSTER, PETER, AND MÜNZENBERG, GOTT-FRIED
Creating superheavy elements. bibl il Scientific American 260:66-72 My '89
ARMCHAIRS See Chairs
ARMED FORCES
See also
Canada—Armed Forces
Great Britain—Armed Forces
Japan—Armed Forces
Korea (South)—Armed Forces
Latin America—Armed Forces
Mercenary troops
National service
Soviet Union—Armed Forces
Syria—Armed Forces
United Nations—Armed Forces
United States—Armed Forces
Western Europe—Armed Forces
Appropriations and expenditures
The drain of a permanent war economy. M. Renner. il USA Today (Periodical) 118:19-21 Jl '89
Journalism
See Journalism, Military
ARMED SERVICES COMMITTEE (HOUSE) See United States. Congress. House. Committee on Armed Services
ARMED SERVICES COMMITTEE (SENATE) See United States. Congress. Senate. Committee on Armed Services
ARMEN, JACOB
about
Third-grader Jacob Armen drums a sense of wonder into the usually cool world of jazz. il por People Weekly 31:57 Ap 24 '89
ARMENDARIS RANCH (N.M.)
Shangri-La or sun-baked wasteland? G. Weiss. il map Business Week p54-6 Ag 7 '89
ARMENIA (SOVIET UNION)
See also
Earthquakes—Armenia (Soviet Union)
Relief work—Armenia (Soviet Union)
Description and travel
Faucet sales and crush syndrome [cover story] M. J. Arlen. il The Nation 248:548-50+ Ap 24 '89
Nationalism
Agony and hope in Armenia. R. L. Deats. The Christian Century 106:81-2 Ja 25 '89
Armenian earthquakes and Soviet tremors. G. J. Libaridian. Society 26:59-63 Mr/Ap '89
Faucet sales and crush syndrome [cover story] M. J. Arlen. il The Nation 248:548-50+ Ap 24 '89
Fires of nationalism. A. Wilson-Smith. il Maclean's 102:43+ O 30 '89
From the rubble. J. Lloyd. il National Review 41:31-2 Ja 27 '89
Life in a weary land. J. Kohan. il Time 133:83 Ja 2 '89
Nightmare of the generals [Soviet generals held captive by Azerbaijanis] Time 134:48 S 18 '89
On the edge of civil war [feud between Armenia and Azerbaijan] P. Hofheinz. il maps Time 134:51 O 23 '89
Trouble in the Transcaucasus [dispute between Armenians and Azerbaijanis over Karabakh] M. Saroyan. bibl f il map The Bulletin of the Atomic Scientists 45:16-18+ Mr '89
ARMEY, RICHARD K.
Debunking the privatization myth: restoring government to its proper role. USA Today (Periodical) 117:33-5 Ja '89
about
Armey's aesthetic. T. Noah. The New Republic 201:14+ S 11 '89
This congressman beat the system. R. Fitzgerald. il por Reader's Digest 134:125-8 Ap '89
ARMIES
See also
Argentina—Army
El Salvador—Army
Great Britain. Army
Guatemala—Army
India—Army
Israel—Army
Soviet Union—Army

ARMIES—See also—cont.
    Switzerland—Army
    United States. Army
ARMINIANISM
              Great Britain
Arminius and the Arminians. D. MacCulloch. il por *History Today* 39:27-34 O '89
              Netherlands
Arminius and the Arminians. D. MacCulloch. il por *History Today* 39:27-34 O '89
ARMINIUS, JACOBUS, 1560-1609
              about
Arminius and the Arminians. D. MacCulloch. il por *History Today* 39:27-34 O '89
ARMITAGE, KAROLE
              about
Motivating factors. D. Kazanjian. il pors *Vogue* 179:516-17+ S '89
ARMOR, DAVID J.
After busing: education and choice. *Current (Washington, D.C.)* 316:14-20 O '89
ARMORED VEHICLES, MILITARY *See* Motor vehicles, Military
ARMORIES
              Great Britain
    See also
    Royal Armouries (Great Britain)
ARMS (ADJUSTABLE RATE MORTGAGES) *See* Mortgages
ARMS (LIMBS) *See* Arm
ARMS (ROBOTIC) *See* Manipulators (Mechanism)
ARMS AND ARMOR
    See also
    Bulletproof vests
A modern armor maker dresses men in knights' clothing [L. Sowers] R. Mashburn. bibl (p183) il pors *Smithsonian* 20:116-20+ D '89
ARMS AND THE MAN [drama] *See* Shaw, Bernard, 1856-1950
ARMS CONTROL *See* Disarmament
ARMS COPRODUCTION *See* Munitions—International aspects
ARMS RACE *See* Nuclear weapons
ARMS SMUGGLING *See* Smuggling
ARMS TRADE *See* Munitions—Export-import trade
ARMSTRONG, ALEXANDRA
The college crunch. il *Ms.* 17:118 Ja/F '89
Investment quandary. il *Ms.* 17:76 Mr '89
ARMSTRONG, LAWRENCE E., AND LIND, ROBERT H.
Movers and shakers. il *Runner's World* 24:80-2 Jl '89
ARMSTRONG, LOUIS, 1900-1971
              about
Papa, Satchmo, and the Babe. G. C. Ward. il *American Heritage* 40:14+ My/Je '89
The Satchmo few people knew. J. L. Collier. il pors *TV Guide* 37:16-18 Jl 29-Ag 4 '89
Satchmo's jazz genius hits high note in new revealing book on him. il pors *Jet* 75:31 F 20 '89
ARMSTRONG, PENNY, AND FELDMAN, SHERYL
Midwives: tapping every woman's strength. il *American Health* 8:74-6+ Ja/F '89
ARMSTRONG, ROBERT L.
              about
As Omaha's tough-talking housing boss, Robert Armstrong helps tenants grab for their bootstraps. M. Brower. il pors *People Weekly* 31:93-4+ My 15 '89
ARMSTRONG, RODNEY
The Boston Athenaeum and its furnishings. il *Antiques* 136:302-15 Ag '89
ARMSTRONG, THOMAS NEWTON, 1932-
Folk, or art? il *Antiques* 135:282-4 Ja '89
ARMSTRONG, WILLIAM
Should the Congress adopt the "Tender Offer Disclosure and Fairness Act of 1987"? [excerpts from address, June 17, 1988] *Congressional Digest* 68:77+ Mr '89
ARMSTRONG-JONES, DAVID ALBERT CHARLES *See* Linley, David Albert Charles Armstrong-Jones, Viscount, 1961-
ARMSTRONG WORLD INDUSTRIES INC.
Armstrong may get strong-armed. G. G. Marcial. *Business Week* p134 F 20 '89
The Belzbergs, again. T. Jaffe. il *Forbes* 144:316 S 4 '89
ARMY ENGINEER CORPS *See* United States. Army. Corps of Engineers
ARMY NURSE CORPS *See* United States. Army Nurse Corps
ARMY RESERVE (U.S.) *See* United States. Army Reserve
ARMYWORMS
              Control
A baculovirus blocks insect molting by producing ecdysteroid UDP-glucosyl transferase. D. R. O'Reilly and L. K. Miller. bibl f il *Science* 245:1110-12 S 8 '89
ARNAULT, BERNARD
              about
Avant le deluge at Moet Hennessy Louis Vuitton. S. Toy. il *Business Week* p44 Ap 24 '89
King of chic—and artful deals. S. Tully. il por *Fortune* 119:40 Ja 2 '89
A luxury fight to the finish. S. Greenhouse. il pors *The New York Times Magazine* p38-9+ D 17 '89

The new king of luxury. C. Dickey. il por *Newsweek* 114:40-2 Ag 7 '89
ARNDT, ALICE
For a yellow color. il por *Americana* 17:34-7 S/O '89
ARNELL, PETER
              about
SoHo salon. M. Filler. il pors *House & Garden* 161:170-3 O '89
ARNESS, JAMES
              about
James Arness. il por *People Weekly* 31 Special Issue:32-3 Summ '89
ARNETTE, JEANNETTA
              about
'I learned to be really perky'. D. Hudson. por *TV Guide* 37:21 S 16-22 '89
ARNIE BECKER (FICTIONAL CHARACTER)
Attention, Arnie Becker: your motions in courtrooms—not bedrooms—would be more help. L. Brenner. il *TV Guide* 37:10-11 Je 17-23 '89
ARNOLD, JAMES W.
Ecumenical jury winners at Montreal. *America* 161:252-3 O 21 '89
ARNOLD, PATRICK M.
In search of the hero: masculine spirituality and liberal Christianity [cover story] il *America* 161:206-10 O 7 '89
State of the question [discussion of October 7, 1989 article, In search of the hero: masculine spirituality and liberal Christianity] *America* 161:304-6 N 4 '89
ARNOLD, PERI E., 1942-
Fifteen presidential decisions that shaped America. il *American History Illustrated* 24:36-42 Ap '89
ARNOLD, TOM
              about
Why did America's funniest housewife leave home? B. Robinson. il pors *Redbook* 174:54+ N '89
ARNOLD, VAL
              about
A tale of two cities: a designer's Los Angeles and San Francisco abodes. I. Borger. il *Architectural Digest* 46:214-21+ My '89
ARNOLD, WILFRED NIELS
Absinthe. bibl il *Scientific American* 260:112-17 Je '89
ARNOLDO MONDADORI EDITORE, SPA
A firestorm scorches De Benedetti's media empire. J. Rossant. il pors *Business Week* p68 D 25 '89-Ja 1 '90
Mondadori posts 11.8% increase in book and magazine sales. H. R. Lottman. *Publishers Weekly* 236:12 N 17 '89
ARNOTT, ANN
Defensive driving. il *Essence* 19:94+ Mr '89
AROMA THERAPY
Aromatherapy arrives. il *Health (New York, N.Y.)* 21:63 N '89
Nature's therapy. S. Lord. il *Vogue* 179:195-6 Mr '89
Scents and sensibility. J. Stone. il *Discover* 10:26+ D '89
AROMAS *See* Odors
AROMATIC PLANT OILS *See* Essences and essential oils
ARON, LEON
What *glasnost* has destroyed. *Commentary* 88:30-4 N '89
ARONIE, NANCY SLONIM
Meet Beau, my very own golden boy. il por *Good Housekeeping* 209:124 O '89
ARONOFF, STEVEN
              about
Growth stocks with more climb left [interview] K. Nickel. il por *Fortune* 120:28+ N 6 '89
ARONOWITZ, STANLEY
Labor's 'deal' is undone. il *The Progressive* 53:18-19 D '89
ARONSFELD, C. C.
The prince of liars who told the truth. il *History Today* 39:7-9 Ap '89
ARONSON, BERNARD
              about
Baker's bipartisan point man. D. Waller. il por *Newsweek* 113:40 Mr 20 '89
Policy circles. G. Black. *The Nation* 248:256-7 F 27 '89
The right stuff. *The New Republic* 200:9-10 F 27 '89
ARONSON, GEOFFREY
The co-opting of CASE. il *The Nation* 249:678+ D 4 '89
ARONSON, STEVEN M. L.
Lady of the canyon. il pors *Architectural Digest* 46:120-7+ F '89
Portrait of the artists: Eric Fischl and April Gornik on Long Island. il pors *Architectural Digest* 46:234-9+ Ap '89
ARONSON, STEVEN M. L., AND TIGER, VIRGINIA
Wired!! [cover story] il *New York* 22:26-33 Ja 30 '89
ARONSON & FOGLER
Finding plays without fancy footwork. G. G. Marcial. il *Business Week* p124 My 1 '89
AROUCH, SALAMO
              about
Lords of the ring. M. Rochlin. il pors *Harper's Bazaar* 122:103 D '89
AROUND THE WORLD BALLOON ASCENSIONS *See* Balloon ascensions
AROUND THE WORLD FLIGHTS *See* Aviation—World flights

AROUND THE WORLD IN 80 DAYS [television program]
See Television program reviews—Single works
AROUND THE WORLD VOYAGES See Voyages around
the world
AROUND THE WORLD YACHT RACES See Yacht racing
ARPAIA, LELLO
about
Endangered species. M. Barrier. il por *Nation's Business*
77:18 O '89
ARQUITECTONICA INTERNATIONAL CORPORATION
Good neighbors [Walner House in Glencoe] K. D. Stein.
il *Architectural Record* 177:72-81 mid-Ap '89
ARRANGEMENT OF FLOWERS See Flower arrangement
ARRANGEMENT OF FURNITURE See Furniture arrangement
ARRAS, JOHN
about
Tough cases, hard choices. A. Rosenfeld. il pors *New York*
22:32-7 Ja 9 '89
ARRAY OF LOW-ENERGY X-RAY IMAGING SENSORS
See Artificial satellites—Astronomical use
ARREST
See also
Bail
Preventive detention
ARRHYTHMIA
It's not a heart attack—but it may be worse. J. Rothfeder.
il *Business Week* p96-7 Jl 10 '89
Therapy
See also
Defibrillators
Backfire drugs [Enkaid and Tambocor, used to treat mild
arrhythmia, may cause fatalities] J. Ziegler. il *American
Health* 8:18 S '89
Heart-rhythm drugs found risky for many [encainide and
flecainide] R. Weiss. *Science News* 135:260 Ap 29 '89
The imperfect art of healing [anti-arrhythmia drugs increase
risk of heart attack] *U.S. News & World Report* 106:10-11
My 8 '89
Quieting electrical storms of the heart [ventricular arrhythmia;
excerpt from Heart rhythms] J. Rothfeder. il *Prevention
(Emmaus, Pa.)* 41:62-8 S '89
ARRIBA (COMPUTER PROGRAM) See Personal information
management software
ARRICALE, FRANK C.
To teach or not? il *Commonweal* 116:165-6 Mr 24 '89
ARRIGONI, WILLIAM
Seahorses [cover story] il *Sea Frontiers* 35:358-65 N/D '89
ARRINGTON & HOLLOWELL
Atlanta minority law firm shares resources with white firm
in unique bar program [Arrington & Hollowell and Hurt,
Richardson, Garner, Todd & Cadenhead] il *Jet* 76:24 O
2 '89
ARROW CRABS See Crabs
ARROW DYNAMICS, INC.
Roller coaster king Ron Toomer has a job he can't stomach.
il por *People Weekly* 32:101-3 Jl 24 '89
ARSA (AIRPORT RADAR SERVICE AREAS) See Radar
in aviation
ARSENIC
Arsenic and old lace [B. Moore accused of poisonings in
Burlington, N.C.] E. Salholz. il por *Newsweek* 114:24 Ag
14 '89
Arsenic in the gas giants [research by Keith S. Noll] *Sky
and Telescope* 78:133 Ag '89
ARSENIDES
See also
Gallium arsenide semiconductors
THE ARSENIO HALL SHOW [television program] See
Television program reviews—Single works
ARSON
Halloween fright night [Detroit] il *Newsweek* 114:49 N 13
'89
Quebec fire storm [language disputes and arson] L. Van
Dusen. il por *Maclean's* 102:12-13 F 6 '89
ART
See also
3-D art
Aesthetics
Anatomy, Artistic
Apocalyptic art
Art deco
Art nouveau
Artists
Arts
Arts and crafts
Arts and crafts movement
Bronzes
Carousel art
Christian art and symbolism
Classicism in art
Computers—Art use
Copyright—Art
Costume
Crop art
Cubism
Decoration and ornament
Design
Drawing

Eclecticism in art
Electricity—Art use
Etching
Figurative art
Folk art
Frescoes
Graffiti
Graphic arts
Holography—Art use
Illumination of books and manuscripts
Illustration
Imitation art
Impressionism (Art)
Inflatable art
Information systems—Art use
Junk art
Landscape painting
Light in art
Lithographs
Miniature painting
Mural painting and decoration
Mural painting and decoration, Exterior
National socialism and art
Object art
Painting
Pastel drawing
Pen drawing
Photography, Artistic
Posters
Postimpressionism (Art)
Pottery
Public art
Publishers and publishing—Art
Realism in art
Roadside art
Romanticism in art
Sculpture
Signatures (Art)
Television broadcasting—Art programs
Video art
Videotapes—Art use
Watercolor painting
Vasari diary. Vasari. See issues of Art News
Appreciation
See also
Art critics and criticism
A landmark painting [H. Frankenthaler's Mountains and
sea] M. S. Doherty. il *American Artist* 53:5 O '89
Awards
See also
Archibald Prize
Bibliography
Art. J. Russell. il *The New York Times Book Review* 94:9+
D 3 '89
Art books. J. Russell. il *The New York Times Book Review*
94:13+ Je 11 '89
Art books and videos. See issues of American Artist
Book reviews. See issues of Art News
Deck the shelves. P. S. Prescott. il *Newsweek* 114:82-4+
D 11 '89
Painting churches. K. Larson. il *New York* 22:88+ D 18
'89
Review of books. See issues of Art in America
Censorship
Armey's aesthetic [views of Congressman R. K. Armey] T.
Noah. *The New Republic* 201:14+ S 11 '89
Art and taxpayers. A. C. Danto. *The Nation* 249:192-3 Ag
21-28 '89
Art for law's sake. R. A. Posner. *The American Scholar*
58:513-20 Aut '89
Art wars: artists and politicans get worked up about the
NEA. H. Goldstein. il *Utne Reader* p14+ N/D '89
Artistic freedom, public anger. R. Berenson. il *National Review*
41:46 O 13 '89
Arts grants under fire [J. Helms leads Senate vote against
controversial art] C. McGuigan. il por *Newsweek* 114:23
Ag 7 '89
Congress passes compromise NEA bill. H. Fields. il *Publishers
Weekly* 236:10 O 20 '89
Congress rejects Helms amendment. W. Robinson. *Art in
America* 77:41 N '89
Congress votes for new censorship. il *Art in America* 77:33
S '89
Days of rage [NEA rescinds funding for Witnesses: against
our vanishing] K. Larson. il *New York* 22:80+ N 27 '89
Disaster at the NEA [rescinds funding for AIDS exhibit
Witnesses: against our vanishing] R. Brustein. *The New
Republic* 201:28-30 D 11 '89
A dispute over a photography exhibit raises once again
the relationship of art to conventional standards of taste.
R. M. Adams. il *Smithsonian* 20:12 O '89
Fallout from Helms Amendment. B. Wallis. *Art in America*
77:29 O '89
The First Amendment and the NEA. R. Brustein. *The New
Republic* 201:27-9 S 11 '89
Flag-burning & other modes of expression. W. Berns.
Commentary 88:37-41 O '89

ART—Censorship—cont.

House sets up commission to address Helms NEA proposal. H. Fields. *Publishers Weekly* 236:10 O 6 '89

Jesse Helms on the meaning of art. F. Bruning. il *Maclean's* 102:9 Ag 14 '89

A loony parody of cultural democracy [J. Helms' attack on the National Endowment for the Arts] R. Hughes. il *Time* 134:82 Ag 14 '89

Notes from the editor . . . M. S. Doherty. *American Artist* 53:10 S '89

Ol' Jesse's dirty word [amendment prohibiting NEA funding of obscene art] *The Nation* 249:441 O 23 '89

Sex, politics, religion & art. J. Cobb. *Common Cause Magazine* 15:22 N/D '89

Shadowboxing with the arts. S. H. Madoff. il *Art News* 88:204 S '89

Shock art: your tax dollars at work. D. Coran. il *Christianity Today* 33:69-70 S 8 '89

Should Congress censor art? [Helms Amendment] M. Horn. il por *U.S. News & World Report* 107:22-4 S 25 '89

Summer, storm [classic drama among artist, patron and public] M. Greenfield. il *Newsweek* 114:76 S 4 '89

Testing the new arts rules [NEA rescinds funds and later decides to support AIDS exhibit Witnesses: against our vanishing] *Newsweek* 114:43 N 27 '89

The war on culture. C. S. Vance. bibl f il *Art in America* 77:39+ S '89

What is pornography? [symposium] il *Art News* 88:138-43 O '89

When taxes pay for art. C. McGuigan. il *Newsweek* 114:68 Jl 3 '89

Anecdotes, facetiae, satire, etc.

Uncivil liberties. C. Trillin. il *The Nation* 249:518 N 6 '89

Collaboration

See also
Group Material (Group)
Tim Rollins + K.O.S. (Group)

Combined operations. E. Heartney. il *Art in America* 77:140-7 Je '89

Collections
See Art—Collectors and collecting

Collectors and collecting

See also
Art as an investment
Art in the home

The art of the interior [collecting paintings of interiors] M. Guralnick. il *House & Garden* 161:158 F '89

Art talk. A. S. Bamberger. See issues of Antiques & Collecting Hobbies beginning December 1987

Courtship of a collector [Prado to receive major loan of Thyssen-Bornemisza Collection] F. Jarque. il por *Art News* 88:65+ My '89

Driven to collect [W. P. Chrysler, Jr.] S. Greenspan. il por *House & Garden* 161:32+ Je '89

Flesh and spirit [New York home of S. Pivar] M. E. Haus. il por *Art News* 88:75-6+ Ja '89

From soup to sèvres [auction of works from the estate of J. T. Dorrance at Sotheby's] S. Greenspan. il *House & Garden* 161:244+ O '89

Private eyes: the modern Medicis [private collectors' museums] T. Gold. il *Harper's Bazaar* 122:98+ My '89

"They reflect me" [I. Sonnabend] C. Brown. il por *Forbes* 143:148+ My 1 '89

A treacherous market. D. Wechsler. il *Forbes* 144:292-4 N 27 '89

Trustees and trust [museum trustees who are also art collectors] A. Decker. il *Art News* 88:49+ D '89

Competitions

See also
Children's art—Competitions

Competition winners revisited [Realism today: American Artist Competition winners] V. R. Rivers. il *American Artist* 53:58-60 Je '89

Editorial. M. S. Doherty. *American Artist* 53:12 My '89

Notes from the editor . . . [juried art competitions] M. S. Doherty. il *American Artist* 53:10+ Ag '89

Conferences

See also
Art trade—Conferences

Art and Design in Action: show guide [Dearborn, Mich.; special section] il *American Artist* 53:67-8+ N '89

Art and Design in Action: Washington, DC, show guide [special section] il *American Artist* 53:71-2+ Ja '89

Conservation and restoration

See also
Drawing—Conservation and restoration
Painting—Conservation and restoration
Public art—Conservation and restoration

Old masters, new tricks [computerized art restoration in Italy] P. Elmer-Dewitt. il *Time* 134:84+ D 18 '89

The watchful eye in paper conservation. V. B. Hill. il *American Artist* 53:22+ Ag '89

Critics and criticism
See Art critics and criticism

Exhibitions

See also
Art galleries and museums

Art Show (New York, N.Y.)
Chicago International Art Exposition
Washington Square Art Show

Around the galleries. See issues of Americana beginning May/June 1984

Art. A. C. Danto. See issues of The Nation beginning October 20, 1984

Art. K. Larson. See issues of New York

Artsmart. See issues of Harper's Bazaar beginning December 1986

The billion-dollar blockbuster [art prices pushing up exhibition expenses] N. Stapen. il *Art News* 88:39-40 S '89

Britain's treasure house of art: the Fitzwilliam Collection. B. L. Brown. il *USA Today (Periodical)* 118:68-83 Jl '89

A British university collection travels [Treasures from the Fitzwilliam Museum] A. E. Ledes. il *Antiques* 135:818 Ap '89

Bulletin board. See issues of American Artist

Calendar. See issues of Antiques

Current and coming. A. E. Ledes. See issues Antiques beginning April 1988

Exhibits. L. S. Hurwitz. See issues of American Artist

International. See issues of Art News beginning Summer 1985

Museums; Galleries [New York City; fall preview] K. Larson and E. Newhall. il *New York* 22:66+ S 11 '89

Nation. See issues of Art News

On exhibit. See issues of Americana

On view. See issues of House & Garden beginning October 1986

Review of exhibitions. See issues of Art in America

Will high costs curtail museum exhibitions? D. Grant. il *American Artist* 53:10+ O '89

Expertising

See also
Archaeometry

Art talk. A. S. Bamberger. il *Antiques & Collecting Hobbies* 94:18 S '89

A Duke fit for a King [A. van Dyck's portrait of the Duke and Duchess of Buckingham] G. Barker. il por *Art News* 88:87+ D '89

A problematic Poussin [Louvre charged in misattribution of Olympos et Marsyas] G. Danto. il *Art News* 88:70+ Ap '89

Federal aid
See Art and state

Forgeries

See also
Art—Expertising

Art talk. A. S. Bamberger. il *Antiques & Collecting Hobbies* 94:18 Ap '89

The Ryder cover-up [tampering with paintings of A. P. Ryder] W. I. Homer. il por *Art News* 88:158-61 O '89

Scholarly sleuth. E. Beck. il por *Art News* 88:83-4 O '89

Galleries and museums
See Art galleries and museums

History
Study and teaching

See also
Yale University. Dept. of Art History

Art History 101. J. Gardner. *National Review* 41:43-6 D 8 '89

International aspects

The global issue: a symposium [cover story] il *Art in America* 77:86-9+ Jl '89

The peripatetic artist: 14 statements. il *Art in America* 77:130-7+ Jl '89

Laws and regulations

See also
Art trade—Laws and regulations
Artists' rights

Missing and found works

Lost and found [C. de Villalpando's St. Francis before the Pope] R. J. Stroessner and T. Dewalt. il *Americas* 41 no1:60-2 '89

Medical recovery [mural series by W. C. Palmer found] J. Herzfeld. il *Art News* 88:14 Ja '89

Return of the "Bohemian girl" [M. Wolf recovers E. Schiele drawing confiscated by Nazis] A. Decker. il *Art News* 88:74+ Ap '89

Mutilation, defacement, etc.

Dutch disaster [vandalism of paintings at the Dordrechts Museum] M. K. Talley, Jr. il *Art News* 88:60-1 Summ '89

Hammering the body politic, blacks wreck a portrait of a blond, white Jesse Jackson [Washington, D.C.] il *People Weekly* 32:79 D 18 '89

Jackson cites reality in portrait of him as white. il por *Jet* 77:5 D 18 '89

Picking up the pieces [restoration of damage to L. da Vinci's The Virgin and child with St. Anne and John the Baptist at the National Gallery in London] B. Taylor. il *Art News* 88:43+ F '89

Photographs and photography

Photographing your artwork [slides of paintings] S. Marcus. *American Artist* 53:32-3+ F '89

ART—*cont.*

Prices

See also

Art as an investment

The $430-million week [auctions of contemporary and impressionist paintings at Sotheby's and Christie's] B. B. Stretch. il *Art News* 88:25 Ja '89

Adventures in the rich art trade. P. C. Newman. il *Maclean's* 102:33 My 22 '89

The anatomy of a deal [A. Bond's purchase of van Gogh's Irises at auction] R. Hughes. il *Time* 134:66+ N 27 '89

The anxious acquisitors. L. Rosenbaum. il *Art News* 88:144-51 Mr '89

Art asking prices in galleries are rarely firm. il *Antiques & Collecting Hobbies* 93:18+ F '89

The billion-dollar blockbuster [art prices pushing up exhibition expenses] N. Stapen. il *Art News* 88:39-40 S '89

British Rail's runaway Renoir [sale of impressionist and modern pictures and sculptures] G. Barker. *Art News* 88:39 Summ '89

The frenzied art market. il *World Press Review* 36:48 F '89

Fruit, flowers, and a sweet Madonna [high prices at sales of old masters paintings] G. Barker. il *Art News* 88:44 O '89

Henry Moore: more means less. R. W. Walker. *Art News* 88:41 Ap '89

Late Picasso: going cheap. G. Barker. il *Art News* 88:25-6 F '89

The market for Norman Rockwell's work. D. Grant. *American Artist* 53:10+ F '89

A modernist surprise [sale of R. Jonson painting] B. B. Stretch. il *Art News* 88:45-6 N '89

New frontiers for West [B. West] R. W. Walker. il *Art News* 88:46 N '89

Painting by numbers [sale of Picasso's Au lapin agile at Sotheby's] L. Black. il *Maclean's* 102:80 N 27 '89

Paying the price in the print market. D. Grant. *American Artist* 53:12+ Ap '89

Price-tag update: court test due [New York dealer R. Feldman refuses to post prices] W. Robinson. *Art in America* 77:23 Ja '89

Sold! [cover story] R. Hughes. il *Time* 134:60-5 N 27 '89

Sotheby's art market trends. See issues of Forbes beginning November 2, 1987

Spring fever. B. B. Stretch. il *Art News* 88:37-9 Summ '89

A treacherous market. D. Wechsler. il *Forbes* 144:292-4 N 27 '89

What's wrong with this painting? [undervaluation of Latin American painting] R. J. Stroessner and T. Dewalt. il *Américas* 41 no2:58-60 '89

Will high costs curtail museum exhibitions? D. Grant. il *American Artist* 53:10+ O '89

Your $20 million may stretch a little further now. J. H. Dobrzynski. il *Business Week* p150-1 D 25 '89-Ja 1 '90

Yves Klein's market: flying high. R. W. Walker. il por *Art News* 88:37 My '89

Private collections

See Art—Collectors and collecting

Psychological aspects

See also

Stendhal syndrome

Reproductions

Art chic [Metropolitan Museum of Art] J. Levine. il *Forbes* 144:94+ Ag 21 '89

Social aspects

Making art as if the world mattered: some models of creative partnership. S. Gablik. il *Utne Reader* p71-6 Jl/Ag '89

". . . nothing will destroy our culture while people are free to create . . ." [interview with M. S. Forbes] J. F. Cooper. il por *Forbes* 144:20+ O 2 '89

Storage

Too much art? S. E. Weil. il *Art News* 88:232 O '89

Study and teaching

See also

Art—Appreciation

Art—History—Study and teaching

Art schools

Art teachers

Discipline-based art education

Drawing—Study and teaching

Metropolitan Museum of Art (New York, N.Y.). Henry R. Luce Center for the Study of American Art

Painting—Study and teaching

Tim Rollins + K.O.S. (Group)

Art education: a curriculum dilemma. L. N. Peeno. bibl f *Design for Arts in Education* 90:41-3 N/D '88

Discipline: science and art as reflective activities. T. Ewens. bibl f *Design for Arts in Education* 90:2-14 Mr/Ap '89

Teaching our children to see. R. Coles. il por *Art News* 88:246 Ap '89

Aids and devices

Art and computers: is there room in the studio for both? C. H. Welter. bibl f *Design for Arts in Education* 91:18-22 N/D '89

Directories

1989 directory of art schools and workshops. il *American Artist* 53:83-4+ Mr '89

Supply and demand

Too much art? S. E. Weil. il *Art News* 88:232 O '89

Taxation

See Taxation of works of art

Technique

See also

Painting—Technique

Terminology

What's the good word? [need for artists to know the correct terminology when selling their pictures] F. J. Goodman. il *American Artist* 53:98-101 S '89

Themes

See also

Aegean Islands in art

AIDS (Disease) in art

America in art

American flag in art

Angels in art

Animals in art

Aphrodite (Greek deity) in art

Architecture in art

Art galleries and museums in art

Art trade in art

Artists in art

Astronomy in art

Auschwitz (Poland: Concentration camp) in art

Automobiles in art

Bagpipe in art

Balloon ascensions in art

Bark in art

Baseball in art

Bayonne (N.J.) in art

Birdhouses in art

Birds in art

Blacks in art

Boats in art

Books in art

Brooklyn (New York, N.Y.) in art

California in art

Canada in art

Circus in art

Concentration camps in art

Connecticut in art

Constellations in art

Country houses in art

Crucifixion in art

D-Day Invasion, 1944, in art

Dance in art

Death in art

Deserts in art

Dinosaurs in art

Diomede Islands in art

Dogs in art

Don Quixote (Fictional character) in art

Education in art

Egypt in art

Feminist art

Fish in art

Flowers in art

Food in art

Fruit in art

Gardens and gardening in art

Golem in art

Golf in art

Grief in art

Guns in art

Headache in art

Heart in art

Hercules (Roman mythology)—Art

Homeless in art

Horses in art

Hudson River Valley (N.Y. and N.J.) in art

Human figure in art

Indians (American) in art

Labor in art

Lakes in art

Leaves in art

Light in art

Luncheons in art

Madewood Plantation (Napoleonville, La.) in art

Marianne (French national symbol) in art

Mars (Planet) in art

Marsyas (Greek deity) in art

Mastectomy in art

Melancholy in art

Miss Liberty (Symbol) in art

Moscow (Soviet Union) in art

Music in art

Nature in art

New Jersey in art

New York (N.Y.) in art

Niagara River (N.Y. and Ont.) in art

Nuclear warfare in art

Nude in art

Phonograph records in art

Physicians and patients in art

Plants in art

Politics in art

ART—Themes—See also—*cont.*
    Primitivism in art
    Rainbow in art
    Refuse and refuse disposal in art
    Rooms in art
    Roses in art
    Royal Canadian Mounted Police in art
    Russian River (Calif.) in art
    Ships in art
    Siva (Hindu deity) in art
    Skeleton in art
    Skinheads in art
    Slaughtering and slaughterhouses in art
    Socialism in art
    Space flight in art
    Sphinxes in art
    Squid in art
    Stonehenge (England) in art
    Suffolk (England) in art
    Swimming in art
    Telephone calls in art
    Time in art
    Tornadoes in art
    Trenton Falls (N.Y.) in art
    Tulips in art
    United States in art
    Venice (Italy) in art
    Western States in art
    Wilderness areas in art
    Witchcraft in art
    Women in art
    Words in art

Transportation
  See Transportation of works of art

Australia
  See also
  Archibald Prize
Nostalgia and self-congratulation. J. Turner. il *Art News* 88:47 Mr '89

Austria
Austria: soul search: in the wake of neo-expressionism. F. Protzman. il *Art News* 88:148-50 S '89

Belgium
  See also
  Ghent (Belgium)—Art
Belgium: ironic visions and solitary quests. B. Grauman. il *Art News* 88:137-9 S '89

Brazil
  See also
  São Paulo (Brazil)—Art

California
  See also
  Los Angeles (Calif.)—Art
  San Diego (Calif.)—Art
  San Francisco Bay Area (Calif.)—Art
  Santa Barbara (Calif.)—Art

China
  See also
  Beijing (China)—Art

Connecticut
  See also
  Old Lyme (Conn.)—Art

France
  See also
  Paris (France)—Art
France: let them have art. G. Danto. il *Art News* 88:136-9 N '89
France: the revolution continues: a new age of patronage. B. Grauman. il *Art News* 88:132-6 S '89

Germany
  See also
  Berlin (Germany)—Art

Germany (East)
  See also
  Berlin (Germany: East)—Art

Germany (West)
  See also
  Munich (Germany)—Art
Elephant-walk follies. D. Galloway. il *Art in America* 77:68-73+ S '89
West Germany: the no-trend trend: vitality and idiosyncrasy. C. Sabisch. il *Art News* 88:151-5 S '89

Great Britain
  See also
  Plymouth (England)—Art
Great Britain: neo, no: still faithful to the old guard. A. Graham-Dixon. il *Art News* 88:122-6 S '89

Haiti
Revolution on the walls. A. W. Barnett. il *Art in America* 77:67-9+ Jl '89

Hawaii
The artists of Hawaii. V. R. Rivers. il *American Artist* 53:54-9+ Mr '89

Illinois
  See also
  Chicago (Ill.)—Art

Israel
Romancing the stones. M. Ronnen. il *Art News* 88:224 O '89

Italy
  See also
  Siena (Italy)—Art
Italy: trash and treasure: the essence of alchemy. J. Turner. il *Art News* 88:143-7 S '89

Japan
Through the looking glass. J. Koplos. il *Art in America* 77:98-107+ Jl '89

Louisiana
  See also
  New Orleans (La.)—Art

Maine
  See also
  Vinalhaven (Me.)—Art

Netherlands
The Netherlands: from isolation to internationalism. J. Lamoree. il *Art News* 88:156-8 S '89

New Jersey
  See also
  Bayonne (N.J.)—Art

New Mexico
  See also
  Santa Fe (N.M.)—Art
Artists of different cultures in the New Mexico light. A. Hines. il *American Artist* 53:60-5+ D '89

New York (State)
  See also
  East Hampton (N.Y.)—Art
  New York (N.Y.)—Art

Scandinavia
Scandinavia: on the edge between twilight and minimalism. G. Sandqvist. il *Art News* 88:159-63 S '89

Soviet Union
  See also
  Moscow (Soviet Union)—Art
  Suprematism (Art)
Canvases of their own. R. Hughes. il *Time* 133:116-18 Ap 10 '89
Moscow and the Hudson [exhibition of American painting in Moscow] K. Larson. il *New York* 22:79-80 O 16 '89

Spain
Spain: learning to absorb the shock of the new. R. Cembalest. il *Art News* 88:127-31 S '89

Sweden
Sweden's royal treasures. il *History Today* 39:12-13 Ap '89

Switzerland
Switzerland: activism to eclecticism: stirring the alpine calm. E. Beck. il *Art News* 88:140-2 S '89

United States
  See Art

Washington (D.C.)
  See Washington (D.C.)—Art

Washington (State)
  See also
  Seattle (Wash.)—Art

Western Europe
Inside Europe [cover story; special section] il *Art News* 88:121-63 S '89

ART, ABSTRACT
  See also
  Abstract expressionism
  Constructivism
  Minimal art
  Suprematism (Art)
In the latest abstract painting, the old is new. J. Perl. il *Vogue* 179:214+ Ag '89
Swamp things. C. Ratcliff. il *Vogue* 179:282+ Ap '89

Exhibitions
  See also
  Museo de Arte Abstracto Español (Cuenca, Spain)
True colors [exhibit of monochrome paintings in Lyon, France] M. Hafif. bibl f il *Art in America* 77:128-39+ Je '89

ART, AFRICAN
Africa's artistic resurrection [Christian art] R. N. Ostling. il *Time* 133:76-9 Mr 27 '89

Exhibitions
  See also
  Museum Rietberg (Zurich, Switzerland)
Resonant images from Africa [Icons: ideals and power in the art of Africa at the National Museum of African Art] K. M. Burke. il *Smithsonian* 20:252 N '89

ART, AMERICAN
  See also
  Americana
  Art, Black
  Art in Embassies (Program)
  Artists, American
  Drawing, American
  Fluxus (Art movement)
  Indians of North America—Art
  Painting, American
  Pottery, American
  Sculpture, American

ART, AMERICAN—cont.

Exhibitions

See also
Hess Collection Winery
Metropolitan Museum of Art (New York, N.Y.). American Wing
Metropolitan Museum of Art (New York, N.Y.). Henry R. Luce Center for the Study of American Art
National Museum of American Art (U.S.)
Thomas Gilcrease Institute of American History and Art
Whitney Museum of American Art

Competition winners revisited [Realism today: American Artist Competition winners] V. R. Rivers. il *American Artist* 53:58-60 Je '89

Craft Today USA [international traveling exhibit opens in Paris] B. Werther. il *American Craft* 49:32-9 O/N '89

Her infinite variety [Making their mark: women artists move into the mainstream, 1970-85] S. Allison. il *Life* 12:64-8 Je '89

Museum biennials and other controversies [Whitney Biennials and other shows of contemporary American art] D. Grant. *American Artist* 53:12+ Mr '89

A new exhibition proves that even when abstraction dominates, the figure remains irresistible [Bay Area figurative art, 1950-1965] J. Tarshis. il *Vogue* 179:210+ D '89

The Potamkin Collection of American art. L. Bantel. il *Antiques* 136:292-301 Ag '89

Two American artists' colonies [En plein air: the art colonies at East Hampton and Old Lyme, 1880-1930] A. E. Ledes. *Antiques* 136:42+ Jl '89

Under Western eyes [Binational and Carnegie International shows] P. Plagens. bibl f il *Art in America* 77:32-7+ Ja '89

ART, ANCIENT
See also
Geoglyphs

ART, ASIAN
Exhibitions
See also
Arthur M. Sackler Gallery (Washington, D.C.)
Museum Rietberg (Zurich, Switzerland)

ART, AUSTRALIAN
The unknown art of Australia. B. W. Smith. il *The Courier (Unesco)* 41:23-6 D '88

ART, AUSTRALIAN (ABORIGINAL) *See* Australian aborigines—Art

ART, AUSTRIAN
Exhibitions
Austria: soul search: in the wake of neo-expressionism. F. Protzman. il *Art News* 88:148-50 S '89

ART, BELGIAN
See also
Painting, Belgian
Exhibitions
Belgium: ironic visions and solitary quests. B. Grauman. il *Art News* 88:137-9 S '89

ART, BLACK
See also
Harlem renaissance
Exhibitions
Across generations, a creative legacy [Anacostia Museum retrospective Inspiration: 1961-1989] K. M. Burke. il *Smithsonian* 19:151 Ja '89

Black satire and bleeding hearts [R. Colescott show and Art as a verb exhibit] B. W. Bloch. il *The New Leader* 72:22-3 My 1 '89

ART, BRAZILIAN
São Paulo diary. E. Leffingwell. il *Art in America* 77:55-7+ Ja '89
Exhibitions
Courting the carnivalesque [P.S. 1's Brazil projects] D. V. Gast. il *Art in America* 77:66-7+ Ja '89

ART, BRITISH
Exhibitions
Great Britain: neo, no: still faithful to the old guard. A. Graham-Dixon. il *Art News* 88:122-6 S '89

ART, CANADIAN
See also
Indians of North America—Art
Exhibitions
See also
Canadian Biennial of Contemporary Art

ART, CATALAN
Romanesque treasures of Catalonia. E. Carbonell i Esteller. il *The Courier (Unesco)* 42:29-31 My '89

ART, CHINESE
See also
China trade art
Painting, Chinese
Pottery, Chinese

ART, CHRISTIAN *See* Christian art and symbolism

ART, CLASSICAL
See also
Art, Greek
Classicism in art
Neoclassicism (Art)

ART, COMMERCIAL
See also
Advertising art
Fashion drawing
Illustration

Pix: commercial applications of realist art [special section] il *American Artist* 53:21+ S '89

ART, DECORATIVE *See* Decoration and ornament

ART, DUTCH
See also
Painting, Dutch
Exhibitions
The Netherlands: from isolation to internationalism. J. Lamoree. il *Art News* 88:156-8 S '89

ART, EGYPTIAN
Exhibitions
Art à la carte [permanent exhibit Inside ancient Egypt at Field Museum] K. Best. il *Travel Holiday* 171:86 F '89

ART, ENGLISH
See also
Drawing, English
Painting, English
Pottery, English

ART, ESKIMO *See* Eskimos—Art

ART, EUROPEAN
See also
Painting, European
Pottery, European
Exhibitions
See also
Hess Collection Winery
Royal Ontario Museum. Samuel European Galleries

Inside Europe [cover story; special section] il *Art News* 88:121-63 S '89

ART, FANTASTIC
The telltale heart [paintings by G. Bruvel] N. Guccione. il *Omni (New York, N.Y.)* 12:88-93 D '89

ART, FINNISH
See also
Sculpture, Finnish

ART, FRENCH
See also
Painting, French
Pottery, French
Sculpture, French
Situationists International (Group)
Exhibitions
France: let them have art. G. Danto. il *Art News* 88:136-9 N '89

France: the revolution continues: a new age of patronage. B. Grauman. il *Art News* 88:132-6 S '89

The museum as studio [show based on collections of the Musée d'Art Moderne de la Ville de Paris] B. Adams. il *Art in America* 77:63+ O '89

ART, GERMAN
See also
Brücke (Group)
Drawing, German
Painting, German
Exhibitions
Elephant-walk follies. D. Galloway. il *Art in America* 77:68-73+ S '89

German exchange [second half of the Binationale] P. Plagens. il *Art in America* 77:42-5+ Ap '89

German expressionism: Los Angeles County Museum of Art. P. Clothier. il *Art News* 88:154 F '89

Memories of modernism [Berlin show] M. Hübl. il *Art News* 88:181 My '89

Under Western eyes [Binational and Carnegie International shows] P. Plagens. bibl f il *Art in America* 77:32-7+ Ja '89

West Germany: the no-trend trend: vitality and idiosyncrasy. C. Sabisch. il *Art News* 88:151-5 S '89

ART, GREEK
See also
Art, Hellenistic
Sculpture, Greek
Exhibitions
The icon cometh [Holy image, holy space: icons and frescoes from Greece] E. Knippers. il *Christianity Today* 33:55 Ap 7 '89

ART, HELLENISTIC
Greek visions [C. Samios' textile designs based on Hellenic art] J. P. Gage. il *House & Garden* 161:72 F '89

ART, HISPANIC AMERICAN
Exhibitions
See also
Museum of International Folk Art (Santa Fe, N.M.). Hispanic Heritage Wing

Hispanic art in the United States: the Brooklyn Museum. T. Wall. il *Art News* 88:170 D '89

Sex and politics [Hispanic art in the United States at the Brooklyn Museum] K. Larson. il *New York* 22:51-2 Jl 17 '89

ART, INDIAN (AMERICAN) *See* Indians of North America—Art

ART, IRANIAN
Exhibitions
A conqueror's enchanting legacy [Timur and the princely vision at the Arthur M. Sackler Gallery] K. M. Burke. il *Smithsonian* 20:180 Ap '89

ART, ISRAELI
Exhibitions
"Fresh paint" in Israel: a mixed catch. M. Ronnen. il *Art News* 88:157 Ja '89
In the shadow of conflict: Israeli art 1980-1989: Jewish Museum. H. A. Weinberg. il *Art News* 88:205 O '89
Romancing the stones. M. Ronnen. il *Art News* 88:224 O '89

ART, ITALIAN
See also
Arte Povera (Art movement)
Painting, Italian
Exhibitions
Chauvinism and chic [Italian art in the 20th century at the Royal Academy of Arts] W. Feaver. il *Art News* 88:138-45 My '89
Italy: trash and treasure: the essence of alchemy. J. Turner. il *Art News* 88:143-7 S '89
Pentimenti [Italian art 1900-1945 at the Palazzo Grassi in Venice] M. E. Vetrocq. bibl f il *Art in America* 77:57+ S '89
Raw talk, but cooked painting [Italian art in the 20th century at the Royal Academy of Arts] R. Hughes. il *Time* 133:77-8 Ap 3 '89

ART, JAPANESE
See also
Mono-ha (Group)
Painting, Japanese
Suminagashi
Collectors and collecting
East meets West Side: James and Marilyn Marinaccio's Japanese ethos. A. Berman. il pors *Architectural Digest* 46:304-9+ N '89
Exhibitions
See also
Los Angeles County Museum of Art. Pavilion for Japanese Art
Against nature: Japanese art in the eighties: San Francisco Museum of Modern Art. C. Tamblyn. il *Art News* 88:188+ S '89
The arts of war and peace [Japan: the shaping of daimyo culture 1185-1868] P. S. Prescott. il *Newsweek* 113:59 Ja 2 '89
No more tributes to Mount Fuji [Against nature: Japanese art in the eighties at the San Francisco Museum of Modern Art] E. M. Gomez. il *Time* 134:68-9 Jl 31 '89

ART, JEWISH
See also
Art, Israeli
Menorah
Exhibitions
See also
Fenster Museum of Jewish Art (Tulsa, Okla.)
Golem!: Danger, deliverance and art: Jewish Museum. R. Cembalest. il *Art News* 88:150+ F '89

ART, LATIN AMERICAN
See also
Art, Pre-Columbian
Art. V. G. Stoddart. See issues of *Américas* through January/February 1989
Exhibitions
Art in Latin America: Hayward Gallery. W. Feaver. il *Art News* 88:179 N '89
Art in the limelight [modern art] A. Sanjurjo de Casciero. il *Américas* 41 no1:52-7 '89

ART, MADAGASCAN
Exhibitions
Art à la carte [Madagascar: island of the ancestors at the American Museum of Natural History] C. Mac Connie. il *Travel Holiday* 171:92 My '89

ART, MEXICAN AMERICAN
See also
Border Art Workshop. Taller de Arte Fronterizo
Living on the border. D. Joselit. bibl f il *Art in America* 77:120-9 D '89
Exhibitions
Heart gallery [Lo del corazón at the Mexican Museum of San Francisco] il *Psychology Today* 23:52+ Ja/F '89

ART, MIDDLE EASTERN
Exhibitions
See also
Arthur M. Sackler Gallery (Washington, D.C.)

ART, MODERN
See also
Abstract expressionism
Art, Abstract
Art deco
Arte Povera (Art movement)
Body art
Conceptual art
Constructivism
Cubism
Dadaism

Environment (Art)
Expressionism (Art)
Fluxus (Art movement)
Impressionism (Art)
Minimal art
Mono-ha (Group)
Performance art
Photo-realism
Pop art
Postmodernism (Art)
Situationists International (Group)
Suprematism (Art)
Surrealism
Wearable art
Combined operations. E. Heartney. il *Art in America* 77:140-7 Je '89
Consistency is no longer a concern, finds Richard B. Woodward. Not confined to a signature style, many artists are exploring diversity. R. B. Woodward. il *Vogue* 179:98+ Jl '89
Panic in art. *The New Republic* 201 [Reprint v1]:20-1 N 6 '89 [N 7 '14]
The shock of modern art [excerpt from Oil painting techniques and materials] H. Speed. il *Utne Reader* p68-9 Jl/Ag '89
Three folds in the fabric and four autobiographical asides as allegories (or interruptions). R. Morris. il *Art in America* 77:142-51 N '89
Collectors and collecting
Artful independence: up-to-date backdrop for a contemporary collection in Dallas [residence decorated by Jay Spectre] M. Ennis. il *Architectural Digest* 46:212-19 O '89
"The big hit" [Brentwood home of C. and M. Einstein] P. Clothier. il pors *Art News* 88:113-14+ D '89
The big picture [Los Angeles home of J. and M. Nathanson] P. Viladas. il *House & Garden* 161:160-7 S '89
A California collection: sleek spaces for art in Beverly Hills [home decorated for G. and J. Lushing by Illya Hendrix and Thomas Allardyce] B. D. Colen. il *Architectural Digest* 46:126-33 D '89
Director Billy Wilder puts his legendary $22 million-or-so art collection on the auction block. S. K. Reed. il pors *People Weekly* 32:154+ N 13 '89
The happy look [collection of N. and I. Braman] E. Turner. il por *Art News* 88:105+ Mr '89
A life in pictures [20th century collector B. Wilder] P. Viladas. il pors *House & Garden* 161:154-9+ Ap '89
Making room for art [J. and E. Spiegel's Manhattan apartment designed by Peter Shelton and Lee Mindel] J. Giovannini. il *House & Garden* 161:132-9 D '89
Parquet and pop [Paris home of H. Bokanowski] G. Wen. il por *Art News* 88:97-8+ S '89
Playing for keeps [M. Schwartz's collection of eighties art in Manhattan loft] J. Saltz. il pors *House & Garden* 161:162-9 O '89
Portrait of Picasso's tailor [M. Sapone's collection] D. H. Minassian. il pors *Architectural Digest* 46:62+ F '89
Western tilt [B. Berkus' Santa Barbara home] P. Clothier. il por *Art News* 88:95-6+ Summ '89
Exhibitions
See also
Canadian Biennial of Contemporary Art
Carnegie International
Centro per l'Arte Contemporaneo Luigi Pecci (Prato, Italy)
Contemporary Museum (Honolulu, Hawaii)
Hungarian Ludwig Museum for International Contemporary Art
Instituto Valenciano de Arte Moderno (Spain)
Los Angeles County Museum of Art
Magiciens de la Terre (Exhibition)
Massachusetts Museum of Contemporary Art and Architecture
Metropolitan Museum of Art (New York, N.Y.). Lila Acheson Wallace Wing
Musée d'Art Moderne de la Ville de Paris
Musée du Jeu de Paume (Paris, France)
Museum of Modern Art (New York, N.Y.)
Salon (Exhibition)
Whitney Museum of American Art. Biennial Exhibition
The '80s: stop making sense [Los Angeles Museum of Contemporary Art's exhibition A forest of signs; cover story] H. Drohojowska. il *Art News* 88:146-51 O '89
Against nature: Japanese art in the eighties: San Francisco Museum of Modern Art. C. Tamblyn. il *Art News* 88:188+ S '89
Art [Refigured painting: the German image 1960-88] A. C. Danto. *The Nation* 248:531-4 Ap 17 '89
Art in the limelight [Latin American art] A. Sanjurjo de Casciero. il *Américas* 41 no1:52-7 '89
Artists in residences [installations in private houses in Santa Barbara, Calif. and Ghent, Belgium] K. Baker. il *House & Garden* 161:38+ Ja '89
A big influence [independent curator C. Leigh] H. Muschamp. il por *Vogue* 179:98+ Ja '89
Bilderstreit: a quarrel between images. J. Hendrickson. il *Art News* 88:192 S '89
Blind ambition [Refigured painting: the German image 1960-88] K. Larson. il *New York* 22:63-4 Mr 6 '89

ART, MODERN—Exhibitions—*cont.*

Casting a *glasnost* glow on once-obscured artists [traveling exhibit entitled 10 + 10: contemporary Soviet and American painters] S. Meisler. bibl (p183) il *Smithsonian* 20:130-6+ D '89

Chauvinism and chic [Italian art in the 20th century at the Royal Academy of Arts] W. Feaver. il *Art News* 88:138-45 My '89

Courting the carnivalesque [P.S. 1's Brazil projects] D. V. Gast. il *Art in America* 77:66-7+ Ja '89

The East Building's anniversary of art. il *Southern Living* 24:38-9 D '89

Epoca Nueva: meadows Art Museum [contemporary Spanish art] J. Kutner. il *Art News* 88:216-17 Ap '89

"Fresh paint" in Israel: a mixed catch. M. Ronnen. il *Art News* 88:157 Ja '89

German exchange [second half of the Binationale] P. Plagens. il *Art in America* 77:42-5+ Ap '89

Getting your motor revved up [Twentieth-century art: selections for the tenth anniversary of the East Building] E. M. Gomez. il *Art News* 88:48+ My '89

Her infinite variety [Making their mark: women artists move into the mainstream, 1970-85] S. Allison. il *Life* 12:64-8 Je '89

Hispanic art in the United States: the Brooklyn Museum. T. Wall. il *Art News* 88:170 D '89

In the shadow of conflict: Israeli art 1980-1989: Jewish Museum. H. A. Weinberg. il *Art News* 88:205 O '89

Ingres and the modernists. E. Hayt-Atkins. il *Art News* 88:139 F '89

Inside Europe [cover story; special section] il *Art News* 88:121-63 S '89

Memories of modernism [Berlin show] M. Hübl. il *Art News* 88:181 My '89

Monstrous mutants, departing souls [Refigured painting: the German image 1960-88] N. Grimes. il *Art News* 88:162 My '89

Moscow and the Hudson [exhibition of American painting in Moscow] K. Larson. il *New York* 22:79-80 O 16 '89

Museum biennials and other controversies [Whitney Biennials and other shows of contemporary American art] D. Grant. *American Artist* 53:12+ Mr '89

New British painting: Contemporary Arts Center. M. Bloomfield. il *Art News* 88:185 Mr '89

A new exhibition proves that even when abstraction dominates, the figure remains irresistible [Bay Area figurative art, 1950-1965] J. Tarshis. il *Vogue* 179:210+ D '89

No more tributes to Mount Fuji [Against nature: Japanese art in the eighties at the San Francisco Museum of Modern Art] E. M. Gomez. il *Time* 134:68-9 Jl 31 '89

Pentimenti [Italian art 1900-1945 at the Palazzo Grassi in Venice] M. E. Vetrocq. bibl f il *Art in America* 77:57+ S '89

Pilgrims' process [4 Americans at the Brooklyn Museum] K. Larson. il *New York* 22:76-7 Mr 13 '89

Raw talk, but cooked painting [Italian art in the 20th century at the Royal Academy of Arts] R. Hughes. il *Time* 133:77-8 Ap 3 '89

Rehabilitating the Russian avant-garde. J. E. Bowlt. il *Art News* 88:116-19 F '89

Sculpted essences [modern sculpture] M. Stevens. il *The New Republic* 201:28-30 S 4 '89

A shift in perspective. R. Smith. il *Vogue* 179:230+ My '89

Under Western eyes [Binational and Carnegie International shows] P. Plagens. bibl f il *Art in America* 77:32-7+ Ja '89

Unesco—40 years, 40 artists, 40 countries. il *The Courier (Unesco)* 41:18-19 N '88

ART, NEOCLASSICAL *See* Neoclassicism (Art)

ART, ORIENTAL
See also
Art, Japanese

ART, PORTUGUESE
Portuguese art in the maritime era. R. D. F. D. Moreira. il *The Courier (Unesco)* 42:35-6 Ap '89

ART, PRE-COLUMBIAN
Rightful owners [court decisions involving Cypriot mosaics and Peruvian pre-Columbian art] R. W. Walker and L. Nilson. il *Art News* 88:51+ O '89

ART, PREHISTORIC
Ice Age art idea toppled [research by Francesco d'Errico] R. Lewin. *Science* 243:1435 Mr 17 '89

Letters [discussion of July 1989 article, Visual thinking in the Ice Age] R. White. *Scientific American* 261:12+ D '89

Visual thinking in the Ice Age [Aurignacian period body ornaments] R. White. bibl il *Scientific American* 261:92-9 Jl '89

ART, PRIMITIVE
See also
Art, Pre-Columbian
Art, Prehistoric
Cave drawings and paintings
Petroglyphs

ART, RENAISSANCE
See also
Painting, Renaissance

ART, ROMANESQUE
Romanesque treasures of Catalonia. E. Carbonell i Esteller. il *The Courier (Unesco)* 42:29-31 My '89

ART, ROMANTIC *See* Romanticism in art

ART, RUSSIAN
See also
Icons
Painting, Russian
Suprematism (Art)

Collectors and collecting
Glasnost in the galleries: the surge in Soviet art. L. Zinn. il *Business Week* p157 My 15 '89

The making of a market [interest in contemporary Soviet art] R. W. Walker. il *Art News* 88:138-43 Mr '89

Exhibitions
Marketing *perestroika*. A. Wallach. il *Art in America* 77:53-5+ Ap '89

Rehabilitating the Russian avant-garde. J. E. Bowlt. il *Art News* 88:116-19 F '89

ART, SCANDINAVIAN
Exhibitions
Scandinavia: on the edge between twilight and minimalism. G. Sandqvist. il *Art News* 88:159-63 S '89

ART, SHAKER
Exhibitions
See also
Shaker Museum (Old Chatham, N.Y.)

ART, SPANISH
Exhibitions
See also
Museo de Arte Abstracto Español (Cuenca, Spain)
Epoca Nueva: meadows Art Museum [contemporary Spanish art] J. Kutner. il *Art News* 88:216-17 Ap '89

Spain: learning to absorb the shock of the new. R. Cembalest. il *Art News* 88:127-31 S '89

ART, SWEDISH
Exhibitions
Sweden's royal treasures. il *History Today* 39:12-13 Ap '89

ART, SWISS
Exhibitions
Switzerland: activism to eclecticism: stirring the alpine calm. E. Beck. il *Art News* 88:140-2 S '89

ART, TIBETAN
See also
Sculpture, Tibetan

ART, UKRAINIAN
Exhibitions
Treasures trapped in light [exhibition of Ukrainian artistic treasures in York, England] A. Morgan. il *History Today* 39:5 Ap '89

ART, VICTORIAN
See also
Pre-Raphaelites

ART AND ARCHITECTURE
See also
Architecture in art
The great outdoors. M. Malone. il *Newsweek* 114:76+ O 23 '89

Exhibitions
Corporate trophies [New urban landscape exhibit at World Financial Center] A. Schwartzman. il *Art in America* 77:34-7+ F '89

Gimme shelter [New urban landscape show at the World Financial Center] P. Viladas. il *Art News* 88:81-2 Ja '89

ART AND CHILDREN
See also
Children's art
Bring out the artist in your child. C. Katchen. il *Parents* 64:80+ Je '89

Teaching our children to see. R. Coles. il por *Art News* 88:246 Ap '89

ART AND FASHION *See* Fashion and art

ART AND INDUSTRY
See also
Advertising art
Chase Art Fund
British Rail's runaway Renoir [sale of impressionist and modern pictures and sculptures] G. Barker. *Art News* 88:39 Summ '89

Corporate art [artist E. King] D. C. Bacon. il por *Nation's Business* 77:20 N '89

Corporate trophies [New urban landscape exhibit at World Financial Center] A. Schwartzman. il *Art in America* 77:34-7+ F '89

Pitchers at an exhibition [cover story] H. I. Schiller. il *The Nation* 249:37+ Jl 10 '89

ART AND LITERATURE
Once there were five beautiful virgins . . . [novelists' interpretations of drawings by Ronald Searle] il *The New York Times Book Review* 94:16-17 D 3 '89

ART AND MASS MEDIA *See* Mass media and art

ART AND MENTAL ILLNESS
Exhibitions
Wölfli's asylum art. A. Temkin. bibl f il por *Art in America* 77:132-41+ Mr '89

ART AND MORALS
Poisoned genius [P. Picasso] J. Garvey. il *Commonweal* 116:40-1 Ja 27 '89

ART AND MUSIC
See also
Music in art
David Hockney's melodic palette. il por *U.S. News & World Report* 107:70-1 N 13 '89

ART AND PHOTOGRAPHY
See also
Art—Photographs and photography
Photography, Artistic
Exhibitions
The influence of the pictorialists on the art of photography [On the art of fixing a shadow: 150 years of photography] M. Fox. il *Antiques* 136:120-31 Jl '89

ART AND POETRY
A certain slant of light: drawings by Will Barnet, poems by Emily Dickinson. S. Marcus. il *American Artist* 53:56-61 N '89

ART AND PSYCHOANALYSIS See Psychoanalysis and art
ART AND RELIGION
See also
Artists—Religious life
Christian art and symbolism
The Protestant struggle with the image. D. Morgan. il *The Christian Century* 106:308-11 Mr 22-29 '89
Sacred arts [works of J. Schnabel and others] H. Muschamp. il por *Vogue* 179:420-5 Ap '89
Shock art: your tax dollars at work. D. Coran. il *Christianity Today* 33:69-70 S 8 '89
Stalking the spiritual in the visual arts [J. Dillenberger's The visual arts and Christianity in America; cover story] D. Morgan. il *The Christian Century* 106:1152-5 D 6 '89

ART AND SCIENCE
See also
Chaos (Science) in art
Scientific illustration
Discipline: science and art as reflective activities. T. Ewens. bibl f *Design for Arts in Education* 90:2-14 Mr/Ap '89
Images of pain: headache art lends a hand to science [cover story] I. Wickelgren. il *Science News* 136:136-7 Ag 26 '89

ART AND SOCIETY See Art—Social aspects
ART AND STATE
See also
National Endowment for the Arts
Public art
Art, intrigue and human rights [U.S. confiscation of paintings by Cuban artist N. Guillen Landrian] E. Shorris. il *The Nation* 249:14-18 Jl 3 '89
A letter to President Bush. M. Esterow. il *Art News* 88:168 Ja '89
Notes from the editor . . . M. S. Doherty. *American Artist* 53:10 S '89
Austria
Double departure [resignation of directors] F. Protzman. *Art News* 88:77 O '89
Vienna: complexity, contradictions [handling of return of works of art stolen by Nazis] A. Decker. il *Art News* 88:63 My '89
Germany (East)
Report from East Berlin. D. Galloway. il *Art in America* 77:45-7+ Jl '89
Germany (West)
Beuys butter battle [suit over J. Beuys' Fettecke settled] J. Dornberg. il por *Art News* 88:23 Ap '89
Chancellor Kohl on "heirless" art [discussion of September 1988 article, The mounting embarrassment of Germany's Nazi treasures] J. Dornberg. il por *Art News* 88:17 Summ '89
Great Britain
Museums falling down. M. A. Roberts. il *Art News* 88:69-70 N '89
Thatcherism: capital strains. P. Failing. il *Art News* 88:48 Mr '89
Soviet Union
Casting a *glasnost* glow on once-obscured artists. S. Meisler. bibl (p183) il *Smithsonian* 20:130-6+ D '89
Culture and *glasnost*. P. Young. il *Maclean's* 102:42-3 Jl 31 '89
"In a neutral zone" [Soviet artists V. Mironenko, A. Roiter and K. Zvezdochetov visit the U.S.] S. Hochfield. il pors *Art News* 88:47-8 D '89
Marketing *perestroika*. A. Wallach. il *Art in America* 77:53-5+ Ap '89
Perestroika shock. J. Gambrell. il *Art in America* 77:124-31+ F '89
Rebels with a balance: Soviet artists and athletes want to keep more of the dollars they earn abroad. D. Rinehart. il *Maclean's* 102:20-1 Jl 3 '89
Rehabilitating the Russian avant-garde. J. E. Bowlt. il *Art News* 88:116-19 F '89
United States
See Art and state
Western Europe
If Mapplethorpe had lived in Europe. il *U.S. News & World Report* 107:12 Jl 24 '89

ART AND TELEVISION
Drawing for the small screen [children's illustrator M. Hague's art used on thirtysomething] O. David. *Publishers Weekly* 235:103 Ja 20 '89

ART AND THE PRESS See Art news
ART AND THE VISUALLY HANDICAPPED
Please touch the art works [Bringing folk art closer, exhibit geared to visually handicapped] J. Seligmann. il por *Newsweek* 114:77+ N 6 '89

ART AND WAR
See also
France—History—Revolution, 1789-1799—Art
United States—History—War with Mexico, 1845-1848—Art
Vietnamese War, 1957-1975—Art
World War, 1914-1918—Art

ART APPRECIATION See Art—Appreciation
ART AS A PROFESSION
1989 business supplement [special section] il *American Artist* 53:69-83 Je '89
An approach to success. L. Garon. il *American Artist* 53:66-71 Jl '89
Artists' career development. D. Grant. *American Artist* 53:12+ S '89
The artist's second career. D. Grant. *American Artist* 53:84+ Mr '89
Artists' second careers. D. Grant. *American Artist* 53:14+ Ag '89
Beginning a career as a watercolorist [J. Cartier] J. R. Kemp. il por *American Artist* 53:72-5+ Jl '89
A curious relationship [artists and dealers] I. C. Karp. il *Art in America* 77:51+ Mr '89
He upped and quit [sculptor P. Tadlock] W. P. Barrett. il pors *Forbes* 144:282+ O 16 '89
Success stories [cover story; special section] D. Grant. il *American Artist* 53:48-53 D '89

ART AS AN INVESTMENT
Art goes to Wall Street. D. R. Katz. il *Esquire* 112:53-4 Jl '89
Collectors' items: artful investments. A. Feinberg. *Harper's Bazaar* 122:42+ Ja '89
Old collectors never die . . . H. L. Rinker. il *Antiques & Collecting Hobbies* 94:26+ Mr '89
A taste for art and money [investment fraud by R. Polo] C. Dickey. il por *Newsweek* 113:68 My 29 '89
When art is acquired primarily as an investment, will it not be subject to the vagaries of the stock market? R. M. Adams. il *Smithsonian* 19:12 F '89
Your $20 million may stretch a little further now. J. H. Dobrzynski. il *Business Week* p150-1 D 25 '89-Ja 1 '90

ART ASSOCIATIONS See Art clubs and societies
ART ATTACK (GROUP)
Radical surgery [condemned Washington, D.C. house turned into public art] S. Staggs. il *Art News* 88:23 My '89

ART AUCTIONS See Art trade
ART BRUT See Art and mental illness
ART CENTER (EUROPE) See Art Center College of Design (Pasadena, Calif.). European campus
ART CENTER COLLEGE OF DESIGN (PASADENA, CALIF.)
Bike to the future [students create innovative bicycles] B. Weber. il *The New York Times Magazine* p82 F 12 '89

ART CENTER COLLEGE OF DESIGN (PASADENA, CALIF.). EUROPEAN CAMPUS
Art Center College of Design (Europe). J. Dornberg. il *Art News* 88:91-2 N '89

ART CENTERS
See also
Centers for the performing arts
Metropolitan Museum of Art (New York, N.Y.). Henry R. Luce Center for the Study of American Art
Architecture
Brave new world [Headlands Center for the Arts, Calif.] K. D. Stein. il *Architectural Record* 177:118-25 mid-S '89
The ranch artistically reconsidered [Anderson Ranch Arts Center, Aspen, Colorado, designed by Harry Teague] J. S. Russell. il *Architectural Record* 177:74-7 Ap '89
California
See also
Headlands Center for the Arts (Calif.)
Colorado
See also
Anderson Ranch Arts Center
Minnesota
See also
Walker Art Center
Ohio
See also
Wexner Center for the Visual Arts (Columbus, Ohio)
Tennessee
See also
Joe L. Evins Appalachian Center for Crafts
Virginia
See also
Torpedo Factory Art Center (Alexandria, Va.)

ART CLUBS AND SOCIETIES
See also
American Craft Council

ART CLUBS AND SOCIETIES—See also—*cont.*
>   Glass Art Society
>   Oil Pastel Association
>   Situationists International (Group)
> A directory of pastel societies. M. E. Stegmaier. il *American Artist* 53:30-5 Jl '89

ART COLLECTORS AND COLLECTING *See* Art—Collectors and collecting
ART COMPETITIONS *See* Art—Competitions
ART CONFERENCES *See* Art—Conferences
ART CRITICS AND CRITICISM
>   *See also*
>   Baudrillard, Jean, 1929-
>   Danto, Arthur Coleman, 1924-
>   Photography—Criticism, interpretation, etc.
> Having it all: uncritical critics in today's art world. J. Gardner. il *National Review* 41:47-50 My 19 '89
> Public rights and critics' failures. A. E. Elsen. il *Art News* 88:174 F '89

ART DECO
>   *See also*
>   Teco ware
> Art déco revisited: a Beverly Hills residence marked by period flair [decorated by Illya Hendrix for A. Kraines] il *Architectural Digest* 46:154-9 Ag '89
> Critical success: Gene Siskel and Marlene Iglitzen's art déco Chicago apartment [decorated by Bruce Gregga] C. T. Buckley. il pors *Architectural Digest* 46:256-61+ O '89
> Déco interpretations: Karl Springer on the Upper East Side. J. Thurman. il por *Architectural Digest* 46:228-35 N '89
> F. Schumacher and Company and the art moderne style. R. E. Slavin, III. il *Antiques* 135:964-73 Ap '89
> Think architecture is boring? Take a shot at Miami Beach's art deco district. L. Dennis. il *Popular Photography* 96:32-3 O '89

ART DONATIONS AS TAX DEDUCTIONS *See* Income tax—Deductions
ART EDUCATION *See* Art—Study and teaching
ART EXHIBITIONS *See* Art—Exhibitions
ART FAIRS *See* Art—Exhibitions; Arts and crafts—Exhibitions
ART GALLERIES AND MUSEUMS
>   *See also*
>   National Gallery of Art (U.S.)
>   Sculpture gardens and parks
> Private eyes: the modern Medicis [private collectors' museums] T. Gold. il *Harper's Bazaar* 122:98+ My '89
> Securing gallery representation. E. Feit. il *American Artist* 53:69-73 Je '89

Acquisitions
> The anxious acquisitors. L. Rosenbaum. il *Art News* 88:144-51 Mr '89
> Museum accessions. E. H. Gustafson. See occasional issues of *Antiques*
> Nothing to hide [discussion of Summer 1989 article, An outrageous anomaly] A. E. Elsen. il *Art News* 88:190 D '89
> An outrageous anomaly [Getty Museum refuses to disclose source of Aphrodite sculpture] A. E. Elsen. il *Art News* 88:196 Summ '89
> Unanswered questions [Museum of Modern Art's private deal to obtain van Gogh's Portrait of Joseph Roulin] T. McGhee. il *Art News* 88:56+ O '89
> When art is acquired primarily as an investment, will it not be subject to the vagaries of the stock market? R. M. Adams. il *Smithsonian* 19:12 F '89

Architecture
> The delirious palace [Pavilion for Japanese Art at Los Angeles County Museum of Art designed by B. Goff] B. Adams. il *Art in America* 77:136-45 D '89
> 'French history, right here' [renovation on the Louvre] R. Marshall. il *Newsweek* 113:40+ Mr 27 '89
> Kimbell times two [addition designed by R. Giurgola] J. Kutner. il *Art News* 88:56 O '89
> Museum roof as flying carpet [Newport Beach Art Museum] il *Architectural Record* 177:53 O '89
> New chapter for Morgan Library [expansion] M. Alexander. il *Art in America* 77:37 Je '89
> Order out of chaos [Chrysler Museum; cover story] C. Pearson. il *Architectural Record* 177:114-19 Jl '89
> Pei's pyramid—new jewel of the Seine. S. M. Alsop. il *Architectural Digest* 46:29+ Ap '89
> Post impressionism [renovation of the Jeu de Paume] B. Grauman. il *Art News* 88:58 Ja '89
> The riddle of the pyramid [I. M. Pei's addition to the Louvre] R. Kimball. il *Architectural Record* 177:58-61 Ja '89
> Who's afraid of James Stirling? D. Ketcham. il por *Art News* 88:98-103 F '89

Crowd control
> "Please have your tickets ready for 'Degas'" [Metropolitan Museum of Art] M. Esterow. il *Art News* 88:198 Mr '89

Deaccessioning
> Market fever at MOMA [sale of seven paintings to obtain van Gogh's Portrait of Joseph Roulin] W. Robinson. il *Art in America* 77:33 D '89
> Picassos for sale? [plans by Haags Gemeentemuseum director R. H. Fuchs to sell works by Monet and Picasso] J. Turner. il *Art News* 88:84-5+ D '89

Directories
> Guide to galleries, museums, artists [cover story; special issue] il *Art in America* 77:45-51+ Ag '89

Directors
> *See* Museum directors

Finance
>   *See also*
>   Art galleries and museums—Gifts, legacies, etc.
> The billion-dollar blockbuster [art prices pushing up exhibition expenses] N. Stapen. il *Art News* 88:39-40 S '89
> A letter to President Bush. M. Esterow. il *Art News* 88:168 Ja '89
> Will high costs curtail museum exhibitions? D. Grant. il *American Artist* 53:10+ O '89

Fires and fire prevention
> Gallery building gutted [Chicago] P. Wolff. il *Art News* 88:43 Summ '89

Gifts, legacies, etc.
> Tainted money. P. Gardner. il *Art News* 88:180-3 Ap '89

Lighting
> Living on borrowed light [architectural use of daylight] J. S. Russell. il *Architectural Record* 177:150-3 My '89

Management
>   *See also*
>   Art galleries and museums—Trustees, boards, committees, etc.
>   Museum directors

Public relations
> Party palace: the high life at the gilded Metropolitan Museum [cover story] J. Taylor. il *New York* 22:20-30 Ja 9 '89

Thefts
> *See* Art thefts

Tours
> *See* Art tours

Trustees, boards, committees, etc.
> Trustees and trust [museum trustees who are also art collectors] A. Decker. il *Art News* 88:49+ D '89

Alabama
>   *See also*
>   Birmingham Museum of Art (Ala.)

Austria
>   *See also*
>   Graphische Sammlung Albertina
>   Kunsthistorisches Museum (Vienna, Austria)
>   Museum Moderner Kunst (Vienna, Austria)

Belgium
>   *See also*
>   Musées Royaux d'Art et d'Histoire (Belgium)
>   Rubenshuis (Antwerp, Belgium)

California
>   *See also*
>   Hess Collection Winery
>   J. Paul Getty Museum
>   Los Angeles County Museum of Art
>   Newport Harbor Art Museum (Newport Beach, Calif.)
>   Severin Wunderman Foundation Museum

Canada
>   *See also*
>   National Gallery of Canada
> Tribal rights [handling of Canadian Indian artifacts] S. Jennings. il *Art News* 88:70-1 N '89

Colorado
>   *See also*
>   Denver Art Museum

Connecticut
>   *See also*
>   Yale University. Art Gallery

Florida
>   *See also*
>   Lannan Museum (Lake Worth, Fla.)
>   Palm Beach Community College. Lannon Gallery

France
>   *See also*
>   Hermès Museum
>   Musée Carnavalet (Paris, France)
>   Musée d'Art Moderne de la Ville de Paris
>   Musée des Arts Décoratifs (Strasbourg, France)
>   Musée du Jeu de Paume (Paris, France)
>   Musée du Louvre
>   Musée Nissim de Camondo (Paris, France)

Germany (West)
>   *See also*
>   Flower Automat Gallery (Berlin, Germany: West)
>   Museumsinsel Hombroich (Neuss, Germany)
> Chancellor Kohl on "heirless" art [discussion of September 1988 article, The mounting embarrassment of Germany's Nazi treasures] J. Dornberg. il por *Art News* 88:17 Summ '89

Great Britain
>   *See also*
>   Kettle's Yard Gallery
>   Leighton House Art Gallery and Museum (London, England)
>   National Gallery (Great Britain)
>   National Portrait Gallery (Great Britain)
>   Tate Gallery
>   Victoria and Albert Museum

ART GALLERIES AND MUSEUMS—Great Britain—*cont.*
Museums falling down. M. A. Roberts. il *Art News* 88:69-70
N '89

Thatcherism: capital strains. P. Failing. il *Art News* 88:48
Mr '89

Hungary

See also
Hungarian Ludwig Museum for International Contemporary Art

Illinois

See also
Art Institute of Chicago

Indiana

See also
Indianapolis Museum of Art

Italy

See also
Castello di Rivoli (Turin, Italy)
Centro per l'Arte Contemporaneo Luigi Pecci (Prato, Italy)

Maryland

See also
Baltimore Museum of Art
Walters Art Gallery

Massachusetts

See also
Massachusetts Museum of Contemporary Art and Architecture
Museum of Fine Arts (Boston, Mass.)

Minnesota

See also
Walker Art Center

Netherlands

See also
Dordrechts Museum (Netherlands)
Haags Gemeentemuseum (Netherlands)
Kasteel het Nijenhuis (Heino, Netherlands)
Kröller-Müller National Museum (Otterlo, Netherlands)
Rijksmuseum (Netherlands)

New Hampshire

See also
Hood Museum of Art

New Mexico

See also
Museum of International Folk Art (Santa Fe, N.M.)

New York (State)

See also
Artists Space (New York, N.Y.)
Chocolate Milk Art Gallery
Galerie St. Etienne
Heckscher Museum
Metropolitan Museum of Art (New York, N.Y.)
Paula Cooper Gallery
Queens Museum
Shaker Museum (Old Chatham, N.Y.)
Solomon R. Guggenheim Museum
Storm King Art Center
Whitney Museum of American Art

Ohio

See also
Contemporary Arts Center (Cincinnati, Ohio)

Ontario

See also
Thomson Gallery (Toronto, Ont.)

Pennsylvania

See also
Pennsylvania Academy of the Fine Arts

Rhode Island

See also
Redwood Library and Athenaeum (Newport, R.I.)

Southern States

Stop and shop at a museum. il *Southern Living* 24:26-7
F '89

Soviet Union

See also
Pushkin Museum of Fine Arts (Moscow, Soviet Union)

Spain

See also
Instituto Valenciano de Arte Moderno (Spain)
Museo de Arte Abstracto Español (Cuenca, Spain)

Texas

See also
Archer M. Huntington Art Gallery (Austin, Tex.)
Kimbell Art Museum

United States

See Art galleries and museums

Virginia

See also
Chrysler Museum
Maier Museum of Art (Lynchburg, Va.)
Virginia Museum of Fine Arts

Washington (State)

See also
Seattle Art Museum

ART GALLERIES AND MUSEUMS IN ART

Exhibitions

The museum as studio [show based on collections of the
Musée d'Art Moderne de la Ville de Paris] B. Adams.
il *Art in America* 77:63+ O '89

Silvia Kolbowski at Postmasters [show based on Metropolitan
Museum's American Wing] J. Zinsser. il *Art in America*
77:265-6 Ap '89

ART HISTORIANS

See also
Daulte, François, 1928-

ART HISTORY *See* Art—History

ART IN BOOKSTORES

Drawing in customers with art [in-store galleries] A. Symons.
il *Publishers Weekly* 236:62-4 S 1 '89

ART IN CONSTRUCTION (FIRM)

Getting plastered. H. S. MacIsaac. il *House & Garden* 161:56
Ja '89

ART IN EMBASSIES (PROGRAM)

The art of diplomacy. J. A. Lewis. il *Art News* 88:34 Ja
'89

ART IN MOTION PICTURES

Art lovers [I. Adjani in film Camille Claudel] A.-E. Moutet.
il *pors Vogue* 179:498-503+ Mr '89

Mondo Longo [R. Longo's Arena brains] C. Lewis. il *Art
in America* 77:35+ Mr '89

ART IN PRISONS

Build a jail, buy some art [sculpture on grounds of Massachusetts prisons] M. Starr. il *Newsweek* 113:35 Mr 20
'89

ART IN RESTAURANTS

The man upstairs [B. Lamotte's paintings in La Grenouille's
private dining room] W. Goodman. il *pors New York*
22:54-9 Je 19 '89

ART IN SHOPPING CENTERS

Gardens of art [sculpture in The Gardens shopping mall,
Palm Beach Gardens] S. Guy. il *Horizon (Tuscaloosa,
Ala.)* 32:27-8 Ja/F '89

ART IN THE HOME

See also
Antiques
Garden ornaments

Adolfo in New York. B. Morris. il por *Architectural Digest*
46:132-7 S '89

Argentine elan: Amalia Lacroze de Fortabat in Buenos Aires.
J. Gruen. il por *Architectural Digest* 46:202-7+ Mr '89

The art of Arnold Scaasi: a colorful collection on eastern
Long Island. R. Fizdale and A. Gold. il por *Architectural
Digest* 46:174-9 S '89

Art of Eastover: Clare and Eugene Thaw in upstate New
York. S. M. Alsop. il por *Architectural Digest* 46:118-25+
Je '89

Artful independence: up-to-date backdrop for a contemporary
collection in Dallas [residence decorated by Jay Spectre]
M. Ennis. il *Architectural Digest* 46:212-19 O '89

Artist in residence: Count and Countess de Clavière d'Hust
on Long Island. S. Stephens. il pors *Architectural Digest*
46:156-61+ D '89

Artists in residences [installations in private houses in Santa
Barbara, Calif. and Ghent, Belgium] K. Baker. il *House
& Garden* 161:38+ Ja '89

Baring the Burdens. R. Koenig. il pors *Vogue* 179:318-25+
Ag '89

"The big hit" [Brentwood home of C. and M. Einstein]
P. Clothier. il pors *Art News* 88:113-14+ D '89

The big picture [Los Angeles home of J. and M. Nathanson]
P. Viladas. il *House & Garden* 161:160-7 S '89

A California collection: sleek spaces for art in Beverly Hills
[home decorated for G. and J. Lushing by Illya Hendrix
and Thomas Allardyce] B. D. Colen. il *Architectural Digest*
46:126-33 D '89

Canyon hideout [N. Tanen's house in Santa Monica Canyon
filled with folk art] P. Viladas. il *House & Garden*
161:120-5+ Ja '89

Capricious collections by the shore [S. Chase's Del Mar
beach house] M. Webb. il *Architectural Digest* 46:244-9
My '89

Carolyne Roehm: an opulent aesthetic for the designer's
Manhattan residence [decorated by Vincent Fourcade] Suzy.
il por *Architectural Digest* 46:112-19 S '89

Catch of the day [A. Helou's London house decorated with
fishing tackle and art] R. Koenig. il por *House & Garden*
161:54-5 Ja '89

The collectors: neoclassical aesthetic: fashion designer Gaston
Choron in Wiesbaden. D. H. Minassian. il por *Architectural
Digest* 46:240-6+ Ap '89

Contemporary Southwest [Santa Fe adobe home of S. S.
Lewis] R. Morris. il *Architectural Digest* 46:148-55 Ap
'89

Cosmopolitan mise-en-scéne [Manhattan apartment of L. and
A. Blanco decorated by Juan Montoya] C. McGee. il
Architectural Digest 46:186-91 Ap '89

Critical success: Gene Siskel and Marlene Iglitzen's art déco
Chicago apartment [decorated by Bruce Gregga] C. T.
Buckley. il pors *Architectural Digest* 46:256-61+ O '89

David Ireland's art doesn't just hang on a wall—it is the
wall. R. Lacayo. il pors *People Weekly* 31:135+ Ap 10
'89

ART IN THE HOME—*cont.*

Dealer's choice [M. Boone] J. J. Buck. il por *Vogue* 179:336-45+ F '89

Déco interpretations: Karl Springer on the Upper East Side. J. Thurman. il por *Architectural Digest* 46:228-35 N '89

East meets West Side: James and Marilyn Marinaccio's Japanese ethos. A. Berman. il pors *Architectural Digest* 46:304-9+ N '89

Eastern soul [Palos Verdes Peninsula home decorated by Anthony Machado] I. Borger. il *Architectural Digest* 46:308-14+ My '89

Easton meets Midwest [Chicago house decorated by David Easton] J. Edelstein and L. Wren. il *House & Garden* 161:112-19 F '89

An educated palette [Manhattan loft of R. Rosenblum and J. Kaplowitz] J. Russell. il pors *House & Garden* 161:136-9+ Je '89

Evolution of a classic: a Fifth Avenue signature by the late Melanie Kahane. S. Stephens. il *Architectural Digest* 46:242-9+ N '89

Flesh and spirit [New York home of S. Pivar] M. E. Haus. il por *Art News* 88:75-6+ Ja '89

The happy look [modern art collection of N. and I. Braman] E. Turner. il por *Art News* 88:105+ Mr '89

Honoring their Cherokee heritage [Kay and Ron Hendricks' log house in north Georgia] C. Engle. il *Southern Living* 24:90-2 O '89

In memory of his wife, Joe Furey created an unusual artwork that may not survive [decoration of Brooklyn, N.Y. apartment] R. Arias. il pors *People Weekly* 32:104-5 S 4 '89

A life in pictures [20th century collector B. Wilder] P. Viladas. il pors *House & Garden* 161:154-9+ Ap '89

Making room for art [J. and E. Spiegel's Manhattan apartment designed by Peter Shelton and Lee Mindel] J. Giovannini. il *House & Garden* 161:132-9 D '89

A Manhattan sampler [remodeled brownstone owned by M. Malcé and J. Kelter] S. M. L. Aronson. il pors *Architectural Digest* 46:158-63+ Je '89

Matching flowers to art. T. A. Steadman. il *Southern Living* 24:58-60 Ja '89

Noble Roman [F. Forquet's Rome apartment] M. Mewshaw. il por *House & Garden* 161:128-39+ My '89

On the Côte d'Azur: Martin and Toni Sosnoff's villa above Nice [1925 house decorated by Timothy Macdonald] J. Gruen. il *Architectural Digest* 46:88-93 Ja '89

Parquet and pop [Paris home of H. Bokanowski] G. Wen. il por *Art News* 88:97-8+ S '89

Playing for keeps [M. Schwartz's collection of eighties art in Manhattan loft] J. Saltz. il pors *House & Garden* 161:162-9 O '89

Roman revival [A. Magistretti's apartment] J. Turner. il por *House & Garden* 161:114-19+ Ja '89

Rustic frame for a modern collection: the Connecticut house of Katharine and Nicholas Fox Weber [18th century farmhouse and converted barn] R. W. B. Lewis. il *Architectural Digest* 46:200-5+ Je '89

Surreal note in Belgium: artist Roger Nellens' collection at Knokke. E. White. il *Architectural Digest* 46:142-9+ D '89

Vass horizons [Manhattan loft] J. Etra. il por *House & Garden* 161:60-9+ Ja '89

A very private collection [Manhattan apartment decorated by S. Parish] J. Richardson. il *House & Garden* 161:154-61 O '89

Western tilt [B. Berkus' Santa Barbara home] P. Clothier. il por *Art News* 88:95-6+ Summ '89

ART INSTITUTE OF CHICAGO

Big job on little rooms [Thorne Miniature Rooms] B. Lau. il *Americana* 17:30-3 My/Je '89

ART INSTITUTE OF CHICAGO. SCHOOL

Art for whose sake? [furor over American flag on floor at exhibition] S. Marlin. *National Review* 41:21-2 Ap 21 '89

Flag furor [S. Tyler's What is the proper way to display a U.S. flag?] S. Hochfield. il por *Art News* 88:43-4+ Summ '89

ART LITERATURE

See also
Art—Bibliography
Publishers and publishing—Art literature

ART LOANS

How to borrow a Rodin [Museum Loan Program from Pew Charitable Trusts will fund inter-museum loans in Philadelphia] S. Staggs. il *Art News* 88:50+ Ap '89

ART MARKET *See* Art trade

ART MATERIALS *See* Artists' materials

ART METAL WORK

See also
Cloisonné
Goldsmithing
Jewelry
Metal sculpture
Tole painting

Dirk van Erp: artistry in metal. B. E. Johnson. bibl f il *Antiques & Collecting Hobbies* 94:32-3+ O '89

Heady metal [G. A. Leavitt] L. Stains. il por *Home Mechanix* 85:14-16+ Je '89

Luster of the past [work produced by Edward F. Caldwell & Co.] M. B. Caldwell. il *House & Garden* 161:96+ N '89

Precious metals [work of M. Zimmermann] D. Saatchi. il por *House & Garden* 161:146-51+ Je '89

ART MUSEUMS *See* Art galleries and museums

ART NEWS

Artworld. See issues of Art in America

The sampler: a selection of previews, reviews, sundries, and suggestions. See issues of Americana

ART NOUVEAU

See also
Art deco

Benson's burners [fixtures by W. A. S. Benson] M. Filler. il *House & Garden* 161:52 Ja '89

Fathers and sons [Prague house of J. Mucha] S. Staggs. il *Art News* 88:83-4+ My '89

Exhibitions

Munich's design for living [Art nouveau in Munich: masters of the Jugendstil] M. Makela. bibl f il *Art in America* 77:144-51 F '89

ART OBJECTS

See also
Art in the home
Censers
Display of antiques, art objects, etc.

Conservation and restoration

See Art—Conservation and restoration

Reproductions

See Art—Reproductions

Taxation

See Taxation of works of art

Transportation

See Transportation of works of art

ART OBJECTS, CHINESE

See also
China trade art

ART OF LIVING *See* Conduct of life

ART OF THE WESTERN WORLD [television program] See Television program reviews—Single works

ART ORGANIZATIONS *See* Art clubs and societies

ART OWNERSHIP

Time share [B. Shahn painting, The jury box, owned jointly by four couples] *The New Yorker* 65:26-7 Jl 3 '89

ART PATRONAGE

See also
Art and industry
Arts and industry

The fine art of giving [interview with P. Mellon] S. Allis. il por *Time* 134:86-7 S 18. '89

The Force behind the Whitney [J. Force] A. Berman. il pors *American Heritage* 40:102-13 S/O '89

Patronage and the publication of botanical illustration [Nature's mirror exhibit; cover story] B. G. Callery. il *Antiques* 136:268-81 Ag '89

Private eyes: the modern Medicis [private collectors' museums] T. Gold. il *Harper's Bazaar* 122:98+ My '89

Summer, storm [classic drama among artist, patron and public] M. Greenfield. il *Newsweek* 114:76 S 4 '89

ART PUBLISHING *See* Publishers and publishing—Art

ART SALES *See* Art trade

ART SCHOOLS

See also
Art Center College of Design (Pasadena, Calif.)
Art Institute of Chicago. School
Greenwich House Pottery

Spotlight on schools. *Teen* 33:109 My '89

Directories

1989 directory of art schools and workshops. il *American Artist* 53:83-4+ Mr '89

Switzerland

See also
Art Center College of Design (Pasadena, Calif.). European campus

ART SHOW (NEW YORK, N.Y.)

Art dealers are puttin' on the glitz. J. H. Dobrzynski. il *Business Week* p83 F 27 '89

ART SHOWS *See* Art—Exhibitions

ART STUDIOS *See* Artists' studios

ART TEACHERS

Certification

The Florida state initial teacher certification test: a case study. C. M. Dorn. bibl f *Design for Arts in Education* 90:37-42 Mr/Ap '89

ART THEFTS

Court orders return of looted art [Cypriot mosaics] *Art in America* 77:256 O '89

Heisting buyers on their own petards. il *U.S. News & World Report* 106:16 My 15 '89

Litigators of the lost art [Cypriot mosaics] S. Mannheimer. il *The Saturday Evening Post* 261:62-8 O '89

Missing masterpieces. C. Dickey. il *Newsweek* 113:65-8 My 29 '89

The portrait of a scandal [Louvre implicated in receiving stolen goods in case of Murillo's Gentleman of Seville] C. Dickey. il por *Newsweek* 113:55 Ja 9 '89

Raiders of the lost art, the nonmovie [Cypriot mosaics] il *U.S. News & World Report* 106:13 Je 12 '89

ART THEFTS—*cont.*

A secret cache [art from Paris museums stolen by F. Fielder] B. Grauman. il *Art News* 88:59-60 Summ '89

The smell of fine art [combating theft by spraying paintings with scents detectible only by dogs] il *Discover* 10:12 Ag '89

Unfit for hanging [E. Manet's Bouquet of peonies stolen from Heckscher Museum] R. Cembalest. il *Art News* 88:16 F '89

ART TOURS

Raider of the lost art [tours of the Metropolitan Museum by P. D. Magriel] M. Filler. il por *House & Garden* 161:36+ Ap '89

ART TRADE

> See also
> Art galleries and museums
> Chicago International Art Exposition
> Indian Market (Santa Fe, N.M.)
> Lagniappe (Firm)
> Photographs—Marketing
> Prisunic Gallery
> Ronald Feldman Fine Arts, Inc.
> Street art
> W. Graham Arader III Gallery
> Washington Square Art Show

1989 business supplement [special section] il *American Artist* 53:69-83 Je '89

Art dealers are puttin' on the glitz [New York City's Art Show tries to draw buyers from auction houses] J. H. Dobrzynski. il *Business Week* p83 F 27 '89

The art market. See issues of Art News

Best bids. B. Felner. See occassional issues of New York beginning November 14, 1988

But will it fit over the couch? [spec sheet for custom made paintings] L. Pozzi. *Harper's* 279:35 S '89

Creating mail-order art. D. Grant. il *American Artist* 53:10+ N '89

A curious relationship [artists and dealers] I. C. Karp. il *Art in America* 77:51+ Mr '89

The greatest [1760 mahogany secretary built by J. Goddard sold at auction for over twelve million dollars] *The New Yorker* 65:39-40 O 9 '89

What's the good word? [need for artists to know the correct terminology when selling their pictures] F. J. Goodman. il *American Artist* 53:98-101 S '89

Conferences

Can a socialist win in a free market? Pavel Khoroshilov as Leo Castelli? [Art bridge conference in Moscow] M. Esterow. il pors *Art News* 88:51-2+ S '89

Ethical aspects

The antiquities boom: who pays the price? [cover story] W. Grimes. il pors *The New York Times Magazine* p16-19+ Jl 16 '89

The art that tourists bring home may reflect declining standards of craftsmanship, but also innovation. R. M. Adams. il *Smithsonian* 20:12 My '89

Buying at auction is not recommended for inexperienced collectors. A. S. Bamberger. il *Antiques & Collecting Hobbies* 94:18 D '89

Cast in doubt [sale of unauthorized bronze casts] S. Hochfield. il *Art News* 88:108-15 F '89

Court orders return of looted art [Cypriot mosaics] *Art in America* 77:256 O '89

Curators in court [P. Rosenberg and J.-D. Ludmann] B. Grauman. il *Art News* 88:72-4 Ap '89

Even the Met has been taken. C. Brown. il *Forbes* 144:294+ D 11 '89

In Indiana, a battle over stolen mosaics [Cypriot mosaics] D. Tsiantar. il *Newsweek* 113:66-7 My 29 '89

Litigators of the lost art [Cypriot mosaics] S. Mannheimer. il *The Saturday Evening Post* 261:62-8 O '89

Nothing to hide [discussion of Summer 1989 article, An outrageous anomaly] A. E. Elsen. il *Art News* 88:190 D '89

An outrageous anomaly [Getty Museum refuses to disclose source of Aphrodite sculpture] A. E. Elsen. il *Art News* 88:196 Summ '89

A problematic Poussin [Louvre charged in misattribution of Olympos et Marsyas] G. Danto. il *Art News* 88:70+ Ap '89

Raiders of the lost art, the nonmovie [Cypriot mosaics] il *U.S. News & World Report* 106:13 Je 12 '89

Rightful owners [court decisions involving Cypriot mosaics and Peruvian pre-Columbian art] R. W. Walker and L. Nilson. il *Art News* 88:51+ O '89

Scandals rock French museums. W. Robinson. il por *Art in America* 77:21+ F '89

Trustees and trust [museum trustees who are also art collectors] A. Decker. il *Art News* 88:49+ D '89

Who owns the Nataraja? [British court rules that Siva bronze bought by Canadian collector belongs to India] S. E. Weil. il *Art News* 88:188 My '89

International aspects

The frenzied art market. il *World Press Review* 36:48 F '89

Sold! [cover story] R. Hughes. il *Time* 134:60-5 N 27 '89

Laws and regulations

Art asking prices in galleries are rarely firm. il *Antiques & Collecting Hobbies* 93:18+ F '89

Price-tag update: court test due [New York dealer R. Feldman refuses to post prices] W. Robinson. *Art in America* 77:23 Ja '89

Terminology

Cracking the cryptic code of the auction world. J. H. Dobrzynski. il *Business Week* p98 Jl 10 '89

Canada

Adventures in the rich art trade. P. C. Newman. il *Maclean's* 102:33 My 22 '89

An artistic bottom line. P. Chisholm. il *Maclean's* 102:36-7 Mr 27 '89

Spirits in the gallery [work of native Canadians] P. Young. il *Maclean's* 102:78+ N 13 '89

France

> See also
> Hôtel Drouot (Paris, France)

An art market for the '90s? T. Godfrey. il *Art in America* 77:44-5+ O '89

The French touch [crafts] C. Petkanas. il *House & Garden* 161:156+ Jl '89

Great Britain

> See also
> Christie's (London, England)
> Sotheby's (Firm)

Italy

A sculptor's heaven on earth is Italy's city of holy stone [Pietrasanta] I. Shenker. il *Smithsonian* 19:106-12+ F '89

Soviet Union

Can a socialist win in a free market? Pavel Khoroshilov as Leo Castelli? [Art bridge conference in Moscow] M. Esterow. il pors *Art News* 88:51-2+ S '89

Culture and *glasnost*. P. Young. il *Maclean's* 102:42-3 Jl 31 '89

Glasnost in the galleries: the surge in Soviet art. L. Zinn. il *Business Week* p157 My 15 '89

The making of a market [interest in contemporary Soviet art] R. W. Walker. il *Art News* 88:138-43 Mr '89

Marketing *perestroika*. A. Wallach. il *Art in America* 77:53-5+ Ap '89

Perestroika shock. J. Gambrell. il *Art in America* 77:124-31+ F '89

Rebels with a balance: Soviet artists and athletes want to keep more of the dollars they earn abroad. D. Rinehart. il *Maclean's* 102:20-1 Jl 3 '89

ART TRADE IN ART

Exhibitions

Jiri Georg Dokoupil: Robert Miller. L. Holst. il *Art News* 88:159 D '89

ART TREASURES, PROTECTION OF *See* Cultural property—Protection

ARTE POVERA (ART MOVEMENT)

Exhibitions

Mario Merz [Guggenheim show] A. C. Danto. *The Nation* 249:613-16 N 20 '89

Toward Arte Povera: Padiglione d'Arte Contemporanea. S. Caley. il *Art News* 88:187-8 Summ '89

ARTE PUBLICO PRESS

Arte Publico: keeping Hispanic literature alive. J. Barbato. *Publishers Weekly* 235:42 Je 9 '89

ARTEC, INC.

Doing business with videotex [use of Prodigy network in video cassette marketing] M. Antonoff. il *Personal Computing* 13:77 My '89

ARTEMISIA *See* Wormwood

ARTEMISININ

Weeding out malaria. D. L. Klayman. il *Natural History* p18+ O '89

ARTERBURN, STEPHEN, 1953-

What would Jesus do about AIDS? por *Christianity Today* 33:10 F 3 '89

ARTERIES

Diseases

> See also
> Arteriosclerosis

Therapy

> See also
> Blood vessels—Surgery
> Cardiac catheterization

Angioplasty deemed unnecessary for many [balloon angioplasty] R. Weiss. *Science News* 135:148 Mr 11 '89

Arterial Rotorooters chop up cholesterol. B. Carpenter. il *High Technology Business* 9:9 Mr '89

Balloon trial [questionable value of percutaneous transluminal coronary angioplasty after heart attacks] T. Appenzeller. *Scientific American* 260:32+ My '89

Clot-busters bring bioelectrical benefits [research by Eli S. Gang and others] R. Weiss. *Science News* 136:182 S 16 '89

Implantation of vascular grafts lined with genetically modified endothelial cells. J. M. Wilson and others. bibl f il *Science* 244:1344-6 Je 16 '89

Inhibitors of angiotensin-converting enzyme prevent myointimal proliferation after vascular injury [use of cilazapril after balloon catheterization] J. S. Powell and others. bibl f il *Science* 245:186-8 Jl 14 '89

ARTERIES—Diseases—Therapy—*cont.*
Lasers take lead in angioplasty treatment. *High Technology Business* 9:37-8 Ap '89
Now in vivo: altering endothelial cells. R. Cowen. *Science News* 135:373 Je 17 '89
Recombinant gene expression in vivo within endothelial cells of the arterial wall. E. G. Nabel and others. bibl f il *Science* 244:1342-4 Je 16 '89
Surgery
See Blood vessels—Surgery
ARTERIOSCLEROSIS
See also
Intermittent claudication
Happy hearts [depression linked with coronary artery disease; research by Robert M. Carney] *Prevention (Emmaus, Pa.)* 41:10-12 F '89
The heart of depression [link with coronary artery disease; research by Robert M. Carney] *Science News* 135:13 Ja 7 '89
Causes
Lipoprotein(a)'s role in heart attacks explored [research by Richard Lawn] J. L. Marx. *Science* 243:316 Ja 20 '89
Meet apo A-I and apo B. *Prevention (Emmaus, Pa.)* 41:19-20 S '89
The mysteries of lipoprotein(a). G. Utermann. bibl f il *Science* 246:904-10 N 17 '89
Nutritional aspects
See also
Cholesterol
ARTHRITIS
See also
Ankylosing spondylitis
Lyme disease
Arthritis—at your age? S. Young. il *Glamour* 87:62+ Ag '89
Heart of an Ironman [triathlete G. Yates] J. G. Hubbell. il pors *Reader's Digest* 134:13-14+ Mr '89
Living with arthritis [cover story] M. Beck. il *Newsweek* 113:64-70 Mr 20 '89
Causes
Joints feel the weight [osteoarthritis linked to obesity] il *Prevention (Emmaus, Pa.)* 41:10 F '89
Nutritional aspects
The anti-arthritis diet [use of fish oil] G. L. Blackburn. il *Prevention (Emmaus, Pa.)* 41:34-5+ F '89
Therapy
See also
Ibuprofen
Arthritis relief [use of hydroxychloroquine and sulfasalazine to slow rheumatoid arthritis] il *Prevention (Emmaus, Pa.)* 41:8+ O '89
Arthritis: what works [excerpt] D. Sobel and A. C. Klein. il *Good Housekeeping* 209:138-9+ O '89
Conquering the crippler of joints. J. Carey. il *U.S. News & World Report* 106:79 Ja 30 '89
Folk belief in deep-down relief [radon] J. Adler. il *Newsweek* 113:70 Mr 20 '89
For arthritis, try fitness. il *Prevention (Emmaus, Pa.)* 41:10+ S '89
Relief for sore joints [special section] il *New Choices for the Best Years* 29:58-60+ S '89
ARTHROPODS
See also
Horseshoe crabs
Sexual behavior—Arthropods
ARTHROPODS, FOSSIL
See also
Trilobites
The early radiation and relationships of the major arthropod groups. D. E. G. Briggs and R. A. Fortey. bibl f il *Science* 246:241-3 O 13 '89
ARTHUR, ARIELLE EMMETT- *See* Emmett-Arthur, Arielle
ARTHUR, MAVIS E., 1945-
(jt. auth) *See* Caruso, James R., 1932-, and Arthur, Mavis E., 1945-
ARTHUR, PAUL
The Academy Awards: back in the envelope, please. il *USA Today (Periodical)* 118:93 Jl '89
Hollywood: the dustbin of history. il *USA Today (Periodical)* 117:35 My '89
The place is the thing. il *USA Today (Periodical)* 118:93 N '89
Survival of the fittest. il *USA Today (Periodical)* 117:67 Ja '89
Tales of the Naked City. il *USA Today (Periodical)* 117:93 Mr '89
Voices from the underground. il *USA Today (Periodical)* 118:33 S '89
ARTHUR A. ADLER (FIRM)
The president's haberdasher. D. Wise. il *Gentlemen's Quarterly* 59:35+ My '89
ARTHUR ANDERSEN & COMPANY
Why Andersen dumped Price. D. Greising. *Business Week* p47 O 9 '89
ARTHUR GUINNESS & SONS PLC
See also
Guinness plc

ARTHUR M. SACKLER GALLERY (WASHINGTON, D.C.)
Islamic paintings at the Sackler enchant the eye [H. Vever collection] C. Bond. il *Smithsonian* 19:122-7 Ja '89
ARTHUR YOUNG & COMPANY
When one plus one equals no. 1 [Ernst & Whinney's merger with Arthur Young] J. M. Laderman. *Business Week* p92+ Je 5 '89
ARTHURIAN ROMANCES
Adaptations
A Connecticut Yankee in hell [work of M. Twain] J. Kaplan. il *American Heritage* 40:97-102+ N '89
Crossway's crossover novelist [S. Lawhead's Arthurian saga] B. Summer. il por *Publishers Weekly* 236:28+ O 6 '89
ARTHUS-BERTRAND, YANN
Above Kenya [photographs] il *Life* 12:90-5 Ag '89
ARTICHOKES
See also
Cooking—Vegetables
Artichokes. J. Del Valle. il *Gourmet* 49:92-3+ Ap '89
ARTICLES FOR PERIODICALS *See* Periodical articles
ARTIFACTS, INDIAN (AMERICAN) *See* Indians of North America—Antiquities
ARTIFACTS, PROTECTION OF *See* Cultural property—Protection
ARTIFICIAL BODY PARTS *See* Prosthesis
ARTIFICIAL BONE *See* Bone, Artificial
ARTIFICIAL CELLS *See* Cells, Artificial
ARTIFICIAL CHROMOSOMES *See* Chromosomes, Artificial
ARTIFICIAL COMETS *See* Comets, Artificial
ARTIFICIAL EAR *See* Ear, Artificial
ARTIFICIAL FERTILIZATION IN VITRO *See* Fertilization in vitro
ARTIFICIAL FINGERNAILS *See* Nails (Anatomy), Artificial
ARTIFICIAL FOG *See* Fog, Artificial
ARTIFICIAL FOOD *See* Food, Artificial
ARTIFICIAL FOOT *See* Foot, Artificial
ARTIFICIAL FRUIT *See* Fruit, Artificial
ARTIFICIAL FUR *See* Fur, Artificial
ARTIFICIAL GILLS *See* Gills, Artificial
ARTIFICIAL HEART *See* Heart, Artificial
ARTIFICIAL HIP JOINT *See* Hip joint, Artificial
ARTIFICIAL INSEMINATION
See also
Ova—Transplantation
ARTIFICIAL INSEMINATION, HUMAN
See also
Surrogate mothers
Single mothers by choice. J. Seligmann. il *Newsweek* 114 Special Issue:40+ Wint '89/Spr '90
This is what you thought: 50% say doctors should turn down lesbians for artificial insemination [survey results] il *Glamour* 87:141 Ag '89
ARTIFICIAL INTELLIGENCE
See also
Discovery systems (Computers)
Expert systems (Computers)
Hypertext
IntelliCorp Inc.
Machine translating
Massively parallel supercomputers
Natural language processing
Neural network computers
Self organizing systems
Symbolics Inc.
Artificial intelligence [careers] D. P. Wash. il *Occupational Outlook Quarterly* 33:2-7 Summ '89
Artificial intelligence and the Chinese Room: an exchange [theories of J. Searle] E. Motzkin. il *The New York Review of Books* 36:44-5 F 16 '89
Conscious technology: the co-evolution of mind and machine [excerpt from Future mind; cover story] J. C. Glenn. il por *The Futurist* 23:15-20 S/O '89
The creative computer [Q1 algebra; work of B. Williams] B. Lawren. il *Omni (New York, N.Y.)* 11:28+ Je '89
Four in race for sub AI deal. *High Technology Business* 9:32 Je '89
The intelligence transplant. M. L. Minsky. il por *Discover* 10:52-6+ O '89
Interview: Hans Moravec. E. Regis. por *Omni (New York, N.Y.)* 11:74-6+ Ag '89
Japan & AI: $38.4 billion in 1995? *High Technology Business* 9:39 Mr '89
Machine dreams [Japan's Fifth Generation project] H. Ullman. il *The New Republic* 201:12-14 Jl 17-24 '89
Manufacturing intelligence [smart factories] P. Wallich. il *Scientific American* 261:100+ D '89
A Pandora's box of minds, machines and metaphysics [views of R. Penrose] A. K. Dewdney. il *Scientific American* 261:140+ D '89
PCs for the year 2000 [work of A. Kay] M. Rogers. il por *Newsweek* 114:36 O 2 '89
Predictions for 1989. *High Technology Business* 9:38 My '89
Research targets machines that learn. *High Technology Business* 9:39 F '89
Robots with human intelligence. il *The Futurist* 23:52-3 Mr/Ap '89

ARTIFICIAL INTELLIGENCE—*cont.*
Smart factories: America's turn? O. Port. il *Business Week* p142-5+ My 8 '89
Telepower: the emerging global brain. J. N. Pelton. il por *The Futurist* 23:9-14 S/O '89

Conferences
Wires that think [International Joint Conference on Artificial Intelligence] P. Wallich. *Scientific American* 261:20 N '89

ARTIFICIAL ISLANDS
Island for new international airport rises in Osaka Bay. J. Ott. il *Aviation Week & Space Technology* 130:71-2 My 8 '89

ARTIFICIAL JOINTS *See* Joints, Artificial
ARTIFICIAL LEATHER *See* Leather, Artificial
ARTIFICIAL LEG *See* Leg, Artificial
ARTIFICIAL LIGHT GARDENING
Get the garden going [bedding plants from seed] il *Southern Living* 24:48-9 Ja '89
Land of the midnight melons? [fiber optic transmission of rays to Arctic crops in indoor gardens; work of Dennis R. St. George] *Science News* 136:412 D 23-30 '89

ARTIFICIAL LIGHTING *See* Lighting
ARTIFICIAL MEMBRANES *See* Membranes (Technology)
ARTIFICIAL NAIL REMOVERS *See* Nails (Anatomy), Artificial—Removers
ARTIFICIAL PACEMAKER (HEART) *See* Pacemaker, Artificial (Heart)
ARTIFICIAL REEFS *See* Reefs, Artificial
ARTIFICIAL SATELLITES

See also
Energetics Satellite Corporation
Eosat (Firm)
General Electric Co. Astro Space Division
Long-Duration Exposure Facility (Artificial satellite)
Tethered Satellite System
Lockheed renovates clean room for work on large satellites. il *Aviation Week & Space Technology* 130:303 Je 12 '89
Lunar flash mystery: solved or deepened? [satellite hypothesis] il *Sky and Telescope* 78:461 N '89
NASA to build 'Small Explorer' satellites. J. Eberhart. *Science News* 135:229 Ap 15 '89

Accidents
U.S., USSR test new strategic satellites; Soviet intelligence spacecraft explodes. C. Covault. il *Aviation Week & Space Technology* 131:26-7 Ag 14 '89

Astronomical use
See also
Cosmic Background Explorer (Artificial satellite)
Gamma Ray Observatory (Artificial satellite)
Hipparcos (Artificial satellites)
Hubble Space Telescope
Astronomy in orbit [table] *Sky and Telescope* 77:243 Mr '89
Ball will build radio astronomy payload for Submillimeter Wave Satellite. il *Aviation Week & Space Technology* 131:50 S 18 '89
Distribution and detection of positrons from an orbiting nuclear reactor [observations by Solar Maximum Mission satellite] E. W. Hones and P. R. Higbie. bibl f il *Science* 244:448-51 Ap 28 '89
Diverse recipes shine in the sun's corona [Solar Max data; research by Keith T. Strong] J. Eberhart. *Science News* 135:358 Je 10 '89
Geomagnetic origin for transient particle events from nuclear reactor-powered satellites [experiment on Solar Maximum Mission satellite] G. H. Share and others. bibl f il *Science* 244:444-8 Ap 28 '89
Granat astronomy satellite launched from Cosmodrome [Soviet spacecraft] J. M. Lenorovitz. *Aviation Week & Space Technology* 131:34 D 11 '89
How a star is born [Submillimeter Wave Astronomy Satellite project by Gary Melnick] K. Hartley. il *Astronomy* 17:14 D '89
Infrared miners [Infrared Astronomy Satellite] S. J. Nadis. il *Omni (New York, N.Y.)* 11:26 My '89
Little missions, big returns. S. P. Maran. il *Astronomy* 17:34-40 Ja '89
Man-made transients observed by the gamma-ray spectrometer on the Solar Maximum Mission satellite. E. Rieger and others. bibl f il *Science* 244:441-4 Ap 28 '89
Pegasus will launch U.S. minisatellite to survey X-rays [Array of Low-Energy X-Ray Imaging Sensors] *Aviation Week & Space Technology* 131:55 S 18 '89
R.I.P. Solar Max: the satellite's last days. J. Eberhart. il *Science News* 136:357 D 2 '89
Reactors in space threaten high-energy astronomy. il *Sky and Telescope* 77:464-5 My '89
Reactors threaten space science [Soviet satellites interfering with orbiting scientific satellites] R. G. Nichols. il *Astronomy* 17:16 O '89
Reentry of Solar Max satellite to pose falling debris hazard. C. Covault. il *Aviation Week & Space Technology* 131:23-4 O 16 '89
Shocks and bubbles around hot stars [IRAS images; research by Dave Van Buren and Richard McCray] il *Sky and Telescope* 77:240-1 Mr '89

Solar blast [Solar Maximum Mission's attempt to track coronal mass ejection] J. Eberhart. il *Science News* 135:331 My 27 '89
Solar-cycle peak threatens Max to the max [Solar Maximum Mission satellite] J. Eberhart. *Science News* 135:87 F 11 '89
Solar Max: 1980-89. R. G. Nichols. il *Sky and Telescope* 78:600-1 D '89
Solar Max satellite reenters atmosphere over Indian Ocean. *Aviation Week & Space Technology* 131:46 D 11 '89
Solar Max snaps a big, brilliant flare. il *Science News* 135:164 Mr 18 '89
Soviet heavyweight astronomy satellite to be launched with international payload [Granat satellite with French Sigma telescope] J. M. Lenorovitz. il *Aviation Week & Space Technology* 131:31 N 27 '89
Telescope offspring. il *Ad Astra* 1:7 D '89
The ups and downs of solar flares [Solar Maximum Mission satellite data] J. Eberhart. *Science News* 135:391 Je 24 '89
When the sun went wild [flare activity recorded by the Solar Maximum Mission satellite] il *Sky and Telescope* 77:590-1 Je '89
Why won't NASA talk to scientists [effect of new ethics law on discussions of Advanced X-ray Astrophysics Facility] M. M. Waldrop. il *Science* 245:699 Ag 18 '89

Atmospheric entry
Reentry of Solar Max satellite to pose falling debris hazard. C. Covault. il *Aviation Week & Space Technology* 131:23-4 O 16 '89
Solar Max satellite reenters atmosphere over Indian Ocean. *Aviation Week & Space Technology* 131:46 D 11 '89

Biological use
See also
Artificial satellites—Cosmos missions

Communication use
See Communications satellites

Control
GAO says computer problems keep USAF satellite control system behind schedule. *Aviation Week & Space Technology* 131:23 Ag 21 '89

Cosmos missions
An astronautical ark [Biosatellite program] R. Spangenburg and D. Moser. il *Ad Astra* 1:32-5 S '89
Soviets sign space pact, launch military satellites. C. Covault. il *Aviation Week & Space Technology* 130:24-5 Ja 9 '89
U.S., USSR test new strategic satellites; Soviet intelligence spacecraft explodes. C. Covault. il *Aviation Week & Space Technology* 131:26-7 Ag 14 '89

Defects
Satellite failure reduces storm warning capability [failure of GOES-West's imager] map *Aviation Week & Space Technology* 130:30 Ja 30 '89
Secret CIA satellite launched by shuttle Columbia observed 'tumbling' by astronomers in 7 countries. il *Aviation Week & Space Technology* 131:35 O 9 '89

Design
NASA's reusable satellite program. W. H. Ganoe. il *Ad Astra* 1:45 My '89

Earth sciences use
See also
Artificial satellites—Meteorological use
Artificial satellites—Oceanographic use
Mission to Planet Earth (Project)
SPOT (Artificial satellites)
A catbird's seat on Amazon destruction [monitoring of illegal agricultural burning by remote sensing satellites] F. Golden. il *Science* 246:201-2 O 13 '89
Commercial satellites [used for spying; cover story; special section] bibl f il map *The Bulletin of the Atomic Scientists* 45:12-16+ S '89
Death postponed for Landsat satellites. il *Science News* 135:172 Mr 18 '89
Decaying orbit [possible Landsat/Spot satellite merger] E. Corcoran. il *Scientific American* 260:72-3 Mr '89
Early data: losing our memory? [Landsat] E. Marshall. *Science* 244:1250 Je 16 '89
Eosat urges U.S. to fund Landsat 7 to capture minor share of data market. T. M. Foley. *Aviation Week & Space Technology* 130:89+ My 1 '89
France defines satellite to complement Spot series. il *Aviation Week & Space Technology* 131:48 O 23 '89
Growth of Greenland ice sheet: measurement. H. J. Zwally and others. bibl f il *Science* 246:1587-9 D 22 '89
Hot times in Lascar [use of Landsat infrared images to predict Lascar volcano eruption; research by Peter Francis] il *Discover* 10:10 Ag '89
How politics killed Landsat. B. Forman. il *Omni (New York, N.Y.)* 11:22+ Ap '89
Landsat/Spot merger talks spark debate on commercial space venture [with editorial comment] C. Covault. il *Aviation Week & Space Technology* 130:7, 20-1 Ja 23 '89
Landsat: cliff-hanging, again. E. Marshall. il *Science* 246:321-2 O 20 '89
Landsat wins a reprieve. E. Marshall. *Science* 243:1429 Mr 17 '89
Landsats: drifting toward oblivion? E. Marshall. *Science* 243:999 F 24 '89

ARTIFICIAL SATELLITES—Earth sciences use—*cont.*

Landsat's tale of woe. J. V. Taranik. il *Ad Astra* 1:3 Ap '89

Large-scale, low-amplitude bedforms (chevrons) in the Selima sand sheet, Egypt [Landsat images] T. A. Maxwell and C. V. Haynes. bibl f il map *Science* 243:1179-82 Mr 3 '89

Monitoring the fate of the forests from space. W. Booth. il *Science* 243:1428-9 Mr 17 '89

Remote sensing is looking down. M. R. Chartrand. *Ad Astra* 1:23 My '89

Remote sensing of the earth: a synoptic view. J. R. Schott. bibl f il *Physics Today* 42:72-9 S '89

Remotely incensed: the search for profits [Landsat; cover story] C. E. Knox. il *Ad Astra* 1:22-4+ Ap '89

Spotting erosion from space [research by Jerry C. Ritchie] R. Monastersky. *Science News* 136:61 Jl 22 '89

White House reverses order to halt Landsat operations. T. M. Foley. il *Aviation Week & Space Technology* 130:30-1 Mr 13 '89

Electronic equipment

See also
Computers—Space flight use

Lockheed develops threat warning system for U.S. military satellites [Satellite On-board Attack Warning System] B. W. Henderson. il *Aviation Week & Space Technology* 131:61+ Jl 3 '89

Launching

America's private road to heaven. il *U.S. News & World Report* 107:11+ S 11 '89

Are we serious about a commercial launch industry? B. Forman. *Ad Astra* 1:3 Je '89

Ariane planning complicated by launcher, payload delays. il *Aviation Week & Space Technology* 131:123 O 9 '89

Arianespace plans 1989 launches to clear backlog of payloads. J. M. Lenorovitz. il *Aviation Week & Space Technology* 130:28-9 Ja 30 '89

Arianespace weighs marketing satellite launches for Pegasus. *Aviation Week & Space Technology* 130:56 Je 19 '89

Commercial launches: getting the business? I. Klotz. il *Ad Astra* 1:16-19 Ap '89

Last Titan 34D, Transtage launches classified military spacecraft. E. H. Kolcum. il *Aviation Week & Space Technology* 131:41 S 11 '89

The launch triad. C. Stadd. il *Ad Astra* 1:3 Mr '89

Titan 4, Delta 2 launches generate confidence in military space operations. E. H. Kolcum. il *Aviation Week & Space Technology* 130:40-1 Je 19 '89

Titan 4 matures [cover story; special section] il *Aviation Week & Space Technology* 131:32-4+ Jl 17 '89

The winged horse [Pegasus booster] R. G. Nichols. il *Ad Astra* 1:32-6 F '89

Winging it into space [Pegasus booster] S. F. Brown. il *Popular Science* 234:126-8+ My '89

Maintenance and repair

Astrotech provides range of payload services from expanded facility. E. H. Kolcum. *Aviation Week & Space Technology* 131:79 Ag 21 '89

Great telescope, bad service plan [Hubble Space Telescope] M. M. Waldrop. il *Science* 246:1551-3 D 22 '89

NASA's $60,000 epoxy drops [Hubble Space Telescope] M. M. Waldrop. *Science* 243:1281 Mr 10 '89

Meteorological use

See also
Nimbus satellites

Advanced weather sensor enhances next-generation defense satellite [Aerojet ElectroSystems' Special Sensor Microwave Imager Sounder] B. W. Henderson. il *Aviation Week & Space Technology* 131:47+ Ag 14 '89

Arianespace launches JCSAT, Meteosat; nine Ariane missions planned for 1989. J. M. Lenorovitz. il *Aviation Week & Space Technology* 130:29-30 Mr 13 '89

Climate and the earth's radiation budget [cover story] V. Ramanathan and others. bibl f il *Physics Today* 42:22-7+ My '89

Cloud-radiative forcing and climate: results from the Earth Radiation Budget Experiment. V. Ramanathan and others. bibl f il maps *Science* 243:57-63 Ja 6 '89

Clouds clearing from climate predictions [Earth Radiation Budget Experiment; research by V. Ramanathan] R. Monastersky. *Science News* 135:6 Ja 7 '89

Clouds in the greenhouse [data from Earth Radiation Budget Satellite] A. C. Revkin. map *Discover* 10:24 Je '89

Cloudy concerns [role of clouds in global warming; cover story] R. Monastersky. il *Science News* 136:106-7+ Ag 12 '89

Europe delays Soho spacecraft work until U.S. approves joint project MOU [solar and heliospheric satellite] J. M. Lenorovitz. il *Aviation Week & Space Technology* 131:31-2 N 13 '89

High school students study Hurricane Gilbert [use of GOES satellite] R. J. Summers. il *Weatherwise* 42:95-6 Ap '89

Hurricane hunters. H. Brandli. il *Popular Mechanics* 166:68-70+ S '89

Interview: Verner Suomi. P. Bagne. por *Omni (New York, N.Y.)* 11:60-2+ Jl '89

Monitoring the fate of the forests from space. W. Booth. il *Science* 243:1428-9 Mr 17 '89

Relay satellite, gas release payload scheduled for Pegasus winged booster. C. Covault. il *Aviation Week & Space Technology* 130:59 Ja 9 '89

Satellite failure reduces storm warning capability [failure of GOES-West's imager] map *Aviation Week & Space Technology* 130:30 Ja 30 '89

Satellite pictures on a home computer. T. L. Wilfong. il *Weatherwise* 42:339-40 D '89

Weather satellite GOES blind. *Science News* 135:77 F 4 '89

Where did AMPTE's ions go? [research by John B. Cladis and William E. Francis] R. Monastersky. *Science News* 135:319 My 20 '89

Military use

See also
Anti-satellite weapons
Artificial satellites—Cosmos missions
LACE (Artificial satellite)
Relay Mirror Experiment (Artificial satellite)
Strategic Defense Initiative

Advanced weather sensor enhances next-generation defense satellite [Aerojet ElectroSystems' Special Sensor Microwave Imager Sounder] B. W. Henderson. il *Aviation Week & Space Technology* 131:47+ Ag 14 '89

Alpha missile defense laser is fired for first time [Zenith Star project] il *Aviation Week & Space Technology* 130:23-4 Ap 17 '89

Commercial satellites [used for spying; cover story; special section] bibl f il map *The Bulletin of the Atomic Scientists* 45:12-16+ S '89

Final launch preparations under way for signal intelligence satellite mission [shuttle Discovery] il *Aviation Week & Space Technology* 131:24 N 6 '89

First USAF/McDonnell Douglas Delta 2 launch begins new military space era [Navstar launch; with editorial comment] E. H. Kolcum. il *Aviation Week & Space Technology* 130:7, 18-19 F 20 '89

GAO says computer problems keep USAF satellite control system behind schedule. *Aviation Week & Space Technology* 131:23 Ag 21 '89

Hawks among the doves [Russian military satellites] H. Banks. il *Forbes* 144:44+ N 13 '89

Last Titan 34D, Transtage launches classified military spacecraft. E. H. Kolcum. il *Aviation Week & Space Technology* 131:41 S 11 '89

Lockheed develops threat warning system for U.S. military satellites [Satellite On-board Attack Warning System] B. W. Henderson. il *Aviation Week & Space Technology* 131:61+ Jl 3 '89

Military space establishment moves toward major changes. B. A. Smith. il *Aviation Week & Space Technology* 130:121+ Mr 20 '89

New missile-warning satellite to be launched on first Titan 4 [cover story; special section] il *Aviation Week & Space Technology* 130:34-5+ F 20 '89

New SDI surveillance satellite to use upgraded Titan 2 booster [Midcourse Space Experiment spacecraft] C. Covault. il *Aviation Week & Space Technology* 131:31 S 25 '89

Night launch of Discovery boosts secret military satellite into orbit. E. H. Kolcum. *Aviation Week & Space Technology* 131:29 N 27 '89

The not-so-secret mission of Atlantis. J. Banke. il *Ad Astra* 1:7+ F '89

Orbiting of advanced imaging satellite bolsters U.S. intelligence capabilities [shuttle mission 28] E. H. Kolcum and C. Covault. il *Aviation Week & Space Technology* 131:30-1 Ag 14 '89

Relay satellite, gas release payload scheduled for Pegasus winged booster. C. Covault. il *Aviation Week & Space Technology* 130:59 Ja 9 '89

SDI Delta Star satellite readied for targeting research flight. *Aviation Week & Space Technology* 129:32 Mr 6 '89

SDIO begins measuring booster plumes with Delta Star sensors. E. H. Kolcum. il *Aviation Week & Space Technology* 130:26-7 Ap 3 '89

Secret CIA satellite launched by shuttle Columbia observed 'tumbling' by astronomers in 7 countries. il *Aviation Week & Space Technology* 131:35 O 9 '89

Soviet using Plesetsk site to launch military satellites. il *Aviation Week & Space Technology* 131:22-3 Jl 3 '89

Space cameras and security risks [use of Spot satellite for spying; views of Carnegie Endowment for Peace] E. Marshall. *Science* 243:472-3 Ja 27 '89

Space labs solicit research by business. *High Technology Business* 9:35-6 F '89

Spy satellites: entering a new era. D. Charles. il *Science* 243:1541-3 Mr 24 '89

Spying from space. M. Krepon. *Foreign Policy* 75:92-108 Summ '89

Tacsat requirements sent to Joint Chiefs of Staff [tactical satellite system] il *Aviation Week & Space Technology* 131:29-30 N 13 '89

Titan 4, Delta 2 launches generate confidence in military space operations. E. H. Kolcum. il *Aviation Week & Space Technology* 130:40-1 Je 19 '89

Titan 4 matures [cover story; special section] il *Aviation Week & Space Technology* 131:32-4+ Jl 17 '89

ARTIFICIAL SATELLITES—*cont.*
Navigational use
See also
Global Positioning System
Glonass (Global Navigation Satellite System)
First USAF/McDonnell Douglas Delta 2 launch begins new military space era [Navstar launch; with editorial comment] E. H. Kolcum. il *Aviation Week & Space Technology* 130:7, 18-19 F 20 '89
Judge fines Rockwell $5.5 million for concealing Navstar double-billing. M. A. Dornheim. *Aviation Week & Space Technology* 130:24-5 Mr 13 '89
USAF assessing liftoff failure of Delta 2 vehicle [Navstar satellite] *Aviation Week & Space Technology* 130:40 My 29 '89
Nuclear power plants
See Artificial satellites—Power supply
Oceanographic use
The big picture of the Pacific's undulations [Geosat data] R. A. Kerr. *Science* 243:739-40 F 10 '89
Hughes may build lightsat to gather ocean data [SeaWiFS spacecraft] J. R. Asker. *Aviation Week & Space Technology* 131:24 O 16 '89
Recent ocean warming: are satellites right? [research by Alan E. Strong] R. Monastersky. *Science News* 135:247 Ap 22 '89
Orbits
European space program managers increase expectations for Hipparcos' useful lifetime. *Aviation Week & Space Technology* 131:58 N 13 '89
Hipparcos failure stuns Europeans. S. Mitton. il *Astronomy* 17:14 N '89
Hipparcos: in the low-orbit blues. M. M. Waldrop. *Science* 245:808 Ag 25 '89
Hipparcos remains in transfer orbit, reducing useful astronomy data. J. M. Lenorovitz. il *Aviation Week & Space Technology* 131:28 S 4 '89
Hipparcos satellite's mission success will depend on lifetime in transfer orbit. *Aviation Week & Space Technology* 131:44 O 23 '89
Satellite viewing [Space Birds computer program] J. L. Wilson. il *Ad Astra* 1:30 Ap '89
Power supply
Courting disaster in orbit [nuclear power] G. E. Brown, Jr. il *The Bulletin of the Atomic Scientists* 45:7-9 Ap '89
Detailing Soviet gamma-ray 'garbage'. F. Flam. *Science News* 135:260 Ap 29 '89
Distribution and detection of positrons from an orbiting nuclear reactor [observations by Solar Maximum Mission satellite] E. W. Hones and P. R. Higbie. bibl f il *Science* 244:448-51 Ap 28 '89
A flap over reactors in orbit. M. D. Lemonick. il *Time* 133:80 F 20 '89
Gamma-ray observations of orbiting nuclear reactors [cover story] J. R. Primack. bibl f *Science* 244:407-8 Ap 28 '89
Geomagnetic origin for transient particle events from nuclear reactor-powered satellites [experiment on Solar Maximum Mission satellite] G. H. Share and others. bibl f il *Science* 244:444-8 Ap 28 '89
Let's ban nuclear reactors from orbit. J. R. Primack. il *Technology Review* 92:27-8 My/Je '89
Man-made transients observed by the gamma-ray spectrometer on the Solar Maximum Mission satellite. E. Rieger and others. bibl f il *Science* 244:441-4 Ap 28 '89
NASA to modify GRO satellite operations to cut interference from Soviet reactors [Gamma Ray Observatory] *Aviation Week & Space Technology* 130:52 My 15 '89
Observations of nuclear reactors on satellites with a balloon-borne gamma-ray telescope. T. J. O'Neill and others. bibl f il *Science* 244:451-4 Ap 28 '89
Reactors in space threaten high-energy astronomy. il *Sky and Telescope* 77:464-5 My '89
Reactors threaten space science [Soviet satellites interfering with orbiting scientific satellites] R. G. Nichols. il *Astronomy* 17:16 O '89
Scientists call for policy on space nuclear reactors. R. G. O'Lone. il *Aviation Week & Space Technology* 130:23 Ja 23 '89
Space reactors and arms control. C. Norman. il *Science* 243:476 Ja 27 '89
Stable orbit [space reactors] T. Beardsley. *Scientific American* 260:14+ F '89
Public health use
Satellite medicine. P. Jovanovic. il *World Health* p18-19 Ja/F '89
Surveillance use, Military
See Artificial satellites—Military use
Tracking
Satellite viewing [Space Birds computer program] J. L. Wilson. il *Ad Astra* 1:30 Ap '89
ARTIFICIAL SATELLITES, EFFECT OF RADIATION ON
Detailing Soviet gamma-ray 'garbage'. F. Flam. *Science News* 135:260 Ap 29 '89
NASA to modify GRO satellite operations to cut interference from Soviet reactors [Gamma Ray Observatory] *Aviation Week & Space Technology* 130:52 My 15 '89

Reactors in space threaten high-energy astronomy. il *Sky and Telescope* 77:464-5 My '89
Reactors threaten space science [Soviet satellites interfering with orbiting scientific satellites] R. G. Nichols. il *Astronomy* 17:16 O '89
ARTIFICIAL SATELLITES, EUROPEAN
See also
Hipparcos (Artificial satellites)
Arianespace launches JCSAT, Meteosat; nine Ariane missions planned for 1989. J. M. Lenorovitz. il *Aviation Week & Space Technology* 130:29-30 Mr 13 '89
ARTIFICIAL SATELLITES, FRENCH
See also
SPOT (Artificial satellites)
France defines satellite to complement Spot series. il *Aviation Week & Space Technology* 131:48 O 23 '89
Open skies tested. D. F. Robertson. il *Ad Astra* 1:7 Je '89
ARTIFICIAL SATELLITES, ISRAELI
Military intelligence—SPOT is not enough. J. Richelson. bibl f il *The Bulletin of the Atomic Scientists* 45:26-7 S '89
ARTIFICIAL SATELLITES, RUSSIAN
See also
Artificial satellites—Cosmos missions
Glonass (Global Navigation Satellite System)
Morsviazsputnik
Detailing Soviet gamma-ray 'garbage'. F. Flam. *Science News* 135:260 Ap 29 '89
Granat astronomy satellite launched from Cosmodrome. J. M. Lenorovitz. *Aviation Week & Space Technology* 131:34 D 11 '89
Hawks among the doves [military satellites] H. Banks. il *Forbes* 144:44+ N 13 '89
NASA to modify GRO satellite operations to cut interference from Soviet reactors [Gamma Ray Observatory] *Aviation Week & Space Technology* 130:52 My 15 '89
Open skies tested. D. F. Robertson. il *Ad Astra* 1:7 Je '89
Reactors in space threaten high-energy astronomy. il *Sky and Telescope* 77:464-5 My '89
Reactors threaten space science [Soviet satellites interfering with orbiting scientific satellites] R. G. Nichols. il *Astronomy* 17:16 O '89
Soviet heavyweight astronomy satellite to be launched with international payload [Granat satellite with French Sigma telescope] J. M. Lenorovitz. il *Aviation Week & Space Technology* 131:31 N 27 '89
Soviet using Plesetsk site to launch military satellites. il *Aviation Week & Space Technology* 131:22-3 Jl 3 '89
Soviets book new commercial payloads, grant greater access to space facilities [Kayser-Threde microgravity missions] J. M. Lenorovitz. *Aviation Week & Space Technology* 131:121+ O 9 '89
ARTIFICIAL SKIN *See* Skin, Artificial
ARTIFICIAL SMOKE *See* Smoke, Artificial
ARTIFICIAL SWEETENERS *See* Sugar substitutes
ARTIFICIAL TEETH *See* Dentures
ARTIFICIAL VEGETABLES *See* Vegetables, Artificial
ARTIFICIAL WETLANDS *See* Wetlands, Artificial
ARTILLERY
See also
Projectiles
ARTISANS
The French touch [crafts] C. Petkanas. il *House & Garden* 161:156+ Jl '89
ARTIST DESCENDING A STAIRCASE [drama] See Stoppard, Tom
ARTISTIC ANATOMY *See* Anatomy, Artistic
ARTISTIC PHOTOGRAPHY *See* Photography, Artistic
ARTISTS
See also
Aged as artists
Alcohol and artists
Art as a profession
Authors as artists
Chimpanzees as artists
Cooking by artists
Drugs and artists
Elephants as artists
Farmers as artists
Homeless as artists
Prisoners as artists
Women artists
Attitudes
The peripatetic artist: 14 statements. il *Art in America* 77:130-7+ Jl '89
Directories
Guide to galleries, museums, artists [cover story; special issue] il *Art in America* 77:45-51+ Ag '89
Economic conditions
See also
Pollock-Krasner Foundation
Health and hygiene
See also
AIDS (Disease) and artists
Art supply labels [toxicity] K. K. Gracey and A. W. Simpson. il *Consumers' Research Magazine* 72:2 S '89

ARTISTS—Health and hygiene—*cont.*
New federal legislation on art material labeling. J. T. Luke.
  American Artist 53:24+ Je '89
Possible ban of some artists' materials [cadmium and lead]
  il *American Artist* 53:22+ N '89
Read the label [passage of Art Materials Labeling Act] P.
  Kessler. il *Art News* 88:40 Mr '89
Toxicity of artists' materials. J. T. Luke. *American Artist*
  53:22+ Jl '89

Housing
See also
  Brooklyn Loft Tenants (Organization)

Language
What's the good word? [need for artists to know the correct
  terminology when selling their pictures] F. J. Goodman.
  il *American Artist* 53:98-101 S '89

Religious life
Our task is to create worlds. E. Antonucci. il *Commonweal*
  116:334-5 Je 2 '89

Salaries, pensions, etc.
See also
  Artists—Taxation

Sexual behavior
Affairs of the art [artists' models who were also mistresses]
  E. MacSweeney. il *Harper's Bazaar* 122:168-73 D '89

Taxation
Free tax advice for artists. D. Grant. *American Artist* 53:12+
  D '89

Travel
Integrating studio work and outdoor painting. T. T. Heidel.
  il por *American Artist* 53:44-7+ D '89

ARTISTS, AMERICAN
See also
  Adams, Dennis, 1948-
  Allen, Terry, 1943-
  Archer, Dave
  Baldessari, John, 1931-
  Barton, Nancy
  Belcher, Alan
  Bellows, George, 1882-1925
  Berlin, Beatrice, 1922-
  Bickerton, Ashley, 1959-
  Black artists
  Bourgeois, Louise
  Bramwell
  Brill, Glenn
  Buck, John E., 1946-
  Buczak, Brian, 1954-1987
  Burden, Chris, 1946-
  Burgess, Lowry, 1940-
  Byron, Michael
  Calder, Alexander, 1898-1976
  Chandler, Robin
  Colson, Greg
  Conal, Robbie
  DeWoody, James
  DiFranza, Americo, 1919-
  Dufour, Paul
  Dwyer, Nancy
  Fehlau, Fred
  Flynt, Henry
  Fogel, Seymour, 1911-1984
  Folwell, Samuel, 1764?-1813
  Gerberich, Stephen J.
  Glier, Mike, 1953-
  Guyton, Tyree
  Hamilton, Ann
  Hammons, David
  Haveron, Bill
  Herd, Stan
  Higgison, Peyton
  Hiller, Susan, 1940-
  Holder, Geoffrey
  Indiana, Robert, 1928-
  Ireland, David
  Jenkins, Jeffrey
  Kidd, Julia
  Kirkpatrick, Joey
  Kohlmeyer, Ida, 1912-
  Kolbowski, Silvia
  Koons, Jeff, 1955-
  Kottler, Howard, 1930-1989
  Kruger, Barbara
  La Farge, John, 1835-1910
  Lawler, Louise
  Levine, Sherrie, 1947-
  Locke, Donald
  Logé, Dan
  Longo, Robert
  Mace, Flora Carrie
  McNeil, Dean
  Mock, Richard Basil
  Mullican, Matt, 1951-
  Noble, John A.
  O'Hagan, Desmond, 1960-
  Oliver, Kermit
  Patterson, William
  Ray, Man, 1890-1976

  Remington, Deborah, 1935-
  Ringgold, Faith
  Rockwell, Norman, 1894-1978
  Rollins, Timothy
  Rosler, Martha, 1943-
  Ryan, Anne, 1889-1954
  Samaras, Lucas, 1936-
  Seager, Sarah
  Shaw, Richard, 1941-
  Staller, Eric
  Steinworth, Skip
  Stevens, May, 1924-
  Syrop, Mitchell, 1953-
  Thompson, Bradbury, 1911-
  Trotsky
  Tuska, John
  Tyler, Scott
  Ukeles, Mierle Laderman
  Warren, Wally
  Watts, Robert, 1923-1988
  White, Susan Chrysler
  Williams-Cacicedo, Jean
  Wojnarowicz, David, 1954-
  Wolfe, Steve
  Zimmermann, Marie
Emerging artists [cover story; special section] il *American
  Artist* 53:35-47 Ag '89
Ten artists respond to a southern plantation [Madewood;
  cover story] M. S. Doherty. il *American Artist* 53:32-43
  Ja '89

Photographs and photography
Timothy Greenfield-Sanders at Mary Boone. W. Robinson.
  il *Art in America* 77:259-60 Ap '89

ARTISTS, BELGIAN
See also
  Broodthaers, Marcel, 1924-1976
  Lafontaine, Marie-Jo

ARTISTS, BRAZILIAN
See also
  Oiticica, Hélio, 1937-1980

ARTISTS, COLOMBIAN
See also
  Botero, Fernando, 1932-

ARTISTS, ENGLISH
See also
  Delany, Mary Granville Pendarves, 1700-1788
  Gilbert and George
  Long, Richard, 1945-
  Mee, Margaret, 1909-1988

ARTISTS, FILIPINO
See also
  Medalla, David

ARTISTS, FRENCH
See also
  Boltanski, Christian, 1944-
  Calle, Sophie
  Cocteau, Jean, 1889-1963
  Gruau, René, 1910-
  Kern, Pascal
  Palissy, Bernard, 1510-1589 or 90

ARTISTS, GERMAN
See also
  Richter, Gerhard

ARTISTS, HONDURAN
See also
  Alvarado-Juarez, Francisco

ARTISTS, INDIAN (AMERICAN)
Soul of the plains. T. Gold. il *Harper's Bazaar* 122:20+
  Jl '89

ARTISTS, ITALIAN
See also
  Bianchi, Domenico, 1955-
  Chiarini, Doriana
  Fornasetti, Piero, 1913-1988
  Giulio, Romano, 1499?-1546
  Michelangelo Buonarroti, 1475-1564
  Seguso, Archimede

ARTISTS, JAPANESE
See also
  Kusama, Yayoi, 1929-
  Yamaguchi, Katsuhiro

ARTISTS, MENTALLY ILL *See* Art and mental illness

ARTISTS, MEXICAN
See also
  Quezada, Abel

ARTISTS, RUSSIAN
See also
  Artists Union (Soviet Union)
Canvases of their own. R. Hughes. il *Time* 133:116-18 Ap
  10 '89

ARTISTS, SPANISH
See also
  Barrionuevo, Bola
  Picasso, Pablo, 1881-1973

ARTISTS, SWISS
See also
  Bill, Max, 1908-
  Oppenheim, Meret, 1913-1985

ARTISTS, SWISS—See also—*cont.*
　Wölfli, Adolf, 1864-1930
ARTISTS' AND AUTHORS' COLONIES
　　See also
　　Old Lyme (Conn.)
ARTISTS AS TEACHERS
　　See also
　　Arts Partners (Organization)
ARTISTS IN ART
　Art: artists by artists. R. Rosenblum. il *Architectural Digest* 46:132-7+ Jl '89
　Color Close-ups [work of C. Close] C. Finch. il *Art in America* 77:112-19+ Mr '89
　A conditional paradise [W. Beckman's double portraits of himself and his wife] C. Belz. il pors *Art in America* 77:136-41 Ja '89
ARTISTS' MATERIALS
　　See also
　　Easels
　　Makeup as art material
　　National Art Materials Trade Association
　　Paint
　　Painting supports
　　Pens
　　Turpentine
　Art mart. See issues of American Artist
　An Etch A Sketch revival: is it an adult art form for baby boomers? S. Morris. il *Omni (New York, N.Y.)* 11:100-1 Ag '89
　Holiday shopping. il *American Artist* 53:28-9 N '89
　New materials. See issues of Art News
　Technical page. See issues of American Artist
　　　　　Labeling
　Art supply labels [toxicity] K. K. Gracey and A. W. Simpson. il *Consumers' Research Magazine* 72:2 S '89
　New federal legislation on art material labeling. J. T. Luke. *American Artist* 53:24+ Je '89
　Read the label [passage of Art Materials Labeling Act] P. Kessler. il *Art News* 88:40 Mr '89
　Toxicity of artists' materials. J. T. Luke. *American Artist* 53:22+ Jl '89
　　　　Laws and regulations
　Possible ban of some artists' materials [cadmium and lead] il *American Artist* 53:22+ N '89
　　　　　　Storage
　Colorful traveling case [artist's kit for children] L. Okrend. il *Workbench* 45:30-2 N/D '89
ARTISTS' MODELS See Models, Artists'
ARTISTS' RIGHTS
　Public rights and critics' failures. A. E. Elsen. il *Art News* 88:174 F '89
ARTISTS SPACE (NEW YORK, N.Y.)
　Days of rage [NEA rescinds funding for Witnesses: against our vanishing] K. Larson. il *New York* 22:80+ N 27 '89
　Disaster at the NEA [rescinds funding for AIDS exhibit Witnesses: against our vanishing] R. Brustein. *The New Republic* 201:28-30 D 11 '89
　Testing the new arts rules [NEA rescinds funds and later decides to support AIDS exhibit Witnesses: against our vanishing] *Newsweek* 114:43 N 27 '89
ARTISTS' STUDIOS
　　See also
　　Chesterwood (Stockbridge, Mass.)
　　Rubenshuis (Antwerp, Belgium)
　Al Held's Catskill pastoral: the artist's studio and house in Woodstock, New York. D. Solomon. il por *Architectural Digest* 46:170-3+ Je '89
　Artful garage conversion: new studio shares space with storage. T. Jackson. il *Better Homes and Gardens* 67:64 My '89
　Artist's dialogue: Cesar [studio in Paris and house in the south of France] M. Peppiatt. il por *Architectural Digest* 46:27+ F '89
　Caro country: the artist's New York State sculpture studio and fields [designed by Donald Clinton] K. Wilken. il por *Architectural Digest* 46:192-7+ Ag '89
　A downtown aesthetic: the residence and studio of artist Jennifer Bartlett. D. Solomon. il por *Architectural Digest* 46:316-21+ N '89
　Lofty ambitions [R. Bleckner's Manhattan loft] L. Kaylin. il pors *Gentlemen's Quarterly* 59:208-11+ F '89
　Portrait of the artists: Eric Fischl and April Gornik on Long Island [farmhouse renovated by Lee Skolnick] S. M. L. Aronson. il pors *Architectural Digest* 46:234-9+ Ap '89
　Rodchenko in Moscow: miraculous survival of the constructivist's historic studio. M. Ruthven. il pors *Architectural Digest* 46:53+ O '89
　Sanctuary for art [converted church in Bellport, Long Island; interview with M. Morley] D. Kazanjian. il por *House & Garden* 161:150-5+ My '89
　　　Photographs and photography
　Photographs of artists' studios. il *American Artist* 53:76-8 Ag '89
ARTISTS UNION (SOVIET UNION)
　Whither the Artists Union? J. Gambrell. *Art in America* 77:132 F '89

ARTISTS' WIVES
　　　Caricatures and cartoons
　Home is where the art is [excerpts from Great housewives of art] S. Swain. il *Ms.* 17:72-3 Ap '89
ARTRA GROUP INCORPORATED
　Cleverness isn't enough. M. Berss. il *Forbes* 144:216 Jl 24 '89
　Scrapping over a food packager [Envirodyne] G. G. Marcial. *Business Week* p146 Mr 20 '89
ARTS
　　See also
　　Art
　　Graphic arts
　　Performing arts
　　Video art
　Artsmart. See issues of Harper's Bazaar beginning December 1986
　Cross country. See issues of Horizon (Tuscaloosa, Ala.)
　How high the brow? [views of L. W. Levine on American culture] D. Gates. il *Newsweek* 113:51 F 20 '89
　　　　　Administration
　　See Arts—Management
　　　　　　Archives
　Our collective knowledge. M. Rhodes. il *Horizon (Tuscaloosa, Ala.)* 32:5 Mr/Ap '89
　　　　　　Awards
　　See also
　　National Medal of Arts
　　Praemium Imperiale
　　　　　Economic aspects
　USArts: strategies for the 80's. See issues of Horizon (Tuscaloosa, Ala.)
　　　　　Federal aid
　　See Arts and state
　　　　　Management
　　See also
　　Arts administrators
　　　　　Study and teaching
　Preparing arts administrators of the future: the need for interprofessional education. L. F. Ettinger and J. Hutchens. bibl f *Design for Arts in Education* 90:32-6 Mr/Ap '89
　　　　　Social aspects
　Crises in society: the role of the arts. L. Ultan. bibl f *Design for Arts in Education* 90:14-21 My/Je '89
　Life and death and the arts. A. Coppola. *Design for Arts in Education* 91:43-5 S/O '89
　　　　Study and teaching
　　See also
　　Art schools
　　Arts Partners (Organization)
　　Arts teachers
　　California Institute of the Arts
　　Getty Center for Education in the Arts
　Advertising, art, and arts education: an uneasy association [effect of television upon children] L. Barton. bibl f *Design for Arts in Education* 90:14-19 N/D '88
　Artists or teachers? Arts education in independent schools. R. A. Lloyd. *Design for Arts in Education* 90:42-5 Ja/F '89
　Arts education in the 1990s: are we ready to move forward? F. Lazarus. *Design for Arts in Education* 90:33-8 Jl/Ag '89
　Arts educators should work with the arts community. G. C. Wenner. *The Education Digest* 54:54-7 F '89
　The arts in education program: a state's perspective [Maine] E. M. Bither and S. J. Kestenbaum. *Design for Arts in Education* 90:35-7 Ja/F '89
　A comprehensive arts curriculum model. B. Reimer. il *Design for Arts in Education* 90:2-16 Jl/Ag '89
　The corporation and arts education: a new merger? S. S. Madeja. *Design for Arts in Education* 90:20-4 N/D '88
　Crises in society: the role of the arts. L. Ultan. bibl f *Design for Arts in Education* 90:14-21 My/Je '89
　The education reform movement and its critics: implications for arts education [favoring Western civilization] J. B. Riddell. bibl f *Design for Arts in Education* 90:2-13 N/D '88
　Equality and excellence education in arts [Massachusetts] E. Lazarus. bibl f *Design for Arts in Education* 90:30-2 Jl/Ag '89
　Forum: the new administration and arts education. *Design for Arts in Education* 90:16-23 Ja/F '89
　The importance of community-based art education programs for adults. M. Y. Roberts. bibl f *Design for Arts in Education* 90:43-8 Jl/Ag '89
　The K-12 arts agenda: next challenges for higher education [teacher education] R. Glidden. *Design for Arts in Education* 91:11-14 S/O '89
　Managing the influence of television through the discipline of video. W. Kennedy. bibl f *Design for Arts in Education* 90:26-8 Mr/Ap '89
　National conditions and policy imperatives. S. Hope. bibl f *Design for Arts in Education* 91:15-35 S/O '89
　The NEA: looking back, and looking ahead. S. Lipman. *Design for Arts in Education* 90:2-9 My/Je '89
　The next century: the impact of social and economic trends on the arts in education. J. K. Urice. bibl f *Design for Arts in Education* 90:36-43 My/Je '89

ARTS—Study and teaching—*cont.*
Policies, agendas, and arts education research. D. B. Pankratz. bibl f *Design for Arts in Education* 90:2-13 My/Je '89
Reformation and responsibilities: a memo to members of the arts education establishment. B. Wilson. bibl f *Design for Arts in Education* 90:27-35 My/Je '89
The simplest and hardest of education reforms. N. King. *Design for Arts in Education* 91:2-9 N/D '89
Stalking [the] deep coherence: curricular design in the arts. N. S. Fichter. bibl f *Design for Arts in Education* 91:2-10 S/O '89
A symposium on skills, knowledge, and creativity in the curriculum. C. H. Ball; E. Boardman; K. A. Hamblen. bibl f *Design for Arts in Education* 90:22-6 My/Je '89
Television, cultural history, and arts education. H. Hoffa. *Design for Arts in Education* 90:15-22 Mr/Ap '89
Time in the curriculum: the dilemma for arts education, K-6. R. McGoff. *Design for Arts in Education* 90:44-6 N/D '88
Toward civilization: next responsibilities [report issued by National Endowment for the Arts] F. Hodsoll. *Design for Arts in Education* 90:10-15 Ja/F '89
What every arts administrator should know about arts education. M. Yaffe. *Design for Arts in Education* 90:29-31 Mr/Ap '89

Bibliography
Art and power. S. Hope. *Design for Arts in Education* 90:49-52 Jl/Ag '89

Alabama
See also
Mobile (Ala.)—Arts

Florida
See also
Palm Beach County (Fla.)—Arts
South Florida Cultural Consortium

Massachusetts
See also
Massachusetts Council on the Arts and Humanities

New York (State)
See also
New York (N.Y.)—Arts

Scotland
See also
Glasgow (Scotland)—Arts

Soviet Union
Critics' choice: a Soviet sampler. il *Time* 133:3 Ap 10 '89
Freedom waiting for vision. J. Kohan. il *Time* 133:108-9 Ap 10 '89

United States
See Arts

Wisconsin
See also
Milwaukee (Wis.)—Arts

ARTS, ASIAN AMERICAN
The arts and the Asian American community. N. Rosca. il *Change* 21:52-5 N/D '89

ARTS, BLACK
See also
Harlem renaissance
Palm Beach County Minority Cultural Consortium
Afro-American art and the corporate dollar. J. R. Barras. il *American Visions* 4:30-4 Je '89
Arts scene. See issues of American Visions

ARTS, INDUSTRIAL *See* Industrial arts
ARTS, PRACTICAL *See* Industrial arts
ARTS ADMINISTRATION *See* Arts—Management
ARTS ADMINISTRATORS
Casting call for artsy business types. M. Silver. il *U.S. News & World Report* 107:58 Ag 7 '89
What every arts administrator should know about arts education. M. Yaffe. *Design for Arts in Education* 90:29-31 Mr/Ap '89

Education
See Arts—Management—Study and teaching
ARTS AND CHRISTIANITY *See* Arts and religion
ARTS AND CRAFTS
See also
Appliqué work
Art metal work
Artisans
Arts and crafts movement
Baskets
Christmas projects
Collage
Eggs, Decorated
Folk art
Glass blowing and working
Inlay
Jewelry
Lace
Lacquer and lacquering
Marbling
Needlework
Paper making
Papier-mâché
Pottery
Pyrography
Stencil work

Tapestry
Textile crafts
Weaving
Wood carving
Woodworking
Cottage crafts with country heart. J. Williams and J. Severson. il *Better Homes and Gardens* 67:91-102+ S '89
Crafter's almanac. J. Williams and J. Severson. il *Better Homes and Gardens* 67:16+ Mr '89
Everything's bloomin' tulips! [handcrafted home furnishings] J. Williams and J. Severson. il *Better Homes and Gardens* 67:45-54+ Mr '89
Getting crafty! J. Kelman. il *Ladies' Home Journal* 106:120+ O '89
Goin' to the dogs [crafts projects] J. Williams and J. Severson. il *Better Homes and Gardens* 67:75-8+ Ag '89
Portfolio. See issues of American Craft

Bibliography
Books. See issues of American Craft

Collectors and collecting
Living with crafts and collectibles [Jim and Lynn Williams entertain] J. Severson. il *Better Homes and Gardens* 67:47-54+ Ja '89

Conferences
Forced dialogue: Do craft symposia serve the field? V. S. Lynn. *American Craft* 49:14 Je/Jl '89
Schedule announced for third Grove Park Inn National Arts and Crafts Conference. *Antiques & Collecting Hobbies* 94:36-7 O '89

Exhibitions
Calendar. See issues of American Craft
Craft Today USA [international traveling exhibit opens in Paris] B. Werther. il *American Craft* 49:32-9 O/N '89
Gallery. See issues of American Craft
High attendance, diversity at Chicago New Art Forms Expo. J. Tognini. il *American Craft* 49:10+ D '89/Ja '90
Traveler's market. D. P. Marshall. il *Travel Holiday* 172:24+ O '89

Photographs and photography
Crafts fairs: they're great places to collect pictures. L. Dennis. il *Popular Photography* 96:20+ Je '89

Marketing
See Art trade

Safety devices and measures
Rx for safe crafting. A. Atkins. *Better Homes and Gardens* 67:46 N '89

Appalachian region
See also
Southern Highland Handicraft Guild

Colorado
Still alive in southern Colorado, crafts of Spanish pioneers. il map *Sunset (Central West edition)* 182:32+ My '89

Massachusetts
Massachusetts waterfowl decoys [cover story] R. Moir and J. Parker. bibl f il *Antiques* 136:516-27 S '89

Maui (Hawaii)
Maui treasure hunting for arts and crafts. il map *Sunset (Central West edition)* 182:102-3+ My '89

New York (State)
See also
Roycroft Shop

Prince Edward Island
Anger on the Island [dispute over Anne of Green Gables merchandising] R. Corelli. il *Maclean's* 102:40 Jl 10 '89

Tennessee
See also
Joe L. Evins Appalachian Center for Crafts
ARTS AND CRAFTS AND CHILDREN
See also
Christmas projects
Fun summer crafts. V. A. Snell and M. L. Poe. il *Good Housekeeping* 208:78-9 Je '89
ARTS AND CRAFTS LITERATURE

Authorship
Creating articles for the crafts market. M. Flathers. *The Writer* 102:24-6 Ag '89
ARTS AND CRAFTS MOVEMENT
American picture frames of the arts and crafts period, 1870-1920. S. Smeaton. bibl f il *Antiques* 136:1124-37 N '89
The arts and crafts architect's studio in Carmel [C. S. Greene] B. P. Greene. il por *Architectural Digest* 46:92+ My '89
The arts and crafts movement past and present [cover story; special section] il *Antiques & Collecting Hobbies* 94:32-8+ O '89
New house, classic craft [home based on designs of C. and H. Greene] P. Harper. il *Home Mechanix* 85:66-8+ F '89
Red House in Kent [home of W. Morris] E. Lambert. il *Architectural Digest* 46:126+ Ap '89
Square roots [Hudson Valley home of Mark McDonald and Ralph Cutler] C. Vogel. il *The New York Times Magazine* p64-5 F 19 '89
ARTS AND CRAFTS TRADE *See* Art trade
ARTS AND ENTERTAINMENT NETWORK
At MIPCOM: a buyer's life [Cannes exhibition] P. Ainslie. il pors *Channels (New York, N.Y.: 1986)* 9:36-40 Mr '89

ARTS AND INDUSTRY
 See also
 Art and industry
Afro-American art and the corporate dollar. J. R. Barras.
 il *American Visions* 4:30-4 Je '89
Art and taxes [corporate and private support for opera]
 M. Mayer. il *Opera News* 53:14-17 Ap 15 '89
Arts exchange. See issues of Horizon (Tuscaloosa, Ala.)
 beginning May 1986
USArts: strategies for the 80's. See issues of Horizon
 (Tuscaloosa, Ala.)
A yen for the arts [Japanese as patrons of the arts in America]
 il *U.S. News & World Report* 107:18 S 25 '89
ARTS AND RELIGION
 See also
 Image (Periodical)
The passion and the arts in worship [cover story; special
 section] il *The Christian Century* 106:308-16 Mr 22-29
 '89
ARTS AND SOCIETY *See* Arts—Social aspects
ARTS AND STATE
 See also
 American Council for the Arts
 United States. Commission of Fine Arts
 Canada
 See also
 Canada. Dept. of Communications
 China
Kickoff [effect of Tiananmen Square occupation on Chinese
 arts] R. Philp. il *Dance Magazine* 63:7 Ag '89
 Iran
A new Iranian revolution. V. Petrossian. *World Press Review*
 36:60 F '89
ARTS AND THE ENVIRONMENT
The visionary arts movement. il *Utne Reader* p66-7 Jl/Ag
 '89
ARTS AND THE HANDICAPPED
 See also
 Arts therapy
ARTS EDUCATION *See* Arts—Study and teaching
LES ARTS FLORISSANTS (CHAMBER ORCHESTRA)
Flourishing Arts [performance of Atys at the Brooklyn
 Academy of Music] M. Swed. il *Opera News* 53:20+ My
 '89
Lully is in bloom again [performance of Atys at the Brooklyn
 Academy of Music] P. G. Davis. il *New York* 22:60+
 Je 5 '89
Musical events:
 Charpentier's Advent and Christmas. A. Porter. *The
 New Yorker* 65:70 D 25 '89
 Performance of Atys at Brooklyn Academy of Music.
 A. Porter. *The New Yorker* 65:90-2 Je 12 '89
ARTS MANAGEMENT *See* Arts—Management
ARTS PARTNERS (ORGANIZATION)
Conditioning artists for teaching. C. B. Fowler. *Design for
 Arts in Education* 90:30-4 Ja/F '89
ARTS TEACHERS
Artists or teachers? Arts education in independent schools.
 R. A. Lloyd. *Design for Arts in Education* 90:42-5 Ja/F
 '89
 Education
The K-12 arts agenda: next challenges for higher education.
 R. Glidden. *Design for Arts in Education* 91:11-14 S/O
 '89
 Education in service
A state strategy for teacher training: the Tennessee Arts
 Academy. J. W. Giles and C. R. Curtis. *Design for Arts
 in Education* 90:39-42 Jl/Ag '89
ARTS THERAPY
Arts therapy: creativity that heals. S. DeVore. il *Current
 Health 2* 15:20-2 Ap '89
ARTSOFT (FIRM)
The ArtSoft connection. D. Towers. il *Dance Magazine* 63:98-9
 Ap '89
ARTZT, EDWIN LEWIS
 about
P&G's worldly new boss wants a more worldly company.
 Z. Schiller. il por *Business Week* p40-1 O 30 '89
Will the real Vince Lombardi please stand up? il por *Fortune*
 120:38 N 6 '89
ARUBA
 See also
 Restoration ecology—Aruba
 Description and travel
Phenomena, comment and notes. J. P. Wiley, Jr. il
 Smithsonian 20:30+ My '89
 Politics and government
 See also
 Campaign management—Aruba
ARUMS
 See also
 Skunk cabbages
ARURI, TAYSEER
 about
Appeals for Tayseer Aruri. *Physics Today* 42:15+ My '89
Dissenting opinions about Tayseer Aruri [letters] *Physics
 Today* 42 pt1:13+ Ag '89

Israeli physicists, and others, comment on case of Palestinian
 physicist. W. Sweet. *Physics Today* 42:83-5 S '89
ARVIN INDUSTRIES, INC.
Early casualties. K. L. Fisher. il *Forbes* 144:168 D 25 '89
ARYAN NATION *See* Neo-Nazis
ASATS *See* Anti-satellite weapons
ASBELL, BERNARD
 (ed) See Paterno, Joe. The man who said no to $1 million
ASBESTOS
The panic in Gramercy Park [contamination from steam
 pipe explosion and water main break] il *U.S. News &
 World Report* 107:14 S 18 '89
Ruptured lives: how the Gramercy Park steam-pipe blast
 spewed misery with the asbestos. E. Pooley. il *New York*
 22:50-4+ O 30 '89
 Disposal
 See also
 Dec-Tam Corporation
Asbestos makers run out of breathing room. B. Bremner.
 il *Business Week* p36+ N 20 '89
The asbestos rip-off [cover story] M. Fumento. il *The
 American Spectator* 22:21-6 O '89
Coping with lead and asbestos. S. Greenberg. il *The Mother
 Earth News* 117:26+ My/Je '89
"Monster in the closet". L. Whitaker. il *Time* 133:53 F
 6 '89
 Laws and regulations
Asbestos angst. V. Novak. *Common Cause Magazine* 15:7-8
 Ja/F '89
Asbestos: the long goodbye. *Newsweek* 114:61 Jl 17 '89
Erecting a fire wall against asbestos [EPA ban] *U.S. News
 & World Report* 107:10-11 Jl 17 '89
ASBESTOS INDUSTRY
 See also
 Celotex Corporation
 Suits and claims
Asbestos makers run out of breathing room. B. Bremner.
 il *Business Week* p36+ N 20 '89
Just when Manville thought it was safe . . . [furious pace
 of settling claims] S. D. Atchison. *Business Week* p36
 N 20 '89
A lion of the Texas bar snarls at KKR and Drexel [S.
 Susman builds asbestos case stemming from Jim Walter
 Corp. LBO] M. Ivey. il por *Business Week* p73+ O 9
 '89
ASBESTOSIS *See* Lungs—Dust diseases
ASCETICISM
 See also
 Monasticism
ASCHER, BARBARA LAZEAR
A brother's death. il *The New York Times Magazine* p30+
 N 19 '89
ASCORBIC ACID *See* Vitamin C
ASDA *See* Aviakompaniya Sverkhdalnykh Avialiniy
ASEA AB
 See also
 ASEA Brown Boveri AB
ASEA BROWN BOVERI AB
An insider caper in Liechtenstein [helps SEC uncover insider
 trading during ABB's friendly takeover bid for Combustion
 Engineering] J. Kapstein. *Business Week* p58-9 D 11 '89
ASEAN
ASEAN postministerial conference, Bandar Seri Begawan
 [statements, July 6-7, 1989] J. A. Baker, III. *Department
 of State Bulletin* 89:58-61 S '89
ASEAN togetherness in pharmaceuticals. T. Yoshida. il *World
 Health* p29 N '89
Vitthya Vejjajiva [advice to George Bush] V. Vejjajiva.
 National Review 41:26-7 F 10 '89
ASEXUAL REPRODUCTION
 See also
 Clones (Biology)
Successful sex [favorable mutation in a sexual population]
 T. Beardsley. *Scientific American* 261:18 Ag '89
ASH, JOHN, 1948-
In a rainy country [poem] *The New Yorker* 65:46-7
 D 25 '89
ASH, ROY
Should the "balanced budget constitutional amendment" be
 adopted? [excerpts from statement, October 15, 1987]
 Congressional Digest 68:277+ N '89
ASH, TIMOTHY GARTON *See* Garton Ash, Timothy
ASH, VOLCANIC *See* Volcanic ash, tuff, etc.
ASH WEDNESDAY
Ash Wednesday meditation:
 Stirring the ashes. J. P. Wind. il *The Christian Century*
 106:102 F 1-8 '89
Ashes to ashes. P. J. Ryan. il *America* 160:94 F 4 '89
ASHBERY, JOHN
In another time [poem] *The New Yorker* 65:81 Ap
 24 '89
Notes from the air [poem] *The New Yorker* 65:44-5
 O 30 '89
Still-life with stranger [poem] *The New Yorker* 65:48
 S 18 '89

ASHBROOK, JAMES B., 1925-
Brain and gender: the missing data [discussion of January 4-11, 1989 article, Ways of knowing God: gender and the brain] *The Christian Century* 106:263-4 Mr 8 '89
Ways of knowing God: gender and the brain. il *The Christian Century* 106:14-15 Ja 4-11 '89
ASHBY, HAL
about
Obituary
American Film il por 14:72 Mr '89
Rolling Stone por p21 F 23 '89. J. Ressner
ASHCRAFT, AARON E.
A plea for 'orphan drugs'. por *Newsweek* 114:12 O 30 '89
ASHCROFT, MARY ELLEN
Is reel life real? il *Christianity Today* 33:29-30 F 17 '89
ASHE, ARTHUR
Is Proposition 42 racist? por *Ebony* 44:138-40 Je '89
about
Arthur Ashe remembers the forgotten men of sport—America's early black athletes [interview] S. K. Reed. il pors *People Weekly* 31:243-4+ Mr 6 '89
Ashe applauds ATP move to avoid South Africa. por *Jet* 76:48 S 18 '89
Ashe sees bright future for blacks in pro tennis. il pors *Jet* 76:48-50 Ag 28 '89
Athletes are exploited, Ashe tells N.C. Central. por *Jet* 77:50 N 13 '89
Word star. P. Giddings. il por *Essence* 20:38 My '89
ASHER, DON
My summer swing: on the road with a fifties big band. il *Harper's* 278:70-6 Je '89
ASHER, GERALD
Gourmet holidays: Montreal. il *Gourmet* 49:64-9+ My '89
Single malt scotch whisky. il *Gourmet* 49:94-9+ D '89
Wine journal. See issues of Gourmet
ASHEVILLE (N.C.)
Architecture
A new house in the Asheville style. il *Southern Living* 24:184-5 N '89
Historic houses, sites, etc.
See also
Biltmore House and Gardens (Asheville, N.C.)
Hotels, motels, etc.
The Grove Park Inn & the arts & crafts movement. B. E. Johnson. il *Antiques & Collecting Hobbies* 94:34-8 O '89
ASHLAND (OR.)
Theater
See also
Oregon Shakespearean Festival
ASHLAND OIL, INC.
Ashland Oil may refine its assets. G. G. Marcial. il *Business Week* p104 D 11 '89
ASHLEY, ELIZA JANE
about
Thirty-four years at the governor's mansion. R. Brown. il pors *Ebony* 44:52+ Jl '89
ASHLEY, FRANKLIN
'I've been through . . . several layers of hell'. il pors *TV Guide* 37:16-20 O 14-20 '89
ASHLEY, KIMBERLY
about
Black UA homecoming queen wins by write-in campaign; stirs a furor. il por *Jet* 77:18 N 6 '89
ASHLEY, MARC
Kauai: next link on the chain. il *The Saturday Evening Post* 261:92-5 Ja/F '89
ASHRY, MOHAMED T. EL- *See* El-Ashry, Mohamed T.
ASHTON, ALAN
What corporate America wants from PCs. por *Personal Computing* 13:216 O '89
ASHTON, SIR FREDERICK, 1904-1988
about
Les illuminations [ballet] Reviews
The New Leader 72:20-1 N 27 '89. L. A. Jacobs
Monotones [ballet] Reviews
The New Leader 72:20-1 N 27 '89. L. A. Jacobs
A wedding bouquet [ballet] Reviews
The New Leader 72:20-1 N 27 '89. L. A. Jacobs
ASHTON, JENNIFER
In your South American dream [poem] *The New Republic* 200:37 My 1 '89
ASHTON-TATE, INC.
dBase IV is a godsend—to the competition [glitches] P. Cole. il *Business Week* p102 N 13 '89
dBugs in dBase IV spread to the bottom line. P. Cole. il *Business Week* p135-6 Jl 17 '89
Is Ashton-Tate born again? [with editorial comment by Fred Abatemarco] C. Strehlo. il *Personal Computing* 13:5, 66-9+ Mr '89
ASHWORTH, GORDON
about
Caught in Starr wars. P. Kaihla. il pors *Maclean's* 102:12-13 Jl 3 '89
A flurry of scandals. R. Corelli. il pors *Maclean's* 102:12-13 Jl 10 '89

ASIA
See also
Asians
East and West
East Asia
Environmental policy—Asia
Investments, American—Asia
Journalism—Asia
Labor unions—Asia
Loans, Bank—Asia
Power resources—Asia
Public health—Asia
South Asia
Southeast Asia
Trade routes—Asia
United Nations—Asia
Regional report: Asia/Pacific. A. Giarelli. See issues of World Press Review beginning October 1986
Commerce
United States
See United States—Commerce—Asia
Description and travel
Pacific and Asian passages. G. Hesse. il *Travel Holiday* 171:73-4+ Ap '89
Economic conditions
The challenge of Asia in the 1990s [cover story] il *Fortune* 120 no13 Special Issue:10-11 Fall '89
Economic relations
See also
Asian Pacific Economic Cooperation (Organization)
When ideology bows to economics. D. Stanglin. il *U.S. News & World Report* 106:30-1 F 6 '89
Foreign relations
Containment's last gasp. P. H. Kreisberg. *Foreign Policy* 75:146-63 Summ '89
The scramble for Asia. *World Press Review* 36:19-20 My '89
Soviet Union
See Soviet Union—Foreign relations—Asia
United States
See United States—Foreign relations—Asia
Industries
The Pac Rim 150. il *Fortune* 120 no13 Special Issue:125-6+ Fall '89
ASIA AND THE UNITED STATES
A few pointers. J. M. Fallows. il *The Atlantic* 264:24+ N '89
ASIAN AMERICAN ARTS *See* Arts, Asian American
ASIAN AMERICAN COLLEGE STUDENTS
Asian and Pacific Americans: behind the myths [cover story; special issue; with editorial comment by Paula Y. Bagasao] il *Change* 21:4-5+ N/D '89
Berkeley's changing student population. R. Buderi. il *Science* 245:694-6 Ag 18 '89
ASIAN AMERICAN COLLEGE TEACHERS
Beyond affirmative action: empowering Asian American faculty. S. Chan. il *Change* 21:48-51 N/D '89
ASIAN AMERICAN FREE LABOR INSTITUTE
The AFL-CIO meddles in the Philippines. K. Scipes. il *The Progressive* 53:33 N '89
ASIAN AMERICAN LITERATURE
Bibliography
Discovering a rich resource: literature by and about Asian Americans. R. C. Leong. *Change* 21:64-8 N/D '89
ASIAN AMERICAN STUDIES
Opening the American mind and body: the role of Asian American studies. S. Hune. il *Change* 21:56-63 N/D '89
ASIAN AMERICANS
Asia in a day [Seattle] H. Lockman. il *Travel Holiday* 172:90-5 Ag '89
Asian Americans as the "model minority". B. H. Suzuki. il *Change* 21:12-19 N/D '89
False modesty. R. Ueda. *The New Republic* 201:16-17 Jl 3 '89
Civil rights
Asian mysteries. D. Seligman. il *Fortune* 120:274+ Jl 31 '89
Education
See also
Asian American college students
Asian and Pacific Americans: behind the myths [cover story; special issue; with editorial comment by Paula Y. Bagasao] il *Change* 21:4-5+ N/D '89
Concern in Washington [discrimination in college admissions] C. Holden. il *Science* 245:694-5 Ag 18 '89
The new 'open door' at Berkeley [charges of quotas] *U.S. News & World Report* 106:13-14 Je 5 '89
Prejudice against excellence. G. F. Will. por *Conservative Digest* 15:15 Jl/Ag '89
Quotas on campus: the new phase. D. Seligman. il *Fortune* 119:205+ Ja 30 '89
Political activities
The invisible success story. S. Rothenberg. il *National Review* 41:43-4+ S 15 '89
Statistics
The demographics of diversity. J. Hsia and M. Hirano-Nakanishi. il map *Change* 21:20-7 N/D '89

ASIAN COCKROACHES See Cockroaches
ASIAN COOKING See Cooking, Asian
ASIAN PACIFIC ECONOMIC COOPERATION (ORGANIZATION)
Is a grand alliance in the making on the Pacific Rim? B. Javetski and S. Hutcheon. il *Business Week* p70 N 6 '89
Pacific overtures. C. P. Work. il *U.S. News & World Report* 107:65+ N 20 '89
ASIAN REFUGEES See Refugees, Asian
ASIANA AIRLINES
Asiana pursues international authority as key to profits. J. Ott. il *Aviation Week & Space Technology* 130:56+ My 8 '89
Korean Air, Asiana order U.S. transports valued at $1.35 billion. J. Ott. *Aviation Week & Space Technology* 130:17 Ap 17 '89
Korea's Asiana grows domestically, plans expansion into overseas market. P. Proctor. il *Aviation Week & Space Technology* 131:142 O 9 '89
ASIANIMPROV RECORDS (FIRM)
East and West. D. Ouellette. il *Down Beat* 56:61 Ag '89
ASIANS

Australia
Advance Australia fair. W. McGurn. *National Review* 41:45 S 15 '89

United States
See also
    Asian Americans
Let's let Asians in. K. Labich. il *Fortune* 120:89-90 Jl 17 '89
Utah increases access to services for the Asian elderly. *Aging* no359:26 '89
ASID See American Society of Interior Designers
ASIMOV, ISAAC, 1920-
For mutual survival we must bring our world together [address, January 1989; cover story] il por *The Humanist* 49:5-8+ S/O '89
If they turned me loose on the moon . . . il por *TV Guide* 37:6-7+ Jl 15-21 '89
Isaac Asimov. il *Video* 13:62+ S '89
The never-ending fight. il por *The Humanist* 49:7-8+ Mr/Ap '89
The unknown solar system. il *Discover* 10:38-43 O '89
    about
Isaac Asimov speaks [interview; cover story] B. Moyers. il pors *The Humanist* 49:5-13+ Ja/F '89
ASINOF, ELIOT, 1919-
On the spot [cover story] il pors *The New York Times Magazine* p28-31+ Mr 26 '89
Pete Rose can't lose. il pors *Sport (New York, N.Y.)* 80:54-6 Ap '89
ASLET, CLIVE, 1955-
Ancestral style. il *House & Garden* 161:188-97 Mr '89
Architecture: Quinlan Terry: a Palladian country house in Kentucky. il por *Architectural Digest* 46:282-7 O '89
ÅSLUND, ANDERS, 1952-
    about
At the top of Washington's reading list. A. Platt. il *Newsweek* 114:23 O 2 '89
ASOCIACION NACIONAL PRO PERSONAS MAYORES
National centers on minority aging. il *Aging* no359:33-4 '89
ASOYAN, BORIS
Racism in the Soviet Union. *World Press Review* 36:85 O '89
ASPARAGUS
    See also
    Cooking—Vegetables
ASPARTAME See Sugar substitutes
ASPARTATE AMINOTRANSFERASE See Transaminases
ASPARTATE RECEPTORS See Chemoreceptors
ASPEN
Colorado aspen loop. il map *Sunset (Central West edition)* 183:26+ O '89
ASPEN (COLO.)
For the ultimate in nouvelle lang syne, the truly hip schuss Aspen. S. Schindehette. il *People Weekly* 31:115-17 Ja 16 '89
A time to remember [Aspen as World Championships host in 1950] N. Howe. il *Skiing* 41:106-8 Ja '89

Architecture
Inventing a new Colorado vernacular [S. Conger design] G. Greene. il por *Architectural Digest* 46:330+ O '89

Description
Welcome to Aspen. T. Chiu. il *Life* 12:70-2+ D '89
THE ASPERN PAPERS [opera] See Argento, Dominick
THE ASPERN PAPERS [television program] See Television program reviews—Single works
ASPHALT DRIVEWAYS See Driveways
ASPIN, LES
    about
The Democrats give Les Aspin a bloody nose. D. Griffiths. *Business Week* p57 Ag 14 '89
House defense leader attacks Air Force plan to add $1.4 billion to B-1B program. P. A. Gilmartin. *Aviation Week & Space Technology* 130:31 My 29 '89

ASPIRIN
Aspirin and heart attacks [Physicians' Health Study] il *FDA Consumer* 23:2-3 O '89
Aspirin and heart disease: a final report [research by Julie E. Buring] R. Cowen. *Science News* 136:55 Jl 22 '89
Aspirin on trial [effect on risk of heart attack and stroke] J. Poppy. il *Esquire* 111:89-91 Mr '89
Heart teamwork [use of aspirin and streptokinase to reduce heart-attack deaths; research by Samuel Z. Goldhaber] il *Prevention (Emmaus, Pa.)* 41:14 Ja '89
ASQUITH MOTOR CARRIAGE COMPANY
Asquith Motor Carriage. R. Hutton. il *Car and Driver* 34:33 My '89
ASSAD, HAFEZ
    about
Following an independent course [interview] K. Prager and others. por *Time* 133:30 Ap 3 '89
ASSASSINATION
    See also
    Henry III, King of France, 1551-1589—Assassination
    Herrhausen, Alfred—Assassination
    Kennedy, John F. (John Fitzgerald), 1917-1963—Assassination
    Moawad, René—Assassination
    Palme, Olof, 1927-1986—Assassination
    Romero, Oscar A. (Oscar Arnulfo), 1917-1980—Assassination
Arsenal [guns used in assassination attempts] D. C. Craig. il *Life* 12:156-7+ Fall '89
Building a better coup [CIA wants clarification on political assassinations] C. S. Manegold. il *Newsweek* 114:55 O 30 '89
Mr. Webster has it exactly wrong [CIA policy on assassinations] W. F. Buckley. *National Review* 41:62-3 N 24 '89
Reopening a deadly debate: the CIA wants to have a freer hand during coups. J. Peterzell. il *Time* 134:54 O 30 '89
We shoot people, don't we? [U.S. ban on assassination] M. Kinsley. il *Time* 134:118 O 23 '89
ASSAULT AND BATTERY
John Wayne's daughter Aissa is brutally beaten, and her ex-husband is soon to stand trial. M. Green. il pors *People Weekly* 31:106-8 My 29 '89
ASSAULT RIFLES
Ban the guns? W. F. Buckley. *National Review* 41:54-5 Ap 21 '89
Carnage control. il *Commonweal* 116:195-6 Ap 7 '89
Gub control [assault rifle ban] H. Hertzberg. *The New Republic* 200:4+ Ap 10 '89
Gunning for assault rifles [import ban] J. V. Lamar, Jr. il *Time* 133:39 Mr 27 '89
His object a gentler L.A., a councilman buys up AK-47s [N. Holden's cash-for-guns scheme to combat crime] il por *People Weekly* 31:120 F 13 '89
The lesson of Stockton. D. E. Petzal. il *Field & Stream* 94:19+ My '89
Lock and load for the gunfight of '89 [ban on imports of AK-47 assault rifles] il *U.S. News & World Report* 106:9 Mr 27 '89
Mad about guns [New York City's proposed ban on assault rifles] M. Kempton. *The New York Review of Books* 36:62 D 21 '89
Media fallout. D. E. Petzal. il *Field & Stream* 94:18+ Jl '89
The NRA comes under the gun [on the defensive as opposition to assault weapons grows] R. Sandza. il *Newsweek* 113:28-30 Mr 27 '89
Playing with guns [G. Bush vacillates on ban] G. F. Will. il *Newsweek* 113:78 Mr 27 '89
The right to bear AK-47s. il *Scholastic Update (Teachers' edition)* 122:14 N 3 '89
The right to bear (and die by) arms. F. Bruning. il *Maclean's* 102:13 Je 19 '89
The shots heard 'round the Congress [J. T. Wesbecker's Louisville murder spree with AK-47] il *U.S. News & World Report* 107:15 S 25 '89
Survey results, and a tale of confusion. D. E. Petzal. *Field & Stream* 94:16-17 S '89
ASSEMBLER LANGUAGE (COMPUTER LANGUAGE)
QuickC smooths QuicAssembler programming. M. Blaszczak. il *Byte* 14:292+ N '89
Sourcer magic disassembles machine code [Sourcer] B. Smith. *Byte* 14:104 F '89
Three assemblers for MS-DOS [Microsoft Macro Assembler; Borland Turbo Assembler; SLR Systems OPTASM] M. Blaszczak. il *Byte* 14:205-9 F '89
ASSEMBLIES OF GOD
Assemblies of God celebrates 75 years. R. Frame. il *Christianity Today* 33:45 S 22 '89
ASSEMBLY LANGUAGE (COMPUTER LANGUAGE) See Assembler language (Computer language)
ASSEMBLY LINE METHODS
    See also
    Automobile factories
    Team work in industry

ASSERTIVENESS (PSYCHOLOGY)
How to say no and make it stick. M. M. Kennedy. il *Glamour* 87:93 D '89
ASSES, DOMESTIC *See* Donkeys
ASSESSMENT
See also
Appraisers
ASSESSMENT OF COLLEGES AND UNIVERSITIES *See* Colleges and universities—Evaluation
ASSESSMENT OF EDUCATION *See* Education—Evaluation
ASSET ALLOCATION, TACTICAL *See* Tactical asset allocation (Investments)
ASSET ALLOCATION FUNDS *See* Investment trusts
ASSET-BACKED FINANCING
Shouldering arms [M. Markus' idea to securitize U.S. armament loans] M. Schifrin. il por *Forbes* 143:208-9 Ap 17 '89
ASSET DISPOSAL
Grabbing the drug bounty. H. Jensen. il *Maclean's* 102:49-50 O 23 '89
ASSET MANAGEMENT ACCOUNTS *See* Cash management accounts
ASSISTANCE IN EMERGENCIES
See also
First aid in illness and injury
Relief work
Rescue work
A disaster brings out the best in people. Why? G. Cowley. il *Newsweek* 114:40+ N 6 '89
Three Samaritans [American youths assist injured woman during visit to Switzerland] B. O'Sullivan. il *Reader's Digest* 135:55-6+ O '89
You to the rescue. il *Current Health 2* 15:22-4 F '89
ASSOCIATION (BIOLOGY) *See* Symbiosis
ASSOCIATION FOR COMPUTING MACHINERY. SPECIAL INTEREST GROUP ON COMPUTER GRAPHICS
Art in the computer age [SIGGRAPH 1989 Art Show] R. F. Malina. il *Technology Review* 92:71-2+ O '89
ASSOCIATION FOR DRUG ABUSE PREVENTION AND TREATMENT
Yolanda Serrano [work in AIDS prevention in New York City] K. Dobie. il pors *Ms.* 17:79-83 Ja/F '89
ASSOCIATION OF AMERICAN PUBLISHERS
Meetings
Unperturbed publishers hear predictions for next decade [annual meeting] M. Reuter. il *Publishers Weekly* 235:18-20 Ap 21 '89
ASSOCIATION OF AMERICAN PUBLISHERS. INTERNATIONAL TRADE GROUP
AAP forms International Trade Group. M. Reuter. *Publishers Weekly* 235:14 My 5 '89
Debut for the AAP International Trade Group. G. Feldman. *Publishers Weekly* 235:60 Je 30 '89
ASSOCIATION OF AMERICAN PUBLISHERS. PROFESSIONAL AND SCHOLARLY PUBLISHING DIVISION
A wide-ranging look at problems and prospects for the professional community [annual meeting] G. Feldman. il *Publishers Weekly* 235:61-4 Mr 10 '89
ASSOCIATION OF AMERICAN UNIVERSITY PRESSES
AAUP in Cincinnati. J. F. Baker and C. B. Grannis. il *Publishers Weekly* 236:37-9 Jl 14 '89
ASSOCIATION OF AMERICAN UNIVERSITY PRESSES BOOK SHOW *See* Book exhibits
ASSOCIATION OF AMERICAN WEATHER OBSERVERS
Weather is for sharing [interview with S. Steinke] il pors *Weatherwise* 42:148-50 Je '89
ASSOCIATION OF EUROPEAN AIRLINES
AEA international traffic grows; departure delays reach 28.3%. il *Aviation Week & Space Technology* 131:59 D 4 '89
European airlines report delays in flight operations. J. M. Lenorovitz. *Aviation Week & Space Technology* 130:107 My 8 '89
European airlines will study forming a single ATC system. *Aviation Week & Space Technology* 130:71 F 27 '89
ASSOCIATION OF GRADUATE STUDENT EMPLOYEES
Graduate students make history [University of California-Berkeley recognizes Association of Graduate Student Employees] P. Selvin. *The Progressive* 53:19 O '89
ASSOCIATION OF NATIONAL SECURITY ALUMNI
Spy society. S. Hornik. il *Common Cause Magazine* 15:10 S/O '89
ASSOCIATION OF PROFESSIONAL BALL PLAYERS OF AMERICA
Baseball alumni wars. G. Castle. il *Sport (New York, N.Y.)* 80:14 Jl '89
ASSOCIATION OF SOUTHEAST ASIAN NATIONS *See* ASEAN
ASSOCIATION OF SPACE EXPLORERS
Planetary Congress. il *Ad Astra* 1:39 D '89
Questions, questions [Planetary Congress] *The New Yorker* 65:41-2 N 27 '89
ASSOCIATION OF TENNIS PROFESSIONALS
Ashe applauds ATP move to avoid South Africa. por *Jet* 76:48 S 18 '89
ATP directive: all systems go. H. Jordan. il por *World Tennis* 36:106 My '89
ATP's tour de force. P. M. Coan. *World Tennis* 37:86+ D '89

How much is too much? A. Wolff. il *Sports Illustrated* 71:80-2+ D 11 '89
A net gain for men's tennis? A. Fins. il *Business Week* p76 D 18 '89
Power games grip men's tour. G. M. Heldman. il *World Tennis* 36:16-17 F '89
ASSOCIATIONS, INSTITUTIONS, ETC.
See also
Clubs
Environmental associations
Professional associations
ASSOCIATIVE LEARNING IN ANIMALS *See* Animal learning
ASSYRO-BABYLONIAN JEWELRY *See* Jewelry, Assyro-Babylonian
ASSYRO-BABYLONIAN MATHEMATICS *See* Mathematics, Assyro-Babylonian
ASTAIRE, FRED
about
From atom bombs to Fred Astaire. A. P. Sanoff. il por *U.S. News & World Report* 106:63 My 22 '89
ASTAPHAN, JAMIE
about
A deepening scandal. B. Wickens. pors *Maclean's* 102:49-50 Je 5 '89
A revealing inquiry. M. Noden. il por *Sports Illustrated* 70:19 Je 5 '89
The saga behind the shame. J. Brant. il pors *Runner's World* 24:78-80 Ap '89
ASTEROIDS
See also
Space flight—Asteroid missions
2060 Chiron = Comet Kowal? il *Sky and Telescope* 78:14 Jl '89
Ad asteroid. M. R. Chartrand. *Ad Astra* 1:23 Ja '89
Apocalypse, how? [probability of impact with planet earth] J. Bosveld. il *Omni (New York, N.Y.)* 12:36+ D '89
An asteroid whizzes past earth [1989 FC] R. W. Sinnott. il *Sky and Telescope* 78:30 Jl '89
Carbonaceous meteorites and asteroids. J. Eberhart. *Science News* 136:334 N 18 '89
Chiron becomes a comet. il *Astronomy* 17:14 S '89
Chiron's brightening hints it's a comet. J. Eberhart. il *Science News* 135:247 Ap 22 '89
A combination of impact and volcano is dismissed. *Science* 243:479 Ja 27 '89
Earth gains a neighbor [1989 FC] il *Astronomy* 17:10 Ag '89
Largest radar detects dumbbell in space [Steven Ostro detects fused asteroid] *Science* 246:999 N 24 '89
Meteors from asteroids. il *Sky and Telescope* 77:245-6 Mr '89
The next doomsday impact. C. R. Chapman and D. Morrison. *Astronomy* 17:8 N '89
Pulverized asteroids and the zodiacal light. il *Sky and Telescope* 77:242-4 Mr '89
Radar reveals an asteroid's strange shape [research by Steven J. Ostro] J. Eberhart. il *Science News* 136:343 N 25 '89
Sing the asteroid electric [work of Floyd Herbert] il *Sky and Telescope* 77:356-7 Ap '89
Stop to consider the stones that fall from the sky. J. S. Trefil. il map *Smithsonian* 20:80-8+ S '89
Unexpected asteroid: a close call from space. *Science News* 135:287 My 6 '89
Uranus and Vesta naked-eye. A. MacRobert. il *Sky and Telescope* 78:66 Jl '89
Orbits
Need one more thing to worry about? [1989FC passes unusually close to earth] *Newsweek* 113:64 My 1 '89
Visit to a small planet [passes close to earth] il *U.S. News & World Report* 106:16 My 1 '89
Whew! That was close [1989FC orbits close to earth] M. D. Lemonick. il *Time* 133:52 My 1 '89
Spectra and spectroscopy
Phyllosilicate absorption features in main-belt and outer-belt asteroid reflectance spectra. F. Vilas and M. J. Gaffey. bibl f il *Science* 246:790-2 N 10 '89
ASTERS
Asters again. A. Lacy. il *Organic Gardening* 36:60-4 N '89
ASTHMA
Don't treat asthma casually! C. Slom. il *McCall's* 117:147+ O '89
Getting a grasp on asthma's grip [American asthma report] J. Seligman. il *Newsweek* 114:60-1 S 4 '89
Life with asthma. C. Gloeckner. il *Current Health 2* 15:10-11 Ap '89
Causes
Breathing easy is no sweat [exercise-induced asthma] J. Silberner. il *U.S. News & World Report* 106:74 F 20 '89
Swimming lapse [exercise-induced asthma] M. Madsen. il *Women's Sports & Fitness* 11:13-14 Ap '89
Viral infections cause spasms [development of asthma from respiratory infections; views of William Busse] *USA Today (Periodical)* 118:2-3 O '89
Mortality
The baffling rise in asthma deaths. *Newsweek* 112:79 My 22 '89

ASTHMA—cont.

Therapy

The breathe-easy guide to asthma relief. A. Weinstein. il *Prevention (Emmaus, Pa.)* 41:57-65 F '89

Breathing easier [use of fish oil] il *Prevention (Emmaus, Pa.)* 41:10 Ap '89

ASTON, NIGEL

Turbulent priests? The Church and the Revolution. bibl il *History Today* 39:20-5 My '89

ASTON MARTIN (AUTOMOBILE) *See* Sports cars

ASTOR, BROOKE

I do, I do, I do. il por *House & Garden* 161:78-80 Je '89

A landscape of people. il por *Architectural Digest* 46:92+ N '89

ASTRA AIRPLANES *See* Airplanes, Business

ASTRAGALUS *See* Milk vetch

ASTRAL CONVERTIBLE [dance] *See* Dance reviews—Single works

ASTROARCHEOLOGY *See* Astronomy, Ancient

ASTROCHEMISTRY

See also
  Matter, Interstellar
  Nucleosynthesis

Carbon ratio shows Halley may be alien [research by Susan Wyckoff] F. Flam. *Science News* 135:214 Ap 8 '89

Halley is an alien [carbon ratio; research by Susan Wyckoff] T. Waters. il *Discover* 10:26-7 Ag '89

Soccer-ball molecules in space. il *Sky and Telescope* 77:358 Ap '89

Spectral reflectance properties of hydrocarbons: remote-sensing implications. E. A. Cloutis. bibl f il *Science* 245:165-8 Jl 14 '89

Tracking an elusive carbon [cover story] C. Vaughan. il *Science News* 135:56-7 Ja 28 '89

Was Halley's comet interstellar? [research by Susan Wyckoff] *Sky and Telescope* 78:573-4 D '89

ASTROCYTES

Astrocytes. H. K. Kimelberg and M. D. Norenberg. bibl il *Scientific American* 260:66-72+ Ap '89

Brain region and gene specificity of neuropeptide gene expression in cultured astrocytes. H. Shinoda and others. bibl f il *Science* 245:415-17 Jl 28 '89

ASTROLOGY

Astrology in high places. D. R. Hales. il *McCall's* 117:83-6 O '89

Dr. Zodiac [theories of S. Percy] D. Sobel. il pors *Omni (New York, N.Y.)* 12:60-2+ D '89

Horoscope. See issues of 'Teen

Horoscope. D. Kempton-Smith. See issues of Seventeen beginning March 1985 through February 1990

Horoscope. M. Lutin. See issues of Vogue beginning January 1989 through November 1989

Horoscopes. J. M. Woolfolk. See issues of Harper's Bazaar beginning December 1988

Redbook's astrology guide: month-by-month predictions for 1989. S. Omarr. il *Redbook* 172:75-82 Ja '89

A sign of the times [many tennis pros born under the sign of Leo] L. Shiras. il *World Tennis* 37:82 Ag '89

Sign time. A. J. Grice. See issues of Essence

Starcast. M. L. Fiel. See issues of Mademoiselle

Starmate match-ups. 'Teen 33:63-4 N '89

Your astrology defense kit. A. Fraknoi. il *Sky and Telescope* 78:146-50 Ag '89

Great Britain

History

The political magic of John Dee. I. Seymour. bibl il por *History Today* 39:29-35 Ja '89

ASTRONAUT MANEUVERING UNIT *See* Space flight—Extravehicular activity

ASTRONAUTICS *See* Space flight

ASTRONAUTS

See also
  Acton, Loren
  Aldrin, Buzz
  Association of Space Explorers
  Romanenko, Yuri, 1944-

Astronaut wanted, no experience needed [selecting British astronaut for Juno mission aboard Soviet Mir space station] C. A. Simpson. il *Ad Astra* 1:5 O '89

Footprints on the moon [Project Apollo flights; cover story] D. MacKinnon and J. Baldanza. il *American History Illustrated* 24:18-23 Summ '89

Memorials on the moon [craters named for astronauts] H. Masursky and M. Strobell. il *Sky and Telescope* 77:265 Mr '89

NASA's next generation. A. R. Oberg. il *Omni (New York, N.Y.)* 11:26+ Ja '89

President's message [civilians aboard shuttle] C. D. Walker. il *Ad Astra* 1:2 Ap '89

Shuttle scientists: an endangered species? [astronauts to be given priority over payload specialists] J. Eberhart. *Science News* 135:71 F 4 '89

Space coloristics [cosmonauts' reporting concerning earth's surface] V. Vasyutin and A. A. Tishchenko. bibl il *Scientific American* 261:84-90 Jl '89

Anecdotes, facetiae, satire, etc.

Last word [interview with Jose Jimenez] B. Dana. il *Omni (New York, N.Y.)* 11:110 Jl '89

Attitudes

Lunar reflections [memories of Apollo astronauts] J. Goldberg. il *Omni (New York, N.Y.)* 11:34-6+ Jl '89

Food

See Space flight—Food problems

Health and hygiene

See also
  Weightlessness

Training

See also
  Young Astronaut Program (Japan)

ASTRONOMERS

See also
  Barnard, Edward Emerson, 1857-1923
  Brahe, Tycho, 1546-1601
  Burckhalter, Charles, 1849-1923
  Hubble, Edwin Powell, 1889-1953
  Lassell, William, 1799-1880
  Lunine, Jonathan I.
  Metcalf, Joel Hastings, 1866-1925
  Rumrill, Harry Barlow
  Russell, Henry Norris, 1877-1957
  Seymour, Percy
  Tombaugh, Clyde, 1906-
  Women astronomers

Turning pro: the good, the bad, and the ugly. S. Odenwald. il *Sky and Telescope* 77:124 F '89

ASTRONOMERS, AMATEUR

See also
  Children as astronomers

Affecting eternity [friendship with J. R. Gill] R. D. Hicks. il *Sky and Telescope* 77:236 Mr '89

Amateur astronomers. S. J. O'Meara. See issues of Sky and Telescope

Amateur news. See issues of Astronomy beginning July 1988

The amateur's universe. J. Newton and P. Teece. *Astronomy* 17:8 Ap '89

Commercial telescope optics: buyer beware! P. Ceravolo. il *Sky and Telescope* 78:564 D '89

Deep-sky wonders. W. S. Houston. il *Sky and Telescope* 77:570-2 My '89

Gleanings for ATM's. R. W. Sinnott. See issues of Sky and Telescope

In defense of casual astronomy. A. Dyer. il *Sky and Telescope* 77:580 Je '89

John Dobson: a man with a mission [interview] S. J. O'Meara. por *Sky and Telescope* 78:530-2 N '89

Reader reports. See issues of Astronomy beginning February 1988

A salesman for the heavens wants to rope you in [J. Dobson] D. Moser. bibl (p174) il pors *Smithsonian* 20:102-6+ Ap '89

Sharing astronomy across the Atlantic. D. Abbou. *Astronomy* 17:99 F '89

StarTrails. D. H. Levy. See issues of Sky and Telescope beginning January 1988

Supernova hunter; ed. by Robert Reeves. R. O. Evans. il *Astronomy* 17:94-7 N '89

Time and the amateur astronomer. A. MacRobert. il *Sky and Telescope* 77:378-9 Ap '89

ASTRONOMICAL DISTANCES

See also
  Stars—Distances

Far-out star. il *Sky and Telescope* 78:573 D '89

How far to the galaxies? [cover story] V. Kiernan. il *Astronomy* 17:48-54 Je '89

Virgo Cluster distance refined. il *Astronomy* 17:10 O '89

ASTRONOMICAL EQUIPMENT

See also
  Binoculars
  Coronagraph
  Image processing—Astronomical use
  Radio telescopes
  Spectrograph
  Telescopes

Astronomy products. See issues of Astronomy beginning October 1988

Don't forget the bug spray! D. J. Eicher. il *Astronomy* 17:66-7 Ag '89

The universe as afterthought. M. Harwit. *Astronomy* 17:8 Ag '89

Advertising

StarTrails [Sky and telescope advertisements] D. H. Levy. *Sky and Telescope* 77:548-9 My '89

Directories

Astronomy equipment directory 1989. il *Astronomy* 17:AED1-AED24 O '89

Dealers and manufacturers. *Sky and Telescope* 78 Resource Guide:18-23 S '89

ASTRONOMICAL ILLUSTRATION *See* Astronomy in art

ASTRONOMICAL LEAGUE

Back to the basics. S. J. O'Meara. il *Sky and Telescope* 78:528-30 N '89

ASTRONOMICAL MEASUREMENTS
Moments of discovery [trying to comprehend light-years] P. M. Leschak. il *Astronomy* 17:98 F '89

ASTRONOMICAL MODELS
Clumps in the machine [computer modeling of galaxy cluster; research by Adrian Melott and Sergei Shandarin] il *Discover* 10:12 S '89
Dance of the Planets [computer orrery] J. E. Mosley. il *Sky and Telescope* 78:642 D '89
From fireball to galaxies: making late waves [late phase transitions in models of the universe] I. Peterson. *Science News* 135:262 Ap 29 '89
Making sunshine [missing solar neutrinos] I. Peterson. il *Science News* 136:280-1 O 28 '89
Pumping gas to fuel a galaxy's active core [computer simulation by Lars Hernquist] I. Peterson. *Science News* 136:150 S 2 '89
Supercomputing the universe. D. Johnson. il *Astronomy* 17:48-54 D '89
Your own piece of the solar system [with editorial comment by Richard Berry] F. Miller, Jr. il *Astronomy* 17:6, 73-7 Mr '89

ASTRONOMICAL NAMES *See* Astronomy—Nomenclature
ASTRONOMICAL OBSERVATIONS *See* Astronomy—Observations

ASTRONOMICAL OBSERVATORIES
See also
  Joint Observatory for Cometary Research
  Kitt Peak National Observatory
  Lone Star Observatory (Tex.)
  McDonald Observatory
  National Optical Astronomy Observatories
  National Radio Astronomy Observatory (U.S.)
  Owens Valley Radio Observatory
  Pettinger-Guiley Observatory
  United States Naval Observatory
The Back River deep-sky project. J. C. Vickers. il *Sky and Telescope* 78:109-11 Jl '89
Build a backyard observatory. S. Chomniak. il *Astronomy* 17:90-4 Je '89
The case of cosmic rays [new Utah observatory to study muons from Cygnus X-3 and Hercules X-1; cover story] G. Taubes. il *Discover* 10:52-8+ S '89
Court rules against light polluter [yard light interferes with astronomical observatory] il *Astronomy* 17:16 Jl '89
Historic refractor back in use [Alvan Clark refractor near Burlington, Iowa] il *Astronomy* 17:18 Mr '89
A "lift-off roof" observatory. K. N. Chandler. il *Sky and Telescope* 77:96 Ja '89
Lights out in Flagstaff. *Astronomy* 17:12+ Jl '89
The magic of an observatory. C. Hamilton. *Astronomy* 17:105 My '89
Michigan light victory [light pollution and John Rogers Observatory] il *Astronomy* 17:16 Ap '89
Observatories. *Sky and Telescope* 78 Resource Guide:7-8 S '89
An observatory from a kit [Hexadome] T. B. Hunter. il *Sky and Telescope* 77:492-3 My '89
A portable observatory [Ace Dome] J. M. Doggett. il *Sky and Telescope* 78:480-1 N '89

Location
Biology versus astronomy: the battle for Mount Graham [impact of proposed observatory on red squirrels] E. Pennisi. il *BioScience* 39:10-13 Ja '89
Mount Graham telescopes get the green light. il *Sky and Telescope* 77:130 F '89

Antarctic regions
Cosmic fire, terrestrial ice [cosmic background radiation project at South Pole] D. H. Smith. il *Sky and Telescope* 78:471-4 N '89
International Antarctic observatory proposed. il *Sky and Telescope* 78:457-8 N '89
An observatory at 90° south [Amundsen-Scott South Pole Station] D. H. Smith. il *Sky and Telescope* 77:598-602 Je '89

Australia
Spectra galore [UCL Echelle Spectrograph at the Anglo-Australian Telescope] il *Sky and Telescope* 77:585-6 Je '89

Chile
Extreme astronomy [observing in the Chilean Andes] S. Brunier. il por map *Sky and Telescope* 78:366-9 O '89
A sharp, new eye scans the southern sky [European Southern Observatory's New Technology Telescope] il *Science News* 135:324 My 27 '89
A telescope for tomorrow [New Technology Telescope; cover story] D. Fischer. il *Sky and Telescope* 78:248-52 S '89

Hawaii
Active-optics camera tested [imaging system built for the Canada-France-Hawaii Telescope] il *Sky and Telescope* 78:12-13 Jl '89
Keck telescope mirror is in production. M. M. Waldrop. il *Science* 243:1010-11 F 24 '89
Mars from Mauna Kea. W. K. Hartmann. il *Sky and Telescope* 77:474 My '89

India
Probing the heliosphere from India. S. K. Alurkar and R. V. Bhonsle. il map *Sky and Telescope* 78:151 Ag '89

New Zealand
Black Birch observatory under fire in New Zealand. il *Sky and Telescope* 78:9-10 Jl '89

North America
1989 directory of observatories, planetariums, and museums. il *Astronomy* 17:50-7 My '89

Puerto Rico
Improvements for Arecibo. il *Sky and Telescope* 77:467-8 My '89

Soviet Union
25-meter Soviet telescope planned for 2000. M. Sigov. il *Astronomy* 17:14+ O '89
Canadians visit the Soviet Union [amateur astronomers] il *Astronomy* 17:18 Je '89

Sweden
Will Tycho's observatory be restored? [Uraniborg] B. Haggman. il *Astronomy* 17:10 N '89

ASTRONOMICAL OBSERVATORIES, AIRBORNE *See* Airplanes in astronomy

ASTRONOMICAL PHOTOGRAPHY
See also
  Earth—Photographs and photography
  Eclipses, Lunar—Photographs and photography
  Galaxies—Photographs and photography
  Jupiter (Planet)—Photographs and photography
  Mars (Planet)—Photographs and photography
  Moon—Photographs and photography
  Nebulae—Photographs and photography
  Sky—Photographs and photography
  Sun—Photographs and photography
Astrophotography's rise and fall. D. Di Cicco. il *Sky and Telescope* 78:124 Ag '89
The Back River deep-sky project. J. C. Vickers. il *Sky and Telescope* 78:109-11 Jl '89
Enhanced-color astrophotography [cover story] T. Hallas and D. Mount. il *Sky and Telescope* 78:216-18 Ag '89
The faint light of deep-sky objects. il *Astronomy* 17:106-7 D '89
Gallery. See issues of Sky and Telescope beginning March 1988
Great astrophotos in less than an hour. R. Bunge. il *Astronomy* 17:78-83 Ag '89
Images. See occasional issues of Sky and Telescope beginning June 1987
Improving color prints. J. Riffle. il *Sky and Telescope* 78:326-7 S '89
The joy of color printing. L. Myers. il *Astronomy* 17:86-91 N '89
Photographing the deep sky amid city lights [increasing contrast] H. A. Entrop. il *Sky and Telescope* 77:108-10 Ja '89
The secrets of my astrophotography success. K. Zussman. il *Astronomy* 17:68-73 Je '89
Tuesday's mail. D. Di Cicco. il *Sky and Telescope* 77:111 Ja '89

Equipment
Astronomy tests the Northern Lites cold camera. R. Reeves. il *Astronomy* 17:86-9 Jl '89
Astrophotos the easy way [piggyback astrophotography] R. Reeves. il *Astronomy* 17:70-5 S '89
Deep-sky photography without guiding. R. Arbour. il *Sky and Telescope* 78:538-9+ N '89
How I made a Schmidt camera. L. Lai. il *Sky and Telescope* 77:664-5+ Je '89
Secrets of city astrophotography. K. R. Brasch. il *Astronomy* 17:90-5 Ja '89
Temperature control of a hypering tank. D. C. Cole. il *Sky and Telescope* 78:658-61+ D '89
Working against the grain of fast films [composite prints] L. Myers. il *Astronomy* 17:88-91 F '89

History
Barnard's 'dark' dilemma. G. L. Verschuur. il pors *Astronomy* 17:30-8 F '89

ASTRONOMICAL PHOTOMETRY *See* Photometry, Astronomical

ASTRONOMICAL RESEARCH
The universe as afterthought. M. Harwit. *Astronomy* 17:8 Ag '89
Who gets the credit? D. H. Levy. *Astronomy* 17:8 O '89

Federal aid
Academy group observes astronomy in cloudy period of budget cuts. I. Goodwin. il *Physics Today* 42:45-6 D '89
U.S. astronomy's diminished funds. il *Sky and Telescope* 78:244 S '89

Soviet Union
UFO update [SETI projects] P. McCarthy. il *Omni (New York, N.Y.)* 12:89 N '89

ASTRONOMICAL SOCIETIES
See also
  American Astronomical Society
  Astronomical League
  Astronomical Society of the Pacific
1989 directory of astronomy clubs. il *Astronomy* 17:70-5 My '89
National societies; Astronomy clubs. *Sky and Telescope* 78 Resource Guide:9-15 S '89
StarTrails. D. H. Levy. *Sky and Telescope* 77:203 F '89

ASTRONOMICAL SOCIETY OF THE PACIFIC
Where the earth touches the sky. S. Cole. il *Astronomy* 17:106-9 O '89

ASTRONOMICAL SPECTROSCOPY
See also
Asteroids—Spectra and spectroscopy
Galaxies—Spectra and spectroscopy
Infrared astronomy
Nebulae—Spectra and spectroscopy
Neptune (Planet)—Spectra and spectroscopy
Quasars—Spectra and spectroscopy
Stars—Spectra and spectroscopy
Sun—Spectra and spectroscopy
Ultraviolet astronomy
Low-budget stellar spectroscopy [Multi-Telescope Telescope]
I. Peterson. *Science News* 136:12 Jl 1 '89

ASTRONOMY
See also
Airplanes in astronomy
Arcs (Astronomy)
Artificial satellites—Astronomical use
Asteroids
Astrophysics
Automobiles in astronomy
Black holes (Astronomy)
CD-ROM (Compact disc-Read only memory)—Astronomical use
Comets
Computers—Astronomical use
Conjunctions (Astronomy)
Constellations
Counterglow
Dark matter (Astronomy)
Doppler effect
Eclipses, Lunar
Eclipses, Solar
Galaxies
Gamma ray astronomy
Great Attractor (Astronomy)
Halos (Astronomy)
Herbig-Haro objects
Image processing—Astronomical use
Information systems—Astronomical use
Infrared astronomy
Lasers—Astronomical use
Life on other planets
Longitude
Lunar bases—Astronomical use
Meteorites
Meteors
Milky Way
Nebulae
Occultations
Olbers' paradox
Planetariums
Planetesimal hypothesis
Planets
Precession
Quasars
Radar in astronomy
Radio astronomy
Satellites
Sky
Solar system
Space astronomy
Stars
Sun
Telephone in astronomy
Telescopes
Television broadcasting—Astronomy programs
Ultraviolet astronomy
Universe
Videotapes—Astronomical use
X ray astronomy
Zodiacal light
Astronews. See issues of Astronomy
Forum. See issues of Astronomy
News notes. See issues of Sky and Telescope
Sky reporter. S. P. Maran. See occasional issues of Natural History through May 1989

Almanacs
1989 almanac for skygazers. F. Schaaf. il *The Mother Earth News* 115:94-6+ Ja/F '89
Sky-gazer's almanac 1989. il *Sky and Telescope* 77:59-62 Ja '89

Awards
See also
Tinsley Prize
Urey Prize
AAS announces 1989 Russell Lecturer; Heineman, Warner and Pierce prizes. il *Physics Today* 42 pt1:81-2 Ag '89

Bibliography
Astronomy books. See issues of Astronomy beginning July 1988
Books and the sky. M. D. Boring. See issues of Sky and Telescope

Charts, diagrams, etc.
See also
Stars—Atlases
Astronomy's 1989 sky guide. R. Burnham. il map *Astronomy* 17:78-89 Ja '89
Celestial events. T. D. Nicholson. See issues of Natural History
Desktop planetarium [Voyager] W. Harwood. il *High Technology Business* 9:48 Ap '89
Hand-held star guides [Bushnell Starwatcher's Decoder Set] B. Luzader. il *Sky and Telescope* 78:260-1 S '89
Moon over Miami [planetarium software Solarsim and Sky Travel] J. L. Wilson. *Ad Astra* 1:38 F '89
Oppolzer's great canon of eclipses. W. H. C. Carton. il por *Sky and Telescope* 78:475-8 N '89
Sky almanac. See issues of Astronomy beginning July 1988
Southern stars. See alternate issues of Sky and Telescope
Star chart. See issues of Earth Science beginning Spring 1988
A star-hop from Capella. A. MacRobert. il *Sky and Telescope* 77:140-2 F '89
Stars for [the month] See issues of Sky and Telescope
Stars on your ceiling. il *Sunset (Central West edition)* 182:62-3 Ja '89
To bin or not to bin. G. Lovi. il *Sky and Telescope* 77:175-6 F '89
Voyager: excellent software. B. Bond. il *Astronomy* 17:104 Mr '89
The world's biggest star catalogue [Hubble Space Telescope Guide star catalog] R. Villard. il *Sky and Telescope* 78:583-9 D '89

Conferences
See also
Planets—Conferences
1989 summer meetings and events. il *Astronomy* 17:76-7 My '89
Astrofest '89. S. J. O'Meara. il *Sky and Telescope* 78:647-9 D '89
Astrofest whets amateur spirit. il *Astronomy* 17:16 D '89
A big year for Riverside. il *Astronomy* 17:18 S '89
Clear skies for Winter Star Party [February 1989] R. Berry. il *Astronomy* 17:20 My '89
Irish amateurs gather at Birr Castle [Whirlpool Star Party] T. O'Hanlon. *Astronomy* 17:18 Mr '89
Meetings and events. See issues of Astronomy beginning July 1988
StarTrails [Texas Star Party] D. H. Levy. il *Sky and Telescope* 78:307-8 S '89
Telescopes highlight Stellafane. il *Astronomy* 17:16 N '89
Texas Star Party survives rain. il *Astronomy* 17:18 O '89

Directories
Sky & telescope's astronomy resource guide. il *Sky and Telescope* 78 Resource Guide:1-23 S '89

History
Astronomy from Brooklyn Heights. D. Trombino. il *Sky and Telescope* 78:305-7 S '89
Henry Norris Russell. D. H. DeVorkin. bibl il por *Scientific American* 260:126-33 My '89
The legacy of Edwin Hubble. B. Jones. il pors *Astronomy* 17:38-44 D '89
A life devoted to astronomy [C. Burckhalter] K. Bracher. il por *Astronomy* 17:50-4 O '89

International aspects
International news. See occasional issues of Sky and Telescope beginning December 1986

Nomenclature
See also
International Star Registry
Memorials on the moon [craters named for astronauts] H. Masursky and M. Strobell. il *Sky and Telescope* 77:265 Mr '89
To name a star, for a price [International Star Registry] L. A. Shore. il *Astronomy* 17:114-15+ D '89

Observations
Backyard astronomy. A. MacRobert. See occasional issues of Sky and Telescope beginning August 1983
Celestial calendar. A. MacRobert. See issues of Sky and Telescope beginning October 1984
Cluttered night vision. D. M. Ludlum. *Country Journal* 16:19 Mr/Ap '89
Don't forget the bug spray! D. J. Eicher. il *Astronomy* 17:66-7 Ag '89
Eye on the sky. D. Byrd. See issues of Astronomy beginning July 1988
Finding the best observing site. T. B. Hunter. il *Astronomy* 17:92-3 D '89
Miles of predawn sky [studying the sky while running] T. B. Hunter. il *Astronomy* 17:90 Ap '89
The never-ending nova hunt. D. H. Kaiser. *Astronomy* 17:90-1 Ap '89
Observer's page. D. Di Cicco. See issues of Sky and Telescope
Observing among the smokestacks [night sky] G. Coburn. il *Astronomy* 17:104-5 My '89
The prize in the sky. M. Chibnik. *Astronomy* 17:98-9 S '89
Reader reports. See issues of Astronomy beginning February 1988

ASTRONOMY—Observations—*cont.*

Seeking stellar flares in a deceptive sky [research by Bradley E. Schaefer] F. Flam. *Science News* 135:118 F 25 '89

Sky almanac. See issues of Astronomy beginning July 1988

Space pollution obscures night sky. il *Earth Science* 42:9 Spr '89

Start new year "starry eyed". *USA Today (Periodical)* 118:14 D '89

StarTrails. D. H. Levy. See issues of Sky and Telescope beginning January 1988

Through the eyepiece. R. Shaffer. See issues of Astronomy beginning July 1988

Tricks of an observer's trade. S. Forrest. il *Astronomy* 17:98-9 Ag '89

Who will miss the night sky? [light pollution] D. L. Crawford. *Astronomy* 17:8 Mr '89

Periodicals
See also
Sky and telescope (Periodical)

Research
See Astronomical research

Study and teaching
See also
Project STAR

Is an astronomy degree useful? R. Lopes. il *Sky and Telescope* 78:236 S '89

Mr. Killoran's fifth-grade cosmos. R. Dier. il *Astronomy* 17:98 S '89

China
China: astronomy in a redeveloping nation. H. P. Coyle. *Sky and Telescope* 77:199-201 F '89

France
History
Astronomy in the French Revolution. R. Barthalot. il *Sky and Telescope* 78:21-3 Jl '89

Great Britain
Britain reveals astronomy plan. D. Dickson. *Science* 243:471 Ja 27 '89

Ireland
Irish amateurs gather at Birr Castle [Whirlpool Star Party] T. O'Hanlon. *Astronomy* 17:18 Mr '89

New Zealand
The sky from New Zealand. il *Astronomy* 17:91+ S '89

Soviet Union
Stalin's purge of Soviet astronomers. R. A. McCutcheon. il *Sky and Telescope* 78:352-7 O '89

Western Europe
See also
European Southern Observatory (Organization)

European amateurs study Titan [28 Sagittarii occultation] A. J. Hollis and J. Mitton. il *Astronomy* 17:52-4 N '89

ASTRONOMY, ANCIENT

The double polestar of the past [computer program] A. Kammerer. il *Sky and Telescope* 77:531-3 My '89

First light at an Irish tomb [roof slit designed to catch sun's rays at solstice; research by Tom P. Ray] *Science News* 135:88 F 11 '89

Irish mist [tomb aligned with winter solstice; research by Tom P. Ray] J. Horgan. il *Scientific American* 260:22+ Ap '89

A place in the sun for the early Irish [tomb sited to receive sun on winter solstice] il *U.S. News & World Report* 106:13-14 F 6 '89

World's oldest (and quietest) observatory? [Irish tomb aligned with winter solstice; research by Tom P. Ray] il *Sky and Telescope* 78:241-2 S '89

ASTRONOMY, CHINESE

Dem bones, dem bones [oracle bone shows evidence of shorter days; work of Kevin D. Pang] A. Fisher. *Popular Science* 235:12 S '89

A Far-Eastern perspective. G. Lovi. il *Sky and Telescope* 78:59-60 Jl '89

The observation of sunspots. R. K. G. Temple. *The Courier (Unesco)* 41:9 O '88

Oracle bone shows a once-shorter day [work of Kevin D. Pang] I. Peterson. *Science News* 135:374 Je 17 '89

Turtle logic [engraved tortoise shell shows rotation of earth is slowing; research by Kevin Pang] T. Waters. il *Discover* 10:16 D '89

ASTRONOMY, GREEK

Stargazing with Homer. G. Lovi. il *Sky and Telescope* 77:57-8 Ja '89

ASTRONOMY, INDIAN (AMERICAN)

Amateur astroarchaeologists [Tenabo site] il *Astronomy* 17:16-17 Ja '89

Ancient art adds to supernova mystery [American Indian petroglyphs in New Mexico] il *Earth Science* 42:5 Fall '89

Sun dagger misses its mark [Anasazi petroglyphs in Chaco Canyon] J. Palca. *Science* 244:1538 Je 30 '89

ASTRONOMY, ROMAN

M31 and its forgotten Roman poet [Andromeda galaxy in poems of R. F. Avienus] il *Sky and Telescope* 78:243-4 S '89

ASTRONOMY, SPHERICAL AND PRACTICAL
See also
Azimuth

ASTRONOMY, SUMERIAN

Neptune déjà vu [views of Zecharia Sitchin] M. Teich. il *Omni (New York, N.Y.)* 12:90-1 N '89

ASTRONOMY (PERIODICAL)

Behind the scenes. R. Berry. See issues of Astronomy

ASTRONOMY IN ART

Capturing the universe on paper. il *Astronomy* 17:91 Ag '89

Exhibitions
Tom Marioni at Margarete Roeder. K. Johnson. il *Art in America* 77:167-8 F '89

ASTRONOMY IN POETRY

M31 and its forgotten Roman poet [Andromeda galaxy in poems of R. F. Avienus] il *Sky and Telescope* 78:243-4 S '89

Stargazing with Homer. G. Lovi. il *Sky and Telescope* 77:57-8 Ja '89

ASTROPHOTOGRAPHY *See* Astronomical photography

ASTROPHYSICS
See also
Astronomical spectroscopy
Black holes (Astronomy)
Cosmic rays
Harvard-Smithsonian Center for Astrophysics
Institute for Advanced Study (Princeton, N.J.)
Magnetic fields (Astrophysics)
Pulsars
Quasars
Red shift
Rockets—Physics use
Solar wind
Stars—Evolution
Universe
University of California, Berkeley. Center for Particle Astrophysics
Wormholes (Astrophysics)

An astrophysical guide to the weather on earth [Piecewise Parabolic Method developed by Paul Woodward] B. A. Cipra. il *Science* 246:212-13 O 13 '89

Astrophysics. bibl f il *Physics Today* 42:S7-S12 Ja '89

The heliosphere as an astrophysical laboratory for particle acceleration. T. Terasawa and M. Scholer. bibl f il *Science* 244:1050-7 Je 2 '89

Conferences
The first Texas Symposium on Relativistic Astrophysics. E. L. Schucking. bibl f il *Physics Today* 42 pt1:46-52 Ag '89

ASTROTECH INTERNATIONAL CORPORATION

Astrotech provides range of payload services from expanded facility. E. H. Kolcum. *Aviation Week & Space Technology* 131:79 Ag 21 '89

ASTUTO, TERRY A.

(jt. auth) *See* Clark, David L. (David Louis), 1929-, and Astuto, Terry A.

ASW *See* Anti-submarine warfare

ASYLMURATOVA, ALTYNAI
about
Freed by *glasnost*, the Kirov Ballet arrives in America this month with new prima ballerina Altynai Asylmuratova. D. Daniel. por *Vogue* 179:84-5 Jl '89

ASYLUM, RIGHT OF

As the huddled masses roll across El Norte [U.S. policy] il *U.S. News & World Report* 106:10-11 Ja 30 '89

The battering ram at the golden door [Central American refugees] A. Fins. il *Business Week* p52-3+ F 6 '89

Closing the door. E. Mortimer. il *World Press Review* 36:22 N '89

Haven maven [terminology] W. Safire. il *The New York Times Magazine* p8+ Jl 2 '89

Newcomers meet hard hearts [Nicaraguans seek U.S. asylum] *America* 160:131 F 18 '89

No sanctuary [Central American refugees] T. Reader. *The Nation* 249:193 Ag 21-28 '89

Roundup on the Rio Grande [Central Americans] J. Juffer. il *The Progressive* 53:32-3 Ap '89

AT LAST INC.

Copie Lilien: hefty sales in hefty kids' togs. R. Duffy. il por *Business Week* p98 My 8 '89

AT&T *See* American Telephone & Telegraph Co.

AT&T BELL LABS

AT&T "microscopic parallel processor" hits 24 GHz [quantum effect transistor] *Byte* 14:17 Ag '89

Commercial labs set pace in U.S. photonics research. il *Aviation Week & Space Technology* 130:60-1 Ja 30 '89

"The Japanese are not superhuman" [interview with A. Penzias] G. F. Gilder. il por *Forbes* 143:122+ Mr 20 '89

AT&T CREDIT CORP.

Benefits for the back office, too [team work concept] J. P. Hoerr. il *Business Week* p59 Jl 10 '89

ATARI CORP.

Court games [antitrust suits against Nintendo by Atari and Tengen] G. Keizer. il *Compute!* 11:84 Ap '89

A game of legal punch-out [Atari sues Nintendo] il *Newsweek* 113:50 Ja 2 '89

The other guys: zap or be zapped. M. Rogers. il *Newsweek* 113:66-7 Mr 6 '89

ATARI CORP.—*cont.*
There's a rumble in the video arcade [Nintendo gets hit with antitrust suits from Tengen and Atari] M. Shao. il *Business Week* p37 F 20 '89

ATC *See* Air traffic control; American Trade Consortium

ATE *See* Automatic test equipment

ATHABASCA RIVER (ALTA.)
The forest fight [environmental concerns over proposed pulp mill] R. Corelli. il *Maclean's* 102:60 N 13 '89

ATHEISM
I was an atheist in a foxhole [Vietnam War] P. K. Paulsen. *The Humanist* 49:28-30 S/O '89

ATHENAEUM (BOSTON, MASS.) *See* Boston Athenaeum

ATHENS COUNTY (OHIO)
Description and travel
Athens County, Ohio. T. Krautwurst. il map *The Mother Earth News* 117:74-81 My/Je '89

ATHENS INTERNATIONAL MARATHON *See* Marathon running

ATHEROSCLEROSIS *See* Arteriosclerosis

ATHLETE PRODUCT ENDORSEMENTS *See* Advertising—Testimonials

ATHLETES
See also
    Automobile racing drivers
    Baseball players
    Basketball players
    Black athletes
    Boxers
    Cyclists
    Discrimination in sports
    Football players
    Golfers
    Hockey players
    Intelligence—Athletes
    Motorcyclists
    Runners
    Skiers
    Sports halls of fame
    Tennis players
    Women athletes
    See also names of athletes
Faces in the crowd. See issues of Sports Illustrated
Make this guy a scout [C. L. Brannen compiles scrapbooks on athletes] R. Harper. il *Sport (New York, N.Y.)* 80:76 Jl '89
Out of the shadows [effect of opening of Berlin Wall on East German athletes] W. O. Johnson and A. Verschoth. il *Sports Illustrated* 71:16-21 N 27 '89
Age
The peak years [research by Richard Schulz and Christine Curnow] J. C. Horn. il *Psychology Today* 22:62-3 D '88
Awards
See Sports—Awards
Crime
An American disgrace [lawlessness among college athletes; special section] il *Sports Illustrated* 70:16-26+ F 27 '89
Hazard to your health [columnist excoriated after criticizing Georgia Tech's handling of violent incident involving football players] R. S. Johnson. por *Sports Illustrated* 70:77 F 27 '89
A national disgrace [lawlessness among college athletes] il *Reader's Digest* 135:136-42 Ag '89
Education
Academics and athletics: 'What price victory?' [Tennessee high school teacher J. A. McGhee fights dismissal after being pressured to raise basketball player's grade] P. A. Zirkel. il *Phi Delta Kappan* 70:564-5 Mr '89
Jan Kemp [professor's stand against college athletes' low academic standards at the University of Georgia] S. Kanfer. il por *People Weekly* 32 Special Issue:124 Fall '89
Jocks with books [Duke and Notre Dame] J. Adler. il *Newsweek* 113:60-1 Ja 9 '89
National Collegiate Athletic Association [address, January 9, 1989] C. B. Reed. *Vital Speeches of the Day* 55:372-3 Ap 1 '89
Smart moves [effects of sports participation upon academic achievement of female and minority high school students] G. Chalkley. il *American Health* 8:32 D '89
Ethics
See Sports—Ethical aspects
Health and hygiene
See also
    Alcohol and sports
    Blood boosting
    Drugs and sports
Athlete's oxygen just gas [research by David Winter, Jr.] *Science News* 136:39 Jl 15 '89
Hot air [results of study on oxygen and athletic performance] *Women's Sports & Fitness* 11:10 O '89
Let's skip the bit about shrunken heads [re-energizing therapy based on crystals] T. Mulgannon. il *Sport (New York, N.Y.)* 80:83 My '89
Nutrition
See also
    Sports drinks

Carbo-loading: the tool for extra fuel. E. Coleman. il *Women's Sports & Fitness* 11:16+ Je '89
Dietary habits [triathletes] L. Applegate. il *Runner's World* 24:66 My '89
Does protein build muscles? [research by Peter Lemon] P. McCarthy. il *American Health* 8:96 N '89
Sugar: a performance boost or sweet nothing? E. Coleman. il *Women's Sports & Fitness* 11:20-1 Jl/Ag '89
Photographs and photography
The Olympics. il *Life* 12:148-54+ Ja '89
Psychology
See Sports—Psychological aspects
Retirement
The second time around [second careers of five retired athletes] R. Fimrite. il pors *Sports Illustrated* 70:110-14+ Ja 9 '89
Salaries, pensions, etc.
See also
    Amateurism (Sports)
Hard bargainers [toughest pro sports team officials] G. Castle. il *Sport (New York, N.Y.)* 80:16 D '89
Locker-room tycoons. M. Goodman. *Utne Reader* p116-18 N/D '89
Rebels with a balance: Soviet artists and athletes want to keep more of the dollars they earn abroad. D. Rinehart. il *Maclean's* 102:20-1 Jl 3 '89
The Sport 100 salary survey [cover story; special section] N. Cohen. il *Sport (New York, N.Y.)* 80:75-7+ Je '89
Anecdotes, facetiae, satire, etc.
How cheap can you get? R. Reilly. por *Sports Illustrated* 71:160 N 6 '89
Training
See also
    Anaerobic training
    Circuit training
    Cross training
    Interval training
    Plyometrics
    Tempo training
Overload, don't overtrain. S. McKee. il *Psychology Today* 23:70 N '89
Travel
Anecdotes, facetiae, satire, etc.
The boys on the bus. F. Lidz. il *Sports Illustrated* 71:58-62+ Jl 3 '89
Uniforms
See Sports uniforms
Vision
See Vision

ATHLETES' AGENTS *See* Sports agencies and agents

ATHLETES AND DRUGS *See* Drugs and sports

ATHLETES AS BROKERS
A bear in the ring and a bull on Wall Street, Leland Hardy is a broker with a convincing pitch. A. Abrahams. il pors *People Weekly* 32:109-10 S 18 '89
He's bullish on boxing [boxer and account executive L. Hardy] il por *Sports Illustrated* 71:8 Jl 3 '89

ATHLETIC ABILITY
Coming on strong [tennis players' ability] M. Bloom. il *World Tennis* 37:52-4 O '89
Master of my fate [maximizing cycling potential] M. Shermer. il *Bicycling* 30:73-5 Je '89
NBA stars are the best athletes in pro sports. R. Aregood. il *TV Guide* 37:14-15 Mr 25-31 '89
Why the obsession with race? [NBC special Black athletes—fact & fiction] S. Smith. il por *Sports Illustrated* 70:12 My 8 '89

ATHLETIC BUILDINGS *See* Gymnasiums

ATHLETIC CLUBS *See* Sports clubs

ATHLETIC DIRECTORS
See also
    Women athletic directors

ATHLETIC SCHOLARSHIPS *See* Scholarships and fellowships

ATHLETIC SHOE INDUSTRY *See* Shoe industry

ATHLETIC SHOES *See* Footwear

ATHLETICS
See also
    Athletes
    Coaches (Athletics)
    College athletics
    Francophone Games
    Gymnastics
    Olympic Games
    Pan American Games
    School athletics
    Track and field athletics

ATHOS (GREECE)
A little piece of heaven. A. Clancy. il *Gentlemen's Quarterly* 59:221-2+ N '89

ATISANOE, SALEVAA *See* Konishiki, Yasokichi

ATKIN, J. MYRON
Can educational research keep pace with education reform? bibl f il *Phi Delta Kappan* 71:200-5 N '89

ATKINS, CHET, 1924-
about
Chet Atkins. B. Milkowski. il por *Down Beat* 56:24 My '89

ATKINS, GARY L., 1949-
Forced march in the military. il *The Nation* 248:16-18 Ja 2 '89
ATKINSON, CONRAD, 1940-
about
Conrad Atkinson at Ronald Feldman. E. Heartney. *Art in America* 77:165-6 Je '89
ATKINSON, JAY
Silent night. il *Runner's World* 24:96 D '89
ATKINSON, JEFF
about
The rat that roared. B. Wischnia. il pors *Runner's World* 24:40-4+ O '89
ATKINSON, KATHIE
Death, where is thy sting? [photograph] il *Natural History* p80-1 Ag '89
ATKINSON, RICHARD C.
A question of information policy. *Science* 246:33 N 10 '89
ATKINSON, RICK
The West Point story [excerpt from The long gray line; cover story] il pors *U.S. News & World Report* 107:44-54 O 9 '89
about
A moving new book helps West Point '66 bind the wounds of war and changing times. L. Kramer. il pors *People Weekly* 32:92-3+ O 30 '89
ATLANTA (GA.)
Air pollution
Leaves of gas [role of hydrocarbons in urban smog; research by William Chameides] il *Discover* 10:20 F '89
Tree pollution [role of hydrocarbons in urban smog; research by William Chameides] J. W. Merline. il *Consumers' Research Magazine* 72:38 Ja '89
Architecture
See also
Atlanta (Ga.)—Buildings
Banks
See also
Citizens & Southern Corp.
Blacks
Atlanta. R. D. Turner. il *Ebony* 44:38-40+ Ag '89
Buildings
Spatial craft [Herman Miller showroom; cover story] K. D. Stein. il *Architectural Record* 177:98-107 Je '89
Contracts, Municipal
See Atlanta (Ga.)—Municipal contracts
Crime
The 'Catwoman' case. B. Wickens. il *Maclean's* 102:39 Jl 31 '89
The 'Catwoman' of Atlanta [A. L. McGraw] por *Newsweek* 113:29 My 8 '89
Festivals
Gifts that go on giving [Festival of Trees] *Southern Living* 24:43 D '89
Gardens and gardening
A shaded glade of green. L. A. Weathers. il *Southern Living* 24:68-9 My '89
Historic houses, sites, etc.
See also
Martin Luther King, Jr. National Historic Site and Preservation District
Housing
An Atlanta prison gets converted [R. Scott's GlenCastle conversion for the working poor] B. Spring. il por *Christianity Today* 33:53-4 Ap 7 '89
Housing Dept.'s Kemp takes Atlanta fact-finding tour. il por *Jet* 75:46 Mr 6 '89
Mad Housers help homeless. L. S. Bates. il *The Progressive* 53:15 My '89
Missions
One of Atlanta's bravest [work of L. Adamson] P. Yancey. il pors *Christianity Today* 33:12-13 N 17 '89
Municipal contracts
Atlanta: keeping affirmative action alive. K. D. Thompson. il *Black Enterprise* 20:48 S '89
Atlanta set-aside plan boasts booming business. il *Jet* 75:53 F 20 '89
Which program will be next? [minority set-aside program] D. Lynch. il *Black Enterprise* 19:36 My '89
Politics and government
Maynard Jackson enters Atlanta mayor's race against former campaign aide. il por *Jet* 75:4 Mr 6 '89
Maynard Jackson gears for 3rd term as Atlanta mayor. il por *Jet* 77:5 O 23 '89
The unbeatable Jackson [M. H. Jackson] L. Copeland. il por *American Visions* 4:42 O '89
Race relations
A turn in Atlanta. V. S. Naipaul. il *The New York Review of Books* 35:52-7 Ja 19 '89
Religious institutions and affairs
See also
Atlanta (Ga.)—Missions
An Atlanta prison gets converted [R. Scott's GlenCastle conversion for the working poor] B. Spring. il por *Christianity Today* 33:53-4 Ap 7 '89
Social history
Once upon a Christmas [excerpt from Christmas gift!] F. Sams. il *Good Housekeeping* 209:172-3+ D '89

Sports
Atlanta. K. Hannon. il *Sport (New York, N.Y.)* 80:70-4 Ag '89
Stores
See also
Underground Atlanta
Theater
Theater in Atlanta. G. G. Seibert. *America* 161:16+ Jl 1-8 '89
ATLANTA BALLET
Atlanta Ballet celebrates sixty. H. C. Smith. il *Dance Magazine* 63:20-1 O '89
Reviews:
A night in Russia program at the Atlanta Civic Center. H. C. Smith. *Dance Magazine* 63:86-7 Ap '89
ATLANTA CAMPAIGN, 1864
1864. A. Nielsen. il *American Heritage* 40:36-7 S/O '89
ATLANTA JOURNAL 500 *See* Automobile racing
ATLANTA UNIVERSITY
See also
Clark Atlanta University
ATLANTIC (PERIODICAL)
745 Boylston Street. il *The Atlantic* 264:4 Jl '89
ATLANTIC AND PACIFIC TEA COMPANY *See* Great Atlantic & Pacific Tea Company, Inc.
ATLANTIC CITY (N.J.)
Economic conditions
Boardwalk of broken dreams [cover story] P. Painton. il *Time* 134:64-9 S 25 '89
Hotels, motels, etc.
See also
Casinos
Trump Plaza Hotel & Casino (Atlantic City, N.J.)
Trump Taj Mahal Casino Resort (Atlantic City, N.J.)
Politics and government
Atlantic City mayor Usry is arrested for bribery; mayors group backs him. il por *Jet* 76:13-14 Ag 14 '89
ATLANTIC FLIGHTS *See* Aviation—Transatlantic flights
ATLANTIC MONTHLY PRESS
Atlantic Monthly uncovers buried riches [publication of G. Kinder's book on the recovery of the SS Central America] *Publishers Weekly* 236:48-9 N 24 '89
Cross-culture shock [long-distance editing of J. McIntyre Varawa's book on Fijian marriage] L. Fleischer. *Publishers Weekly* 235:207 F 24 '89
ATLANTIC OCEAN
See also
Gulf Stream
Petroleum—Atlantic Ocean
Carbon dioxide transport by ocean currents at 25°N latitude in the Atlantic Ocean. P. Brewer and others. bibl f il *Science* 246:477-9 O 27 '89
ATLANTIC RICHFIELD CO.
Arco: democracy in an age of standards [computer use] il *Personal Computing* 13:85+ S '89
Cleaner gasoline comes on line [EC-1] A. Dane. il *Popular Mechanics* 166:38 N '89
Fill 'er up with gas lite [Arco's Emission Control-1] il *Time* 134:56 Ag 28 '89
What worries Arco's chief the most [interview with L. Cook] il por *Fortune* 120:102 O 9 '89
ATLANTIC SALMON FISHING *See* Salmon fishing
ATLANTIC STATES
See also
Allegheny Mountains region
Automobile touring—Atlantic States
Beaches—Atlantic States
Hotels, motels, etc.—Atlantic States
ATLANTIQUE CITY *See* Antiques—Exhibitions
ATLANTIS (SPACE SHUTTLE VEHICLE) *See* Space vehicles
ATLAS, JAMES
Golden boy. bibl f il *The New York Review of Books* 36:42-6 Je 29 '89
The kids are fine. *The New Republic* 201:13-14 S 4 '89
A memorable ride. il *The New York Times Magazine* p14+ F 5 '89
Thatcher puts a lid on. il *The New York Times Magazine* p36-8+ Mr 5 '89
What is Fukuyama saying? And to whom is he saying it? il por *The New York Times Magazine* p38-40+ O 22 '89
ATLAS, JOHN, AND DREIER, PETER
The phony case against rent control. il *The Progressive* 53:26-7+ Ap '89
Tenants' rights movement presses for quality affordable housing. il *Utne Reader* p66-7 My/Je '89
ATLAS (GROUP)
Atlas airline groups adapt operations to cope with market changes, new aircraft. *Aviation Week & Space Technology* 130:95 F 13 '89
ATLAS (LAUNCH VEHICLE) *See* Space vehicles—Propulsion systems
ATLAS SWIMMING POOL COMPANY
Wet dreams. E. Stern. il *Gentlemen's Quarterly* 59:61 N '89
ATLASES
See also
Anatomy—Atlases

ATLASES—See also—cont.
    Stars—Atlases
Buying travel books and atlases [Gallup survey] L. A. Wood.
    il *Publishers Weekly* 235:64 Ja 20 '89
PC-Globe+. K. Sternberg. il *Compute!* 11:74 Ag '89
Whereabouts [entering students given free atlases at Tufts
    University] *The New Yorker* 65:29-30 F 20 '89
        Bibliography
What's new in maps & atlases. J. Crichton. il *Publishers
    Weekly* 235:91-4 Ja 20 '89

ATMOSPHERE
    See also
    Biosphere
    Carbon dioxide
    Counterglow
    Haze
    International Conference on the Changing Atmosphere:
        Implications for Global Security
    Jupiter (Planet)—Atmosphere
    Mars (Planet)—Atmosphere
    Mercury (Planet)—Atmosphere
    Moon—Atmosphere
    Neptune (Planet)—Atmosphere
    Ozone
    Planets—Atmosphere
    Pluto (Planet)—Atmosphere
    Saturn (Planet)—Atmosphere
    Saturn (Planet)—Satellites—Atmosphere
    Venus (Planet)—Atmosphere
    Winds
Carbon monoxide and the burning earth. R. E. Newell and
    others. bibl il map *Scientific American* 261:82-8 O '89
The changing atmosphere [human activity is altering the
    complex mixture of gases] T. E. Graedel and P. J. Crutzen.
    bibl il *Scientific American* 261:58-64+ S '89
Lack of data is frustrating [incomplete ecosystem knowledge
    hampers ability to deal with atmosphere and climate;
    views of Hal Mooney and Peter Vitousek] *USA Today
    (Periodical)* 117:6 Je '89
Simple experiments in atmospheric physics. C. F. Bohren.
    See issues of Weatherwise
Trouble in the atmosphere: does your cup of coffee cause
    forest fires? C. A. Moore. il *International Wildlife* 19:38-45
    Mr/Ap '89

ATMOSPHERE, UPPER
    See also
    Airglow
    International Conference on the Changing Atmosphere:
        Implications for Global Security
    Magnetosphere
    Noctilucent clouds
    Ozone
    Rockets—Meteorological use
Changing composition of the global stratosphere. M. McElroy
    and R. J. Salawitch. bibl f il *Science* 243:763-70 F 10
    '89
Effects of the large June 1975 meteoroid storm on earth's
    ionosphere [very low frequency radio wave propagation
    anomalies] P. Kaufmann and others. bibl f il map *Science*
    246:787-90 N 10 '89
Energetic electrons and ozone loss. R. Monastersky. *Science
    News* 135:335 My 27 '89

ATMOSPHERE-OCEAN INTERACTION *See* Ocean-
atmosphere interaction
ATMOSPHERE-SOIL INTERACTION *See* Soil-atmosphere
interaction
ATMOSPHERIC AEROSOLS *See* Aerosols

ATMOSPHERIC CIRCULATION
Far-off clues to nearby weather [drought research by Kevin
    Trenberth] B. Carpenter. il map *U.S. News & World Report*
    106:56 Ja 16 '89
Persistent circulation patterns [1988] A. J. Wagner. il
    Weatherwise 42:18-21 F '89
The summer of '88 [research by Kevin E. Trenberth] L.
    Burnham. *Scientific American* 260:21 Mr '89

ATMOSPHERIC ELECTRICITY
    See also
    Auroras
    Lightning
    Thunderstorms

ATMOSPHERIC METHANE *See* Methane
ATMOSPHERIC MODELS *See* Meteorological models
ATMOSPHERIC NUCLEATION
    See also
    Condensation (Meteorology)
ATMOSPHERIC OPTICS *See* Meteorological optics
ATMOSPHERIC POLLUTION *See* Air pollution
ATMOSPHERIC PRESSURE
    See also
    Airplanes—Pressurization
    Southern Oscillation
Wobbling world [theory that Chandler wobble is caused
    by atmospheric oscillation; research by Sultan Hameed
    and Robert Currie] S. Vogel. il *Discover* 10:24 Ag '89
        Physiological effects
    See also
    Decompression (Physiology)

ATMOSPHERIC RESEARCH
    See also
    Artificial satellites—Meteorological use
    Computers—Meteorological use
    International Geosphere-Biosphere Program
    Meteorology
    Ocean-atmosphere interaction
    Rockets—Meteorological use
    United States. National Oceanic and Atmospheric Admin-
        istration
Issues in atmospheric science [cover story; special section;
    with editorial comment by John I. Brauman] bibl f il
    maps *Science* 243:709, 745-81 F 10 '89

ATMOSPHERIC TEMPERATURE
    See also
    Greenhouse effect
'88 set warm record; '89 looks cooler. R. Monastersky. *Science
    News* 135:84-5 F 11 '89
1988 ties for warmest year. R. A. Kerr. il *Science* 243:891
    F 17 '89
Hot spots and cold spots [1988] D. H. Hickcox. il *Weatherwise*
    42:42-6 F '89

ATMOSPHERIC TURBULENCE
Airborne infrared system provides advance warning of tur-
    bulence. il *Aviation Week & Space Technology* 130:130-1
    Je 19 '89
All shook up [airspeed] J. M. McClellan. il *Flying* 116:106+
    N '89

ATMOSPHERIC WAVES
Hurricane prediction: catching the waves [research by Richard
    L. Pfeffer] D. E. Loupe. *Science News* 136:262 O 21 '89
ATMS *See* Automated teller machines
ATOMIC BATTERIES *See* Nuclear batteries
ATOMIC BEAMS
Atomic fountain springs from a light touch [work of Steven
    Chu] I. Peterson. il *Science News* 136:117 Ag 19 '89
Chilling an atom in solitary confinement. I. Amato. *Science
    News* 136:103 Ag 12 '89
Ion sits still for sharp 'picture' of its optical transition.
    B. G. Levi. il *Physics Today* 42:17-18 S '89
Laser optics of neutral atomic beams. V. I. Balykin and
    V. S. Letokhov. bibl f il *Physics Today* 42:23-8 Ap '89

ATOMIC BLASTING
    See also
    Project Chariot
ATOMIC BOMB SHELTERS
        Anecdotes, facetiae, satire, etc.
A bunker mentality in New Brunswick [fallout shelter for
    government officials] A. Fotheringham. il *Maclean's* 102:48
    Jl 31 '89

ATOMIC BOMBS
    See also
    Hydrogen bombs
        Historiography
After the bomb, a mushroom cloud of metaphors [chronicling
    the explosion of the first atomic bomb in New Mexico
    in 1945] J. Gleick. il *The New York Times Book Review*
    94:1+ My 21 '89
        History
    See also
    Hiroshima (Japan)—Bombardment, 1945
    Nagasaki (Japan)—Bombardment, 1945
Bumbling toward the bomb [1939 letter from A. Einstein
    to President Roosevelt] W. J. Lanouette. bibl f il por
    The Bulletin of the Atomic Scientists 45:7-11 S '89
Cool Hand Nuke [Paul Newman as Gen. L. Groves in
    Fat Man and Little Boy] R. Scheer. il *Esquire* 112:170-1
    O '89
The Cuban missiles [discussion of March 1989 article, Nuclear
    revisionism] P. Glynn. *Commentary* 88:9-12 Ag '89
Do nuclear weapons matter? [views of M. Bundy] S. Hoff-
    mann. bibl f il *The New York Review of Books* 36:28-31
    F 2 '89
'Do nuclear weapons matter?': an exchange [discussion of
    February 2, 1989 article] S. Hoffmann. il *The New York
    Review of Books* 36:57-8 Ap 27 '89
Fatal fiction: a weapon to end all wars [how early science
    fiction helped shape U.S. conceptions of nuclear weapons;
    cover story] H. B. Franklin. bibl f il *The Bulletin of
    the Atomic Scientists* 45:18-25 N '89
The making of Fat Man and Little Boy [motion picture;
    interview with D. Schultz] D. K. Mano. il *National Review*
    41:63-7 N 10 '89
Nuclear revisionism [views of M. Bundy] P. Glynn.
    Commentary 87:42-7 Mr '89
The race to build the bomb. D. O. Relin. il *Scholastic
    Update (Teachers' edition)* 122:11-13 O 6 '89
The untaming of the bomb. S. Budiansky. il *U.S. News
    & World Report* 106:8-9 Je 12 '89
What to do with B Reactor? [old reactors at Hanford] K.
    D. Steele. il *The Bulletin of the Atomic Scientists* 45:21
    O '89
What's unusable—and indispensable? [interview with M.
    Bundy] H. Trewhitt. il por *U.S. News & World Report*
    106:43-4 Ja 9 '89

ATOMIC BOMBS—cont.

Testing
See Nuclear weapons—Testing

ATOMIC BOMBS IN LITERATURE See Nuclear warfare in literature

ATOMIC BOMBS IN MOTION PICTURES See Nuclear warfare in motion pictures

ATOMIC BOMBS IN TELEVISION See Nuclear warfare in television

ATOMIC CLOCKS
Atomic fountain springs from a light touch [work of Steven Chu] I. Peterson. il Science News 136:117 Ag 19 '89

Atomic timekeeping. R. Henson. il Technology Review 92:12-13 Ag/S '89

Basic measurements lead to Physics Nobel [N. F. Ramsey for separated oscillatory fields technique] R. Pool. il pors Science 246:327-8 O 20 '89

Ion sits still for sharp 'picture' of its optical transition. B. G. Levi. il Physics Today 42:17-18 S '89

Physics [Nobel Prize awarded to N. Ramsey for separated oscillatory fields technique and to H. Dehmelt and W. Paul for devising ways of trapping ions] il pors Time 134:74 O 23 '89

Physics Nobel: traps, clocks, quantum leaps [to N. F. Ramsey for separated oscillatory fields technique] E. Peterson. Science News 136:262 O 21 '89

Ramsey, Dehmelt, Paul win Nobel for helping to set high standards [ion trap techniques] B. G. Levi. il pors Physics Today 42:17-19 D '89

ATOMIC ENERGY See Nuclear energy

ATOMIC ENERGY AGENCY See International Atomic Energy Agency

ATOMIC ENERGY COMMISSION (UNITED NATIONS) See United Nations. Atomic Energy Commission

ATOMIC FACILITIES See Nuclear facilities

ATOMIC FORCE MICROSCOPES
Imaging crystals, polymers, and processes in water with the atomic force microscope. B. Drake and others. bibl f il Science 243:1586-9 Mr 24 '89

Making 'movies' of biological molecules [work of Calvin F. Quate and others] I. Amato. il Science News 135:180 Mr 25 '89

Seeing atoms [cover story] A. Fisher. il Popular Science 234:102-7 Ap '89

ATOMIC FUELS See Nuclear fuels

ATOMIC HYDROGEN See Hydrogen

ATOMIC MEDICINE See Nuclear medicine

ATOMIC NUCLEI

Energy levels
See Energy levels (Quantum mechanics)
Spin
See Nuclear spin

ATOMIC PHYSICS See Nuclear physics

ATOMIC POWER See Nuclear energy

ATOMIC POWER INDUSTRY See Nuclear industry

ATOMIC POWER PLANTS See Nuclear power plants

ATOMIC POWER WORKERS See Nuclear power workers

ATOMIC POWERED ARTIFICIAL SATELLITES See Artificial satellites—Power supply

ATOMIC POWERED SHIPS See Nuclear ships

ATOMIC POWERED SPACE VEHICLES See Space vehicles—Power supply

ATOMIC POWERED SUBMARINES See Nuclear submarines

ATOMIC RESEARCH See Nuclear research

ATOMIC RESEARCH LABORATORIES See Nuclear research laboratories

ATOMIC WARFARE See Nuclear warfare

ATOMIC WARFARE IN ART See Nuclear warfare in art

ATOMIC WARFARE IN LITERATURE See Nuclear warfare in literature

ATOMIC WARFARE IN MOTION PICTURES See Nuclear warfare in motion pictures

ATOMIC WARFARE IN TELEVISION See Nuclear warfare in television

ATOMIC WEAPONS See Nuclear weapons

ATOMS

See also
Electronegativity
Electrons
Neutrinos
Neutrons
Protons

Microclusters. M. A. Duncan and D. H. Rouvray. bibl il Scientific American 261:110-15 D '89

Beams
See Atomic beams
Measurement
Atom counting at surfaces [use of multiphoton resonance ionization] D. L. Pappas and others. bibl f il Science 243:64-6 Ja 6 '89

New probes reveal atomic structures [position sensing atom probe] il Popular Mechanics 166:14 My '89

Space arrangement
See Stereochemistry

ATP See Adenosine triphosphate

ATPASE See Adenosine triphosphatase

ATR-42 AIRPLANES See Airplanes, Jet

ATRESIA, BILIARY See Biliary atresia

ATRIAL NATRIURETIC FACTOR
Atrial natriuretic peptide inhibits a cation channel in renal inner medullary collecting duct cells. D. B. Light and others. bibl f il Science 243:383-5 Ja 20 '89

New type of receptor found. J. L. Marx. Science 244:1140-1 Je 9 '89

The protein kinase domain of the ANP receptor is required for signaling. M. Chinkers and D. L. Garbers. bibl f il Science 245:1392-4 S 22 '89

ATRIUM (HEART) See Heart

ATTACHÉ CASES See Briefcases

ATTACHED HOUSES See Row houses

ATTARDI, GIUSEPPE
(jt. auth) See King, Michael P., and Attardi, Giuseppe

ATTENBOROUGH, RICHARD
about
Deification of a Tramp. N. Mills. il por American Film 14:13 Je '89

Richard Attenborough [interview] C. Vieler-Porter. il pors The Unesco Courier 42:4-7 Ag '89

ATTENTION
See also
Distraction
Listening

Boron/brain connection [may affect alertness; research by James G. Penland] il Prevention (Emmaus, Pa.) 41:8+ S '89

How colds affect your performance [improved concentration; research by Tami McGraw and others] J. Davidson. Psychology Today 23:20 D '89

People can't be programmed [research by Michael Dawson] USA Today (Periodical) 118:12-13 Ag '89

Scientists give the nod to more sleep time [alertness and vigilance testing by Timothy Roehrs and others] K. Fackelmann. Science News 136:260 O 21 '89

The wandering mind of youth [minds wander less as people get older; research by Alicia Grodsky and Leonard Giambra] P. Chance. Psychology Today 22:22 D '88

ATTENTION DEFICIT DISORDER
See also
Hyperactivity

Michael's orchestra. E. Berlin. Ladies' Home Journal 106:108 O '89

ATTENTION DEFICIT HYPERACTIVITY DISORDER See Hyperactivity

ATTENTION SEEKING
Your child's need for attention. L. Salk. il McCall's 116:57 Ja '89

ATTIC LADDERS See Ladders

ATTICS, REMODELED
Attic built-in [cabinets in bathroom] P. Brown and P. Brown. il Workbench 45:30-3+ Mr/Ap '89

An attic for all seasons. T. O. Bakke. il Popular Science 235:80-1 Ag '89

Look up, look down. B. Saxhaug. il Good Housekeeping 208:195-7 Ap '89

Shope Reno Wharton: "architectural furniture" revitalizes a Connecticut attic. il Architectural Digest 46:92-3 Ap '89

Upstairs getaway for the whole family. il Sunset (Central West edition) 181:116 D '89

ATTILA, KING OF THE HUNS, D. 453
about
Ross Perot as literary critic. J. Queenan. il Forbes 143:90+ Ap 17 '89

ATTITASH (N.H.: RESORT) See Resorts—New Hampshire

ATTITUDES
See also
Optimism
Political attitudes
Public opinion
Stereotype (Psychology)

ATTORNEY, POWER OF See Power of attorney

ATTORNEYS See Lawyers

ATTORNEYS GENERAL
See also
National Association of Attorneys General

Filling the deregulatory vacuum [state attorneys general; cover story] M. J. Green. il The Nation 249:441+ O 23 '89

ATTRACTING OF BIRDS See Birds, Attracting of

ATTRACTING OF BUTTERFLIES See Butterfly gardens

ATTRACTING OF WILDLIFE See Wildlife, Attracting of

ATTRACTION, INTERPERSONAL See Interpersonal attraction

ATVS See All terrain vehicles

ATWATER, HARVEY LEROY See Atwater, Lee, 1951-

ATWATER, LEE, 1951-
From two new party chairmen: plans to woo and keep the black vote. il American Visions 4:17-18 Je '89

about
Ambitious visions for a GOP majority. G. Borger. il por U.S. News & World Report 106:18-19 Ja 23 '89

ATWATER, LEE, 1951—about—cont.

Anatomy of a smear. G. Borger. il pors *U.S. News & World Report* 106:40-1 Je 19 '89

Attaché case full of blues. G. Hirshey. il pors *Rolling Stone* p19-20 Mr 9 '89

Atwater to the rescue. J. McLaughlin. *National Review* 41:54 Ja 27 '89

Atwatergate. H. Hertzberg. *The New Republic* 201:4 Jl 3 '89

Bushwaterism. *The New Republic* 201:5-6 Jl 17-24 '89

Dirtball politics. T. Morganthau. il pors *Newsweek* 113:32-3 Je 19 '89

Ditch the cheerleaders, Lee. A. F. Lewis. il por *Ms.* 17:86 Ap '89

The GOP blues. M. Kempton. il *The New York Review of Books* 36:4 Mr 16 '89

How to spread a smear. M. B. Carlson. il pors *Time* 133:33 Je 19 '89

Howard students force Atwater's resignation, and push other demands. il *Jet* 75:37 Mr 27 '89

Lee Atwater's GOP offensive is off and stumbling. R. Fly. por *Business Week* p31 Ap 17 '89

Mission accomplished. F. Barnes. il *The New Republic* 201:8-10 Jl 3 '89

Now Willie Horton stalks the GOP. il *U.S. News & World Report* 106:13 Mr 20 '89

Playing hardball. E. Alterman. il pors *The New York Times Magazine* p30-1+ Ap 30 '89

The power of negative thinking [interview] W. Greider. il pors *Rolling Stone* p51-3+ Ja 12 '89

Saying no to Lee Atwater. J. V. Lamar, Jr. il por *Time* 133:27 Mr 20 '89

Students fight naming of Atwater to Howard board. *Jet* 75:11 Mr 20 '89

"Ten steps, then we shoot," says Ron Brown. "I've got my AK-47," replies Lee Atwater. "What've you got?". M. Kelly. il pors *Gentlemen's Quarterly* 59:142-7+ Jl '89

ATWOOD, DONALD J.

about

Atwood eyes tighter scrutiny of weapons development. *Aviation Week & Space Technology* 130:23 My 15 '89

Once more, with feeling: Atwood takes the baton. D. F. Bond. *Aviation Week & Space Technology* 131:25 D 18-25 '89

Senators criticize Defense nominee for statement on acquisition chief. P. A. Gilmartin. *Aviation Week & Space Technology* 130:7, 29 Ap 10 '89

ATWOOD, MARGARET, 1939-

Cat's eye [fiction] il *Seventeen* 48:310-13+ Ag '89

My brother [fiction] *Harper's* 278:36+ Mr '89

about

Reflected in Margaret Atwood's Cat's eye, girlhood looms as a time of cruelty and terror. K. Hubbard. il pors *People Weekly* 31:205-6 Mr 6 '89

Witch craft. C. Peri. il pors *Mother Jones* 14:28-31+ Ap '89

ATYS [opera] See Lully, Jean Baptiste, 1632-1687

AU, ALEX

about

Mixed blessings. E. F. Cone. por *Forbes* 143:10 F 20 '89

AU, MACY

(jt. auth) See Chalfie, Martin, and Au, Macy

AU PAIR EMPLOYEES See Household employees

AU REVOIR LES ENFANTS [film] See Motion picture reviews—Single works

AUCHINCLOSS, LOUIS

Wildcat mountain. il por *Architectural Digest* 46:29+ Je '89

AUCOIN, KEVYN

about

Master of makeup. il por *Harper's Bazaar* 122:38 Je '89

AUCTION COMPANY OF AMERICA

The man with the hammer [J. Gall] D. C. Bacon. il por *Nation's Business* 77:16 D '89

AUCTIONS

See also

Art trade

Automobile auctions

Horse auctions

Armchair auctions [mail and telephone auctions] N. Santelmann. il *Forbes* 143:314+ My 29 '89

Best bids. B. Felner. See occassional issues of New York beginning November 14, 1988

Fair warning . . . [New York City] B. Felner. il *New York* 22:128+ My 1 '89

Heavy metal [Transit Authority's Auction and Tag Sale] *The New Yorker* 65:46-7 D 11 '89

His Oscars Gone with the wind, art director Lyle Wheeler fights to regain more than statuettes [attempts to halt auction of trophies] S. K. Reed. il pors *People Weekly* 31:91-2 Mr 27 '89

House sale [Sotheby auction of only New York City home designed by P. Johnson] *The New Yorker* 65:29-30 My 29 '89

Making the most of government auctions. D. LaMaute. il *Black Enterprise* 19:49-50 F '89

Old glories [prices for American furniture] S. Pennington. il *House & Garden* 161:140-1 Ja '89

A school of one's own [bidding on vacant high school building] B. Greene. il *Esquire* 111:37-8 Ja '89

This Hollywood landmark could be gone with the wind [Ambassador Hotel] K. Kerwin. il *Business Week* p38 Mr 27 '89

Uncle Sam's garage [government auctions] K. Davis. il *Changing Times* 43:120 O '89

'Willi Smith' Day held to aid needy N.Y. groups. il *Jet* 75:14-15 Mr 20 '89

World's biggest garage sale. R. J. Maturi. il *Changing Times* 43:65-7 Ap '89

France

Castle cast-offs [estate auction at Château de Cheverny in Loire Valley] C. Petkanas. il *House & Garden* 161:96+ My '89

Great Britain

Science artifacts on the block [London auction arranged by P. Cook] D. Dickson. il por *Science* 244:649 My 12 '89

AUDI (AUTOMOBILE) See Automobiles, Foreign

AUDI AG

Can Audi start winning races in the showroom, too? [U.S. market] J. B. Treece and J. Templeman. il *Business Week* p47 My 29 '89

AUDIENCES

See also

Motion picture audiences

Opera audiences

Television audiences

AUDIO AMPLIFIERS See Amplifiers

AUDIO DISC PLAYERS See Compact disc players

AUDIO DISC RECORDERS See Compact disc recorders and recording

AUDIO DISCS See Compact discs

AUDIO DISTORTION See Amplifiers—Noise; Audio systems—Noise

AUDIO ENGINEERING

See also

Motion picture theaters—Electronic sound control

Sound—Recording and reproducing

Theater—Electronic sound control

The explorers. W. Berger. il *Stereo Review* 54:84-9 Je '89

"Just the facts, please". K. C. Pohlmann. *Stereo Review* 54:22 D '89

Anecdotes, facetiae, satire, etc.

Audio fetish finalists. il *High Fidelity (New York, N.Y.)* 39:41-3 Je '89

AUDIO ENGINEERING SOCIETY

AES report [annual convention] R. Heller. *Theatre Crafts* 23:30-3 F '89

The next revolution(s). K. C. Pohlmann. *Stereo Review* 54:28 S '89

AUDIO EQUIPMENT INDUSTRY

See also

Carver Corp.

Finial Technology (Firm)

JBL Incorporated

Sonic Solutions (Firm)

American audio classics [cover story] M. Smolen. il *Stereo Review* 54:68-74 Je '89

Quality control

The question of reliability. L. Klein. il *Radio-Electronics* 60:89-90+ F '89

East Asia

Eastern standards [cover story] M. Smolen. il *Stereo Review* 54:42-8 Jl '89

Japan

See also

Akai Electric Co., Ltd.

Nakamichi Corp.

Yamaha International Corp.

Western Europe

A tradition of excellence [cover story] M. Smolen. il *Stereo Review* 54:48-54 Ag '89

AUDIO EQUIPMENT STORES

Ethical aspects

Cat 'n mouse tips for dealing with audio/video salespeople [cover story] G. Brockhouse. il *High Fidelity (New York, N.Y.)* 39:40-3+ Mr '89

AUDIO PUBLISHERS See Tape recording industry

AUDIO SYSTEMS

See also

Amplifiers

Automobiles—Audio systems

Boats and boating—Audio systems

Karaokes

Loudspeakers

Phonograph

Radio receivers

Tape recorders and recording

1989 equipment buying guide [cover story; special section] il *Stereo Review* 54:67-70+ F '89

Audio. F. Vizard. See issues of Popular Mechanics beginning October 1986

Audio Q&A. I. Masters. See issues of Stereo Review beginning October 1986

Audio update. L. Klein. See issues of Radio-Electronics beginning January 1987

AUDIO SYSTEMS—*cont.*

Good listening. C. Begole. See occasional issues of Glamour
Technology for the nineties [special section] il *Rolling Stone*
p83-6+ Je 15 '89

Upgrading your system. J. D. Hirsch. il *Stereo Review* 54:50-7
F '89

Cabinets

Stereo cabinet. B. Kieffer. il *The Family Handyman* 39:88-90+
My '89

Systems [audio system in a home office] R. Day. il *Stereo
Review* 54:100-1 O '89

Systems [G. Haserot's system] R. Day. il *Stereo Review*
54:96-7 Mr '89

Systems [Leo Gutman's audio system] R. Day. il *Stereo
Review* 54:56-7 Jl '89

Caricatures and cartoons

Rodrigues Cartoon Caption Contest. il *Stereo Review* 54:27
Ja '89

The winner of the Rodrigues Caption Contest. W. Livingstone.
il *Stereo Review* 54:18 Jl '89

Compatibility

Compatibility. I. Masters. il *Stereo Review* 54:98-102 N '89

Component interdependence. J. D. Hirsch. il *Stereo Review*
54:36-7 Mr '89

Control

Fingertip control [touch-sensitive buttons for car stereo] F.
Vizard. il *Popular Mechanics* 166:50+ Jl '89

Remote controls. J. D. Hirsch. il *Stereo Review* 54:26+ Ag
'89

Design

Design for listening. W. Berger. il *Stereo Review* 54:102-6
D '89

The high end. R. Hodges. See issues of Stereo Review
beginning June 1984

Equipment

See also
Headphones

AudioSource EQ Ten equalizer/analyzer. J. D. Hirsch. il
Stereo Review 54:54+ Mr '89

Carrier current audio transmitter [cover story] W. Sheets
and R. F. Graf. il *Radio-Electronics* 60:55+ Ja '89

Holiday gifts [audiophiles] W. Livingstone. il *Stereo Review*
54:113-16+ D '89

New products. See issues of Stereo Review

Exhibitions

1988 Japan Audio Fair. B. Harrell. il *Stereo Review* 54:95-8
Ja '89

The ultimate music boxes [Consumer Electronics Show] M.
Rogers. il *Newsweek* 113:48-9 Ja 23 '89

Installation

How to pick an autosound installer [cars] B. C. Fishkind.
il *High Fidelity (New York, N.Y.)* 39:33-5+ My '89

Systems. R. Day. il *Stereo Review* 54:62-5 Ag '89

Systems [J. Basile's system] R. Day. il *Stereo Review* 54:84-5
Ja '89

Systems [the Duncans of Lincoln, Neb.] R. Day. il *Stereo
Review* 54:112-13 N '89

The yellow room. R. Hodges. il *Stereo Review* 54:172 D
'89

Noise

See also
Dolby noise reduction system

The audibility of distortion. I. Masters. il *Stereo Review*
54:72-8 Ja '89

Prices

The $120,000 stereo. M. Porter. il *Gentlemen's Quarterly*
59:136+ F '89

Ask before you buy. B. C. Fishkind. il *High Fidelity (New
York, N.Y.)* 39:18 Jl '89

The audio mating game. H. Fantel. il *Rolling Stone* p125-6
S 21 '89

Budget edge. il *Rolling Stone* p111-12+ Je 15 '89

The price is right [low cost components] H. Fantel. il *Rolling
Stone* p73 Ja 12 '89

Sky-hi fidelity for the audio fanatic. S. Woolley. il *Business
Week* p158-9 F 20 '89

Specifications

Frequency response: what do the numbers really mean? L.
Klein. il *Radio-Electronics* 60:71-2 Ag '89

Terminology

The basics: names and numbers. I. Masters. il *Stereo Review*
54:27-8+ N '89

Testing

American audio classics [cover story] M. Smolen. il *Stereo
Review* 54:68-74 Je '89

Hardware for home entertainment [special section] il
Consumer Reports 54:155-71 Mr '89

Proton's protean little box [AI-3000] I. Berger. il *Video* 12:34-5
Ja '89

The right stuff for a hi-fi system. il *Consumer Reports*
54:688-90 N '89

Sight and sound: best buys '89. H. Fantel. il *Opera News*
54:56 N '89

Technical talk. J. D. Hirsch. See issues of Stereo Review

Test reports. See issues of High Fidelity (New York, N.Y.)
through July 1989

Test reports. J. D. Hirsch and C. Stark. See issues of Stereo
Review

Test we must, yes, we must! [need for laboratory evaluations]
M. Riggs. il *High Fidelity (New York, N.Y.)* 39:5 Ja '89

AUDIO-VIDEO RECEIVERS

Testing

All-pro receivers. L. B. Johnson. il *Video* 13:76-8+ D '89

Harman Kardon HK-990 Vxi AM/FM audio-video receiver.
R. Long. il *High Fidelity (New York, N.Y.)* 39:23+ Mr
'89

JVC RX-801V audio/video surround-sound receiver. J. D.
Hirsch. il *Stereo Review* 54:60+ O '89

Kenwood KR-V9010 audio/video receiver. J. D. Hirsch. il
Stereo Review 54:93-4+ N '89

Mitsubishi M-AV1 audio/video receiver. J. D. Hirsch. il
Stereo Review 54:32+ Jl '89

Sansui RZ-5000 AM/FM audio-video receiver. R. Long. il
High Fidelity (New York, N.Y.) 39:38+ Ja '89

Sight and sound: complete packages. H. Fantel. *Opera News*
53:41 Mr 18 '89

System integration. J. D. Hirsch. il *Stereo Review* 54:28
Je '89

AUDIOCASSETTE BOOKS *See* Talking books
AUDIOCASSETTE RECORDINGS *See* Tape recordings
AUDIOCASSETTE TAPE *See* Tape, Magnetic
AUDIOVISUAL EQUIPMENT

See also
Business presentations—Aids and devices
Combination disc players
Compact disc interactive
Compact disc players
Compact disc recorders and recording
Compact discs
Videodisc players
Videodiscs
Videotape recorders and recording
Videotapes

Currents. See issues of High Fidelity (New York, N.Y.)
through July 1989

Control

Better remote control. K. McManus and W. Giese. il *Changing
Times* 43:22 My '89

JVC audio/video selector [JX-S900U] il *Video* 13:30+ My
'89

Luxman TP-117 tuner/preamplifier and multiroom system
controller. J. D. Hirsch. il *Stereo Review* 54:64+ S '89

A perfect friendship [cover story] C. Sarver. il *High Fidelity
(New York, N.Y.)* 39:42-8 My '89

Secrets of the universals. I. Berger. il *Video* 12:44-7+ F
'89

Sony video/audio selector [SB-V1000] il *Video* 12:32+ F '89

System integration. J. D. Hirsch. il *Stereo Review* 54:28
Je '89

Design

Dark victory [Eurostyle] M. Porter. il *Gentlemen's Quarterly*
59:213-14 O '89

A perfect friendship [cover story] C. Sarver. il *High Fidelity
(New York, N.Y.)* 39:42-8 My '89

AUDIOVISUAL INSTRUCTION

See also
Educational technology
Motion pictures in education
Television in education
Videotapes—Educational use

AUDIT COMMITTEES

Giving the watchdog fangs. D. Wechsler. il *Forbes* 144:130+
N 13 '89

AUDITING

See also
Audit committees
Curriculum auditing
Tax auditing

Nasty surprises [requiring audited quarterly reports] P. Wang.
il *Forbes* 143:72 Ja 23 '89

Standards

Still pussyfooting. S. N. Chakravarty. il *Forbes* 144:51 Ag
21 '89

AUDITIONS, DANCE *See* Dance—Auditions
AUDITIONS, TELEVISION *See* Television performers—
Auditions
AUDITIONS, THEATER *See* Theater—Auditions
AUDITORIUMS

See also
Concert halls

AUDITORY PERCEPTION *See* Sound perception
AUDITORY SYSTEM *See* Hearing
**AUDUBON PARK AND ZOOLOGICAL GARDEN (NEW
ORLEANS, LA.)**

New Orleans uncages an urban Eden. C. Maddox. il *Southern
Living* 24:30-1 Ag '89

AUDUBON SOCIETY *See* National Audubon Society
AUEL, JEAN M.

about

Auel signs major three-book deal with Crown, Bantam. G.
Feldman. il por *Publishers Weekly* 236:34-5 D 22 '89

AUER, J. JEFFREY

Prime Minister Margaret Thatcher [address, October 19, 1988]
Vital Speeches of the Day 55:276-82 F 15 '89

AUERBACH, ARNOLD See Auerbach, Red, 1917-
AUERBACH, RED, 1917-
about
The pride of the Celtics. J. Schwartz. il por *Gentlemen's Quarterly* 59:156+ N '89
AUGUST, BILLE
about
Pelle the conqueror [film] Reviews
America 160:88+ F 4 '89. R. A. Blake
National Review 41:54-6+ My 5 '89. J. Simon
The New Republic 200:26-7 Ja 23 '89. S. Kauffmann
New York 22:54-5 Ja 9 '89. D. Denby
Newsweek il 113:54 Ja 9 '89. D. Ansen
People Weekly il 31:19 Ja 16 '89. P. Travers
Time il 133:94 Ja 2 '89. R. Schickel
Video 13:59+ Ag '89. J. Bernard
AUGUST, MARILYN
Frenchman on the fringe. il por *World Tennis* 37:59-62 Je '89
AUGUST
The August almanac. il *The Atlantic* 264:12 Ag '89
AUGUSTA (GA.)
Description
Augusta returns to the river [Riverwalk] C. Griffith-Roberts. il *Southern Living* 24:100-1 My '89
AUGUSTA NATIONAL (GA.: GOLF COURSE) See Golf courses
AUGUSTINE, NORMAN R.
U.S. credibility and viability in worldwide competition [address, May 25, 1989] *Vital Speeches of the Day* 55:693-7 S 1 '89
AUKERMAN, DALE
The execution of Ronnie Dunkins. il *The Christian Century* 106:783-5 Ag 30-S 6 '89
AULBY, MIKE
about
Does Planned Parenthood know about this? D. Herbst. il por *Sport (New York, N.Y.)* 80:15 O '89
AULT, GEORGE C., 1891-1948
about
Summer nights at Russell's Corners. S. Schwartz. *The Atlantic* 263:84+ My '89
AUMILLER, LARRY
about
It's a good thing McNeil's big bears get plenty to eat. B. Norton. il pors *Smithsonian* 20:56-60+ Ap '89
AUNESE, SAL
about
This is for you, Sal. B. Newman. il *Sports Illustrated* 71:22-5 O 9 '89
AUNG SAN SUU KYI
about
A country under the boot. D. Benjamin. il por *Time* 134:36-7 Ag 21 '89
AUNG-THWIN, MAUREEN
Burmese days. bibl f *Foreign Affairs* 68:143-61 Spr '89
THE AUNTS [drama] See Bonasorte, Gary
AURA SYSTEMS, INC.
Look, Ma, no bearings. K. K. Wiegner. il *Forbes* 143:136+ My 1 '89
Short-pulse thrusters for SDI require new instrumentation [magnetic suspension test stand for Lightweight Exoatmospheric Projectile] M. A. Dornheim. il *Aviation Week & Space Technology* 131:53+ Ag 28 '89
AURARIA HIGHER EDUCATION CENTER (COLO.)
Opening doors. M. Gaskie. il *Architectural Record* 177:102-7 Ag '89
AUREOLE (NEW YORK, N.Y.: RESTAURANT) See New York (N.Y.)—Restaurants, nightclubs, bars, etc.
AURICULIN See Atrial natriuretic factor
AURORA BOREALIS See Auroras
AURORAS
Brilliant aurorae produced by solar flare. D. J. Eicher. il *Astronomy* 17:95+ Jl '89
The dynamic aurora [cover story] S.-I. Akasofu. bibl il *Scientific American* 260:90-7 My '89
A jam-jar magnetometer as "aurora detector". R. J. Livesey. il *Sky and Telescope* 78:426-32 O '89
Nature's incredible night show. L. Ponte. il *Reader's Digest* 135:86-91 D '89
The northern lights head south. T. D. Nicholson. il *Natural History* p104-8 N '89
Return of the northern lights. F. Schaaf. il *The Mother Earth News* 119:75-7 S/O '89
Photographs and photography
March's spectacular aurora. il *Astronomy* 17:92-3 Jl '89
AUSABLE INSTITUTE OF ENVIRONMENTAL STUDIES
The earth groans, and Christians are listening. K. G. Streiffert. il *Christianity Today* 33:38+ S 22 '89
AUSCHWITZ (POLAND: CONCENTRATION CAMP)
Auschwitz and the nuns. W. F. Buckley. *National Review* 41:63 O 13 '89
The Auschwitz Carmel. *America* 161:179 S 30 '89
Auschwitz ire [controversial Carmelite convent] il *Time* 134:49 Ag 21 '89
Cardinal Glemp's memory lapse [Carmelite convent] J. M. Wall. *The Christian Century* 106:867 O 4 '89

Close enough to step on toes: tensions between Jews & Catholics [Carmelite convent controversy] L. Klenicki and E. D. Mallon. il *Commonweal* 116:521-6 O 6 '89
Détente at a death camp [dispute over Carmelite convent] K. L. Woodward. il *Newsweek* 114:58 O 2 '89
The ghosts of an ancient plague [controversial Carmelite convent] il *U.S. News & World Report* 107:10 S 11 '89
The Glemp controversy [Carmelite convent] *The Christian Century* 106:808 S 13-20 '89
Harsh homily [J. Glemp's remarks concerning Carmelite convent] *Time* 134:77 S 11 '89
Mea culpa, Auschwitz [agreement to move Carmelite convent] il *Time* 134:25 O 2 '89
Missing [downplaying of the Jewish nature of the Auschwitz horror] A. J. Blinken. *The New Republic* 201:15-16 O 16 '89
Peace signals from the papal chimney [Pope John Paul II calls for removal of Carmelite convent] il *U.S. News & World Report* 107:14 O 2 '89
Polish memories [convent controversy] J. Neusner. il *National Review* 41:27-8 O 27 '89
A sign of contradiction [Auschwitz convent controversy] J. T. Pawlikowski. il *Commonweal* 116:485-8 S 22 '89
The Vatican and the Jews [support for relocation of Carmelite convent] il *The Christian Century* 106:873 O 4 '89
Whose Auschwitz? [dispute over Carmelite convent] il *National Review* 41:18+ S 29 '89
Whose Holocaust? [controversy over Carmelite convent] R. Watson. il *Newsweek* 114:35-6 S 11 '89
AUSCHWITZ (POLAND: CONCENTRATION CAMP) IN ART
Auschwitz [paintings by J. P. Czarnecki] il *Life* 12:79-80+ S '89
AUSIMONT (FIRM)
Why Wall Street is furioso at Raul Gardini [deal to buy out minority holders of Ausimont] J. Rossant and W. Glasgall. il por *Business Week* p48 F 20 '89
AUSPITZ, JOSIAH LEE
Where philosophy matters. *Commentary* 87:54-60 Je '89
AUSTER, LAWRENCE
The Regents' Round Table. il *National Review* 41:18+ D 8 '89
AUSTER, PAUL, 1947-
about
PW interviews. M. Thiébaux. por *Publishers Weekly* 235:80-1 Mr 3 '89
AUSTER, STANLEY
about
The egg cream. J. Berendt. il por *Esquire* 112:48 D '89
The secret of life. *The New Yorker* 65:37-8 My 15 '89
AUSTERLITZ, BATTLE OF, 1805
Military *perestroika* [reenactment] D. G. Chandler. il *History Today* 39:3-4 N '89
AUSTIN, PENELOPE
Heedless [poem] *The New Republic* 200:34 Je 12 '89
AUSTIN (MINN.)
Social conditions
A company town decays [effect of strike against Hormel] B. Koeppel. il *The Progressive* 53:12-13 F '89
AUSTIN (TEX.)
Architecture
They love houses. E. Wood. il *Southern Living* 24:148+ Ap '89
Crime
An apparent murder attempt on a venerable oak tree makes Texans fear for their roots [poisoning of the Treaty Oak] il *People Weekly* 32:116-17 Jl 17 '89
Description
Powerful fun in T-bird Town. il *Rolling Stone* p24 Jl 13-27 '89
Galleries and museums
See also
Archer M. Huntington Art Gallery (Austin, Tex.)
History
See also
Treaty Oak (Austin, Tex.)
Parks and playgrounds
See also
Wild Basin Wilderness Preserve (Tex.)
Poor
The homeless take to the water. D. Claitor. il *The Progressive* 53:10-11 F '89
Wildlife
Good evening, fellow bat lovers [Mexican freetail bats] J. Schwartz. il *Newsweek* 114:63 Jl 3 '89
AUSTRALIA
See also
Art—Australia
Astronomical observatories—Australia
Australians
Automobile racing—Australia
Aviation and state—Australia
Ayers Rock (Australia)
Booksellers and bookselling—Australia
Botany—Australia
Brookfield Conservation Park (Australia)
Collective bargaining—Airlines—Australia
Education—Australia

AUSTRALIA—See also—*cont.*
    Environmental policy—Australia
    Gardens and gardening—Australia
    Geology—Australia
    Great Barrier Reef (Australia)
    Investments, Australian
    Islands—Australia
    Kakadu National Park (Australia)
    Morale, National—Australia
    Motion pictures—Australia
    Motorcycle racing—Australia
    Natural resources—Australia
    Northern Territory (Australia)
    Opera—Australia
    Otway Basin (Australia)
    Paleontology—Australia
    Petroleum—Australia
    Prisons—Australia
    Publishers and publishing—Australia
    Queensland (Australia)
    Revegetation—Australia
    Rich—Australia
    Science—Australia
    Space centers—Australia
    Strikes—Air pilots—Australia
    Technology—Australia
    Uluru National Park (Australia)
    University extension—Australia
    Wildlife—Australia
    Zoos—Australia

Centennial celebrations, etc.
Nostalgia and self-congratulation. J. Turner. il *Art News* 88:47 Mr '89

Civilization
Unknown Australia [cover story; special issue] il *The Courier (Unesco)* 41:3-38 D '88

Defenses
See also
Airplanes, Military—Australia
Australia. Royal Australian Air Force
Aviation, Military—Australia

Description and travel
See also
Cycling—Australia
G'day, wimp [Back of Beyond vacation] T. Friend. il *Esquire* 112:61-2 S '89
Off in the wild Down Under. P. M. Prince. il map *Travel Holiday* 171:60-7 Ap '89
Outback odyssey. D. Holing. il *New Choices for the Best Years* 29:50-6 S '89
Slouching through Australia [camel trip] C. J. Hadley. il *The Saturday Evening Post* 261:82-5+ Mr '89
Unknown Australia [cover story; special issue] il *The Courier (Unesco)* 41:3-38 D '88

Economic conditions
See also
Cost and standard of living—Australia
Australia's Down Under economy. il *U.S. News & World Report* 107:70 N 20 '89

Economic policy
Up from Down Under. L. Kraar. il *Fortune* 120 no13 Special Issue:54 Fall '89

History
Steps to nationhood. il *The Courier (Unesco)* 41:8-9 D '88

Industries
See also
Aerospace Technologies of Australia Pty. Ltd.
Airlines—Australia
Australian Jet Charter (Firm)
Bond Corporation Holdings Ltd.
Broken Hill Proprietary Co., Ltd.
Corporations—Acquisitions and mergers—Australia
Hawker de Havilland Australia Pty. Ltd.
Memtec Ltd.
Motion picture industry—Australia
Qantas Airways Ltd.
Wine industry—Australia

Maps
Aussie jumble [map puzzle] il *National Geographic World* 172:24 D '89

Native peoples
See also
Australian aborigines

Photographs and photography
A photographer's guide to Australia. P. Skinner. il *Petersen's Photographic Magazine* 17:68-70 Ja '89

Population
See also
Asians—Australia

Religious institutions and affairs
Talking about religion Down Under. M. E. Marty. *The Christian Century* 106:708-9 Ag 2-9 '89

Social life and customs
Dallas Down Under. M. Lewis. *The New Republic* 200:14+ My 22 '89

AUSTRALIA. ROYAL AUSTRALIAN AIR FORCE
Military preparedness in the South Pacific: Australia [cover story; special section] il map *Aviation Week & Space Technology* 130:34-5+ F 6 '89
AUSTRALIA IN ADVERTISING
G'night, mate. J. Levine. il *Forbes* 144:286+ D 11 '89
AUSTRALIAN ABORIGINES
Aboriginality [Burnum Burnum] *The New Yorker* 65:31-3 S 4 '89

Art
Dreamtime stories. V. Tippett. il *The Courier (Unesco)* 41:12-15 D '88

Exhibitions
Aboriginal art: symptom or success? T. Fry and A.-M. Willis. bibl f il *Art in America* 77:108-17+ Jl '89
Beautiful Dreamings [exhibit at the Asia Society] A. Wallach. il *Ms.* 17:60-4 Mr '89
Dreamings of life [Dreamings: the art of aboriginal Australia] C. Liotta. il *Art News* 88:26 Ap '89

Civil rights
A cry of desperation [deaths of aborigines in police custody] W. E. Smith. il *Time* 133:34 Ja 9 '89
AUSTRALIAN ART *See* Art, Australian
AUSTRALIAN AUTHORS *See* Authors, Australian
AUSTRALIAN BOOK SOURCE (FIRM)
Australian books in the U.S.: two small companies find success. il *Publishers Weekly* 235:38-40 Mr 24 '89
AUSTRALIAN COOKING *See* Cooking, Australian
AUSTRALIAN GRAND PRIX *See* Automobile racing—Australia
AUSTRALIAN JET CHARTER (FIRM)
Charter operators gain ground in Pacific, despite red tape. P. Proctor. il *Aviation Week & Space Technology* 131:87+ O 2 '89
AUSTRALIAN LITERATURE
See also
Publishers and publishing—Australian literature
AUSTRALIAN OPERA COMPANY *See* Opera—Australia
AUSTRALIAN REVEGETATION CORPORATION
How to stop the desert's march. J. Cribb. *World Press Review* 36:32 Ap '89
AUSTRALIAN RULES FOOTBALL
Ten things you always wanted to know about Australian rules football. S. Jantz. il *Sport (New York, N.Y.)* 80:80 Ja '89
AUSTRALIAN TENNIS PLAYERS *See* Tennis players
AUSTRALIAN WINES *See* Wine
AUSTRALIANS
Who are the Australians? G. Bolton. il *The Courier (Unesco)* 41:4-8+ D '88

United States
Inside with the INS [experience of Australian tourist] G. Rodoreda. il *The Progressive* 53:50 My '89
AUSTRIA
See also
Alps
Americans—Austria
Architecture—Austria
Art—Austria
Art and state—Austria
Dance festivals—Austria
Funeral rites and ceremonies—Austria
Immigration and emigration—Austria
Jews—Austria
Lake Constance
Lech (Austria)
Music festivals—Austria
Opera—Austria
Prostitution—Austria
Salzburg (Austria)
Suicide—Austria
United States—Diplomatic and consular service—Austria
Vienna (Austria)

Industries
See also
Oesterreichische Industrieholding Aktiengesellschaft

Kings and rulers
See also
House of Habsburg

Politics and government
See also
Politics, Corruption in—Austria
Socialist Party (Austria)
AUSTRIA FUND
Watch on the Danube. J. Queenan. il *Forbes* 144:174 S 4 '89
AUSTRIAN ART *See* Art, Austrian
AUTHEIL (FRANCE)
Historic houses, sites, etc.
Architectural digest visits: Yves Montand. C. Aillaud. il pors *Architectural Digest* 46:82-7+ Ja '89
AUTHORITARIANISM
See also
Fascism
Totalitarianism
AUTHORITY (RELIGION)
See also
Catholic Church—Authority

AUTHORS

See also

Authorship
Black authors
Celebrities as authors
Chemists as authors
Clothing and dress—Authors
Copyright
Executives as authors
Homeless as authors
Judges as authors
Literary agencies and agents
Literature
Physicians as authors
Prisoners as authors
Psychotherapists as authors
Royalties
Women authors
Youth as authors

The early line on 1989: books. il *People Weekly* 31:72-3 Ja 9 '89
PW interviews. See issues of Publishers Weekly

Attitudes

Anywhere, with the best of company [authors select literary or historical characters as traveling companions] il *The New York Times Book Review* 94:31-3 Je 11 '89
Dateline 1999 [predictions of science fiction authors] E. Bryant. il *Omni (New York, N.Y.)* 11:22+ Ja '89
Words for Salman Rushdie. il *The New York Times Book Review* 94:1+ Mr 12 '89

Biography

Public or purloined? [disposition of writers' letters] F. Busch. il *Harper's* 279:58-61 Ag '89

Conferences

See Authors' conferences

Correspondence, reminiscences, etc.

Public or purloined? [disposition of letters] F. Busch. il *Harper's* 279:58-61 Ag '89
Where does a writer's family draw the line? J. M. Smith. il por *The New York Times Book Review* 94:1+ N 5 '89

Photographs and photography

The face on the back of the book. J. Kaufman. il *The New York Times Book Review* 94:1+ Je 25 '89

Political activities

Ballantine releases updated edition of 'Dangerous dossiers' [H. Mitgang book on FBI surveillance of authors and Freedom of Information Act] B. Levine. il *Publishers Weekly* 235:27 Mr 17 '89
Doves & hawks [discussion of March 1989 article, On not being a dove] J. Updike. *Commentary* 88:2-4 Ag '89
On not being a dove [Vietnam War] J. Updike. *Commentary* 87:22-30 Mr '89
Thanks to protesters, a runaway best seller [S. Rushdie's Satanic verses] L. Shapiro. il *Newsweek* 113:32-3 Mr 6 '89
Writers speak out and step out [supporting S. Rushdie's Satanic verses] C. Reid. il *Publishers Weekly* 235:16-17 Mr 10 '89

Professional ethics

See Literary ethics

Promotion tours

See Books—Advertising

Psychology

Envy, the writer's disease. B. Friedman. il *The New York Times Book Review* 94:1+ N 26 '89
Fighting writer's block. D. O'Hehir. *The Writer* 102:12-14+ F '89
O muse! You do make things difficult! D. Ackerman. il *The New York Times Book Review* 94:1+ N 12 '89
Storied objects [writing at home surrounded by personal possessions] A. Gurganus. il pors *House & Garden* 161:46+ My '89
A time to backburner. D. W. Trebilcock. *The Writer* 102:9-10 Je '89
Writers beware writers [friendships] A. Broyard. il *The New York Times Book Review* 94:14 My 21 '89

Public relations

See Authors and readers

Reading

Favorite authors' favorite books. *Ladies' Home Journal* 106:62 Jl '89
Read any bad books lately? L. Shea. il *Esquire* 112:90-1 Jl '89

Religious life

Creativity's sacred sources. P. King. *Psychology Today* 23:68+ D '89

Salaries, pensions, etc.

See also

Authors—Taxation

Freelance writers claim nonpayment by 'Inside books'. C. Reid. *Publishers Weekly* 235:25 Je 30 '89
A literary illusion. A. Smith. il *Esquire* 111:77-8 F '89

Taxation

Anecdotes, facetiae, satire, etc.

Sour tax notes. D. Seligman. il *Fortune* 119:164 Mr 27 '89

Travel

Anecdotes, facetiae, satire, etc.

It's not all absinthe and croissants. P. Margoshes. *The Writer* 102:5-6 Jl '89

AUTHORS, AMERICAN

See also

Abbey, Edward, 1927-1989
Algonquin Round Table
Asimov, Isaac, 1920-
Bansemer, Roger, 1948-
BenShea, Noah
Berg, A. Scott (Andrew Scott)
Black authors
Branch, Taylor
Brodkey, Harold
Bromfield, Louis, 1896-1956
Brownmiller, Susan
Campbell, Joseph, 1904-1987
Caro, Robert A.
Carter, Forrest, d. 1979
Carver, Raymond
Clark, Mary Higgins
Crane, Stephen, 1871-1900
Croly, Herbert David, 1869-1930
Dickson, Paul
Dreiser, Theodore, 1871-1945
Duberman, Martin B.
Eiseley, Loren C., 1907-1977
Elliott, George P., 1918-1980
Frazier, Ian
Friedman, Bruce Jay, 1930-
Gossett, Hattie, 1942-
Griffin, John Howard, 1920-1980
Halliburton, Richard
James, Henry, 1843-1916
Kennedy, William, 1928-
Kerouac, Jack, 1922-1969
Kidder, Tracy
Leaming, Barbara
Lebowitz, Fran
Lopez, Barry Holstun, 1945-
Mailer, Norman
Marshall, James, 1942-
Matthiessen, Peter
McGinniss, Joe
McGrath, Thomas, 1916-
McKibben, Bill
McManus, Patrick F.
Mencken, H. L. (Henry Louis), 1880-1956
Mills, Enos, 1870-1922
Nestle, Joan, 1940-
O'Rourke, P. J.
Poe, Edgar Allan, 1809-1849
Randall, Margaret, 1936-
Rhodes, Richard
Rose, Phyllis, 1942-
Schulberg, Budd
Seuss, Dr.
Shaw, Irwin, 1913-1984
Sontag, Susan, 1933-
Stein, Gertrude, 1874-1946
Steptoe, John, 1950-1989
Trilling, Diana
Twain, Mark, 1835-1910
Van Allsburg, Chris
Welty, Eudora, 1909-
Whedbee, Charles Harry
Whiting, Robert
Wolfe, Tom
Wolff, Geoffrey, 1937-
Wolff, Tobias, 1945-
Wright, Richard, 1908-1960

Aspirations. il *Publishers Weekly* 235:46-8 Ja 6 '89
Ballantine releases updated edition of 'Dangerous dossiers' [H. Mitgang book on FBI surveillance of authors and Freedom of Information Act] B. Levine. il *Publishers Weekly* 235:27 Mr 17 '89
Literary lights on the Potomac. D. Cutler. il *Publishers Weekly* 235:112-14 My 12 '89
Pages. il *People Weekly* 32:87 S 4 '89

Biography

Book reviews. R. S. Phillips. *America* 160:14+ Ja 7-14 '89

AUTHORS, AUSTRALIAN

See also

Base, Graeme, 1958-

Why Australian writers keep their heads down. C. See. il *The New York Times Book Review* 94:1+ My 14 '89

AUTHORS, BLACK See Black authors

AUTHORS, CANADIAN

See also

Hutchison, Bruce

AUTHORS, CHINESE

See also

Bai Hua

AUTHORS, CUBAN

See also

Moore, Carlos

AUTHORS, CZECH
See also
Urbánek, Zdeněk
Czech writers: politicians in spite of themselves. J. Škvorecký. *The New York Times Book Review* 94:1+ D 10 '89

AUTHORS, ECUADORIAN
See also
Montalvo, Juan, 1832-1889

AUTHORS, ENGLISH
See also
Ackerley, J. R. (Joe Randolph), 1896-1967
Browne, Anthony
Chesterton, G. K. (Gilbert Keith), 1874-1936
Dahl, Roald
Dickens, Charles, 1812-1870
Glendinning, Victoria
Greene, Graham, 1904-
Hardy, Thomas, 1840-1928
Hart, Alan, 1935-
Hughes, Frieda
Hurne, Ralph
Kipling, Rudyard, 1865-1936
Lewis, C. S. (Clive Staples), 1898-1963
Nesbit, E. (Edith), 1858-1924
Orwell, George, 1903-1950
Potter, Beatrix, 1866-1943
Reid Banks, Lynne, 1929-

AUTHORS, FRENCH
See also
Bataille, Georges, 1897-1962
Flaubert, Gustave, 1821-1880
Tournier, Michel

AUTHORS, GERMAN
See also
Benjamin, Walter, 1892-1940
Goethe, Johann Wolfgang von, 1749-1832
Grass, Günter, 1927-
Grimm, Jacob, 1785-1863
Grimm, Wilhelm, 1786-1859

AUTHORS, HANDICAPPED
Driven by an unquenchable spirit, a Massachusetts woman writes an impossible book [confinement of cerebral palsy patient R. Sienkiewicz-Mercer to Belchertown State School] L. Smith. il pors *People Weekly* 32:107+ S 11 '89
I raise my eyes to say yes [confinement of cerebral palsy patient to Belchertown State School in Massachusetts; excerpts] R. Sienkiewicz-Mercer and S. B. Kaplan. il *Glamour* 87:280-1+ O '89

AUTHORS, HISPANIC AMERICAN
See also
Hijuelos, Oscar

AUTHORS, IRISH
See also
Joyce, James, 1882-1941
Wilde, Oscar, 1854-1900
Yeats, W. B. (William Butler), 1865-1939

AUTHORS, JAPANESE
See also
Nakae, Chōmin, 1847-1901

AUTHORS, JEWISH
See also
BenShea, Noah
Tarr, Herbert
Writing as a Jew. H. Bartov. *Commentary* 87:24-7 Je '89

AUTHORS, MEXICAN AMERICAN
La boom [women] M. DiLeo. il *Mother Jones* 14:15 O '89

AUTHORS, RUSSIAN
See also
Serge, Victor, 1890-1947
Solzhenitsyn, Aleksandr, 1918-
Tolstoy, Leo, graf, 1828-1910
Glasnost writing: so where's the golden age? C. R. Whitney. il *The New York Times Book Review* 94:1+ Mr 19 '89

AUTHORS, TRINIDADIAN
See also
Naipaul, V. S. (Vidiadhar Surajprasad), 1932-

AUTHORS, WOMEN *See* Women authors

AUTHORS AND EDITORS
Writing for life style magazines (II). il *The Writer* 102:28-30 Ja '89
Writing for Mother Jones. J. A. Cabello. il *The Writer* 102:28 O '89
Writing for Vegetarian times. L. Moll. il *The Writer* 102:25-6 Ap '89
Writing successful proposals for the romance market. T. Carter. *The Writer* 102:23-5 My '89
The year of the young reader. *The Writer* 102:20-5 Je '89

AUTHORS AND PUBLISHERS
See also
Copyright
Literary agencies and agents
Royalties
Auel signs major three-book deal with Crown, Bantam. G. Feldman. il por *Publishers Weekly* 236:34-5 D 22 '89
Authors concerned about Dodd, Mead liquidation. *Publishers Weekly* 235:20 Ja 6 '89

Barry Lopez finds a new home at Knopf. por *Publishers Weekly* 235:30-1 Je 23 '89
Better times for black writers? W. Nixon. il *Publishers Weekly* 235:35-40 F 17 '89
Big books, big bucks. P. Painton. il *Time* 133:44-6 Je 12 '89
Computing for dollars [selling articles to computer magazines] C. Walnum. il *The Writer* 102:20-2 Mr '89
Court aids freelancers in work-for-hire ruling [case of Community for Creative Non-Violence vs. J. E. Reid] H. Fields. *Publishers Weekly* 235:11 Je 16 '89
Cross-culture shock [long-distance editing by Atlantic Monthly Press of J. McIntyre Varawa's book on Fijian marriage] L. Fleischer. *Publishers Weekly* 235:207 F 24 '89
Delacorte's Dutch treat [return of E. Leonard] M. Simson. il *Publishers Weekly* 236:24 O 20 '89
Dodd, Mead operations suspended over arbitration [dispute with authors] C. Reid. *Publishers Weekly* 235:11 Mr 31 '89
How to write a how-to that sells. G. Luttmann. *The Writer* 102:19-20+ Jl '89
The Joy Luck Club: Chinese magic, American blessings and a publishing fairy tale. G. Feldman. il por *Publishers Weekly* 236:24-6 Jl 7 '89
Lawyers see little impact from High Court's work-for-hire ruling [Community for Creative Non-Violence v. Reid] H. Fields. *Publishers Weekly* 235:10-11 Je 23 '89
Literary cross-pollination [using literary magazines to identify potential book authors] W. Nixon. il *Publishers Weekly* 235:30+ Mr 31 '89
Market newsletter. See issues of The Writer
Money: the curse of the publishing class. J. F. Baker. *Publishers Weekly* 235:6 Je 9 '89
Philip Roth and Bill Cosby move houses for high stakes. pors *Publishers Weekly* 236:42-3 S 8 '89
Reading between the lines [self-licensing of paperback rights can institutionalize half-royalties] L. Chu. il *Publishers Weekly* 235:48 F 17 '89
Sampling a cookbook manuscript [authors of The simple secrets of Vietnamese cooking invite prospective publishers to a buffet] D. Brainard. *Publishers Weekly* 236:33 S 8 '89
Sell your hidden gold with a query [query letters] T. Jenkins. *The Writer* 102:18-20+ Ag '89
Sparks fly as Colleen McCullough leaves Harper for Hearst. G. Feldman. *Publishers Weekly* 236:40 Jl 21 '89
Supreme Court hears work-for-hire arguments [case brought by Community for Creative Non-Violence against J. E. Reid] H. Fields. *Publishers Weekly* 235:14 Ap 14 '89
This month's special market lists. See issues of The Writer
Three surefire ways to write and sell nonfiction. S. S. Baker. *The Writer* 102:11-13 Mr '89
What authors want from publishers [National Writers Union campaign] J. Tasini. por *Publishers Weekly* 235:46 F 10 '89
Where to sell manuscripts. See issues of The Writer
Work for hire: round two [authors fight for full copyright] A. Dubro. por *Publishers Weekly* 235:80 Je 30 '89
Writing for the trades. H. Scott. *The Writer* 102:22-5 F '89

Anecdotes, facetiae, satire, etc.
Book sightings: a new source of author income? J. Kelman. por *Publishers Weekly* 235:65 Mr 17 '89
Homer and his publishers. J. Queenan. il *The American Spectator* 22:39 D '89
'No author is a man of genius to his publisher'. W. Cole. *The New York Times Book Review* 94:1+ S 3 '89
The postman didn't ring even once [lost manuscript] J. E. Scalia. *The Writer* 102:7-8 My '89
Pubquips: homilies for the writing trade. E. Sommer. *The Writer* 102:7-8 Mr '89
Slaying dragons: a writer's fantasy. J. Van Wicklen. *The Writer* 102:9-10 D '89

Bibliography
Writers and the market—II. C. Goodrich. *The Nation* 249:24-6+ Jl 3 '89

AUTHORS AND READERS
The gap between the writer and the reader. N. Gordimer. bibl f il *The New York Review of Books* 36:59-61 S 28 '89
Selling travelers on guidebooks [reader complaints] T. Brosnahan. por *Publishers Weekly* 235:95 Ja 20 '89
Think of the reader. P. Anthony. *The Writer* 102:11-13+ Ag '89
The treason of the critics. I. Howe. *The New Republic* 200:28-31 Je 12 '89
Writing back [correspondence from fans] A. Dillard. *Harper's* 278:28-9 Je '89

AUTHORS AS ARTISTS
Exhibitions
"Literary vision" at Jack Tilton. G. Henry. *Art in America* 77:171-2 Je '89

AUTHORS AS GARDENERS
A writer's garden. M. Piercy. il por *Organic Gardening* 36:72 Je '89

AUTHORS AS PHOTOGRAPHERS
Eudora Welty, inquiring photographer [interview] H. Cole and S. Srinivasan. il *The New York Times Book Review* 94:1+ O 22 '89
Southern exposure [E. Welty's photographs] G. Jaynes. il por *Life* 12:58-60+ N '89
AUTHORS' CONFERENCES
Black writers debate 'being human in the 20th century' [Celebration of Black Writing] M. Coffey. il *Publishers Weekly* 235:16-17 F 17 '89
Making the best use of a writers' workshop. W. E. Stafford. *The Writer* 102:15-18 Ap '89
Why writers workshops? [with list of 1989 conferences] J. Oak. *The Writer* 102:26-34 My '89
AUTHORS' CONTRACTS See Authors and publishers
AUTHORS' FAMILIES
Where does a writer's family draw the line? J. M. Smith. il por *The New York Times Book Review* 94:1+ N 5 '89
AUTHORS' LOUNGE (BANGKOK, THAILAND: BAR) See Bangkok (Thailand)—Restaurants, nightclubs, bars, etc.
AUTHORS' MARKETS See Authors and publishers
AUTHORS' ORGANIZATIONS
See also
PEN
Textbook Authors Association
AUTHORS' RIGHTS
See also
Copyright
Public lending rights (of authors)
Royalties
McMurtry and others decry continuing use of McCarran Act. H. Fields. *Publishers Weekly* 235:15 My 26 '89
AUTHORSHIP
See also
Anthropological literature—Authorship
Arts and crafts literature—Authorship
Authors
Autobiography
Business writing
Children's literature—Authorship
Creative writing
Dedications (in books)
Detective and mystery stories—Authorship
Drama—Technique
Educational literature—Authorship
Fiction—Authorship
Fiction—Technique
Freelance writing
Historical fiction—Authorship
Horror tales—Authorship
Humor—Authorship
Journalism
Literature—Technique
Motion picture authorship
Nature literature—Authorship
Outlines (Authorship)
Periodical articles
Physics literature—Authorship
Picture books for children—Authorship
Plagiarism
Plots (Drama, novel, etc.)
Poetry—Authorship
Science fiction—Authorship
Scientific literature—Authorship
Short story
Spy stories—Authorship
Television authorship
Textbooks—Authorship
Travel literature—Authorship
Word processors and processing—Authors' use
Young adults' literature—Authorship
Youth as authors
The more they write, the more they write [productivity] J. Parini. il *The New York Times Book Review* 94:1+ Jl 30 '89
Off the cuff. See issues of The Writer
On writing: let there be less. A. Krystal. il *The New York Times Book Review* 94:1+ Mr 26 '89
Write till you drop. A. Dillard. il *The New York Times Book Review* 94:1+ My 28 '89
Writing on the go. D. Gilbert. *The Writer* 102:27-8 Mr '89
Anecdotes, facetiae, satire, etc.
The wrong stuff. M. G. Stoddard. il *The Saturday Evening Post* 261:56-7+ O '89
Bibliography
The writer's library. See occasional issues of The Writer
Collaboration
The celebs' golden mouthpiece [ghostwriter W. Novak] M. Smilgis. il por *Time* 134:82 N 27 '89
Ken Kesey's eclectic writing acid test [collaboration with University of Oregon students results in novel, Caverns] D. Weddle. il por *Rolling Stone* p119-20+ O 5 '89
Remember this: write what you don't know [University of Oregon students collaborate on novel] K. Kesey. *The New York Times Book Review* 94:1+ D 31 '89

Competitions
See Literature—Competitions
Copy preparation
Let's do it over. P. A. Whitney. *The Writer* 102:13-15+ D '89
Rewriting your novel. S. L. Stebel. *The Writer* 102:17-19 Je '89
Psychological aspects
See Authors—Psychology
AUTISM
M*A*S*H's William Christopher and wife Barbara find love and pain with an autistic son [interview] D. Bacon. il pors *People Weekly* 32:79-80+ N 13 '89
Mixed blessing [autistic son] W. Christopher and B. Christopher. il pors *Ladies' Home Journal* 106:144+ My '89
New evidence: autism is a brain disorder [abnormal cerebellum; research by Eric Courchesne] W. Herbert. *Psychology Today* 23:22 Je '89
This man is an island [J. Sullivan, model for character in film Rain Man] D. Chu. il pors *People Weekly* 31:36-41 Ja 23 '89
Genetic aspects
Genetic evidence for autism [research by Susan E. Folstein] I. Wickelgren. *Science News* 135:349 Je 3 '89
Therapy
The little girl without a smile [mother's attempts to help daughter overcome autism] C. Legrand. il *Reader's Digest* 135:107-12 Ag '89
Remodeling the autistic child. B. Bower. il *Science News* 136:312-13 N 11 '89
AUTOBIOGRAPHY
Autobiography and the craft of embellishment. A. P. Sanoff. il *U.S. News & World Report* 107:64 O 23 '89
A brush with history [cover story; special section; with editorial comment by Byron Dobell] il *American Heritage* 40:7, 47-52+ D '89
My father's autobiography. D. Cole. il *Psychology Today* 22:56-7 D '88
Bibliography
Our stories, our selves. D. Gates. il *Newsweek* 113:64-5 Ja 23 '89
AUTODESK INC.
Autodesk confounds the venture capitalists. R. A. Shaffer. il *Personal Computing* 13:45-6 Ap '89
AUTOFOCUS CAMERAS See Cameras
AUTOFOCUS CAMERAS, SINGLE-LENS REFLEX See Cameras, Single-lens reflex
AUTOGIROS
Testing
Space case [Air and Space 18-A] A. Laboda. il *Flying* 116:62-6+ My '89
AUTOGRAPHS
Collectors and collecting
Assembly line of dreams [fees charged for baseball players' autographs] T. Callahan. il *Time* 133:78 My 15 '89
Collect autographs. J. M. Taylor. il *Americana* 17:13-15 Jl/Ag '89
The foul ball in the closet [signatures on baseball signed by 1938 Yankees turn out to have been forged] D. Seligman. il *Fortune* 120:141-2 Jl 3 '89
The handwriting's off the wall. J. Queenan. il *Forbes* 144:186+ O 2 '89
Yours, truly. D. V. Gast. il *New Choices for the Best Years* 29:82+ N '89
AUTOIMMUNE DISEASES See Immunologic diseases
AUTOLOGOUS BLOOD TRANSFUSION See Blood—Transfusion
AUTOMATA, CELLULAR See Cellular automata
AUTOMATED TELLER MACHINES
Are ATMs easy targets for crooks? P. Cole. il *Business Week* p30 Mr 6 '89
Cash on the run. C. Torcellini. il *Forbes* 143:145 My 1 '89
Change agents [inventor D. Wetzel] D. Moreau. il por *Changing Times* 43:108 Ja '89
AUTOMATIC CONTROL
See also
Self organizing systems
AUTOMATIC DATA PROCESSING, INC.
Rich prospects, poor bedfellows [ADP taking stock quote market away from Quotron] F. Meeks. il *Forbes* 143:72+ Ap 3 '89
AUTOMATIC FILM WINDERS See Photography—Equipment
AUTOMATIC IMPLANTABLE DEFIBRILLATORS See Defibrillators
AUTOMATIC SPEECH RECOGNITION SYSTEMS See Speech processing systems
AUTOMATIC TEST EQUIPMENT
Automatic test equipment. A. C. Stover. il *Radio-Electronics* 60:61-4 O '89
AUTOMATION
See also
Airlines—Automation
Airlines—Reservation systems—Automation
Airplane factories—Automation
Allen-Bradley Co.
Automobile factories—Automation

AUTOMATION—See also—cont.
    Automobile service stations—Automation
    Carnivals—Automation
    Clothing factories—Automation
    Computer industry—Automation
    Computer integrated manufacturing
    Concrete industry—Automation
    Construction industry—Automation
    Customer service—Automation
    Drugstores—Automation
    Flexible manufacturing systems
    Honeywell Inc.
    Hotels, motels, etc.—Automation
    Libraries—Automation
    Lotteries—Automation
    Machine vision
    Offices—Automation
    Piano industry—Automation
    Railroads—Automation
    Research libraries—Automation
    Robots—Industrial use
    Saline water conversion—Automation
    Television industry—Automation
    Travel agencies and agents—Automation
    United States Postal Service—Automation
    Word processors and processing
Bosses ignore worker concerns [views of Ann Majchrzak] il *USA Today (Periodical)* 118:4-5 Ag '89
Manufacturing intelligence [smart factories] P. Wallich. il *Scientific American* 261:100+ D '89
Research targets machines that learn. *High Technology Business* 9:39 F '89
Smart factories: America's turn? O. Port. il *Business Week* p142-5+ My 8 '89
AUTOMATONS *See* Robots
AUTOMOBILE ACCIDENTS *See* Traffic accidents
AUTOMOBILE ALARMS *See* Automobiles—Alarms
AUTOMOBILE ASSEMBLY PLANTS *See* Automobile factories
AUTOMOBILE AUCTIONS
    See also
    Manheim Exotic Auction
The auction [Monterey Vintage Sports and Race Car Auction] R. Homan. il *Road & Track* 41:89 D '89
Mary Wilson to have her Beatles' limo auctioned. il por *Jet* 76:14 Ap 10 '89
AUTOMOBILE BATTERIES *See* Storage batteries
AUTOMOBILE BOAT TRAILERS
Easy riders. S. Stapleton. il *Motor Boating & Sailing* 164:60-4+ O '89
Package deals. J. Skorupa. il *Popular Mechanics* 166:68-71 Mr '89
Trailer to go [Calkins trailer kit] M. Morris. il *Home Mechanix* 86:106-7+ Ap '89
    Maintenance and repair
Trailering checklist. S. Stapleton. il *Motor Boating & Sailing* 163:44-5 My '89
    Security measures
Trailer security update. B. Stearns. il *Field & Stream* 93:124+ Ap '89
    Towing
Adventures in pulling your weight. J. Skorupa. il *Popular Mechanics* 166:18+ F '89
Top 10 tow vehicles for 1990. T. P. Banse. *Motor Boating & Sailing* 164:64+ O '89
AUTOMOBILE BODIES *See* Automobiles—Bodies
AUTOMOBILE BODIES, REMODELED *See* Automobiles, Remodeled
AUTOMOBILE BODY WORK *See* Automobiles—Maintenance and repair
AUTOMOBILE BRAKES *See* Brakes, Automobile
AUTOMOBILE BROKERS
A better way to buy a car? il *Consumer Reports* 54:593-5 S '89
AUTOMOBILE BUYING *See* Automobiles—Purchasing
AUTOMOBILE CAMPING *See* Camping
AUTOMOBILE CLUBS
    See also
    American Automobile Association
    Sports Car Club of America
Best deals in auto clubs. E. Henry. il *Changing Times* 43:41-4 F '89
AUTOMOBILE COVERS *See* Automobiles—Equipment
AUTOMOBILE DEALERS
    See also
    Black automobile dealers
    Hendrick Management Corporation
    Longo Toyota (Firm)
    Southeast Toyota Distributors
For Rolls-Royce owners across America, all roads lead to Zionsville, Indiana [H. Albers] il por *People Weekly* 31:117 Ap 17 '89
    Advertising
Car ads: low-interest loans and other offers. il *Consumers' Research Magazine* 72:16-17 Je '89
How do you build a luxury image? [Infiniti dealer R. Rosenthal and Lexus dealer J. Taylor] J. Flint. il pors *Forbes* 143:60-3 Ap 3 '89

    Anecdotes, facetiae, satire, etc.
Lube job. G. Schwartz. il *New York* 22:27 F 13 '89
Ten best dealers stories. A. St. Antoine. il *Car and Driver* 34:47-50 Ja '89
    Chain and franchise operations
    See also
    JM Family Enterprises Inc.
    Customer relations
Dealing with a car dealer shouldn't be so demeaning. J. B. Treece. il *Business Week* p83 Je 12 '89
    Finance
Gloom in the showroom. J. B. Treece. il *Business Week* p30-1 O 16 '89
AUTOMOBILE DRIVERS
    See also
    Aged automobile drivers
    Alcohol and automobile drivers
    Children as automobile drivers
    Drugs and automobile drivers
    Taxicab drivers
    Teenage automobile drivers
    Women automobile drivers
Stopped by the cops? Roadside advice for you and your kids. M. W. Clark. *Better Homes and Gardens* 67:148 D '89
    Anecdotes, facetiae, satire, etc.
Be a nerd . . . in the privacy of your own car. W. Jeanes. il *Car and Driver* 35:3 O '89
He drives me crazy. M. Haskell. il *The New York Times Magazine* p26+ S 24 '89
    Licenses
No pass, no drive [requiring school attendance for driver's license] J. Rachlin and J. P. Shapiro. il *U.S. News & World Report* 106:49-51 Je 5 '89
The quick fix or a lasting solution? [requiring school attendance for obtaining driver's license] C. Pipho. il *Phi Delta Kappan* 70:502-3 Mr '89
    Anecdotes, facetiae, satire, etc.
License to manhood. P. Theroux. il *Parents* 64:52+ Ja '89
    Psychology
    See also
    Fear of automobile driving
    Anecdotes, facetiae, satire, etc.
Power under my hood. B. Ehrenreich. il *Mother Jones* 14:7-8 My '89
    Stunt drivers
    See Automobile driving—Stunt driving
    Vision
    See Vision
AUTOMOBILE DRIVING
    See also
    Automobile drivers
    Automobile touring
    Automobiles—Speed
    Fear of automobile driving
    Traffic accidents
    Traffic congestion
    Truck driving
Are you a good driver? [quiz] A. Arnott. il *McCall's* 116:148 My '89
Defensive driving. A. Arnott. il *Essence* 19:94+ Mr '89
Driver's notebook. See issues of Motor Trend beginning January 1987
Safe summer driving tips. A. Arnott. *McCall's* 116:72 Ag '89
When a woman drives alone. S. Nelson. il *Reader's Digest* 134:157-60 Ap '89
    Animal hazards
Car/pool. A. Meyer. il *The Mother Earth News* 119:40+ S/O '89
Not tonight, deer [cars hitting deer] P. Bedard. il *Car and Driver* 34:22 F '89
When two worlds collide [cars hitting deer in New York State] D. J. Decker and K. M. Loconti. il *The Conservationist* 44:44-7 N/D '89
    International aspects
The dawn patrol [driving through cities at dawn] W. Jeanes. il *Car and Driver* 35:7 S '89
Itala 35/45: from China to Paris. Again. R. Hutton. il *Car and Driver* 34:38 Je '89
    Study and teaching
    See also
    Automobile driving simulators
    Automobile racing—Study and teaching
Can you drive? Are you sure? W. Jeanes. il *Car and Driver* 34:7 My '89
Quick studies [B. Bondurant's course for teenagers] B. Visnic. il pors *Car and Driver* 35:141-3 O '89
    Anecdotes, facetiae, satire, etc.
Driving ambition. B. Stepko. il *Seventeen* 48:56+ Mr '89
    Stunt driving
Fare's fare, but when cabdriver Chuck Hollom goes off the meter, criminals had better look out [San Francisco] W. Plummer. il pors *People Weekly* 32:97-8 S 25 '89
    Winter driving
A new look at an old snow job. W. Jeanes. il *Car and Driver* 34:5 Mr '89

AUTOMOBILE DRIVING—Winter driving—cont.

Simplifying your options [choosing a car for ski country driving] B. Glenne. il *Skiing* 42:50+ Ja '89

Street-smart winter driving. G. Witzenburg. il *Reader's Digest* 134:25-8 Ja '89

Winter driving. D. Chaikin. il *Home Mechanix* 85:68-9+ Ja '89

New York (State)

When two worlds collide [cars hitting deer] D. J. Decker and K. M. Loconti. il *The Conservationist* 44:44-7 N/D '89

Ontario
Anecdotes, facetiae, satire, etc.

Our man in Ontario [attempt to drive a Lada Samara from Ann Arbor, Mich., to Wyoming, N.Y., via Canada] M. Smith. il *Car and Driver* 34:101 Je '89

Western Europe

Notes from abroad. B. W. Yates. il *Car and Driver* 34:29 Je '89

AUTOMOBILE DRIVING SIMULATORS

Simulated experience. R. Ceppos. il *Car and Driver* 35:20 Jl '89

AUTOMOBILE DRIVING VIDEO GAMES *See* Video games

AUTOMOBILE EMISSION STANDARDS *See* Automobiles—Environmental aspects

AUTOMOBILE ENGINEERING

1990 import cars: technical highlights. N. Bissoon Dath. il *Car and Driver* 35:72+ N '89

Big is back—with a high-tech advantage. D. McCosh and B. Nadel. il *Popular Science* 235:62-6 O '89

Continental drift [European influence on American models] L. A. Ealey. il *House & Garden* 161:184-5 Ap '89

Driving into the next decade. B. A. Stertz and J. B. White. il *Consumers' Research Magazine* 72:17-19 S '89

The engineering story [1990 imports] il *Popular Mechanics* 166:103-6 D '89

Fine tuning [1990 models] il *Popular Mechanics* 166:71-5 O '89

GM/Hughes: vaulting into technology. M. Keller. il *Motor Trend* 41:117 Ja '89

The new 1990 American cars: good as the imports? D. Sherman. il *Popular Science* 235:57-61 O '89

The real Masters of the Universe [address, March 2, 1989] G. Greenwald. *Vital Speeches of the Day* 55:528-30 Je 15 '89

Surprising cars you'll drive tomorrow. E. Henry. il *Changing Times* 43:79-81+ O '89

Technical highlights [1990 cars] N. Bissoon Dath. il *Car and Driver* 35:54-6 O '89

Technologue. R. Grable. See issues of Motor Trend

When engineers don't [hands-on approach of Japanese engineers] A. Assenza. il *Car and Driver* 35:22 Ag '89

AUTOMOBILE ENGINES

See also
Automobiles, Racing—Engines
Diesel engines, Automotive
Gas turbines, Automotive

Physics 101, the hard way [attempt to install a Chevy V-8 engine in a Porsche 911] M. Anson. il *Motor Trend* 41:29 My '89

Air supply

See also
Automobile engines—Superchargers

Belts

One belt does it all [serpentine belt system] B. Markovich. il *Home Mechanix* 85:70 Ja '89

Camshafts

Variable valve timing. R. Grable. il *Motor Trend* 41:121-2 Jl '89

Cooking use

Under the hood [food cooks on trip from Manhattan to the Bronx; work of C. Maynard and B. Scheller] *The New Yorker* 65:26-7 Ag 14 '89

Cooling

See also
Automobiles—Radiators

The 50% solution. B. Markovich. il *Home Mechanix* 85:22 S '89

Cooling system savvy. R. Freudenberger. il *The Mother Earth News* 117:50+ My/Je '89

Warm interior, warm engine. P. Weissler. il *Home Mechanix* 85:78-81 O '89

Your car's cooling system: what's wrong, and where. B. Cerullo. *Popular Science* 234:77 Ja '89

Cylinders

4-valves/cylinder. R. Taylor. *Motor Trend* 41:120-1 Ag '89

Design

See also
Paganelli & Company
PAS, Inc.

1990 import cars: technical highlights. N. Bissoon Dath. il *Car and Driver* 35:72+ N '89

A dozen motor factories—under one roof [Ford's flexible manufacturing plant in Romeo, Mich.] D. Woodruff. il *Business Week* p90+ N 20 '89

Engines for the millennium. D. Simanaitis. il *Road & Track* 40:114-15+ Jl '89

The flexible engine [variable stroke designed by J. Scalzo] S. F. Brown. il *Popular Science* 235:82-4 N '89

Honda's fire-breathing VTEC Integra. J. K. Yamaguchi. il *Road & Track* 40:161-2 Ag '89

Say, Smokey: what's the car engine of the future? [views of S. Yunick] il pors *Popular Science* 234:105-9+ Mr '89

Technical highlights [1990 cars] N. Bissoon Dath. il *Car and Driver* 35:54-6 O '89

V10. D. Sherman. il *Popular Science* 234:122-3 Je '89

Yesterday, today [Chrysler's V6] D. McCosh. il *Popular Science* 235:14 Ag '89

Detonation

Knocking out engine knocks. P. Stenquist. il *Popular Mechanics* 166:113-16 F '89

Ping pong. C. Maxwell. il *The Family Handyman* 39:100 Ap '89

Energy usage

Bush won't get any mileage from this auto compromise [Corporate Average Fuel Economy standards] R. Fly. *Business Week* p43 My 15 '89

Bush's first big chance to score environmental points [Corporate Average Fuel Economy rules] S. Payne and V. Cahan. il *Business Week* p41 Ap 10 '89

CAFE days are here again. B. Nagy. il *Motor Trend* 41:118-19 S '89

The CAFE society. W. Jeanes. il *Car and Driver* 35:5 Jl '89

Comparing for economy: 1990 EPA mileage estimates. il *Consumers' Research Magazine* 72:20-6 N '89

Driving into the next decade. B. A. Stertz and J. B. White. il *Consumers' Research Magazine* 72:17-19 S '89

Environmental delusions. R. J. Samuelson. il *Newsweek* 113:45 My 29 '89

Free lunch [renting a high mileage Chevrolet Sprint] P. Egan. il *Road & Track* 40:28+ Ag '89

I take pen in hand . . . [upward revision of Corporate Average Fuel Economy standards] B. W. Yates. il *Car and Driver* 35:16 Ag '89

Japan will feast at the CAFE [stricter fuel efficiency standards] *U.S. News & World Report* 106:11 My 29 '89

Last chance CAFE [purpose of skipshift device in 1989 Corvette] J. R. Nerad. il *Motor Trend* 41:16-17 Ja '89

More CAFE. R. Coorsh. *Consumers' Research Magazine* 72:4 Jl '89

The road to fuel efficiency in the passenger vehicle fleet. S. E. Plotkin. bibl f il *Environment* 31:18-20+ Jl/Ag '89

Who's in charge here? [Corporate Average Fuel Economy] W. Jeanes. il *Car and Driver* 35:7 Ag '89

With friends like this . . . [American companies not allowed to count imports when figuring fuel efficiency] J. Flint. il *Forbes* 143:48 Je 26 '89

Environmental aspects

See Automobiles—Environmental aspects

Exhaust

See also
Automobiles—Environmental aspects

Fan belts

Emergency fan belts: too quick a fix. il *Consumer Reports* 54:491 Ag '89

Filters

Filter fitness [oil, air and fuel filters] B. Markovich. il *Home Mechanix* 85:38 O '89

Replacing PCV valves and filters. P. Brand. il *The Family Handyman* 39:84 O '89

Fuel

See also
Alcohol as fuel
Gasoline

Alternative fuels. D. Simanaitis. il *Road & Track* 41:72-3+ N '89

The any-fuel engine. D. McCosh. il *Popular Science* 234:73+ F '89

Bumpy road ahead for gas guzzlers [alternative fuels] il *U.S. News & World Report* 107:16+ Ag 28-S 4 '89

The bumpy road to 'clean fuels' [methanol] il *U.S. News & World Report* 106:10-11 Je 26 '89

The case for methanol. C. L. Gray and J. A. Alson. bibl il *Scientific American* 261:108-14 N '89

Coalaholics [methanol-powered cars from Chevrolet, Ford and Chrysler] M. Allen. il *Popular Mechanics* 166:60-2 N '89

Fill'er up with methyl. G. Cowley. il *Newsweek* 113:67 My 1 '89

Fuel fantasies [alternative fuels for cars] J. Flint. il *Forbes* 143:66-7 My 29 '89

Fuel for thought. T. Beardsley. *Scientific American* 261:20 D '89

Fuels in your future. M. Knepper. il *Popular Mechanics* 166:55-7 N '89

Gasoline: the unclean fuel? E. Marshall. il *Science* 246:199-201 O 13 '89

The methanol car in your future. A. Kupfer. il *Fortune* 120:71+ S 25 '89

Methanol may be clean, but it's a dirty word to big oil. M. Ivey. il *Business Week* p106 S 4 '89

AUTOMOBILE ENGINES—*cont.*

Fuel consumption

See Automobile engines—Energy usage

Fuel feeding

The any-fuel engine. D. McCosh. il *Popular Science* 234:73+ F '89

Painless injection. B. Markovich. il *Home Mechanix* 85:24+ N '89

Hoses

Emergency hose repairs. il *The Family Handyman* 39:78 Jl/Ag '89

Finding vacuum leaks. M. J. Schultz. il *Popular Mechanics* 166:107-10 S '89

Lubrication and lubricants

See Automobiles—Lubrication and lubricants

Manifolds

Finding vacuum leaks. M. J. Schultz. il *Popular Mechanics* 166:107-10 S '89

Mufflers

Brake & muffler shops. il *Consumer Reports* 54:138-42 D '89

Getting your brakes and muffler fixed. il *Consumer Reports* 54:528-33 Ag '89

Starting

See Automobiles—Starting

Superchargers

See also

Automobiles, Racing—Engines—Superchargers

20th anniversary Pontiac Trans Am. C. Csere. il *Car and Driver* 34:106-9+ Je '89

'89 Mercury Cougar XR7. D. C. Ross. il *Motor Trend* 41:46-50 Ja '89

1989 Car of the Year [Ford Thunderbird SC; cover story] il *Motor Trend* 41:48-56+ F '89

Bang for the buck! [top 10 performance coupes] J. Karr. il *Motor Trend* 41:42-6+ N '89

Bentley Turbo R. P. Bingham. il *Motor Trend* 41:97-100 F '89

Buick future cars. D. McCosh. il *Popular Science* 235:17-18 Jl '89

Callaway Twin-Turbo Corvette [cover story] R. Ceppos. il *Car and Driver* 34:50-3+ My '89

Chrysler LeBaron GTC. B. Visnic. il *Car and Driver* 35:121+ Jl '89

Chrysler's TC by Maserati. il *Road & Track* 40:100-2+ Je '89

Chrysler's TC by Maserati. J. Karr. il *Motor Trend* 41:120-2+ Ap '89

Coupes [Acura Legend, Buick Regal, Cutlass Supreme, Thunderbird Super Coupe] D. McCosh. il *Popular Science* 234:42-4+ Ja '89

Dodge Daytona CS. D. C. Ross. il *Motor Trend* 41:67-8+ Ag '89

Dodge Daytona Shelby. J. Phillips, III. il *Car and Driver* 35:83-4 O '89

Eagle Talon TSi AWD. L. Griffin. il *Car and Driver* 35:102-6+ Jl '89

Evolution IROC II [Chevrolet/Motor trend development of car based on the Camaro] D. C. Ross. il *Motor Trend* 41:64-8+ D '89

Fast-track sedans [Audi 200, BMW535i, Ford Taurus SHO, Nissan Maxima SE] D. Sherman. il *Popular Science* 234:28-30+ Mr '89

Ferrari Mondial T. P. Frère. il *Road & Track* 40:176-7 Jl '89

Flat-out fastest American cars II, the sequel [Chevy Camaro IROC-Z and Corvette, Ford Mustang LX and Taurus SHO, Olds Cutlass Calais Quad 4 H.O., Plymouth Laser RS, Dodge Shelby CSX, and Pontiac McLaren Turbo and Trans Am; cover story] R. Grable. il *Motor Trend* 41:42-7+ Je '89

Ford Thunderbird Super Coupe. R. Ceppos. il *Car and Driver* 34:59-61+ Mr '89

French impressions [CxAuto Citroën CX 25 GTI Turbo] T. C. Browne. il *Road & Track* 40:69-70+ Ag '89

Honda Legend V6Ti. Y. Ishiwatari. il *Car and Driver* 34:30 Mr '89

Ital Design Aztec. R. Hutton. il *Car and Driver* 34:87-8 Mr '89

Koenig Competition Cabrio. J. Lamm. il *Road & Track* 40:96-7+ My '89

Lancia Delta HF Integrale 16V. R. Hutton. il *Car and Driver* 35:29 Ag '89

Lancia Delta HG Integrale 16V. P. Frère. il *Road & Track* 41:159-60 O '89

Long-term test: Oldsmobile Calais, Mazda 626 4WS Turbo, Buick Regal Custom. il *Popular Mechanics* 166:48+ Ja '89

Lotus Esprit Turbo. il *Road & Track* 40:72-4+ My '89

Lotus Esprit Turbo SE. il *Road & Track* 41:142-3+ N '89

Lotus Esprit Turbo SE. J. Karr. il *Motor Trend* 41:64-8+ Jl '89

Lotus Esprit Turbo SE. J. Phillips, III. il *Car and Driver* 35:86-7+ D '89

Maserati 430. il *Road & Track* 40:84-6 F '89

Mazda 323 GTX. J. Miller. il *Motor Trend* 41:106+ Mr '89

Mazda MX-6 4WS. B. Nagy. il *Motor Trend* 41:100-2+ Ap '89

Mazda RX-7s [RX-7 Turbo II and RX-7 Convertible] J. R. Nerad. il *Motor Trend* 41:96-9+ Ag '89

Mercury Cougar XR7. J. Lamm. il *Road & Track* 40:100 Jl '89

Miata mania [Millen Turbo MX-5 version; cover story] R. Homan. il *Road & Track* 41:52-9 N '89

Mitsubishi Eclipse GSX. il *Road & Track* 40:50-3 Ag '89

Mitsubishi Eclipse GSX & Eagle Talon TSi. D. Fuller. il *Motor Trend* 41:80-2+ Jl '89

Mitsubishi Mirage Turbo. A. St. Antoine. il *Car and Driver* 35:91-3+ Ag '89

MVS Venturi. P. Bedard. il *Car and Driver* 34:85-7+ My '89

MVS Venturi: *oui*, wheee! P. Frère. il *Road & Track* 40:126-30 My '89

Nissan 300ZX Turbo. il *Road & Track* 41:68-9+ D '89

Nissan 300ZX Turbo. C. Csere. il *Car and Driver* 35:46-9+ N '89

Nissan 300ZX Twin Turbo. J. Karr. il *Motor Trend* 41:126-8+ N '89

Nissan March Super Turbo. Y. Ishiwatari. il *Car and Driver* 35:32-3 S '89

Nissan Skyline GTS-t. Y. Ishiwatari. il *Car and Driver* 35:28-9 O '89

Peugeot Oxia. G. Perini. il *Car and Driver* 35:28 S '89

Pontiac 20th-Anniversary Trans Am. R. Grable. il *Motor Trend* 41:50-2+ Mr '89

Pontiac Grand Prix STE Turbo. P. Berg. il *Car and Driver* 35:40-4 O '89

Pontiac McLaren Turbo Grand Prix. il *Road & Track* 40:110-13 Ap '89

Pontiac Turbo Grand Prix. J. Miller. il *Motor Trend* 41:54-6+ Ag '89

Pontiac Turbo Trans Am. il *Road & Track* 40:92-4 Ja '89

Porsche 959. P. Bingham. il *Motor Trend* 41:74-9+ Ja '89

Porsches in Provence [Carrera 4, 944 S2 and 911 Turbo; cover story] il *Road & Track* 40:42-53 F '89

Power coupes [Isuzu Impulse Turbo GT, Mitsubishi Eclipse, Mustang GT, Plymouth Laser] D. McCosh. il *Popular Science* 234:28-9+ Ap '89

Rat racer reborn [A-T Engineering Honda CRX Si Turbo] T. West. il *Road & Track* 40:74+ Jl '89

Saab 900 Turbo. A. Assenza. il *Car and Driver* 34:59 F '89

Saab 9000 CD Turbo. J. Miller. il *Motor Trend* 41:101-3+ F '89

Saab 9000 Talladega. R. Hutton. il *Car and Driver* 35:33 Jl '89

Shelby CSX. il *Road & Track* 40:88-9+ Jl '89

Shelby CSX. C. Csere. il *Car and Driver* 34:89-91+ Ap '89

Shelby CSX. J. Karr. il *Motor Trend* 41:160-2+ My '89

Sizzling performance—without sticker shock [Plymouth Turbo Laser, Nissan 240SX and Mitsubishi Eclipse] S. Toy and W. J. Hampton. il *Business Week* p105 F 6 '89

Subaru Rex Combi Super Charger ECVT. D. Simanaitis. il *Road & Track* 40:70 Mr '89

Supes are super. D. Simanaitis. il *Road & Track* 40:115+ F '89

Toyota Celica All-Trac Turbo. P. Berg. il *Car and Driver* 35:54-6+ N '89

Toyota Supra Turbo. il *Road & Track* 40:68-70 F '89

Toyota Supra Turbo. B. Visnic. il *Car and Driver* 34:140-1 Ap '89

Tracking the Orient Express [Bentley Turbo R races the Orient Express from Venice to Paris] W. Jeanes. il *Car and Driver* 34:104-9 Mr '89

Turbo to go [1989 and 1987 Shelby CSX] D. McCosh. il *Popular Science* 235:28-30+ Ag '89

Two-seat heat [Nissan 300ZX, Mazda RX-7 and Porsche 944 S2] D. Sherman. il *Popular Science* 235:38-40+ S '89

Two times four equals great [Ford Mustang and Probe, Honda Prelude, Mazda MX-6, Mitsubishi Eclipse Turbo, Nissan 240SX, Subaru XT6 and Toyota Celica GT-S; cover story] C. Csere. il *Car and Driver* 35:36-9+ Jl '89

Volkswagen Corrado. P. Bedard. il *Car and Driver* 35:125-7+ N '89

Volkswagen Corrado. J. R. Nerad. il *Motor Trend* 41:110-12 Mr '89

Volkswagen Corrado G60. il *Road & Track* 41:66-70 N '89

Volkswagen Corrado G60. C. Csere. il *Car and Driver* 34:119-22+ Ja '89

Volvo 740 Turbo. R. Homan. il *Road & Track* 40:123 Mr '89

Valves

4-valves/cylinder. R. Taylor. *Motor Trend* 41:120-1 Ag '89

Replacing PCV valves and filters. P. Brand. il *The Family Handyman* 39:84 O '89

Technical highlights [Infiniti Q45's variable valve timing] N. Bissoon Dath. il *Car and Driver* 35:63 S '89

Variable valve timing. R. Grable. il *Motor Trend* 41:121-2 Jl '89

AUTOMOBILE EQUIPMENT See Automobiles—Equipment
AUTOMOBILE EQUIPMENT INDUSTRY
   See also
   A. O. Smith Corp.
   Acustar Inc.
   Arvin Industries, Inc.
   Eaton Corporation
   Johnson Controls Inc.
   Ohio Crankshaft (Firm)
   SPX (Firm)
The changing distribution of U.S. motor vehicle parts sup-
   pliers. J. M. Rubenstein. il maps *Focus (New York, N.Y.:
   1950)* 38:10-14+ Wint '88
                Acquisitions and mergers
Few is more. K. L. Fisher. il *Forbes* 143:406 My 1 '89
A poison-pill play that may pay off [SPX] G. G. Marcial.
   Business Week p86 Ja 23 '89
                International aspects
Beware the gaijin raider. *Newsweek* 113:48 Ap 17 '89
Boone Pickens, samurai warrior [bid for Koito Manufacturing]
   M. Ivey. il por *Business Week* p90+ My 8 '89
Kamikaze capitalism [T. B. Pickens buys into Koito Manufac-
   turing] M. Lewis. *The New Republic* 200:19-20 My 1 '89
T. Boone's declaration of yen-dependence [bid for seat on
   the board of Koito Manufacturing] M. Tharp. il por *U.S.
   News & World Report* 106:51 My 1 '89
A Texas raider rocks Club Japan [T. B. Pickens buys into
   Koito Manufacturing] *U.S. News & World Report* 106:15
   Ap 17 '89
                Export-import trade
When U.S. joint ventures with Japan go sour [auto parts]
   S. Phillips. il *Business Week* p30-1 Jl 24 '89
                Finance
Automotive. J. Flint. il *Forbes* 143:90-2 Ja 9 '89
Unlevel playing field. N. Alster. il *Forbes* 143:53+ Je 26
   '89
                Management
Maintaining competitiveness [address, January 19, 1989] R.
   D. Tuttle. *Vital Speeches of the Day* 55:598-600 Jl 15
   '89
                Securities
Few is more. K. L. Fisher. il *Forbes* 143:406 My 1 '89
Parts is parts, but those for autos should sell steadily. il
   Money 18:8 Ja '89
                Canada
   See also
   Magna International Inc.
                Japan
Unlevel playing field. N. Alster. il *Forbes* 143:53+ Je 26
   '89
When U.S. joint ventures with Japan go sour [auto parts]
   S. Phillips. il *Business Week* p30-1 Jl 24 '89
AUTOMOBILE EQUIPMENT STORES
                Management
Productivity in the retail auto and home supply store industry.
   P. S. Wilder. bibl f il *Monthly Labor Review* 112:36-40
   Ag '89
AUTOMOBILE FACTORIES
Three plants, three futures. L. Turner. il *Technology Review*
   92:38-45 Ja '89
                Automation
A dozen motor factories—under one roof [Ford's flexible
   manufacturing plant in Romeo, Mich.] D. Woodruff. il
   Business Week p90+ N 20 '89
A factory that practically runs itself [Lansdale, Pa. Ford
   plant] il por *Business Week* p145 My 8 '89
                Employees
   See Automobile industry workers
                Environmental aspects
Lethal Lordstown: workers fight poison at a GM plant.
   J. Slaughter. il *The Progressive* 53:28-9+ Mr '89
                Location
The changing distribution of U.S. motor vehicle parts sup-
   pliers. J. M. Rubenstein. il maps *Focus (New York, N.Y.:
   1950)* 38:10-14+ Wint '88
                Germany (West)
Industrial chic [BMW plant in Regensburg] W. Baldwin.
   il *Forbes* 144:96 N 27 '89
                Sweden
Volvo's back-to-the-future factory [Uddevalla plant] D. Bartal.
   il *U.S. News & World Report* 107:42 Ag 21 '89
Volvo's radical new plant: 'the death of the assembly line'?
   J. Kapstein. il *Business Week* p92-3 Ag 28 '89
AUTOMOBILE FILTERS See Automobile engines—Filters
AUTOMOBILE HEADLIGHTS See Automobiles—Lighting
AUTOMOBILE INDUSTRY
   See also
   American Motors Corp.
   Automobile dealers
   Automobile factories
   Black automobile dealers
   Blacks in the automobile industry
   Buick Motor Division
   Cadillac Motor Car Division
   Chevrolet Motor Division
   Chrysler Corp.
   Classic Motor Carriages (Firm)
   Collective bargaining—Automobile industry

   Collective labor agreements—Automobile industry
   De Tomaso Industries, Inc.
   Diamond-Star Motors Corporation
   Ford Motor Co.
   General Motors Corp.
   New Avanti Motor Corporation
   Oldsmobile Division
   PAS, Inc.
   Saab-Scania of America, Inc.
   Saturn Corporation
   Subaru-Isuzu Automotive Inc.
   Subaru of America, Inc.
   Volkswagen of America Inc.
Detroit report. D. C. Ross. See issues of Motor Trend
For your information. See issues of Car and Driver
Inside Detroit. J. Dunne. See issues of Popular Mechanics
   beginning January 1986 through September 1989
                Acquisitions and mergers
Will the Big Three buy Chrysler? [Chrysler executives
   leveraging a buyout] il *Motor Trend* 41:29 O '89
                International aspects
A bid for upward mobility [Ford bids on Jaguar and Saab]
   A. Gabor. il *U.S. News & World Report* 107:46 O 2
   '89
Ford is kicking Saab's tires. R. A. Melcher. il *Business
   Week* p52 S 18 '89
Ford's sporty new number [acquisition of Jaguar] il *Time*
   134:83 N 13 '89
Have you driven a Jag, lately? [Ford buys Jaguar] D. Pauly.
   il *Newsweek* 114:64 N 13 '89
The hole in Ford's doughnut [pursuit of Jaguar and luxury
   model market] J. Flint. il *Forbes* 144:50+ N 13 '89
How Chrysler's $30,000 sports car got sideswiped [venture
   with Maserati] J. Rossant. il *Business Week* p68+ Ja 23
   '89
A Jaguar buyer may be in for a long, slow drive [GM
   or Ford] M. Maremont. il *Business Week* p48-9 N 13
   '89
The law of the jungle catches up with Jaguar [Ford's bid]
   R. A. Melcher. il *Business Week* p54 O 2 '89
Make love, not war. J. Flint. il *Forbes* 144:46+ O 2 '89
Would you pay $2 billion for a sick cat? [GM and Ford
   go after Jaguar] M. Maremont. il *Business Week* p58
   O 23 '89
                Advertising
Auto erotica. B. Lippert. il *Vogue* 179:430 Mr '89
Consider the urushi tree—is it not like a luxury car? [Hill
   Holliday's campaign for Nissan's Infiniti] L. Armstrong.
   il *Business Week* p84+ S 4 '89
Detroit tries to rev up [cover story] J. B. Treece and W.
   Zellner. il *Business Week* p78-82 Je 12 '89
Do not try these maneuvers [lack of proof supporting proposal
   that car advertising contributes to accidents] R. Ceppos.
   il *Car and Driver* 34:26-7 My '89
Eastern standard [ads for Infiniti] B. Kanner. il *New York*
   22:28+ S 25 '89
From here to Infiniti: Nissan's 'high concept' pitch. il
   Newsweek 114:38 S 25 '89
Infiniti's art of Pacific persuasion. K. R. Sheets. il *U.S.
   News & World Report* 107:67 N 13 '89
Murphy does $multimillion car commercials in Japan [Eddie
   Murphy] por *Jet* 77:36 O 23 '89
Singer Tina Turner completes Chrysler ads. il pors *Jet* 76:57
   S 18 '89
What price perfection? [Porsche] J. Levine. il *Forbes* 144:228-9
   O 30 '89
                Awards
   See also
   Motor Trend Awards
                Cooperation
Teaming up in Detroit [GM and Chrysler teamup] *Newsweek*
   114:59 O 16 '89
                Employees
   See Automobile industry workers
                Ethical aspects
The strange case of William Favre [intrigue surrounding
   Ferrari replica builder] B. W. Yates. il pors *Car and
   Driver* 35:77+ D '89
                Export-import trade
   See Automobiles—Export-import trade
                Finance
Automotive. J. Flint. il *Forbes* 143:90-2 Ja 9 '89
The coming car crunch. R. J. Samuelson. il *Newsweek* 114:62
   O 16 '89
Detroit hasn't downshifted fast enough. G. Koretz and J.
   B. Treece. il *Business Week* p24 D 4 '89
Detroit hits the brakes. K. R. Sheets. il *U.S. News & World
   Report* 107:50-1 D 4 '89
Detroit's blues are consumer gold. C. P. Work. il *U.S. News
   & World Report* 106:46-7 Ap 17 '89
Domestics reach decade's end. M. Keller. *Motor Trend* 41:146
   D '89
How a hard landing in Detroit will dent the economy.
   G. Koretz. il *Business Week* p16 Jl 17 '89
How Motown lost its big mo. S. C. Gwynne. il *Time* 134:34
   Jl 31 '89
Motor City madness. J. B. Treece. il *Business Week* p22-3
   Mr 6 '89

AUTOMOBILE INDUSTRY—Finance—*cont.*
Now carmakers are really burning rubber. J. B. Treece.
il *Business Week* p68-9 Ja 9 '89
Running low on gas. S. C. Gwynne. il *Time* 134:70-2 N
20 '89
Running scared. J. Flint. il *Forbes* 144:38-9 Ag 21 '89
A short skid would hardly put a dent in Detroit. J. B.
Treece. il *Business Week* p104 S 11 '89

History
Miscellaneous ramblings [1980s] T. L. Bryant. il *Road &
Track* 41:43-4 D '89
Tucker: a man and his car. M. Mueller. il pors *American
History Illustrated* 23:36-41 Ja '89

International aspects
See also
New United Motor Mfg., Inc.
Driving toward a world car? F. Washington and D. Pauly.
il *Newsweek* 113:48-9 My 1 '89
International report. See issues of Motor Trend
Universal Motors takes over. *World Press Review* 36:36-7
Ja '89
Will Detroit cut itself loose from 'captive' imports? J. B.
Treece. il *Business Week* p34 S 4 '89

Laws and regulations
See Automobiles—Laws and regulations

Management
At Toyota, rank loses its privileged titles. J. Impoco. il
U.S. News & World Report 107:40-1 Ag 21 '89
The auto industry enters the 1990s [special section] il
Technology Review 92:27-34+ Ja '89
For auto workers, it's team spirit vs. suspicion. W. Zellner.
il *Business Week* p60-1 Jl 10 '89
From the top [views of D. A. Fraser, R. A. Lutz, D. E.
Petersen, and R. C. Stempel] il pors *Car and Driver* 35:93-6+
O '89
GM and UAW: together again for the first time. M. Keller.
il *Motor Trend* 41:146 Ap '89
Help wanted, room to advance—out the door [American
managers quit at Mazda's U.S. plant] W. Zellner. il *Business
Week* p42 O 30 '89
How a top boss manages his day [R. A. Lutz of Chrysler]
A. L. Taylor, III. il pors *Fortune* 119:95-7+ Je 19 '89
Into the future of the management game. M. Keller. il *Motor
Trend* 41:130 Ag '89
Japan's gung-ho U.S. car plants. L. Kraar. il map *Fortune*
119:98-100+ Ja 30 '89
Mass production or messy production? W. Jeanes. il *Car
and Driver* 34:7 F '89
Of excellence and excitement. W. Jeanes. il *Car and Driver*
35:3 N '89
Shaking up Detroit: how Japanese carmakers are beating
the Big Three on their own turf [cover story] J. B. Treece.
il *Business Week* p74-80 Ag 14 '89
The UAW rebels teaming up against teamwork. W. Zellner.
il *Business Week* p110+ Mr 27 '89
Why U.S. carmakers are losing ground. A. L. Taylor. il
Fortune 120:96-7+ O 23 '89

Marketing
See also
Automobile dealers
Detroit tries to rev up [cover story] J. B. Treece and W.
Zellner. il *Business Week* p78-82 Je 12 '89
The Lumina has its brights off. J. B. Treece. il *Business
Week* p31 Ag 28 '89
Luxury cars: new leaders in an upscale upheaval. A. L.
Taylor, III. il *Fortune* 119:66-70+ Ap 10 '89
Motor City madness. J. B. Treece. il *Business Week* p22-3
Mr 6 '89
Putting on the clout [women automobile customers] M. Keller.
il *Motor Trend* 41:144 Mr '89
Shuttle consultancy [Chrysler hires L. Cutler as vice president
of consumer affairs] M. E. Kirk. il por *Forbes* 143:324
Ja 9 '89
Somebody's wrong [Japanese planning to increase production
at American plants without reducing imports] J. Flint.
il *Forbes* 144:118 S 18 '89

Quality control
Buy American? Are you sure we should do that? B. W.
Yates. il *Car and Driver* 35:14 D '89
Counterparts [using cars to judge quality in other products]
P. Egan. il *Road & Track* 40:26+ Ap '89
The new 1990 American cars: good as the imports? D.
Sherman. il *Popular Science* 235:57-61 O '89

Securities
The bulls build their case for buying the Big Three automakers.
P. Sellers. il *Fortune* 120:33-4 O 9 '89
Driving with a rearview mirror. M. Berss. il *Forbes*
144:114-16+ S 18 '89

Taxation
One company's taxes [General Motors] L. Saunders. *Forbes*
143:298 Ja 9 '89

China
Chinese cars. D. Abrahamson. il *Car and Driver* 34:30-1
Ap '89

France
See also
Peugeot SA
Renault (Regie Nationale des Usines Renault)

French supercars [Mondial de l'Automobile] D. McCosh.
il *Popular Science* 234:22+ Ja '89

Germany (West)
See also
Audi AG
Bayerische Motoren Werke AG
Daimler-Benz AG
Porsche AG
Infiniti and Lexus: characters in a German nightmare. J.
Templeman. il *Business Week* p64 O 9 '89

Great Britain
See also
Jaguar plc
Rover Group plc

Italy
See also
Fiat SpA
Officine Alfieri Maserati SpA
Paganelli & Company

Japan
See also
Honda Motor Co., Ltd.
Mazda Motor Corporation
Mitsubishi Motors Corp.
Nissan Motor Co. Ltd.
Toyota Motor Corporation
Japan thinks there's room for vroom in the U.S. [sports
cars] D. Woodruff. il *Business Week* p42 F 27 '89
Japan will feast at the CAFE [stricter fuel efficiency standards]
U.S. News & World Report 106:11 My 29 '89
Japanese carmakers flash their cash at the EC. T. Peterson
and A. Borrus. il *Business Week* p43+ F 13 '89
Japan's gung-ho U.S. car plants. L. Kraar. il map *Fortune*
119:98-100+ Ja 30 '89
Japan's new cars [Tokyo Motor Show] S. Solo. il *Fortune*
120:82-4+ D 4 '89
Miscellaneous ramblings [reaction of Daimler-Benz to
introduction of Japanese luxury cars] T. L. Bryant. il
Road & Track 41:37-8 S '89
Of excellence and excitement. W. Jeanes. il *Car and Driver*
35:3 N '89
Shaking up Detroit: how Japanese carmakers are beating
the Big Three on their own turf [cover story] J. B. Treece.
il *Business Week* p74-80 Ag 14 '89
Somebody's wrong [Japanese planning to increase production
at American plants without reducing imports] J. Flint.
il *Forbes* 144:118 S 18 '89
When engineers don't [hands-on approach of Japanese
engineers] A. Assenza. il *Car and Driver* 35:22 Ag '89
Why U.S. carmakers are losing ground. A. L. Taylor. il
Fortune 120:96-7+ O 23 '89
You know who is flooring it again [carmakers increase capital
spending] A. Borrus. il *Business Week* p66 O 9 '89

Korea (South)
See also
Daewoo Corporation

Mexico
A free-for-all for carmakers south of the border [easing of
Mexico's local content restrictions] S. Baker. il *Business
Week* p32 O 16 '89

Sweden
See also
Saab-Scania AB
Volvo AB

United States
See Automobile industry

Western Europe
See also
Ford of Europe Inc.
General Motors Europe AG
Agnelli on cars, greens, and Japan. R. I. Kirkland, Jr. il
pors *Fortune* 120:133+ Jl 31 '89
Detroit's Euro-boom. J. Marcom, Jr. il *Forbes* 143:38-9 Mr
20 '89
Don't tread on us—please [Ford and GM poised to be
winners in European car market] J. Flint. il *Forbes* 143:92
Je 12 '89

AUTOMOBILE INDUSTRY WORKERS
See also
Black automobile industry workers
Strikes—Automobile industry workers
United Automobile, Aerospace and Agricultural Imple-
ment Workers of America
I built a Buick [Buick Reatta Craft Centre] M. Allen. il
Popular Mechanics 166:62-4 F '89

Health and hygiene
See also
Workers Against Toxic Chemical Hazards

Salaries, pensions, etc.
1914 [H. Ford initiates five-dollar day for employees] A.
Nielsen. il *American Heritage* 40:38-40 F '89

Training
The bitter split in organized labor [multiskilling] il *Fortune*
119:66 F 13 '89
Constant improvement? Or speedup? [Mazda's emphasis on
kaizen concept fosters union discontent at Michigan plant]
J. Flint. il *Forbes* 143:92+ Ap 17 '89

AUTOMOBILE INSURANCE *See* Insurance, Automobile

AUTOMOBILE JUNKYARDS
Rising from the wreckage [replacement parts from junkyards] M. Lamm. il *Road & Track* 41:86 O '89

AUTOMOBILE LAWS AND REGULATIONS *See* Automobiles—Laws and regulations

AUTOMOBILE LIGHTING *See* Automobiles—Lighting

AUTOMOBILE LOANS
See also
  Ford Motor Credit Co.
Car ads: low-interest loans and other offers. il *Consumers' Research Magazine* 72:16-17 Je '89
Cheap loans vs. rebates. J. Goldwasser. il *Changing Times* 43:53-4 Mr '89
Good rates for good risks. E. Henry. il *Changing Times* 43:47 My '89
Those high-profile low car loans. *Modern Maturity* 32:24 O/N '89

AUTOMOBILE MAGAZINE
Case of the purloined pix [photos of GM's Saturn] il *Time* 134:74 N 27 '89

AUTOMOBILE MANUALS *See* Automobiles—Handbooks, manuals, etc.

AUTOMOBILE MODELS
Control
Scale sensations [race car models] D. Kott. il *Road & Track* 40:150+ My '89

AUTOMOBILE MUSEUMS
See also
  Patrick Collection (Birmingham, England)

AUTOMOBILE OIL FILTERS *See* Automobile engines—Filters

AUTOMOBILE OWNERSHIP
See also
  Automobiles—Purchasing
Connecting the dots [neighborhood cars] P. Egan. il *Road & Track* 41:20+ O '89
Don't look back [1964 Corvair] A. Finder. il *Gentlemen's Quarterly* 59:45+ My '89
Driving passions. K. D. Thompson. il *Black Enterprise* 20:89-90 N '89
Kin ship ['82 Honda Civic] J. Sedgwick. il *Gentlemen's Quarterly* 59:48+ Ag '89
My affair with fantasy [1974 MGB] M. Norman. il *Gentlemen's Quarterly* 59:61+ Mr '89
The painful end of a secret affair [car owned for twelve years] A. Fotheringham. il *Maclean's* 102:52 Ag 21 '89
Remembrances of cars past. J. R. Nerad. il *Motor Trend* 41:10 F '89
Sudden conversions [MG TC buffs] P. Egan. il *Road & Track* 41:26+ D '89
Which cars do consumers like most? il *Consumers' Research Magazine* 72:13-15 N '89
Who likes their cars? il *Consumers' Research Magazine* 72:24 F '89
Would you buy that car again? il *Consumer Reports* 54:240-1 Ap '89
Year of shame [1962 Rambler station wagon owned by author as a teenager] E. Serotta. il *Road & Track* 40:68-70 Ja '89

AUTOMOBILE PAINTING *See* Automobiles—Painting

AUTOMOBILE PARKING
See also
  Chuck's Parking (Firm)
  Garages
Anecdotes, facetiae, satire, etc.
Confessions of a valet parking attendant. B. J. Hoffman. il *Motor Trend* 41:204-5 My '89
A ridiculous addiction [obsession with good parking spots] G. Owens. por *Newsweek* 114:7 D 4 '89

AUTOMOBILE PARTS
See also
  Automobile junkyards
Boxes of treasure [old parts] P. Egan. il *Road & Track* 40:20+ Mr '89
Rising from the wreckage [replacement parts from junkyards] M. Lamm. il *Road & Track* 41:86 O '89
Prices
The war over bent fenders [high priced auto parts] il *Consumer Reports* 54:201 Ap '89

AUTOMOBILE PARTS INDUSTRY *See* Automobile equipment industry

AUTOMOBILE RACE TRACKS *See* Speedways

AUTOMOBILE RACING
See also
  Automobile racing drivers
  Automobile rallies
  Automobiles, Racing
  Championship Auto Racing Teams (Organization)
  Drag racing
  International Motor Sports Association
  Midget automobile racing
  Speedways
About the sport. J. Rusz. *See* issues of Road & Track
About time, fella [D. Waltrip wins Daytona 500] S. Moses. il por *Sports Illustrated* 70:46-7 F 27 '89
Birdman of Dawsonville [B. Elliott] L. Griffin. il pors *Car and Driver* 34:175-7+ Ap '89

Bump and run [A. Unser, Jr. wins Long Beach Grand Prix after rear-ending M. Andretti] S. Moses. il pors *Sports Illustrated* 70:33 Ap 24 '89
A bumper-car Indy. S. Moses. il *Sports Illustrated* 70:32-4+ Je 5 '89
The cars, the people, the money [Monterey races and Pebble Beach concours] T. C. Browne. il *Road & Track* 40:44-9 Ja '89
Close call for a millionaire [R. Wallace wins NASCAR title with 15th place finish in Atlanta Journal 500] S. Moses. il por *Sports Illustrated* 71:90-1 N 27 '89
Daytona's park-in [Jim Busby Porsche team wins 24 Hours of Daytona] S. Moses. il *Sports Illustrated* 70:30-1 F 13 '89
Des Moines set to stage a street race [Greater Des Moines Grand Prix] T. Swan. il map *Popular Mechanics* 166:44 Je '89
Dirty driving [R. Wallace in the Daytona 500] T. Gabriel. il pors *Rolling Stone* p68-70+ Ag 10 '89
"Gentlemen, start your engines . . ." [Indy 500 preview] R. Miller. il *Sport (New York, N.Y.)* 80:60-2+ Je '89
Japan race project on track [Indianapolis 500] il *The Saturday Evening Post* 261:46-7 N/D '89
Just desert [A. Prost wins United States Grand Prix at Phoenix] R. Walker. il *Road & Track* 41:82-5 S '89
Life on a small but fast track [Holland (N.Y.) International Speedway] J. McCallum. il pors *Sports Illustrated* 71:58+ Ag 14 '89
A long day at Nelson Ledges. T. Swan. il *Popular Mechanics* 166:36-7 O '89
Miscellaneous ramblings [vintage race scheduled for the Ford GT40] T. L. Bryant. il *Road & Track* 40:35 My '89
Motor sports: racing through 1988. W. Jeanes. il *Sports Illustrated* 70:37+ F 13 '89
Motorsport. *See* issues of Motor Trend
One bright day in May [E. Fittipaldi wins Indianapolis 500] T. West. il por *Road & Track* 41:96-7+ S '89
One family's mountain [R. Unser wins Pikes Peak Auto Hill climb] S. Moses. il por *Sports Illustrated* 71:22-3 Jl 17 '89
Persistence of vision [regular drivers at Road Atlanta] P. Egan. il *Road & Track* 40:104-6+ F '89
Porsche redux [24 Hours of Daytona] J. Rusz. il *Road & Track* 40:154+ My '89
The races [Aston Martin tribute at Monterey Historic Automobile Races] P. Egan. il *Road & Track* 41:82-5+ D '89
Racing is what they were built for [vintage racing] N. Santelmann. il *Forbes* 144:106+ Jl 10 '89
Red, white and blue racing [Corvette Challenge] T. Swan. il *Popular Mechanics* 166:38 F '89
Rocket Rick burns up the track [R. Mears earns Indy pole position] S. Moses. il por *Sports Illustrated* 70:69-70 My 22 '89
Sport. L. Griffin. *See* issues of Car and Driver
Time & place. *See* issues of Road & Track
Wheels of fortune [R. Wallace-B. Elliott NASCAR rivalry] K. Hannon. il pors *Sport (New York, N.Y.)* 80:72-4+ Mr '89

Economic aspects
See also
  Formula One Constructor's Association
Arms race on wheels [Grand Prix racing becomes corporate sport] R. Behar. il *Forbes* 143:60+ F 20 '89
Cosbys backing race car driver Willy T. Ribbs in championship auto racing. il pors *Jet* 77:16-17 D 4 '89
Fast cars and tough racing for fair money [Barber Saab Pro Series] D. Fuller. il *Motor Trend* 41:127-31 Ap '89
Fast lane for Phoenix [Iceberg U.S.A. Grand Prix] S. Moses. il *Sports Illustrated* 70:28-9 Je 12 '89
Indy oldie [D. Simon] J. Zweig. il por *Forbes* 143:178+ Je 12 '89
Money fuels the Honda wonder [Grand Prix racing] H. J. Steinbreder. il *Sports Illustrated* 71:58-9 Ag 21 '89
Porsche's racing plans. P. Frère. il *Road & Track* 40:163 F '89
The price of admission. J. Rusz. il *Road & Track* 40:114+ Ap '89
Rick Hendrick: man on the fast track. J. Ingram. il pors *Motor Trend* 41:116-19+ Ag '89
History
'80s racing. L. Franck. il *Sport (New York, N.Y.)* 80:85 O '89
Flying lady [E. Junek] B. Visnic. il pors *Car and Driver* 35:141-4+ Jl '89
Indy: families of the 500. P. Bedard. il *Sports Illustrated* 70:51+ My 8 '89
Miscellaneous ramblings [D. Seaman] T. L. Bryant. il *Road & Track* 41:47 N '89
Motorsport memories. B. Cahier and others. il *Motor Trend* 41:130-2+ My '89
A racer of the purest kind [J. Surtees] M. Nicks. il pors *Road & Track* 40:74-6+ Je '89
Ten best race teams in history. L. Griffin and O. Bolus. il *Car and Driver* 34:105-9 Ja '89
The trinity [Grand Prix drivers J. Stewart, P. Courage and J. Rindt] C. Fox. il pors *Car and Driver* 34:139-40+ Mr '89
Years ago. *See* issues of Road & Track

AUTOMOBILE RACING—cont.

International aspects

The 1988 Grand Prix season: setting records [title won by A. Senna for McLaren-Honda team] J. Thompson. il por *Road & Track* 40:126-7+ Ap '89

A farewell to Turbos: Formula One races into the new atmospheric age. B. Cahier and B. Nagy. il *Motor Trend* 41:110-12+ Jl '89

Original Senna [world driving champion] D. Phipps. il pors *Car and Driver* 34:125+ F '89

Prix view [1989 Formula 1 season preview] R. Walker. il *Road & Track* 40:162-4 Je '89

Photographs and photography

Speed work. L. Griffin. il *Car and Driver* 35:171+ N '89

Psychological aspects

Like a burning coal [urge to race cars] R. Ceppos. il *Car and Driver* 35:16 N '89

Study and teaching

Driving ambition [list of schools] J. Rusz. il *Road & Track* 40:98-9+ Mr '89

Race Car Handling Analysis Seminar. M. Anson. il *Motor Trend* 41:184 My '89

A school where you pass the test at 125 MPH [Skip Barber Racing School] E. Schine. il *Business Week* p108 Je 12 '89

Sports Car Club of America National Racing School. J. Karr. il *Motor Trend* 41:118-19+ O '89

Australia

Winners & losers [A. Senna wins Japanese Grand Prix and A. Prost wins Australian Grand Prix] I. Ireland. il por *Road & Track* 40:106-8+ Mr '89

Belgium

Splash & dash [A. Senna wins Belgian Grand Prix] I. Ireland. il *Road & Track* 41:132-5 D '89

Brazil

Red hot! [N. Mansell wins Brazilian Grand Prix] I. Ireland. il *Road & Track* 40:102-4+ Jl '89

The ultimate fast lane [Brazilian Grand Prix] S. McBride. il *Travel Holiday* 171:72-6 Mr '89

Canada

Boots 'n brollies [T. Boutsen wins Canadian Grand Prix] I. Ireland. il *Road & Track* 41:114-15+ O '89

Racing at Trembling Mountain with Terry and the Pirates [Rothmans-Porsche Turbo Cup] D. Fuller. il *Motor Trend* 41:123-6+ O '89

France

24 Heures du Mans. P. Bingham. il *Motor Trend* 41:132-5+ Je '89

The patient war [24 Hours of Le Mans] T. West. il *Road & Track* 41:56-60+ O '89

Textbook Prost [wins French Grand Prix] I. Ireland. il pors *Road & Track* 41:120-1+ O '89

History

Reims remembered. I. Ireland. il *Road & Track* 40:90-2+ Mr '89

Remembrance of things fast [Porsche 917s at Le Mans] H. L. Bergandi. il *Road & Track* 40:95-7 Je '89

Germany (West)

Deutsche treat [Group A touring car racing] J. Rusz. il *Road & Track* 40:78+ Ag '89

Senna's surprise [A. Senna wins German Grand Prix] I. Ireland. il pors *Road & Track* 41:120-2+ N '89

Great Britain

Alain alone [A. Prost wins British Grand Prix] R. Walker. il por *Road & Track* 41:112-13+ N '89

Hungary

Mansell the magician [Hungarian Grand Prix] I. Ireland. il *Road & Track* 41:124-5+ D '89

Italy

The 1989 Mille Miglia historic rally. W. Jeanes. il *Car and Driver* 35:99+ S '89

Encore, encore! [A. Senna wins San Marino Grand Prix] R. Walker. il pors *Road & Track* 40:108-10+ Ag '89

Mille Miglia '89. T. C. Browne. il *Road & Track* 41:52-6 S '89

New beginnings [G. Berger wins Italian Grand Prix, A. Prost wins Portuguese Grand Prix] R. Walker. il por *Road & Track* 40:110-11+ Ja '89

History

Targa Florio. B. Cahier. il *Motor Trend* 41:112-15+ Je '89

Japan

Winners & losers [A. Senna wins Japanese Grand Prix and A. Prost wins Australian Grand Prix] I. Ireland. il por *Road & Track* 40:106-8+ Mr '89

Mexico

Senna's single [wins Mexican Grand Prix] R. Walker. il por *Road & Track* 41:78-81 S '89

History

The Carrera Panamericana. T. Madigan. il *Motor Trend* 41:104-11 Ja '89

La Carrera Panamericana. J. R. Nerad. il map *Motor Trend* 41:72-6+ Jl '89

Monaco

Quibbles & bits [A. Senna wins Monaco Grand Prix] I. Ireland. il por *Road & Track* 40:114-16+ Ag '89

Portugal

New beginnings [G. Berger wins Italian Grand Prix, A. Prost wins Portuguese Grand Prix] R. Walker. il por *Road & Track* 40:110-11+ Ja '89

Spain

Down to the wire [A. Prost wins Spanish Grand Prix] R. Walker. il por *Road & Track* 40:126-8 F '89

United States

See Automobile racing

AUTOMOBILE RACING DRIVERS

See also

Andretti, Mario
Andretti, Michael
Berger, Gerhard
Boutsen, Thierry
Courage, Piers
Elliott, Bill
Fittipaldi, Emerson
Flaig, Dick
Hill, Eddie
Hurt, Bob
Lockhart, Frank
Mansell, Nigel
Mears, Rick
Miller, Ak
Prost, Alain
Ribbs, Willy T.
Rindt, Jochen, 1942-1970
Robinson, Shawna
Schwab, Gary
Seaman, Dick
Senna, Ayrton
Simon, Dick
Stewart, Jackie
Surtees, John
Unser, Al, Jr.
Wallace, Rusty
Waltrip, Darrell

Indy: families of the 500. P. Bedard. il *Sports Illustrated* 70:51+ My 8 '89

Motorsport. See issues of Motor Trend

Persistence of vision [regular drivers at Road Atlanta] P. Egan. il *Road & Track* 40:104-6+ F '89

Ten best race teams in history. L. Griffin and O. Bolus. il *Car and Driver* 34:105-9 Ja '89

Psychology

See Automobile racing—Psychological aspects

AUTOMOBILE RACING VIDEO GAMES *See* Video games
AUTOMOBILE RADIOS *See* Automobiles—Radio equipment

AUTOMOBILE RALLIES

History

Classy reunion [veterans of Cannonball runs] B. W. Yates. il *Car and Driver* 34:16-17 Ja '89

Mexico

La Carrera Panamericana. J. R. Nerad. il map *Motor Trend* 41:72-6+ Jl '89

AUTOMOBILE RENTING *See* Automobiles—Leasing and renting

AUTOMOBILE RESEARCH

See also

Automobiles, Experimental

AUTOMOBILE SALES PERSONNEL

See also

Automobile dealers

Productivity in the retail auto and home supply store industry. P. S. Wilder. bibl f il *Monthly Labor Review* 112:36-40 Ag '89

Training

Two days in boot camp—learning to love Lexus [Toyota] W. Zellner. il *Business Week* p87 S 4 '89

AUTOMOBILE SEARCHES *See* Searches and seizures

AUTOMOBILE SERVICE STATIONS

See also

AutoSpa Corporation
Jiffy Lube International Inc.
Truck service stations

Franchises under the hood. M. Whittemore. *Nation's Business* 77:54 S '89

It's not just a fill-up anymore—it's an event. M. Ivey. il *Business Week* p90+ Je 19 '89

Survivor's guide to quick lubes. E. Henry. il *Changing Times* 43:41-3+ Ap '89

Automation

Do-it-yourself gas pumps. J. Wilson. *High Technology Business* 9:10 Ap '89

AUTOMOBILE SHOWS *See* Automobiles—Exhibitions

AUTOMOBILE SPEED RECORDS

The glory and the dream [driver F. Lockhart dies attempting to set land speed record in 1928] J. A. Wren. il por *Road & Track* 40:106-7 My '89

King of the salt [D. Vesco] P. Lyons. il pors *Cycle* 40:48-51+ D '89

Rocket Oldsmobile [record for production car with front drive and 4-cylinder engine set at Bonneville] D. Fuller. il *Motor Trend* 41:126-7+ Mr '89

AUTOMOBILE STYLING *See* Automobiles—Design
AUTOMOBILE SUPPLIES *See* Automobiles—Equipment
AUTOMOBILE SUPPLY INDUSTRY *See* Automobile equipment industry
AUTOMOBILE TELEPHONES *See* Cellular radio in automobiles
AUTOMOBILE TIRES *See* Tires, Automobile
AUTOMOBILE TOOLS *See* Tools
AUTOMOBILE TOURING
   10 easy weekend drives. il *Glamour* 87:181-3 O '89
   All-American highways. R. Mears. il por maps *Popular Mechanics* 166:66-8+ My '89
   Crumbling highways and congested byways: can you steer clear? H. Gieseking. il *Travel Holiday* 172:12-13 Jl '89
   I-80. K. Emmons. il *Life* 12:96-102+ Fall '89
   Road tripping circa 2015. T. Blankenhorn. il *Road & Track* 40:54-6 My '89
   Vacationing in your car. *Consumers' Research Magazine* 72:18 Jl '89
      Arizona
   Curing the interstate blues. P. Berg. il *Car and Driver* 35:158 Ag '89
      Atlantic States
   Ferrari fun in the Florida sun [driving a Ferrari 328GTS from N.J. to Fla.] J. R. Nerad. il *Motor Trend* 41:70-2+ S '89
      California
   Gold country [in footsteps of Gold Rush ancestor] R. F. Snow. il *American Heritage* 40:30+ My/Je '89
   Hidden detours off Interstate 5. il map *Sunset (Central West edition)* 183:48+ S '89
   Holiday on Highway 1. B. Visnic. il *Car and Driver* 34:192 Ap '89
   A redwood "tunnel to the sea" [State Highway 128] il *Sunset (Central West edition)* 182:16+ My '89
   The road least traveled [Highway 1] D. M. Roth. il map *Travel Holiday* 172:62-3 O '89
   A road still good as gold [California 49] L. Griffin. il *Car and Driver* 34:154 Mr '89
   Where cowboys drive longhorns. And MR2s [Lion's Trail near Caliente] J. Phillips, III. il *Car and Driver* 35:168 D '89
      Florida
   Space available. L. Griffin. il *Car and Driver* 34:242 Je '89
      Florida Keys (Fla.)
   Romancing the Keys. M. Chabon. il *Vogue* 179:234-5+ D '89
      France
   The Champagne region. T. C. Browne. il map *Road & Track* 40:68-70+ Ap '89
   Porsches in Provence [Carrera 4, 944 S2 and 911 Turbo; cover story] il *Road & Track* 40:42-53 F '89
      Great Britain
   Britain's Derbyshire: heather and hedgerows. L. Griffin. il *Car and Driver* 34:196 My '89
      Great Lakes region
   Great Lakes and ghosts [touring in a Ford Bronco II] M. B. Lewis. il *Car and Driver* 34:187 Ja '89
      Italy
   Italian Lake District. D. Simanaitis. il map *Road & Track* 40:80+ My '89
      Kentucky
   Bluegrass. R. F. Snow. il *American Heritage* 40:26+ Ap '89
      Maui (Hawaii)
   Munchkin Maui the magnificent. L. Griffin. il *Car and Driver* 35:154 S '89
      Ohio
   Our secrets revealed. Well, some of them. L. Griffin. il *Car and Driver* 35:172 O '89
      Southern States
   Open road. *The New Yorker* 65:32-3 My 8 '89
      Texas
   The longest 28 miles. S. Bonassin. il *Southern Living* 24:66 Ag '89
      United States
   See Automobile touring
      Western Europe
   Alpine fling. B. W. Yates. il *Car and Driver* 35:158 Jl '89
      Wyoming
   Powder River country. O. M. Hall. il map *American Heritage* 40:43-51 Ap '89
AUTOMOBILE TRAFFIC *See* City traffic
AUTOMOBILE TRAILERS
      See also
   Automobile boat trailers
      Electric wiring
   Trailer wiring made easy; Troubleshooting trailer wiring. P. Brand. il *The Family Handyman* 39:70+ Mr '89
      Towing
   Picking the right hitch. S. L. White. il *Field & Stream* 94:114+ S '89
AUTOMOBILE TRIPS *See* Automobile touring
AUTOMOBILE WARRANTY *See* Warranty
AUTOMOBILE WHEELS *See* Automobiles—Wheels
AUTOMOBILE WINCHES *See* Winches
AUTOMOBILE WORKERS *See* Automobile industry workers; Black automobile industry workers

AUTOMOBILES
      See also
   Convertibles (Automobiles)
   Jeep automobiles
   Limousines
   Sports cars
   Station wagons
   Trucks
   The 10 best cars for cyclists [survey results] S. Martin. il *Bicycling* 30:40-2+ D '89
   The 1989 cars [cover story; special issue] il *Consumer Reports* 54:203-15+ Ap '89
   1990 new cars [cover story; special section] il *Car and Driver* 35:38-44+ O '89
   Automotive newsfront. D. McCosh. See issues of Popular Science beginning January 1986
   The Black enterprise 1990 auto guide [special section] il *Black Enterprise* 20:83+ N '89
   Buick Reatta [owners report] M. Lamm. il *Popular Mechanics* 166:48-9 D '89
   Cars for 1990. il *Ebony* 45:132-3+ N '89
   Detroit for 1990. K. Zino. il *Road & Track* 41:90-1+ O '89
   Detroit report. D. C. Ross. See issues of Motor Trend
   For your information. See issues of Car and Driver
   Freewheeling. See issues of Popular Mechanics beginning January 1986
   Garage. See issues of The Family Handyman beginning July/August 1987
   Motor trend's top 10 [cover story; special section; with editorial comment by Jack R. Nerad] il *Motor Trend* 41:8, 41-6+ N '89
   The new 1990s, from Acura to ZR-1. J. B. Treece. il *Business Week* p178-9 N 13 '89
   New car special report [cover story; special section] il *Consumers' Research Magazine* 72:11-29 N '89
   Owners reports [Ford Probe, Jaguar XJ6, Lincoln Continental and Cadillac Allanté] M. Lamm. il *Popular Mechanics* 166:74-7 Je '89
   Say, Smokey: what's the car engine of the future? [views of S. Yunick] il pors *Popular Science* 234:105-9+ Mr '89
   Ten best [cover story; special section] il *Car and Driver* 34:29-35+ Ja '89
   They're here! [1990 cars from Detroit] D. Chaikin. il *Home Mechanix* 85:104-8 N '89
   USA 1990 buyer's guide [cover story; special section] il *Motor Trend* 41:43-7+ O '89
      Acceleration
   Driver error! [sudden acceleration] P. Bedard. il *Car and Driver* 35:71-2+ Jl '89
   Miscellaneous ramblings [report on sudden acceleration issued by National Highway Traffic Safety Administration] T. L. Bryant. il *Road & Track* 40:35-6 Je '89
   NHTSA blames sudden acceleration on "pedal misapplication". il *Motor Trend* 41:34+ Je '89
   Sudden acceleration. J. W. Merline. il *Consumers' Research Magazine* 72:38 Je '89
      Accessories
   See Automobiles—Equipment
      Accidents
   See Traffic accidents
      Advertising
   See Automobile industry—Advertising
      Air bags
   Airbag armistice. T. Orme. *Motor Trend* 41:38-9 D '89
   The drive for safety. S. Shane. *Travel Holiday* 171:6 F '89
   Ford and Chrysler move to air bags. il *Consumer Reports* 54:209 Ap '89
   Hot air bags [Talley Industries] R. Addis. il *Forbes* 143:10 Mr 20 '89
   Proper restraint. M. Knepper. il *Home Mechanix* 85:72-3+ S '89
      Air conditioning
   Air conditioning system checkup. il *The Family Handyman* 39:97 Je '89
   Cooling out in your car [Freon substitute] W. J. Cook. il *U.S. News & World Report* 107:82 N 6 '89
   Try convertibles [ban on auto air conditioners that use CFCs in Vermont] *Time* 133:92 My 22 '89
      Airplane combinations
   See Aerocars
      Alarms
   These alarms do more than just scream. D. H. Dunn. il *Business Week* p104 Ag 21 '89
      Anecdotes, facetiae, satire, etc.
   Confessions of an automotive idiot. J. U. Bacon. il *Motor Trend* 41:128 Ag '89
   I have seen the future . . . W. Jeanes. il *Car and Driver* 34:5 Ja '89
      Audio systems
      See also
   Automobiles—Radio equipment
   The autophile. B. C. Fishkind. See issues of High Fidelity (New York, N.Y.) beginning March 1989 through July 1989
   Blaupunkt New York SCD-08 car tuner/CD player. R. Long. il *High Fidelity (New York, N.Y.)* 39:30-3 Jl '89

AUTOMOBILES—Audio systems—*cont.*
Car stereo. See occasional issues of Stereo Review
The evolution of car stereo. L. Klein. il *Radio-Electronics* 60:70-1 S '89
Fingertip control [touch-sensitive buttons] F. Vizard. il *Popular Mechanics* 166:50+ Jl '89
Hi-fi hits the road. W. Wolfe and M. Smolen. il *Stereo Review* 54:80-5 My '89
How to pick an autosound installer. B. C. Fishkind. il *High Fidelity (New York, N.Y.)* 39:33-5+ My '89
Pioneer DEH-66 car stereo receiver/CD player. R. Long. il *High Fidelity (New York, N.Y.)* 39:46+ Ja '89
Running on stereo. H. Fantel. il *Rolling Stone* p175 My 18 '89
Shake, rattle and roar [boom cars] C. Gorman. il *Time* 133:52 Mr 6 '89
Sony CDX-R77 car tuner/CD player. R. Long. il *High Fidelity (New York, N.Y.)* 39:33-5 Jl '89
Sound advice for the '90s [Sony Disc Jockey changer for cars] B. J. Hoffman. il *Motor Trend* 41:186 My '89
Sound shots. B. C. Fishkind. il *High Fidelity (New York, N.Y.)* 39:37-40 My '89
Stereo to go. K. C. Pohlmann. il *Stereo Review* 54:42 N '89
Traveling [cover story] K. C. Pohlmann. il *Stereo Review* 54:73-9 My '89
Wanted: car audio standards! J. D. Hirsch. il *Stereo Review* 54:34-5 F '89

Maintenance and repair
Sound advice. B. Markovich. il *Home Mechanix* 85:28 Ag '89

Awards
See also
Motor Trend Awards
Anecdotes, facetiae, satire, etc.
Ten best 1988 winners and losers. B. W. Yates. il *Car and Driver* 34:90-4 Ja '89

Batteries
See Storage batteries

Bibliography
Reviews. See issues of Road & Track

Bodies
Body dimensions. il *Consumer Reports* 54:268-70 Ap '89

Bodies, Remodeled
See Automobiles, Remodeled

Brakes
See Brakes, Automobile

Braking
See Automobiles—Stopping

Bumpers
With an instinct for the extinct, John Kearney brings back the dinosaurs—bumper-to-bumper. il por *People Weekly* 32:94 O 16 '89

Business use
See Automobiles in business

Camping equipment
See also
Automobile trailers

Care
See Automobiles—Maintenance and repair

Cleaning
See also
Hanna Car Wash Systems (Firm)
Auto polishes. il *Consumer Reports* 54:142-5 D '89
Car care. R. Taylor. See issues of Motor Trend beginning March 1989
Inviting interiors. B. Markovich. il *Home Mechanix* 85:12 Je '89
Restoring faded paint. P. Stenquist. il *Popular Mechanics* 166:145-8 Ap '89
Spring-cleaning for your car. E. Henry. *Changing Times* 43:101 My '89
Straight-stick Maytag. P. Bedard. il *Car and Driver* 35:18 Ag '89
These car washes clean even the inside of the gas cap [detailers] J. B. Treece. il *Business Week* p100 Ap 17 '89
Understanding car waxes. P. Brand and M. J. Schultz. il *The Family Handyman* 39:76-8 Jl/Ag '89

Clubs
See Automobile clubs

Collectors and collecting
Big ones that got away [previously owned cars that are now collector's items] P. Egan. il *Road & Track* 40:20+ My '89
Collecting old Mustangs. J. Heasley. il *Popular Mechanics* 166:46-7 Ag '89
Investments that really accelerate. R. Brandt. il *Business Week* p172 O 30 '89
Muscle fever. N. Santelmann. il *Forbes* 143:192-4 Mr 20 '89
Retrospect. T. C. Browne. See issues of Motor Trend beginning January 1988

Collisions with animals
See Automobile driving—Animal hazards

Corrosion and anticorrosives
Building a better body. J. Decker. il *Home Mechanix* 85:70-2+ My '89

Countering corrosion. B. Markovich. il *Home Mechanix* 86:32 Ap '89
Rust protection. A. T. Diaz. il *Better Homes and Gardens* 67:102-3 Ja '89

Cost of operation
The case for hanging on to your aging family car for 100,000 miles. R. J. Klein. il *Money* 18:165-6 Mr '89

Defects
See also
Automobiles—Recall
Car trouble. E. Henry. il *Changing Times* 43:63-4+ N '89
Life with a lemon. A. Assenza. il *Car and Driver* 35:25 O '89

Design
See also
Automobiles—Safety devices and measures
Automobiles, Foreign—Design
Automobiles, Racing—Design
Convertibles (Automobiles)—Design
Sports cars—Design
California Camaro. J. Lamm. il *Road & Track* 40:96-7+ Ap '89
Cars for a new decade. T. Swan and J. Dunne. il *Popular Mechanics* 166:63-70 O '89
Charting the changes [1990 models] B. Visnic. il *Car and Driver* 35:48-53 O '89
Continental drift [European influence on American models] L. A. Ealey. il *House & Garden* 161:184-5 Ap '89
Designs on tomorrow. T. Swan. il *Popular Mechanics* 166:35 Mr '89
Ford LTD Crown Vic, 1991. J. Dunne. il *Popular Mechanics* 166:24 F '89
Millennium Mustangs. J. Dunne. il *Popular Mechanics* 166:62-3 Ag '89
New graphics tools let designers see the future. il *Popular Mechanics* 166:15 D '89
Talk of the Town Car [Lincoln] P. Viladas. il *House & Garden* 161:232 S '89
Upwardly mobile [National Automobile Design Contest] D. Adcroft. il *Omni (New York, N.Y.)* 11:48-51 Mr '89

Doors
Jammed door latch fix. P. Brand. il *The Family Handyman* 39:73-4 N/D '89

Driving
See Automobile driving

Economic aspects
See also
Automobiles—Cost of operation
Automobiles—Purchasing

Electric equipment
Plug in power [accessories that can be used with car battery] B. Markovich. il *Home Mechanix* 85:74-6+ Je '89
See also
Automobiles—Navigation systems
Radar detectors

Electronic equipment
Computer aids steering [steer-by-wire system; work of Petros Ioannou] *USA Today (Periodical)* 117:10 Je '89
Working on the highway. J. Kluger. il *Discover* 10:34+ Ap '89

Emission standards
See Automobiles—Environmental aspects

Environmental aspects
Afield [special section] M. Mardon. il *Sierra* 74:22-8 My/Je '89
Bush Clean-Air plan: tough but doable. T. Orme. il *Motor Trend* 41:34-5 O '89
Can bicycles save the world? J. Bosveld. *Omni (New York, N.Y.)* 11:33 F '89
Cars and pollution: rethinking transportation. M. Renner. *Current (Washington, D.C.)* 313:32-40 Je '89
Clean Air isn't a clean deal. M. Keller. *Motor Trend* 41:154 N '89
Detroit's big worry for the 1990s: the greenhouse effect. D. Woodruff. il *Business Week* p103+ S 4 '89
Emissions making world "car sick" [views of Michael Renner] il *USA Today (Periodical)* 117:9 Je '89
Fuel additives offer solution to auto pollution. *High Technology Business* 9:30 Je '89
Gasoline: the unclean fuel? E. Marshall. il *Science* 246:199-201 O 13 '89
A (not quite) Clean Air Act [House subcommittee mandates stricter automobile emission standards] il *U.S. News & World Report* 107:23 O 16 '89
Pushing pedalers: bicycles may be the key to unlocking our traffic woes. M. D. Lowe. il *Utne Reader* p90-2 Mr/Ap '89
Report on reports: Air pollution, the automobile, and public health. R. Wilson. *Environment* 31:25-7 My '89
Rethinking the auto: blueprints for a cleaner, greener future. M. Renner. il *Utne Reader* p82-9 Mr/Ap '89
Rethinking the future of global transportation. M. Renner. il *USA Today (Periodical)* 118:23-6 S '89
Smart cars and smart policies [address, March 28, 1989] R. B. Smith. *Vital Speeches of the Day* 55:534-7 Je 15 '89
This is one game of chicken Detroit can't win [auto emissions] V. Cahan. *Business Week* p32 O 16 '89

AUTOMOBILES—Environmental aspects—*cont.*

To live and breathe in L.A. J. E. Basu. il maps *American Health* 8:52-4+ S '89

Tradeoff time. J. Flint. il *Forbes* 144:68+ D 11 '89

Transportation tomorrow. M. Renner. il por *The Futurist* 23:14-16+ Mr/Ap '89

Yearning to breathe free [stricter emission standards adopted by a House Energy and Commerce subcommittee] J. Greenwald. il *Time* 134:51-2 O 16 '89

Equipment

See also

Automobile equipment industry

Automobiles—Audio systems

Automobiles—Radio equipment

Automobiles—Safety devices and measures

Tires, Automobile

8 new products from the Auto Parts Show. il *Home Mechanix* 85:80-3 My '89

Car options: why you should kick the tires—hard. J. B. Treece. il *Business Week* p97 Jl 10 '89

The cover story. R. Taylor. il *Motor Trend* 41:146 N '89

From burlwood steering wheel to concert-quality stereo, the latest car accessories redefine the limits of luxury. D. Barry. il *Vogue* 179:250 D '89

Getting in gear. R. Ives. *Travel Holiday* 171:42-3 Mr '89

Goin' mobile [bicycle carriers] F. Zahradnik. il *Bicycling* 30:136-41 Jl '89

Helpful hardware. il *Home Mechanix* 85:86+ O '89

Mass production or messy production? W. Jeanes. il *Car and Driver* 34:7 F '89

New bike racks: designs for almost every vehicle. il *Sunset (Central West edition)* 183:66-8 O '89

Take it along [car-top carrier] L. Green. il *Home Mechanix* 86:90+ Mr '89

What to get for the car that has everything. S. Esters. il *Black Enterprise* 20:95-6 N '89

What's new: cars. See issues of Popular Science beginning February 1988

Which options to choose. il *Consumer Reports* 54:212-13 Ap '89

Exhibitions

1989 Frankfurt Motor Show. il *Car and Driver* 35:26 D '89

Auto-topia [Geneva Auto Show] T. C. Browne. il *Road & Track* 40:94-8 Jl '89

The battle of Paris. T. West. il *Road & Track* 40:53-5 Ja '89

Chicago Auto Show: all that glitters. T. West. il *Road & Track* 40:108+ My '89

The Concours [Pebble Beach Concours d'Elegance] B. Hall. il *Road & Track* 41:90-1 D '89

Detroit Auto Show. J. Keebler. il *Road & Track* 40:186-9 Ap '89

Dream today, drive tomorrow [North American International Auto Show] J. Dunne. il *Popular Mechanics* 166:69-72 Ap '89

French supercars [Mondial de l'Automobile] D. McCosh. il *Popular Science* 234:22+ Ja '89

Geneva '89: from Alfa to Omega. M. Cotton. il *Motor Trend* 41:18-19 Je '89

Geneva Auto Show. R. Hutton. il *Car and Driver* 34:42 Je '89

Japan's new cars [Tokyo Motor Show] S. Solo. il *Fortune* 120:82-4+ D 4 '89

Miscellaneous ramblings [Greater Los Angeles Auto Show] T. L. Bryant. il *Road & Track* 40:39-40 Ap '89

New American dreams [concept cars from the Detroit and Los Angeles auto shows] R. Ceppos and A. Assenza. il *Car and Driver* 34:65-71 Ap '89

New American realities [new production cars at the Detroit and Los Angeles auto shows] R. Ceppos. il *Car and Driver* 34:75-6 Ap '89

North American International Auto Show. D. C. Ross. il *Motor Trend* 41:20-1 Ap '89

Paris Auto Show. R. Hutton. il *Car and Driver* 34:24 Ja '89

Showstoppers: Detroit's high-tech cars for the '90s. D. McCosh. il *Popular Science* 234:108-10 Ap '89

Time & place. See issues of Road & Track

Export-import trade

See also

Jeep automobiles—Export-import trade

Can Audi start winning races in the showroom, too? [U.S. market] J. B. Treece and J. Templeman. il *Business Week* p47 My 29 '89

The coming traffic jam in the luxury lane [Toyota Lexus and Nissan Infiniti] W. Zellner. il *Business Week* p78 Ja 30 '89

A free-for-all for carmakers south of the border [easing of Mexico's local content restrictions] S. Baker. il *Business Week* p32 O 16 '89

Here come Japan's new luxury cars [Toyota's Lexus] A. L. Taylor, III. il *Fortune* 120:62-6 Ag 14 '89

Infiniti and Lexus: characters in a German nightmare. J. Templeman. il *Business Week* p64 O 9 '89

Japan thinks there's room for vroom in the U.S. [sports cars] D. Woodruff. il *Business Week* p42 F 27 '89

Japan will feast at the CAFE [stricter fuel efficiency standards] *U.S. News & World Report* 106:11 My 29 '89

Luxury cars: new leaders in an upscale upheaval. A. L. Taylor, III. il *Fortune* 119:66-70+ Ap 10 '89

Miscellaneous ramblings [reaction of Daimler-Benz to introduction of Japanese luxury cars] T. L. Bryant. il *Road & Track* 41:37-8 S '89

The road to Infiniti [W. Bruce, general manager of Nissan division] S. Kichen. il por *Forbes* 143:104 Ja 23 '89

Somebody's wrong [Japanese planning to increase production at American plants without reducing imports] J. Flint. il *Forbes* 144:118 S 18 '89

What's driving car prices up? il *Consumers' Research Magazine* 72:27-9 N '89

Will Detroit cut itself loose from 'captive' imports? J. B. Treece. il *Business Week* p34 S 4 '89

With friends like this . . . [American companies not allowed to count imports when figuring fuel efficiency] J. Flint. il *Forbes* 143:48 Je 26 '89

Anecdotes, facetiae, satire, etc.

Our man in Ontario [attempt to drive a Lada Samara from Ann Arbor, Mich., to Wyoming, N.Y., via Canada] M. Smith. il *Car and Driver* 34:101 Je '89

Four wheel drive

See also

Automobiles, Foreign—Four wheel drive

Jeep automobiles

Sports cars—Four wheel drive

4WD in demand. D. Sherman. *Skiing* 41:12+ F '89

Eagle Talon TSi AWD. L. Griffin. il *Car and Driver* 35:102-6+ Jl '89

Long-term test [Pontiac 6000 STE] il *Popular Mechanics* 166:120+ Je '89

Long-term update [Mazda MX-5 Miata and Eagle Talon TSi AWD] il *Road & Track* 41:109 N '89

Mitsubishi Eclipse GSX & Eagle Talon TSi. D. Fuller. il *Motor Trend* 41:80-2+ Jl '89

Pontiac 6000 STE AWD. D. Batchelor. il *Motor Trend* 41:89-93+ Jl '89

Front wheel drive

Evolutionary, not revolutionary [GM-10 line] J. Flint. il *Forbes* 143:43 My 1 '89

Fuel

See Automobile engines—Fuel

Fuel systems

See Automobile engines—Fuel feeding

Fuel tanks

See also

Kuhlman Corporation

Gas mileage

See Automobile engines—Energy usage

Gearing

See also

Automobiles—Steering gear

Handbooks, manuals, etc.

Video car repair. P. Brand. il *The Family Handyman* 39:72-3 Ja '89

Heating and ventilation

Warm interior, warm engine. P. Weissler. il *Home Mechanix* 85:78-81 O '89

History

See also

Automobiles, Antique

Automobiles, Racing—History

Convertibles (Automobiles)—History

Sports cars—History

50 years of Mercury [cover story] F. M. H. Gregory. il *Motor Trend* 41:40-5 Ja '89

Chrysler Turbine Car [1963 car] P. Bedard. il *Car and Driver* 34:147-9+ My '89

Fins de siècle [40th anniversary of the Cadillac Coupe De Ville] S. Loveday. il *Vogue* 179:264 F '89

Happy birthday Mustang! [25th anniversary; cover story; special section] il *Popular Mechanics* 166:56-74 Ag '89

Motor trend's 40th anniversary [cover story; special section] il *Motor Trend* 41:68-72+ My '89

Mustang moments. R. Ceppos. il *Car and Driver* 34:115+ Ap '89

Remembrances of cars past. J. R. Nerad. il *Motor Trend* 41:10 F '89

Retrospect. T. C. Browne. See issues of Motor Trend beginning January 1988

Ten best performance cars of all time. C. Csere. il *Car and Driver* 34:38-41+ Ja '89

Tucker: a man and his car. M. Mueller. il pors *American History Illustrated* 23:36-41 Ja '89

Years ago. See issues of Road & Track

Photographs and photography

Auto focus: cars and society. il *Popular Photography* 96:46-7 My '89

Classic cars. J. Zuckerman. il *Petersen's Photographic Magazine* 17:14-15+ Mr '89

Hubcaps

See also

Hubcap City (Firm)

AUTOMOBILES—cont.

Insurance

See Insurance, Automobile

Laws and regulations

See also

Automobiles—Environmental aspects

President's Select Committee on Automotive Regulation and Economics

Traffic regulations

The feds and your next car. *Changing Times* 43:82 O '89

We the geeks [comparing auto regulations with gun laws] P. Bedard. il *Car and Driver* 35:17 S '89

Leakage

Finding vacuum leaks. M. J. Schultz. il *Popular Mechanics* 166:107-10 S '89

Plugging power steering leaks. P. Stenquist. il *Popular Mechanics* 166:133-6 Je '89

Leasing and renting

See also

Automotive Answer, Inc.

Avis, Inc.

National Car Rental System, Inc.

$650 a day, 75 cents per mile [exotic cars] N. Santelmann. il *Forbes* 144:130-1 S 4 '89

Car-rental companies: the best and the worst. *Consumer Reports* 54:477-80 Jl '89

Free CDW insurance [credit card collision insurance on rentals] K. McCormally. il *Changing Times* 43:120 S '89

Free lunch [renting a high mileage Chevrolet Sprint] P. Egan. il *Road & Track* 40:28+ Ag '89

Good reasons to lease your next car. K. McCormally. il *Changing Times* 43:77-83 S '89

The lease frontier. P. A. Humphrey. il *Ms.* 18:38+ O '89

Leasing vs. buying a car. S. Nielsen. il *Good Housekeeping* 208:236 Ap '89

Leasing your wheels. J. B. Quinn. il *Newsweek* 112:65 My 22 '89

Leave the coverage to us [credit card collision insurance causes rental rates to rise] B. Rudolph. il *Time* 133:46 Ja 16 '89

New leases to lure you. E. Henry. il *Changing Times* 43:128 N '89

To buy or to lease a car? M. Rowland. il *Working Woman* 14:61-2+ Ja '89

When the payments never stop. J. Flint. il *Forbes* 143:148-9 Mr 6 '89

Who needs expensive coverage? [collision damage waiver on rentals] il *Consumer Reports* 54:478-9 Jl '89

Advertising

"Naaging" guidelines: keeping car-rental ads honest. il *Travel Holiday* 172:14-15 Jl '89

Shut up and show us your rates [proposed guidelines] G. Eichler. il *Esquire* 111:78 Je '89

Wheels of fortune [advertising by National] B. Kanner. il *New York* 22:14+ F 20 '89

Ethical aspects

The collision over collision waivers. A. Fins and C. Power. il *Business Week* p96+ My 1 '89

"Naaging" guidelines: keeping car-rental ads honest [eliminating collision damage waivers] il *Travel Holiday* 172:14-15 Jl '89

The truth about insurance you need (and don't need) in a rented car. E. Henry. il *Changing Times* 43:24 Ap '89

Your money: insurance for rental cars. E. N. Berg. *Modern Maturity* 32:29 Ap/My '89

Lighting

Adding a third brake light. il *The Family Handyman* 39:74 Ja '89

Out of the dark ages [headlights] J. Tomerlin. il *Road & Track* 41:102-3+ O '89

This bright idea could make GE a billion [high intensity discharge headlights] M. Mallory. il *Business Week* p120 D 4 '89

Lubrication and lubricants

See also

AutoSpa Corporation

Jiffy Lube International Inc.

Minit-Lube (Firm)

Motor oils. K. K. Gracey. *Consumers' Research Magazine* 72:2 Ja '89

Survivor's guide to quick lubes. E. Henry. il *Changing Times* 43:41-3+ Ap '89

Synthesizing oils is a slippery job. R. Pool. il *Science* 246:444-6 O 27 '89

Maintenance and repair

See also

Automobile service stations

Radio broadcasting—Automobile repair programs

12 tools for fixing your eighties car. M. Allen. il *Popular Mechanics* 166:65-7 S '89

Auto Q&A. P. Weissler. See issues of Home Mechanix beginning January 1985

Car care. R. Taylor. See issues of Motor Trend beginning March 1989

Car care made easy [Home mechanix Car of the Year awarded to Nissan Maxima; special section] il *Home Mechanix* 85:57-64+ My '89

Car-care quiz. S. Mercaldo. *Popular Science* 235:88+ Ag '89

Car-care quiz. S. Mercaldo. il *Popular Science* 234:148+ My '89

Car clinic. M. J. Schultz. See issues of Popular Mechanics

Dollar-saving car questions. R. Sikorsky. *Reader's Digest* 135:157-8+ Ag '89

Facts, not fables. E. Henry. il *Changing Times* 43:122 S '89

Fast fixes. See issues of The Family Handyman beginning January 1986

Fit & trim. P. Weissler. il *Home Mechanix* 85:60-2+ Ag '89

Frequency-of repair records, 1983-1988. il *Consumer Reports* 54:242-59 Ap '89

Frequency-of-repair records, 1983-1988. il *Consumer Reports* 54:174-211 D '89

Is your car ready for winter? [special section] il *Home Mechanix* 85:71-2+ O '89

The kindness of Druids. P. Egan. il *Road & Track* 40:20+ F '89

Nathalie & the MG [father and daughter repair 1974 MGB] G. Sidline. il *Good Housekeeping* 209:66+ S '89

Perfect plastic parts. B. Markovich. il *Home Mechanix* 85:24 Jl '89

Preparing your car for summer vacation. W. W. Watt. il *Consumers' Research Magazine* 72:13-17 Jl '89

Preventive maintenance. B. Markovich. See issues of Home Mechanix beginning September 1988

Roadside remedies. P. Weissler. il *Home Mechanix* 86:96-9 Mr '89

Saturday mechanic. See issues of Popular Mechanics

Say, Smokey. S. Yunick. See issues of Popular Science

Taking care of your car. S. Mercaldo. See issues of Popular Science through April 1989

Technologue. R. Grable. See issues of Motor Trend

Trust me, ignorance is bliss. J. Miller. il *Motor Trend* 41:120 O '89

Truth . . . or consequences. P. Weissler. il *Home Mechanix* 85:63-6+ Je '89

Tune-ups your car can live without. E. Henry. il *Changing Times* 43:57-60 Je '89

What's your auto IQ? [quiz] A. C. Mallozzi. il *Good Housekeeping* 209:166 Ag '89

Your auto: tuning it up for winter. A. M. Thompson. il *New Choices for the Best Years* 29:93-5 O '89

Materials

Perfect plastic parts. B. Markovich. il *Home Mechanix* 85:24 Jl '89

Names

Clone cars. T. Wilkinson. il *Home Mechanix* 85:70-3+ Je '89

Counterparts [using cars to judge quality in other products] P. Egan. il *Road & Track* 40:26+ Ap '89

Navigation systems

Brainy cars are on the way [views of Robert L. French] il *USA Today (Periodical)* 118:6 D '89

Cars that know where they're going [cover story] R. L. French. il por *The Futurist* 23:29-36 My/Je '89

Just what we need. Automatic roads [onboard navigation systems] B. W. Yates. il *Car and Driver* 34:19 F '89

Smart cars and smart policies [address, March 28, 1989] R. B. Smith. *Vital Speeches of the Day* 55:534-7 Je 15 '89

Smart highways. D. McCosh. il *Popular Science* 235:76-9+ N '89

Street smarts [Ali-Scout navigation system] W. Baldwin. il *Forbes* 144:298+ N 13 '89

Options

See Automobiles—Equipment

Ownership

See Automobile ownership

Painting

After-the-wash touch-up. R. Taylor. *Motor Trend* 41:123-5 Jl '89

If Leonardo had driven a Chevy, would The Last Supper have been the first meal on wheels? [artists in Seattle, Wash. paint original designs on cars] S. K. Reed. il *People Weekly* 32:57-9 Jl 31 '89

Scratch repair. P. Brand. il *The Family Handyman* 39:77 S '89

Parts

See Automobile parts

Periodicals

See also

Road & track (Periodical)

Photographs and photography

Auto focus [cover story] il *Popular Photography* 96:44-51 My '89

Mustang corral. R. Ceppos. il *Car and Driver* 34:125-6 Ap '89

Polishing

See Automobiles—Cleaning

Prices

1990 cars: how to buy a car you'll love [cover story; special section] il *Changing Times* 43:28-35+ D '89

Get 'em while they're cold. A. Assenza. il *Car and Driver* 35:19 D '89

AUTOMOBILES—cont.

Styling

See Automobiles—Design

Taxation

A tax on sin: the six-cylinder car. D. E. Koshland, Jr. Science 243:281 Ja 20 '89

Terminology

New-car lingo: a buyer's guide to today's technological wonders. M. Knepper. il Better Homes and Gardens 67:176 My '89

Rev up your auto vocabulary. A. Arnott. il McCall's 116:116 Ap '89

Testing

See also

Automobiles, Experimental—Testing
Automobiles, Foreign—Testing
Automobiles, Home-built—Testing
Automobiles, Remodeled—Testing
Automobiles, Three wheel—Testing
Automobiles, Used—Testing
Convertibles (Automobiles)—Testing
Sports cars—Testing

20th anniversary Pontiac Trans Am. C. Csere. il Car and Driver 34:106-9+ Je '89

'89 Mercury Cougar XR7. D. C. Ross. il Motor Trend 41:46-50 Ja '89

302 versus 302 [1970 Ford Mustang Boss 302 vs. 1989 Ford Mustang GT] P. Lyons. il Car and Driver 34:128-9+ Ap '89

1989 Car of the Year [Ford Thunderbird SC; cover story] il Motor Trend 41:48-56+ F '89

Affordable four-doors: perfect cars for young families. M. Knepper. il Better Homes and Gardens 67:187-8+ N '89

Bang for the buck! [top 10 performance coupes] J. Karr. il Motor Trend 41:42-6+ N '89

Barnstorming with Buick. T. Swan. il Popular Mechanics 166:48-9 Jl '89

Best sellers. R. Taylor. il Popular Mechanics 166:60-3+ Jl '89

The big American sedan [Oldsmobile 88 Royale, Ford LTD Crown Victoria, Dodge Dynasty and Chevrolet Caprice] il Consumer Reports 54:178-85 Mr '89

Big is back—with a high-tech advantage. D. McCosh and B. Nadel. il Popular Science 235:62-6 O '89

Buick Park Avenue Ultra. N. Bissoon Dath. il Car and Driver 34:158-9 My '89

Buick Regal Custom. B. Hartford. il Popular Mechanics 166:50 Ja '89

Buick Skylark Custom. N. Bissoon Dath. il Car and Driver 34:138-9 Ap '89

Cadillac Brougham. M. DeMere. il Motor Trend 41:90-1 O '89

Cadillac Fleetwood. A. St. Antoine. il Car and Driver 34:55-7+ Ap '89

Caprice comments [Chevrolet Caprice] J. Dunne. il Popular Mechanics 166:30 Ag '89

Chevrolet Beretta GTZ. R. Ceppos. il Car and Driver 35:69-71+ D '89

Chevrolet Beretta GTZ. D. C. Ross. il Motor Trend 41:72+ O '89

Chevrolet Corsica LTZ. D. C. Ross. il Motor Trend 41:93-6 Ap '89

Chevrolet Lumina. J. Rusz. il Road & Track 40:99+ Ag '89

Chevrolet Lumina Euro. R. Ceppos. il Car and Driver 35:55-8 Ag '89

Chevrolet Lumina Euro Coupe. D. C. Ross. il Motor Trend 41:93-5 O '89

Chrysler LeBaron GTC. B. Visnic. il Car and Driver 35:121+ Jl '89

Chrysler LeBaron Sedan. J. R. Nerad. il Motor Trend 41:64-5 O '89

Civil war [Ford Taurus vs. Chevy Lumina] T. Swan. il Popular Mechanics 166:57-9 D '89

Coupes [Acura Legend, Buick Regal, Cutlass Supreme, Thunderbird Super Coupe] D. McCosh. il Popular Science 234:42-4+ Ja '89

Coupes de grâce. L. Frank. il Popular Mechanics 166:120-4+ My '89

Crash tests for small cars. il Consumers' Research Magazine 72:23 My '89

Dodge Daytona CS. D. C. Ross. il Motor Trend 41:67-8+ Ag '89

Dodge Daytona Shelby. J. Phillips, III. il Car and Driver 35:83-4 O '89

Eagle Premier ES Limited. L. Griffin. il Car and Driver 34:133-4 Je '89

Eagle Summit LX. B. Visnic. il Car and Driver 35:130-1+ Ag '89

Fast-track sedans [Audi 200, BMW535i, Ford Taurus SHO, Nissan Maxima SE] D. Sherman. il Popular Science 234:28-30+ Mr '89

Ford Escort LX. A. Assenza. il Car and Driver 35:124+ Ag '89

Ford LTD Crown Victoria LX vs. Chevrolet Caprice Classic Brougham LS. D. C. Ross. il Motor Trend 41:88-92+ Ag '89

Ford Probe LX. R. Ceppos. il Car and Driver 35:69+ O '89

Ford Probe LX. J. Miller. il Motor Trend 41:69-70 O '89

Ford Taurus SHO. D. C. Ross. il Motor Trend 41:48-51+ Jl '89

Ford Thunderbird Super Coupe. R. Ceppos. il Car and Driver 34:59-61+ Mr '89

Four small economy cars [Eagle Summit, Nissan Sentra, Toyota Tercel and Ford Escort] il Consumer Reports 54:336-44 My '89

Four sporty cars [Plymouth Laser, Nissan 240SX, Honda CRX Si, and Subaru XT] il Consumer Reports 54:631-7 O '89

Go to work in style [Chevrolet Corsica, Ford Escort LX, Mazda MPV, Yugo GV] D. Chaikin. il Home Mechanix 85:64-7 Ja '89

How CU tests and rates cars. il Consumer Reports 54:218-19 Ap '89

I built a Buick [Buick Reatta Craft Centre] M. Allen. il Popular Mechanics 166:62-4 F '89

Life with Continental [long-term test] B. Visnic. il Car and Driver 35:117-19+ Ag '89

Lincoln Town Car. R. Ceppos. il Car and Driver 35:76-7 O '89

Lincoln Town Car. J. Miller. Motor Trend 41:85-7 O '89

Long haulers [Pontiac Trans Am GTA, Ford Thunderbird Super Coupe, Pontiac 6000 STE, Winnebago Chieftan, and Ford Club Wagon] M. Allen. il Popular Mechanics 166:62-4+ S '89

Long-term test [Pontiac 6000 STE, Ford Festiva and Dodge Caravan] il Popular Mechanics 166:120+ Je '89

Long-term test: Oldsmobile Calais, Mazda 626 4WS Turbo, Buick Regal Custom. il Popular Mechanics 166:48+ Ja '89

Mercury Cougar XR7. J. Lamm. il Road & Track 40:100 Jl '89

Motown muscle. T. Swan and M. Allen. il Popular Mechanics 166:53-7+ Ja '89

New spirit in family cars [Dodge Spirit ES, Toyota Camry, Chevrolet Corsica LT, Ford Tempo] D. McCosh. il Popular Science 234:48-50+ Je '89

Oldmobile Cutlass Supreme. J. R. Nerad. il Motor Trend 41:118-20+ N '89

Oldsmobile Cutlass Calais International Series Coupe. D. Fuller. il Motor Trend 41:120-3+ Mr '89

Oldsmobile Cutlass Calais International Series H.O. Quad 4. il Road & Track 40:82-5+ Mr '89

Oldsmobile Touring Sedan. P. Bedard. il Car and Driver 35:115-18 S '89

Oldsmobile Troféo. A. Assenza. il Car and Driver 35:72+ O '89

Oldsmobile Trofeo. D. Simanaitis. il Road & Track 40:150-1 Jl '89

Plymouth Acclaim LX. D. C. Ross. il Motor Trend 41:197-8+ My '89

Plymouth Laser RS. B. Visnic. il Car and Driver 34:93-4 My '89

Pontiac 20th-Anniversary Trans Am. R. Grable. il Motor Trend 41:50-2+ Mr '89

Pontiac Grand Prix. T. Orme. il Motor Trend 41:79-81 O '89

Pontiac Grand Prix STE Turbo. P. Berg. il Car and Driver 35:40-4 O '89

Pontiac McLaren Turbo Grand Prix. il Road & Track 40:110-13 Ap '89

Pontiac Sunbird GT Sport Coupe. R. Grable. il Motor Trend 41:55-8+ S '89

Pontiac Turbo Grand Prix. J. Miller. il Motor Trend 41:54-6+ Ag '89

Pontiac Turbo Trans Am. il Road & Track 40:92-4 Ja '89

Power coupes [Isuzu Impulse Turbo GT, Mitsubishi Eclipse, Mustang GT, Plymouth Laser] D. McCosh. il Popular Science 234:28-9+ Ap '89

Road tests: Mitsubishi Galant, Peugeot 405, Ford Tempo, Chevrolet Corsica. il Consumer Reports 54:55-62 Ja '89

Road tests of the Ford Probe, the Dodge Daytona, the Ford Mustang, and the Chevrolet Camaro. il Consumer Reports 54:102-11 F '89

Sensible speed [Audi 80 Quattro, BMW 325i, Ford Taurus SHO, Nissan Maxima SE, and Sterling 827S] C. Csere. il Car and Driver 34:46-8+ Mr '89

Shelby CSX. il Road & Track 40:88-9+ Jl '89

Shelby CSX. C. Csere. il Car and Driver 34:89-91+ Ap '89

Shelby CSX. J. Karr. il Motor Trend 41:160-2+ My '89

Showdown [Audi V8 Quattro, BMW 735i, Cadillac STS, Infiniti Q45, Jaguar Sovereign, Lexus LS 400, and Mercedes-Benz 420SEL] P. Bedard. il Car and Driver 35:41-3+ D '89

Sizzling performance—without sticker shock [Plymouth Turbo Laser, Nissan 240SX and Mitsubishi Eclipse] S. Toy and W. J. Hampton. il Business Week p105 F 6 '89

Summary judgments of the 1989 cars. il Consumer Reports 54:220-39 Ap '89

Take a car to lunch [Road & track staff favorites] P. Egan. il Road & Track 41:30+ S '89

Ten best cars. W. Jeanes. il Car and Driver 34:30-5 Ja '89

AUTOMOBILES—Testing—cont.

Three nice cars trapped inside unhappy bodies [Ford Thunderbird, Pontiac Grand Prix, and Chrysler Le Baron] il *Consumer Reports* 54:511-17 Ag '89

Turbo to go [1989 and 1987 Shelby CSX] D. McCosh. il *Popular Science* 235:28-30+ Ag '89

Two new family sedans [Dodge Spirit and Hyundai Sonata] il *Consumer Reports* 54:588-92 S '89

Two times four equals great [Ford Mustang and Probe, Honda Prelude, Mazda MX-6, Mitsubishi Eclipse Turbo, Nissan 240SX, Subaru XT6 and Toyota Celica GT-S; cover story] C. Csere. il *Car and Driver* 35:36-9+ Jl '89

Versatile vehicles [Nissan Axxess, Plymouth Laser, and Chevrolet Suburban] D. Chaikin. il *Home Mechanix* 85:64-70 Jl '89

Weenie with a black belt [Ford Taurus SHO] P. Bedard. il *Esquire* 111:60 Mr '89

When dependability counts [Geo Prizm, Oldsmobile Cutlass Calais, Ford LTD Crown Victoria] D. Chaikin. il *Home Mechanix* 85:78-81+ F '89

Which cars do better in a crash? il *Consumer Reports* 54:208-11 Ap '89

Yesteryear's luxury in a cushy new Chrysler [New Yorker Landau] J. B. Treece. il *Business Week* p134 Ja 9 '89

Anecdotes, facetiae, satire, etc.

Beretta versus Beretta [car vs. gun] B. McCall. il *Car and Driver* 34:86-9 F '89

Theft

See also

Automobiles—Security measures

After the fact [LoJack Retrieve] D. Kott. il *Road & Track* 41:133 N '89

Extra-credit assignment [high school teacher-organized auto theft ring] M. Anson. il *Motor Trend* 41:6 Je '89

To catch a thief [LoJack tracking equipment] C. Torcellini. il *Forbes* 143:202 Ap 17 '89

Tires

See Tires, Automobile

Towing

Disco-towing [New York Dept. of Transportation's program to clear away illegally parked cars near discotheques] il *The New Yorker* 65:30-1 My 22 '89

Traction

See also

Automobiles, Foreign—Traction

Getting unstuck. P. Brand. il *The Family Handyman* 39:86 F '89

Tire siping question. P. Brand. il *The Family Handyman* 39:84-5 F '89

Trailers

See Automobile trailers

Transmission

See also

Automobiles, Foreign—Transmission

Sports cars—Transmission

Warranty

See Warranty

Washing

See Automobiles—Cleaning

Wheels

Hope for hop. P. Brand. il *The Family Handyman* 39:96 My '89

Keep your wheels in line. B. Markovich. il *Home Mechanix* 86:24 Mr '89

Windshields

Sun stopper [layered glass in the Chevrolet Lumina reflects heat] B. Nadel. il *Popular Science* 235:66 O '89

What do phonograph records have in common with windshield wipers? [reflection optics] J. Walker. il *Scientific American* 261:106-9 Jl '89

Maintenance and repair

Improving your outlook. B. Markovich. il *Home Mechanix* 85:22 D '89

AUTOMOBILES, ANTIQUE

1911 American LaFrance Roadster. B. R. Kimes. il *Road & Track* 41:94-100 D '89

1922 Hispano-Suiza H6B Skiff Labourdette. S. MacMinn. il *Road & Track* 41:124-30+ S '89

1937 Alfa Romeo 8C 2900 B Touring Spider. P. Hill. il *Road & Track* 40:170-6 My '89

1937 Bugatti Type 57SC by Corsica. R. T. Devlin and M. T. Lynch. il *Road & Track* 40:134-40 F '89

Four-wheel steer? 4WD? They're old hat! [1923 Holle] D. Nye. il *Road & Track* 40:150 Je '89

Houston, the Model A has landed [watching the 1969 moon landing on TV while sitting in a 1929 Ford] J. Calabro. il *Road & Track* 40:144+ Jl '89

Itala 35/45: from China to Paris. Again. R. Hutton. il *Car and Driver* 34:38 Je '89

Secrets of the Model T. A. B. Stephenson. il *American Heritage* 40:73-7 Jl/Ag '89

AUTOMOBILES, ELECTRIC

Lessons of Sunraycer [cover story] H. G. Wilson and others. il *Scientific American* 260:90-7 Mr '89

AUTOMOBILES, EXPERIMENTAL

'89 Buick auto show car a '91 Park Avenue. il *Motor Trend* 41:31 F '89

California Camaro. J. Lamm. il *Road & Track* 40:96-7+ Ap '89

Dodge Viper RT/10 [cover story] J. Keebler. il *Road & Track* 40:44-53 Ap '89

Dream today, drive tomorrow [North American International Auto Show] J. Dunne. il *Popular Mechanics* 166:69-72 Ap '89

New American dreams [concept cars from the Detroit and Los Angeles auto shows] R. Ceppos and A. Assenza. il *Car and Driver* 34:65-71 Ap '89

Showstoppers: Detroit's high-tech cars for the '90s. D. McCosh. il *Popular Science* 234:108-10 Ap '89

Surprising cars you'll drive tomorrow. E. Henry. il *Changing Times* 43:79-81+ O '89

This is a test [Pontiac Banshee] A. Girdler. il *Road & Track* 40:114-16 Mr '89

Top 10 cars of the future. il *Motor Trend* 41:92-4+ N '89

Toyota's conceptual GT for tomorrow. J. K. Yamaguchi. il *Road & Track* 41:144-5 D '89

Viper green light likely. K. Zino. il *Road & Track* 41:158-9 O '89

History

'50s fantasies. J. R. Nerad. il *Motor Trend* 41:106-9 D '89

Alfa Romeo B.A.T. 9d. S. MacMinn. il *Road & Track* 40:122-9 Ag '89

Testing

Coalaholics [methanol-powered cars from Chevrolet, Ford and Chrysler] M. Allen. il *Popular Mechanics* 166:60-2 N '89

Crystal-ball Buicks. A. Assenza. il *Car and Driver* 35:112+ Jl '89

Driving the futurebird [Pontiac's Banshee] T. Swan. il *Popular Mechanics* 166:38 Ja '89

Evolution IROC II [Chevrolet/Motor trend development of car based on the Camaro] D. C. Ross. il *Motor Trend* 41:64-8+ D '89

Peugeot Oxia. G. Perini. il *Car and Driver* 35:28 S '89

Pontiac Banshee. J. Miller. il *Motor Trend* 41:114-16 Mr '89

AUTOMOBILES, FLYING *See* Aerocars

AUTOMOBILES, FOREIGN

See also

Convertibles (Automobiles)

Sports cars

Station wagons, Foreign

The 1989 cars [cover story; special issue] il *Consumer Reports* 54:203-15+ Ap '89

1990 import cars [special section] il *Car and Driver* 35:37-41+ N '89

The Black enterprise 1990 auto guide [special section] il *Black Enterprise* 20:83+ N '89

Cars for 1990. il *Ebony* 45:132-3+ N '89

For Rolls-Royce owners across America, all roads lead to Zionsville, Indiana [dealer H. Albers] il por *People Weekly* 31:117 Ap 17 '89

For your information. See issues of Car and Driver

Foreign intrigue. R. Taylor. il *Popular Mechanics* 166:97-100+ D '89

Imports. B. Hartford. See issues of Popular Mechanics

International report. See issues of Motor Trend

The Japanese go head to head in family sedans. il *Fortune* 120:104 O 23 '89

Japan's new cars [Tokyo Motor Show] S. Solo. il *Fortune* 120:82-4+ D 4 '89

The new 1990s, from Acura to ZR-1. J. B. Treece. il *Business Week* p178-9 N 13 '89

Owners reports [Ford Probe, Jaguar XJ6, Lincoln Continental and Cadillac Allanté] M. Lamm. il *Popular Mechanics* 166:74-7 Je '89

Awards

See also

Motor Trend Awards

Collectors and collecting

Cost of everything, value of nothing. P. Egan. il *Road & Track* 41:20+ N '89

Defects

See also

Automobiles, Foreign—Recall

Design

1990 import cars: charting the changes. J. Phillips, III. il *Car and Driver* 35:64-7+ N '89

1990 import cars: technical highlights. N. Bissoon Dath. il *Car and Driver* 35:72+ N '89

Audi unveils new sporty Coupe. il *Motor Trend* 41:21 Ja '89

The coming traffic jam in the luxury lane [Toyota Lexus and Nissan Infiniti] W. Zellner. il *Business Week* p78 Ja 30 '89

Continental drift [European influence on American models] L. A. Ealey. il *House & Garden* 161:184-5 Ap '89

Daihatsu gets its Applause. J. K. Yamaguchi. il *Road & Track* 41:179 N '89

The engineering story [1990 imports] il *Popular Mechanics* 166:103-6 D '89

The Europeans are losing their lock on luxury [Lexus, Infiniti and Maxima] D. Barry. il *Vogue* 179:320 O '89

French supercars [Mondial de l'Automobile] D. McCosh. il *Popular Science* 234:22+ Ja '89

AUTOMOBILES, FOREIGN—Design—*cont.*

Honda's fire-breathing VTEC Integra. J. K. Yamaguchi. il *Road & Track* 40:161-2 Ag '89

Hopeful Opel [introduction of Vectra] P. Frère. il *Road & Track* 40:150+ Ja '89

Lexus tech. L. Frank. il *Popular Mechanics* 166:70-1+ Ja '89

Lexus—first look. J. Rusz. il *Road & Track* 40:148-9 Ja '89

New names for luxury [Toyota Lexus and Nissan Infiniti] D. Sherman. il *Popular Science* 234:80-1 Ja '89

Nissan's Infiniti joins luxury car wars. T. Swan. il *Popular Mechanics* 166:64 Mr '89

The road to Infiniti [W. Bruce, general manager of Nissan division] S. Kichen. il por *Forbes* 143:104 Ja 23 '89

Taking the classic approach [Toyota Lexus and Nissan Infiniti luxury cars] M. Keller. il *Motor Trend* 41:213 My '89

Four wheel drive

Audi 90 Quattro 20V. P. Berg. il *Car and Driver* 34:150-2 Je '89

Audi Coupe Quattro. il *Road & Track* 41:62+ S '89

Audi Coupe Quattro. B. Nagy. il *Motor Trend* 41:61-4 S '89

Audi Coupe Quattro. B. Visnic. il *Car and Driver* 35:121-5 S '89

Audi V8 Quattro. D. Fuller. il *Motor Trend* 41:80-5 D '89

Counterattack [Subaru Legacy] S. N. Chakravarty. il *Forbes* 144:56+ N 13 '89

German gripper [Opel Vectra] D. Scott. il *Popular Science* 234:141 Ap '89

Lancia Delta HF Integrale 16V. R. Hutton. il *Car and Driver* 35:29 Ag '89

Lancia Delta HG Integrale 16V. P. Frère. il *Road & Track* 41:159-60 O '89

Mitsubishi Eclipse GSX. il *Road & Track* 40:50-3 Ag '89

Mitsubishi Eclipse GSX & Eagle Talon TSi. D. Fuller. il *Motor Trend* 41:80-2+ Jl '89

Mitsubishi Galant GSX. J. Miller. il *Motor Trend* 41:136-7 D '89

Peugeot 405X4. R. Hutton. il *Car and Driver* 35:28-9 N '89

Peugeot launches two 405 4wd models. P. Frère. il *Road & Track* 40:199-201 Je '89

Sensible speed [Audi 80 Quattro, BMW 325i, Ford Taurus SHO, Nissan Maxima SE, Peugeot 405Mi16 and Sterling 827S] C. Csere. il *Car and Driver* 34:46-8+ Mr '89

Subaru Legacy. R. Homan. il *Road & Track* 40:65+ Ag '89

Subaru Legacy. Y. Ishiwatari. il *Car and Driver* 34:34-5 My '89

Subaru Legacy LS. J. Miller. il *Motor Trend* 41:97-101 Jl '89

Subaru Legacy LS 4WD. R. Ceppos. il *Car and Driver* 34:139-41+ Je '89

Toyota Celica All-Trac. B. Nagy. il *Motor Trend* 41:110-14 N '89

Toyota Celica All-Trac Turbo. P. Berg. il *Car and Driver* 35:54-6+ N '89

Upscale Subaru [Legacy] J. K. Yamaguchi. il *Road & Track* 40:202 My '89

History

Bitten by the Bug [Volkswagen Beetle] il *National Geographic World* 172:12-15 D '89

Mini happy returns. R. Hutton. il *Car and Driver* 35:73+ Ag '89

Return of the Jaguar [Mark 2] R. Ryan. il *Gentlemen's Quarterly* 59:92+ O '89

Ownership

See Automobile ownership

Prices

Habit dies hard [Detroit cars cheaper than foreign makes] J. Flint. il *Forbes* 143:264+ My 29 '89

Here come Japan's new luxury cars [Toyota's Lexus] A. L. Taylor, III. il *Fortune* 120:62-6 Ag 14 '89

How do you build a luxury image? [Infiniti dealer R. Rosenthal and Lexus dealer J. Taylor] J. Flint. il pors *Forbes* 143:60-3 Ap 3 '89

Luxury cars: new leaders in an upscale upheaval. A. L. Taylor, III. il *Fortune* 119:66-70+ Ap 10 '89

Where have all the cheap cars gone? M. Keller. il *Motor Trend* 41:130 Jl '89

Purchasing

1990 cars: how to buy a car you'll love [cover story; special section] il *Changing Times* 43:28-35+ D '89

Top 10 new car buys: import. il *Motor Trend* 41:86-9 N '89

Rear wheel drive

Hot rides in rear-wheel drive. B. Hartford. il *Popular Mechanics* 166:30 Ap '89

Recall

Recalling the 'perfect' car [Lexus LS 400] il *Newsweek* 114:48 D 18 '89

Steering gear

Four-wheel steer? 4WD? They're old hat! [1923 Holle] D. Nye. il *Road & Track* 40:150 Je '89

Long-term test: Oldsmobile Calais, Mazda 626 4WS Turbo, Buick Regal Custom. il *Popular Mechanics* 166:48+ Ja '89

Mazda MX-6 4WS. B. Nagy. il *Motor Trend* 41:100-2+ Ap '89

Steering a new course [four wheel steering] il *Newsweek* 113:77 Ja 30 '89

Testing

1989 Import Car of the Year [Mitsubishi Galant GS] il *Motor Trend* 41:86-91+ Mr '89

1990 Acura Integra. J. Dinkel. il *Road & Track* 40:130+ Je '89

1990 Acura Integra. B. Nagy. il *Motor Trend* 41:82-4+ Je '89

1990 Honda Accord. D. Simanaitis. il *Road & Track* 41:151+ N '89

1990 Mazda 323 series. D. Kott. il *Road & Track* 41:157-8 N '89

Acura Integra. T. Swan. il *Popular Mechanics* 166:56 O '89

Acura Integra 3-door GS. J. Karr. il *Motor Trend* 41:89-92 S '89

Acura Integra GS. il *Road & Track* 41:110-13+ S '89

Acura Integra GS. P. Bedard. il *Car and Driver* 35:63-6+ Ag '89

Acura Integra GS. A. St. Antoine. il *Car and Driver* 34:79-81+ Je '89

Acura Legend Coupe L [long-term test] D. Kott. il *Road & Track* 40:62+ Mr '89

Acura Legend Coupe LS [long term test] G. Coppock. il *Motor Trend* 41:77 D '89

Affordable four-doors: perfect cars for young families. M. Knepper. il *Better Homes and Gardens* 67:187-8+ N '89

Aiming higher [Nissan Infiniti and Toyota Lexus] M. Morris and D. Chaikin. il *Home Mechanix* 85:79-81 S '89

Audi Coupe. R. Hutton. il *Car and Driver* 34:28-9 Mr '89

Audi V-8. P. Frère. il *Road & Track* 40:98-9 Ja '89

Audi V8. W. Jeanes. il *Car and Driver* 34:141+ Ja '89

Audi V8. J. R. Nerad. il *Motor Trend* 41:64-6 F '89

Audi V8. J. Phillips, III. il *Car and Driver* 35:120-3+ O '89

Bang for the buck! [top 10 performance coupes] J. Karr. il *Motor Trend* 41:42-6+ N '89

Bentley Turbo R. P. Bingham. il *Motor Trend* 41:97-100 F '89

Best sellers. R. Taylor. il *Popular Mechanics* 166:60-3+ Jl '89

BMW 525i. R. Ceppos. il *Car and Driver* 35:83-5+ Jl '89

BMW 525i. J. Miller. il *Motor Trend* 41:46-8+ S '89

BMW 535i. il *Road & Track* 40:122-6 Ja '89

BMW 535i. L. Griffin. il *Car and Driver* 34:128-9+ Ja '89

BMW 535i. B. Nagy. il *Motor Trend* 41:85-8 Ap '89

BMW M5. G. Perini. il *Car and Driver* 34:27 F '89

Celica comeback. D. McCosh. il *Popular Science* 235:53+ N '89

Citroën XM. R. Hutton. il *Car and Driver* 35:142+ D '89

Citroën's revolutionary XM on the road. P. Frère. il *Road & Track* 41:145+ D '89

Country club Camry for the junior affluent [Lexus ES250] T. Orme. il *Motor Trend* 41:98-101+ S '89

Coupes [Acura Legend, Buick Regal, Cutlass Supreme, Thunderbird Super Coupe] D. McCosh. il *Popular Science* 234:42-4+ Ja '89

Coupes de grâce. L. Frank. il *Popular Mechanics* 166:120-4+ My '89

Crash tests for small cars. il *Consumers' Research Magazine* 72:23 My '89

Cressida vs. Maxima [Toyota vs. Nissan] J. Miller. il *Motor Trend* 41:102-4+ Je '89

Daihatsu Charade CLS. A. Assenza. il *Car and Driver* 35:127-9 S '89

Daihatsu Charade CLS versus Suzuki Swift GTi. il *Road & Track* 40:108-10+ Je '89

The disappointing Peugeot 405. E. Henry. *Changing Times* 43:122+ Mr '89

Driving Lexus and Infiniti. R. Stepler. il *Popular Science* 235:29-30 S '89

East vs. West [Lexus LS 400, Mercedes-Benz 560SEL, Infiniti Q45, Audi V8 and BMW 735iL] D. Sherman. il *Popular Science* 235:78-83+ D '89

Fall firsts [1990 Lexus, Infiniti, and Mercedes-Benz SL] il *Popular Mechanics* 166:51-3+ S '89

Fast-track sedans [Audi 200, BMW535i, Ford Taurus SHO, Nissan Maxima SE] D. Sherman. il *Popular Science* 234:28-30+ Mr '89

Faster fives [BMW's 5-Series models] D. Sherman. il *Popular Science* 234:52 Ja '89

Ford Fiesta [European Ford] R. Hutton. il *Car and Driver* 34:38 My '89

Four small economy cars [Eagle Summit, Nissan Sentra, Toyota Tercel and Ford Escort] il *Consumer Reports* 54:336-44 My '89

Geo Metro LSi. B. Visnic. il *Car and Driver* 34:187+ Je '89

Geo Prizm. M. DeMere. il *Motor Trend* 41:73-5 Ap '89

Geo Prizm LSi. A. Assenza. il *Car and Driver* 34:81-5 Ap '89

AUTOMOBILES, FOREIGN—Testing—cont.

Geo Storm GSi. D. C. Ross. il *Motor Trend* 41:98+ O '89

Go to work in style [Yugo GV] D. Chaikin. il *Home Mechanix* 85:64-7 Ja '89

Honda Accord. J. Miller. il *Motor Trend* 41:114-16+ O '89

Honda Accord EX [cover story] L. Griffin. il *Car and Driver* 35:38-41+ N '89

Honda Civic Si. L. Griffin. il *Car and Driver* 34:117 F '89

Honda Legend V6Ti. Y. Ishiwatari. il *Car and Driver* 34:30 Mr '89

Hopped-up Hyundai. D. McCosh. il *Popular Science* 235:24+ D '89

How CU tests and rates cars. il *Consumer Reports* 54:218-19 Ap '89

Hyundai Excel GLS. A. Assenza. il *Car and Driver* 35:109-12 D '89

Hyundai Sonata. A. Assenza. il *Car and Driver* 34:117-19+ My '89

Hyundai Sonata. D. Batchelor. il *Motor Trend* 41:93-6+ Je '89

Hyundai Sonata. D. Simanaitis. il *Road & Track* 40:85-6 Jl '89

Import report. D. Chaikin and B. Markovich. il *Home Mechanix* 86:64-6+ Ap '89

Infiniti M30. A. Assenza. il *Car and Driver* 35:83 N '89

Infiniti M30. M. Knepper. il *Motor Trend* 41:102-3 S '89

Infiniti Q-Series. P. Bedard. il *Car and Driver* 34:112-13+ Ja '89

Infiniti Q45. R. Ceppos. il *Car and Driver* 35:59-62+ S '89

Infiniti Q45. J. Dinkel. il *Road & Track* 41:105+ S '89

Infiniti Q45. J. Miller. il *Motor Trend* 41:72-4+ Ag '89

Infiniti unveiled. D. Clendenin. il *Road & Track* 40:50-2 Ja '89

Isuzu I-Mark RS. A. Assenza. il *Car and Driver* 34:123+ Mr '89

Isuzu I-Mark RS. J. Miller. il *Motor Trend* 41:58-60 Ja '89

Jaguar Vanden Plas. W. Jeanes. il *Car and Driver* 35:83+ Ag '89

Jaguar XJ6. J. Miller. il *Motor Trend* 41:154-6+ My '89

Japan's best [Acura Legend, Mazda 929, Nissan Maxima, and Toyota Cressida] il *Consumer Reports* 54:451-7 Jl '89

Lada Samara. B. W. Yates. il *Car and Driver* 34:95-7+ Je '89

Lancia Dedra replaces Prisma. P. Frère. il *Road & Track* 40:160-1 Ag '89

Lexus ES 250 & LS 400. J. Miller. il *Motor Trend* 41:69-71+ Ja '89

Lexus ES250. B. Visnic. il *Car and Driver* 35:85 N '89

Lexus ES250 and LS400. A. Assenza. il *Car and Driver* 34:138-40 Ja '89

Lexus LS 400. P. Egan. il *Road & Track* 41:117-19+ S '89

Lexus LS 400. J. Karr. il *Motor Trend* 41:81-5 Ag '89

Lexus LS400. P. Bedard. il *Car and Driver* 35:50-3+ S '89

Life with Hyundai [Excel long-term test] A. Assenza. il *Car and Driver* 34:111-13 F '89

Life with Mazda 626 [long-term test] B. Visnic. il *Car and Driver* 34:113+ Mr '89

The little transmission that could [Subaru Justy ECVT] E. Henry. il *Changing Times* 43:100 My '89

Long-term Mazda MX-6 LX: the distant cousin of GT. D. C. Ross. il *Motor Trend* 41:102 Ap '89

Long-term test: Oldsmobile Calais, Mazda 626 4WS Turbo, Buick Regal Custom. il *Popular Mechanics* 166:48+ Ja '89

Long-term update [Nissan 240SX SE, Mitsubishi Galant GS and Peugeot 405 Mi16] il *Road & Track* 41:135 O '89

Long-term update [Mitsubishi Galant GS] J. Keebler. il *Road & Track* 40:78 Mr '89

Maserati 430. il *Road & Track* 40:84-6 F '89

Mazda 323 GTX. J. Miller. il *Motor Trend* 41:106+ Mr '89

Mazda 323 Protegé. R. Ceppos. il *Car and Driver* 35:129-31+ O '89

Mazda 323 Protegé LX. M. Brockman. il *Motor Trend* 41:122+ D '89

Mazda 929S. R. Ceppos. il *Car and Driver* 35:89 N '89

Mazda Familia. Y. Ishiwatari. il *Car and Driver* 35:26-7 Jl '89

Mazda MX-6 4WS. B. Nagy. il *Motor Trend* 41:100-2+ Ap '89

Mazda Persona. Y. Ishiwatari. il *Car and Driver* 34:36-7 Ap '89

Mercedes-Benz 190E 2.6. il *Road & Track* 40:48-50+ My '89

Miscellaneous ramblings [Jaguar XJ6] T. L. Bryant. il *Road & Track* 41:37-8 O '89

Mitsubishi Galant GS. il *Road & Track* 40:128+ Mr '89

Mitsubishi Mirage Turbo. A. St. Antoine. il *Car and Driver* 35:91-3+ Ag '89

Neo Geo [Prizm] B. Nadel. il *Popular Science* 234:140 Ap '89

New spirit in family cars [Dodge Spirit ES, Toyota Camry, Chevrolet Corsica LT, Ford Tempo] D. McCosh. il *Popular Science* 234:48-50+ Je '89

Nissan Cefiro. Y. Ishiwatari. il *Car and Driver* 34:31 Mr '89

Nissan March Super Turbo. Y. Ishiwatari. il *Car and Driver* 35:32-3 S '89

Nissan Maxima SE. il *Road & Track* 40:146-50 Ap '89

Nissan Skyline GTS-t. Y. Ishiwatari. il *Car and Driver* 35:28-9 O '89

Nissan Stanza GXE. D. C. Ross. il *Motor Trend* 41:98+ D '89

Nissan's Porsche-chaser [GT-R coupe and Skyline series] J. K. Yamaguchi. *Road & Track* 41:162-3 S '89

One-upmanship [Audi V8, BMW 535i and Mercedes-Benz 300E] il *Road & Track* 41:90-1+ N '89

Opel Vectra/Vauxhall Cavalier. R. Hutton. il *Car and Driver* 34:22-3 Ja '89

Power coupes [Isuzu Impulse Turbo GT, Mitsubishi Eclipse, Mustang GT, Plymouth Laser] D. McCosh. il *Popular Science* 234:28-9+ Ap '89

Proper Protegé [Mazda] B. Nadel. il *Popular Science* 235:58+ N '89

Recollections of an ICOY princess [Import Car of the Year tests] J. Manfredi. *Motor Trend* 41:142 Mr '89

Road tests: Mitsubishi Galant, Peugeot 405, Ford Tempo, Chevrolet Corsica. il *Consumer Reports* 54:55-62 Ja '89

Saab 9000 CD Turbo. J. Miller. il *Motor Trend* 41:101-3+ F '89

Saab 9000 Talladega. R. Hutton. il *Car and Driver* 35:33 Jl '89

Sensible speed [Audi 80 Quattro, BMW 325i, Ford Taurus SHO, Nissan Maxima SE, Peugeot 405Mi16 and Sterling 827S] C. Csere. il *Car and Driver* 34:46-8+ Mr '89

Showdown [Audi V8 Quattro, BMW 735i, Cadillac STS, Infiniti Q45, Jaguar Sovereign, Lexus LS 400, and Mercedes-Benz 420SEL] P. Bedard. il *Car and Driver* 35:41-3+ D '89

Sizzling performance—without sticker shock [Plymouth Turbo Laser, Nissan 240SX and Mitsubishi Eclipse] S. Toy and W. J. Hampton. il *Business Week* p105 F 6 '89

Škoda Favorit 136LX. R. Hutton. il *Car and Driver* 35:36 S '89

Sterling 827SLi. il *Road & Track* 40:58-60+ Je '89

Sterling 827SLi. M. Anson. il *Motor Trend* 41:189-90+ My '89

Sterling 827SLi. B. Visnic. il *Car and Driver* 34:162+ My '89

Style for a song [Hyundai Sonata] B. Markovich. il *Home Mechanix* 85:76 Ag '89

Subaru Justy ECVT. D. Kott. il *Road & Track* 40:62+ Ap '89

Subaru Justy GL ECVT. D. Fuller. il *Motor Trend* 41:124-5+ N '89

Subaru Rex Combi Super Charger ECVT. D. Simanaitis. il *Road & Track* 40:70 Mr '89

Subaru's ECVT on the road [Justy] D. McCosh. il *Popular Science* 234:20+ My '89

Summary judgments of the 1989 cars. il *Consumer Reports* 54:220-39 Ap '89

Suzuki Sprint grows tail. J. K. Yamaguchi. il *Road & Track* 41:162 O '89

Suzuki Swift GTi. A. Assenza. il *Car and Driver* 34:103-5+ F '89

Suzuki Swift GTi. B. Nagy. il *Motor Trend* 41:65-8 S '89

Ten best cars. W. Jeanes. il *Car and Driver* 34:30-5 Ja '89

Toyota Supra Turbo. il *Road & Track* 40:68-70 F '89

Toyota Supra Turbo. B. Visnic. il *Car and Driver* 34:140-1 Ap '89

Tracking the Orient Express [Bentley Turbo R races the Orient Express from Venice to Paris] W. Jeanes. il *Car and Driver* 34:104-9 Mr '89

Two new family sedans [Dodge Spirit and Hyundai Sonata] il *Consumer Reports* 54:588-92 S '89

Two times four equals great [Ford Mustang and Probe, Honda Prelude, Mazda MX-6, Mitsubishi Eclipse Turbo, Nissan 240SX, Subaru XT6 and Toyota Celica GT-S; cover story] C. Csere. il *Car and Driver* 35:36-9+ Jl '89

Two ways to say BMW in Japanese [Toyota Lexus LS400 and Nissan Infiniti Q45] L. Armstrong. il *Business Week* p155 D 18 '89

Volkswagen Fox GL Sport. D. Kott. il *Road & Track* 40:64 Ja '89

Volkswagen Jetta GLI 16V. W. Jeanes. il *Car and Driver* 35:127+ Jl '89

Volvo 740 GLE. il *Road & Track* 40:120-2+ Mr '89

Volvo 740 Turbo. R. Homan. il *Road & Track* 40:123 Mr '89

Volvo 740GLE 16-valve. B. Visnic. il *Car and Driver* 34:128-9 Mr '89

Voyage to Infiniti. B. Nagy. il *Motor Trend* 41:53-5 Ja '89

When dependability counts [Geo Prizm, Oldsmobile Cutlass Calais, Ford LTD Crown Victoria] D. Chaikin. il *Home Mechanix* 85:78-81+ F '89

When more is more [Maxima] B. Markovich. il *Home Mechanix* 85:79 Ja '89

AUTOMOBILES, FOREIGN—Testing—*cont.*
Which cars do better in a crash? il *Consumer Reports* 54:208-11 Ap '89
World's best cars [Ferrari Testarossa, Mazda MX-5 Miata, Mercedes-Benz 300E, Corvette ZR-1, and Porsche 911 Carrera 4; cover story] il *Road & Track* 40:40-51 Jl '89

Traction

Grip, don't slip. S. F. Brown. il *Popular Science* 234:71+ Ja '89

Transmission

The little transmission that could [Subaru Justy ECVT] E. Henry. il *Changing Times* 43:100 My '89
Subaru Justy ECVT. D. Kott. il *Road & Track* 40:62+ Ap '89
Subaru Justy GL ECVT. N. Bissoon Dath. il *Car and Driver* 34:95-7 Mr '89
Subaru Justy GL ECVT. D. Fuller. il *Motor Trend* 41:124-5+ N '89
Subaru revives the variable transmission [Justy ECVT] il *Consumer Reports* 54:500-1 Ag '89
Subaru's ECVT on the road [Justy] D. McCosh. il *Popular Science* 234:20+ My '89
Technical highlights [Subaru's continuously variable transmission] N. Bissoon Dath. il *Car and Driver* 34:99-100 Mr '89

Used automobiles

See Automobiles, Used

AUTOMOBILES, HOME-BUILT

See also
Classic Motor Carriages (Firm)

Testing

Piontek Sport-Tech. C. Csere. il *Car and Driver* 35:131+ D '89

AUTOMOBILES, MINIATURE *See* Automobile models

AUTOMOBILES, POLICE

Electronic equipment

The electronic cop [Custom Electronics Model DXT Mobile Data Terminal used by Mesa, Ariz. police] D. C. Ross. il *Motor Trend* 41:70 Je '89

Speed

High-speed heat! [cars used by the Border Patrol and Arizona police] D. C. Ross. il *Motor Trend* 41:64-8+ Je '89

Testing

Saleen Mustang SB/S. J. Miller. il *Motor Trend* 41:120-1 D '89

AUTOMOBILES, RACING

See also
International Motorsports Hall of Fame
About the sport. J. Rusz. See issues of Road & Track
Motorsport. See issues of Motor Trend
Sport. L. Griffin. See issues of Car and Driver

Collectors and collecting

Racing is what they were built for [vintage racing] N. Santelmann. il *Forbes* 144:106+ Jl 10 '89

Design

Birth of an Eagle [D. Gurney's HF89] L. Griffin. il pors *Car and Driver* 34:175+ My '89
Electramotive Nissan GTP. D. Fuller. il *Motor Trend* 41:128-32 Mr '89
The Indytech 500. P. Stenquist. il *Popular Mechanics* 166:128-31 My '89
PM ponies [Saleen Mustang SSC modified for racing] M. Allen. il *Popular Mechanics* 166:60-1 Ag '89
Some technicalities from 1988 [Formula 1 cars] P. Van Valkenburgh. il *Road & Track* 40:134+ Ap '89

Engines

Prix view: the engines [1989 Formula 1 cars] D. Simanaitis. il *Road & Track* 40:166-8+ Je '89

Superchargers

Why ban super- or turbocharging? P. Frère. il *Road & Track* 40:162 Mr '89

Four wheel drive

Fact or fiction: front drive vs. rear drive [Dodge Daytona Shelby Zs] P. Brand. il *Motor Trend* 41:90-1+ Ap '89

Front wheel drive

Fact or fiction: front drive vs. rear drive [Dodge Daytona Shelby Zs] P. Brand. il *Motor Trend* 41:90-1+ Ap '89

History

See also
Automobiles, Antique
1948 Cisitalia Type 360 Grand Prix. R. T. Devlin and M. T. Lynch. il *Road & Track* 40:156-62 Ap '89
1949 Maserati A6GCS. D. Batchelor. il *Road & Track* 40:102-7 Ja '89
1952 Mercedes-Benz 300SL. J. Thompson. il *Road & Track* 40:50-7 Je '89
1953 Pegaso Z-102 BS Touring Spyder. R. T. Devlin and M. T. Lynch. il *Road & Track* 41:128-34 O '89
1954 BRM V16 Mark II. D. Nye and P. Hill. il *Road & Track* 41:166-72 N '89
1955 Mercedes-Benz 300SL Gullwing. H. Rasmussen. il *Motor Trend* 41:111-14 Ag '89
The cars, the people, the money [Monterey races and Pebble Beach concours] T. C. Browne. il *Road & Track* 40:44-9 Ja '89
Cobra revisited: long ago and not so far away. T. C. Browne. il por *Road & Track* 40:54-6 Ap '89

Miscellaneous ramblings [vintage race scheduled for the Ford GT40] T. L. Bryant. il *Road & Track* 40:35 My '89
The races [Aston Martin tribute at Monterey Historic Automobile Races] P. Egan. il *Road & Track* 41:82-5+ D '89
Remembrance of things fast [Porsche 917s at Le Mans] H. L. Bergandi. il *Road & Track* 40:95-7 Je '89
Thunder from the past [Ford GT40s] P. Hill. il *Road & Track* 40:56-61+ Ag '89
War horses [Ford Mustangs] R. Taylor. il *Popular Mechanics* 166:59+ Ag '89

Maintenance and repair

Dialing it in [adjustments made to the Electramotive Nissan GTP ZX Turbo during a race] T. West. il *Road & Track* 40:60-2+ F '89
Diary of an Indy car team [Kraco Racing] G. Medley. il *Motor Trend* 41:108-15+ S '89
Racing concours. R. Taylor. il *Motor Trend* 41:202 My '89

Models

See Automobile models

Testing

A drive in the ultimate GTP Car [Electramotive Nissan] R. Grable. il *Motor Trend* 41:128-31 Mr '89
Nissan Saurus. J. Bird. il *Motor Trend* 41:102-3 Jl '89
Nissan Saurus. Y. Ishiwatari. il *Car and Driver* 35:30 Ag '89
A pair of Pontiacs at Talladega. R. Grable. il *Motor Trend* 41:96-7+ Ja '89

Tires

See Tires, Automobile

AUTOMOBILES, REBODIED *See* Automobiles, Remodeled

AUTOMOBILES, REMODELED

Bearbaiter [Spoilers Plus redesigns Beretta] C. Gromer. il *Popular Mechanics* 166:72-3 Mr '89
Physics 101, the hard way [attempt to install a Chevy V-8 engine in a Porsche 911] M. Anson. il *Motor Trend* 41:29 My '89
PM ponies [Saleen Mustang SSC modified for racing] M. Allen. il *Popular Mechanics* 166:60-1 Ag '89

Anecdotes, facetiae, satire, etc.

Ten best ugly cars. B. Visnic. il *Car and Driver* 34:53-7 Ja '89
Ugly cars, the sequel. B. Visnic. il *Car and Driver* 34:123-5+ Je '89

Testing

ASC/McLaren Mustang [convertible] J. Oldham. il *Popular Mechanics* 166:61-2 My '89
Callaway Twin-Turbo Corvette [cover story] R. Ceppos. il *Car and Driver* 34:50-3+ My '89
French impressions [CxAuto Citroën CX 25 GTI Turbo] T. C. Browne. il *Road & Track* 40:69-70+ Ag '89
Koenig Cabrio [remodeled Ferrari] N. Bissoon Dath. il *Car and Driver* 34:56-7 F '89
Koenig Competition Cabrio. J. Lamm. il *Road & Track* 40:96-7+ My '89
Lingenfelter Corvettes. N. Bissoon Dath. il *Car and Driver* 35:136+ D '89
Miata mania [Millen Turbo MX-5 version; cover story] R. Homan. il *Road & Track* 41:52-9 N '89
Rat racer reborn [A-T Engineering Honda CRX Si Turbo] T. West. il *Road & Track* 40:74+ Jl '89
Saleen Mustang SSC [cover story] A. Assenza. il *Car and Driver* 34:42-7 My '89
Topless Testarossa [Koenig Ferrari] R. Grable. il *Motor Trend* 41:64-6+ Ap '89

AUTOMOBILES, RESTORED

Burning the candle at neither end [restoring cars as a way to save gasoline] P. Egan. il *Road & Track* 40:16+ Ja '89

AUTOMOBILES, SOLAR

Lessons of Sunraycer [cover story] H. G. Wilson and others. il *Scientific American* 260:90-7 Mr '89

AUTOMOBILES, THREE WHEEL

Testing

Pendulum trike [Micro designed by Edmund Jephcott] D. Scott. il *Popular Science* 235:63 N '89

AUTOMOBILES, TOY *See* Toys

AUTOMOBILES, USED

The care and feeding of the beater. J. R. Nerad. il *Motor Trend* 41:34 My '89
Don't look back [1964 Corvair] A. Finder. il *Gentlemen's Quarterly* 59:45+ My '89
Kin ship ['82 Honda Civic] J. Sedgwick. il *Gentlemen's Quarterly* 59:48+ Ag '89
Life with a lemon. A. Assenza. il *Car and Driver* 35:25 O '89
Nathalie & the MG [father and daughter repair 1974 MGB] G. Sidline. il *Good Housekeeping* 209:66+ S '89
The painful end of a secret affair [car owned for twelve years] A. Fotheringham. il *Maclean's* 102:52 Ag 21 '89
Year of shame [1962 Rambler station wagon owned by author as a teenager] E. Serotta. il *Road & Track* 40:68-70 Ja '89

Auctions

See Automobile auctions

Prices

Bargain exotics [cover story] P. Bohr. il *Road & Track* 41:48-57 D '89

AUTOMOBILES, USED—Prices—cont.
New methodology reduces importance of used cars in the revised CPI [Consumer Price Index] J. H. Kellar. il *Monthly Labor Review* 111:34-6 D '88
Ten best grinmobiles. P. Bedard. il *Car and Driver* 34:69-73 Ja '89
What's your old car really worth? M. Spaniola. il *The Family Handyman* 39:81-2 O '89
With deals this good, why settle for new? J. B. Treece. il *Business Week* p81 Jl 3 '89

Purchasing
1989 models as used cars. il *Consumer Reports* 54:146-73 D '89
Bombs away! L. Thatcher. il *Seventeen* 48:138+ Ag '89
Buying a used car: an expert's tips on where, what, and how. T. Swan. il *Better Homes and Gardens* 67:122+ Je '89
How to find a good used car. il *Consumer Reports* 54:273-6 Ap '89
Where to find a street smart car. R. Sikorsky. *Consumers' Research Magazine* 72:16 O '89
Why I voted for a used car. A. P. Tobias. il *Time* 134:69 N 6 '89

Testing
302 versus 302 [1970 Ford Mustang Boss 302 vs. 1989 Ford Mustang GT] P. Lyons. il *Car and Driver* 34:128-9+ Ap '89
1950-1965 Porsche 356 Coupes. P. Bohr. il *Road & Track* 41:88-9+ S '89
Jaguar E-Types. P. Bohr. il *Road & Track* 40:59+ My '89
Mazda RX-7. P. Bohr. il *Road & Track* 40:72-4+ F '89

AUTOMOBILES IN ART
Auto focus: cars as art. il *Popular Photography* 96:48-9 My '89
Bitten by the Bug [Volkswagen Beetle] il *National Geographic World* 172:12-15 D '89
Ten best cartifacts. R. Ceppos. il *Car and Driver* 34:61-5 Ja '89
Ten best kid's drawings. M. B. Lewis. il *Car and Driver* 34:82-6 Ja '89

Exhibitions
In a Nebraska wheat field stands Carhenge, attracting a bumper crop of tourists—and trouble [Alliance, Neb. monument created from used automobiles by J. Reinders] M. Neill. il por *People Weekly* 32:196-7 D 11 '89

AUTOMOBILES IN ASTRONOMY
StarTrails [astronomical observing] D. H. Levy. il *Sky and Telescope* 78:650-1 D '89

AUTOMOBILES IN BUSINESS
Leasing and renting
The leased advantages. J. Candler. il *Nation's Business* 77:40+ My '89

AUTOMOBILES IN MOTION PICTURES
The Batmobile. P. Bingham. il *Motor Trend* 41:56-9+ Jl '89
Batmobile combines Stealth bomber with '68 Chevy. il *Popular Mechanics* 166:13 O '89
Ten best car movies. A. Assenza. il *Car and Driver* 34:77-81 Ja '89

AUTOMOBILES IN TELEVISION
The case of the missing Peugeot [Columbo] il *TV Guide* 36:12 F 4-10 '89

AUTOMOTIVE ANSWER, INC.
What, me quit? [J. Ryder] D. Wechsler. il pors *Forbes* 143:162+ Ap 3 '89

AUTOMOTIVE DIESEL ENGINES *See* Diesel engines, Automotive

AUTOMOTIVE ELECTRONICS *See* Automobiles—Electronic equipment

AUTOMOTIVE ENGINEERING *See* Automobile engineering

AUTOMOTIVE GAS TURBINES *See* Gas turbines, Automotive

AUTOMOTIVE INDUSTRIES
See also
Automobile equipment industry
Automobile industry
Truck industry

AUTOMOTIVE JOURNALISM *See* Journalism, Automotive

AUTONOMEN
Germany's radical counterculture. M. Bauerlein. il *Utne Reader* p30+ Jl/Ag '89

AUTONOMY
See also
National liberation movements
United Nations. Decolonization Committee
United Nations. Special Committee on the Situation with Regard to the Implementation of the Declaration on the Granting of Independence to Colonial Countries and Peoples

AUTONOMY (PSYCHOLOGY) *See* Self reliance

AUTOPSIES
See also
Medical examiners (Law)
Autopsies answer final questions. il *USA Today (Periodical)* 118:10 O '89

AUTORADIOGRAPHY
Imaging of memory-specific changes in the distribution of protein kinase C in the hippocampus [associative learning experiment] J. L. Olds and others. bibl f il *Science* 245:866-9 Ag 25 '89

AUTOSPA CORPORATION
Lube job, anyone? D. Wechsler. il por *Forbes* 143:83-4 Ap 3 '89

AUTOWINDERS (PHOTOGRAPHY) *See* Photography—Equipment

AUTRY (GENE) WESTERN HERITAGE MUSEUM *See* Gene Autry Western Heritage Museum

AUTUMN
See also
November
October
Fall preview [cover story; special section] il *People Weekly* 32:74-7+ S 4 '89

Photographs and photography
Autumn [cover story] J. Kotsilibas-Davis. il *Travel Holiday* 172:38-43 O '89

AUTUMN LEAVES, COLOR OF *See* Color of leaves

AUVERS-SUR-OISE (FRANCE)
Description
The artistry of Auvers. L. Daly. il *The Atlantic* 264:78-82 Jl '89

AUXILIARY EQUIPMENT ON BOATS *See* Boats and boating—Equipment

AUXILIARY POWER SUPPLY (AIRPLANES) *See* Airplanes, Jet—Auxiliary power supply

AUXINS
The Diageotropica mutant of tomato lacks high specific activity auxin binding sites. G. R. Hicks and others. bibl f il *Science* 245:52-4 Jl 7 '89
Rapid redistribution of auxin-regulated RNAs during gravitropism. B. A. McClure and T. Guilfoyle. bibl f il *Science* 243:91-3 Ja 6 '89

AVALANCHES
See also
Landslides
Avalanche! [B. Woods and K. Cathcart buried in Colorado avalanche] R. D. LeBlanc. il *Reader's Digest* 135:129-33 D '89
The increasing perils of downhill racing [study by K. Smith] *Focus (New York, N.Y.: 1950)* 38:30 Wint '88

AVANT-GARDE (AESTHETICS)
See also
Situationists International (Group)

AVANT-GARDE ART *See* Art, Modern

AVANT-GARDE FILMS *See* Motion pictures—Experimental films

AVANTEK, INC.
Avantek pursues separate MMIC strategy rather than participate in Pentagon's program. il *Aviation Week & Space Technology* 131:93-4 S 18 '89

AVANTI AIRPLANES *See* Airplanes, Business

AVANTI MOTOR CORPORATION
See also
New Avanti Motor Corporation

AVARICE
Gonna party like it's 1999. A. Heard. il *Mother Jones* 14:29-31+ N '89
Greed does not explain it [America's greatness] M. Novak. il *Forbes* 143:56 Ap 3 '89
Is greed dead? R. Henkoff. il *Fortune* 120:40-3+ Ag 14 '89
Less is more. H. Fehren. *U.S. Catholic* 54:39-41 F '89

AVDEL (FIRM)
Rivets and revelation [Textron's acquisition of Avdel prompts FTC antitrust case concerning blind rivets] H. Banks. *Forbes* 143:153 Je 12 '89

AVEDON, JOHN F.
Tibet today [excerpts] il *Utne Reader* p34+ Mr/Ap '89

AVELINO, JOSÉ FRANCISCO
about
Assassination in Brazil. B. Tyson. *The Christian Century* 106:384-7 Ap 12 '89

AVELINO, KIM H.
What a beautiful baby. il por *Parents* 64:132-4+ O '89

AVELLANA, MARIA BRITO- *See* Brito-Avellana, Maria

AVERAGE
Are you an "average" person? [statistics on American life] B. Cutler. *Reader's Digest* 135:189-90+ S '89

AVERAGES, STOCK *See* Stocks—Price indexes and averages

AVERBUCH, GLORIA, 1951-
Doing the double juggle. il *Ms.* 17:115-16 Ja/F '89
Never again. il *Runner's World* 24:10-11 Ag '89
Package deal. il *Runner's World* 24:50+ N '89
Rebel without a pause. il pors *Runner's World* 24:32-4 Ap '89
Running at age 40 and beyond. il *Women's Sports & Fitness* 11:18 N/D '89

AVERINTSEV, SERGEI S.
The idea of Holy Russia; tr. by J. Crowfoot. il *History Today* 39:37-44 N '89
Poetry, freedom and revolution. il *The Unesco Courier* 42:36-9 Je '89

AVERMECTINS
See also
Ivermectin
AVERY, BYLLYE Y.
about
The 1989 Essence Awards [with editorial comment by Susan L. Taylor] il pors *Essence* 20:57-60+, 69 O '89
AVERY, CARYL
How do you build intimacy in an age of divorce? [cover story] il *Psychology Today* 23:27-31 My '89
How good should you look? pors *Ladies' Home Journal* 106:119-21+ Je '89
Jackie: a mother's journey. il *Ladies' Home Journal* 106:142-4+ Mr '89
AVERY, JAMES
A guide to gemstones [excerpt from The right jewelry for you]; ed. by Karen Jackson. il *Good Housekeeping* 208:167 F '89
AVERY, INC.
Nelson Peltz: shopping to chase the blues. K. Deveny. il pors *Business Week* p143 Je 26 '89
AVERY ISLAND (LA.)
Salt and pepper flavor this island. il map *Southern Living* 24:34-5 Mr '89
AVGAS *See* Airplane engines—Fuel
AVIAEXPORT (SOVIET UNION) *See* Soviet Union. Aviaexport
AVIAKOMPANIYA SVERKHDALNYKH AVIALINIY
Soviets attempt to set up competitor for Aeroflot. J. T. McKenna and R. G. O'Lone. *Aviation Week & Space Technology* 131:42-3 D 11 '89
AVIARIES
Bringing birds up close [outdoor home aviaries] il *Sunset (Central West edition)* 183:60-1 Ag '89
A little piece of paradise in Houston [Tropical Bird House at the Houston Zoological Gardens] il *Southern Living* 24:21 D '89
Some rather close-up bird-watching at six walk-through aviaries in the Bay Area, Fresno, Salt Lake City, Denver. il *Sunset (Central West edition)* 182:14-16 F '89
AVIATION
See also
Air navigation
Air travel
Airlines
Airplanes
Airports
Airships
Balloon ascensions
Children and aviation
Computers—Aviation use
Hang gliding
Image processing—Aviation use
Information systems—Aviation use
Optoelectronics—Aviation use
Press and aviation
Private flying
Radar in aviation
Tomography—Aviation use
Videotapes—Aviation use
Aviation. F. Mackerodt. See issues of Popular Mechanics beginning April 1987
High-flying ideas [views of Robert W. Simpson] il *Technology Review* 92:80 O '89
News briefs. See issues of Aviation Week & Space Technology
Ready, fire, aim [interview with B. Goldwater] P. Garrison. il pors *Flying* 116:78-80+ D '89
Reporting points. See issues of Flying
The shooting gallery. G. Baxter. il *Flying* 116:92+ Ap '89
Stocking stuffers. il *Flying* 116:32-4 D '89
Unicom. See issues of Flying beginning February 1989
Accident prevention
See Aviation—Safety devices and measures
Accidents
See also
Airplanes—Collision avoidance systems
Airplanes, Jet—Fires and fire prevention
Airplanes, Military—Fires and fire prevention
Bermuda Triangle
Drugs and airplane accidents
Helicopters—Accidents
Iranian air disaster, 1988
Korean Air Lines Flight 007 disaster, 1983
Pan American Flight 103 disaster, 1988
United States. National Transportation Safety Board
737-400 crash investigation turns to engine instruments [British Midland Airways jet] *Aviation Week & Space Technology* 130:67 Ja 23 '89
Accident investigators seek cause of Fokker 100 landing gear failure [KLM flight to Geneva] *Aviation Week & Space Technology* 130:64 Mr 13 '89
After the crash, cash [General Electric offering rewards for scattered engine parts from Sioux City, Iowa plane crash] il *Newsweek* 114:32 O 23 '89
Aftermath. P. Garrison. See issues of Flying
Airworthiness directives issued following Fokker 100 gear failure [KLM landing accident at Geneva] *Aviation Week & Space Technology* 130:267 Mr 20 '89

Aloha 737 fuselage skin, structures undergo detailed fatigue inspections [April 1988 accident] il *Aviation Week & Space Technology* 131:129-30 S 18 '89
Aloha Airlines probe raises questions about FAA surveillance of maintenance [fuselage failure on Boeing 737 in April 1988] *Aviation Week & Space Technology* 131:77+ Ag 28 '89
ALPA claims Gander probe relied on some faulty, fabricated data [1985 crash] D. Hughes. *Aviation Week & Space Technology* 131:66-7 Jl 3 '89
Benefit of the doubt [role of pilot in crash of Surinam Airways DC-8 in June 1989] L. Morgan. map *Flying* 116:114-15 O '89
The best and worst of times at Boeing. il *U.S. News & World Report* 106:14-15 Mr 6 '89
A bizarre and suspicious flight [T. Root loses consciousness while piloting Cessna 210] G. J. Church. il por map *Time* 134:21 Jl 24 '89
Black flight attendants recall plane crash horror [United flight 232] il *Jet* 76:16 Ag 14 '89
A blackened year [explosion of French jet over Sahara Desert and USAir 737 crash at New York City's LaGuardia Airport] D. Jenish. il *Maclean's* 102:59 O 2 '89
Blowout over the Pacific [cargo door failure on Honolulu-Auckland flight] R. Lacayo. il *Time* 133:28-9 Mr 6 '89
Board suggests changing cargo door latch design [United Flight 811] *Aviation Week & Space Technology* 131:29 Ag 28 '89
Board urges closer review of special approach procedures, pilots' skills [Trans-Colorado Airlines crash in January 1988] *Aviation Week & Space Technology* 131:111+ Jl 31 '89
Brace! Brace! Brace! [United Airlines DC-10 crashes while making emergency landing in Iowa] E. Magnuson. il *Time* 134:12-15 Jl 31 '89
By the book [NTSB review of general aviation accident data for 1986] J. M. McClellan. il *Flying* 116:118-20 Jl '89
Canadian justice rules out new effort to find cause of DC-8 crash at Gander [W. Z. Estey] D. Hughes. *Aviation Week & Space Technology* 131:29 Jl 31 '89
Canadian Transport minister orders independent review of Gander crash [1985 crash] D. Hughes. *Aviation Week & Space Technology* 130:67 Ap 3 '89
Capt. Al Haynes [recording of conversation between control tower and Flight 232 before crash in Sioux City, Iowa] il por *People Weekly* 32:102-3 D 25 '89-Ja 1 '90
Close look at cargo door workings fails to reveal cause of accident [United Flight 811 accident in February 1989] il *Aviation Week & Space Technology* 130:86-7+ My 22 '89
Congressman Leland dies in plane crash during mission to feed the hungry. il *Jet* 76:10-13+ Ag 28 '89
Cracks in geriatric aircraft [Boeing 737s and other passenger planes] E. Marshall. il *Science* 243:595-7 F 3 '89
Crash course in Denver [TV newsrooms cover Sioux City air crash, July 1989] J. M. Robins. il *Channels (New York, N.Y.: 1986)* 9:16 O '89
Crash of 737-400 prompts stricter CFM56 engine checks [British Midland Airways jet] D. A. Brown. il *Aviation Week & Space Technology* 130:60-1 Ja 16 '89
Death in the Pacific [United Airlines Flight 811] il *Maclean's* 102:24 Mr 6 '89
Death over the desert [terrorist bomb responsible for explosion of UTA jet over Niger] map *Time* 134:25 O 2 '89
Delta accepts responsibility for crash, dismisses flight crew [failure to set flaps and slats properly blamed for August 1988 crash at Dallas/Ft. Worth] J. T. McKenna. *Aviation Week & Space Technology* 131:76-7 Ag 7 '89
Doomsday flight [crash landing of United DC-10 in Sioux City, Iowa] H. Jensen. il *Maclean's* 102:24-5 Jl 31 '89
Douglas asks NTSB to reopen probe of Northwest MD-82 crash [charging that pilots disconnected warning system that could have prevented August 1987 crash in Detroit] C. Fotos. *Aviation Week & Space Technology* 130:106 My 1 '89
Emergency landing damage on B-1B limited to radome, bulkhead, engines. W. B. Scott. il *Aviation Week & Space Technology* 131:43+ O 30 '89
Experts concerned about effect of airline growth on safety. J. Ott. il *Aviation Week & Space Technology* 131:70+ D 18-25 '89
F-117A crash reports cite pilot fatigue, disorientation [Stealth fighter accidents in 1986 and 1987] W. B. Scott. *Aviation Week & Space Technology* 130:22-3 My 15 '89
FAA orders inspections of CF6-6 powerplants [result of Sioux City DC-10 accident in July 1989] *Aviation Week & Space Technology* 131:33 O 2 '89
Fatal flight in Ethiopia [crash kills Congressman M. Leland] C. S. Manegold. il por map *Newsweek* 114:37 Ag 21 '89
Fatal subtraction [suspicious crash that killed Gulf Power executive J. Horton] J. Carney. il por *Time* 133:87 My 22 '89
The 'fear of death' lawsuits [legal action after Flight 232 crash at Sioux City, Iowa] K. Springen. il *Newsweek* 114:27 Ag 7 '89

AVIATION—Accidents—*cont.*

Five die on Lexington as student pilot crashes. *Aviation Week & Space Technology* 131:31 N 6 '89

Flight 811: a nightmare in the sky [cargo door rips open] G. Hackett. il *Newsweek* 113:26 Mr 6 '89

Flight rules for future Paris shows unaffected by Soviet MiG-29 crash. il *Aviation Week & Space Technology* 130:36-7 Je 26 '89

Flying straight into trouble [mysterious flight of T. L. Root] J. S. Kunen. il por *People Weekly* 32:20-3 Jl 31 '89

Flying Tigers 747-200 freighter crashes on approach to airport in Malaysian capital. *Aviation Week & Space Technology* 130:24 F 27 '89

Germany's burden [NATO flight training in German air space] *Aviation Week & Space Technology* 130:9 F 6 '89

Gripen crash delays flight test program. il *Aviation Week & Space Technology* 130:22 F 13 '89

Growing concerns about airline safety [special section] il *Aviation Week & Space Technology* 131:28-32 O 9 '89

'Here I was sitting at the edge of eternity' [passenger accounts of Flight 232 crash in Sioux City, Iowa; cover story] il *Life* 12:28-32+ S '89

High tech and human error above the clouds. il *U.S. News & World Report* 106:8-9 Ja 23 '89

Hit and run at La Guardia [USAir Flight 5050] B. Turque. il *Newsweek* 114:25-6 O 2 '89

Home on a wing and a prayer [passengers recount details of United Airlines Flight 811 after cargo door ripped open] W. Plummer. il *People Weekly* 31:38-43 Mr 13 '89

Horror in the skies [aging fleet; cover story] W. Hoffer. il *Popular Mechanics* 166:67-70+ Je '89

'I had to turn away' [tapes of conversations between crew and controllers of UAL flight 232 in Sioux City, Iowa] *Newsweek* 114:37 Ag 28 '89

Infrequent fliers. P. Body. il *Flying* 116:76-8+ My '89

Investigators assess role of apparent pilot errors in crash of USAir 737-400 [LaGuardia Airport; with editorial comment] J. T. McKenna. *Aviation Week & Space Technology* 131:11, 32-3 O 2 '89

Investigators detail failure of Aloha 737's fuselage [April 1988 accident] il *Aviation Week & Space Technology* 131:76-8 S 4 '89

Investigators find reconstructed tail of DC-10 riddled with damage [disintegration of engine in Iowa crash] J. Ott. il *Aviation Week & Space Technology* 131:22-3 Ag 7 '89

Investigators probe crash of Fokker F-28 in Canada. *Aviation Week & Space Technology* 130:67 Ap 3 '89

Investigators seek cause of blast that destroyed UTA DC-10 over Niger. *Aviation Week & Space Technology* 131:25 S 25 '89

Investigators study blade fracture's role in 737 crash [British Midland aircraft] *Aviation Week & Space Technology* 130:31 F 20 '89

Investigators suspect faulty repair as cause of 727 fuselage failure [Eastern Air Lines jet forced to make emergency landing] il *Aviation Week & Space Technology* 130:107 Ja 2 '89

It's safer, better to fly. il *Consumers' Research Magazine* 72:25-7 Mr '89

"Just ten more minutes . . ." [H. Balick, victim of plane crash, rescued by helicopter] J. McDermott. il *Reader's Digest* 134:89-94 My '89

Leaders of Canada's Liberal Party may seek hearings on Gander crash [1985 crash] D. Hughes. *Aviation Week & Space Technology* 130:24-5 F 27 '89

Metro 3 crashed during special approach to airport in Colorado [January 1988] *Aviation Week & Space Technology* 130:75+ Jl 10 '89

"My baby really didn't have a chance . . . it has to be a miracle" [family survives United Flight 232 crash in Sioux City, Iowa; ed. by Beth Weinhouse] L. Michaelson. il *Redbook* 174:130-2+ N '89

My moment of courage [surviving Sioux City DC-10 crash] R. Ness. il por *Ladies' Home Journal* 106:28+ N '89

A mysterious plane crash [flight by T. L. Root] A. Miller. il por *Newsweek* 114:19 Jl 24 '89

NASA shuttle commander involved in near collision with Pan Am A310 [D. M. Walker] *Aviation Week & Space Technology* 130:105 My 22 '89

New qualms about the DC-10 [United Airlines Flight 232 crash in Sioux City, Iowa] J. Birnbaum. il *Time* 134:20 Ag 7 '89

NTSB, GE inquiry into United DC-10 crash focuses on fan disk recovered from Iowa farm field [July 1989 crash landing] il map *Aviation Week & Space Technology* 131:84 O 16 '89

NTSB probes Aloha 737's maintenance records [fuselage failure during April 1988 flight] *Aviation Week & Space Technology* 131:131+ S 11 '89

NTSB raps Aloha, aviation system for fuselage failure [Boeing 737 in April 1988] J. Ott. il *Aviation Week & Space Technology* 130:24-6 My 29 '89

NTSB receives reports of 737 trim problems [investigation of crash of USAir Flight 5050 at LaGuardia Airport] *Aviation Week & Space Technology* 131:73 N 13 '89

NTSB says CF6-6s may require new inspection techniques [investigation of Sioux City crash in July 1989] *Aviation Week & Space Technology* 131:73 N 13 '89

NTSB seeks to verify reports of 737 rudder trim problems [probe of USAir Flight 5050 crash at LaGuardia Airport] *Aviation Week & Space Technology* 131:69 O 23 '89

NTSB urges increase in frequency of fatigue testing of transports [investigation of fuselage failure on Aloha Airlines 737 in April 1988] *Aviation Week & Space Technology* 131:83-6 N 13 '89

On the trail of terrorists [FBI investigation of Pan Am Flight 103 bombing] S. Emerson. il *U.S. News & World Report* 106:36 F 13 '89

Operations: crew of Aloha Flight 243 [aircraft brought down safely after loss of upper fuselage; aerospace laureate] il *Aviation Week & Space Technology* 130:17 Ja 2 '89

Pain behind the camera [covering crash of Pan Am 103 on local TV] K. Frankola. por *Newsweek* 113:9 F 6 '89

Playing hardball [responding to bombing of Pan Am Flight 103] *National Review* 41:13+ Ja 27 '89

Probe faults commander, pilot in B-1B crash at Ellsworth AFB [November 1988 crash] C. R. Barr. *Aviation Week & Space Technology* 130:71-2 Mr 13 '89

Probe focuses on failure of fan disk in DC-10 crash [crash landing at Sioux City, Iowa] J. Ott. il *Aviation Week & Space Technology* 131:30-1 Jl 31 '89

RAF, German Air Force jets collide over Germany. K. F. Mordoff. *Aviation Week & Space Technology* 130:29 Ja 23 '89

Rescue coordination, drills helped speed evacuation of survivors [United Airlines DC-10 crash at Sioux City, Iowa] D. Hughes. *Aviation Week & Space Technology* 131:31+ Jl 31 '89

Restricted instrument landing systems hamper B-1B crews, crash documents show [November 1988 crash at Ellsworth AFB] B. M. Greeley, Jr. *Aviation Week & Space Technology* 130:29 F 6 '89

Review the Gander crash [call for Canada to investigate 1985 crash] *Aviation Week & Space Technology* 130:7 F 13 '89

Safety Board analyzes how Aloha 737 fuselage failed [April 1988 accident] *Aviation Week & Space Technology* 131:145-6+ O 9 '89

Safety Board blames lax crew behavior but also faults Delta, FAA for Dallas crash [August 1988] J. Ott. *Aviation Week & Space Technology* 131:103-4 O 2 '89

Safety Board cites captain's failure to monitor approach as key in crash [Trans-Colorado Airlines crash in January 1988] *Aviation Week & Space Technology* 131:103+ Jl 17 '89

Safety Board cites copilot's flying, captain's drug use in Metro 3 crash [Trans-Colorado Airlines crash in January 1988] *Aviation Week & Space Technology* 130:103-4 Je 26 '89

Safety Board examines Aloha's maintenance of aging 737s [investigation of fuselage failure during April 1988 flight] *Aviation Week & Space Technology* 131:117+ S 25 '89

Safety Board investigates two midair collisions of general aviation aircraft [over New England] *Aviation Week & Space Technology* 130:95 Je 26 '89

Safety Board recommends upgrade in corrosion control research [investigation of fuselage failure on Aloha Airlines 737 in April 1988] *Aviation Week & Space Technology* 131:70-1 N 6 '89

Safety Board urges FAA to revamp maintenance, inspection training [investigation of fuselage failure on Aloha Airlines 737 in April 1988] *Aviation Week & Space Technology* 131:77+ O 23 '89

Safety experts cite similarities between DC-8, 747 crashes [bombing of Pan Am Flight 103 and crash of Arrow Air DC-8 at Gander, Nfld. in 1985; minority report of Canadian Aviation Safety Board] D. Hughes. il *Aviation Week & Space Technology* 130:58-9 F 6 '89

The search for a fail-safe jet [DC-10 crash in Iowa] il *U.S. News & World Report* 107:10 Jl 31 '89

Seeking answers [Canadian investigations of Air Ontario crash in March 1989 and 1985 Gander crash] G. W. Taylor. il *Maclean's* 102:10-12 Jl 31 '89

Show stopper [safety concerns over stunt demonstrations] L. Morgan. il *Flying* 116:86+ Ja '89

Showdown in "Sue City" [suits filed after United DC-10 crash] A. Sachs. il *Time* 134:42 Ag 7 '89

Sioux City DC-10 accident may force extensive inspection of CF6 engines. M. Mecham. *Aviation Week & Space Technology* 131:28-9 Ag 28 '89

Sioux City hearings focus on history of failed disk [United Airlines DC-10 crash in July 1989] C. Fotos. *Aviation Week & Space Technology* 131:56 N 6 '89

South Korea, Libya begin joint probe of DC-10 crash in Tripoli. *Aviation Week & Space Technology* 131:77 Ag 7 '89

Soviet MiG-29 fighter crashes during flight demonstration [Paris Air Show] il *Aviation Week & Space Technology* 130:60-1 Je 12 '89

Soviets say engine stall caused crash of MiG-29 at Le Bourget [Paris Air Show] il *Aviation Week & Space Technology* 130:32-3 Je 19 '89

AVIATION—Accidents—*cont.*

The stunt pilot [D. Rahm] A. Dillard. il *Esquire* 111:118-23 Ja '89

Sweden's first Gripen prototype destroyed in crash on landing. il *Aviation Week & Space Technology* 130:25 F 6 '89

Tarnished wings [airlines plan to overhaul jets] J. Greenwald. il *Time* 133:40-1 Mr 13 '89

The technology of terror [terrorists' bombs] W. J. Cook. il *U.S. News & World Report* 106:24 Mr 6 '89

Terror at 30,000 feet [Flight 772 from Chad to Paris crashes in Niger] E. Salholz. il map *Newsweek* 114:30 O 2 '89

The Thanksgiving they'll never forget [survivors of Flight 232 crash in Sioux City, Iowa] R. Wright. il *Good Housekeeping* 209:32+ N '89

Tragedy and luck [United Airlines Flight 232 crash lands in Sioux City, Iowa] T. Morganthau. il *Newsweek* 114:18-21 Jl 31 '89

Transport Canada Gander crash review focuses on safety issues, not causes [1985 crash] *Aviation Week & Space Technology* 130:66 Mr 13 '89

Transport Canada official resigns as Gander controversy intensifies [resignation of C. LaFrance over report on 1985 crash] D. Hughes. *Aviation Week & Space Technology* 130:33 Mr 27 '89

Transport Canada technical document questions icing theory in Gander crash [1985 crash] D. Hughes. *Aviation Week & Space Technology* 130:267 Mr 20 '89

Two Canadian Snowbirds crash into Lake Ontario. *Aviation Week & Space Technology* 131:34 S 11 '89

Two killed as USAir 737 slides off runway [LaGuardia Airport] J. T. McKenna. *Aviation Week & Space Technology* 131:25 S 25 '89

United 747 accident [nine killed as cargo door blows out; special section] il *Aviation Week & Space Technology* 129:18-22 Mr 6 '89

United DC-10 crashes in Sioux City, Iowa. D. Hughes and M. A. Dornheim. il map *Aviation Week & Space Technology* 131:96-7 Jl 24 '89

United officials tell NTSB AD procedures not followed [hearings on Flight 811 cargo door accident in February 1989] B. W. Henderson. *Aviation Week & Space Technology* 130:107 My 1 '89

Up in the air [dissension over Canadian investigation of 1985 Gander crash] B. Wallace. il por *Maclean's* 102:54 Ap 3 '89

USAF investigators report on crash that destroyed B-1B on approach [November 1988 crash at Ellsworth AFB] *Aviation Week & Space Technology* 129:72-3 Mr 6 '89

USAir 737 flight transcripts confirm autothrottle cutoff, rudder deflection [crash on takeoff at LaGuardia Airport] C. Fotos. il *Aviation Week & Space Technology* 131:84-5 N 27 '89

USAir 737 severs power lines during approach to Kansas City [thunderstorm activity] *Aviation Week & Space Technology* 131:33 S 18 '89

The vapor trails of terror in Africa [bombing of French jet over Niger] il *U.S. News & World Report* 107:13 O 2 '89

VFR in IMC: taking it to the limit [flying VFR in instrument meteorological conditions; NTSB accident statistics] J. M. McClellan. *Flying* 116:38 S '89

The 'virgin terrorist' [Kim Hyun Hee stands trial for bombing KAL Flight 858 in 1987] S. Begley. il por *Newsweek* 113:8 Mr 20 '89

Warsaw Pact unable to track MiG that crashed in Belgium after pilot ejected over Poland. il *Aviation Week & Space Technology* 130:28 Jl 10 '89

Was President Zia murdered? J. Barron. *Reader's Digest* 135:59-63 Ag '89

'We're going to crash' [Air Ontario Flight 363] il *Maclean's* 102:14 Mr 20 '89

Years after a crash that killed 248 soldiers, families still seek answers [D. Phillips wants truth about Gander, Nfld. crash that killed son returning from Sinai peacekeeping mission] C. E. Cohen. il pors *People Weekly* 32:65-7 D 18 '89

Altitude flying

AltAlert beats altitude busts. J. M. McClellan. il *Flying* 116:20 Ja '89

Beat the heat [high density altitude takeoffs] J. M. McClellan. il *Flying* 116:104-6 Ag '89

Pressure group: it's your altitude [altitude chamber flight at Andrews Air Force Base] P. Scott. il *Flying* 116:36+ Ag '89

The road warrior [low altitude VFR scud running] P. Garrison. *Flying* 116:84-5 My '89

Bird hazards

GAO criticizes Defense Dept. testing of aircraft for bird strikes. *Aviation Week & Space Technology* 131:62-3 Ag 7 '89

Charts

See Aviation charts

Cold weather conditions

See Aviation—Winter flying

Collectibles

"Off we go into the wild blue yonder . . .". H. L. Rinker. il *Antiques & Collecting Hobbies* 94:20+ N '89

Communication systems

See also
Communications satellites—Aviation use

Army pursues voice-controlled avionics to improve helicopter pilot performance. B. W. Henderson. il *Aviation Week & Space Technology* 130:43+ My 22 '89

Beam it up, Scotty [Weathertrak and Airborne Flight Information System access for Lasertrak FP100 owners] A. Laboda. il *Flying* 116:115 Jl '89

Digital network could improve aircraft links to operations, ATC. P. J. Klass. il *Aviation Week & Space Technology* 131:121+ N 20 '89

New communication, navigation systems will increase North Atlantic capacity. D. Hughes. il *Aviation Week & Space Technology* 131:115+ N 20 '89

Competitions

See also
Airplane racing

Conferences

See also
European Civil Aviation Conference

Aerospace calendar. See issues of Aviation Week & Space Technology

Calendar. See issues of Flying beginning August 1985

Economic aspects

See also
Airlines—Fares

Aviation economic impact study begins campaign for more airport capacity. J. Ott. il *Aviation Week & Space Technology* 131:68 Jl 3 '89

Exhibitions

See also
National Air and Space Museum

Additional exhibit space, larger flight displays planned for 1991 Dubai Air Show. D. A. Brown. il *Aviation Week & Space Technology* 130:28 F 13 '89

Age of *aerostroika* [Soviets at air shows] W. Garvey. il *Flying* 116:8 N '89

Airshow Canada [Soviet displays; special section; with editorial comment] il *Aviation Week & Space Technology* 131:11, 30-2 Ag 21 '89

Airshow Canada sponsors hope to make display top event in North America. R. G. O'Lone. *Aviation Week & Space Technology* 130:41+ Ap 10 '89

Calendar. See issues of Flying beginning August 1985

China Expo attendance drops; companies eye trunkliner project. P. Proctor. il *Aviation Week & Space Technology* 131:28 O 23 '89

Fine red whines and other delicacies of the 1989 Paris Air Show. N. Moll. il *Flying* 116:74-8+ O '89

First Airshow Canada will feature Soviet An-225, MiG-29 aircraft. *Aviation Week & Space Technology* 131:25 Ag 7 '89

Flight rules for future Paris shows unaffected by Soviet MiG-29 crash. il *Aviation Week & Space Technology* 130:36-7 Je 26 '89

Focus on Mideast markets: Dubai Air Show [special section] il *Aviation Week & Space Technology* 130:18-20 F 6 '89

From antiques to Antonovs [Soviet cargo plane highlight of Oshkosh '89] G. Baxter. il *Flying* 116:86-8+ N '89

Ghost story [World War II aircraft of Confederate Air Force] N. Moll. il *Flying* 116:68-72+ F '89

Growing pains [trip to airshow revives daughter's interest in airplanes] G. Baxter. il *Flying* 116:122+ S '89

HAI convention: new helicopter developments [special section] il *Aviation Week & Space Technology* 130:16-19 Ja 23 '89

Helicopter heaven: the HAI show. il *Flying* 116:15-16 Ap '89

Launch of new MDX reflects industry confidence in helicopter market [Helicopter Assn. International show] C. A. Shifrin. il *Aviation Week & Space Technology* 130:54-6 F 6 '89

Oshkosh: a day in the life. N. Moll. il *Flying* 116:62-4+ Jl '89

Paris Air Show 1989 [cover story; special section] il *Aviation Week & Space Technology* 130:60-7 Je 12 '89

Paris Air Show 1989 [cover story; special section; with editorial comment by Donald E. Fink] il *Aviation Week & Space Technology* 130:19, 28-35+, 46-7+ Je 19 '89

Paris when it sizzles [1989 Paris Air Show] il *Flying* 116:10-11 O '89

Report from Le Bourget: Paris Air Show 1989 (I) [cover story; special section; with editorial comment] il *Aviation Week & Space Technology* 130:19, 44-6+ Je 26 '89

Report from Le Bourget: Paris Air Show 1989 (II) [cover story; special section] il *Aviation Week & Space Technology* 131:34-7+ Jl 3 '89

Report from Paris [1989 Paris Air Show] F. Mackerodt. il *Popular Mechanics* 166:54 O '89

Soviet displays, kit-built aircraft highlight EAA show at Oshkosh [with editorial comment] E. H. Phillips. il *Aviation Week & Space Technology* 131:7, 24-5 Ag 7 '89

Soviet shuttle will appear at Paris show. *Aviation Week & Space Technology* 130:32 My 15 '89

Soviets display export version of Mi-24 at helicopter trade show [Helitech '89 in England] il *Aviation Week & Space Technology* 131:30 S 25 '89

AVIATION—Exhibitions—*cont.*

Soviets plan high profile at 1989 Paris Air Show [with editorial comment] J. M. Lenorovitz. il map *Aviation Week & Space Technology* 130:15, 44-6+ My 1 '89

Soviets will bring Su-25 Frogfoot to Paris; orbiter may join it. *Aviation Week & Space Technology* 130:22 Ap 17 '89

The sport hounds of Bartlesville [Biplane Expo '89] G. Baxter. il *Flying* 116:82-6+ S '89

Strong Soviet presence enlivens Canadian air show. R. G. O'Lone. *Aviation Week & Space Technology* 131:33 Ag 14 '89

Why not take the X-29 to Farnborough? *Aviation Week & Space Technology* 131:9 S 25 '89

Fog hazards

Fog bound. R. Mazziotti. il *Flying* 116:100 Ja '89

Takeoff minimums [low-visibility IFR takeoffs] J. M. McClellan. il *Flying* 116:106-7 S '89

Glacier flying

Daredevil pilots take glacier flying to new heights [Alaska; cover story] J. Krakauer. bibl (p147) il *Smithsonian* 19:96-100+ Ja '89

Handbooks, manuals, etc.

See also
Aviation charts

History

See also
Airplanes, Antique
Aviation—Transatlantic flights—History

Charting Jeppesen [interview with E. B. Jeppesen] N. Moll. il pors *Flying* 116:36-41 Ja '89

Eyewitness report from the right seat of the Wright Flyer. G. Dickin. il *Flying* 116:82-6 O '89

Hot weather conditions

See Aviation—Summer flying

Ice hazards

The Bonanza's weeping wing [TKS anti-ice system] A. Laboda. il *Flying* 116:22 Mr '89

Frost bite [crash of Continental DC-9 at Denver in 1987] P. Garrison. *Flying* 116:122+ Jl '89

Investigators probe crash of Fokker F-28 in Canada. *Aviation Week & Space Technology* 130:67 Ap 3 '89

Starship 1 begins final tests to certify pneumatic deicers. E. H. Phillips. *Aviation Week & Space Technology* 130:105 Ja 2 '89

Transport Canada technical document questions icing theory in Gander crash [1985 crash] D. Hughes. *Aviation Week & Space Technology* 130:267 Mr 20 '89

Instrument flying

Churning up the soup [helicopter IFR flying] J. M. McClellan. il *Flying* 116:30-1 D '89

Grave expectations [flying an approach into low IFR weather] J. M. McClellan. il *Flying* 116:39-40 O '89

Keeping IFR currency in check. J. M. McClellan. il *Flying* 116:40-1 Ag '89

Quick ticket [IFR training programs] A. Laboda. il *Flying* 116:28-9 Mr '89

Restricted instrument landing systems hamper B-1B crews, crash documents show [November 1988 crash at Ellsworth AFB] B. M. Greeley, Jr. *Aviation Week & Space Technology* 130:29 F 6 '89

Takeoff minimums [low-visibility takeoffs] J. M. McClellan. il *Flying* 116:106-7 S '89

USAF investigators report on crash that destroyed B-1B on approach [November 1988 crash at Ellsworth AFB] *Aviation Week & Space Technology* 129:72-3 Mr 6 '89

International aspects

See also
Helicopter Association International

Laws and regulations

See also
Air pilots—Legal status, laws, etc.
Air traffic control
Airspace (International law)
United States. Federal Aviation Administration

Airline deregulation and public policy. S. A. Morrison and C. Winston. bibl f *Science* 245:707-11 Ag 18 '89

Airline reregulation? J. W. Merline. il *Consumers' Research Magazine* 72:38 N '89

Congress pushes White House to boost airline competition. M. Mecham. *Aviation Week & Space Technology* 131:106-7 S 25 '89

Crashing Eastern [unions urging re-regulation of airlines] il *National Review* 41:12 Ap 7 '89

Memo to the airlines: deregulation's days are numbered. S. Payne. *Business Week* p59 N 13 '89

The not so friendly skies [effects of airline deregulation] G. Rebeck. il *Utne Reader* p12-13 N/D '89

Plane truth [case for reregulation] R. Kuttner. *The New Republic* 201:21-3 Jl 17-24 '89

Regulation bills prompt carriers to counterattack. M. Mecham. *Aviation Week & Space Technology* 131:70-1 N 13 '89

Should airlines be reregulated? K. Labich. il *Fortune* 119:82-4+ Je 19 '89

Who wins the air wars? [deregulation's effect on passengers] C. Friday and J. Schwartz. il *Newsweek* 114:41 S 18 '89

Medical aspects

Is there a doctor on board? [air travel] C. Perlmutter. il *Prevention (Emmaus, Pa.)* 41:56-64 Ap '89

Meteorological aspects

See Meteorology, Aviation

Mountain flying

Point of know return [1987 crash of twin-engine Caribou in Yukon river valley during attempted go-around from single-engine approach] P. Garrison. *Flying* 116:24+ D '89

Power struggle [too much weight and inadequate horsepower create dangerous situation] T. Benoit. il *Flying* 116:124 Je '89

Ridge runners [ridge soaring in sailplanes over Allegheny Mountains] N. Moll. il *Flying* 116:58-62+ Ag '89

Snow storm [cocaine and lack of skill blamed for crash of commuter airliner on approach to Durango, Colo.] P. Garrison. *Flying* 116:30-2 N '89

Night flying

Critics fault U.S. Army helicopter training with night vision goggles. *Aviation Week & Space Technology* 130:23 Mr 27 '89

ITT solves complex problems to produce image intensifiers [night vision goggles] B. D. Nordwall. il *Aviation Week & Space Technology* 130:91+ My 22 '89

New goggles improve night vision but do not match daylight conditions. B. D. Nordwall. il *Aviation Week & Space Technology* 130:86-7 Ap 10 '89

Overwater flying

Monarch Airlines will expand EROPS 757 service to Far East [extended range overwater operations] D. A. Brown. *Aviation Week & Space Technology* 130:71 Ja 9 '89

Pulling out the stops [new planes designed for long-haul routes] G. Eichler. il *Esquire* 112:60 Ag '89

Periodicals

See also
Aviation week & space technology
Flying and popular aviation (Periodical)

Physiological aspects

See also
Jet lag

Air travail [cabin air; research by M. N. Emmerman] J. Poppy. il *Esquire* 112:141-2+ S '89

Air traveler's syndrome: do's & don'ts [getting blood clots on flights of four hours or more] A. C. Mallozzi. il *Good Housekeeping* 209:176 Jl '89

Flying can be a pain in the neck. K. Schaefer. il *Nation's Business* 77:73 S '89

Rain hazards

See Aviation—Storm hazards

Safety devices and measures

See also
Air traffic control
Airplane engines, Jet—Inspection
Airplanes—Collision avoidance systems
Airplanes, Jet—Inspection
Airplanes, Military—Escape devices
Parachutes
Radar in aviation
United States. National Transportation Safety Board

Board asks FAA to help form model safety department. *Aviation Week & Space Technology* 131:104 O 2 '89

Check mate! [checklists] P. Garrison. il *Flying* 116:70-2+ My '89

Experts concerned about effect of airline growth on safety. J. Ott. il *Aviation Week & Space Technology* 131:70+ D 18-25 '89

FAA and NASA design program to improve human performance. *Aviation Week & Space Technology* 130:115 My 29 '89

FAA officials say Eastern safety matches that of other airlines. C. Fotos. *Aviation Week & Space Technology* 131:80-1 Ag 7 '89

Growing concerns about airline safety [special section] il *Aviation Week & Space Technology* 131:28-32 O 9 '89

How safe are you in the air? A. Ramirez. il *Fortune* 119:75-6 My 22 '89

It's safer, better to fly. il *Consumers' Research Magazine* 72:25-7 Mr '89

New approach to airline safety. W. E. Sheeline. il *Fortune* 119:8 Mr 27 '89

Safety in the air. L. Dahl. *World Press Review* 36:78 O '89

SETP identifies safe flying practices to be observed by demonstration pilots. W. B. Scott. *Aviation Week & Space Technology* 131:137 N 20 '89

Scholarships and fellowships

Scholarships: smart training money. *Flying* 116:115-16 N '89

Storm hazards

See also
Wind shear

Heaven's gate [thunderstorms] J. M. McClellan. il *Flying* 116:108-9 My '89

Lunch break [takeoff decision with thunderstorms predicted] J. M. McClellan. il *Flying* 116:104 Ja '89

NASA tests indicate heavy rainfall can reduce lift at high angles of attack [transport aircraft wings] E. H. Phillips. il *Aviation Week & Space Technology* 131:64-5 Ag 28 '89

AVIATION—Storm hazards—*cont.*
NASA will study heavy rain effects on wing aerodynamics [cover story] E. H. Phillips. il *Aviation Week & Space Technology* 130:38-9+ F 13 '89
Squeeze play [ATC turn command sends Piper Seneca into thunderstorm] P. Steeves. il *Flying* 116:128-9 S '89
USAir 737 severs power lines during approach to Kansas City [thunderstorm activity] *Aviation Week & Space Technology* 131:33 S 18 '89
Waiting for Gilbert [sheltering airplanes during hurricane] G. Baxter. il *Flying* 116:84-5 Ja '89
Wind socked [shift in wind results in rough landing] J. Emmerling. il *Flying* 116:102 Ap '89

Study and teaching
See also
Academy of Civil Aviation (Soviet Union)
Airplanes, Training
Bolivar Aviation
Flight simulators
FlightSafety International, Inc.
Imagineering Systems Corporation
National Test Pilot School
Naval Strike Warfare Center (U.S.)
Parks College of Saint Louis University
Sierra Academy of Aeronautics
Spartan School of Aeronautics
University of North Dakota. Center for Aerospace Sciences

Airline safety [special section] D. Hughes. il *Aviation Week & Space Technology* 131:86-7+ O 16 '89
A balk down memory lane [mnemonics] P. Garrison. *Flying* 116:38-9 O '89
The boys from Bremen [Lufthansa pilot training program] W. Garvey. il *Flying* 116:72-7 Je '89
Critics fault U.S. Army helicopter training with night vision goggles. *Aviation Week & Space Technology* 130:23 Mr 27 '89
Double-barrelled rating [multiengine training] N. Moll. il *Flying* 116:58-60+ Ap '89
EW officers get intensive training for complex, modern warfare role [Air Force electronic warfare officers] il *Aviation Week & Space Technology* 131:84-6 S 11 '89
Father knows best [Piper Training Center courses] N. Moll. il *Flying* 116:100 Ag '89
Helicopter instructors make better hovers. N. Moll. il *Flying* 116:32 Ag '89
Indecent exposure: CFI liability [flight instructors] A. Laboda. il *Flying* 116:36-7 O '89
A learn-to-fly primer [cover story] N. Moll. il *Flying* 116:59-61 Je '89
Marine training prepares crews for combined operations. il *Aviation Week & Space Technology* 130:48-9 F 27 '89
The next best thing [learning to fly a new airplane] L. Morgan. il *Flying* 116:128-9 Ag '89
Old dogs, new tricks [flight schools] il *Flying* 116:28 F '89
Quick ticket [IFR training programs] A. Laboda. il *Flying* 116:28-9 Mr '89
Self-test pattern. J. M. McClellan. il *Flying* 116:22+ Jl '89
Spin cycle [spin training] W. Garvey. il *Flying* 116:21-2 Jl '89
Splash party [floatplanes] A. Laboda. il *Flying* 116:104+ My '89
Teaching teamwork [Continental Air Lines course] N. Moll. il *Flying* 116:84-5 Ap '89
Trump begins training flight crews for northeast shuttle. J. T. McKenna. *Aviation Week & Space Technology* 130:77 Ja 30 '89
Twist and shout [questioning need for helicopter pilots to learn piston throttle control] J. M. McClellan. il *Flying* 116:110-11 Je '89

Aids and devices
Guide to stepping up [General Aviation Manufacturers Association Transition training master syllabus] il *Flying* 116:113-14 N '89
Vertical video [Sporty's So you want to fly helicopters?] J. M. McClellan. il *Flying* 116:30 My '89

Anecdotes, facetiae, satire, etc.
Oh solo mio. A. Harr. il *Flying* 116:86+ D '89

Stunt flying
See also
Airplanes, Aerobatic
Blue Angels (Flight squadron)
Snowbirds (Flight squadron)

SETP identifies safe flying practices to be observed by demonstration pilots. W. B. Scott. *Aviation Week & Space Technology* 131:137 N 20 '89
Show stopper [safety concerns over stunt demonstrations] L. Morgan. il *Flying* 116:86+ Ja '89
The stunt pilot [D. Rahm] A. Dillard. il *Esquire* 111:118-23 Ja '89

Summer flying
Beat the heat [high density altitude takeoffs] J. M. McClellan. il *Flying* 116:104-6 Ag '89

Taxation
Weathering tax time. F. George. il *Flying* 116:90-2+ S '89

Transatlantic flights
History
Bridging the Atlantic [early flights with Pan Am; cover story] R. K. Schrader. il *American History Illustrated* 24:34-47 My '89
It's the heroes who give us specialized fields of collecting [medals commemorating C. Lindbergh's flight] E. Rochette. il *Antiques & Collecting Hobbies* 93:66-7 Ja '89

History—Anecdotes, facetiae, satire, etc.
Wings ahoy! [75th anniversary of the flying boat] B. McCall. il *The New Yorker* 65:30-3 My 1 '89

Visual flight rules
See Airplanes—Piloting

Volcano hazards
A perilous passage through volcanic ash [KLM Royal Dutch Airlines' loss of engine power near Redoubt Volcano] R. Monastersky. *Science News* 136:407 D 23-30 '89

Wind hazards
See Aviation—Storm hazards

Winter flying
See also
Aviation—Ice hazards

Low temperatures, high pressure ground most flights in Alaska. B. W. Henderson. il *Aviation Week & Space Technology* 130:27 F 6 '89
USAF, McDonnell Douglas prepare to deploy F-15E for winter testing. W. B. Scott. il *Aviation Week & Space Technology* 130:79+ Ja 2 '89

World flights
Concorde cruising speed. W. F. Buckley. il *National Review* 41:26-8+ My 19 '89
Full circle [Concorde flight] W. F. Buckley. *National Review* 41:37-40 Je 2 '89

Alaska
Daredevil pilots take glacier flying to new heights [cover story] J. Krakauer. bibl (p147) il *Smithsonian* 19:96-100+ Ja '89
Low temperatures, high pressure ground most flights in Alaska. B. W. Henderson. il *Aviation Week & Space Technology* 130:27 F 6 '89

California
FAA awards California grant to study applications for commercial tilt-rotor. *Aviation Week & Space Technology* 131:25 Jl 31 '89

France
History
High flyers: women aviators in pre-war France. S. Reynolds. bibl il *History Today* 39:36-41 Ap '89

Soviet Union
See also
Academy of Civil Aviation (Soviet Union)
Soviet aircraft [tables] il *Aviation Week & Space Technology* 130:152-3 Mr 20 '89

Western Europe
Come together [1992 integration] N. Moll. il map *Flying* 116:86-90+ Jl '89

AVIATION, MILITARY
See also
Afghanistan—Russian invasion, 1979-1989—Aerial operations
Air bases
Aircraft carriers
Airplanes, Military
Close air support
El Salvador—Civil War, 1980- —Aerial operations
Helicopters—Military use
United States. Air Force
Vietnamese War, 1957-1975—Aerial operations
Military [special section] il *Aviation Week & Space Technology* 130:45+ Mr 20 '89

History
See also
Airplanes, Military—History
Korean War, 1950-1953—Aerial operations
World War, 1939-1945—Aerial operations

Australia
See also
Australia. Royal Australian Air Force
Military preparedness in the South Pacific: Australia [cover story; special section] il map *Aviation Week & Space Technology* 130:34-5+ F 6 '89

Canada
See also
Snowbirds (Flight squadron)

Japan
Japan plans to purchase 112 aircraft under $29-billion defense budget. il *Aviation Week & Space Technology* 131:36 S 11 '89

Korea (South)
South Korea: nation at a crossroads [special section] J. D. Morrocco. il maps *Aviation Week & Space Technology* 130:176-7+ Je 12 '89

Maine
Start of Tomahawk flights renews controversy in Maine [cruise missile testing] D. Hughes. il *Aviation Week & Space Technology* 130:28-9 Ja 23 '89
When cruise missiles zoom across Maine. T. DePaul. *The Progressive* 53:12-13 Ja '89

AVIATION, MILITARY—cont.
New Zealand
See also
New Zealand. Royal New Zealand Air Force
New Zealand upgrades forces to face low-intensity fighting.
P. Proctor. il *Aviation Week & Space Technology* 130:47+
F 6 '89

AVIATION AND HEALTH *See* Aviation—Physiological
aspects

AVIATION AND STATE
See also
United States. Congress. House. Committee on Public
Works and Transportation. Subcommittee on Aviation
United States. Federal Aviation Administration
Air transportation [address, May 11, 1989] R. J. Aaronson.
Vital Speeches of the Day 55:592-4 Jl 15 '89
Aviation interests unite. *Flying* 116:16-17 My '89
Big Brother is watching you. L. Morgan. il *Flying* 116:136-7
Jl '89
How 'Sam the Hammer' could nail the airlines [S. Skinner]
S. Payne. il por *Business Week* p126-7 Je 26 '89
Senators press Skinner on civil aviation agenda [Transporta-
tion Secretary-designate S. K. Skinner] M. Mecham. *Aviation
Week & Space Technology* 130:70-1 Ja 30 '89
Skinner speaks. *Flying* 116:22 Je '89
Taxes, liability top political agenda. il *Flying* 116:10 F '89
Washington roundup. See issues of Aviation Week & Space
Technology

Anecdotes, facetiae, satire, etc.
Life in Washington is American life, regardless of our local
variations. C. Fotos. *Aviation Week & Space Technology*
131:88 D 18-25 '89

International aspects
See also
Airspace (International law)
International Air Transport Association
International Civil Aviation Organization
Air service rights will be key issue for U.S. carriers in
Europe. il *Aviation Week & Space Technology* 130:157+
Je 12 '89
Aviation's role in shaping today's world [address, June 20,
1989] E. J. McAllister. *Department of State Bulletin* 89:33-5
O '89
European Aviation Conference, U.S. fail to agree on extending
fare pact. il *Aviation Week & Space Technology* 131:66
Ag 14 '89
Skinner's proposal to expand service by foreign airlines gets
mixed response. J. Ott. *Aviation Week & Space Technology*
131:57 O 30 '89
Surging demand prompts U.S., Japan to boost capacity 30%.
J. Ott. il *Aviation Week & Space Technology* 131:20-1
N 13 '89
U.S. airlines establish new European flights before 1992 market
restructuring. J. T. McKenna. il *Aviation Week & Space
Technology* 131:79+ N 20 '89
U.S. airport executives seek change in bilateral negotiations.
C. Fotos. il *Aviation Week & Space Technology* 130:112
Ap 24 '89

Australia
Australia eases landing rights policy, putting more pressure
on Qantas. P. Proctor. il *Aviation Week & Space Technology*
130:97 Je 26 '89

Belgium
Belgium will sell British Airways, KLM 20% stakes in new
Sabena. *Aviation Week & Space Technology* 130:95 Je
26 '89

Canada
ALPA claims Gander probe relied on some faulty, fabricated
data [1985 crash] D. Hughes. *Aviation Week & Space
Technology* 131:66-7 Jl 3 '89
Canadian justice rules out new effort to find cause of DC-8
crash at Gander [W. Z. Estey] D. Hughes. *Aviation Week
& Space Technology* 131:29 Jl 31 '89
Canadian Transport minister orders independent review of
Gander crash [1985 crash] D. Hughes. *Aviation Week &
Space Technology* 130:67 Ap 3 '89
Government to sell 41.1 million shares of Air Canada stock,
finish privatization. N. C. Kernstock. il *Aviation Week
& Space Technology* 130:171-2 Je 19 '89
Leaders of Canada's Liberal Party may seek hearings on
Gander crash [1985 crash] D. Hughes. *Aviation Week &
Space Technology* 130:24-5 F 27 '89
Regaining altitude [fewer airlines charging higher fares] J.
Daly. il *Maclean's* 102:46-8 N 6 '89
Review the Gander crash [call for Canada to investigate
1985 crash] *Aviation Week & Space Technology* 130:7
F 13 '89
Seeking answers [investigations of Air Ontario crash in March
1989 and 1985 Gander crash] G. W. Taylor. il *Maclean's*
102:10-12 Jl 31 '89
Transport Canada Gander crash review focuses on safety
issues, not causes [1985 crash] *Aviation Week & Space
Technology* 130:66 Mr 13 '89
Transport Canada official resigns as Gander controversy
intensifies [resignation of C. LaFrance over report on 1985
crash] D. Hughes. *Aviation Week & Space Technology*
130:33 Mr 27 '89

Transport Canada technical document questions icing theory
in Gander crash [1985 crash] D. Hughes. *Aviation Week
& Space Technology* 130:267 Mr 20 '89
Up in the air [dissension over investigation of 1985 Gander
crash] B. Wallace. il por *Maclean's* 102:54 Ap 3 '89

China
See also
China. Civil Aviation Administration
China aviation: at a critical crossroads [cover story; special
section; with editorial comment] D. E. Fink and P. Proctor.
il *Aviation Week & Space Technology* 131:23, 48-9+ D
11 '89
MiG-29 crash, turmoil in China mar start of show [Paris
Air Show] il *Aviation Week & Space Technology* 130:60-3
Je 12 '89

France
France funds weapon detectors, issues new airport ID cards.
J. M. Lenorovitz. il *Aviation Week & Space Technology*
130:64 Ja 16 '89

Germany (West)
Commission approves subsidies for Airbus. *Aviation Week
& Space Technology* 130:67 Mr 13 '89
Daimler accepts German constraints on its buyout of MBB.
Aviation Week & Space Technology 131:31 S 18 '89
German Cartel Office raises antitrust issues in MBB takeover
[acquisition by Daimler-Benz] *Aviation Week & Space
Technology* 130:271 Mr 20 '89
U.S. criticizes E.C. plan to shield MBB from fluctuations
in exchange rate. M. Mecham. *Aviation Week & Space
Technology* 130:91 Mr 27 '89

Great Britain
See also
Great Britain. Civil Aviation Authority
Change of transport ministers leaves new rules for British
airports in doubt. D. A. Brown. *Aviation Week & Space
Technology* 131:82-3 Ag 7 '89
Put teeth into air safety recommendations [report on British
Airtours Boeing 737 fire in August 1985] *Aviation Week
& Space Technology* 130:7 Ap 17 '89

Ireland
Dublin trims international, domestic competition between
Irish carriers. J. Ott. *Aviation Week & Space Technology*
131:107-8 O 2 '89

Japan
Deregulation, privatization spur JAL to diversify operations.
J. Ott. il *Aviation Week & Space Technology* 130:42-3
My 8 '89

Northern Ireland
Britain to assume Short's debt as step toward sale. *Aviation
Week & Space Technology* 129:30 Mr 6 '89
Britain will recapitalize Short Brothers prior to sale. *Aviation
Week & Space Technology* 130:28 Ja 16 '89

Philippines
Philippine Airlines readies itself for privatization. P. Proctor.
il map *Aviation Week & Space Technology* 131:99+ Ag
21 '89

Scandinavia
Nordic nations face need to find links with European Community. *Aviation Week & Space Technology* 130:118 Je
12 '89

Sweden
Swedish defense planners seek more funds, cost cuts on
Gripen. D. A. Brown. *Aviation Week & Space Technology*
130:25-6 Ja 30 '89

United States
See Aviation and state

Western Europe
1992: unifying Europe's markets [special section; with editorial
comment by Donald E. Fink] il map *Aviation Week &
Space Technology* 130:51, 78-9+ Je 12 '89
Boeing agrees to 747-400 design changes sought by European
aviation authorities. *Aviation Week & Space Technology*
131:58 N 6 '89
EEC delays action on aircraft that fail to meet noise limits.
E. H. Phillips. il *Aviation Week & Space Technology* 130:30
F 13 '89
Europe may exempt business jets from Stage 2 nonaddition
rule [noise regulation] il *Aviation Week & Space Technology*
131:53+ O 2 '89
European Court ruling could ban bilateral air fare agreements.
Aviation Week & Space Technology 130:32 Ap 17 '89
GE-powered 747-400 gets initial approval in Europe after
Boeing accepts design changes. *Aviation Week & Space
Technology* 130:105 My 22 '89
High costs, political rows hinder Europe's combat aircraft
programs. D. A. Brown. il *Aviation Week & Space
Technology* 130:95-6 Mr 20 '89
Study finds Europe must boost R&D spending to remain
competitive. il *Aviation Week & Space Technology* 130:79-80
Ja 30 '89
U.S. airlines establish new European flights before 1992 market
restructuring. J. T. McKenna. il *Aviation Week & Space
Technology* 131:79+ N 20 '89

AVIATION ASSOCIATIONS
See also
Air Transport Association of America
Airborne Law Enforcement Association
Association of European Airlines

AVIATION ASSOCIATIONS—See also—*cont.*
Experimental Aircraft Association
General Aviation Manufacturers Association
Helicopter Association International
International Air Transport Association
National Biplane Association
National Business Aircraft Association
Partnership for Improved Air Travel
Aerospace calendar. See issues of Aviation Week & Space Technology
Calendar. See issues of Flying beginning August 1985

AVIATION CHARTS
Charting Jeppesen [interview with E. B. Jeppesen] N. Moll. il pors *Flying* 116:36-41 Ja '89
Motion pictures [Argus 5000 moving map] N. Moll. il *Flying* 116:66-7 Ja '89
Simplified Q Service. J. M. McClellan. il *Flying* 116:24 O '89

AVIATION CLUBS
See also
Confederate Air Force

AVIATION COMMUNICATIONS *See* Aviation—Communication systems

AVIATION COMPOSITES COMPANY, LTD.
Lawsuit against Rutans could test liability of designers, test pilots. *Aviation Week & Space Technology* 130:61 Ja 23 '89

AVIATION EDUCATION *See* Aviation—Study and teaching

AVIATION ENGINEERING
See also
Computers—Aviation use
Eidetics International (Firm)
New USAF contracts speed up aerospace component redesign. B. W. Henderson. *Aviation Week & Space Technology* 131:74 Ag 21 '89

AVIATION EQUIPMENT
See also
Air navigation—Aids and devices
Airplanes—Radio equipment
Airplanes, Business—Electronic equipment
Airplanes, Jet—Electronic equipment
Airplanes, Military—Electronic equipment
Airplanes, Training—Electronic equipment
Altimeters
Flight recorders
Image processing—Aviation use
Inertial guidance systems

AVIATION FUEL *See* Airplane engines—Fuel

AVIATION METEOROLOGY *See* Meteorology, Aviation

AVIATION MUSEUMS
See also
Air Force Museum (China)
Museum of Flight (Seattle, Wash.)
Museum of Flying (Santa Monica, Calif.)
National Air and Space Museum
Space museums

AVIATION POLICY *See* Aviation and state

AVIATION RECORDS
See also
Airplane speed records

AVIATION RESEARCH
See also
Air Force Wright Aeronautical Laboratories
Eidetics International (Firm)
Langley Research Center (U.S.)
United States. National Aeronautics and Space Administration
Government, industry mount major effort to characterize aging aircraft issues. il *Aviation Week & Space Technology* 131:60-1+ Jl 24 '89
Independent labs play key role in aerospace testing, verification. W. B. Scott. il *Aviation Week & Space Technology* 130:110-11 My 22 '89
Laurels 1988 [cover story; special section] il *Aviation Week & Space Technology* 130:11-18 Ja 2 '89

Japan
Industry, government join in HSCT research. J. Ott. *Aviation Week & Space Technology* 130:53 My 8 '89
International engine manufacturers expect to work on Japan's HSCT propulsion effort [high-speed civil transport] S. W. Kandebo. *Aviation Week & Space Technology* 131:39-40 D 11 '89
Japan to set up R&D programs on advanced engines, heat-resistant materials for supersonic transport. *Aviation Week & Space Technology* 131:138 O 9 '89

Soviet Union
See also
Central Aero-Hydrodynamic Institute (Soviet Union)
Central Institute for Aviation Motors (Moscow, Soviet Union)

Western Europe
Study finds Europe must boost R&D spending to remain competitive. il *Aviation Week & Space Technology* 130:79-80 Ja 30 '89

AVIATION SCHOOLS *See* Aviation—Study and teaching

AVIATION SUBCOMMITTEE (SENATE) *See* United States. Congress. Senate. Committee on Commerce, Science, and Transportation. Subcommittee on Aviation

AVIATION WEEK & SPACE TECHNOLOGY
Spies are us [unauthorized photos published] il *Discover* 10:10 Mr '89

AVIATION WORKERS
See also
Aerospace industries—Employees
Air pilots
Air traffic controllers (Persons)
Airlines—Employees
Airplane mechanics (Persons)
FAA and NASA design program to improve human performance. *Aviation Week & Space Technology* 130:115 My 29 '89

AVIBRAS INDUSTRIA AEROESPACIAL SA
Brazil, China form space launch venture [INSCOM] E. H. Kolcum. il *Aviation Week & Space Technology* 130:35 My 29 '89

AVIENUS, RUFUS FESTUS, 4TH CENT.
about
M31 and its forgotten Roman poet. il *Sky and Telescope* 78:243-4 S '89

AVILA, MISSY
about
Karen Severson swore she'd find her best friend's murderer—now she stands accused of the crime. K. Kingsbury. il pors *People Weekly* 32:147-8+ S 18 '89

AVILDSEN, JOHN G.
about
The Karate Kid, part III [film] Reviews
People Weekly il 32:13-14 Jl 10 '89. R. Novak
Lean on me [film] Reviews
Commonweal 116:245 Ap 21 '89. T. O'Brien
The Education Digest 55:20-2 N '89. I. A. Hyman
New York 22:73-5 Mr 20 '89. D. Denby
People Weekly 31:19-20 Mr 20 '89. T. Cunneff
Time il 133:82 Mr 13 '89. R. Schickel
Video il 13:78+ N '89. J. Young

AVILES, RICK
about
Street smart. K. Dieckmann. il por *New York* 22:28 N 27 '89

AVIONICS
See also
Airplanes, Business—Electronic equipment
Airplanes, Jet—Electronic equipment
Airplanes, Military—Electronic equipment
Airplanes, Training—Electronic equipment
Computers—Aviation use
Helicopters—Electronic equipment
Avionics. See issues of Aviation Week & Space Technology

AVIONICS INDUSTRY
See also
Bendix Corp.
CTA, Inc.
Eventide Avionics (Firm)
Loral Corp.
Narco Avionics (Firm)
Norden Systems Inc.
Ovonic Imaging Systems Inc.
Sundstrand Corporation

Acquisitions and mergers
France
European aerospace industry enters period of restructuring. J. M. Lenorovitz. il *Aviation Week & Space Technology* 131:34-5 Jl 3 '89
France prepares to merge four state-controlled avionics firms. J. M. Lenorovitz. *Aviation Week & Space Technology* 130:78 Ja 30 '89

Ethical aspects
GAO advises Air Force to cancel Loral's advanced radar warning receiver contract [allegations of illegally receiving information about competing Litton system] *Aviation Week & Space Technology* 130:23 My 22 '89
Litton gets share of ALR-56M program in Ill Wind plea agreement by Loral. D. F. Bond. *Aviation Week & Space Technology* 131:115 D 18-25 '89
Litton protest raises questions about new Loral operation [USAF award for F-16 radar warning receivers] P. J. Klass. *Aviation Week & Space Technology* 130:57 F 6 '89
Operation Ill Wind whips through Loral. M. D. Oneal. il *Business Week* p68 Je 12 '89
Sundstrand prepares to pay the piper—and the Pentagon. M. D. Oneal and P. Dwyer. il *Business Week* p35-6 Ja 23 '89
U.S. joins ex-employee in accusing Singer of fraud. *Aviation Week & Space Technology* 130:263 Mr 20 '89
USAF urges GAO to reconsider criticism of Loral contract award [Litton protest of contract] B. W. Henderson. *Aviation Week & Space Technology* 130:31 Je 5 '89

Finance
Defense electronic industry expects little sales growth. D. Hughes. il *Aviation Week & Space Technology* 130:66+ My 29 '89
Upgrades and civil avionics to counter budget squeeze. B. D. Nordwall. il *Aviation Week & Space Technology* 130:249-50 Mr 20 '89

AVIONICS INDUSTRY—*cont.*
Marketing
Avionics manufacturers target aging aircraft for instrument, TCAS sales. il *Aviation Week & Space Technology* 131:89+ Jl 24 '89
Canada
See also
Garrett Canada Ltd.
France
See also
Sextant Avionique (Firm)
United States
See Avionics industry
Western Europe
Post-1992 prospects spark restructuring in electronics and equipment groups. il *Aviation Week & Space Technology* 130:167-8+ Je 12 '89

AVIONS MARCEL DASSAULT BREGUET AVIATION *See* Dassault Breguet Aviation (Avions Marcel)

AVIRGAN, TONY
Panama contras? *The Nation* 249:263-5 S 18 '89

AVIS, INC.
With its ESOP, Avis tries even harder. H. Collingwood. il *Business Week* p122 My 15 '89

AVISE, JOHN C.
Nature's family archives. *Natural History* p24+ Mr '89

AVISE, JOHN C., AND NELSON, WILLIAM S.
Molecular genetic relationships of the extinct dusky seaside sparrow. bibl f il map *Science* 243:646-8 F 3 '89

AVNI, YORAM
about
Obituary
Physics Today 42:133-4 Mr '89. A. P. Lightman and others

AVOCADO INDUSTRY
Export-import trade
Death, intrigue and avocados [Mexico accuses Nucal de Mexico of being part of Israeli scheme to control export market] M. A. Lerner. il *Newsweek* 114:37 Ag 14 '89
Mexico
See also
Nucal de Mexico (Firm)

AVON BOOKS (FIRM)
Avon to launch trade paper line. il *Publishers Weekly* 236:24 Ag 25 '89

AVON PRODUCTS, INC.
Barrio makeover [selling products to Hispanic migrant women] R. Kirk. il *Ms.* 17:73-5 My '89
Can Avon get Wall Street to answer the door? K. Deveny. il por *Business Week* p123-4 Mr 20 '89
Ding-dong, raider calling [I. Jacobs] K. Deveny. *Business Week* p51+ Ag 14 '89
How d'ya say "liquidator" in Japanese? [I. Jacobs plays Tokyo-New York arbitrage in raids on Shaklee and Avon] S. Flack. il por *Forbes* 143:39-40 Je 12 '89
A takeover of Avon could mean a makeover for Amway. W. Zellner. il *Business Week* p38-9 My 22 '89

AVONDALE INDUSTRIES INC.
Big easy survivor. il *Forbes* 143:193 Ja 9 '89

AVONLEA TRADITIONS INC.
Anger on the Island [dispute over Anne of Green Gables merchandising] R. Corelli. il *Maclean's* 102:40 Jl 10 '89

AVOURIS, PHAEDON
(jt. auth) See Lyo, In-Whan, and Avouris, Phaedon

AVRIL, PROSPER
about
Haiti goes back. A. Wilentz. *The Nation* 249:669-70 D 4 '89
Haiti's prospects under Prosper Avril. S. Rodman. il por *The New Leader* 72:5-7 S 4 '89
Little priest, big general. S. Rodman. il *National Review* 41:24-5 S 29 '89

AVS *See* American Vacuum Society

AVTEK CORPORATION
Lacadre to certify Avtec 400A aircraft. E. H. Phillips. *Aviation Week & Space Technology* 131:138 N 20 '89

AVTEX FIBERS INC.
New source expected to prevent shortage of rayon for NASA, defense rockets [North American Rayon Corp.] *Aviation Week & Space Technology* 131:24 N 27 '89

AVX CORP.
Living dangerously. A. A. Lappen. il por *Forbes* 143:100+ Je 26 '89

AWACS (AIRBORNE WARNING AND CONTROL SYSTEM) *See* Airplanes, Military—Radar equipment

AWAD, JOSEPH
Stonework [poem] *America* 160:422 My 6 '89

AWAD, MUBARAK E.
about
The PLO: terrorists or freedom fighters? [interview] por *Christianity Today* 33:62 Ja 13 '89

AWAHUN INDIANS *See* Aguaruna Indians
AWAKENING FROM SLEEP *See* Wakening from sleep
AWARDS *See* Rewards, prizes, etc.
AWARDS OF MERIT *See* Certificates of merit
AWE *See* Wonder
AWNINGS
Made in the shade. il *Home Mechanix* 85:40-2+ My '89

Sun control with style. il *Southern Living* 24:122-3 Jl '89

AX, EMANUEL
about
Emanuel Ax plays Haydn sonatas. R. Freed. por *Stereo Review* 54:123-4 S '89

AXAF (ADVANCED X-RAY ASTROPHYSICS FACILITY) *See* Artificial satellites—Astronomical use

AXEL, GABRIEL
about
Babette's feast [film] Reviews
Video il 13:60 Ap '89. R. Gehr

AXES
Axes, heads and other tales. il *Workbench* 45:104 S/O '89

AXON, GORDON V.
Gems: be on your guard. il *Consumers' Research Magazine* 72:24-8 Je '89

AXONS
Electrophysiologic responses in hamster superior colliculus evoked by regenerating retinal axons. S. A. Keirstead and others. bibl f il *Science* 246:255-7 O 13 '89
A squid for all seasons [cultured in Texas for axon research] M. Kemp. il *Discover* 10:66-70 Je '89
Subplate neurons pioneer the first axon pathway from the cerebral cortex. S. K. McConnell and others. bibl f il *Science* 245:978-82 S 1 '89

AXTHELM, PETE
Smelling the roses, pricked by a thorn. il pors *Gentlemen's Quarterly* 59:234-9+ My '89

AYA *See* Fumihito, Prince of Japan, 1965-
AYERS-ALLEN, PHYLICIA *See* Rashad, Phylicia
AYERS ROCK (AUSTRALIA)
Rock dreams. R. Davidson. il *Mother Jones* 14:39-40 O '89

AYKROYD, DAN
about
A haunted humorist. B. D. Johnson. il pors *Maclean's* 102:54-5 Je 26 '89

AYLWIN, PATRICIO
about
Fall of the patriarch. T. Rosenberg. il *The New Republic* 201:20-3 D 18 '89
A vote for change in Chile. J. Contreras. il por *Newsweek* 114:40 D 18 '89

AYR MOUNT (HILLSBOROUGH, N.C.: PLANTATION) *See* Plantations—North Carolina

AYRES, IAN
Colleges in collusion. *The New Republic* 201:19-20 O 16 '89

AYRES, RICHARD E.
Should the Congress adopt the "Acid Deposition Control Act of 1987"? [excerpt from statement, July 9, 1987] *Congressional Digest* 68:58+ F '89

AYRES CORPORATION
Ayres Corp. developing low-cost, multimission Vigilante aircraft. E. H. Phillips. il *Aviation Week & Space Technology* 131:52-3 S 4 '89

AYUPOVA, ZHANNA
about
Dancescape. N. Alovert. il por *Dance Magazine* 63:6 N '89

AYVAZIAN, ANDREA
No payment enclosed: why I resist war taxes [cover story] il *The Progressive* 53:19-21 Ap '89

AZAD, ABDUL KALAM, 1888-1958
about
Makers of modern India. S. Gopal. il pors *The Courier (Unesco)* 42:10-11 F '89

AZCARRAGA, EMILIO
about
And in this corner coin box: an all-sports daily. S. Baker and D. Lieberman. il pors *Business Week* p30 Ag 21 '89

AZERBAIJAN (SOVIET UNION)
See also
Nagorno-Karabakh Autonomous Oblast (Soviet Union)
Nationalism
Agony and hope in Armenia. R. L. Deats. *The Christian Century* 106:81-2 Ja 25 '89
Fires of nationalism. A. Wilson-Smith. il *Maclean's* 102:43+ O 30 '89
Nightmare of the generals [Soviet generals held captive by Azerbaijanis] *Time* 134:48 S 18 '89
On the edge of civil war [feud between Armenia and Azerbaijan] P. Hofheinz. il maps *Time* 134:51 O 23 '89
Trouble in the Transcaucasus [dispute between Armenians and Azerbaijanis over Karabakh] M. Saroyan. bibl f il map *The Bulletin of the Atomic Scientists* 45:16-18+ Mr '89

AZIDES
Explosive molecular ionic crystals. W. L. Faust. bibl f il *Science* 245:37-42 Jl 7 '89

AZIDOTHYMIDINE
AZT causes cancer in lab animals. *Science News* 136:396 D 16 '89
AZT helps in early AIDS. *Science News* 136:102 Ag 12 '89
AZT reverses AIDS dementia in children. B. J. Culliton. il *Science* 246:21-3 O 6 '89

AZIDOTHYMIDINE—*cont.*
AZT slows HIV infection. *FDA Consumer* 23:5 N '89
AZT still on trial. J. Cherfas. *Science* 246:882 N 17 '89
Drug combo: double whammy with a bonus [AZT and interferon for AIDS patients with Kaposi's sarcoma; research by H. Clifford Lane] *Science News* 136:141 Ag 26 '89
Drug-resistant strains of AIDS virus found. J. L. Marx. *Science* 243:1551-2 Mr 24 '89
Early AZT use slows progression to AIDS. K. Fackelmann. *Science News* 136:135 Ag 26 '89
Fighting AIDS all the way. L. Josephs. il *The New York Times Magazine* p42+ O 8 '89
Gout drug might cut AZT dosage by half [probenecid; research by David M. Kornhauser] S. Hart. *Science News* 136:167 S 9 '89
HIV with reduced sensitivity to zidovudine (AZT) isolated during prolonged therapy. B. A. Larder and others. bibl f il *Science* 243:1731-4 Mr 31 '89
Interferon-α but not AZT suppresses HIV expression in chronically infected cell lines. G. Poli and others. bibl f il *Science* 244:575-7 My 5 '89
Multiple mutations in HIV-1 reverse transcriptase confer high-level resistance to zidovudine (AZT). B. A. Larder and S. D. Kemp. bibl f il *Science* 246:1155-8 D 1 '89
A new AIDS alert [early intervention with AZT] N. Underwood. *Maclean's* 102:55 Ap 3 '89
New hope [AZT slows onset of AIDS] il *Time* 134:56 Ag 14 '89
A new reprieve for AIDS victims [AZT slows onset of disease] *U.S. News & World Report* 107:13+ Ag 28-S 4 '89
NIH offers AZT to exposed workers. W. Booth. *Science* 243:1137 Mr 3 '89
Now that AIDS is treatable, who'll pay the crushing cost? N. J. Freundlich. il *Business Week* p115+ S 11 '89
Promising drug for children with AIDS [research by Pim Brouwers] *Science News* 135:88 F 11 '89
The virus strikes back [AZT-resistant strains] P. Gadsby. il *Discover* 10:20 Jl '89
Wider use of AIDS drugs advocated [AZT can delay development of AIDS] J. L. Marx. *Science* 245:811 Ag 25 '89
Prices
AIDS profiteering. P. C. Montgomery. il *Common Cause Magazine* 15:9 Ja/F '89
AIDS: the high cost of hope. il *Scholastic Update (Teachers' edition)* 122:12 N 3 '89
How much for a reprieve from AIDS? [Burroughs Wellcome lowers price] C. Gorman. il *Time* 134:81-2 O 2 '89
AZIMUTH
Directions—earth and sky. G. Lovi. il *Sky and Telescope* 77:399-400 Ap '89
AZIZ, BARBARA NIMRI
Buddhist nuns. il *Natural History* p40-9 Mr '89
AZIZA, CLAUDE
Creatures from inner space. il *The Unesco Courier* 42:12-13 O '89
AZORES
See also
Fishing—Azores
AZT *See* Azidothymidine
AZTECS
Food
Before the Conquest. R. Sokolov. il *Natural History* p76-9 Ag '89
How to eat like an Aztec. R. Sokolov. *Natural History* p110+ N '89
AZUL [film] *See* Motion picture reviews—Single works
AZZI, JENNIFER
about
A Cardinal virtue. D. S. Looney. il pors *Sports Illustrated* 71:94-6 N 20 '89

B

B., AGNES
about
A fresh approach to fashion and life in Paris. C. Aillaud. il por *Architectural Digest* 46:34+ S '89
B-1B AIRPLANES *See* Airplanes, Military
B-52 AIRPLANES *See* Airplanes, Military
B-52'S (MUSICAL GROUP)
After a decade off the radar screen, the funky B-52's are frequently flying again. M. Small. il *People Weekly* 32:191+ D 11 '89
B-52's' cosmic homecoming. P. Puterbaugh. il *Rolling Stone* p27 N 30 '89
B.A.D. (MUSICAL GROUP) *See* Big Audio Dynamite (Musical group)
B.A.S.S. INC.
Angling for bass and bucks. R. Woodbury. il *Time* 133:56 Je 5 '89
B A T INDUSTRIES PLC
A British war—on Yankee soil [Goldsmith-BAT takeover fight] T. Smart and M. Maremont. il *Business Week* p33 S 11 '89

'Goldfinger' is back [Sir J. Goldsmith's bid] L. Reibstein. il por *Newsweek* 114:48-9 Jl 24 '89
Jimmy Goldsmith, leading indicator. C. P. Work. il por *U.S. News & World Report* 107:43-4 Jl 24 '89
A raider returns [J. Goldsmith's bid] J. DeMont. il por *Maclean's* 102:34 Jl 24 '89
Smoke signals on BAT and American Brands. G. G. Marcial. il *Business Week* p98 S 11 '89
Storming a British blue chip [J. Goldsmith's bid] R. A. Melcher. il por *Business Week* p18-19 Jl 24 '89
Take that, Jimmy Goldsmith [BAT Industries sell-off] R. A. Melcher. il *Business Week* p60-1 O 9 '89
That's a reach, Sir James [J. Goldsmith's bid] J. Castro. il por *Time* 134:36-7 Jl 24 '89
Up to B.A.T.? [J. Coxon and Cigna Corp. to benefit in battle for BAT Industries] J. Zweig. il por *Forbes* 144:102 Ag 21 '89
B. ALTMAN & CO.
Debacle on 34th Street: how takeover debt helped kill off the venerable B. Altman chain. B. Rudolph. il por *Time* 134:77 D 11 '89
B CELLS
Transformation and plasmacytoid differentiation of EBV-infected human B lymphoblast by *ras* oncogenes. S. Seremetis and others. bibl f il *Science* 243:660-3 F 3 '89
B. DALTON BOOKSELLERS
Dalton acquires Scribner name, sees more stores. *Publishers Weekly* 235:15 My 26 '89
Why B. Dalton had second thoughts [controversy over sale of S. Rushdie's Satanic verses; interview with L. Riggio] J. F. Baker. *Publishers Weekly* 235:14-15 Mr 10 '89
B.F. GOODRICH CO.
See also
Uniroyal Goodrich Tire Co.
Goodrich looks steel-belted. G. G. Marcial. *Business Week* p132 My 15 '89
B.L. STRYKER [television program] *See* Television program reviews—Single works
B. MANISCHEWITZ CO.
Man oh Manischewitz [A. E. Levine puts LBO deal together] K. Kerwin. il por *Business Week* p25 Jl 24 '89
B. SMITH'S (NEW YORK, N.Y.: RESTAURANT) *See* New York (N.Y.)—Restaurants, nightclubs, bars, etc.
B STARS
Polar winds and excretion disks [B[e] supergiants; research by Franz-Josef Zickgraf and Roberta M. Humphreys] I. Peterson. *Science News* 136:12 Jl 1 '89
BAADER-MEINHOF GROUP *See* Red Army Faction
BABA RAM DASS *See* Ram Dass
BABAR (FICTIONAL CHARACTER)
Babar's triumphs [animated feature film] G. Hayden. il *Maclean's* 102:48 Ag 7 '89
BABAR: THE MOVIE [film] *See* Motion picture reviews—Single works
BABB, KRISTEN
about
Woman to watch. K. Millman. por *Women's Sports & Fitness* 11:55 Jl/Ag '89
BABBITT, BRUCE E.
First word. por *Omni (New York, N.Y.)* 11:6 S '89
BABE DIDRIKSON ZAHARIAS MEMORIAL MUSEUM (BEAUMONT, TEX.)
Beaumont remembers Babe. il *Southern Living* 24:22-3 O '89
BABEL, TOWER OF *See* Tower of Babel
BABETTE *See* March, Babette
BABETTE'S FEAST [film] *See* Motion picture reviews—Single works
BABIES *See* Infants
BABILONIA, TAI
A skating star's long fall from grace [cover story]; ed. by Lois Armstrong. il pors *People Weekly* 31:86-8+ Ap 17 '89
BABIN, CHARLES E.
Down but not out. il por *Forbes* 144:235 S 18 '89
How, and why, to play a housing rebound. il por *Forbes* 144:256 O 30 '89
BABOONS
Nice nitpickers [non-aggressive behavior leads to successful mating in olive baboons; research by Shirley Strum] il *Discover* 10:16 N '89
Sex and friendship among baboons [research by Shirley C. Strum] B. Bower. *Science News* 135:251 Ap 22 '89
Food and feeding
Junk food monkeys [olive baboons in Masai Mara Game Reserve feeding on humans' garbage] R. M. Sapolsky. il *Discover* 10:48-51 S '89
Weight and measurements
Upscale baboons [Kenya's Amboseli National Park] J. Altmann and A. Samuels. il *Natural History* p60-3 My '89
BABY ANIMALS *See* Animals, Infancy of
BABY BARS
San Francisco's Bellini Bar encourages its baby customers to hit the bottle, and burp. il *People Weekly* 31:153 My 15 '89

BABY BELLS *See* Telephone companies
BABY BOOM GENERATION
See also
　Children of baby boomers
Age vs. wage: how baby boomers may cool inflation. G. Koretz. il *Business Week* p26 F 6 '89
The age wave—and how to ride it. C. Farrell. il *Business Week* p112+ O 16 '89
The aging of America [economic impact of baby boomers; address, June 21, 1989] R. Christian. *Vital Speeches of the Day* 56:29-32 O 15 '89
Amid prosperity, unequal prospects [report by Frank Levy and Richard Michel] S. Nazar. il *U.S. News & World Report* 107:73 N 20 '89
The baby-boomer retirement blues. il *Black Enterprise* 20:51 O '89
Boomers at fortysomething. il *Business Week* p142-3 S 25 '89
The geezer boom. M. Beck. il *Newsweek* 114 Special Issue:62-3+ Wint '89/Spr '90
The gray '90s. il *Psychology Today* 22:8-9 D '88
The great boomer bust. K. Butler. il *Mother Jones* 14:32-8 Je '89
How we will live [retirement] S. Dentzer. il *U.S. News & World Report* 107:62-4 D 25 '89-Ja 1 '90
Paté poverty: downwardly mobile baby boomers lust after luxury. K. Butler. il *Utne Reader* p72-80 S/O '89
The Pepsi Generation heads for the corner office. J. Carey. il *Business Week* p170 S 25 '89
The workaholic generation [cover story] W. Kiechel. il *Fortune* 119:50-4+ Ap 10 '89
Political activities
George Bush's play for the baby-boomers. D. Baer. *U.S. News & World Report* 106:32 Je 26 '89
Religious life
The pivotal generation. P. Rinehart. il *Christianity Today* 33:21-6 O 6 '89
Sports
The boom in golf as baby boomers hit the links. W. C. Symonds. il *Business Week* p76-7+ Mr 27 '89
BABY BUST GENERATION
25 and taking over: the high-expectation, low-sweat generation. N. Angier. il *Mademoiselle* 95:214-15+ Ag '89
BABY CARE *See* Infants—Care and hygiene
BABY CARRIAGES
Stroll models [running strollers] M. Cimons. il *Runner's World* 24:74-5 Je '89
BABY CRIBS *See* Cribs (Beds)
BABY DOLLS *See* Dolls
BABY FOOD *See* Infants—Nutrition
BABY, IT'S YOU [film] *See* Motion picture reviews—Single works
BABY M CASE
Baby M. B. Darrach. il *People Weekly* 32 Special Issue:76 Fall '89
BABY PRODUCTS *See* Infants—Equipment
BABY SITTERS
The baby-sitter bind. K. Levine. il *Parents* 64:74+ Mr '89
Child care: smarter sitters [views of Cynthia Vlasich] S. Christenson. il *American Health* 8:120 Mr '89
Choosing a baby-sitter. K. Karlsrud and D. Schultz. il *Parents* 64:201 My '89
Leaving a child in charge. M. R. Skrocki. *McCall's* 117:71 N '89
Sitting pretty [New York City agencies] M. Morgan. il *New York* 22:102+ My 1 '89
Super sitters. L. Salk. il *McCall's* 116:69+ Je '89
Think before you (baby)sit. C. Purdy. il *Current Health 2* 16:22-3 N '89
What to look for in a sitter. L. MacCallum. il *Glamour* 87:92 Mr '89
Anecdotes, facetiae, satire, etc.
How we survived our first night out. J. Leonard. il *Parents* 64:97-8+ N '89
BABY SITTERS' COOPERATIVES
Shared baby-sitting. J. T. Gibson. il *Parents* 64:207 Je '89
BABY SITTERS IN LITERATURE
Children's books: inside the Baby-sitters Club [series by A. M. Martin] N. R. Kleinfield. *The New York Times Book Review* 94:42 Ap 30 '89
Games for girls: fun without bloodshed [suggested game based on Ann M. Martin's The Baby-sitters Club series] O. S. Card. il *Compute!* 11:12 Ag '89
BABY SWITCHING *See* Child switching
BABYLON (ANCIENT CITY)
Neo-Nebuchadnezzar [restoration] B. Weber. il *The New York Times Magazine* p94 N 26 '89
BACARD, ANDRÉ
A Hippocratic oath for scientists. il *The Humanist* 49:43 Jl/Ag '89
The second genesis: future technologies and humanism. il por *The Humanist* 49:9-11+ S/O '89
BACCALAUREATE ADDRESSES
Big man on campus [G. Bush's commencement addresses] F. Barnes. *The New Republic* 200:13-14 Je 5 '89
Camille Cosby warns Spelman grads about use of sex and money. il por *Jet* 76:4 Je 12 '89

Comedy of errors? [discussion of October 2, 1989 article, 'A gangsterdom of the spirit'] *The Nation* 249:406 O 16 '89
'A gangsterdom of the spirit' [E. L. Doctorow's controversial speech at Brandeis University] *The Nation* 249:348 O 2 '89
Rhonda Williams delivers historic graduation speech at University of Maryland. por *Jet* 76:19 Je 19 '89
BACH, CALEB
Taut strings. il pors *Américas* 41 no1:20-3 '89
BACH, CARL PHILIPP EMANUEL, 1714-1788
about
Ups and downs. W. H. Youngren. il *The Atlantic* 263:105-7 Ja '89
BACH, JOHANN SEBASTIAN, 1685-1750
about
Mass appeal. P. G. Davis. il *New York* 22:152 O 23 '89
Parallel bars [Conversations with fear and hope after death] P. G. Davis. il pors *New York* 22:78 Ap 17 '89
BACHE, ELLYN
Cutting weight [story] il *Seventeen* 48:190-1+ My '89
BACHELDER, ROBERT S.
Welfare and warfare: a dispute [discussion of December 14, 1988 article, Blinded by metaphor: churches and welfare reform] *The Christian Century* 106:419-21 Ap 19 '89
BACHELORS *See* Single men
BACHER, RENÉE
Member of the wedding. il *Seventeen* 48:34+ Mr '89
The ring cycle. il *The New York Times Magazine* p20+ Ag 13 '89
BACHMAN, DAVID
China's politics: conservatism prevails. bibl f *Current History* 88:257-60+ S '89
BACHMAN, RICHARD *See* King, Stephen, 1947-
BACILLUS
Chromosomal rearrangement generating a composite gene for a developmental transcription factor [Bacillus subtilis] P. Stragier and others. bibl f il *Science* 243:507-12 Ja 27 '89
Switch protein alters specificity of RNA polymerase containing a compartment-specific sigma factor [Bacillus subtilis] L. Kroos and others. bibl f il *Science* 243:526-9 Ja 27 '89
BACK PACKS *See* Backpacks and backpacking
BACK PORCHES *See* Porches
BACK RIVER (N.W.T.)
Follow your bliss [interview with canoeist R. Perkins] P. Edidin. il pors *Psychology Today* 23:62-4 My '89
Near-perfect paddle [women canoe length of the Back River] D. A. Buettner. il *Women's Sports & Fitness* 11:60 My '89
BACK TO THE FUTURE, PART II [film] *See* Motion picture reviews—Single works
BACKACHE
8 ways to prevent back pain. il *Glamour* 87:50 F '89
Back talk: advice for suffering spines. E. Zamula. il *FDA Consumer* 23:28-35 Ap '89
Can you avoid aches and pain? [views of Joseph A. Kopta] il *USA Today (Periodical)* 118:3 O '89
Expert's guide to relieving back pain. J. Alper. il *McCall's* 116:101-2+ Mr '89
Four weeks to a pain-free back [University of Miami's Comprehensive Pain and Rehabilitation Center] G. Maleskey. il *Prevention (Emmaus, Pa.)* 41:40-8 Mr '89
Good moves for bad backs. J. Hendley. il *Working Woman* 14:70 D '89
I am Joe's aching back. J. Pekkanen. il *Reader's Digest* 135:131-6 N '89
Liz Taylor's aching back and yours! G. McBride. il por *Ladies' Home Journal* 106:80+ Je '89
Tips to prevent aches and pains. *USA Today (Periodical)* 117:3 F '89
Your basic back. il *Mademoiselle* 95:212-13 Ag '89
BACKDRAFT DETECTORS *See* Draft detectors (Air infiltration measurement)
BACKGROUND IN PHOTOGRAPHY *See* Photography—Setting and scenery
BACKLIST BOOKS *See* Publishers and publishing—Backlist books
BACKMANN, RENÉ, AND BLANCHET, PIERRE
Why the carnage does not stop. *World Press Review* 36:24-5 O '89
BACKPACK HUNTING *See* Hunting
BACKPACKING BOOTS *See* Hiking boots
BACKPACKS AND BACKPACKING
Backpacking [tips on packing food] il *American Health* 8:108 Jl/Ag '89
Packing it in [food] C. Taylor. il *The Mother Earth News* 118:76+ Jl/Ag '89
Take a hike! B. A. Jacobs. il *Black Enterprise* 20:79-80+ Ag '89
Thoughtless packing. S. Netherby. *Field & Stream* 94:76 My '89
BACKS (CAMERAS) *See* Photography—Electronic equipment; Photography—Equipment
BACKSCATTER RADAR SYSTEM *See* Radar defense networks

BACKTROLLING *See* Trawls and trawling
BACKUS, JIM

about

Obituary
    People Weekly il por 32:54 Jl 17 '89
BACKWARD SPEECH *See* Speech
BACKYARD CAMPING *See* Camping
BACKYARDS *See* Home grounds
BACON, FRANCIS, 1909-

about

Angst of the spirit. E. MacSweeney. il *Harper's Bazaar* 122:174-5+ O '89
The painted face. J. Brown. il *Vogue* 179:420-5 O '89
The taste for Bacon. B. Taylor. il por *Art News* 88:57 Ja '89
Unnerving art [cover story] M. Kimmelman. il por *The New York Times Magazine* p40-3+ Ag 20 '89
BACON
Bacon: the food you hate to love. il *Consumer Reports* 54:647-9 O '89
What's known about the risk [nitrosamines] il *Consumer Reports* 54:648 O '89
BACQUE, JAMES

about

Ike's revenge? por *Time* 134:19 O 2 '89
Sullying the allies. D. Turbide. il por *Maclean's* 102:75 N 13 '89
BACTERIA

See also

Bacillus
Escherichia coli
Mutation—Bacteria
Mycobacterium
Probiotics
Pseudomonas
Thiobacillus

The bacteria that hate women. M. Beck. il *Ladies' Home Journal* 106:118-19+ Ag '89

Resistance and sensitivity

Inhibition of a class C β-lactamase by a specific phosphonate monoester. R. F. Pratt. bibl f il *Science* 246:917-19 N 17 '89
A Salmonella locus that controls resistance to microbicidal proteins from phagocytic cells. P. I. Fields and others. bibl f il *Science* 243:1059-62 F 24 '89
BACTERIA, EFFECT OF ANTIBIOTICS ON *See* Bacteria—Resistance and sensitivity
BACTERIA, HALOPHILIC

See also

Halobacteria
BACTERIA, MARINE
Symbiotic marine bacteria chemically defend crustacean embryos from a pathogenic fungus. M. S. Gil-Turnes and others. bibl f il *Science* 246:116-18 O 6 '89
BACTERIA, METHANOGENIC
Peatlands: a global warming threat? [research by Joseph B. Yavitt and R. Kelman Wieder] J. Raloff. *Science News* 136:143 Ag 26 '89
BACTERIA, NITROGEN FIXING
Sunshine fuels a bacterial relationship [research by Ralph W. F. Hardy] I. Wickelgren. il *Science News* 135:36 Ja 21 '89
BACTERIA, PATHOGENIC

See also

Borrelia
Salmonella
Staphylococci

Coordinate regulation and sensory transduction in the control of bacterial virulence. J. F. Miller and others. bibl f il *Science* 243:916-22 F 17 '89
BACTERIA, PETROLEUMLYTIC
Exxon bets on bugs in Alaska cleanup. M. Crawford. *Science* 245:704 Ag 18 '89
Microbes recruited in Valdez cleanup. *Science News* 135:383 Je 17 '89
Valdez 'bugs' chomp away. *Science News* 136:38 Jl 15 '89
Where was Chakrabarty's "bug"? G. Byrne. *Science* 244:919 My 26 '89
BACTERIA, PHOTOSYNTHETIC

See also

Halobacteria
Rhodobacter
Rhodopseudomonas

Sunshine fuels a bacterial relationship [research by Ralph W. F. Hardy] I. Wickelgren. il *Science News* 135:36 Ja 21 '89
BACTERIAL ANTIGENS *See* Antigens and antibodies
BACTERIAL CHEMOTAXIS *See* Chemotaxis
BACTERIAL DEGRADATION *See* Biodegradation
BACTERIAL DISEASES

See also

Chlamydia infections
Streptococcal infections
Toxic shock syndrome
Typhoid fever

BACTERIAL GENETICS *See* Microbial genetics
BACTERIAL MEMBRANES *See* Membranes (Biology)
BACTERIAL PROTEINS

See also

Flagellin
Porin
Streptavidin

Epithelial cell surfaces induce Salmonella proteins required for bacterial adherence and invasion. B. B. Finlay and others. bibl f il *Science* 243:940-3 F 17 '89
Function of a bacterial activator protein that binds to transcriptional enhancers. D. L. Popham and others. bibl f il *Science* 243:629-35 F 3 '89
Hydrophobic organization of membrane proteins [Rhodobacter] D. C. Rees and others. bibl f il *Science* 245:510-13 Ag 4 '89
The location of DNA in RecA-DNA helical filaments. E. H. Egelman and X. Yu. bibl f il *Science* 245:404-7 Jl 28 '89
Proton motive force involved in protein transport across the outer membrane of Aeromonas salmonicida. K. R. Wong and J. T. Buckley. bibl f il *Science* 246:654-6 N 3 '89
Sindbis virus: an efficient, broad host range vector for gene expression in animal cells. C. Xiong and others. bibl f il *Science* 243:1188-91 Mr 3 '89
BACTERIAL VIRUSES *See* Bacteriophages
BACTERIOLOGY

See also

Computers—Biological use
Fermentation
Mouth—Microbiology
Toxins and antitoxins

BACTERIOPHAGES
Control of enzyme activity by an engineered disulfide bond. M. Matsumura and B. W. Matthews. bibl f il *Science* 243:792-4 F 10 '89
DNA looping generated by DNA bending protein IHF and the two domains of lambda integrase. L. Moitoso De Vargas and others. bibl f il *Science* 244:1457-61 Je 23 '89
Enhancement of bacteriophage T4 late transcription by components of the T4 DNA replication apparatus. D. R. Herendeen and others. bibl f il *Science* 245:952-8 S 1 '89
Generation of a large combinatorial library of the immunoglobulin repertoire in phage lambda. W. D. Huse and others. bibl f il *Science* 246:1275-81 D 8 '89
Splicing on-off switches into proteins [disulfide bond; research by Brian W. Matthews and Masazumi Matsumura] *Science News* 135:123 F 25 '89
BACTERIORHODOPSIN *See* Pigments (Biology)
BACULOVIRUSES
Baculovirus for biocontrol and biotech. R. Lewis. il *BioScience* 39:431-4 Jl/Ag '89
First field test of engineered virus [weakened baculoviruses to be sprayed onto cabbages] *Science News* 136:46 Jl 15 '89
BACZYNSKI, JERZY, AND KRZEMINSKI, ADAM
The defeated party plays for time. *World Press Review* 36:29-30 Ag '89
BAD BREATH *See* Halitosis
BAD HABITS *See* Habits
BAD MOODS *See* Moods
BADASH, LAWRENCE
The age-of-the-earth debate. il *Scientific American* 261:90-4+ Ag '89
BADEN-BADEN (GERMANY)
The ultimate spa: Baden-Baden offers a tradition of soothing elegance. H. Basch and S. Slater. *Travel Holiday* 172:92-3 O '89
BADER, ELEANOR J.
March on Washington. il *The Humanist* 49:26-8+ Jl/Ag '89
BADER, LOIS A.
Communicating with teachers—honestly. bibl f il *Phi Delta Kappan* 70:626-9 Ap '89
BADER FAMILY FARM
Successful family farm [cover story] D. Mowitz. il *Successful Farming* 87:54-6 S '89
BADFINGER (MUSICAL GROUP)
Badfinger. P. Puterbaugh. il *Rolling Stone* p52 Ag 10 '89
BADMINTON HOUSE (AVON, ENGLAND) *See* Historic houses, sites, etc.—Great Britain
BADOVINUS, WAYNE

about

Pig sweaters versus sleeping bags. C. Siler. il por *Forbes* 144:211-12 S 18 '89
BAECHLER, DONALD, 1956-

about

Donald Baechler at Paul Kasmin and Tony Shafrazi. S. Ellis. il *Art in America* 77:170-1 Je '89
BAER, DONALD
The next George Wallace. il pors *Gentlemen's Quarterly* 59:292-7+ D '89
BAER, JOSHUA
Space and design: a brief history of the Navajo chief's blanket. bibl f il *Antiques* 136:528-41 S '89

BAER, RICHARD A.
The High Court's "S" word. il *Christianity Today* 33:20-1 S 8 '89

BAFFIN ISLAND (N.W.T.)
Industries
See also
Whaling—Baffin Island (N.W.T.)

BAG LADIES *See* Homeless women

BAGASAO, PAULA Y.
Student voices: breaking the silence. il *Change* 21:28-37 N/D '89

BAGBY, ALBERT MORRIS
about
Amazin' Albert (I). F. Bowers. il pors *Opera News* 53:12-14+ F 4 '89
Amazin' Albert (II). F. Bowers. il por *Opera News* 53:32-7 F 18 '89

BAGBY FOUNDATION FOR THE MUSICAL ARTS
Amazin' Albert (II). F. Bowers. il por *Opera News* 53:32-7 F 18 '89

BAGDAD CAFE [film] *See* Motion picture reviews—Single works

BAGDADE, AL
(jt. auth) *See* Bagdade, Susan, and Bagdade, Al

BAGDADE, SUSAN, AND BAGDADE, AL
Classics in china. *See* occasional issues of Antiques & Collecting Hobbies beginning March 1985 through May 1989

BAGDIKIAN, BEN
The lords of the global village [cover story; with editorial comment] *The Nation* 248:799-800, 805-8+ Je 12 '89
Missing from the news. il *The Progressive* 53:32-4 Ag '89

BAGET, ANDRE, AND BAGET, LISA
Kite festivals. il *Petersen's Photographic Magazine* 17:30-3 Ap '89

BAGET, LISA
(jt. auth) *See* Baget, Andre, and Baget, Lisa

BAGGAGE *See* Luggage

BAGLEY, BRUCE MICHAEL
Dateline drug wars: Colombia: the wrong strategy. *Foreign Policy* 77:154-71 Wint '89/'90

BAGNE, PAUL
Interview: Verner Suomi. por *Omni (New York, N.Y.)* 11:60-2+ Jl '89

BAGPIPE IN ART
History at the margins: bagpipers in medieval manuscripts. D. Stephens. bibl il *History Today* 39:42-8 Ag '89

BAGS
See also
Camera bags, cases, etc.
Duffel bags
Shopping bags
ABA launches group buying for store bags. J. Mutter. *Publishers Weekly* 235:18 My 19 '89
Bag and baggage [reprint from March 1959 issue] T. Trueblood. il *Field & Stream* 94:28+ My '89
On the road [tote bags for men] F. Rogers. il *The New York Times Magazine* p64 Je 25 '89
Tropical tote. il *Sunset (Central West edition)* 183:54-5 Ag '89

BAGWORMS
Bagworms earned their name. L. A. Weathers. il *Southern Living* 24:40 Ag '89

BAHAMAS
See also
Fishing—Bahamas
Green Turtle Cay (Bahamas)
Narcotics laws and regulations—Bahamas
Nassau (Bahamas)
Samana Cay (Bahamas)
Yacht clubs—Bahamas
Description and travel
See also
Cruising—Bahamas
The Caribbean & Bahamas: beaches & beyond. R. J. Christmas. il *Travel Holiday* 171:25-6+ Ap '89
Industries
See also
Crayfish fisheries—Bahamas

BAHAR, ANN
Miniatures. *See* issues of Antiques & Collecting Hobbies beginning March 1985

BAHIAN COOKING *See* Cooking, Brazilian

BAHLS, JANE EASTER
Patenting genetic 'inventions'. il *High Technology Business* 9:10 Je '89
Save the world! Earn big money! *Sierra* 74:18+ Jl/Ag '89
Two for one: a working idea. il *Nation's Business* 77:28-30 Je '89
U.S. shoe firms thrive in high-quality market. il *Nation's Business* 77:38-40 F '89
(jt. auth) *See* Bahls, Steven C., and Bahls, Jane Easter

BAHLS, STEVEN C., AND BAHLS, JANE EASTER
Courts clamp down on boards. il *Nation's Business* 77:52-3 D '89

BAHRAIN
See also
Public health—Bahrain

BAHRO, RUDOLF, 1935-
about
Theology not ecology [interview] N. Gardels. il *New Perspectives Quarterly* 6:36-9 Spr '89

BAI HUA
about
Two dissidents challenge 'feudal communism' [interview] J. L. Du Sablon. il pors *World Press Review* 36:26-7 F '89

BAICHUN XIAO
about
Reborn in the U.S.A. S. Seixas. il pors *Money* 18:64-6+ Ag '89

BAIDA, PETER
Men who made the rules. il *American Heritage* 40:18+ F '89

BAIER, SUE, AND SCHOMAKER, ZIMMETH
Woman in bed number 10 [condensation] il *Reader's Digest* 134:199-205+ F '89

BAIL
The no-bail solution. R. F. Nagel. *The New Republic* 200:13-14 Ap 24 '89

BAILARD, BIEHL & KAISER
Can you buy insurance against a recession? G. G. Marcial. il *Business Week* p76 Ap 17 '89

BAILEY, FERESHTEH
about
Outwitting the hackers. S. Kauffman. il por *Nation's Business* 77:17 S '89

BAILEY, JAMES
The global zeitgeist checklist: Japan. *The New Republic* 200:25 Je 26 '89

BAILEY, JAMES, 1938-
Photo-electronics. *See* issues of Popular Photography beginning July 1988

BAILEY, JANET
Built to last. il *Health (New York, N.Y.)* 21:60-3+ O '89
Dancin' and romancin' [cover story] il *Health (New York, N.Y.)* 21:39-43 Ja '89
Friendly persuasion: how to help your husband help himself. *Redbook* 172:110-11+ Ap '89
The lure of the rogue. il *Health (New York, N.Y.)* 21:62-5+ D '89
Mind over mother. *Harper's Bazaar* 122:165+ O '89
Sports shy. il *Health (New York, N.Y.)* 21:56-61 Je '89

BAILEY, JANET
about
Fingers of speech. S. Nelton. il por *Nation's Business* 77:12+ Jl '89

BAILEY, JOHNNY
about
New standard for yardage. M. McKenzie. il por *Sports Illustrated* 71:96 O 23 '89

BAILEY, MILTON
about
Gold country. R. F. Snow. il *American Heritage* 40:30+ My/Je '89

BAILEY, ROBERT C.
The Efe: archers of the African rain forest. il maps *National Geographic* 176:664-86 N '89

BAILEY, SAMMY
about
A boy sides with Dr. Seuss's Lorax, and puts a town at loggerheads. R. Arias. il pors *People Weekly* 32:67-8 O 23 '89

BAILEY, VAREL
about
'Declare rural America a third-world country!'. C. Tevis. il por map *Successful Farming* 87:13-14 Ag '89

BAILEY, VICTOR
about
Blindfold test. B. Milkowski. il por *Down Beat* 56:46 My '89

BAILEY, WES
about
The great talk-show hoax. B. G. Harrison. *Mademoiselle* 95:62 Ja '89

BAIN, DAVID HAWARD
Manifest Destiny's man of the hour: Frederick Funston. bibl (p164) il pors *Smithsonian* 20:134-6+ My '89

BAIN, GEORGE
Media watch. *See* occasional issues of Maclean's

BAINBRIDGE, J. S., JR.
Frogs that sweat—not bullets, but a poison for darts. il *Smithsonian* 19:70-4+ Ja '89

BAINBRIDGE, JOHN
London journal. *See* occasional issues of Gourmet

BAINBRIDGE ISLAND (WASH.)
See also
Flower gardens and gardening—Bainbridge Island (Wash.)

BAIRD, FORREST E.
My dream house and my boy; ed. by Linda Lawrence. il *Reader's Digest* 135:9-10+ O '89

BAIRD, ROBERT
about
A margin for the electronic broker. R. D. R. Hoffmann. il por *Personal Computing* 13:90-2 O '89

BAIT
See also
Earthworms
Mealworms
Among the liver eaters [channel catfish] J. M. Vance. il *Field & Stream* 94:16-17 Je '89
The best bass bait [crayfish] K. Etling. il *Outdoor Life* 183:64-5+ Je '89
Going live. B. Stearns. il *Field & Stream* 93:68+ Mr '89
How to use strip baits. P. B. Wright. il *Motor Boating & Sailing* 164:74 D '89
Skeeter and the great bait debate. W. G. Tapply. il *Field & Stream* 94:44-5+ Je '89
Small bait, big fish. P. B. Wright. il *Motor Boating & Sailing* 163:102 Mr '89
Summer smallmouth secrets [live crayfish bait] W. Ryan. il *Outdoor Life* 183:78-9+ My '89
Why fish bite. P. B. Wright. il *Motor Boating & Sailing* 164:37 O '89
BAIT, ARTIFICIAL *See* Fishing lures, flies, etc.
BAIT BOXES
A floating bait box. P. Butler and M. Butler. il *Outdoor Life* 183:30+ Je '89
BAIT CASTING REELS *See* Fishing tackle
BAIT TRAPS *See* Fish traps
BAITS, DEER *See* Deer baits
BAJA 1000 (RACE) *See* Motor vehicle racing—Baja California (Mexico: Peninsula)
BAJA CALIFORNIA (MEXICO: PENINSULA)
See also
Cabo San Lucas (Mexico)
Fishing—Baja California (Mexico: Peninsula)
Motor vehicle racing—Baja California (Mexico: Peninsula)
Description and travel
Baja California: Mexico's land apart. D. Belt. il maps *National Geographic* 176:714-45 D '89
Photographs and photography
A photographer's guide to Baja. P. Skinner. il map *Petersen's Photographic Magazine* 18:44-8 S '89
BAJA CALIFORNIA NORTE (MEXICO)
Politics and government
Democracy wins a round [P. R. I. concedes gubernatorial race] G. D. Garcia. il *Time* 134:67 Jl 17 '89
Mexico: true concessions [PRI loses to PAN in Baja] S. McGuire. il *Newsweek* 114:36 Jl 17 '89
BAKER, ANITA
about
Anita Baker on love. P. Garland. por *Stereo Review* 54:108 Mr '89
Anita Baker suffers a miscarriage in Detroit. il por *Jet* 75:17 F 27 '89
Anita Baker tells how fame takes toll on her. por *Jet* 76:63 Jl 3 '89
Anita Baker tells why she kept her marriage and pregnancy a secret [cover story] C. Waldron. il pors *Jet* 75:28-32 F 6 '89
Hot voice, cool head [cover story] B. Allen. il pors *Ms.* 17:42-5 Je '89
A personal and private look at Anita Baker [cover story] L. Norment. il pors *Ebony* 44:29-30+ Jl '89
BAKER, BETH
Rubber stamp. *Common Cause Magazine* 15:7-8 Jl/Ag '89
BAKER, BRENT
Media's liberal slant on the news. il *USA Today (Periodical)* 118:64-6 Jl '89
(jt. auth) See Bozell, L. Brent, III, and Baker, Brent
BAKER, CHET
about
At long last, jazz. R. Seidenberg. il pors *American Film* 14:50-4 My '89
Farewell, my unlovelies. R. Merkin. il *Gentlemen's Quarterly* 59:112+ Ap '89
Hall of Fame. O. Cordle. il por *Down Beat* 56:20 Ag '89
BAKER, CHRISTOPHER
Requiem for a heavyweight? il *National Wildlife* 27:38-43 Je/Jl '89
BAKER, DAVID, 1954-
After the reunion [poem] *The Nation* 249:100 Jl 17 '89
BAKER, DEXTER F.
about
Keeping the cow, selling the milk. H. Banks. il por *Forbes* 143:40-1 Mr 20 '89
BAKER, GINGER
about
Ginger Baker. D. Browne. il por *Rolling Stone* p54-5 Ag 10 '89
Voted least likely to survive the '60s, rocker Ginger Baker now faces 50 with a smile. S. Dougherty. il pors *People Weekly* 31:133-4+ Je 19 '89
BAKER, GRAHAM
about
Alien nation [film] Reviews
Video il 13:60 Ag '89. J. Walker

BAKER, JACK
about
Gardens: subtropical artistry: Jack Baker's exuberant creation near Santa Barbara. M. Frank. il pors *Architectural Digest* 46:284-9+ My '89
BAKER, JAMES A., III
After the NATO summit: challenges for the West in a changing world [address and excerpts from question-and-answer session, June 8, 1989] *Department of State Bulletin* 89:55-61 Ag '89
ASEAN postministerial conference, Bandar Seri Begawan [statements, July 6-7, 1989] *Department of State Bulletin* 89:58-61 S '89
Certification for narcotics source and transit countries [text of letter, March 1, 1989] *Department of State Bulletin* 89:68 My '89
The challenge of change in U.S.-Soviet relations [address, May 4, 1989] *Department of State Bulletin* 89:36-9 Jl '89
Challenges ahead for NATO and developments in East-West relations [statement, June 20, 1989] *Department of State Bulletin* 89:61-4 Ag '89
The international agenda and the FY 1990 budget request [statement, February 21, 1989] *Department of State Bulletin* 89:16-21 Ap '89
International conference on Cambodia held in Paris [statement, July 30, 1989; with text of conference statement, August 30, 1989] il *Department of State Bulletin* 89:25-7 O '89
James A. Baker, III, sworn in as Secretary of State [remarks, January 27, 1989] il por *Department of State Bulletin* 89:8-9 Ap '89
MAI pledging conference, Tokyo, July 4, 1989 [address] *Department of State Bulletin* 89:56-8 S '89
Namibian independence and troop withdrawal from Angola [statement, March 31, 1989] *Department of State Bulletin* 89:29 My '89
New horizons in Europe [address, March 6, 1989] *Department of State Bulletin* 89:56-9 My '89
A new Pacific partnership: framework for the future [address, June 26, 1989] *Department of State Bulletin* 89:64-6 Ag '89
News conference of June 29. *Department of State Bulletin* 89:63-5 S '89
News conference of September 19. *Department of State Bulletin* 89:39-43 N '89
Points of mutual advantage [address, October 16, 1989] *Vital Speeches of the Day* 56:66-70 N 15 '89
Power for good: American foreign policy in the new era [address, April 14, 1989] *Department of State Bulletin* 89:8-11 Je '89
President's visit to Canada [news conference, February 10, 1989] il *Department of State Bulletin* 89:28-31 Ap '89
Principles and pragmatism [address, May 22, 1989] *Vital Speeches of the Day* 55:549-51 Jl 1 '89
Principles and pragmatism: American policy toward the Arab-Israeli conflict [address, May 22, 1989] *Department of State Bulletin* 89:24-7 Jl '89
Secretary addresses panel on global climate change [remarks, January 30, 1989] *Department of State Bulletin* 89:13 Ap '89
Secretary Baker's and Foreign Minister van den Broek's news conference, The Hague, July 17, 1989. *Department of State Bulletin* 89:50-3 S '89
Secretary Baker's news briefing, Bonn, May 30, 1989. il *Department of State Bulletin* 89:34-7 Ag '89
Secretary Baker's news briefing, Feb. 23, 1989. il *Department of State Bulletin* 89:1-4 My '89
Secretary Baker's news briefing, London, June, 1, 1989. il pors *Department of State Bulletin* 89:41-4 Ag '89
Secretary Baker's news conference, Budapest, July 12, 1989. il por *Department of State Bulletin* 89:43-6 S '89
Secretary Baker's news conference, Paris, July 15, 1989. *Department of State Bulletin* 89:3-6 S '89
Secretary Baker's news conference, Warsaw, July 10, 1989. il *Department of State Bulletin* 89:29-32 S '89
Secretary-designate's confirmation hearings [statement, January 17, 1989] *Department of State Bulletin* 89:10-16 Ap '89
Secretary meets with Israeli foreign minister [remarks, March 13, 1989] *Department of State Bulletin* 89:63 My '89
Secretary meets with NATO allies [remarks, February 11-17, 1989] *Department of State Bulletin* 89:38-42 Ap '89
Secretary meets with Soviet foreign minister [remarks and question-and-answer session, March 7, 1989] *Department of State Bulletin* 89:59-60 My '89
Secretary's news briefings in New York [September 25-29, 1989] il pors *Department of State Bulletin* 89:31-8 N '89
Secretary's news conference [May 23, 1989] *Department of State Bulletin* 89:21-4 Jl '89
Secretary's news conference, the White House, Sept. 21, 1989. il por *Department of State Bulletin* 89:1-4 N '89
Secretary's trip to Moscow and NATO [remarks, news conferences, etc., May 10-12, 1989] *Department of State Bulletin* 89:29-36 Jl '89
Times full of promise [excerpts from address, October 23, 1989] *Aviation Week & Space Technology* 131:7 O 30 '89

BAKER, JAMES A., III—*cont.*

U.S. and Latin America: a shared destiny [address; with text of question and answer session, May 1, 1989] *Department of State Bulletin* 89:5-8 Je '89

U.S.-Mexico Binational Commission meets in Mexico City [statement, news conference, and text of joint communique, August 7, 1989] il por *Department of State Bulletin* 89:76-84 O '89

about

Aiming for the heights. H. Mackenzie. il pors *Maclean's* 102:31-3 O 2 '89

Baker and the bureaucrats are already crossing swords at State. B. Javetski. por *Business Week* p51 F 27 '89

Baker: sheepdog diplomacy? M. G. Warner. il *Newsweek* 113:40 Ap 17 '89

Baker takes a risky step to center stage in the Middle East. S. Reed. il *Business Week* p82 O 23 '89

Baker's 'useless' advice. por *Newsweek* 113:42 Je 5 '89

The banker plan. *The New Republic* 200:7-8 Mr 6 '89

Blind men's bluff [cover story] M. Kondracke. *The New Republic* 200:20+ Mr 6 '89

Bush's Mr. Smooth runs into rough water. *Newsweek* 113:17 F 13 '89

Capitol gains. A. Stanley. il por *Vogue* 179:496-7+ Mr '89

A false start in the Middle East. E. V. Rostow. *Commentary* 88:24-7 O '89

First steps toward a policy. M. Kramer. il por *Time* 133:41 Mr 27 '89

Happy campers, for a change. S. Talbott. pors *Time* 134:24 Ag 28 '89

Inching ever closer together. B. Javetski. il *Business Week* p40-1 O 9 '89

James A. Baker, III, Secretary of State. *Department of State Bulletin* 89:9 Ap '89

James Baker: pragmatist at State. R. Evans and R. D. Novak. il pors *Reader's Digest* 135:213-14+ N '89

Jim Baker, ministering to the media [cover story] T. Bethell. il *National Review* 41:24-7 My 5 '89

Jim Baker's conflict-of-interest problems. W. Greider. il *Rolling Stone* p43-5 Ap 20 '89

Letter from Washington. Cato. *National Review* 41:9 Mr 24 '89

Letter from Washington. E. Drew. *The New Yorker* 65:72-82 Je 26 '89

A letter to Mr. Baker. il *America* 161:335-6 N 18 '89

Master handler. A. R. Dowd. por *Fortune* 119:54 Ja 2 '89

Mr. Inside, Mr. Outside. J. Barry. pors *Newsweek* 113:28 F 27 '89

An overture to Congress. M. G. Warner. il por *Newsweek* 113:26 Ja 23 '89

Peace later. M. Kondracke. *The New Republic* 200:10-12 Mr 27 '89

Playing for the edge [cover story; with interview] M. Kramer. il pors map *Time* 133:26-33 F 13 '89

The politics of diplomacy. H. Anderson. il *Newsweek* 114:20-1 O 2 '89

The pragmeologues. D. Seligman. il *Fortune* 119:165 My 8 '89

The quiet sage steering Bush's foreign policy. H. Trewhitt. il por *U.S. News & World Report* 106:22-4 F 20 '89

Raining on Baker's parade. M. B. Carlson. il por *Time* 133:18-19 F 27 '89

Regrets only. *The New Republic* 200:8 Je 19 '89

Secretary Baker's interview on "Evans and Novak," Paris, July 15, 1989 [transcript of program] il *Department of State Bulletin* 89:7-10 S '89

Secretary Baker's interview on "Face the nation" (excerpts), Feb. 26, 1989. il *Department of State Bulletin* 89:10-13 My '89

Secretary Baker's interview on "Good morning, America," Brussels, May 30, 1989 [transcript of program] *Department of State Bulletin* 89:29-30 Ag '89

Secretary Baker's interview on "Meet the press," Rome, May 28, 1989 [transcript of program] il *Department of State Bulletin* 89:12-15 Ag '89

Secretary Baker's interview on "This week with David Brinkley", Paris, July 16, 1989 [transcript of program] *Department of State Bulletin* 89:10-12 S '89

Secretary's interview for "American interests" [transcript of program, April 22, 1989] M. Kondracke. *Department of State Bulletin* 89:14-19 Je '89

Secretary's interview on "Face the nation" [transcript of program, May 14, 1989] *Department of State Bulletin* 89:27-9 Jl '89

Secretary's interview on "MacNeil/Lehrer newshour" [transcript of program, March 24, 1989] *Department of State Bulletin* 89:23-5 My '89

Secretary's interview on "Meet the press" [transcript of program, February 19, 1989] *Department of State Bulletin* 89:21-4 Ap '89

Secretary's interview on "Newsmaker Saturday" [transcript of program, June 3, 1989] *Department of State Bulletin* 89:67-9 Ag '89

Secretary's interview on the "MacNeil/Lehrer newshour" [transcript of program, July 19, 1989] *Department of State Bulletin* 89:66-9 S '89

Secretary's interview on "This week with David Brinkley" [transcript of program, March 26, 1989] *Department of State Bulletin* 89:25-7 My '89

Secretary's interview on "This week with David Brinkley" [transcript of program, April 9, 1989] *Department of State Bulletin* 89:12-14 Je '89

Sparring partners. M. Kondracke. *The New Republic* 201:14-16 N 13 '89

START deals cut at Jackson Hole. J. Mendelsohn. il pors *The Bulletin of the Atomic Scientists* 45:25-7 D '89

Straight talk from the U.S. C. Ogden. il por *Time* 133:32 Je 5 '89

Teflon John and Jim. T. Eastland. il *The American Spectator* 22:40-1 Je '89

True friends and false. *Commonweal* 116:357 Je 16 '89

Vision problems at State . . . C. Ogden. il por *Time* 134:22 S 25 '89

Visit to the Soviet Union, 1989

Agenda for Baker-Shevardnadze. *National Review* 41:11-12 My 5 '89

Agreement to disagree. A. Wilson-Smith. il pors *Maclean's* 102:25-6 My 22 '89

Madison Avenue, Moscow [M. Gorbachev's proposal to J. Baker] G. J. Church. il pors *Time* 133:33-4 My 22 '89

The naysayer and new détente [J. A. Baker's Soviet visit yields new arms proposals] H. Trewhitt. il pors *U.S. News & World Report* 106:18-19 My 22 '89

Secretary's trip to Moscow and NATO [remarks, news conferences, etc., May 10-12, 1989] J. A. Baker, III. *Department of State Bulletin* 89:29-36 Jl '89

Will the allies leave Bush behind? B. Javetski and D. Griffiths. il pors *Business Week* p30-1 My 15 '89

Visit to Western Europe, 1989

Secretary meets with NATO allies [remarks, February 11-17, 1989] J. A. Baker, III. *Department of State Bulletin* 89:38-42 Ap '89

BAKER, JERRY

about

The grass is always greener on Jerry Baker's lawn because he feeds it beer, soap and ammonia [interview] J. Greenwalt. il pors *People Weekly* 31:85+ Je 19 '89

BAKER, JOHN

about

A reunion in friendship. il pors *Sports Illustrated* 71:12+ N 27 '89

BAKER, JOSEPHINE, 1906-1975

about

Feathers. T. Tobias. il *New York* 22:53 Jl 17 '89

Josephine Baker's naughty jiggle makes a comeback: Jazz Age princess. M. Aloff. il pors *Dance Magazine* 63:32-4 Jl '89

Josephine Baker's war on racism [excerpt from Jazz Cleopatra] P. Rose. il pors *American Visions* 4:25-8 O '89

PW interviews [biographer P. Rose] K. Weber. por *Publishers Weekly* 236:36-7 S 22 '89

The St. Louis Woman of Paris. G. C. Ward. il *American Heritage* 40:14+ N '89

Anecdotes, facetiae, satire, etc.

A film bio of Josephine Baker is in the works—and Vogue has a few casting suggestions. J. Mullen. il por *Vogue* 179:276 Je '89

BAKER, KENNETH, 1946-

Artists in residences. il *House & Garden* 161:38+ Ja '89

Vintage images of a fifty-year-old miracle. il *Architectural Digest* 46:186+ My '89

BAKER, KRISTIN

about

Breaking barriers in the barracks. P. Cary. il pors *U.S. News & World Report* 107:26-7 Ag 21 '89

Manning the barricades no more, West Point names Kristin Baker to head the long gray line. S. K. Reed. il pors *People Weekly* 32:50-1 Ag 28 '89

'No slack': a woman's touch at West Point. por *Newsweek* 114:20 Ag 21 '89

BAKER, MARTHA

about

Between the lines. il por *New York* 22:6 Ag 21 '89

BAKER, PAULINE H.

The American challenge in Southern Africa. bibl f *Current History* 88:209-12+ My '89

BAKER, RAY STANNARD, 1870-1946

See also

Grayson, David, 1870-1946

BAKER, ROBERT

about

Go with the flow. M. Barrier. il por *Nation's Business* 77:37-8 My '89

BAKER, ROBERT

about

Couple on the firing line. R. L. Haywood. il pors *Ebony* 44:142+ Ag '89

BAKER, RUSSELL, 1925-

Brown-bagging it to Buckingham. il pors *The New York Times Magazine* p16-19+ Ja 1 '89

Paper boy [excerpt from The good times] il por *Life* 12:17-18+ Ap '89

The roots of my ambition [condensed from The good times] il por *Reader's Digest* 135:115-18 N '89

BAKER, RUSSELL, 1925——cont.
about
'It's almost impossible to get it right'. C. McGuigan. *Newsweek*
113:65 Je 12 '89
BAKER, RUSSELL, 1925-, AND PETERS, CHARLES, 1926-
The prince and his courtiers: at the White House, the Kremlin,
and the Reichschancellery. *The Washington Monthly* 21:38+
F '89
BAKER, SAMM SINCLAIR
Three surefire ways to write and sell nonfiction. *The Writer*
102:11-13 Mr '89
BAKER, SUSAN, AND GORE, TIPPER, 1948-
Some reasons for 'wilding'. pors *Newsweek* 113:6-7 My 29
'89
BAKER, SUZANNE J., AND OTHERS
Chromosome 17 deletions and p53 gene mutations in colorec-
tal carcinomas. bibl f il *Science* 244:217-21 Ap 14 '89
BAKER, VERONICA
about
Couple on the firing line. R. L. Haywood. il pors *Ebony*
44:142+ Ag '89
BAKER & McKENZIE
U. of Chicago bans law firm's recruiting after racist comments.
Jet 75:30 F 20 '89
BAKER, FENTRESS & CO.
Discount hunter [closed end fund strategy on a personal
computer] D. Churbuck. il *Forbes* 143:252-3 Je 26 '89
BAKER HUGHES INCORPORATED
Baker Hughes lops off a weak limb. T. Vogel. *Business
Week* p34 My 29 '89
BAKERS AND BAKERIES
See also
Caraway's (Firm)
Dunkin' Donuts Incorporated
Greyston Bakery
Just Desserts Inc.
Keim Family Bakery
Mrs. Fields Cookies
Natural Ovens of Manitowoc Inc.
Pepperidge Farm, Inc.
France
The fall and rise of French bread [B. Ganachaud's Paris
bakery] N. Barry. il por *Gourmet* 49:56-9+ Mr '89
Flour power [French bread bakers] C. Petkanas. il *Harper's
Bazaar* 122:200+ D '89
BAKES, ANNIE
about
Piston's Rodman hit with paternity, palimony suits. il pors
Jet 76:52 Jl 3 '89
Rebounding into court. il pors *People Weekly* 32:75 Ag
7 '89
BAKHASH, SHAUL
What Khomeini did. il *The New York Review of Books*
36:16-19 Jl 20 '89
BAKING
See also
Bread
Cake
Cookies
Gingerbread
Pastry
Pie
Deck the halls. il *Seventeen* 48:118-23 D '89
Gastronomie sans argent [holiday baking] il *Gourmet* 49:130-1+
N '89
The LHJ cooking school [layer cake, raspberry soufflé, and
apple pie] il *Ladies' Home Journal* 106:179-80+ S '89
BAKING SODA *See* Sodium bicarbonate
BAKKE, TIMOTHY O.
What's new: home. See issues of Popular Science beginning
January 1989
BAKKER, C. G.
(jt. auth) See Schwartz, Alan W., and Bakker, C. G.
BAKKER, JIM
about
Amid tears and jeers, justice makes prison pen pals out
of Zsa Zsa Gabor and Jim Bakker. R. Micheli and L.
Marx. il pors *People Weekly* 32:129-30 N 6 '89
The day of reckoning delayed. R. N. Ostling. il por *Time*
134:76-7 S 11 '89
A guilty evangelist. B. Wickens. il por *Maclean's* 102:55-6
O 16 '89
Having a devil of a time. il por *Newsweek* 114:61 S 11
'89
Healing the church—after Bakker. T. C. Muck. il *Christianity
Today* 33:16 N 17 '89
Jim & Tammy Faye Bakker. D. Barry. il pors *People Weekly*
32 Special Issue:70-1 Fall '89
Jim Bakker and the Eternal Revenue Service. G. Wacker.
il pors *The Christian Century* 106:1053-5 N 15 '89
Judgment day. il por *Time* 134:65 O 16 '89
The living legacy of Jim Bakker. il por *U.S. News & World
Report* 107:14 N 6 '89
The remnants of PTL. K. A. Lawton. il por *Christianity
Today* 33:36-8 O 6 '89
Trial and tribulation. N. Underwood. il por *Maclean's* 102:63
S 11 '89

Unholy roller coaster [cover story] M. Brower. il pors *People
Weekly* 32:98-100+ S 18 '89
The wrath of "Maximum Bob". A. L. Sanders. il por *Time*
134:62 N 6 '89
BAKKER, ROBERT T.
about
Uncovering the mystery of the dinosaur. E. Ziegler. il *Reader's
Digest* 135:163-8 D '89
BAKKER, TAMMY
about
Jim & Tammy Faye Bakker. D. Barry. il pors *People Weekly*
32 Special Issue:70-1 Fall '89
Unholy roller coaster [cover story] M. Brower. il pors *People
Weekly* 32:98-100+ S 18 '89
BAKSHI, RALPH
about
The last angry mouse. R. Powers. il por *Gentlemen's Quarterly*
59:106+ Ag '89
BAKSHIAN, ARAM, AND SCHAD, GEOFFREY D.
Hyderabad: shadow of empire [cover story] bibl il *History
Today* 39:19-28 Ja '89
BAKULA, SCOTT
about
He's praying for a Quantum leap—right into the movies.
E. Kiester. por *TV Guide* 37:14-15 D 23-29 '89
BALABAN, BOB
about
Parents [film] Reviews
Maclean's il 102:55 F 13 '89. B. D. Johnson
The Nation 248:206-7 F 13 '89. S. Klawans
The New Yorker 65:95-7 Mr 6 '89. P. Kael
Newsweek il 113:79 F 13 '89. D. Ansen
People Weekly il 31:14+ Ja 30 '89. P. Travers
Video il 13:62 Je '89. I. Robbins
BALABAN, JOHN, 1943-
Words for my daughter [poem] *Harper's* 278:42 Ja
'89
BALAGNA, DIANE
about
Housekeeping services. il pors *Home Office Computing* 7:42
Je '89
BALAGUER, JOAQUÍN, 1907-
about
In the land of the blind caudillo. M. Kurlansky. il pors
The New York Times Magazine p24-6+ Ag 6 '89
BALANCE (PHYSIOLOGY) *See* Equilibrium (Physiology)
BALANCE OF NATURE *See* Ecology
BALANCE OF PAYMENTS
See also
Balance of trade
Capital movements
America's economic dependence. F. G. Rohatyn. *Foreign
Affairs* 68 Special Issue:53-65 ['89]
Hogwash [debtor status of U.S.] M. S. Forbes, Jr. il *Forbes*
144 Special Issue:29 O 23 '89
The imbalance of payments. E. Corcoran and P. Wallich.
il *Scientific American* 261:104+ D '89
Picking up Reagan's tab. D. D. Hale. *Foreign Policy* 74:145-67
Spr '89
Time to trade in our old notions about deficits. P. C. Roberts.
il *Business Week* p30 N 13 '89
The U.S. role in a changing world economy. P. D. Nigro.
il *USA Today (Periodical)* 117:21-2 My '89
Great Britain
Britain's mixed blessing [balanced budget] J. Marcom, Jr.
il *Forbes* 143:43-4 Mr 6 '89
BALANCE OF POWER
After a cruise to nowhere [superpowers] K. Auchincloss.
il *Newsweek* 114:39 D 11 '89
The American perspective, five key questions [address, March
31, 1989] B. O. Wireman. *Vital Speeches of the Day*
55:538-40 Je 15 '89
America's true power [prestige] J. Lukacs. il *American Heritage*
40:74-9 Mr '89
Are we underestimating America's future? K. E. House. il
Reader's Digest 134:185-6+ My '89
Axis, Ltd. [Germany and Japan; cover story] M. Sayle. il
The New Republic 200:22-4+ Je 5 '89
Broken Axis [Germany and Japan; cover story] *The New
Republic* 200:7-9 Je 5 '89
Consequences of Soviet decline [views of Kurt M. Campbell]
The Futurist 23:39-40 Ja/F '89
Economic and military security [address, February 22, 1989]
P. M. Kennedy. *Vital Speeches of the Day* 55:594-7 Jl
15 '89
Economic growth and military power: erosion of the super-
powers. W. Goldstein. *Current (Washington, D.C.)* 309:23-31
Ja '89
Gorbachev's challenge to the West [address, April 11, 1989]
E. W. Lefever. *Vital Speeches of the Day* 55:588-91 Jl
15 '89
Hour of power? [Japan; special section] il *Newsweek* 113:14-18+
F 27 '89
Is the cold war really over? O. Harries. il *National Review*
41:40+ N 10 '89
Notes and comment [encouraging national modesty without
diminishing national pride] *The New Yorker* 65:31-2 My
8 '89

BALANCE OF POWER—*cont.*
Sunset on the superpowers. S. V. Roberts. il *U.S. News & World Report* 107:12-13 D 11 '89
Superpower sweepstakes. R. J. Samuelson. il *Newsweek* 113:43 F 20 '89
U.S. role in the world. A. Brummer. il *World Press Review* 36:16-17+ S '89
Will America become #2? A. K. Selimuddin. il *USA Today (Periodical)* 118:14-16 S '89

Bibliography
Can the US remain number one? [cover story] P. M. Kennedy. il *The New York Review of Books* 36:36-42 Mr 16 '89

BALANCE OF POWER (VIDEO GAME)
Grow up! D. Atkin. il *Compute!* 11:94-6+ D '89
Video scans. B. Lindstrom. il *Omni (New York, N.Y.)* 11:122 Je '89

BALANCE OF TRADE
America's bright global future [excerpt from America in the global '90s] A. H. Kiplinger and K. Kiplinger. il *Changing Times* 43:111-12+ O '89
America's oil-chill factor [rising imports increase trade deficit] K. R. Sheets. il *U.S. News & World Report* 106:54-5 Mr 27 '89
And now, back to the issues: budget, trade, banking and debtors [address, November 10, 1988] W. C. Butcher. *Vital Speeches of the Day* 55:241-3 F 1 '89
Are U.S. companies dangerously addicted to foreign equipment? G. Koretz. il *Business Week* p22 Mr 27 '89
Attacking the deficits now will bring years of prosperity. C. F. Bergsten. il por *Fortune* 119:19+ Ja 2 '89
Exports have the vapors. M. J. Mandel. il *Business Week* p37-8 My 22 '89
Ins and outs on America's trade list [trade deficit] R. F. Black. il *U.S. News & World Report* 107:43-4 Ag 21 '89
The news on trade remains mixed. H. Banks. *Forbes* 144:37 S 18 '89
Of cultural gaps and trade talks [effect of Japanese citizens' habits on balance of trade] C. P. Work. *U.S. News & World Report* 107:58 S 18 '89
Oil imports are setting an ambush for the economy. G. Koretz. il *Business Week* p26 Mr 13 '89
One bad apple can spoil the ledgers. R. J. Black. *U.S. News & World Report* 107:67 N 6 '89
The political realities of trade. H. Banks. *Forbes* 143:33 My 15 '89
The real trade culprits lie closer to home [trade deficit] R. F. Black. il *U.S. News & World Report* 106:52 My 22 '89
Stop bashing Japan for U.S. deficits. T. Kataoka. il *USA Today (Periodical)* 117:26-8 Ja '89
Straight talk about deficits. M. Friedman. *Reader's Digest* 134:105-7 Mr '89
Time to trade in our old notions about deficits. P. C. Roberts. il *Business Week* p30 N 13 '89
The trade deficit is still heading the right way. V. Brownstein. il *Fortune* 119:27-8 F 13 '89
A trade gap worth a smile [U.S. leads competition in service industries] C. P. Work. il *U.S. News & World Report* 107:66-7+ N 6 '89
U.S. trade balance. *Congressional Digest* 68:3-4 Ja '89
What you won't hear in Paris [economic summit] R. Thomas. il *Newsweek* 114:38-40 Jl 17 '89
Who sets the standards? [product standards] J. R. Hayes. il *Forbes* 143:110+ Ap 17 '89
Will we ever close the trade gap? [cover story] il *Business Week* p86-9+ F 27 '89

Japan
The hard life. J. M. Fallows. il *The Atlantic* 263:16+ Mr '89
How can Japan reduce surplus? [views of Bela Balassa and Marcus Noland] *USA Today (Periodical)* 117:11 Ap '89
Japan is investing at full blast. H. Banks. *Forbes* 143:41 Ja 9 '89
Our Japan problem. M. Kondracke. *The New Republic* 201:11-12+ Jl 31 '89

Korea (South)
No more Mr. Cheap Guy. J. Flint. il *Forbes* 144:102-3 O 30 '89

United States
See Balance of trade
BALANCE SHEETS *See* Financial statements
BALANCHINE, GEORGE, 1904-1983
about
Apollo [ballet] Reviews
The New Yorker 65:77-9 Mr 13 '89. A. Croce
Danses concertantes [ballet] Reviews
New York il 22:69 My 22 '89. T. Tobias
Jewels [ballet] Reviews
The New Leader il 72:23 F 6 '89. L. A. Jacobs
The red shoes dance modern. il por *U.S. News & World Report* 106:16 F 27 '89
BALAR, LUV RAGHAVJI
Who cares? il *World Health* p18 Mr '89
BALCOMB, MARY N.
The watercolor page: Sheila Savannah. il por *American Artist* 53:76-9+ S '89

BALCONY GARDENS, ROOF GARDENS, ETC.
Another country [Peter and Olga Gee's loft and roof garden in New York's SoHo] M. Bethany. il *New York* 22:84-8+ Jl 3-10 '89
BALD EAGLES *See* Eagles
BALDANZA, JOSEPH
(jt. auth) See MacKinnon, Douglas, and Baldanza, Joseph
BALDESSARI, JOHN, 1931-
about
Novel ideas. R. B. Woodward. il *Art News* 88:127 Ap '89
BALDNESS
The pleasure dome [shaved head] M. Sager. il *Gentlemen's Quarterly* 59:282-5+ Ap '89
Stressed tresses [stress] R. Wiest. il *American Health* 8:20-2 S '89
BALDNESS REMEDIES
Bald-faced hair scam [indictment against Philip P. West and Wayne P. Kreklewich] il *FDA Consumer* 23:34-5 Mr '89
Beyond the fringe: late word from the war on baldness. N. Brown. il *Nation's Business* 77:79 Je '89
Minoxidil—better known under its brand name Rogaine—has been found to have about a 60 percent success rate for women with thinning hair. R. M. Henig. *Vogue* 179:560+ S '89
Thin, thinning, gone [treating women with minoxidil] E. Baum. *Health (New York, N.Y.)* 21:74-6 Ja '89

Advertising
Hair today [low-key ads for Rogaine] B. Kanner. il *New York* 22:20+ O 30 '89
BALDOR ELECTRIC CO.
Baldor's success: made in the U.S.A. A. Farnham. il *Fortune* 120:101-2+ Jl 17 '89
BALDOVIN, JOHN F.
Liturgy in time of trouble. *America* 161:337-8 N 18 '89
BALDRIDGE, RITA
about
A mother's revenge. M. Cohen. il por *Ladies' Home Journal* 106:140-1+ S '89
BALDRIGE, LETITIA
Entertaining etiquette. il *McCall's* 116:57 Ap '89
BALDWIN, ALEC
about
Smart Alec. il pors *Esquire* 112:142-7 N '89
BALDWIN, BRUCE A.
Outmaneuver manipulators. il *Reader's Digest* 134:118-20 Ap '89
BALDWIN, ENOCH, AND SCHULTZ, PETER G.
Generation of a catalytic antibody by site-directed mutagenesis. bibl f il *Science* 245:1104-7 S 8 '89
BALDWIN, J. (JAMES)
The compleat country workshop. il pors *Country Journal* 16:59-64 N/D '89
BALDWIN, JAMES *See* Baldwin, J. (James)
BALDWIN, JAMES, 1924-1987
about
A memory of James Baldwin. M. McCarthy. il *The New York Review of Books* 36:48-9 Ap 27 '89
BALDWIN, ROBERT F.
To market, to market. il *Country Journal* 16:51-4 Jl/Ag '89
BALDWIN, WILLIAM, FL. 1547
about
The English novel unsheathes its claws. A. Broyard. il *The New York Times Book Review* 94:12 F 5 '89
BALDWIN HILLS ENTERTAINMENT COMPLEX (LOS ANGELES, CALIF.) *See* Los Angeles (Calif.)—Motion picture theaters
BALENCIAGA
about
Couture report: the four schools of design. J. J. Buck. il *Vogue* 179:324-5+ O '89
BALERS, LEAF *See* Leaf balers
BALHI, DJAMEL
about
World tour. J. Henderson. il por *Runner's World* 24:16 Je '89
BALI (INDONESIA)
See also
Irrigation—Bali (Indonesia)
Description and travel
Travel. T. Friend. il *Vogue* 179:164+ Je '89
BALICK, HOWARD
about
"Just ten more minutes . . .". J. McDermott. il *Reader's Digest* 134:89-94 My '89
BALINESE DANCE *See* Dance, Balinese
BALINESE MUSIC *See* Music, Balinese
BALK, FAIRUZA
about
More dangerous than Oz. B. D. Johnson. *Maclean's* 102:83 N 20 '89
BALKAN PENINSULA
See also
Albania
History
See also
World War, 1914-1918—Balkan Peninsula

BALKAN PENINSULA—*cont.*

Nationalism

Europe's third world. R. D. Kaplan. il *The Atlantic* 264:16-18+ Jl '89

BALKWILL, DAVID L.

(jt. auth) See Fliermans, Carl B., and Balkwill, David L.

BALL, AIMEE LEE

The daddy track. il *New York* 22:52-7+ O 23 '89

Learning to love life at the top. il *Working Woman* 14:78-80+ Je '89

Mentors & protégés: portraits of success [special section] il *Working Woman* 14:134-8+ O '89

Sarandon, seriously [cover story] pors *Mother Jones* 14:30-3+ F/Mr '89

Swan's way. il pors *New York* 22:40-4 Je 5 '89

White lies: cocaine—the dirty little secret in the age of clean. il *Mademoiselle* 95:266-9+ Ap '89

BALL, CHARLES H.

A symposium on skills, knowledge, and creativity in the curriculum. *Design for Arts in Education* 90:22-3 My/Je '89

BALL, DESMOND

A sad record. il *The Bulletin of the Atomic Scientists* 45:41-2 My '89

BALL, JOAN

The National PTA's stand on corporal punishment. *The Education Digest* 54:23-5 Ap '89

BALL, LAURIE

Metamorphosis to individual responsibility: a search for curriculum. bibl f *Design for Arts in Education* 91:36-42 S/O '89

BALL, LUCILLE, 1911-1989

about

I loved Lucy. J. Brochu. il pors *Ladies' Home Journal* 106:120-2+ Ag '89

Lucille Ball. il pors *People Weekly* 31 Special Issue:22-3 Summ '89

Lucy: the life behind the laughter [cover story] S. Schindehette. il pors *People Weekly* 32:66-70+ Ag 14 '89

Obituary

American Film il por 14:14 Jl/Ag '89. T. Carson

Maclean's il por 102:61 My 8 '89. B. D. Johnson

The Nation 248:685 My 22 '89

Newsweek il pors 113:75 My 8 '89. J. Kroll

People Weekly il pors 31:46-56 My 8 '89. B. Darrach

Time il por 133:101 My 8 '89. W. A. Henry

U.S. News & World Report il pors 106:14 My 8 '89

BALL, WILLIAM BENTLEY

Should the Senate approve the "Americans with Disabilities Act of 1989"? [excerpts from testimony, May 10, 1989] *Congressional Digest* 68:295+ D '89

BALL AEROSPACE (FIRM)

Ball Aerospace stresses simplicity in space-based motion sensor design [Remote Attitude Measurement Sensor] W. B. Scott. il *Aviation Week & Space Technology* 130:100-2 Je 5 '89

Ball Aerospace Systems developing compact toroidal liquid oxygen tank [for orbital transfer vehicles] il *Aviation Week & Space Technology* 130:107 Je 5 '89

Ball develops multi-anode microchannel array for Space Telescope, defense uses. W. B. Scott. il *Aviation Week & Space Technology* 130:296-7 Je 12 '89

Pegasus, Ball to launch communication satellites into geosynchronous orbit. il *Aviation Week & Space Technology* 130:64 Je 12 '89

BALL CORPORATION

Ball will build radio astronomy payload for Submillimeter Wave Satellite. il *Aviation Week & Space Technology* 131:50 S 18 '89

USAF developing better camouflage to protect bases from enemy attack. W. B. Scott. il *Aviation Week & Space Technology* 131:85+ S 25 '89

BALL GAMES

See also

Pesapallo (Game)

BALL THROWING

See also

Passing (Football)

Pitching (Baseball)

BALLANTINE, BETTY

(jt. auth) See Ballantine, Ian, and Ballantine, Betty

BALLANTINE, IAN, AND BALLANTINE, BETTY

From the two-bit beginning. il *The New York Times Book Review* 94:25+ Ap 30 '89

BALLANTINE BOOKS, INC.

Ballantine's new translations of Chinese classics. M. Wu. *Publishers Weekly* 236:58-9 O 6 '89

Have laser gun, Ballantine reps will travel—faster and smarter [speeding inventory and ordering] J. Mutter. il *Publishers Weekly* 235:53-5 F 17 '89

BALLANTYNE, SARA

about

Innerviews [interview] il por *Women's Sports & Fitness* 11:56 Jl/Ag '89

BALLARD, DEL, JR.

about

Life in the slow lane. D. S. Looney. il por *Sports Illustrated* 70:92 My 1 '89

BALLARD, RAE

Eve to her daughters [poem] *The Christian Century* 106:436 Ap 26 '89

BALLARD, ROBERT D.

The Bismarck found. il maps *National Geographic* 176:622-37 N '89

BALLARD, SARAH

Always fair weather. il pors *Sports Illustrated* 70 Special Issue:71-4 F '89

Britannia rules again. il pors *Sports Illustrated* 71:60-4+ Jl 10 '89

Building a new life. il pors *Sports Illustrated* 70:57-8+ My 15 '89

Fabric of the game. il *Sports Illustrated* 70 Special Issue:108-16+ Ap '89

From Baja with love. il pors *Sports Illustrated* 70 Special Issue:65-7 F '89

A show that has the goods. il *Sports Illustrated* 70:36-40 F 20 '89

BALLAY, UTE

Nineteenth-century Bohemian glass [cover story] il *Antiques & Collecting Hobbies* 94:42-5 My '89

BALLENGER, NOELLA, AND TULLEY, JALIEN

Funlights. il *Petersen's Photographic Magazine* 17:58-60 Ap '89

BALLESTEROS, SEVE

about

Superior 'Sevvy'. L. Rubenstein. il por *Maclean's* 102:54-5 Ap 10 '89

BALLET

See also

American Ballet Theatre

American Festival Ballet

Atlanta Ballet

Ballet Chicago

Ballet Florida

Ballet Hispanico of New York

Ballet West

BalletMet

Boston Ballet

California Ballet Company

Cincinnati Ballet

Cincinnati/New Orleans City Ballet

Colorado Ballet

Dance Theatre of Harlem

Des Moines Ballet

Feld Ballet

Joffrey Ballet

Louisville Ballet

Miami City Ballet

Milwaukee Ballet

Mobile Ballet

Motion pictures—Dance films

New York City Ballet

NorthWest Ballet

Oakland Ballet

Omaha Ballet

Pacific Ballet Theatre

Pacific Northwest Ballet

Pennsylvania and Milwaukee Ballet

Pittsburgh Ballet Theatre

San Francisco Ballet

Spokane Ballet

State Ballet of Missouri

Television broadcasting—Ballet programs

Tulsa Ballet Theatre

Dance magazine special summer events calendar 1989. il *Dance Magazine* 63:SC1-SC4+ My '89

Performance calendar. See issues of Dance Magazine

Presstime news. See issues of Dance Magazine

Special section: Nutcracker and holiday performance calendar. il *Dance Magazine* 63:115-19+ D '89

Bibliography

Dancebooks. See issues of Dance Magazine

Competitions

See also

Bruhn Prize

Prix de Lausanne

Memories of a Moscow mole: competing for gold and glory in Moscow. M. E. Willis. il *Dance Magazine* 63:54-7 D '89

Directories

Dance directory. See issues of Dance Magazine

History

Dancescape [200th anniversary celebration of pastoral ballet La fille mal gardée] R. C. Lamont. il *Dance Magazine* 63:9 Jl '89

Not just a Tin Lizzie [effect of Ford Foundation grants to American ballet companies in the 1960s] C. Barnes. *Dance Magazine* 63:106 O '89

Some ballet called Swan Lake. C. Barnes. il *Dance Magazine* 63:138+ My '89

Names

The naming of names [significance in naming of ballet companies, dancers, choreographers, and ballets] C. Barnes. *Dance Magazine* 63:82 Jl '89

BALLET—cont.
Study and teaching
See also
Harid Conservatory
National Ballet School (Canada)
School of American Ballet
Vaganova Choreographic Institute (Leningrad, Soviet Union)
Education. M. Horosko. See issues of Dance Magazine
Pirouettes: placed and paced [A. Alonso's technique] M. Horosko. il *Dance Magazine* 63:68-9 S '89
Argentina
A new regime reopens the Teatro Colon in Argentina. C. Hardy. il *Dance Magazine* 63:16 O '89
Belgium
See also
Royal Ballet of Flanders
Brazil
See also
Ballet of the Teatro Municipal
Canada
See also
Alberta Ballet Company
Ballet British Columbia
Ballet de Montréal
Les Grands Ballets Canadiens
National Ballet of Canada
Royal Winnipeg Ballet
Chile
See also
Ballet de Santiago
Denmark
See also
Royal Danish Ballet
Finland
See also
Finnish National Ballet
France
See also
Paris Opera Ballet
Germany (West)
See also
Hamburg Ballet
Stuttgart Ballet
Great Britain
See also
English National Ballet
London Festival Ballet
Royal Ballet
Hungary
See also
Hungarian State Opera and Ballet
Ireland
See also
Irish National Ballet
Korea (South)
See also
Universal Ballet Company
Monaco
See also
Ballets de Monte Carlo
Netherlands
See also
Dutch National Ballet
New York (State)
Dance [New York City; fall preview] R. Gilbert. il *New York* 22:116+ S 11 '89
Scotland
See also
Scottish Ballet
Soviet Union
See also
Bolshoi Academy Ballet
Bolshoi Ballet
Kirov Ballet
Leningrad Theater of Contemporary Ballet
Moscow Classical Ballet
History
Before Balanchine: Kasyan Goleizovsky's Russian revolution (I). G. Manor. il pors *Dance Magazine* 63:56-60 Ja '89
Before Balanchine: Kasyan Goleizovsky's Russian revolution (II). G. Manor. il pors *Dance Magazine* 63:60-4 F '89
From St. Petersburg to Leningrad: Lupukhov's legacy. N. Alovert. il pors *Dance Magazine* 63:42-6 Mr '89
History—Exhibitions
Ballet archeology à la Russe. J. R. Acocella. il *Art in America* 77:51+ D '89
Golden girl [100 years of Russian ballet, 1830-1930] *The New Yorker* 65:39-41 O 16 '89
Spain
See also
Ballet del Teatro Lírico Nacional de la Zarzuela
Sweden
See also
Cullberg Ballet
Royal Swedish Ballet

Switzerland
See also
Basel Ballet
Ukraine
See also
Donetsk Ballet
United States
See Ballet
Venezuela
See also
Ballet Nacional de Caracas
Western Europe
Report from Europe: festive dancing [opera ballets included in various festivals] S. Whyte. il *Dance Magazine* 63:50-3 D '89

BALLET, WATER *See* Synchronized swimming
BALLET BRITISH COLUMBIA
Ballet upstarts. M. Crabb. il *Maclean's* 102:74 D 4 '89
Reviews:
Performances in Vancouver. C. Valleskey. *Dance Magazine* 63:53-4 Ag '89
BALLET CHICAGO
Reviews:
Spring season at the Civic Opera House. C. Survant. il *Dance Magazine* 63:77-8 S '89
BALLET COMPANIES *See* Ballet
BALLET COSTUME *See* Costume, Theatrical
BALLET DANCERS *See* Dancers
BALLET DE MONTRÉAL
Toussaint company is squeezed for funds. K. Greenaway. il *Dance Magazine* 63:22 O '89
BALLET DE SANTIAGO
Chile launches choreography search. C. Hardy. il *Dance Magazine* 63:8+ Ja '89
BALLET DEL TEATRO LÍRICO NACIONAL DE LA ZARZUELA
Reviews:
November season at the Teatro de la Zarzuela, Madrid. L. Kumin. *Dance Magazine* 63:108-10 My '89
BALLET FESTIVALS *See* Dance festivals
BALLET FLORIDA
All the right moves. S. Guy. il *Horizon (Tuscaloosa, Ala.)* 32:21-2 Ja/F '89
BALLET HISPANICO OF NEW YORK
Reviews:
Performances in New York City. R. A. Thom. il *Dance Magazine* 63:22+ F '89
BALLET MUSIC
See also
Compact discs—Ballet music
Phonograph records—Ballet music
BALLET NACIONAL CLÁSICO
See also
Ballet del Teatro Lírico Nacional de la Zarzuela
BALLET NACIONAL DE CARACAS
Reviews:
Performances in Madrid. L. Kumin. *Dance Magazine* 63:33-4 Mr '89
BALLET OF THE DOLLS
Reviews:
Performances in Minneapolis, Minn. J. Timmis. *Dance Magazine* 63:80-1 S '89
BALLET OF THE TEATRO MUNICIPAL
Reviews:
1988 season in Rio de Janeiro. A. J. Faro. *Dance Magazine* 63:34 Mr '89
BALLET REVIEWS
Dancing. A. Croce. See occasional issues of The New Yorker
Reviews. See issues of Dance Magazine
Single works
Apollo
  The New Yorker 65:77-9 Mr 13 '89. A. Croce
L'après-midi d'un faune
  Dance Magazine il 63:32-4 O '89. L. Garafola
La bayadère
  Dance Magazine il 63:76-7 O '89. L. Svedin
  Dance Magazine il 63:77-8 O '89. M. E. Willis
Bum's rush
  The New Yorker 65:94 Je 12 '89. A. Croce
Carmina Burana
  Dance Magazine 63:100-1 F '89. J. Williams
Le corsaire
  New York il 22:56-7 Jl 24 '89. T. Tobias
Danses concertantes
  New York il 22:69 My 22 '89. T. Tobias
Don Quixote
  Dance Magazine 63:86 F '89. E. Aschengreen
  Dance Magazine 63:88-9 N '89. I. M. Fanger
Echo
  New York il 22:53-4 Jl 17 '89. T. Tobias
Everlast
  The New Yorker 65:95-6 Je 12 '89. A. Croce
La fille mal gardée
  Dance Magazine il 63:9 Jl '89. R. C. Lamont
A fool for you
  Dance Magazine il 63:59 O '89. J. Gruen
The gilded bat
  Dance Magazine il 63:8 N '89. E. Kendall

BALLET REVIEWS—Single works—cont.
Giselle
    Dance Magazine il 63:84-5 D '89. H. Koegler
Les illuminations
    The New Leader 72:20-1 N 27 '89. L. A. Jacobs
Impressing the czar
    The New Leader il 72:20 N 27 '89. L. A. Jacobs
Jewels
    The New Leader il 72:23 F 6 '89. L. A. Jacobs
Lady of the camellias
    Dance Magazine il 63:26 Mr '89. R. Libermann
Love song waltzes
    New York il 22:81-2 Mr 13 '89. T. Tobias
Martin
    American Visions il pors 4:34-9 D '89. D. Moore
The master and Margarita
    Dance Magazine 63:53+ Jl '89. V. Vanslov
Monotones
    The New Leader 72:20-1 N 27 '89. L. A. Jacobs
Les noces
    The New Yorker 65:86-7 Jl 17 '89. A. Croce
The Nutcracker
    Dance Magazine il 63:115-19+ D '89
    The New Leader 72:21-2 Ja 9 '89. L. A. Jacobs
    Vogue il 179:192+ D '89. D. Daniel
Oscar
    Dance Magazine 63:100+ My '89. C. Swift
Peer Gynt
    Dance Magazine 63:105-7 My '89. H. Koegler
Petrushka
    Dance Magazine il 63:78-9 O '89. M. E. Willis
Potemkin
    Dance Magazine il 63:52-3 Jl '89. A. Degen
The Shakers
    Dance Magazine il 63:10-11 Mr '89. G. R. Hubbard
The sleeping beauty
    The New Yorker 65:89-92 Ag 7 '89. A. Croce
Swan Lake
    Dance Magazine 63:94-5 Mr '89. C. Hardy
    Dance Magazine il 63:138+ My '89. C. Barnes
    Dance Magazine il 63:44-9 My '89. L. Horn
    The New Leader 72:23 Je 12-26 '89. L. A. Jacobs
    New York il 22:70 My 29 '89. T. Tobias
    The New Yorker 65:105-7 My 29 '89. A. Croce
La sylphide
    New York il 22:121-2 S 25 '89. T. Tobias
Tagore
    Dance Magazine il 63:52 Ag '89. P. Citron
A wedding bouquet
    The New Leader 72:20-1 N 27 '89. L. A. Jacobs
BALLET WEST
    Dancescape [premiere of The gilded bat] E. Kendall. il Dance
    Magazine 63:8 N '89
    Reviews:
        1988-89 season in Salt Lake City. D. Stowe. il Dance
        Magazine 63:24-5 Ja '89
BALLETMET
    Reviews:
        Last program of the 1988-89 season in Columbus, Ohio.
        B. Zuck. il Dance Magazine 63:72-3 S '89
BALLETS DE MONTE CARLO
    Making a home in Monte Carlo: life on the moneyed
    merry-go-round. O. Stuart. il Dance Magazine 63:42-3
    Ag '89
BALLETS RUSSES
    Diaghilev sits out WWI in Spain: Iberian idyll. J. R. Acocella.
    il pors Dance Magazine 63:45-8 Je '89
    Diaghilev tantalizes the ballet world [revivals of works from
    repertoire] R. Johnson. il Dance Magazine 63:17 N '89
BALLIETT, WHITNEY
    Goodbye, Michael. The New Yorker 65:133-7 N 6 '89
    Jazz. See occasional issues of The New Yorker
    Profiles [L. Bellson] il The New Yorker 65:41-6 Je 19 '89
BALLOON ASCENSIONS
        See also
        Sky Endeavors (Firm)
    Armand Hammer, 90, who doesn't have time to retire or
    die [helping M. Forbes get permission for motorcycle and
    balloon trip to China] A. Hammer. il por Forbes 143:20
    Ja 23 '89
    Bagging it. W. Garvey. il Flying 116:8-9 O '89
    Balloonist [J. Nott to attempt first non-stop voyage around
    the world] The New Yorker 65:39-40 O 2 '89
    Tapas, bulls and kings [Forbes Friendship Tour of Spain]
    R. Morais. il pors map Forbes 144:140-6+ Ag 7 '89
BALLOON ASCENSIONS IN ART
    A rising career for Roger Bansemer [artist who published
    his own book on ballooning] M. E. Stegmaier. il por
    American Artist 53:58-63+ Ag '89
BALLOON BOMBS
    On wings of forgiveness [J. Takeshita meets relatives of
    American civilians killed in explosion of Japanese balloon
    bomb in Oregon during World War II] J. Fincher. il
    Reader's Digest 134:85-90 Mr '89
BALLOON DILATATION, ARTERIAL See Arteries—Dis-
    eases—Therapy

BALLOON RACING
    Managing a different kind of float [chase crew member]
    K. Madigan. il Business Week p130 S 11 '89
BALLOONS
        See also
        Balloon ascensions
    Beware balloons. C. Loomis. il Parents 64:13 F '89
    A Christmas tree that will leave you breathless [balloon
    tree] il Sunset (Central West edition) 181:96 D '88
    Why are the first few puffs the hardest when you blow
    up a balloon? J. Walker. bibl il Scientific American 261:136-9
    D '89
                    Medical use
    Balloon angioplasty finds other applications. il Popular
    Mechanics 166:16 Ap '89
    Defusing a bomb in the brain [use of balloon angioplasty
    to treat aneurysms; work of Grant Hieshima] G. McBride.
    il American Health 8:9-10 D '89
                    Research use
    Aeronauts to astronauts. R. J. Duhse. il Ad Astra 1:25 Ap
    '89
    Balloon-launched scale orbiter to gather data for Hermes
    spaceplane program. Aviation Week & Space Technology
    131:58 S 18 '89
    A balloonful of earth to help study Mars. Science News
    135:223 Ap 8 '89
    German microgravity drop capsule approved for operational
    service [Mikroba balloon-launched system] Aviation Week
    & Space Technology 130:29 Jl 10 '89
    Little missions, big returns. S. P. Maran. il Astronomy 17:34-40
    Ja '89
    Observations of nuclear reactors on satellites with a balloon-
    borne gamma-ray telescope. T. J. O'Neill and others. bibl
    f il Science 244:451-4 Ap 28 '89
    Photogenic science [studying the tropical forest canopy by
    hot air balloon; work of Francis Hallé] J. Horgan. il
    Scientific American 261:20+ D '89
    Seeing in the ultraviolet [work of Bruno Milliard] il Sky
    and Telescope 78:459 N '89
    Treed [exploring the tropical forest canopy by hot air balloon;
    work of Francis Halle and others] B. Weber. il The New
    York Times Magazine p86 D 17 '89
    U.S. places new emphasis on high-altitude balloons [cover
    story] B. D. Nordwall. il Aviation Week & Space Technology
    131:34-6 O 23 '89
BALLPARKS See Stadiums
BALLROOM DANCING
        See also
        American Ballroom Theater
    Cheek to cheek is doubly chic, the second time around
    [cover story] A. Kelvin. il Smithsonian 19:84-90+ Mr '89
    Dancin' and romancin' [cover story] J. Bailey. il Health
    (New York, N.Y.) 21:39-43 Ja '89
                    Study and teaching
    Beyond the box step [learning ballroom dancing as a child
    in the sixties] W. B. Logan. il House & Garden 161:82+
    N '89
BALLS
        See also
        Footballs
        Golf balls
        Wiffle balls
BALLS (PARTIES)
    Gonna party like it's 1999. A. Heard. il Mother Jones
    14:29-31+ N '89
    The stars have a (masked) ball as the Phantom starts stalking
    in Hollywood [celebrating premiere of musical] il People
    Weekly 31:50-1 Je 5 '89
BALLY MANUFACTURING CORP.
    Leader of the pack [Independence Bank of Chicago courts
    Bally Manufacturing] M. M. McDowell. il Black Enterprise
    20:22 D '89
    No dice for Drexel? [possibly barred from doing business
    with Bally in N.J.] J. Crudele. il New York 22:22 Ja
    23 '89
    Will three be Bally's lucky number? [restructuring bids] J.
    F. Siler. il Business Week p48 Ag 14 '89
BALSA AIRPLANE MODELS See Airplane models
BALSA BURNING (CRAFT) See Pyrography
BALTER, LAWRENCE
    Understanding kids. See issues of Ladies' Home Journal
    beginning February 1984
BALTER, MARIE
                    about
    Return of Marie Balter. T. Armbrister. il por Reader's Digest
    135:123-7 Jl '89
BALTIC FREEDOM DAY
    Baltic Freedom Day [proclamation, June 14, 1989] G. Bush.
    Department of State Bulletin 89:80 Ag '89
BALTIC SEA REGION
                    Description and travel
    The Baltic: arena of power [cover story] P. J. Vesilind.
    il map National Geographic 175:602-35 My '89
                    Politics and government
    The Baltic: arena of power [cover story] P. J. Vesilind.
    il map National Geographic 175:602-35 My '89

BALTIC STATES
See also
Estonia
Latvia

Economic policy

Will economic success buy the Baltics their freedom? R. Brady. il *Business Week* p74-5 D 11 '89

Nationalism

The Baltic States in an era of Soviet reform [address, March 11, 1989] P. J. Dobriansky. *Department of State Bulletin* 89:35-9 Je '89

The Baltics: the old flags are unfurled. D. Stanglin. il map *U.S. News & World Report* 106:51-3 Ap 3 '89

A chain of freedom. il *Time* 134:20 S 4 '89

Cry independence. J. Kohan. il map *Time* 134:28-32 Ag 21 '89

A double standard. A. Nagorski. il *Newsweek* 114:35-6 D 18 '89

The language of unrest. W. R. Doerner. il *Time* 134:40 S 11 '89

The limits of freedom. M. Nemeth. il *Maclean's* 102:25 S 11 '89

Minority report [views of C. Milosz] C. Hitchens. *The Nation* 248:259 F 27 '89

Now, about those Baltic Republics. E. V. Rostow. map *The New Leader* 72:8-9 O 30 '89

Perestroika in the twilight zone. J. Trimble. il *U.S. News & World Report* 107:39+ S 11 '89

Restive republics. A. Wilson-Smith. il *Maclean's* 102:22-3 My 29 '89

The scientist in the Kremlin. S. Talbott. il *Time* 134:37 S 25 '89

Stirrings in the melting pot [Bensonhurst, Brooklyn and the Baltic States] H. Rainie. il *U.S. News & World Report* 107:8-9 S 11 '89

Unrest in the Baltics. il *World Press Review* 36:8+ O '89

'Until we are free again'. F. Coleman. il map *Newsweek* 114:28-30 S 4 '89

Will economic success buy the Baltics their freedom? R. Brady. il *Business Week* p74-5 D 11 '89

Politics and government

Washington's captive policy. S. Talbott. il *Time* 134:50 N 20 '89

BALTIMORE, DAVID, 1938-

Conquering the gene. il *Discover* 10:74-6+ O '89

The lost opportunity in AIDS research. il *Technology Review* 92:24-5 F/Mr '89

Mapping the genetic wilderness. il por *Technology Review* 92:20 N/D '89

Self-regulation of science: reflections on a day spent testifying at a congressional hearing. il por *Technology Review* 92:20+ Ag/S '89

The worsening climate for biological research. por *Technology Review* 92:22+ My/Je '89

about

Baltimore case reopened. *Science News* 135:278 My 6 '89

Baltimore cleared of all fraud charges. B. J. Culliton. il por *Science* 243:727 F 10 '89

Baltimore to succeed Lederberg? B. J. Culliton. il por *Science* 245:1441 S 29 '89

Conduct unbecoming? P. Weiss. il pors *The New York Times Magazine* p40-1+ O 29 '89

The Dingell probe finally goes public. B. J. Culliton. *Science* 244:643-6+ My 12 '89

Dingell v. Baltimore. B. J. Culliton. pors *Science* 244:412-14 Ap 28 '89

Fraud debate aired on Capitol Hill. K. Fackelmann. *Science News* 135:294-5 My 13 '89

NIH finds scientific errors but no fraud. K. Fackelmann. *Science News* 135:85 F 11 '89

Whose notes are they? B. J. Culliton. il *Science* 244:765 My 19 '89

BALTIMORE (MD.)

City planning

Baltimore, Maryland, USA: would H.L. Mencken recognize it? J. M. Rubenstein. bibl il maps *Focus (New York, N.Y.: 1950)* 39:30-2 Spr '89

Education

Baltimore mayor Schmoke cites city's Read-A-Thon. il por *Jet* 76:23-4 Ag 28 '89

Baltimore, the city that reads. B. Prete. *Publishers Weekly* 236:71-2 Ag 4 '89

Galleries and museums

See also
Baltimore Museum of Art
Walters Art Gallery

Housing

Mitchell family home in Baltimore up for auction due to default on loan. *Jet* 76:9 Jl 3 '89

Newspapers

See also
Baltimore sun

Sports

Baltimore & Washington. T. Loverro. il *Sport (New York, N.Y.)* 80:74-8 S '89

Father and son [watching sports events] W. Gildea. *Reader's Digest* 134:127-30 Ja '89

Stores

See also
Colwill-McGehee Antique Decorative and Fine Arts (Firm)

BALTIMORE MUSEUM OF ART

The gem of Baltimore celebrates 75. il *Southern Living* 24:43 My '89

BALTIMORE SUN

Brown-bagging it to Buckingham [reporting on Queen Elizabeth's coronation] R. Baker. il pors *The New York Times Magazine* p16-19+ Ja 1 '89

BALTZELL, E. DIGBY (EDWARD DIGBY), 1915-

Blue-blood blues. *The New Republic* 200:15-16 Ap 3 '89

BALTZELL, E. DIGBY (EDWARD DIGBY), 1915-, AND SCHNEIDERMAN, HOWARD G.

Social class in the Oval Office [discussion of September/October 1988 article] *Society* 26:10-15 Mr/Ap '89

BALTZELL, EDWARD DIGBY *See* Baltzell, E. Digby (Edward Digby), 1915-

BALTZELL, JAN C.

about

Jan C. Baltzell at Giannetta. W. P. Scott. il *Art in America* 77:269 Ap '89

BALYKIN, VICTOR I., AND LETOKHOV, V. S.

Laser optics of neutral atomic beams. bibl f il *Physics Today* 42:23-8 Ap '89

BALZER, ROBERT LAWRENCE

Concerning food and wine. See alternate issues of *Travel Holiday* through April 1989

BAM *See* Brooklyn Academy of Music

BAMBERGER, ALAN S.

Art talk. See issues of *Antiques & Collecting Hobbies* beginning December 1987

BAMBERGER, MICHAEL

Just having a fling. il pors *Sports Illustrated* 70:54+ Ja 30 '89

My brother, my teammate. il pors *Sports Illustrated* 70:54+ Mr 13 '89

BAMBOO

Bamboo and human evolution. G. G. Pope. il map *Natural History* p48-57 O '89

Bye-bye bamboo. il *Sunset (Central West edition)* 183:210 N '89

BAMBOO FENCES *See* Fences

BAMPTON, ROSE

about

The subject is Rose [cover story] J. W. Freeman. il pors *Opera News* 53:8-13 Mr 18 '89

BAN, S. D.

(jt. auth) See Burnett, W. M., and Ban, S. D.

BANACH-TARSKI PARADOX

The circle can be squared! [proof by Miklós Laczkovich] B. A. Cipra. *Science* 244:528 My 5 '89

A matter fabricator provides matter for thought. A. K. Dewdney. il *Scientific American* 260:116-19 Ap '89

Squaring the circle [proof by Miklós Laczkovich] R. Ruthen. *Scientific American* 261:22+ Jl '89

The straight side of sliced circles [work of Miklós Laczkovich] *Science News* 136:31 Jl 8 '89

BANANA INDUSTRY

See also
Seaside Banana Gardens

Costa Rica

Will the circle be unbroken? [infertility in banana workers through use of pesticide dibromochloropropane] D. Weir and C. Matthiessen. il *Mother Jones* 14:20-7 Je '89

BANANA TREES

Pot luck: bananas indoors and out. L. J. Goldstein. il *Organic Gardening* 36:30 D '89

BANANA WORKERS

Health and hygiene

Will the circle be unbroken? [infertility in Costa Rican banana workers through use of pesticide dibromochloropropane] D. Weir and C. Matthiessen. il *Mother Jones* 14:20-7 Je '89

BANANAS

Growin' bananas [techniques of D. Richardson and P. Turner of Seaside Banana Gardens] L. Hollenhorst. il por *Organic Gardening* 36:54-6+ S '89

Disease and pest resistance

The best banana bred [hybrid banana resistant to black sigatoka disease; work of P. Rowe] S. Brownlee. il *The Atlantic* 264:22+ S '89

BANC ONE CORP.

How Banc One moved to the front of the line. S. Phillips. il por *Business Week* p76 Jl 3 '89

BANCO DE CREDITO DEL PERU

Bankers' trust [designed by Arquitectonica; cover story] K. D. Stein. il *Architectural Record* 177:90-9 F '89

BANCO DE OCCIDENTE SA

Getting banks to just say 'no' [campaign against laundering drug money] P. Dwyer and P. Engardio. il *Business Week* p16-17 Ap 17 '89

BANCROFT, BARBARA

about

Mutual delights. il pors *Harper's Bazaar* 122:154-7 O '89

BANDANNAS See Scarves
BANDELIER NATIONAL MONUMENT (N.M.)
Logging poses threat to Bandelier. il *National Parks* 63:10 N/D '89
Rock steady. D. Roberts. il *Mother Jones* 14:49-51 Ap '89
BANDLER, MICHAEL J.
Jobeth Williams: "We still have hope". por *Ladies' Home Journal* 106:124-5 N '89
Mister Rogers: everybody's neighbor. il pors *Parents* 64:118-20+ Mr '89
"Whatever happens to me, I'm going to be happy". il pors *Redbook* 174:42+ N '89
BANDLER, RICHARD
about
The Bandler method. F. Clancy and H. Yorkshire. il pors *Mother Jones* 14:22-8+ F/Mr '89
BANDOW, DOUG
Leaving Korea. *Foreign Policy* 77:77-93 Wint '89/'90
BANDS (MUSIC)
See also
Big bands (Music)
Jazz groups
Lesbian and Gay Big Apple Corps Marching Band
Lincoln High School Band (East Saint Louis, Ill.)
Polka bands
Rock groups
Temple Band
The funkiest half-time show [Florida A&M's Marching 100] D. Winbush. il *Time* 134:14-15 S 18 '89
A man named Fay [Ozark, Ala. high school band director in 1950's] L. Wells. il por *Southern Living* 24:84+ O '89
The oldest American bands. il *Country Journal* 16:46 Jl/Ag '89
BANDSAWS See Saws and sawing
BANE, DON
Writing about science. *The Writer* 102:25-7 N '89
BANE, MARY JO, AND ELLWOOD, DAVID T.
One fifth of the nation's children: why are they poor? bibl f il *Science* 245:1047-53 S 8 '89
BANE, WILLIAM
about
Consultant in a bind. D. Churbuck. il por *Forbes* 144:285-6 N 13 '89
BANFF NATIONAL PARK (ALTA.)
An identity crisis [debate over expansion of skiing operation] J. Howse. il *Maclean's* 102:48 F 27 '89
Of moose and men. J. Maxwell. il *Esquire* 112:50+ N '89
BANFF TELEVISION FESTIVAL See Television festivals—Alberta
BANGKOK (THAILAND)
Architecture
Exotic themes in Bangkok [residence decorated by Chantaka Puranananda for M. Viravaidya; cover story] W. Warren. il *Architectural Digest* 46:150-5 D '89
Description
Bangkok by day and night. G. Powell. il *World Press Review* 36:62 Ag '89
"Somerset Maugham did not sleep here". L. Gubernick. il *Forbes* 144:290-2 D 11 '89
Hotels, motels, etc.
The jewel of the Chao Phraya [Oriental Hotel] T. D. Allman. il *Gentlemen's Quarterly* 59:160-5+ Ja '89
Restaurants, nightclubs, bars, etc.
The Authors' Lounge. R. Brookhiser. il *The American Spectator* 22:46 D '89
Tongue Thai'd in Bangkok. D. G. Gordon. il *Travel Holiday* 172:52-7 O '89
BANGKOK STOCK EXCHANGE
Thailand Inc. G. Eisenstodt. il *Forbes* 144:113+ N 27 '89
BANGLADESH
See also
Flood prevention and control—Bangladesh
Climate
Bad-luck land. E. Mandelstam. il *Scholastic Update (Teachers' edition)* 121:21 Mr 10 '89
Industries
See also
Salvage (Ships)—Bangladesh
Politics and government
The struggle for development in Bangladesh. C. Baxter. bibl f *Current History* 88:437-40+ D '89
BANGLES (MUSICAL GROUP)
Heroines take a fall [concert] H. Gleason. il *Rolling Stone* p26 Je 15 '89
BANI-SADR, ABU AL-HASAN
An Islamic victory. *New Perspectives Quarterly* 6:50-1 Spr '89
BANISHMENT See Exiles
BANK ACCOUNTING See Banks and banking—Accounting
BANK ACCOUNTS
See also
Cash management accounts
Certificates of deposit
Checks
Escrow accounts
Where to keep your cash (I). il *Consumer Reports* 54:153 Mr '89

Insurance
See also
Federal Deposit Insurance Corporation
Federal Savings and Loan Insurance Corporation
The $100 billion blunder. A. Bladen. il *Forbes* 143:167 F 6 '89
Avoiding another S&L crisis. M. S. Forbes, Jr. il *Forbes* 143:27 My 15 '89
Financial reform [address, August 29, 1989] W. L. Hoskins. *Vital Speeches of the Day* 56:111-14 D 1 '89
Just how safe is your bank? J. Blyskal and M. Hodge. il *New Choices for the Best Years* 29:43-5 Jl '89
New name, same rules: how to make the most of deposit insurance. J. Bodnar. il *Changing Times* 43:22 O '89
Too little, too late. W. Niskanen and C. England. il *National Review* 41:38-9 My 19 '89
What's behind the S&L crisis? F. L. Smith. il *Consumers' Research Magazine* 72:24-7 My '89
Who is to blame for the S&L crisis? D. Seligman. il *Fortune* 119:152 Mr 13 '89
Interest (Economics)
Boring was better [CDs] D. R. Katz. il *Esquire* 111:63-4 F '89
CDs that are fast on their feet [adjustable or variable rate CDs] S. Woolley. *Business Week* p180 My 22 '89
Certificates of deposit: it pays to shop around. P. N. Strassels. il *Nation's Business* 77:62 Jl '89
Don't ditch your old CD just for some sexy young rate. D. H. Dunn. *Business Week* p172 Mr 20 '89
An end to the fast talk in bank ads? C. Yang. il *Business Week* p97 Jl 3 '89
Going-out-of-business sale [Ginnie Mae outlook brightens as CD rates go down] B. Weberman. il *Forbes* 144:229 S 18 '89
The latest threat to the thrifts: rising interest rates. F. A. Miller. il *Business Week* p104-5 F 27 '89
Why settle for 6.5% when you can get 9.5%? [money market accounts vs. money market funds] M. Sivy. *Money* 18:76-7 O '89
Joint accounts
Joint bank accounts: the hidden dangers. *Consumer Reports* 54:458 Jl '89
Taxation
Read their lips: no S&L tax [proposed savers' fee] il *Newsweek* 113:50 F 6 '89
BANK ARCHITECTURE See Bank buildings
BANK BUILDINGS
Bankers' trust [Banco de Credito designed by Arquitectonica; cover story] K. D. Stein. il *Architectural Record* 177:90-9 F '89
New directions [Bridgeport Center, Conn.] D. Dietsch. il *Architectural Record* 177:70-7 Ag '89
Temples of thrift [New York City] *The New Yorker* 65:27-8 Mr 6 '89
BANK CHECKS See Checks
BANK CREDIT CARDS See Credit cards
BANK DEBIT CARDS See Debit cards
BANK DEPOSITS See Bank accounts
BANK ETHICS See Banks and banking—Ethical aspects
BANK FAILURES
The big fix [savings and loan crisis; cover story] J. R. Adams. il *The American Spectator* 22:21-4 Mr '89
Breaking the banks. B. Burgower. *Ladies' Home Journal* 106:24 Je '89
Capital crimes [savings and loan crisis] M. B. Zuckerman. il *U.S. News & World Report* 107:72 O 2 '89
The downfall of a thrift [Midwest Federal Savings and Loan Association] J. Hammer. il por *Newsweek* 113:54 F 27 '89
Fast money and fraud [Empire Savings & Loan] A. Pusey. il pors *The New York Times Magazine* p30-2+ Ap 23 '89
"Help! My bank just failed". J. P. Goodman. il por *Ladies' Home Journal* 106:22+ Je '89
Just how safe is your bank? J. Blyskal and M. Hodge. il *New Choices for the Best Years* 29:43-5 Jl '89
Thrifts on the slide. *Commonweal* 116:3-4 Ja 13 '89
BANK FEES See Banks and banking—Service charges
BANK HOLDING COMPANIES
See also
Banc One Corp.
BankAmerica Corp.
Citicorp
Citizens & Southern Corp.
Equimark Corp.
First Bank System Inc.
First City Bancorporation of Texas, Inc.
Hibernia Corporation
MCorp
NCNB Corp.
Republic New York Corp.
Society Corp.
Texas Commerce Bancshares, Inc.
Texop Bancshares
Union Planters Corporation
Valley National Corp.

BANK HOLDING COMPANIES—*cont.*
Acquisitions and mergers
Dixie's new superbanks. J. Egan. il map *U.S. News & World Report* 106:43-4 My 15 '89
The hometown boys [Texop Bancshares] J. H. Taylor. il por *Forbes* 144:253-4 O 16 '89
It's back to square 2 for Texas Commerce [failed bid for MCorp banks] M. Ivey. il por *Business Week* p125-6 Jl 17 '89
Why Hugh McColl is courting an Atlanta belle [NCNB goes after Citizens & Southern Corp.] D. Foust and S. Ticer. il por *Business Week* p19-20 Ap 17 '89
Why Robert Abboud wants MCorp in his corral. T. Vogel. il por *Business Week* p31 Ap 10 '89
Laws and regulations
See Banks and banking—Laws and regulations
BANK LOANS See Loans, Bank
BANK MANAGEMENT
For tomorrow's bank managers [address, August 25, 1989] T. P. Rideout. *Vital Speeches of the Day* 56:153-5 D 15 '89
BANK NOTES
See also
U.S. Banknote Company L. P.
BANK OF AMERICA NATIONAL TRUST & SAVINGS ASSN.
See also
BankAmerica Corp.
BANK OF CANADA
Marching bravely towards recession [high interest rates] D. Francis. il *Maclean's* 102:19 O 2 '89
BANK OF CRETE
The looting of Greece [G. Koskotas implicates government in scandal] R. Ajemian. il pors *Time* 133:32-5 Mr 13 '89
"No mud touches me" [A. Papandreou denies corruption charges leveled by G. Koskotas] W. R. Doerner. il por *Time* 133:37 Mr 20 '89
Out of office, into the dock? [A. Papandreou implicated by G. Koskotas] por *Time* 134:38 S 25 '89
BANK OF ENGLAND MUSEUM
The Bank of England Museum and Sweetings. J. Bainbridge. il *Gourmet* 49:36+ My '89
The new lady of Threadneedle Street. il *History Today* 39:62 Ja '89
BANK OF MONTREAL
Stepping aside [M. W. Barrett to succeed W. Mulholland] P. Chisholm. il pors *Maclean's* 102:40 Ja 30 '89
BANK OF NOVA SCOTIA
Apartheid and the Canada connection [involvement in financing Minorco's bid for Consolidated Gold Fields] P. C. Newman. il *Maclean's* 102:29 F 13 '89
Banking on Time [role of Toronto Dominion and Bank of Nova Scotia in Paramount Communications' hostile bid for Time Inc.] P. Chisholm and J. DeMont. il *Maclean's* 102:34-5 Jl 10 '89
BANK OF THE UNITED STATES (1816-1836)
The president vs. the Senate [A. Jackson] B. A. Weisberger. il *American Heritage* 40:22+ S/O '89
BANK PLANTING See Hillside gardens and gardening
BANK RATES See Interest (Economics)
BANK RESERVES See Banks and banking—Reserves
BANK ROBBERIES
Are ATMs easy targets for crooks? P. Cole. il *Business Week* p30 Mr 6 '89
Pushing his luck—and his blood pressure—an aged bank robber is caught red-handed [J. Kelm in Denver, Colo.] il por *People Weekly* 31:108 Ap 17 '89
History
The banker who robbed banks [L. Pope] J. Morgenstern. il pors *The New York Times Magazine* p54-6+ N 12 '89
BANK SECRECY See Confidential communications—Banking
BANK STOCKS See Banks and banking—Securities
BANKAITIS-DAVIS, BUNKI, AND TOBIN, KATRIN
Tour de France diary; ed. by Lewis Rothlein. il pors *Women's Sports & Fitness* 11:24-8 N/D '89
BANKAMERICA CORP.
Watch out: here comes Bank of America again. J. B. Levine. il por *Business Week* p129-30 F 20 '89
BANKE, JIM
The not-so-secret mission of Atlantis. il *Ad Astra* 1:7+ F '89
STS-29 mission report. il *Ad Astra* 1:15+ My '89
STS-30 mission report. il *Ad Astra* 1:41-2 S '89
We're back! il *Ad Astra* 1:8-12 Ja '89
BANKERS
See also
Journalists as bankers
Recruiting
Big bucks vs. a job for life: why top talent is defecting [Western firms raid Japanese banks and brokerages] T. Holden. il *Business Week* p58 Ja 9 '89
BANKING See Banks and banking
BANKING ETHICS See Banks and banking—Ethical aspects
BANKOWSKI, ZBIGNIEW
Ethics and health. il *World Health* p2-6 Ap '89

Genetics, medicine and ethics [cover story] il *World Health* p3-5 D '88
BANKRUPTCY
See also
Bank failures
Business failures
Why it's not smart—even if legal—to welsh on your debts. *Money* 18:18+ Mr '89
Anecdotes, facetiae, satire, etc.
Let's rake a deal [reverse bankruptcy and fraternal equalization rescission] B. Stein. il *The American Spectator* 22:37 O '89
BANKS, ANN
Alone at home: 10 safety tips for working parents & their kids [excerpt] *Redbook* 173:110+ O '89
BANKS, ERNIE
about
Cubs' Ernie Banks recalls greatest sports moments. il por *Jet* 76:50 S 11 '89
BANKS, HOWARD
What's ahead for business. See issues of Forbes beginning January 16, 1984
BANKS, JEFFREY, 1954-
about
The designer's eye for timeless fashion photography. J. Gruen. il por *Architectural Digest* 46:78+ S '89
BANKS, JONATHAN
about
On hot doughnuts—and jealousy. J. Marion. il por *TV Guide* 37:21 S 2-8 '89
BANKS, LYNNE REID See Reid Banks, Lynne, 1929-
BANKS, PETER M., AND RIDE, SALLY K.
Soviets in space [cover story] bibl il *Scientific American* 260:32-40 F '89
BANKS, RUSSELL, 1940-
about
Russell Banks's tale of family violence hits close to home. K. Hubbard. il pors *People Weekly* 32:135+ N 13 '89
Who to blame, who to forgive. W. Brown. il pors *The New York Times Magazine* p52-3+ S 10 '89
BANKS, BLOOD See Blood banks
BANKS, COIN
A banking success [making musical banks] J. Hanning. il por *The Mother Earth News* 115:46 Ja/F '89
A good old-fashioned piggy bank. il *The Family Handyman* 39:52 N/D '89
Collectors and collecting
Banks that move [mechanical banks] F. Donegan. il *Americana* 17:18-21 Mr/Ap '89
BANKS, FOOD See Food banks
BANKS, GENE See Gene banks
BANKS AND BANKING
See also
Agricultural credit
Bank holding companies
Bankers
Black banks and banking
Central banks
Checks
Chemical Bank
Citibank N.A.
Computers—Banking use
Confidential communications—Banking
Credit
Development banks
Federal Reserve banks
Federal Reserve System (U.S.)
Free banking
Interest (Economics)
Investment banking
Journalists as bankers
Loans, Bank
Piano music in banks
Savings and loan associations
Savings banks
Thrift institutions
Women's banks and banking
Eight forecasts for U.S. banking. B. P. Beckwith. il por *The Futurist* 23:27-33 Mr/Ap '89
Is your bank safe? M. Daly. *Better Homes and Gardens* 67:124-5 My '89
Money & banking. See issues of Business Week
Accounting
A colossal case of apples and oranges [banks disclosing information about their lending to highly leveraged transactions] P. Wang. il *Forbes* 143:48+ Mr 20 '89
The Fed lifts the Brady plan out of its sickbed [relaxing reserve accounting rules] M. McNamee and W. Glasgall. il *Business Week* p43 O 9 '89
What did Boston Co. know and when did it know it? K. H. Hammonds. por *Business Week* p87 F 6 '89
Acquisitions and mergers
International aspects
And now, Tex-Mex banking [Mexicans snap up small Texas banks] M. Ivey and S. Baker. il *Business Week* p140 O 9 '89

BANKS AND BANKING—Acquisitions and mergers—*cont.*

Japan

The birth of a behemoth [Mitsui Taiyo Kobe Bank] T. Holden. il *Business Week* p52 S 11 '89

Advertising

An end to the fast talk in bank ads? C. Yang. il *Business Week* p97 Jl 3 '89

No more Mr. Nice Guy. K. Hannon. il *Forbes* 144:140 D 25 '89

Automated teller machines

See Automated teller machines

Branch banking

See also

Banks and banking, International

Customer relations

A banker tells the secrets of the vault [interview with E. Mrkvicka] E. M. MacDonald. il pors *Money* 18:95-6+ Je '89

Humbled banks make nice again. R. W. Casey. il *Working Woman* 14:65-7 Mr '89

My banker wouldn't back my building [futile attempt to obtain mortgage for office space] J. DeParle. il *The Washington Monthly* 20:30-1 Ja '89

Debit cards

See Debit cards

Ethical aspects

American Express slings mud—and gets splattered [smear campaign against financier E. Safra] W. Glasgall and J. Meehan. il por *Business Week* p102+ Ag 14 '89

Bank shot: Edmond Safra turns the tables on American Express. J. Taylor. il pors *New York* 22:42-7 S 18 '89

Battling crime through the banks. D. Francis. il *Maclean's* 102:13 My 29 '89

City of Angels, indeed [Los Angeles banks involved in laundering drug money] il *U.S. News & World Report* 106:14 Ap 10 '89

A drug crackdown in the Alps [Switzerland] C. Dickey. il *Newsweek* 113:40 Ap 10 '89

The drug-money hunt [money laundering crackdown] P. R. Range. il map *U.S. News & World Report* 107:22-5 Ag 21 '89

Getting banks to just say 'no' [campaign against laundering drug money] P. Dwyer and P. Engardio. il *Business Week* p16-17 Ap 17 '89

Hiding the drug money [Canada; cover story; special section; with editorial comment by Kevin Doyle] H. Jensen. il *Maclean's* 102:2, 42-4+ O 23 '89

License to loot [R. Tamraz of Almashrek Bank in Beirut] Z. Sawaya. il por *Forbes* 143:157 Mr 6 '89

Finance

See also

Bank failures

Banks and banking, International—Finance

The 100 safest banks. J. Gilbert and E. M. MacDonald. il *Money* 18:31-2+ O '89

Banks and thrifts. T. Pouschine. il *Forbes* 143:94-7 Ja 9 '89

Banks look solid—if not rock-solid. F. A. Miller. il *Business Week* p104-5 Ja 9 '89

The giants retrench. F. A. Miller. il *Business Week* p94-5 Ap 3 '89

Just how safe is your bank? J. Blyskal and M. Hodge. il *New Choices for the Best Years* 29:43-5 Jl '89

Statistics

See also

Banks and banking, International—Finance—Statistics

Bank scoreboard. F. A. Miller. il *Business Week* p96-105 Ap 3 '89

Float

Congress cuts out lengthy check-holds. *Modern Maturity* 32:93 F/Mr '89

Foreign branches

See Banks and banking, International

Foreign business

See Banks and banking, International

History

See also

Bank of the United States (1816-1836)

Holding companies

See Bank holding companies

Insurance, Surety and fidelity

See Insurance, Surety and fidelity

Insurance of accounts

See Bank accounts—Insurance

Laws and regulations

See also

Community Reinvestment Act of 1977

Federal Deposit Insurance Corporation

United States. Federal Home Loan Bank Board

Evolution of banking legislation; Federal agencies involved. *Congressional Digest* 68:164-5+ Je/Jl '89

Financial reform [address, August 29, 1989] W. L. Hoskins. *Vital Speeches of the Day* 56:111-14 D 1 '89

Let the Glass-Steagall wall come tumbling down. L. J. Nathans and D. Foust. il *Business Week* p116 D 18 '89

One toe over the line [ruling permits bank holding companies to buy and sell corporate bonds] il *Time* 133:51 Ja 30 '89

Time to bank on the future [competing internationally through deregulation] M. B. Zuckerman. il *U.S. News & World Report* 107:64 Jl 10 '89

Management

See Bank management

Real estate operations

Suddenly, all this terra doesn't feel so firma. J. Meehan. il *Business Week* p64 O 23 '89

Thumb in the dike [Valley National] J. H. Taylor. il por *Forbes* 144:76 Ag 21 '89

Reserves

Banks are getting those third world jitters again [push for higher reserves] J. Meehan and W. Glasgall. il *Business Week* p200+ S 25 '89

The Fed lifts the Brady plan out of its sickbed [relaxing reserve accounting rules] M. McNamee and W. Glasgall. il *Business Week* p43 O 9 '89

What are they waiting for? [reserve boosts by banks with third world loans] P. Duggan. il *Forbes* 144:45-6 O 2 '89

Securities

Banking gets leaner and meaner. J. Meehan. il *Business Week* p106-7 O 16 '89

Banking on regionals. C. Poole. il *Forbes* 144:190 S 4 '89

Big bank stocks rise on hopes of a third world deal. J. Mendes. il *Fortune* 120:39+ Jl 31 '89

Chicago bank stock basket. T. Jaffe. il *Forbes* 144:124 Ag 21 '89

Even 'good banks' can be bad buys [Class B Chemical stock] J. M. Laderman. *Business Week* p60 Ja 9 '89

A sight seeing tour of regional bank stocks. A. Kupfer. il *Fortune* 119:40 Ja 30 '89

Securities handling

See also

Cash management accounts

Let the Glass-Steagall wall come tumbling down. L. J. Nathans and D. Foust. il *Business Week* p116 D 18 '89

One toe over the line [ruling permits bank holding companies to buy and sell corporate bonds] il *Time* 133:51 Ja 30 '89

Tough new kid on the block [competition in investment banking] M. Berss. il *Forbes* 144:42-3 O 2 '89

Service charges

Advice to one-stop bankers: shop around. P. Sharif. *Black Enterprise* 19:33-4 Mr '89

Congress moves to ensure affordable banking. il *Modern Maturity* 32:9 O/N '89

Shopping for the best bank. M. Rowland. *Working Woman* 14:94 Ap '89

Services

See also

Bank accounts

Brokers—Banking services

Credit cards

Debit cards

Home banking services

Private banking

Supermarkets—Banking services

Advice to one-stop bankers: shop around. P. Sharif. *Black Enterprise* 19:33-4 Mr '89

Do you know where your mortgage is? Or whether your property taxes and insurance premiums have been paid? il *Consumer Reports* 54:441 Jl '89

Getting the most out of your bank. P. Sharif. il *Black Enterprise* 19:46-8 Jl '89

How good is your bank? B. G. Quint. il *Glamour* 87:151 Ap '89

Suits and claims

Taking the banker to court [lender liability] C. Friday and L. Reibstein. il *Newsweek* 113:44 My 8 '89

Africa

See also

African Development Bank

Arizona

See also

Valley National Corp.

Belgium

See also

Banque Bruxelles Lambert SA

British Columbia

See also

Vancouver (B.C.)—Banks

California

See also

Far East National Bank

GBC Bancorp

Los Angeles (Calif.)—Banks

Wells Fargo Bank, National Association

History

Opportunities [success of banker D. O. Mills during the California Gold Rush] J. S. Gordon. il *American Heritage* 40:20+ N '89

Canada

See also

Bank of Canada

Bank of Nova Scotia

Hongkong Bank of Canada

Royal Trust Company of Canada

BANKS AND BANKING—Canada—*cont.*
Bankers against Tories [American Express bids for bank
  status] M. Clark. il *Maclean's* 102:16 F 6 '89
Breaking barriers. P. Chisholm. il *Maclean's* 102:24-5 F 13
  '89
Canada's growing economic outreach [views of M. Cornelissen]
  P. C. Newman. il *Maclean's* 102:42 Ja 23 '89
Hiding the drug money [cover story; special section; with
  editorial comment by Kevin Doyle] H. Jensen. il *Maclean's*
  102:2, 42-4+ O 23 '89
A new plan for debt [Canadian banks wary of Brady plan
  for Latin America] J. DeMont. il *Maclean's* 102:32-3 Mr
  27 '89

Colombia
See also
Banco de Occidente SA
Delaware
See also
Wilmington Trust Co.
East Asia
The top banks. il *Fortune* 120 no13 Special Issue:135-6
  Fall '89
Your banker in Asia. F. S. Worthy. il *Fortune* 120 no13
  Special Issue:68 Fall '89
Florida
See also
Barnett Banks, Inc.
France
See also
Banque Nationale de Paris
Lazard Frères et Cie
Georgia
See also
Citizens & Southern Corp.
Germany (West)
See also
Bundesbank
Commerzbank Aktiengesellschaft
Deutsche Bank AG
Great Britain
See also
London (England)—Banks
Greece
See also
Bank of Crete
Hong Kong
See also
Hongkong and Shanghai Banking Corporation
Illinois
See also
Chicago (Ill.)—Banks
Continental Bank, N.A.
Israel
"If I were a rich man . . .". M. Schifrin. *Forbes* 143:56+
  Ap 17 '89
Japan
See also
Dai-Ichi Kangyo Bank, Ltd.
Mitsui Taiyo Kobe Bank
Norinchukin Bank
Sumitomo Bank, Ltd.
Big bucks vs. a job for life: why top talent is defecting
  [Western firms raid Japanese banks and brokerages] T.
  Holden. il *Business Week* p58 Ja 9 '89
Lebanon
See also
Almashrek Bank
Banque du Liban
Louisiana
See also
Hibernia Corporation
Whitney National Bank
Mexico
And now, Tex-Mex banking [Mexicans snap up small Texas
  banks] M. Ivey and S. Baker. il *Business Week* p140
  O 9 '89
New York (State)
See also
New York (N.Y.)—Banks
North Fork Bank & Trust Co.
North Carolina
See also
NCNB Corp.
Ohio
See also
Banc One Corp.
Ontario
See also
Toronto Dominion Bank
Pennsylvania
See also
Equibank
Mellon Bank NA
Peru
See also
Banco de Credito del Peru

Québec (Province)
See also
Montreal (Québec)—Banks
Southeastern States
Too much of a good thing. J. H. Taylor. il *Forbes* 144:195+
  D 11 '89
Soviet Union
A Soviet cure for the S&L mess. J. Mois. il por *Fortune*
  120:207+ N 6 '89
Switzerland
See also
Crédit Suisse
Crackdown on the Swiss laundry. C. Gorman. il *Time* 133:53
  Ap 24 '89
A drug crackdown in the Alps. C. Dickey. il *Newsweek*
  113:40 Ap 10 '89
Texas
And now, Tex-Mex banking [Mexicans snap up small Texas
  banks] M. Ivey and S. Baker. il *Business Week* p140
  O 9 '89
Texas' born-again banks find a savior: consumers. M. Ivey
  and K. Kelly. il *Business Week* p160+ N 27 '89
United States
See Banks and banking
Western Europe
The drug war—European style [money laundering crackdown]
  B. Riemer. *Business Week* p31-2 O 2 '89
BANKS AND BANKING, COOPERATIVE
See also
Credit unions
BANKS AND BANKING, INTERNATIONAL
See also
Citibank N.A.
Citicorp
Development banks
Export-Import Bank of the United States
Iranian seizure of United States embassy, 1979-1981—
  Economic aspects
Money—International aspects
World Bank
Love 'em and leave 'em [agricultural lending] M. Fritz.
  il *Forbes* 144:48 N 13 '89
Time to bank on the future [competing internationally through
  deregulation] M. B. Zuckerman. il *U.S. News & World
  Report* 107:64 Jl 10 '89
Finance
Statistics
The 100 biggest banks outside the U.S. J. Park and J.
  C. Viebranz. il *Fortune* 120:320-4 Jl 31 '89
The world's 50 biggest banks. il *Fortune* 120:286 Jl 31 '89
The world's biggest banks enjoyed a bountiful year. W.
  Glasgall. il *Business Week* p114-15 Je 26 '89
Taxation
An offer they can't refuse [IRS ruling limits tax advantages
  banks get for writing off foreign loan losses] L. Saunders.
  il *Forbes* 143:144 My 29 '89
BANNED BOOKS WEEK
In praise of banned books [events in Los Angeles] L. See.
  Publishers Weekly 236:49 O 27 '89
BANNENBERG, JON
  about
Even the model costs $50,000. G. Burks. il por *Forbes*
  144 Special Issue:372 O 23 '89
BANNER, JAMES M., JR.
Organizing the humanities. il *Change* 21:44-51 Mr/Ap '89
BANNERS
Don't ban the banners [stadiums] R. Telander. por *Sports
  Illustrated* 71:100 O 30 '89
Japanese banners as sun screens. il *Sunset (Central West
  edition)* 182:162 My '89
BANNOURA, BASSAM
  about
Palestinian Christians join intifada tax protest. L. Cryderman.
  il por *Christianity Today* 33:42 D 15 '89
BANQUE BRUXELLES LAMBERT SA
Buy American [views of R. Leuschel] P. Fuhrman. il por
  Forbes 144:64 Jl 10 '89
BANQUE DU LIBAN
An oasis of sanity. P. Fuhrman. il por *Forbes* 144:100+
  O 2 '89
BANQUE NATIONALE DE PARIS
A marriage of giants to defend French finance [joining Union
  des Assurances de Paris with Banque Nationale de Paris]
  B. Riemer. il por *Business Week* p46 Ap 10 '89
BANSE, TIMOTHY P.
Engine room. *See* issues of Motor Boating & Sailing
BANSEMER, ROGER, 1948-
  about
A rising career for Roger Bansemer. M. E. Stegmaier. il
  por *American Artist* 53:58-63+ Ag '89
BANTA CORPORATION
Banta Corp. R. Abelson. il *Fortune* 120:86 Ag 28 '89
BANTAM AUDIO PUBLISHING
Bantam targets retail market with young adult line. P. Sweeting
  and J. Zinsser. *Publishers Weekly* 235:49 My 5 '89
Random, Bantam to distribute audiotapes through video
  stores. *Publishers Weekly* 236:27 D 1 '89

BANTAM BOOKS, INC.
Auel signs major three-book deal with Crown, Bantam. G. Feldman. il por *Publishers Weekly* 236:34-5 D 22 '89
Vestron teams with Bantam. P. Sweeting. il *Publishers Weekly* 235:30 F 3 '89
BANTAM DOUBLEDAY DELL PUBLISHING GROUP INC.
Harlequin sues Bantam on promotional materials. C. Reid. *Publishers Weekly* 235:14 Ap 14 '89
Hoeft is new president of Bantam Doubleday Dell. D. Maryles. por *Publishers Weekly* 236:9 N 17 '89
BANTEL, LINDA
The Potamkin Collection of American art. il *Antiques* 136:292-301 Ag '89
BAPTISM
Against R.C.I.A. [Rite of Christian Initiation for Adults; with reply by R. D. Duggan; cover story] A. M. Greeley. il *America* 161:231-7 O 14 '89
Professing faith. P. J. Ryan. *America* 160:95 F 4 '89
State of the question [discussion of October 14, 1989 article, Against R.C.I.A.] A. M. Greeley. *America* 161:328-30 N 11 '89
With a few tears and a splash of the river Jordan, England's littlest Princess is christened [Beatrice] M. Dougherty. il pors *People Weekly* 31:44-5 Ja 9 '89
BAPTIST WORLD CENTER (NASHVILLE, TENN.)
$10 million headquarters signals new course for National Baptist Convention, U.S.A. Inc. [cover story] C. L. Sanders. il pors *Ebony* 44:68-70+ O '89
National Baptists build a headquarters. R. Waddle. *The Christian Century* 106:805-7 S 13-20 '89
BAPTISTS
United States
See also
Abyssinian Baptist Church (New York, N.Y.)
$10 million headquarters signals new course for National Baptist Convention, U.S.A. Inc. [cover story] C. L. Sanders. il pors *Ebony* 44:68-70+ O '89
Baptists back Thompson in Proposition 42 fight [National Baptist Convention] il por *Jet* 75:50 F 27 '89
Baptists take few chances in Las Vegas [Southern Baptist Convention] K. H. Sidey. il *Christianity Today* 33:50-1 Jl 14 '89
Fragmentation grows for Southern Baptists [Las Vegas convention] B. Leonard. *The Christian Century* 106:644-6 Jl 5-12 '89
Growing up Baptist. M. E. Snodgrass. il *Ms.* 17:66-7 Mr '89
National Baptists build a headquarters. R. Waddle. *The Christian Century* 106:805-7 S 13-20 '89
Pastors given rare glimpse of North Korea [Korean-American Southern Baptist pastors attend Easter service] D. Burton. *Christianity Today* 33:63 Je 16 '89
Sanders gives his church $1/4 million in tithes [football player's gifts to Paradise Baptist Church, Wichita, Kan.] il por *Jet* 76:51 S 25 '89
SBC fundamentalists aim to defuse debate [Southern Baptist Convention in Las Vegas] S. Hastey. *The Christian Century* 106:548-50 My 24-31 '89
Vermont: 'whitest state in America' gets first black church [New Alpha Missionary Baptist Church] C. Waldron. il pors *Jet* 75:14-15+ Mr 13 '89
BAR ASSOCIATIONS
See also
American Bar Association
BAR CLAMPS *See* Clamps
BAR CODING
See also
Bookland EAN system
By using bar coding on busy bees, scientist Stephen Buchmann becomes an unstung hero [use in monitoring activities] il *People Weekly* 31:105 My 22 '89
Probing secrets of small critters: fuchsia mice and bar-coded bees. L. Ware. il *Audubon* 91:12 Ja '89
Wider uses for bar codes. L. Davis. il *Nation's Business* 77:34+ Mr '89
Japan
New uses for bar codes. *The Futurist* 23:47 N/D '89
BAR COOKIES *See* Cookies
BAR DU THÉÂTRE (NEW YORK, N.Y.) *See* New York (N.Y.)—Restaurants, nightclubs, bars, etc.
BAR HARBOR (ME.)
Description
Bar Harbor, RFD. R. Sassaman. il por *Country Journal* 16:76-80 S/O '89
BAR MITZVAH
Herman Gollob's bar mitzvah. B. Greene. por *Esquire* 112:33-4 Jl '89
BARACH, PHILIP
about
If the shoe fits, sell it? S. Phillips. *Business Week* p42+ Mr 13 '89
BARAKA, AMINA
Soweto song [poem] *Essence* 19:129 F '89
BARAŃCZAK, STANISLAW, 1946-
The confusion of tongues [cover story] il *The New Leader* 72:16-18 F 6 '89

BARATTA, ANTHONY
about
Custom of the country. G. Harrell. il *House & Garden* 161:116-21+ Ag '89
BARBACH, LONNIE GARFIELD, 1946-
Are you too inhibited in bed? *Redbook* 172:112-13+ Mr '89
BARBARA BUSH FOUNDATION FOR FAMILY LITERACY
Barbara Bush Foundation for Family Literacy launched at White House. H. Fields. *Publishers Weekly* 235:12 Mr 24 '89
BARBARA FELDMAN AND DANCERS
Reviews:
Performances in New Haven, Conn. D. Scott. il *Dance Magazine* 63:56-8 Ag '89
BARBARA PIASECKA JOHNSON-GDAŃSK SHIPYARD COMPANY
Lech's American angel [heiress B. Johnson bails out shipyard; cover story] D. Margolick. il pors *The New York Times Magazine* p28-31+ O 8 '89
BARBARA THOMAS ENTERPRISES INC.
Make room for the children. N. Thomas-Cote. por *Nation's Business* 77:13 O '89
BARBASH, JACK
John R. Commons: pioneer of labor economics [cover story] bibl f *Monthly Labor Review* 112:44-9 My '89
BARBATO, JOSEPH
Independent publishing. See occasional issues of Publishers Weekly beginning October 23, 1987
BARBECUE COOKING
Backyard barbecue cookbook. il *McCall's* 116:119-24+ Je '89
Backyard barbecue Italian style. J. W. Wilson. il *New Choices for the Best Years* 29:64-9 Ag '89
Barbecue: Texas-style. il *Ladies' Home Journal* 106:146-8+ Jl '89
Barbecuing goes gourmet. L. Shapiro. il *Newsweek* 114:60-1 Jl 3 '89
Best-ever barbecues. il *Better Homes and Gardens* 67:117-18 Ag '89
Down-home backyard barbecues. J. Stern and M. Stern. il *Redbook* 173:117-22+ Ag '89
Easy-on-dad barbecue: start in microwave, finish on grill. il *McCall's* 116:133 Je '89
Great grilling! 3 easy menus for summer barbecues. B. Johnson. il *Better Homes and Gardens* 67:131-7+ Je '89
Great outdoors. C. Idone. il *The New York Times Magazine* p71-2 My 14 '89
Grill it! C. Koury. il *Parents* 64:173-6+ Je '89
In La Jolla, it's bring-your-own-barbecue for buffet on the beach. il *Sunset (Central West edition)* 181:80-1, 150+ D '88
Keep the home fires burning. B. Kafka. il *Gourmet* 49:40 Ag '89
Lean pork on the barbecue . . . chops or tenderloin. il *Sunset (Central West edition)* 182:176 Ap '89
Mastering the art of outdoor cooking. M. Thompson and others. il *The Family Handyman* 39:47-50+ Je '89
Micro-way: super-easy barbecue. il *McCall's* 116:109 Ag '89
A Middle Eastern-style dinner from the grill. il *Gourmet* 49:90-2+ Je '89
The new American picnic [Fourth of July barbecue] J. B. Hurley. il *Prevention (Emmaus, Pa.)* 41:72-6+ Jl '89
The new BBQ [cutting calories] M. Burros. il *American Health* 8:102+ Jl/Ag '89
New grill in town. M. Burros. il *The Mother Earth News* 118:82 Jl/Ag '89
Nouvelle barbecue [with recipes by Ellen Brown] K. Hamilton. il *Health (New York, N.Y.)* 21:76-9+ Je '89
Over the coals. C. Kummer. il *The Atlantic* 263:83-6 Je '89
Piled high and hot off the grill . . . turkey or pork sandwiches. il *Sunset (Central West edition)* 183:110 Jl '89
Quick & easy: breads on the barbecue. M. Langan. il *McCall's* 116:135 Je '89
Quick! Grill a meal. il *Southern Living* 24:106 Ag '89
Savory grilled vegetables [low calorie] il *McCall's* 116:126 Jl '89
Shellfish spectacular. il *Sunset (Central West edition)* 183:70-1 Jl '89
Timesaving barbecue [microwaved] il *Southern Living* 24:192 Ap '89
Ultimate skewering . . . beef, fish, or chicken. il *Sunset (Central West edition)* 182:130-1 My '89
Anecdotes, facetiae, satire, etc.
Mmm, mmm, simulacrum. F. Gannon. il *Harper's* 278:55-7 My '89
Equipment
BBQ grill table. S. Kingman and P. Kingman. il *The Family Handyman* 39:80-1 Je '89
Charcoal storage bin. T. Wolfe. il *Flower and Garden* 33:60 My/Je '89
What's new in barbecue. B. Johnson. il *Better Homes and Gardens* 67:138 Je '89
BARBECUE GRILLS
The gas barbecue. il *Sunset (Central West edition)* 182:198+ Je '89

BARBECUE GRILLS—*cont.*
Grill in style. R. N. Hoffman. il *Workbench* 45:32-4 Jl/Ag '89
Mastering the art of outdoor cooking. M. Thompson and others. il *The Family Handyman* 39:47-50+ Je '89
Safety devices and measures
Barbecues for safe grilling. il *Current Health 2* 15:22-3 My '89
BARBECUE RESTAURANTS
Searching for BBQ bliss, the pickings are easy [top ten barbecue places in the U.S.] A. Richman. il *People Weekly* 32:34-44 Ag 28 '89
BARBECUE SAUCES *See* Sauces
BARBED WIRE FENCES
Fences that kill [barbed wire barrier used to keep out wild animals in Botswana] F. Carbone. *World Press Review* 36:80 O '89
BARBEE, ROBERT, AND SCHULLERY, PAUL
Yellowstone: the smoke clears. il *National Parks* 63:18-21 Mr/Ap '89
BARBER, DESIRÉE
about
Amid a raging debate, one woman chooses abortion. D. Grogan and others. il *People Weekly* 32:89-90+ Jl 24 '89
BARBER, JOHN LYSBERG NOËL *See* Barber, Noël
BARBER, NOËL
Singapore in the thirties. il map *Gourmet* 49:100+ My '89
BARBER, SAMUEL, 1910-1981
about
Barber Down Under. T. W. Libbey, Jr. il *High Fidelity (New York, N.Y.)* 39:56 F '89
BARBER, VIRGINIA
about
Quality lit. K. Pryor. il por *New York* 22:26 Mr 27 '89
THE BARBER OF SEVILLE [opera] *See* Rossini, Gioacchino, 1792-1868
BARBER POLES
The barber pole: symbol with a past and a future. P. Krumholz. il *Antiques & Collecting Hobbies* 94:69-72 Mr '89
BARBIE DOLLS
As a tiny plastic star turns 30, the real Barbie and Ken reflect on life in the shadow of the dolls [B. Segal and K. Handler] M. Green. il pors *People Weekly* 31:186-7+ Mr 6 '89
Hot date: Barbie and G.I. Joe. B. Kantrowitz. il *Newsweek* 113:59 F 20 '89
The jewelry designer's crush on Schiaparelli—and Barbie [Billy Boy] E. White. il por *Architectural Digest* 46:94+ S '89
Wow! Barbie is thirty! M. Forrest. il *Antiques & Collecting Hobbies* 94:22-5 S '89
BARBIER, EDWARD B.
Sustaining agriculture on marginal land: a policy framework. bibl f il *Environment* 31:12-17+ N '89
BARBOUR, J. PIUS
about
The activism of interpretation: black pastors and public life. K. B. Jones. *The Christian Century* 106:817-18 S 13-20 '89
BARBOUR, SPIDER
Overnight sensation. il *Natural History* p24+ My '89
BARBOUTI, IHSAN
about
The mysterious "Doctor B.". J. Birnbaum. il por *Time* 133:40+ F 27 '89
BARBUDA (ANTIGUA AND BARBUDA)
See also
Land tenure—Barbuda (Antigua and Barbuda)
BARCELONA (SPAIN)
City planning
Barcelona's Olympic buildup. J. Garcia. *World Press Review* 36:55 Ap '89
Description
Welcome to Barcelona. J. Valls-Russell. il *The New Leader* 72:9-10 Ja 9 '89
BARCLAYSAMERICAN/FINANCIAL INC.
Primerica adds another feather to its cap. J. Friedman. il *Business Week* p98 D 11 '89
BARCO VARGAS, VIRGILIO
about
Dateline drug wars: Colombia: the wrong strategy. B. M. Bagley. *Foreign Policy* 77:154-71 Wint '89/'90
Seize the time against cocaine kings. G. F. Gugliotta. il *U.S. News & World Report* 107:21 S 11 '89
BARD, MITCHELL
Israel: some surprising polls. *Commentary* 88:45-7 Ag '89
BARDEN CORP.
SKF may find its high-tech bearings. G. G. Marcial. *Business Week* p106 D 4 '89
BARDO, JOHN
about
An innocent life, a heartbreaking death. P. Axthelm. il por *People Weekly* 32:60-2+ Jl 31 '89
BARDOT, BRIGITTE
about
Taking some pity on Brigitte Bardot. B. Amiel. il *Maclean's* 102:9 Ag 28 '89

Anecdotes, facetiae, satire, etc.
Charly's loss, Bardot's gain [actress orders castration of neighbor's donkey] A. Fotheringham. il *Maclean's* 102:56 Ag 7 '89
BARDWICK, JUDITH M., 1933-
En route or just in a holding pattern? il *Working Woman* 14:118-19 O '89
BAREIRO SAGUIER, RUBÉN
The birth of a language. il *The Courier (Unesco)* 42:24-5 My '89
BARENBOIM, DANIEL
about
Clashing egos at the Paris Opera. R. Marshall. il por *Newsweek* 113:66 Ja 30 '89
Imbroglio at the Bastille. B. Villien. il *Opera News* 54:30-3 Jl '89
Letter from Europe. J. Kramer. *The New Yorker* 65:81-94 My 1 '89
Music. E. W. Said. *The Nation* 248:498-500 Ap 10 '89
Musical events:
New York concerts. A. Porter. *The New Yorker* 65:93-4 Mr 6 '89
Second storming of the Bastille. O. Friedrich. il por *Time* 133:75 Ja 30 '89
Viewpoint. J. L. Poole. *Opera News* 53:4 Mr 4 '89
BARGAINING (INDUSTRIAL) *See* Collective bargaining
BARGAINS
Sales & bargains. L. Fleischer. *See* issues of New York
BARGE CRUISING *See* Cruising
BARILE, NANCY, D. 1989
about
'Hit Man' Hearns' brother charged in shooting of 'girlfriend' in Michigan. il pors *Jet* 76:51-2 Je 26 '89
BARING BROTHERS & CO. LTD.
The sixth great power returns. J. Willoughby. il por *Forbes* 143:135 F 20 '89
BARITEAU, CORINNE ADRIA
Baby's first Christmas [poem] *McCall's* 117:95 D '89
Infant power . . . [poem] *Good Housekeeping* 209:184 Jl '89
BARK IN ART
Bark with a bite [R. Carroll's egg tempera paintings] E. Agar. il *American Artist* 53:92-7 S '89
BARKENTIN, MARJORIE
about
Ulysses in Nighttown [drama] Reviews
The Nation 248:247-8 F 20 '89. T. M. Disch
BARKER, BOB
about
Speaking up for 'abused' animals, Bob Barker is hit with a lawsuit. L. Smith. il por *People Weekly* 32:75-6 S 18 '89
BARKER, NICHOLAS
about
Creative collaborators. il pors *Harper's Bazaar* 122:116-21 Je '89
BARKER, THEO
Business as usual? London and the industrial revolution. bibl il *History Today* 39:45-51 F '89
BARKER, WENDY
Requiescat, for my father [poem] *The American Scholar* 58:578-80 Aut '89
BARKER TEXAS HISTORY CENTER (AUSTIN, TEX.)
Texas Music Collection
See Texas Music Collection
BARKHO, LEON Y.
Restoring ancient Hatra. il *World Press Review* 36:55 Mr '89
BARKIN, ELLEN
about
Barkin up the right tree. R. Corliss. por *Time* 134:86 O 23 '89
Ellen Barkin. por *People Weekly* 32:80-1 D 25 '89-Ja 1 '90
Ellen Barkin and the man behind her new look. C. Krupp. pors *Glamour* 87:192 O '89
BARKIN, ROGER M.
The changing role of fathers. il *USA Today (Periodical)* 118:56-7 Jl '89
BARKLEY, IRAN
about
Stonehands rules again. B. Newman. il pors *Sports Illustrated* 70:18-19 Mr 6 '89
BARKSDALE, JAMES F.
about
Companies should "create capital" [interview] E. Schultz. il por *Fortune* 120:48+ Jl 31 '89
BARLAM, CATHY
Women on the verge: the surge in borderline personality disorder. il *Mademoiselle* 95:140 N '89
BARLETT, DONALD L.
about
Two reporters you don't want on your tail. J. Alter. il pors *Newsweek* 113:71+ Ap 24 '89
BARLOW, LINDA
Great storytelling. *The Writer* 102:14-17 Ag '89

BARLOW, MARILYN
about
Seeds selected from the past. J. Parente. il *Americana* 17:12
Mr/Ap '89
BARN AGAIN! (PROGRAM)
Batten down the hatches. J. Walter. il *Successful Farming*
87:33 D '89
Old barn, young muscle. J. Walter. il *Successful Farming*
87:46-7 F '89
On the farm: Barn Again! J. D. Reed. il *Time* 133:87-8
F 20 '89
BARN OWLS *See* Owls
BARN SWALLOWS *See* Swallows
BARNARD, CHARLES N.
A lifetime of ritual. il *National Wildlife* 28:6-8 D '89/Ja
'90
Travelog. See issues of Modern Maturity
BARNARD, EDWARD EMERSON, 1857-1923
about
Barnard's 'dark' dilemma. G. L. Verschuur. il pors *Astronomy*
17:30-8 F '89
BARNARD, ROBERT
I could have died laughing. il *The Writer* 102:15-18 F '89
BARNARD COLLEGE
Holding court [Centennial Hall dorm] C. Pearson. il
Architectural Record 177:112-15 O '89
BARNES, BARBARA, AND LESLIE, MARY
A program to improve local school site management. *The
Education Digest* 55:32-4 N '89
BARNES, BRIAN M.
Freeze avoidance in a mammal: body temperatures below
0°C in an Arctic hibernator [cover story] bibl f il *Science*
244:1593-5 Je 30 '89
BARNES, CLIVE, 1927-
Attitudes. See issues of Dance Magazine beginning May
1989
BARNES, DUNCAN
Up front. See issues of Field & Stream
BARNES, FRED, 1943-
The Bush league. il *Vogue* 179:292+ Ap '89
Mistakes new presidents make. il *Reader's Digest* 134:38-43
Ja '89
National capital, national shame. il por *Reader's Digest*
135:106-11 N '89
No longer dismissed as weirdos, animal-rights groups are
now threatening medical research. *Vogue* 179:542 S '89
Politics. *Vogue* 179:144 Je '89
BARNES, JOHN A.
Cable TV's costly monopoly game. il *Reader's Digest*
135:97-100 O '89
Why cable costs too much. *The Washington Monthly*
21:12-14+ Je '89
BARNES, JOHN A., AND HADDEN, JEFFREY
New deal. *The New Republic* 200:20+ My 1 '89
BARNES, JULIAN
Prince of poets. il *The New York Review of Books* 36:10+
N 9 '89
Shipwreck [story] il *The New Yorker* 65:40-50 Je 12
'89
about
PW interviews. A. Smith. il por *Publishers Weekly* 236:73-4
N 3 '89
BARNES, KATE
Time out [poem] *Country Journal* 16:22 Ja '89
BARNES, RANDY
about
A show of strength. J. E. Vader. il pors *Sports Illustrated*
70:62-4+ My 15 '89
BARNES, ROGER E.
(jt. auth) See Stephens, Brooke M., and Barnes, Roger E.
BARNES, STEVE
The crusade of Dr. Elders. il pors *The New York Times
Magazine* p38-41+ O 15 '89
BARNES, SUSAN KELLY
about
Constant growth is one reward at a start-up. M. Aaland.
il por *Working Woman* 14:61 My '89
BARNES, THOMAS
about
New brooms against deadly weapons. P. C. Newman. il
Maclean's 102:28 Ja 9 '89
BARNES & NOBLE
California court upholds limits on trade books in college
stores [case of Marin County Community College bookstore
managed by Barnes & Noble] C. Reid. *Publishers Weekly*
235:18 Ap 28 '89
BARNES FOUNDATION (MERION, PA.)
New prospects at the Barnes? W. Robinson. il por *Art in
America* 77:21+ Mr '89
BARNES-SVARNEY, PATRICIA
Amber reveals the past. il *Earth Science* 41:13-15 Wint
'88
Righting the risk of radon. il map *Earth Science* 42:17-18
Fall '89
BARNET, RICHARD J.
Holding big businesses accountable. *Utne Reader* p68-9 Ja/F
'89

BARNET, ROBERT J.
Health care in the United States: rights and reality. *America*
160:268-71 Mr 25 '89
BARNET, WILL, 1911-
about
A certain slant of light: drawings by Will Barnet, poems
by Emily Dickinson. S. Marcus. il *American Artist* 53:56-61
N '89
BARNETT, ALAN W.
Revolution on the walls. il *Art in America* 77:67-9+ Jl '89
BARNETT, BOB
Our changing football heroes. il *The Saturday Evening Post*
261:36+ Ja/F '89
BARNETT, DORIS
about
Calif. lottery moves to get back $3.4 mil. win by Los Angeles
woman. por *Jet* 76:25 My 22 '89
Los Angeles nurse finally named $3M lottery winner. il
pors *Jet* 76:24 Ap 24 '89
New ruling favors Barnett in Calif. lottery battle. por *Jet*
76:36 Je 26 '89
BARNETT, FRANK, AND BARNETT, SHARAN
How entrepreneurial couples work together. il pors *Working
Woman* 14:77-80 Ap '89
BARNETT, MARGUERITE
Missouri Youth 2000 Conference [address, November 30,
1988] *Vital Speeches of the Day* 55:349-52 Mr 15 '89
BARNETT, MARY, D. 1984
about
Fray erupts when white woman wills estate worth $476,000
to black man. *Jet* 76:4 My 22 '89
BARNETT, ROBERT A.
Taking a reasonable approach to our food dilemmas. il *Working
Woman* 14:129-30+ My '89
BARNETT, SHARAN
(jt. auth) See Barnett, Frank, and Barnett, Sharan
BARNETT, STEPHEN
Preserving newspapers or monopoly? [cover story] *The Nation*
249:513+ N 6 '89
BARNETT BANKS, INC.
"Do we know how to run something like this?". J. H.
Taylor. il por *Forbes* 144:79-80 N 27 '89
BARNETTE, JAMES
about
'We will not fight another war'. R. Chepesiuk. il por *The
Progressive* 53:17 N '89
BARNEY'S, NEW YORK
The Store of the Year. I. Daria. il *Money* 18:136-40+ N
'89
BARNHARDT, REBECCA
Creating the pot of gold. il *Petersen's Photographic Magazine*
18:98-9 N '89
BARNS, CONVERTED *See* Houses, Remodeled
BARNS AND STABLES
See also
Milking parlors
Swine houses
Pull tie stalls to pack the barn [dairy barn] J. R. Borcherding.
il *Successful Farming* 87:56-7 F '89
Architecture
Horse show [stable at Cellular Farm, North Castle, N.Y.]
M. Gaskie. il *Architectural Record* 177:120-3 Jl '89
Conservation and restoration
See also
Barn Again! (Program)
A barn is more than a building, it is a shrine to our agrarian
past [cover story] J. Doherty. il *Smithsonian* 20:30-43
Ag '89
Fires and fire prevention
Fireproof barn for fancy cows. J. R. Borcherding. il *Successful
Farming* 87:46 O '89
BARNSLEY (ENGLAND)
Economic conditions
From misery to self-reliance. A. Phillips. il *Maclean's* 102:37+
My 8 '89
BARNSTONE, WILLIS, 1927-
In praise of Wang Meng. *The Nation* 249:502-3 O 30 '89
BARNUM, P. T. (PHINEAS TAYLOR), 1810-1891
about
The farm where the elephants plowed! E. Rochette. il *Antiques
& Collecting Hobbies* 94:61-2 Jl '89
BARNUM, PHINEAS TAYLOR *See* Barnum, P. T. (Phineas
Taylor), 1810-1891
BARNUM (P.T.) MUSEUM (BRIDGEPORT, CONN.) *See*
P.T. Barnum Museum (Bridgeport, Conn.)
BARNWELL, MICHELE R.
My Semester at Sea. il pors *Essence* 20:23+ Ag '89
BAROCCI, NANCY
about
That's Italian in Illinois. D. Weil. il por *Working Woman*
14:58-60 Ag '89
BAROID CORPORATION
Simmons' sleeper. T. Jaffe. *Forbes* 143:285 Je 26 '89
BAROL, BILL
The Carrig-Rohane frame. il *American Heritage* 40:30-1 D
'89
Chantilly. il *American Heritage* 40:26-7 N '89
The Navajo blanket. *American Heritage* 40:24 Jl/Ag '89

BAROL, BILL—*cont.*

The pillar-and-scroll clock. *American Heritage* 40:24 Ap '89
Tucker porcelain. il *American Heritage* 40:28-9 My/Je '89
The Wurlitzer 1015. il *American Heritage* 40:28-9 S/O '89

BARON, CLIFFORD
about
Up links. E. G. Carter. il *Gentlemen's Quarterly* 59:31 Jl '89

BARON, HANNELORE, 1926-1987
about
Hannelore Baron: Schlesinger and Solomon R. Guggenheim Museum. B. A. MacAdam. il *Art News* 88:195 O '89

BARON-FAUST, RITA
Sexually transmitted diseases: are you at risk? il *McCall's* 116:105-6+ Ap '89
Why doctors mistreat women: special medical report. *Redbook* 173:114-15+ My '89

BARONE, JEANINE
11 ways to eat safer fish. *American Health* 8:112-13 Je '89
Making health a family affair. il *Working Woman* 14:179-80+ N '89
Riding to lose (weight, that is). *Bicycling* 30:104+ My '89

BARONE, THOMAS
Ways of being at risk: the case of Billy Charles Barnett. il *Phi Delta Kappan* 71:147-51 O '89

BAROODY, ELIZABETH
Costume jewelry: the basics in bangles and beads. il *Antiques & Collecting Hobbies* 94:26-9 S '89
The joy of Jasper: Wedgwood's finest legacy. il *Antiques & Collecting Hobbies* 94:30-2 Je '89

BAROU, JEAN-PIERRE
An interview with Andrei Sakharov. il *The New York Review of Books* 36:6-7 Mr 2 '89

BAROWITZ, ELLIOTT, 1936-
about
Elliott Barowitz at Ingber. W. Thompson. il *Art in America* 77:175 Je '89

BARR, DANNY
about
Hail to the chief's pilot. W. Garvey. il por *Flying* 116:8-9 Ag '89

BARR, DAVE
about
Life as a 'grinder'. H. Quinn. il por *Maclean's* 102:64 Ap 10 '89

BARR, DAVID, 1939-
about
A universal gesture. S. Yolles. il *Art News* 88:13 Ja '89

BARR, DONALD J.
From the publisher. See issues of Sports Illustrated beginning December 9, 1985

BARR, ROSEANNE
My life as a woman [excerpt from Roseanne; cover story] il pors *People Weekly* 32:60-2+ O 2 '89
about
The real Roseanne [cover story] K. Casey. il pors *Ladies' Home Journal* 106:137-9+ S '89
Roseanne. R. Crane. il pors *Good Housekeeping* 209:60+ Jl '89
Roseanne Barr: the funniest "housewife" in America. M. Collins. il pors *Redbook* 172:34+ F '89
Roseanne Barr wows the crowd at ABA's closing banquet. M. J. O'Brien. il por *Publishers Weekly* 235:41 Je 30 '89
Roseanne nay! P. Freundlich. por *Esquire* 112:99 Ag '89
Roseanne: no-holds-Barred [interview] F. Robbins. il por *Ladies' Home Journal* 106:102+ F '89
Roseanne unchained [cover story; interview] J. Jerome. il pors *People Weekly* 32:84-6+ O 9 '89
Roseanne yea! P. Nelson. por *Esquire* 112:98 Ag '89
Slightly to the left of normal [interview] E. Dutka. il por *Time* 133:82-3 My 8 '89
Temper! Temper! Behind Roseanne's backstage battles [cover story] il pors *TV Guide* 37:4-6 My 20-26 '89
TV's battle of the sexes: with Roseanne, it's no holds Barred [cover story] J. Hicks. il pors *TV Guide* 37:2-5 Ja 28-F 3 '89
Why did America's funniest housewife leave home? B. Robinson. il pors *Redbook* 174:54+ N '89

BARRA, ALLEN
The incredible shrinking epic. il *American Film* 14:40-3+ Mr '89
Tuesday Weld. il pors *American Film* 14:62-4 Ja/F '89
Ye shall pass. il *Sport (New York, N.Y.)* 80:58-60+ S '89

BARRACUDA FISHING
Chased out of the sea [catching barracuda while swimming off Fort Lauderdale] B. Masselink. il *Sea Frontiers* 35:256 Jl/Ag '89

BARRAL, ROBERT
Vermont French light. il *American Health* 8:140+ Mr '89

BARREIRO, DAN
The Twin Cities. il *Sport (New York, N.Y.)* 80:76-9 D '89

BARREL VAULT STRUCTURES See Shells (Structural engineering)

BARRELL, BILL, 1932-
about
Bill Barrell: Ingber; Gallery Jupiter. G. Henry. il *Art News* 88:135-6 Ja '89

BARRELS
The dog house [made from plastic barrels] B. Tarrant. il *Field & Stream* 94:94+ Je '89

BARRETO, LUIS FILIPE
The dawn of a new age. il maps *The Courier (Unesco)* 42:4-7 Ap '89

BARRETT, ANDREA
The seducer [story] il *Mademoiselle* 95:140+ O '89

BARRETT, CAROL
The falling of hair [poem] *The Christian Century* 106:279 Mr 15 '89

BARRETT, DAVID
about
Challenge seeker. B. Wallace. il por *Maclean's* 102:21-2 D 4 '89
The NDP drafts a star. M. Clark. il por *Maclean's* 102:20 O 9 '89

BARRETT, GARY W.
A sustainable society. *BioScience* 39:754 D '89

BARRETT, GRAHAM
A kinder, gentler Nicaragua? *World Press Review* 36:28 Jl '89

BARRETT, HELEN
Anything for a baby [story] il *Redbook* 173:64+ Je '89

BARRETT, KATHERINE, AND GREENE, RICHARD
Money news. See issues of Ladies' Home Journal beginning March 1983 through April 1989
The baby chase. il *Ladies' Home Journal* 106:114+ N '89
"I thought I could make it home". il *Reader's Digest* 134:148-50 Mr '89
Necessary evil? il *Redbook* 173:160-1+ S '89
A stepfamily Christmas. il *Ladies' Home Journal* 106:100+ D '89

BARRETT, MARTHA BARRON
Double lives: what it's like to be lesbian today [excerpt from Invisible lives] il *Glamour* 87:316-17+ S '89

BARRETT, MATTHEW WILLIAM
Canada [address, December 7, 1988] *Vital Speeches of the Day* 55:345-6 Mr 15 '89
about
Stepping aside. P. Chisholm. il pors *Maclean's* 102:40 Ja 30 '89

BARRETT, PETER
Fishing. See issues of Field & Stream beginning February 1984

BARRETT, ROBERT D.
about
Operation Ill Wind may have scared up a canary. P. Dwyer. il pors *Business Week* p37 F 6 '89

BARRETT, SPENCER C. H.
Waterweed invasions. bibl il map *Scientific American* 261:90-7 O '89

BARRETT, TOM HANS, 1930-
about
Can Goodyear pull out of its skid? Z. Schiller. il *Business Week* p41 Mr 20 '89

BARRETT, WAYNE
about
The N.Y.C. scandals of Ed Koch [cover story] M. J. Green. *The Nation* 248:397 Mr 27 '89

BARRETT, WAYNE M.
Globe-trotting athletes. il *USA Today (Periodical)* 118:81 N '89
Margaret Bourke-White: new vistas in photojournalism. il por *USA Today (Periodical)* 118:54-63 S '89

BARRETT-CONNOR, ELIZABETH
Conquering jet lag. il *Travel Holiday* 171:18-19 Ap '89

BARRIER, PHYLLIS M.
Boning up on calcium. il *Nation's Business* 77:57 D '89
Cancer and your diet. il *Nation's Business* 77:69 Ja '89
Should you go on a very-low-calorie diet? il *Nation's Business* 77:61 Jl '89

BARRIER ISLANDS
Only fools build on shifting sands. R. L. Di Silvestro. il map *Audubon* 91:106-12+ Mr '89

BARRIER REEF, GREAT (AUSTRALIA) See Great Barrier Reef (Australia)

BARRIO, CONSTANCE GARCíA- See García-Barrio, Constance

BARRIONUEVO, BOLA
about
Bola Barrionuevo at Galeria Mar Estrada. K. Bradley. il *Art in America* 77:185 D '89

BARRO, ROBERT J.
Rational-expectationist. *National Review* 41:49-50 Ja 27 '89

BARRON, ERIC J., AND PETERSON, WILLIAM H.
Model simulation of the Cretaceous ocean circulation. bibl f il *Science* 244:684-6 My 12 '89

BARRON, JOHN, 1930-
Our Moscow embassy mess. *Reader's Digest* 134:193-6+ F '89
Tracking China's master spy. il *Reader's Digest* 135:97-102 D '89

BARRON, JOHN, 1930——cont.
Was President Zia murdered? *Reader's Digest* 135:59-63 Ag '89
BARRON, SUSAN, 1945-
Framer's art. il por *House & Garden* 161:150-7+ D '89
BARRON, ZELDA
about
Shag: the movie [film] Reviews
People Weekly 32:12 Ag 7 '89. R. Novak
BARROW, SCOTT
about
. . . and bring the kids. L. Rosch. il pors *Working Woman* 14:118-21+ Je '89
BARROWMAN, MIKE
about
On top of the world. B. Anderson. il pors *Sports Illustrated* 71:40-1 Ag 14 '89
BARROWS, STANLEY
about
Recalling a golden era in Manhattan design. P. Carlsen. il por *Architectural Digest* 46:350+ N '89
BARRY, DAVE
Halloween's here! il *Reader's Digest* 135:89-90 O '89
How to redo your house for under $650,000 [condensed from Homes and other black holes] il *Reader's Digest* 134:93-6 Ap '89
The ideal summer books: huge, scary, waterproof. il *The New York Times Book Review* 94:3 Je 11 '89
Jim & Tammy Faye Bakker. il pors *People Weekly* 32 Special Issue:70-1 Fall '89
Little League blues. il *Reader's Digest* 135:56-8 Ag '89
about
Madcap airs all [interview] J. Birnbaum. il por *Time* 134:68-9 Jl 3 '89
BARRY, DAVID
The Europeans are losing their lock on luxury. il *Vogue* 179:320 O '89
BARRY, GENE
about
Though grayer, and wider in the saddle, Gene Barry and Hugh O'Brian ride again. il pors *People Weekly* 32:106-7 Ag 28 '89
BARRY, JOHN M.
Anatomy of a smear. il pors *Esquire* 112:215-20+ O '89
BARRY, JOSEPH B., 1759 OR 60-1838
about
Joseph B. Barry, Philadelphia cabinetmaker. D. L. Fennimore and R. T. Trump. bibl f il *Antiques* 135:1212-25 My '89
BARRY, LYNDA
1619 East Crowley. See issues of Mother Jones beginning February/March 1989
Kid stuff: our panel of young experts rate the summer movies. il *American Film* 14:72 S '89
BARRY, MARION, 1936-
about
The bizarre and troubling escapades of Mayor Barry. T. Gest. il por *U.S. News & World Report* 106:31 Ja 9 '89
A bright, broken promise. M. Riley. il por *Time* 133:60-2 Je 26 '89
A capital offense. R. Lacayo. il por *Time* 133:27 Ja 16 '89
Contempt for the little colony. C. Hitchens. il *Harper's* 279:70-6 O '89
The mayor's new drug crisis. L. Martz. por *Newsweek* 113:25 Ja 9 '89
National capital, national shame. F. Barnes. il por *Reader's Digest* 135:106-11 N '89
Scandal at the top. W. Lowther. il por *Maclean's* 102:36 Ja 16 '89
Trying to stop, Jesse, stop. J. N. Baker. il pors *Newsweek* 114:29 Jl 17 '89
Washington's mayor with nine lives, Marion Barry, risks another amid rumors of scandal. M. Brower. il por *People Weekly* 31:48-9 Ja 16 '89
'You predict sun and it's raining like hell' [interview] M. Miller. por *Newsweek* 113:18-19 Mr 13 '89
BARRY, NAOMI
Escoffier. il por *Gourmet* 49:124+ O '89
The fall and rise of French bread. il por *Gourmet* 49:56-9+ Mr '89
Gourmet holidays: Mauritius. il maps *Gourmet* 49:96-101+ N '89
Hello Dolley—on the trail of the Madisons. il por *Gourmet* 49:130+ D '89
BARRY, PAMELA
Christmas carol [story] il *Good Housekeeping* 208:80+ Ja '89
BARRY, ROSEMARY
Paris: remembering the Revolution. il *Travel Holiday* 172:36-47 Jl '89
BARRY, TOM, 1950-, AND PREUSCH, DEB
Ambassadors of Zion. *The Christian Century* 106:79-81 Ja 25 '89
BARRY, WILLIAM A.
The Kingdom of God: what role do we play? *America* 161:165-6 S 23 '89

Should religion concern itself with political and social questions? *America* 161:61-2+ Jl 29-Ag 5 '89
BARRYMORE, DREW
The secret Drew Barrymore [cover story; ed. by Todd Gold. il pors *People Weekly* 31:70-2+ Ja 16 '89
about
Celebs speak out on addiction. L. E. Brooks. pors *'Teen* 33:30+ S '89
'I wanted people to know I had a problem'. E. Warren. il pors *TV Guide* 37:16-18 Mr 25-31 '89
BARRYMORE, JOHN, 1882-1942
about
Where John Barrymore once hid from fans, Paul Rudnick has found the actor's ghost—and medieval inspiration. P. Rudnick. il por *Vogue* 179:130-2 Jl '89
BARS AND BARROOMS
See also
Baby bars
Dry bars
Sports bars
Topless nightclubs, bars, etc.
In praise of taverns [American spectator's Great American saloon series] J. Walljasper. il *Utne Reader* p34 Jl/Ag '89
Interview: James Schaefer. A. J. S. Rayl. il pors *Omni (New York, N.Y.)* 12:106-8+ D '89
Lookin' for science in all the wrong places [J. M. Schaefer's study of the relationship between drinking and country music] J. Stone. il *Discover* 10:96-9 Mr '89
Caribbean region
Ruminiscences. R. Brookhiser. il *The American Spectator* 22:33 S '89
Great Britain
Charles Dickens got crocked here. S. V. Gold. il map *The American Spectator* 22:36-7 Ag '89
Outer Banks (N.C.)
Papagayo. D. Shiflett. *The American Spectator* 22:37 Ap '89
Washington (D.C.)
See Washington (D.C.)—Restaurants, nightclubs, bars, etc.
BARS FOR THE HOME
Bar essentials. E. Fried. il *Black Enterprise* 20:108 S '89
Here's to your well-stocked bar. D. Moreau. il *Changing Times* 43:99-101 D '89
BARSUKOV, VALERIY L.
about
A Soviet perspective [interview] S. F. Brown. *Popular Science* 235:75 Jl '89
BART (BEAR) *See* Bears in motion pictures
BARTA'A (ISRAEL)
A thin green line. D. L. Kirp. il *Mother Jones* 14:16-17+ My '89
BARTEL, PAUL
about
Scenes from the class struggle in Beverly Hills [film] Reviews
America 161:116 Ag 26-S 2 '89. R. A. Blake
American Film il 14:92 Ap '89. L. Loud
The Nation 248:860-1 Je 19 '89. S. Klawans
The New Republic 201:26+ Jl 10 '89. S. Kauffmann
Newsweek il 113:68 Je 12 '89. D. Ansen
Time il 133:73 Je 12 '89. R. Corliss
Video il 13:76+ N '89. I. Robbins
Vogue il 179:204 My '89
BARTER
See also
Educational Assistance Limited
Real estate exchanges
The ancient art of bartering revived. L. Wu. il *Home Office Computing* 7:12 Mr '89
BARTH, JACK
Celebrating the celebactor. il *Film Comment* 25:46 N/D '89
This decade in review. il *Film Comment* 25:50-1 Ja/F '89
BARTH, JIM
about
The Barth balance. C. Hurst. il pors *Home Office Computing* 7:51-3 Je '89
BARTH, LAURIE
about
The Barth balance. C. Hurst. il pors *Home Office Computing* 7:51-3 Je '89
BARTHALOT, RAYMONDE
Astronomy in the French Revolution. il *Sky and Telescope* 78:21-3 Jl '89
BARTHÉ, RICHMOND, 1901-1989
about
Obituary
Jet il pors 75:52 Ap 3 '89
BARTHELME, DONALD
Tickets [story] *The New Yorker* 65:32-4 Mr 6 '89
about
Obituary
The New York Times Book Review il por 94:9 S 3 '89. J. Barth
The New Yorker 65:23-4 Ag 14 '89

BARTHELME, FREDERICK
With Ray and Judy [story] *The New Yorker* 65:34-8
Ap 24 '89
BARTHOLOMEW, REGINALD, 1936-
U.S. efforts against the spread of chemical weapons [statement,
June 22, 1989] *Department of State Bulletin* 89:74-7 S
'89
BARTLETT, ALBERT
Exile [poem] *America* 161:109 Ag 26-S 2 '89
BARTLETT, BO
about
Bo Bartlett at P.P.O.W. K. Johnson. *Art in America* 77:174
Je '89
BARTLETT, JAMES Y.
The Pinehurst tradition. il *Travel Holiday* 172:50-7 N '89
BARTLETT, JENNIFER, 1941-
about
A downtown aesthetic: the residence and studio of artist
Jennifer Bartlett. D. Solomon. il por *Architectural Digest*
46:316-21+ N '89
BARTLETT, KAY
Are you an innumerate? il por *The Saturday Evening Post*
261:36 S '89
BARTLETT, STEVE
Should President Bush's minimum wage proposal be adopted?
[excerpts from address, March 23, 1989] *Congressional
Digest* 68:144+ My '89
BARTLETT MAINE ESTATE WINERY
They call it "Nouveau Blueberry" [blueberry wine] il *Audubon*
91:62 Jl '89
BARTLETT'S FAMILIAR QUOTATIONS
For editor Justin Kaplan, updating Bartlett's is as easy as
shopping for a new quote. M. Neill. il por *People Weekly*
31:141-2 Ap 10 '89
BARTLEY, DIANE
A man with a mission. il pors *The Saturday Evening Post*
261:58-61+ N/D '89
BARTLEY, ROBERT L.
How Reaganomics made the world work. il *National Review*
41:30-4 Ap 21 '89
Supply-sider. il *National Review* 41:46-7 Ja 27 '89
BARTLEY, SHIRLEY
Nine steps for outlining nonfiction. *The Writer* 102:22-4
Ap '89
BARTOCCI, BARBARA
Let go and live. *Reader's Digest* 135:103-6 O '89
When he's unfaithful: how some women cope. *McCall's*
116:49-50+ My '89
BARTÓK, BÉLA, 1881-1945
about
Bluebeard's castle [opera] Reviews
The Nation 248:314-6 Mr 6 '89. E. W. Said
New York il 22:54 Ja 30 '89. P. G. Davis
The New Yorker 64:98+ F 6 '89. A. Porter
Newsweek il 113:70 Ja 30 '89. K. Ames
Opera News il 53:30-1, 33 Ja 21 '89
Opera News il 53:8-14 Ja 21 '89. N. Rorem
BARTON, CLARA, 1821-1912
about
Clara Barton: founder of the American Red Cross. C. Schurr.
il pors *American History Illustrated* 24:50-8+ N/D '89
BARTON, DEBBIE
Fun family food. il *American Health* 8:98+ My '89
BARTON, LAURIE
Advertising, art, and arts education: an uneasy association.
bibl f *Design for Arts in Education* 90:14-19 N/D '88
BARTON, NANCY
about
Nancy Barton at American Fine Arts. H. Cotter. *Art in
America* 77:261 Ap '89
BARTON, RALPH, 1891-1931
about
A case of melancholia. J. Updike. il *The New Yorker* 65:112-20
F 20 '89
BARTON, WILLIAM, AND CAPOBIANCO, MICHAEL
Harvesting the near-earthers [cover story] il *Ad Astra* 1:24-30+
N '89
BARTON (CLARA) NATIONAL HISTORIC SITE (MD.)
See Clara Barton National Historic Site (Md.)
BARTON NELSON, INC.
Barton Nelson, Inc. R. Koselka and others. il *Forbes*
144:213-14 D 11 '89
BARTOV, HANOCH
Writing as a Jew. *Commentary* 87:24-7 Je '89
BARTSCH, JIM
A balancing act in three exposures. il *Petersen's Photographic
Magazine* 18:94-5 D '89
Cross-polarization of light. il *Petersen's Photographic Magazine*
17:58-9 F '89
BARTUSIAK, MARCIA, 1950-
Einstein's unfinished symphony. il *Discover* 10:62-9 Ag '89
The sunspot syndrome [with editorial comment by Paul
Hoffman] il *Discover* 10:4, 44-8+ N '89
BARYLSKI, MICHAEL
Scenic roads. il *The Conservationist* 44:16-21 S/O '89

BARYSHNIKOV, MIKHAIL, 1948-
about
Baryshnikov takes on Swan Lake: something old, something
new. L. Horn. il *Dance Magazine* 63:44-9 My '89
Baryshnikov's stewardship. C. Barnes. il por *Dance Magazine*
63:106 S '89
Baryshnikov's transformation. J. Kroll. il por *Newsweek*
113:76-7 Mr 20 '89
Dancing:
Resignation of M. Baryshnikov and overview of recently
completed season. A. Croce. *The New Yorker* 65:84-6
Jl 17 '89
Swan Lake. A. Croce. *The New Yorker* 65:105-7 My
29 '89
A Metamorphosis indeed: Baryshnikov's bug bit. N. V. Dalva.
il por *Dance Magazine* 63:49 Je '89
On dance. L. A. Jacobs. *The New Leader* 72:23 Je 12-26
'89
Swan song. T. Tobias. il *New York* 22:70 My 29 '89
Together at a tense moment, two titans of dance turn crisis
into creation. M. Small. il pors *People Weekly* 32:42-3
O 16 '89
Turning point. E. Levin. il pors *Life* 12:50-2+ N '89
BARZELATTO, JOSÉ
Research in human reproduction. il *World Health* p18-21
Ap '89
BARZUN, JACQUES, 1907-
Is democratic theory for export? *Society* 26:16-23 Mr/Ap
'89
The paradoxes of creativity. *The American Scholar* 58:337-51
Summ '89
BASALT
Effect of water on the composition of partial melts of
greenstone and amphibolite. J. S. Beard and G. E. Lofgren.
bibl f il *Science* 244:195-7 Ap 14 '89
Flood basalts and hot-spot tracks: plume heads and tails.
M. A. Richards and others. bibl f il map *Science* 246:103-7
O 6 '89
Heady theory for largest eruptions [work of Mark A. Richards]
Science News 136:271 O 21 '89
BASE, GRAEME, 1958-
about
Graeme Base's new mystery for kids has the whole family
scratching their heads. il por *People Weekly* 32:103 D
18 '89
BASEBALL
See also
American Women's Baseball Association
Baseball players
Batting (Baseball)
Boardwalk and Baseball (Amusement park)
Home runs (Baseball)
Pesapallo (Game)
Pitching (Baseball)
Softball
Strikeouts (Baseball)
Anecdotes, facetiae, satire, etc.
Play ball! il *The Mother Earth News* 118:128 Jl/Ag '89
Dictionaries
A new guide to baseball slang is a dinger of a read [work
of P. Dickson] J. Friedman. il pors *People Weekly* 31:93+
My 1 '89
Paul Dickson talks about language for his baseball dictionary.
G. Corcoran. il por *Publishers Weekly* 235:42 F 17 '89
Equipment
See also
Baseball bats
Baseball caps
Baseball gloves
Bases (Baseball equipment)
Worth Inc.
History
The creation myths of Cooperstown. S. J. Gould. il *Natural
History* p14+ N '89
Exhibitions
Art à la carte [Let's play ball exhibit at the Royal Ontario
Museum] C. Mac Connie. il *Travel Holiday* 171:104 Ap
'89
Study and teaching
The College of Cardinals [roving instructors in St. Louis
farm system] J. Garrity. il pors *Sports Illustrated* 71:64-8+
Ag 14 '89
Aids and devices
Playing ball and chain [Stride Tutors, hitting aid invented
by White Sox centerfielder D. Gallagher] N. Dawidoff.
il por *Sports Illustrated* 70:81 My 22 '89
Cuba
Castro's curveball. J. D. Truby. *Harper's* 278:32+ My '89
Dominican Republic
Baseball scout Epy Guerrero looks for rough diamonds amid
hunger and poverty. W. Plummer. il pors *People Weekly*
31:127-8+ Ap 10 '89
Japan turns the double play [scouts from Japan in Dominican
Republic] G. Black. il *The Nation* 248:370+ Mr 20 '89
Soviet Union
First steppes in baseball. C. Bogert. il *Newsweek* 113:41
Ap 17 '89

BASEBALL, CHILDREN'S
See also
   Frank Bolling Adaptive Baseball League
   Little League baseball
BASEBALL, COLLEGE
The college baseball boom. D. Knobler. il *Sport (New York, N.Y.)* 80:48+ Ap '89
Innerviews [interview with J. Croteau, only female college player] il por *Women's Sports & Fitness* 11:64 S '89
Who's on first? [J. Croteau, only woman playing college baseball] E. Gibson. il por *Seventeen* 48:54 S '89

Tournaments
Chewing up their foes [Wichita State wins College World Series] J. Garrity. il *Sports Illustrated* 70:71 Je 19 '89
BASEBALL, HIGH SCHOOL
An American classic [pitcher J. Peters of Brenham, Tex. wins 51st consecutive game; cover story] R. Reilly. il pors *Sports Illustrated* 70:16-21 My 8 '89
Felled by the fall [pitcher K. Lomon of Cameron, Okla. takes 53-game winning streak into state tournament] J. Rodewald. il por *Sports Illustrated* 71:16 O 9 '89
In the heart of Texas, Jon Peters is a pitcher of perfection [sets record of 51 straight victories] il por *People Weekly* 31:128 My 15 '89
BASEBALL, PROFESSIONAL
See also
   Association of Professional Ball Players of America
   Baseball fans
   Baseball managers
   Baseball players
   Baseball records
   Batting (Baseball)
   Collective bargaining—Baseball, Professional
   Home runs (Baseball)
   Pitching (Baseball)
   Rotisserie League Baseball
   Strikeouts (Baseball)
The A's find ways. E. M. Swift. il *Sports Illustrated* 70:36-8+ My 29 '89
As the boys of Zimmer dare to dream, a nostalgic editor returns to his field of futility [takes father and son to watch Chicago Cubs game] R. Novak. il por *People Weekly* 32:52-4 O 9 '89
Baseball 1989. il *Sports Illustrated* 70 Special Issue:8-14+ Ap '89
Baseball at midseason. P. Gammons. il *Sports Illustrated* 71:30-2+ Jl 17 '89
The Bay and before. R. Angell. *The New Yorker* 65:58-60+ D 11 '89
Beers with . . . Jack McKeon [interview with coach of the San Diego Padres] S. Delsohn. il pors *Sport (New York, N.Y.)* 80:19+ Jl '89
Birdland [Toronto overtakes Baltimore in AL East] F. Lidz. il pors *Sports Illustrated* 71:22-5 S 11 '89
Can you help the Mets by watching on TV? [Strong Baseball Principal; work of N. D. Mermin] R. Pool. il por *Science* 244:773-4 My 19 '89
The days dwindle down [pennant races] W. Shapiro. il *Time* 134:96 O 2 '89
The face of genius [Cub manager D. Zimmer] L. Montville. il pors *Sports Illustrated* 71:58-62+ S 25 '89
A flight to the finish [Baltimore vs. Toronto] P. Gammons. il *Sports Illustrated* 71:48-50 O 2 '89
He's an Angel now [California manager D. Rader] P. Gammons. il pors *Sports Illustrated* 71:34-9 Ag 7 '89
Hopes of glory [Montreal] D. Burke. il *Maclean's* 102:46-7 Ag 7 '89
Inside baseball. P. Gammons. See issues of Sports Illustrated published during the baseball season beginning April 14, 1986 through October 9, 1989
The keys to this season? Jack Clark's bat and Jesse Orosco's pranks. L. Feldman. il *TV Guide* 37:10-12+ Ap 8-14 '89
Last ups [Mets vs. Phillies in last game of season at Shea Stadium] *The New Yorker* 65:41 O 16 '89
The myths of autumn [cover story; special section; with editorial comment by Kevin Doyle] il *Maclean's* 102:2, 44-8+ O 2 '89
Northern challenge [Blue Jays and Expos] D. Turner. il *Maclean's* 102:56 Ap 3 '89
O you beautiful Birds [Baltimore] S. Wulf. il *Sports Illustrated* 70:26-8+ Je 19 '89
Oh, what a relief it is [Toronto clinches American League East title] P. Gammons. il *Sports Illustrated* 71:106-7 O 9 '89
Oh, what a show! [R. Henderson sparks Oakland past Toronto in American League playoffs; cover story] P. Gammons. il pors *Sports Illustrated* 71:30-3+ O 16 '89
On the stick [San Francisco Giants; cover story] R. Fimrite. il pors *Sports Illustrated* 71:18-23 Jl 10 '89
One Giant step [San Francisco vs. Chicago in National League playoffs] R. Fimrite. il *Sports Illustrated* 71:38-40+ O 16 '89
Orioles, Blue Jays, put black managers on spot. il pors *Jet* 77:51 O 16 '89
The passions of fall ball [Oakland and San Francisco win championship series] B. Came. il *Maclean's* 102:52-3 O 16 '89

Quantum baseball [Strong Baseball Principle; work of N. D. Mermin; cover story] I. Peterson. il por *Science News* 136:88-9 Ag 5 '89
Rangers risin' [cover story] W. Nack. il pors *Sports Illustrated* 70:16-23 My 1 '89
Reflections on the game [excerpts from Baseball lives] M. Bryan. il *Sports Illustrated* 70:74-8+ Ap 24 '89
Returning to glory [Montreal Expos] T. Frayne. il *Maclean's* 102:34 Je 26 '89
Scary show at Shea [Mets sweep weekend series with Montreal] H. Hersch. il *Sports Illustrated* 71:22-5 Ag 14 '89
Season in the shadows. S. Wulf. por *Sports Illustrated* 71:96 N 13 '89
A series to shout about [Cubs vs. Cardinals] P. Gammons. il *Sports Illustrated* 71:42-4+ S 18 '89
The Sport 1989 baseball preview [cover story; special section] il *Sport (New York, N.Y.)* 80:22-30+ Ap '89
A team that's hard to top [Montreal Expos] P. Gammons. il *Sports Illustrated* 71:28-31 Jl 31 '89
These Reds look Rosy. D. S. Looney. il *Sports Illustrated* 70:42-3 Je 5 '89
This one's still up in the air [San Francisco takes two of three from Houston] S. Wulf. il *Sports Illustrated* 71:26-30+ Ag 14 '89
To rise again [Baltimore Orioles and Atlanta Braves rebuild in tradition of 1983 New York Mets] D. Knobler. il *Sport (New York, N.Y.)* 80:47-8+ S '89
To the vanquished, go . . . [Chicago Cubs] T. Callahan. il *Newsweek* 114:65 O 2 '89
Too much, too soon [Oakland takes two of three from California Angels] P. Gammons. il *Sports Illustrated* 71:22-7 Ag 21 '89

Accidents and injuries
After a courageous comeback, a star pitcher breaks his arm but keeps his faith intact; ed. by Liz McNeil. D. Dravecky. il pors *People Weekly* 32:69-70+ S 11 '89
Giant comeback cut short [pitcher D. Dravecky] J. Carvalho. il por *Christianity Today* 33:54+ O 20 '89
Gripping saga [B. Ojeda regains pitching grip] B. Weber. il pors *The New York Times Magazine* p98 F 19 '89
'It felt like I lost my arm' [D. Dravecky breaks arm during comeback from cancer surgery] il por *Newsweek* 114:65 Ag 28 '89
A victim of careless gardening, Bob Ojeda is back in the ball game with the finger he nearly cut off [interview] M. Huzinec. il pors *People Weekly* 31:107-8+ Mr 27 '89
Where have all the players gone? S. Wulf and R. Demak. il *Sports Illustrated* 71:22-5+ Ag 28 '89

All-star games
MVP Bo Jackson powers AL to All-star game victory. il pors *Jet* 76:46 Jl 31 '89

Awards
See also
   Gold Glove Award
A hero lives here [World Series MVP D. Stewart] P. Gammons. il pors *Sports Illustrated* 71:28-31 N 6 '89
Orel in MVP-Land. K. Garrett. il pors *Sport (New York, N.Y.)* 80:35 Mr '89

Betting
See Baseball betting

Bibliography
Diamonds are forever. D. Todd. il *Maclean's* 102:56 Je 12 '89
Four for baseball's good old days. V. Gold. *The American Spectator* 22:35-7 O '89
In short/baseball. il *The New York Times Book Review* 94:36-7 Ap 23 '89
Outside baseball. W. Sheed. il *The New York Review of Books* 36:49-53 O 12 '89

Collectibles
From grand slams to grand scams. il *U.S. News & World Report* 107:17 O 30 '89

Economic aspects
See also
   Baseball players—Salaries, pensions, etc.
Another winner for the Bush family? [G. W. Bush buys Texas Rangers] K. Kelly. il por *Business Week* p166 My 22 '89
Baseball's owners want to play softball [revenue sharing proposal] A. Bernstein. il *Business Week* p52 D 18 '89
The Blue Jays have a lot to crow about [soaring profits and attendance] B. Bremner. il *Business Week* p40 O 16 '89
Buffalo's Rich baseball legacy [Bisons owner R. Rich] G. Macnow. il por *Nation's Business* 77:42-5 F '89
For the Orioles, less is more—it's first place. J. Carey. il *Business Week* p34 Jl 10 '89
If the Mariners don't shape up, they may get shipped out. W. C. Symonds. il por *Business Week* p36 S 11 '89
The New Jersey Yankees? N. Cohen. il *Sport (New York, N.Y.)* 80:14 Mr '89
Rich makes his pitch [owner of Buffalo Bisons R. E. Rich] I. Muchnick. il por *The New York Times Magazine* p18-19+ Jl 30 '89
Rusty the Mortician [E. W. Rose of the Texas Rangers] J. H. Taylor. il por *Forbes* 144:60+ Jl 24 '89
The selling of spring [spring training] R. Fimrite. il *Sports Illustrated* 70:58-60+ Mr 27 '89

BASEBALL, PROFESSIONAL—Economic aspects—cont.
Spring training is big business. E. Cohen. il *Sport (New York, N.Y.)* 80:14 Ap '89
Watching the bottom line. D. Jenish. il *Maclean's* 102:51-2 O 2 '89

Ethical aspects

All the odds against him [P. Rose] C. Leerhsen. il por *Newsweek* 114:74-5 Jl 10 '89
The case against Pete Rose [account of former bookmaker R. Peters; cover story] J. Lieber and C. Neff. il pors *Sports Illustrated* 71:10-20+ Jl 3 '89
Charlie Hustle's final play [P. Rose banned from baseball] M. B. Carlson. il por *Time* 134:64 S 4 '89
Closing in on Charlie Hustle [P. Rose betting case] C. Leerhsen. il por *Newsweek* 114:23 Jl 3 '89
The Cobb gambling scandal [alleged wagering on fixed game in 1919] il por *Sports Illustrated* 70:20 Je 12 '89
The darkening cloud over Pete [P. Rose gambling case] T. Callahan. por *Time* 134:57 Jl 3 '89
The end of the affair [P. Rose receives lifetime ban] C. Leerhsen. il por *Newsweek* 114:58-9 S 4 '89
A game of chance [P. Rose] R. Dolphin. il por *Maclean's* 102:52-3 Ap 17 '89
Glenn Davis [anti-alcohol stand] S. Kanfer. il por *People Weekly* 32 Special Issue:125 Fall '89
Henderson blames drunks for '88 Yankee downfall. por *Jet* 75:50 Mr 20 '89
Hit, field and cheat. R. Skolnik. il *TV Guide* 37:18-19 Je 10-16 '89
Hotdogging with relish [Oakland in playoff series with Toronto] P. Gammons. il *Sports Illustrated* 71:34 O 16 '89
An idol banned [P. Rose] J. Lieber and C. Neff. il pors *Sports Illustrated* 71:29-30 S 4 '89
Morals and immortals [urging election of F. Jenkins and G. Perry to Hall of Fame] P. Gammons. il por *Sports Illustrated* 70:78 Ja 23 '89
Parker: double standard in his, Pete Rose cases. il pors *Jet* 76:48 Jl 24 '89
Pete Rose. il por *People Weekly* 32:86-7 D 25 '89-Ja 1 '90
The Rose probe [Cincinnati Reds manager linked to baseball betting] C. Neff. il por *Sports Illustrated* 70:13 Mr 27 '89
Rose probe (cont.) [alleged betting by Cincinnati Reds manager] C. Neff. il por *Sports Illustrated* 70:11-12 My 8 '89
Rose probe (cont.) [alleged sports betting by Cincinnati Reds manager] C. Neff. il por *Sports Illustrated* 70:13+ Ap 17 '89
Rose's grim vigil [gambling allegations; cover story] C. Neff and J. Lieber. il pors *Sports Illustrated* 70:52-4+ Ap 3 '89
The sad ordeal of Mr. Baseball [gambling allegations surrounding P. Rose] T. Callahan. il por *Time* 133:85 Ap 3 '89
Shoeless Joe: his legend survives the man and the scandal [1919 Black Sox scandal] W. Plummer. il pors *People Weekly* 32:99-101 Ag 7 '89
Too good to be left out [J. Jackson, banished for role in 1919 Black Sox scandal, should be elected to Hall of Fame] N. Dawidoff. por *Sports Illustrated* 70:118 Je 12 '89
Troubled times [P. Rose case] M. Nichols. il por *Maclean's* 102:42 Jl 10 '89
Up to speed [drug taking charges against P. Rose] R. Wright. *The New Republic* 201:42 Jl 31 '89
Waiting for the final chapter [P. Rose betting scandal interferes with R. Kahn's biography] C. Leerhsen. il pors *Newsweek* 113:71 Ap 10 '89
Why pick on Pete? [P. Rose case emblematic of American obsession with gambling; cover story] G. J. Church. il por *Time* 134:16-21 Jl 10 '89

Anecdotes, facetiae, satire, etc.

Baseball: not the movie [P. Rose gambling scandal] J. Leo. il *U.S. News & World Report* 107:54 Jl 10 '89

History

See also
National Baseball Hall of Fame and Museum
'80s baseball. D. Knobler. il *Sport (New York, N.Y.)* 80:54-6+ O '89
Baseball's closest calls. M. G. Stoddard. il *The Saturday Evening Post* 261:30+ Jl/Ag '89
The 'Belles of the Ball Game' were a hit with their fans [All-American Girls Professional Baseball League commemorated at Baseball Hall of Fame] J. Fincher. il *Smithsonian* 20:88-94+ Jl '89
Do the people in Seattle feel the same way about the Pilots? [Brooklyn Dodgers nostalgia] S. Miller. il *Sport (New York, N.Y.)* 80:82 Ja '89
Negro League stars feted as baseball's legends. il *Jet* 76:48+ Jl 10 '89
The once and future champs. J. W. Poses. il *Sport (New York, N.Y.)* 80:64-7 Ag '89
That's Earl, folks! [retired Orioles manager E. Weaver] M. Lupica. il *Esquire* 111:53-4+ My '89
A visit to Edd Roush [excerpt from Spring training] W. K. Zinsser. *The American Scholar* 58:113-16 Wint '89
What I learned from the Pirates. R. Bendiner. il *American Heritage* 40:116-19 S/O '89

The year of the blue snow [reunion of 1964 Philadelphia team that blew the pennant] S. Wulf. il *Sports Illustrated* 71:76-86 S 25 '89

International aspects

Gloves across the water: put the world in World Series. R. Fimrite. por *Sports Illustrated* 70 Special Issue:120 Ap '89

Minor leagues

Baseball lives [statistician W. Weiss; excerpt] M. Bryan. il por *Sports Illustrated* 70:80+ Ap 24 '89
Buffalo's Rich baseball legacy [Bisons owner R. Rich] G. Macnow. il por *Nation's Business* 77:42-5 F '89
The College of Cardinals [roving instructors in St. Louis farm system] J. Garrity. il pors *Sports Illustrated* 71:64-8+ Ag 14 '89
Dodgers vs. Giants? That means Bakersfield vs. San Jose. il map *Sunset (Central West edition)* 182:66+ Ap '89
The farm report. J. Scher. il *Sport (New York, N.Y.)* 80:52-3 Ap '89
Rich makes his pitch [owner of Buffalo Bisons R. E. Rich] I. Muchnick. il por *The New York Times Magazine* p18-19+ Jl 30 '89
Take us out to the ball game [Billings Mustangs] J. McCallum. il *Sports Illustrated* 71:32-4+ Jl 24 '89

Anecdotes, facetiae, satire, etc.

The great potato pick-off play [prank played by catcher D. Bresnahan of the Williamsport Bills] M. Bowden. il *Reader's Digest* 134:103-7 Je '89

Organization and administration

See also
Senior Professional Baseball Association
After the death of Bart Giamatti, his friend Fay Vincent steps in as the commissioner's pinch hitter. K. Gross. il pors *People Weekly* 32:56-7 S 18 '89
All my Padres [San Diego] S. Wulf. il *Sports Illustrated* 70 Special Issue:42-6+ Ap '89
Baseball meets Harvard Law [vice president of the Oakland Athletics, S. Alderson] A. P. Sanoff. il por *U.S. News & World Report* 107:48-9 Jl 31 '89
Baseball picks a pioneer [B. White appointed president of the National League] T. Callahan. il por *Time* 133:76 F 13 '89
Bill White selected as National League prexy. il por *Jet* 75:51 F 20 '89
Bill White: the National League's new boss. il pors *Ebony* 44:44+ My '89
Breaking into the majors [black executive C. J. Cottrell becomes Texas Rangers limited partner] J. Coleman and C. C. Williams. il por *Black Enterprise* 20:18 S '89
For the love of the game: an open letter to new baseball commissioner Fay Vincent. P. Gammons. il por *Sports Illustrated* 71:92 S 25 '89
A gentleman and a scholar [commissioner B. Giamatti] F. Deford. il por *Sports Illustrated* 70:86-90+ Ap 17 '89
A man in command [commissioner F. Vincent's actions after earthquake] S. Wulf. il pors *Sports Illustrated* 71:30-2+ O 30 '89
The new Mister Clean [commissioner F. Vincent] R. Corelli. il por *Maclean's* 102:50 O 2 '89
Of many things [views of A. B. Giamatti] G. W. Hunt. *America* 160:338 Ap 15 '89
On the money [commissioner P. Ueberroth] D. Okrent. il pors *Sports Illustrated* 70:41+ Ap 10 '89
On the spot [Yankee manager D. Green; cover story] E. Asinof. il pors *The New York Times Magazine* p28-31+ Mr 26 '89
The price of Peter's principles [commissioner P. Ueberroth and collusion issue] P. Schmuck. por *Sport (New York, N.Y.)* 80:10 Ja '89
Professor Hardball [B. Giamatti; cover story] B. Welling and W. C. Symonds. il pors *Business Week* p84-8 Ap 3 '89
Stepping up to the plate: a new baseball league? B. Welling. il *Business Week* p48 Ag 21 '89
Throwing a curve ball at city hall [relocation threats] il *U.S. News & World Report* 107:20 O 23 '89

Player trades

A wanted man [Seattle's M. Langston] R. Fimrite. il pors *Sports Illustrated* 70:34-6 Ap 24 '89

Psychological aspects

Knowing the score. J. Schwartz. il *Gentlemen's Quarterly* 59:272+ S '89
Tommy Lasorda's "Sermon on the mound" [condensed from Out of the blue; ed. by Jerry B. Jenkins. O. Hershiser. il por *Reader's Digest* 135:63-5 S '89

Scouting

Baseball lives [Chicago Cubs scout H. Alexander; excerpt] M. Bryan. il por *Sports Illustrated* 70:76-8 Ap 24 '89
Baseball scout Epy Guerrero looks for rough diamonds amid hunger and poverty [Dominican Republic] W. Plummer. il pors *People Weekly* 31:127-8+ Ap 10 '89
Japan turns the double play [scouts from Japan in Dominican Republic] G. Black. il *The Nation* 248:370+ Mr 20 '89
Top secret [effect of advance scouting reports on the World Series] D. Knobler. il *Sport (New York, N.Y.)* 80:72-4 N '89

BASEBALL, PROFESSIONAL—cont.

Social aspects

The elements of surprise [lack of surprise in domed stadiums] C. Gordon. il *Maclean's* 102:11 Ag 21 '89

The game without violins or apologies [cover story] L. Eisenberg. il *Esquire* 111:130-41 Ap '89

Giamatti: talking baseball [excerpts from Take time for paradise] A. B. Giamatti. il por *Newsweek* 114:87-8 N 6 '89

Spring training

Baseball's back: spring training preview. il *Sport (New York, N.Y.)* 80:22-9+ Mr '89

He shoots baseball cards: a dentist with a passion for spring training [S. Levy] S. Martin. il por map *Petersen's Photographic Magazine* 18:32-5 My '89

The second hundred years [visiting spring training sites in Florida] P. Oliver. il map *Travel Holiday* 171:62-7 F '89

The selling of spring. R. Fimrite. il *Sports Illustrated* 70:58-60+ Mr 27 '89

Spring training is big business. E. Cohen. il *Sport (New York, N.Y.)* 80:14 Ap '89

Spring's old sweet song. J. D. Reed. il *Time* 133:10+ Ap 17 '89

State of the art. R. Angell. il *The New Yorker* 65:54+ My 8 '89

Touching base with the boys of spring. R. Hoffman. il *Business Week* p174 Mr 20 '89

Statistics

Are their days numbered? [using BFS statistics to predict pitchers' longevity; research by Craig Wright] A. Kim. il *Sports Illustrated* 70:46-8+ My 22 '89

Ballpark figures [based on 1988 season] il *Sports Illustrated* 70 Special Issue:104-7 Ap '89

Baseball lives [minor league statistician W. Weiss; excerpt] M. Bryan. il por *Sports Illustrated* 70:80+ Ap 24 '89

Baseball's LQ test [Leadoff Quotient] E. Cohen. il *Sport (New York, N.Y.)* 80:15 Ag '89

Move over, ERA [opponent runners average considered more reliable pitching yardstick than earned run average] T. Singer. il *Sport (New York, N.Y.)* 80:14 My '89

Television broadcasting

See Cable television—Sports; Television broadcasting—Sports

Umpiring

Call to glory [woman umpire P. Postema] R. Brown. il pors *Ms.* 17:34 Ap '89

You're a what? Umpire. M. Stanton. il *Occupational Outlook Quarterly* 33:32-5 Summ '89

Uniforms

Baseball lives [Orioles fan S. Vardavas borrows B. Robinson's uniform for Halloween costume; excerpt] M. Bryan. il por *Sports Illustrated* 70:78+ Ap 24 '89

Fabric of the game. S. Ballard. il *Sports Illustrated* 70 Special Issue:108-16+ Ap '89

World Series

Athletics sweep Giants to win 1989 World Series. il *Jet* 77:51 N 13 '89

Baseball calls time [earthquake disrupts San Francisco-Oakland Series] T. Callahan. il *Newsweek* 114:48 O 30 '89

Calling a game [O. Hershiser pitching in Game 2 of 1988 World Series]; ed. by Peter Gammons. M. Scioscia. il *Sports Illustrated* Special Issue:34-9 Ap '89

The earthquake game. M. Nemeth. il *Maclean's* 102:64 O 30 '89

The earthquake: the day the World Series stopped [cover story; special section] il *Sports Illustrated* 71:22-32+ O 30 '89

A hero lives here [MVP D. Stewart] P. Gammons. il pors *Sports Illustrated* 71:28-31 N 6 '89

In the West: play "Baysball!" [San Francisco Giants vs. Oakland Athletics] L. Griggs. il *Time* 134:79 O 23 '89

On a roll [Oakland takes 2-0 lead against San Francisco] S. Wulf. il *Sports Illustrated* 71:34-9 O 23 '89

Orel in MVP-Land. K. Garrett. il pors *Sport (New York, N.Y.)* 80:35 Mr '89

Swept away [Oakland sweeps San Francisco] S. Wulf. il *Sports Illustrated* 71:24-7 N 6 '89

Tale of two cities [Oakland vs. San Francisco] R. Corelli. il *Maclean's* 102:61 O 23 '89

Two cities wild for 'Baysball' [San Francisco and Oakland] H. Caen. il *Newsweek* 114:70 O 23 '89

Anecdotes, facetiae, satire, etc.

Inside the World Series: the laughs that go with the drama. D. Granger. il *TV Guide* 37:2-4 O 14-20 '89

History

Mets: 1969. M. Starr. il *Newsweek* 114:59 Jl 3 '89

Top secret [effect of advance scouting reports] D. Knobler. il *Sport (New York, N.Y.)* 80:72-4 N '89

World Series goats and controversies. B. James. il *Sports Illustrated* 71:51+ O 9 '89

Italy

The bad news orsi. P. Jordan. il *Gentlemen's Quarterly* 59:353+ S '89

Japan

Hitting hard. T. Koppel. il *Maclean's* 102:54 O 2 '89

Japan turns the double play [scouts from Japan in Dominican Republic] G. Black. il *The Nation* 248:370+ Mr 20 '89

The master of besaboru [American player W. Cromartie] R. Whiting. il por *Sports Illustrated* 71:68-9 Ag 21 '89

The pain of perfection [excerpt from You gotta have wa] R. Whiting. il *Sports Illustrated* 70:76-80+ My 15 '89

Wa is hell [views of Robert Whiting] B. Hillenbrand. il *Time* 134:87 S 25 '89

Latin America

¡Plei bol! [Caribbean Series] P. Gammons. il *Sports Illustrated* 70:16-21 F 20 '89

BASEBALL, SEMI-PRO

History

The best little ballpark in Texas (or anywhere else) [Kokernot Field] N. Dawidoff. il *Sports Illustrated* 71:58-64+ Jl 31 '89

BASEBALL ALUMNI TEAM

Baseball alumni wars. G. Castle. il *Sport (New York, N.Y.)* 80:14 Jl '89

BASEBALL BATS

See also
Softball bats

End of an era [wood bats being replaced by aluminum; cover story] P. Gammons. il *Sports Illustrated* 71:16-23 Jl 24 '89

Sculpting a Louisville Slugger [excerpt from Baseball lives] M. Bryan. il *Harper's* 278:34-5 My '89

BASEBALL BETTING

All the odds against him [P. Rose] C. Leerhsen. il por *Newsweek* 114:74-5 Jl 10 '89

Bettin' baseball: the key to diamond dollars: pick your spots. D. Sheridan. il *Sport (New York, N.Y.)* 80:72-3 Jl '89

The case against Pete Rose [account of former bookmaker R. Peters; cover story] J. Lieber and C. Neff. il pors *Sports Illustrated* 71:10-20+ Jl 3 '89

Charlie Hustle's final play [P. Rose banned from baseball] M. B. Carlson. il por *Time* 134:64 S 4 '89

Closing in on Charlie Hustle [P. Rose betting case] C. Leerhsen. il por *Newsweek* 114:23 Jl 3 '89

The darkening cloud over Pete [P. Rose gambling case] T. Callahan. por *Time* 134:57 Jl 3 '89

The end of the affair [P. Rose receives lifetime ban] C. Leerhsen. il por *Newsweek* 114:58-9 S 4 '89

A game of chance [P. Rose] R. Dolphin. il por *Maclean's* 102:52-3 Ap 17 '89

An idol banned [P. Rose] J. Lieber and C. Neff. il pors *Sports Illustrated* 71:29-30 S 4 '89

Parker: double standard in his, Pete Rose cases. il pors *Jet* 76:48 Jl 24 '89

Pete Rose. il por *People Weekly* 32:86-7 D 25 '89-Ja 1 '90

Playoff payoffs. D. Sheridan. il *Sport (New York, N.Y.)* 80:82-4 N '89

The Rose probe [Cincinnati Reds manager linked to baseball betting] C. Neff. il por *Sports Illustrated* 70:13 Mr 27 '89

Rose probe (cont.) [alleged betting by Cincinnati Reds manager] C. Neff. il por *Sports Illustrated* 70:11-12 My 8 '89

Rose probe (cont.) [alleged sports betting by Cincinnati Reds manager] C. Neff. il por *Sports Illustrated* 70:13+ Ap 17 '89

Rose's grim vigil [cover story] C. Neff and J. Lieber. il pors *Sports Illustrated* 70:52-4+ Ap 3 '89

The sad ordeal of Mr. Baseball [gambling allegations surrounding P. Rose] T. Callahan. il por *Time* 133:85 Ap 3 '89

Troubled times [P. Rose case] M. Nichols. il por *Maclean's* 102:42 Jl 10 '89

Waiting for the final chapter [P. Rose betting scandal interferes with R. Kahn's biography] C. Leerhsen. il pors *Newsweek* 113:71 Ap 10 '89

Why pick on Pete? [P. Rose case emblematic of American obsession with gambling; cover story] G. J. Church. il por *Time* 134:16-21 Jl 10 '89

Anecdotes, facetiae, satire, etc.

Baseball: not the movie [P. Rose gambling scandal] J. Leo. il *U.S. News & World Report* 107:54 Jl 10 '89

History

The Cobb gambling scandal [alleged wagering on fixed game in 1919] il por *Sports Illustrated* 70:20 Je 12 '89

BASEBALL CAPS

The discreet charm of the ball cap. R. Merkin. il *Gentlemen's Quarterly* 59:143+ O '89

BASEBALL CARDS

He shoots baseball cards: a dentist with a passion for spring training [S. Levy] S. Martin. il por map *Petersen's Photographic Magazine* 18:32-5 My '89

It's all in the cards. R. Brody. il *New Choices for the Best Years* 29:86+ Ap '89

It's in the cards. J. Schuster. il *Sport (New York, N.Y.)* 80:48-52+ My '89

Making a profitable nostalgia trip. D. Francis. il *Maclean's* 102:9 Ja 23 '89

Sociology 101 in a shoe box. D. Rea. por *Newsweek* 113:8 Mr 27 '89

Take me out to the card game. E. C. Baig. il *Fortune* 119:16 Mr 27 '89

What a card! [F. Willard's collection] M. Long. il por *Gentlemen's Quarterly* 59:148-9 Jl '89

BASEBALL COMMISSIONER *See* Baseball, Professional—Organization and administration

BASEBALL FANS

Baseball diamonds are a girl's best friend [taking daughter to watch Mets games] R. Schoenstein. il *New Choices for the Best Years* 29:80+ O '89

Baseball lives [R. Maris' fan A. Strasberg; excerpt] M. Bryan. il por *Sports Illustrated* 70:85+ Ap 24 '89

Do the people in Seattle feel the same way about the Pilots? [Brooklyn Dodgers nostalgia] S. Miller. il *Sport (New York, N.Y.)* 80:82 Ja '89

A fan's view of Bay's ball [San Francisco Bay Area] R. Fimrite. il *Sports Illustrated* 71:40-1 O 23 '89

Knowing the score. J. Schwartz. il *Gentlemen's Quarterly* 59:272+ S '89

The second hundred years [visiting spring training sites in Florida] P. Oliver. il map *Travel Holiday* 171:62-7 F '89

There's still hope, Elva [Chicago Cubs fan E. K. Reyburn dies at age 108] R. Telander. por *Sports Illustrated* 71:128 O 9 '89

Touching base with the boys of spring. R. Hoffman. il *Business Week* p174 Mr 20 '89

What I learned from the Pirates. R. Bendiner. il *American Heritage* 40:116-19 S/O '89

Why home plate is where his heart is. W. D. Leight. *Mademoiselle* 95:111 O '89

Religious life

Who's first? Good Catholics, good fans. K. Holland. *Commonweal* 116:582-3 N 3 '89

BASEBALL FANS IN DRAMA

A winning revival about a losing team [Bleacher bums about Cubs fans in 1969] R. Berler. il *Sports Illustrated* 70:16 Je 26 '89

BASEBALL FIELDS IN MOTION PICTURES

For Field of dreams fans who trek to Don Lansing's Iowa farm, the diamond is forever. M. Donovan. il pors *People Weekly* 32:120-1 O 23 '89

Infield of dreams [Iowa field transformed for Field of dreams] J. McCormick. il *Newsweek* 113:68 Je 12 '89

BASEBALL GLOVES

The great glove shark [San Diego infielder T. Flannery] J. E. Vader. il por *Sports Illustrated* 70:89 Je 5 '89

BASEBALL IN ART

Exhibitions

Diamonds are forever: artists & baseball. P. H. Gordon. il *USA Today (Periodical)* 117:76-85 My '89

BASEBALL IN LITERATURE

Undying words from the front office [B. Giamatti's book Take time for paradise] il por *U.S. News & World Report* 107:12 D 18 '89

Exhibitions

Diamonds are forever: artists & baseball. P. H. Gordon. il *USA Today (Periodical)* 117:76-85 My '89

BASEBALL IN MOTION PICTURES

Baseball like it oughta be [interview with W. P. Kinsella] A. Knight. il *American Film* 14:76 My '89

Born again baseball [Field of dreams] H. Jacobson. il *Film Comment* 25:78-9 My/Je '89

No, but I saw the game. R. Angell. *The New Yorker* 65:41+ Jl 31 '89

What is it with guys and baseball? R. Rosenbaum. il *Mademoiselle* 95:66+ Jl '89

BASEBALL LITERATURE

See also

Baseball, Professional—Bibliography

BASEBALL MANAGERS

See also

Berra, Yogi, 1925-

Gaston, Cito

Lasorda, Tom

McKeon, Jack

Rader, Doug

Robinson, Frank

Rose, Pete, 1941-

Weaver, Earl

Williams, Jimy

Zimmer, Don, 1931-

Toronto, Baltimore game pits two black managers [C. Gaston and F. Robinson] il pors *Jet* 76:46 Jl 17 '89

Toronto hires Cito Gaston as fourth black manager. il por *Jet* 76:46+ Je 19 '89

Anecdotes, facetiae, satire, etc.

The lost art of baseball prediction. J. Leo. il *U.S. News & World Report* 106:66 My 1 '89

Dismissal

Coming to terms [Blue Jays former manager J. Williams] M. Gray. por *Maclean's* 102:54 O 16 '89

BASEBALL PLAYERS

See also

Abbott, Jim

Andersen, Larry

Association of Professional Ball Players of America

Banks, Ernie

Blue, Vida

Boggs, Wade

Boone, Bob

Bresnahan, Dave

Brown, Chris, 1961-

Burke, Tim, 1959-

Canseco, José

Cepeda, Orlando, 1937-

Clark, Will

Clyde, David

Cobb, Ty, 1886-1961

Cone, David

Conigliaro, Tony

Cromartie, Warren

Croteau, Julie

Darling, Ron

Davis, Glenn

DiMaggio, Joe

Distefano, Benny

Dravecky, Dave

Fisk, Carlton, 1947-

Fletcher, Scott

Franco, John, 1960-

Gaetti, Gary

Gallagher, Dave

Garvey, Steve

Gossage, Rich, 1951-

Gott, Jim

Gray, Pete, 1915-

Griffey, Ken, Jr.

Griffey, Ken, Sr.

Gwynn, Chris

Gwynn, Tony

Harrell, Matt

Harrell, Phil

Henderson, Rickey

Hernandez, Keith, 1953-

Hershiser, Orel

Jackson, Bo

Jackson, Joe, 1887 or 8-1951

Jenkins, Ferguson, 1943-

Johnson, Randy

Jones, Kiki

Langston, Mark

LaValliere, Mike

Lomon, Kevin

Magrane, Joe

Major League Baseball Players Association

Mantle, Mickey, 1931-

Maris, Roger, 1934-1985

Mattingly, Don

Mays, Willie, 1931-

McDonald, Ben

McGriff, Fred

Mitchell, Kevin

Moore, Donnie, 1954-1989

Morgan, Mike

Ojeda, Bob, 1957-

Parker, Dave, 1951-

Perry, Gaylord

Peters, Jon

Puckett, Kirby

Reuschel, Rick

Robinson, Brooks, 1937-

Rose, Pete, 1941-

Rose, Petey

Roush, Edd, 1893-1988

Ruth, Babe, 1895-1948

Ryan, Nolan

Salkeld, Roger

Sandberg, Ryne

Sanders, Deion

Sheffield, Gary

Smith, Lonnie

Smith, Michele

Staub, Rusty, 1944-

Stewart, Dave

Strawberry, Darryl

Swan, Craig

Tabler, Pat

Tettleton, Mickey

Van Slyke, Andy

Walker, Greg

Welch, Bob, 1956-

Williams, Mitch

Williams, Ted, 1918-

Wilson, Glenn

Wilson, Mookie, 1956-

Winfield, Dave, 1951-

Assembly line of dreams [fees charged for autographs] T. Callahan. il *Time* 133:78 My 15 '89

Best of the best [first basemen] D. Knobler. il *Sport (New York, N.Y.)* 80:23-6 My '89

The big spin. S. Rosenbloom. il *Sport (New York, N.Y.)* 80:40-2+ O '89

Bosox boys gone batty. M. Starr. il pors *Newsweek* 113:58 F 20 '89

The boys of spring [rookies] D. Knobler. il *Sport (New York, N.Y.)* 80:24-5 Mr '89

The foul ball in the closet [signatures on baseball signed by 1938 Yankees turn out to have been forged] D. Seligman. il *Fortune* 120:141-2 Jl 3 '89

BASEBALL PLAYERS—cont.
The keys to this season? Jack Clark's bat and Jesse Orosco's pranks. L. Feldman. il *TV Guide* 37:10-12+ Ap 8-14 '89
Lefties and longevity: look again [disagreement between Stanley Coren and Max Anderson] R. Weiss. *Science News* 136:180 S 16 '89
Life on the lip of a volcano [relief pitchers] G. F. Will. il *Newsweek* 113:80 Ap 10 '89
Negro League stars feted as baseball's legends. il *Jet* 76:48+ Jl 10 '89
Not just a tall tale [rookie pitchers] H. Hersch. il pors *Sports Illustrated* 70:42-4+ Mr 20 '89
Old catchers never die . . . P. Korn. il pors *Sport (New York, N.Y.)* 80:44-9 Jl '89
The power rabbits [J. Canseco and other strong hitters who run well; cover story] D. Knobler. il pors *Sport (New York, N.Y.)* 80:22-4+ Jl '89
Presenting . . . Tim McCarver's all-star screwball team [baseball's colorful eccentrics] T. McCarver. il *TV Guide* 37:21-2 Jl 8-14 '89
They don't make 'em like they used to [catchers; cover story] P. Gammons. il *Sports Illustrated* 70 Special Issue:26-30+ Ap '89

Accidents and injuries
See Baseball, Professional—Accidents and injuries

Awards
See Baseball, Professional—Awards

Health and hygiene
Armed with a miracle [San Francisco Giants pitcher D. Dravecky returns after arm surgery to remove tumor] il pors *Sports Illustrated* 71:18 Ag 21 '89
Catchers die young, infielders live longest [research by John Waterbor] S. McKee. il *American Health* 8:18 Ap '89

Names
Is there an echo in here? [players with same name] S. Wulf. il por *Sports Illustrated* 71:84 Jl 10 '89

Anecdotes, facetiae, satire, etc.
'He welted the sphere a prodigious biff' [nicknames] D. D. Jackson. il *Smithsonian* 20:184 Ap '89

Photographs and photography
The boy in the photograph. D. I. Fine. il por *The New York Times Magazine* p28+ Ap 2 '89
The game without violins or apologies [cover story] L. Eisenberg. il *Esquire* 111:130-41 Ap '89
He shoots baseball cards: a dentist with a passion for spring training [S. Levy] S. Martin. il por map *Petersen's Photographic Magazine* 18:32-5 My '89
Life at home [major league catchers] il *Sports Illustrated* 70 Special Issue:16-25 Ap '89

Psychology
See Baseball, Professional—Psychological aspects

Religious life
Giant comeback cut short [pitcher D. Dravecky] J. Carvalho. il por *Christianity Today* 33:54+ O 20 '89
The Gospel and Gaetti [religious conversion changes G. Gaetti of the Minnesota Twins] H. Hersch. il por *Sports Illustrated* 71:42-4+ Ag 21 '89

Retirement
See also
Baseball Alumni Team

Salaries, pensions, etc.
See also
Collective bargaining—Baseball, Professional
Baseball's $2 million club [black players] il *Ebony* 44:134-6+ My '89
Baseball's owners want to play softball [revenue sharing proposal] A. Bernstein. il *Business Week* p52 D 18 '89
A crucial inning for baseball. W. C. Symonds. il por *Business Week* p90 O 23 '89
The man with the golden arm [O. Hershiser] J. Nocera. il pors *Newsweek* 113:42-4+ Ap 10 '89
The price of Peter's principles [commissioner P. Ueberroth and collusion issue] P. Schmuck. por *Sport (New York, N.Y.)* 80:10 Ja '89
Rich man's game. P. Gammons. il *Sports Illustrated* 71:60-2 D 11 '89
Richest of the rich [California Angels win bidding war for M. Langston] F. Lidz. il pors *Sports Illustrated* 71:64-6+ D 11 '89
Twins' Kirby Puckett cracks $3 million mark. il por *Jet* 77:52 D 11 '89

Anecdotes, facetiae, satire, etc.
It's Back to the Bambino [B. Ruth back as free agent] L. Montville. il por *Sports Illustrated* 71:100 D 18 '89

Sexual behavior
Facing the music [storm over W. Bogg's love life; cover story] E. M. Swift. il pors *Sports Illustrated* 70:38-40+ Mr 6 '89
Garvey scores! M. Lupica. il *Esquire* 112:37-8+ Jl '89

Trades
See Baseball, Professional—Player trades

Training
See also
Baseball, Professional—Spring training
Throwing old gracefully [N. Ryan] R. Givens. il por *Newsweek* 114:65 Ag 28 '89

BASEBALL RECORDS
See also
Softball records
An American classic [high school pitcher J. Peters of Brenham, Tex. wins 51st consecutive game; cover story] R. Reilly. il pors *Sports Illustrated* 70:16-21 My 8 '89
In the heart of Texas, Jon Peters is a pitcher of perfection [sets high school record of 51 straight victories] il por *People Weekly* 31:128 My 15 '89
A mound of unbreakable marks [pitching records] G. Castle. il *Sport (New York, N.Y.)* 80:18 S '89

BASEBALL SCOUTS *See* Baseball, Professional—Scouting
BASEBALL STADIUMS *See* Stadiums
BASEBALL VIDEO GAMES *See* Video games
BASEL (SWITZERLAND)
Music
See also
Opera—Switzerland

BASEL BALLET
Back in the U.S.A.: big times for Basel [cover story] W. Como. il *Dance Magazine* 63:40-5 F '89
In the doldrums [performances at City Center] T. Tobias. il *New York* 22:75-6 F 20 '89
Reviews:
Performances at City Center, New York City. C. Hardy. il *Dance Magazine* 63:66+ My '89

BASEL CONVENTION ON THE CONTROL OF TRANS-BOUNDARY MOVEMENTS OF HAZARDOUS WASTE AND THEIR DISPOSAL (1989)
Ending the traffic in toxic waste. *UN Chronicle* 26:71 Je '89
Managing toxic waste. T. Land. *The New Leader* 72:4 N 27 '89
New accord would control waste exports. J. Raloff. *Science News* 135:197 Ap 1 '89
The toxic-waste convention. il *World Press Review* 36:10 My '89

BASEMENTS
See also
Wine cellars
Skunk in the cellar! A. B. C. Whipple. il *Reader's Digest* 134:155-8 Mr '89

Waterproofing
See Waterproofing

BASEMENTS, REMODELED
Basement finishing options [interview with C. Knutson-Lycholat] il por *Home Mechanix* 85:18+ D '89
Look up, look down. B. Saxhaug. il *Good Housekeeping* 208:195-7 Ap '89
Once the furnace monster lived there. Now it's a bright playroom-office. il *Sunset (Central West edition)* 182:180+ My '89
Welcome to our basement [cover story; special section] G. Branson. il *Workbench* 45:37-44+ S/O '89

BASES (BASEBALL EQUIPMENT)
Safe on base [sliding injuries reduced by use of breakaway bases] *Women's Sports & Fitness* 11:12+ N/D '89

BASES (MILITARY) *See* Military bases
BASES (MISSILE) *See* Guided missile bases
BASHFULNESS
Why you're shy. M.-L. Kamberg. il *Current Health 2* 16:27-9 N '89

BASHIN, BRYAN JAY
Please don't eat the trees. il *Sierra* 74:22-4 Jl/Ag '89

BASHLINE, SYLVIA
Bounty. See issues of Field & Stream

BASIA
about
A Polish samba queen wins the West; her style is from Rio, but her heart's in Jaworzno. A. Abrahams. il pors *People Weekly* 31:85-6 Ja 30 '89

BASIC (COMPUTER LANGUAGE)
The 25th birthday of BASIC. W. H. Gates. il *Byte* 14:268-70+ O '89
Language sojourn [using QuickBasic] J. Pournelle. il *Byte* 14:111-12+ Ap '89
QuickBASIC comes to the Macintosh [Macintosh QuickBASIC 1.0] N. C. Shammas. il *Byte* 14:223-4+ Ja '89

BASIC TRAINING CAMPS *See* Military training camps
BASIDIOMYCETES
Fungal duo teaches evolutionary lesson [research by Jeffrey D. Palmer] B. Bower. *Science News* 135:318 My 20 '89

BASIE, COUNT, 1904-1984
about
The AJO tribute to Count Basie: Cooper Union/New York. M. Bourne. il *Down Beat* 56:54-5 My '89

BASIE, WILLIAM *See* Basie, Count, 1904-1984
BASIL
Growing basil indoors. C. Shirley. il *Organic Gardening* 36:26-7 O '89

BASILE, JOE
about
Systems. R. Day. il *Stereo Review* 54:84-5 Ja '89

BASINGER, KIM
about
Flix chick picks stix; or, Kim Basinger buys Braselton. il por *People Weekly* 31:125 Ap 17 '89

BASIX CORP.
"If something could go wrong, it did" [D. Beldock's BASIX]
E. Giltenan. il por *Forbes* 143:70+ My 29 '89
BASKERVILLE, LEZLI
about
Former Gray aide denies she's object of FBI probe. por
Jet 76:6 Je 19 '89
BASKET MAKING *See* Baskets
BASKETBALL
See also
Basketball players
Dribbling (Basketball)
Free throw shooting (Basketball)
Midnight Basketball League
Rebounding (Basketball)
Three-point shooting (Basketball)
Wheelchair basketball
Faked out by Zethel [Army team plays All American Red
Heads] S. Toperoff. il *The New York Times Magazine*
p22+ Je 11 '89
No dunkin'. No dough. Just nuts. J. Queenan. il *Gentlemen's
Quarterly* 59:207-8+ N '89
What's wrong with U.S. basketball? [competing on the inter-
national level] R. Waterman. il *Sport (New York, N.Y.)*
80:36 Je '89
Ethical aspects
A sanctuary no more [summer program at St. Cecilia church
in Detroit shut down] R. Sullivan. il *Sports Illustrated*
71:12 Ag 28 '89
History
The basketball man [J. Naismith] B. Broeg. il pors *The
Saturday Evening Post* 261:58-9+ Ap '89
Soviet Union
A Soviet hoopster in the Promised Land [S. Marciulionis
signs with the NBA] P. De Jonge. il pors *The New York
Times Magazine* p64+ N 5 '89
BASKETBALL, COLLEGE
See also
Basketball coaches
Basketball players
Basketball records
Black college basketball conference standings. See issues of
Jet published during the college basketball season
The bluegrass isn't so blue [Kentucky under new coach
R. Pitino] C. Kirkpatrick. il pors *Sports Illustrated* 71:54-6+
D 11 '89
College basketball. See issues of Sports Illustrated published
during the college basketball season beginning December
8, 1986
College basketball preview 1989-90 [cover story; special sec-
tion] il *Sports Illustrated* 71:46-52+ N 20 '89
Guru of the glass [Auburn coach S. Smith's ability to develop
rebounders] T. Kertes. il por *Sport (New York, N.Y.)*
80:68-71 Mr '89
Heavy traffic in the Pac-10. A. Wolff. il *Sports Illustrated*
70:62-3 Ja 30 '89
Illini on the rise [Illinois vs. Michigan] C. Kirkpatrick. il
Sports Illustrated 70:12-15 Ja 23 '89
The Knight I knew [excerpt from Playing for Knight]; ed.
by John Garrity. S. Alford. il pors *The Saturday Evening
Post* 261:66-8+ N/D '89
The NBA's entrance exam [college programs that best prepare
players for the pros] T. Kertes. il *Sport (New York, N.Y.)*
80:40-1+ Ja '89
On the brink again [Indiana] W. F. Reed. il *Sports Illustrated*
70:42-5 Mr 13 '89
Playing the cerebral game [Princeton coach P. Carril] S.
Toperoff. il *The Atlantic* 264:115-18 N '89
Rising in the East [Seton Hall and Providence] A. Wolff.
il por *Sports Illustrated* 70:36-8+ Ja 16 '89
Scouting reports: women. J. Jennings. il *Sports Illustrated*
71:98 N 20 '89
The Sport 1989-90 college hoops preview [cover story] T.
Kertes. il *Sport (New York, N.Y.)* 80:36-40+ D '89
Accidents and injuries
By the skin of his neck [fractured vertebra ends season
for Ohio State player J. Burson] H. Hersch. il pors *Sports
Illustrated* 70:46-9 Mr 6 '89
Ethical aspects
Dodging a bullet [Kentucky put on probation; cover story]
C. Kirkpatrick. il *Sports Illustrated* 70:24-6+ My 29 '89
Former basketball player sues Creighton University [K. Ross]
por *Jet* 76:50 Ag 14 '89
Foul play by the book [allegations against coach J. Valvano]
H. F. Waters. por *Newsweek* 114:62 Ag 14 '89
The ordeal of Jim Valvano [allegations against North Carolina
State] J. Feinstein. il por *Sports Illustrated* 70:34-6 Ja
30 '89
Playing to win in Vegas [UNLV basketball program] T.
Gup. il por *Time* 133:56-7 Ap 3 '89
Tempest at Mizzou [troubles of Missouri coach N. Stewart]
A. Wolff. il pors *Sports Illustrated* 70:24-6+ F 20 '89
Under the volcano [charges against University of Kentucky]
H. Nuwer. il *Sport (New York, N.Y.)* 80:50-3+ F '89
History
'80s basketball. T. Kertes. il *Sport (New York, N.Y.)* 80:62-4+
O '89

The coach and his champion [retired UCLA coach J. Wooden]
A. Wolff. il pors *Sports Illustrated* 70:94-8+ Ap 3 '89
Recruiting
My brother, my teammate [Philadelphia players J. and C.
Warley determined to attend college together] M. Bamber-
ger. il pors *Sports Illustrated* 70:54+ Mr 13 '89
Rules
How I fell for the bomb [three-point shot] A. Wolff. por
Sports Illustrated 70:84 F 20 '89
Television broadcasting
See Television broadcasting—Sports
Tournaments
Coaches, ad nauseam [too much attention given to coaches
at NCAA basketball tournament] J. Feinstein. por *Sports
Illustrated* 70:102 Ap 10 '89
The cream rises [NCAA] A. Wolff. il *Sports Illustrated* 70:18-23
Mr 27 '89
Face-off! [ACC-Big East Challenge] C. Kirkpatrick. il *Sports
Illustrated* 71:18-23 D 18 '89
Fearless Final Fourcast. T. Kertes. il *Sport (New York, N.Y.)*
80:66-70 Ap '89
Great escape [Georgetown vs. Princeton in NCAAs] A. Wolff.
il *Sports Illustrated* 70:24-5 Mr 27 '89
Heeling process [North Carolina wins Atlantic Coast Confer-
ence tournament] J. Feinstein. il *Sports Illustrated* 70:18-21
Mr 20 '89
The Jayhawks take flight [Kansas wins Dodge NIT] A. Wolff.
il *Sports Illustrated* 71:32-4+ D 4 '89
Mister Clutch [Michigan beats Seton Hall for NCAA
championship; cover story] C. Kirkpatrick. il *Sports
Illustrated* 70:16-23 Ap 10 '89
Q. What makes better TV than the World Series or Super
Bowl? A. This week's NCAA finals. J. Feinstein. il *TV
Guide* 37:10-12 Ap 1-7 '89
The right man for the job [S. Fisher given Univ. of Michigan
head coaching job after leading team to NCAA cham-
pionship] A. Wolff. il pors *Sports Illustrated* 70:58-60+
Ap 17 '89
Seton Hall on the map [NCAA runnerup] P. McKillop.
il *Newsweek* 113:63 Ap 17 '89
Team Turmoil triumphs [Missouri beats Oklahoma to win
Big Eight tournament] C. Kirkpatrick. il *Sports Illustrated*
70:22-5 Mr 20 '89
Tennessee waltzes in Tacoma [women's NCAA Final Four]
J. Garrity. il *Sports Illustrated* 70:80 Ap 10 '89
Terrific Whitewater journey [Univ. of Wisconsin at
Whitewater wins Division III championship] P. Putnam.
il *Sports Illustrated* 70:74+ Mr 27 '89
Up, up and away! [NCAA regionals; special section] il *Sports
Illustrated* 70:36-46+ Ap 3 '89
Wolverines NCAA title triumph of the orphaned. il *Jet*
76:50 Ap 24 '89
Anecdotes, facetiae, satire, etc.
The NCAAs from A to Z. C. Kirkpatrick. il por *Sports
Illustrated* 70:136 Mr 20 '89
Economic aspects
Baskets full of money [CBS pays $1 billion to keep NCAA
basketball tournament] H. J. Steinbreder. il *Sports Illustrated*
71:66-7 D 4 '89
Share the wealth, NCAA. A. Wolff. por *Sports Illustrated*
71:128 N 20 '89
History
The Final 4 [NCAA tournament] D. Kindred. il *Sports
Illustrated* 70:49+ Mr 20 '89
Magic vs Bird: 10 years ago they first met in a memorable
NCAA title game. W. Ladson and R. Harper. il pors
Sport (New York, N.Y.) 80:76-7 Ap '89
BASKETBALL, HIGH SCHOOL
Lady coach shows D.C. high school's boys basketball team
its way to victory [W. Oates] il pors *Jet* 75:48-9 Ja 23
'89
Making a fast break out of the ghetto [program founded
by B. Doss at Upward Bound Academy] J. Tabor. il
pors *Time* 133:14-15+ F 6 '89
Unlikely champs [St. Anthony's of Jersey City, N.J.] il pors
Life 12:68-70+ My '89
Ethical aspects
Academics and athletics: 'What price victory?' [Tennessee
teacher J. A. McGhee fights dismissal after being pressured
to raise basketball player's grade] P. A. Zirkel. il *Phi
Delta Kappan* 70:564-5 Mr '89
Tournaments
The Iowa girl stands tall [1988 six-on-six state tournament]
K. Cook. il *Sports Illustrated* 70:76-84+ F 13 '89
BASKETBALL, PROFESSIONAL
See also
Basketball fans
Basketball players
Naismith Memorial Basketball Hall of Fame
All things being equal [playoff preview] V. E. Smith. il
Newsweek 113:62-4 My 8 '89
The Bad Boys get better [Detroit vs. Chicago in Eastern
Conference finals] J. McCallum. il *Sports Illustrated* 70:29-31
Je 5 '89
Beers with . . . Doug Moe [interview with Denver Nuggets
coach] B. Diddlebock. il pors *Sport (New York, N.Y.)*
80:21-2 F '89

BASKETBALL, PROFESSIONAL—cont.

The best little division in basketball [Central Division] K. Simpson. il *Sport (New York, N.Y.)* 80:48-52 Ja '89

Cleveland's Cavaliers now class of the NBA. por *Jet* 75:50 Ja 16 '89

Fast new pace [Indiana Pacers] H. Hersch. il *Sports Illustrated* 71:34-6+ D 25 '89-Ja 1 '90

The final agenda [Lakers vs. Pistons] J. McCallum. il *Sports Illustrated* 70:30-2+ Je 12 '89

Free-for-all! [playoff preview; cover story] A. Cotton. il *Sport (New York, N.Y.)* 80:28-30 My '89

High anxiety [Knicks] E. Pooley. il *New York* 22:60-4+ My 8 '89

Hub of emotion [L. Bird and Boston Celtics struggling; cover story] J. McCallum. il pors *Sports Illustrated* 71:42-4+ D 11 '89

Into the deep: at playoff time, an NBA team's bench warrants special attention. T. Pluto. il *Sport (New York, N.Y.)* 80:54-6+ Je '89

Is anybody happy here? [Portland Trail Blazers] J. McCallum. il por *Sports Illustrated* 70:22-4+ Ja 16 '89

Less is more [Golden State takes playoff lead over Utah] A. Wolff. il *Sports Illustrated* 70:22-3 My 8 '89

Look who's on top [Cleveland] H. Hersch. il *Sports Illustrated* 70:92-5 Ja 9 '89

Motor City madmen [Detroit Pistons] J. Coplon. il *Rolling Stone* p68-72+ My 4 '89

NBA preview [special section] il *Sports Illustrated* 71:44-8+ N 6 '89

A new face, but the same old Magic [L.A. Lakers sweep playoff series with Seattle] J. McCallum. il *Sports Illustrated* 70:16-21 My 22 '89

A perfect fit [Detroit coach C. Daly] J. McCallum. il pors *Sports Illustrated* 71:52-4+ D 18 '89

Pistons sweep to title, Dumars cops MVP award. il *Jet* 76:46-7 Jl 3 '89

The power of the press [New York Knicks; cover story] J. McCallum. il por *Sports Illustrated* 70:22-6 F 13 '89

Pushed to the brink [Lakers vs. Detroit in NBA finals] B. Newman. il *Sports Illustrated* 70:22-5 Je 19 '89

A real Bulls market [Chicago in playoffs] J. McCallum. il *Sports Illustrated* 70:20-1 My 29 '89

. . . risen again [Phoenix Suns] B. Newman. il *Sports Illustrated* 70:38-41 F 27 '89

Simply perfect [L.A. Lakers sweep Phoenix to reach NBA finals; cover story] B. Newman. il *Sports Illustrated* 70:24-9 Je 5 '89

Sitting Bulls they weren't [Chicago takes 3-1 lead over New York in Eastern semifinals] H. Hersch. il *Sports Illustrated* 70:22-3 My 22 '89

The Sport 1989-90 NBA preview [cover story] B. Ryan. il *Sport (New York, N.Y.)* 80:52-6+ N '89

Sports [Knicks coach S. Jackson] E. Pooley. il por *New York* 22:148-9 S 11 '89

Three's company [three-point shooting] D. Herbst. il *Sport (New York, N.Y.)* 80:20-4 D '89

The transformation of Pat Riley [cover story] D. K. Shah. il pors *Gentlemen's Quarterly* 59:136-41+ Ja '89

'Un-fath-om-able' [M. Jordan leads Chicago over Cleveland in playoffs; cover story] J. McCallum. il pors *Sports Illustrated* 70:26-8+ My 15 '89

What drives the Pistons. F. Waitzkin. il *The New York Times Magazine* p30-3+ Ja 8 '89

Wild Bill [B. Musselman, coach of the Minnesota Timberwolves] N. Karlen. il por *Gentlemen's Quarterly* 59:306-11+ D '89

Accidents and injuries

General Hospital [ailments of players from 1988 Olympic team] H. Hersch. il *Sports Illustrated* 70:22 F 6 '89

See Larry run [L. Bird plays in exhibition game seven months after foot surgery] L. Montville. il pors *Sports Illustrated* 71:26-9 Jl 3 '89

Ten things you never knew about Bill Walton's injuries. S. Rosenbloom and W. Ladson. por *Sport (New York, N.Y.)* 80:83 Mr '89

Aesthetics

Choreography on the court. E. Zimmer. il *Dance Magazine* 63:48-9 Ag '89

All-star games

Utah's Mailman delivers in 39th NBA All-star game. il por *Jet* 75:51 F 27 '89

Awards

The 1989 Sport NBA Finals MVP: Joe Dumars. il pors *Sport (New York, N.Y.)* 80:82 S '89

Man in the slow lane [finals MVP J. Dumars of champion Detroit] B. Newman. il pors *Sports Illustrated* 70:28-30+ Je 26 '89

Who's Most Valuable? J. McCallum. il *Sports Illustrated* 70:42-4+ Ap 17 '89

Benefit games

Magic's fund-raiser nets a cool $1 million for UNCF. il por *Jet* 76:28-9 S 4 '89

Betting

See Basketball betting

Draft

Life at the top [NBA draft preview] T. Kertes. il *Sport (New York, N.Y.)* 80:31-7 Jl '89

Take your pick. H. Hersch. *Sports Illustrated* 70:60 Je 26 '89

Economic aspects

The L.A. Clippers' full-court mess [owner D. Sterling] P. Cole. il *Business Week* p64 F 13 '89

Playing the global game. E. F. Cone. il *Forbes* 143:90-1 Ja 23 '89

The slam-dunk comes to small-town America. B. Bremner. il *Business Week* p82 Mr 6 '89

Ethical aspects

The sad tale of Sweet Pea [L. Daniels shot during reported drug dispute] il por *Sports Illustrated* 70:12 My 22 '89

History

'80s basketball. T. Kertes. il *Sport (New York, N.Y.)* 80:62-4+ O '89

Big George [G. Mikan of the Minneapolis Lakers] R. Fimrite. il pors *Sports Illustrated* 71:128-34+ N 6 '89

Mountains of men [former players W. Reed and W. Unseld now coaching] T. Loverro. il pors *Sport (New York, N.Y.)* 80:58-62 F '89

NBA playoffs: big wins on the way to the title. B. Ryan. il *Sports Illustrated* 70:5+ Ap 24 '89

The pride of the Celtics [R. Auerbach] J. Schwartz. il por *Gentlemen's Quarterly* 59:156+ N '89

International aspects

Playing the global game. E. F. Cone. il *Forbes* 143:90-1 Ja 23 '89

Organization and administration

See also

Continental Basketball Association

National Basketball Association

World Basketball League

Blacks buy NBA Nuggets; 1st black-owned pro team. il pors *Jet* 76:51+ Jl 24 '89

Blacks conclude deal to buy NBA Denver Nuggets. *Jet* 77:51 N 6 '89

Crossing the last sports color line [black owners of Denver Nuggets] il *Newsweek* 114:52 Jl 24 '89

The NBA scores a first in the front office [black businessmen B. Lee and P. Bynoe buy Denver Nuggets] K. H. Hammonds and W. C. Symonds. il pors *Business Week* p26 Jl 24 '89

Nuggets buy makes history. Will it crumble barrier? P. Raybon. il pors *Black Enterprise* 20:17-18 S '89

Play it again, Bill [Bill Byrne starting women's league in 1990] L. Rothlein. il *Women's Sports & Fitness* 11:77-8 Ap '89

Sale of Denver Nuggets to two blacks is delayed [B. M. Lee and P. C. B. Bynoe] pors *Jet* 77:37 O 30 '89

The Wayne and Lenny show [Cleveland's black general manager W. Embry and coach L. Wilkens] M. Lupica. pors *Esquire* 111:61-3+ Je '89

Welcome to the owners' club [B. M. Lee purchases Denver Nuggets and becomes first black owner of a major league team] M. Jaffe. il por *Sports Illustrated* 71:12 Jl 24 '89

Photographs and photography

Super strobo basketball: bringing light to the pros who shoot the NBA. D. Mazzapica. il *Petersen's Photographic Magazine* 18:20-3+ Je '89

Player trades

And the winner is . . . [Dallas trades M. Aguirre to Detroit for A. Dantley] J. McCallum. il pors *Sports Illustrated* 70:34-6 Mr 6 '89

Psychological aspects

The night the Lakers got psyched out of a victory. P. King. il *TV Guide* 37:8-9 Je 3-9 '89

Rules

In the nick of time [24-second clock] L. Montville. il *Sports Illustrated* 71:104-6+ N 6 '89

Securities

See also

Boston Celtics Limited Partnership

Television broadcasting

See Television broadcasting—Sports

Italy

How do you say 'slam dunk' in Italian? [American players] J. Rossant. il *Business Week* p48 Ag 28 '89

Sitting pretty in Rome [American D. Ferry] C. Kirkpatrick. il pors *Sports Illustrated* 71:26-8+ O 9 '89

BASKETBALL BETTING

Home cookin' [home court advantage in NBA playoffs] D. Sheridan. il *Sport (New York, N.Y.)* 80:123-4 Je '89

A sanctuary no more [summer program at St. Cecilia church in Detroit shut down] R. Sullivan. il *Sports Illustrated* 71:12 Ag 28 '89

BASKETBALL COACHES

See also

Carlesimo, P. J.

Carril, Pete

Collins, Doug

Daly, Chuck

Fisher, Steve

Hurley, Bob

Jackson, Stu

Knight, Bobby

Moe, Doug

Musselman, Bill

Oates, Wanda

BASKETBALL COACHES—See also—*cont.*
Pitino, Rick
Reed, Willis
Riley, Pat
Schuler, Mike
Smith, Sonny
Stewart, Norm
Tarkanian, Jerry, 1930-
Thompson, John
Unseld, Wes
Valvano, Jim
Wilkens, Lenny
Wooden, John R.
Coaches, ad nauseam [too much attention given to coaches at NCAA tournament] J. Feinstein. por *Sports Illustrated* 70:102 Ap 10 '89
Women coaches win big in male basketball. D. C. Lyons. il *Ebony* 44:113-14+ Ap '89
Dismissal
Call it coaching roulette [college coaches] *Newsweek* 113:63 Ap 17 '89
Jordan denies any role in Bulls' coach firing [D. Collins fired by Chicago Bulls] il pors *Jet* 76:46 Jl 24 '89
BASKETBALL FANS
Miraculous conversion [baseball fan reconsiders pro basketball] S. Wulf. il *Sports Illustrated* 70:86 Mr 6 '89
BASKETBALL HALL OF FAME *See* Naismith Memorial Basketball Hall of Fame
BASKETBALL NEWSLETTERS
Green achers [Celtic scene] M. Ventre. *Sport (New York, N.Y.)* 80:85 My '89
BASKETBALL PLAYERS
See also
Abdul-Jabbar, Kareem, 1947-
Aguirre, Mark
Anderson, Kenny
Azzi, Jennifer
Benjamin, Benoit
Berry, Ricky, d. 1989
Bird, Larry
Bol, Manute
Burson, Jay
Cass, Cami
Daniels, Lloyd
Dantley, Adrian
Duckworth, Kevin
Dumars, Joe
Eaton, Mark
Ferry, Danny
Frazier, Walt, III
Frazier, Walt, 1945-
Gathers, Hank
Jackson, Chris
Johnson, Earvin, 1959-
Johnson, Kevin, 1966-
Jordan, Michael
Kemp, Shawn
Kerr, Steve
Koncak, Jon
Love, Bob
Mahorn, Rick
Malone, Karl
Marciulionis, Sarunas
Mikan, George
National Basketball Players Association
Nevitt, Chuck
Nixon, Norm
Olajuwon, Akeem
Perry, Chana
Reed, Willis
Richmond, Mitch
Robertson, Oscar
Robinson, David
Robinson, Rumeal
Rodman, Dennis
Ross, Kevin
Salley, John
Sampson, Ralph
Schintzius, Dwayne
Stinson, Andrea
Thomas, Isiah
Unseld, Wes
Warley, Carlin
Warley, Jason
Washington, Kermit
White, Randy
Big men, big problems [pro centers] P. Korn. il pors *Sport (New York, N.Y.)* 80:71-3+ Ap '89
Failure most foul [NBA's worst free throw shooters] J. McCallum. il *Sports Illustrated* 70:96-8+ Mr 20 '89
The lost generation [college scoring champs from 1971 to 1984] A. Wolff. il *Sports Illustrated* 71:100-11 N 20 '89
NBA stars are the best athletes in pro sports. R. Aregood. il *TV Guide* 37:14-15 Mr 25-31 '89
No longer the center of things. M. Littwin. il *TV Guide* 37:8-9 Ap 29-My 5 '89
The Sport all-time NBA all-star team. B. Ryan. il *Sport (New York, N.Y.)* 80:52-5 Mr '89

Which college stars should make good pros. H. Brown. il *TV Guide* 37:22-3 Mr 11-17 '89
Accidents and injuries
See Basketball, College—Accidents and injuries; Basketball, Professional—Accidents and injuries
Awards
See Basketball, Professional—Awards
Salaries, pensions, etc.
Millions from heaven [Atlanta Hawks' J. Koncak] R. Telander. il pors *Sports Illustrated* 71:56-8+ N 6 '89
Trades
See Basketball, Professional—Player trades
BASKETBALL RECORDS
Gathers 'round the rim [Loyola Marymount defeats U.S. International in highest scoring game ever] H. Hersch. il pors *Sports Illustrated* 70:68-9 F 13 '89
BASKETS
Door decor [vine basket and wreath] D. Temple. il *Flower and Garden* 33:57 S/O '89
BASKETS, MINIATURE
See also
Indians of North America—Baskets, Miniature
BASKIN, GORDON
about
The spoils of victory. K. Moore. il pors *Sports Illustrated* 70:50-3+ Ap 10 '89
BASKIN, RICHARD
about
Sing [film] Reviews
People Weekly il 31:17 Ap 17 '89. R. Novak
Time 133:83 Ap 17 '89. R. Corliss
BASLER, KONRAD, AND HAFEN, ERNST
Ubiquitous expression of *sevenless*: position-dependent specification of cell fate. bibl f il *Science* 243:931-4 F 17 '89
BASLER, WARREN
about
Gooney squadron. G. Baxter. il por *Flying* 116:84-6 Mr '89
BASQUE COOKING *See* Cooking, Basque
BASQUETTE, LINA
about
Profiles. B. Paris. il por *The New Yorker* 64:54-73 F 13 '89
BASQUIAT, JEAN-MICHEL, 1960-1988
about
Farewell, my unlovelies. R. Merkin. il *Gentlemen's Quarterly* 59:112+ Ap '89
The price of fame. A. Decker. il pors *Art News* 88:96-101 Ja '89
BASS, ANNE
about
The flowering of Fort Worth. C. Burden. il por *House & Garden* 161:84-91+ F '89
BASS, ARTHUR C.
about
Can Arthur Bass rouse Cooper from its sickbed? J. O. Hamilton. il por *Business Week* p33 Ap 10 '89
BASS, GEORGE FLETCHER, 1932-
Civilization under the sea. bibl il por *Modern Maturity* 32:58-64 Ap/My '89
BASS, RICK, 1958-
After oil [excerpt from Oil notes] *Harper's* 278:27-8+ My '89
A dog in the hand. il pors *Esquire* 112:150-4+ O '89
BASS, ROBERT M.
about
Bob Bass may have to settle for a quick profit on this one. J. F. Siler. il por *Business Week* p48+ O 9 '89
It's the end of an era for S&L rescues—but what an end. C. Yang. il por *Business Week* p40 Ja 9 '89
Secret agent. J. P. Newport, Jr. il por *Fortune* 119:50 Ja 2 '89
Time-Warner: three's a crowd: Bob Bass may stop the merger. K. Kelly and D. Lieberman. il por *Business Week* p38 Ap 3 '89
BASS
See also
Cooking—Fish
The mouth that swims [largemouth bass] A. J. McClane. il *Field & Stream* 93:40+ F '89
BASS (ROBERT M.) GROUP INC. *See* Robert M. Bass Group Inc.
BASS BOATS *See* Fishing boats
BASS BROTHERS ENTERPRISES INC.
Fat city [Bass Brothers invest in Darling-Delaware] H. Rudnitsky. il *Forbes* 144:70 Jl 10 '89
How the Basses caught their billions [stock positions] C. Palmeri. il *Forbes* 144 Special Issue:404-5 O 23 '89
BASS FISHERIES (COMMERCIAL) *See* Fisheries
BASS FISHING
See also
B.A.S.S. Inc.
Anatomy of a lily pad patch. B. Ignizio. il *Field & Stream* 94:40-1+ Je '89
Bass between a rock and a hard place [light lines and small baits] K. Jackson. il *Outdoor Life* 184:74-5+ Ag '89

BASS FISHING—*cont.*
Bass in the brush. M. Hicks. il *Field & Stream* 93:64-5+ F '89
The bass of summer. J. Dean. il *Outdoor Life* 184:51-3+ Jl '89
Bass on a fly. J. Bashline. il *Field & Stream* 94:34+ Je '89
Beat the heat bass. J. Gibbs. il *Outdoor Life* 184:24+ Jl '89
The best bass bait [crayfish] K. Etling. il *Outdoor Life* 183:64-5+ Je '89
Bugging summer smallmouths. T. Davis. il *Field & Stream* 94:46-7+ Ag '89
Buzzing for white bass. K. Schultz. il *Field & Stream* 94:32-3 S '89
Canada's "secret" smallmouths [New Brunswick] K. Schultz. il map *Field & Stream* 93:27+ Ja '89
Cold-current smallmouths. K. Etling. il *Outdoor Life* 184:88-9+ N '89
Cold-water surface bass [night fishing] J. Potts. il *Outdoor Life* 183:60-1+ F '89
Confidence water [large lakes] J. Doggett. il *Field & Stream* 94:56+ Jl '89
Count on clouds. J. Doggett. il *Field & Stream* 94:39+ S '89
Cross-country bass fishing. B. Whitaker. il *Outdoor Life* 183:72-3+ Je '89
The dawn and dusk syndrome. C. Hauptman. il *Field & Stream* 94:18 S '89
The dock side of bassing. N. Ward. il *Outdoor Life* 183:66-7+ Je '89
Fall's finer side [gear] J. Doggett. il *Field & Stream* 94:54+ O '89
Footloose on vacation lakes. P. Barrett. il *Field & Stream* 94:56-7+ Ag '89
The gentleman from Kentucky [spotted bass fishing] P. Barrett. il *Field & Stream* 94:69-70 My '89
Getting down to bassness. C. Hauptman. il *Field & Stream* 94:74+ N '89
The glass key. C. Hauptman. il *Field & Stream* 93:64-5+ Ap '89
Go with the flow [smallmouth bass fishing] B. W. Dalrymple. il *Field & Stream* 94:48-9+ Je '89
How to catch the biggest bass in any lake. J. E. Phillips. il *Outdoor Life* 183:74-5+ Mr '89
Is it too hot to fish? C. Hauptman. il *Field & Stream* 94:44-5+ Ag '89
Keep the heat on fall bass [largemouth] J. Dean. il *Outdoor Life* 184:68-9+ O '89
The new all-American fish [striped bass] il map *Field & Stream* 93:30-1+ Ja '89
Out of bed bass [views of D. Brauer] K. Etling. il *Outdoor Life* 183:71-3+ My '89
Perfectly clear. J. Doggett. il *Field & Stream* 94:47+ My '89
Plastic worms for summer bass. K. Schultz. il *Field & Stream* 94:41+ Jl '89
Rising to the occasion [catching smallmouth and largemouth bass with topwater lures] J. Bashline. il *Field & Stream* 94:20-1 O '89
School days. K. Schultz. il *Field & Stream* 94:40-1+ O '89
Serpents on the surface [snake lures] C. Hauptman. il *Field & Stream* 93:43+ Mr '89
Snowbird bass [Dixie] S. Price. il map *Field & Stream* 93:40-1+ Ja '89
The striper tug of war [sport and commercial fishermen on Chesapeake Bay] L. Williamson. il *Outdoor Life* 184:56-7 Ag '89
Summer smallmouth secrets [live crayfish bait] W. Ryan. il *Outdoor Life* 183:78-9+ My '89
Three ploys for trophy-bass [largemouth] C. Hauptmann; A. H. Putnam; E. J. Mendus. il *Field & Stream* 94:56-7 D '89
Through the slot [slot regulations for bass and trout] J. Bashline. il *Field & Stream* 93:18 Ja '89
Timber tactics [fishing flooded trees] K. Schultz. il *Field & Stream* 94:76+ N '89
Tips for taking early-season bass. K. Schultz. il *Field & Stream* 93:76+ Ap '89
Top lures for shallow bass [spinner baits] K. Schultz. il *Field & Stream* 94:82+ My '89
Ultralight largemouths. J. Dean. il *Outdoor Life* 183:84-5+ Ap '89
Walleye systems for bass. J. Gibbs. il *Outdoor Life* 183:20+ Ja '89
Where to hook a hawg next year [best places in America to fish for trophy largemouth bass] L. Larsen. il *Outdoor Life* 184:70-1+ D '89

Anecdotes, facetiae, satire, etc.
On becoming a bassman. B. R. Hooten. il *Field & Stream* 93:30+ Mr '89

Competitions
See Fishing—Competitions
BASS TOURNAMENTS *See* Fishing—Competitions
BASSET HOUNDS
See also
Basseting (Sport)

BASSETING (SPORT)
The hare and the beagle. M. Cohen. il *Gentlemen's Quarterly* 59:49+ D '89
BASTIAN, LOIS BRUNNER
Fiestas de Octubre. il *Travel Holiday* 171:50-7 Je '89
BASTIDA, JOAQUíN SOROLLA Y *See* Sorolla y Bastida, Joaquín, 1863-1923
BASTILLE (PRISON)
Celebrating the Bastille: fact and fable. C. P. Reynolds. il *Gourmet* 49:28+ Jl '89
BASTILLE OPÉRA *See* Opéra Bastille
BASTROP COUNTY (TEX.)
Crime
Knowing Johnny Jenkins [controversial rare book dealer who was mysteriously murdered] C. Trillin. *The New Yorker* 65:79-97 O 30 '89
BASU, JANET ELSE
To live and breathe in L.A. il maps *American Health* 8:52-4+ S '89
BAT *See* Baseball Alumni Team
BAT MITZVAH
"My amazing Lisa" [Down syndrome teenager L. Grossman's Bat mitzvah]; ed. by Susan Lapinski. A. S. Grossman. il por *Redbook* 172:56+ Ap '89
BATAILLE, GEORGES, 1897-1962
about
Fontana's base materialism. Y.-A. Bois. bibl f il *Art in America* 77:238-49+ Ap '89
Bibliography
The attraction of repulsion. A. Nehamas. *The New Republic* 201:31-6 O 23 '89
BATCHELLER, GORDON
(jt. auth) See Odell, David, and Batcheller, Gordon
BATE, ROBERT T.
about
A growing force in the shrinking business. W. C. Symonds. il por *Business Week* Special Issue:75 Je 16 '89
BATEMAN, ANYA
I'm sick of the F word. *Reader's Digest* 134:96-8 F '89
BATEMAN, JASON
about
Why them? . . . and what it's like being a TV heartthrob [cover story] S. Littwin. il pors *TV Guide* 37:4-6+ Ap 22-28 '89
BATEMAN, JUSTINE
about
Justine Bateman becomes the latest celebrity to be menaced by an obsessive fan. B. Hewitt. il por *People Weekly* 32:112-13 S 25 '89
BATES, ARTIE ANN
about
Coal miner's doctor. J. Ralston. il pors *McCall's* 116:70+ S '89
BATES, CAROLINE
Gourmet holidays: Society Islands. il map *Gourmet* 49:58-63+ F '89
Gourmet holidays: Society Islands. il map *Gourmet* 49:36-41+ Ja '89
Sonoma County: fresh from the farm. il map *Gourmet* 49:86-91+ S '89
Spécialités de la maison. See issues of Gourmet
BATES, DAISY
about
Former Arkansas gov. Orval Faubus honors Daisy Bates. pors *Jet* 76:30 Ag 21 '89
BATES, DAVID, 1952-
about
David Bates: Modern Art Museum. J. Kutner. il *Art News* 88:155 Ja '89
BATES, KAREN GRIGSBY
My dollars count. por *Essence* 20:148 O '89
BATES, LINCOLN S.
Mad Housers help homeless. il *The Progressive* 53:15 My '89
BATES, ROBERT H.
Is liberalism still possible? *National Review* 41:17 D 31 '89
BATES, STEPHEN
First, this message. *The New Republic* 201:16+ O 16 '89
Ignore a menorah. *The New Republic* 201:14-16 Jl 31 '89
BATESON, CAROL
about
Dec-Tam corporation: selling peace of mind. J. David and K. File. il por *Working Woman* 14:124+ O '89
BATH COUNTY (VA.)
Firefighters
Rural firemen [volunteers] D. McCaig. il *Country Journal* 16:79-83 Mr/Ap '89
BATH TUBS *See* Bathtubs
BATHHOUSES
See also
Cabanas
BATHING *See* Baths
BATHING SUITS
Back from the bikini brink. R. Zoglin. il *Time* 134:82 Jl 17 '89
"I don't want to look fat". il *Ladies' Home Journal* 106:138-9 Je '89

BATHING SUITS—cont.
New swimsuits hark back to the 1940s—try them on for thighs! il People Weekly 31:128-9 Je 12 '89
The perfect swimsuit for your body. il Glamour 87:216-23 Je '89
Suit yourself: taking the trauma out of swimwear shopping. il American Health 8:33-4+ My '89
Swimsuit anxiety. L. F. McCarthy. il Health (New York, N.Y.) 21:43+ My '89
Swimsuit makeovers. W. Gavin. il Parents 64:157-9 Je '89
History
In the swim. W. O. Johnson. il Sports Illustrated 70 Special Issue:20-4+ F '89
Photographs and photography
25th anniversary swimsuit issue. il Sports Illustrated 70 Special Issue:20-4+ F '89
The fanciest dive [Sports illustrated swimsuit issue] J. Adler. il Newsweek 113:53-4 F 13 '89
SI's swimsuit issue: more than meets the eye. D. Lieberman. il Business Week p52 Ja 16 '89
Spectacular swimwear [cover story] S. Lucas. il Petersen's Photographic Magazine 18:24-9+ Jl '89
Tapping a market [swimsuit magazines] J. DeMont. il Maclean's 102:28 F 20 '89
BATHROOM CABINETS See Cabinets (Furniture)
BATHROOM FIXTURES
See also
Plumbing
Toilets
Towel racks, rings, etc.
6 great products for kitchens and baths. A. Arnott. il Home Mechanix 85:66-7 O '89
King for a day in a small room with a view [high tech bathroom fixtures in Japan] M. Walsh. il Time 133:80 F 13 '89
Advertising
Dear John. B. Kanner. il New York 22:12-13 Jl 17 '89
BATHROOM SCALES See Scales (Weighing instruments)
BATHROOM SHELVES See Shelves and racks
BATHROOM VANITIES (FURNITURE) See Vanities (Furniture)
BATHROOM VENTILATORS See Ventilators
BATHROOMS
See also
Powder rooms
Public comfort stations
Architects review: baths. il Architectural Digest 46:58+ Ag '89
Bath masters space and style. il Southern Living 24:138 My '89
Bath with a view. il Sunset (Central West edition) 183:62-3 S '89
Bathroom remodeling. A. Rooze. il The Family Handyman 39:64-5 Jl/Ag '89
Bathroom remodeling [special section] il Popular Mechanics 166:93+ Ap '89
Baths: Bentley Larosa Salasky: reorganizing a New York space. il Architectural Digest 46:99 Ap '89
Big new bathroom borrows space from spare bedroom. il Sunset (Central West edition) 183:112 N '89
Bigger, better baths [cover story; special section] il Home Mechanix 85:45-54+ O '89
Bringing daylight and a mini-kitchen into the master bathroom. il Sunset (Central West edition) 182:74 Ja '89
A cut above the rest [Carol and Gary Gebhard's remodeled family bathroom] il Better Homes and Gardens 67:93 O '89
Dazzling baths [excerpt from Country floors—decorating with tiles] R. Siegal. il Redbook 173:122-4 Jl '89
Easy ways to more bathroom space. il Good Housekeeping 208:200+ Ap '89
Finishing a bathroom. il Workbench 45:50-3 S/O '89
Glorified bathrooms. P. Langdon. il The Atlantic 264:102+ O '89
Living near the water. J. Scandura. il Working Woman 14:138-9 Ap '89
Remodeling the old bathroom—starting from scratch [cover story] D. Johnson. il The Family Handyman 39:30-8 O '89
Small space baths. W. L. Nolan. il Better Homes and Gardens 67:87-8+ N '89
Snug-fit bath. il Better Homes and Gardens 68:87 F '89
Splendor in the bath. il McCall's 116:95 Ap '89
Suite retreat. C. Poole. il Home Mechanix 86:78-80+ Mr '89
Sumptuous bathrooms. il Ebony 45:78-80+ N '89
Tight space, tight budget. il Sunset (Central West edition) 182:134 Je '89
Lighting
Lighting up your bathroom. il McCall's 116:95 Ap '89
Japan
King for a day in a small room with a view [high tech bathroom fixtures] M. Walsh. il Time 133:80 F 13 '89
BATHS
See also
Japanese baths
Mud baths
Public baths

Shower baths
Whirlpool baths
Beauty and the bath. J. Gordon. il Good Housekeeping 208:118+ My '89
Delicious immersions. L. J. Sass. il Health (New York, N.Y.) 21:54-7 Ja '89
Rub-a-dub-dub [toddlers] J. T. Gibson. il Parents 64:226 O '89
BATHS, WHIRLPOOL See Whirlpool baths
BATHTUBS
New tub wouldn't just drop in. il Sunset (Central West edition) 182:146-7 Ap '89
Repair porcelain enamel. il The Family Handyman 39:52-3 S '89
BÁTIZ, ENRIQUE
about
Mexico in music. R. Freed. por Stereo Review 54:158 N '89
BATMAN (FICTIONAL CHARACTER)
Batman [movie; cover story] B. Zehme. il pors Rolling Stone p38-42+ Je 29 '89
Batmania. B. Barol. il Newsweek 113:70-4 Je 26 '89
Betting on Batman. B. Eder. il Video 13:80-1+ D '89
Bush as Batman? Wait for the sequel. F. Bruning. il Maclean's 102:9 Jl 17 '89
Gotham great grows grim. D. S. Husler. il Christianity Today 33:65 My 12 '89
Movies [M. Keaton] E. G. Carter. il pors Vogue 179:128-30 Je '89
My son, the Batman: a proud memoir by the artist who sired Gotham's defender; ed. by Michael Alexander. B. Kane. il pors People Weekly 32:33-4+ Jl 31 '89
Return to Gotham City [movie] J. Kroll. il Newsweek 113:68-9 Ja 23 '89
Tim Burton, Batman and the Joker [movie] J. Morgenstern. il por The New York Times Magazine p44-6+ Ap 9 '89
With help from some wily haircutters, Batman leaves his mark on cropped crusaders. il People Weekly 32:74 Jl 17 '89
Would Batman vote Republican? M. Sieff. National Review 41:55-7 S 15 '89
Collectibles
Holy bootlegger! What a lot of phony Batstuff! G. Jacobson. il Business Week p70 Jl 17 '89
BATMAN [film] See Motion picture reviews—Single works
BATON ROUGE (LA.)
Galleries and museums
See also
LSU Rural Life Museum and Burden Research Plantation
BATOR, FRANCIS M.
Must we retrench? bibl f il Foreign Affairs 68:93-123 Spr '89
BATS
Good evening, fellow bat lovers [Mexican freetail bats in Austin, Tex.] J. Schwartz. il Newsweek 114:63 Jl 3 '89
Night flyers. T. Engel. il The Conservationist 43:32-5 My/Je '89
Food and feeding
Fatal attraction? [demise of long-nosed bat linked to disappearance of agave] K. Heacox. il International Wildlife 19:38-43 My/Je '89
The regeneration gap [disappearance of saguaro and long-nosed bats from Saguaro National Monument] J. Erickson. il National Parks 63:30-3 Jl/Ag '89
BATS, BASEBALL See Baseball bats
BATS, SOFTBALL See Softball bats
BATTAGLIA, CARL
A Texan for Tancredi. il pors Opera News 53:16-18 Ja 21 '89
Transported in time [cover story] il por Opera News 53:8-10+ Ja 7 '89
BATTELLE, PHYLLIS
Raquel Welch: starting over. il pors Ladies' Home Journal 106:46+ My '89
BATTELLE MEMORIAL INSTITUTE
Keep the HSCT on track. Aviation Week & Space Technology 131:11 S 18 '89
Lack of U.S. interest derails international HSCT consortium. J. Ott. il Aviation Week & Space Technology 131:28-9 S 11 '89
BATTERED WIVES See Wife abuse
BATTERED WOMEN See Abused women
BATTERIES, AUTOMOBILE See Storage batteries
BATTERIES, BOAT See Storage batteries
BATTERIES, ELECTRIC See Electric batteries
BATTERIES, STORAGE See Storage batteries
BATTERIES NOT INCLUDED [film] See Motion picture reviews—Single works
BATTERS FACED PER START See Baseball, Professional—Statistics
BATTERY BOOSTER CABLES See Storage batteries—Booster cables
BATTERY CHARGING See Electric batteries—Charging
BATTERY PARK CITY (NEW YORK, N.Y.)
Where the skyline meets the shore. B. Angelo. il Time 134:82-3 O 23 '89

BATTERY TECHNOLOGIES INC.
China's headlong rush to capitalism. P. C. Newman. il *Maclean's* 102:38 Je 12 '89

BATTIN, PATRICIA M.
Crumbling books. il *Change* 21:6+ S/O '89

BATTING (BASEBALL)
Bat those eyes! [crossed eye-hand dominance in baseball players; research by Jose Portal and Paul Romano] S. McKee. il *American Health* 8:16 O '89
The game teachers play [R. Watt's scientific research] S. A. Booth. il por *Rolling Stone* p152-6 Mr 23 '89
Oh-and-two: when the count goes to two strikes, the pitcher-hitter battle really gets interesting. D. Knobler. il *Sport (New York, N.Y.)* 80:98-100+ Je '89
Playing ball and chain [Stride Tutors, hitting aid invented by White Sox centerfielder D. Gallagher] N. Dawidoff. il por *Sports Illustrated* 70:81 My 22 '89
Way above average [W. Clark and T. Gwynn compete for NL batting title] B. Newman. il pors *Sports Illustrated* 71:24-6+ S 25 '89

BATTLE MOUNTAIN (NEV.)
Invisible gold [mining] J. Seabrook. *The New Yorker* 65:45-6+ Ap 24 '89

BATTLEFIELD TOURS
See also
Major & Mrs. Holt's Battlefield Tours (Firm)

BATTLEFIELDS
See also
Antietam National Battlefield (Md.)
Custer Battlefield National Monument (Mont.)
Gettysburg National Military Park (Pa.)
Manassas National Battlefield Park (Va.)
Yorktown Battlefield (Va.)
Back to the battlefields [World War II veterans visit Pacific] K. Castle. il *Travel Holiday* 172:60-71 S '89
Fighting for the past [preserving Civil War battlefields] T. A. Lewis. il map *Audubon* 91:56-72 S '89
Save or pave? [Civil War battlefields; cover story] R. M. Williams. il *Americana* 17:23-9 My/Je '89
Great Britain
Charles, Cromwell and Channon [highway threatens Naseby battlefield] *History Today* 39:4-5 Ap '89

BATTLES
See also
United States—History—Civil War, 1861-1865—Campaigns and battles
War
World War, 1914-1918—Campaigns and battles
World War, 1939-1945—Campaigns and battles

BATTLESHIPS See Warships

BATTLETECH (VIDEO GAME)
BattleTech: the Crescent Hawk's Inception. B. Guerra. il *Compute!* 11:136 O '89
Mall MechWarrior. D. Stover. il *Popular Science* 235:17 S '89

BATY, CHARLIE
about
Little Charlie and the Nightcats. D. Whiteis. il por *Down Beat* 56:15 D '89

BATZDORFF, SUSANNE M.
Catholics and Jews: can we bridge the abyss? [adaptation of address, October 16, 1988] *America* 160:223-4+ Mr 11 '89

BAU, HAIM H.
(jt. auth) See Foster, Kenneth R., and Bau, Haim H.

BAUBIOLOGIE
Baubiologie: Germany's natural home movement. E. Maciocha. il *Utne Reader* p78-9 My/Je '89

BAUDRILLARD, JEAN, 1929-
about
After utopia: the primitive society of the future [interview] N. Gardels. il *New Perspectives Quarterly* 6:52-4 Summ '89
The work of Roy Lichtenstein in the age of Walter Benjamin's and Jean Baudrillard's popularity [cover story] C. Ratcliff. il *Art in America* 77:110-23+ F '89

BAUER, ERWIN A., AND BAUER, PEGGY
Rivers of life [photograph] il *Natural History* p90-1 Ja '89

BAUER, GARY L.
about
Should public officials' private lives matter? [interview] il *U.S. News & World Report* 107:23 S 11 '89

BAUER, MARIA
The cats of Cairo. il *Opera News* 53:38-9 My '89

BAUER, MARTY
about
Why Marty Bauer wears the black hat. K. Turan. il por *Gentlemen's Quarterly* 59:89-90+ F '89

BAUER, PEGGY
(jt. auth) See Bauer, Erwin A., and Bauer, Peggy

BAUER, SCOTT
Black on black on black. il *Petersen's Photographic Magazine* 18:84-5 O '89

BAUER (EDDIE) INC. See Eddie Bauer Inc.

BAUER BENEDEK AGENCY
Why Marty Bauer wears the black hat. K. Turan. il por *Gentlemen's Quarterly* 59:89-90+ F '89

BAUHAUS
Art: painters of the Bauhaus. D. Solomon. il *Architectural Digest* 46:242-7+ O '89

BAULIEU, ETIENNE-EMILE
Contragestion and other clinical applications of RU 486, an antiprogesterone at the receptor [cover story] bibl f il *Science* 245:1351-7 S 22 '89
about
Dispute surfaces over paternity of RU 486. J. Cherfas. *Science* 246:994 N 24 '89
Etienne-Emile Baulieu: in the eye of the storm. J. Cherfas. il pors *Science* 245:1323-4 S 22 '89
A new pill, a fierce battle. S. Greenhouse. il por *The New York Times Magazine* p22-4+ F 12 '89

BAUM, EILEEN
Thin, thinning, gone. *Health (New York, N.Y.)* 21:74-6 Ja '89

BAUM, HERBERT MERRILL
Mandatory labeling of food products [address, March 2-3, 1989] *Vital Speeches of the Day* 55:458-61 My 15 '89

BAUM, RICHARD, AND SMITH, ROBERT W. (ROBERT WILLIAM), 1952-
Neptune's forgotten ring. il por *Sky and Telescope* 77:610-11 Je '89

BAUMANN, MELISSA
Namibia on edge. il *Mother Jones* 14:18+ O '89

BAUMANN, PAUL DAVID
Never a question of easy grace. il por *Commonweal* 116:395-400 Jl 14 '89

BAUMBER, MICHAEL
Cromwell's soldier-admirals. bibl il pors *History Today* 39:42-7 O '89

BAUMGAERTNER, JILL P.
From an old house in Illinois [poem] *The Christian Century* 106:654 Jl 5-12 '89
Jephthah's daughter [poem] *The Christian Century* 106:590 Je 7-14 '89
A literary roundup. il *The Christian Century* 106:1048-50 N 15 '89
The resurrection of the body. *The Christian Century* 106:302-3 Mr 22-29 '89

BAUMGARTEN, JON A.
(jt. auth) See Risher, Carol, and Baumgarten, Jon A.

BAUMGARTNER, FRED
Spectrum monitor (I) [cover story] il *Radio-Electronics* 60:33-6+ S '89
Spectrum monitor (II). il *Radio-Electronics* 60:46-8 O '89

BAUMGOLD, JULIE
In the kingdom of the brain [cover story] il pors *New York* 22:36-43 F 6 '89
That party [cover story] il pors *New York* 22:30-41 O 2 '89

BAUMOL, WILLIAM J.
Is there a U.S. productivity crisis? bibl f il *Science* 243:611-15 F 3 '89

BAUR, FRANK
about
Keynote Kid. B. Newman. il pors *Sports Illustrated* 71:106-10+ S 4 '89

BAUSCH, PINA
about
The evolution of Pina Bausch [interview] S. de Nussac. il por *World Press Review* 36:91 O '89

BAUSCH, RICHARD, 1945-
The fireman's wife [story] il *The Atlantic* 264:102-4+ N '89
Letter to the lady of the house [story] *The New Yorker* 65:48-52 O 23 '89

BAUTCH, RICHARD
American archbishops visit Vietnam. *America* 160:132-3 F 18 '89
The great experiment. *America* 160:316-17 Ap 8 '89
The new Irish immigrant. *America* 160:236-7 Mr 18 '89
South Africa: the growing tolerance of intolerance [interview with N. Tutu-Seavers] *America* 160:450-1+ My 13 '89

BAVARIA (GERMANY)
See also
Iron Age—Bavaria (Germany)

BAVENDAM, FRED
Even for ethereal phantasms, it's a dog-eat-dog world. bibl (p135) il *Smithsonian* 20:94-101 Ag '89

BAWER, BRUCE, 1956-
The talkies. See issues of The American Spectator

BAXTER, CHARLES
Scheherazade [story] il *Harper's* 278:62-4 Je '89

BAXTER, CRAIG
The struggle for development in Bangladesh. bibl f *Current History* 88:437-40+ D '89

BAXTER, FRANK E.
about
The house that Boyd built. R. King. il por *Forbes* 144:222 S 18 '89
Life after Boyd? And how. E. Schine. il por *Business Week* p143 Mr 20 '89

BAXTER, GORDON, 1923-
Bax seat. See issues of Flying

BAXTER, MEREDITH See Birney, Meredith Baxter

BAY, WILLOW
about
Life after Lauder. S. N. Chakravarty. il por *Forbes* 144:128 N 13 '89

BAY AREA (CALIF.) See San Francisco Bay Area (Calif.)

BAY AREA RIDGE TRAIL (CALIF.)
New trail takes you up for Bay views. il *Sunset (Central West edition)* 182:20+ Je '89

BAY OF PIGS INVASION See Cuba—History—Invasion, 1961

BAY SHORE STAKES See Horse racing

BAY WINDOWS See Windows

LA BAYADÈRE [ballet] See Ballet reviews—Single works

BAYAN, LAUREN
Kidnapping
The search for Lauren. N. C. Livingstone and D. Halevy. il pors *Reader's Digest* 135:77-84 Ag '89

BAYAN (ORGANIZATION)
Filipina activist fights repression [Z. Uy] J. Jiji and D. Bernstein. *The Progressive* 53:14 Ap '89

BAYE, BETTY WINSTON
Back to school. il *Essence* 19:68-70+ Mr '89
Fighting back. il *Essence* 20:59+ N '89

BAYER, PETER BRANDON
A life in limbo. il por *The New York Times Magazine* p48+ Ap 2 '89

BAYER, WILLIAM
about
PW interviews. M. Harris. il por *Publishers Weekly* 235:45-6 Je 9 '89

BAYER AG
All's well in Wellsburg. M. Vitez. il *New Choices for the Best Years* 29:10 Je '89
A couple of collective tons later, the citizens of Wellsburg, W. Va., are no longer in Fat City [Bayer Wellness Program] M. Brower. il *People Weekly* 31:44-6 F 20 '89
Fit city [Bayer Wellness Program in Wellsburg, W. Va.] D. Zevin. il *American Health* 8:45 Mr '89
The town that lost two tons [Bayer Wellness Program] D. Grady. il *Ladies' Home Journal* 106:46+ Je '89
Wellness in Wellsburg. P. Stone. il *The Mother Earth News* 115:16+ Ja/F '89

BAYERISCHE MOTOREN WERKE AG
The company behind the image. P. Fuhrman. il *Forbes* 144:89+ N 27 '89

BAYH, BIRCH, 1928-
Let's tear off their hoods. por *Newsweek* 113:8 Ap 17 '89

BAYLEY, JOHN, 1925-
Living with Trollope. il *The New York Review of Books* 36:6-8 Ag 17 '89
The master at home. il *The New York Review of Books* 36:21-3 D 7 '89

BAYMILLER, JOANNA
Blueprint for the 90s. il *Theatre Crafts* 23:35-9+ D '89

BAYÓN, MIGUEL
A winner from Spain. il por *World Press Review* 36:60 Ap '89

BAYONNE (N.J.)
Art
Bayonne [A. Melamid and V. Komar admire the work of J. A. Noble] *The New Yorker* 65:32-3 Ap 24 '89
Description
Bayonne. S. V. Roberts. il *U.S. News & World Report* 107:56+ D 18 '89

BAYONNE (N.J.) IN ART
Exhibitions
Komar & Melamid at Ronald Feldman Fine Arts. N. Princenthal. *Art in America* 77:206 S '89

BAYREUTH FESTIVAL See Music festivals—Germany (West)

BAYS AND GULFS
See also
Delaware Bay (Del. and N.J.)
Golfo Dulce (Costa Rica)
Morro Bay (Calif.)

BAYSIDE BOAT & BREAKFAST (FIRM)
Thanks to Boat & Breakfast, Bay Area landlubbers can enjoy the high life on the high seas [owner R. Harris] J. Boudreau. il pors *People Weekly* 32:107-8 O 16 '89

BAYWATCH [television program] See Television program reviews—Single works

BAZAN, ERNESTO
Refugees [photographs] il *Life* 12:94-100 Ap '89

BAZELL, ROBERT
Cancer warp. *The New Republic* 201:12-14 D 18 '89
Hype-energy physics. *The New Republic* 200:7-8 Ap 24 '89
Potemkin cleanup. *The New Republic* 201:22 S 18-25 '89

BAZILEVSKIY, ALEKSANDR T.
The planet next door. il *Sky and Telescope* 77:360-6+ Ap '89

BBC
Mind's Eye lands BBC catalogue [radio dramas] P. Sweeting. il *Publishers Weekly* 235:61 Ja 6 '89

BBC BROWN, BOVERI & COMPANY, LTD.
See also
ASEA Brown Boveri AB

BCE MOBILE COMMUNICATIONS INC.
Canada Bell belle. T. Jaffe. *Forbes* 144:304-5 O 16 '89

BCL ENTERTAINMENT CORPORATION
It's only rock 'n' roll, but he likes it [M. Cohl] L. Gubernick. il por *Forbes* 143:114+ My 29 '89
The music man [promoter of Rolling Stones tour M. Cohl] T. Powis. il por *Maclean's* 102:53+ S 11 '89

BEACH, AMY MARCY CHENEY, 1867-1944
about
New-world symphonies. P. G. Davis. pors *New York* 22:88-9 F 6 '89

BEACH, MRS. H. H. A. See Beach, Amy Marcy Cheney, 1867-1944

BEACH, HUGH
The case for the third zero. *The Bulletin of the Atomic Scientists* 45:14-15 D '89

BEACH, RANDALL
Sally Jessy Raphaël on the move. il pors *The Saturday Evening Post* 261:58-9+ S '89

BEACH ARCHITECTURE
See also
Boardwalks
Cabanas
Architecture: Franklin D. Israel: Kathryn and Robert Altman's Malibu residence. P. Goldberger. il pors *Architectural Digest* 46:120-5+ Jl '89
Breaking the code [Chatham House; cover story] P. M. Sachner. il *Architectural Record* 177:100-5 mid-Ap '89
Capricious collections by the shore [S. Chase's Del Mar beach house] M. Webb. il *Architectural Digest* 46:244-9 My '89
David Rockwood: a steel-and-glass bay-front house in Portland. D. Gantenbein. il por *Architectural Digest* 46:72-7 Ag '89
Double standards [Walter Chatham's Seaside, Fla. beach house] C. Vogel. il *The New York Times Magazine* p56-7 Ap 30 '89
It's an easy-going all-year retreat [Stinson Beach, Calif.] il *Sunset (Central West edition)* 183:96-7 O '89
Long Island symmetry: reworking a designer's 1920s residence in Southampton [home of A. E. Smith] P. Warner. il *Architectural Digest* 46:138-43 Jl '89
Maui vacation house is a five-unit compound. il *Sunset (Central West edition)* 182:80 Ja '89
Nassau via New York [homes of I. and T. A. Kramer decorated by Mark Hampton] Suzy. il *Architectural Digest* 46:142-51 Mr '89
Newlyweds Ian Irving and Carolina Estrada have transformed a small house at the shore with big-impact color. J. Etra. il pors *Vogue* 179:260-1+ Ag '89
On Stinson Beach: Pacific spaces for John and Elinor McGuire [house designed by Joseph Esherick and decorated by Andrew Delfino] J. Chatfield-Taylor. il pors *Architectural Digest* 46:206-13 My '89
Planned for privacy on a shallow beach lot [Washington State] il *Sunset (Central West edition)* 183:124 O '89
Robert A. M. Stern: new interpretation of the shingle style on Long Island. K. Andersen. il por *Architectural Digest* 46:66-71+ Ag '89
Seaside sensation [cover story] il *Home Mechanix* 86:44-8+ Ap '89
Spacious, bold on a very tight beach lot. il *Sunset (Central West edition)* 183:122 O '89
Vacation cottage with seaside lounging in mind [Washington State] il *Sunset (Central West edition)* 183:118+ O '89
Wedging it in [Hermosa Beach, Calif.] il *Sunset (Central West edition)* 183:106-7 O '89

BEACH BOYS (MUSICAL GROUP)
'Pet' project due on CD. J. Ressner. il *Rolling Stone* p23 Mr 23 '89

BEACH EQUIPMENT
The toys of summer. B. Young. il *Rolling Stone* p157+ Jl 13-27 '89

BEACH EROSION See Coast changes

BEACH VOLLEYBALL
Beach volleyball nets big bucks. J. D. Reed. il *Time* 134:71 Ag 28 '89

BEACHAM, STEPHANIE
Photographs and photography
Stream of consciousness—"Sister Kate". G. Bernstein. il *Petersen's Photographic Magazine* 18:10 O '89

BEACHES
See also
National seashores
Weekending at eight great beaches. D. Butwin. il *Working Woman* 14:127-8 Je '89
Anecdotes, facetiae, satire, etc.
Post-baby beach days. J. Leonard. il *Parents* 64:90-2 Jl '89
Sanitation
Beachless summer [Atlantic beaches fouled by waste] C. V. Reynolds. il *Discover* 10:38 Ja '89
Hype tide [medical waste and beaches] A. Burdick. *The New Republic* 200:15-18 Je 12 '89
Medical waste just one threat to beaches. il *National Parks* 63:9-10 Ja/F '89
Atlantic States
Beachless summer [beaches fouled by waste] C. V. Reynolds. il *Discover* 10:38 Ja '89
Hype tide [medical waste and beaches] A. Burdick. *The New Republic* 200:15-18 Je 12 '89

BEACHES—Atlantic States—*cont.*
Medical waste just one threat to beaches. il *National Parks* 63:9-10 Ja/F '89

California
See also
Huntington Beach (Calif.)

Caribbean region
Best beaches in the Caribbean. J. Anthony. il *Changing Times* 43:112-17 D '89

Florida
The inundation of our coastlines [effects of rising sea level on south Florida] H. R. Wanless. bibl il maps *Sea Frontiers* 35:264-71 S/O '89

Long Island (N.Y.)
Some Long Island seashells. H. Foglino and R. Foglino. il *The Conservationist* 44:22-5 Jl/Ag '89

Massachusetts
See also
Cape Cod National Seashore (Mass.)
Revere Beach (Mass.)

South Africa
Stopping apartheid on the beach. il *U.S. News & World Report* 107:14+ N 27 '89

South Carolina
Back to the beach [Myrtle Beach] C. F. Wall. il *Southern Living* 24:116+ My '89

South Padre Island (Tex.)
South Padre's magic shrinking beaches. D. Chaney. il *The Saturday Evening Post* 261:84-7 O '89

Washington (State)
Oil spill taints Olympic beaches [Olympic National Park] il *National Parks* 63:8-9 Mr/Ap '89

Yucatan (Mexico: State)
Beachcombing for Yucatán's treasures. il map *Sunset (Central West edition)* 182:64+ Mr '89

BEACHES [film] See Motion picture reviews—Single works
BEACON LANES (NEW YORK, N.Y.)
End of the lane. S. Goldberg. il *New York* 22:28 D 11 '89
BEACONS
See also
Lighthouses
BEACONS OF JAZZ AWARDS
Buck Clayton, Roy Eldridge. C. Deffaa. il pors *Down Beat* 56:48 F '89
BEADWORK
Fancy footwork [beaded sneakers by M. Lightfeather] J. O'Dwyer. il por *Americana* 16:6 Ja/F '89
BEAGLES (DOGS)
A gun-shy cure that works [using tape recordings on beagles] L. Mueller. il *Outdoor Life* 184:30+ O '89
Littlebit's first hunt [cottontails] B. Tarrant. il *Field & Stream* 94:110+ N '89
BEAL, DOONE
Gourmet holidays: a corner of Provence. il map *Gourmet* 49:44-9+ Jl '89
Nevis. il map *Gourmet* 49:60-3+ Mr '89
Vence. il map *Gourmet* 49:86-91+ Ap '89
BEAL, EILEEN
Mr. Cowan's pottery: how one man's vision shaped a generation of potters. il por *Antiques & Collecting Hobbies* 94:55-7+ O '89
BEALL, CYNTHIA
(jt. auth) See Goldstein, Melvyn C., and Beall, Cynthia
BEAMS, ATOMIC *See* Atomic beams
BEAMS, ELECTRON *See* Electron beams
BEAMS, ION *See* Ion bombardment
BEANS
See also
Cooking—Vegetables
Soybeans
About shell beans. S. Pacher. il *The Mother Earth News* 120:26-8+ N/D '89
About snap beans. S. Pacher. il *The Mother Earth News* 118:24-5+ Jl/Ag '89
Bean bounty [growing dried beans; cover story] B. Keough. il *Organic Gardening* 36:30-2+ F '89
Cut your cholesterol 30 points in 30 days [eating oat bran and beans; research by James W. Anderson] A. Roblin. il *Prevention (Emmaus, Pa.)* 41:36-7+ F '89
Full of beans . . . and better for it [beneficial properties of antinutrients; research by Lilian U. Thompson] R. Green. il *Health (New York, N.Y.)* 21:58-61 D '89
New genes for complete-protein beans [research by Samuel Sun] I. Wickelgren. *Science News* 135:300 My 13 '89
BEANS, CANNED
Baked beans. il *Consumer Reports* 54:231-4 D '89
Baked beans. il *Consumer Reports* 54:14-17 Ja '89
BEAR, MARK F.
(jt. auth) See Dudek, Serena M., and Bear, Mark F.
THE BEAR [film] See Motion picture reviews—Single works
BEAR HUNTING
The bear guardian [Minnesota] P. M. Leschak. il *Outdoor Life* 184:54-5+ Jl '89
Bear tales [cover story] H. V. Stent. il *Outdoor Life* 183:72-3+ Ja '89
Bears by invitation [black bears; cover story] M. Strandlund. il *Outdoor Life* 184:82-3+ N '89

Bears on your own [black bears] J. E. Churchill. il *Outdoor Life* 183:80-1+ Ap '89
Fair chase bears. J. Barsness. il *Field & Stream* 93:62-3+ Ap '89
Heroes, bears and true baloney. J. Skow. il *Time* 134:122 N 13 '89
BEAR, STEARNS & CO. INC.
'Ace' Greenberg tries to trade up. B. Nussbaum. il por *Business Week* p120-4 Mr 13 '89
A bear in the ring and a bull on Wall Street, Leland Hardy is a broker with a convincing pitch. A. Abrahams. il pors *People Weekly* 32:109-10 S 18 '89
He's bullish on boxing [boxer and account executive L. Hardy] il por *Sports Illustrated* 71:8 Jl 3 '89
BEARD, GEOFFREY W.
Grinling Gibbons. bibl f il por *Antiques* 135:1444-55 Je '89
BEARD, JAMES
(jt. auth) See Albright, David, and Beard, James
BEARD, JAMES S., AND LOFGREN, GARY E.
Effect of water on the composition of partial melts of greenstone and amphibolite. bibl f il *Science* 244:195-7 Ap 14 '89
BEARDS

Anecdotes, facetiae, satire, etc.
Big new contest! E. Zern. il *Field & Stream* 93:140 Mr '89
Exit laughing. E. Zern. il *Field & Stream* 94:117 Je '89
More beard stuff. E. Zern. il *Field & Stream* 94:168 S '89
More beard stuff! E. Zern. il *Field & Stream* 94:104 Jl '89
BEARINGS (MACHINERY)
See also
Barden Corp.
Magnetic suspension
Trucks—Bearings
BEARS
See also
Pandas
Polar bears
Audubon Wildlife Adventures: Grizzly Bears [computer program] T. A. Summers. il *Home Office Computing* 7:69 Jl '89
Bare facts about bear acts. R. Cheek. il *Field & Stream* 93:62-3+ F '89
Bear of the clouds [effects of deforestation on the Latin American spectacled bear] P. Steinhart. il map *Audubon* 91:92-4+ Jl '89
Bear tales [cover story] H. V. Stent. il *Outdoor Life* 183:72-3+ Ja '89
End of the line for French bears? J. Mills. il *International Wildlife* 19:4-11 Ja/F '89
Home, sweet-smelling home [homing in black bears] L. L. Rogers. il *Natural History* p60-7 S '89
It's a good thing McNeil's big bears get plenty to eat [work of L. Aumiller with brown bears in Alaska's McNeil River State Game Sanctuary] B. Norton. il pors *Smithsonian* 20:56-60+ Ap '89
Sleeping beauties [hibernating black bears; study by Ralph Nelson and others] A. C. Revkin. bibl (p84) il *Discover* 10:62-5 Ap '89
Wildlife Adventures: Grizzly Bears [computer program] K. Sternberg. il *Compute!* 11:66 Jl '89
Yellowstone grizzlies: the new breed. P. Schullery. il *National Parks* 63:24-9+ N/D '89

Food and feeding
Please don't eat the trees [damage caused by black bears in the commercial forests of the Northwest] B. J. Bashin. il *Sierra* 74:22-4 Jl/Ag '89

Photographs and photography
Leap of faith [brown bear catching sockeye salmon] J. Foott. il *Natural History* p112-13 O '89
BEARS, TOY See Teddy bears
BEARS IN MOTION PICTURES
Animal magnetism [The bear] B. D. Johnson. il *Maclean's* 102:94+ O 30 '89
The bear facts. il *Time* 134:97 O 30 '89
It's a grizzly story, but Bart the filmmaking bear is clawing his way to the top [star of the movie The bear] I. Lacher. il *People Weekly* 32:87-8 N 6 '89
Quest for fur [training bears for J.-J. Annaud's film The bear] A. Thompson. il por *Film Comment* 25:2+ S/O '89
Sneak preview [J.-J. Annaud's use of live bears in The bear] T. Skari. il *Life* 12:89-91 Spr '89
BEARSE, AMANDA
about
Four earrings in one ear. J. Marion. il pors *TV Guide* 37:20 Jl 8-14 '89
BÉART, EMMANUELLE
about
Offbeat sex appeal. M. Matousek. pors *Harper's Bazaar* 122:54+ Ap '89
BEASLEY, PHOEBE
about
Newest 'in' artist is tops in two fields. H. Nipson. il pors *Ebony* 44:128-30+ O '89

BEASLEY, WILLIAM HOWARD, III
about
Bad news for Beasley. R. Reiff. il por *Forbes* 143:180 Je
12 '89
BEASTIE BOYS (MUSICAL GROUP)
The Beasties: def, not dumb [release of Paul's Boutique]
D. Handelman. il *Rolling Stone* p89-90 Ag 10 '89
License renewed. F. Goodman. il *Rolling Stone* p19 Je 15
'89
BEAT CULTURE
On the road to nowhere [J. Kerouac's On the road] S.
Birkerts. il *Harper's* 279:74-6 Jl '89
BEATHARD, BOBBY
about
A season at the beach. il por *Sports Illustrated* 71:125 S
11 '89
BEATIFICATION
Catholics and Jews: can we bridge the abyss? [Holocaust
martyr E. Stein; adaptation of address, October 16, 1988]
S. M. Batzdorff. *America* 160:223-4+ Mr 11 '89
BEATLES
Fixing a hole [unreleased recordings] J. Ressner. il *Rolling
Stone* p20 F 9 '89
The second coming [excerpt from Beatles '64] A. J. S. Rayl.
il *Rolling Stone* p110-17 Jl 13-27 '89
Telling the children how it was. A. Fotheringham. il *Maclean's*
102:56 F 27 '89
Tracking the Beatles [book by M. Lewisohn] J. Ressner.
il *Rolling Stone* p15-17 F 9 '89
BEATNIKS *See* Beat culture
BEATRICE, PRINCESS OF YORK, 1988-
about
For her public, the Princess shows three new teeth and
a stiff lower lip, but don't worry—Bea's happy. il por
People Weekly 31:124 My 8 '89
A new peek at two princesses provides royal watchers some
relief from the blahs. S. Schindehette. il pors *People Weekly*
31:64-6 Ap 10 '89
Queen Mum turns 89 as Baby Bea hits the big one. M.
H. J. Farrell. il pors *People Weekly* 32:40-2 Ag 21 '89
With a few tears and a splash of the river Jordan, England's
littlest Princess is christened. M. Dougherty. il pors *People
Weekly* 31:44-5 Ja 9 '89
BEATRICE COMPANY
Has the Beatrice LBO gone pffft? C. J. Loomis. il *Fortune*
120:113+ Jl 31 '89
BEATRICE M. TINSLEY PRIZE *See* Tinsley Prize
BEATTIE, ANN
What was mine [story] il *Esquire* 112:220-2+ N '89
BEATTIE, MELODY
about
Melody Beattie helps anguished readers kick the dependency
habit. J. D. Reed. il pors *People Weekly* 32:89-91 Ag
7 '89
BEATTY, J. KELLY
SETI's guiding light. il *Omni (New York, N.Y.)* 11:24 Mr
'89
BEATTY, JACK
Brigadoon, USA. il *The Atlantic* 264:102-6 S '89
The exorbitant anachronism. il *The Atlantic* 263:40-2+ Je
'89
Reagan's gift. il *The Atlantic* 263:58-62+ F '89
BEATTY, PATRICIA
Writing the historical novel for young readers. *The Writer*
102:17-19 Mr '89
BEAU BRUMMEL (FIRM)
Beau Brummel meets the beau monde. H. Sterne. il
Gentlemen's Quarterly 59:78+ Mr '89
BEAU GESTE (NEW YORK, N.Y.: RESTAURANT) *See* New
York (N.Y.)—Restaurants, nightclubs, bars, etc.
BEAUBIEN, MICHAEL
Saving my marriage. por *Essence* 19:6 Mr '89
BEAUCHAMP, BENOIT, AND OTHERS
Cretaceous cold-seep communities and methane-derived car-
bonates in the Canadian Arctic. bibl f il map *Science*
244:53-6 Ap 7 '89
BEAUCHEMIN, TIMOTHY A., AND KRAMER, ORIN S.
Auto insurance reform for consumers [cover story] il
Consumers' Research Magazine 72:11-15 O '89
BEAUDOIN, LAURENT
about
Building for the future with a worldwide view. D. Jenish.
il por *Maclean's* 102:20-1 D 25 '89
A down-home hero. D. Burke. il por *Maclean's* 102:30+
S 11 '89
Flying high with the little engine that could. P. C. Newman.
il *Maclean's* 102:38 Mr 27 '89
BEAUFORT, CAROLINE, DUCHESS OF
about
Badminton Court. P. Kinmonth. il por *Vogue* 179:426-35
O '89
BEAUFORT (S.C.)
Cemeteries
See also
Beaufort National Cemetery (S.C.)

BEAUFORT NATIONAL CEMETERY (S.C.)
Black Civil War heroes in S.C. reburied there with military
honors ceremony. D. M. Cheers. il *Jet* 76:22-4 Je 19
'89
BEAUJOLAIS (WINE) *See* Wine
BEAUMONT, JOSÉ F.
Connecting to the continent. il *World Press Review* 36:79
O '89
BEAUMONT (TEX.)
Education
Attracting bright adolescents to teaching careers [program
developed by Lamar University and Beaumont School
District] M. J. Cooper and others. il *Phi Delta Kappan*
70:566-7 Mr '89
Galleries and museums
See also
Babe Didrikson Zaharias Memorial Museum (Beaumont,
Tex.)
BEAUTICIANS
See also
Hairstylists
Beauty's power elite [Paris salons] A. Bogart. il *Harper's
Bazaar* 122:118-19+ Ja '89
BEAUTICONTROL COSMETICS
See Dick and Jinger sell. W. P. Barrett. il pors *Forbes*
144:48-9 Ag 7 '89
BEAUTY *See* Aesthetics
BEAUTY, PERSONAL
See also
Baths
Beauty shops
Body image
Cosmetics
Exercise
Hair
Hairstyling
Hand—Care
Leg—Care
Lips
Makeup
Manicuring
Pedicure
Powder (Face, toilet, etc.)
Skin—Care and hygiene
10 little luxuries. il *Redbook* 173:136-7 O '89
10 ways to make (not break) your look. il *Essence* 19:62-5
Ap '89
15 little holiday beauty triumphs. il *Glamour* 87:194-9 D
'89
All-star holiday beauty secrets. il *McCall's* 117:15+ D '89
American beauty [C. Crawford] B. Sherman. il pors *Harper's
Bazaar* 122:58-63+ Jl '89
America's 10 most beautiful women [cover story; special
section] il *Harper's Bazaar* 122:158+ S '89
Basic black [black women] il *Teen* 33:48 N '89
Beauty & fashion journal. See issues of Ladies' Home Journal
beginning January 1988
Beauty & health report. S. Young. See issues of Glamour
Beauty and fashion makeovers. C. Straley and W. Gavin.
il *Parents* 64:150-2+ S '89
Beauty answers. See issues of Vogue
Beauty at a fair price [B. Dautresme, general manager of
L'Oréal SA] il pors *Harper's Bazaar* 122:192-3+ Mr '89
Beauty binge for two [moms and daughters] il *Teen* 33:66-7
D '89
Beauty escapes. il *Glamour* 87:260-3 Mr '89
Beauty heartbreakers. il *Mademoiselle* 95:236-9 Ap '89
Beauty notebook. See issues of Good Housekeeping
Beauty overkill. il *Glamour* 87:246-9 My '89
Beauty playoffs. il *Teen* 33:76-9 Ap '89
Beauty Q & A. See issues of Mademoiselle
Beauty Q and A. See issues of Seventeen beginning October
1987
Beauty questions. See issues of Glamour
Beauty secrets of the elite [Britain's blue bloods] P. Barron.
il *Harper's Bazaar* 122:50+ S '89
Beauty smarts [tips for summer] il *Ladies' Home Journal*
106:198-202 My '89
Beauty talk. See issues of Mademoiselle
Beauty time-savers. C. Straley. il *Parents* 64:158-61 My '89
Beauty workshop. See issues of Mademoiselle
Beautystyle. A. Robinson and D. Schefer. See issues of Vogue
beginning July 1985 through July 1988
Bedtime beauties. il *Teen* 33:88-9 Ap '89
The best in beauty [special section] il *Harper's Bazaar*
122:178-91+ Ap '89
Better than ever [winners of the "I look great for my age"
contest] il *Ladies' Home Journal* 106:32+ Ap '89
Big on beauty (and fashion!). il *Good Housekeeping* 209:148-51
O '89
Body be beautiful/89 [special section] il *Good Housekeeping*
208:89+ My '89
Boost your beauty score. il *Teen* 33:64-5 F '89
Boost your romantic potential. il *McCall's* 116:36-9 F '89
Care for the caretaker [beauty treatments at Gurney's Inn
in Montauk, N.Y.] D. Raskin. il *American Health* 8:90+
Ap '89

BEAUTY, PERSONAL—*cont.*
A day in the life of the American beauty. L. J. Johnson. il *Ladies' Home Journal* 106:127-34 Mr '89
Dear beauty editor. See issues of 'Teen
The doctors' guide to beauty [panel discussion] L. J. Johnson. il *Ladies' Home Journal* 106:126-32 F '89
Easy summer beauty. il *Glamour* 87:210-15 Je '89
Everything you always wanted to know about beauty and fashion. L. J. Johnson. il *Ladies' Home Journal* 106:149-56 O '89
Facing up to the 90's [views of K. Lagerfeld] L. Wells. il por *The New York Times Magazine* p66-7 S 24 '89
Flourishes. L. Wells. il *The New York Times Magazine* p42 Ja 8 '89
Follow that girl! 24 stop-traffic beauty tips from real, live women. il *Mademoiselle* 95:204-7 O '89
For your eyes only? The beauty secrets men love—or loathe. E. Welty. il *Mademoiselle* 95:178-81 F '89
Future beauty. S. Lord. il *Vogue* 179:406-9 O '89
Get a rich girl's looks (on a working girl's pay). il *Mademoiselle* 95:110-13 Ja '89
Get glowing! il *Teen* 33:72-3 Je '89
Good-bye '80s, hello '90s [special section] il *Ladies' Home Journal* 106:236-46 N '89
Grooming guide: his & hers [black men and women] L. Norment. il *Ebony* 44:46+ Ap '89
Harvard makeovers. L. Barrett. il *Essence* 20:76-9 Ag '89
Hayley Mills—a healthy attitude. J. Jones. il pors *Redbook* 172:12+ F '89
Healthy, sexy beauty. il *Glamour* 87:246-51 O '89
Holiday health and beauty guide [special section] il *Ladies' Home Journal* 106:39-40+ D '89
How to look younger . . . now! [women in their 30s, 40s, and 50s] il *McCall's* 116:19-24 Ag '89
Images. See issues of Vogue beginning November 1987
Look who's looking good [stars from '60s sitcoms; special section] J. Jones. il *Redbook* 172:85-91 Ja '89
Looking great in bed. il *Essence* 19:78-9+ F '89
Makeover of the month. See issues of Good Housekeeping
Makeup makeovers. il *McCall's* 116:19-22 My '89
Malibu U. [special section] il *Teen* 33:82-3+ My '89
Models' secrets. il *Essence* 19:84-6 F '89
Mothers & daughters [special section] il *Harper's Bazaar* 122:154-65+ O '89
Moving from the East to the West, as Claire Scovell found out, doesn't just mean a change of climate. C. Scovell. il *Vogue* 179:162-4 Ag '89
Neat tricks [minimalist grooming] S. Shapiro. il *Ms.* 18:43-4+ O '89
New school . . . new you [makeovers] il *Teen* 33:106-7 Ag '89
The new top models. il *Glamour* 87:252-7 My '89
New year, new you. il *Seventeen* 48:64-5 Ja '89
Over-40 special [cover story; special issue] il *Harper's Bazaar* 122:28+ Ag '89
Please make me over! See occasional issues of Glamour
Prosaic to professional [makeover for S. Jungstedt] G. Lee. il pors *Harper's Bazaar* 122:22+ Je '89
Real-life beauty. A. G. Britton. il por *American Health* 8:110-11 Mr '89
The right look: you can have it. il *Redbook* 173:116-19 Jl '89
Salon secrets. il *Good Housekeeping* 209:100-3 Ag '89
School beauty rules [what's in, what's out] il *Teen* 33:114-15 Ag '89
School-day smart to after-dark spark. il *Teen* 33:72-5 Mr '89
Seductively simple [black women] il *Essence* 20:68-71 S '89
Sitting pretty [Forester Sisters] il *Redbook* 174:114-17 N '89
Spa splurge. H. Platt. il *Seventeen* 48:92-8 Ja '89
Summer beauty myths. il *McCall's* 116:23-6 Je '89
Take your looks from day to night. il *Seventeen* 48:122-7 N '89
'Teen's great-looks guide. il *Teen* 33:77-84 Ag '89
Ten back-to-school makeovers [Fair Lawn, N.J. teachers] il *McCall's* 116:21-4 S '89
The ten most beautiful black women of 1989. il *Ebony* 44:146-8+ O '89
Think soft! il *Mademoiselle* 95:190-3 O '89
The top 10 beauty foods. il *Mademoiselle* 95:202-5 N '89
Top 10 summer beauty boosters. il *Teen* 33:64-5 Je '89
Trade secrets: look your business best. il *Harper's Bazaar* 122:53+ Mr '89
What if . . .? [makeovers of celebrities] L. Wells. il *The New York Times Magazine* p85-91 S 17 '89
Your beauty game plan. il *Teen* 33:70-1 Je '89
You're on: diary of a 14-hour day. N. Malkin. il *Working Woman* 14:156+ O '89

Children
Sexism and summer camp or: Am I crazy??!! [young girl's appearance anxiety] E. Berg. il *Parents* 64:86-8 Ag '89
Economic aspects
Low-cost beauty steals. il *Teen* 33:56-7 Jl '89
Exhibitions
See also
International Beauty Show

History
For beauty's sake. il *'Teen* 33:20 Je '89
Men
Damn! [morning survival guide] A. Tardio. il *Gentlemen's Quarterly* 59:466-74 S '89
Grooming guide: his & hers [black men and women] L. Norment. il *Ebony* 44:46+ Ap '89
Grooming the groom. A. Tardio. il *Gentlemen's Quarterly* 59:194-5 Je '89
Mission impossible: boyfriend makeover. il *Seventeen* 48:80-5 Jl '89
Psychological aspects
Beauty and the beasts [feminism and standards of beauty] R. E. Tyrrell. il *The American Spectator* 22:10 O '89
Face to face with the new me [makeovers] D. Sobel. il *The New York Times Magazine* p26+ Ap 9 '89
Nobody's perfect [special section] il *Harper's Bazaar* 122:82-103+ Ja '89
Pushing a feature. J. Shields. il *Vogue* 179:163-4 Ap '89
Should you change your looks for a lover? D. Heyn. *Mademoiselle* 95:54 Ja '89
BEAUTY AND THE BEAST [television program] See Television program reviews—Single works
BEAUTY CONTESTS
See also
Miss America Pageant
Miss Teenage America Pageant
Miss Universe Pageant
Campus queens at black colleges. il *Ebony* 44:54+ Ap '89
Daphne Maxwell Reid still bitter over snub as beauty queen at Northwestern U. il pors *Jet* 77:25 N 13 '89
History
Let Tom Edison be the judge. il *U.S. News & World Report* 106:13 Je 5 '89
Soviet Union
Here she comes, Miss U.S.S.R.! And Yulia Sukhanova even wins a fight to visit the decadent West. H. Shapiro. il pors *People Weekly* 32:42-3 S 25 '89
BEAUTY CONTESTS IN MOTION PICTURES
Beth's beauties [Miss Firecracker; cover story] K. Jaehne. il pors *Film Comment* 25:9-12+ My/Je '89
BEAUTY OPERATORS See Beauticians
BEAUTY PRODUCTS See Cosmetics
BEAUTY QUEENS See Beauty contests
BEAUTY RESORTS See Health resorts, watering places, etc.
BEAUTY SHOPS
See also
Beauticians
Beauty's power elite [Paris salons] A. Bogart. il *Harper's Bazaar* 122:118-19+ Ja '89
In the hands of a pro [services offered by nail salons] L. Daigneault. il *Health (New York, N.Y.)* 21:67 Ag '89
Is your nail salon safe? A. P. Lynn. il *Glamour* 87:55 N '89
When every minute counts, the salon that can save you time is worth every penny. L. Cunliffe. il *Vogue* 179:202+ O '89
World-class skin care [salons] il *Harper's Bazaar* 122:182-5 Ap '89
Advertising
The ad says, "hair" [photography for hairstyling salon] U. Puga. il *Petersen's Photographic Magazine* 18:80-1 Je '89
Chain and franchise operations
See also
Charlene's (Firm)
BEAUVAIS, EDWARD R.
about
America West has the hub—now it needs the spokes. E. Schine. il por *Business Week* p104 D 18 '89
America West is flying high again—but for how long? S. Toy. il por *Business Week* p41-2 F 6 '89
BEAUVAIS, STEVE
Pigs in sheep's clothing: how to spot a secret sexist. il *Glamour* 87:116+ Je '89
THE BEAVER (FICTIONAL CHARACTER)
The Beaver. il *People Weekly* 31 Special Issue:68 Summ '89
BEAVER CREEK (COLO.: RESORT) See Resorts—Colorado
BEAVERKILL RIVER (N.Y.)
Welcome, world, to Trout Town U.S.A., where all the flies are fit to be tied [flyfishing] J. Friedman. il *People Weekly* 32:92-4+ Jl 3 '89
BEAVERS
The world of Lily Pond [Harriman State Park; condensation] H. Ryden. il *Reader's Digest* 135:189-92+ Ag '89
BEBE MILLER AND COMPANY
Bebe Miller comes home. E. Zimmer. il pors *Dance Magazine* 63:34-8 D '89
BECK, AARON T.
Love is never enough. *Reader's Digest* 134:57-8+ Ap '89
When your spouse wants to argue [condensed from Love is never enough] il *Reader's Digest* 135:101-4 S '89
BECK, CHARLES
Discover dahlias. il *Organic Gardening* 36:54-5 O '89
BECK, JEFF
about
Guitar slingers shoot it out. T. Drozdowski. il pors *Rolling Stone* p28 N 30 '89

BECK, JOE
about
Joe Beck. B. Milkowski. il por *Down Beat* 56:15 D '89
BECK, MARILYN
Getting even . . . Hollywood-style. il *TV Guide* 37:4-6+ Je 10-16 '89
Hollywood's most outrageous homes. il *TV Guide* 37:10-12+ Ag 12-18 '89
What TV doesn't tell you about the Oscars [cover story] il *TV Guide* 37:4-7 Mr 25-31 '89
BECK, MELINDA
The bacteria that hate women. il *Ladies' Home Journal* 106:118-19+ Ag '89
BECK, NOELLE
about
Why didn't Chevy chase her? J. Marion. il por *TV Guide* 37:25 Ag 12-18 '89
BECK, PETER J.
Whose island story? il map *History Today* 39:8-11 F '89
BECKER, BORIS
about
Boom Boom [cover story] C. Kirkpatrick. il pors *Sports Illustrated* 71:22-7 S 18 '89
Break point for Becker [cover story] N. Amdur. il pors *World Tennis* 36:32-5 Mr '89
Datelines. C. Shmerler. il por *World Tennis* 37:58-60 D '89
Mr. Kramer and Mr. Becker. H. W. Wind. il *The New Yorker* 65:85-96+ O 16 '89
The promised land [cover story] S. Flink. il pors *World Tennis* 37:16+ N '89
Wunderbar! A. Wolff. il pors *Sports Illustrated* 71:14-21 Jl 17 '89
BECKER, DAN
Solar power supply. il *Radio-Electronics* 60:47-51 Ag '89
Wireless security system. il *Radio-Electronics* 60:47-52+ Ap '89
BECKER, ELIZABETH
Killing fields II. *The New Republic* 200:10+ Ja 2 '89
The progress of peace in Cambodia. bibl f *Current History* 88:169-72+ Ap '89
BECKER, GARY STANLEY, 1930-
Economic viewpoint. See issues of Business Week
BECKER, HAROLD
about
Sea of love [film] Reviews
Commonweal 116:565 O 20 '89. P. D. Baumann
National Review il 41:61-2 N 10 '89. J. Simon
New York il 22:70-1 S 18 '89. D. Denby
The New Yorker il 65:100+ S 18 '89. T. Rafferty
Newsweek il 114:81 S 18 '89. D. Ansen
People Weekly il 32:14 S 18 '89. R. Novak
Rolling Stone il p35 O 5 '89. P. Travers
BECKER, JAMEE See Guilbert, Jamee Becker
BECKER, JASPER
Toward a new Asian equation. *World Press Review* 36:12-13 My '89
BECKER, MICHAEL M.
about
Playing for real. N. Hass. il pors *New York* 22:60-2+ D 11 '89
BECKER, NORMAN
Homeowners' clinic. See issues of Popular Mechanics beginning June 1984
BECKER, PETER L., AND OTHERS
Regulation of calcium concentration in voltage-clamped smooth muscle cells. bibl f il *Science* 244:211-14 Ap 14 '89
BECKER, THOMAS W.
Industry's stake in space education. *Ad Astra* 1:13 Ja '89
BECKER, ARNIE (FICTIONAL CHARACTER) See Arnie Becker (Fictional character)
BECKETT, EDWIN H. A.
Maturing NATO could benefit by ending cooperative military procurement barriers. por *Aviation Week & Space Technology* 130:73-4 Ap 3 '89
BECKETT-YOUNG, KATHLEEN
Inventing spring's colors. il *Health (New York, N.Y.)* 21:56-63 Mr '89
BECKMAN, STAN, 1931-
about
Stan Beckman. D. C. Hines. il por *American Artist* 53:80-5+ S '89
BECKMAN, WILLIAM
about
A conditional paradise. C. Belz. il pors *Art in America* 77:136-41 Ja '89
BECKWITH, BURNHAM P. (BURNHAM PUTNAM), 1904-
Eight forecasts for U.S. banking. il por *The Futurist* 23:27-33 Mr/Ap '89
BECKWITH, KAREN, 1950-
about
. . . and bring the kids. L. Rosch. il pors *Working Woman* 14:118-21+ Je '89
BED AND BREAKFAST ACCOMMODATIONS
B&Bs go upscale. P. Plawin. il *Changing Times* 43:71-4 Ag '89

An expert offers the ABCs of getting into the B&B biz [interview with P. Hardy] J. Wuorio. il por *Money* 18:18 D '89
To B&B or not to B&B [apprenticeship program at Wildwood Inn, Ware, Mass.] C. McLaughlin. il *New Choices for the Best Years* 29:10-11 Mr '89
Urban B&Bs. il *New Choices for the Best Years* 29:18 O '89
BED LINENS See Bedding
BED WETTING See Urine—Incontinence
BEDARD, PATRICK
[Column] See issues of Car and Driver
Indy: families of the 500. il *Sports Illustrated* 70:51+ My 8 '89
Two's company, three's a pedestrian. il *Esquire* 112:64 S '89
Weenie with a black belt. il *Esquire* 111:60 Mr '89
BEDARD, ROGER L.
Challenges to the field: working together. *Design for Arts in Education* 91:35-7 N/D '89
BEDDING
See also
Blankets, Electric
Coverlets
Mattress pads
Pillow cases
Quilts and quilting
Bedtime story [children's beds] N. Wing. il *Parents* 64:150-2+ Ap '89
BEDDOW, MARGERY
New hips for a veteran dancer. il pors *Dance Magazine* 63:46-50 S '89
BEDE, JIM
about
Bede ayes. G. Baxter. il por *Flying* 116:108+ D '89
Homebuilt machbuster [cover story] W. Garvey. il *Popular Mechanics* 166:68-71 D '89
BEDFORD, SYBILLE
Une vie de château [story] *The New Yorker* 65:38-48 F 20 '89
BEDFORD (N.Y.)
Historic houses, sites, etc.
Belle Epoque weekends [1918 carriage house designed by Jean-Paul Beaujard] A. Tapert. il *House & Garden* 161:128-37 N '89
BEDFORD-STUYVESANT (NEW YORK, N.Y.) IN MOTION PICTURES
Do the right thing: a jarring look at racism. J. M. Wall. *The Christian Century* 106:739-40 Ag 16-23 '89
Doing the controversial thing [S. Lee's film Do the right thing] A. P. Sanoff. por *U.S. News & World Report* 107:51 Jl 10 '89
How hot is too hot? [S. Lee's Do the right thing; special section] il *Newsweek* 114:64-6 Jl 3 '89
Insight to riot [S. Lee's Do the right thing] D. Handelman. il por *Rolling Stone* p104-5+ Jl 13-27 '89
Spike Lee explores racial conflict in 'Do the right thing' [cover story] T. S. Moore. il pors *Jet* 76:36-9 Jl 10 '89
Spike Lee inflames the critics with a film he swears is The right thing. J. S. Kunen. il pors *People Weekly* 32:67-8 Jl 10 '89
Spike Lee replies: "Say it ain't so, Joe" [discussion of June 26, 1989 article, Spiked?] J. Klein. il por *New York* 22:6 Jl 17 '89
Spike Lee's Bed-Stuy BBQ [Do the right thing; interview] M. Glicksman. il pors *Film Comment* 25:12-16+ Jl/Ag '89
Spiked? [effect of S. Lee's film Do the right thing on D. Dinkins's mayoral campaign] J. Klein. il pors *New York* 22:14-15 Je 26 '89
Spike's riot [S. Lee; cover story] P. Orenstein. il pors *Mother Jones* 14:32-5+ S '89
The world according to Spike Lee [Do the right thing; cover story] M. Morrison. por *National Review* 41:24-5 Ag 4 '89
BEDNARSKI, STANISLAW
about
The almost-perfect-market thesis. J. Clements. il por *Forbes* 143:150-1 F 6 '89
BEDOUINS
The importance of hugging [link between absence of childhood affection and violence in Bedouin society; excerpt from The Lucifer principle] H. Bloom. il *Omni (New York, N.Y.)* 11:30+ F '89
BEDQUILTS See Quilts and quilting
BEDROOM FURNITURE
See also
Beds
BEDROOMS
See also
Children's rooms
Guest rooms
White House (Washington, D.C.). Lincoln Bedroom
Bedtime stories. M. D. Glass. il *Ladies' Home Journal* 106:148-54 Mr '89
Bedtime story. D. L. Caringer. il *Better Homes and Gardens* 68:103-5 F '89

BEDROOMS—cont.

The best beds. C. Donovan. il *The New York Times Magazine* p88-92 N 12 '89

Dreamy bedrooms. il *Good Housekeeping* 208:102-9 F '89

Finishing a bedroom. il *Workbench* 45:54-5 S/O '89

Master bedroom over the garage. il *Sunset (Central West edition)* 182:144 Mr '89

Mini-wall with lights and bookshelves. il *Sunset (Central West edition)* 182:118 F '89

Remodeling made the master bedroom into a sunlit suite. il *Sunset (Central West edition)* 182:86-7 Ja '89

Sew-easy decorating. D. L. Caringer and R. E. Dittmer. il *Better Homes and Gardens* 67:35-7 Ag '89

Their new bedroom is an "executive suite". il *Sunset (Central West edition)* 182:172 Ap '89

View, storage, light . . . the stairwell is the key. il *Sunset (Central West edition)* 182:132 Je '89

Wardrobes and seats . . . built-ins were the answer. il *Sunset (Central West edition)* 182:156 My '89

BEDS

See also
Bedding
Cribs (Beds)
Murphy beds

Beds that slide out, swing down, or otherwise come out of hiding. il *Sunset (Central West edition)* 182:96+ Ja '89

Bedtime story. D. B. Cowin. il *House & Garden* 161:224-9 S '89

Bedtime story [children's beds] N. Wing. il *Parents* 64:150-2+ Ap '89

Crumbs in the covers [eating in bed] L. Wells. il *The New York Times Magazine* p99-100 N 12 '89

Great legs [coffee table and master bed] L. M. Dalsgaard. il *Home Mechanix* 85:48-52 Ja '89

Henry Ford slept here [constructing reproduction wicker bed for Ford Estate] K. P. Crombie. il *Workbench* 45:42-6 Mr/Ap '89

New products: bedside manners. il *Architectural Record* 177:114-15 mid-Ap '89

BEDSPREADS See Coverlets

BEDTIME

Smoothing out bedtime [young children] L. G. Katz. il *Parents* 64:191 Ap '89

Taming toddlers' tantrums [study by Lisa A. Adams and Vaughn I. Rickert] *Science News* 136:332 N 18 '89

BEDWELL, DON

Reflections on a tragedy. il *Travel Holiday* 172:96+ Ag '89

A tragic dilemma [discussion of August 1989 article, Reflections on a tragedy] il *Travel Holiday* 172:8 N '89

BEE, ANTHONY, D. 1989

about

Security manager for Guy dead following dispute with New Edition's crew member. il *Jet* 76:18 Jl 24 '89

BEE CULTURE

See also
American Beekeeping Federation

BEE-EATERS

Avian altruism [cover story] K. Fackelmann. *Science News* 135:364-5 Je 10 '89

BEE GEES (MUSICAL GROUP)

Bee Gees hope to break 'Fever' grip. A. White. il *Rolling Stone* p32-3 O 5 '89

The Bee Gees search for life after disco. C. Durkee. il *People Weekly* 32:36-41 Ag 7 '89

BEE STINGS See Insect bites and stings

BEEBA'S CREATIONS INC.

Is Beeba tailored for a takeover? G. G. Marcial. *Business Week* p98 S 11 '89

BEEBE, HERMAN K.

about

"Dad would make a deal with the devil". R. Woodbury. il por *Time* 133:71 F 20 '89

BEEBE, LUCIUS MORRIS, 1902-1966

about

Luscious Lucius. R. Merkin. il *Gentlemen's Quarterly* 59:195+ S '89

BEEBE, THOMAS P., JR., AND OTHERS

Direct observation of native DNA structures with the scanning tunneling microscope. bibl f il *Science* 243:370-2 Ja 20 '89

BEECH AIRCRAFT CORP.

Beech craftmasters. J. M. McClellan. *Flying* 116:26 Ap '89

Beech plans to boost production, introduces Model 350 Super King Air. E. H. Phillips. il *Aviation Week & Space Technology* 131:41-2 O 16 '89

Optimistic data, schedule blamed for Starship certification delays. E. H. Phillips. *Aviation Week & Space Technology* 131:30 D 4 '89

Starship 1 begins final tests to certify pneumatic deicers. E. H. Phillips. *Aviation Week & Space Technology* 130:105 Ja 2 '89

The Starship chronicles. J. M. McClellan. il *Flying* 116:56-60+ Mr '89

BEECH-NUT NUTRITION CORP.

Bad apples: in the executive suite [bogus apple juice case] il *Consumer Reports* 54:294-6 My '89

BEECHAM GROUP PLC

See also
SmithKline Beecham plc

SmithKline thinks Beecham can cure what ails it. J. Weber, Jr. and M. Maremont. il *Business Week* p22 Ap 17 '89

BEEF

See also
Cooking—Meat

An egg's an egg, but slightly less so [cholesterol levels] J. Silberner. il *U.S. News & World Report* 106:61 Je 5 '89

BEEF BOURGUIGNON See Stew

BEEF CATTLE See Cattle

BEEF CATTLE INDUSTRY See Cattle industry

BEEF GRADING See Meat—Grading

BEEF PROCESSING INDUSTRY See Meat industry

BEEF STEW See Stew

BEEHLER, BRUCE MCP.

The birds of paradise [cover story] bibl il map *Scientific American* 261:116-23 D '89

BEENE, GEOFFREY

about

The cultivated Beene. W. Goodman. il por *House & Garden* 161:88-95+ D '89

BEEPER PAGERS See Paging devices

BEER, JAKOB LIEBMANN See Meyerbeer, Giacomo, 1791-1864

BEER, LAWRENCE WARD, 1932-

The United States-Japan partnership [address, November 21, 1988] *Vital Speeches of the Day* 55:167-70 Ja 1 '89

BEER

See also
Brewing industry
Cooking—Beer
Stout (Beverage)

Beer from a stone [Samuel Smith's beer] W. Grimes. il *Esquire* 111:30 My '89

Fresh from the vat [tours of fine breweries] K. Zimmermann. il *Americana* 17:56-60 Jl/Ag '89

Physics lite [studies by C. F. Bohren] W. Sones. il por *Discover* 10:56-60 Ag '89

Tapping into the oat-bran market [Otto's Original Oat Bran Beer] il *Newsweek* 114:65 N 13 '89

These days, some like it dry. T. Segal. il *Business Week* p136 Ag 14 '89

This brew's for you. E. Fried. il *Black Enterprise* 20:84 Ag '89

Prices

A warning shot from the king of beers [Anheuser] J. F. Siler. il *Business Week* p124 D 18 '89

BEER CANS

Can overboard! [throwing beer cans into ocean from tuna fishing boat off Tahiti] C. Safina. il *Sea Frontiers* 35:384 N/D '89

The crowned heads of Britain in a can [new beer can for Guinness stout works like a keg tap] il *U.S. News & World Report* 107:19 Ag 21 '89

BEERS, C. DAVID

Storytelling and Native American CDAs. il *Children Today* 18:24-5 Mr/Ap '89

BEERS, DAVID

Master of disaster [cover story] il pors *Mother Jones* 14:28-9+ O '89

Rethinking suburbia: blueprints for a new kind of community. il *Utne Reader* p98 Mr/Ap '89

BEES

The apian way [genes linked to honeybee behavior] il *Discover* 10:6 Ja '89

Beekeepers gather for sweet talk. F. D. Cavinder. il *The Saturday Evening Post* 261:14 Ap '89

The big sting [Africanized honey bees] J. Alper. il *Health (New York, N.Y.)* 21:52-4+ Ap '89

Disco-bee [robot bee designed by Wolfgang H. Kirchner and Axel Michelsen] J. Horgan. *Scientific American* 260:31-2 Je '89

Freedom fighters [Sonoran Desert digger bees] J. Alcock. il *Natural History* p68-74 Mr '89

Hearing in honey bees: detection of air-particle oscillations. W. F. Towne and W. H. Kirchner. bibl f il *Science* 244:686-8 My 12 '89

Honey bees listen to the dance [research by William F. Towne] B. Bower. *Science News* 135:318 My 20 '89

Hormonal and genetic control of behavioral integration in honey bee colonies. G. E. Robinson and others. bibl f il *Science* 246:109-12 O 6 '89

New dancer in the hive [robot honeybee; cover story] R. Weiss. il *Science News* 136:282-3 O 28 '89

Stopping killer bees with Star Wars [Africanized honey bees] J. Schlefer. *Technology Review* 92:2 My/Je '89

Texans devise battle plan for bee invasion [Africanized honeybees] R. Weiss. *Science News* 136:389 D 16 '89

Anecdotes, facetiae, satire, etc.

Last word [Dragnet vs. killer bees] K. Thornock. il *Omni (New York, N.Y.)* 11:124 Mr '89

Diseases and pests

Attraction of the parasitic mite Varroa to the drone larvae of honey bees by simple aliphatic esters. Y. Le Conte and others. bibl f il *Science* 245:638-9 Ag 11 '89

BEES—Diseases and pests—*cont.*

Baby bee odor lures cradle-robbing mites. S. Hart. *Science News* 136:103 Ag 12 '89

Identification

By using bar coding on busy bees, scientist Stephen Buchmann becomes an unstung hero [use in monitoring activities] il *People Weekly* 31:105 My 22 '89

Hive technology [tracking killer bees; work of Howard T. Kerr] J. Horgan. il *Scientific American* 260:22 Ja '89

Probing secrets of small critters: fuchsia mice and bar-coded bees. L. Ware. il *Audubon* 91:12 Ja '89

Larvae

See Larvae

BEES, GEOGRAPHY *See* Geography—Competitions

BEES, SPELLING *See* Spelling—Competitions

BEETHOVEN, LUDWIG VAN, 1770-1827

about

The "authentic" Beethoven. E. Salzman. il *Stereo Review* 54:126 My '89

Beethoven lite. P. G. Davis. il por *New York* 22:60-1 Ag 28 '89

Beethoven's nine, times two. E. Salzman. il pors *Stereo Review* 54:128 Ja '89

Making Beethoven the old-fashioned way. S. Cantrell. il *High Fidelity (New York, N.Y.)* 39:61+ Ap '89

Roger Norrington's Beethoven. P. Mattick, Jr. *The Nation* 249:326-8 S 25 '89

BEETHOVEN PROJECT *See* Center for Successful Childhood Development (Chicago, Ill.)

BEETLES

See also

Ladybirds

Beetlejuice genes now in biotechnicolor [click beetles; research by Keith V. Wood and William D. McElroy] R. Weiss. il *Science News* 135:308 My 20 '89

Beetlemania [excerpt from Other people's trades]; tr. by Raymond Rosenthal. P. Levi. *Harper's* 278:27-8 F '89

Complementary DNA coding click beetle luciferases can elicit bioluminescence of different colors. K. V. Wood and others. bibl f il *Science* 244:700-2 My 12 '89

Guardians of the underworld [burying beetles] M. P. Scott and J. F. A. Traniello. il *Natural History* p32-7 Je '89

Kittyboo colors [gene tagging with luciferase from click beetles; research by Keith Wood and others] il *Discover* 10:12 N '89

Control

Dealing with Japanese beetles. L. A. Weathers. il *Southern Living* 24:58 Je '89

Larvae

See Larvae

Sexual behavior

See Sexual behavior—Insects

BEETS

See also

Cooking—Vegetables

About beets. S. Pacher. il *The Mother Earth News* 117:32-4+ My/Je '89

BEGGING AND BEGGARS

From Dickens to Beckett in Grand Central [stories created by beggars in New York City] A. Broyard. il *The New York Times Book Review* 94:12 Mr 12 '89

Give to beggars for Christ's sake [with readers' comments] E. Wojcicki. *U.S. Catholic* 54:14-20 Ap '89

This is what you thought: 43% say they never give to panhandlers [survey results] il *Glamour* 87:175 Mr '89

What's your opinion? [beggars and the homeless] D. O. Relin. il *Scholastic Update (Teachers' edition)* 121:3+ F 10 '89

BEGINNINGS, LITERARY

Beginnings. P. A. Whitney. *The Writer* 102:9-12 Ap '89

'Chug, chug, chug' and other great first liners [quiz] il *The New York Times Book Review* 94:52 N 12 '89

First lines [quiz] W. M. Kneupper. *The Writer* 102:27+ O '89

BEGLEITER, STEVEN

Fathers & sons [excerpt] il *Parents* 64:143-5 Je '89

about

Capturing a love he missed out on, a photographer pays homage to dads and sons. il por *People Weekly* 31:123-6 Je 19 '89

BEGLEY, ADAM

Ann Getty: publish and perish? il pors *The New York Times Magazine* p36-7+ O 22 '89

BEGLEY, ED, JR.

about

She-devil. J. Ressner. il *American Film* 15:64 D '89

BEGLEY, SHARON

The first wildlife artists. il *International Wildlife* 19:22-7 Mr/Ap '89

BEGOLE, CHRISTINE

Good listening. See occasional issues of Glamour

New options for working at home. il *Glamour* 87:324-5+ S '89

New tech. See occasional issues of Glamour

BEHAVIOR, ANIMAL *See* Animals—Habits and behavior

BEHAVIOR, ORGANIZATIONAL *See* Organizational behavior

BEHAVIOR (PSYCHOLOGY)

See also

Addictive behavior

Brats

Conditioned responses

Helping behavior

Obsessive-compulsive behavior

Passive-aggressive personality

Self destructive behavior

Social norm

Type A behavior

Type T behavior

Clinical versus actuarial judgment [diagnosing and predicting human behavior] R. M. Dawes and others. bibl f *Science* 243:1668-74 Mr 31 '89

How the mind was designed [sociobiology] G. Cowley. il *Newsweek* 113:56-8 Mr 13 '89

Understanding behavior in escalation situations. B. M. Staw and J. Ross. bibl f il *Science* 246:216-20 O 13 '89

BEHAVIOR MODIFICATION

A clean break with bad habits. E. Kiester and S. V. Kiester. il *Reader's Digest* 135:165-6+ O '89

Relax, you'll run faster [behavioral imagery technique; study by Scot Machlus and Richard O'Brien] J. C. Horn. il *Psychology Today* 23:22 Ja/F '89

Remodeling the autistic child. B. Bower. il *Science News* 136:312-13 N 11 '89

The trusting heart [modifying hostile behavior; excerpt] R. B. Williams. il *Psychology Today* 23:36-7+ Ja/F '89

BEHAVIOR PROBLEMS (CHILDREN) *See* Problem children

BEHAVIOR THERAPY *See* Behavior modification

BEHAVIORAL GENETICS

What a child is given. D. Franklin. il *The New York Times Magazine* p36-41+ S 3 '89

BEHAVIORAL PHARMACOLOGY *See* Psychopharmacology

BEHRENS, BOLKE, AND SCHULTE-DOINGHAUS, ULI

Europe tries to stay on track. *World Press Review* 36:56 Ap '89

BEHRING, KENNETH

about

After Fallingwater: a California house inspired by Frank Lloyd Wright. J. Chatfield-Taylor. il *Architectural Digest* 46:214-21 Mr '89

BEHRINGER, RICHARD R., AND OTHERS

Synthesis of functional human hemoglobin in transgenic mice. bibl f il *Science* 245:971-3 S 1 '89

BEIER, EUGENE W.

(jt. auth) See Wolfenstein, Lincoln, and Beier, Eugene W.

BEIJING (CHINA)

Art

The naked and the damned [nude art show] S. Staggs. il *Art News* 88:24+ Ap '89

Description

Beijing pumps up its bicycles for Bush. *U.S. News & World Report* 106:15 Mr 6 '89

Letter from Beijing. F. C. Shapiro. *The New Yorker* 65:97-103 My 8 '89

Life in two capitals. L. Doder. il *Maclean's* 102:37 My 29 '89

Streets

The street of the glazed tile factory [Liulichang Street] P. Clément. il *The Unesco Courier* 42:38-41 Ag '89

Tiananmen Square student occupation, 1989

See Tiananmen Square (China) student occupation, 1989

BEIJING INSTITUTE OF AERONAUTICAL MATERIALS

Aerospace Materials Institute turns to commercial sector to fund growth. *Aviation Week & Space Technology* 131:89 D 11 '89

BEIJING PLANETARIUM

Beijing: projecting into the future. Wen Xueshi. il *Sky and Telescope* 77:201-2 F '89

BEIRUT (LEBANON)

The agony of Beirut. J. Bierman. il *Maclean's* 102:20-2 Ag 28 '89

Beirut days: life and death. S. Issa. il map *Newsweek* 114:58+ N 13 '89

Beirut diary. I. A. Hijazi. il por *The New York Times Magazine* p30-3+ My 28 '89

A Beirut family's survival guide. il *U.S. News & World Report* 107:16 Ag 28-S 4 '89

Bloody chaos in Beirut. H. Anderson. il *Newsweek* 113:43 My 1 '89

A city of banditry and extortion. F. Ajami. il *U.S. News & World Report* 106:33 Ap 10 '89

Death throes of a capital. J. Bartholet and S. Issa. il *Newsweek* 114:24-6 Ag 21 '89

Muddling through in Beirut. V. Gryzinski. il *World Press Review* 36:72 D '89

A preview of the apocalypse [continued fighting in Beirut] J. Smolowe. il map *Time* 134:23-4 Ag 28 '89

Public health

War against the heart [study by Abla M. Sibai] *Science News* 136:284 O 28 '89

BEIRUT AIRPLANE HIJACKING, 1985
Portrait of a patriot [Navy Seabee R. Stethem killed by terrorists] H. Hurt. il por *Reader's Digest* 135:65-9 Jl '89
To catch a terrorist [U.S. captures Arab airplane hijacker F. Yoonis] S. Emerson. il por *Reader's Digest* 135:107-11 O '89
BEISH, JEFF D., AND OTHERS
The red planet shows off. il *Sky and Telescope* 77:30-5 Ja '89
BEISWINGER, GEORGE L., 1924-
How to complain effectively. il *McCall's* 116:42 Ja '89
BEITZEL, JEFF
about
House of the specialty. C. Csere. il por *Car and Driver* 34:109 Je '89
BEJCEK, BRUCE E., AND OTHERS
Transformation by v-sis occurs by an internal autoactivation mechanism. bibl f il *Science* 245:1496-9 S 29 '89
BEKEY, MICHELLE
The rocky road to launching a business. il por *Working Woman* 14:41-2+ Je '89
BEKOFF, MARC
Assessing publication impact. *BioScience* 39:586 O '89
BEL CANTO OPERA (COMPANY)
Musical events:
J. Peri's Euridice. A. Porter. *The New Yorker* 65:77 My 8 '89
A slight case of opera [performance of The white rose] P. G. Davis. il *New York* 22:62-3 Je 19 '89
BEL GEDDES, NORMAN, 1893-1958
about
The shaping of things to come. L. W. Speck. il por *Omni (New York, N.Y.)* 12:86-95 O '89
BELAFONTE, HARRY
Talking back to Jackie. il por *New York* 22:40 O 16 '89
BÉLAND, PIERRE
about
Doomed canaries of Tadoussac. J. R. Luoma. il por map *Audubon* 91:92-7 Mr '89
BELASCO, WARREN
The two taste cultures. il *Psychology Today* 23:29+ D '89
BELAU *See* Palau
BELCHER, ALAN
about
Alan Belcher at Josh Baer. J. Zinsser. *Art in America* 77:145 Mr '89
BELCHER, JOHN W., AND OTHERS
Plasma observations near Neptune: initial results from Voyager 2. bibl f il *Science* 246:1478-83 D 15 '89
BELDOCK, D. T.
about
"If something could go wrong, it did". E. Giltenan. il por *Forbes* 143:70+ My 29 '89
BELFIELD, WENDELL O.
about
Dysplasia's end. L. Mueller. il pors *Outdoor Life* 183:46+ Ap '89
BELFOND (PIERRE) EDITIONS *See* Editions Pierre Belfond
BELGE DE CONSTRUCTIONS AÉRONAUTIQUES SA
Belgium will use equipment provided under offset pact to expand industry [F-16 deal with General Dynamics] il *Aviation Week & Space Technology* 130:57 F 13 '89
BELGIAN ART *See* Art, Belgian
BELGIAN COOKING *See* Cooking, Belgian
BELGIAN GRAND PRIX *See* Automobile racing—Belgium
BELGIAN PAINTING *See* Painting, Belgian
BELGIAN SHOES INC.
Gloves for the feet. S. Dinkel. il *Gentlemen's Quarterly* 59:70 D '89
BELGIUM
See also
Americans—Belgium
Anti-Semitism—Belgium
Art—Belgium
Automobile racing—Belgium
Aviation and state—Belgium
Bruges (Belgium)
Brussels (Belgium)
Ghent (Belgium)
Knokke-le-Zoute (Belgium)
Stone Age—Belgium
Terrorism—Belgium
Commerce
United States
See United States—Commerce—Belgium
Defenses
See also
Airplanes, Military—Belgium
Industries
See also
Banque Bruxelles Lambert SA
Belge de Constructions Aéronautiques SA
Sabena World Airlines
Religious institutions and affairs
See also
Muslims—Belgium

BELIEF AND DOUBT
See also
Faith
Faith and reason
Skepticism
Truth
BELIEF IN GOD *See* Faith
BELIZE
See also
Fish—Belize
Antiquities
See also
Caracol site (Belize)
How Maya culture withstood colonial force [Tipu and Lamanai sites; research by Elizabeth Graham] B. Bower. *Science News* 136:373 D 9 '89
Late Maya culture gets an island lift [Marco Gonzalez site excavations by Elizabeth Graham and David M. Pendergast] B. Bower. *Science News* 136:20 Jl 8 '89
On the fringes of conquest: Maya-Spanish contact in colonial Belize [Tipu and Lamanai sites] E. Graham and others. bibl f il map *Science* 246:1254-9 D 8 '89
BELKIN, LISA
Lone Star fakes. il pors *The New York Times Magazine* p66+ D 10 '89
BELL, ALEXA
Asking him out: what the guys say, what do you say? il *'Teen* 33:28+ Je '89
BELL, ALISON
From hugs to happiness: the affection connection. il *'Teen* 33:20-1+ O '89
BELL, BEVERLY K.
A golf great cut down in her prime. il por *Women's Sports & Fitness* 11:60 O '89
BELL, BILL
about
Games. S. Morris. il *Omni (New York, N.Y.)* 11:128 F '89
BELL, CURRER *See* Brontë, Charlotte, 1816-1855
BELL, DANIEL
about
Reflections of a bourgeois Menshevik [interview] L. Greenfeld. *Society* 26:10-20 S/O '89
BELL, DAVID A.
Liberté, egalité, have a nice day. *The New Republic* 200:22-5 Ja 23 '89
BELL, EDDIE
about
Bell to use market research for Harper's new paperback line. M. Reuter. por *Publishers Weekly* 235:15 F 10 '89
BELL, ELLIS *See* Brontë, Emily, 1818-1848
BELL, HUBERT T.
about
Guarding the nation's vice presidents. H. J. Massaquoi. il pors *Ebony* 44:166+ Je '89
BELL, LARRY GENE
about
Beauty and the beast. E. H. Methvin. il pors *Reader's Digest* 134:132-8 F '89
BELL, MARVIN, 1937-
Comb and rake [poem] *The Atlantic* 263:70 Je '89
I, or someone like me [poem] *The New Republic* 201:40 O 16 '89
An old trembling [poem] *The New Yorker* 65:60 Ag 21 '89
Victim of himself [poem] *The Atlantic* 263:61 My '89
BELL, NANCY
FY 1990 budget: Bush's words, Reagan's numbers. il *BioScience* 39:292-6 My '89
The government's role in investigating scientific misconduct. *BioScience* 39:79 F '89
Science issues in the 101st Congress. *BioScience* 39:369 Je '89
Science regains the White House. il *BioScience* 39:435 Jl/Ag '89
BELL, PATRICIA J.
Cuernavaca and Taxco. il *Gourmet* 49:64-9+ F '89
Travel journal. See issues of Gourmet beginning January 1989
BELL, PEGGY KIRK
about
For the love of the game. D. Young. il pors *Southern Living* 24:78+ O '89
BELL, QUENTIN
about
The scion of Bloomsbury in Sussex. E. Lambert. il por *Architectural Digest* 46:72+ D '89
BELL, ROBERT MAURICE, 1944-
(jt. auth) See Hannun, Yusuf A., and Bell, Robert Maurice, 1944-
BELL, TERREL HOWARD
Memo to the Secretary of Education: how to make education a top priority. por *Change* 20:20-3 N/D '88
BELL, TRUDY E.
The besieged bays of the world. il maps *Sea Frontiers* 35:238-45 Jl/Ag '89

BELL, VANESSA, 1879-1961
about
Painting Charleston. J. Johnston. bibl f il pors *Art in America* 77:152-63+ D '89
BELL, WARREN
about
'Drugs almost destroyed my career'. L. Norment. il pors *Ebony* 44:124-5 Ag '89
BELL (JAN) MARKETING INC. *See* Jan Bell Marketing Inc.
BELL & HOWELL CO.
Bob Bass may have to settle for a quick profit on this one [disappointing results of Bell & Howell leveraged buyout] J. F. Siler. il por *Business Week* p48+ O 9 '89
BELL ATLANTIC CORP.
A telco-cable survey sparks controversy [E. C. Parker's survey funded by Bell Atlantic] J. Stilson. il por *Channels (New York, N.Y.: 1986)* 9:17+ S '89
BELL CANADA ENTERPRISES INC.
David and Goliath dial a busy signal [CALL-NET vs. Bell Canada] D. Francis. il *Maclean's* 102:11 Ap 3 '89
BELL COMMUNICATIONS RESEARCH, INC.
Beyond the telephone: new ways to communicate [cover story] S. B. Weinstein and P. W. Shumate, Jr. il pors *The Futurist* 23:8-12 N/D '89
On the cutting edge of tomorrow's technology. P. W. Shumate, Jr. and S. B. Weinstein. il *USA Today (Periodical)* 118:30-2 S '89
BELL HELICOPTER TEXTRON INC.
680 rotor system enhances Bell Model 222 performance [cover story] N. C. Kernstock. il *Aviation Week & Space Technology* 130:36-7+ My 15 '89
Avionics system lets helicopter crews focus on search, rescue. N. C. Kernstock. il *Aviation Week & Space Technology* 130:50-1+ Ap 24 '89
Bell, Boeing push V-22 flight test program [Osprey tilt-rotor aircraft; cover story] D. A. Brown. il *Aviation Week & Space Technology* 131:38-40 O 16 '89
Bell-Boeing V-22 tilt-rotor prototype makes first flight. C. A. Shifrin. il *Aviation Week & Space Technology* 130:20-1 Mr 27 '89
European firms agree to join Bell-Boeing in marketing V-22 [tilt-rotor aircraft] *Aviation Week & Space Technology* 130:37 Je 19 '89
McDonnell Douglas/Bell team introduces its LHX concept [special section] il *Aviation Week & Space Technology* 129:56-9+ Mr 6 '89
V-22 prepared for further expansion of flight envelope [Osprey tilt-rotor prototype; cover story] C. A. Shifrin. il *Aviation Week & Space Technology* 130:34-6+ Ap 10 '89
BELL LABORATORIES *See* AT&T Bell Labs
BELL TELEPHONE LABORATORIES, INCORPORATED
See also
AT&T Bell Labs
BELLA LUNA (NEW YORK, N.Y.: RESTAURANT) *See* New York (N.Y.)—Restaurants, nightclubs, bars, etc.
BELLACK, ALISON R., AND HALLIN, CARLYN K.
Business, home, and school: cooperating to develop lifelong readers. il *Phi Delta Kappan* 70:415 Ja '89
BELLAGIO (ITALY)
Gardens and gardening
Garden exploring along Italy's Lake Como. il map *Sunset (Central West edition)* 182:254 My '89
BELLAH, ROBERT NEELY, 1927-
about
Habits of the hearth [interview] R. Clapp. il pors *Christianity Today* 33:20-4 F 3 '89
BELLANCA, ANTONIA
about
Flowers. R. West. il *American Health* 8:28 Je '89
BELLARDO, PAUL
about
A store on History Street. B. Bibby. il por *New York* 22:20 Je 26 '89
BELLCORE *See* Bell Communications Research, Inc.
BELLEVUE (WASH.)
Parks and playgrounds
See also
Newcastle Beach Park (Bellevue, Wash.)
BELLEVUE HOSPITAL
Life and death: scenes from a hospital emergency ward [cover story] R. Falco. il *USA Today (Periodical)* 118:41-53 Jl '89
Murder in the safest places [death of Dr. K. Hinnant] R. Rosenblatt. il *U.S. News & World Report* 106:6-7 Ja 23 '89
The tragedy at Bellevue [murder of Dr. K. Hinnant] E. Salholz. il pors *Newsweek* 113:27 Ja 23 '89
BELLEZZA, LEONARD
about
Guarantees with nothing behind them. A. A. Lappen. il *Forbes* 144:41-2 Jl 24 '89
BELLI, HUMBERTO
Election nearing. il *The New Republic* 201:16-19 N 27 '89
BELLI, REMO
about
Remo Belli: an industry innovator reflects. H. Nolan. il *Down Beat* 56:62 D '89

BELLINGER, DANIEL
Winslow Homer, "Mink Pond," 1891 [poem] *America* 161:208 O 7 '89
BELLINI, VINCENZO, 1801-1835
about
Il pirata [opera] Reviews
The New Yorker 65:97-8 My 1 '89. A. Porter
BELLINI (FIRM)
San Francisco's Bellini Bar encourages its baby customers to hit the bottle, and burp. il *People Weekly* 31:153 My 15 '89
BELLM, DAN
And sew it goes. por *Mother Jones* 14:34-5 Ja '89
Quetzalandia. il *Mother Jones* 14:49-50 D '89
A woman who knew Latin. *The Nation* 248:891-3 Je 26 '89
BELLO, JUDITH HIPPLER
(jt. auth) *See* Holmer, Alan F., and Bello, Judith Hippler
BELLOFATTO, VIVIAN, AND CROSS, GEORGE A. M.
Expression of a bacterial gene in a trypanosomatid protozoan. bibl f il *Science* 244:1167-9 Je 9 '89
BELLOW, SAUL
about
At 73, Nobel laureate Saul Bellow decides he wants to be a paperback writer. A. Chambers. il pors *People Weekly* 31:65-6+ Mr 27 '89
A conversation with Saul Bellow. S. S. Steinberg. il por *Publishers Weekly* 235:59-60 Mr 3 '89
None die of heartburn. il por *Esquire* 111:192-3 Je '89
BELLOWS, GEORGE, 1882-1925
about
George Bellows, great printmaker. il *USA Today (Periodical)* 117:8-9 Ap '89
The use and abuse of realism. B. W. Bloch. *The New Leader* 72:22-3 O 2-16 '89
BELLPORT (N.Y.)
Historic houses, sites, etc.
Sanctuary for art [converted church; interview with M. Morley] D. Kazanjian. il por *House & Garden* 161:150-5+ My '89
Social life and customs
The UnHampton. M. Gross. il map *New York* 22:30-2+ Jl 3-10 '89
BELL'S PALSY
"I fear I'm losing my husband" [A. Murcia's illness] A. Jillian. il pors *Redbook* 173:83-4 Jl '89
BELLSON, LOUIS, 1924-
about
Profiles. W. Balliett. il *The New Yorker* 65:41-6 Je 19 '89
BELLSOUTH CORPORATION
BellSouth is on a ringing streak. S. Gannes. il por *Fortune* 120:66-7+ O 9 '89
For Craig McCaw, it's do-or-die time [battle for LIN Broadcasting] C. Hawkins and R. D. Hof. il *Business Week* p34 D 4 '89
This cellular hookup could jam the competition [LIN and BellSouth's merger] J. J. Keller. il *Business Week* p45 S 25 '89
BELLY BUTTON *See* Umbilical cord
BELLY DANCING
Anahid. *The New Yorker* 65:23-4 Jl 31 '89
Get fit-with a twist. il *Mademoiselle* 95:38 Ag '89
BELMONT STAKES *See* Horse racing
BELOFF, MAX, BARON
Leo Amery, the last imperialist. bibl il pors *History Today* 39:13-18 Ja '89
BELOUS, RICHARD S.
How human resource systems adjust to the shift toward contingent workers. bibl f il *Monthly Labor Review* 112:7-12 Mr '89
BELOUSOV-ZHABOTINSKII REACTION
Oscillating chemical waves process images [research by Lothar Kuhnert and others] *Science News* 135:94 F 11 '89
BELSINGER, SUSAN, AND DILLE, CAROLYN
Spirited vegetables. il *Gourmet* 49:182+ Je '89
BELSKY, JAY, 1952-
Ordeal on I-80. il *The New York Times Magazine* p24+ F 19 '89
BELT SANDERS *See* Sanding and sanding equipment
BELTER, JOHN HENRY, 1804-1863
about
The Belter chair. D. Bourdon. il *American Heritage* 40:24-5 Mr '89
BELTER FURNITURE *See* Furniture, Rococo
BELTS (CLOTHING)
The belt [men's] J. Berendt. il *Esquire* 112:26+ Jl '89
BELTS (MACHINERY)
See also
Automobile engines—Belts
Automobile engines—Fan belts
BELUGA WHALES *See* Whales
BELUSHI, JOHN, 1949-1982
about
Dead men don't act. M. Rochlin. por *American Film* 14:72 Jl/Ag '89
Finally, the Belushi story. R. Zoglin. il por *Time* 133:90-1 Ap 24 '89

BELUSHI, JOHN, 1949-1982—about—*cont.*
John Belushi. il pors *People Weekly* 31 Special Issue:70-1 Summ '89
BELZ, CARL, 1937-
A conditional paradise. il pors *Art in America* 77:136-41 Ja '89
BELZBERG FAMILY

about

The Belzberg brats. S. Flack. il *Forbes* 144:41-2 N 13 '89
The Belzbergs, again. T. Jaffe. il *Forbes* 144:316 S 4 '89
Hoist by their own greenmail [takeover of H. H. Robertson] K. Hannon. il *Forbes* 143:156 My 29 '89
BELZER, ELLEN J.
12 ways to better team building. il *Working Woman* 14:12+ Ag '89
BEN & JERRY'S HOMEMADE INC.
A call to pig out for peace [support for 1% for Peace] il *Newsweek* 113:45 My 8 '89
I scream, you scream . . . E. Larson. il *Utne Reader* p64-6+ Ja/F '89
Purveying yuppie porn. J. Queenan. il pors *Forbes* 144:60+ N 13 '89
BEN-ABRAHAM, AVI
Putting death on ice. il *The Saturday Evening Post* 261:60-2+ Ap '89
BEN HILL GRIFFIN INC.
The last of the citrus barons [B. H. Griffin] T. Trussell. il pors *Nation's Business* 77:46+ F '89
BEN-HORIN, DANIEL
(jt. auth) See Whitmyer, Claude, and Ben-Horin, Daniel
BEN JELLOUN, TAHAR, 1944-
The spirit of '89. il *The Unesco Courier* 42:48-9 Je '89
BEŇAČKOVA, GABRIELA

about

Connoisseur's choice. Y. S. Graff. il pors *Opera News* 54:32-3+ S '89
BENBRIDGE, HENRY, 1743-1812

about

Museum accessions. E. H. Gustafson. il *Antiques* 136:1022 N '89
BENCE, EVELYN, 1952-
Rhubarb [poem] *America* 160:534 Je 3 '89
BENCHES

See also
Garden benches
Potting benches
Settees
Workbenches

Backyard bench. H. Wicks. il *Home Mechanix* 86:36+ Mr '89
Classic in teak. A. Hontoir. il *Workbench* 45:50-3 My/Je '89
Five-board bench [Shaker bench] R. N. Hoffman. il *Workbench* 45:74-6+ S/O '89
Movable seats. D. B. Cowin. il *House & Garden* 161:200-3 My '89
Southwestern bench. B. Kieffer. il *The Family Handyman* 39:62-5 Ja '89
Super-simple porch seat. il *Better Homes and Gardens* 67:63 Je '89
BENCHMARK TESTING (COMPUTERS) See Computers—Testing
BENDA, MARY KRISTA
Disarmament at dawn [poem] *America* 161:31 Jl 15-22 '89
BENDAH, DAVID

about

The prince of get rich quick. M. S. Gill. il por *Rolling Stone* p107-8+ F 9 '89
BENDER (MATTHEW) & CO. See Matthew Bender & Co.
BENDERLY, BERYL LIEFF
Attackers from inner space. il *Health (New York, N.Y.)* 21:44-7+ D '89
Filling the bills. il *Health (New York, N.Y.)* 21:32+ My '89
Palate training. il *Health (New York, N.Y.)* 21:56-7+ Jl '89
Saving the children. il *Health (New York, N.Y.)* 21:74-5 D '89
BENDINER, ROBERT
What I learned from the Pirates. il *American Heritage* 40:116-19 S/O '89
BENDIX CORP.
Bendix/King gears up to meet demand for T/CAS in 1990s [traffic alert and collision avoidance systems] E. H. Kolcum. il *Aviation Week & Space Technology* 130:109+ F 20 '89
BENDJEDID CHADLI See Chadli, Bendjedid
BENDS See Decompression (Physiology)
BENEDETTO, M. WILLIAM
The mad rush to merchant banking. por *Fortune* 120:121-2 Jl 17 '89
BENEDICT, SAINT, ABBOT OF MONTE CASSINO

about

How to find God here, there, and everywhere. J. Chittister. il *U.S. Catholic* 54:6-7 F '89
BENEDICT, SAINT, OF NURSIA See Benedict, Saint, Abbot of Monte Cassino

BENEDICTINES
How to find God here, there, and everywhere. J. Chittister. il *U.S. Catholic* 54:6-7 F '89
BENEFICIAL INSECTS See Insects
BENEFIT AUCTIONS See Auctions
BENEFIT PERFORMANCES

See also
Basketball, Professional—Benefit games
Dance—Benefit performances
Earthquake Relief concert, 1989
Rock concerts—Benefit performances

BENEFITS, EMPLOYEE See Fringe benefits
BENEFITS, LIVING (INSURANCE) See Living benefits (Insurance)
BENEJ, RICK

about

The game. *The New Yorker* 65:28-30 Mr 6 '89
BENESH, PETER
Canada's white whales are dying. *World Press Review* 36:56 Ja '89
BÉNÉTEAU (FIRM)
Safe harbor. K. Weisman. il por *Forbes* 144:58+ S 4 '89
BENETTON SPA
Benetton targets a new customer—Wall Street [American depositary receipts] J. Rossant and A. Dunkin. il *Business Week* p32-3 My 29 '89
BENFEY, CHRISTOPHER E. G., 1954-
The courage of Stephen Crane. il *The New York Review of Books* 36:31-4 Mr 16 '89
BENFEY, PHILIP N., AND CHUA, N.-H. (NAM-HAI)
Regulated genes in transgenic plants. bibl f il *Science* 244:174-81 Ap 14 '89
BENFORD, GREGORY, 1941-
Leviathan [fiction] *Omni (New York, N.Y.)* 12:57-8 N '89
BENGAL LANCERS See Great Britain. Army. Bengal Lancers
BENHAM, JAMES

about

How Jim Benham pioneered the idea of the supersafe mutual fund. F. W. Frailey. il por *Changing Times* 43:140 N '89
BENHAM CAPITAL MANAGEMENT GROUP
How Jim Benham pioneered the idea of the supersafe mutual fund. F. W. Frailey. il por *Changing Times* 43:140 N '89
BENIHANA NATIONAL CORPORATION
Rocky's road. E. Schmuckler. il por *Forbes* 143:80+ Mr 20 '89
BENIN

Politics and government

Pass the ammunition. P. R. Michaud. *The New Republic* 200:14 Mr 13 '89
BENIRSCHKE, ROLF

about

Ex-jock Rolf Benirschke, whose number once almost came up, puts his spin on Wheel of fortune. S. Schindehette. il pors *People Weekly* 31:51-2+ Ja 23 '89
Inflammatory bowel disease: incurable and difficult to diagnose. B. Rosenstein. il por *USA Today (Periodical)* 117:91-2 Mr '89
BENJAMIN, BENOIT

about

Big men, big problems. P. Korn. il pors *Sport (New York, N.Y.)* 80:71-3+ Ap '89
BENJAMIN, RICHARD

about

My stepmother is an alien [film] Reviews
Video 13:63 Jl '89. J. Walker
BENJAMIN, WALTER, 1892-1940

about

The work of Roy Lichtenstein in the age of Walter Benjamin's and Jean Baudrillard's popularity [cover story] C. Ratcliff. il *Art in America* 77:110-23+ F '89
BENNET, JAMES
If it's not on the budget this year, it doesn't exist. *The Washington Monthly* 21:28-9 N '89
BENNET, JOHN
Mr. Reed's house [story] *The New Yorker* 65:36-42 My 22 '89
BENNETT, ALAN, 1934-

about

Bringing down the house. C. Worthington. il por *Harper's Bazaar* 122:46-7+ S '89
Single spies [drama] Reviews
The New York Review of Books il 36:24-9 Ap 13 '89. N. G. A. Annan, Baron
BENNETT, HELEN
Two of us is one too many. il *The New York Times Magazine* p22+ O 22 '89
BENNETT, JACK FRANKLIN, 1924-

about

Parting predictions from Exxon's Jack Bennett [interview] W. Glasgall. por *Business Week* p73 Ja 30 '89
BENNETT, JAMES GORDON, 1795-1872

about

Celebrity journalists. B. A. Weisberger. il *American Heritage* 40:20+ Mr '89

BENNETT, LERONE, 1928-
(ed) See Johnson, John H. How to get your way
(ed) See Johnson, John H. The untold story of how publisher made millions with a $500 loan
BENNETT, NEIL G.
(jt. auth) See Bloom, David E., and Bennett, Neil G.
BENNETT, PAT
about
After 20 years, an abandoned wife makes her ex pay his due. D. Chu. il pors *People Weekly* 31:79-82 F 20 '89
BENNETT, RALPH KINNEY
Brilliant Pebbles: amazing new missile killer. *Reader's Digest* 135:128-33 S '89
Communism in crisis. por *Reader's Digest* 135:99-104 Jl '89
The growing menace of chemical weapons. il *Reader's Digest* 135:82-7 Jl '89
Tom Clancy's dream come true. il por *Reader's Digest* 134:126-31 F '89
BENNETT, ROBERT S.
about
Bob Bennett: on the trail of the 'Keating Five'. T. Smart. il por *Business Week* p60 D 11 '89
BENNETT, THOMAS, D. 1989
about
Family doesn't know father died in N.Y. hospital till daughter finds its bill. il por *Jet* 75:19 F 13 '89
BENNETT, WILLIAM, 1941-
Sun: the new wisdom. il *Vogue* 179:204-6 Je '89
BENNETT, WILLIAM G.
about
Circus Circus rakes in the bread bread. R. Grover. il *Business Week* p80-2 F 27 '89
BENNETT, WILLIAM IRA
Overactive machinery. il *The New York Times Magazine* p59-60 My 7 '89
The salt alarm. il *The New York Times Magazine* p30-1 Ja 22 '89
(jt. auth) See Hanson, Amy Axt, and Bennett, William Ira
BENNETT, WILLIAM JOHN, 1943-
Restoring authority [adaptation of address, May 3, 1989] il *New Perspectives Quarterly* 6:4-7 Summ '89
William J. Bennett [advice to George Bush] *National Review* 41:20-1 F 10 '89
about
Back in the bully pulpit. H. Sidey. il por *Time* 133:19 Ja 23 '89
Bennett: 'It's their fight right now' [interview] M. Miller. il *Newsweek* 114:32 S 11 '89
Bennett the drug czar: an agenda. F. Barnes. il *The American Spectator* 22:14-15 Ap '89
Bennett's bad job. *National Review* 41:14-15 F 10 '89
Bennett's drug war. T. Morganthau. il por *Newsweek* 114:16-18 Ag 21 '89
Cowboy in the capital: drug czar Bill Bennett. H. Kohn. il *Rolling Stone* p41-2+ N 2 '89
Creating a generation of "aliterates". S. Ohanian. *The Education Digest* 54:29-32 F '89
Czar without a throne? J. McLaughlin. *National Review* 41:19 Mr 10 '89
Drug czar in search of a throne [cover story] W. McGurn. il por *National Review* 41:22-4 Je 16 '89
The drug czar: no "Walter Wallflower". E. Marshall. por *Science* 243:1287 Mr 10 '89
The drug warrior [cover story] T. Morganthau and M. Miller. il pors map *Newsweek* 113:20-4 Ap 10 '89
Fighting on two fronts. il *Time* 134:29 Ag 14 '89
General Bennett. F. Barnes. *The New Republic* 201:14+ S 18-25 '89
Good place for a test case. il *Time* 133:24 Ap 3 '89
The man who would be czar. G. Witkin and M. Satchell. il pors *U.S. News & World Report* 106:40-1 Mr 6 '89
Mr. Bennett's war. *National Review* 41:13-14 S 15 '89
Rangel raps Bush for his snubbing drug czar status. por *Jet* 75:4 Mr 6 '89
Some things you do because they're right [interview] J. Cook. il por *Forbes* 144:118+ N 13 '89
Taking on the legalizers. T. Morganthau. il *Newsweek* 114:46-8 D 25 '89
Unveiling Bennett's battle plan. M. Miller. il por *Newsweek* 113:6 Ap 24 '89
BENNETT, WILLIAM RICHARDS, 1932-
about
The Crown's case. H. Quinn. il por *Maclean's* 102:36-7 My 1 '89
A victory for Bennett. J. DeMont. il por *Maclean's* 102:28-9 My 22 '89
BENNEY, PAUL
about
Paul Benney at P.P.O.W. H. Cotter. il *Art in America* 77:197-8 N '89
BENNINGTON (VT.)
Buildings
Strong medicine [dentists' offices designed by Burr & McCallum] P. M. Sachner. il *Architectural Record* 177:94-7 O '89

BENNINK, JACK R.
(jt. auth) See Yewdell, Jonathan W., and Bennink, Jack R.
BENNY'S BURRITOS (NEW YORK, N.Y.: RESTAURANT)
See New York (N.Y.)—Restaurants, nightclubs, bars, etc.
BENOIST, JEAN-MARIE
Thatcherism across the Channel. map *National Review* 41:23-5 N 10 '89
BENOIT, BOB, AND BRAUN, JOSEPH A., 1947-
The mentor as an expert coach: a model for rural school districts. il *Phi Delta Kappan* 70:488-9 F '89
BENOIT, TOM
Power struggle. il *Flying* 116:124 Je '89
BENOT, YVES
In the Antilles, 'liberty for all'. il *The Unesco Courier* 42:18-23 Je '89
BENOVIC, JEFFREY L., AND OTHERS
β-adrenergic receptor kinase: primary structure delineates a multigene family. bibl f il *Science* 246:235-40 O 13 '89
BENSHEA, NOAH
Baking a bestseller [N. BenShea's Jacob the baker] L. Fleischer. *Publishers Weekly* 235:64 Ja 13 '89
BENSKY, LARRY
Little big one. *The Nation* 249:553 N 13 '89
BENSON, BENJAMIN
Do you keep too many secrets? il *Nation's Business* 77:42+ Ag '89
BENSON, GEORGE
about
George Benson tells how he copes with fame, family, career and the stresses of show business [cover story] R. E. Johnson. il pors *Jet* 76:56-9 My 1 '89
BENSON, HERBERT
about
The prayer war. S. Kiesling and T. G. Harris. *Psychology Today* 23:65-6 O '89
BENSON, JOHN, 1945-
Enterprise past and present. il *History Today* 39:5-7 Ag '89
BENSON, ROBERT L.
about
Centerline: Robert L. Benson. M. Sommers. il por *Theatre Crafts* 23:28-9 My '89
BENSON, TEDD
Revival of the timber-framed house. bibl il *Country Journal* 16:49-56 S/O '89
BENSON, W. A. S. (WILLIAM ARTHUR SMITH), 1854-1924
about
Benson's burners. M. Filler. il *House & Garden* 161:52 Ja '89
BENSON, WILLIAM ARTHUR SMITH *See* Benson, W. A. S. (William Arthur Smith), 1854-1924
BENSONHURST (NEW YORK, N.Y.)
Race relations
Anatomy of a racial murder [death of Y. Hawkins] J. Derevlany. il pors *Seventeen* 48:108-11+ D '89
Brotherhood week [reaction of D. Dinkins and other mayoral candidates to murder of Y. Hawkins] J. Klein. il por *New York* 22:36+ S 11 '89
The business of us all [racial murders of Y. Hawkins and E. Till] *Commonweal* 116:484-5 S 22 '89
Death on a mean street [murder of Y. Hawkins] F. Trippett. il *Time* 134:28 S 11 '89
Fighting the power [racial murder and New York mayoral race] A. Logan. il *The New Yorker* 65:108+ S 11 '89
Meditating on Bensonhurst [racial murder of Y. Hawkins] *America* 161:131 S 9-16 '89
N.Y. gunman surrenders in Hawkins slaying; blacks riot on Brooklyn Bridge. il *Jet* 76:7-8 S 18 '89
New York youth killed in racial attack by whites. il *Jet* 76:52 S 11 '89
A racist ambush in New York [death of Y. Hawkins] J. N. Baker. il por *Newsweek* 114:25 S 4 '89
Stirrings in the melting pot [Bensonhurst, Brooklyn and the Baltic States] H. Rainie. il *U.S. News & World Report* 107:8-9 S 11 '89
The two racisms [murder of Y. Hawkins] M. E. Dyson. *The Nation* 249:300-1 S 25 '89
What really happened in Bensonhurst [murder of Y. Hawkins; cover story] M. Stone. il pors map *New York* 22:46-56 N 6 '89
BENT, BRUCE
about
Change agents. D. Moreau. il por *Changing Times* 43:132 Mr '89
BENTHIC CURRENTS *See* Ocean currents
BENTLEY, DAVID R.
(jt. auth) See Klose, Monika, and Bentley, David R.
BENTLEY, HELEN DELICH, 1923?-
The plane drain: the FSX deal and other transfers of technology. il por *Conservative Digest* 15:54-7 Jl/Ag '89
U.S. competition in emerging technology areas [address, August 8, 1989] *Vital Speeches of the Day* 56:2-5 O 15 '89
BENTLEY (AUTOMOBILE) *See* Automobiles, Foreign
BENTLEY-LAROSA-SALASKY DESIGN
Below the surface [interiors] J. S. Russell. il *Architectural Record* 177:108-13 Ag '89

BENTON, JIM
about
Success brings cartoonist Jim Benton a pile of funny money. S. K. Reed. il pors *People Weekly* 31:81-2 My 8 '89
BENTON, THOMAS HART, 1889-1975
about
American frontiers. D. Solomon. il pors *House & Garden* 161:124-7 Je '89
An art of conflict. P. T. Reynolds. il por *Americana* 17:22-5 Mr/Ap '89
Benton's enduring American art (I). C. J. Goodman. il pors *American Artist* 53:30-7+ D '89
Corn king. K. Larson. il *New York* 22:154+ D 4 '89
Framing America. C. Ratcliff. il pors *Harper's Bazaar* 122:114+ Ap '89
Solving the Benton puzzle. G. C. Ward. il por *American Heritage* 40:12+ Jl/Ag '89
Tarted up till the eye cries Uncle. R. Hughes. il *Time* 133:80-1 My 1 '89
Thomas Hart Benton. A. E. Ledes. il *Antiques* 135:820+ Ap '89
Thomas Hart Benton [cover story] H. Adams. il pors *USA Today (Periodical)* 118:32-44 N '89
A Thomas Hart Benton bash. P. Plagens. il *Newsweek* 113:81 My 15 '89
Thomas Hart Benton came from Missouri—and he showed 'em [cover story] V. Klinkenborg. bibl (p174) il pors *Smithsonian* 20:82-101 Ap '89
BENTON (KY.)
Sanitary affairs
Cleansing waters [artificial wetlands as sewage treatment facility] M. Klockenbrink. il map *American Health* 8:72 S '89
BENTON & BOWLES
See also
D'Arcy Masius Benton & Bowles, Inc.
BENTSEN, CALVIN
about
Oh, give me a home where wild rhinos roam. M. Vollers. il por *Time* 133:12+ Je 26 '89
Texas rancher Calvin Bentsen, a former big-game hunter, takes his best shot at saving the rhinos. K. Demaret. il pors *People Weekly* 32:103-4 D 11 '89
BENTSEN, LLOYD
about
Covert campaigns. P. Montgomery. *Common Cause Magazine* 15:7-8 My/Je '89
Lloyd Bentsen is having a ball bashing George Bush. D. Harbrecht and H. Gleckman. il por *Business Week* p57 O 23 '89
Members only. V. Kemper. *Common Cause Magazine* 15:6-7 N/D '89
BENVENISTE, JACQUES
about
Benveniste criticism is diluted. D. Dickson. *Science* 245:248 Jl 21 '89
Dilutions of grandeur. A. C. Revkin. il *Discover* 10:74-5 Ja '89
BENZ, OBIE
about
Heavy petting [film] Reviews
Mother Jones il 14:50 S '89. J. Farber
Psychology Today il 23:67-8 O '89. M. Nelson
BENZAIA, DIANA
Help your hearing. il *The Saturday Evening Post* 261:16+ Mr '89
Hold on to your hearing. il *The Saturday Evening Post* 261:40+ Ja/F '89
Is it Lyme disease? [excerpt from Protect yourself from Lyme disease] il *Health (New York, N.Y.)* 21:72-5 Je '89
The revolution in diabetes care. *McCall's* 117:151-2 O '89
BENZENE
Biggest benzene risks hide close to home [Environmental Protection Agency study] J. Raloff. *Science News* 136:245 O 14 '89
A dream come true [ring revealed by scanning tunneling microscope] J. Kluger. il *Discover* 10:56 Ja '89
EPA limits industrial benzene emissions. J. Raloff. *Science News* 136:165 S 9 '89
BENZODIAZEPINE RECEPTORS *See* Drug receptors
BEQUESTS *See* Wills
BEQUETTE, FRANCE
Pollution unlimited. il *The Courier (Unesco)* 42:24-30 Mr '89
BEQUIA (SAINT VINCENT AND THE GRENADINES)
Description and travel
Bequia: Mykonos west. J. Quale. il *Vogue* 179:318 N '89
Bliss on Bequia. J. Iaconetti. il *Travel Holiday* 171:10+ Ap '89
BERARD, CHRISTIAN, 1902-1949
about
A legacy of fantasy and grace. D. Harris. il por *Architectural Digest* 46:42+ Ap '89
BERBERIAN, TEDDY
about
A boy's best friend. M. Clary. il por *McCall's* 116:75-6 Je '89

BERCOVICI, DAVE, AND OTHERS
Three-dimensional spherical models of convection in the earth's mantle. bibl f il *Science* 244:950-5 My 26 '89
BEREAN SAVINGS ASSOCIATION
Stand & deliver. K. Dumas. il por *Black Enterprise* 19:276-8+ Je '89
BEREAVEMENT *See* Grief
BERECZ, JÁNOS
about
From Big Brother to Big Mac [interview] N. Gardels. il *New Perspectives Quarterly* 5:12-17 Wint '88/'89
BEREND, IVÁN T. (IVÁN TIBOR), 1930-
Hungary breaks loose. il *The Bulletin of the Atomic Scientists* 45:27-31 Je '89
BERENDT, JOHN
Classics. See issues of Esquire
BERENSON, MARGARET MATHEWS- *See* Mathews-Berenson, Margaret
BERENSON, RUTH
Artistic freedom, public anger. il *National Review* 41:46 O 13 '89
BERENSTAIN, JAN, 1923-
(jt. auth) See Berenstain, Stan, 1923-, and Berenstain, Jan, 1923-
BERENSTAIN, STAN, 1923-, AND BERENSTAIN, JAN, 1923-
It's all in the family. See occasional issues of Good Housekeeping
BERESFORD, BRUCE
about
Driving Miss Daisy [film] Reviews
Maclean's 102:52 D 25 '89. B. D. Johnson
The New Yorker 65:74-6 D 25 '89. P. Kael
Newsweek il 114:68-9 D 18 '89. D. Ansen
People Weekly il 32:15-16 D 18 '89. R. Novak
Time il 134:91 D 18 '89. R. Schickel
Her alibi [film] Reviews
The New Republic 200:24 Mr 6 '89. S. Kauffmann
People Weekly il 31:15 F 6 '89. P. Travers
Video il 13:79 O '89. M. Pierson
BERG, A. SCOTT (ANDREW SCOTT)
Wuthering Heights. il pors *The New York Times Magazine* p46-8+ F 19 '89
about
PW interviews. L. See. por *Publishers Weekly* 235:49-50 Mr 24 '89
BERG, ANDREW SCOTT *See* Berg, A. Scott (Andrew Scott)
BERG, BARBARA J.
"My blankie and me" [with editorial comment by Ann Pleshette Murphy] il *Parents* 64:6, 94-8+ Jl '89
Staying in love. il *Parents* 64:95-9 Je '89
Working mother overload. *Redbook* 172:92-3+ Mr '89
BERG, CHUCK
Dexter Gordon: making his great leap forward [interview; reprint] il por *Down Beat* 56:82-3 S '89
BERG, CONSTANCE DEMUTH
One summer in Constable country. il *American Artist* 53:38-43+ Jl '89
BERG, ELIZABETH
A dog's tale. il *Ladies' Home Journal* 106:42+ Ja '89
Snow days. il *Parents* 64:102-4 F '89
A wake-up call. il *The New York Times Magazine* p12+ Jl 30 '89
BERG, ERIC N.
Your money: insurance for rental cars. *Modern Maturity* 32:29 Ap/My '89
BERG, FLOYD
about
Floyd Berg. M. S. Doherty. il por *American Artist* 53:74-5 Ag '89
BERG, KAREN, AND GILMAN, ANDREW
How to stay cool under fire [excerpt from Get to the point] il *Working Woman* 14:41+ N '89
BERG, MILTON
about
Meet big, bad bear Milton Berg. L. J. Nathans. il por *Business Week* p82 Je 19 '89
BERG, NATE
about
Nate Berg, 12, approaches 500 fishing days—the mind reels. il por *People Weekly* 32:65 Ag 14 '89
BERG PARTNERS
Meet big, bad bear Milton Berg. L. J. Nathans. il por *Business Week* p82 Je 19 '89
BERGAMO (ITALY)
Music
See also
Opera—Italy
BERGANTZ, GEORGE W.
Underplating and partial melting: implications for melt generation and extraction. bibl f il *Science* 245:1093-5 S 8 '89
BERGÉ, PIERRE
about
Clashing egos at the Paris Opera. R. Marshall. il por *Newsweek* 113:66 Ja 30 '89
Imbroglio at the Bastille. B. Villien. il *Opera News* 54:30-3 Jl '89

BERGÉ, PIERRE—about—cont.
Letter from Europe. J. Kramer. *The New Yorker* 65:81-94 My 1 '89
Second storming of the Bastille. O. Friedrich. il por *Time* 133:75 Ja 30 '89
Viewpoint. J. L. Poole. *Opera News* 53:4 Mr 4 '89
BERGEN, CANDICE
about
Candice. C. Kramer. il pors *McCall's* 117:20-2+ O '89
Candice Bergen: finally getting it all together at 42. C. Reid. il pors *Good Housekeeping* 208:72+ Mr '89
Candice Bergen: she's no dummy. D. Cavett. por *TV Guide* 37:7-9 D 23-29 '89
Class act. pors *Harper's Bazaar* 122:138-41 Ag '89
Hard Candy. B. Zehme. il por *Rolling Stone* p18+ Ja 26 '89
"I didn't know how to be a mom". V. J. Radovsky. il pors *Redbook* 172:44+ Ap '89
Shedding a glacial identity. H. F. Waters. il por *Newsweek* 113:55 Mr 13 '89
BERGEN BRUNSWIG CORP.
A drug wholesaler that looks as if it's on steroids. G. G. Marcial. il *Business Week* p88 F 6 '89
BERGER, BRUCE, 1938-
Visitation [poem] *Wilderness* 52:69 Spr '89
BERGER, GERHARD
about
New beginnings. R. Walker. il por *Road & Track* 40:110-11+ Ja '89
BERGER, JOHN, 1926-
Muck and its entanglements. *Harper's* 278:60-1 My '89
BERGER, JOSEPH
The view from St. Patrick's. il pors *The New York Times Magazine* p38-40+ Mr 26 '89
BERGER, LISA, AND OTHERS
Shaping up your company [excerpt from Cashing in] il *Working Woman* 14:47-8+ My '89
BERGER, MARILYN
about
60 minutes in the garden. C. K. Gandee. il pors *House & Garden* 161:110-17 Je '89
BERGER, PHILIP A.
about
NIMH assigns blame for tainted studies. M. Barinaga. *Science* 245:812 Ag 25 '89
BERGER, SUZANNE, AND OTHERS
Toward a new industrial America. il map *Scientific American* 260:39-47 Je '89
BERGER, WARREN
The explorers. il *Stereo Review* 54:84-9 Je '89
Speaker of the house. il *Stereo Review* 54:91-5 Mr '89
BERGLAS, STEVEN
The success syndrome. il *American Health* 8:56-9 Ap '89
BERGLIE, CAROLE
(jt. auth) See Geffen, Alice M., and Berglie, Carole
BERGLUND, MARIANNE
about
Bringing out the best. A. Smith. il por *Women's Sports & Fitness* 11:62-3 S '89
BERGMAN, DAVID, 1950-
Death and the young man [poem] *The New Republic* 201:30 O 23 '89
A father's blessings [poem] *The American Scholar* 58:103-4 Wint '89
My father almost ascending [poem] *The American Scholar* 58:102 Wint '89
BERGMAN, INGRID, 1915-1982
Archives
Mother and daughter [I. Rossellini visits archive at Wesleyan College] *The New Yorker* 65:44-6 O 23 '89
BERGMAN, YOLANDA
about
A self-styled food cop polices the coolest fridges in L.A. N. Geeslin. il pors *People Weekly* 31:87-8 Mr 27 '89
BERGREEN, LAURENCE
about
Irving Berlin's life, his biographer finds, was as rich in myth as in music [interview] M. H. J. Farrell. il pors *People Weekly* 32:63-4+ O 9 '89
BERGSTEN, C. FRED, 1941-
Attacking the deficits now will bring years of prosperity. il por *Fortune* 119:19+ Ja 2 '89
BERING STRAIT
Thaw on the Bering Strait. J. Mettke. il *World Press Review* 36:58 Ja '89
BERINSTEIN, NEIL, AND OTHERS
Activation of an excluded immunoglobulin allele in a human B lymphoma cell line. bibl f il *Science* 244:337-9 Ap 21 '89
BERIO, LUCIANO
about
Un re in ascolto [opera] Reviews
Opera News il 53:47 My '89. N. Goodwin
BERIRO, SHERLEE
about
Above Beverly Hills. H. Drohojowska. il *Architectural Digest* 46:230-7 My '89

BERIRO, SIMON
about
Above Beverly Hills. H. Drohojowska. il *Architectural Digest* 46:230-7 My '89
BERKE, DEBORAH, 1954-
about
Model houses. M. Filler. il por *House & Garden* 161:44 Ap '89
BERKE, JUDITH
Triple toe loop [poem] *The Atlantic* 263:73 Mr '89
BERKELEY, BILL
One party fits all. *The New Republic* 200:15-17 Mr 6 '89
War without end. *The New Republic* 200:14+ My 8 '89
BERKELEY (CALIF.)
Description
Berkeley. M. Horn. il *U.S. News & World Report* 107:59+ D 18 '89
Education
Teen sexuality [Berkeley High School] G. H. Colt. il *Life* 12:24-30 Jl '89
Historic houses, sites, etc.
How do you remodel an architectural icon? il *Sunset (Central West edition)* 183:110 O '89
Politics and government
Holding office is kid's stuff for 8-year-old Teddy Andrews [Youth Commissioner] il pors *People Weekly* 31:91-2 My 8 '89
Social conditions
Going Berserkeley. K. Wells. *Reader's Digest* 134:173-4+ Je '89
BERKLEY, CHARLES
about
The town that said "No" to racism. A. Cassidy. il pors *Good Housekeeping* 208:62+ F '89
BERKLEY, WILLIAM R., 1945-
about
Boy wonder grows up. E. F. Cone. il por *Forbes* 143:49+ F 20 '89
BERKLEY (W. R.) CORP. See W. R. Berkley Corp.
BERKLEY PUBLISHING GROUP
Berkley loses in appeals court over 'Red October' [suit by Naval Institute Press] M. Reuter. *Publishers Weekly* 235:9 Je 9 '89
BERKMAN, MARSHALL LEE
about
Educating Marshall Berkman. K. Hannon. il por *Forbes* 144:72 O 30 '89
BERKMAN, MEREDITH
College bound: a guide to the guides. *Seventeen* 48:184+ Mr '89
Scenes: looking for young love in all the new places. il *New York* 22:46-8+ Jl 3-10 '89
BERKMAN, SUE
No-sweat exercise. il *Ladies' Home Journal* 106:94+ Ag '89
The Weight Watchers New Year's diet. *Ladies' Home Journal* 106:49-50+ Ja '89
BERKOFF, STEVEN
about
Metamorphosis [drama] Reviews
America 160:454 My 13 '89. G. G. Seibert
Dance Magazine il 63:49 Je '89. N. V. Dalva
The Nation 248:535 Ap 17 '89. M. Hodgson
The New Leader 72:22-3 Ap 3-17 '89. L. A. Jacobs
New York il 22:78 Mr 20 '89. J. Simon
The New Yorker 65:87-8 Mr 20 '89. M. Kramer
Newsweek il 113:76-7 Mr 20 '89. J. Kroll
Time il 133:90 Mr 20 '89. W. A. Henry
BERKOWITZ, BRUCE D., 1956-
Corollaries. *The Bulletin of the Atomic Scientists* 45:39-40 My '89
BERKOWITZ, EDWARD D., AND DEAN, DAVID H.
Should the Senate approve the "Americans with Disabilities Act of 1989"? [excerpts from testimony, May 9, 1989] *Congressional Digest* 68:304+ D '89
BERKSHIRE HATHAWAY INC.
Warren Buffett makes money by making nice [friendly stake in Gillette] L. Jereski. il por *Business Week* p58 Ag 7 '89
Would you believe a $10,000 stock? G. Weiss. il por *Business Week* p96 S 4 '89
BERKSHIRE HILLS (MASS.)
Description and travel
Tapping the source [sugaring season in western Mass.] D. Grant. il *New York* 22:70+ Mr 20 '89
BERKSON, BILL
Ambassador of light. il por *Art in America* 77:170-5 N '89
David Ireland's accommodations [cover story] il por *Art in America* 77:178-87+ S '89
BERKUS, BARRY A.
about
Western tilt. P. Clothier. il por *Art News* 88:95-6+ Summ '89
BERLE, MILTON
Waiting [story] il por *Ladies' Home Journal* 106:104+ S '89

BERLE, MILTON—*cont.*
about
Milton Berle. il pors *People Weekly* 31 Special Issue:42-3 Summ '89
Mr. TV's message on the medium. il por *U.S. News & World Report* 106:14 My 22 '89
BERLE, PETER A. A., 1937-
The Audubon view. See issues of Audubon beginning November 1985
BERLIN, ANN
(jt. auth) See Taylor, Valerie, and Berlin, Ann
BERLIN, BEATRICE, 1922-
about
Beatrice Berlin. K. Haber. il pors *American Artist* 53:64-7 My '89
BERLIN, EVELYN
Michael's orchestra. *Ladies' Home Journal* 106:108 O '89
BERLIN, IRVING, 1888-1989
about
Obituary
National Review 41:22 O 27 '89. J. P. Hart
Newsweek il por 114:75 O 2 '89. B. Barol
Opera News il pors 54:56-7 D 9 '89. D. Harris
People Weekly il pors 32:63-4+ O 9 '89. M. H. J. Farrell
Time il por 134:84 O 2 '89. M. Walsh
BERLIN, SIR ISAIAH
about
Isaiah Berlin at eighty. J. Brodsky. il por *The New York Review of Books* 36:44-5 Ag 17 '89
BERLIN (GERMANY)
Art
Memories of modernism. M. Hübl. il *Art News* 88:181 My '89
Streets
See also
Friedrichstrasse (Berlin, Germany)
BERLIN (GERMANY: EAST)
East Berlin diary; tr. by Phillip Boehm. C. Hein. il *The New York Times Magazine* p34-7+ D 17 '89
Art
Report from East Berlin. D. Galloway. il *Art in America* 77:45-7+ Jl '89
Description
As the Wall came tumbling down. J. Agee. il *The New York Times Magazine* p42-3+ N 26 '89
Music
See also
Opera—Germany (East)
BERLIN (GERMANY: WEST)
Galleries and museums
See also
Flower Automat Gallery (Berlin, Germany: West)
Housing
Americans in Berlin. D. Dietsch. il *Architectural Record* 177:82-95 Jl '89
Markets
West Berlin: a cheerfully irrelevant outpost [Polish flea market] P. R. Range. il *U.S. News & World Report* 107:48 N 6 '89
Music
See also
Deutsche Oper Berlin
Opera—Germany (West)
Politics and government
Blitzkrieg by the ultra-right [city elections] J. Smolowe. il *Time* 133:47 F 13 '89
Religious institutions and affairs
The hazards of an unusable past. J. M. Wall. *The Christian Century* 106:195-6 F 22 '89
Street traffic
Keeping an 'eye' on traffic [computer system] A. Wormnes. il *World Press Review* 36:57 Mr '89
Street smarts [Ali-Scout navigation system] W. Baldwin. il *Forbes* 144:298+ N 13 '89
BERLIN FILM FESTIVAL *See* Motion picture festivals—Germany (West)
BERLIN JAZZ FESTIVAL *See* Music festivals—Germany (West)
BERLIN PHILHARMONIC ORCHESTRA
Abbado takes Berlin. N. Lebrecht. il por *Opera News* 54:16-17 D 23 '89
Now, a grab for new chairs [choosing successor to H. von Karajan] M. Walsh. il pors *Time* 133:90-1 My 8 '89
BERLIN QUESTION, 1945-
Berlin: forty years on. R. E. Hunter. *Foreign Affairs* 68:41-52 Summ '89
BERLIN WALL, 1961-1989
Adjusting to change. J. Bierman. il *Maclean's* 102:28+ N 27 '89
After the Wall. *The New Republic* 201:7-8 D 4 '89
After the Wall. il *Time* 134:44 N 13 '89
Anniversary of the Berlin Wall [statement, August 12, 1989] G. Bush. *Department of State Bulletin* 89:41 O '89
As the Wall came tumbling down. J. Agee. il *The New York Times Magazine* p42-3+ N 26 '89
Bring down the Wall. E. Mortimer. *World Press Review* 36:31 My '89

Consider the Wall. *Commonweal* 116:659-60 D 1 '89
Crossing the divide. *The Nation* 249:665 D 4 '89
Dateline East Germany: the wall behind the Wall. D. Hamilton. *Foreign Policy* 76:176-97 Fall '89
The death of the old order [cover story; with editorial comment by Stephen Budiansky] D. Stanglin and P. R. Range. il *U.S. News & World Report* 107:9, 20-2+ N 20 '89
East Berlin diary; tr. by Phillip Boehm. C. Hein. il *The New York Times Magazine* p34-7+ D 17 '89
Euphoria & beyond. C. Wilpert. *Commonweal* 116:695-7 D 15 '89
Fall of the Berlin Wall fits Rev. King's dream. il por *Jet* 77:53-4 N 27 '89
The fall of the Wall [reflections of M. von Chielanski-Lallinger] M. Ryan. il por *People Weekly* 32:46-9 N 27 '89
Free at last! [cover story; special section] il map *Maclean's* 102:44-8+ N 20 '89
Freedom! [opening of Berlin Wall; cover story; special section] il *Time* 134:24-30+ N 20 '89
The German revolution. T. Garton Ash. il *The New York Review of Books* 36:14+ D 21 '89
Glasnost as a verb: to open a Wall. *America* 161:367-8 N 25 '89
The Gorbachev tease [hints at tearing down Berlin Wall] M. Peretz. *The New Republic* 201:14+ Jl 10 '89
Gorbachev's doctrine. D. Schorr. *The New Leader* 72:4 N 13 '89
Hallelujah! W. F. Buckley. *National Review* 41:54 D 22 '89
If the Wall came tumbling down. P. Schneider. il *The New York Times Magazine* p22-4+ Je 25 '89
Must walls of hostility continue to divide? J. E. Will. il *The Christian Century* 106:1191-2 D 20-27 '89
A new day in Berlin. M. Tyan. il *People Weekly* 32:70-3 D 4 '89
Notes and comment. *The New Yorker* 65:39 N 27 '89
Out of the shadows [effect of opening of Berlin Wall on East German athletes] W. O. Johnson and A. Verschoth. il *Sports Illustrated* 71:16-21 N 27 '89
The party at the Wall. B. Owen. il *National Review* 41:20-1 D 22 '89
A postcard from Berlin. M. B. Zuckerman. il *U.S. News & World Report* 107:80 D 11 '89
Seeing is believing [East Germans in Berlin] C. Hope. *The New Republic* 201:14-16 D 18 '89
Tearing down the Wall. S. Manning. il *Scholastic Update (Teachers' edition)* 122:13 O 20 '89
The Wall comes down [cover story; special section] il maps *Newsweek* 114:24-32+ N 20 '89
When will the Wall fall? H. Anderson. il *Newsweek* 113:43 Ja 30 '89
Reporters and reporting
How TV helped tear down the Berlin Wall. D. Schorr. il *TV Guide* 37:10-11 D 23-29 '89
BERLIN WALL, 1961-1989, IN ADVERTISING
A batch of really off-the-Wall ads [television commercials] il *U.S. News & World Report* 107:11-12 D 18 '89
BERLINER, DAVID C.
(jt. auth) See Gage, N. L. (Nathaniel Lees), 1917-, and Berliner, David C.
BERLOW, ALAN
Habeas corpse. *The New Republic* 201:12+ O 30 '89
Never again? il *Harper's* 279:62-8 O '89
Who's the puppet? *The New Republic* 201:16-18 O 2 '89
BERLUSCONI, SILVIO
about
A firestorm scorches De Benedetti's media empire. J. Rossant. il pors *Business Week* p68 D 25 '89-Ja 1 '90
Four titans carve up European TV [cover story] W. Fisher and M. Shapiro. il *The Nation* 248:37+ Ja 9-16 '89
BERMAN, AVIS
Antiques: Chinese censers. il *Architectural Digest* 46:186-91+ Ag '89
Art: sporting prints. il *Architectural Digest* 46:210-15+ Ap '89
East meets West Side: James and Marilyn Marinaccio's Japanese ethos. il pors *Architectural Digest* 46:304-9+ N '89
The Force behind the Whitney. il pors *American Heritage* 40:102-13 S/O '89
The fraktur. *American Heritage* 40:28 F '89
Juliana Force and folk art. il *Antiques* 136:542-53 S '89
A passion for living. il por *Modern Maturity* 32:56-61+ Je/Jl '89
Space exploration. il pors *Art News* 88:130-5 N '89
Two masterworks of American architecture. il por *Architectural Digest* 46:314+ O '89
BERMAN, CLAIRE
Stepparenting: how to make it work. *McCall's* 117:97+ N '89
BERMAN, MILDRED
Revere Beach: a peculiarly American seaside resort. bibl il map *Focus (New York, N.Y.: 1950)* 39:4-8 Fall '89
BERMAN, WILLIAM
Should the Congress adopt the "Clean Air Act amendments of 1987"? [excerpts from statement, September 30, 1987] *Congressional Digest* 68:42+ F '89

BERMANN, KARL
Unlikely Managua is again Mecca for international book trade. il *Publishers Weekly* 236:12-13 Ag 18 '89
BERMANT, DAVID
about
"If it doesn't work, it isn't art". C. Brown. il por *Forbes* 143:142 My 15 '89
BERMUDA
See also
British—Bermuda
Gardens and gardening—Bermuda
Historic houses, sites, etc.—Bermuda
Sports—Bermuda
Description and travel
Bermuda beckons. J. White. il *Black Enterprise* 20:141-2 O '89
A sporting good time in Bermuda. C. Males. il *Travel Holiday* 171:9-10+ F '89
Photographs and photography
A photographer's guide to Bermuda. J. Marvullo. il map *Petersen's Photographic Magazine* 18:50-3+ Jl '89
BERMUDA TRIANGLE
The Bermuda Triangle. il *National Geographic World* 172:9-11 D '89
BERN, MARSHALL W., AND GRAHAM, RONALD L.
The shortest-network problem. bibl il map *Scientific American* 260:84-9 Ja '89
BERN (SWITZERLAND)
Fountains
Tempest in a fountain [work of artist M. Oppenheim] E. Beck. il *Art News* 88:75-6 O '89
BERNARD, JEFFREY
The man who put the grouch into Groucho's. R. Ryan. il por *Gentlemen's Quarterly* 59:31+ Ja '89
BERNARD, JOSEF
Capacitors (I). il *Radio-Electronics* 60:49-53 My '89
Capacitors (II). il *Radio-Electronics* 60:56-9 Ag '89
BERNARD, RUEL
(jt. auth) See Kane, Brian A., and Bernard, Ruel
BERNARD L. MADOFF INVESTMENT SECURITIES
Living off the spread [B. L. Madoff takes advantage of New York Stock Exchange rule that protects specialists] R. L. Stern. il *Forbes* 144:66-7 Jl 10 '89
BERNARDIN, JOSEPH L., CARDINAL
Abortion: Catholics must change hearts as well as laws. *U.S. Catholic* 54:31-3 D '89
BERNATH, PETER F., AND OTHERS
Detection of C₅ in the circumstellar shell of IRC+10216. bibl f il *Science* 244:562-4 My 5 '89
BERNAYS, MINNA, 1865-1941
about
Sigmund and Minna? The biographer as voyeur. P. Gay. por *The New York Times Book Review* 94:1+ Ja 29 '89
BERNBAUM, GLENN
about
Society's café. M. Filler. il pors *House & Garden* 161:100+ O '89
BERNDT, BRUCE C., 1939-
Srinivasa Ramanujan. *The American Scholar* 58:234-44 Spr '89
BERNE CONVENTION FOR THE PROTECTION OF LITERARY AND ARTISTIC WORKS
Berne Convention Implementation Act of 1988 [statement, October 31, 1988] R. Reagan. *Department of State Bulletin* 89:35 Ja '89
BERNER, ROBERT A., 1935-, AND LASAGA, ANTONIO C.
Modeling the geochemical carbon cycle. bibl il *Scientific American* 260:74-81 Mr '89
BERNEY, LOUIS
News of the world [story] *The New Yorker* 65:36-42 Ap 3 '89
BERNHARD, SANDRA
You can be too thin. il *Mademoiselle* 95:128-9 Jl '89
about
Gal pals Sandra Bernhard and Madonna monkey around to save the jungle. il pors *People Weekly* 31:54-6 Je 12 '89
BERNHARDT, SARAH, 1844-1923
about
Bernhardt in America. J. Kobler. il pors *American Heritage* 40:52-4+ Jl/Ag '89
BERNHEIM, ANTOINE
about
Tough guys with a genteel manner. P. Berman. il por *Forbes* 144:75-80 Jl 10 '89
BERNICK, HOWARD B., 1952-
about
Washing the gray out at Alberto-Culver. J. F. Siler. il pors *Business Week* p138 Je 26 '89
BERNIER, ANDRÉ, AND SCHMIES, HOWARD
Building an automated recording anemometer. il *Weatherwise* 42:164-6 Je '89
BERNIER, OLIVIER
Building an empire. il *House & Garden* 161:40+ D '89
BERNIER, ROSAMOND
Eloquent bouquets. il *House & Garden* 161:96-101+ D '89

BERNOULLIAN EFFECT
The fascinating physics of fizz [work of A. Prosperetti] W. F. Allman. il por *U.S. News & World Report* 107:77 N 20 '89
BERNS, BEN, 1936-
about
Boundless landscapes. L. Anderson. il *American Artist* 53:86-91+ S '89
BERNS, WALTER, 1919-
Flag-burning & other modes of expression. *Commentary* 88:37-41 O '89
BERNSEN, CORBIN
about
Hear Corbin coo. il pors *Life* 12:60-1 Je '89
BERNSTAM, MIKHAIL S.
(jt. auth) See Rabushka, Alvin, and Bernstam, Mikhail S.
BERNSTEIN, ADAM
about
Budget genius. J. Farber. por *Rolling Stone* p99-100 Ag 10 '89
BERNSTEIN, ALBERT J., AND ROZEN, SYDNEY CRAFT
13 ways to re-energize your staff. il *Working Woman* 14:45-6 Ap '89
BERNSTEIN, ALFRED
about
In Loyalties, Carl Bernstein digs up a past best remembered. S. Dougherty. il pors *People Weekly* 31:89-90+ Ap 10 '89
Loyalties [excerpt] C. Bernstein. il pors *Rolling Stone* p82-3+ Mr 9 '89
Still taking the Fifth. D. Horowitz. *Commentary* 88:53-5 Jl '89
This boy's life. E. Pooley. il pors *New York* 22:38-43 F 13 '89
BERNSTEIN, CARL
Loyalties [excerpt] il pors *Rolling Stone* p82-3+ Mr 9 '89
about
In Loyalties, Carl Bernstein digs up a past best remembered. S. Dougherty. il pors *People Weekly* 31:89-90+ Ap 10 '89
Still taking the Fifth. D. Horowitz. *Commentary* 88:53-5 Jl '89
This boy's life. E. Pooley. il pors *New York* 22:38-43 F 13 '89
Woodward and Bernstein: what they think of Watergate now [interview] J. Kalter. il pors *TV Guide* 37:6-8 O 28-N 3 '89
BERNSTEIN, CHARLES
Wet verse at the New Yorker. *Harper's* 279:28+ N '89
BERNSTEIN, DENNIS
(jt. auth) See Jiji, Jessica, and Bernstein, Dennis
BERNSTEIN, GARY
Pro talk. See issues of Petersen's Photographic Magazine
BERNSTEIN, HARRIET
(jt. auth) See Abrams, Malcolm, and Bernstein, Harriet
BERNSTEIN, HARRIET TYSON- See Tyson-Bernstein, Harriet
BERNSTEIN, JEREMY, 1929-
Besso. *The New Yorker* 65:86-92 F 27 '89
BERNSTEIN, LEONARD, 1918-
about
Bernstein at seventy. J. Ardoin. *National Review* 41:62-4 Ja 27 '89
Bernstein's Mahler. R. Freed. il por *Stereo Review* 54:145 S '89
Family ties. P. G. Davis. il *New York* 22:129-30 N 6 '89
Lenny explains. W. F. Buckley. *National Review* 41:71 Ja 27 '89
Mahler from a master. D. Hurwitz. il por *High Fidelity (New York, N.Y.)* 39:62-3 Ja '89
Musical America's 1989 Musician of the Year: Leonard Bernstein. il pors *High Fidelity (New York, N.Y.)* 39:11 Ap '89
Musical events:
American premiere of Arias and barcarolles song cycle. A. Porter. *The New Yorker* 65:95-7 O 23 '89
BERNSTEIN, LESTER
Time Inc. means business [cover story] il *The New York Times Magazine* p22-5+ F 26 '89
BERNSTEIN, LORI R., AND COLBURN, NANCY H.
AP1/jun function is differentially induced in promotion-sensitive and resistant JB6 cells. bibl f il *Science* 244:566-9 My 5 '89
BERNSTEIN, MARGARET
Pressing on. il *Black Enterprise* 19:142-4+ Je '89
BERNSTEIN, MARK
John Patterson rang up success with the Incorruptible Cashier. bibl f (p174) il por *Smithsonian* 20:150-2+ Je '89
BERNSTEIN, PAULA, 1933-
Approaching a better job sideways. il *New Choices for the Best Years* 29:48-50 D '89
BERNSTEIN, RICHARD
A journey of conscience. il *The New York Times Magazine* p22-5+ Ap 16 '89
BERNSTEIN, RICHARD K.
about
A medical messiah? S. S. Hall. il pors *New Choices for the Best Years* 29:31-6 Ap '89

BERNSTEIN, ROBERT
about
What goes up must come down. J. Zweig. pors *Forbes* 143:200 Mr 20 '89

BERNSTEIN, ROBERT L., 1923-
about
Bernstein retiring from Random; Vitale is new chairman. C. Reid and J. F. Baker. pors *Publishers Weekly* 236:8 N 17 '89
Cerf to Newhouse. *The Nation* 249:623-4 N 27 '89
The Random House shuffle. J. Alter. il pors *Newsweek* 114:74 N 13 '89

BERNSTEIN, SAM
about
Money. S. Anderson. il *Cycle* 40:7 Ag '89

BERNSTEIN, SYLVIA
about
In Loyalties, Carl Bernstein digs up a past best remembered. S. Dougherty. il pors *People Weekly* 31:89-90+ Ap 10 '89
Loyalties [excerpt] C. Bernstein. il pors *Rolling Stone* p82-3+ Mr 9 '89
This boy's life. E. Pooley. il pors *New York* 22:38-43 F 13 '89

BERNSTEIN (SANFORD C.) & CO., INC. *See* Sanford C. Bernstein & Co., Inc.

BERRA, YOGI, 1925-
about
Yogi: it's not over, but it is. T. Callahan. il por *Newsweek* 114:83 O 16 '89

BERREBY, DAVID
Contagious fortune. il *Ms.* 17:30+ My '89

BERRIE (RUSS) & CO., INC. *See* Russ Berrie & Co., Inc.

BERRIEN, JAMES S.
about
James Berrien: sailing along in a sea of challengers. il por *Business Week* p99 Ag 21 '89

BERRIES
See also
Blackberries
Cranberries
Mulberries
Raspberries

BERRIGAN, PHILIP, 1923-
about
"Serving justice". C. Moekle. il por *American Health* 8:67 Ap '89

BERRY, ANDREA L.
The farming doctor. il por *American Visions* 4:44-5 Ag '89

BERRY, CARMEN RENEE
When helping hurts. *Essence* 19:75-6+ Mr '89

BERRY, CHUCK, 1926-
about
Two Chess mates at their very best. D. Fricke. il pors *Rolling Stone* p40-1 Ja 26 '89

BERRY, LAURIE
about
Laurie Berry's 252-word story may seem an under-a-Cheever, but it ended up a big winner. por *People Weekly* 31:107 Je 19 '89

BERRY, R. STEPHEN
Our energy future: time horizons and instability. *Environment* 31:5+ Jl/Ag '89

BERRY, RICHARD, 1946-
Behind the scenes. See issues of Astronomy

BERRY, RICKY, D. 1989
about
Ricky Berry of Sacramento Kings commits suicide. por *Jet* 76:55-6 S 4 '89

BERRY, THOMAS
about
A new story of creation. K. L. Woodward. il por *Newsweek* 113:70-2 Je 5 '89
Thomas Berry and a new creation story. M. Hope and J. Young. il por *The Christian Century* 106:750-3 Ag 16-23 '89

BERRY, WENDELL, 1934-
The futility of global thinking [adaptation of address, June 1989] *Harper's* 279:16-19+ S '89
The lowland grove [poem] *Wilderness* 53:55 Wint '89
True integration. il *Mother Jones* 14:16+ Je '89

BERRY DESSERTS *See* Desserts

BERRYMAN, PHILLIP
The battle for the Catholic Church. por *The Christian Century* 106:523-6 My 17 '89

BERSCH, SUZANNE
Quick-fix revitalizers. il *Harper's Bazaar* 122:16+ Ja '89

BERT RIGBY, YOU'RE A FOOL [film] *See* Motion picture reviews—Single works

BERTA, ANNALISA, AND OTHERS
Skeleton of the oldest known pinniped, Enaliarctos mealsi. bibl f il *Science* 244:60-2 Ap 7 '89

BERTELS, THOMAS MORE, SISTER
about
Agriculture's hell-raising nun. J. Midgett. il por *Successful Farming* 87:33 F '89

BERTELSMANN AG
Press conference in Gütersloh: Bertelsmann's usual good news. M. Reuter. il *Publishers Weekly* 236:14 O 20 '89
Reinhard Mohn. il *The Nation* 248:810 Je 12 '89
World's fastest press runs Cosby title at three copies a second [integrated book manufacturing machine] J. P. Frank. il *Publishers Weekly* 235:67-8 Mr 17 '89

BERTHOLD, ERIC A.
Borderlines. il *House & Garden* 161:178 Ap '89
Yankee preserve. il *House & Garden* 161:98-103+ Je '89

BERTHOT, JAKE, 1939-
about
States of grace. M. Moorman. il por *Art News* 88:118-22 Ja '89

BERTHOUD PASS SKI AREA (COLO.) *See* Resorts— Colorado

BERTINELLI, VALERIE, 1960?-
about
'I'm not so beautiful that I'm hard to reach'. E. Warren. il pors *TV Guide* 37:19-20+ N 4-10 '89

BERTOLLI, PAUL
about
A family dinner with Alice Waters and Paul Bertolli. M. Damsker. il pors *Organic Gardening* 36:46-9 O '89

BERTON, PIERRE, 1920-
The golden age of steel. il *Maclean's* 102:18-19 Ag 21 '89

BERTONCINI, GENE
about
Goodbye, Michael. W. Balliett. *The New Yorker* 65:133-7 N 6 '89

BERTRAM, ROBERT W.
The storyteller visits the vineyard. *The Christian Century* 106:255-6 Mr 8 '89

BERTRAND, LYNNE
The American canvas. il por *National Parks* 63:32-6+ S/O '89

BERTRAND, YANN ARTHUS- *See* Arthus-Bertrand, Yann

BERTY, ANNE
A trip along the Séptima. il *The Unesco Courier* 42:18-21 Ag '89

BERUMEN, JULIO
about
Julio Berumen. il por *People Weekly* 32:54 D 25 '89-Ja 1 '90
A loving father eases the recovery of Julio Berumen, the quake's littlest survivor. M. Brower. il pors *People Weekly* 32:74-5 D 4 '89

BESANCON, ALAIN
Can Poland ever be free? *Commentary* 87:15-20 Ap '89

BESANT, ANNIE, 1847-1933
about
The odyssey of Annie Besant. J. Oppenheim. bibl il pors *History Today* 39:12-18 S '89

BESIDE HERSELF [drama] *See* Pintauro, Joseph

BESPALOFF, ALEXIS
Wine. See occasional issues of New York

BESSELL, TED
about
Trapped in a nice-guy image since That girl, Ted Bessell's no patsy as Tracey Ullman's director. F. A. Bernstein. il pors *People Weekly* 31:117+ Ap 3 '89

BESSIE, CORNELIA
about
Cornelia & Michael Bessie Books. R. A. Carter. il pors *Publishers Weekly* 235:46-8 Ja 13 '89

BESSIE, SIMON MICHAEL
about
Cornelia & Michael Bessie Books. R. A. Carter. il pors *Publishers Weekly* 235:46-8 Ja 13 '89

BESSIE (CORNELIA & MICHAEL) BOOKS *See* Cornelia & Michael Bessie Books

BESSO, MICHELANGELO, 1873-1955
about
Besso. J. Bernstein. *The New Yorker* 65:86-92 F 27 '89

BESSON, PAUL
See you in court. il *Black Enterprise* 20:74-6 N '89

BEST BOOKS *See* Books and reading—Best books

BEST DRESSED LISTS *See* Clothing and dress—Celebrities

BEST SELLERS
1988 top sellers: the year's most successful new children's books. il *Publishers Weekly* 235:43 Ap 28 '89
1988's hardcover bestsellers. D. Maryles. bibl il *Publishers Weekly* 235:23-7 Mr 10 '89
All-time bestselling hardcover children's books; All-time best-selling paperback children's books. *Publishers Weekly* 236:28-9 O 27 '89
Best sellers. See issues of The New York Times Book Review
Longest-running hardcover bestsellers for 1988. *Publishers Weekly* 235:53 Ja 6 '89
Longest-running paperback bestsellers for 1988. *Publishers Weekly* 235:55 Ja 6 '89
Paperback best sellers. See issues of The New York Times Book Review
Paperback top sellers. P. Kaganoff. bibl *Publishers Weekly* 235:28 Mr 10 '89
Publishers weekly children's bestsellers. See occasional issues of Publishers Weekly beginning February 26, 1988

BEST SELLERS—cont.
Publishers weekly hardcover bestsellers. See issues of Publishers Weekly
Publishers weekly paperback bestsellers. See issues of Publishers Weekly
Religious bestsellers [new list from Evangelical Christian Publishers Association and Christian Booksellers Association] L. Sibley. *Publishers Weekly* 235:39 Mr 3 '89
So big: the all-time mass market bestsellers [paperbacks] il *Publishers Weekly* 235:S31 My 26 '89
The top of the charts. il *Publishers Weekly* 235:54 Ja 6 '89

Anecdotes, facetiae, satire, etc.
Belles lettres. L. H. Lapham. *Harper's* 278:10-11 Je '89
BETA (SECURITIES MEASUREMENT)
How savvy fund investors tally the risk. J. Meehan. *Business Week* p118 O 2 '89
BETA BLOCKERS (DRUGS) *See* Adrenergic blocking agents
BETA-CAROTENE *See* Carotene
BETA RAYS
See also
Double-beta decay
BETHANY, MARILYN
Design. See occassional issues of New York beginning February 20, 1984
BETHE, HANS ALBRECHT, 1906-
Chop down the nuclear arsenals. il *The Bulletin of the Atomic Scientists* 45:11-15 Mr '89
BETHELL, TOM
Capitol ideas. See issues of The American Spectator
Criminals belong in jail. *The Washington Monthly* 21:68-9 F '89
Golden State opportunity. il *National Review* 41:34+ N 10 '89
Jim Baker, ministering to the media [cover story] il *National Review* 41:24-7 My 5 '89
Socialism by the textbook. il *National Review* 41:36-8 O 13 '89
A tale of two cities. il *National Review* 41:30-3+ F 10 '89
BETHLEHEM
O little town [visit on Christmas Eve] C. N. Barnard. il map *Modern Maturity* 32:46-52 D '89/Ja '90
BETHLEHEM STEEL CORP.
Bethlehem-Steelworkers contract. il *Monthly Labor Review* 112:43-4 Jl '89
Forging the new Bethlehem. G. L. Miles. il por *Business Week* p108-10 Je 5 '89
BETHUNE, JOHN
Books with a bedside manner. il *Publishers Weekly* 235:35-6+ Ap 21 '89
BETHUNE-COOKMAN COLLEGE
Bill and Camille Cosby give $1.5 million to Meharry and Bethune-Cookman colleges. il pors *Jet* 75:5-6 Ja 9 '89
BETRAYED [film] *See* Motion picture reviews—Single works
BETSKY, AARON
Booming L.A.: brave new urbanism? il *Architectural Record* 177:71+ F '89
Heavy metal. il *Architectural Record* 177:86-93 mid-S '89
BETTER, NANCY MARX
Call of the wild. il *House & Garden* 161:46+ Je '89
BETTER HOMES AND GARDENS (PERIODICAL)
Editor's letter. D. Jordan. See issues of Better Homes and Gardens beginning November 1984
BETTER HOMES FOUNDATION
Helping homeless families. M. Daly. il *Better Homes and Gardens* 67:27-8 My '89
Helping homeless families [Great American Yard Sale and National Home Furnishings Sale; with editorial comment by David Jordan] M. Daly. il *Better Homes and Gardens* 67:8, 18+ S '89
Helping homeless families [quilt made by Long Island women] M. Daly. il *Better Homes and Gardens* 67:35-6 Ap '89
Helping homeless families: how we're putting your money to work right now. M. Daly. il *Better Homes and Gardens* 67:21-2+ Mr '89
Homeless families in America [with editorial comment by David Jordan] M. Daly. il *Better Homes and Gardens* 67:8, 29-30 D '89
Homeless families in America: what we all can do to help. M. Daly. il *Better Homes and Gardens* 67:199+ N '89
BETTI, JOHN A.
about
Betti nominated to become new acquisition chief. por *Aviation Week & Space Technology* 130:20 Jl 10 '89
BETTING *See* Gambling
BETTING, BASEBALL *See* Baseball betting
BETTING, BASKETBALL *See* Basketball betting
BETTING, BOXING *See* Boxing betting
BETTING, FOOTBALL *See* Football betting
BETTING, HORSE RACE *See* Horse race betting
BETTING, SPORTS *See* Sports betting
BETTS, RICHARD K., 1947-
NATO's mid-life crisis. bibl f *Foreign Affairs* 68:37-52 Spr '89
BETTY CLUB
No name tags, please! Everyone at the annual Betty Picnic is on a first-name basis. il *People Weekly* 32:89 Jl 17 '89

BEUM, ROBERT
524 [poem] *The Christian Century* 106:101 F 1-8 '89
First grade: end of term [poem] *The Christian Century* 106:621 Je 21-28 '89
Rain years [poem] *The Christian Century* 106:646 Jl 5-12 '89
BEUYS, JOSEPH, 1921-1986
about
Beuys butter battle. J. Dornberg. il por *Art News* 88:23 Ap '89
BEVERAGE CONTAINERS
See also
Beer cans
Drinking vessels
Sharpening the edge [steel beverage cans vs. aluminum] E. Corcoran. il *Scientific American* 260:72-3 F '89
BEVERAGE INDUSTRY
See also
Brewing industry
Liquor industry
Soft drink industry
Wine industry
Finance
Beverages and tobacco. E. Giltenan. il *Forbes* 143:100+ Ja 9 '89
BEVERAGES
See also
Alcoholic beverages
Bottled water
Cider
Coffee
Egg creams
Eggnog
Kefir
Lemonade
Punch (Beverage)
Sports drinks
Tea (Beverage)
Festive beverages. il *Better Homes and Gardens* 67:141-2 D '89
Fruit drinks for fitness. E. Fried. il *Black Enterprise* 19:64 Jl '89
Get a headstart on the beverage. il *Southern Living* 24:148 My '89
Keeping your head crystal clear. E. Fried. il *Black Enterprise* 20:126 N '89
Micro-way: holiday party drinks. il *McCall's* 117:123 D '89
Spirited drinks without spirits [Christmas drinks] il *McCall's* 116:71 Ja '89
Tropical coolers. C. Lyons. il *Ebony* 44:96-8+ Jl '89
Zero-proof solutions. M. Simmons. il *New Choices for the Best Years* 29:70-3 My '89
BEVERLY, ELIZABETH
A silence that is not hollow. il por *Commonweal* 116:491-4 S 22 '89
BEVERLY HILLS (CALIF.)
Architecture
Above Beverly Hills [home of S. and S. Beriro designed by Kalef Alaton] H. Drohojowska. il *Architectural Digest* 46:230-7 My '89
Architectural digest visits: Joan Rivers [interior by Louis Malkin] J. Allen. il pors *Architectural Digest* 46:134-9+ F '89
Buildings
Poor little rich man [D. T. Sterling] D. Wechsler. il por *Forbes* 144:196+ N 27 '89
Children
Those Beverly Hills kids. H. Dresner. por *Newsweek* 114:10 D 25 '89
Economic conditions
Rich but dumb. T. Noah. *The New Republic* 201:46 D 25 '89
Historic houses, sites, etc.
See also
Pickfair (Beverly Hills, Calif.: Historic house)
Art déco revisited: a Beverly Hills residence marked by period flair [decorated by Illya Hendrix for A. Kraines] il *Architectural Digest* 46:154-9 Ag '89
Housing
Beverly Hills HUD [subsidized housing for the elderly] T. Noah. *The New Republic* 201:14-16 Ag 21 '89
Restaurants, nightclubs, bars, etc.
Short-order chic [Fountain Coffee Room] P. Viladas. il *House & Garden* 161:62 S '89
Spécialités de la maison:
Pastel. C. Bates. il *Gourmet* 49:22+ Jl '89
Pazzia. C. Bates. il *Gourmet* 49:40+ N '89
To live and dine in L.A. [Rex, Pazzia and Fennel] D. Shaw. il por *Gentlemen's Quarterly* 59:161+ Ap '89
Savings and loan associations
See also
Columbia Savings & Loan Assoc.
Stores
See also
Madeleine Gallay (Firm)
Dressing the part [relationship between film industry and clothing stores on Rodeo Drive] C. Fleming. il *American Film* 14:48-51 S '89

BEVERLY HILLS (CALIF.)—cont.
Streets
See also
Rodeo Drive (Beverly Hills, Calif.)
BEVILACQUA, MICHAEL P.
(jt. auth) See Rice, G. Edgar, and Bevilacqua, Michael P.
BEVILACQUA, MICHAEL P., AND OTHERS
Endothelial leukocyte adhesion molecule 1: an inducible receptor for neutrophils related to complement regulatory proteins and lectins. bibl f il *Science* 243:1160-5 Mr 3 '89
BEYER, ANDREW
about
The daily double. G. Norman. il pors *Sports Illustrated* 70:92-6+ Je 5 '89
BEYER, KENNY
about
Weigh to go! N. Amdur. il pors *World Tennis* 37:42-3 O '89
BEYOND WORD WRITER (WORD PROCESSOR PROGRAM) See Word processors and processing—Programming
BFS (BATTERS FACED PER START) See Baseball, Professional—Statistics
BHAGWATI, JAGDISH N., 1934-
about
"Pressure has its uses". L. Minard. il por *Forbes* 143:96+ Je 12 '89
BHALERAO, VIJAYA R.
The mini-doctors of Bombay. il *World Health* p20-3 D '88
BHARADWAT, RADHA
India's dream makers. il *Scholastic Update (Teachers' edition)* 121:24-5 Mr 10 '89
BHC COMMUNICATIONS, INC.
The new Herb Siegel play. T. Jaffe. *Forbes* 144:172 D 25 '89
BHONSLE, RAJARAM V.
(jt. auth) See Alurkar, Sadanand K., and Bhonsle, Rajaram V.
BHOPAL (INDIA)
See also
Bhopal poisonous gas disaster, India, 1984
BHOPAL POISONOUS GAS DISASTER, INDIA, 1984
Suits and claims
Bhopal's over—at least for Union Carbide. *Newsweek* 113:54 F 27 '89
Damages for a deadly cloud. il *Time* 133:53 F 27 '89
Poison gas, up two bucks. *The Nation* 248:289 Mr 6 '89
Union Carbide's Bhopal bill. R. W. King. *Business Week* p40 F 27 '89
BHUMIBOL ADULYADEJ, KING OF THAILAND
about
King Bhumibol's reign. B. Crossette. il pors *The New York Times Magazine* p30-2+ My 21 '89
BHUTTO, BENAZIR
The education and stormy career of Islam's leading lady [excerpt from Daughter of destiny] il pors *People Weekly* 31:218-20+ Mr 6 '89
The policies of Pakistan [address, June 7, 1989] *Vital Speeches of the Day* 55:551-3 Jl 1 '89
Visit of Pakistan's prime minister [remarks, June 6, 1989] il por *Department of State Bulletin* 89:63-4 O '89
about
Benazir Bhutto's victory. il *World Press Review* 36:11 Ja '89
Can Pakistan's superwoman survive? E. MacFarquhar. il pors *U.S. News & World Report* 106:38-9+ Ap 17 '89
The double life of Benazir Bhutto [cover story] I. Buruma. il *The New York Review of Books* 36:8-11 Mr 2 '89
The Indian subcontinent [cover story; special issue] il maps *Scholastic Update (Teachers' edition)* 121:3-26 Mr 10 '89
A nation divided. I. Buruma. il pors *The New York Times Magazine* p26-30+ Ja 15 '89
Pakistan under Benazir Bhutto. W. L. Richter. bibl f *Current History* 88:433-6+ D '89
Pakistan's steel magnolia. il por *U.S. News & World Report* 106:14 Je 12 '89
Priming the minister. K. Starr. il pors *Vogue* 179:416-19+ Ap '89
Visit to the United States, 1989
Bhutto's diplomatic debut. A. Platt. il por *Newsweek* 113:46 Je 19 '89
The policies of Pakistan [address, June 7, 1989] B. Bhutto. *Vital Speeches of the Day* 55:551-3 Jl 1 '89
A rosy reception for Bhutto. K. Makihara. il por *Time* 133:40 Je 19 '89
Visit of Pakistan's prime minister [remarks, June 6, 1989] G. Bush; B. Bhutto. il por *Department of State Bulletin* 89:63-4 O '89
BI RESEARCH (NEWSLETTER)
Fantasy and reality. D. Machan. il por *Forbes* 144:282+ N 27 '89
The same . . . but different. M. Hulbert. il *Forbes* 143:408 My 1 '89

BIA *See* Brick Institute of America
BIALER, SEWERYN
Can Gorbachev radicalize *perestroika*? il *U.S. News & World Report* 107:39-40 Ag 7 '89
Communism turned upside down. il *U.S. News & World Report* 106:31 Je 19 '89
The deal that still lives in infamy. *U.S. News & World Report* 107:68-9 Ag 28-S 4 '89
Gorbachev and the Soviet military. il *U.S. News & World Report* 106:40+ Mr 13 '89
Out of misery, a flicker of hope. il *U.S. News & World Report* 106:42 Mr 27 '89
Reform: Moscow vs. Beijing. il *U.S. News & World Report* 106:32-3 F 6 '89
BIALER, STEWART
about
Different strokes: eleven kids from Brooklyn try life on a kibbutz. J. Taylor. il por *New York* 22:56-8+ Je 12 '89
BIALIK, MAYIM
about
Mayim Bialik. por *Seventeen* 48:112 Ap '89
Mayim Bialik, who strolls Beaches as baby Bette Midler. T. Gold. il pors *People Weekly* 31:63-4 F 6 '89
BIANCHI, DOMENICO, 1955-
about
Domenico Bianchi: Sperone Westwater. M. R. Rubinstein. il *Art News* 88:173 S '89
BIANCHI, MARCO E., AND OTHERS
Specific recognition of cruciform DNA by nuclear protein HMG1. bibl f il *Science* 243:1056-9 F 24 '89
BIANCHI, ROBERT, 1945-
Islam and democracy in Egypt. bibl f *Current History* 88:93-5+ F '89
BIANCO, LISA
about
Beware of paper tigers. J. C. Simpson. il pors *Time* 133:104-5 Mr 27 '89
BIAS ATTACKS *See* Hate crimes
BIATHLON (RUNNING AND CYCLING)
Tough stuff for the masses: mainstreaming the Ironman. J. Silverman. il *Health (New York, N.Y.)* 21:86-8 Ag '89
BIATHLON (SKIING AND SHOOTING)
Heading for an 'off' year [year without a nordic world championship] P. Robbins. il *Skiing* 42:42+ S '89
The thawing of the biathlon. J. Hanc. il *Sport (New York, N.Y.)* 80:15 Ag '89
BIBA (SACRAMENTO, CALIF.: RESTAURANT) See Sacramento (Calif.)—Restaurants, nightclubs, bars, etc.
BIBB, ELIZABETH
Vision quest: the Seventeen career quiz. *Seventeen* 48:205-6+ Mr '89
BIBENDUM (LONDON, ENGLAND: RESTAURANT) See London (England)—Restaurants, nightclubs, bars, etc.
BIBLE
See also
Adultery in the Bible
Biblical literacy
Cities and towns—Biblical teaching
Dreams in the Bible
Enemy in the Bible
Gentiles in the Bible
Hospitality in the Bible
Leprosy in the Bible
Money in the Bible
Poor in the Bible
Prophets
Sex in the Bible
Shepherds in the Bible
High-tech Bible [Franklin Computer's Electronic Bible] R. N. Ostling. il *Time* 134:82 O 30 '89
The vice president's Bible [D. Quayle] R. Pulliam. il por *The Saturday Evening Post* 261:26 Ap '89
Bibliography
The best books on the Good Book. G. M. Costello. *U.S. Catholic* 54:57-9 S '89
Books on the Bible. D. J. Harrington. *America* 161:404-9 D 2 '89
Concordances
QuickVerse Bible Concordance [computer program] S. Hudson. il *Compute!* 11:70-1 Jl '89
Criticism, interpretation, etc.
The Bible is more offensive than you think. K. Guentert. *U.S. Catholic* 54:18-20 S '89
Living by the Word. See issues of The Christian Century beginning April 5, 1989
The Word. P. J. Ryan. See issues of America beginning November 21, 1987
Literary character
Hans Frei and the meaning of biblical narrative [cover story] W. C. Placher. *The Christian Century* 106:556-9 My 24-31 '89
Publication and distribution
Believers push forward despite legal limbo [Soviet Union] K. A. Lawton. il *Christianity Today* 33:63-4+ N 17 '89
Putting out the Word. J. P. Frank. il *Publishers Weekly* 236:72+ O 6 '89

BIBLE—cont.

Study and teaching

The "Good Book" gets a bad rap in school. K. Blomquist. il *Christianity Today* 33:52 F 3 '89

Scripture from scratch [cover story] W. J. O'Malley. *America* 160:77-81 F 4 '89

Why Catholics can't get enough of the Bible [cover story; special issue; with editorial comment by Robert E. Burns] il *U.S. Catholic* 54:2, 6-50+ S '89

Translations

See Bible—Versions

Versions

Missions and the translatable Gospel [L. Sanneh's Translating the message; cover story] J. B. Carman. *The Christian Century* 106:786+ Ag 30-S 6 '89

The revised RSV. *The Christian Century* 106:584 Je 7-14 '89

BIBLE. N.T.

Bibliography

Shaking loose Biblical fruit. L. Sibley. il *Christianity Today* 33:34-5 F 17 '89

Criticism, interpretation, etc.

F. F. Bruce: a mind for what matters [interview] W. W. Gasque and L. Gasque. il por *Christianity Today* 33:22-5 Ap 7 '89

It is necessarily so. R. N. Longenecker. il *Christianity Today* 33:11 N 17 '89

Rich wisdom: New Testament teachings on wealth [cover story; special section] il *Christianity Today* 33:27-40 My 12 '89

Gospels

Do the Gospels put words in Jesus' mouth? [work by the Jesus Seminar] B. Doyle. il *U.S. Catholic* 54:32-5 S '89

BIBLE. N.T. EPISTLES OF PAUL

F. F. Bruce: a mind for what matters [interview] W. W. Gasque and L. Gasque. il por *Christianity Today* 33:22-5 Ap 7 '89

BIBLE. N.T. LUKE

This bridge called my back [bent woman in Luke 13] G. E. Ziegenhals. *The Christian Century* 106:343-4 Ap 5 '89

BIBLE. N.T. PAUL, EPISTLES OF See Bible. N.T. Epistles of Paul

BIBLE. NEW TESTAMENT See Bible. N.T.

BIBLE. O.T.

Criticism, interpretation, etc.

Land or life: a biblical dilemma [O. Yosef's views in rabbinical debate over Israeli occupation] R. N. Ostling. il por *Time* 134:67 S 18 '89

What you don't know about the Old Testament could fill a book [interview with L. Hoppe] il *U.S. Catholic* 54:26-31 S '89

BIBLE. O.T. GENESIS

Genesis 1 [discussion of November 1988 article, Evolution and the Bible] L. Kass. *Commentary* 87:2+ Ap '89

BIBLE. O.T. PSALMS

How I learned to stop hating and start loving the Psalms. P. Yancey. il *Christianity Today* 33:28-32 O 6 '89

BIBLE. O.T. SONG OF SOLOMON

The cantata of love [book by Blaise Arminjon] P. V. Ahern. *America* 160:53 Ja 28 '89

BIBLE. OLD TESTAMENT See Bible. O.T.

BIBLE AS LITERATURE See Bible—Literary character

BIBLE SOCIETIES

See also
Society of Biblical Literature

BIBLE STORIES

See also
Sodom and Gomorrah (Biblical story)
Videotapes—Bible stories

Four stories that shape the Christian character. J. Shea. il *U.S. Catholic* 54:39-43 S '89

BIBLE STUDY See Bible—Study and teaching

BIBLICAL LITERACY

It is written in the polls [growth in biblical literacy] M. E. Marty. *The Christian Century* 106:607 Je 7-14 '89

BIBLIOGRAPHY

See also
Reading lists

BIBLIOTHÈQUE DE FRANCE

An architect for Mitterrand's new library [D. Perrault] N. Marmer. il *Art in America* 77:31 O '89

BIBLIOTHÈQUE NATIONALE (FRANCE)

See also
Bibliothèque de France

A library in action [preservation of manuscripts] F. Callu. il *The Courier (Unesco)* 42:10-11 My '89

BIBY (SWEDEN: COUNTRY ESTATE) See Country estates—Sweden

BICARBONATE OF SODA See Sodium bicarbonate

BICARBONATES

Possible role of carbamates in neurotoxicity and neurotransmitter inactivation [discussion of August 19, 1988 article, Beta-N-methylamino-L-alanine neurotoxicity: requirement for bicarbonate as a cofactor] J. H. Weiss and D. W. Choi. *Science* 243:1615 Mr 24 '89

BICKERTON, ASHLEY, 1959-

about

Nature's nobleman. K. Larson. il *New York* 22:128-9 N 13 '89

BICKFORD, DENNIS

(jt. auth) See Wicks, George G., and Bickford, Dennis

BICOUVARIS, MARY VASSILIKOU

about

1989 Teacher of the Year. M. S. Miller. il por *Good Housekeeping* 208:152+ My '89

BICYCLE ACCIDENTS See Cycling—Accidents and injuries

BICYCLE BRAKES See Brakes, Bicycle

BICYCLE CARRIERS, AUTOMOBILE See Automobiles—Equipment

BICYCLE CHAINS

Chain reactions [cleaning and lubrication] J. Langley. il *Bicycling* 30:82+ S '89

BICYCLE INDUSTRY

See also
Cannondale Corporation
Huffy Corporation

BICYCLE PUMPS See Air pumps

BICYCLE RACING

See also
Biathlon (Running and cycling)
Bicycle rallies
Cyclists
Human powered vehicle racing
Triathlon

Are RAAM riders crazy? M. Shermer. *Bicycling* 30:108+ Ag '89

The art of the wheel [Tour de Trump] G. Drake. il por *Bicycling* 30:26-8+ Ag '89

Bringing out the best [M. Berglund, winner of Women's Cycling Classic] A. Smith. il por *Women's Sports & Fitness* 11:62-3 S '89

CoreStates [10th place finish of G. LeMond] T. Blumenthal. il *Bicycling* 30:14 S '89

Dirty tricks [cyclocross] T. Chauran. *Bicycling* 30:80+ D '89

The fast (dirt) track [mountain bike racing] S. Martin. il *Bicycling* 30:42 O/N '89

A full-time cycling team: US cycling shifts its gear after the poor showing in Seoul. T. Blumenthal. il *Women's Sports & Fitness* 11:66 Mr '89

Le Grand LeMond [Sportsman of the Year; winner of Tour de France; cover story] E. M. Swift. il pors map *Sports Illustrated* 71:54-8+ D 25 '89-Ja 1 '90

How to watch a cycling race. M. Ratner. il *Women's Sports & Fitness* 11:18-19 My '89

The human machine [energy efficiency of riders in Race Across America] C. Kyle. il *Bicycling* 30:196+ My '89

Humility and a pinch of purpose [A. Hampsten] C. Carpenter-Phinney. il pors *Bicycling* 30:90-2+ Ap '89

If Columbus had a bike [Soviet cycling team's U.S. visit] V. Senatorov. il *Bicycling* 30:164-5 Ap '89

Innerviews [interview with mountain racer S. Ballantyne] il por *Women's Sports & Fitness* 11:56 Jl/Ag '89

Joy ride [Casper Classic] J. McCallum. il *Sports Illustrated* 71:53-4+ Jl 17 '89

LeMond's ultimate challenge. G. Drake. il pors *Bicycling* 30:60-2+ My '89

Little big wheels [children's races] S. Martin. il *Bicycling* 30:100-2 Je '89

The outer limits [Race Across America] T. Blumenthal. il *Bicycling* 30:36-9 D '89

RAAM tough [Race Across America champ S. Notorangelo] C. Patterson. il por *Women's Sports & Fitness* 11:57-8 N/D '89

The 'Seoul searching' begins [poor performance of American cycling team] G. Drake. il *Bicycling* 30:52-6 Ja/F '89

She goes round in circles [C. Paraskevin-Young] T. D'Ottavio. il por *American Health* 8:86 My '89

Tiny and tough [L. Brambini, winner of Ore-Ida Women's Challenge] *Women's Sports & Fitness* 11:15 O '89

Tour de Tundra: cyclist Amy McClean caps the grueling Iditabike. Y. Samer. il *Women's Sports & Fitness* 11:56-7 Je '89

Unveiling Nelson Vails. K. Cobb. il por *American Health* 8:84 My '89

Uphill racer [I. Thompson] T. Blumenthal. il pors *Women's Sports & Fitness* 11:24-7 S '89

Waiting for the black Merckx [lack of black bicycle racers] M. E. Mantell. il *Bicycling* 30:90-1+ My '89

The wheels of fortune [Tour de Trump] E. M. Swift. il *Sports Illustrated* 70:32-4+ My 22 '89

Woman to watch: cyclocross champion Lisa Muhich. B. Cooper. il por *Women's Sports & Fitness* 11:61 My '89

Photographs and photography

Reachable racers. J. A. Dickerson. il *Petersen's Photographic Magazine* 18:68-71 Jl '89

Rules

What is the UCI? [International Cycling Union] M. E. Mantell. il *Bicycling* 30:64+ Je '89

BICYCLE RACING—*cont.*

Study and teaching
See Cycling—Study and teaching

Television broadcasting
See Television broadcasting—Sports

France
Beating the clock—and all the odds—cyclist Greg LeMond triumphs in the Tour de France. C. Nolan and others. il pors *People Weekly* 32:51-3 Ag 7 '89

Following the Tour de France. M. Kenyon. il *Gourmet* 49:72+ Jl '89

Never say die [G. LeMond wins Tour de France; cover story; with editorial comment by James C. McCullagh] P. Kimmage. il pors *Bicycling* 30:10, 30-4+ O/N '89

Tour de France. G. Duclos-Lassalle. il map *National Geographic* 176:132-7 Jl '89

Tour de France diary [U.S. women's cycling team]; ed. by Lewis Rothlein. B. Bankaitis-Davis and K. Tobin. il pors *Women's Sports & Fitness* 11:24-8 N/D '89

A Tour of honor [Tour de France] D. Walsh. il *Bicycling* 30:46-8+ Jl '89

Vive LeMond! [winner of Tour de France; cover story] F. Lidz. il pors *Sports Illustrated* 71:12-17 Jl 31 '89

World beater [G. LeMond wins World Championship Professional Road Race] G. Drake. il por *Bicycling* 30:28-32+ D '89

Italy
Giro heroes [Giro d'Italia] G. Drake. il *Bicycling* 30:24+ S '89

BICYCLE RACING IN LITERATURE
The greatest cycling novel ever written [R. Hurne's The yellow jersey] M. E. Mantell. il *Bicycling* 30:82+ Ap '89

BICYCLE RACING IN MOTION PICTURES
'Breaking away' revisited [10 years since release of film depicting Bloomington, Indiana's Little 500] S. Martin. il *Bicycling* 30:62-3+ Ap '89

BICYCLE RALLIES
Road rallies. R. Guest. *Bicycling* 30:76 Jl '89

BICYCLE TIRES See Tires, Bicycle

BICYCLES
See also
Cycling

ATB update [all-terrain high tech features] D. Abramowski. il *Home Mechanix* 85:66-9+ Ag '89

The best gears of your life: how to buy the right bike. A. Willard-Cross. il *American Health* 8:80+ My '89

Bicycle buyer's bible. C. Patterson. il *Women's Sports & Fitness* 11:46-8+ Ap '89

Bicycle warranties. J. Langley. *Bicycling* 30:74+ Mr '89

Buying that first bike [children] G. Drake. *Bicycling* 30:84+ Je '89

Campagnolo's first mountain bike group [Euclid] F. Zahradnik. il *Bicycling* 30:26 Ja/F '89

Frame flex. C. Kyle. il *Bicycling* 30:76+ S '89

How to choose the right bike. J. Kukoda. il *Bicycling* 30:96-8 Ja/F '89

Hybrid bikes [touring bicycles] D. Cuerdon. il *Bicycling* 30:241 Ap '89

A new generation of bicycles offers more comfort and convenience. M. Herman. il *Utne Reader* p92 Mr/Ap '89

Pedaling into the future. M. D. Lowe. il *The Futurist* 23:18 Mr/Ap '89

Plain-vanilla bikes for family riding fun. M. Silver. il *U.S. News & World Report* 106:61-3 Mr 6 '89

Show time. F. Zahradnik. il *Bicycling* 30:168 Ja/F '89

Tot rods [children] J. Kukoda. il *Bicycling* 30:26-7 D '89

What makes the new bikes so boss. P. Kranz. il *Business Week* p100 Ja 30 '89

Aerodynamics
LeMond's aero edge. F. Zahradnik. il *Bicycling* 30:36-7 O/N '89

Testing in a tempest [wind tunnel test] F. Zahradnik. il *Bicycling* 30:100+ O/N '89

Anecdotes, facetiae, satire, etc.
The Liberator. A. Liere. il *Field & Stream* 94:25+ My '89

Brakes
See Brakes, Bicycle

Cleaning
Wash and wax. J. Langley. il *Bicycling* 30:208+ Ap '89

Collectors and collecting
New bike collectors. J. Kukoda. il *Bicycling* 30:48-50+ My '89

Re-cycling the past [P. Dodge] E. Siff. il por *Gentlemen's Quarterly* 59:83 O '89

Design
Bike to the future [students at Art Center College of Design create innovative bicycles] B. Weber. il *The New York Times Magazine* p82 F 12 '89

Transport [designers G. Bliss and J. Van der Tuin] *The New Yorker* 65:50-1 S 25 '89

Electronic equipment
See also
Cyclecomputers

Environmental aspects
Vicious cycles? [all terrain bicycles] D. Coello. il *Sierra* 74:50-4 My/Je '89

Equipment
Clothing & accessory checklist. F. Zahradnik. il *Bicycling* 30:100-2 Ja/F '89

Component preview. F. Zahradnik. il *Bicycling* 30:96+ D '89

The equipment you'll need. *Bicycling* 30:162 Mr '89

Group dynamics [Dura-Ace Integrated-8 and Deore XT-II components from Shimano] E. Pavelka; J. Kukoda. il *Bicycling* 30:140-3 Ja/F '89

How not to waste time on your indoor trainer. S. Martin. il *Bicycling* 30:124-6 Ja/F '89

Kid's stuff. il *Bicycling* 30:106-8+ Je '89

Made for shade [sunglasses] J. Davis and F. Zahradnik. il *Bicycling* 30:56-8+ Je '89

New products. F. Zahradnik. See issues of Bicycling

Take a ride in the great indoors [wind trainers] J. Lehrer. il *Women's Sports & Fitness* 11:14 O '89

Towing your toddler. G. Drake. il *Bicycling* 30:94+ Je '89

Velosaurus. G. Drake. il *Bicycling* 30:186 Jl '89

A wardrobe of accessories for the fashionable cyclist. V. S. Sussman. il *U.S. News & World Report* 107:63 Ag 21 '89

Women's products. S. Weaver. il *Bicycling* 30:40-4+ Ag '89

Fenders
Mounting mudguards. J. Langley. il *Bicycling* 30:104+ O/N '89

Gearing
See also
Bicycles—Transmission

Index shifting systems [guidelines for installing and adjusting index rear derailleur systems] J. Langley. il *Bicycling* 30:208+ Mr '89

The low-tech solution: kids have a way of reducing any bike to a one-speed. C. Kyle. il *Bicycling* 30:146 Ag '89

Smart shifting. F. Berto. il *Bicycling* 30:204-6 Ap '89

Lighting
Lighten up. J. Kukoda. il *Bicycling* 30:128-9 Ja/F '89

Take back the night. J. Langley. il *Bicycling* 30:88-92 O/N '89

Lubrication and lubricants
Bicycle grease. F. Berto. il *Bicycling* 30:190+ My '89

Maintenance and repair
Basic bike care. J. Langley. il *Bicycling* 30:108-10 Ja/F '89

Be the master of your machine. J. Lehrer. il *Women's Sports & Fitness* 11:16+ Jl/Ag '89

Crash course [post-accident inspection] J. Langley. il *Bicycling* 30:114+ Ag '89

Pre-event checkup. J. Langley. il *Bicycling* 30:146+ Jl '89

Materials
Fiber frames for all-terrain bikes. N. Mayersohn. il *Popular Mechanics* 166:40+ F '89

Inside the Kestrel MX-Z [carbon fiber mountain bike] B. Feldman. il *Bicycling* 30:204+ Mr '89

The one-pound frame [metal matrix composites] F. Zahradnik. *Bicycling* 30:144 Ja/F '89

Titanium: the miracle metal. J. Kukoda. il *Bicycling* 30:110-14 Jl '89

Pedals
A pedal revolution. F. Berto. il *Bicycling* 30:172-7+ Ap '89

Periodicals
See also
Bicycling (Periodical)

Police use
Long leg of the law [Seattle police] S. Martin. il *Bicycling* 30:42 O/N '89

The pedal patrol. il *U.S. News & World Report* 107:10 Ag 7 '89

Saddles
Not-so-hot seat [impotence in cyclists; research by Harin Padma-Nathan] L. Schroepfer. il *American Health* 8:40 O '89

Safety devices and measures
Bike safety: rules for the road. il *Ladies' Home Journal* 106:58 Je '89

How to get your child to wear a helmet. S. Sorensen. il *Bicycling* 30:88+ Je '89

Safe cycling. il *Current Health 2* 15:20-1 Mr '89

Steering gear
Bullet bars [aero bars] S. Martin. il *Bicycling* 30:102-6 Ag '89

Frontal adjustments [road and mountain bikes] J. Langley. il *Bicycling* 30:202+ My '89

Testing
'89 buyer's guide [cover story] il *Bicycling* 30:65+ Mr '89; Addendum. 30:184 My '89

ABM American [mountain bike] J. Kukoda. il *Bicycling* 30:112-13 D '89

Bicycle built for cruise [Montague BiFrame folding mountain bike] A. Laboda. il *Flying* 116:34 N '89

Bruce Gordon Rock 'n Road. J. Kukoda. il *Bicycling* 30:184+ Je '89

Campagnolo Euclid [mountain bicycle] J. Kukoda. il *Bicycling* 30:194-6+ Mr '89

Cannondale tandem. F. Zahradnik. il *Bicycling* 30:178+ My '89

Compact cruisers [Moulton-folding bikes] J. Kukoda. il *Bicycling* 30:194+ Ap '89

BICYCLES—Testing—*cont.*

Fuso Lux [racing bike by D. Moulton] J. Kukoda. il *Bicycling* 30:188+ Je '89

GT Crossover series [road/mountain bicycles] J. Kukoda. il *Bicycling* 30:114-15 D '89

Guest test II [Terry Chröm, Ryan Vanguard, Masi 3V Volumetrica; special section] J. Kukoda. il *Bicycling* 30:60+ Ja/F '89

Hybrids: bikes for all reasons. J. Kukoda. il *Bicycling* 30:78-80+ Ag '89

Kestrel 200SC [racing bike] F. Zahradnik. il *Bicycling* 30:44+ My '89

LeMond TSX [racing bike] G. Drake. il *Bicycling* 30:72+ S '89

Nishiki Alien [mountain bike] F. Zahradnik. il *Bicycling* 30:142+ Jl '89

Road test [Diamond Back Axis XT, Bridgestone Comp MB-3, and Muddy Fox Courier Comp mountain bikes] F. Zahradnik; J. Kukoda. il *Bicycling* 30:94-9 O/N '89

Specialized Stumpjumper [mountain bike] F. Zahradnik. il *Bicycling* 30:194+ Je '89

Three pounds of performance [Cannondale SR400 racer] F. Zahradnik. il *Bicycling* 30:136-9 Ja/F '89

Titanium put to the test [road and mountain bikes] J. Kudoda. il *Bicycling* 30:116-18+ Jl '89

Trek 1100 [racing bike] J. Kukoda. il *Bicycling* 30:174+ My '89

Trek 5000 [carbon fiber road bike] G. Drake. il *Bicycling* 30:46+ Mr '89

Univega Range Rover ES [mountain bike] S. Martin. il *Bicycling* 30:170+ My '89

What the editors ride. il *Bicycling* 30:47-8+ O/N '89

Theft

So long, Horse: sometimes losing a bicycle can be like losing a friend. M. Westerman. *Bicycling* 30:76 O/N '89

Transmission

Fixed gearing. J. Kukoda. il *Bicycling* 30:176-7 Mr '89

Transportation

The 10 best cars for cyclists [survey results] S. Martin. il *Bicycling* 30:40-2+ D '89

Taking your bike on a plane or train. il *Sunset (Central West edition)* 182:62 Je '89

Wheels

Rim replacement. J. Langley. il *Bicycling* 30:198+ Je '89

Spoke tensiometers. J. Langley. il *Bicycling* 30:208+ My '89

Wheels of the future [3- and 4-spoke composite] C. Kyle. il *Bicycling* 30:190+ Ap '89

BICYCLES, EXERCISE *See* Exercising equipment

BICYCLES, RESTORED

Recycling the classics [balloon tire bikes] N. Mayersohn. il *Popular Mechanics* 166:64-6+ Jl '89

BICYCLES, USED

'Have I got a deal for you'. J. Langley. il *Bicycling* 30:184+ Ap '89

BICYCLING *See* Cycling

BICYCLING (PERIODICAL)

Inside. J. C. McCullagh. See issues of Bicycling

What the editors ride. il *Bicycling* 30:47-8+ O/N '89

BICYCLING CLOTHES *See* Clothing and dress—Sports clothes

BICYCLING HELMETS *See* Helmets

BICYCLING SHOES *See* Cycling shoes

BIDDING ON ART *See* Art trade

BIDEL, SUSAN

Millionaire bachelors: the 20 most wanted. il *Harper's Bazaar* 122:46+ Ja '89

BIDINOTTO, ROBERT JAMES

The law criminals love. *Reader's Digest* 135:57-62 S '89

BIEBER, OWEN

American business should put America's future first [address, June 18, 1989] *Vital Speeches of the Day* 55:613-20 Ag 1 '89

BIEDERMAN, HARRY R.

Snow domes. il *Antiques & Collecting Hobbies* 93:28-31 Ja '89

BIEDERMEIER FURNITURE

Collectors and collecting

SoHo salon [Manhattan loft of P. Arnell and S. Nolan] M. Filler. il pors *House & Garden* 161:170-3 O '89

BIELEFELDT, TALBOT

Give us your tires, your Coors cans . . . il *Sierra* 74:74-7 Mr/Ap '89

BIENSTOCK (N.S.) INC. *See* N.S. Bienstock Inc.

BIERDS, LINDA

For the sake of retrieval [poem] *The Atlantic* 264:58 O '89

The shakers [poem] *The New Yorker* 65:44-5 Ap 10 '89

BIERDZ, THOM

about

Thom Bierdz: small-town boy finds big-city success! [interview] por *'Teen* 33:52 Mr '89

BIERMAN, MARSHA

about

A reel revolutionary. P. Hoover. il por *Women's Sports & Fitness* 11:78 Ap '89

BIERMAN, ROBERT

about

Vampire's kiss [film] Reviews

American Film il 14:67-8 Je '89. J. E. Fitch

New York 22:68-9 Je 19 '89. D. Denby

The New Yorker 65:105-6 Je 12 '89. P. Kael

People Weekly il 31:17-18 Je 12 '89. R. Novak

BIEVER-MONDAVI, MARGRIT

about

View from Wappo Hill: Robert and Margrit Mondavi's Napa Valley vineyard. B. D. Colen. il pors *Architectural Digest* 46:276-83 My '89

BIEWENER, ANDREW A.

Mammalian terrestrial locomotion and size. bibl f il *BioScience* 39:776-83 D '89

Scaling body support in mammals: limb posture and muscle mechanics. bibl f il *Science* 245:45-8 Jl 7 '89

BIFFEN, JOHN, 1930-

United we fall? *National Review* 41:25-6 Je 30 '89

BIFOCAL CONTACT LENSES *See* Contact lenses

BIG [film] *See* Motion picture reviews—Single works

BIG AUDIO DYNAMITE (MUSICAL GROUP)

Back from the brink of death, former Clash rocker Mick Jones is reborn as the man from B.A.D. S. Dougherty. il pors *People Weekly* 32:99-100 N 20 '89

BIG BANDS (MUSIC)

Big bang. K. Whitehead. il *Down Beat* 56:41-4 D '89

My summer swing: on the road with a fifties big band. D. Asher. il *Harper's* 278:70-6 Je '89

BIG BANG SCHTROUMPFS

Pollution parable [T. J. Thordarson designs pollution monster for French theme park] B. Weber. il *The New York Times Magazine* p86 F 26 '89

BIG BANG THEORY *See* Universe

BIG BUSINESS

See also

Competition

Advice to small companies: think big [interview with A. D. Chandler] R. Koselka. il por *Forbes* 144:204-5+ N 13 '89

Is your company too big? [cover story] J. A. Byrne. il *Business Week* p84-8+ Mr 27 '89

BIG CYPRESS NATIONAL PRESERVE (FLA.)

N.P.S. double cross [no more hunting] L. Williamson. il *Outdoor Life* 183:34+ F '89

Searching for the one true cat [Florida panthers] C. Flowers. il *National Wildlife* 27:24-8 O/N '89

THE BIG PICTURE [film] *See* Motion picture reviews—Single works

BIG SCREEN TELEVISION *See* Television projection

BIG SOUTH FORK NATIONAL RIVER AND RECREATION AREA (TENN. AND KY.)

New life, old dreams on the Cumberland Plateau. D. Young. il *Southern Living* 24:50-5 Ag '89

BIG SUR MARATHON *See* Marathon running

BIG SUR RIVER (CALIF.)

Rock-hopping on a day's hike up the Big Sur River. il map *Sunset (Central West edition)* 183:18-19 S '89

BIG THICKET NATIONAL PRESERVE (TEX.)

Preserve protectors take heart. S. McCarthy. il *Sierra* 74:91-2 N/D '89

The wild boar is a formidable foe and an admirable pest. J. Tabor. il *Smithsonian* 20:114-18+ S '89

BIG TOP PEE-WEE [film] *See* Motion picture reviews—Single works

BIGELOW, KATHRYN

about

Blue steel [film] Reviews

American Film 14:59 S '89. N. Mills

Rolling Stone il p47-8 S 21 '89. P. Travers

Genre bender. K. Turan. il por *Gentlemen's Quarterly* 59:162+ O '89

BIGGIN HILL AIRPORT *See* London (England)—Airports

BIGGS, BARTON

about

A last hurrah for stocks? [interview] J. Mendes. il por *Fortune* 120:46-8 Ag 28 '89

BIGGS, FRIEDERIKE

about

Above it all. J. Reginato. il por *House & Garden* 161:152-9+ Je '89

BIGGS, JEREMY

about

Above it all. J. Reginato. il por *House & Garden* 161:152-9+ Je '89

BIGHORN RIVER (WYO. AND MONT.)

Bighorn of plenty. W. G. Tapply. il map *Field & Stream* 93:32-3+ Ja '89

BIGOTRY *See* Prejudice

BIKING *See* Cycling

BIKKEMBERGS, DIRK

about

A look on the wild side. J. Cocks. il pors *Time* 133:68 Ja 16 '89

BILE DUCTS

Abnormalities

See also

Biliary atresia

BILE PIGMENTS
See also
Bilirubin
BILIARY ATRESIA
Still grieving after the death of his young son, Eddie Rabbitt finds solace in country music [Timmy Rabbitt] T. Allis. il pors *People Weekly* 31:83-4 Ap 17 '89
BILIARY CALCULI *See* Gallstones
BILINGUAL EDUCATION
The language of power. Y. T. De Mola. *America* 160:364-5 Ap 22 '89
BILINGUALISM
An Anglo rebellion [English-speaking Quebecers consider alternatives in upcoming provincial election] M. Rose. il *Maclean's* 102:13 Ag 28 '89
Bilingualism in America: English should be the only language. S. I. Hayakawa. il *USA Today (Periodical)* 118:32-4 Jl '89
A choice of words [Paraguay] D. Einhorn and S. O. Einhorn. il *Américas* 41 no1:42-7 '89
The divided nation [Meech Lake constitutional accord in Canada; cover story; special section; with editorial comment by Kevin Doyle] il *Maclean's* 102:4, 18-23+ Mr 20 '89
English: the language of liberty [English as official language] J. R. Joelson. *The Humanist* 49:35-6 Jl/Ag '89
The failures of Robert Bourassa [Quebec] J. Stewart. por *Maclean's* 102:64 Ja 2 '89
Killing fields in Old Montreal. P. C. Newman. il *Maclean's* 102:29 F 20 '89
Legislating assimilation: the English-only movement. M. R. Halton. il *The Christian Century* 106:1119-21 N 29 '89
Linguistic backlash [Confederation of Regions Party wages anti-French campaign in New Brunswick] G. Allen. *Maclean's* 102:17 Ag 28 '89
Quebec fire storm [language disputes and arson] L. Van Dusen. il por *Maclean's* 102:12-13 F 6 '89
The return to two solitudes [Canada] B. Bergman. il *Maclean's* 102:26+ N 6 '89
Say it in English. E. Salholz. il *Newsweek* 113:22-3 F 20 '89
'To remind them that we're here' [Montreal's English-speaking community] S. Page. *World Press Review* 36:42 F '89
Uncertain survival [Ontario francophones] G. W. Taylor. il *Maclean's* 102:30 N 6 '89
War over words [Quebec's move to restrict use of English signs; special section] il por *Maclean's* 102:38-42 Ja 2 '89

Anecdotes, facetiae, satire, etc.
Drawing the line [English-only crusade] B. Ehrenreich. il *Mother Jones* 14:7-8 Je '89
We're number 1 in language debates [Canada] C. Gordon. il *Maclean's* 102:39 Ja 9 '89
BILIRUBIN
. . . and toxic chemicals from the blood [enzyme filters] J. Raloff. *Science News* 135:271 Ap 29 '89
BILL, MAX, 1908-
about
Max Bill's birthday blues. E. Beck. por *Art News* 88:45+ F '89
BILL AND TED'S EXCELLENT ADVENTURE [film] *See* Motion picture reviews—Single works
BILL COLLECTING *See* Collecting of accounts
BILL EVANS TRIO
Natural flow: the Bill Evans Trio [reprint] J. A. Tynan. il por *Down Beat* 56:61 S '89
BILL MELENDEZ PRODUCTIONS
He's a howling success at bringing comics to life [B. Melendez] M. Barrier. il por *Nation's Business* 77:16+ O '89
BILL OF RIGHTS (U.S.) *See* United States. Constitution. 1st-10th amendments
BILL PAYMENT *See* Payment of accounts
BILL PAYMENT SERVICES, BANK *See* Banks and banking—Services
BILL T. JONES/ARNIE ZANE & COMPANY
Bill T. Jones choreographs an anguished tribute to his late partner, a victim of AIDS. M. Small. il pors *People Weekly* 32:44-6 Jl 31 '89
Modern dancers reach out to prisoners and to homeless men. R. Johnson. il *Dance Magazine* 63:15 S '89
Pressing forward [performances at the Joyce Theater] T. Tobias. il *New York* 22:82-3 Ap 3 '89
Reviews:
Performances at the Joyce Theater, New York City. L. Garafola. *Dance Magazine* 63:54-5 Jl '89
BILLARD, MARY
Jawing with Jay Leno. il pors *Gentlemen's Quarterly* 59:220-5+ Ag '89
BILLBOARDS
The great outdoors. B. Kanner. il *New York* 22:20+ S 4 '89
Open roads: keeping America's scenic roads free of billboard blight. E. T. McMahon. il *National Parks* 63:14-15 N/D '89
BILLFISH FISHING
See also
Marlin fishing
Sailfish fishing

The sweet gulf [Golfo Dulce, Costa Rica] B. Stearns. il *Field & Stream* 94:64-6 Ag '89
The Wright rules for billfish. P. B. Wright. il *Motor Boating & Sailing* 163:78+ My '89
BILLFISH FOUNDATION
Winners [W. Rockefeller] L. Rudeen. il por *Motor Boating & Sailing* 163:30 My '89
BILLIARD CUES *See* Pool cues
BILLIARD TABLES *See* Pool tables
BILLIARDS, POCKET *See* Pool (Game)
BILLING
When time is money [Timeslips III] S. P. Andrus. il *Personal Computing* 13:208 N '89
BILLING SERVICES, BANK *See* Banks and banking—Services
BILLINGTON, JAMES H., 1929-
Keeping the faith in the USSR after a thousand years. bibl (p174) il *Smithsonian* 20:130-6+ Ap '89
about
Scholarly Librarian of Congress to knock on publishers' doors. H. Fields. il por *Publishers Weekly* 235:26 Ja 13 '89
BILLIONAIRES
See also
Getty, Gordon P.
The billionaires. il *Fortune* 120:44-6+ S 11 '89
The Forbes four hundred: billionaires. il *Forbes* 144 Special Issue:152+ O 23 '89
Un-American riches [foreign billionaires] *Forbes* 144 Special Issue:336-7 O 23 '89
A wealth of billionaires [cover story; special section] il *Forbes* 144:117-19+ Jl 24 '89
Where are the microchip billionaires? G. F. Gilder. il *Forbes* 144 Special Issue:378-80+ O 23 '89
Anecdotes, facetiae, satire, etc.
How to be happy on less than a billion. K. Fury. il *Working Woman* 14:236 S '89
Canada
A small compact of rich families. A. Fotheringham. il *Maclean's* 102:80 O 23 '89
BILLIONAIRES' WIVES
For richer and richer. N. Cooper. il *Ladies' Home Journal* 106:184-6+ My '89
BILLY, THE KID
about
Did Billy really die a kid? G. Byrne. il por *Science* 243:610 F 3 '89
Modern technology meets Billy the Kid. il por *Newsweek* 113:28 Je 5 '89
BILLY BOY
about
The jewelry designer's crush on Schiaparelli—and Barbie. E. White. il por *Architectural Digest* 46:94+ S '89
BILLY HILL (MUSICAL GROUP)
Billy Hill [release of I am just a rebel] A. Nash. il *Stereo Review* 54:136 D '89
BILOXI (MISS.)
Crime
The murder—and the mayor [Mayor P. Halat accused of hiring hit man to murder Judge V. Sherry] J. N. Baker. il por *Newsweek* 114:32 O 23 '89
BILTMORE HOUSE AND GARDENS (ASHEVILLE, N.C.)
A Vanderbilt Christmas [cover story] P. L. Hudson. il map *Americana* 17:28-35 N/D '89
BILZERIAN, PAUL A.
about
The feds finger an upstart raider, too. D. Pauly. il por *Newsweek* 113:48 Ja 2 '89
Is getting rich quick becoming a crime? C. Byron. il por *New York* 22:25-6 Je 12 '89
A raider's days of reckoning. il por *Time* 134:45 Jl 10 '89
Wall Street is glued to the Bilzerian trial. M. Galen. il por *Business Week* p33 My 15 '89
BINAISA, GODFREY
about
A survivor—barely—as Uganda's president, Godfrey Binaisa finds life in Brooklyn a beach. P. Chin. il pors *People Weekly* 31:139-40+ My 1 '89
BINARY PULSARS *See* Pulsars
BINARY STARS *See* Stars, Double
BINARY WEAPONS *See* Chemical and biological weapons
BINAZZI, LAPO, 1943-
about
"A stone of Florence". J. Turner. il por *Art News* 88:97-8 Mr '89
BINDER, LAURIE
about
Laurie Binder. B. Wischnia. il por *Runner's World* 24:51 F '89
BINDER, LEONARD
The changing American role in the Middle East. *Current History* 88:65-8+ F '89
BINDING SITES (BIOCHEMISTRY)
See also
Allosterism
Chemoreceptors
Drug receptors
Hormone receptors
Molecular recognition

BINDING SITES (BIOCHEMISTRY)—See also—*cont.*
Protein receptors
Cognate DNA binding specificity retained after leucine zipper exchange between GCN4 and C/EBP. P. Agre and others. bibl f il *Science* 246:922-6 N 17 '89
A cold remedy not to be sneezed at [identification of ICAM-1, rhinovirus receptor site] il *U.S. News & World Report* 106:14 Mr 20 '89
The cold war heats up [identification of rhinovirus receptor site] R. Trubo. il *American Health* 8:12 N '89
Coming closer to a common-cold cure [rhinovirus receptor molecule ICAM-1] il *Newsweek* 113:60 Mr 20 '89
The Diageotropica mutant of tomato lacks high specific activity auxin binding sites. G. R. Hicks and others. bibl f il *Science* 245:52-4 Jl 7 '89
The DNA binding domain of the rat liver nuclear protein C/EBP is bipartite [support for leucine zipper hypothesis] W. H. Landschulz and others. bibl f il *Science* 243:1681-8 Mr 31 '89
DNA looping generated by DNA bending protein IHF and the two domains of lambda integrase. L. Moitoso De Vargas and others. bibl f il *Science* 244:1457-61 Je 23 '89
Domain separation in the activation of glycogen phosphorylase α. E. J. Goldsmith and others. bibl f il *Science* 245:528-32 Ag 4 '89
Drosophila nuclear proteins bind to regions of alternating C and T residues in gene promoters. D. S. Gilmour and others. bibl f il *Science* 245:1487-90 S 29 '89
Evidence that the leucine zipper is a coiled coil. E. K. O'Shea and others. bibl f il *Science* 243:538-42 Ja 27 '89
Function of a bacterial activator protein that binds to transcriptional enhancers. D. L. Popham and others. bibl f il *Science* 243:629-35 F 3 '89
Functionally distinct NF-κB binding sites in the immunoglobulin κ and IL-2 receptor α chain genes. S. L. Cross and others. bibl f il *Science* 244:466-9 Ap 28 '89
Generation of a catalytic antibody by site-directed mutagenesis. E. Baldwin and P. G. Schultz. bibl f il *Science* 245:1104-7 S 8 '89
High-resolution epitope mapping of hGH-receptor interactions by alanine-scanning mutagenesis. B. C. Cunningham and J. A. Wells. bibl f il *Science* 244:1081-5 Je 2 '89
Identification of a zinc finger protein that binds to the sterol regulatory element. T. B. Rajavashisth and others. bibl f il *Science* 245:640-3 Ag 11 '89
Identification of an AUUUA-specific messenger RNA binding protein. J. S. Malter. bibl f il *Science* 246:664-6 N 3 '89
Inhibition of DNA binding proteins by oligonucleotide-directed triple helix formation. L. J. Maher, III and others. bibl f il *Science* 245:725-30 Ag 18 '89
Kappa B-specific DNA binding proteins: role in the regulation of human interleukin-2 gene expression. B. Hoyos and others. bibl f il *Science* 244:457-60 Ap 28 '89
Leucine repeats and an adjacent DNA binding domain mediate the formation of functional cFos-cJun heterodimers [proposed function of the leucine zipper] T. Turner and R. Tjian. bibl f il *Science* 243:1689-94 Mr 31 '89
The MHC-binding and gp120-binding functions of CD4 are separable. D. Lamarre and others. bibl f il *Science* 245:743-6 Ag 18 '89
Molecular modeling of the HIV-1 protease and its substrate binding site. I. T. Weber and others. bibl f il *Science* 243:928-31 F 17 '89
Neural cadherin: role in selective cell-cell adhesion. S. Miyatani and others. bibl f il *Science* 245:631-5 Ag 11 '89
New family of adhesion proteins discovered. J. L. Marx. *Science* 243:1144 Mr 3 '89
Parallel association of Fos and Jun leucine zippers juxtaposes DNA binding domains. R. Gentz and others. bibl f il *Science* 243:1695-9 Mr 31 '89
Peptide binding and release by proteins implicated as catalysts of protein assembly. G. C. Flynn and others. bibl f il *Science* 245:385-90 Jl 28 '89
Portrait of a virus [foot-and-mouth disease; research by David Stuart and others] il *Discover* 10:10 Je '89
Preferential heterodimer formation by isolated leucine zippers from Fos and Jun. E. K. O'Shea and others. bibl f il *Science* 245:646-8 Ag 11 '89
A protein that binds to a cis-acting element of wheat histone genes has a leucine zipper motif. T. Tabata and others. bibl f il *Science* 245:965-7 S 1 '89
Recognition of thymine·adenine base pairs by guanine in a pyrimidine triple helix motif. L. C. Griffin and P. B. Dervan. bibl f il *Science* 245:967-71 S 1 '89
Rhinovirus receptor found; colds carry on [identification of ICAM-1] R. Weiss. *Science News* 135:165 Mr 18 '89
The role of cis-acting promoter elements in tissue-specific albumin gene expression. P. Maire and others. bibl f il *Science* 244:343-6 Ap 21 '89
Scissors-grip model for DNA recognition by a family of leucine zipper proteins. C. R. Vinson and others. bibl f il *Science* 246:911-16 N 17 '89

Signal peptide for protein secretion directing glycophospholipid membrane anchor attachment. I. W. Caras and G. N. Weddell. bibl f il *Science* 243:1196-8 Mr 3 '89
Similarity between the transcriptional silencer binding proteins ABF1 and RAP1 [Saccharomyces] J. F. X. Diffley and B. Stillman. bibl f il *Science* 246:1034-8 N 24 '89
Snuffed sniffles [discovery of ICAM-1 receptor site for rhinoviruses] *Time* 133:61 Mr 20 '89
Steroid binding at σ-"opioid" receptors [discussion of April 8, 1988 article, Steroid binding at σ receptors suggests a link between endocrine, nervous, and immune systems] T.-P. Su and others. bibl f il *Science* 246:1635-8 D 22 '89
Three-dimensional solution structure of a single zinc finger DNA-binding domain [cover story] M. S. Lee and others. bibl f il *Science* 245:635-7 Ag 11 '89
Transcriptional regulation in mammalian cells by sequence-specific DNA binding proteins [RNA polymerase II transcription initiation] P. J. Mitchell and R. Tjian. bibl f il *Science* 245:371-8 Jl 28 '89
BINDINGS, SKI See Ski bindings
BING, DAVE
about
Bing saves school sports. V. Lynn. por *Black Enterprise* 20:34 O '89
BING, STANLEY
The Bing report. See issues of Esquire beginning July 1989
The strategist. See issues of Esquire through June 1989
BINGAMAN, JEFF
Should the Congress adopt the "Textile and Apparel Trade Act of 1987"? [excerpts from address, September 13, 1988] *Congressional Digest* 68:17+ Ja '89
BINGE BUYING See Compulsive shopping
BINGE-PURGE SYNDROME See Bulimia
BINGHAM, WALTER
Super Bowl: the quarterly report. il *Sports Illustrated* 70:51+ Ja 9 '89
BINGO
Bingo! Are Indian tribes hitting the jackpot? S. D. Atchison. il *Business Week* p115 Ap 24 '89
Laws and regulations
Gambling and guns [St. Regis reserve] M. Clark. il *Maclean's* 102:21+ S 18 '89
BINNEY & SMITH INC.
Brand-new start [Magic Markers to be marketed by Binney & Smith] E. F. Cone. il *Forbes* 143:10 Mr 6 '89
BINNS, RUTH ANNE
about
Nature's aid. K. Martin. il pors *Organic Gardening* 36:68-72+ Ja '89
BINOCULAR VISION See Vision
BINOCULARS
Big binoculars for wide-field views. C. Crossen. *Astronomy* 17:104-5 F '89
Binocular buyer's guide [cover story] il *Petersen's Photographic Magazine* 18:62-9+ S '89
Binoculars. il *Consumer Reports* 54:30-4 D '89
Copernicus Binoc-U-Mount. R. Burnham. il *Astronomy* 17:104-5 Mr '89
High-class glass. D. E. Petzal. il *Field & Stream* 94:80+ N '89
Holiday trash-scopes. G. Lovi. il *Sky and Telescope* 78:617-18 D '89
How to size up binoculars. il *Consumer Reports* 54:444-50 Jl '89
Ideal binoculars. R. Kimber. *Country Journal* 16:97-9 N/D '89
Let's take a closer look. N. Schreiber. il *New Choices for the Best Years* 29:79-81 Ap '89
Point of view [to observe nature] J. Madson. il *National Wildlife* 27:42-4 O/N '89
Seeing in the almost dark [low-light binoculars] D. Petersen. il *The Mother Earth News* 117:70-3 My/Je '89
These binoculars aren't just for the birds. S. Woolley. il *Business Week* p116 My 29 '89
BINS
Charcoal storage bin. T. Wolfe. il *Flower and Garden* 33:60 My/Je '89
BINUR, YORAM
Palestinian like me: notes from an undercover Jewish journalist [excerpt from My enemy, my self] il pors *Utne Reader* p34-45 S/O '89
BIOACOUSTICS
Predation on ocean krill [discussion of July 15, 1988 article, Acoustical detection of high-density krill demersal layers in the submarine canyons off Georges Bank] C. H. Greene and others. *Science* 243:237-3a Ja 13 '89
BIOCHEMICAL REDUCTION See Reduction, Biochemical
BIOCHEMISTRY
See also
Binding sites (Biochemistry)
Chemotaxis
Molecules
Pigments (Biology)
Synergism
Synthesis

BIODEGRADABLE PLASTICS See Plastics—Degradability
BIODEGRADATION
Bacteria that eat TNT [research by Pat Unkefer] M. M. Soviero. *Popular Science* 235:116 N '89
Explosive bacteria [biodegradation of explosive wastes; research by Pat Unkefer] *Discover* 10:18 O '89
Genetic engineering of bacteria from managed and natural habitats. S. E. Lindow and others. bibl f *Science* 244:1300-7 Je 16 '89
Shredders and riparian vegetation [relationship between plant litter and aquatic invertebrate growth] K. W. Cummins and others. bibl f il *BioScience* 39:24-30 Ja '89
Super microbes attack hazardous waste. *High Technology Business* 9:29 Jl/Ag '89
X-ray microanalysis of leaf-litter decomposition in lakes [scanning microscope] J. A. Perry and others. bibl f il *BioScience* 39:260-3 Ap '89
BIODIVERSITY See Diversity (Biology)
BIOELASTICS
Lab-made proteins stretch like life [work of Dan W. Urry] I. Amato. *Science News* 136:398 D 16 '89
BIOELECTRICITY See Electrophysiology
BIOENERGETICS
See also
Muscle strength
The human machine [energy efficiency of riders in Race Across America] C. Kyle. il *Bicycling* 30:196+ My '89
BIOENGINEERING
See also
Ergonomics
BIOETHICS
See also
Animal experimentation
Gene therapy—Ethical aspects
Genetic research—Ethical aspects
Medical ethics
Reproduction—Moral and religious aspects
Ethics and health [special issue] il *World Health* p2-25 Ap '89
France introduces bioethics law. D. Dickson. *Science* 243:1284 Mr 10 '89
BIOFEEDBACK TRAINING
What biofeedback does (and doesn't) do. L. Miller. il *Psychology Today* 23:22-4 N '89
Anecdotes, facetiae, satire, etc.
Alpha/theta meditation goggles. M. C. Worley. il *Radio-Electronics* 60:53-7 Ap '89
BIOGAS See Refuse as fuel
BIOGEN INCORPORATED
Biogen's new moneymaking genes. L. Jereski. il por *Business Week* p94 Je 19 '89
BIOGEOCHEMICAL CYCLES
See also
Carbon cycle (Biogeochemistry)
Detritus
BIOGEOGRAPHY
See also
Animal introduction
Trees—Geographical distribution
A 48-million-year-old aphid-host plant association and complex life cycle: biogeographic evidence [aphid subtribe Melaphidina and sumac host plant] N. A. Moran. bibl f il map *Science* 245:173-5 Jl 14 '89
Biologists disagree over bold signature of nature [species-richness gradient; views of George Stevens] R. Lewin. il *Science* 244:527-8 My 5 '89
Gauging the biological impacts of the greenhouse effect. J. P. Cohn. il *BioScience* 39:142-6 Mr '89
Macroecology: the division of food and space among species on continents. J. H. Brown and B. A. Maurer. bibl f il *Science* 243:1145-50 Mr 3 '89
Nature under glass [greenhouse effect] J. R. Udall. il map *Sierra* 74:34-40 Jl/Ag '89
BIOGRAPHY
See also
Authors—Biography
Authors, American—Biography
Autobiography
Crime and criminals—Biography
Executives—Biography
Obituaries
Public officers—Biography
Publishers and publishing—Biography
Women—Biography
BIOLOGICAL ACOUSTICS See Bioacoustics
BIOLOGICAL AND CHEMICAL WEAPONS See Chemical and biological weapons
BIOLOGICAL ARCHITECTURE See Baubiologie
BIOLOGICAL ASSAY
See also
Draize test
Immunoassay
BIOLOGICAL CLOCKS See Biological rhythms
BIOLOGICAL CONTROL OF INSECTS See Insect control
BIOLOGICAL CONTROL SYSTEMS
See also
Biofeedback training
Cellular control mechanisms

BIOLOGICAL CYCLES See Biological rhythms
BIOLOGICAL EQUIPMENT
See also
Microscopes
Biologist's toolbox. See issues of BioScience beginning February 1985
BIOLOGICAL FORM See Morphology
BIOLOGICAL LITERATURE
See also
Information systems—Biological use
Publishers and publishing—Biological literature
BIOLOGICAL LUMINESCENCE See Bioluminescence
BIOLOGICAL PRODUCTIVITY See Productivity, Biological
BIOLOGICAL RESEARCH
See also
Fluorescent indicators in biological research
Genetic research
Jackson Laboratory (Bar Harbor, Me.)
Medical research
BioBriefs. See issues of BioScience
The coming pluralization of biology and the stewardship of systematics. E. O. Wilson. *BioScience* 39:242-5 Ap '89
The worsening climate for biological research. D. Baltimore. por *Technology Review* 92:22+ My/Je '89
Federal aid
Wanted: $25 million for mouse house [rebuilding Jackson Lab after fire] B. J. Culliton. il *Science* 245:697-8 Ag 18 '89
International aspects
See also
Human Frontiers Science Program
Mexico
See also
National Research Institute for Biotic Resources (Mexico)
BIOLOGICAL RESOURCES See Natural resources
BIOLOGICAL RHYTHMS
See also
Cell cycle
Jet lag
Photoperiodism
Ace in the hole Stefania Follini never caved in [spends 130 days isolated in cave in New Mexico] T. Allis. il por *People Weekly* 31:52-3 Je 12 '89
Are you a day or night person? [views of Gordon Deckert and Frank Holloway] il *USA Today (Periodical)* 117:11 Mr '89
Are you out of sync with each other? [differing circadian rhythms; research by Jeffry Larson] K. Locitzer. il *Psychology Today* 23:66 Jl/Ag '89
Beat the clock. S. Nelson. il *Seventeen* 48:145-6+ Ap '89
The body chaotic. G. Taubes. il *Discover* 10:62-7 My '89
Body-wise: safe solutions for night work [research by Charles Czeisler] S. Chollar. il *Psychology Today* 23:26 N '89
Body's clock keeps insomniacs wide awake [research by Mary Morris] K. Fackelmann. *Science News* 136:13 Jl 1 '89
Bright light induction of strong (type O) resetting of the human circadian pacemaker. C. A. Czeisler and others. bibl f il *Science* 244:1328-33 Je 16 '89
A cave dweller's chronicle: fifty-six days and counting [interview with S. Follini] A. R. Oberg. il *Omni (New York, N.Y.)* 11:50-2+ Je '89
Circadian system controlling release of sperm in the insect testes [gypsy moth] J. M. Giebultowicz and others. bibl f il *Science* 245:1098-100 S 8 '89
Clockwork in the brain [transplantation of suprachiasmatic nucleus restores circadian rhythm in hamsters; work of Martin R. Ralph and others] J. A. Miller. il *BioScience* 39:75-8 F '89
Getting in sync psychologically [tennis players' circadian rhythms] J. E. Loehr. il *World Tennis* 36:72 F '89
Illuminating jet lag [research by Charles Czeisler and Richard Kronauer] R. Pool. il *Science* 244:1256-7 Je 16 '89
Is it healthy to be chaotic? R. Pool. bibl il *Science* 243:604-7 F 3 '89
A light touch changes the biological clock [research by Charles A. Czeisler] K. Fackelmann. *Science News* 135:374 Je 17 '89
Molecular cloning of genes under control of the circadian clock in Neurospora. J. J. Loros and others. bibl f il *Science* 243:385-8 Ja 20 '89
Notes from the underground [S. Follini emerges from New Mexico cave, ending isolation experiment] S. Begley. il pors *Newsweek* 113:64 Je 5 '89
Recent awakenings in melatonin research [work of Margarita L. Dubocovich] R. Weiss. *Science News* 136:317 N 11 '89
Safety gets short shrift on long night shift [behavioral effects of circadian rhythms; research by Charles Czeisler] R. Weiss. *Science News* 135:37 Ja 21 '89
Signals [salmon fishing by biological rhythms] M. Hilbert. il *Field & Stream* 94:22+ D '89
Stefania Follini goes down under. L. Morgan. il *Seventeen* 48:34 D '89
Tennis in good time [effects of circadian rhythms] M. Bloom. il *World Tennis* 36:70-1 F '89
The times of your life [effects of long term isolation studied by S. Follini in New Mexico cave] A. Toufexis. il por *Time* 133:66-7 Je 5 '89

BIOLOGICAL RHYTHMS—*cont.*
Voluntary solitary [S. Follini spends eighteen weeks in New Mexico cave] M. Heenan. il por *Ad Astra* 1:35 O '89
Your finest hour [effects of circadian rhythms on cycling] R. Eichner. il *Bicycling* 30:122-5 My '89
BIOLOGICAL SOCIETIES
See also
American Institute of Biological Sciences
BIOLOGICAL STRUCTURE *See* Morphology
BIOLOGICAL TRANSPORT
See also
Blood-brain barrier
Calcium channels
Chloride channels
Glucose transport
Ion channels
Ionophores
Potassium channels
Protein transport
Sodium channels
Movement protein of tobacco mosaic virus modifies plasmodesmatal size exclusion limit. S. Wolf and others. bibl f il *Science* 246:377-9 O 20 '89
Osteoclastic bone resorption by a polarized vacuolar proton pump. H. C. Blair and others. bibl f il *Science* 245:855-7 Ag 25 '89
Proton motive force involved in protein transport across the outer membrane of Aeromonas salmonicida. K. R. Wong and J. T. Buckley. bibl f il *Science* 246:654-6 N 3 '89
BIOLOGICAL WARFARE *See* Chemical and biological weapons
BIOLOGISTS
See also
Béland, Pierre
People and places. See issues of BioScience
Supply and demand
Searching for researchers. B. Holland. il *World Press Review* 36:54 Ja '89
BIOLOGY
See also
Adaptation (Biology)
Biometry
Cells
Clones (Biology)
Computers—Biological use
Cytology
Developmental biology
Diversity (Biology)
Ecology
Electrophysiology
Embryology
Environment
Ethnobiology
Eugenics
Evolution
Homology (Biology)
Image processing—Biological use
Information systems—Biological use
Life (Biology)
Marine biology
Membranes (Biology)
Molecular biology
Morphogenesis
Mutation
Natural history
Pattern (Biology)
Phylogeny
Polymorphism (Biology)
Population biology
Predation (Biology)
Regeneration (Biology)
Reproduction
Robots—Biological use
Sex (Biology)
Soil biology
Space biology
Symbiosis
Symmetry (Biology)
Zoology
Contributions of bird studies to biology. M. Konishi and others. bibl f il *Science* 246:465-72 O 27 '89
Golden opportunities seen in biology [National Research Council report] M. Barinaga. *Science* 246:1115 D 1 '89
Awards
1989 AIBS Distinguished Service Award to Alfred E. Harper. por *BioScience* 39:499 Jl/Ag '89
Bibliography
Books. See occasional issues of BioScience
Classification
See also
Species
Linnaeus: interactive taxonomy using the Macintosh computer and HyperCard. K. W. Estep and others. bibl f il *BioScience* 39:635-8 O '89
Conferences
Calendar. See alternate issues of BioScience

Periodicity
See Biological rhythms
Philosophy
The science of metamorphoses [J. Loeb] R. C. Lewontin. bibl f il *The New York Review of Books* 36:18-22 Ap 27 '89
Social aspects
See also
Sociobiology
Study and teaching
See also
Biology teachers
Colleges and universities—Departments of biology
News on science education. J. S. Weis. *BioScience* 39:763 D '89
BIOLOGY IN LITERATURE
Biology in science fiction. E. Van Dommelen. bibl f il *BioScience* 39:729-31 N '89
BIOLOGY TEACHERS
What makes a good teacher? C. G. Reed. il *BioScience* 39:555-7 S '89
BIOLUMINESCENCE
Beetlejuice genes now in biotechnicolor [click beetles; research by Keith V. Wood and William D. McElroy] R. Weiss. il *Science News* 135:308 My 20 '89
Complementary DNA coding click beetle luciferases can elicit bioluminescence of different colors. K. V. Wood and others. bibl f il *Science* 244:700-2 My 12 '89
Kittyboo colors [gene tagging with luciferase from click beetles; research by Keith Wood and others] il *Discover* 10:12 N '89
Starlight on the reef [brittle stars glow with displeasure when touched; cover story] M. S. Grober. il *Natural History* p72-6+ O '89
BIOMAGNETISM *See* Magnetic fields—Physiological effects
BIOMASS ENERGY
See also
Wood as fuel
Refuse to riches. J. Yeaple. *Popular Science* 234:155 My '89
BIOMATHEMATICS
The body chaotic. G. Taubes. il *Discover* 10:62-7 My '89
BIOMECHANICS
See also
Comparative biomechanics
Human locomotion
The mechanics of rock climbing, or Surviving the ultimate physics exam. J. Walker. il *Scientific American* 260:118-21 Je '89
Therapeutic use
See Bodywork (Biomechanics)
BIOMEDICAL ENGINEERING
See also
Medical electronics
BIOMEDICAL ETHICS *See* Medical ethics
BIOMEDICAL RESEARCH *See* Medical research
BIOMETRY
Putting the finger on security. C. Garcia. il *Time* 133:79 Ap 3 '89
BIOMOLECULES *See* Molecules
BIOMUSE SYSTEM
Muscle melodies and brain refrains: turning bioelectric signals into music [work of Hugh S. Lusted and R. Benjamin Knapp] I. Amato. il *Science News* 135:202-3 Ap 1 '89
BIONDI, FRANK JOSEPH, JR.
The meaning of achievement. por *Channels (New York, N.Y.: 1986)* 9:34-5+ Jl/Ag '89
about
Is Viacom ready to channel the world? D. Lieberman. il pors *Business Week* p72-4 D 18 '89
BIONET *See* Information systems—Genetic research use
BIOPHYSICS
See also
Medical physics
Biological physics. bibl f *Physics Today* 42:S17-S19 Ja '89
BIOPOLYMERS
In search of the plastic potato. R. Pool. il *Science* 245:1187-9 S 15 '89
BIOPROSTHESIS *See* Prosthesis
BIOREGIONALISM
Bioregionalism: saving the earth, one small piece at a time. S. Zuckerman. il *Utne Reader* p86 N/D '89
BIORESOURCES *See* Natural resources
BIORHYTHMS *See* Biological rhythms
BIOSENSORS
See also
Silicon microphysiometers
Biological recognition repackaged. R. Lewis. il *BioScience* 39:288-91 My '89
Cell-like biosensor opens ionic floodgates [work of Frances S. Ligler] I. Amato. *Science News* 135:117 F 25 '89
Sweet semiconductor snags bacteria [Mark D. Bednarski] I. Amato. *Science News* 136:398 D 16 '89
BIOSPHERE
See also
Gaia hypothesis
International Geosphere-Biosphere Program

BIOSPHERE—cont.

The management of the biosphere [address, July 19, 1989] P. C. Cato. *Vital Speeches of the Day* 56:53-5 N 1 '89

Our planet, our health [cover story] G. Scott. bibl il *Current Health 2* 16:4-7+ D '89

Regional and global impacts on the biosphere. T. E. Graedel. bibl f il *Environment* 31:8-13+ Ja/F '89

BIOSPHERE II

Building an ecosystem from scratch. M. H. Turner. il *BioScience* 39:147-50 Mr '89

BIOSPHERE RESERVES

Biosphere reserves: what, where and why? il map *Focus (New York, N.Y.: 1950)* 39:17-19 Spr '89

Mexico

See also

Sian Ka'an Biosphere Reserve (Mexico)

BIOSYNTHESIS *See* Synthesis

BIOTECHNOLOGY EQUIPMENT *See* Biological equipment

BIOTECHNOLOGY RESEARCH *See* Genetic research

BIOTECHNOLOGY RESEARCH (PLANTS) *See* Plant genetics

BIOTELEMETRY

Around the Mall and beyond [capture and tracking of a clouded leopard in Royal Chitwan National Park, Nepal] E. Dinerstein. il *Smithsonian* 20:24+ Ap '89

Blueprinting big bucks [study on hunting trophy whitetails; cover story]; ed. by Kathy Etling. S. Demarais and B. Zaiglin. il *Outdoor Life* 184:61-3+ O '89

By using bar coding on busy bees, scientist Stephen Buchmann becomes an unstung hero [use in monitoring activities] il *People Weekly* 31:105 My 22 '89

Catching a ghost [monitoring snow leopards in Nepal] R. Jackson and G. Ahlborn. il *International Wildlife* 19:30-3 My/Je '89

Hive technology [tracking killer bees; work of Howard T. Kerr] J. Horgan. il *Scientific American* 260:22 Ja '89

Hunting for an elusive hunter [field studies of American martens in Wyoming] S. Buskirk and H. Harlow. il *National Wildlife* 28:20-3 D '89/Ja '90

King of the marsh [tracking rhinoceros in Royal Chitwan National Park, Nepal; cover story] E. Dinerstein. il *International Wildlife* 19:4-11 Mr/Ap '89

Probing secrets of small critters: fuchsia mice and bar-coded bees. L. Ware. il *Audubon* 91:12 Ja '89

Stopping killer bees with Star Wars [Africanized honey bees] J. Schlefer. *Technology Review* 92:2 My/Je '89

Stubborn hunter in a harsh land [tracking caribou herds and wolf packs in Denali National Park and Preserve] L. D. Mech. il map *National Wildlife* 27:20-4 Ag/S '89

A Yankee coat fits the coyote well [New England; cover story] R. Wolkomir and J. Wolkomir. il *National Wildlife* 27:34-8 Ap/My '89

BIOTIN

Structural origins of high-affinity biotin binding to streptavidin. P. C. Weber and others. bibl f il *Science* 243:85-8 Ja 6 '89

BIOTRODES *See* Biosensors

BIPEDAL LOCOMOTION IN HUMANS *See* Human locomotion

BIPHENYL COMPOUNDS

See also

Polychlorinated biphenyls

BIPLANE EXPO *See* Aviation—Exhibitions

BIPLANES

See also

National Biplane Association

BIPOLAR INTEGRATED CIRCUITS

Speed demons [emitter coupled logic] K. K. Wiegner. il *Forbes* 143:302-3 Ja 9 '89

BIPOLAR INTEGRATED TECHNOLOGY (FIRM)

Speed demons. K. K. Wiegner. il *Forbes* 143:302-3 Ja 9 '89

BIPPUS, SUNNY

about

Always fair weather. S. Ballard. il pors *Sports Illustrated* 70 Special Issue:71-4 F '89

BIRA, SHAGDARYN

The secret history of the Mongols. il *The Unesco Courier* 42:36-9 S '89

BIRAN, YOAV

Why Israel fears a PLO state. *World Press Review* 36:20 F '89

BIRD, ELIZABETH

Invasion of the mind snatchers. il *Psychology Today* 23:64-6 Ap '89

BIRD, JUNIUS BOUTON, 1907-1982

about

Portrait of an archeologist. J. Hyslop. il pors *Natural History* p84+ F '89

BIRD, LARRY

about

An ailing Bird, a retiring Kareem. il por *Newsweek* 113:62 My 8 '89

Hub of emotion [cover story] J. McCallum. il pors *Sports Illustrated* 71:42-4+ D 11 '89

Magic vs Bird: 10 years ago they first met in a memorable NCAA title game. W. Ladson and R. Harper. il pors *Sport (New York, N.Y.)* 80:76-7 Ap '89

See Larry run. L. Montville. il pors *Sports Illustrated* 71:26-9 Jl 3 '89

Who's the best—Bird, Magic or Air Jordan? M. Littwin. il pors *TV Guide* 37:20-1+ F 11-17 '89

BIRD, RICHARD

about

It's another day, another marathon, as Richard Bird ends a record year on the run. J. Friedman. il pors *People Weekly* 31:103+ Ap 24 '89

BIRD, SAMUEL R.

about

The courage of Sam Bird. B. T. Collins. il *Reader's Digest* 134:49-54 My '89

BIRD, VAL

"I saved my baby from crib death"; ed. by Judith Kelman. il por *Redbook* 173:42+ My '89

BIRD, WILLIAM L.

Enterprise and meaning: sponsored film, 1939-1949. bibl il *History Today* 39:24-30 D '89

BIRD [film] *See* Motion picture reviews—Single works

BIRD ATTRACTING *See* Birds, Attracting of

BIRD CAGES

Cages that soar [work of K. Marquis] T. Sweeney. il por *Home Mechanix* 85:26-7 F '89

BIRD CALLING

Duck calling simplified. N. Strung. il *Field & Stream* 94:56 N '89

Turkey calling is going to the birds. S. Grenoble. il *Outdoor Life* 183:56-7+ F '89

Turkey hunting's cutting edge. K. Etling. il *Outdoor Life* 183:72-3+ Mr '89

BIRD CALLS *See* Birds—Song

BIRD COMMUNICATION

The owl that traded a hoot for a hiss [burrowing owl] M. Rowe. il *Natural History* p32-3 My '89

The ravens' feast. B. Heinrich. il *Natural History* p44-51 F '89

BIRD CONTROL

See also

Ducks, Wild—Control

Woodpeckers—Control

BIRD DOGS *See* Hunting dogs

BIRD FEEDERS

Bird feeder. A. Hontoir. il *Workbench* 45:58-60+ My/Je '89

A winter gift for birds or bird-watchers. il *Sunset (Central West edition)* 181:170+ D '88

BIRD HUNTING *See* Game bird shooting; Water bird shooting

BIRD INTRODUCTION

Hidden complexities in the risks of extinction [reintroducing birds to Guam; work of Stuart Pimm] R. Lewin. *Science* 243:1294 Mr 10 '89

BIRD NAMES *See* Birds—Nomenclature

BIRD POACHING *See* Poaching

BIRD POPULATIONS

See also

Population genetics—Birds

As trees fall in the tropics, songbirds fall silent. il *U.S. News & World Report* 107:52 Ag 7 '89

Birding by the numbers. S. Stuller. il *The Atlantic* 263:88-9+ My '89

Hidden complexities in the risks of extinction [reintroducing birds to Guam; work of Stuart Pimm] R. Lewin. *Science* 243:1294 Mr 10 '89

Vanishing songbirds [views of Richard Coles] il *The Futurist* 23:51 Jl/Ag '89

BIRD SANCTUARIES

Alaska

Gunning for bald eagles [Alaska Chilkat Bald Eagle Preserve] il *Newsweek* 113:33 F 27 '89

Louisiana

See also

Avery Island (La.)

Martha's Vineyard (Mass.)

See also

Felix Neck Wildlife Sanctuary (Mass.)

Mexico

See also

Rasa Island (Mexico)

BIRD SHOOTING *See* Game bird shooting; Water bird shooting

BIRD SONGS *See* Birds—Song

BIRD STUDY

See also

National Audubon Society

Birding by the numbers. S. Stuller. il *The Atlantic* 263:88-9+ My '89

Birdland. F. Graham. See issues of Audubon through January 1989

Computerized canaries [British Trust for Ornithology monitoring system] T. Beardsley. *Scientific American* 260:34 Ap '89

Contributions of bird studies to biology. M. Konishi and others. bibl f il *Science* 246:465-72 O 27 '89

A lark of a way to see the world. J. Leo. il *U.S. News & World Report* 106:58 Je 12 '89

My mother-in-law is for the birds. S. H. Shetterly. il *New Choices for the Best Years* 29:89-92 Mr '89

BIRD STUDY—*cont.*
Anecdotes, facetiae, satire, etc.
Birding, southern style. P. G. Quinnett. il *Audubon* 91:34-7 My '89

Going to the birds. P. F. McManus. il *Outdoor Life* 184:118+ Jl '89
Competitions
The World Series of Birding. A. Mapes. il *The Conservationist* 43:20-5 Mr/Ap '89

BIRD WATCHING *See* Bird study
BIRDCAGES *See* Bird cages
BIRDHOUSES IN ART
Laura Foreman's houses have something to say; no longer are they just for the birds. B. Johnson. il pors *People Weekly* 31:143-4 Je 19 '89

BIRDIE AFRICA *See* Ward, Michael Moses
BIRDING *See* Bird study
BIRDS

See also
Aviaries
Embryology—Birds
Eye—Birds
Hearing—Birds
Nervous system—Birds
Scarecrows
Shore birds
Vision—Birds
Water birds
See also names of birds

Birdland. F. Graham. See issues of Audubon through January 1989

Accidents and hazards
See also
Aviation—Bird hazards
Brain
See Brain
Care
See also
University of Minnesota. Raptor Center
Behind the gauze mask [Jains run Charity Birds Hospital in India] D. R. Ward. il *International Wildlife* 19:14-19 Ja/F '89

Thoroughly modern Polly. S. L. Gerstenfeld. il *Parents* 64:250 D '89
Caricatures and cartoons
Pufted tuffins (and other backward birds). T. M. Shortt. il *International Wildlife* 19:12-13 Jl/Ag '89
Collisions with airplanes
See Aviation—Bird hazards
Coloration
See Color of birds
Diseases and pests
The numbers game puts birds at risk [avian disease at Alamosa and Monte Vista refuges in Colorado] F. Graham. il map *Audubon* 91:18+ Ja '89
Ecology
In the struggle to protect our planet, ornithologists and their grass-roots flock have insights worth following. J. P. Wiley, Jr. il *Smithsonian* 20:34+ D '89
Exhibitions
See also
American Museum of Natural History. Whitney Wing
Food and feeding
See also
Bird feeders
Alimentary, my dear hoatzin [research by Stuart D. Strahl] R. Cowen. il *Science News* 136:269-70 O 21 '89

The birds of paradise [diet's influence on sexual behavior; cover story] B. M. Beehler. bibl il map *Scientific American* 261:116-23 D '89

Foregut fermentation in the hoatzin, a neotropical leaf-eating bird [cover story] A. Grajal and others. bibl f il *Science* 245:1236-8 S 15 '89

Goose prelude to global warming [destruction of wetland vegetation due to delayed migration of snow geese; research by Robert Jefferies] J. A. Miller. *BioScience* 39:673 N '89

What's a hoatzin? [only bird with foregut fermentation; research by Stuart D. Strahl] J. Horgan. il *Scientific American* 261:30 D '89
Habits and behavior
See also
Parental behavior in birds
Sexual behavior—Birds
Avian altruism [bee-eaters; cover story] K. Fackelmann. *Science News* 135:364-5 Je 10 '89
Handbooks, manuals, etc.
A field guide to field guides to wild birds. P. McWilliams. il *Country Journal* 16:14+ F '89
Identification
See Bird study
Migration
As trees fall in the tropics, songbirds fall silent. il *U.S. News & World Report* 107:52 Ag 7 '89

Vanishing songbirds [views of Richard Coles] il *The Futurist* 23:51 Jl/Ag '89

Nests
Nesting instincts [bird nest finders V. Pitzrick and E. Brooks] R. E. Bonney. il *National Wildlife* 27:28 Ap/My '89
Nomenclature
The ethnobiologist's dilemma. J. M. Diamond. *Natural History* p26+ Je '89

This-fellow frog, name belong-him dakwo [Papua New Guinea] J. M. Diamond. *Natural History* p16+ Ap '89
Photographs and photography
Winging it [work of D. Guravich] D. Matthews. il *Popular Photography* 96:42-7 Je '89
Protection
See also
Bird sanctuaries
Birds, Attracting of
National Audubon Society
Song
Categorical perception of a natural stimulus continuum: birdsong [swamp sparrows] D. A. Nelson and P. Marler. bibl f il *Science* 244:976-8 My 26 '89

From bird song to neurogenesis [study of the canary brain] F. Nottebohm. il *Scientific American* 260:74-9 F '89

Living with your neighbors' fowl habits [peacocks] W. Maus. *Flower and Garden* 33:64+ Mr/Ap '89

Of birds and brains [quail-chick chimeras produce modified songs; research by Evan Balaban and others] il *Discover* 10:14 F '89

What, when, where, and why warblers warble [cover story] D. E. Kroodsma. il *Natural History* p50-9 My '89

Who listens to the mockingbird? R. Breitwisch. il *Natural History* p6+ Je '89
Antarctic regions
See also
Penguins
Canada
Grondin: wings over Canada. J. Watson. il *International Wildlife* 19:38-43 Ja/F '89
Caribbean region
Polly wants to be saved [work of P. Butler] S. Begley. il *Newsweek* 114:65 D 18 '89
Christmas Island (Pacific Ocean)
Ghosts of Christmas [effects of El Niño; study by Ralph and Elizabeth Schreiber] L. Oliwenstein. il *Discover* 10:22 Ag '89
Colorado
The numbers game puts birds at risk [avian disease at Alamosa and Monte Vista refuges] F. Graham. il map *Audubon* 91:18+ Ja '89
Falkland Islands
Albatross alley [cover story] I. J. Strange. il *Natural History* p26-33 Jl '89

March of the feathered thugs: Johnny Rook birds in the Falklands wreak havoc on an albatross colony. T. De Roy. il *International Wildlife* 19:52-9 Mr/Ap '89
Florida
Murder most fowl: the Florida duck war [Muscovy ducks in St. Augustine Beach] il *Newsweek* 113:32 Ja 2 '89
Gardiners Island (N.Y.)
Lord of ospreys [R. Gardiner of Gardiners Island] F. Graham. il *Audubon* 91:10+ S '89
Great Britain
Anecdotes, facetiae, satire, etc.
Noble notes [pelicans in St. James Park] F. Graham. il *Audubon* 91:14 Jl '89
Guam
Cold-blooded killers [birds eaten by brown tree snakes] *Discover* 10:16 Ag '89

Hidden complexities in the risks of extinction [reintroducing birds to Guam; work of Stuart Pimm] R. Lewin. *Science* 243:1294 Mr 10 '89
Hawaii
Integrated conservation strategy for Hawaiian forest birds [discussion of April 1988 article, Conservation of Hawaii's vanishing avifauna] J. M. Scott and others. bibl f *BioScience* 39:475-9 Jl/Ag '89

Let it pau out? [controversy surrounding efforts to save the Hawaiian crow] F. Graham. *Audubon* 91:14+ N '89
Hudson Bay region
Goose prelude to global warming [destruction of wetland vegetation due to delayed migration of snow geese; research by Robert Jefferies] J. A. Miller. *BioScience* 39:673 N '89
Idaho
Lone ranger of the Rockies [boreal owls in Frank Church-River of No Return Wilderness] P. H. Hayward and G. D. Hayward. il *Natural History* p78-85 N '89

Swan song [trumpeter swans] F. Graham. *Audubon* 91:18-19 My '89

To save the swans [trumpeter swans] il *Life* 12:109-11 Ap '89
India
Behind the gauze mask [Jains run Charity Birds Hospital] D. R. Ward. il *International Wildlife* 19:14-19 Ja/F '89
Kenya
Honey hunters follow birds to reach bees [research by H. A. Isack and H.-U. Reyer] *Science News* 135:172 Mr 18 '89

BIRDS—Kenya—*cont.*
Honeyguides and honey gatherers: interspecific communication in a symbiotic relationship. H. A. Isack and H.-U. Reyer. bibl f il *Science* 243:1343-6 Mr 10 '89

Latin America
See also
Cracids (Birds)

Maui (Hawaii)
A seabird in the house of the sun [dark-rumped petrels] T. Simons and G. C. Whittow. il *Natural History* p50-3 Mr '89

Michigan
Mack Lake, Michigan [Kirtland's warblers] R. H. Mohlenbrock. il map *Natural History* p90-5 O '89

Midway Islands
Northern Hemisphere albatrosses. J. Kenyon. bibl il *Sea Frontiers* 35:342-7 N/D '89

Montana
Bluebirds liked it hot. H. Power. maps *Natural History* p61 Ja '89

New Jersey
The birds and the B&B's [Cape May] R. Norris. il map *Travel Holiday* 171:55-9 Ap '89
The World Series of Birding. A. Mapes. il *The Conservationist* 43:20-5 Mr/Ap '89

New York (State)
Birdmen of Harlem [raising pigeons on tenement roofs] J. W. Miller. il *The New York Times Magazine* p48-9+ N 19 '89
Increasing ducks in New York. D. Carroll. il *The Conservationist* 43:12-15 Mr/Ap '89
Nesting instincts [bird nest finders V. Pitzrick and E. Brooks] R. E. Bonney. il *National Wildlife* 27:28 Ap/My '89

North America
The last watering holes on the prairie [loss of wetland habitat for waterfowl] G. L. Krapu. il *Natural History* p66-9 Ja '89
Portrait of a deepening crisis [loss of wetlands endangers water birds] P. Steinhart. il *National Wildlife* 27:4-13 O/N '89
Waterfowl for tomorrow: the North American Waterfowl Management Plan. D. Odell and G. Batcheller. il map *The Conservationist* 43:6-11 Mr/Ap '89

North Carolina
Anecdotes, facetiae, satire, etc.
Birding, southern style. P. G. Quinnett. il *Audubon* 91:34-7 My '89

North Dakota
Dimples on a black desert [wetland conservation efforts hampered by farmers] T. Williams. il *Audubon* 91:36-8+ S '89

Papua New Guinea
The ethnobiologist's dilemma. J. M. Diamond. *Natural History* p26+ Je '89
This-fellow frog, name belong-him dakwo. J. M. Diamond. *Natural History* p16+ Ap '89

Prince William Sound (Alaska)
A soiled symbol [bald eagles affected by Exxon Valdez oil spill] J. R. Luoma. il *Audubon* 91:101 S '89

Rhode Island
Dark side of a classic beauty [control of mute swan population] W. Williams. il *National Wildlife* 27:42-8 F/Mr '89

Seal Island (Me.)
Man to puffins: please come back and stay [work of Steve Kress] M. Satchell. il *U.S. News & World Report* 107:51-2 Ag 7 '89

South America
The terror bird still screams. K. H. Redford and P. Shaw. il *International Wildlife* 19:14-16 My/Je '89
Tudor's tutors [G. Tudor's illustrations for book The birds of South America] F. Graham. *Audubon* 91:20+ N '89
Photographs and photography
Watch the birdie! [work of J. S. Dunning] A. Meadows. il por *Américas* 41 no2:61-3 '89

Southern States
A bird for Miss Alma. E. C. Murray. il *Southern Living* 24:89 F '89

Texas
A clearcutting ban for the birds [red cockaded woodpeckers in national forests] P. Larmer. il *Sierra* 74:28-30 Mr/Ap '89

Venezuela
Rhapsody in red [scarlet ibises] C. S. Luthin. il *International Wildlife* 19:46-51 Jl/Ag '89

Washington (State)
After an oil spill: saving the birds. D. B. Lewis. il *Sea Frontiers* 35:200-5 Jl/Ag '89
Hands against the darkness [cleaning oil-soaked birds after spill] A. E. Simonov. il *The Mother Earth News* 118:8 Jl/Ag '89

BIRDS, ATTRACTING OF
See also
Bird feeders
Farming in the Flyways (Program)
Attracting barn swallows. il *Country Journal* 16:41 My/Je '89
Attracting spring birds. P. Macneale. il *Flower and Garden* 33:101-3 Mr/Ap '89

Birds in the winter garden. J. Glattstein. il *Flower and Garden* 33:20+ N/D '89
He's on wild path in CRP. J. Walter. il *Successful Farming* 87:72 S '89

BIRDS, FOSSIL
Call that bird 'Sir' [Diatryma] R. Monastersky. *Science News* 136:332 N 18 '89
Sixth find is a feathered friend [Archaeopteryx specimen from West Germany] P. Shipman. il *Discover* 10:63 Ja '89

BIRDS, PREDATORY *See* Birds of prey

BIRDS IN ART
Grondin: wings over Canada. J. Watson. il *International Wildlife* 19:38-43 Ja/F '89
Tudor's tutors [G. Tudor's illustrations for book The birds of South America] F. Graham. *Audubon* 91:20+ N '89

BIRDS IN VIDEOTAPES
Jane Talkington's Kitty video gives hungry cats a view that forever fascinates. il *People Weekly* 32:99 N 13 '89

BIRDS OF PARADISE
The birds of paradise [diet's influence on sexual behavior; cover story] B. M. Beehler. bibl il map *Scientific American* 261:116-23 D '89

BIRDS OF PREY
See also
Condors
Eagles
Falcons
Hawks
Ospreys
Owls
The terror bird still screams [South America] K. H. Redford and P. Shaw. il *International Wildlife* 19:14-16 My/Je '89

BIRDSALL, JESSE
about
He's 'Getting it right'. C. Mundy. il por *Rolling Stone* p38 Je 1 '89

BIRDWATCHING *See* Bird study
BIREFRINGENCE *See* Refraction, Double
BIRGENEAU, ROBERT J.
about
AAPT top honors awarded to French and Birgeneau. pors *Physics Today* 42:126-8 Mr '89

BIRINYI, LASZLO, JR.
about
Is any stock shock-proof? These come close. G. G. Marcial. il *Business Week* p180 N 6 '89

BIRKERTS, SVEN
On the road to nowhere. il *Harper's* 279:74-6 Jl '89
BIRKIN, ANDREW
about
Burning secret [film] Reviews
People Weekly il 31:19 Ja 16 '89. P. Travers
BIRMAN, IGOR' IĀKOVLEVICH
about
How to dismantle communism [interview] P. Lubin. il *National Review* 41:29-33 D 8 '89
BIRMINGHAM, STEPHEN
Stephen Birmingham's one-upmanship guide [cover story] il *TV Guide* 37:6-9 Mr 11-17 '89
BIRMINGHAM (ALA.)
Economic conditions
No longer the South's Johannesburg. V. E. Smith. il *Newsweek* 113:44 F 6 '89
Firefighters
Birmingham firehouse [Supreme Court decision permitting white firemen to bring suit against the city for job discrimination] *Commonweal* 116:387-8 Jl 14 '89
Galleries and museums
See also
Birmingham Museum of Art (Ala.)
Libraries
Library with a southern accent [Tutwiler Collection of Southern History and Literature maintained by the public library] il *Southern Living* 24:46 Mr '89
Monuments, statues, etc.
Vandals desecrate King's statue in Birmingham park. il *Jet* 76:32 My 29 '89
Politics and government
Backtracking in Birmingham? [charges of racial harassment] B. Turque. il *Newsweek* 114:25 Jl 3 '89
Race relations
Backtracking in Birmingham? [charges of racial harassment] B. Turque. il *Newsweek* 114:25 Jl 3 '89
BIRMINGHAM (ENGLAND)
Galleries and museums
See also
Patrick Collection (Birmingham, England)
BIRMINGHAM MUSEUM OF ART (ALA.)
A case of the Wedgwood blues [Beeson collection] il *Southern Living* 24:30 F '89
BIRMINGHAM STEEL CORP.
Why a big steelmaker is mimicking the minimills [Birmingham vs. LTV] il *Business Week* p92 Mr 27 '89
BIRNBAUM, LARRY
Bill Evans: the art of the fisherman. il pors *Down Beat* 56:20-2 Ja '89

BIRNBAUM, LARRY—*cont.*
The Kinsey Report. il *Down Beat* 56:46-7 F '89
BIRNBAUM, NORMAN
Fighting off the beer-hall boys. il *The Nation* 248:588-9+ My 1 '89
BIRNBAUM, STEPHEN
Travel news. See issues of Good Housekeeping
BIRNEY, DAVID
about
Once a devoted Hollywood duo, Meredith Baxter and David Birney call it quits after 15 years. K. Hubbard. il pors *People Weekly* 31:59-60 Mr 13 '89
BIRNEY, MEREDITH BAXTER
about
Meredith Baxter Birney: starting over at 42. N. Gittelson. il pors *McCall's* 117:109-12 O '89
Once a devoted Hollywood duo, Meredith Baxter and David Birney call it quits after 15 years. K. Hubbard. il pors *People Weekly* 31:59-60 Mr 13 '89
BIRSH, ANDY
Spécialités de la maison. See issues of Gourmet beginning May 1986
BIRTH *See* Childbirth
BIRTH, MULTIPLE
See also
Quintuplets
Triplets
Twins
The baby-baby-baby boom!!! D. R. Hales. il *Redbook* 172:94-7 Ja '89
BIRTH CERTIFICATES *See* Registers of births, etc.
BIRTH CONTROL
See also
Abortifacients
Abortion
Contraceptives
Planned Parenthood Federation of America
Contraception: a special report [special section] il *Mademoiselle* 95:168-71+ D '89
The Trojan wars. J. Alper. il *Health (New York, N.Y.)* 21:78-9 N '89

International aspects
See also
United Nations Fund for Population Activities
Research in human reproduction [WHO's Special Programme of Research, Development and Research Training in Human Reproduction] J. Barzelatto. il *World Health* p18-21 Ap '89

Laws and regulations
Family planning and the law. A.-M. Dourlen-Rollier. il *World Health* p7-9 Ap '89

Moral and religious aspects
The blessings of fertility. M. Shivanandan. *America* 161:474-7 D 23-30 '89
Building a creative conscience [Catholic ethics]; tr. by Ingrid Knapp. B. Häring. il *Commonweal* 116:433-6 Ag 11 '89
Does God condemn contraception? [questioning Vatican position] B. Häring. *Commonweal* 116:69-71 F 10 '89
Islam and family planning. M. Mahran. il *World Health* p22-3 Ap '89
Paul VI was right [discussion of July 15, 1988 article, Anniversary waltz] *Commonweal* 116:386+ Jl 14 '89
Reinventing the brake [family planning and Catholic Church in the Philippines] J. Miller. *Commonweal* 116:105-7 F 24 '89
Who can pass judgment on the Joneses? R. E. Burns. *U.S. Catholic* 54:2 Je '89

Algeria
Birth-spacing. O. Zémor. il *World Health* p17 D '88

China
Background on China. M. Morain. *The Humanist* 49:33+ Jl/Ag '89

Developing countries
Disconnections and anomalies [restrictions on aid] M. Morain. *The Humanist* 49:31 S/O '89

Indonesia
Background on Indonesia. M. Morain. *The Humanist* 49:33 Jl/Ag '89
A global leader of a new kind; A part of the fabric of life. M. Morain. il *The Humanist* 49:31 My/Je '89

Philippines
Reinventing the brake. J. Miller. *Commonweal* 116:105-7 F 24 '89

Thailand
The good news: Thailand controls a baby boom [work of Mechai Viravaidya] il por *Time* 133:50 Ja 2 '89
BIRTH DEFECTS
See also
Biliary atresia
Fetus—Diseases
Hypoplastic left heart syndrome
Neural tube—Diseases
Spina bifida
Accutane: under attack. J. Kaplan. *Vogue* 179:112-13 Ja '89
Facing the future [Canadian thalidomide victims seek compensation] A. Steacy. il *Maclean's* 102:41 F 20 '89

Faith of a family: the Tony Melendez story [thalidomide victim; condensed from A gift of hope]; ed. by Mel White. T. Melendez. il *Reader's Digest* 134:209-12+ Je '89
The man who would not quit [thalidomide victim D. L. Stevens] J. G. Hubbell. il pors *Reader's Digest* 134:115-18 F '89
A miracle goes sour [Accutane] C. Raymond. il *Discover* 10:72 Ja '89
What a beautiful baby. K. H. Avelino. il por *Parents* 64:132-4+ O '89
When the spirit takes wing [Provera victim D. Able born without arms or legs] M. Grant. il pors *People Weekly* 31:50-5 My 15 '89
BIRTH ORDER
Were you born for each other? [significance in choosing a mate] P. M. Withers. *McCall's* 116:56+ F '89
BIRTH RATE
See also
Baby boom generation
Baby bust generation
Birth control
Population
The birth dearth confirmed. E. Rubenstein. *National Review* 41:13 My 5 '89
The changing face of out-of-wedlock births. B. J. Wattenberg. il *U.S. News & World Report* 107:29 Jl 3 '89
A confederacy of dunces [views of R. J. Herrnstein on IQ and falling birth rates] G. Cowley. il por *Newsweek* 112:80+ My 22 '89
Future shock [population trends point to labor shortage and increase in minority birth rate; cover story] D. E. Bloom and N. G. Bennett. *The New Republic* 200:18-20+ Je 19 '89
IQ and falling birth rates. R. J. Herrnstein. il *The Atlantic* 263:72-6+ My '89

Developing countries
Lower birth rates spell a brighter future for the third world. B. J. Wattenberg. il *U.S. News & World Report* 107:23 D 18 '89

United States
See Birth rate
BIRTH TECHNOLOGY *See* Reproduction
BIRTH TRAUMA *See* Childbirth—Complications
BIRTH WEIGHT
Cesareans don't help lowest-weight babies [study by Michael H. Malloy] S. Hart. *Science News* 136:182 S 16 '89
BIRTHDAY CARDS
Special Days [custom birthday card computer program] J. Zornberg. il *Home Office Computing* 7:90-1 Ja '89
BIRTHDAY PARTIES
See also
Jeremy's Place (Firm)
4 fabulous birthday parties. R. G. McKenzie. il *Parents* 64:145-9 My '89
Alexis' birthday party with Martha Stewart. B. Rodriguez. il por *Organic Gardening* 36:38-40+ O '89
Ali-Dada's Arabian night [M. S. Forbes celebrates in Morocco] M. Dougherty. il pors *People Weekly* 32:34-9 S 4 '89
And now, our 2¢ about that $2 million birthday bash [Malcolm Forbes' Morocco party] M. S. Forbes. il *Forbes* 144:20-1 O 16 '89
As singers sang to help their own, the sweet tones and high notes were all for Ella [E. Fitzgerald] il por *People Weekly* 31:56-7 My 15 '89
Children's party planner [suggestions from Maureen Smith Williams] P. Schiller. il *McCall's* 116:45-6+ Ag '89
Happy birthday parties: fun for kids; easy on parents. B. Johnson. il *Better Homes and Gardens* 67:149-52 My '89
In defence of the freedom to spend [M. S. Forbes] B. Amiel. il *Maclean's* 102:17 O 23 '89
It's your party [M. S. Forbes' 70th birthday celebration] *The New Republic* 201:4+ S 11 '89
Jackson saluted at his gala 48th birthday bash in D.C. il pors *Jet* 77:6-7 O 23 '89
New standards of wretched excess [M. Forbes' party in Morocco] F. Bruning. il *Maclean's* 102:9 S 11 '89
Party hearty Elton John lights 40 candles in the wind for his manager's birthday [party for J. Reid] il pors *People Weekly* 32:40-1 S 25 '89
A survival guide to birthdays [with editorial comment by Ann Pleshette Murphy] P. Theroux. il *Parents* 64:8, 58-61 My '89
That party [M. S. Forbes' party; cover story] J. Baumgold. il pors *New York* 22:30-41 O 2 '89
Whitney Houston holds a lavish birthday gala. il pors *Jet* 76:60-1 S 11 '89
Who you gonna call if you want your kid's party to gel? Try faux Ghostbuster Peter Mosen. il por *People Weekly* 32:115 Jl 17 '89
BIRTHDAYS
Drafted at the age of nine [link between birth date and hockey ability; research by Roger Barnsley] J. C. Horn. il *Psychology Today* 23:22+ Ja/F '89
BIRTHMARKS
Dye laser clears children's birthmarks [research by Oon Tian Tan] K. Fackelmann. *Science News* 135:118 F 25 '89
Erasing port-wine stains [use of tunable dye laser] S. Begley. il *Newsweek* 113:65 F 27 '89

BIRTHMARKS—*cont.*
Latest ways to remove scars and birthmarks. L. Holland. il *Good Housekeeping* 209:179 Jl '89
BISCUITS
Down-home muffins & biscuits. il *Good Housekeeping* 208:158-9 Ap '89
From our kitchen to yours. K. Adams. *Southern Living* 24:179 S '89
Hospitality is the common thread in these breads. D. A. Campbell. il *Southern Living* 24:72-3 S '89
BISHIP, PAUL
Understanding trapping in New York. il *The Conservationist* 44:38-43 N/D '89
BISHOP, J. MICHAEL, 1936-
about
Cancer gene research wins Medicine Nobel. J. L. Marx. il pors *Science* 246:326-7 O 20 '89
Gene-tracking leads to Nobel Prize. A. McKenzie. *Science News* 136:244 O 14 '89
Medicine. il pors *Time* 134:73 O 23 '89
BISHOP, JOHN
about
Bishops, king and queen. L. Griffin. il pors *Car and Driver* 35:161-2+ O '89
BISHOP, MAURICE
Assassination
In Grenada, victors' justice. *The Progressive* 53:15-16 Mr '89
BISHOP, MICHAEL, 1945-
Hunkered down on Pine Mountain. il por *The Mother Earth News* 115:75-7 Ja/F '89
Reading the silks [fiction] il *Omni (New York, N.Y.)* 11:48-50+ Ag '89
BISHOP, PEG
about
Bishops, king and queen. L. Griffin. il pors *Car and Driver* 35:161-2+ O '89
BISHOP, ROBERT CHARLES
Double wedding ring quilts. il *Antiques* 135:732-41 Mr '89
about
Just folks. A. Prud'Homme. il por *New York* 22:40 Ap 10 '89
BISHOP, ROY
The standard lens. il por *Petersen's Photographic Magazine* 17:16-18+ Ja '89
BISHOP, TOM
about
Fantasy and reality. D. Machan. il por *Forbes* 144:282+ N 27 '89
The same . . . but different. M. Hulbert. il *Forbes* 143:408 My 1 '89
BISHOP DESMOND TUTU SOUTHERN AFRICAN REFUGEE SCHOLARSHIP FUND
Cry freedom [interview with M. Tutu] C. G. Fraser. por *Essence* 20:34 S '89
BISHOPS
See also
Catholic Church. National Conference of Catholic Bishops
Synod of Bishops (1987)
The archbishops go to Rome. T. J. Reese. *America* 160:187-8 Mr 4 '89
Audition for tragedy [U.S. archbishops meet with the Pope in Rome] J. McNeal. *Commonweal* 116:228-31 Ap 21 '89
Discussions in Rome [U.S. archbishops and Vatican officials] T. J. Reese. *America* 160:260-1 Mr 25 '89
Get with the program [U.S. archbishops meet with the Pope in Rome] K. L. Woodward. *Newsweek* 113:60 Mr 20 '89
Of many things [Thomas J. Reese's Archbishop: inside the power structure of the American Catholic Church] G. W. Hunt. *America* 160:442 My 13 '89
U.S. bishops visit Pope. *The Christian Century* 106:345 Ap 5 '89
Appointment, call and election
All the Pope's men [naming of conservative Catholic bishops] R. N. Ostling. il por *Time* 133:62 Ja 16 '89
Autocracy isn't the Catholic style. P. S. Kaufman. il *Commonweal* 116:110-14 F 24 '89
Liberation theology and the Peruvian Church [cover story] J. A. McCoy. *America* 160:526-30 Je 3 '89
The Peruvian Church and liberation theology [discussion of June 3, 1989 article, Liberation theology and the Peruvian Church] J. A. McCoy. *America* 161:84-5+ Ag 12-19 '89
Roman inroads [new Soviet bloc bishops] *Time* 134:43 Ag 7 '89
Vatican under fire [European theologians protest appointment of conservative archbishops] *Time* 133:57 F 6 '89
Political activities
Bishops shouldn't take a vow of silence. R. E. Burns. *U.S. Catholic* 54:2 Jl '89
BISHOP'S UNIVERSITY
North Hatley's old world charm [class of 1964 reunion] A. Fotheringham. il *Maclean's* 102:76 O 9 '89
BISMARCK, MONA, GRÄFIN VON, 1897-1983
about
Mona Bismarck on Capri. W. Weaver. il por *Architectural Digest* 46:32+ F '89

BISMARCK (BATTLESHIP)
The Bismarck found. R. D. Ballard. il maps *National Geographic* 176:622-37 N '89
Sink the Führer twice! [sunken ship found by Robert Ballard] il *U.S. News & World Report* 106:11-12 Je 26 '89
Stalking the Bismarck a second time. il map *Newsweek* 114:32 Jl 3 '89
BISMUTH
See also
Triphenyl bismuth
BISON, AMERICAN
See also
Buffalo hunting
National Bison Range (Mont.)
Bison, elk deaths high in Yellowstone. il *National Parks* 63:11 My/Je '89
Sifting ashes in Yellowstone [management of bison and elk in wake of forest fires] T. Williams. il *Audubon* 91:30-2+ N '89
BISSELL, EMILY
about
"Stamping" out tuberculosis: the story of Christmas seals. K. Doyle. il por *American History Illustrated* 24:66-8 N/D '89
BISSELL, GEORGE
about
Gentleman scamster. R. L. Stern. il por *Forbes* 143:104+ F 20 '89
BISSET, JACQUELINE
about
With two steamy new roles, Jackie Bisset is on a burn from Brazil to Beverly Hills. M. Dougherty. il pors *People Weekly* 31:124-6 Je 12 '89
BISSOONDATH, NEIL, 1955-
about
PW interviews. B. Slopen. por *Publishers Weekly* 235:79-80 Ja 6 '89
BITES, ANIMAL *See* Animal bites
BITES, DOG *See* Dog bites
BITES, INSECT *See* Insect bites and stings
BITHER, EVE M., AND KESTENBAUM, STUART J.
The arts in education program: a state's perspective. *Design for Arts in Education* 90:35-7 Ja/F '89
BITNER, JOANN
about
A therapist who's been there urges sympathy for the 'other woman' [interview] S. Adelson. il pors *People Weekly* 32:116+ O 30 '89
BITOMSKY, HARTMUT
about
In the eye of the beholder: poetic documentaries about technology. K. Rosenberg. il *Technology Review* 92:62-8 F/Mr '89
BITREX
A good idea in bad taste [L. Tylczak pushes for the addition of Bitrex to household products to reduce risk of childhood poisoning] M. G. Stoddard. il por *The Saturday Evening Post* 261:38-9 S '89
BITS (DRILLING AND BORING)
Router bits. J. Truini. il *Popular Mechanics* 166:65-8 F '89
Will the real Mr. Forstner please stand up. P. McCafferty. il *Workbench* 45:25-6 N/D '89
Sharpening
See Sharpeners and sharpening
BITTLE, CAMILLA R.
Birthday blessings [story] il *Good Housekeeping* 208:122-3 Ap '89
BIVALVES *See* Mollusks
BIX (COMPUTER NETWORK)
Out my computer window. H. Kenner. il *Harper's* 279:76-80 N '89
BIX (SAN FRANCISCO, CALIF.: RESTAURANT) *See* San Francisco (Calif.)—Restaurants, nightclubs, bars, etc.
BIZNET *See* American Business Network
BJERKLIE, DAVID
The electronic transformation of maps. il *Technology Review* 92:54-63 Ap '89
BJÖRK, GLENN R., AND OTHERS
Prevention of translational frameshifting by the modified nucleoside 1-methylguanosine. bibl f il *Science* 244:986-9 My 26 '89
BJORKEN, JAMES D.
Feynman and partons. bibl f il *Physics Today* 42:56-9 F '89
BJORKLUND, BARBARA
(jt. auth) *See* Bjorklund, David F., 1949-, and Bjorklund, Barbara
BJORKLUND, DAVID F., 1949-, AND BJORKLUND, BARBARA
As they grow/7 through 10. See issues of Parents beginning January 1987 through January 1990
BL PLC
See also
Rover Group plc
BLACK, BILL
Washington, D.C., contemplates the SRO as affordable housing. il *Architectural Record* 177:43 F '89

BLACK, CARL

Old light in a new world. il pors *House & Garden* 161:176-81+
N '89

BLACK, CARLA F.

Prepaid legal plans come on strong. il *Consumers' Research Magazine* 72:19-22 Jl '89

Tiny Town's big comeback. il map *Americana* 17:28-33 Jl/Ag '89

BLACK, CATHLEEN

about

Beyond macho: the power of womanly management [excerpt from Tender power] S. S. Cohen. il pors *Working Woman* 14:77-83 F '89

BLACK, CLINT

about

Clint Black. D. Handelman. il por *Rolling Stone* p25 S 21 '89

That new Black magic. J. P. Smith. il por *New York* 22:24 O 2 '89

Women want all of Clint Black—including his fingernails. S. Dougherty. il pors *People Weekly* 32:101+ S 11 '89

BLACK, CONRAD M.

about

An emerging media baron. J. DeMont. *Maclean's* 102:28 Jl 17 '89

Media barons are making pilgrimages to Jerusalem. J. Rossant and N. Sandler. il por *Business Week* p50 My 15 '89

BLACK, CORAL S.

Take the plunge! il por *Women's Sports & Fitness* 11:66 Jl/Ag '89

BLACK, GEORGE

Is there life after Thatcher? *The Nation* 248:620-2 My 8 '89

Japan turns the double play. il *The Nation* 248:370+ Mr 20 '89

Look—we've come through. il *The Nation* 249:166-8+ Ag 7-14 '89

Policy circles. *The Nation* 248:256-7 F 27 '89

'Shame'. *The Nation* 248:328-9 Mr 13 '89

Spitting distance. *The Nation* 248:5 Ja 2 '89

BLACK, GEORGIA, D. 1951

about

The man who lived 30 years as a woman. il pors *Jet* 75:29 F 20 '89

BLACK, SIR JAMES WHYTE, 1924-

Drugs from emasculated hormones: the principle of syntoptic antagonism. bibl f il *Science* 245:486-93 Ag 4 '89

BLACK, KATHRYN STECHERT

The good we do. il *New Choices for the Best Years* 29:62-5 D '89

BLACK, KENT

In plains English. il por *Harper's Bazaar* 122:88+ O '89

The well-tempered robot. il *House & Garden* 161:146-9+ D '89

BLACK, LYDIA

Russia's American adventure. il map *Natural History* p46-57 D '89

BLACK, ROXANNE

about

Roxanne Black's Long Distance Love. T. Kauchak. il por *Seventeen* 48:68 Je '89

BLACK, SHIRLEY TEMPLE, 1928-

about

America's baby. G. C. Ward. il *American Heritage* 40:12+ Mr '89

Shirley Temple Black sets the record straight. H. Yorkshire. il pors *McCall's* 116:88+ Mr '89

Collectibles

Happy birthday, Shirley! M. Forrest. il pors *Antiques & Collecting Hobbies* 94:30-2 Ap '89

BLACK, THOMAS E.

Digi-compass. il *Radio-Electronics* 60:43-5+ N '89

BLACK

Black on black on black [creating a photograph made up entirely of black] S. Bauer. il *Petersen's Photographic Magazine* 18:84-5 O '89

Dark forces [impact of black uniforms on temper of a team; research by Tom Gilovich and Mark G. Frank] S. Boxer. il *Sports Illustrated* 70:52-4+ Ap 17 '89

Dressing thin: the real black magic. N. Malkin. il *Harper's Bazaar* 122:90-1 Ja '89

Noir has gone too far. L. Lague. il *People Weekly* 32 Special Issue:110-11 Fall '89

BLACK & DECKER CORP.

Black & Decker cuts a neat dovetail joint [merger with Emhart] J. Weber, Jr. il por *Business Week* p52-3 Jl 31 '89

The new power in Black & Decker. J. Huey. il por *Fortune* 119:89-91+ Ja 2 '89

BLACK & DECKER MFG. CO.

See also

Black & Decker Corp.

BLACK ACTORS AND ACTRESSES

See also

Blacks in motion pictures

Blacks in television

See also names of black actors and actresses

Black actors are still ignored: Esther Rolle. por *Jet* 76:22 S 11 '89

John Amos raps critics of interracial cast in Shakespeare's '12th night'. il por *Jet* 76:63 Jl 17 '89

The new wave of black starlets [cover story] R. Brown and others. il *Ebony* 44:29-30+ Mr '89

BLACK AMBASSADORS

See also

Perkins, Edward J.

BLACK AMERICAN WEST MUSEUM

How Paul Stewart mines lost 'gold' with a tape recorder. E. C. White. bibl (p135) il pors *Smithsonian* 20:58-64+ Ag '89

BLACK AND BLUE [musical] See Musicals, revues, etc.—Reviews—Single works

BLACK AND WHITE FILMS *See* Photography—Films

BLACK ARCHITECTS

See also

Hazel, William Augustus, d. 1929

BLACK ARCHIVES OF MID-AMERICA

The Black Archives of Mid-America, Inc. J. Helms-Mindell. il *American Visions* 4:56 Ap '89

BLACK ART *See* Art, Black

BLACK ARTISTS

See also

Basquiat, Jean-Michel, 1960-1988

Brown, Frederick, 1945-

Burke, Selma, 1900-

Chandler, Robin

Colescott, Robert, 1925-

Gilliam, Sam, 1933-

Guyton, Tyree

Hammons, David

Holder, Geoffrey

Lewis, Norman, 1909-1979

Locke, Donald

Nassy, Josef

Traylor, Bill, 1854-1947

Trotsky

Black artists today: a case of exclusion. P. Failing. il *Art News* 88:124-31 Mr '89

BLACK ARTS *See* Arts, Black

BLACK ASTRONAUTS

See also

Jemison, Mae C.

BLACK ATHLETES

See also names of black athletes

Arthur Ashe remembers the forgotten men of sport—America's early black athletes [interview] S. K. Reed. il pors *People Weekly* 31:243-4+ Mr 6 '89

Blacks in . . . the greatest sports events of all time. il *Ebony* 44:120-2+ O '89

Sports. See issues of Jet

What black sports heroes are doing to help black kids. L. Ransom. il *Jet* 76:48+ My 1 '89

Why the obsession with race? [NBC special Black athletes—fact & fiction] S. Smith. il por *Sports Illustrated* 70:12 My 8 '89

Word star [books by A. Ashe] P. Giddings. il por *Essence* 20:38 My '89

Education

Athletes are exploited, Ashe tells N.C. Central. por *Jet* 77:50 N 13 '89

Baptists back Thompson in Proposition 42 fight [National Baptist Convention] il por *Jet* 75:50 F 27 '89

Central State U. designs high school, B.A. degree program for Mike Tyson. il por *Jet* 77:28 N 6 '89

Former basketball player sues Creighton University [K. Ross] por *Jet* 76:50 Ag 14 '89

Is Proposition 42 racist? J. B. Johnson; A. Ashe. il *Ebony* 44:138-40 Je '89

A new Proposition [NCAA's Proposition 42 stiffens rules governing awarding of scholarships] W. F. Reed. il *Sports Illustrated* 70:16-19 Ja 23 '89

Out of bounds [questions regarding the NCAA's Proposition 42 to tighten restrictions on scholarships] *The New Republic* 200:10-11 F 20 '89

Race becomes the game [J. Thompson challenges NCAA's Proposition 42 which tightens restrictions on scholarships] J. Kroll. il por *Newsweek* 113:56-9 Ja 30 '89

Thompson's walkout spurs review of Proposition 42. il *Jet* 75:50 F 13 '89

Tightening the rules [NCAA's Proposition 42 tightens scholarship requirements] il *Newsweek* 113:58 Ja 23 '89

When is the playing field too level? [NCAA's Proposition 42 tightens restrictions on scholarships] A. P. Sanoff. il *U.S. News & World Report* 106:68-9 Ja 30 '89

Salaries, pensions, etc.

Black sports millionaires for 1989. il *Jet* 76:46-9 My 8 '89

BLACK ATHLETES—FACT & FICTION [television program] See Television program reviews—Single works

BLACK AUTHORS

See also

Baldwin, James, 1924-1987

Campbell, Bebe Moore

Golden, Marita

Gossett, Hattie, 1942-

BLACK AUTHORS—See also—*cont.*
    Himes, Chester, 1909-1984
    Kenan, Randall
    Morrison, Toni, 1931-
    Naylor, Gloria
    Steptoe, John, 1950-1989
    Troupe, Quincy
    Walker, Alice, 1944-
    Wideman, John Edgar
    Wright, Richard, 1908-1960
  Better times for black writers? W. Nixon. il *Publishers Weekly* 235:35-40 F 17 '89

Reading
  The write stuff. P. Giddings. il *Essence* 20:30 Ag '89
BLACK AUTOMOBILE DEALERS
    See also
    Dick Gidron Cadillac & Ford Inc.
  B.E. 100s: auto dealers. il *Black Enterprise* 19:211+ Je '89
  The rise of black auto dealers. F. Rice. il *Fortune* 120:68-71 Ag 14 '89
BLACK AUTOMOBILE INDUSTRY WORKERS
  GM settles six-year suit [employment opportunities for blacks] G. Huskisson. il *Black Enterprise* 19:36 My '89
BLACK BACHELORS *See* Single men
BLACK BAKERS AND BAKERIES
    See also
    Champ Cookies (Firm)
    Quality Croutons Inc.
BLACK BANKS AND BANKING
    See also
    Black savings and loan associations
    Independence Bank of Chicago
  Vaulting into new ventures. M. A. Fortune. il *Black Enterprise* 19:245-6+ Je '89
BLACK BASEBALL LEAGUES *See* Baseball, Professional—History
BLACK BASEBALL MANAGERS *See* Baseball managers
BLACK BASEBALL PLAYERS *See* Baseball players
BLACK BEAR HUNTING *See* Bear hunting
BLACK BEARS *See* Bears
BLACK BISHOPS
    See also
    Ford, Louis Henry
    Morris, Samuel Solomon, d. 1989
    Reid, Frank M., d. 1989
    Walker, John Thomas
BLACK BOXERS *See* Boxers
BLACK BUSINESS CONSULTANTS
    See also
    SJA (Firm)
BLACK BUSINESS ENTERPRISES
    See also
    American Health and Beauty Aids Institute
    Black entrepreneurs
  17th annual report on black business [cover story; special issue; with editorial comment by Earl G. Graves] il map *Black Enterprise* 19:13-14, 100-2+ Je '89
  An agenda for the 1990s [Black enterprise Board of Economists report] J. Davidson. il *Black Enterprise* 19:152-4+ Je '89
  Atlanta: keeping affirmative action alive. K. D. Thompson. il *Black Enterprise* 20:48 S '89
  Atlanta set-aside plan boasts booming business. il *Jet* 75:53 F 20 '89
  Big biz in Boston [city contracts and affirmative action] B. W. O'Connor. il *Black Enterprise* 20:18 Ag '89
  Black companies look for niches in the 1990s. M. Simms. il *Black Enterprise* 20:51 D '89
  Black enterprise lists TLC Group as largest black-owned business. *Jet* 76:17 My 29 '89
  A blow to affirmative action [Supreme Court strikes down Richmond, Va. minority set-aside law] A. Sachs. il *Time* 133:60 F 6 '89
  A build-down for black contractors [Supreme Court ruling against minority set-aside program in Richmond, Va.] *U.S. News & World Report* 106:13 F 6 '89
  The coming of the next generation. E. G. Graves. il *Black Enterprise* 19:7 Ap '89
  Contracts [special section] il *Black Enterprise* 19:154-6+ F '89
  Court in the middle [Supreme Court strikes down set-aside program for minority firms in Richmond, Va.] *National Review* 41:14 F 24 '89
  Houston Convention Bureau affirmative-action plan. L. Gite. il *Black Enterprise* 20:28 N '89
  Making it. See issues of Black Enterprise
  NAACP's Gibson urges new tactics to keep set asides. por *Jet* 75:29 Mr 13 '89
  A negative on affirmative action [Supreme Court ruling on Richmond, Va. minority set-aside law] R. Stodghill, II and P. Dwyer. *Business Week* p40 F 6 '89
  The next generation takes over at the B.E. 100s [Black enterprise] A. Edmond, Jr. *Black Enterprise* 19:54 Ap '89
  'Now we're on our own' [Supreme Court strikes down Richmond, Va. minority set-aside law] T. Jacoby. il *Newsweek* 113:64-5 F 6 '89
  Perseverance pays, HUD Secretary Jack Kemp tells Central State U. students. il pors *Jet* 76:16+ Je 19 '89

  Racial preference in court (again) [Supreme Court to decide legality of minority set-asides in Richmond, Va.] T. Eastland. *Commentary* 87:32-8 Ja '89
  Ruling delivers hard blow to set-asides [Supreme Court decision] N. McCall. il *Black Enterprise* 19:17-18 Ap '89
  'Stigmatic harm' [Supreme Court's nullification of the Richmond, Va. minority set-aside program] *The Nation* 248:183-4 F 13 '89
  Supreme Court set aside ruling not 'devastating' blow to black businesses. il *Jet* 75:4 F 13 '89
  Which program will be next? [minority set-aside program in Atlanta] D. Lynch. il *Black Enterprise* 19:36 My '89
  Why blacks like Mike Milken. J. Lieblich. il por *Fortune* 119:10 My 22 '89

Federal aid
    See also
    United States. Minority Business Development Agency
  Bush taps Joshua Smith to lead business commission. por *Jet* 76:37 Ag 14 '89
  Paving the path to 8(a) contracts. A. Poinsett. il *Black Enterprise* 19:160 F '89
  SBA drafts new 8(a) rules. K. D. Thompson. il *Black Enterprise* 20:22 N '89

International aspects
  Ready for the world. F. McCoy. il *Black Enterprise* 19:162-4+ Je '89

Africa
  Africa. F. McCoy. il *Black Enterprise* 19:164+ Je '89

Canada
  Canada. F. McCoy. il *Black Enterprise* 19:174 Je '89

Caribbean region
  Caribbean; S. America. F. McCoy. il *Black Enterprise* 19:176 Je '89

East Asia
  Asia. F. McCoy. il *Black Enterprise* 19:170 Je '89

Great Britain
  To be young, British and black. D. Pitts. il *Black Enterprise* 20:86-8+ D '89

South Africa
  A free-market cure for apartheid ills. J. Jones. il *U.S. News & World Report* 107:47 Ag 7 '89

Western Europe
  Europe. F. McCoy. il *Black Enterprise* 19:172 Je '89
BLACK BUSINESSMEN
    See also
    Black business enterprises
    Black entrepreneurs
    Black executives
  On the move. See issues of Black Enterprise
BLACK BUSINESSWOMEN *See* Businesswomen
BLACK CANDIDATES, POLITICAL *See* Black political candidates
BLACK CARTOONISTS
    See also
    Cowan, Denys
  Serious business. F. McCoy and A. Edmond, Jr. il por *Black Enterprise* 20:86-8+ S '89
BLACK CAUCUS *See* Congressional Black Caucus
BLACK CELEBRITIES
  10 most exciting couples. L. Norment. il *Ebony* 44:164-6+ F '89
  20 people to watch in '89. il *Ebony* 44:27+ Ja '89
  Favorite hobbies of famous faces. il *Ebony* 44:54+ Mr '89
  Fifty, fabulous and flaunting it. R. D. Turner. il *Ebony* 44:34+ O '89
  How celebrities will celebrate Christmas. R. D. Turner. il *Ebony* 45:31-2+ D '89
  'How we met' [black celebrity couples] il *Ebony* 44:158-61 F '89
  'My brush with death'. il *Ebony* 44:96+ My '89
  'My first love'. L. B. Randolph. il *Ebony* 44:144+ F '89
  People. See issues of Jet
  People are talking about . . . See issues of Jet
  The ten most beautiful black women of 1989. il *Ebony* 44:146-8+ O '89
  Who left what behind: wills of famous blacks. R. Brown. il *Ebony* 44:136+ F '89

Health and hygiene
  Fitness in the fast lane. il *Ebony* 44:120+ Jl '89
Photographs and photography
  The best photos of 1989. il *Jet* 77:31-4+ D 25 '89-Ja 1 '90
  Memorable photos from the Ebony files. See issues of Ebony beginning June 1984

Religious life
  Why are so many celebrities turning to God? il *Jet* 76:12-14 Jl 3 '89

Sports
  Bill Cosby's all-stars shock Eddie Murphy's all-stars team 30-18 [softball game] il pors *Jet* 76:56-8 Jl 3 '89
BLACK CELEBRITIES' FAMILIES
  Growing up with a famous mother. il *Ebony* 44:122+ My '89
  Second generation: children tell why they follow in their parents' footsteps. il *Jet* 76:58-60 Je 19 '89
BLACK CHILDREN
  Readin', ritin' & rage: how schools are destroying black boys. D. J. Dent. il *Essence* 20:54-6+ N '89

BLACK CHILDREN—cont.

Adoption

See Adoption and adopted children

Economic conditions

Teaching your children the financial facts of life [cover story; with editorial comment by Earl G. Graves] P. Sharif. il *Black Enterprise* 20:9, 56-8+ D '89

Education

See Blacks—Education

Management and training

Raising kids strong [special section] il *Essence* 20:73-4+ D '89

Raising sons under siege. M. Golden. il *Essence* 20:104 N '89

Religious life

Giving children spiritual gifts that last a lifetime. A. Iadavaia-Cox and L. Tarrant-Reid. il *Essence* 20:78+ D '89

BLACK CHILDREN'S LITERATURE See Children's literature

BLACK CHOREOGRAPHERS See Choreographers

BLACK CHURCHES

See also

First African Baptist Church

The invisible church. J. A. Smith. il *Christianity Today* 33:32-4 Mr 3 '89

Joining the AIDS fight. J. N. Baker and R. Elam. il *Newsweek* 113:26-7 Ap 17 '89

Vermont: 'whitest state in America' gets first black church [New Alpha Missionary Baptist Church] C. Waldron. il pors *Jet* 75:14-15+ Mr 13 '89

Finance

On solid rock: the black church's economic clout. B. W. O'Connor. il *Black Enterprise* 19:50 Je '89

BLACK CLASSIC PRESS

Black and in print. J. R. Barras. il por *American Visions* 4:48-9 O '89

BLACK CLERGY

See also

Black missionaries

The church and the drug crisis: ministers mobilize against 'the death of a race'. il *Ebony* 44:160+ Ag '89

Riverside Church in N.Y. gets 1st black sr. pastor [J. Forbes] por *Jet* 75:23 F 20 '89

Political activities

The activism of interpretation: black pastors and public life [work of J. P. Barbour] K. B. Jones. *The Christian Century* 106:817-18 S 13-20 '89

The education of Reverend Butts [leader of Abyssinian Baptist Church in Harlem] E. Pooley. il pors *New York* 22:42-9 Je 26 '89

Rev. Calvin Butts installed as pastor of Abyssinian Baptist Church in New York. il pors *Jet* 77:12-13 D 11 '89

'We will not fight another war' [peace activist J. Barnette] R. Chepesiuk. il por *The Progressive* 53:17 N '89

BLACK COLLECTIBLES

Racist artifacts become popular collectors' items. il *Jet* 77:30 N 27 '89

BLACK COLLEGE PRESIDENTS

See also

Cheek, James Edward, 1932-

Cole, Johnnetta B.

Cole, Thomas W.

Sudarkasa, Niara

BLACK COLLEGE STUDENTS

Blacks get own yearbook at Univ. of Pa.; It's a 1st for Ivy League schools. il *Jet* 76:22 Ag 21 '89

Campus racism. W. E. Williams. *National Review* 41:36-8 My 5 '89

The new racism on campus. T. Sowell. il por *Fortune* 119:115-16+ F 13 '89

The recoloring of campus life. S. Steele. il *Harper's* 278:47-55 F '89

The sources of racial discrimination [disparity in achievement levels; views of Thomas Sowell] W. F. Buckley. *National Review* 41:70 S 29 '89

Student-aid smarts! *Essence* 20:103 Ag '89

BLACK COLLEGE STUDENTS, WOMEN See Women college students

BLACK COLLEGES AND UNIVERSITIES

See also

Bethune-Cookman College

Central Intercollegiate Athletic Association

Central State University (Ohio)

Florida A & M University

Howard University

Lincoln University (Pa.)

Meharry Medical College

Morehouse College

Southern University

Spelman College

Texas Southern University

Black by popular demand. S. Tifft. il *Time* 133:59 Mr 20 '89

Black colleges are tools of affirmative action: Kenneth Tollett of Howard. por *Jet* 75:33 Mr 6 '89

Black universities: in demand and in trouble. E. Alterman. il *The New York Times Magazine* p60-3+ N 5 '89

Giving students a taste of the executive life. S. M. Williams. *Black Enterprise* 19:181-2 F '89

Federal aid

Black schools facing new student loan default plan. *Jet* 76:9 Je 19 '89

Bush asks Congress for $60 million to aid black colleges and universities. il *Jet* 75:16-18 Ap 3 '89

Goodwin leads fed. effort to aid black universities [R. K. Goodwin] por *Jet* 76:16 Ag 7 '89

Navy awards $14 million to foster math, science degrees at universities. il *Jet* 77:18 O 16 '89

Finance

See also

Black colleges and universities—Gifts, legacies, etc.

United Negro College Fund

Gifts, legacies, etc.

Bill and Camille Cosby: first family of philanthropy [cover story] R. E. Johnson. il pors *Ebony* 44:25-6+ My '89

Bill and Camille Cosby give $1.5 million to Meharry and Bethune-Cookman colleges. il pors *Jet* 75:5-6 Ja 9 '89

Central State U. honors Cosby family generosity at Cleveland Classic. pors *Jet* 76:10 S 11 '89

Cosby's $20 million gift: a source of funds—and hope. K. D. Thompson. il por *Black Enterprise* 19:27 F '89

Howard U. gets Warner Communications grant. il *Jet* 75:47 Mr 13 '89

Oprah Winfrey gives gift of $1 million to Morehouse to help educate black men. il por *Jet* 76:4 Je 5 '89

BLACK COMEDIANS

See also

Cosby, Bill, 1937-

Foxx, Redd

Hall, Arsenio

McDonald, Bob

Murphy, Eddie

Pryor, Richard

Wayans, Keenen

BLACK COMPOSERS

See also

Davis, Anthony

BLACK CONDUCTORS (MUSIC)

See also

Harvey, Raymond

Morgan, Michael

The maestros. D. Narine. il *Ebony* 44:54+ F '89

BLACK CONGRESSMEN

See also

Congressional Black Caucus

Conyers, John, 1929-

Crockett, George W., Jr.

Gray, William H., III

Leland, Mickey

Payne, Donald M.

Top of Capitol Hill. L. B. Randolph. il *Ebony* 45:144-6+ D '89

BLACK CONSTRUCTION WORKERS

N.Y. construction hiring rule voided. K. Osborne. *Black Enterprise* 20:28 D '89

BLACK CONSUMERS

Don't ignore impact of ethnic market on U.S. economy: NAMD prexy. il *Jet* 76:23 Je 26 '89

Economic racism. J. Malveaux. il *Essence* 20:116 S '89

A long way from 'Aunt Jemima'. M. Mabry. il *Newsweek* 114:34-5 Ag 14 '89

My dollars count. K. G. Bates. por *Essence* 20:148 O '89

BLACK COOKING See Cooking, Black

BLACK COOKS

See also

Ashley, Eliza Jane

Lewis, Edna

BLACK CRIMINALS See Blacks—Crime

BLACK CULTURE See Blacks—Culture

BLACK CYCLISTS See Cyclists

BLACK DANCE See Dance, Black

BLACK DIALECTS See Black-English dialects

BLACK DRAMA

30th anniversary showing of 'Raisin in the sun' winning rave reviews. il *Jet* 75:38-9 F 20 '89

Look beyond the mad rush to be number one [A raisin in the sun] J. E. Wideman. il *TV Guide* 37:32-4 Ja 28-F 3 '89

A raisin in the sun: the uncut version. D. G. Peerman. *The Christian Century* 106:71-3 Ja 25 '89

BLACK EDUCATION See Blacks—Education

BLACK EDUCATORS

See also

Clark, Kenneth Bancroft

National Alliance of Black School Educators

BLACK ENGINEERS

Engineering growth. W. M. Woodard. *Black Enterprise* 20:22 D '89

The push for blacks in technology [charts] il *Black Enterprise* 19:61 My '89

BLACK-ENGLISH DIALECTS

"Broadcast English" for nonstandard dialect speakers [black high school students] J. F. Robbins. *The Education Digest* 54:52-3 F '89

'Talkin' white'. W. L. Aponte. por *Essence* 19:11 Ja '89

BLACK ENTERTAINERS
Making money from the grave. D. Narine. il *Ebony* 44:142+ Je '89
New child stars. R. E. McKinney. il *Ebony* 44:88+ Je '89
Parents who manage money and fame of young stars. C. Waldron. il *Jet* 77:16-18 D 25 '89-Ja 1 '90

BLACK ENTERTAINMENT TELEVISION
BET faces music, comes up with talk. K. Beck. por *Channels (New York, N.Y.: 1986)* 9:58-60 Je '89
BET: tuning into viewers. K. Osborne. il *Black Enterprise* 19:24 Ap '89

BLACK ENTREPRENEURS
See also
   Black intrapreneurs
The B.E. guide to growing a business [special section] il *Black Enterprise* 19:125-6+ Je '89
Cutting deals at conventions. M. M. McDowell. il *Black Enterprise* 20:114-16+ O '89
Doing business on the home front. M. Scott. il *Black Enterprise* 19:68-70 Ap '89
Exploring new frontiers [Black Enterprise Franchise 50; cover story; special section; with editorial comment by Earl G. Graves] W. M. Woodard. il *Black Enterprise* 20:9, 53-4+ S '89
Go west, young entrepreneur. S. L. Hilliard and J. Shiver. il *Black Enterprise* 19:112+ Je '89
Good entrepreneur, bad manager? T. Bachemin. il *Black Enterprise* 19:54-6+ Mr '89
A hot decade for franchising. il *Black Enterprise* 20:39 S '89
How to make a million dollars. C. Whitaker. il *Ebony* 44:134+ S '89
Student entrepreneurs on campus. L. Williams. il *Black Enterprise* 19:169-72 F '89

BLACK EXECUTIVE SEARCH CONSULTANTS
The Black enterprise executive recruiter directory. W. M. Wise. il *Black Enterprise* 19:105-8 F '89

BLACK EXECUTIVES
Lighting the way for youth [mentorship roles] Y. R. Lamb. il *Black Enterprise* 19:205-7 F '89
Return of the top 25. D. T. Dingle. il *Black Enterprise* 19:95-6+ F '89
When the boss is black. il *Time* 133:60-1 Mr 13 '89

Age
Taking charge [managers under 35; cover story] K. D. Thompson and others. il pors *Black Enterprise* 20:42-4+ Ag '89

Health and hygiene
The body starts here [special section] il *Black Enterprise* 19:51-5+ Jl '89

Nutrition
Diet right. E. Iverem. il *Black Enterprise* 19:58-9 Jl '89

Promotion
Branch office big shot. C. Legette. il *Black Enterprise* 19:129-30+ F '89
The corporate 'color bar'. D. Nora. *World Press Review* 36:35 My '89

Relocation
Branch office big shot. C. Legette. il *Black Enterprise* 19:129-30+ F '89

Training
B.E. guide to fellowships and executive training programs. S. S. Harrison. il *Black Enterprise* 19:119-20+ F '89
Peak performance [cover story; with editorial comment by Earl G. Graves] D. T. Dingle. il *Black Enterprise* 19:8, 64-6+ My '89
Syllabus for success. M. N.-K. Collison. il *Black Enterprise* 19:113-14+ F '89

Travel
See Business travel

BLACK-EYED PEA COOKING See Cooking—Vegetables
BLACK-EYED SUSANS
Coneflowers are at home in the garden. L. B. Trigg. il *Southern Living* 24:38-9 Ag '89

BLACK FAMILY
The 10 biggest myths about the black family [reprint from August 1986 issue] L. Bennett. il *Ebony* 45:114+ N '89
Arkansas family produces 18 black college graduates [survey of black families] il *Jet* 76:22-4+ Ag 7 '89
The family. See issues of American Visions beginning April 1989
Scapegoating the black family [cover story; special issue; with editorial comment] il *The Nation* 249:111, 115-20+ Jl 24-31 '89
The Toni award [T. Morrison's views] *The New Republic* 200:9-10 Je 19 '89

BLACK FAMILY IN TELEVISION
'Generations' soap opera debuts with large cast of blacks [cover story] il *Jet* 75:60-2 Ap 3 '89

BLACK FARMERS
Watermelon king remembered [R. Chatham] P. S. Prather. il por *American Visions* 4:38-9 Ag '89

BLACK FBI AGENTS See United States. Federal Bureau of Investigation

BLACK FILMMAKERS HALL OF FAME
Celebs pay tribute to Lola Falana at recent Filmmakers Hall gala. il por *Jet* 75:24-5+ Mr 20 '89

BLACK FIREFIGHTERS
Birmingham firehouse [Supreme Court decision permitting white firemen to bring suit against the city for job discrimination] *Commonweal* 116:387-8 Jl 14 '89
Fighting the fires of racism [discriminatory practices of the International Association of Fire Fighters] P. Rockwell. il *The Nation* 249:714-16+ D 11 '89

BLACK FOOTBALL COACHES See Football coaches
BLACK FOOTBALL OWNERS See Football, Professional—Organization and administration
BLACK FOOTBALL PLAYERS See Football players
BLACK FOREIGN SERVICE OFFICERS See United States. Dept. of State. Foreign Service
BLACK FRIARS See Dominicans (Religious order)
BLACK GOVERNMENT EMPLOYEES
Blacks in government hit federal job bias. il *Jet* 76:26 S 11 '89
Blacks lacking on staffs of U.S. senators: report. il *Jet* 75:12-13 Mr 27 '89

Dismissal
Atlanta suit to examine black-on-black bias [firing of IRS employee T. L. Morrow] *Jet* 76:7 Je 12 '89

BLACK GOVERNORS
See also
   Wilder, L. Douglas
BLACK HAIR CARE See Hair—Care
BLACK HAIRSTYLING See Hairstyling
BLACK HAIRSTYLISTS
Black hairdresser turns six-chair salon into a multimillion $ business [C. Miles] il pors *Jet* 76:28-30+ Je 12 '89

BLACK HILLS (S.D. AND WYO.)
See also
   Mount Rushmore National Memorial (S.D.)
   Thunderhead Mountain (S.D.)
Disputed land. J. Naughton. il *Scholastic Update (Teachers' edition)* 121:8-10 My 26 '89

BLACK HISTORIANS
See also
   Williams, George Washington, 1849-1891
BLACK HISTORY See Blacks—History
BLACK HISTORY MONTH
Coca-Cola USA to award $130,000 in scholarships [Share the Dream Scholarship Sweepstakes] il *Jet* 75:32 Mr 6 '89
History in the making. J. L. Jackson. il por *Harper's Bazaar* 122:138-9+ F '89

BLACK HISTORY TRAIL (WASHINGTON, D.C.)
Historic-trail blazer [W. A. Hutt] il map *National Geographic World* 162:30 F '89

BLACK HOCKEY PLAYERS See Hockey players
BLACK HOLES (ASTRONOMY)
Black hole in the making? [V404 Cygni] il *Sky and Telescope* 78:460-1 N '89
Carrying fuel into the galactic center [Paul T. P. Ho identifies stream of gas] I. Peterson. *Science News* 135:21 Ja 14 '89
Feeding the hole [stream of gas near Milky Way; research by Paul Ho] il *Discover* 10:14 Je '89
Feeding the monster in the middle [Milky Way's black hole; research by Paul Ho] M. M. Waldrop. il *Science* 243:478 Ja 27 '89
More black-hole candidates. *Sky and Telescope* 78:13 Jl '89
No black holes? *Sky and Telescope* 78:572-3 D '89

BLACK ILLUSTRATORS
See also
   Cowan, Denys
   Pinkney, Jerry, 1939-
   Steptoe, John, 1950-1989
BLACK INSURANCE COMPANIES
See also
   Golden State Mutual Life Insurance Co.
   Supreme Life Insurance Company
Fortify or die. il *Black Enterprise* 19:285-6+ Je '89

BLACK INTRAPRENEURS
Making entrepreneurship an inside job. P. Watkins. il *Black Enterprise* 19:136-8+ F '89

BLACK INVENTORS
Reclaiming some talents lost to time [The real McCoy: African-American invention and innovation, 1619-1930 at the Anacostia Museum] K. M. Burke. il *Smithsonian* 20:212 S '89

BLACK JOCKEYS See Jockeys
BLACK JOURNALISM See Black press
BLACK JOURNALISTS
See also
   Bell, Warren
   Herbert, Bob
   Page, Clarence
   Tubbs, Vincent, d. 1989
Daily news case update [racial discrimination] T. Chapelle. il *Black Enterprise* 20:20 Ag '89

BLACK JUDGES
See also
   Dixon, Herbert
   Hastings, Alcee L.
   Posten, William
   Stout, Juanita Kidd
   Walton, Reggie B.

BLACK JUDGES—*cont.*
3 blacks get judgeships in Arkansas from governor. il *Jet* 77:22 O 9 '89
U.S. Appeals Court judges: from protest to power. il *Ebony* 44:68+ Ag '89
BLACK JURORS *See* Jury
BLACK LABOR *See* Blacks—Employment
BLACK LANDMARKS *See* Historic houses, sites, etc.
BLACK LAW CLERKS
Thurgood Marshall hires two black Ivy League law clerks. il pors *Jet* 77:4+ N 13 '89
BLACK LAW FIRMS
See also
    Arrington & Hollowell
Atlanta minority law firm shares resources with white firm in unique bar program [Arrington & Hollowell and Hurt, Richardson, Garner, Todd & Cadenhead] il *Jet* 76:24 O 2 '89
BLACK LAWYERS
See also
    Baskerville, Lezli
    Branton, Wiley A., 1923-1988
    Brown, Ron
    DePriest, Darryl
    Espy, Michael
    Everett, Ralph
U. of Chicago bans law firm's recruiting after racist comments [Baker & McKenzie] *Jet* 75:30 F 20 '89
BLACK LEADERSHIP
See also
    African American Summit
30 leaders of the future. il *Ebony* 45:68-70+ N '89
The 100 most influential black Americans. il *Ebony* 44:182+ My '89
Black leaders tell what they want President Bush to do first. R. L. Haywood. il *Jet* 75:4-6 Ja 30 '89
Eyes on the prizes, not the people [cover story] S. Anderson. il *The Nation* 249:405+ O 16 '89
His truth is marching on [former aides to Martin Luther King Jr.] il *Ebony* 44:44+ Ja '89
Passing the torch. P. Ruffins. il *Black Enterprise* 19:46-7 Ja '89
The racism scam: how liberal black leaders perpetuate dependence. P. B. McGuigan. il por *Conservative Digest* 15:53-5+ Mr/Ap '89
BLACK LITERATURE
See also
    Black authors
    Black drama
    Blacks in literature
    Booksellers and bookselling—Black literature
    Harlem renaissance
    Publishers and publishing—Black literature
Whose canon is it, anyway? [place among classics] H. L. Gates. *The New York Times Book Review* 94:1+ F 26 '89
Bibliography
Ebony book shelf. See issues of Ebony
Summer reading. il *American Visions* 4:39-43 Je '89
Conferences
Black writers debate 'being human in the 20th century' [Celebration of Black Writing] M. Coffey. il *Publishers Weekly* 235:16-17 F 17 '89
BLACK LOBBYISTS AND LOBBYING
See also
    TransAfrica (Organization)
BLACK MARKETS
Capitalism on the sly [Soviet Union] J. Trimble. il *U.S. News & World Report* 107:27 N 20 '89
The paradox of *perestroika*: a raging black market. P. Galuszka. il *Business Week* p66+ Je 5 '89
BLACK MARRIED COUPLES *See* Married couples
BLACK MAYORS
See also
    Barry, Marion, 1936-
    Bradley, Tom
    Dinkins, David, 1927-
    Ford, Johnny Lawrence, 1942-
    Jackson, Maynard H.
    Sawyer, Eugene
    Schmoke, Kurt
    Usry, James L.
    Young, Coleman
Are black mayors losing their popularity? S. Booker. *Jet* 76:14-17 Jl 10 '89
Hope, not fear: New York may be the next city to elect a black mayor [Democratic candidate D. Dinkins] R. Lacayo. il por *Time* 134:20-1 S 25 '89
How coalition politics put blacks in power as mayors across nation. W. Wofford, Jr. il *Jet* 77:14-16+ N 27 '89
Mayoral candidates spell victory: c-o-a-l-i-t-i-o-n. P. Ruffins. il *Black Enterprise* 19:47-8 Je '89
BLACK MEDICAL COLLEGES
See also
    Morehouse School of Medicine

BLACK MEMORABILIA *See* Black collectibles
BLACK MIDDLE CLASS
An agenda for the black middle class [cover story] D. T. Dingle. il *Black Enterprise* 20:52-4+ N '89
Between two worlds [cover story] R. Lacayo. il *Time* 133:58-62+ Mr 13 '89
Race and money. W. L. Updegrave. il *Money* 18:152-7+ D '89
Staying in the community. B. M. Campbell. il *Essence* 20:96-8+ D '89
The two black Americas [cover story] M. Kondracke. *The New Republic* 200:17-20 F 6 '89
BLACK MILITANTS
The fugitive [former black militant H. Ferguson] P. Blauner. il pors *New York* 22:32-7 Ag 7 '89
BLACK MILLIONAIRES *See* Millionaires
BLACK MINISTERS *See* Black clergy
BLACK MISSIONARIES
A new era for black missionaries. V. Becker. il *Christianity Today* 33:38+ O 20 '89
BLACK MODELS (PERSONS)
See also
    Iman
    Swainson, Sharon C.
Models' secrets. il *Essence* 19:84-6 F '89
BLACK MONDAY *See* Stock market crash, 1987
BLACK MOSHANNON STATE PARK (PA.)
Whirlybirds not welcome [National Guard helicopters] S. D. Borowitz. il *Sierra* 74:90-1 N/D '89
BLACK MOTION PICTURE DIRECTORS
See also
    Lane, Charles
    Lee, Spike
    Palcy, Euzhan
    Townsend, Robert
    Wayans, Keenen
BLACK MUSIC
See also
    Blues music
    Center for Black Music Research
    Compact discs—Black music
    Gospel music
    Phonograph records—Black music
    Rap music
    Soul Train Music Awards
    Soulbeat Entertainment Network
    Spirituals (Songs)
Are white singers taking over blues and soul? il *Jet* 75:60-2+ Mr 6 '89
Are whites taking over rhythm & blues? D. Narine. il *Ebony* 44:90+ Jl '89
Economic aspects
Rhythm and blues, on the upbeat [payment of retroactive royalties to singers] A. Levine. il *U.S. News & World Report* 106:59-60 Ja 16 '89
BLACK MUSICIANS
See also names of black musicians
Bush rhythm & blues bash headlined by black stars [final concert of the Bush inauguration] il *Jet* 75:59 F 6 '89
Classical sounds. P. Williams-Jones. il *American Visions* 4:58-9 D '89
False note [Detroit Symphony agrees to hire more blacks] *The New Republic* 200:9 Mr 27 '89
A limit to affirmative action? [black bassist R. Robinson hired by Detroit Symphony Orchestra] J. Blanton. *Commentary* 87:28-32 Je '89
Statues, portraits, etc.
Frederick Brown: Marlborough [portraits of blues musicians] C. Lyon. il *Art News* 88:164-5 N '89
To Fred Brown, blues are more than a color on his palette [portraits of blues singers] D. Grogan. il pors *People Weekly* 32:96-8 O 2 '89
BLACK MUSLIMS
Muslim dopebusters: the brightest point of light [work of the Nation of Islam; interview with A. Muhammed] il *New Perspectives Quarterly* 6:32-6 Summ '89
The Muslims to the rescue [anti-drug patrol in Washington, D.C.'s Mayfair Mansions housing project] il *Ebony* 44:136+ Ag '89
BLACK NEWSPAPERS *See* Black press
BLACK NURSES AND NURSING
Nurse Corps chief [Brigadier General C. Adams-Ender] D. M. Cheers. il pors *Ebony* 44:64+ Je '89
BLACK ORGANIZATIONS
See also
    International Society on Hypertension in Blacks
    National Association for the Advancement of Colored People
    National Black Republican Council
    National Rainbow Coalition
    National Urban League
    People United to Serve Humanity (Organization)
Cruising with a cause. B. Peurifoy-Green. il *Black Enterprise* 19:61-2 Jl '89
Fighting back [community youth programs across the country] B. W. Baye. il *Essence* 20:59+ N '89

BLACK OSCAR NOMINEES (AWARDS)
Black Oscar Nominees gala celebrates movie talents. il *Jet* 76:52+ Ap 17 '89
BLACK PARENT-CHILD RELATIONSHIP *See* Parent-child relationship
BLACK PERIODICALS
See also
Ebony (Periodical)
Essence (Periodical)
Johnson Publishing Company, Inc.
BLACK PHOTOGRAPHERS
See also
Mathews, Everette
McLemore, Lamonte
Parks, Gordon
BLACK PHYSICIANS
See also
Cruzat, Roscoe Modesta, d. 1989
Elders, Joycelyn
Freeman, Harold P.
Lawless, Theodore K., d. 1971
Rabb, Maurice F.
Smith, Robert
Williams, Irving
Reagan treated at Ft. Huachuca hospital black medics made famous in WW II. il *Jet* 76:52-4 Jl 31 '89
Salaries, fees, etc.
A family's finances [J. Wood; cover story] L. Gite. il pors *Black Enterprise* 20:72-4+ O '89
BLACK POETS
See also
Brown, Sterling Allen, 1901-1989
Hughes, Langston, 1902-1967
BLACK POLICE
Black elected FOP prexy in Prince Georges County [D. Jones] por *Jet* 77:14 D 25 '89-Ja 1 '90
BLACK POLICEWOMEN *See* Policewomen
BLACK POLITICAL CANDIDATES
Crossing the color line [black leaders campaign for white votes] G. Borger. il *U.S. News & World Report* 107:22-4 N 6 '89
The end of the Civil War [state and city elections] M. Barone. il *U.S. News & World Report* 107:45-6+ N 20 '89
Moderates' day? [blacks win state and city elections] *The Nation* 249:668-9 D 4 '89
The new black politics [winning candidates] H. Fineman. il *Newsweek* 114:52-3 N 20 '89
Politics. See issues of Jet
The politics of race [New York City, Virginia, and Cleveland] H. Fineman. il *Newsweek* 114:32-4 N 6 '89
There were other elections in November '88. *American Visions* 4:22+ F '89
White lies, bad polls [white voters misinforming pollsters concerning black candidates] *Time* 134:56 N 20 '89
BLACK POWER
See also
Blacks—Political activities
Agenda 2000. L. Anderson. por *Essence* 20:132 D '89
New spirit infuses black America. S. Muwakkil. il *Utne Reader* p93-4 S/O '89
BLACK PRESIDENTIAL ADVISERS
Bush breaks tradition and names many black advisers. il por *Jet* 75:7 F 27 '89
Young black aides at White House highlight change of new Bush administration. il por *Jet* 76:8 My 1 '89
BLACK PRESS
See also
Amsterdam news (New York, N.Y.)
Black journalists
Pressing on. M. Bernstein. il *Black Enterprise* 19:142-4+ Je '89
BLACK PRIESTS
Double dose of divinity [twin Catholic priests C. and C. Smith] R. Brown. il pors *Ebony* 44:52+ Ja '89
Sexual behavior
Stallings denies charge of a homosexual relationship. por *Jet* 76:38 S 25 '89
BLACK PROFESSIONALS
Making your money work for them [black professionals' contributions to worthy causes] A. Reid-Dove. il *Black Enterprise* 19:321-2+ Je '89
Networking news. See issues of Black Enterprise beginning November 1987
New dilemma for black professionals: 'living together' or marriage? R. Brown. il *Ebony* 45:96+ D '89
Our legacy of achievement. E. G. Graves. il *Black Enterprise* 20:9 Ag '89
Racism and blacks who've 'made it'. D. C. Lyons. il *Ebony* 44:112+ O '89
The ten top-paying jobs for blacks. D. Narine. il *Ebony* 45:122+ D '89
You can go home again [moving back to the South] B. Lane. il *American Visions* 4:24-7 Ap '89
BLACK PROMOTERS AND PROMOTING
See also
King, Don, 1929-

BLACK PUBLIC OFFICERS
Blacks in the Bush administration. S. Booker. il pors *Ebony* 44:42+ Jl '89
Bush's black appointees. il *American Visions* 4:14-15 Ag '89
Guess who's (not) coming to dinner [rejected civil rights nominee W. Lucas and other black Republicans undercut by White House] W. McGurn. il *National Review* 41:18-19 S 1 '89
BLACK PUBLIC PROSECUTORS
See also
Partee, Cecil A.
BLACK PUBLISHERS AND PUBLISHING *See* Blacks in publishing
BLACK RADIO PROGRAMS *See* Radio broadcasting—Black programs
BLACK RADIO STATIONS *See* Radio stations, Black
BLACK RAIN [film] See Motion picture reviews—Single works
BLACK RUNNERS *See* Runners
BLACK SABBATH (MUSICAL GROUP)
Black Sabbath. K. Richardson. il *High Fidelity (New York, N.Y.)* 39:52-4 Jl '89
BLACK SAVINGS AND LOAN ASSOCIATIONS
See also
Berean Savings Association
Black S&Ls and thrift reform: the purge begins. A. Edmond, Jr. il *Black Enterprise* 20:33+ N '89
Feeling the heat. A. Kimbrough. il *Black Enterprise* 19:265-6+ Je '89
BLACK SCHOOL ADMINISTRATORS
Education
See School management and organization—Study and teaching
BLACK SCHOOL SUPERINTENDENTS AND PRINCIPALS
His pupils want someone to lean on, but Joe Clark may simply want out [considering resignation after reaction to striptease show at Eastside High] D. Van Biema and G. Moses. il pors *People Weekly* 31:51-3 Mr 27 '89
The make-believe world of "Lean on me" [methods of Paterson, N.J. principal J. Clark] I. A. Hyman. *The Education Digest* 55:20-2 N '89
Principal Joe Clark leaving school for lecture circuit. por *Jet* 76:22 Jl 31 '89
Selection and appointment
Kerns named S.C. school district superintendent. por *Jet* 76:30 My 8 '89
BLACK SHABBOS (MUSICAL GROUP)
Three nice boys from Queens shine as Black Shabbos, heavy metal's Henny Young-men. S. Dougherty. il *People Weekly* 32:78-9 Jl 31 '89
BLACK SHERIFFS
A reunion in friendship [former Giants quarterback Y. A. Tittle to make campaign appearance for Wake County, N.C. sheriff J. Baker, whose hit in 1964 helped end Tittle's career] il pors *Sports Illustrated* 71:12+ N 27 '89
BLACK SIGATOKA DISEASE
The best banana bred [hybrid banana resistant to black sigatoka disease; work of P. Rowe] S. Brownlee. il *The Atlantic* 264:22+ S '89
BLACK SINGERS
See also
Phonograph records—Black music
See also names of black singers
Love songs are back—with a handsome look. il *Ebony* 45:122+ N '89
BLACK SINGLE MOTHERS *See* Single mothers
BLACK SORROWS (MUSICAL GROUP)
The Black Sorrows. J. Ressner. il *Rolling Stone* p18 S 7 '89
BLACK SPARROW PRESS
Penniless poet to laureate of lowlife [C. Bukowski] il por *U.S. News & World Report* 106:52 Ja 9 '89
BLACK STATE OFFICERS
Current elected state officials. R. Brown. il *Ebony* 45:42 N '89
BLACK STOCKHOLDERS
When profits meet principles. N. S. Charles. il *Black Enterprise* 19:83-4+ My '89
BLACK STUDENTS
See also
Colleges and universities—Desegregation
Colleges and universities—Segregation
Public schools—Segregation
Awards
See also
ACT-SO Awards
Project Excellence Awards
Scholarships and fellowships
See Scholarships and fellowships
BLACK STUDIES
Save black studies! il *Ebony* 44:70-1 Mr '89
What culture should mean. L. S. Robinson. *The Nation* 249:319-21 S 25 '89
BLACK SUFFRAGE
Jackson to appear on 'A different world' in new segment on voting. il por *Jet* 76:62 Ap 10 '89
Kennedy justice [Equal Access to Voting Act of 1989] *The New Republic* 200:9 Je 5 '89

BLACK SUFFRAGE—cont.
NAACP sues 5 S. Carolina cities over voting systems. il Jet 76:32 Jl 24 '89
A veteran of Mississippi's 'Freedom Summer' remembers the cause—and the danger [drive for black voter registration conducted by SNCC in 1964]; ed. by Jane Sugden. L. Guyot. il pors People Weekly 32:61-2+ S 18 '89

BLACK TEACHERS
Supply and demand
The disappearing black teacher. C. Whitaker. il Ebony 44:122+ Ja '89

BLACK TELEVISION CHARACTERS See Blacks in television
BLACK TELEVISION PROGRAMS See Television broadcasting—Black programs
BLACK TELEVISION STATIONS See Television stations, Black
BLACK TENNIS PLAYERS See Tennis players
BLACK THEATRICAL AGENCIES AND AGENTS
Parents who manage money and fame of young stars. C. Waldron. il Jet 77:16-18 D 25 '89-Ja 1 '90

BLACK TIRE DEALERS
The titan of tires [Goodyear dealer M. Brown] M. E. Howard. il pors Black Enterprise 20:68-70+ S '89

BLACK UNIVERSITIES See Black colleges and universities
BLACK VELVET BAND
Black Velvet Band. J. Ressner. il Rolling Stone p17 O 19 '89

BLACK VETERANS
Black veterans of WWII honor unknown soldiers. il Jet 77:28 N 20 '89
Home-front vets [Vietnam veteran] J. L. Howe. por Essence 20:12 My '89

BLACK VOTE See Black suffrage; Blacks—Political activities
BLACK-WHITE MARRIAGE See Interracial marriage
BLACK WIDOW SPIDERS See Spiders
BLACK WOMEN
See also
Beauty, Personal
National Council of Negro Women
1989 bachelorettes: smart, pretty and available. il Ebony 44:132-4+ Jl '89
In the spirit. S. L. Taylor. See issues of Essence
No chocolates for breakfast. J. Jordan. il The Progressive 53:11 Ap '89
Scapegoating the black family [cover story; special issue; with editorial comment] il The Nation 249:111, 115-20+ Jl 24-31 '89
Sexism comes in all colors. J. Morgan. Utne Reader p48-9 N/D '89
Attitudes
Here's what you think [results of Essence reader opinion poll] il Essence 20:70-2+ Je '89
Awards
See also
Candace Awards
The 1989 Essence Awards [with editorial comment by Susan L. Taylor] il pors Essence 20:57-60+, 69 O '89
Economic conditions
Economics and you. J. Malveaux. See issues of Essence beginning August 1987
Mind over money. M. E. Jackson and G. Pollard. il Essence 20:94+ Jl '89
Money moves. P. Martin. See issues of Essence beginning March 1988
The racialization of poverty. M. B. Wilkerson and J. H. Gresham. il The Nation 249:126-30+ Jl 24-31 '89
Tighten your money belt. P. Martin. il Essence 19:105-6 Mr '89
You, men and money. A. Edwards. Essence 20:55-6+ Ag '89
Education
See also
Upward Bound Academy
Back to school. B. W. Baye. il Essence 19:68-70+ Mr '89
Employment
Atlanta suit to examine black-on-black bias [firing of IRS employee T. L. Morrow] Jet 76:7 Je 12 '89
Dealing with job discrimination. J. Malveaux. il Essence 20:118 My '89
Hard times for Freedom Quilters [Freedom Quilting Bee in Alabama] N. Callahan. The Christian Century 106:317-18 Mr 22-29 '89
Work it out! B. Nivens. See occasional issues of Essence
History
My white father [excerpt from Telling memories among southern women] S. Tucker. Harper's 279:36+ N '89
Health and hygiene
Total well-being. See issues of Essence
History
Coincoin: plantation owner before the nation was born. P. S. Prather. il American Visions 4:46-7 F '89
Don't bury my heart [discussion of May 22, 1989 article, What can the white man . . . say to the black woman?] A. Walker. The Nation 249:226 S 4-11 '89
Ida B. Wells-Barnett: an Afro-American prophet. E. M. Townes. The Christian Century 106:285-6 Mr 15 '89

What can the white man . . . say to the black woman? [address, April 8, 1989] A. Walker. il The Nation 248:691-2 My 22 '89
Housing
Va. woman gets $120,000 in civil rights lawsuit [F. Bradley of Alexandria] Jet 77:9 N 13 '89
Legal status, laws, etc.
Black feminists. C. Kocol. The Humanist 49:35-6 S/O '89
Black women's plight cited at pro-choice rally in D.C. il Jet 76:13 Ap 24 '89
How will the abortion ruling affect blacks? R. L. Haywood. il Jet 76:12-15 Jl 24 '89; Correction. 76:8 Ag 14 '89
Our big choice [black women and abortion] E. Strothers. por Essence 20:116 Jl '89
Our bodies, their laws [abortion and reproductive rights] L. Villarosa. il Essence 20:24+ O '89
Which way black America? Anti-abortion or pro-choice. P. Carr; F. Wattleton. il Ebony 44:134+ O '89
Nutrition
Fat is a black women's issue [overeating] R. Powers. il Essence 20:75+ O '89
Foods: eat right for life! il Essence 19:80-1 Ja '89
How healthy is your diet? [quiz] il Essence 20:81-3 Je '89
Photographs and photography
Black womanhood honored in photo portrait exhibit [I dream a world] il Jet 75:8-9 F 27 '89
I dream a world [excerpts; with introd. by M. Angelou] B. Lanker. il National Geographic 176:206-25 Ag '89
'Ordinary women of grace' [B. Lanker's I dream a world at the Corcoran Gallery] M. McLoughlin. il U.S. News & World Report 106:50-5+ F 13 '89
A singer and his camera [work of L. McLemore] il por Ebony 45:92-4+ N '89
Political activities
NOW proposes new party; black activists respond. il Jet 76:14-15 Ag 14 '89
Rise up! S. L. Taylor. il Essence 20:41 Jl '89
A season in hell [D. Brazile, staff member during M. Dukakis presidential campaign] G. E. Curry. il pors Ms. 18:58-60+ O '89
Psychology
Angry. J. Malveaux. Essence 20:64+ My '89
Just between us. G. G. Grant. See issues of Essence beginning May 1983
The powers that free; ed. by Bebe Moore Campbell. I. Vanzant. il por Essence 20:80-2+ O '89
Unwind! Relax and enjoy life. A. Mascelli. il Essence 19:59-62 Ja '89
Sexual behavior
See Sexual behavior
Travel
Travel. See issues of Essence
BLACK WOMEN AND AIDS (DISEASE) See AIDS (Disease) and women
BLACK WOMEN BISHOPS See Women bishops
BLACK WOMEN CLERGY See Women clergy
BLACK WOMEN ENTREPRENEURS See Women entrepreneurs
BLACK WOMEN EXECUTIVES See Women executives
BLACK WOMEN IN RESTAURANT MANAGEMENT See Women in restaurant management
BLACK WOMEN IN TELEVISION See Women in television
BLACK WOMEN IN THE MOTION PICTURE INDUSTRY See Women in the motion picture industry
BLACK WOMEN IN THE TELEVISION INDUSTRY See Women in the television industry
BLACK WOMEN PRISON WARDENS See Women prison wardens
BLACK WOMEN SUPERVISORS See Women supervisors
BLACK WORKERS See Blacks—Employment
BLACK YOUTH
30 leaders of the future. il Ebony 45:68-70+ N '89
Fighting back [community youth programs across the country] B. W. Baye. il Essence 20:59+ N '89
Three lives [growing up black in New York City] M. Stone. il pors New York 22:35-42 Ja 30 '89
We are not 'lost'. A. M. Copeland. por Essence 19:128 Ja '89
What black sports heroes are doing to help black kids. L. Ransom. il Jet 76:48+ My 1 '89
Crime
See Juvenile delinquents and delinquency
Employment
Too good for manual labor. W. Raspberry. il Reader's Digest 135:155-6 N '89
Health and hygiene
Fitness lowers young blacks' blood pressure [study by Gregory A. Harshfield] K. Fackelmann. Science News 136:214 S 30 '89
Travel
Trips for teens. R. J. Christmas. il Essence 19:22+ Ja '89
BLACKADAR, ALFRED
Using your computer. See issues of Weatherwise beginning June 1984

BLACKALLER, TOM
about
Obituary
Motor Boating & Sailing il por 164:15 N '89. P. A. Janssen
Sports Illustrated por 71:18 S 18 '89. S. Ballard
BLACKBEARD, 1680?-1718
about
The quest for Blackbeard's cup. L. Fleischer. *Publishers Weekly* 235:74 F 3 '89
BLACKBERRIES
Picking
Blackberrying. K. Stewart. il *Gourmet* 49:62-3+ Ag '89
BLACKBERRY DESSERTS See Desserts
BLACKBIRDS
Sexual behavior
See Sexual behavior—Birds
BLACKBODY RADIATION
See also
Cosmic background radiation
BLACKBURN, ALBERT W.
U.S. should establish independent FAA based on Britain's CAA model. por *Aviation Week & Space Technology* 130:119-20 My 1 '89
BLACKBURN, GEORGE L.
Nutritional medicine. See issues of Prevention (Emmaus, Pa.) beginning August 1988
BLACKBURN, ROBIN, 1940-
Upheaval in the East: is the socialist bloc ready for socialism? [cover story] *The Progressive* 53:18-22 Jl '89
BLACKBURN, TAYE
Call me Cinderella [story] il *'Teen* 33:58+ S '89
BLACKER, COIT D.
The new United States-Soviet détente. bibl f *Current History* 88:321-4+ O '89
BLACKFLIES
See also
Onchocerciasis
BLACKFORD, JOHN
Technology. See occasional issues of Personal Computing beginning July 1987
BLACKHAWK (CALIF.)
Stores
See also
FJ's (Firm)
BLACKLISTING
Postscript on Lucy [L. Ball's testimony before House Committee on Un-American Activities] *The Nation* 248:685 My 22 '89
The real blacklist [Hollywood blacklisting period] J. Farah. *National Review* 41:42-3 O 27 '89
BLACKMAN, CINDY
about
Cindy Blackman. B. Milkowski. il por *Down Beat* 56:29 D '89
BLACKMAN, MARCIA A., AND OTHERS
Influence of the major histocompatibility complex on positive thymic selection of $V_\beta 17a^+$ T cells. bibl f il *Science* 244:214-17 Ap 14 '89
BLACKMUN, HARRY A.
about
The confusion of Justice Blackmun. W. F. Buckley. *National Review* 41:55 Ag 18 '89
BLACKOUTS (ELECTRIC POWER) See Electric power failures
BLACKS
See also
Black Muslims
Blacks and mass media
Chinese and blacks
Drugs and blacks
Intelligence—Blacks
Japanese and blacks
Jews and blacks
Labor unions—Blacks
National Caucus and Center on Black Aged
Smoking and blacks
Vietnamese War, 1957-1975—Blacks
The 100 most influential black Americans. il *Ebony* 44:182+ My '89
Our men in crisis [cover story; with editorial comment by Susan L. Taylor] il *Essence* 20:47, 49-52+ N '89
Attitudes
Who's hot, who's not in 1989 [Ebony poll] il *Ebony* 44:200-2+ My '89
Awards
See also
American Black Achievement Awards
Communications Excellence to Black Audiences Awards
Caricatures and cartoons
Strictly for laughs. See issues of Ebony
Charities
The arts—and more [corporations support black charities] J. R. Barras. il *American Visions* 4:35 Je '89
Bill Cosby and black leaders urge affluent blacks to give money. il por *Jet* 75:30-1 Ja 23 '89
Blacks donate to charity as much as whites: study. *Jet* 77:4 D 11 '89

Making your money work for them [black professionals' contributions to worthy causes] A. Reid-Dove. il *Black Enterprise* 19:321-2+ Je '89
What black sports heroes are doing to help black kids. L. Ransom. il *Jet* 76:48+ My 1 '89
Civil rights
See also
African American Summit
Alabama—Race relations
Arizona—Race relations
Atlanta (Ga.)—Race relations
Bensonhurst (New York, N.Y.)—Race relations
Birmingham (Ala.)—Race relations
Boston (Mass.)—Race relations
Cambridge (Mass.)—Race relations
Chicago (Ill.)—Race relations
Civil rights demonstrations
Columbia (Mo.)—Race relations
Conway (S.C.)—Race relations
Cranston (R.I.)—Race relations
Denver (Colo.)—Race relations
Forsyth County (Ga.)—Race relations
Georgia—Race relations
Lansdowne (Pa.)—Race relations
Martin Luther King, Jr. Center for Nonviolent Social Change
Miami (Fla.)—Race relations
Mobile (Ala.)—Race relations
New York (N.Y.)—Race relations
North Augusta (S.C.)—Race relations
Philadelphia (Miss.)—Race relations
Pulaski (Tenn.)—Race relations
Richmond (Va.)—Race relations
Southern States—Race relations
United States—Race relations
Affirmative action. D. T. Dingle. il *Black Enterprise* 20:42-6+ S '89
Are equal rights only a dream? M. Schwelien. il *World Press Review* 36:32-4 My '89
Black leaders tell what they want President Bush to do first. R. L. Haywood. il *Jet* 75:4-6 Ja 30 '89
Challenge for the year 2000. O. Davis. *The Nation* 249:144-8 Jl 24-31 '89
Equal justice under siege: coping with the runaway Supreme Court. C. Benson. il *Ebony* 45:54+ D '89
Gottwald's cap. *Commonweal* 116:67-8 F 10 '89
Hitting the wall [Supreme Court decisions] R. W. Wilkins. il *Mother Jones* 14:12+ N '89
Major issues facing African-Americans [address, August 6, 1989] J. E. Jacob. *Vital Speeches of the Day* 56:7-12 O 15 '89
NAACP confab ignites blacks to unite against erosion of civil rights. il *Jet* 76:4-8 Jl 31 '89
Notes and comment [philosophy of E. Burke applied to recent Supreme Court decisions] *The New Yorker* 65:21-2 Jl 31 '89
Protection against racial discrimination [Supreme Court reconsidering Runyon v. McCrary] R. F. Drinan. *America* 160:52 Ja 28 '89
Racism: can we heal the wounds? [cover story; special issue] il *Scholastic Update (Teachers' edition)* 121:2-12+ Ap 7 '89
The racism scam: how liberal black leaders perpetuate dependence. P. B. McGuigan. il por *Conservative Digest* 15:53-5+ Mr/Ap '89
Retreat on civil rights? S. Holmes. il *American Visions* 4:20-4 O '89
Should Congress pass laws to protect flag and gains of blacks? W. Wofford, Jr. il *Jet* 76:6-9 Jl 17 '89
Supreme Court splits on two landmark bias cases. il *Jet* 76:4-5 Jl 3 '89
Willie Horton and me. A. Walton. il por *The New York Times Magazine* p52-3+ Ag 20 '89
Exhibitions
Valentine Museum's Jim Crow [Racism and reaction in the New South, Richmond, 1865-1940] E. Chappell. *The Nation* 249:102-4 Jl 17 '89
History
See also
Civil Rights Act of 1964
Civil rights demonstrations—History
Civil Rights Memorial (Montgomery, Ala.)
National Civil Rights Center (Memphis, Tenn.)
The '64 civil rights murders: the struggle continues [honoring J. Chaney, M. Schwerner and A. Goodman; cover story] J. Kornbluth. il pors *The New York Times Magazine* p16-19+ Jl 23 '89
Back on the bus [events commemorating 25th anniversary of the murder of civil rights workers J. E. Chaney, A. Goodman and M. H. Schwerner] P. Dray. il pors *Mother Jones* 14:37-9+ N '89
Civil rights movement led Lawson to her PBS career [J. Lawson] *Jet* 77:38 D 18 '89
Fire this time [film Mississippi burning; cover story] R. Corliss. il *Time* 133:56-62 Ja 9 '89
The greening of a martyr [interview with T. Branch] A. P. Sanoff. il por *U.S. News & World Report* 106:22 Ja 23 '89

BLACKS—Civil rights—History—*cont.*

Hollywood and civil rights [shortcomings of Mississippi burning] D. Bogle. il *Essence* 19:32 Mr '89

Hollywood: the dustbin of history [Mississippi burning] P. Arthur. il *USA Today (Periodical)* 117:35 My '89

Honor trio killed by KKK in Mississippi vote drive [M. Schwerner, J. Chaney and A. Goodman] il pors *Jet* 76:6-7 Jl 10 '89

Hot writers [biography of M. L. King by T. Branch] A. DeCurtis. il pors *Rolling Stone* p117-18+ My 18 '89

Ida B. Wells-Barnett: an Afro-American prophet. E. M. Townes. *The Christian Century* 106:285-6 Mr 15 '89

In the churches, in the streets: Taylor Branch on 'the King years'. R. Westbrook. *The Christian Century* 106:351-4 Ap 5 '89

'It must never happen again' [Philadelphia, Miss. relives 1964 murders of Andrew Goodman, James Chaney and Michael Schwerner] A. Murr. il *Newsweek* 113:26-7 Ja 9 '89

Josephine Baker's war on racism [excerpt from Jazz Cleopatra] P. Rose. il pors *American Visions* 4:25-8 O '89

Martin Luther King: the preacher as virtuoso [cover story] M. E. Marty. *The Christian Century* 106:348-50 Ap 5 '89

Mississippi theater won't show controversial movie [Philadelphia, Miss. theater won't show Mississippi burning] il *Jet* 75:51 Ja 23 '89

Out of sight, out of mind. J. Alter. il *Newsweek* 113:52-3 Ja 23 '89

Outcast to hero [R. Flowers Jr.] J. Wooten. il pors *TV Guide* 37:36-8 Ja 14-20 '89

The second time around: will history repeat itself and rob blacks of the gains of the 1960s? [reprint from October 1981] L. Bennett. il *Ebony* 44:46+ O '89

Since Mississippi burned [impact of 1964 murder of three civil rights workers on residents of Philadelphia, Miss.] D. McWhorter. il *People Weekly* 31:36-43 Ja 9 '89

The struggle for equality. L. Eskin. il *Scholastic Update (Teachers' edition)* 121:17-19 Ap 7 '89

Where is the rage? J. Jordan. il *The Progressive* 53:12-13 O '89

Crime

Crime and race. P. M. Buchanan. il *Conservative Digest* 15:36-7 Jl/Ag '89

Do the right thing—suppress crime. J. O'Sullivan. *National Review* 41:13 O 13 '89

Root causes. *National Review* 41:16+ Je 2 '89

Crimes against

How to keep from getting ripped off. D. Fortune. il *Ebony* 44:62+ Mr '89

Culture

An old look is new again [black street fashions] N. Darnton. il *Newsweek* 114:78-9 O 16 '89

Study and teaching

See Black studies

Economic conditions

See also

Blacks—Employment

Advising the new administration [Black enterprise Board of Economists report] C. C. Williams. il *Black Enterprise* 19:48-53 Ja '89

"The American dilemma has not been solved" [A common destiny: blacks and American society report] D. M. Watts. il *Black Enterprise* 20:26 O '89

Between two worlds [middle class; cover story] R. Lacayo. il *Time* 133:58-62+ Mr 13 '89

Black enterprise annual money management issue [special issue] il *Black Enterprise* 20:53-4+ O '89

Black progress 'stagnant' since '70s, report says [A common destiny: blacks and American society] il *Jet* 76:28-9 Ag 14 '89

Blacks and poverty [charts] il *Black Enterprise* 20:49 N '89

Capital improvements [results of Black enterprise survey] M. E. Howard. il *Black Enterprise* 20:53-4+ Ag '89

The drive for economic equality: the new civil rights movement. A. Poinsett. il *Ebony* 44:74+ Ag '89

Economic perspectives. A. F. Brimmer. See issues of Black Enterprise

Facts and figures. See issues of Black Enterprise

How to live above your means . . . and get away with it. A. Poinsett. il *Ebony* 45:46+ D '89

HUD director hosts black finance show on network [T. R. Daniels] por *Jet* 76:24 My 8 '89

Keeping it in the family. D. LaMaute. il *Black Enterprise* 19:56-8+ Ja '89

The limits of tolerance. R. W. Wilkins. il *Mother Jones* 14:60 Ja '89

Opportunity foreclosure zones. J. D. Kasarda. il *New Perspectives Quarterly* 6:16-21 Summ '89

Personal finance. See issues of Black Enterprise

Pride and prejudice: an examination of the economics of black America [conference at Hillsdale College] W. J. Koshelnyk. il *Conservative Digest* 15:23-6 Jl/Ag '89

Race and money. W. L. Updegrave. il *Money* 18:152-7+ D '89

Racism and poverty [report A common destiny: blacks and American society] R. J. Samuelson. il *Newsweek* 114:46 Ag 7 '89

Two go-getters skip the basics in their rush toward riches [Mark and Toya Evans] L. Luciano. il *Money* 18:177-8 Ap '89

Education

See also

Black athletes—Education

Black college students

Black colleges and universities

Colleges and universities—Desegregation

Colleges and universities—Segregation

National Alliance of Black School Educators

Penn Center of the Sea Islands (Saint Helena Island, S.C.)

Public schools—Desegregation

Public schools—Segregation

Sister Thea Bowman Black Catholic Educational Foundation

Arkansas family produces 18 black college graduates [survey of black families] il *Jet* 76:22-4+ Ag 7 '89

Bill Cosby makes academic deal with Texas students [Carver Elementary Academy, Amarillo] il pors *Jet* 77:33 N 20 '89

The billionaire and the students [Kansas City, Mo., students helped to stay drug free by E. M. Kauffman] D. Narine. il pors *Ebony* 44:146+ Ag '89

The color of learning [influence of ethnicity upon learning styles of black preschool children; work of Janice Hale-Benson] L. Troiano. il *American Health* 8:76 D '89

Court ruling rekindles controversy over SATs [question of race bias] C. Holden. il *Science* 243:885-7 F 17 '89

Detroit minister and wife send 8 daughters through college; 2 M.D.s, 3 Ph.D.s [H. and J. Green] W. Wofford, Jr. il pors *Jet* 75:22-3 F 13 '89

Eastside story [views of principal J. Clark] Y. Kramer and R. Kramer. il *The American Spectator* 22:21-4 Ag '89

Education and employment. il *Black Enterprise* 20:53 D '89

Giving computers an ethnic edge [educational software for black children] K. Moses. il *American Visions* 4:12 D '89

How do you spell "wound," as in gunshot? [teacher helps inner city child write a play] J. Murphy. il *U.S. Catholic* 54:36-9 O '89

The impact of education on business growth. B. E. Anderson. *Black Enterprise* 19:31-2 Jl '89

Lesson plans: eleven ways to help your child excel in school. D. C. Williams. il *Essence* 20:100 Ag '89

Liberal establishment on Tory Row [neighborhood opposition forces departure of predominantly black Commonwealth Day School from Cambridge, Mass.] E. W. Wagner. il *National Review* 41:19-21 D 31 '89

Mama and Miss Jordan [relationships with mother and high school teacher] M. H. Futrell. il *Reader's Digest* 135:75-80 Jl '89

Readin', ritin' & rage: how schools are destroying black boys. D. J. Dent. il *Essence* 20:54-6+ N '89

The score before the game starts [question of bias in Scholastic Aptitude Test] *Newsweek* 113:58 Ja 30 '89

A smouldering race issue [blacks seek school reform in Nova Scotia] G. Allen. il *Maclean's* 102:14 F 27 '89

Steve Wolf's class act: straight talk in the schoolroom [chairman of UAL Corp. speaks to black students in Chicago] J. E. Ellis. il *Business Week* p57 F 6 '89

Stop blaming the tests [question of SAT's bias] J. Leo. il *U.S. News & World Report* 106:80 Mr 20 '89

Teaching as though life hangs in the balance [Zion Christian School in Seattle] S. Ulstein. il *Christianity Today* 33:10-11 Ap 21 '89

We can educate all our children [urban public schools] C. Clayton. *The Nation* 249:132-5 Jl 24-31 '89

Whitest city in Illinois graduates only black teen from high school. il por *Jet* 76:14 Je 26 '89

Employment

See also

Black business enterprises

Black businessmen

Black entrepreneurs

Black executives

Black youth—Employment

Blacks—Occupations

The 50 best places for blacks to work [cover story] il *Black Enterprise* 19:73-8+ F '89

Affirmative action. D. T. Dingle. il *Black Enterprise* 20:42-6+ S '89

Affirmative action in vogue? M. A. Fortune. il *Black Enterprise* 19:20 Ap '89

Big biz in Boston [city contracts and affirmative action] B. W. O'Connor. il *Black Enterprise* 20:18 Ag '89

Birmingham firehouse [Supreme Court decision permitting white firemen to bring suit against the city for job discrimination] *Commonweal* 116:387-8 Jl 14 '89

Black FBI agent loses case at Justice Dept. [D. Rochon case] *Jet* 76:7 Jl 24 '89

Blacks and employment. il *Black Enterprise* 19:33 Ja '89

BLACKS—Employment—*cont.*

Blacks in government hit federal job bias. il *Jet* 76:26 S 11 '89

Chambers warns of dire impact of recent rulings by U.S. Supreme Court [affirmative action] por *Jet* 76:38 Ag 21 '89

Daily news case update [racial discrimination] T. Chapelle. il *Black Enterprise* 20:20 Ag '89

Education and employment. il *Black Enterprise* 20:53 D '89

False note [Detroit Symphony agrees to hire more blacks] *The New Republic* 200:9 Mr 27 '89

Fed. probe of job bias in Fairfax, Va., government. il *Jet* 76:38 Jl 17 '89

Fighting the fires of racism [discriminatory practices of the International Association of Fire Fighters] P. Rockwell. il *The Nation* 249:714-16+ D 11 '89

Fractured gospel. *The New Republic* 201:4 S 4 '89

GM settles six-year suit [employment opportunities for blacks] G. Huskisson. il *Black Enterprise* 19:36 My '89

A limit to affirmative action? [black bassist R. Robinson hired by Detroit Symphony Orchestra] J. Blanton. *Commentary* 87:28-32 Je '89

N.Y. construction hiring rule voided. K. Osborne. *Black Enterprise* 20:28 D '89

NAACP/LDEF sues Shoney's. L. Brown. *Black Enterprise* 20:20 Ag '89

Retreat on civil rights? S. Holmes. il *American Visions* 4:20-4 O '89

Wage and salary. il *Black Enterprise* 19:63 F '89

Wounds of race [Supreme Court affirmative action decisions] H. Hertzberg. *The New Republic* 201:4+ Jl 10 '89

Hairstyling

See Hairstyling

Health and hygiene

See also

AIDS (Disease) and blacks

Blacks—Medical care

International Society on Hypertension in Blacks

Sickle cell anemia

F-F-F-Fortysomething? E. V. Tait. il *Essence* 20:16+ N '89

Health & science notes. See issues of American Visions beginning February 1989

House call: expert advice on health and fitness. See issues of Ebony beginning October 1988

The life expectancy gap widens for blacks, whites. il *Jet* 76:37 Ap 10 '89

Nighttime danger for blacks [connection between high nocturnal blood pressure and heart damage; research by Michael Murphy and Roberto Lang] il *USA Today (Periodical)* 118:8 O '89

Special section on health and fitness. il *Ebony* 44:102+ Jl '89

History

See also

Black American West Museum

Black History Month

Black History Trail (Washington, D.C.)

Harlem renaissance

Slavery

United States—History—Revolution, 1775-1783—Blacks

United States—History—Civil War, 1861-1865—Blacks

World War, 1939-1945—Blacks

The 50 most important figures in black American history. L. Bennett. il *Ebony* 44:176-8+ F '89

The 1980's: a look back. B. Allen. il *Essence* 20:82-4 D '89

Black history: wise words of famous blacks. il *Jet* 75:36-8 F 27 '89

On the road to glory [historical black sites] W. M. T. Walls. il *Black Enterprise* 19:209-10 F '89

This week in black history. See issues of Jet

Collectibles

See Black collectibles

Historiography

Stalking George W. Williams. J. H. Franklin. il por *American Visions* 4:28-31 Ap '89

Study and teaching

See Black studies

Hospital care

Family doesn't know father died in N.Y. hospital till daughter finds its bill [T. Bennett dies at Jamaica Hospital] il por *Jet* 75:19 F 13 '89

Housing

Financing options for today's home buyers. G. James-Gallagher and R. E. Barnes. il *Black Enterprise* 20:41-2 N '89

Practical tips for first time homebuyers. G. J. Gallagher. il *Black Enterprise* 19:25-6 Jl '89

Staying in the community. B. M. Campbell. il *Essence* 20:96-8+ D '89

An unlikely source. K. D. Thompson. *Black Enterprise* 19:15 Ja '89

Using your home as an investment. P. Sharif. il *Black Enterprise* 19:57-8+ Ap '89

Working for our cities [B. Lindsey, executive director of the Fort Lauderdale Housing Authority] D. Young. il pors *Southern Living* 24:141-2+ S '89

Income

See Blacks—Economic conditions

Language

See also

Black-English dialects

Medical care

'Dr. Bob' [work of R. Smith in Miss.] R. D. Turner. il pors *Ebony* 44:102+ S '89

Expert doubts success rate of transplants in blacks [views of Clive Callender on kidney transplants] il *Jet* 76:51 Je 19 '89

Migration

You can go home again [moving back to the South] B. Lane. il *American Visions* 4:24-7 Ap '89

Mortality

The cost of cancer [comparing survival rates of whites and blacks] il *Black Enterprise* 19:43 Ap '89

Museums

See also

Alex Haley House Museum

Black Archives of Mid-America

Harriet Tubman Historical and Cultural Museum (Macon, Ga.)

National African-American Heritage Memorial Museum

National Civil Rights Center (Memphis, Tenn.)

Names

Names can hurt [odd names bestowed on black children] C. M. Jackson. por *Essence* 19:134 Ap '89

Nutrition

Eating your way to good health. R. E. McKinney. il *Ebony* 44:75-6+ My '89

Tasty foods for a healthy heart. il *Ebony* 44:110+ Jl '89

Occupations

The 10 top careers for blacks in the '90s. il *Ebony* 44:39-40+ F '89

Building a bridge to a new career. A. Edmond, Jr. il *Black Enterprise* 19:96-8+ My '89

Careers and opportunities 1989. il *Black Enterprise* 19:67-70 F '89

Careers of tomorrow you can prepare for today. A. Edmond, Jr. il *Black Enterprise* 20:58-60+ Ag '89

Math, engineering, law offer best jobs for '90s. il *Jet* 75:33 F 27 '89

Speaking of people. See issues of Ebony

The ten top-paying jobs for blacks. D. Narine. il *Ebony* 45:122+ D '89

White collar, blue collar love [black professional women in love with blue collar men] L. B. Randolph. il *Ebony* 44:48+ My '89

Photographs and photography

Memorable photos from the Ebony files. See issues of Ebony beginning June 1984

Political activities

See also

African American Summit

Black clergy—Political activities

Black congressmen

Black political candidates

Black public officers

Joint Center for Political Studies (U.S.)

National Black Republican Council

Back to the party of Lincoln? [G. Bush courts blacks and appoints L. W. Sullivan as Secretary of Health and Human Services] R. Lacayo. il pors *Time* 133:79 Ja 2 '89

Black leaders gather at White House to discuss their concerns with Bush. il por *Jet* 77:26 D 11 '89

Black politics: the growing pains are growing. D. Harbrecht. il *Business Week* p52-4 F 13 '89

Blacks agonize over abortion. J. N. Baker. il *Newsweek* 114:63 D 4 '89

Blacks and Republicans. W. A. Keyes. il *Conservative Digest* 15:47-9 Jl/Ag '89

Blacks slated for major participation in inaugural. il *Jet* 75:12-13 Ja 23 '89

Blackstabbers [special interests pursue black vote] R. Blow. *The New Republic* 200:16-18 My 29 '89

Bush inaugural events symbolic of the change in new administration [special section] il pors *Jet* 75:4-14+ F 6 '89

Bush promises 'a new breeze'. L. B. Randolph. il pors *Ebony* 44:132-4+ Ap '89

Courting black power [special interests pursue black vote] V. Novak. il *Common Cause Magazine* 15:17-22 Mr/Ap '89

Dems win Congress but will they lose blacks? il *Black Enterprise* 19:13 Ja '89

Divided we fell: race and the '88 election. J. Williams. il pors *American Visions* 4:31+ F '89

Drugs, Democrats and priorities [call for blacks to fight drug plague] M. Waters. *The Nation* 249:141-4 Jl 24-31 '89

Eyeing the prize: GOP sets sights on blacks. K. D. Thompson. il *Black Enterprise* 19:35 My '89

Eyes on the prizes, not the people [cover story] S. Anderson. il *The Nation* 249:405+ O 16 '89

From two new party chairmen: plans to woo and keep the black vote. R. Brown; L. Atwater. il *American Visions* 4:16-18 Je '89

BLACKS—Political activities—*cont.*

Getting serious about blacks [conservatives and Republicans] P. Weyrich. il *Conservative Digest* 15:11-14 Jl/Ag '89

The GOP's plan for Jesse. il por *Newsweek* 113:6 F 13 '89

The inward turn of black Americans. M. Barone. il *U.S. News & World Report* 106:32-3 My 8 '89

Party of Lincoln [Republican Party seeks black support] F. Barnes. *The New Republic* 200:10-12 Mr 20 '89

Playing the politics of race [R. Brown to be Democratic Party chairman while Republicans woo blacks] H. Fineman. il por *Newsweek* 113:20 F 6 '89

Politics. See issues of Jet

The return of segregation [black election districts] M. Cooper. il *U.S. News & World Report* 107:24 N 6 '89

The road to 1992 [blacks and the election of G. Bush] E. G. Graves. il *Black Enterprise* 19:7 Ja '89

Strength in numbers. E. G. Graves. il *Black Enterprise* 20:11 N '89

Ticker tape U.S.A. S. Booker. See issues of Jet

Washington page. See issues of Black Enterprise

Psychology

Being black and feeling blue. S. Steele. *The American Scholar* 58:497-508 Aut '89

Bouncing back from dead-end situations [black role models] D. Narine. il *Ebony* 44:40+ O '89

The Ebony advisor. See issues of Ebony

Free your mind [interview with N. Akbar] J. Nelson. por *Essence* 19:69-70+ F '89

Race identity

African-American or black: what's in a name? il *Ebony* 44:76+ Jl '89

Atlanta suit to examine black-on-black bias [firing of IRS employee T. L. Morrow] *Jet* 76:7 Je 12 '89

Being black and feeling blue. S. Steele. *The American Scholar* 58:497-508 Aut '89

Birth certificate says she's white, but woman gets a judge to declare her black [M. C. Walker] por *Jet* 76:36 S 18 '89

Black and Latino. R. Santiago. por *Essence* 20:12 N '89

Broad coalition seeks 'African American' name. il *Jet* 75:53 Ja 16 '89

By any other name [African-American] K. D. Thompson. il por *Black Enterprise* 19:22 Ap '89

Cambridge diarist [J. Jackson's campaign for term African-American to replace black] M. Peretz. *The New Republic* 200:43 F 6 '89

The delicate roots of identity. *U.S. News & World Report* 107:17-18 O 30 '89

From 'black' to 'African-American'? *Newsweek* 113:28 Ja 2 '89

In search of a good name [black vs. African-American] R. Lacayo. il *Time* 133:32 Mr 6 '89

Just say Afro. S. Thernstrom. *The New Republic* 200:10+ Ja 23 '89

Loaded terms [African-American] E. K. Braxton. *Commonweal* 116:328-9 Je 2 '89

New spirit infuses black America. S. Muwakkil. il *Utne Reader* p93-4 S/O '89

Readin', ritin' & rage: how schools are destroying black boys. D. J. Dent. il *Essence* 20:54-6+ N '89

Seize the time. D. E. Byrd. por *Essence* 20:134 N '89

What to call people of color. B. Lyles. por *Newsweek* 113:8-9 F 27 '89

Religious life

See also
Black churches
Catholic Church—Blacks
Church and race relations

The invisible church. J. A. Smith. il *Christianity Today* 33:32-4 Mr 3 '89

The prolife credibility gap [alienation of black support] S. Perkins. il por *Christianity Today* 33:21-2 Ap 21 '89

Retirement

The baby-boomer retirement blues. il *Black Enterprise* 20:51 O '89

A welcome mat for minorities? [retirement communities] A. Winter. *Modern Maturity* 32:14 Ag/S '89

Scholarships and fellowships

See Scholarships and fellowships

Segregation

See also
Apartheid
Church and race relations
Colleges and universities—Segregation
Public schools—Desegregation
Public schools—Segregation

The crisis of caste. C. V. Woodward. il *The New Republic* 201:38+ N 6 '89

No Jim Crow. H. Pearson. por *Essence* 20:8 D '89

Study: blacks segregated despite their status. *Jet* 75:27 F 27 '89

Valentine Museum's Jim Crow [Racism and reaction in the New South, Richmond, 1865-1940] E. Chappell. *The Nation* 249:102-4 Jl 17 '89

White S.C. restaurateur refuses to admit blacks; state NAACP files lawsuit [B. Salter] *Jet* 76:28 O 2 '89

Segregation, Resistance to

See Civil rights demonstrations

Sexual behavior

See Sexual behavior

Social conditions

See also
Black middle class
Blacks—Segregation

Agenda 2000. L. Anderson. por *Essence* 20:132 D '89

"The American dilemma has not been solved" [A common destiny: blacks and American society report] D. M. Watts. il *Black Enterprise* 20:26 O '89

An American dilemma revisited [report A common destiny: blacks and American society] *U.S. News & World Report* 107:8-9 Ag 7 '89

The black pathology biz. I. Reed. il *The Nation* 249:597-8 N 20 '89

Black progress 'stagnant' since '70s, report says [A common destiny: blacks and American society] il *Jet* 76:28-9 Ag 14 '89

Confronting minority failure [address, January 26, 1989] R. D. Lamm. *Vital Speeches of the Day* 55:433-5 My 1 '89

The crisis of caste. C. V. Woodward. il *The New Republic* 201:38+ N 6 '89

The future of black men. W. Strickland. il *Essence* 20:50-2+ N '89

Harping on racism. R. W. Wilkins. il *Mother Jones* 14:6-8 D '89

The inward turn of black Americans. M. Barone. il *U.S. News & World Report* 106:32-3 My 8 '89

Major issues facing African-Americans [address, August 6, 1989] J. E. Jacob. *Vital Speeches of the Day* 56:7-12 O 15 '89

Other victims in the Park: they are the 'invisible' blacks who are slandered by our mindless, sometimes racist generalities. M. Greenfield. il *Newsweek* 113:86 My 15 '89

The pain of being black [interview with T. Morrison] B. Angelo. il por *Time* 133:120-2 My 22 '89

Passages: 1989-2000 [address, January 30, 1989] V. Jordan. *Vital Speeches of the Day* 55:406-8 Ap 15 '89

Race: the issue [cover story] J. Klein. il *New York* 22:32-8 My 29 '89

Racism and poverty [report A common destiny: blacks and American society] R. J. Samuelson. il *Newsweek* 114:46 Ag 7 '89

Scapegoating the black family [cover story; special issue; with editorial comment] il *The Nation* 249:111, 115-20+ Jl 24-31 '89

Steps to help the urban black man. J. P. Newport, Jr. il *Fortune* 120:164-6+ D 18 '89

The surprising news about the underclass. D. Whitman. il *U.S. News & World Report* 107:73+ D 25 '89-Ja 1 '90

The Toni award [T. Morrison's views] *The New Republic* 200:9-10 Je 19 '89

The two black Americas [cover story] M. Kondracke. *The New Republic* 200:17-20 F 6 '89

Unfinished business [report A common destiny: blacks and American society] W. Shapiro. il *Time* 134:12-15 Ag 7 '89

Statistics

The biggest secret of race relations: the new white minority. il *Ebony* 44:84+ Ap '89

New York has the most blacks: nearly 3 million. *Jet* 76:10 Jl 10 '89

Taxation

Staying ahead of the IRS. B. M. Stephens and R. E. Barnes. il *Black Enterprise* 20:69-70+ D '89

Travel

Cruising with a cause. B. Peurifoy-Green. il *Black Enterprise* 19:61-2 Jl '89

Africa

Africa up close. S. Rule. il *The New York Times Magazine* p36+ Ap 30 '89

Alabama

Hard times for Freedom Quilters [Freedom Quilting Bee] N. Callahan. *The Christian Century* 106:317-18 Mr 22-29 '89

Arkansas

See also
Little Rock (Ark.)—Blacks

California

See also
Los Angeles (Calif.)—Blacks
San Francisco Bay Area (Calif.)—Blacks
Watts (Los Angeles, Calif.)

Florida

See also
Ocoee (Fla.)—Blacks

Georgia

See also
Atlanta (Ga.)—Blacks

Great Britain

See also
Parliamentary Black Caucus

To be young, British and black. D. Pitts. il *Black Enterprise* 20:86-8+ D '89

BLACKS—*cont.*

Massachusetts
See also
Martha's Vineyard (Mass.)—Blacks

Mississippi
The new Mississippi: is it really better than 'up north'? C. Whitaker. il *Ebony* 44:30+ Ag '89
Rural exchange program makes links [Project Self-Help and Awareness between white Wisconsin people and black people in rural Mississippi] J. Miller. il por *The Progressive* 53:12-13 Ap '89
Weaving a new spell in Mississippi. S. R. Gregg. il map *American Visions* 4:30-7 Ag '89

New England
History
Leafing through history [black landmarks] B. W. O'Connor. il *Black Enterprise* 20:105-6 S '89

New York (State)
See also
Harlem (New York, N.Y.)
New York (N.Y.)—Blacks
New York has the most blacks: nearly 3 million. *Jet* 76:10 Jl 10 '89

Pennsylvania
See also
Philadelphia (Pa.)—Blacks

Saint Helena Island (S.C.)
History
Treasures on an island. N. L. Mohr. il *American Visions* 4:29-31 O '89

South Africa
See also
Apartheid
South Africa goes black. A. Sparks. *World Press Review* 36:64 Je '89

Southern States
A tale of eight cities: go south to surprises. R. Brown. il map *Ebony* 44:46+ Ag '89
You can go home again [moving back to the South] B. Lane. il *American Visions* 4:24-7 Ap '89
History
The man who changed his skin [white author J. H. Griffin's four weeks as an itinerant southern black in 1959] E. Sharpe, Jr. il pors *American Heritage* 40:44-55 F '89
My white father [excerpt from Telling memories among southern women] S. Tucker. *Harper's* 279:36+ N '89
A partnership of the heart [work of surgeon A. Blalock and black assistant V. T. Thomas] K. McCabe. il por *Reader's Digest* 135:91-6 O '89

Soviet Union
Black Russian. Y. Khanga. il pors *Essence* 20:59-60+ Ag '89

United States
See Blacks

Washington (D.C.)
See Washington (D.C.)—Blacks
BLACKS, FAMOUS *See Black celebrities*
BLACKS AND MASS MEDIA
See also
Communications Excellence to Black Audiences Awards
A case of 'severe bias'. P. Raybon. por *Newsweek* 114:11 O 2 '89
In our image. J. H. Clarke. por *Essence* 20:158 S '89
BLACKS AND POLITICS *See Blacks—Political activities*
BLACKS AND THE PRESS
Beat the devil. A. Cockburn. il *The Nation* 249:113-14 Jl 24-31 '89
The black pathology biz. I. Reed. il *The Nation* 249:597-8 N 20 '89
Mainstreaming minorities [inclusion of minorities in news stories that are not specifically concerned with minority issues at Gannett] *Harper's* 279:16 Ag '89
BLACKS IN ADVERTISING
A long way from 'Aunt Jemima'. M. Mabry. il *Newsweek* 114:34-5 Ag 14 '89
My dollars count. K. G. Bates. por *Essence* 20:148 O '89
BLACKS IN ART
The dark legacy of the Enlightenment. G. Wills. il *The New York Review of Books* 36:9-11 Mr 30 '89
Mocking black stereotypes, a black artist makes waves [work of R. Colescott] R. Lacayo. il pors *People Weekly* 31:149+ My 22 '89
Exhibitions
Art [work of R. Colescott] A. C. Danto. *The Nation* 248:709-13 My 22 '89
Black satire and bleeding hearts [R. Colescott show and Art as a verb exhibit] B. W. Bloch. il *The New Leader* 72:22-3 My 1 '89
Colescott on black & white. K. Johnson. il *Art in America* 77:148-53+ Je '89
An eye on ethnicity [work of W. Reiss; cover story] B. Jacob. il por *American Visions* 4:14-19 O '89
An immigrant artist captured the faces of the New World [works of R. Winold at the National Portrait Gallery] J. H. Heminway. il pors *Smithsonian* 20:172-8+ N '89
BLACKS IN BASEBALL MANAGEMENT *See Baseball, Professional—Organization and administration*

BLACKS IN BASKETBALL MANAGEMENT *See Basketball, Professional—Organization and administration*
BLACKS IN BUSINESS *See Black businessmen*
BLACKS IN CABLE TELEVISION *See Cable television, Black*
BLACKS IN FOOTBALL MANAGEMENT *See Football, Professional—Organization and administration*
BLACKS IN LITERATURE
Bibliography
Ebony book shelf. See issues of Ebony
Good reads for black kids. G. Evans. il *American Visions* 4:50-2 D '89
BLACKS IN MOTION PICTURES
See also
Black Filmmakers Hall of Fame
Black Oscar Nominees (Awards)
Blacks in the motion picture industry
Tyler, Texas Black Film Collection
Why Hollywood ignores black love and intimacy. A. Collier. il *Ebony* 44:41-4 Ap '89
BLACKS IN POLITICS *See Blacks—Political activities*
BLACKS IN PUBLISHING
See also
Johnson Publishing Company, Inc.
Just-Us-Books
Book marks. P. Giddings. il *Essence* 19:26 Mr '89
Independent black publishing. J. A. Pinkney. bibl *American Visions* 4:50-4 Ap '89
BLACKS IN RETAIL TRADE
Pay dirt: underground mall boosts black business [Underground Atlanta] A. S. Harris. il *Black Enterprise* 20:20 S '89
BLACKS IN TELEVISION
See also
Blacks in the television industry
Blacks and 50 years of TV: ten memorable moments. D. C. Lyons. il *Ebony* 44:70+ S '89
Kim Fields: what happened to child stars after TV fame? [cover story] il pors *Jet* 75:56-9 Ja 23 '89
Minority view: seeing white, being black [interview with L. Gossett] R. Hofler. il por *Life* 12:90 Mr '89
Motown Production of 'Lonesome dove' gets 18 Emmy nominations. il *Jet* 76:64 Ag 21 '89
Raiding Cosby for her stars, Debbie Allen turns Pollyanna into a black musical. Polly. J. Park. il pors *People Weekly* 32:102-4 Ag 28 '89
Television. See issues of Jet
That enchanting Amen ensemble. H. Yorkshire. il *McCall's* 116:138+ Ap '89
Tim Reid and Daphne Maxwell Reid return in new TV series 'Snoops' [cover story] pors *Jet* 76:58-60 S 18 '89
TV series today make most blacks look rich: report. *Jet* 76:61 S 18 '89
What TV stars are doing now until the next season starts. il *Jet* 76:58-60 Je 5 '89
Who's new and who's back on TV. il *Ebony* 44:94+ O '89
BLACKS IN THE AIR FORCE *See United States. Air Force—Blacks*
BLACKS IN THE ARMY *See United States. Army—Blacks*
BLACKS IN THE AUTOMOBILE INDUSTRY
Ford and PUSH sign $2.5 billion deal. H. Manly. il *Black Enterprise* 19:18 Mr '89
Ford and PUSH sign affirmative action pact. il *Jet* 75:8+ Ja 9 '89
Forest Farmer: Chrysler's component parts president. C. Whitaker. il pors *Ebony* 44:90-2+ Mr '89
NAACP and Chrysler sign a fair share pact at confab. il *Jet* 76:7-8 Jl 31 '89
Will power [W. South, systems support manager for Saab-Scania of America] S. M. Williams. il por *Black Enterprise* 20:71-2 N '89
BLACKS IN THE FOOD INDUSTRY
Food, glorious food. M. A. Fortune. il *Black Enterprise* 19:74-6+ My '89
BLACKS IN THE GENETIC RESEARCH INDUSTRY
Getting in on the biotech revolution. F. Brown, Jr. *American Visions* 4:12+ Je '89
BLACKS IN THE GREETING CARD INDUSTRY
Sentimental returns. Y. R. Lamb. il *Black Enterprise* 20:79-80+ D '89
BLACKS IN THE MASS MEDIA INDUSTRY
FCC distress-sale policy overturned. S. M. Williams. *Black Enterprise* 19:54 Je '89
BLACKS IN THE MOTION PICTURE INDUSTRY
See also
Black Filmmakers Hall of Fame
Tyler, Texas Black Film Collection
Black theater gets new run [Baldwin Entertainment Complex, Los Angeles] S. Herbert. *Black Enterprise* 20:18 Ag '89
Hollywood's dirty little secret. J. Horowitz. il *American Visions* 4:16-21 Ag '89
Knocking on Hollywood's door [cover story] B. Sharkey. il pors *American Film* 14:22-7+ Jl/Ag '89
They've gotta have it [cover story; with editorial comment by Earl G. Graves] P. Johnson. il *Black Enterprise* 19:7, 36-8+ Jl '89

BLACKS IN THE NAVY *See* United States. Navy—Blacks
BLACKS IN THE PHONOGRAPH RECORD INDUSTRY
Black music's new hit doctors [T. Riley, A. Reid, and K. Edmonds] S. Bloom. il pors *Rolling Stone* p32 My 18 '89
L.A. & Babyface [black producers A. Reid and K. Edmonds] il pors *Ebony* 44:134+ Je '89
BLACKS IN THE RADIO INDUSTRY
See also
Radio stations, Black
NAACP challenges the affirmative action plans of TV, radio stations. *Jet* 76:26 Je 12 '89
BLACKS IN THE TELEVISION INDUSTRY
See also
Cable television, Black
Television stations, Black
60 minutes' man [E. Bradley] J. Schwartz. il por *Gentlemen's Quarterly* 59:141-4 My '89
After Seoul, Barcelona [NBC's J. Gilbert to oversee Olympic coverage] T. Paige. il por *Black Enterprise* 19:16 Ja '89
'Drugs almost destroyed my career' [black TV anchorman W. Bell] L. Norment. il pors *Ebony* 44:124-5 Ag '89
NAACP challenges the affirmative action plans of TV, radio stations. *Jet* 76:26 Je 12 '89
BLACKS IN THE TOY AND GAME INDUSTRY
Black toymakers brace for increased competition. D. Whittingham-Barnes. il *Black Enterprise* 20:24 D '89
BLACKSMITHS AND BLACKSMITHING
Conferences
'Expressive Iron' at Penland. J. Pehoski. il *American Craft* 49:72 Ag/S '89
BLACKSTONE, MIKE
about
Attention, Walter Mitty! Here's a sky-high dogfight for any would-be air ace. R. Arias. il pors *People Weekly* 32:70-2 N 20 '89
BLACKSTONE GROUP
Carving up mortgages [collateralized mortgage obligation residuals] B. Weberman. il *Forbes* 143:165 Mr 6 '89
Teaching a Tokyo whiz kid the art of the deal [H. Kondo from Nikko Securities] J. Friedman. il por *Business Week* p83 Ja 16 '89
BLACKWELL, BILL
about
She wore serious satin and tulle, but Debbie Harmon made her 'I do's' sheer sitcom. M. Dougherty. il pors *People Weekly* 31:150-1 My 22 '89
BLACKWELL, CHRIS
about
"I don't loon off all the time". P. Newcomb. il por *Forbes* 144:344+ N 13 '89
Now it's Chris Blackwell, corporate hipster. R. A. Melcher and D. Lieberman. il por *Business Week* p49 Ag 14 '89
BLACKWELL, RICHARD
The five best—and worst—dressed in the soaps. il *TV Guide* 37:28-31 N 4-10 '89
Mr. Blackwell's fashion guide: TV stars to watch—and ignore—if you want to look sharp [cover story] il *TV Guide* 37:10-13 Jl 22-28 '89
BLACQUE, TAUREAN
about
With two houses and a big heart, Generations star Taurean Blacque becomes a single father to nine. C. Sanz. il pors *People Weekly* 32:101-2+ O 9 '89
BLADDER
Cancer
Causes
Bladder cancers: one in four due to jobs [study by Debra T. Silverman] J. Raloff. *Science News* 136:230 O 7 '89
Diseases
See also
Cystitis
Urine—Incontinence
BLADE RUNNER [film] *See* Motion picture reviews—Single works
BLADE WORKS PRODUCTS INC.
Cutting through start-up problems. K. Smith. por *Nation's Business* 77:9 Ap '89
BLADEN, ASHBY
Observations. See occasional issues of Forbes
BLADES, AIRPLANE ENGINE *See* Airplane engines, Jet—Blades
BLADES, SAW *See* Saws and sawing
BLAGOVESHCHENSK (SOVIET UNION)
Watermelon diplomacy on the border [Sino-Soviet thaw along Amur River] J. Trimble. il map *U.S. News & World Report* 106:33 My 15 '89
BLAGOVOLIN, S.
A Soviet view: defense only. *World Press Review* 36:23-4 F '89
BLAH NA NA (MUSICAL GROUP)
Blah Na Na! For the blahs [rock and roll band formed by teachers in Eden, N.C.] J. M. Carter. il *Phi Delta Kappan* 71:84-5 S '89
BLAHOUS, CHARLES P.
about
Blahous will be APS Congressional Scientist Fellow in 1989-90. por *Physics Today* 42:109-10 S '89

BLAIR, ALISTAIR
about
Young fogey. J. McLaughlin. il por *Harper's Bazaar* 122:81 S '89
BLAIR, ERIC *See* Orwell, George, 1903-1950
BLAIR, HARRY C., AND OTHERS
Osteoclastic bone resorption by a polarized vacuolar proton pump. bibl f il *Science* 245:855-7 Ag 25 '89
BLAIR, S. ROBERT
about
Nova's sell-off. J. DeMont. por *Maclean's* 102:37 Jl 10 '89
BLAIR (D. L.) INC. *See* D. L. Blair Inc.
BLAIR (JOHN) & COMPANY *See* John Blair & Company
BLAIR (JOHN F.), PUBLISHER *See* John F. Blair, Publisher
BLAKE, AMANDA, 1929-1989
about
Friends—and her doctor—say A.I.D.S., not cancer, killed Gunsmoke's Amanda Blake. J. Stark. il pors *People Weekly* 32:68-9 N 20 '89
Obituary
People Weekly il por 32:100 S 4 '89
BLAKE, ERNIE, D. 1989
about
The laird of Taos Ski Valley. N. Howe. il *Skiing* 41:48 F '89
Obituary
Skiing il por 42:38 S '89. E. Bowen
BLAKE, JUDITH
Number of siblings and educational attainment. bibl f il *Science* 245:32-6 Jl 7 '89
BLAKE, RANDOLPH
(jt. auth) *See* Nawrot, Mark, and Blake, Randolph
BLAKE, RICHARD A.
An autopsy on 'Temptation'. *America* 160:199-201 Mr 4 '89
BLAKE, ROBERT, 1598-1657
about
Cromwell's soldier-admirals. M. Baumber. bibl il pors *History Today* 39:42-7 O '89
BLAKE, WILLIAM, 1757-1827
about
William Blake and August's fiery meteors. D. W. Olson and M. S. Olson. il *Sky and Telescope* 78:192-4 Ag '89
BLAKELY, MARY KAY
Coma. il por *Life* 12:80-4+ Ag '89
Halfway to heaven! [excerpt from Wake me when it's over] il por *Redbook* 173:126-7+ Jl '89
Memories of Frank. il *Psychology Today* 23:48-50+ O '89
BLAKES HOTEL (LONDON, ENGLAND) *See* London (England)—Hotels, motels, etc.
BLAKESLEE, SANDRA
Memories are made of this. il *New Choices for the Best Years* 29:41-2+ N '89
The return of the mind. il por *American Health* 8:94-6 Mr '89
(jt. auth) *See* Wallerstein, Judith S., and Blakeslee, Sandra
BLAKEY, ART
about
John Coltrane-Cecil Taylor-Art Blakey: Philharmonic Hall, Lincoln Center, New York City [reprint] I. A. Baraka. il *Down Beat* 56:62 S '89
BLAKEY, G. ROBERT, 1936-
about
G. Robert Blakey versus Michael Milken. J. Queenan. il por *Forbes* 143:57+ My 1 '89
BLALOCK, ALFRED, 1899-1964
about
A partnership of the heart. K. McCabe. il por *Reader's Digest* 135:91-6 O '89
BLANCH, ENRIC BALASCH
Turkish kaleidoscope. il *World Press Review* 36:76 D '89
BLANCHARD, BOB, AND WATROUS, SUSAN
Daniel Ellsberg [interview; cover story] il por *The Progressive* 53:17-21 S '89
BLANCHARD, KENNETH H.
about
One minute management [interview] S. F. Edwards. por *Home Office Computing* 7:62 S '89
BLANCHARD, MARY ELLEN
about
Woman to watch. S. Robb. por *Women's Sports & Fitness* 11:58 O '89
BLANCHET, PIERRE
(jt. auth) *See* Backmann, René, and Blanchet, Pierre
BLANCHETTE, CRAIG
about
Hell on wheels. K. Moore. il pors *Sports Illustrated* 71:44-6+ Jl 17 '89
BLANCO, ANTONIO
about
Cosmopolitan mise-en-scéne. C. McGee. il *Architectural Digest* 46:186-91 Ap '89
BLANCO, LENORA
about
Cosmopolitan mise-en-scéne. C. McGee. il *Architectural Digest* 46:186-91 Ap '89

BLANCO (TEX.)
Historic houses, sites, etc.
Hill Country hideaway [1860s guest house] E. Wood. il *Southern Living* 24:124-5 My '89
BLANCORNELAS, JESÚS
about
To the left of zero. W. Murray. *The New Yorker* 65:57-66 Jl 31 '89
BLAND, JOHN
He gave quinine to the world. il *World Health* p28-9 D '88
BLAND, WARREN
about
A criminal lack of common sense. J. Leo. il *U.S. News & World Report* 107:56 Ag 21 '89
BLANDFORD, LINDA
Anatomy of a sitcom. il *The New York Times Magazine* p34-7+ Ap 2 '89
A prince of Hollywood. il pors *The New York Times Magazine* p56-7+ D 3 '89
BLANDFORD, ROGER D., AND OTHERS
Gravitational lens optics. bibl f il *Science* 245:824-30 Ag 25 '89
BLANDIANA, ANA
A star in my street [poem] *Harper's* 279:16+ D '89
about
Ceauşescu: no Little prince. *Harper's* 279:16+ D '89
BLANK, JOSEPH P.
Arnie and Ginger. *Reader's Digest* 134:9-10+ Ja '89
BLANKET CHESTS *See* Chests
BLANKETS
See also
Indian blankets, rugs, etc. (American)
BLANKETS, ELECTRIC
Are electric blankets safe? il *Consumer Reports* 54:715-16 N '89
Electric blankets & mattress pads. il *Consumer Reports* 54:711-14 N '89
BLANNING, T. C. W.
The abortive crusade. bibl il *History Today* 39:33-8 My '89
BLANTON, JAMES
A limit to affirmative action? *Commentary* 87:28-32 Je '89
BLAQUIER, NELLY ARRIETA DE
about
Nelly Arrieta de Blaquier's South American silver. J. Gruen. il por *Architectural Digest* 46:102+ O '89
BLASKO, LARRY
A decade into the Big Bang. il por *Compute!* 11:42 O '89
BLASPHEMY
On blasphemy: advice for the Ayatollah [S. Rushdie's novel The satanic verses] R. Goetz. *The Christian Century* 106:253-5 Mr 8 '89
The sins of Salman [S. Rushdie's Satanic verses] M. Walzer. *The New Republic* 200:13-15 Ap 10 '89
BLATTY, WILLIAM PETER
about
That old devil William Blatty is filming a new Exorcist like a man possessed. M. Dougherty. il pors *People Weekly* 32:44-6 Ag 14 '89
BLAU, MELINDA
Caregiving: coping with a chronically ill spouse. *McCall's* 117:108+ N '89
In it together. il *New York* 22:44-8+ S 4 '89
BLAU, RICHARD
about
Safari. *The New Yorker* 65:35-6 Mr 20 '89
BLAU, ROBERT
about
Safari. *The New Yorker* 65:35-6 Mr 20 '89
BLAUGRUND, ANNETTE
American artists at the 1889 Exposition Universelle in Paris. bibl f il *Antiques* 136:1158-69 N '89
BLAUNER, PETER
All-star family feud. il pors *New York* 22:34-7 F 13 '89
Big Ben: has Police Commissioner Ward become a liability to Koch? il pors *New York* 22:48-50+ Ap 3 '89
Fonzie on the spot: the HUD revelations tarnish the 'new' D'Amato. il pors *New York* 22:42-8 N 13 '89
The fugitive. il pors *New York* 22:32-7 Ag 7 '89
O pioneers. il *New York* 22:68-70+ D 25 '89-Ja 1 '90
Rock noir: Lou Reed reckons with Andy Warhol in 'Songs for 'Drella'. il pors *New York* 22:44-9 N 27 '89
The wild and crazy gangster: Michael Markowitz's twisted American dream. il pors *New York* 22:52-6+ O 9 '89
BLAUSTEIN, RICHARD
about
From offices of excellence. D. Young. il pors *Southern Living* 24:142+ Ap '89
BLAUSTEIN, SUSAN
Letter from the Philippines. *The New Yorker* 65:95-106 D 18 '89
Looking to the private sector. il *The Nation* 248:226-8 F 20 '89
Old war, China card & Sihanouk. il *The Nation* 249:485-6+ O 30 '89
Restoring Cambodian culture. *The Nation* 249:426-9 O 16 '89

BLAYLOCK, JAMES P.
Unidentified objects [fiction] il *Omni (New York, N.Y.)* 11:42-4+ Jl '89
BLAZE [film] See Motion picture reviews—Single works
BLAZERS (JACKETS)
Men's & women's blazers. il *Consumer Reports* 54:7-11 D '89
BLEACHER BUMS [drama] See Mantegna, Joe, 1948?-
BLEACHING OF TEETH *See* Dentistry
BLECHMAN, BARRY M.
Cost reduction dubious. il *The Bulletin of the Atomic Scientists* 45:38-9 My '89
Triad, schmiad. *The New Republic* 200:15-17 F 6 '89
BLECKNER, ROSS, 1949-
about
Lofty ambitions. L. Kaylin. il pors *Gentlemen's Quarterly* 59:208-11+ F '89
Ross Bleckner at Mary Boone. R. Storr. il *Art in America* 77:145-6 Mr '89
BLEDSOE, TEMPESTT
about
At 15 . . . she had the clout to can the beer scene. H. Polskin. il pors *TV Guide* 37:24-6 O 7-13 '89
Clifton Davis and Tempestt Bledsoe star in TV movie. A. Collier. il pors *Jet* 77:22-3+ O 16 '89
Tempestt gets a new 'do. il pors *Seventeen* 48:72 O '89
BLEEDING *See* Hemorrhage
BLEHL, VINCENT FERRER
Prelude to the making of a saint [cover story] pors *America* 160:213-16 Mr 11 '89
BLEIER, ROCKY
Unforgettable Art Rooney. il por *Reader's Digest* 135:15-16+ N '89
BLENDERS (APPLIANCES)
See also
Drink mixers (Appliances)
Blenders & milkshake makers. il *Consumer Reports* 54:261-4 D '89
Butter tub fur blender [fly tying use] R. Drew. il *Field & Stream* 94:14 Je '89
BLENKARN, DONALD
about
The Kings of the Hills. il pors *Maclean's* 102:60-1 Jl 3 '89
BLEOMYCIN
Sequence-specific isotope effects on the cleavage of DNA by bleomycin. J. W. Kozarich and others. bibl f il *Science* 245:1396-9 S 22 '89
BLESS, ROBERT C.
Space station Freedom: bad news for astronomy. *Sky and Telescope* 77:460 My '89
BLESSED VIRGIN MARY, SAINT *See* Mary, Blessed Virgin, Saint
BLESSING, LEE
about
Eleemosynary [drama] Reviews
New York il 22:74+ My 22 '89. J. Simon
Time il 133:110 My 22 '89. W. A. Henry
A walk in the woods [drama] Reviews
Theatre Crafts il 23:20 O '89
BLETILLA *See* Orchids
BLEY, PAUL
about
Paul Bley. J. Woodard. il por *Down Beat* 56:14 Ag '89
BLICK, NICHOLAS CHRISTIE- *See* Christie-Blick, Nicholas
BLIGHT, JAMES G.
A joint U.S.-Soviet reexamination of the Cuban Missile Crisis. il *USA Today (Periodical)* 117:70-2 Mr '89
BLIND
See also
Guide dogs
Music and the blind
"Blindness isn't a handicap—it's a nuisance" [blind couple, M. and P. Maurer, raising children] D. Scoblionkov. il pors *McCall's* 117:49-52 O '89
Civil rights
Language and the future of the blind [address, July 8, 1989] M. Maurer. *Vital Speeches of the Day* 56:16-22 O 15 '89
Equipment
High-tech aids offer new options to deaf, blind. il *The Futurist* 23:50-1 S/O '89
Recreation
See also
Deaf-Blind Trailblazers (Organization)
Travel
Blind passengers protest exit row seating policy. C. Fotos. *Aviation Week & Space Technology* 130:94-5 Mr 27 '89
Lives at stake [FAA rule excluding blind airline passengers from seats in exit rows] *Aviation Week & Space Technology* 130:9 Ap 3 '89
BLIND DATING *See* Dating (Social customs)
BLIND POOLS (SECURITIES)
Never, but never, give a sucker an even break [securities fraud charges against A. Kimmes implicate M. Blinder] R. L. Stern and others. il pors *Forbes* 143:46-50 Ja 9 '89

BLIND POOLS (SECURITIES)—*cont.*
The penny stock scandal [cover story] P. Engardio and G. DeGeorge. il *Business Week* p74-7+ Ja 23 '89
BLIND RIVETS *See* Rivets and riveting
BLIND WITNESS [television program] See Television program reviews—Single works
BLINDER, ALAN S.
Economic viewpoint. See issues of Business Week
BLINDER, EVA J.
Innovations here and still to come. il *Channels (New York, N.Y.: 1986)* 9:46-8 My '89
BLINDER, MEYER
about
Meyer, meet RICO. J. Zweig. il por *Forbes* 143:168 Je 26 '89
Never, but never, give a sucker an even break. R. L. Stern and others. il pors *Forbes* 143:46-50 Ja 9 '89
BLINDER, ROBINSON & COMPANY
Meyer, meet RICO [penny stock swindler M. Blinder] J. Zweig. il por *Forbes* 143:168 Je 26 '89
Never, but never, give a sucker an even break [securities fraud charges against A. Kimmes implicate M. Blinder] R. L. Stern and others. il pors *Forbes* 143:46-50 Ja 9 '89
BLINDNESS
See also
Blind
Color blindness
Leber's hereditary optic neuropathy
Onchocerciasis
Retinopathy of prematurity
Gone blind. O. Friedrich. il *Harper's* 278:73-80 Mr '89
Prevention
See also
National Society to Prevent Blindness
BLINDS
Slat drift and other conundrums. P. Patton. il *Esquire* 112:31 Ag '89
BLINKEN, ANTONY J.
L'édifice, c'est moi. *The New Republic* 200:16+ My 15 '89
Missing. *The New Republic* 201:15-16 O 16 '89
BLINKING *See* Eye—Movements
BLISS, CATHY
Teen to teen. See issues of 'Teen beginning February 1989 through December 1989
about
Get-ups to go! il pors *'Teen* 33:78-81 S '89
Miss Teenage America 1989: taking it to the top. il pors *'Teen* 33:60-1 F '89
BLISS, GEORGE
about
Transport. *The New Yorker* 65:50-1 S 25 '89
BLISS, SHEPHERD
about
Of hawks and men: a weekend in the male wilderness. J. Tevlin. il *Utne Reader* p50-7+ N/D '89
BLISTERS
Between a sock and a hard place [foot blisters] J. Ellis. il *Runner's World* 24:28 Ag '89
If you get blisters, check your socks [acrylic fibers more effective than cotton in preventing foot blisters; views of Kirk M. Herring] il *Prevention (Emmaus, Pa.)* 41:12+ Jl '89
BLIVEN, NAOMI
Aristocrats. il *The New Yorker* 65:81-8+ D 25 '89
BLIZZARDS *See* Snowstorms
THE BLOB [film] See Motion picture reviews—Single works
BLOCH, BRADLEY W.
Black satire and bleeding hearts. il *The New Leader* 72:22-3 My 1 '89
Mixed movement at the Whitney. il *The New Leader* 72:21-2 Jl 10-24 '89
The obsession of the long-distance runner. il *Gentlemen's Quarterly* 59:312-13+ N '89
Pigments of the imagination. il *The New Leader* 72:22-3 S 4 '89
Thinking pictures. *The New Leader* 72:22-3 N 27 '89
The use and abuse of realism. *The New Leader* 72:22-3 O 2-16 '89
Where Warhol failed. il *The New Leader* 72:22-3 Mr 20 '89
BLOCH, FELIX S.
about
The Bloch case. *World Press Review* 36:8-9 S '89
A case of espionage. H. Mackenzie. il por *Maclean's* 102:27 Ag 7 '89
First the verdict, then the trial. B. Van Voorst. il pors *Time* 134:16 Ag 7 '89
High spy at State? *Time* 134:16 Jl 31 '89
Making a case against Bloch. R. Moreau. il por *Newsweek* 114:32 Ag 7 '89
More secrets from the life of Felix Bloch. il *Newsweek* 114:40 O 23 '89
My lunch with Felix. B. Van Voorst. il por *Time* 134:16 S 4 '89
A spy in high places? H. Anderson. il por *Newsweek* 114:36 Jl 31 '89
Stategate. *National Review* 41:10-12 S 1 '89

Summer spy scoops. D. Schorr. *The New Leader* 72:3-4 Ag 7-21 '89
Suspected spy Felix Bloch leads G-men and the press on a wild spook chase. B. Hewitt. il por *People Weekly* 32:42-3 Ag 14 '89
Tinker, tailor, soldier, deputy chief of mission. B. Duffy. il por *U.S. News & World Report* 107:21 Ag 7 '89
Vienna waltz. *The Nation* 249:228-9 S 4-11 '89
BLOCH, GORDON BAKOULIS
6 steps to lifelong health. *Working Woman* 14:153-4 Ap '89
Curing the empty-bed syndrome. il *Working Woman* 14:57-9 F '89
Sports and your career. il *Working Woman* 14:137-8+ Je '89
BLOCH, JEAN
Words as weapons: romantic literature and the Revolution. bibl il *History Today* 39:45-50 My '89
BLOCH, SONNY, AND LICHTENSTEIN, GRACE
Smart ways to afford a home of your own. il *Reader's Digest* 134:132-6 Je '89
BLOCK, ADAM
Pure Bono [interview; cover story] il pors *Mother Jones* 14:32-7+ My '89
BLOCK, JEAN LIBMAN
Bess Myerson: the inside story. il pors *Good Housekeeping* 208:70+ Ap '89
"The best time of my life is now" [cover story] il pors *Good Housekeeping* 209:155+ N '89
Six women who beat the odds. il *Good Housekeeping* 209:16+ Jl '89
"We had to kidnap our son from the hospital". il pors *Good Housekeeping* 209:144-5+ O '89
BLOCK, MICKEY
Me and the Preacher Man [condensed from Before the dawn]; ed. by William R. Kimball. *Reader's Digest* 134:33-7 Ja '89
BLOCK, WALTER, 1941-
Analyzing the welfare system [address, October 29, 1988] *Vital Speeches of the Day* 55:333-7 Mr 15 '89
BLOCK DRUG CO.
In anonymity they thrive. R. Phalon. il *Forbes* 144:72+ D 25 '89
BLOCK ISLAND (R.I.)
See also
Architecture, Domestic—Block Island (R.I.)
Description and travel
Block Island. G. Trotta. il map *Gourmet* 49:76-81+ My '89
BLOCKBUSTER ENTERTAINMENT CORP.
Will this video chain stay on fast-forward? P. Engardio and A. Fins. il *Business Week* p72+ Je 12 '89
BLOCKS (TOYS)
Blocks! Much more than a toy. H. Cuffaro. il *Good Housekeeping* 209:156 S '89
Box of blocks. M. Wells. il *Workbench* 45:42-3 N/D '89
BLOCKSTEIN, DAVID E.
Biodiversity bill update. *BioScience* 39:677 N '89
BLODGETT, BARBARA
about
Awakening from a coma, a Washington woman meets her miraculous baby boy. M. Green. il pors *People Weekly* 31:38-40+ F 27 '89
BLOEMBERGEN, NICOLAAS, 1920-
about
Bloembergen elected vice president; Crasemann to head nominating group. il pors *Physics Today* 42:93-4 Ja '89
BLOMGREN, JENNIFER
Vestibular disorders: causes and effects of a hidden problem. il *Children Today* 18:14-17 Jl/Ag '89
BLOMSTEDT, HERBERT, 1927-
about
Blomstedt's resplendent Strauss. D. Hall. por *Stereo Review* 54:103-4 Mr '89
The maestro's greatest loyalty. D. Neff. il por *Christianity Today* 33:62 Mr 3 '89
BLONSKY, MARSHALL
A literary high-wire act. il por *The New York Times Magazine* p42-3+ D 10 '89
BLOOD
See also
Fear of blood
Hemorrhage
Alcohol content
How reliable is breath-alcohol testing? D. A. Labianca. il *USA Today (Periodical)* 118:71-2 S '89
Circulation
See also
Blood-brain barrier
Blood flow
Blood pressure
Coagulation
See also
Anticoagulants
Thrombin
Thrombosis
Blood clotting may increase with age [research by Robert Rosenberg] J. L. Marx. *Science* 243:316 Ja 20 '89

BLOOD—Coagulation—*cont.*
The involvement of platelet activating factor in ovulation. A. O. Abisogun and others. bibl f il *Science* 243:381-3 Ja 20 '89

Collection and preservation
See also
Blood banks

Dialysis
See Hemodialysis

Diseases
See also
Anemia
Hemophilia
Leukemia
Sickle cell anemia

Fats
See Blood—Lipids

Flow
See Blood flow

Formation
See Blood cells—Growth

Lipids
See also
Apolipoproteins
Cholesterol
Hypertension, heart disease and diuretics. R. Weiss. *Science News* 136:254 O 14 '89

Parasites
See also
Plasmodium (Parasite)

Pigments
See also
Hemoglobin

Proteins
See also
Hemoglobin
Immunoglobulins
Myoglobin
Serum albumin
Neutrophil Mac-1 and MEL-14 adhesion proteins inversely regulated by chemotactic factors. T. K. Kishimoto and others. bibl f il *Science* 245:1238-41 S 15 '89

Testing
See also
Drug abuse—Testing
An assay for circulating antibodies to a major etiologic virus of human non-A, non-B hepatitis. G. Kuo and others. bibl f il *Science* 244:362-4 Ap 21 '89
Blood test linked to alcoholism risk [work of Gerald C. Mueller] *Science News* 135:13 Ja 7 '89
Breaking a fever in the blood [detecting non-A, non-B hepatitis] *U.S. News & World Report* 106:16+ My 1 '89
The burden of proof: donated blood runs a costly gauntlet of tests. E. Corcoran. il *Scientific American* 260:79-80 Ap '89
Coming soon: safer blood [test for non-A, non-B hepatitis virus] J. Langone. il *Time* 133:66 My 1 '89
Do you know your cholesterol level? D. Blumenthal. il *FDA Consumer* 23:24-7 Mr '89
HDL at your finger tips [cholesterol screening] J. Ziegler. il *American Health* 8:14 D '89
Hepatitis B mutants hide in blood [research by Girish N. Vyas] I. Wickelgren. *Science News* 135:52 Ja 28 '89
High 'I do' blood-test dues [mandatory AIDS testing for marriage license applicants in Illinois] *Science News* 135:357 Je 10 '89
HIV can linger years with no antibodies [research by David T. Imagawa] R. Weiss. *Science News* 135:340 Je 3 '89
HTLV-I: a new AIDS-like threat? R. Montagna. il por map *The Saturday Evening Post* 261:82-4+ Jl/Ag '89
The loss of a husband and father [misdiagnosis of AIDS; case of E. Young] C. SerVaas. il por *The Saturday Evening Post* 261:94+ Jl/Ag '89
Mail-order AIDS tests: FDA confronts the implications. R. Weiss. *Science News* 135:268 Ap 29 '89
More questions than answers: a gay man takes the AIDS test. J. Green. il *Gentlemen's Quarterly* 59:152+ D '89
The mystery of 'silent' AIDS infections [deficiencies of standard test] J. Seligmann. il *Newsweek* 113:59 Je 12 '89
Not necessarily non-A, non-B hepatitis. C. SerVaas. *The Saturday Evening Post* 261:100-1 Jl/Ag '89
Notes and comment [blood test required as part of health insurance application] *The New Yorker* 65:27-8 My 22 '89
The one-two-threes of a complete blood count. D. Farley. il *FDA Consumer* 23:28-31 S '89
Path to hepatitis C yields test, clues [research by Michael Houghton] I. Wickelgren. *Science News* 135:246-7 Ap 22 '89
Plasma HIV reflects AIDS progression. K. Fackelmann. *Science News* 136:389 D 16 '89
Safeguarding the supply [computer program designed to interpret blood test data; work of Jack Smith] *USA Today (Periodical)* 118:4 O '89
Screening for the high risk [cholesterol] H. J. Ullmann. il *The Saturday Evening Post* 261:82-3+ Ja/F '89
Silent AIDS [deficiencies of antibody test] *Time* 133:61 Je 12 '89

Testing newborns for cystic fibrosis [measuring immunoreactive trypsinogen; work of Frank J. Accurso] S. Hart and A. McKenzie. *Science News* 136:233 O 7 '89
Top 10 laboratory tests: blood will tell [cover story] D. Farley. *FDA Consumer* 23:22-7 Jl/Ag '89
Turning up the dirt in cholesterol screens [unsafe public cholesterol screenings; report by Richard P. Kusserow] D. E. Loupe. *Science News* 136:359 D 2 '89

Transfusion
See also
Blood boosting
Global Blood Safety Initiative (Program)
AIDS, blood and money [lawsuits against blood banks] J. Hammer. il *Newsweek* 113:43 Ja 23 '89
Bad blood? [AIDS and blood supply] M. Cimons. *Essence* 20:21-2 S '89
The burden of proof: donated blood runs a costly gauntlet of tests. E. Corcoran. il *Scientific American* 260:79-80 Ap '89
Challenging the traditional transfusion. T. L. Crenshaw. il *The Saturday Evening Post* 261:66-8 Ap '89
Danger from blood transfusions [cancer surgery; views of Dale H. Rice] il *USA Today (Periodical)* 117:5 F '89
HTLV-I: a new AIDS-like threat? R. Montagna. il por map *The Saturday Evening Post* 261:82-4+ Jl/Ag '89
Justice in Milwaukee [AIDS victim J. Carroll wins suit against Blood Center of Southeast Wisconsin] H. G. Miller. il pors *The Saturday Evening Post* 261:44-8+ My/Je '89
A life in limbo [hemophiliac tests positive for AIDS] P. B. Bayer. il por *The New York Times Magazine* p48+ Ap 2 '89
The loss of a husband and father [misdiagnosis of AIDS; case of E. Young] C. SerVaas. il por *The Saturday Evening Post* 261:94+ Jl/Ag '89
Marrow rebuilt with umbilical-cord blood [work of Arleen D. Auerbach] A. McKenzie. *Science News* 136:293 N 4 '89
Not necessarily non-A, non-B hepatitis. C. SerVaas. *The Saturday Evening Post* 261:100-1 Jl/Ag '89
A surgical patient's transfusion survival guide [intraoperative autologous transfusions] T. L. Crenshaw. il por *The Saturday Evening Post* 261:60+ Mr '89
Transfusions: it's a bloody shame [intraoperative autologous transfusion as alternative to traditional transfusion] T. L. Crenshaw. il por *The Humanist* 49:16-20+ My/Je '89

BLOOD AS A COMMERCIAL PRODUCT
See also
PSICOR Inc.

BLOOD BANKS
Suits and claims
AIDS, blood and money. J. Hammer. il *Newsweek* 113:43 Ja 23 '89
Justice in Milwaukee [AIDS victim J. Carroll wins suit against Blood Center of Southeast Wisconsin] H. G. Miller. il pors *The Saturday Evening Post* 261:44-8+ My/Je '89

BLOOD BOOSTING
EPO is not the way to go [too risky for use by athletes] R. Goldingay. il *Women's Sports & Fitness* 11:10 Jl/Ag '89

BLOOD-BRAIN BARRIER
Across the great divide. M. S. Glucksman. il *Omni (New York, N.Y.)* 11:30+ Ap '89
Brain man [somatic cell therapy; work of E. A. Neuwelt] M. S. Glucksman. il *Omni (New York, N.Y.)* 11:28 My '89
The mammalian choroid plexus. R. Spector and C. E. Johanson. bibl il *Scientific American* 261:68-74 N '89

BLOOD BROTHERS [musical] See Musicals, revues, etc.—Reviews—Single works

BLOOD CELL AGGREGATION
Histamine is an intracellular messenger mediating platelet aggregation. S. P. Saxena and others. bibl f il *Science* 243:1596-9 Mr 24 '89

BLOOD CELLS
See also
Erythrocytes
Leukocytes
Lymphocytes

Growth
See also
Colony-stimulating factors
Erythropoietin
Lineage-specific requirement of *c-abl* function in normal hematopoiesis [chronic myelogenous leukemia] D. Caracciolo and others. bibl f il *Science* 245:1107-10 S 8 '89

BLOOD CLOT ANTICOAGULANTS See Anticoagulants
BLOOD CLOTS See Thrombosis
BLOOD CLOTTING See Blood—Coagulation
BLOOD DOPING See Blood boosting
BLOOD FLOW
A better gauge for measuring how heart patients are doing [InterFlo Medical Inc.] W. C. Symonds. il *Business Week* p54 Jl 31 '89
Fluid flow stimulates tissue plasminogen activator secretion by cultured human endothelial cells. S. L. Diamond and others. bibl f il *Science* 243:1483-5 Mr 17 '89

BLOOD FLOW—*cont.*
Neuroanatomical correlates of anticipatory anxiety [study of brain blood flow by positron emission tomography] E. M. Reiman and others. bibl f il *Science* 243:1071-4 F 24 '89
A novel vasodilatory peptide from the salivary glands of the sand fly Lutzomyia longipalpis. J. M. C. Ribeiro and others. bibl f il *Science* 243:212-14 Ja 13 '89
PET pictures produce a palette of anxiety [research by Eric M. Reiman] B. Bower. il *Science News* 135:116-17 F 25 '89
Pulmonary blood flow regulation in an aquatic snake [diving by Acrochordus granulatus] H. B. Lillywhite and J. A. Donald. bibl f il *Science* 245:293-5 Jl 21 '89

BLOOD GROUPS
What's your type? [work of K. Landsteiner] il *Current Health 2* 16:12-13 O '89

BLOOD LACTATE RESPONSE TRAINING *See* Tempo training

BLOOD PRESSURE
See also
Hypertension
Fish oil lowers even normal blood pressure [research by Constance Kies] J. Raloff. *Science News* 136:181 S 16 '89

BLOOD SUGAR
See also
Hypoglycemia

BLOOD TESTS *See* Blood—Testing
BLOOD TRANSFUSIONS *See* Blood—Transfusion
BLOOD VESSELS
See also
Arteries
Capillaries
Cardiovascular system

Diseases
See also
Aneurysms
Raynaud's disease

Growth
See Angiogenesis

Surgery
See also
Cardiac catheterization
Can operation avoid strokes? [carotid endarterectomy; views of John Byer] *USA Today (Periodical)* 117:14 F '89
Drill unclogs blood vessels [work of Robert Ginsburg] il *USA Today (Periodical)* 118:4-5 O '89
"Medical research saved my son's life" [animal research necessary for development of endovascular embolization procedure] K. Barrett and R. Greene. il *Redbook* 173:161 S '89

Transplantation
Implantation of vascular grafts lined with genetically modified endothelial cells. J. M. Wilson and others. bibl f il *Science* 244:1344-6 Je 16 '89

BLOODROCK (MUSICAL GROUP)
Bloodrock. D. Fricke. il *Rolling Stone* p56 Ag 10 '89

BLOOM, ALLAN DAVID
about
Educational misconceptions of a democratic public. W. Feinberg. *The Education Digest* 55:7-10 O '89
Learning by story. N. Postman. il *The Atlantic* 264:119-24 D '89

BLOOM, BARBARA
about
Barbara Bloom at Jay Gorney. K. Johnson. il *Art in America* 77:169 D '89

BLOOM, DAVID E., AND BENNETT, NEIL G.
Future shock [cover story] *The New Republic* 200:18-20+ Je 19 '89

BLOOM, HOWARD
The importance of hugging [excerpt from The Lucifer principle] il *Omni (New York, N.Y.)* 11:30+ F '89

BLOOM, JANE E.
Employment of older refugees: New York State initiatives. il *Aging* no359:27-8 '89

BLOOM, JANE L.
(jt. auth) *See* Uva, Mary Deery, and Bloom, Jane L.

BLOOM, LLOYD
about
A question of fairness. R. Telander. por *Sports Illustrated* 70:114 My 1 '89
Tough message. il pors *Time* 133:78 Ap 24 '89

BLOOM, MARC, 1947-
Broadcast news. il *Runner's World* 24:66-70 N '89
Coming on strong. il *World Tennis* 37:52-4 O '89
The fats of life. il *World Tennis* 37:92-5 S '89
Forever young. il *Runner's World* 24:36-41 My '89
The gentle man of Verona. il pors *Runner's World* 24:60-5 N '89
Life in the Filutze lane. il pors *Runner's World* 24:68-72 Je '89
Missed opportunity. il por *Runner's World* 24:60-2+ Ja '89
Revival of the fittest. il *Runner's World* 24:30-5 Ja '89
Tennis in good time. il *World Tennis* 36:70-1 F '89
That old college try. il *Runner's World* 24:36-8 S '89
Where the pros train. il *New York* 22:48-57 S 18 '89

Workout for one. il *Health (New York, N.Y.)* 21:42-3 Ap '89
(ed) *See* Scott, Dave. Commit to get fit

BLOOM COUNTY (COMIC STRIP) *See* Comic books, strips, etc.

BLOOMFIELD, HAROLD H., 1944-, AND VETTESE, SIRAH
Healthy love [excerpt from Lifemates]; ed. by Robert B. Kory. il *Health (New York, N.Y.)* 21:24+ F '89
How to have an affair with your husband [excerpt from Lifemates]; ed. by Robert B. Kory. il *Ladies' Home Journal* 106:52+ Ap '89

BLOOMINGDALE'S
The big deal at Bloomingdale's: Marvin Traub makes a run at the top. M. Gross. il pors *New York* 22:56-60+ O 16 '89
Bloomie's may be on JMB's Christmas list. D. Greising. il *Business Week* p54 D 25 '89-Ja 1 '90
Campeau's big sell-off [proposed sale of Bloomingdale's] P. Chisholm. il por *Maclean's* 102:48 S 18 '89
The empire shrinks back [Campeau Corp. forced to sell] J. Castro. il *Time* 134:54 S 25 '89
The four-hour spa [E. Bruck visits Estée Lauder Spa at Bloomingdale's in Manhattan] L. Washer. il *Working Woman* 14:111-12 F '89
Look who wants to try Bloomie's on for size [Crown American] M. Schroeder. il por *Business Week* p30 O 2 '89
A retail marriage not made in heaven [Campeau Corp. forced to sell Bloomingdale's] il *U.S. News & World Report* 107:18 S 25 '89

BLOOMINGTON (MINN.)
Stores
See also
Mall of America (Bloomington, Minn.)

BLOOMSBURY GROUP
Doing the Charleston [country retreat] B. Taylor. il *Art News* 88:87-8 S '89
Painting Charleston [country retreat for D. Grant, V. Bell and the Bloomsbury artists] J. Johnston. bibl f il pors *Art in America* 77:152-63+ D '89
The scion of Bloomsbury in Sussex [Q. Bell] E. Lambert. il por *Architectural Digest* 46:72+ D '89

BLOSSOM END ROT OF TOMATOES *See* Tomatoes—Diseases and pests

BLOUIN, BONNIE
A skateboarder's guide to unstoked parents. *Harper's* 279:22+ Ag '89

BLOUIN, KAREN
Travel without trauma. il *Essence* 20:102+ D '89

BLOUNT, JOAN ACKERMANN- *See* Ackermann-Blount, Joan
BLOUNT, MEL
about
Blount, Shell and Wood welcomed into NFL Hall. il pors *Jet* 76:57 Ag 21 '89

BLOUNT, RICK
Reading, 'riting & running. il pors *Runner's World* 24:26-8 Ja '89

BLOUNT, ROY
It gripes me to say this. il *The New York Times Magazine* p40+ Ap 16 '89
No sense lending my body an ear. il *The Atlantic* 263:34-5 Ja '89
Tomorrow doesn't wait. il *The Atlantic* 264:50+ N '89
The way mama tells it. il *The Atlantic* 264:30+ Jl '89

BLOW, RICHARD
Blackstabbers. *The New Republic* 200:16-18 My 29 '89

BLOWERS (MACHINERY)
See also
Snow blowers, throwers, etc.
Power blowers [leaf blowers] M. Ferrara. il *Organic Gardening* 36:63-6 O '89
Power blowers: rev 'em up to clean the farm. D. Mowitz. il *Successful Farming* 87:24-5 F '89

BLOXHAM, JEREMY, AND GUBBINS, DAVID
The evolution of the earth's magnetic field. bibl il maps *Scientific American* 261:68-75 D '89

BLUE, CHARLES
Whaleback anticline. il *Earth Science* 42:19-21 Fall '89

BLUE, VIDA
about
Former hurler Vida Blue takes a bride on mound. il pors *Jet* 77:56-7 O 9 '89

BLUE ANGELS (FLIGHT SQUADRON)
Rhapsody in Blue. P. Scott. il *Flying* 116:98-100+ Jl '89

BLUE ARROW GROUP *See* Blue Arrow plc
BLUE ARROW PLC
Betting on the man who built Manpower. G. G. Marcial. il *Business Week* p106 D 4 '89
For Mitchell Fromstein, how sweet it is. R. A. Melcher and J. E. Ellis. il por *Business Week* p32 Ja 30 '89

BLUE CHIP MARKETING GROUP
In the Blue Chips. M. Barrier. il pors *Nation's Business* 77:54 F '89

BLUE CHIP STOCKS *See* Stocks
BLUE COLLAR WORKERS *See* Labor
BLUE CROSS & BLUE SHIELD ASSOCIATION
The covered city [catastrophic health insurance plan in Montgomery County, Md.] il *Esquire* 111:70 F '89

BLUE-GREEN ALGAE See Algae
BLUE JAYS See Jays
BLUE LAWS See Sunday—Laws and regulations
BLUE RIDGE MOUNTAINS
Head for the hills. H. Leifermann. il *New Choices for the Best Years* 29:58-64 Mr '89
BLUE RODEO (MUSICAL GROUP)
Blue Rodeo. M. Goldberg. il *Rolling Stone* p29 O 5 '89
Urban cowboys. N. Jennings. il *Maclean's* 102:58-9 Ap 17 '89
BLUE STEEL [film] See Motion picture reviews—Single works
BLUE WHALES See Whales
BLUEBEARD'S CASTLE [opera] See Bartók, Béla, 1881-1945
BLUEBERRIES
See also
Cooking—Fruit
BLUEBERRY INDUSTRY
Taming the wild blueberry [Maine] F. Graham. il map *Audubon* 91:48-69 Jl '89
BLUEBERRY PANCAKES See Pancakes, waffles, etc.
BLUEBERRY WINE See Wine
BLUEBIRDS
Bluebirds are funny. V. Lampron. il *Southern Living* 24:118 Ap '89
Bluebirds liked it hot [Montana] H. Power. maps *Natural History* p61 Ja '89
BLUEFISH
Bluefish—a great marine resource. A. Ristori. il *The Conservationist* 44:18-21 Jl/Ag '89
BLUEFISH FISHING
Bluefish—a great marine resource. A. Ristori. il *The Conservationist* 44:18-21 Jl/Ag '89
BLUEGILL FISHING
Besting big bluegills. J. Fallon. il *Field & Stream* 94:54+ Ag '89
BLUEPRINTS
Ask the sun to help you [blueprinted fabric] il *Sunset (Central West edition)* 183:122+ N '89
Blueprint your photos [Sun-Fun Squares and Quilt Squares kits] K. Geller-Shinn. il *Petersen's Photographic Magazine* 17:10 Mr '89
Blueprinting to create one-of-a-kind wrapping paper. il *Sunset (Central West edition)* 183:82 D '89
BLUES See Depression, Mental
BLUES MUSIC
See also
Compact discs—Blues music
Phonograph records—Blues music
Are white singers taking over blues and soul? il *Jet* 75:60-2+ Mr 6 '89
Are whites taking over rhythm & blues? D. Narine. il *Ebony* 44:90+ Jl '89
Frederick Brown: Marlborough [portraits of blues musicians] C. Lyon. il *Art News* 88:164-5 N '89
Living legends [photos] A. DeCurtis. il *Rolling Stone* p89-93+ S 21 '89
To Fred Brown, blues are more than a color on his palette [portraits of singers] D. Grogan. il pors *People Weekly* 32:96-8 O 2 '89
Willie Dixon. R. Wolmuth. il pors *People Weekly* 32:120-1+ S 11 '89
Willie Dixon and the wisdom of the blues. A. DeCurtis. il pors *Rolling Stone* p109+ Mr 23 '89
Archives
See also
Jazz-Blues-Gospel Hall of Fame Archive
Illinois
See also
Chicago (Ill.)—Music
BLUESTEIN, BARRY
about
Season to Taste Books: a comfy (and kitschy) culinary store. M. McQuade. il pors *Publishers Weekly* 236:45-6 S 8 '89
BLUESTEIN, HOWARD
about
Tornado tracker. M. B. Roman. il por *Discover* 10:50-6 Je '89
BLUESTONE, BARRY
about
America's great U-turn [interview] il *New Perspectives Quarterly* 6:35-7 Fall '89
BLUFORD, LUCILE
about
Kansas City Call publisher gets honorary degree at U. of Mo.; locked out in '39. il por *Jet* 76:16 My 22 '89
BLUHM, NORMAN, 1920-
about
Norman Bluhm at Washburn. H. Cotter. il *Art in America* 77:213-14 O '89
BLUM, DAVID
Hollywood Shakespeare [cover story] il *New York* 22:28-35 Je 19 '89
Profiles [Y.-Y. Ma] il *The New Yorker* 65:41-2+ My 1 '89
Spying on 'Spy' [cover story] il pors *New York* 22:32-41 Ap 17 '89
Where were you in '68? il *New York* 22:112-18+ F 27 '89

BLUM, MAYA SIEBER- See Sieber-Blum, Maya
BLUM, NANCEE S.
(jt. auth) See Walz, Thomas H., and Blum, Nancee S.
BLUM, RICHARD C.
about
"How do you put a lien on an elephant?". M. Berss. il por *Forbes* 144:114+ O 30 '89
BLUM (RICHARD C.) & ASSOCIATES See Richard C. Blum & Associates
BLUME, DELORYS
(jt. auth) See Blume, Robert A., and Blume, Delorys
BLUME, ROBERT A., AND BLUME, DELORYS
The crime of punishment. il pors *The Humanist* 49:12-15+ N/D '89
BLUMENFELD, YORICK
The Ideal Palace: Ferdinand Cheval's fantasy in the Rhône Valley. il *Architectural Digest* 46:108-13+ Ja '89
BLUMENTHAL, DALE
Artificial nail remover poses poisoning risk. il *FDA Consumer* 23:22-3 Je '89
Catching fish in all the wrong places. il *FDA Consumer* 23:22-3 F '89
Complex carbohydrates [cover story] il *FDA Consumer* 23:13-17 Ap '89
Do you know your cholesterol level? il *FDA Consumer* 23:24-7 Mr '89
The health-diet link: charting a rising awareness. il *FDA Consumer* 23:22-7 O '89
A new look at food labeling. il *FDA Consumer* 23:14-17 N '89
An unwanted souvenir: lead in ceramic ware. il *FDA Consumer* 23:18-21 D '89/Ja '90
BLUMENTHAL, DALE, AND HOLLAND, LULA
Orange juice: pure or adulterated. il *FDA Consumer* 23:32-3 D '89/Ja '90
BLUMENTHAL, EILEEN, 1948-
Cambodia's royal dance [cover story] il *Natural History* p55-63 Ap '89
BLUMENTHAL, MICHAEL
A courage born of broken promises. il *The New York Times Magazine* p14+ Jl 23 '89
BLUMENTHAL, TIM
Uphill racer. il pors *Women's Sports & Fitness* 11:24-7 S '89
BLUMENTHAL, W. MICHAEL
about
Michael Blumenthal. J. Weber, Jr. il por *Business Week* Special Issue:118 Ap 14 '89
This is hardly the turning point Unisys had in mind. J. Weber, Jr. il por *Business Week* p82+ Ag 28 '89
BLUNT, ANTHONY, 1907-1983
Bibliography
The upper class and the underworld. N. G. A. Annan, Baron. il *The New York Review of Books* 36:24-9 Ap 13 '89
BLURBS, BOOK See Books—Advertising
BLUSHER APPLICATION See Makeup
BLUTH, DON
about
All dogs go to heaven [film] Reviews
American Film il 15:17 D '89. R. Lloyd
Newsweek il 114:72-3 N 20 '89. B. Barol
People Weekly il 32:21 D 4 '89. R. Novak
Time il 134:91 N 20 '89. R. Corliss
The land before time [film] Reviews
Video il 13:80 N '89. M. Meyer
BLY, NELLIE, 1867-1922
about
Celebrity journalists. B. A. Weisberger. il *American Heritage* 40:20+ Mr '89
BLY, ROBERT
about
Connecting with the wild man inside all males [interview] K. Thompson. *Utne Reader* p58 N/D '89
Mano a mano. M. Ventura. il *American Health* 8:64-5 Ja/F '89
The wild man [interview] A. Meyer. *American Health* 8:67-8 Ja/F '89
BLYSKAL, JEFF
You can fight city hall. il *Reader's Digest* 134:103-7 Ja '89
(jt. auth) See Hodge, Marie, and Blyskal, Jeff
BLYSKAL, JEFF, AND HODGE, MARIE
Weekend getaways. il *New York* 22:148-9 My 1 '89
Where to complain. il *New York* 22:70-3 My 1 '89
Your airline survival guide [cover story] il *New York* 22:30-41 Ag 28 '89
BLYSKAL, MARIE HODGE See Hodge, Marie
BLYTH, JEFF
about
Cheetah [film] Reviews
People Weekly il 32:13 S 4 '89. R. Novak
BLYTH, MYRNA
Editor's journal. See issues of Ladies' Home Journal
BLYTH, SAM
about
One alternative: buy the train. D. Jenish. *Maclean's* 102:22 Ag 21 '89

BLYTH SUMMER FESTIVAL (ONT.) *See* Drama festivals—Ontario
BLYTHEVILLE (ARK.)
Economic conditions
Blytheville's bounty [Japanese-U.S. joint steel mill] il *Time* 133:52 Je 5 '89
BMI *See* Book Manufacturers' Institute
BMI JAZZ COMPOSERS WORKSHOP
BMI Jazz Composers Workshop. S. Stein. il *Down Beat* 56:13 Ap '89
BML ASSOCIATES INC.
M&M Products purchased by Boston minority firm. il *Jet* 76:16-17 Jl 17 '89
Negotiations end between M&M Products and BML. il *Jet* 76:36 Ag 14 '89
With M&M buy, B.M.L. moves into hair-care business. N. McCall. il *Black Enterprise* 20:17 Ag '89
BMW *See* Bayerische Motoren Werke AG
BMW (AUTOMOBILE) *See* Automobiles, Foreign
BOADI, E. GYIMAH- *See* Gyimah-Boadi, E.
BOAM, JEFFREY
about
Jeffrey Boam's two scripts make him a Lethal box office weapon after a long Crusade for success. M. H. J. Farrell. il pors *People Weekly* 32:47-8 S 4 '89
BOAR HUNTING *See* Wild boar hunting
BOARD GAMES *See* Games
BOARD OF REGENTS OF THE UNIVERSITY OF THE STATE OF NEW YORK *See* University of the State of New York. Board of Regents
BOARDING SCHOOLS *See* Private schools
BOARDMAN, EUNICE
A symposium on skills, knowledge, and creativity in the curriculum. *Design for Arts in Education* 90:23-5 My/Je '89
BOARDMAN, PAULINE
about
Relative affinity. il pors *Harper's Bazaar* 122:160-3 O '89
BOARDMAN, SAMANTHA
about
Relative affinity. il pors *Harper's Bazaar* 122:160-3 O '89
BOARDMAN, SERENA
about
Relative affinity. il pors *Harper's Bazaar* 122:160-3 O '89
BOARDS, CUTTING *See* Cutting boards
BOARDS OF DIRECTORS *See* Corporations—Directors
BOARDS OF EDUCATION *See* School boards
BOARDSAILING
In search of nuclear winds [windsurfing in Columbia River Gorge] M. Beauchamp. il *Forbes* 144:214-15 S 18 '89
Where there's a wind, there's a way. K. Robberson. il *Women's Sports & Fitness* 11:36-7 Je '89
Windsurfing for grownups. E. Sharp. il *Motor Boating & Sailing* 163:64-7+ My '89
BOARDWALK AND BASEBALL (AMUSEMENT PARK)
Batter up at the Boardwalk. il *Southern Living* 24:47-8 Mr '89
BOARDWALKS
Down by the boardwalk. B. Barol. il *Newsweek* 114:58-60 Ag 14 '89
Last of the West's beach boardwalks [Santa Cruz] il *Sunset (Central West edition)* 183:136 Ag '89
BOARS, WILD *See* Wild boars
BOASTFULNESS
Too big for the country. K. McCafferty. il *Field & Stream* 94:50-1+ Jl '89
BOAT ACCESSORIES *See* Boats and boating—Equipment
BOAT ALARMS *See* Boats and boating—Alarms
BOAT BUILDING *See* Boatbuilding
BOAT BUYING *See* Boats and boating—Purchasing
BOAT CLUBS
See also
Yacht clubs
BOAT DECORATION
Aboard the Impromptu [yacht decorated by S. Chase] I. Borger. il *Architectural Digest* 46:144-9 Ag '89
Seaworthy style [Valentino's yacht decorated by Peter Marino] G. Y. Dryansky. il pors *House & Garden* 161:122-5 Ag '89
Thoroughly modern Hatteras [54] L. Rudeen. il *Motor Boating & Sailing* 163:72-5+ Ja '89
Viking's tour de force [72-foot flagship] S. Stapleton. il *Motor Boating & Sailing* 163:62-7+ Mr '89
BOAT DOCKS *See* Docks, wharves, etc.
BOAT ENGINES *See* Marine engines; Motor boat engines
BOAT HANDLING *See* Boats and boating—Handling
BOAT LIVING
See also
Houseboats
Citizens of the world [Couvreux family] G. Jaynes. il *Life* 12:15 O '89
BOAT LOANS
Affordable dreams. S. Bernardo. il *Motor Boating & Sailing* 163:82-3+ Ja '89
Easy money. S. Bernardo. il *Motor Boating & Sailing* 163:90-3+ F '89

BOAT MODELS *See* Ship and boat models
BOAT OWNERSHIP
See also
Boats and boating—Purchasing
Gone with the wind [sailboat owners] J. A. Fishman. il *Motor Boating & Sailing* 163:94-7+ F '89
On board with Mario Andretti. L. Rudeen. il pors *Motor Boating & Sailing* 163:66-9+ Ja '89
Anecdotes, facetiae, satire, etc.
Wet behind the ears. P. F. McManus. il *Outdoor Life* 183:128+ F '89
BOAT PAINT, ANTIFOULING *See* Paint, Protective
BOAT PEOPLE (REFUGEES) *See* Refugees, Vietnamese
BOAT PROPELLERS *See* Boats and boating—Propellers
BOAT RACING
See also
Boat rallies
Canoe racing
Hydroplane racing
Motor boat racing
Rowing
Sailboat racing
Yacht racing
Calendar. See issues of Motor Boating & Sailing beginning October 1988
BOAT RALLIES
Newport jet set [rally from Narragansett Bay to Nantucket] P. Whittell. il *Motor Boating & Sailing* 164:46-7 S '89
BOAT REPAIRING *See* Boats and boating—Maintenance and repair
BOAT SHOWS *See* Boats and boating—Exhibitions
BOAT SIGNALS *See* Signals and signaling
BOAT SPEED RECORDS
Landed Gentry [Eagle sets transatlantic record] D. Wallace. il por *Motor Boating & Sailing* 164:54-7+ O '89
Shipwrecked [disastrous effort to set trans-Atlantic speed record] D. Pike. il *Motor Boating & Sailing* 164:54-7+ Jl '89
Thursday's child triumphs [W. Luhrs breaks record from New York to San Francisco via Cape Horn] L. Rudeen. il por map *Motor Boating & Sailing* 163:66-71+ Ap '89
Winners [G. Kolesnikovs breaks record from New York to San Francisco via Cape Horn] L. Rudeen. il por *Motor Boating & Sailing* 164:20 Ag '89
BOAT TOWING *See* Boats and boating—Towing; Fishing boats—Towing
BOAT TRADE *See* Boating industry
BOAT TRAILERS *See* Automobile boat trailers
BOATBUILDING
See also
Boats and boating—Materials
Broward Marine, Inc.
Genmar Industries Inc.
Hulls (Naval architecture)
Keels
Murray Chris-Craft Sportdecks Inc.
O'Day Corporation
Shannon Boat Company
The happy clam [folding cartop boat] L. D. Warren. il *The Mother Earth News* 116:62-5 Mr/Ap '89
History
The roaring twenties [excerpt from Speedboat] D. W. Fostle. il *Motor Boating & Sailing* 163:78-81+ Ja '89
France
See also
Bénéteau (Firm)
BOATING ETIQUETTE *See* Etiquette
BOATING INDUSTRY
See also
Brunswick Corp.
Acquisitions and mergers
Chris-Craft comes back [acquired by OMC] P. A. Janssen. il *Motor Boating & Sailing* 163:15+ Ap '89
Did Irv Jacobs sandbag Outboard Marine? [auction for assets of Murray Chris-Craft] G. DeGeorge. *Business Week* p38+ F 20 '89
Has Brunswick gone overboard in powerboats? J. F. Siler. il *Business Week* p27 Ag 7 '89
BOATS, TOY *See* Toys
BOATS, USED
Selling
Trade-in tips. L. Rudeen. il *Motor Boating & Sailing* 164:34+ Ag '89
BOATS AND BOATING
See also
Boat living
Boat speed records
Boatbuilding
Boating industry
Canoes and canoeing
Catamarans
Children and boating
Condominiums (Boat docking)
Cruisers (Pleasure boats)
Cruising
Ferries
Fishing boats
Gondolas

BOATS AND BOATING—See also—*cont.*
>   Houseboats
>   Ice boats and ice boating
>   Jet boats
>   Kayaks and kayaking
>   Marinas
>   Motor boats
>   Navigation
>   River trips
>   Running rapids
>   Sailboats
>   Sailing
>   Seamanship
>   Sightseeing boats
>   Trimarans
>   Tugboats
>   Yachts and yachting

1989 new boat directory. J. Wooldridge. il *Motor Boating & Sailing* 163:99-138 Ja '89
Better blow-ups [inflatable boats] B. McKeown. il *Outdoor Life* 183:28+ Mr '89
Boating. B. McKeown. See issues of Outdoor Life beginning May 1983
Boating. B. Stearns. See issues of Field & Stream
Boating '89 [special section] il *Popular Mechanics* 166:83-4+ F '89
Cruising after dark. H. Halsted. il *Motor Boating & Sailing* 163:42+ Ap '89
The happy clam [folding cartop boat] L. D. Warren. il *The Mother Earth News* 116:62-5 Mr/Ap '89
New boats. See issues of Motor Boating & Sailing
The new wave in family boating. M. Morris. il *Home Mechanix* 86:69-72+ Mr '89
Scenes. See issues of Motor Boating & Sailing
Time machines [replicas of classic boats] J. Clemans. il *Motor Boating & Sailing* 164:38-43+ Ag '89
Trends '90 [special section] il *Motor Boating & Sailing* 164:54-65 S '89
Up front. See issues of Motor Boating & Sailing

Accidents
Floating free [running aground] B. McKeown. il *Outdoor Life* 184:16-17 Jl '89
Killer encounters [attacked by killer whales] M. Benson. il *Motor Boating & Sailing* 164:50-1+ N '89
Making up for bus left unpaid, Griffin O'Neal goes to jail. il por *People Weekly* 31:117 F 6 '89
Man overboard maneuvers. S. Stapleton. il *Motor Boating & Sailing* 163:38+ Ap '89

Alarms
Early warning systems [engine room alarms] E. Dennis. il *Motor Boating & Sailing* 163:111-12 Ap '89

Anchoring
See Anchorage

Audio systems
Sailing, sailing . . . [Pioneer's Nautica line] il *High Fidelity (New York, N.Y.)* 39:12 My '89

Batteries
See Storage batteries

Design
Design board. See issues of Motor Boating & Sailing

Electric equipment
A.C. power without a generator. B. Gladstone. il *Motor Boating & Sailing* 163:83-5 Je '89

Electric generators
The care and feeding of gen/sets [diesels] E. Dennis. il *Motor Boating & Sailing* 164:95-6 N '89
Quiet power. C. Husick. *Motor Boating & Sailing* 164:111-12 N '89

Electronic equipment
See also
>   Loran
>   Radiotelephone on ships, boats, etc.
>   Sonar

Electronics Q&A. G. West. See issues of Motor Boating & Sailing
Electrons afloat. B. McKeown. il *Outdoor Life* 183:24+ F '89
New electronics. See issues of Motor Boating & Sailing
Smart boats. M. Benson. il *Motor Boating & Sailing* 163:82-6+ Ap '89

Engines
See Marine engines; Motor boat engines

Equipment
See also
>   Anchors

Boatkeeper's guide to docking aids. B. Gladstone. il *Motor Boating & Sailing* 163:83-6 My '89
Chandlery. See issues of Motor Boating & Sailing
Deck the hulls. B. Gladstone and others. il *Motor Boating & Sailing* 164:65-72 D '89
Gadgets to go. B. McKeown. il *Outdoor Life* 184:33-4 S '89
Gilt-edged gifts. J. Chwasky. il *Motor Boating & Sailing* 164:20-3 N '89
Great gear. J. Chwasky. il *Motor Boating & Sailing* 164:28-9 D '89
Great gear. J. Wooldridge. il *Popular Mechanics* 166:104-6+ F '89

High-tech gear. D. Fales. il *Motor Boating & Sailing* 163:58-61 Mr '89
Three winter projects to improve your boat [adding a TV antenna, improving plumbing, and building a chart table] il *Motor Boating & Sailing* 163:117-20 F '89
What's new. See issues of Outdoor Life
The whole sea catalog. D. Davis. il *Motor Boating & Sailing* 163:101-8 F '89

Exhibitions
Calendar. See issues of Motor Boating & Sailing beginning October 1988
New York National Boat Show directory '89 [cover story; special section] il *Motor Boating & Sailing* 163:52+ Ja '89
Showboating in Biscayne Bay [Miami International Boat Show] J. Skorupa. il *Popular Mechanics* 166:32 Jl '89
Suspending reality. P. A. Janssen. il *Motor Boating & Sailing* 163:17 Mr '89
Welcome to the Show [Miami Boat Show; special section] il *Motor Boating & Sailing* 163:89-97+ F '89

Generators
See Boats and boating—Electric generators

Handling
Boat handling. H. Halsted. See issues of Motor Boating & Sailing
Boatkeeper's guide to docking aids. B. Gladstone. il *Motor Boating & Sailing* 163:83-6 My '89
Docking in a new marina. S. Stapleton. il *Motor Boating & Sailing* 164:30-1 Ag '89
Running in reverse. S. Stapleton. il *Motor Boating & Sailing* 163:38+ Mr '89

History
Now: the nineties [boating] P. A. Janssen. il *Motor Boating & Sailing* 164:15 D '89

Hulls
See Hulls (Naval architecture)

Ice hazards
Buying and installing your own de-icer [storing boats in the water] B. Gladstone. il *Motor Boating & Sailing* 164:87 O '89

Interior decoration
See Boat decoration

Keels
See Keels

Launching
Easy riders. S. Stapleton. il *Motor Boating & Sailing* 164:60-4+ O '89

Laws and regulations
Notices to boatmen. E. S. Maloney. See issues of Motor Boating & Sailing

Leasing and renting
Boatkeeper's guide to trouble-free chartering. B. Gladstone. il *Motor Boating & Sailing* 164:91-4 Ag '89

Lubrication and lubricants
Engine blood test. T. P. Banse. il *Motor Boating & Sailing* 164:72 S '89
Oil burners: causes & cures. T. P. Banse. il *Motor Boating & Sailing* 163:110 Ap '89

Maintenance and repair
Boatkeeper. B. Gladstone. See issues of Motor Boating & Sailing
Boatyard. B. Gladstone. See issues of Motor Boating & Sailing
Get set—go. B. McKeown. il *Outdoor Life* 183:74+ Ap '89
Spring commissioning checklist. B. Gladstone and others. *Motor Boating & Sailing* 163:81-4 Mr '89

Materials
Classic wooden boats [excerpt from Wood, water and light] B. Mendlowitz. il *Oceans* 22:46-53 Mr/Ap '89
Fiberglassing over wood. B. Gladstone. il *Motor Boating & Sailing* 164:89-91 N '89
Repairing fiberglass keels. L. W. Taylor. il *Motor Boating & Sailing* 163:87 Je '89

Mooring
See Anchorage

Options
See Boats and boating—Equipment

Painting
The bottom line on bottom paints [marine antifouling paints] B. Gladstone. il *Motor Boating & Sailing* 163:105-8 Ap '89

Photographs and photography
Classic wooden boats [excerpt from Wood, water and light] B. Mendlowitz. il *Oceans* 22:46-53 Mr/Ap '89

Prices
Ten new boats for under $587.86 a month. P. Whittell. il *Motor Boating & Sailing* 163:74-9 Mr '89

Propellers
Prop blades do the twist [Autoprop] D. Scott. il *Popular Science* 234:49 My '89
Twin wheels keep on turning [Land & Sea Torque-Shift and Volvo Penta Duoprop] J. Skorupa. il *Popular Mechanics* 166:38+ S '89

Psychological aspects
Follow your bliss. P. A. Janssen. il *Motor Boating & Sailing* 163:23 F '89

BOATS AND BOATING—Psychological aspects—*cont.*
Anecdotes, facetiae, satire, etc.
Nautical dementia. P. F. McManus. il *Outdoor Life* 183:162-3+ Ap '89

Purchasing
Picking the perfect boat. B. McKeown. il *Outdoor Life* 184:44+ N '89

Radio equipment
See also
Cellular radio on ships, boats, etc.
Radiotelephone on ships, boats, etc.
Safety devices and measures
See also
Life preservers
Lighthouses
Rule of the road at sea
Signals and signaling
Boating safety checklist. il *Outdoor Life* 183:41 Ja '89
The security of float plans. H. Halstead. il *Motor Boating & Sailing* 163:46 My '89
Special skill. B. McKeown. il *Outdoor Life* 183:26+ Je '89
What to grab when your boat sinks. J. A. Fishman. il *Motor Boating & Sailing* 164:51+ N '89
Winners [J. Muetzel's involvement in boating safety education] L. Rudeen. il por *Motor Boating & Sailing* 163:24 Ap '89

Security measures
See also
Boats and boating—Alarms
Signals and signaling
See Signals and signaling
Steering gear
Straight talk on power steering. T. P. Banse. il *Motor Boating & Sailing* 163:89-90 My '89
Storage
Storing your boat in the water. B. Gladstone. il *Motor Boating & Sailing* 164:85-6+ O '89
Storm hazards
Battening for a blow [preparations by boat owners in Texas for Hurricane Gilbert] F. Sargeant. il *Motor Boating & Sailing* 164:32+ S '89
Heading to weather. S. Stapleton. il *Motor Boating & Sailing* 164:32 N '89
Hell and high water: forty-three hours from Cancun to Key West in hurricane-whipped seas. E. Sharp. *Motor Boating & Sailing* 164:107-11 S '89
Running in angry seas. S. Stapleton. il *Motor Boating & Sailing* 164:36 O '89
Surviving Hurricane Hugo. B. Prentiss. il *Motor Boating & Sailing* 164:34+ D '89
Testing
Boat Show '89. il *Motor Boating & Sailing* 163:84+ Ja '89
Showboating in Biscayne Bay [Miami International Boat Show] J. Skorupa. il *Popular Mechanics* 166:32 Jl '89
When less is more [dinghies] J. Chwasky. il *Motor Boating & Sailing* 164:48-9 Ag '89
Towing
Abandon ship! A galleon runs aground in a highway wreck [J. Fiondella's replica of Spanish galleon overturns on road] il por *People Weekly* 32:206 D 4 '89
Tender towing. S. Stapleton. il *Motor Boating & Sailing* 164:24 S '89
Transportation
See also
Automobile boat trailers
Californian . . . here I come [three-day delivery of a Carver 48 from Sarasota to Miami] D. Fales. il *Motor Boating & Sailing* 163:58-61+ Ap '89
A custom boat cart. P. Butler and M. Butler. il *Outdoor Life* 183:46+ Mr '89
Water supply
On tap: cleaner, better tasting water. B. Gladstone. il *Motor Boating & Sailing* 164:73-6 Jl '89
Three winter projects to improve your boat [adding a TV antenna, improving plumbing, and building a chart table] il *Motor Boating & Sailing* 163:117-20 F '89
BOATS IN ART
Exhibitions
Now voyagers [The boat show: fantastic vessels, fictional voyages at the Renwick Gallery] L. Hammel. il *American Craft* 49:34-41 Ag/S '89
Vessels borne on fantasy [The boat show: fantastic vessels, fictional voyages at the Renwick Gallery] K. M. Burke. il *Smithsonian* 20:125 Jl '89
BOATS IN MOTION PICTURES
James Bond's sizzling new boats [filming Licence to kill] P. Whittell. il *Motor Boating & Sailing* 163:62-5+ Ap '89
BOB BONDURANT SCHOOL OF HIGH PERFORMANCE DRIVING *See* Automobile driving—Study and teaching
BOB LARSON MINISTRIES
Questions raised about Bob Larson campaign [evangelical radio programs] L. Cryderman. il *Christianity Today* 33:47-8 Mr 3 '89
BOB MARSHALL WILDERNESS (MONT.)
Big Sky hike. J. Zumbo. il *Outdoor Life* 183:88-90+ Mr '89
BOBBY GOULD IN HELL [drama] *See* Mamet, David

BOBBY KEBOBBY (NEW YORK, N.Y.: RESTAURANT) *See* New York (N.Y.)—Restaurants, nightclubs, bars, etc.
BOBCATS
The bobcat. T. Williams. il *Country Journal* 16:86-90 Mr/Ap '89
Anecdotes, facetiae, satire, etc.
A good deed undoes. P. F. McManus. il *Outdoor Life* 183:144+ My '89
BOBWHITE SHOOTING *See* Quail shooting
BOCHCO, STEVEN
about
Prime-time renegade. N. Koch. il pors *Channels (New York, N.Y.: 1986)* 9:56-60 N '89
BOCK, PAUL, 1922-
Religious responses to AIDS. il *USA Today (Periodical)* 117:66-7 My '89
BODE, KEN
After Hart, Tower, Wright . . . the backlash is starting against those trials by media. il *TV Guide* 37:21-3 O 7-13 '89
BODEANS (MUSICAL GROUP)
The BoDeans' blue-collar cool-out [Milwaukee] C. Mundy. il *Rolling Stone* p52 Jl 13-27 '89
The BoDeans: songs from Home. R. Givens. il *Stereo Review* 54:124+ N '89
BODETT, TOM
Everything that counts [story] il *Redbook* 174:74+ N '89
A sudden fortune [story] il *Redbook* 174:58+ N '89
about
"We'll leave the light on for ya". D. Raffel. il por *Redbook* 174:60 N '89
BODLEY HEAD LTD.
Loss of Bodley Head fuels U.K. disquiet over conglomeration. V. Menkes. *Publishers Weekly* 236:8 Jl 7 '89
BODT, BRIAN SCHOFIELD- *See* Schofield-Bodt, Brian
BODY, HUMAN *See* Human body
BODY AND MIND *See* Mind and body
BODY AND SOUL (SONG)
A classic turns 50 [C. Hawkins' recording] K. Whitehead. il por *Down Beat* 56:60-1 N '89
BODY ART
Exhibitions
Rudolf Schwarzkogler at Burnett Miller. F. Colpitt. il *Art in America* 77:180-1 D '89
BODY FAT *See* Fat
BODY FLUIDS
See also
Amniotic fluid
Blood
Cerebrospinal fluid
Perspiration
Urine
Water in the body
BODY HEAT *See* Temperature, Animal and human
BODY IMAGE
Body hate. D. Heyn. il *Ms.* 18:34+ Jl/Ag '89
Body image, body love [views of R. Freedman] C. Valentino. il *American Health* 8:60-2 Je '89
Body love. K. McCoy. il *Seventeen* 48:48+ D '89
Body zones. S. Lord. il *Vogue* 179:362-7 My '89
Good-looking: the new definition: be fit, adopt a good attitude, and eat right [teenagers] il *Current Health 2* 16:28-9 S '89
Helping your kids to eat right and have good body images. R. Israeloff. il *Working Woman* 14:219-22 S '89
How good should you look? C. Avery. pors *Ladies' Home Journal* 106:119-21+ Je '89
Life at large [excerpt from Bodylove] R. J. Freedman. il *Health (New York, N.Y.)* 21:40+ Ap '89
The lust for thin. J. Schneller. il *Mademoiselle* 95:222-3+ Mr '89
Obsessed by thighs? Hair? Breasts? Fat? il *Glamour* 87:210-15 N '89
Thin thighs, heavy heart. D. Kent. il *Mademoiselle* 95:166+ S '89
Who, him? Worry about his body? D. Seeley. il *Mademoiselle* 95:258-9+ Ap '89
Why are girls obsessed with their weight? L. Morgan. il *Seventeen* 48:118-19+ N '89
BODY LANGUAGE *See* Communication, Nonverbal
BODY ODORS *See* Odors
BODY PARTS, ARTIFICIAL *See* Prosthesis
BODY RHYTHMS *See* Biological rhythms
BODY SHOP INTERNATIONAL PLC
The Body Shop. M. Kelly. por *Utne Reader* p76 Ja/F '89
The naked truth [A. Roddick's shops] il pors *Seventeen* 48:138-43 O '89
BODY SIZE
Cost accounting for lizards [size differences among lizards of the Galapagos Islands; research by Howard L. Snell] J. A. Miller. il *BioScience* 39:674-5 N '89
Hidden complexities in the risks of extinction [reintroducing birds to Guam; work of Stuart Pimm] R. Lewin. *Science* 243:1294 Mr 10 '89
Mammalian terrestrial locomotion and size. A. A. Biewener. bibl f il *BioScience* 39:776-83 D '89

BODY SIZE—*cont.*
Scaling body support in mammals: limb posture and muscle mechanics. A. A. Biewener. bibl f il *Science* 245:45-8 Jl 7 '89
BODY TEMPERATURE *See* Temperature, Animal and human
BODY TYPES, HUMAN *See* Somatotypes
BODY WEIGHT *See* Weight (Physiology)
BODYBUILDING
The ballerinas and the bodybuilders: body and soul [encounter between Soviet dancers and bodybuilders in Philadelphia] T. Tobias. il *Dance Magazine* 63:46 Jl '89

Competitions
Carla Dunlap: more than muscle. M. Greenwood-Robinson. il por *Women's Sports & Fitness* 11:62 Je '89
Grammy award [54 year old D. D. Allen wins Ms. Los Angeles '88 title] C. O'Connor. il por *Women's Sports & Fitness* 11:58 Je '89

Psychological aspects
Steroids built Mike Keys up; then they tore him down [teen's suicide linked to use of anabolic steroids] M. Brower. il pors *People Weekly* 31:107-8 Mr 20 '89
BODYGUARDS
Body double. il *Vogue* 179:535 Mr '89
Stand by me: inside the world of rock & roll bodyguards. J. Ressner. il *Rolling Stone* p56-60+ Ap 6 '89
BODYWORK (BIOMECHANICS)
When classes are not enough: body therapies [dancers] M. Myers and M. Horosko. il *Dance Magazine* 63:47-51 Jl '89
BOE, MARILYN J.
Sorting Mother's things [poem] *The Christian Century* 106:78 Ja 25 '89
Wild swans at Christmas [poem] *The Christian Century* 106:1200 D 20-27 '89
BOEHLER, KAREN
Lifeboat to safer shores. il *Ad Astra* 1:8-12 Mr '89
Paper trails to contrails. il *Ad Astra* 1:39-41 Je '89
BOEHLERT, BART
Collecting vintage dresses with contemporary flair. il pors *Architectural Digest* 46:60+ S '89
BOEHM, HELEN
Toys and games to learn by. il *Psychology Today* 23:62-4 S '89
BOEHM, PHILLIP
(tr) See Hein, Christoph. East Berlin diary
BOEING CO.
Accidents, delays in 747-400 program prompt Boeing to review operations. il *Aviation Week & Space Technology* 129:21-2 Mr 6 '89
Airframe makers exploit boom by adding production capacity. il *Aviation Week & Space Technology* 130:95+ My 29 '89
Airlines cite delays of up to three months in Boeing 747-400 deliveries. R. G. O'Lone. il *Aviation Week & Space Technology* 130:61 F 6 '89
Airport cramp [7x7 or 767-X] H. Banks. il *Forbes* 144:85 Jl 24 '89
All Nippon buys 20 747-400s, a record order. C. Fotos. il *Aviation Week & Space Technology* 130:69-70 F 27 '89
A beleaguered Boeing may be on Lockheed's tail. G. G. Marcial. il *Business Week* p130 Mr 13 '89
The best and worst of times at Boeing. il *U.S. News & World Report* 106:14-15 Mr 6 '89
Boeing 720B testbed begins new phase of avionic evaluations. P. J. Klass. il *Aviation Week & Space Technology* 131:50-1 N 6 '89
Boeing 737-500 rolled out; first flight set for June 30. il *Aviation Week & Space Technology* 130:163 Je 19 '89
Boeing: a backlog strains its assembly line. M. Shao. il *Business Week* p35-6 My 8 '89
Boeing achieves major advance in space solar cell efficiency. B. W. Henderson. il *Aviation Week & Space Technology* 131:61+ O 23 '89
Boeing Aerospace wins SDI contract for RF-driven free electron laser. P. A. Gilmartin. il *Aviation Week & Space Technology* 131:21 O 23 '89
Boeing agrees to 747-400 design changes sought by European aviation authorities. *Aviation Week & Space Technology* 131:58 N 6 '89
Boeing borrows skilled workers from Lockheed for 747-400 program. R. G. O'Lone. il *Aviation Week & Space Technology* 130:66 Mr 13 '89
Boeing expanding facilities for standard-body transports. *Aviation Week & Space Technology* 130:93 Mr 27 '89
Boeing foresees problems despite record orders. *Aviation Week & Space Technology* 131:26 Jl 31 '89
Boeing machinists strike hits economy, airline fleet plans. R. G. O'Lone. il *Aviation Week & Space Technology* 131:126-7 N 20 '89
Boeing modifies 720B to serve as advanced avionics testbed. B. W. Henderson. il *Aviation Week & Space Technology* 130:83-5+ Mr 27 '89
Boeing: new dents in a sterling record [flaws in fire extinguisher systems] *Newsweek* 113:51 F 13 '89
Boeing pleads guilty to trafficking in classified documents, pays $5-million fine. *Aviation Week & Space Technology* 131:38 N 20 '89

Boeing records $1.4-billion sales increase in 1988. *Aviation Week & Space Technology* 130:61 F 6 '89
Boeing seeks decision on 767 version to challenge MD-11 A340. R. G. O'Lone. il *Aviation Week & Space Technology* 130:21 F 13 '89
Boeing selects design for 777 candidate. R. G. O'Lone and J. T. McKenna. il *Aviation Week & Space Technology* 131:106-7 D 18-25 '89
Boeing sets new mark with orders totaling $31.2 billion. *Aviation Week & Space Technology* 130:27 My 29 '89
The Boeing strike: both sides are flying. A. Bernstein and others. il *Business Week* p44 N 6 '89
Boeing takes steps to prevent fire extinguisher malfunctions. *Aviation Week & Space Technology* 130:71 F 27 '89
Boeing told to solve Peace Shield problems [system for Saudi Arabia] D. Hughes. *Aviation Week & Space Technology* 131:114 D 18-25 '89
Boeing upgrades high-speed civil transport study effort. R. G. O'Lone. il *Aviation Week & Space Technology* 130:108 My 22 '89
Boeing will produce two new 747-400 versions. R. G. O'Lone. il *Aviation Week & Space Technology* 131:102-3 O 2 '89
Boeing's happy, harrowing times [cover story] A. Ramirez. il *Fortune* 120:40-4+ Jl 17 '89
Britain accepting fraction of Boeing's offset claims [purchase of E-3A Airborne Warning and Control System aircraft] D. A. Brown. il *Aviation Week & Space Technology* 131:76-7 Jl 17 '89
British Airways starts transatlantic service with new Boeing 747-400s. C. A. Shifrin. il *Aviation Week & Space Technology* 131:62-3+ Ag 14 '89
Commercial airframe makers take conservative approach. R. G. O'Lone. il *Aviation Week & Space Technology* 130:197-9 Mr 20 '89
Delays force Boeing to revise 747-400 delivery schedules. R. G. O'Lone. *Aviation Week & Space Technology* 130:73 Ja 30 '89
E-6A Tacamo tail damage prompts delivery delay [submarine communications aircraft] M. A. Dornheim. il *Aviation Week & Space Technology* 130:28-9 Ap 17 '89
FAA probes Boeing's reporting of faulty wiring in 757 extinguisher systems. C. Fotos. *Aviation Week & Space Technology* 130:66 Ja 23 '89
Frank Shrontz. M. Shao. il por *Business Week* Special Issue:129 Ap 14 '89
GE-powered 747-400 gets initial approval in Europe after Boeing accepts design changes. *Aviation Week & Space Technology* 130:105 My 22 '89
Grounding a high-flying giant [machinists strike] L. Griggs. il *Time* 134:57 O 16 '89
Huge aircraft order signals revitalization of United. il *Aviation Week & Space Technology* 130:34-5+ My 1 '89
MD90, 737 transport orders set stage for Delta's increased share of U.S. market. il *Aviation Week & Space Technology* 131:35+ N 20 '89
No progress reported in second week of strike. R. G. O'Lone. il *Aviation Week & Space Technology* 131:18-19 O 16 '89
Strike at Boeing cripples production of transports. R. G. O'Lone. *Aviation Week & Space Technology* 131:136-7 O 9 '89
Striking machinists return to work at Boeing; restoring full production may take six weeks. R. G. O'Lone. *Aviation Week & Space Technology* 131:85 N 27 '89
Trying times at Boeing. M. Shao. il *Business Week* p34-6 Mr 13 '89
Turbulent fortunes. J. Daly. il *Maclean's* 102:30-1 Mr 13 '89
U.S. permits Boeing to transfer four 757s to Chinese airlines. *Aviation Week & Space Technology* 131:96 Jl 17 '89
West Germany's LTU expands fleet with Boeing 767-300ERs. B. A. Smith. il *Aviation Week & Space Technology* 130:92-3 Mr 27 '89
Why Boeing's hard line didn't pay off [strike ends] A. Bernstein. il *Business Week* p33 D 4 '89
BOEING CO. BOEING VERTOL COMPANY (DIV.)
Bell, Boeing push V-22 flight test program [Osprey tilt-rotor aircraft; cover story] D. A. Brown. il *Aviation Week & Space Technology* 131:38-40 O 16 '89
Bell-Boeing V-22 tilt-rotor prototype makes first flight. C. A. Shifrin. il *Aviation Week & Space Technology* 130:20-1 Mr 27 '89
Boeing and Sikorsky near completion of U.S. Army special operations aircraft. S. W. Kandebo. il *Aviation Week & Space Technology* 131:53+ N 27 '89
Boeing rolls out MH-47E Special Operations helicopter. il *Aviation Week & Space Technology* 131:37 D 11 '89
European firms agree to join Bell-Boeing in marketing V-22 [tilt-rotor aircraft] *Aviation Week & Space Technology* 130:37 Je 19 '89
V-22 prepared for further expansion of flight envelope [Osprey tilt-rotor prototype; cover story] C. A. Shifrin. il *Aviation Week & Space Technology* 130:34-6+ Ap 10 '89
BOEING VERTOL COMPANY (DIV.) *See* Boeing Co. Boeing Vertol Company (Div.)
BOEKE, DUFFY
"A judge split my children—body and soul"; ed. by John Duggleby. il por *Redbook* 173:26+ S '89

BOELDT, JANET WHEELER
To-do or not to-do? il *New Choices for the Best Years* 29:88 Ag '89

BOESAK, ALLAN AUBREY, 1946-
about
Polling the Israelites: Boesak on sanctions. A. Welsh-Huggins. *The Christian Century* 106:924-5 O 18 '89

BOESKY, IVAN F.
about
The phantom of Wall Street: how Ivan Boesky's bitter legacy haunts Mike Milken and his former firm. C. Byron. il pors *New York* 22:52-6 D 4 '89
The transformation of Ivan Boesky. A. Miller. il pors *Newsweek* 114:60 N 27 '89

BOFF, CLODOVIS
about
Left-wing miracles. D. Lee. *National Review* 41:34 S 29 '89

BOFF, LEONARDO
about
Of many things. G. W. Hunt. *America* 160:98 F 11 '89

BOFORS NOBEL AB
Gandhi's Watergate? [arms sale scandal] *Newsweek* 114:42 O 23 '89

BOG PEOPLE
In search of Denmark's bog people [cycling trip] G. Thomson. il map *Bicycling* 30:68-72+ Ag '89

BOGART, ANNE
Beauty's power elite. il *Harper's Bazaar* 122:118-19+ Ja '89
Regal air. il pors *Harper's Bazaar* 122:378-9 S '89
Secrets of the sleek chic. il *Harper's Bazaar* 122:36+ Ap '89
Soirées on the Seine. il pors *Harper's Bazaar* 122:199+ D '89
Western Europe: the Tex-Mex invasion. il *Harper's Bazaar* 122:48+ F '89

BOGART, JAMES P., AND OTHERS
Temperature and sperm incorporation in polyploid salamanders. bibl f il *Science* 246:1032-4 N 24 '89

BOGART, PAUL
about
Torch song trilogy [film] Reviews
Film Comment il 25:9-12+ Ja/F '89. J. Scott
Glamour il 87:140 F '89. J. G. Boyum
Maclean's il 102:53 F 20 '89. B. D. Johnson
National Review 41:46-8 Mr 24 '89. J. Simon
Newsweek il 113:58 Ja 2 '89. D. Ansen
People Weekly il 31:12+ Ja 9 '89. P. Travers

BOGDAN, CORNELIU, 1921-1990
Crossing the European divide. bibl f *Foreign Policy* 75:56-75 Summ '89

BOGDANOVICH, PETER, 1939-
about
The passions of Peter Bogdanovich [cover story] J. Wadler. il pors *People Weekly* 31:56-8+ Ja 23 '89

BOGEN, DANIEL K.
Simulation software for the Macintosh. bibl f il *Science* 246:138-42 O 6 '89

BOGEN, DON
The machines [poem] *The New Republic* 201:50-1 S 18-25 '89
Necklace [poem] *The New Republic* 200:34 Ap 3 '89

BOGGS, WADE
about
Bosox boys gone batty. M. Starr. il pors *Newsweek* 113:58 F 20 '89
Facing the music [cover story] E. M. Swift. il pors *Sports Illustrated* 70:38-40+ Mr 6 '89
Gwynn vs. Boggs. D. Knobler. il por *Sport (New York, N.Y.)* 80:28 Ag '89

BOGGUSS, SUZY
about
Suzy Bogguss. A. Nash. por *Stereo Review* 54:76 Jl '89

BOGHOSIAN, VARUJAN, 1926-
about
The Vergil of things. J. P. Hart. il *National Review* 41:55-6 O 13 '89

BOGLE, DONALD
Hollywood and civil rights. il *Essence* 19:32 Mr '89

BOGOMOLOV, OLEG TIMOFEYEVICH
Goodbye, Stalin hello, marketplace. il *World Press Review* 36:13+ D '89

BOGOSIAN, ERIC
about
Talking big. A. DeCurtis. por *Rolling Stone* p95-7 F 9 '89
Why I wear what I wear: Eric the dark [interview] S. Mansfield. il pors *Gentlemen's Quarterly* 59:94+ D '89

BOGOTÁ (COLOMBIA)
Streets
A trip along the Séptima. A. Berty. il *The Unesco Courier* 42:18-21 Ag '89

BOGS
Bucks of the big bogs. N. Nelson. il *Field & Stream* 94:42-3+ S '89
Peatlands: a global warming threat? [research by Joseph B. Yavitt and R. Kelman Wieder] J. Raloff. *Science News* 136:143 Ag 26 '89

Peatlands as source of acid rain [study by Lee F. Klinger] R. Monastersky. *Science News* 136:413 D 23-30 '89
Great Britain
The world's oldest road [Sweet Track of England: a 6,000-year-old wooden walkway discovered in a peat bog] J. Coles. il maps *Scientific American* 261:100-6 N '89

BOHANNON, JOHN
Eating out of hand. il *The Saturday Evening Post* 261:30+ S '89
A survivor's guide to New York City. il *The Saturday Evening Post* 261:26+ Ja/F '89

LA BOHÈME [opera] See Puccini, Giacomo, 1858-1924

BOHEMIAN GLASS See Glassware

BOHEMIANISM
See also
Beat culture
Hippies

BOHJALIAN, CHRISTOPHER A.
A neighborly sort of way. il *Reader's Digest* 134:71-2 Ja '89

BOHLEN, S. R., AND MEZGER, K.
Origin of granulite terranes and the formation of the lowermost continental crust. bibl f il *Science* 244:326-9 Ap 21 '89

BÖHME, J., AND OTHERS
Transgenic mice with I-A on islet cells are normoglycemic but immunologically intolerant. bibl f il *Science* 244:1179-83 Je 9 '89

BOHREN, CRAIG F., 1940-
Simple experiments in atmospheric physics. See issues of Weatherwise
about
Physics lite. W. Sones. il por *Discover* 10:56-60 Ag '89

BOILER ROOM SCAMS See Fraud

BOILING
Air bubble growth in water. C. F. Bohren. il *Weatherwise* 42:280-1 O '89
Boil and bubble, toil and trouble. C. F. Bohren. il *Weatherwise* 42:104-8 Ap '89

BOIS, YVE-ALAIN
Fontana's base materialism. bibl f il *Art in America* 77:238-49+ Ap '89

BOIS BLANC ISLAND (MICH.)
See also
Education—Bois Blanc Island (Mich.)

BOISE INTERAGENCY FIRE CENTER
Fighting fires bit by byte. S. Begley. il *Newsweek* 114:53 Ag 28 '89

BOIVIN, PAOLA
David is Goliath. il por *Sport (New York, N.Y.)* 80:62-3 N '89

BOJAR, KAREN
Broadening community service to include low-income students. il *Change* 21:22-3 S/O '89

BOK, SISSELA
The survival value of trust. por *American Health* 8:120+ S '89

BOKANOWSKI, HELENE
about
Parquet and pop. G. Wen. il por *Art News* 88:97-8+ S '89

BOKOR, J.
Ultrafast dynamics at semiconductor and metal surfaces. bibl f il *Science* 246:1130-4 D 1 '89

BOKSEN, BERT
about
Brokers in the boondocks. M. Schifrin. il pors *Forbes* 143:228+ Je 26 '89

BOL, MANUTE
about
Sudanese family worries about NBA's Manute Bol. il por *Jet* 76:49 Jl 17 '89

BOLAND, EAVAN
Dark flowers [poem] *The New Yorker* 65:56 S 25 '89
Three poems [poem] *The New Yorker* 65:33 My 29 '89
White hawthorn in the west of Ireland [poem] *The New Yorker* 65:111 Mr 27 '89

BOLEN, ERIC G., AND OTHERS
Playa lakes: prairie wetlands of the Southern High Plains. bibl f il map *BioScience* 39:615-23 O '89

BOLGER, JAMES
Inspecting for a safe home. *Consumers' Research Magazine* 72:29-30 O '89

BOLIDO (NEW YORK, N.Y.: NIGHTCLUB) See New York (N.Y.)—Restaurants, nightclubs, bars, etc.

BOLINAS (CALIF.)
Health facilities
See also
Commonweal Cancer Help Program

BOLING, KATHARINE
Apple country. il *Southern Living* 24:162 N '89

BOLÍVAR, SIMÓN, 1783-1830
The republican dream [excerpts from address, 1819] il *The Unesco Courier* 42:34-5 Je '89
Fiction
New from García Márquez. S. Cato. il por *World Press Review* 36:60 Je '89

BOLIVAR AVIATION
Swimming, volleyball and the flight life. A. Laboda. il *Flying* 116:112 N '89
BOLIVIA
See also
Drug abuse—Bolivia
Labor unions—Tin miners—Bolivia
Loans, Bank—Bolivia
Medical care—Bolivia
Narcotics laws and regulations—Bolivia
Public health—Bolivia
Radio broadcasting—Bolivia
Rain forests—Bolivia
Native peoples
See Indians of South America—Bolivia
Politics and government
See also
Political campaigns—Bolivia
Religious institutions and affairs
See also
Church and civil rights—Bolivia
Church and narcotics trade—Bolivia
Missions—Bolivia
BOLKIAH, MUDA HASSANAL *See* Hassanal Bolkiah, Sultan of Brunei, 1946-
BOLLETTIERI, NICK
Tennis workshop. il *World Tennis* 37:46-7 Ag '89
Tennis workshop: the drop shot. il *World Tennis* 37:72-3 Jl '89
Tennis workshop: the high ball. il *World Tennis* 36:44-5 Ja '89
Tennis workshop: the lob. il *World Tennis* 36:36-7 Mr '89
Tennis workshop: the serve. il *World Tennis* 36:44-5 My '89
Tennis workshop: the service return. il *World Tennis* 36:84-5 Ap '89
Tennis workshop: the short angle. il *World Tennis* 36:64-5 F '89
Tennis workshop: the slice backhand. il *World Tennis* 37:44-5 Je '89
Workshop: high backhand volley. il *World Tennis* 37:56-7 D '89
Workshop: inside-out forehand. il *World Tennis* 37:70-1 O '89
Workshop: overhead. il *World Tennis* 37:72-3 N '89
Workshop: the topspin lob. il *World Tennis* 37:104-5 S '89
BOLLING, FRANK
about
Going to bat for special children. D. Young. il pors *Southern Living* 24:100+ Jl '89
BOLLING (FRANK) ADAPTIVE BASEBALL LEAGUE *See* Frank Bolling Adaptive Baseball League
BOLLS, NATHAN J.
The chemicals of half-life. *BioScience* 39:138 Mr '89
BOLOGNA CHILDREN'S BOOK FAIR *See* Book fairs
BOLOGNESI, DANI
Progress in vaccines against AIDS. bibl f *Science* 246:1233-4 D 8 '89
BOLSA DE VALORES DE SÃO PAULO
Blame it on Nahas [stock market crash] J. Ryser. *Business Week* p40 Jl 3 '89
BOLSA DE VALORES DO RIO DE JANEIRO
Blame it on Nahas [stock market crash] J. Ryser. *Business Week* p40 Jl 3 '89
BOLSHOI ACADEMY BALLET
Michael Shannon, a California beach boy who's making waves with the Bolshoi Ballet. il por *People Weekly* 32:74 Ag 21 '89
Shannon shines with Soviets. M. E. Willis. por *Dance Magazine* 63:50 Ag '89
BOLSHOI BALLET
London critics give Grigorovich the cold shoulder. M. Hunt. il *Dance Magazine* 63:23 N '89
Reviews:
Stars of the Bolshoi Ballet, Glassboro, N.J. G. Parks. il *Dance Magazine* 63:84-5 N '89
BOLSTAD, GUNNAR
Light at the end of the tunnel. il *World Health* p8-10 My '89
BOLT, ALAN
about
The long march of Alan Bolt. J. Peters. *The Nation* 248:855-8 Je 19 '89
BOLT, RICHARD
Safeguards controversy, continued [discussion of December 1988 article, Plutonium for all: leaks in global safeguards] il *The Bulletin of the Atomic Scientists* 45:38-40 Je '89
BOLT, ROBERT
about
Robert Bolt. G. Carpenter. il por *American Film* 14:60-2 S '89
BOLTANSKI, CHRISTIAN, 1944-
about
Art. A. C. Danto. *The Nation* 248:210-12 F 13 '89
The art world. A. Gopnik. *The New Yorker* 65:107-11 F 20 '89

Boltanski: the uses of contradiction [cover story] N. Marmer. bibl f il *Art in America* 77:168-81+ O '89
Speak, memory. K. Larson. il *New York* 22:76-7 Ja 23 '89
BOLTON, GEOFFREY
Who are the Australians? il *The Courier (Unesco)* 41:4-8+ D '88
BOLTON, JOHN R.
The concept of the 'unitary UN' [address, June 29, 1989] *Department of State Bulletin* 89:74-5 O '89
BOLTON LANDING (N.Y.)
Hotels, motels, etc.
Steal away to Sagamore. R. J. Christmas. il *Black Enterprise* 19:62-3 Ja '89
BOLZE, DORENE
about
Earth angel. P. Pacheco. il pors *Harper's Bazaar* 122:54-7 Jl '89
BOMB DETECTORS
Airlines say FAA moving too fast on plan to install bomb detectors. M. Mecham. *Aviation Week & Space Technology* 131:96-7 Jl 17 '89
Antiterrorist bomb scanners installed [thermal neutron analyzer] il *Popular Mechanics* 166:16 D '89
British, Czechs push for tighter controls on plastic explosives [proposal at International Civil Aviation Organization assembly] D. Hughes. *Aviation Week & Space Technology* 131:26 S 25 '89
Caught in the net [neural network bomb detectors; work of Patrick Shea] T. Waters. il *Discover* 10:30 N '89
Congressmen, industry leaders say U.S. should pay for bomb detectors. C. Fotos. *Aviation Week & Space Technology* 130:69 Ap 3 '89
A daunting new quest to secure the skies [aftermath of Pan Am Flight 103 bombing] il *U.S. News & World Report* 106:9-10 Ja 9 '89
A deceptive killer [methods of detecting plastic explosives] *Time* 133:27 Ja 9 '89
Easier detection of plastic explosives urged by Security Council. *UN Chronicle* 26:19 S '89
Extra flight insurance. il *High Technology Business* 9:8-9 Ap '89
FAA fights back on plastic explosives. M. M. Waldrop. il *Science* 243:165-6 Ja 13 '89
FAA orders U.S. airlines to install bomb detectors [thermal neutron analysis device] J. Ott. *Aviation Week & Space Technology* 131:68-9 S 4 '89
FAA seeks detectors requiring little human judgment to find explosives. C. Fotos. il *Aviation Week & Space Technology* 130:65-7 Ja 16 '89
FAA's bomb scanner: an awkward Goliath? [thermal neutron analysis device developed by Tsahi Gozani] E. Marshall. il *Science* 245:926-7 S 1 '89
High-speed X-ray CT scanner could meet FAA's explosive detection requirements. B. W. Henderson. il *Aviation Week & Space Technology* 131:78-9 N 13 '89
House passes security bill, raising possibility of federal TNA funding [thermal neutron analysis system] *Aviation Week & Space Technology* 131:108-9 O 2 '89
Increasing TNA sensitivity causes higher number of false alarms [thermal neutron analysis bomb detection device] B. W. Henderson. il *Aviation Week & Space Technology* 131:127-8 S 18 '89
It's a bomb all right [thermal neutron bomb detectors] J. Drummond. il *Forbes* 144:41-2 S 4 '89
Kaboom! G. Slutsker. il *Forbes* 143:120-1 F 20 '89
Snaring hidden explosives with a neural net [research by Patrick M. Shea] R. Cowen. *Science News* 136:6 Jl 1 '89
Thermedics begins production of portable bomb detection unit [EGIS system] D. Hughes. *Aviation Week & Space Technology* 130:164-6 Je 19 '89
TNA system at JFK detects 94-99% of explosives in first weeks of test [thermal neutron analysis system] J. T. McKenna. *Aviation Week & Space Technology* 131:143 O 9 '89
Transportation Dept. will require wider use of advanced bomb detectors. *Aviation Week & Space Technology* 130:69 Ap 17 '89
U.S., industry officials debate funding for new security gear. J. Ott. *Aviation Week & Space Technology* 130:118 F 20 '89
X-ray backscatter equipment provides automatic screening for explosives. D. Hughes. il *Aviation Week & Space Technology* 130:65+ Ap 17 '89
BOMB SHELTERS *See* Atomic bomb shelters
BOMBA (FICTIONAL CHARACTER)
Collectibles
Bomba the Jungle Boy: the series. L. C. May. il *Antiques & Collecting Hobbies* 94:40+ Jl '89
BOMBARDIER INC.
Bombardier, GEC-Fokker team lead field of suitors for Northern Ireland's Short Brothers. *Aviation Week & Space Technology* 130:31 Mr 13 '89
Bombardier of Canada wins competition to buy Short Brothers. *Aviation Week & Space Technology* 130:63 Je 12 '89
Building for the future with a worldwide view [L. Beaudoin] D. Jenish. il por *Maclean's* 102:20-1 D 25 '89

BOMBARDIER INC.—*cont.*
A down-home hero. D. Burke. il por *Maclean's* 102:30+
S 11 '89
Flying high with the little engine that could. P. C. Newman.
il *Maclean's* 102:38 Mr 27 '89
BOMBARDMENT, ION *See* Ion bombardment
BOMBAY (INDIA)
Public health
The mini-doctors of Bombay. V. R. Bhalerao. il *World Health*
p20-3 D '88
Stations
See also
Victoria Terminus (Bombay, India)
BOMBECK, ERMA
about
Two from the heart [interview] M. Lodge. il pors *Ladies'
Home Journal* 106:78+ D '89
BOMBERS (AIRPLANES) *See* Airplanes, Military
BOMBING, AERIAL
See also
Afghanistan—Russian invasion, 1979-1989—Aerial opera-
tions
Bombing and gunnery ranges
World War, 1939-1945—Aerial operations
BOMBING AND GUNNERY RANGES
Korea (South)
Protests threaten to cripple USAF training operations [Koon-
Ni gunnery range] J. D. Morrocco. il *Aviation Week &
Space Technology* 130:239+ Je 12 '89
BOMBING MANEUVERS *See* Military maneuvers
BOMBINGS, TERRORIST *See* Terrorism
BOMBS
See also
Atomic bombs
Balloon bombs
Hydrogen bombs
BON JOVI, JON
about
Jon Bon Jovi gives his home to non-Jovi Judy Frappier.
il pors *People Weekly* 31:135 Ap 17 '89
No Don Juan Bon Jovi, Jon marries his high school sweetheart
in a Vegas chapel. il pors *People Weekly* 31:46 My 22
'89
BON JOVI (MUSICAL GROUP)
Bon fire. K. Richardson. *High Fidelity (New York, N.Y.)*
39:75 Ja '89
Bon voyage [Soviet tour; cover story] R. Tannenbaum. il
Rolling Stone p52-4+ F 9 '89
The boys in the band: Bon Jovi. il *'Teen* 33:41 F '89
BONADUCE, DANNY
about
Spinning off his Partridge past, Danny Bonaduce rocks Philly
as a raunchy midnight deejay. T. Cunneff. il pors *People
Weekly* 31:97-9 F 27 '89
BONAFE, EDDIE
about
The piano is Eddie's key. N. Epstein and M. Fay. il pors
Life 12:102-4 Ap '89
BONAPARTE, JOSÉPHINE *See* Josephine, Empress, consort
of Napoleon I, Emperor of the French, 1763-1814
BONAPARTE, NAPOLÉON *See* Napoleon I, Emperor of the
French, 1769-1821
BONASORTE, GARY
about
The aunts [drama] Reviews
New York il 22:107 O 16 '89. J. Simon
The New Yorker 65:111 O 16 '89. E. Oliver
BONAVOGLIA, ANGELA
Where there's a skill, there's a way. il *Ms.* 18:67-8 O '89
BOND, ALAN
about
The anatomy of a deal. R. Hughes. il *Time* 134:66+ N
27 '89
Atop Down Under. A. Farnham. il por *Fortune* 119:54+
Ja 2 '89
Sailing close to the wind. M. Rose. il por *Maclean's* 102:58+
D 4 '89
Suddenly, Alan Bond is losing his gilt edge. S. Hutcheon.
il por *Business Week* p46-7 My 29 '89
These days, they don't call it 'Down Under' for nothing.
S. Hutcheon. il por *Business Week* p66+ N 6 '89
BOND, CHRISTOPHER, 1939-
Should the Congress adopt the "Financial Institutions Reform,
Recovery, and Enforcement Act of 1989"? [excerpts from
address, April 17, 1989] *Congressional Digest* 68:184+ Je/Jl
'89
BOND, JAMES, 1900-1989
about
Bird, James Bird. *Discover* 10:13 Jl '89
Obituary
Audubon il 91:12+ My '89. F. Graham
BOND, JONATHAN
about
The ad brats. J. Taylor. il pors *New York* 22:50-6 N 13
'89

BOND, JULIAN
about
Court papers say Bond denies fathering baby. por *Jet* 77:55
N 27 '89
BOND, JAMES (FICTIONAL CHARACTER) *See* James Bond
(Fictional character)
BOND CORPORATION HOLDINGS LTD.
Atop Down Under [A. Bond] A. Farnham. il por *Fortune*
119:54+ Ja 2 '89
Bond Centre, Hong Kong. M. F. Schmertz. il *Architectural
Record* 177:76-9 Ja '89
Sailing close to the wind. M. Rose. il por *Maclean's* 102:58+
D 4 '89
Suddenly, Alan Bond is losing his gilt edge. S. Hutcheon.
il por *Business Week* p46-7 My 29 '89
These days, they don't call it 'Down Under' for nothing.
S. Hutcheon. il por *Business Week* p66+ N 6 '89
BOND FUNDS *See* Investment trusts
BOND MARKET *See* Bonds
BONDHOLDERS
Bondholders are mad as hell—and they're not going to take
it anymore. C. Farrell. il *Business Week* p82-3 F 6 '89
The bondholders' cold new world. G. Hector. il *Fortune*
119:83-4+ F 27 '89
The rape of the bondholder. A. Sloan. il *Forbes* 143:67-9
Ja 23 '89
BONDING, PARENTAL-INFANT *See* Parent-child relationship
BONDING (INSURANCE) *See* Insurance, Surety and fidelity
BONDS
See also
Banks and banking—Securities handling
Bondholders
Brokers
Convertible bonds
Junk bonds
Mortgage bonds and notes
Municipal bonds
Zero coupon bonds
Are bonds a good bet? M. Hodge and J. Blyskal. il *New
Choices for the Best Years* 29:69-71+ S '89
The basics of bonds. il *Consumer Reports* 54:579 S '89
Bonds' January effect? M. Hulbert. il *Forbes* 144:254 O
30 '89
Capital markets. B. Weberman. See issues of Forbes
Don't join the bondwagon! M. K. Evans. il *Gentlemen's
Quarterly* 59:197+ Ap '89
For bonds, glad tidings in the year to come. L. Light. il
Business Week p132-3 D 25 '89-Ja 1 '90
Let's call them bundle bonds. B. Weberman. il *Forbes* 143:333
Ja 9 '89
One toe over the line [ruling permits bank holding companies
to buy and sell corporate bonds] il *Time* 133:51 Ja 30
'89
The outlook for bonds. P. Sharif. *Black Enterprise* 20:58
O '89
The rape of the bondholder. A. Sloan. il *Forbes* 143:67-9
Ja 23 '89
A roaring bull market for bonds, at last. T. Thompson.
il *U.S. News & World Report* 107:78+ D 4 '89
Default
When vultures get food poisoning [investing in distressed
companies] H. Rudnitsky. il *Forbes* 144:53+ O 16 '89
Insurance
Investors are developing a taste for this poison [poison put
insurance] L. Light. il *Business Week* p78 Jl 10 '89
Prices
Bearish on bonds [bond market timer letters] M. Hulbert.
il *Forbes* 143:168 F 6 '89
The discount window [closed-end bond funds] B. Weberman.
il *Forbes* 144:307 S 4 '89
Fixed income with a hedge [indexed bonds] R. Addis. il
Forbes 143:246 Je 26 '89
The next best thing to bond market nirvana. C. Farrell.
il *Business Week* p102+ Je 26 '89
Rating
Bond ratings are a security blanket that sometimes gets
ripped away. D. Moreau. il *Changing Times* 43:18 Je
'89
Bondholders are mad as hell—and they're not going to take
it anymore. C. Farrell. il *Business Week* p82-3 F 6 '89
The bondholders' cold new world. G. Hector. il *Fortune*
119:83-4+ F 27 '89
Redemption
Bondholders brace for the great roundup [calls] L. J. Nathans.
il *Business Week* p77 Jl 3 '89
Corporate America wants out from under its junk pile. L.
Light. il *Business Week* p80-1 Ag 21 '89
Good zeros, bad zeros. B. Weberman. il *Forbes* 144:367
N 13 '89
Yield curve strategies. B. Weberman. il *Forbes* 144:337 Jl
24 '89
Yields
Blue-chip bonds look like a 'buyer's dream'. D. Zigas. il
Business Week p103 D 4 '89
Cannibal bond funds [bond funds that pay lavish dividends
but eat up principal] W. Baldwin. il *Forbes* 144:166+ S
4 '89

BONDS—Yields—*cont.*

The case for bonds. B. G. Malkiel. il *Forbes* 143:180-5 Je 26 '89

The case for stocks. D. N. Dreman. il *Forbes* 143:156 My 15 '89

Doesn't honesty sell? [SEC crackdown on bond unit trusts] B. Weberman. il *Forbes* 144:297 O 16 '89

Fixed income review. E. Hardy. il *Forbes* 144:156 D 25 '89

How to capture high yields at low risk [funds] C. Willis. il *Money* 18:41-2 Ja '89

How to steer your investments around a twisting yield curve. il *Money* 18:7 F '89

The long bet. B. Weberman. il *Forbes* 143:113 Ja 23 '89

Long-term bonds are too risky now. J. J. Curran. il *Fortune* 120 no10 Special Issue:22 Fall '89

Riding the wave of long bond yields. W. L. Updegrave. il *Money* 18:100-1+ Ap '89

Spread watch. B. Weberman. il *Forbes* 143:187 Je 12 '89

There's been a lot of bang in bonds, and a few pops are left. J. J. Curran. il *Fortune* 119:49-50 Je 19 '89

"Watch out for the old squeezeroo". M. Sivy. il *Money* 18:80+ D '89

What's an inverted yield curve? And why should you care? J. Bodnar. il *Changing Times* 43:20 My '89

Why short-term rates are so sweet. L. J. Nathans. il *Business Week* p86 Ja 16 '89

Yield curve strategies. B. Weberman. il *Forbes* 144:337 Jl 24 '89

Yield inversion. T. Jaffe. *Forbes* 143:340 Ja 9 '89

Yield versus total return [bond funds] J. Clements. il por *Forbes* 144:162-3 S 4 '89

Yielding to total return [closed-end bond funds vs. open-end] J. Clements. il *Forbes* 144:312+ D 11 '89

BONDS, CHEMICAL *See* Chemical bonds
BONDS, FIDELITY *See* Insurance, Surety and fidelity
BONDS, GOVERNMENT *See* Government securities
BONDS, HOSPITAL *See* Hospitals—Securities
BONDS, HOUSING *See* Mortgage bonds and notes
BONDS, MORTGAGE *See* Mortgage bonds and notes
BONDS, SURETY *See* Insurance, Surety and fidelity
BONDURANT, BOB, 1933-

about

Quick studies. B. Visnic. il pors *Car and Driver* 35:141-3 O '89

BONDURANT (BOB) SCHOOL OF HIGH PERFORMANCE DRIVING *See* Automobile driving—Study and teaching
BONE, JAMES

The price of peacekeeping. *World Press Review* 36:57 D '89

BONE

See also
Dislocations
Fractures
Maxilla & Mandible (Firm)
Skeleton
Skull

The basics of bone [excerpt from Preventing osteoporosis] K. H. Cooper. il *Health (New York, N.Y.)* 21:80-2 Ap '89

Blood-lead climbs as old bones decline [aged women at risk] J. Raloff. *Science News* 135:181 Mr 25 '89

Exercising bones. J. Kaplan. il *Vogue* 179:246+ Mr '89

Cancer
Causes

Asbestos again? [cobalt chrome artificial joints may cause bone cancer] L. Scheer. il *Forbes* 143:162+ Je 12 '89

Therapy

All-out attack on deadly bone cancer [research by Robert B. Marcus Jr. on Ewing's sarcoma] K. Fackelmann. *Science News* 135:230 Ap 15 '89

Radioactive drugs ease bone-tumor pain. I. Wickelgren. *Science News* 135:373 Je 17 '89

Diseases

See also
Osteoporosis

Growth

Substances found to promote bone growth. *High Technology Business* 9:30 My '89

Surgery

See also
Ilizarov method

BONE, ARTIFICIAL

Stone to bone [use of hydroxyapatite; work of Richard J. Lagow] P. E. Ross. *Scientific American* 261:31+ D '89

BONE JEWELRY *See* Jewelry
BONE MARROW *See* Marrow
BONE MARROW DERIVED CELLS *See* B cells
BONE ORACLES *See* Oracle bones
BONE RESORPTION *See* Absorption (Physiology)
BONEFISH FISHING

Best of the Bahamas. A. J. McClane. il map *Field & Stream* 93:42+ Ja '89

Playing in the bonefish league [T. Williams] J. Skorupa. il pors *Popular Mechanics* 166:28-9 Mr '89

The ugly, inedible fish that hooked a president. P. Engardio. il *Business Week* p108 Mr 6 '89

BONES, FOSSIL *See* Paleontology
BONET, LISA

about

Bonet sues drugstore over published picture of baby. il por *Jet* 76:27 Jl 3 '89

Lisa Bonet returns to 'The Cosby show' with TV husband and child prodigy [cover story] il pors *Jet* 76:60-2 S 25 '89

BONETTI, MATTIA

about

Barbarians at play. C. K. Gandee. il pors *House & Garden* 161:132-5 Jl '89

BONFIRES

Putting up the Christmas lights, Louisiana-style. M. A. Sternberg. il *Smithsonian* 20:146-51 D '89

BONGARTZ, ROY

Halls of fame. il *Americana* 17:56-9 My/Je '89

BONILLA DE GIROLDI, ADELA

about

The widow of a slain rebel leader looks back in anguish after the failed coup in Panama. B. Hewitt. il pors *People Weekly* 32:101-2 O 30 '89

BONKER, DON L.

Should the Congress adopt the "Textile and Apparel Trade Act of 1987"? [excerpts from address, September 16, 1987] *Congressional Digest* 68:31 Ja '89

BONNABEL, DAVID

about

Duped by a mysterious con man, a Florida couple 'find' a missing son only to lose him again. W. Plummer. il pors *People Weekly* 32:59-60 Ag 14 '89

BONNAIRE, SANDRINE

about

Offbeat sex appeal. M. Matousek. pors *Harper's Bazaar* 122:54+ Ap '89

BONNAMY, ALAIN

In the heart of an ancient capital. il *The Unesco Courier* 42:30-3 Ag '89

BONNARD, PIERRE, 1867-1947

about

A rue with a view. B. Adams. il *Harper's Bazaar* 122:116+ D '89

BONNE TERRE MINE (FIRM)

In the depths of a flooded mine, Doug and Cathy Goergens found a Missouri mecca for scuba divers. D. Chu. il pors *People Weekly* 32:81+ N 6 '89

BONNER, ELENA

about

An evening with the Sakharovs [interview] A. W. Bouis and J.-C. Bouis. il pors *Life* 12:96-8+ Jl '89

BONNER, RAYMOND

Choices. *The New Yorker* 65:43-8+ D 25 '89

Famine. map *The New Yorker* 65:85-96+ Mr 13 '89

BONNEVILLE LAND SPEED RECORDS *See* Land speed records
BONNEY, WILLIAM H. *See* Billy, the Kid
BONO

about

Pure Bono [interview; cover story] A. Block. il pors *Mother Jones* 14:32-7+ My '89

BONO, SONNY

about

Mayor Sonny Bono resists a recall, telling Palm Springs voters, 'You got me, Babe'. T. Gold. il pors *People Weekly* 32:53-4 O 2 '89

Now Sonny Bono is singing 'I want you, Babe'. R. Grover. il por *Business Week* p44 My 8 '89

BONSAI

Bonsai: a way of looking at trees with different eyes. O. Tanner. bibl (p229) il *Smithsonian* 20:138-48+ O '89

Bonsai landscape pruning. P. Chan. il *Organic Gardening* 36:27-9 Je '89

BONUS SYSTEM

The changing basis for pay. R. M. Kanter. bibl *Society* 26:54-65 S/O '89

BOO, KATHERINE

It's not just Washington. *The Washington Monthly* 20:37+ Ja '89

(jt. auth) See Goldsmith, Suzanne, and Boo, Katherine

BOODRO, MICHAEL

Radical cheek. il por *Art News* 88:114-17 Ja '89

BOOK ADVERTISING *See* Books—Advertising
BOOK AWARDS *See* Literary prizes
BOOK BINDING *See* Bookbinding
BOOK BLURBS *See* Books—Advertising
BOOK BUYING

The Gallup survey. L. A. Wood. See occasional issues of Publishers Weekly

BOOK CENSORSHIP *See* Censorship
BOOK CLUBS

See also
Book-of-the-Month Club, Inc.
Doubleday Book & Music Clubs

BOOK COLLECTING *See* Books—Collectors and collecting
BOOK COMPANY

Coles of Canada launches upscale line of bookstores. B. Slopen. *Publishers Weekly* 236:14 S 22 '89

BOOK CONTRACTS *See* Authors and publishers

BOOK COVERS

Book jackets go high-deco in the display space war. J. P. Frank. il *Publishers Weekly* 235:60-1 Je 2 '89

Competitive market spurs new mass market cover ideas. J. P. Frank. il *Publishers Weekly* 236:30+ N 17 '89

Component producers face capacity crunch in 1989 [jackets and covers] J. P. Frank. *Publishers Weekly* 235:77-8 F 3 '89

The face on the back of the book [book jacket photographs] J. Kaufman. il *The New York Times Book Review* 94:1+ Je 25 '89

New engraving process debuts at Dynamic Graphic [Dyna-Etch] J. P. Frank. il *Publishers Weekly* 235:44 Je 16 '89

When Elaine Duillo paints it, a romance novel's cover is worth a thousand steamy words. M. Neill. il pors *People Weekly* 31:141+ My 15 '89

BOOK CRITICS AND CRITICISM *See* Book reviews and reviewing

BOOK DESIGN

See also
Book covers

Book design & manufacturing. J. P. Frank. *See* alternate issues of Publishers Weekly

Graphics changes/cost-savings liven professional books. J. P. Frank. il *Publishers Weekly* 235:40+ Je 16 '89

Exhibitions

See Book exhibits

BOOK DISCARDING

Moving day: the books I left behind. A. Broyard. il *The New York Times Book Review* 94:1+ N 19 '89

Phenomena, comment and notes. J. P. Wiley, Jr. *Smithsonian* 20:32+ O '89

BOOK DISTRIBUTORS *See* Book wholesalers and distributors

BOOK EXHIBITS

See also
Book fairs

Bookbinders' officers selected; awards dinner scheduled. il *Publishers Weekly* 236:40 Ag 18 '89

Design does matter: the 1989 AAUP Book Show. C. B. Grannis. *Publishers Weekly* 236:25-6 S 22 '89

Prizewinners in the N.Y. Book Show range over many new subcategories. J. P. Frank. il *Publishers Weekly* 236:32-3 D 1 '89

To Russia, with books [USIA exhibit titled Many-booked America] Y. Richmond. por *Publishers Weekly* 235:76 F 3 '89

BOOK FAIRS

Anatomy of a book festival [Southern Festival of Books] *Publishers Weekly* 236:28 D 15 '89

Bologna '89 [Children's Book Fair; special section] il *Publishers Weekly* 235:25-6+ Mr 24 '89

Bologna: an American commitment. H. R. Lottman. il *Publishers Weekly* 235:32-4+ My 19 '89

Finding room at the fair [Frankfurt Book Fair; cover story] il *Publishers Weekly* 236:59-60+ S 15 '89

Frankfurt '89: quiet but crowded. H. R. Lottman. *Publishers Weekly* 236:10+ O 27 '89

Frankfurt '89: when less is more. H. R. Lottman. il *Publishers Weekly* 236:39-40+ N 3 '89

Frankfurt for the Americans. J. F. Baker. il *Publishers Weekly* 236:48+ N 3 '89

International book fairs 1990. *Publishers Weekly* 236:90 S 15 '89

Jerusalem. H. R. Lottman. il *Publishers Weekly* 235:35-42 Ja 13 '89

Jerusalem: building relationships [Jerusalem International Book Fair] D. Maryles. il *Publishers Weekly* 235:25-9 Ap 21 '89

Liber: Spain's summer fair. H. R. Lottman. il *Publishers Weekly* 236:22-3 Ag 4 '89

London '89: a growing internationalism. V. Menkes. il *Publishers Weekly* 235:33-6 My 5 '89

McGraw-Hill and Wiley quit Iran Fair but decry book boycotts. C. Reid. *Publishers Weekly* 235:104 My 12 '89

Promise and problems at Guadalajara Book Fair [Feria Internacional de Libro] P. Schuman. il *Publishers Weekly* 235:24+ Ja 6 '89

Regional trade shows take shape: 1989 schedule. il *Publishers Weekly* 236:40-2 Jl 14 '89

Small presses at Expo '89 show 'increasing sophistication'. J. Barbato. il *Publishers Weekly* 235:16 Ap 14 '89

Third Latin American Fair focuses on new writers. J. Ponce de León. il *Publishers Weekly* 235:18 My 26 '89

This year in Moscow. F. Kobrak. il *Publishers Weekly* 236:23-4 O 13 '89

Transpacific [Singapore International Book Fair] S. A. Taylor. *Publishers Weekly* 236:38 O 20 '89

U.K. publishers vote Rushdie support, reject Teheran boycott. V. Menkes. *Publishers Weekly* 235:104 My 12 '89

U.S. visitors to the fair find 'nothing to die for' [Bologna Children's Book Fair] D. E. Roback. il *Publishers Weekly* 235:37-8 My 19 '89

Unlikely Managua is again Mecca for international book trade. K. Bermann. il *Publishers Weekly* 236:12-13 Ag 18 '89

Photographs and photography

New York Is Book Country. il *Publishers Weekly* 236:15 O 6 '89

BOOK INDUSTRIES

See also
Book Manufacturers' Institute
Book packagers
Book wholesalers and distributors
Bookbinding
BookCrafters, Inc.
Books—Marketing
Books—Prices
Booksellers and bookselling
Dynamic Graphic Finishing Inc.
Ecological Fibers (Firm)
Literary agencies and agents
Narragansett Coated Papers (Firm)
Paper industry
Printing industry
Publishers and publishing

Book design & manufacturing. J. P. Frank. *See* alternate issues of Publishers Weekly

Component producers face capacity crunch in 1989 [jackets and covers] J. P. Frank. *Publishers Weekly* 235:77-8 F 3 '89

History

Making books: design and production changes over the years [paperbacks] J. P. Frank. il *Publishers Weekly* 235:S16+ My 26 '89

Laws and regulations

See also
Copyright

United States

See Book industries

BOOK INVENTORY SYSTEMS (FIRM)

Book Inventory Systems: the quiet bookstore helper. A. Symons. il *Publishers Weekly* 235:45-7 Mr 24 '89

BOOK JACKETS *See* Book covers

BOOK LISTS *See* Reading lists

BOOK MANUFACTURERS' INSTITUTE

BMI elects officers; honors Child as 'Master Bookman' [annual conference] il *Publishers Weekly* 235:78+ F 3 '89

BOOK MANUFACTURING INDUSTRY *See* Book industries

BOOK-OF-THE-MONTH CLUB, INC.

BOMC's Riger is president of Doubleday Clubs. M. Reuter. por *Publishers Weekly* 235:34-5 Ap 7 '89

Inside the Club. J. Kaplan. il *The New York Times Magazine* p62+ Je 11 '89

BOOK PACKAGERS

Vampire agents at play [headline related books] J. Hammer. il *Newsweek* 114:64 S 11 '89

BOOK PRICES *See* Books—Prices

BOOK PRIZES *See* Literary prizes

BOOK PRODUCERS *See* Book packagers

BOOK PROMOTION *See* Books—Advertising

BOOK RACKS *See* Bookends and bookracks

BOOK RARITIES *See* Rare books

BOOK RESTORATION *See* Books—Conservation and restoration

BOOK REVIEWS AND REVIEWING

See also
Inside books (Periodical)

Four candid reviewers discuss 'good, bad, overlooked' books [panel discussion sponsored by the Association of American Publishers and PEN American Center] C. Reid. *Publishers Weekly* 235:332 Ja 27 '89

Have Christian books been censored? S. Charles. il *Publishers Weekly* 235:58 Mr 3 '89

Nasty reviews: easy to give, hard to take. W. H. Pritchard. *The New York Times Book Review* 94:1+ My 7 '89

To catch a thief [man attempts to get books from publishers by posing as a reviewer for Business week] L. Fleischer. *Publishers Weekly* 235:76 Ja 6 '89

The trouble with reviews [small presses] J. Barbato. il *Publishers Weekly* 235:28-9 Ap 14 '89

The writers of wrong: a novelist carves the critics [cover story] J. McInerney. il por *Esquire* 112:104-8+ Jl '89

Anecdotes, facetiae, satire, etc.

Reiterating some minor complaints [newspaper reviews of author's latest work] A. Fotheringham. il *Maclean's* 102:88 D 4 '89

BOOK SALES REPRESENTATIVES, PUBLISHERS' *See* Publishers and publishing—Employees

BOOK SERIES *See* Serial publication of books

BOOK SHELVES *See* Bookcases

BOOK SHOWS *See* Book exhibits

BOOK THEFTS

See also
Booksellers and bookselling—Security measures

BOOK WHOLESALERS AND DISTRIBUTORS

See also
Book Inventory Systems (Firm)
Ingram Book Company
Kampmann & Company
National Book Network Inc.
Publishers Group West

Going to market [commitment to regional publishing] M. Raymond. il *Publishers Weekly* 236:22-3 O 20 '89

BOOK WHOLESALERS AND DISTRIBUTORS—*cont.*

How to choose a distributor [points considered by Master-Media] S. S. Stautberg. por *Publishers Weekly* 236:429 Ag 11 '89

Ingram forms publisher fulfillment service [other wholesalers fear conflict of interest] M. Reuter. *Publishers Weekly* 235:17-18 Ap 28 '89

Scaling the small press hurdle: getting titles onto the shelves. M. Jones. il *Publishers Weekly* 235:37-41 Ap 14 '89

Directories

PW's annual Yuletide guide to the wholesalers. J. Mutter and M. J. O'Brien. il *Publishers Weekly* 236:44-6 O 27 '89

History

Getting them out: distribution, how it's done, and how it's doing [paperbacks] M. Jones. il *Publishers Weekly* 235:S22+ My 26 '89

BOOKBASE

BookBase: a tailor-made ordering alternative. M. J. O'Brien. il *Publishers Weekly* 235:52-3 Ja 13 '89

BOOKBINDERS' GUILD OF NEW YORK BOOK SHOW
See Book exhibits

BOOKBINDING

Arcata improves its round-backing capability. J. P. Frank. il *Publishers Weekly* 235:62 Je 2 '89

BOOKCASES

Build a better bookcase. A. Weaver and V. Weaver. il *Workbench* 45:41-4 Jl/Ag '89

Build a home library [cover story] K. Collier. il *The Family Handyman* 39:32-9 Jl/Ag '89

Revolving bookcase. B. Kieffer. il *The Family Handyman* 39:64-9 Mr '89

BOOKCHIN, MURRAY, 1921-

Death of a small planet [cover story] il *The Progressive* 53:19-23 Ag '89

We can't heal the environment without remaking our society. il *Utne Reader* p80-2 N/D '89

BOOKCRAFTERS, INC.

BookCrafters takes over assets of Stein & Day. *Publishers Weekly* 235:14 Mr 24 '89

BookCrafters to publish Stein & Day titles. C. Reid. il *Publishers Weekly* 236:124 Jl 28 '89

Tentative pact gives BookCrafters control of Stein & Day backlist. C. Reid. *Publishers Weekly* 235:12 F 17 '89

BOOKENDS AND BOOKRACKS

Sturdy bookends. il *Workbench* 45:54-5 Mr/Ap '89

BOOKER, SIMEON

Ticker tape U.S.A. See issues of Jet

BOOKER [television program] See Television program reviews—Single works

BOOKER PRIZE

Roald Dahl lambastes Booker for giving elitist awards. V. Menkes. *Publishers Weekly* 236:19 D 15 '89

BOOKERS (TELEVISION WORKERS)

Talking people into talking. R. Givens. il *Newsweek* 114:44-5 Jl 17 '89

BOOKLAND EAN SYSTEM

Bookland EAN comes to the book world. J. Mutter. il *Publishers Weekly* 235:441-4 Ja 27 '89

BOOKLETS See Pamphlets

BOOKPAGE (NEWSPAPER)

'BookPage' aims for greater coverage. B. Summer. il *Publishers Weekly* 236:27-8 Ag 18 '89

BOOKRACKS See Bookends and bookracks

BOOKS

See also
Best sellers
Manuscripts
Out of print books
Paperback books
Picture books
Rare books
Royalties
Scrapbooks
Talking books
Textbooks

Advertising

See also
BookPage (Newspaper)
Franklin Spier Inc.

Booksellers talk to publicists. J. Mutter. *Publishers Weekly* 235:53-4 Ap 28 '89

Breakfasts [book and author breakfast speakers] il *Publishers Weekly* 235:46-8 Je 30 '89

Pocket pockets sales brochures. J. Mutter. *Publishers Weekly* 236:28 N 17 '89

Promoting religious books. M. Cullar. il *Publishers Weekly* 235:31-3 Mr 3 '89

Routledge boosts its sales and image in Iowa [book week at University of Iowa bookstore] J. Mutter. il *Publishers Weekly* 235:112-13 Ja 20 '89

Savvy marketer learns about publishing . . . and vice versa? [experiences of P. C. Gallagher] M. Reuter. il por *Publishers Weekly* 236:13 Ag 4 '89

Sound bites from Never-never Land. P. Yancey. il *Christianity Today* 33:56 Ap 21 '89

The South rises—to the occasion of an 'Encycloparty' [promotional event for the Encyclopedia of southern culture] M. J. O'Brien. il *Publishers Weekly* 236:40 Ag 25 '89

Talk-show prep [C. Brown works with author P. Reynolds] L. See. *Publishers Weekly* 236:201 Jl 28 '89

Anecdotes, facetiae, satire, etc.

Essential reading [blurbs] M. Kinsley. *The New Republic* 201:4 D 18 '89

The favor of Erik Nielsen's silence [former Canadian politician's shunning of all interviews about memoirs] S. MacLeod. por *Maclean's* 102:64 S 11 '89

A model author. M. Richler. il *Gentlemen's Quarterly* 59:145+ N '89

Care

See Books—Conservation and restoration

Censorship

See Censorship

Collectors and collecting

See also
Children's literature—Collectors and collecting
Libraries, Private
Rare books

An antiquarian bookseller looks at new books. A. S. Bamberger. il *Antiques & Collecting Hobbies* 93:19+ Ja '89

Conservation and restoration

AAUP-ARL survey finds strong university press commitment to acid-free paper. *Publishers Weekly* 235:68+ Mr 17 '89

Crumbling books. P. M. Battin. il *Change* 21:6+ S/O '89

An end to the yellowing pages [publishers agree to first printings of quality hard cover trade books on acid-free paper] il *Newsweek* 113:80 Mr 20 '89

House unit hears testimony on availability of acid-free paper. H. Fields. *Publishers Weekly* 235:17 My 26 '89

Microwaves that save manuscripts [deacidification] D. Sergent. il *The Courier (Unesco)* 42:9 My '89

Paper progress. J. I. Mattill. il *Technology Review* 92:11 Ap '89

Top firms pledge use of acid-free paper in hardcover first printings. il *Publishers Weekly* 235:12 Mr 31 '89

Toward the totally acid-free book. J. P. Frank. il *Publishers Weekly* 236:28-9 Jl 21 '89

Dedications

See Dedications (in books)

Design

See Book design

Discarding

See Book discarding

Exhibitions

See Book exhibits

Export-import trade

1992 and all that [round table discussion on the implications for American publishers of the European Economic Community] il *Publishers Weekly* 235:21-8 F 3 '89

AAP report hits book embargo of South Africa as 'misguided'. C. Reid. *Publishers Weekly* 236:8+ D 1 '89

Balancing the books: U.S. export ratio rises; world figures reported. C. B. Grannis. il *Publishers Weekly* 235:42-5 Je 2 '89

Exports increase 40% in number, 25% in value. H. Fields. *Publishers Weekly* 235:9 Mr 31 '89

The international PSP market: an update. F. Kobrak. *Publishers Weekly* 236:44-5 N 10 '89

Manufacture

See Book industries

Marketing

See also
Book wholesalers and distributors
Bookland EAN system
Booksellers and bookselling
Catalogs, Publishers'
Paperback books—Marketing

AAP-PSP market-driven publishing strategies. L. Conley. *Publishers Weekly* 235:47-8 F 10 '89

Creative marketing [Christian Booksellers Association convention] W. Griffin. *Publishers Weekly* 236:18 Ag 18 '89

Direct-response selling for the 1990s [strategies for publishers] P. Hodges. il *Publishers Weekly* 235:260+ My 12 '89

Do awards sell books? [children's literature] A. Meeker. il *Publishers Weekly* 236:32+ Ag 25 '89

A history of book marketing [1940s and 1950s] R. A. Carter. il *Publishers Weekly* 235:54-6 Ja 13 '89

A history of book marketing [1960s through the 1980s] R. A. Carter. il *Publishers Weekly* 235:34-7 My 26 '89

In search of older readers [over-50 book market] J. Crichton. il por *Publishers Weekly* 236:20+ Jl 7 '89

An open market for Australia? L. Vardey. por *Publishers Weekly* 236:100 S 15 '89

Rights. P. S. Nathan. See issues of Publishers Weekly

Shatzkin's report on small press distribution arouses debate. M. Reuter. *Publishers Weekly* 236:9-10 S 8 '89

Targeting the hand-sell [Houghton Mifflin's Network puts books in sellers' hands] R. Burroughs. il *Publishers Weekly* 235:52-4 My 19 '89

Microscopic and miniature editions

Hand-scribed missals: calligraphed masterpieces in miniature [work of S. Mitchell] A. Bahar. il por *Antiques & Collecting Hobbies* 94:60-3 D '89

BOOKS—*cont.*

Preservation
See Books—Conservation and restoration

Prices
See also
Net Book Agreement (Great Britain)
H & R to offer free freight, new discount schedule. *Publishers Weekly* 236:9 Ag 25 '89
Pocket and Warner announce retail incentive plans [end of antitrust campaign by independent booksellers] J. Mutter. *Publishers Weekly* 235:19-20 Ja 6 '89
Title output and prices. C. B. Grannis. il *Publishers Weekly* 235:36-9 Mr 10 '89
Titles and prices, 1988; final figures. C. B. Grannis. il *Publishers Weekly* 236:24-7 S 29 '89
Traditional booksellers suffer by French price-fix law, study shows. H. R. Lottman. *Publishers Weekly* 235:16 Mr 24 '89

Statistics
See Publishers and publishing—Statistics

Transportation
H & R to offer free freight, new discount schedule. *Publishers Weekly* 236:9 Ag 25 '89

BOOKS, FILMED *See* Motion picture adaptations
BOOKS, STAGED *See* Theatrical adaptations
BOOKS, TELEVISED *See* Television adaptations

BOOKS AND READING
See also
Authors—Reading
Black authors—Reading
Book buying
Book reviews and reviewing
Books as gifts
Children's reading
College students—Reading
Detective and mystery stories
Executives—Reading
Fiction
Libraries
Libraries, Private
Literature
Men—Reading
National Book Week
Prisoners—Reading
Reading aloud
Reference books
Television and reading

About books. A. Broyard. See occasional issues of The New York Times Book Review beginning November 11, 1984 through May 21, 1989
Books & things. M. Richler. See issues of Gentlemen's Quarterly
Branch libraries [reading under a shade tree] E. A. Peeples. bibl il *Country Journal* 16:30-1 Jl/Ag '89
Bullcrit. R. Rosen. il *New York* 22:44-7 F 6 '89
Competitive reading. L. Lipking. *The New Republic* 201:28-30+ O 2 '89
Don't wait to see the movie. T. C. Muck. il *Christianity Today* 33:13 N 3 '89
The Gallup survey. L. A. Wood. See occasional issues of Publishers Weekly
Moving day: the books I left behind. A. Broyard. il *The New York Times Book Review* 94:1+ N 19 '89
NEA study finds 56% of Americans claim to read some literature. H. Fields. *Publishers Weekly* 236:9-10 Ag 25 '89
On writing: let there be less. A. Krystal. il *The New York Times Book Review* 94:1+ Mr 26 '89
Waiter, there's a paragraph in my soup! J. Epstein. *The American Scholar* 58:327-9+ Summ '89

Anecdotes, facetiae, satire, etc.
The ideal summer books: huge, scary, waterproof. D. Barry. il *The New York Times Book Review* 94:3 Je 11 '89
The night The Forsyte saga struck back. B. Watson. il *Smithsonian* 20:184 Je '89
The unsung unread. L. Grossberger. il *Vogue* 179:230+ F '89

Best books
See also
Best sellers
Books as gifts
Great books of the Western world
Best of '88. il *Time* 133:95 Ja 2 '89
Books [fall releases] R. Koenig. il *New York* 22:132+ S 11 '89
Books for vacation reading. il *The New York Times Book Review* 94:34-41 Je 11 '89
The books of summer: an all-star lineup. J. Warner. il *Business Week* p14-16 My 29 '89
Books we like. *New Choices for the Best Years* 29:76-7 N '89
Celebrations. il *Publishers Weekly* 235:49-52 Ja 6 '89
Editors' choice: the best books of 1989. il *The New York Times Book Review* 94:3+ D 3 '89
Notable books of the year. il *The New York Times Book Review* 94:48-9+ D 3 '89
Notable paperbacks. *The New York Times Book Review* 94:78-80 D 3 '89

Past present [lesser known works] G. Cravens. *The Nation* 249:574-5 N 13 '89
The pick of 1988. il *Maclean's* 102:60-1+ Ja 2 '89
Reads: paperbacks by the sack for when the pressure's off. R. Koenig. il *New York* 22:138+ Jl 3-10 '89
Stories for an endless summer. M. McLoughlin. il *U.S. News & World Report* 107:56-8 Jl 3 '89
Summer reading. il *Utne Reader* p118-25+ Jl/Ag '89
Summer reading. il *Time* 133:65-6+ Je 19 '89
Summer reads: just your type. il *Seventeen* 48:125-6 Ag '89
Ten best books [1980s] N. Connors. il *Seventeen* 48:68 D '89
Winter reading [special section] il *Utne Reader* p103-15 Ja/F '89

Bibliography
See also
Best sellers
Books and reading—Best books
Book reviews. See issues of The Humanist
Books. See issues of The American Scholar
Books. See issues of Américas
Books. See issues of Business Week
Books. See issues of The Christian Century
Books. See issues of Maclean's
Books. See issues of The New Yorker
Books. See alternate issues of USA Today (Periodical)
Books. See issues of Vogue beginning March 1985
Books. L. Mathews. See issues of Glamour
Books. J. Maynard. See issues of Mademoiselle beginning January 1985
Books in brief. See issues of National Review
Brief reviews. P.-L. Adams. See issues of The Atlantic
[Column] G. M. Costello. See issues of U.S. Catholic beginning January 1985
Fall book roundup: islands and memoirs. D. Diehl. il *Modern Maturity* 32:82+ O/N '89
Forecasts. See issues of Publishers Weekly
Leafing through fall '89 books. G. Feldman. il *Publishers Weekly* 236:339-407+ Ag 11 '89
The leaves of autumn. il *Newsweek* 114:76-8+ S 18 '89
Nation books, 1988. *The Nation* 248:23-4 Ja 2 '89
New books for a new year [spring announcements] B. Levine. il *Publishers Weekly* 235:342-82+ Ja 27 '89; Addendum. 235:44 Mr 24 '89
A new world of pathos and comedy. D. Diehl. il *Modern Maturity* 32:32-3 Ap/My '89
The New Yorker lists at this season some books by its contributors published during the year. *The New Yorker* 65:114-15 D 18 '89
Noted with pleasure. See issues of The New York Times Book Review beginning January 1, 1984
People picks & pans. See issues of People Weekly
Pink and green: fall's bestsellers and big books that may be. G. Feldman. il *Publishers Weekly* 235:73-4+ Je 30 '89
Recent arrivals. See issues of The Christian Century
The right books. C. Williamson. See issues of National Review through August 4, 1989
The rites of spring: a new season's hopefuls leap (and lurch) into view. G. Feldman. il *Publishers Weekly* 236:32+ D 15 '89
Summer announcements. il *Publishers Weekly* 235:45-76+ Ap 7 '89
Writers & writing. B. Gewen. See occasional issues of The New Leader
The writer's library. See occasional issues of The Writer

Study and teaching
See Literature—Study and teaching

Latin America
Best sellers in the Americas. M. del C. Prodoscimi. il *Américas* 41 no2:54-6 '89
Best sellers in the Americas. M. del C. Prodoscimi. *Américas* 41 no1:50-1 '89

BOOKS AS GIFTS
10 best new picturebooks for kids. C. Weston. il *Redbook* 174:32+ D '89
Books for Christmas. il *The American Spectator* 22:27-32 D '89
Books for Christmas. *America* 161:356-61 N 18 '89
Books for grown-ups [Christmas gifts] L. Rosenberg. il *Parents* 64:235-6+ N '89
Children's books for Christmas. F. McNulty. il *The New Yorker* 65:134-44 N 27 '89
Christmas books 1989 [special issue] il *The New York Times Book Review* 94:3+ D 3 '89
Christmas books: beyond Santa Claus [children's books] A. E. Johnson. *The New York Times Book Review* 94:19 D 24 '89
Critics' choices for Christmas [cover story] *Commonweal* 116:677-87 D 1 '89
'Dear Scrooge . .' [holiday books for children] R. Donahue. il *Publishers Weekly* 236:34-7 O 27 '89
Deck the shelves [art and picture books] P. S. Prescott. il *Newsweek* 114:82-4+ D 11 '89
Gift books for fall. il *Publishers Weekly* 236:35+ S 1 '89
Great gifts for small people. D. Diehl. il *Modern Maturity* 32:54-8+ D '89/Ja '90

BOOKS AS GIFTS—*cont.*

Health books to give and get. C. Slom. *McCall's* 117:98 D '89

A holiday compendium. P. Crowley. il *Country Journal* 16:11-12 N/D '89

A holiday harvest [travel books for Christmas] il *Travel Holiday* 172:80-1 N '89

In 'fruitcake weather' [children's books] J. Baumgold. il *New York* 22:80 D 18 '89

The Mother Earth news country home library [Christmas list] il *The Mother Earth News* 120:90+ N/D '89

O little town of Plugsville [books about English language] W. Safire. il *The New York Times Magazine* p24+ D 3 '89

Of cats, myths and pizza [Christmas gifts for children] S. Kanfer. il *Time* 134:100+ D 11 '89

Pages of pleasure [holiday gifts] il *Maclean's* 102:60-2 D 18 '89

Regional digest: the best regional garden books for gift giving. il *Flower and Garden* 33:14-18 N/D '89

Santa Claus bags a varied collection of science books for children. P. Morrison and P. Morrison. il *Scientific American* 261:144-53 D '89

Season's readings: gifts to delight and instruct. J. H. Dobrzynski. il *Business Week* p160 D 18 '89

Tidings of color and joy [Christmas gifts] il *Time* 134:88-9 D 18 '89

'Tis the season. L. Sibley. il *Christianity Today* 33:38-9 N 17 '89

Under our trees. il *House & Garden* 161:78+ D '89

BOOKS FROM TELEVISION PROGRAMS See Television and literature

BOOKS IN ADVERTISING

Ads in books are back. J. F. Baker. *Publishers Weekly* 235:96 My 12 '89

Advertising in books draws diverse responses [Whittle Communications' series of short hardcover books by prominent authors] C. Reid. il *Publishers Weekly* 235:11-12 My 5 '89

BOOKS IN ART

Exhibitions

Steve Wolfe at Diane Brown. K. Johnson. il *Art in America* 77:204-5 S '89

BOOKS ON CASSETTE See Talking books

BOOKSELLERS AND BOOKSELLING

   See also

   American Booksellers Association

   Art in bookstores

   Book fairs

   Books—Marketing

   Books—Prices

   Catalogs, Booksellers'

   College bookstores

   Computers—Bookselling use

Chain reaction [FTC charges that chains get preferential treatment from publishers] C. Goodrich. *The Nation* 248:596-8 My 1 '89

Christmas business survey: tidings of joy—and jumpiness. J. Mutter and M. J. O'Brien. il *Publishers Weekly* 236:20-2+ D 22 '89

Curling up with a good bookstore. S. D. Atchison. il *Business Week* p138 Ag 14 '89

The Gallup survey. L. A. Wood. See occasional issues of *Publishers Weekly*

PW annual business survey: summer of '89: few worries, much happiness. J. Mutter and M. J. O'Brien. il *Publishers Weekly* 236:38-41 Ag 25 '89

Rattling the chains [independent bookstores] J. D. Reed. il *Time* 134:95+ O 23 '89

Riggio foresees 'golden age' in bookselling. J. Mutter. *Publishers Weekly* 236:8+ N 24 '89

The Rushdie crisis: a report from the front lines [independent booksellers] M. J. O'Brien. il *Publishers Weekly* 236:45-8 S 29 '89

Six houses win one point in first FTC skirmish [charge that chains get preferential treatment not accorded independent bookstores] H. Fields. *Publishers Weekly* 235:14 Ap 21 '89

Six publishers charged with price bias by FTC [policies favoring bookstore chains over independents] *Publishers Weekly* 235:19 Ja 6 '89

Through the holidays: good tidings for many. J. Mutter and M. J. O'Brien. il *Publishers Weekly* 235:71-3 F 3 '89

The year in bookselling. J. Mutter. il *Publishers Weekly* 235:56-7 Ja 6 '89

Acquisitions and mergers
Great Britain

W. H. Smith merges specialist bookselling chain with Waterstone's. V. Menkes. *Publishers Weekly* 236:14 Ag 4 '89

Advertising

See Books—Advertising

Black literature

Book biz: a community best-seller [C. Villarosa's Hue-Man Experience Bookstore in Denver] il por *Ms.* 18:85 S '89

Denver's black "bookstore and more" [Hue-Man Experience Bookstore] M. L. Small. il *American Visions* 4:42-5 F '89

Chain and franchise operations

   See also

   B. Dalton Booksellers

   Barnes & Noble

   Book Company

   Brentano's, Inc.

   Crown Books Corporation

   Little Professor Book Centers

   Quinby's (Firm)

   Waldenbooks

Books with easy hooks: selling to the chains [children's market] R. Burroughs. il *Publishers Weekly* 235:37+ Ap 28 '89

Children's literature

   See also

   Quinby's (Firm)

Books with easy hooks: selling to the chains. R. Burroughs. il *Publishers Weekly* 235:37+ Ap 28 '89

Children's booksellers and teachers: partners in literacy. S. Wilensky-Lanford. il *Publishers Weekly* 235:101-3 Ja 20 '89

A higher profile than ever: children's books at ABA [special section] D. E. Roback. il *Publishers Weekly* 235:62-4+ Je 30 '89

A potpourri of fact and fiction from Down Under [Australian booksellers] A. Ullin. il *Publishers Weekly* 235:37-8 Mr 24 '89

'Save the books' fund helps quake-damaged bookstores replace children's books [San Francisco Bay Area] B. Stander. *Publishers Weekly* 236:44-5 N 24 '89

Selling children's books in the bookstore [survey results] D. E. Roback. il *Publishers Weekly* 236:34-6+ N 24 '89

Snapshots of the children's regional booksellers associations. il *Publishers Weekly* 236:194-6 Jl 28 '89

Comic books, strips, etc.

   See also

   Geppi's Comic World (Firm)

Computer literature

Booksellers: learning from expert customers. C. T. Anthony. il *Publishers Weekly* 236:28+ N 24 '89

Cookbooks

Season to Taste Books: a comfy (and kitschy) culinary store [Chicago] M. McQuade. il pors *Publishers Weekly* 236:45-6 S 8 '89

Dance literature

London's dance book shop [Dance Books, Ltd.] D. Cox. *Dance Magazine* 63:69-70 D '89

Equipment

Shelf-awareness: getting a fix on fixtures. M. Jones. il *Publishers Weekly* 236:18+ Jl 21 '89

Ethical aspects

At stake: the freedom to imagine [booksellers pull S. Rushdie's Satanic verses off shelves in wake of murder order issued by Khomeini] L. Shapiro. il *Newsweek* 113:36-7 F 27 '89

Feminist literature

Judith's Room: New York City again has a women's bookstore. M. McQuade. il *Publishers Weekly* 235:59 Ap 21 '89

New Words: the collective works [women's bookstore in Cambridge, Mass.] J. Rosen. il *Publishers Weekly* 235:56-9 Ap 21 '89

A Room of One's Own finds a niche of its own [Madison, Wis.] M. E. Guthrie. il *Publishers Weekly* 236:66-8 Ag 4 '89

Finance

What to do (or not do) when the local economy goes bust. R. Burroughs. il *Publishers Weekly* 236:27-9 Jl 7 '89

Garden literature

   See also

   Capability's Books (Firm)

Hunting down antique gardening books. il *Sunset (Central West edition)* 181:160 D '88

Guidebooks

The crowded world of travel books [special section] J. Crichton. il *Publishers Weekly* 235:36-8+ Ja 20 '89

Homosexual literature

   See also

   Different Light (Firm)

Reflections on a growing market. J. Ponce de León. *Publishers Weekly* 236:24 D 8 '89

International aspects

   See also

   International Booksellers Federation

Book world reacts to Khomeini's threats [death threat against novelist S. Rushdie; special section; with editorial comment by John F. Baker] *Publishers Weekly* 235:22, 26-8+ Mr 3 '89

Book world unites to fight threats to Rushdie and free speech [special section] *Publishers Weekly* 235:12+ Mr 10 '89

New Age materials

'Convergence' at the bookstore. M. Jones. il *Publishers Weekly* 236:32-4 N 3 '89

Order processing

   See also

   BookBase

BOOKSELLERS AND BOOKSELLING — Order processing —cont.

Computers in bookstores: the effect on special ordering. A. Symons. il *Publishers Weekly* 236:19-22 O 13 '89

Have laser gun, Ballantine reps will travel—faster and smarter [speeding inventory and ordering] J. Mutter. il *Publishers Weekly* 235:53-5 F 17 '89

On-line on the road: Harper & Row sales reps computerize [using laptops] J. Mutter. il *Publishers Weekly* 235:50-1 Ja 13 '89

Paperback books

See also
Paperback books—Marketing

Periodical selling

Magazines: ups and downs. S. Schwartzman. il *Publishers Weekly* 235:21-2+ Mr 31 '89

Political literature

The light of the Midnight Special [Los Angeles leftist political bookstore] M. Jones. il *Publishers Weekly* 236:50-2 N 24 '89

Protests mount over 'political harassment' of Los Angeles store [Libros Revolución bookstore] L. See. *Publishers Weekly* 235:22 Ap 21 '89

Professional literature

Reaching the trade: advice from two publishers turned booksellers. J. Kapitan and B. Szabo. il pors *Publishers Weekly* 235:26+ Je 16 '89

Rare books

See also
Jenkins Company

Regional literature

Trails West rounds up western readers [Louisville, Colo. bookstore] S. Sherman. il *Publishers Weekly* 235:41+ My 5 '89

Religious literature

See also
Christian Booksellers Association

Remainders

New dimensions in remaindering. W. Nixon. il *Publishers Weekly* 235:23-4+ Ap 28 '89

Russian literature

Glasnost by the book [Russian language bookseller Victor Kamkin] J. Lowenstein. il *Nation's Business* 77:57-8 Ag '89

Science fiction

A Change of Hobbit changes its digs once again [Santa Monica] M. Jones. il por *Publishers Weekly* 235:34-6 Je 23 '89

Secondhand books

Battle to keep a bookstore in town [attempt to prohibit A Time for Books in San Carlos, Calif.] L. See. *Publishers Weekly* 236:66 S 1 '89

Hunting down antique gardening books. il *Sunset (Central West edition)* 181:160 D '88

Textbook publishers and authors clash over comp copy proposals. C. Reid. il *Publishers Weekly* 236:12 O 20 '89

Security measures

FBI gives bookstore threats top priority [relating to S. Rushdie's Satanic verses] H. Fields. il *Publishers Weekly* 235:12 Mr 17 '89

Sidelines

1990 calendars. il *Publishers Weekly* 235:29-30+ Mr 17 '89

The New York International Gift Fair. M. A. Tennenhouse. il *Publishers Weekly* 236:31-2 S 22 '89

Social aspects

Booksellers rally around the homeless. M. Jones. il *Publishers Weekly* 236:51 N 24 '89

Statistics

1988 sales finish strongly. J. P. Dessauer. il *Publishers Weekly* 235:47 Mr 10 '89

Videotapes

Margins and returns still bedevil video publishers in bookstores [panel at Home Video Show] P. Sweeting. il *Publishers Weekly* 235:33 Ap 14 '89

More book-video tie-ins on display at VSDA meeting. A. Wickstrom. il *Publishers Weekly* 236:46+ S 1 '89

Video publishers showing renewed interest in bookstore distribution. P. Sweeting. il *Publishers Weekly* 235:30-1+ F 3 '89

Atlantic States

See also
Mid-Atlantic Booksellers Association

Australia

A potpourri of fact and fiction from Down Under [children's booksellers] A. Ullin. il *Publishers Weekly* 235:37-8 Mr 24 '89

California

See also
Different Light (Firm)
Northern California Booksellers Association

Battle to keep a bookstore in town [attempt to prohibit A Time for Books in San Carlos] L. See. *Publishers Weekly* 236:66 S 1 '89

A bookstore older than the movies [Fowler Brothers in Los Angeles] L. See. *Publishers Weekly* 235:33 My 26 '89

A Change of Hobbit changes its digs once again [Santa Monica] M. Jones. il por *Publishers Weekly* 235:34-6 Je 23 '89

Earthquake: four stores face uncertain future. M. Reuter and others. *Publishers Weekly* 236:10-11 N 3 '89

John Cole's Bookshop [La Jolla] W. Brisick. il por *Publishers Weekly* 236:95+ S 15 '89

The light of the Midnight Special [Los Angeles leftist political bookstore] M. Jones. il *Publishers Weekly* 236:50-2 N 24 '89

Protests mount over 'political harassment' of Los Angeles store [Libros Revolución bookstore] L. See. *Publishers Weekly* 235:22 Ap 21 '89

Quake update: damaged stores reopen; Debt forgiveness asked [San Francisco Bay Area] J. Mutter and M. J. O'Brien. *Publishers Weekly* 236:10 D 1 '89

'Save the books' fund helps quake-damaged bookstores replace children's books [San Francisco Bay Area] B. Stander. *Publishers Weekly* 236:44-5 N 24 '89

Canada

See also
Book Company

Colorado

Book biz: a community best-seller [C. Villarosa's Hue-Man Experience Bookstore in Denver] il por *Ms.* 18:85 S '89

Denver's black "bookstore and more" [Hue-Man Experience Bookstore] M. L. Small. il *American Visions* 4:42-5 F '89

Trails West rounds up western readers [Louisville, Colo. bookstore] S. Sherman. il *Publishers Weekly* 235:41+ My 5 '89

France

A birthday at kilometer zero [Shakespeare and Company] R. Ryan. il por *Gentlemen's Quarterly* 59:49+ N '89

Traditional booksellers suffer by French price-fix law, study shows. H. R. Lottman. *Publishers Weekly* 235:16 Mr 24 '89

Great Britain

See also
Booksellers Association of Great Britain and Ireland
Net Book Agreement (Great Britain)
Sherratt & Hughes
W. H. Smith & Son (Holdings) plc
Waterstone's Booksellers

London's dance book shop [Dance Books, Ltd.] D. Cox. *Dance Magazine* 63:69-70 D '89

Hawaii

The Honolulu book shops: bookselling in paradise. W. Brisick. il *Publishers Weekly* 235:51-3 Ap 28 '89

Illinois

Season to Taste Books: a comfy (and kitschy) culinary store [Chicago] M. McQuade. il pors *Publishers Weekly* 236:45-6 S 8 '89

Indiana

High Court bars pretrial RICO seizure of books [obscene materials] H. Fields. *Publishers Weekly* 235:19 Mr 10 '89

Iowa

Prairie Lights Books: a beacon in the Midwest [Iowa City] C. S. Drum. il *Publishers Weekly* 235:95-6+ Ap 7 '89

Ireland

See also
Booksellers Association of Great Britain and Ireland

Maryland

Glasnost by the book [Russian language bookseller Victor Kamkin] J. Lowenstein. il *Nation's Business* 77:57-8 Ag '89

Massachusetts

New Words: the collective works [women's bookstore in Cambridge] J. Rosen. il *Publishers Weekly* 235:56-9 Ap 21 '89

The Odyssey Book Shop: a long voyage home [South Hadley] K. McCune. il *Publishers Weekly* 235:63-5 Mr 3 '89

The sharp vision of the World Eye [bookstore in Greenfield] K. O. Fakih. il *Publishers Weekly* 236:38-41 D 15 '89

Middle Western States

See also
Upper Midwest Booksellers Association

New England

See also
New England Booksellers Association

New Mexico

The smart moves of Los Llanos Bookstore [Santa Fe] M. Jones. il por *Publishers Weekly* 236:425-6+ Ag 11 '89

New York (State)

See also
Different Light (Firm)
New York Regional Booksellers Association

Bookworks: a bookselling thoroughbred [Saratoga Springs] J. Angelo. il *Publishers Weekly* 236:24-6 D 1 '89

The Corner Bookstore: a folksy New York storefront in the fancy part of town. M. J. O'Brien. il *Publishers Weekly* 235:187-90 F 24 '89

Dalton acquires Scribner name, sees more stores [negotiating revival of Manhattan store] *Publishers Weekly* 235:15 My 26 '89

Future dims for New York City's St. Marks Bookstore. C. Reid. *Publishers Weekly* 236:10 Ag 18 '89

BOOKSELLERS AND BOOKSELLING—New York (State)
—*cont.*

Good-bye to all that [closing of Scribners] R. D. Story. il *New York* 22:27 Ja 23 '89

Judith's Room: New York City again has a women's bookstore. M. McQuade. il *Publishers Weekly* 235:59 Ap 21 '89

Rodale Press bails out St. Mark's Bookstore in Manhattan. C. Reid. il *Publishers Weekly* 236:12 S 22 '89

Some Scribners memories. R. M. Elman. por *Publishers Weekly* 235:439 Ja 27 '89

Waldenbooks to open Brentano's in Scribner's amid controversy [New York City] C. Reid. *Publishers Weekly* 236:13 S 29 '89

Southeastern States

See also

Southeast Booksellers Association

Soviet Union

Moscow bookstore, with sales of $250,000, starts second year. *Publishers Weekly* 236:9 D 8 '89

United States

See Booksellers and bookselling

Washington (D.C.)

Bookstores from A to Z. D. Cutler. il *Publishers Weekly* 235:125-7 My 12 '89

Sidney Kramer Books: the big turnaround. H. Fields. il *Publishers Weekly* 235:128-9 My 12 '89

Western States

See also

Mountains and Plains Booksellers Association

Wisconsin

A Room of One's Own finds a niche of its own [Madison] M. E. Guthrie. il *Publishers Weekly* 236:66-8 Ag 4 '89

BOOKSELLERS AND PUBLISHERS

Targeting the hand-sell [Houghton Mifflin's Network puts books in sellers' hands] R. Burroughs. il *Publishers Weekly* 235:52-4 My 19 '89

BOOKSELLERS ASSOCIATION OF GREAT BRITAIN AND IRELAND

British booksellers support Rushdie, Net Book Agreement [annual meeting] V. Menkes. *Publishers Weekly* 235:16 Je 9 '89

BOOKSHELVES *See* Bookcases

BOOKSTORES *See* Booksellers and bookselling

BOOKSTORES, COLLEGE *See* College bookstores

BOOKWORKS (SARATOGA SPRINGS, N.Y.: BOOKSTORE) *See* Booksellers and bookselling—New York (State)

BOONE, BOB

about

Old catchers never die . . . P. Korn. il pors *Sport (New York, N.Y.)* 80:44-9 Jl '89

BOONE, DEBBY, AND FERRER, GABRIEL

Debby Boone and family send you . . . hugs, laughter, love: "Mommy, read me a story". il pors *Redbook* 173:28 My '89

BOONE, MARY

about

Dealer's choice. J. J. Buck. il por *Vogue* 179:336-45+ F '89

BOONE (MARY) GALLERY *See* Mary Boone Gallery

BOORSTIN, DANIEL J. (DANIEL JOSEPH), 1914-

Can patriotism be legislated? il *U.S. News & World Report* 106:26 F 13 '89

The luxury of retrospect. *Life* 12:37 Fall '89

Our only American ritual. il *U.S. News & World Report* 106:35 Ja 30 '89

BOOSLER, ELAYNE, 1952?-

about

Why she's not a Johnny Carson fan. I. Rudolph. por *TV Guide* 37:19 O 7-13 '89

BOOSTER CABLES *See* Storage batteries—Booster cables

BOOSTERS FOR GUIDED MISSILES *See* Guided missiles—Propulsion systems

BOOT CAMPS *See* Military training camps

BOOTBLACKS *See* Shoeshine business

BOOTES (CONSTELLATION) *See* Constellations

BOOTH, CHARLES, 1840-1916

about

Retrieved riches: Charles Booth's Life and labour of the people in London. R. O'Day. bibl il por map *History Today* 39:29-35 Ap '89

BOOTH, PHILIP

Dillard School of Performing Arts. *Down Beat* 56:23-4 Je '89

BOOTH, STEPHEN A.

Electronics. See issues of Popular Mechanics beginning February 1985

Hot house. il *Rolling Stone* p104-6+ Je 15 '89

Photography. See issues of Popular Mechanics beginning January 1986

BOOTH, WILLIAM

The joys of a big brain. il *Psychology Today* 23:57 Ap '89

BOOTHBY, NEIL

about

An American doctor in the schools of hell. B. Duffy. il pors map *U.S. News & World Report* 106:32-5 Ja 16 '89

BOOTHROYD, G. (GEOFFREY), 1932-

about

Pssst! Want a secret for making superproducts? O. Port. il pors *Business Week* p106+ O 2 '89

BOOTHROYD, GEOFFREY *See* Boothroyd, G. (Geoffrey), 1932-

BOOTHROYD DEWHURST INC.

Pssst! Want a secret for making superproducts? O. Port. il pors *Business Week* p106+ O 2 '89

BOOTS

See also

Cowboy boots

Hiking boots

Ski boots

Tony Lama Company

Boots are better. B. McKeown. il *Outdoor Life* 184:86-8+ S '89

These boots are made for . . . commuting? [Sorel boot] M. Porter. il *Gentlemen's Quarterly* 59:27 Ja '89

BOOZ, ALLEN & HAMILTON INC.

Living with a laptop [B. Moeller] M. Antonoff. il pors *Personal Computing* 13:94-5+ F '89

BORA BORA (FRENCH POLYNESIA)

Description and travel

Gourmet holidays: Society Islands. C. Bates. il map *Gourmet* 49:58-63+ F '89

BORAN (AFRICAN PEOPLE)

Honey hunters follow birds to reach bees [research by H. A. Isack and H.-U. Reyer] *Science News* 135:172 Mr 18 '89

Honeyguides and honey gatherers: interspecific communication in a symbiotic relationship. H. A. Isack and H.-U. Reyer. bibl f il *Science* 243:1343-6 Mr 10 '89

BORCHARDT, JOHN

How to make business travel more productive. il *Working Woman* 14:99-100+ S '89

BORDAS, BONNIE

about

When Bonnie Bordas leads a wilderness tour, there's no male call at all. D. Chu. il pors *People Weekly* 31:135-6+ My 8 '89

BORDEAUX WINES *See* Wine

BORDEN, SARAH

about

The deb of the minute. M. Gross. il pors *New York* 22:42-5 Ag 28 '89

BORDEN, INC.

First it was poison pills—now it's 'people pills' [resignation pact for top managers] C. Farrell. *Business Week* p33-4 Ja 16 '89

Moving into senior management [K. Johnson, vice president of consumer affairs] J. Ciabattari. il pors *Working Woman* 14:104-6+ My '89

Remaking Elsie. N. Alster. il por *Forbes* 144:106+ D 25 '89

BORDER ART WORKSHOP. TALLER DE ARTE FRONTERIZO

Border Art Workshop/Taller de Arte Fronterizo. C. Fusco. *The Nation* 248:602-4 My 1 '89

Living on the border. D. Joselit. bibl f il *Art in America* 77:120-9 D '89

BORDER PATROL (U.S.) *See* United States. Border Patrol

BORDERLINE PERSONALITY DISORDER

Crossing the 'borderline' of child abuse [research by Judith L. Herman] B. Bower. *Science News* 135:246 Ap 22 '89

Women on the verge: the surge in borderline personality disorder. C. Barlam. il *Mademoiselle* 95:140 N '89

BORDERS, GARDEN *See* Garden borders

BORDES, PAMELLA

about

Hookers aren't the only ones for sale. B. Amiel. il *Maclean's* 102:9 My 8 '89

More sex please, we're British. A. Stanley. il pors *Time* 133:31 Ap 3 '89

Raising an uncommon furor in the Commons, powerful Brits heed an Indian love call. P. Chin. il pors *People Weekly* 31:52-3 Ap 3 '89

Strange bedfellows. A. Phillips. il por *Maclean's* 102:31+ Ap 3 '89

BORDEWICH, FERGUS M.

Decision time in Hong Kong. il *Reader's Digest* 134:121-6 Je '89

BORDIA, ANIL

A new policy for education. il *The Courier (Unesco)* 42:16-21 F '89

BORDIN, GELINDO

about

The gentle man of Verona. M. Bloom. il pors *Runner's World* 24:60-5 N '89

BOREAL OWLS *See* Owls

BOREAS INTERNATIONAL

The man who would be magnate [Y. Fromer] M. Schifrin. il por *Forbes* 144:41-4 S 18 '89

BOREN, SUSAN

about

Rounding out with lateral moves. L. Dusky. il por *Working Woman* 14:112 O '89

BORENSTEIN, NATHANIEL S.
My life as a NATO collaborator [cover story] il *The Bulletin of the Atomic Scientists* 45:14-20 Ap '89

BORG, BJÖRN, 1956-
about
A break down [cover story] N. Amdur. il pors *World Tennis* 36:28-9 Ap '89

BORG, ERIK, AND COUNTER, S. ALLEN
The middle-ear muscles. bibl il *Scientific American* 261:74-80 Ag '89

BORG, PARKER W.
Building a flexible framework for new information services [address, October 19, 1988] *Department of State Bulletin* 89:33-5 Ja '89
Telecommunications and economic development in the Caribbean [address, November 30, 1988] *Department of State Bulletin* 89:17-20 Mr '89

BORGER, IRENE
Aboard the Impromptu. il *Architectural Digest* 46:144-9 Ag '89
Eastern soul. il *Architectural Digest* 46:308-14+ My '89
The Moroccan moods of Laise Adzer. il por *Architectural Digest* 46:168-73 S '89
The pleasures of Partemi: restoring a ruined castellino on the Tuscan coast. il por *Architectural Digest* 46:178-85 Ap '89

BORGMAN, RUTH ELIZABETH
The body snatchers. *Omni (New York, N.Y.)* 12:41 D '89

BORING, MOLLIE D.
Books and the sky. See issues of Sky and Telescope

BORING See Drilling and boring (Earth and rocks)

BORING MACHINERY See Drilling and boring machinery

BORIS, ROBERT
about
Buy & cell [film] Reviews
People Weekly 31:16+ F 13 '89. S. Haller

BORISH, JEFFREY
The basics of concert hall acoustics. il *High Fidelity (New York, N.Y.)* 39:40-7 Jl '89

BORJA CEVALLOS, RODRIGO, 1935-
about
Ecuador swings toward social democracy. C. M. Conaghan. bibl f *Current History* 88:137-41+ Mr '89

BORK, ROBERT H., 1927-
The case against political judging [cover story] il por *National Review* 41:23-8 D 8 '89
Should a constitutional amendment to prevent flag desecration be approved? [excerpts from testimony, July 19, 1989] *Congressional Digest* 68:212+ Ag/S '89
about
The remaking of Robert Bork. M. Pertschuk and W. Schaetzel. il *The Nation* 249:750-2 D 18 '89
'The tempting of America'. G. F. Will. il *Newsweek* 114:96 D 4 '89

BORLAND, HAL, 1900-1978
Winter's moon. il *Audubon* 91:37 Ja '89

BORLAND INTERNATIONAL INC.
VROOMM: Borland says memory technology will make future programs better, not bigger [Virtual Real-Time Object-Oriented Memory Manager] *Byte* 14:17-18 Ag '89

BORN, C. ALLEN
about
Shareholders say 'thanks' to these CEOs. D. Foust and M. Roman. il pors *Business Week* p48 My 1 '89

BORN, JORGE, III
about
Can business save Argentina? J. Ryser and R. A. Kessler. il pors *Business Week* p46-8 S 18 '89

BORN ON THE FOURTH OF JULY [film] See Motion picture reviews—Single works

BORN YESTERDAY [drama] See Kanin, Garson, 1912-

BORNEMISZA, HANS HEINRICH THYSSEN- See Thyssen-Bornemisza, Hans Heinrich, Baron, 1921-

BORNEO
See also
Kinabalu National Park (Borneo)
Rain forests—Borneo
Wildlife—Borneo
Description and travel
Borneo. F. Gebhart. il *Travel Holiday* 172:72-9 S '89
Industries
See also
Tourist trade—Borneo

BORNS, BETSY
Arresting appeal. pors *Harper's Bazaar* 122:50+ F '89

BORON IN THE BODY
Belief in boron: an element of strength [osteoporosis prevention; work of Forrest H. Nielsen] I. Wickelgren. *Science News* 135:204 Ap 1 '89
Boron/brain connection [may affect alertness; research by James G. Penland] il *Prevention (Emmaus, Pa.)* 41:8+ S '89

BOROS, MONICA C. ROTHSCHILD- See Rothschild-Boros, Monica C.

BORRA, AGOSTINO
A simple cure for diarrhoea. il *World Health* p14-15 N '89

BORRELIA
At the drop of a tick [Lyme disease; cover story] I. Wickelgren. il *Science News* 135:184-7 Mr 25 '89
Lyme on the lam [antibodies unable to recognize Borrelia bacteria; research by Tom Schwan] il *Discover* 10:10 S '89

BORROWING OF MONEY See Credit; Loans, Personal

BORST, FRANÇOIS
(jt. auth) See Scherrer, Jean-Raoul, and Borst, François

BORTLE, JOHN E.
Comet digest. See issues of Sky and Telescope through April 1989

BORUCH, MARIANNE
Maps [poem] *The New Yorker* 65:36 Jl 3 '89

BOSCAWEN, EDWARD
about
Gardens: High Beeches: preserving a woodland heritage in Sussex. E. Lambert. il *Architectural Digest* 46:150-3+ Ag '89

BOSCH, JUAN, 1909-
about
In the land of the blind caudillo. M. Kurlansky. il pors *The New York Times Magazine* p24-6+ Ag 6 '89

BOSCH, MARNIX L., AND OTHERS
Identification of the fusion peptide of primate immunodeficiency viruses. bibl f il *Science* 244:694-7 My 12 '89

BOSCH, ORLANDO
about
Caught up in Miami's Cuban politics. B. Turque. il por *Newsweek* 114:24 S 4 '89

BOSCHI PALACE (KORCULA, YUGOSLAVIA) See Palaces—Yugoslavia

BOSCHWITZ, RUDY
Should the Congress adopt the "High Risk Occupational Disease Notification and Prevention Act of 1987"? [excerpts from address, March 24, 1988] *Congressional Digest* 68:113+ Ap '89

BOSCO, KALAME IYAMUSE
Shaka Zulu, a living legend. il *The Unesco Courier* 42:44-7 S '89

BOSCOBEL RESTORATION
Boscobel in Garrison-on-Hudson, New York. F. W. Stanyer. bibl f il *Antiques* 136:1356-65 D '89

BOSKET, WILLIE, JR.
about
"I won't kill, I'll just maim". R. Behar. il por *Time* 133:30-1 My 29 '89

BOSKIN, MICHAEL J.
about
Boskin: "I have a lot of strong principles". R. Hornik. il por *Time* 133:48 Ja 30 '89
Masterminding the U.S. economy. A. R. Dowd. il por *Fortune* 119:46 Ja 2 '89
Michael Boskin isn't just another ignored economist. H. Gleckman. il por *Business Week* p128-9 Je 26 '89

BOSLOUGH, JOHN
Searching for the secrets of gravity. il *National Geographic* 175:562-83 My '89

BOSONS See Particles (Nuclear physics)

BOSQUE DEL APACHE NATIONAL WILDLIFE REFUGE (N.M.)
Watching the sandhills in New Mexico and Arizona. il *Sunset (Central West edition)* 182:46 Ja '89

BOSS-EMPLOYEE RELATIONS See Psychology, Industrial

BOSSA NOVA
Bye-bye Brazil [A. C. Jobim] E. Pooley. il por *New York* 22:30 Mr 20 '89

BOSSELMAN, ROBERT A., AND OTHERS
Germline transmission of exogenous genes in the chicken. bibl f il *Science* 243:533-5 Ja 27 '89

BOSTON (MASS.)
Airports
Court grounds Logan fees. il *Flying* 116:12 N '89
Massport drops PACE to avoid loss of U.S. aid [landing fee schedule at Logan International Airport] *Aviation Week & Space Technology* 130:109 Ja 2 '89
Massport suspends Logan's higher fees. *Flying* 116:12-13 Mr '89
Architecture
See also
Boston (Mass.)—Buildings
Build Boston (Organization)
Bridges
See also
Harvard Bridge
Buildings
Two on the town [Heritage on the Garden] P. M. Sachner. il maps *Architectural Record* 177:122-7 My '89
Crime
See also
Stuart, Charles—Murder case
Education
Curbing teen violence [Barron Assessment and Counseling Center] R. Levine. il *American Health* 8:108 Ap '89

BOSTON (MASS.)—cont.

Express highways
See Express highways—Massachusetts
Galleries and museums
See also
Isabella Stewart Gardner Museum
Museum of Fine Arts (Boston, Mass.)
Harbor
Boston's toilet: the true story. A. Wolff. il *Audubon* 91:26-30+
Mr '89
Historic houses, sites, etc.
Back Bay reflections [W. Hodgins' 1872 townhouse] G. Harrell.
il por *House & Garden* 161:206-9 S '89
Back Bay Victorian [Boston town house decorated by Bruce
Gregga for B. and F. Herman] D. Roberts. il *Architectural
Digest* 46:152-9 Mr '89
Behind the Federal facade [houses designed by C. Bullfinch]
A. O. Boulton. il pors *American Heritage* 40:68-75 My/Je
'89
The hub of the solar system [walking tour of literary sites]
P. Davison. il map *American Heritage* 40:54-6+ Ap '89
Hospitals
See also
Brigham and Women's Hospital (Boston, Mass.)
Massachusetts Eye and Ear Infirmary
New England Medical Center Hospital
Housing
See also
Project Family Independence
Look for the union label [housing trust fund in contract
of Local 26 of Hotel Workers Union] P. Dreier. il *The
Progressive* 53:30 Ap '89
Renovation and the housing crisis. J. Schlefer. *Technology
Review* 92:3+ O '89
Industries
Boston faces reality [early evening tabloid TV] K. Haley.
il *Channels (New York, N.Y.: 1986)* 9:86-7 F '89
Intellectual life
The hub of the solar system [walking tour of literary sites]
P. Davison. il map *American Heritage* 40:54-6+ Ap '89
Labor
New believers [union organizers] B. McKibben. il *Mother
Jones* 14:38-41+ Ap '89
Libraries
See also
Boston Athenaeum
Municipal contracts
Big biz in Boston [city contracts and affirmative action]
B. W. O'Connor. il *Black Enterprise* 20:18 Ag '89
Music festivals
See Music festivals—Massachusetts
Newspapers
See also
Boston globe
Poor
See also
Project Family Independence
In Boston, a busing plan that works [nightly busing of the
homeless to Braintree] *Newsweek* 113:27 Mr 6 '89
Lashanda Daniels's outstanding essay on the homeless was
no academic exercise—she'd been there. W. Plummer.
il pors *People Weekly* 32:39-40 Jl 31 '89
Protests, demonstrations, etc.
Jackson marches against drugs at rally in Boston. il por
Jet 76:31 Jl 3 '89
Public health
The rats are coming [effect of Central Artery project] S.
Allis. il *Time* 133:63 F 27 '89
Race relations
Tale of two cities. *Time* 134:28 S 11 '89
Religious institutions and affairs
Help wanted: a few good fishers of men [TV ad campaign
for priests] *Newsweek* 113:61 Je 26 '89
Sanitary affairs
Boston's toilet: the true story. A. Wolff. il *Audubon* 91:26-30+
Mr '89
Mud-slinging over sewage technology [EPA vs. Boston and
San Diego] M. Sun. il *Science* 246:440-3 O 27 '89
Schools
See Boston (Mass.)—Education
Sports
Boston. B. Ryan. il *Sport (New York, N.Y.)* 80:54-8 Jl '89
Stores
Traveler's market. D. P. Marshall. il *Travel Holiday* 172:34-9
S '89
Streets
See also
Newbury Street (Boston, Mass.)
Water pollution
Boston's toilet: the true story. A. Wolff. il *Audubon* 91:26-30+
Mr '89
**BOSTON (MASS.). ISABELLA STEWART GARDNER
MUSEUM** *See* Isabella Stewart Gardner Museum
BOSTON ATHENAEUM
The Boston Athenaeum and its furnishings. R. Armstrong.
il *Antiques* 136:302-15 Ag '89
Museum accessions [portraits by G. Stuart and E. Tarbell
acquired] E. H. Gustafson. il *Antiques* 136:240 Ag '89

BOSTON BALLET
Boston Ballet to celebrate silver anniversary. I. M. Fanger.
il *Dance Magazine* 63:7 Mr '89
Reviews:
J. Gelfand debuts in Don Quixote. I. M. Fanger. *Dance
Magazine* 63:88-9 N '89
Performances at Wang Center. I. M. Fanger. il *Dance
Magazine* 63:25-6 Ja '89
BOSTON CELTICS LIMITED PARTNERSHIP
The greening of the Celtics [purchase of TV station] il
Newsweek 114:60 O 16 '89
BOSTON CHILDREN'S BOOK COLLABORATIVE
Children's book group flourishes in Boston. A. Meeker.
Publishers Weekly 236:32 Ag 25 '89
BOSTON COMPANY, INC.
What did Boston Co. know and when did it know it?
[accounting errors] K. H. Hammonds. por *Business Week*
p87 F 6 '89
BOSTON EARLY MUSIC FESTIVAL AND EXHIBITION
Musical events. A. Porter. *The New Yorker* 65:93-6 Je 19
'89
BOSTON EARLY MUSIC FESTIVAL ORCHESTRA
Musical events:
Concert version of Mozart's Idomeneo. A. Porter. *The
New Yorker* 65:72-4 Jl 3 '89
BOSTON GLOBE
Boston's accidental demibillionaires. M. Fritz. il por *Forbes*
144 Special Issue:112+ O 23 '89
BOSTON MARATHON *See* Marathon running
BOSTON MUSEUM OF FINE ARTS *See* Museum of Fine
Arts (Boston, Mass.)
BOSTON UNIVERSITY
At Boston University, Biotech 101 is no breeze [investment
in Seragen] L. Jereski. *Business Week* p30-1 Ap 10 '89
Crusader on the Charles [J. Silber; cover story] H. Epstein.
il pors *The New York Times Magazine* p26-9+ Ap 23
'89
Letting the losses run [investment in Seragen Inc.] D. Wechs-
ler. il *Forbes* 143:116 Ap 17 '89
Rewriting the code of conduct on campus. J. Rachlin. il
U.S. News & World Report 106:56 Ja 9 '89
Silber bullet [J. Silber's plans to have Boston University
manage the Chelsea school system] D. P. Hamilton. *The
New Republic* 201:18-19 D 4 '89
BOSTON UNIVERSITY. SCHOOL OF THEATRE ARTS
Boston University. il *Theatre Crafts* 23:51+ N '89
BOSTWICK, BARRY
about
Look who else is on this month. L. Eisenberg. por *TV
Guide* 37:12+ N 4-10 '89
BOSVELD, JANE
Midnight dreams. il *Harper's Bazaar* 122:188-93+ O '89
(jt. auth) See Gackenbach, Jayne, 1946-, and Bosveld, Jane
BOSWELL, JAMES G., II
about
"Let the growth come by itself". R. King. il pors *Forbes*
143:98+ Ap 17 '89
BOSWELL, JOHN
about
The unwanted children of times past [interview] A. P. Sanoff.
il por *U.S. News & World Report* 106:62 My 1 '89
BOSWELL, ROBERT, 1953-
The proximity [story] *Esquire* 112:123-4+ Jl '89
Rain [story] *The New Yorker* 65:48-58 N 20 '89
BOSWELL (J.G.) COMPANY *See* J.G. Boswell Company
BOTANICAL EXPLORATION
Field notes for better gardens. B. Yinger. il *Flower and
Garden* 33:78-80+ Ja/F '89
The New Deal and the guru [Russian mystic N. Roerich
sent on scientific expedition to North China and Manchuria
by Roosevelt administration's H. A. Wallace] C. J. Errico
and J. S. Walker. il pors *American Heritage* 40:92-5+
Mr '89
BOTANICAL GARDENS
International aspects
Research amid the camellias. S. Begley. il *Newsweek* 113:58-9
My 15 '89
Great Britain
See also
Royal Botanic Gardens (Kew, England)
New York (State)
See also
New York Botanical Garden
Texas
See also
Moody Gardens (Galveston, Tex.)
San Antonio Botanical Gardens
BOTANICAL ILLUSTRATION *See* Flowers in art
BOTANICAL MAGAZINE (LONDON, ENGLAND) *See* Cur-
tis's botanical magazine
BOTANICAL RESEARCH
See also
Computers—Botanical use
Research amid the camellias [botanical gardens] S. Begley.
il *Newsweek* 113:58-9 My 15 '89
BOTANICAL SOCIETY OF AMERICA
Botanical awards. *BioScience* 39:59 Ja '89

BOTANICALS *See* Botany, Medical
BOTANY
See also
Angiosperms
Clones (Botany)
Cryptogams
Ethnobotany
Forest vegetation
Fungi
Leaves
Morphogenesis
Paleobotany
Phyllotaxis
Plants
Roots
Seeds
Anatomy
See also
Plant cells and tissues
Awards
Botanical awards. *BioScience* 39:59 Ja '89
Classification
Where the wild things grow [C. Linne's plant classification system] J. Bosveld. il *Omni (New York, N.Y.)* 11:56-61 Ap '89
Ecology
See also
Forest ecology
Plant succession
Bootstrapping in ecosystems [reciprocal interactions between plants and soils] D. A. Perry and others. bibl f il *BioScience* 39:230-7 Ap '89
Periodicals
See also
Curtis's botanical magazine
Physiology
See also
Chloroplasts
Photosynthesis
Amazon River Valley
Out of Amazonia [botanical illustrator M. Mee] B. Maddox. il por *Ms.* 18:54-7 O '89
Arizona
Workman Creek Falls, Arizona. R. H. Mohlenbrock. il map *Natural History* p86-9 Mr '89
Australia
'Living fossils'. il *The Courier (Unesco)* 41:30-1 D '88
Illinois
Some plants slept [drought] R. H. Mohlenbrock. il *Natural History* p58-60 Ja '89
Kauai (Hawaii)
Living on the edge [botanist M. Doyle's studies of gunnera in Alakai Swamp] J. Nielsen. il pors *National Wildlife* 27:20-3 O/N '89
Korea (South)
In pursuit of a hardy camellia. B. Yinger. il map *Flower and Garden* 33:104-6 Mr/Ap '89
On site with hardy camellias: Sochong Island, Korea. B. Yinger. il *Flower and Garden* 33:62-6 My/Je '89
New York (State)
See also
New York (N.Y.)—Botany
Pennsylvania
Hunting for giants [tree hunters T. Grisez and M. Hobaugh comb Pennsylvania for champion specimens] C. Fergus. il pors *Country Journal* 16:56-61 Ja '89
BOTANY, MEDICAL
See also
Aloe
8 medical miracles from nature. S. Lally. il *Prevention (Emmaus, Pa.)* 41:33-41 N '89
Aloe: the healing plant. B. Dunham. il *Flower and Garden* 33:37 N/D '89
Botanical beauty [natural cosmetics] il *Harper's Bazaar* 122:152-3+ F '89
Immuni-tea [effects of astragalus on T cell activity; research by Giora Mavligit and Da-Tong Chu] J. Barone. il *American Health* 8:100 O '89
Just another day in paradise [M. Plotkin's work with the Tirió Indians of Suriname] D. D. Jackson. il *Reader's Digest* 134:166-8+ Ap '89
Natural herbal remedies. M. Morrison. il *Redbook* 174:18 D '89
Searching for medicinal wealth in Amazonia [M. Plotkin's work with Tirió Indians of Suriname] D. D. Jackson. bibl (p171) il pors *Smithsonian* 19:94-103 F '89
Weeding out malaria [artemisinin] D. L. Klayman. il *Natural History* p18+ O '89
BOTERO, FERNANDO, 1932-
about
Fernando Botero's 'obsession' [interview] A. Abelleyra. il *World Press Review* 36:61 Ag '89
BOTHA, PIETER W.
about
Botha's untimely stroke. M. Nemeth. il por *Maclean's* 102:28 Ja 30 '89
The end of an era: President Botha bids a resentful goodbye. A. Bilski. il por *Maclean's* 102:22 Ag 28 '89

A glimmer of peace. C. Erasmus. il por *Maclean's* 102:26 Jl 24 '89
An heir apparent in the march to Pretoria. por *Newsweek* 113:35 F 13 '89
In the teeth of the 'Great Crocodile'. S. Reiss. il pors *Newsweek* 113:39 Mr 27 '89
Return of the Great Crocodile. B. W. Nelan. il por *Time* 133:56 Mr 27 '89
Showdown in Cape Town. M. Nemeth. por *Maclean's* 102:30 Mr 27 '89
Teatime in Pretoria. C. S. Manegold. il *Newsweek* 114:24 Jl 24 '89
An unlikely tea for two. B. W. Nelan. il pors *Time* 134:29 Jl 24 '89
BOTHWELL, JOHN H.
about
One Gundarev revelation: the strange case of officer Bothwell. D. Wise. il por *The New York Times Magazine* p82 S 17 '89
BOTSTEIN, LEON, 1946-
about
Your own world. J. Groch. il por *American Health* 8:65-6 Ap '89
BOTSWANA
See also
Kalahari Desert
Wildlife—Botswana
Wildlife management—Botswana
BOTTÉRO, JEAN
Gilgamesh, the king who did not wish to die. il *The Unesco Courier* 42:18-21 S '89
BOTTLED WATER
Calories in H$_2$O [sparkling water] il *Prevention (Emmaus, Pa.)* 41:12 Ag '89
Labeling
Body Toddy [mineral water claimed to be health cure] il *FDA Consumer* 23:33-4 D '89/Ja '90
BOTTLED WATER INDUSTRY
France
See also
Source Perrier SA
BOTTLES
See also
Beverage containers
Medicine bottles
Perfume bottles
Wine bottles
BOTTOM BOUNCERS *See* Fishing lures, flies, etc.
BOTTOM FISH FISHERIES (COMMERCIAL) *See* Fisheries
BOTTOM LINE (NEW YORK, N.Y.: NIGHTCLUB) *See* New York (N.Y.)—Restaurants, nightclubs, bars, etc.
BOTULISM
Don't trifle with truffles. il *FDA Consumer* 23:36 Jl/Ag '89
BOUCHARD, BENOÎT
about
The minister of VIA. M. Clark. il por *Maclean's* 102:24 Ag 21 '89
Up in the air. B. Wallace. il por *Maclean's* 102:54 Ap 3 '89
BOUCHARD, FRED
(ed) *See* Lyons, Emilio. The Sax Doctor rides again
BOUCHARD, LUCIEN
about
'I understand impatience' [interview] L. Van Dusen. *Maclean's* 102:46 Je 26 '89
BOUCHER, NORMAN
Whose woods these are [cover story; with editorial comment by T. H. Watkins] il map *Wilderness* 53:16-41 Fall '89
BOUCHER, RICK
RICO: a racketeering law run amok. il *USA Today (Periodical)* 118:48-9 N '89
BOUCICAULT, DION, 1820-1890
about
The shaughraun [drama] Reviews
Theatre Crafts il 23:10 Ja '89. M. Sommers
BOUDIER, CHRISTIAN
A two-pronged diplomacy. *World Press Review* 36:24-5 Mr '89
BOUDIN, LEONARD B., 1912-1989
about
Obituary
The Nation 249:740-1 D 18 '89
National Review 41:15 D 22 '89
BOUDOIR PHOTOGRAPHY *See* Erotic photography
BOUIS, ANTONINA W.
(tr) *See* Dovlatov, Sergeĭ. Driving gloves
(tr) *See* Dovlatov, Sergeĭ. The photo album
BOUIS, ANTONINA W., AND BOUIS, JEAN-CLAUDE
An evening with the Sakharovs [interview] il pors *Life* 12:96-8+ Jl '89
BOUIS, JEAN-CLAUDE
(jt. auth) *See* Bouis, Antonina W., and Bouis, Jean-Claude
BOULDER (COLO.)
Parks and playgrounds
Trout fishing and inner-tubing near downtown Boulder. il *Sunset (Central West edition)* 183:16-17 Jl '89

BOULEVARD ANTIQUE CENTER (OAK PARK, ILL.)
The collecting life [interview with J. Toomey] il por *Antiques & Collecting Hobbies* 94:40-2 O '89
BOULT, SIR ADRIAN CEDRIC, 1889-1983
about
Encores. R. Freed. pors *Stereo Review* 54:162 D '89
BOULTON, ALEXANDER ORMOND
Behind the Federal facade. il pors *American Heritage* 40:68-75 My/Je '89
The best of Georgian. il por *American Heritage* 40:110-17 F '89
The Gothic awakening. il *American Heritage* 40:140-8 N '89
BOULWARE, LEMUEL R.
about
A look back at "Boulwarism". P. Brimelow. il pors *Forbes* 143:246+ My 29 '89
BOUNCING OF CHECKS *See* Checks, Fraudulent
BOUNDARIES
See also
Alaska—Boundaries
Mexico—Boundaries
Poland—Boundaries
Siberia (Soviet Union)—Boundaries
Territorial waters
United States—Boundaries
BOUNDARY LAYER
See also
Laminar flow
Large eddy breakup devices
BOUNDARY LAYER (METEOROLOGY)
What is clean air? [Amazon Boundary Layer Experiment] S. A. Motley. il *Technology Review* 92:8+ Ja '89
BOUNDARY WATERS CANOE AREA (MINN.)
The bear guardian. P. M. Leschak. il *Outdoor Life* 184:54-5+ Jl '89
BOUNDAS, LOUISE GOOCH
Speaking my piece. See issues of Stereo Review beginning May 1987
BOUNTIES
After the crash, cash [General Electric offering rewards for scattered engine parts from Sioux City, Iowa plane crash] il *Newsweek* 114:32 O 23 '89
BOUNTY MUTINY, 1789
HMS Pandora. J. Murray. il map *Sea Frontiers* 35:328-35 N/D '89
Trouble in Christian's paradise [Pitcairn Island] H. Shapiro. il por map *People Weekly* 31:42-9 Ap 17 '89
Collectibles
Heritage of the Bounty: collectibles from Pitcairn Island. S. Pendleton. il *Antiques & Collecting Hobbies* 94:41-4 Jl '89
BOUQUETS
The bouquet beautiful [bridal bouquets] N. Doerner. il *McCall's* 116:34 My '89
BOURASSA, ROBERT, 1933-
about
A campaign setback. M. Rose. il *Maclean's* 102:12-13 S 4 '89
Campaigning in Quebec. M. Rose. il por *Maclean's* 102:14-15 Ag 21 '89
The failures of Robert Bourassa. J. Stewart. por *Maclean's* 102:64 Ja 2 '89
Heading for the polls. B. Wallace. il por *Maclean's* 102:14-15 Je 19 '89
Qualified victory. M. Rose. il por *Maclean's* 102:16-18 O 9 '89
The re-election of a barefaced opportunist. P. C. Newman. il *Maclean's* 102:44 O 9 '89
Storm clouds over Quebec [cover story; special section; with editorial comment by Kevin Doyle] il pors *Maclean's* 102:2, 16-22+ S 25 '89
Trouble on the Quebec front. B. Wallace. *Maclean's* 102:12 Je 26 '89
War over words. il por *Maclean's* 102:38-42 Ja 2 '89
BOURBON-PARMA, ZITA VON *See* Zita, Empress, consort of Charles I, Emperor of Austria, 1892-1989
BOURBON WHISKEY *See* Whiskey
BOURDON, DAVID, 1934-
The Belter chair. il *American Heritage* 40:24-5 Mr '89
BOURGEOIS, LOUISE
about
Intimate strangeness. K. Larson. il *New York* 22:64 Ap 17 '89
Louise Bourgeois at Galerie Lelong and Robert Miller. K. Johnson. il *Art in America* 77:139 Jl '89
BOURGOIS, PHILIPPE
Just another night on crack street. il *The New York Times Magazine* p52-3+ N 12 '89
BOURKE, JARON
Mergermania. *The Nation* 249:495 O 30 '89
BOURKE-WHITE, MARGARET, 1904-1971
about
The day she shot Joseph Stalin . . . over and over. E. Caldwell. il por *TV Guide* 37:22-3 Ap 22-28 '89
Margaret Bourke-White: new vistas in photojournalism. W. M. Barrett. il por *USA Today (Periodical)* 118:54-63 S '89

BOURNE, MICHAEL
Fusion: jazz-rock-classical [reprint] il *Down Beat* 56:79-80 S '89
Gerry Mulligan: singing a song of Mulligan. il pors *Down Beat* 56:23-5 Ja '89
Mike Mainieri & Steps Ahead: hitting it heavy. il pors *Down Beat* 56:20-2 Jl '89
Willem Breuker, & Kompany: Euro-bop, with a twist. il pors *Down Beat* 56:28-30 My '89
William Paterson College. *Down Beat* 56:23 Je '89
BOURNE, RANDOLPH SILLIMAN, 1886-1918
In a schoolroom. *The New Republic* 201 [Reprint v1]:23-4 N 6 '89 [N 7 '14]
BOURQUE, JOSEPH
Fed up with charity. por *Newsweek* 114:10 S 4 '89
BOUTIQUES *See* Clothing stores
BOUTON, KATHERINE
The Nobel pair. il pors *The New York Times Magazine* p28-9+ Ja 29 '89
BOUTONNIERES
The boutonniere. J. Berendt. il *Esquire* 112:56 N '89
The last detail. W. Irvine. il *Gentlemen's Quarterly* 59:43 N '89
BOUTSEN, THIERRY
about
Boots 'n brollies. I. Ireland. il *Road & Track* 41:114-15+ O '89
BOUTTE, ALVIN J.
about
Banking on new territory. M. M. McDowell. il por *Black Enterprise* 19:256-8+ Je '89
BOVARD, JAMES
The agricultural swamp. il *National Review* 41:46-8 F 10 '89
The alarming truth about the World Bank. *Reader's Digest* 134:108-12 Je '89
The failure of federal job training. *Society* 26:57-64 My/Je '89
BOVIN, ALEXANDER
The doors swing open. il *World Press Review* 36:13-14 My '89
BOVINE LEUKEMIA VIRUS *See* Leukemia viruses
BOVINE SOMATOTROPIN, SYNTHETIC *See* Pituitary hormones, Synthetic
BOW AND ARROW
See also
Archery
BOW HUNTING *See* Hunting with bow and arrow
BOWDEN, CHARLES
The importance of being nothing. il *National Parks* 63:26-31 S/O '89
BOWDEN, MARK
The great potato pick-off play. il *Reader's Digest* 134:103-7 Je '89
BOWEN, EZRA
High Rustler, Alta, Utah. il *Skiing* 42:12 D '89
BOWEN, RICHARD A.
Tracking down bugs using a spectrum analyzer. il *Radio-Electronics* 60:33-7 Je '89
BOWEN HOUSE, ROSELAND COTTAGE (WOODSTOCK, CONN.)
The Gothic awakening. A. O. Boulton. il *American Heritage* 40:140-8 N '89
BOWER, JOHN, 1949-
Pollution-free housing. bibl il *The Mother Earth News* 116:98-100 Mr/Ap '89
BOWER, MARVIN
about
The U.S. Business Hall of Fame. W. Guzzardi. il por *Fortune* 119:134 Mr 13 '89
BOWERMASTER, JON, 1954-
20 years, and 50 miles, down the road. il *The New York Times Magazine* p22-5 Jl 2 '89
Peak moments. il *Harper's Bazaar* 122:90+ F '89
The sky is the limit. *Harper's Bazaar* 122:65+ Jl '89
BOWERS, CATHY SMITH- *See* Smith-Bowers, Cathy
BOWERS, FAUBION
Amazin' Albert (I). il pors *Opera News* 53:12-14+ F 4 '89
Amazin' Albert (II). il por *Opera News* 53:32-7 F 18 '89
BOWERS, RICHARD L.
about
"I learn on the job". W. P. Barrett. il por *Forbes* 144:49-50 Ag 7 '89
BOWERSOCK, G. W. (GLEN WARREN), 1936-
Herodotus, Alexander, and Rome. *The American Scholar* 58:407-14 Summ '89
BOWERSOCK, GLEN WARREN *See* Bowersock, G. W. (Glen Warren), 1936-
BOWERY SAVINGS BANK
Bowery follies [1985 federal bailout arranged by R. Ravitch] C. Byron. il por *New York* 22:14+ My 29 '89
BOWIE, DAVID
about
Bowie's bicoastal blitz. J. Ressner. il por *Rolling Stone* p24 Ag 10 '89
Bowie's Tin Machine. P. Puterbaugh. il por *Stereo Review* 54:129 S '89

BOWIE, DAVID—about—*cont.*
The dark soul of a new machine. D. Fricke. il *Rolling Stone* p137-9 Je 15 '89
The wooing of David Bowie. J. Guterman. *Rolling Stone* p28 My 18 '89

BOWIE, ROBERT
White on green [poem] *America* 160:562 Je 10 '89

BOWIE, ROBERT R.
A promising future. *The Bulletin of the Atomic Scientists* 45:41 My '89

BOWKER'S LEGAL PUBLISHING PREVIEW (NEWSLETTER)
Bowker aims to help lawyers make book-buying easier. J. Wisdom. il *Publishers Weekly* 236:51 S 8 '89

BOWL GAMES (FOOTBALL) *See* Football, College—Bowl games

BOWLDS, LARRY S.
Tracking the early Permian. il pors *Earth Science* 42:16-19 Summ '89

BOWLES, PAUL, 1910-
about
Pipe dreams. R. Craft. bibl f il *The New York Review of Books* 36:6+ N 23 '89

BOWLING
See also
National Bowling Hall of Fame and Museum
Scott and Matthew Higa make their mark as bowling's youngest twin strike force [7 year old bowlers] il pors *People Weekly* 31:98-9 Ja 30 '89

BOWLING, PROFESSIONAL
Does Planned Parenthood know about this? [M. Aulby] D. Herbst. il por *Sport (New York, N.Y.)* 80:15 O '89
Tournaments
Life in the slow lane [D. Ballard wins Firestone Tournament of Champions] D. S. Looney. il por *Sports Illustrated* 70:92 My 1 '89

BOWLING ALLEYS
See also
Beacon Lanes (New York, N.Y.)
The bowling bumper cushion spares frustrated alley cats the indignity of gutter balls [DBA-Glancer Bowling Cushions developed by Z. Sheinberg and A. Wortman] il pors *People Weekly* 32:157 D 11 '89

BOWLING CLOTHES *See* Clothing and dress—Sports clothes

BOWLT, JOHN E.
Rehabilitating the Russian avant-garde. il *Art News* 88:116-19 F '89

BOWMAN, BARBARA T.
Educating language-minority children: challenges and opportunities. il *Phi Delta Kappan* 71:118-20 O '89

BOWMAN, DEWITT F.
about
California's new crusader for shareholder rights. T. Carson and J. B. Levine. il por *Business Week* p72-3 Ja 30 '89

BOWMAN (SISTER THEA) BLACK CATHOLIC EDUCATIONAL FOUNDATION *See* Sister Thea Bowman Black Catholic Educational Foundation

BOWNE & CO., INC.
Survivor. T. Jaffe. *Forbes* 144:317 S 4 '89

BOX, CHARLES
about
Charles Box elected first black Rockford, Il., mayor. il por *Jet* 76:25 Ap 24 '89

BOX, CLOYCE K., 1924-
about
Third down and long. E. F. Cone. por *Forbes* 143:10 F 20 '89

BOX TURTLES *See* Turtles

BOXER, SARAH
Dark forces. il *Sports Illustrated* 70:52-4+ Ap 17 '89
Inside our sleeping minds. bibl il *Modern Maturity* 32:48-54 O/N '89

BOXER SHORTS *See* Underwear

BOXERCISE
Uppercutting old notions [for women] C. Leerhsen. il *Newsweek* 114:66-7 Ag 7 '89

BOXERS
See also
Ali, Muhammad, 1942-
Barkley, Iran
Bruno, Frank
Camacho, Hector
Chávez, Julio César
Dokes, Michael
Duran, Roberto
Foreman, George
Hardy, Leland
Haugen, Greg
Hearns, Thomas
Hill, Virgil
Holmes, Larry
Holyfield, Evander
Johansson, Ingemar
Jones, Roy
Kalambay, Sumbu
Kilrain, Jake
Lasisi, Joe

Leonard, Sugar Ray
Louis, Joe, 1914-1981
Mancini, Boom Boom
Marcus, Egerton
Mayweather, Roger
McCarthy, Steve
Moore, Archie, 1913-
Nunn, Michael
Patterson, Tracy
Ramirez, Jose Luis
Randall, Ricky
Robinson, Sugar Ray
Rodrigues, Adilson
Schmeling, Max, 1905-
Seales, Sugar Ray
Spinks, Leon
Stewart, Alex
Sullivan, John L., 1858-1918
Tyson, Mike
Whitaker, Pernell, 1964?-
Williams, Carl
Wilson, Tony
Women boxers
Ali says former champs 'are all the greatest'. il por *Jet* 77:54 N 20 '89
They're perfect, so far [unblemished pro records of 1988 Olympians] R. O'Brien. il *Sports Illustrated* 70:47 My 15 '89
What has six legs and stings like a bee? The Weaver brothers, boxing's only triple threat. il *People Weekly* 32:148-9 N 13 '89
You can count them out [opponents who go down so that the hometown heroes can go up] R. Reilly. il *Sports Illustrated* 71:86-96+ O 16 '89
Economic conditions
See Boxing—Economic aspects
Training
Dear Mike . . . [trainer E. Futch] G. Smith. il pors *Sports Illustrated* 70:58-64+ F 27 '89

BOXERS (DOGS)
One of the family. A. McCarthy. il *Commonweal* 116:135-6 Mr 10 '89

BOXES, CASES, ETC.
See also
Bait boxes
Briefcases
Gun cases
Jewelry boxes, cases, etc.
Light boxes
Mailboxes
Saffron boxes
Snuffboxes, bottles, etc.
Colorful traveling case [artist's kit for children] L. Okrend. il *Workbench* 45:30-2 N/D '89
Shaker boxes. N. Barrett, Jr. il *Popular Mechanics* 166:140-1+ My '89
Collectors and collecting
The original box. H. L. Rinker. il *Antiques & Collecting Hobbies* 93:27 Ja '89

BOXING
See also
Boxercise
Another classic [S. R. Leonard and T. Hearns fight to a draw; cover story] P. Putnam. il pors *Sports Illustrated* 70:18-21 Je 19 '89
The beatings go on [M. Tyson KOs C. Williams] P. Putnam. pors *Sports Illustrated* 71:18-19 Jl 31 '89
'Belt the body' [P. Whitaker wins IBF lightweight title from G. Haugen] P. Putnam. il pors *Sports Illustrated* 70:44-5 F 27 '89
The boxer the champs won't fight [M. Nunn] J. Stravinsky. il pors *The New York Times Magazine* p32-4+ Ag 13 '89
British boxer's mom takes bout into her own hands [T. Wilson's mother enters ring against S. McCarthy] il por *Jet* 77:52-3 O 16 '89
Fat City for rusty pugs [H. Camacho beats R. Mancini] W. Nack. il pors *Sports Illustrated* 70:36-7 Mr 20 '89
Heavyweight division, R.I.P. J. Ryan. il *Sport (New York, N.Y.)* 80:13 O '89
The Hit Man [T. Hearns to face S. R. Leonard] R. Wiley. il pors *Sports Illustrated* 70:48-50+ Je 5 '89
Holyfield KO's Dokes, moves toward Tyson bout. il por *Jet* 75:51 Mr 27 '89
In your face, José Luis [P. Whitaker vs. J. L. Ramírez for lightweight championship] P. Putnam. il pors *Sports Illustrated* 71:66-7 Ag 28 '89
The last Olympian [R. Jones defeats R. Randall] C. Gammon. il pors *Sports Illustrated* 70:42-4+ My 15 '89
Lean and mean [E. Holyfield KOs A. Rodrigues in heavyweight bout] P. Putnam. il pors *Sports Illustrated* 71:24-6+ Jl 24 '89
Leonard dances to win as Duran has 'no mas'. il pors *Jet* 77:51-2 D 25 '89-Ja 1 '90
Leonard-Hearns, again. D. Miller. il pors *Sport (New York, N.Y.)* 80:69-71 Jl '89
Leonard, Hearns rematch finally will take place. pors *Jet* 75:50 F 20 '89

BOXING—*cont.*

Leonard-Hearns war ends 8-year wait. il pors *Jet* 76:48-50 Je 12 '89

One angry man [E. Holyfield defeats A. Stewart] P. Putnam. il pors *Sports Illustrated* 71:38-9 N 13 '89

One for the ages [S. R. Leonard defeats R. Duran] P. Putnam. il pors *Sports Illustrated* 71:24-5 D 18 '89

One more time! [S. R. Leonard vs. R. Duran] J. Torres. pors *TV Guide* 37:34-6 D 2-8 '89

Patterson's son captures first pro boxing title. il por *Jet* 76:50 My 8 '89

Smashing! [M. Tyson KOs F. Bruno] P. Putnam. il pors *Sports Illustrated* 70:14-17 Mr 6 '89

Stars provide fireworks for Leonard-Duran fans. il *Jet* 77:53-4 D 25 '89-Ja 1 '90

Stonehands rules again [R. Duran beats I. Barkley for WBC middleweight title] B. Newman. il pors *Sports Illustrated* 70:18-19 Mr 6 '89

Stop meeting like this [J. C. Chávez KOs R. Mayweather for WBC super lightweight title] P. Putnam. il pors *Sports Illustrated* 70:75 My 22 '89

Sugar Ray Leonard and Thomas Hearns battle to a draw in title brawl. il pors *Jet* 76:53-4 Je 26 '89

Take cover, Mike Tyson—Frank Bruno's got a secret weapon. A. Coren. il *TV Guide* 37:8-9 F 25-Mr 3 '89

Tale of the tape [M. Tyson vs. football lineman T. Mandarich] il pors *Sports Illustrated* 70:14 My 29 '89

There's no place like home [V. Hill defends light heavy title against J. Lasisi] K. Cook. il pors *Sports Illustrated* 70:90 Je 5 '89

This time Nunn chose not to run [IBF middleweight champ M. Nunn vs. S. Kalambay] P. Putnam. il pors *Sports Illustrated* 70:80 Ap 3 '89

Tyson destroys 'Truth' in 1½ min. Atlantic City bout. il pors *Jet* 76:52+ Ag 7 '89

Tyson's return a triumph, KO's Frank Bruno in five. il pors *Jet* 75:51-2 Mr 13 '89

You're next, Tyson [E. Holyfield KOs M. Dokes] P. Putnam. il pors *Sports Illustrated* 70:34-5 Mr 20 '89

Anecdotes, facetiae, satire, etc.

Hey, Tyson, I'm The Man! L. Montville. il *Sports Illustrated* 71:116 O 2 '89

Economic aspects

An oil heiress looks for pay dirt at the track [fight promoter and race horse breeder J. Abercrombie] T. Vogel. il por *Business Week* p162 My 22 '89

Tyson no 'slave,' King testifies against Cayton. por *Jet* 75:47 Mr 6 '89

We've grown accustomed to his face [manager and promoter L. Duva] B. Newman. il pors *Sports Illustrated* 70:84-8+ Ap 10 '89

Ethical aspects

Fight on [hockey teams turn to boxing trainers for expertise] J. Ryan. il *Sport (New York, N.Y.)* 80:11 My '89

History

'80s boxing. J. Ryan. il *Sport (New York, N.Y.)* 80:76-7 O '89

1889 [J. L. Sullivan vs. J. Kilrain in country's last bareknuckle match] A. Nielson. il por *American Heritage* 40:30+ Jl/Ag '89

Larry Holmes' champion season [historical video called Champions forever] C. Meth. il por *Video* 13:18 D '89

Periodicals

See also
Ring (Periodical)

Psychological aspects

A Ray of hope [mental techniques of boxer R. Mancini applied to tennis] J. E. Loehr. il pors *World Tennis* 37:36-8+ Ag '89

Television broadcasting

See Cable television—Sports

Training

See Boxers—Training

BOXING BETTING

A fighting chance. D. Sheridan. il *Sport (New York, N.Y.)* 80:75-6 Ag '89

BOXING IN LITERATURE

Budd Schulberg in Great Gatsby land. A. Fotheringham. il *Maclean's* 102:56 Ag 28 '89

BOXING VIDEO GAMES *See* Video games

BOY MEETS GIRL (MUSICAL GROUP)

Boy Meets Girl: a star-quality couple! D. McCue. il pors *'Teen* 33:45 Jl '89

Boy Meets Girl! Boy loses girl! But now they're back together, and singing in an altared state. il pors *People Weekly* 31:69 Ja 16 '89

BOY SCOUTS OF AMERICA

Adventures of a reluctant Forty-sixer [hiking in the Adirondacks] L. P. Fortin. il *The Conservationist* 44:10-15 N/D '89

Good scouts indeed [Wilderness Scouts fight Boy Scouts over right to retain name] P. W. Moser. il pors *Sports Illustrated* 70:46-9 F 6 '89

Anecdotes, facetiae, satire, etc.

Send a preacher to camp [week at a Boy Scout camp] W. H. Willimon. *The Christian Century* 106:1006-8 N 8 '89

BOYCOTT

See also
Blacklisting
Nestle SA—Infant formula boycott case

Activism in the checkout line: the rising tide of boycotts. L. Savan. il *Utne Reader* p87-9 S/O '89

Boycott targets TV sponsors [Christian Leaders for Responsible Television] J. Maxwell. il *Christianity Today* 33:47-9 Ag 18 '89

Boycott the Germans. R. E. Tyrrell. *The American Spectator* 22:8-9 Ag '89

Bringing Satan to heel [interview with D. Wildmon] D. Winbush. il por *Time* 133:54-5 Je 19 '89

Just say no: boycotts at the barricades [prochoice boycott of Domino's Pizza and prolife boycott of Maxwell House coffee] *Newsweek* 114:21 Ag 14 '89

McGraw-Hill and Wiley quit Iran Fair but decry book boycotts. C. Reid. *Publishers Weekly* 235:104 My 12 '89

U.K. publishers vote Rushdie support, reject Teheran boycott. V. Menkes. *Publishers Weekly* 235:104 My 12 '89

BOYD, BLANCHE M., 1945-

The way it should be remembered. il *The New York Times Magazine* p44+ N 19 '89

BOYD, J. MITCHELL

about

Shoney's needs a recipe for succession. W. Konrad. il por *Business Week* p52 D 25 '89-Ja 1 '90

BOYD, JAMES, 1929-

What happens to a senator's day. *The Washington Monthly* 21:48-9 F '89

BOYD, JAYNE

about

Two-timing. B. Greene. pors *Esquire* 111:57-9 Je '89

BOYD, JOAN

about

Two-timing. B. Greene. pors *Esquire* 111:57-9 Je '89

BOYD, JOHN D.

Star time [poem] *America* 160:85 F 4 '89

Tea time [poem] *America* 160:85 F 4 '89

BOYD, MONA SUE

Summer sense in a sandwich. il *American Health* 8:100-2 Jl/Ag '89

Summer sense in a sandwich. il *The Mother Earth News* 118:78+ Jl/Ag '89

BOYD, RICHARD N., 1940-, AND OTHERS

Optimum chemical sites and techniques for searches for negatively charged rare particles. bibl f il *Science* 244:1450-7 Je 23 '89

BOYER, ERNEST L.

A memo to the new Secretary of Education. *The Education Digest* 54:3-6 Mr '89

Memo to the Secretary of Education: how to give education a vision and voice of credibility. por *Change* 20:24-6 N/D '88

School reform [address, June 5, 1989] *Vital Speeches of the Day* 55:741-4 O 1 '89

The third wave of school reform [excerpt from The blackboard fumble; cover story] il *Christianity Today* 33:16-19 S 22 '89

BOYER, PAUL S.

Arms race as sitcom plot. il *The Bulletin of the Atomic Scientists* 45:6-8 Je '89

BOYETT, JOSEPH H., AND CONN, HENRY P.

How does your staff measure up? [excerpt from Maximum performance management] il *Working Woman* 14:26+ Je '89

BOYFRIENDS AND GIRLFRIENDS *See* Women and men

BOYLE, GERT

about

Gert Boyle has a vested interest in George Bush's fishing fortunes. H. Shapiro. il pors *People Weekly* 32:143-4 S 18 '89

BOYLE, GREGORY J.

about

The priest who loves gangsters [cover story] E. Shorris. il *The Nation* 249:737+ D 18 '89

BOYLE, T. CORAGHESSAN

East is east [fiction] il *Rolling Stone* p126-30+ O 5 '89

Peace of mind [story] il *Harper's* 278:65-71 Ja '89

Thawing out [story] il *Gentlemen's Quarterly* 59:187-8+ My '89

BOYLE FAMILY

about

Four by four. il *Esquire* 111:120-3 My '89

BOYLES, DENIS

See you in Kisumu. il *Esquire* 112:34+ Ag '89

BOYS

See also
Sex differences

War babies: a mother refuses her son toy guns. J. Zandy. il *Utne Reader* p120-1 N/D '89

BOYS (MUSICAL GROUP)

Introducing: The Boys. il *Ebony* 44:104+ Mr '89

BOYS CHOIR OF HARLEM

Sing a song of self-esteem. A. Ellis. il *American Visions* 4:54+ D '89

BOYS CLUB (MUSICAL GROUP)
Girls love the Boys Club! K. Turman. il *'Teen* 33:46 F '89

BOYS' CLUBS
See also
Boy Scouts of America

BOYSEN, JAN
Mrs. Delany's fabulous flowers. il por *International Wildlife* 19:44-5 Jl/Ag '89
A nation of symbols. il *National Wildlife* 28:26-8 D '89/Ja '90

BOYTE, HARRY CHATTEN, 1945-
People power transforms a St. Louis housing project. il por *Utne Reader* p46-7 Jl/Ag '89

BOYUM, JOY GOULD, 1934-
Movies. See issues of Glamour

BOZELL, L. BRENT, III, AND BAKER, BRENT
Henry Luce, call your medium. *National Review* 41:37 S 15 '89

BPD *See* Borderline personality disorder

BPD (FIRM)
LTV, BPD consider building increased-lift Scout 2 launcher. J. M. Lenorovitz. *Aviation Week & Space Technology* 130:25 Ap 10 '89

BRACCO, LORRAINE
about
Lorraine Bracco. J. C. Johnson. por *Mademoiselle* 95:248-9 Ap '89

BRACES, ORTHODONTIC *See* Orthodontics

BRACEWELL, RONALD NEWBOLD, 1921-
The Fourier transform. bibl il *Scientific American* 260:86-9+ Je '89

BRACEY, GERALD W.
The $150 million redundancy. bibl f il *Phi Delta Kappan* 70:698-702 My '89
Research. See alternate issues of Phi Delta Kappan beginning March 1984

BRACH, PAUL, 1924-
An act of salvation. il *Art in America* 77:130-5 Ja '89

BRACHER, KATHERINE
A life devoted to astronomy. il por *Astronomy* 17:50-4 O '89

BRACKMAN, JACOB
Carly Simon's Vineyard. il pors *House & Garden* 161:182-7+ N '89

BRACY, ARNOLD
about
The Moscow bug hunt. J. Peterzell. il pors *Time* 134:26-8 Jl 10 '89

BRADBURY, MALCOLM, 1932-
The courtship dance: on giving and getting books. il *The New York Times Book Review* 94:7+ D 3 '89
Speaking the prince's English. il *The New York Times Magazine* p46+ S 24 '89

BRADEMAS, JOHN
about
Public pensions play tougher. F. H. Katayama. il por *Fortune* 119:16 F 27 '89

BRADEN, VIC
about
Teaching tennis to toads. L. Jaroff. il por *Time* 134:84-6 O 16 '89

BRADFORD (ENGLAND)
Cemeteries
Bradford's living dead [Undercliffe Cemetery] A. Hills. il *History Today* 39:3 O '89

BRADLEY, BILL
Aftershocks. *The New Republic* 201:15-16 N 27 '89
Should the Congress adopt the "Financial Institutions Reform, Recovery, and Enforcement Act of 1989"? [excerpts from address, April 19, 1989] *Congressional Digest* 68:181+ Je/Jl '89
The West should not bankroll *perestroika*. *USA Today (Periodical)* 118:22-4 Jl '89
about
Political pair: a win-win situation. A. L. Ball. il pors *Working Woman* 14:137-8 O '89

BRADLEY, DIANNE F.
Alcohol and drug education in elementary schools. *The Education Digest* 54:61-3 Mr '89

BRADLEY, ED
about
60 minutes' man. J. Schwartz. il por *Gentlemen's Quarterly* 59:141-4 My '89

BRADLEY, FELISHA
about
Va. woman gets $120,000 in civil rights lawsuit. *Jet* 77:9 N 13 '89

BRADLEY, GEORGE, 1953-
Ideal city [poem] *The New Yorker* 65:36 Mr 6 '89
Nostalgie de la boue [poem] *The New Yorker* 65:40 O 30 '89

BRADLEY, IAN C.
Gerrard Winstanley: England's pioneer Green? bibl il *History Today* 39:12-17 Ag '89

BRADLEY, JOHN ED
Goodness gracious! [cover story] il pors *Esquire* 111:136-42+ Mr '89

BRADLEY, MEL
about
Mel Bradley hosts inaugural dinner at Twin Oaks Estate. il por *Jet* 75:13-14 F 6 '89

BRADLEY, PAT
After beating what seemed bad odds, a top pro is back up to par; ed. by Andrew Abrahams. il pors *People Weekly* 32:80+ S 18 '89

BRADLEY, TOM
about
Bradley: down and nearly out? E. Schine. *Business Week* p29 Ag 7 '89
Hard times for Teflon Tom. E. M. Reingold. por *Time* 133:35 My 22 '89
L.A.'s teflon mayor. M. Reese. il por *Newsweek* 113:33 Ap 10 '89
Letter from Los Angeles. J. Didion. *The New Yorker* 65:88+ Ap 24 '89
Tom Bradley wins an unprecedented fifth term as mayor of L.A. il por *Jet* 76:4 My 1 '89

BRADLEY FIGHTING VEHICLES *See* Motor vehicles, Military

BRADLEY'S (NEW YORK, N.Y.: BAR) *See* New York (N.Y.)—Restaurants, nightclubs, bars, etc.

BRADY, CHARLES
Hast thou entered into the storehouses of the snow? [poem] il *America* 161:460 D 16 '89

BRADY, JAMES S.
about
Sarah Brady. S. Weller. il pors *Ms.* 17:84-7 Ja/F '89

BRADY, MATHEW B., CA. 1823-1896
about
Photograph by Brady. il por *American History Illustrated* 24:42-3 S/O '89

BRADY, MICHAEL J.
about
Phoenix Airlines may get its wings clipped. D. Foust. il por *Business Week* p114 Mr 13 '89

BRADY, NICHOLAS F., 1930-
Dealing with the international debt crisis [remarks, March 10, 1989] *Department of State Bulletin* 89:53-6 My '89
OECD Council ministerial held in Paris [statement and text of final communique, May 31 and June 1, 1989] *Department of State Bulletin* 89:78-83 S '89
Request for U.S. contributions to multilateral development banks [statement, April 17, 1989] *Department of State Bulletin* 89:21-30 Je '89
about
Brady's long-term plans will collide with the deficit. H. Gleckman. por *Business Week* p33 Ja 23 '89
The debt plan Brady floated is still, well, floating. M. McNamee. por *Business Week* p51 My 8 '89
Enter the Brady plan. B. Rudolph. il por *Time* 133:54 Mr 20 '89
The Fed gets one of Brady's boys. M. McNamee. por *Business Week* p102 D 11 '89
The new spelling of relief. D. Pauly. il por *Newsweek* 113:32 Mr 20 '89
The Nick & Dick show: what next? C. Hutton. il pors *Fortune* 119:12 Ja 30 '89
The old boy and the new boys. C. Bruck. *The New Yorker* 65:81-90+ My 8 '89
The pick-and-shovel work of Nick Brady. S. Dentzer. il por *U.S. News & World Report* 106:23-4 Mr 20 '89
The quiet crusader [cover story] H. Gleckman. il pors *Business Week* p80-3+ S 18 '89
Washington's new, softer line on Latin debt. M. McNamee. il por *Business Week* p58 Mr 20 '89
Who is Nick Brady? Why it matters. L. S. Richman. il por *Fortune* 119:59-60+ My 22 '89

BRADY, ROBERT, 1946-
about
Robert Brady: masked gods. C. White. il por *American Craft* 49:30-7 D '89/Ja '90

BRADY, SARAH
about
Sarah Brady. S. Weller. il pors *Ms.* 17:84-7 Ja/F '89

BRAGANTI, NANCY, 1941-
(jt. auth) See Devine, Elizabeth, 1938-, and Braganti, Nancy, 1941-

BRAGG, BILLY
about
Billy Bragg: of Labour and love. D. Fricke. por *Rolling Stone* p18 Ja 12 '89

BRAGG, FORRESTINE A.
I read and write. por *Essence* 20:148 My '89

BRAGG, MELVYN, 1939-
Love story [excerpt from Richard Burton] pors *Ladies' Home Journal* 106:103-5+ Ja '89
about
PW interviews. M. Field. por *Publishers Weekly* 235:83-4 F 3 '89

BRAGGING *See* Boastfulness

BRAHE, TYCHO, 1546-1601
about
Who first saw the zodiacal light? D. W. Olson. il *Sky and Telescope* 77:146-8 F '89

BRAHE, TYCHO, 1546-1601—about—*cont.*
Will Tycho's observatory be restored? B. Haggman. il *Astronomy* 17:10 N '89
BRAHIC, A., AND HUBBARD, WILLIAM B.
The baffling ring arcs of Neptune. il *Sky and Telescope* 77:606-9 Je '89
BRAIKER, HARRIET B., 1948-
The power of self-talk. il *Psychology Today* 23:23-7 D '89
What all career women need to know about drinking. il *Working Woman* 14:72-5+ Ag '89
BRAILSFORD, HENRY NOEL, 1873-1958
The empire of the East. *The New Republic* 201 [Reprint v1]:14-15 N 6 '89 [N 7 '14]
BRAIN
See also
Cerebrospinal fluid
Consciousness
Cybernetics
Electroencephalography
Human information processing
Hypothalamus
Intelligence
Laterality
Magnetoencephalography
Memory
Mind
Mind and body
Mind gyms
Nervous system
Neuropsychology
Pituitary body
Sleep
The horse is dead [brain-compatible approach to restructuring schools] L. A. Hart. bibl f il *Phi Delta Kappan* 71:237-42 N '89
How the mind was designed [sociobiology] G. Cowley. il *Newsweek* 113:56-8 Mr 13 '89
The mammalian choroid plexus. R. Spector and C. E. Johanson. bibl il *Scientific American* 261:68-74 N '89

Abnormalities
The anatomy of memory loss [abnormality in the hippocampal formation of amnesia patients; research by Gary A. Press] *Science News* 136:204 S 23 '89
Islands of genius [link between savant syndrome and cerebral cortex abnormalities] R. Robotham. il *Omni (New York, N.Y.)* 11:18+ S '89
New evidence: autism is a brain disorder [abnormal cerebellum; research by Eric Courchesne] W. Herbert. *Psychology Today* 23:22 Je '89

Analysis and chemistry
See also
Chemoreceptors
Drug receptors
Hormone receptors
Protein receptors
Are neural nets like the human brain? L. Roberts. *Science* 243:481-2 Ja 27 '89
Imaging of memory-specific changes in the distribution of protein kinase C in the hippocampus [associative learning experiment] J. L. Olds and others. bibl f il *Science* 245:866-9 Ag 25 '89
Neurobiology gets computational. E. Pennisi. il *BioScience* 39:283-7 My '89
A pertussis toxin-sensitive G protein in hippocampal long-term potentiation. J. W. Goh and P. S. Pennefather. bibl f il *Science* 244:980-3 My 26 '89
The role of excitatory amino acids and NMDA receptors in traumatic brain injury. A. I. Faden and others. bibl f il *Science* 244:798-800 My 19 '89

Cancer
Causes
UFO update [Michael Persinger's theory that UFO investigation causes brain tumors] P. Huyghe. il *Omni (New York, N.Y.)* 11:73 F '89

Diseases
See also
Alzheimer's disease
Brain damage
Cerebral palsy
Cerebrovascular disease
Parkinson's disease
Tay-Sachs disease
The infant brain [cell culture pinpoints onset of infection; research by Arye Rubenstein and William Lyman] G. Montgomery. il *Discover* 10:30+ Ag '89
Possible role of carbamates in neurotoxicity and neurotransmitter inactivation [discussion of August 19, 1988 article, Beta-N-methylamino-L-alanine neurotoxicity: requirement for bicarbonate as a cofactor] J. H. Weiss and D. W. Choi. *Science* 243:1615 Mr 24 '89
Prions linked to nerve regulation [research by Gerald D. Fischbach] R. Weiss. *Science News* 136:308 N 11 '89
Slow viruses. T. Kiely. il *Technology Review* 92:11-12 O '89
Why a man may mistake his wife for a cat [study of cognitive disabilities by Antonio R. Damasio] R. Weiss. *Science News* 136:309 N 11 '89

Growth
From bird song to neurogenesis [study of the canary brain] F. Nottebohm. il *Scientific American* 260:74-9 F '89
Of birds and brains [quail-chick chimeras produce modified songs; research by Evan Balaban and others] il *Discover* 10:14 F '89
The return of the mind [M. Diamond's theory that brain's plasticity allows it to keep growing into old age] S. Blakeslee. il por *American Health* 8:94-6 Mr '89
Synapse formation in the developing brain. R. E. Kalil. bibl il *Scientific American* 261:76-9+ D '89
Taxonomic differences in the scaling of brain on body weight among mammals. M. D. Pagel and P. H. Harvey. bibl f il *Science* 244:1589-93 Je 30 '89
What makes bigger brains? [research by Paul Harvey and Mark Pagel] R. Lewin. *Science* 244:1544 Je 30 '89

Hemorrhage
Japanese stroke clues [increased risk of cerebral hemorrhage from low cholesterol] K. Fackelmann. il *Science News* 135:250+ Ap 22 '89

Innervation
A biochemical correlate of the critical period for synaptic modification in the visual cortex. S. M. Dudek and M. F. Bear. bibl f il *Science* 246:673-5 N 3 '89
Electrophysiologic responses in hamster superior colliculus evoked by regenerating retinal axons. S. A. Keirstead and others. bibl f il *Science* 246:255-7 O 13 '89
Inescapable versus escapable shock modulates long-term potentiation in the rat hippocampus [evidence that controllability modulates plasticity] T. J. Shors and others. bibl f il *Science* 244:224-6 Ap 14 '89
Limbic seizures increase neuronal production of messenger RNA for nerve growth factor. C. M. Gall and P. J. Isackson. bibl f il *Science* 245:758-61 Ag 18 '89
Long-term potentiation in the motor cortex. A. Iriki and others. bibl f il *Science* 245:1385-7 S 22 '89
Model of the origin of rhythmic population oscillations in the hippocampal slice. R. D. Traub and others. bibl f il *Science* 243:1319-25 Mr 10 '89
The neostriatal mosaic: striatal patch-matrix organization is related to cortical lamination. C. R. Gerfen. bibl f il *Science* 246:385-8 O 20 '89
Neural connections between the lateral geniculate nucleus and visual cortex in vitro. N. Yamamoto and others. bibl f il *Science* 245:192-4 Jl 14 '89
Neuronal correlates of subjective visual perception. N. K. Logothetis and J. D. Schall. bibl f il *Science* 245:761-3 Ag 18 '89
Pathological changes induced in cerebrocortical neurons by phencyclidine and related drugs. J. W. Olney and others. bibl f il *Science* 244:1360-2 Je 16 '89
Protection of dentate hilar cells from prolonged stimulation by intracellular calcium chelation. H. E. Scharfman and P. A. Schwartzkroin. bibl f il *Science* 246:257-60 O 13 '89
Regenerated nerves send first messages. R. Weiss. il *Science News* 136:244 O 14 '89
Selective loss of hippocampal granule cells in the mature rat brain after adrenalectomy. R. Sloviter and others. bibl f il *Science* 243:535-8 Ja 27 '89
Subplate neurons pioneer the first axon pathway from the cerebral cortex. S. K. McConnell and others. bibl f il *Science* 245:978-82 S 1 '89
Tracking down the neurons of perception [research by Jeffrey D. Schall and Nikos K. Logothetis] I. Amato. il *Science News* 136:118 Ag 19 '89
Transneuronal transfer of herpes virus from peripheral nerves to cortex and brainstem. G. Ugolini and others. bibl f il *Science* 243:89-91 Ja 6 '89

Localization of functions
See also
Laterality
Split brain
The biology of obsessions and compulsions. J. L. Rapoport. il *Scientific American* 260:82-9 Mr '89
Brain and gender: the missing data [discussion of January 4-11, 1989 article, Ways of knowing God: gender and the brain] J. B. Ashbrook. *The Christian Century* 106:263-4 Mr 8 '89
Brain and immunity: mapping the link [periaqueductal gray matter of mesencephalon mediates opiate-induced immunosuppression; work of Richard J. Weber and Agu Pert] K. Fackelmann. *Science News* 136:36 Jl 15 '89
Brain changes [area in the brain responsible for sense of touch shows adaptability to injury; work of Michael Merzenich] J. Rubin. *Psychology Today* 23:26 Mr '89
Doping the immune system [morphine-induced immunosuppression in rats; research by Richard Weber and Agu Pert] *Discover* 10:14 D '89
Flipping the main switch in the central reward system? [cocaine and the brain] C. Holden. il *Science* 246:1378-9 D 15 '89
A leap in the light: faith, science, & the imagination. W. J. O'Malley. il *Commonweal* 116:141-3+ Mr 10 '89
Mapping neuronal inputs to REM sleep induction sites with carbachol-fluorescent microspheres. J. J. Quattrochi and others. bibl f il *Science* 245:984-6 S 1 '89

BRAIN—Localization of functions—*cont.*

Mental rotation of the neuronal population vector [motor cortex of monkeys] A. P. Georgopoulos and others. bibl f il *Science* 243:234-6 Ja 13 '89

The mind in motion [PET scans by Steven Petersen and Peter T. Fox; cover story] G. Montgomery. il *Discover* 10:58-61+ Mr '89

Mind meets brain [cognitive neuroscience] J. Rubin. il *Technology Review* 92:13-14 Ja '89

Monkey think, monkey do [mental rotation of neuronal population vector in motor cortex; work of Apostolos Georgopoulos] L. Oliwenstein. il *Discover* 10:20 Je '89

Neural integration of information specifying structure from stereopsis and motion. M. Nawrot and R. Blake. bibl f il *Science* 244:716-18 My 12 '89

Ocular dominance column development: analysis and simulation [visual cortex] K. D. Miller and others. bibl f il *Science* 245:605-15 Ag 11 '89

On creativity [cover story] N. McAleer. il *Omni (New York, N.Y.)* 11:42-4+ Ap '89

Organization of the human brain. M. S. Gazzaniga. bibl f il *Science* 245:947-52 S 1 '89

The periaqueductal gray matter mediates opiate-induced immunosuppression [mesencephalon] R. J. Weber and A. Pert. bibl f il *Science* 245:188-90 Jl 14 '89

The real revenge of the nerds [over-developed frontal lobes; theory by David Forrest] L. Miller. il *Psychology Today* 23:20+ Je '89

Recognizing faces and expressions [research by Michael Hasselmo] J. Rubin. *Psychology Today* 23:22 My '89

Recording and interpretation of cerebral magnetic fields. R. Hari and O. V. Lounasmaa. bibl f il *Science* 244:432-6 Ap 28 '89

Rhinos in the heart of darkness [language information in the brain stored in various locations; research by Rosaleen A. McCarthy and E. K. Warrington] A. H. Rosenfeld. il *Psychology Today* 23:26 Mr '89

Seeking the source of emotions [amygdala research by Nathan A. Fox] *Science News* 136:175 S 9 '89

A specialization for speech perception. A. M. Liberman and I. G. Mattingly. bibl f il *Science* 243:489-94 Ja 27 '89

A specialization for speech perception? [discussion of January 27, 1989 article, A specialization for speech perception] A. M. Liberman and I. G. Mattingly. *Science* 244:1530-1 Je 30 '89

Thinking in circles [mental rotation of neuronal population vector in monkey motor cortex; work of Apostolos Georgopoulos] T. Appenzeller. *Scientific American* 260:26-7 Mr '89

Tonotopic organization of the auditory cortex: pitch versus frequency representation. C. Pantev and others. bibl f il *Science* 246:486-8 O 27 '89

Visuomotor coordination in reaching and locomotion. A. P. Georgopoulos and S. Grillner. bibl f *Science* 245:1209-10 S 15 '89

Anecdotes, facetiae, satire, etc.

Excuse me, there's branches on my dendrites. K. Fury. il *Working Woman* 14:102 Ag '89

Mathematical models

The chaotic brain: new models of behavior [nonlinear mathematical models] J. Alper. *Psychology Today* 23:21 My '89

Surgery

See also
Split brain

Skull's angels [neurosurgeons] S. Fishman. il *Rolling Stone* p94-5+ Mr 9 '89

Tomography

See Tomography—Medical use

Transplantation

Brain repair [adrenal gland transplants for Parkinson's disease] A. Hollister. il *Life* 12:76-80+ My '89

Clockwork in the brain [transplantation of suprachiasmatic nucleus restores circadian rhythm in hamsters; work of Martin R. Ralph and others] J. A. Miller. il *BioScience* 39:75-8 F '89

New trial evaluates Parkinsonian therapy. R. Lewin. *Science* 243:892 F 17 '89

The ten-minute pain transplant [chromaffin cell grafts suppress pain in rats] D. Stein. il *Omni (New York, N.Y.)* 11:22+ Je '89

Transplants offer promise [adrenal medulla transplants as treatment for Parkinson's disease] *USA Today (Periodical)* 118:11-12 O '89

Wounds and injuries

See Brain damage

BRAIN ANEURYSMS *See* Aneurysms
BRAIN-BLOOD BARRIER *See* Blood-brain barrier
BRAIN CELLS *See* Nerve cells
BRAIN DAMAGE

See also
Autism

A brother's keeper [former Red Sox baseball star T. Conigliaro irreversibly brain damaged] M. Lupica. il por *Esquire* 111:77-80 Mr '89

Coming back from head injury [Central Park jogger] D. R. Hales and R. E. Hales. il *American Health* 8:9-10+ N '89

Driven off the road by brain disease [research by Larry E. Tune] B. Bower. *Science News* 135:318 My 20 '89

Pathological changes induced in cerebrocortical neurons by phencyclidine and related drugs. J. W. Olney and others. bibl f il *Science* 244:1360-2 Je 16 '89

R.T.'s topsy-turvy world [role of mental rotation in recognition of common objects; research by Martha Farah and Katherine Hammond] J. Rubin. il *Psychology Today* 22:20 D '88

The role of excitatory amino acids and NMDA receptors in traumatic brain injury. A. I. Faden and others. bibl f il *Science* 244:798-800 My 19 '89

BRAIN DAMAGED CHILDREN *See* Mentally handicapped children

BRAIN DRAIN

Beltway brain drain: why civil servants are making tracks. S. B. Garland. il *Business Week* p60-1 Ja 23 '89

Brain drain in reverse [Taiwan's U.S.-trained returnees] A. Tanzer. il *Forbes* 143:114-15 Ap 17 '89

The great British brain drain. D. Foote. il *Newsweek* 114:60 Jl 17 '89

A new Operation Brain Drain [raising U.S. immigration quotas for Europeans and better-educated workers] il *U.S. News & World Report* 107:14-16 Jl 24 '89

Scholar slip [Britain's brain drain] A. Ryan. *The New Republic* 201:14-16 D 4 '89

BRAIN LESIONS *See* Brain damage

BRAIN STEM

Brain may be the villain [stress ulcers; research by Daniel Hernandez] *USA Today (Periodical)* 117:16 F '89

Transneuronal transfer of herpes virus from peripheral nerves to cortex and brainstem. G. Ugolini and others. bibl f il *Science* 243:89-91 Ja 6 '89

BRAIN STIMULATION *See* Brain—Innervation

BRAIN WAVES

See also
Electroencephalography

Anecdotes, facetiae, satire, etc.

Alpha/theta meditation goggles. M. C. Worley. il *Radio-Electronics* 60:53-7 Ap '89

BRAINARD, DULCY

Reader's Digest launching direct-mail nonfiction series. il *Publishers Weekly* 235:37-8 My 26 '89

Sampling a cookbook manuscript. *Publishers Weekly* 236:33 S 8 '89

BRAINERD, ELIZABETH L., AND OTHERS

Air ventilation by recoil aspiration in polypterid fishes. bibl f il *Science* 246:1593-5 D 22 '89

BRAINERD, PAUL

The need to focus on communication by design. por *Personal Computing* 13:238 O '89

BRAINSTEM *See* Brain stem

BRAINTREE (MASS.)

Poor

In Boston, a busing plan that works [nightly busing of the homeless to Braintree] *Newsweek* 113:27 Mr 6 '89

BRAINWASHING

See also
Deprogramming

Brainwashed or converted? [suit against Unification Church by former members] L. D. Streiker. *The Christian Century* 106:721-3 Ag 2-9 '89

BRAKE LIGHTS, AUTOMOBILE *See* Automobiles—Lighting

BRAKES, AUTOMOBILE

See also
Automobiles—Stopping

Grip, don't slip. S. F. Brown. il *Popular Science* 234:71+ Ja '89

Types of brakes. *Consumers' Research Magazine* 72:14 Jl '89

Anecdotes, facetiae, satire, etc.

Change the weather. P. Bedard. il *Car and Driver* 35:16 D '89

Maintenance and repair

Are your brakes safe? K. Zino. il *Better Homes and Gardens* 67:60 Mr '89

Brake & muffler shops. il *Consumer Reports* 54:138-42 D '89

Getting your brakes and muffler fixed. il *Consumer Reports* 54:528-33 Ag '89

BRAKES, BICYCLE

Fat-tire stoppers [mountain bike brakes] il *Bicycling* 30:186+ My '89

Stop watch [repairs] J. Langley. il *Bicycling* 30:116+ D '89

BRAKES, MOTORCYCLE

Braided-steel brake lines. il *Cycle* 40:63-4 Jl '89

BRAKING OF AUTOMOBILES *See* Automobiles—Stopping

BRAMAN, IRMA

about

The happy look. E. Turner. il por *Art News* 88:105+ Mr '89

BRAMAN, NORMAN

about

The happy look. E. Turner. il por *Art News* 88:105+ Mr '89

BRAMBINI, LISA

about

Tiny and tough. *Women's Sports & Fitness* 11:15 O '89

BRAMWELL

about

Walter Bramwell Young's high-stylus jewelry is music to fashionable ears. il por *People Weekly* 32:67 S 18 '89

BRAMWELL, ELIZABETH

about

In the boss' shadow. G. Button. il por *Forbes* 144:238+ N 27 '89

BRAN

See also

Cooking—Grain

All about oat bran. il *McCall's* 117:91-3 O '89

Beyond oat bran [rice bran] il *Prevention (Emmaus, Pa.)* 41:12+ Je '89

Big G is growing fat on oat cuisine [General Mills' cereals gain on Kellogg's] R. Mitchell. il *Business Week* p29 S 18 '89

Bran works wonders! L. Lindner and G. Zyla. il *Redbook* 174:16 N '89

Crazy about oat bran [controlling cholesterol] D. Tonnessen. il *Health (New York, N.Y.)* 21:32+ Ap '89

Cut your cholesterol 30 points in 30 days [eating oat bran and beans; research by James W. Anderson] A. Roblin. il *Prevention (Emmaus, Pa.)* 41:36-7+ F '89

Eating for whole health [benefits of oat bran and whole foods] R. Rodale. il *Prevention (Emmaus, Pa.)* 41:28+ Ap '89

How I made $812 in the oat bran craze. P. W. Moser. il *Fortune* 120:125+ O 9 '89

The new bran in town [cholesterol-lowering effects of beta glucans found in rice bran] R. A. Barnett and M. Behen. *American Health* 8:101+ N '89

The next wave of high-fiber grains [rice and corn bran in controlling cholesterol] J. Silberner. il *U.S. News & World Report* 106:73 My 22 '89

The oat bran craze. B. T. Hunter. il *Consumers' Research Magazine* 72:8-9 Jl '89

Rice bran recipes to lower cholesterol. il *The Saturday Evening Post* 261:92-3 Jl/Ag '89

The scoop on bran. B. Goldman. il *Better Homes and Gardens* 67:41 N '89

Should you eat more oat bran? il *Glamour* 87:262 N '89

Taking oat bran to heart [lowering cholesterol] J. W. Anderson. il *The Saturday Evening Post* 261:18+ Jl/Ag '89

Tapping into the oat-bran market [Otto's Original Oat Bran Beer] il *Newsweek* 114:65 N 13 '89

Toasting good health [bran muffins and breads] J. B. Hurley. il *Prevention (Emmaus, Pa.)* 41:67-70+ O '89

Anecdotes, facetiae, satire, etc.

Bing's oat bran life plan. S. Bing. il *Esquire* 111:32+ F '89

BRANAGH, KENNETH

about

Henry V [film] Reviews

American Film il por 15:62-3 N '89. R. Seidenberg *Maclean's* il por 102:89-90 N 20 '89. B. D. Johnson *The Nation* 249:724-6 D 11 '89. S. Klawans *The New Republic* 201:28-30 D 4 '89. S. Kauffmann *New York* il por 22:74+ N 27 '89. D. Denby *The New Yorker* 65:104-5 N 27 '89. P. Kael *Rolling Stone* il p49 N 30 '89. P. Travers

Kenneth. G. Fuller. il pors *Film Comment* 25:2+ N/D '89

King Ken comes to conquer. R. Corliss. il pors *Time* 134:119-20 N 13 '89

BRANCH, ANDREA D., AND OTHERS

An ultraviolet-sensitive RNA structural element in a viroid-like domain of the hepatitis delta virus. bibl f il *Science* 243:649-52 F 3 '89

BRANCH, SHELLY J.

On the upbeat: two young conductors. il pors *American Visions* 4:22-6 Ag '89

BRANCH, TAYLOR

Black fear: law and justice in rural Georgia. *The Washington Monthly* 21:70-2 F '89

Blacks and Jews: the uncivil war [with editorial comment by Lee Eisenberg] il *Esquire* 111:25, 89-90+ My '89

about

The greening of a martyr [interview] A. P. Sanoff. il por *U.S. News & World Report* 106:22 Ja 23 '89

Hot writers. A. DeCurtis. il pors *Rolling Stone* p117-18+ My 18 '89

In the churches, in the streets: Taylor Branch on 'the King years'. R. Westbrook. *The Christian Century* 106:351-4 Ap 5 '89

BRAND, DOLLAR See Abdullah Ibrahim

BRAND NAME PRODUCTS

See also

Motion picture product placement

Private brands

But in the office, no. J. Levine. il *Forbes* 144:272-3 O 16 '89

Growing pains—and gains [established brand names used on new products] B. Kanner. il *New York* 22:22+ Mr 13 '89

Who makes it? G. Williams. il *Home Mechanix* 85:72-3+ F '89

BRAND NAMES See Trade marks and trade names

BRANDAUER, KLAUS MARIA

about

'King of the mountain'. J. Riedl. il por *World Press Review* 36:61 My '89

BRANDED MERCHANDISE See Brand name products

BRANDEIS, LOUIS DEMBITZ, 1856-1941

about

Men who made the rules. P. Baida. il *American Heritage* 40:18+ F '89

BRANDEIS UNIVERSITY

Comedy of errors? [discussion of October 2, 1989 article, 'A gangsterdom of the spirit'] *The Nation* 249:406 O 16 '89

'A gangsterdom of the spirit' [E. L. Doctorow's controversial commencement speech] *The Nation* 249:348 O 2 '89

BRANDEIS UNIVERSITY. DEPT. OF THEATER ARTS

Brandeis University. il *Theatre Crafts* 23:54+ N '89

BRANDENBURG, JIM

White wolf: living with an Arctic legend [condensation] il *Reader's Digest* 134:126-32 Mr '89

BRANDER, BRUCE

World Vision. il *Petersen's Photographic Magazine* 18:24-6+ Je '89

BRANDL, JOHN

Dear constituent: here's where I stand. *Commonweal* 116:661-2 D 1 '89

BRANDO, MARLON, 1924-

about

Brando. M. Kram. il pors *Esquire* 112:156-62+ N '89

Brando says studio sold him out on 'Dry white season'. il por *Jet* 77:63 O 23 '89

Brando's back—and better than ever. R. Rosenbaum. il pors *Mademoiselle* 95:102+ O '89

Playing the Godfather to Matthew Broderick means another mob scene for Brando. il por *People Weekly* 31:97 Je 26 '89

BRANDON, HENRY

about

Of many things. G. W. Hunt. *America* 160:210 Mr 11 '89

BRANDON, WILLIAM

The man nobody remembered [story] il *The Saturday Evening Post* 261:60-3+ S '89

BRANDT, DAVID

The Spacecause success story. *Ad Astra* 1:13 Mr '89

Spacepac's election results. *Ad Astra* 1:15 Ap '89

BRANDT, E. H.

Levitation in physics [cover story] bibl f il *Science* 243:349-55 Ja 20 '89

BRANDT, WARREN, 1918-

about

Warren Brandt [excerpt] N. F. Weber. il *American Artist* 53:48-53+ Mr '89

BRANDT, WILLIAM

about

William Brandt: putting small businesses back in the black. L. Therrien. il por *Business Week* p99 Ag 21 '89

BRANDY

See also

Grappa

Brandy: the best of spirits. J. F. Mariani. il *Motor Boating & Sailing* 164:34-5 N '89

Oregon original [S. McCarthy's fruit brandies] F. J. Prial. il *The New York Times Magazine* p56 F 5 '89

BRANDYWINE FUND

Will the pendulum swing again? [views of F. Friess] J. Clements. il por *Forbes* 144:360+ N 13 '89

BRANFORD-HORRY HOUSE (CHARLESTON, S.C.) See Charleston (S.C.)—Historic houses, sites, etc.

BRANGHAM, SUZANNE

about

The hidden fortune in ugly-duckling real estate. L. Touby. il por *Working Woman* 14:98 My '89

BRANIFF, INC.

Braniff files for Chapter 11, slashes flights. *Aviation Week & Space Technology* 131:34 O 2 '89

Braniff halts passenger service, plans attempt as charter carrier. *Aviation Week & Space Technology* 131:72 N 13 '89

Braniff may be at the end of the runway. G. DeGeorge. il *Business Week* p49-50 N 13 '89

Braniff operates reduced schedule, plans to accept 95 Airbus A320s [bankruptcy reorganization plan] *Aviation Week & Space Technology* 131:139 O 9 '89

Braniff takes off on a wing and a prayer. il *Newsweek* 113:40 Ja 16 '89

Braniff will use 50 A320s to expand service from Kansas City to coasts. il *Aviation Week & Space Technology* 130:63 Ja 9 '89

Flying first class at Braniff. J. H. Taylor. il *Forbes* 144:49+ O 30 '89

Kansas City rebuilding after Braniff bankruptcy. C. Fotos. *Aviation Week & Space Technology* 131:56-7 D 4 '89

On a wing and a dare [expansion plans] il *Time* 133:46 Ja 16 '89

This engine maker is finally seeing a patch of blue [International Aero Engines' Braniff deal] R. W. King. *Business Week* p39-40 Ja 23 '89

BRANNEN, CHARLES L.
about
Make this guy a scout. R. Harper. il *Sport (New York, N.Y.)* 80:76 Jl '89

BRANSCOMB, LEWIS M., 1926-
about
Rethinking the military's role in the economy: an interview with Harvey Brooks and Lewis Branscomb. S. Hackman and R. Howard. il pors *Technology Review* 92:54-60+ Ag/S '89

BRANSON, BRANLEY ALLAN
On the road with mushrooms. il *Travel Holiday* 171:22-5 F '89

BRANSON, LOUISE
Poaching the pandas. *World Press Review* 36:53 Mr '89

BRANSON (MO.)
Description
Down toward Arkansas. L. Walker. *The New Yorker* 65:105-6+ S 18 '89

BRANTLEY, ROBIN
Goodbye, long hair—so long, fast times. il pors *TV Guide* 37:8-10 Ag 5-11 '89

BRANTON, WILEY A., 1923-1988
about
Famed civil rights lawyer Wiley Branton leaves entire estate to his widow. il por *Jet* 76:5 My 29 '89
Obituary
Jet il pors 75:12-14 Ja 9 '89

BRANWYN, GARETH, AND CLABAUGH, GAVIN
Computer scan. See issues of The Futurist beginning January/February 1989

BRAQUE, GEORGES, 1882-1963
about
The Adam and Eve of modernism. R. Hughes. il *Time* 134:93-4 O 2 '89
The art world. A. Gopnik. *The New Yorker* 65:132-6+ O 23 '89
Braque, Picasso and early cubism. A. C. Danto. *The Nation* 249:540-4 N 6 '89
Cubiquitous. J. D. Flam. il pors *Art News* 88:144-9 D '89
Cubism's odd couple. D. Solomon. il pors *House & Garden* 161:58+ S '89
Double vision. B. Adams. il pors *Harper's Bazaar* 122:142-3+ Ag '89
The legacy of cubism [interview with W. S. Rubin] M. Horn. il pors *U.S. News & World Report* 107:68 O 23 '89
Married . . . with cubism. S. Schwartz. *The New Republic* 201:28-30 D 25 '89
Picasso, Braque, and an art revolution. J. Perl. il pors *Vogue* 179:722-7 S '89
Present at the creation. P. Plagens. il *Newsweek* 114:73 O 2 '89
Rubin's cube. K. Larson. il *New York* 22:77-8 O 9 '89
To find originality. L. J. O'Donovan. *America* 161:299-300 N 4 '89

BRAS See Brassieres

BRASCH, KLAUS R.
Secrets of city astrophotography. il *Astronomy* 17:90-5 Ja '89

BRASELTON (GA.)
Flix chick picks stix; or, Kim Basinger buys Braselton. il por *People Weekly* 31:125 Ap 17 '89

BRASS INSTRUMENT MUSIC
See also
Canadian Brass (Ensemble)
Compact discs—Brass instrument music

BRASS RUBBINGS [drama] See Pinsent, Gordon, 1930-

BRASSICA
See also
Broccoli
Cabbages
Cauliflower
Kale
Flashy brassicas [cover story] V. Mattern. il *Organic Gardening* 36:28-32 O '89
To stymie cancer, eat broccoli raw [study by Lloyd D. Campbell and Bogdan A. Slominski] *Science News* 136:351 N 25 '89

BRASSIERES
See also
Rigby & Peller (Firm)
Sports bra round-up. C. Cummins. il *Women's Sports & Fitness* 11:66-71 Ap '89
History
Ooh-la-la! The bra [cover story] C. Dowling. il *Life* 12:88-92+ Je '89

BRATS
The day of the brat. R. Merkin. il *Gentlemen's Quarterly* 59:47-8 Ja '89

BRAUDEL, FERNAND
Alexis de Tocqueville's Recollections. *Society* 26:67-72 Mr/Ap '89

BRAUER, CARL M., 1946-
Staffing a new president. *Current (Washington, D.C.)* 310:28-35 F '89

BRAUER, DENNY
about
Out of bed bass. K. Etling. il *Outdoor Life* 183:71-3+ My '89

BRAUER, RALPH
Learning from Millie. por *Newsweek* 114:10 N 20 '89

BRAUN, BARBARA
The new look in art books. il *Publishers Weekly* 236:12-14+ S 1 '89

BRAUN, JOSEPH A., 1947-
(jt. auth) See Benoit, Bob, and Braun, Joseph A., 1947-

BRAUN, KATHRYN A.
about
Rapid evolution can mean quick success . . . or failure. M. Aaland. *Working Woman* 14:58+ My '89

BRAUN, SHEILA
about
One point of light. D. Finkel. il pors *Esquire* 112:123-8+ O '89

BRAUN, THEODORE A.
When a church supports a lesbian seminarian. *The Christian Century* 106:516-17 My 17 '89

BRAVERMAN, KATE
about
From the tropic of L.A. [interview] C. Garcia. il por *Time* 134:18-19 N 20 '89

BRAVERY See Courage

BRAVO (FIRM)
Will a new Bravo be too basic? C. Capuzzi. il *Channels (New York, N.Y.: 1986)* 9:42-6 Ja '89

BRAWLEY, TAWANA
Assault case
A cry for help. M. A. Gillespie. il por *Ms.* 17:32-3 Ja/F '89
Reporters and reporting
Tawana Brawley case explored in books from Bantam, HBJ. M. Coffey. il *Publishers Weekly* 235:34-5 Ap 14 '89

BRAXTON, ANTHONY
about
Anthony Braxton. G. Santoro. *The Nation* 248:642-4 My 8 '89
Anthony Braxton: the dynamics of creativity [interview] B. Shoemaker. il pors *Down Beat* 56:20-2 Mr '89

BRAXTON, EDWARD K.
Loaded terms. *Commonweal* 116:328-9 Je 2 '89

BRAY, MICHAEL
about
Psycho drama. P. Hoban. il pors *New York* 22:40-2+ Je 19 '89

BRAYBECK, MARY M.
Merging spheres. *Commonweal* 116:175-7 Mr 24 '89

BRAZEL, SANDRA W.
(jt. auth) See Cerveny, Randall S., and Brazel, Sandra W.

BRAZELTON, T. BERRY, 1918-
Working parents [cover story] il por *Newsweek* 113:66-70 F 13 '89
about
Somersaults and sympathy. B. Kantrowitz. il por *Newsweek* 113:72 F 13 '89

BRAZIL
See also
AIDS (Disease)—Brazil
Amazon River
Amazon River Valley
Anti-nuclear movement—Brazil
Arembepe (Brazil)
Automobile racing—Brazil
Carnival (Pre-Lenten festival)—Brazil
Child welfare—Brazil
Crime and criminals—Brazil
Dams—Brazil
Drug laws and regulations—Brazil
Environmental movement—Brazil
Environmental policy—Brazil
Express highways—Brazil
Family—Brazil
Information systems—Brazil
Labor unions—Rubber industry workers—Brazil
Labor unions—Brazil
Land reform—Brazil
Loans, Bank—Brazil
Marajó Island (Brazil)
Mount Roraima
Nuclear energy—Brazil
Paleontology—Brazil
Police—Brazil
Poor—Brazil
Privatization—Brazil
Public health—Brazil
Rain forests—Brazil
Rio de Janeiro (Brazil)
Rondônia (Brazil)
São Paulo (Brazil)
Securities—Laws and regulations—Brazil
Socialism—Brazil
Squatter settlements—Brazil
Videotapes—Brazil
Women—Brazil

BRAZIL—*cont.*
Civilization
Jorge Amado: where peoples and cultures have mingled [interview] il *The Unesco Courier* 42:4-7 Jl '89
Commerce
Japan
Jungle road to Tokyo [U.S. soybean growers concern over Brazilian highway's impact on trade with Japan] P. Duggan. il map *Forbes* 143:96 My 29 '89
United States
See United States—Commerce—Brazil
Cultural relations
Portugal
Camões and Brazil. J. Montello. il *The Courier (Unesco)* 42:28-9 Ap '89
Defenses
See also
Airplanes, Military—Brazil
Bomb potential for South America. D. Albright. bibl f il map *The Bulletin of the Atomic Scientists* 45:16-20 My '89
Brazil's nuclear shakeup: military still in control. A. R. Britto de Castro and others. bibl f il *The Bulletin of the Atomic Scientists* 45:22-5 My '89
Description and travel
Brazil [via rail] D. V. Gast. il map *New Choices for the Best Years* 29:53-6 Ap '89
Economic policy
Brazil: a nation in search of a miracle. J. A. Page. *America* 161:273-4 O 28 '89
Brazil on the tightrope toward democracy. J. De Onis. *Foreign Affairs* 68:127-43 Fall '89
Brazil's transition to democracy. R. Roett. bibl f *Current History* 88:117-20+ Mr '89
Foreign relations
United States
See United States—Foreign relations—Brazil
Industries
See also
Avibras Industria Aeroespacial SA
Bunge & Born
Embraer Empresa Brasileira de Aeronautica SA
Forest products industry—Brazil
Gold mines and mining—Brazil
Soybean industry—Brazil
TV Globo LTDA
Native peoples
See Indians of South America—Brazil
Politics and government
See also
Elections—Brazil
Political campaigns—Brazil
Political candidates—Brazil
Press and politics—Brazil
Brazil's transition to democracy. R. Roett. bibl f *Current History* 88:117-20+ Mr '89
Race relations
Jorge Amado: where peoples and cultures have mingled [interview] il *The Unesco Courier* 42:4-7 Jl '89
Religious institutions and affairs
See also
Candomblé
Catholic Church—Brazil
Church and social problems—Brazil
Religious conferences—Brazil
BRAZIL NUTS
Nuts about selenium. R. A. Barnett. il *American Health* 8:149 Mr '89
BRAZILE, DONNA L.
about
A season in hell. G. E. Curry. il pors *Ms.* 18:58-60+ O '89
BRAZILIAN ART *See* Art, Brazilian
BRAZILIAN COOKING *See* Cooking, Brazilian
BRAZILIAN GRAND PRIX *See* Automobile racing—Brazil
BRAZILIAN PHYSICAL SOCIETY
FAS and Brazilian physicists discuss improved nuclear safeguards. W. Sweet. *Physics Today* 42:57-8 Ap '89
BRAZILIAN POETRY
Camões and Brazil. J. Montello. il *The Courier (Unesco)* 42:28-9 Ap '89
BRAZILIAN SCULPTURE *See* Sculpture, Brazilian
BRAZOS RIVER VALLEY (TEX.)
Description and travel
Roll on, Brazos. L. Thomas. il map *Southern Living* 24:82-7 My '89
BREACH OF CONTRACT
The journalist and the murderer (I) [convicted murderer J. MacDonald's suit against author J. McGinniss] J. Malcolm. *The New Yorker* 65:38-42+ Mr 13 '89
The journalist and the murderer (II) [convicted murderer J. MacDonald's suit against author J. McGinniss] J. Malcolm. *The New Yorker* 65:49-50+ Mr 20 '89
McGinniss: a travesty of libel [J. MacDonald's breach of contract suit against J. McGinniss] M. Garbus. *Publishers Weekly* 235:69 Ap 21 '89

BREAD
See also
Biscuits
Cinnamon rolls
Cornbread
Crackers
Gingerbread
Muffins
Baking bread. C. Taylor. il *The Mother Earth News* 115:78-80+ Ja/F '89
Braid a bread [jam-and-cheese loaf] il *Southern Living* 24:176 O '89
Breads and pastries from our ancestors. D. A. Campbell. il *Southern Living* 24:192-4 N '89
Breads Italian style. M. Langan. il *McCall's* 116:135 Mr '89
Easy brunch breads. il *Better Homes and Gardens* 67:160-1 Je '89
Easy turkey rolls. il *Redbook* 174:26 N '89
Flour power [French bread bakers] C. Petkanas. il *Harper's Bazaar* 122:200+ D '89
From our kitchen to yours [making bread] K. Adams. *Southern Living* 24:203 N '89
Gift breads [Christmas] B. Ojakangas. il *Ladies' Home Journal* 106:178-80+ D '89
Good food, good health: the puzzling bread picture. D. Haverstock. il *Better Homes and Gardens* 67:50+ O '89
Harvest loaf. il *Sunset (Central West edition)* 183:78-9 O '89
Holiday bread wreath. il *Good Housekeeping* 209:74 N '89
Holiday sourdough. il *Sunset (Central West edition)* 181:146+ D '88
Holiday-spanning bread [panettone] C. Kummer. il *The Atlantic* 263:84+ Mr '89
How do you say "brown bag bread" in Italian? [panettone] il *Sunset (Central West edition)* 182:96-7 Mr '89
Leaf, loaf, and ladle. K. Haedrich. il *Country Journal* 16:60-4 F '89
Loafing around. L. Land. il *The New York Times Magazine* p73-4 S 24 '89
Old-time breads go light. H. A. Dorrough. il *Southern Living* 24:184-6 Mr '89
Quick & easy: breads on the barbecue. M. Langan. il *McCall's* 116:135 Je '89
Quick! Breads for soup. il *Southern Living* 24:130 F '89
Raisin bread in the round. il *Southern Living* 24:188 S '89
Recipe of the week [walnut bread] il *Jet* 75:38 F 13 '89
Return of the Ginger-Kids . . . and our 1967 Christmas bread [cover story] il *Sunset (Central West edition)* 183:64-7 D '89
Savor summer with a bread. il *Southern Living* 24:168 Je '89
Savory breads. K. Haedrich. il *Country Journal* 16:88-92+ N/D '89
Shortcut breads. il *Better Homes and Gardens* 67:141-2 Mr '89
Using quick-rise yeast. il *Better Homes and Gardens* 67:150 Ap '89
Wheat-free bread [pumpkin rice bread] il *Better Homes and Gardens* 67:137 Mr '89
Contamination
Bread of dreams [effects of malnutrition and adulterated bread on the poor of medieval Europe; cover story] P. Camporesi. il *History Today* 39:14-21 Ap '89
BREAD (MUSICAL GROUP)
Bread. M. Azerrad. il *Rolling Stone* p55-6 Ag 10 '89
BREAD MAKERS (APPLIANCES)
Bread makers. *Consumer Reports* 54:298-9 D '89
BREAD PUDDING *See* Puddings
BREADMAKERS (APPLIANCES) *See* Bread makers (Appliances)
BREAK DANCING
See also
New York Express (Dance group)
BREAKFAST FOODS *See* Cereal foods
BREAKFASTS
See also
Brunches
School breakfasts
A.M. cuisine. B. Goldman. il *Better Homes and Gardens* 67:137-41+ My '89
Another dietary advantage to fiber [research by Allen S. Levine] *Science News* 136:412 D 23-30 '89
The best quick breakfasts for active women. G. Shockey. il *Women's Sports & Fitness* 11:34-5+ Ap '89
Breakfast for a pair. il *Southern Living* 24:174-5 S '89
Breakfast of champions. M. Mohler and M. D. Rosen. il *Ladies' Home Journal* 106:80 S '89
Breakfast sandwiches [microwaved] il *Southern Living* 24:130-1 Ja '89
Breakfasts & brunches [special section] il *Southern Living* 24:121+ Ap '89
The food and cancer connection: breakfast tips to reduce the risk. il *Redbook* 172:146+ Mr '89
Good-bye, June Cleaver [working mother's anxiety over fixing breakfast for her children] L. Flaherty. il *Ladies' Home Journal* 106:62+ Jl '89

BREAKFASTS—*cont.*
Guide to great breakfasts [special section] il *McCall's* 117:81-3+ N '89
A holiday weekend breakfast. il *Gourmet* 49:132-4+ N '89
Jump-start your day. E. Hackman. il *American Health* 8:118-19+ Ap '89
Quick and cool, these are breakfast salads. il *Sunset (Central West edition)* 183:94 Ag '89
Quick breakfasts [microwave] J. B. Hurley. *Prevention (Emmaus, Pa.)* 41:84 O '89
Quick-fix breakfasts [microwaving] C. Koury and J. Galton. il *Parents* 64:183-4+ S '89
Rise and dine. I. Chalmers. il *Modern Maturity* 32:68-72 O/N '89
Wake up to breakfast for two. il *Southern Living* 24:163 Je '89
Would you believe . . . it's breakfast! C. Koury. il *Parents* 64:140-2+ F '89

BREAKING IN [film] See Motion picture reviews—Single works

BREAST
Beauty and the breast [décolletage] il *Vogue* 179:518-21 Mr '89
Curves ahead. L. Heller. il *Redbook* 173:81-5 Ag '89
Exercise and your breasts. A. P. Lynn. il *Glamour* 87:50 O '89

Anecdotes, facetiae, satire, etc.
The boob trap. E. Welty. il *Mademoiselle* 95:188-9+ Je '89

Cancer
The 184 best breast cancer doctors [surgeons and oncologists] M. Abrams. *Good Housekeeping* 208:77-80+ Ap '89
Battling the beast within [J. Ireland] H. G. Miller. il pors *The Saturday Evening Post* 261:44-5 Jl/Ag '89
Breast cancer: most common, most curable. R. G. Somers. il *USA Today (Periodical)* 118:49-50 S '89
Breast cancer update [results of survey on female doctors' attitudes] S. Bulow-Hube. *Ladies' Home Journal* 106:96+ Jl '89
Enzyme suggests breast cancer spread [cathepsin-D; research by Henri Rochefort] J. Raloff. *Science News* 136:325 N 18 '89
"I can't have breast cancer—I'm only 35!". M. Dawson. il *Ladies' Home Journal* 106:104+ N '89
In Time flies when you're alive, actor Paul Linke turns the last years of his wife's life into art [F. Linke's battle with breast cancer] J. Kaufman. il pors *People Weekly* 32:59-60 Ag 21 '89
Marker predicts breast cancer recurrence [haptoglobin-related protein] R. Weiss. *Science News* 136:164 S 9 '89
Reducing the risk of breast cancer. N. Peterson. il *McCall's* 116:101-2+ S '89
Shattered for the second time [J. Ireland fights cancer and son's drug addiction] B. Kantrowitz. pors *Newsweek* 113:66 My 8 '89
The triumph of Bonnie Lovette. L. Marsa. il pors *Good Housekeeping* 209:72+ Ag '89
A triumph of love [J. Eikenberry] J. Cullen. il pors *Ladies' Home Journal* 106:34+ Ja '89
"Why I kept my cancer a secret". M. F. Hoyt. il pors *Good Housekeeping* 208:154-5+ Je '89
Why me? [interview with J. Ireland] il pors *Life* 12:108-9+ Je '89
Young women, crucial choices. S. Gilbert. *Glamour* 87:242-3+ N '89

Causes
Beyond bucks [possible cancer risk linked to silicone breast implants] D. M. Podolsky. il *American Health* 8:12 D '89
Birth-control pills and breast cancer. A. B. Eagan. il *Ms.* 17:41 Ap '89
Does the pill cause breast cancer? il *Consumer Reports* 54:498-9+ Ag '89
Estrogen effects assessed [risk of breast cancer in postmenopausal women] *Science News* 136:86 Ag 5 '89
Estrogen use linked to breast cancer. J. L. Marx. *Science* 245:593 Ag 11 '89
Hard looks at hormones [estrogen and progestin may increase risk] J. Langone. il *Time* 134:56 Ag 14 '89
The miracles and misfires of medicine [progestin and estrogen increase risk in postmenopausal women] *U.S. News & World Report* 107:16+ Ag 14 '89
The new breast-implant scare [silicone's possible link to cancer] C. Marks. *Mademoiselle* 95:124+ F '89
New perils of the pill? A. Toufexis. il *Time* 133:73 Ja 16 '89
The pill and breast cancer: what doctors say now. L. Holland. il *Good Housekeeping* 208:245-6 My '89
Rad risks in young breasts. *Science News* 136:311 N 11 '89
A scare for pill users. G. Cowley. il *Newsweek* 113:62 Ja 16 '89
Who should stop using the pill? G. Kolata. *Glamour* 87:250-1+ My '89

Diagnosis
See also
Breast—Examination
Mammography

Breast cancer risk linked to dense tissue [research by Audrey F. Saftlas] K. Fackelmann. *Science News* 135:213 Ap 8 '89
The disease women fear most. S. L. Englebardt. il *Reader's Digest* 134:61-3 Ja '89
Women beware of breast cancer. C. Tevis. il *Successful Farming* 87:72 O '89

Genetic aspects
Gene signals relapse of breast, ovarian cancers [research by Dennis Slamon] J. L. Marx. il *Science* 244:654-5 My 12 '89
Studies of the HER-2/*neu* proto-oncogene in human breast and ovarian cancer. D. J. Slamon and others. bibl f il *Science* 244:707-12 My 12 '89

Nutritional aspects
Animal protein and breast cancer. *Prevention (Emmaus, Pa.)* 41:9-10 Ag '89
Should she or shouldn't she? [link between alcohol and breast cancer] L. Abraham. il *Discover* 10:73 Ja '89
Study refines diet's link to breast cancer [research by Paolo Toniolo] J. Raloff. *Science News* 135:102 F 18 '89

Prevention
Hypertension in pregnancy cuts cancer risk [role of alpha fetoprotein; research by Herbert I. Jacobson] J. Raloff. *Science News* 136:263 O 21 '89

Psychological aspects
Can psychotherapy delay cancer deaths? [research by David Spiegel] M. Barinaga. il *Science* 246:448-9 O 27 '89
Cancer: facts vs. feelings. M. Kaufman. por *Newsweek* 113:10 Ap 24 '89
Group therapy aids cancer survival [work of David Spiegel] *Science News* 136:302 N 4 '89
'I refused to be a victim to cancer'. S. Jordan. il por *New Choices for the Best Years* 29:16+ Ap '89

Surgery
See also
Mastectomy
Prognosis: excellent following lumpectomy and radiation [J. Cox] C. SerVaas. por *The Saturday Evening Post* 261:46+ Jl/Ag '89
Tempering the trauma [research shows lumpectomy and mastectomy are equally effective] *U.S. News & World Report* 106:17 Ap 10 '89

Therapy
Breast cancer: beating the odds. *Harper's Bazaar* 122:136+ Ag '89
Breast-cancer care: a state-of-the-art treatment site [Memorial Sloan-Kettering Cancer Center] *Vogue* 179:228 D '89
Breast cancer: playing the odds [additional therapy for mastectomy patients] il *Newsweek* 113:46-7 Mr 6 '89
Drugs give slight edge in breast cancer. K. Fackelmann. *Science News* 135:135 Mr 4 '89
New treatment may reduce breast surgeries [chemotherapy followed by lumpectomy and radiation; work of Gianni Bonadonna] R. Weiss. *Science News* 135:325-6 My 27 '89
Tamoxifen and breast cancer: new choices. M. Weber. *Vogue* 179:114 Ja '89
Treatment trends. N. E. Gupta and H. Sobol. *Ladies' Home Journal* 106:98+ Jl '89

Diseases
The case of the suspect lump [fibrocystic breast disease] E. Padus. *Prevention (Emmaus, Pa.)* 41:112-14+ Ag '89

Examination
See also
Mammography
The breast self-exam. il *McCall's* 116:102 S '89
A lifesaving exam. il *Parents* 64:16 N '89
Screening rules to live by. il *Ladies' Home Journal* 106:107 N '89
Video breast self-examination. il *Glamour* 87:240+ F '89

Surgery, Plastic
See Surgery, Plastic

Wounds and injuries
Frontal assault [women athletes] M. Madsen. il *Women's Sports & Fitness* 11:10 Ja/F '89

BREAST EXERCISES See Exercise

BREAST FEEDING
See also
Milk, Human

BREAST IMPLANTS See Surgery, Plastic

BREAST MILK See Milk, Human

BREAST PUMPING
Imagery boosts breast milk [research by Stephen D. K. Feher] *Science News* 135:71 F 4 '89

BREAST X RAYS See Mammography

BREATH ODOR See Halitosis

BREATH TESTS
How reliable is breath-alcohol testing? D. A. Labianca. il *USA Today (Periodical)* 118:71-2 S '89

BREATHED, BERKE
about
Has this Opus drawn to an end? il por *Newsweek* 113:65 My 15 '89
A hooligan who wields a pen [interview] D. S. Levy. il por *Time* 134:10+ D 25 '89

BREATHING *See* Respiration
BREATHING EQUIPMENT *See* Respirators
BREATHING EXERCISES
Breathe away your chains of pain [hyperventilation] G. McVeigh. il *Prevention (Emmaus, Pa.)* 41:58-64 D '89
For less stress—breathe right. M. Rhodes. il *Redbook* 173:14 Je '89
BREAUX, JOHN B., 1944-
Should the Congress adopt the "High Risk Occupational Disease Notification and Prevention Act of 1987"? [excerpts from address, March 28, 1988] *Congressional Digest* 68:122+ Ap '89
BRECHT, BERTOLT, 1898-1956
about
The shrillest Stalinist. R. Grenier. il *National Review* 41:53-4 N 24 '89
BRECKER, MICHAEL
about
Michael Brecker: re-charged sax. R. Tolleson. il por *Down Beat* 56:56-7 N '89
BREDER, HANS, 1935-
about
Hans Breder at Schreiber/Cutler. G. Henry. il *Art in America* 77:153 Ja '89
BREEDEN, RICHARD
about
Bush's man on the Street. T. Smart. il por *Business Week* p27 Ag 28 '89
BREEDERS' CUP (RACES) *See* Horse racing
BREEDING, CINDILOU
about
Hit-and-run: a family's nightmare. D. M. Mazie. il *Reader's Digest* 135:152-7 D '89
BREEDING
See also
Cats—Breeding
Cattle—Breeding
Elephants—Breeding
Horses—Breeding
Iguanas—Breeding
Inbreeding
Livestock—Breeding
Mice—Breeding
Reproduction
Rhinoceros—Breeding
Swine—Breeding
Doling out DNA [DNA fingerprinting for captive breeding programs; cover story] R. Weiss. il *Science News* 135:72-4 F 4 '89
Glass menageries [use of cryopreservation in captive breeding] T. Beardsley. il *Scientific American* 261:36+ O '89
A technique originally developed for overcoming human infertility may also help endangered species [in vitro fertilization] R. M. Adams. *Smithsonian* 19:12 Ja '89
BREEDLOVE, SARAH *See* Walker, Madame C. J., 1867-1919
BREEN, JOSEPH IGNATIUS, 1890-1965
about
No trollops, no tomcats [excerpt from The dame in the kimono] L. J. Leff and J. Simmons. il por *American Film* 15:40-3+ D '89
BREEST, GÜNTHER
about
Watch on the Elbe. T. W. Libbey, Jr. il *High Fidelity (New York, N.Y.)* 39:55 Ja '89
BREFELDIN
Brefeldin A specifically inhibits presentation of protein antigens to cytotoxic T lymphocytes. J. W. Yewdell and J. R. Bennink. bibl f il *Science* 244:1072-5 Je 2 '89
BREGA, DOUG
about
Be prolific. il *American Artist* 53:49 D '89
BREGENZ FESTIVAL *See* Music festivals—Austria
BREGGIN, PETER ROGER, 1936-
about
The anti-shrinks. M. DiLeo. pors *Mother Jones* 14:13 Jl/Ag '89
BREGMAN, WALTER
about
Trouble in paradise. D. Machan. il pors *Forbes* 143:144+ My 15 '89
BREILLAT, CATHERINE
about
36 fillette [film] Reviews
The Nation 248:174 F 6 '89. S. Klawans
The New Republic 200:24 F 6 '89. S. Kauffmann
New York 22:83 F 6 '89. D. Denby
People Weekly 31:19-20 Ja 16 '89. P. Travers
BREITE FAMILY
about
Seizing the moment. R. Lacayo. il *Time* 134:43 O 16 '89
BREITWISCH, RANDALL
Who listens to the mockingbird? il *Natural History* p6+ Je '89
BREMER, L. PAUL, III
Countering terrorism in the 1980s and 1990s [address, November 22, 1988] *Department of State Bulletin* 89:61-4 F '89
Terrorism: its evolving nature [statement, February 9, 1989] *Department of State Bulletin* 89:74-8 My '89

BREN, DONALD L.
about
Bleak ranch. E. Schmuckler. il por *Forbes* 144 Special Issue:14 O 23 '89
BRENDEL, ALFRED
Schubert's last sonatas. bibl f il *The New York Review of Books* 36:32-6 F 2 '89
'Schubert's last sonatas': an exchange [discussion of February 2, 1989 article] il *The New York Review of Books* 36:42-3 Mr 16 '89
about
Extreme occasions. E. W. Said. *The Nation* 248:898-900 Je 26 '89
BRENER, MILTON E.
Baltic odyssey. il por map *Opera News* 54:18-21 D 23 '89
BRENER, PABLO
about
Mexican contrarian. R. King. il por *Forbes* 144:88+ S 4 '89
BRENNAN, CHRISTINE
To be young, gifted & fast [cover story] il pors *Runner's World* 24:42-7 Mr '89
BRENNAN, EDWARD A.
about
The Big Store's big trauma. B. Bremner and M. D. Oneal. il por *Business Week* p50-1+ Jl 10 '89
BRENNAN, GEORGEANNE, 1943-
Holiday dinner. il *Organic Gardening* 36:37-41 D '89
BRENNAN, HAROLD J., 1903-1989
about
Obituary
American Craft il por 49:64+ D '89/Ja '90. J. Prip
BRENNAN, THOMPSON
about
Cop art. B. Weber. il *The New York Times Magazine* p94 Ap 30 '89
BRENNER, BARBARA
It's never too early to make a friend. il *Good Housekeeping* 209:81+ S '89
Preschool and your child. il *Good Housekeeping* 209:98+ S '89
BRENNER, DANIEL
Congress, the FCC, and Judge Greene [address, November 10, 1988] *Vital Speeches of the Day* 55:250-3 F 1 '89
Telecommunications and the world information revolution [address, July 19, 1989] *Vital Speeches of the Day* 56:88-91 N 15 '89
BRENNER, DOUGLAS
Clean sweep. il *House & Garden* 161:118-23 Je '89
Eire apparent. il por *House & Garden* 161:90+ S '89
Green secrets of Venice. il *House & Garden* 161:114 N '89
Hard-hatted woman. il pors *House & Garden* 161:38+ My '89
BRENNER, LOIS
Attention, Arnie Becker: your motions in courtrooms—not bedrooms—would be more help. il *TV Guide* 37:10-11 Je 17-23 '89
BRENNER, LYNN
13 ways to save on car insurance. *Better Homes and Gardens* 67:166 O '89
BRENNER, MARC A.
Help yourself to happy feet. il *Women's Sports & Fitness* 11:58 S '89
BRENNER, ROBERT
Fragile paper treasures. il *Antiques & Collecting Hobbies* 94:56-9 D '89
BRENT, JONATHAN
about
Northwestern UP looks to the trade. T. Unsworth. *Publishers Weekly* 236:31 O 13 '89
BRENT, LANA JANE LEWIS- *See* Lewis-Brent, Lana Jane
BRENTANO'S, INC.
Waldenbooks to open Brentano's in Scribner's amid controversy [New York City] C. Reid. *Publishers Weekly* 236:13 S 29 '89
BRENTON, HOWARD, 1942-
Iranian nights [drama] Reviews
Newsweek il 113:43 My 1 '89
BRENTWOOD (LOS ANGELES, CALIF.)
Architecture
"The big hit" [home of C. and M. Einstein] P. Clothier. il pors *Art News* 88:113-14+ D '89
A creative collaboration: softening a modern house in Los Angeles [home of S. Harris and P. J. Witt decorated by John Saladino] M. Frank. il pors *Architectural Digest* 46:130-7 Ag '89
Restaurants, nightclubs, bars, etc.
Spécialités de la maison:
Daily Grill. C. Bates. il *Gourmet* 49:42+ Je '89
BRESKIN, DAVID
Michael Jordan, in his own orbit [cover story] il pors *Gentlemen's Quarterly* 59:318-23+ Mr '89
BRESLAU, KAREN
Old Volk's home. *The New Republic* 200:16+ My 1 '89
BRESLER, JUDITH
(jt. auth) *See* Lerner, Ralph E., 1943-, and Bresler, Judith

BRESLER, ROBERT J., 1937-
Bush and the deficit dilemma. il *USA Today (Periodical)* 117:7 My '89
The complexities of affirmative action. il *USA Today (Periodical)* 118:7 S '89
Confronting the Sandinistas. il *USA Today (Periodical)* 118:5 N '89
The decline of civility. il *USA Today (Periodical)* 117:7 Mr '89
Defense strategy for the 1990's. il *USA Today (Periodical)* 117:7 Ja '89
Is the cold war over? *USA Today (Periodical)* 118:7 Jl '89

BRESLIN, CATHERINE
Day of reckoning. il *Ms.* 17:46-52 Je '89
Tokyo Prep. il *New York* 22:50-2 Mr 6 '89

BRESLIN, LYNNE
Tokyo collage. il *Architectural Record* 177:84-93 O '89

BRESNAHAN, DAVE
about
The great potato pick-off play. M. Bowden. il *Reader's Digest* 134:103-7 Je '89

BRESSAN, SERGE
Doping for the competitive edge. il *World Press Review* 36:59 Je '89

BRESSON, HENRI CARTIER- *See* Cartier-Bresson, Henri, 1908-

BREST, MARTIN
about
Midnight run [film] Reviews
Video il 13:74+ My '89. I. Robbins

BRETT, BOB
about
A fusion of power [interview] N. Amdur. il pors *World Tennis* 36:34-5 Mr '89

BRETT, GUY
Hélio Oiticica: reverie and revolt [cover story] bibl f il pors *Art in America* 77:110-21+ Ja '89
Impromptus: David Medalla. bibl f il pors *Art in America* 77:156-63+ N '89

BRETTING, HENRY LYMAN, JR.
about
Folding napkins to ring up sales. M. Barrier. il por *Nation's Business* 77:58-9 Jl '89

BRETTING (C. G.) MFG. CO. *See* C. G. Bretting Mfg. Co.

BREUKER, WILLEM
about
Willem Breuker, & Kompany: Euro-bop, with a twist. M. Bourne. il pors *Down Beat* 56:28-30 My '89

BREWER, DAVID
about
Recording the sky on videotape [interview] M. B. Pepin. il *Astronomy* 17:86-9 S '89

BREWER, PETER, AND OTHERS
Carbon dioxide transport by ocean currents at 25°N latitude in the Atlantic Ocean. bibl f il *Science* 246:477-9 O 27 '89

BREWER, SCOTT
about
Thurgood Marshall hires two black Ivy League law clerks. il pors *Jet* 77:4+ N 13 '89

BREWER (ME.)
Parks and playgrounds
Wherever he goes, architect Robert Leathers leaves another new playground behind [volunteer-built playground] N. Geeslin. il pors *People Weekly* 32:63+ S 25 '89

BREWERY TOURS
Fresh from the vat. K. Zimmermann. il *Americana* 17:56-60 Jl/Ag '89

BREWIN, BOB
Charge of the 'telcos'. il *Video* 12:142 Ja '89
Whittle while you learn. il *Video* 13:122 My '89

BREWING INDUSTRY
See also
Adolph Coors Co.
Anheuser-Busch, Inc.
Mass. Bay Brewing Company
Miller Brewing Company
S&P Company
Stroh Brewery Company
Home brews [microbreweries] F. J. Prial. il *The New York Times Magazine* p57 Ag 6 '89
Acquisitions and mergers
Coors may take a gulp of a rival brew [Stroh Brewery] S. D. Atchison. il *Business Week* p70 Ag 21 '89
One last call for fading beer brands [S&P launches antitrust suit against Adolph Coors Co.'s acquisition of Stroh Brewery] L. Armstrong. il *Business Week* p68 O 16 '89
International aspects
A sip of Stroh's could turn into a gulp. D. Woodruff. il *Business Week* p37 My 15 '89
Canada
In search of a bigger gulp [merger of Molson and Carling] B. Came. il *Maclean's* 102:36 Ja 30 '89
Advertising
Beer ads: fuel for the drug bonfire. N. Fleishman and D. Fleishman. il pors *The Humanist* 49:18-19+ N/D '89

How the owl drove a wedge between Stroh and Audubon [beer company pulls ads from TV show on Pacific Northwest old growth forests] V. Cahan. *Business Week* p99 S 18 '89
Miller guy life [spring break beer ads] T. Riordan. *The New Republic* 200:16-17 Mr 27 '89
Nonalcoholic sports [beer commercials on TV] L. Cryderman. *Christianity Today* 33:15 S 22 '89
Antitrust cases
One last call for fading beer brands [S&P launches antitrust suit against Adolph Coors Co.'s acquisition of Stroh Brewery] L. Armstrong. il *Business Week* p68 O 16 '89
Finance
Why the beer market went flat. il *U.S. News & World Report* 107:16+ N 6 '89
Marketing
A sophisticated sampler for Joe Six-Pack [California breweries marketing Microbrew Discovery Pack] *Newsweek* 113:44 Ja 23 '89
Canada
See also
Carling O'Keefe Limited
John Labatt Limited
Molson Breweries
Molson Companies Limited
Great Britain
See also
Guinness plc
Samuel Smith's (Firm)
Japan
Have Japan's brewers been drinking too much? R. Neff. il *Business Week* p43-4 Ag 28 '89

BREWIS, HEATHER
about
Winners. S. Wilson. il por *Motor Boating & Sailing* 163:26+ Mr '89

BREYTENBACH, BREYTEN
Erogenous South Africa [fiction] *Harper's* 279:38-9 Jl '89
about
True confessions of an exiled Afrikaner. G. Marzorati. il pors *The New York Times Magazine* p32-3+ Ag 27 '89

BRIA, GEORGE
Think small when growing tomatoes. il *The Saturday Evening Post* 261:90 Jl/Ag '89

BRIALY, JEAN-CLAUDE
about
Acts of culture: Jean-Claude Brialy's château in the Marne Valley. C. Aillaud. il por *Architectural Digest* 46:94-9+ Ja '89

BRIAND, FRÉDÉRIC, AND COHEN, JOEL E.
Habitat compartmentation and environmental correlates of food chain length [discussion of November 13, 1987 article, Environmental correlates of food chain length] il *Science* 243:238-40 Ja 13 '89

BRIBERY
See also
Payola
Pentagon procurement scandal
Politics, Corruption in
When somebody wants a payoff [East Asia] F. S. Worthy. il *Fortune* 120 no13 Special Issue:117-18+ Fall '89

BRICK CONSTRUCTION
Brick Institute of America Brick in Architecture Award. il *Architectural Record* 177:54-5 Ag '89

BRICK HOUSES
In the brick tradition. il *Southern Living* 24:116 Ja '89

BRICK INSTITUTE OF AMERICA
Brick Institute of America Brick in Architecture Award. il *Architectural Record* 177:54-5 Ag '89

BRICK PAVEMENTS *See* Pavements

BRICK VENEER
A veneer too thin? J. S. Russell. il *Architectural Record* 177:116-19 Mr '89

BRICKELL, EDIE
about
Edie Brickell & New Bohemians. B. Stepko. il pors *Seventeen* 48:105-6 Ap '89
Edie Brickell stands by her band. B. Balfour. il por *Mademoiselle* 95:92 Ag '89
Who she is is who she is. S. Pond. il pors *Rolling Stone* p44-6+ My 4 '89

BRICKELL (EDIE) AND THE NEW BOHEMIANS (MUSICAL GROUP) *See* Edie Brickell and the New Bohemians (Musical group)

BRICKEN, FAY
about
A man named Fay. L. Wells. il por *Southern Living* 24:84+ O '89

BRICKLAYERS
Bricklayer's boy. A. Lubrano. il *Gentlemen's Quarterly* 59:171-2+ Je '89

BRICKLIN, DAN
about
Birthing the visible calculator [interview] il pors *Byte* 14:326-8 D '89

BRICKLIN, MARK
Prevention system. See issues of Prevention (Emmaus, Pa.) beginning March 1988
BRIDAL BOUQUETS See Bouquets
BRIDAL GOWNS See Wedding clothes
BRIDAL SHOWERS
A bridal shower. il Gourmet 49:92-4+ My '89
BRIDES See Weddings
BRIDESMAIDS
Member of the wedding. R. Bacher. il Seventeen 48:34+ Mr '89
BRIDGE (GAME)
Playing for real [bridge masters M. Becker and R. Rubin become options traders] N. Hass. il pors New York 22:60-2+ D 11 '89

Tournaments
Men win a point at bridge [Bridge Battle of the Sexes] M. Starr. il Newsweek 113:82 Ap 24 '89
BRIDGE LOANS
Big bucks at the end of the bridge. D. P. Wiener. il U.S. News & World Report 107:68 O 2 '89
BRIDGE TO SILENCE [television program] See Television program reviews—Single works
BRIDGEHAMPTON (N.Y.)

Description
Bridgehampton perspectives. M. M. Thomas. il Architectural Digest 46:58+ Je '89
BRIDGEPORT (CONN.)

Buildings
New directions [Bridgeport Center] D. Dietsch. il Architectural Record 177:70-7 Ag '89

Education
See also
Upward Bound Academy

Galleries and museums
See also
P.T. Barnum Museum (Bridgeport, Conn.)

History
The farm where the elephants plowed! E. Rochette. il Antiques & Collecting Hobbies 94:61-2 Jl '89

Savings and loan associations
See also
People's Bank
BRIDGES, C. DAVID

about
New round in Dingell v. NIH? J. Palca. Science 245:349 Jl 28 '89
NIH sees plagiarism in vision paper. B. J. Culliton. Science 245:120-2 Jl 14 '89
BRIDGES, HUDSON
Along the avenues. See occasional issues of Gourmet
BRIDGES, LINDA
The past as prologue. National Review 41:22-3 Je 2 '89
BRIDGES, TODD

about
Bail is set at $2 mil. for Bridges; faces more charges. por Jet 75:12 Mr 20 '89
Bridges held on attempted murder charge in L.A. por Jet 75:54 F 20 '89
Bridges' mother blames son's problems on drugs. il por Jet 75:52 F 27 '89
Jury acquits Todd Bridges of charges of attempted murder, manslaughter. il por Jet 77:36-7 N 27 '89
Todd Bridges tells how Hollywood destroyed his life and how God is rebuilding it. il pors Jet 76:28-30 Ap 10 '89
BRIDGES
See also
Brooklyn Bridge (New York, N.Y.)
Covered bridges
Earthquakes and bridges
San Francisco Bay (Calif.)—Bridges

China
The segmental arch bridge [ancient China] R. K. G. Temple. il The Courier (Unesco) 41:19-20 O '88
BRIDGES, NATURAL
See also
Rainbow Bridge (Utah and Ariz.)
Ohio natural bridges. M. C. Hansen. il map Earth Science 41:10-12 Wint '88
BRIDGES, WOODEN
See also
Covered bridges
Wood bridges: back in favor. il Country Journal 16:14 F '89
BRIDGESTONE CORP.
Can Bridgestone make the climb? [acquisition of Firestone] Z. Schiller. il Business Week p78-9 F 27 '89
Why Bridgestone's chairman is making tracks to Akron [T. Eguchi transferred to Firestone] Z. Schiller. il por Business Week p32-3 N 20 '89
BRIDGLAND, FRED
The ivory dispute. World Press Review 36:69 S '89
BRIEFCASES
The attaché case. J. Berendt. il Esquire 111:36 F '89
BRIGADA S (MUSICAL GROUP)
Hot, hot, hot: Brigada S. P. Hofheinz. il Time 133:110-11 Ap 10 '89

BRIGEOIS, EVELYNE, 1946-
The watercolor page. il por American Artist 53:54-7 Ja '89
BRIGGS, ASA, 1921-
Manningham Mills, Bradford. il por History Today 39:62-3 O '89
BRIGGS, DEREK E. G.
(jt. auth) See Aldridge, Richard J. (Richard John), and Briggs, Derek E. G.
BRIGGS, DEREK E. G., AND FORTEY, RICHARD A.
The early radiation and relationships of the major arthropod groups. bibl f il Science 246:241-3 O 13 '89
BRIGGS, JOHN
Interview: Reese Jenkins. il por Omni (New York, N.Y.) 11:82-4+ Ap '89
BRIGGS, NANCY

about
Lunch is being served at the world's smallest restaurant; reservations available in 1990. il pors People Weekly 32:150 N 20 '89
BRIGHAM AND WOMEN'S HOSPITAL (BOSTON, MASS.)
Ambulatory Services Building, Brigham and Women's Hospital. M. Gaskie. il Architectural Record 177:79-83 Ap '89
BRIGHAM YOUNG UNIVERSITY
Will this tortoise beat the hares? [Brigham Young vs. Univ. of Utah in cold fusion race] J. Carey and W. C. Symonds. il por Business Week p103 My 8 '89
BRIGHT, CHRIS
Chinese head tax haunts Canada. il por The Progressive 53:13-14 Ap '89
BRIGHT, HARVEY R., 1920-

about
Bum Bright goes for the long bomb. K. Kelly. il por Business Week p98+ F 6 '89
BRIGHT, MARY

about
Curtain call. H. S. MacIsaac. il por House & Garden 161:60+ N '89
BRIGHT CHILDREN See Children, Gifted
BRIGHTNESS CONTROL See Lighting—Control
BRILL, DAVID L.
Raising day [photographs] il Country Journal 16:57-9 S/O '89
BRILL, GLENN

about
Glenn Brill/Allrich Gallery. C. White. il American Craft 49:74-83 Je/Jl '89
BRILL, STEVEN

about
Scandal in the courts. M. Greenfield. il Newsweek 114:68 Ag 21 '89
BRILL, WINSTON J.

about
Breaking biotech barriers in botany. L. Therrien. il por Business Week Special Issue:78 Je 16 '89
BRILLIANT, LARRY

about
The man who found himself. J. Queenan. Forbes 143:138 My 29 '89
BRILLIANT PEBBLES (DEFENSE SYSTEM)
Brilliant Pebbles: amazing new missile killer [work of L. Wood and G. Canavan] R. K. Bennett. Reader's Digest 135:128-33 S '89
Brilliant Pebbles becomes focus of strategic review. Aviation Week & Space Technology 130:47-9 Ap 3 '89
Brilliant Pebbles shines in phase one SDI test. il Popular Mechanics 166:14 O '89
Defense cubed. J. J. Frelk. National Review 41:34-5 My 5 '89
Defense Dept. postpones decision on Brilliant Pebbles until November. P. A. Gilmartin. Aviation Week & Space Technology 131:23-4 Ag 14 '89
Heavenly Pebbles. Commonweal 116:292-3 My 19 '89
Pebbles go bam-bam. F. Barnes. The New Republic 200:12+ Ap 17 '89
Promise of Brilliant Pebbles casts doubt on SDI plan. T. M. Foley. il Aviation Week & Space Technology 130:260-1 Mr 20 '89
SDI officials plan to boost Brilliant Pebbles funding. P. A. Gilmartin. Aviation Week & Space Technology 131:21 N 27 '89
Sharp rise in Brilliant Pebbles interceptor funding accompanied by new questions about technical feasibility. T. M. Foley. il Aviation Week & Space Technology 130:20-1 My 22 '89
Smart rocks, Brilliant Pebbles, genius dust? G. Chapman. il The Bulletin of the Atomic Scientists 45:10-11+ N '89
Throwing stones at "Brilliant Pebbles". J. Jacky. il Technology Review 92:20-1+ O '89
Too Brilliant by half. il The New Republic 200:7-9 My 29 '89
The waning technological glitter of Star Wars. S. Budiansky. il U.S. News & World Report 107:53-4 Jl 3 '89
BRILLIANT TRACES [drama] See Johnson, Cindy Lou
BRIM, ORVILLE GILBERT, 1923-
Losing and winning. Current (Washington, D.C.) 311:12-15 Mr/Ap '89

BRIMMER, ANDREW F.
Economic perspectives. See issues of Black Enterprise
BRINCKERHOFF, CONSTANCE E., AND OTHERS
Autocrine induction of collagenase by serum amyloid A-like and β_2-microglobulin-like proteins. bibl f il *Science* 243:655-7 F 3 '89
BRINCKERHOFF, RICHARD F.
Resource centers for science teachers. *The Education Digest* 54:36-9 Mr '89
BRINGLE, MARY LOUISE
Confessions of a glutton [cover story] *The Christian Century* 106:955-8 O 25 '89
BRINK, PETER
about
Preserving the South's past, city to town. D. Young. il pors *Southern Living* 24:90-1+ F '89
BRINKER, RUTH
about
Open heart, Open Hand. il por *Time* 133:21 Ja 9 '89
BRINKLEY, CHRISTIE
about
Christie Brinkley. C. Krupp. il por *Glamour* 87:226-7+ F '89
Rich and famous. B. Newman. il pors *Sports Illustrated* 70 Special Issue:161+ F '89
BRINKLEY, JOEL, 1952-
Inside the intifada [cover story] il *The New York Times Magazine* p36-9+ O 29 '89
The soldiers: anger and frustration [cover story] il *The New York Times Magazine* p30-3+ My 7 '89
BRINLEY, MARYANN BUCKNUM
When the urge to spend strikes. il *McCall's* 116:39-41 Jl '89
BRINT, STEVEN
Italy observed. *Society* 26:71-6 Jl/Ag '89
BRISICK, WILLIAM
The Honolulu book shops: bookselling in paradise. il *Publishers Weekly* 235:51-3 Ap 28 '89
John Cole's Bookshop. il por *Publishers Weekly* 236:95+ S 15 '89
BRISKET COOKING See Cooking—Meat
BRISSON, JEAN-PAUL
Aeneas, Rome's man of destiny. il *The Unesco Courier* 42:22-7 S '89
BRISTER, BUBBY
about
"Let's play football!". J. D. Miller. il pors *Sport (New York, N.Y.)* 80:22-3+ O '89
BRISTOL, HORACE
Travels with Steinbeck; ed. by Jack Kelly. il pors *People Weekly* 31:66-8+ My 1 '89
BRISTOL (ENGLAND)
Labor
History
A social contract? Master against servant in the Court of Requests [case of notary W. Yeamans and his apprentice T. Alford] P. S. Seaver. il *History Today* 39:50-6 S '89
BRISTOL AEROSPACE LTD.
Bristol remanufacturing Canadian Forces F-5s. il *Aviation Week & Space Technology* 131:60+ N 27 '89
BRISTOL-MYERS CO.
Filling Bristol-Myers' prescription [Squibb merger] J. Weber, Jr. and S. Benway. il pors *Business Week* p80-1 Ag 14 '89
Friendly medicine [merger of Bristol-Myers and Squibb] *Time* 134:39 Ag 7 '89
A risky lifeline for AIDS victims [distributes unproven drug] *U.S. News & World Report* 107:14 Jl 24 '89
BRISTOW HELICOPTERS LTD.
Aerospatiale takes first civilian order for Super Puma Mk. 2 helicopters. il *Aviation Week & Space Technology* 130:73 Je 26 '89
BRITAIN See Great Britain
BRITISH
Anecdotes, facetiae, satire, etc.
Uncivil liberties. C. Trillin. il *The Nation* 249:230 S 4-11 '89
Bermuda
History
Colonising Bermuda—defending Virginia [seventeenth century] C. W. Brown. bibl il maps *History Today* 39:36-41 Ja '89
Lebanon
A shattered deal [release of British hostages in Beirut jeopardized by S. Rushdie affair] il *Newsweek* 113:5 Mr 13 '89
Nicaragua
History
Nicaragua's English connection [indigenous people on Atlantic coast] A. Hills. il *History Today* 39:3-4 Ag '89
Spain
An Anglo-Spanish nightmare. R. Alan. *The New Leader* 72:10-11 N 13 '89
United States
The great British brain drain. D. Foote. il *Newsweek* 114:60 Jl 17 '89
Scholar slip [Britain's brain drain] A. Ryan. *The New Republic* 201:14-16 D 4 '89

History
Colonising Bermuda—defending Virginia [seventeenth century] C. W. Brown. bibl il maps *History Today* 39:36-41 Ja '89
Editorial [question of colonial regionalism] W. Garrett. *Antiques* 136:1319 D '89
Remapping American culture [D. H. Fischer traces regionalism back to early English settlers] A. P. Sanoff. il maps *U.S. News & World Report* 107:60-4 D 4 '89
BRITISH ACTORS AND ACTRESSES See Actors and actresses
BRITISH AEROSPACE PLC
AMR Eagle places 100 orders, options for Jetstream aircraft. *Aviation Week & Space Technology* 130:167 Je 19 '89
British Aerospace decides to proceed with Jetstream 41 development program [turboprop commuter aircraft] *Aviation Week & Space Technology* 130:111 My 29 '89
British Aerospace launches BAe 1000 business jet. C. A. Shifrin. il *Aviation Week & Space Technology* 131:43+ O 16 '89
British Aerospace, Thomson-CSF consider making joint bid for Ferranti International Signal. *Aviation Week & Space Technology* 131:32 O 16 '89
British aircraft maker reports first profit. *Aviation Week & Space Technology* 131:33 S 18 '89
Pan Am will use Jetstreams to bolster Miami operations. J. T. McKenna. *Aviation Week & Space Technology* 131:82-3 N 27 '89
Top British Aerospace, Daimler officials discuss collaboration in aerospace markets. *Aviation Week & Space Technology* 130:56 Ap 17 '89
Unit set up to finance Saudi military buys from Britain. *Aviation Week & Space Technology* 131:24 D 4 '89
BRITISH AIRWAYS PLC
Belgium will sell British Airways, KLM 20% stakes in new Sabena. *Aviation Week & Space Technology* 130:95 Je 26 '89
British Airways profits set new company record. *Aviation Week & Space Technology* 130:125 My 29 '89
British Airways seeks larger share of first-class market. C. A. Shifrin. il *Aviation Week & Space Technology* 130:106 My 8 '89
British Airways starts transatlantic service with new Boeing 747-400s. C. A. Shifrin. il *Aviation Week & Space Technology* 131:62-3+ Ag 14 '89
British Airways, United Airlines will expand cooperative services. map *Aviation Week & Space Technology* 130:69 Mr 13 '89
Davis ups buyout bid for United but pilot offer still stronger. J. Ott and C. A. Shifrin. il *Aviation Week & Space Technology* 131:126-7 S 11 '89
From 'Bloody Awful' to bloody awesome. C. Power. il por *Business Week* p97+ O 9 '89
Growing up with Concorde: supersonic maintenance. *Flying* 116:14 D '89
Helping time fly [in-flight videotapes] J. Marcom, Jr. il *Forbes* 143:149-50 Mr 6 '89
BRITISH ART See Art, British
BRITISH ASTRONAUTS See Astronauts
BRITISH BROADCASTING CORPORATION See BBC
BRITISH CIVIL AVIATION AUTHORITY See Great Britain. Civil Aviation Authority
BRITISH COLUMBIA
See also
Abortion clinics—British Columbia
Columbia River
Earthquakes—British Columbia
Educational laws and regulations—British Columbia
Finance—British Columbia
Fishing—British Columbia
Music festivals—British Columbia
Oil pollution—British Columbia
Pacific Rim National Park (B.C.)
Port Kells (B.C.)
Public welfare—British Columbia
Rogers Pass (B.C.)
Vancouver (B.C.)
Vancouver Island (B.C.)
Victoria (B.C.)
Water pollution—British Columbia
Commercial policy
China's pain is Vancouver's gain. P. C. Newman. il *Maclean's* 102:43 O 2 '89
Free trade [address, November 22, 1988] T. Siddon. *Vital Speeches of the Day* 55:222-4 Ja 15 '89
Fisheries
See Fisheries—Canada
Industries
See also
Coal mines and mining—British Columbia
Gold mines and mining—British Columbia
Real estate business—Canada
Shellfish fisheries—Canada
Politics and government
See also
Social Credit Party (B.C.)
A New Democrat sweep [byelections] H. Quinn. il *Maclean's* 102:14 Mr 27 '89

BRITISH COLUMBIA—Politics and government—*cont.*
Vander Zalm besieged [cabinet resignation and byelection loss in Cariboo] B. Bergman. il por *Maclean's* 102:26-7 O 2 '89
Bibliography
Leaders in Lotusland. J. Pifer. il *Maclean's* 102:85-6 D 4 '89
BRITISH COLUMBIA SOCIAL CREDIT PARTY *See* Social Credit Party (B.C.)
BRITISH COMMONWEALTH OF NATIONS *See* Commonwealth of Nations
BRITISH COMMUNICATIONS SATELLITES *See* Communications satellites, British
BRITISH-DUTCH WARS, 1652-1784 *See* Anglo-Dutch Wars, 1652-1784
BRITISH GRAND PRIX *See* Automobile racing—Great Britain
BRITISH HELICOPTERS *See* Helicopters
BRITISH HOROLOGICAL INSTITUTE
The British Horological Institute. R. Cavendish. il *History Today* 39:62 Je '89
BRITISH IMPERIALISM *See* Imperialism
BRITISH JEWELRY *See* Jewelry, British
BRITISH MIDLAND AIRWAYS LTD.
Two British carriers launch efforts to boost international market shares. C. A. Shifrin. *Aviation Week & Space Technology* 131:125 S 18 '89
BRITISH MUSEUM
See also
Elgin marbles
A celebrated Roman vase has become a 20th-century phoenix [Portland Vase restoration] I. Shenker. bibl (p122) il *Smithsonian* 20:52-4+ Jl '89
BRITISH PETROLEUM CO. PLC
BP: making the best of it [buys back half of Kuwait's shares] M. Maremont. *Business Week* p48 Ja 16 '89
British royalty [new royalty trust may signal new takeovers] T. Mack. il *Forbes* 143:92 Ap 3 '89
Exxon's legal problems are washing up on BP's beach. S. Phillips. il *Business Week* p193 S 25 '89
BRITISH PHOTOGRAPHERS *See* Photographers, British
BRITISH PUBLISHERS ASSOCIATION
U.K. publishers vote Rushdie support, reject Teheran boycott. V. Menkes. *Publishers Weekly* 235:104 My 12 '89
BRITISH RAIL PENSION FUND
British Rail's runaway Renoir [sale of impressionist and modern pictures and sculptures] G. Barker. *Art News* 88:39 Summ '89
BRITISH RAILWAYS
See also
British Rail Pension Fund
BRITISH SATELLITE BROADCASTING (FIRM)
Hollywood reaps a windfall from television's richest endeavor. K. Pearce. il *Channels (New York, N.Y.: 1986)* 9:9 Mr '89
U.S. reenters commercial launch arena with private Delta mission [launch of television relay spacecraft Marcopolo] E. H. Kolcum. il *Aviation Week & Space Technology* 131:24-5 S 4 '89
BRITISH SOCCER FANS *See* Soccer fans
BRITISH SPACEPLANE *See* Spaceplane, British
BRITISH TELECOM PLC
British Telecom is getting less British all the time [buying McDonnell Douglas Corp.'s electronic data communications operations] M. Maremont. il *Business Week* p62 Ag 14 '89
Craig McCaw goes establishment [selling British Telecom a stake in McCaw Cellular Communications] J. J. Keller. il por *Business Week* p40-1 F 6 '89
BRITISH VIRGIN ISLANDS
See also
Guana Island (British Virgin Islands)
Necker Island (British Virgin Islands)
Resorts—Mosquito Island (British Virgin Islands)
Description and travel
See also
Cruising—British Virgin Islands
BRITO, CLAUDIO J.
Compact disks. il *World Health* p18-20 Ag/S '89
BRITO-AVELLANA, MARIA
about
Maria Brito-Avellana: Galerie 99. E. Turner. il *Art News* 88:187 Mr '89
BRITTAIN, DONALD
about
Obituary
Maclean's il por 102:40 Jl 31 '89. C. Mollins
BRITTAIN, VICTORIA
Algerian journalists rebel. il *World Press Review* 36:58 Ag '89
BRITTAN, LEON
about
'Subsidy' becomes a dirty word. J. Kapstein. il *Business Week* p48 Je 19 '89
BRITTLE STARS
Starlight on the reef [brittle stars glow with displeasure when touched; cover story] M. S. Grober. il *Natural History* p72-6+ O '89

BRITTO DE CASTRO, ANTONIO RUBENS, AND OTHERS
Brazil's nuclear shakeup: military still in control. bibl f il *The Bulletin of the Atomic Scientists* 45:22-5 My '89
BRIVE (NEW YORK, N.Y.: RESTAURANT) *See* New York (N.Y.)—Restaurants, nightclubs, bars, etc.
BROAD, ELI
about
Eli Broad's revenge. K. Kerwin. il *Business Week* p35 N 20 '89
BROAD, INC.
Eli Broad's revenge [buying core financial services assets of Integrated Resources] K. Kerwin. il *Business Week* p35 N 20 '89
BROADBENT, EDWARD
about
Party politics. M. Clark. il por *Maclean's* 102:10-11 Ja 23 '89
Passing on the flame; Searching for an heir. M. Clark. il por *Maclean's* 102:10-12 Mr 13 '89
BROADCASTING LAW *See* Television laws and regulations
BROADCASTING RATING COUNCIL
See also
Electronic Media Rating Council
BROADFOOT, A. L., AND OTHERS
Ultraviolet spectrometer observations of Neptune and Triton. bibl f il *Science* 246:1459-66 D 15 '89
BROADWAY THEATER DISTRICT (NEW YORK, N.Y.) *See* New York (N.Y.)—Theater
BROADWAY VIDEO (FIRM)
Up all night [L. Michaels] C. Reece. il pors *Channels (New York, N.Y.: 1986)* 9:39-41 N '89
BROCCOLI
See also
Cooking—Vegetables
Last call for broccoli. L. A. Weathers. il *Southern Living* 24:51 F '89
BROCCOLI RABE
See also
Cooking—Vegetables
BROCHU, JIM
I loved Lucy. il pors *Ladies' Home Journal* 106:120-2+ Ag '89
BROCHURES *See* Pamphlets
BROCK, DAVID
Air America's flyboys. il *The American Spectator* 22:37-8 D '89
The world of narcoterrorism. il *The American Spectator* 22:24-8 Je '89
BROCK, JOEL D., AND OTHERS
Liquids, crystals and liquid crystals [cover story] bibl f il *Physics Today* 42:52-9 Jl '89
BROCKHOUSE, GORDON
Cat 'n mouse tips for dealing with audio/video salespeople [cover story] il *High Fidelity (New York, N.Y.)* 39:40-3+ Mr '89
The CD bit wars. il *High Fidelity (New York, N.Y.)* 39:41-5 Ap '89
BROCKWAY, DON
How to shoot scenics [cover story] il pors *Popular Photography* 96:48-59+ N '89
BROCKWAY, GEORGE P.
The dismal science. *See* issues of The New Leader
Pollution—going once, going twice . . . *The New Leader* 72:14-15 O 30 '89
The truth about inflation. il *The New Leader* 72:13-14 F 6 '89
BRODER, DAVID S.
about
Androgyny and Dr. Broder. T. Eastland. il *The American Spectator* 22:28-9 Mr '89
BRODER, SAMUEL, 1945-
about
Cancer prevention strategy at the NCI [interview] C. SerVaas. il por *The Saturday Evening Post* 261:50-1+ My/Je '89
Dare to dialogue on cancer [interview] C. SerVaas. il pors *The Saturday Evening Post* 261:42-6+ Jl/Ag '89
BRODERICK, CATHY
about
Winning is the best revenge. L. Romano. il pors *Good Housekeeping* 208:46+ Ap '89
BRODEUR, JACQUES, AND MCNEIL, JEREMY N.
Seasonal microhabitat selection by an endoparasitoid through adaptive modification of host behavior. bibl f il *Science* 244:226-8 Ap 14 '89
BRODEUR, PAUL
The hazards of electromagnetic fields (I). *The New Yorker* 65:51-2+ Je 12 '89
The hazards of electromagnetic fields (II). *The New Yorker* 65:47-9+ Je 19 '89
The hazards of electromagnetic fields (III). *The New Yorker* 65:39-42+ Je 26 '89
about
An electromagnetic storm. G. Cowley. il por *Newsweek* 114:77 Jl 10 '89
Feeling fatigued and forgetful? The power line next door may be the source of your burnout [interview] D. Mathison. il pors *People Weekly* 32:137-8+ N 27 '89

BRODICK CASTLE (SCOTLAND)
Scotland's Brodick Castle kitchen. L. Langseth-Christensen. il *Gourmet* 49:82-3+ My '89

BRODKEY, HAROLD
about
America's most-awaited writer profits from an impatient wife. P. Freeman. il pors *People Weekly* 31:56-7+ Ja 9 '89
The Brodkey question. C. Iannone. *Commentary* 87:58-61 Ap '89

BRODKIN, HERBERT HARRISON
about
An enduring virtuoso. W. A. Henry. il por *Channels (New York, N.Y.: 1986)* 9:66-8 N '89

BRODOVITCH, ALEXEY, 1898-1971
about
The Russian revolutionary. E. Hartney. il *Harper's Bazaar* 122:324-5+ S '89

BRODSKY, JOSEPH, 1940-
Isaiah Berlin at eighty. il por *The New York Review of Books* 36:44-5 Ag 17 '89
A song [poem] *The New Yorker* 65:40 Mr 27 '89
about
Joseph Brodsky's Nobel Prize; tr. by Barry J. Rubin. Y. Kovalenko and E. Polianovsky. il *The New Republic* 200:38-40 F 20 '89

BRODY, ROBERT
E.T., phone Toronto. il *Omni (New York, N.Y.)* 12:38 O '89
It's all in the cards. il *New Choices for the Best Years* 29:86+ Ap '89

BROEG, BOB, 1918-
The basketball man. il pors *The Saturday Evening Post* 261:58-9+ Ap '89

BROEK, HANS VAN DEN
Secretary Baker's and Foreign Minister van den Broek's news conference, The Hague, July 17, 1989. *Department of State Bulletin* 89:50-3 S '89

BROEKAERT, WILLEM F., AND OTHERS
A chitin-binding lectin from stinging nettle rhizomes with antifungal properties. bibl f il *Science* 245:1100-2 S 8 '89

BROEKEL, RAY, 1923-
The great American candy bar. il *Antiques & Collecting Hobbies* 94:27-9 Mr '89

BROGI, PAOLO
Secrets of Pisa's Tower. *World Press Review* 36:75 D '89

BROILING
Quick! Broil an entrée. il *Southern Living* 24:204 N '89

BROKAW, CHARLES J.
Direct measurements of sliding between outer doublet microtubules in swimming sperm flagella. bibl f il *Science* 243:1593-6 Mr 24 '89

BROKEN BONES See Fractures

BROKEN HILL PROPRIETARY CO., LTD.
The price was right [acquires Pacific Resources] E. McGlinn. il *Forbes* 143:10 F 20 '89

BROKEN HOMES
See also
Children of divorced parents

BROKERS
See also
A. G. Edwards & Sons, Inc.
Airline ticket brokers
Athletes as brokers
Automobile brokers
Banks and banking—Securities handling
Bear, Stearns & Co. Inc.
Bernard L. Madoff Investment Securities
Blinder, Robinson & Company
Charles Schwab & Co., Inc.
Commodity brokers
Cyrus J. Lawrence Incorporated
D.A. Campbell Company
Dean Witter Reynolds Inc.
Drexel Burnham Lambert Incorporated
Foreign exchange brokers
Gamco Investors (Firm)
Government securities dealers
Haas Securities Corporation
Investors Center Inc.
Jefferies Group Inc.
Kidder, Peabody & Co., Incorporated
Mass media brokers
Mortgage brokers
OTC Net Inc.
Over-the-counter securities markets
PaineWebber Group Inc.
Paulson Investment Company
Power Securities Corporation
Prudential-Bache Securities Inc.
Raymond James & Associates, Inc.
Real estate agencies and agents
Robinson Humphrey Company Inc.
Shearson Lehman Hutton Inc.
Smith Barney, Harris Upham & Co. Incorporated
Soft dollar brokers
Specialists (Stock exchange firms)
Stuart-James Company Inc.
Thomson McKinnon Inc.
Money's second annual all pro stockbrokers: 1989. J. Ellis. il *Money* 18:112-14+ O '89

Accounting
Brokers' statements: close, but no cigar. W. Giese. il *Changing Times* 43:47-9+ Mr '89

Acquisitions and mergers
The captains who didn't go down with the ship [Prudential-Bache takes over Thomson McKinnon] G. Morgenson. il *Forbes* 144:39-41 Ag 21 '89
Is Shearson no. 1 on Amex' sell list? G. G. Marcial. *Business Week* p130 Mr 13 '89

Advertising
Basic training on Wall Street. B. Kanner. il *New York* 22:24+ My 15 '89

Banking services
See also
Cash management accounts
Let the Glass-Steagall wall come tumbling down. L. J. Nathans and D. Foust. il *Business Week* p116 D 18 '89

Commissions
See also
Soft dollar brokers
Are analysts putting their mouths where the money is? W. Konrad. il *Business Week* p118 D 18 '89
Beware the big producer. G. Morgenson. il *Forbes* 143:226-7 Je 26 '89
The business that brokers would love to ditch [commissions on trades for institutions] J. M. Laderman. il *Business Week* p106 Mr 27 '89
Climbing high with discount brokers. E. Schultz. il *Fortune* 120 no10 Special Issue:219-20+ Fall '89
How to elude the sharp bite of those submerged fees. A. Rock. il *Money* 18:183-4 Ap '89
When discounts don't count. W. Giese. il *Changing Times* 43:50-1+ F '89
The wide spread phenomenon [high o-t-c transaction costs] R. L. Stern. il *Forbes* 143:232+ Je 26 '89
Will you save money with a discount broker? il *Consumers' Research Magazine* 72:14-17 Mr '89

Customer relations
Avoid the half full in full service. E. Schultz. il *Fortune* 119:52 Je 19 '89
Battling your broker just got a bit easier [SEC rules] L. Zinn. *Business Week* p142 Je 5 '89
Big-time managers for small-fry investors. E. Schultz. il *Fortune* 120:34+ D 4 '89
Getting the most from a full-service broker. il *Fortune* 120 no10 Special Issue:222 Fall '89
How lonely brokers are rewriting the book on service. T. Segal. il *Business Week* p154-5 Mr 13 '89
How to get the most out of a broker. P. Lynch. il *Money* 18:132 Ja '89
The joys of haggling. E. Giltenan. il *Forbes* 143:236 Je 26 '89
Those cold calls leave him cold. J. R. Graham. por *Fortune* 119:326 Ap 24 '89
Wall Street's other arbs [stockholders vs. brokers in arbitration] E. Giltenan. il *Forbes* 143:196-7 Mr 20 '89
What to do when your broker says 'buy'. D. P. Wiener. il *U.S. News & World Report* 106:62-4 Je 19 '89
When you switch brokers, your assets need help passing from one hand to the other. M. C. Paulson. il *Changing Times* 43:18 S '89

Dismissal
Does the plant-closing law apply to brokerages? M. Galen. il *Business Week* p146 My 22 '89
A sad time for brokers [layoffs] P. Chisholm. il *Maclean's* 102:40-1 D 18 '89
Wall Street runs scared. J. Friedman. il *Business Week* p24-5 My 1 '89

Ethical aspects
Are analysts putting their mouths where the money is? W. Konrad. il *Business Week* p118 D 18 '89
Beware of penny stocks [excerpt from Investor alert!] il *Consumers' Research Magazine* 72:26-8 Ap '89
Beware the big producer. G. Morgenson. il *Forbes* 143:226-7 Je 26 '89
'The business nobody wants to talk about' [stock loan abuses] J. Friedman. il *Business Week* p196+ S 25 '89
Charlie Keating in the Show Me state [American Continental Corp.'s bankruptcy hits broker R. Ruppert] G. Morgenson. il por *Forbes* 143:12 My 29 '89
Dean Witter braces for a backlash in Boston [arrest of broker W. F. Curran] K. H. Hammonds. il por *Business Week* p86 Mr 6 '89
False securities [charges against Haas Securities] J. Crudele. il *New York* 22:25-6 F 6 '89
The final frenzy of a penny stock shop [Investors Center] D. Zigas. il por *Business Week* p128 Mr 13 '89
Five years of hard putting [B. L. Jefferies] J. Nocera. il por *Esquire* 112:67-8+ D '89
The fugitive king of penny stocks [J. C. Schidlowski] D. Zigas. il pors *Business Week* p124-5+ N 20 '89
Have the penny stock police caught a live one? [Power Securities] P. Engardio. il por *Business Week* p132 F 20 '89

BROKERS—Ethical aspects—*cont.*

Life after Boyd? And how [Jefferies Group] E. Schine. il por *Business Week* p143 Mr 20 '89

"Like a slaughter-house for hogs" [Mafia manipulation of penny stocks] R. L. Stern and C. Poole. il *Forbes* 144:42-4 D 25 '89

Meyer, meet RICO [penny stock swindler M. Blinder] J. Zweig. il por *Forbes* 143:168 Je 26 '89

The most brazen of the penny hustlers? [Power Securities] P. Engardio. il por *Business Week* p130+ N 20 '89

Never, but never, give a sucker an even break [securities fraud charges against A. Kimmes implicate M. Blinder] R. L. Stern and others. il pors *Forbes* 143:46-50 Ja 9 '89

A penny-stock scam [Haas Securities] C. Friday and J. Hammer. il por *Newsweek* 113:51 My 1 '89

The penny stock scandal [cover story] P. Engardio and G. DeGeorge. il *Business Week* p74-7+ Ja 23 '89

The SEC casts a net at penny stocks' biggest fish [Stuart-James] S. D. Atchison. il *Business Week* p128 Ap 24 '89

This penny-stock scam packs a one-two punch [brokers cross investors into another favorite stock] D. Zigas. *Business Week* p154 My 8 '89

The war on penny stocks. J. B. Quinn. il *Newsweek* 113:52 Ap 10 '89

Finance

Roaring '80s turn grinding '90s. J. Greenwald. il *Time* 133:58 My 1 '89

A sweeter ride for discount brokers. J. Friedman. il *Business Week* p100 Ag 14 '89

Tough new kid on the block [competition in investment banking] M. Berss. il *Forbes* 144:42-3 O 2 '89

Wall Street runs scared. J. Friedman. il *Business Week* p24-5 My 1 '89

You might call it the insecurities industry. J. Friedman. il *Business Week* p111 Ja 9 '89

Information services

See also
Stockbrokers Society

Monitoring

In tapes we trust: Wall Street bugs itself. C. Byron. il *New York* 22:40-1 O 23 '89

Recruiting

Big bucks vs. a job for life: why top talent is defecting [Western firms raid Japanese banks and brokerages] T. Holden. il *Business Week* p58 Ja 9 '89

Resignation

The body count keeps growing at Kidder Peabody. J. R. Norman and J. Friedman. il *Business Week* p128-9 F 20 '89

Securities

A good broker is also a good investment. J. Friedman. il *Business Week* p136 Ag 14 '89

Perrin Long: the loner everybody listens to. J. Friedman. il por *Business Week* p58 Jl 24 '89

Canada

See also
Merrill Lynch Canada Inc.
Midland Doherty Financial Corp.

A sad time for brokers [layoffs] P. Chisholm. il *Maclean's* 102:40-1 D 18 '89

Great Britain

See also
Baring Brothers & Co. Ltd.

Big Bang: big bust, big lessons. R. A. Melcher. il *Business Week* p38-9 Mr 6 '89

Japan

See also
Nikko Securities Co. Ltd.
Nomura Securities Co. Ltd.

Big bucks vs. a job for life: why top talent is defecting [Western firms raid Japanese banks and brokerages] T. Holden. il *Business Week* p58 Ja 9 '89

The Japanese connection [T. Pickens' takeover of Clemente Global Growth Fund thwarted by web of Japanese ties] R. Phalon. il pors *Forbes* 143:172+ Ap 3 '89

An onslaught from the West: foreign traders and methods are rocking Japan's stock markets. T. Holden. il *Business Week* p140-1 Mr 20 '89

Salomon just can't lose—in Tokyo. T. Holden. il *Business Week* p94 Je 12 '89

Tokyo brokers beat a retreat from the Street. W. Glasgall. il *Business Week* p42-3 F 13 '89

Switzerland

See also
Ellis AG

BROMEGRASS *See* Grasses

BROMELIADS

Exotic bromeliads thrive indoors [cover story] S. Bender. il *Southern Living* 24:88-90 Ja '89

BROMFIELD, LOUIS, 1896-1956
about

The most famous farm in America. M. Hoy. il por *Audubon* 91:64-7 N '89

BROMLEY, A. M.

Smart love. *Harper's Bazaar* 122:200-1 Ap '89

BROMLEY, D. ALLAN (DAVID ALLAN), 1926-
about

Bromley in line for science adviser. M. Crawford. por *Science* 244:283 Ap 21 '89

Bromley speaks. T. M. Powledge. por *Science* 246:1176 D 1 '89

Bromley targets superconductors. M. Crawford. *Science* 246:321 O 20 '89

Bush picks science adviser. I. Wickelgren. *Science News* 135:263 Ap 29 '89

A conversation with D. Allan Bromley. B. J. Culliton. il por *Science* 246:203-4 O 13 '89

Global warming becomes hot issue for Bromley. M. Sun. il por *Science* 246:569 N 3 '89

Meet D. Allan Bromley [interview] J. Carey. il por *Business Week* Special Issue:44 Je 16 '89

President Bush picks Yale's Bromley for Cabinet-level science adviser. I. Goodwin. il por *Physics Today* 42:39-41 Je '89

Science adviser gets first formal look. B. J. Culliton. por *Science* 245:247-8 Jl 21 '89

Science gains a voice. T. Beardsley. *Scientific American* 261:14 Jl '89

Science regains the White House. N. Bell. il *BioScience* 39:435 Jl/Ag '89

Senate committee quizzes Bromley. M. Crawford. *Science* 245:349 Jl 28 '89

Senate quiz show: Bromley passes but he faces tougher tests ahead. I. Goodwin. por *Physics Today* 42:65-7 S '89

BROMLEY, DAVID ALLAN *See* Bromley, D. Allan (David Allan), 1926-

BROMODEOXYURIDINE

5-bromo-2'-deoxyuridine blocks myogenesis by extinguishing expression of MyoD1. S. J. Tapscott and others. bibl f il *Science* 245:532-6 Ag 4 '89

BROMON AIRCRAFT COMPANY

Bromon Aircraft suspends operations, orders suppliers to stop BR2000 work [twin-turboprop transport] *Aviation Week & Space Technology* 131:18 O 30 '89

BRONFMAN, CHARLES R.
about

Closing credits. J. Daly. *Maclean's* 102:34 Ap 24 '89

BRONFMAN, EDGAR M., JR.
about

Give me a Chivas and natural soda. P. Sherrid. il pors *U.S. News & World Report* 107:42-3 Jl 17 '89

The maverick boss at Seagram [cover story] A. Rothman. il pors *Business Week* p90-3+ D 18 '89

BRONFMAN FAMILY
about

The house that prohibition built. A. Rothman. il *Business Week* p96 D 18 '89

Reshaping an empire. D. Jenish. *Maclean's* 102:43 My 29 '89

BRONNER, OSCAR
about

A minor revolution in Austria. J. Dempsey. il *World Press Review* 36:60 Ja '89

BRONNER SLOSBERG ASSOCIATES

Slaying the market. B. Kanner. il *New York* 22:26+ D 18 '89

BRONSON, CHARLES, 1920-
about

Architectural digest visits: Charles Bronson and Jill Ireland. J. Ireland. il por *Architectural Digest* 46:98-103+ Jl '89

Why me? [interview with J. Ireland] il pors *Life* 12:108-9+ Je '89

BRONSON, HAROLD
about

The gold in oldies. F. Meeks. il pors *Forbes* 143:68+ My 1 '89

BRONTË, CHARLOTTE, 1816-1855
about

Reader, I married him. J. Thurman. *The New Yorker* 65:109-14 Mr 20 '89

Anecdotes, facetiae, satire, etc.

The sisters Brontë and the sisters Collins: a study in stunning literary parallels. R. Hacker and J. Kaufman. pors *The New York Times Book Review* 94:12-13 Ag 20 '89

BRONTË, EMILY, 1818-1848

Anecdotes, facetiae, satire, etc.

The sisters Brontë and the sisters Collins: a study in stunning literary parallels. R. Hacker and J. Kaufman. pors *The New York Times Book Review* 94:12-13 Ag 20 '89

BRONX (NEW YORK, N.Y.)

Art

See also
Tim Rollins + K.O.S. (Group)

Crime

N.Y. couple charged with abusing their 9 children [H. McMillan] il por *Jet* 76:38 S 11 '89

Criminal justice, Administration of

The new DA in town [R. T. Johnson] K. Osborne. por *Black Enterprise* 19:16 Ja '89

Galleries and museums

See also
North Wind Undersea Institute

BRONX (NEW YORK, N.Y.)—cont.

Gardens and gardening

See also

New York Botanical Garden

Hospitals

See also

Montefiore Hospital and Medical Center (New York, N.Y.)

Housing

A South Bronx landscape. C. J. Vergara. il *The Nation* 248:302-6 Mr 6 '89

Social work

The lives of teenage mothers [Kingsbridge Heights Community Center] E. Marek. il *Harper's* 278:56-8+ Ap '89

Sports

Miracle on Hoe Avenue [Community Tennis Center in the South Bronx helps inner city children] P. M. Coan. il pors *World Tennis* 37:36-41+ O '89

BRONZE AGE

Abu Dhabi (United Arab Emirates: Emirate)

Yesterday's Abu Dhabi. A. Bingham. il *History Today* 39:3-4 O '89

Turkey

Kestel: an early Bronze Age source of tin ore in the Taurus Mountains, Turkey. K. A. Yener and others. bibl f il map *Science* 244:200-3 Ap 14 '89

BRONZE FOUNDING

Ethical aspects

Cast in doubt [sale of unauthorized bronze casts] S. Hochfield. il *Art News* 88:108-15 F '89

BRONZES

See also

Bronze founding

Collectors and collecting

Bronzes. G. Michael. il *Antiques & Collecting Hobbies* 94:35 N '89

Exhibitions

Touched in bronze [B. Hunt] S. Westfall. il *Art in America* 77:250-5+ Ap '89

Forgeries

Cast in doubt [sale of unauthorized bronze casts] S. Hochfield. il *Art News* 88:108-15 F '89

BROODTHAERS, MARCEL, 1924-1976

about

Broodthaers's not-art art. P. Plagens. il *Newsweek* 113:73 My 8 '89

Triumph of the mussels. P. Hammond. il *Art News* 88:217 O '89

BROOK, PETER, 1925-

about

The Mahabharata [drama] Reviews

The Unesco Courier il pors 42:4-9+ S '89

BROOK TROUT FISHING See Trout fishing

BROOKE, MELISSA

about

Voice of the Beehive, sisters from L.A. who have London all abuzz about their stinging pop songs. il pors *People Weekly* 31:88 Mr 13 '89

BROOKE, MICHAEL

Tricks of the egg trade. il *Natural History* p50-4 Ap '89

BROOKES, TIM

A sense of direction. il *The New York Times Magazine* p18+ Ap 30 '89

BROOKES, WARREN T.

Commentary. See issues of Nation's Business beginning October 1988

The global warming panic [cover story] il *Forbes* 144:96-100+ D 25 '89

BROOKFIELD CONSERVATION PARK (AUSTRALIA)

Digging is their game [hairy-nosed wombats] S. Montgomery. il *International Wildlife* 19:46-50 Mr/Ap '89

BROOKGREEN GARDENS

The Brookgreen Gardens sculpture collection. E. Agar. il *American Artist* 53:62-7+ Je '89

BROOKHISER, RICHARD

The long goodbye. il *National Review* 41:18-19 N 24 '89

Poetry out loud. il *The Atlantic* 263:43-5 F '89

Poison pens. il *National Review* 41:30-3 S 1 '89

Public opinion and the jogger. Commentary 88:50-2 Jl '89

Writing about American politics. *The American Scholar* 58:257-64 Spr '89

BROOKLANDS BOOKS (FIRM)

Miscellaneous ramblings [H. N. Manney and J. Dowdeswell] T. L. Bryant. il pors *Road & Track* 40:35-6 Jl '89

BROOKLINE (MASS.)

Politics and government

Verities. R. Kuttner. *The New Republic* 200:46 Ja 30 '89

BROOKLYN (NEW YORK, N.Y.)

Arts

See also

Brooklyn Academy of Music

Clubs

The health club with a heart. B. G. Harrison. *Mademoiselle* 95:145 S '89

Crime

The wild and crazy gangster: Michael Markowitz's twisted American dream. P. Blauner. il pors *New York* 22:52-6+ O 9 '89

Education

Different strokes: eleven kids from Brooklyn try life on a kibbutz [project initiated by teacher S. Bialer] J. Taylor. il por *New York* 22:56-8+ Je 12 '89

The great white hope [T. Guinzburg sponsors Brownsville, Brooklyn class] M. Webb. il pors *New York* 22:50-3 Ja 16 '89

Firefighters

High school grad thanks retired firefighter who rescued her 14 years ago [L. Greene thanks M. Bunch, former Brooklyn fireman] il pors *Jet* 76:23 Jl 17 '89

Housing

See also

Brooklyn Loft Tenants (Organization)

Music

See also

Brooklyn Philharmonic Symphony Orchestra

Parks and playgrounds

See also

Prospect Park (New York, N.Y.)

Population

Jeans in the genes [S. Toussie and other successful Syrians in the jeans business] P. Patton. il por *New York* 22:40-4+ My 22 '89

Restaurants, nightclubs, bars, etc.

Food with thought [chef E. Lewis of Gage & Tollner] J. Gruder. il por *Harper's Bazaar* 122:116-17 O '89

Making Brooklyn cook again [E. Lewis at Gage & Tollner] S. Wyndham. il por *New York* 22:24 Jl 31 '89

River brats [River Cafe] B. Kafka. il *Vogue* 179:342 Ap '89

Spécialités de la maison:

Gage & Tollner, Peter Luger, Gargiulo's Restaurant. A. Birsh. il *Gourmet* 49:54+ S '89

Bensonhurst

See Bensonhurst (New York, N.Y.)

Brooklyn Heights

See Brooklyn Heights (New York, N.Y.)

Park Slope

See Park Slope (New York, N.Y.)

BROOKLYN (NEW YORK, N.Y.) IN ART

Depicting urban landscapes with pastels. M. Wickes. il por *American Artist* 53:60-3 Mr '89

Douglas Safranek [egg tempera paintings] L. S. Hurwitz. il *American Artist* 53:36-7 Ag '89

BROOKLYN ACADEMY OF MUSIC

Opera blooms in Brooklyn. O. Friedrich. il *Time* 133:73-4 F 13 '89

BROOKLYN BOTANIC GARDEN. STEINHARDT CONSERVATORY

Reconstructing a Victorian legacy. il *Architectural Record* 177:110-15 N '89

BROOKLYN BRIDGE (NEW YORK, N.Y.)

Strung up [replacing 177,000 feet of steel cable] B. Weber. il *The New York Times Magazine* p150 D 3 '89

BROOKLYN BRIDGE (NEW YORK, N.Y.). ANCHORAGE

See Anchorage (New York, N.Y.)

BROOKLYN HEIGHTS (NEW YORK, N.Y.)

Astronomy from Brooklyn Heights. D. Trombino. il *Sky and Telescope* 78:305-7 S '89

BROOKLYN LOFT TENANTS (ORGANIZATION)

Loft Tenants. *The New Yorker* 64:25-6 Ja 16 '89

BROOKLYN PHILHARMONIA See Brooklyn Philharmonic Symphony Orchestra

BROOKLYN PHILHARMONIC SYMPHONY ORCHESTRA

Musical events:

Brooklyn Academy of Music concert. A. Porter. *The New Yorker* 65:90-1 My 22 '89

BROOKLYN UNION GAS CO.

"We had to get more sophisticated". J. Cook. il por *Forbes* 143:57+ Mr 20 '89

BROOKS, AVERY

about

Avery Brooks. M. Southgate. pors *Essence* 19:74-6+ Ap '89

BROOKS, CLEANTH, 1906-

John Crowe Ransom: as I remember him. *The American Scholar* 58:211-33 Spr '89

BROOKS, ELIZABETH W.

about

Nesting instincts. R. E. Bonney. il *National Wildlife* 27:28 Ap/My '89

BROOKS, GERTRUDE

Penelope [story] il *Good Housekeeping* 208:116-17 Mr '89

BROOKS, GINNY

about

A useful family space. M. McClintock. il pors *Country Journal* 16:40-6 F '89

BROOKS, GWENDOLYN

To those of my sisters who kept their naturals [poem] *Essence* 19:129 F '89

BROOKS, HARVEY

about

Rethinking the military's role in the economy: an interview with Harvey Brooks and Lewis Branscomb. S. Hackman and R. Howard. il pors *Technology Review* 92:54-60+ Ag/S '89

BROOKS, JAMES L., 1940-
about
Don't worry, be unhappy. S. Mitchell. il pors *American Film* 14:44-9 My '89
BROOKS, LOUISE, 1906-1985
about
Our wild Miss Brooks [excerpt from Louise Brooks] B. Paris. il pors *American Film* 15:38-41+ N '89
BROOKS, LOUISE EMERSON
Celebs speak out on addiction. pors *'Teen* 33:30+ S '89
BROOKS, MEL
Mel Brooks: of Woody, the Great Caesar, flop sweat and cigar smoke. il por *People Weekly* 31 Special Issue:106-7 Summ '89
BROOKS, PHIL
about
A useful family space. M. McClintock. il pors *Country Journal* 16:40-6 F '89
BROOKS, WALTER R., 1886-1958
Do ye ken Wilbur Pope— [story] il *The Saturday Evening Post* 261:36-8+ Ap '89
BROOKS, CREEKS, ETC.
See also
Spruce Creek (Pa.)
Black earth, spring creeks. P. Kaminsky. il *Field & Stream* 94:50-1+ D '89
The enchantment of creeks. P. Steinhart. il *Reader's Digest* 135:17-19 Ag '89
Evolution of a spring creek fisherman. N. Lyons. il *Field & Stream* 93:16-17 Ap '89
Go with the flow [smallmouth bass fishing] B. W. Dalrymple. il *Field & Stream* 94:48-9+ Je '89
The meaning of creeks. P. Steinhart. il *Audubon* 91:22-4 My '89
Trout in the spring runoff. J. Gierach. il *Field & Stream* 93:70-1+ Ap '89
Unlock your trout stream. T. Rosenbauer. il *Outdoor Life* 183:82-3+ My '89
BROOKS BROTHERS
Brooks Brothers in arms. N. Darnton. il *Newsweek* 114:84 D 4 '89
BROOKSIDE NURSERIES
Loam sweet loam [manufactured soil by Bud and David Bulpitt] J. Stone. il *Discover* 10:26+ O '89
BROS (MUSICAL GROUP)
O.K. in the U.K., the brothers Goss, known as Bros, are still looking for respect in the States. il *People Weekly* 32:92 D 11 '89
BROSNAHAN, LIAM
The Nick of time [poem] il *McCall's* 117:11-13 D '89
BROSNAHAN, TOM
Selling travelers on guidebooks. por *Publishers Weekly* 235:95 Ja 20 '89
BROSNAN, PIERCE
about
"I have faith my wife will live". V. J. Radovsky. il pors *Redbook* 173:36+ My '89
BROSSE, JACQUES
The sacred tree. il *The Courier (Unesco)* 42:4-9 Ja '89
BROTAK, EDWARD
Audio visuals. *Weatherwise* 42:335 D '89
Audio visuals about the weather. *Weatherwise* 42:216 Ag '89
Tornado tapes. *Weatherwise* 42:102 Ap '89
BROTH *See* Soups
BROTHER BEYOND (MUSICAL GROUP)
Beyond belief. C. Connors. il *Seventeen* 48:206+ Ag '89
BROTHERHOOD CRUSADE (ORGANIZATION)
Brotherhood Crusade salutes Motown's Berry Gordy. il pors *Jet* 75:32 Ja 30 '89
BROTHERS, JOYCE
Dr. Joyce Brothers answers your questions. See issues of Good Housekeeping
If you want to be a better parent . . . here are the TV moms and dads you should learn from. il *TV Guide* 37:22-5 Mr 4-10 '89
Memories of love make a spouse's death both more heart-breaking and, in the end, more bearable; ed. by Angela Blessing. il pors *People Weekly* 31:86-8+ Je 26 '89
The shows that'll make you feel better. il *TV Guide* 37:12-15 Jl 29-Ag 4 '89
Why we need to laugh. il *TV Guide* 37:18-19 N 11-17 '89
BROTHERS, MILTON J., 1926-1989
about
Memories of love make a spouse's death both more heart-breaking and, in the end, more bearable; ed. by Angela Blessing. J. Brothers. il pors *People Weekly* 31:86-8+ Je 26 '89
BROTHERS *See* Siblings
BROTHERS (IN RELIGIOUS ORDERS, CONGREGATIONS, ETC.)
See also
Benedictines
Christian Brothers

BROTHERS AND SISTERS *See* Siblings
BROTHERS GRIMM
See also
Grimm, Jacob, 1785-1863
Grimm, Wilhelm, 1786-1859
BROUGHTON, CONNIE
Serving refugee children and families in Head Start [cover story] il *Children Today* 18:6-10 S/O '89
BROUGHTON, HENARE R.
The well-being of the Maori. il *World Health* p20-1 Je '89
BROUN, HEYWOOD HALE, 1918-
The Algonquin—nights at the Round Table. il *Architectural Digest* 46:184+ N '89
BROUN, JANICE A.
No *glasnost* yet for religion in Bulgaria. *The Christian Century* 106:1124-5 N 29 '89
Religious nationalism strains Yugoslavia. *The Christian Century* 106:885-8 O 4 '89
BROUWER, ARIE R.
about
NCC leader stuns board. G. Spohn. por *Christianity Today* 33:52 Je 16 '89
NCC moves painfully toward *perestroika*. D. Heim. *The Christian Century* 106:547-8 My 24-31 '89
BROUWER, KURT
How to invest like a millionaire. il *Forbes* 143:210-13 Je 26 '89
BROW, ROBERT
The taming of a New Age prophet. il *Christianity Today* 33:28-30 Je 16 '89
What I was doing at the hospital. il *Christianity Today* 33:31-2 Ap 21 '89
BROWARD COUNTY (FLA.)
Police
Making an arresting TV debut, deputy sheriff Linda Canada puts the cuffs on fame in Fox's Cops. P. Jordan. il pors *People Weekly* 31:89-90 Ap 24 '89
Watch the Farrah lookalike make a real drug bust [Cops] J. Weisman. il *TV Guide* 37:18-19 Je 17-23 '89
BROWARD MARINE, INC.
Breakthrough at Broward [high-speed megayachts] S. Stapleton. il *Motor Boating & Sailing* 163:84-7+ F '89
BROWBACK, VIRGINIA BARTON
Ukrainian odyssey. il map *Modern Maturity* 32:58-9+ Ag/S '89
BROWDER, TAMARA
about
The boys on the varsity get a real kick out of homecoming queen Tamara Browder. il por *People Weekly* 32:113 N 13 '89
BROWER, BROCK
Bud McFarlane: semper fi. il pors *The New York Times Magazine* p26-8 Ja 22 '89
BROWER, KENNETH, 1944-
The destruction of dolphins [cover story] il *The Atlantic* 264:35-8+ Jl '89
Losing paradise. il map *Wilderness* 53:20-8 Wint '89
The Navajo nation. il map *The Atlantic* 263:79-83 Mr '89
Save our sea mammals. il *Omni (New York, N.Y.)* 11:26+ Je '89
Sea of trouble. il *Omni (New York, N.Y.)* 11:20+ Ap '89
Starry blight. il *Omni (New York, N.Y.)* 11:22+ My '89
State of the reef. il *Audubon* 91:56-81 Mr '89
BROWER, MICHAEL
In search of the elusive Stealth bomber. il *Technology Review* 92:41-5 My/Je '89
BROWER, W. A.
Bebop's children. il *American Visions* 4:44+ O '89
BROWN, ABE
The here-and-now story of cocaine. il *Current Health 2* 16:11-13 D '89
Medical terms—what do those words mean? il *Current Health 2* 15:28-9 My '89
BROWN, ANEETA SPELTS
Love letters from grandma. il *New Choices for the Best Years* 29:98+ S '89
BROWN, ANN C.
Stock trends. See issues of Forbes
BROWN, ARNOLD, 1927-
(jt. auth) See Weiner, Edith, and Brown, Arnold, 1927-
BROWN, ARTHUR M., 1932-
(jt. auth) See Yatani, Atsuko, and Brown, Arthur M., 1932-
BROWN, AZBY, 1956-
Japan's moonhouses. il *Omni (New York, N.Y.)* 11:17 Jl '89
BROWN, BERTRAM WYATT- *See* Wyatt-Brown, Bertram
BROWN, BEVERLY LOUISE
Britain's treasure house of art: the Fitzwilliam Collection. il *USA Today (Periodical)* 118:68-83 Jl '89
Palladio and Veronese at the Villa Barbaro in Maser, Italy. bibl f il *Antiques* 135:298-309 Ja '89
BROWN, BLAIR
about
Blair Brown, television's Molly Dodd, returns to the stage—her first love. R. Short. por *Vogue* 179:486+ S '89
Where I grew up: Blair Brown [interview] L. Konner. il pors *Glamour* 87:172 Mr '89

BROWN, BOBBY

about

Bobby Brown. B. M. Cooper. pors *Essence* 20:70-2+ My '89

Bobby Brown: is he the hottest new R&B singer? [cover story] T. S. Moore. il pors *Jet* 76:22-4 Jl 3 '89

Bobby Brown: success on his own. pors *'Teen* 33:57 N '89

Bobby Brown's Cruel beguiles fans—but not the cop who nabbed him for dirty dancing. S. Dougherty. il pors *People Weekly* 31:108-10 Ap 10 '89

Bobby Brown's uneasy passage. R. Tannenbaum. il pors *Rolling Stone* p68-9+ S 7 '89

The new heroes of hip-hop. D. Gates. il pors *Newsweek* 113:66 Ap 10 '89

BROWN, BOBBY RAY

Defining coal's future [address, June 19, 1989] *Vital Speeches of the Day* 56:87-8 N 15 '89

BROWN, BRACK

Beyond techno-talk. *Ad Astra* 1:3 O '89

BROWN, C. WALTON

Colonising Bermuda—defending Virginia. bibl il maps *History Today* 39:36-41 Ja '89

BROWN, CHARNELE

about

Hubby's advice? Wipe that smile off your face! J. Marion. il por *TV Guide* 37:18 Jl 29-Ag 4 '89

BROWN, CHIP

Blood circle. il *Esquire* 112:122-8+ Ag '89

Family ties. il *House & Garden* 161:128-35 Je '89

The light in August. il por *Esquire* 111:116-18+ Ap '89

Why I never trust a woman under 30. il *Mademoiselle* 95:188+ N '89

BROWN, CHRIS, 1961-

about

Tale of a trade. F. Lidz. il por *Sports Illustrated* 70:44 Je 26 '89

BROWN, CHRISTEN

about

Talk-show prep. L. See. *Publishers Weekly* 236:201 Jl 28 '89

BROWN, CLAUDE, 1937-

about

Three lives. M. Stone. il pors *New York* 22:35-42 Ja 30 '89

BROWN, COLIN, 1932-

The other half of the gospel? il *Christianity Today* 33:26-9 Ap 21 '89

BROWN, CRAIG

Fay Weldon. il por *Vogue* 179:182+ Ja '89

He's traveled the world—in fact and fiction. por *Vogue* 179:88+ Jl '89

In part II of the Warhol diaries, Andy shares his views on the afterlife with Craig Brown. il pors *Vogue* 179:362-4 Ag '89

BROWN, CYNTHIA G., 1943-, AND GOLDMAN, ROBERT K.

Torture, memory and justice. il *The Nation* 248:408+ Mr 27 '89

BROWN, DAVID E. (DAVID EARL), 1938-

Return of the natives. il *Wilderness* 52:40-52 Wint '88

BROWN, DEBORAH A., AND OTHERS

Mechanism of membrane anchoring affects polarized expression of two proteins in MDCK cells. bibl f il *Science* 245:1499-501 S 29 '89

BROWN, DENISE SCOTT *See* Scott Brown, Denise, 1931-

BROWN, DENNIS

Serving 'em right. il *Women's Sports & Fitness* 11:72-5 Ap '89

BROWN, DWIGHT

Jammin' in Montreux. il *Black Enterprise* 19:80-2 Ap '89

BROWN, EDMUND G., 1905-

Private mercy [excerpt from Public justice, private mercy]; ed. by Dick Adler. il *Common Cause Magazine* 15:28-33 Jl/Ag '89

BROWN, EDMUND GERALD *See* Brown, Jerry, 1938-

BROWN, ELAINE

Free Winnie! por *Essence* 20:128 Je '89

BROWN, FRED, JR.

Gathering together in their name. il *American Visions* 4:12-13 Ag '89

Getting in on the biotech revolution. *American Visions* 4:12+ Je '89

BROWN, FREDERICK, 1945-

about

Frederick Brown: Marlborough. C. Lyon. il *Art News* 88:164-5 N '89

To Fred Brown, blues are more than a color on his palette. D. Grogan. il pors *People Weekly* 32:96-8 O 2 '89

BROWN, GEORGE ALBERT

about

Flying through airline loopholes [interview] J. Popkin. il por *U.S. News & World Report* 107:61 Jl 31 '89

BROWN, GEORGE E., JR.

Courting disaster in orbit. il *The Bulletin of the Atomic Scientists* 45:7-9 Ap '89

Project 2061: a congressional view. *Science* 245:340 Jl 28 '89

BROWN, HANK

(jt. auth) *See* Haskins, Ron, and Brown, Hank

BROWN, HILTON

Looking at art [reprint of December 1982 article] bibl f il *American Artist* 53:34+ Ap '89

BROWN, HUBIE

Which college stars should make good pros. il *TV Guide* 37:22-3 Mr 11-17 '89

BROWN, IRVING, 1911-1989

about

Obituary

National Review 41:18 Ap 7 '89

BROWN, J. D.

Customized adventures. il *American Health* 8:56-7 N '89

BROWN, JAMES

about

Brown: concurrent terms. M. Goldberg. il por *Rolling Stone* p20 Mr 9 '89

James Brown sent to another prison for having $48,000 in checks in his possession. por *Jet* 76:53 Ag 14 '89

James Brown: tragic downfall of a black hero. R. E. Johnson. il pors *Jet* 75:56-61 Ja 16 '89

Jesse Jackson calls for release of James Brown. pors *Jet* 75:10 Mr 13 '89

Soul brother no. 155413. A. Stanley. il *Time* 133:40 F 20 '89

Wife and fans outraged by 6-year prison term handed to James Brown. il pors *Jet* 75:18+ Ja 9 '89

Wrestling with the devil: the struggle for the soul of James Brown [cover story] M. Goldberg. il pors *Rolling Stone* p36-7+ Ap 6 '89

BROWN, JAMES H., AND MAURER, BRIAN A.

Macroecology: the division of food and space among species on continents. bibl f il *Science* 243:1145-50 Mr 3 '89

BROWN, JERRY, 1938-

about

Jerry Brown: a California comeback [interview] L. Wright. il por *Newsweek* 113:6 F 27 '89

Jerry Brown rises from the ashrams. R. D. Hof. il por *Business Week* p36 F 13 '89

Tanned, rested, and ready. R. Brownstein. il *The New Republic* 200:23+ Ja 30 '89

That was Zen, this is now. R. Lacayo. por *Time* 133:20 F 27 '89

BROWN, JIM, 1936-

Jim Brown on life and love in Hollywood [excerpt from Out of bounds] il pors *Ebony* 45:60+ D '89

about

Jim Brown's book talks about his encounters with the rich and famous. L. Ransom. il pors *Jet* 77:46-50 O 30 '89

BROWN, JOHN C., AND JOLLEY, VON D.

Plant metabolic responses to iron-deficiency stress. bibl f il *BioScience* 39:546-51 S '89

BROWN, JOHN GEORGE, 1831-1913

about

American sentimental painting. A. E. Ledes. il *Antiques* 135:598+ Mr '89

Remembering a neglected artist. D. Grant. il *American Artist* 53:64+ S '89

BROWN, JONATHAN

The painted face. il *Vogue* 179:420-5 O '89

The unliberal imagination. il *The New Republic* 200:30-5 My 15 '89

BROWN, JOSEPH E., 1929-

Monarchs of the mist [excerpt] il *National Parks* 63:46-7 S/O '89

Rogue waves. bibl (p84) il *Discover* 10:46-50+ Ap '89

Scared smokeless. il *Reader's Digest* 134:117-21 My '89

BROWN, JULIE

about

Earth girls didn't come easy for the unsinkable Julie Brown, but success has been topsy-turvy. M. Dougherty. il pors *People Weekly* 31:124-6 Je 5 '89

Queen of the Valley. J. Lazar. il por *Vogue* 179:212 My '89

BROWN, JULIE

about

Born to run at the mouth. And dance. And flash her $200 purple lingerie. H. Polskin. il por *TV Guide* 37:20-1 Jl 15-21 '89

BROWN, KENNETH L.

Human rights issues in Africa [statement, February 7, 1989] *Department of State Bulletin* 89:27-32 My '89

BROWN, LARRY, 1951-

about

Books from Oxford and Algonquin question idea of a 'good' war. C. Goodrich. il pors *Publishers Weekly* 235:31-2 Je 23 '89

BROWN, LAURENCE D.

Books. *See* issues of Phi Delta Kappan beginning September 1985

BROWN, LES, 1928-

The public eye. *See* issues of Channels (New York, N.Y.: 1986)

BROWN, LESTER RUSSELL, 1934-

The grain drain: the waning of food security [excerpt from State of the world: 1989] il por *The Futurist* 23:9-16 Jl/Ag '89

BROWN, LESTER RUSSELL, 1934——cont.
The world food crisis. il *USA Today (Periodical)* 117:51-3 Mr '89
BROWN, LESTER RUSSELL, 1934-, AND OTHERS
A world at risk. il pors *Country Journal* 16:44-8 My/Je '89
BROWN, LILLIAN
How to make a big impact on the small screen [excerpt from Your public best] il por *Working Woman* 14:80-4 D '89
about
Putting your best self forward. S. Nelton. il pors *Nation's Business* 77:46-7 Ag '89
BROWN, LUTHER
Dates for dad. por *Essence* 19:10 F '89
BROWN, MARY, 1929-
Christmas plant legends. il *Flower and Garden* 33:47-9 N/D '89
BROWN, MATT
about
The titan of tires. M. E. Howard. il pors *Black Enterprise* 20:68-70+ S '89
BROWN, MERRILL
The business side. See issues of Channels (New York, N.Y.: 1986) beginning January/February 1986
BROWN, MICHAEL FOBES
Dark side of the shaman. *Natural History* p8+ N '89
BROWN, MICHAEL H.
A toxic ghost town. il *The Atlantic* 264:23-4+ Jl '89
BROWN, MILDRED
about
Obituary
Jet il pors 77:23 N 27 '89
BROWN, NOEL
Our biological heritage under siege [address, August 6, 1989] *BioScience* 39:725-8 N '89
BROWN, NORMAN
Beyond the fringe: late word from the war on baldness. il *Nation's Business* 77:79 Je '89
Putting your finger on what makes you itch. il *Nation's Business* 77:75 Ap '89
BROWN, ORAL
about
Underwriting the future: two women will send 146 kids to college. R. Brown. il pors *Ebony* 44:74+ Ap '89
BROWN, PAT *See* Brown, Edmund G., 1905-
BROWN, PATRICIA LEIGH
Lessons from the sandbox. il pors *The New York Times Magazine* p26-30+ Jl 23 '89
BROWN, PAUL M.
about
Soup-can physics. C. Poole. il *Forbes* 143:142 Mr 6 '89
BROWN, PETER H.
'There was no sex diary': Jennifer Levin wasn't asking for trouble. il pors *TV Guide* 37:24-7 S 23-29 '89
BROWN, PHYLLIS GEORGE *See* George, Phyllis
BROWN, POLLY
Rites of man. il *Mother Jones* 14:25-31 S '89
BROWN, RICHARD, 1945-
Home for Christmas [photographs; excerpt from A Vermont Christmas] il *Good Housekeeping* 208:96-9 Ja '89
BROWN, ROBERT K., 1932-
about
War is swell? J. Zweig and P. Klebnikov. il por *Forbes* 144:223 S 18 '89
BROWN, ROBERT MCAFEE, 1920-
Christians can be good and angry [with readers' comments] *U.S. Catholic* 54:14-15 N '89
about
What every North American should know about liberation theology [interview] por *U.S. Catholic* 54:21-8 Ap '89
BROWN, ROBERT W.
The National Scholars Program. *Ad Astra* 1:30 Je '89
BROWN, ROGER, 1941-
about
Roger Brown: Phyllis Kind. R. Bass. il *Art News* 88:159 D '89
BROWN, RON
From two new party chairmen: plans to woo and keep the black vote. il *American Visions* 4:16+ Je '89
about
Brown seeks DNC chair. K. D. Thompson. il por *Black Enterprise* 19:30 F '89
Democrat Brown. *The Nation* 248:219-20 F 20 '89
The Democrats' next dilemma. P. R. Range. il por *U.S. News & World Report* 106:23 F 6 '89
'Democrats should pick Ron Brown,' state some powerful white backers. il por *Jet* 75:8 Ja 30 '89
Diarist. J. Bennet. *The New Republic* 200:50 Je 19 '89
Donkey serenade. J. Klein. il por *New York* 22:10-11 Ja 30 '89
Meet Ron Brown, pillar of the establishment. R. Fly. il por *Business Week* p54 F 13 '89
A move to 'Stop Ron'. il por *Newsweek* 113:4 Ja 23 '89
A new act in the Democratic Party. K. D. Thompson. por *Black Enterprise* 19:29 Ap '89
Party games. V. Novak. por *Common Cause Magazine* 15:7 My/Je '89

Playing the politics of race. H. Fineman. il por *Newsweek* 113:20 F 6 '89
Ron Brown: chairman of the Democratic National Committee. il pors *Ebony* 44:36+ My '89
Ron Brown is voted first black to chair Dem. Party. il por *Jet* 75:4+ F 27 '89
Ron Brown sets priorities, names his senior staff. il por *Jet* 76:5 My 1 '89
Ron Brown's first test. il por *Newsweek* 113:7 F 20 '89
Ron Brown's party line. R. Kuttner. il pors *The New York Times Magazine* p44+ D 3 '89
Running as his own man. W. Isaacson. il por *Time* 133:56-8 Ja 30 '89
Solomon with a computer. M. B. Zuckerman. il *U.S. News & World Report* 106:84 F 20 '89
"Ten steps, then we shoot," says Ron Brown. "I've got my AK-47," replies Lee Atwater. "What've you got?". M. Kelly. il pors *Gentlemen's Quarterly* 59:142-7+ Jl '89
BROWN, RUSTY
Call to glory. il pors *Ms.* 17:34 Ap '89
BROWN, RUTH
about
Knowing all there is to know of rhythm and blues, Ruth Brown makes her comeback on Broadway. S. Dougherty. il pors *People Weekly* 31:261-3+ Mr 6 '89
BROWN, SCOTT
about
Greenwich time [cover story] P. Green. il *House & Garden* 161:120-7 N '89
BROWN, STERLING ALLEN, 1901-1989
about
The last New Negro. D. Pinckney. il por *The New York Review of Books* 36:14-16 Mr 16 '89
BROWN, STUART F.
What's new: recreation. See occasional issues of Popular Science beginning December 1985
BROWN, TERRY
about
Infinite pattern. D. Dietsch. il *Architectural Record* 177:94-7 mid-S '89
BROWN, THOMAS WILSON
about
Thomas Brown: no small act. il pors *'Teen* 33:55 N '89
BROWN, TINA
about
High gloss news. T. Mathews. il pors *Newsweek* 113:54-6+ My 1 '89
BROWN, TRISHA
about
Astral convertible [dance] Reviews
Dance Magazine il 63:54 Jl '89. C. Hardy
New York 22:82 Ap 3 '89. T. Tobias
The New York Times Magazine il por p110 Mr 12 '89. B. Weber
Dancing:
Performances at City Center. A. Croce. *The New Yorker* 65:108 Ap 3 '89
BROWN, VALERIE S.
Drug talk: what your friends don't tell you. il *'Teen* 33:22+ Je '89
Stamp out insecurity (yes, you can!). il *'Teen* 33:18+ Ap '89
BROWN, VIRGINIA M.
Choices [story] il *'Teen* 33:32+ Jl '89
BROWN, WESLEY
Who to blame, who to forgive. il pors *The New York Times Magazine* p52-3+ S 10 '89
BROWN, WILLIAM S.
(jt. auth) See Nicklos, Lee B., and Brown, William S.
BROWN, WILLIE LEWIS, JR.
Willie L. Brown Jr. [advice to George Bush] *National Review* 41:24-5 F 10 '89
BROWN, MURPHY (FICTIONAL CHARACTER) *See* Murphy Brown (Fictional character)
BROWN (TRISHA) DANCE COMPANY *See* Trisha Brown Dance Company
BROWN BEARS *See* Bears
BROWN COUNTY PUBLISHING COMPANY
Do you sincerely want to publish? R. Koselka. il pors *Forbes* 144:68+ S 18 '89
BROWN DWARF STARS *See* Stars, Dwarf
BROWN FAMILY
about
Keeping it all in the family. B. D. Fromson. il *Fortune* 120:86-7+ S 25 '89
BROWN-FORMAN CORP.
Kansas hooch in Scandinavian bottles [marketing strategy for Icy vodka] J. Levine. il *Forbes* 144:131 Ag 7 '89
Keeping it all in the family. B. D. Fromson. il *Fortune* 120:86-7+ S 25 '89
BROWN-FORMAN DISTILLERS CORP.
See also
Brown-Forman Corp.
BROWN GROUP, INC.
Three easy steps. K. L. Fisher. il *Forbes* 144:253 O 30 '89

BROWN TIDE
The besieged bays of the world. T. E. Bell. il maps *Sea Frontiers* 35:238-45 Jl/Ag '89
BROWN TREE SNAKES *See* Snakes
BROWN TROUT *See* Trout
BROWN TROUT FISHING *See* Trout fishing
BROWN V. BOARD OF EDUCATION DECISION *See* United States. Supreme Court—Decisions
BROWNE, ANTHONY
about
Anglo-Indian impressions. S. M. Alsop. il por *Architectural Digest* 46:222-6+ Mr '89
BROWNE, CHRISTOPHER
about
Waltzing with the wallflowers [interview] S. Smith. il por *Fortune* 119:43+ Ap 10 '89
BROWNE, HARRY, 1933-
about
Put your eggs in several baskets. M. Hulbert. il *Forbes* 143:168 Mr 6 '89
BROWNE, JACKSON
about
As Jackson Browne's 'World' turns. A. DeCurtis. il pors *Rolling Stone* p24-5 O 5 '89
Jackson Browne. R. Givens. il por *Stereo Review* 54:113 O '89
BROWNE, MARY T.
about
Extra-ordinary perception [interview] O. J. Lipstein. il pors *American Health* 8:60-5 D '89
BROWNE, T. C.
Retrospect. See issues of Motor Trend beginning January 1988
BROWNELL, KELLY D.
When and how to diet. il *Psychology Today* 23:40-4+ Je '89
BROWNELL, ROBERT L., JR.
(jt. auth) See Ralls, Katherine, and Brownell, Robert L., Jr.
BROWNIES (CAKE)
Brownies plain and fancy. C. Koury. il *Parents* 64:166-7+ Mr '89
Sweet treats to bake 'n eat! [Valentine's Day] C. Thomas and S. Young. il *'Teen* 33:30-1 F '89
BROWNING, COLLEEN, 1929-
The evolution of a painting. il *American Artist* 53:54-9 Jl '89
BROWNING, DON S.
Rethinking homosexuality. *The Christian Century* 106:911-16 O 11 '89
BROWNING, GRAEME
about
China will always be risky business [interview] C. P. Work. il por *U.S. News & World Report* 107:43 Jl 31 '89
BROWNING, KURT
about
The split-second skill of a figure skating prodigy. D. Jenish. il por *Maclean's* 102:38-9 D 25 '89
BROWNING, TIM
Spirits in stone [cover story] il *National Parks* 63:37-9 S/O '89
BROWNLEE, SHANNON
The best banana bred. il *The Atlantic* 264:22+ S '89
BROWNLEE, W. ELLIOT, 1941-
Taxation: the American way. *Current (Washington, D.C.)* 315:11-17 S '89
BROWNMILLER, SUSAN
Hedda speaks out [discussion of April 1989 article, Madly in love] il *Ms.* 17:12 My '89
Madly in love. il *Ms.* 17:56-9+ Ap '89
Waverly Place [fiction] il *Ladies' Home Journal* 106:118-19+ F '89
about
PW interviews. P. Kaganoff. il por *Publishers Weekly* 235:449-50 Ja 27 '89
BROWNOUTS (ELECTRIC POWER) *See* Electric power failures
BROWN'S HOTEL (LONDON, ENGLAND) *See* London (England)—Hotels, motels, etc.
BROWNSTEIN, BERNARD H., AND OTHERS
Isolation of single-copy human genes from a library of yeast artificial chromosome clones. bibl f il *Science* 244:1348-51 Je 16 '89
BROWNSTEIN, HENRY
(jt. auth) See Goldstein, Paul, and Brownstein, Henry
BROWNSTEIN, LARRY
Best city skylines. il *Petersen's Photographic Magazine* 18:48-50 D '89
BROWNSTEIN, RONALD
Tanned, rested, and ready. il *The New Republic* 200:23+ Ja 30 '89
BROWNWORTH, VICTORIA A.
Stonewall + 20. *The Nation* 249:5-6 Jl 3 '89
BROYARD, ANATOLE
About books. See occasional issues of The New York Times Book Review beginning November 11, 1984 through May 21, 1989

Intoxicated by my illness. il *The New York Times Magazine* p32+ N 12 '89
Moving day: the books I left behind. il *The New York Times Book Review* N 19 '89
Travel. il *The New York Times Book Review* 94:22 D 3 '89
BRUBACH, HOLLY
Between times. *The New Yorker* 65:100-2+ Ap 24 '89
For better or for worse? *The New Yorker* 65:86-90 Jl 10 '89
Modernism outmoded. *The New Yorker* 65:102-9 N 20 '89
School of Chanel. *The New Yorker* 65:71-6 F 27 '89
Selling Montana. *The New Yorker* 64:110+ Ja 23 '89
Visionaries. il *The New Yorker* 65:64+ Ag 28 '89
BRUBAKER, STANLEY C.
Constitutional law [discussion of December 1988 article, Rewriting the Constitution] *Commentary* 87:2-4+ My '89
BRUCAN, SILVIU, 1916-
The strategic imperative of reform. il *New Perspectives Quarterly* 5:18-23 Wint '88/'89
BRUCE, F. F. (FREDERICK FYVIE), 1910-
about
F. F. Bruce: a mind for what matters [interview] W. W. Gasque and L. Gasque. il por *Christianity Today* 33:22-5 Ap 7 '89
BRUCE, FREDERICK FYVIE See Bruce, F. F. (Frederick Fyvie), 1910-
BRUCE, LAWRENCE E.
First word. por *Omni (New York, N.Y.)* 11:4 Ag '89
BRUCE, LIZA
about
Creative collaborators. il pors *Harper's Bazaar* 122:116-21 Je '89
BRUCE, MICHAEL G.
Guiding our paths. *Phi Delta Kappan* 71:252-4 N '89
Power to parents. il *Phi Delta Kappan* 70:413-14 Ja '89
Primary education. il *Phi Delta Kappan* 71:82-3 S '89
BRUCE, ROBERT See Robert I, King of Scotland, 1274-1329
BRUCE, ROBERT W., III
about
Value is where you find it. J. Clements. il por *Forbes* 143:62+ Mr 20 '89
BRUCE, SCOTT
about
Lunch box [cover story] H. J. LaFleche. il por *Antiques & Collecting Hobbies* 94:24-5+ Jl '89
BRUCE, TERRY L.
about
Let the lobbying commence. A. Plattner. il por *U.S. News & World Report* 106:54 Je 12 '89
BRUCE, WILLIAM
about
The road to Infiniti. S. Kichen. il por *Forbes* 143:104 Ja 23 '89
BRUCH, CRIS
about
Cris Bruch: Fuller Elwood. L. Smallwood. il *Art News* 88:219-20 Ap '89
BRUCH, DANIEL
about
LCMS pastor could face heresy charges. W. Thorkelson. *Christianity Today* 33:43 Ap 21 '89
BRUCK, CONNIE
Billion-dollar mind. *The New Yorker* 65:76-88 Ag 7 '89
The old boy and the new boys. *The New Yorker* 65:81-90+ My 8 '89
BRUCK, EVA
about
The four-hour spa. L. Washer. il *Working Woman* 14:111-12 F '89
BRÜCKE (GROUP)
Burning bridges [Brücke: German expressionist prints from the Granvil and Marcia Specks Collection] C. Moser. il *Art in America* 77:64-5+ N '89
BRUCKEL, JANE
about
The case of the harrowing back pain. A. Roblin. il *Prevention (Emmaus, Pa.)* 41:102+ Je '89
BRUCKNER, ANTON, 1824-1896
about
New views on Bruckner. D. Hurwitz. il *High Fidelity (New York, N.Y.)* 39:56-7 Jl '89
BRUEMMER, FRED
Ancient spell of the sea unicorn. il *International Wildlife* 19:38-43 N/D '89
Arctic treasures: what ruler could resist the allure of white falcons, giant moles, and unicorns? il *Natural History* p38-47 Je '89
Diary of a bear-watcher. il *International Wildlife* 19:46-51 S/O '89
BRUGES (BELGIUM)
Processions
The Procession of Holy Blood. D. C. Marsh. il map *Travel Holiday* 171:64-71 Mr '89
BRUHN PRIZE
American and Dane win Bruhn Prize; ABT backs out at last minute. M. Crabb. il *Dance Magazine* 63:17 Ag '89

BRUMBERG, ABRAHAM
Moscow: the struggle for reform. bibl f il *The New York Review of Books* 36:37-42 Mr 30 '89
BRUMBERG, ELAINE
5 ways to clean your face [excerpt from Take care of your skin] il *Health (New York, N.Y.)* 21:84-5+ Ag '89
BRUMLIK, DONALD C.
about
The playboy and the 'teddy bear' taking aim at Del Webb. T. Carson. *Business Week* p43-4 Ja 9 '89
BRUMMELL, BEAU, 1778-1840
about
Fine & dandy. P. Kinmonth. il *Vogue* 179:334-9 Ag '89
BRUMMELL, GEORGE BRYAN *See* Brummell, Beau, 1778-1840
BRUMMER, ALEX
U.S. role in the world. il *World Press Review* 36:16-17+ S '89
BRUNCHES
A.M. cuisine. B. Goldman. il *Better Homes and Gardens* 67:137-41+ My '89
Bountiful brunch. J. Nash. il *Essence* 20:95-8+ My '89
Breakfasts & brunches [special section] il *Southern Living* 24:121+ Ap '89
Corn, cheese, chilies: Santa Fe brunch [cover story] il *Sunset (Central West edition)* 182:98-9 Ap '89
Dad's Day brunch. il *Seventeen* 48:174 Je '89
Easy brunch breads. il *Better Homes and Gardens* 67:160-1 Je '89
Family-style weekend brunch. il *McCall's* 117:93 N '89
In Montana, a hike with hot cider break, then a sausage-and-egg brunch. il *Sunset (Central West edition)* 181:78-9 D '88
Summer brunch New Orleans style. R. F. Guste. il *New Choices for the Best Years* 29:64-7 Jl '89
BRUNDTLAND, GRO HARLEM
Global change and our common future [address, May 2, 1989; with editorial comment by Timothy O'Riordan] bibl f il por *Environment* 31:inside cover, 16-20+ Je '89
How to secure our common future. *Scientific American* 261:190 S '89
about
Norway's radical daughter. N. R. Gibbs. il por *Time* 134:42-4 S 25 '89
Reflections on 'Our common future' [interview] N. Myers. il por *International Wildlife* 19:14-15 N/D '89
The test of our civilization [interview] N. Gardels. il *New Perspectives Quarterly* 6:4-8 Spr '89
BRUNEI
See also
Government publicity—Brunei
BRUNER, RICHARD W.
How citizens can beat the gun lobby [cover story] il *The Nation* 248:433+ Ap 3 '89
BRUNET, PATRICK
about
The heirs of Madame Guillotine. D. Lawday. il por *U.S. News & World Report* 107:46-8 Jl 17 '89
Patrick Brunet, whose ancestor guillotined Louis XVI, swears he's no chip off the old block. T. Allis. il pors *People Weekly* 31:128+ Je 5 '89
BRUNETTE HAIR *See* Hair
BRUNIER, SERGE
Extreme astronomy. il por map *Sky and Telescope* 78:366-9 O '89
BRUNING, FRED
An American view. See issues of Maclean's
BRUNNER, EMIL, 1889-1966
about
Emil Brunner: a centennial perspective [cover story] I. J. Hesselink. il por *The Christian Century* 106:1171-4 D 13 '89
BRUNNER, HANNES
about
Hannes Brunner: Vera Engelhorn. L. Holst. il *Art News* 88:208-9 Ap '89
BRUNO, C. C.
Why I am homeless. il por *The Humanist* 49:10-11+ My/Je '89
BRUNO, FRANK
about
British boxer Frank Bruno ducks questions of marriage. il por *Jet* 76:38 My 15 '89
British champ Frank Bruno steels himself for Iron Mike. J. Friedman. il pors *People Weekly* 31:101-2 F 20 '89
Smashing! P. Putnam. il pors *Sports Illustrated* 70:14-17 Mr 6 '89
Take cover, Mike Tyson—Frank Bruno's got a secret weapon. A. Coren. il *TV Guide* 37:8-9 F 25-Mr 3 '89
Tyson's return a triumph, KO's Frank Bruno in five. il pors *Jet* 75:51-2 Mr 13 '89
BRUNS, REBECCA
Puerto Vallarta [cover story] il map *Travel Holiday* 172:38-49 N '89
BRUNS, ROGER, AND KENNEDY, BRYAN
"The dream of yesterday is the reality of tomorrow". il pors *American History Illustrated* 24:24-9+ Summ '89

El presidente gringo. il por map *American History Illustrated* 23:14-21+ F '89
BRUNSON, SUSAN
about
The oldest living American? R. E. McKinney. il pors *Ebony* 44:86+ S '89
BRUNSWICK CORP.
Boating may buoy Brunswick. G. G. Marcial. *Business Week* p206 S 25 '89
Has Brunswick gone overboard in powerboats? J. F. Siler. il *Business Week* p27 Ag 7 '89
BRUSH, STEPHEN G.
Prediction and theory evaluation: the case of light bending. bibl f *Science* 246:1124-9 D 1 '89
BRUSH
Bass in the brush. M. Hicks. il *Field & Stream* 93:64-5+ F '89
BRUSH FIRES
See also
Fire ecology
Combustible grass winning the West [cheat grass; research by Dwight Billings] J. Raloff. *Science News* 136:127 Ag 19 '89
If you live in wildfire country [California] il *Sunset (Central West edition)* 183:96+ S '89
Letter from Los Angeles. J. Didion. *The New Yorker* 65:92-9 S 4 '89
BRUSHER, MARGARET
about
Ann Arbor Antiques Market. J. Weber. il por *Antiques & Collecting Hobbies* 94:47-8+ Ag '89
BRUSHES
See also
Cosmetic brushes
Hairbrushes
BRUSKE, EDWARD
Man in space. il *National Parks* 63:32-8 Ja/F '89
BRUSSELS (BELGIUM)
Airports
Mail war. F. Vaysse. il *World Press Review* 36:62 S '89
Description
Gourmet holidays: Brussels. A. M. Zwack. il map *Gourmet* 49:72-9+ S '89
A new boomtown sprouts as Western Europe unites. D. Lawday. il *U.S. News & World Report* 107:32-3 O 9 '89
Galleries and museums
See also
Musées Royaux d'Art et d'Histoire (Belgium)
Restaurants, nightclubs, bars, etc.
Cooking up profits in Europe [A. Conway's eateries] A. McKenzie. por *Black Enterprise* 20:79-80 N '89
Terrorism
See Terrorism—Belgium
BRUSTEIN, ROBERT, 1927-
Robert Brustein on theater. See occasional issues of The New Republic
BRUVEL, GIL
about
The telltale heart. N. Guccione. il *Omni (New York, N.Y.)* 12:88-93 D '89
BRUXISM
Avoid the daily grind [views of Richard Glass] il *USA Today (Periodical)* 118:14 O '89
BRYAN, C. D. B. (COURTLANDT DIXON BARNES)
Shingle style revival: new life for a rambling Connecticut residence. il pors *Architectural Digest* 46:152-7+ Je '89
BRYAN, COURTLANDT DIXON BARNES *See* Bryan, C. D. B. (Courtlandt Dixon Barnes)
BRYAN, KATHERINE
about
Family ties. C. Cozzone. il pors *Harper's Bazaar* 122:114-17 Ag '89
BRYAN, MIKE
Reflections on the game [excerpts from Baseball lives] il *Sports Illustrated* 70:74-8+ Ap 24 '89
Sculpting a Louisville Slugger [excerpt from Baseball lives] *Harper's* 278:34-5 My '89
BRYANT, BEAR
about
The Bear trap. W. M. Adler. il por *Esquire* 112:204-6+ S '89
BRYANT, CLORA
about
One jazzy lady. J. Malveaux. il pors *New Choices for the Best Years* 29:54-8 N '89
BRYANT, EDWARD
Dateline 1999. il *Omni (New York, N.Y.)* 11:22+ Ja '89
Mod dogs [fiction] *Omni (New York, N.Y.)* 12:62+ N '89
BRYANT, MILES T.
Does teacher evaluation diminish creativity? *The Education Digest* 54:20-1 Mr '89
BRYANT, PAUL W. *See* Bryant, Bear
BRYANT, PAUL WILLIAM, JR.
about
The Bear trap. W. M. Adler. il por *Esquire* 112:204-6+ S '89

BRYANT, RENE K.
Mr. Egan and my drowned lobsters. il *Gourmet* 49:196+ My '89
BRYANT, THOS L.
Miscellaneous ramblings. See issues of Road & Track beginning November 1988
BRYCE, JAMES BRYCE, 1ST VISCOUNT, 1838-1922
about
Presidents: the power and the mediocrity. S. R. Graubard. il *The New York Times Book Review* 94:1+ Ja 15 '89
BRYCE CANYON NATIONAL PARK (UTAH)
Utility to trade coal leases near Bryce [Nevada Power Company] *National Parks* 63:11 My/Je '89
BRYN, TRACEY
about
Voice of the Beehive, sisters from L.A. who have London all abuzz about their stinging pop songs. il pors *People Weekly* 31:88 Mr 13 '89
BRYSON, BILL
Glasgow isn't Paris, but . . . il *The New York Times Magazine* p34-8+ Jl 9 '89
Life's little gambles. il *Reader's Digest* 135:61-2+ D '89
You must remember this. il *Gentlemen's Quarterly* 59:169+ Ap '89
about
Continental drifter. C. S. Smith. il por *New York* 22:26 S 18 '89
BRZEZINSKI, ZBIGNIEW
Post-Communist nationalism. il map *Foreign Affairs* 68:1-25 Wint '89/'90
Will the Soviet empire self-destruct? il *The New York Times Magazine* p38+ F 26 '89
about
Communism in crisis. R. K. Bennett. por *Reader's Digest* 135:99-104 Jl '89
This 'unique chance': assessing the new Poland [interview] H. Mackenzie. il por *Maclean's* 102:30 Ag 28 '89
Vindication of a hard-liner [interview] S. Talbott and R. T. Zintl. il por *Time* 134:10+ D 18 '89
Watching a failed order die [interview] L. Kramer. il por *People Weekly* 32:49 N 27 '89
Zbig deal in Cambodia. *The Nation* 248:109 Ja 30 '89
BRZOSKA, MICHAEL
Behind the German export scandals. bibl f il *The Bulletin of the Atomic Scientists* 45:32-5 Jl/Ag '89
BSA *See* Bronner Slosberg Associates
BSN SA
Is BSN's stomach as big as its eyes? F. J. Comes. il por *Business Week* p55+ Ja 9 '89
The race to stock Europe's common supermarket [BSN buys European operations of RJR Nabisco with more food deals to follow] S. Toy and R. A. Melcher. il *Business Week* p80+ Je 26 '89
BSTAN-'DZIN-RGYA-MTSHO *See* Dalai Lama XIV, 1935-
BTR PLC
White knight or raider? [H. Kravis' stake] S. Flack. il *Forbes* 144:46 S 18 '89
BUATTA, MARIO, 1935-
about
America the Buatta-ful. M. Bethany. il pors *New York* 22:62-3 Mr 27 '89
War at the Armory. S. Greenspan. il *House & Garden* 161:76+ S '89
BUBA, TONY
about
Lightning over Braddock: a Rustbowl fantasy [film] Reviews *American Film* il por 14:11-12 Je '89. P. Aufderheide
BUBBLE MEMORY DEVICES (COMPUTERS) *See* Computers—Memory systems
BUBBLES
See also
Foams
Soap bubbles and films
The fascinating physics of fizz [work of A. Prosperetti] W. F. Allman. il por *U.S. News & World Report* 107:77 N 20 '89
How to build a Hele-Shaw cell and watch bubbles playing tag in a viscous fluid [air bubbles] J. Walker. bibl il *Scientific American* 261:116-19 O '89
BUBEL, NANCY
The vegetable garden. See issues of Country Journal beginning October 1986
BUBER, MARTIN, 1878-1965
about
A (Jewish) double helix. C. Raphael. *Commentary* 87:56-8 My '89
BUBER, MORDEKHAI MARTIN *See* Buber, Martin, 1878-1965
BUBLEY, ESTHER
about
A nation of zombies. K. Dieckmann. bibl f il *Art in America* 77:55-7+ N '89
BUBRICK, ELIZABETH SLOAN- *See* Sloan-Bubrick, Elizabeth
BUCCANEERS *See* Pirates
BUCHA, PAUL
about
On the waterfront. S. J. Madden. il por *Fortune* 119:112 F 13 '89

BUCHAN, BARBARA
about
They never gave up. R. Hoffer. il pors *Sports Illustrated* 71:117-27+ D 25 '89-Ja 1 '90
BUCHAN, VIVIAN
The four P's for free lancers. *The Writer* 102:30 S '89
Welcome change. *Reader's Digest* 134:145 F '89
BUCHANAN, EDWARD
about
This raider may have beaten 'em by joining 'em. G. G. Marcial. il *Business Week* p88 F 13 '89
BUCHANAN, JAMES M., 1919-
What is the 'right' amount of saving? *National Review* 41:32 Je 16 '89
BUCHANAN, LISA K.
The bite [story] il *Mademoiselle* 95:132+ D '89
BUCHANAN, PATRICK M.
Crime and race. il *Conservative Digest* 15:36-7 Jl/Ag '89
BUCHANAN, ROBERT E.
The watercolor page. il por *American Artist* 53:44-7 Mr '89
BUCHANAN, WILLIAM J., 1926-
The bizarre wind of Unishima. il *Reader's Digest* 135:71-6 Ag '89
BUCHER, LLOYD
about
21 years after losing the Pueblo, Lloyd Bucher wins honors for its crew. M. Brower. il pors *People Weekly* 32:26-7 Jl 31 '89
BUCHLOH, H. D.
The whole earth show [interview with J.-H. Martin] il *Art in America* 77:150-9+ My '89
BUCHMANN, STEPHEN
about
By using bar coding on busy bees, scientist Stephen Buchmann becomes an unstung hero. il *People Weekly* 31:105 My 22 '89
BÜCHNER, GEORG, 1813-1837
about
Danton's death [drama] Reviews
    The New York Review of Books il 36:40-2 O 12 '89. J. Kott
BUCHWALD, ART
A born-again nonsmoker. por *The Saturday Evening Post* 261:28 Jl/Ag '89
BUCK, DANIEL, AND MEADOWS, ANNE
Quest for the holy trail. il map *Américas* 41 no1:14-19 '89
BUCK, JERRY
"I was paralyzed! What was wrong with me?". il pors *Redbook* 173:84+ My '89
BUCK, JIM
about
Building to last. M. King. il por *Nation's Business* 77:17-18 N '89
BUCK, JOHN E., 1946-
about
John Buck at Carlo Lamagna. K. Johnson. il *Art in America* 77:166 F '89
BUCK HUNTING *See* Deer hunting
BUCKELS, JIM
about
Creating imaginary places. M. E. Stegmaier. il pors *American Artist* 53:56-9+ O '89
BUCKEYE *See* Horse chestnut
BUCKINGHAM, GEORGE VILLIERS, 1ST DUKE OF, 1592-1628
about
A Duke fit for a King. G. Barker. il por *Art News* 88:87+ D '89
BUCKLER, CHARLES
about
A research tool in the war against AIDS. P. Honan. il por *Personal Computing* 13:182-4 O '89
BUCKLEY, CHRISTOPHER TAYLOR, 1952-
Washington memoirs: bombshell or bust. il *The New York Times Book Review* 94:1+ O 1 '89
BUCKLEY, J. THOMAS
(jt. auth) See Wong, Kevin R., and Buckley, J. Thomas
BUCKLEY, PATRICIA TAYLOR
A penthouse with period grace. il *Architectural Digest* 46:250-7 N '89
BUCKLEY, PRISCILLA L.
Experiencing Nika. *National Review* 41:56-8 Mr 10 '89
Floating through Europe. il *National Review* 41:48-9 D 31 '89
Ice sizzle & totem poles. *National Review* 41:65-6 Ja 27 '89
BUCKLEY, WILLIAM F. (WILLIAM FRANK), 1925-
Concorde cruising speed. il *National Review* 41:26-8+ My 19 '89
Full circle. *National Review* 41:37-40 Je 2 '89
. . . makes a difference where you are. il *Personal Computing* 13:23-4 O '89
Notes & asides. See issues of National Review
On the right. See issues of National Review
A toast to Bill Rusher [address, December 9, 1988] *National Review* 41:19-20 Ja 27 '89

BUCKLEY, WILLIAM F. (WILLIAM FRANK), 1925- — *cont.*
Where we stand. il *National Review* 41:25-6 D 22 '89
BUCKLEY, WILLIAM THOMAS
Bad blood. *Redbook* 173:104-5+ Je '89
The feel-full pill. il *Health (New York, N.Y.)* 21:28-9+ Ja '89
BUCKSEY, COLIN
about
Dealers [film] Reviews
People Weekly il 32:19-20 N 27 '89. R. Novak
BUCKTAILS (FISHING FLIES) *See* Fishing lures, flies, etc.
BUCZAK, BRIAN, 1954-1987
about
Brian Buczak at Emily Harvey. E. Heartney. *Art in America* 77:188-9 N '89
BUDAPEST (HUNGARY)
Cemeteries
Totems and taboos: thoughts in a Budapest graveyard. L. Wieseltier. *The New Republic* 201:21+ Ag 7-14 '89
Description
Budapest reborn. S. May. il *World Press Review* 36:62 Jl '89
High times in Hungary. R. Alleman. il *Vogue* 179:589-90+ S '89
Hungary hearts. T. Aczel. *The New Republic* 201:13-15 D 25 '89
The Queen of Budapest. R. Polt. il map *Travel Holiday* 171:82-7 Mr '89
The way we are [Christmas in Budapest with friends] L. Wyse. il *Good Housekeeping* 209:208 Jl '89
Galleries and museums
See also
Hungarian Ludwig Museum for International Contemporary Art
BUDAPEST STOCK EXCHANGE
A Wall Street in Budapest. M. Dini. il *World Press Review* 36:49 Ap '89
BUDD, JIM
Touché for a Mexican Lampooner. il por *Américas* 41 no1:38-41 '89
BUDD, JOHN F., 1923-
Omissions hurt CEO ethics rating [address, March 29, 1989] *Vital Speeches of the Day* 55:478-80 My 15 '89
BUDD, MERV
about
Missionaries to Nepal, Colombia find freedom. K. H. Sidey. il pors *Christianity Today* 33:47+ Ap 7 '89
BUDDE, RAY
Education by charter. il *Phi Delta Kappan* 70:518-20 Mr '89
BUDDHISM
See also
Fasts and feasts—Buddhism
Zen Buddhism
Canada
God and profits [Buddhist firms flourish in Nova Scotia] il *Maclean's* 102:34-5 Mr 27 '89
Tibet
See also
Dalai Lama XIV, 1935-
United States
See also
Vajradhatu (Organization)
Buddhism in America: can it blend with our philosophy and culture? Y. B. Oh. il *USA Today (Periodical)* 118:84-5 Jl '89
BUDDHIST MONKS
With no margarine for error, eight Buddhist monks practice a butter way to honor the gods [butter sculpting at the American Museum of Natural History] il *People Weekly* 31:81 F 27 '89
BUDDHIST NUNS
Buddhist nuns. B. N. Aziz. il *Natural History* p40-9 Mr '89
BUDDHIST PRESS
See also
Vajradhatu sun (Newspaper)
BUDDHISTS
Health and hygiene
See also
AIDS (Disease) and Buddhists
BUDGET
See also
Astronomical research—Federal aid
Biological research—Federal aid
Colleges and universities—Federal aid
Horticultural research—Federal aid
National Economic Commission (U.S.)
National Institutes of Health (U.S.)—Appropriations and expenditures
National Science Foundation (U.S.)—Appropriations and expenditures
Nuclear research—Federal aid
Off-budget programs
Physics—Federal aid
Research—Federal aid
Surplus (Budget)

United States—Appropriations and expenditures
United States. Congress. Senate. Committee on the Budget
United States. Congressional Budget Office
United States. Dept. of Agriculture—Appropriations and expenditures
United States. Dept. of Defense—Appropriations and expenditures
United States. Dept. of Energy—Appropriations and expenditures
United States. Dept. of Housing and Urban Development—Appropriations and expenditures
United States. Dept. of State—Appropriations and expenditures
United States. Forest Service—Appropriations and expenditures
United States. National Aeronautics and Space Administration—Appropriations and expenditures
United States. Office of Management and Budget
Advanced budget fudging. H. Banks. *Forbes* 143:33 Je 12 '89
All rich nations need their debt. R. L. Heilbroner. *The Nation* 248:81-2 Ja 23 '89
And now, back to the issues: budget, trade, banking and debtors [address, November 10, 1988] W. C. Butcher. *Vital Speeches of the Day* 55:241-3 F 1 '89
Are the economy's real problems being overlooked? [views of Peter L. Bernstein] G. Koretz. *Business Week* p26 Ja 9 '89
Attacking the deficits now will bring years of prosperity. C. F. Bergsten. il por *Fortune* 119:19+ Ja 2 '89
Balanced budget constitutional amendment. il *Congressional Digest* 68:257-88 N '89
The blame game begins. D. Goodgame. il por *Time* 133:26 Ja 16 '89
Blink or go broke. *Time* 134:68 N 20 '89
The bottom line: Gramm-Rudman isn't working. H. Gleckman. il *Business Week* p36 Ap 10 '89
Bring back big spending. il *The New Republic* 200:7-8 Mr 27 '89
Budget battle lines drawn in red ink. A. Holzinger. il *Nation's Business* 77:50-1 F '89
A budget deal in record time. D. Pauly. il *Newsweek* 113:36 Ap 24 '89
Budget fix hits research grants. M. Crawford. *Science* 246:1115 D 1 '89
Budget poker [final Reagan budget] *National Review* 41:15 F 10 '89
Bush and Congress: budget ballet. L. Smith. *Fortune* 119:8 Mr 13 '89
Bush and the deficit dilemma. R. J. Bresler. il *USA Today (Periodical)* 117:7 My '89
Bush marching to his own beat. D. Gergen. il por *U.S. News & World Report* 106:20-3 F 20 '89
Bush plays budget chicken. E. Salholz. il por *Newsweek* 113:26-7 Ja 16 '89
Bush v. Congress: a formula. W. F. Buckley. *National Review* 41:55 Mr 24 '89
Bush's budget test. A. J. Glass. il *The New Leader* 72:3-4 F 20 '89
Bush's cautious spending plans. M. McDonald. *Maclean's* 102:12 F 20 '89
Darman: the collapse of a grand strategy. E. Clift. por *Newsweek* 114:54 N 20 '89
Days of reckoning: deficit woes weigh heavily on science budgets. I. Goodwin. il *Physics Today* 42:49-50 N '89
The deficit: an exchange [discussion of June 1, 1989 article, A deficit of civic courage] B. M. Friedman. *The New York Review of Books* 36:73-4 S 28 '89
Deficit figuring doesn't add up. C. R. Morris. il *The New York Times Magazine* p36+ F 12 '89
A deficit of civic courage. B. M. Friedman. il *The New York Review of Books* 36:23-6 Je 1 '89
The deficit time bomb [address, March 13, 1989] J. P. Grace. *Vital Speeches of the Day* 55:390-4 Ap 15 '89
Deja voodoo all over again [budget deficit] M. B. Zuckerman. il *U.S. News & World Report* 107:84 O 9 '89
Did Darman diddle while the deficit burned? H. Gleckman. il por *Business Week* p56-7 D 11 '89
Divided we fail [deficit] M. B. Zuckerman. il *U.S. News & World Report* 106:71 Je 5 '89
Doing right by the budget. M. W. Karmin. *U.S. News & World Report* 107:47 Jl 24 '89
Double trouble ahead from inflation and the budget. V. Brownstein. il *Fortune* 119:21-2 Mr 13 '89
Enter the Bush team. L. Walczak and R. Fly. il por *Business Week* p24-6 Ja 30 '89
F.D.R. changed, and so can you [advice for G. Bush] R. Lekachman. il por *The Nation* 248:117-18 Ja 30 '89
Fighting or friendly? [101st Congress] N. Amidei. *Commonweal* 116:5-6 Ja 13 '89
The fine mess created by skid-row politics [budget deficit] G. Borger and S. Dentzer. il *U.S. News & World Report* 107:32+ O 16 '89
Firemen first, or, How to beat a budget cut. C. Peters. il *The Washington Monthly* 21:42-3 F '89
Fixing the deficit: where there's no will, there's no way. D. Harbrecht. il *Business Week* p31 O 2 '89

BUDGET—*cont.*

Forget those phony problems [views of M. Friedman] M. Magnet. *Fortune* 120:68-9 Jl 3 '89

A Fortune proposal for balancing the budget. il *Fortune* 119:92-3 Ja 16 '89

The fudge factor [budget deficit] R. Kuttner. *The New Republic* 200:22-4 Je 19 '89

Fueling up a brawl [proposal to increase gas tax to reduce the deficit] J. Greenwald. il *Time* 133:42-3 Ja 23 '89

Getting back to the spirit of Gramm-Rudman. A. S. Blinder. il *Business Week* p16 O 30 '89

Go ahead! You try making a budget. R. S. Klein and R. J. Morse. il *U.S. News & World Report* 106:42-3 Mr 6 '89

Gramm-Rudman: a potent weapon for spending restraint. D. J. Mitchell. il *USA Today (Periodical)* 118:22-4 N '89

Gramm-Rudman avoided, for now. C. Norman. *Science* 244:281 Ap 21 '89

The great deficit debate [special section] il *National Review* 41:46-51 Ja 27 '89

Has Bush blown his best chance for progress on the deficit? H. Gleckman. il *Business Week* p39 My 1 '89

Have we really been bingeing? D. Henwood. il *The Nation* 248:43-4 Ja 9-16 '89

Hoping for more market magic [G. Bush's address] L. Reibstein. il por *Newsweek* 113:32-3 F 20 '89

How America can triumph [cover story] L. S. Richman. il *Fortune* 120:52-4+ D 18 '89

How the budget deficit affects you. J. Malveaux. il *Essence* 19:106 Ja '89

Incredible but true: the budget deficit will shrink. V. Brownstein. il *Fortune* 120:21+ N 20 '89

Is our eye on the wrong ball? [preoccupation with deficit] D. A. Levy. il por *Forbes* 143:232 Ap 17 '89

Is the deficit really so bad? [cover story] J. Rauch. il *The Atlantic* 263:36-42 F '89

Is the deficit too high? Yes. Should it be higher? Maybe. A. S. Blinder. il *Business Week* p17 F 20 '89

Knocking the teeth out of Gramm-Rudman: round III. H. Gleckman and D. Harbrecht. il *Business Week* p43 S 18 '89

Leave it to cleaver [Gramm-Rudman deficit reduction targets] R. Hornik. il *Time* 134:53 O 30 '89

Legislating deficit cuts. W. Lowther. il *Maclean's* 102:53 My 1 '89

Let him have it [line item veto] M. Kinsley. *The New Republic* 201:4+ N 20 '89

Letter from Washington [G. Bush's budget] Cato. *National Review* 41:12 F 24 '89

Live! Stupid budget tricks! E. Clift. il *Newsweek* 114:29-30 O 23 '89

The month in Congress [address, February 9, 1989] G. Bush. il *Congressional Digest* 68:65-6 Mr '89

The month in Congress [excerpts from message to Congress, January 9, 1989] R. Reagan. il *Congressional Digest* 68:33-4 F '89

Mumbo jumbo on the budget. R. Thomas. il *Newsweek* 113:48 F 27 '89

New plan to slash deficit [report by Council on Competitiveness] N. S. Charles. il *Black Enterprise* 19:24 Mr '89

New spending talk worries GOP whip [views of R. Cheney] D. C. Bacon. il por *Nation's Business* 77:6 F '89

No apology needed [deficit] E. Rubenstein. il *National Review* 41:16 F 10 '89

No-fuss budget. A. C. Brown. il *Forbes* 143:158 My 15 '89

Of deficits and diplomacy. S. Talbott. il *Time* 133:26 Mr 6 '89

President's budget message [address, February 9, 1989] G. Bush. *Vital Speeches of the Day* 55:290-4 Mr 1 '89

Quack! Quack! Quack! [tax increases] *Time* 134:48 D 4 '89

Read my tips [deficit] M. K. Evans. il *Gentlemen's Quarterly* 59:241+ Mr '89

Read our lips. il *The New Republic* 200:9-10 Ja 30 '89

Reaganism with a human face. il *The Progressive* 53:7-8 Ap '89

Reaganomics with a human face [G. Bush's address] W. Shapiro. il por *Time* 133:32-4 F 20 '89

Reagan's budget, Bush's battle. H. Gleckman. il *Business Week* p32-4 Ja 23 '89

The real bottom line [deficit] M. B. Zuckerman. il *U.S. News & World Report* 106:92 Mr 20 '89

A "secret" budget proposal [Reagan's 1990 budget proposal] C. W. Weinberger. il *Forbes* 143:31 F 20 '89

Straight talk about deficits. M. Friedman. *Reader's Digest* 134:105-7 Mr '89

Tame the budget beast. C. Cox. il por *Conservative Digest* 15:6-7+ Jl/Ag '89

A tax windfall could help pare the deficit . . . and sinking rates might chop it even more. G. Koretz. il *Business Week* p20 My 29 '89

Time to trade in our old notions about deficits. P. C. Roberts. il *Business Week* p30 N 13 '89

To keep the tax promise, try a lottery. A. Rabushka and M. S. Bernstam. pors *Fortune* 119:126 F 27 '89

Tory budget, Whig reasoning [Bush budget] *National Review* 41:11 Mr 24 '89

The trillion dollar man [R. Darman; cover story] H. Gleckman. il pors *Business Week* p100-3+ Mr 13 '89

Voodoo deficits. A. Evans-Pritchard. il *The American Spectator* 22:14-15 F '89

'Voodoo economics' in Washington [bipartisan agreement] *U.S. News & World Report* 106:16+ Ap 24 '89

Wait till next year. W. Shapiro. il por *Time* 133:19 Ap 24 '89

Waiting for the whistle to blow. A. Bladen. il *Forbes* 143:216 Mr 20 '89

Who's afraid of George Bush? R. Fly and others. il por *Business Week* p30-1 F 20 '89

Why budget-by-crisis may be for the best. H. Gleckman. il *Business Week* p73 Jl 17 '89

Terminology

Glossary. il *Congressional Digest* 68:259-60 N '89

Canada

See also
Canada—Armed Forces—Appropriations and expenditures

Back to a chilling financial future. D. Francis. il *Maclean's* 102:9 Ap 17 '89

Belt-tightening. R. Laver. il *Maclean's* 102:10-12 F 13 '89

Canada [address, December 7, 1988] M. W. Barrett. *Vital Speeches of the Day* 55:345-6 Mr 15 '89

Canada tackles its deficit. H. M. Waller. il *The New Leader* 72:8-9 O 2-16 '89

Courtroom chaos [Mountie R. Jordan alleges political interference at budget leak trial] M. Clark. il por *Maclean's* 102:20 N 20 '89

Damage control [budget leak controversy] T. Tedesco. il pors *Maclean's* 102:14-16 Je 12 '89

Deficits and the national debt [address, February 23, 1989] T. D'Aquino. *Vital Speeches of the Day* 55:427-9 My 1 '89

Doubts over deficit cuts. D. Jenish. il *Maclean's* 102:42-3 My 15 '89

Entertainment disguised as news [budget story on The journal] G. Bain. il *Maclean's* 102:58 Ap 24 '89

The honeymoon will end on budget night. P. C. Newman. il *Maclean's* 102:33 Mr 6 '89

Penny-pinching times. M. Clark. il *Maclean's* 102:12-13 Ap 17 '89

A pessimistic and enraging budget. P. C. Newman. il *Maclean's* 102:48 My 8 '89

A search for savings. B. Wallace. il *Maclean's* 102:15 Ap 3 '89

The subtleties of inside information [leaked budget] G. Bain. il *Maclean's* 102:48 My 22 '89

The tax squeeze [furor over leaked budget; cover story; special section; with editorial comment by Kevin Doyle] il *Maclean's* 102:2, 10-12+ My 8 '89

What is the deficit? [cover story; special section; with editorial comment by Kevin Doyle] il *Maclean's* 102:4, 40-1+ My 1 '89

Wilson's trials [leaks of Finance Minister M. Wilson's budget; with editorial comment by Kevin Doyle] T. Tedesco. il *Maclean's* 102:2, 10-11+ Je 5 '89

Anecdotes, facetiae, satire, etc.

Watergate envy: it's a scandal [furor over budget leaks couched in Watergate terminology] C. Gordon. il *Maclean's* 102:9 Je 26 '89

Great Britain

See also
Great Britain—Armed Forces—Appropriations and expenditures

Britain deals with a surplus. A. Phillips. il *Maclean's* 102:52 My 1 '89

Britain's mixed blessing [balanced budget] J. Marcom, Jr. il *Forbes* 143:43-4 Mr 6 '89

Voodoo deficits. A. Evans-Pritchard. il *The American Spectator* 22:14-15 F '89

Italy

La dolce deficit. R. Ball. il *Time* 134:58 O 16 '89

Japan

See also
Japan—Armed Forces—Appropriations and expenditures

Nicaragua

A dose of reality for the Sandinistas. il *Newsweek* 113:38 F 13 '89

Soviet Union

See also
Soviet Union—Armed Forces—Appropriations and expenditures

Gorbanomics. R. Parker. *The New Republic* 200:18-20 F 27 '89

Moscow in the red. A. Wilson-Smith. il *Maclean's* 102:36-7 Mr 20 '89

Moscow's hard choices. L. Minard. il *Forbes* 143:39-40 Mr 20 '89

United States

See Budget

BUDGET, BUSINESS *See* Corporations—Finance

BUDGET, CITY *See* Municipal finance

BUDGET, COLLEGE AND UNIVERSITY *See* Colleges and universities—Finance

BUDGET, HOUSEHOLD
Calculating your finances. W. M. Woodard. il *Black Enterprise* 20:63-4+ O '89
Celebrating a bright financial future. M. Rowland. il *Working Woman* 14:63-4+ F '89
Experts who can solve your budget problems [budget counselors and financial planners] S. Nielsen. il *Good Housekeeping* 209:177 Jl '89
How to buy the things you want most: five ways to stretch your paycheck. B. G. Quint. il *Glamour* 87:139+ S '89
How to stay ahead of your paycheck. M. Rowland. il *Working Woman* 14:91-2+ Ap '89
Money. M. Daly. See issues of Better Homes and Gardens
Tighten your money belt. P. Martin. il *Essence* 19:105-6 Mr '89
To free money for what matters most, analyze expenses. C. Willis. il *Money* 18:68-70 F '89
BUDGET, MUNICIPAL See Municipal finance
BUDGET, PERSONAL See Finance, Personal
BUDGET, STATE See State finance
BUDGET ANALYSTS
Budget analysts: so much to do, so little to do it with. E. McGregor. il *Occupational Outlook Quarterly* 33:33-6 Spr '89
BUDGET COMMITTEE (SENATE) See United States. Congress. Senate. Committee on the Budget
BUDGET MOTELS See Hotels, motels, etc.
BUDGYK, MARKO
about
Junk buy update. E. Hardy. il *Forbes* 144:158 D 25 '89
BUEHL, OLIVIA
Warm elegance in ski country. il *New Choices for the Best Years* 29:34-6 Je '89
BUELL, ERIK
about
American dreamer. K. Cameron. il por *Cycle* 40:53-4 Ap '89
BUELL, JOHN
Two cheers for patriotism. il *Utne Reader* p96-7 S/O '89
BUELL MOTOR COMPANY
American dreamer. K. Cameron. il por *Cycle* 40:53-4 Ap '89
BUENA VISTA TELEVISION
Syndication's Magic Kingdom. K. Masters. il *Channels (New York, N.Y.: 1986)* 9:39-42 Ja 16 '89
BUENOS AIRES (ARGENTINA)
Description
After the last tango. J. Hooper. il *Esquire* 111:140-5 F '89
BUFFALO (N.Y.)
Religious institutions and affairs
God and man in Buffalo [B. Graham and humanists contrasted; cover story] T. C. Muck. il por *Christianity Today* 33:21-6 Ja 13 '89
Sports
Buffalo's Rich baseball legacy [Bisons owner R. Rich] G. Macnow. il por *Nation's Business* 77:42-5 F '89
Rich makes his pitch [owner of Buffalo Bisons R. E. Rich] I. Muchnick. il por *The New York Times Magazine* p18-19+ Jl 30 '89
BUFFALO BOB SMITH See Smith, Bob, 1917-
BUFFALO HUNTING
A firing squad for buffalo [bison hunt in Montana] S. Begley. il *Newsweek* 113:51 Mr 6 '89
Montana hunters, confronting targets big, slow and unwary, take aim at Yellowstone's bison [hunters allowed to shoot bison who wander out of park] D. Grogan. il *People Weekly* 31:110-11 F 27 '89
BUFFALOES, AMERICAN See Bison, American
BUFFET MEALS
A Glorious buffet [recipes developed by caterer Glorious Foods] il *Ladies' Home Journal* 106:164-5+ D '89
Happy New Year! il *The Mother Earth News* 115:52-5 Ja/F '89
A light buffet for special occasions. H. A. Dorrough. il *Southern Living* 24:196+ N '89
A New Year's open-house buffet. il *Gourmet* 49:66-72+ Ja '89
BUFFETS, SIDEBOARDS, ETC. (FURNITURE)
Bonus buffet. E. Thompson and E. Thompson. il *Popular Mechanics* 166:93 Je '89
Dining room duo. B. Kieffer. il *The Family Handyman* 39:66-8+ S '89
Sideboard workbench. P. McCafferty. il *Popular Science* 234:84-7 Ja '89
BUFFETT, WARREN E.
about
And now, a look at the old one. B. D. Fromson. il por *Fortune* 120 no10 Special Issue:98 Fall '89
He doesn't walk on water? J. Zweig. il por *Forbes* 144:144 S 4 '89
Warren Buffett makes money by making nice. L. Jereski. il por *Business Week* p58 Ag 7 '89
Worrying about Warren. D. Seligman. il *Fortune* 120:273-4 Jl 31 '89
Would you believe a $10,000 stock? G. Weiss. il por *Business Week* p96 S 4 '89
BUFFUM, CHARLES
There's crack on my block. il *Glamour* 87:128 D '89

BUGAJSKI, JANUSZ, 1954-
Solidarity in power. *The New Republic* 201:12-14 S 11 '89
BUGATTI, CARLO, 1855 OR 6-1940
about
The silver of Carlo Bugatti. A. Duncan. bibl f il por *Antiques* 136:1344-55 D '89
BUGBEE, DICK
about
Sounding off on security systems [interview] A. Cala. il por *Home Mechanix* 85:20-1+ N '89
BUGGING See Electronics in criminal investigation, espionage, etc.; Lasers in criminal investigation, espionage, etc.
BUGGING OF TELEPHONES See Wiretapping
BUHRKE, RICH
about
When's the last time this guy saw a game? G. Castle. il *Sport (New York, N.Y.)* 80:105 F '89
BUICK MOTOR DIVISION
Barnstorming with Buick. T. Swan. il *Popular Mechanics* 166:48-9 Jl '89
Buick on the (American) road back. M. Keller. il *Motor Trend* 41:146 Je '89
I built a Buick [Buick Reatta Craft Centre] M. Allen. il *Popular Mechanics* 166:62-4 F '89
BUILD BOSTON (ORGANIZATION)
Annual Build Boston conference continues to grow in national importance. C. K. Hoyt. il *Architectural Record* 177:27 Ja '89
BUILDING
See also
Acoustics, Architectural
Brick construction
Carpentry
Ceilings
Concrete construction
Earthquakes and building
Environmental engineering (Buildings)
House construction
Housing
Insulation (Heat)
Roofs and roofing
Stone construction
Structural engineering
Underground structures
Walls
Wood construction
Contracts and specifications
Expert panel explores the pros and cons of computerized building specifications (I). C. K. Hoyt. il *Architectural Record* 177:159+ Je '89
An expert panel explores the pros and cons of computerized building specifications (II). C. K. Hoyt. il *Architectural Record* 177:131+ Ag '89
Software reviews for architects [Electronic Sweet's and Auto CAD release 10 with ADE 3] il *Architectural Record* 177:137+ Mr '89
Costs
Congress's initiatives seen as threats to small architectural firms and the costs of construction. P. Hoffmann. il *Architectural Record* 177:21 Ap '89
Construction costs: moderation in the face of unexpectedly strong demand. C. K. Hoyt. il *Architectural Record* 177:42 O '89
Construction costs: no inflation here. C. K. Hoyt. il *Architectural Record* 177:42 My '89
Construction costs: the best of both worlds? C. K. Hoyt. il *Architectural Record* 177:44 Jl '89
Construction costs: the Southeast pulls ahead. il *Architectural Record* 177:27 F '89
Estimating your estimates. C. C. Munroe, III. il por *Architectural Record* 177:44 My '89
Managing costs with Excel [home-based construction consultant R. West] K. J. Novak. il *Home Office Computing* 7:32+ N '89
When liability insurance can cover your construction-cost estimate problems [architects] A. Kornblut. por *Architectural Record* 177:31 Ap '89
Finance
See also
Housing finance
Mortgages
Inspection
See Building inspection
Terminology
Lingo to learn: build your construction vocabulary. *Better Homes and Gardens* 67:126-7 N '89
BUILDING, ADOBE See Adobe buildings
BUILDING COSTS See Building—Costs
BUILDING FITTINGS
New products. See issues of Architectural Record
Product reports 1990 [cover story; special issue; with editorial comment by Joan F. Blatterman] il *Architectural Record* 177:25-9+ D '89
BUILDING INDUSTRY See Construction industry
BUILDING INSPECTION
Inspecting for a safe home. J. Bolger. *Consumers' Research Magazine* 72:29-30 O '89

BUILDING INSPECTION—*cont.*
What to look for in a house. il *Changing Times* 43:52
My '89
BUILDING LAWS AND REGULATIONS
See also
Building inspection
Plumbing—Laws and regulations
Zoning
How to sabotage the homeless. J. Mehrten. il *Conservative
Digest* 15:6-7+ My/Je '89
Innovative exteriors: has technology left building codes
behind? J. S. Russell. *Architectural Record* 177:20-1 D
'89
BUILDING LOTS *See* Building sites
BUILDING MANAGEMENT *See* Real estate management
BUILDING MATERIALS
See also
Asbestos
Concrete
Concrete blocks
Insulation (Heat)
Lumber
Roofs and roofing
Stucco
New products. See issues of Architectural Record
Product reports 1990 [cover story; special issue; with editorial
comment by Joan F. Blatterman] il *Architectural Record*
177:25-9+ D '89
Technology comes home [special section] T. O. Bakke. il
Popular Science 235:63-9 Ag '89
BUILDING MATERIALS INDUSTRY
See also
Champion Building Systems Inc.
Di Giorgio Corp.
Eljer Industries
H. H. Robertson Co.
Jim Walter Corp.
Ply-Gem Industries, Inc.
Acquisitions and mergers
How a hot-growth company got decked [Amre's acquisition
of Champion Building Systems Inc.] T. Mason. il *Business
Week* p34+ F 13 '89
Finance
Construction. J. Willoughby. il *Forbes* 143:120-1+ Ja 9 '89
BUILDING SITES
See also
Hillside architecture
Buying your vacation lot: let a checklist be your guide.
Better Homes and Gardens 67:84 Je '89
Less-is-more lots. W. L. Nolan. il *Better Homes and Gardens*
67:106 My '89
On the waterfront. P. Whittell. il *Motor Boating & Sailing*
164:60-2+ D '89
BUILDING STONE INSTITUTE
Building Stone Institute 1989 Tucker Awards. il *Architectural
Record* 177:52-3 S '89
BUILDING STONES
Sandstone and cousins. il *Sunset (Central West edition)*
183:102-4 N '89
BUILDINGS
See also
Adobe buildings
Architecture
Bank buildings
Concert halls
Embassies (Buildings)
Office buildings
Public buildings
School buildings
Environmental engineering
See Environmental engineering (Buildings)
Equipment
See Building fittings
Management
See Real estate management
Models
See Architectural models
BUILDINGS, HISTORIC *See* Historic houses, sites, etc.
BUILDINGS, PREFABRICATED
See also
Houses, Prefabricated
School buildings, Prefabricated
BUILDINGS, REMODELED
See also
School buildings, Remodeled
Reach for natural light: mandate for old cabinet shop [convert-
ed to single-family residence] il *Sunset (Central West edition)*
182:102+ F '89
Sanctuary for art [converted church in Bellport, Long Island;
interview with M. Morley] D. Kazanjian. il por *House
& Garden* 161:150-5+ My '89
BUILDINGS, ROUND
See also
Geodesic domes

BUILDINGS, UNDERGROUND *See* Underground structures
BUILDINGS, WRECKING OF *See* Wrecking
BUILDINGS IN ART *See* Architecture in art
BUILT IN FURNITURE *See* Furniture, Built in
BUJONES, FERNANDO
about
Reviews:
C. Gregory and F. Bujones at City Center. A. Murphy.
Dance Magazine 63:82-4 Ja '89
BUKOVSKY, VLADIMIR
Vladimir Bukovsky [advice to George Bush] il *National Review*
41:22-3 F 10 '89
BUKOWSKI, CHARLES
about
Penniless poet to laureate of lowlife. il por *U.S. News &
World Report* 106:52 Ja 9 '89
BULBS
See also
Crocuses
Forcing (Plants)
Fritillarias
Tulips
Blooming color [miniature bulbs] T. James. il *New Choices
for the Best Years* 29:76-80 S '89
Bulbs go wild [cover story] M. Damsker. il *Organic Gardening*
36:30-2+ S '89
The bulbs of summer. L. A. Weathers. il *Southern Living*
24:66 Ap '89
Drilling for bulbs? A brighter idea than you'd think [planting
tool] il *Sunset (Central West edition)* 183:194-5 O '89
Five-year-olds have a bulb-planting party. They make Christ-
mas gifts. il *Sunset (Central West edition)* 183:156 D '89
Indoor gardening. C. Siler. il *Parents* 64:247+ O '89
Naturalizing spring flowering bulbs [special section] il *Flower
and Garden* 33:25-30+ S/O '89
Playing up little bulbs. il *Sunset (Central West edition)* 183:198
N '89
Simply sensational summer bulbs. D. A. Jimerson. il *Better
Homes and Gardens* 67:95-6+ Ap '89
Spring fragrance from bulbs you plant in September. il *Sunset
(Central West edition)* 183:186 S '89
BULGARIA
See also
Civil rights—Bulgaria
Narcotics trade—Bulgaria
Religious liberty—Bulgaria
Turks—Bulgaria
Politics and government
The three holdouts against change. J. Borrell. il *Time* 134:51
N 6 '89
BULGARIAN FOLK MUSIC PHONOGRAPH RECORDS
See Phonograph records—Bulgarian folk music
BULIMAREXIA *See* Bulimia
BULIMIA
The big fat lie: when thin does you in. E. Karlsberg. il
'Teen 33:28-9+ Jl '89
Eating disorders and pregnancy. P. A. Hillard. il *Parents*
64:202+ N '89
New treatment for bulimia [cholecystokinin; research by
Thomas D. Geracioti and Rodger A. Liddle] A. H. Rosen-
feld. il *Psychology Today* 23:28 Mr '89
A tragic obsession. D. Jenish. il *Maclean's* 102:52+ O 9
'89
Turning around bulimia with therapy [research by Barbara
Bauer and Wayne Anderson] P. King. il *Psychology Today*
23:14 S '89
BULK BUYING
ABA launches group buying for store bags. J. Mutter.
Publishers Weekly 235:18 My 19 '89
BULL, BART
L.A. international. il *Vogue* 179:332-5 F '89
The real thing. il pors *Vogue* 179:232-7 Je '89
Tracey Ullman: just being herselves. il por *Vogue* 179:386+
My '89
BULL, SANDY
about
The return of Sandy Bull. D. Fricke. il por *Rolling Stone*
p33 My 18 '89
BULL (FIRM) *See* Groupe Bull
BULL DURHAM [film] *See* Motion picture reviews—Single
works
BULL HN INFORMATION SYSTEMS INC.
"We still have more to do". C. Siler. il *Forbes* 144:183
D 11 '89
BULLARD, THOMAS E.
about
UFO update. D. S. Rogo. il *Omni (New York, N.Y.)* 12:121
O '89
BULLDOGS
Rad dog! Rad dog! When it comes to skateboarding, Sidney
the bulldog is a wheelie big star. il *People Weekly* 31:80
Je 12 '89
BULLET WOUNDS *See* Gunshot wounds
BULLETIN BOARDS
See also
Computer bulletin boards

BULLETIN OF THE ATOMIC SCIENTISTS
The "atomic" scientists. L. Ackland. *The Bulletin of the Atomic Scientists* 45:2 O '89
Clock power [impact on savings rate of perceived threat of nuclear war; research by Joel Slemrod] L. Ackland. *The Bulletin of the Atomic Scientists* 45:2 Je '89
Today's Bulletin. *The Bulletin of the Atomic Scientists* 45:3 O '89
Why detente may raise the savings rate [imminence of nuclear war] G. Koretz. il *Business Week* p18 Mr 6 '89

BULLETPROOF VESTS
Lightweight armor [Spectra Shield] J. Free. il *Popular Science* 234:30 Je '89

BULLETS
See also
Cartridges
Shot
Nonlethal bullets that kill [rubber-clad metal balls used by Israelis to quell Palestinian uprising] il *Time* 133:33 Ja 30 '89
October slugfest. B. Brister and D. E. Petzal. il *Field & Stream* 94:62+ O '89
Trajectories
See Trajectories

BULLFINCH, CHARLES
about
Behind the Federal facade. A. O. Boulton. il por *American Heritage* 40:68-75 My/Je '89

BULLHEAD FISHING
Just a bullhead. W. Ryan. il *The Conservationist* 44:34-7 Jl/Ag '89

BULLIES *See* Bullying

BULLOCK, GEORGE, 1782 OR 3-1818
about
Master of cabinetry. M. Filler. il por *House & Garden* 161:146-9+ Mr '89

BULLYING
Battling the school-yard bully. D. F. Bjorklund and B. Bjorklund. il *Parents* 64:195 Ap '89
Besting bullies. D. Calkins. il *American Health* 8:124 S '89

BULOW, LEAH A.
Stencil stationery! il *The Mother Earth News* 120:24 N/D '89

BULOW HAMMOCK (FLA.)
Mind in a forest [excerpts from Bulow Hammock] D. R. Wallace. il *Sierra* 74:62-7 My/Je '89

BULOW-HUBE, SANDRA
Breast cancer update. *Ladies' Home Journal* 106:96+ Jl '89

BULTMAN, JUDITH
Diary of a tragedy. il por *Parents* 64:105-10 My '89

BUMPERS, DALE
Should the Senate-passed Immigration Act of 1989 be approved? [excerpts from debate, July 12, 1989] *Congressional Digest* 68:247+ O '89

BUMPERS, AUTOMOBILE *See* Automobiles—Bumpers

BUM'S RUSH [ballet] *See* Ballet reviews—Single works

BUNCH, MARVIN
about
High school grad thanks retired firefighter who rescued her 14 years ago. il pors *Jet* 76:23 Jl 17 '89

BUNDESBANK
The Bundesbank brakes. P. Fuhrman. il *Forbes* 143:56+ Ja 9 '89
Why should Europe dance to Germany's economic tune? B. Riemer. il *Business Week* p76 O 23 '89

BUNDY, MCGEORGE
Ending a common danger. *The New York Times Magazine* p54-6+ Ag 20 '89
Negotiating skills needed. il *The Bulletin of the Atomic Scientists* 45:33-4 My '89
about
The Cuban missiles [discussion of March 1989 article, Nuclear revisionism] P. Glynn. *Commentary* 88:9-12 Ag '89
Do nuclear weapons matter? S. Hoffmann. bibl f il *The New York Review of Books* 36:28-31 F 2 '89
'Do nuclear weapons matter?': an exchange [discussion of February 2, 1989 article] S. Hoffmann. il *The New York Review of Books* 36:57-8 Ap 27 '89
Nuclear revisionism. P. Glynn. *Commentary* 87:42-7 Mr '89
What's unusable—and indispensable? [interview] H. Trewhitt. il por *U.S. News & World Report* 106:43-4 Ja 9 '89

BUNDY, THEODORE ROBERT
about
The Bundy carnival. D. Gelman. il por *Newsweek* 113:66 F 6 '89
Bundy told Dobson, "It was pornography". *Christianity Today* 33:43 F 17 '89
Burning question. *The New Republic* 200:4+ F 20 '89
A condemned man's last bequest. P. Axthelm and M. Ryan. il pors *People Weekly* 31:44-51 F 6 '89
Crime: that's entertainment. J. Leo. il por *U.S. News & World Report* 106:53 F 6 '89
Final attraction: men who charm women—to death. A. Rule. il pors *Redbook* 172:104-6+ F '89
"I deserve punishment". J. V. Lamar, Jr. il por *Time* 133:34 F 6 '89

A killer's final hour. M. Nichols. il por *Maclean's* 102:54 F 6 '89
Notes and comment. *The New Yorker* 65:23-4 F 27 '89
Reflections on Bundy. *National Review* 41:17-18 F 24 '89

BUNGALOWS
The California bungalow [Pasadena] il *Esquire* 112:132 S '89
New house, classic craft [home based on designs of C. and H. Greene] P. Harper. il *Home Mechanix* 85:66-8+ F '89

BUNGE, MARY BARTLETT, AND OTHERS
Perineurium originates from fibroblasts: demonstration in vitro with a retroviral marker. bibl f il *Science* 243:229-31 Ja 13 '89

BUNGE, ROBERT
Great astrophotos in less than an hour. il *Astronomy* 17:78-83 Ag '89

BUNGE & BORN
Can business save Argentina? J. Ryser and R. A. Kessler. il pors *Business Week* p46-8 S 18 '89

BUNGEE JUMPING
Boing! W. P. Barrett. il *Forbes* 144:233+ O 30 '89
The wonderful world of bungee jumping. E. Grinnan. il por *Seventeen* 48:132 Ag '89

BUNGY JUMPING *See* Bungee jumping

BUNIONS
Things that go bump in your foot. R. Getty. il *Women's Sports & Fitness* 11:14 S '89

BUNIS, KITTY
about
Life in the stress lane: diary of a wired day. N. Angier. il pors *Mademoiselle* 95:192-5+ F '89

BUNKLEY-WILLIAMS, LUCY, AND WILLIAMS, ERNEST H.
Hangers-on. il *Natural History* p40-1 Ja '89

BUNTE, DONNA
about
Real-life beauty. A. G. Britton. il por *American Health* 8:110-11 Mr '89

BUONARROTI, MICHEL ANGELO *See* Michelangelo Buonarroti, 1475-1564

BUOYS
Inland navigation. S. Stapleton. il *Motor Boating & Sailing* 164:32 D '89

BUPRENORPHINE
Buprenorphine suppresses cocaine self-administration by rhesus monkeys [possible use in treatment of cocaine addiction] N. K. Mello and others. bibl f il *Science* 245:859-62 Ag 25 '89
Lukewarm turkey [drug firms balk at pursuing buprenorphine, a heroin addiction treatment] J. Horgan. *Scientific American* 260:32 Mr '89

BURACHEVSKY, YAKOV
about
Freedom and skepticism: snapshots of the *glasnost* era. N. Marcus. il por *Scholastic Update (Teachers' edition)* 121:18-20 My 5 '89

THE 'BURBS [film] *See* Motion picture reviews—Single works

BURCHFIELD, HARRY
about
Rising star. J. Watson. il pors *National Wildlife* 27:46-9 O/N '89

BURCKHALTER, CHARLES, 1849-1923
about
A life devoted to astronomy. K. Bracher. il por *Astronomy* 17:50-4 O '89

BURCKHARDT, JACOB, 1818-1897
about
Landlord blues [film] Reviews
The Nation 248:862 Je 19 '89. S. Klawans

BURCKHARDT, RUDY
about
Better. *The New Yorker* 65:43-4 D 4 '89

BURDEN, CARTER
The flowering of Fort Worth. il por *House & Garden* 161:84-91+ F '89
about
Baring the Burdens. R. Koenig. il pors *Vogue* 179:318-25+ Ag '89

BURDEN, CHRIS, 1946-
about
Best of Burden. K. Larson. il *New York* 22:65-6 S 18 '89
Chris Burden: Institute of Contemporary Art. N. Stapen. il *Art News* 88:175 N '89
He has forsaken the violent art of his youth, but Chris Burden is still out to startle. M. Small. il pors *People Weekly* 32:55-6+ Ag 28 '89

BURDEN, ERNEST E., 1934-
Awards program reveals the latest techniques. il *Architectural Record* 177:29+ Ja '89

BURDEN, SUSAN
about
Baring the Burdens. R. Koenig. il pors *Vogue* 179:318-25+ Ag '89

BURDEN RESEARCH PLANTATION See LSU Rural Life Museum and Burden Research Plantation

BURDICK, ALAN
Hype tide. *The New Republic* 200:15-18 Je 12 '89

BURDICK, BRUCE, 1933-
about
Teaming up in love and work. L. Rosch. il pors *Working Woman* 14:92-3 Jl '89

BURDICK, SUSAN KOSAKOWSKY
about
Teaming up in love and work. L. Rosch. il pors *Working Woman* 14:92-3 Jl '89

BURDICK GROUP (FIRM)
Teaming up in love and work [office of B. and S. Burdick] L. Rosch. il pors *Working Woman* 14:92-3 Jl '89

BUREAU OF ENGRAVING AND PRINTING See United States. Bureau of Engraving and Printing

BUREAUCRACY
See also
President's Private Sector Survey on Cost Control (U.S.)
Firemen first, or, How to beat a budget cut. C. Peters. il *The Washington Monthly* 21:42-3 F '89
Who runs Japan? C. Rapoport. il *Fortune* 120:113-14 Ag 28 '89

BUREAUCRATS See Government employees; Public officers

BURG, DALE
Why men make awful wives. il *Harper's Bazaar* 122:118-19+ F '89

BURG, STEVEN L., 1950-
The Soviet Union's nationalities question. bibl f map *Current History* 88:341-4+ O '89

BURGER, RICHARD L.
Long before the Inca. il map *Natural History* p66-73 F '89

BURGER KING CORPORATION
Can a new CEO pull Burger King out of the fire? [B. Gibbons] P. Engardio. il *Business Week* p40 My 22 '89
The publican at Burger King [B. Gibbons] P. Sellers. il por *Fortune* 119:68 Mr 13 '89
Trying to get Burger King out of the flames [Grand Met executive B. J. Gibbons] M. Maremont. il por *Business Week* p29-30 Ja 30 '89
Tuition payments cut job turnover [downtown Detroit] S. D. Rinella and R. J. Kopecky. il por *Nation's Business* 77:25-6 Ag '89

BURGESS, ANTHONY, 1917-
The ecstasy of Gerard Manley Hopkins. il *The New York Times Book Review* 94:15 Ag 27 '89

BURGESS, DAVID LOWRY See Burgess, Lowry, 1940-

BURGESS, JOHN P.
Church in East Germany helps create die Wende. *The Christian Century* 106:1140-2 D 6 '89

BURGESS, LOWRY, 1940-
about
A lunar cube. S. Staggs. il *Art News* 88:13-14 Ja '89

BURGESS, MICHAEL
about
Doubling up on a dream. G. Hayden. por *Maclean's* 102:43 Mr 27 '89

BURGESS SHALE FOSSILS
Burgess Shale faunas and the Cambrian explosion [cover story] S. Conway Morris. bibl f il map *Science* 246:339-46 O 20 '89
PW interviews [S. J. Gould] W. Smith. por *Publishers Weekly* 236:32-3 O 13 '89
We're all lucky to be here [S. J. Gould's evolutionary theory] J. Adler. il por *Newsweek* 114:68 N 20 '89

BURGH ISLAND (ENGLAND)
Description and travel
Agatha's murder island. R. Ryan. il *Gentlemen's Quarterly* 59:93+ N '89

BURGHARDT, WALTER J.
Intellectual and Catholic? Or Catholic intellectual [address, February 1989] *America* 160:420-5 My 6 '89

BURGI, ADRIANA
Hot lines. il *New York* 22:134-46 My 1 '89

BURGIN, CHRISTINE
about
The new dealers. A. Virshup. il pors *Harper's Bazaar* 122:80+ D '89

BURGIN, TONI, AND OTHERS
The fossils of Monte San Giorgio. bibl il map *Scientific American* 260:74-81 Je '89

BURGIN, VICTOR, 1941-
about
Victor Burgin at John Weber. J. Zinsser. il *Art in America* 77:179 D '89

BURGIS, ROSEMARY L.
The Overlord Embroidery. il *American Heritage* 40:108-13 My/Je '89

BURGLAR ALARMS See Alarms

BURGLAR ALARMS, AUTOMOBILE See Automobiles—Alarms

BURGLARY AND BURGLARS
See also
Art thefts
The 'Catwoman' case [Atlanta burglar] B. Wickens. il *Maclean's* 102:39 Jl 31 '89

The 'Catwoman' of Atlanta [A. L. McGraw] por *Newsweek* 113:29 My 8 '89
Death of black in small Texas town questioned [J. O. King] il *Jet* 77:5 D 11 '89
The missing lists [series of break-ins at offices of environmental organizations in Canada] A. Steacy. il *Maclean's* 102:58 My 15 '89

Anecdotes, facetiae, satire, etc.
Conan and me. B. Persky. il *Esquire* 111:34+ My '89

BURGLARY PROTECTION
See also
Alarms
Locks and keys
Burglarproofing your home. C. Schaeffer. il *Changing Times* 43:69-72 Ja '89
High-tech home security [cover story] H. Friedman. il *Radio-Electronics* 60:33-7+ Ap '89
Home security [special section] il map *Popular Science* 235:76-80+ O '89
Preventing burglaries. J. W. Merline. il *Consumers' Research Magazine* 72:38 Ja '89

BURGOO (STEW) See Stew

BURGOWER, BARBARA
Breaking the banks. *Ladies' Home Journal* 106:24 Je '89
A living nightmare. il pors *Ladies' Home Journal* 106:74+ Mr '89

BURGUNDY (FRANCE)
Wine industry
See Wine industry—France

BURGUNDY (WINE) See Wine

BURIAL
See also
Cryonics
Funeral rites and ceremonies
Hawaiians—Mortuary customs
Indians of North America—Mortuary customs
Man, Prehistoric—Mortuary customs
Mummies
Grave misunderstandings [changing mortuary customs; research by Aubrey Cannon] B. Bower. il *Science News* 136:330-1 N 18 '89

BURIED TREASURE See Treasure trove

BURKE, BILL
about
In the culture of fitness. por *Runner's World* 24:52 Ja '89

BURKE, CHRIS
about
For Chris Burke, the first actor with Down syndrome to star on TV, Life goes on in a big way. K. McMurran. il pors *People Weekly* 32:61-2+ O 16 '89
"My son will always amaze me"; ed. by Sara Nelson. M. Burke. il pors *Redbook* 174:48+ N '89
Takes guts [cover story] J. B. McDaniel. il pors *Life* 12:70-2+ N '89

BURKE, DANIEL B.
about
The brass at Cap Cities/ABC: rethinking TV [interview] M. Brown and P. Ainslie. il pors *Channels (New York, N.Y.: 1986)* 9:93-5 F '89

BURKE, DELTA
about
Delta Burke and Gerald McRaney: their first screen kiss turned into real-life love. S. Littwin. il pors *TV Guide* 37:32-5 Ja 14-20 '89
Delta Burke: "The man who taught me to love again" [cover story] V. Scott. pors *Good Housekeeping* 208:76+ F '89
Of hearts, flowers and wedding bliss [cover story] S. Schindehette. il pors *People Weekly* 31:86-7+ Je 12 '89
The ultimate prime-time love story [cover story] G. Esterly. il pors *TV Guide* 37:4-5+ O 7-13 '89

BURKE, ED, 1949-
What ails you? il *Bicycling* 30:152-3 Ap '89

BURKE, EDMUND, 1729?-1797
about
Notes and comment. *The New Yorker* 65:21-2 Jl 31 '89

BURKE, MARIAN
"My son will always amaze me"; ed. by Sara Nelson. il pors *Redbook* 174:48+ N '89

BURKE, SELMA, 1900-
about
The 1989 Essence Awards [with editorial comment by Susan L. Taylor] il pors *Essence* 20:57-60+, 69 O '89

BURKE, TIM, 1959-
about
An All-star father. R. Demak. il pors *Sports Illustrated* 71:69 Jl 24 '89
All-star pitcher Tim Burke goes home a winner with a baby boy. il pors *People Weekly* 32:82-3 Ag 7 '89

BURKE, TOM
The year of the Greens. bibl f il *Environment* 31:18-20+ N '89

BURKES, JEFFREY
about
Tooth of the crime. N. Hirschfeld. il por *New York* 22:22 Je 19 '89

BURKHOLDER, STEVE
And why they let anyone be an informant. *The Washington Monthly* 20:19-20 Ja '89

BURKINA FASO
See also
Medicine—Burkina Faso
Politics and government
See also
Populism—Burkina Faso
BURKITT'S LYMPHOMA *See* Lymphatic system—Cancer
BURLAND, JAN
Tilling the earth. il *Country Journal* 16:64-8 Mr/Ap '89
BURLEIGH, A. PETER
FY 1990 assistance request for the Middle East [statement, March 9, 1989] *Department of State Bulletin* 89:66-8 My '89
BURLESON, DONALD
about
Virus hacker nailed. P. Scisco. il *Compute!* 11:7 Ja '89
BURLESQUE
See also
Striptease
BURLEY, ANNE-MARIE
The once and future German question. bibl f *Foreign Affairs* 68:65-83 Wint '89/'90
BURLEY, PETER
A farrago of nonsense? The French Revolution in the cinema. bibl il *History Today* 39:51-6 My '89
BURLINGTON (N.C.)
Crime
Arsenic and old lace [B. Moore accused of poisonings] E. Salholz. il por *Newsweek* 114:24 Ag 14 '89
BURLINGTON (VT.)
Politics and government
The Greens of Vermont [mayoral race] J. N. Baker. il *Newsweek* 113:33 F 27 '89
Religious institutions and affairs
Vermont: 'whitest state in America' gets first black church [New Alpha Missionary Baptist Church] C. Waldron. il pors *Jet* 75:14-15+ Mr 13 '89
BURLINGTON NORTHERN INC.
Railroaded [clearcutting by Plum Creek Timber Company spurred on by LBO fever] A. Porterfield. il *Common Cause Magazine* 15:21-3 S/O '89
BURLINGTON RESOURCES INC.
Hidden values for 1989. B. D. Fromson. il *Fortune* 119:28 Ja 2 '89
BURMA
See also
Civil rights—Burma
Guerrillas—Burma
Karens—Burma
Narcotics laws and regulations—Burma
Narcotics trade—Burma
Foreign relations
United States
See United States—Foreign relations—Burma
Politics and government
Burma: political situation and human rights [statement, March 2, 1989] D. F. Lambertson. map *Department of State Bulletin* 89:40-3 My '89
Burmese days. M. Aung-Thwin. bibl f *Foreign Affairs* 68:143-61 Spr '89
A country under the boot. D. Benjamin. il por *Time* 134:36-7 Ag 21 '89
Crisis in Burma. D. I. Steinberg. *Current History* 88:185-8+ Ap '89
Life in the hills. W. Law-Yone. il *The Atlantic* 264:24+ D '89
A rich country gone wrong. S. Sesser. *The New Yorker* 65:55-6+ O 9 '89
BURMESE COOKING *See* Cooking, Burmese
BURN, DIANE
about
The pleasures of Partemi: restoring a ruined castellino on the Tuscan coast. I. Borger. il por *Architectural Digest* 46:178-85 Ap '89
BURNE, KEVIN, AND OTHERS
Faculty development from the inside. pors *Change* 21:43-9 My/Je '89
BURNELLI, VINCENT, D. 1964
about
Burnelli's lifting fuselage. P. Garrison. il por *Flying* 116:80+ Ap '89
BURNERS
See also
Cooktops
Halogen burners
BURNES, KAREN
about
They've run her off the road—but never off a story. D. Hill. il por *TV Guide* 37:36-7 Ja 21-27 '89
BURNETT, CAROL
about
Carol Burnett. il pors *People Weekly* 31 Special Issue:56-7 Summ '89
Carol Burnett: "Talk to your kids—I finally did". A. W. Petrucelli. il *Redbook* 172:96-7+ F '89
Julie and Carol together again. E. Sirkin and D. Lamanna. il pors *Ladies' Home Journal* 106:62+ D '89

BURNETT, JOHN
Magic and murder in Matamoros. *The Christian Century* 106:815-16 S 13-20 '89
BURNETT, W. M., AND BAN, S. D.
Changing prospects for natural gas in the United States. bibl f il *Science* 244:305-10 Ap 21 '89
BURNEY, DEREK
Canada and the United States in a global context [address, September 22, 1989] *Vital Speeches of the Day* 56:43-5 N 1 '89
about
Men of credentials. H. Mackenzie. il pors *Maclean's* 102:62-3 Jl 3 '89
BURNEY COMPANY
Basic training for value investors [interview with T. Rosenberg] E. Schultz. il por *Fortune* 119:29-31 Ja 2 '89
BURNHAM, DAVID, 1933-
The abuse of power: misuse of the I.R.S. [cover story] il *The New York Times Magazine* p24-7+ S 3 '89
BURNHAM, GREGORY
Subtotals [story] *Harper's* 279:37-8 Jl '89
BURNHAM, JANE
The watercolor page. por *American Artist* 53:44-7 Jl '89
BURNHAM, MARGARET
The Great Society didn't fail. il *The Nation* 249:122-4 Jl 24-31 '89
BURNHAM BROADCASTING COMPANY
Make no little plans. P. Noglows. il *Channels (New York, N.Y.: 1986)* 9:67 Ap '89
BURNING-IN (PHOTOGRAPHY) *See* Photography—Processing
BURNING OF LAND
See also
Shifting cultivation
Carbon monoxide and the burning earth. R. E. Newell and others. bibl il map *Scientific American* 261:82-8 O '89
Farmers playing with fire [burning of grass seed threatens air quality in Willamette Valley, Or.] J. Stiak. il *Sierra* 74:92-3 Mr/Ap '89
William Wharton, author of Dad, seeks to avenge his daughter's horrible death [K. Rodewald killed in automobile crash caused by smoke cloud from grass fires in Oregon's Willamette Valley] M. Green. il pors *People Weekly* 32:122-4 N 27 '89
BURNING QUESTIONS [television program] *See* Television program reviews—Single works
BURNING SECRET [film] *See* Motion picture reviews—Single works
BURNOUT, OCCUPATIONAL *See* Job stress
BURNS, BREE
Fake food. il *Theatre Crafts* 23:30+ Ap '89
BURNS, DAVID D.
How to deal with difficult people [condensed from The feeling good handbook] *Reader's Digest* 135:113-15 D '89
BURNS, GEORGE, 1896-
about
Amazing Gracie. M. G. Stoddard. il pors *The Saturday Evening Post* 261:58-9 Mr '89
George Burns, humor's elder statesman. S. Roman. por *Video* 13:14 Jl '89
The Man with the pictures. W. Safire. il *The New York Times Magazine* p14+ Je 18 '89
BURNS, JERE
about
Gaining fame as Dear John's hunk lout is no sweat for Jere Burns. S. Schindehette. il pors *People Weekly* 31:145-6 Ap 10 '89
'I'm a bad boy'. J. Marion. il por *TV Guide* 37:22 F 18-24 '89
BURNS, KHEPHRA
Jazz. il por *Essence* 20:70-9 N '89
Skiers for all seasons. il *Essence* 20:100+ N '89
BURNS, M. ANTHONY
about
Suddenly, Ryder's engine is sputtering. P. Engardio. il *Business Week* p56 Je 19 '89
BURNS, MONIQUE
Summer spirit: 20 travel money savers and the best of the cultural festivals. il *Essence* 19:27+ Ap '89
BURNS, PAT
about
Third-degree Burns. A. Murphy. il *Sports Illustrated* 70:50-3 F 27 '89
BURNS, RALPH, 1949-
Barbed wire [poem] *The Atlantic* 264:60 Ag '89
BURNS, ROBERT
about
Steep sleep. M. Beauchamp. il por *Forbes* 143:209 Ap 17 '89
BURNS, ROBERT E., 1927-
The examined life. See issues of U.S. Catholic
BURNS, THOMAS J.
The second greatest Christmas story ever told. il *Reader's Digest* 135:65-70 D '89
BURNS, THOMAS J., 1942-
Tests to target dependability. il *Nation's Business* 77:26+ Mr '89

BURNS, WILLIAM F.
An overview of U.S. arms control objectives [statement, October 18, 1988] *Department of State Bulletin* 89:41-4 Ja '89
Prohibition of chemical weapons conference held in Paris [statement, January 11, 1989] *Department of State Bulletin* 89:9-10 Mr '89
BURNS AND SCALDS
Burns, eye injuries from tanning devices. il *FDA Consumer* 23:3-4 O '89
BURNSVILLE (N.C.)
Architecture
Home in the mountains. il *Southern Living* 24:130-2 Je '89
BURNUM BURNUM
about
Aboriginality. *The New Yorker* 65:31-3 S 4 '89
BURR, DONALD C.
about
Donald Burr may be ready to take to the skies again. J. A. Byrne. il por *Business Week* p74-5 Ja 16 '89
BURR TRAIL (UTAH)
BLM report cites harm in paving Burr Trail. *National Parks* 63:12-13 Mr/Ap '89
BURRILL, G. STEVEN
about
High-tech guru Steven Burrill [interview] M. Mandell. il por *High Technology Business* 9:20-3 N/D '89
BURRIS, KEITH
Nothing inevitable about democracy. *The Christian Century* 106:807 S 13-20 '89
BURROS, MARIAN
Express-lane cook [excerpts from Twenty minute menus] il *Working Woman* 14:146-8 O '89
Georgia on my mind. il *The New York Times Magazine* p41-2 F 5 '89
Gourmet classics in 20 minutes. il *Ladies' Home Journal* 106:170-2+ S '89
The new BBQ. il *American Health* 8:102+ Jl/Ag '89
New grill in town. il *The Mother Earth News* 118:82 Jl/Ag '89
BURROS, DOMESTIC See Donkeys
BURROUGHS, ROBERT
Books with easy hooks: selling to the chains. il *Publishers Weekly* 235:37+ Ap 28 '89
Fitting into the conglomerate picture. il *Publishers Weekly* 236:138-40 Jl 28 '89
Targeting the hand-sell. il *Publishers Weekly* 235:52-4 My 19 '89
What to do (or not do) when the local economy goes bust. il *Publishers Weekly* 236:27-9 Jl 7 '89
BURROUGHS, WILLIAM S., 1914-
about
Caravan of Dreams launches audio line. P. Sweeting. il por *Publishers Weekly* 235:34 F 3 '89
BURROUGHS (JOHN) MEDAL See John Burroughs Medal
BURROUGHS CORPORATION
See also
Unisys Corp.
BURROUGHS WELLCOME CO.
AIDS profiteering [AZT] P. C. Montgomery. il *Common Cause Magazine* 15:9 Ja/F '89
How much for a reprieve from AIDS? [Burroughs Wellcome lowers price of AZT] C. Gorman. il *Time* 134:81-2 O 2 '89
BURROWING BY FISH See Fish—Habits and behavior
BURROWING OWLS See Owls
BURROWS, E. G. (EDWIN GLADDING), 1917-
In late October [poem] *Wilderness* 53:71 Fall '89
BURROWS, EDWIN GLADDING See Burrows, E. G. (Edwin Gladding), 1917-
BURSON, JAY
about
By the skin of his neck. H. Hersch. il pors *Sports Illustrated* 70:46-9 Mr 6 '89
BURSTALL, JAMES
Alexandre has influenced hairstyles the world over for nearly fifty years. il pors *Vogue* 179:285+ S '89
In her own fashion. il pors *House & Garden* 161:114-17 Jl '89
BURSTEIN, DANIEL
A yen for New York: what the Japanese own—what they're after [cover story] il *New York* 22:26-36 Ja 16 '89
BURT, BERNARD I.
The new American spa. il *American Health* 8:87-8 Ap '89
BURT, JAMES C.
about
James Burt's 'love surgery' was supposed to boost pleasure, but some patients say it brought pain. M. Brower. il por *People Weekly* 31:97-6+ Mr 27 '89
The love surgeon. J. A. Hennessee. il *Mademoiselle* 95:206-7+ Ag '89
"My gynecologist butchered me!"; ed. by Judith Kelman. G. Harness. il por *Redbook* 173:22+ Jl '89
BURT, RICHARD
Nuclear and space talks open round 11 [statement, June 20, 1989] *Department of State Bulletin* 89:73-4 Ag '89

Status of the Strategic Arms Reduction Talks [statement, August 3, 1989] *Department of State Bulletin* 89:17-19 O '89
BURTCHAELL, JAMES TUNSTEAD
Anecdotes, facetiae, satire, etc.
Forged teaching [revised Catholic loyalty oath] M. E. Marty. *The Christian Century* 106:455 Ap 26 '89
BURTON, GARY
about
Blindfold test. F. Bouchard. il por *Down Beat* 56:47 Ag '89
Gary Burton: good vibes. R. Givens. por *Stereo Review* 54:116 Mr '89
Gary Burton: vibes alive! [interview] B. Milkowski. il pors *Down Beat* 56:20-3 Ap '89
BURTON, JAKE
about
Jake and the Rad Man. D. White. il pors *Skiing* 42:238-40+ D '89
BURTON, JONATHAN
The Vietnam Film Project. *The Nation* 248:825-7 Je 12 '89
BURTON, KATHY
(jt. auth) See Yanker, Gary, and Burton, Kathy
BURTON, PHILLIP, 1926-1983
about
Beware the gerrymander, my son. J. H. Fund. il *National Review* 41:34-6 Ap 7 '89
BURTON, REBECCA S.
Rugby: a gentlewoman's sport. il *Women's Sports & Fitness* 11:66 Je '89
BURTON, RICHARD, 1925-1984
about
Love story [excerpt from Richard Burton] M. Bragg. pors *Ladies' Home Journal* 106:103-5+ Ja '89
PW interviews [biographer M. Bragg] M. Field. por *Publishers Weekly* 235:83-4 F 3 '89
Richard Burton: great actor whose talents were often wasted. K. Turan. il pors *TV Guide* 37:12-14+ N 25-D 1 '89
BURTON, TIM
about
Batman [film] Reviews
Commonweal il 116:503 S 22 '89. P. D. Baumann
Film Comment il 25:76+ N/D '89. A. White
Life il 12:84-6 Spr '89. L. Nickson
The Nation 249:100-1 Jl 17 '89. S. Klawans
National Review 41:55-7 S 15 '89. M. Sieff
National Review 41:46+ Ag 18 '89. J. Simon
The New Republic 201:24 Jl 31 '89. S. Kauffmann
New York il 22:45-6 Jl 17 '89. D. Denby
The New Yorker 65:83-5 Jl 10 '89. P. Kael
Newsweek il 113:68-9 Ja 23 '89. J. Kroll
Newsweek il 113:70-4 Je 26 '89. B. Barol
People Weekly il 32:13 Jl 3 '89. R. Novak
Rolling Stone il p38-42+ Je 29 '89. B. Zehme
Theatre Crafts il 23:21 Ag/S '89. A. Pirani
Time il 133:60-2 Je 19 '89. R. Corliss
Video il 13:80-1+ D '89. B. Eder
Vogue il 179:128-30 Je '89. E. G. Carter
Tim Burton, Batman and the Joker. J. Morgenstern. il por *The New York Times Magazine* p44-6+ Ap 9 '89
BURTON SNOWBOARDS (FIRM)
Jake and the Rad Man [J. Burton and B. LaMar] D. White. il pors *Skiing* 42:238-40+ D '89
BURUMA, IAN
After Hirohito: what remains sacred. il por *The New York Times Magazine* p28-9+ My 28 '89
The bartered bride. il *The New York Review of Books* 36:7-11 Je 1 '89
The double life of Benazir Bhutto [cover story] il *The New York Review of Books* 36:8-11 Mr 2 '89
From Hirohito to Heimat. *The New York Review of Books* 36:31-2+ O 26 '89
Japan's emperor of film. il pors *The New York Times Magazine* p42-5+ O 29 '89
A nation divided. il pors *The New York Times Magazine* p26-30+ Ja 15 '89
BURY, MAIRI
about
Mount Stewart vistas: the Northern Ireland estate of Lady Mairi Bury. P. Lauritzen. il *Architectural Digest* 46:222-7+ Ap '89
BURYING BEETLES See Beetles
BUS DRIVERS
See also
Drugs and bus drivers
BUS HIJACKING
Capital standoff [C. Yacoub charged in hijacking of bus from Montreal to Ottawa] P. Kopvillem. il *Maclean's* 102:10-11 Ap 17 '89
No one called in the helicopters [hijacked bus on Canada's Parliament Hill] C. Gordon. il *Maclean's* 102:35 My 1 '89
'Today's word is revenge' [attack on Israeli bus puts latest peace proposals in jeopardy] A. Platt. il *Newsweek* 114:34 Jl 17 '89

BUS HIJACKING—*cont.*
The widening gulf [Palestinian attack on Israeli bus throws peace endeavors into chaos] B. Came. il *Maclean's* 102:21 Jl 17 '89

BUS LINES
See also
Greyhound Lines, Inc.

BUS TERMINALS
See also
Port Authority of New York and New Jersey. Bus Terminal

BUS TRAVEL
California caravan: the Parlor Car way. M. C. Lehrer. il *USA Today (Periodical)* 117:36-41 My '89
Planes, trains, etc. P. Egan. il *Road & Track* 40:22+ Jl '89

Anecdotes, facetiae, satire, etc.
The boys on the bus [athletes] F. Lidz. il *Sports Illustrated* 71:58-62+ Jl 3 '89

Photographs and photography
A nation of zombies [works by E. Bubley] K. Dieckmann. bibl f il *Art in America* 77:55-7+ N '89

BUSCAGLIA, LEO F.
Our dinner table university [condensed from Papa, my father] il *Reader's Digest* 135:78-80 S '89
"Papa was so proud" [excerpt from Papa, my father] il pors *Redbook* 173:24+ Je '89

BUSCH, AUGUST A., III
about
Even August Busch can only handle so much beer. J. F. Siler. il por *Business Week* p182+ S 25 '89

BUSCH, CHARLES
about
The lady in question [drama] Reviews
New York il 22:44 Ag 7 '89. J. Simon

BUSCH, FREDERICK, 1941-
Public or purloined? il *Harper's* 279:58-61 Ag '89

BUSCH, PHYLLIS S., 1909-
Surviving and thriving—plants and animals in winter. il *The Conservationist* 43:26-33 Ja/F '89

BUSCHEL, BRUCE
The battle is with himself [cover story] il pors *Gentlemen's Quarterly* 59:224-9+ My '89

BUSES
See also
School buses
Trolleys
Hijacking
See Bus hijacking
Theft
See also
Bus hijacking

BUSES (COMPUTERS) *See* Computers—Buses

BUSEY, GARY
A near-fatal motorcycle crash changes an actor's life, but not his refusal to wear a helmet; ed. by Jack Kelley. il pors *People Weekly* 31:65-6+ My 15 '89

BUSEY, JAMES B.
about
Busey embarks on plan to boost FAA safety inspectors, shift duties. J. Ott. il *Aviation Week & Space Technology* 131:108-9 D 18-25 '89

BUSFIELD, TIMOTHY
about
Nerdysomething no more [interview] S. Fried. il pors *Gentlemen's Quarterly* 59:120+ Mr '89

BUSH, BARBARA, 1925-
Millie's six-pack [cover story] il pors *Life* 12:32-4+ My '89
about
America's need to read. L. Smith. il por *Harper's Bazaar* 122:70-1 Ja '89
Anna Perez boards Bush administration as First Lady's press secretary. por *Jet* 75:12 F 6 '89
'B.B.' style. C. Donovan. il pors *The New York Times Magazine* p38-9 Jl 30 '89
Barbara and George—their love story [excerpt from Simply Barbara Bush] D. Radcliffe. il pors *Good Housekeeping* 209:156-7+ N '89
Barbara Bush discusses racism, poverty in Ebony. il pors *Jet* 76:22 Ag 28 '89
Barbara Bush: down-to-earth First Lady. M. B. Carlson. il por *Reader's Digest* 134:83-7 Ap '89
Barbara Bush . . . her lifestyle, her look. il pors *Good Housekeeping* 208:184-5 My '89
Barbara Bush speaks out [cover story] L. B. Randolph. il pors *Ebony* 44:52-4+ S '89
Barbara Bush's hand-made rug. il por *Good Housekeeping* 209:40+ Ag '89
"The best time of my life is now" [cover story] J. L. Block. il pors *Good Housekeeping* 209:155+ N '89
The Bushes of Kennebunkport [interview] D. Kazanjian. il pors *House & Garden* 161:140-5 Je '89
A favorite 'grandmother'. M. McDonald. il por *Maclean's* 102:30 Ja 23 '89
First Lady teaches kids at D.C. non-profit center. il por *Jet* 75:24 F 20 '89
A First Lady who cares. B. Kantrowitz and A. McDaniel. il pors *Newsweek* 114:43-4 Jl 10 '89

George Bush [interview] M. Wilhelm and L. Y. Jones. il pors *People Weekly* 32:42-7 D 25 '89-Ja 1 '90
How good should you look? C. Avery. pors *Ladies' Home Journal* 106:119-21+ Je '89
'I've got George Bush' [interview] T. M. DeFrank and A. McDaniel. il por *Newsweek* 113:25 Ja 23 '89
Letter to the First Lady. K. Fury. *Working Woman* 14:136 F '89
Making a home in the White House. G. Hackett. il pors *Newsweek* 113:32-3 Ja 16 '89
The natural. J. Reed. il pors *Vogue* 179:312-18 Ag '89
Our nation's new First Lady. L. Eskin. il por *Scholastic Update (Teachers' edition)* 121:7 Ja 13 '89
Reading along with Barbara Bush: the endings are mostly happy. E. R. Lipson. il por *The New York Times Book Review* 94:36+ My 21 '89
The Silver Fox [cover story] M. B. Carlson. il pors *Time* 133:22-6 Ja 23 '89
Welcome to the Bushes'. D. Radcliffe. il pors *The Saturday Evening Post* 261:42+ N/D '89
What's a First Lady to do? An open letter to Barbara Bush. A. Hornaday. *Ms.* 17:98 Ja/F '89
With Barbara Bush present, literacy event raises $215,000. il por *Publishers Weekly* 235:10 Je 9 '89

BUSH, DOROTHY *See* LeBlond, Dorothy Bush
BUSH, GEORGE, 1924-
See also
Bush-Gorbachev summit conference, 1989
The American adventure. il por *Popular Mechanics* 166:22-3 My '89
American hostages in the Middle East [remarks, statement, etc., July 31-August 7, 1989] *Department of State Bulletin* 89:66-9 O '89
Anniversary of the Berlin Wall [statement, August 12, 1989] *Department of State Bulletin* 89:41 O '89
Baltic Freedom Day [proclamation, June 14, 1989] *Department of State Bulletin* 89:80 Ag '89
A boy goes to war. il pors *Life* 12:70-2+ S '89
Bush: 'moving beyond containment' [excerpts from address, May 12, 1989] *Aviation Week & Space Technology* 130:9 My 22 '89
Bush: 'the inescapable challenge' [excerpts from address, July 20, 1989] *Aviation Week & Space Technology* 131:13 Jl 31 '89
Captive Nations Week, 1989 [proclamation, July 6, 1989] *Department of State Bulletin* 89:91 S '89
Change in the Soviet Union [address, May 12, 1989] *Department of State Bulletin* 89:16-17 Jl '89
Commitment to democracy and economic progress in Latin America [address, May 2, 1989] il por *Department of State Bulletin* 89:1-2 Je '89
"Dear Doro . . . Devotedly, Dad". il pors *Good Housekeeping* 208:120-1+ Ap '89
Emergency package for Colombia's drug flight [statement, August 25, 1989] *Department of State Bulletin* 89:47 O '89
Encouraging political and economic reforms in Poland [address, April 17, 1989] *Department of State Bulletin* 89:3-5 Je '89
European security negotiations open in Vienna [conventional armed forces; statements and text of Western position paper, March 9, 1989] *Department of State Bulletin* 89:33 My '89
The events in Eastern Europe [address, November 22, 1989] *Vital Speeches of the Day* 56:130-2 D 15 '89
Excellence in education: President Bush's strategy. *The Education Digest* 54:3-6 Ja '89
Extending the limits of our frontiers [address, July 20, 1989; with editorial comment by Charles D. Walker] il pors *Ad Astra* 1:2, 38-40 S '89
First report on Cyprus [message to Congress, March 1, 1989] *Department of State Bulletin* 89:43 Ap '89
FSX coproduction prohibition disapproved by president [letter to the Senate, July 31, 1989] *Department of State Bulletin* 89:32 O '89
The future of Europe [address, May 21, 1989] *Department of State Bulletin* 89:18-19 Jl '89
Helsinki Human Rights Day, 1989 [proclamation, August 1, 1989] *Department of State Bulletin* 89:42 O '89
Inaugural address [January 20, 1989] *Vital Speeches of the Day* 55:258-60 F 15 '89
The inaugural address of President Bush [January 20, 1989; cover story] il por *Department of State Bulletin* 89:1-3 Ap '89
James A. Baker, III, sworn in as Secretary of State [remarks, January 27, 1989] il por *Department of State Bulletin* 89:8 Ap '89
Letter from the president. il por *Parents* 64:45 Mr '89
The month in Congress [address, February 9, 1989] il *Congressional Digest* 68:65-6 Mr '89
National drug control strategy [address, September 5, 1989] *Vital Speeches of the Day* 55:738-40 O 1 '89
News conference of August 15 (excerpts). *Department of State Bulletin* 89:13-15 O '89
News conference of January 27 (excerpts). *Department of State Bulletin* 89:4-5 Ap '89
News conference of June 27 (excerpts). *Department of State Bulletin* 89:54-6 S '89

BUSH, GEORGE, 1924—cont.

News conferences of June 5 and 8 (excerpts). *Department of State Bulletin* 89:46-52 Ag '89

Nuclear and space talks open round 11 [statement, June 19, 1989] *Department of State Bulletin* 89:73 Ag '89

Nuclear cooperation with EURATOM [letter to Congress, March 9, 1989] *Department of State Bulletin* 89:44 Je '89

Outlines of a new world of freedom [address, September 25, 1989] il pors *Department of State Bulletin* 89:27-31 N '89

Panama elections [statements, April 27-May 11, 1989] *Department of State Bulletin* 89:66-72 Jl '89

President addresses joint session of the Congress [excerpts, February 9, 1989] *Department of State Bulletin* 89:3-4 Ap '89

President Bush visits Europe [special section] il pors *Department of State Bulletin* 89:22-53 S '89

President Bush's news conference, Paris, July 16, 1989. il por *Department of State Bulletin* 89:17-21 S '89

President holds session with news reporters [excerpts, February 16, 1989] *Department of State Bulletin* 89:5-6 Ap '89

President meets with French president [news conference, May 21, 1989] il por *Department of State Bulletin* 89:79-83 Ag '89

President meets with Irish prime minister [statement, March 17, 1989] *Department of State Bulletin* 89:39 Je '89

President meets with Prime Minister Mulroney [question-and-answer session, May 4, 1989] *Department of State Bulletin* 89:45-7 Jl '89

President meets with South African antiapartheid activist [statement, June 30, 1989] il pors *Department of State Bulletin* 89:71 S '89

President visits Europe; attends North Atlantic Council meeting [cover story; special section] il pors *Department of State Bulletin* 89:11-45 Ag '89

President's budget message [address, February 9, 1989] *Vital Speeches of the Day* 55:290-4 Mr 1 '89

President's trip to Japan, China, and South Korea [special section] il pors *Department of State Bulletin* 89:1-22 My '89

President's visit to Canada [remarks and news conference, February 10, 1989] il por *Department of State Bulletin* 89:26-8 Ap '89

Second report on Cyprus [message to Congress, June 5, 1989] *Department of State Bulletin* 89:89 S '89

Security strategy for the 1990s [address, May 24, 1989] *Department of State Bulletin* 89:19-21 Jl '89

Soviets withdraw from Afghanistan [statement, February 16, 1989] *Department of State Bulletin* 89:48 Ap '89

Steel trade liberalization program [statement, July 25, 1989] *Department of State Bulletin* 89:35 O '89

U.S. international activities in science and technology [message to Congress, April 5, 1989] *Department of State Bulletin* 89:51-2 Je '89

U.S., Japan agree to codevelop FSX aircraft [statement, April 28, 1989] *Department of State Bulletin* 89:48-9 Jl '89

U.S. severs diplomatic contact with Noriega regime [statement, September 1, 1989] *Department of State Bulletin* 89:69 N '89

U.S. support for democracy and peace in Central America [statements, March 24, 1989; cover story] il por map *Department of State Bulletin* 89:55-9 Je '89

United States and NATO [address, May 31, 1989] *Vital Speeches of the Day* 55:546-9 Jl 1 '89

Upcoming elections in Nicaragua [statement, July 19, 1989] *Department of State Bulletin* 89:92 S '89

Visit of Australian prime minister [remarks, June 27, 1989] il por map *Department of State Bulletin* 89:60-2 O '89

Visit of Egyptian president [remarks, April 3, 1989] il por *Department of State Bulletin* 89:40 Je '89

Visit of Israeli prime minister [remarks, April 6, 1989] il por *Department of State Bulletin* 89:42-3 Je '89

Visit of Japanese prime minister [remarks, February 2, 1989] il por *Department of State Bulletin* 89:32 Ap '89

Visit of Japanese prime minister [remarks, September 1, 1989] il por *Department of State Bulletin* 89:51-3 N '89

Visit of King Hussein I [remarks, April 19, 1989] il por map *Department of State Bulletin* 89:53-4 Jl '89

Visit of Pakistan's prime minister [remarks, June 6, 1989] il por *Department of State Bulletin* 89:63-4 O '89

Visit of Zaire's president [remarks, June 29, 1989] il por map *Department of State Bulletin* 89:15-17 O '89

World Trade Week, 1989 [proclamation, May 5, 1989] *Department of State Bulletin* 89:51 Jl '89

about

The 1988 election. N. J. Ornstein and M. Schmitt. *Foreign Affairs* 68 Special Issue:39-52 ['89]

Advice to the president: don't count on nuclear weapons. J. Wales and M. H. Halperin. il *The Bulletin of the Atomic Scientists* 45:7-8 Mr '89

An agenda for President Bush. L. Smith and A. R. Dowd. il por *Fortune* 119:82-4+ Ja 16 '89

American foreign policy: the Bush agenda. R. M. Nixon. *Foreign Affairs* 68 Special Issue:199-219 ['89]

Avoiding trouble. F. Barnes. *The New Republic* 201:9-10+ O 2 '89

Barbara and George—their love story [excerpt from Simply Barbara Bush] D. Radcliffe. il pors *Good Housekeeping* 209:156-7+ N '89

The benefits of benign neglect. M. Ruby. il *U.S. News & World Report* 107:68 Jl 31 '89

"The best time of my life is now" [cover story] J. L. Block. il pors *Good Housekeeping* 209:155+ N '89

Black leaders tell what they want President Bush to do first. R. L. Haywood. il *Jet* 75:4-6 Ja 30 '89

Bless me, father. D. Goodgame. il pors *Time* 133:22-3 My 8 '89

Blue-blood blues. E. D. Baltzell. *The New Republic* 200:15-16 Ap 3 '89

Bush and the conservatives. R. E. Tyrrell. *The American Spectator* 22:10-11 S '89

Bush as Batman? Wait for the sequel. F. Bruning. il *Maclean's* 102:9 Jl 17 '89

Bush at the helm. M. McDonald. il por *Maclean's* 102:18-19 F 6 '89

Bush clarifies position on tuition tax credits. K. A. Lawton. *Christianity Today* 33:55 My 12 '89

Bush conducts a historic meeting with Black Caucus. il por *Jet* 76:6-7 Je 12 '89

Bush league. J. Klein. il pors *New York* 22:16+ Mr 13 '89

Bush looks ahead to the 1990s [interview] M. B. Zuckerman and others. il por *U.S. News & World Report* 107:34 D 25 '89-Ja 1 '90

Bush marching to his own beat. D. Gergen. il por *U.S. News & World Report* 106:20-3 F 20 '89

Bush names Morehouse Medical School prexy to Cabinet post. il pors *Jet* 75:4 Ja 9 '89

The Bush presidency: cautious to a fault. H. Gleckman and R. Fly. il por *Business Week* p64-5 My 8 '89

Bush's challenge: the first 100 days. S. Manning. il por *Scholastic Update (Teachers' edition)* 121:4-5 Ja 13 '89

Bush's first foreign crisis. il por *Newsweek* 113:16-18 My 8 '89

Bush's first quarter. K. T. Walsh. il pors *U.S. News & World Report* 106:24-7 My 1 '89

Bush's lukewarm welcome. L. I. Barrett. il *Time* 133:18 Ja 23 '89

Bush's plans to defeat the forces of sleaze. K. T. Walsh. il *U.S. News & World Report* 106:16-17 Ja 23 '89

Bush's plea: 'A lot is happening'. L. Martz. il por *Newsweek* 113:26-8 Mr 20 '89

Bush's second inaugural speech. D. Gergen. il *U.S. News & World Report* 106:87 F 13 '89

Bush's shovel brigade. S. V. Roberts. il *U.S. News & World Report* 107:14-16 Ag 7 '89

Can the EPA chief clean up Bush's image? V. Cahan. il pors *Business Week* p135-6 D 11 '89

Caught up in Miami's Cuban politics. B. Turque. il por *Newsweek* 114:24 S 4 '89

Clark Kent, please call your office. il *Newsweek* 113:28 F 27 '89

Collision course: Bush and the Fed. M. McNamee and H. Gleckman. il *Business Week* p34-6 F 27 '89

Contempt for the little colony. C. Hitchens. il *Harper's* 279:70-6 O '89

The contratution. *The Nation* 248:723-4 My 29 '89

Counseling the president [special section] il *National Review* 41:20-8 F 10 '89

Courting the conservatives. M. Duffy. il por *Time* 134:33 O 16 '89

The dawning of the Bush method. S. V. Roberts. il por *U.S. News & World Report* 106:34-5 Ap 17 '89

A day in the life of President Bush. R. Rosenblatt. il pors *U.S. News & World Report* 106:26-7 Je 26 '89

The Democrats [discussion of February 1989 article, Why the Democrats lost again] J. Muravchik. *Commentary* 87:2-5 Je '89

A design, but is it grand? H. Trewhitt. il *U.S. News & World Report* 106:42-4 My 1 '89

The Duke did his best. R. E. Tyrrell. *The American Spectator* 22:10 Ja '89

Encore for Iran-contra? L. Howard. il pors *Newsweek* 113:9 Ja 30 '89

Experienced conservatives for Bush. E. J. Feulner. il *The American Spectator* 22:28-9 Ja '89

F.D.R. changed, and so can you. R. Lekachman. il por *The Nation* 248:117-18 Ja 30 '89

Farewell and hail. *National Review* 41:11 F 10 '89

The first 100 Zs. H. Hertzberg. *The New Republic* 200:4 My 8 '89

Fishing for leadership. D. Thompson. il por *Time* 133:91-2 My 22 '89

For Bush, Central America won't be a crusade. S. Baker and others. il *Business Week* p50 Ja 16 '89

The foreign policy thing: how long will Bush's luck hold out? D. Harbrecht and B. Javetski. il por *Business Week* p63 D 25 '89-Ja 1 '90

Four bore years. F. Barnes. *The New Republic* 200:12+ Mr 27 '89

Frenetic caution. F. Barnes. *The New Republic* 201:10-11 Ag 28 '89

The frenetic president. G. Hackett. il por *Newsweek* 113:19 F 6 '89

BUSH, GEORGE, 1924——about—cont.

George Bush [interview] M. Wilhelm and L. Y. Jones. il pors *People Weekly* 32:42-7 D 25 '89-Ja 1 '90

George Bush & environmental leadership. J. D. Hair. il *National Wildlife* 27:30 F/Mr '89

George Bush moves in. J. D. Isaacs. il *The Bulletin of the Atomic Scientists* 45:3-4 Ja/F '89

George Bush's balky start. D. Gergen. il *U.S. News & World Report* 106:34 Ja 30 '89

George Bush's opportunity. il *The Progressive* 53:6-7 F '89

A green Blueprint for Bush. M. J. McCloskey. il *Sierra* 74:36-8 Ja/F '89

Guidelines for President Bush. T. Bethell. il *The American Spectator* 22:11-13 Ja '89

Has Bush assigned Kemp a mission impossible? R. Stodghill, II. por *Business Week* p51 Ja 9 '89

Hidden agenda. F. Barnes. *The New Republic* 200:14-16 F 20 '89

Hitting the ground running. M. Duffy. il pors *Time* 133:30-1 F 6 '89

An Ike-Jack model for President Bush. R. S. Cline. il *Conservative Digest* 15:60-1 Jl/Ag '89

Illegal money and the '88 campaign. F. Wertheimer. il *Common Cause Magazine* 15:44 Mr/Ap '89

An interview with Bush. R. M. Smith and others. il por *Newsweek* 113:32 Ja 30 '89

The invisible man. *Commonweal* 116:291-2 My 19 '89

Is Bush a true WASP? E. Thomas. il por *Newsweek* 114:23 S 25 '89

Is Bush losing the struggle for Europe's hearts and minds? B. Javetski and D. Griffiths. il *Business Week* p61 My 8 '89

It's not always fair weather. J. O'Sullivan. *National Review* 41:5 S 29 '89

Leadership into the next American century [interview; cover story; with editorial comment by James R. Whelan] J. R. Whelan and W. P. Hoar. il pors *Conservative Digest* 15:4, 6-11 S/O '89

Lessons of campaign '88. F. Barnes. il *The American Spectator* 22:14-16 Ja '89

Letter from Washington. E. Drew. *The New Yorker* 65:77-85 F 27 '89

Letter from Washington. E. Drew. *The New Yorker* 65:74-81 Jl 31 '89

Letter from Washington. E. Drew. *The New Yorker* 65:121-4+ N 27 '89

Letter from Washington. E. Drew. *The New Yorker* 65:87-93 My 15 '89

Letter from Washington. E. Drew. *The New Yorker* 65:100-4+ O 30 '89

Letter from Washington. E. Drew. il *The New Yorker* 65:81-92 Ag 28 '89

Letter from Washington. E. Drew. *The New Yorker* 65:72-82 Je 26 '89

The 'liberation' of George Bush [with interview] T. Morganthau. il pors *Newsweek* 113:28-9 Ja 16 '89

Looking back from 2000: what exactly did Bush do? D. Gergen. il por *U.S. News & World Report* 106:26-7 My 1 '89

Man of a thousand lights. R. Z. Hallow. *National Review* 41:19-20 My 19 '89

Manipulating the media and America: the negative 1988 presidential campaign. R. L. Fischer. il *USA Today (Periodical)* 117:20-2 Mr '89

Master handler. A. R. Dowd. por *Fortune* 119:54 Ja 2 '89

Memo to Bush: don't take your economic luck for granted. M. McNamee. il *Business Week* p27 Ja 30 '89

Minority report. C. Hitchens. *The Nation* 248:402 Mr 27 '89

Mr. Consensus [cover story] M. Duffy. il pors *Time* 134:16-22 Ag 21 '89

A NATO balancing act. D. Goodgame. il por *Time* 133:39 Je 5 '89

New deal? T. Beardsley. *Scientific American* 260:12+ Ja '89

The new look [cover story; special section; with editorial comment by Kevin Doyle] il pors *Maclean's* 102:2, 26-36 Ja 23 '89

Notes and comment. *The New Yorker* 65:27-8 My 29 '89

Nouns and pronouns. L. H. Lapham. *Harper's* 278:8-9 Ja '89

Old bland-dad. T. Noah. *The New Republic* 200:17-19 Ap 3 '89

Ollie North's eleventh-hour stratagem. T. Morganthau. il pors *Newsweek* 113:24 Ja 9 '89

Ollie's trial: the Bush factor. L. Martz. il por *Newsweek* 113:20 Ap 17 '89

Open letter to George Bush. *Consumer Reports* 54:20-1 Ja '89

The past as prologue. L. Bridges. *National Review* 41:22-3 Je 2 '89

The pastel president. G. F. Will. il *Newsweek* 113:86 Ap 24 '89

Paying the price for political errors [Iran-contra affair] M. Barone. il *U.S. News & World Report* 106:30 My 1 '89

Pebbles go bam-bam. F. Barnes. *The New Republic* 200:12+ Ap 17 '89

Playing with guns. G. F. Will. il *Newsweek* 113:78 Mr 27 '89

The post-Hollywood style of George Bush. W. Greider. il *Rolling Stone* p33-4 Ap 6 '89

The power of negative thinking [interview with L. Atwater] W. Greider. il pors *Rolling Stone* p51-3+ Ja 12 '89

The presidency (administration of George Bush). H. Sidey. See issues of Time beginning January 23, 1989

President Bush. il *World Press Review* 36:6+ Mr '89

President Bush and school choice. *America* 160:99 F 11 '89

President Bush and the world of science. T. H. Cole. il *Popular Mechanics* 166:48 Mr '89

Reagan, Bush, and the liberal revolution [address, December 8, 1988] E. H. Crane. *Vital Speeches of the Day* 55:265-8 F 15 '89

Reagan's gift. J. Beatty. il *The Atlantic* 263:58-62+ F '89

Right-wing activists take aim at Bush. J. M. Wall. *The Christian Century* 106:163-4 F 15 '89

The road to 1992. E. G. Graves. il *Black Enterprise* 19:7 Ja '89

Robbing the future. R. W. Wilkins. il *Mother Jones* 14:6+ S '89

Rude awakening. D. Goodgame. il por *Time* 133:22-4 Mr 20 '89

Say a prayer for Gorbachev. H. Sidey. il pors *Time* 134:19 Ag 7 '89

Short honeymoon? J. Klein. il *New York* 22:16+ F 6 '89

A slow start for Bush. D. Schorr. *The New Leader* 72:3-4 F 6 '89

A small town goes prime-time. S. Allis. il *Time* 133:14+ Ja 9 '89

Spurious George. H. Fairlie. il *The New Republic* 200:12-14 My 8 '89

The stovepipe problem. il por *Time* 134:35 N 6 '89

Sworn to run. K. Hosler. il por *Runner's World* 24:30-1+ D '89

A tale of two candidates. M. A. Kramer. *Change* 20:9+ N/D '88

A talk with the new commander in chief. R. Rosenblatt and others. il por *U.S. News & World Report* 106:27 Ja 30 '89

Tar baby. F. Barnes. *The New Republic* 200:12-13 F 13 '89

Teflon II. F. Barnes. *The New Republic* 201:11-13 Jl 10 '89

"There's been a certain liberation" [interview] S. Talbott and others. il por *Time* 133:26 Ja 30 '89

This is 'ready on day one'? T. M. DeFrank and others. por *Newsweek* 114:30 O 23 '89

Vic Damone in Eastern Europe. J. Klein. il por map *New York* 22:24-5 N 27 '89

Welcome to the Bushes'. D. Radcliffe. il pors *The Saturday Evening Post* 261:42+ N/D '89

What Bush should do. R. J. Samuelson. il *Newsweek* 113:45 Ja 23 '89

What can we expect from George Bush? J. Walljasper. il pors *Utne Reader* p142-3 Mr/Ap '89

What liberals haven't learned & why. F. F. Siegel. il *Commonweal* 116:16-20 Ja 13 '89

Where's George? J. Klein. il por *New York* 22:24-5 Ap 24 '89

A White House of many mansions. D. Baer. il por *U.S. News & World Report* 106:14-17 Ja 23 '89

Why George Bush should break his promise. C. W. Colson. il *Christianity Today* 33:64 Ap 7 '89

Why I am not Ronald Reagan, by G. Bush. E. Clift. il por *Newsweek* 113:18 F 20 '89

Why the Democrats lost again. J. Muravchik. *Commentary* 87:13-22 F '89

Will the allies leave Bush behind? B. Javetski and D. Griffiths. il pors *Business Week* p30-1 My 15 '89

A working holiday. H. Mackenzie. il pors *Maclean's* 102:10-11 S 11 '89

The world is waiting for Bush to lead. B. Javetski and J. Pearson. il *Business Week* p86-7 Je 5 '89

Yale's most famous graduate [interview] il por *U.S. News & World Report* 107:68 O 16 '89

The year of living timorously. G. Borger. il por *U.S. News & World Report* 107:26-7 N 13 '89

Addresses, messages, etc.

Andean strategy [antidrug plan] H. Jensen. il por *Maclean's* 102:26-8 S 18 '89

The big drug bust. *America* 161:155 S 23 '89

Big man on campus [commencement addresses] F. Barnes. *The New Republic* 200:13-14 Je 5 '89

Drugs, lies & TV [televised war on drugs speech] R. Clark. *The Nation* 249:408-9 O 16 '89

Hoping for more market magic [budget address] L. Reibstein. il por *Newsweek* 113:32-3 F 20 '89

'A journey into tomorrow' [speech on space program] J. Schwartz and M. Hager. il por *Newsweek* 114:31 Jl 31 '89

Letter from Washington [televised address on war on drugs] E. Drew. *The New Yorker* 65:102-4 O 2 '89

Notes and comment [address on the drug problem] *The New Yorker* 65:33-4 S 18 '89

Now it's Bush's war [televised address on drugs] T. Morganthau. il pors *Newsweek* 114:22-4 S 18 '89

BUSH, GEORGE, 1924—Addresses, messages, etc.—*cont.*
Reaganomics with a human face. W. Shapiro. il por *Time* 133:32-4 F 20 '89
The struggle with ourselves [war against drugs] H. Sidey. il por *Time* 134:32 S 18 '89

Anecdotes, facetiae, satire, etc.
Back in the tall cotton. M. Ivins. il por *The Progressive* 53:40 Mr '89
Exhaust-op and the p.-rind flap. D. McGrath. il por *The Nation* 249:456-8 O 23 '89
A grateful nation [small problems and annoyances that G. Bush should solve] C. Murphy. il *The Atlantic* 263:16+ Ja '89
How the savings and loans were saved. G. Keillor. *The New Yorker* 65:42 O 16 '89
A midwinter's nightmare: looking back on the Bush years. A. S. Blinder. il *Business Week* p22 Ja 23 '89
My reply to George. B. Ehrenreich. il *Mother Jones* 14:7-8 F/Mr '89
Now, something completely different. R. N. Perle. il *U.S. News & World Report* 106:31 Je 12 '89
Ode to a silver foot: a sampler of Bushspeak. il por *Newsweek* 113:40 My 29 '89
Pro-life pro. P. Roth. il *The New York Review of Books* 36:5 Ag 17 '89

Caricatures and cartoons
From CIA to KGB (kinder, gentler Bush) [cover story] M. Ivins. il por *Mother Jones* 14:32-7 Ap '89

Clothing and dress
Pomp and circumstance. R. La Ferla. il pors *The New York Times Magazine* p80-1 Ap 30 '89
The president's haberdasher [Arthur A. Adler men's shop] D. Wise. il *Gentlemen's Quarterly* 59:35+ My '89

Correspondence
Anecdotes, facetiae, satire, etc.
Dear Willie Horton [imaginary thank-you notes] J. Bennet. *The New Republic* 200:15-16 Ja 30 '89

Financial disclosure
The president and his money. G. Anrig, Jr. il pors *Money* 18:81-2+ Je '89

Homes
The Bushes of Kennebunkport [interview with B. Bush] D. Kazanjian. il pors *House & Garden* 161:140-5 Je '89

Inaugural address
Go fly a kite. H. Fairlie. *The New Republic* 200:16-17 F 13 '89
Inaugural address [January 20, 1989] G. Bush. *Vital Speeches of the Day* 55:258-60 F 15 '89
The inaugural address of President Bush [January 20, 1989; cover story] G. Bush. il por *Department of State Bulletin* 89:1-3 Ap '89
Marking Bush's inaugural. W. Safire. il *The New York Times Magazine* p10+ F 5 '89
Mr. Bush lifts off. *National Review* 41:13-14 F 24 '89
The nice age. H. Hertzberg. *The New Republic* 200:4 F 13 '89

Inauguration
All hat and no cows. A. Stanley. il *Vogue* 179:462 Ap '89
Attaché case full of blues. G. Hirshey. il pors *Rolling Stone* p19-20 Mr 9 '89
Blacks slated for major participation in inaugural. il *Jet* 75:12-13 Ja 23 '89
Bush bash. A. Ferguson. il *The American Spectator* 22:33+ Mr '89
Bush inaugural events symbolic of the change in new administration [special section] il pors *Jet* 75:4-14+ F 6 '89
Bush promises 'a new breeze'. L. B. Randolph. il pors *Ebony* 44:132-4+ Ap '89
Bush reaches out [special section] il pors *Newsweek* 113:22-9+ Ja 30 '89
A celebration of power. M. McDonald. il pors *Maclean's* 102:20-2 Ja 30 '89
Feather dusters. T. Noah. *The New Republic* 200:42 F 13 '89
First in 200 years: black generals head military at Bush's inaugural ceremony. il por *Jet* 75:24-5 Ja 23 '89
Grand kids. il pors *Life* 12:36-8+ Mr '89
Homeless couple given $50 tickets to attend a coveted inaugural ball [R. and V. Gaines] il pors *Jet* 75:14 F 13 '89
The inauguration [cover story; special section] il pors *U.S. News & World Report* 106:18-22+ Ja 30 '89
"A new breeze is blowing" [cover story; special section] il pors *Time* 133:16-21+ Ja 30 '89
Notes and comment. *The New Yorker* 64:23-4 F 6 '89
Quadrennial. *The New Yorker* 64:24-5 F 13 '89
Rhythm & blue bloods. P. J. O'Rourke. il *Rolling Stone* p43+ Mr 9 '89

Anecdotes, facetiae, satire, etc.
From CIA to KGB (kinder, gentler Bush) [cover story] M. Ivins. il por *Mother Jones* 14:32-7 Ap '89
Schlock City. A. Heard. *The New Republic* 200:13-14 F 13 '89

Language
My sentence-fragment thing. *Harper's* 279:16-18 Ag '89

Read his lips? Sometimes you have to read the president's mind to find out what he really means. M. Neill. il *People Weekly* 32:94-5 O 2 '89

Pets
Millie's six-pack [cover story] B. Bush. il pors *Life* 12:32-4+ My '89

Press relations
Bush and the media. B. Kantrowitz. por *Newsweek* 113:5 Ja 9 '89
Bush undoes pummeling pundits by his candor, humor, happiness. M. S. Forbes. *Forbes* 143:19-20 My 15 '89
Covering the Bush White House. L. Zuckerman. il *Time* 133:54-5 Ja 30 '89
George Bush's dirty big secrets [stories ignored by the establishment press] il *Utne Reader* p59-60 S/O '89
Hardship post. F. Barnes. *The New Republic* 200:7-9 My 8 '89
Malice toward none. M. Newman. il *The New Republic* 200:16-17 F 20 '89
Meet Brit Hume, ABC's newest rising star. A. Stanley. il por *Vogue* 179:106 Jl '89
Memo to President Bush: how to use TV—and keep from being abused by it. R. M. Nixon. il pors *TV Guide* 37:26-7+ Ja 14-20 '89
The not-playing-for-prime-time presidency. K. T. Walsh. il por *U.S. News & World Report* 106:22-3 Ap 17 '89
Playing the media game. T. M. DeFrank. il pors *Newsweek* 113:21 Ap 17 '89
The president and the press. J. Alter. il por *Newsweek* 113:68 F 6 '89
The press and the prez (a stormy affair). B. G. Harrison. *Mademoiselle* 95:82 Je '89
Read my cliché. L. Zuckerman. il por *Time* 133:64 Ja 16 '89
Smile, and sharpen your knives. H. Sidey. il *Time* 133:33 F 6 '89
Why Bush's press strategy is failing. M. Hertsgaard. il *Rolling Stone* p83-4 Jl 13-27 '89
Winkle-pickers of the press. W. Safire. il *The New York Times Magazine* p16+ Jl 9 '89

Public relations
The art of presidential persuasion. M. L. Whicker and T. W. Areson. il *USA Today (Periodical)* 117:12-14 My '89
Black leaders gather at White House to discuss their concerns with Bush. il por *Jet* 77:26 D 11 '89
The by-the-numbers presidency. F. Barnes. il *The New Republic* 201:34+ N 6 '89
Caving in. F. Barnes. *The New Republic* 201:8+ Jl 17-24 '89
Counterpunching Gorbachev [Bush's policies overshadowed by Soviet arms proposals on eve of NATO summit] S. V. Roberts. il por *U.S. News & World Report* 106:16-17 My 29 '89
Eichmann with a smile [comments on U.S. aid to El Salvador] *The Nation* 249:701 D 11 '89
Escape from the inferno. J. Friedman. il pors *People Weekly* 31:32-7 Mr 27 '89
The honeymoon's still on: a Newsweek poll. il *Newsweek* 113:27 Mr 20 '89
The "just folks" presidency. H. Sidey. il por *Time* 133:24 Ap 17 '89
The moment-maker [S. Rogich] F. Barnes. *The New Republic* 201:11-12 D 11 '89
What they say about Bush [cover story; special section] il *World Press Review* 36:11-14+ S '89

Reading
Merry Christmas, Mr. President! L. Eisenberg. il *Esquire* 112:37+ D '89

Relations with Congress
The 30¢ gap [minimum wage bill vetoed] por *Time* 133:58 Je 26 '89
Alan Keyes. A. Keyes. il *National Review* 41:27-8 F 10 '89
The big schmooze. F. Barnes. *The New Republic* 200:10+ Mr 13 '89
The blame game begins [budget] D. Goodgame. il por *Time* 133:26 Ja 16 '89
Blink or go broke [budget battles] *Time* 134:68 N 20 '89
A budget deal in record time. D. Pauly. il *Newsweek* 113:36 Ap 24 '89
Bush and Congress: budget ballet. L. Smith. *Fortune* 119:8 Mr 13 '89
Bush plays budget chicken. E. Salholz. il por *Newsweek* 113:26-7 Ja 16 '89
Bush pulls a Clean-Air victory out of the air. V. Cahan and R. Fly. *Business Week* p43 O 2 '89
Bush risks his chips on Tower. T. M. DeFrank. il *Newsweek* 113:19 F 20 '89
Bush v. Congress: a formula. W. F. Buckley. *National Review* 41:55 Mr 24 '89
Bush's budget test. A. J. Glass. il *The New Leader* 72:3-4 F 20 '89
Bush's cautious spending plans. M. McDonald. *Maclean's* 102:12 F 20 '89
Bush's fence-sitting has both sides throwing stones. D. Harbrecht and others. il *Business Week* p90 N 27 '89
By George, it's me [photos of congressmen in the Lincoln Bedroom taken by G. Bush] il *Life* 12:84-5 Ap '89

BUSH, GEORGE, 1924—Relations with Congress—*cont.*
Capital gains: as the Democrats squabble, Bush may score. D. Harbrecht and R. Fly. il *Business Week* p58 S 25 '89

Capitol showdown [with editorial comment by Kevin Doyle] M. Nemeth. il pors *Maclean's* 102:2, 22-3 Mr 6 '89

Congress II. *National Review* 41:13 D 31 '89

Darman: the collapse of a grand strategy. E. Clift. por *Newsweek* 114:54 N 20 '89

Did Darman diddle while the deficit burned? H. Gleckman. il por *Business Week* p56-7 D 11 '89

The Dodd Doctrine [bipartisan accord on aid to contras] W. McGurn. il *National Review* 41:27-8 S 15 '89

Fearless leader. F. Barnes. *The New Republic* 201:11-13 N 27 '89

Fetal position. Z. R. Eisenstein. *The Nation* 249:588-9 N 20 '89

For now, the Chinese students can stay [veto of legislation to extend visas of Chinese students] P. Wingert and D. Waller. il *Newsweek* 114:98 D 11 '89

Has Bush blown his best chance for progress on the deficit? H. Gleckman. il *Business Week* p39 My 1 '89

Holier than everyone [J. Tower nomination as Secretary of Defense reviewed in the Senate] L. Martz. il por *Newsweek* 113:22-3 Mr 13 '89

In the wake of the Tower wars. G. Borger. il pors *U.S. News & World Report* 106:44-6 Mr 13 '89

Is this goodbye? [Defense Secretary nomination of J. Tower rejected by Senate Armed Services Committee; cover story; special section] il pors *Time* 133:18-22+ Mr 6 '89

Legislating deficit cuts. W. Lowther. il *Maclean's* 102:53 My 1 '89

Let him have it [line item veto] M. Kinsley. *The New Republic* 201:4+ N 20 '89

Let's make a deal. J. D. Isaacs. il *The Bulletin of the Atomic Scientists* 45:3 Je '89

Letter from Washington. Cato. *National Review* 41:11 Mr 10 '89

Letter from Washington. Cato. *National Review* 41:11 Ja 27 '89

Letter from Washington [Defense Secretary nominee J. Tower's confirmation fight] E. Drew. *The New Yorker* 65:97-100+ Mr 20 '89

Letter from Washington [budget] Cato. *National Review* 41:12 F 24 '89

The limits of bipartisanship [deal over contra aid] *National Review* 41:12 Ap 21 '89

Listen, can we talk? [economic program] L. Reibstein. il *Newsweek* 113:46-7 Mr 27 '89

Lloyd Bentsen is having a ball bashing George Bush. D. Harbrecht and H. Gleckman. il por *Business Week* p57 O 23 '89

Lucky George. F. Barnes. *The New Republic* 201:9-10 D 18 '89

Missed opportunity [decision not to submit a recess appointment of W. Lucas as head of Justice Department's Civil Rights Division] *National Review* 41:14 S 15 '89

A new Congress gets down to business. S. Manning. il por *Scholastic Update (Teachers' edition)* 121:6-8 F 24 '89

Newtered [N. Gingrich] F. Barnes. il *The New Republic* 200:8-10 Ap 24 '89

Now for the hard part. F. Barnes. *The New Republic* 201:13-14 Ag 21 '89

An overture to Congress. M. G. Warner. il por *Newsweek* 113:26 Ja 23 '89

The Reagan difference. *National Review* 41:14 Ap 7 '89

Reagan's budget, Bush's battle. H. Gleckman. il *Business Week* p32-4 Ja 23 '89

'Republicans are thirsting for blood' [hard feelings over J. Tower nomination] R. Fly and D. Harbrecht. il por *Business Week* p39 Mr 20 '89

The rise and rise of George Bush [dealing with the Democrats] D. Gergen and K. T. Walsh. il por *U.S. News & World Report* 107:25+ S 18 '89

Rostenkowski adds a twist to the tax tango. H. Gleckman. il *Business Week* p61 Je 26 '89

Saint George and the congressional dragon [opposition to J. Tower nomination] *National Review* 41:10-11 Mr 24 '89

Secretary's interview on "This week with David Brinkley" [deal over contra aid; interview with J. A. Baker; transcript of program, March 26, 1989] *Department of State Bulletin* 89:25-7 My '89

A setback for Bush [Senate rejects J. Tower nomination] J. Bierman. il pors *Maclean's* 102:34-5 Mr 20 '89

Ship of fools. *The Progressive* 53:7-8 Mr '89

So much for bipartisanship [J. Tower nomination as Secretary of Defense] R. Lacayo. il pors *Time* 133:20-1 Mr 13 '89

Storming the Tower. G. Borger. il pors *U.S. News & World Report* 106:37-9 Mr 6 '89

Tax paranoia is causing gridlock on the Hill. H. Gleckman. il *Business Week* p43 My 29 '89

Time for make-nice politics [bipartisanship] G. Borger. il por *U.S. News & World Report* 106:22-3 F 6 '89

To Congress, Bush looked like a pushover. D. Harbrecht and R. Fly. il *Business Week* p27-8 Ag 21 '89

Tory budget, Whig reasoning [Bush budget] *National Review* 41:11 Mr 24 '89

The Tower precedent [rejection of J. Tower as Defense Secretary] S. Garment. *Commentary* 87:42-8 My '89

Tower's troubles [Secretary of Defense-designate's confirmation fight; cover story] T. Morganthau. il pors *Newsweek* 113:16-20+ Mr 6 '89

Trouble on the home front [attempt at bipartisanship in foreign relations] S. Talbott. il *Time* 133:45 F 20 '89

U.S. support for democracy and peace in Central America [bipartisan accord; statements and text of accord, March 24, 1989; texts of joint declarations of Central American presidents, January 16, 1988 and February 14, 1989; cover story] G. Bush. il por map *Department of State Bulletin* 89:55-9 Je '89

'Voodoo economics' in Washington [bipartisan budget agreement] *U.S. News & World Report* 106:16+ Ap 24 '89

Wait till next year [budget deal] W. Shapiro. il por *Time* 133:19 Ap 24 '89

Washington notebook. D. Schorr. il *The New Leader* 72:3-4 Mr 6 '89

White House, Hill clash over airline takeovers [with editorial comment] M. Mecham. *Aviation Week & Space Technology* 131:7, 16-17 O 23 '89

Who's afraid of George Bush? R. Fly and others. il por *Business Week* p30-1 F 20 '89

Why Bush's trickle-up theory is sailing through Congress. H. Gleckman and D. Harbrecht. il *Business Week* p47 O 16 '89

Religion
Religion in the Bush White House. R. G. Hutcheson. *The Christian Century* 106:37-8 Ja 18 '89

White House religion. K. A. Lawton. il por *Christianity Today* 33:36-7 F 17 '89

Speechwriters and speechwriting
Get me rewrite [need for G. Bush to improve foreign policy speeches] M. Kondracke. *The New Republic* 200:10+ Je 12 '89

High Noonan. M. Dowd. il por *Vogue* 179:338-41 D '89

Read Bush's lips. J. Saltzman. il *USA Today (Periodical)* 117:15 My '89

Sports
Anecdotes, facetiae, satire, etc.
Tackling the Bush pentathlon. H. Hurt. il pors *Newsweek* 114:21-2 Ag 21 '89

Staff
Back to the party of Lincoln? [G. Bush courts blacks and appoints L. W. Sullivan as Secretary of Health and Human Services] R. Lacayo. il pors *Time* 133:79 Ja 2 '89

Blacks in the Bush administration. S. Booker. il pors *Ebony* 44:42+ Jl '89

Bush: a ladies' man? P. Simpson. *Ms.* 18:67+ O '89

Bush breaks tradition and names many black advisers. il por *Jet* 75:7 F 27 '89

The Bush league. F. Barnes. il *Vogue* 179:292+ Ap '89

Bush makes some science appointments. B. J. Culliton and E. Marshall. il por *Science* 243:24 Ja 6 '89

Bush rolls right. F. Barnes. *The New Republic* 200:9-10 F 6 '89

Bush's black appointees. il *American Visions* 4:14-15 Ag '89

Bush's farmer in the White House [C. Evans] G. Vincent. il por *Successful Farming* 87:34AF mid-F '89

Cashing in on kiss-and-tell. M. Greenfield. il *Newsweek* 113:70 Ja 23 '89

The conservative vicar of domestic policy [J. Sununu] K. T. Walsh. *U.S. News & World Report* 107:27 O 9 '89

Empty-office syndrome is hurting Bush's mandate. R. Fly. il *Business Week* p37 Je 12 '89

Enter the Bush team. L. Walczak and R. Fly. il por *Business Week* p24-6 Ja 30 '89

Fraudulence I. R. E. Tyrrell. il *The American Spectator* 22:10 Ap '89

The great right hope [J. Sununu; cover story] P. Osterlund. il *National Review* 41:24-6 Mr 24 '89

Help wanted: 3,000 appointees. Right-wing purity not required. R. Fly. *Business Week* p49 Ja 23 '89

'Help wanted' at the White House. il *Newsweek* 113:25 Je 5 '89

How Bush is keeping the radical right inside the tent. R. Fly. il *Business Week* p45 Je 19 '89

John Sununu: the right-hand man. D. Tibbetts. il pors *Conservative Digest* 15:43+ Ja/F '89

Off on the wrong foot [legal counsel C. B. Gray] B. Turque and A. McDaniel. il por *Newsweek* 113:30+ Ap 10 '89

Politics. F. Barnes. *Vogue* 179:144 Je '89

The restoration. J. Klein. il pors *New York* 22:14+ Ja 23 '89

Seeing Crimson. D. Wisenberg. il *Common Cause Magazine* 15:7 S/O '89

Sununu and improved [J. Sununu] F. Barnes. il *The New Republic* 200:13-14 My 29 '89

Sununu: the making of a scapegoat. E. Salholz. il por *Newsweek* 113:23 Mr 13 '89

The trying times of John Sununu. D. Baer. il pors *U.S. News & World Report* 106:49-50 Mr 13 '89

BUSH, GEORGE, 1924—Staff—cont.

Wanted: a few good leaders for the Bush team. R. Fly. il *Business Week* p25 Mr 6 '89

With friends like these . . . [criticism of former president R. Reagan] B. Turque. il por *Newsweek* 113:40 Ap 24 '89

With Sununu, a different story? Cato. *National Review* 41:26 My 5 '89

Young black aides at White House highlight change of new Bush administration. il por *Jet* 76:8 My 1 '89
Anecdotes, facetiae, satire, etc.

Jockey, scheme and pray. S. Waldman. il *Newsweek* 113:24 Ap 3 '89

Visit to Belgium, 1989

Arrival remarks, Brussels, May 28, 1989. G. Bush. il por *Department of State Bulletin* 89:15-16 Ag '89

Visit to Canada, 1989

In Reagan's footsteps. T. Tedesco. il por *Maclean's* 102:14 F 6 '89

President's visit to Canada [remarks and news conferences, February 10, 1989] G. Bush; B. Mulroney; J. A. Baker. il pors *Department of State Bulletin* 89:26-31 Ap '89

A symbolic visit. T. Tedesco. il por *Maclean's* 102:10-12 F 20 '89

Visit to China, 1989

An act of defiance [dissenter Fang Lizhi barred from state dinner; cover story] O. Schell. il pors *The New York Times Magazine* p26-7+ Ap 16 '89

Beijing [interviews, statement, etc., February 16-27, 1989] il pors *Department of State Bulletin* 89:10-17 My '89

Chinese bar physicist from Bush dinner [dissident Fang Lizhi] M. Sun. il por *Science* 243:1282 Mr 10 '89

The furious flap over Fang Lizhi [Washington and Beijing clash over Chinese dissident] S. MacLeod. por *Time* 133:38 Mr 13 '89

Notes and comment [exclusion of Fang Lizhi from G. Bush's banquet in Beijing] *The New Yorker* 65:34-5 Mr 20 '89

Visit to East Asia, 1989

Bush faces life in Asia. L. Martz. il por *Newsweek* 113:28-30 Mr 6 '89

President's trip to Japan, China, and South Korea [special section] G. Bush. il pors *Department of State Bulletin* 89:1-22 My '89

Visit to Europe, 1989

Affable abroad. F. Barnes. *The New Republic* 201:11-12 Ag 7-14 '89

From patrons to partners. W. Isaacson. il por *Time* 134:19 Jl 24 '89

George Bush: what I did on my summer vacation [call for European unity] *National Review* 41:10-11 Ag 18 '89

The green summit. L. Martz. il *Newsweek* 114:12-15 Jl 24 '89

President Bush visits Europe [special section] G. Bush. il pors *Department of State Bulletin* 89:22-53 S '89
Reporters and reporting

CS. F. Barnes. *The New Republic* 201:42 Ag 7-14 '89

Visit to France, 1989

Mellow George and the don't worry, be happy summit. R. Fly and B. Riemer. por *Business Week* p32 Jl 31 '89

Summit of the Arch [Paris summit; cover story; special section] il pors *Department of State Bulletin* 89:1-21 S '89

Visit to Germany (West), 1989

Remarks and question-and-answer session, Bonn, May 30, 1989. H. Kohl. *Department of State Bulletin* 89:33-4 Ag '89

United States and NATO [address, May 31, 1989] G. Bush. *Vital Speeches of the Day* 55:546-9 Jl 1 '89

Visit to Great Britain, 1989

Remarks and question-and-answer session, London, June 1, 1989. M. Thatcher. il pors *Department of State Bulletin* 89:40-1 Ag '89

Secretary Baker's news briefing, London, June, 1, 1989. J. A. Baker, III. il pors *Department of State Bulletin* 89:41-4 Ag '89

Visit to Hungary, 1989

A bloc turned upside down. H. Anderson. il por map *Newsweek* 114:30-3 Jl 17 '89

High-wire act. H. Sidey. il pors *Time* 134:16-18 Jl 24 '89

Hungary for love. F. Barnes. *The New Republic* 201:8-10 Jl 31 '89

President Bush visits Europe [special section] G. Bush. il pors *Department of State Bulletin* 89:22-53 S '89

Unquiet on the Eastern front. D. Stanglin. il map *U.S. News & World Report* 107:31-3 Jl 17 '89

Wooing the East. H. Jensen. il pors *Maclean's* 102:22-3 Jl 24 '89

Visit to Italy, 1989

Arrival remarks, Rome, May 26, 1989; Dinner toast, Rome, May 27, 1989. G. Bush. *Department of State Bulletin* 89:11-12 Ag '89

Visit to Japan, 1989

Bush faces life in Asia. L. Martz. il por *Newsweek* 113:28-30 Mr 6 '89

Bush's bow to Japan. R. J. Samuelson. il *Newsweek* 113:37 F 6 '89

Tokyo [news conferences, etc., February 16-25, 1989] G. Bush. il pors *Department of State Bulletin* 89:1-9 My '89

Visit to Korea (South), 1989

Has Bush helped paint Roh into a corner? L. Nakarmi. il pors *Business Week* p61-2 Mr 13 '89

Seoul [remarks, address, etc. February 16-27, 1989] G. Bush. il pors *Department of State Bulletin* 89:17-22 My '89

Visit to Poland, 1989

A bloc turned upside down. H. Anderson. il por map *Newsweek* 114:30-3 Jl 17 '89

Economy tour. *The Nation* 249:155-6 Ag 7-14 '89

High-wire act. H. Sidey. il pors *Time* 134:16-18 Jl 24 '89

Hungary for love. F. Barnes. *The New Republic* 201:8-10 Jl 31 '89

A July surprise for Gorby? B. Javetski and R. Fly. il por *Business Week* p60-2 Jl 17 '89

Lack of Solidarity [cover story] J. D. Sachs. *The New Republic* 201:20-1 Ag 7-14 '89

President Bush visits Europe [special section] G. Bush. il pors *Department of State Bulletin* 89:22-53 S '89

Unquiet on the Eastern front. D. Stanglin. il map *U.S. News & World Report* 107:31-3 Jl 17 '89

Wooing the East. H. Jensen. il pors *Maclean's* 102:22-3 Jl 24 '89

Reporters and reporting

Now starring 'President Bush'. A. Cockburn. *The Nation* 249:194 Ag 21-28 '89

Visit to the Netherlands, 1989

President's remarks to residents, Leiden, July 17, 1989. G. Bush. il pors *Department of State Bulletin* 89:47-9 S '89

Secretary Baker's and Foreign Minister van den Broek's news conference, The Hague, July 17, 1989. J. A. Baker; H. van den Broek. *Department of State Bulletin* 89:50-3 S '89

Visit to Western Europe, 1989

After the NATO summit: challenges for the West in a changing world [address and excerpts from question-and-answer session, June 8, 1989] J. A. Baker, III. *Department of State Bulletin* 89:55-61 Ag '89

Bush and NATO [Brussels summit] il *World Press Review* 36:8 Jl '89

Bush includes combat aircraft cuts in NATO arms proposal [Brussels summit; special section] il map *Aviation Week & Space Technology* 130:16-21 Je 5 '89

Bush makes his mark [peace initiative at NATO summit] J. Bierman. il por *Maclean's* 102:24-5+ Je 12 '89

Bush pulls one out of a hat [arms proposal at NATO summit] B. Javetski. il por *Business Week* p22-3 Je 12 '89

Bush's bold bid to rescue NATO [U.S. troop cuts] H. Trewhitt. il por *U.S. News & World Report* 106:26-9 Je 12 '89

Bush's chintzy offer at Vienna [conventional arms reductions] R. Leavitt. *The Bulletin of the Atomic Scientists* 45:13 O '89

Bush's new look for the NATO alliance [troop reduction proposal] H. Anderson. il por *Newsweek* 113:34-5 Je 12 '89

By the numbers [arms proposals at NATO summit] *The Nation* 248:835-6 Je 19 '89

Challenges ahead for NATO and developments in East-West relations [statement, June 20, 1989] J. A. Baker, III. *Department of State Bulletin* 89:61-4 Ag '89

Crowing before sunrise [NATO summit] *Commonweal* 116:355-6 Je 16 '89

"Here we go, on the offensive" [troop reduction initiative at NATO meeting] G. J. Church. il por *Time* 133:28-31+ Je 12 '89

The NATO compromise: dangerous. *National Review* 41:12-13 Je 30 '89

One for the Gipper [proposals at NATO summit] il *The New Republic* 200:7-8 Je 19 '89

President visits Europe; attends North Atlantic Council meeting [cover story; special section] G. Bush. il pors *Department of State Bulletin* 89:11-45 Ag '89

Secretary's news conference [May 23, 1989] J. A. Baker, III. *Department of State Bulletin* 89:21-4 Jl '89

BUSH, GEORGE W.

about

Another winner for the Bush family? K. Kelly. il por *Business Week* p166 My 22 '89

The brothers Bush. M. Hosenball. *The New Republic* 200:19-21 Ap 3 '89

Junior is his own Bush now. L. I. Barrett. il por *Time* 134:60-2 Jl 31 '89

BUSH, JEB

The capital gains mandate. il *The American Spectator* 22:32 Je '89

How to keep pressure on the Sandinistas. il *The American Spectator* 22:16-17 Jl '89

about

The brothers Bush. M. Hosenball. *The New Republic* 200:19-21 Ap 3 '89

BUSH, MARVIN

My second chance. il pors *Ladies' Home Journal* 106:138-9+ Mr '89

BUSH, NEIL
about
The brothers Bush. M. Hosenball. *The New Republic* 200:19-21 Ap 3 '89

BUSH, PRESCOTT S., 1895-1972
about
Old bland-dad. T. Noah. *The New Republic* 200:17-19 Ap 3 '89

BUSH (BARBARA) FOUNDATION FOR FAMILY LITERACY *See* Barbara Bush Foundation for Family Literacy

BUSH FAMILY
about
The Bush clan: inaugurating a new family dynasty? E. Clift. il *Newsweek* 113:24-5 Ja 23 '89
A First Family that just won't quit [cover story] S. Schindehette. il *People Weekly* 31:52-3+ Ja 30 '89
Grand kids. il pors *Life* 12:36-8+ Mr '89
A pride of would-be pols. G. Borger. il *U.S. News & World Report* 106:32-3 Ja 30 '89

BUSH-GORBACHEV SUMMIT CONFERENCE, 1989
After the Malta summit; A rusting Iron Curtain. J. Bierman. il *Maclean's* 102:30-3 D 11 '89
As the world turns. *Commonweal* 116:612-13 N 17 '89
A burial for the cold war at sea? D. Stanglin. il *U.S. News & World Report* 107:18-19+ D 4 '89
Bush's summit favors to Gorbachev. R. N. Perle. il *U.S. News & World Report* 107:27 D 18 '89
A chance to redraw the map. J. Barry. il *Newsweek* 114:49 N 20 '89
Designing 'a new era' [with interview with G. Bush] T. M. DeFrank and A. McDaniel. il *Newsweek* 114:22-4 D 18 '89
Easier said than done [goals set at Malta] M. Duffy. il *Time* 134:36-8 D 18 '89
Europe's grand drama: waiting for Bush to make his entrance. B. Javetski. il *Business Week* p66+ N 27 '89
The events in Eastern Europe [address, November 22, 1989] G. Bush. *Vital Speeches of the Day* 56:130-2 D 15 '89
A game of one-on-one. H. Sidey. il *Time* 134:38 D 18 '89
Getting behind Gorby. B. Javetski and D. Harbrecht. il *Business Week* p40-2 N 13 '89
Going to meet the man. M. Duffy. il *Time* 134:30-1 D 4 '89
The goodies Gorbachev brought home from Malta. R. Brady. il *Business Week* p42-3 D 18 '89
Heading toward an early summit. R. Watson. il *Newsweek* 114:28-9 S 18 '89
How to deal with Gorbachev. W. F. Buckley. *National Review* 41:54 D 31 '89
Malta summit [special section] il *Newsweek* 114:34-42+ D 4 '89
No time for showboating. R. Watson. il *Newsweek* 114:30-1 N 27 '89
Pax Bush. B. Javetski and D. Harbrecht. il *Business Week* p40-1 D 18 '89
The road to Malta. S. Talbott. il *Time* 134:32+ D 4 '89
The saltwater summit. G. J. Church. il *Time* 134:32-5 N 13 '89
The seaborne summit meeting. A. Bilski. *Maclean's* 102:28 N 13 '89
Star of Malta [G. Bush] F. Barnes. *The New Republic* 201:12-13 D 25 '89
The summit on the sea. R. Watson. il *Newsweek* 114:50-1 N 13 '89
Summits of '89. il *The New Republic* 201:7-9 D 25 '89
Super partners [cover story; special section] il *Newsweek* 114:28-36+ D 11 '89
Turning visions into reality [cover story; special section] il *Time* 134:34-42+ D 11 '89
What Gorbachev wants from the summit at sea. J. Trimble. il *U.S. News & World Report* 107:22-3 N 13 '89
The winds of Malta. *America* 161:440 D 16 '89
Terminology
Floating naming game. W. Safire. il *The New York Times Magazine* p16+ N 26 '89

BUSHELL, RANDY J.
about
When it sounds too good to be true. G. Slutsker. il *Forbes* 143:256-7 Je 26 '89

BUSHNELL, CANDACE
Dating for dollars: the gold diggers of 1989. il *Mademoiselle* 95:176-7 N '89
From the heartland. il *Health (New York, N.Y.)* 21:62-5+ Jl '89
Grand illusions. il *Health (New York, N.Y.)* 21:72-7+ S '89
Hot times from 9 to 5: the new social life is strictly an office affair. il *Mademoiselle* 95:162-3+ Jl '89
The language of brows. il *Health (New York, N.Y.)* 21:62-7 F '89
The no-regrets ultimatum. il *Mademoiselle* 95:186+ Ap '89
Visionary facts, visible differences [cover story] il *Health (New York, N.Y.)* 21:66-73 D '89

BUSHNELL, PETER G., AND HOLLAND, KIM N.
Tunas. il *Sea Frontiers* 35:42-8 Ja/F '89

BUSINESS
See also
Advertising
Aged and business
Airplanes in business
Big business
Capitalism
Christmas business
Competition
Computers—Business use
Conflict of interests (Business)
Corporations
Entrepreneurs
Goodwill in business
Home-based business
Humor in business
Ideas in business
Image processing—Business use
Industry
Information systems—Business use
Inventories
Location in business and industry
Mail order business
New Age movement and business
Photocopying—Business use
Real estate business
Retail trade
Selling
Sex in business
Sex oriented business
Small business
Stock exchanges
Tape recordings—Business use
Telecommunication in business
Telephone in business
Trade marks and trade names
Trucks in business
Video games—Business use
Videotapes—Business use
Word processors and processing—Business use
Youth and business

Business week's 1989 hip parade. il *Business Week* p37 Ja 16 '89
Most of '88. il *Time* 133:88 Ja 2 '89
Awards
See also
Malcolm Baldrige National Quality Award
Small Business Person of the Year Awards
Bibliography
Books & business [special section] il *The New York Times Book Review* 94:25-8+ O 29 '89
Rating the season's business books [Canada] P. C. Newman. il *Maclean's* 102:48 D 11 '89
The ten best business books of the year. D. Demong. il *Business Week* p18+ D 11 '89
Conferences
Anecdotes, facetiae, satire, etc.
Enduring conferences. M. Skapinker. il *World Press Review* 36:50 Mr '89
Finance
See Corporations—Finance
History
Advice to small companies: think big [interview with A. D. Chandler] R. Koselka. il por *Forbes* 144:204-5+ N 13 '89
Business: the decade of the deal [1980s] J. Egan. il *U.S. News & World Report* 107:98 D 25 '89-Ja 1 '90
A new era of rapid rise and ruin [past five years' departures from Fortune 500] J. P. Newport, Jr. il *Fortune* 119:77+ Ap 24 '89
Photographs and photography
Sixty years of American business: an anniversary photo essay. il *Business Week* pP1-P32 S 25 '89
Information services
Risks and opportunities for international business [study by Frost & Sullivan's Political Risk Services] il *USA Today (Periodical)* 118:5 Ag '89
International aspects
See also
Banks and banking, International
Corporations, International
Export-import trade
B-schools get a global vision. J. Main. il *Fortune* 120:78-80+ Jl 17 '89
Blunders abroad. C. F. Valentine. il *Nation's Business* 77:54+ Mr '89
Going global. il *Business Week* Special Issue:9-16+ O 20 '89
How 21 men got global in 35 days [Noel Tichy's Global Leadership Program] J. Main. il *Fortune* 120:71+ N 6 '89
Irresistible international revolution [views of W. Wriston] M. Magnet. por *Fortune* 120:66-7 Jl 3 '89
When in Tokyo . . . F. Marsh. *World Press Review* 36:55 My '89
Periodicals
See also
American City Business Journals, Inc.

BUSINESS—Periodicals—See also—*cont.*
  Business week
  Financial planning (Periodical)
  Financial times of Canada
  Forbes (Periodical)
  House organs
  Wall Street journal
    Anecdotes, facetiae, satire, etc.
Is it coercive, mimetic and normative? [academic journals]
  J. Queenan. il *Forbes* 144:237+ O 16 '89
    Political aspects
    See also
  Chamber of Commerce of the United States of America
  Industry and state
  Lobbyists and lobbying
  Political action committees
Business: applaud the cooperation, but be prepared for the
  conflict. *Nation's Business* 77:80 Mr '89
A business guide to Bush country. A. R. Dowd. il *Fortune*
  120:93-4+ Jl 17 '89
Business should speak up. M. Novak. il *Forbes* 143:120
  My 1 '89
Buyouts: the LBO lobby makes its move on Washington
  [cover story] M. Holland and V. Novak. il *Common Cause
  Magazine* 15:13-20 S/O '89
Congressional alert. See issues of Nation's Business
Cue the Green god, Ted [cover story] G. Vidal. il *The
  Nation* 249:153+ Ag 7-14 '89
How big business bankrolls the left. W. T. Poole. il *National
  Review* 41:34-7 Mr 10 '89
How business bosses saved a sick city [Cleveland] M. Magnet.
  il *Fortune* 119:106-10 Mr 27 '89
Politics & policy. See issues of Fortune beginning March
  5, 1984
Risks and opportunities for international business [study
  by Frost & Sullivan's Political Risk Services] il *USA Today
  (Periodical)* 118:5 Ag '89
    Psychological aspects
    See Psychology, Industrial
    Public relations
    See also
  Business and mass media
  Business and television
  Business and the press
  Customer relations
  Fur industry—Public relations
  Home-based business—Public relations
  Petroleum industry—Public relations
  Railroads—Public relations
Integrating public relations into the marketing mix [address,
  August 7, 1989] C. Howard. *Vital Speeches of the Day*
  56:93-6 N 15 '89
The public is willing to take business on [Business week/Harris
  poll] il *Business Week* p29 My 29 '89
Putting your best self forward [views of L. Brown] S. Nelton.
  il pors *Nation's Business* 77:46-7 Ag '89
Shape up your firm's image. S. Dark. il *Nation's Business*
  77:42+ Jl '89
    Security measures
    See Industry—Security measures
    Social aspects
    See also
  Corporations—Charitable contributions
The best of public service [1988] il *Business Week* p126
  Ja 9 '89
Doing well by doing good [encouraging volunteer work] A.
  Miller. il *Newsweek* 114:38 Jl 10 '89
Ethical business: oxymoron? . . . Or last best hope for
  planet earth? [cover story; special section] il *Utne Reader*
  p53-62+ Ja/F '89
Ethical shopping [Shopping for a better world, a guide to
  supermarket shopping] J. Queenan. il *Forbes* 143:80+ Ap
  17 '89
Fighting back. R. Grover. il *Business Week* p34-5 My 22
  '89
Framing the public agenda [address, September 29, 1988]
  R. D. Pagán, Jr. *Vital Speeches of the Day* 55:177-80
  Ja 1 '89
Listen here, Mr. Big! [emphasis on corporate responsibility
  by consumers] C. Gorman. il *Time* 134:40-1 Jl 3 '89
A new era of activism: who will frame the agenda? R.
  D. Pagán, Jr. il por *The Futurist* 23:12-16 My/Je '89
Saintly companies that make heavenly profits [special section]
  J. David and K. File. il *Working Woman* 14:122-4+ O
  '89
Shopping for a better world [guide to socially responsible
  supermarket shopping] il *USA Today (Periodical)* 117:4-5
  Ap '89
U.S. business isn't about to be society's savior. R. Kuttner.
  il *Business Week* p29 N 6 '89
An untapped resource [business encouragement to volunteer
  work] R. Thompson. il *Nation's Business* 77:50+ Mr '89
Volunteer jobs with solid payoffs. T. Thompson. il *U.S.
  News & World Report* 106:76-7 Ap 24 '89
When companies care. T. Armbrister. *Reader's Digest*
  134:25-6+ Ap '89

    Terminology
How 'managing' is managing. W. Safire. il *The New York
  Times Magazine* p18+ F 19 '89
BUSINESS AIRPLANE INDUSTRY *See* Airplane industry
BUSINESS AIRPLANES *See* Airplanes, Business
BUSINESS AND ALCOHOLISM *See* Alcohol and employment
BUSINESS AND ART *See* Art and industry
BUSINESS AND CONVICT LABOR *See* Convict labor
BUSINESS AND DAY CARE *See* Day care and industry
BUSINESS AND EDUCATION
    See also
  Business Council for Effective Literacy
  Corporate Community School (Chicago, Ill.)
  Corporate Executive Fellows Program
  Educational Assistance Limited
  Interns (Business)
  Satellite learning centers
Advanced bio class? That's over in Hitachi Hall [Japanese
  companies setting up labs at U.S. colleges] D. P. Oran.
  il *Business Week* p73-4 Ag 7 '89
At Boston University, Biotech 101 is no breeze [investment
  in Seragen] L. Jereski. *Business Week* p30-1 Ap 10 '89
Business and education reform [address, January 27, 1989]
  P. Townley. *Vital Speeches of the Day* 55:354-6 Ap 1
  '89
The business-education link. J. Dawes. il por *Nation's Business*
  77:27 Je '89
Business goes to college [backing university labs] N. J.
  Freundlich. il *Business Week* Special Issue:50+ Je 16 '89
Business, home, and school: cooperating to develop lifelong
  readers [project in Pinellas County, Fla.] A. R. Bellack
  and C. K. Hallin. il *Phi Delta Kappan* 70:415 Ja '89
Can business throw a net under Hispanic dropouts? T. Mason.
  il *Business Week* p151+ F 20 '89
Century 21 education [address, October 11, 1988] J. F.
  Alibrandi. *Vital Speeches of the Day* 55:247-50 F 1 '89
CEOs for 4-year-olds [Smart Start] J. Lieblich. il *Fortune*
  119:8 Mr 27 '89
Computers and preschoolers: Head Start/IBM Partnership.
  L. Tsantis and others. il *Children Today* 18:21-3 Ja/F
  '89
Conflict over conflict of interest [research fund recipients;
  guidelines drafted by the National Institutes of Health]
  J. Palca. *Science* 245:1440 S 29 '89
Coping with the coming labor shortage [address, May 11,
  1989] G. M. Smith. *Vital Speeches of the Day* 55:669-71
  Ag 15 '89
Corporate takeover on campus [high tuition costs attributed
  to increased funding of corporate-sponsored research; cover
  story] L. Minsky and D. F. Noble. il *The Nation* 249:477+
  O 30 '89
The corporation and arts education: a new merger? S. S.
  Madeja. *Design for Arts in Education* 90:20-4 N/D '88
Education as funny business. C. E. Finn. il *National Review*
  41:34-5+ F 24 '89
Education: the competitor's key [views of Chamber of Com-
  merce chairman J. L. Clendenin] R. T. Gray. il pors
  Nation's Business 77:60+ Je '89
First, this message. S. Bates. *The New Republic* 201:16+
  O 16 '89
The forgotten half [undereducated work force; cover story]
  D. Whitman. il *U.S. News & World Report* 106:44-9+
  Je 26 '89
Giving students a taste of the executive life. S. M. Williams.
  Black Enterprise 19:181-2 F '89
Harvard chases biotech bucks [Medical Science Partners to
  market biotechnology research of Harvard Medical School]
  J. Wiener. il *The Nation* 248:12-16 Ja 2 '89
Helping out at school. R. R. Roha. il *Changing Times*
  43:124 S '89
Hire education [adopt-a-class program at P.S. 175 in Harlem]
  K. Emmons. il *Omni (New York, N.Y.)* 11:18+ Je '89
How to help America's schools [Fortune's second education
  summit] N. J. Perry. il *Fortune* 120:137-40+ D 4 '89
Human resources [address, January 19, 1989] A. H. Magazine.
  Vital Speeches of the Day 55:502-7 Je 1 '89
Ignorance threatens companies [views of W. Woodside] M.
  Magnet. por *Fortune* 120:69-70 Jl 3 '89
The impact of education on business growth. B. E. Anderson.
  Black Enterprise 19:31-2 Jl '89
Industry's stake in space education. T. W. Becker. *Ad Astra*
  1:13 Ja '89
Intellectual exports [M.I.T.'s Industrial Liaison Program] T.
  Beardsley. *Scientific American* 261:17+ S '89
Is academic freedom bad for business? [denial of tenure
  to MIT professor D. Noble] K. Hart. il por *The Bulletin
  of the Atomic Scientists* 45:28-31+ Ap '89
Letting the losses run [Boston University's investment in
  Seragen Inc.] D. Wechsler. il *Forbes* 143:116 Ap 17 '89
A local business invests in the kids [work-study program
  offered by Wegmans' supermarkets in Rochester, N.Y.]
  il *U.S. News & World Report* 106:60 Ja 26 '89
Mergermania. J. Bourke. *The Nation* 249:495 O 30 '89
Million-dollar professors: should the ivory tower be a gold
  mine? J. F. Siler. il *Business Week* p90-2 Ag 21 '89
MIT-industry links draw congressional attention. M. Crawford.
  il *Science* 244:1136 Je 9 '89

BUSINESS AND EDUCATION—*cont.*

NIH grapples with conflict of interest. J. Palca. il *Science* 245:23 Jl 7 '89

Performance of U.S. educational system threatens defense base, economic position. S. W. Kandebo. *Aviation Week & Space Technology* 131:34-5 D 18-25 '89

The power of ideas and information [address, February 2, 1989] J. Sculley. *Vital Speeches of the Day* 55:565-9 Jl 1 '89

The role of business in educational reform [address, December 8, 1988] V. R. Ruggiero. *Vital Speeches of the Day* 55:286-8 F 15 '89

Saving the schools: how business can help. N. J. Perry. *Current (Washington, D.C.)* 310:20-6 F '89

Science, technology, and public knowledge [having high school teachers spend time in university and industrial research laboratories] G. Pallrand. bibl f il *Phi Delta Kappan* 70:460-4 F '89

The selling of our schools [cover story] T. Moore. il *U.S. News & World Report* 107:34-6+ N 6 '89

Sending companies to school. D. Gergen. il *U.S. News & World Report* 107:112 N 6 '89

Shiseido grant: more than skin deep [Japanese funding of Massachusetts General Hospital-Harvard University's Cutaneous Biology Research Center] M. Sun. *Science* 245:810-11 Ag 25 '89

Smart approaches to productivity. W. T. Brookes. il *Nation's Business* 77:97 O '89

Steve Wolf's class act: straight talk in the schoolroom [chairman of UAL Corp. speaks to black students in Chicago] J. E. Ellis. il *Business Week* p57 F 6 '89

Technology is reshaping both work and workers. J. Sculley. por *Personal Computing* 13:218 O '89

Thinking globally: educating Americans for the 21st century. P. R. Piccigallo. il *USA Today (Periodical)* 118:29-31 N '89

Today, class, we'll learn about soap [7-Eleven store operated by students in Union City, Calif. high school] L. Wright. *Newsweek* 113:63 Mr 20 '89

Tuition payments cut job turnover [Burger King in downtown Detroit] S. D. Rinella and R. J. Kopecky. il por *Nation's Business* 77:25-6 Ag '89

What companies can do [encouraging children to read] B. Prete. *Publishers Weekly* 236:47-8 O 27 '89

What the boardroom has to offer the schoolroom. E. Flax. *Working Woman* 14:26+ D '89

The will to take leadership [increasing America's competitiveness; address, March 22, 1989] L. A. Iacocca. *Vital Speeches of the Day* 55:454-8 My 15 '89

Would you hire them? [business' role in improving education; cover story] N. C. Baker. il *Nation's Business* 77:16-19+ Ap '89

Youth Opportunity: a private sector investment in prevention [summer work at Domino's Pizza Inc.'s Whatley Farm in Ann Arbor, Mich.] C. H. Tice. il *Children Today* 18:20-3 Mr/Ap '89

BUSINESS AND GOVERNMENT *See* Industry and state
BUSINESS AND MASS MEDIA

Putting your best self forward [views of L. Brown] S. Nelton. il pors *Nation's Business* 77:46-7 Ag '89

BUSINESS AND POLITICS *See* Business—Political aspects
BUSINESS AND SOCIETY *See* Business—Social aspects
BUSINESS AND SPORTS

> *See also*
> Industry—Recreation programs

Arms race on wheels [Grand Prix racing becomes corporate sport] R. Behar. il *Forbes* 143:60+ F 20 '89

Business secrets of Tommy Lasorda [interview] B. Dumaine. il pors *Fortune* 120:130-2+ Jl 3 '89

Corporate sponsorships: the new name of the game. C. Pesmen. il *Sport (New York, N.Y.)* 80:82 Je '89

Dream jobs [running as a livelihood] B. Wischnia. il *Runner's World* 24:82-6+ Je '89

Golf's old greats are really swinging again [Senior Tour] W. C. Symonds. il *Business Week* p122-3 Je 26 '89

How to quit losing in the Olympics. D. J. Morrow. il *Fortune* 119:265-6+ Ap 24 '89

Indy oldie [D. Simon] J. Zweig. il por *Forbes* 143:178+ Je 12 '89

Money fuels the Honda wonder [Grand Prix racing] H. J. Steinbreder. il *Sports Illustrated* 71:58-9 Ag 21 '89

Not just kid stuff anymore [corporate sponsorship of adult participation in childhood games] T. Barrett. il *Newsweek* 114:70 O 30 '89

Pass the gravy, please [Georgia Tech's solicitation of corporate sponsors for home football games] D. Kindred. il por *Sports Illustrated* 70:96 My 15 '89

Playing the global game [basketball] E. F. Cone. il *Forbes* 143:90-1 Ja 23 '89

Porsche's racing plans. P. Frère. il *Road & Track* 40:163 F '89

Sports tie-ins help firms score. G. Macnow. il *Nation's Business* 77:36-8 S '89

Superbike shuffle [difficulty in finding sponsors for the World Superbike Series] J. Greening. il *Cycle* 40:82 Jl '89

Tobacco green [Norton Formula 1 team backed by Imperial Tobacco] J. Greening. il *Cycle* 40:114 My '89

Warning: sports stars may be hazardous to your health [cigarette ads; cover story] J. DeParle. il *The Washington Monthly* 21:34-44+ S '89

What's as gory as hockey and as upscale as squash? [Major Indoor Lacrosse League] R. Duffy. il *Business Week* p42 Ap 17 '89

What's next—the Mazda Fed-Ex Big Mac Pine-Sol Bowl? M. Durslag. il *TV Guide* 37:12-14 D 30 '89-Ja 5 '90

Why more companies are ponying up for polo. G. DeGeorge. il *Business Week* p148+ Mr 13 '89

BUSINESS AND STATE *See* Industry and state
BUSINESS AND TELEVISION

> *See also*
> American Business Network

How to make a big impact on the small screen [excerpt from Your public best] L. Brown. il por *Working Woman* 14:80-4 D '89

Why business is glued to the tube [private networks] K. Kelly. il *Business Week* p160 Mr 20 '89

BUSINESS AND THE AGED *See* Aged and business
BUSINESS AND THE ARTS *See* Arts and industry
BUSINESS AND THE COMMUNITY *See* Business—Social aspects
BUSINESS AND THE ENVIRONMENT *See* Industry and the environment
BUSINESS AND THE NEW AGE MOVEMENT *See* New Age movement and business
BUSINESS AND THE PRESS

> *See also*
> Investment banking—Press relations

Bolstering your high-tech image. M. Spaeth. il *High Technology Business* 9:26+ Ja '89

Forbes's publicity machine. J. Alter. il por *Newsweek* 114:50-1 Ag 28 '89

Smart ways to handle the press. S. P. Sherman. il *Fortune* 119:69-70+ Je 19 '89

Western Europe

Europe's press isn't taking 'no comment' for an answer anymore. B. Riemer and J. Templeman. il *Business Week* p49 F 6 '89

BUSINESS AND WEATHER *See* Industry and weather
BUSINESS ARBITRATION *See* Arbitration, Commercial
BUSINESS CARDS

Charged with practicing the art of the steal, Ed Zito plays his own Trump Card against Donald [photographic business cards] il pors *People Weekly* 32:111 Ag 7 '89

BUSINESS CLASS AIRLINE SERVICE *See* Airlines—Passenger service
BUSINESS CLOTHES *See* Clothing and dress—Businessmen; Clothing and dress—Businesswomen
BUSINESS COMMUNICATION *See* Communication in management
BUSINESS CONDITIONS

> *See also*
> Business cycles
> Business depression
> Business failures
> Business forecasting
> Economic conditions
> Inflation (Finance)
> Productivity, Industrial

Economic trends. See issues of Business Week

Economy and business notes. See issues of World Press Review

International business. See issues of Business Week

BUSINESS CONSULTANTS

> *See also*
> Agricultural consultants
> Booz, Allen & Hamilton Inc.
> Business etiquette consultants
> Engineering consultants
> Executive search consultants
> Franchise consultants
> Interconsult (Firm)
> Investment advisers
> Kissinger Associates Inc.
> Marketing consultants
> Outplacement consultant services
> Public relations consultants
> R.F. Schiffmann Associates
> Somers H. White Company, Inc.
> Theater consultants

Under the eye of the consultant. P. Amend. il *Working Woman* 14:37-8 O '89

International aspects

The ever-bigger boom in consulting. A. B. Fisher. il *Fortune* 119:113+ Ap 24 '89

Salaries, pensions, etc.

Would you make more as a consultant? A. M. Russell. il *Working Woman* 14:74 Ja '89

Canada

Free trade's selling points. T. Tedesco. il *Maclean's* 102:66-7 Jl 3 '89

BUSINESS CONVENTIONS *See* Conventions
BUSINESS COOPERATION

> *See also*
> Automobile industry—Cooperation
> Drug industry—Cooperation

BUSINESS COOPERATION—See also—*cont.*
  Electronic industries—Cooperation
  Television industry—Cooperation
BUSINESS COUNCIL FOR EFFECTIVE LITERACY
Business defines its role. B. Prete. il *Publishers Weekly* 235:20-1 My 26 '89
BUSINESS CRIMES *See* Commercial crimes
BUSINESS CYCLES
  See also
    Business depression
A kinder, gentler business cycle? J. Warner. il *Business Week* p50+ Mr 6 '89
To keep profits on a roll, stay tuned to the business cycle. W. L. Updegrave. il *Money* 18:169-70+ My '89
While cyclical stocks go begging, the companies are getting rich. J. Mendes. il *Fortune* 119:37-8 Ap 10 '89
BUSINESS DECISION MAKING *See* Decision making
BUSINESS DEPRESSION
Are we headed for the fabled soft landing? H. Gleckman. il *Business Week* p27-8 Ap 24 '89
As the economy slows, investors should prepare for rough weather. M. Sivy. il *Money* 18:39-43 S '89
Bill Helming business. B. Helming. il *Successful Farming* 87:6 Ag '89
Borrowing to the bitter end. A. Bladen. il *Forbes* 144:310 S 4 '89
Breaking the inflation-recession cycle [address, September 19, 1989] W. L. Hoskins. *Vital Speeches of the Day* 56:158-60 D 15 '89
Business. B. Helming. il *Successful Farming* 87:7 S '89
Business. B. Helming. il *Successful Farming* 87:11 N '89
Business. B. Helming. il *Successful Farming* 87:12 O '89
Caution lights. J. Daly. il *Maclean's* 102:27 Ja 9 '89
Counting the recession risks. S. Nasar. il *U.S. News & World Report* 107:64 N 27 '89
Dangerous shapes [inverted yield curve pushes up short term rates] J. Willoughby. il *Forbes* 143:39-40 Ja 23 '89
Dollar signs floating in the crystal ball [Canada] P. C. Newman. il *Maclean's* 102:52 Ja 2 '89
Don't be lulled [Friday the 13th stock plunge] G. Shilling. il *Forbes* 144:370 N 13 '89
Economists find a new straw floating in the wind [world dollar base] K. Pennar. il *Business Week* p30 O 9 '89
The economy/18-month forecast [special section] il *Fortune* 120:62-70+ Jl 17 '89
The fairy-tale economy. D. Pauly. il *Newsweek* 114:44 S 11 '89
False confidence. A. Bladen. il *Forbes* 143:118 Ja 23 '89
A Greenspan recession? M. S. Forbes, Jr. il *Forbes* 143:27 Ap 3 '89
Greenspan's moment of truth: can he manage a soft landing without skidding into a recession? [cover story] M. McNamee. il pors *Business Week* p58-62+ Jl 31 '89
How bad will the next downturn be? Flip a coin. G. S. Becker. il *Business Week* p17 Ap 10 '89
How severe will the coming downturn be? H. Banks. il *Forbes* 144:33-4 D 11 '89
How soft a 'soft landing'? S. Dentzer. il *U.S. News & World Report* 107:42-4 Ag 14 '89
How to tell when a recession is coming. M. C. Paulson. il *Changing Times* 43:18 Mr '89
If manufacturing slows much more, watch out for recession. J. C. Cooper and K. Madigan. il *Business Week* p37-8 N 6 '89
Inflation II: the sequel [possiblity of a recession] R. E. Norton. il *U.S. News & World Report* 106:18-20+ Ap 3 '89
Is it inflation? Recession? or just spring fever? J. M. Laderman. il *Business Week* p70-1 Ap 10 '89
Is the patient dead yet, doctor? H. Banks. il *Forbes* 144:33-4 Ag 21 '89
Is your portfolio weatherproofed? E. Schultz. il *Fortune* 120:30 S 25 '89
The job juggernaut is squelching fears of recession. J. C. Cooper and K. Madigan. il *Business Week* p29-30 Ja 23 '89
The lowdown on the slowdown. A. C. Brown. il *Forbes* 143:190 Je 12 '89
Mirror, mirror, on the wall, will the economy really fall? [views of A. G. Shilling] J. C. Cooper. il por *Business Week* p80 D 25 '89-Ja 1 '90
A new, improved index says recession isn't a threat. G. Koretz. il *Business Week* p24 Je 19 '89
The next recession. R. J. Samuelson. il *Newsweek* 113:49 Ap 17 '89
No recession—yet [views of S. Hymans] R. Bailey. il por *Forbes* 143:86-7 Ap 17 '89
The ominous warning signs of recession. W. Greider. il *Rolling Stone* p37+ Mr 9 '89
Painting without numbers. H. Banks. il *Forbes* 144:10 N 27 '89
The peek-a-boo recession. R. Thomas. il *Newsweek* 114:60 N 20 '89
Put your eggs in several baskets [advice from H. Browne] M. Hulbert. il *Forbes* 143:168 Mr 6 '89
Recession? J. K. Galbraith. *The Nation* 248:364-5 Mr 20 '89
Recession is not a solution. A. Etzioni. il *The New Leader* 72:15-16 Mr 20 '89

A recessionist's portfolio. A. G. Shilling. il por *Forbes* 144:234 S 18 '89
Sagging growth is the worry of the week. J. C. Cooper and K. Madigan. il *Business Week* p19-20 Ag 7 '89
Searching for the runway. L. Reibstein. il *Newsweek* 114:40 Jl 17 '89
A silver lining in a stormy recession [views of W. E. Simon] M. Magnet. il por *Fortune* 120:71-2 Jl 3 '89
Surviving the slowdown: diversity is key. K. Madigan. il *Business Week* p57-8 Jl 3 '89
Tangling with the U.S. economic octopus. R. W. Haseltine. il *USA Today (Periodical)* 118:28-30 Jl '89
Welcome to the third world, Uncle Sam. A. Bladen. il *Forbes* 143:167 Mr 6 '89
When will a recession hit? L. S. Richman. il *Fortune* 119:80-2+ F 13 '89
Why smokestack America doesn't quake at the word 'recession'. M. Schroeder. il *Business Week* p100-1+ S 11 '89
Why this quartet is singing the recession blues. G. Koretz. *Business Week* p12 Ap 17 '89
With a Republican in office, a recession may be lurking . . . and if it comes, the poor will really take a hit. M. J. Mandel. il *Business Week* p20 Ap 10 '89
The wolf at the door doesn't look so scary. K. Pennar. il *Business Week* p73-4 Mr 27 '89
                   Anecdotes, facetiae, satire, etc.
A midwinter's nightmare: looking back on the Bush years. A. S. Blinder. il *Business Week* p22 Ja 23 '89
BUSINESS DEPRESSION, 1901
Jacob Schiff and the Northern Pacific corner [battle with J. P. Morgan for control of company] J. S. Gordon. il por *American Heritage* 40:86-7 Jl/Ag '89
BUSINESS DEPRESSION, 1929-1939
  See also
    Okies
The Great Depression. E. Whitford. il *Scholastic Update (Teachers' edition)* 121:16-17 F 10 '89
A tale of two crashes. D. N. Dreman. il *Forbes* 143:214 Mr 20 '89
                   Photographs and photography
Telling the news from Desolation Row. il *Time* 134 Special Issue:36-7 Fall '89
BUSINESS DISTRICTS
Downtown redevelopment [integration of theaters] S. Lieberman. il *Theatre Crafts* 23:40-3+ D '89
Main Street revisited [work of AIA Regional/Urban Design Assistant Team in Healdsburg, Calif.] W. Hoffer. il *Nation's Business* 77:36-8+ Ja '89
BUSINESS EDUCATION
  See also
    Business ethics—Study and teaching
    Business management—Study and teaching
    Business schools
    Corporate Executive Fellows Program
    Hotel management—Study and teaching
    Junior Achievement, Inc.
    Professional education
Fast-track business courses. M. Conroy. il *Better Homes and Gardens* 67:21 Ja '89
BUSINESS ENTERPRISE TRUST
Worrying about Warren. D. Seligman. il *Fortune* 120:273-4 Jl 31 '89
BUSINESS ENTERPRISES
  See also
    Black business enterprises
    Enterprise zones
    French Canadian business enterprises
    Hispanic American business enterprises
    Korean American business enterprises
    Minority business enterprises
    Palestinian Arab business enterprises
    Syrian American business enterprises
The truth behind get-rich-quick ads [business opportunity classifieds] E. King. il *Home Office Computing* 7:61-2 N '89
BUSINESS ENTERTAINING
Business and pleasure: champagne tasting and toasting. E. Sahatjian. il *Working Woman* 14:107-10+ D '89
Guest work: the good (business) guest's guide to being wined and dined. S. Richardson. il *Working Woman* 14:114+ D '89
A little plastic can help small companies, too [corporate travel and entertainment cards] S. Woolley. il *Business Week* p180 My 22 '89
Lunch with the boss—how not to blow it. L. Lague. il *Glamour* 87:128 S '89
Mingling successfully for fun and profit [excerpt from How to work a room] S. RoAne. il *Glamour* 87:111 Mr '89
Nutrition power in working lunches. J. Hendley. il *Working Woman* 14:63 Jl '89
Sampling a cookbook manuscript [authors of The simple secrets of Vietnamese cooking invite prospective publishers to a buffet] D. Brainard. *Publishers Weekly* 236:33 S 8 '89
'Tis the season for new-job networking. M. M. Kennedy. il *Glamour* 87:94 D '89

BUSINESS ENTERTAINING—cont.

Taxation

Court cancels a Super Bowl bid [denial of tax deduction for corporate entertainment expenses] G. W. Padwe. il *Nation's Business* 77:60 Jl '89

It's your party [M. S. Forbes' 70th birthday celebration] *The New Republic* 201:4+ S 11 '89

BUSINESS ETHICS

See also
Accounting ethics
Advertising ethics
Aerospace industries—Ethical aspects
Airlines—Ethical aspects
Appraisers—Ethical aspects
Art trade—Ethical aspects
Audio equipment stores—Ethical aspects
Automobile industry—Ethical aspects
Automobiles—Leasing and renting—Ethical aspects
Avionics industry—Ethical aspects
Banks and banking—Ethical aspects
Booksellers and bookselling—Ethical aspects
Bribery
Brokers—Ethical aspects
Business intelligence
Cable television—Ethical aspects
Cigarette industry—Ethical aspects
Clam fisheries—Ethical aspects
Cleaning services—Ethical aspects
Clothing industry—Ethical aspects
Commercial crimes
Commodity brokers—Ethical aspects
Competition
Credit bureaus—Ethical aspects
Direct selling—Ethical aspects
Drug industry—Ethical aspects
Electronic industries—Ethical aspects
Electronics stores—Ethical aspects
Employment agencies—Ethical aspects
Fraud
Frequent flier programs—Ethical aspects
Guides—Ethical aspects
Insurance companies—Ethical aspects
Investment banking—Ethical aspects
Jewelers—Ethical aspects
Milk industry—Ethical aspects
Motion picture industry—Ethical aspects
Nepotism
Nuclear industry—Ethical aspects
Nurseries (Horticulture)—Ethical aspects
Phonograph record industry—Ethical aspects
Publishers and publishing—Ethical aspects
Real estate agencies and agents—Ethical aspects
Shoe industry—Ethical aspects
Soft dollar brokers—Ethical aspects
Television industry—Ethical aspects
Theatrical agencies and agents—Ethical aspects
Timesharing (Real estate)—Ethical aspects
Tourist trade—Ethical aspects
Videotape industry—Ethical aspects

Confronting ethical dilemmas [address, September 19, 1989] D. Grier. *Vital Speeches of the Day* 56:100-4 D 1 '89

Do you disagree with your boss's ethics? B. J. Goodman. il *Glamour* 87:107-8 Ag '89

Ethical business: oxymoron? . . . Or last best hope for planet earth? [cover story; special section] il *Utne Reader* p53-62+ Ja/F '89

Fun and games—and ethics [family business people] S. Nelton. il *Nation's Business* 77:38 N '89

Omissions hurt CEO ethics rating [address, March 29, 1989] J. F. Budd. *Vital Speeches of the Day* 55:478-80 My 15 '89

Public relations and ethical leadership [address, June 15, 1989] J. Paluszek. *Vital Speeches of the Day* 55:747-50 O 1 '89

The right way [address, January 19, 1989] J. E. Perrella. *Vital Speeches of the Day* 55:375-6 Ap 1 '89

Rules of the road to Red Square [code of ethics for investing in the U.S.S.R. developed by Alexander Slepak] E. Pomice. il *U.S. News & World Report* 107:63 N 27 '89

Anecdotes, facetiae, satire, etc.

The Bing ethics test. S. Bing. il *Esquire* 111:68 My '89

Study and teaching

Money, power and fame [teaching Harvard MBAs] A. Etzioni. por *Newsweek* 114:10 S 18 '89

No easy answers. R. Thompson. il *Nation's Business* 77:38-9 Jl '89

BUSINESS ETIQUETTE

Business etiquette: 5 bloopers that can cost you a lot. M. M. Kennedy. il *Glamour* 87:125 Mr '89

The etiquette of ambition. M. C. Williams. il *Mademoiselle* 95:108+ Je '89

Kissing in the boardroom. *Harper's* 279:27+ S '89

Miss Manners on office etiquette [interview with J. Martin] B. Dumaine. il por *Fortune* 120:155+ N 6 '89

BUSINESS ETIQUETTE CONSULTANTS

Mind your manners—by hiring an expert. G. DeGeorge. il *Business Week* p128 S 18 '89

BUSINESS EXECUTIVES See Black executives; Executives; Women executives

BUSINESS EXPANSION

See also
Capital investments

To grow or not to grow? [women's businesses] L. Sagalyn. il *Working Woman* 14:66 Ag '89

You can plan to expand or just let it happen to you. L. J. Moore. il *U.S. News & World Report* 107:73+ O 23 '89

BUSINESS FAILURES

See also
Bank failures
Default (Finance)
Trade claims (Debt)
Workout investments

Advantage, Lorenzo [Chapter 11 strategy at Eastern] G. DeGeorge and S. Payne. il por *Business Week* p24-6 Jl 10 '89

All that floats is not equal [Shannon Boat Co.] C. Brown. il por *Forbes* 143:84+ Ap 3 '89

Allegheny's battle to come back from the abyss. M. Schroeder. il *Business Week* p130+ Je 26 '89

Authors concerned about Dodd, Mead liquidation. *Publishers Weekly* 235:20 Ja 6 '89

Back from the dead [Public Service of New Hampshire] il *Forbes* 143:134 Ja 9 '89

Bankrupt Kampmann & Co. faces counter suits. C. Reid. *Publishers Weekly* 235:15 Ap 21 '89

Bankruptcy snarls device seizure [unsterile eye surgery devices manufactured by Trueline Instruments] il *FDA Consumer* 23:35-6 Mr '89

BookCrafters takes over assets of Stein & Day. *Publishers Weekly* 235:14 Mr 24 '89

BookCrafters to publish Stein & Day titles. C. Reid. il *Publishers Weekly* 236:124 Jl 28 '89

A boss they love to hate [F. Lorenzo and Eastern Air Lines strike] J. Schwartz. il por *Newsweek* 113:20-4 Mr 20 '89

Braniff files for Chapter 11, slashes flights. *Aviation Week & Space Technology* 131:34 O 2 '89

Braniff halts passenger service, plans attempt as charter carrier. *Aviation Week & Space Technology* 131:72 N 13 '89

Braniff may be at the end of the runway. G. DeGeorge. il *Business Week* p49-50 N 13 '89

Braniff operates reduced schedule, plans to accept 95 Airbus A320s. *Aviation Week & Space Technology* 131:139 O 9 '89

Brothers, are you spared a dime? [Hunts] K. Kelly. il pors *Business Week* p38 N 20 '89

Chain of troubles: the LBO that went bust [Revco] E. Pomice. *U.S. News & World Report* 106:69 F 13 '89

Charlie Keating in the Show Me state [American Continental Corp.'s bankruptcy hits broker R. Ruppert] G. Morgenson. il por *Forbes* 143:12 My 29 '89

Charming their bankers [Shape Inc.] R. Behar. il *Forbes* 143:43-4 F 20 '89

Closing down is not a failure as long as you do it right. T. Thompson. il *U.S. News & World Report* 107:84+ O 23 '89

Court frees $75 million from escrow after talks between Eastern, creditors. C. Fotos. *Aviation Week & Space Technology* 131:98 Jl 24 '89

Creditors pose key threat to Eastern revival effort. J. T. McKenna. *Aviation Week & Space Technology* 130:106-7 Ap 24 '89

Debacle on 34th Street: how takeover debt helped kill off the venerable B. Altman chain. B. Rudolph. il por *Time* 134:77 D 11 '89

Diced and sliced [Cuisinarts in Chapter 11] K. Hannon. il por *Forbes* 144:68+ O 2 '89

Dodd, Mead operations suspended over arbitration [dispute with authors] C. Reid. *Publishers Weekly* 235:11 Mr 31 '89

Don't blame me [L. Funston's failed leveraged buyout of O'Day Corp.] A. A. Lappen. il por *Forbes* 144:102-3+ S 4 '89

Down-and-out investing. J. B. Quinn. il *Newsweek* 114:46 Jl 3 '89

Eastern adds flights, signs $210-million Midway pact. C. Fotos. *Aviation Week & Space Technology* 131:74-5 Ag 7 '89

Eastern Air Lines. *Monthly Labor Review* 112:44 S '89

Eastern asks court's permission to break contract with pilots. *Aviation Week & Space Technology* 130:92 Je 26 '89

Eastern building pilot corps amid strike, bankruptcy battles. C. Fotos. il *Aviation Week & Space Technology* 131:101-2 Jl 31 '89

Eastern, creditors divided on new reorganization plan. J. T. McKenna. *Aviation Week & Space Technology* 131:68-9 O 23 '89

Eastern: does anybody win? W. Woods. il por *Fortune* 119:14 Ap 10 '89

Eastern expands systemwide flight operations; bankruptcy court to hear arguments on trustee. *Aviation Week & Space Technology* 130:62 Jl 10 '89

Eastern goes bust. J. Castro. il por *Time* 133:52-3 Mr 20 '89

BUSINESS FAILURES—cont.

Eastern seeks creditors' approval of recovery plan. J. T. McKenna. *Aviation Week & Space Technology* 130:104-5 My 1 '89

Eastern struggles to expand service, fend off lawsuits. E. H. Kolcum. *Aviation Week & Space Technology* 130:268-9 Mr 20 '89

Ernest Fleischer finally tastes humble pie [filing for bankruptcy for L.F. Rothschild Holdings] D. Zigas. il por *Business Week* p67 Jl 17 '89

Fewer businesses calling it quits. D. C. Bacon. il *Nation's Business* 77:6 My '89

Fewer companies have bad cases of strained finances. G. Koretz. il *Business Week* p26 Ja 9 '89

Flying first class at Braniff. J. H. Taylor. il *Forbes* 144:49+ O 30 '89

For Charlie Keating, the best defense is a lawsuit [declares American Continental bankrupt as feds close in on Lincoln Savings & Loan] K. Kerwin. il por *Business Week* p32+ My 1 '89

GAO will review Ritchie, Lorenzo plans for Eastern. J. T. McKenna. *Aviation Week & Space Technology* 131:100-1 Jl 31 '89

Getting refunds when a travel firm folds. H. Gieseking. il *Travel Holiday* 171:76-7 Je '89

Great Japanese mistakes. C. Rapoport. il *Fortune* 119:108-11 F 13 '89

How a real estate highflier flamed out [Residential Resources Mortgage Investments Corp.] D. Zigas. il *Business Week* p90 Mr 6 '89

How not to run a franchise [Convenient Food Mart] R. Koselka. *Forbes* 144:244 N 27 '89

How to reward the criminals [A. H. Robins' use of bankruptcy law to avoid Dalkon Shield suits] R. Shereff. *The Nation* 248:192-5 F 13 '89

"If something could go wrong, it did" [D. Beldock's BASIX] E. Giltenan. il por *Forbes* 143:70+ My 29 '89

Is your health club healthy? C. Schaeffer. *Changing Times* 43:116+ S '89

Judge releases books in Connecticut warehouse [publishers able to remove books from Key Book Services] C. Reid. *Publishers Weekly* 236:10 Ag 4 '89

Kampmann bankruptcy order threatens 65 firms. C. Reid. *Publishers Weekly* 236:10-11 Jl 21 '89

Kansas City rebuilding after Braniff bankruptcy. C. Fotos. *Aviation Week & Space Technology* 131:56-7 D 4 '89

LBOs: let's bail out. J. Greenwald. il *Time* 134:50-1 Ag 14 '89

Look before you laugh at 'Chapter 11' investments. L. Zinn. il *Business Week* p100 Ap 10 '89

Now the Texas plague is spreading to insurance. M. Ivey. *Business Week* p38-9 F 27 '89

OMAC, Inc., files voluntary petition for bankruptcy. *Aviation Week & Space Technology* 130:25 Mr 13 '89

Pilot supply may be key issue in talks on Eastern recovery. J. T. McKenna. *Aviation Week & Space Technology* 130:315 Je 12 '89

Presidential Airways' woes show code sharing no guarantee of success. C. Fotos. *Aviation Week & Space Technology* 131:43-4 D 11 '89

PSNH: down to the last lines in Chapter 11. L. Jereski. il *Business Week* p36 O 2 '89

Recovery strategy poses major risks for Eastern. J. T. McKenna. *Aviation Week & Space Technology* 130:103 My 8 '89

Sifting ashes on Wall Street: turnaround artists prosper rescuing failed LBOs. D. Pauly. il *Newsweek* 114:42-3 S 4 '89

Stable Jerry [former Crazy Eddie pitchman J. Carroll] J. Queenan. il pors *Forbes* 144:350 N 13 '89

A stacked deck? [trading in bankruptcy claims discriminates against small creditors] D. Fanning. il *Forbes* 143:126-7 Je 12 '89

Strike forces Eastern into bankruptcy court [special section; with editorial comment] il *Aviation Week & Space Technology* 130:7, 16-23 Mr 13 '89

Suicide pact at Eastern Air Lines [filing for bankruptcy during strike; with interview with F. A. Lorenzo] T. Moore and C. P. Work. il por *U.S. News & World Report* 106:18-21 Mr 20 '89

Technology licenses: new law closes bankruptcy loophole. M. Shea-Stonum and D. Sloan. il *High Technology Business* 9:15 Mr '89

Tentative pact gives BookCrafters control of Stein & Day backlist. C. Reid. *Publishers Weekly* 235:12 F 17 '89

Tentative pact joins Kampmann & Co. with National Book Network. C. Reid. *Publishers Weekly* 235:16 My 26 '89

Tough times for Mr. Levittown [suburban housing pioneer W. Levitt] M. T. Kaufman. il pors *The New York Times Magazine* p42-4+ S 24 '89

Unions, investor plead for time to negotiate pact to buy Eastern. *Aviation Week & Space Technology* 130:113 Je 5 '89

When vultures get food poisoning [investing in distressed companies] H. Rudnitsky. il *Forbes* 144:53+ O 16 '89

Whodunit [failure of detective agency Sahlen & Associates] K. Hannon. il *Forbes* 143:40-1 Je 26 '89

Will corporate debt force the Fed to scrap zero inflation? K. Pennar. il *Business Week* p22 O 23 '89

Workout artist [bankruptcy lawyer J. Zweibel] J. Zweig. il por *Forbes* 144:274-5 Jl 24 '89

BUSINESS FLYING *See* Airplanes in business

BUSINESS FORECASTING

See also
> SEI Center for Advanced Studies in Management
> Stocks—Price forecasting

The 21st-century manager. R. Farmanfarmaian. il *Working Woman* 14:73+ N '89

1990s key ideas [cover story; special section] il *Fortune* 120:48-51+ Jl 3 '89

An agenda for the 1990s [Black enterprise Board of Economists report] J. Davidson. il *Black Enterprise* 19:152-4+ Je '89

Business outlook. See issues of Business Week

Experts are keeping their seatbelts loosely fastened. J. C. Cooper and K. Madigan. il *Business Week* p76-7+ D 25 '89-Ja 1 '90

Fortune forecast. See issues of Fortune

Growing fast on the 500's fringe [Fortune 500] P. Nulty. il *Fortune* 119:69-70+ Ap 24 '89

Industry and technology leaders in 2003. *The Futurist* 23:54-5 Jl/Ag '89

Industry outlook: 1989 [cover story; special section] il *Business Week* p63-71+ Ja 9 '89

The password is 'flexible'. il *Business Week* p152+ S 25 '89

Promising industries for 1990. B. Dumaine. il *Fortune* 120 no10 Special Issue:151-2+ Fall '89

A scoreboard to help you play by the numbers. il *Business Week* p155-62+ D 25 '89-Ja 1 '90

The shape of 1990: a new projection. *Nation's Business* 77:8 O '89

Small business: an upbeat '89 [cover story] R. Thompson. il *Nation's Business* 77:10-12+ Ja '89

An upbeat mood suddenly strikes small business. G. Koretz. il *Business Week* p26 N 27 '89

Who will do well? C. Hutton and E. Prewitt. il *Fortune* 120:67-70 Jl 17 '89

Winners for slow times. S. Caminiti and others. il *Fortune* 119:60+ Ja 16 '89

BUSINESS FORMS *See* Forms, blanks, etc.

BUSINESS GIFTS *See* Gifts in business

BUSINESS HALL OF FAME

The U.S. Business Hall of Fame. W. Guzzardi. il *Fortune* 119:130-6 Mr 13 '89

Wisdom from the giants of business. W. Guzzardi. il *Fortune* 120:78-82+ Jl 3 '89

BUSINESS HOURS

See also
> Hours of labor
> Sunday—Laws and regulations

Canada

Even shopkeepers need a day off. C. Gordon. il *Maclean's* 102:13 D 11 '89

BUSINESS IN DRAMA

Burned by the market crash, Jerry Sterner finds another way to make a Wall Street hit. A. Chambers. il pors *People Weekly* 32:123+ D 4 '89

Jerry Sterner: rolling in Other people's money. il por *Business Week* p69 D 4 '89

The word from the playwright of Wall Street [interview with J. Sterner] R. Eisenberg. il por *Money* 18:12 O '89

BUSINESS IN LITERATURE

Merger mystery [book by D. Aaron] B. Van Voorst. il por *Time* 133:54 F 27 '89

BUSINESS IN MOTION PICTURES

Enterprise and meaning: sponsored film, 1939-1949. W. L. Bird. bibl il *History Today* 39:24-30 D '89

Financial questions [Working girl] D. Seligman. il *Fortune* 119:124 F 13 '89

BUSINESS INSURANCE *See* Insurance, Business

BUSINESS INTELLIGENCE

Case of the purloined pix [photos of GM's Saturn sold to Automobile magazine] il *Time* 134:74 N 27 '89

How to get the scoop on your competition [excerpt from Monitoring the competition] L. M. Fuld. il *Working Woman* 14:39-42 Ja '89

Learn your firm's inside story. M. Stevens. il *Nation's Business* 77:59-60 Ag '89

That's Sam Spade leafing through the ledgers [using private eyes in takeover battles] R. Grover. il *Business Week* p95+ My 29 '89

Using 'spies to win a war': corporations turn to detectives to catch workers with drug problems. J. Schwartz. il *Newsweek* 114:56-7 N 6 '89

BUSINESS INTERNS *See* Interns (Business)

BUSINESS JOURNALISM *See* Journalism, Commercial

BUSINESS LETTERS *See* Business writing

BUSINESS LIABILITY *See* Liability (Law)

BUSINESS LIQUIDATION *See* Liquidation

BUSINESS LITERATURE

See also
> House organs
> Publishers and publishing—Business literature

BUSINESS LOBBY *See* Lobbyists and lobbying
BUSINESS LOCATION *See* Location in business and industry
BUSINESS MANAGEMENT

See also

Agricultural chemicals industry—Management
Airlines—Management
Architectural firms—Management
Arts—Management
Automobile equipment industry—Management
Automobile equipment stores—Management
Automobile industry—Management
Bank management
Black executives
Business expansion
Business intelligence
Business planning
Cable television—Management
Chemical industries—Management
Clothing industry—Management
Communication in management
Computers—Business use
Conflict of interests (Business)
Construction industry—Management
Corporate turnarounds
Corporations—Directors
Corporations, International—Management
Crisis management in business
Decision making
Department stores—Management
Diversification in industry
Electronic industries—Management
Executives
Factory management
Fisheries—Management
Hotel management
Inventories
Leveraged buyouts
Location in business and industry
Marketing
Munitions—Management
Nuclear industry—Management
Office management
Organizational change
Participative management
Personnel management
Productivity, Industrial
Real estate management
Retail trade—Management
Savings and loan associations—Management
Service industries—Management
Shoe industry—Management
Steel industry—Management
Team work in industry
Television industry—Management
Tire industry—Management
Valve industry—Management
Women executives

41st annual report on American industry [cover story; special issue] il *Forbes* 143:77-9+ Ja 9 '89
The 1990 guide to small business [special section] bibl il *U.S. News & World Report* 107:72-3+ O 23 '89
The B.E. guide to growing a business [special section] il *Black Enterprise* 19:125-6+ Je '89
Big ideas for your small business. D. M. Kehrer. il *Changing Times* 43:56-60 N '89
Born to run the show? The management test [women] A. Gates. il *Mademoiselle* 95:166+ Mr '89
Breaking the cycle that stifles innovation [views of Deborah J. Dougherty] A. Kozlov. il *Psychology Today* 23:18 O '89
Companies that compete best [cover story] B. Saporito. il *Fortune* 119:36-8+ My 22 '89
The corporate elite [cover story] il *Business Week* Special Issue:9-16+ O 20 '89
The corporation. See issues of Business Week
The Darman diet for bloated business [views of R. Darman] H. Gleckman. *Business Week* p102 Mr 13 '89
The excuse industry [explanations for lack of American success in global competition] R. J. Samuelson. il *Newsweek* 114:74 D 11 '89
Five steps to profits. C. Gottlieb. *Fortune* 119:14 Ja 30 '89
A formula for the future [address, October 19, 1988] I. W. Gorr. *Vital Speeches of the Day* 55:190-2 Ja 1 '89
Good entrepreneur, bad manager? T. Bachemin. il *Black Enterprise* 19:54-6+ Mr '89
How the kinder, more cooperative corporation wins [excerpt from When giants learn to dance] R. M. Kanter. *Working Woman* 14:118-20 My '89
I came, I saw, I blundered [foreign owners of U.S. companies] W. McWhirter. il *Time* 134:72+ O 9 '89
The importance of long-term thinking. C. W. Weinberger. il *Forbes* 144:31 Jl 24 '89
Is your company too big? [cover story] J. A. Byrne. il *Business Week* p84-8+ Mr 27 '89

A lesson learned and a lesson forgotten [American businessmen H. Sarasohn and C. Protzman instruct Japanese in management techniques during U.S. occupation] R. C. Wood. il pors *Forbes* 143:70-2+ F 6 '89
Lessons of leadership. See issues of Nation's Business
Life after debt: how LBOs do it. B. D. Fromson. il *Fortune* 119:91-2+ Mr 13 '89
The manager as a developer [address, November 5, 1988] G. M. Durst. *Vital Speeches of the Day* 55:309-14 Mr 1 '89
Managers' shoptalk. See issues of Working Woman beginning October 1984
The message of the market [stock plunges reflect business' response to competition] R. J. Samuelson. il *Newsweek* 114:64-8 O 30 '89
Needed: less bureaucracy [views of Thomas J. Peters] *USA Today (Periodical)* 117:14 Ap '89
New ways to exercise power [decentralization] T. A. Stewart. il *Fortune* 120:52-4+ N 6 '89
Professionalizing: a necessary hurdle [family businesses] J. L. Ward. il por *Nation's Business* 77:38-9 N '89
Sudden success [cover story; special section] il *Working Woman* 14:77-80+ Je '89
U.S. credibility and viability in worldwide competition [address, May 25, 1989] N. R. Augustine. *Vital Speeches of the Day* 55:693-7 S 1 '89
Why cowboy management is bad for American business [excerpt from When giants learn to dance] R. M. Kanter. il por *Working Woman* 14:134-6+ Ap '89

Bibliography

Ross Perot as literary critic. J. Queenan. il *Forbes* 143:90+ Ap 17 '89

Study and teaching

See also

Black executives—Training
Business schools
Entrepreneurs—Training
Executives—Training
Junior Achievement, Inc.

Action learning. D. Pine. *Psychology Today* 23:25-6 Jl/Ag '89

Germany (West)

Taking over the helm of Germany Inc. J. Templeman and G. E. Schares. il por *Business Week* p66-7 D 18 '89

Hungary

See also

International Management Center (Budapest, Hungary)

Japan

Dear Betty Harragan [Japanese management practices in the U.S.] B. L. Harragan. il *Working Woman* 14:50+ S '89
The delicate art of doing business in Japan. T. Holden. il *Business Week* p120 O 2 '89
Great Japanese mistakes. C. Rapoport. il *Fortune* 119:108-11 F 13 '89
How the Japanese manage risk. B. Harrison. il *Technology Review* 92:16 Ja '89
Learning from Japan's success. L. Tarshis. il *Scholastic Update (Teachers' edition)* 122:18-19 D 8 '89
A lesson learned and a lesson forgotten [American businessmen H. Sarasohn and C. Protzman instruct Japanese in management techniques during U.S. occupation] R. C. Wood. il pors *Forbes* 143:70-2+ F 6 '89

Soviet Union

See also

Higher Commercial Management School (Moscow, Soviet Union)

'We need yuppies in Moscow' [Soviet managers attend business course in U.S.] C. Leinster. il *Fortune* 120:153+ N 20 '89

BUSINESS MEETINGS *See* Corporations—Meetings
BUSINESS MEMOS *See* Memorandums
BUSINESS MENTORS

CEF fellowship program adds mentorship touch [Corporate Executive Fellows Program] B. Watson. il *Black Enterprise* 19:19 Ja '89
Help for women entrepreneurs [SBA's mentor program] B. Stein. il *Home Office Computing* 7:12 My '89
How tough critics may be mentors in disguise [excerpt from The critical edge] H. Weisinger. il *Working Woman* 14:102-4 Je '89
Lighting the way for youth. Y. R. Lamb. il *Black Enterprise* 19:205-7 F '89
Mentors & protégés: portraits of success [special section] A. L. Ball. il *Working Woman* 14:134-8+ O '89
With a little help from her friends [mentoring program started by Oregon chapter of the American Leadership Forum] J. C. Johnson. il *Nation's Business* 77:28 Ja '89

BUSINESS NAMES *See* Corporations—Names
BUSINESS ORGANIZATION *See* Business management
BUSINESS PATRONAGE OF ART *See* Art and industry
BUSINESS PATRONAGE OF THE ARTS *See* Arts and industry
BUSINESS PLANNING

See also

Computers—Business use
Organizational change
Product planning

BUSINESS PLANNING—*cont.*

Advance planning: the key to success in a business start-up. M. Rowland. *Working Woman* 14:58 Jl '89

The corporation. See issues of Business Week

A hard look at executive vision. W. Kiechel. il *Fortune* 120:207+ O 23 '89

How to prepare a business plan. M. Rowland. il *Working Woman* 14:89-90+ O '89

Intuition & strategic planning. W. H. Agor. il por *The Futurist* 23:20-3 N/D '89

A well-grounded plan can launch your business. S. Woolley. il *Business Week* p124-5 D 4 '89

Your business plan: road map to success. S. F. Edwards. il *Home Office Computing* 7:49-50 Ap '89

BUSINESS POLITICAL ACTION COMMITTEES See Political action committees

BUSINESS PRESENTATIONS

Acing the last-minute presentation. V. Randall. *Working Woman* 14:18-19 Ag '89

How to grab—and hold—an audience. D. H. Dunn. il *Business Week* p118 Ap 3 '89

How to make the pitch they can't resist. D. Walton. il *Working Woman* 14:102-4+ D '89

Aids and devices

Buyer's guide: presentation graphics [Draw Applause; 35mm Express; Graphics Gallery; Freelance Plus; Graph Plus; Harvard Graphics; Pixie] il *Personal Computing* 13:121-3+ F '89

Create inexpensive, yet high-quality presentations [Pinstripe Presenter and PFS: First Graphics] R. Geist and H. Geist. il *Home Office Computing* 7:34-5 Je '89

Create professional slides and presentations [Freelance Plus] R. Geist and H. Geist. il *Home Office Computing* 7:86-8 N '89

Dazzling artwork from dull numbers [presentation graphics software] D. P. Wiener. il *U.S. News & World Report* 106:63 Ja 9 '89

The desktop presentation star [Aldus Persuasion 1.0] M. Antonoff. il *Personal Computing* 13:188-9 Jl '89

The layman's guide to presentation design. R. Raskin. il *Home Office Computing* 7:37-9 Jl '89

Mac desktop presentation software [StandOut! 1.0, PowerPoint 2.00A, and Cricket Presents 1.0] L. Stevens. il *Byte* 14:203-5 Ap '89

Perspective Junior [presentation graphics program] J. Nimersheim. il *Compute!* 11:114+ O '89

Pinstripe Presenter [chart producing program] S. Anzovin. il *Compute!* 11:71 My '89

PowerPoint. B. Hunt. *Home Office Computing* 7:71-3 Ap '89

Presentation-graphics software. R. Raskin. il *Home Office Computing* 7:40-3 Jl '89

Presentations with punch. C. O'Malley. il *Personal Computing* 13:108-11+ Ja '89

Prodigious presentation power from Xerox [Xerox Presents] L. Kleinman. il *Personal Computing* 13:184-5 Je '89

Xerox Graph gives data its due [presentation graphics software] L. Kleinman. il *Personal Computing* 13:196+ N '89

BUSINESS RECESSION See Business depression

BUSINESS RELOCATION See Location in business and industry

BUSINESS REPORTS See Corporation reports

BUSINESS SCHOOLS

See also

Florida A & M University. School of Business and Industry

Harvard University. Graduate School of Business Administration

University of Chicago. Graduate School of Business

University of North Carolina at Chapel Hill. Graduate School of Business Administration

Wharton School

Give your business skills a B-school brush-up. L. Helm. il *Business Week* p88 Jl 24 '89

Curriculum

See also

Business ethics—Study and teaching

B-schools get a global vision. J. Main. il *Fortune* 120:78-80+ Jl 17 '89

Chicago's B-school goes touchy-feely. D. Greising. il *Business Week* p140 N 27 '89

Evaluation

B-schools: the up-and-comers. M. Roman. il *Business Week* p168-9 O 30 '89

How to pick a business school. W. Kiechel. il *Fortune* 120:225-6+ D 18 '89

Graduates

Getting down to business [special section] *Harper's Bazaar* 122:28+ Je '89

Gray suits in Oz [MBAs in Hollywood] N. Koch. il *Channels (New York, N.Y.: 1986)* 9:88 Ja '89

M.B.A.s with blue collars [manufacturers should recruit best and brightest young managers] A. G. Shilling. il por *Forbes* 144:300 O 16 '89

What B-school doesn't teach you about startups. il *Business Week* p40-1 Jl 24 '89

Anecdotes, facetiae, satire, etc.

Where I'm at right now. S. Bing. il *Esquire* 111:84 Je '89

Great Britain

See also

University of Cambridge. Institute of Management Studies

Hungary

See also

International Management Center (Budapest, Hungary)

Poland

The long road to capitalism. M. Schifrin. il *Forbes* 144:44 S 18 '89

Soviet Union

See also

Higher Commercial Management School (Moscow, Soviet Union)

BUSINESS SECRETS See Trade secrets

BUSINESS SUCCESS See Success

BUSINESS TRAINING FILMS See Motion pictures in industry

BUSINESS TRAVEL

See also

Automobiles in business

Frequent flier programs

Midway Airlines, Inc.

Accept nothing less than first class [black businessmen] E. G. Graves. il *Black Enterprise* 19:9 Mr '89

The B.E. guide to executive travel [special section] il *Black Enterprise* 19:69-70+ Mr '89

The business traveler. G. Eichler. See issues of Esquire beginning July 1986

Going places. E. C. Ray. il *Essence* 19:19+ Mr '89

How to make business travel more productive. J. Borchardt. il *Working Woman* 14:99-100+ S '89

In a cellular state of mind [computers and business travel] N. Sullivan. il *Home Office Computing* 7:116 N '89

A little plastic can help small companies, too [corporate travel and entertainment cards] S. Woolley. il *Business Week* p180 My 22 '89

On leaving [going on assignment and leaving children at home] D. Sobel. il *Ladies' Home Journal* 106:54+ Je '89

On the road again [traveling with a computer] W. Rash, Jr. il *Byte* 14:123-4 S '89

A room of her own [Reeves hotel for businesswomen in London] N. R. Gibbs. il *Time* 134:58-9 Ag 21 '89

Travel lights. M. Porter. il *Gentlemen's Quarterly* 59:247+ Mr '89

Psychological aspects

So it's come to this [study by Steve Barnett] G. Eichler. il *Esquire* 111:62 My '89

BUSINESS TRIPS See Business travel

BUSINESS WEEK

From typesetter to insider trader? [J. J. Lynch nabbed for trading on Business week column] C. Welles. *Business Week* p47-8 D 18 '89

The last 60 years—and a look ahead. J. W. Patten and S. B. Shepard. il *Business Week* p10 S 25 '89

To catch a thief [man attempts to get books from publishers by posing as a reviewer for Business week] L. Fleischer. *Publishers Weekly* 235:76 Ja 6 '89

BUSINESS WRITING

Better business writing that gets results. J. Pharriss. il *Working Woman* 14:128+ D '89

How to write letters that win jobs. M. Swain and R. Swain. il *Working Woman* 14:120-3 Ap '89

The Mulvihill perplexity [use of salutations] W. Safire. il *The New York Times Magazine* p10+ Je 25 '89

The perfect marriage—the message and the mechanics. C. Cohl. il *Home Office Computing* 7:8 Mr '89

BUSINESSLAND, INC.

More than just salesmen. R. A. Shaffer. il *Personal Computing* 13:45-6 D '89

Next means business now [agreement with Businessland] R. A. Shaffer. il *Personal Computing* 13:47-8 Jl '89

Steve Jobs gets the keys to the office PC market [link with Businessland] R. Brandt. il por *Business Week* p80-1 Ap 10 '89

Steve Jobs's hard sell [deal with Businessland] *Newsweek* 113:49 Ap 10 '89

The stubborn maverick of retail [D. A. Norman] C. O'Malley. por *Personal Computing* 13:76 Jl '89

Time to look at the retailers. R. A. Shaffer. il *Forbes* 144:128 D 25 '89

BUSINESSMEN

See also

Clothing and dress—Businessmen

Entrepreneurs

Executives

Faces behind the figures. See issues of Forbes

Fortune people. See issues of Fortune beginning May 9, 1988

Making it. See issues of Nation's Business beginning September 1985

What is business? [address, March 17, 1989] E. A. Opitz. *Vital Speeches of the Day* 55:497-500 Je 1 '89

BUSINESSMEN (AMERICAN) IN FOREIGN COUNTRIES See Americans—Foreign countries

BUSINESSMEN AS ARCHEOLOGISTS See Executives as archeologists

BUSINESSMEN AS PUBLIC OFFICERS *See* Executives as public officers

BUSINESSWOMEN
See also
Clothing and dress—Businesswomen
Women entrepreneurs
Women executives
Making it. See issues of Nation's Business beginning September 1985
On the move. See issues of Black Enterprise
Trade secrets: look your business best. il *Harper's Bazaar* 122:53+ Mr '89
Women who go for it! [A. Perez, T. F. Weekley, W. Matthews, and D. G. Robinson] B. M. Campbell. il pors *Essence* 20:48-50+ Ag '89

Travel
See Business travel
BUSINESSWOMEN (AMERICAN) IN FOREIGN COUNTRIES *See* Americans—Foreign countries
BUSINESSWOMEN'S ORGANIZATIONS
Where women can get business know-how. J. H. Pratt. il *Home Office Computing* 7:47-9 My '89
BUSING FOR SCHOOL INTEGRATION
After busing: education and choice. D. J. Armor. *Current (Washington, D.C.)* 316:14-20 O '89
BUSING OF THE HOMELESS *See* Homeless—Transportation
BUSKIRK, STEVEN, AND HARLOW, HENRY
Hunting for an elusive hunter. il *National Wildlife* 28:20-3 D '89/Ja '90
BUSONI, FERRUCCIO, 1866-1924
about
Arlecchino [opera] Reviews
The New Yorker 64:68+ Ja 16 '89. A. Porter
BUSS, JANICE E., AND OTHERS
Activation of the cellular proto-oncogene product p21Ras by addition of a myristylation signal. bibl f il *Science* 243:1600-3 Mr 24 '89
BUSS, TERRY
about
Driveway surfaces: concrete vs. asphalt [interview] il pors *Home Mechanix* 85:16-21+ Jl '89
BUSSCHE, GASTÓN VON DEM
Gabriela Mistral: poet and humanist. pors *The Unesco Courier* 42:49 N '89
BUSTS *See* Portrait sculpture
BUTADIENE
A rotationally resolved fluorescence excitation spectrum of all-trans-1,4-diphenyl-1,3-butadiene. J. F. Pfanstiel and others. bibl f il *Science* 245:736-8 Ag 18 '89
BUTANEDIAMINE
Ripe for a change [used to prolong shelf life of tomatoes; work of Peter J. Davies] T. Beardsley. *Scientific American* 261:26+ Jl '89
BUTCHER, CHARLES
about
Life begins—again—at 72. R. Koselka. il por *Forbes* 144:64-5 S 18 '89
BUTCHER, SUSAN
about
An intense drive. C. Szirak. il por *Women's Sports & Fitness* 11:66-7 Mr '89
BUTCHER, WILLARD C.
And now, back to the issues: budget, trade, banking and debtors [address, November 10, 1988] *Vital Speeches of the Day* 55:241-3 F 1 '89
BUTCHER CO., INC.
Life begins—again—at 72. R. Koselka. il por *Forbes* 144:64-5 S 18 '89
BUTENSKY, AVE
Riding the rumble seat into the '90s. por *Channels (New York, N.Y.: 1986)* 9:88 F '89
BUTLER, ABBEY J.
about
Background check. L. Gubernick. *Forbes* 143:14-15 F 20 '89
BUTLER, ALICE, AND OTHERS
A family of putative potassium channel genes in Drosophila. bibl f il *Science* 243:943-7 F 17 '89
BUTLER, BILL
about
Staying alive. S. Stapleton. il pors *Motor Boating & Sailing* 164:48-51+ N '89
BUTLER, FRANCELIA, 1913-
Scorned but not defeated. il *The Progressive* 53:50 Je '89
BUTLER, KATY
The great boomer bust. il *Mother Jones* 14:32-8 Je '89
Paté poverty: downwardly mobile baby boomers lust after luxury. il *Utne Reader* p72-80 S/O '89
BUTLER, M. CALDWELL
about
Right cross. F. Barnes. *The New Republic* 201:10-12 O 16 '89
BUTLER, MARSHALL D., 1927-
about
Living dangerously. A. A. Lappen. il por *Forbes* 143:100+ Je 26 '89
BUTLER, OCTAVIA E.
Birth of a writer. por *Essence* 20:74+ My '89

BUTLER, PAUL
about
Polly wants to be saved. S. Begley. il *Newsweek* 114:65 D 18 '89
BUTLER, PRISCILLA, 1909-
My white father [excerpt from Telling memories among southern women] S. Tucker. *Harper's* 279:36+ N '89
BUTLER, RICHARD
about
Nazi retreat. B. Reed. *The New Republic* 200:10-11 Ap 3 '89
BUTLER, STUART M.
A conservative war on poverty. il *National Review* 41:27-30 N 10 '89
Freeing health care. il *National Review* 41:34-6 D 22 '89
Stuart Butler [advice to George Bush] il *National Review* 41:25-6 F 10 '89
BUTOH
Heart of darkness [M. Tanaka and K. Appel's Can we dance a landscape?] T. Tobias. por *New York* 22:124+ N 6 '89
Variations on a theme of butoh. L. Garafola. il *Dance Magazine* 63:66-8 Ap '89
BUTOW, RONALD A.
(jt. auth) See Perlman, Philip S., and Butow, Ronald A.
BUTOWSKY, HARRY A.
Vacations for the mind. il *Ad Astra* 1:15-20 Je '89
BUTSON, ANN MARIE RADASKIEWICZ
Inside the classroom. por *Newsweek* 113:8 Je 5 '89
BUTTE COUNTY (CALIF.)
Criminal justice, Administration of
Jailing mothers for drug abuse [screening newborns] S. LaCroix. il *The Nation* 248:585-6+ My 1 '89
BUTTENWIESER, HELEN LEHMAN, 1905-1989
about
Obituary
The Nation 249:741 D 18 '89
BUTTER
See also
Margarine
Peanut butter
Butter & margarine. il *Consumer Reports* 54:249-53 D '89
Butter vs. margarine. il *Consumer Reports* 54:551-6 S '89
BUTTER MOLDS
Collectors and collecting
Collecting butter & cheese making tools. F. Johnson. il *Antiques & Collecting Hobbies* 94:46-9 Je '89
BUTTER PRINTS *See* Butter molds
BUTTER SCULPTURE
With no margarine for error, eight Buddhist monks practice a butter way to honor the gods [butter sculpting at the American Museum of Natural History] il *People Weekly* 31:81 F 27 '89
BUTTER SUBSTITUTES
Shake-on 'butter' is no great shakes. il *Consumer Reports* 54:489 Ag '89
BUTTERFIELD, DEBORAH, 1949-
about
Equestrian mysteries. M. Tucker. il *Art in America* 77:154-7+ Je '89
BUTTERFIELD, PAUL, 1942-1987
about
Father and son: an interview with Muddy Waters and Paul Butterfield [reprint] D. DeMicheal. pors *Down Beat* 56:68-71 S '89
BUTTERFLIES
See also
Caterpillars
Development
See Insects—Development
Migration
My butterfly mystery [monarch butterflies] J. Weiner. il *Reader's Digest* 135:134-6 S '89
Photographs and photography
Butterflies. J. Zuckerman. il *Petersen's Photographic Magazine* 18:54-7 Je '89
On the wing. K. B. Sandved. il *Harper's* 279:43 O '89
Sexual behavior
See Sexual behavior—Insects
BUTTERFLIES, ATTRACTING OF *See* Butterfly gardens
BUTTERFLY GARDENS
See also
Callaway Gardens. Day Butterfly Center
Butterfly gardens are soaring [live butterfly exhibits] R. Snyder. il *Flower and Garden* 33:50+ Mr/Ap '89
BUTTERNUT SQUASH COOKING *See* Cooking—Vegetables
BUTTERWORTH, BRENT
Last word. por *Omni (New York, N.Y.)* 12:156 D '89
BUTTOCKS EXERCISES *See* Exercise
BUTTON, JOHN, 1929-1982
about
Ambassador of light. B. Berkson. il por *Art in America* 77:170-5 N '89
BUTTONS
See also
Campaign buttons, posters, etc.
Tender Buttons (Firm)
The button. J. Berendt. il *Esquire* 112:72 S '89

BUTTONS—cont.
Collectors and collecting
A nostalgic look at buttons [antiques from Tender Buttons] il *Good Housekeeping* 209:198-9 S '89

Police uniform buttons. B. Manas. il *Antiques & Collecting Hobbies* 94:52-3 My '89

Well, button my lips if Dalton Stevens hasn't gone and stuck 'em on every ol' thing. il por *People Weekly* 32:141 D 4 '89

BUTTS, CALVIN O., III
about
The education of Reverend Butts. E. Pooley. il pors *New York* 22:42-9 Je 26 '89

Rev. Calvin Butts installed as pastor of Abyssinian Baptist Church in New York. il pors *Jet* 77:12-13 D 11 '89

BUTWIN, DAVID
Coward's Jamaica. il pors *Oceans* 22:54-7 Mr/Ap '89

Weekending at eight great beaches. il *Working Woman* 14:127-8 Je '89

BUTYRIC ACID
See also
Aminobutyric acid

BUXTON FESTIVAL *See* Music festivals—Great Britain
BUY & CELL [film] See Motion picture reviews—Single works
BUYBACKS (STOCKS) *See* Stocks—Repurchase
BUYER PROTECTION *See* Consumer protection

BUYERS (RETAIL TRADE)
Selling Montana [store buyers choosing from C. Montana's spring collection] H. Brubach. *The New Yorker* 64:110+ Ja 23 '89

BUYING *See* Bulk buying; Compulsive shopping; Consumption (Economics); Purchasing, Household; Shopping
BUYING POWER *See* Income
BUYOUTS, LEVERAGED *See* Leveraged buyouts
BUZZSAW BERKELEY [musical] See Musicals, revues, etc.—Reviews—Single works

BYARS, JAMES LEE, 1932-
about
Gilt trip. K. Larson. il *New York* 22:106-7 Ap 10 '89

BYBEE, JIM
Build REACTS: the Radio-Electronics Advanced Control System (XI). il *Radio-Electronics* 60:65-8 Ja '89

BYERS, JACK
about
High risks, distant payoffs. E. Dyson. il *Forbes* 144:114-16+ D 11 '89

BYERS, JOHN A.
Pronghorns in—and out of—a rut. il *Natural History* p38-49 Ap '89

BYNOE, PETER C. B.
about
Blacks buy NBA Nuggets; 1st black-owned pro team. il pors *Jet* 76:51+ Jl 24 '89

Blacks conclude deal to buy NBA Denver Nuggets. *Jet* 77:51 N 6 '89

The NBA scores a first in the front office. K. H. Hammonds and W. C. Symonds. il pors *Business Week* p26 Jl 24 '89

Nuggets buy makes history. Will it crumble barrier? P. Raybon. il pors *Black Enterprise* 20:17-18 S '89

Sale of Denver Nuggets to two blacks is delayed. pors *Jet* 77:37 O 30 '89

BYPASS SURGERY, CORONARY *See* Heart—Surgery
BYPASS SURGERY, GASTRIC *See* Stomach—Surgery
BYPASS TELEPHONE SYSTEMS *See* Telephone bypass systems

BYRD, DAVID EARL
Seize the time. por *Essence* 20:134 N '89

BYRD, DEBORAH
Do brown dwarfs really exist? il *Astronomy* 17:18-24 Ap '89

Eye on the sky. See issues of Astronomy beginning July 1988

BYRD, DONALD
about
Byrd bits on CD. R. Welburn. *Down Beat* 56:30 N '89

Donald Byrd's solo on Each time I think of you—a trumpet transcription. J. T. Cohen. il *Down Beat* 56:54 Mr '89

BYRD, MAX
Which viewpoint—and why. *The Writer* 102:12-14 O '89

BYRD, RICHARD EVELYN, 1888-1957
about
Richard E. Byrd. J. B. Graves. il pors *Conservative Digest* 15:24-7+ Ja/F '89

BYRD, ROBERT C.
Should the Senate-passed Immigration Act of 1989 be approved? [excerpts from debate, July 13, 1989] *Congressional Digest* 68:237+ O '89

BYRD, WILLIAM, 1674-1744
about
The best of Georgian. A. O. Boulton. il por *American Heritage* 40:110-17 F '89

BYRD ANTARCTIC EXPEDITION
Richard E. Byrd. J. B. Graves. il pors *Conservative Digest* 15:24-7+ Ja/F '89

BYRNE, BETH
about
Goal getter. L. Rothlein. il por *Women's Sports & Fitness* 11:78-9 Ap '89

BYRNE, DAVID
about
Byrne compiles Brazil LP. M. Goldberg. il por *Rolling Stone* p16 Ja 12 '89

David Byrne's Brazil. S. Stein. il por *Down Beat* 56:13 Jl '89

Rei Momo. A. DeCurtis. il *Rolling Stone* p111+ N 30 '89

Talking godheads. R. F. Thompson. il por *Rolling Stone* p78 Jl 13-27 '89

BYRNE, JOHN, 1949-, AND MARTINEZ, CECILIA
Ghastly science. bibl *Society* 27:22-4 N/D '89

BYRON, CHRISTOPHER
The bottom line. See issues of New York beginning May 29, 1989

Feeding frenzy. il *New York* 22:24-8 Je 26 '89

The phantom of Wall Street: how Ivan Boesky's bitter legacy haunts Mike Milken and his former firm. il pors *New York* 22:52-6 D 4 '89

Sweatshirt justice: how the war on crime is expanding to crush some rights. il *New York* 22:42-4+ O 2 '89
about
Between the lines. il por *New York* 22:8 My 29 '89

BYRON, ELLEN
Bring home the joy! il *Redbook* 174:118-19+ D '89

BYRON, GLORIA
Making money talk (I). il *Dance Magazine* 63:44-7 O '89

Making money talk (II). il *Dance Magazine* 63:40-3 N '89

BYRON, MICHAEL
about
Michael Byron at Phyllis Kind and Randolph Street. S. Taylor. il *Art in America* 77:183 Je '89

BYRON, WILLIAM J.
Empowerment and progress in the Campaign for Human Development. *America* 160:350-2 Ap 15 '89

A walk on the demand side [address, May 14, 1989] *Vital Speeches of the Day* 55:627-9 Ag 1 '89

BYTE (PERIODICAL)
15 years and counting. il *Byte* 14:397-8 S '89

Benchmarks at a glance: 1989. S. Diehl. il *Byte* 14 Special Issue:49-53 Fall '89

A billion bits of Byte. F. Langa. *Byte* 14:8 S '89

The Byte Awards. il *Byte* 14:327-30+ Ja '89

BYTE INFORMATION EXCHANGE (COMPUTER NETWORK) *See* BIX (Computer network)

BYZANTINE EMPIRE
Byzantium: the emperor's new clothes? [cover story] A. P. Kazhdan. bibl il map *History Today* 39:26-34 S '89

The idea of Holy Russia; tr. by J. Crowfoot. S. S. Averintsev. il *History Today* 39:37-44 N '89

C

C (COMPUTER LANGUAGE)
C++ users await next release. *Byte* 14:11-12 Ja '89

Power to the programmer [Watcom C 386] F. Hommel. il *Byte* 14:199-200+ D '89

QuickC smooths QuicAssembler programming. M. Blaszczak. il *Byte* 14:292+ N '89

Smoothing out C [optimizing compilers] S. Apiki and J. Udell. il *Byte* 14:170-8+ F '89

Think C goes OOP. T. Thompson. il *Byte* 14:81-2 O '89

C-130 AIRPLANES *See* Airplanes, Military transport
C.A.F. *See* Confederate Air Force

C.F. MONROE COMPANY
The decorated opal ware of C. F. Monroe. R. V. Simpson. il *Antiques & Collecting Hobbies* 94:36-40 S '89

C. G. BRETTING MFG. CO.
Folding napkins to ring up sales [T. Bretting wins Small Business Person of the Year Award] M. Barrier. il por *Nation's Business* 77:58-9 Jl '89

C I T GROUP HOLDINGS, INC.
Dai-Ichi's move on CIT: it's bold—and about time. T. Holden. il *Business Week* p202 S 25 '89

C³I (COMMAND, CONTROL, COMMUNICATIONS AND INTELLIGENCE NETWORK) *See* Communications, Military
CAB DRIVERS *See* Taxicab drivers

CABALA
Jewish mysticism in dispute [views of M. Idel and G. G. Scholem] R. Alter. *Commentary* 88:53-9 S '89

CABANAS
Far out pavilions [Lance Boge's fabric cabanas] D. B. Cowin. il *House & Garden* 161:140 Ag '89

CABARETS
Isn't it romantic? J. Pearlman. il *Harper's Bazaar* 122:189+ N '89

CABBAGE LOOPERS
The pathway of infection of Autographa californica nuclear polyhedrosis virus in an insect host. B. A. Keddie and others. bibl f il *Science* 243:1728-30 Mr 31 '89

CABBAGES
See also
Coleslaw
Cooking—Vegetables
Sauerkraut
Vegetables that think they're flowers [ornamentals; cover
story] L. B. Trigg. il *Southern Living* 24:50-1 O '89
Diseases and pests
First field test of engineered virus [weakened baculoviruses
to be sprayed onto cabbages] *Science News* 136:46 Jl 15
'89
CABELLO, JO ANN
Writing for Mother Jones. il *The Writer* 102:28 O '89
CABERNET SAUVIGNON (WINE) *See* Wine
CABINET (CANADA) *See* Canada. Cabinet
CABINET (GREAT BRITAIN) *See* Great Britain. Cabinet
CABINET (U.S.) *See* United States. Cabinet
CABINETMAKERS
See also
Barry, Joseph B., 1759 or 60-1838
Bullock, George, 1782 or 3-1818
Furness, Frank, 1839-1912
Goddard, John, 1723-1785
Linley, David Albert Charles Armstrong-Jones, Viscount,
1961-
Editorial. W. Garrett. il *Antiques* 135:1177 My '89
CABINETS (FURNITURE)
See also
Audio systems—Cabinets
Kitchen cabinets
Medicine cabinets
Vanities (Furniture)
Attic built-in [cabinets in bathroom] P. Brown and P. Brown.
il *Workbench* 45:30-3+ Mr/Ap '89
Build a home library [cover story] K. Collier. il *The Family
Handyman* 39:32-9 Jl/Ag '89
Building a three-drawer plan box. D. Yerman. il *Theatre
Crafts* 23:84-7 D '89
Changing times: 3-in-1 cabinet grows with your child. R.
Barnhart. il *Home Mechanix* 85:40-5 F '89
Divider and three-level cabinet. il *Sunset (Central West
edition)* 182:161 Ap '89
Hang a cabinet [corner cabinet] il *Southern Living* 24:130
My '89
Heirloom curio cabinet [Queen Anne] G. E. Derzinski. il
Workbench 45:30-6 S/O '89
Hiding and otherwise dealing with television. il *Sunset (Central
West edition)* 182:106 F '89
Lock 'em up [gun wall cabinet] P. Butler and M. Butler.
il *Outdoor Life* 184:44+ O '89
Lockable storage cabinet [workshops] S. Kingman and P.
Kingman. il *The Family Handyman* 39:84-5 My '89
Make space for yourself. il *Good Housekeeping* 208:190+
Ap '89
CABINS
See also
Log cabins, houses, etc.
1,200 square feet of efficiency on a rugged site. il *Sunset
(Central West edition)* 183:132 O '89
This little cabin hangs from 4 columns. il *Sunset (Central
West edition)* 182:130-2 Mr '89
Vacation cabin [built by owners Bill and Nina Stull] T.
Jackson. il *Better Homes and Gardens* 67:77-82 Je '89
Vacation house as summer camp [waterfront cabin on San
Juan Island] il *Sunset (Central West edition)* 183:94-5 O
'89
CABINS, AIRPLANE *See* Airplanes, Jet—Cabins
CABLE & WIRELESS PLC
Digital highwayman. J. Marcom, Jr. il *Forbes* 144:268-70
D 11 '89
CABLE LABS *See* Cable Television Laboratories Inc.
CABLE NEWS NETWORK
CNN takes on the big boys. J. N. Maclean. il *Reader's
Digest* 135:148-52 Ag '89
From 'chicken noodle network' to global powerhouse. S.
Ticer. il *Business Week* p106 Jl 17 '89
Going up against the Big Three [The world today] W. A.
Henry. il *Time* 134:86 O 30 '89
Here comes the judge—Catherine Crier now presides at a
news desk [co-anchor on The world today] J. Park. il
pors *People Weekly* 32:59-60 N 6 '89
In the battle for viewers at school, Turner takes on Whittle
[News Access service] F. Moore. il *Channels (New York,
N.Y.: 1986)* 9:14 Ap '89
Leading a stylish revolution in the fashion media [E. Klensch]
P. Warner. il por *Architectural Digest* 46:29+ S '89
Newsworld's U.S. model. D. Turbide. il *Maclean's* 102:42
Ag 7 '89
Residuals woes plague ESPN, CNN [advertisements beamed
into Latin America] J. Loftus. il *Channels (New York,
N.Y.: 1986)* 9:10 S '89
Vet Bernard Shaw, rookie newcomer, co-anchor CNN's 'The
world today' newscast. pors *Jet* 77:23 O 30 '89
CABLE RADIO
Music-by-wire: here comes digital radio. S. A. Booth. il
Popular Mechanics 166:26-7 F '89

CABLE TELEVISION
See also
Acton Corp.
Bravo (Firm)
Cable Television Laboratories Inc.
Cablevision Systems Corporation
Colony Communications
Continental Cablevision Inc.
Daniels & Associates Inc.
Discovery Channel
Falcon Communications
Greater Rochester Cablevision
Group W Cable, Inc.
Home Box Office
Law in cable television
Lifetime (Firm)
Manhattan Cable TV Services
Multichannel multipoint distribution service
New York Times Cable
NuCable Resources Corporation
Psychics in cable television
Sex in cable television
Storer Communications, Inc.
Tele-Communications, Inc.
Telephone companies—Cable television activities
Turner Broadcasting System, Inc.
Turner Network Television
USA Cable Network
Viacom International Inc.
Violence in cable television
Women in cable television
Breaking through [satellite master antenna television] R. Katz.
il *Channels (New York, N.Y.: 1986)* 9:92 D '89
Cable changes the system from within [operators] J. Stilson.
il *Channels (New York, N.Y.: 1986)* 9:90-1 D '89
A Carnegie Hall for the couch-potato crowd [pay-per-view
TV] P. Simons-Ellis. il *U.S. News & World Report* 107:62
N 27 '89
Descrambling pay-per-view [with editorial comment by Judith
Sawyer] F. Lovece. il *Video* 12:6, 48-50+ F '89
Hooray for pay television. P. W. Huber. il *Forbes* 144:136
D 25 '89
MSOs: the new frontiers [multiple system operators; special
section] il *Channels (New York, N.Y.: 1986)* 9:43+ Mr
'89
Pay-per-view starts perking. R. Zoglin. il *Time* 133:73 Mr
6 '89
Swinging for the fences? [pay-per-view] R. Katz. il *Channels
(New York, N.Y.: 1986)* 9:82 D '89
To watch is O.K., but to air is divine [public access cable
television] M. Kiernan. il *U.S. News & World Report*
107:112+ O 16 '89
Acquisitions and mergers
The Baby Bells toddle toward cable [Pacific Telesis' stake
in Group W Cable] R. D. Hof. il *Business Week* p40
My 8 '89
Going with the cash flow. P. Noglows. il *Channels (New
York, N.Y.: 1986)* 9:64 D '89
Llewellyn plugs into $420 million NYT cable deal. K. D.
Thompson. por *Black Enterprise* 19:17 Mr '89
The meaning of the merger [impact of Time-Warner merger
on cable operations] H. Solomon. il *Channels (New York,
N.Y.: 1986)* 9:62-3 Je '89
New blood for cable [InterMedia Partners] P. Noglows. il
Channels (New York, N.Y.: 1986) 9:45 O '89
Off the beach, back into cable [deal-maker J. Marcus] J.
Stilson. por *Channels (New York, N.Y.: 1986)* 9:20 N
'89
Time-Warner is wired for cable wars. D. Lieberman. il
Business Week p44 Ap 17 '89
Why GE is firming up its cable connection. D. Lieberman.
Business Week p134 Je 5 '89
Black music
See also
Soulbeat Entertainment Network
Children's programs
See also
YTV Canada Inc.
The best children's shows on cable. J. Morrow. il *TV Guide*
37:16-17+ F 25-Mr 3 '89
New kids' shows worth watching. M. Silver. il *U.S. News
& World Report* 107:64-5 Ag 21 '89
Comedy programs
See also
Comedy Channel
HA! The Comedy Network
Red-faced in Moscow? Would Billy Crystal get his laughs?
[taping a special] B. Crystal. il por *TV Guide* 37:14-15+
O 21-27 '89
Conversation programs
Even for cable, his lunatic talk show is cheap, but it's
paying big dividends for L.A.'s Mr. Pete [P. Chaconas]
R. Arias. il pors *People Weekly* 31:61-2 Je 19 '89
What's up with the doc. E. Grinnan. il por *Seventeen* 48:34
D '89
Ethical aspects
Wired [loaded politics of cable TV] T. W. Hazlett. *The
New Republic* 200:11-13 My 29 '89

CABLE TELEVISION—cont.

Export-import trade

American cable is lassoing foreign markets. W. C. Symonds. il *Business Week* p70-1 Ag 14 '89

Fashion programs

Leading a stylish revolution in the fashion media [E. Klensch] P. Warner. il por *Architectural Digest* 46:29+ S '89

Show and television [model C. Crawford to host House of style] P. Sikowitz. il por *Harper's Bazaar* 122:43 N '89

Finance

Cable. il *Channels (New York, N.Y.: 1986)* 9:40 Jl/Ag '89

Cable's balance of power [special section] il *Channels (New York, N.Y.: 1986)* 9:47+ Je '89

In the race for viewers, the networks fall further behind. R. Grover and D. Lieberman. il *Business Week* p80-1 Ja 9 '89

Who's picking up the check? J. Stilson. il *Channels (New York, N.Y.: 1986)* 9:76-9 D '89

Wrong channel [pay-per-view] W. Heuslein. il *Forbes* 143:10 My 29 '89

Financial programs

See also
Consumer News & Business Channel
Financial News Network Inc.

Franchise operations

Cable TV's costly monopoly game. J. A. Barnes. il *Reader's Digest* 135:97-100 O '89

Refranchising: cities fight back. H. Solomon. il *Channels (New York, N.Y.: 1986)* 9:46-9 Mr '89

Why cable costs too much. J. A. Barnes. *The Washington Monthly* 21:12-14+ Je '89

Wired [loaded politics of cable TV] T. W. Hazlett. *The New Republic* 200:11-13 My 29 '89

Game shows

Remote control. il *'Teen* 33:53 Mr '89

Laws and regulations

Awakening cable. M. Brown. il *Channels (New York, N.Y.: 1986)* 9:28 Je '89

Charge of the 'telcos' [fiber optic television vs. cable] B. Brewin. il *Video* 12:142 Ja '89

The coming battle over your TV set [telephone companies vs. cable operators] J. Dreyfuss. il *Fortune* 119:104-7 F 13 '89

Grabbing an electronic bonanza [telephone companies enter cable business; cover story] S. W. Dean, Jr. and R. L. Shayon. il *The Nation* 249:369+ O 9 '89

The gravy train may stop for cable TV operators. M. Lewyn and T. Smart. *Business Week* p59 D 18 '89

The latest telco debate [telephone companies entering cable business] M. Brown. il *Channels (New York, N.Y.: 1986)* 9:28 Mr '89

Learning to play in sweet harmony [broadcast stations and local cable systems] F. Lovece. il *Channels (New York, N.Y.: 1986)* 9:68-70 Ja '89

Setting cable free: did Congress unleash a monster? T. Smart. il *Business Week* p136 Je 5 '89

Telecom apartheid. P. W. Huber. il *Forbes* 144:268 N 27 '89

Tune in, turn on, sort out. J. Greenwald. il *Time* 133:68 My 29 '89

Washington casts a regulatory spell. P. Pagano. il *Channels (New York, N.Y.: 1986)* 9:38+ D '89

Why broadcasters woke up. M. Brown. il *Channels (New York, N.Y.: 1986)* 9:80 N '89

Management

10 to watch. il *Channels (New York, N.Y.: 1986)* 9:65-6+ Je '89

The meaning of achievement. J. J. Collins. por *Channels (New York, N.Y.: 1986)* 9:34 Jl/Ag '89

MSO problems and prospects [profiles of top 20 operators] il *Channels (New York, N.Y.: 1986)* 9:58-62 Mr '89

Marketing

Cable turns on to tune-in promotion. M. Burgi. il *Channels (New York, N.Y.: 1986)* 9:60-1 Ap '89

Cable's promotion puzzle [special section] il *Channels (New York, N.Y.: 1986)* 9:65-71 S '89

New customers at $50 a head, not $2,500 [Continental Cablevision] J. A. Trachtenberg. il *Forbes* 143:144-5 Mr 6 '89

Righting cable's image wrongs. K. Haley. il *Channels (New York, N.Y.: 1986)* 9:68-9 Jl/Ag '89

Motion pictures

See also
American Movie Classics (Firm)

Cablers' antidote for syndex chaos [syndicated-exclusivity rule] R. Katz. il *Channels (New York, N.Y.: 1986)* 9:70-1 S '89

Old gold [old films on TNT; special section] il *Film Comment* 25:29-48 Jl/Ag '89

Shifting windows: an indie dilemma [Hollywood films appearing on basic cable in advance of independent TV stations] R. Marich. il *Channels (New York, N.Y.: 1986)* 9:76-8 Ja '89

Who's got the theatrical window? [videotapes vs. pay-per-view; chart] il *Channels (New York, N.Y.: 1986)* 9:96 F '89

News

See also
Cable News Network
Newsworld

Dangerous liaisons [Whittle Communications' newscast with commercials for school classrooms] L. P. Sheinfeld. il *Film Comment* 25:70-2 S/O '89

The home town report. C. Reece. il *Channels (New York, N.Y.: 1986)* 9:57+ S '89

Is the classroom for blackboards or billboards? [controversy over Channel One] il *Consumer Reports* 54:286 My '89

The news show that's sweet revenge for the purists [World monitor] J. Weisman. il *TV Guide* 37:24-5 Ap 15-21 '89

Pay attention, class [P. Charren hopes to stop Whittle Communications' "Educational Network"] E. Watters. il por *Mother Jones* 14:18 D '89

S-TV (school TV) [Channel One] T. Kauchak. il *Seventeen* 48:48 S '89

School daze [controversy over commercials on Channel One news show used in schools] *The New Republic* 200:7-8 Ap 10 '89

Teacher or Trojan horse? [Whittle expands Channel One] L. Zuckerman. il *Time* 133:56 Je 19 '89

Today, class, we'll learn about soap [controversy over commercials on Channel One show used in schools] M. Starr. il *Newsweek* 113:62-3 Mr 20 '89

Whittle while you learn [controversy over Channel One] B. Brewin. il *Video* 13:122 My '89

Whittling the message into the medium [Whittle Communications' plans to broadcast news show with commercials in classrooms] E. Pomice. il *U.S. News & World Report* 106:52+ F 20 '89

Wooing a captive audience [Whittle Communications provides schools with television equipment in exchange for mandatory watching of Channel One] J. E. Gallagher. il *Time* 133:88 F 20 '89

Programming

Cable. il *TV Guide* 37:12-14+ S 9-15 '89

Cable networks plan double feature future. J. Stilson. il *Channels (New York, N.Y.: 1986)* 9:31 O '89

Cable TV's fresh pitch. A. Gabor and C. P. Work. il *U.S. News & World Report* 106:56-7 Ja 30 '89

Is cable now worth the money? D. Handler. il *TV Guide* 37:24-6 Ap 8-14 '89

The search for identity. M. Brown. il *Channels (New York, N.Y.: 1986)* 9:34 Ja '89

Who's picking up the check? J. Stilson. il *Channels (New York, N.Y.: 1986)* 9:76-9 D '89

Rap music

Top hip-hop [Yo! MTV raps] J. Malanowski. il por *Rolling Stone* p77-8 Jl 13-27 '89

Rates

Cable rate flux [Ohio; table] il *Channels (New York, N.Y.: 1986)* 9:88 Je '89

Cable TV's costly monopoly game. J. A. Barnes. il *Reader's Digest* 135:97-100 O '89

Why cable costs too much. J. A. Barnes. *The Washington Monthly* 21:12-14+ Je '89

Ratings

A headlock on pay-per-view [boxing and wrestling dominate top 20 events of decade; table] il *Channels (New York, N.Y.: 1986)* 9:100 N '89

Religious programs

Will cable operators unplug Christian TV? il *Christianity Today* 33:36+ F 3 '89

Rock music

See also
MTV Networks Inc.
MuchMusic Network
Soulbeat Entertainment Network
Video Jukebox Network, Inc.

Dig in, Robert [R. Meyrowitz] P. Newcomb. il por *Forbes* 143:328 My 29 '89

Shopping services

See Electronic shopping

Sports

See also
Entertainment and Sports Programming Network
Madison Square Garden Network
Southeastern Sports Network
Sports Network
Sports News Network (Cable television)
SportsChannel America

Give this plan an 'F' [SportsChannel America televising high school football games] R. Reilly. por *Sports Illustrated* 71:100 S 18 '89

A headlock on pay-per-view [boxing and wrestling dominate top 20 events of decade; table] il *Channels (New York, N.Y.: 1986)* 9:100 N '89

Late-night score wars [CNN's Sports Tonight and ESPN's SportsCenter] A. Wolff. il *Sports Illustrated* 70:74 Je 26 '89

Left out in the cold [National Hockey League TV rights held by SportsChannel America] A. Murphy. il *Sports Illustrated* 70:81 F 20 '89

CABLE TELEVISION—Sports—cont.

The upstart (slam!) who's reinventing (pow!) the tube (grrr!) [V. McMahon and professional wrestling on pay-per-view television] J. Hammer. il pors *Gentlemen's Quarterly* 59:280-5+ N '89

Whole lot of Carays going on [three generations of play-by-play announcers] D. S. Looney. il *Sports Illustrated* 71:87 Ag 14 '89

Would you pay to watch the Super Bowl? N. Hickey. il *TV Guide* 37:31-2+ N 25-D 1 '89

Wrong channel [pay-per-view] W. Heuslein. il *Forbes* 143:10 My 29 '89

The Yankee dollar [Cablevision and MSG battle over cable rights to Yankee baseball] C. Byron. il *New York* 22:20+ Je 5 '89

Syndicated programs

Cablers' antidote for syndex chaos [syndicated-exclusivity rule] R. Katz. il *Channels (New York, N.Y.: 1986)* 9:70-1 S '89

In the eye of the storm [Tribune Co. fights syndicated exclusivity rules; interview with J. Dowdle] K. Haley. il pors *Channels (New York, N.Y.: 1986)* 9:62-3 Ja 16 '89

Norman Lear, meet Adam Smith [Greater Rochester Cablevision owned by Time Warner competes with Act III Broadcasting's independent station in syndicated market] P. Newcomb. il *Forbes* 144:206+ N 27 '89

Off-net hours: life after cable? H. Solomon. il *Channels (New York, N.Y.: 1986)* 9:48-50 Ja 16 '89

Syndication on the wire. il *Channels (New York, N.Y.: 1986)* 9:64 Ja 16 '89

What's syndex? Will it affect you? [syndicated exclusivity reimposed by the Federal Communications Commission] N. Hickey. il *TV Guide* 37:12 D 23-29 '89

Weather forecasts

See also

Weather Channel

Canada

See also

MuchMusic Network

Newsworld

Rogers Communications Inc.

Sports Network

YTV Canada Inc.

Wiring the world. D. Jenish. il *Maclean's* 102:32-3 Jl 17 '89

China

China star [Y.-S. Kan] *The New Yorker* 64:20-2 Ja 9 '89

France

See also

Canal Plus (Firm)

United States

See Cable television

Western Europe

See also

Sky Television plc

Four titans carve up European TV [cover story] W. Fisher and M. Schapiro. il *The Nation* 248:37+ Ja 9-16 '89

CABLE TELEVISION, BLACK

See also

Black Entertainment Television

Llewellyn plugs into $420 million NYT cable deal. K. D. Thompson. por *Black Enterprise* 19:17 Mr '89

CABLE TELEVISION ADVERTISING

Cable closes in on the classifieds [NuCable Resources] J. Loftus. il por *Channels (New York, N.Y.: 1986)* 9:52-4 Mr '89

Cable nets go it alone [production of on-air promos] R. Katz. il *Channels (New York, N.Y.: 1986)* 9:76 N '89

Mutual aid society [joint promotion of Storer Cable and KLRT in Little Rock, Ark.] A. Snyder. il *Channels (New York, N.Y.: 1986)* 9:22-3 Ja '89

Residuals woes plague ESPN, CNN [advertisements beamed into Latin America] J. Loftus. il *Channels (New York, N.Y.: 1986)* 9:8 Jl/Ag '89

Time purchasing

Cable's smarter sell [special section] il *Channels (New York, N.Y.: 1986)* 9:57-62 Ap '89

Media mixing in the rep business. L. Collins. il *Channels (New York, N.Y.: 1986)* 9:90-1 N '89

A surprisingly good year for the masses. D. Kalish. il *Channels (New York, N.Y.: 1986)* 9:28+ D '89

CABLE TELEVISION ADVERTISING AND CHILDREN

Dangerous liaisons [Whittle Communications' newscast with commercials for school classrooms] L. P. Sheinfeld. il *Film Comment* 25:70-2 S/O '89

Is the classroom for blackboards or billboards? [controversy over Channel One] il *Consumer Reports* 54:286 My '89

Pay attention, class [P. Charren hopes to stop Whittle Communications' "Educational Network"] E. Watters. il por *Mother Jones* 14:18 D '89

School daze [controversy over commercials on Channel One news show used in schools] *The New Republic* 200:7-8 Ap 10 '89

Teacher or Trojan horse? [Whittle expands Channel One] L. Zuckerman. il *Time* 133:56 Je 19 '89

Today, class, we'll learn about soap [controversy over commercials on Channel One show used in schools] M. Starr. il *Newsweek* 113:62-3 Mr 20 '89

Whittle while you learn [controversy over Channel One] B. Brewin. il *Video* 13:122 My '89

Whittling the message into the medium [controversy over commercials on Channel one] E. Pomice. il *U.S. News & World Report* 106:52+ F 20 '89

Wooing a captive audience [controversy over commercials on Channel One] J. E. Gallagher. il *Time* 133:88 F 20 '89

CABLE TELEVISION AND CHILDREN

Locking out sex and violence on cable. M. Meyer. il *Video* 13:61-2 Ap '89

CABLE TELEVISION AND POLITICS

The greening of Ted Turner [cover story] J. Lanham. il pors *The Humanist* 49:5-7+ N/D '89

CABLE TELEVISION AND WOMEN

If at first you don't succeed . . . [Lifetime] M. Burgi. il *Channels (New York, N.Y.: 1986)* 9:66-7 S '89

CABLE TELEVISION IN EDUCATION

Dangerous liaisons [Whittle Communications' newscast with commercials for school classrooms] L. P. Sheinfeld. il *Film Comment* 25:70-2 S/O '89

In the battle for viewers at school, Turner takes on Whittle [News Access service] F. Moore. il *Channels (New York, N.Y.: 1986)* 9:14 Ap '89

Is the classroom for blackboards or billboards? [controversy over Channel One] il *Consumer Reports* 54:286 My '89

Pay attention, class [P. Charren hopes to stop Whittle Communications' "Educational Network"] E. Watters. il por *Mother Jones* 14:18 D '89

S-TV (school TV) [Channel One] T. Kauchak. il *Seventeen* 48:48 S '89

School daze [controversy over commercials on Channel One news show used in schools] *The New Republic* 200:7-8 Ap 10 '89

Teacher or Trojan horse? [Whittle expands Channel One] L. Zuckerman. il *Time* 133:56 Je 19 '89

Today, class, we'll learn about soap [controversy over commercials on Channel One show used in schools] M. Starr. il *Newsweek* 113:62-3 Mr 20 '89

Whittle while you learn [controversy over Channel One] B. Brewin. il *Video* 13:122 My '89

Whittling the message into the medium [Whittle Communications' plans to broadcast news show with commercials in classrooms] E. Pomice. il *U.S. News & World Report* 106:52+ F 20 '89

Wooing a captive audience [Whittle Communications provides schools with television equipment in exchange for mandatory watching of Channel One news program] J. E. Gallagher. il *Time* 133:88 F 20 '89

CABLE TELEVISION LABORATORIES INC.

Cable Labs swings into the future. J. M. Robins. il *Channels (New York, N.Y.: 1986)* 9:50-1 Mr '89

CABLE TELEVISION SATELLITES *See* Communications satellites—Television broadcasting use

CABLES

See also

Computer cables

Electric cables

Telephone cables

CABLESOFT INC.

A real Live Wire [LiveWire board delivers quotes from Financial News Network] R. Bel Bruno. il *Personal Computing* 13:38 Ja '89

CABLEVISION SYSTEMS CORPORATION

A cable mogul's daring dance on the high wire [C. Dolan] D. Lieberman. il por *Business Week* p133-4+ Je 5 '89

Can a maverick run a giant? [C. F. Dolan] C. Reece. il por *Channels (New York, N.Y.: 1986)* 9:49-50+ Je '89

The Yankee dollar [Cablevision and MSG battle over cable rights to Yankee baseball] C. Byron. il *New York* 22:20+ Je 5 '89

CABO SAN LUCAS (MEXICO)

Description

Numero Uno [marlin fishing off Cabo San Lucas in a Barattucci 82-foot sportsfisher] N. Rabinowitz. il *Motor Boating & Sailing* 163:52-7+ Ap '89

CABOT, LOUIS W.

Sci-humanists unite [address, January 26, 1989] *Vital Speeches of the Day* 55:467-70 My 15 '89

CACHE MEMORY

ALR revs up MCA [MicroFlex 7000] B. Catchings and M. L. Van Name. il *Byte* 14:165-9 S '89

ALR's other 80486s: the PowerCache 4 duo. il *Byte* 14:112-13 N '89

Better than cache in the bank? [Western Digital Speedkit caching controller] H. Eglowstein. il *Byte* 14:204+ S '89

Caching in. il *Byte* 14:328-9 N '89

Caching in on memory systems. B. Glass. il *Byte* 14:281-5 Mr '89

Cold cache for your hard disk [hyperStore-816 and Smart Cache PM3011] S. Miastkowski. *Byte* 14:86+ O '89

Disk caching. B. Glass. il *Byte* 14:297-301 O '89

EMS with a cache [Elite 16 Plus HyperCache] J. Holtzman. il *Byte* 14:181-2+ Jl '89

CACHE MEMORY—*cont.*
Risking pushed-chip performance [Dyna 30MHz 386 Cache Tower System] J. Pepper. il *Personal Computing* 13:190-1 S '89

CACHECTIN *See* Tumor necrosis factor

CACICEDO, JEAN WILLIAMS- *See* Williams-Cacicedo, Jean

CACTUS
See also
Christmas cactus
Brumley Ridge, Utah [spineless hedgehog cactus] R. H. Mohlenbrock. il map *Natural History* p68-71 S '89
The regeneration gap [disappearance of saguaro and long-nosed bats from Saguaro National Monument] J. Erickson. il *National Parks* 63:30-3 Jl/Ag '89

Photographs and photography
Cactus flower. T. A. Wiewandt. il *National Wildlife* 27:46-51 Ag/S '89

Theft
Lassoing the cactus bandit [saguaro theft and conservation efforts in Arizona] J. Houston. il *Omni (New York, N.Y.)* 11:22 Ag '89

CACTUS RUSTLERS *See* Cactus—Theft

CAD (COMPUTER-AIDED DESIGN) *See* Computer graphics

CADDEN, VIVIAN
Mothers on a diplomatic mission. il *McCall's* 116:86+ Ap '89
Raisa. il pors *McCall's* 116:110+ F '89
(jt. auth) See Schoumacher, Stephanie, and Cadden, Vivian

CADENCE DESIGN SYSTEMS INC.
The hot box syndrome. K. K. Wiegner. il por *Forbes* 143:178+ Ap 17 '89
Sure, he's wild and crazy—like a fox [J. B. Costello] R. D. Hof. il por *Business Week* p132 O 30 '89

CADES COVE (TENN.)
A frosty morning at Cades Cove. J. T. Black. il *Southern Living* 24:24+ O '89

CADETS
See also
Women cadets

CADHERINS
Neural cadherin: role in selective cell-cell adhesion. S. Miyatani and others. bibl f il *Science* 245:631-5 Ag 11 '89

CADIGAN, PAT
Shoot the moon [fiction] il *Omni (New York, N.Y.)* 11:68-70+ Jl '89

CADILLAC MOTOR CAR DIVISION
Fins de siècle [40th anniversary of the Cadillac Coupe De Ville] S. Loveday. il *Vogue* 179:264 F '89
Polishing Cadillac's image [Allanté] M. Keller. il *Motor Trend* 41:136 F '89
The prestige deficit. P. Bedard. il *Car and Driver* 34:15 Ja '89

CADMIUM POISONING
Prevention
Possible ban of some artists' materials. il *American Artist* 53:22+ N '89

CADMIUM SULFIDE
Semiconductor studies get a rise from yeast. F. Flam. *Science News* 135:231 Ap 15 '89

CADY, MARLENE L. S.
The pure joy of being alive [cover story] il pors *People Weekly* 32:64-71 Jl 3 '89

CADY TWINS *See* Siamese twins

CAEDMON AUDIO (FIRM)
JFK Jr. to narrate 'Profiles in courage' for Harper Audio. il pors *Publishers Weekly* 236:28 D 1 '89

CAEIRO, ALBERTO *See* Pessoa, Fernando, 1888-1935

CAEN, HERB
Infinite riches in a little room. il por *Architectural Digest* 46:52+ My '89
Two cities wild for 'Baysball'. il *Newsweek* 114:70 O 23 '89

CAENORHABDITIS ELEGANS MUTATION *See* Mutation—Nematodes

CAENORHABDITIS ELEGANS NERVOUS SYSTEM *See* Nervous system—Nematodes

CAESAR, SID
about
31 years later, New York renders unto Sid that which is Caesar's—laughter. il por *People Weekly* 32:92-3 Jl 10 '89
Sid Caesar. il pors *People Weekly* 31 Special Issue:30-1 Summ '89
Theater [Sid Caesar & Company: Does anybody know what I'm talking about?] J. Simon. *New York* 22:131-2 N 13 '89
The theatre [Sid Caesar & Company: Does anybody know what I'm talking about?] E. Oliver. *The New Yorker* 65:106 N 13 '89

CAESAREAN SECTION *See* Cesarean section

CAFARO, J. J.
about
Buffing up an old classic. F. Washington. il por *Newsweek* 113:46 Ap 3 '89
The car that won't die. S. Kichen. il pors *Forbes* 144:176+ O 2 '89

CAFARO, TERRI L., AND NEUMAIER, DIANE, 1946-
La bicentenaire II [photographs] il *Art in America* 77:55-9 O '89

CAFE (CORPORATE AVERAGE FUEL ECONOMY) STANDARD *See* Automobile engines—Energy usage

CAFE BEAUJOLAIS (MENDOCINO, CALIF.) *See* Mendocino (Calif.)—Restaurants, nightclubs, bars, etc.

CAFE BEL CANTO (NEW YORK, N.Y.) *See* New York (N.Y.)—Restaurants, nightclubs, bars, etc.

CAFFEINE
Caffeine addiction. il *Glamour* 87:236 F '89
Coffee and conception [research by Allen Wilcox and others] P. King. *Psychology Today* 23:25 N '89
A cup of infertility? [linked to use of caffeine; research by Allen Wilcox] J. Rivkin. il *American Health* 8:124 Je '89
Latest infertility suspect: caffeine. il *Newsweek* 113:60 Ja 23 '89
The new diet buzzword—caffeine! E. Kunes. il *Mademoiselle* 95:230 O '89
Panic by the cupful [effect on panic disorder; research by Michael F. Breslow] L. Schroepfer. il *American Health* 8:46 Je '89
The weight-loss perk [effect on metabolism] K. Hamilton. il *Health (New York, N.Y.)* 21:32+ Jl '89
What's brewin'? [effects on health and athletic performance] L. Applegate. il *Runner's World* 24:22-4 N '89

CAFFEINE-FREE COFFEE *See* Coffee

CAGE, JOHN
about
The avant-garde composer returns to a lost love. D. Sylvester. il por *Architectural Digest* 46:134+ Ap '89
Year of the Cage in Cambridge. F. Bouchard. *Down Beat* 56:11 Jl '89

CAGE, NICOLAS
about
Vampire's kiss: Nicolas Cage bites back. J. E. Fitch. il pors *American Film* 14:67-8 Je '89

CAGES
See also
Bird cages

CAGNEY, KATE
Health kick. *The Nation* 249:301 S 25 '89

CAGNEY & LACEY [television program] *See* Television program reviews—Single works

CAHALL, CHRISTINA ORR- *See* Orr-Cahall, Christina, 1947-

CAHILL, LINDA
Jalapa moves ahead. il *Américas* 41 no1:7 '89

CAHILL, MICHAEL O'CONNELL- *See* O'Connell-Cahill, Michael

CAHILL, SUSAN
Challenges facing U.S. Catholics. *Commonweal* 116:621 N 17 '89

CAHILL, TIM
Born again. il *Life* 12:32-4+ Je '89
Into the eye of a hurricane [condensed from Jaguars ripped my flesh] il *Reader's Digest* 135:81-4 S '89

CAHN, LILLIAN
about
Goat cheese, anyone? P. Berman. il pors *Forbes* 144:220-1 S 18 '89

CAHN, MILES
about
Goat cheese, anyone? P. Berman. il pors *Forbes* 144:220-1 S 18 '89

CAHN, PATRICIA
(jt. auth) See Cahn, Robert, and Cahn, Patricia

CAHN, ROBERT, AND CAHN, PATRICIA
Reorganizing conservation efforts in New Zealand. bibl f il maps *Environment* 31:18-20+ Ap '89

CAHOUET, FRANK V.
about
Selling your problems to others. il por *Forbes* 143:97 Ja 9 '89

CAHUACHI SITE (PERU) *See* Peru—Antiquities

CAILLET, LAURENCE
The Pavilion of the Second Moon. il *The Unesco Courier* 42:24-31 D '89

CAIN, CHRISTOPHER
about
Young guns [film] Reviews
Video il 12:60-1 F '89. D. Wheeler

CAIN, JOY DUCKETT
Debbi Morgan: feeling good. il pors *Essence* 20:105-6+ S '89
Florence Griffith Joyner: life in the fast lane [cover story] pors *Essence* 19:48-50+ Mr '89
The Jackie nobody knows [cover story] pors *Essence* 20:62-4+ Ag '89

CAIN, STEPHEN ALEXIS
Military budget: one more for the Gipper. il *The Bulletin of the Atomic Scientists* 45:5-6 Jl/Ag '89

CAIN, WILLIAM E., 1952-
(jt. auth) See Graff, Gerald, 1937-, and Cain, William E., 1952-

CAINE, MICHAEL, 1933?-
about
A 'Dirty' job. A. White. il por *Rolling Stone* p44 F 9 '89

CAINE, SHAKIRA
about
Don't call it a Caine mutiny, but Michael's wife, Shakira, is shaking her baubles, bangles and beads. J. Stark. il pors *People Weekly* 32:105-6 N 27 '89

CAIRNS, JOHN, 1923-
Speaking at length. *BioScience* 39:632-3 O '89

CAIRNS, SCOTT
Embalming [poem] *The New Republic* 200:34 Je 26 '89
The mummy viewed [poem] *The New Republic* 201:36 N 13 '89
Still waiting [poem] *The New Republic* 200:34 Ja 2 '89

CAIRO (EGYPT)
Description
Coping with Cairo. W. P. Barrett. il *Forbes* 143:156-8 Ap 3 '89
Galleries and museums
See also
Egyptian Museum
Music
See also
Opera—Egypt
Streets
In the heart of an ancient capital. A. Bonnamy. il *The Unesco Courier* 42:30-3 Ag '89

CAISSE DE DÉPÔT ET PLACEMENT DU QUÉBEC
Quebec's powerful secret weapon. D. Francis. il *Maclean's* 102:23 O 30 '89

CAJORI, CHARLES
about
Charles Cajori at the New York Studio School. L. Campbell. *Art in America* 77:202 My '89

CAJUN COOKING *See* Cooking, Cajun
CAJUN MUSIC
See also
Radio broadcasting—Cajun music

CAKE
See also
Brownies (Cake)
Cheesecake
Coffee cake
Cupcakes
Fruitcake
Gingerbread
A big beautiful cake that you can bake [tiered cakes for up to 112 people] il *Sunset (Central West edition)* 182:208-10+ My '89
Cakes: delicious legacies [cover story] P. Y. Cordell. il *Southern Living* 24:86-9 Mr '89
Cakes for giving. il *Southern Living* 24:106-7 D '89
A century of classic cakes. il *Ladies' Home Journal* 106:182-4+ O '89
A chocolate fantasy. S. Payne. il *Southern Living* 24:120-2+ F '89
A contest and a cake [Great New Delectations Contest and chocolate cake] N. Hazelton. *National Review* 41:48+ Je 16 '89
Double-chocolate mousse cake. il *Good Housekeeping* 209:46 S '89
Dried cherries and dark chocolate combine in a glossy layer cake. il *Sunset (Central West edition)* 182:190 Ap '89
Easy Easter basket cake. il *Redbook* 172:28 Ap '89
Fall cakes . . . fragrant and fruity with tart apples. il *Sunset (Central West edition)* 182:112-13 Ja '89
Fantastic cakes. A. Johnson. il *Parents* 64:151-2+ My '89
From our kitchen to yours. K. Adams. *Southern Living* 24:204 Mr '89
Light cornbread and a moist, springy cake [four-spice wine savarin] il *Sunset (Central West edition)* 182:112-13 Ja '89
Luscious strawberry cake. il *Southern Living* 24:133 Jl '89
Nothing but chocolate. il *Ladies' Home Journal* 106:228-30+ My '89
Queen's cake . . . treasured recipe from old Finland. il *Sunset (Central West edition)* 183:100 Ag '89
Rites of passage III [receiving lamb cake as Confirmation Day present] M. E. Marty. il *The Christian Century* 106:735 Ag 2-9 '89
Show-off chocolate cake. il *Good Housekeeping* 209:50 D '89
What's cooking? Fun for all! [Christmas tree cakes] il *Redbook* 174:26 D '89

CAL-A-VIE (VISTA, CALIF.: SPA) *See* Health resorts, watering places, etc.—California
CALABRESE, RAYMOND L.
Ethics for principals. *The Education Digest* 54:16-19 Mr '89
Student alienation and academic achievement. *The Education Digest* 54:7-9 My '89

CALADIUMS
Delightful, dependable caladiums. T. A. Steadman. il *Southern Living* 24:42-3 Jl '89

CALAH (ANCIENT CITY)
The golden treasures of Nimrud. P. Elmer-Dewitt. il *Time* 134:80-1 O 30 '89

CALAMITIES *See* Disasters
CALANO, JAMES, AND SALZMAN, JEFF
How delegation can lead your team to victory. *Working Woman* 14:86-7+ Ag '89
How to be the boss they all want to work for [excerpt from Careertracking] il *Working Woman* 14:94-5+ Ja '89
Ten ways to fire up your creativity [excerpt from Career tracking] *Working Woman* 14:94-5 Jl '89

CALATHEAS
Calatheas: beyond green. L. B. Trigg. il *Southern Living* 24:44-5 D '89

CALATRAVA, SANTIAGO, 1951-
about
Perfect pitch. J. S. Russell. il *Architectural Record* 177:108-17 mid-S '89

CALAVERAS BIG TREES STATE PARK (CALIF.)
Notes and comment [felling of Discovery Tree redwood in 1853] *The New Yorker* 64:23-4 F 13 '89

CALAVERAS FAULT *See* Faults (Geology)
CALAWAY, JAMES C.
about
Fed up. S. Hornik. il por *Common Cause Magazine* 15:6 Jl/Ag '89

CALBERT, CATHLEEN
When nights were full of sex and churches [poem] *The New Republic* 201:32 D 25 '89

CALCAVECCHIA, MARK
about
Giving out high marks. J. Diaz. il pors *Sports Illustrated* 70:20-1 Mr 6 '89
High noon at Troon. R. Reilly. il por *Sports Illustrated* 71:20-2+ Jl 31 '89

CALCIO STORICO (FLORENCE, ITALY)
Patriotic gore. P. Jordan. il *Gentlemen's Quarterly* 59:71+ Je '89

CALCITE
Great Basin calcite vein and the Pleistocene time scale [discussion of December 2, 1988 article, A 250,000-year climatic record from Great Basin vein calcite: implications for Milankovitch theory] I. J. Winograd and others. *Science* 246:262-3 O 13 '89

CALCIUM BLOCKING AGENTS
See also
Nimodipine
Verapamil
CALCIUM CARBONATE
See also
Calcite
Coccolithophores
Calcium carbonate found in 'Mars' meteorites [research by James L. Gooding] *Astronomy* 17:14 Je '89
Mollusk teaches ceramics to scientists [rugged shell of the red abalone; research by Mehmet Sarikaya] I. Amato. *Science News* 136:383 D 9 '89

CALCIUM CHANNELS
The cycling of calcium as an intracellular messenger. H. Rasmussen. bibl il *Scientific American* 261:66-73 O '89
Localization and mobility of ω-conotoxin-sensitive Ca^{2+} channels in hippocampal CA1 neurons. O. T. Jones and others. bibl f il *Science* 244:1189-93 Je 9 '89
Modulation of calcium channels in cardiac and neuronal cells by an endogenous peptide. G. Callewaert and others. bibl f il *Science* 243:663-6 F 3 '89
Primary structure of the β subunit of the DHP-sensitive calcium channel from skeletal muscle. P. Ruth and others. bibl f il *Science* 245:1115-18 S 8 '89
Rapid β-adrenergic modulation of cardiac calcium channel currents by a fast G protein pathway. A. Yatani and A. M. Brown. bibl f il *Science* 245:71-4 Jl 7 '89
Specific block of calcium channel expression by a fragment of dihydropyridine receptor cDNA. I. Lotan and others. bibl f il *Science* 243:666-9 F 3 '89
Splice variants of the α subunit of the G protein G_s activate both adenylyl cyclase and calcium channels. R. Mattera and others. bibl f il *Science* 243:804-7 F 10 '89

CALCIUM CHELATES *See* Chelation
CALCIUM IN THE BODY
Activation of salivary secretion: coupling of cell volume and $[Ca^{2+}]_i$ in single cells. J. K. Foskett and J. E. Melvin. bibl f il *Science* 244:1582-5 Je 30 '89
Bad to the bone. G. L. Blackburn. il *Prevention (Emmaus, Pa.)* 41:99-100+ Mr '89
Block of stretch-activated ion channels in Xenopus oocytes by gadolinium and calcium ions. X.-C. Yang and F. Sachs. bibl f il *Science* 243:1068-71 F 24 '89
Boning up on calcium. P. M. Barrier. il *Nation's Business* 77:57 D '89
Calcium tablets: bone up on the basics. K. Devereaux. il *Women's Sports & Fitness* 11:22 My '89
Coping with your calcium needs. il *McCall's* 117:102 O '89

CALCIUM IN THE BODY—*cont.*

Does voltage affect excitation-contraction coupling in the heart? [discussion of May 19, 1989 article, Regulation of calcium release is gated by calcium current, not gating charge, in cardiac myocytes] M. Näbauer and others. bibl f *Science* 246:1640 D 22 '89

Fluoride-calcium combo builds better bones [research by Charles Y. C. Pak] K. Fackelmann. *Science News* 135:36 Ja 21 '89

Free calcium at rest during "catch" in single smooth muscle cells [mussels] N. Ishii and others. bibl f il *Science* 243:1367-8 Mr 10 '89

Keep your bones straight and strong. L. Heller. il *Redbook* 172:22 Mr '89

New fluoride-calcium treatment for bone loss. *Prevention (Emmaus, Pa.)* 41:14+ Je '89

Protection of dentate hilar cells from prolonged stimulation by intracellular calcium chelation. H. E. Scharfman and P. A. Schwartzkroin. bibl f il *Science* 246:257-60 O 13 '89

Regulation of calcium concentration in voltage-clamped smooth muscle cells. P. L. Becker and others. bibl f il *Science* 244:211-14 Ap 14 '89

Regulation of calcium release is gated by calcium current, not gating charge, in cardiac myocytes. M. Näbauer and others. bibl f il *Science* 244:800-3 My 19 '89

Saving premature babies [work of Laura Hillman] il *USA Today (Periodical)* 118:4 O '89

The truth about calcium. P. Mann. il *Reader's Digest* 134:70-4 Mr '89

CALCIUM PHOSPHATES
    See also
        Hydroxyapatite

CALCOMP INC.

Simpler designs, simpler factories. P. Cole. il *Business Week* Special Issue:150 Je 16 '89

CALCULATING MACHINES *See* Calculators

CALCULATORS

New wave of calculators reflect technological evolution. S. Esters. il *Black Enterprise* 19:39-40 Ap '89
    Financial services use

Give a calculating gift. K. McCormally. il *Changing Times* 43:81-2+ D '89

Mastering the math behind your money [using a calculator for time value computations] C. Willis. il *Money* 18:129-30+ My '89

CALCULI, BILIARY *See* Gallstones
CALCULI, URINARY *See* Kidney stones
CALCULUS
    Study and teaching

Miracle worker at Garfield High [calculus teacher J. Escalante; condensed from Escalante] J. Mathews. il pors *Reader's Digest* 134:165-70+ Ja '89

CALCUTTA (INDIA)
    Description

PW interviews [G. Grass] T. Weyr. il por *Publishers Weekly* 235:54-5 Je 16 '89

CALDER, ALEXANDER, 1898-1976
    about

Around the Mall and beyond. E. Park. il *Smithsonian* 20:24-6+ O '89

CALDER, JOHN
    about

John Calder: a sturdy survivor. J. Barbato. *Publishers Weekly* 235:254 My 12 '89

CALDER (JOHN) LTD. *See* John Calder Ltd.
CALDERAS *See* Craters
CALDERWOOD, JAMES L.

Borders [poem] *The American Scholar* 58:39-40 Wint '89

CALDWELL, ERSKINE, 1903-1987

The day she shot Joseph Stalin . . . over and over. il por *TV Guide* 37:22-3 Ap 22-28 '89

CALDWELL, MARGARET B.

In the American mold. il *House & Garden* 161:174-7+ My '89

Luster of the past. il *House & Garden* 161:96+ N '89

CALDWELL, ZOE
    about

Taking the stage. pors *Harper's Bazaar* 122:150-3+ Ag '89

CALDWELL (EDWARD F.) & COMPANY *See* Edward F. Caldwell & Company

CALE, DAVID

The sex life. *Harper's* 278:36 F '89

CALE, WILLIAM G., AND OTHERS

Inferring process from pattern in natural communities. bibl f il *BioScience* 39:600-5 O '89

CALENDARS
    See also
        Church calendar
        Datebooks

1990 calendars. il *Publishers Weekly* 235:29-30+ Mr 17 '89

Calendars for 1990. G. Turim. il *Americana* 17:21-3 N/D '89

Calendars for kids. J. Moyer. il *Parents* 64:254+ D '89

Great 1990 gift calendars. P. A. Seefeldt. il *Good Housekeeping* 209:271 N '89

An heirloom advent calendar. il *The Family Handyman* 39:50-1 N/D '89

Sneeze calendar [chart listing types of pollen by geographic location] il *American Health* 8:16 Jl/Ag '89
    Anecdotes, facetiae, satire, etc.

Lunar timekeeper [Tranquillity calendar] J. Siggins. il *Omni (New York, N.Y.)* 11:96-102 Jl '89

CALFED INC.

Out of the fire [J. Torell's departure] K. Hannon. il *Forbes* 144:10 O 2 '89

Unhealthy growth. J. Heins. il *Forbes* 143:56 F 20 '89

CALGARY (ALTA.)
    Politics and government

Alberta's 'loose cannon' [Mayor R. Klein to run as Conservative in next provincial election] J. Howse. il por *Maclean's* 102:12 Ja 23 '89

CALGARY OLYMPICS, 1988 *See* Olympic Games—1988— Winter Olympics

CALHOUN, CRAIG J., 1952-

Revolution and repression in Tiananmen Square. *Society* 26:21-38 S/O '89

CALIARI, PAOLO *See* Veronese, 1528-1588
CALIFANO, JOSEPH A., 1931-

Tough talk for Democrats. il *The New York Times Magazine* p28-9+ Ja 8 '89

CALIFORNIA
    See also
        Agriculture—California
        Air pollution—California
        Airports—California
        Architecture—California
        Architecture, Domestic—California
        Aviation—California
        Banks and banking—California
        Big Sur River (Calif.)
        Booksellers and bookselling—California
        Butte County (Calif.)
        Carrizo Plain (Calif.)
        Cascade Range
        Central Valley (Calif.)
        Clark Mountain (Calif.)
        Coachella Valley (Calif.)
        Colleges and universities—California
        Crime and criminals—California
        Criminal justice, Administration of—California
        Dance—California
        Dance festivals—California
        Earthquakes—California
        Education—California
        Educational laws and regulations—California
        El Capitan (Calif.)
        Environmental policy—California
        Express highways—California
        Gardens and gardening—California
        Geology—California
        Geothermal resources—California
        Golden Gate National Recreation Area (Calif.)
        Groundwater pollution—California
        Health resorts, watering places, etc.—California
        Hotels, motels, etc.—California
        Huntington Beach (Calif.)
        Insurance law—California
        John Muir Trail (Calif.)
        Klamath River (Or. and Calif.)
        Lake Tahoe (Calif. and Nev.)
        Lake Tahoe region (Calif. and Nev.)
        Lassen Volcanic National Park (Calif.)
        Livermore Valley (Calif.)
        Los Angeles County (Calif.)
        Marin County (Calif.)
        Mendocino County (Calif.)
        Mojave Desert (Calif.)
        Mono Lake (Calif.)
        Monterey County (Calif.)
        Monterey Peninsula (Calif.)
        Morro Bay (Calif.)
        Motion picture festivals—California
        Mount Shasta (Calif.)
        Music festivals—California
        Napa County (Calif.)
        Napa Valley (Calif.)
        Newspapers—California
        Organic farming—California
        Paleontology—California
        Point Reyes National Seashore (Calif.)
        Prisons—California
        Public health—California
        Radioactive pollution—California
        Redwood National Park (Calif.)
        Resorts—California
        Restaurants—California
        Rivers—California
        Roads—California
        Sacramento River (Calif.)
        Sacramento-San Joaquin Delta (Calif.)
        San Diego Bay (Calif.)
        San Francisco Bay (Calif.)
        San Francisco Bay Area (Calif.)

CALIFORNIA—See also—*cont.*

Santa Clara County (Calif.)
Santa Monica Mountains National Recreation Area (Calif.)
Sequoia National Forest (Calif.)
Sierra Nevada Mountains (Calif. and Nev.)
Skiing—California
Solar energy—California
Sonoma County (Calif.)
Taxation—California
Trials—California
Vegetable gardens and gardening—California
Volcanoes—California
White Mountain Peak (Calif.)
Wild Horse Sanctuary (Calif.)
Wilderness areas—California
Wildflowers—California
Wildlife—California
Wildlife conservation—California
Yosemite National Park (Calif.)
Zoos—California

Brush fires
See Brush fires

Description and travel
See also
Automobile touring—California
Cycling—California
Motorcycling—California
California caravan: the Parlor Car way [bus tour] M. C. Lehrer. il *USA Today (Periodical)* 117:36-41 My '89
Rafting. H. Fairlie. *The New Republic* 201:43 N 13 '89

Industries
See also
Brewing industry
Fruit industry
Gold mines and mining—California
Pacific Gas & Electric Co.
Perfume industry
Publishers and publishing
Shellfish culture
Tourist trade—California
Wine industry
California, here I come [investment attractions] R. J. Maturi. *Changing Times* 43:30 O '89

Parks and reserves
See also
Calaveras Big Trees State Park (Calif.)
Mount Diablo State Park (Calif.)
Point Lobos State Reserve (Calif.)

Politics and government
Aftershocks. B. Bradley. *The New Republic* 201:15-16 N 27 '89
Golden State opportunity [gubernatorial race] T. Bethell. il *National Review* 41:34+ N 10 '89
How to make boring beautiful. M. B. Carlson. il *Time* 133:20 Ap 24 '89
Is this any way to run a state? [government by initiative] M. Reese. *Newsweek* 114:27 Jl 31 '89
Jerry Brown: a California comeback [interview with state Democratic Party chairman] L. Wright. il por *Newsweek* 113:6 F 27 '89
Jerry Brown rises from the ashrams. R. D. Hof. il por *Business Week* p36 F 13 '89
Tanned, rested, and ready [J. Brown running for state Democratic Party chairman] R. Brownstein. il *The New Republic* 200:23+ Ja 30 '89
That was Zen, this is now [J. Brown elected chairman of state Democrats] R. Lacayo. por *Time* 133:20 F 27 '89

Religious institutions and affairs
See also
Calvary Chapel

Social conditions
California: American dream, American nightmare [cover story; special section] M. Reese and J. Foote. il map *Newsweek* 114:22-9 Jl 31 '89
California's other bedeviling problems. L. J. Lord and P. Dworkin. il *U.S. News & World Report* 107:36 O 30 '89

CALIFORNIA. PUBLIC EMPLOYEES' RETIREMENT SYSTEM
Bang for the buck [D. Hanson] N. J. Perry. il por *Fortune* 119:37 Ja 2 '89
California's new crusader for shareholder rights [D. F. Bowman] T. Carson and J. B. Levine. il por *Business Week* p72-3 Ja 30 '89
Public pensions play tougher [nominee J. Brademas appointed Texaco director] F. H. Katayama. il por *Fortune* 119:16 F 27 '89
Will California's anti-China syndrome spread? [forcing pension funds to divest] M. Shao. il *Business Week* p33 Jl 24 '89

CALIFORNIA. STATE TEACHERS' RETIREMENT SYSTEM
Will California's anti-China syndrome spread? [forcing pension funds to divest] M. Shao. il *Business Week* p33 Jl 24 '89

CALIFORNIA. UNIVERSITY *See* University of California (System)

CALIFORNIA, LOWER *See* Baja California (Mexico: Peninsula)

CALIFORNIA BALLET COMPANY
California Ballet at twenty: staking a claim. W. E. Fark. il por *Dance Magazine* 63:52-5 Ja '89

CALIFORNIA CONSERVATION CORPS
For whom the corps toils. T. Moore. il *U.S. News & World Report* 106:24-5 F 13 '89

CALIFORNIA IN ART
Art: early California watercolors. T. S. Hines. il *Architectural Digest* 46:296-301+ My '89

CALIFORNIA INSTITUTE OF THE ARTS
Liberal arts. R. Rugoff. il *Vogue* 179:328-33+ Ag '89

CALIFORNIA KIWIFRUIT COMMISSION
Kiwi crunch. J. Schlax. il por *Forbes* 143:157 My 1 '89

CALIFORNIA LOTTERY WINNERS *See* Lottery winners

CALIFORNIA PARLOR CAR TOURS
California caravan: the Parlor Car way. M. C. Lehrer. il *USA Today (Periodical)* 117:36-41 My '89

CALIFORNIA PIZZA KITCHEN
Flax and Rosenfield: taking pizza way past pepperoni. P. Cole. il pors *Business Week* p98 My 8 '89

CALIFORNIA SEA LIONS *See* Seals (Animals)

CALIFORNIA STATE RAILROAD MUSEUM
Sacramento's Railroad Museum. D. Darvishian. il *Travel Holiday* 172:64-6+ O '89

CALIFORNIA WINES *See* Wine

CALIFORNIA ZEPHYR (TRAIN) *See* Railroads—Trains

CALIFORNIANS
Californians keep out! [backlash in Seattle] J. Bonfante. il *Time* 134:38-9 N 13 '89
West Coasting. il map *Seventeen* 48:40-5 F '89

Anecdotes, facetiae, satire, etc.
The Los Angeles man. C. Scovell. il *Gentlemen's Quarterly* 59:139-40 Ag '89

CALIO, JIM, AND RACHLIN, JILL
Hollywood's rising stars. il *Ladies' Home Journal* 106:138+ N '89

CALISHER, HORTENSE
In praise of Wang Meng. *The Nation* 249:500-2 O 30 '89

CALISTOGA (CALIF.)
Description
My game is mud. P. Mehlman. il *Gentlemen's Quarterly* 59:302-7 O '89

CALISTRO, PADDY
California perfume boom. il *Harper's Bazaar* 122:30+ My '89

CALKINS, ANNIE
(jt. auth) See Parrett, William H., and Calkins, Annie

CALL ACCOUNTING SYSTEMS *See* Telephone call accounting systems

CALL-NET TELECOMMUNICATIONS LTD.
David and Goliath dial a busy signal [CALL-NET vs. Bell Canada] D. Francis. il *Maclean's* 102:11 Ap 3 '89

CALL OPTIONS *See* Put and call transactions

CALL PROCESSING SYSTEMS
Intelligent telephone networks. *Radio-Electronics* 60:4 Ag '89

CALL WAITING (TELEPHONE SERVICE)
Call-waiting etiquette. P. Edwards and S. Edwards. il *Home Office Computing* 7:48 N '89

CALLAHAN, JEAN
Seeking meaning. il *Glamour* 87:326 S '89

CALLAHAN, JOHN
Hell on wheels [excerpt from Don't worry, he won't get far on foot] il por *Mother Jones* 14:38-40+ My '89
about
Almost charmed. L. Fleischer. *Publishers Weekly* 235:66 Mr 17 '89
Paralyzed at 21, cartoonist John Callahan finds laughter the best medicine for his rage. R. Arias. il pors *People Weekly* 31:102+ Je 12 '89

CALLAHAN, MAUREEN
Coping with chronic pain. il *Parents* 64:202+ Ap '89
Good food, good health: what's what in vegetable oils. il *Better Homes and Gardens* 67:45 Je '89
Hives at first bite. il *Parents* 64:210+ Mr '89

CALLAHAN, NANCY
Hard times for Freedom Quilters. *The Christian Century* 106:317-18 Mr 22-29 '89

CALLAHAN, PETER J.
about
Peter Callahan: an acquiring mind. A. Rothman. il por *Business Week* p139-40 My 15 '89

CALLAHAN, SIDNEY CORNELIA
Getting our heads together. il *Commonweal* 116:635-42 N 17 '89

CALLAHAN, WILLIAM P.
about
This gumshoe does his legwork in wing tips. J. Friedman. *Business Week* p98 My 29 '89

CALLAS, MARIA, 1923-1977
about
Maria Callas. T. Eckert, Jr. il pors *High Fidelity (New York, N.Y.)* 39:46-50 F '89

CALLAWAY GARDENS. DAY BUTTERFLY CENTER
Butterfly paradise. B. Day. il *The Saturday Evening Post* 261:62-3 Jl/Ag '89
Step into the world of butterflies. il *Southern Living* 24:30-1 My '89

CALLE, SOPHIE
about
Sophie Calle: the prying eye. R. L. Pincus. il *Art in America* 77:192-7 O '89

CALLENDAR, NEWGATE
Spies & thrillers. See occasional issues of The New York Times Book Review beginning November 6, 1988

CALLER ID (TELEPHONE SERVICE)
Is Caller ID the wrong number? il *U.S. News & World Report* 107:10 D 18 '89

CALLERY, BERNADETTE G.
Patronage and the publication of botanical illustration [cover story] il *Antiques* 136:268-81 Ag '89

CALLERY, SEAN
The clay moves awry . . . il *Commonweal* 116:519-21 O 6 '89

CALLEWAERT, GEERT, AND OTHERS
Modulation of calcium channels in cardiac and neuronal cells by an endogenous peptide. bibl f il *Science* 243:663-6 F 3 '89

CALLEY, WILLIAM LAWS
about
William Calley. C. Unger. il pors *People Weekly* 32:152-8 N 20 '89

CALLIGRAPHY
Collectors and collecting
Fine lines [calligraphy drawings] M. Guralnick. il *House & Garden* 161:50+ Je '89
Hand-scribed missals: calligraphed masterpieces in miniature [work of S. Mitchell] A. Bahar. il por *Antiques & Collecting Hobbies* 94:60-3 D '89

CALLONI, STELLA
Noriega speaks out. *World Press Review* 36:52-3 D '89

CALLOW, SIMON
The mighty Gambon. por *Vogue* 179:352-3+ My '89

CALLOWAY, CAB, 1907-
about
Cab Calloway stable after emergency surgery in N.Y. il por *Jet* 75:65 Ja 16 '89

CALLOWAY, D. WAYNE
about
Those highflying Pepsico managers. B. Dumaine. il por *Fortune* 119:78-80+ Ap 10 '89

CALLOWAY, STEPHEN
Restoration drama. il por *House & Garden* 161:120-3+ D '89
Rethinking the past. il *House & Garden* 161:42+ Je '89
about
The decorative dandy. R. Koenig. il por *House & Garden* 161:42+ Mr '89

CALLS FOR ANIMALS See Animal calling
CALLS FOR BIRDS See Bird calling
CALLS OF BIRDS See Birds—Song

CALLU, FLORENCE
A library in action. il *The Courier (Unesco)* 42:10-11 My '89

CALMARK FINANCIAL CORPORATION
The playboy and the 'teddy bear' taking aim at Del Webb [U. Sheinbaum and D. Brumlik] T. Carson. *Business Week* p43-4 Ja 9 '89

CALMAT CO.
A buyout guru shares two takeover visions [views of L. Smith] G. G. Marcial. il por *Business Week* p146 Mr 20 '89

CALMENSON, STEPHANIE
Where's Rufus? [story] il *Parents* 64:131+ Ap '89

CALMODULIN
Inhibition of postsynaptic PKC or CaMKII blocks induction but not expression of LTP. R. Malinow and others. bibl f il *Science* 245:862-6 Ag 25 '89

CALONYCTION ACULEATUM See Moonflowers

CALORIES, FOOD
See also
Low calorie cooking
Calories count. J. Scala. il *Dance Magazine* 63:64-5 Ja '89
Calories in H_2O [sparkling water] il *Prevention (Emmaus, Pa.)* 41:12 Ag '89
The fat-fighter's bible (I). il *Prevention (Emmaus, Pa.)* 41:83-5+ My '89
The fat-fighter's bible (II). il *Prevention (Emmaus, Pa.)* 41:77-8+ Je '89
The fat-fighter's bible (III). il *Prevention (Emmaus, Pa.)* 41:65-8+ Jl '89
The fat-fighter's bible (IV). il *Prevention (Emmaus, Pa.)* 41:83-8 Ag '89
Putting fat in its place. L. E. Koszuta. il *Current Health 2* 16:14-16 N '89
Rev up [reducing fat calories] L. Moll. il *Health (New York, N.Y.)* 21:45-6 Je '89
This fast food won't slow down your diet. E. Kunes. il *Mademoiselle* 95:260 S '89

CALORIMETERS AND CALORIMETRY
Analysis of the published calorimetric evidence for electrochemical fusion of deuterium in palladium. G. M. Miskelly and others. bibl f il *Science* 246:793-6 N 10 '89

CALOTYPES
Negative and positive [work of W. H. Talbot] il *American History Illustrated* 24:30 S/O '89
William Henry Fox Talbot: Metropolitan Museum. R. B. Woodward. il *Art News* 88:168-9 N '89

CALTA, MARIALISA
All about New Year's Eve. il *The New York Times Magazine* p14+ D 31 '89

CALVARY CHAPEL
Church, parachurch locked in legal battle [Calvary Chapel vs. Gospel Films over videocassette distribution rights for evangelistic film Fury to freedom] B. Bird. il *Christianity Today* 33:40-3 Ag 18 '89

CALVARY CHURCH (CHARLOTTE, N.C.)
Fatigue fatigue. M. E. Marty. *The Christian Century* 106:767 Ag 16-23 '89

CALVERT, ANNIVORY
about
Giving birth to a scandal. por *Time* 133:23 Je 26 '89
Mom of Detroit mayor's son wants FBI probe of police. por *Jet* 76:8 Jl 10 '89

CALVES
Prices
A calf named 'Opportunity' [feeder-calf prices; cover story] B. Eftink. il *Successful Farming* 87:11 Ap '89
Treatment
Fight animal welfare emotion with emotionalism. *Successful Farming* 87:41 D '89

CALVIN, JEAN, 1509-1564
Bibliography
The life and thought of Calvin. D. K. McKim. il *Christianity Today* 33:53 Mr 17 '89

CALVIN, JOHN See Calvin, Jean, 1509-1564

CALVINISM
See also
Arminianism

CAMACHO, HECTOR
about
Fat City for rusty pugs. W. Nack. il pors *Sports Illustrated* 70:36-7 Mr 20 '89

CAMACHO, RENE GONZALES
about
Khalilah Ali marries in her Flossmoor mansion. il pors *Jet* 77:15 O 30 '89

CAMARENA SALAZAR, ENRIQUE
Murder case
Guadalajara vice [M. Mann's TV miniseries The drug wars: Camarena] M. Christensen. il por *Rolling Stone* p53 N 30 '89
When jailbirds are also fat cats [luxurious treatment of suspects] *U.S. News & World Report* 107:13 Jl 31 '89

CAMBARERI, EDWARD B., AND OTHERS
Repeat-induced G-C to A-T mutations in Neurospora. bibl f il *Science* 244:1571-5 Je 30 '89

CAMBODIA
See also
Cambodians
Military assistance, American—Cambodia
United Nations—Cambodia
Vietnamese—Cambodia
Cultural policy
Restoring Cambodian culture. S. Blaustein. *The Nation* 249:426-9 O 16 '89
Economic policy
Looking to the private sector. S. Blaustein. il *The Nation* 248:226-8 F 20 '89
Foreign relations
United States
See United States—Foreign relations—Cambodia
Vietnam
As China agonizes, the U.S. wavers and Cambodia waits. L. Lief. il *U.S. News & World Report* 107:34 Jl 3 '89
Better times for a ravaged land. W. Stewart. il *Time* 133:42 My 15 '89
Cambodia and Vietnam: trapped in an eddy of history? [address, September 8, 1989] R. H. Solomon. por *Department of State Bulletin* 89:47-51 N '89
Cambodia's line of death. C. S. Manegold. il map *Newsweek* 113:30 Je 26 '89
Efforts toward a Cambodian settlement [statement and text of UN General Assembly resolution, November 3, 1988] V. A. Walters. *Department of State Bulletin* 89:65-8 F '89
Hanoi declares 'victory' in Cambodia. *Newsweek* 113:41 Ap 17 '89
Hanoi's struggle for respect. il *U.S. News & World Report* 107:11 O 9 '89
Killing fields II. E. Becker. *The New Republic* 200:10+ Ja 2 '89
Leaving the killing fields [Vietnamese withdrawal] M. Nemeth. il *Maclean's* 102:24-5 O 9 '89
The progress of peace in Cambodia. E. Becker. bibl f *Current History* 88:169-72+ Ap '89
Signs of progress towards settlement of Kampuchean conflict seen. il *UN Chronicle* 26:22-3 S '89
Sihanouk on the high wire. A. Platt. il pors *Newsweek* 113:45 My 15 '89

CAMERA BAGS, CASES, ETC.

A bag for every reason: the nature photographer's guide to creative equipment hauling. J. Shaw. il *Popular Photography* 96:28+ Jl '89

The middle-size bag battle: are you going vertical slim or conventional boxy? H. Keppler. il *Popular Photography* 96:22-4 N '89

CAMERA BATTERIES *See* Electric batteries

CAMERA INDUSTRY *See* Photographic industry

CAMERA LENSES *See* Lenses, Photographic

CAMERA SHUTTERS

Just how accurate is your exposure system? The simple answers are based on complex tests. L. White. il *Popular Photography* 96:76+ S '89

Long live 35mm cameras with mechanical shutters and TTL metering! C. W. Kennedy. il *Popular Photography* 96:78-9+ Ag '89

Control

Does your new AF camera focus faster than a speeding bullet? L. White. il *Popular Photography* 96:70 N '89

Need a cable release? Where's the damned socket? il *Popular Photography* 96:29+ F '89

Only the human eye focuses faster, but how long does your AF SLR take to trip the shutter? B. Schwalberg. il *Popular Photography* 96:75+ Jl '89

CAMERA STORES

There are good dealers like good car salesmen, but the rotters can spoil it for everyone. H. Keppler. il *Popular Photography* 96:42+ Jl '89

CAMERA SUPPORTS

Dreaming of a no-shake SLR? Try these ideas until it arrives [monopods] C. W. Kennedy. il *Popular Photography* 96:112+ Ja '89

CAMERA TRIPODS

Bogen 3021 & 3050 tripods. il *Petersen's Photographic Magazine* 18:80 N '89

Cullmann Magic 2. D. Brooks. il *Petersen's Photographic Magazine* 17:40+ F '89

Cullmann Titan tripods. il *Petersen's Photographic Magazine* 18:64 My '89

Me and my Benbo. S. Drafahl and J. Drafahl. il *Petersen's Photographic Magazine* 18:76-7 Jl '89

Sinar Bron Foba Superball. il *Petersen's Photographic Magazine* 18:50 My '89

Tripodmania: the readers strike back! [discussion of November 1988 article, Tripodmania] B. Schwalberg. il *Popular Photography* 96:77+ F '89

CAMERAS

See also
3-D cameras
Disposable cameras
Eastman Kodak Co.
Video cameras

How I made a Schmidt camera. L. Lai. il *Sky and Telescope* 77:664-5+ Je '89

Know before you go. M. Grimm and T. Grimm. il *Travel Holiday* 171:6+ My '89

Lens-shutter AF [Dallas PMA Show] il *Popular Photography* 96:56-7+ My '89

Real photographers don't use compacts . . . or do they? G. Lewis. il *Petersen's Photographic Magazine* 18:60-2 Jl '89

Three new Olympus cameras. il *Petersen's Photographic Magazine* 18:8 O '89

Two views: one yaw-free, the other nearly so [Photokina] il *Popular Photography* 96:132 Ja '89

Anecdotes, facetiae, satire, etc.

Point and shoot follies. D. Richards. il *Popular Photography* 96:50-1 O '89

Collectors and collecting

Collecting cameras. J. Schneider. See issues of Popular Photography beginning March 1988

Mickey Mouse cameras. E. S. Lothrop. il *Popular Photography* 96:52-3 Jl '89

Control

See also
Camera shutters—Control

Design

The man behind the O [N. Sakai] H. Gaffin. il pors *Popular Photography* 96:34 D '89

Photography's march of time. R. Dolphin. il *Maclean's* 102:51-2 Ap 24 '89

Equipment

See Photography—Equipment

Films

See Photography—Films

History

Photography for everyman [Kodak cameras developed by G. Eastman] il *American History Illustrated* 24:64-5 S/O '89

Portraits. S. A. Booth. il *Popular Mechanics* 166:58-61+ Ja '89

Second-wave half-frame 35s: once they got done copying, they gave us some character. J. Schneider. il *Popular Photography* 96:34+ Jl '89

Mounting

You are there! [use of remote-control, helmet-mounted camera] R. Doyle. il *Petersen's Photographic Magazine* 18:14-16 Ag '89

Testing

35mm compact camera buyer's guide. il *Petersen's Photographic Magazine* 18:57-8+ D '89

40 top cameras [cover story] il *Popular Photography* 96:66-106 D '89

Astronomy tests the Northern Lites cold camera. R. Reeves. il *Astronomy* 17:86-9 Jl '89

Cambo Master view. D. Brooks. il *Petersen's Photographic Magazine* 17:34+ Ap '89

Canon Sure Shot Zoom. K. Geller-Shinn. il *Petersen's Photographic Magazine* 17:62-3 Ja '89

Canon Sure Shot Zoom XL [compact camera] K. Geller-Shinn. il *Petersen's Photographic Magazine* 18:90-1 S '89

Canon's new point & zoom [Canon Sure Shot Zoom XL] il *Popular Photography* 96:38 O '89

A close-up on classic cameras [Leica, Rollei and Hasselblad] J. W. Verity. il *Business Week* p147 N 20 '89

Compact 35mm cameras. il *Consumer Reports* 54:219-25 D '89

Fuji Discovery 500 Zoom [compact 35mm lens/shutter] K. Geller-Shinn. il *Petersen's Photographic Magazine* 17:46-7 Mr '89

Horseman 450 EX [monorail camera] D. Brooks. il *Petersen's Photographic Magazine* 18:59-61+ S '89

How to check your new camera. il *Popular Photography* 96:107+ D '89

Jay Maisel directs the compacts [Kodak S100EF camera and others] il *Petersen's Photographic Magazine* 17:56-7 Mr '89

Konica A4 compact. K. Geller-Shinn. il *Petersen's Photographic Magazine* 18:43-4 Ag '89

Konica Z-up 80 [automatic focus compact] K. Geller-Shinn. il *Petersen's Photographic Magazine* 17:41-3 F '89

Leica point & shoot 35 [AF-C1] H. Keppler. il *Popular Photography* 96:62 Je '89

Mamiya 6 [rangefinder camera] D. Brooks. il *Petersen's Photographic Magazine* 18:46-7+ Jl '89

Minolta Freedom Zoom 90. K. Geller-Shinn. il *Petersen's Photographic Magazine* 18:66-7 Jl '89

Nikon Zoom-Touch 500 [35mm compact] B. Hurter. il *Petersen's Photographic Magazine* 17:70-1 Ap '89

Olympus Infinity Twin. K. Geller-Shinn. il *Petersen's Photographic Magazine* 18:72-3 Je '89

Ricoh's compact quartet. K. Geller-Shinn. il *Petersen's Photographic Magazine* 18:78-80 O '89

Sharp shooting. S. A. Booth. il *Popular Mechanics* 166:54-5 Ag '89

Summer fun with waterproof & weatherproof cameras. il *Petersen's Photographic Magazine* 18:30-2+ Jl '89

Things look up for looking down [Canon Sure Shot Ace] S. A. Booth. il *Rolling Stone* p113 Mr 9 '89

What are all those charts and graphs, and where do they come from? L. White. il *Popular Photography* 96:66 Jl '89

Zone VI Classic [folding bed wood field camera] D. Brooks. il *Petersen's Photographic Magazine* 17:54-6 F '89

CAMERAS, INSTANT PRINT

See also
Polaroid Corp.

CAMERAS, MINIATURE

Is this camera really necessary? Strictly speaking, maybe not, but it's a lot of fun [miniature press cameras] J. Schneider. il *Popular Photography* 96:28-9+ Mr '89

CAMERAS, SINGLE-LENS REFLEX

Byzantine puzzle: when is a discontinued camera a discontinued camera? H. Keppler. il *Popular Photography* 96:22+ O '89

In search of the potential SLR buyer. J. Augustine. *Petersen's Photographic Magazine* 18:4 S '89

Is there a future for SLRs? J. Augustine. il *Petersen's Photographic Magazine* 18:4 Ag '89

Readers respond to autofocus. J. Augustine. il *Petersen's Photographic Magazine* 17:4 F '89

SLR world. H. Keppler. See issues of Popular Photography beginning September 1987

What drew Canon to Motorola? Passion, of course [microprocessor for EOS camera] N. Gross. il *Business Week* p118 N 13 '89

Design

Long live 35mm cameras with mechanical shutters and TTL metering! C. W. Kennedy. il *Popular Photography* 96:78-9+ Ag '89

Testing

35mm SLR cameras. il *Consumer Reports* 54:212-18 D '89

40 top cameras [cover story] il *Popular Photography* 96:66-106 D '89

Affordable AF SLR camera shootout! Canon EOS 750 vs. Minolta Maxxum 3000i vs. Nikon N4004S. il *Petersen's Photographic Magazine* 18:72-5+ O '89

Bronica ETRSi. il *Petersen's Photographic Magazine* 18:65 My '89

Bronica ETRSi [645 SLR] D. Brooks. il *Petersen's Photographic Magazine* 17:52-4 Mr '89

CAMPAIGN FUNDS
See also
Political action committees
Watergate case

Andrew Young taking fund-raising nationally [campaign to become first black governor of Georgia] *Jet* 77:15 N 13 '89

Congress and the culture of money. H. Fineman. il *Newsweek* 113:21 Je 5 '89

Fed up [J. C. Calaway's views on congressional fundraising] S. Hornik. il por *Common Cause Magazine* 15:6 Jl/Ag '89

Fellow Republicans [Progressive readers receive fund raising letters from Republican Party] E. Knoll. *The Progressive* 53:4 D '89

It's money that matters [author's Senate campaigns in Wisconsin; cover story] E. Garvey. il *The Progressive* 53:17-21 Mr '89

Money matters. B. Phillips. il *Scholastic Update (Teachers' edition)* 121:20-1 F 24 '89

Party games [costs of R. Brown's campaign to become chairman of Democratic National Committee] V. Novak. por *Common Cause Magazine* 15:7 My/Je '89

Public relations and ethical leadership [address, June 15, 1989] J. Paluszek. *Vital Speeches of the Day* 55:747-50 O 1 '89

The seduction of Senator Alan Cranston [Lincoln Savings & Loan Assn. scandal] P. Dwyer. il pors *Business Week* p82-4 D 4 '89

Stacking the deck [advantages of incumbent in Pennsylvania congressional race] E. Howard. il por *Common Cause Magazine* 15:24-6 Ja/F '89

Unanswered letters [Progressive editor receives fund raising letter from Republican Party] E. Knoll. *The Progressive* 53:4 N '89

The White House connection [use of HUD and EPA monies to fund Republican campaigns during the Reagan administration; cover story] M. Waas. *The Nation* 249:585+ N 20 '89

Laws and regulations

Campaign '89: the decisive fight. F. Wertheimer. il *Common Cause Magazine* 15:42-3 Ja/F '89

The Capitol charity ball [use of voter registration drives and charities to solicit soft money campaign funds] G. Borger. il *U.S. News & World Report* 107:19+ D 18 '89

Coming to terms with campaign reform. R. England. il *The American Spectator* 22:22-5 N '89

Covert campaigns [vice presidential fundraising committees] P. Montgomery. *Common Cause Magazine* 15:7-8 My/Je '89

Debtor's prison [L. LaRouche sentenced for tax evasion and fraud] por *Time* 133:33 F 6 '89

Demand-side reform. *The New Republic* 201:7-8 Ag 7-14 '89

End the Washington money chase! [special section] il *Common Cause Magazine* 15:41-7 S/O '89

Funny money [presidential compliance committees] P. C. Montgomery. il *Common Cause Magazine* 15:28-31 My/Je '89

The GOP stokes a new fire to roast Democrats. D. Harbrecht and R. Fly. il *Business Week* p39 Jl 10 '89

Illegal money and the '88 campaign. F. Wertheimer. il *Common Cause Magazine* 15:44 Mr/Ap '89

Old softie [A. Cranston's use of voter registration drives to generate campaign funds] R. Kuttner. *The New Republic* 201:17-19 D 11 '89

Playing the politics of reform. H. Fineman. il *Newsweek* 114:18 Jl 10 '89

A running start for campaign finance reform. J. Denny. il *Common Cause Magazine* 15:39-40 Mr/Ap '89

So you want to reform Congress? F. Barnes. il *The American Spectator* 22:14-16 S '89

Urge your senators to act on campaign finance reform [House Ways and Means Committee vetoes proposal for consumer rebates from utilities] *Common Cause Magazine* 15:31 N/D '89

White House balks at honoraria ban while momentum builds in Congress; Campaign finance reform. J. Denny. *Common Cause Magazine* 15:38-9 My/Je '89

Will Congress come clean? J. Denny. il *Common Cause Magazine* 15:39-40 Jl/Ag '89

Canada

Questions of privilege [H. R. Argue faces charges of misused Senate funds] B. Wallace and D. Jenish. il por *Maclean's* 102:17 N 27 '89

CAMPAIGN ISSUES
See also
Abortion
Education and state
Student aid

CAMPAIGN MANAGEMENT

Handling the handlers. A. McCarthy. *Commonweal* 116:7 Ja 13 '89

Master handler [J. A. Baker] A. R. Dowd. por *Fortune* 119:54 Ja 2 '89

The new breed of campaign manager [J. Cowart deploys personal computers] K. A. Frenkel. il por *Personal Computing* 13:108-10 O '89

The power of negative thinking [interview with L. Atwater] W. Greider. il pors *Rolling Stone* p51-3+ Ja 12 '89

Aruba

Politics under the palms. E. Clift. il *Newsweek* 113:27 Ja 9 '89

CAMPAIGN ORGANIZERS *See* Campaign management
CAMPAIGN WORKERS

A season in hell [D. Brazile, staff member during M. Dukakis presidential campaign] G. E. Curry. il pors *Ms.* 18:58-60+ O '89

CAMPAIGNS, MONEY RAISING *See* Fund raising
CAMPAIGNS, POLITICAL *See* Political campaigns
CAMPAIGNS, PRESIDENTIAL *See* Presidential campaigns
CAMPANILE (LOS ANGELES, CALIF.: RESTAURANT)
See Los Angeles (Calif.)—Restaurants, nightclubs, bars, etc.

CAMPBELL, BEBE MOORE

Good friends [story] il *Essence* 20:91-2+ S '89

When old men went out of my life [excerpt from Sweet summer] il pors *Essence* 20:58-60+ Je '89

(ed) See Vanzant, Iyanla. The powers that free

about

PW interviews. L. See. por *Publishers Weekly* 235:82-3 Je 30 '89

CAMPBELL, DENNIS M., 1945-

Why should anyone believe? Apologetics and theological education. *The Christian Century* 106:136-8 F 1-8 '89

CAMPBELL, DONALD

about

Rockwell's model doc, Donald Campbell, gives his last shot and retires. il por *People Weekly* 31:114-15 Mr 27 '89

CAMPBELL, DONALD B., AND OTHERS

Styles of volcanism on Venus: new Arecibo high resolution radar data. bibl f il *Science* 246:373-7 O 20 '89

CAMPBELL, DOUGLAS

about

Global phone plays. R. King. il por *Forbes* 144:192+ S 18 '89

CAMPBELL, GORDON

about

Making time a commodity. S. R. Reed. por *Personal Computing* 13:81 Jl '89

CAMPBELL, JOHN, 1949-

about

Better late than never. R. Robinson. il pors *Runner's World* 24:62-5 Ag '89

CAMPBELL, JOSEPH, 1904-1987

about

Bill Moyers angrily defends Joseph Campbell against charges that his wisdom was only a myth. A. Chambers. il pors *People Weekly* 32:64+ N 27 '89

Continued interest in Campbell sparks new market for audio & video publishers. J. Tangorra. *Publishers Weekly* 236:64 O 6 '89

The faces of Joseph Campbell. B. Gill. il *The New York Review of Books* 36:16+ S 28 '89

Joseph Campbell: an exchange [discussion of September 28, 1989 article, The faces of Joseph Campbell] B. Gill. il *The New York Review of Books* 36:57-61 N 9 '89

The power of myth: lessons from Joseph Campbell. B. C. Lane. il *The Christian Century* 106:652-4 Jl 5-12 '89

CAMPBELL, JULE

about

Lights, camera, action! F. Deford. il pors *Sports Illustrated* 70 Special Issue:51-2+ F '89

CAMPBELL, KURT M., 1957-

The soldiers' summit. bibl f *Foreign Policy* 75:76-91 Summ '89

CAMPBELL, LAWRENCE, 1914-

Color coordinates. il *Art in America* 77:188-93 S '89

CAMPBELL, LIZA

Ozbek: on the fringe. il por *Vogue* 179:166-7+ Ja '89

CAMPBELL, MARTIN

about

Criminal law [film] Reviews
  The Humanist il 49:47-8 Jl/Ag '89. H. M. Geduld
  People Weekly il 31:13+ Je 5 '89. R. Novak

CAMPBELL, NAOMI

about

Fight knight. V. Woods. il pors *Vogue* 179:330-7+ D '89

The Naomi show. il pors *Mademoiselle* 95:122-3 F '89

CAMPBELL, NINA

about

A queen of chintz does Fergie's new palace. il por *People Weekly* 32:127 N 20 '89

The well-appointed decorator [cover story] C. K. Gandee. il pors *House & Garden* 161:108-15+ Mr '89

CAMPBELL, PETER

about

An audacious gambler bucks the trends. P. C. Newman. il *Maclean's* 102:41 Ja 30 '89

CAMPBELL, T. COLIN, 1934-

about

The world's healthiest diet. S. S. Lang. il map *American Health* 8:105-7+ S '89

CAMPBELL (D.A.) COMPANY *See* D.A. Campbell Company

CAMPBELL COUNTY (TENN.)

Education

Academics and athletics: 'What price victory?' [high school teacher J. A. McGhee fights dismissal after being pressured to raise basketball player's grade] P. A. Zirkel. il *Phi Delta Kappan* 70:564-5 Mr '89

CAMPBELL-EWALD CO.

See also

Lintas: Worldwide (Firm)

CAMPBELL SOUP COMPANY

'Deathwatch' investments. D. Pauly. il por *Newsweek* 113:62 Ap 24 '89

Holly Driscoll had a fine idea, but it left her in the soup [collecting Campbell Soup labels to obtain van for school in Washburn, Wis.] il por *People Weekly* 31:97 My 22 '89

M'm! M'm! Bad! trouble at Campbell Soup. J. Weber, Jr. il *Business Week* p68-70 S 25 '89

CAMPEAU, ROBERT, 1923-

about

Campeau is up on that high wire again. C. Hawkins and S. Phillips. il por *Business Week* p108-10 My 15 '89

Campeau's big sell-off. P. Chisholm. il por *Maclean's* 102:48 S 18 '89

Campeau's day of reckoning. A. Walmsley. il pors *Maclean's* 102:38-40 S 25 '89

The Canadian who sparked the crash. P. C. Newman. il *Maclean's* 102:75 O 30 '89

A desperate Campeau grabs a Canadian lifeline. C. Hawkins. il por *Business Week* p44 S 25 '89

The price of a reprieve. A. Walmsley. il pors *Maclean's* 102:36-9 O 2 '89

Robert Campeau. C. Hawkins. por *Business Week* Special Issue:114 Ap 14 '89

The spectacular fall of a titan. P. C. Newman. il *Maclean's* 102:44 S 25 '89

Waiting for Christmas. J. DeMont. il por *Maclean's* 102:54-5+ D 4 '89

Walking a fine line. P. Chisholm. il por *Maclean's* 102:50-1 Ja 2 '89

CAMPEAU CORPORATION

The big deal at Bloomingdale's: Marvin Traub makes a run at the top. M. Gross. il pors *New York* 22:56-60+ O 16 '89

Breathing easier. A. Dunkin and C. Hawkins. il *Business Week* p28-9 O 2 '89

Campeau is up on that high wire again. C. Hawkins and S. Phillips. il por *Business Week* p108-10 My 15 '89

Campeau's big sell-off [proposed sale of Bloomingdale's] P. Chisholm. il por *Maclean's* 102:48 S 18 '89

Campeau's day of reckoning [loan from Olympia & York] A. Walmsley. il pors *Maclean's* 102:38-40 S 25 '89

The Canadian who sparked the crash [decline in value of R. Campeau's junk bonds before Friday the 13th plunge] P. C. Newman. il *Maclean's* 102:75 O 30 '89

A desperate Campeau grabs a Canadian lifeline [capital infusion by Olympia & York] C. Hawkins. il por *Business Week* p44 S 25 '89

The empire shrinks back. J. Castro. il *Time* 134:54 S 25 '89

The price of a reprieve. A. Walmsley. il pors *Maclean's* 102:36-9 O 2 '89

A retail marriage not made in heaven [forced to sell Bloomingdale's] il *U.S. News & World Report* 107:18 S 25 '89

Robert Campeau. C. Hawkins. por *Business Week* Special Issue:114 Ap 14 '89

The spectacular fall of a titan. P. C. Newman. il *Maclean's* 102:44 S 25 '89

Waiting for Christmas. J. DeMont. il por *Maclean's* 102:54-5+ D 4 '89

Walking a fine line [R. Campeau] P. Chisholm. il por *Maclean's* 102:50-1 Ja 2 '89

CAMPECHE, JOSÉ, 1752-1809

about

The San Juan master. B. Adams. il *Art in America* 77:51+ Ja '89

CAMPERS, TRUCK

Room with a view [Al Weber's Mark 5 Minicruiser] S. L. White. il *Field & Stream* 93:126+ Ap '89

Testing

Long haulers [Winnebago Chieftan] M. Allen. il *Popular Mechanics* 166:62-4+ S '89

A winner fit for the Gipper [Newell motorhomes] L. Griffin. il *Car and Driver* 34:107-9+ My '89

CAMPERS (TRAILERS) *See* Automobile trailers

CAMPFIRES

Campfires [reprint from June 1965 issue] T. Trueblood. il *Field & Stream* 94:28+ Jl '89

CAMPGROUNDS *See* Camp sites, facilities, etc.

CAMPING

See also

Backpacks and backpacking

Camp sites, facilities, etc.

Campfires

Camps

Cooking, Outdoor

Camping overnight. C. Fergus. il *Country Journal* 16:50-2 My/Je '89

The great outdoors [camping in national parks] il maps *U.S. News & World Report* 106:65-7+ My 8 '89

The great sleep-out [backyard camping] D. Kennedy. il *Parents* 64:170 Ag '89

On the road with mushrooms [RV camping] B. A. Branson. il *Travel Holiday* 171:22-5 F '89

Parked in the middle of nowhere [retirees with RVs migrate to Quartzsite, Ariz. for the winter] J. Ackermann-Blount. il map *Time* 133:108-9 My 22 '89

Anecdotes, facetiae, satire, etc.

A cure for old age [excerpt from Whatchagot stew] P. F. McManus. il *Outdoor Life* 184:152+ N '89

Equipment

See also

Backpacks and backpacking

Sleeping bags

Tents

Camp clues: pack these tips! il *'Teen* 33:48+ My '89

Getting into gear for your next trip. il *U.S. News & World Report* 106:70-1 My 8 '89

What's new. See issues of Outdoor Life

Maintenance and repair

Camping gear care. J. Kukoda. il *Bicycling* 30:89-90 Ja/F '89

Don't toss it, fix it. C. Leigh. *Outdoor Life* 184:109 Jl '89

Outfits, supplies, etc.

See Camping—Equipment

Siberia (Soviet Union)

How I spent my summer vacation. S. Talbott. il map *Life* 12:16+ Jl '89

United States

See Camping

Western Europe

Tooling around the continent [van camping] T. Gindick. il *Travel Holiday* 171:52-9 My '89

Western States

New guides to western camping. *Sunset (Central West edition)* 183:30 O '89

CAMPING OUTFITS *See* Camping—Equipment

CAMPINS, HUMBERTO, AND KRIDER, E. PHILIP

Surface discharges on natural dielectrics in the solar system. bibl f il *Science* 245:622-4 Ag 11 '89

CAMPION, NARDI REEDER

Half a century of sex education. il *The New York Times Magazine* p22+ Mr 26 '89

CAMPOLO, ANTHONY

about

Campolo's views challenged. R. Frame. por *Christianity Today* 33:43 S 8 '89

CAMPORESI, PIERO

Bread of dreams. il *History Today* 39:14-21 Ap '89

CAMPOS, ALVARO DE *See* Pessoa, Fernando, 1888-1935

CAMPS

See also

Church camps

Music camps

Dream camps [bicycle racing] K. Kendrick. *Bicycling* 30:164 Mr '89

Happy campers [children's summer camps] S. Berkman. il *Good Housekeeping* 208:100 Je '89

Summer camp '89 [running camps] il *Runner's World* 24:76-8 Je '89

Summer camp: off to a great start. C. Winters. il *Parents* 64:82+ My '89

Anecdotes, facetiae, satire, etc.

Send a preacher to camp [week at a Boy Scout camp] W. H. Willimon. *The Christian Century* 106:1006-8 N 8 '89

International aspects

Directory assistance [tennis camps] R. Ingber. il *World Tennis* 36:48-57 Ja '89

Alabama

See also

U.S. Space Camp (Huntsville, Ala.)

California

See also

Mother's Camp (Calif.)

Connecticut

See also

Hole-in-the-Wall Gang Camp

Florida Keys (Fla.)

See also

Seacamp (Fla.)

Illinois

See also

Camp Algonquin (Elgin, Ill.)

North Dakota

Top-flight camp [summer camp at Center for Aerospace Sciences at Univ. of North Dakota] il *National Geographic World* 163:18-21 Mr '89

Texas

Kenny, Emmo & the Newk [participating in Tennis Fantasies camp] A. N. Eden. il pors *World Tennis* 37:31-3+ N '89

Vermont

See also

Circus Smirkus

CAMPS FOR PROBLEM CHILDREN
> See also
>> Camp Algonquin (Elgin, Ill.)

CAMPUS CRUSADE FOR CHRIST
Ten-year run for Jesus [film distributed by Campus Crusade for Christ] il *Christianity Today* 33:52 O 20 '89

CAMPUS QUEENS *See* Beauty contests

CAMSHAFTS
> See also
>> Automobile engines—Camshafts
>> Motorcycle engines—Camshafts

CAN WE DANCE A LANDSCAPE? [dance] *See* Dance reviews—Single works

CANADA, LINDA
> *about*
Making an arresting TV debut, deputy sheriff Linda Canada puts the cuffs on fame in Fox's Cops. P. Jordan. il pors *People Weekly* 31:89-90 Ap 24 '89

CANADA
> See also
>> Abortion—Laws and regulations—Canada
>> Abortion clinics—Canada
>> Advertising—Canada
>> Affinity cards—Canada
>> Aged market—Canada
>> Agricultural administration—Canada
>> Agriculture—Canada
>> AIDS (Disease)—Canada
>> Air pollution—Canada
>> Airports—Canada
>> Alberta
>> Americans—Canada
>> Antitrust law—Canada
>> Art galleries and museums—Canada
>> Automobile racing—Canada
>> Aviation and state—Canada
>> Banks and banking—Canada
>> Billionaires—Canada
>> Birds—Canada
>> British Columbia
>> Business hours—Canada
>> Cable television—Canada
>> Canadian Rockies (B.C. and Alta.)
>> Cancer research—Canada
>> Capital gains tax—Canada
>> Censorship—Canada
>> Charities—Canada
>> Child molesting—Canada
>> China—Diplomatic and consular service—Canada
>> Chinese—Canada
>> Church colleges and universities—Canada
>> Collective bargaining—Nurses—Canada
>> Colleges and universities—Canada
>> Colombians—Canada
>> Compensation (Law)—Canada
>> Corporations—Acquisitions and mergers—Laws and regulations—Canada
>> Country music—Canada
>> Courts—Canada
>> Crime and criminals—Canada
>> Czechs—Canada
>> Dams—Canada
>> Dance concerts—Canada
>> Day care—Canada
>> Debts, Public—Canada
>> Deportation—Canada
>> Drug abuse—Canada
>> Drug laws and regulations—Canada
>> Economic assistance, Domestic—Canada
>> Energy policy—Canada
>> Engineering—Canada
>> Environmental associations—Canada
>> Environmental marketing—Canada
>> Environmental movement—Canada
>> Environmental policy—Canada
>> Eskimos
>> Espionage, Russian—Canada
>> Family—Canada
>> Financial institutions—Laws and regulations—Canada
>> Firearms—Laws and regulations—Canada
>> Fishing—Canada
>> Football, College—Canada
>> Foreign students—Canada
>> Gambling—Canada
>> Gangs—Canada
>> Gas pipelines—Canada
>> Golf—Canada
>> Golf courses—Canada
>> Government and the press—Canada
>> Government entertaining—Canada
>> Greenmail—Canada
>> Health education—Canada
>> Health facilities—Canada
>> Hippies—Canada
>> Homosexuality—Canada
>> Hospitals—Canada
>> Hotels, motels, etc.—Canada
>> Hours of labor—Canada
>> Housing—Canada
>> Immigration and emigration—Canada
>> Indians of North America—Canada
>> Industry and state—Canada
>> Industry and the environment—Canada
>> Insider trading—Canada
>> Insurance, Health—Canada
>> Insurance, Unemployment—Canada
>> Insurance, Workers' compensation—Canada
>> Interest (Economics)—Canada
>> Investments, American—Canada
>> Investments, British—Canada
>> Investments, Canadian
>> Investments, Chinese—Canada
>> Investments, Foreign—Canada
>> Investments, French—Canada
>> Investments, Hong Kong—Canada
>> Investments, Japanese—Canada
>> Japanese—Canada
>> Journalism—Canada
>> Juvenile justice, Administration of—Canada
>> Manitoba
>> Maritime Provinces
>> Mass media—Canada
>> Medical care—Canada
>> Medical ethics—Canada
>> Men's liberation movement—Canada
>> Middle classes—Canada
>> Minorities—Canada
>> Morale, National—Canada
>> Motion picture laws and regulations—Canada
>> Motion pictures—Canada
>> Mountains—Canada
>> Narcotics laws and regulations—Canada
>> Narcotics trade—Canada
>> New Brunswick
>> Newfoundland
>> Nova Scotia
>> Nuclear power plants—Canada
>> Nuclear research—Canada
>> Ontario
>> Paleontology—Canada
>> Paper money—Canada
>> Parent and child (Law)—Canada
>> Poles—Canada
>> Police—Canada
>> Pollution—Canada
>> Prices—Canada
>> Prince Edward Island
>> Privatization—Canada
>> Prolife movement—Canada
>> Public opinion—Canada
>> Public prosecutors—Canada
>> Québec (Province)
>> Railroad tunnels—Canada
>> Railroads—Canada
>> Real estate investment—Canada
>> Research—Canada
>> Rural development—Canada
>> Russians—Canada
>> Saint Lawrence River
>> Sales tax—Canada
>> Sanitary landfills—Canada
>> Saskatchewan
>> Satanism—Canada
>> Science and state—Canada
>> Securities—Canada
>> Servicewomen—Canada
>> Shopping—Canada
>> Smoking—Laws and regulations—Canada
>> Smoking and employment—Canada
>> Social security—Canada
>> Sports—Canada
>> Sports and state—Canada
>> Stadiums—Canada
>> Strikes—Nurses—Canada
>> Strikes—Radio workers—Canada
>> Strikes—Television workers—Canada
>> Suicide—Canada
>> Sunday—Laws and regulations—Canada
>> Taxation—Canada
>> Technology—Canada
>> Television advertising—Canada
>> Television and politics—Canada
>> Television broadcasting—Canada
>> Terrorism—Canada
>> Theater—Canada
>> Trade fairs—Canada
>> Trade waste—Disposal—Canada
>> Traffic accidents—Canada
>> Trusts and trustees—Canada
>> United States—Diplomatic and consular service—Canada
>> Veterinary medicine—Canada
>> Vietnamese—Canada
>> War crime trials—Canada
>> Wilderness areas—Canada
>> Wildlife conservation—Canada
>> Women—Canada

CANADA—See also—*cont.*
Youth—Canada
Yukon Territory
Canada [cover story] il *Department of State Bulletin* 89:7-12
O '89

Appropriations and expenditures
See also
Budget—Canada

Armed Forces
See also
Military bases, Canadian
Appropriations and expenditures
Canada's defense budget cancels key programs in 1987 white
paper. D. Hughes. *Aviation Week & Space Technology*
130:28 My 8 '89
The defence gap. M. Clark. il *Maclean's* 102:10-12 My 22
'89
Military manoeuvres [base closings] M. Clark. il *Maclean's*
102:19 My 8 '89
On the defensive. J. Daly. il *Maclean's* 102:36 Jl 10 '89
Forces in Europe
The defence gap [budget cuts] M. Clark. il *Maclean's* 102:10-12
My 22 '89
Should Canada bring the boys home? T. Rauf and J. M.
Lamb. il *The Bulletin of the Atomic Scientists* 45:36-8
S '89

Women
See Servicewomen—Canada

Capital
See also
Ottawa (Ont.)

Climate
Canadian weather. See issues of Weatherwise
A cold blast of winter. P. Kaihla. il *Maclean's* 102:14 F
13 '89

Commerce
East Asia
China's pain is Vancouver's gain. P. C. Newman. il *Maclean's*
102:43 O 2 '89
France
See France—Commerce—Canada
Great Britain
See Great Britain—Commerce—Canada
Iran
See also
Iran-contra affair—Canadian participation
Netherlands
Fokker initiates North American service with Inter-Canadian.
C. Fotos. il *Aviation Week & Space Technology* 130:98
F 13 '89
South Africa
Canada in a hot seat [business transactions questioned at
Commonwealth meeting] M. Nemeth. il por *Maclean's*
102:21 F 20 '89
Soviet Union
See Soviet Union—Commerce—Canada
United States
See United States—Commerce—Canada
Western Europe
Canadian firms concerned that 1992 may hinder marketing
efforts in Europe [aerospace] il *Aviation Week & Space
Technology* 130:139+ Je 12 '89
Champagne diplomacy [Ontario Premier D. Peterson leads
business delegation to France] J. Daly. *Maclean's* 102:39+
Ap 17 '89

Commercial policy
See also
Tariff—Canada
Brave new world [free trade agreement goes into effect]
M. Clark. il *Maclean's* 102:12-13 Ja 9 '89
Business [U.S.-Canada free trade agreement] il *Maclean's*
102:66-70+ Jl 3 '89
The call for a referendum [Maclean's/Decima poll on free
trade agreement with the U.S.] *Maclean's* 102:13 Ja 2
'89
The costs of free trade [unemployment] J. DeMont. il
Maclean's 102:28 Ap 10 '89
Free trade [address, November 22, 1988] T. Siddon. *Vital
Speeches of the Day* 55:222-4 Ja 15 '89
A free trade anniversary [Canada-U.S.; special section] il
Maclean's 102:44-50+ D 18 '89
Opening with a bang [first week in the free trade era]. T.
Tedesco and M. Clark. il *Maclean's* 102:15 Ja 16 '89
Signing away Canada's soul [free trade agreement with the
U.S.; adaptation of address, May 1988] R. Davies. il
Harper's 278:43-7 Ja '89
A warm welcome from up north. il *U.S. News & World
Report* 106:46 My 29 '89
Words of conciliation [interview with Ontario premier D.
Peterson] T. Tedesco. il por *Maclean's* 102:16 Ja 30 '89

Cultural policy
See also
Canada. Dept. of Communications
Culture in crisis. P. Young. il por *Maclean's* 102:58-60 My
8 '89
Standing on guard [Canada-U.S. free trade accord] J. DeMont.
il *Maclean's* 102:50 D 18 '89

Cultural relations
Canada at the summit [Francophonie summit in Senegal]
B. Wallace. il *Maclean's* 102:17 My 29 '89
France
See France—Cultural relations—Canada
United States
See United States—Cultural relations—Canada

Defenses
See also
Airplanes, Military—Canada
Military bases, Canadian
North Atlantic Treaty Organization
Nuclear submarines, Canadian
Remotely piloted vehicles—Canada
Warships—Canada

Description and travel
See also
Cruising—Canada
Canada [special section] M. Ingebretsen. il *Better Homes
and Gardens* 67:154+ Mr '89
Canada [Via Rail] B. Keating. il map *New Choices for the
Best Years* 29:56-9 Ap '89

Diplomatic and consular service
The honorary consuls [Canada's volunteer diplomats] G.
Allen. il *Maclean's* 102:18-19 Ja 30 '89
United States
A fiery reception [Canadian embassy in Washington] C. Wood.
il por *Maclean's* 102:52-3 Mr 6 '89
Men of credentials [American ambassador E. Ney and
Canadian counterpart D. Burney] H. Mackenzie. il pors
Maclean's 102:62-3 Jl 3 '89

Economic conditions
See also
Cost and standard of living—Canada
Debt—Canada
Inflation (Finance)—Canada
Unemployment—Canada
Caution lights. J. Daly. il *Maclean's* 102:27 Ja 9 '89
Dollar signs floating in the crystal ball. P. C. Newman.
il *Maclean's* 102:52 Ja 2 '89
The return of the West. T. Fennell. il *Maclean's* 102:44-6
S 18 '89

Economic policy
See also
Bank of Canada
Budget—Canada
Canada. Centre for Sustainable Economic Development

Economic relations
Canada's fictional role at summits. A. Fotheringham. il
Maclean's 102:52 Jl 24 '89

Foreign opinion
American
A different kind of 'north-south' dialogue. C. Wood. il *World
Press Review* 36:36-8 Ag '89
Portrait of two nations [cover story; special section; with
editorial comment by Kevin Doyle] il *Maclean's* 102:4,
23-8+ Jl 3 '89
American—Anecdotes, facetiae, satire, etc.
Different—in a manner of speaking. A. Fotheringham. il
Maclean's 102:84 Jl 3 '89

Foreign relations
China
See also
China—Diplomatic and consular service—Canada
Rage and sorrow [response to violence in Beijing] M. Nemeth.
il *Maclean's* 102:28-9 Je 19 '89
Communist countries
Double standards on Canada's left. B. Amiel. il *Maclean's*
102:9 S 25 '89
France
See France—Foreign relations—Canada
Jordan
See also
Hussein, King of Jordan, 1935-—Visit to Canada, 1989
Latin America
A crash course for Mulroney [Nicaragua's decision to cancel
ceasefire overshadows announcement of Canada's intention
to join OAS] H. Mackenzie. il pors *Maclean's* 102:32-3+
N 6 '89
A seat at the table [Canada prepares to join the OAS]
R. Laver. il *Maclean's* 102:24 O 16 '89
Middle East
Divisive diplomacy [cabinet minister J. Clark seeks stronger
ties with PLO] M. Nemeth. por *Maclean's* 102:40 Mr
20 '89
Talking to the PLO; A personal triumph [Canada upgrades
relations] L. Van Dusen. il por *Maclean's* 102:10-12 Ap
10 '89
Soviet Union
See Soviet Union—Foreign relations—Canada
United States
See United States—Foreign relations—Canada

Forest fires
See Forest fires

Governors-general
See also
Hnatyshyn, Ramon

CANADA—*cont.*

History
1914-1945
See also
World War, 1939-1945—Canada
Industries
See also
Aerospace industries—Canada
Air Canada
Airlines—Acquisitions and mergers—Canada
Airlines—Canada
Alberta-Pacific Forest Industries Inc.
American Barrick Resources Corp.
American Express Canada, Inc.
Art trade—Canada
Battery Technologies Inc.
BCE Mobile Communications Inc.
BCL Entertainment Corporation
Bell Canada Enterprises Inc.
Black business enterprises—Canada
Bombardier Inc.
Book Company
Brewing industry—Acquisitions and mergers—Canada
Bristol Aerospace Ltd.
Brokers—Canada
Business consultants—Canada
CALL-NET Telecommunications Ltd.
Campeau Corporation
Canadair Ltd.
Canadian Airlines International
Canadian Manufacturing Advanced Technology Exchange
Canadian National Railway Company
Canadian Pacific Limited
Cantel Inc.
Carling O'Keefe Limited
CKO Inc.
Clothing industry—Canada
Computer industry—Canada
Concert Productions International
Connaught Biosciences Inc.
Consolidated-Bathurst Inc.
Corona Corp.
Corporations—Acquisitions and mergers—Canada
Cundill Value Fund
DeHavilland Aircraft of Canada, Limited
Doman Industries Ltd.
Dominion Textile Inc.
Edper Enterprises
Falconbridge Limited
Famous Players Ltd.
Financial institutions—Acquisitions and mergers—Canada
First City Financial Corporation
Fish industry—Canada
Fisheries—Canada
Four Seasons Hotels Limited
Furniture industry—Canada
Gainers Inc.
Garrett Canada Ltd.
Gas industry—Canada
Grocery trade—Acquisitions and mergers—Canada
Harper & Collins Publishers Ltd.
Hollinger, Inc.
IKOY Partnership
Imperial Oil Limited
Inter-Canadian (Firm)
Investment trusts—Canada
Irving Industrial Group
Irving Oil Company
John Labatt Limited
Journey's End Motels
LAC Minerals Ltd.
Law firms—Acquisitions and mergers—Canada
Loblaw Companies Ltd.
Maclean Hunter Ltd.
MacMillan Bloedel Limited
Magna International Inc.
Mass media brokers—Canada
Mass media industry—Acquisitions and mergers—Canada
Mass media industry—Canada
Midland Doherty Financial Corp.
Mining industry—Acquisitions and mergers—Canada
Molson Breweries
Molson Companies Limited
Motion picture industry—Canada
Munitions—Canada
National Money Mart Inc.
National Sea Products Ltd.
Newspaper publishers and publishing—Acquisitions and mergers—Canada
Newspaper publishers and publishing—Canada
Noranda Inc.
Northern Telecom Ltd.
Nova Corporation of Alberta
Olympia & York Developments Ltd.
Pacific Western Airlines Ltd.
Petro-Canada Inc.
Petroleum industry—Acquisitions and mergers—Canada

Petroleum industry—Canada
Pollution control industries—Canada
Poultry industry—Canada
Pratt & Whitney Aircraft of Canada Ltd.
Prime Resources Corporation
Principal Group Ltd.
Printing industry—Canada
Publishers and publishing—Canada
Quebecor Inc.
Real estate business—Canada
Rogers Communications Inc.
Sea Industries Ltd.
Seagram Company Ltd.
Selkirk Communications Limited
Shell Canada Ltd.
Shellfish fisheries—Canada
Sobeys Stores, Ltd.
Southam Inc.
Steinberg Inc.
Television industry—Canada
Texaco Canada Inc.
Thomson Newspapers Ltd.
TransCanada PipeLines Limited
Tridel Enterprises Inc.
Triple Five Corporation
Triton Alliance Corporation
Via Rail Canada Inc.
Wardair Inc.
Business watch. P. C. Newman. See issues of Maclean's
Opting out of the 21st century [free trade agreement accelerating the de-industrialization of Canada] P. C. Newman. il *Maclean's* 102:38 O 23 '89
The winners and the losers [Canada-U.S. free trade agreement] P. Chisholm. il *Maclean's* 102:48-9 D 18 '89
Bibliography
Rating the season's business books. P. C. Newman. il *Maclean's* 102:48 D 11 '89
Languages
Canada: struggling to keep its identity [French language question] D. Strait. il *Scholastic Update (Teachers' edition)* 122:29 S 22 '89
The divided nation [Meech Lake constitutional accord; cover story; special section; with editorial comment by Kevin Doyle] il *Maclean's* 102:4, 18-23+ Mr 20 '89
The return to two solitudes [bilingualism] B. Bergman. il *Maclean's* 102:26+ N 6 '89
Anecdotes, facetiae, satire, etc.
We're number 1 in language debates. C. Gordon. il *Maclean's* 102:39 Ja 9 '89
Monetary policy
See Bank of Canada
Moral conditions
A retreat from ideals [Maclean's/Decima poll] C. Wood. il *Maclean's* 102:36-7 Ja 2 '89
Nationalism
See also
Federal and provincial relations (Canada)
Canada: struggling to keep its identity [French language question] D. Strait. il *Scholastic Update (Teachers' edition)* 122:29 S 22 '89
Canadian conundrums: nationalism, socialism, and free trade. A. Stark. il *The American Spectator* 22:20-2 Ap '89
The forces of division. G. W. Taylor. il *Maclean's* 102:30+ N 20 '89
Signing away Canada's soul [free trade agreement with the U.S.; adaptation of address, May 1988] R. Davies. il *Harper's* 278:43-7 Ja '89
Photographs and photography
Maclean's fourth national Photo Contest winners. il *Maclean's* 102:75-8 N 27 '89
Politics and government
See also
Campaign funds—Canada
Canada—Prime ministers
Canada. Cabinet
Canada. Constitution
Canada. Parliament
Confederation of Regions Party (Canada)
Elections—Canada
Federal and provincial relations (Canada)
Liberal Party (Canada)
Liberalism—Canada
Political attitudes—Canada
Political candidates—Canada
Political ethics—Canada
Political patronage—Canada
Politics, Corruption in—Canada
Press and politics—Canada
Referendum—Canada
Reform Party of Canada
Socialism—Canada
Column. A. Fotheringham. See issues of Maclean's
Shaping the future [Canada and U.S. styles of government contrasted] M. Janigan. il *Maclean's* 102:58-9 Jl 3 '89
Anecdotes, facetiae, satire, etc.
Ottawa's usual air of unreality. A. Fotheringham. il *Maclean's* 102:76 O 16 '89

CANADA—Politics and government—Anecdotes, facetiae, satire, etc.—*cont.*

The political look of 1989. A. Fotheringham. il *Maclean's* 102:48 Ja 16 '89

Where second best is good enough. A. Fotheringham. il *Maclean's* 102:56 Je 19 '89

Population

See also
Immigrants—Canada
Migration, Internal—Canada

Premiers

See Canada—Prime ministers

Prime ministers

Dissension in 'the Club' [premiers discuss Meech Lake constitutional accord] B. Wallace. il *Maclean's* 102:14 Mr 13 '89

The nation's agenda [premiers attack federal policies] B. Wallace. il *Maclean's* 102:14 S 4 '89

Stepping back from the brink [debate over constitutional accord at First Ministers' conference; special section] il *Maclean's* 102:22-6+ N 20 '89

Provinces

See also
Federal and provincial relations (Canada)

Race relations

An angry racial backlash [cover story; special section; with editorial comment by Kevin Doyle] il *Maclean's* 102:4, 14-21+ Jl 10 '89

Religious institutions and affairs

See also
Buddhism—Canada
Catholic Church—Canada
Church and race relations—Canada
Church and state—Canada
Evangelical churches—Canada
United Church of Canada

Social conditions

See also
Sexual behavior—Canada

Statistics

Profiles in numbers. S. Steele. il *Maclean's* 102:51 Jl 3 '89

CANADA. AIR FORCE *See* Canada. Royal Canadian Air Force

CANADA. BUREAU OF COMPETITION POLICY

A warning from Ottawa. B. Wallace. il por *Maclean's* 102:38 Ja 30 '89

CANADA. CABINET

Anecdotes, facetiae, satire, etc.

Cromwell rules in the nation's capital. A. Fotheringham. il *Maclean's* 102:68 Ap 3 '89

CANADA. CENTRE FOR SUSTAINABLE ECONOMIC DEVELOPMENT

Boss of the outdoors [appointment of M. Strong] B. Wallace. por *Maclean's* 102:15 Ja 23 '89

CANADA. COMMUNICATIONS SECURITY ESTABLISHMENT

Is Big Brother listening? L. Van Dusen. *Maclean's* 102:14 Jl 24 '89

CANADA. CONSTITUTION

An assault on Meech [interview with Newfoundland's premier C. Wells] G. Allen. il por *Maclean's* 102:26 O 16 '89

A battle joined [P. Trudeau enters debate over constitutional accord; cover story; special section] il pors *Maclean's* 102:20-2+ N 6 '89

Dissension in 'the Club' [premiers discuss Meech Lake constitutional accord] B. Wallace. il *Maclean's* 102:14 Mr 13 '89

The divided nation [Meech Lake constitutional accord; cover story; special section; with editorial comment by Kevin Doyle] il *Maclean's* 102:4, 18-23+ Mr 20 '89

A parallel accord [Manitoba politicians near agreement on Meech Lake constitutional accord] G. W. Taylor. il *Maclean's* 102:15+ Jl 24 '89

Revisiting Meech Lake. T. Tedesco. il *Maclean's* 102:16 Jl 17 '89

Stepping back from the brink [debate over constitutional accord at First Ministers' conference; special section] il *Maclean's* 102:22-6+ N 20 '89

Storm clouds over Quebec [separatism issue in provincial election campaign; cover story; special section; with editorial comment by Kevin Doyle] il pors *Maclean's* 102:2, 16-22+ S 25 '89

Stormy weather [Manitoba premier G. Filmon withdraws support for Meech Lake constitutional accord] B. Wallace. il por *Maclean's* 102:12-14 Ja 16 '89

Test in the West [public hearings on Meech Lake constitutional accord in Manitoba] R. Laver. il por *Maclean's* 102:12-14 Ap 24 '89

Trouble on the Quebec front [R. Bourassa vs. J. Chrétien on constitutional accord] B. Wallace. *Maclean's* 102:12 Je 26 '89

Troubled waters [Meech Lake constitutional accord] B. Wallace. il *Maclean's* 102:18-19 O 9 '89

Under the gun [pressure on New Brunswick and Manitoba to support Meech Lake constitutional accord; with interview with F. McKenna] il por *Maclean's* 102:10-13 F 27 '89

CANADA. DEPT. OF COMMUNICATIONS

Culture in crisis. P. Young. il por *Maclean's* 102:58-60 My 8 '89

CANADA. NATIONAL ENERGY BOARD *See* National Energy Board (Canada)

CANADA. NATIONAL FILM BOARD *See* National Film Board of Canada

CANADA. NATIONAL GALLERY *See* National Gallery of Canada

CANADA. OFFICE OF THE MINISTER OF STATE FOR MULTICULTURALISM

Anecdotes, facetiae, satire, etc.

Subsidizing the hyphenated Canadian. S. MacLeod. por *Maclean's* 102:48 Ja 9 '89

CANADA. PARLIAMENT. HOUSE OF COMMONS

The Kings of the Hills [contrasting MP D. Blenkarn of Canada with Congressman J. Dingell of the United States] il pors *Maclean's* 102:60-1 Jl 3 '89

The rookies on the hill. M. Clark. il *Maclean's* 102:14-15 Ja 9 '89

A Tory game plan. B. Wallace. il por *Maclean's* 102:10-11 S 25 '89

Anecdotes, facetiae, satire, etc.

Helping taxpayers by using fewer 'jerks'. S. MacLeod. por *Maclean's* 102:64 Mr 13 '89

CANADA. PARLIAMENT. SENATE

By popular demand [S. Waters' Alberta nomination election victory part of drive to reform Senate; special section] il por *Maclean's* 102:24-5+ O 30 '89

The winds of change [Alberta plans to elect a senator] J. Howse. il *Maclean's* 102:15 F 13 '89

CANADA. RADIO-TELEVISION AND TELECOMMUNICATIONS COMMISSION *See* Canadian Radio-Television and Telecommunications Commission

CANADA. REVENUE CANADA

Diagnosis: a severe case of the wobblies [Satanic verses case; interview with J. Clark] A. Fotheringham. il *Maclean's* 102:56 Mr 27 '89

Ducking the Rushdie challenge [Satanic verses case] A. Fotheringham. il *Maclean's* 102:64 Mr 6 '89

CANADA. ROYAL CANADIAN AIR FORCE

Harvard graduate [American receives Royal Canadian Air Force training on AT-6 Harvard during World War II] L. Morgan. il *Flying* 116:82+ F '89

CANADA. ROYAL CANADIAN MOUNTED POLICE *See* Royal Canadian Mounted Police

CANADA. SPACE AGENCY

Canada establishes Space Agency to oversee major programs, research. il *Aviation Week & Space Technology* 130:132 Mr 20 '89

CANADA. SUPREME COURT

The final appeal [C. Daigle's fight for an abortion] L. Van Dusen. il por *Maclean's* 102:10-11 Ag 14 '89

Decisions

Abortion agony [okays abortion sought by C. Daigle over objections of former boyfriend] B. Wallace and L. Van Dusen. il por *Maclean's* 102:12-14 Ag 21 '89

Abortion deadlock [refuses to rule on fetal rights] N. Underwood. il *Maclean's* 102:48 Mr 20 '89

Court fails to block abortion [case of C. Daigle] L. Mackey. *Christianity Today* 33:65 S 8 '89

Nelles's legal gain [rules in favor of nurse S. Nelles over baby murder mystery at Sick Children's Hospital] B. Wickens. il por *Maclean's* 102:42 Ag 28 '89

The Pez is golden [ruling favors Corona Corp. in claim dispute] J. DeMont. il por *Maclean's* 102:39 Ag 21 '89

A unanimous view [ruling in C. Daigle case denying partner's right to prevent an abortion] L. Van Dusen. il por *Maclean's* 102:16 N 27 '89

CANADA. TRANSPORT CANADA

Up in the air [dissension over investigation of 1985 Gander crash] B. Wallace. il por *Maclean's* 102:54 Ap 3 '89

CANADA AND THE UNITED STATES

See also
Canada—Foreign opinion—American
United States—Foreign opinion—Canadian

Canadians cope, Americans conquer. A. Fotheringham. *World Press Review* 36:36 Ap '89

The continental divide [interview with S. M. Lipset] P. Kaihla. *Maclean's* 102:39 O 30 '89

A different kind of 'north-south' dialogue. C. Wood. il *World Press Review* 36:36-8 Ag '89

Portrait of two nations [cover story; special section; with editorial comment by Kevin Doyle] il *Maclean's* 102:4, 23-8+ Jl 3 '89

Anecdotes, facetiae, satire, etc.

Different—in a manner of speaking. A. Fotheringham. il *Maclean's* 102:84 Jl 3 '89

CANADA DEPOSIT INSURANCE CORPORATION

Keeping the money safe. *Maclean's* 102:34 Jl 31 '89

CANADA GOOSE SHOOTING *See* Goose shooting

CANADA IN ART

Seasons of the Canadian soul [wilderness paintings] R. M. Peck. il *International Wildlife* 19:44-51 My/Je '89

CANADA POST CORPORATION

The man for the job [D. Lander] G. W. Taylor. il por *Maclean's* 102:36 O 9 '89

CANADA POST CORPORATION—cont.

The power of Canada Post. G. W. Taylor. il *Maclean's* 102:32-4 O 9 '89

Profits in the mail. J. Daly. il *Maclean's* 102:36 Je 19 '89

CANADA-U.S.S.R. BUSINESS COUNCIL

A blue-ribbon trade mission. M. Gray. *Maclean's* 102:45 N 13 '89

CANADAIR LTD.

Canadair group expands operations to meet new program requirements [Airbus subcontracting and Regional Jet program] D. Hughes. il *Aviation Week & Space Technology* 130:75-7 My 15 '89

Canadair RJ: go ahead. il *Flying* 116:9 Jl '89

Canadair ships Airbus fuselage sections to France on Soviet An-124 transports. il *Aviation Week & Space Technology* 131:135 N 20 '89

Canadair to build Challenger 601-S. *Flying* 116:20 S '89

Canadair to resume CL-227 flights after completing technical review [remotely piloted vehicle] il *Aviation Week & Space Technology* 130:78-9 My 15 '89

Canadair's CL-215 [firefighter aircraft spurned in U.S.] A. Laboda. il *Flying* 116:58 Ja '89

CANADIAN (TRAIN) *See* Railroads—Trains

CANADIAN AIRLINES INTERNATIONAL

The end of Ward's dream [Wardair sold to Pacific Western Airlines] P. Chisholm. il pors *Maclean's* 102:34-5 Ja 30 '89

PWA Corp. to lay off 1,900 airline personnel [combining Canadian Airlines International and Wardair into one airline] *Aviation Week & Space Technology* 131:45 D 11 '89

CANADIAN BIENNIAL OF CONTEMPORARY ART

The shock of the new. G. MacKay. il *Maclean's* 102:75 O 23 '89

CANADIAN BRASS (ENSEMBLE)

Horns of plenty. P. Young. il *Maclean's* 102:49 Ag 21 '89

CANADIAN BROADCASTING CORPORATION

The CBC's future [launching of Newsworld; cover story; special section; with editorial comment by Kevin Doyle] il *Maclean's* 102:2, 34-42 Ag 7 '89

Closing down the options for Mulroney [successor to Pierre Juneau] A. Fotheringham. il *Maclean's* 102:48 Ja 23 '89

Faulty reception [strike] D. Turbide. il *Maclean's* 102:54 Mr 27 '89

The new helmsmen [G. Veilleux and P. Watson; with interview with P. Watson] R. Corelli. il pors *Maclean's* 102:60-1 O 9 '89

CANADIAN CENTRE FOR ARCHITECTURE (MONTREAL, QUÉBEC)

A capital of design. P. Young. il por *Maclean's* 102:54-5 My 22 '89

The fire behind a fight for livable cities [P. Lambert] D. Jenish. il por *Maclean's* 102:18-19 D 25 '89

Hard-hatted woman [founder P. Lambert] D. Brenner. il pors *House & Garden* 161:38+ My '89

L'architecture parlante. S. Stephens. il *Architectural Record* 177:57+ Ag '89

A Montreal must-see if you're interested in architecture. il *Sunset (Central West edition)* 183:60-1 N '89

CANADIAN COINS *See* Coins

CANADIAN EMBASSY BUILDINGS *See* Embassies (Buildings)

CANADIAN ESKIMOS *See* Eskimos

CANADIAN FICTION

See also

Governor General's Literary Award (Canada)

CANADIAN FOOTBALL LEAGUE

A game of survival. D. Burke. il *Maclean's* 102:45 Ag 14 '89

CANADIAN FOREST FIRES *See* Forest fires

CANADIAN FURNITURE *See* Furniture, Canadian

CANADIAN GRAND PRIX *See* Automobile racing—Canada

CANADIAN ICE BREAKING VESSELS *See* Ice breaking vessels, Canadian

CANADIAN LAWYER (PERIODICAL)

Rating the judiciary. N. Underwood. il *Maclean's* 102:56 My 22 '89

CANADIAN MANUFACTURING ADVANCED TECHNOLOGY EXCHANGE

Shaping a new industrial Canada [address, September 11, 1989] B. M. McGourty. *Vital Speeches of the Day* 56:104-8 D 1 '89

CANADIAN MUSEUM OF CIVILIZATION

Canada's visionary new museum. S. Rao. il *World Press Review* 36:61 Jl '89

A grand folly in Ottawa [work of architect D. Cardinal] K. Andersen. il por *Time* 134:64 Jl 10 '89

'Oh, Canada . . .'. P. Johnston. il *History Today* 39:4-5 Ag '89

Showcasing Canada. P. Young. il *Maclean's* 102:38-9 Jl 10 '89

CANADIAN NATIONAL RAILWAY COMPANY

One of the world's biggest railways. D. Francis. il *Maclean's* 102:11 My 1 '89

CANADIAN NUCLEAR SUBMARINES *See* Nuclear submarines, Canadian

CANADIAN ODEON THEATRES LTD.

See also

Cineplex Odeon Corporation

CANADIAN OPERA COMPANY

Women of passion [performances of Tosca and The Makropulos case] J. Pearce. il *Maclean's* 102:59 F 6 '89

CANADIAN PACIFIC LIMITED

A confused agenda for selling the country [rumored takeover target of Britain's Hanson Trust] A. Fotheringham. il *Maclean's* 102:56 Ag 14 '89

Taming a mountain [opening of tunnel through Rogers Pass] J. DeMont. *Maclean's* 102:45+ My 15 '89

CANADIAN PREMIERS *See* Canada—Prime ministers

CANADIAN RADIO-TELEVISION AND TELECOMMUNICATIONS COMMISSION

Assuring the regulators [Maclean Hunter Ltd.'s purchase of Selkirk Communications] J. DeMont. il *Maclean's* 102:36 Je 12 '89

David and Goliath dial a busy signal [CALL-NET vs. Bell Canada] D. Francis. il *Maclean's* 102:11 Ap 3 '89

CANADIAN ROCKIES (B.C. AND ALTA.)

See also

Banff National Park (Alta.)

Big ice. D. Thomson. il *Sierra* 74:57 My/Je '89

CANADIAN SECURITY INTELLIGENCE SERVICE

The looking-glass trade. R. Laver. il *Maclean's* 102:12-14 Jl 24 '89

CANADIAN UNION OF PUBLIC EMPLOYEES

Faulty reception [CBC strike] D. Turbide. il *Maclean's* 102:54 Mr 27 '89

CANADIANS

See also

French Canadians

The Honor Roll [cover story; special section; with editorial comment by Kevin Doyle] D. Jenish. il *Maclean's* 102:4, 15-39 D 25 '89

El Salvador

Under suspicion [human rights activist K. Ridd] A. Bilski. il por *Maclean's* 102:52 D 4 '89

Foreign countries

Breaking away [travel to exotic destinations] R. Dolphin. il *Maclean's* 102:46-7 Mr 13 '89

Soviet Union

Canadians visit the Soviet Union [amateur astronomers] il *Astronomy* 17:18 Je '89

United States

The Maple Leaf Mafia [Canadians in Hollywood] B. D. Johnson. il *Maclean's* 102:78-80+ Jl 3 '89

Southern bargains: Canadians cash in on U.S. prices. A. Walmsley. il *Maclean's* 102:54 D 18 '89

CANADY, ROBERT LYNN, AND HOTCHKISS, PHYLLIS R.

It's a good score! Just a bad grade. il *Phi Delta Kappan* 71:68-71 S '89

CANAL, ANTONIO *See* Canaletto, 1697-1768

CANAL, GIOVANNI ANTONIO *See* Canaletto, 1697-1768

CANAL + (FIRM) *See* Canal Plus (Firm)

CANAL BAR (NEW YORK, N.Y.) *See* New York (N.Y.)—Restaurants, nightclubs, bars, etc.

CANAL CAPITAL (FIRM)

Cash cows, so where's the cash? J. Clements. il por *Forbes* 144:246-7 O 30 '89

CANAL CRUISING *See* Cruising

CANAL PLUS (FIRM)

TV de triomphe. J. Marcom, Jr. il *Forbes* 144:124 O 16 '89

CANALETTO, 1697-1768

about

The far-reaching eye of Venice's Antonio Canaletto. D. Hofstadter. bibl (p245) il *Smithsonian* 20:78-86+ N '89

Venice observed. R. Bernier. il *Vogue* 179:418-23+ N '89

Visions of Venice. E. Heartney. il *Harper's Bazaar* 122:158-9+ N '89

CANALS

China

The first contour transport canal [ancient China] R. K. G. Temple. il *The Courier (Unesco)* 41:32-3 O '88

Panama

See also

Panama Canal

CANAPÉS *See* Appetizers

CANARIES

Brain

See Brain

CANARY, JOANNE

Games for growing. il *Parents* 64:120-4 My '89

CANAVAN, GREG

about

Brilliant Pebbles: amazing new missile killer. R. K. Bennett. *Reader's Digest* 135:128-33 S '89

CANBY, THOMAS Y.

Reshaping our lives: advanced materials. il *National Geographic* 176:746-81 D '89

CANBY, VINCENT

What's so funny about Japan. il pors *The New York Times Magazine* p26-9+ Je 18 '89

CANCER

See also
Bladder—Cancer
Bone—Cancer
Brain—Cancer
Breast—Cancer
Cancer research
Cervix—Cancer
Colon (Anatomy)—Cancer
Colorectal cancer
Esophagus—Cancer
Eye—Cancer
Hodgkin's disease
Kaposi's sarcoma
Kidneys—Cancer
Larynx—Cancer
Leukemia
Liver—Cancer
Lungs—Cancer
Lymphatic system—Cancer
Metastasis
Mouth—Cancer
Ovaries—Cancer
Pancreas—Cancer
Precancerous conditions
Prostate gland—Cancer
Skin—Cancer
Synovioma
Throat—Cancer
Thyroid gland—Cancer
Vagina—Cancer

Causes

See also
Bladder—Cancer—Causes
Bone—Cancer—Causes
Brain—Cancer—Causes
Breast—Cancer—Causes
Cervix—Cancer—Causes
Daminozide
Liver—Cancer—Causes
Lungs—Cancer—Causes
Mouth—Cancer—Causes
Nitrosamines
Oncogenic viruses
Radiation—Physiological effects
X rays—Physiological effects
The Alar debate [with reply by M. Stanton Evans] E. Groth, III. *Consumers' Research Magazine* 72:28-30 Jl '89
Are electric blankets safe? il *Consumer Reports* 54:715-16 N '89
Are Lake Michigan fish dangerous to your health? J. Gibbs. il *Outdoor Life* 184:72-4+ D '89
Can chlorine cause cancer? [views of Richard J. Bull] *USA Today (Periodical)* 117:14-16 F '89
Cancer warp. R. Bazell. *The New Republic* 201:12-14 D 18 '89
Chemically fingerprinting DNA damage [work of Miral Dizdaroglu] J. Raloff. *Science News* 135:199 Ap 1 '89
Chlorination: residues cloud water safety. J. Raloff. *Science News* 135:342 Je 3 '89
A corrosive fight over California's toxics law [Safe Drinking Water and Toxic Enforcement Act] L. Roberts. il *Science* 243:306-9 Ja 20 '89
Does everything cause cancer? [Alar in apples and other carcinogens; cover story; special section] il *Consumers' Research Magazine* 72:11-18 My '89
Ectopic expression of the serotonin 1c receptor and the triggering of malignant transformation. D. Julius and others. bibl f il *Science* 244:1057-62 Je 2 '89
Forewarned is fairly warned [California's Safe Drinking Water and Toxic Enforcement Act] C. Russell. il *Sierra* 74:36-8+ N/D '89
The hazards of electromagnetic fields (I). P. Brodeur. *The New Yorker* 65:51-2+ Je 12 '89
The hazards of electromagnetic fields (II). P. Brodeur. *The New Yorker* 65:47-9+ Je 19 '89
Is risk assessment conservative? L. Roberts. *Science* 243:1553 Mr 24 '89
Pesticides, risk, and applesauce [discussion of March 10, 1989 article, Pesticides and kids, and March 24, 1989 article, Is risk assessment conservative?] L. Roberts. il *Science* 244:755-7 My 19 '89
Power play [link between ELF fields and cancer; with editorial comment by Paul Hoffman] D. Noland. il *Discover* 10:4, 62-8 D '89
Reduction of intestinal carcinogen absorption by carcinogen-specific secretory immunity. L. K. Silbart and D. F. Keren. bibl f il *Science* 243:1462-4 Mr 17 '89
Rust never sleeps [iron imbalances] J. Scandura. *American Health* 8:151-2 Mr '89
Suckers for science [conflicting results of carcinogenic risk studies] E. Kunes. *Omni (New York, N.Y.)* 11:25 Jl '89
This is what you thought: 70% say the government should do more to protect us from dangerous foods and drugs [survey results] il *Glamour* 87:161 O '89
Too much fuss about pesticides? il *Consumer Reports* 54:655-8 O '89

Warning: if you eat Great Lakes fish . . . *Science News* 135:300 My 13 '89
What about pesticides and other chemicals? *Consumers' Research Magazine* 72:34 Jl '89
Why are rats and actresses dictating U.S. food policy? R. Krumme. *Successful Farming* 87:18-19 Je '89
World cancer patterns. S. Whelan. il *World Health* p25-7 Je '89

Diagnosis

See also
Breast—Cancer—Diagnosis
Cervix—Cancer—Diagnosis
Lungs—Cancer—Diagnosis
Skin—Cancer—Diagnosis

Genetic aspects

See also
Breast—Cancer—Genetic aspects
Colorectal cancer—Genetic aspects
Eye—Cancer—Genetic aspects
Kidneys—Cancer—Genetic aspects
Larynx—Cancer—Genetic aspects
Lungs—Cancer—Genetic aspects
Lymphatic system—Cancer—Genetic aspects
Ovaries—Cancer—Genetic aspects
16 cancers that run in families—will you inherit? M. Castleman. il *Redbook* 173:150-1+ S '89
Activation of the cellular proto-oncogene product p21Ras by addition of a myristylation signal. J. E. Buss and others. bibl f il *Science* 243:1600-3 Mr 24 '89
Antisense RNA-induced reduction in murine TIMP levels confers oncogenicity on Swiss 3T3 cells. R. Khokha and others. bibl f il *Science* 243:947-50 F 17 '89
AP1/*jun* function is differentially induced in promotion-sensitive and resistant JB6 cells [activation by tetradecanoylphorbol acetate] L. R. Bernstein and N. H. Colburn. bibl f il *Science* 244:566-9 My 5 '89
Banking on your DNA [waiting for discovery of gene probes for cancer] S. Begley. il *Newsweek* 114:64 Ag 21 '89
Cancer gene research wins Medicine Nobel [J. M. Bishop and H. Varmus] J. L. Marx. il pors *Science* 246:326-7 O 20 '89
Cancer roadblock on cholesterol pathway [research by William R. Schafer] R. Cowen. *Science News* 136:70-1 Jl 29 '89
Cancer's bad seeds [oncogenes] S. Brownlee. il *U.S. News & World Report* 107:58-9 D 11 '89
Conquering the gene. D. Baltimore. il *Discover* 10:74-6+ O '89
Dynamic expression pattern of the *myc* protooncogene in midgestation mouse embryos. P. Schmid and others. bibl f il *Science* 243:226-9 Ja 13 '89
Fibroblasts transformed with v-*src* show enhanced formation of an inositol tetrakisphosphate. R. M. Johnson and others. bibl f il *Science* 246:121-4 O 6 '89
Gene-tracking leads to Nobel Prize [oncogenes; work of J. M. Bishop and H. Varmus] A. McKenzie. *Science News* 136:244 O 14 '89
Genetic and pharmacological suppression of oncogenic mutations in *RAS* genes of yeast and humans. W. R. Schafer and others. bibl f il *Science* 245:379-85 Jl 28 '89
How DNA viruses may cause cancer. J. L. Marx. il *Science* 243:1012-13 F 24 '89
Induction of mesoderm by a viral oncogene in early Xenopus embryos. M. Whitman and D. A. Melton. bibl f il *Science* 244:803-6 My 19 '89
Many gene changes found in cancer [stepwise accumulation of mutations affecting both oncogenes and suppressor genes] J. L. Marx. bibl il *Science* 246:1386-8 D 15 '89
Medicine [J. M. Bishop and H. E. Varmus awarded Nobel Prize for study of oncogenes] il pors *Time* 134:73 O 23 '89
A new cancer clue [tissue inhibitor of metalloproteinase] R. Dolphin. il *Maclean's* 102:50 Mr 6 '89
The oncogene connection. J. L. Marx. *Science* 245:253 Jl 21 '89
The product of the *mos* proto-oncogene as a candidate "initiator" for oocyte maturation [Xenopus] N. Sagata and others. bibl f il *Science* 245:643-6 Ag 11 '89
Specific expression of nuclear proto-oncogenes before entry into meiotic prophase of spermatogenesis [mice] H. Wolfes and others. bibl f il *Science* 245:740-3 Ag 18 '89
Transformation and plasmacytoid differentiation of EBV-infected human B lymphoblast by *ras* oncogenes. S. Seremetis and others. bibl f il *Science* 243:660-3 F 3 '89
Tumor suppressor genes: the puzzle and the promise. R. Sager. bibl f il *Science* 246:1406-12 D 15 '89
Turning cancer off [*ras* protein structure; work of Sung-Hou Kim] G. Montgomery. il *Discover* 10:66-7 Ja '89

Immunological aspects

Bringing home the bacon [nitric oxide secreted by macrophages; research by Michael Marletta and Dennis Stuehr] S. Vogel. il *Discover* 10:42 Jl '89
New frontiers [research in Canada] A. Steacy. il *Maclean's* 102:45-6 Jl 24 '89

Mortality

The cost of cancer [comparing survival rates of whites and blacks] il *Black Enterprise* 19:43 Ap '89

CANCER—*cont.*

Nutritional aspects

See also

Breast—Cancer—Nutritional aspects
Colon (Anatomy)—Cancer—Nutritional aspects
Lungs—Cancer—Nutritional aspects
Ovaries—Cancer—Nutritional aspects

The anticancer dessert book [views of Michael Pariza] R. A. Barnett. il *American Health* 8:121-2+ Jl/Ag '89

Cancer and your diet. P. M. Barrier. il *Nation's Business* 77:69 Ja '89

Carrot 'chemo'? Beta-carotene may shrink oral precancers. il *Prevention (Emmaus, Pa.)* 41:8 N '89

Cheese source of dietary anticancer agent [research by Michael W. Pariza] J. Raloff. *Science News* 135:87 F 11 '89

Cole's role [anticancer coleslaw] J. Duke and R. A. Barnett. il *American Health* 8:100+ O '89

Cut your cancer risk by more than 50%. D. Webb. il *Redbook* 172:96-9+ Ap '89

Diet, cancer, and common sense. T. Mendoza. il *Current Health 2* 16:18-21 N '89

The diet-cancer link. *McCall's* 117:106 O '89

Does everything cause cancer? [Alar in apples and other carcinogens; cover story; special section] il *Consumers' Research Magazine* 72:11-18 My '89

Eat to beat cancer: our 50 food picks. S. Zarrow. il *Prevention (Emmaus, Pa.)* 41:66-72 F '89

Fighting cancer with carrots. C. Sherman. il *New Choices for the Best Years* 29:59-63 O '89

Fish oil slows some developing cancers [research by T. Colin Campbell] J. Raloff. *Science News* 135:390 Je 24 '89

The food and cancer connection: breakfast tips to reduce the risk. il *Redbook* 172:146+ Mr '89

Give me five! [Nutrition and Cancer Prevention Program in California] R. A. Barnett. il *American Health* 8:141-2 Ap '89

Got a light? This carrot keeps going out [research by Harinder Garewal] R. Weiss. *Science News* 135:348 Je 3 '89

Is broccoli more toxic than dioxin? [views of B. Ames on natural poisons in food and manmade carcinogens] L. Lamb. il *Utne Reader* p11-12 Mr/Ap '89

A man with a mission [P. Greenwald] D. Bartley. il pors *The Saturday Evening Post* 261:58-61+ N/D '89

The new anticancer agenda. S. Levin. il *Mademoiselle* 95:143-4 Mr '89

New hope from the fish-oil factor. G. L. Blackburn. il *Prevention (Emmaus, Pa.)* 41:29-30+ Je '89

Nuts about selenium [Brazil nuts] R. A. Barnett. il *American Health* 8:149 Mr '89

Ode to Cheez Whiz [natural poisons and carcinogens present in food; views of B. Ames] J. Hooper. il *Health (New York, N.Y.)* 21:44+ O '89

Pouring it on for good health [Cheez Whiz spread found to contain altered fatty acids which may help in cancer prevention] il *Newsweek* 113:70 Mr 6 '89

Raw, raw, raw! [uncooked fruits and vegetables may offer greater protection against cancer; research by Blossom Patterson] R. A. Barnett. il *American Health* 8:130+ S '89

Take five [Nutrition and Cancer Prevention Program in California] S. M. Smith. il *Health (New York, N.Y.)* 21:66-71+ S '89

To stymie cancer, eat broccoli raw [study by Lloyd D. Campbell and Bogdan A. Slominski] *Science News* 136:351 N 25 '89

Vegetarians vs. cancer. il *Prevention (Emmaus, Pa.)* 41:8 D '89

Prevention

See also

Breast—Cancer—Prevention
Cancer inhibiting substances
Colon (Anatomy)—Cancer—Prevention
Skin—Cancer—Prevention

Cancer Board attacks tobacco. B. J. Culliton. *Science* 243:889 F 17 '89

Cancer prevention strategy at the NCI [interview with S. Broder] C. SerVaas. il por *The Saturday Evening Post* 261:50-1+ My/Je '89

Panel steps up cancer war [recommendations of the National Cancer Advisory Board] *Science News* 135:85 F 11 '89

Psychological aspects

See also

Breast—Cancer—Psychological aspects

The character of controversy [link between disease and personality; work of R. Grossarth-Maticek] J. Fischman. il *Psychology Today* 22:27 D '88

Depression and cancer: no clear connection [disease causation; research by Alan B. Zonderman] S. Hart. *Science News* 136:150 S 2 '89

Health's character [link between personality and disease; research by R. Grossarth-Maticek] H. J. Eysenck. il pors *Psychology Today* 22:28-32+ D '88

Survivors of childhood cancer [study of teenagers by Gregory Fritz and Judith R. Williams] *Children Today* 18:4 Ja/F '89

Wish me well. R. Shereff. il *Ms.* 18:26+ O '89

Surgery

See also

Breast—Cancer—Surgery
Liver—Cancer—Surgery

After a courageous comeback, a star pitcher breaks his arm but keeps his faith intact; ed. by Liz McNeil. D. Dravecky. il pors *People Weekly* 32:69-70+ S 11 '89

Armed with a miracle [San Francisco Giants pitcher D. Dravecky returns after arm surgery to remove tumor] il pors *Sports Illustrated* 71:18 Ag 21 '89

Danger from blood transfusions [cancer surgery; views of Dale H. Rice] il *USA Today (Periodical)* 117:5 F '89

The man in green [surgeon J. Coleman] J. Stone. il *Discover* 10:88-91 O '89

Therapy

See also

Bone—Cancer—Therapy
Breast—Cancer—Therapy
Cancer inhibiting substances
Colon (Anatomy)—Cancer—Therapy
Commonweal Cancer Help Program
Hodgkin's disease—Therapy
Leukemia—Therapy
Lymphatic system—Cancer—Therapy
Ovaries—Cancer—Therapy
Prostate gland—Cancer—Therapy
Salick Health Care, Inc.
Thyroid gland—Cancer—Therapy

Accelerated medicine [proton therapy] G. Levoy. il *Omni (New York, N.Y.)* 11:26+ Mr '89

America's top cancer clinics [programs sponsored by the National Cancer Institute] S. Lally. *Prevention (Emmaus, Pa.)* 41:49-60 My '89

A blistering debate [heroin for terminal cancer] R. Dolphin. il *Maclean's* 102:41 F 27 '89

Brave new gene therapy [Steven Rosenberg's cancer experiments] S. Begley. il *Newsweek* 113:65 F 13 '89

Cancer: beyond standard therapy. R. Rodale. il *Prevention (Emmaus, Pa.)* 41:30+ My '89

A cancer fighter starts showing its mettle [interleukin-2] J. O. Hamilton. il *Business Week* p96+ Ja 16 '89

Chiseling away at tumors with protons [work of James M. Slater] *Science News* 135:46 Ja 21 '89

Coming: a historic experiment [human gene transplant planned by National Institutes of Health] D. Thompson. il *Time* 133:64 F 13 '89

Compelling cancer cells to self-destruct [use of anti-APO-1] S. Hart. *Science News* 136:69 Jl 29 '89

Cranking up cancer treatments [use of colony-stimulating factors] R. Weiss. *Science News* 135:380 Je 17 '89

Dare to dialogue on cancer [interview with S. Broder] C. SerVaas. il pors *The Saturday Evening Post* 261:42-6+ Jl/Ag '89

Easing the sting of chemotherapy [research by Thomas G. Burish] K. Fackelmann. *Science News* 135:238 Ap 15 '89

Fighting cancer with designer cells [immunotherapy using tumor-infiltrating lymphocytes; work of S. A. Rosenberg] B. J. Culliton. il por *Science* 244:1430-3 Je 23 '89

From wrinkle cream to cancer cure? [retinoids] N. J. Freundlich. il *Business Week* p146 F 20 '89

Gene test begins [patient with advanced melanoma receives infusion of his own white blood cells containing a foreign gene] B. J. Culliton. il *Science* 244:913 My 26 '89

Gene transfer test: so far, so good [treatment of advanced melanoma with tumor-infiltrating lymphocytes; work of Steven A. Rosenberg] B. J. Culliton. *Science* 245:1325 S 22 '89

Gene-transfer trial begins in humans [work of Steven A. Rosenberg] K. Fackelmann. *Science News* 135:324 My 27 '89

Groups seek human gene-transfer delay [opposition to cancer experiment] R. Weiss. *Science News* 135:68 F 4 '89

Human gene therapy: after a lot of looking, now the leap. J. Carey. il *Business Week* p133+ My 1 '89

Immunology's designer genes [tumor-infiltrating lymphocytes; work of S. A. Rosenberg] S. Brownlee. il por *U.S. News & World Report* 107:65-6 O 30 '89

An ingenious way to fix genes [patient receives genetically engineered cells; work of Steven Rosenberg] il *U.S. News & World Report* 106:12-13 Je 5 '89

Labeled therapy [gene transfer experiment may improve a cancer treatment] T. Beardsley. *Scientific American* 260:24-5 F '89

Medical breakthroughs to conquer cancer. S. Lally. il *Prevention (Emmaus, Pa.)* 41:44-52 Ja '89

Monoclonal antibody-mediated tumor regression by induction of apoptosis [leukemia cells] B. C. Trauth and others. bibl f il *Science* 245:301-5 Jl 21 '89

Multidrug resistance in cancer. N. Kartner and V. Ling. bibl il *Scientific American* 260:44-51 Mr '89

Neutron healing [research by Lionel Cohen] *Prevention (Emmaus, Pa.)* 41:19-20 N '89

New frontiers [research in Canada] A. Steacy. il *Maclean's* 102:45-6 Jl 24 '89

Rifkin battles gene transfer experiment. L. Roberts. *Science* 243:734 F 10 '89

Shedding light on cancer [photodynamic therapy] I. Wickelgren. il *Science News* 135:26-8 Ja 14 '89

CANCER—Therapy—*cont.*

A shiny new weapon in the war on cancer: light [light-activated drugs] S. Yanchinski and N. J. Freundlich. il *Business Week* p106-7 My 29 '89

Vital opinions. G. Kolata. il *The New York Times Magazine* p46-7 Ap 16 '89

When they say it's cancer [value of second opinions] G. Kolata. *Reader's Digest* 135:151-3 S '89

Zapping tumors with microwaves. il *High Technology Business* 9:4 Je '89

Zeroing in on cancer [On-line Portal Imaging designed to improve accuracy of radiation therapy] M. Brosnahan. *Maclean's* 102:57 O 16 '89

Vaccines and vaccination

Cancer vaccines show promise at last. J. L. Marx. il *Science* 245:813-15 Ag 25 '89

Reduction of intestinal carcinogen absorption by carcinogen-specific secretory immunity. L. K. Silbart and D. F. Keren. bibl f il *Science* 243:1462-4 Mr 17 '89

CANCER CELLS

See also

Metastasis

Activation of an excluded immunoglobulin allele in a human B lymphoma cell line. N. Berinstein and others. bibl f il *Science* 244:337-9 Ap 21 '89

Compelling cancer cells to self-destruct [use of anti-APO-1] S. Hart. *Science News* 136:69 Jl 29 '89

Identification of monocyte chemotactic activity produced by malignant cells. D. T. Graves and others. bibl f il *Science* 245:1490-3 S 29 '89

An inducible endothelial cell surface glycoprotein mediates melanoma adhesion. G. E. Rice and M. P. Bevilacqua. bibl f il *Science* 246:1303-6 D 8 '89

Monoclonal antibody-mediated tumor regression by induction of apoptosis [leukemia cells] B. C. Trauth and others. bibl f il *Science* 245:301-5 Jl 21 '89

Multidrug resistance in cancer. N. Kartner and V. Ling. bibl il *Scientific American* 260:44-51 Mr '89

Repression of the IgH enhancer in teratocarcinoma cells associated with a novel octamer factor. M. J. Lenardo and others. bibl f il *Science* 243:544-6 Ja 27 '89

Tumor resistance: weakening the pulse [research by Thomas P. Miller] R. Weiss. *Science News* 135:348 Je 3 '89

Culture

AIDS-Kaposi's sarcoma-derived cells express cytokines with autocrine and paracrine growth effects. B. Ensoli and others. bibl f il *Science* 243:223-6 Ja 13 '89

Whose spleen is it? [J. Moore case] D. Andrews. il por *Technology Review* 92:14 N/D '89

CANCER GENES *See* Cancer—Genetic aspects

CANCER IN ANIMALS

Cancer care in the kennel. J. Seligmann. il *Newsweek* 113:64-5 Ap 3 '89

CANCER IN CHILDREN

See also

Leukemia

Never say die. N. E. Gupta. il *Ladies' Home Journal* 106:142-3+ Ap '89

Survivors of childhood cancer [study of teenagers by Gregory Fritz and Judith R. Williams] *Children Today* 18:4 Ja/F '89

CANCER INHIBITING SUBSTANCES

See also

Bleomycin

Cancer—Nutritional aspects

Tissue inhibitor of metalloproteinases

Tumor necrosis factor

Anticancer tobacco? [transient gene expression system developed by Biosource Genetics] J. E. Rodgers. il *American Health* 8:16 S '89

Calicheamicin $\gamma_1{}^I$ and DNA: molecular recognition process responsible for site-specificity. N. Zein and others. bibl f il *Science* 244:697-9 My 12 '89

Cancer-fighting tobacco plants? [transient gene expression system developed at Biosource Genetics Corp.] K. Fackelmann. *Science News* 135:238 Ap 15 '89

Carotenoids: colorful cancer protection. J. Raloff. *Science News* 136:294 N 4 '89

Nontoxic drugs halt cancer spread in mice [anti-metastatic compounds; research by George Martin] J. Raloff. il *Science News* 135:228 Ap 15 '89

CANCER PATIENTS

See also

Vital Options (Organization)

Civil rights

Whose life is it, anyway? [patients' rights in Japan and U.S.] N. Darnton. il *Newsweek* 113:61 Ja 23 '89

Dental care

Cancer's second strike. C. Sears. il *American Health* 8:38 N '89

Employment

First, you beat the cancer [facing discrimination] J. Silberner. il *U.S. News & World Report* 107:97-8+ N 6 '89

Family relationships

Cancer claimed the heart of this family. C. Tevis. il *Successful Farming* 87:62 S '89

"I wish I could hold you more" [B. Wagner videotapes messages for his children before his death] B. Remsberg. il *Reader's Digest* 134:147-52 Je '89

In Time flies when you're alive, actor Paul Linke turns the last years of his wife's life into art [F. Linke's battle with breast cancer] J. Kaufman. il pors *People Weekly* 32:59-60 Ag 21 '89

The prodigal son [former radical reconciles with terminally ill father] P. Collier. il *Reader's Digest* 135:64-8 Ag '89

A sense of direction [reflections on father's death] T. Brookes. il *The New York Times Magazine* p18+ Ap 30 '89

Sweet sorrow [mother's battle with lung cancer] A. Rosen. il *Ms.* 18:24-5 N '89

Home care

Cancer comes home. S. Fishman. il *The New York Times Magazine* p70-1 Je 11 '89

CANCER PRODUCING SUBSTANCES *See* Cancer—Causes

CANCER RESEARCH

See also

International Agency for Research on Cancer

Memorial Sloan-Kettering Cancer Center

National Cancer Institute (U.S.)

A philanthropist against cancer [A. Hammer] C. SerVaas. il por *The Saturday Evening Post* 261:100-1 Ap '89

Ethical aspects

NIH probes researcher's fundraising [case of leukemia researcher R. I. Glazer] C. Holden. *Science* 243:1000 F 24 '89

Federal aid

Cancer warp. R. Bazell. *The New Republic* 201:12-14 D 18 '89

Canada

New frontiers. A. Steacy. il *Maclean's* 102:45-6 Jl 24 '89

CANCER VIRUSES *See* Oncogenic viruses

CANCOGNI, ANNA

(tr) *See* Eco, Umberto. Umberto Eco: a memo to Roone

CANCÚN (MEXICO)

"Féliz Navidad". R. S. Peffer. il *Travel Holiday* 172:90+ D '89

Lolling on the Yucatán. W. G. Flanagan. il *Forbes* 144:274-6 N 27 '89

Weathering the storm [effect of Hurricane Gilbert] G. Young. il *Travel Holiday* 171:85-6 My '89

CANDACE AWARDS

NCBW honors 10 blacks with Candace Awards during New York gala. il *Jet* 76:12+ Ag 7 '89

CANDID PHOTOGRAPHY

Hometown: Hollywood [work of D. Strick] M. Kiwak. il *Petersen's Photographic Magazine* 18:27-9 My '89

Real photographers don't use compacts . . . or do they? G. Lewis. il *Petersen's Photographic Magazine* 18:60-2 Jl '89

CANDIDATES, POLITICAL *See* Political candidates

CÀNDITO, MÌMMO

Elections bring new faces to power. *World Press Review* 36:22-3 Jl '89

CANDLES AND CANDLEHOLDERS

See also

Menorah

Votive candles

Yellow candelabra. il *Workbench* 45:60 S/O '89

CANDLESTICK PARK (SAN FRANCISCO, CALIF.)

Sticking it to the Stick. R. Fimrite. por *Sports Illustrated* 71:102 Ag 21 '89

CANDOMBLÉ

Talking godheads [D. Byrne's Ilé aiyé on PBS] R. F. Thompson. il por *Rolling Stone* p78 Jl 13-27 '89

CANDU NUCLEAR POWER PLANT (CANADA) *See* Nuclear power plants—Canada

CANDY

See also

Chocolate

Cracker Jack

Fudge (Candy)

Candy man [S. Nekos makes Easter chocolates at the Nekos Pharmacy in Kingston, N.Y.] *The New Yorker* 65:34-5 Mr 27 '89

Unsweetened stress [link between stress and desire for sweets; research by Neil Grunberg] B. Fischman. il *Psychology Today* 23:72 Mr '89

Valentine candies. il *Better Homes and Gardens* 68:143-4 F '89

Packaging

Collectors and collecting

The great American candy bar. R. Broekel. il *Antiques & Collecting Hobbies* 94:27-9 Mr '89

CANDY AMERICANA MUSEUM (LITITZ, PA.)

Candy is dandy. J. J. Devanney. il *Americana* 17:6 N/D '89

CANDY INDUSTRY

See also

Godiva Chocolatier

Hershey Foods Corp.

La Maison du Chocolat (Firm)

Tootsie Roll Industries, Inc.

Switzerland

See also

Du Rhône Chocolatier

CANE POLES (FISHING) *See* Fishing tackle
CANE WEAVING
How to weave a cane seat. T. Klenck. il *Popular Mechanics* 166:79-80 F '89
CANE WORKERS *See* Sugar workers
CANETTI, NICOLAI
about
Looking out for number one. D. Machan. il por *Forbes* 144:242+ O 2 '89
CANETTI INC.
Looking out for number one. D. Machan. il por *Forbes* 144:242+ O 2 '89
CANIFF, MILTON ARTHUR, 1907-1988
about
Steve Canyon hangs up his uniform. il *Flying* 116:17 Je '89
CANINE, CRAIG
Freezer birds. il *The Atlantic* 263:18+ F '89
CANINE DISTEMPER VIRUS *See* Distemper virus
CANING *See* Cane weaving
CANION, JOSEPH R. *See* Canion, Rod
CANION, ROD
about
A genius for sales. D. Pauly. il por *Newsweek* 114:43 O 2 '89
How Compaq gets there firstest with the mostest. M. Ivey. il por *Business Week* p146-7+ Je 26 '89
Soft dollars, hard choices. N. Alster. il por *Forbes* 144:106-7+ S 4 '89
Stepping out from IBM's shadow. P. Honan. por *Personal Computing* 13:79 Jl '89
CANNABIS *See* Marijuana
CANNADINE, DAVID, 1950-
Winston agonistes. bibl f il por *The New York Review of Books* 36:36-42 Je 15 '89
CANNAVINO, JAMES A.
about
Defending the realm. C. O'Malley. por *Personal Computing* 13:71 Jl '89
CANNED BEANS *See* Beans, Canned
CANNED FISH *See* Fish, Canned
CANNED FOOD *See* Food, Canned
CANNED FOOD COOKING *See* Cooking—Canned food
CANNED MUSHROOMS *See* Mushrooms, Canned
CANNED SOUPS *See* Soups, Canned
CANNED TOMATOES *See* Tomatoes, Canned
CANNELL, PETER B.
about
The thin file strategy. R. Phalon. il por *Forbes* 143:221-2 Je 26 '89
CANNELL (PETER B.) & COMPANY *See* Peter B. Cannell & Company
CANNERIES
Alaska
See also
Wards Cove Packing Co.
CANNES FILM FESTIVAL
Americans abroad. H. Jacobson. il *Film Comment* 25:67-9 Jl/Ag '89
Jésus of Cannes. B. D. Johnson. il *Maclean's* 102:54-5 My 29 '89
Riviera refuge. M. Corliss. il *Film Comment* 25:66+ Jl/Ag '89
CANNIBALISM
The dark side of the Anasazi [evidence of a cannibalistic ritual at Yellow Jacket, Colo. site; work of John Cater] il *Discover* 10:12 Ap '89
CANNING, GEORGE, 1770-1827
about
George Canning's left buttock and the origin of species. S. J. Gould. *Natural History* p18+ My '89
CANNING AND PRESERVING
See also
Food, Canned
Pectins
Pickles and relishes
Everyone can can. D. G. Howard. il *The Saturday Evening Post* 261:26+ S '89
From our kitchen to yours. K. Adams. il *Southern Living* 24:166 Je '89
Putting a few things by. N. Hauser. il *American Health* 8:142+ S '89
CANNON, CORNELIA JAMES
about
A message in a bottle: or, Honeymoon on Cannon Mountain. M. C. Schlesinger. il pors map *American Heritage* 40:106-9 Ap '89
CANNON, DYAN
about
A new husband and a new film help Dyan Cannon put her ex, Cary Grant, behind her at last. D. Grogan. il pors *People Weekly* 31:44-5 My 22 '89
CANNON, MAUREEN
Brushstrokes [poem] *Good Housekeeping* 209:180 Ag '89
Circa '89 [poem] *National Review* 41:36 D 31 '89
Laughter [poem] *Good Housekeeping* 208:228 Je '89

My daughter's house [poem] il *Good Housekeeping* 208:194 Mr '89
CANNON, WALTER BRADFORD, 1871-1945
about
A message in a bottle: or, Honeymoon on Cannon Mountain. M. C. Schlesinger. il pors map *American Heritage* 40:106-9 Ap '89
CANNON GROUP INC.
Puzzle in Movieland: the case of the mystery moguls [G. Parretti and F. Fiorini] J. Rossant. il pors *Business Week* p80-1+ Mr 13 '89
CANNON MOUNTAIN (MONT.)
A message in a bottle: or, Honeymoon on Cannon Mountain [1901 climb by newlyweds W. B. and C. J. Cannon] M. C. Schlesinger. il pors map *American Heritage* 40:106-9 Ap '89
CANNONDALE CORPORATION
Ten-speed to grow on. R. Koselka. il por *Forbes* 144:224+ N 27 '89
CANOE HUNTING *See* Hunting
CANOE RACING
The best just became better [J. Lugbill wins fifth world white water crown] D. S. Looney. il por *Sports Illustrated* 71:53 Jl 3 '89
Paddling the straight and narrow [white water racer J. Lugbill] D. S. Looney. il pors *Sports Illustrated* 70:56+ Je 19 '89
CANOE TRIPS *See* Canoes and canoeing
CANOES AND CANOEING
See also
Kayaks and kayaking
Running rapids
Amazing Glades [canoe trip in the Florida Everglades] S. Lechner. il *Sierra* 74:134-40 Ja/F '89
Every sportsman's secret weapon. E. A. Bauer. il *Outdoor Life* 183:90-1+ Ap '89
Follow your bliss [interview with R. Perkins] P. Edidin. il pors *Psychology Today* 23:62-4 My '89
Near-perfect paddle [women canoe length of the Back River] D. A. Buettner. il *Women's Sports & Fitness* 11:60 My '89
A question of trust [taking girlfriend's daughter canoeing] P. Mandelbaum. il *The New York Times Magazine* p14+ Ag 6 '89
Quietly by canoe. R. Reid. il *Sierra* 74:112-13 My/Je '89
Ride the rivers [canoe trips in the national parks] C. M. Toops. il *National Parks* 63:39-41 Mr/Ap '89
Safety devices and measures
Canoeing our rivers. V. Chambers. il *The Conservationist* 44:8-11 Jl/Ag '89
CANOLA OIL
The canola caper. J. Novack. il *Forbes* 144:132 O 16 '89
CANON INC.
What drew Canon to Motorola? Passion, of course [microprocessor for EOS camera] N. Gross. il *Business Week* p118 N 13 '89
CANON LAW
Barriers to the sacraments. J. M. Champlin. il *Commonweal* 116:559-61 O 20 '89
Bishops and theologians [bishops approve Doctrinal responsibilities statement] T. J. Reese. *America* 161:4-6 Jl 1-8 '89
CANONIZATION
See also
Beatification
Campaigns for sainthood can make a lot of enemies. T. Unsworth. il *U.S. Catholic* 54:34-8 N '89
Prelude to the making of a saint [J. H. Newman; cover story] V. F. Blehl. pors *America* 160:213-16 Mr 11 '89
CANOPY, FOREST CROWN *See* Forest crown canopy
CANOVA, PAT
The reclamation of Holland. il map *Sea Frontiers* 35:154-64 My/Je '89
CANOVAS, ISABEL
about
Only Isabel Canovas could convince women to slip on a banana peel or put a snail on their wrist. V. Woods. il por *Vogue* 179:86+ Ag '89
CANS
See also
Beer cans
Sharpening the edge [steel beverage cans vs. aluminum] E. Corcoran. il *Scientific American* 260:72-3 F '89
Recycling
See also
We Can (Organization)
The can people [poor collect aluminum cans in New York City] E. Barnes. il *Life* 12:98-102 Ag '89
CANSECO, JOSÉ
about
Across the Bay: waiting for Jose. R. Fimrite. il por *Sports Illustrated* 71:23 Jl 10 '89
The battle is with himself [cover story] B. Buschel. il pors *Gentlemen's Quarterly* 59:224-9+ My '89
The power rabbits [cover story] D. Knobler. il pors *Sport (New York, N.Y.)* 80:22-4+ Jl '89
The summer of his discontent. P. Gammons. il pors *Sports Illustrated* 71:72-4+ O 2 '89

CANSON, SUZANNE DE, D. 1986
about
The portrait of a scandal. C. Dickey. il por *Newsweek* 113:55 Ja 9 '89
CANTATA AND CANTATAS
See also
Compact discs—Cantatas
CANTEKIN, ERDEM
about
Corporate-funded research may be hazardous to your health. K. Hart. *The Bulletin of the Atomic Scientists* 45:32 Ap '89
CANTEL INC.
Let the Second Force be with you [E. S. Rogers] P. C. Newman. il *Maclean's* 102:46 Mr 20 '89
CANTER, CAROL
The four faces of Tahoe. il map *Travel Holiday* 171:88-95 Mr '89
CANTER, LEE
Assertive Discipline—more than names on the board and marbles in a jar. bibl f il *Phi Delta Kappan* 71:57-61 S '89
CANTHARIDIN
Spanish fly's lure: ardor or armor? [aphrodisiac for pyrochroid beetles; research by Jerrold Meinwald] J. Raloff. *Science News* 136:189 S 16 '89
CANTICUM CANTICORUM *See* Bible. O.T. Song of Solomon
CANTO, JACQUELINE
about
Prop art. B. Kanner. il por *New York* 22:20+ N 27 '89
CANTON, KATIA
House of miracles. il *Art in America* 77:73+ D '89
CANTON (MISS.)
Housing
See also
MadCAAP (Organization)
CANTORIAL [drama] *See* Levin, Ira
CANTRELL, SCOTT
A man for all seasons. il pors *High Fidelity (New York, N.Y.)* 39:46-8 Mr '89
Rooted, but not in the past. il pors *High Fidelity (New York, N.Y.)* 39:48-50 Jl '89
CANTWELL, DAN
about
Fifty years of changing minds & structures. T. Unsworth. il *Commonweal* 116:365-7 Je 16 '89
CANTWELL, KEVIN
The Darwin decades [poem] *The New Republic* 201:32 Jl 17-24 '89
Spelling lesson [poem] *America* 160:266 Mr 25 '89
CANTWELL, MARY
The barn collectors. il pors *House & Garden* 161:126-35 F '89
Gentleman's quarters. il por *House & Garden* 161:78-81+ Ja '89
The quality quandary. il *House & Garden* 161:64+ Ap '89
Writer's turf. il por *House & Garden* 161:108+ O '89
CANVAS
Draped with canvas. il *Southern Living* 24:113 Jl '89
CANYON, STEVE (FICTIONAL CHARACTER) *See* Steve Canyon (Fictional character)
CANYON RANCH SPA (TUCSON, ARIZ.) *See* Health resorts, watering places, etc.—Arizona
CANYONS
See also
Columbia River Gorge (Or. and Wash.)
Grand Canyon (Ariz.)
CAP D'ANTIBES (FRANCE)
Historic houses, sites, etc.
Villa America [summer home of G. and S. Murphy in the 1920s] J. Robinson. il *Gourmet* 49:70+ Jl '89
CAP MARTIN (FRANCE)
Historic houses, sites, etc.
Legends of Villa Cypris. D. H. Minassian. il *Architectural Digest* 46:126-31 Ja '89
CAPA, CORNELL, 1918-
about
Indelible images. R. Cembalest. il pors *Art News* 88:174-9 Ap '89
CAPABILITY'S BOOKS (FIRM)
Capability's cultivates a gardening clientele. M. Jones. il *Publishers Weekly* 235:42-4 F 10 '89
CAPACITANCE METERS *See* Electric meters
CAPACITORS *See* Electric capacitors
CAPACITY, INDUSTRIAL *See* Industrial capacity
CAPACITY AND DISABILITY
Demonstrating the disability of depression [research by Kenneth B. Wells] B. Bower. *Science News* 136:132 Ag 26 '89
CAPASSO, CARL
about
Bess Myerson: the inside story. J. L. Block. il pors *Good Housekeeping* 208:70+ Ap '89
How Bess got out of the mess. J. Kasindorf. il pors *New York* 22:38-48 Ja 16 '89
Miss America wins again. il por *Time* 133:80 Ja 2 '89

CAPE COD (MASS.)
See also
Architecture, Domestic—Cape Cod (Mass.)
Gardens and gardening—Cape Cod (Mass.)
CAPE COD NATIONAL SEASHORE (MASS.)
Interior may lift Cape Cod ORV ban. il *National Parks* 63:8-9 S/O '89
CAPE HATTERAS NATIONAL SEASHORE (N.C.)
Hatteras jetty plans set back, not halted. il *National Parks* 63:11 Ja/F '89
CAPE MAY (N.J.)
Historic houses, sites, etc.
A stick style curiosity on the Jersey coast [Emlen Physick House] V. J. Scully. il por *Architectural Digest* 46:34+ Mr '89
Hotels, motels, etc.
The birds and the B&B's. R. Norris. il map *Travel Holiday* 171:55-9 Ap '89
CAPE VERDE
Diplomatic and consular service
United States
Lopes in line to lead elite corps of envoys. por *Jet* 76:9 Jl 24 '89
CAPE YORK SPACE AGENCY (AUSTRALIA)
Cape York update. M. T. Rigby. *Ad Astra* 1:42 F '89
CAPECCHI, MARIO R.
Altering the genome by homologous recombination. bibl f il *Science* 244:1288-92 Je 16 '89
CAPERS
Caper questions. il *Sunset (Central West edition)* 183:136 Jl '89
CAPERTON, GASTON
about
Can anybody govern West Virginia? M. Schroeder. il por *Business Week* p40 D 4 '89
Selling hope in West Virginia. S. C. Gwynne. il por *Time* 133:37 My 22 '89
CAPILLARIES
Mechanics of stimulated neutrophils: cell stiffening induces retention in capillaries. G. S. Worthen and others. bibl f il *Science* 245:183-6 Jl 14 '89
Stiffened cells lodge in lung capillaries [neutrophils; research by G. Scott Worthen and others] S. Hart. *Science News* 136:39 Jl 15 '89
CAPILLARY ELECTROPHORESIS *See* Electrophoresis
CAPITAL
See also
Human capital
Liquidity (Economics)
CAPITAL, VENTURE *See* Venture capital
CAPITAL CITIES/ABC INC.
The brass at Cap Cities/ABC: rethinking TV [interview with J. Sias, T. Murphy and D. Burke] M. Brown and P. Ainslie. il pors *Channels (New York, N.Y.: 1986)* 9:93-5 F '89
How they do it. J. Loftus. il *Channels (New York, N.Y.: 1986)* 9:44-6 Ap '89
In the nick of Time? [rumor of Cap Cities/ABC bid for Time Inc.] S. N. Chakravarty. il *Forbes* 144:14 Jl 10 '89
CAPITAL COSTS
The cost of capital. E. Corcoran and P. Wallich. il *Scientific American* 261:79-81 O '89
The excuse industry [explanations for lack of American success in global competition] R. J. Samuelson. il *Newsweek* 114:74 D 11 '89
How capital costs cripple America. L. S. Richman. il *Fortune* 120:50-2+ Ag 14 '89
CAPITAL EQUIPMENT INDUSTRY *See* Industrial equipment industry
CAPITAL GAINS TAX
See also
Real property—Taxation
101 more reasons not to cut capital-gains taxes. A. S. Blinder. il *Business Week* p18 S 4 '89
Bill me later [House votes to cut tax] G. J. Church. il *Time* 134:22-3 O 9 '89
Bribery is bad policy. R. J. Samuelson. il *Newsweek* 113:45 Mr 6 '89
Bush goes long. H. Gleckman. il *Business Week* p26-7 F 13 '89
Capital gained [House Democrats support cut in capital gains tax] *The Nation* 249:443-4 O 23 '89
Capital gains and other tax tricks. M. W. Karmin. *U.S. News & World Report* 107:50 Jl 3 '89
Capital gains: as the Democrats squabble, Bush may score. D. Harbrecht and R. Fly. il *Business Week* p58 S 25 '89
The capital-gains cut isn't dead—it's just playing possum. R. Fly and D. Harbrecht. il *Business Week* p57 N 6 '89
The capital-gains cut: who would benefit? *Newsweek* 114:26 S 18 '89
Capital-gains cuts: new look, same dim prospects. H. Gleckman. *Business Week* p43 My 15 '89
The capital gains mandate. J. Bush. il *The American Spectator* 22:32 Je '89

CAPITAL GAINS TAX—*cont.*

The capital-gains quandary: here's a way out, Mr. Bush. H. Gleckman. il *Business Week* p121-2 F 20 '89

The capital gains tax cut. P. L. Spencer. il *Consumers' Research Magazine* 72:30-2 N '89

Capital gains tax cut: 'not dead yet'. A. R. Dowd. il *Fortune* 120:18 Jl 31 '89

Capital ideas. E. Rubenstein. il *National Review* 41:28 S 29 '89

Capital pains [political tradeoffs behind tax cut] L. Saunders. il *Forbes* 144:46 Jl 10 '89

Capital tax cuts. R. Coorsh. il *Consumers' Research Magazine* 72:4 N '89

A capitalist's guide to capital gains. M. Kinsley. il *Time* 134:108 N 6 '89

Capitol gains [House votes to cut tax] *National Review* 41:18-19 O 27 '89

The Capitol gains of the well-to-do [Democratic Congress addresses tax cuts] M. Barone. il *U.S. News & World Report* 107:26-7+ O 2 '89

Capitol pains on capital gains. J. Egan. il *U.S. News & World Report* 107:42-3 Ag 7 '89

The class warfare fizzles [House vote on cutting tax] E. Clift. il *Newsweek* 114:37 O 9 '89

Common sense about capital gains. W. T. Brookes. por *Nation's Business* 77:48 Ja '89

A commonsense approach to taxing capital gains. A. S. Blinder. il *Business Week* p30 D 25 '89-Ja 1 '90

Congress caused the crash [threat to tax cut responsible for Friday the 13th stock market drop] *National Review* 41:14-15 N 10 '89

Congress should look to a tax cut, not an increase, to curb the deficit. il *Nation's Business* 77:92 Je '89

Darman: the collapse of a grand strategy. E. Clift. por *Newsweek* 114:54 N 20 '89

De-taxification [tax cut] D. Corn. *The Nation* 249:480-1 O 30 '89

Decision for Congress: penalize success or create opportunity. il *Nation's Business* 77:88 Ap '89

Did Darman diddle while the deficit burned? H. Gleckman. il por *Business Week* p56-7 D 11 '89

Ditch the capital-gains tax once and for all. P. C. Roberts. il *Business Week* p21 Ap 3 '89

Easing the pain of a capital gain [interview with P. Nirdlinger] M. Henkenius. il por *Home Mechanix* 85:17-19 Ag '89

Gaining on a gains cut. *Newsweek* 114:34 S 25 '89

How to get the Dow to 3000 [cut capital gains tax and interest rates] M. S. Forbes, Jr. il *Forbes* 144:29 N 13 '89

How to keep more profit when you sell a mutual fund. G. Anrig, Jr. il *Money* 18:131-2 Ag '89

Investors' wish list for Washington. J. Egan. il *U.S. News & World Report* 106:83 F 13 '89

Losing big on capital gains. D. Goodgame. il *Time* 134:53 Ag 14 '89

A lower tax rate on capital gains. il *Nation's Business* 77:70 F '89

Not only the rich are capitalists now. M. Novak. il *Forbes* 144:98 S 4 '89

The push to trim capital-gains tax. J. C. Szabo. il *Nation's Business* 77:56-7 Jl '89

A rich man's tax? E. Rubenstein. *National Review* 41:15 Ap 21 '89

Room at the trough [tax break] C. Byron. il *New York* 22:24-5 O 16 '89

Rostenkowski adds a twist to the tax tango. H. Gleckman. il *Business Week* p61 Je 26 '89

Section 89 among House GOP targets. D. C. Bacon. por *Nation's Business* 77:6 Jl '89

Talking chop [Democratic support of capital gains tax cut] *The New Republic* 201:4+ O 23 '89

A tax break geared to high rollers. H. Gleckman. il *Business Week* p47 Ag 14 '89

A tax cut! What it'll mean to you. *Successful Farming* 87:14 N '89

Tax deform. R. S. McIntyre. *The New Republic* 201:18-21 Ag 21 '89

Tax strategy [funds and capital gains] W. Baldwin. il *Forbes* 144:186+ S 4 '89

Them's the breaks [George Bush's tax proposals] *The New Republic* 200:7-8 F 27 '89

There is a better way. M. S. Forbes, Jr. il *Forbes* 143:27 Ja 23 '89

These swaps can keep you a step ahead of the taxman. S. Woolley. *Business Week* p180 N 13 '89

This penny-stock scam packs a one-two punch [brokers cross investors into another favorite stock] D. Zigas. *Business Week* p154 My 8 '89

'Tis the season of the mutual fund tax boomerang. M. Meyer. il *Money* 18:51 N '89

The trickle-up effect of a capital-gains tax cut. R. Kuttner. il *Business Week* p32 Ag 14 '89

Ways without means [views of D. Rostenkowski] *National Review* 41:11 Ag 18 '89

What will the folks back in Chicago think? [D. Rostenkowski softens position on rollback] *Newsweek* 113:54 Je 19 '89

Where are the Democrats? *The New Republic* 201:4 S 18-25 '89

Why Bush's trickle-up theory is sailing through Congress. H. Gleckman and D. Harbrecht. il *Business Week* p47 O 16 '89

A winnable fight. M. S. Forbes, Jr. il *Forbes* 143:29 Ap 17 '89

Your best strategies to cash in on a cut in capital-gains taxes. P. Wang. *Money* 18:21 N '89

Canada

The billion-dollar tax deadline [capital gains tax on trusts] D. Francis. il *Maclean's* 102:13 D 25 '89

CAPITAL GOODS *See* Durable goods, Industrial

CAPITAL GOODS INVESTMENT *See* Capital investments

CAPITAL GROUP INC.

Gordon Crawford. N. Koch. por *Channels (New York, N.Y.: 1986)* 9:53-4 Jl/Ag '89

CAPITAL INVESTMENTS

See also

Investment tax credit

Bush goes long. H. Gleckman. il *Business Week* p26-7 F 13 '89

Business investment could still have some steam left. K. Madigan. il *Business Week* p27 D 11 '89

The capital spending boom that won't end. H. Banks. il *Forbes* 144:33 S 4 '89

Capital spending isn't growing where it counts. G. Koretz. il *Business Week* p23 Je 26 '89

Dr. Brady's cure for corporate myopia [plan to cut corporate taxes in order to increase capital investment] S. Dentzer. il *U.S. News & World Report* 107:48+ S 25 '89

The Fed's brakes aren't slowing capital spending. M. J. Mandel. il *Business Week* p74 Mr 27 '89

The importance of long-term thinking. C. W. Weinberger. il *Forbes* 144:31 Jl 24 '89

Investment is fine—it's the critics who are wrong. P. C. Roberts. il *Business Week* p16 Ag 21 '89

Keeping up with Japan [shortage of capital in U.S. due to lack of savings] D. Gergen. il *U.S. News & World Report* 106:68 Mr 6 '89

Lean times loom on the factory floor. M. W. Karmin. il *U.S. News & World Report* 107:72 N 20 '89

The "net savings" illusion. A. Reynolds. il *Forbes* 143:169 F 6 '89

The new look of capital spending. K. Ballen. il *Fortune* 119:115-16+ Mr 13 '89

Services are supplying the steam for business investment. M. F. Allyn. il *Fortune* 119:37-8 Je 5 '89

The sliding investment myth [views of Frank de Leeuw] T. May, Jr. il *Fortune* 119:18 My 22 '89

Surprising strength in capital spending. H. Banks. *Forbes* 144:33 D 25 '89

There's nothing fickle about the Fed's war on inflation . . . and if rates rise, capital spending will take the biggest hit. G. Koretz. il *Business Week* p22 S 18 '89

The urge for new equipment will keep business investment growing. V. Brownstein. il *Fortune* 120:33+ D 18 '89

Japan

How do you shut the darn thing off? A. Tanzer. il *Forbes* 144:38-40 N 13 '89

Japan is investing at full blast. H. Banks. *Forbes* 143:41 Ja 9 '89

Japan is like a kid in a candy store—a rich kid. T. Holden. il *Business Week* p50-1 D 4 '89

Japan's big knack for coming back. C. Rapoport. il *Fortune* 120:131+ N 6 '89

Japan's secret weapon. J. M. Fallows. il *U.S. News & World Report* 107:46 D 25 '89-Ja 1 '90

CAPITAL MOVEMENTS

Latin America

Can this flight be grounded? [exodus of capital from Latin debtor nations] M. McNamee. il *Business Week* p74 Ap 10 '89

The dirty little debt secret. D. Pauly. il *Newsweek* 113:46 Ap 17 '89

CAPITAL PRESERVATION FUND

How Jim Benham pioneered the idea of the supersafe mutual fund. F. W. Frailey. il por *Changing Times* 43:140 N '89

CAPITAL PUNISHMENT

See also

Electrocution

Executions and executioners

Guillotine

Hanging

Bad news for death row [Supreme Court okays execution of juvenile and retarded criminals] A. L. Sanders. il *Time* 134:48-9 Jl 10 '89

Burning question. *The New Republic* 200:4+ F 20 '89

The death penalty debate. *America* 160:443 My 13 '89

Execute an 8-year-old? The Johnny Penry case [mentally retarded adult awaiting execution in Texas] R. F. Drinan. *The Christian Century* 106:199-200 F 22 '89

Execute Ronald Monroe? [Louisiana case] W. F. Buckley. *National Review* 41:63 S 15 '89

The execution of Ronnie Dunkins. D. Aukerman. il *The Christian Century* 106:783-5 Ag 30-S 6 '89

Girl 13, raps death penalty at White House event for children's anti-drug group [views of C. Charles] il pors *Jet* 76:31 O 2 '89

CAPITAL PUNISHMENT—cont.

High Court ruling upholds states' rights to execute young killers, retarded. *Jet* 76:4 Jl 10 '89

The juice ain't no use: why the death penalty won't work in D.C. J. DeParle. *The Washington Monthly* 21:32-3 My '89

Only two weeks to live [impending execution of R. Monroe in Louisiana] G. Carroll and A. Press. il por *Newsweek* 114:62-4 Ag 21 '89

O'Sullivan's first law [Amnesty International's opposition to death penalty shows abandonment of political neutrality] J. O'Sullivan. *National Review* 41:14 O 27 '89

Politicians, voters and voltage. R. M. Cohen. il *Time* 133:96 F 13 '89

Pressure in New York for death penalty. R. F. Drinan. *The Christian Century* 106:582-3 Je 7-14 '89

Private mercy [execution of R. A. Lindsey; excerpt from *Public justice, private mercy*]; ed. by Dick Adler. E. G. Brown. il *Common Cause Magazine* 15:28-33 Jl/Ag '89

Ronald Monroe fights a Louisiana verdict of murder for a crime many think he did not commit. J. S. Kunen. il por *People Weekly* 32:95-6+ Ag 28 '89

So what if the death penalty deters? S. Goldberg. *National Review* 41:42+ Je 30 '89

Too young to die? [case of H. Wilkins; cover story] R. Rosenbaum. il pors *The New York Times Magazine* p32-5+ Mr 12 '89

South Africa

South Africa's 'death wish'. J. Carlin. *World Press Review* 36:57 Ag '89

CAPITAL RESEARCH COMPANY

Capital gains [office designed by R. A. M. Stern in New York City] P. M. Sachner. il *Architectural Record* 177:98-103 mid-S '89

CAPITAL SPENDING *See* Capital investments

CAPITALISM

See also
    Big business
    Small business

Boredom, virtue, and democratic capitalism. M. Novak. *Commentary* 88:34-7 S '89

The capitalism/socialism debate in East Asia. S. N. G. Davies. bibl *Society* 26:29-37 Mr/Ap '89

Capitalism and freedom. R. J. Samuelson. il *Newsweek* 113:46 Je 12 '89

The death of radicalism. R. E. Tyrrell. il *The American Spectator* 22:10 Jl '89

Economics made easy. R. J. Samuelson. il *Newsweek* 114:64 N 27 '89

The irony of capitalism. R. J. Samuelson. il *Newsweek* 113:44 Ja 9 '89

The larger context. M. Novak. See issues of *Forbes* beginning February 6, 1989

Revolutionary nostalgia [Europe] D. Singer. il *The Nation* 249:598-600 N 20 '89

Risk, safety and capitalism [special section] bibl *Society* 27:4-31 N/D '89

The specter of capitalism. D. Singer. il *The Nation* 249:202-5 Ag 21-28 '89

Testing time for both socialism and capitalism. A. Chambraud. il *World Press Review* 36:11-13 D '89

The triumph of capitalism. R. L. Heilbroner. *The New Yorker* 64:98-109 Ja 23 '89

The triumph of capitalism [cover story; special section; with editorial comments by Nathan Gardels and Stanley K. Sheinbaum] il *New Perspectives Quarterly* 6:2-52, 64 Fall '89

Victorian values/Jewish values. G. Himmelfarb. *Commentary* 87:23-31 F '89

Who's burying whom? A. Cockburn. *The Nation* 248:222 F 20 '89

CAPITALISM AND CHRISTIANITY *See* Christianity and economics

CAPITALISTS AND FINANCIERS

The five-percenters, Moscow's pet capitalists [privileged foreign businessmen acting as go-betweens; cover story] P. Berman. il *Forbes* 143:93-7 F 6 '89

Rich for a day. J. S. Gordon. il *American Heritage* 40:16+ Ap '89

CAPITOL (WASHINGTON, D.C.)

Capitol Hill. P. M. Jones. il *Scholastic Update (Teachers' edition)* 121:4-5 F 24 '89

CAPITOLS

See also
    Nebraska—Capitol

CAPLIN, CANDACE HOFFINGER

Don't tell me secrets. *Glamour* 87:168-9 Mr '89

CAPOBIANCO, MICHAEL

(jt. auth) See Barton, William, and Capobianco, Michael

CAPOEIRA (DANCE)

Capoeira [teacher J. Vieira] *The New Yorker* 65:38-9 My 15 '89

CAPON, ROSS

Going nowhere: gridlock and the politics of transportation [excerpt from *Winning America*] il *Utne Reader* p86-7 Mr/Ap '89

CAPONE, FRANCO

A new galaxy vs. old theories. *World Press Review* 36:67 D '89

CAPONIGRO, ANGELA

about

Reviews:
    Performances at Cunningham Studio, New York City. J. Lewis. il por *Dance Magazine* 63:68 O '89

CAPONIGRO (ANGELA) DANCE ENSEMBLE *See* Angela Caponigro Dance Ensemble

CAPOTE, TRUMAN, 1924-1984

about

Tru confessions. R. Leivenberg. il pors *Harper's Bazaar* 122:362-3+ S '89

CAPOTOSTO, ROSARIO

Workshop basics. See issues of *Popular Mechanics* beginning January 1986 through April 1989

CAPPA, CHARLES

Build a PVC-pipe 50mm finder. il *Astronomy* 17:72-3 N '89

CAPPELLA SISTINA (VATICAN) *See* Vatican. Cappella Sistina

CAPRA, FRANK, 1897-

about

It's a wonderful life [film] Reviews
    Common Cause Magazine il 15:26-30 S/O '89. J. Cobb
    Modern Maturity il 32:38-43 D '89/Ja '90. N. Dillon

CAPRI ISLAND (ITALY)

See also
    Country estates—Capri Island (Italy)

CAPRIATI, JENNIFER

about

Test of a champion. J. E. Loehr. il pors *World Tennis* 37:30+ S '89

Woman to watch: tennis prodigy Jennifer Capriati. J. Young. il por *Women's Sports & Fitness* 11:57 Je '89

CAPS (HATS)

See also
    Baseball caps

Capping it off. il *Vogue* 179:132 Mr '89

Capping off a springtime look. il *Gentlemen's Quarterly* 59:234 Ap '89

CAPSICUM *See* Peppers

CAPSL (COMPUTER LANGUAGE)

The language of lasers. K. Quirk. il *Byte* 14 Special Issue:203-6+ Fall '89

CAPTAINS OF SHIPS *See* Shipmasters

CAPTIVE ANIMALS *See* Zoos

CAPTIVE BREEDING PROGRAMS (ANIMALS) *See* Breeding

CAPTIVE INSURANCE COMPANIES *See* Insurance companies—Captive companies

CAPTIVE NATIONS WEEK

Captive Nations Week, 1989 [proclamation, July 6, 1989] G. Bush. *Department of State Bulletin* 89:91 S '89

CAPUCILLI, TERESE

about

A woman under the influence. J. Gruen. pors *Dance Magazine* 63:52-4 Mr '89

CAPUTO, PHILIP

Death goes to school. il *Esquire* 112:136-8+ D '89

CAPUZZO, MICHAEL

Journey of a cult child. il pors *Reader's Digest* 134:109-14 My '89

CAR AND DRIVER (PERIODICAL)

The fugiting of tempus. B. W. Yates. il *Car and Driver* 35:14-15 N '89

CAR AUCTIONS *See* Automobile auctions

CAR CLUBS *See* Automobile clubs

CAR MANUALS *See* Automobiles—Handbooks, manuals, etc.

CAR SEATS (SAFETY SEATS) *See* Automobiles—Safety devices and measures

CAR TALK [radio program] See Radio program reviews—Single works

CAR TELEPHONES *See* Cellular radio in automobiles

CARACARAS

March of the feathered thugs: Johnny Rook birds in the Falklands wreak havoc on an albatross colony. T. De Roy. il *International Wildlife* 19:52-9 Mr/Ap '89

CARACCIOLO, DANIELE, AND OTHERS

Lineage-specific requirement of *c-abl* function in normal hematopoiesis. bibl f il *Science* 245:1107-10 S 8 '89

CARACOL SITE (BELIZE)

From a remote jungle site, a trail of striking clues [excavation by A. and D. Chase] N. Epstein. bibl (p183) il pors map *Smithsonian* 20:98-104+ D '89

Maya mañana. A. Hills. il *History Today* 39:4-5 S '89

CARAS, INGRID W., AND WEDDELL, GREGORY N.

Signal peptide for protein secretion directing glycophospholipid membrane anchor attachment. bibl f il *Science* 243:1196-8 Mr 3 '89

CARAVAN (NEW YORK, N.Y.: RESTAURANT) *See* New York (N.Y.)—Restaurants, nightclubs, bars, etc.

CARAVAN AIRPLANES *See* Airplanes, Light

CARAVAN OF DREAMS

Caravan of Dreams launches audio line [W. S. Burroughs lecture] P. Sweeting. il por *Publishers Weekly* 235:34 F 3 '89

CARAVANS
See also
Wagon trains
LA CARAVELLE (NEW YORK, N.Y.: RESTAURANT) See
New York (N.Y.)—Restaurants, nightclubs, bars, etc.
CARAWAY'S (FIRM)
A single mom bets it all on herself [owner A. Marchette]
S. Seixas. il pors *Money* 18:127-32 Ap '89
CARAY, HARRY
about
Beers with . . . Harry Caray [interview] J. Schuster. il por
Sport (New York, N.Y.) 80:19-20 O '89
Holy cow! It's Harry Caray. C. P. Miller. il pors *The Saturday
Evening Post* 261:54-5+ O '89
CARAY FAMILY
about
Whole lot of Carays going on. D. S. Looney. il *Sports
Illustrated* 71:87 Ag 14 '89
CARBACHOL
Mapping neuronal inputs to REM sleep induction sites with
carbachol-fluorescent microspheres. J. J. Quattrochi and
others. bibl f il *Science* 245:984-6 S 1 '89
CARBAMYLCHOLINE See Carbachol
CARBIDES
See also
Silicon carbide
CARBO, MARIE
An evaluation of Jeanne Chall's response to 'Debunking
the great phonics myth' [discussion of November 1988
and March 1989 articles] bibl f il *Phi Delta Kappan* 71:152-7
O '89
Learning to read: the great debate 20 years later—a response
to 'Debunking the great phonics myth' [discussion of
November 1988 article; with editorial comment by Pauline
B. Gough] bibl f il *Phi Delta Kappan* 70:498, 521-38
Mr '89
about
The 'great' debate—can both Carbo and Chall be right?
R. L. Turner. bibl f il *Phi Delta Kappan* 71:276-83 D
'89
CARBOHYDRATE METABOLISM
Bonk [glucose depletion during cycling] S. Johnson. *Bicycling*
30:48 S '89
Carbohydrate loading [dancers] J. Scala. il *Dance Magazine*
63:64-5 Mr '89
Fill 'er up [glycogen burning] G. Sheehan. il *Runner's World*
24:16 N '89
High-carbohydrate diet may pose heart risks [insulin resis-
tance] K. Fackelmann. *Science News* 136:185 S 16 '89
The right stuff [glycogen burning] E. Coleman. *Bicycling*
30:174 Mr '89
CARBOHYDRATES
Beyond pasta. E. Coleman. *Bicycling* 30:74 Jl '89
Carbo-loading: the tool for extra fuel. E. Coleman. il *Women's
Sports & Fitness* 11:16+ Je '89
Carbohydrates and depression. R. J. Wurtman and J. J.
Wurtman. il map *Scientific American* 260:68-75 Ja '89
Complex carbohydrates [cover story] D. Blumenthal. il *FDA
Consumer* 23:13-17 Ap '89
Eat for energy. R. A. Barnett. il *Working Woman* 14:129+
F '89
Eat healthy, eat thin. il *Glamour* 87:286-7 O '89
The feel-full pill [fenfluramine used to suppress cravings]
W. T. Buckley. il *Health (New York, N.Y.)* 21:28-9+ Ja
'89
Fill up on complex carbohydrates [excerpt from Good fat/bad
fat] G. C. Griffin and W. P. Castelli. il *The Saturday
Evening Post* 261:12-13+ O '89
Raising your carbo consciousness. O. Anderson. il *Women's
Sports & Fitness* 11:18 O '89
Twinkie power. E. Coleman. il *Bicycling* 30:56-7 Ag '89
CARBON
See also
Fullerenes
Graphite
Liquid carbon
Epitaxial growth of diamond films on Si(111) at room
temperature by mass-selected low-energy C^+ beams. J. L.
Robertson and others. bibl f il *Science* 243:1047-50 F
24 '89
Isotopes
Ancient ocean upheaval marks the spot [Precambrian-
Cambrian boundary in Yunnan Province, China; research
by Martin Brasier] R. Monastersky. *Science News* 136:61
Jl 22 '89
Carbon-14 in methane sources and in atmospheric methane:
the contribution from fossil carbon. M. Wahlen and others.
bibl f il *Science* 245:286-90 Jl 21 '89
Carbon ratio shows Halley may be alien [research by Susan
Wyckoff] F. Flam. *Science News* 135:214 Ap 8 '89
Food chains: the carbon link [cover story] S. Hart. il map
Science News 136:168-70 S 9 '89
Halley is an alien [research by Susan Wyckoff] T. Waters.
il *Discover* 10:26-7 Ag '89
Was Halley's comet interstellar? [research by Susan Wyckoff]
Sky and Telescope 78:573-4 D '89

Spectra and spectroscopy
Diode-laser absorption spectroscopy of supersonic carbon
cluster beams: the v_3 spectrum of C_5. J. R. Heath and
others. bibl f il *Science* 244:564-6 My 5 '89
CARBON-14 DATING See Radiocarbon dating
CARBON COMPOUNDS
See also
Hydrocarbons
Organic compounds
Synthesis
All-carbon molecules: evidence for the generation of cy-
clo[18]carbon from a stable organic precursor. F. Diederich
and others. bibl f il *Science* 245:1088-90 S 8 '89
CARBON CYCLE (BIOGEOCHEMISTRY)
Carbon dioxide: where does it all go? [research by Pieter
P. Tans] R. Monastersky. *Science News* 136:132 Ag 26
'89
A light meal at sea [study of carbon cycle by Kenneth
Mopper] *Science News* 136:284 O 28 '89
Modeling the geochemical carbon cycle. R. A. Berner and
A. C. Lasaga. bibl il *Scientific American* 260:74-81 Mr
'89
CARBON DIOXIDE
See also
Greenhouse effect
Plants, Effect of carbon dioxide on
Trees, Effect of carbon dioxide on
Carbon dioxide transport by ocean currents at 25°N latitude
in the Atlantic Ocean. P. Brewer and others. bibl f il
Science 246:477-9 O 27 '89
Carbon dioxide: where does it all go? [research by Pieter
P. Tans] R. Monastersky. *Science News* 136:132 Ag 26
'89
Domestic calculations. J. R. Udall. il *Sierra* 74:33 Jl/Ag
'89
Flowering plants leave earth cold [research by Tyler Volk]
Science News 135:188 Mr 25 '89
Modeling the geochemical carbon cycle. R. A. Berner and
A. C. Lasaga. bibl il *Scientific American* 260:74-81 Mr
'89
New way to switch earth between hot and cold [ocean
dissolved carbon dioxide; research by Edward Boyle] R.
A. Kerr. il *Science* 243:480 Ja 27 '89
Nyos, the killer lake, may be coming back. R. A. Kerr.
il *Science* 244:1541-2 Je 30 '89
Scandinavian, Siberian, and Arctic Ocean glaciation: effect
of Holocene atmospheric CO_2 variations. D. R. Lindstrom
and D. R. MacAyeal. bibl f il *Science* 245:628-31 Ag
11 '89
CARBON IN SEA WATER See Sea water
CARBON MONOXIDE
Carbon monoxide and the burning earth. R. E. Newell and
others. bibl il map *Scientific American* 261:82-8 O '89
Monoxide heart risk. *Science News* 136:342 N 25 '89
CARBON STARS
Detection of C_5 in the circumstellar shell of IRC+10216.
P. F. Bernath and others. bibl f il *Science* 244:562-4 My
5 '89
CARBON TETRACHLORIDE
Just when the ozone war looked winnable . . . V. Cahan.
il *Business Week* p56 Je 12 '89
CARBONACEOUS CHONDRITES See Meteorites
CARBONATES
See also
Bicarbonates
Carbon copies [Cretaceous cold-seep communities in the
Canadian Arctic; research by Renoit Beauchamp] *Discover*
10:15 Ag '89
Cretaceous cold-seep communities and methane-derived car-
bonates in the Canadian Arctic. B. Beauchamp and others.
bibl f il map *Science* 244:53-6 Ap 7 '89
Methane key to Arctic mystery mounds [research by Benoit
Beauchamp] R. Monastersky. *Science News* 135:215 Ap
8 '89
Uranium-series dated authigenic carbonates and Acheulian
sites in southern Egypt. B. J. Szabo and others. bibl f
il maps *Science* 243:1053-6 F 24 '89
CARBONATITES
Temperature measurements in carbonatite lava lakes and
flows from Oldoinyo Lengai, Tanzania. M. Krafft and
J. Keller. bibl f il *Science* 245:168-70 Jl 14 '89
CARBONDALE (ILL.)
Religious institutions and affairs
When a church supports a lesbian seminarian [United Church
of Christ] T. A. Braun. *The Christian Century* 106:516-17
My 17 '89
CARBONE, FABRIZIO
Fences that kill. *World Press Review* 36:80 O '89
CARBONELL I ESTELLER, EDUARD
Romanesque treasures of Catalonia. il *The Courier (Unesco)*
42:29-31 My '89
CARBONIFEROUS PERIOD See Paleobotany—Carboniferous;
Paleontology—Carboniferous
CARBOXYLIC ACIDS
Effect of carboxylic acid side chains on the absorption
maximum of visual pigments. E. A. Zhukovsky and D.
D. Oprian. bibl f il *Science* 246:928-30 N 17 '89

CARBOXYLIC ACIDS—cont.

Indole-2-carboxylic acid: a competitive antagonist of potentiation by glycine at the NMDA receptor. J. E. Huettner. bibl f il *Science* 243:1611-13 Mr 24 '89

Orthogonal self-assembled monolayers: alkanethiols on gold and alkane carboxylic acids on alumina. P. E. Laibinis and others. bibl f il *Science* 245:845-7 Ag 25 '89

CARBURETORS

The problems of carburetors [motorcycles] *Cycle* 40:32-3 D '89

Productivity in the carburetors, pistons, and valves industry. J. W. Ferris and V. L. Klarquist. bibl f il *Monthly Labor Review* 112:43-6 F '89

CARCINOGENS *See* Cancer—Causes

CARCINOMA *See* Cancer

CARD, ORSON SCOTT

Gameplay. See issues of Compute! beginning May 1988

CARDIAC ARRHYTHMIA *See* Arrhythmia

CARDIAC ARRHYTHMIA DEFIBRILLATORS *See* Defibrillators

CARDIAC CATHETERIZATION

Arterial Rotorooters chop up cholesterol. B. Carpenter. il *High Technology Business* 9:9 Mr '89

A better gauge for measuring how heart patients are doing [InterFlo Medical Inc.] W. C. Symonds. il *Business Week* p54 Jl 31 '89

CARDIAC DISEASES *See* Heart—Diseases

CARDIAC MUSCLE *See* Heart—Muscle

CARDIAC PACEMAKERS *See* Pacemaker, Artificial (Heart)

CARDIAC PATIENTS *See* Cardiacs

CARDIACS

Dental care

The heart part [failure of dentists to treat with antibiotics to prevent endocarditis] C. Sears. il *American Health* 8:44 Je '89

Employment

Early return to work possible [heart attack patients] *USA Today (Periodical)* 118:4 O '89

Psychology

See Heart—Diseases—Psychological aspects

Rehabilitation

See Heart—Diseases—Therapy

CARDIFF GIANT

The creation myths of Cooperstown. S. J. Gould. il *Natural History* p14+ N '89

CARDINAL, DOUGLAS

about

Canada's visionary new museum. S. Rao. il *World Press Review* 36:61 Jl '89

A grand folly in Ottawa. K. Andersen. il por *Time* 134:64 Jl 10 '89

CARDINAL INDUSTRIES INC.

Cardinal sin. E. Schmuckler. il por *Forbes* 143:14 Ap 17 '89

Cardinal's shaky foundation. S. Phillips. *Business Week* p42+ Mr 20 '89

CARDINAL INVESTMENT (FIRM)

Rusty the Mortician [E. W. Rose] J. H. Taylor. il por *Forbes* 144:60+ Jl 24 '89

CARDINAL POINTS

See also

North (Direction)

CARDIOMYOPATHY *See* Heart—Diseases

CARDIOPULMONARY RESUSCITATION *See* Resuscitation

CARDIOVASCULAR SYSTEM

See also

Blood vessels

Heart

Diseases

Prevention

Exercising choice [research by Lars-Göran Ekelund] T. Beardsley. *Scientific American* 260:24 F '89

CARDOSO, LYNN

I'm just wild about horses! il por *Women's Sports & Fitness* 11:66 O '89

CARDOZO, NANCY B.

Big fat lies: the new weight-loss scams. il *Mademoiselle* 95:128-9+ Ja '89

CARDOZO, YVETTE, AND HIRSCH, BILL

Antarctic tourism '89 [cover story] bibl il map *Sea Frontiers* 35:282-91 S/O '89

CARDS

See also

Bridge (Game)

Poker (Game)

Solitaire (Game)

Tarot

CARDS, ADVERTISING *See* Advertising cards

CARDS, BASEBALL *See* Baseball cards

CARDS, BUSINESS *See* Business cards

CARDS, GREETING *See* Greeting cards

CARDS, HOCKEY *See* Hockey cards

CAREER COUNSELING *See* Vocational guidance

CAREER COUNSELING FIRMS *See* Employment agencies

CAREER CRIMINALS *See* Recidivists

CAREER EDUCATION *See* Vocational-technical education

CAREER PLATEAUS

Dear Betty Harragan. B. L. Harragan. il *Working Woman* 14:49-50 Ap '89

The plateau payoff. A. Edwards. il *Working Woman* 14:114-16+ O '89

En route or just in a holding pattern? J. M. Bardwick. il *Working Woman* 14:118-19 O '89

When the next step up is just beyond your reach. T. Thompson. il *U.S. News & World Report* 107:71-2 S 25 '89

Anecdotes, facetiae, satire, etc.

High plains drifter. S. Bing. il *Esquire* 111:108 Mr '89

CAREER STRESS *See* Job stress

CAREER SWITCHING *See* Occupational mobility

CAREERS *See* Occupations; Professions

CAREERS FOR WOMEN *See* Women—Occupations

CAREERTRACK INC.

Are you a difficult person? D. Owen. il *The Atlantic* 264:73-80 O '89

CAREY, ART

Road warrior. il *Gentlemen's Quarterly* 59:83+ D '89

CAREY, BILL

I visited Nicaragua. il por *The Humanist* 49:20-2+ S/O '89

CAREY, CATHY

Drug label mix-ups lead to recalls, lawsuits. il *FDA Consumer* 23:33-4 Mr '89

Mary Mallon's trail of typhoid. il por *FDA Consumer* 23:18-21 Je '89

Three jailed for selling drug that killed 38 babies. il *FDA Consumer* 23:33-4 Jl/Ag '89

CAREY, JACQUELINE

about

Model stats. il pors *'Teen* 33:26 O '89

CAREY, JOHN

Spiral effect. il *National Wildlife* 27:52-9 Ap/My '89

CAREY, JOHN

Adopting new technologies. bibl *Society* 26:10-16 Jl/Ag '89

CAREY, LAURA

On alienation and the ESL student. il *Phi Delta Kappan* 71:74-5 S '89

CAREY, MICHAEL R.

Confessions of a lay collaborator [cover story] *America* 160:500-2 My 27 '89

CAREY-THOMAS AWARDS

Small houses sweep Carey-Thomas Awards. C. Reid. il *Publishers Weekly* 236:20-1 D 15 '89

CARGILL, INC.

Eggshells everywhere. J. Willoughby. il *Forbes* 143:254+ My 29 '89

CARGO AIRLINES *See* Air freight service

CARGO AIRPLANES *See* Airplanes, Freight

CARIBBEAN BASIN INITIATIVE

Sugar lumps [U.S. sugar program] P. C. Montgomery. il *Common Cause Magazine* 15:10-11 Ja/F '89

U.S. consumers, and the Caribbean, are getting a sour deal on sugar. P. Magnusson. il *Business Week* p41 My 8 '89

CARIBBEAN COOKING *See* Cooking, Caribbean

CARIBBEAN CORAL REEFS *See* Coral reefs and islands

CARIBBEAN NATIONAL FOREST (PUERTO RICO)

Of buccaneers and biodiversity. D. R. Wallace. il maps *Wilderness* 53:38-51 Wint '89

CARIBBEAN REEF SHARKS *See* Sharks

CARIBBEAN REGION

See also

Bars and barrooms—Caribbean region

Beaches—Caribbean region

Birds—Caribbean region

Carnival (Pre-Lenten festival)—Caribbean region

Conservation of resources—Caribbean region

Economic assistance, American—Caribbean region

Festivals—Caribbean region

Jamaica

Marriage law—Caribbean region

Music festivals—Caribbean region

Narcotics laws and regulations—Caribbean region

Real estate investment—Caribbean region

Resorts—Caribbean region

Trails—Caribbean region

United Nations—Caribbean region

Description and travel

See also

Cruising—Caribbean region

America's Caribbean [special section] M. Ingebretsen. il map *Better Homes and Gardens* 67:211-12+ N '89

The Caribbean & Bahamas: beaches & beyond. R. J. Christmas. il *Travel Holiday* 171:25-6+ Ap '89

The Caribbean demystified. il *Glamour* 87:198-90+ My '89

CARIBBEAN REGION—Description and travel—*cont.*
Catch the Caribbean spirit [special section] il *Black Enterprise* 19:103-5+ My '89
Island travel. L. Wolfe and J. Cecil. il *New York* 22:66-70+ N 6 '89
Islands. K. Showker. il *Southern Living* 24:21+ Mr '89
The secret Caribbean [special section] il map *Vogue* 179:304-5+ N '89
What's hot, what's happening in the Caribbean. il *Glamour* 87:167-8+ N '89

Foreign relations
United States
See United States—Foreign relations—Caribbean region

Industries
See also
Black business enterprises—Caribbean region
Telecommunication—Caribbean region
Tourist trade—Caribbean region

Photographs and photography
Back to the Caribbean. J. Augustine. il *Petersen's Photographic Magazine* 18:34-7 N '89
A photographer's guide to the Caribbean [cover story] J. Augustine. il map *Petersen's Photographic Magazine* 18:38-44+ My '89

CARIBOU
Beating the drum for caribou [Gwich'in people bordering Arctic National Wildlife Refuge oppose oil development] M. Peale. il *Sierra* 74:32+ My/Je '89
Stubborn hunter in a harsh land [tracking caribou herds and wolf packs in Denali National Park and Preserve] L. D. Mech. il map *National Wildlife* 27:20-4 Ag/S '89

CARICATURES AND CARTOONS
See also
Comic books, strips, etc.
Motion pictures—Animated films
Political cartoons
Television advertising—Cartoons
Television broadcasting—Cartoons
Videotapes—Animated films

CARIES, DENTAL *See* Dental caries
CARILLO, MARY
about
Working girl. C. Shmerler. il pors *World Tennis* 37:64-7 Je '89
CARILLON IMPORTERS LTD.
Absolut marketing [vodka] E. McGlinn. il por *Forbes* 144:282+ D 11 '89
Breaking the last taboo [M. Roux's erotic ad for La Grande Passion liqueur] I. Bosch. il *Mother Jones* 14:49 My '89
CARING
See also
Helping behavior
The good we do. K. S. Black. il *New Choices for the Best Years* 29:62-5 D '89
"Mommy, are homeless people bad?". J. G. Fitzpatrick. il *Parents* 64:95-8+ F '89
Raising kids who care. A. Kohn. il *Ladies' Home Journal* 106:112 D '89
CARING EDUCATION *See* Social education
CARINGTON, PETER ALEXANDER RUPERT *See* Carrington, Peter Alexander Rupert Carington, 6th Baron, 1919-
CARL, IRIS M.
Essential mathematics for the twenty-first century. *The Education Digest* 55:40-2 D '89
CARLESIMO, P. J.
about
Rising in the East. A. Wolff. il por *Sports Illustrated* 70:36-8+ Ja 16 '89
CARLIN, DAVID R., JR.
Of several minds. See alternate issues of Commonweal beginning May 31, 1985
CARLIN, DIANE
about
The case of the shaky diagnosis. A. Roblin. il *Prevention (Emmaus, Pa.)* 41:103-4+ Mr '89
CARLIN, JOHN
The group. *The New Republic* 201:21-3 N 27 '89
South Africa's 'death wish'. *World Press Review* 36:57 Ag '89
'The very worst and the very best'. *World Press Review* 36:26-7 Mr '89
CARLING O'KEEFE LIMITED
In search of a bigger gulp [merger of Molson and Carling] B. Came. il *Maclean's* 102:36 Ja 30 '89
CARLISLE, CARLA
London. il *Esquire* 112:185+ D '89
CARLISLE, KIM
Hypoxics, zoomers, and other drill sharpeners. il *Women's Sports & Fitness* 11:14+ Jl/Ag '89
Janet Evans: good as gold. il pors *Women's Sports & Fitness* 11:28-33 Ap '89
Take a turn for the better. il *Women's Sports & Fitness* 11:20-1 Je '89
CARLOS, LAURIE
about
Star quality. M. Southgate. por *Essence* 19:26 Ja '89

CARLSEN, GREGG
Archome. il por *The Mother Earth News* 119:66-71+ S/O '89
CARLSEN, PETER
Elements of style. il *Architectural Digest* 46:212-19 N '89
Interior landscapes. il *Architectural Digest* 46:172-9 Ag '89
Manhattan variations. il *Architectural Digest* 46:138-43 Ag '89
On the Sound: breezy style for a Long Island estate. il *Architectural Digest* 46:128-33 F '89
Recalling a golden era in Manhattan design. il por *Architectural Digest* 46:350+ N '89
CARLSON, ALLAN C.
Helping children: income tax reform. *Current (Washington, D.C.)* 314:12-15 Jl/Ag '89
CARLSON, ANN
about
Reviews:
A. Carlson's site specific piece at the Minneapolis Sculpture Garden. C. LeFevre. il *Dance Magazine* 63:78 D '89
Sloss, Kerr, Rosenberg & Moore [dance] Reviews *Newsweek* il 114:52 Ag 14 '89. L. Shapiro
CARLSON, CURTIS LEROY
about
Still hungry at 75. G. Button. il por *Forbes* 144:302+ D 11 '89
CARLSON, DAVID R.
Why was Flight 655 shot down? *Harper's* 279:26-8 N '89
CARLSON, GRETCHEN ELIZABETH
about
Miss America—was last year's voting suspect? L. DePaulo. il pors *TV Guide* 37:4-7 S 2-8 '89
On the road with Miss America. A. Cook. il pors *Ladies' Home Journal* 106:38+ S '89
CARLSON, MARGARET B.
As State Department spokesperson, Margaret Tutwiler has won even the press's respect. il por *Vogue* 179:276+ O '89
Barbara Bush: down-to-earth First Lady. il por *Reader's Digest* 134:83-7 Ap '89
Fallen angel. il *The New Republic* 200:18-21 Je 12 '89
One of the boys. *The New Republic* 200:11-13 Je 5 '89
CARLSON, PAUL
about
25 years later, life still springs from death. il por *Christianity Today* 33:56+ N 17 '89
CARLSON, RON, 1947-
A sign of love [story] il por *McCall's* 116:58+ Ja '89
Weathering heights. il map *Harper's* 279:40-1 Jl '89
CARLSON, TIM
Air Time. il pors *Sport (New York, N.Y.)* 80:53-6 Ja '89
Beat the Baja. il map *Sport (New York, N.Y.)* 80:66-9 My '89
CARLSON, TIMOTHY
Lights! Camera! Tragedy! il *TV Guide* 37:8-11 Ag 26-S 1 '89
'You learn . . . about pain and humility and failing'. il pors *TV Guide* 37:42-5 Ja 7-13 '89
CARLSON COMPANIES, INC.
Still hungry at 75 [C. Carlson] G. Button. il por *Forbes* 144:302+ D 11 '89
CARLSSON-PAIGE, NANCY, AND LEVIN, DIANE E.
Why children's television should be regulated. *The Education Digest* 55:37-9 S '89
CARLTON, DAVID, 1938-
Were we wrong in 1939? [with reply by J. P. Roche] il *National Review* 41:44+ S 29 '89
CARLTON, LARRY
about
Larry Carlton comes back. C. Stern. il por *Rolling Stone* p23 Je 15 '89
CARLTON, SUSAN
Bright chefs, big City. il pors *Health (New York, N.Y.)* 21:78-81 F '89
CARLTON COMMUNICATIONS PLC
Is this one for real? J. Marcom, Jr. il por *Forbes* 144:252 Jl 24 '89
CARLUCCI, FRANK CHARLES
about
In the bullpen. J. Zweig. por *Forbes* 143:180 Je 12 '89
CARLYLE GROUP
In the bullpen [F. Carlucci] J. Zweig. por *Forbes* 143:180 Je 12 '89
CARLYLE RESTAURANT (NEW YORK, N.Y.) *See* New York (N.Y.)—Restaurants, nightclubs, bars, etc.
CARLZON, JAN
about
Can SAS keep flying with the big birds? J. Kapstein. il por *Business Week* p142+ N 27 '89
CARMAN, JOHN BRAISTED
Missions and the translatable Gospel [cover story] *The Christian Century* 106:786+ Ag 30-S 6 '89
CARMEL, DAN
about
Taking a flyer on direct mail. K. H. Hammonds. il por *Business Week* p41 Jl 24 '89

CARMEL (CALIF.)

Historic houses, sites, etc.
The arts and crafts architect's studio in Carmel [C. S. Greene] B. P. Greene. il por Architectural Digest 46:92+ My '89
CARMELITES
Auschwitz and the nuns. W. F. Buckley. National Review 41:63 O 13 '89
The Auschwitz Carmel. America 161:179 S 30 '89
Auschwitz ire [controversial Carmelite convent] il Time 134:49 Ag 21 '89
Cardinal Glemp's memory lapse [convent at Auschwitz] J. M. Wall. The Christian Century 106:867 O 4 '89
Catholics and Jews: can we bridge the abyss? [Holocaust martyr E. Stein; adaptation of address, October 16, 1988] S. M. Batzdorff. America 160:223-4+ Mr 11 '89
Détente at a death camp [dispute over convent at Auschwitz] K. L. Woodward. il Newsweek 114:58 O 2 '89
The ghosts of an ancient plague [controversial convent at Auschwitz] il U.S. News & World Report 107:10 S 11 '89
The Glemp controversy [convent at Auschwitz] The Christian Century 106:808 S 13-20 '89
Harsh homily [J. Glemp's remarks concerning Carmelite convent at Auschwitz] Time 134:77 S 11 '89
Mea culpa, Auschwitz [agreement to move Carmelite convent] il Time 134:25 O 2 '89
Peace signals from the papal chimney [Pope John Paul II calls for removal of Carmelite convent at Auschwitz] il U.S. News & World Report 107:14 O 2 '89
Polish memories [Auschwitz convent controversy] J. Neusner. il National Review 41:27-8 O 27 '89
A sign of contradiction [Auschwitz convent controversy] J. T. Pawlikowski. il Commonweal 116:485-8 S 22 '89
The Vatican and the Jews [support for relocation of convent from Auschwitz] il The Christian Century 106:873 O 4 '89
Whose Auschwitz? [dispute over convent] il National Review 41:18+ S 29 '89
Whose Holocaust? [controversy over convent at Auschwitz] R. Watson. il Newsweek 114:35-6 S 11 '89
CARMEN, ERIC

about
An Indian summer for Eric Carmen. D. Wild. il por Rolling Stone p54 Jl 13-27 '89
CARMEN SANDIEGO (VIDEO GAMES)
Compute! choice [Where in Time is Carmen Sandiego?] K. Sternberg. il Compute! 11:72-4 D '89
CARMICHAEL, HOAGY, 1899-1982

about
The classic Hoagy Carmichael. J. McDonough. Down Beat 56:30 Je '89
CARMICHAEL, NELSON

about
Nelson Carmichael: the bumpy road to the top. L. Tejada-Flores. il pors Skiing 42:72-6+ D '89
CARMICHEL, JIM
Shooting. See issues of Outdoor Life
CARMINA BURANA [ballet] See Ballet reviews—Single works
CARNAC MEGALITHS (FRANCE) See Megalithic monuments—France
CARNARVON FAMILY

about
Ancestral style. C. Aslet. il House & Garden 161:188-97 Mr '89
CARNATION CO.
Heating up the bottle battle [controversy over TV ads for Carnation and Gerber infant formulas; cover story] F. A. Oski. The Nation 249:665+ D 4 '89
CARNEGIE, ANDREW, 1835-1919

about
The centennial of Andrew Carnegie's "Gospel of wealth". J. M. McShane. America 161:211-13 O 7 '89
CARNEGIE, DALE, 1888-1955

about
S&S issues unabridged Carnegie. P. Sweeting. il Publishers Weekly 235:62 Ja 6 '89
CARNEGIE HALL (NEW YORK, N.Y.)
A bath every century, need it or not [cleaning exterior] B. Weber. il The New York Times Magazine p94 Ag 20 '89
CARNEGIE INSTITUTION OF WASHINGTON OBSERVATORIES See Observatories of the Carnegie Institution of Washington
CARNEGIE INTERNATIONAL
Pittsburgh: ironic and ionic at the Carnegie. H. Schwalb. il Art News 88:159 F '89
Under Western eyes. P. Plagens. bibl f il Art in America 77:32-7+ Ja '89
CARNEGIE-MELLON UNIVERSITY. SOFTWARE ENGINEERING INSTITUTE
Soft machine [cover story] J. S. Russell. il Architectural Record 177:78-83 Mr '89
CARNES, BEN

about
Choctaw with a mission. G. S. Phillips. il por The Progressive 53:14-15 Jl '89

CARNEY, ART

about
The all-out art of Art Carney. M. Zolotow. il por Reader's Digest 135:76-80 O '89
O'pal o'mine! por People Weekly 31 Special Issue:151 Summ '89
CARNEY, RAYMOND
Complex characters. il Film Comment 25:30-3 My/Je '89
Unfinished business. Film Comment 25:48-9 My/Je '89
CARNEY, RICHARD P.

about
Buy on weakness. J. Clements. il por Forbes 144:150-1 S 4 '89
CARNIVAL (PRE-LENTEN FESTIVAL)
Larger than life [B. Kern's floats for New Orleans Mardi Gras parade] B. Weber. il The New York Times Magazine p70 Ja 22 '89

Brazil
Samba time! [Rio de Janeiro] S. A. Teixeira. il The Unesco Courier 42:38-41 D '89

Caribbean region
Hot, hot, hot. N. S. Charles. il Black Enterprise 19:104-5 My '89

Soviet Union
Farewell to winter [Maslenitsa] H. Yvert-Jalu. il The Unesco Courier 42:32-7 D '89
CARNIVAL CRUISE LINES INC.
Carnival tries sailing upstream. A. Fins. il Business Week p82-3+ S 25 '89
How Carnival stacks the decks. F. Rice. il Fortune 119:108-10+ Ja 16 '89
CARNIVAL OF SOULS [film] See Motion picture reviews—Single works
CARNIVALS

See also
Conklin Shows (Firm)

Automation
This way to the egress [computer use by Conklin Shows] P. Scisco. il Compute! 11:107 Ja '89
CARNIVORES
How meat-eaters rule each other [Kalahari Desert; cover story] D. Owens and M. Owens. il International Wildlife 19:4-11 Jl/Ag '89
CARO, ANTHONY, 1924-

about
Caro. M. Filler. il por House & Garden 161:174-5 Mr '89
Caro country: the artist's New York State sculpture studio and fields. K. Wilken. il por Architectural Digest 46:192-7+ Ag '89
CARO, ROBERT A.
The Johnson years: a congressman goes to war. por The New Yorker 65:62-4+ N 6 '89
The Johnson years: buying and selling. The New Yorker 65:43-8+ D 18 '89

about
A Texas-size L.B.J. obsession. R. Z. Sheppard. il pors Time 134:98-9 N 13 '89
CARO, TIM
The brotherhood of cheetahs [cover story] il Natural History p50-9 Je '89
THE CAROL BURNETT SHOW [television program] See Television program reviews—Single works
CAROL PUBLISHING GROUP
Carol Publishing goes to the videotape [fall catalog] J. Mutter. il Publishers Weekly 236:25-6 Ag 18 '89
New Era wins pre-pub review of Hubbard bio. Publishers Weekly 236:332 Ag 11 '89
CAROLI, BETTY BOYD
America's First Ladies. il American History Illustrated 24:26-31+ My '89
CAROLINE ISLANDS

See also
Palau
CAROLINGIANS
Alcuin and the 'new Athens'. M. Alberi. il por History Today 39:35-41 S '89
CARON, GLENN

about
Clean and sober [film] Reviews
Video il 13:76 My '89. J. Young
The Moonlighting mess—behind the feuding that almost killed the show [cover story] L. Farr. il pors TV Guide 37:2-4+ Ja 14-20 '89
CAROTENE
Beta carotene: the protective nutrient. J. Scala. il Dance Magazine 63:62-3 Ap '89
Carrot 'chemo'? Beta-carotene may shrink oral precancers. il Prevention (Emmaus, Pa.) 41:8 N '89
Got a light? This carrot keeps going out [research by Harinder Garewal] R. Weiss. Science News 135:348 Je 3 '89
CAROTENOIDS
Carotenoids: colorful cancer protection. J. Raloff. Science News 136:294 N 4 '89

CAROTID ARTERY SURGERY See Blood vessels—Surgery
CAROUSEL ANIMALS See Carousel art
CAROUSEL ART
Joseph Lutter carves carousel horses by giving rein to his gifts. H. Shapiro. il pors *People Weekly* 32:167-8 D 11 '89
CAROUSELS
Merrily round and round [New Orleans' City Park] il *Southern Living* 24:18 Jl '89
CARPAL TUNNEL SYNDROME
Computeritis. R. Trubo. il *Glamour* 87:56+ D '89
Light at the end of the carpal tunnel. D. M. Pagnanelli. il *Nation's Business* 77:69 Ag '89
Preventing strain injuries [device developed by John LaCourse] *USA Today (Periodical)* 117:8-9 F '89
A twist of the wrist [reducing risk when playing in sports] L. Rogak. il *American Health* 8:34 D '89
CARPENTER, GERALD
Robert Bolt. il por *American Film* 14:60-2 S '89
CARPENTER, HUMPHREY
Mary Poppins, force of nature. *The New York Times Book Review* 94:29 Ag 27 '89
CARPENTER, JAKE BURTON See Burton, Jake
CARPENTER, LIZ
Catching up with the Johnson women. il pors *Good Housekeeping* 208:88+ Ja '89
Lost horizons. il *Ms.* 17:86-7 Mr '89
CARPENTER, MARY
Homeopathic chic. il *Health (New York, N.Y.)* 21:52-5+ Mr '89
CARPENTER, MATT
about
King of the mountain. M. Will-Weber. il por *Runner's World* 24:83 F '89
CARPENTER, MICHAEL ALAN, 1947-
about
Michael Carpenter. J. Friedman. il por *Business Week* Special Issue:154 Ap 14 '89
CARPENTER, RICHARD C.
Greece adrift. il *National Review* 41:17-18 D 8 '89
CARPENTERS' SQUARES
Rafter layout with a framing square. R. Capotosto. il *Popular Mechanics* 166:69-70 F '89
A very versatile square. T. H. Jones. il *Home Mechanix* 85:24-6 S '89
CARPENTRY
See also
Joints (Carpentry)
Woodworking
Notes on carpentry and craft. J. Higgins. *The Writer* 102:9-10 Ag '89
Tools
See Tools
CARPET CLEANING See Rugs and carpets—Care
CARPETS See Rugs and carpets
CARR, ANNE E.
about
Does God want to be your macho man? [interview] por *U.S. Catholic* 54:16-22 My '89
CARR, FRED
about
Milken's shadow hovers over Fred Carr. K. Kerwin. il por *Business Week* p24 Ap 17 '89
This could be the end of a beautiful friendship. K. Kerwin and Z. Schiller. il pors *Business Week* p33-4 S 4 '89
CARR, JOSEPH J.
Choosing the right shortwave antenna. il *Radio-Electronics* 60:61-5 Jl '89
CARR, PAMELA
Which way black America? Anti-abortion or pro-choice. il por *Ebony* 44:134+ O '89
CARR, ROBYN
Informed risk [fiction] il por *Good Housekeeping* 208:225-8+ My '89
CARR, TEMPLE ST. CLAIR
about
Bygone bijoux. K. Bruno. il por *Harper's Bazaar* 122:60 N '89
CARR, TERRY
A marriage gone wrong. por *Newsweek* 113:6 My 8 '89
CARR, WILLIAM F.
Lead me safely through death [cover story] *America* 160:264-7 Mr 25 '89
CARRADINE, CALISTA
about
Calista Carradine grows up. R. Tierney. il por *American Film* 14:80 Je '89
CARRADINE, DAVID
about
Mata Hari [film] Reviews
American Film il por 14:80 Je '89. R. Tierney
CARREFOUR (FIRM)
Cherchez la store [opens hypermarket in Philadelphia] D. Fong. il *Forbes* 143:311+ Ja 9 '89
CARRELL, STEVE
Allergic reactions. il *Better Homes and Gardens* 67:32+ Mr '89

CARRERA, MICHAEL
Sex: preventing teen pregnancy. il *American Health* 8:72 O '89
about
Giving teenagers a new view of their future. M. Ludtke. il por *Time* 133:12+ My 1 '89
CARRERA SÉPTIMA (BOGOTÁ, COLOMBIA: STREET) See Bogotá (Colombia)—Streets
CARRERAS, JOSÉ, 1946-
about
'A little bit of wonder'. K. Ames. il por *Newsweek* 113:74 My 1 '89
CARRÈRE, ENRIQUE JORGE CONTOU- See Contou-Carrère, Enrique Jorge
CARRIAGE HORSES See Horses
CARRIAGE HOUSES, CONVERTED See Houses, Remodeled
CARRIAGES, BABY See Baby carriages
CARRIEDO, RUBEN
about
Using research data to shape our schools [interview] D. B. Strother. il por *Phi Delta Kappan* 70:480-3 F '89
CARRIER, MARK
about
Safeties first. A. Murphy. il pors *Sports Illustrated* 71:78-80 S 4 '89
CARRIER CURRENT TRANSMISSION
Carrier current audio transmitter [cover story] W. Sheets and R. F. Graf. il *Radio-Electronics* 60:55+ Ja '89
Carrier current receiver. W. Sheets and R. F. Graf. il *Radio-Electronics* 60:55+ F '89
Current events [CarrierNET, system for local area networks] R. L. Mitchell. il *Byte* 14:97 Mr '89
CARRIER PIGEONS See Pigeons
CARRIÈRE, JEAN-CLAUDE
about
Jean-Claude Carrière: the Mahabharata, the great history of mankind [interview] il pors *The Unesco Courier* 42:4-9+ S '89
The Mahabharata [drama] Reviews
The Unesco Courier il pors 42:4-9+ S '89
CARRIERS, AIRCRAFT See Aircraft carriers
CARRIERS, CAR-TOP See Automobiles—Equipment
CARRIERS OF INFECTION
See also
Animals as carriers of infection
Milk as carrier of infection
Mosquitoes as carriers of infection
Ticks as carriers of infection
CARRIL, PETE
about
Playing the cerebral game. S. Toperoff. il *The Atlantic* 264:115-18 N '89
CARRINGTON, PETER ALEXANDER RUPERT CARING-TON, 6TH BARON, 1919-
about
Government/military: Lord Carrington, Paul H. Nitze, Marshal Sergei Fedorovich Akhromeyev. il pors *Aviation Week & Space Technology* 130:18 Ja 2 '89
CARRINGTON, TERRI LYNE
about
A new generation of black beauties. il pors *Ebony* 44:152+ S '89
A prodigy with a future as well as a past, Terri Lyne Carrington is drumming up a brilliant career. L. Wohlfert. il pors *People Weekly* 31:162-3 Ap 10 '89
Terri Lyne Carrington: real-life heartbeats. B. Milkowski. il pors *Down Beat* 56:20-2 Je '89
CARRIZO PLAIN (CALIF.)
Carrizo Plain, land of extremes. il map *Sunset (Central West edition)* 183:35+ N '89
Plain dealing. D. Holing. il map *Sierra* 74:142-7 Ja/F '89
CARROLL, DAN
Increasing ducks in New York. il *The Conservationist* 43:12-15 Mr/Ap '89
CARROLL, DEVIN
Humanism for Kids. *The Humanist* 49:37 N/D '89
Sexual morality for young humanists and their parents. *The Humanist* 49:41-2+ Jl/Ag '89
CARROLL, E. JEAN
Pretty poison: Anne Crawford skewers Hollywood. il *Mademoiselle* 95:202-3+ O '89
CARROLL, ETHNA
One of the great seductresses of Irish history [story] *The New Yorker* 65:37-42 Je 5 '89
CARROLL, JERRY
about
Stable Jerry. J. Queenan. il pors *Forbes* 144:350 N 13 '89
CARROLL, JOHN
about
Justice in Milwaukee. H. G. Miller. il pors *The Saturday Evening Post* 261:44-8+ My/Je '89
CARROLL, JOHN E. (JOHN EDWARD), 1944-
The acid challenge to security. bibl f il *The Bulletin of the Atomic Scientists* 45:32-4 O '89
CARROLL, JONATHAN, 1949-
Mr. Fiddlehead [story] il *Omni (New York, N.Y.)* 11:68-70+ F '89

CARROLL, PAM
Houses of the future today. il *Working Woman* 14:82+ N '89
The paperless office comes true. il *Working Woman* 14:73-4+ O '89

CARROLL, PETER
Frances Moore Lappé's diet for a better world. il pors *Utne Reader* p42-8 My/Je '89

CARROLL, RICHARD
about
Bark with a bite. E. Agar. il *American Artist* 53:92-7 S '89

CARROLL COUNTY (GA.)
Public health
Scientists nab water-polluting parasite [Cryptosporidium infection] K. Fackelmann. *Science News* 135:343 Je 3 '89

CARRONADE (WEAPON)
The rise and fall of the carronade [18th century naval gun] J. E. Talbott. bibl il *History Today* 39:24-30 Ag '89

CARROTS
"Visionary" carrots take root [Beta III carrot] il *The Saturday Evening Post* 261:26 Jl/Ag '89

CARRY-ON LUGGAGE See Luggage

CARS (AUTOMOBILES) See Automobiles

CARS (RAILROAD) See Railroads—Cars

CARSEY, JULIAN NANCE
about
PW interviews [biographer J. Coleman] C. Goodrich. il por *Publishers Weekly* 236:52-3 S 8 '89

CARSEY, MARCY
about
Can this TV team go five for five? R. Grover. il pors *Business Week* p77 Je 19 '89

CARSEY-WERNER COMPANY
Can this TV team go five for five? R. Grover. il pors *Business Week* p77 Je 19 '89

CARSON, BUD
about
Nipped in the Bud. P. Zimmerman. il por *Sports Illustrated* 71:36-8+ O 9 '89

CARSON, CIARÁN, 1948-
Ambition [poem] *The New Yorker* 65:58-9 N 6 '89
Bedtime story [poem] *The New Yorker* 65:44 S 4 '89

CARSON, CYNTHIA
about
Her challenge: win new dairy consumers. J. R. Borcherding and P. Smith. il por *Successful Farming* 87:35 O '89

CARSON, JOHNNY, 1925-
about
Heeeeere's Johnny! S. Kanfer. il por *Time* 133:66 Je 26 '89
Johnny Carson. il pors *People Weekly* 31 Special Issue:20-1 Summ '89
Johnny Carson [excerpt from King of the night] L. Leamer. il pors *Good Housekeeping* 209:104-5+ Jl '89

CARSON, RACHEL, 1907-1964
The edge of the sea [excerpt] il *The Conservationist* 44:55 S/O '89
The enduring sea. il *Audubon* 91:47 Mr '89
about
Remembering Rachel Carson. J. D. DuPont. il *The Conservationist* 44:54 S/O '89

CARSON, SHARON
about
A conversation with Sharon Carson. C. Movalli. il *American Artist* 53:32-7+ N '89

CARSON, TOM
Television. See issues of American Film beginning May 1989

CARSON PIRIE SCOTT & CO.
Some unwelcome shoppers may drop in on Carson Pirie. B. Bremner. il *Business Week* p39-40 Ap 3 '89

CARSTAIRS, SHARON
about
Out of the wilderness. B. Wallace. *Maclean's* 102:14 Ja 16 '89

CARSTARPHEN, META G.
Rare films: the Tyler, Texas treasure trove. il *American Visions* 4:36-8 Je '89

CART See Championship Auto Racing Teams (Organization)

CARTAGENA (COLOMBIA)
Description
Cartagena nights. B. McDowell. il maps *National Geographic* 175:494-509 Ap '89

CARTE DE VISITE PHOTOGRAPHS
Cartes de visite. il *American History Illustrated* 24:38-9 S/O '89

CARTELS
International aspects
See also
Organization of Petroleum Exporting Countries

CARTER, ANNE BABSON
Bells on Taiwan [poem] *The Nation* 249:396 O 9 '89

CARTER, ANTHONY
about
Reaching for the ring. R. Wiley. il pors *Sports Illustrated* 71:48-52 Ag 14 '89

CARTER, ASHTON B.
Testing weapons in space. bibl il *Scientific American* 261:33-40 Jl '89

CARTER, BENNY
about
Benny Carter: a legend in process. M. Seidel. il pors *Down Beat* 56:24-6 D '89

CARTER, BETH W.
Splash! Science can be fun. il *Parents* 64:136-40 Je '89

CARTER, BETTY
about
Betty Carter: look what we've got! J. T. Jones, IV. il pors *Down Beat* 56:24-6 Ag '89

CARTER, BILL
No laughing matter. il pors *The New York Times Magazine* p50+ N 5 '89

CARTER, CAROL
about
Introspective reflections [cover story] J.-P. Wolf. il por *American Artist* 53:50-5 O '89

CARTER, CAROL SMITH- See Smith-Carter, Carol

CARTER, CHARLA
The essence of Provence. il por *House & Garden* 161:126-31+ Jl '89

CARTER, DANIEL C., AND OTHERS
Three-dimensional structure of human serum albumin. bibl f il *Science* 244:1195-8 Je 9 '89

CARTER, DOMINIC
about
The Carter campaign. C. S. Smith. il por *New York* 22:36 N 13 '89

CARTER, E. GRAYDON
The joker. il pors *Rolling Stone* p46-8+ N 2 '89
about
Spying on 'Spy' [cover story] D. Blum. il pors *New York* 22:32-41 Ap 17 '89

CARTER, ELLIOTT, 1908-
about
Musical events:
Birthday tributes to E. Carter in New York City. A. Porter. *The New Yorker* 64:54-5 Ja 2 '89
Turin's Settembre Musica. A. Porter. *The New Yorker* 65:126-9 N 6 '89
Uneasy pieces. P. G. Davis. il por *New York* 22:58-9 Ja 9 '89

CARTER, FORREST, D. 1979
about
Big sales for New Mexico's 'Little Tree'. il *Publishers Weekly* 235:49 My 19 '89

CARTER, HELLE
about
Virginia's Shirley Plantation. J. S. Wamsley. il *Architectural Digest* 46:126-31+ Je '89

CARTER, HILL
about
Virginia's Shirley Plantation. J. S. Wamsley. il *Architectural Digest* 46:126-31+ Je '89

CARTER, JACQUE
Grouper sex in Belize. il *Natural History* p60-9 O '89

CARTER, JAMES EARL See Carter, Jimmy, 1924-

CARTER, JESSIE
about
100 pounds lighter—and loving it. il pors *Ebony* 45:104+ D '89

CARTER, JIMMY, 1924-
about
Carter redux [cover story] W. King. il pors *The New York Times Magazine* p38-41+ D 10 '89
Hail to the ex-chief. S. W. Cloud. il pors *Time* 134:60-3 S 11 '89
What happened to Jimmy Carter. G. P. Brockway. il *The New Leader* 72:11-13 N 27 '89
Religion
The preacher as ex-president. J. M. Wall. *The Christian Century* 106:1035-6 N 15 '89
Visit to Panama, 1989
Mr. Ex-President. H. Hertzberg. *The New Republic* 200:4 Je 5 '89

CARTER, JOHN MACK
Editor's notebook. See issues of Good Housekeeping

CARTER, JOHN MARSHALL
Blah Na Na! For the blahs. il *Phi Delta Kappan* 71:84-5 S '89

CARTER, KARLYN S.
Helping give students a sense of audience. *The Education Digest* 55:43-6 O '89

CARTER, LUTHER J.
Current controversies over the Waste Isolation Pilot Plant. bibl f *Environment* 31:5+ S '89

CARTER, NELL
about
Nell Carter takes charge of life, love and career. il por *Jet* 76:59 S 25 '89

CARTER, RON
about
Award-winning director faces layoff. D. Helland. il *Down Beat* 56:12 Ag '89

CARTER, RON, 1937-
about
Class act. P. Brock. il por *Gentlemen's Quarterly* 59:158-9 Ja '89
CARTER, TAHTI
Writing successful proposals for the romance market. *The Writer* 102:23-5 My '89
CARTER-SCOTT, CHÉRIE
Are you a negaholic? [excerpt] *Harper's Bazaar* 122:103+ Ja '89
CARTIER, GEORGES
Libraries to the rescue. il *The Courier (Unesco)* 42:6-8 My '89
CARTIER, JANICE
about
Beginning a career as a watercolorist. J. R. Kemp. il por *American Artist* 53:72-5+ Jl '89
CARTIER (FIRM)
Opulent objects by Cartier [Musée du Petit Palais in Paris] A. E. Ledes. il *Antiques* 136:958+ N '89
Tiffany tries the Cartier formula. F. Rice. il *Fortune* 120:141+ N 20 '89
CARTIER-BRESSON, HENRI, 1908-
about
Cartier-Bresson's real thing. M. Esterow. il por *Art News* 88:132-5 Summ '89
Profiles (I). D. Hofstadter. por *The New Yorker* 65:59-60+ O 23 '89
Profiles (II). D. Hofstadter. il *The New Yorker* 65:49-52+ O 30 '89
CARTOGRAPHY
See also
Contours (Cartography)
Geographic information systems
Road maps, guides, etc.
Mapping the world. L. Eskin. il *Scholastic Update (Teachers' edition)* 122:8-9 S 22 '89
Portugal
Japan in early Portuguese maps. A. P. Marques. il maps *The Courier (Unesco)* 42:14-16 Ap '89
Of caravels and cartographers . . . L. de Albuquerque. il *The Courier (Unesco)* 42:10-13 Ap '89
CARTON, WILHELM H. C.
Oppolzer's great canon of eclipses. il por *Sky and Telescope* 78:475-8 N '89
CARTOONISTS
See also
Barton, Ralph, 1891-1931
Benton, Jim
Black cartoonists
Breathed, Berke
Callahan, John
Caniff, Milton Arthur, 1907-1988
Feiffer, Jules
Groening, Matt
Jones, Chuck, 1912-
Keane, Glen, 1954-
Larson, Gary
Laxman, R. K.
Oliphant, Patrick
Quezada, Abel
Rodrigues, Charles
Schulz, Charles M.
Smith, Elwood H., 1941-
Trudeau, G. B., 1948-
CARTOONISTS, HANDICAPPED
Almost charmed [publication of J. Callahan's autobiography] L. Fleischer. *Publishers Weekly* 235:66 Mr 17 '89
Hell on wheels [excerpt from Don't worry, he won't get far on foot] J. Callahan. il por *Mother Jones* 14:38-40+ My '89
Paralyzed at 21, cartoonist John Callahan finds laughter the best medicine for his rage. R. Arias. il pors *People Weekly* 31:102+ Je 12 '89
CARTOONS *See* Motion pictures—Animated films; Television advertising—Cartoons; Television broadcasting—Cartoons; Videotapes—Animated films
CARTRIDGE TAPE RECORDERS *See* Tape recorders and recording
CARTRIDGES
The .280 vs. the .270. J. Carmichel. il *Outdoor Life* 183:22+ Ap '89
The big boom in big bores (I). J. Carmichel. il *Outdoor Life* 184:38+ O '89
The big boom in big bores (II). J. Carmichel. il *Outdoor Life* 184:34+ N '89
Birth of the .270. J. Carmichel. il *Outdoor Life* 183:56+ Mr '89
The mighty lites. B. Brister. il *Field & Stream* 94:106+ S '89
The old Suzy-Q [rifle cartridges] D. E. Petzal. il *Field & Stream* 94:60+ Je '89
CARTRIDGES, PHONOGRAPH *See* Phonograph—Pickup
CARTS
A custom boat cart. P. Butler and M. Butler. il *Outdoor Life* 183:46+ Mr '89
Serving cart. M. Ferrara. il *Organic Gardening* 36:71-3 O '89

CARTWHEEL (GALAXY) *See* Galaxies
CARTWRIGHT, GEORGE
about
George Cartwright. B. Shoemaker. il por *Down Beat* 56:48+ N '89
CARTWRIGHT, LENORA T., D. 1989
about
Obituary
Jet por 76:7 Ag 21 '89
CARTWRIGHT ELECTRONICS, INC.
Cartwright develops missile attack warning for high-speed tactical aircraft. *Aviation Week & Space Technology* 131:93 S 11 '89
CARUANA, CLAUDIA
The advice network. il *Parents* 64:208+ Ap '89
CARUCCI, VIC
Spying at the Super Bowl: the inside story. il *TV Guide* 37:14-17 Ja 21-27 '89
CARUSO, JAMES R., 1932-, AND ARTHUR, MAVIS E., 1945-
Home editing comes of age. il *Video* 12:44-8+ Mr '89
Simple tricks for great F/X. il *Video* 13:40-3 Ap '89
CARUSO, LAURA
The high ground. il *Ms.* 17:52-3 Ja/F '89
CARVEN, MADAME
about
Madame Carven: eighteenth-century splendor in her Avenue Foch house. C. Aillaud. il por *Architectural Digest* 46:180-3+ S '89
CARVER, BOB
about
Eliminating the static. M. Barrier. il pors *Nation's Business* 77:63-4+ S '89
CARVER, CRAIG M., 1947-
Word histories. See alternate issues of The Atlantic beginning October 1988
CARVER, MAXWELL
Brain bogglers. See issues of Discover beginning November 1987
CARVER, RAYMOND
Afterglow [poem] *The New Yorker* 65:36 Ap 24 '89
Lemonade [poem] il *Esquire* 112:78-9 Jl '89
Proposal [poem] *Harper's* 278:32 Mr '89
about
Raymond Carver: a still, small voice. J. McInerney. il por *The New York Times Book Review* 94:1+ Ag 6 '89
Raymond Carver had his cake and ate it too. T. Wolff. il por *Esquire* 112:240-2+ S '89
CARVER, SALLY S.
Postcards. See issues of Antiques & Collecting Hobbies beginning March 1985 through May 1989
CARVER CORP.
Eliminating the static. M. Barrier. il pors *Nation's Business* 77:63-4+ S '89
CARVEY, DANA
about
Hans and Franz get pumped. P. Serrani. il pors *Gentlemen's Quarterly* 59:230-5 Ag '89
CARVING (ART INDUSTRIES)
See also
Pumpkin faces
Stone carving
Wood carving
CARVING (MEAT, ETC.)
The art of carving—turkey. Z. E. Zakroff. il *Gourmet* 49:128-9+ N '89
Cut-ups. il *Home Mechanix* 85:56 D '89
CARY, ERNESTINE
(jt. auth) See Jessup, Shelby P., and Cary, Ernestine
CAS *See* Certificates of annuity
CASA *See* Construcciones Aeronauticas SA
CASA TOSCANINI (MILAN, ITALY): HISTORIC HOUSE)
See Milan (Italy)—Historic houses, sites, etc.
CASABLANCA (MOROCCO)
Mosques
See also
Great Mosque Hassan II (Casablanca, Morocco)
CASADY, KERI
(jt. auth) See Netter, Patrick, and Casady, Keri
CASANI, JOHN R.
We need nuclear power in space. *Astronomy* 17:8 Je '89
CASAS, PENELOPE
Spain in a stew. il *The New York Times Magazine* p69-70 O 15 '89
CASBERGUE, RENÉE M., AND GREENE, JANE FELL
Sensory perception and reading disability. *The Education Digest* 54:33-5 Mr '89
CASCADE RANGE
Easy Eden. B. Groff. il *Sierra* 74:61 My/Je '89
Heat flow and hydrothermal circulation in the Cascade Range, north-central Oregon. S. E. Ingebritsen and others. bibl f il maps *Science* 243:1458-62 Mr 17 '89
CASCIERO, ANNICK SANJURJO DE *See* Sanjurjo de Casciero, Annick
CASE, JOYCE
She reaches for her pen, not her plate. il pors *Prevention (Emmaus, Pa.)* 41:107-8+ O '89

CASE, PETER
about
Peter Case's "Blue guitar": unchained. P. Puterbaugh. il por *Stereo Review* 54:71 Ag '89
CASE *See* Computer-aided software engineering
CASE (J. I.) COMPANY *See* J. I. Case Company
CASE METHOD
The case for the case study [political science] S. Goldsmith and K. Boo. *The Washington Monthly* 21:18-20+ Je '89
Discussion method teaching. W. M. Welty. bibl il *Change* 21:40-9 Jl/Ag '89
THE CASE OF THE HILLSIDE STRANGLERS [television program] *See* Television program reviews—Single works
CASES *See* Boxes, cases, etc.
CASEY, JOHN, 1939-
At Dartmouth the clash of '89. il *The New York Times Magazine* p28-30+ F 26 '89
CASEY, JOHN G.
(jt. auth) *See* Mason, John M., and Casey, John G.
CASEY, KATHRYN
The real Roseanne [cover story] il pors *Ladies' Home Journal* 106:137-9+ S '89
A thousand days of tears. il pors *Ladies' Home Journal* 106:120-2+ F '89
CASEY, ROBERT W.
Humbled banks make nice again. il *Working Woman* 14:65-7 Mr '89
CASEY'S GENERAL STORES INC.
Clear signs to sell short. G. G. Marcial. *Business Week* p108 Mr 27 '89
CASEY'S TOP 40 [radio program] *See* Radio program reviews—Single works
CASH AMERICA INVESTMENTS (FIRM)
Pawn scheme. T. Jaffe. il *Forbes* 144:140 Jl 10 '89
CASH COW (TERM)
Nice, Bossy. W. Safire. il *The New York Times Magazine* p26 N 5 '89
CASH DISCOUNTS *See* Discount, Cash
CASH FLOW
Cash flow can be the investor's best guide to a stock's true worth. A. Rock. *Money* 18:161-2 Mr '89
Cashing in on cash-rich companies. J. Kosnett. il *Changing Times* 43:29-33 Jl '89
Earnings, schmernings—look at the cash. J. M. Laderman. il *Business Week* p56-7 Jl 24 '89
Eyeing companies with lots of cash [interview with M. Hawkins of Southeastern Asset Management] A. E. Serwer. il por *Fortune* 119:37-9 F 13 '89
The money magician at Philip Morris [H. Storr] L. J. Nathans. il por *Business Week* p78 Ap 10 '89
A peculiar beauty contest [concentration on cash flow vs. earnings in stock valuation as highlighted in Time Inc. merger] D. Wechsler. il *Forbes* 144:43-4+ Jl 10 '89
Soft dollars [software companies' cash flow] D. Churbuck. il *Forbes* 143:126-7 My 1 '89
There's cash flow, and there's cash flow [views of D. Yackt-man] J. Clements. il por *Forbes* 144:138+ S 18 '89
To free money for what matters most, analyze expenses. C. Willis. il *Money* 18:68-70 F '89
While cyclical stocks go begging, the companies are getting rich. J. Mendes. il *Fortune* 119:37-8 Ap 10 '89
Why 'cash flow' might still be magic words. L. J. Nathans. il *Business Week* p114 D 25 '89-Ja 1 '90
CASH FLOW TAX
Live from New York: it's the American Economic Assn. K. Pennar. il *Business Week* p24 Ja 16 '89
CASH MANAGEMENT
Managing your cash. P. N. Strassels. il *Nation's Business* 77:56 F '89
Managing your company's money [interview with B. Michels] N. Sullivan. por *Home Office Computing* 7:60 S '89
Where to keep your cash (II). il *Consumer Reports* 54:260 Ap '89
CASH MANAGEMENT ACCOUNTS
Cash-management checklist. J. F. Wasik. il *Home Office Computing* 7:18 Jl '89
CASH REGISTERS
See also
Point-of-sale systems
History
John Patterson rang up success with the Incorruptible Cashier. M. Bernstein. bibl f (p174) il por *Smithsonian* 20:150-2+ Je '89
CASHEW NUTS
Contamination
Buggy nuts [insect filth discovered in shipments produced by International Nut] il *FDA Consumer* 23:31-2 My '89
CASHIN, SHERYLL
about
Thurgood Marshall hires two black Ivy League law clerks. il pors *Jet* 77:4+ N 13 '89
CASHMERE
Expensive habits: cashmere. P. Mayle. il *Gentlemen's Quarterly* 59:51+ O '89
CASIANO, MANUEL A., JR.
about
Malaret and Casiano: a voguish women's mag that speaks Spanish. P. Finch. il pors *Business Week* p107 Je 5 '89

CASINO CONTROL COMMISSION (N.J.) *See* New Jersey. Casino Control Commission
CASINO GAMBLING *See* Gambling
CASINOS
See also
Circus Circus Enterprises Inc.
Del E. Webb Corp.
Golden Nugget, Inc.
Mirage (Las Vegas, Nev.: Casino)
Players Club International Inc.
Resorts International Inc.
Riverside Resort Hotel & Casino
Trump Plaza Hotel & Casino (Atlantic City, N.J.)
Trump Taj Mahal Casino Resort (Atlantic City, N.J.)
Boardwalk of broken dreams [Atlantic City; cover story] P. Painton. il *Time* 134:64-9 S 25 '89
Acquisitions and mergers
The Merv and Don boardwalk game [Resorts having financial difficulties] il por *U.S. News & World Report* 107:17 N 27 '89
Merv Griffin's last Resort may be bankruptcy. R. Grover. il *Business Week* p34 N 20 '89
The new Merv Griffin show [Resorts deal sours] K. Hannon. il *Forbes* 144:10 Ag 21 '89
The Wheel of Fortune turns badly for Merv Griffin. L. Reibstein. il por *Newsweek* 114:62 N 27 '89
The wheel of misfortune? [M. Griffin's deal for Resorts turns sour] R. Grover. il *Business Week* p35-6 Ja 16 '89
Finance
How Trump plays monopoly [D. Trump's lease deal with B. Guccione freezes out Pratt Hotel as Atlantic City competitor] H. Rudnitsky. il *Forbes* 143:128 Ap 17 '89
Laws and regulations
See also
New Jersey. Casino Control Commission
Bahamas
See also
Crystal Palace Resort & Casino (Nassau, Bahamas)
CASIRAGHI, STEFANO
about
Rough water roulette. P. Whittell. il por *Motor Boating & Sailing* 164:46-9+ D '89
CASLER, LAWRENCE
Hypnotize students and improve their ability to learn. il *USA Today (Periodical)* 118:88-90 S '89
CASOLO, JENNIFER JEAN
about
Home for the holidays—from El Salvador. por *Newsweek* 114:52 D 25 '89
Notes and comment. *The New Yorker* 65:42-4 D 11 '89
CASPARI (LAURA) LTD./SHE, INC. *See* Laura Caspari Ltd./SHE, Inc.
CASS, CAMI
about
Enjoying a quiet success. W. F. Reed. il por *Sports Illustrated* 70:108 Ja 9 '89
CASSATT, MARY, 1844-1926
about
Long-lasting impressions. J. A. Lewis. il *Harper's Bazaar* 122:48+ Je '89
Mary Cassatt in the 1890's: the color prints in context. N. M. Mathews. bibl f il *Antiques* 136:860-71 O '89
CASSAVAS
Put a cassava in your tank [genetically altered yeast cells produce ethanol] il *Discover* 10:10 F '89
CASSAVETES, JOHN
about
Cassavetes [special section] il pors *Film Comment* 25:29-39+ My/Je '89
Obituary
American Film il por 14:40-3+ My '89. M. Meisel
People Weekly il por 31:65 F 20 '89
CASSEROLE COOKING
See also
Skillet cooking
Better-than-ever casseroles. il *Good Housekeeping* 209:152-62+ O '89
Clever ways with casseroles. il *Southern Living* 24:200+ Mr '89
Fish casseroles. S. Bashline. il *Field & Stream* 94:40 My '89
Oldies but goodies! Eight '50s casseroles updated. il *Redbook* 173:157-60+ O '89
One-dish dinners [microwaving] il *Good Housekeeping* 209:265-6 N '89
Recipe of the week [enchilada casserole] il *Jet* 75:38 Mr 13 '89
Vegetable casseroles. il *Better Homes and Gardens* 67:159-60 S '89
Vegetable casseroles for wholesome summer meals. il *Sunset (Central West edition)* 183:114+ Jl '89
CASSETTE BOOKS *See* Talking books
CASSETTE DECKS *See* Tape recorders and recording
CASSETTE RECORDERS *See* Tape recorders and recording
CASSETTE RECORDERS, VIDEO *See* Videotape recorders and recording

CASSETTE RECORDINGS See Tape recordings
CASSETTE RECORDINGS, VIDEO See Videotapes
CASSETTE TAPE See Tape, Magnetic
CASSIAN, NINA, 1924-
Poetry [poem]; tr. by William Jay Smith. *The New Yorker* 64:71 Ja 30 '89
CASSIDY, ANNE
The town that said "No" to racism. il pors *Good Housekeeping* 208:62+ F '89
CASSIDY, JO
Lupus: master of disguise. il *Current Health 2* 16:26-7 D '89
Silent signals. il *Current Health 2* 16:14-16 O '89
CASSIDY, JOHN
Comment as cautious as the president himself. il *World Press Review* 36:11-12 S '89
War among Washington's blacks. *World Press Review* 36:34 My '89
CASSIDY, MICHAEL, 1945-
about
Hope for a peaceful end to apartheid [interview] il por *Christianity Today* 33:55-6 N 17 '89
CASSILLY, BOB
about
Armed and fiberglass. B. Weber. il por *The New York Times Magazine* p86 Ap 16 '89
CASSINI FLIGHTS TO SATURN See Space flight to Saturn
CASSINO (ITALY), BATTLE OF, 1944
Letter from Cassino. W. Murray. *The New Yorker* 65:112-20 My 15 '89
CASSIOPEIA (CONSTELLATION) See Constellations
CASSIRER, NADINE GORDIMER See Gordimer, Nadine, 1923-
CASSON, LIONEL, 1914-
Think that taxes take a big bite today? il *Smithsonian* 19:122-7 Mr '89
CASSONI, VITTORIO
about
Can Cassoni get Olivetti off the slippery slope? J. Rossant and T. Peterson. il por *Business Week* p99+ Je 12 '89
CASSOULET
A cassoulet to celebrate the new wine . . . not too seriously. il *Sunset (Central West edition)* 183:142+ N '89
CAST IRON
Cast iron [ancient China] R. K. G. Temple. il *The Courier (Unesco)* 41:10-11 O '88
Collectors and collecting
Cast-iron collectibles. W. C. Ketchum. il *Better Homes and Gardens* 67:112 Ap '89
CASTAÑEDA, JORGE
about
Bordering on friends [interview] A. Dabrowski. il por *Time* 134:56-8 Ag 7 '89
CASTE
India
Different castes, different lives: growing up in India. S. Tefft. il *Scholastic Update (Teachers' edition)* 121:14-15 Mr 10 '89
CASTELBAJAC, JEAN-CHARLES DE
about
A frisky French designer makes a teddy-bear coat for adults. il por *People Weekly* 31:83 Ja 30 '89
CASTELBAJAC, KATE DE
about
Kate de Castelbajac. C. Petkanas. il pors *Harper's Bazaar* 122:108-13+ F '89
CASTELLANOS, ROSARIO
about
A woman who knew Latin. D. Bellm. *The Nation* 248:891-3 Je 26 '89
CASTELLI, WILLIAM P.
(jt. auth) See Griffin, Glen C., and Castelli, William P.
CASTELLO DI RIVOLI (TURIN, ITALY)
Turin's most surprising museum. M. Peppiatt. il *Architectural Digest* 46:124+ My '89
CASTERS, GLIDES, ETC. (HARDWARE)
Easy rollers [motorized spheres] D. Scott. il *Popular Science* 234:31 Je '89
Uses for rigid-swivel based casters [theater scenery] E. Littlefield. il *Theatre Crafts* 23:97 Ap '89
CASTILLO, ENRIQUE ALVAREZ DEL See Alvarez del Castillo, Enrique
CASTING (FISHING)
Becoming a fly angler, step by step. P. Barrett. il *Field & Stream* 93:117-19 Ap '89
Distance casting. K. Schultz. il *Field & Stream* 94:82-3 D '89
Evolution of a spring creek fisherman. N. Lyons. il *Field & Stream* 93:16-17 Ap '89
Fly fishing slow currents. J. Gierach. il *Field & Stream* 94:56-7+ My '89
Practice makes adequate. G. Hill. il *Field & Stream* 94:11 Je '89
Shorten up! J. Bashline. il *Field & Stream* 93:32+ Ap '89
The two-fly cast. K. McCafferty. il *Field & Stream* 94:26+ Je '89

Welcome, world, to Trout Town U.S.A., where all the flies are fit to be tied [flyfishing the Beaverkill River in New York State] J. Friedman. il *People Weekly* 32:92-4+ Jl 3 '89
Zen and the art of fly-fishing. J. Cramer. il *Time* 134:52 Ag 7 '89
Anecdotes, facetiae, satire, etc.
A fly-fishing primer. P. J. O'Rourke. il *Field & Stream* 93:22+ Ap '89
CASTING (SCULPTURE)
See also
Bronze founding
A sculptor's heaven on earth is Italy's city of holy stone [Pietrasanta] I. Shenker. il *Smithsonian* 19:106-12+ F '89
CASTING CENTER See Walt Disney World (Fla.). Casting Center
CASTING OF TELEVISION PROGRAMS See Television production and direction
CASTING REELS See Fishing tackle
CASTLE, GEORGE
The Goose again. il pors *Sport (New York, N.Y.)* 80:38-40 Mr '89
CASTLE, KATHY
(jt. auth) See Castle, Ken, and Castle, Kathy
CASTLE, KEN
Back to the battlefields. il *Travel Holiday* 172:60-71 S '89
The dog days of winter. il *Travel Holiday* 171:60-1 Ja '89
Head over wheels. il *Travel Holiday* 171:18-21 Ja '89
Splash! il *Travel Holiday* 172:74-81 Jl '89
To go or not to go? il *Travel Holiday* 171:16-17+ F '89
CASTLE, KEN, AND CASTLE, KATHY
Living the high life in the low season. il *Travel Holiday* 172:74-8 Ag '89
CASTLE, NICK, JR.
about
Tap [film] Reviews
Ebony il 44:46+ F '89
The New Republic 200:32 Mr 20 '89. S. Kauffmann
The New Yorker 64:74-5 F 6 '89. A. Croce
Newsweek 113:79 F 13 '89. D. Ansen
People Weekly il 31:16 F 13 '89. R. Novak
CASTLE & COOKE, INC.
Pineapple play: the action in Castle & Cooke. G. G. Marcial. il *Business Week* p132 My 15 '89
Will the circle be unbroken? [infertility in Costa Rican banana workers through use of pesticide dibromochloropropane] D. Weir and C. Matthiessen. il *Mother Jones* 14:20-7 Je '89
CASTLEMAN, MICHAEL
16 cancers that run in families—will you inherit? il *Redbook* 173:150-1+ S '89
The chicken-soup solution. il *New Choices for the Best Years* 29:46-7+ N '89
CASTLEREAGH, ROBERT STEWART, VISCOUNT, 1769-1822
about
George Canning's left buttock and the origin of species. S. J. Gould. *Natural History* p18+ My '89
CASTLES
France
See also
Château de Montgeoffroy (France)
Acts of culture: Jean-Claude Brialy's château in the Marne Valley [interior by Michel van Leempoel] C. Aillaud. il por *Architectural Digest* 46:94-9+ Ja '89
Castle cast-offs [estate auction at Château de Cheverny in Loire Valley] C. Petkanas. il *House & Garden* 161:96+ My '89
A castle under the Louvre. P. Miller. il *National Geographic* 176:102-7 Jl '89
Château de Cornillon: antiquarian Bernard Steinitz's feudal castle on the Loire [cover story] C. Styles-McLeod. il *Architectural Digest* 46:72-81+ Ja '89
Château de La Lorie: Marquise de Saint-Genys in the Haut-Anjou. B. D. Colen. il *Architectural Digest* 46:154-8+ Ja '89
Meditative explorations in a French manor house [Zao Wou-ki's château] Countess Du Saillant. il por *Architectural Digest* 46:116+ O '89
Three faces of the 16th-century Château de Fleury. S. M. Alsop. il por *Architectural Digest* 46:106+ D '89
Great Britain
See also
Highclere Castle
Scotland
See also
Brodick Castle (Scotland)
Spain
See also
Fundación Casa Ducal de Medinaceli
CASTNER, JAMES L.
Life as a leaf. il *International Wildlife* 19:18-21 Mr/Ap '89
CASTRATION
Animals
Anecdotes, facetiae, satire, etc.
Charly's loss, Bardot's gain [actress orders castration of neighbor's donkey] A. Fotheringham. il *Maclean's* 102:56 Ag 7 '89

CASTRILLO, JOSÉ-LUIS, AND OTHERS
Purification of growth hormone-specific transcription factor GHF-1 containing homeobox. bibl f il *Science* 243:814-17 F 10 '89
CASTRO, CARMEN DE LARA *See* Lara Castro, Carmen de
CASTRO, FIDEL, 1927-
about
After Castro [cover story] S. Landau. il por *Mother Jones* 14:20-6+ Jl/Ag '89
The Albania of the Caribbean. R. Grenier. il *National Review* 41:41-3 My 5 '89
Castro: dilemmas of the last idealist. T. Szulc. *New Perspectives Quarterly* 5:50-1 Wint '88/'89
'Castro lives in a cloud'. C. S. Manegold. il por *Newsweek* 114:36 Ag 7 '89
Castro's curveball. J. D. Truby. *Harper's* 278:32+ My '89
Courting a Queen. M. Nemeth. il pors *Maclean's* 102:18-19 Ap 17 '89
The graying of a revolution. C. A. Robbins. il pors *U.S. News & World Report* 106:37-41 Ja 9 '89
Human rights situation in Cuba [statement, August 2, 1989] R. Schifter. *Department of State Bulletin* 89:41-3 O '89
Reading between the lines in Havana. pors *U.S. News & World Report* 106:13 Ap 17 '89
The revolution at 30. S. McGuire. il por *Newsweek* 113:36-7 Ja 9 '89
The trial that shook Cuba [cover story] J. Preston. il pors *The New York Review of Books* 36:24-31 D 7 '89
CASTRO, JOSEPH
about
Caution urged on DNA fingerprinting. C. Norman. *Science* 245:699 Ag 18 '89
DNA typing is called flawed. R. Lewin. il *Science* 245:355 Jl 28 '89
DNA typing on the witness stand. R. Lewin. il *Science* 244:1033-5 Je 2 '89
Misprints. J. Kinoshita. *Scientific American* 261:12+ Ag '89
A trial of high-tech detectives. D. Thompson. il por *Time* 133:63 Je 5 '89
CASUALTIES OF WAR [film] *See* Motion picture reviews—Single works
CASUALTY LOSS DEDUCTIONS *See* Income tax—Loss deductions
CAT (COMPUTERIZED AXIAL TOMOGRAPHY) *See* Tomography
CAT FOOD *See* Cats—Food and feeding
CATALAN ART *See* Art, Catalan
CATALASE
Growing old together: fruit flies and you [effects of catalase production on cell aging in Drosophila; research by Glenn Bewley] il *Discover* 10:8 Ap '89
CATALOG HOUSES *See* Mail order business
CATALOG SHOWROOMS
See also
Service Merchandise Co., Inc.
CATALOGING
See also
Manuscripts—Cataloging
Catalogue your collection. M. J. Youngken. il *Americana* 16:16+ Ja/F '89
CATALOGS, BOOKSELLERS'
The book of Jason [J. Epstein's Reader's catalog] D. Smith. il pors *New York* 22:26-31 Ag 7 '89
CATALOGS, COMMERCIAL
See also
Spiegel, Inc.
But will they ever know Zytel from Lycra? [Du Pont and Deere & Co. introduce new mail order catalogs] S. B. Weiner. il *Forbes* 143:150+ Je 26 '89
Buy catalog. I. Dunn-Lee. il *Essence* 20:48 My '89
Forget the mall—it's in the mail. L. Laurence. il *New Choices for the Best Years* 29:72-3+ F '89
How the busy go shopping. M. Rowland. il *Working Woman* 14:47-8+ Ja '89
Machine dreams [kitchen equipment] B. Shacochis. il *Gentlemen's Quarterly* 59:358+ O '89
Outdoor catalogs: a divertissement. H. Middleton. il *Southern Living* 24:40+ Ja '89
Shop by mail catalogs. See issues of Glamour
Special delivery [tool catalogs] J. Truini. il *Popular Mechanics* 166:142 My '89
'Up to the chin' in catalogs [Christmas season] A. Miller. il *Newsweek* 114:57-8 N 20 '89
CATALOGS, PUBLISHERS'
Carol Publishing goes to the videotape [fall catalog] J. Mutter. il *Publishers Weekly* 236:25-6 Ag 18 '89
CATALOGS, SEED AND PLANT
A garden catalog collection. S. McInerney. il *Country Journal* 16:39-43 N/D '89
Gardening by mail. il *Better Homes and Gardens* 67:110 Ja '89
A guide to garden wishbooks. il *The Mother Earth News* 115:56-7 Ja/F '89
Looking for rare fruits? [Fruit, berry and nut inventory published by Seed Savers Exchange] *Sunset (Central West edition)* 183:196 O '89

Spellbound by seeds. R. Page. il *Country Journal* 16:34-6 Ja '89
These seed catalogs go beyond the garden variety. R. D. Hof. il *Business Week* p154 Ap 24 '89
Where to buy the less usual potatoes. il *Sunset (Central West edition)* 182:132 Ja '89
Where to find new plants '89. il *Flower and Garden* 33:56-7+ Ja/F '89
CATALOGS, TRADE *See* Catalogs, Commercial
CATALONIA (SPAIN)
Civilization
A thousand years of Catalan history. F. Vallverdú. il *The Courier (Unesco)* 42:26-8 My '89
Nationalism
Thriving without a state. D. H. Rosenthal. il *The Atlantic* 263:20+ Je '89
CATALYSTS AND CATALYSIS
See also
Chemzymes
Enzymes
Ribozymes
The design and catalytic properties of a simplified ribonuclease P RNA. D. S. Waugh and others. bibl f il *Science* 244:1569-71 Je 30 '89
New catalysts scavenge NO_x emissions. J. Raloff. *Science News* 135:271 Ap 29 '89
Peptide binding and release by proteins implicated as catalysts of protein assembly. G. C. Flynn and others. bibl f il *Science* 245:385-90 Jl 28 '89
Polymer synthesis and organotransition metal chemistry. R. H. Grubbs and W. Tumas. bibl f il *Science* 243:907-15 F 17 '89
CATALYTIC ANTIBODIES
Catalytic antibodies do greasy work. I. Amato. *Science News* 135:28 Ja 14 '89
Catalytic antibodies with lipase activity and *R* or *S* substrate selectivity. K. D. Janda and others. bibl f il *Science* 244:437-40 Ap 28 '89
Catalytic hydrolysis of vasoactive intestinal peptide by human autoantibody. S. Paul and others. bibl f il *Science* 244:1158-62 Je 9 '89
Enzymatic catalysts in organic synthesis. C.-H. Wong. bibl f il *Science* 244:1145-52 Je 9 '89
Generation of a catalytic antibody by site-directed mutagenesis. E. Baldwin and P. G. Schultz. bibl f il *Science* 245:1104-7 S 8 '89
Teaching antibodies new tricks [cover story] I. Amato. il *Science News* 136:152-3+ S 2 '89
Turning antibodies into chemists [work of Peter G. Schultz] I. Amato and J. Raloff. *Science News* 135:252 Ap 22 '89
Turning plants into antibody factories [work of Andrew Hiatt] *Science News* 136:334 N 18 '89
CATALYTIC RNA *See* Ribozymes
CATAMARAN RACING
See also
America's Cup races
CATAMARANS
Braving the Northwest Passage. J. MacInnis. il map *National Geographic* 175:584-601 My '89
Getting respect. K. Weisman. il *Forbes* 144:98-9 Ag 21 '89
The girl who loved cat sailing. J. Renfro. il por *Women's Sports & Fitness* 11:42-3 Je '89
CATANESE, ANTHONY JAMES
Architectural education: bridging the teaching/practice gap. por *Architectural Record* 177:47 Jl '89
CATAPANO, FRED
Science Q & A. il *The Atlantic* 263:32 Mr '89
CATARACTS (EYE DEFECT)
Nutritional aspects
Vitamins C and E may prevent cataracts [research by James McD. Robertson] I. Wickelgren. *Science News* 135:308 My 20 '89
Surgery
Check out eye doctor referrals. J. Wood. *Modern Maturity* 32:24 F/Mr '89
Lifting the clouds of cataracts. E. Hale. il *FDA Consumer* 23:26-8+ D '89/Ja '90
CATARACTS (WATERFALLS) *See* Ocean cataracts; Waterfalls
CATASTROPHE OPTICS
A drop of water becomes a gateway into the world of catastrophe optics. J. Walker. il *Scientific American* 261:176-9 S '89
CATASTROPHES *See* Disasters
CATASTROPHIC EXTINCTION OF SPECIES *See* Mass extinction of species
CATASTROPHIC HEALTH INSURANCE *See* Insurance, Health
CATASTROPHIC THINKING
"He's late. He's been in an accident. He's dead in a ditch. And I'll never, ever meet another man . . . ". E. Kaye. il *Mademoiselle* 95:176+ Ap '89
CATATONIA
The wolf at the door [lupus-induced catatonia] E. Rosenthal. il *Discover* 10:34+ F '89
CATBIRD PRESS
Humor and Czech writers are the calling cards from Catbird. J. Barbato. *Publishers Weekly* 236:28 O 13 '89

CATCH AND RELEASE FISHING See Fish protection
CATCHERS (BASEBALL PLAYERS) See Baseball players
CATE, MARSIE
about
The smart moves of Los Llanos Bookstore. M. Jones. il por *Publishers Weekly* 236:425-6+ Ag 11 '89
CATECHOLAMINES
See also
Dopamine
Norepinephrine
CATER, DAVID
Escaping the maze. il *Health (New York, N.Y.)* 21:64-9 Je '89
CATERERS AND CATERING
Affairs to remember. J. Freiman. il *Harper's Bazaar* 122:132+ Je '89
Mind your own business: Seventeen's guide to starting up a summer catering career. il *Seventeen* 48:119-20+ My '89
Ways to save on catering costs. S. Nielsen. il *Good Housekeeping* 208:251 My '89
CATERPILLAR INC.
Can Caterpillar inch its way back to heftier profits? B. Bremner. il *Business Week* p75+ S 25 '89
Cat aye. T. Jaffe. il *Forbes* 143:284 Je 26 '89
Caterpillar could turn into a butterfly. G. Weiss. il *Business Week* p59 Ag 7 '89
CATERPILLAR TRACTOR CO.
See also
Caterpillar Inc.
CATERPILLARS
See also
Bagworms
Gypsy moths
Inchworms
Tent caterpillars
Food and feeding
Caterpillar disguise: you are what you eat [work of Erick Greene with Nemoria arizonaria] I. Wickelgren. il *Science News* 135:70 F 4 '89
Caterpillars and polymorphisms [discussion of February 3, 1989 article, A diet-induced developmental polymorphism in a caterpillar] E. Greene. bibl f *Science* 246:1639-40 D 22 '89
A diet-induced developmental polymorphism in a caterpillar [Nemoria arizonaria; cover story] E. Greene. bibl f il *Science* 243:643-6 F 3 '89
Is diet destiny? [developmental polymorphism in caterpillars; research by Erick Greene] *Newsweek* 113:62 F 13 '89
CATEY, DAN
about
Neighbors are partners in his Hereford herd. L. F. Hoffman. por *Successful Farming* 87:44 F '89
CATFISH
See also
Cooking—Fish
Some catfishes of New York. E. Stegemann. il *The Conservationist* 44:38-45 Jl/Ag '89
CATFISH CULTURE See Fish culture
CATFISH FISHING
Among the liver eaters [channel catfish] J. M. Vance. il *Field & Stream* 94:16-17 Je '89
Boiling cats [waters below dams] B. Taylor. il *Outdoor Life* 184:72-3+ Ag '89
Cat with a million friends [channel catfish in Manitoba] P. Barrett. il *Field & Stream* 94:58-9+ Jl '89
CATHAY PACIFIC AIRWAYS LTD.
Cathay Pacific orders 10 A330s to replace L-1011s. J. M. Lenorovitz. il *Aviation Week & Space Technology* 130:91 Ap 10 '89
The right kind of problem. A. Tanzer. il *Forbes* 143:134+ Mr 20 '89
CATHCART, KEITH
about
Avalanche! R. D. LeBlanc. il *Reader's Digest* 135:129-33 D '89
CATHEDRAL OF ST. JOHN THE DIVINE (NEW YORK, N.Y.)
The gospel according to Verity [carving central entryway figures] B. Weber. il *The New York Times Magazine* p86 Jl 9 '89
Notes and comment [programs honoring M. L. King] *The New Yorker* 64:23-4 Ja 30 '89
CATHEDRALS
France
The Gothic revolution. il *National Geographic* 176:108-19 Jl '89
Ivory Coast
See also
Our Lady of Peace (Cathedral: Yamoussoukro, Ivory Coast)
New York (State)
See also
Cathedral of St. John the Divine (New York, N.Y.)
CATHEPSIN
Enzyme suggests breast cancer spread [cathepsin-D; research by Henri Rochefort] J. Raloff. *Science News* 136:325 N 18 '89

CATHERINE II, THE GREAT, EMPRESS OF RUSSIA, 1729-1796
about
Catherine the Great's Chinese jewel box. P. Lauritzen. il *Architectural Digest* 46:174-9 O '89
A Russian folly: visiting Catherine the Great's baroque roller coaster near Leningrad. P. Lauritzen. il por *Architectural Digest* 46:146-9+ My '89
CATHETERIZATION
See also
Cardiac catheterization
CATHODE RAY TUBE DISPLAY TERMINALS See Video display terminals
CATHOLIC AUTHORS
See also
Chesterton, G. K. (Gilbert Keith), 1874-1936
Endō, Shūsaku, 1923-
Girzone, Joseph F.
Keneally, Thomas
Kennedy, William, 1928-
CATHOLIC CHURCH
See also
Beatification
Canon law
Catholic traditionalist movement
Catholicism
Catholics
Fasts and feasts—Catholic Church
Laity—Catholic Church
Nuns
Papacy
Synod of Bishops (1987)
Vatican Council (2nd: 1962-1965)
The Church and its public life [address, May 18, 1989; cover story] M. O. Steinfels. *America* 160:550-8 Je 10 '89
Of many things [top Catholic news stories of 1980s] G. W. Hunt. *America* 161:462 D 23-30 '89
Who are the Catholic 'fundamentalists'? [cover story] J. A. Coleman. il *Commonweal* 116:42-7 Ja 27 '89
Attendance
See Church attendance
Authority
See also
Catholic Church—Teaching office
Loyalty oaths—Catholic Church
Popes—Infallibility
Academic freedom and the Catholic University of America [implications of Curran case] F. R. McManus. *America* 160:506-9 My 27 '89
The archbishops go to Rome. T. J. Reese. *America* 160:187-8 Mr 4 '89
Audition for tragedy [U.S. archbishops meet with the Pope in Rome] J. McNeal. *Commonweal* 116:228-31 Ap 21 '89
The battle for the Catholic Church [P. Lernoux's People of God] P. Berryman. por *The Christian Century* 106:523-6 My 17 '89
The Cologne Declaration [text of statement signed by German-speaking theologians; cover story] *Commonweal* 116:102-4 F 24 '89
Conflict in context. *Commonweal* 116:101 F 24 '89
The Curran decision [court upholds ban on his teaching theology at Catholic University of America] *America* 160:259 Mr 25 '89
Curran loses—so does Catholic education [suit against Catholic University of America] S. Maloney. *The Christian Century* 106:278-9 Mr 15 '89
Discussions in Rome [U.S. archbishops and Vatican officials] T. J. Reese. *America* 160:260-1 Mr 25 '89
Get with the program [U.S. archbishops meet with the Pope in Rome] K. L. Woodward. *Newsweek* 113:60 Mr 20 '89
In rejoinder: what next at Catholic U? [special section] il *Commonweal* 116:270-5+ My 5 '89
The Pope wins in court [removal of C. Curran from theology faculty at Catholic University upheld] R. N. Ostling. por *Time* 133:70 Mr 13 '89
The Pope's critics. J. Duquesne. il por *World Press Review* 36:56 Je '89
A reverence for fundamentalism. P. Lernoux. il *The Nation* 248:513-16 Ap 17 '89
The taming of a New Age prophet [M. Fox] R. Brow. il *Christianity Today* 33:28-30 Je 16 '89
U.S. bishops visit Pope. *The Christian Century* 106:345 Ap 5 '89
Verdicts yet to come [C. Curran vs. Catholic University; with excerpts from court decision] *Commonweal* 116:163-5+ Mr 24 '89
Blacks
See also
Imani Temple African-American Catholic Congregation
Black Catholics vs. the Church [problems in Detroit and Washington, D.C.] R. N. Ostling. il por *Time* 134:57 Jl 10 '89
Catholic bishops OK plan to recruit, retain blacks. il *Jet* 77:24-5 N 27 '89
Preaching the word & doing it: black Catholics in America. A. Raboteau. il *Commonweal* 116:631-2+ N 17 '89

CATHOLIC CHURCH—Blacks—*cont.*

Troubles they've seen: African-American Catholics. A. Levine. il *Commonweal* 116:550-1 O 20 '89

Clergy

See also

Bishops
Black priests
Catholic Church. National Conference of Catholic Bishops
Jesuits
Popes
Priests
Salesians

Teaching orders and the efficacy of school. P. Ellis. *America* 161:262-5 O 21 '89

Titles

God's children should be on a first-name basis. R. Tillemans. *U.S. Catholic* 54:37 Ag '89

Conferences

See Religious conferences

Converts

See Converts, Catholic

Devotions

See Catholic Church—Prayer books and devotions

Discipline

See also

Penance

Education

See also

Catholic Church. Congregation for Catholic Education
Catholic colleges and universities
Catholic schools
Jesuits—Education

Challenges facing U.S. Catholics. K. L. Woodward. *Commonweal* 116:618 N 17 '89

Converting the baptized [cover story] W. J. O'Malley. *America* 161:180-2+ S 30 '89

Scripture from scratch [cover story] W. J. O'Malley. *America* 160:77-81 F 4 '89

Why Catholics can't get enough of the Bible [cover story; special issue; with editorial comment by Robert E. Burns] il *U.S. Catholic* 54:2, 6-50+ S '89

Eucharist

Barred from Communion [prochoice assemblywoman L. Killea of San Diego] *The Christian Century* 106:1193-4 D 20-27 '89

Catholics won't settle for half a Mass [priestless liturgies; with readers' comments] T. Unsworth. *U.S. Catholic* 54:13-19 Je '89

Challenges facing U.S. Catholics. A. McCarthy. *Commonweal* 116:618-19 N 17 '89

Eucharist and tradition in the Middle Kingdom [China] E. LaVerdiere. *America* 161:162-4 S 23 '89

Eucharistic exposition: an obsolete relic? [cover story] K. McDonnell. il *America* 160:166-9 F 25 '89

A mistake in San Diego [Bishop L. T. Maher bars Assembly-woman L. Killea from receiving Communion because of pro-choice stand on abortion] *America* 161:416 D 9 '89

Standing in the way of worship. P. E. Dinter. il *Commonweal* 116:367-70 Je 16 '89

Standing in the way of worship [discussion of June 16, 1989 article] P. E. Dinter. *Commonweal* 116:495+ S 22 '89

Why settle for Communion? [in the absence of priests] G. Huck. *Commonweal* 116:37-9 Ja 27 '89

Foreign relations

See Catholic Church—Relations (Diplomatic)

Government

Autocracy isn't the Catholic style. P. S. Kaufman. il *Commonweal* 116:110-14 F 24 '89

The Pope's critics. J. Duquesne. il por *World Press Review* 36:56 Je '89

Infallibility

See also

Catholic Church—Teaching office
Popes—Infallibility

Liturgy and ritual

See also

Baptism
Catholic Church—Eucharist
Forty hours' devotion
Mass
Sacraments
Sign of peace (Catholic liturgy)

30 ways to decode liturgy lingo. K. Guentert. il *U.S. Catholic* 54:20-4 Jl '89

Liturgy in time of trouble. J. F. Baldovin. *America* 161:337-8 N 18 '89

Priestless rites: Catholic bishops okay services led by nuns and lay people. il *Time* 134:98 N 20 '89

Scripture: now starring in a liturgy near you. L. Jacquet. il *U.S. Catholic* 54:44-6 S '89

To found traditions of Catholic Church music. J. P. Swain. il *America* 161:186-9 S 30 '89

When laity lead. J. Figueroa. *Commonweal* 116:470-1 S 8 '89

Marriage

See Marriage—Catholic Church

Missions

See Missions

Music

See Religious music

Parishes

See Parishes

Prayer books and devotions

Are Catholics ashamed of their devotions? [interview with R. Orsi; cover story] por *U.S. Catholic* 54:6-13 N '89

Of thee (and thy, and thou) I sing. M. Finley. *America* 160:76 F 4 '89

Relations

Church of England

John Paul's ecumenical warning [opposition to women priests threatens Anglican-Catholic union] R. N. Ostling. il *Time* 133:96 My 8 '89

Episcopal Church

Of many things [M. Dally's account of acceptance of married Episcopal priest into Catholic priesthood] J. W. Donohue. *America* 160:362 Ap 22 '89

Judaism

Auschwitz and the nuns. W. F. Buckley. *National Review* 41:63 O 13 '89

The Auschwitz Carmel. *America* 161:179 S 30 '89

Auschwitz ire [controversial Carmelite convent] il *Time* 134:49 Ag 21 '89

Cardinal Glemp's memory lapse [Carmelite convent at Auschwitz] J. M. Wall. *The Christian Century* 106:867 O 4 '89

Close enough to step on toes: tensions between Jews & Catholics [Auschwitz convent controversy] L. Klenicki and E. D. Mallon. il *Commonweal* 116:521-6 O 6 '89

Détente at a death camp [dispute over Carmelite convent at Auschwitz] K. L. Woodward. il *Newsweek* 114:58 O 2 '89

The ghosts of an ancient plague [controversial Carmelite convent at Auschwitz] il *U.S. News & World Report* 107:10 S 11 '89

The Glemp controversy [Carmelite convent at Auschwitz] *The Christian Century* 106:808 S 13-20 '89

Harsh homily [J. Glemp's remarks concerning Carmelite convent at Auschwitz] *Time* 134:77 S 11 '89

Mea culpa, Auschwitz [agreement to move Carmelite convent] il *Time* 134:25 O 2 '89

Peace signals from the papal chimney [Pope John Paul II calls for removal of Carmelite convent at Auschwitz] il *U.S. News & World Report* 107:14 O 2 '89

Polish memories [Auschwitz convent controversy] J. Neusner. il *National Review* 41:27-8 O 27 '89

Pope John Paul II and the Jews. K. L. Woodward. il por *Newsweek* 114:36 S 11 '89

A sign of contradiction [Auschwitz convent controversy] J. T. Pawlikowski. il *Commonweal* 116:485-8 S 22 '89

The Vatican and the Jews [support for relocation of Carmelite convent from Auschwitz] il *The Christian Century* 106:873 O 4 '89

Whose Auschwitz? [dispute over Carmelite convent] il *National Review* 41:18+ S 29 '89

Whose Holocaust? [controversy over Carmelite convent at Auschwitz] R. Watson. il *Newsweek* 114:35-6 S 11 '89

Orthodox Eastern Church

Why the Orthodox Church has been such a mystery to Roman Catholics. J. Garvey. il *U.S. Catholic* 54:26-30 D '89

Protestant churches

Beyond protocol: the quest for unity [meeting Pope John Paul II] T. Hoyt, Jr. *The Christian Century* 106:926-7 O 18 '89

Ethical issues and ecumenism. T. P. Rausch. *America* 160:30-3 Ja 21 '89

Relations (Diplomatic)

Poland

No longer Poles apart. R. N. Ostling. il *Time* 134:44 Jl 31 '89

Soviet Union

See also

Gorbachev, Mikhail—Visit to the Vatican, 1989

Roman inroads [new Soviet bloc bishops] *Time* 134:43 Ag 7 '89

Rites and ceremonies

See also

Sacraments

Against R.C.I.A. [Rite of Christian Initiation for Adults; with reply by R. D. Duggan; cover story] A. M. Greeley. il *America* 161:231-7 O 14 '89

State of the question [discussion of October 14, 1989 article, Against R.C.I.A.] A. M. Greeley. *America* 161:328-30 N 11 '89

Societies

See also

Opus Dei (Society)
Society of the Sacred Heart

Teaching office

Bishops and theologians [bishops approve Doctrinal responsibilities statement] T. J. Reese. *America* 161:4-6 Jl 1-8 '89

CATHOLIC CHURCH—Teaching office—*cont.*

The Cologne Declaration [text of statement signed by German-speaking theologians; cover story] *Commonweal* 116:102-4 F 24 '89

A university perspective on the 'oath of fidelity'. Q. L. Quade. *America* 160:348-9 Ap 15 '89

Theology

See Theology

Tradition (Theology)

See Tradition (Theology)

Brazil

See also

Church and social problems—Brazil

Turning back the clock in Brazil. *America* 161:336 N 18 '89

Canada

A breach of faith [sex charges against priests in Newfoundland] G. Allen. il *Maclean's* 102:16-17 Mr 13 '89

A Church in crisis [sex scandals involving priests in Newfoundland] G. Allen. il *Maclean's* 102:66 N 27 '89

Sins of the flesh [sex charges against priests in Newfoundland] G. W. Taylor. il *Maclean's* 102:10-12 Jl 17 '89

Chile

Chile: a watershed in Church/state relations. J. Torrens. *America* 161:268-70+ O 28 '89

China

China friendships after June 4. E. J. Malatesta. *America* 161:132 S 9-16 '89

The Church in China [interview with J. Ching and H. Küng] P. H. Samway. *America* 160:374-6+ Ap 22 '89

Eucharist and tradition in the Middle Kingdom. E. LaVerdiere. *America* 161:162-4 S 23 '89

Czechoslovakia

Catholics under communism: the case of Czechoslovakia [cover story] P. Ramet. il *The Christian Century* 106:202-5 F 22 '89

Religion in Czechoslovakia, 1989. M. J. Lavelle. *America* 161:375-7 N 25 '89

East Timor (Indonesia)

See also

John Paul II, Pope, 1920——Visit to East Timor (Indonesia), 1989

Eastern Europe

Roman inroads [new Soviet bloc bishops] *Time* 134:43 Ag 7 '89

The triumph of John Paul II. S. Kanfer. il pors *Life* 12:34-40+ D '89

El Salvador

See also

Church and social problems—El Salvador

Barbarity in El Salvador [Jesuits murdered] *The Christian Century* 106:1112-13 N 29 '89

Celluloid evangelism [motion picture Romero] S. Ulstein. il por *Christianity Today* 33:77-8 N 3 '89

Death in El Salvador [murder of six Jesuit priests] J. Sobrino. il *Commonweal* 116:693-5 D 15 '89

Demonizing D'Aubuisson [role in assassination of Archbishop O. Romero] J. Morley. il *The Nation* 248:624-6 My 8 '89

The El Salvador horror [need for papal intervention] *The New Republic* 201:7-9 D 11 '89

Grave thoughts [conversation with Jesuit priest I. Ellacuria nine months before his murder] M. Massing. *The New Republic* 201:12-14 D 11 '89

In cold blood [murder of six Jesuit priests] *Time* 134:44 N 27 '89

In solidarity with the slain Jesuits of El Salvador [address, November 22, 1989] J. A. O'Hare. *America* 161:443-6 D 16 '89

In the name of God, stop the killing [Jesuit priests] R. A. Hyde. *The Christian Century* 106:1144 D 6 '89

'Now you be quiet, Oscar' [death squad killings] *America* 161:415 D 9 '89

Of many things [murder of Jesuits] T. H. Stahel. *America* 161:390 D 2 '89

Romero: evolution of a martyr [motion picture] D. G. Peerman. il *The Christian Century* 106:870-2 O 4 '89

France

See also

France—History—Revolution,   1789-1799—Catholic Church

L'affaire Touvier: opening old wounds. T. Morgan. il pors *The New York Times Magazine* p32-3+ O 1 '89

Another way to peace. C. Guicherd. il *Commonweal* 116:704-6 D 15 '89

The Church in France since the second Vatican Council. H. Madelin. il *America* 160:582-4+ Je 17-24 '89

The French Church in crisis [interview with J. Gaillot]; tr. by James P. Jurich. P. H. Samway. *America* 160:576-8+ Je 17-24 '89

Scandalous sanctuary [P. Touvier, French war criminal arrested] R. Marshall. il por *Newsweek* 113:44 Je 5 '89

A yawning chasm: French laity and bishops. G. Vahanian. *The Christian Century* 106:39 Ja 18 '89

Haiti

See also

Church and social problems—Haiti

Exalted violence [J.-B. Aristide expelled by Salesians] *The Nation* 248:76-7 Ja 23 '89

Hong Kong

The Hong Kong Church faces 1997. M. H. Kelleher. il *America* 161:63-4 Jl 29-Ag 5 '89

Hungary

In the realm of St. Stephen. T. P. O'Malley. *America* 161:312 N 11 '89

Ireland

Cardinal Ó Fiaich: my vision of a new Ireland [cover story] T. P. O'Mahony. *America* 160:238-40 Mr 18 '89

Latin America

See also

Church and social problems—Latin America

The Church in South America [cover story; special section] il *America* 161:266-70+ O 28 '89

Speaking in Latin tongues [cover story] D. Martin. il *National Review* 41:30-5 S 29 '89

Trying to hold on to the Medellín legacy [Notre Dame conference marks 20th anniversary of Latin American Bishops' Conference] D. G. Peerman. *The Christian Century* 106:403-4 Ap 19 '89

Bibliography

Books on Catholicism and inter-American affairs. A. F. Deck. *America* 161:279-81 O 28 '89

Mexico

See also

Church and social problems—Mexico

Church behind the scenes. M. W. Foley. *Commonweal* 116:549-50 O 20 '89

Nicaragua

Vagaries of religious experience in Nicaragua [cover story] T. C. Wright. il *America* 161:158-61 S 23 '89

Northern Ireland

Cardinal Ó Fiaich: my vision of a new Ireland [cover story] T. P. O'Mahony. *America* 160:238-40 Mr 18 '89

Peru

See also

Church and social problems—Peru

Philippines

Reinventing the brake [family planning] J. Miller. *Commonweal* 116:105-7 F 24 '89

Poland

Can Poland ever be free? A. Besançon. *Commentary* 87:15-20 Ap '89

Faith goes legal in Warsaw. L. Cryderman. *Christianity Today* 33:15 Jl 14 '89

God, man (and Marx) [legalization of Church] il *U.S. News & World Report* 106:11-12 My 29 '89

The triumph of John Paul II. S. Kanfer. il pors *Life* 12:34-40+ D '89

Puerto Rico

Political crossroads for islands of enchantment. J. F. Talbot. *America* 161:142-4 S 9-16 '89

Ukraine

From underground, a Church blooms. F. Coleman. il *Newsweek* 114:92+ D 4 '89

Gorby's bow to the Roman legions. il pors *U.S. News & World Report* 107:15 D 11 '89

United States

See also

Campaign for Human Development

Catholic Church. National Conference of Catholic Bishops

Catholics—United States

Parishes

65 [special issue] il *Commonweal* 116:611-32+ N 17 '89

The archbishops go to Rome. T. J. Reese. *America* 160:187-8 Mr 4 '89

Audition for tragedy [U.S. archbishops meet with the Pope in Rome] J. McNeal. *Commonweal* 116:228-31 Ap 21 '89

The Church: looking to the future [cover story] J. H. Fichter. *America* 160:189-92 Mr 4 '89

Confessions of an erstwhile evangelizer. R. E. Burns. *U.S. Catholic* 54:2 N '89

Data and mystery: a decade of studies on Catholic leadership [Lilly Foundation research] J. R. Kelly. *America* 161:345-6+ N 18 '89

Discussions in Rome [U.S. archbishops and Vatican officials] T. J. Reese. *America* 160:260-1 Mr 25 '89

Fifty years of changing minds & structures [priest D. Cantwell of Chicago] T. Unsworth. il *Commonweal* 116:365-7 Je 16 '89

Get with the program [U.S. archbishops meet with the Pope in Rome] K. L. Woodward. *Newsweek* 113:60 Mr 20 '89

Of many things [Thomas J. Reese's Archbishop: inside the power structure of the American Catholic Church] G. W. Hunt. *America* 160:442 My 13 '89

A survey of research on Church life today [Lilly Endowment study of U.S. Catholic leaders] T. Schier. *America* 161:351-2 N 18 '89

U.S. bishops visit Pope. *The Christian Century* 106:345 Ap 5 '89

The view from St. Patrick's [J. Cardinal O'Connor] J. Berger. il pors *The New York Times Magazine* p38-40+ Mr 26 '89

CATHOLIC CHURCH—United States—*cont.*
History
The Catholic experience at taming pluralism [cover story] J. M. McShane. il *The Christian Century* 106:443-6 Ap 26 '89
Join it, work it, fight it [public Catholicism] D. J. O'Brien. il *Commonweal* 116:624-30 N 17 '89
Vietnam
American archbishops visit Vietnam. R. Bautch. *America* 160:132-3 F 18 '89
Western Europe
Standing in the way of worship. P. E. Dinter. il *Commonweal* 116:367-70 Je 16 '89
Standing in the way of worship [discussion of June 16, 1989 article] P. E. Dinter. *Commonweal* 116:495+ S 22 '89
Vatican under fire [European theologians protest appointment of conservative archbishops] *Time* 133:57 F 6 '89
CATHOLIC CHURCH. CONGREGATION FOR CATHOLIC EDUCATION
From Rome with hope [international congress on Catholic higher education] E. A. Malloy. *America* 160:548-9+ Je 10 '89
Good news, but . . . [draft document on higher education] *Commonweal* 116:325-6 Je 2 '89
Loading the blunderbuss [draft of papal document on higher education] *Commonweal* 116:35-6 Ja 27 '89
Rome and higher education [A draft document on Catholic higher education] *America* 160:339 Ap 15 '89
The Vatican and Catholic universities. J. A. O'Hare. *America* 160:503-5 My 27 '89
CATHOLIC CHURCH. CONGREGATION FOR THE DOCTRINE OF THE FAITH
Catholic oaths and academic freedom. M. B. Lukens. *The Christian Century* 106:982-4 N 1 '89
Inflating the oath. J. A. Coriden. il *Commonweal* 116:455-6 S 8 '89
New loyalty oath. *The Christian Century* 106:377 Ap 12 '89
Of many things [Harvey Cox's The silencing of Leonardo Boff] G. W. Hunt. *America* 160:98 F 11 '89
On Bernard Häring's new book. B. Häring. *America* 161:339-40 N 18 '89
Profession of faith and the 'oath of fidelity'. L. M. Orsy. *America* 160:345-7+ Ap 15 '89
A university perspective on the 'oath of fidelity'. Q. L. Quade. *America* 160:348-9 Ap 15 '89
The Vatican heresy [Instruction on respect for human life in its origins and on the dignity of procreation] W. Michalsky. il *The Humanist* 49:27+ N/D '89
Anecdotes, facetiae, satire, etc.
Forged teaching [revised loyalty oath] M. E. Marty. *The Christian Century* 106:455 Ap 26 '89
CATHOLIC CHURCH. NATIONAL CONFERENCE OF CATHOLIC BISHOPS
Bishops and theologians [bishops approve Doctrinal responsibilities statement] T. J. Reese. *America* 161:4-6 Jl 1-8 '89
Bishops meet in Baltimore. T. J. Reese. *America* 161:369 N 25 '89
Bishops on bishops [upcoming elections] T. J. Reese. *America* 161:290-3 N 4 '89
Bishops, politicians and abortion [cover story] R. J. McManus. *America* 161:294-6+ N 4 '89
Bishops' principles for Middle East peace. C. A. Kimball. *The Christian Century* 106:972-3 N 1 '89
Catholic bishops OK plan to recruit, retain blacks. il *Jet* 77:24-5 N 27 '89
Favor debt cancellation [statement on third world debt] *The Christian Century* 106:976-7 N 1 '89
It's not all that complicated [Relieving third world debt] *America* 161:263-4 O 28 '89
Of many things [Reflections on the morale of priests] G. W. Hunt. *America* 160:26 Ja 21 '89
Those turbulent bishops [New York times' criticism of positions taken by Catholic bishops] R. J. Neuhaus. il *National Review* 41:32-3 D 31 '89
Triple play [statements on the Middle East, AIDS, and third world debt] *Commonweal* 116:581-2 N 3 '89
The U.S. bishops' statements on AIDS. *America* 161:391 D 2 '89
U.S. Catholic Bishops convene. *The Christian Century* 106:1080-1 N 22 '89
CATHOLIC CHURCH AND ABORTION *See* Abortion—Moral and religious aspects
CATHOLIC CHURCH AND AIDS (DISEASE) *See* AIDS (Disease)—Religious aspects
CATHOLIC CHURCH AND BIRTH CONTROL *See* Birth control—Moral and religious aspects
CATHOLIC CHURCH AND CHILDREN *See* Church work with children
CATHOLIC CHURCH AND CIVIL RIGHTS *See* Church and civil rights
CATHOLIC CHURCH AND COMMUNISM *See* Communism and religion
CATHOLIC CHURCH AND ECONOMICS *See* Christianity and economics

CATHOLIC CHURCH AND ETHICS *See* Christian ethics
CATHOLIC CHURCH AND HOMOSEXUALITY *See* Homosexuality and Christianity
CATHOLIC CHURCH AND NARCOTICS TRADE *See* Church and narcotics trade
CATHOLIC CHURCH AND OTHER RELIGIONS *See* Christianity and other religions
CATHOLIC CHURCH AND POLITICS *See* Religion and politics
CATHOLIC CHURCH AND RACE RELATIONS *See* Church and race relations
CATHOLIC CHURCH AND REPRODUCTION *See* Reproduction—Moral and religious aspects
CATHOLIC CHURCH AND SCIENCE *See* Religion and science
CATHOLIC CHURCH AND SEX *See* Sex and religion
CATHOLIC CHURCH AND SOCIAL PROBLEMS *See* Church and social problems
CATHOLIC CHURCH AND SOCIALISM *See* Socialism and religion
CATHOLIC CHURCH AND THE DYING *See* Church work with the dying
CATHOLIC CHURCH AND THE PRESS *See* Church and the press
CATHOLIC CHURCH AND WOMEN *See* Women and religion
CATHOLIC COLLEGE STUDENTS *See* College students
CATHOLIC COLLEGES AND UNIVERSITIES
See also
Catholic University of America
Georgetown University
Seton Hall University
Sister Thea Bowman Black Catholic Educational Foundation
University of Notre Dame
The mission and ministry of Jesuits in higher education [address, June 5, 1989; cover story] F. H. T. Rhodes. *America* 161:54-60 Jl 29-Ag 5 '89
The Order of Education [Jesuit schools] K. L. Woodward. il *Newsweek* 113:59 Je 19 '89
Sex (how about love?) on Catholic campuses [with discussion; cover story] D. J. O'Brien. *Commonweal* 116:169-77 Mr 24 '89
Laws and regulations
Catholic oaths and academic freedom. M. B. Lukens. *The Christian Century* 106:982-4 N 1 '89
From Rome with hope [international congress on Catholic higher education] E. A. Malloy. *America* 160:548-9+ Je 10 '89
Good news, but . . . [draft document on higher education from the Vatican Congregation for Catholic Education] *Commonweal* 116:325-6 Je 2 '89
Loading the blunderbuss [draft of papal document on higher education] *Commonweal* 116:35-6 Ja 27 '89
New loyalty oath. *The Christian Century* 106:377 Ap 12 '89
Rome and higher education [A draft document on Catholic higher education] *America* 160:339 Ap 15 '89
A university perspective on the 'oath of fidelity'. Q. L. Quade. *America* 160:348-9 Ap 15 '89
The Vatican and Catholic universities. J. A. O'Hare. *America* 160:503-5 My 27 '89
CATHOLIC CONVERTS *See* Converts, Catholic
CATHOLIC EDUCATION *See* Catholic colleges and universities; Catholic schools
CATHOLIC ETHICS *See* Christian ethics
CATHOLIC LAITY *See* Laity—Catholic Church
CATHOLIC LEADERSHIP *See* Christian leadership
CATHOLIC MISSIONS *See* Missions
CATHOLIC PARISHES *See* Parishes
CATHOLIC PRESS
See also
Commonweal (Periodical)
U.S. Catholic (Periodical)
A survey of research on Church life today [Lilly Endowment study of U.S. Catholic leaders] T. Schier. *America* 161:351-2 N 18 '89
CATHOLIC-PROTESTANT MARRIAGE *See* Interfaith marriage
CATHOLIC SCHOOL TEACHERS *See* Nuns as teachers
CATHOLIC SCHOOLS
Catholic schools: a golden twilight? A. M. Greeley. *America* 160:106+ F 11 '89
Convent school [Manhattan's Notre Dame School operated by Sisters of St. Ursula] J. W. Donohue. *America* 160:288-95+ Ap 1 '89
Don't sell Catholic schools short [with readers' comments] A. M. Greeley. *U.S. Catholic* 54:14-20 Mr '89
Intellectual decapitalization. *America* 161:252 O 21 '89
The lessons of St. Joe's [St. Joseph of the Palisades High School, West New York, N.J.] A. DePalma. il por *The New York Times Magazine* p34-7 F 5 '89
Of more than parochial interest. J. Rachlin and P. Glastris. il *U.S. News & World Report* 106:61-2 My 22 '89
Teaching orders and the efficacy of school. P. Ellis. *America* 161:262-5 O 21 '89

CATHOLIC SCHOOLS—*cont.*

Those were the days [V. V. Harrison's book describing changes since Vatican II in secondary schools operated by Society of the Sacred Heart] J. W. Donohue. il *America* 161:258-61 O 21 '89

Unlikely champs [St. Anthony's of Jersey City, N.J. deemed best high school basketball team in America] il pors *Life* 12:68-70+ My '89

Why Catholic schools outperform all others [interview with J. S. Coleman; cover story] por *U.S. Catholic* 54:6-12 Jl '89

Federal aid

The 'education president' meets with Catholic educators. S. P. McHenry. *America* 161:52-3 Jl 29-Ag 5 '89

President Bush and school choice. *America* 160:99 F 11 '89

CATHOLIC THEOLOGY See Theology

CATHOLIC TRADITIONALIST MOVEMENT

The Lefebvrite-feminist coalition? M. McGough. il *The American Spectator* 22:28-9 Ag '89

CATHOLIC UNIVERSITY OF AMERICA

Academic freedom and the Catholic University of America [implications of Curran case] F. R. McManus. *America* 160:506-9 My 27 '89

The Curran decision [court upholds ban on his teaching theology] *America* 160:259 Mr 25 '89

Curran loses—so does Catholic education. S. Maloney. *The Christian Century* 106:278-9 Mr 15 '89

In rejoinder: what next at Catholic U? [special section] il *Commonweal* 116:270-5+ My 5 '89

The Pope wins in court [removal of C. Curran from theology faculty upheld] R. N. Ostling. por *Time* 133:70 Mr 13 '89

Verdicts yet to come [C. Curran vs. Catholic University; with excerpts from court decision] *Commonweal* 116:163-5+ Mr 24 '89

CATHOLICISM

See also

Anti-Catholicism

There's no such thing as a Catholic fundamentalist. E. LaVerdiere. il *U.S. Catholic* 54:36-8 S '89

Who are the Catholic 'fundamentalists'? [cover story] J. A. Coleman. il *Commonweal* 116:42-7 Ja 27 '89

CATHOLICISM IN LITERATURE See Religion in literature

CATHOLICS

See also

Clothing and dress—Catholics

The empty convent. H. Fehren. *U.S. Catholic* 54:39-41 Jl '89

Intellectual life

American Catholic intellectual life [cover story; special section] *America* 160:412-26+ My 6 '89

Getting our heads together. S. C. Callahan. il *Commonweal* 116:635-42 N 17 '89

Japan

The message the Japanese have missed [views of S. Endo] P. Yancey. il *Christianity Today* 33:56 Mr 17 '89

A silence that is not hollow [works of S. Endo] E. Beverly. il por *Commonweal* 116:491-4 S 22 '89

Northern Ireland

A 20th anniversary with nothing to celebrate. M. Skelton. il *Christianity Today* 33:36-7 Mr 17 '89

Daughters of Derry [Catholic women] N. McCafferty. il *Ms.* 18:72-7 S '89

United States

American Catholic intellectual life [cover story; special section] *America* 160:412-26+ My 6 '89

Challenges facing U.S. Catholics [special section] il *Commonweal* 116:617-32+ N 17 '89

[Column] H. Fehren. See issues of U.S. Catholic

The examined life. R. E. Burns. See issues of U.S. Catholic

How to get through to a lapsed Catholic [cover story] J. Deedy. il *U.S. Catholic* 54:6-13 Ap '89

On the margins of the Church: a sociological note [surveys by ABC News and Gallup] A. M. Greeley. il *America* 160:194-5+ Mr 4 '89

Seeking meaning [lapsed Catholic creates own rituals] J. Callahan. il *Glamour* 87:326 S '89

Who's first? Good Catholics, good fans. K. Holland. *Commonweal* 116:582-3 N 3 '89

Why Catholics can't get enough of the Bible [cover story; special issue; with editorial comment by Robert E. Burns] il *U.S. Catholic* 54:2, 6-50+ S '89

Political activities

Of many things [Catholics in Congress] G. W. Hunt. *America* 160:74 F 4 '89

CATHOLICS AND JEWS See Christianity and other religions

CATHOLICS AND OTHER RELIGIONS See Christianity and other religions

CATION CHANNELS See Ion channels

CATLIN, GEORGE, 1796-1872

about

Going back to the past, using collotype art. J. P. Frank. il *Publishers Weekly* 236:62-4 Ag 4 '89

CATLIN COBB AND DANCERS

Reviews:

Performances at Bessie Schönberg Theater. J. Lewis. *Dance Magazine* 63:22 Ja '89

CATO

Letter from Washington. See issues of National Review

CATO, PHILLIP C.

The management of the biosphere [address, July 19, 1989] *Vital Speeches of the Day* 56:53-5 N 1 '89

CATO, SUSANA

New from García Márquez. il por *World Press Review* 36:60 Je '89

CATO INSTITUTE

An end to monetary instability? [privatizing money] P. Brimelow. il *Forbes* 143:120+ Ap 3 '89

CATON-JONES, MICHAEL

about

Scandal [film] Reviews

American Film il 14:10-11 Mr '89. A. Barra

The American Spectator il 22:37-8 Jl '89. B. Bawer

Commonweal 116:371-2 Je 16 '89. T. O'Brien

Film Comment il 25:56-8+ Mr/Ap '89. G. Fuller

Gentlemen's Quarterly il 59:328-31 Mr '89

Glamour il 87:226+ Ap '89. D. Denicolo

Maclean's il 102:58-9 My 22 '89. B. D. Johnson

The Nation 248:787-8 Je 5 '89. S. Klawans

National Review 41:53-4+ Je 30 '89. J. Simon

The New Leader 72:20-1 My 1 '89. J. Morrone

The New Republic 200:24-5 My 29 '89. S. Kauffmann

New York il 22:78+ My 8 '89. D. Denby

The New Yorker 65:121-2 My 15 '89. P. Kael

Newsweek il 113:76 My 1 '89. J. Kroll

People Weekly 31:12 My 22 '89. S. Haller

Rolling Stone p40 Ap 20 '89. J. Kaplan

Rolling Stone il p39 My 18 '89. P. Travers

Time il 133:68 My 1 '89. R. Corliss

Video il 13:76 N '89. I. Robbins

Vogue il 179:506-9 Mr '89. A. Waugh

CATROUX, FRANÇOIS

about

Haut Catroux. C. Petkanas. il *House & Garden* 161:160-7+ Ap '89

CATS

Are cats smart? P. W. Moser. il *Reader's Digest* 135:112-16 O '89

Attack of the killer cats [study by Peter Churcher and John Lawton on predatory habits] L. Jaroff. il *Time* 134:46 Jl 31 '89

The cat's meow. il *Seventeen* 48:182+ Mr '89

Home is where the cat is. P. La Farge. il *Parents* 64:120-2 O '89

The inscrutable cat; The cat's meow. L. Spiotta-DeMare. il *American Health* 8:128 S '89

Anecdotes, facetiae, satire, etc.

Our son the cat. K. Fury. il *New Choices for the Best Years* 29:92 Ja '89

Breeding

Domestic cat bears exotic kitten [endangered Indian desert cat born at Cincinnati Zoo] il *Science News* 135:172 Mr 18 '89

Wild child [Indian desert cat born to surrogate domestic mother at Cincinnati Zoo] il *Discover* 10:12 Jl '89

Care

See also

Last Post (Conn.)

The aging pet. R. Kidd. *The Mother Earth News* 118:34-6 Jl/Ag '89

Exercising your cat and dog. S. L. Gerstenfeld. il *Parents* 64:202 F '89

On the move with your cat. A. R. Marder. il *Prevention (Emmaus, Pa.)* 41:110+ S '89

Diseases and pests

See also

Rabies

Feline leukemia. R. Kidd. il *The Mother Earth News* 119:34+ S/O '89

Equipment

Jane Talkington's Kitty video gives hungry cats a view that forever fascinates [videotape of birds] il *People Weekly* 32:99 N 13 '89

Eye

See Eye—Animals

Food and feeding

Beware of well-fed felines. P. B. Churcher and J. H. Lawton. il *Natural History* p40-7 Jl '89

Hold the tuna [risk of mercury poisoning from cat food] V. Adler. *American Health* 8:110 Jl/Ag '89

A tuna a day makes the cat slow to play [research by Katherine A. Houpt] *Science News* 135:111 F 18 '89

Photographs and photography

Cats now officially no. 1, these were always—as these charming photos show—the pet of choice for some Americans. il *Good Housekeeping* 208:61 Je '89

Vision

See Vision—Animals

Wounds and injuries

How cats survive falls from New York skyscrapers [research by Wayne Whitney and Cheryl Mehlhaff] J. M. Diamond. il *Natural History* p20-6 Ag '89

CATS, EFFECT OF TEMPERATURE ON

Hot car caveat [views of Michael Garvey] M. Behen. *American Health* 8:118 Je '89

CATS, WILD
See also
Bobcats
Leopards
Pumas
Servals
CATS AND CHILDREN See Children and animals
CATS AS CARRIERS OF INFECTION
Annals of medicine [cat-related outbreak of Q fever in Nova Scotia] B. Roueché. *The New Yorker* 65:100-5 S 4 '89
CATS IN MOTION PICTURES
Wherefore art thou Romeo, if Juliet is a castrated cat? [adaptation of Shakespeare play directed by A. Acosta] J. Stark. il por *People Weekly* 31:281-3 Mr 6 '89
CATSIMATIDIS, JOHN
about
"They hated me". J. Flint. il por *Forbes* 144:240-1 O 30 '89
CATSKILL MOUNTAINS REGION (N.Y.)
See also
Architecture, Domestic—Catskill Mountains region (N.Y.)
CATSUP
See also
H. J. Heinz Co.
CATTAILS
Tuttle Marsh, Michigan. R. H. Mohlenbrock. il maps *Natural History* p72+ Je '89
CATTLE
See also
Beef
Calves
Cows
Bovine madness [cattle burps as source of atmospheric methane] J. Stone. il *Discover* 10:38+ F '89
Breeding
The big picture [integrated reproductive management] B. Eftink and J. Walter. il *Successful Farming* 87:42-3 F '89
Double muscle, double trouble? C. Peterson, Jr. il *Successful Farming* 87:36-7 Ap '89
Get nosy, cattlemen [genetic tracking] V. Ehmke. il *Successful Farming* 87:34 S '89
Neighbors are partners in his Hereford herd [D. Catey] L. F. Hoffman. por *Successful Farming* 87:44 F '89
Confinement methods
See also
Cattle feedlots
Diseases and pests
Bovine leukemia's hidden toll [research by Harris A. Lewin] *Science News* 135:123 F 25 '89
Healthy herds major problem of beef producers. D. Eaheart. *Successful Farming* 87:10 N '89
Trespassers will be poisoned [endophyte-infected tall fescue] K. Clay. il *Natural History* p8+ S '89
Feeding
See also
Cattle feedlots
Grazing
All milo is not created equal. *Successful Farming* 87 no4:38 Mr '89
Combine grain, steal the stalks! il *Successful Farming* 87:48X N '89
Leaner and meatier [use of beta agonists for hogs and beef] J. R. Borcherding and C. Peterson, Jr. il *Successful Farming* 87:40 D '89
Mutilation
UFO update. P. Noonan. il *Omni (New York, N.Y.)* 12:121 D '89
Prices
Buy cows, not heifers. L. Stalcup. il *Successful Farming* 87:30 mid-Mr '89
Theft
A new kind of rustler hits the heartland. J. M. Schrof. il *U.S. News & World Report* 107:45 Ag 7 '89
CATTLE BARNS See Barns and stables
CATTLE DRIVES
Cattle driving for fun [Wyoming] S. Cohen. il map *Travel Holiday* 171:68-71 F '89
CATTLE FARM MANAGEMENT
The big picture [integrated reproductive management] B. Eftink and J. Walter. il *Successful Farming* 87:42-3 F '89
Cattleman's nightmare [drought] V. Ehmke. il *Successful Farming* 87:38 Ag '89
CATTLE FEEDLOTS
See also
Commercial Cattle Feeders of Iowa
A calf named 'Opportunity' [feeder-calf prices; cover story] B. Eftink. il *Successful Farming* 87:11 Ap '89
Feeders, cow-calf producers stress different factors. *Successful Farming* 87:35 My '89
Feedlots using creative means to stay full. *Successful Farming* 87:32H Ag '89
CATTLE INDUSTRY
See also
Commercial Cattle Feeders of Iowa
Feeders, cow-calf producers stress different factors. *Successful Farming* 87:35 My '89

CATTLE RANCHES See Ranches
CATTLE RUSTLERS See Cattle—Theft
CATTO, HENRY
Anthony agonistes. il *National Review* 41:34-7+ S 1 '89
CATTON, WILLIAM ROBERT, 1926-
Choosing which danger to risk. *Society* 27:6-8 N/D '89
CATV SYSTEM See Cable television; Cable television, Black
CAUCASUS COOKING See Cooking, Caucasus
CAUCUSES
See also
Congressional Black Caucus
Democratic Leadership Council
House Democratic Caucus (U.S.)
Great Britain
See also
Parliamentary Black Caucus
CAUDILL, JEFFERY C.
Plasma display globe. il *Radio-Electronics* 60:62-4 Ja '89
CAULFIELD, H. J. (HENRY JOHN), 1936-
about
'I think we can be the next IBM'. D. Foust. il por *Business Week* Special Issue:86 Je 16 '89
CAULFIELD, HENRY JOHN See Caulfield, H. J. (Henry John), 1936-
CAULIFLOWER
Setting the record straight on cauliflower. il *Sunset (Central West edition)* 183:180+ S '89
CAUNITZ, WILLIAM J.
about
Police story. C. S. Smith. il por *New York* 22:30 Mr 13 '89
CAUSA (ORGANIZATION)
Moon struck. S. Hornik. *Common Cause Magazine* 15:11-12 Mr/Ap '89
CAUSATION
The perception of intention [study of preschool children] V. Dasser and others. bibl f *Science* 243:365-7 Ja 20 '89
CAUSE AND EFFECT See Causation
CAUSES OF DEATH See Death—Causes
CAUVIN, JEAN See Calvin, Jean, 1509-1564
CAVANAGH, WALTER
about
You gotta give a card like Walter some credit. il por *People Weekly* 31:69 Ja 30 '89
CAVAZOS, LAURO FRED, 1927-
Building bridges for at-risk children. *The Education Digest* 55:16-19 N '89
The huge problem in American schools [address, December 6, 1988] *Vital Speeches of the Day* 55:236-8 F 1 '89
Restructuring American education through choice [address, May 19, 1989] *Vital Speeches of the Day* 55:514-16 Je 15 '89
about
The do-nothing Education Secretary. por *Newsweek* 114:56 O 2 '89
Go to the rear of the class. S. Tifft. il por *Time* 133:76 My 29 '89
Lauro's themes. *The New Republic* 201:7-8 Jl 10 '89
Shortest education presidency? *National Review* 41:11-12 Mr 24 '89
CAVE DRAWINGS AND PAINTINGS
The bones from Brazil [evidence of earlier New World migration date; work of Maria Beltrão and Niède Guidon] H. Pringle. il *Omni (New York, N.Y.)* 11:26+ Ap '89
The first wildlife artists. S. Begley. il *International Wildlife* 19:22-7 Mr/Ap '89
CAVENDISH, ANDREW ROBERT BUXTON See Devonshire, Andrew Robert Buxton Cavendish, 11th Duke of, 1920-
CAVES
South Dakota
See also
Jewel Cave National Monument (S.D.)
Western States
Going underground. il map *Sunset (Central West edition)* 183:58-63 Jl '89
CAVETT, DICK
Candice Bergen: she's no dummy. por *TV Guide* 37:7-9 D 23-29 '89
CAVIAR
Caviar that doesn't cost you royally. T. Segal. il *Business Week* p180 N 13 '89
CAVINDER, FRED D., 1931-
Beekeepers gather for sweet talk. il *The Saturday Evening Post* 261:14 Ap '89
CAVITANDS
Building up better synthetic receptors [research by Donald J. Cram] I. Amato. il *Science News* 135:327 My 27 '89
CAVITATION
The chemical effects of ultrasound. K. S. Suslick. bibl il *Scientific American* 260:80-6 F '89
CAVITIES, DENTAL See Dental caries
CAWTHORN, ROBERT E.
Are U.S. multi-nationals ready for the U.S. of Europe? [address, May 16, 1989] *Vital Speeches of the Day* 55:654-7 Ag 15 '89

CAWTHORN, ROBERT E.—*cont.*
about
Please pass the Maalox. J. Novack. il por *Forbes* 144:114-15
Ag 7 '89
CAYAPO INDIANS
The Amazon's savvy Indians. M. Simons. il map *The New
York Times Magazine* p36-7+ F 26 '89
CAYMAN ISLANDS
Industries
See also
Turtle fisheries—Cayman Islands
CAYTON, BILL
about
Tyson no 'slave,' King testifies against Cayton. por *Jet* 75:47
Mr 6 '89
CBA *See* Christian Booksellers Association; Continental Basket-
ball Association
CBC *See* Canadian Broadcasting Corporation
CBI *See* Caribbean Basin Initiative
CBN *See* Christian Broadcasting Network, Inc.
CBS INC.
Baskets full of money [pays $1 billion to keep NCAA
basketball tournament] H. J. Steinbreder. il *Sports Illustrated*
71:66-7 D 4 '89
CBS has won the World Series . . . now it could lose
its shirt. L. Shames. il *The New York Times Magazine*
p20-4 Jl 23 '89
Dan Rather's difficult days. J. Rovin. il pors *Ladies' Home
Journal* 106:80+ Ja '89
A day in the life of the evening news [D. Rather broadcast]
D. O. Relin. il por *Scholastic Update (Teachers' edition)*
122:7-9 S 8 '89
Days of distress at CBS. R. Zoglin. il *Time* 134:91 D 25
'89
The Greek in purgatory [Jimmy the Greek] M. Lupica. il
Esquire 111:43-4+ Ja '89
Howard Stringer. D. Lieberman. il por *Business Week* Special
Issue:130 Ap 14 '89
It's going, going, going . . . [network baseball coverage curtailed
in new contract] C. Smith. il por *Sports Illustrated* 70:104
Ap 17 '89
Last laugh [SBK sells former CBS music publishing division
to Thorn EMI] L. Gubernick. il por *Forbes* 143:41-2 F
20 '89
'No excuses' for Stringer's CBS team [interview with H.
Stringer] il pors *Channels (New York, N.Y.: 1986)* 9:86-7
Je '89
On network falls and balls [deal for baseball rights] M.
Brown. il *Channels (New York, N.Y.: 1986)* 9:40 F '89
Picking up the pieces [fall promotion campaigns] J. Flinn.
il *Channels (New York, N.Y.: 1986)* 9:14 Je '89
Pilson's progress [Sports president N. Pilson] A. Snyder.
il por *Channels (New York, N.Y.: 1986)* 9:58-62 Jl/Ag
'89
Rather strange: behind Dan's odd behavior. R. Townley.
il pors *TV Guide* 37:4-7 F 25-Mr 3 '89
Truth and consequences [CBS's alleged use of faked footage
of Afghan war] il *Time* 134:98 O 9 '89
Winning Diane: how ABC's Roone Arledge snatched her
away from CBS [cover story] E. Klein. il pors *New York*
22:36-43 Mr 13 '89
CBS INC. MAGAZINES DIVISION
Living out every manager's dream [buying and then selling
off former CBS magazine group] P. G. Diamandis. il
por *Fortune* 120:109+ O 9 '89
CBS RECORDS INC.
Even for Walter Yetnikoff, this will be a stretch: can Sony's
ace juggle both Columbia and CBS Records? D. Lieberman.
il por *Business Week* p144-5 O 30 '89
Revenge of the antisuits [Sony's takeover] S. N. Chakravarty.
il *Forbes* 144:49+ D 11 '89
Watch on the Elbe [G. Breest leaves Deutsche Grammophon
to head CBS Masterworks] T. W. Libbey, Jr. il *High
Fidelity (New York, N.Y.)* 39:55 Ja '89
CCA *See* Club Corp. of America
CCC *See* California Conservation Corps
CCDS *See* Charge coupled devices (Electronics)
CCM *See* Christian contemporary music
CCNY *See* City College of New York
CD-ROM (COMPACT DISC-READ ONLY MEMORY)
CDs come to consumers [CD-ROM from Egghead] P. Scisco.
Compute! 11:10 Ja '89
Compact-disc recorder [Meridian Data's system] J. Free. il
Popular Science 235:19-21 S '89
Compact disks for PCs put a library at your fingertips.
K. H. Hammonds. il *Business Week* p112 Ja 23 '89
Gadgets no more: computers take hold in education and
research. D. Stanton. *Compute!* 11:106 N '89
Multimedia: seeing is deceiving. P. Saffo. il *Personal
Computing* 13:181-2 Ag '89
New titles show diversity of CD-ROM. *Byte* 14:18+ D '89
Tomorrow's vision builds on today's reality. W. H. Gates.
por *Personal Computing* 13:212 O '89
The world on CD-ROMs. J. Pournelle. il *Byte* 14:103-4+
S '89

Astronomical use
The world's biggest star catalogue [Hubble Space Telescope
Guide star catalog] R. Villard. il *Sky and Telescope* 78:583-9
D '89
Dictionaries
Words! [Oxford English Dictionary] J. Pournelle. *Byte* 14:116+
O '89
Encyclopedias
Compton's debuts CD-ROM encyclopedia. J. Zinsser. il
Publishers Weekly 236:56 N 3 '89
Games
CD-ROM is no game—or is it? P. Scisco. il *Compute!* 11:8
My '89
Health use
Compact disks [Pan American Health Organization project]
C. J. Brito. il *World Health* p18-20 Ag/S '89
Reference books
Electronic bookshelf. R. Scibilia. il *Popular Mechanics*
166:112-13 O '89
Scientific use
Research à la Mac [Mac Portable and IIci] D. E. Crabb.
il *Byte* 14:153-4 N '89
CD-V *See* Compact disc video
CD4 PROTEINS
Activators of protein kinase C induce dissociation of CD4,
but not CD8, from p56[lck]. T. R. Hurley and others. bibl
f il *Science* 245:407-9 Jl 28 '89
AIDS predictors [measures of a drug's efficacy] K. Fackelmann.
il *Science News* 136:298-9 N 4 '89
AIDS research focuses on CD4. *High Technology Business*
9:30 Jl/Ag '89
AIDS viral burden far exceeds estimates [patients harbor
HIV in CD4-positive T4 cells; research by Miltiades C.
Psallidopoulos] R. Weiss. *Science News* 136:54 Jl 22 '89
Biogen's new moneymaking genes. L. Jereski. il por *Business
Week* p94 Je 19 '89
Conserved repetitive epitope recognized by CD4[+] clones from
a malaria-immunized volunteer. E. H. Nardin and others.
bibl f il *Science* 246:1603-6 D 22 '89
Docking site decoy, antibody fragment wed [immunoadhesins;
research by Daniel J. Capon] R. Weiss. *Science News*
135:86 F 11 '89
The Fc and not CD4 receptor mediates antibody enhancement
of HIV infection in human cells. J. Homsy and others.
bibl f il *Science* 244:1357-60 Je 16 '89
Fusion factor in AIDS cells identified [role of leukocyte
adhesion receptor LFA-1 in syncytium formation; research
by James E. K. Hildreth and Rimas J. Orentas] *Science
News* 135:366 Je 10 '89
Identification of the fusion peptide of primate im-
munodeficiency viruses. M. L. Bosch and others. bibl
f il *Science* 244:694-7 My 12 '89
Involvement of a leukocyte adhesion receptor (LFA-1) in
HIV-induced syncytium formation. J. E. K. Hildreth and
R. J. Orentas. bibl f il *Science* 244:1075-8 Je 2 '89
The MHC-binding and gp120-binding functions of CD4 are
separable. D. Lamarre and others. bibl f il *Science* 245:743-6
Ag 18 '89
New AIDS drugs take careful aim. J. Palca. il *Science*
246:1559-60 D 22 '89
A possible design for 'mopping up' AIDS [Chimeric CD4]
Newsweek 113:58 F 20 '89
The reservoir for HIV-1 in human peripheral blood is a
T cell that maintains expression of CD4. S. M. Schnittman
and others. bibl f il *Science* 245:305-8 Jl 21 '89
Synergism between HIV gp120 and gp120-specific antibody
in blocking human T cell activation. R. S. Mittler and
M. K. Hoffmann. bibl f il *Science* 245:1380-2 S 22 '89
T cell signaling. R. M. Perlmutter. bibl f il *Science* 245:344
Jl 28 '89
CDC *See* Centers for Disease Control (U.S.); Control Data
Corp.
CDF *See* Children's Defense Fund (U.S.)
CDI (COMPACT DISC INTERACTIVE) *See* Compact disc
interactive
CDM (COLD DARK MATTER) *See* Dark matter (Astronomy)
CDS *See* Certificates of deposit
CEAUŞESCU, NICOLAE
about
Curtain still down. A. Daniels. por *National Review* 41:21-3
D 22 '89
The last great Stalinist. M. R. Meyer. il por *Newsweek* 114:30+
Ag 21 '89
Romania: breaking the silence. W. Pfaff. il *The New York
Review of Books* 36:8-9 Ap 27 '89
Romania: defying the tyrant. W. Pfaff. il *The New York
Review of Books* 36:43 Ag 17 '89
Romania, Romania. T. R. Swick. *Commonweal* 116:263-4
My 5 '89
Where Stalinism still thrives. R. Knight. por *U.S. News
& World Report* 107:35 D 4 '89
CEBA AWARDS *See* Communications Excellence to Black
Audiences Awards
CECALA, KATHY PETERSEN
Meeting God in others. il *Commonweal* 116:400-2 Jl 14
'89

CECCOBELLI, BRUNO, 1952-
about
Bruno Ceccobelli: Jack Shainman. M. R. Rubinstein. il *Art News* 88:161 Summ '89
CECH, THOMAS R.
(jt. auth) See Latham, John A., and Cech, Thomas R.
(jt. auth) See McSwiggen, James A., and Cech, Thomas R.
about
Catalytic RNA wins Chemistry Nobel. M. M. Waldrop. il pors *Science* 246:325 O 20 '89
Chemistry. il pors *Time* 134:73 O 23 '89
RNA researchers earn Chemistry Nobel. I. Amato. *Science News* 136:262 O 21 '89
CECIL, JENNIFER
Traveling single [cover story] il *New York* 22:44-50+ F 13 '89
(jt. auth) See Wolfe, Linda, and Cecil, Jennifer
CECIL, JENNIFER, AND ROBBINS, MICHAEL W.
Great escapes. il *New York* 22:52-6+ Ap 24 '89
CECIL HOTEL (ALEXANDRIA, EGYPT) *See* Alexandria (Egypt)—Hotels, motels, etc.
CEDAR SHINGLES *See* Shingles and shingling
CEDARS-SINAI MEDICAL CENTER (LOS ANGELES, CALIF.)
Miracle baby [I. Roe, born at 23½ weeks] S. M. Halpern. il pors *Ms.* 18:56-60+ S '89
CEILING FANS *See* Fans, Electric
CEILINGS
How to hang a suspended ceiling. K. Collier. il *The Family Handyman* 39:75-6+ Je '89
CELA, CAMILO JOSÉ, 1916-
about
Cela vie. M. Ugarte. *The Nation* 249:646+ N 27 '89
A risky life. por *Time* 134:86 O 30 '89
CELANT, GERMANO, 1940-
about
Guggenheim lassoes jet-set curator. B. Wallis. *Art in America* 77:25 Ja '89
CELEBRITIES
See also
    Alcohol and celebrities
    Black celebrities
    Children of celebrities
    Clothing and dress—Celebrities
    Drugs and celebrities
    Fans (Persons)
    Walk of Fame (Hollywood, Calif.)
7 stars say what makes a good friend [women] il *Redbook* 173:22+ O '89
Adolescence lives at L.A.'s all-gal celeb pajama bash [hosted by A. Willis] P. Lansden. il pors *People Weekly* 32:147-8 N 27 '89
After the loving, counting the cost [celebrity breakups; cover story; special section] S. Schindehette. il *People Weekly* 32:68-70+ Ag 7 '89
America's 10 most beautiful women [cover story; special section] il *Harper's Bazaar* 122:158+ S '89
Astrology in high places. D. R. Hales. il *McCall's* 117:83-6 O '89
Best friends, all the way. L. Stover. il *Mademoiselle* 95:212-17 S '89
The best of the best [results of Roper poll] il *Ladies' Home Journal* 106:103-5 Jl '89
Can you read this headline? If not, these celebs put on a Wild West hoedown for you [benefit for Literacy Volunteers of New York City] il *People Weekly* 32:80-1 D 18 '89
Celebrating the celebactor [play themselves in movies] J. Barth. il *Film Comment* 25:46 N/D '89
Champions of synthetic fiber, angry human stars make the fur fly at a benefit for animal rights. il *People Weekly* 31:266-7 Mr 6 '89
Diary of a mad decade [excerpts from The Andy Warhol diaries]; ed. by Pat Hackett. A. Warhol. il pors *People Weekly* 31:100-2+ My 8 '89
Easy! Makeup hints from Hollywood [views of makeup artist Joe Blasco] il *Redbook* 174:14+ D '89
The end of celebrity. D. Hurley. il *Psychology Today* 22:50-3+ D '88
A fete honoring Clint, Julio and Bette Davis turns into a blast from the past [fund raiser for the Motion Picture and Television Country House and Hospital] il *People Weekly* 31:106-7 Ja 23 '89
Hollywood garden tour. L. Fears. il *Ladies' Home Journal* 106:126-30 Jl '89
Hollywood hair [hair extensions] C. Krupp. il *Glamour* 87:191 O '89
Hollywood puts on the dog—and ponies up—to do battle with AIDS [Art against AIDS] il *People Weekly* 31:118-19 F 13 '89
Hollywood's sheikh elite shows up to toast the restored Lawrence of Arabia. il *People Weekly* 31:36-7 F 27 '89
The hot issue [cover story; special issue] il *Rolling Stone* p51-4+ My 18 '89
If I could turn back time [May-December celebrity couples] il *People Weekly* 32:147+ D 25 '89-Ja 1 '90
Inquirer. See issues of 'Teen beginning November 1983

Island fantasies [who or what Canadians would take along to a desert island; Maclean's/Decima poll] il *Maclean's* 102:32 Ja 2 '89
Loose lips [views of L. Smith] C. Jahr. il por *Ladies' Home Journal* 106:110-12+ Ja '89
Makeovers of the mind: L.A.'s new intellectuals. D. Denicolo. il *Glamour* 87:164 Ag '89
Male bodies! Who rates a 10 in the swimsuit competition? il *Glamour* 87:111 Jl '89
A new breed of celebrity [TV journalists] J. Saltzman. *USA Today (Periodical)* 118:67 Jl '89
Notes from an endless night [excerpts from The Andy Warhol diaries]; ed. by Pat Hackett. A. Warhol. il pors *People Weekly* 31:106-8+ My 15 '89
Nymphs and satyrs [worship of celebrity] L. H. Lapham. *Harper's* 279:8-10 Ag '89
People. C. Krupp. See issues of Glamour
People to watch. il *U.S. News & World Report* 107:83-4+ D 25 '89-Ja 1 '90
Personal milestones: what stands out [women celebrities] il *Glamour* 87:170 Ap '89
Post people. See issues of The Saturday Evening Post
Private lives [special issue; with editorial comment by Lee Eisenberg] *Esquire* 111:35, 103-4+ Je '89
The really, really big stars come out to spend the night together with Mick Jagger and the Stones. il *People Weekly* 32:56 N 6 '89
Restaurants of the stars. il *Ladies' Home Journal* 106:184-6+ Ap '89
Ronald Reagan is full of bologna [deli sandwiches named for celebrities] J. Queenan. il *Gentlemen's Quarterly* 59:161-2 Ag '89
The satanic diaries [A. Warhol's diaries] M. Gross. il pors *New York* 22:48-56 My 29 '89
Scent-sational ideas [favorite perfumes] il *Redbook* 173:10 Ag '89
September spells severance for Harry Hamlin and other soon-to-be single celebs. il *People Weekly* 32:93-4+ S 18 '89
Specialties of the house [recipes from celebrity hangouts] il *Redbook* 172:104-7+ Ja '89
Specs appeal. il *Ladies' Home Journal* 106:27 Je '89
The stars have a (masked) ball as the Phantom starts stalking in Hollywood [celebrating premiere of musical] il *People Weekly* 31:50-1 Je 5 '89
Stars in the kitchen. il *Redbook* 172:133-8 Mr '89
Summer loves [women's crushes on male celebrities] il *Ladies' Home Journal* 106:48+ Ag '89
Superstar hair. L. J. Johnson. il *Ladies' Home Journal* 106:126-31 Ag '89
A tip of the man-watcher's hat to the also-rans. il *People Weekly* 32:126-7 D 18 '89
Tracking the rich and famous [R. Leach] H. G. Miller. por *The Saturday Evening Post* 261:30-1 My/Je '89
Wedding styles of the stars: psst! The bridesmaids are armed! D. Denicolo. il *Glamour* 87:178-9 Je '89
What do you read to your children? [famous parents share their children's most cherished books] T. Reinhold. bibl il *Redbook* 173:20 Jl '89
What if . . .? [makeover] L. Wells. il *The New York Times Magazine* p85-91 S 17 '89
When valet king Chuck Pick parks their wheels, Hollywood heavies count it a lucky brake. T. Allis. il pors *People Weekly* 31:116-17 Ap 24 '89
Wishing on a star [involvement in Starlight Foundation] L. Gross. il *McCall's* 117:64+ N '89
Women we love [cover story; special section] il *Esquire* 112:86-101 Ag '89
Agencies and agents
See Theatrical agencies and agents
Anecdotes, facetiae, satire, etc.
Field of bad dreams. il *People Weekly* 32:170-1 D 25 '89-Ja 1 '90
'Hall, Jerry, body odor of, 141' [indexes to A. Warhol diaries] il por *Newsweek* 114:66 Ag 7 '89
Personal glimpses. See issues of Reader's Digest
Attitudes
Great expectations [celebrities discuss most wanted videotapes for Christmas] J. Bernard. il *Video* 13:62-3 D '89
Turned on for fifty years [celebrities' favorite shows] J. Dunn and others. il *Rolling Stone* p29-30+ D 14-28 '89
What's your wish list for women in the 90's, and what do you want for yourself? il *Glamour* 87:320-1 Ap '89
Civil rights
All my children [lawyer L. Marks] P. Newcomb. il por *Forbes* 144:287 N 27 '89
They are hip, hot—and dead [late celebrities used in advertising] J. Hammer and K. Springen. il *Newsweek* 114:34 Jl 10 '89
Trouble for copycats [B. Midler wins suit against Young & Rubicam over sound-alike ad] P. Young. il por *Maclean's* 102:92 N 20 '89
A U.S. patent on famous voices [B. Midler wins suit against Young & Rubicam's use of her singing style] il por *U.S. News & World Report* 107:19 N 13 '89
Economic conditions
The hired and the mighty [perks of Hollywood] E. Stern. il *Gentlemen's Quarterly* 59:242-7+ Je '89

CELEBRITIES—Economic conditions—cont.

The magic kingdom [Forbes top 40] P. Newcomb. il Forbes 144:139-44+ O 2 '89

Michael Jackson earns $125 million and remains highest paid entertainer [Forbes list] il por Jet 76:26+ O 2 '89

The price was right [business deals] il People Weekly 32:164-6+ D 25 '89-Ja 1 '90

Health and hygiene
See also

AIDS (Disease) and celebrities

Housing

"Can I get a bulldozer down the driveway?" [teardowns of houses in Los Angeles] E. Paris. il Forbes 144 Special Issue:48-9+ O 23 '89

Gandee at large [decorator W. Fernandez] C. K. Gandee. il por House & Garden 161:218 N '89

Hollywood's most outrageous homes. M. Beck. il TV Guide 37:10-12+ Ag 12-18 '89

Million-dollar "birthday cakes" [historic homes demolished in wealthy Los Angeles neighborhoods] N. R. Gibbs. il Time 133:79 My 1 '89

My favorite room [actresses] M. Glass and K. Reisler. il Ladies' Home Journal 106:134-40 F '89

Uncensored: inside seven bachelor pads. B. E. Ellis. il Mademoiselle 95:164-71 F '89

Wall-to-wall Waldo means California cool to the likes of Merv and Liz [work of decorator W. Fernandez] H. Shapiro. il pors People Weekly 31:131-2 My 1 '89

Photographs and photography

Mrs. Leonard, can Elmore come out and play? Childhood homes of famous grown-ups. il Esquire 111:168-9 Je '89

Mortality

They went that-a-way [excerpt] M. S. Forbes. il The Saturday Evening Post 261:12+ My/Je '89

Nutrition

A self-styled food cop polices the coolest fridges in L.A. [Y. Berman, owner of Yolanda Enterprises, Inc.] N. Geeslin. il pors People Weekly 31:87-8 Mr 27 '89

What's cooking in Hollywood? J. McCollister. il The Saturday Evening Post 261:18+ My/Je '89

Pets

Life-styles of the rich and furry. il Glamour 87:192 Mr '89

Photographs and photography

Best friends [excerpt] P. Rattazzi. il Good Housekeeping 209:48 Ag '89

Photographs and photography

26 years of famous weddings. M. Fiore. il Good Housekeeping 208:46+ Je '89

Click! Click! Click! il People Weekly 32:130-1+ D 25 '89-Ja 1 '90

Double exposure [excerpts] R. McDowall. il Good Housekeeping 209:162-7 N '89

Hot numbers. il Life 12:34-43 Ja '89

If the camera never lies, then passport photos always tell the truth. Here, the real identities of the rich and famous. G. Doppelt. il Vogue 179:447 N '89

Lasting impressions. il Life 12:68-70+ Fall '89

Notorious. il Life 12:126-30+ Ja '89

The paparazzi have long been considered the foot soldiers of photography. B. Houston-Montgomery. il Vogue 179:274-5 Je '89

People classics. il People Weekly 31:70-80+ Mr 6 '89

Point, shoot, hob, nob. E. Nemy. il Popular Photography 96:30-1 Ja '89

Rolling stone: the photographs [excerpt] il Rolling Stone p57-62 O 19 '89

Some women [work of R. Mapplethorpe; cover story] J. Didion. il por Esquire 112:214-23 S '89

Yes! There is a Santa Claus. il Good Housekeeping 209:160-1 D '89

Political activities
See also

Hollywood Women's Political Committee

Flix mix in politix [Hollywood activism; cover story] F. Barnes. The New Republic 201:20+ O 30 '89

A sea of stars [Housing Now! march in Washington, D.C.] A. Ferguson. il National Review 41:26 N 10 '89

Speaking out for a place to call home [march on Washington, D.C., to protest the plight of the homeless] J. Park. il People Weekly 32:40-3 O 23 '89

Taking to the streets [celebrities march in support of Roe v. Wade abortion decision in Washington, D.C.] S. Schindehette. il People Weekly 31:40-5 Ap 24 '89

Press relations

The art of the deals. J. Alter. il Newsweek 113:58-9 Ja 9 '89

Barbara Walters's theater of revenge. M. C. Miller. Harper's 279:40-1+ N '89

Cover stories. E. Diamond. il New York 22:20+ O 9 '89

Psychology

Fame means stress. il Psychology Today 22:54-5 D '88

Recreation

Wish-list weekends. L. Saroyan. il Working Woman 14:112-13+ Je '89

Sports

Celebrity cyclists [cover story] D. Cuerdon. il Bicycling 30:56-8+ D '89

For the ultimate in nouvelle lang syne, the truly hip schuss Aspen. S. Schindehette. il People Weekly 31:115-17 Ja 16 '89

Michael Jordan launches project to help students in black colleges [celebrity golf tournament to benefit United Negro College Fund] il pors Jet 76:22-5 Ag 14 '89

The not ready for prime time hockey players [Celebrity All-stars vs. Bruins Legends] S. Harris. il Sport (New York, N.Y.) 80:83 Ap '89

People players [golf] il Maclean's 102:57 Ap 10 '89

Prince Rainier marks his 40-year reign with a Monaco gala [pro-celebrity tennis tournament] D. Bacon. il por People Weekly 32:96-9 Jl 24 '89

Stars provide fireworks for Leonard-Duran fans. il Jet 77:53-4 D 25 '89-Ja 1 '90

Tennis, anyone? Sporting a new 'do, Ronald Reagan joins Nancy at courtside [Nancy Reagan Tennis Tournament] il pors People Weekly 32:46-7 O 23 '89

The word of mouth on Ted Danson's Hawaiian celeb bash: it was a ball [fund raiser for the American Oceans Campaign] il por People Weekly 32:113-15 O 16 '89

Statues, portraits, etc.

Personality paper dolls. M. Jailer. il Antiques & Collecting Hobbies 93:51-3 F '89

Using Rick Tweddell's Vegiform molds, gardeners can say, 'Let us now raise famous men'. il por People Weekly 32:91 O 2 '89

Travel

Travel secrets of the rich and famous. il Glamour 87:163-4 Je '89

Soviet Union

People. H. G. Chua-Eoan. il Time 133:106-7 Ap 10 '89

CELEBRITIES AND THE ENVIRONMENT

Earth angels. T. Gold. il Harper's Bazaar 122:66-7+ Ja '89

Gal pals Sandra Bernhard and Madonna monkey around to save the jungle [benefit at the Brooklyn Academy of Music to save rain forests] il pors People Weekly 31:54-6 Je 12 '89

The greening of Hollywood. J. McDowell. il Time 133:76 Je 12 '89

Ted Danson's crusade [American Oceans Campaign] T. Green. il por Oceans 22:18-20+ Mr/Ap '89

The word of mouth on Ted Danson's Hawaiian celeb bash: it was a ball [fund raiser for the American Oceans Campaign] il por People Weekly 32:113-15 O 16 '89

CELEBRITIES AS AIR PILOTS

Clifton Davis lives his fantasy of being pilot. il por Jet 75:33 Ja 9 '89

CELEBRITIES AS AUTHORS

The stars of the trike-and-tantrum set [children's books] G. Cerio. il Newsweek 114:74 D 4 '89

CELEBRITIES AS POETS

Bard of Beverly Hills [J. Stewart] T. Gold. il por Harper's Bazaar 122:71+ O '89

Hollywood's new Brat Pack of poets. il Newsweek 114:74 S 18 '89

CELEBRITIES' FAMILIES
See also

Black celebrities' families

Family valentines. il Good Housekeeping 208:112-15 F '89

Hollywood's proud new papas. D. Lamanna. il Ladies' Home Journal 106:46-7 Mr '89

Tough guys talk about mom. il New Choices for the Best Years 29:48-50+ My '89

CELEBRITIES FOR A DRUG-FREE AMERICA

Ben Vereen becomes warrior in fight against drugs. il por Jet 77:11 D 11 '89

CELEBRITY See Fame

CELEBRITY PRODUCT ENDORSEMENTS See Advertising—Testimonials

CELESTE, RICHARD F.

Workers welfare [address, March 22, 1989] Vital Speeches of the Day 55:490-2 Je 1 '89

CELESTIAL MASERS See Masers, Celestial

CELESTIAL SEASONINGS INC.

Why Celestial Seasonings wasn't Kraft's cup of tea. S. D. Atchison. il por Business Week p76 My 8 '89

CELGENE CORPORATION

All they can eat. S. J. Madden. il Fortune 119:191-2 Ja 30 '89

CELIAC DISEASE

Nutritional aspects

Case of the 'nervous stomach' [case of R. Smith] A. Roblin. Prevention (Emmaus, Pa.) 41:112+ D '89

CELIBACY

Benched: life after sex. F. King. il por Ms. 17:43-5 My '89

Beyond the stiff upper lip [excerpt from The sexual Christian] T. Stafford. il Christianity Today 33:30-4 Ja 13 '89

CELIBIDACHE, SERGIU, 1912-
about

Extreme occasions. E. W. Said. The Nation 248:898-900 Je 26 '89

CELIS, PÉREZ See Pérez Celis

CELL ADHESION See Adhesion

CELL AGGREGATION
See also

Blood cell aggregation

CELL AGING *See* Aging
CELL COMMUNICATION *See* Cells—Communication
CELL CYCLE
The cell cycle coming under control. J. L. Marx. il *Science* 245:252-5 Jl 21 '89
Cell cycle-dependent regulation of phosphorylation of the human retinoblastoma gene product. K. Mihara and others. bibl f il *Science* 246:1300-3 D 8 '89
Frontiers in biology: the cell cycle [cover story; special section; with editorial comment by Daniel E. Koshland] il *Science* 246:545, 603-40 N 3 '89
CELL DEATH
Activation-driven programmed cell death and T cell receptor ζη expression. M. Mercep and others. bibl f il *Science* 246:1162-5 D 1 '89
Compelling cancer cells to self-destruct [use of anti-APO-1] S. Hart. *Science News* 136:69 Jl 29 '89
Monoclonal antibody-mediated tumor regression by induction of apoptosis [leukemia cells] B. C. Trauth and others. bibl f il *Science* 245:301-5 Jl 21 '89
CELL DEGENERATION *See* Cell death
CELL DIFFERENTIATION *See* Differentiation (Biology)
CELL DIVISION (BIOLOGY)
See also
Mitogens
Checkpoints: controls that ensure the order of cell cycle events. L. H. Hartwell and T. A. Weinert. bibl f il *Science* 246:629-34 N 3 '89
Directing cell division during development. P. H. O'Farrell and others. bibl f il *Science* 246:635-40 N 3 '89
Dominoes and clocks: the union of two views of the cell cycle. A. W. Murray and M. W. Kirschner. bibl f il *Science* 246:614-21 N 3 '89
G₁ events and regulations of cell proliferation. A. B. Pardee. bibl f il *Science* 246:603-8 N 3 '89
Mitosis. J. R. McIntosh and M. P. Koonce. bibl f il *Science* 246:622-8 N 3 '89
The mitotic spindle. J. R. McIntosh and K. L. McDonald. bibl il *Scientific American* 261:48-56 O '89
Plasticity and differentiation of embryonic retinal cells after terminal mitosis [chick eye] R. Adler and M. Hatlee. bibl f il *Science* 243:391-3 Ja 20 '89
Role of phosphatidylinositol kinase in PDGF receptor signal transduction. S. R. Coughlin and others. bibl f il *Science* 243:1191-4 Mr 3 '89
S phase of the cell cycle. R. A. Laskey and others. bibl f il *Science* 246:609-14 N 3 '89
Specific expression of nuclear proto-oncogenes before entry into meiotic prophase of spermatogenesis [mice] H. Wolfes and others. bibl f il *Science* 245:740-3 Ag 18 '89
CELL FUSION *See* Cell hybridization
CELL HYBRIDIZATION
Activation-driven programmed cell death and T cell receptor ζη expression [hybridomas] M. Mercep and others. bibl f il *Science* 246:1162-5 D 1 '89
Fusion factor in AIDS cells identified [role of leukocyte adhesion receptor LFA-1 in syncytium formation; research by James E. K. Hildreth and Rimas J. Orentas] *Science News* 135:366 Je 10 '89
Involvement of a leukocyte adhesion receptor (LFA-1) in HIV-induced syncytium formation. J. E. K. Hildreth and R. J. Orentas. bibl f il *Science* 244:1075-8 Je 2 '89
Isolation of human transcribed sequences from human-rodent somatic cell hybrids. P. Liu and others. bibl f il *Science* 246:813-15 N 10 '89
CELL INTERACTION *See* Cells—Communication
CELL JUNCTIONS *See* Junctions (Physiology)
CELL LYSIS *See* Lysis
CELL MEMBRANES *See* Membranes (Biology)
CELL MOVEMENT *See* Cells—Motility
CELL ORGANELLES
See also
Golgi apparatus
Lysosomes
Microtubules
Mitochondria
Peroxisomes
Ribosomes
CELL REGULATION *See* Cellular control mechanisms
CELL TRANSFORMATION *See* Gene transfer
CELL WALLS *See* Membranes (Biology)
CELLARS *See* Basements
CELLARS, WINE *See* Wine cellars
CELLISTS
See also
Haimovitz, Matt
Ma, Yo-Yo, 1955-
Starker, Janos, 1924-
CELLO MUSIC
See also
Compact discs—Cello music
The cello in jazz. C. White. il *Down Beat* 56:62-3 F '89
Musical events:
Various concertos performed in New York. A. Porter. *The New Yorker* 65:144-6 D 4 '89
CELLS
See also
Astrocytes

Blood cells
Cancer cells
Chromaffin cells
Chromatin
Chromosomes
Cytology
Differentiation (Biology)
Epithelium
Fibroblasts
Keratinocytes
Macrophages
Mast cells
Membranes (Biology)
Myoblasts
Nematocysts
Nerve cells
Phagocytes and phagocytosis
Pigments (Biology)
Plant cells and tissues
Commitment of mouse fibroblasts to adipocyte differentiation by DNA transfection. S. Chen and others. bibl f il *Science* 244:582-5 My 5 '89
Interleukin-1 mitogenic activity of fibroblasts and smooth muscle cells is due to PDGF-AA. E. W. Raines and others. bibl f il *Science* 243:393-6 Ja 20 '89
Sporozoite vaccine induces genetically restricted T cell elimination of malaria from hepatocytes. S. L. Hoffman and others. bibl f il *Science* 244:1078-81 Je 2 '89
Viral alteration of cell function. M. B. A. Oldstone. bibl il *Scientific American* 261:42-8 Ag '89
Communication
Dictyostelium discoideum: a model system for cell-cell interactions in development. P. Devreotes. bibl f il *Science* 245:1054-8 S 8 '89
Lectins as cell recognition molecules. N. Sharon and H. Lis. bibl f il *Science* 246:227-34 O 13 '89
Culture
Arachidonic acid and other fatty acids directly activate potassium channels in smooth muscle cells. R. W. Ordway and others. bibl f il *Science* 244:1176-9 Je 9 '89
Fluid flow stimulates tissue plasminogen activator secretion by cultured human endothelial cells. S. L. Diamond and others. bibl f il *Science* 243:1483-5 Mr 17 '89
High-level recombinant gene expression in rabbit endothelial cells transduced by retroviral vectors. J. A. Zwiebel and others. bibl f il *Science* 243:220-2 Ja 13 '89
The power of plastics [use in transplantation of liver cells; work of Joseph Vacanti] L. Oliwenstein. il *Discover* 10:18 D '89
Whose spleen is it? D. Andrews. il por *Technology Review* 92:14 N/D '89
Fusion
See Cell hybridization
Metabolism
Detection of cell-affecting agents with a silicon biosensor [silicon microphysiometer] J. W. Parce and others. bibl f il *Science* 246:243-7 O 13 '89
Listening to the breaths of 1,000 cells [silicon microphysiometer] *Science News* 136:286 O 28 '89
Motility
The neuronal growth-associated protein GAP-43 induces filopodia in non-neuronal cells. M. X. Zuber and others. bibl f il *Science* 244:1193-5 Je 9 '89
Physiology
See also
Endocytosis
Folliculo-stellate cells of the pituitary gland. E. K. Perryman. bibl f il *BioScience* 39:81-8 F '89
CELLS, ARTIFICIAL
Artificial cells aid patients [research by Thomas M. S. Chang] *USA Today (Periodical)* 117:11 Je '89
Cell "factories" churn out goods [research by James M. Lee and Bernard J. Van Wie] il *USA Today (Periodical)* 117:11-12 Je '89
Patient, heal thyself—with lab-grown cells. N. J. Freundlich. il *Business Week* p148+ Mr 20 '89
CELLULAR AGING *See* Aging
CELLULAR AUTOMATA
A cellular universe of debris, droplets, defects and demons. A. K. Dewdney. il *Scientific American* 261:102-5 Ag '89
The soul of a new machine [E. Fredkin's desalinator] G. Cowley. il por *Newsweek* 113:53 My 29 '89
Your own universe [Rudy Rucker's Cellular Automata Laboratory computer program] T. Waters. il *Discover* 10:24 D '89
CELLULAR CONTROL MECHANISMS
See also
Calmodulin
Cells—Communication
COOH-terminal-modified interleukin-3 is retained intracellularly and stimulates autocrine growth. C. E. Dunbar and others. bibl f il *Science* 245:1493-6 S 29 '89
Functions of sphingolipids and sphingolipid breakdown products in cellular regulation. Y. A. Hannun and R. M. Bell. bibl f il *Science* 243:500-7 Ja 27 '89
G₁/S transition in normal human T-lymphocytes requires the nuclear protein encoded by c-*myb*. A. M. Gewirtz and others. bibl f il *Science* 245:180-3 Jl 14 '89

CELLULAR CONTROL MECHANISMS—*cont.*

Histone H5 in the control of DNA synthesis and cell proliferation. J.-M. Sun and others. bibl f il *Science* 245:68-71 Jl 7 '89

Induction of mesoderm by a viral oncogene in early Xenopus embryos. M. Whitman and D. A. Melton. bibl f il *Science* 244:803-6 My 19 '89

Sphingomyelin synthase and PKC activation [discussion of January 27, 1989 article, Functions of sphingolipids and sphingolipid breakdown products in cellular regulation] Y. A. Hannun and R. M. Bell. il *Science* 246:1050 N 24 '89

CELLULAR DIFFERENTIATION *See* Differentiation (Biology)

CELLULAR RADIO

See also
Fort Mojave Telecommunications, Inc.
Gila River Telecommunications, Inc.
McCaw Cellular Communications Inc.
Mobilnet Inc.

Cellular cautions. M. Mandell. il *High Technology Business* 9:48 F '89

Have phone, will travel. E. Pomice. il *U.S. News & World Report* 107:40-1 Jl 24 '89

In a cellular state of mind. N. Sullivan. il *Home Office Computing* 7:116 N '89

Acquisitions and mergers

The cellular bidding war will get even hotter [McCaw's offer for LIN] R. D. Hof. il *Business Week* p39-40 Je 19 '89

For Craig McCaw, it's do-or-die time [battle for LIN Broadcasting] C. Hawkins and R. D. Hof. il *Business Week* p34 D 4 '89

This cellular hookup could jam the competition [LIN and BellSouth's merger] J. J. Keller. il *Business Week* p45 S 25 '89

Will McCaw be ensnared by the net of his dreams? [LIN acquisition] R. D. Hof. map *Business Week* p43-4 D 18 '89

Winning is only the first step [McCaw Cellular gains control of LIN Broadcasting] F. Meeks. il pors map *Forbes* 144:80-3 D 25 '89

International aspects

Craig McCaw goes establishment [selling British Telecom a stake in McCaw Cellular Communications] J. J. Keller. il por *Business Week* p40-1 F 6 '89

Export-import trade

Motorola is pounding on Japan's 'open door'. N. Gross. il *Business Week* p58 My 8 '89

A sanctions scare finally makes the Japanese jump [Motorola's cellular phone deal] P. Magnusson. *Business Week* p28-9 Jl 10 '89

Tokyo answers the call [Japan opens up its mobile phone market] *Time* 134:46 Jl 10 '89

Licenses

The great cellular giveaway [rural cellular licenses] H. Rudnitsky. il *Forbes* 144:40-1 D 25 '89

The phone flushaway [FCC lottery for distribution of cellular telephone licenses] D. Ellen. *The New Republic* 201:13-15 O 9 '89

Smoke on the line [D. Segress wins cellular licenses for American Indian-owned companies] F. Meeks. il *Forbes* 144:114+ S 4 '89

Marketing

Cincinnati Microwave tries to strengthen its signal [cellular co-marketing deal with GTE] M. Mallory. *Business Week* p29-30 Mr 6 '89

Prices

Cellular phones to match your car—and wallet. D. H. Dunn. il *Business Week* p166 Je 26 '89

Securities

Hello, reality calling. R. D. Hof. il *Business Week* p22-3 Ag 7 '89

Operator, can you connect me to the real world? [American investors are bidding up British cellular shares] J. Marcom, Jr. il *Forbes* 144:142 S 18 '89

Testing

Have phone, will travel [portable Motorola Micro TAC] S. A. Booth. il *Popular Mechanics* 166:52-3 O '89

Canada

See also
BCE Mobile Communications Inc.
Cantel Inc.

Great Britain

A mobile phone in every home. H. Dixon. il *World Press Review* 36:36+ O '89

Operator, can you connect me to the real world? [American investors are bidding up British cellular shares] J. Marcom, Jr. il *Forbes* 144:142 S 18 '89

Japan

Motorola is pounding on Japan's 'open door'. N. Gross. il *Business Week* p58 My 8 '89

A sanctions scare finally makes the Japanese jump [Motorola's cellular phone deal] P. Magnusson. *Business Week* p28-9 Jl 10 '89

Tokyo answers the call [Japan opens up its mobile phone market] *Time* 134:46 Jl 10 '89

CELLULAR RADIO IN AUTOMOBILES

Cellular phones to match your car—and wallet. D. H. Dunn. il *Business Week* p166 Je 26 '89

"Gotta go, I'm heading into the canyon". G. Slutsker. il *Forbes* 143:138+ Mr 6 '89

Talk to me, baby. B. Young. il *Rolling Stone* p176 My 18 '89

Working on the highway. J. Kluger. il *Discover* 10:34+ Ap '89

CELLULAR RADIO ON SHIPS, BOATS, ETC.

1990 buyer's guide: communications [VHFs, SSBs, and cellular phones] G. West. il *Motor Boating & Sailing* 164:70-2+ O '89

CELLULAR RADIO TRANSMISSION

"Gotta go, I'm heading into the canyon". G. Slutsker. il *Forbes* 143:138+ Mr 6 '89

CELLULOSE

Cellulose and the evolution of plant life [plant cell walls] L. C. Duchesne and D. W. Larson. bibl f il *BioScience* 39:238-41 Ap '89

CELMINS, VIJA, 1939-

about

Vija Celmins at David McKee. K. Johnson. *Art in America* 77:146 Mr '89

CELOTEX CORPORATION

A lion of the Texas bar snarls at KKR and Drexel [S. Susman builds asbestos case stemming from Jim Walter Corp. LBO] M. Ivey. il por *Business Week* p73+ O 9 '89

CELSING, FREDRIK VON

about

Swedish fantasies. C. Petkanas. il por *House & Garden* 161:126-33+ Ag '89

CELTIC SCENE (NEWSLETTER) *See* Basketball newsletters

CEMENT

See also
Concrete

CEMENT INDUSTRY

See also
CalMat Co.
Lone Star Industries, Inc.

CEMETERIES

Hot tombs [purchasing desirable burial plots; cover story] M. Specter. *The New Republic* 201:22-5 S 11 '89

Great Britain

See also
Bradford (England)—Cemeteries
Highgate Cemetery (London, England)

Hungary

See also
Budapest (Hungary)—Cemeteries

Returning home [S. Schwarcz buried in family cemetery] C. Fenyvesi. por *Organic Gardening* 36:99 Ap '89

Middle East

See also
Jerusalem—Cemeteries

CENEDELLA, JOAN

Parent-teacher conference. il *Good Housekeeping* 209:132+ S '89

CENSERS

Collectors and collecting

Antiques: Chinese censers. A. Berman. il *Architectural Digest* 46:186-91+ Ag '89

CENSORSHIP

See also
Art—Censorship
Banned Books Week
Freedom of information
Freedom of the press
Government and the press
Humor—Censorship
Motion pictures—Censorship
Obscenity (Law)
Photography—Censorship
Television broadcasting—Censorship
Textbooks—Censorship

Bad Astra: the other side of the Spectrum [court rules against predistribution review policy in case of high school underground newspaper in Renton, Wash.] P. A. Zirkel. bibl f il *Phi Delta Kappan* 70:734-5+ My '89

A boy sides with Dr. Seuss's Lorax, and puts a town at loggerheads [parents of S. Bailey call for removal of title from school reading list in Laytonville, Calif.] R. Arias. il pors *People Weekly* 32:67-8 O 23 '89

Combating censorship in the U.S. H. F. Pilpel. il *USA Today (Periodical)* 117:84-5 Ja '89

Comedy of errors? [discussion of October 2, 1989 article, 'A gangsterdom of the spirit'] *The Nation* 249:406 O 16 '89

For goodness sake? [S. King's books banned in public school libraries] H. Wornom. por *Omni (New York, N.Y.)* 12:16+ D '89

'A gangsterdom of the spirit' [E. L. Doctorow's controversial commencement speech at Brandeis University] *The Nation* 249:348 O 2 '89

Have Christian books been censored? [rejection by book reviewers] S. Charles. il *Publishers Weekly* 235:58 Mr 3 '89

CENSORSHIP—*cont.*

In praise of censure. G. Wills. il *Time* 134:71-2 Jl 31 '89
Lesbian writer fights feminist censors [J. Nestle] H. Metz. il por *The Progressive* 53:16-17 Ag '89
Our own ayatollahs. E. Knoll. *The Progressive* 53:4 Ap '89
Print in prison. E. Knoll. *The Progressive* 53:4 Jl '89
Random notes [American Booksellers Association convention] D. Klinghoffer. *National Review* 41:44 Jl 14 '89
Religious fanatics and censorship. J. R. Joelson. il *The Humanist* 49:33 My/Je '89
Researchers irked by changes to testimony [Office of Management and Budget] E. Marshall. *Science* 244:648 My 12 '89
School paper's story on teen mother who's class valedictorian is barred [C. M. Dixon] il por *Jet* 76:31 My 8 '89
Student journalists fight for free expression [Supreme Court ruling permits censorship of student press in Hazelwood, Mo. case] L. Eskin. il *Scholastic Update (Teachers' edition)* 122:19-21 S 8 '89
Tea and toleration [difference in attitudes between Great Britain and the U.S.] *The New Republic* 201:6 Ag 21 '89
The top 10 censored stories of 1988 [underreported or overlooked by the media; views of Project Censored] il *Utne Reader* p59-63 S/O '89

International aspects

See also
Rushdie, Salman—Satanic verses case

Canada

Diagnosis: a severe case of the wobblies [Satanic verses case; interview with J. Clark] A. Fotheringham. il *Maclean's* 102:56 Mr 27 '89
Ducking the Rushdie challenge [Satanic verses case] A. Fotheringham. il *Maclean's* 102:64 Mr 6 '89

Great Britain

Her majesty's censors [M. Thatcher] M. Friedman. il *The Progressive* 53:30-3 F '89
Tea and toleration [difference in attitudes between Great Britain and the U.S.] *The New Republic* 201:6 Ag 21 '89
Thatcher puts a lid on. J. Atlas. il *The New York Times Magazine* p36-8+ Mr 5 '89

Grenada

Groups condemn confiscation of books by Grenada. C. Reid. *Publishers Weekly* 235:36 Ap 7 '89

Poland

Up from the underground in Poland. A. Husarska. il *The New York Times Book Review* 94:1+ O 8 '89

Soviet Union

Jamming: the end of an era? S. Leinwoll. il *Radio-Electronics* 60:75-7 Je '89
The Soviet jamming system and the future of jamming. S. Leinwoll. il *Radio-Electronics* 60:78-9 O '89

United States

See Censorship

CENSUS

See also
United States—Census
CENTAUR (LAUNCH VEHICLE) *See* Space vehicles—Propulsion systems

CENTAUR PARTNERS

America's no. 1 tipster [stock market journalist D. Dorfman] J. Egan. il por *U.S. News & World Report* 107:59-60 Ag 21 '89
Background check [A. J. Butler's offer for Pennwalt] L. Gubernick. *Forbes* 143:14-15 F 20 '89

CENTENARIANS

Elsie Frum remembers a train's desperate whistle 100 years ago—and the great Johnstown flood. B. Johnson. il pors *People Weekly* 31:85-8 Je 5 '89
I'm 109 and guess what . . . I'm a great, great, great, great granny [A. Pagel] J. Hayes. il pors *Life* 12:89-92 Ap '89
The oldest living American? [S. Brunson] R. E. McKinney. il pors *Ebony* 44:86+ S '89
Still hungry for knowledge at 105, Gertrude Palmer is one for the books [named Senior Adult Student of the Year in Lemon Grove, Calif.] il pors *People Weekly* 31:116-17 Mr 20 '89
Wed when the West was wild, Ernie and Maud Scott celebrate 80 years of staying hitched [longest-wed living couple in the world] il pors *People Weekly* 31:99 Je 26 '89

CENTENNIAL GROUP, INC.

The Ron and John show [R. White and J. Joseph] R. King. il pors *Forbes* 143:103+ Je 26 '89

CENTER FOR BLACK MUSIC RESEARCH

Dr. Samuel A. Floyd Jr.: man with a mission. il pors *Ebony* 44:194-5 My '89

CENTER FOR INTERNATIONAL PRIVATE ENTERPRISE

Openings abroad for enterprise. A. Holzinger. il *Nation's Business* 77:66+ N '89

CENTER FOR NONVIOLENT ALTERNATIVES

A lifetime devoted to nonviolence [M. Swann] B. Tober. por *The Progressive* 53:16 D '89
CENTER FOR PARTICLE ASTROPHYICS *See* University of California, Berkeley. Center for Particle Astrophysics

CENTER FOR SUCCESSFUL CHILDHOOD DEVELOPMENT (CHICAGO, ILL.)

Right from the beginning. *Newsweek* 113:49 F 20 '89

CENTER FOR TAPESTRY ARTS (NEW YORK, N.Y.)

Urban tapestry [cover story] P. Scheinman. il *American Craft* 49:42-7 Ag/S '89

CENTER FOR UTILIZATION OF LOCAL PLANETARY RESOURCES

Road map of space resources [views of John Lewis] il *Ad Astra* 1:6 N '89

CENTER ON RELIGION & SOCIETY (NEW YORK, N.Y.)

Unpleasant business [Rockford Institute locks out R. J. Neuhaus] *National Review* 41:12+ Je 16 '89
CENTERPIECES *See* Table decoration
CENTERS (BASKETBALL PLAYERS) *See* Basketball players

CENTERS FOR DISEASE CONTROL (U.S.)

Agent Orange: Congress impatient for answers [Centers for Disease Control study vs. Stellman study] M. Barinaga. il *Science* 245:249-50 Jl 21 '89

CENTERS FOR THE PERFORMING ARTS

See also
Alaska Center for the Performing Arts (Anchorage, Alaska)
Brooklyn Academy of Music
Caravan of Dreams
Cornell University. Center for Theatre Arts
Metropolitan Performing Arts Center (Spokane, Wash.)
Morton H. Meyerson Symphony Center (Dallas, Tex.)
Symphony Space (New York, N.Y.)
Blueprint for the 90s [cover story; special section; with editorial comment by John Calhoun] il *Theatre Crafts* 23:7, 24-8+ D '89

France

See also
La Villette (Paris, France)

Hong Kong

See also
Hong Kong Cultural Centre

CENTRAL AERO-HYDRODYNAMIC INSTITUTE (SOVIET UNION)

Aerodynamic Institute aids effort to develop fuel-efficient transports. il *Aviation Week & Space Technology* 130:52+ Je 5 '89

CENTRAL AFRICA

See also
Rain forests—Central Africa
Sudan
Uganda

CENTRAL AMERICA

See also
Belize
Colleges and universities—Central America
Costa Rica
Economic assistance, American—Central America
El Salvador
Guatemala
Honduras
Indians of Central America
Military assistance, American—Central America
Military assistance, Russian—Central America
Nicaragua
Panama
United Nations—Central America

Foreign relations

Soviet Union

See Soviet Union—Foreign relations—Central America

United States

See United States—Foreign relations—Central America

Politics and government

Blown opportunities in Central America [failure of George Bush to enact policies] C. A. Robbins. il *U.S. News & World Report* 106:28 F 27 '89
Catching the administration napping [Nicaragua's pledge of reforms prompts Central American neighbors to remove U.S.-backed contras] *Newsweek* 113:43 F 27 '89
Central America. *World Press Review* 36:9-10 Ap '89
Central America: Bush may be reduced to a supporting player. B. Javetski and A. Arana. il *Business Week* p60 Ap 3 '89
Crimping the accords [latest U.S. aid package for Nicaragua contradicts U.S. support for regional peace plan] *Commonweal* 116:227-8 Ap 21 '89
The deal in Central America. E. Abrams. *Commentary* 87:29-32 My '89
Disarming the rebels [accord signed by Central American presidents] M. Nemeth. il *Maclean's* 102:33+ Ag 21 '89
The "disposal problem" [Tela plan to disband contras] J. Smolowe. il *Time* 134:32 Ag 21 '89
A done deal. *The New Republic* 200:5-6 Ap 24 '89
El Salvador [discussion of May 1989 article, The deal in Central America] E. Abrams. *Commentary* 88:8-9 S '89
Enlarging the cloth [Tela agreement disbanding and resettling the contras] *Commonweal* 116:451-2 S 8 '89
Look out, gringo [Bush administration policies] M. Kondracke. *The New Republic* 201:12-13 S 4 '89
Now the Sandinistas can't blame it on the contras. B. Javetski and S. Baker. il *Business Week* p47 Ag 21 '89

CENTRAL AMERICA—Politics and government—*cont.*

Planning for peace [summit of Central American presidents] A. Bilski. il *Maclean's* 102:29 F 27 '89

Plans for UN observers in Central America 'in suspense'. map *UN Chronicle* 26:13-14 S '89

Security Council adopts resolution on Central American peace [text of resolution and statement, July 28, 1989] H. S. Okun. *Department of State Bulletin* 89:73-4 O '89

'Strongest support' for peace plan for Central America expressed by Assembly. il *UN Chronicle* 26:65 Mr '89

Termination time [move to disband contras] *The Nation* 249:227-8 S 4-11 '89

U.S. support for democracy and peace in Central America [bipartisan accord; statements and text of accord, March 24, 1989; texts of joint declarations of Central American presidents, January 16, 1988 and February 14, 1989; cover story] G. Bush. il por map *Department of State Bulletin* 89:55-9 Je '89

UN observers asked to verify Central American peace plan. il *UN Chronicle* 26:30 Je '89

UN pursues peace process in Central America [special section] il *UN Chronicle* 26:15-20 D '89

What can Central America expect from the Bush administration? F. B. Morris. il *The Christian Century* 106:472-5 My 3 '89

Religious institutions and affairs
See also
Evangelical churches—Central America

CENTRAL AMERICA (STEAMSHIP)

Atlantic Monthly uncovers buried riches [publication of G. Kinder's book] *Publishers Weekly* 236:48-9 N 24 '89

The sinking that shook America. il *U.S. News & World Report* 107:15 S 25 '89

CENTRAL AMERICA AND ISRAEL *See* Israel and Central America

CENTRAL AMERICA AND THE UNITED STATES
See also
Student exchange programs

CENTRAL AMERICAN REFUGEES *See* Refugees, Central American

CENTRAL ARIZONA PROJECT

Earth last! [D. Foreman and others of Earth First! charged with attempted sabotage of the Central Arizona Project] D. Russell. *The Nation* 249:77 Jl 17 '89

CENTRAL ASIA
See also
Afghanistan
Tibet

CENTRAL ASSET ACCOUNTS *See* Cash management accounts

CENTRAL BANKS

As central banks put on the brakes, inflation will skid . . . C. Farrell. *Business Week* p34 S 25 '89

The shadow bankers [currency brokers control dollar's fate] B. Powell. il *Newsweek* 114:47-8 O 23 '89

Showdown on the dollar: central banks are attacking the greenback. J. Daly. il *Maclean's* 102:39 O 9 '89

CENTRAL CAPITAL CORPORATION

Canadian imperialism [R. Cohen and L. Ellen buy into U.S. Trust Co.] J. Willoughby. il por *Forbes* 143:52 Ja 9 '89

CENTRAL EUROPE
See also
Literature and state—Central Europe

Civilization

Notes on your Central Europe—and mine; tr. by James A. Tucker. G. Konrád. *Harper's* 278:22-4 F '89

Defenses

Central European security. H. Owen and E. C. Meyer. il *Foreign Affairs* 68:22-40 Summ '89

Politics and government

The telltale scar. C. Miłosz. *The New Republic* 201:27-9 Ag 7-14 '89

CENTRAL FREIGHT LINES INC.

Central Freight Lines Inc. R. Koselka and others. il *Forbes* 144:214+ D 11 '89

CENTRAL INSTITUTE FOR AVIATION MOTORS (MOSCOW, SOVIET UNION)

Propulsion research center focuses on developing fuel-efficient aircraft. il *Aviation Week & Space Technology* 130:40-3 Je 5 '89

CENTRAL INTELLIGENCE AGENCY (U.S.) *See* United States. Central Intelligence Agency

CENTRAL INTERCOLLEGIATE ATHLETIC ASSOCIATION

The CIAA celebrates its 77th year. il *Ebony* 44:176-8 My '89

CENTRAL NERVOUS SYSTEM *See* Nervous system

CENTRAL NEWSPAPERS, INC.

Indianapolis intrigue [B. SerVaas' role in Central Newspapers going public] E. Schmuckler. il por *Forbes* 144:222-3 S 18 '89

The Quayle family newspapers: black, white—and green all over. J. F. Siler. il por *Business Week* p29 Ag 28 '89

CENTRAL PARK (NEW YORK, N.Y.)
See also
Central Park wilding attack, 1989

Riches [Cirque Grégoire's production of Bateaux des rêves] *The New Yorker* 65:27-8 Je 19 '89

Conservatory Garden

Central Park's Conservatory Garden and a revolutionary exhibition. H. Bridges. il *Gourmet* 49:48+ Je '89

Shakespeare Garden

Shakespeare in the Park. P. Hagan. il *House & Garden* 161:200-3+ O '89

CENTRAL PARK WILDING ATTACK, 1989

Boys will be boys? L. C. Pogrebin. il *Ms.* 18:24 S '89

The Central Park rape: has it made us angry? Scared? Or smart? L. Mosedale. il *Glamour* 87:212-13+ Ag '89

A city transfixed by a brutal act. F. Bruning. il *Maclean's* 102:9 My 22 '89

A clockwork orange in Central Park [gang of youths rapes woman jogger] il *U.S. News & World Report* 106:10 My 8 '89

Coming back from head injury. D. R. Hales and R. E. Hales. il *American Health* 8:9-10+ N '89

Crime & its remedies. *Commonweal* 116:292 My 19 '89

Crime and responsibility [rape of woman by teenagers in New York City] C. Krauthammer. il *Time* 133:104 My 8 '89

Dangerous times. N. Underwood. il *Maclean's* 102:54+ My 8 '89

Don't blame "society" [rape of woman jogger in New York City] C. Krauthammer. *Reader's Digest* 135:54-5 Ag '89

Going 'wilding' in the city [rape of jogger in Central Park] D. Gelman. il *Newsweek* 113:65 My 8 '89

Going 'wilding': terror in Central Park [rape of jogger] *Newsweek* 113:27 My 1 '89

The jogger: running for her life. B. G. Harrison. *Mademoiselle* 95:122 Ag '89

Madness in the heart of the city [cover story] J. S. Kunen. il *People Weekly* 31:106-11 My 22 '89

Meltdown in our cities [crimes by black youths] M. B. Zuckerman. il *U.S. News & World Report* 106:74 My 29 '89

Never again. G. Averbuch. il *Runner's World* 24:10-11 Ag '89

Opinions, but no solutions. G. Hackett and P. McKillop. il *Newsweek* 113:40 My 15 '89

Other victims in the Park: they are the 'invisible' blacks who are slandered by our mindless, sometimes racist generalities. M. Greenfield. il *Newsweek* 113:86 My 15 '89

The rape in Central Park. *The Nation* 248:721 My 29 '89

Root causes. *National Review* 41:16+ Je 2 '89

Sexism comes in all colors. J. Morgan. *Utne Reader* p48-9 N/D '89

Society loves a good victim. L. Jackson. por *Newsweek* 114:8 Jl 24 '89

Violations: the legacy of the Central Park rape. J. Neimark. il *Mademoiselle* 95:226-7+ S '89

What really happened in Central Park [cover story] M. Stone. il map *New York* 22:30-43 Ag 14 '89

Who pays for the boys' night out? R. E. Burns. *U.S. Catholic* 54:2 Ag '89

Wilding in the night [woman gang-raped by teenagers in New York City] N. R. Gibbs. il *Time* 133:20-1 My 8 '89

The 'wilding' of the vanities [attack on jogger] A. Fotheringham. il *Maclean's* 102:64 My 8 '89

You can't cure the wilding sickness. C. W. Colson. il *Christianity Today* 33:80 S 8 '89

Reporters and reporting

Anatomy of a horror. E. Diamond. il *New York* 22:41-5 My 15 '89

Evil running wild. T. Eastland. il *The American Spectator* 22:32 Jl '89

Public opinion and the jogger [New York times coverage] R. Brookhiser. *Commentary* 88:50-2 Jl '89

CENTRAL PARK ZOO

Zoo story [design by Kevin Roche, John Dinkeloo & Associates] J. S. Russell. il *Architectural Record* 177:84-9 F '89

CENTRAL SERVICES ORGANIZATION *See* Bell Communications Research, Inc.

CENTRAL STATE UNIVERSITY (OHIO)

Central St. fetes Tyson with honorary doctorate [M. Tyson] il pors *Jet* 76:14 My 15 '89

Central State pioneers in innovative programs for well-rounded grads. *Jet* 76:18 My 29 '89

Central State U. designs high school, B.A. degree program for Mike Tyson. il por *Jet* 77:28 N 6 '89

Central State U. honors Cosby family generosity at Cleveland Classic. pors *Jet* 76:10 S 11 '89

Perseverance pays, HUD Secretary Jack Kemp tells Central State U. students. il pors *Jet* 76:16+ Je 19 '89

CENTRAL VACUUM CLEANING SYSTEMS *See* Vacuum cleaning

CENTRAL VALLEY (CALIF.)
See also
Carrizo Plain (Calif.)

Looking ahead to the 'fourth wave'. M. A. Lerner and J. Gordon. il *Newsweek* 114:27-9 Jl 31 '89

CENTRE FOR SUSTAINABLE ECONOMIC DEVELOPMENT (CANADA) *See* Canada. Centre for Sustainable Economic Development

CENTRE NATIONAL D'ÉTUDES SPATIALES (FRANCE)
Landsat/Spot merger talks spark debate on commercial space venture [with editorial comment] C. Covault. il *Aviation Week & Space Technology* 130:7, 20-1 Ja 23 '89

CENTRO DE ARTE REINA SOFIA (MADRID, SPAIN)
A new reign in Spain. V. Combalía. il *Art News* 88:58+ Ja '89

CENTRO PER L'ARTE CONTEMPORANEO LUIGI PECCI (PRATO, ITALY)
The warehouse effect. J. Turner. il *Art News* 88:63-4 Ja '89

CENTRUST SAVINGS BANK
CenTrust's offbeat plan to be a plain old thrift [radical restructuring] G. DeGeorge. il por *Business Week* p36 S 18 '89
Even for a go-go banker, there are certain no-nos. G. DeGeorge. il por *Business Week* p140-1 My 22 '89
A spendthrift thrift gets its ears boxed. G. DeGeorge. *Business Week* p46 D 25 '89-Ja 1 '90

CENTURION GOLD LTD.
Fool's gold? [recent investments by C. Seaman] S. Flack. il por *Forbes* 144:150+ D 25 '89

CENTURY CITY (LOS ANGELES, CALIF.)
Restaurants, nightclubs, bars, etc.
Spécialités de la maison:
Langan's Brasserie. C. Bates. il *Gourmet* 49:42+ Je '89

CENTURY HUTCHINSON LTD.
RH-Century deal creates major U.K. trade group. V. Menkes. *Publishers Weekly* 235:9 Je 23 '89

CENTURY PLANTS *See* Agave

CENTURY RIDES (CYCLING)
Century training secrets. G. Drake. il *Bicycling* 30:48-51 Ag '89
The double century. C. Kostman. *Bicycling* 30:160-1 Ap '89
Riding your first century. S. J. Henry. il *Women's Sports & Fitness* 11:16-17 Ap '89
Take the AT&T Century Challenge. N. Pena. *Bicycling* 30:52+ Ag '89

CENTURY SHARES TRUST
Portfolio insurance. J. Clements. il por *Forbes* 144:160 D 25 '89

CEPAD *See* Evangelical Committee for Aid and Development in Nicaragua

CEPEDA, ORLANDO, 1937-
about
Didn't you used to be . . . W. Ladson. il por *Sport (New York, N.Y.)* 80:84 Mr '89

CEPHALOPODS
See also
Octopuses
Squid

CEPHALOSPORIN
Alliterative prescriptions pose problems. *Science News* 135:237 Ap 15 '89

CEQ *See* Council on Environmental Quality (U.S.)

CERAMIC AIRPLANE ENGINES *See* Airplane engines, Jet—Materials

CERAMIC FIGURINES *See* Figurines

CERAMIC MEMBRANES (TECHNOLOGY)
Membranes could remove coal pollutants. *High Technology Business* 9:38 Mr '89

CERAMIC OXIDES
Anomalous scattering study of the Bi distribution in the 2212 superconductor: implications for Cu valency. P. Lee and others. bibl f il *Science* 244:62-3 Ap 7 '89
The axial oxygen atom and superconductivity in $YBa_2Cu_3O_7$. S. D. Conradson and I. D. Raistrick. bibl f il *Science* 243:1340-3 Mr 10 '89
The dogged push to overcome resistance [work of S. Jin] E. T. Smith. il por *Business Week* Special Issue:84 Je 16 '89
High-temperature supercurrents may not be forever. A. Khurana. bibl f il *Physics Today* 42:17-21 Mr '89
Magnon-exchange pairing and superconductivity [discussion of February 19, 1988 article, The magnon pairing mechanism of superconductivity in cuprate ceramics] G. Chen and W. A. Goddard, III. *Science* 243:547-8 Ja 27 '89
Submicrometer superconducting $YBa_2Cu_3O_{6+x}$ particles made by a low-temperature synthetic route. H. S. Horowitz and others. bibl f il *Science* 243:66-9 Ja 6 '89
Superconducting ceramics [Ceracon process] *USA Today (Periodical)* 117:9-10 Je '89
What you see isn't always what you get [research by Aloysius J. Arko] *Science News* 135:143 Mr 4 '89

CERAMIC SCULPTURE
Crack pots. D. Gimelson. il *Harper's Bazaar* 122:80 O '89
A harvest of ceramics [work of A. Gordon and C. Potter] C. Petkanas. il pors *House & Garden* 161:28+ Ag '89
Exhibitions
Common clay: a Soviet sojourn brings *glasnost* to ceramic art. J. Tognini. il *American Craft* 49:10-11 O/N '89
Jun Kaneko/Brendan Walter Gallery. M. McCloud. il *American Craft* 49:80-1 Ag/S '89

Robert Brady: masked gods [retrospective at the Crocker Art Museum in Sacramento] C. White. il por *American Craft* 49:30-7 D '89/Ja '90
Prices
Christie's sale a success [auction of contemporary ceramics and glass] il *American Craft* 49:12 Ap/My '89

CERAMIC SPHERES
Tiny bubbles [hollow ceramic spheres for insulation] G. Davis. il *Popular Science* 235:42 O '89

CERAMIC TILE LAYING *See* Tile laying

CERAMIC TILES *See* Tiles

CERAMICS
See also
Pottery
Better materials through clusters [work of Richard W. Siegel] I. Amato. *Science News* 135:284 My 6 '89
Ceramic matrix composites improve. *High Technology Business* 9:36 Ja '89
Ceramics take new shapes. il *High Technology Business* 9:4-5 My '89
Mollusk teaches ceramics to scientists [rugged shell of the red abalone; research by Mehmet Sarikaya] I. Amato. *Science News* 136:383 D 9 '89
Polymers, fractals, and ceramic materials. D. W. Schaefer. bibl f il *Science* 243:1023-7 F 24 '89

CERAVOLO, PETER
Commercial telescope optics: buyer beware! il *Sky and Telescope* 78:564 D '89

CERCLE DE L'UNION INTERALLIÉE
Cercle de l'Union Interalliée. Suzy. il *Architectural Digest* 46:148-53+ Ja '89

CEREAL FOODS
See also
Cooking—Grain
Box treats. L. Applegate. il *Runner's World* 24:20-1 F '89
Breakfast cereals. il *Consumer Reports* 54:254-60 D '89
Cereal: breakfast food or nutritional supplement? [cover story] il *Consumer Reports* 54:638-45 O '89
The cereal guide. il *Women's Sports & Fitness* 11:45 Ap '89
Good morning sugar, salt, and fat. T. Mendoza. il *Current Health 2* 15:22-5 Mr '89
Power breakfast in a bowl: a quick guide to cold cereals. il *Glamour* 87:174 Ja '89
Advertising
The breakfast drug [FDA reviews use of psyllium to determine if it is a food or drug] J. Newman. *American Health* 8:82+ D '89
Can cereal cut cholesterol levels? il *Consumer Reports* 54:646 O '89
Does this cereal belong in the medicine cabinet? [P&G claims that General Mills' cholesterol-reducing Benefit is a drug; Metamucil also contains psyllium] R. Mitchell and others. il *Business Week* p22-3 Jl 24 '89
Marketing
Big G is growing fat on oat cuisine [General Mills' cereals gain on Kellogg's] R. Mitchell. il *Business Week* p29 S 18 '89

CEREALS *See* Grain

CEREBELLUM *See* Brain

CEREBRAL CORTEX *See* Brain

CEREBRAL DOMINANCE *See* Laterality

CEREBRAL LESIONS *See* Brain damage

CEREBRAL PALSY
Driven by an unquenchable spirit, a Massachusetts woman writes an impossible book [confinement of R. Sienkiewicz-Mercer to Belchertown State School] L. Smith. il pors *People Weekly* 32:107+ S 11 '89
I raise my eyes to say yes [confinement to Belchertown State School in Massachusetts; excerpts] R. Sienkiewicz-Mercer and S. B. Kaplan. il *Glamour* 87:280-1+ O '89

CEREBROSPINAL FLUID
Looking for Lyme in the nervous system [research by John J. Halperin] I. Wickelgren. *Science News* 135:390 Je 24 '89
The mammalian choroid plexus. R. Spector and C. E. Johanson. bibl il *Scientific American* 261:68-74 N '89

CEREBROVASCULAR DISEASE
"I nearly lost my marriage" [actor T. Danson's wife, C. Coates, suffers stroke while giving birth] V. J. Radovsky. il pors *Redbook* 173:46+ Je '89
My body, myself. P. West. *Harper's* 279:26-8 Ag '89
Not your typical family-business wife [M. Forthman] S. Nelton. il por *Nation's Business* 77:40 Ag '89
Stroke: the brain disrupted [cover story] M.-L. Kamberg. il *Current Health 2* 15:3-9 F '89
The volunteer angel of San Antonio [stroke victim G. Cisneros] H. Hylton. il pors *New Choices for the Best Years* 29:76-7+ Ja '89
Causes
Aspirin on trial [effect on risk of heart attack and stroke] J. Poppy. il *Esquire* 111:89-91 Mr '89
What blocks blood to the brain? [stroke] *USA Today (Periodical)* 117:15-16 F '89
Diagnosis
Tests that can predict heart attacks and strokes. A. C. Mallozzi. il *Good Housekeeping* 209:249-50 O '89

CEREBROVASCULAR DISEASE—cont.
Nutritional aspects
Japanese stroke clues [increased risk of cerebral hemorrhage from low cholesterol] K. Fackelmann. il *Science News* 135:250+ Ap 22 '89
Prevention
Can operation avoid strokes? [carotid endarterectomy; views of John Byer] *USA Today (Periodical)* 117:14 F '89
New drug can avert strokes [ticlopidine] *USA Today (Periodical)* 117:12 F '89
Therapy
Innovative approaches to plasminogen activator therapy. E. Haber and others. bibl f il *Science* 243:51-6 Ja 6 '89
Keeping on [mother's recovery from stroke] S. L. Taylor. il *Essence* 20:43 Je '89
The long haul. M. Konner. il *The New York Times Magazine* p55-6 Jl 9 '89
New therapies brighten stroke horizon. R. Weiss. *Science News* 136:292 N 4 '89
Viper venom for stroke. il *Prevention (Emmaus, Pa.)* 41:16+ My '89
CEREMONIES *See* Rites and ceremonies
CERF, BENNETT, 1898-1971
about
Cerf to Newhouse. *The Nation* 249:623-4 N 27 '89
CERF, STEVEN R.
The other Frau. il *Opera News* 54:38-9+ D 9 '89
CERN *See* European Organization for Nuclear Research
CERN ACCELERATORS *See* Accelerators (Electrons, etc.)
CERNIGLIA, JOSEPH
about
Trading the Big Apple for an orchard. R. Duffy. il por *Business Week* p91 Je 26 '89
CERNIGLIA (JOSEPH) WINERY INC. *See* Joseph Cerniglia Winery Inc.
CERNUDA, RAMON
about
Art, intrigue and human rights. E. Shorris. il *The Nation* 249:14-18 Jl 3 '89
CERNY, ANN
(jt. auth) *See* Cerny, George, and Cerny, Ann
CERNY, GEORGE, AND CERNY, ANN
Cooperative games. pors *The Humanist* 49:35+ Mr/Ap '89
CERTIFICATES OF ANNUITY
Taxation
Is the tax-free CD too good to be true? il *Money* 18:16+ My '89
CERTIFICATES OF CREDIT CARD RECEIVABLES
You love plastic. Are your ready for 'plastic bonds'? L. J. Nathans. *Business Week* p182 Jl 17 '89
CERTIFICATES OF DEPOSIT
See also
Junk certificates of deposit
Boring was better. D. R. Katz. il *Esquire* 111:63-4 F '89
CDs that are fast on their feet [adjustable or variable rate CDs] S. Woolley. *Business Week* p180 My 22 '89
Certificates of deposit. K. K. Gracey. *Consumers' Research Magazine* 72:2 Mr '89
Certificates of deposit: it pays to shop around. P. N. Strassels. il *Nation's Business* 77:62 Jl '89
Don't ditch your old CD just for some sexy young rate. D. H. Dunn. *Business Week* p172 Mr 20 '89
Going-out-of-business sale [Ginnie Mae outlook brightens as CD rates go down] B. Weberman. il *Forbes* 144:229 S 18 '89
How to shop for CDs. il *Consumer Reports* 54:392 Je '89
Savings: don't reach for long-term CDs quite yet. J. Gilbert and E. M. MacDonald. il *Money* 18:33 Ja '89
Sick CDs [sick S&Ls] B. Weberman. il *Forbes* 143:165 F 6 '89
When your CD's time is up. K. McCormally. *Changing Times* 43:120-1 S '89
Where to keep your cash (I). il *Consumer Reports* 54:153 Mr '89
Your IRA: 9% bank CDs are the deals to beat. il *Money* 18:36 F '89
CERTIFICATES OF MERIT
Certificates and More [computer program] L. Frey. il *Compute!* 11:130+ D '89
CERTIFICATES OF PARTICIPATION
Sort-of bonds. B. Weberman. il *Forbes* 143:225 Ap 17 '89
CERTIFICATION
See also
Airplane engines, Jet—Standards
Airplanes, Business—Standards
Airplanes, Jet—Standards
Airships—Standards
Art teachers—Certification
Teachers—Certification
CERVENY, RANDALL S.
Weather of the pharaohs. il *Weatherwise* 42:307-14 D '89
CERVENY, RANDALL S., AND BRAZEL, SANDRA W.
Sherlock Holmes and the weather [cover story] il *Weatherwise* 42:80-4 Ap '89
CERVICAL CAPS
Preventing pregnancy with the cervical cap. K. Fackelmann. *Science News* 136:101 Ag 12 '89

CERVIX
Cancer
Don't let it happen to you! A. Fischer. *Redbook* 174:20+ N '89
"I'm trying to save women's lives" [interview with S. Dey] V. J. Radovsky. il pors *Redbook* 174:18+ N '89
Virus type predicts risky cancer return [human papillomavirus] K. Fackelmann. *Science News* 136:310 N 11 '89
Causes
More cervical cancer in passive smokers [research by Martha L. Slattery] K. Fackelmann. *Science News* 135:166 Mr 18 '89
Yet another deadly link [cigarette smoke and cervical cancer] *Time* 133:82 Mr 27 '89
Diagnosis
See also
Pap test
New test may replace Pap smear [quantitative fluorescent image analysis developed by Jeffrey Smith and George Hemstreet] il *USA Today (Periodical)* 117:7 F '89
CÉSAR, 1921-
about
Artist's dialogue: Cesar. M. Peppiatt. il por *Architectural Digest* 46:27+ F '89
CESAREAN SECTION
The cesarean epidemic. M. L. Grisanti. il *New York* 22:56-61 F 20 '89
Cesareans don't help lowest-weight babies [study by Michael H. Malloy] S. Hart. *Science News* 136:182 S 16 '89
Status symbol: affluent women have cesareans more often than poor women do. J. Horgan. *Scientific American* 261:36 O '89
Vaginal birth after a cesarean. P. A. Hillard. il *Parents* 64:179-80 Ap '89
CESARI, JOE
about
Gold amid the coal. N. Dawidoff. il por *Sports Illustrated* 70:44-6+ Ja 16 '89
CESIUM
Swedish moose a la cesium 137 [high concentration of radiation in muscle tissue following Chernobyl accident] il *Environment* 31:22-3 My '89
CESIUM IODIDE
X-ray diffraction to 302 gigapascals: high-pressure crystal structure of cesium iodide. H. K. Mao and others. bibl f il *Science* 246:649-51 N 3 '89
CESS, R. D., AND OTHERS
Interpretation of cloud-climate feedback as produced by 14 atmospheric general circulation models. bibl f il *Science* 245:513-16 Ag 4 '89
CESSNA AIRCRAFT COMPANY
Cessna foresees large market for new, $2.4-million CitationJet. E. H. Koicum. il *Aviation Week & Space Technology* 131:38 O 9 '89
Cessna pistons still on hold [liability concerns] *Flying* 116:8 Jl '89
Cessna plans to boost Citation production. *Aviation Week & Space Technology* 131:28 Jl 17 '89
Citation 5 provides larger cabin, improved performance. E. H. Phillips. il *Aviation Week & Space Technology* 130:246-7+ Je 12 '89
CETACEA
See also
Dolphins
Whales
Cetaceans. B. Würsig. bibl f il *Science* 244:1550-7 Je 30 '89
CETRON, MARVIN J.
The growing threat of terrorism. il por *The Futurist* 23:20-4 Jl/Ag '89
Preparing education for the year 2000. *The Education Digest* 54:3-6 Ap '89
CETRON, MARVIN J., AND DAVIES, OWEN
100 years of attitude [excerpt from American renaissance] il *Omni (New York, N.Y.)* 12:18+ O '89
Future trends [excerpt from American renaissance] il por *Omni (New York, N.Y.)* 12:112-14+ O '89
How to get the jump on the next ten years. il *Glamour* 87:252-7+ O '89
CETUS CORPORATION
A cancer fighter starts showing its mettle [interleukin-2] J. O. Hamilton. il *Business Week* p96+ Ja 16 '89
CEVALLOS, RODRIGO BORJA *See* Borja Cevallos, Rodrigo, 1935-
CEYLON *See* Sri Lanka
CÉZANNE, PAUL, 1839-1906
about
The counterlife. M. Stevens. il *The New Republic* 200:29-32 Ap 17 '89
'The father of us all'. P. Plagens. il *Newsweek* 113:68 F 27 '89
In the thick of it. S. Geist. il *Vogue* 179:226+ F '89
Modern art's first wild man. J. G. Swank. il *Christianity Today* 33:64-5 F 3 '89

CF *See* Cystic fibrosis
CF AIRFREIGHT, INC.
Consolidated Freightways to acquire Emery Air Freight for $230 million. R. G. O'Lone. *Aviation Week & Space Technology* 130:119 F 20 '89
CFCS *See* Chlorofluorocarbons
CFE TALKS *See* Disarmament—Conferences
CHA, YUAN, AND OTHERS
Hydrogen tunneling in enzyme reactions. bibl f il *Science* 243:1325-30 Mr 10 '89
CHABON, MICHAEL
Footloose. il por *Vogue* 179:266+ My '89
A model world [story] *The New Yorker* 65:41-8+ My 8 '89
More than human [story] il *Gentlemen's Quarterly* 59:175-6+ Je '89
Ocean Avenue [story] *The New Yorker* 65:52-5 N 6 '89
Romancing the Keys. il *Vogue* 179:234-5+ D '89
CHABROL, CLAUDE, 1930-
about
Story of women [film] Reviews
Film Comment il 25:16-18+ S/O '89. M. Pally
Harper's Bazaar il por 122:98 N '89. W. Fisher
Mademoiselle il 95:104+ N '89. R. Rosenbaum
The Nation 249:576-7 N 13 '89. S. Klawans
The New Republic 201:24-5 O 30 '89. S. Kauffmann
New York il 22:70+ O 30 '89. D. Denby
Rolling Stone p36 N 2 '89. P. Travers
CHACE, JAMES
Answering 'the German question'. *The New Republic* 201:19-20+ D 11 '89
Dithering in Nicaragua. bibl f il *The New York Review of Books* 36:46-51 Ag 17 '89
CHACE, SUSAN, 1942-
My generation. il *Seventeen* 48:99-106 O '89
CHACONAS, PETER
about
Even for cable, his lunatic talk show is cheap, but it's paying big dividends for L.A.'s Mr. Pete. R. Arias. il pors *People Weekly* 31:61-2 Je 19 '89
CHADLI, BENDJEDID
about
Algeria tries untying the knots of socialism. S. Toy. il por *Business Week* p49 Jl 31 '89
CHADWICK, DOUGLAS H.
Never snicker at a snipe. il *National Wildlife* 27:12-15 Ag/S '89
Sagebrush country: America's outback. il map *National Geographic* 175:52-71+ Ja '89
CHADWICK, GEORGE W.
about
New-world symphonies. P. G. Davis. pors *New York* 22:88-9 F 6 '89
CHAFETS, ZE'EV
Fear and loathing in Israel. il map *U.S. News & World Report* 107:36-8 Jl 10 '89
CHAFIN, DEWEY
about
Courting death, Appalachia's old-time religionists praise the Lord and pass the snakes. D. Grogan. il pors *People Weekly* 31:79+ My 1 '89
CHAGALL [dance] *See* Dance reviews—Single works
CHAGNON, NAPOLEON A., 1938-
about
Warfare over Yanomamö Indians. W. Booth. il *Science* 243:1138-40 Mr 3 '89
Yanomamö survival [discussion of March 3, 1989 article, Warfare over Yanomamö Indians] W. Booth. *Science* 244:11 Ap 7 '89
CHAIKOVSKY, P. I. *See* Tchaikovsky, Peter Ilich, 1840-1893
CHAIN LETTERS
Anecdotes, facetiae, satire, etc.
Chain of fools. J. Queenan. *The New Republic* 201:8 Jl 17-24 '89
CHAIN SAWS AND SAWING *See* Saws and sawing
CHAIN STORES
See also
Booksellers and bookselling—Chain and franchise operations
Department stores
Supermarkets
CHAINS
See also
Bicycle chains
CHAIR CANING *See* Cane weaving
CHAIRS
See also
La-Z-Boy Chair Co.
The 11 most uncomfortable chairs. S. Greenspan. il *House & Garden* 161:30+ Ja '89
Adirondack chair. T. Clauss. il *Outdoor Life* 184:42+ Ag '89
Chairs, with style [wood chairs] il *Southern Living* 24:174+ N '89
Classic chair-table. il *Home Mechanix* 86:41 Ap '89
Contemporary comfort [Morris chairs] B. Kieffer. il *The Family Handyman* 39:74-80 O '89

Easy does it [armchairs] R. Capotosto. il *Popular Mechanics* 166:80-4 Ja '89
Fold-over library chair. R. Freudenberger. il *The Mother Earth News* 119:78-9 S/O '89
The man in the perfect chair [designer J. Hutton] P. Patton. il por *Esquire* 111:104-7 Ja '89
Plein air chairs. D. B. Cowin. il *House & Garden* 161:124+ S '89
Sack-back Windsor chair (I). R. Marquis. il *Workbench* 45:58-62+ Ja/F '89
Sack-back Windsor chair (II). R. Marquis. il *Workbench* 45:82-7 Mr/Ap '89
Sitting well: how to shop for dining chairs. *Better Homes and Gardens* 67:64 Ap '89
Slipper chairs. C. Vogel. il *The New York Times Magazine* p56-7 Je 25 '89
Stand by your chair [rocking chairs] P. Patton. il *Esquire* 112:60 O '89
A traveling rocker. P. Butler and M. Butler. il *Outdoor Life* 183:63+ Ja '89
Anecdotes, facetiae, satire, etc.
Fit only for the fire: the Adirondack chair. M. Kernan. il *Smithsonian* 20:192 D '89
Collectors and collecting
The Belter chair. D. Bourdon. il *American Heritage* 40:24-5 Mr '89
Collectibles to cherish [children's chairs] il *Southern Living* 24:168-9 Ap '89
Maintenance and repair
See also
Cane weaving
How to fix a loose spindle chair. T. Klenck. il *Popular Mechanics* 166:105-6 Ja '89
Prices
Sitting pretty [chairs of government officials] V. Novak. il *Common Cause Magazine* 15:7 Mr/Ap '89
CHAISSON, ERIC
The cosmological imperative. *Astronomy* 17:8 F '89
CHAKA, ZULU CHIEF, 1787?-1828
about
Shaka Zulu, a living legend. K. I. Bosco. il *The Unesco Courier* 42:44-7 S '89
CHAKRABARTY, ANANDA M., 1938-
about
Where was Chakrabarty's "bug"? G. Byrne. *Science* 244:919 My 26 '89
CHALFIE, MARTIN, AND AU, MACY
Genetic control of differentiation of the Caenorhabditis elegans touch receptor neurons. bibl f il *Science* 243:1027-33 F 24 '89
CHALIAPIN, FEODOR, 1873-1938
Photographs and photography
Le grand Chaliapin. il *Opera News* 54:16-17 S '89
CHALK'S INTERNATIONAL AIRLINES
Merv Griffin may ground the seaplanes Miami Vice made famous. A. Fins. il *Business Week* p36 D 4 '89
CHALL, JEANNE STERNLICHT, 1921-
Learning to read: the great debate 20 years later—a response to 'Debunking the great phonics myth'. bibl f il *Phi Delta Kappan* 70:521-38 Mr '89
The uses of educational research: comments on Carbo. bibl f *Phi Delta Kappan* 71:158-60 O '89
about
An evaluation of Jeanne Chall's response to 'Debunking the great phonics myth' [discussion of November 1988 and March 1989 articles] M. Carbo. bibl f il *Phi Delta Kappan* 71:152-7 O '89
The 'great' debate—can both Carbo and Chall be right? R. L. Turner. bibl f il *Phi Delta Kappan* 71:276-83 D '89
Learning to read: the great debate 20 years later—a response to 'Debunking the great phonics myth' [discussion of November 1988 article; with editorial comment by Pauline B. Gough] M. Carbo. bibl f il *Phi Delta Kappan* 70:498, 521-38 Mr '89
CHALLENGER (RESEARCH SHIP)
Oceanographic ships [stamps] A. L. Rice. bibl il *Sea Frontiers* 35:14-17 Ja/F '89
CHALLENGER (SPACE SHUTTLE) EXPLOSION, 1986
A thousand days of tears [J. Scobee, widow of astronaut D. Scobee] K. Casey. il pors *Ladies' Home Journal* 106:120-2+ F '89
Reporters and reporting
NASA's legal folly [battle to block release of recording of astronauts' voices] M. Stevens. *Ad Astra* 1:48 My '89
The return of the shuttle syndrome? F. Jerome. il *Technology Review* 92:65-6 Ja '89
CHALLENGER AIRPLANES *See* Airplanes, Business
CHALMERS, IRENA
Rise and dine. il *Modern Maturity* 32:68-72 O/N '89
CHAMBER MUSIC
See also
Compact discs—Chamber music
Da Camera Society
String quartets
CHAMBER MUSIC SOCIETY OF LINCOLN CENTER
Family ties. P. G. Davis. il *New York* 22:129-30 N 6 '89

CHAMBER OF COMMERCE OF THE UNITED STATES OF AMERICA
Education: the competitor's key [views of chairman J. L. Clendenin] R. T. Gray. il pors *Nation's Business* 77:60+ Je '89
Free-market economics: antidote for war and poverty. il *Nation's Business* 77:71 D '89
Herman J. Russell named to U.S. Chamber board. por *Jet* 76:6 Je 5 '89
How the good guys won the battle of Section 89. il *Nation's Business* 77:101 N '89
New challenges, new opportunities [annual report] il *Nation's Business* 77:81-5 My '89
A plan for competitiveness and continued economic growth [Keeping America on top policy statement] il *Nation's Business* 77:80 Ja '89
CHAMBER OF COMMERCE OF THE UNITED STATES OF AMERICA. AMERICAN BUSINESS NETWORK
See American Business Network
CHAMBER ORCHESTRAS
See also
Les Arts Florissants (Chamber orchestra)
Chamber Music Society of Lincoln Center
New York Chamber Ensemble
New York Chamber Symphony
Orpheus Chamber Orchestra
CHAMBERLAIN, JOHN ANGUS, 1927-
about
John Chamberlain at Pace. N. Princenthal. il *Art in America* 77:165 Je '89
CHAMBERLAIN, NEVILLE, 1869-1940
about
The last lion: alone [excerpt] W. Manchester. il pors *Conservative Digest* 15:63+ Jl/Ag '89
Postscript to Munich [interview with A. Douglas-Home] J. Ranelagh. *National Review* 41:30-1 Je 2 '89
Were we wrong in 1939? [with reply by J. P. Roche] D. Carlton. il *National Review* 41:44+ S 29 '89
CHAMBERLAIN, RICHARD
about
23 years after Dr. Kildare, Richard Chamberlain's back in practice [cover story] L. Eisenberg. il pors *TV Guide* 37:2-3+ N 11-17 '89
CHAMBERS, DENNIS
about
Dennis Chambers. B. Milkowski. il por *Down Beat* 56:28 D '89
CHAMBERS, JANE, 1937-1983
about
The quintessential image [drama] Reviews
New York il 22:77-8 Ag 14 '89. J. Simon
CHAMBERS, JOSEPH
about
Trouble brews over charges of "liberalism". D. Disch. por *Christianity Today* 33:42-3 F 17 '89
CHAMBERS, JULIUS LEVONNE
about
Chambers warns of dire impact of recent rulings by U.S. Supreme Court. por *Jet* 76:38 Ag 21 '89
CHAMBERS, RAYMOND G.
about
Ready to roll. R. King. il por *Forbes* 144 Special Issue:118-19+ O 23 '89
CHAMBERS, ROBERT
about
Art imitates death in The preppie murder. J. S. Kunen. il pors *People Weekly* 32:36-9 S 25 '89
'There was no sex diary': Jennifer Levin wasn't asking for trouble. P. H. Brown. il pors *TV Guide* 37:24-7 S 23-29 '89
Wasted lives: the shocking case of "the preppie murder" [excerpt from Wasted] L. Wolfe. il pors *Redbook* 173:170-2+ S '89
CHAMBERS, ROBERT B.
Simulating shattered glass. il *Theatre Crafts* 23:84 Ja '89
CHAMBERS, VIRGIL
Canoeing our rivers. il *The Conservationist* 44:8-11 Jl/Ag '89
CHAMBERS, WHITTAKER
about
Whittaker Chambers, journalist. T. Teachout. il *The American Spectator* 22:17-20 Jl '89
CHAMBERS DEVELOPMENT COMPANY
Talking trash. E. F. Cone. il por *Forbes* 143:14 Ap 17 '89
CHAMBERS OF COMMERCE
See also
Chamber of Commerce of the United States of America
CHAMBRAUD, ANDRÉ
Testing time for both socialism and capitalism. il *World Press Review* 36:11-13 D '89
CHAMONIX (FRANCE)
Valley high! C. Cooper. il *Skiing* 41:64-9+ Mr '89
CHAMORRO, VIOLETA BARRIOS DE
about
Don't call her comrade. J. Moody. il por *Time* 133:62-4 Je 12 '89
If not the Sandinistas . . . il por *Time* 134:49 N 13 '89

Money isn't everything. R. Watson. il por *Newsweek* 114:47 O 9 '89
Turning to the voters in Nicaragua [cover story] F. D. Colburn. il pors *The New Leader* 72:5-7 N 13 '89
CHAMP COOKIES (FIRM)
Black cookie co. in D.C. gets presidential push. il *Jet* 76:36 S 11 '89
CHAMPAGNE
See also
Cooking—Wine
Britain's boast. F. J. Prial. il *The New York Times Magazine* p64 My 14 '89
Business and pleasure: champagne tasting and toasting. E. Sahatjian. il *Working Woman* 14:107-10+ D '89
Champagne etiquette. il *Home Mechanix* 85:54 D '89
Elegant effervescence [Taittingers] R. Levio. il *Harper's Bazaar* 122:48 Ap '89
Magnum force. A. Richman. il *Gentlemen's Quarterly* 59:270+ Je '89
Popping your cork. S. Dooley. il *Harper's Bazaar* 122:36+ Ja '89
The red, the white, and the bubbly. A. Bespaloff. il *New York* 22:50-1 Ja 2 '89
Vintage celebrations. S. Dooley. il *Harper's Bazaar* 122:131+ Je '89
Waiter, a magnum of your best Portland champagne. S. Toy. il *Business Week* p92+ D 11 '89
CHAMPION BUILDING SYSTEMS INC.
How a hot-growth company got decked [Amre's acquisition of Champion Building Systems Inc.] T. Mason. il *Business Week* p34+ F 13 '89
CHAMPION INTERNATIONAL CORP.
Fight for Pigeon River [conflict between Champion International Corp. in Canton, N.C. and Tennessee environmentalists over pollution control] M. Satchell. il map *U.S. News & World Report* 107:27-8+ D 4 '89
CHAMPION PRODUCTS INC.
The price was right [Sara Lee acquires Champion Products] W. Heuslein. il *Forbes* 143:10 My 15 '89
CHAMPIONS FOREVER [film] See Motion picture reviews—Single works
CHAMPIONSHIP AUTO RACING TEAMS (ORGANIZATION)
CART charts a new course. J. Rusz. il *Road & Track* 40:99+ F '89
Factory fracas [lineup for Indy Car World Series] J. Rusz. il *Road & Track* 40:120-5+ Je '89
CHAMPLAIN, LAKE *See* Lake Champlain
CHAMPLIN, JOSEPH M.
Barriers to the sacraments. il *Commonweal* 116:559-61 O 20 '89
CHAMPOLLION, JEAN FRANÇOIS, 1790-1832
about
Champollion, a hero of the Enlightenment [interview with J. Lacouture] il por *The Unesco Courier* 42:4-9 O '89
CHAMPS *See* Charged massive particles
CHAN, JOHNNY
about
Chan is bluffing (we think). P. Alson. il por *Esquire* 111:166-8+ My '89
CHAN, PETER
Bonsai landscape pruning. il *Organic Gardening* 36:27-9 Je '89
CHAN, SUCHENG
Beyond affirmative action: empowering Asian American faculty. il *Change* 21:48-51 N/D '89
CHANCE, PAUL
Free spirits. il *Psychology Today* 23:16 Ap '89
Kids without friends. il *Psychology Today* 23:28-31 Ja/F '89
A neat gift idea. il *Psychology Today* 22:58-9 D '88
The other 90%. il *Psychology Today* 23:20-1 N '89
Seeing is believing. il *Psychology Today* 23:26 Ja/F '89
CHANCE
See also
Luck
Probabilities
CHANCES ARE [film] See Motion picture reviews—Single works
CHANDA, NAYAN
Civil war in Cambodia? *Foreign Policy* 76:26-43 Fall '89
CHANDLER, ALFRED DUPONT
about
Advice to small companies: think big [interview] R. Koselka. il por *Forbes* 144:204-5+ N 13 '89
CHANDLER, ANDREA RAY
Third time's a charm: making your autumn garden work. il *Flower and Garden* 33:34-7 Jl/Ag '89
CHANDLER, COLBY H.
Manufacturing [address, April 6, 1989] *Vital Speeches of the Day* 55:461-4 My 15 '89
CHANDLER, CYNTHIA K., AND KOLANDER, CHERYL A.
Helping students accentuate positive thoughts. *The Education Digest* 54:52-4 Ja '89

CHANDLER, ROBIN
about
Pieces of Robin Chandler. E. Strickland. il por *American Visions* 4:40-3 D '89
CHANDLER, THEODORE A.
Redistributing work to shrink class size. *The Education Digest* 54:44-5 F '89
CHANDLER WOBBLE *See* Polar wander
CHANDRA MAHARAJ, SWAMI
Of guns and a guru. M. McDonald. il pors *Maclean's* 102:28-9 Mr 27 '89
CHANEL, COCO, 1883-1971
about
The billionaires behind Chanel [cover story] P. Berman. il pors *Forbes* 143:104-8 Ap 3 '89
Collaborating on the spirit of a new age. D. Harris. il pors *Architectural Digest* 46:42+ S '89
Couture report: the four schools of design. J. J. Buck. il *Vogue* 179:324-5+ O '89
School of Chanel. H. Brubach. *The New Yorker* 65:71-6 F 27 '89
CHANEL, GABRIELLE *See* Chanel, Coco, 1883-1971
CHANEL (FIRM)
The billionaires behind Chanel [cover story] P. Berman. il pors *Forbes* 143:104-8 Ap 3 '89
In a clash of symbols, Chanel's top model falls from the runway [I. de la Fressange selected to be model for bust of Marianne] M. H. J. Farrell. il pors *People Weekly* 32:51+ Ag 14 '89
CHANEY, DALE
South Padre's magic shrinking beaches. il *The Saturday Evening Post* 261:84-7 O '89
Southwest skiing: lodes of fun. il *The Saturday Evening Post* 261:86-7+ N/D '89
CHANEY, JAMES EARL, 1943-1964
about
The '64 civil rights murders: the struggle continues [cover story] J. Kornbluth. il pors *The New York Times Magazine* p16-19+ Jl 23 '89
Back on the bus. P. Dray. il pors *Mother Jones* 14:37-9+ N '89
Honor trio killed by KKK in Mississippi vote drive. il pors *Jet* 76:6-7 Jl 10 '89
CHANEY, JOHN
A slap at blacks. il por *Sports Illustrated* 70:18-19 Ja 23 '89
CHANEY, WILLIAM R.
about
Fast break at Tiffany's. M. Roman. il por *Business Week* p102+ O 9 '89
CHANG, MICHAEL
about
Feat of clay [with editorial comment by Neil Amdur] S. Flink. il pors *World Tennis* 37:4, 56-7+ Ag '89
Giant killers. C. Kirkpatrick. il pors *Sports Illustrated* 70:34-6+ Je 19 '89
I was a teenage U.S. hope. R. Wetzsteon. il pors *Sport (New York, N.Y.)* 80:60-2+ Jl '89
Rising star Michael Chang breaks records, not rackets. S. K. Reed. il por *People Weekly* 31:59-60 My 29 '89
Strokes of genius. P. Cohen. il pors *World Tennis* 36:62-4 Ap '89
Youth will be served. T. Callahan. il pors *Time* 133:90 Je 26 '89
CHANG, MICHAEL P., AND OTHERS
Second cytotoxic pathway of diphtheria toxin suggested by nuclease activity. bibl f il *Science* 246:1165-8 D 1 '89
CHANGE
See also
Political change
Social change
Technological innovations
No escaping modern times. R. Rosenblatt. il *U.S. News & World Report* 107:10-11 O 2 '89
CHANGE (PERIODICAL)
Contributing to Change. T. J. Marchese. *Change* 21:4 Ja/F '89
CHANGE (PSYCHOLOGY)
. . . and other rites of passage. S. G. Sheehy. il *Working Woman* 14:90-2 Je '89
Can men change? J. Stone. il *Glamour* 87:164 Mr '89
Do kids ever change? J. Segal and Z. Segal. il *Parents* 64:212 Je '89
How to make the most of change in your life [quiz] J. Wonder and P. Donovan. il *Glamour* 87:262-5+ Je '89
Lifestyle changes control disease [views of James R. Gavin and Leann Olansky] *USA Today (Periodical)* 117:12-13 F '89
Personal milestones: what stands out [women celebrities] il *Glamour* 87:170 Ap '89
Ready, willing and wary. D. Merkin. il *The New York Times Magazine* p12+ Jl 16 '89
Should you change your looks for a lover? D. Heyn. *Mademoiselle* 95:54 Ja '89
Turning points to better health. R. Rodale. il *Prevention (Emmaus, Pa.)* 41:30+ Mr '89

Welcome change. V. Buchan. *Reader's Digest* 134:145 F '89
What bugs you about boys? [advice on getting guys to change] il *Seventeen* 48:70-1 Jl '89
When it's time for a change [finding a mentor] A. Gottlieb. *McCall's* 117:113-14 N '89
CHANGE OF ADDRESS
Mail and the moving man. R. Phalon. il *Forbes* 143:133-4 F 6 '89
When you move, tell your friends. And the IRS. L. Wiener. il *U.S. News & World Report* 107:121 O 16 '89
CHANGE OF HOBBIT (SANTA MONICA, CALIF.: BOOKSTORE) *See* Booksellers and bookselling—California
CHANGE OF LIFE IN WOMEN *See* Menopause
CHANGE OF SEX
Sexual stunts of clownfish [cover story] D. G. Fautin. il *Natural History* p42-7 S '89
CHANGELINGS *See* Child switching
CHANHASSEN DINNER THEATRE
6,500 'I do's' make for one sturdy marriage for Susan Goeppinger and fellow actor David Anders [18 year run of musical I do, I do] P. Freeman. il pors *People Weekly* 31:89-90 My 1 '89
CHANNEL CATFISH FISHING *See* Catfish fishing
CHANNEL FREQUENCY ALLOCATION, TELEVISION *See* Television frequency allocation
CHANNEL ONE [television program] See Television program reviews—Single works
CHANNEL TUNNEL *See* English Channel tunnel
CHANNELERS
A linguistic "nay" to channeling [work of Sarah Thomason] M. Roberts. il *Psychology Today* 23:64-5 O '89
CHANNELING (PHYSICS)
The channeling of electrons and positrons. A. H. Sørensen and E. Uggerhøj. bibl il *Scientific American* 260:96-102 Je '89
CHANNELS (HYDRAULIC ENGINEERING)
See also
Aqueducts
CHANNELS (PERIODICAL)
Covering our bets. M. Brown. *Channels (New York, N.Y.: 1986)* 9:6 My '89
Forward progress. M. Brown. *Channels (New York, N.Y.: 1986)* 9:6 S '89
The new age of marketing. J. A. Berger. *Channels (New York, N.Y.: 1986)* 9:6 Ja '89
CHANNON, SIR HENRY, 1897-1958
about
All's well that's Boswell. T. Mallon. il *Gentlemen's Quarterly* 59:75+ D '89
CHANT, BEN
Street smarts. il *New York* 22:68-9 My 1 '89
CHANTERELLE (NEW YORK, N.Y.: RESTAURANT) *See* New York (N.Y.)—Restaurants, nightclubs, bars, etc.
CHANTIERS BÉNÉTEAU (FIRM) *See* Bénéteau (Firm)
CHANUKAH *See* Hanukkah
CHAO, B. FONG
Length-of-day variations caused by El Niño-Southern Oscillation and Quasi-Biennial Oscillation. bibl f il *Science* 243:923-5 F 17 '89
CHAOS (SCIENCE)
See also
Strange attractors
The body chaotic. G. Taubes. il *Discover* 10:62-7 My '89
Can butterflies cause tornadoes? G. Charles. il *World Press Review* 36:54 Ag '89
Chaos on computers [Chaos Demonstrations program] *Science* 246:1172 D 1 '89
Chaos study could affect computers, networks. *Byte* 14:16+ My '89
Chaos theory: how big an advance? R. Pool. il *Science* 245:26-8 Jl 7 '89
The chaotic brain: new models of behavior [nonlinear mathematical models] J. Alper. *Psychology Today* 23:21 My '89
Does chaos permeate the solar system? R. A. Kerr. il *Science* 244:144-5 Ap 14 '89
Ecologists flirt with chaos. R. Pool. il *Science* 243:310-13 Ja 20 '89
Ergodic theory, randomness, and "chaos". D. S. Ornstein. bibl f il *Science* 243:182-7 Ja 13 '89
First direct view of solar system chaos [Hyperion observations by James Klavetter] *Science* 246:998-9 N 24 '89
Is it chaos, or is it just noise? [patterns in epidemics] R. Pool. bibl il *Science* 243:25-8 Ja 6 '89
Is it healthy to be chaotic? R. Pool. bibl il *Science* 243:604-7 F 3 '89
Is something strange about the weather? [researchers using tools from the study of chaos] R. Pool. bibl il *Science* 243:1290-3 Mr 10 '89
The love of randomness. D. K. Mano. *National Review* 41:58-9 O 13 '89
The mixing of fluids [cover story] J. M. Ottino. il *Scientific American* 260:56-7+ Ja '89
Nonlinear thinking [chaotic theories of G. Mayer-Kress] J. Horgan. *Scientific American* 260:26+ Je '89
Playing dice with the solar system. A. M. Killian. il *Sky and Telescope* 78:136-8+ Ag '89

CHAOS (SCIENCE)—*cont.*
Predicting chaos [work of Ian Stewart] H. Kenner. il *Byte* 14:340+ Jl '89
Quantum chaos: enigma wrapped in a mystery. R. Pool. *Science* 243:893-5 F 17 '89
Shooting for the moon [role of chaos in business; address, April 27, 1989] R. A. Ferchat. *Vital Speeches of the Day* 55:727-31 S 15 '89
Terminal chaos. il *Discover* 10:12 F '89

CHAOS (SCIENCE) IN ART
Exhibitions
Art [Strange attractors: signs of chaos at New Museum of Contemporary Art] K. Larson. il *New York* 22:149-50 O 23 '89
Art imitates chaos [Chicago and New York exhibits] R. Pool. il *Science* 245:27 Jl 7 '89

CHAPIN, LAUREN
"All I ever wanted was my mother's love": the sad life of a child star; ed. by Ace Collins. il pors *Redbook* 173:28+ Ag '89
about
After Father knows best, it was drugs, jail, depression. M. Littwin. il pors *TV Guide* 37:6-8 Je 17-23 '89
"I'm not ashamed of my past" [interview] L. Woods. por *Redbook* 173:30 Ag '89

CHAPLAINS, MILITARY
Legend of the four chaplains [courage displayed by Lieutenants Fox, Goode, Poling, and Washington during sinking of the S. S. Dorchester in World War II] L. Elliott. il *Reader's Digest* 134:65-70 Je '89

CHAPLIN, CHARLIE, 1889-1977
about
132 takes/th-th-that's all folks. C. Jones. il por *Film Comment* 25:2-3 Mr/Ap '89
Chaplin's admirers tip their hats for his 100th. il por *People Weekly* 31:50-1 My 1 '89
Charlie Chaplin, stranger and brother. M. Oms. il pors *The Unesco Courier* 42:38-43 O '89
Deification of a Tramp. N. Mills. il por *American Film* 14:13 Je '89
Double event. H. M. Geduld. il *The Humanist* 49:39-40 Ja/F '89
Funny man of the century. il pors *U.S. News & World Report* 106:16 Ap 24 '89
Notes and comment. *The New Yorker* 64:19 Ja 9 '89
Out from the shadow of the Little Tramp. S. Chaplin. il pors *People Weekly* 31:101-4 Mr 20 '89
Sunnyside [film] Reviews
  The New Republic 200:28 My 22 '89. S. Kauffmann
A woman of Paris [film] Reviews
  The New Republic 200:28-9 My 22 '89. S. Kauffmann

CHAPLIN, SYDNEY
Out from the shadow of the Little Tramp. il pors *People Weekly* 31:101-4 Mr 20 '89

CHAPMAN, CLARK R., AND MORRISON, DAVID, 1940-
The next doomsday impact. *Astronomy* 17:8 N '89

CHAPMAN, GARY, 1952-
Smart rocks, Brilliant Pebbles, genius dust? il *The Bulletin of the Atomic Scientists* 45:10-11+ N '89

CHAPMAN, GRAHAM
about
Obituary
  People Weekly il pors 32:52-4 O 30 '89. S. Schindehette

CHAPMAN, IAN
about
Craig to head all Murdoch book business; Chapman resigns from Collins; authors' reaction uncertain. por *Publishers Weekly* 235:10+ F 3 '89

CHAPMAN, JEFFERSON, AND OTHERS
Strawberry fields, almost forever. il maps *Natural History* p50-8 S '89

CHAPMAN, MAX, JR.
about
Nomura seeks a Yankee skipper. J. Friedman. il por *Business Week* p96 S 4 '89

CHAPMAN, TRACY
about
Crossroads for Tracy Chapman. P. Garland. por *Stereo Review* 54:129 D '89
This year's Grammys: the women have their day. D. Hiltbrand. il pors *TV Guide* 37:6-7+ F 18-24 '89
Tracy Chapman. R. Givens. il por *Newsweek* 114:65-6 O 16 '89
Tracy Chapman at the 'Crossroads'. F. Goodman. il *Rolling Stone* p135-6 O 5 '89

CHAPPAQUIDDICK INCIDENT, JULY 1969 *See* Kennedy, Edward Moore, 1932——Chappaquiddick incident, July 1969

CHAPPELL, EDWARD
Minnesota's 'Way to independence'. *The Nation* 249:763-6 D 18 '89
Museums. *The Nation* 249:655-60 N 27 '89
Valentine Museum's Jim Crow. *The Nation* 249:102-4 Jl 17 '89

CHAPPELL, THOMAS M.
about
Hearts, minds and market share. L. Jereski. il por *Forbes* 143:80+ Ap 3 '89

CHAPPLE, STEVE
Montana: not a movie. il *Mother Jones* 14:40-1 S '89

CHAPUT-ROLLAND, SOLANGE
about
One senator's crusade. L. Van Dusen. il por *Maclean's* 102:35 O 30 '89

CHARACTER
See also
Individuality
Personality
Typology (Psychology)
Measuring character in the headlines. J. M. Wall. *The Christian Century* 106:275-6 Mr 15 '89

CHARACTER EDUCATION *See* Moral education

CHARACTER SETS (COMPUTER SCIENCE)
The ABCs of digital type. J. Collins. il *Byte* 14:403-8 N '89
A complete circuit [character generator] R. Grossblatt. il *Radio-Electronics* 60:28-9+ Jl '89
A custom-character generator [EPROM character sets for LED displays] R. Grossblatt. il *Radio-Electronics* 60:80-2+ Mr '89
Let's start programming! [EPROM character sets for LED displays] R. Grossblatt. il *Radio-Electronics* 60:72-3+ My '89

CHARACTERIZATION
The birth of a series character [detective fiction] G. C. Chesbro. *The Writer* 102:14-16 Mr '89
Creating short fiction from character: five rules. L. Nevai. *The Writer* 102:11-13 Ja '89
The human factor. I. Howe. *The New Republic* 200:30-4 My 8 '89
The major role of minor characters in fiction. H. A. Ostrom. *The Writer* 102:9-11+ F '89
Plot and character in suspense fiction. J. Aiken. *The Writer* 102:9-13 My '89
Where to find supporting characters. J. Daniels. *The Writer* 102:27-8 D '89
Who are these people? Knowing your fiction characters. S. Levitin. *The Writer* 102:15-17 N '89

CHARACTERS IN ADVERTISING *See* Advertising characters

CHARACTERS IN LITERATURE
See also
Alice in Wonderland (Fictional character)
Animals in literature
Anne of Green Gables (Fictional character)
Babar (Fictional character)
Blacks in literature
Bomba (Fictional character)
Characterization
Curious George (Fictional character)
Eloise (Fictional character)
Ilya of Murom (Fictional character)
James Bond (Fictional character)
Lucy Marsden (Fictional character)
Mary Poppins (Fictional character)
Moby Dick (Fictional character)
Oliver Twist (Literary character)
Perry Mason (Fictional character)
Phantom of the Opera (Fictional character)
Sherlock Holmes (Fictional character)
Wizard of Oz (Fictional character)
Women in literature
Anywhere, with the best of company [authors select literary or historical characters as traveling companions] il *The New York Times Book Review* 94:31-3 Je 11 '89

CHARACTERS IN MOTION PICTURES
See also
Batman (Fictional character)
E.T. (Fictional character)
Freddy Krueger (Fictional character)
Ghostbusters (Fictional characters)
Goofy (Fictional character)
Grumpy (Fictional character)
James Bond (Fictional character)
Mickey Mouse (Fictional character)
Munchkins (Fictional characters)
Phantom of the Opera (Fictional character)
Sherlock Holmes (Fictional character)
Shirley Valentine (Fictional character)
Snow White (Fictional character)
Wizard of Oz (Fictional character)
Women in motion pictures
Celebrating the celebactor [celebrities play themselves in movies] J. Barth. il *Film Comment* 25:46 N/D '89

CHARACTERS IN MUSICALS, REVUES, ETC.
See also
Phantom of the Opera (Fictional character)

CHARACTERS IN RADIO
See also
Mama Montego (Fictional character)

CHARACTERS IN TELEVISION
See also
Abby Perkins (Fictional character)
ALF (Fictional character)
Arnie Becker (Fictional character)
Batman (Fictional character)
Blacks in television

CHARACTERS IN TELEVISION—See also—*cont.*
Children in television
Columbo (Fictional character)
J.R. Ewing (Fictional character)
Mary Richards (Fictional character)
Mighty Mouse (Fictional character)
Mothers in television
Murphy Brown (Fictional character)
Rebecca Howe (Fictional character)
Roseanne Conners (Fictional character)
Women in television
Youth in television
LE CHARDONNAY (WEST HOLLYWOOD, CALIF.: RESTAURANT) *See* West Hollywood (Calif.)—Restaurants, nightclubs, bars, etc.
CHARDONNAY WINES *See* Wine
CHARGE COUPLED DEVICES (ELECTRONICS)
See also
Metal oxide semiconductors
Active-optics camera tested [imaging system built for the Canada-France-Hawaii Telescope] il *Sky and Telescope* 78:12-13 Jl '89
Amateurs record Mars with CCD. il *Astronomy* 17:92 F '89
Crab close up [CCD images by Sidney van den Bergh and Christopher J. Pritchet] il *Sky and Telescope* 77:586 Je '89
Deep space [observation of extremely faint, bluish galaxies by J. Anthony Tyson] il *Sky and Telescope* 78:455-6 N '89
Interpreting CCD images of Mars. S. M. Larson. il *Sky and Telescope* 77:472 My '89
Monster CCD's get the big picture [Kitt Peak] il *Sky and Telescope* 78:343-4 O '89
CHARGED MASSIVE PARTICLES
Weighing the CHAMPions of the universe [research by Sheldon L. Glashow] I. Peterson. *Science News* 136:214 S 30 '89
CHARGES, ELECTRIC *See* Electric charges
CHARGING, BATTERY *See* Electric batteries—Charging
CHARISMA
The charisma merchants. D. Machan. il *Forbes* 143:100-1 Ja 23 '89
CHARISMATIC MOVEMENT *See* Pentecostalism
CHARITABLE CONTRIBUTIONS AS TAX DEDUCTIONS
See Income tax—Deductions
CHARITABLE GIFT ANNUITIES
A way to give—and keep on receiving. T. Segal. *Business Week* p164 Je 26 '89
CHARITABLE TRUSTS *See* Trusts and trustees—Charitable trusts
CHARITIES
See also
Affinity cards
Blacks—Charities
Charitable gift annuities
Congressmen—Charitable contributions
Corporations—Charitable contributions
Fund raising
Giving
Relief work
Trusts and trustees—Charitable trusts
The Capitol charity ball [use of voter registration drives and charities to solicit soft money campaign funds] G. Borger. il *U.S. News & World Report* 107:19+ D 18 '89
Cards that send two messages [cards that aid charitable causes] A. C. Mallozzi. *Good Housekeeping* 209:271 N '89
Fed up with charity. J. Bourque. por *Newsweek* 114:10 S 4 '89
For goodness' sake [special section] N. R. Gibbs. il *Time* 133:20-4 Ja 9 '89
Gift list [Forbes four hundred contributors to charities] il *Forbes* 144 Special Issue:124-5 O 23 '89
Giving back. See alternate issues of Changing Times beginning January 1989
Marcia Anderson and Jim Diebold marry for money—the dollars their guests gave to charity. P. Freeman. il pors *People Weekly* 31:139+ Je 19 '89
New guidelines for giving. M. T. Smith. il *Money* 18:141-4+ D '89
Sweet charity. J. Anthony. il *Mother Jones* 14:51-2+ D '89
The thoughts that count. A. Matthews. il *Forbes* 143:126-8 F 20 '89
Bibliography
On discovering philanthropy: an informal guide to the core literature. R. L. Payton. il *Change* 20:32-7 N/D '88
Directors
An executive's guide to volunteering. P. Kruger. *Working Woman* 14:86-8 D '89
History
The centennial of Andrew Carnegie's "Gospel of wealth". J. M. McShane. *America* 161:211-13 O 7 '89
Trustees, boards, committees, etc.
Serve on that board? R. R. Roha. *Changing Times* 43:126-7 Mr '89

Canada
Struggling for dollars. N. Underwood. il *Maclean's* 102:50 S 25 '89
CHARITY
See also
Love (Theology)
Should I have let him in? T. J. Craughwell. il *Commonweal* 116:702-3 D 15 '89
CHARLATANS *See* Quacks and quackery
CHARLEMAGNE, EMPEROR, 742-814
about
Alcuin and the 'new Athens'. M. Alberi. il por *History Today* 39:35-41 S '89
CHARLENE'S (FIRM)
Black hairdresser turns six-chair salon into a multimillion $ business [C. Miles] il pors *Jet* 76:28-30+ Je 12 '89
CHARLES, PRINCE OF WALES, 1948-
A vision of Britain—architecture in crisis [excerpt] il pors *Architectural Digest* 46:32-4+ O '89
about
Charles and Diana: portrait of a marriage [excerpt from King Charles III] A. Holden. il pors *Ladies' Home Journal* 106:115-17+ F '89
Charles and the 'carbuncle'. por *Newsweek* 114:37 S 18 '89
Charles: England's designing prince. M. Filler. il pors *House & Garden* 161:158-61+ Mr '89
Charles's new duds turn a fashion frog princely. S. Schindehette. il pors *People Weekly* 31:184-5 Mr 6 '89
The prince and the architects. C. Knevett. il *Architectural Record* 177:57+ O '89
The rush-rush routine of Charles and Diana [cover story] I. Seward. il pors *The Saturday Evening Post* 261:42-7 S '89
Seeking greener pastures. R. Knight. il por *U.S. News & World Report* 106:54 Je 19 '89
Speaking the prince's English. M. Bradbury. il *The New York Times Magazine* p46+ S 24 '89
Whose Britain is it? J. Adler. il por *Newsweek* 114:84-6 N 13 '89
The winds of Windsorism [cover story] H. Muschamp. *The New Republic* 201:30-5 D 11 '89
CHARLES, CAROLINE
about
Caroline Charles: the practical charms of a very English apartment in Knightsbridge. E. Lambert. il por *Architectural Digest* 46:128-31 S '89
CHARLES, CHANTEE
about
Girl 13, raps death penalty at White House event for children's anti-drug group. il pors *Jet* 76:31 O 2 '89
CHARLES, DANIEL
Exporting trouble—West Germany's freewheeling nuclear business. bibl f il *The Bulletin of the Atomic Scientists* 45:21-7 Ap '89
Keeping semiconductors safe for democracy. il *The Bulletin of the Atomic Scientists* 45:8-10 N '89
CHARLES, GILBERT
Can butterflies cause tornadoes? il *World Press Review* 36:54 Ag '89
CHARLES, HENRIETTA E.
Flying high. il *American Visions* 4:8+ Ap '89
CHARLES, JOSH
about
Putting a romantic spin on Dead Poets Society, Josh Charles finds his career alive and kicking. A. Abrahams. il por *People Weekly* 32:55-6 Jl 3 '89
CHARLES, NICHOLAS S.
Hot, hot, hot. il *Black Enterprise* 19:104-5 My '89
When profits meet principles. il *Black Enterprise* 19:83-4+ My '89
CHARLES, RAY
about
Ray Charles comes to town. J. Gruen. il por *Dance Magazine* 63:59 O '89
What'd I say—a conversation with Ray Charles [cover story] J. Levenson. il pors *Down Beat* 56:16-19 Ja '89
CHARLES, STACI
Have Christian books been censored? il *Publishers Weekly* 235:58 Mr 3 '89
CHARLES COUNTY (MD.)
Child welfare
Specialized foster family care: a community-based program for children with special needs. M. Luginbill and A. Spiegler. il *Children Today* 18:5-9 Ja/F '89
CHARLES SCHWAB & CO., INC.
After cost cuts, what? J. Heins. il por *Forbes* 143:46 My 1 '89
Are you ready for robobroker? [TeleBroker system] B. Hager. il *Money* 18:14+ O '89
Charles Schwab's little red book [disaster planning before Bay Area earthquake] il *Fortune* 120:104 N 20 '89
The little guy is back. Ask Schwab. G. G. Marcial. *Business Week* p80 Jl 10 '89
A sweeter ride for discount brokers. J. Friedman. il *Business Week* p100 Ag 14 '89

CHARLES STARK DRAPER PRIZE See Draper Prize
CHARLES THE GREAT See Charlemagne, Emperor, 742-814
CHARLESTON (S.C.)
Climate
Charleston, S.C. rebounds from $2-billion destruction by Hugo; Jackson tours state. D. M. Cheers. il *Jet* 77:5-6+ O 9 '89
A hurricane's haunting legacy [wake of Hugo] D. Gelman. il *Newsweek* 114:68-9 O 23 '89
The way it should be remembered [impact of Hurricane Hugo] B. M. Boyd. il *The New York Times Magazine* p44+ N 19 '89
Description
Charleston. M. Elder. il *Gourmet* 49:68-73+ Ap '89
Charleston by foot, buggy, boat. *Southern Living* 24:23 S '89
Gardens and gardening
Charleston charm, minimal maintenance. il *Southern Living* 24:50 Jl '89
Historic houses, sites, etc.
John Philip Kassebaum's unparalleled ceramics in Charleston [Branford-Horry House] J. S. Wamsley. il pors *Architectural Digest* 46:86+ D '89
Tourist trade
Working for our cities [V. Turner-Maybank, director of the Office of Tourism Management] D. Young. il pors *Southern Living* 24:141-2+ S '89
CHARLESTON (S.C.). SPOLETO FESTIVAL U.S.A. See Spoleto Festival U.S.A.
CHARLESTON (W. VA.)
Monuments, statues, etc.
Lincoln walks in Charleston. il por *Southern Living* 24:32 Je '89
CHARLESTON MANOR (LEWES, ENGLAND)
Doing the Charleston. B. Taylor. il *Art News* 88:87-8 S '89
Painting Charleston [country retreat for D. Grant, V. Bell and the Bloomsbury artists] J. Johnston. bibl f il pors *Art in America* 77:152-63+ D '89
CHARLOTTE (N.C.)
Churches (Buildings)
See also
Calvary Church (Charlotte, N.C.)
Economic conditions
Falling for the Huck Finn factor. J. McCormick. il *Newsweek* 113:48 F 6 '89
CHARLOTTE'S WEB [musical] See Musicals, revues, etc.— Reviews—Single works
CHARNEY, ROSALIND
The 6 nutrition mistakes moms make. il *Redbook* 173:168+ O '89
CHARON (SATELLITE) See Pluto (Planet)—Satellites
CHARPENTIER, MARC ANTOINE, 1634-1704
about
Musical events:
Charpentier's Advent and Christmas. A. Porter. *The New Yorker* 65:70 D 25 '89
CHARREN, PEGGY
about
Pay attention, class. E. Watters. il por *Mother Jones* 14:18 D '89
CHARTER AIRLINES See Airlines—Non-scheduled operations
CHARTERHOUSE INC.
From the Mekong to Motown [S. Plum of Charterhouse Inc. bids on Income Opportunity Realty Trust] M. Schifrin. il por *Forbes* 143:324+ My 29 '89
CHARTERING OF BOATS See Boats and boating—Leasing and renting; Fishing boats—Leasing and renting; Motor boats—Leasing and renting; Yachts and yachting—Leasing and renting
CHARTIST (NEWSLETTER)
Bullish beachcomber [D. Sullivan] P. Brimelow. il por *Forbes* 144:118-19 O 30 '89
Relative strength is absolutely hot. M. Hulbert. il *Forbes* 144:117 Ag 21 '89
CHARTRAND, MARK R.
Space basics. See issues of Ad Astra beginning January 1989
CHARTS, ASTRONOMICAL See Astronomy—Charts, diagrams, etc.
CHARTS, AVIATION See Aviation charts
CHARTS, NAUTICAL See Nautical charts
CHARVET (FIRM)
Expensive habits: the Charvet shirt. P. Mayle. il *Gentlemen's Quarterly* 59:53+ Je '89
CHARYBDOTOXIN
Mutant potassium channels with altered binding of charybdotoxin, a pore-blocking peptide inhibitor. R. MacKinnon and C. Miller. bibl f il *Science* 245:1382-5 S 22 '89
CHASE, ARLEN
about
From a remote jungle site, a trail of striking clues. N. Epstein. bibl (p183) il pors map *Smithsonian* 20:98-104+ D '89
CHASE, BARRIE
about
An agile aesthetic: dancer Barrie Chase's country cottage in Los Angeles. M. Frank. il por *Architectural Digest* 46:248-55+ O '89

CHASE, DIANE
about
From a remote jungle site, a trail of striking clues. N. Epstein. bibl (p183) il pors map *Smithsonian* 20:98-104+ D '89
CHASE, JOHN, 1953-
California architecture. il *Art News* 88:138-43 D '89
CHASE, ROBERT
Lightwright for lighting designers. il *Theatre Crafts* 23:28-9 F '89
CHASE, STEVE
about
Aboard the Impromptu. I. Borger. il *Architectural Digest* 46:144-9 Ag '89
Capricious collections by the shore. M. Webb. il *Architectural Digest* 46:244-9 My '89
CHASE ART FUND
Launching a $300 million art fund. B. B. Stretch. *Art News* 88:37+ My '89
CHASE-RIBOUD, BARBARA, 1936-
about
Word star. P. Giddings. il por *Essence* 19:30 F '89
CHASNOV, MARC
The ice is right. il *Runner's World* 24:24 Jl '89
CHASTAIN, BILL
Beers with . . . Andy Van Slyke [interview] il pors *Sport (New York, N.Y.)* 80:19-20 Ap '89
Beers with . . . Joe Magrane [interview] il pors *Sport (New York, N.Y.)* 80:19-21 S '89
CHASTAIN, DEBORAH
about
Queen of the range. B. Eftink. il por *Successful Farming* 87:46-7 Ja '89
CHASTAIN, THOMAS
The think tank murder. il *Discover* 10:96+ O '89
about
Morrow to release first new Perry Mason novel in 15 years. *Publishers Weekly* 235:66+ F 3 '89
CHASTITY
See also
Celibacy
Kids get the message: it's okay to say no [abstinence programs] K. H. Sidey. il *Christianity Today* 33:40 O 6 '89
CHATAWAY, CHRISTOPHER
about
Britain's biggest new radio star. R. A. Melcher. il por *Business Week* p114 My 22 '89
CHÂTEAU DE CHEVERNY (FRANCE) See Castles—France
CHÂTEAU DE CORNILLON (FRANCE) See Castles—France
CHÂTEAU DE FLEURY (FRANCE) See Castles—France
CHÂTEAU DE LA LORIE (ANGERS, FRANCE) See Castles—France
CHÂTEAU DE MONTGEOFFROY (FRANCE)
The kitchen at Montgeoffroy. L. Langseth-Christensen. il *Gourmet* 49:50-1+ Jl '89
CHÂTELET, ANNE-MARIE
Under the roofs of Paris. il *The Unesco Courier* 42:42-5 Ag '89
CHATFIELD-TAYLOR, JOAN
Ace Architects: historical gamesmanship in San Francisco. il *Architectural Digest* 46:84-7+ Ag '89
After Fallingwater: a California house inspired by Frank Lloyd Wright. il *Architectural Digest* 46:214-21 Mr '89
Classic David Hayes. il por *Architectural Digest* 46:210-17 S '89
Contemporary traditions on Lake Tahoe. il *Architectural Digest* 46:270-5+ O '89
Cottage industry: a versatile poolhouse near San Francisco. il *Architectural Digest* 46:302-7 My '89
On Stinson Beach: Pacific spaces for John and Elinor McGuire. il pors *Architectural Digest* 46:206-13 My '89
A rare collection of classic Hollywood costume sketches. il por *Architectural Digest* 46:250+ S '89
CHATFIELD-TAYLOR, ROBERT
about
The Jack O'Connor letters (I). il pors *Outdoor Life* 183:66-7+ F '89
The Jack O'Connor letters (II). il pors *Outdoor Life* 183:80-1+ Mr '89
CHATHAM, ROBERT, D. 1929
about
Watermelon king remembered. P. S. Prather. il por *American Visions* 4:38-9 Ag '89
CHATHAM (MASS.)
Historic houses, sites, etc.
Architectural digest visits: Julie Harris. D. Roberts. il por *Architectural Digest* 46:140-5+ Je '89
CHATHAM HALL (CHATHAM, VA.: SCHOOL) See Private schools
CHATSWORTH FOODS LTD.
Brand name nobility. J. Marcom, Jr. il por *Forbes* 144:318+ N 13 '89
CHATSWORTH HOUSE (DERBYSHIRE, ENGLAND)
Brand name nobility. J. Marcom, Jr. il por *Forbes* 144:318+ N 13 '89
CHATTOOGA RIVER
The Chattooga River: a weekend white-water adventure. il map *Southern Living* 24:30+ S '89

CHATTOPADHYAYA, KAMALADEVI, 1903-1988
about
Obituary
  American Craft il por 49:66 Je/Jl '89. R. Kalapesi
CHATWIN, BRUCE
Brief interludes [excerpt from What am I doing here] por *Vogue* 179:326-7 Ag '89
On George Ortiz. *The New York Review of Books* 36:62 S 28 '89
The Songlines quartet. il *The New York Review of Books* 35:50-1 Ja 19 '89
about
Obituary
  Harper's Bazaar por 122:74+ Ag '89. K. Black
  The New York Review of Books il por 36:4 Mr 2 '89. M. Ignatieff
CHAU, VINCENT, AND OTHERS
A multiubiquitin chain is confined to specific lysine in a targeted short-lived protein. bibl f il *Science* 243:1576-83 Mr 24 '89
CHAUCER, GEOFFREY, D. 1400
about
Chaucer and the moon's speed. D. W. Olson and L. E. Jasinski. il *Sky and Telescope* 77:376-7 Ap '89
CHAUNER, WALT
A touch of class: how to go from wide-track to a narrow stance. il *Skiing* 41:137-41 Ja '89
CHAURAN, TIM
Dirty tricks. *Bicycling* 30:80+ D '89
CHAUTAUQUA OPERA
Summer idyll [general director L. Jackson; cover story] P. J. Smith. il pors *Opera News* 53:10-12 Je '89
CHAVES, EDUARDO O. C.
(jt. auth) See Fogelman, Ilana, and Chaves, Eduardo O. C.
CHÁVEZ, JULIO CÉSAR
about
Stop meeting like this. P. Putnam. il pors *Sports Illustrated* 70:75 My 22 '89
CHAVÍN CULTURE
Long before the Inca. R. L. Burger. il map *Natural History* p66-73 F '89
CHEAPSKATES *See* Stinginess
CHEAT GRASS *See* Grasses
CHEATHAM, DOC
about
Doc Cheatham. D. Helland. il por *Down Beat* 56:14 Mr '89
CHECCHI, AL
about
Front man. S. Flack. il *Forbes* 144:69 Jl 10 '89
Landing Northwest. R. Grover and R. Mitchell. il por *Business Week* p24-5 Jl 3 '89
The odd couple chasing Northwest Airlines. R. Grover. il pors *Business Week* p126 Ap 24 '89
Wings Holdings chief pledges to keep Northwest growing. C. Fotos. *Aviation Week & Space Technology* 130:90-1 Je 26 '89
Wings Holdings' purchase of Northwest could become blueprint for future LBOs. *Aviation Week & Space Technology* 131:22 Ag 14 '89
CHECHIK, JEREMIAH
about
National Lampoon's Christmas vacation [film] Reviews
  People Weekly il 32:17-18 D 11 '89. R. Novak
CHECK CASHING SERVICES
Canada
  See also
  National Money Mart Inc.
CHECK CLEARING *See* Banks and banking—Float
CHECKERS (GAME)
  See also
  International Checker Hall of Fame
Tournaments
Squares [International Goodwill Checkers Invitational Tournament] *The New Yorker* 65:22-3 Jl 31 '89
CHECKMATES [drama] See Milner, Ron, 1938-
CHECKPOINT SYSTEMS, INC.
Checking out Checkpoint. G. G. Marcial. *Business Week* p118 Je 5 '89
CHECKS
  See also
  John H. Harland Co.
Bits in the bank [CheckFree] P. Scisco. il *Compute!* 11:7 Mr '89
Check fraud [problems with credit card numbers written on checks] J. W. Merline. il *Consumers' Research Magazine* 72:2 D '89
CheckFree [computer program] G. McClure. il *Compute!* 11:72-3 Jl '89
Checkless checkwriting [CheckFree] R. Cullen. il *Home Office Computing* 7:32+ My '89
Quicken [computer program] S. Anzovin. il *Compute!* 11:72 Ap '89
Quicken vs. Checkwrite Plus. R. Cullen. il *Home Office Computing* 7:28-9 Ag '89
Stocking-stuffer software. K. Davis. *Changing Times* 43:122-3 D '89

Forgeries
Desktop forgery [cover story] D. Churbuck. il *Forbes* 144:246-9+ N 27 '89
Stop payment
Who's at risk for a lost check? *Consumer Reports* 54:74 F '89
CHECKS, FRAUDULENT
Quick checks [point-of-sale systems that verify checks and credit cards] J. Wynn. il *Nation's Business* 77:45-6 D '89
CHECKS AND BALANCES (GOVERNMENT) See Separation of powers
CHECKSFIELD, JAMES
about
The case of the singing CPA. *Newsweek* 114:41 Jl 17 '89
CHECKUPS, MEDICAL See Physical examinations
CHEEK, JAMES EDWARD, 1932-
about
Howard's Cheek to end 20-year career there to take new ambassadorship. il pors *Jet* 76:4-5 Ap 24 '89
James Cheek bows out as candidate for envoy post. por *Jet* 76:5 My 15 '89
CHEERLEADERS See Cheerleading
CHEERLEADING
Full of good cheers [college squads] L. Hart. il *Life* 12:114-16 O '89
Anecdotes, facetiae, satire, etc.
As thousands cheer [J. Jones's attempt to alter image of Dallas Cowboys Cheerleaders] M. Ivins. il *The Progressive* 53:35 Ag '89
Competitions
Chicago cheerleading team wins world competition [Abbott Park Cheerleading Team] il *Jet* 76:14 My 1 '89
It's 'Gimme a yea!' as thousands of cheerleaders cartwheel into the national championships. M. Neill. il *People Weekly* 31:99-101 Ja 23 '89
CHEERS See Cheerleading
CHEERS [television program] See Television program reviews—Single works
CHEESE
  See also
  Cooking—Cheese
Cheese source of dietary anticancer agent [research by Michael W. Pariza] J. Raloff. *Science News* 135:87 F 11 '89
Collecting butter & cheese making tools. F. Johnson. il *Antiques & Collecting Hobbies* 94:46-9 Je '89
Entertaining with cheese. S. La Rosa. il *McCall's* 116:57-8+ My '89
Fresh mozzarella . . . make it and eat it right now. il *Sunset (Central West edition)* 182:92-3 Je '89
Fromages. il *Gourmet* 49:154 Jl '89
Marinated cheeses. il *Sunset (Central West edition)* 182:66-7 Ja '89
The original "Big Cheese" [citizens of Cheshire, Mass. present 1,235 pound cheese to T. Jefferson] R. Sassaman. il *American History Illustrated* 23:34-5 Ja '89
Say fromage! il *Seventeen* 48:280-2+ Mr '89
CHEESE APPETIZERS See Appetizers
CHEESE INDUSTRY
  See also
  Coach Farm
CHEESE SOUPS See Soups
CHEESE SPREADS See Spreads (Food)
CHEESE STORES See Food stores
CHEESEBURGERS See Hamburgers
CHEESECAKE
Cheesecake-bar buffet. *Parents* 64:117 Ag '89
Cheesecakes flirt with flavor. S. Payne. il *Southern Living* 24:110-11 Ap '89
Say cheesecake! J. T. Hazard. il *Ladies' Home Journal* 106:192-4+ Ap '89
Sour cream cheesecake. B. Johnson. il *Better Homes and Gardens* 67:130 Mr '89
CHEETAH [film] See Motion picture reviews—Single works
CHEETAHS
The brotherhood of cheetahs [Serengeti National Park; cover story] T. Caro. il *Natural History* p50-9 Je '89
Cheetahs: wild cats in danger [cover story] il *National Geographic World* 161:3-7 Ja '89
Photographs and photography
Curiosity killed the hat. G. G. Dimijian. il *Natural History* p62-5 N '89
CHEFS See Cooks
CHELALA, CESAR A.
Bolivia's health couriers. il *World Health* p18-19 D '88
They condone torture. il *World Health* p24-5 Ap '89
CHELATION
Protection of dentate hilar cells from prolonged stimulation by intracellular calcium chelation. H. E. Scharfman and P. A. Schwartzkroin. bibl f il *Science* 246:257-60 O 13 '89
CHELMINSKI, RUDOLPH
France's Mitterrand: a study in ambition. il pors *Reader's Digest* 134:141-6 Ap '89
The winning edge. il por *Reader's Digest* 135:175-6+ D '89

CHELSEA (LONDON, ENGLAND)
Historic houses, sites, etc.
Chelsea collector [S. Hoppen's converted carriage house] J. Etra. il *House & Garden* 161:140-5 Mr '89
CHELSEA (MASS.)
Education
Silber bullet [J. Silber's plans to have Boston University manage the Chelsea school system] D. P. Hamilton. *The New Republic* 201:18-19 D 4 '89
CHELSEA (NEW YORK, N.Y.)
Better [walk with photographer R. Burckhardt as guide] *The New Yorker* 65:43-4 D 4 '89
CHELSEA POTTERY See Pottery, English
CHELTENHAM (ENGLAND)
Music
See also
Opera—Great Britain
CHEMDESIGN (FIRM)
Hitching a ride on the fax boom. G. G. Marcial. *Business Week* p84 Je 19 '89
CHEMED CORP.
Growth with a dividend. T. Jaffe. *Forbes* 143:414 My 1 '89
CHEMICAL ADDITIVES IN FOOD See Food additives
CHEMICAL AND BIOLOGICAL WEAPONS
The buildup that was [Reagan administration] S. Wright. bibl f il *The Bulletin of the Atomic Scientists* 45:52-6 Ja/F '89
Chemical warfare: a forgotten lesson [reputed plan to use gas in 1945 attack on Iwo Jima] J. E. van C. Moon. bibl f il *The Bulletin of the Atomic Scientists* 45:40-3 Jl/Ag '89
Retargeting research on biological weapons. K. R. Yamamoto. il *Technology Review* 92:23-4 Ag/S '89
"They may not be weapons at all" [untested binaries] H. Kestin. il *Forbes* 144:45-6 S 18 '89
Disposal
Chemical weapons disposal program [statement, April 4, 1989] M. L. Friedersdorf. *Department of State Bulletin* 89:19-21 Je '89
Export-import trade
Anger and recrimination [government knowledge of West German firms' participation in construction of Libyan gas plant] J. O. Jackson. il *Time* 133:34 Ja 30 '89
Bonn finally comes clean [Imhausen-Chemie implicated in Libya's chemical weapons plant] M. G. Warner and T. Waldrop. il *Newsweek* 113:32 Ja 23 '89
The curious case of chemical warfare [German exports] M. Ledeen. *Commentary* 88:37-41 Jl '89
How Qadaffi built his deadly chemical plant. J. Templeman and D. Lee. il *Business Week* p50-1 Ja 23 '89
Libya's chemical weapons plant [State Dept. statement, January 1, 1989] *Department of State Bulletin* 89:71 Mr '89
More German dealing in the poison trade [selling chemical weapons to Iran] *Newsweek* 114:28 Jl 10 '89
The new merchants of death [West German link to manufacture of chemical weapons by Libya] il *World Press Review* 36:13-14 Mr '89
On second thought [Imhausen-Chemie's role in building Libyan gas plant] W. R. Doerner. il *Time* 133:30-1 Ja 23 '89
A self-inflicted wound [West Germany's role in Libyan poison gas scandal] M. R. Meyer. il *Newsweek* 113:42 Ja 30 '89
International aspects
Bad chemical reactions [disarmament meeting to convene in Paris] J. L. Galloway. il *U.S. News & World Report* 106:30-1 Ja 16 '89
Biological weapons proliferation [statement, May 17, 1989] H. A. Holmes. *Department of State Bulletin* 89:43-5 Jl '89
Bush's folly [treaty banning chemical weapons] *National Review* 41:20-1 O 27 '89
Chemical arms ban still uncertain [Paris conference] D. Dickson. il *Science* 243:301-2 Ja 20 '89
Chemical disarmament: the superpowers propose a major arms cutback. J. Bierman. il *Maclean's* 102:26 O 9 '89
CIA details chemical weapons spread [testimony by William H. Webster before the Senate Committee on Government Operations] C. Norman. il *Science* 243:888 F 17 '89
Clearing the air [proposed global ban on chemical weapons] T. Beardsley. il *Scientific American* 260:17-18 Mr '89
Conference against chemical weapons [government-industry conference in Canberra, Australia; statement, September 19, 1989] R. A. Clarke. *Department of State Bulletin* 89:45-7 N '89
Conference on chemical weapons use [White House statement, October 21, 1988] *Department of State Bulletin* 89:16 Ja '89
Foreign policy implications of biological weapons [statement, July 26, 1989] H. A. Holmes. *Department of State Bulletin* 89:22-4 O '89
The growing menace of chemical weapons. R. K. Bennett. il *Reader's Digest* 135:82-7 Jl '89
Heading toward an early summit [Bush-Gorbachev] R. Watson. il *Newsweek* 114:28-9 S 18 '89

Joint statement on chemical weapons, Sept. 23, 1989 [U.S. and Soviet Union] il *Department of State Bulletin* 89:8-9 N '89
Leave the taboo alone. M. Greenfield. il *Newsweek* 113:64 Ja 9 '89
Limited progress reported on chemical weapons ban. il *UN Chronicle* 26:30-1 D '89
Mother knows best . . . But is anyone listening? J. D. Isaacs. il *The Bulletin of the Atomic Scientists* 45:3-4 Ap '89
The new face of war [cover story; special section] il *World Press Review* 36:11-14+ Mr '89
Paris conference calls for complete ban on chemical weapons. *UN Chronicle* 26:58-9 Je '89
A poisonous threat [chemical weapons conference in Paris] A. Phillips. il *Maclean's* 102:20-2 Ja 23 '89
Prohibition of chemical weapons conference held in Paris [address, news conference, text of final declaration and statement, January 7-11, 1989] G. P. Shultz; W. F. Burns. *Department of State Bulletin* 89:4-10 Mr '89
The search for a poison antidote [convening Paris meeting to stop proliferation] J. Smolowe. il *Time* 133:22 Ja 16 '89
Turning off the gas [global, comprehensive, and verifiable ban on chemical weapons] *Commonweal* 116:548-9 O 20 '89
U.S. efforts against the spread of chemical weapons [statement, June 22, 1989] R. Bartholomew. *Department of State Bulletin* 89:74-7 S '89
The 'winds of death'. R. Watson. il *Newsweek* 113:22-5 Ja 16 '89
Security measures
Breathing room [proposal by Raymond Cohen and Robin Ranger] *The New Republic* 200:8-9 F 27 '89
Iran
More German dealing in the poison trade [selling chemical weapons to Iran] *Newsweek* 114:28 Jl 10 '89
Iraq
Flanders Fields revisited [Iraqi use of poison gas against Kurds] I. O'Keeffe. il *World Press Review* 36:12-13 Mr '89
'If hypocrisy could kill'. L. Infante. il *World Press Review* 36:21 Mr '89
The poor man's atomic bomb [use of poison gas against the Kurds] A. C. Revkin. il *Discover* 10:76 Ja '89
A precarious refuge in Iran [Iraqi Kurds] F. A. Reed. il *Maclean's* 102:25 Ja 16 '89
Libya
Anger and recrimination [government knowledge of West German firms' participation in construction of Libyan gas plant] J. O. Jackson. il *Time* 133:34 Ja 30 '89
Bonn finally comes clean [Imhausen-Chemie implicated in Libya's chemical weapons plant] M. G. Warner and T. Waldrop. il *Newsweek* 113:32 Ja 23 '89
Chemical reaction [U.S. fighters shoot down Libyan MiGs] E. Magnuson. il por *Time* 133:18-21 Ja 16 '89
Does he or doesn't he? D. White and P. Marsh. il *World Press Review* 36:16-17 Mr '89
Gunning for Gadhafi [U.S. shoots down two jets and claims Libya will soon make chemical weapons] J. Bierman. il *Maclean's* 102:18-19 Ja 16 '89
How Qadaffi built his deadly chemical plant. J. Templeman and D. Lee. il *Business Week* p50-1 Ja 23 '89
Hypocritical warfare [downing of Libyan MiGs and controversy over alleged chemical weapons plant] *The Nation* 248:73 Ja 23 '89
Libya [U.S. downing of two Libyan MiG-23s over the Mediterranean] *Business Week* p50 Ja 16 '89
Libyan planes fall, questions rise. *America* 160:27 Ja 21 '89
Libya's chemical weapons plant [State Dept. statement, January 1, 1989] *Department of State Bulletin* 89:71 Mr '89
The mysterious "Doctor B." [role of I. Barbouti in construction of Libyan gas plant] J. Birnbaum. il por *Time* 133:40+ F 27 '89
The new merchants of death [West German link to manufacture of chemical weapons by Libya] il *World Press Review* 36:13-14 Mr '89
On second thought [Imhausen-Chemie's role in building Libyan gas plant] W. R. Doerner. il *Time* 133:30-1 Ja 23 '89
A poisonous threat. A. Phillips. il *Maclean's* 102:20-2 Ja 23 '89
A self-inflicted wound [West Germany's role in Libyan poison gas scandal] M. R. Meyer. il *Newsweek* 113:42 Ja 30 '89
Showdown with Libya [cover story; special section] il por *Newsweek* 113:16-25 Ja 16 '89
The U.S. vs. Libya. *World Press Review* 36:8 F '89
The uphill fight to contain chemical weapons. L. Lief. il *U.S. News & World Report* 106:42 Ja 9 '89
A war of nerves. H. Evans. il *U.S. News & World Report* 106:72 Ja 16 '89
Middle East
The curious case of chemical warfare [German exports] M. Ledeen. *Commentary* 88:37-41 Jl '89

CHEMICAL BANK

Back to the velvet-roped lines [cancels home banking system] P. Elmer-Dewitt. il *Time* 133:49 Ja 9 '89

The banker plan [disclosure of J. Baker's Chemical Bank holdings clouds his policy on Latin American debt relief] *The New Republic* 200:7-8 Mr 6 '89

Even 'good banks' can be bad buys [Class B Chemical stock] J. M. Laderman. *Business Week* p60 Ja 9 '89

Jim Baker's conflict-of-interest problems. W. Greider. il *Rolling Stone* p43-5 Ap 20 '89

CHEMICAL BONDS

See also

Binding sites (Biochemistry)
Electronegativity
Ligands

The chemistry of solid-state electronics. E. Yablonovitch. bibl f il *Science* 246:347-51 O 20 '89

Crystal versus solution structures of enzymes: NMR spectroscopy of a crystalline serine protease. S. O. Smith and others. bibl f il *Science* 244:961-4 My 26 '89

Major enhancement of the affinity of an enzyme for a transition-state analog by a single hydroxyl group. W. M. Kati and R. Wolfenden. bibl f il *Science* 243:1591-3 Mr 24 '89

A rare ménage à trois [three-atom bond made by John E. McMurry and others] *Science News* 136:373 D 9 '89

CHEMICAL ELEMENTS

See also

Carbon
Helium
Hydrogen
Iodine
Nitrogen
Nucleosynthesis
Periodic table
Transuranium elements

CHEMICAL ENGINEERING

See also

Leaching

High tech frontiers in the energy industry [address, November 30, 1988] R. F. Tucker. *Vital Speeches of the Day* 55:437-41 My 1 '89

CHEMICAL EQUIPMENT

See also

Spectrometers

New equipment roundup dazzles scientists [Pittsburgh Conference & Exposition on Analytical Chemistry and Applied Spectroscopy] R. Pool. il *Science* 243:1554-6 Mr 24 '89

CHEMICAL FACTORIES *See* Chemical plants
CHEMICAL HYPERSENSITIVITY *See* Environmental illness

CHEMICAL INDUSTRIES

See also

Agricultural chemicals industry
Air Products and Chemicals, Inc.
Aristech Chemical Corporation
ChemDesign (Firm)
Chemed Corp.
Chemical plants
Chemical workers
Dexter Corp.
Dow Chemical Co.
E. I. Du Pont de Nemours & Co.
FMC Corporation
Georgia Gulf Corporation
Great Lakes Chemical Corp.
H.B. Fuller Company
Huntsman Chemical Corporation
Kerr-McGee Corp.
Lubrizol Corp.
Monsanto Company
Orchem (Firm)
Pennwalt Corp.
Petrochemical industry
Quantum Chemical Corp.
Rohm & Haas Co.
RPM Inc. (Ohio)
Uniroyal Chemical Co., Inc.
W.R. Grace & Co.
Wellman, Inc.

Acquisitions and mergers

Background check [A. J. Butler's offer for Pennwalt] L. Gubernick. *Forbes* 143:14-15 F 20 '89

A chemical maker's secret admirer? [Sherwin-Williams' interest in Dexter Corp.] G. G. Marcial. *Business Week* p76 Ja 30 '89

International aspects

On the prowl in America [Rhone-Poulenc] J. Zweig. il por *Forbes* 143:154 My 1 '89

Why Wall Street is furioso at Raul Gardini [deal to buy out minority holders of Ausimont] J. Rossant and W. Glasgall. il por *Business Week* p48 F 20 '89

Export-import trade

The chemical connection [Operation Primavera reveals U.S.-manufactured chemicals used in Colombian cocaine production] W. R. Doerner. il *Time* 133:44-5 F 20 '89

Cocaine chemistry [chemicals exported by the U.S. used in cocaine manufacture] P. Andreas. *The New Republic* 201:12+ N 20 '89

Finance

Chemicals. R. Simon. il *Forbes* 143:103-5 Ja 9 '89

A winning formula for chemical makers. J. H. Cutaia. il *Business Week* p74 Ja 9 '89

Laws and regulations

See Chemicals—Laws and regulations

Management

A formula for the future [address, October 19, 1988] I. W. Gorr. *Vital Speeches of the Day* 55:190-2 Ja 1 '89

Monsanto is teaching old workers new tricks. J. E. Ellis. il por *Business Week* p67 Ag 21 '89

France

See also

Rhone-Poulenc SA

Germany (West)

See also

Bayer AG
Hoechst AG
Imhausen-Chemie (Firm)
Rheineisen Chemical Products

Italy

See also

Montedison SpA

Japan

Absorbing Japanese technology. R. DiCicco. il *High Technology Business* 9:9 N/D '89

United States

See Chemical industries

CHEMICAL INSTRUMENTS *See* Chemical equipment

CHEMICAL PLANTS

Accidents and explosions

See also

Bhopal poisonous gas disaster, India, 1984

Profiting from disaster [explosion at Phillips Petroleum polyethylene plant outside Houston] A. A. Lappen. il *Forbes* 144:203+ N 27 '89

"Pull me out" [K. Rodriguez rescued from machine] P. Michelmore. il *Reader's Digest* 135:120-5 Ag '89

Environmental aspects

See also

Love Canal case

The toxic avenger strikes at corporate polluters [work of M. Kaltofen] M. Satchell. il por *U.S. News & World Report* 106:28 Je 26 '89

CHEMICAL POLLUTION *See* Pollution
CHEMICAL POLLUTION OF THE AIR *See* Air pollution

CHEMICAL REACTIONS

See also

Acetylation
Belousov-Zhabotinskii reaction
Catalysts and catalysis
Electron transfer reactions
Hydrolysis
Methylation
Oxidation reduction reaction
Phosphorylation
Proteolysis

Chemical cartography: finding the keys to the kinetic labyrinth. G. W. Flynn. bibl f il *Science* 246:1009-15 N 24 '89

The chemical effects of ultrasound. K. S. Suslick. bibl il *Scientific American* 260:80-6 F '89

Chemical waves curl around tiny globes [study of oscillating reactions by Kenneth Showalter and Jerzy Maselko] I. Amato. *Science News* 136:6-7 Jl 1 '89

Neural networks predict reactions [research by David W. Elrod] J. Raloff. *Science News* 135:271 Ap 29 '89

CHEMICAL RESEARCH

See also

Gordon Research Conferences

Why Monsanto is plunking down its chips on R&D. J. E. Ellis. il por *Business Week* p66-7 Ag 21 '89

Japan

Absorbing Japanese technology. R. DiCicco. il *High Technology Business* 9:9 N/D '89

CHEMICAL SYNTHESIS *See* Synthesis

CHEMICAL WARFARE

See also

Chemical and biological weapons

CHEMICAL WASTE DISPOSAL *See* Hazardous substances—Disposal; Trade waste—Disposal
CHEMICAL WASTES *See* Trade waste

CHEMICAL WORKERS

Productivity trends in agricultural chemicals. H. Brand and K. Bryant. bibl f il *Monthly Labor Review* 112:21-8 Mr '89

CHEMICALS

See also

Agricultural chemicals
Herbicides
Pesticides
Trade waste

The chemicals of half-life. N. J. Bolls. *BioScience* 39:138 Mr '89

CHEMICALS—cont.

Biodegradation
See Biodegradation

Export-import trade
See Chemical industries—Export-import trade

Laws and regulations
A corrosive fight over California's toxics law [Safe Drinking Water and Toxic Enforcement Act] L. Roberts. il *Science* 243:306-9 Ja 20 '89
Forewarned is fairly warned [California's Safe Drinking Water and Toxic Enforcement Act] C. Russell. il *Sierra* 74:36-8+ N/D '89
Lets apply common sense to chemicals [address, February 21, 1989] R. E. Heckert. *Vital Speeches of the Day* 55:476-8 My 15 '89

Physiological effects
Is broccoli more toxic than dioxin? [views of B. Ames on natural poisons in food and manmade carcinogens] L. Lamb. il *Utne Reader* p11-12 Mr/Ap '89
Ode to Cheez Whiz [natural poisons and carcinogens present in food; views of B. Ames] J. Hooper. il *Health (New York, N.Y.)* 21:44+ O '89

Safety devices and measures
See also
International Program on Chemical Safety

Testing
Alternatives to animals in toxicity testing. A. M. Goldberg and J. M. Frazier. bibl il *Scientific American* 261:24-30 Ag '89

CHEMISTRY
See also
Astrochemistry
Catalysts and catalysis
Chelation
Chemical research
Computers—Chemical use
Decomposition (Chemistry)
Diffusion
Electrochemistry
Fermentation
Geochemistry
Lasers—Chemical use
Magnetic resonance imaging—Chemical use
Photochemistry
Photographic chemistry
Polymers
Solubility
Stereochemistry
Ultrasonic waves—Chemical use

Awards
Chauvinism in Nobel nominations [views of Bo G. Malmstrom] C. Holden. *Science* 243:471 Ja 27 '89

Conferences
New equipment roundup dazzles scientists [Pittsburgh Conference & Exposition on Analytical Chemistry and Applied Spectroscopy] R. Pool. il *Science* 243:1554-6 Mr 24 '89

Study and teaching
See also
Colleges and universities—Departments of chemistry

CHEMISTRY, ANALYTIC
See also
Chromatographic analysis
Colorimetry
Lasers—Chemical use
Oil analysis
Proteins—Analysis
Separation (Technology)
Spectrum analysis
Water—Analysis

CHEMISTRY, ATMOSPHERIC See Atmosphere

CHEMISTRY, ORGANIC
See also
Enzymes
Organic compounds
Synthesis

CHEMISTRY, PHYSICAL AND THEORETICAL
See also
Boiling
Colloids
Coordination (Chemistry)
Crystallization
Electronegativity
Surface chemistry
Thermodynamics
Chemical physics. bibl f il *Physics Today* 42:S20-S21 Ja '89

CHEMISTRY, TECHNICAL
See also
Separation (Technology)

CHEMISTS
See also
Altman, Sidney
Cram, Donald J., 1919-
Pons, Stanley
Wrighton, Mark S., 1949-

CHEMISTS AS AUTHORS
The mark of the chemist [excerpt from Other people's trades]; tr. by Raymond Rosenthal. P. Levi. il *Discover* 10:70-5 F '89

CHEMORECEPTORS
See also
Drug receptors
Hormone receptors
Serotonin receptors
Activation of bacterial porin gene expression by a chimeric signal transducer in response to aspartate. R. Utsumi and others. bibl f il *Science* 245:1246-9 S 15 '89
Analysis of ligand binding specificity of receptor chimeras [discussion of June 3, 1988 article, Chimeric α_2-,β_2-adrenergic receptors: delineation of domains involved in effector coupling and ligand binding specificity] B. K. Kobilka and others. *Science* 243:236-7 Ja 13 '89
Autonomic regulation of a chloride current in heart. R. D. Harvey and J. R. Hume. bibl f il *Science* 244:983-5 My 26 '89
β-adrenergic receptor kinase: primary structure delineates a multigene family. J. L. Benovic and others. bibl f il *Science* 246:235-40 O 13 '89
Building up better synthetic receptors [cavitands; research by Donald J. Cram] I. Amato. il *Science News* 135:327 My 27 '89
Cnidocyte mechanoreceptors are tuned to the movements of swimming prey by chemoreceptors [cover story] G. M. Watson and D. A. Hessinger. bibl f il *Science* 243:1589-91 Mr 24 '89
Ethanol inhibits NMDA-activated ion current in hippocampal neurons. D. M. Lovinger and others. bibl f il *Science* 243:1721-4 Mr 31 '89
Indole-2-carboxylic acid: a competitive antagonist of potentiation by glycine at the NMDA receptor. J. E. Huettner. bibl f il *Science* 243:1611-13 Mr 24 '89
Molecular characterization of the human B_2-adrenergic receptor. L. J. Emorine and others. bibl f il *Science* 245:1118-21 S 8 '89
Muscarinic modulation of cardiac rate at low acetylcholine concentrations. D. DiFrancesco and others. bibl f il *Science* 243:669-71 F 3 '89
NMDA antagonists differentiate epileptogenesis from seizure expression in an in vitro model. S. F. Stasheff and others. bibl f il *Science* 245:648-51 Ag 11 '89
Rapid β-adrenergic modulation of cardiac calcium channel currents by a fast G protein pathway. A. Yatani and A. M. Brown. bibl f il *Science* 245:71-4 Jl 7 '89
Receptor gene found for brain protein [D2 dopamine receptor; research by Olivier Civelli] B. Bower. *Science News* 135:6 Ja 7 '89
The role of excitatory amino acids and NMDA receptors in traumatic brain injury. A. I. Faden and others. bibl f il *Science* 244:798-800 My 19 '89
Self-assembling molecular receptors [research by Alanna Schepartz] *Science News* 136:222 S 30 '89
Tonic activation of NMDA receptors by ambient glutamate enhances excitability of neurons. P. Sah and others. bibl f il *Science* 246:815-18 N 10 '89
What tells anemones to kill their enemies? [research by Glen M. Watson and David A. Hessinger] R. Weiss. *Science News* 135:182 Mr 25 '89

CHEMOTAXIS
Activation of bacterial porin gene expression by a chimeric signal transducer in response to aspartate. R. Utsumi and others. bibl f il *Science* 245:1246-9 S 15 '89
Endothelial cell gene expression of a neutrophil chemotactic factor by TNF-α, LPS, and IL-1β. R. M. Strieter and others. bibl f il *Science* 243:1467-9 Mr 17 '89
Identification of monocyte chemotactic activity produced by malignant cells. D. T. Graves and others. bibl f il *Science* 245:1490-3 S 29 '89
The neutrophil-activating protein (NAP-1) is also chemotactic for T lymphocytes. C. G. Larsen and others. bibl f il *Science* 243:1464-6 Mr 17 '89
Neutrophil Mac-1 and MEL-14 adhesion proteins inversely regulated by chemotactic factors. T. K. Kishimoto and others. bibl f il *Science* 245:1238-41 S 15 '89
Thymotaxin, a chemotactic protein, is identical to β_2-microglobulin. C. Dargemont and others. bibl f il *Science* 246:803-6 N 10 '89

CHEMOTHERAPY
See also
Breast—Cancer—Therapy
Cancer—Therapy
Cancer inhibiting substances
Heart—Diseases—Therapy
Hodgkin's disease—Therapy
Psychopharmacology
Easing chemo-therapy [antivomiting drug ondansetron] *Prevention (Emmaus, Pa.)* 41:14 D '89
A kinder cure [combating chemotherapy-induced nausea with ondansetron] *Discover* 10:12 O '89
The purine path of chemotherapy [Nobel Prize lecture, December 8, 1988] G. B. Elion. bibl f il *Science* 244:41-7 Ap 7 '89

CHEMZYMES
Building chemicals the new-fashioned way [work of Elias J. Corey] I. Amato. *Science News* 135:388 Je 24 '89

"Chemzymes" mimic biology in miniature [work of E. J. Corey] M. M. Waldrop. por *Science* 245:354-5 Jl 28 '89

CHEN, GUANHUA, AND GODDARD, WILLIAM A., III
Magnon-exchange pairing and superconductivity [discussion of February 19, 1988 article, The magnon pairing mechanism of superconductivity in cuprate ceramics] *Science* 243:547-8 Ja 27 '89

CHEN, JAMES
The long-play Dobsonian. il *Astronomy* 17:70 N '89

CHEN, JENNIFER H., AND OTHERS
A cAMP-regulated chloride channel in lymphocytes that is affected in cystic fibrosis. bibl f il *Science* 243:657-60 F 3 '89

Is regulation of a chloride channel in lymphocytes affected in cystic fibrosis? [discussion of February 3, 1989 article, A cAMP-regulated chloride channel in lymphocytes that is affected in cystic fibrosis] *Science* 246:1049-50 N 24 '89

CHEN, MILTON, AND MARSH, WILLIAM
Belying the myths about instructional television. *The Education Digest* 55:60-3 D '89

CHEN, SUZIE, AND OTHERS
Commitment of mouse fibroblasts to adipocyte differentiation by DNA transfection. bibl f il *Science* 244:582-5 My 5 '89

CHEN, ZHONGGUO, AND OTHERS
Protein-RNA interactions in an icosahedral virus at 3.0 Å resolution. bibl f il *Science* 245:154-9 Jl 14 '89

CHEN MIN
Choreographer flees China when students are massacred. il por *Dance Magazine* 63:22 Ag '89

CHENEY, RICHARD B.
about

Cheney assures allies of U.S.'s continued commitment to NATO. *Aviation Week & Space Technology* 131:24 D 4 '89

Cheney calls for major realignment of Pentagon's procurement system. *Aviation Week & Space Technology* 130:21-2 Jl 10 '89

Cheney hoists 'red flag' against B-2, orders cost and technical review. P. A. Gilmartin. il *Aviation Week & Space Technology* 130:28-31 My 1 '89

Cheney pledges swift action on pressing defense issues. J. D. Morrocco. por *Aviation Week & Space Technology* 130:262-3 Mr 20 '89

Cheney proposes canceling major U.S. weapon programs. il *Aviation Week & Space Technology* 130:9, 18-23 Ap 24 '89

Cheney's pre-emptive strike. *National Review* 41:12-13 D 22 '89

Dick Cheney's chance to get the Pentagon in step. H. Gleckman. il *Business Week* p32-3 D 4 '89

Does Cheney have enough artillery to scrap with the brass? D. Griffiths. *Business Week* p43 Mr 27 '89

Happy campers, for a change. S. Talbott. pors *Time* 134:24 Ag 28 '89

Kick-starting the presidency of George Bush. il por *U.S. News & World Report* 106:10 Mr 20 '89

Letter from Washington. Cato. *National Review* 41:8 Je 16 '89

Making procurers cleaner and leaner. *U.S. News & World Report* 107:10+ Jl 24 '89

New spending talk worries GOP whip. D. C. Bacon. il por *Nation's Business* 77:6 F '89

On the second shot, a straight arrow. il por *Time* 133:24 Mr 20 '89

The politician at the Pentagon. G. Borger. il por *U.S. News & World Report* 107:24-5 O 2 '89

Rookie of the Year? *The New Republic* 200:7-8+ Ap 17 '89

A setback for Bush. J. Bierman. il pors *Maclean's* 102:34-5 Mr 20 '89

Time for a new speechwriter. J. D. Isaacs. por *The Bulletin of the Atomic Scientists* 45:5-6 N '89

Tortoise? *The Nation* 248:436-7 Ap 3 '89

Voodoo economics at the Pentagon. P. Cary. *U.S. News & World Report* 106:29 My 15 '89

CHENG, NIEN, 1915-
Massacre in Peking. il *National Review* 41:28-31 Ag 4 '89

about

A voice of hope for China. C. Reeve. il por *New Choices for the Best Years* 29:10 S '89

CHENG GANG
The Chinese view of Tibet. map *Utne Reader* p36 Mr/Ap '89

CHENG-MAYER, CECILIA, AND OTHERS
Differential effects of *nef* on HIV replication: implications for viral pathogenesis in the host. bibl f il *Science* 246:1629-32 D 22 '89

CHENGDU (CHINA)
Description

Mainland China's perfect metropolis. D. E. Manry. il *Travel Holiday* 171:12+ Ja '89

CHENGDU AIRCRAFT CORPORATION
Chengdu Aircraft Corp. builds export F-7M, upgraded F-7-3. il *Aviation Week & Space Technology* 131:82-3 D 11 '89

CHENGDU ENGINE COMPANY
Chengdu Engine Co. increases industrial turbine, overseas subcontract work as military orders fall. il *Aviation Week & Space Technology* 131:88-9 D 11 '89

CHEPESIUK, RONALD
Citizens tackle toxic dump. il *The Progressive* 53:12-13 Je '89

Fighting anarchy in Colombia [cover story] il *The New Leader* 72:5-8 S 18 '89

'We will not fight another war'. il por *The Progressive* 53:17 N '89

CHER, 1946-
about

Architectural digest visits: Cher. S. M. L. Aronson. il pors *Architectural Digest* 46:160-7+ Mr '89

The Cher effect [cover story; special section; with interview] il pors *Maclean's* 102:38-42+ Mr 6 '89

Solo again, Cher no longer acts in concert with Rob Camilletti. il pors *People Weekly* 31:77 Je 19 '89

Where's Cher? [cover story] J. Gissen. il pors *Ladies' Home Journal* 106:36+ Jl '89

CHERIMOYA
See also
Cooking—Fruit

CHERKASSKY, SHURA
about

Charm school. P. G. Davis. il por *New York* 22:144+ D 4 '89

CHERMAYEFF, IVAN, 1932-
about

Barn appeal: Ivan and Jane Clark Chermayeff's country house. S. Stephens. il *Architectural Digest* 46:146-51 Je '89

CHERMAYEFF, JANE CLARK
about

Barn appeal: Ivan and Jane Clark Chermayeff's country house. S. Stephens. il *Architectural Digest* 46:146-51 Je '89

CHERNOBYL (UKRAINE)
See also
Chernobyl nuclear disaster, 1986

CHERNOBYL NUCLEAR DISASTER, 1986
Chernobyl: 3 years after. il *FDA Consumer* 23:38-9 Ap '89

The Chernobyl cover-up. M. D. Lemonick. il *Time* 134:73 N 13 '89

Chernobyl fallout. S. Shulman. il *Technology Review* 92:12-13 F/Mr '89

Chernobyl: what really happened. W. Sweet. bibl il *Technology Review* 92:42-52 Jl '89

Chernobyl's legacy [World Association of Nuclear Operators] D. Rinehart. il *Maclean's* 102:52 My 29 '89

Sheepfarming after Chernobyl [Great Britain] B. Wynne. bibl f il maps *Environment* 31:10-15+ Mr '89

Swedish moose a ka cesium 137 [high concentration of radiation in muscle tissue] il *Environment* 31:22-3 My '89

Ukraine fallout debate. D. R. Marples. bibl f il *The Bulletin of the Atomic Scientists* 45:9-11 D '89

CHERNOVSKY, HERSH
Of ice and men. il *Runner's World* 24:96 Ja '89

CHEROKEE INDIANS
Strawberry fields, almost forever [prehistoric Native Americans] J. Chapman and others. il maps *Natural History* p50-8 S '89

CHEROKEE NATIONAL FOREST (TENN.)
Paint Rock, North Carolina. R. H. Mohlenbrock. il maps *Natural History* p64-7 Ag '89

Taking heart from upper East Tennessee. B. Wallach. il map *Focus (New York, N.Y.: 1950)* 38:22-8 Wint '88

CHERRIES
See also
Cooking—Fruit

Tart treats. M. Damsker. il *Organic Gardening* 36:28-32 N '89

CHERRINGTON, MARK
The pirate scientist. il por *Weatherwise* 42:205-7 Ag '89

CHERRY, DON
about

Don Cherry: globetrotter in the mainstream. J. Woodard. il pors *Down Beat* 56:23-5 N '89

Not your average family. J. Hooper. il pors *The New York Times Magazine* p48-50+ D 10 '89

CHERRY, DON
about

Don Cherry's outrageous credo. T. Frayne. il *Maclean's* 102:80 N 6 '89

CHERRY, EAGLE-EYE
about

Not your average family. J. Hooper. il pors *The New York Times Magazine* p48-50+ D 10 '89

CHERRY, KELLY
Remembering [poem] *The American Scholar* 58:428 Summ '89

CHERRY, NENEH
about

British accents. D. A. Keeps. il pors *Harper's Bazaar* 122:358+ S '89

CHERRY, NENEH—about—cont.

Music and mothering. D. DeNicolo; E. Zimmerman. il pors *Glamour* 87:178 N '89

Neneh Cherry, Britain's rising new rapper, is a self-styled Buffalo girl. K. Leston. il pors *Vogue* 179:154+ O '89

Neneh Cherry's popular stance. S. Pond. il pors *Rolling Stone* p76-8+ Ag 10 '89

Not your average family. J. Hooper. il pors *The New York Times Magazine* p48-50+ D 10 '89

Rising star Neneh Cherry discovers that the lowly deer tick is a showstopper, too. S. Dougherty. il por *People Weekly* 32:124-5 O 9 '89

CHERRY DESSERTS See Desserts

CHERRY TOMATOES See Tomatoes

CHERRY TREES

Cherry. S. D. Garber. il *Focus (New York, N.Y.: 1950)* 39:28-9 Spr '89

CHESANING (MICH.)

Stores

See also

Fancy That Antiques & Uniques (Firm)

CHESAPEAKE BAY (MD. AND VA.)

See also

Fishing—Chesapeake Bay (Md. and Va.)

Fisheries

See Fisheries

Shellfish fisheries

See Shellfish fisheries

CHESAPEAKE BAY GALLERY See Mariner's Museum (Newport News, Va.). Chesapeake Bay Gallery

CHESAPEAKE BAY REGION (MD. AND VA.)

Description and travel

Rite of passage [Eastern Shore; cover story] R. S. Peffer. il map *Travel Holiday* 172:40-51 Ag '89

CHESAPEAKE BAY RETRIEVERS See Retrievers

CHESBRO, GEORGE C.

The birth of a series character. *The Writer* 102:14-16 Mr '89

CHESHIRE (MASS.)

History

The original "Big Cheese" [citizens present 1,235 pound cheese to T. Jefferson] R. Sassaman. il *American History Illustrated* 23:34-5 Ja '89

CHESLEY, JACQUELINE

about

Painting with oil sticks [cover story] E. Feit. il *American Artist* 53:44-9 Ap '89

CHESS, CARON, AND HANCE, BILLIE JO

Opening doors: making risk communication agency reality. bibl f il *Environment* 31:10-15+ Je '89

CHESS

See also

Computer chess

Living Chess Game (Marostica, Italy)

Chairwomen of the chessboard [the Polgars] R. Givens. il *Newsweek* 113:63+ Mr 27 '89

From street kids to Royal Knights [B. Hall coaches team at J.H.S. 99 in East Harlem] J. Coudert. il por *Reader's Digest* 134:141-6 Je '89

Mink [player who takes on challengers in Washington Square, N.Y.] *The New Yorker* 65:38-9 Je 12 '89

The winning edge [G. Kasparov] R. Chelminski. il por *Reader's Digest* 135:175-6+ D '89

Economic aspects

More computers—and humans—are saying 'checkmate'. M. Schroeder. il *Business Week* p50 N 6 '89

CHESSON, KATHLEEN KLINE- See Kline-Chesson, Kathleen

CHEST PAIN

Chest pains: what do they mean? J. Stone. il *The New York Times Magazine* p53-4 F 19 '89

Getting to the heart of panic disorder. K. Fackelmann. *Science News* 135:39 Ja 21 '89

CHESTERTON, G. K. (GILBERT KEITH), 1874-1936

The quick one [story] il *The Saturday Evening Post* 261:34-7+ N/D '89

The quick one [story] il *The Saturday Evening Post* 261:36-8+ O '89

The quick one [story] il *The Saturday Evening Post* 261:48-51+ S '89

about

Coming to terms with Chesterton. T. Teachout. *The American Scholar* 58:105-12 Wint '89

The newer, thinner me. P. Yancey. il *Christianity Today* 33:56 Ag 18 '89

CHESTERTON, GILBERT KEITH See Chesterton, G. K. (Gilbert Keith), 1874-1936

CHESTERTOWN (MD.)

Description

Chestertown. L. L. Creighton. il *U.S. News & World Report* 107:45-7 D 18 '89

CHESTERWOOD (STOCKBRIDGE, MASS.)

Chesterwood: a sculptor's studio. D. Sherwood. il *Gourmet* 49:76-9+ Je '89

CHESTS

See also

Cooler chests

Blanket chest [Shaker design] R. N. Hoffman. il *Workbench* 45:32-3 My/Je '89

Shaker blanket chest. K. Collier. il *The Family Handyman* 39:94-8 Ap '89

Walnut foyer chest. A. Weaver and V. Weaver. il *Workbench* 45:36-8+ Mr/Ap '89

Collectors and collecting

Antiques: Pennsylvania German chests. R. Conniff. il *Architectural Digest* 46:276-81+ O '89

CHEUNG, LILIAN

(jt. auth) See Gee, Molly, and Cheung, Lilian

CHEVAL, FERDINAND, 1836-1924

about

The Ideal Palace: Ferdinand Cheval's fantasy in the Rhône Valley. Y. Blumenfeld. il *Architectural Digest* 46:108-13+ Ja '89

The postman's palace. B. Weber. il por *The New York Times Magazine* p122 S 10 '89

LE CHEVAL BLANC (NEW YORK, N.Y.: RESTAURANT)

See New York (N.Y.)—Restaurants, nightclubs, bars, etc.

CHEVALIER (OA) HOLDINGS LTD.

A fast ride on Hong Kong's high-tech wave. D. J. Yang. il por *Business Week* p111 My 22 '89

CHEVROLET MOTOR DIVISION

Chevrolet tries to get the lead out. J. B. Treece. il por *Business Week* p39 My 22 '89

The Lumina has its brights off. J. B. Treece. il *Business Week* p31 Ag 28 '89

CHEVRON CORPORATION

Can Ken Derr turn Chevron around? T. Mack. il por *Forbes* 144:49+ N 27 '89

Chevron gets its act together. *Money* 18:42 S '89

Pollution prevention: the Chevron story [Richmond, Calif. refinery] G. Karras. bibl f *Environment* 31:4-5+ O '89

Pressure on a U.S. oil power. G. G. Marcial. *Business Week* p142 O 9 '89

What does Liedtke want? [Pennzoil's stake in Chevron] M. Ivey and M. Shao. il por *Business Week* p42-3 D 25 '89-Ja 1 '90

CHEWING GUM

See also

Wm. Wrigley Jr. Co.

Chewing pays off [plaque and cavities reduced with use of xylitol gum; research by Kauko Makinen] il *Prevention (Emmaus, Pa.)* 41:22 Mr '89

Advertising

Two-timing [original Doublemint Twins J. and J. Boyd] B. Greene. pors *Esquire* 111:57-9 Je '89

CHEZ JOSEPHINE (NEW YORK, N.Y.: RESTAURANT)

See New York (N.Y.)—Restaurants, nightclubs, bars, etc.

CHEZ NICO (LONDON, ENGLAND: RESTAURANT) *See* London (England)—Restaurants, nightclubs, bars, etc.

CHÉZ-ZAM (FIRM)

Safari. *The New Yorker* 65:35-6 Mr 20 '89

CHI CHI RODRIGUEZ YOUTH FOUNDATION

Chi Chi's children. S. Cronkite. il *Life* 12:48-50+ Ag '89

CHIANG, HUI-LING, AND OTHERS

A role for a 70-kilodaton heat shock protein in lysosomal degradation of intracellular proteins. bibl f il *Science* 246:382-5 O 20 '89

CHIANTI (WINE) *See* Wine

CHIARELLA, TOM

Berard's luck [story] *The New Yorker* 65:42-9 O 2 '89

CHIARELLO, MICHAEL

about

Culinary crossroads. D. Welch. il por *Health (New York, N.Y.)* 21:74-9+ Ap '89

CHIARINI, DORIANA

about

Doriana Chiarini at Ala. A. F. Collins. il *Art in America* 77:153-4 Mr '89

CHIAROSCURO

Painting values accurately. F. Covino. il *American Artist* 53:64-7 Mr '89

CHIAUZZI, EMIL

Breaking the patterns that lead to relapse. il *Psychology Today* 23:18-19 D '89

CHICAGO (ILL.)

Airports

Completion near on O'Hare's $2.1-billion expansion project. J. Ott. *Aviation Week & Space Technology* 130:113 Je 5 '89

Architecture

Architecture: Stanley Tigerman [house in Chicago suburbs; cover story] R. A. M. Stern. il por *Architectural Digest* 46:146-51+ F '89

Good neighbors [Walner House in Glencoe and private residence in Chicago] K. D. Stein. il *Architectural Record* 177:72-81 mid-Ap '89

Art

See also

Chicago International Art Exposition

Brushed-aside artists have their day [exhibit by homeless artists] D. Neff. il por *Christianity Today* 33:62 D 15 '89

Banks

See also

Continental Bank, N.A.

Independence Bank of Chicago

CHICAGO (ILL.)—Banks—See also—*cont.*
  Shorebank Corporation (Chicago, Ill.)
  Chicago bank stock basket. T. Jaffe. il *Forbes* 144:124 Ag 21 '89

Bookstores
See Booksellers and bookselling—Illinois

Buildings
See also
  Hancock Center (Chicago, Ill.)
Able to leap the Sears Tower in a single bound? [125 story skyscraper to be built] D. Greising. il *Business Week* p94 Je 5 '89
And, now, another tall story [125 story skyscraper to be built] il *U.S. News & World Report* 106:14-15 Je 12 '89
Chicago style [303 West Madison Street] M. Gaskie. il *Architectural Record* 177:92-5 S '89

Buses
See Chicago (Ill.)—Transit systems

Crime
Bus drivers: dealing while driving [school bus drivers arrested on drug charges] *Newsweek* 114:50 D 11 '89
A change of command for the Chicago Mob [death of J. Ferriola] *Newsweek* 113:34 Mr 27 '89
A sour scam in Chicago [Peoples Gas Light & Coke Co. employees accused in stolen gas meter scam] T. Padgett. il *Newsweek* 114:84 N 6 '89

Criminal justice, Administration of
Comedian Bob McDonald gets jail term for scam. il pors *Jet* 77:25 D 25 '89-Ja 1 '90
Jailed for a rape that never happened, Gary Dotson has his name cleared at last. M. Brower. il pors *People Weekly* 32:80-1 Ag 28 '89

Dance
Reviews:
  Modern dance performances. C. Survant. il *Dance Magazine* 63:58 Je '89
  Work of J. Erkert and A. Osgood at MoMing Dance and Arts Center. C. Survant. il *Dance Magazine* 63:82-3 D '89

Description
Chicago's badlands [cycling] F. Staub. il *Bicycling* 30:82 O/N '89
His kind of town [tour guide B. Young] E. Stern. il pors *Gentlemen's Quarterly* 59:138+ S '89

Education
See also
  Center for Successful Childhood Development (Chicago, Ill.)
  Corporate Community School (Chicago, Ill.)
AIDS in America's schoolhouses: learning the hard lessons [cover story; with editorial comment by Pauline B. Gough] D. L. Kirp and S. Epstein. il *Phi Delta Kappan* 70:578, 584-93 Ap '89
Can parents save schools? C. Leslie. il *Newsweek* 114:74 O 16 '89
Chicago parents 1, bureaucrats 0 [community control of schools] J. Rachlin. il *U.S. News & World Report* 106:51-2 F 6 '89
Mayor Sawyer supports Chicago public schools. il por *Jet* 75:8 F 13 '89
Reconstructing the nation's worst schools. H. J. Walberg and others. il *Phi Delta Kappan* 70:802-5 Je '89
School order and safety as community issues. J. Menacker and others. bibl f il *Phi Delta Kappan* 71:39-40+ S '89
Site-managed schools: the Chicago plan [excerpt from Organizing for learning] J. J. Lane and H. J. Walberg. *The Education Digest* 55:28-31 N '89
Steve Wolf's class act: straight talk in the schoolroom [chairman of UAL Corp. speaks to black students] J. E. Ellis. il *Business Week* p57 F 6 '89
War between the classes [South Loop Elementary School] T. Padgett. il *Newsweek* 113:64 My 1 '89
A watchdog guards the public schools [teacher G. Schmidt] M. Ervin. por *The Progressive* 53:16-17 N '89

Elections
See Chicago (Ill.)—Politics and government

Galleries and museums
See also
  Art Institute of Chicago
  Field Museum of Natural History
Gallery building gutted [fire] P. Wolff. il *Art News* 88:43 Summ '89

Health facilities
See also
  Claretian Medical Center

Historic houses, sites, etc.
Easton meets Midwest [Chicago house decorated by David Easton] J. Edelstein and L. Wren. il *House & Garden* 161:112-19 F '89

Housing
See also
  Shorebank Corporation (Chicago, Ill.)
HUD Sec. Kemp visits as Chicago gives control of housing unit to tenants. il por *Jet* 76:26 My 29 '89
"The tenants could do a better job of managing" [Chicago housing project] M. M. McDowell. il *Black Enterprise* 19:16 Jl '89

Music
See also
  Chicago Opera Theater
  Chicago Symphony Orchestra
  Lyric Opera Center for American Artists
  Lyric Opera of Chicago
  Southend Musicworks, Inc.
Alumni tribute to Walter Dyett: Jazz Showcase, Dusable High School/Chicago. J. Cunniff. il *Down Beat* 56:51-2 Je '89
This blue city. P. Schneider. il pors *Esquire* 111:38 F '89

Music festivals
See Music festivals—Illinois

Newspapers
See also
  Chicago sun-times (Newspaper)
  Chicago tribune
  Substance (Newspaper)

Politics and government
Battling an old bugaboo [election of R. M. Daley as mayor] L. I. Barrett. il pors *Time* 133:26-7 Ap 17 '89
Black vs. white in Chicago. T. B. Edsall. il *The New York Review of Books* 36:21-3 Ap 13 '89
Chicago alderman Evans to run for mayor after Sawyer's primary defeat. il pors *Jet* 75:4-5 Mr 20 '89
Chicago blacks back Tim Evans, Harold Washington Party candidate for mayor. R. E. Johnson. il pors *Jet* 75:4+ Ap 3 '89
Chicago's sonny days [Mayor R. M. Daley] il *U.S. News & World Report* 107:30 Ag 21 '89
Eugene Sawyer faces an Hispanic, two whites, in Chicago mayoral race. por *Jet* 75:26 Ja 23 '89
In Chicago, it's back to the future [R. M. Daley's race for mayor] J. McCormick. il por *Newsweek* 113:26 F 6 '89
Jackson backs Sawyer in Chicago mayoral primary. il pors *Jet* 75:6 F 13 '89
Jackson strikes out [involvement in mayoral primary] J. McCormick. il pors *Newsweek* 113:24 Mr 13 '89
The old man's Irish eyes are smiling [M. Royko's views on mayoral candidate R. M. Daley] il por *U.S. News & World Report* 106:12-13 Mr 13 '89
'Points of challenge' [J. Jackson's involvement in mayoral primary] *The Nation* 248:433 Ap 3 '89
Primogeniture in the Windy City [R. M. Daley wins Democratic mayoral nomination] G. Scott. il por *Time* 133:24 Mr 13 '89
Race after Washington [mayoral contest] P. Greene. il *Commonweal* 116:199-201 Ap 7 '89
Racial politics—Chicago's raw nerve [R. M. Daley vs. E. Sawyer in mayoral race] D. Johnson. il pors *The New York Times Magazine* p34-8+ F 19 '89
Richard Daley wins Chicago mayoral race; blacks fail to unite behind Tim Evans. il pors *Jet* 76:8-9 Ap 24 '89
Richard M. Daley calls for racial 'harmony' at inaugural. il por *Jet* 76:12-13 My 8 '89
Skin deep. F. Barnes. *The New Republic* 200:10-11 Ap 10 '89
A wet mayor or what? [R. Daley's election] J. R. Coyne, Jr. *National Review* 41:20-1 Ap 21 '89

Poor
Brushed-aside artists have their day [exhibit by homeless artists] D. Neff. il por *Christianity Today* 33:62 D 15 '89
Helping the homeless [P. Crowley's work at women's shelter] C. Reeve. il por *New Choices for the Best Years* 29:16 F '89

Prisons and reformatories
The church picnic goes to jail [work of Mother York] R. Clapp. il por *Christianity Today* 33:14-15 Je 16 '89

Public health
Measles busters: Chicago's vaccine plan. J. N. Baker. il *Newsweek* 114:22 Ag 21 '89

Race relations
Black vs. white in Chicago. T. B. Edsall. il *The New York Review of Books* 36:21-3 Ap 13 '89
Blacks and Jews: the uncivil war [with editorial comment by Lee Eisenberg] T. Branch. il *Esquire* 111:25, 89-90+ My '89
Chicago suffers racially from isolation, report says. *Jet* 77:8 O 16 '89
Racial politics—Chicago's raw nerve [R. M. Daley vs. E. Sawyer in mayoral race] D. Johnson. il pors *The New York Times Magazine* p34-8+ F 19 '89
Richard M. Daley calls for racial 'harmony' at inaugural. il por *Jet* 76:12-13 My 8 '89
Skin deep. F. Barnes. *The New Republic* 200:10-11 Ap 10 '89
A wet mayor or what? [R. Daley's election] J. R. Coyne, Jr. *National Review* 41:20-1 Ap 21 '89

Religious institutions and affairs
See also
  Claretian Medical Center
COGIC bishop Louis Ford lauded during 54th anniv. of his church in Chicago. il pors *Jet* 76:18 Jl 31 '89
Fifty years of changing minds & structures [priest D. Cantwell] T. Unsworth. il *Commonweal* 116:365-7 Je 16 '89

CHICAGO (ILL.)—Religious institutions and affairs—*cont.*

In Chicago, two angry priests declare a holy war on drugs [M. Pfleger and G. Clements put pressure on stores to stop selling drug paraphernalia] W. Plummer. il pors *People Weekly* 32:102-3 S 4 '89

Restaurants, nightclubs, bars, etc.

Oprah invites you to dinner [dishes from Eccentric restaurant] E. Byron. il por *Redbook* 173:102-3+ Ag '89

Steve Langlois is out to prove that haute cuisine and oat cuisine are not the same in the Midwest [executive chef at Prairie] D. Chu. il pors *People Weekly* 32:143-4 N 27 '89

Suiting science to a T (shirt), two Chicago bar owners set up a Stephen Hawking Fan Club [Gold Star Sardine Bar] il *People Weekly* 32:111 S 11 '89

What's a sports bar anyway? M. Kiefer. il *Sport (New York, N.Y.)* 80:64 Mr '89

Social work

See also

Genesis House

Mothers Against Gangs (Organization)

Sports

Chicago. M. Kiefer. il *Sport (New York, N.Y.)* 80:62-6 Mr '89

Stores

See also

Convito Italiano (Firm)

Chicago law maker tells grocers to learn English [W. Henry] por *Jet* 77:15 D 25 '89-Ja 1 '90

Chicago style! [boutiques] il *Essence* 20:46 O '89

Streets

Chicago names street for Lou Rawls; brother dies before ceremony. il pors *Jet* 76:61 Je 26 '89

Theater

See also

Willow Street Carnival (Comedy troupe)

Transit systems

Monday morning miracle [commuters communicate on Chicago bus]; ed. by Philip Yancey. P. Wigand. il *Reader's Digest* 134:9+ Mr '89

World's fair, 1893

See World's Columbian Exposition (1893: Chicago, Ill.)

CHICAGO (ILL.). HOUSING AUTHORITY

Can business save public housing? [work of V. Lane] R. Henkoff. il por *Fortune* 120:121+ N 20 '89

Can Chicago beat the odds? J. McCormick. il por *Newsweek* 113:24-6 Ja 2 '89

High noon at the housing project [work of V. Lane] il pors *Ebony* 44:130+ Ag '89

Kemp OKs use of vacant apartments for homeless. il por *Jet* 77:52 N 27 '89

The man who's giving Chicago's projects some r-e-s-p-e-c-t [V. Lane] B. Bremner. por *Business Week* p88 Je 12 '89

CHICAGO (ILL.). UNIVERSITY *See* University of Chicago

CHICAGO (MUSICAL GROUP)

Chicago: jazz-rock pioneers [reprint] H. Siders. il *Down Beat* 56:81-2 S '89

CHICAGO AUTO SHOW *See* Automobiles—Exhibitions

CHICAGO BOARD OF TRADE

A bid to salvage a go-go legacy [L. Melamed suggests areas for reform in wake of FBI investigation] W. McWhirter. il por *Time* 133:52 F 6 '89

Big trouble in the pits [indictment of commodities traders] T. Padgett. il *Newsweek* 114:36 Ag 14 '89

A blast from the past for the Chicago Board of Trade? [L. Rosenthal] D. Greising. il por *Business Week* p137 D 25 '89-Ja 1 '90

Commodities sting [FBI investigation] J. J. Curran. il *Fortune* 119:12 F 13 '89

Crackdown on the Chicago boys [FBI uncovers widespread fraud in commodity markets] C. Gorman. il *Time* 133:52 Ja 30 '89

Ferruzzi trading "illogical" for many months. *Successful Farming* 87:48P N '89

Future shock is rattling the futures pits. K. A. Behof. il *Business Week* p93-4 Ap 17 '89

Futures shock: fraud charges shake the Chicago exchanges. D. Greising. il *Business Week* p44-5 Ag 14 '89

How scandal may change Chicago. *Successful Farming* 87:16 mid-Mr '89

In the futures pits, life is no longer a bowl of cherries [FBI uncovers fraud in Chicago's commodity exchanges] C. P. Work and R. F. Black. il *U.S. News & World Report* 106:44-5 F 6 '89

An Italian 'peasant' who would be soybean king [Ferruzzi chairman R. Gardini's attempt to corner U.S. soybean market] E. Pomice. il por *U.S. News & World Report* 107:44-5 Ag 7 '89

Life in the pits will never be the same [FBI sting of Chicago's trading system] K. A. Behof. il *Business Week* p32-4 F 6 '89

Life is the pits in Chicago's pits [probe of futures markets] il *U.S. News & World Report* 107:11-12 Ag 14 '89

More shoes drop in the pits [probe of futures markets] D. Pauly. il *Newsweek* 113:50 F 6 '89

A pall over the futures pits? Hell, no. K. A. Behof. il *Business Week* p91 Ap 3 '89

Pit players [P. Kern of Norman Kern & Company] D. Sherman. il pors *Ms.* 18:62-4+ N '89

Snakes in the pits [FBI busts traders] C. Gorman. il *Time* 134:52+ Ag 14 '89

The sting in the pits [FBI probe uncovers fraud] J. McCormick. il *Newsweek* 113:54 Ja 30 '89

Why the pits are sick over soybeans [directive, in response to Ferruzzi Group maneuvers, sends prices tumbling] D. Greising. il *Business Week* p76+ Jl 31 '89

You can almost hear a sigh of relief in the pits. K. A. Behof. il *Business Week* p33 F 20 '89

CHICAGO BOARD OPTIONS EXCHANGE

Will the Amex and Philly team up against Chicago? [merge options trading] L. J. Nathans. il *Business Week* p78 Jl 31 '89

CHICAGO CITY BALLET

See also

Ballet Chicago

CHICAGO GROUP *See* Morgan Stanley Asset Management/Chicago Group

CHICAGO HEIGHTS (ILL.)

Housing

Uncle Sam's NIMBY attack [Justice Dept. suing for discrimination against mentally disabled] J. P. Shapiro. il *U.S. News & World Report* 107:24 S 18 '89

CHICAGO INTERNATIONAL ART EXPOSITION

Fair city. D. Saatchi. il *House & Garden* 161:74+ My '89

CHICAGO LYRIC OPERA *See* Lyric Opera of Chicago

CHICAGO MARATHON *See* Marathon running

CHICAGO MERCANTILE EXCHANGE

A bid to salvage a go-go legacy [L. Melamed suggests areas for reform in wake of FBI investigation] W. McWhirter. il por *Time* 133:52 F 6 '89

Big trouble in the pits [indictment of commodities traders] T. Padgett. il *Newsweek* 114:36 Ag 14 '89

Commodities sting [FBI investigation] J. J. Curran. il *Fortune* 119:12 F 13 '89

Crackdown on the Chicago boys [FBI uncovers widespread fraud in commodity markets] C. Gorman. il *Time* 133:52 Ja 30 '89

Future shock is rattling the futures pits. K. A. Behof. il *Business Week* p93-4 Ap 17 '89

Futures shock: fraud charges shake the Chicago exchanges. D. Greising. il *Business Week* p44-5 Ag 14 '89

How scandal may change Chicago. *Successful Farming* 87:16 mid-Mr '89

In the futures pits, life is no longer a bowl of cherries [FBI uncovers fraud in Chicago's commodity exchanges] C. P. Work and R. F. Black. il *U.S. News & World Report* 106:44-5 F 6 '89

Leo Melamed. K. A. Behof. il por *Business Week* Special Issue:123 Ap 14 '89

Life in the pits will never be the same [FBI sting of Chicago's trading system] K. A. Behof. il *Business Week* p32-4 F 6 '89

Life is the pits in Chicago's pits [probe of futures markets] il *U.S. News & World Report* 107:11-12 Ag 14 '89

More shoes drop in the pits [probe of futures markets] D. Pauly. il *Newsweek* 113:50 F 6 '89

A pall over the futures pits? Hell, no. K. A. Behof. il *Business Week* p91 Ap 3 '89

Snakes in the pits [FBI busts traders] C. Gorman. il *Time* 134:52+ Ag 14 '89

The sting in the pits [FBI probe uncovers fraud] J. McCormick. il *Newsweek* 113:54 Ja 30 '89

Was George Soros sheared by Shearson? [futures loss] D. Greising. il por *Business Week* p45 N 6 '89

You can almost hear a sigh of relief in the pits. K. A. Behof. il *Business Week* p33 F 20 '89

CHICAGO OPERA THEATER

Chicago. J. Von Rhein. il *Opera News* 54:38 Ag '89

CHICAGO PACIFIC CORP.

Can Maytag clean up around the world? [acquisition of Chicago Pacific Corp.] B. Bremner. il *Business Week* p86-7 Ja 30 '89

CHICAGO SUN-TIMES (NEWSPAPER)

Can the Chicago sun-times reverse its slide? J. F. Siler. il *Business Week* p82 N 27 '89

Mr. Lonelyhearts [taking over A. Landers' column] J. Zaslow. il *The New York Times Magazine* p59-60+ O 29 '89

Two Chicago newspapers complete negotiations. *Monthly Labor Review* 112:52 F '89

CHICAGO SYMPHONY ORCHESTRA

Lost in Crete [performance of Eighth symphony by D. Shostakovich] P. G. Davis. il *New York* 22:144+ F 27 '89

CHICAGO TRIBUNE

Discrimination isn't comic [replaces Kudzu with Pogo] M. E. Marty. *The Christian Century* 106:215 F 22 '89

Two Chicago newspapers complete negotiations. *Monthly Labor Review* 112:52 F '89

CHICANO AUTHORS *See* Authors, Mexican American

CHICANOS *See* Mexican Americans

CHICHÉN ITZÁ (MEXICO)

The first place to stop when you visit Yucatán ruins. il *Sunset (Central West edition)* 183:52 D '89

CHICHESTER-MILES, IAN
about
Leopard makes leap for bizjet market. N. Moll. il por *Flying* 116:20-2 Ap '89
CHICHILNISKY, GRACIELA
about
Unwelcome Recruit. J. Zweig. il por *Forbes* 143:149 My 15 '89
CHICK BRAIN *See* Brain
CHICK EMBRYOS *See* Embryology—Birds
CHICK EYE *See* Eye—Birds
CHICKEN COOKING *See* Cooking—Poultry
CHICKEN INDUSTRY *See* Poultry industry
CHICKEN SALADS *See* Salads
CHICKEN SANDWICHES *See* Sandwiches
CHICKEN SOUP [television program] *See* Television program reviews—Single works
CHICKENS *See* Poultry
CHICO (CALIF.)
Housing
Living in sin? Not in her apartments, vows Christian landlady Evelyn Smith [K. Phillips and G. Randall file discrimination charges] M. Brower. il pors *People Weekly* 32:113-14 D 11 '89
CHICORY
See also
Cooking—Vegetables
Pan de zucchero
CHIDESTER, WILLIAM
about
Relative strength is absolutely hot. M. Hulbert. il *Forbes* 144:117 Ag 21 '89
CHIEF EXECUTIVE OFFICERS (CORPORATIONS) *See* Executives
CHIELANSKI-LALLINGER, MANUELA VON
about
The fall of the Wall. M. Ryan. il por *People Weekly* 32:46-9 N 27 '89
CHILD, JULIA
Julia Child's Christmas Eve [excerpt from The way to cook] il por *Ladies' Home Journal* 106:162-3+ D '89
Julia Child's sweet indulgences. il *Ladies' Home Journal* 106:282-4+ N '89
about
The energetic epicure. P. Garfinkel. il por *New Choices for the Best Years* 29:10 Ap '89
Food for thought. M. Barrier. il pors *Nation's Business* 77:29+ D '89
A holiday bird and a free-range chat with Julia. G. Jaynes. il pors *Life* 12:95-8+ D '89
Julia Child— cooking at 76. C. K. Gandee. il pors *House & Garden* 161:174 Je '89
Once more, it's 'Bon appétit!'. L. Shapiro. il pors *Newsweek* 114:114-15+ O 9 '89
CHILD ABUSE
See also
Child molesting
Steinberg, Lisa, d. 1987—Child abuse case
The abuse of America's incarcerated children. *Utne Reader* p63 S/O '89
The battered child [Supreme Court rules social worker not liable in case of J. DeShaney] *The New Republic* 200:7-8 Mr 20 '89
Child abuse: a 'cycle of violence'? [research by Cathy Spatz Widom] *Science News* 136:61 Jl 22 '89
Child abuse hysteria: a warning for educators. L. D. Spiegel. *The Education Digest* 54:55-8 Ja '89
Child abuse: the interrogation. P. Klass. il *The New York Times Magazine* p53-4 F 26 '89
Crossing the 'borderline' of child abuse [research by Judith L. Herman] B. Bower. *Science News* 135:246 Ap 22 '89
The cycle of violence. C. S. Widom. bibl f il *Science* 244:160-6 Ap 14 '89
Multiple personalities. B. Wickens. il *Maclean's* 102:60-1 N 27 '89
N.Y. couple charged with abusing their 9 children [H. McMillan] il por *Jet* 76:38 S 11 '89
"Poor Joshua!" [Supreme Court absolves Wisconsin child welfare agency in case of J. DeShaney] il por *Time* 133:56 Mr 6 '89
Poor Joshua [Supreme Court rules Wisconsin child welfare agency not liable for injuries caused by father of J. DeShaney] P. A. Zirkel. bibl f il *Phi Delta Kappan* 70:828-9 Je '89
Prisoners of childhood. C. Tavris. *Vogue* 179:380+ Mr '89
Report cards can hurt you [poor grades trigger child abuse] A. Toufexis. il *Time* 133:75 My 1 '89
Reverend father [daughter of abusive minister] D. Loring. *The Humanist* 49:21-3+ Jl/Ag '89
School prevention of suicide, violence, and abuse. E. Guetzloe. *The Education Digest* 54:46-9 F '89
Solomon's choice [mishandling of cases by social workers] D. Zegart. il *Ms.* 17:78-83 Je '89
"The teacher called me stupid, Mommy!" [emotionally abused students] M. H. Christensen. il *Redbook* 173:144-5+ O '89
Violence begets violence [research by Elise Lake] *USA Today (Periodical)* 118:3 D '89

When words hurt [parents' use of verbal abuse] B. M. Campbell. il *Essence* 20:88 Jl '89
Whose responsibility is it, anyway? [child welfare worker liability] J. P. Shapiro. il *U.S. News & World Report* 106:29-30 Ja 9 '89
Whose rights are we protecting, anyway? [with discussion] K. Dorros and P. Dorsey. il *Children Today* 18:6-11+ My/Je '89
"Why did I hit my daughter?". D. Lennard. il *Redbook* 173:50+ Je '89
Witness to child abuse. J. Simms. il *Parents* 64:90+ My '89
CHILD-ADULT RELATIONSHIP
See also
Generation gap
Parent-child relationship
Youth-adult relationship
Brighter afternoons for latchkey children [involving seniors in day care programs] il *Aging* no359:20-1 '89
Every woman needs a champion. C. G. Vogel. il pors *Good Housekeeping* 208:158+ My '89
Hands across the ages [aged working with children; cover story] A. Korpivaara. il *New Choices for the Best Years* 29:41-3+ Ag '89
I won't grow up. G. Sheehan. il *Runner's World* 24:14 Ja '89
Leading questions. P. Theroux. il *Parents* 64:71-2 Mr '89
Old hands [senior citizens working at a day care center in Union City, N.J.] C. Dowling. il *Life* 12:102-4+ D '89
A question of trust [taking girlfriend's daughter canoeing] P. Mandelbaum. il *The New York Times Magazine* p14+ Ag 6 '89
Starting a senior center latchkey program. *Children Today* 18:5 Jl/Ag '89
What a neighbor will do [condensed from Out of the Ozarks] W. Childress. il *Reader's Digest* 135:125-7 S '89
CHILD CARE *See* Children—Care and hygiene; Day care
CHILD CARE CENTERS *See* Day care
CHILD CARE TAX CREDITS *See* Tax credits
CHILD CUSTODY *See* Custody of children
CHILD EVANGELISM FELLOWSHIP INC.
Doctrine splits Child Evangelism Fellowship. J. Maxwell. *Christianity Today* 33:49 Mr 17 '89
CHILD EVANGELISM MINISTRIES, INC.
Doctrine splits Child Evangelism Fellowship. J. Maxwell. *Christianity Today* 33:49 Mr 17 '89
CHILD GUIDANCE *See* Child psychology
CHILD LABOR *See* Children—Employment
CHILD MOLESTING
See also
Incest
Breaking silence: Glamour readers talk about childhood sexual abuse, and how it changed their lives. L. Mosedale. il *Glamour* 87:246-9+ My '89
Child-abuse evidence debated [variations in girls' genitals] D. Nathan. *Ms.* 17:81-2 Mr '89
Child sexual abuse prevention programs: what makes them effective in protecting children? S. Kraizer and others. bibl f *Children Today* 18:23-7 S/O '89
How best to heal a shattered child [interview with K. Hagans] L. J. Moore. por *U.S. News & World Report* 106:68-9 Ap 10 '89
Making history—of a dubious sort [McMartin Preschool trial] *U.S. News & World Report* 106:20 My 1 '89
The sex-abuse puzzle [doubts about child witnesses] D. Gelman. il *Newsweek* 114:99-100 N 13 '89
Victims of abuse: paying the price for the sins of others [child molestation and Catholic teaching] M. B. Mann. *U.S. Catholic* 54:36-8 Jl '89
"We have a problem". J. Marks. il *Parents* 64:83-7 Mr '89
Canada
The abuse of children [cover story; special section; with editorial comment by Kevin Doyle] il *Maclean's* 102:2, 56-62+ N 27 '89
A breach of faith [sex charges against Newfoundland priests] G. Allen. il *Maclean's* 102:16-17 Mr 13 '89
Charges of a coverup [Mount Cashel Orphanage, St. John's, Nfld.] N. Underwood. *Maclean's* 102:66+ D 4 '89
Scandal on the Rock [inquiry into sexual abuse involving Christian Brothers at Mount Cashel Orphanage, St. John's, Nfld.] N. Underwood. il *Maclean's* 102:61 O 2 '89
Sex and scandal [former resident S. Earle testifies about sexual abuse at Mount Cashel Orphanage, St. John's, Nfld.] N. Underwood. il por *Maclean's* 102:84 O 30 '89
Sins of the flesh [priests and sex crimes in Newfoundland] G. W. Taylor. il *Maclean's* 102:10-12 Jl 17 '89
CHILD NEGLECT *See* Child abuse
CHILD ORIENTED BUSINESS *See* Youth market
CHILD PLACEMENT *See* Adoption and adopted children; Foster home care
CHILD PORNOGRAPHY LAWS *See* Obscenity (Law)
CHILD PSYCHIATRY
Research on child and adolescent mental disorders. B. A. Hamburg. *Science* 246:738 N 10 '89
When child's play isn't fun. P. Klass. il *The New York Times Magazine* p31-2 Ag 6 '89

CHILD PSYCHOLOGY
See also
Aggressiveness in children
Anger in children
Anxiety in children
Children and death
Fear in children
Imagination in children
Infant psychology
Lying in children
Maternal deprivation
Moral development
Parent-child relationship
Parent education
Play
Problem children
Vitality in children
The child psychologist. L. Salk. See issues of McCall's beginning March 1986
Child's aggression may foretell heart risk [research by Saundra MacD. Hunter] K. Fackelmann. *Science News* 136:15 Jl 1 '89
Coping with stress. L. G. Katz. il *Parents* 64:174 F '89
Deceptive successes in young children [research by Michael Lewis] B. Bower. *Science News* 135:343 Je 3 '89
Growing up sad. B. Bower. il *Science News* 136:90-1 Ag 5 '89
Kids who beat the odds. C. Safran. il *Reader's Digest* 134:197-8+ Mr '89
Kids without friends [problems caused by rejection] P. Chance. il *Psychology Today* 23:28-31 Ja/F '89
Lonely teardrops: when kids have trouble making friends. J. K. Rosemond. il *Better Homes and Gardens* 67:27 Mr '89
Moving without misery. L. G. Katz. il *Parents* 64:210 Je '89
The perception of intention [study of preschool children] V. Dasser and others. bibl f *Science* 243:365-7 Ja 20 '89
Reading, thinking, and testing. G. W. Bracey. *Phi Delta Kappan* 71:248-9 N '89
The state of the kids [special section; with editorial comment by Joel Gurin] il *American Health* 8:43-6+, 110 O '89
Type-A tots: when pushing kids leads to stress. A. Atkins. il *Better Homes and Gardens* 67:36+ N '89
Understanding kids. L. Balter. See issues of Ladies' Home Journal beginning February 1984
When kids see you fight [parents' quarrels] N. Rubin. il *Parents* 64:73-6+ Jl '89
When sadness turns to childhood depression. L. M. Smelser. *The Education Digest* 55:52-3 S '89

CHILD RAISING *See* Children—Management and training
CHILD RAISING, COST OF *See* Children—Cost of raising
CHILD SNATCHING *See* Custody kidnapping
CHILD SUPPORT *See* Support (Domestic relations)
CHILD SWITCHING
Every mother's nightmare comes true when a hospital nursery mix-up sends two babies home with the wrong parents [N. Kirks and W. Mailett born at Kaiser Permanente Medical Center in Los Angeles, Calif.] M. Brower. il pors *People Weekly* 31:123-4 Ap 3 '89
Every parent's nightmare: a hospital nursery swap throws two Florida families into disarray [A. Twigg and K. Mays switched at birth in Hardee Memorial Hospital in Wauchula] M. Green. il pors *People Weekly* 32:77-8+ D 11 '89
Whose little girl is Kimberly? [A. Twigg and K. Mays switched at birth in Hardee Memorial Hospital, Wauchula, Fla.] M. Jacobbi. il pors *Good Housekeeping* 208:122-3+ Mr '89

CHILD TESTIMONY *See* Witnesses
CHILD WELFARE
See also
Adoption and adopted children
Child abuse
Child molesting
Children's Defense Fund (U.S.)
Custody of children
Day care
Foster home care
Homeless children
Indian Child Welfare Act of 1978
National Task Force on the Next Generation (U.S.)
Orphans and orphanages
Parent and child (Law)
Social work with youth
FYI. See issues of Children Today
How to raise money for the class of 2000 [proposal for government bonds to fund child welfare programs; cover story] F. A. Oski. *The Nation* 248:217+ F 20 '89
The least of these. A. McCarthy. *Commonweal* 116:663 D 1 '89
Politicians discover children. K. A. Lawton. il *Christianity Today* 33:34-6 Mr 17 '89
Programs that can make a difference. J. N. Baker. il *Newsweek* 114:28 S 11 '89
A promise at risk [cover story] S. C. Taylor. il *Modern Maturity* 32:32-6+ Ag/S '89

Solomon's choice [mishandling of child abuse cases by social workers] D. Zegart. il *Ms.* 17:78-83 Je '89
Whose responsibility is it, anyway? [child welfare worker liability] J. P. Shapiro. il *U.S. News & World Report* 106:29-30 Ja 9 '89
Whose rights are we protecting, anyway? [victims of child abuse; with discussion] K. Dorros and P. Dorsey. il *Children Today* 18:6-11+ My/Je '89

International aspects
See also
Convention on the Rights of the Child
Declaration of the Rights of the Child
UNICEF
The best mankind has to give [cover story; special section] il *UN Chronicle* 26:40-51 S '89

Public opinion
Dear President Bush . . . [results of survey] K. Greer. il *Better Homes and Gardens* 67:19-20 Ag '89

Alabama
See also
Mobile (Ala.)—Child welfare

Brazil
Death without weeping [mother love in shantytowns of Brazil] N. Scheper-Hughes. *Natural History* p8+ O '89

Iraq
Iraq: an accusation of torture. *Newsweek* 113:39 Mr 13 '89
Suffer the littlest children [atrocities] *U.S. News & World Report* 106:13+ Mr 13 '89

Maryland
See also
Charles County (Md.)—Child welfare
Prince Georges County (Md.)—Child welfare

Michigan
See also
LIFE Program

New York (State)
See also
New York (N.Y.)—Child welfare

Ohio
See also
Portsmouth (Ohio)—Child welfare

Southern States
Southern success stories. il *Children Today* 18:4-5 Mr/Ap '89

United States
See Child welfare

Washington (State)
Court backs two-mom family [lesbians recognized as legal parents] K. Monagle. il *Ms.* 18:69 O '89

Western Europe
History
Before birth control [child abandonment in ancient and medieval Europe; views of John Boswell] L. George. *American Health* 8:114-15 Jl/Ag '89
The unwanted children of times past [child abandonment in ancient and medieval Europe; interview with J. Boswell] A. P. Sanoff. il por *U.S. News & World Report* 106:62 My 1 '89

Wisconsin
The battered child [Supreme Court rules social worker not liable in case of J. DeShaney] *The New Republic* 200:7-8 Mr 20 '89
"Poor Joshua!" [Supreme Court absolves Wisconsin child welfare agency in case of J. DeShaney] il por *Time* 133:56 Mr 6 '89
Poor Joshua [Supreme Court rules Wisconsin child welfare agency not liable for injuries caused by father of J. DeShaney] P. A. Zirkel. bibl f il *Phi Delta Kappan* 70:828-9 Je '89

CHILD WELFARE WORKERS *See* Social workers
CHILDBIRTH
See also
Cesarean section
Hospitals—Maternity care
Midwives
Obstetrics
Postpartum depression
Pregnancy
All-in-the-family birth [sibling-attended birth] L. Mosedale. il *Health (New York, N.Y.)* 21:85-6+ S '89
As they grow/pregnancy and birth. P. A. Hillard. See issues of Parents
Bethlehem today [delivering a baby in apartment of impoverished immigrant family in Chicago on Christmas] K. P. Glynn. il *America* 161:441-2 D 16 '89
Giving birth—together. A. P. Murphy. il *Parents* 64:8 Ja '89
Not tonight, honey . . . [lovelife after childbirth] S. F. Enos. il *Ladies' Home Journal* 106:42 Ja '89
Present at birth. R. B. McCall. il *Parents* 64:136 Ja '89
The whys of hard labor [ability to cope with pain; research by Nancy K. Lowe] V. Brower. il *American Health* 8:120 Je '89
Womb with a view [techniques for remembering your own birth] K. Harary. il *Omni (New York, N.Y.)* 11:39-40+ Ag '89

CHILDBIRTH—*cont.*

Complications

A happy ending [assisting at difficult birth leads to training of birth attendants in the Middle East] G. Hafez. il *World Health* p13-15 Jl '89

Maternal death: a preventable tragedy. il *UN Chronicle* 26:46-7 S '89

Preterm labor. P. A. Hillard. il *Parents* 64:190+ S '89

CHILDBIRTH IN LITERATURE

Pioneer work [Fran Hosken's Universal childbirth picture book] M. Morain. *The Humanist* 49:33 N/D '89

CHILDBIRTH IN TELEVISION

Baby boom! [cover story] A. Meisler. il pors *TV Guide* 37:4-7+ D 30 '89-Ja 5 '90

CHILDHOOD *See* Children

CHILDHOOD AUTISM *See* Autism

CHILDHOOD OBESITY *See* Obesity

CHILDHOOD POISONING *See* Poisons and poisoning

CHILDREN

See also
Advertising and children
Aggressiveness in children
Anger in children
Anxiety in children
Art and children
Beauty, Personal—Children
Birth order
Birth rate
Black children
Boys
Bullying
Cable television advertising and children
Cable television and children
Christmas gifts for children
City children
Cooking by children
Cosmetics for children
Cycling with children
Dance and children
Eskimos—Children
Family
Family size
Farm children
Fathers
Fear in children
Gifts for children
Homeless children
Imagination in children
Infants
Lying in children
Missing children
Mothers
Motion pictures—Children's films
Music and children
Only child
Orphans and orphanages
Parents
Problem children
Refugee children
School children
Siblings
Single parent families
Socially handicapped children
Stepparents and stepchildren
Telephone and children
Television advertising and children
Television and children
Triplets
Twins
Vitality in children
Youth

Career first, children later [survey of college women by Kristine Baber] il *USA Today (Periodical)* 117:8-9 Mr '89

Kids did it! See issues of National Geographic World

Mother & child. M. A. Littell. See issues of Good Housekeeping beginning March 1987

What I miss about being a kid. E. Berg. il *Parents* 64:116-18 My '89

Accidents

See Accidents; Poisons and poisoning

Adoption

See Adoption and adopted children

Attitudes

Ask the kids [advice to working mothers] *Ladies' Home Journal* 106:76 Ag '89

How to have a happy marriage [advice from fourth graders] il *Good Housekeeping* 208:64 Je '89

Bedtime

See Bedtime

Bibliography

Book reviews. See issues of Children Today

Care and hygiene

See also
Baby sitters
Child psychology
Child welfare
Children—Medical care

Children—Preparation for hospital and medical care
Dependent care (Employee benefits)
Parent education
Physical education and training
Sick children

Ask Dr. Mom. M. R. Neifert. See issues of McCall's beginning May 1986

Child care news. See issues of Parents beginning February 1989

Child's play [excerpt from The family fitness handbook] B. Glover. il *Runner's World* 24:60-6 Je '89

Choking prevention. K. K. Gracey. *Consumers' Research Magazine* 72:2 Ap '89

Falling investments in children's health [developing nations] il *The Futurist* 23:51 My/Je '89

First word [child health crisis in developing countries] L. E. Bruce. por *Omni (New York, N.Y.)* 11:4 Ag '89

Good housekeeping child care '89 [special section] il *Good Housekeeping* 209:79+ S '89

Have fun with fitness. C. Straley. il *Parents* 64:32 Ap '89

A parent's guide to children's health [special section] il *McCall's* 117:59+ N '89

Physically fit families. D. F. Bjorklund and B. Bjorklund. il *Parents* 64:215 Je '89

Q&A. See issues of Parents

Serious fun [fitness programs and equipment for children] il *American Health* 8:30 N '89

U.S. youth gaining weight, losing stamina [study by Wynn F. Updyke] D. E. Loupe. *Science News* 136:199 S 23 '89

Civil rights

See also
Children's Defense Fund (U.S.)
Convention on the Rights of the Child
Declaration of the Rights of the Child
Parent and child (Law)

Clothing and dress

See Clothing and dress—Children

Cost of raising

The high cost of child care [Canada] A. Walmsley. *Maclean's* 102:60 N 6 '89

Keeping ahead of baby costs. *Glamour* 87:154 Ap '89

Creativity

See Creativity

Crime

See Juvenile delinquents and delinquency

Crimes against

See also
Child abuse
Child molesting
Parents of murdered children
Safety education

The day death came into Carrie Edmondson's yard [caught in Miami shootout] S. J. Hedges. il *U.S. News & World Report* 106:22-3 Ap 10 '89

Death goes to school [P. Purdy's shooting rampage in Stockton, Calif. in January 1989] P. Caputo. il *Esquire* 112:136-8+ D '89

Death on the playground [P. Purdy kills children in school yard in Stockton, Calif.] J. N. Baker. il por *Newsweek* 113:35 Ja 30 '89

The impact of Stockton [schoolyard murders gives momentum to gun control] J. Hammer. il *Newsweek* 113:8 F 20 '89

The littlest victim [interview with five year old murder witness J. Royal] V. Gladstone. il pors *Life* 12:16+ O '89

The littlest witness may testify about her friend's killing [four year old J. Royal to testify against M. Ward in Miami murder trial] M. Brower. il pors *People Weekly* 31:108-10 Ap 24 '89

A nation of certified killers [murderer P. Purdy's firearms transaction record] J. D. McNamara. il *Harper's* 278:58-9 My '89

Slaughter in a school yard [P. Purdy shoots children in Stockton, Calif.] il *Time* 133:29 Ja 30 '89

Day care

See Day care

Development

See Children—Growth and development

Diseases

See also
AIDS (Disease) and children
Allergy
Asthma
Cancer in children
Cystic fibrosis
Diarrhea
Epilepsy
Hypertension
Infants, Newborn—Diseases
Lead poisoning
Lungs—Diseases
Meningitis
Pneumonia
Tay-Sachs disease
Whooping cough

Care for winter illnesses [views of Martha Lepow] C. Slom. il *McCall's* 117:59 N '89

CHILDREN—Diseases—*cont.*

CMV a risk in child care [research by Stuart Adler] J. Raloff. *Science News* 136:327 N 18 '89

Disease of the month [seasonality of childhood illnesses] P. Klass. il *Discover* 10:32+ My '89

Kids' diseases doctors miss. P. Skalka. il *Ladies' Home Journal* 106:80+ F '89

"Mommy, I don't feel good" [day care diseases; views of Selma Deitch] D. Sobel. il *Ladies' Home Journal* 106:68 Ag '89

Smallest aerosol pollutants linked to disease [research by C. A. Pope] J. Raloff. *Science News* 135:277 My 6 '89

When to call the doctor; ed. by Marilyn Mercer. H. Harris. il *Good Housekeeping* 209:110+ S '89

Vaccines and vaccination

Childhood diseases aren't just kids' stuff. P. Paul. il *Current Health 2* 15:26-7 My '89

EPI: a dream come true [Western Pacific region] H. Mehta. il *World Health* p12-13 N '89

Health watch: the return of childhood diseases. il *Ladies' Home Journal* 106:80+ S '89

Old diseases still a threat [views of Philip Rettig] il *USA Today (Periodical)* 118:5 O '89

Economic conditions

See also
Children's allowances
First Children's Bank

Curing kids who want it all [teaching money management] M. Silver. il *U.S. News & World Report* 106:83-5 Mr 20 '89

Kids & money. D. Sobel. il *Ladies' Home Journal* 106:94 Ap '89

Kids and cash. P. Theroux. il *Parents* 64:62+ Ap '89

Teach your kids about money. M. Hodge. il *Reader's Digest* 134:54-8 Ja '89

Economic value

Kids as capital. J. Rauch. il *The Atlantic* 264:56-61 Ag '89

Education

See also
Elementary education
Experimental education
Moral education
Play
Preschool education
Readiness for school
Safety education
School age
Sex education
Social education
Teaching

Dr. Salk talks to parents about kids and school. L. Salk. il *McCall's* 116:53-6 S '89

How 3-year-olds learn best. J. Marzollo. il *Parents* 64:124-6+ Mr '89

Preparing your child for the 21st century [special section] S. Schoumacher and V. Cadden. il *McCall's* 116:41+ S '89

School days. F. Roberts. See issues of Parents beginning January 1983

Employment

The family that works together . . . P. N. Strassels. il *Nation's Business* 77:80 Je '89

A future denied: children who work. il *UN Chronicle* 26:44-5 S '89

Photographs and photography

Time exposures [work of L. W. Hine] E. F. Provenzo. il *Society* 26:87-9 S/O '89

Philippines

An Asian tale: young girls, red roses. S. Mydans. il *The New York Times Magazine* p44-7+ Ap 2 '89

Food

See Children—Nutrition

Growth and development

See also
Child psychology
Infants—Growth and development
Moral development

10 myths about child development. J. Segal. il *Parents* 64:81-4+ Jl '89

As they grow. See issues of Parents

As your child grows. A. R. New. il *Better Homes and Gardens* 67:46+ Je '89

Delay of gratification in children. W. Mischel and others. bibl f il *Science* 244:933-8 My 26 '89

It's never too early to make a friend. B. Brenner. il *Good Housekeeping* 209:81+ S '89

Pediatric peptide spurs growth hormone [research by Arthur Felix] I. Amato and J. Raloff. *Science News* 135:252 Ap 22 '89

Preschool self-control and pretzel logic [research by Walter Mischel] B. Bower. *Science News* 135:325 My 27 '89

Reading, thinking, and testing. G. W. Bracey. *Phi Delta Kappan* 71:248-9 N '89

Social butterflies. P. Theroux. il *Parents* 64:47-9 Jl '89

Social graces [two-year-olds] B. Weissbourd. il *Parents* 64:198 S '89

That magic touch. N. S. Schwartzberg. il *Parents* 64:87-90+ F '89

"We have a problem" [developing child's social skills] J. Marks. il *Parents* 64:63-6 D '89

Where does the time go? [passage from baby to child] E. Berg. il *Parents* 64:58+ D '89

Hairstyling

See Hairstyling

Health

See Children—Care and hygiene

Hospital care

See also
Children—Hospitals
Children—Preparation for hospital and medical care
Infants, Newborn—Hospital care

Children, families and hospitals [survey by the Association for the Care of Children's Health] il *Children Today* 18:4-5 Jl/Ag '89

Disease of the month [seasonality of childhood illnesses] P. Klass. il *Discover* 10:32+ My '89

When your toddler is hospitalized. J. T. Gibson. il *Parents* 64:187 Ap '89

Hospitals

See also
Children's Hospital National Medical Center
Hospital for Sick Children (Toronto, Ont.)

Clifton Davis, 'Amen' TV star visits children at La Rabida Hospital. il pors *Jet* 76:24-5 My 15 '89

Housing

Adults-only housing hears the pitter-patter of little feet. R. Stodghill, II and G. DeGeorge. il *Business Week* p39-40 Mr 13 '89

Home rule [condominium refuses to permit daughter J. Swartz to live with father in Margate, Fla.] I. Nelson. il por *New Choices for the Best Years* 29:12-13 Ap '89

Opening the door to kids [amendment to the Fair Housing Act] A. L. Sanders. il *Time* 134:75 S 18 '89

A welcome mat for kids [Fair Housing Act of 1988] W. Giese. il *Changing Times* 43:22 F '89

Imprisonment

See Juvenile delinquents and delinquency—Imprisonment; Refugee children—Imprisonment

Institutional care

See also
Orphans and orphanages

Intelligence

See Intelligence

Kidnapping

See Kidnapping

Language

How adults could learn languages as well as children [study by Elissa L. Newport and Ted Supalla] J. Rubin. il *Psychology Today* 23:21 Ap '89

"I love the way you talk". A. P. Murphy. il *Parents* 64:7 N '89

Language development. B. Weissbourd. il *Parents* 64:213 N '89

Let's talk. J. Segal and Z. Segal. il *Parents* 64:148 Ag '89

Listening and learning [effect of reading stories aloud on children's vocabulary; research by Warwick Elley] G. W. Bracey. il *Phi Delta Kappan* 71:77 S '89

Toward a unified theory of literacy learning and instructional practices [cover story] D. Taylor. bibl f il *Phi Delta Kappan* 71:184-93 N '89

Law

See also
Children—Employment
Children's Defense Fund (U.S.)
Guardian and ward
Juvenile delinquents and delinquency
Parent and child (Law)

Management and training

See also
Child abuse
Child psychology
Children's allowances
Children's chores
Corporal punishment
Moral education
Overprotective parents
Parent-child relationship
Parent education
Problem children
Toilet training

10 strategies for getting kids to mind [views of Willard L. Johnson and Russell E. Hedge] il *Ladies' Home Journal* 106:126-7 My '89

The 10 worst things you can say to your kids (and how to stop saying them). A. Van der Meer. il *Redbook* 174:32+ N '89

The 12 building blocks of discipline. T. Harms. il *Parents* 64:76-8+ Ag '89

The age of independence [with editorial comment by Ann Pleshette Murphy] F. B. Maynard. il *Parents* 64:6, 122-5+ Ap '89

Bringing up baby [books on child care and parenting] R. M. Gilinsky. il *Publishers Weekly* 235:20+ Je 9 '89

CHILDREN—Management and training—*cont.*

Bringing up daddy [cover story; with editorial comment by Lisa Grunwald] bibl il *Esquire* 112:35, 116-20+ N '89

Can you praise a child too much? F. B. Maynard. il *Parents* 64:93-6 S '89

Children without limits. P. Theroux. il *Parents* 64:62+ Je '89

Domesticating your 'wild' one [toddlers] J. K. Rosemond. il *Better Homes and Gardens* 67:25 N '89

Dr. Spock had it right: studies suggest that kids thrive when parents set firm limits. B. Brophy. il *U.S. News & World Report* 107:49-51 Ag 7 '89

How kids raise their parents. J. Segal and Z. Segal. il *Parents* 64:192 Ap '89

How not to turn into your mother: for your child to grow up free, you have to remember all the ways in which you didn't. N. Eberle. il *Glamour* 87:160+ My '89

How to handle family fights [excerpt from When families fight] J. Rubin and C. Rubin. il *Ladies' Home Journal* 106:70+ Ja '89

How to outwit your two-year-old. D. K. Salmon. il *Parents* 64:135-6+ D '89

Indulged? Or just plain spoiled? [views of Bruce J. McIntosh] K. Henderson. il *Psychology Today* 23:28 Je '89

Is married better? [sisters exchange places] S. Nelson and L. Nelson. il pors *Glamour* 87:274-5+ O '89

'It's all up to us'. B. Spock. il por *Newsweek* 114 Special Issue:106-7 Wint '89/Spr '90

Morning walks with Alex [mother and son] P. A. Hall. il *Parents* 64:90+ O '89

Mother knows best. J. Gaylin. il *Parents* 64:57-60+ Ja '89

The new discipline. A. Kohn. il *Ladies' Home Journal* 106:190 N '89

The "no fair" solution. C. Hyde. il *Parents* 64:78+ D '89

Parenting. J. K. Rosemond. See issues of Better Homes and Gardens beginning June 1985

Parents' journal. M. Mohler and M. D. Rosen. See issues of Ladies' Home Journal beginning September 1987

Preparing your child to enjoy work [excerpt from Kids who succeed] B. N. Feldman. il *Working Woman* 14:155-6 My '89

Pride and prejudice. D. F. Bjorklund and B. Bjorklund. il *Parents* 64:180 F '89

Q&A. See issues of Parents

Respecting house rules [children] L. G. Katz. il *Parents* 64:200 S '89

Say it with silence. S. Isaacs. il *Parents* 64:134-7 Mr '89

Setting limits. L. G. Katz. il *Parents* 64:215 N '89

Spare the rod, spare the child [adult emotional problems can result from harsh discipline as a child; research by Sandra Holmes and Lee Robins] N. Jordan. il *Psychology Today* 23:16 Je '89

Stress-busting strategies for fast-track families. il *American Health* 8:60-1 O '89

Success, family-style. S. Berglas. *American Health* 8:107 Ap '89

Take the bite out of discipline. B. Weissbourd. il *Parents* 64:209 Je '89

Taming toddlers' tantrums [study by Lisa A. Adams and Vaughn I. Rickert] *Science News* 136:332 N 18 '89

Teaching children responsibility. L. Salk. il *McCall's* 117:29 O '89

Understanding kids [disciplining a fresh child] L. Balter. il *Ladies' Home Journal* 106:110 D '89

War babies: a mother refuses her son toy guns. J. Zandy. il *Utne Reader* p120-1 N/D '89

Whining, dawdling, tantrums, and other toddler problems—solved! P. Schneider. il *Parents* 64:81-4+ N '89

Wouldn't you like your kids to be closer? A. Faber and E. Mazlish. il *Redbook* 172:98-9+ F '89

"You can do it!". S. Isaacs. il *Parents* 64:114-18 F '89

Anecdotes, facetiae, satire, etc.

Our son the cat. K. Fury. il *New Choices for the Best Years* 29:92 Ja '89

Bibliography

Books for grown-ups [Christmas gifts] L. Rosenberg. il *Parents* 64:235-6+ N '89

Books on child care and parenting. B. Stander and B. Levine. il *Publishers Weekly* 235:28+ Je 9 '89

In short/parents and children. il *The New York Times Book Review* 94:26-7 N 26 '89

Medical care

See also

Pediatricians

Crimes of faith? [denial of medical care to children] D. Neff. *Christianity Today* 33:17 Je 16 '89

Doctor visits made easy. D. B. King. il *Parents* 64:237-8 D '89

Getting kids to take their medicine [views of Barton D. Schmitt] S. Mahler. il *McCall's* 117:62 N '89

God's will vs. doctor's orders. C. Levine. il *Parents* 64:220+ Mr '89

Help for kids who get sick at night [after-hours pediatric clinics] L. J. Moore. il *U.S. News & World Report* 107:86 N 13 '89

"My right to be there" [mother's role in child's medical care] J. Gaylin. il *Parents* 64:74-6 N '89

Pediatricians answer 20 nagging questions. L. Yarrow. il *Parents* 64:82-4+ Ja '89

Rx for a healthy summer [views of Mark D. Windome] E. Grossman. il *Good Housekeeping* 208:71-2 Je '89

Small patient, big emergency [Pediatric Emergency Medical Services Training Program; work of Jane Ball] B. Portnow. *American Health* 8:120+ Je '89

Nutrition

See also

Baby bars

Obesity

School breakfasts

School lunches

The 6 nutrition mistakes moms make. R. Charney. il *Redbook* 173:168+ O '89

The 29 foods kids love best. il *Good Housekeeping* 209:84+ S '89

Are our children well-nourished? K. S. Feld. il *American Health* 8:108+ My '89

The battle against heart disease begins with children. il *The Saturday Evening Post* 261:12-13+ S '89

Building a low-fat kid. J. Poppy. il *Esquire* 112:93-5 N '89

Cholesterol checks for children? J. Carey. il *U.S. News & World Report* 106:74 Ap 24 '89

Cholesterol's littlest (known) risk group. E. Stark. il *Psychology Today* 23:28+ S '89

Dangers in the vegetable patch [pesticides] S. Begley. il *Newsweek* 113:74-5 Ja 30 '89

Eating right from the start. J. T. Gibson. il *Parents* 64:122 Ja '89

Facts about kids and cholesterol; ed. by Florence Isaacs. J. H. Moller. il *Good Housekeeping* 209:101+ S '89

Food: the family dinner. E. Satter. il *American Health* 8:58-9 O '89

The foods that are poisoning your child [pesticide residues] A. Fischer. il *Redbook* 173:116+ My '89

Heart-healthy children. R. E. Kowalski. il *Parents* 64:177+ O '89

Helping kids with high cholesterol [excerpt from Cholesterol and children] R. E. Kowalski. il *Psychology Today* 23:30 S '89

Helping your kids to eat right and have good body images. R. Israeloff. il *Working Woman* 14:219-22 S '89

High cholesterol in children. il *The Saturday Evening Post* 261:42-3 Ap '89

A mother's crusade [M. Streep's campaign against pesticide residues; cover story] J. C. McCullagh. il pors *Organic Gardening* 36:32-7 Ap '89

Ms. Streep goes to Washington to stop a bitter harvest [pesticide residues in children's food; interview] B. Johnson. il pors *People Weekly* 31:50-1 Mr 20 '89

New foods confuse parents [views of Donald McCormick] *USA Today (Periodical)* 117:10 F '89

NRDC on Alar. R. M. Whyatt. bibl f *Science* 245:910-11 S 1 '89

Palate training. B. L. Benderly. il *Health (New York, N.Y.)* 21:56-7+ Jl '89

Pesticide/food risk greatest under age 6. J. Raloff. *Science News* 135:133 Mr 4 '89

Pesticide residues safe for children, too. *FDA Consumer* 23:2 My '89

Pesticides and kids. L. Roberts. il *Science* 243:1280-1 Mr 10 '89

Pesticides, risk, and applesauce [discussion of March 10, 1989 article, Pesticides and kids, and March 24, 1989 article, Is risk assessment conservative?] L. Roberts. il *Science* 244:755-7 My 19 '89

Raising vegetarian kids. L. J. Davis. il *Parents* 64:190 Jl '89

Reducing risk of colon cancer [study by Theresa B. Young] il *USA Today (Periodical)* 117:6 F '89

Rescuing the family meal. E. Satter. il *American Health* 8:93-8 My '89

Sour logic [high intake of aspartame] R. Gautier. *American Health* 8:153+ Mr '89

Sugar and the boob tube [influence of television commercials upon eating habits; research by Nancy Cotugna] P. McCarthy. *American Health* 8:146-7 Ap '89

Test cases [getting a family to eat what you cook] A. Ward. il *The New York Times Magazine* p49-50 Ag 13 '89

Wake up kids to the benefits of breakfast. M. S. Williams. il *McCall's* 117:91 N '89

Watch those vegetables, Ma [pesticide danger] A. Toufexis. il *Time* 133:57 Mr 6 '89

"We have a problem". J. Marks. il *Parents* 64:67+ Ap '89

Anecdotes, facetiae, satire, etc.

Remembrance of Cheerios past [father and daughter] E. Larson. il *Parents* 64:268+ N '89

Obesity

See Obesity

Only child

See Only child

Perception

See Perception

Photographs and photography

Angels! [work of I. Penn] H. Muschamp. il *Vogue* 179:278-87 D '89

CHILDREN—Photographs and photography—*cont.*
Shoot! Here are some of the biggest mistakes that parent photographers make. il *Ladies' Home Journal* 106:110 D '89

Political activities
See also
Children as public officers

Preparation for hospital and medical care
Lollipop draws consumer group's ire [presurgical sedative laced with fentanyl] *Science News* 135:156 Mr 11 '89
A no-tears trip to the hospital [six-year-old prepares for a myringotomy] L. Kotrosits. il *Parents* 64:85-6+ Je '89
When your child goes to the hospital. S. Richmond. il *Changing Times* 43:116 O '89

Psychology
See Child psychology

Recreation
See also
Arts and crafts and children
Christmas projects
Games
Play
Play groups
Playgrounds
Toys
The art of taking lessons. D. F. Bjorklund and B. Bjorklund. il *Parents* 64:213 My '89
Here's how to beat back the midsummer doldrums with some style. D. Stanton. il *Compute!* 11:12 Jl '89
Kids: hot or not, keep them busy [New York City] L. Schnurnberger. il *New York* 22:120+ Jl 3-10 '89
Kids of summer 1989 [special section] il *Good Housekeeping* 208:69+ Je '89
The lazy days of summer. J. Segal and Z. Segal. il *Parents* 64:162 Jl '89
Mother's children. See issues of The Mother Earth News
Superfun special [special section] il *National Geographic World* 165:17-20 My '89
Superfun special [special section] il *National Geographic World* 169:17-20 S '89
Superfun special [special section] il *National Geographic World* 161:17-20 Ja '89
Time out of school [correlation between out-of-school activities and reading proficiency; research by Richard Anderson and others] G. W. Bracey. il *Phi Delta Kappan* 70:408-9 Ja '89

Religious life
See also
Church work with children
Religious education
Sunday schools

Self reliance
See Self reliance

Self respect
See Self respect

Sexual behavior
See also
Sex education
Sex role

Anecdotes, facetiae, satire, etc.
A pretty girl is like a malady [boy attributes myopia to hours spent reading about sex] P. Freundlich. il *Esquire* 111:122-6 F '89

Social development
See Children—Growth and development

Speech
See Children—Language

Sports
See also
Bicycle racing
Bowling
Cycling
School athletics
Skiing, Children's
Tennis
Choosing a sports program for your child. C. E. Trunzo. il *Working Woman* 14:226+ S '89
How you play the game. P. Jones. il *Good Housekeeping* 208:74+ Je '89
Not fan-made [importance of participation] G. Sheehan. il *Runner's World* 24:18 Je '89
The sporting life. D. Elkind. il *Parents* 64:207 S '89
Sports, kids, fun, and safety; ed. by Barbara Raymond. M. A. Nelson. il *Good Housekeeping* 209:82+ S '89

Surgery
See also
Children—Preparation for hospital and medical care
Less pain for the littlest patients [use of painkillers during and after surgery] J. Carey. il *U.S. News & World Report* 106:62-3 F 27 '89

Taxation
See also
Gifts to minors
The family that works together . . . P. N. Strassels. il *Nation's Business* 77:80 Je '89
A gift to savings-bond owners from the IRS [delayed reporting of interest] L. Wiener. il *U.S. News & World Report* 107:72 S 18 '89

Hooray for child labor! H. Wheelwright. il *Money* 18:198 Je '89
The kiddie-tax form. il *Money* 18:93 Ja '89
Passing the bucks to your kids. R. R. Roha. il *Changing Times* 43:65-6+ Mr '89
The squeeze on the littlest taxpayers. *U.S. News & World Report* 106:82 Mr 27 '89

Training
See Children—Management and training

Travel
See also
Travel with children

Writing
See also
Humanism for Kids (Program)

California
See also
Beverly Hills (Calif.)—Children

Developing countries
See also
UNICEF
Children are paying the third world debt with their lives. *Utne Reader* p62 S/O '89
Debt: killer of third world children. il *UN Chronicle* 26:48 S '89
Falling investments in children's health. il *The Futurist* 23:51 My/Je '89
First word [child health crisis] L. E. Bruce. por *Omni (New York, N.Y.)* 11:4 Ag '89

Indiana
Profiling Indiana's children. *Children Today* 18:3-4 Jl/Ag '89

Kauai (Hawaii)
Children of the Garden Island [30-year resilience study] E. E. Werner. bibl il map *Scientific American* 260:106-8+ Ap '89

Mozambique
An American doctor in the schools of hell [child psychologist N. Boothby treats Mozambicans] B. Duffy. il pors map *U.S. News & World Report* 106:32-5 Ja 16 '89

United States
See Children

Vietnam
See also
Vietnamese War, 1957-1975—Children

CHILDREN, ABANDONED *See* Homeless children
CHILDREN, EXCEPTIONAL
See also
Children, Gifted
Children, Handicapped
Learning disabilities
Problem children

Education
See Special education

CHILDREN, GIFTED
See also
Children as musicians
Confessions of a whiz kid. S. R. Arbetter. il *Current Health 2* 15:25-7 F '89

Anecdotes, facetiae, satire, etc.
Young Einsteins. G. Schwartz. il *New York* 22:43 S 25 '89

Education
Ethics education for the gifted. A. Roeper. *The Education Digest* 54:37-9 F '89
The families of gifted underachievers [research by Sylvia Rimm and Barbara Lowe] G. W. Bracey. il *Phi Delta Kappan* 70:563 Mr '89
"Is my daughter learning too fast?". F. Roberts. il *Parents* 64:52 O '89

CHILDREN, HANDICAPPED
See also
Cerebral palsy
Deaf children
Mentally handicapped children
Parents of the handicapped
Socially handicapped children
When the spirit takes wing [Provera victim D. Able born without arms or legs] M. Grant. il pors *People Weekly* 31:50-5 My 15 '89

Education
See also
Gateway Education Center (Greensboro, N.C.)
Easing the adjustment to mainstreaming programs. H. Margolis and P. P. McCabe. *The Education Digest* 55:58-61 S '89
The latest Supreme Court special education case: not moot but Muth. P. A. Zirkel. bibl f *Phi Delta Kappan* 71:250-1 N '89
"Report card" on children with handicaps [Collaborative study of children with special needs] il *Children Today* 18:3-4 Mr/Ap '89
Robotic arms aid handicapped kids [increases learning ability; work of Richard Howell] il *USA Today (Periodical)* 117:6-7 F '89
Sink or swim in the mainstream [placement of hearing-impaired students R. and J. Visco in Pittsburgh] P. A. Zirkel. bibl f il *Phi Delta Kappan* 70:411-13 Ja '89

CHILDREN, HANDICAPPED—cont.
Recreation
See Handicapped—Recreation
CHILDREN, HANDICAPPED, AND ANIMALS See Handicapped and animals
CHILDREN, HYPERACTIVE See Hyperactivity
CHILDREN, ILLEGITIMATE See Illegitimacy
CHILDREN, MENTALLY SUPERIOR See Children, Gifted
CHILDREN AND ADULTS See Child-adult relationship
CHILDREN AND ALCOHOL See Alcohol and youth
CHILDREN AND ANIMALS
Choosing the right puppy. S. L. Gerstenfeld. il *Parents* 64:244 Je '89
Costumed cows and other critters [4-H Club of Maryland sponsors costume parade at State Fair] il *National Geographic World* 167:26-9 Jl '89
Home is where the cat is. P. La Farge. il *Parents* 64:120-2 O '89
Pet-associated injuries: the trouble with children's best friends. P. M. Wishon and A. Huang. bibl il *Children Today* 18:24-7 My/Je '89
Pet peeves and praises. D. F. Bjorklund and B. Bjorklund. il *Parents* 64:151 Ag '89
Pets teach kids to care: studies confirm the facts. A. Atkins. il *Better Homes and Gardens* 67:182 S '89
Summer care for pets [views of Michael Garvey] S. Berkman. il *Good Housekeeping* 208:80 Je '89
What kids learn from pets. S. L. Gerstenfeld. il *Parents* 64:234 Mr '89
CHILDREN AND AVIATION
Growing pains [trip to airshow revives daughter's interest in airplanes] G. Baxter. il *Flying* 116:122+ S '89
The little yellow airplane [boy's first flight in Piper Cub] J. Doub. il *Reader's Digest* 135:197-8+ O '89
CHILDREN AND BOATING
Family cruising. P. A. Janssen. il *Motor Boating & Sailing* 163:15 Je '89
Paddle tales [whitewater rafting trip for Pittsburgh, Pa. physical education students] il *National Geographic World* 164:23-7 Ap '89
CHILDREN AND BUSINESS See Youth and business
CHILDREN AND CHRISTMAS
See also
Rudolph the Red-Nosed Reindeer (Fictional character)
Santa Claus
Easing holiday woes. L. Salk. il *McCall's* 117:61 D '89
Mixed blessings [Christian-Jewish household] J. Hope. il *Parents* 64:252 D '89
CHILDREN AND COMPUTERS See Computers and youth
CHILDREN AND DEATH
"Good-bye, daddy" [reflections on father's death] M. Mayo. il *Parents* 64:114-15 Je '89
How do you talk to a child about death? J. Viorst. *Redbook* 173:32+ My '89
In praise of Mister Rogers [response to child grieving over grandmother's death] B. H. Edgington. il *Parents* 64:120 Mr '89
Teaching kids how to grieve [program in Watts for children whose lives have been touched by murder] S. Doherty. il *Newsweek* 114:73 N 13 '89
"We have a problem" [child fears getting AIDS after uncle dies] J. Marks. il *Parents* 64:50+ Jl '89
When a parent dies. J. Segal. il *Parents* 64:112-13+ Je '89
Bibliography
Helping children cope with death. M. Mayo. il *Parents* 64:228+ Je '89
CHILDREN AND DRUGS See Drugs and youth
CHILDREN AND FIREARMS
A message from Brian [ten year old son accidentally killed by handgun] D. D. Darling. il *por Ladies' Home Journal* 106:22+ My '89
Tiny fingers on the trigger [Florida proposal authorizing prison terms for parents whose children misuse guns] il *U.S. News & World Report* 107:11-12 Jl 3 '89
With a new law, Florida heeds a child's plaintive cry to 911: 'I shot her—I didn't mean to'. M. Green. il *People Weekly* 32:56-8+ Jl 10 '89
CHILDREN AND GRANDPARENTS See Grandparents
CHILDREN AND MASS MEDIA See Mass media and youth
CHILDREN AND PARENTS See Parent-child relationship
CHILDREN AND PEACE
See also
Children as the Peacemakers Foundation
CHILDREN AND PETS See Children and animals
CHILDREN AND SCIENCE
Splash! Science can be fun [water experiments for children] B. W. Carter. il *Parents* 64:136-40 Je '89
CHILDREN AND SICKNESS
See also
Sick children
CHILDREN AND THE ENVIRONMENT
See also
Young Naturalist Foundation
The case for natural schools. M. Wells. il *Country Journal* 16:34-9 Mr/Ap '89

The children's cleanup crusade [students from Jackson Elementary School in Salt Lake City, Utah lobby to establish state Superfund] B. A. Lewis. il *Sierra* 74:62-6 Mr/Ap '89
Kids crusade to save our streams. P. Michelmore. il *Reader's Digest* 134:98-102 Je '89
CHILDREN AND WAR
See also
Children as soldiers
Children of War (Organization)
United States—History—Civil War, 1861-1865—Children
Vietnamese War, 1957-1975—Children
An American doctor in the schools of hell [child psychologist N. Boothby treats Mozambicans] B. Duffy. il *pors* map *U.S. News & World Report* 106:32-5 Ja 16 '89
CHILDREN AS ACTORS AND ACTRESSES
"All I ever wanted was my mother's love": the sad life of a child star [television performer on Father knows best]; ed. by Ace Collins. L. Chapin. il *pors Redbook* 173:28+ Ag '89
Annie [11-year-old D. Findley gets the part in Annie 2 after nationwide auditions] C. Dowling. il *pors Life* 12:42-9 N '89
Attention, kids: Sesame Street wants you . . . if you've got the right stuff. A. D. Plate. il *TV Guide* 37:16-18 Jl 15-21 '89
Education
Welcome back to school—we'd like to beat you up [TV actors] R. Waldron. il *TV Guide* 37:14-16 My 20-26 '89
CHILDREN AS AIR PILOTS
Top-flight camp [summer camp at Center for Aerospace Sciences at Univ. of North Dakota] il *National Geographic World* 163:18-21 Mr '89
CHILDREN AS ASTRONOMERS
Mr. Killoran's fifth-grade cosmos. R. Dier. il *Astronomy* 17:98 S '89
The prize in the sky. M. Chibnik. *Astronomy* 17:98-9 S '89
CHILDREN AS AUTOMOBILE DRIVERS
A young driver humbles the car [seven-year-old J. Richer's drive tells us a lot about our relationship with the car] C. Gordon. il *Maclean's* 102:50 My 29 '89
CHILDREN AS CIRCUS PERFORMERS
See also
Circus Smirkus
Canadian stars [Le Cirque du Soleil; cover story] il *National Geographic World* 167:4-9 Jl '89
CHILDREN AS COLLECTORS
The collector. S. Katz. il *Ladies' Home Journal* 106:122+ My '89
Kids as collectors. J. Gaylin. il *Parents* 64:124-8 O '89
CHILDREN AS CONSUMERS See Youth market
CHILDREN AS DISC JOCKEYS
Little Ricky Rocko, the world's youngest deejay, proves you're never too small to rock and roll [9 year old S. Rogoway at KKRZ-FM in Portland, Or.] S. K. Reed. il *pors People Weekly* 31:91-2 Ja 16 '89
CHILDREN AS ENTERTAINERS
New child stars [black children] R. E. McKinney. il *Ebony* 44:88+ Je '89
Parents who manage money and fame of young stars. C. Waldron. il *Jet* 77:16-18 D 25 '89-Ja 1 '90
CHILDREN AS FARMERS See Farm children
CHILDREN AS GUESTS See Guests
CHILDREN AS HISTORIANS
Threads of Lancashire history [Young Historians Scheme's History Day in Britain] D. Gregory. il *History Today* 39:4-5 O '89
CHILDREN AS INVENTORS
See also
Invent America! (Program)
CHILDREN AS MUSICIANS
Prepubescent punk [Old Skull punk band] A. Block. il *Mother Jones* 14:13 O '89
Third-grader Jacob Armen drums a sense of wonder into the usually cool world of jazz. il *por People Weekly* 31:57 Ap 24 '89
Those precocious young bloods in Old Skull are the only punk rockers with a 9 o'clock bedtime. il *People Weekly* 32:113 S 18 '89
CHILDREN AS PHOTOGRAPHERS
Jana Taylor gives new focus to the lives of inner-city kids [teaching photography in Los Angeles] S. Schindehette. il *pors People Weekly* 31:126-7+ Ap 3 '89
World Photo Contest winners. il *National Geographic World* 162:12-16 F '89
CHILDREN AS PRISONERS See Juvenile delinquents and delinquency—Imprisonment; Refugee children—Imprisonment
CHILDREN AS PUBLIC OFFICERS
Holding office is kid's stuff for 8-year-old Teddy Andrews [Youth Commissioner of Berkeley, Calif.] il *pors People Weekly* 31:91-2 My 8 '89
CHILDREN AS SOLDIERS
Children in combat. E. Egan. il *Commonweal* 116:104-5 F 24 '89

CHILDREN AS THE PEACEMAKERS FOUNDATION
Organization urges kids to wage peace instead of war. *Jet*
77:14 O 23 '89
CHILDREN AS TRACTOR DRIVERS
About 65% of farm boys drive tractors before age 12. il
Successful Farming 87:18H-18I mid-F '89
CHILDREN AS WITNESSES *See* Witnesses
CHILDREN IN TAPE RECORDINGS
Record the sounds of childhood. K. Gunst and J. Rudolph.
il *Parents* 64:73-6 D '89
CHILDREN IN TELEVISION
See also
The Beaver (Fictional character)
Kim Fields: what happened to child stars after TV fame?
[cover story] il pors *Jet* 75:56-9 Ja 23 '89
CHILDREN IN THE RADIO INDUSTRY
See also
Children as disc jockeys
CHILDREN OF ALCOHOLICS
Images of a brief moment [memories of father] C. Flowers.
il *The New York Times Magazine* p20+ Jl 9 '89
My father was an alcoholic. D. Grady. il *Reader's Digest*
135:31-2 S '89
Not just my brother's problem. E. Harris. il *Glamour*
87:218-19+ F '89
Prisoners of childhood. C. Tavris. *Vogue* 179:380+ Mr '89
Under the influence. S. R. Sanders. il *Harper's* 279:68-75
N '89
When parents abuse alcohol. J. P. Comer. il *Parents* 64:198
Mr '89
Why a comedian? Louie Anderson recalls his tormented
life with father [excerpt from Dear dad] L. Anderson.
il pors *TV Guide* 37:24-7 O 14-20 '89
CHILDREN OF BABY BOOMERS
Is life too fast for baby boomers' kids? D. Harrington-Lueker.
The Education Digest 55:29-31 O '89
CHILDREN OF CELEBRITIES
5 beautiful moms say, "Go for it all!". K. C. Engles. il
por *Redbook* 173:123-7 My '89
The Bear trap [P. W. Bryant, son of late Alabama coach]
W. M. Adler. il por *Esquire* 112:204-6+ S '89
Carol Burnett: "Talk to your kids—I finally did". A. W.
Petrucelli. il *Redbook* 172:96-7+ F '89
Celebrity kids haul out their finest Halloween hijinks for
a charity fashion show [benefit for Los Angeles Children's
Museum] il *People Weekly* 32:38-9 O 30 '89
Growing up with a famous mother. il *Ebony* 44:122+ My
'89
"It's hard being the child of movie stars" [J. L. Curtis;
cover story] M. Morrison. il pors *Redbook* 173:98+ O
'89
Like mother . . . like daughter [cover story] J. Ardmore.
il *Good Housekeeping* 209:110-11+ Jl '89
Second generation: children tell why they follow in their
parents' footsteps. il *Jet* 76:58-60 Je 19 '89
Photographs and photography
Capturing a love he missed out on, a photographer pays
homage to dads and sons [work of S. Begleiter] il por
People Weekly 31:123-6 Je 19 '89
Fathers & sons [excerpt] S. Begleiter. il *Parents* 64:143-5
Je '89
CHILDREN OF CLERGYMEN
Reverend father [daughter of abusive minister] D. Loring.
The Humanist 49:21-3+ Jl/Ag '89
CHILDREN OF COOKS
All in the family. J. Nathan. il *The New York Times Magazine*
p71-2 Ap 30 '89
CHILDREN OF DIVORCED PARENTS
Children after divorce [cover story] J. S. Wallerstein. il *The
New York Times Magazine* p18-21+ Ja 22 '89
Children and divorce: helping kids handle the news. J. K.
Rosemond. il *Better Homes and Gardens* 67:26+ Ag '89
Children of the aftershock [views of J. S. Wallerstein] B.
Kantrowitz. il por *Newsweek* 113:61 F 6 '89
Children's divorce trauma [study by Judith Wallerstein] *Society*
26:3 Mr/Ap '89
Dealing with divorce. J. Segal and Z. Segal. il *Parents* 64:201
S '89
A family divided: time bombs of divorce [excerpt from
Second chances] J. S. Wallerstein and S. Blakeslee. il
American Health 8:49-52 Je '89
I couldn't forgive my father. il *Good Housekeeping* 209:52+
N '89
I was an unwed stepmother. E. Mehren. por *Newsweek*
114:12-13 O 23 '89
The lasting wounds of divorce [study by J. S. Wallerstein]
A. Toufexis. il *Time* 133:61 F 6 '89
Learning to live with a past that failed [cover story; with
interview with Judith S. Wallerstein] D. Van Biema. il
People Weekly 31:78-80+ My 29 '89
Living together: bad for the kids [research by Marla Beth
Isaacs and George Leon] P. King. *Psychology Today* 23:77
Mr '89
My parents put me in the middle of their divorce [adult
daughter] il *Good Housekeeping* 208:16+ Mr '89
The painless-divorce myth. D. Neff. *Christianity Today* 33:17
My 12 '89

The post-divorce family, legal practice, and the child's needs
for stability. A. P. Derdeyn. bibl il *Children Today* 18:12-14
My/Je '89
Protecting the children of divorce. D. Trueman. il *USA
Today (Periodical)* 117:74-5 My '89
PW interviews [views of J. S. Wallerstein] B. Levine. por
Publishers Weekly 235:50+ F 10 '89
A question of trust [taking girlfriend's daughter canoeing]
P. Mandelbaum. il *The New York Times Magazine* p14+
Ag 6 '89
"We have a problem" [child vents anger on other children]
J. Marks. il *Parents* 64:51-2+ Ag '89
Weekend dads. J. T. Gibson. il *Parents* 64:188 Mr '89
When a marriage ends: how men, women and children cope.
J. S. Wallerstein and S. Blakeslee. *McCall's* 116:78+ Mr
'89
When the bough breaks . . . P. Theroux. il *Parents* 64:59-60
F '89
When your best friend's parents get divorced. J. Schneller.
il *Seventeen* 48:113-14+ Mr '89
Kidnapping
See Custody kidnapping
Religious life
See also
Church work with children of divorced parents
Interfaith divorce. D. Neff. il *Christianity Today* 33:14-15
F 17 '89
"A judge split my children—body and soul" [ex-husband
gets spiritual custody of daughters]; ed. by John Duggleby.
D. Boeke. il por *Redbook* 173:26+ S '89
CHILDREN OF EX-CONVICTS
Is a rap sheet a legacy? A. Hjelmeland. por *Newsweek* 113:10
My 15 '89
CHILDREN OF EXECUTIVES
The coming of the next generation [black business] E. G.
Graves. il *Black Enterprise* 19:7 Ap '89
Fathers and sons: no easy business. S. Nelton. il *Nation's
Business* 77:16 F '89
Give your daughter a chance. S. Nelton. il *Nation's Business*
77:72 Je '89
The next generation takes over at the B.E. 100s [Black
enterprise] A. Edmond, Jr. *Black Enterprise* 19:54 Ap '89
CHILDREN OF HOLOCAUST SURVIVORS
Past present [W. Grimm's Dear Mili] L. Metzger. *The Nation*
249:801-2 D 25 '89
CHILDREN OF INTERFAITH PARENTS
Interfaith divorce. D. Neff. il *Christianity Today* 33:14-15
F 17 '89
"A judge split my children—body and soul" [ex-husband
gets spiritual custody of daughters]; ed. by John Duggleby.
D. Boeke. il por *Redbook* 173:26+ S '89
Mixed blessings [Christian-Jewish household] J. Hope. il
Parents 64:252 D '89
CHILDREN OF INTERRACIAL PARENTS
Children of mixed parentage: how can professionals respond?
F. Wardle. bibl f il *Children Today* 18:10-13 Jl/Ag '89
Growing up beige. R. Stevens. il *Scholastic Update (Teachers'
edition)* 121:9 Ap 7 '89
Twins: 1 black, 1 white, born to interracial pair [T. and
D. Gantt] il pors *Jet* 76:16-17 Jl 31 '89
CHILDREN OF MISSIONARIES
Education
Growing up a world away [cover story] R. A. Tucker. il
Christianity Today 33:17-21 F 17 '89
CHILDREN OF PRISONERS
My dad's on death row. S. Laney. il *Seventeen* 48:68+ My
'89
CHILDREN OF SERVICEMEN
"I'll always believe she's my daughter" [U.S. government
wants blood test to prove paternity of Tuyet Mai]; ed.
by Laura Huntoon. B. Huntoon. il pors *Redbook* 174:79-80+
D '89
Mary Nguyen's G.I. dad has never seen her face, but Revlon
thinks it's a winner [Most Unforgettable Woman of the
Year] M. H. J. Farrell. il pors *People Weekly* 32:54-5
Ag 7 '89
CHILDREN OF THE RICH
Drowning in wealth. P. Edidin. il *Psychology Today* 23:32-5+
Ap '89
CHILDREN OF WAR (ORGANIZATION)
Teens make their own peace. L. Eskin. il *Scholastic Update
(Teachers' edition)* 121:12 Mr 24 '89
CHILDREN OF WORKING PARENTS
See also
After school programs
Day care
Dependent care (Employee benefits)
Alone at home: 10 safety tips for working parents & their
kids [excerpt] A. Banks. *Redbook* 173:110+ O '89
Brighter afternoons for latchkey children [involving seniors
in day care programs] il *Aging* no359:20-1 '89
Families today. A. Clark-Stewart. il *Good Housekeeping*
208:110-11+ O '89
How educators can help latchkey children. L. Long. *The
Education Digest* 54:53-7 Mr '89
Kids at work! il *Good Housekeeping* 209:118 S '89
L.A. law helps latchkey pupils; extends hours for after-school
play. il *Jet* 75:38 Ja 16 '89

CHILDREN OF WORKING PARENTS—*cont.*

Latchkey kids risk substance use [study by Jean L. Richardson] *Science News* 136:188 S 16 '89

On their own: what to tell your latchkey kids. D. Sobel. il *Ladies' Home Journal* 106:72 Ag '89

Pick the best after-school care [latchkey children] E. Klavan. il *Parents* 64:72+ S '89

Stop ironing the diapers. B. Ehrenreich. il *Ms.* 17:30-1 Ap '89

Vote to continue programs for latchkey kids in L.A. il *Jet* 77:52 O 9 '89

"Why my mom works". K. Levine. il *Parents* 64:77-80 O '89

Working parents [cover story] T. B. Brazelton. il por *Newsweek* 113:66-70 F 13 '89

Yes, you can work at home. R. Cohen. il *Parents* 64:64+ Jl '89

CHILDREN'S ALLOWANCES

Kids and money. D. M. Topolnicki. il *Good Housekeeping* 208:173 Ja '89

CHILDREN'S ART

Art mailbag. il *National Geographic World* 167:3 Jl '89

Art mailbag [drawings by children] il *National Geographic World* 170:3 O '89

Circus art mailbag. il *National Geographic World* 169:16 S '89

Family folk art designed by kids. J. Williams and J. Severson. il *Better Homes and Gardens* 67:105-7 Ap '89

Prehistoric mailbag [children's drawings of dinosaurs] il *National Geographic World* 161:10-11 Ja '89

Space mailbag. il *National Geographic World* 171:30-1 N '89

Competitions

Here are the top-winning cards in the 1989 Mother's Day contest! il *Good Housekeeping* 208:56+ My '89

Ten best kid's drawings [automobiles] M. B. Lewis. il *Car and Driver* 34:82-6 Ja '89

CHILDREN'S ART MATERIALS *See* Artists' materials

CHILDREN'S BEDS *See* Beds

CHILDREN'S BOOKS *See* Children's literature

CHILDREN'S BOOKSTORES *See* Booksellers and bookselling—Children's literature

CHILDREN'S CAMPS *See* Camps

CHILDREN'S CHORES

Chores with a purpose. J. P. Comer. il *Parents* 64:205 S '89

Get your kids to help at home [condensed from How to get kids to help at home] E. Anson. il *Reader's Digest* 135:27-8+ Ag '89

Kids and chores: why an early start is so important. J. K. Rosemond. il *Better Homes and Gardens* 67:27+ Je '89

CHILDREN'S CLOTHES *See* Clothing and dress—Children

CHILDREN'S CLUBS

See also

4-H clubs

Wilderness Scouts of America

CHILDREN'S COSTUMES *See* Costume

CHILDREN'S CRIBS *See* Cribs (Beds)

CHILDREN'S DEFENSE FUND (U.S.)

Profiles [M. Edelman] C. Tomkins. il por *The New Yorker* 65:48-50+ Mr 27 '89

CHILDREN'S ETIQUETTE *See* Etiquette

CHILDREN'S FISHING *See* Fishing

CHILDREN'S FRIENDS *See* Friendship

CHILDREN'S FURNITURE *See* Furniture, Children's

CHILDREN'S GAMES *See* Games

CHILDREN'S GARDENS AND GARDENING

Cultivate a budding gardener. A. B. Miles. il *Parents* 64:78-9+ Ap '89

Garden of delights [parent and child garden together] C. Jabs. il *Good Housekeeping* 208:84+ Je '89

Growing people. il *The Mother Earth News* 118:38+ Jl/Ag '89

Homegrown [cover story] M. J. Phillips. il *Flower and Garden* 33:20-1 My/Je '89

CHILDREN'S HAIRSTYLING *See* Hairstyling

CHILDREN'S HOMES, INSTITUTIONAL *See* Orphans and orphanages

CHILDREN'S HOSPITAL NATIONAL MEDICAL CENTER

Emergency treatment! True cases from the files of an extraordinary children's hospital [excerpt from In the blink of an eye] A. Doelp. il *Redbook* 172:82-3+ F '89

Race against death [trauma unit; condensed from In the blink of an eye] A. Doelp. il *Reader's Digest* 135:221-4+ N '89

CHILDREN'S HOSPITALS *See* Children—Hospitals

CHILDREN'S HUNTING *See* Hunting

CHILDREN'S LITERATURE

See also

Booksellers and bookselling—Children's literature

Boston Children's Book Collaborative

Children's periodicals

Children's reading

Children's stories

Computer picture books for children

Fairy tales

Picture books for children

Publishers and publishing—Children's literature

Scientific literature for children

Story telling

Young adults' literature

Favorite authors' favorite books. *Ladies' Home Journal* 106:62 Jl '89

It's all right to be innocent again. L. Rosenberg. il *The New York Times Book Review* 94:46 My 21 '89

Publishers weekly children's bestsellers. See occasional issues of Publishers Weekly beginning February 26, 1988

Authorship

See also

Picture books for children—Authorship

Ann Martin stirs up a tiny tempest in Preteen Land with her best-selling Baby-sitters Club. K. McMurran. il pors *People Weekly* 32:55-6 Ag 21 '89

Ballyhooing birthdays: four children's classics and how they grew. M. McQuade. il *Publishers Weekly* 236:28-30 S 29 '89

Coming attractions. il *Publishers Weekly* 236:132-7 Jl 28 '89

Fascinating Fergie facts [cover story] il *Redbook* 173:132 S '89

Flying starts: new faces of 1989. il *Publishers Weekly* 236:26-30+ D 22 '89

Lynne Reid Banks. A. Smith. il por *Publishers Weekly* 236:30+ O 27 '89

PW interviews [J. Marshall] L. S. Marcus. il por *Publishers Weekly* 236:202-3 Jl 28 '89

Rhinoceroses in the living room [work of C. Van Allsburg] S. Allis. il por *Time* 134:108 N 13 '89

A royal mum writes for children [Sarah, Duchess of York] A. Smith. il por *Publishers Weekly* 236:34+ S 29 '89

The stars of the trike-and-tantrum set [celebrity authors] G. Cerio. il *Newsweek* 114:74 D 4 '89

Van Allsburg's express. K. Heron. il por *The New York Times Magazine* p12-15 D 24 '89

When truth isn't stranger than fiction. M. L. Johnson. *The Writer* 102:26-7 F '89

Writing the historical novel for young readers. P. Beatty. *The Writer* 102:17-19 Mr '89

The year of the young reader. *The Writer* 102:20-5 Je '89

Awards

See also

Picture books for children—Awards

Do awards sell books? A. Meeker. il *Publishers Weekly* 236:32+ Ag 25 '89

Bibliography

The 1988 Cuffies: the top picks from children's booksellers. il *Publishers Weekly* 235:105 Ja 20 '89

1988 top sellers: the year's most successful new children's books. il *Publishers Weekly* 235:43 Ap 28 '89

All-time bestselling hardcover children's books; All-time bestselling paperback children's books. *Publishers Weekly* 236:28-9 O 27 '89

Best kids' books of '89. C. Loomis. il *Parents* 64:124-6+ D '89

Bringing architecture alive for young readers. il *Sunset (Central West edition)* 183:80 D '89

Children's books. See issues of The New York Times Book Review

Childrens books: fall 1989 [religious books] il *Publishers Weekly* 236:54-6 O 6 '89

Children's books for Christmas. F. McNulty. il *The New Yorker* 65:134-44 N 27 '89

Children's books spring 1989. B. Stander. il *Publishers Weekly* 235:145-85 F 24 '89

Children's books—spring 1989 [religious books] il *Publishers Weekly* 235:56-7 Mr 3 '89

Christmas books: beyond Santa Claus. A. E. Johnson. *The New York Times Book Review* 94:19 D 24 '89

'Dear Scrooge . .' [holiday books] R. Donahue. il *Publishers Weekly* 236:34-7 O 27 '89

Fall 1989 children's books. il *Publishers Weekly* 236:145-87 Jl 28 '89

Forecasts. See issues of Publishers Weekly

Good reads for black kids. G. Evans. il *American Visions* 4:50-2 D '89

Great gifts for small people. D. Diehl. il *Modern Maturity* 32:54-8+ D '89/Ja '90

In 'fruitcake weather'. J. Baumgold. il *New York* 22:80 D 18 '89

Of cats, myths and pizza [Christmas gifts] S. Kanfer. il *Time* 134:100+ D 11 '89

OK, kids, get serious. L. Shapiro. il *Newsweek* 114:72-4+ D 4 '89

Collectors and collecting

Children's book collections. S. Stan. il *Publishers Weekly* 236:26-8+ Ag 25 '89

Conferences

See also

International Board on Books for Young People

'Other lands, other cultures': Jewish Book Council discusses children's books in translation. B. List. il *Publishers Weekly* 235:142-3 F 24 '89

CHILDREN'S LITERATURE—cont.

Illustration
See Illustration

Marketing
See Books—Marketing

Psychological aspects
Taming the Wild Things [work of M. Sendak] M. H. Lystad. bibl f il *Children Today* 18:16-19 Mr/Ap '89

Technique
Calling it quits. L. Lowry. *The Writer* 102:13-14+ Ap '89
Common failings in juvenile fiction—and how to correct them. J. Giblin. *The Writer* 102:15-18 Jl '89
Fantasy for young readers. S. R. Murphy. *The Writer* 102:19-20+ S '89

Themes
Children's books: inside the Baby-sitters Club [series by A. M. Martin] N. R. Kleinfield. *The New York Times Book Review* 94:42 Ap 30 '89
It's so much easier to write about the rich. M. J. Harris. il *The New York Times Book Review* 94:46 N 12 '89
Kiddie litter. J. R. Dunlap. il *The American Spectator* 22:19-21 D '89

CHILDREN'S MUSEUM OF INDIANAPOLIS
Kids' museum is second home. M. Osburn. il *American Visions* 4:52-4 O '89
Putting on a happy face. M. Gaskie. il *Architectural Record* 177:78-81 Ag '89

CHILDREN'S MUSEUMS
See also
　　Children's Museum of Indianapolis
Children's museums. K. Stechert. il *Better Homes and Gardens* 67:112-13 Ja '89
Playgrounds for the mind. il *Newsweek* 113:50-2 Je 12 '89

CHILDREN'S MUSIC
See also
　　Lullabies
　　Videotapes—Children's music
Buzz off, Big Bird! Pack it in, Pee-wee! The big names on little lips are Sharon, Lois and Bram. T. Allis. il *People Weekly* 31:127-8 My 1 '89
Raffi. C. Ricci. il pors *Parents* 64:134-6+ N '89

CHILDREN'S OPINIONS See Children—Attitudes

CHILDREN'S PARTIES
See also
　　Birthday parties
　　Halloween parties
"Come to my party . . . and wait till you see the treats mom made!". il *Good Housekeeping* 209:120+ S '89
A cookie tea for ladies of all ages [mother-daughter event] S. Payne. il *Southern Living* 24:62-3 D '89
The test-tube generation celebrates its first decade [anniversary of the opening of Bourn Hall Clinic] il *People Weekly* 31:77 Je 5 '89

CHILDREN'S PERIODICALS
Tapping the kiddie market. L. Zuckerman. il *Time* 133:74 Ap 24 '89

History
Desk-top publishing [explosion of adolescent printing in years after Civil War] P. E. Petrik. bibl il *History Today* 39:12-26 O '89

CHILDREN'S POETRY
See also
　　Lullabies

CHILDREN'S PROGRAMS (TELEVISION) See Cable television—Children's programs; Television broadcasting—Children's programs

CHILDREN'S QUESTIONS AND ANSWERS
Ask me [student reluctance to ask questions in class; research by Hans van der Meij] G. W. Bracey. il *Phi Delta Kappan* 70:410 Ja '89
Leading questions. P. Theroux. il *Parents* 64:71-2 Mr '89
"Mommy, why is she different?" [answers to sensitive questions children ask] L. Derman-Sparks and others. il *Parents* 64:120-3 D '89
"What makes a rainbow, mom?". R. Chevat. il *Good Housekeeping* 208:94-5 Je '89
Why in the world? See occasional issues of National Geographic World

CHILDREN'S READING
See also
　　Children's literature
　　Reading aloud
　　Year of the Young Reader, 1989
Children's booksellers and teachers: partners in literacy. S. Wilensky-Lanford. il *Publishers Weekly* 235:101-3 Ja 20 '89
Eager readers. B. Weissbourd. il *Parents* 64:190 Mr '89
How to get your kid to love to read [views of Christine Behrmann] P. Colman. il *Ladies' Home Journal* 106:58 Je '89
The love of books. J. Segal and Z. Segal. il *Parents* 64:216 D '89
When kids won't read: tips for inspiring the most reluctant reader. A. Atkins. il *Better Homes and Gardens* 67:51+ Je '89

Anecdotes, facetiae, satire, etc.
A pretty girl is like a malady [boy attributes myopia to hours spent reading about sex] P. Freundlich. il *Esquire* 111:122-6 F '89

Awards
See also
　　Mott's Apple Awards

Projects
Business, home, and school: cooperating to develop lifelong readers [project in Pinellas County, Fla.] A. R. Bellack and C. K. Hallin. il *Phi Delta Kappan* 70:415 Ja '89
'Reading rainbow''s 7th season: 1989 titles. il *Publishers Weekly* 235:106 Ja 20 '89
What companies can do. B. Prete. *Publishers Weekly* 236:47-8 O 27 '89

CHILDREN'S ROOMS
Go with your deco-rating. il *'Teen* 33:18 My '89
A room to grow in. N. Wing. il *Parents* 64:134-6+ F '89
Snazzy bedrooms for kids. K. McManus. *Changing Times* 43:24 N '89
The sound-, light-, and sleep-show in your room. M.-L. Kamberg. il *Current Health 2* 15:26-7 Ja '89
Space makers. N. Wing. il *Parents* 64:156-8 S '89

CHILDREN'S SAFETY SEATS (AUTOMOBILES) See Automobiles—Safety devices and measures

CHILDREN'S STORIES
See also
　　Story telling

Single works
See name of author for full entry
Barney is big. Weiss, Nicki, 1951-
Bear and Mrs. Duck. Winthrop, Elizabeth
Budgie the little helicopter. Sarah, Duchess of York, 1959-
Christmas at Piety Corner. Gilligan, Edmund
Here comes the cat! Vagin, Vladimir Vasil'evich, 1937-, and Asch, Frank
Maxine in the middle. Keller, Holly
Monster manners. Cole, Joanna
One hungry monster. O'Keefe, Susan Heyboer
Where's Rufus? Calmenson, Stephanie
Who put the pepper in the pot? Cole, Joanna

CHILDREN'S STORIES (BY CHILDREN)
AmandaStories, Vol.1 [Hypercard children's stories] G. Solomon. il *Home Office Computing* 7:88 F '89
KidWriter Gold. N. Rentschler. il *Compute!* 11:67 S '89
KidWriter Golden Edition. M. B. Eltgroth. il *Home Office Computing* 7:85 Ap '89
The Puzzle Storybook. J. Zornberg. il *Home Office Computing* 7:87-8 O '89
Super Story Tree. C. S. Holzberg. il *Compute!* 11:122-3 N '89

CHILDREN'S TANTRUMS See Temper

CHILDREN'S TAPE RECORDINGS See Tape recordings—Children's use

CHILDREN'S TELEVISION WORKSHOP
Joan Ganz Cooney created Sesame Street 20 years ago. Now it's an institution. D. Moreau. il por *Changing Times* 43:88 Jl '89

CHILDREN'S VIDEOTAPES See Videotapes—Children's use

CHILDRESS, MARK
The wild life. il *Southern Living* 24:104 Jl '89

CHILDRESS, WILLIAM
What a neighbor will do [condensed from Out of the Ozarks] il *Reader's Digest* 135:125-7 S '89

CHILDS, ANTONY
about
Capital venture. D. Streitfeld. il por *House & Garden* 161:76-81+ Ag '89

CHILDS, DAVID, 1933-
East Germany: coping with Gorbachev. bibl f *Current History* 88:385-8+ N '89

CHILDS, LUCINDA
about
The new Lucinda Childs. I. M. Fanger. il pors *Dance Magazine* 63:48-53 O '89

CHILDS, TONI
about
This year's Grammys: the women have their day. D. Hiltbrand. il pors *TV Guide* 37:6-7+ F 18-24 '89
Toni Childs. E. Miller. por *Seventeen* 48:60 Ja '89
'Wild weed' Toni Childs takes root. M. Meyer. por *Rolling Stone* p16 Ja 26 '89

CHILDS (LUCINDA) DANCE COMPANY See Lucinda Childs Dance Company

CHILE
See also
　　Advertising, Political—Chile
　　Astronomical observatories—Chile
　　Civil rights—Chile
　　Easter Island
　　Geology—Chile
　　Opera—Chile
　　Resorts—Chile
　　Volcanoes—Chile

Antiquities
Skepticism fades over pre-Clovis man [Tom Dillehay's Monte Verde excavations] R. Lewin. *Science* 244:1140 Je 9 '89

CHILE—cont.
Commerce
United States
See United States—Commerce—Chile
Commercial policy
A letter from Santiago. J. A. Briggs. il *Forbes* 143:92-6 My 15 '89
Description and travel
Where the people are nice and the trains run on time. G. A. Wagner. *Harper's* 278:17 Ja '89
Economic policy
A tale of two countries: why Chile booms as Peru swoons. C. Roberts. il *Business Week* p18 My 29 '89
Foreign relations
United States
See United States—Foreign relations—Chile
Industries
See also
Fruit industry—Chile
Wine industry—Chile
Native peoples
See Indians of South America—Chile
Politics and government
See also
Elections—Chile
Political campaigns—Chile
Socialism—Chile
¡Adios, General! [cover story] M. Morrison. il *The American Spectator* 22:16-20 My '89
Adiós, General: saying good-bye to Pinochet. A. Dorfman. il *Harper's* 279:72-6 D '89
Chile: transition to democracy? J. H. Wolfe. il *USA Today (Periodical)* 117:25 Ja '89
Chile's return to democracy. P. Constable and A. Valenzuela. *Foreign Affairs* 68:169-86 Wint '89/'90
Sixteen years under Pinochet. M. Montecino. il por *The Progressive* 53:34-7 D '89
Religious institutions and affairs
See also
Catholic Church—Chile
Church and civil rights—Chile
CHILE AND THE UNITED STATES
See also
United States—Foreign opinion—Chilean
CHILEAN WINE PALMS See Palms
CHILES, JAMES R.
Flying cars were a dream that never got off the ground. il *Smithsonian* 19:144-6+ F '89
CHILES, LAWTON
about
Putting children before politics. D. Olin. il por *New Choices for the Best Years* 29:16+ Jl '89
CHILES, LOIS
about
Picture perfect. C. Seipp. il pors *Harper's Bazaar* 122:118-21+ Ag '89
CHILI
Five Wyoming farm and ranch families start Chugwater Chili. il *Successful Farming* 87:22-3 mid-F '89
Recipe of the week [chili and rice skillet] il *Jet* 75:38 Mr 20 '89
CHILI PEPPER COOKING See Cooking—Vegetables
CHILI PEPPERS See Peppers
CHILKAT BALD EAGLE PRESERVE See Bird sanctuaries—Alaska
CHILTON, KENNETH W.
(jt. auth) See Warren, Melinda, and Chilton, Kenneth W.
CHIMERAS (BIOLOGY) See Mosaics (Biology)
CHIMES
Audience chime system [signaling start of a performance in a theater] B. Koenig. il *Theatre Crafts* 23:76-7 O '89
CHIMNEY CLEANING
Care and feeding of chimneys. K. McManus. *Changing Times* 43:24+ N '89
Controlling creosote. S. Benado. *Popular Science* 234:51 Mr '89
CHIMNEY SWEEPS See Chimney cleaning
CHIMNEYS
Fires and fire prevention
Avoiding chimney fires. il *Consumers' Research Magazine* 72:28 O '89
Maintenance and repair
What to do about fireplace problems. J. Seisler. il *Consumers' Research Magazine* 72:25-8 O '89
CHIMPANZEES
Calls in the wild [study by Christopher Boehm] *Science News* 135:223 Ap 8 '89
Easy does it! [mothers and infant chimps] il *National Geographic World* 171:16-17 N '89
Reach out and branch someone [branch dragging by pygmy chimps; research by Ellen J. Ingmanson] B. Bower. *Science News* 135:251 Ap 22 '89
Suffer the little chimps [J. Goodall bitten at Laboratory for Experimental Medicine Surgery in Primates] A. Cockburn. *The Nation* 248:222-3 F 20 '89
To save the wild chimps [U.S. lab chimps not affected by new protective regulations] *Science News* 135:155 Mr 11 '89

CHIMPANZEES AS ARTISTS
At Chicago's Lincoln Park Zoo, artistic elephants and chimps are living the easel life. il *People Weekly* 32:108-9 Ag 28 '89
CHIN, JAMES
Understanding the figures. il *World Health* p8-9 O '89
CHIN, LARRY WU-TAI
about
Tracking China's master spy. J. Barron. il *Reader's Digest* 135:97-102 D '89
CHINA
See also
Agricultural administration—China
Aihui (China)
Air pollution—China
Airplanes, Training—China
Americans—China
Amur River (China and Soviet Union)
Arts and state—China
Astronomy—China
Aviation and state—China
Beijing (China)
Birth control—China
Bridges—China
Cable television—China
Canals—China
Chengdu (China)
Chinese
Civil rights—China
College education and state—China
Colleges and universities—China
Concentration camps—China
Copyright infringement—China
Criminal law—China
Cybernetics—China
Dance concerts—China
Day care—China
Economic assistance—China
Economic conversion—China
Education—China
Energy policy—China
Environment—China
Environmental policy—China
Family—China
Foreign correspondents—China
Foreign students—China
Forests and forestry—China
Freedom of information—China
Geology—China
Government and the press—China
Great Wall of China
Guangdong Province (China)
Harbin (China)
Huizhou (China)
Hunan Province (China)
Ice—China
Investments, American—China
Investments, Canadian—China
Investments, Chinese
Investments, Foreign—China
Investments, Hong Kong—China
Literature and state—China
Loans, Bank—China
Manchuria (China)
Military assistance, American—China
Mount Everest (China and Nepal)
Narcotics trade—China
Natural gas—China
Nepotism—China
Paleontology—China
Paper money—China
Police—China
Public health—China
Qinghai Province (China)
Science—China
Sex education—China
Shanghai (China)
Space research—China
Stele (Archeology)—China
Student movement—China
Student protests, demonstrations, etc.—China
Taiwan
Technology—China
Television broadcasting—China
Theater buildings—China
Wildlife conservation—China
Women—China
Youth—China
Youth movement—China
Zhejiang Province (China)
Air Force
China modernizes military aircraft in atmosphere of fiscal austerity. il *Aviation Week & Space Technology* 131:55+ D 11 '89
Anniversaries, etc.
Symbols of danger [celebrations marking 40th anniversary of Communist rule] J. Bierman. il *Maclean's* 102:27+ O 9 '89

CHINA—cont.

Antiquities
See also
Great Wall of China
Oracle bones

Armed Forces
See also
China. People's Liberation Army

Bibliography
Book reviews. D. E. Soled. *Current History* 88:285-6+ S '89
Keeping up with the new China. J. K. Fairbank. il *The New York Review of Books* 36:17-20 Mr 16 '89

Civilization
The Chinese scientific genius [cover story; special issue] R. K. G. Temple. il *The Courier (Unesco)* 41:3-34 O '88
'We shouldn't be so afraid': China's anti-West campaign may be self-defeating. D. Elliott. il *Newsweek* 114:54 O 9 '89

Commerce
France
See France—Commerce—China
Soviet Union
See Soviet Union—Commerce—China
United States
See United States—Commerce—China

Commercial policy
The lure of the Gold Coast. L. Doder. il *Maclean's* 102:38 My 29 '89

Cultural policy
In praise of Wang Meng. W. Barnstone. *The Nation* 249:502-3 O 30 '89

Cultural relations
United States
See United States—Cultural relations—China

Defenses
See also
Airplanes, Military—China
China—Air Force
Guided missiles, Chinese
Known Chinese nuclear tests, 1964-1988 [table] il *The Bulletin of the Atomic Scientists* 45:48 O '89

Description and travel
See also
Cycling—China
Motorcycling—China
China on my mind. W. Cross. il *New Choices for the Best Years* 29:36-42 My '89
Free to fly inside the cage. M. Kramer. il *Time* 134:64-8+ O 2 '89
Travel writing: why I bother [book prefigures events in Tiananmen Square] P. Theroux. il *The New York Times Book Review* 94:7-8 Jl 30 '89

Diplomatic and consular service
Canada
Dissident diplomats [Chinese envoys defect to Canada following Tiananmen Square massacre] T. Tedesco. il *Maclean's* 102:21 Je 26 '89
United States
The Chinese ambassador defends his government [views of Han Xu] W. F. Buckley. *National Review* 41:71 S 29 '89

Economic conditions
See also
Inflation (Finance)—China

Economic policy
Are the hardliners squandering China's chances for growth? D. J. Yang. il *Business Week* p58 N 20 '89
Behind China's anger [cover story] J. Wallace. il *U.S. News & World Report* 106:20-3 Je 5 '89
Capitalism has no patent on the market [interview with Hu Qili] N. Gardels. por *New Perspectives Quarterly* 5:7-11 Wint '88/'89
China begins a new Long March. D. J. Yang. il map *Business Week* p38-41+ Je 5 '89
China gropes toward a way out [cover story] P. Kwong and D. Miščevič. il *The Nation* 249:73+ Jl 17 '89
China prepares for a bitter harvest [effects of student crackdown] E. MacFarquhar. il *U.S. News & World Report* 107:34-5 Jl 10 '89
China puts on the brakes. D. Elliott and L. Magida. il *Newsweek* 113:33 Ap 3 '89
China's economic moves make sense. L. C. Thurow. il por *Fortune* 119:323-4+ Je 5 '89
China's economy is careening out of control. D. J. Yang. il *Business Week* p54+ Ap 3 '89
China's slipping economy. R. Franklin. *World Press Review* 36:56 N '89
'Democracy' is not enough [student uprising] A. Cockburn. *The Nation* 248:802 Je 12 '89
'For a socialist country, China is lucky'. D. Elliott. il *Newsweek* 112:48 My 22 '89
The genie is out of Beijing's bottle [students' push for freedom] D. J. Yang and D. Lee. il *Business Week* p48 My 29 '89
Inflation and economic reform in China. B. Naughton. bibl f *Current History* 88:269-72+ S '89

Marriage of convenience. D. Doder. il pors *U.S. News & World Report* 106:30-2 My 15 '89
The new Chinese warlords. E. Salem. *World Press Review* 36:50 Ja '89
Quick step backward. L. do Rosario. *World Press Review* 36:60-1 D '89
Reform: Moscow vs. Beijing. S. Bialer. il *U.S. News & World Report* 106:32-3 F 6 '89
Two different roads to reform. E. Wickert. il *World Press Review* 36:16-17 My '89
Who's minding the store in China? D. Lee and J. Becker. il *Business Week* p58-9 Ag 14 '89
Why there's still promise in China. F. S. Worthy. il *Fortune* 119:95-6+ F 27 '89

Economic relations
The shock waves from Beijing. B. Javetski. il *Business Week* p76-7 Je 26 '89
Testing the power of dollar diplomacy [effects of Beijing crackdown] H. Trewhitt. il *U.S. News & World Report* 107:30-1 Jl 3 '89

Foreign relations
See also
Espionage, Chinese
Tuning up Chinese foreign policy. Xie Yixian. *World Press Review* 36:14 My '89
The uncertain future of Chinese foreign policy. S. I. Levine. bibl f *Current History* 88:261-4+ S '89
'We shouldn't be so afraid': China's anti-West campaign may be self-defeating. D. Elliott. il *Newsweek* 114:54 O 9 '89
Canada
See Canada—Foreign relations—China
Great Britain
See Great Britain—Foreign relations—China
Soviet Union
See Soviet Union—Foreign relations—China
Taiwan
China deal. L. Hahn. *The New Republic* 201:10-11 O 30 '89
Turning quantitative change into qualitative change [address, August 1, 1989] Y.-M. Shaw. *Vital Speeches of the Day* 55:713-15 S 15 '89
You can't go home again. M. McSherry. il *National Review* 41:37-8+ D 22 '89
Tibet
'A' is for autonomy. E. N. Luttwak. *The New Republic* 200:15-16 Ap 17 '89
A bow to Tibet [Dalai Lama wins Peace Prize] por *Time* 134:44 O 16 '89
China's hard line in Tibet. G. Deshingkar. *World Press Review* 36:18-19 Je '89
China's Nobel rebuke [Peace Prize awarded to Dalai Lama] *Newsweek* 114:54 O 16 '89
A firestorm in Shangri-La. H. Anderson. il *Newsweek* 113:36-8 Mr 20 '89
Honoring a god-king [Dalai Lama awarded Nobel Peace Prize] R. Corelli. il por *Maclean's* 102:58 O 16 '89
Inside Tibet [special section] il *Utne Reader* p33-46 Mr/Ap '89
Massacre in the Forbidden Kingdom [riot in Lhasa] C. Meindersma. il *Reader's Digest* 135:126-30 O '89
Tibet. *Business Week* p60 Mr 20 '89
Tibet's agony [Dalai Lama awarded Nobel Peace Prize] M. Moynihan. *The New Republic* 201:10-11 N 20 '89
Unrest in Tibet. J. T. Dreyer. bibl f *Current History* 88:281-4+ S '89
You don't have to be a Buddhist to dig the Dalai Lama. M. S. Forbes. por *Forbes* 144:19-20 S 4 '89
Tibet—History
Roots of Tibet's clash with China. W. Gasperini. *Utne Reader* p35 Mr/Ap '89
United States
See United States—Foreign relations—China

History
The Long March to revolution. L. Eskin. il por *Scholastic Update (Teachers' edition)* 121:21 My 5 '89
Ming dynasty, 1368-1644
The merchants of Huizhou: commerce and Confucianism [cover story] M. Dillon. bibl il map *History Today* 39:24-30 F '89
Ch'ing dynasty, 1644-1912
The merchants of Huizhou: commerce and Confucianism [cover story] M. Dillon. bibl il map *History Today* 39:24-30 F '89
19th century
China: rethinking the Revolution [influence of French Revolution] Zhilian Zhang. il *The Unesco Courier* 42:44-7 Je '89
1912-1937
See also
Long March, 1934-1935
1949-1976
The beatification of comrade Zhou Enlai. D. Wilson. il pors *History Today* 39:7-10 Mr '89
The incredible shrinking man [Mao Zedong] J. Mirsky. il *The New York Review of Books* 36:18-20 Je 29 '89

CHINA—History—*cont.*
Cultural Revolution, 1966-1969
Beware the dunce caps [concern that current unrest will lead to repeat of Cultural Revolution] W. R. Doerner. il *Time* 133:47 My 29 '89

Industries
See also

Aerospace industries—China
Airlines—China
Airplane industry—China
Automobile industry—China
Chengdu Aircraft Corporation
Chengdu Engine Company
China Great Wall Industry Corporation
Electric battery industry—China
Liming Engine Manufacturing Corporation
Nanchang Aircraft Manufacturing Company
Nut industry—China
Publishers and publishing—China
Shanghai Aviation Industrial Corporation
Shenyang Aircraft Corporation
Steel industry—China
Stone Group Corporation
Tourist trade—China

Intellectual life
The Chinese intellectuals and the revolt. P. Link. il *The New York Review of Books* 36:38-41 Je 29 '89
The Chinese intelligentsia: training the new elite. F. Strebeigh. il *Current (Washington, D.C.)* 318:32-40 D '89
'Intellectuals are waking up'. D. Elliott. il *Newsweek* 113:34 Mr 6 '89
The price China has paid: an interview with Liu Binyan [with introduction by Merle Goldman] N. Gardels. il *The New York Review of Books* 35:31+ Ja 19 '89
Training China's new elite. F. Strebeigh. il *The Atlantic* 263:72-80 Ap '89
Two dissidents challenge 'feudal communism' [interview with Liu Binyan and Bai Hua] J. L. Du Sablon. il pors *World Press Review* 36:26-7 F '89

Kings and rulers
See also

K'ang-hsi, Emperor of China, 1654-1722
Pu Yi, 1906-1967

Military policy
See also

China—Defenses

China's "new thinking" on nuclear arms. J. Prados. bibl f il *The Bulletin of the Atomic Scientists* 45:32-5 Je '89
The military in China. H. W. Jencks. bibl f *Current History* 88:265-8+ S '89

Photographs and photography
Above China. L. Kohl. il maps *National Geographic* 175:278-311 Mr '89
A day in the life of China [excerpts; cover story] il *Time* 134:30-8+ O 2 '89

Politics and government
See also

Communism—China
Communist Party (China)
Politics, Corruption in—China
Tiananmen Square (China) student occupation, 1989

Another little red book. S. Burton. il por *Time* 134:47 S 18 '89
Bad days in Beijing [review of last 10 years] M. Liu. il *Newsweek* 114:34-5 Jl 31 '89
The battle over the Chairman [rising prestige of Mao] R. Wilkinson. il *Newsweek* 114:14 Ag 14 '89
Beijing spring [student protests] M. S. Serrill. il *Time* 133:36-8 My 8 '89
Beijing's bad-times bash. E. MacFarquhar. il *U.S. News & World Report* 107:33-5 O 2 '89
China. *Business Week* p56 O 2 '89
China and the U.S.S.R.: the changing face of communism [cover story; special issue] il map *Scholastic Update (Teachers' edition)* 121:2-12+ My 5 '89
China's despair and China's hope; tr. by Perry Link. Fang Lizhi. il *The New York Review of Books* 36:3-4 F 2 '89
China's need for leadership. B. M. Frolic. *World Press Review* 36:17-18+ Jl '89
Deng's hard-liners and their enemies list. E. MacFarquhar. il pors *U.S. News & World Report* 106:24-6 Je 5 '89
Deng's 'pact with the devil'. C. S. Manegold. il por *Newsweek* 114:33 S 18 '89
Deng's pyrrhic victory [cover story] Liu Binyan. *The New Republic* 201:21-4 O 2 '89
A dilemma for Washington [China's repressive policies] R. Holbrooke. il *Newsweek* 113:32 Je 12 '89
Fighting the founders [cover story] S. Talbott. il *Time* 133:16-19 Je 5 '89
The flowering of dissent in Deng's Republic. il *U.S. News & World Report* 106:12 Mr 13 '89
The Goddess of Democracy deconstructed. B. Lee and L. O.-F. Lee. il *New Perspectives Quarterly* 6:58-61 Fall '89
The Great Wall endures [interview with Liu Binyan] O. Schell and N. Gardels. il *New Perspectives Quarterly* 5:42-6 Wint '88/'89
Happy birthday, now shut up. S. V. Lawrence. il *U.S. News & World Report* 107:36 O 2 '89

Last days of China's old guard [cover story] M. Hopkins. il *The New Leader* 72:7-8 N 27 '89
The making of Deng's successor. S. Burton. il por *Time* 134:44 O 9 '89
Marriage of convenience. D. Doder. il pors *U.S. News & World Report* 106:30-2 My 15 '89
The new truth in China [with editorial comment] M. Hopkins. il *The New Leader* 72:2, 5-7 Jl 10-24 '89
The People's Republic of China, 1989 [cover story; special issue] bibl f map (inside back cover) *Current History* 88:257-97 S '89
The price China has paid: an interview with Liu Binyan [with introduction by Merle Goldman] N. Gardels. il *The New York Review of Books* 35:31+ Ja 19 '89
Reflections on the revolution in China. C. Krauthammer. il *Time* 133:90 Je 5 '89
Two dissidents challenge 'feudal communism' [interview with Liu Binyan and Bai Hua] J. L. Du Sablon. il pors *World Press Review* 36:26-7 F '89
Vengeance in China. M. Goldman. il *The New York Review of Books* 36:5-9 N 9 '89
The view from the Forbidden City. W. Lord. il por *Newsweek* 114:36 D 18 '89
Why China's rulers fear democracy. J. K. Fairbank. il *The New York Review of Books* 36:32-3 S 28 '89
Zhao fights for his political life. J. Mirsky. *World Press Review* 36:15-16 My '89
Zhao's fall, China's loss. J. H. Fincher. *Foreign Policy* 76:3-25 Fall '89

Bibliography
Keeping up with the new China. J. K. Fairbank. il *The New York Review of Books* 36:17-20 Mr 16 '89

Race relations
"Beat the black devils!" [Chinese students march against African students in Nanjing] S. Burton. il *Time* 133:37 Ja 9 '89
China: 'Kill the black devils' [Chinese college students protest against African students in Nanjing] M. Beck. il *Newsweek* 113:35 Ja 9 '89
The fallout from Nanjing [continued anti-African demonstrations by Chinese students] M. S. Serrill. il *Time* 133:38 Ja 16 '89
More than just Chinese racism [anti-African demonstrations by Chinese students] R. Seidelman. il *The Nation* 248:195-6 F 13 '89
The roots of racism are rubbed raw [Chinese college students protest against African students in Nanjing] il *U.S. News & World Report* 106:10-11 Ja 9 '89

Religious institutions and affairs
See also

Catholic Church—China
Christians—China
Church and state—China
House churches—China
Protestant churches—China

Religion in China [cover story] W. R. Garrett. il *The Christian Century* 106:748-9 Ag 16-23 '89

Social conditions
See also

Women—China

Free to fly inside the cage. M. Kramer. il *Time* 134:64-8+ O 2 '89
Watching China. A. Tan. il por *Glamour* 87:302-3 S '89

CHINA. ARMY *See* China. People's Liberation Army
CHINA. CIVIL AVIATION ADMINISTRATION
CAAC continues restructuring effort; regionals pursue international routes. il *Aviation Week & Space Technology* 131:63-4 D 11 '89

CHINA. PEOPLE'S LIBERATION ARMY
An Army in the middle [student protests] H. Anderson. il *Newsweek* 113:33 Je 5 '89
The Chinese Army's uneasy truce with itself. H. Anderson. il *Newsweek* 113:19 Je 19 '89
Commanding Mao's gun. D. Stanglin. il *U.S. News & World Report* 106:25 Je 5 '89
The military in China. H. W. Jencks. bibl f *Current History* 88:265-8+ S '89

CHINA (PORCELAIN) *See* Pottery
CHINA AIRLINES LTD.
Taiwan's China Airlines seeks links with trade partners. J. Ott. il *Aviation Week & Space Technology* 130:61+ My 8 '89

CHINA AND HONG KONG
Apprehension in Hong Kong [killings in Beijing] A. Phillips. *Maclean's* 102:27 Je 19 '89
A bad omen for Hong Kong [crackdown on students in mainland China] C. S. Manegold. il *Newsweek* 113:27 Je 19 '89
The Bank. A. Tanzer. il por *Forbes* 144:43-4 D 11 '89
Biting the hands that feed them [effects of violence on China's economic ties] il *U.S. News & World Report* 106:26 Je 19 '89
Britain's Hong Kong headache has just begun to throb. D. J. Yang. il *Business Week* p83 Jl 17 '89
Britain's shame. M. Elliott. *The New Republic* 201:15-16 Ag 7-14 '89
Broken China [effects of crackdown on students] *The New Republic* 200:5-6 Je 26 '89

CHINA AND HONG KONG—cont.

A colony living on the edge of chaos. D. Lee. il *Business Week* p34-5 Je 19 '89

Decision time in Hong Kong. F. M. Bordewich. il *Reader's Digest* 134:121-6 Je '89

Exodus creates church leadership shortage. S. Mumper. il *Christianity Today* 33:42+ N 3 '89

Fear and anger in Hong Kong [Beijing massacre shakes the colony] W. Stewart. il *Time* 133:22 Je 19 '89

Fear and trembling in Hong Kong [violence in Beijing] J. Elliott. *World Press Review* 36:18 Jl '89

Fear in the colony [Hong Kong reacts to Beijing crackdown] T. Fennell. il *Maclean's* 102:32-4 Je 19 '89

Hong Kong [address, October 16, 1989] Sir D. Wilson. *Vital Speeches of the Day* 56:140-3 D 15 '89

Hong Kong: bound and adrift. B. Wallach. il map *Focus (New York, N.Y.: 1950)* 39:17-25 Fall '89

The Hong Kong Church faces 1997 [Catholic Church] M. H. Kelleher. il *America* 161:63-4 Jl 29-Ag 5 '89

Hong Kong gone. W. McGurn. *National Review* 41:22-3 Ap 21 '89

Hong Kong? Just watch China. B. Crozier. *National Review* 41:20 Mr 10 '89

Hong Kong on borrowed time. M. Scott. il *The New York Times Magazine* p30-2+ O 22 '89

Hong Kong's contrarians [buying stocks] J. Mendes. il *Fortune* 120:30 Jl 17 '89

Hong Kong's future seems even more in doubt [effects of student protests in China] D. J. Yang and D. Lee. il *Business Week* p41+ Je 12 '89

Hong Kong's lost confidence [repression in China] P. Hazan. il *World Press Review* 36:61 S '89

The long goodbye [Hong Kong residents who wish to leave and boat people who have arrived] R. Brookhiser. il *National Review* 41:18-19 N 24 '89

Next door and eight years away. J. Greenwald. il *Time* 133:29 Je 5 '89

Preparing for 1997 [Canadian B. Strayer helps draft bill of rights for Hong Kong] J. Keating. *Maclean's* 102:73-4 N 20 '89

A tale of two cities: Hong Kong & Shanghai. N. R. Clifford. il *Commonweal* 116:453-5 S 8 '89

The tragedy of Hong Kong. M. Novak. il *Forbes* 144:80-1 Ag 21 '89

What will happen when the Chinese take back their 'fragrant harbor'? S. Karnow. bibl (p174) il map *Smithsonian* 20:40-8+ Ap '89

Will the last one to leave please turn out the lights? [reaction to Beijing crackdown] E. MacFarquhar. il *U.S. News & World Report* 107:36-7 Ag 21 '89

CHINA AND THE SOVIET UNION *See* Soviet Union and China

CHINA AND THE UNITED STATES

See also
Educational exchanges
Exchanges, Literary and scientific

CHINA BEACH [television program] See Television program reviews—Single works

CHINA CLUB (PARIS, FRANCE: RESTAURANT) *See* Paris (France)—Restaurants, nightclubs, bars, etc.

CHINA GENERAL PLASTICS CORP.

Taiwan's U.S. strategy. R. Simon. il *Forbes* 143:43-4 My 29 '89

CHINA GREAT WALL INDUSTRY CORPORATION

Brazil, China form space launch venture [INSCOM] E. H. Kolcum. il *Aviation Week & Space Technology* 130:35 My 29 '89

CHINA GRILL (NEW YORK, N.Y.) *See* New York (N.Y.)—Restaurants, nightclubs, bars, etc.

CHINA IN MOTION PICTURES

Student-crushing China cows Natural History Museum [film The first emperor of China not shown by American Museum of Natural History] M. S. Forbes. il *Forbes* 144:20 Ag 7 '89

A tale by two cultures [making of The first emperor of China] T. R. Miller. il *Natural History* p66-9 Jl '89

CHINA IN TELEVISION

All the rage in China [River dirge series] F. Wakeman. il *The New York Review of Books* 36:19-21 Mr 2 '89

CHINA LAKE NAVAL WEAPONS CENTER (U.S.) *See* Naval Weapons Center (U.S.)

CHINA MOON CAFE (SAN FRANCISCO, CALIF.) *See* San Francisco (Calif.)—Restaurants, nightclubs, bars, etc.

CHINA TRADE ART

China's polished art [export silver] M. Guralnick. il *House & Garden* 161:78+ My '89

CHINA TRADE PORCELAIN

Collectors and collecting

Chinese export porcelain. S. Jones. il *Antiques & Collecting Hobbies* 94:26-8+ Jl '89

A Rubens crucifixion on a Chinese export porcelain dish. N. Pearce. bibl f il *Antiques* 136:844-7 O '89

CHINA XI'AN STUDIO *See* Xi'an Film Studio

CHINATOWN (NEW YORK, N.Y.)

Chinatown—one man's meat. C. Trillin. il por *Architectural Digest* 46:116+ N '89

CHINATOWN (SEATTLE, WASH.)

Asia in a day. H. Lockman. il *Travel Holiday* 172:90-5 Ag '89

CHINESE

Getting to the heart of the Chinese [Chinese men more sensitive than Caucasian men to propranolol] *Science News* 135:156 Mr 11 '89

Canada

Assault on racism [anti-Asian sentiment in Vancouver] H. Quinn. il *Maclean's* 102:16+ Ap 24 '89

Chinese head tax haunts Canada [experience of J. Wing in 1923] C. Bright. il por *The Progressive* 53:13-14 Ap '89

Prosperity and parochialism [influx of Hong Kong Chinese into Vancouver, B.C.] J. L. Graff. il *Time* 133:51 My 22 '89

Rage and sorrow [response to violence in Beijing] M. Nemeth. il *Maclean's* 102:28-9 Je 19 '89

A watchdog for the Asian connection [D. Lam] P. C. Newman. il *Maclean's* 102:35 Ap 24 '89

France

Meditative explorations in a French manor house [Zao Wou-ki's château] Countess Du Saillant. il por *Architectural Digest* 46:116+ O '89

North America

Religious life

Destination: North America [Hong Kong residents] *Christianity Today* 33:44 N 3 '89

United States

See also
Chinatown (New York, N.Y.)
Chinatown (Seattle, Wash.)
Chinese Americans

Biologist monitors human rights [work of Fu Xin-yuan] M. Sun. por *Science* 245:592 Ag 11 '89

Children of Tiananmen [Shen Tong and Wuer Kaixi] O. Schell. il pors *Rolling Stone* p185-8+ D 14-28 '89

The hopes of China [symposium] il *Mother Jones* 14:21-6+ D '89

New diplomacy by Fax Americana [broadcasting information to China via fax machine and telephone] S. V. Roberts. il *U.S. News & World Report* 106:32-4 Je 19 '89

Notes and comment [Chinese student recounts story of the Goddess of Democracy] il *The New Yorker* 65:43-4 O 23 '89

Notes and comment [views of Chinese journalists in the U.S. on student protests in China] *The New Yorker* 65:35-7 Je 12 '89

Economic conditions

Reborn in the U.S.A. [Baichun Xiao family] S. Seixas. il pors *Money* 18:64-6+ Ag '89

CHINESE AMERICAN RESTAURANTS *See* Restaurants, American

CHINESE AMERICAN SCIENTISTS *See* Scientists, Chinese American

CHINESE AMERICANS

See also
Chinatown (New York, N.Y.)
Chinatown (Seattle, Wash.)

Hawaii celebrates a Chinese bicentennial. *Sunset (Central West edition)* 182:66 F '89

Education

What price glory? [toll that high achievement takes on students; research by Stanley Sue] L. Troiano. il *American Health* 8:119 Mr '89

Political activities

A voice of hope for China [views of Nien Cheng] C. Reeve. il por *New Choices for the Best Years* 29:10 S '89

Religious life

Out of Chinatown and back again. W. N. Pang. il *Christianity Today* 33:29-31 Mr 3 '89

CHINESE AND BLACKS

"Beat the black devils!" [Chinese students march against African students in Nanjing] S. Burton. il *Time* 133:37 Ja 9 '89

China: 'Kill the black devils' [Chinese college students protest against African students in Nanjing] M. Beck. il *Newsweek* 113:35 Ja 9 '89

The fallout from Nanjing [continued anti-African demonstrations by Chinese students] M. S. Serrill. il *Time* 133:38 Ja 16 '89

More than just Chinese racism [anti-African demonstrations by Chinese students] R. Seidelman. il *The Nation* 248:195-6 F 13 '89

Not like here [New York Express break dancers touring China] *The New Yorker* 64:25-7 F 13 '89

The roots of racism are rubbed raw [Chinese college students protest against African students in Nanjing] il *U.S. News & World Report* 106:10-11 Ja 9 '89

CHINESE ASTRONOMY *See* Astronomy, Chinese

CHINESE CENSERS *See* Censers

CHINESE COOKING *See* Cooking, Chinese

CHINESE DEFECTORS *See* Defectors

CHINESE DISSENTERS *See* Dissenters

CHINESE FICTION

Bibliography

Stories from the Ice Age. J. Mirsky. bibl f il *The New York Review of Books* 36:27-8+ O 26 '89

CHINESE FOLK DANCE COMPANY
Companies on the East and West coasts keep their dance traditions alive: regional Chinese dance, American-style. N. Woronov. il *Dance Magazine* 63:28-30 Ag '89
CHINESE LACQUERWARE *See* Lacquer and lacquering
CHINESE LITERATURE
See also
Publishers and publishing—Chinese literature
Translations into English
Ballantine's new translations of Chinese classics. M. Wu. *Publishers Weekly* 236:58-9 O 6 '89
CHINESE MATHEMATICS *See* Mathematics, Chinese
CHINESE MEDICINE *See* Medicine, Chinese
CHINESE PAINTING *See* Painting, Chinese
CHINESE PEOPLE'S LIBERATION ARMY *See* China. People's Liberation Army
CHINESE POTTERY *See* Pottery, Chinese
CHINESE PROPAGANDA *See* Propaganda, Chinese
CHINESE REFUGEES *See* Refugees, Chinese
CHINESE ROOM THOUGHT EXPERIMENT
Artificial intelligence and the Chinese Room: an exchange [theories of J. Searle] E. Motzkin. il *The New York Review of Books* 36:44-5 F 16 '89
CHINESE SPACE VEHICLES *See* Space vehicles, Chinese
CHINESE STUDENTS IN CANADA *See* Foreign students—Canada
CHINESE STUDENTS IN THE UNITED STATES *See* Foreign students—United States
CHING, CYRUS S., 1876-1967
about
Cyrus S. Ching: pioneer in industrial peacemaking. A. H. Raskin. il *Monthly Labor Review* 112:22-35 Ag '89
CHING, JULIA
about
The Church in China [interview] P. H. Samway. *America* 160:374-6+ Ap 22 '89
CH'ING DYNASTY, 1644-1912 *See* China—History—Ch'ing dynasty, 1644-1912
CH'ING SHÊNG-TSU *See* K'ang-hsi, Emperor of China, 1654-1722
CHINKERS, MICHAEL, AND GARBERS, DAVID L.
The protein kinase domain of the ANP receptor is required for signaling. bibl f il *Science* 245:1392-4 S 22 '89
CHINMOY, SRI
about
Not explainable. *The New Yorker* 65:25-7 F 27 '89
CHINOOK SALMON FISHING *See* Salmon fishing
CHINZAN-SO (EDGEWATER, N.J.: RESTAURANT) *See* Edgewater (N.J.)—Restaurants, nightclubs, bars, etc.
CHIP CARDS *See* Smart cards
CHIP CIRCUIT COPYRIGHT *See* Copyright—Integrated circuits
CHIP CIRCUITS *See* Integrated circuits
CHIPAUX, FRANÇOISE
Islam in Syria and Iraq. *World Press Review* 36:32 Jl '89
CHIPKIN, HARVEY
Monuments to millions. il *Harper's Bazaar* 122:104+ O '89
CHIPLEY (GA.) *See* Pine Mountain (Ga.)
CHIPMUNKS
Alice and the chipmunk. J. M. Laskas. *Reader's Digest* 134:107-8 My '89
CHIPPERS, GARDEN *See* Garden equipment
CHIPPEWA INDIANS
Mississippi of the North [protests over fishing rights in Wisconsin] D. Parmentier. il por *The Humanist* 49:17-19+ S/O '89
Spearing fish, playing 'chicken' [confrontation over fishing rights in Wisconsin] J. Oberly. il *The Nation* 248:844-5+ Je 19 '89
State of the Band, January 14, 1989 [Mille Lacs Chippewa Band; address] A. Gashbow. *Vital Speeches of the Day* 55:409-13 Ap 15 '89
The Wisconsin fishing war [spearfishing] il *Sports Illustrated* 70:16 My 15 '89
CHIPS AND TECHNOLOGIES, INC.
Making time a commodity [G. Campbell] S. R. Reed. por *Personal Computing* 13:81 Jl '89
CHIRAC, JACQUES, 1932-
The same rights for all, East and West. *World Press Review* 36:18 D '89
Soviet change and Western security. *Current (Washington, D.C.)* 315:27-32 S '89
CHIROPRACTIC
Public opinion
Inside chiropractic [survey results] G. Maleskey. il *Prevention (Emmaus, Pa.)* 41:60-4 O '89
CHISEL PLOWING *See* Tillage
CHISMAN, FORREST, 1944-
The federal role in adult literacy. *The Education Digest* 55:11-14 O '89
CHISWICK HOUSE (MIDDLESEX, ENGLAND)
Chiswick House—polishing a family jewel. A. R. B. C. Devonshire, 11th Duke of. il *Architectural Digest* 46:28+ Ag '89
CHITIN
See also
Chitosan

A chitin-binding lectin from stinging nettle rhizomes with antifungal properties. W. F. Broekaert and others. bibl f il *Science* 245:1100-2 S 8 '89
CHITOSAN
Crab-shell derivative retards rancidity [chitosan compound, NCMC, developed by John R. Vercellotti and Allen J. St. Angelo] J. Raloff. *Science News* 136:189 S 16 '89
CHITTENDEN, MARGARET
Writing the romantic novel you'd like to read. *The Writer* 102:19-21 Ap '89
CHITTICK, WILLIAM, AND CLAWSON, PATRICK
A love poem. *The New Republic* 201:35 S 4 '89
CHITTISTER, JOAN
How to find God here, there, and everywhere. il *U.S. Catholic* 54:6-7 F '89
CHLAMYDIA INFECTIONS
Diagnosis
Quick new test for chlamydia. *Prevention (Emmaus, Pa.)* 41:18+ My '89
CHLOÉ (FIRM)
Paris originals [work of M. Sitbon] M. Gross. il por *New York* 22:28+ My 15 '89
CHLORAMPHENICOL
Two veterinarians guilty in antibiotic case [W. A. Jacobs and S. S. Takhar] M. Segal. il *FDA Consumer* 23:33-4 N '89
CHLORIDE CHANNELS
Acetylcholine and GABA mediate opposing actions on neuronal chloride channels in crayfish. C. Pfeiffer-Linn and R. M. Glantz. bibl f il *Science* 245:1249-51 S 15 '89
Activation of apical chloride channels in the gastric oxyntic cell. J. R. Demarest and others. bibl f il *Science* 245:402-4 Jl 28 '89
Autonomic regulation of a chloride current in heart. R. D. Harvey and J. R. Hume. bibl f il *Science* 244:983-5 My 26 '89
Blood cells yield cystic fibrosis clues [cyclic adenosine monophosphate-regulated chloride channel in lymphocytes; research by Jennifer H. Chen and others] *Science News* 135:110 F 18 '89
A cAMP-regulated chloride channel in lymphocytes that is affected in cystic fibrosis. J. H. Chen and others. bibl f il *Science* 243:657-60 F 3 '89
Cl⁻ channels in CF: lack of activation by protein kinase C and cAMP-dependent protein kinase. T.-C. Hwang and others. bibl f il *Science* 244:1351-3 Je 16 '89
Is regulation of a chloride channel in lymphocytes affected in cystic fibrosis? [discussion of February 3, 1989 article, A cAMP-regulated chloride channel in lymphocytes that is affected in cystic fibrosis] J. H. Chen and others. *Science* 246:1049-50 N 24 '89
Persistence of abnormal chloride conductance regulation in transformed cystic fibrosis epithelia. A. M. Jetten and others. bibl f il *Science* 244:1472-5 Je 23 '89
Purification and reconstitution of chloride channels from kidney and trachea [plasma membranes] D. W. Landry and others. bibl f il *Science* 244:1469-72 Je 23 '89
Regulation of chloride channels by protein kinase C in normal and cystic fibrosis airway epithelia. M. Li and others. bibl f il *Science* 244:1353-6 Je 16 '89
CHLORIDES
See also
Carbon tetrachloride
CHLORINATION OF WATER
Can chlorine cause cancer? [views of Richard J. Bull] *USA Today (Periodical)* 117:14-16 F '89
Chlorination: residues cloud water safety. J. Raloff. *Science News* 135:342 Je 3 '89
CHLORINE
See also
Chlorination of water
CHLORINE COMPOUNDS
See also
Organochlorine compounds
CHLORINE MONOXIDE
Rate of formation of the ClO dimer in the polar stratosphere: implications for ozone loss. S. P. Sander and others. bibl f il *Science* 245:1095-8 S 8 '89
CHLOROFLUOROCARBONS
See also
Hydrochlorofluorocarbons
Call for strong ozone protection [Helsinki declaration] *Science News* 135:367 Je 10 '89
Can we repair the sky? [chlorofluorocarbons and the ozone shield] il *Consumer Reports* 54:322-6 My '89
Cooling out in your car [Freon substitute for air conditioners] W. J. Cook. il *U.S. News & World Report* 107:82 N 6 '89
Deadly danger in a spray can. M. D. Lemonick. il *Time* 133:42 Ja 2 '89
Economics of preserving the ozone layer [views of Douglas G. Cogan] il *The Futurist* 23:40-1 Ja/F '89
Europe recognizes the ozone threat [banning of chlorofluorocarbons] D. Dickson and E. Marshall. *Science* 243:1279 Mr 10 '89
Europe to ban CFCs by 2000. *Science News* 135:148 Mr 11 '89

CHLOROFLUOROCARBONS—*cont.*

First aid for the ozone layer [European Community agrees to ban CFCs] M. D. Lemonick. il *Time* 133:50 Mr 13 '89

Getting by without CFC's. A. Wilson. il *The Mother Earth News* 120:110-14+ N/D '89

Good news for greenhouse worriers [research by James Hansen] *Science News* 136:367 D 2 '89

Highest disregard [use of CFCs by the electronics industry] D. Hayes. il *Mother Jones* 14:32-6+ D '89

Just when the ozone war looked winnable . . . V. Cahan. il *Business Week* p56 Je 12 '89

The man who knew too much [S. Rowland] E. Edelson. il por *Popular Science* 234:60-5+ Ja '89

My adventures in the ozone layer. S. F. Singer. *National Review* 41:34-8 Je 30 '89

Ozone defense [Helsinki accord calls for ban on certain chlorofluorocarbons] il *Time* 133:63 My 15 '89

Ozone hole's reappearance linked to chlorofluorocarbons [data of Total Ozone Mapping Spectrometer on Nimbus 7 satellite] il *Aviation Week & Space Technology* 131:28 O 30 '89

The poles in peril [ozone layer] R. Dolphin. *Maclean's* 102:50 F 27 '89

Potential replacement for ozone killer [development of chemical blend by Du Pont] *Science News* 135:94 F 11 '89

Saving the ozone layer; Ozone depletion worsens. il *UN Chronicle* 26:70-1 Je '89

The sky is the limit [ozone hole] J. Bowermaster. *Harper's Bazaar* 122:65+ Jl '89

The sky's the limit [foam insulation boards] C. Pearson. il *Architectural Record* 177:134-5 O '89

Total ban asked on ozone-killing chemicals [Helsinki declaration] il *UN Chronicle* 26:56-7 S '89

Try convertibles [ban on auto air conditioners that use CFCs in Vermont] *Time* 133:92 My 22 '89

The two faces of ozone. R. Monastersky. il *Science News* 136:154-5 S 2 '89

Unpopular packaging [Canadians protest chlorofluorocarbons] M. Nichols. *Maclean's* 102:51 D 25 '89

Upstairs, downstairs—the ozone dilemma. B. Hogan and B. Allen. il *The Conservationist* 44:16-21 N/D '89

A worse fridge [effect of ban] J. W. Merline. *Consumers' Research Magazine* 72:38 D '89

CHLOROPHYLL
See also
Chloroplasts

CHLOROPICRIN
U.S. physicians probe deaths in Soviet Georgia [use of riot control agent chloropicrin by Soviet troops] C. Norman. il *Science* 244:1133 Je 9 '89

CHLOROPLASTS
Knotty evolutionary tree in plant world [Prochlorothrix] R. Monastersky. *Science News* 135:71 F 4 '89

The manganese site of the photosynthetic water-splitting enzyme. G. N. George and others. bibl f il *Science* 243:789-91 F 10 '89

CHLOROSIS (PLANTS)
Iron deficiency. L. A. Weathers. il *Southern Living* 24:62 My '89

Plant metabolic responses to iron-deficiency stress. J. C. Brown and V. D. Jolley. bibl f il *BioScience* 39:546-51 S '89

CHMELKA, B. F., AND PINES, A.
Some developments in nuclear magnetic resonance of solids [cover story] bibl f il *Science* 246:71-7 O 6 '89

CHOATE, JUDITH, 1940-, AND GREEN, JANE
Special deliveries [excerpt from The gift-giver's cookbook] il *Health (New York, N.Y.)* 21:80-3+ N '89

CHOCK FULL O'NUTS CORPORATION
From takeout to takeover target. il *Money* 18:7 My '89

CHOCOLAT [film] See Motion picture reviews—Single works

CHOCOLATE
See also
Cooking—Chocolate
Du Rhône Chocolatier
Godiva Chocolatier
Hershey Foods Corp.
Candy man [S. Nekos makes Easter chocolates at the Nekos Pharmacy in Kingston, N.Y.] *The New Yorker* 65:34-5 Mr 27 '89

Lace eggs [white chocolate with mousse filling] il *Sunset (Central West edition)* 182:158 Mr '89

Terminology
Chocolate glossary. *Better Homes and Gardens* 67:159 O '89

CHOCOLATE CAKE See Cake
CHOCOLATE CHIP COOKIES See Cookies
CHOCOLATE DESSERTS See Desserts
CHOCOLATE MILK ART GALLERY
Chocolate Milk. *The New Yorker* 65:25-6 Ag 14 '89

CHOCOLATE STORES
See also
Fudge Factory (Firm)
La Maison du Chocolat (Firm)

THE CHOCOLATE WAR [film] See Motion picture reviews—Single works

CHOCTAW INDIANS
Choctaw with a mission [activist B. Carnes in Oklahoma] G. S. Phillips. il por *The Progressive* 53:14-15 Jl '89

CHOI, DENNIS W.
(jt. auth) See Weiss, John H., and Choi, Dennis W.

CHOICE (PSYCHOLOGY)
See also
Decision making
Risk taking (Psychology)
A chicken sexer's tough choices. G. K. Brushaber. il *Christianity Today* 33:13 Ap 7 '89

An economic animal [use of rats to test economic theories; work of John H. Kagel and Raymond C. Battalio] E. Corcoran. *Scientific American* 260:73 Mr '89

CHOICE OF COLLEGE See College choice
CHOICE OF SCHOOL See School choice
CHOIRS
Choir director Joyce Garrett battles D.C.'s mean streets with the power of positive singing [Eastern High School choir] R. Arias. il por *People Weekly* 31:99-100 Je 12 '89

Song of Eastern High [J. Garrett prepares high school choir in Washington, D.C. for International Youth and Music Festival] K. McCabe. il *Reader's Digest* 135:51-6 S '89

CHOJNA, BOGDAN
about
Have I got a deal for you. K. Wandycz. il por *Forbes* 144:44-5 O 2 '89

CHOKES, SHOTGUN See Shotguns—Chokes
CHOKING
See also
Heimlich maneuver
Choking prevention. K. K. Gracey. *Consumers' Research Magazine* 72:2 Ap '89

CHOL, ANGELO
about
One teen's bout with hunger. E. Whitford. il por *Scholastic Update (Teachers' edition)* 121:3 Ja 27 '89

CHOLAME (CALIF.)
Monuments, statues, etc.
Obsessed by James Dean, Japan's Seita Onishi makes a monument to that fallen rebel his cause. il por *People Weekly* 32:66-7 Ag 7 '89

CHOLECYSTOKININ
New treatment for bulimia [research by Thomas D. Geracioti and Rodger A. Liddle] A. H. Rosenfeld. il *Psychology Today* 23:28 Mr '89

Pigging out [blocking cholecystokinin in pigs increases appetite; work of Jerome Pekas] *Discover* 10:20 My '89

Why you can—or can't—eat another bite [role in regulating appetite] C. Hacinli. il *Mademoiselle* 95:96+ Jl '89

CHOLECYSTOKININ RECEPTORS See Hormone receptors
CHOLERA
Vaccines and vaccination
Immune response to cholera toxin epitope inserted in Salmonella flagellin. S. M. C. Newton and others. bibl f il *Science* 244:70-2 Ap 7 '89

CHOLERA TOXIN
Immune response to cholera toxin epitope inserted in Salmonella flagellin. S. M. C. Newton and others. bibl f il *Science* 244:70-2 Ap 7 '89

Role of prostaglandins and cAMP in the secretory effects of cholera toxin. J. W. Peterson and L. G. Ochoa. bibl f il *Science* 245:857-9 Ag 25 '89

CHOLESTEROL
A 30-day plan to lower your cholesterol. A. Ulene. il por *Good Housekeeping* 208:77+ Mr '89

All about your cholesterol numbers [excerpt from Good fat, bad fat] G. C. Griffin and W. P. Castelli. il *Prevention (Emmaus, Pa.)* 41:55-9 Mr '89

Australian convicted in 'Cho Low' fraud [P. Foster's mail order scheme selling Chinese tea to lower cholesterol] il por *FDA Consumer* 23:35 D '89/Ja '90

The battle against heart disease begins with children. il *The Saturday Evening Post* 261:12-13+ S '89

Behind the battle over cholesterol. S. Gannes. il *Fortune* 120:101+ D 18 '89

Beyond oat bran [rice bran] il *Prevention (Emmaus, Pa.)* 41:12+ Je '89

Blood pressure is rising in the cholesterol debate. N. J. Freundlich. il *Business Week* p128 O 9 '89

The breakfast drug [FDA reviews use of psyllium in cereal to determine if it is a food or drug] J. Newman. *American Health* 8:82+ D '89

Building a low-fat kid. J. Poppy. il *Esquire* 112:93-5 N '89

Can cereal cut cholesterol levels? il *Consumer Reports* 54:646 O '89

Cancer roadblock on cholesterol pathway [research by William R. Schafer] R. Cowen. *Science News* 136:70-1 Jl 29 '89

Cholesterol and your family. R. E. Kowalski. il por *Parents* 64:169+ O '89

Cholesterol checks for children? J. Carey. il *U.S. News & World Report* 106:74 Ap 24 '89

Cholesterol confusion [views of T. J. Moore] G. Cowley. il *Newsweek* 114:68-9 S 18 '89

Cholesterol control: your guide to a healthy heart. B. Weinhouse. il *Ladies' Home Journal* 106:83+ My '89

CHOLESTEROL—*cont.*

The cholesterol myth [excerpt from Heart failure; cover story] T. J. Moore. il *The Atlantic* 264:37-40+ S '89

Cholesterol quiz. il *FDA Consumer* 23:39 F '89

Coffee alert: decaf brews raise cholesterol. *Time* 134:56 N 27 '89

Cook away your cholesterol. J. B. Hurley. il *Prevention (Emmaus, Pa.)* 41:83-4+ S '89

Cookies the heart can love [foodmakers replace tropical oils with less saturated fats] A. Toufexis. il *Time* 133:71 Ja 23 '89

Crazy about oat bran. D. Tonnessen. il *Health (New York, N.Y.)* 21:32+ Ap '89

Cut your cholesterol 30 points in 30 days [eating oat bran and beans; research by James W. Anderson] A. Roblin. il *Prevention (Emmaus, Pa.)* 41:36-7+ F '89

Decaf coffee: the cholesterol connection. *Newsweek* 114:78 N 27 '89

Diabetic diet [use of olive oil to lower cholesterol; research by Abhimanyu Garg] il *Prevention (Emmaus, Pa.)* 41:10 Ja '89

Diuretic dilemma [Swedish study] *Time* 134:103 O 9 '89

Do you know your cholesterol level? D. Blumenthal. il *FDA Consumer* 23:24-7 Mr '89

Do you know your HDL? J. Raloff. il *Science News* 136:171-3 S 9 '89

Does cholesterol screening help? *USA Today (Periodical)* 118:14 O '89

Does this cereal belong in the medicine cabinet? [P&G claims that General Mills' cholesterol-reducing Benefit is a drug; Metamucil also contains psyllium] R. Mitchell and others. il *Business Week* p22-3 Jl 24 '89

Don't go back to butter [views of T. Moore] A. Purvis. il *Time* 134:108+ O 9 '89

The egg news is scrambled. J. Seligmann. il *Newsweek* 113:60 My 29 '89

The egg scramble [lowered cholesterol eggs] S. McKee. il *American Health* 8:132 S '89

Egging on cholesterol-wary diners [research by Gary R. Beecher] *Science News* 135:349 Je 3 '89

An egg's an egg, but slightly less so. J. Silberner. il *U.S. News & World Report* 106:61 Je 5 '89

Eggs . . . reconsidered. il *Glamour* 87:360 Ap '89

The enigma of cholesterol. N. Underwood. il *Maclean's* 102:55-6 O 9 '89

Face the fats. L. Applegate. il *Runner's World* 24:22+ Ag '89

Facts about kids and cholesterol; ed. by Florence Isaacs. J. H. Moller. il *Good Housekeeping* 209:101+ S '89

Fat blockers [role of heparin in cholesterol absorption; research by Louis Lange] *Discover* 10:18 N '89

Fats and figures. *World Tennis* 37:44-5 O '89

Fear of eggs. il *Consumer Reports* 54:650-2 O '89

Foods that fight cholesterol. A. Simon. il *The Saturday Evening Post* 261:30-2 Mr '89

Genetic and pharmacological suppression of oncogenic mutations in *RAS* genes of yeast and humans. W. R. Schafer and others. bibl f il *Science* 245:379-85 Jl 28 '89

The GH heart-healthy food book. il *Good Housekeeping* 208:191+ Je '89

Good food, good health: unscrambling the facts about eggs. B. Goldman. il *Better Homes and Gardens* 67:45-6 Ap '89

Have a heart [P. Sokolof's campaign against products using coconut and palm oils] S. J. Madden. il por *Fortune* 119:117+ Ja 16 '89

HDL at your finger tips [cholesterol screening] J. Ziegler. il *American Health* 8:14 D '89

Heart-healthy children. R. E. Kowalski. il *Parents* 64:177+ O '89

Heartfelt splash of olive oil. il *Prevention (Emmaus, Pa.)* 41:14+ O '89

High cholesterol in children. il *The Saturday Evening Post* 261:42-3 Ap '89

High cholesterol: the lowdown. il *Harper's Bazaar* 122:98+ F '89

High-fat diets that lower cholesterol [study by Jean T. Snook] J. Raloff. *Science News* 136:318 N 11 '89

Identification of a zinc finger protein that binds to the sterol regulatory element. T. B. Rajavashisth and others. bibl f il *Science* 245:640-3 Ag 11 '89

Japanese stroke clues [increased risk of cerebral hemorrhage from low cholesterol] K. Fackelmann. il *Science News* 135:250+ Ap 22 '89

Keeping your ticker running like clockwork. L. Zinn. il *Business Week* p114-15 My 29 '89

The lazy diet [reducing cholesterol without radical changes; research by Rita Dougherty] P. McCarthy. *American Health* 8:124+ Je '89

Life in the fats lane. C. Hacinli. *Mademoiselle* 95:98 Jl '89

Low cholesterol around the clock. C. Koury. il *Parents* 64:181-3+ O '89

Low-cholesterol eggs are coming. *USA Today (Periodical)* 117:13-14 Ap '89

A man with a mission—and millions to back it up—takes on brand name cholesterol [P. Sokolof's campaign against products using coconut and palm oils] il por *People Weekly* 31:112 F 6 '89

Meet apo A-I and apo B. *Prevention (Emmaus, Pa.)* 41:19-20 S '89

Mind over cholesterol [special section] bibl il *Psychology Today* 23:21+ S '89

Myocardial infraction? [interpretation of cholesterol studies] K. Wright. *Scientific American* 261:30 N '89

The new bran in town [effects of beta glucans found in rice bran] R. A. Barnett and M. Behen. *American Health* 8:101+ N '89

A new look at low-cholesterol diets. il *Prevention (Emmaus, Pa.)* 41:10 Je '89

The next wave of high-fiber grains [rice and corn bran] J. Silberner. il *U.S. News & World Report* 106:73 My 22 '89

The oat bran craze. B. T. Hunter. il *Consumers' Research Magazine* 72:8-9 Jl '89

Psyllium beats cholesterol. il *Prevention (Emmaus, Pa.)* 41:9-10 D '89

Revealing the finicky functions of fish oil. I. Wickelgren. *Science News* 135:183 Mr 25 '89

Rice bran recipes to lower cholesterol. il *The Saturday Evening Post* 261:92-3 Jl/Ag '89

Screening for the high risk. H. J. Ullmann. il *The Saturday Evening Post* 261:82-3+ Ja/F '89

Skinny eggs and other dream foods [low-cholesterol products] C. Hudson. il *Health (New York, N.Y.)* 21:30+ S '89

Smoker's "high" [smoking may increase levels] J. C. Horn. *American Health* 8:16+ Je '89

Splash on the olive oil and cut your cholesterol. A. Roblin. il *Prevention (Emmaus, Pa.)* 41:33-7 Ja '89

Stalking the goodness of corn. R. Rodale. il *Prevention (Emmaus, Pa.)* 41:23+ Ja '89

Taking aim at doctors' dire warnings, Thomas Moore triggers a cholesterol debate. M. H. J. Farrell. il pors *People Weekly* 32:125-6 N 13 '89

Taking oat bran to heart. J. W. Anderson. il *The Saturday Evening Post* 261:18+ Jl/Ag '89

Toasting good health [bran muffins and breads] J. B. Hurley. il *Prevention (Emmaus, Pa.)* 41:67-70+ O '89

Too little cholesterol? [HDL levels] *Prevention (Emmaus, Pa.)* 41:16 My '89

The truth about cholesterol. *McCall's* 117:94 O '89

The truth about cholesterol [cover story] S. Findlay and J. Silberner. il *U.S. News & World Report* 107:82-5+ N 27 '89

Try a healthier way of cooking [excerpt from The American Heart Association low-fat, low-cholesterol cookbook] S. M. Grundy. *Redbook* 173:16 Ag '89

Turning up the dirt in cholesterol screens [unsafe public cholesterol screenings; report by Richard P. Kusserow] D. E. Loupe. *Science News* 136:359 D 2 '89

The ups and downs of your cholesterol. G. L. Blackburn. il *Prevention (Emmaus, Pa.)* 41:108+ S '89

The use of palm and coconut oils in America's food has triggered a debate that is as much about politics as it is about health. L. M. Kase. *Vogue* 179:150+ Je '89

What's your HDL level? [guidelines] L. Husten. il *American Health* 8:20 Ap '89

Working women take one benefit to heart [higher HDL cholesterol than non-working women in West Germany; study by Ursula Haertel] K. Fackelmann. *Science News* 135:389 Je 24 '89

CHOLESTYRAMINE

Candy-coated cholesterol cutter. M. Behen. il *American Health* 8:18+ Jl/Ag '89

CHOLINE

See also
Acetylcholine

CHOLINERGIC NEURONS *See* Nerve cells

CHOMNIAK, STEVEN

Build a backyard observatory. il *Astronomy* 17:90-4 Je '89

CHONDRITES *See* Meteorites

CHONDRODYSPLASIA

Identification of the molecular defect in a family with spondyloepiphyseal dysplasia. B. Lee and others. bibl f il *Science* 244:978-80 My 26 '89

CHOO, QUI-LIM, AND OTHERS

Isolation of a cDNA clone derived from a blood-borne non-A, non-B viral hepatitis genome. bibl f il *Science* 244:359-62 Ap 21 '89

CHOP (TERM)

Chop on, chop at, chop-chop. W. Safire. il *The New York Times Magazine* p22+ N 12 '89

CHOPP, REBECCA S., 1952-

Palm Sunday Christianity. *The Christian Century* 106:277-8 Mr 15 '89

CHORAL GROUPS AND SOCIETIES

See also
Boys Choir of Harlem
Choirs
Collegiate Chorale
New Amsterdam Singers
Pro Arte Chorale and Orchestra
Red Army Chorus

CHORAL GROUPS AND SOCIETIES—See also—*cont.*
Sine Nomine Singers
Tallis Scholars (Musical group)
CHOREOGRAPHERS
See also
Ailey, Alvin
Balanchine, George, 1904-1983
Brown, Trisha
Clark, Michael
Cunningham, Merce
Duncan, Jeff, 1930-1989
Feld, Eliot
Forsythe, William
Goleizovsky, Kasyan
Goode, Joe
Hawkins, Erick
Holder, Geoffrey
Hu, Jia-lu
Jones, Bill T.
Kylián, Jiři
Lopukhov, Fyodor Vasilievich, 1887?-1973
Morris, Mark
Patrelle, Francis
Robbins, Jerome
Russell, Paul
Shawn, Michael
Taylor, Paul, 1930-
Van Schayk, Toer
West, Daniel
Women choreographers
Zane, Arnie
Attitudes [posthumous fame] C. Barnes. il *Dance Magazine* 63:98 Je '89
Neoromanticism, men, and the eighties: dancing the difference. P. Kelly and O. Stuart. il *Dance Magazine* 63:34-8 Ja '89
West Coast show cases black choreographers. D. Gere. il *Dance Magazine* 63:16 N '89
CHOREOGRAPHY
See also
Dance notation
Conquering the elements: choreography on ice. S. C. Turner and R. Harris. il *Dance Magazine* 63:34-9 F '89
On six hundred thousand choreographers. M. Louis. *Dance Magazine* 63:102-3 D '89
Competitions
Chile launches choreography search. C. Hardy. il *Dance Magazine* 63:8+ Ja '89
CHORES
See also
Children's chores
CHORIONIC VILLI SAMPLING
The earliest prenatal test. P. A. Hillard. il *Parents* 64:151-2 Jl '89
Harbinger tests. M. Krance. il *American Health* 8:14 Jl/Ag '89
CHOROID PLEXUS *See* Brain
CHORON, GASTON
about
The collectors: neoclassical aesthetic: fashion designer Gaston Choron in Wiesbaden. D. H. Minassian. il por *Architectural Digest* 46:240-6+ Ap '89
A CHORUS OF DISAPPROVAL [film] See Motion picture reviews—Single works
CHOU, EN-LAI *See* Zhou Enlai, 1898-1976
CHOUINARD, YVON
about
The man is the message. F. Meeks. il por *Forbes* 143:148+ Ap 17 '89
CHOW, YEI CHING
about
A fast ride on Hong Kong's high-tech wave. D. J. Yang. il por *Business Week* p111 My 22 '89
CHOWDER
Super bowl. B. Shacochis. il *Gentlemen's Quarterly* 59:386+ Mr '89
CHOY, CHRISTINE
about
Who killed Vincent Chin? [film] Reviews
Mother Jones 14:54 Jl/Ag '89. D. Sachs
CHRÉTIEN, JEAN
about
Chrétien tests the pool. P. Kaihla. il por *Maclean's* 102:22 O 9 '89
Jean Chrétien's race for the fastest track. P. C. Newman. il *Maclean's* 102:28 Je 5 '89
The leaders in waiting. R. Laver. il pors *Maclean's* 102:10-12 Mr 6 '89
Ready to run. R. Laver. il por *Maclean's* 102:10-12 Je 26 '89
Anecdotes, facetiae, satire, etc.
All the comedy that's fit to print [delay in announcing leadership bid] A. Fotheringham. il *Maclean's* 102:112 N 20 '89
CHRIS-CRAFT INDUSTRIES, INC.
The thorn in Steve Ross's side [H. Siegel wants deal for his stake in Warner] R. Grover. il por *Business Week* p51 Ag 14 '89

CHRIST *See* Jesus Christ
CHRIST THE KING, FEAST OF *See* Jesus Christ the King, Feast of
CHRISTAKOS, CANDICE
about
Reviews:
C. Christakos at Nikolais/Louis ChoreoSpace, New York City. G. Solomons. *Dance Magazine* 63:68 O '89
CHRISTEN INDUSTRIES
Orders mounting for Huskys. il *Flying* 116:16 My '89
CHRISTENING *See* Baptism
CHRISTENSEN, CAREN
about
Saga of a business start-up (I). L. Washer. il pors *Working Woman* 14:45-6+ D '89
CHRISTENSEN, CORINE
about
The Bandler method. F. Clancy and H. Yorkshire. il pors *Mother Jones* 14:22-8+ F/Mr '89
CHRISTENSEN, HAROLD, 1904-1989
Obituary
Dance Magazine por 63:28 My '89. S. C. Steinberg
CHRISTENSEN, JOHN N., AND OTHERS
Rates of tectonometamorphic processes from rubidium and strontium isotopes in garnet. bibl f il *Science* 244:1465-9 Je 23 '89
CHRISTENSEN, JON
The wings of conservation. il *Sierra* 74:32-5 Ja/F '89
CHRISTENSEN, LILLIAN LANGSETH- *See* Langseth-Christensen, Lillian
CHRISTENSEN, MARILYN HOLM
"The teacher called me stupid, Mommy!". il *Redbook* 173:144-5+ O '89
CHRISTENSEN, NORMAN L., AND OTHERS
Interpreting the Yellowstone fires of 1988. bibl f il *BioScience* 39:678-85 N '89
CHRISTENSEN, TERRY N.
about
Hollywood's hottest hired gun. R. Grover. il por *Business Week* p132 N 13 '89
CHRISTENSEN, TIM
about
Battle to keep a bookstore in town. L. See. *Publishers Weekly* 236:66 S 1 '89
CHRISTENSEN, WHITE, MILLER, FINK & JACOBS
Hollywood's hottest hired gun [T. N. Christensen] R. Grover. il por *Business Week* p132 N 13 '89
CHRISTENSON, GARY D.
Why Joan Rivers and Betty White keep playing games. il *TV Guide* 37:10-12 Ja 14-20 '89
CHRISTIAN, FLETCHER, 1764-1793
about
Trouble in Christian's paradise. H. Shapiro. il por map *People Weekly* 31:42-9 Ap 17 '89
CHRISTIAN, MARC
about
Lovers, liars and other strangers. pors *Newsweek* 113:61 F 27 '89
The price of betrayal. P. Chin. il pors *People Weekly* 31:180-3 Mr 6 '89
CHRISTIAN, RICHARD S.
about
Obituary
Physics Today 42:98-100 Ja '89. F. T. Cole and others
CHRISTIAN, ROBERT
The aging of America [economic impact of baby boomers; address, June 21, 1989] *Vital Speeches of the Day* 56:29-32 O 15 '89
CHRISTIAN ART AND SYMBOLISM
See also
Church decoration and ornament
Icons
Jesus Christ—Crucifixion—Art
Votive sculpture
Africa's artistic resurrection. R. N. Ostling. il *Time* 133:76-9 Mr 27 '89
Holy art! [work of H. Finster] D. Handelman. il por *Rolling Stone* p64-6+ Ap 20 '89
The Protestant struggle with the image. D. Morgan. il *The Christian Century* 106:308-11 Mr 22-29 '89
Sacred arts [works of J. Schnabel and others] H. Muschamp. il por *Vogue* 179:420-5 Ap '89
CHRISTIAN BOOK PUBLISHING *See* Publishers and publishing—Religious literature
CHRISTIAN BOOKSELLERS ASSOCIATION
Belle, book and candle [annual convention] W. Griffin. il *Publishers Weekly* 236:15-16+ Ag 18 '89
Religious bestsellers. L. Sibley. *Publishers Weekly* 235:39 Mr 3 '89
CHRISTIAN BROADCASTING NETWORK, INC.
Planning ahead? [Washington, D.C. radio station WNTR purchased] V. Novak. il *Common Cause Magazine* 15:6 S/O '89
CHRISTIAN BROTHERS
Charges of a coverup [sexual and physical abuse at Mount Cashel Orphanage, St. John's, Nfld.] N. Underwood. *Maclean's* 102:66+ D 4 '89

CHRISTIAN BROTHERS—*cont.*
Scandal on the Rock [inquiry into sexual abuse involving Christian Brothers at Mount Cashel Orphanage, St. John's, Nfld.] N. Underwood. il *Maclean's* 102:61 O 2 '89
Sex and scandal [former resident S. Earle testifies about sexual abuse at Mount Cashel Orphanage, St. John's, Nfld.] N. Underwood. il por *Maclean's* 102:84 O 30 '89

CHRISTIAN CAMPS *See* Church camps

CHRISTIAN COLLEGES *See* Church colleges and universities

CHRISTIAN CONTEMPORARY MUSIC
The hymnal is not enough. C. H. Kraft. por *Christianity Today* 33:8 Ap 7 '89
Supermom Sandi Patti [cover story] H. G. Miller. il pors *The Saturday Evening Post* 261:44-5+ Ja/F '89
Wilderness reclamation [interview with R. Matthews] D. Coran. il por *Christianity Today* 33:63 D 15 '89

CHRISTIAN CONVERTS *See* Converts

CHRISTIAN DEMOCRATIC PARTY (ITALY)
Italy's DC recycles Forlani. S. F. Senigallia. il *The New Leader* 72:9-10 Mr 6 '89

CHRISTIAN DEMOCRATIC UNION (GERMANY: WEST)
Fighting off the beer-hall boys. N. Birnbaum. il *The Nation* 248:588-9+ My 1 '89
Kohl isn't quite out, but he sure is down. J. Templeman. il por *Business Week* p52 S 11 '89

CHRISTIAN DIOR (FIRM)
"Maybe I should have left sooner" [career of C. Nicholas] D. Machan. il pors *Forbes* 143:320+ My 29 '89

CHRISTIAN EDUCATION *See* Religious education

CHRISTIAN ETHICS
See also
Christianity and economics
Church and social problems
Clergy—Ethics
Humility
Love (Theology)
Righteousness
Sin
Sociology, Christian
Building a creative conscience [Catholic ethics]; tr. by Ingrid Knapp. B. Häring. il *Commonweal* 116:433-6 Ag 11 '89
Ethical issues and ecumenism. T. P. Rausch. *America* 160:30-3 Ja 21 '89
Fit for the reign of God. P. Perkins. il *The Christian Century* 106:618 Je 21-28 '89
Four stories that shape the Christian character. J. Shea. il *U.S. Catholic* 54:39-43 S '89
A matter of conscience. H. Fehren. *U.S. Catholic* 54:39-41 N '89
Morality vs. moralism [address, January 26, 1989] P. B. Henry. *Vital Speeches of the Day* 55:295-7 Mr 1 '89
Of many things [John Mahoney's The making of moral theology] G. W. Hunt. *America* 160:50 Ja 28 '89
Of many things [Richard A. McCormick's The critical calling: reflections on moral dilemmas since Vatican II] G. W. Hunt. *America* 161:178 S 30 '89
On Bernard Häring's new book. B. Häring. *America* 161:339-40 N 18 '89
A providential lesson on the need for rules. J. M. Wall. *The Christian Century* 106:611-12 Je 21-28 '89
Why "safe" is not enough. H. Smith. *Christianity Today* 33:15 F 3 '89

Bibliography
Practicing ethics & spirituality. L. Cunningham. *Commonweal* 116:572-4 O 20 '89

CHRISTIAN FEMINISM *See* Women and religion

CHRISTIAN GIVING
Give to beggars for Christ's sake [with readers' comments] E. Wojcicki. *U.S. Catholic* 54:14-20 Ap '89
Jubilee time. M. E. Marty. *The Christian Century* 106:999 N 1 '89

CHRISTIAN IDENTITY (MOVEMENT)
Lausanne group addresses anti-Semitism. il *Christianity Today* 33:56 Je 16 '89

CHRISTIAN LEADERS FOR RESPONSIBLE TELEVISION
Boycott targets TV sponsors. J. Maxwell. il *Christianity Today* 33:47-9 Ag 18 '89
Prime-time shoot-out. D. Neff. il *Christianity Today* 33:14 O 6 '89

CHRISTIAN LEADERSHIP
Data and mystery: a decade of studies on Catholic leadership [Lilly Foundation research] J. R. Kelly. *America* 161:345-6+ N 18 '89
Lay leadership in the 1990's [Catholic Church; cover story] E. C. Sellner. *America* 161:133-8 S 9-16 '89
On the margins of the Church: a sociological note [surveys of U.S. Catholics by ABC News and Gallup] A. M. Greeley. il *America* 160:194-5+ Mr 4 '89
Put faith back into management. L. Thompson. por *Christianity Today* 33:10 My 12 '89
A survey of research on Church life today [Lilly Endowment study of U.S. Catholic leaders] T. Schier. *America* 161:351-2 N 18 '89

CHRISTIAN LIFE
See also
Christian ethics
Faith
Humility

Prayer
A chicken sexer's tough choices. G. K. Brushaber. il *Christianity Today* 33:13 Ap 7 '89
Don't worry, be still. J. Garvey. il *Commonweal* 116:489-90 S 22 '89
The examined life. R. E. Burns. See issues of U.S. Catholic
Exchange of values [nature of discipleship] T. Sine. por *Christianity Today* 33:52 Mr 17 '89
The fear of insignificance. D. Taylor. il *Christianity Today* 33:25-6 F 3 '89
Have I done well? [excerpt from Tough questions Christians ask] D. Neff. il *Christianity Today* 33:22-8 F 17 '89
Living by the Word. See issues of The Christian Century beginning April 5, 1989
Q: Who made me? J. Garvey. *U.S. Catholic* 54:25-7 Jl '89
Reading life backwards. T. K. Jones. il *Christianity Today* 33:28-31 S 22 '89
Taking our lumps. M. E. Marty. *The Christian Century* 106:511 My 10 '89
The Word. P. J. Ryan. See issues of America beginning November 21, 1987

CHRISTIAN LITERATURE
See also
Publishers and publishing—Religious literature
Have Christian books been censored? [rejection by book reviewers] S. Charles. il *Publishers Weekly* 235:58 Mr 3 '89

Bibliography
Religious bestsellers [new list from Evangelical Christian Publishers Association and Christian Booksellers Association] L. Sibley. *Publishers Weekly* 235:39 Mr 3 '89
'Tis the season. L. Sibley. il *Christianity Today* 33:38-9 N 17 '89

CHRISTIAN LOVE *See* Love (Theology)

CHRISTIAN MISSIONS *See* Missions

CHRISTIAN RECONSTRUCTION MOVEMENT
The Reconstructionist Movement on the new Christian right [cover story] A. D. Shupe. *The Christian Century* 106:880-2 O 4 '89
The theonomic urge. R. Frame. il *Christianity Today* 33:38-40 Ap 21 '89

CHRISTIAN RENEWAL *See* Church renewal

CHRISTIAN SCHOOLS *See* Church schools

CHRISTIAN SCIENCE CHURCH *See* Church of Christ, Scientist

CHRISTIAN SCIENCE MONITOR
A conscientious objector [K. Fanning] R. Loth. il por *New Choices for the Best Years* 29:16+ S '89

CHRISTIAN SOCIOLOGY *See* Sociology, Christian

CHRISTIAN WITNESS *See* Witness bearing (Christianity)

CHRISTIANITY
See also
Bible
Catholicism
Christian ethics
Christian Reconstruction movement
Church
Church history
Ecumenical movement
Fundamentalism
God
Grace (Theology)
Homosexuality and Christianity
Jesus Christ
Kingdom of God
Prophecy (Christianity)
Sociology, Christian
Sunday
Theology
Christianity's future. S. L. Dunn. il por *The Futurist* 23:34-7 Mr/Ap '89
The new Christendom. *World Press Review* 36:33-4 Mr '89
Religion scorned. W. F. Buckley. *National Review* 41:55 Ap 21 '89

CHRISTIANITY AND AIDS (DISEASE) *See* AIDS (Disease)—Religious aspects

CHRISTIANITY AND CULTURE
Filling in the gaps of liberal culture [Robert Booth Fowler's Unconventional partners: religion and liberal culture in the United States] M. E. Marty. *The Christian Century* 106:1019-20+ N 8 '89
Impolite disenglobments [views of S. Hauerwas] M. E. Marty. *The Christian Century* 106:487 My 3 '89
Living in the new Dark Ages [excerpt from Against the night]; ed. by Ellen Santilli Vaughn. C. W. Colson. il *Christianity Today* 33:30-3 O 20 '89

CHRISTIANITY AND DEMOCRACY
We can't make it without religious values. M. Thatcher. il por *The Saturday Evening Post* 261:60-1 Jl/Ag '89

CHRISTIANITY AND ECONOMICS
Capitalism and technology in global perspective: a dispute [discussion of May 3, 1989 article, The theological challenge of globalization] M. L. Stackhouse. *The Christian Century* 106:690-3 Jl 19-26 '89
The centennial of Andrew Carnegie's "Gospel of wealth". J. M. McShane. *America* 161:211-13 O 7 '89

CHRISTIANITY AND ECONOMICS—*cont.*

Favor debt cancellation [U.S. Catholic bishops' statement on third world debt] *The Christian Century* 106:976-7 N 1 '89

Forgive us our debts . . . [third world] P. Henriot. *America* 161:420-2+ D 9 '89

How do we solve the global debt crisis? [statement by Interfaith Action for Economic Justice] J. W. Skillen. *The Christian Century* 106:1004-6 N 8 '89

It's not all that complicated [Relieving third world debt; a statement released by the U.S. bishops] *America* 161:263-4 O 28 '89

The last socialist? [John Paul II; cover story] J. Gray. il *National Review* 41:27-9+ Je 30 '89

"Let not the rich man boast of his riches" [R. Van Kampen] M. Berss. il por *Forbes* 144 Special Issue:44-6 O 23 '89

Liberals and Catholics: political economy in our time. M. Novak. *Current (Washington, D.C.)* 311:20-3 Mr/Ap '89

A 'new moon' sensitivity. L. O. Sanneh. *The Christian Century* 106:811 S 13-20 '89

The Pope of enterprise [John Paul II] M. Novak. il *Forbes* 143:70-1 Je 26 '89

Rich wisdom: New Testament teachings on wealth [cover story; special section] il *Christianity Today* 33:27-40 My 12 '89

Sharp dealing. P. J. Ryan. *America* 161:151 S 9-16 '89

Structures of interest, structures of love: a response to Michael Novak [discussion of January 28, 1989 article, Structures of virtue, structures of sin: a theology of natural liberty] M. Novak. *America* 160:369-71 Ap 22 '89

Structures of virtue, structures of sin: a theology of natural liberty [address, May 5, 1988; cover story] M. Novak. *America* 160:54-60 Ja 28 '89

Triple play [U.S. Catholic bishops' statement on third world debt] *Commonweal* 116:581-2 N 3 '89

Mexico

The great experiment [Living Bridges International arranges debt exchange with Catholic priest E. Gonzalez Torres] R. Bautch. *America* 160:316-17 Ap 8 '89

CHRISTIANITY AND HUMANISM

Death of a secular humanist. M. Rosenbaum. *The Christian Century* 106:167-8 F 15 '89

God and man in Buffalo [B. Graham and humanists contrasted in Buffalo, N.Y.; cover story] T. C. Muck. il por *Christianity Today* 33:21-6 Ja 13 '89

A humanistic approach toward religionists. T. E. Jones. *The Humanist* 49:25+ Ja/F '89

Humanists and theists. T. A. Webb. por *The Humanist* 49:18-20+ Jl/Ag '89

The never-ending fight. I. Asimov. il por *The Humanist* 49:7-8+ Mr/Ap '89

Reverend father [daughter of abusive minister] D. Loring. *The Humanist* 49:21-3+ Jl/Ag '89

CHRISTIANITY AND JUSTICE *See* Religion and justice

CHRISTIANITY AND LAW *See* Religion and law

CHRISTIANITY AND OCCULT SCIENCES *See* Christianity and occultism

CHRISTIANITY AND OCCULTISM

See also

Christianity and the New Age movement

Keeping an eye on the cults [Rockford Conference on Discernment and Evangelism] *Christianity Today* 33:50 N 17 '89

Salt substitutes. T. C. Muck. il *Christianity Today* 33:14-15 F 3 '89

CHRISTIANITY AND OTHER RELIGIONS

See also

Catholic Church—Relations—Judaism

International Christian Embassy Jerusalem (Organization)

International Jewish Committee on Interreligious Consultations

Lausanne Consultation on Jewish Evangelism

Catholics and Jews: can we bridge the abyss? [Holocaust martyr E. Stein; adaptation of address, October 16, 1988] S. M. Batzdorff. *America* 160:223-4+ Mr 11 '89

Christian claims in a pluralistic society. A. M. Watts. *The Christian Century* 106:222-3 Mr 1 '89

Christian fulfillment and Jewish-Christian dialogue. I. C. Rottenberg. *The Christian Century* 106:387-91 Ap 12 '89

The Church in China [interview with J. Ching and H. Küng] P. H. Samway. *America* 160:374-6+ Ap 22 '89

Close enough to step on toes: tensions between Jews & Catholics. L. Klenicki and E. D. Mallon. il *Commonweal* 116:521-6 O 6 '89

The dangers of dialogue [Christians and Jews] R. J. Neuhaus. *National Review* 41:38 Ag 18 '89

Document angers Jewish community [Willowbank Declaration on the Christian Gospel and the Jewish People] P. P. Wong. il *Christianity Today* 33:48 S 22 '89

Father Coughlin and the Jews: a broadcast remembered [justifying Kristallnacht] R. Modras. *America* 160:219-22 Mr 11 '89

God's true brew. J. Garvey. il *Commonweal* 116:231-2 Ap 21 '89

Good news from missionaries: God was already there [interview with J. Donders] por *U.S. Catholic* 54:26-33 Ja '89

Jews and Christians: striving to shape America's future. R. F. Thiemann. il *USA Today (Periodical)* 118:84-7 S '89

A lost chance to save the Jews? [failure of German Christianity] C. C. O'Brien. il *The New York Review of Books* 36:27-8+ Ap 27 '89

Missions and the translatable Gospel [L. Sanneh's Translating the message; cover story] J. B. Carman. *The Christian Century* 106:786+ Ag 30-S 6 '89

Moral heroes of our time: Christian rescuers [saving Jews under Nazism] E. Fogelman. *America* 161:426-8+ D 9 '89

New Jewish secretariat [forum for dialogue with Christian bodies] *The Christian Century* 106:873-4 O 4 '89

Offense and counter-offense [controversy over The satanic verses] E. D. Mallon. il *America* 160:327-9 Ap 8 '89

Righteous Gentiles. P. J. Ryan. il *America* 160:519 My 27 '89

Rushdie furor highlights the nature of Islamic faith [interview with S. Johnson] il pors *Christianity Today* 33:38-9 Ap 7 '89

Whither Israel? K. A. Lawton. il *Christianity Today* 33:57+ Ja 13 '89

CHRISTIANITY AND POLITICS *See* Religion and politics

CHRISTIANITY AND SEX *See* Sex and religion

CHRISTIANITY AND SOCIAL PROBLEMS *See* Church and social problems

CHRISTIANITY AND SOCIALISM *See* Socialism and religion

CHRISTIANITY AND TECHNOLOGY *See* Religion and technology

CHRISTIANITY AND THE ARTS *See* Arts and religion

CHRISTIANITY AND THE ENVIRONMENT *See* Religion and the environment

CHRISTIANITY AND THE NEW AGE MOVEMENT

Christianity today talks to Frank Peretti [author of Piercing the darkness] M. G. Maudlin. por *Christianity Today* 33:58-9 D 15 '89

Confronting the New Age. D. Groothuis. il *Christianity Today* 33:36-9 Ja 13 '89

The taming of a New Age prophet [M. Fox] R. Brow. il *Christianity Today* 33:28-30 Je 16 '89

CHRISTIANITY AND THE WORLD *See* Church and the world

CHRISTIANITY IN LITERATURE *See* Religion in literature

CHRISTIANITY TODAY (PERIODICAL)

Bad-news bearers [news stories on clergy scandals] L. Cryderman. il *Christianity Today* 33:12 Ap 21 '89

The CT brain trust. T. C. Muck. il *Christianity Today* 33:13 S 8 '89

CHRISTIANO, DONNA

Abortion: just the facts, not the hype. il *Glamour* 87:228-31 N '89

CHRISTIANS

Africa

The church in Africa [interview with T. Adeyemo] il por *Christianity Today* 33:52-3 O 20 '89

Cambodia

Christians face uncertain future in Cambodia. M. Adeney. il *Christianity Today* 33:48 N 3 '89

China

See also

Three-Self Movement (China)

The church seeks a new place in China. K. H. Sidey. il *Christianity Today* 33:55-6 S 8 '89

Communist crackdown worries Chinese church. K. H. Sidey. il *Christianity Today* 33:40-2 Jl 14 '89

Let a hundred lilies bloom. D. Elliott. il *Newsweek* 113:59 Ap 10 '89

Developing countries

The new Christendom. *World Press Review* 36:33-4 Mr '89

Eastern Europe

Echoes of *glasnost*. K. A. Lawton. il maps *Christianity Today* 33:26-8 O 20 '89

Ethiopia

New growth for Ethiopian church. il *Christianity Today* 33:51 O 6 '89

Germany

Angel of light [church's reaction to Hitler] T. Stafford. il *Christianity Today* 33:16-19 S 8 '89

A lost chance to save the Jews? [failure of German Christianity] C. C. O'Brien. il *The New York Review of Books* 36:27-8+ Ap 27 '89

Germany (East)

East Germans seek out 'free space'. J. M. Wall. *The Christian Century* 106:219-20 Mr 1 '89

Germany (West)

The German past and unusable churches. A. G. Roeber. *The Christian Century* 106:407-8 Ap 19 '89

The hazards of an unusable past. J. M. Wall. *The Christian Century* 106:195-6 F 22 '89

Haiti

Haitian Christians press on amid poverty, violence. D. Disch. il *Christianity Today* 33:46+ My 12 '89

Hong Kong

Exodus creates church leadership shortage. S. Mumper. il *Christianity Today* 33:42+ N 3 '89

Iran

Iranian Christians flee persecution [refuge in Pakistan] H. Martyn. *The Christian Century* 106:461-2 My 3 '89

CHRISTIANS—*cont.*

Israel

An elusive peace. K. A. Lawton. il *Christianity Today* 33:34-6 Ap 21 '89

No taxation without representation [Palestinian Christians] M. Ward. *America* 161:464-5 D 23-30 '89

Palestinian Christians join intifada tax protest. L. Cryderman. il por *Christianity Today* 33:42 D 15 '89

Korea (North)

Pastors given rare glimpse of North Korea [Korean-American Southern Baptist pastors attend Easter service] D. Burton. *Christianity Today* 33:63 Je 16 '89

Lebanon

Lebanon's last battle? K. H. Sidey. *Christianity Today* 33:46-8 Je 16 '89

Middle East

See also

Middle East Council of Churches

Nicaragua

One Nicaraguan Christian's perspective [interview with G. Parajón] por *Christianity Today* 33:48 Mr 3 '89

Paraguay

Church leaders greet coup with hope, prayer. A. L. Sherman. il *Christianity Today* 33:48 Mr 17 '89

Soviet Union

Believers push forward despite legal limbo. K. A. Lawton. il *Christianity Today* 33:63-4+ N 17 '89

Cross meets Kremlin. R. N. Ostling. il pors *Time* 134:74-6 D 4 '89

In solitary cells on winter nights [interview with I. Ratushinskaya and I. Geraschenko] E. S. Vaughn. il pors *Christianity Today* 33:26-9 D 15 '89

New U.S. policy may stem flow of Soviet Christians. il *Christianity Today* 33:52+ N 3 '89

The Pope and the pol. K. L. Woodward. il pors *Newsweek* 114:87-90 D 4 '89

Russian revolution? A. Deyneka and P. Deyneka. il *Christianity Today* 33:22-5 O 20 '89

Soviet exodus strains church resources. K. A. Lawton. il *Christianity Today* 33:50 Je 16 '89

U.S. denies refugee status to Soviets. il *Christianity Today* 33:58 Mr 3 '89

WCC takes its agenda to the Soviet Union. M. VanElderen. *The Christian Century* 106:773-5 Ag 30-S 6 '89

Turkey

Believers in Turkey claim their legal rights. B. G. Baker. il *Christianity Today* 33:44 Ap 7 '89

United States

So little change, so much difference [Andrew Greeley's Religious indicators 1940-1985] R. J. Neuhaus. *National Review* 41:20 Mr 24 '89

Vietnam

Vietnam's doi moi could help Christians. R. Reimer. *Christianity Today* 33:48-9 N 3 '89

CHRISTIANS AND JEWS *See* Christianity and other religions

CHRISTIANS AND MUSLIMS *See* Christianity and other religions

CHRISTIANS FOR BIBLICAL EQUALITY (ORGANIZATION) *See* Men, Women and God: Christians for Biblical Equality (Organization)

CHRISTIC INSTITUTE

Christic Institute woes [ordered to pay legal fees to defendants in conspiracy suit] *The Christian Century* 106:224 Mr 1 '89

Media campaigns in the courts [ordered to pay defendants' costs in conspiracy suit] *National Review* 41:13-14 Mr 10 '89

CHRISTIC INSTITUTE SOUTH

Love takes you a long way [activist lawyer L. Pitts] W. H. Willimon. *The Christian Century* 106:460-1 My 3 '89

CHRISTIE, GEORGE A.

Construction economy outlook: three roads to more volume. il por *Architectural Record* 177:37+ N '89

Construction economy update: a kind and gentle letdown in 1988 leads to the seeds of a possible turnaround in 1990 [with editorial comment by Mildred F. Schmertz] il *Architectural Record* 177:5, 25+ Ap '89

Construction economy update: a smaller-than-expected step backward. il *Architectural Record* 177:33+ S '89

CHRISTIE, MACDONALD J., AND OTHERS

Expression of a cloned rat brain potassium channel in Xenopus oocytes. bibl f il *Science* 244:221-4 Ap 14 '89

CHRISTIE, WILLIAM

about

Flourishing Arts. M. Swed. il *Opera News* 53:20+ My '89

CHRISTIE-BLICK, NICHOLAS

(jt. auth) See Levy, Marjorie, and Christie-Blick, Nicholas

CHRISTIE'S (LONDON, ENGLAND)

The $430-million week [auctions of contemporary and impressionist paintings] B. B. Stretch. il *Art News* 88:25 Ja '89

Christie's sale a success [auction of contemporary ceramics and glass] il *American Craft* 49:12 Ap/My '89

Director Billy Wilder puts his legendary $22 million-or-so art collection on the auction block. S. K. Reed. il pors *People Weekly* 32:154+ N 13 '89

The pleasure of the chase [auction of S. Wagstaff's silver collection] C. McGuigan. il pors *Newsweek* 113:62-3 Ja 30 '89

CHRISTINA *See* Scholl, Rochelle

CHRISTMAN, CATHERINE

Kitchen-counter intelligence. il *New Choices for the Best Years* 29:75+ My '89

Travel take-alongs. il *New Choices for the Best Years* 29:84+ Ag '89

CHRISTMAS, JUNE JACKSON, AND CHRISTMAS, RACHEL J.

Getting help. *Essence* 20:52+ Je '89

CHRISTMAS, RACHEL J.

The Caribbean & Bahamas: beaches & beyond. il *Travel Holiday* 171:25-6+ Ap '89

Clubhouse comfort. il *Black Enterprise* 19:72+ Mr '89

Steal away to Sagamore. il *Black Enterprise* 19:62-3 Ja '89

Trips for teens. il *Essence* 19:22+ Ja '89

Walk this way. il *Black Enterprise* 19:117-18 My '89

(jt. auth) See Christmas, June Jackson, and Christmas, Rachel J.

CHRISTMAS

See also

Advent

Children and Christmas

Jesus Christ—Nativity

Rudolph the Red-Nosed Reindeer (Fictional character)

Santa Claus

Television broadcasting—Christmas programs

Across the editor's desk [memorable childhood Christmas on the farm] L. J. Kruse. il *Successful Farming* 87:2 D '89

The best gifts you can give: choose from this lovely assortment of intangibles. J. Stone. il *Glamour* 87:116 D '89

Bethlehem on a budget. T. Stafford. il *Christianity Today* 33:34-5 D 15 '89

Bethlehem today [delivering a baby in apartment of impoverished immigrant family in Chicago on Christmas] K. P. Glynn. il *America* 161:441-2 D 16 '89

Bring home the joy! [tradition] E. Byron. il *Redbook* 174:118-19+ D '89

A calendar meditation: Christmas 1989. T. H. Stahel. *America* 161:439 D 16 '89

Celebrate a Kentucky Christmas. J. T. Black. il map *Southern Living* 24:40+ D '89

Christmas 1888 in 1988 [Western States] il *Sunset (Central West edition)* 181:62-5 D '88

A Christmas alphabet [excerpt] C. Wells. il *Good Housekeeping* 209:148-51 D '89

Christmas in July. T. Peters. il *The Mother Earth News* 120:10 N/D '89

Christmas in the Upcountry [museum houses in South Carolina] C. Engle. il *Southern Living* 24:64-8+ D '89

Christmas meant football and turkey—and a swig o' cranberry bog; ed. by Herma M. Rosenthal. W. Marsalis. il pors *TV Guide* 37:12-14 D 16-22 '89

Christmas wonders. J. Shea. il *U.S. Catholic* 54:20-5 D '89

December's stickiest situations. il *Glamour* 87:69 D '89

Dickens to Dungeness: Fisherman's Wharf holiday doings. il *Sunset (Central West edition)* 181:16-18 D '88

Energy up—stress-level down! [excerpt from Positive living and health] il *Redbook* 174:126-7+ D '89

Finding Christmas. G. Logsdon. il *Country Journal* 16:82-7 N/D '89

The gifts heaven sent: five true stories to touch your heart. G. Kopecky. il *Redbook* 174:108-9+ D '89

Gifts that go on giving [Festival of Trees] *Southern Living* 24:43 D '89

Hassle-free holidays. A. Arnott. il *Home Mechanix* 85:52-3 D '89

Holiday harmony. G. Schwartz. *Seventeen* 48:42 D '89

Holiday stress [results of poll] I. Groller. il *Parents* 64:33 D '89

Holiday visits: home is where the guilt is [adult daughters] E. Welty. *Mademoiselle* 95:102 D '89

How celebrities will celebrate Christmas. R. D. Turner. il *Ebony* 45:31-2+ D '89

If there is no God, then Scrooge was right. J. M. Wall. *The Christian Century* 106:1163-4 D 13 '89

Interfaith anxiety [Jewish-gentile marriages face Christmas and Hanukkah] il *Psychology Today* 22:6+ D '88

K.C.'s Christmas is in the cards [Kansas City] W. Mueller. il *The Saturday Evening Post* 261:82-5 N/D '89

Light from light. P. J. Ryan. il *America* 161:459 D 16 '89

Lighting the way to Christmas [San Antonio] il *Southern Living* 24:35 D '89

My holiday memories [former patients] E. E. Rosenbaum. il *New Choices for the Best Years* 29:90+ D '89

A New Orleans Noel. E. Laborde. il *New Choices for the Best Years* 29:19-24 D '89

Newport in winter. C. Davidson. il *American Heritage* 40:33+ D '89

Once upon a Christmas [excerpt from Christmas gift!] F. Sams. il *Good Housekeeping* 209:172-3+ D '89

People who work on Christmas. il *Good Housekeeping* 209:106+ D '89

Physics and Christmas. *National Review* 41:15 D 31 '89

Rebel without a Claus [college freshman returns home] B. Stepko. il *Seventeen* 48:44+ D '89

Rejoice! S. L. Taylor. il *Essence* 20:49 D '89

CHRISTMAS—cont.

The spirit of Christmas South. G. Norman. il *Southern Living* 24:84 D '89

Spirit! Ring in the season [J. Amory] M. Matousek. il pors *Harper's Bazaar* 122:154-7+ D '89

A stepfamily Christmas. K. Barrett and R. Greene. il *Ladies' Home Journal* 106:100+ D '89

A survival guide for the holidays. il *Consumer Reports* 54:678-9 N '89

'Tis the season to be fighting. C. Rubin and J. Rubin. il *Psychology Today* 22:36-9 D '88

The way we are [Christmas in Budapest with friends] L. Wyse. il *Good Housekeeping* 209:208 Jl '89

Ways to reduce holiday stress. S. Seliger. il *McCall's* 116:100+ Ja '89

Collectibles

See also
  Santa Claus—Collectibles

Fragile paper treasures [antique tree ornaments] R. Brenner. il *Antiques & Collecting Hobbies* 94:56-9 D '89

Economic aspects

See also
  Christmas business
  Christmas shopping

Photographs and photography

Home for Christmas [excerpt from A Vermont Christmas] R. Brown. il *Good Housekeeping* 208:96-9 Ja '89

Traveler's camera. L. Dennis. il *Popular Photography* 96:24+ D '89

The twelve days of Christmas. il *Ladies' Home Journal* 106:129-32+ D '89

France

Christmas in Provence. E. Jones. il *Gourmet* 49:108-9+ D '89

Provincial pleasures [H. and I. Ornano's 18th century house in Sologne] C. Petkanas. il pors *Harper's Bazaar* 122:178-85 D '89

Mexico

"Féliz Navidad" [Cancun] R. S. Peffer. il *Travel Holiday* 172:90+ D '89

Norway

The year I met Santa [Americans in Norway, 1951] K. St. Vincent. il pors *Good Housekeeping* 209:62+ D '89

United States

See Christmas

Western Europe

Festive days, festive nights! [cover story] M. McHugh. il map *Travel Holiday* 172:36-47 D '89

CHRISTMAS AND CHILDREN *See* Children and Christmas

CHRISTMAS BEVERAGES *See* Beverages

CHRISTMAS BREADS *See* Bread

CHRISTMAS BUSINESS

286 Christmas winner [80286-based personal computers] P. Scisco. il *Compute!* 11:6 My '89

. . . but the rest of the holiday flicks look mostly ho-ho-hum. R. Grover. il *Business Week* p51 N 13 '89

Calling all Scrooges. E. Pomice. il *U.S. News & World Report* 107:53 D 11 '89

Christmas business survey: tidings of joy—and jumpiness. J. Mutter and M. J. O'Brien. il *Publishers Weekly* 236:20-2+ D 22 '89

Stores may have themselves a very little Christmas. B. Bremner. il *Business Week* p78-9 N 27 '89

Superelf plans for Xmas [Toys "R" Us] F. Rice. il *Fortune* 120:151 S 11 '89

Through the holidays: good tidings for many [bookseller survey] J. Mutter and M. J. O'Brien. il *Publishers Weekly* 235:71-3 F 3 '89

'Twas the day before Christmas, and all through the mall . . . A. Dunkin. il *Business Week* p41 Ja 9 '89

Waiting for Christmas [Campeau Corp.] J. DeMont. il por *Maclean's* 102:54-5+ D 4 '89

CHRISTMAS CACTUS

Caring for holiday cacti. N. L. Shepherd. il *Flower and Garden* 33:43-4 N/D '89

CHRISTMAS CAKE *See* Cake

CHRISTMAS CARDS

Balsa burning. il *Sunset (Central West edition)* 181:102-3 D '88

Cards that send two messages [cards that aid charitable causes] A. C. Mallozzi. *Good Housekeeping* 209:271 N '89

Keep those Christmas cards coming! M. A. Rodgers. il *McCall's* 117:105 D '89

One-of-a-kind appliqués as Christmas cards. il *Sunset (Central West edition)* 183:134 N '89

The perfect Christmas card. J. Elliott. il *The New York Times Magazine* p10+ D 24 '89

CHRISTMAS CATALOGS *See* Catalogs, Commercial

CHRISTMAS COOKIES *See* Cookies

CHRISTMAS COOKING

See also
  Christmas dinners
  Christmas entertaining
  Cooking, Ornamental
  Food as gifts

15 easy, elegant holiday recipes [cover story] L. Holderness. il *Better Homes and Gardens* 67:140-6+ N '89

Deck the halls. il *Seventeen* 48:118-23 D '89

Favorite holiday recipes. M. Simmons. il *New Choices for the Best Years* 29:66-70+ D '89

A Glorious buffet [recipes developed by caterer Glorious Foods] il *Ladies' Home Journal* 106:164-5+ D '89

Holiday entrées. S. Dosier. il *Southern Living* 24:56-9 D '89

Holiday party baskets. il *Good Housekeeping* 209:174-84+ D '89

Holiday treats. M. Horosko. il *Dance Magazine* 63:58-9 D '89

In La Jolla, it's bring-your-own-barbecue for buffet on the beach. il *Sunset (Central West edition)* 181:80-1, 150+ D '88

* In Montana, a hike with hot cider break, then a sausage-and-egg brunch. il *Sunset (Central West edition)* 181:78-9 D '88

Marie Osmond's all-out holiday celebration. N. Gittelson. il por *McCall's* 116:23-4+ Ja '89

Old-fashioned Christmas cookbook. il *McCall's* 117:109-14+ D '89

CHRISTMAS CRIBS

Christmas in July [crèche and menorah decision issued by the Supreme Court] *America* 161:27 Jl 15-22 '89

Court and crèche [Supreme Court ruling on religious symbols on public property] *The Christian Century* 106:713 Ag 2-9 '89

Ignore a menorah [Supreme Court rules on public religious displays] S. Bates. *The New Republic* 201:14-16 Jl 31 '89

Is the Court hostile to religion? [Christmas crèche-menorah display decision] R. N. Ostling. il *Time* 134:80 Jl 17 '89

CHRISTMAS DECORATIONS

See also
  Christmas wreaths

American country Christmas [excerpt] M. E. Emmerling and C. Mead. il *Good Housekeeping* 209:139-47 D '89

Bright felt ornaments go together in a snap. il *Sunset (Central West edition)* 183:93 D '89

Caroler's night-light and glowing centerpieces . . . with simple cutout stars. il *Sunset (Central West edition)* 181:101 D '88

Celebrate and decorate with Martha Stewart [excerpt from Martha Stewart's Christmas] M. Stewart. il *Redbook* 174:101-7 D '89

Christmas east and west [Vermont and Idaho homes] K. Reisler. il *Ladies' Home Journal* 106:148-51 D '89

Citrus rings and apple wreaths. il *Sunset (Central West edition)* 183:62-3 D '89

Clothespin ornaments. il *National Geographic World* 172:18-19 D '89

Country Christmas. M. Melendez. il *McCall's* 116:38-41 Ja '89

Deck the halls made easy. il *Glamour* 87:226-9 D '89

Fragile paper treasures [antique tree ornaments] R. Brenner. il *Antiques & Collecting Hobbies* 94:56-9 D '89

Glittery or colorful stars . . . just cut and fold paper plates [tree ornaments] il *Sunset (Central West edition)* 183:88 D '89

Glory be! [tree trimming tips from three decorators] il *Redbook* 174:116-17 D '89

Holiday sparkle welcomes friends. L. Hallam. il *Southern Living* 24:88-90 D '89

Holiday totems [angel and Santa] il *Sunset (Central West edition)* 181:68-9 D '88

The holly and the ivy. il *Ladies' Home Journal* 106:152-3 D '89

Merry Christmas [ornaments for the tree] J. W. Anglund. il *Good Housekeeping* 209:124+ D '89

Old-World Christmas [chalets in New Glarus, Wis. modeled after ones in Switzerland] il *Good Housekeeping* 209:162-5 D '89

On the tree, each gift bag holds a tiny toy. il *Sunset (Central West edition)* 181:104-5 D '88

They started life as basic glass balls [Christmas tree ornaments] il *Sunset (Central West edition)* 181:76-7 D '88

A Vanderbilt Christmas [Biltmore Estate; cover story] P. L. Hudson. il map *Americana* 17:28-35 N/D '89

White flowers for the holidays [lilies and spider mums] il *Southern Living* 24:60-1 D '89

Windows and young artists . . . quick and magical decorations. il *Sunset (Central West edition)* 183:60-1 D '89

You just cut out and stuff lace. il *Sunset (Central West edition)* 181:108 D '88

Care

Keep antique ornaments alive. D. C. Arkins. il *Americana* 17:55-8 N/D '89

Collectors and collecting

Bough wows [antique tree ornaments] L. Rosenkrantz. il *House & Garden* 161:53-4 D '89

CHRISTMAS DECORATIONS, OUTDOOR

Holiday displays [religious symbols on public property] *The Christian Century* 106:1194 D 20-27 '89

Honolulu lights say "Mele Kalikimaka". il map *Sunset (Central West edition)* 181:50 D '88

CHRISTMAS DECORATIONS, OUTDOOR—*cont.*
Pa-rum-pum-pum-pum [Christmas cadets used as decorations at Rockefeller Center] B. Weber. il *The New York Times Magazine* p130 N 19 '89
Tahoe City lights "The Big Tree". il *Sunset (Central West edition)* 181:164 D '88
Traditional plywood cutouts [lawn ornaments] il *Workbench* 45:54-6 N/D '89
CHRISTMAS DEPRESSION SYNDROME *See* Depression, Mental
CHRISTMAS DESSERTS *See* Desserts
CHRISTMAS DINNERS
Christmas dinner [cover story] il *Gourmet* 49:160-8+ D '89
A dinner menu for company. P. Y. Cordell. il *Southern Living* 24:96-8 D '89
A family feast. B. Johnson. il *Better Homes and Gardens* 67:108-14+ D '89
A festive Christmas dinner. C. Lyons. il *Ebony* 45:80-2+ D '89
A holiday bird and a free-range chat with Julia [J. Child] G. Jaynes. il pors *Life* 12:95-8+ D '89
Holiday classics with a big fat difference. J. B. Hurley. il *Prevention (Emmaus, Pa.)* 41:66-70+ D '89
Holiday dinner. G. Brennan. il *Organic Gardening* 36:37-41 D '89
Holiday dinners [special section] il *Southern Living* 24:87+ N '89
Julia Child's Christmas Eve [excerpt from The way to cook] J. Child. il por *Ladies' Home Journal* 106:162-3+ D '89
Pass the buck [venison] A. J. McClane. il *Esquire* 112:50+ D '89
Potluck potpourri. J. Voltz. il *Modern Maturity* 32:70-4+ D '89/Ja '90
Quick, simple, and traditional holiday dinner. il *Sunset (Central West edition)* 183:144 D '89
Season's eatings! from A Christmas carol by Charles Dickens. il *Redbook* 174:110-13+ D '89
We do holidays right! B. Freese. il *Successful Farming* 87:50-1 D '89
Why our Christmas dinner looks better than yours [work of food stylist Karen Gillingham] il *Esquire* 112:166-9 D '89
"Wild" to traditional, beef to buffalo, boneless choices for a holiday roast. il *Sunset (Central West edition)* 181:128-9 D '88
CHRISTMAS ENTERTAINING
See also
Christmas dinners
Chestnuts roasting on an open fire . . . it's a hearthside party. il *Sunset (Central West edition)* 183:58-9 D '89
Company's coming cookbook. il *McCall's* 116:107-12+ Ja '89
Fast feasts: for the holidays, take it out—take it all out [New York City] B. Costikyan. il *New York* 22:66-8+ D 18 '89
Holiday party planner [special section] A. Arnott. il *McCall's* 116:67+ Ja '89
Menus for festive get-togethers. il *Good Housekeeping* 208:114-24+ Ja '89
Merry citrus. il *Sunset (Central West edition)* 183:128-30 D '89
A southern tree-trimming party. il *Gourmet* 49:132-4+ D '89
CHRISTMAS EVE
O little town [visit to Bethlehem] C. N. Barnard. il map *Modern Maturity* 32:46-52 D '89/Ja '90
Putting up the Christmas lights, Louisiana-style [bonfires] M. A. Sternberg. il *Smithsonian* 20:146-51 D '89
Silent night [running on Christmas Eve in home town] J. Atkinson. il *Runner's World* 24:96 D '89
Photographs and photography
The day before Christmas. il *Good Housekeeping* 208:106-9 Ja '89
CHRISTMAS GIFT CATALOGS *See* Catalogs, Commercial
CHRISTMAS GIFT WRAPPING *See* Wrapping of packages
CHRISTMAS GIFTS
See also
Books as gifts
Christmas projects
Christmas shopping
Food as gifts
Gifts in business
Phonograph records as gifts
Video games as gifts
Videotapes as gifts
Wrapping of packages
Baskets for the holidays. il *Gourmet* 49:116-18 D '89
Best buy gifts. il *Consumer Reports* 54:699-705 N '89
Christmas giftbook. il *Good Housekeeping* 209:122+ N '89
Christmas gifts [cover story] C. Pollan. il *New York* 22:59-74+ D 4 '89
Down with the gift Grinch! C. A. Henningsen. il *Ladies' Home Journal* 106:92 D '89
Editors' choice gifts. il *Good Housekeeping* 209:42+ D '89
The fine art of giving. il *Harper's Bazaar* 122:51+ D '89
Garden giftables. il *Flower and Garden* 33:8-9 N/D '89
Gift shopping at science museums in the Bay Area. il *Sunset (Central West edition)* 183:14 D '89

Gifts '90: cheap thrills. D. White. il *Skiing* 42:186-9 D '89
Gifts for gardeners. L. A. Weathers. il *Southern Living* 24:46 D '89
Gifts from the heart. A. Stoddard. il *McCall's* 117:128 D '89
Gilt-edged gifts [for boat owners] J. Chwasky. il *Motor Boating & Sailing* 164:20-3 N '89
Gourmet's Christmas gifts. il *Gourmet* 49:118-23 N '89
Holiday gift guide [computer gifts] H. E. H. Aycock and J. Sloan. il *Compute!* 11:46-8 D '89
Holiday gift guide: what to buy the sports nut who's seen and played everything. R. Leivenberg. il *Sport (New York, N.Y.)* 80:76-7 Ja '89
Holiday gifts [audiophiles] W. Livingstone. il *Stereo Review* 54:113-16+ D '89
Holiday shopping [gifts for artists] il *American Artist* 53:28-9 N '89
On and off the avenue. *The New Yorker* 65:156-64+ D 4 '89
The pleasures of giving. il *The New York Times Magazine* p73-9 N 5 '89
Santa's special helper [donating and distributing gifts for needy families in East Saint Louis, Ill.] R. Swiener. il por *Ladies' Home Journal* 106:18+ D '89
Stocking feats [electronics] M. Porter. il *Gentlemen's Quarterly* 59:186+ D '89
Stocking stuffers [aviation-related gifts] il *Flying* 116:32-4 D '89
Telephone accessories as Christmas gifts? il *Sunset (Central West edition)* 181:90-1 D '88
When good things come in small packages [cover story; special section] il *Video* 13:54-7+ D '89
Anecdotes, facetiae, satire, etc.
Christmas shopping. M. E. Marty. *The Christian Century* 106:1135 N 29 '89
CHRISTMAS GIFTS FOR CHILDREN
See also
Books as gifts
Toys
The children's closet. *The New Yorker* 65:173-6+ D 4 '89
The gift. A. J. Gordon. il *American Visions* 4:27-31 D '89
Great gifts for $10 and under. M. Mohler and M. D. Rosen. il *Ladies' Home Journal* 106:108 D '89
Great gifts for kids [holiday projects; special section] K. Collier. il *The Family Handyman* 39:43-52 N/D '89
Great gifts for under $10. J. Gaylin. il *Parents* 64:94-6+ D '89
On and off the avenue. *The New Yorker* 65:141-53 D 11 '89
CHRISTMAS GIFTS FOR MEN
Christmas shopping: gifts for him. il *Good Housekeeping* 209:120+ D '89
Great ideas for dogs. L. Mueller. il *Outdoor Life* 184:16+ D '89
CHRISTMAS GIFTS FOR PETS
Pets and the holidays. R. Kidd. il *The Mother Earth News* 120:33-4 N/D '89
CHRISTMAS GIFTS FOR THE HOME
21 gift ideas. il *Workbench* 45:58-61 N/D '89
Gadgets under the tree. il *Home Mechanix* 85:74-6+ Ja '89
Gifts for growing workshops: presents to delight any handyperson. il *Better Homes and Gardens* 67:125 N '89
Holiday gift guide. il *Radio-Electronics* 60:51-3+ D '89
Home style: black and white and red-y to wrap. J. Williams and others. il *Better Homes and Gardens* 67:59-60 N '89
Home style: Santa's helpers. J. Williams and others. il *Better Homes and Gardens* 67:21-2+ D '89
If there's a nutrition-minded cook in your kitchen. il *Sunset (Central West edition)* 183:124 D '89
On and off the avenue. *The New Yorker* 65:83-9 D 18 '89
Stocking-stuffers for cooks of all ages. il *Sunset (Central West edition)* 181:120 D '88
Year-end special: great gifts for the home office [cover story] M. Alvich. il *Home Office Computing* 7:56-9 D '89
CHRISTMAS GIFTS FOR WOMEN
Christmas shopping: gifts for her. il *Good Housekeeping* 209:116+ D '89
CHRISTMAS GREENS
See also
Christmas trees
Christmas wreaths
Christmas plant legends. M. Brown. il *Flower and Garden* 33:47-9 N/D '89
Living bouquets for the holidays . . . and afterward. il *Sunset (Central West edition)* 181:162-3 D '88
Mantel spray with no hint of its underpinnings. il *Sunset (Central West edition)* 181:158 D '88
CHRISTMAS IN AMERICA [television program] *See* Television program reviews—Single works
CHRISTMAS IN LITERATURE
See also
Christmas poems
Christmas stories
'Dear Scrooge . .' [holiday books for children] R. Donahue. il *Publishers Weekly* 236:34-7 O 27 '89

CHRISTMAS IN LITERATURE—*cont.*
The second greatest Christmas story ever told [C. Dickens' A Christmas carol] T. J. Burns. il *Reader's Digest* 135:65-70 D '89

CHRISTMAS IN MOTION PICTURES
The holiday evergreens we never grow tired of. K. Turan. il *TV Guide* 37:16-19 D 16-22 '89

CHRISTMAS ISLAND (INDIAN OCEAN)
See also
Wildlife—Christmas Island (Indian Ocean)

CHRISTMAS ISLAND (PACIFIC OCEAN)
See also
Birds—Christmas Island (Pacific Ocean)

CHRISTMAS LETTERS
A Christmas letter to myself. S. M. Richmond. il *Ladies' Home Journal* 106:94 D '89

CHRISTMAS MAIL ORDER BUSINESS *See* Mail order business

CHRISTMAS MUSIC
See also
Phonograph records—Christmas music

CHRISTMAS PAGEANTS
The pageant [excerpt from It was on fire when I lay down on it] R. Fulghum. il *Good Housekeeping* 209:78+ D '89

CHRISTMAS PARTIES *See* Christmas entertaining
CHRISTMAS PLANTS *See* House plants
CHRISTMAS POEMS
Go tell it on the mountain: Christmas and the black spirit. il *Ebony* 45:36-8 D '89

Anecdotes, facetiae, satire, etc.
St. Nicholas: a textual scandal [corrected text of The night before Christmas; cover story] R. R. Lingeman and T. M. Disch. *The Nation* 248:1+ Ja 2 '89

Single works
See name of author for full entry
About nights. Spinelli, Eileen, 1942-
Baby's first Christmas. Bariteau, Corinne Adria
Circa '89. Cannon, Maureen
Clay vessels. McNamee, John
A cup of Christmas tea. Hegg, Tom
December. Ormsby, Eric
Feeding the winter cattle. McDonald, Walter
Greetings, friends! Angell, Roger
Hast thou entered into the storehouses of the snow? Brady, Charles
Holly comes from a cold heaven. Hiestand, Emily
I'm dreaming. Shepherd, J. Barrie
The Nick of time. Brosnahan, Liam
Speakin' o' Christmas. Dunbar, Paul Laurence, 1872-1906
Wild swans at Christmas. Boe, Marilyn J.

CHRISTMAS POINSETTIAS *See* Poinsettias
CHRISTMAS PRESENTS *See* Christmas gifts
CHRISTMAS PROJECTS
See also
Christmas decorations
25 last-minute gifts to craft. J. Williams and J. Severson. il *Better Homes and Gardens* 67:129+ N '89
Christmas gifts to make now. il *Good Housekeeping* 209:106-7+ Ag '89
Christmas naturals [creations of Carol Ann Newman] J. Williams and J. Severson. il *Better Homes and Gardens* 67:35-42+ D '89
Deck the halls. il *Seventeen* 48:118-23 D '89
Festive touches. il *Better Homes and Gardens* 67:106-8+ Jl '89
Fun for kids. R. G. McKenzie. il *Parents* 64:153-6 D '89
Great gifts for kids [holiday projects; special section] K. Collier. il *The Family Handyman* 39:43-52 N/D '89
Great gifts for under $10. J. Gaylin. il *Parents* 64:94-6+ D '89
Heartfelt gestures, handmade gifts. A. Zabar. il *Seventeen* 48:135-8 N '89
Holiday gift workshop [cover story; special section] il *Workbench* 45:30-8+ N/D '89
A holly, jolly Christmas [creations of Theresa Disney] J. Williams and J. Severson. il *Better Homes and Gardens* 67:60-6+ D '89
Kit stuff [cover story] J. Truini. il *Home Mechanix* 85:40-2+ D '89
Make it merry: easy crafts for kids. il *Redbook* 174:120-3 D '89
Make it merry—make it yourself. il *'Teen* 33:70-2 D '89
Max the Dragon's Christmas crafts for kids. il *Ladies' Home Journal* 106:115-16+ D '89
Workshop whimsy. il *Sunset (Central West edition)* 181:68-71 D '88

CHRISTMAS SEALS
History
"Stamping" out tuberculosis: the story of Christmas seals [work of E. Bissell] K. Doyle. il por *American History Illustrated* 24:66-8 N/D '89

CHRISTMAS SHOPPING
See also
Christmas business
Don't get swamped this holiday season [use of credit cards; views of Elgie Holstein] *USA Today (Periodical)* 118:1-2 D '89

Found objects [shopping for antiques] A. De Moubray. il *Vogue* 179:267-9+ D '89

CHRISTMAS STORES
See also
Käthe Wohlfahrt's Christkindlmarkt

CHRISTMAS STORIES
Single works
See name of author for full entry
Blessed to receive. Liebenthal, Jean
Bookends. Sauro, Joan
Christmas at our house. Paquin, Ethel
The Christmas box. Piglia, Paola
Christmas carol. Barry, Pamela
A Christmas story. Keillor, Garrison
A different kind of Christmas. Haley, Alex
Happy after all. Gingher, Marianne
It says here . . . Heath, Aloise Buckley
The man who found Christmas. Doig, David
The skates. Pilcher, Rosamunde, 1924-
The tree that came to stay. Quindlen, Anna

CHRISTMAS TABLE SETTING *See* Table setting
CHRISTMAS TELEVISION PROGRAMS *See* Television broadcasting—Christmas programs
CHRISTMAS TOYS *See* Toys
CHRISTMAS TREE ORNAMENTS *See* Christmas decorations
CHRISTMAS TREES
A Christmas tree that will leave you breathless [balloon tree] il *Sunset (Central West edition)* 181:96 D '88
O Christmas tree. il *Parents* 64:17 D '89
Picking the perfect tree. il *McCall's* 117:41 D '89
Season of the tree [special section] il *National Wildlife* 28:4-13 D '89/Ja '90
Support your family tree. *Ladies' Home Journal* 106:92 D '89
Tabletop trees. il *Sunset (Central West edition)* 183:68-9 D '89
This tree won't drop a needle [pine cone tree] il *Southern Living* 24:53 D '89
Tires, trees, terns, terrapins [planting Christmas trees on Massachusetts beaches to halt erosion] T. Williams. il *Audubon* 91:26-8+ My '89

Breeding
Yuletide tissue cultures. R. Khalaf. il *Forbes* 144:276+ D 11 '89

Decoration
See Christmas decorations
Exhibitions
National treasure Christmas trees [exhibit at the Smithsonian Institution] il *Good Housekeeping* 209:158-9 D '89
Photographs and photography
The Christmas cover story [special effects used to create New York times magazine cover photo; work of Elliot Erwitt and Bran Ferren] B. Weber. il *The New York Times Magazine* p34 D 24 '89

CHRISTMAS WREATHS
Making a picture-perfect wreath. il *Sunset (Central West edition)* 181:82-3 D '88

CHRISTO, JIM
about
Driveway surfaces: concrete vs. asphalt [interview] il pors *Home Mechanix* 85:16-21+ Jl '89

CHRISTOPHER, BARBARA
(jt. auth) See Christopher, William, and Christopher, Barbara
about
M*A*S*H's William Christopher and wife Barbara find love and pain with an autistic son [interview] D. Bacon. il pors *People Weekly* 32:79-80+ N 13 '89

CHRISTOPHER, NICHOLAS
In the country [poem] *The New Yorker* 65:36 Ag 21 '89
Nine cities [poem] *The New Republic* 200:32 Ap 10 '89

CHRISTOPHER, ROBERT C.
Terms of estrangement. il *Newsweek* 113:21 F 27 '89

CHRISTOPHER, WILLIAM
about
M*A*S*H's William Christopher and wife Barbara find love and pain with an autistic son [interview] D. Bacon. il pors *People Weekly* 32:79-80+ N 13 '89

CHRISTOPHER, WILLIAM, AND CHRISTOPHER, BARBARA
Mixed blessing. il pors *Ladies' Home Journal* 106:144+ My '89

CHRISTOPHER COLUMBUS DOLLAR COINS *See* Coins
CHRISTOPHERSON, TERI
Stood up [fiction] il *'Teen* 33:60-2+ Mr '89

CHRIST'S CHURCH FELLOWSHIP
New church body formed. S. Rabey. *Christianity Today* 33:45 Ap 7 '89

CHROMAFFIN CELLS
The ten-minute pain transplant [chromaffin cell grafts suppress pain in rats] D. Stein. il *Omni (New York, N.Y.)* 11:22+ Je '89

CHROMATIN
Drosophila nuclear proteins bind to regions of alternating C and T residues in gene promoters. D. S. Gilmour and others. bibl f il *Science* 245:1487-90 S 29 '89

CHROMATOGRAPHIC ANALYSIS
Identifying cells' chemical personalities [open tubular liquid chromatography; work of James W. Jorgenson and Robert T. Kennedy] I. Amato. *Science News* 135:150 Mr 11 '89
Microcolumn separations and the analysis of single cells [capillary zone electrophoresis and open tubular liquid chromatography] R. T. Kennedy and others. bibl f il *Science* 246:57-63 O 6 '89
Recent developments in analytical chromatography. M. V. Novotny. bibl f il *Science* 246:51-7 O 6 '89

CHROMOPHORES
Effect of carboxylic acid side chains on the absorption maximum of visual pigments. E. A. Zhukovsky and D. D. Oprian. bibl f il *Science* 246:928-30 N 17 '89
Membranes as the energy source in the endergonic transformation of vitamin A to 11-*cis*-retinol. P. S. Deigner and others. bibl f il *Science* 244:968-71 My 26 '89

CHROMOSOME ABNORMALITIES
See also
Down syndrome
Fragile X syndrome
Chromosomal rearrangement generating a composite gene for a developmental transcription factor [Bacillus subtilis] P. Stragier and others. bibl f il *Science* 243:507-12 Ja 27 '89
Chromosome 17 deletions and p53 gene mutations in colorectal carcinomas. S. J. Baker and others. bibl f il *Science* 244:217-21 Ap 14 '89
Cloning of breakpoints of a chromosome translocation identifies the AN2 locus [aniridia] M. Gessler and others. bibl f il *Science* 244:1575-8 Je 30 '89
Cutting away DNA the mitochondrial way [work of Douglas C. Wallace] P. Young. *Science News* 136:85 Ag 5 '89
Cystic fibrosis: cloning and genetics [cover story; special section; with editorial comment by Daniel E. Koshland] *Science* 245:1029, 1059-80 S 8 '89
A direct repeat is a hotspot for large-scale deletion of human mitochondrial DNA [neuromuscular disorders characterized by ocular myopathy and ophthalmoplegia] E. A. Schon and others. bibl f il *Science* 244:346-9 Ap 21 '89
elk, tissue-specific *ets*-related genes on chromosomes X and 14 near translocation breakpoints. V. N. Rao and others. bibl f il *Science* 244:66-70 Ap 7 '89
The gene for enhancer binding proteins E12/E47 lies at the t(1;19) breakpoint in acute leukemias. J. D. Mellentin and others. bibl f il *Science* 246:379-82 O 20 '89
Human genotoxicity: pesticide applicators and phosphine. V. F. Garry and others. bibl f il *Science* 246:251-5 O 13 '89
Identification of the molecular defect in a family with spondyloepiphyseal dysplasia. B. Lee and others. bibl f il *Science* 244:978-80 My 26 '89
Manic depression gene put in limbo [follow-up on Amish study by John Kelsoe] M. Barinaga. il *Science* 246:886-7 N 17 '89
Manic depression: suspect gene acquitted [follow-up on Amish study] A. McKenzie. *Science News* 136:327 N 18 '89
Modifying Mendel one more time [cystic fibrosis findings] P. Young. *Science News* 136:92 Ag 5 '89
The myeloperoxidase gene in acute promyelocytic leukemia [discussion of May 6, 1988 article, Translocation and rearrangement of myeloperoxidase gene in acute promyelocytic leukemia] S. C. Weil and others. il *Science* 244:823-6 My 19 '89
p53: a frequent target for genetic abnormalities in lung cancer. T. Takahashi and others. bibl f il *Science* 246:491-4 O 27 '89
Physical mapping of a translocation breakpoint in neurofibromatosis. J. W. Fountain and others. bibl f il *Science* 244:1085-7 Je 2 '89
T cell receptor gene trans-rearrangements: chimeric γ-δ genes in normal lymphoid tissues. B. Tycko and others. bibl f il *Science* 245:1242-6 S 15 '89
Two NF1 translocations map within a 600-kilobase segment of 17q11.2. P. O'Connell and others. bibl f il *Science* 244:1087-8 Je 2 '89

CHROMOSOME MAPPING *See* Genetic mapping; Genome mapping
CHROMOSOME TRANSLOCATIONS *See* Chromosome abnormalities

CHROMOSOMES
See also
Chromatin
Linkage (Genetics)
Polyploidy
Testis determining factor
Transposons
Chromosomal location and evolutionary rate variation in enterobacterial genes. P. M. Sharp and others. bibl f il *Science* 246:808-10 N 10 '89
Human chromosome 12 is required for elevated HIV-1 expression in human-hamster hybrid cells. C. E. Hart and others. bibl f il *Science* 246:488-91 O 27 '89
A lizard foretold [search for Gymnophthalmus species by chromosome comparison] C. J. Cole and others. map *Natural History* p12+ My '89
S phase of the cell cycle. R. A. Laskey and others. bibl f il *Science* 246:609-14 N 3 '89

Sexy genes [evidence that there may be many more differences in male and female genes] il *Time* 134:43 Ag 7 '89

CHROMOSOMES, ARTIFICIAL
Isolation of single-copy human genes from a library of yeast artificial chromosome clones [Saccharomyces] B. H. Brownstein and others. bibl f il *Science* 244:1348-51 Je 16 '89
Mapping the Drosophila genome with yeast artificial chromosomes. D. Garza and others. bibl f il *Science* 246:641-6 N 3 '89

CHRONAR CORP.
Burnt bulb? J. Cook and R. Addis. il por *Forbes* 144:10 Ag 7 '89

CHRONIC FATIGUE SYNDROME
"Am I sick or am I tired?". P. Dranov. *Ladies' Home Journal* 106:120+ S '89
The baffling case of chronic fatigue [research by Stephen E. Straus] K. Fackelmann. *Science News* 135:4 Ja 7 '89
Chronic fatigue revisited. L. Lamb. *Utne Reader* p26 S/O '89
Chronic fatigue syndrome: solving a medical mystery. K. Roderick. il *Glamour* 87:80 N '89
Sick of being tired? News about fatigue. C. Hacinli. il *Mademoiselle* 95:125-6 F '89
Yuppie flu or overtraining? S. Festa. *Runner's World* 24:56 Ja '89

CHRONIC GRANULOMATOUS DISEASE
Recombinant 47-kilodalton cytosol factor restores NADPH oxidase in chronic granulomatous disease. K. J. Lomax and others. bibl f il *Science* 245:409-12 Jl 28 '89; Correction. 246:987 N 24 '89

CHRONIC MYELOGENOUS LEUKEMIA *See* Leukemia
CHRONICLE BOOKS
'Chronicle' trademark infringement disputes are resolved. C. Reid. *Publishers Weekly* 236:12 O 27 '89
CHRONICLE PUBLICATIONS INC.
'Chronicle' trademark infringement disputes are resolved. C. Reid. *Publishers Weekly* 236:12 O 27 '89
CHRONOBIOLOGY *See* Biological rhythms
CHRONOLOGY
See also
Geological time
CHRYSLER, WALTER PERCY, 1909-1988
about
Driven to collect. S. Greenspan. il por *House & Garden* 161:32+ Je '89

CHRYSLER CORP.
Chrysler Corp.: cautiously planning a PC future. il *Personal Computing* 13:89-90 S '89
Chrysler heads back to earth [selling aerospace and defense operations] W. Zellner. il *Business Week* p46 D 18 '89
Chrysler would prefer a bar by any other name, but Jeep Molnar would rather fight than switch [suit filed against owner of Jeep's Bar in Alpine, Wyo.] il por *People Weekly* 31:63 Ap 3 '89
How a top boss manages his day [R. A. Lutz] A. L. Taylor, III. il pors *Fortune* 119:95-7+ Je 19 '89
How Chrysler's $30,000 sports car got sideswiped [venture with Maserati] J. Rossant. il *Business Week* p68+ Ja 23 '89
Interview: Robert A. Lutz. J. Miller. il pors *Motor Trend* 41:61-5 Ja '89
Is a takeover tailgating Chrysler? G. G. Marcial. il *Business Week* p120 D 18 '89
The list nobody wants to be on [L. Iacocca and R. Hunsucker head list of executives returning least value for most pay] T. Vogel and W. Zellner. il pors *Business Week* p50 My 1 '89
NAACP and Chrysler sign a fair share pact at confab. il *Jet* 76:7-8 Jl 31 '89
The real Masters of the Universe [address, March 2, 1989] G. Greenwald. *Vital Speeches of the Day* 55:528-30 Je 15 '89
Shuttle consultancy [hires L. Cutler as vice president of consumer affairs] M. E. Kirk. il por *Forbes* 143:324 Ja 9 '89
Teaming up in Detroit [GM and Chrysler teamup] *Newsweek* 114:59 O 16 '89
Will the Big Three buy Chrysler? [Chrysler executives leveraging a buyout] il *Motor Trend* 41:29 O '89

CHRYSLER CORP. CHRYSLER-PLYMOUTH DIVISION
Singer Tina Turner completes Chrysler ads. il pors *Jet* 76:57 S 18 '89

CHRYSLER MUSEUM
Chrysler Museum: the next phase. B. Wallis. il *Art in America* 77:29 My '89
The Chrysler opens new doors. il *Southern Living* 24:26 Jl '89
Driven to collect [W. P. Chrysler, Jr.] S. Greenspan. il por *House & Garden* 161:32+ Je '89
Order out of chaos [cover story] C. Pearson. il *Architectural Record* 177:114-19 Jl '89

CHRYSLER-PLYMOUTH DIVISION *See* Chrysler Corp. Chrysler-Plymouth Division
CHRYSLER TECHNOLOGIES CORPORATION
Chrysler heads back to earth. W. Zellner. il *Business Week* p46 D 18 '89

CHU, CHUNG-HUNG
about
Window on China. A. Bahar. il *Antiques & Collecting Hobbies*
93:62-5 F '89
CHU, LYNN
Reading between the lines. il *Publishers Weekly* 235:48 F
17 '89
CHUA, LAWRENCE
Cheek chic. il por *Rolling Stone* Fashion Collection:63+ S
7 '89
CHUA, N.-H. (NAM-HAI)
(jt. auth) See Benfey, Philip N., and Chua, N.-H. (Nam-hai)
CHUA, NAM-HAI See Chua, N.-H. (Nam-hai)
CHUBB, JOHN E.
Can the government govern? [address, November 17, 1988]
Vital Speeches of the Day 55:363-7 Ap 1 '89
CHUBBUCK, IVANA
How to succeed in Hollywood. il *TV Guide* 37:14-16 O
28-N 3 '89
Rejection in Hollywood: how the stars cope. il *TV Guide*
37:16-18 O 7-13 '89
She said she could ride a motorcycle and then . . . crash!
il *TV Guide* 37:23-5 Je 3-9 '89
CHUBINSKY, V.
Darkness at noon; tr. by Barry J. Rubin. il *The New Republic*
200:28-30 F 20 '89
CHUCK'S PARKING (FIRM)
When valet king Chuck Pick parks their wheels, Hollywood
heavies count it a lucky brake. T. Allis. il pors *People
Weekly* 31:116-17 Ap 24 '89
CHUGACH MOUNTAINS (ALASKA)
Deep water, high peaks. C. Noble. il *Sierra* 74:59 My/Je
'89
CHUMA, KIYOFUKU
Spending more on defense. il *World Press Review* 36:19
Ap '89
CHUNG, CONNIE
about
Star wars at the networks. R. Zoglin. il pors *Time* 133:70-1
Ap 3 '89
Switching channels. il pors *Harper's Bazaar* 122:130-1 Ag
'89
Two hearts, beating in prime time [cover story] K. McMurran.
il pors *People Weekly* 31:116-17+ Ap 10 '89
The wooing of Diane Sawyer sparks a fierce network battle.
il pors *People Weekly* 31:124 Ap 10 '89
CHUNG, KOONG-NAH, AND OTHERS
Molecular sorting in the secretory pathway. bibl f il *Science*
243:192-7 Ja 13 '89
CHUNNEL See English Channel tunnel
CHURCH, BENJAMIN, 1734-CA. 1778
about
Benjamin Church: Son of Liberty, Tory spy. M. G. Stoler.
il pors *American History Illustrated* 24:28-35 N/D '89
The Church cryptogram: to catch a Tory spy. M. L. Peterson.
il *American History Illustrated* 24:36-43 N/D '89
CHURCH, FREDERIC EDWIN, 1826-1900
about
Frederic Church and the enterprise of landscape painting
[with editorial comment by Wendell Garrett] F. Kelly.
bibl f il *Antiques* 136:1108-23 N '89
The Hudson River revisited. R. I. C. Fisher. il *American
Artist* 53:48-54+ N '89
In the halcyon days when pictures of the land came first.
J. Sherman. bibl (p229) il por *Smithsonian* 20:88-96+ O
'89
Olana [cover story] F. Donegan. il *Americana* 17:26-32 S/O
'89
CHURCH
See also
Catholic Church
Christianity
House churches
Laity
Mission of the church
Parishes
The business of the church. R. C. Wood. *The Christian
Century* 106:221-2 Mr 1 '89
CHURCH ADVERTISING See Religious advertising
CHURCH AND AIDS (DISEASE) See AIDS (Disease)—
Religious aspects
CHURCH AND ART See Art and religion
CHURCH AND CIVIL RIGHTS
Of many things. J. W. Donohue. *America* 161:74 Ag 12-19
'89
Bolivia
Tribute to a Latin American martyr [L. Espinal, Jesuit
missionary murdered in 1980] M. O'Sullivan. *America*
160:8-11+ Ja 7-14 '89
Chile
Chile: a watershed in Church/state relations. J. Torrens.
America 161:268-70+ O 28 '89
Guatemala
The hidden reality in Guatemala. T. Montgomery-Fate. il
The Christian Century 106:820-2 S 13-20 '89

CHURCH AND DAY CARE
An "accommodating" Court [Supreme Court lets stand a
licensing law that allows child care centers run by religious
organizations to seek an exempt status] D. Neff. *Christianity
Today* 33:15 Mr 3 '89
CHURCH AND DISARMAMENT
Another way to peace [French Catholics] C. Guicherd. il
Commonweal 116:704-6 D 15 '89
CHURCH AND ECONOMIC PROBLEMS See Christianity
and economics
CHURCH AND EDUCATION
See also
Church colleges and universities
Church schools
Public schools and religion
CHURCH AND HOMOSEXUALITY See Church work with
homosexuals; Homosexuality and Christianity
CHURCH AND IMMIGRANTS See Church and social
problems
CHURCH AND LABOR
See also
United Methodist Church—Employees
Christians and the coalfield conflict [Episcopalian involvement
in strike against Pittston] L. Johnson. *The Christian Century*
106:868-9 O 4 '89
Preachers need to spend a day on the job [with readers'
comments] G. F. Pierce. *U.S. Catholic* 54:14-19 D '89
Why work? B. L. Shelley. il *Christianity Today* 33:16-18
Jl 14 '89
CHURCH AND LAW See Religion and law
CHURCH AND NARCOTICS TRADE
Christian veterans, new recruits on the front lines. S. Rabey.
il *Christianity Today* 33:52+ O 6 '89
The church and the drug crisis: ministers mobilize against
'the death of a race'. il *Ebony* 44:160+ Ag '89
The drug war next door. L. Cryderman. il *Christianity Today*
33:14 O 20 '89
In Chicago, two angry priests declare a holy war on drugs
[M. Pfleger and G. Clements put pressure on stores to
stop selling drug paraphernalia] W. Plummer. il pors *People
Weekly* 32:102-3 S 4 '89
Reading the signs of a drug-plagued time. J. M. Wall. *The
Christian Century* 106:803-4 S 13-20 '89
Bolivia
Christians who grow coca [cover story] B. Bird. il *Christianity
Today* 33:40-3 S 8 '89
Colombia
Missionaries assess risks in Colombia. J. Maust. *Christianity
Today* 33:52 O 6 '89
Violence in Colombia unites evangelicals. J. Maust.
Christianity Today 33:49 S 22 '89
Peru
Christians who grow coca [cover story] B. Bird. il *Christianity
Today* 33:40-3 S 8 '89
CHURCH AND PEACE See Religion and peace
CHURCH AND POLITICS See Religion and politics
CHURCH AND RACE RELATIONS
See also
Christian Identity (Movement)
Imani Temple African-American Catholic Congregation
The activism of interpretation: black pastors and public
life [work of J. P. Barbour] K. B. Jones. *The Christian
Century* 106:817-18 S 13-20 '89
Catholic bishops OK plan to recruit, retain blacks. il *Jet*
77:24-5 N 27 '89
Ida B. Wells-Barnett: an Afro-American prophet. E. M.
Townes. *The Christian Century* 106:285-6 Mr 15 '89
Listening to America's ethnic churches [special section] il
Christianity Today 33:25-42 Mr 3 '89
Praying with the Klan [evening of dialogue sponsored by
Tennessee seminary students in 1981] R. Hosmer. *The
Christian Century* 106:494-5 My 10 '89
Preaching the word & doing it: black Catholics in America.
A. Raboteau. il *Commonweal* 116:631-2+ N 17 '89
The prolife credibility gap [alienation of black support] S.
Perkins. il por *Christianity Today* 33:21-2 Ap 21 '89
Tension in Miami. J. Maust. il *Christianity Today* 33:40-1
F 17 '89
Toward a more perfect union of black and white Americans
[Cardinal Joseph Ritter Award Essay Contest; cover story;
special section; with editorial comment by George W.
Hunt] il *America* 160:130, 134-49+ F 18 '89
Troubles they've seen: African-American Catholics. A. Levine.
il *Commonweal* 116:550-1 O 20 '89
Two cheers for heterogeneity [Christopher Ricks' T. S. Eliot
and prejudice] M. E. Marty. *The Christian Century* 106:837
S 27 '89
International aspects
A blaspheming cancer [Vatican document The Church and
racism] *Commonweal* 116:196-7 Ap 7 '89
Racism, fear and reconciliation [Vatican document The
Church and racism; cover story] J. A. Fiorenza. *America*
160:444-6 My 13 '89
Reckoning with a racist world [proclamation by the Vatican's
Commission on Justice and Peace] K. L. Woodward. il
Newsweek 113:50 F 20 '89
'Towards a more fraternal society' [Vatican document The
Church and racism] *America* 160:211-12 Mr 11 '89

CHURCH AND RACE RELATIONS—cont.
Canada
In Toronto, concerns about police racism. L. Mackey. il *Christianity Today* 33:46 Ap 7 '89
South Africa
Charismatic churches and the struggle against apartheid: a dispute [discussion of August 17-24, 1988 article, Charismatics and change in South Africa] I. Hexham and K. O. Poewe-Hexham. *The Christian Century* 106:16+ Ja 4-11 '89
Dissenting on divestment [Evangelical Lutheran Church in America] *The Christian Century* 106:927 O 18 '89
An exceptional protest [Cape Town march] M. Nemeth. il *Maclean's* 102:34+ S 25 '89
Hope for a peaceful end to apartheid [interview with M. Cassidy] il por *Christianity Today* 33:55-6 N 17 '89
The illusion of reform in South Africa. D. Palos and T. Soeldner. *The Christian Century* 106:447-50 Ap 26 '89
A new phase in the antiapartheid struggle? J. W. De Gruchy. *The Christian Century* 106:1078-9 N 22 '89
Polling the Israelites: Boesak on sanctions. A. Welsh-Huggins. *The Christian Century* 106:924-5 O 18 '89
A skeptical view [interview with D. Tutu] J. Bierman. il por *Maclean's* 102:32 Mr 13 '89
South Africa: the growing tolerance of intolerance [interview with N. Tutu-Seavers] R. Bautch. *America* 160:450-1+ My 13 '89
Sticking a needle in apartheid [church sponsored sewing classes] M. S. Van Leeuwen. il *Christianity Today* 33:13 Mr 17 '89

CHURCH AND REFUGEE PROBLEMS See Church and social problems
CHURCH AND REPRODUCTION See Reproduction—Moral and religious aspects
CHURCH AND SLAVERY See Slavery and the church
CHURCH AND SOCIAL PROBLEMS
See also
> Abortion—Moral and religious aspects
> Birth control—Moral and religious aspects
> Campaign for Human Development
> Church and civil rights
> Church and labor
> Church and race relations
> Church work with families
> Church work with homosexuals
> Horace McKenna Center
> Liberation theology
> Sanctuary movement (Refugee aid)
> Slavery and the church
> Socialism and religion
> Sociology, Christian
> World Vision (Organization)

Against complacency. P. J. Ryan. il *America* 161:175 S 23 '89
An Atlanta prison gets converted [R. Scott's GlenCastle conversion for the working poor] B. Spring. il por *Christianity Today* 33:53-4 Ap 7 '89
Challenges facing U.S. Catholics. S. Cahill. *Commonweal* 116:621 N 17 '89
Faith and justice: a delicate balance [care for the poor] A. DiIanni. il *America* 161:32-4+ Jl 15-22 '89
Flesh-and-blood priorities. il *Christianity Today* 33:18-19 Ja 13 '89
Home, street home [homeless; cover story] B. Spring. il *Christianity Today* 33:15-20 Ap 21 '89
If you give a feast, invite the poor. K. Koyama. il *The Christian Century* 106:747 Ag 16-23 '89
The new Irish immigrant [conference sponsored by National Conference of Catholic Bishops' Committee on Migration] R. Bautch. *America* 160:236-7 Mr 18 '89
A 'new moon' sensitivity. L. O. Sanneh. *The Christian Century* 106:811 S 13-20 '89
One point of light [New York City homeless woman M. Davis taken in by S. Braun of Honesdale, Pa.] D. Finkel. il pors *Esquire* 112:123-8+ O '89
The peculiar blessings of poverty. P. Yancey. il *Christianity Today* 33:72 Je 16 '89
A rebirth of virtue: religion and liberal renewal. K. Townsend. *The Washington Monthly* 21:36-7 F '89
Social teaching and social history: learning from the early church [views of G. Theissen] M. M. Mitchell. *The Christian Century* 106:724-5 Ag 2-9 '89
Structures of interest, structures of love: a response to Michael Novak [discussion of January 28, 1989 article, Structures of virtue, structures of sin: a theology of natural liberty] M. Novak. *America* 160:369-71 Ap 22 '89
Structures of virtue, structures of sin: a theology of natural liberty [address, May 5, 1988; cover story] M. Novak. *America* 160:54-60 Ja 28 '89
The success of the sects among Hispanics in the United States. J. J. Diaz Vilar. il *America* 160:174-5+ F 25 '89
Welfare and workfare: a dispute [discussion of December 14, 1988 article, Blinded by metaphor: churches and welfare reform] R. S. Bachelder. *The Christian Century* 106:419-21 Ap 19 '89
Brazil
Assassination in Brazil [land reform activist J. F. Alevino] B. Tyson. *The Christian Century* 106:384-7 Ap 12 '89

Left-wing miracles [views of C. Boff] D. Lee. *National Review* 41:34 S 29 '89
Of many things [Harvey Cox's The silencing of Leonardo Boff] G. W. Hunt. *America* 160:98 F 11 '89
Old friends and new problems. J. B. Malley. *America* 161:275-6 O 28 '89
Developing countries
Kairos international: call to conversion. R. M. Brown. il *The Christian Century* 106:1091-3 N 22 '89
El Salvador
A community of remembrance. S. Hutchinson. *The Christian Century* 106:853-6 S 27 '89
Germany (East)
Questions for the East German church [Dresden conference] J. C. Erlick. *The Christian Century* 106:791-5 Ag 30-S 6 '89
Guatemala
Mass appeal [Catholic priest A. Giron] M. Cooper. il por *Mother Jones* 14:14 D '89
Haiti
Little priest, big general [J.-B. Aristide and P. Avril] S. Rodman. il *National Review* 41:24-5 S 29 '89
India
A pencil in the hand of God [interview with Mother Teresa] E. W. Desmond. por *Time* 134:11+ D 4 '89
Latin America
Blending salt and spice, joining wisdom and prophecy [cover story] B. C. Lane. il *The Christian Century* 106:499-502 My 10 '89
Liberation theology adapts & endures [excerpt from Liberation theology and its critics] A. F. McGovern. il *Commonweal* 116:587-90 N 3 '89
Trying to hold on to the Medellín legacy [Notre Dame conference marks 20th anniversary of Latin American Bishops' Conference] D. G. Peerman. *The Christian Century* 106:403-4 Ap 19 '89
Mexico
The Mexican Church: into the public arena [Catholic Church; cover story] D. Goulet. il *America* 160:318-22 Ap 8 '89
Reviving Mexico City neighborhood by neighborhood. J. H. Fish and J. Kretzmann. il *The Christian Century* 106:1116-18 N 29 '89
Peru
A Christian spirituality of nonviolence. E. W. Ranly. *America* 161:110-11+ Ag 26-S 2 '89
Has God forgotten Peru? R. A. Schroth. il *Commonweal* 116:459-61 S 8 '89
Liberation theology and the Peruvian Church [cover story] J. A. McCoy. *America* 160:526-30 Je 3 '89
Peru in peril. E. W. Ranly. il *The Christian Century* 106:657-9 Jl 5-12 '89
The Peruvian Church and liberation theology [discussion of June 3, 1989 article, Liberation theology and the Peruvian Church] J. A. McCoy. *America* 161:84-5+ Ag 12-19 '89
Squalor in the "City of God" [work of D. Wroughton in Lima] P. Yancey. il *Christianity Today* 33:12-13 F 17 '89
Philippines
Philippine Council celebrates 25 years [National Council of Churches] R. M. Brown. *The Christian Century* 106:69-71 Ja 25 '89

CHURCH AND STATE
See also
> Public schools and religion
> Religion and law
> Religion and politics
> Religious liberty
> Sunday—Laws and regulations
> Taxation, Exemption from
> Williamsburg charter

An "accommodating" Court [Supreme Court lets stand a licensing law that allows child care centers run by religious organizations to seek an exempt status] D. Neff. *Christianity Today* 33:15 Mr 3 '89
A 'Christian nation' in the Far West [declaration by E. Mecham supporters] *U.S. News & World Report* 106:14 Mr 27 '89
Christmas in July [crèche and menorah decision issued by the Supreme Court] *America* 161:27 Jl 15-22 '89
Church and state. E. Doerr. See issues of The Humanist
Court and crèche [Supreme Court ruling on religious symbols on public property] *The Christian Century* 106:713 Ag 2-9 '89
Court rules on clergy malpractice, Sabbath. *Christianity Today* 33:51-2 My 12 '89
Court upholds prayer ban before games [cases before Supreme Court] *Christianity Today* 33:55 Jl 14 '89
Crimes of faith? [denial of medical care to children] D. Neff. *Christianity Today* 33:17 Je 16 '89
Disability bill may go too far for churches [Americans with Disabilities Act of 1989] il *Christianity Today* 33:54-5 Je 16 '89
God's will vs. doctor's orders. C. Levine. il *Parents* 64:220+ Mr '89
The High Court's "S" word [sectarian used as synonym for religious] R. A. Baer. il *Christianity Today* 33:20-1 S 8 '89

CHURCH AND STATE—*cont.*

Holiday displays [religious symbols on public property] *The Christian Century* 106:1194 D 20-27 '89

Ignore a menorah [Supreme Court rules on public religious displays] S. Bates. *The New Republic* 201:14-16 Jl 31 '89

Is the Court hostile to religion? [Christmas crèche-menorah display decision] R. N. Ostling. il *Time* 134:80 Jl 17 '89

Mayor Koch and Cardinal O'Connor: a conversation [excerpts from His Eminence and Hizzoner] E. Koch; J. J. O'Connor. il *Good Housekeeping* 208:148+ My '89

O'Connor fumbles 'Christian nation' case [Justice S. D. O'Connor's letter in support of Arizona Republican Party resolution] E. M. Gaffney, Jr. *The Christian Century* 106:373-5 Ap 12 '89

Our flag is not sacred. R. McKinniss. por *Christianity Today* 33:8 S 8 '89

The prophet motive [book by E. Koch and J. O'Connor] J. Klein. il pors *New York* 22:12+ Mr 20 '89

Right to life, church-state cases before Court [Supreme Court] il *Christianity Today* 33:44+ O 6 '89

Three Court cases. *The Christian Century* 106:976 N 1 '89

'Wall of separation': a principle in crisis? D. Slingluff. *Christianity Today* 33:69+ N 17 '89

Why 'separation' is not the key to church-state relations [cover story; with reply by D. M. Kelley] M. McConnell. il *The Christian Century* 106:43-52 Ja 18 '89

Cambodia

See also
Christians—Cambodia

Canada

'Going to law' in Canada. T. Sinclair-Faulkner. *The Christian Century* 106:68-9 Ja 25 '89

Chile

See also
Catholic Church—Chile

China

See also
Christians—China

No more bad guys? L. Cryderman. il *Christianity Today* 33:16 My 12 '89

Czechoslovakia

See also
Catholic Church—Czechoslovakia

Religion in Czechoslovakia, 1989. M. J. Lavelle. *America* 161:375-7 N 25 '89

Eastern Europe

See also
Catholic Church—Eastern Europe
Christians—Eastern Europe

Echoes of *glasnost*. K. A. Lawton. il maps *Christianity Today* 33:26-8 O 20 '89

Religion and revolution: top story of 1989 [cover story] il *The Christian Century* 106:1187-90 D 20-27 '89

Ethiopia

See also
Christians—Ethiopia

Germany (East)

See also
Christians—Germany (East)
Protestant churches—Germany (East)

Greece

See also
Orthodox Eastern Church—Greece

Haiti

See also
Catholic Church—Haiti

Hong Kong

See also
Catholic Church—Hong Kong

Hungary

See also
Catholic Church—Hungary

Ireland

See also
Catholic Church—Ireland

Japan

Churches and the emperor. P. Park. *The Christian Century* 106:6 Ja 4-11 '89

Korea (South)

Koreans yearn for reunification [trip to North by Moon Ik Hwan] D. G. Peerman. map *The Christian Century* 106:580-2 Je 7-14 '89

Lebanon

See also
Christians—Lebanon

Mexico

See also
Catholic Church—Mexico

Nicaragua

See also
Catholic Church—Nicaragua
Christians—Nicaragua
Evangelical churches—Nicaragua

Philippines

See also
Catholic Church—Philippines

Poland

See also
Catholic Church—Poland

Soviet Union

See also
Christians—Soviet Union
Old Believers
Orthodox Eastern Church, Russian
Pentecostal churches—Soviet Union

The idea of Holy Russia; tr. by J. Crowfoot. S. S. Averintsev. il *History Today* 39:37-44 N '89

No more bad guys? L. Cryderman. il *Christianity Today* 33:16 My 12 '89

Sweden

See also
Lutheran Church—Sweden

Turkey

See also
Christians—Turkey

United States
See Church and state

Vietnam

See also
Catholic Church—Vietnam
Christians—Vietnam

Yugoslavia

See also
Orthodox Eastern Church—Yugoslavia

CHURCH AND THE POOR *See* Church and social problems

CHURCH AND THE PRESS

The great God blackout [Life magazine removes mention of God from cover of copies sold in New York City] M. E. Marty. *The Christian Century* 106:967 O 25 '89

Those turbulent bishops [New York times' criticism of positions taken by Catholic bishops] R. J. Neuhaus. il *National Review* 41:32-3 D 31 '89

CHURCH AND THE WORLD

See also
World Council of Churches

Capitalism and technology in global perspective: a dispute [discussion of May 3, 1989 article, The theological challenge of globalization] M. L. Stackhouse. *The Christian Century* 106:690-3 Jl 19-26 '89

Church/world watch. J. B. Hehir. See occasional issues of Commonweal

The Church and its public life [address, May 18, 1989; cover story] M. O. Steinfels. *America* 160:550-8 Je 10 '89

East-West, North-South [papal letter] J. B. Hehir. il *Commonweal* 116:614-15 N 17 '89

The theological challenge of globalization [cover story] M. L. Stackhouse. il *The Christian Century* 106:468-71 My 3 '89

CHURCH ARCHITECTURE *See* Churches (Buildings)

CHURCH ART *See* Christian art and symbolism

CHURCH ATTENDANCE

A Catholic taste in clothes [dress code at Sacred Heart Church, Dayton, Ohio] il por *Newsweek* 114:27 S 18 '89

Come back, little Sheba [Catholics] H. Fehren. *U.S. Catholic* 54:39-41 Je '89

How to get through to a lapsed Catholic [cover story] J. Deedy. il *U.S. Catholic* 54:6-13 Ap '89

The pivotal generation [baby boomers] P. Rinehart. il *Christianity Today* 33:21-6 O 6 '89

CHURCH CALENDAR

A fixed date for Easter? P. H. Pfatteicher. *The Christian Century* 106:300-1 Mr 22-29 '89

CHURCH CAMPS

A hopeful, happy camper. M. S. Van Leeuwen. il *Christianity Today* 33:13 Jl 14 '89

CHURCH COLLEGES AND UNIVERSITIES

See also
Brigham Young University
Catholic colleges and universities
Eastern College
Liberty University
Philadelphia College of Bible
Westmont College

Abortion: common at Christian colleges? il *Christianity Today* 33:42-3 Jl 14 '89

Playing the oxymoron game. G. K. Brushaber. il *Christianity Today* 33:17 D 15 '89

The university tag. K. H. Sidey. il *Christianity Today* 33:59-61 N 3 '89

Canada

Canada's evangelical schools grow, change. L. Mackey. *Christianity Today* 33:60-1 N 3 '89

CHURCH CONFERENCES *See* Religious conferences

CHURCH COOPERATION *See* Religious cooperation

CHURCH DECORATION AND ORNAMENT

The gospel according to Verity [carving central entryway figures at Cathedral of St. John the Divine] B. Weber. il *The New York Times Magazine* p86 Jl 9 '89

CHURCH DISCIPLINE

See also
Excommunication

CHURCH EMPLOYEES
See also
United Methodist Church—Employees
Salaries, pensions, etc.
Medical costs hit churches. *The Christian Century* 106:713-14 Ag 2-9 '89

CHURCH FINANCE
See also
Black churches—Finance
Evangelical Council for Financial Accountability
Evangelistic work—Finance
Lutheran Church—United States—Finance
National Religious Broadcasters. Ethics and Financial Integrity Commission
Taxation, Exemption from
Tithes
Bethlehem on a budget. T. Stafford. il *Christianity Today* 33:34-5 D 15 '89
Fatigue fatigue [building of 6,500-seat Calvary Church near Charlotte, N.C.] M. E. Marty. *The Christian Century* 106:767 Ag 16-23 '89
Jubilee time. M. E. Marty. *The Christian Century* 106:999 N 1 '89

CHURCH GOVERNMENT
See also
Catholic Church—Government
Sunday monarchists and Monday citizens? W. J. Everett. *The Christian Century* 106:503-5 My 10 '89

CHURCH GROWTH
Religious best-smellers. M. E. Marty. *The Christian Century* 106:943 O 18 '89
Turning around the Lord's business. T. A. Stewart. il *Fortune* 120:116-17+ S 25 '89
Anecdotes, facetiae, satire, etc.
The ultimate church [cover story] T. Raabe. *The Christian Century* 106:717-21 Ag 2-9 '89

CHURCH GROWTH DEVELOPMENT INTERNATIONAL
Many are called [N. Whan's telemarketing service specializes in starting up new churches] R. N. Ostling. il por *Time* 133:79 F 27 '89

CHURCH HISTORY
See also
Bible
Heresy
Christianity as an enfolding circle [interview with J. J. Pelikan] J. Carey. por *U.S. News & World Report* 106:57 Je 26 '89
Bibliography
Theology, history, & transitions. L. Cunningham. *Commonweal* 116:539-41 O 6 '89
Middle Ages
See also
Crusades
Reformation
Primitive and early church
Ascetic enthusiasm: Origen and the early church. R. Williams. bibl il *History Today* 39:31-7 D '89
Social teaching and social history: learning from the early church [views of G. Theissen] M. M. Mitchell. *The Christian Century* 106:724-5 Ag 2-9 '89
Sophisticated primitives then, primitive sophisticates now [adaptation of address; cover story] M. E. Marty. il *The Christian Century* 106:588-91 Je 7-14 '89

CHURCH LEADERSHIP *See* Christian leadership

CHURCH MANAGEMENT
See also
Leadership Network (Firm)
Put faith back into management. L. Thompson. por *Christianity Today* 33:10 My 12 '89
Turning around the Lord's business. T. A. Stewart. il *Fortune* 120:116-17+ S 25 '89

CHURCH MEMBERSHIP
See also
Confirmation
Membership figures. *The Christian Century* 106:776 Ag 30-S 6 '89
Those mainline blues [decline in membership] R. N. Ostling. il *Time* 133:94-6 My 22 '89
Anecdotes, facetiae, satire, etc.
Mess up the computers! M. E. Marty. *The Christian Century* 106:831 S 13-20 '89

CHURCH MONUMENTS SOCIETY
Articles of association: the Church Monuments Society. R. Cavendish. il *History Today* 39:60-1 Mr '89

CHURCH MUSIC *See* Religious music

CHURCH OF CHRIST, SCIENTIST
Crimes of faith? [denial of medical care to children] D. Neff. *Christianity Today* 33:17 Je 16 '89
Healing an ailing church. J. L. Sheler. il *U.S. News & World Report* 107:75-6 N 6 '89

CHURCH OF ENGLAND
See also
Catholic Church—Relations—Church of England
Billy brings 'em in [use of B. Graham's crusades to stimulate clerical vocations] A. McCarthy. il *Commonweal* 116:456-7 S 8 '89

CHURCH OF GOD
Trouble brews over charges of "liberalism". D. Disch. por *Christianity Today* 33:42-3 F 17 '89

CHURCH OF GOD IN CHRIST
COGIC bishop announces new anti-drug campaign. il *Jet* 76:38 Jl 31 '89
COGIC bishop Louis Ford lauded during 54th anniv. of his church in Chicago. il pors *Jet* 76:18 Jl 31 '89

CHURCH OF JESUS CHRIST OF LATTER-DAY SAINTS
See Mormons and Mormonism

CHURCH OF LOVE
The trouble with angels [mail order fraud perpetrated against single men] il *New Choices for the Best Years* 29:13+ Ap '89
Victims of the Church of Love were only the lonely [mail order scam perpetrated by D. S. Lowry] J. Friedman. il por *People Weekly* 31:77-8+ Ja 30 '89

CHURCH OF SCIENTOLOGY *See* Scientology
CHURCH OF SWEDEN *See* Lutheran Church—Sweden
CHURCH OF THE NAZARENE
Nazarenes break ground in social/moral concern. R. Frame. il *Christianity Today* 33:48+ S 8 '89

CHURCH PARISHES *See* Parishes
CHURCH POLITY *See* Church government
CHURCH RELATED COLLEGES *See* Church colleges and universities
CHURCH RELATED SCHOOLS *See* Church schools
CHURCH RENEWAL
See also
Mission of the church
Being 50 is okay. G. K. Brushaber. il *Christianity Today* 33:13 Ja 13 '89

CHURCH SCHOOLS
See also
Catholic schools
Sunday schools
Teaching as though life hangs in the balance [Zion Christian School in Seattle] S. Ulstein. il *Christianity Today* 33:10-11 Ap 21 '89
Transmitting a vision: religion in independent schools. D. R. Heischman. *The Christian Century* 106:417-9 Ap 19 '89
Finance
Bush clarifies position on tuition tax credits. K. A. Lawton. *Christianity Today* 33:55 My 12 '89
Race relations
Christian school racism. T. Penning. *The Education Digest* 55:40-2 N '89
State aid
Election '88. E. Doerr. il *The Humanist* 49:37-8 Ja/F '89

CHURCH SERVICES
See also
Worship

CHURCH UNION
See also
Consultation on Church Union
Ecumenical movement
World Council of Churches

CHURCH UNIVERSAL AND TRIUMPHANT
Paradise under siege [investigation of leader E. C. Prophet] M. P. Harris. il por *Time* 134:61 Ag 28 '89

CHURCH WORK
See also
Christian leadership
Church and social problems
City churches
Evangelistic work
Missions
Revivals
Ministry as more than a helping profession [cover story] S. Hauerwas and W. H. Willimon. il *The Christian Century* 106:282-4 Mr 15 '89

CHURCH WORK WITH ABUSED WOMEN
Battered into submission [wife abuse in the Christian home; excerpt] J. Alsdurf and P. E. Alsdurf. il *Christianity Today* 33:24-7 Je 16 '89

CHURCH WORK WITH AIDS PATIENTS
AIDS epidemic grows, but is the church ready? [Mid-Atlantic Conference on AIDS ministry] D. Porter. *Christianity Today* 33:42 F 17 '89
The faces of fear. C. E. Meirose. il *America* 160:372-3 Ap 22 '89
George's story. R. A. Sirico. *Commonweal* 116:464-5 S 8 '89
Joining the AIDS fight [black churches] J. N. Baker and R. Elam. il *Newsweek* 113:26-7 Ap 17 '89
What would Jesus do about AIDS? S. Arterburn. por *Christianity Today* 33:10 F 3 '89

CHURCH WORK WITH ALCOHOLICS
Dry times at Slick's Bar [Minneapolis] M. A. Kuharski. il pors *Christianity Today* 33:14-15 Mr 17 '89
Twelve steps for women alcoholics. G. Unterberger. *The Christian Century* 106:1150-2 D 6 '89

CHURCH WORK WITH CHILDREN
See also
Child Evangelism Fellowship Inc.
Child Evangelism Ministries, Inc.
Church and day care

CHURCH WORK WITH CHILDREN—See also—cont.
Church camps
Sunday schools
Victims of abuse: paying the price for the sins of others [child molestation and Catholic teaching] M. B. Mann. *U.S. Catholic* 54:36-8 Jl '89

CHURCH WORK WITH CHILDREN OF DIVORCED PARENTS
The biggest divorce. J. Guest. il *Christianity Today* 33:30-2 N 17 '89

CHURCH WORK WITH DRUG ADDICTS
Christian veterans, new recruits on the front lines. S. Rabey. il *Christianity Today* 33:52+ O 6 '89
The church and the drug crisis: ministers mobilize against 'the death of a race'. il *Ebony* 44:160+ Ag '89
COGIC bishop announces new anti-drug campaign. il *Jet* 76:38 Jl 31 '89

CHURCH WORK WITH FAMILIES
The Church and family life: more than avoiding contraceptives [Catholic Church] M. Finley. *America* 161:205 O 7 '89
Families in trouble: how to know when to get help. D. Morris. il *U.S. Catholic* 54:30-6 Ag '89

CHURCH WORK WITH HOMOSEXUALS
Coming out. T. Stafford. il *Christianity Today* 33:16-21 Ag 18 '89
The human rights of homosexuals [Catholic Church] G. C. Zahn. *Commonweal* 116:462-5 S 8 '89

CHURCH WORK WITH PRISONERS
See also
Prison Fellowship Ministries
The church picnic goes to jail [work of Mother York in Chicago] R. Clapp. il por *Christianity Today* 33:14-15 Je 16 '89
Daughter of Manson victims finds forgiveness [S. LaBerge and inmate C. Watson] J. Shaver. il pors *Christianity Today* 33:50-1 S 22 '89
Glasnost in Perm 35? [Soviet labor camp] K. A. Lawton. il *Christianity Today* 33:37-8 O 20 '89

CHURCH WORK WITH PROSTITUTES
Loving a prostitute [Genesis House in Chicago; cover story] J. Hahn. il *The Christian Century* 106:415-16 Ap 19 '89

CHURCH WORK WITH SINGLE MOTHERS
See also
Claretian Medical Center

CHURCH WORK WITH SINGLE PEOPLE
Beyond the stiff upper lip [excerpt from The sexual Christian] T. Stafford. il *Christianity Today* 33:30-4 Ja 13 '89

CHURCH WORK WITH THE AGED
The basics. M. E. Marty. *The Christian Century* 106:191 F 15 '89
Coming to grips with an aging church. F. Hutchison. il *The Christian Century* 106:206-8 F 22 '89

CHURCH WORK WITH THE DYING
Lead me safely through death [St. Joseph's Hospice in London; cover story] W. F. Carr. *America* 160:264-7 Mr 25 '89

CHURCH WORK WITH THE SICK
What I was doing at the hospital. R. Brow. il *Christianity Today* 33:31-2 Ap 21 '89

CHURCH WORK WITH YOUTH
See also
Exodus Youth Services (Washington, D.C.)
The priest who loves gangsters [Los Angeles mission for gang members run by G. J. Boyle; cover story] E. Shorris. il *The Nation* 249:737+ D 18 '89

CHURCH YEAR
See also
Church calendar
Holy Week

CHURCHER, PETER B., AND LAWTON, JOHN H.
Beware of well-fed felines. il *Natural History* p40-7 Jl '89

CHURCHER, SHARON
Radical transformations. il pors *The New York Times Magazine* p30-1+ Jl 16 '89

CHURCHES (BUILDINGS)
See also
Cathedrals
In a right spirit [work of C. Tapley] M. Gaskie. il *Architectural Record* 177:100-11 F '89

Conservation and restoration
Keeping the faith in the USSR after a thousand years. J. H. Billington. bibl (p174) il *Smithsonian* 20:130-6+ Ap '89
Warding off demolition. *The Christian Century* 106:41-2 Ja 18 '89

Colorado
See also
Englewood (Colo.)—Churches (Buildings)

France
See also
Paris (France)—Churches (Buildings)

Great Britain
See also
Church Monuments Society
London (England)—Churches (Buildings)

Louisiana
See also
New Orleans (La.)—Churches (Buildings)

Peru
See also
Arequipa (Peru)—Churches (Buildings)

Soviet Union
Keeping the faith in the USSR after a thousand years. J. H. Billington. bibl (p174) il *Smithsonian* 20:130-6+ Ap '89

Texas
See also
Dallas (Tex.)—Churches (Buildings)

Vermont
See also
Island Pond (Vt.)—Churches (Buildings)

CHURCHES (BUILDINGS), CONVERTED *See* Buildings, Remodeled

CHURCHILL, SIR WINSTON, 1874-1965
What can England do about Hitler? [reprint from October 1938 issue] *Current History* 88:24-5+ Ja '89

about
The last lion: alone [excerpt] W. Manchester. il pors *Conservative Digest* 15:63+ Jl/Ag '89
Winston agonistes. D. Cannadine. bibl f il por *The New York Review of Books* 36:36-42 Je 15 '89

CHURCHILL (MAN.)
Diary of a bear-watcher [polar bears] F. Bruemmer. il *International Wildlife* 19:46-51 S/O '89

CHURCHILL DOWNS (LOUISVILLE, KY.: RACE TRACK)
See Race tracks

CHURCHLAND, PATRICIA SMITH
From Descartes to neural networks. *Scientific American* 261:118 Jl '89

CHURCH'S FRIED CHICKEN, INC.
Chicken that packs a punch [A. Copeland] M. Barrier. il pors *Nation's Business* 77:52+ Jl '89

CHURM, PETER
about
A case of mistaken identity. M. Beauchamp. il por *Forbes* 144:103 Jl 24 '89

CHUTE, DAVID
Toronto wigs out. *Film Comment* 25:70+ N/D '89

CHUTES
See also
Laundry chutes

CHYNA
Photographs and photography
On becoming a short-order chef of lighting. J. Fruchtman. il por *Petersen's Photographic Magazine* 18:28-9 S '89

CIA *See* United States. Central Intelligence Agency
CIAA *See* Central Intercollegiate Athletic Association

CIABATTARI, JANE
Comeback charisma. *Harper's Bazaar* 122:102+ Ja '89
Will the '90s be the age of envy? [cover story] il *Psychology Today* 23:46-50 D '89

CIARCIA, STEVE
Ciarcia's circuit cellar. See issues of Byte through December 1988

CIBA-GEIGY AG
Tempest in a test tube [bidders for Connaught Biosciences] G. W. Taylor. il *Maclean's* 102:42 S 25 '89

CICCARELLI, DINO
about
Rough the passer, go to jail. S. Rosenbloom. il *Sport (New York, N.Y.)* 80:10 Ja '89

CICIPPIO, JOSEPH
Kidnapping
Hostage showdown. R. Watson. il map *Newsweek* 114:14-18 Ag 14 '89
Hostages to terror [cover story; special section; with editorial comment by Kevin Doyle] il pors *Maclean's* 102:2, 20-4+ Ag 14 '89
An unlikely target. il por *Time* 134:19 Ag 14 '89

CIDER
House cider rules. R. Kimber. il *Country Journal* 16:81-4+ S/O '89

CIGAR INDUSTRY
Cuba
Seeing red [Z. Davidoff] M. Kripalani. il por *Forbes* 144 Special Issue:370+ O 23 '89

Switzerland
See also
Davidoff & Cie

CIGARETTE INDUSTRY
See also
American Brands, Inc.
Philip Morris, Inc.
R. J. Reynolds Tobacco Co.
Beverages and tobacco. E. Giltenan. il *Forbes* 143:100+ Ja 9 '89

Advertising
A smokeless cigarette ad? [Philip Morris' Bill of Rights ad campaign stirs controversy] *Newsweek* 114:64 N 13 '89
A smoking issue [laws banning Canadian tobacco advertising] P. Chisholm. il *Maclean's* 102:28 Ja 16 '89
Taxation of advertising: a violation of free speech? W. Murray. il *USA Today (Periodical)* 117:23-4 Mr '89

CIGARETTE INDUSTRY—Advertising—*cont.*

Warning: sports stars may be hazardous to your health [cover story] J. DeParle. il *The Washington Monthly* 21:34-44+ S '89

Caricatures and cartoons

Smoke signals [Doonesbury mocks cigarette ads that entice teens to smoke] P. Theiler. il *Common Cause Magazine* 15:8 S/O '89

Ethical aspects

The $600 million cigarette scam [RJR Nabisco creates bogus profits through trade loading] C. J. Loomis. il *Fortune* 120:89+ D 4 '89

Export-import trade

Fuming over a hazardous export [U.S. cigarettes sold in Asia] B. Rudolph. il *Time* 134:82 O 2 '89

Getting opium to the masses: the political economy of addiction [U.S. cigarette exports to Asia] A. Cockburn. il *The Nation* 249:482-3 O 30 '89

Hazardous to whose health? [U.S. cigarette exports] J. Drummond. il *Forbes* 144:89+ D 11 '89

Smoking gun [C. Yeutter's efforts on behalf of cigarette industry while U.S. Trade Representative] S. Hornik. il *Common Cause Magazine* 15:9 Mr/Ap '89

A trade threat that worked [Japan opens cigarette market to foreigners] G. Eisenstodt and H. Katayama. il *Forbes* 143:38-9 Ap 3 '89

Uncle Sam shouldn't be a traveling salesman for tobacco [cigarette exports to Asia] P. Magnusson. il *Business Week* p61 O 9 '89

Laws and regulations

Fighting fire with P.R. [Tobacco Institute fights cigarette fire safety legislation] M. Levin. il *The Nation* 249:52-5 Jl 10 '89

Marketing

The $600 million cigarette scam [RJR Nabisco creates bogus profits through trade loading] C. J. Loomis. il *Fortune* 120:89+ D 4 '89

The cigarette makers: just wheezing along. S. Ticer. il *Business Week* p58-9 Ja 23 '89

Securities

The cigarette makers: just wheezing along. S. Ticer. il *Business Week* p58-9 Ja 23 '89

Japan

See also
Japan Tobacco Inc.

CIGARETTE SMOKING See Smoking

CIGARETTE VENDING MACHINES See Vending machines

CIGARETTES

See also
Smokeless cigarettes

Cigarettes: the low-tar irony [research by Orestes T. Chortyk] *Science News* 136:398 D 16 '89

Advertising

See Cigarette industry—Advertising

Fire resistance

Fighting fire with P.R. [Tobacco Institute fights cigarette fire safety legislation] M. Levin. il *The Nation* 249:52-5 Jl 10 '89

Taxation

Elasticity, it's wonderful. D. Seligman. *Fortune* 119:123-4 F 13 '89

Higher 'sin' taxes: a low blow to the poor. G. S. Becker. il *Business Week* p23 Je 5 '89

Laying the blame [sin taxes] B. D. Colen. il *Health (New York, N.Y.)* 21:38-9 Ag '89

Smokers may be keeping social security healthy . . . but pricier smokes and drinks may still make economic sense. G. Koretz. il *Business Week* p27 Je 5 '89

Smoking 101 [tax level to maximize federal revenues; research by Michael Grossman] D. Seligman. il *Fortune* 119:134 F 27 '89

Taxing the wages of sin. P. Wallich. *Scientific American* 260:22 Je '89

CIGNA CORPORATION

Up to B.A.T.? [J. Coxon and Cigna Corp. to benefit in battle for BAT Industries] J. Zweig. il por *Forbes* 144:102 Ag 21 '89

CIGUATERA

Fish poisoning. B. T. Hunter. il *Consumers' Research Magazine* 72:8-9 Ap '89

CII HONEYWELL BULL

See also
Groupe Bull

CIKOVSKY, NICOLAI

American paintings in the Manoogian Collection. il *Antiques* 136:132-43 Jl '89

CILAZAPRIL

Inhibitors of angiotensin-converting enzyme prevent myointimal proliferation after vascular injury [use after balloon catheterization] J. S. Powell and others. bibl f il *Science* 245:186-8 Jl 14 '89

CILIA AND CILIARY MOTION

See also
Flagella

CILIARY NEUROTROPHIC FACTOR

Purification, cloning, and expression of ciliary neurotrophic factor (CNTF). L.-F. H. Lin and others. bibl f il *Science* 246:1023-5 N 24 '89

CILIATES

See also
Tetrahymena

CILLUFFO, FRANK J. A.

about
"We were shaking with rage". A. A. Lappen. il pors *Forbes* 144:119+ O 30 '89

CIM *See* Computer integrated manufacturing

CIMARRON COUNTY (OKLA.)

Climate

The Dust Bowl. M. Parfit. bibl (p174) il *Smithsonian* 20:44-54+ Je '89

CIMENT, MICHEL, 1938-

Expatriate. il por *Film Comment* 25:16-19 My/Je '89

Visually speaking [interview with H. Pinter] il por *Film Comment* 25:20-2 My/Je '89

CIMETIDINE

Drugs from emasculated hormones: the principle of syntopic antagonism [Nobel lecture, December 8, 1988] Sir J. W. Black. bibl f il *Science* 245:486-93 Ag 4 '89

Sting operation nabs Iranian counterfeit drug dealer [counterfeit Tagamet dealer J. Naghdi] W. Grigg. il *FDA Consumer* 23:37-8 Ap '89

CIMFLEX TEKNOWLEDGE CORPORATION

A factory that practically runs itself. il por *Business Week* p145 My 8 '89

CIMONS, MARLENE, 1945-

Bad blood? *Essence* 20:21-2 S '89

Stroll models. il *Runner's World* 24:74-5 Je '89

CINADER, EMILY

about
Captain of the Crew. A. Radakovich. il por *Harper's Bazaar* 122:76+ N '89

CINAR *See* Citizens for Nonviolent Action Against Racism

CINCINNATI (OHIO)

Climate

In search of Cincinnati's weather [historical records] S. L. Horstmeyer. il *Weatherwise* 42:320-6 D '89

Galleries and museums

See also
Contemporary Arts Center (Cincinnati, Ohio)

Police

Eavesdropping left and right [Cincinnati Bell implicated in wiretapping scandal] G. Flannery. il *The Nation* 248:516-18+ Ap 17 '89

Stores

Say g'day to the megamall [Forest Fair] S. Phillips. il *Business Week* p29 Mr 6 '89

CINCINNATI BALLET

Reviews:
1988-89 season in Cincinnati. J. Light. *Dance Magazine* 63:74-5 S '89

CINCINNATI BELL INC.

Eavesdropping left and right [implicated in wiretapping scandal] G. Flannery. il *The Nation* 248:516-18+ Ap 17 '89

CINCINNATI MICROWAVE, INC.

Cincinnati Microwave tries to strengthen its signal [cellular co-marketing deal with GTE] M. Mallory. *Business Week* p29-30 Mr 6 '89

CINCINNATI/NEW ORLEANS CITY BALLET

With money at issue, Cincinnati and New Orleans redefine their relations. J. Light. il *Dance Magazine* 63:6 Mr '89

CINEMA *See* Motion pictures

CINEMATOGRAPHERS

See also
Nykvist, Sven, 1922-
Storaro, Vittorio, 1940-

Cinematographers: eye to eye [special section] il *Film Comment* 25:31-4+ S/O '89

CINEMATOGRAPHY *See* Motion picture photography

CINEPHILES (ORGANIZATION)

Profiles [H. Graff] D. Watt. por *The New Yorker* 65:59-60+ N 20 '89

CINEPLEX CORP.

See also
Cineplex Odeon Corporation

CINEPLEX ODEON CORPORATION

Closing credits [C. Bronfman sells stake] J. Daly. *Maclean's* 102:34 Ap 24 '89

Co-starring soon: MCA and Cineplex? G. G. Marcial. *Business Week* p87 Ja 16 '89

Every trick in the books [accounting techniques] D. Wechsler. il por *Forbes* 143:46+ My 29 '89

Fast fade for a cinema king [G. Drabinsky] J. Hammer. il por *Newsweek* 114:61 N 6 '89

A melodrama's final scene [G. Drabinsky gives up struggle to regain control] J. DeMont and P. Chisholm. il por *Maclean's* 102:42-3 D 11 '89

Mogul in distress [G. Drabinsky] B. Bremner. *Business Week* p45 O 9 '89

An Olympian extravaganza [Phantom of the Opera] D. Francis. il *Maclean's* 102:11 F 6 '89

The screen wars [Famous Players vs. Cineplex Odeon] J. Daly. il pors *Maclean's* 102:40-1 My 29 '89

Showdown at Cineplex [G. Drabinsky battles to regain control] J. DeMont. il por *Maclean's* 102:46-7 My 8 '89

CINERAMA, INC.
Ron Perelman's $640 million unsure thing [acquisition and resale of Technicolor, Inc.] R. King. il por *Forbes* 144:42-4+ O 30 '89

CINESANJUAN FESTIVAL *See* Motion picture festivals— Puerto Rico

CINNABAR (FIRM)
Lights! Camera! Hammer and nails! M. Barrier. il por *Nation's Business* 77:12+ Je '89

CINNAMON ROLLS
Homemade cinnamon rolls. J. Taylor. il *Better Homes and Gardens* 67:148 O '89
On a roll . . . il *Seventeen* 48:115+ F '89
Peanuts, popcorn . . . cinnamon rolls? [sold at Anaheim Stadium] E. Cohen. il *Sport (New York, N.Y.)* 80:83 My '89

CIO *See* AFL-CIO

CIOCHON, RUSSELL L.
about
Stalking the giant ape. J. James. il map *Discover* 10:42-6+ F '89

CIPHERS *See* Cryptography

CIRCADIAN RHYTHMS *See* Biological rhythms

THE CIRCLE [drama] *See* Maugham, W. Somerset (William Somerset), 1874-1965

CIRCLE IN FASHION
Gone full circle. il *'Teen* 33:20 Mr '89

CIRCLE K CORP.
Confessions of a convenience man. K. Hannon. il *Forbes* 144:10 O 16 '89
Troubled Circle K is turning this way and that. K. Kerwin. il por *Business Week* p78+ N 20 '89

CIRCLE REPERTORY COMPANY
The Circle is unbroken. M. Wade. il *Horizon (Tuscaloosa, Ala.)* 32:15-16 Ja/F '89

CIRCLE-SQUARING
The circle can be squared! [proof by Miklós Laczkovich] B. A. Cipra. *Science* 244:528 My 5 '89
Squaring the circle [proof by Miklós Laczkovich] R. Ruthen. *Scientific American* 261:22+ Jl '89
The straight side of sliced circles [work of Miklós Laczkovich] *Science News* 136:31 Jl 8 '89

CIRCUIT TRAINING
Aerobic circuit training—a combination of strength and aerobic exercises—is today's state-of-the-art workout. J. Scandura. *Vogue* 179:234+ O '89

CIRCUITS, INTEGRATED *See* Integrated circuits

CIRCULAR SAWS *See* Saws and sawing

CIRCULATION, OCEAN *See* Ocean circulation

CIRCULATORY SYSTEM *See* Cardiovascular system

CIRCUMCISION
Circumcision may protect against the AIDS virus [results of African studies] J. L. Marx. il *Science* 245:470-1 Ag 4 '89
Circumcision—it's not necessary. B. Spock. por *Redbook* 172:53 Ap '89
Circumcision's comeback? [views of American Academy of Pediatrics] V. Brower. il *American Health* 8:126 S '89
Task force says circumcision has benefits [views of American Academy of Pediatrics] *Science News* 135:150 Mr 11 '89

CIRCUMNAVIGATION *See* Voyages around the world

CIRCUS
See also
Peru Amateur Circus (Ind.)
There's a customer born every minute. il por *U.S. News & World Report* 106:15 F 20 '89
Canada
See also
Le Cirque du Soleil
Soviet Union
See also
Moscow Circus

CIRCUS ANIMALS
Training
See Animals—Training

CIRCUS CIRCUS ENTERPRISES INC.
Circus Circus rakes in the bread bread. R. Grover. il *Business Week* p80-2 F 27 '89

CIRCUS IN ART
Circus art mailbag. il *National Geographic World* 169:16 S '89
The evolution of a painting. C. Browning. il *American Artist* 53:54-9 Jl '89

CIRCUS MUSEUMS
See also
P.T. Barnum Museum (Bridgeport, Conn.)

CIRCUS PERFORMERS
See also
Children as circus performers
Clowns
Gebel-Williams, Gunther

CIRCUS SMIRKUS
Feel like clowning around? Step right up to Rob Mermin's big top camp, Circus Smirkus. A. Chambers. il pors *People Weekly* 32:99-101 Ag 14 '89

CIRIELLO, MARIO
Chunnel vision. il *World Press Review* 36:54 Je '89

LE CIRQUE (NEW YORK, N.Y.: RESTAURANT) *See* New York (N.Y.)—Restaurants, nightclubs, bars, etc.

LE CIRQUE DU SOLEIL
Canadian stars [child performers; cover story] il *National Geographic World* 167:4-9 Jl '89

CIRQUE GRÉGOIRE
Riches [production of Bateaux des rêves in Central Park] *The New Yorker* 65:27-8 Je 19 '89

CIRRUS LOGIC (FIRM)
How smart is your disk drive? K. K. Wiegner. il *Forbes* 144:219+ O 30 '89

CISCO (UTAH)
Description
Cisco, Utah—destination or bypass? H. L. Renwick. il map *Focus (New York, N.Y.: 1950)* 39:21-3 Summ '89

CISNEROS, GEORGE
about
The volunteer angel of San Antonio. H. Hylton. il pors *New Choices for the Best Years* 29:76-7+ Ja '89

CISNEROS, HENRY
about
Adios, city hall. T. Vogel. il por *Business Week* p40 F 20 '89

CISNEROS GROUP
Adios, city hall [H. Cisneros] T. Vogel. il por *Business Week* p40 F 20 '89

CISPES *See* U.S. Committee in Solidarity with the People of El Salvador

CISTERNS
Cistern water: soft—and corrosive. *Science News* 135:191 Mr 25 '89

CIT (COMPUTERIZED INDUSTRIAL TOMOGRAPHY) *See* Tomography—Industrial use

CITADEL PRESS
Citadel Press celebrates 30 years in film. il *Publishers Weekly* 236:26 O 13 '89

CITADEL THEATRE (EDMONTON, ALTA.)
A passion for plays. J. Howse. il *Maclean's* 102:62 O 9 '89

CITATION AIRPLANES *See* Airplanes, Business

CITES *See* Convention on International Trade in Endangered Species of Wild Fauna and Flora (1973)

CITIBANK N.A.
Rhodes to Latin America [loan negotiator] J. Zweig. il por *Forbes* 144:142+ S 4 '89

CITICORP
Easy to leave home without it? [Diners Club card] C. Siler. il *Forbes* 144:140 S 4 '89

CITIES AND TOWNS
See also
Business districts
Housing
Location in business and industry
Metropolitan areas
Neighborhoods
Slums
Small towns
Sociology, Urban
Squatter settlements
Streets
Trees in cities
United States. Dept. of Housing and Urban Development
America's boom towns [cover story] M. W. Karmin. il maps *U.S. News & World Report* 107:54-6+ N 13 '89
America's hot cities [cover story; special section] il map *Newsweek* 113:42-9 F 6 '89
The best cities for business [cover story; special section] il *Fortune* 120:56-8+ O 23 '89
The best places to live in America. R. Eisenberg and M. T. Smith. il *Money* 18:124-6+ S '89
Brighter lights for houses in big cities [prices] C. A. Fried. il *Money* 18:71 Je '89
Cities get into the game [sports] G. Macnow. il *Nation's Business* 77:48-9+ N '89
Favorite cities for tomorrow's workers. il *The Futurist* 23:52 Jl/Ag '89
Going home [cover story; special section] il *U.S. News & World Report* 107:44-51+ D 18 '89
Home affordability, city by city. il *Changing Times* 43:51 My '89
The pace of life [link between high speed cities and heart disease] R. Levine. il *Psychology Today* 23:42-6 O '89
Where the men are [six cities with eligible single black men] il *Ebony* 44:98+ F '89
Biblical teaching
City-building and the benefits of Babel. J. W. Aageson. il *The Christian Century* 106:517-18 My 17 '89
Defenses
See also
Civil defense
Finance
See Municipal finance
Growth
See also
Exurbs
Metropolitan areas
Suburbs

CITIES AND TOWNS—Growth—*cont.*
Megacities [studies by Ellen Brennan] A. M. Cunningham. il *Technology Review* 92:12-13 Jl '89
The sky line [mania for skyscrapers and growth in American cities] B. Gill. *The New Yorker* 64:73-7 Ja 9 '89
Third world metropolises are becoming monsters. il *World Press Review* 36:32-4 O '89
Urban growing pains [Denver approves new airport, while Seattle votes for restrictions on building size] G. J. Church. il *Time* 133:33 My 29 '89
A world of megacities. W. Booth. *Science* 243:475-6 Ja 27 '89

History
. . . and man made the town. E. J. Weber. *The American Scholar* 58:79-96 Wint '89

International aspects
City scripts [urban centers of the future] il *Omni (New York, N.Y.)* 12:50-4+ O '89

Names
See Names, Geographical

Photographs and photography
10 most photogenic cities of the world. P. Slaughter. il *Petersen's Photographic Magazine* 18:12-18 O '89
Best city skylines. L. Brownstein. il *Petersen's Photographic Magazine* 18:48-50 D '89
Hometown photo essay. D. Mazzapica. il *Petersen's Photographic Magazine* 18:34-7 S '89

Planning
See City planning

Transit systems
See Local transit

Zone system
See Zoning

Developing countries
Third world metropolises are becoming monsters. il *World Press Review* 36:32-4 O '89

United States
See Cities and towns
CITIES AND TOWNS, MINIATURE *See* Models of cities, towns, etc.
CITIES AND TOWNS, RUINED, EXTINCT, ETC.

Guatemala
See also
Nakbe (Ancient city)

Honduras
See also
Copán (Ancient city)

Iraq
See also
Babylon (Ancient city)
Calah (Ancient city)
Hatra (Iraq)
Mashkan-shapir (Ancient city)

Italy
See also
Pompeii (Ancient city)

Jordan
See also
Petra (Ancient city)

Mexico
See also
Chichén Itzá (Mexico)

Peru
See also
Machu Picchu (Peru)

Turkey
See also
Aphrodisias (Ancient city)
CITIZENS & SOUTHERN CORP.
Why Hugh McColl is courting an Atlanta belle [NCNB goes after Citizens & Southern Corp.] D. Foust and S. Ticer. il por *Business Week* p19-20 Ap 17 '89
CITIZENS ASKING FOR A SAFE ENVIRONMENT
Citizens tackle toxic dump [Sumter, S.C.] R. Chepesiuk. il *The Progressive* 53:12-13 Je '89
CITIZENS' ASSOCIATION FOR SOUND ENERGY
The co-opting of CASE [withdraws opposition to Comanche Peak nuclear plant] G. Aronson. il *The Nation* 249:678+ D 4 '89
CITIZENS' ASSOCIATIONS
See also
Crime prevention—Citizen participation
Special interest groups
CITIZENS FOR NONVIOLENT ACTION AGAINST RACISM
Citizens organize against neo-Nazis. A. Sochocky and C. Siegner. il por *The Progressive* 53:15 Ag '89
CITIZENS FOR RATIONAL TRAFFIC LAWS
Rationalizing the irrational. W. Jeanes. il *Car and Driver* 35:5 D '89
CITIZENSHIP
See also
Aliens
Patriotism
Author wins citizenship battle [case of M. Randall] L. Stapleton. il por *Ms.* 18:71 N '89
"Papa was so proud" [excerpt from Papa, my father] L. F. Buscaglia. il pors *Redbook* 173:24+ Je '89

United States
See Citizenship

Yugoslavia
Between issues [M. Mihajlov stripped of Yugoslav citizenship] *The New Leader* 72:2 Mr 20 '89
CITIZENSHIP EDUCATION
The Civic Achievement Award Program [elementary students] J. Dolenga. *The Education Digest* 55:47-9 O '89
Developing the citizen leader [address, August 18, 1989] S. W. Morse. *Vital Speeches of the Day* 56:79-81 N 15 '89
Promoting civic education. G. H. Wood. *The Education Digest* 54:38-40 Ap '89
Teaching politics as public work [excerpt from Public leadership education] D. Mathews. *The Education Digest* 55:32-4 D '89
CITROËN (AUTOMOBILE) *See* Automobiles, Foreign
CITRUS ANTS *See* Ants
CITRUS FRUIT INDUSTRY
See also
Alico Inc.
CITRUS FRUITS
See also
Cooking—Fruit
Grapefruits
Kumquats
Mandarin oranges
CITRUS FRUITS IN DECORATION *See* Fruits, vegetables, etc. in decoration
CITY (LOS ANGELES, CALIF.: RESTAURANT) *See* Los Angeles (Calif.)—Restaurants, nightclubs, bars, etc.
CITY AGRICULTURE *See* Urban agriculture
CITY AND COUNTRY
See also
Country life
Suburban life
. . . and man made the town. E. J. Weber. *The American Scholar* 58:79-96 Wint '89
In praise of small places [New Yorker abandons urban arena for country life] C. Stinnett. il *Country Journal* 16:72-4 My/Je '89

Anecdotes, facetiae, satire, etc.
From pillar to post. G. Jaynes. il *Life* 12:17 Je '89
CITY AND TOWN LIFE
See also
Suburban life
CITY BUDGET *See* Municipal finance
CITY CHILDREN

Recreation
Reaching out from the inner city [Inner City Outings leader M. Pyeatt] B. Fuller. il por *Sierra* 74:50-4 Jl/Ag '89
CITY CHURCHES
The Church: looking to the future [cover story] J. H. Fichter. *America* 160:189-92 Mr 4 '89
CITY COLLEGE OF NEW YORK
The case of Michael Levin [professor censored for article on black intelligence] D. Seligman. *National Review* 41:38-40 My 5 '89
CITY FAUNA *See* Urban fauna
CITY FLORA *See* Urban flora
CITY FORESTRY *See* Urban forestry
CITY GARDENS AND GARDENING
See also
Charleston (S.C.)—Gardens and gardening
CITY HALLS
See also
Corpus Christi (Tex.)—City hall
Escondido (Calif.)—City hall

Architecture
Civic virtue [special section] P. M. Sachner. il *Architectural Record* 177:102-13 Ja '89
CITY HOUSES
See also
Row houses
Townhouses step back and up from the street [San Francisco] il *Sunset (Central West edition)* 183:126 O '89
CITY HOUSES, REMODELED *See* Houses, Remodeled
CITY LIGHTS [film] See Motion picture reviews—Single works
CITY OF ANGELS [musical] *See* Musicals, revues, etc.—Reviews—Single works
CITY OF PARIS MUSEUM OF MODERN ART *See* Musée d'Art Moderne de la Ville de Paris
CITY OF RIO DE JANEIRO (SHIP)
Raise the Rio! [work of B. Gibson] J. Grissim. il map *Oceans* 22:30-7+ Mr/Ap '89
CITY PARK (NEW ORLEANS, LA.) *See* New Orleans (La.)—Parks and playgrounds
CITY PLANNING
See also
Business districts
Community development
Streets
Traffic engineering
Waterfronts
Dinosaurs haunt our landscape. T. Oppenheimer. il *Utne Reader* p96-7 Mr/Ap '89
The greening of our cities. T. Oppenheimer. il *Utne Reader* p14-15 My/Je '89

CITY PLANNING—cont.

Mixed-use facilities [including theaters] R. Long. il *Theatre Crafts* 23:50-3+ D '89

Nice profits from better city life [commercial developer Maguire Thomas Partners] J. F. Lawrence. il *Fortune* 120:117-19+ O 9 '89

The sky line [mania for skyscrapers and growth in American cities] B. Gill. *The New Yorker* 64:73-7 Ja 9 '89

Sprucing up our cities' streets [views of Gary Greenan] *USA Today (Periodical)* 118:5-6 D '89

Zone system

See Zoning

California

See also
Davis (Calif.)—City planning
Healdsburg (Calif.)—City planning
Los Angeles (Calif.)—City planning

Canada

See also
Canadian Centre for Architecture (Montreal, Québec)

Florida

See also
Key West (Fla.)—City planning
Seaside (Fla.)

Louisiana

See also
New Orleans (La.)—City planning

Maryland

See also
Baltimore (Md.)—City planning
Columbia (Md.)
Ocean City (Md.)—City planning

Massachusetts

See also
Mashpee (Mass.)—City planning

Middle East

See also
Jerusalem—City planning

New York (State)

See also
New York (N.Y.)—City planning

North Carolina

See also
Raleigh (N.C.)—City planning

Ohio

See also
Cleveland (Ohio)—City planning

Ontario

See also
Toronto (Ont.)—City planning

Oregon

See also
Portland (Or.)—City planning

Scotland

See also
Glasgow (Scotland)—City planning

Spain

See also
Barcelona (Spain)—City planning

Virginia

See also
Altavista (Va.)—City planning

Washington (State)

See also
Seattle (Wash.)—City planning

CITY PROVISIONERS, INC.

A laptop brigade that focuses on the customer. C. O'Malley. il *Personal Computing* 13:76-7+ O '89

CITY TRAFFIC

See also
Berlin (Germany: West)—Street traffic
Los Angeles (Calif.)—Street traffic
New York (N.Y.)—Street traffic
Palo Alto (Calif.)—Street traffic
Traffic engineering

The dawn patrol [driving through cities at dawn] W. Jeanes. il *Car and Driver* 35:7 S '89

Helicopters can help unsnarl U.S. city surface gridlock. N. C. Kernstock. il *Aviation Week & Space Technology* 131:89-91 D 18-25 '89

CITY TRANSIT *See* Local transit

CITY TREES *See* Trees in cities

CITY UNIVERSITY OF NEW YORK. CITY COLLEGE *See* City College of New York

CITY UNIVERSITY OF NEW YORK. HUNTER COLLEGE *See* Hunter College

CITYPLACE (DALLAS, TEX.)

The Texas chain store massacre. J. H. Taylor. il *Forbes* 143:54+ F 6 '89

CITYSCAPES (PHOTOGRAPHY) *See* Cities and towns—Photographs and photography

CIUDAD JUAREZ (MEXICO)

Poor

Border crossing. W. P. Norton. il *The Progressive* 53:46 O '89

CIVIC FORUM (CZECHOSLOVAKIA)

Ten-day wonder. T. Omestad. *The New Republic* 201:19-20+ D 25 '89

CIVICS *See* Citizenship education

CIVIL AVIATION ADMINISTRATION (CHINA) *See* China. Civil Aviation Administration

CIVIL COOPERATION BUREAU (SOUTH AFRICA) *See* South Africa. Army. Civil Cooperation Bureau

CIVIL DEFENSE

See also
Atomic bomb shelters
Evacuation of civilians
United States. Federal Emergency Management Agency

Defenseless cowards. T. Bethell. il *The American Spectator* 22:11-13 Mr '89

Medical preparedness and nuclear war [address, April 23, 1988] J. M. Orient. *Vital Speeches of the Day* 55:186-90 Ja 1 '89

History

From 'duck and cover' to 'run like hell' [nuclear warfare] M. McLoughlin. il *U.S. News & World Report* 107:30-1 Ag 7 '89

New Brunswick

Anecdotes, facetiae, satire, etc.
A bunker mentality in New Brunswick [fallout shelter for government officials] A. Fotheringham. il *Maclean's* 102:48 Jl 31 '89

CIVIL DISOBEDIENCE *See* Government, Resistance to

CIVIL ENGINEERING

See also
Public works

CIVIL LIBERTY *See* Liberty

CIVIL RESERVE AIR FLEET (U.S.) *See* United States. Civil Reserve Air Fleet

CIVIL RIGHTS

See also
Asian Americans—Civil rights
Australian aborigines—Civil rights
Authors' rights
Blacks—Civil rights
Blind—Civil rights
Cancer patients—Civil rights
Celebrities—Civil rights
Church and civil rights
Citizenship
Deaf—Civil rights
Employees—Civil rights
Freedom of information
Freedom of speech
Freedom of the press
Handicapped—Civil rights
Hospital patients—Civil rights
Liberty
Mentally handicapped—Civil rights
Minorities—Civil rights
Poor—Civil rights
Right of petition
Right of privacy
Right to counsel
Searches and seizures
Sick—Civil rights
Students—Civil rights
United States. Dept. of Justice. Civil Rights Division
United States Commission on Civil Rights
Women—Equal rights

Are human rights real? [natural human rights theory] T. R. Machan. por *The Humanist* 49:28-9+ N/D '89

Chipping away at civil liberties. J. Leo. il *U.S. News & World Report* 106:61 Je 26 '89

Constitutional rights: a casualty of the drug war? P. Sudo. il *Scholastic Update (Teachers' edition)* 122:17-18 N 17 '89

Demythologizing natural human rights. D. B. McKown. por *The Humanist* 49:21-4+ My/Je '89

For the civil-rights lobby, a time to regroup. S. V. Roberts. *U.S. News & World Report* 107:30 Jl 10 '89

Illogical force [affirmative action and civil rights Supreme Court decisions] H. Schwartz. *The Nation* 249:40-1 Jl 10 '89

Let's try discriminating for once. J. Leo. il *U.S. News & World Report* 107:53 Ag 7 '89

"Ma'am, what you need is a new improved Hoover" [FBI and domestic spying] M. Miller. il por *The Washington Monthly* 20:10-14+ Ja '89

Sweatshirt justice: how the war on crime is expanding to crush some rights. C. Byron. il *New York* 22:42-4+ O 2 '89

The swing to the left in state courts. T. Gest. il *U.S. News & World Report* 107:32 O 23 '89

A threat to freedom? [civil liberties endangered by war on drugs] R. Lacayo. il *Time* 134:28+ S 18 '89

What is conservatism? J. Wadleigh. por *The Humanist* 49:20-6+ N/D '89

When criminal rights go wrong [cover story] P. Savoy. *The Washington Monthly* 21:36-41+ D '89

Conferences

See also
Human Dimension Conferences

International aspects

See also
Captive Nations Week

CIVIL RIGHTS—International aspects—See also—*cont.*
　　United Nations. Commission on Human Rights
　　United Nations. Sub-commission on Prevention of Discrimination and Protection of Minorities
　　Universal Declaration of Human Rights
"Affirmative action": a worldwide disaster [cover story] T. Sowell. *Commentary* 88:21-41 D '89
Beat the devil. A. Cockburn. il *The Nation* 248:874-5 Je 26 '89
Beware of geobaloney. M. Greenfield. il *Newsweek* 114:84 D 25 '89
Big shtick [Bush administration policies] *The Progressive* 53:8-9 Jl '89
CSCE follow-up meeting held in Vienna [text of concluding document; special section] il *Department of State Bulletin* 89:21-54 Mr '89
Declaration on Human Rights, July 15, 1989 [text of Paris economic summit declaration] *Department of State Bulletin* 89:1 S '89
Good news: our human rights policy [address, October 3, 1988] G. Lister. *Department of State Bulletin* 89:36-8 Ja '89
Human rights and policy: the American tradition. P. J. Dobriansky. *Current (Washington, D.C.)* 314:28-37 Jl/Ag '89
International human rights and the Bush administration. R. F. Drinan. *America* 160:242-4 Mr 18 '89
Scientists as detectives: investigating human rights. C. Snow and others. il *Technology Review* 92:42-9+ F/Mr '89
Waltzing in Vienna [human rights agreement] D. Seligman. *Fortune* 119:133-4 F 27 '89

Africa
Human rights issues in Africa [statements, February 7-8, 1989] K. L. Brown; R. W. Farrand. *Department of State Bulletin* 89:27-32 My '89

Argentina
Cry, Argentina [C. S. Menem pardons military personnel convicted of civil rights violations] J. Malamud-Goti. *The Nation* 249:517-18 N 6 '89
Dirty secrets of the 'dirty war'. M. Andersen. *The Nation* 248:339-40+ Mr 13 '89
The generals don't repent. P. Lacefield. *Commonweal* 116:583-4 N 3 '89
Ningún nombre: identifying Argentina's desaparecidos. T. Beardsley. il *Scientific American* 261:18+ N '89
Rabbi Marshall Meyer: a prophet's agenda. R. Hirschfield. *The Christian Century* 106:438-9 Ap 26 '89
Scientists as detectives: investigating human rights. C. Snow and others. il *Technology Review* 92:42-9+ F/Mr '89

Bulgaria
Ethnic Turks in Bulgaria [NATO and State Dept. statements, August 9 and 10, 1989] *Department of State Bulletin* 89:43 O '89
A modern Balkan exodus [ethnic Turks flee] R. Flamini. il *Time* 134:39 Ag 14 '89

Burma
Burma: political situation and human rights [statement, March 2, 1989] D. F. Lambertson. map *Department of State Bulletin* 89:40-3 My '89

Chile
Adiós, General: saying good-bye to Pinochet. A. Dorfman. il *Harper's* 279:72-6 D '89

China
　　See also
　　Tiananmen Square (China) student occupation, 1989
745 Boylston Street [Fang Lizhi] il por *The Atlantic* 264:4 S '89
An act of defiance [Chinese dissenter Fang Lizhi barred from state dinner; cover story] O. Schell. il pors *The New York Times Magazine* p26-7+ Ap 16 '89
Biologist monitors human rights [work of Fu Xin-yuan, visiting scholar in the U.S.] M. Sun. por *Science* 245:592 Ag 11 '89
The China syndrome. *The New Republic* 200:7-9 My 15 '89
China's despair and China's hope; tr. by Perry Link. Fang Lizhi. il *The New York Review of Books* 36:3-4 F 2 '89
China's forbidden subject. M. Hopkins. il *The New Leader* 72:7-9 F 20 '89
Chinese bar physicist from Bush dinner [dissident Fang Lizhi] M. Sun. il por *Science* 243:1282 Mr 10 '89
The Chinese intellectuals and the revolt. P. Link. il *The New York Review of Books* 36:38-41 Je 29 '89
Fang Lizhi: speaking out for human rights. M. Sun. il por *Science* 244:417-18 Ap 28 '89
Fang loses post, gains award. por *Science* 246:1252 D 8 '89
The fate of Fang Lizhi. il por *Sky and Telescope* 78:240-1 S '89
The flowering of dissent in Deng's Republic. il *U.S. News & World Report* 106:12 Mr 13 '89
From Big Bang to big trouble [Fang Lizhi seeks refuge at U.S. embassy] il por *U.S. News & World Report* 106:38 Je 26 '89
The furious flap over Fang Lizhi [Washington and Beijing clash over Chinese dissident] S. MacLeod. por *Time* 133:38 Mr 13 '89

The Goddess of Democracy deconstructed. B. Lee and L. O.-F. Lee. il *New Perspectives Quarterly* 6:58-61 Fall '89
Human rights in China. J. V. Feinerman. bibl f *Current History* 88:273-6+ S '89
'Intellectuals are waking up'. D. Elliott. il *Newsweek* 113:34 Mr 6 '89
A journey of conscience. R. Bernstein. il *The New York Times Magazine* p22-5+ Ap 16 '89
Keeping the faith [address, November 15, 1989]; tr. by James H. Williams and Orville Schell. Fang Lizhi. il por *The New York Review of Books* 36:43-4 D 21 '89
Letters from the other China [letters written to dissident Fang Lizhi in 1987]; tr. by Orville Schell. bibl f il por *The New York Review of Books* 36:32-3 Jl 20 '89
Notes and comment [exclusion of Fang Lizhi from G. Bush's banquet in Beijing] *The New Yorker* 65:34-5 Mr 20 '89
Pantheon to publish autobiography of Chinese dissident next spring [Liu Binyan] por *Publishers Weekly* 235:29-30 My 26 '89
Physicists protest treatment by PRC of Fang Lizhi. W. Sweet. *Physics Today* 42:59 Ap '89
The price China has paid: an interview with Liu Binyan [with introduction by Merle Goldman] N. Gardels. il *The New York Review of Books* 35:31+ Ja 19 '89
Quotations from dissident Fang. il por *Newsweek* 113:26-7 Je 26 '89
Two dissidents challenge 'feudal communism' [interview with Liu Binyan and Bai Hua] J. L. Du Sablon. il pors *World Press Review* 36:26-7 F '89
Vengeance in China. M. Goldman. il *The New York Review of Books* 36:5-9 N 9 '89

Colombia
Dangerous days in the Macarena. A. Weisman. il map *The New York Times Magazine* p40-2+ Ap 23 '89

Cuba
　　See also
　　Political prisoners—Cuba
Art, intrigue and human rights [U.S. confiscation of paintings by Cuban artist N. Guillen Landrian] E. Shorris. il *The Nation* 249:14-18 Jl 3 '89
Cuba: freedom vs. equality. M. Vargas Llosa. il *World Press Review* 36:45 Mr '89
Cuba: the human rights show. A. Neier. il *The New York Review of Books* 36:33-5 Je 15 '89
Human rights in Cuba: an update. *Department of State Bulletin* 89:59-62 Ap '89
Human rights situation in Cuba [statement, August 2, 1989] R. Schifter. *Department of State Bulletin* 89:41-3 O '89
An open letter to Fidel Castro. *The New York Review of Books* 36:41 F 2 '89

Czechoslovakia
Actions speak louder [police crackdown on demonstrators in Prague] il *Time* 133:38 Ja 30 '89
Fighting back in Prague. J. Laber. il *The New York Review of Books* 36:39-41 Ap 27 '89
Fueling demands for Czech reform. H. Schwartz. *The Nation* 248:660-3 My 15 '89
A historic encounter [meeting between V. Havel and A. Dubcek] il pors *Time* 133:48 My 29 '89
"Hundred per cent": a Czech protest anthem. *Utne Reader* p118-19 Ja/F '89
A journey to 'Absurdistan'. J. Fleischman. *The Nation* 249:276+ S 18 '89
The magic flute; tr. by Peter Kussi. B. Hrabal. *The New York Review of Books* 36:39 My 18 '89
Prague diarist. M. Peretz. *The New Republic* 200:43 Je 26 '89
When you visit Prague [letter to F. Mitterrand] V. Havel. *Harper's* 278:22+ My '89

Eastern Europe
　　See also
　　Helsinki Human Rights Day
CSCE Conference on the Human Dimension [statement, May 31, 1989] M. B. Abram. *Department of State Bulletin* 89:88-90 S '89
Helsinki in Paris. W. Korey. il *The New Leader* 72:12-14 Jl 10-24 '89
Independent activists challenge the status quo across Eastern Europe. B. Morton and J. Landy. il *Utne Reader* p81-3+ Ja/F '89
Notes and comment. *The New Yorker* 65:30 Ag 7 '89

El Salvador
'Absolute, diabolical terror'. S. Miles and B. Ostertag. il *Mother Jones* 14:22-7+ Ap '89
Adolf's heirs [electoral victory by Arena] A. Cockburn. *The Nation* 248:655 My 15 '89
Confessions of an assassin [H. Torres Cortez, former member of a death squad] D. Farah and T. Gibb. por *Mother Jones* 14:10+ Ja '89
In freedom's name. A. Cockburn. *The Nation* 249:706-7 D 11 '89
Losing gamble [U.S. military aid continues despite human rights abuses] *The Nation* 249:704 D 11 '89
Sad new El Salvador. M. Massing. il *The New York Review of Books* 36:53-60 My 18 '89
Salvadoran death threats: a dialogue. *Harper's* 278:19-20 Ap '89

CIVIL RIGHTS—El Salvador—cont.

Under suspicion [Canadian human rights activist K. Ridd] A. Bilski. il por *Maclean's* 102:52 D 4 '89

'The very worst and the very best'. J. Carlin. *World Press Review* 36:26-7 Mr '89

Will Bush keep his word with the death squads? P. Kornbluh. *Mother Jones* 14:26-7 Ap '89

Europe

One (forgetful) Europe [address, 1985] T. Garton Ash. *Harper's* 279:30-1 S '89

The same rights for all, East and West. J. Chirac. *World Press Review* 36:18 D '89

France

See also
France. Declaration of the Rights of Man and of the Citizen

Germany (East)

Fighting Honecker's stagnation. D. R. Shanor. il *The New Leader* 72:8-9 Mr 20 '89

Great Britain

Big sister [M. Thatcher] A. Sullivan. *The New Republic* 200:7-8 Ja 2 '89

Britons worry about civil rights. N. Gelb. il *The New Leader* 72:5-6 F 20 '89

Civil liberties imperiled under Thatcher. C. Sugnet. il *Utne Reader* p12-14 My/Je '89

Guatemala

Friendly death squads. *The Progressive* 53:9 N '89

The hidden reality in Guatemala. T. Montgomery-Fate. il *The Christian Century* 106:820-2 S 13-20 '89

Haiti

Haiti goes back. A. Wilentz. *The Nation* 249:669-70 D 4 '89

Hong Kong

Preparing for 1997 [Canadian B. Strayer helps draft bill of rights] J. Keating. *Maclean's* 102:73-4 N 20 '89

Iran

Rafsanjani's no moderate. M. Farhang. il *The Nation* 249:560+ N 13 '89

Iraq

Iraq: an accusation of torture [brutality to children] *Newsweek* 113:39 Mr 13 '89

Suffer the littlest children [atrocities] *U.S. News & World Report* 106:13+ Mr 13 '89

Korea (North)

A party in Pyongyang [World Festival of Youth and Students] B. Martin. il *Newsweek* 114:35 Jl 17 '89

Nicaragua

Deregulating political murder. P. Savoy. il *The Nation* 248:869+ Je 26 '89

Panama

Rights of spring [work of O. de Koster] E. Pall. il por *Mother Jones* 14:16 Ap '89

Paraguay

Hope for Paraguay [human rights activist C. de Lara Castro] W. Steif. *The Progressive* 53:16-17 Jl '89

Philippines

Democracies, yes; justice, not yet. *America* 161:463 D 23-30 '89

Human rights abuses shrouded in Philippines. D. Friesen. *The Christian Century* 106:678-9 Jl 19-26 '89

'Total war' in the Philippines. N. Rosca. il *The Nation* 248:839-42 Je 19 '89

Vigilante justice. J. Ross. *The New Republic* 201:9-21 N 27 '89

Puerto Rico

Island of repression. B. A. Kane. il *The Progressive* 53:35 S '89

Romania

Romania: breaking the silence. W. Pfaff. il *The New York Review of Books* 36:8-9 Ap 27 '89

Romania: defying the tyrant. W. Pfaff. il *The New York Review of Books* 36:43 Ag 17 '89

Romania, Romania. T. R. Swick. *Commonweal* 116:263-4 My 5 '89

Somalia

Somalia pledges human rights reforms. C. Holden. *Science* 243:734 F 10 '89

South Africa

See also
Apartheid

The point system. A. Kopkind. *The Nation* 248:761-2 Je 5 '89

Soviet Union

See also
Political prisoners—Soviet Union

Advancing the Helsinki process. W. Korey. il *The New Leader* 72:7-9 F 6 '89

Changing times: Sakharov in the US on human rights and arms control. I. Goodwin. il *Physics Today* 42:91-5 F '89

Counting the votes and the dead [cover story] K. Vanden Heuvel. il *The Nation* 248:505+ Ap 17 '89

Dateline USSR: on the human rights track. D. K. Shipler. *Foreign Policy* 75:164-81 Summ '89

Gulag? What gulag? M. Kondracke. *The New Republic* 200:8-9+ F 13 '89

Human rights get their biggest boost in a decade. B. Javetski. il *Business Week* p55 Ja 30 '89

Individual rights in the U.S.S.R. [address, July 21, 1989] W. H. Webster. *Vital Speeches of the Day* 55:711-13 S 15 '89

An interview with Andrei Sakharov. J.-P. Barou. il *The New York Review of Books* 36:6-7 Mr 2 '89

A Moscow conference on human rights? *America* 160:51 Ja 28 '89

Moscow: the struggle for reform. A. Brumberg. bibl f il *The New York Review of Books* 36:37-42 Mr 30 '89

The rights of Gorbachev [cover story] I. F. Stone. il *The New York Review of Books* 36:3-4+ F 16 '89

Sakharov's bold challenge [with interview] J. Trimble. il por *U.S. News & World Report* 106:49-50 Ja 30 '89

Turkey

Cruel and usual punishment. J. Laber. il *The New York Review of Books* 36:34-5 Jl 20 '89

Letter from Bodrum. H. Greer. *The American Spectator* 22:42-3 D '89

United States

See Civil rights

Uruguay

Department of amplification [amnesty law sustained in referendum] L. Weschler. *The New Yorker* 65:92-3 My 22 '89

Forgive & forget? [referendum to uphold or overturn law giving amnesty to military responsible for violations of human rights] R. Neild. *Commonweal* 116:358-60 Je 16 '89

The great exception (I) [abuses under military dictatorship, 1973-1985] L. Weschler. il *The New Yorker* 65:43-6+ Ap 3 '89

The great exception (II) [drive for referendum to overturn amnesty for military civil rights abusers] L. Weschler. *The New Yorker* 65:85-102+ Ap 10 '89

Torture, memory and justice. C. G. Brown and R. K. Goldman. il *The Nation* 248:408+ Mr 27 '89

Uruguay confronts its torturers [amnesty law referendum] il *U.S. News & World Report* 106:36-7 Ap 17 '89

Western Europe

Fortress Europe for 1992. A. Rosenbaum. il *The Nation* 249:748-50 D 18 '89

Zimbabwe

'Serious disruptions' in Zimbabwe [Renamo activities] J. L. Phillips. *The Christian Century* 106:1038-9 N 15 '89

CIVIL RIGHTS ACT OF 1964

Ebony special issue examines drug crisis in black America. *Jet* 76:57 Ag 7 '89

Special report: 25 years after the Civil Rights Act of 1964 [cover story; special section] il *Ebony* 44:29-30+ Ag '89

CIVIL RIGHTS COMMISSION (U.S.) *See* United States Commission on Civil Rights

CIVIL RIGHTS DEMONSTRATIONS

March on Washington by students slated for April. *Jet* 75:6 Mr 27 '89

NAACP: China's protests will be small to our's. il *Jet* 76:4 Jl 24 '89

NAACP march protests 'legal lynching' of civil rights in U.S. il *Jet* 76:4-6 S 11 '89

NAACP to hold silent march in Washington to protest new Supreme Court rulings. il *Jet* 76:6 Ag 21 '89

A turn in Atlanta [protest march against racism in Forsyth County] V. S. Naipaul. il *The New York Review of Books* 35:52-7 Ja 19 '89

History

The chemistry of protest [effect of the civil rights movement on Vietnam War protests in the sixties] il *U.S. News & World Report* 106:16 Ap 10 '89

A veteran of Mississippi's 'Freedom Summer' remembers the cause—and the danger [drive for black voter registration conducted by SNCC in 1964]; ed. by Jane Sugden. L. Guyot. il pors *People Weekly* 32:61-2+ S 18 '89

CIVIL RIGHTS DIVISION (DEPT. OF JUSTICE) *See* United States. Dept. of Justice. Civil Rights Division

CIVIL RIGHTS MEMORIAL (MONTGOMERY, ALA.)

Dedicate memorial to 40 who died in civil rights struggle. D. M. Cheers. il *Jet* 77:4-5+ N 20 '89

First she looks inward [work of architect M. Lin] J. Coleman. il pors *Time* 134:90-2+ N 6 '89

Maya Lin lets healing waters flow over her Civil Rights Memorial. D. Grogan. il por *People Weekly* 32:78-80 N 20 '89

CIVIL RIGHTS ORGANIZATIONS

See also
American-Arab Anti-Discrimination Committee
American Civil Liberties Union
Amnesty International
Citizens for Nonviolent Action Against Racism
Legal Defense and Educational Fund
National Association for the Advancement of Colored People
National Urban League
People United to Serve Humanity (Organization)
Southern Christian Leadership Conference
Student Nonviolent Coordinating Committee

How to fight racism. *Scholastic Update (Teachers' edition)* 121:26 Ap 7 '89

CIVIL RIGHTS ORGANIZATIONS—*cont.*
Philippines
See also
Bayan (Organization)
CIVIL SERVICE
See also
Bureaucracy
Government employees
United States. Office of Personnel Management
A kind word for the spoils system. C. Peters. *The Washington Monthly* 21:37-8 F '89
United States
See Civil service
CIVIL SERVICE PENSIONS
See also
California. Public Employees' Retirement System
The comparative value of pensions in the public and private sectors. L. M. Lovejoy. bibl f il *Monthly Labor Review* 111:18-26 D '88
The government's golden handshake. E. Clift. il *Newsweek* 114:27 D 18 '89
A pension for trouble. M. Cooper. il *The Washington Monthly* 21:24-9 Jl/Ag '89
CIVIL WAR
See also
El Salvador—Civil War, 1980-
Spain—History—Civil War, 1936-1939
United States—History—Civil War, 1861-1865
CIVILIAN DEFENSE *See* Civil defense
CIVILITY *See* Courtesy
CIVILIZATION
See also
Acculturation
Animals and civilization
Anthropology
Archeology
Australia—Civilization
Brazil—Civilization
Catalonia (Spain)—Civilization
Central Europe—Civilization
China—Civilization
Computers and civilization
Developing countries—Civilization
Egypt—Civilization
Europe—Civilization
Great books of the Western world
History
Humanism
India—Civilization
Intellectuals and intellectual life
Middle East—Civilization
Ocean and civilization
Plants and civilization
Popular culture
Progress
Renaissance
Social change
Southern States—Civilization
Soviet Union—Civilization
United States—Civilization
Western Europe—Civilization
The education reform movement and its critics: implications for arts education [favoring Western civilization] J. B. Riddell. bibl f *Design for Arts in Education* 90:2-13 N/D '88
Food for thought. G. F. Kreyche. il *USA Today (Periodical)* 117:98 Mr '89
No escaping modern times. R. Rosenblatt. il *U.S. News & World Report* 107:10-11 O 2 '89
Television, cultural history, and arts education. H. Hoffa. *Design for Arts in Education* 90:15-22 Mr/Ap '89
The war and the future of civilization. [World War I] R. G. Usher. *The New Republic* 201 [Reprint v1]:22-3 N 6 '89 [N 7 '14]
CIVILIZATION, ANCIENT
See also
Man, Prehistoric
Mayas
CIVILIZATION, ARAB
Self-determination, Arab style. D. Pryce-Jones. *Commentary* 87:39-46 Ja '89
CIVILIZATION, CHRISTIAN
See also
Christianity and culture
CIVILIZATION, GRECO-ROMAN
Greeks, Romans, Jews & others. J. Griffin. il *The New York Review of Books* 36:6+ Mr 16 '89
CIVILIZATION, ISLAMIC
A third encounter of the close kind [cover story] A. S. Ahmed. il *History Today* 39:4-9 N '89
A Western response. W. M. Watt. il *History Today* 39:5-8 D '89
CIVILIZATION, MINOAN *See* Minoans
CIZEWSKI, LEONARD
The coffee connection. il *The Progressive* 53:46 N '89
CKO INC.
Pulling the plug at CKO. J. Daly. il *Maclean's* 102:65 N 20 '89

CLAASSEN, DIETER
A new British empire. *World Press Review* 36:50 Jl '89
CLABAUGH, GAVIN
(jt. auth) See Branwyn, Gareth, and Clabaugh, Gavin
CLABIR CORP.
Meltdown [marketing strategy backfires for Klondike ice cream bars] K. Hannon. il por *Forbes* 144:130-1 Ag 7 '89
CLAIBORNE, JERRY
about
This coach did it right. W. F. Reed. il por *Sports Illustrated* 71:126 D 11 '89
CLAIBORNE, LIZ
about
Can Ms. Fashion bounce back? [cover story] K. Deveny. il pors *Business Week* p64-7+ Ja 16 '89
CLAIBORNE (LIZ), INC. *See* Liz Claiborne, Inc.
CLAIMS
See also
Insurance—Adjustment of claims
Insurance, Health—Adjustment of claims
CLAIR, DICK
about
Reruns will keep sitcom writer Dick Clair on ice—indefinitely. J. S. Kunen. il pors *People Weekly* 32:57+ Jl 17 '89
CLAIRE'S STORES INC.
A costume jeweler regains its sparkle. G. G. Marcial. *Business Week* p88 F 13 '89
CLAIRVOYANCE
See also
Extrasensory perception
CLAITOR, DIANA
The homeless take to the water. il *The Progressive* 53:10-11 F '89
CLAM FISHERIES
See also
Washington King Clam, Inc.
Ethical aspects
Clamscam [B. Hodgson of Washington King Clam prosecuted for geoduck theft] F. Graham. *Audubon* 91:8+ N '89
CLAMBAKES
Labor Day clambake. il *Gourmet* 49:134-40+ S '89
A New England clambake. J. T. Hazard. il *Ladies' Home Journal* 106:136-8 Jl '89
CLAMPITT, AMY
My cousin Muriel [poem] *The New Yorker* 65:33 F 20 '89
A note from Leiden [poem] *The New Yorker* 65:50 D 4 '89
Nothing stays put [poem] *The New Yorker* 65:40-1 Ap 24 '89
Savannah [poem] *The New Yorker* 64:70 Ja 16 '89
CLAMPS
One-hand clamp [Quick-Grip bar clamp] P. McCafferty. il *Popular Science* 235:79 Ag '89
CLAMS
See also
Clambakes
Cooking—Shellfish
CLANCY, AMBROSE, 1948-
A little piece of heaven. il *Gentlemen's Quarterly* 59:221-2+ N '89
CLANCY, DEIRDRE
about
Deirdre Clancy. M. Sommers. il por *Theatre Crafts* 23:34-9+ F '89
CLANCY, FRANK, AND YORKSHIRE, HEIDI
The Bandler method. il pors *Mother Jones* 14:22-8+ F/Mr '89
CLANCY, TOM, 1947-
about
As his latest flight of fancy goes on sale, novelist Tom Clancy eyes a job in space. P. Alson. il pors *People Weekly* 32:86-8 Ag 28 '89
Berkley loses in appeals court over 'Red October'. M. Reuter. *Publishers Weekly* 235:9 Je 9 '89
Of arms and the man. W. Shapiro. il por *Time* 134:66-8 Ag 21 '89
Paperback fighter. S. Shuger. il *The Washington Monthly* 21:10-14+ N '89
Tom Clancy's dream come true. R. K. Bennett. il por *Reader's Digest* 134:126-31 F '89
CLAPHAM, DAVID E.
(jt. auth) See Kim, Donghee, and Clapham, David E.
CLAPHAM, SIR J. H. (JOHN HAROLD), 1873-1946
about
Words, not numbers: John Harold Clapham. R. Floud. bibl il pors *History Today* 39:42-7 Ap '89
CLAPHAM, JOHN HAROLD *See* Clapham, Sir J. H. (John Harold), 1873-1946
CLARA BARTON NATIONAL HISTORIC SITE (MD.)
Clara Barton National Historic Site. il *American History Illustrated* 24:65 N/D '89
CLARE BOOTHE LUCE FUND
Luce Foundation funds positions for women in physics. *Physics Today* 42:85-6 S '89

CLAREMONT ECONOMICS INSTITUTE
The sky is rising? [J. Rutledge and D. Allen's views in Rust to riches] P. Brimelow. il pors *Forbes* 144:156+ N 13 '89

CLARETIAN MEDICAL CENTER
Baby on board. B. Doyle. il *U.S. Catholic* 54:20-7 Je '89

CLARINET MUSIC
See also
Compact discs—Clarinet music
Play it again, Woody [filmmaker W. Allen as a jazz clarinetist] T. A. Sancton. il por *Time* 134:76-8 O 23 '89

CLARINETISTS
See also
Daniels, Eddie
Wilber, Bob

CLARIS CORPORATION
The three phases of Claris Corporation. S. R. Reed. il *Personal Computing* 13:203-4 Je '89

CLARK, ANNIE TROY
about
Annie Troy Clark. S. Kanfer. il por *People Weekly* 32 Special Issue:23 Fall '89

CLARK, BILL
about
Extra Ordinary. P. Mandell. il pors map *Americana* 17:26-31+ Mr/Ap '89
The fire's always burning at Randall's Ordinary, a Revolutionary inn in Connecticut. N. Geeslin. il pors *People Weekly* 32:143-4 N 13 '89

CLARK, CHARLES, 1933-
Two views of electrocopying: the international view. il por *Publishers Weekly* 236:53 Jl 14 '89

CLARK, CHARLES JOSEPH See Clark, Joe, 1939-

CLARK, CHERI
Disney World and the four dwarfs. il *The Saturday Evening Post* 261:86-7 Mr '89

CLARK, CINDY
about
Extra Ordinary. P. Mandell. il pors map *Americana* 17:26-31+ Mr/Ap '89
The fire's always burning at Randall's Ordinary, a Revolutionary inn in Connecticut. N. Geeslin. il pors *People Weekly* 32:143-4 N 13 '89

CLARK, DAVID L. (DAVID LOUIS), 1929-, AND ASTUTO, TERRY A.
Reagan's final report card. *Society* 26:32-9 My/Je '89

CLARK, DICK, 1929-
about
Dick Clark. il por *People Weekly* 31 Special Issue:59 Summ '89
Dick Clark's last stand. S. Pond. il pors *Rolling Stone* p47-8 My 18 '89

CLARK, ELLEN MCCALLISTER
George Washington's study. bibl f il *Antiques* 135:490-5 F '89

CLARK, GUY
about
Guy Clark and friends. A. Nash. il por *Stereo Review* 54:102 Je '89

CLARK, J. C. D.
The American Revolution: a war of religion? bibl il *History Today* 39:10-16 D '89

CLARK, JAMES M., AND OTHERS
Mammal-like dentition in a Mesozoic crocodylian. bibl f il *Science* 244:1064-6 Je 2 '89

CLARK, JAMES S.
The forest is for burning. il *Natural History* p50-3 Ja '89

CLARK, JOE
about
Eastside story. Y. Kramer and R. Kramer. il *The American Spectator* 22:21-4 Ag '89
Education: the movie [cover story] D. L. Kirp. il pors *Mother Jones* 14:36-45 Ja '89
His pupils want someone to lean on, but Joe Clark may simply want out. D. Van Biema and G. Moses. il pors *People Weekly* 31:51-3 Mr 27 '89
The make-believe world of "Lean on me". I. A. Hyman. *The Education Digest* 55:20-2 N '89
Morgan Freeman stars as tough principal Joe Clark in hit movie, 'Lean on me'. T. S. Moore. il pors *Jet* 75:24-6 Mr 6 '89
Principal Joe Clark leaving school for lecture circuit. por *Jet* 76:22 Jl 31 '89

CLARK, JOE, 1939-
about
Canada in a hot seat. M. Nemeth. il por *Maclean's* 102:21 F 20 '89
Diagnosis: a severe case of the wobblies [interview] A. Fotheringham. il *Maclean's* 102:56 Mr 27 '89
Divisive diplomacy. M. Nemeth. por *Maclean's* 102:40 Mr 20 '89

CLARK, KATHERINE
(ed) See Logan, Onnie Lee. What I know about deliverin' babies come from motherwit, common sense. God gave it to me

CLARK, KENNETH BANCROFT
about
Toni Morrison, Kenneth Clark get honorary degrees during Harvard University graduation. il pors *Jet* 76:13 Je 26 '89

CLARK, KIT
about
When Ed Greer vanished, a myth was born—and a bitter reality for the family he left behind. G. Stone. il pors *People Weekly* 31:109+ Je 5 '89

CLARK, KRISTINE L., 1953-, AND THOMPSON, TERRI
Aerobic videos: ten you can trust. il *Women's Sports & Fitness* 11:44-6+ S '89

CLARK, LEWIS F.
about
Lewis & Nathan Clark: friends and brothers. B. Fuller. il pors *Sierra* 74:148-50+ Ja/F '89

CLARK, MARGOT
Soothing memories. il por *American Artist* 53:60-5+ O '89

CLARK, MARY HIGGINS
The Anastasia syndrome [story] il *Ladies' Home Journal* 106:160+ N '89
A husband beyond compare [condensed from Family portraits] *Reader's Digest* 135:92-4 D '89
about
PW interviews. E. H. O'Neill. por *Publishers Weekly* 235:64-5 My 19 '89
Shedunnit. R. Hoopes. il por *Modern Maturity* 32:52-7 Ag/S '89

CLARK, MICHAEL
about
British accents. E. MacSweeney. il por *Harper's Bazaar* 122:358-9+ S '89

CLARK, NANCY, 1951-
Dairy tales. il *Runner's World* 24:44-8+ Je '89

CLARK, NATHAN
about
Lewis & Nathan Clark: friends and brothers. B. Fuller. il pors *Sierra* 74:148-50+ Ja/F '89

CLARK, RAMSEY, 1927-
Drugs, lies & TV. *The Nation* 249:408-9 O 16 '89

CLARK, ROGER N. (ROGER NELSON)
Drawing Mars from video. il *Sky and Telescope* 77:476 My '89

CLARK, SALLY
Get your money's worth from summer shoes. il *Glamour* 87:126 Jl '89
Straw bargains. il *Glamour* 87:186 Ag '89

CLARK, SANDY
The big shot. il *Southern Living* 24:146 S '89

CLARK, STEPHEN
about
A new way for people to beat the banks. P. C. Newman. il *Maclean's* 102:39 Je 19 '89

CLARK, TOM
CD libraries: sound effects on compact disc. *Theatre Crafts* 23:38+ Ag/S '89

CLARK, WARREN F.
about
A husband beyond compare [condensed from Family portraits] M. H. Clark. *Reader's Digest* 135:92-4 D '89

CLARK, WILL
about
Way above average. B. Newman. il pors *Sports Illustrated* 71:24-6+ S 25 '89

CLARK, WILLIAM, JR.
Burdensharing and Japan. *Department of State Bulletin* 88:30-1 D '88
FY 1990 assistance request for East Asia and the Pacific [statement, February 27, 1989] il *Department of State Bulletin* 89:49-53 My '89
U.S.-Japan relations [statement, October 13, 1988] *Department of State Bulletin* 88:27-30 D '88

CLARK, WILLIAM C., 1948-
Managing planet earth. bibl il maps *Scientific American* 261:46-54 S '89

CLARK ATLANTA UNIVERSITY
Cole sworn in as first Clark Atlanta U. prexy. il pors *Jet* 77:16 O 16 '89

CLARK COLLEGE
See also
Clark Atlanta University

CLARK ESTATES INC.
The Clarks of Cooperstown. W. P. Barrett. il *Forbes* 144:76+ S 18 '89

CLARK FAMILY
about
The Clarks of Cooperstown. W. P. Barrett. il *Forbes* 144:76+ S 18 '89

CLARK MOUNTAIN (CALIF.)
The pastures of Class-L heaven [climbing Clark Mountain in the East Mojave Scenic Area] D. Darlington. il *Sierra* 74:70-3+ S/O '89

CLARK-STEWART, ALISON
Families today. il *Good Housekeeping* 208:110-11+ F '89

CLARKE, ARTHUR C., 1917-
Apollo plus twenty. il *Ad Astra* 1:30-1 Jl/Ag '89
First word. por *Omni (New York, N.Y.)* 12:8 O '89

CLARKE, CAROLINE V.
The $70 billion man. il pors *Black Enterprise* 19:100-2+ Je '89
Financial strategies for unmarrieds. il *Black Enterprise* 20:94-6+ O '89
CLARKE, HENRY DE BRUNNER, JR.
about
Meltdown. K. Hannon. il por *Forbes* 144:130-1 Ag 7 '89
CLARKE, JOHN F.
about
Fusion chief reassigned as program is refocused. M. Crawford. por *Science* 243:303 Ja 20 '89
CLARKE, JOHN HENRIK, 1915-
In our image. por *Essence* 20:158 S '89
CLARKE, LEE BEN
Capitalism is richer, democracy is safer. *Society* 27:17-18 N/D '89
CLARKE, RICHARD A.
Conference against chemical weapons [statement, September 19, 1989] *Department of State Bulletin* 89:45-7 N '89
CLARKE, ROBERT BRADSTREET
about
Clarke retires amid top shake-up at Grolier. *Publishers Weekly* 235:14 F 10 '89
CLARKE, ROBERT L.
Congress and the banking community [address, October 10, 1988] *Vital Speeches of the Day* 55:203-6 Ja 15 '89
CLARKIN, GREG
Children's video attracting new players; distribution called key. *Publishers Weekly* 235:50 My 5 '89
CLARY, MIKE
A boy's best friend. il por *McCall's* 116:75-6 Je '89
CLASS DISTINCTION *See* Social classes
CLASS REUNIONS *See* College reunions; High school reunions
CLASS SIZE
Redistributing work to shrink class size. T. A. Chandler. *The Education Digest* 54:44-5 F '89
CLASSES, SOCIAL *See* Social classes
CLASSIC AUTOMOBILES *See* Automobiles—History
CLASSIC MOTOR CARRIAGES (FIRM)
Kim Basinger by UPS. P. Bedard. il *Car and Driver* 34:20 My '89
CLASSICAL BAND
Music. P. G. Davis. *New York* 22:69 My 29 '89
Musical events:
Debut at Columbia University's Miller Hall. A. Porter. *The New Yorker* 65:99 My 29 '89
CLASSICAL EDUCATION
See also
Humanities
Liberal education
CLASSICAL LITERATURE
See also
Greek literature
Study and teaching
After smashing the Wedgwood. W. R. Connor. *The American Scholar* 58:533-41 Aut '89
CLASSICAL MUSIC *See* Music
CLASSICISM IN ARCHITECTURE
See also
Neoclassicism (Architecture)
Terry: keeper of the faith [English architect] M. Filler. il por *House & Garden* 161:162-3+ Mr '89
CLASSICISM IN ART
Classical realism: the other 20th century. R. Lack. il *Utne Reader* p59 Jl/Ag '89
CLASSICS (BOOKS) *See* Great books of the Western world
CLASSICS IV (MUSICAL GROUP)
Classics IV. W. King. il *High Fidelity (New York, N.Y.)* 39:75 Jl '89
CLASSIFICATION
See also
Biology—Classification
Botany—Classification
Reptiles—Classification
Wine—Classification
CLASSIFIED ADVERTISING *See* Advertising, Classified
CLASSIFIED INFORMATION
See also
Official secrets
Pentagon procurement scandal
As his latest flight of fancy goes on sale, novelist Tom Clancy eyes a job in space [offered job as consultant to the National Space Council] P. Alson. il pors *People Weekly* 32:86-8 Ag 28 '89
The backbone of hidden government [National Security Decision Directives; cover story] E. Pell. *The Nation* 248:833+ Je 19 '89
Black programs must balance cost, time savings with public oversight [top secret defense projects] W. B. Scott. il *Aviation Week & Space Technology* 131:42+ D 18-25 '89
Boeing pleads guilty to trafficking in classified documents, pays $5-million fine. *Aviation Week & Space Technology* 131:38 N 20 '89
Chilly draft [security clearances and government employment] E. Pell. *The Nation* 248:400 Mr 27 '89
Flash point [security restrictions on inertial confinement fusion] J. Horgan. il *Scientific American* 260:18+ Ap '89

Giving in to "graymail" [L. Walsh drops conspiracy charge against O. North] S. Holmes. il pors *Time* 133:24-5 Ja 16 '89
Heard on the Street [Wall Street defense watchers] L. Feinstein. il *Common Cause Magazine* 15:12-15 Jl/Ag '89
Iran-contra: a CIA win [blocking use of classified information in trial of J. Fernandez] *Newsweek* 114:62 D 4 '89
Let common sense prevail in space secrecy. E. H. Kolcum. il *Aviation Week & Space Technology* 131:49-50 D 18-25 '89
Mapping a wet frontier [Sea Beam sonar maps declassified] A. C. Revkin. il *Discover* 10:30 S '89
National insecurity [government's refusal to make available documents requested by O. North] *Commonweal* 116:36-7 Ja 27 '89
Navy relents in battle over mapping sea floor. C. Norman. *Science* 244:25 Ap 7 '89
New North wind? *The Nation* 248:327-8 Mr 13 '89
The North case [dismissal of conspiracy and fraud charges] F. FitzGerald. *The Nation* 248:149 F 6 '89
Ollie's short-lived victory [dropping two major counts against O. North] R. Parry. il por *Newsweek* 113:33 Ja 16 '89
Ollie's true colors. E. Alterman. *The New Republic* 200:13-14 Mr 13 '89
On & on it goes [classified documents in O. North case] W. F. Buckley. *National Review* 41:70 F 10 '89
Public always the last to know [Energy Dept. fighting to avoid giving data on underground nuclear tests to arms control groups] W. J. Lanouette. il *The Bulletin of the Atomic Scientists* 45:11-12 O '89
Seafloor maps no longer secret. *Science News* 135:255 Ap 22 '89
Security blanket [decision to drop conspiracy and fraud charges against O. North] *The Nation* 248:111-12 Ja 30 '89
Soliciting for the secret war: a chronicle [summary of classified documents submitted as evidence in O. North's trial] *Harper's* 278:17-19+ Je '89
Suspect [security clearance procedures; cover story] V. Novak. il *Common Cause Magazine* 15:17-22+ My/Je '89
Top-secret strategy [trial of O. North] G. J. Church. il por *Time* 133:16-17 F 27 '89
When broken arrows show [accidents involving nuclear weapons] S. Plous. il *The Bulletin of the Atomic Scientists* 45:3-4 D '89
Where, oh where have all the scandals gone? [dropping several charges against Iran-contra principal O. North] il por *U.S. News & World Report* 106:11-12 Ja 16 '89
CLASSROOM MANAGEMENT
See also
Class size
Ask me [student reluctance to ask questions in class; research by Hans van der Meij] G. W. Bracey. il *Phi Delta Kappan* 70:410 Ja '89
Assertive Discipline—more than names on the board and marbles in a jar. L. Canter. bibl f il *Phi Delta Kappan* 71:57-61 S '89
In a schoolroom. R. S. Bourne. *The New Republic* 201 [Reprint v1]:23-4 N 6 '89 [N 7 '14]
A teacher development model for classroom management. T. J. Lasley. bibl f il *Phi Delta Kappan* 71:36-8 S '89
CLASSROOMS
A new look at modular classrooms. B. Gossett. *The Education Digest* 54:64-5 Mr '89
CLATHRATE COMPOUNDS *See* Intercalation compounds
CLATHRIN
Clathrin: a role in the intracellular retention of a Golgi membrane protein [yeast] G. S. Payne and R. Schekman. bibl f il *Science* 245:1358-65 S 22 '89
CLAUDEL, CAMILLE, 1864-1943
about
Art lovers. A.-E. Moutet. il pors *Vogue* 179:498-503+ Mr '89
A star reborn. B. Grauman. por *Art News* 88:63 Summ '89
CLAUDICATION, INTERMITTENT *See* Intermittent claudication
CLAUSEN, A. W. (ALDEN WINSHIP)
Economic changes in the U.S.S.R. [address, May 23, 1989] *Vital Speeches of the Day* 55:674-7 S 1 '89
CLAUSEN, ALDEN WINSHIP *See* Clausen, A. W. (Alden Winship)
CLAVIÈRE D'HUST, ANNE-MARIE DE, COMTESSE
about
Artist in residence: Count and Countess de Claviére d'Hust on Long Island. S. Stephens. il pors *Architectural Digest* 46:156-61+ D '89
CLAVIÈRE D'HUST, BERNARD DE, COMTE
about
Artist in residence: Count and Countess de Claviére d'Hust on Long Island. S. Stephens. il pors *Architectural Digest* 46:156-61+ D '89
CLAWSON, PATRICK
(jt. auth) See Chittick, William, and Clawson, Patrick
CLAY, ANDREW DICE
about
The comedy of hate. G. Hirshey. il pors *Gentlemen's Quarterly* 59:226-9+ Ag '89

CLAY, CASSIUS See Ali, Muhammad, 1942-

CLAY, JASON W.

Genocide in our time: 200,000 indigenous people killed last year. *Utne Reader* p112-13 N/D '89

Radios in the rain forest. il *Technology Review* 92:52-7 O '89

CLAY, KEITH

Trespassers will be poisoned. il *Natural History* p8+ S '89

CLAY, WILLIAM

Should President Bush's minimum wage proposal be adopted? [excerpts from address, March 23, 1989] *Congressional Digest* 68:141+ My '89

CLAY

See also

Ceramics

Unexpected leakage through landfill liners [diffusion of chemicals through clay] J. Raloff. *Science News* 135:164 Mr 18 '89

CLAY CENTER (KAN.)

Small-town blues. R. Hornik. il *Time* 133:66-8 Mr 27 '89

CLAY SCULPTURE See Ceramic sculpture

CLAY STUDIO (ORGANIZATION)

The Clay Studio at 15. il *American Craft* 49:15+ Je/Jl '89

CLAY TENNIS COURTS See Tennis courts

CLAYMONT (DEL.)

Religious institutions and affairs

Brother Isidore covers 20 miles a day on his spiritual trek [Franciscan] B. Johnson. il pors *People Weekly* 32:63-4 Ag 7 '89

CLAYS (SHOOTING) See Trapshooting

CLAYSON, ALISON MCKELVEY

Understanding global change. il *The Unesco Courier* 42:48-9 O '89

CLAYTON, BUCK, 1911-

about

Buck Clayton. D. Helland. por *Down Beat* 56:14 S '89

Buck Clayton, Roy Eldridge. C. Deffaa. il pors *Down Beat* 56:48 F '89

CLAYTON, CONSTANCE

We can educate all our children. *The Nation* 249:132-5 Jl 24-31 '89

CLAYTON, JANET

Making playgrounds safer. il *Essence* 20:97 Je '89

Those little brown 'moles'. il *Essence* 20:22 My '89

CLAYTON, ROBERT N.

about

Geophysical Union salutes excellent work in the field. pors *Physics Today* 42:87-91 D '89

CLAYTOR, W. GRAHAM, JR.

about

Is Amtrak turning around? [interview] H. Gieseking. *Travel Holiday* 171:75-6 Ja '89

CLEAGE, PEARL

Bernice King. por *Essence* 19:69-70+ Ja '89

Diana: down-to-earth [cover story] il pors *Essence* 20:70-2+ O '89

In my solitude. por *Essence* 19:56-8+ F '89

CLEAN & LEAN (FIRM)

Hard bodies, soft fabrics: laundry guru Greg Trabert says yes, you can have it all. il por *People Weekly* 31:99 My 15 '89

CLEAN AIR ACT

Air: how clean is clean enough? E. Faltermayer. il map *Fortune* 120:54-6+ Jl 17 '89

Air pollution: it's all legal. G. Easterbrook. il *Newsweek* 114:28-9+ Jl 24 '89

A breath of fresh air from the White House. V. Cahan. il *Business Week* p60 Je 26 '89

Bush Clean-Air plan: tough but doable. T. Orme. il *Motor Trend* 41:34-5 O '89

Bush proposes strong air-cleaning measures. J. Raloff. *Science News* 135:375 Je 17 '89

Bush pulls a Clean-Air victory out of the air. V. Cahan and R. Fly. *Business Week* p43 O 2 '89

Bush's Clean Air bill falls short. *National Parks* 63:10 S/O '89

The Clean Air Act [and the Acid Deposition Control Act] il *Congressional Digest* 68:35-64 F '89

Clean Air and the 100th Congress. P. Byrnes. *Wilderness* 52:23 Wint '88

Clean air? Don't hold your breath. E. Marshall. il *Science* 244:517-20 My 5 '89

Clean Air isn't a clean deal. M. Keller. *Motor Trend* 41:154 N '89

Clean Air reactions [Bush administration proposals] *Environment* 31:2-4 Jl/Ag '89

Clearing the air: Bush's plan. G. Easterbrook. il *Newsweek* 113:34 Je 19 '89

Clearing the air of ozone. M. Warren and K. W. Chilton. bibl *Society* 26:48-58 Mr/Ap '89

Clearing the air, sort of [Bush plan] *The Nation* 249:1 Jl 3 '89

The cost of missed Clean-Air deadlines. il *Nation's Business* 77:70 F '89

Fighting acid rain [Bush plan; cover story; special section; with editorial comment by Kevin Doyle] il map *Maclean's* 102:2, 38-46 Je 26 '89

First hot air, then Clean Air. M. Duffy. il *Time* 134:16 Jl 31 '89

Gasoline: the unclean fuel? E. Marshall. il *Science* 246:199-201 O 13 '89

Looking for a win on Clean Air bills. *National Parks* 63:13 Jl/Ag '89

Mr. Clean's Air Act [interview with H. Waxman] J. Getlin. il pors *Sierra* 74:76-81 N/D '89

New law needed to control toxic air. J. D. Hair. il *International Wildlife* 19:26 Jl/Ag '89

Our dirty air [cover story] M. McLoughlin. il map *U.S. News & World Report* 106:48-9+ Je 12 '89

Smell that fresh air! [George Bush's proposals] G. J. Church. il *Time* 133:16-17 Je 26 '89

The smog of disagreement delaying a new Clean-Air Act. V. Cahan and R. Fly. il *Business Week* p51 My 22 '89

Two cheers for Bush's plan to clean up the Clean Air Act. A. S. Blinder. il *Business Week* p14 Jl 10 '89

Up in smoke. *The Nation* 249:444-5 O 23 '89

The White House effect [Bush proposals] *The Progressive* 53:9-10 O '89

CLEAN AND SOBER [film] See Motion picture reviews—Single works

CLEAN ROOMS

Lockheed renovates clean room for work on large satellites. il *Aviation Week & Space Technology* 130:303 Je 12 '89

CLEANING

See also

Automobiles—Cleaning

Bicycles—Cleaning

House cleaning

Rifles—Cleaning

Rugs and carpets—Care

Stain removal

Vacuum cleaning

CLEANING COMPOSITIONS

See also

Butcher Co., Inc.

Paint and varnish removers

Soap

All-purpose cleaners. il *Consumer Reports* 54:338-40 D '89

Gilt without guilt [formulas for nontoxic products] il *Women's Sports & Fitness* 11:10 O '89

Glass cleaners. il *Consumer Reports* 54:611-14 O '89

CLEANING MACHINERY AND APPLIANCES

See also

Pressure washers

Vacuum cleaners

CLEANING OF FISH See Fish, Dressing of

CLEANING OF LAKES, RIVERS, ETC.

Give us your tires, your Coors cans . . . [cleanup trips down the Rogue River] T. Bielefeldt. il *Sierra* 74:74-7 Mr/Ap '89

Of time and the river [Kalamazoo River] B. Gilbert. il *Sports Illustrated* 71:76-80+ Jl 24 '89

Restoration along the Delaware [work of the Delaware River Basin Commission] C. M. Roberts. il *The Conservationist* 43:2-9 My/Je '89

CLEANING SERVICES

See also

House cleaning services

Molly Maid Inc.

ServiceMaster Limited Partnership

Wright-Way Cleaning Service, Inc.

ZZZZ Best Company

Ethical aspects

How Barry Minkow fooled the auditors. D. Akst. il pors *Forbes* 144:126-7+ O 2 '89

CLEANSING CREAMS See Cosmetics

CLEAR CREEK DISTILLERY

Oregon original [S. McCarthy's fruit brandies] F. J. Prial. il *The New York Times Magazine* p56 F 5 '89

CLEARCUTTING

Ancient forests agreement [Pacific Northwest] P. Byrnes. il *Wilderness* 53:3-4 Wint '89

Ancient forests as victims of myth [Pacific Northwest] *Wilderness* 53:3 Fall '89

California's chain-saw massacre [clearcutting redwood by Pacific Lumber] M. J. Walters. il *Reader's Digest* 135:144-9 N '89

A clearcutting ban for the birds [red cockaded woodpeckers in national forests in Texas] P. Larmer. il *Sierra* 74:28-30 Mr/Ap '89

Coming into clearcut [excerpt from The island within] R. K. Nelson. *Harper's* 279:28+ D '89

Enough is enough [destruction of old growth forest in the Pacific Northwest] J. D. Hair. il *International Wildlife* 19:30 S/O '89

The last stand for old growth? [Pacific Northwest] J. Watson. il *National Wildlife* 28:24-5 D '89/Ja '90

Logging poses threat to Bandelier. il *National Parks* 63:10 N/D '89

Milken, junk bonds and raping redwoods [C. Hurwitz accelerates logging following takeover] B. McKibben. *Rolling Stone* p39-40 Ag 10 '89

New thinking on old growth [Pacific Northwest] W. Booth. il map *Science* 244:141-3 Ap 14 '89

CLEARCUTTING—*cont.*

A raider's ruckus in the redwoods [accelerated logging following Maxxam's takeover of Pacific Lumber] E. Schultz. il por *Fortune* 119:172-3+ Ap 24 '89

Railroaded [clearcutting by Plum Creek Timber Company spurred on by LBO fever] A. Porterfield. il *Common Cause Magazine* 15:21-3 S/O '89

Showdown in the treetops [confrontations over old-growth forests in the Pacific Northwest] M. D. Lemonick. il *Time* 134:58-9 Ag 28 '89

'The spotted owl could wipe us out' [Northwest lumber industry] J. B. Levine. il *Business Week* p94+ S 18 '89

Still at loggerheads [timber industry vs. conservationists in Oregon] il *Time* 134:24 Jl 10 '89

Succession. J. Metzler. il *Sierra* 74:71-2+ N/D '89

Taking heart from upper East Tennessee [Cherokee National Forest] B. Wallach. il map *Focus (New York, N.Y.: 1950)* 38:22-8 Wint '88

A towering fight [proposed logging of Sitka spruce on Vancouver Island] H. Quinn. il *Maclean's* 102:46 Je 5 '89

War in the woods: Swan song [confrontations over destruction of old-growth timber in Flathead National Forest] J. G. Mitchell. il map *Audubon* 91:92-102+ N '89

Watching over the Ouachita. S. McCarthy. il *Sierra* 74:80-1 S/O '89

CLEARING OF LAND
See also
Shifting cultivation

CLEARING OF SECURITIES
No personal checks accepted here. R. L. Stern. il *Forbes* 144:53 D 25 '89

CLEARVISION *See* Extended definition television

CLEARWATER (FLA.)
Criminal justice, Administration of
True confession? [excerpt from transcript of police interrogation of murder suspect T. F. Sawyer] *Harper's* 279:17-20+ O '89

Untrue confessions [T. F. Sawyer confesses to murder after brutal interrogation by police] P. Weiss. il por *Mother Jones* 14:18-20+ S '89

CLEATED SHOES
The hole story. il *Women's Sports & Fitness* 11:41 Mr '89

CLEAVE, JAMES
about
Hongkong Bank's quiet invasion. P. C. Newman. il *Maclean's* 102:42 D 18 '89

CLEESE, JOHN
about
Now for something completely . . . [interview] A. P. Sanoff. por *U.S. News & World Report* 107:105 O 16 '89

Sharp Cleese. V. Woods. il por *Vogue* 179:230+ Ja '89

CLEGG, JOHNNY
about
Warrior against racism. K. McKenna. il por *Scholastic Update (Teachers' edition)* 121:16 Ja 27 '89

CLEMATIS
Clematis is always a surprise. L. B. Trigg. il *Southern Living* 24:64-5 Ap '89

Pruning clematis. J. Glattstein. il *Organic Gardening* 36:30-1 Ap '89

CLEMENS, SAMUEL LANGHORNE *See* Twain, Mark, 1835-1910

CLEMENT, CHARLES R.
A center of crop genetic diversity in western Amazonia. bibl f il maps *BioScience* 39:624-31 O '89

CLÉMENT, JACQUES, CA. 1566-1589
about
The assassination of Henry III. M. Greengrass. il bibl *History Today* 39:11-17 N '89

CLÉMENT, PIERRE
The street of the glazed tile factory. il *The Unesco Courier* 42:38-41 Ag '89

CLEMENTE, ENRIQUE
'This farewell to communism'. il *World Press Review* 36:28-9 Ag '89

CLEMENTE, LILIA C.
about
Feisty Filipina. M. Alpert. il *Fortune* 119:121-2 F 27 '89

The Japanese connection. R. Phalon. il pors *Forbes* 143:172+ Ap 3 '89

CLEMENTE CAPITAL INC.
Feisty Filipina [L. Clemente] M. Alpert. por *Fortune* 119:121-2 F 27 '89

CLEMENTE GLOBAL GROWTH FUND, INC.
The Japanese connection [T. Pickens' takeover thwarted by web of Japanese ties] R. Phalon. il pors *Forbes* 143:172+ Ap 3 '89

CLEMENTS, GEORGE
about
In Chicago, two angry priests declare a holy war on drugs. W. Plummer. il pors *People Weekly* 32:102-3 S 4 '89

CLEMENTS, GEORGE
about
Chickamauga quail. B. Tarrant. il *Field & Stream* 93:181-2 Ap '89

CLEMENTS, KEVIN P.
Will test ban conference self-destruct? bibl f il *The Bulletin of the Atomic Scientists* 45:16-18 Jl/Ag '89

CLENDENIN, JOHN L.
about
BellSouth is on a ringing streak. S. Gannes. il por *Fortune* 120:66-7+ O 9 '89

Education: the competitor's key. R. T. Gray. il pors *Nation's Business* 77:60+ Je '89

CLERGY
See also
Bishops
Black clergy
Catholic Church—Clergy
Chaplains, Military
Children of clergymen
Missionaries
Preaching
Priests
Seminarians
Women clergy

Ministry as more than a helping profession [cover story] S. Hauerwas and W. H. Willimon. il *The Christian Century* 106:282-4 Mr 15 '89

We ask for poor sermons. K. Miller. por *Christianity Today* 33:10 D 15 '89

Age
Being 50 is okay. G. K. Brushaber. il *Christianity Today* 33:13 Ja 13 '89

Appointment, call and election
The accidental parson. T. W. Gillespie. il *Christianity Today* 33:61+ O 20 '89

On making it in the pros [ministry as a gift and art] T. E. Frank. *The Christian Century* 106:103-4 F 1-8 '89

Crime
The victim of a savage attack, a minister's wife is condemned to a long death in life [P. Railey, severely brain damaged after being strangled in Dallas, Tex. home] J. Young. il pors *People Weekly* 31:50-2+ Ja 16 '89

White Harlem minister convicted of sex abuse [case of T. Streitferdt] il por *Jet* 76:32 Je 19 '89

White minister called 'wolf in sheep's clothes' gets 7 years in sex cases [T. Streitferdt] il por *Jet* 76:53 Jl 24 '89

Education
See also
Theological seminaries
Theology—Study and teaching

Ethics
Bad-news bearers [news stories on clergy scandals] L. Cryderman. il *Christianity Today* 33:12 Ap 21 '89

TV evangelists: the scandals may not be over. D. Hill. il *TV Guide* 37:10-11+ Ap 15-21 '89

Leaves of absence
Paternity leave as church praxis [experience of United Methodist Church minister] B. Schofield-Bodt. il *The Christian Century* 106:463-4 My 3 '89

Political activities
See also
Black clergy—Political activities

Psychology
Prescriptions for pastors. M. E. Marty. *The Christian Century* 106:159 F 1-8 '89

Sexual behavior
See also
Ordination of homosexuals

The battle over gay clergy. R. N. Ostling. il *Time* 134:89-90 N 13 '89

Centerfold follies [revelations concerning J. Swaggart in Penthouse] L. Cryderman. *Christianity Today* 33:17 Mr 17 '89

The phallic pulpit. G. Wills. bibl f il *The New York Review of Books* 36:20+ D 21 '89

Pop stars blast evangelists. P. Crescenti. il *Christianity Today* 33:63 Mr 3 '89

When a pastor turns seducer. K. L. Woodward. il *Newsweek* 114:48-9 Ag 28 '89

CLERGY CONFERENCES
See also
Catholic Church. National Conference of Catholic Bishops

CLERGY MALPRACTICE
Court rules on clergy malpractice, Sabbath. *Christianity Today* 33:51-2 My 12 '89

CLERKS (RETAIL TRADE)
See also
United Food and Commercial Workers International Union

CLEVELAND, PAUL M.
U.S.-New Zealand revelations: some parting observations [address, April 12, 1989] *Department of State Bulletin* 89:45-8 Je '89

CLEVELAND (OHIO)
Banks
See also
Society Corp.

City planning
Facing an uncomfortable truth [address, June 15, 1989] J. H. Ross. *Vital Speeches of the Day* 55:690-3 S 1 '89

CLEVELAND (OHIO)—cont.

Crime

The blind high [narcotics trade not just a black problem] M. Drexler. *Utne Reader* p99-100 S/O '89

Description

Greetings from Cleveland Ohio. B. McBride and B. McBride. il *Travel Holiday* 172:52-6 Ag '89

An Indian summer for Eric Carmen. D. Wild. il por *Rolling Stone* p54 Jl 13-27 '89

Industries

How business bosses saved a sick city. M. Magnet. il *Fortune* 119:106-10 Mr 27 '89

Music

See also
Cleveland Opera
Cleveland Orchestra

Cleveland may finally get some satisfaction [Rock Hall of Fame] S. Phillips. il *Business Week* p60 O 2 '89

Music festivals

See Music festivals—Ohio

Police

Fury over an unholy alliance [police accused of teaming up with drug dealer A. Feckner] B. Turque. il por *Newsweek* 113:26 My 8 '89

Politics and government

Forbes, White battle to become Cleveland mayor. il pors *Jet* 77:12 O 23 '89

Religious institutions and affairs

UCC headquarters site. *The Christian Century* 106:520 My 17 '89

CLEVELAND OPERA

Roll over, Wagner [Cleveland Opera to perform S. Copeland's Holy blood and crescent moon] A. Tommasini. il pors *The New York Times Magazine* p40-1+ S 24 '89

CLEVELAND ORCHESTRA

Festive spirits [performances at Carnegie Hall] P. G. Davis. il por *New York* 22:73-4 F 13 '89

Musical events:
Concerts in Carnegie Hall. A. Porter. *The New Yorker* 65:68 F 27 '89

CLIBURN, VAN, 1934-

about

The return of Van Cliburn. O. Friedrich. il por *Time* 134:72 Jl 3 '89

CLICHÉS

Of many things [David Feldman's Who put the butter in the butterfly?] G. W. Hunt. *America* 160:234 Mr 18 '89

Read my cliché [press use of G. Bush's phrases] L. Zuckerman. il por *Time* 133:64 Ja 16 '89

CLICK AGENCY

Follow that girl [Click Agency brings suit against Ford Agency over defection of R. Williams] A. Keteyian. il pors *New York* 22:38-43 Mr 6 '89

CLICK BEETLES See Beetles

CLICKSMAN, MARLAINE

Wonder Brad [interview with B. Dourif] il pors *Film Comment* 25:44-5 N/D '89

CLIFFORD, CATHERINE

From bear teeth to pearls. il *Health (New York, N.Y.)* 21:74-9 Ag '89

CLIFFORD, CATHERINE, AND FARGANIS, SONDRA

Wearing the pants. il *Health (New York, N.Y.)* 21:68-73+ Ap '89

CLIFFORD, GERALDINE JONÇICH

(jt. auth) See Guthrie, James W., and Clifford, Geraldine Jonçich

CLIFFORD, HOWARD

about

Develop an audience. il *American Artist* 53:50 D '89

CLIFFORD, NICHOLAS R.

A tale of two cities: Hong Kong & Shanghai. il *Commonweal* 116:453-5 S 8 '89

CLIFF'S NOTES INC.

Court removes ban on 'Spy notes' parody. il *Publishers Weekly* 236:10 O 6 '89

Doubleday fights block of 'Spy notes' parody. *Publishers Weekly* 236:9 Ag 18 '89

Shakespeare, Dickens & Hillegass. F. Meeks. il por *Forbes* 144:206+ O 30 '89

CLIFT HOTEL (SAN FRANCISCO, CALIF.: RESTAURANT)

See San Francisco (Calif.)—Restaurants; nightclubs, bars, etc.

CLIFTON, FRED J., D. 1984

about

A letter to Fred. L. Clifton. il pors *Essence* 20:65-6 N '89

CLIFTON, LUCILLE, 1936-

A letter to Fred. il pors *Essence* 20:65-6 N '89

CLIMATE

See also
Climatic changes
Droughts
Paleoclimatology
Plants, Effect of climate on
Urban climatology
Weather
See also subhead Climate under names of continents, countries, states, cities, etc.

Lack of data is frustrating [incomplete ecosystem knowledge hampers ability to deal with atmosphere and climate; views of Hal Mooney and Peter Vitousek] *USA Today (Periodical)* 117:6 Je '89

CLIMATE MODELS See Meteorological models

CLIMATE-OCEAN INTERACTION See Ocean-atmosphere interaction

CLIMATE-SOLAR RELATIONSHIPS See Sun and meteorology

CLIMATIC CHANGES

See also
El Niño (Ocean current)
Greenhouse effect
Intergovernmental Panel on Climate Change
International Geosphere-Biosphere Program
La Niña (Ocean current)
Nuclear winter

Amazon River discharge and climate variability: 1903 to 1985. J. E. Richey and others. bibl f il map *Science* 246:101-3 O 6 '89

The forest is for burning [influence of climate on Minnesota forest fires] J. S. Clark. il *Natural History* p50-3 Ja '89

Global change: defining the ill-defined. M. F. Price. bibl f il *Environment* 31:18-20+ O '89

Global climate change through the eons [implications for current habitat management; research by George L. Jacobson] J. A. Miller. *BioScience* 39:673-4 N '89

Planning for our common future. M. W. Holdgate. bibl f *Environment* 31:14-17+ O '89

Preparing for the worst. P. Elmer-Dewitt. il *Time* 133:70-1 Ja 2 '89

Questioning the cooling effects of volcanoes [research by Clifford F. Mass and David A. Portman] F. Flam. *Science News* 135:359 Je 10 '89

Volcanoes can muddle the greenhouse. R. A. Kerr. il *Science* 245:127-8 Jl 14 '89

CLIMATOLOGY See Climate

CLIMBING

See also
Mountaineering
Snow and ice climbing

CLIMBING MACHINES See Exercising equipment

CLIMBING PLANTS

See also
Clematis
Moonflowers

Overhead, on a fence, in a container . . . versatile flowering vines. il *Sunset (Central West edition)* 182:240 My '89

CLIMBING ROSES See Roses

CLINCHY, EVANS

Public school choice: absolutely necessary but not wholly sufficient. il *Phi Delta Kappan* 71:289-94 D '89

CLINE, RAY S.

Commentary: the Cuban missile crisis. bibl f *Foreign Affairs* 68:190-6 Fall '89

CLINE, STEPHEN

Down on the fish farm. il *Sierra* 74:30+ Mr/Ap '89

CLINICAL ECOLOGY

The clinical ecology scam. P. W. Huber. il por *Forbes* 144:232 O 2 '89

CLINICAL LABORATORIES See Medical laboratories

CLINICAL TECHNOLOGIES ASSOCIATES

The opposite of a bitter pill? [method to convert certain drugs to oral form] G. G. Marcial. *Business Week* p132 My 15 '89

CLINICS See Health facilities

CLINTON, GEORGE

about

George Clinton's theory of funk. P. Puterbaugh. il *Rolling Stone* p16 O 5 '89

CLINTON (ILL.)

Education

Helping give students a sense of audience [junior high school magazine] K. S. Carter. *The Education Digest* 55:43-6 O '89

CLIP ART SOFTWARE

Testing

Graphics for the non-artist. S. Morgenstern. il *Home Office Computing* 7:28-9 Mr '89

CLIPPER SHIPS

Technological turkeys. J. S. Gordon. il *American Heritage* 40:18+ My/Je '89

CLIQUES

The power of cliques. N. Rubin. il *Parents* 64:104-8+ N '89

CLOCK RADIOS

Clock radios. il *Consumer Reports* 54:122-6 D '89

Which radios sound the sweetest wake-up call? il *Consumer Reports* 54:558-61 S '89

CLOCKS

See also
Atomic clocks
British Horological Institute

Caveman Clockwork [computer program] S. Hudson. il *Compute!* 11:106+ D '89

Timely face-lifts for clocks, and a hands-on quiz to set your mind ticking. S. Morris. il *Omni (New York, N.Y.)* 11:90-2 Jl '89

CLOCKS—cont.

Collectors and collecting

Antiques: country clocks. R. Conniff. il *Architectural Digest* 46:178-81+ Je '89

The pillar-and-scroll clock. B. Barol. *American Heritage* 40:24 Ap '89

Timely obsessions [P. Reginato's and F. De Chabris' collection of fifties clocks] M. Guralnick. il pors *House & Garden* 161:94+ S '89

Conservation and restoration

The clock strikes back [Engle clock] B. Weber. il *The New York Times Magazine* p66 Ag 6 '89

He fixed it [Seattle street clock restorations by J. Martin] J. Schwarz. il pors map *Americana* 16:57-60 Ja/F '89

Exhibitions

Museum accessions [French pendulum clock donated to the Indianapolis Museum of Art] E. H. Gustafson. il *Antiques* 136:1270 D '89

History

The mechanical clock [ancient China] R. K. G. Temple. il *The Courier (Unesco)* 41:26-7 O '88

Maintenance and repair

I am the clock winder [tower clock of Christ Episcopal Church in Island Pond, Vt.] G. Keizer. il *Reader's Digest* 134:113-17 Ap '89

CLOGGING (DANCE)

"Just clogging". K. S. Edwards and S. Antle. il *Americana* 17:17-20 N/D '89

CLOISONNÉ

The art of the fire: cloisonné enamels [cover story] R. V. Simpson. bibl il *Antiques & Collecting Hobbies* 94:40-1+ Ap '89

CLOMIPRAMINE

Chemistry of compulsive hair pulling [treatment with clomipramine; research by Susan E. Swedo] *Science News* 136:175 S 9 '89

CLONES (BIOLOGY)

See also
Monoclonal antibodies

Amplification and molecular cloning of HTLV-I sequences from DNA of multiple sclerosis patients. E. P. Reddy and others. bibl f il *Science* 243:529-33 Ja 27 '89; Correction. 246:10-11 O 6 '89

Cloning and expression of a Xenopus embryonic gap junction protein. L. Ebihara and others. bibl f il *Science* 243:1194-5 Mr 3 '89

Cloning and sequencing of porcine LH-hCG receptor cDNA: variants lacking transmembrane domain. H. Loosfelt and others. bibl f il *Science* 245:525-8 Ag 4 '89

Cloning of breakpoints of a chromosome translocation identifies the AN2 locus [aniridia] M. Gessler and others. bibl f il *Science* 244:1575-8 Je 30 '89

Conserved repetitive epitope recognized by CD4+ clones from a malaria-immunized volunteer. E. H. Nardin and others. bibl f il *Science* 246:1603-6 D 22 '89

Expression of a cloned rat brain potassium channel in Xenopus oocytes. M. J. Christie and others. bibl f il *Science* 244:221-4 Ap 14 '89

Gene control research gets a boost [TATA protein gene cloned; work of Leonard Guarente] J. L. Marx. il *Science* 245:1329-30 S 22 '89

Human chromosome 12 is required for elevated HIV-1 expression in human-hamster hybrid cells. C. E. Hart and others. bibl f il *Science* 246:488-91 O 27 '89

Identification of the cystic fibrosis gene: cloning and characterization of complementary DNA. J. R. Riordan and others. bibl f il *Science* 245:1066-73 S 8 '89

Immunodeficiency and clonal growth of target cells induced by helper-free defective retrovirus. M. Huang and others. bibl f il *Science* 246:1614-17 D 22 '89

Interleukin-2 receptor β chain gene: generation of three receptor forms by cloned human α and β chain cDNA's. M. Hatakeyama and others. bibl f il *Science* 244:551-6 My 5 '89

Isolation of a cDNA clone derived from a blood-borne non-A, non-B viral hepatitis genome. Q.-L. Choo and others. bibl f il *Science* 244:359-62 Ap 21 '89

Isolation of human transcribed sequences from human-rodent somatic cell hybrids. P. Liu and others. bibl f il *Science* 246:813-15 N 10 '89

Isolation of single-copy human genes from a library of yeast artificial chromosome clones [Saccharomyces] B. H. Brownstein and others. bibl f il *Science* 244:1348-51 Je 16 '89

Mapping the Drosophila genome with yeast artificial chromosomes. D. Garza and others. bibl f il *Science* 246:641-6 N 3 '89

The molecular basis of muscular dystrophy in the *mdx* mouse: a point mutation. P. Sicinski and others. bibl f il *Science* 244:1578-80 Je 30 '89

Molecular cloning of genes under control of the circadian clock in Neurospora. J. J. Loros and others. bibl f il *Science* 243:385-8 Ja 20 '89

Molecular cloning of the thyrotropin receptor. M. Parmentier and others. bibl f il *Science* 246:1620-2 D 22 '89

Mouse lymph node homing receptor cDNA clone encodes a glycoprotein revealing tandem interaction domains. M. H. Siegelman and others. bibl f il *Science* 243:1165-72 Mr 3 '89

The neuron-specific protein PGP 9.5 is a ubiquitin carboxyl-terminal hydrolase. K. D. Wilkinson and others. bibl f il *Science* 246:670-3 N 3 '89

PCR analysis of DNA from multiple sclerosis patients for the presence of HTLV-I [discussion of January 27, 1989 article, Amplification and molecular cloning of HTLV-I sequences from DNA of multiple sclerosis patients] E. P. Reddy and others. il *Science* 246:821-4 N 10 '89

Plant ion-pump gene cloned, sequenced [work of Michael R. Sussman] I. Wickelgren. *Science News* 135:135 Mr 4 '89

Purification and complementary DNA cloning of a receptor for basic fibroblast growth factor. P. L. Lee and others. bibl f il *Science* 245:57-60 Jl 7 '89

Selective amplification and cloning of four new members of the G protein-coupled receptor family. F. Libert and others. bibl f il *Science* 244:569-72 My 5 '89

Thymic requirement for clonal deletion during T cell development. A. M. Fry and others. bibl f il *Science* 246:1044-6 N 24 '89

CLONES (BOTANY)

Ethylene gene control: research ripens [gene for ACC synthase cloned; work of Takahide Sato and Athanasios Theologis] *Science News* 136:188 S 16 '89

Yuletide tissue cultures [Christmas tree breeding] R. Khalaf. il *Forbes* 144:276+ D 11 '89

CLOONEY, GEORGE

about

When Twins' Kelly Preston needs a lift, she gets it from Roseanne's George Clooney. S. Haller. il pors *People Weekly* 31:113-14+ F 13 '89

CLOS-LUCÉ (AMBOISE, FRANCE)

Leonardo's manor house in France. il *Sunset (Central West edition)* 181:24 D '88

CLOSE, CHUCK, 1940-

about

Color Close-ups. C. Finch. il *Art in America* 77:112-19+ Mr '89

CLOSE, GLENN

about

Close-up. K. Bishop. il pors *Vogue* 179:298-303 Ag '89

Glenn Close [interview] J. Ellis. il pors *Life* 12:17-19 F '89

Glenn Close: sitting pretty [cover story] B. Allen. il pors *Ms.* 18:46-50 N '89

She's not Meryl Streep, but she's Close. C. Michener. il pors *Esquire* 112:136-8+ N '89

CLOSE AIR SUPPORT

Budget cuts, cost growth cloud F-16 plans for 1990s. D. F. Bond. *Aviation Week & Space Technology* 131:18-19 D 4 '89

Close air support move in Congress might disrupt production of F-16. D. F. Bond and J. D. Morrocco. il *Aviation Week & Space Technology* 131:22-4 N 13 '89

Congress eases F-16 production curbs; Pentagon debates CAS responsibilities. D. F. Bond. *Aviation Week & Space Technology* 131:32 N 20 '89

Defense Dept. plans CAS review; Congress seeks upgrades agreement. D. F. Bond. il *Aviation Week & Space Technology* 131:31-3 S 11 '89

Design of Su-25 combines simplicity, survivability [Soviet aircraft] il *Aviation Week & Space Technology* 131:43 Jl 3 '89

Falcon Eye Flir, GEC helmet aid F-16 mission flexibility [cover story] W. B. Scott. il *Aviation Week & Space Technology* 130:34-6+ Ap 17 '89

LTV begins flight tests of reengined A-7F for Air Guard mission. D. A. Brown. il *Aviation Week & Space Technology* 131:19-21 D 4 '89

Pentagon proposes testing plan to resolve CAS aircraft dispute. J. D. Morrocco. *Aviation Week & Space Technology* 130:97+ F 20 '89

TAC demonstration bolsters support for F-16 in CAS role. C. A. Shifrin. il *Aviation Week & Space Technology* 130:49-50 Ap 17 '89

USAF to accept plan on modifying F-16, A-10 for close air support. *Aviation Week & Space Technology* 130:28 Mr 13 '89

CLOSE CORPORATIONS See Closely held corporations

CLOSE-UP PHOTOGRAPHY See Photography, Close-up

CLOSED CIRCUIT TELEVISION

Oceanographic use

Live broadcasts from the ocean floor. il *Popular Mechanics* 166:13 Ap '89

Sports

Has racing staked its future on a bad pony? [off-track simulcasting's effect on race track attendance] S. Phillips. il *Business Week* p84+ My 8 '89

CLOSED ECOLOGICAL SYSTEMS

See also
Biosphere II
Biosphere reserves

CLOSED-END FUNDS *See* Investment trusts
CLOSELY HELD CORPORATIONS
The 400 largest private companies in the U.S. il *Forbes* 144:220-2+ D 11 '89
CLOSER THAN EVER [musical] *See* Musicals, revues, etc.—Reviews—Single works
CLOSETS
7 creative closets. il *Redbook* 172:102-7 Mr '89
Bath trio [vanity, linen locker, and mirror-backed shelves] L. M. Dalsgaard. il *Home Mechanix* 85:42-4+ Je '89
Building a simple closet [cover story] D. Johnson. il *The Family Handyman* 39:38-43 Ja '89
Closets! From messy to marvelous. E. Petrowski. il *Good Housekeeping* 208:188+ Ap '89
Useful closet only 6 inches deep. il *Sunset (Central West edition)* 183:94 S '89

Equipment
Clutter busters: closet organizers you can buy. il *Better Homes and Gardens* 67:81 S '89
How to install a closet organizer. il *Popular Mechanics* 166:93-4 O '89
It was a one-pole inefficient closet. il *Sunset (Central West edition)* 183:146-7 O '89
Making space. H. Wicks. il *Home Mechanix* 85:62-4+ F '89

CLOTH *See* Textile fabrics
CLOTHES DRYERS
Clothes dryers. il *Consumer Reports* 54:314-18 D '89
Heat-pump clothes dryer. V. E. Gilmore. il *Popular Science* 235:124+ N '89
The line on dryers. il *Consumer Reports* 54:616-20 O '89
CLOTHES WASHING MACHINES *See* Washing machines
CLOTHESPINS
Clothespin ornaments. il *National Geographic World* 172:18-19 D '89
CLOTHIER, PETER, 1936-
L.A.: outward bound. il *Art News* 88:126-31 D '89
True grit. il por *Art News* 88:102-7 Ja '89
CLOTHING, COLD WEATHER
See also
Coats
All-weather sportswear [treated with polyethylene glycol] il *USA Today (Periodical)* 118:15 D '89
Cold comfort. C. C. Johnson. il *Parents* 64:240+ D '89
Dressing for exercise. D. Lang and L. Lang. il *Current Health 2* 16:14-15 D '89
Dressing for the cold. S. Richmond. il *Changing Times* 43:122 N '89
Guide to insulation material. il *Women's Sports & Fitness* 11:37 O '89
Staying snug on the slopes. R. Stead. il *Business Week* p126 D 4 '89
Sub-zero snowsuit [Expedition Series from Northern Outfitters] G. Davis. il *Popular Science* 235:120-1 N '89
Suit up to work out in the cold. J. Rogoznica. il *Working Woman* 14:118+ F '89
Winter where? [bicycle clothing] L. Fritz. il *Bicycling* 30:48-53 D '89

Care
Clean up on down. R. Ball. il *Field & Stream* 94:137 S '89
CLOTHING, PROTECTIVE
See also
Arms and armor
Clothing, Cold weather
Clothing, Waterproof
Helmets
CLOTHING, SECONDHAND
See also
Garment District (Firm)
Thrift shops and rummage sales
Everything old is new again [new versions of old classics] J. Shields. il *Vogue* 179:138+ Ap '89

Collectors and collecting
Collecting sure things. C. Donovan. il *The New York Times Magazine* p80-1 N 26 '89
Collecting vintage dresses with contemporary flair [L. Hutton] B. Boehlert. il pors *Architectural Digest* 46:60+ S '89
Old clothing. G. Michael. il *Antiques & Collecting Hobbies* 94:62 S '89
CLOTHING, WATERPROOF
Clothed in history. M. Reed. il *Weatherwise* 42:98-9 Ap '89
Dry by design [waterproof/breathable fabrics for skiers] E. Perlman. il *Skiing* 42:112-14+ D '89
Rain or shine. R. Gollin. il *Vogue* 179:97 Ap '89
Take cover. il *Teen* 33:28 Ap '89
Weatherwise sportswear. il *Good Housekeeping* 208:104 My '89
CLOTHING AND DRESS
See also
Bathing suits
Belts (Clothing)
Blazers (Jackets)
Caps (Hats)
Clothing industry
Coats
Costume
Dandies
Dress accessories
Fashion
Fashion designers
Fashion shows
Footwear
Fur coats, wraps, etc.
Gloves
Hats
Hosiery
Jackets
Kimonos
Knickers
Leather garments
Models (Persons)
Pants
Scarves
Sewing
Shirts
Shorts (Clothing)
Shoulder pads
Skirts (Clothing)
Sleepwear
Sweaters
Tailoring
Tights (Clothing)
Underwear
Uniforms
Vests
Wedding clothes
70 great ways to greet summer. il *Glamour* 87:129-37 Jl '89
Beat the heat. W. Gavin. il *Parents* 64:110-12 Jl '89
Beauty & fashion journal. *See* issues of Ladies' Home Journal beginning January 1988
Boyish good looks [menswear for women] B. Boehlert. il *Vogue* 179:78-9 F '89
A dash of haberdashery [menswear for women] il *Glamour* 87:251 Ap '89
Dos & don'ts. *See* issues of Glamour
Everything old is new again [new versions of old classics] J. Shields. il *Vogue* 179:138+ Ap '89
Everything you always wanted to know about beauty and fashion. L. J. Johnson. il *Ladies' Home Journal* 106:149-56 O '89
Fancy-free easy, breezy, even black-tie [Multiples by Sandra Garratt] E. Rogers. il *American Health* 8:38 Ja/F '89
Fashion questions. *See* issues of Glamour
Fashion sense [wraps] il *Essence* 20:32 Jl '89
How to put together your fall wardrobe. il *McCall's* 116:26-9 S '89
In the fashion no! L. Phillips. il *Ms.* 17:42-3 Mr '89
Menswear: a girl's best friend. A. Holch. il *American Health* 8:34-6 Ja/F '89
Mid-summer style. il *Ladies' Home Journal* 106:132-4 Ag '89
Pass/fail summer fashion. il *Glamour* 87:191-6 Je '89
Resort report. L. J. Nonkin. il *Vogue* 179:92-3+ N '89
What went wrong here? How to make it right. *See* issues of Mademoiselle
What's new? What's wise to buy? M. A. C. Fusco. *Redbook* 173:141 S '89

Anecdotes, facetiae, satire, etc.
Fit to be tied [wrap-and-tie clothing] S. Orlean. il *Vogue* 179:370+ F '89

Authors
Royalton flash. il *Vogue* 179:240 Ja '89

Businessmen
The high road. F. Rogers. il *The New York Times Magazine* p76-7 O 1 '89
Shop talk. N. Raoul. *Black Enterprise* 20:139 O '89
Unfit for the occasion [showing Russians how to dress when conducting foreign business] C. Bogert. il *Newsweek* 114:71 D 25 '89

Businesswomen
See also
Laura Caspari Ltd./SHE, Inc.
1989 fall fashion portfolio [cover story; special section] il *Working Woman* 14:143+ S '89
Best new career clothes [cover story; special section] il *Working Woman* 14:129+ Mr '89
Break out of your fashion rut. il *Glamour* 87:288-91 Mr '89
Clothes strategies. J. Mattera. *See* issues of Glamour beginning October 1986
Diamonds are for boardrooms. P. Baldwin and L. Calvacca. *Working Woman* 14:44 Ag '89
Executive style. R. Newland. il *Black Enterprise* 20:129-30+ O '89
Glamour-for-rent. A. Russell. il *Working Woman* 14:69 D '89
Job interview update: navy suit not required. il *Glamour* 87:217-20 Mr '89
Makeovers for success: is how you dress your company's business? [case of B. Smith] P. R. Satran. il por *Glamour* 87:154-5+ Jl '89
Real-life cues to clothes for your job. il *Glamour* 87:203-6 O '89

CLOTHING AND DRESS—Businesswomen—*cont.*

A working wardrobe. S. Dresner. il *New Choices for the Best Years* 29:37-44 Ja '89

Care

Cyclewear comes clean. S. Sorensen. il *Bicycling* 30:128+ My '89

Laundry daze. S. Shapiro. il *Ms.* 17:34+ My '89

Catholics

A Catholic taste in clothes [dress code at Sacred Heart Church, Dayton, Ohio] il por *Newsweek* 114:27 S 18 '89

Celebrities

Call it Dangerous excess as loads of Oscar's ladies bust out and take the plunge. il *People Weekly* 31:136-7 Ap 17 '89

The Coast. G. Stone. il *Gentlemen's Quarterly* 59:199 Mr '89

Courthouse couture. il *People Weekly* 32:106-7 D 25 '89-Ja 1 '90

Dressing the part. il *Teen* 33:52-4 Jl '89

The five best—and worst—dressed in the soaps. R. Blackwell. il *TV Guide* 37:28-31 N 4-10 '89

The good, bad and ugh-ly [cover story] il *People Weekly* 32:64-74 D 11 '89

Mr. Blackwell's fashion guide: TV stars to watch—and ignore—if you want to look sharp [cover story] R. Blackwell. il *TV Guide* 37:10-13 Jl 22-28 '89

The original rebels [celebrities who have influenced fashion] il *Mademoiselle* 95:160-1 Jl '89

Star struck. N. Malkin. il *Vogue* 179:40-1 Ja '89

The Vogue 100. C. Heimel. il *Vogue* 179:262-9 Je '89

Children

See also
At Last Inc.
Bellini (Firm)
Hanna Andersson Corporation

The children's closet [Christmas gifts] *The New Yorker* 65:173-6+ D 4 '89

Child's play [exercise clothes] il *Health (New York, N.Y.)* 21:36+ Ap '89

Guys and dolls at the mall. R. La Ferla. il *The New York Times Magazine* p58-61 Jl 9 '89

How to dress a 2-year-old. T. Gough. il *Parents* 64:207-9 Mr '89

It's a small world. R. La Ferla. il *The New York Times Magazine* p44-8 Ja 15 '89

Vacation clothes. W. Gavin and C. DiGrappa. il *Parents* 64:166 Je '89

The way we were [shopping for back-to-school clothes with children] D. Sobel. il *Ladies' Home Journal* 106:82 S '89

Dancers

No body's perfect. M. Horosko. il *Dance Magazine* 63:56-7 O '89

Detectives

In the trenches. R. La Ferla. il *The New York Times Magazine* p56 Ap 16 '89

Infants

See also
Diapers

Leasing and renting

Glamour-for-rent. A. Russell. il *Working Woman* 14:69 D '89

Rent and rave: look like a million on borrowed time. D. Wise. il *Glamour* 87:176 D '89

Maternity clothes

Maternity dressing: what works for work. S. Young. il *Glamour* 87:89 N '89

The perfect fit [underwear] C. DiGrappa. il *Parents* 64:154-6 N '89

Men

See also
Clothing and dress—Businessmen
Designers' Collective
Hats
Neckties
Shirts
Tuxedos

The bespoke life [custom-made clothes] P. Mayle. il *Gentlemen's Quarterly* 59:422-7+ S '89

Can you turn a guy who's a fashion zero into a 10? *Glamour* 87:93 Ja '89

Classics. J. Berendt. See issues of Esquire

Clothes make the man—nervous. W. D. Leight. *Mademoiselle* 95:116 F '89

Dressing down. R. La Ferla. il *The New York Times Magazine* p29 Ja 1 '89

GQ preview. See issues of Gentlemen's Quarterly

Jocks and nerds [exhibition at Fashion Institute of Technology] *The New Yorker* 65:30-2 Ap 24 '89

Merkin on style. R. Merkin. See issues of Gentlemen's Quarterly beginning March 1988

Past as prologue [designs of J. Abboud and L. Karesh] R. La Ferla. il pors *The New York Times Magazine* p56-7 F 19 '89

Sacking out [suits] R. La Ferla. il *The New York Times Magazine* p54 Ap 9 '89

Sartorially suited [Jocks and nerds exhibit at Fashion Institute of Technology] J. Perl. il *Vogue* 179:274+ Ap '89

Seersucker joins the ranks of the chic. T. Segal. il *Business Week* p184 Jl 17 '89

Tested by time [Jocks and nerds at Fashion Institute of Technology] R. La Ferla. il *The New York Times Magazine* p66-7 Mr 12 '89

Why I wear what I wear. See issues of Gentlemen's Quarterly

Physiological aspects

Are you a fashion victim? K. Haukebo. il *Current Health 2* 15:26-7 Ap '89

Presidents

See also
Bush, George, 1924——Clothing and dress

Prices

At what price young success? [G. Henderson's designs] N. Darnton. il por *Newsweek* 114:87 N 20 '89

Where the deals are. il *Seventeen* 48:230 Ag '89

Women vs. fashion: why clothes cost so much. C. E. Trunzo. il *Ladies' Home Journal* 106:108+ Mr '89

Psychological aspects

See also
Sex and fashion

How to look pulled together when you feel like you're falling apart. il *Glamour* 87:102+ Je '89

"Move over, Phil" [using attitudes to enhance appearance] L. Phillips. il *Ms.* 17:44+ Ja/F '89

Rock musicians

Gonna dress you up [rock couturiers] J. Conlin. il *Rolling Stone* Fashion Collection:51-6+ Ap 20 '89

On the rack & off the wall [stylist F. Williams] J. McLaughlin. il por *Harper's Bazaar* 122:58 N '89

Size

See also
At Last Inc.
T. Deane Inc.

10 foolproof rules for dressing slim. il *McCall's* 117:26-9 N '89

Big on beauty (and fashion!). il *Good Housekeeping* 209:148-51 O '89

Nobody's perfect [special section] il *Harper's Bazaar* 122:82-103+ Ja '89

Your body-guide to new fashion. il *Glamour* 87:80-8 Ja '89

Social aspects

See also
Sex and fashion

Sports clothes

See also
Champion Products Inc.
Columbia Sportswear Company
J. Crew (Firm)
Jodhpurs
Patagonia Inc.
Quiksilver, Inc.
Sports uniforms

All-weather sportswear [treated with polyethylene glycol] il *USA Today (Periodical)* 118:15 D '89

The best and the tightest [running tights] D. Kardong. il *Runner's World* 24:80-3 S '89

Best defense [leather riding suits for motorcyclists] J. P. Burns. il *Cycle* 40:60-6 S '89

BMW Gore-Tex suit and Aerostich Roadcrafter II [motorcycling clothes] il *Cycle* 40:64-7 Ap '89

The bowling shirt. J. Berendt. il *Esquire* 111:26 Ja '89

Child's play [exercise clothes] il *Health (New York, N.Y.)* 21:36+ Ap '89

Close fit [influence of athletic clothes on fashion designer] D. Schefer. il *Vogue* 179:408-15 Ap '89

Clothing & accessory checklist. F. Zahradnik. il *Bicycling* 30:100-2 Ja/F '89

Clothing on the cutting edge [hunting] T. Huggler. il *Outdoor Life* 184:96-7+ N '89

Cycle chic [bicycling clothes] E. Nowport. il *American Health* 8:88+ My '89

Cyclewear comes clean. S. Sorensen. il *Bicycling* 30:128+ My '89

Do clothes a skier make? A. H. Greenberg. il *Skiing* 42:50-1 S '89

Dressing for exercise. D. Lang and L. Lang. il *Current Health 2* 16:14-15 D '89

Dry by design [waterproof/breathable fabrics for skiers] E. Perlman. il *Skiing* 42:112-14+ D '89

Energized! [fluorescent bicycling clothes] S. Sorensen and L. Fritz. il *Bicycling* 30:54-8+ Mr '89

Fitting solutions [ski clothes] H. Brooks. il *Skiing* 42:46+ S '89

Flash pants [bicycling clothes] S. Martin. il *Bicycling* 30:240 My '89

Geared up for downhill [skiing gear] il *Health (New York, N.Y.)* 21:30+ D '89

Get it two-gether [mothers and daughters model activewear] il *Teen* 33:62-4 D '89

The gray ghost [running clothes] B. Julyan. il *Runner's World* 24:96 Ag '89

In action [exercise clothing] L. Wells. il *The New York Times Magazine* p78-80 My 7 '89

Let's dance [workout wear] A. Holch. il *American Health* 8:36-8+ Mr '89

CLOTHING AND DRESS—Sports clothes—cont.

The lure of it all [fishing clothes] F. Rogers. il *The New York Times Magazine* p80-1 Ag 20 '89

The mild ones [motorcycling clothes] F. Rogers. il *The New York Times Magazine* p56-7 S 3 '89

No-sweat wear for working out. M. Galen. il *Business Week* p130 S 18 '89

Oh my! [bicycling underwear] S. Sorensen and L. Fritz. il *Bicycling* 30:154-5 Ap '89

Rawhide [leather motorcycle riding suits after suffering accidents] K. Vreeke. il *Cycle* 40:67 S '89

Reelin' in the year 1989. J. Gibbs. il *Outdoor Life* 184:64-6+ Jl '89

The runner's companion [cover story; special section] K. Delhagen. il *Women's Sports & Fitness* 11:31+ S '89

Second skin. D. Schefer. il *Vogue* 179:252-5 Je '89

Selling true grit [designs by R. Comstock] F. Rogers. il pors *The New York Times Magazine* p58-61 O 8 '89

Show-stopping sweats. il *Health (New York, N.Y.)* 21:40+ O '89

Skin thin [activewear] H. Hansen. il *Vogue* 179:178-9 D '89

Sportin' some style. il *Teen* 33:70-3 Ap '89

Staying snug on the slopes. R. Stead. il *Business Week* p126 D 4 '89

Suit up to work out in the cold. J. Rogoznica. il *Working Woman* 14:118+ F '89

Winter where? [cold weather bicycle clothing] L. Fritz. il *Bicycling* 30:48-53 D '89

Students

American casual seizes Japan. B. Hillenbrand. il *Time* 134:106 N 13 '89

Arguing that sloppy duds make sloppy minds, schools fight to revive stricter dress codes. T. Allis. il *People Weekly* 32:73-4+ O 23 '89

Campus styles '89. il *Ebony* 44:52-4+ O '89

Hey, hairball! You're gone! [dress codes] C. Leslie. il *Newsweek* 114:79 N 27 '89

Robberies push Detroit's school board to propose district-wide dress code. *Jet* 77:29 D 25 '89-Ja 1 '90

Soviet Union

Couture for the comrades. N. Traver. il *Time* 133:128 Ap 10 '89

CLOTHING FACTORIES

Automation

Rags to riches? R. Kazis. il *Technology Review* 92:42-53 Ag/S '89

CLOTHING INDUSTRY

See also
At Last Inc.
Champion Products Inc.
Clothing factories
Columbia Sportswear Company
Crystal Brands Inc.
Designers' Collective
Donna Karan Company
Guess?, Inc.
Halston Enterprises
J. Crew (Firm)
Jordache Enterprises Inc.
Lena Fiore Inc.
Levi Strauss & Co.
Liz Claiborne, Inc.
North Beach Leather (Firm)
Patagonia Inc.
Perry Ellis Sportswear Inc.
Phillips-Van Heusen Corp.
Quiksilver, Inc.
Tailors
Trinder & Boylan Inc.
Tweeds (Firm)
VF Corp.
Warnaco Inc.

Advertising

The attitude sell. G. Howell. il *Vogue* 179:370+ Mr '89

What's it all about, Ralphie? Ralph Lauren and the New Traditionalism. B. Edmondson. il por *Utne Reader* p21-2 Jl/Ag '89

Ethical aspects

A 'blood war' in the jeans trade [Jordache-Guess battle] C. Welles. il *Business Week* p74-5+ N 13 '89

The great jeans war [Guess? vs. Jordache] C. Byron. il *New York* 22:13-14 Jl 24 '89

The IRS follies [IRS embroiled in jeans war between Nakash family of Jordache and Marciano family of Guess?] C. Byron. il *New York* 22:11-12 Ag 7 '89

Export-import trade

See also
Beeba's Creations Inc.

Textile and Apparel Trade Act. il *Congressional Digest* 68:1-32 Ja '89

Finance

Apparel, shoes and textiles. G. Eisenstodt. il *Forbes* 143:86-8 Ja 9 '89

Management

Rags to riches? R. Kazis. il *Technology Review* 92:42-53 Ag/S '89

Marketing

Before the fall [fall collections arriving during the summer] M. Gross. il *New York* 22:30+ Ag 21 '89

Canada

Halting the slump. B. Wickens. il *Maclean's* 102:36+ Ap 10 '89

France

See also
Chanel (Firm)
Chloé (Firm)
Christian Dior (Firm)
Yves Saint Laurent (Firm)

The business of chic [Paris fashion industry] N. Hyde. il *National Geographic* 176:146-57 Jl '89

French fashion goes global. N. Darnton. il *Newsweek* 114:75-6 N 6 '89

Lace at $300 a yard [Paris' haute couture industry] R. Morais. il *Forbes* 144 Special Issue:76-8+ O 23 '89

Selling Montana [store buyers choosing from C. Montana's spring collection] H. Brubach. *The New Yorker* 64:110+ Ja 23 '89

Germany (West)

See also
Escada AG

Great Britain

See also
Harvey Nichols (Firm)

Italy

See also
Benetton SpA

CLOTHING STORES

See also
Alaïa (Firm)
Arthur A. Adler (Firm)
Barney's, New York
Beau Brummel (Firm)
Brooks Brothers
Charvet (Firm)
Comme des Garçons SHIRT (Firm)
Designs, Inc.
Ecru (Firm)
Emporio Armani (Firm)
Gap, Inc.
Garment District (Firm)
Indigo (Firm)
Joseph's (Firm)
Laura Caspari Ltd./SHE, Inc.
Madeleine Gallay (Firm)
Merry-Go-Round Enterprises, Inc.
One Price Clothing Stores, Inc.
Rigby & Peller (Firm)
T. Deane Inc.

Breaking in [elegant boutiques in New York City and Paris] N. Scovell. il *Vogue* 179:550+ Mr '89

Chicago style! [boutiques] il *Essence* 20:46 O '89

A cut above the best [London clothiers] J. McLaughlin. il *Harper's Bazaar* 122:118 S '89

Dressing the part [relationship between film industry and clothing stores on Rodeo Drive] C. Fleming. il *American Film* 14:48-51 S '89

The empire's new clothes [London] S. James. il *Harper's Bazaar* 122:150 S '89

Window shopping [display windows] il *Glamour* 87:220 My '89

Anecdotes, facetiae, satire, etc.

Clothes klutz. B. Ehrenreich. il *Ms.* 17:24-5 Je '89

Fear and clothing [boutiques in New York City] C. Heimel. il *Vogue* 179:538+ Mr '89

Spreedom, now! L. Phillips. il *Ms.* 18:30+ Jl/Ag '89

Architecture

Tailor made [Comme des Garçons SHIRT store, New York City] K. D. Stein. il *Architectural Record* 177:92-3 Ja '89

CLOTHS, FLOOR *See* Floorcloths
CLOTTING OF BLOOD *See* Blood—Coagulation
CLOUDED LEOPARDS *See* Leopards
CLOUDS

See also
Noctilucent clouds

Aerosols, cloud microphysics, and fractional cloudiness. B. A. Albrecht. bibl f il *Science* 245:1227-30 S 15 '89

All about iridescence. T. Schlatter. il *Weatherwise* 42:159-60 Je '89

Climate and the earth's radiation budget [cover story] V. Ramanathan and others. bibl f il *Physics Today* 42:22-7+ My '89

Cloud-radiative forcing and climate: results from the Earth Radiation Budget Experiment. V. Ramanathan and others. bibl f il maps *Science* 243:57-63 Ja 6 '89

Clouds clearing from climate predictions [Earth Radiation Budget Experiment; research by V. Ramanathan] R. Monastersky. *Science News* 135:6 Ja 7 '89

Clouds in the greenhouse [data from Earth Radiation Budget Satellite] A. C. Revkin. map *Discover* 10:24 Je '89

Cloudy concerns [role of clouds in global warming; cover story] R. Monastersky. il *Science News* 136:106-7+ Ag 12 '89

CLOUDS—*cont.*

Count on clouds [bass fishing] J. Doggett. il *Field & Stream* 94:39+ S '89

Direct and remote sensing observations of the effects of ships on clouds. L. F. Radke and others. bibl f il *Science* 246:1146-9 D 1 '89

How clouds heat and cool the earth [research by V. Ramanathan] *USA Today (Periodical)* 117:3 Je '89

How to fix the clouds in greenhouse models. R. A. Kerr. *Science* 243:28-9 Ja 6 '89

Interpretation of cloud-climate feedback as produced by 14 atmospheric general circulation models. R. D. Cess and others. bibl f il *Science* 245:513-16 Ag 4 '89

Pinning down clouds [role in climatic change] J. Horgan. il *Scientific American* 260:22+ My '89

The road warrior [low altitude VFR scud running] P. Garrison. *Flying* 116:84-5 My '89

Warmer clouds could keep earth cooler. R. Monatersky. *Science News* 136:196 S 23 '89

Will it be clear tonight? J. Moeller. il *Astronomy* 17:74-7 D '89

CLOUDS, INTERGALACTIC *See* Matter, Interstellar

CLOUDS, OORT *See* Oort clouds

CLOUGH, CHARLES
about
All fired up about natural gas. J. Friedman. il por *Business Week* p110 D 25 '89-Ja 1 '90

The market is high but cash is a trap [interview] J. Mendes. il por *Fortune* 120:37 O 9 '89

CLOUGH, PATRICIA
The welcome can wear thin. *World Press Review* 36:12 N '89

CLOUTIS, EDWARD A.
Spectral reflectance properties of hydrocarbons: remote-sensing implications. bibl f il *Science* 245:165-8 Jl 14 '89

CLOVIS (CALIF.)
Stores
Detouring to Clovis for antiques. il map *Sunset (Central West edition)* 183:20 S '89

CLOWNFISH
Sexual stunts of clownfish [cover story] D. G. Fautin. il *Natural History* p42-7 S '89

CLOWNS
See also
Irwin, Bill
Clown around town [B. Cozzens] F. Greve. il por *New Choices for the Best Years* 29:11-12 Mr '89

CLOZAPINE
Clozaril approved. *FDA Consumer* 23:2 D '89/Ja '90

Schizophrenia drug gains FDA approval. B. Bower. *Science News* 136:245 O 14 '89

CLUB CORP. OF AMERICA
Driving to become the IBM of golf. W. C. Symonds. il *Business Week* p100-1 Je 19 '89

CLUB MÉDITERRANÉE SA
Club Med: come on down and bring the kids! S. Birnbaum. il *Good Housekeeping* 208:32+ Ja '89

"I am sorry, we have changed" [family image for Club Med] J. Levine. il *Forbes* 144:136-7 S 4 '89

Kicking sand in Club Med's face. S. Toy. il *Business Week* p59+ Ag 14 '89

Scuba duba do. J. O'Reilly. il *New Choices for the Best Years* 29:44-8 F '89

CLUBB, OLIVER EDMUND, 1901-1989
America's China policy [reprint from September 1981 issue] *Current History* 88:35-6+ Ja '89
about
Obituary
The Nation 248:873 Je 26 '89

CLUBS
See also
Art clubs and societies
Astronomical societies
Automobile clubs
Businesswomen's organizations
Club Corp. of America
Country clubs
Health clubs
Investment clubs
Political clubs and associations
Sports clubs
Travel clubs
Venture capital clubs
Warehouse clubs
Yacht clubs
Food service
Club comfort [private clubs] C. Idone. il *The New York Times Magazine* p75-6 Mr 12 '89
New York (State)
See also
Brooklyn (New York, N.Y.)—Clubs
New York (N.Y.)—Clubs
North Woods Club

CLUSTER THEORY (PHYSICS)
Better materials through clusters [work of Richard W. Siegel] I. Amato. *Science News* 135:284 My 6 '89

Microclusters. M. A. Duncan and D. H. Rouvray. bibl il *Scientific American* 261:110-15 D '89

Physics of the photographic latent image [silver halide film] T. Tani. bibl f il *Physics Today* 42:36-41 S '89

CLUSTERS, GALACTIC *See* Galaxies—Clusters

CLYDE, DAVID
about
Didn't you used to be . . . W. Ladson. il por *Sport (New York, N.Y.)* 80:86 My '89

CML GROUP, INC.
CML Group Inc. J. Slovak. il *Fortune* 119:155 Ja 30 '89

CMOS (COLLATERALIZED MORTGAGE OBLIGATIONS)
See Mortgage bonds and notes

CMOS CIRCUITS *See* Metal oxide semiconductors

CMV *See* Cytomegalovirus

CNBC *See* Consumer News & Business Channel

CNES *See* Centre National d'Études Spatiales (France)

CNN *See* Cable News Network

CNTF *See* Ciliary neurotrophic factor

CNW CORP.
Will Japonica bag a railroad—or get derailed? [attack on CNW] G. G. Marcial. il *Business Week* p79 Ap 10 '89

CO-OP & CONDO CONNECTION (DATABASE)
Pulling the plug on a real estate data base. por *Business Week* p41 Jl 24 '89

CO-OPERATIVE COMMONWEALTH FEDERATION
Changing times. B. Bergman. il *Maclean's* 102:26+ D 11 '89

COACH FARM
Goat cheese, anyone? [M. and L. Cahn] P. Berman. il pors *Forbes* 144:220-1 S 18 '89

COACH LEATHERWARE (FIRM)
Goat cheese, anyone? [M. and L. Cahn] P. Berman. il pors *Forbes* 144:220-1 S 18 '89

COACHELLA VALLEY (CALIF.)
Description and travel
Desert song. J. Schwartz. il *Gentlemen's Quarterly* 59:189-91 O '89

COACHES (ACADEMIC) *See* Tutors and tutoring

COACHES (ATHLETICS)
See also
Basketball coaches
Football coaches
Ski coaches
Tennis coaches
Coaches preach: win at any cost [views of Edward J. Shea] il *USA Today (Periodical)* 118:9 D '89

Coaches wanted, unlimited benefits. K. M. Reith. il *Women's Sports & Fitness* 11:64 Jl/Ag '89

Go with a pro. P. Dranov. il *Harper's Bazaar* 122:74+ My '89

Where the boys are [effect of Title IX on women athletic directors and coaches at the college level] M. Goodman. *The Washington Monthly* 21:18-20 Ap '89

With all due respect: some guys don't get it, no matter how much they win. R. Rapoport. il *Sport (New York, N.Y.)* 80:46-50 Mr '89

COAGULATION OF BLOOD *See* Blood—Coagulation

COAKLEY, SHERIDAN
about
Coakley's clan. H. S. MacIsaac. il por *House & Garden* 161:48 Mr '89

COAL
Coal's future. il *The Futurist* 23:54-5 S/O '89

Defining coal's future [address, June 19, 1989] B. R. Brown. *Vital Speeches of the Day* 56:87-8 N 15 '89
Sulfur content
New process rids coal of sulfur. *High Technology Business* 9:38 F '89

COAL-FIRED ELECTRIC POWER PLANTS *See* Electric plants

COAL GASIFICATION
Membranes could remove coal pollutants. *High Technology Business* 9:38 Mr '89

Utah researchers probe coalbed methane. *High Technology Business* 9:36-7 Ap '89

COAL INDUSTRY
See also
Coal mines and mining
Nerco, Inc.
Pittston Company
Environmental aspects
Difficult days ahead [impact of Bush Clean Air proposals] D. Jenish. il *Maclean's* 102:42-3 Je 26 '89

International hearings on mine near Glacier. il *National Parks* 63:12-13 Ja/F '89
Finance
Coal. K. Hannon. il *Forbes* 143:108+ Ja 9 '89

Defining coal's future [address, June 19, 1989] B. R. Brown. *Vital Speeches of the Day* 56:87-8 N 15 '89
Laws and regulations
See Strip mining—Laws and regulations
United States
See Coal industry

COAL LAWS AND REGULATIONS
See also
Strip mining—Laws and regulations

COAL LEASES
Utility to trade coal leases near Bryce [Nevada Power Company] *National Parks* 63:11 My/Je '89

COAL MINERS
See also
Labor unions—Coal miners
Strikes—Coal miners
United Mine Workers of America
Notes from underground. P. F. Gray. il *The Washington Monthly* 21:19-25 D '89
Photographs and photography
In the footsteps of Russell Lee. E. Margolis. il *Society* 26:77-83 Ja/F '89
COAL MINES AND MINING
See also
Coal industry
Coal miners
Strip mining
Environmental aspects
See Coal industry—Environmental aspects
Laws and regulations
See Strip mining—Laws and regulations
Management
Notes from underground. P. F. Gray. il *The Washington Monthly* 21:19-25 D '89
British Columbia
International hearings on mine near Glacier. il *National Parks* 63:12-13 Ja/F '89
Colorado
Photographs and photography
In the footsteps of Russell Lee. E. Margolis. il *Society* 26:77-83 Ja/F '89
COAL SEAM GAS See Coalbed methane
COAL STOVES See Stoves
COALBED METHANE
Coal feat [San Juan Basin Royalty Trust] T. Mack. il *Forbes* 144:198 O 2 '89
Maybe we'll need it someday—maybe [tax credits for coalbed methane development] T. Mack. il *Forbes* 143:42-3 Ja 23 '89
COALE, JOHN P.
about
Courting disaster. J. A. Jenkins. il pors *Gentlemen's Quarterly* 59:214-17+ F '89
COALINGA (CALIF.)
Recreation centers
Aftermath [Coalinga Community Swim Complex] J. Fillip. il *Architectural Record* 177:116-19 N '89
COALITION OF ESSENTIAL SCHOOLS
The politics of school restructuring [cover story] T. Timar. bibl f il *Phi Delta Kappan* 71:264-75 D '89
COALITION TO CEASE OCEAN DUMPING
The lobster man [G. Whidden] J. Howard. il por *Modern Maturity* 32:50 Ag/S '89
COARCTATION OF THE AORTA See Aortic coarctation
COAST CHANGES
The inundation of our coastlines [effects of rising sea level on south Florida] H. R. Wanless. bibl il maps *Sea Frontiers* 35:264-71 S/O '89
Only fools build on shifting sands [beach erosion in Ocean City, Md.] R. L. Di Silvestro. il map *Audubon* 91:106-12+ Mr '89
South Padre's magic shrinking beaches. D. Chaney. il *The Saturday Evening Post* 261:84-7 O '89
Tires, trees, terns, terrapins [planting Christmas trees on Massachusetts beaches to halt erosion] T. Williams. il *Audubon* 91:26-8+ My '89
COAST GUARD (U.S.) See United States. Coast Guard
COAST STARLIGHT (TRAIN) See Railroads—Trains
COASTAL CORPORATION
Coastal warning [rumor of takeover of Columbia Gas by Coastal Corp.] T. Jaffe. *Forbes* 144:140-1 Jl 10 '89
The lasso is tightening around Texas Eastern. M. Ivey. il por *Business Week* p30-1 Ja 30 '89
The man who strikes fear in the heart of the oil patch [O. Wyatt] M. Ivey. il por *Business Week* p120-1+ N 6 '89
Oscar Wyatt. M. Ivey. il por *Business Week* Special Issue:120 Ap 14 '89
COASTAL ECOLOGY See Seashore ecology
COASTAL PROTECTION See Shore protection
COASTS
See also
National seashores
Shore protection
The touch of the sea [cover story; special issue] il *Audubon* 91:10-12+ Mr '89
United States
See Coasts
COATES, CASEY
about
"I nearly lost my marriage". V. J. Radovsky. il pors *Redbook* 173:46+ Je '89
COATES, J. F. (JOHN F.)
The trireme sails again. bibl il *Scientific American* 260:96-103 Ap '89
COATES, JOHN F. See Coates, J. F. (John F.)
COATES, JOSEPH F.
Pressures reshaping retailing in the '90's [address, January 17, 1989] *Vital Speeches of the Day* 55:356-60 Ap 1 '89

COATES, NIGEL, 1949-
about
Body building. N. Shulman. il por *Harper's Bazaar* 122:128 S '89
COATES, W. PAUL
about
Black and in print. J. R. Barras. il por *American Visions* 4:48-9 O '89
COATS, BRUCE A.
In a Japanese garden. il map *National Geographic* 176:638-63 N '89
COATS
See also
Blazers (Jackets)
Fur coats, wraps, etc.
Jackets
Lena Fiore Inc.
Coat tales [work of J. Williams-Cacicedo] M. Porges. il por *American Craft* 49:46-51 O/N '89
Coats: the big chill. il *Teen* 33:22 N '89
A frisky French designer makes a teddy-bear coat for adults [creation of J.-C. de Castelbajac] il por *People Weekly* 31:83 Ja 30 '89
COAXIAL CABLES, TELEPHONE See Telephone cables
COAXIAL CABLES, TELEVISION See Television cables
COBALT CHROME
Asbestos again? [cobalt chrome artificial joints may cause bone cancer] L. Scheer. il *Forbes* 143:162+ Je 12 '89
COBB, ARNETT CLEOPHUS, 1918-1989
about
Obituary
Jet il por 76:18 Ap 10 '89
COBB, CATLIN
about
Reviews:
Performances at Bessie Schönberg Theater. J. Lewis. *Dance Magazine* 63:22 Ja '89
COBB, CHARLES E.
Living with radiation. il maps *National Geographic* 175:402-37 Ap '89
COBB, HUGH
The siege of New England. il map *Weatherwise* 42:262-6 O '89
COBB, KEVIN
Managing your mileage—are you feeling groovy or burning out? il *American Health* 8:79-84 O '89
Unveiling Nelson Vails. il por *American Health* 8:84 My '89
What's cooking, good looking? il *American Health* 8:100-1 Ap '89
COBB, TY, 1886-1961
about
The Cobb gambling scandal. il por *Sports Illustrated* 70:20 Je 12 '89
Three who made history: Cobb, Louis and Howe. J. Lapointe. il pors *Sport (New York, N.Y.)* 80:60 My '89
COBB, VICKI
About new brooms and musical chairs. por *Publishers Weekly* 236:36 D 8 '89
COBB, WILLIAM
The wishes [story] *The New Yorker* 65:50-7 D 11 '89
COBB (CATLIN) AND DANCERS See Catlin Cobb and Dancers
COBBAN, HELENA
(jt. auth) See Smith, Gerard C., and Cobban, Helena
COBBLERS (PIE) See Pie
COBE, PATRICIA
You are what you eat. il *Ladies' Home Journal* 106:164-6+ Mr '89
COBURN, MARCIA FROELKE, 1950-
The prom queen from hell. il pors *Gentlemen's Quarterly* 59:204-7+ Ag '89
COCA
See also
Cocaine
COCA-COLA COMPANY
Coca-Cola USA to award $130,000 in scholarships [Share the Dream Scholarship Sweepstakes] il *Jet* 75:32 Mr 6 '89
The cola superpowers' outrageous new arsenals. S. Ticer. il *Business Week* p162+ Mr 20 '89
Globalization [address, February 9, 1989] R. C. Goizueta. *Vital Speeches of the Day* 55:360-2 Ap 1 '89
"We can't let Pepsi outflesh us!" [Coke-Pepsi war] J. Levine. il *Forbes* 144:270+ N 27 '89
COCA-COLA ENTERPRISES INC.
Bottling is hardly a classic for Coke. W. Konrad. il por *Business Week* p130+ D 11 '89
COCAINE
See also
Crack (Cocaine)
Addiction and IQ [brain cells conditioned to crave cocaine; research by Larry Stein and James Belluzzi] L. Marsa. il *Omni (New York, N.Y.)* 12:24+ O '89
Autopsy on Trans-Colorado captain reveals evidence of cocaine use [crash in January 1988] il *Aviation Week & Space Technology* 131:71+ Jl 3 '89

COCAINE—*cont.*
Brown's Mack a free man, returns to football team. il por *Jet* 77:48 N 27 '89
Buprenorphine suppresses cocaine self-administration by rhesus monkeys [possible use in treatment of cocaine addiction] N. K. Mello and others. bibl f il *Science* 245:859-62 Ag 25 '89
Coca. P. T. White. il map *National Geographic* 175:2-47 Ja '89
Cocaine abuse leaves lingering heart risk [research by Koonlawee Nademanee] K. Fackelman. *Science News* 136:358 D 2 '89
Cocaine babies: the littlest victims [penalties to mothers] il *Newsweek* 114:55 O 2 '89
Cocaine mothers imperil babies' brains [reports by Ira J. Chasnoff and Barry Zuckerman] K. Fackelmann. *Science News* 135:198 Ap 1 '89
Contradictions of cocaine capitalism [cover story] J. Morley. il *The Nation* 249:341-7 O 2 '89
Flipping the main switch in the central reward system? [cocaine and the brain] C. Holden. il *Science* 246:1378-9 D 15 '89
The here-and-now story of cocaine. A. Brown. il *Current Health 2* 16:11-13 D '89
Hollywood's drug scene—how bad is it now? [cover story] G. Dillow. il *TV Guide* 37:4-8 Ag 19-25 '89
The mayor's new drug crisis [Washington's M. Barry] L. Martz. por *Newsweek* 113:25 Ja 9 '89
NTSB asserts captain's cocaine use contributed to crash of Continental Express Metro 3 [Capt. S. Silver; January 1988 crash near Durango, Colo.] C. Fotos. *Aviation Week & Space Technology* 130:59 F 6 '89
On ice for keeps [NHL bans B. Probert after arrest for importing cocaine] B. Newman. il por *Sports Illustrated* 70:26 Mr 13 '89
Past and present cocaine epidemics. C. Holden. *Science* 246:1377 D 15 '89
Racing's cocaine mystery [race horses test positive] il *Sports Illustrated* 70:14 F 27 '89
Safety Board cites captain's failure to monitor approach as key in crash [Trans-Colorado Airlines crash in January 1988] *Aviation Week & Space Technology* 131:103+ Jl 17 '89
Safety Board cites copilot's flying, captain's drug use in Metro 3 crash [Trans-Colorado Airlines crash in January 1988] *Aviation Week & Space Technology* 130:103-4 Je 26 '89
Scandal at the top [revelations about Washington mayor M. Barry] W. Lowther. il por *Maclean's* 102:36 Ja 16 '89
The search for cocaine's methadone [link to dopamine pathways in the brain] D. Hurley. il *Psychology Today* 23:59-60 Jl/Ag '89
A technical fix for cocaine addiction. J. Silberner. il *U.S. News & World Report* 106:61 Ap 17 '89
Washington's mayor with nine lives, Marion Barry, risks another amid rumors of scandal [alleged use] M. Brower. il por *People Weekly* 31:48-9 Ja 16 '89
White lies: cocaine—the dirty little secret in the age of clean. A. L. Ball. il *Mademoiselle* 95:266-9+ Ap '89
Wildfire in the brain [linked to seizures; research by Robert Post] S. Blakeslee. il *American Health* 8:19-20 Ja/F '89
Laws and regulations
See Narcotics laws and regulations
COCAINE TRADE *See* Narcotics trade
COCCIDIOSIS
Scientists nab water-polluting parasite [Cryptosporidium infection in Carroll County, Ga.] K. Fackelmann. *Science News* 135:343 Je 3 '89
COCCOLITHOPHORES
White-water bounty [coccolithophore bloom in Gulf of Maine] C. Mlot. il *BioScience* 39:222-4 Ap '89
COCHRAN, LEONARD
The testing [poem] *The Christian Century* 106:445 Ap 26 '89
COCHRAN, THOMAS B.
Black Sea experiment only a start. il *The Bulletin of the Atomic Scientists* 45:12-16 N '89
COCHRANE, ELIZABETH *See* Bly, Nellie, 1867-1922
COCKBURN, ALEXANDER
Beat the devil. See issues of The Nation
Double exposure [interview with H. Newton] il pors *House & Garden* 161:168-73+ S '89
(jt. auth) See Hecht, Susanna, and Cockburn, Alexander
about
Alexander Cockburn: a voice of moderation. A. Puddington. *National Review* 41:27 N 24 '89
Minority report [discussion of A. Cockburn's Stalinist leanings] C. Hitchens. *The Nation* 249:375 O 9 '89
COCKBURN, BRUCE, 1945-
about
Frontline rocker. N. Jennings. il pors *Maclean's* 102:52-3 F 27 '89
Yo! Canada! D. Ouellette. il por *Mother Jones* 14:12 Ap '89
COCKBURN, PATRICK
Dateline USSR: ethnic tremors. *Foreign Policy* 74:168-84 Spr '89

USSR and its ethnics: the desire for autonomy. *Current (Washington, D.C.)* 315:33-9 S '89
COCKERHAM, JOHN M.
Whistleblowing on U.S. defense contractors is out of control. por *Aviation Week & Space Technology* 130:99+ Ap 10 '89
COCKERHAM (JOHN M.) AND ASSOCIATES, INC. *See* John M. Cockerham and Associates, Inc.
COCKPIT VOICE RECORDERS *See* Flight recorders
COCKPITS, AIRPLANE *See* Airplanes, Business—Cockpits; Airplanes, Jet—Cockpits; Airplanes, Military—Cockpits
COCKPITS, HELICOPTER *See* Helicopters—Cockpits
COCKROACHES
Control
Asian roaches enjoying Florida vacation [study by Richard J. Brenner] R. Weiss. *Science News* 136:405 D 23-30 '89
COCKS, JAY
10 great movies to watch over and over. il *TV Guide* 37:13-17 Ag 5-11 '89
COCKTAIL [film] See Motion picture reviews—Single works
THE COCKTAIL HOUR [drama] See Gurney, A. R. (Albert Ramsdell), 1930-
COCKTAIL SHAKERS
Collectors and collecting
Attitude on the rocks [Campari shaker] P. Patton. il *Esquire* 112:45 D '89
COCKTAILS
A good tall drink [highballs] J. F. Mariani. il *Motor Boating & Sailing* 163:46-7 Mr '89
I'll take Manhattan. J. F. Mariani. il *Motor Boating & Sailing* 163:52+ Ja '89
Macho drinks. J. F. Mariani. il *Motor Boating & Sailing* 163:48 My '89
Popping your cork. S. Dooley. il *Harper's Bazaar* 122:36+ Ja '89
COCOA
See also
Cooking—Chocolate
COCOA BEACH (FLA.)
Architecture
Media magnate Allen Neuharth's dream house has him up a tree [tree house] il por *People Weekly* 31:75 Ja 30 '89
COCOM *See* Coordinating Committee on Multilateral Export Controls
COCONUT
See also
Cooking—Coconut
On Malay Peninsula picking coconuts is monkey business [trained macaques] R. S. Peffer. bibl (p147) il *Smithsonian* 19:110-12+ Ja '89
COCONUT GROVE (MIAMI, FLA.)
Historic houses, sites, etc.
Coconut Grove Tudor: the Miami residence of Maurice and Mercedes Ferré [remodeled by Bernard Zyscovich] B. Dunlop. il *Architectural Digest* 46:108-13+ F '89
COCONUT OIL
Cookies the heart can love [foodmakers replace tropical oils with less saturated fats] A. Toufexis. il *Time* 133:71 Ja 23 '89
Have a heart [P. Sokolof's campaign against products using coconut and palm oils] S. J. Madden. il por *Fortune* 119:117+ Ja 16 '89
A man with a mission—and millions to back it up—takes on brand name cholesterol [P. Sokolof's campaign against products using coconut and palm oils] il por *People Weekly* 31:112 F 6 '89
Putting tropical oils in their place [emphasis should be on reducing total dietary fat] G. L. Blackburn. il *Prevention (Emmaus, Pa.)* 41:30+ Ag '89
The use of palm and coconut oils in America's food has triggered a debate that is as much about politics as it is about health. L. M. Kase. *Vogue* 179:150+ Je '89
COCOON: THE RETURN [film] See Motion picture reviews—Single works
COCOS ISLAND (COSTA RICA)
Description and travel
Cocos Island. T. Koppel. il *Travel Holiday* 172:88-90+ N '89
COCTEAU, JEAN, 1889-1963
about
Dancescape. L. Garafola. il *Dance Magazine* 63:56 Ap '89
In pursuit of Cocteau. R. Winegarten. *The American Scholar* 58:436-43 Summ '89
Severin Wunderman's Jean Cocteau obsession is so strong he sometimes feels he's possessed by the artist's spirit. R. Urquhart. il por *Vogue* 179:182-4 Je '89
COCU *See* Consultation on Church Union
COD
See also
Cooking—Fish
COD FISHERIES (COMMERCIAL) *See* Fisheries
CODEPENDENCE (PSYCHOLOGY)
Codependency. L. J. Moore. il *U.S. News & World Report* 107:73 S 11 '89
Do codependency theories explain women's unhappiness—or exploit their insecurities? C. Tavris. *Vogue* 179:220+ D '89

CODEPENDENCE (PSYCHOLOGY)—cont.
Melody Beattie helps anguished readers kick the dependency habit. J. D. Reed. il pors *People Weekly* 32:89-91 Ag 7 '89

CODEPENDENT BEHAVIOR *See* Codependence (Psychology)

CODES
See also
Cryptography

CODES, SECRET *See* Cryptography

CODETERMINATION IN INDUSTRY *See* Participative management

CODEVILLA, ANGELO M., 1943-
The Soviet threat [discussion of November 1988 article, Is there still a Soviet threat?] *Commentary* 87:2+ Mr '89

CODING, BAR *See* Bar coding

CODING THEORY
See also
Data compression (Computer science)

CODLING MOTHS
Control
Apples, worms, and synthetic mating hormones. il *Sunset (Central West edition)* 182:200-1 Mr '89

CODY, IRON EYES, 1904-
"But you promised". il *Reader's Digest* 134:130-1 Je '89

COE, JIM
about
An expert warns of the dangers of driftnets, lethal curtains that reap fish—and controversy—by the ton [interview] J. H. Blackman. il pors *People Weekly* 31:145-6+ My 15 '89

COE, SUE, 1951-
Slaughterhouse '89. il *The Progressive* 53:33-9 Mr '89
about
Sue Coe: Galerie St. Etienne. E. Heartney. il *Art News* 88:158 D '89

COECHEA, IGNACIO ELLACURIA BEAS *See* Ellacuria Beas Coechea, Ignacio, d. 1989

COED SPORTS
The boys on the varsity get a real kick out of homecoming queen Tamara Browder [Woodward High School in Toledo, Ohio] il por *People Weekly* 32:113 N 13 '89
D.C. girls first to play on boys' football team [S. Wells and L. Ellis] D. M. Cheers. il pors *Jet* 77:28-30 N 13 '89

COEDUCATION
Boys and girls at Deerfield. K. Ames. il *Newsweek* 114:77 O 16 '89

COELENTERATES
See also
Jellyfish
Sponges
Needles and pins. D. F. Donavel. il *Sea Frontiers* 35:18-25 Ja/F '89

COELHO, DUARTE PINTO *See* Pinto Coelho, Duarte

COELHO, TONY, 1942-
about
Coelho under fire. *Newsweek* 112:41 My 22 '89
Fallen angel. M. B. Carlson. il *The New Republic* 200:18-21 Je 12 '89
How many will fall? M. B. Carlson. il pors *Time* 133:34-5 Je 5 '89
Lessons in quitting. T. Eastland. por *Newsweek* 113:8 Je 12 '89
The rise and fall of Tony Coelho. H. Fineman. *Newsweek* 113:20 Je 5 '89
Wright, Coelho and the S&L fiasco. M. Barone. il pors *U.S. News & World Report* 106:21-2 Je 12 '89

COELLO, DENNIS
Vicious cycles? il *Sierra* 74:50-4 My/Je '89

COENZYMES
See also
Methoxatin

COETZEE, DIRK
about
The secrets of South Africa's hit squad. *Newsweek* 114:56 N 27 '89

COEUR D'ALENE (IDAHO)
Protests, demonstrations, etc.
Nazi retreat [planned protest march against R. Butler's Aryan Nation] B. Reed. *The New Republic* 200:10-11 Ap 3 '89

COEVOLUTION *See* Evolution

COFFEE, GERALD L.
Beyond survival: a P.O.W.'s story [condensation] il *Reader's Digest* 135:137-44+ D '89

COFFEE
See also
Caffeine
Cooking—Coffee
Coffee alert: decaf brews raise cholesterol. *Time* 134:56 N 27 '89
Decaf coffee: the cholesterol connection. *Newsweek* 114:78 N 27 '89
What's brewin'? [effects on health and athletic performance] L. Applegate. il *Runner's World* 24:22-4 N '89
Prices
See also
International Coffee Agreement

Another cartel bites the dust. P. Fuhrman. il *Forbes* 144:41-2 O 30 '89
Taste testing
See Coffee tasting

COFFEE CAKE
The coffee klatch. il *Redbook* 173:175-80 S '89

COFFEE FILTERS
See also
Melitta-Werke Bentz & Sohn

COFFEE INDUSTRY
See also
Maxwell House Coffee Company
A new coffee roasting boom in San Francisco [Bay Area] il *Sunset (Central West edition)* 182:76+ Mr '89
Advertising
Drip, drip, drip . . . drip [Maxwell House] J. Levine. il *Forbes* 143:196+ Ap 17 '89
Export-import trade
Another cartel bites the dust. P. Fuhrman. il *Forbes* 144:41-2 O 30 '89
One way to help Colombia [reestablish world coffee agreement] *World Press Review* 36:28 N '89
Marketing
Helmut Radtke: no grind at selling coffee [Melitta] il por *Business Week* p68 S 18 '89
Colombia
Choice tasters. H. Correa G. il *World Press Review* 36:52 Je '89
One way to help Colombia [reestablish world coffee agreement] *World Press Review* 36:28 N '89

COFFEE TABLES *See* Tables

COFFEE TASTING
Choice tasters [Colombia] H. Correa G. il *World Press Review* 36:52 Je '89

COFFEY, KATHY
'In the tongues of men': homilies for women [cover story] il *America* 161:392-4 D 2 '89

COFFIN, WILLIAM SLOANE
about
America's last peacenik [interview] F. Ungeheuer. il por *Time* 133:76-7 Je 5 '89

COFFMAN, JOE M.
(jt. auth) See Palmer, Beverly B., and Coffman, Joe M.

COFFMAN, ROBERT L., AND OTHERS
Antibody to interleukin-5 inhibits helminth-induced eosinophilia in mice. bibl f il *Science* 245:308-10 Jl 21 '89

COFFMAN, ROSIE
about
U.S. rep. convicted for having sex with a minor. il pors *Jet* 76:8 Je 12 '89
U.S. Rep. Lukens gets 30-day jail term, fine in sex with minor case. il pors *Jet* 76:33 Jl 24 '89

COGAN, EDDY
about
King Eddy of the dealmakers. P. C. Newman. il *Maclean's* 102:56 N 13 '89
The leader of the pack. A. Walmsley. il por *Maclean's* 102:48 N 13 '89

COGENERATION *See* Energy cogeneration

COGGER, MICHEL
about
Hi-tech disagreements. P. Kaihla. il por *Maclean's* 102:16-17 Je 26 '89
Questions of ethics. B. Wallace. il por *Maclean's* 102:18+ N 13 '89

COGNAC *See* Brandy

COGNITION
See also
Knowledge, Theory of
Perception
Mind meets brain [cognitive neuroscience] J. Rubin. il *Technology Review* 92:13-14 Ja '89

COGNITIVE SCIENCE *See* Cognition

COGNITIVE THERAPY
Kind ears help some depressed patients [comparison of interpersonal psychotherapy with cognitive behavior therapy; work of Irene Elkin] *Science News* 136:365 D 2 '89
The power of self-talk. H. B. Braiker. il *Psychology Today* 23:23-7 D '89
The thoughts that wound. D. Gelman. il *Newsweek* 113:46-8 Ja 9 '89
Try not to think of a white bear [obsessive thoughts; excerpt from White bears and other unwanted thoughts] D. M. Wegner. il *Psychology Today* 23:64-6 Je '89
"Woulda/coulda/shoulda": how to avoid no-win thinking [excerpt] A. M. Freeman. il *Ladies' Home Journal* 106:124+ O '89

COHABITATION *See* Unmarried couples

COHEN, ARTHUR G.
about
How Arthur Cohen came back. J. D. Greenberg. il por *Forbes* 144:252-3 O 16 '89

COHEN, BARBARA E., 1949-, AND TAYLOR, LOUISE, 1949-
Woman's best friend [excerpts from Dogs and their women] il *Good Housekeeping* 208:106 Mr '89

COHEN, BENJAMIN J.
A global Chapter 11. *Foreign Policy* 75:109-27 Summ '89

COHEN, BENNETT
about
Purveying yuppie porn. J. Queenan. il pors *Forbes* 144:60+ N 13 '89

COHEN, CLAUDIA
about
Star reporter. J. Conant. il pors *Harper's Bazaar* 122:146-7+ N '89

COHEN, DANIEL
Tribal enterprise. il *The Atlantic* 264:32-4+ O '89

COHEN, E. RICHARD, AND TAYLOR, BARRY N.
The fundamental physical constants. il *Physics Today* 42 pt2:BG8-BG8D Ag '89

COHEN, ERWIN V.
Building a sidewalk art booth. il *American Artist* 53:68-72+ My '89
Matting for greater impact (I). il *American Artist* 53:102-4 S '89

COHEN, HERMAN J.
Independence process in Namibia [statement, July 20, 1989] *Department of State Bulletin* 89:43-4 N '89

COHEN, IRWIN
Beers with . . . Angel Cordero [interview] il por *Sport (New York, N.Y.)* 80:41-2 Je '89

COHEN, ISRAEL
about
Why Giant Foods is a gargantuan success. D. Foust. il por *Business Week* p80 D 4 '89

COHEN, JEFFREY
Stop bashing men! il *TV Guide* 37:27-9 Ag 12-18 '89

COHEN, JEFFREY TODD
Donald Byrd's solo on Each time I think of you—a trumpet transcription. il *Down Beat* 56:54 Mr '89

COHEN, JOEL E.
(jt. auth) See Briand, Frédéric, and Cohen, Joel E.

COHEN, MARCIA
A mother's revenge. il por *Ladies' Home Journal* 106:140-1+ S '89

COHEN, MARCIA, 1945-
When a First Lady's husband leaves her for a younger woman. il pors *Good Housekeeping* 208:82+ My '89

COHEN, MARK
The hare and the beagle. il *Gentlemen's Quarterly* 59:49+ D '89

COHEN, MARVIN L.
(jt. auth) See Liu, Amy Y., and Cohen, Marvin L.

COHEN, MICHAEL
Restructuring the system. *Society* 26:40-8 My/Je '89

COHEN, MITCHELL, 1952-
A profusion of land mines. il *Commonweal* 116:275-8 My 5 '89

COHEN, PAUL
It ain't pretty . . . il por *World Tennis* 37:50-2 D '89
Strokes of genius. il pors *World Tennis* 36:62-4 Ap '89
The water way. il pors *World Tennis* 37:58-9 Ag '89

COHEN, PETER
about
For Peter Cohen, it's even lonelier at the top. J. Friedman. il por *Business Week* p90-1 Ap 3 '89
Musical chairs may not do the trick at Shearson. J. Friedman. il por *Business Week* p59-60 D 11 '89
Peter Cohen. J. Friedman. il por *Business Week* Special Issue:112 Ap 14 '89
The Peter principle. J. Queenan and T. Pouschine. il por *Forbes* 144:40-3 Jl 10 '89
The slide of Shearson Lehman. L. Reibstein and C. Friday. il por *Newsweek* 114:70 D 11 '89

COHEN, PHILLIP, 1919-
about
Barbies on the cheap. J. Harris. il por *Forbes* 144:116+ D 25 '89

COHEN, RANDY
Dry. *The New Yorker* 65:34-5 Ap 3 '89
The Emigrants Club. il *The Atlantic* 264:44+ O '89
Write in plain sight. *The Nation* 248:528-9 Ap 17 '89

COHEN, RHEA L.
These friends [poem] *The New Yorker* 65:66 Jl 31 '89

COHEN, RICHARD, 1952-
Yes, you can work at home. il *Parents* 64:64+ Jl '89

COHEN, SHERRY SUIB
Beyond macho: the power of womanly management [excerpt from Tender power] il pors *Working Woman* 14:77-83 F '89
How to be a leader. il *Reader's Digest* 135:98-100 Ag '89

COHEN, STANLEY, 1922-
(jt. auth) See McKanna, James A., and Cohen, Stanley, 1922-

COHEN, STEPHEN F.
The cold war: a presidential agenda. *Current (Washington, D.C.)* 311:32-8 Mr/Ap '89
about
West meets East. il pors *Esquire* 111:62-5 Ja '89

COHEN, STEPHEN F., AND VANDEN HEUVEL, KATRINA
De-Stalinizing the Soviet past [interview with Y. Afanasyev] *Harper's* 279:32+ O '89

COHEN, STEVE
Cattle driving for fun. il map *Travel Holiday* 171:68-71 F '89
Light and shadow [cover story] il map *Travel Holiday* 171:28-34 Je '89

COHEN, STEVEN R.
about
As long as the price is right. L. Gubernick. il por *Forbes* 143:82 My 29 '89

COHEN, VICTOR D.
Exon-Florio an imperfect tool for protecting U.S. technology. por *Aviation Week & Space Technology* 131:68-9 N 6 '89

COHL, CLAUDIA
Editor's note. See issues of Home Office Computing beginning September 1988

COHL, MICHAEL
about
It's only rock 'n' roll, but he likes it. L. Gubernick. il por *Forbes* 143:114+ My 29 '89
The music man. T. Powis. il por *Maclean's* 102:53+ S 11 '89

COHLER, LARRY
Republican racist. *The New Republic* 201:11-14 S 18-25 '89

COHN, AMY
Children's books/animals. il *The New York Times Book Review* 94:38-9 Ja 29 '89

COHN, JEFFREY P.
Beyond the lab rat. il *BioScience* 39:518-22 S '89
Gauging the biological impacts of the greenhouse effect. il *BioScience* 39:142-6 Mr '89
Iguana conservation and economic development [cover story] il *BioScience* 39:359-63 Je '89
Leprosy: out of the Dark Ages. il *FDA Consumer* 23:24-7 S '89
Sealing out decay. il *FDA Consumer* 23:18-21 N '89

COHN, JORDAN E.
The immune system [cover story] bibl il *Current Health 2* 15:4-9 Ap '89
Narcotics: a primer. il *Current Health 2* 15:11-13 Mr '89
The spinal cord: the brain/body connection [cover story] bibl f il *Current Health 2* 15:4-9 My '89

COHN, SY
about
Sy Cohn steers phobic drivers around mental roadblocks. il por *People Weekly* 32:72 N 6 '89

COHOUSING See Housing, Cooperative

COIFFURE See Hairstyling

COIN BANKS See Banks, Coin

COIN COLLECTING See Numismatics

COIN OPERATED MACHINES
See also
Jukeboxes

COIN OPERATED TELEPHONES See Pay telephones

COINAGE See Coins

COINCOIN, MARIA THERESA
about
Coincoin: plantation owner before the nation was born. P. S. Prather. il *American Visions* 4:46-7 F '89

COINS
See also
Tokens
United States. Mint
America's Memorial Day coin! [half-dollar commemorating 75th anniversary of the Battle of Gettysburg] E. Rochette. il *Antiques & Collecting Hobbies* 94:68-9 My '89
The buck starts here, and may stop here, at the nation's money mills. D. Stewart. bibl (p163) il *Smithsonian* 20:36-45 My '89
The Christopher Columbus dollar [proposed] W. F. Buckley. *National Review* 41:55 D 31 '89
Coming up: new heads and tails. S. Dembling. il *The Saturday Evening Post* 261:32+ O '89
The future of pennies: an exchange. J. Rauch; C. Murphy. il *The Atlantic* 264:20+ D '89
A 'loonie' revolt [opposition to replacing Canadian dollar bill with loonie coin] N. Underwood. il *Maclean's* 102:44-5 Je 5 '89
When people cared that Miss Liberty was Irish! [model for Indian-head $10 gold piece] E. Rochette. il *Antiques & Collecting Hobbies* 94:55+ Mr '89
Who says Iowans are unloved? [centennial commemorative half dollar] E. Rochette. il *Antiques & Collecting Hobbies* 93:50+ F '89

Collectors and collecting
See Numismatics

COINS AS AN INVESTMENT
Can you make a mint by investing in old coins? T. Segal. il *Business Week* p140-1 Je 5 '89
Heads you lose, tails you lose [coin investment scams] M. C. Paulson. il *Changing Times* 43:71-6 F '89
Investing in rare coins. il *Consumers' Research Magazine* 72:19-21 My '89
'Wall Street money' flips over the coin market. T. Segal. il *Business Week* p146 D 25 '89-Ja 1 '90

COIT, DAWN G.
Star trek: the continuing saga of a sixties sensation. il *USA Today (Periodical)* 117:88-90 Ja '89

COKE OVENS
See also
Dunlap Coke Ovens Park (Tenn.)
COKELY, STEVE
about
Blacks and Jews: the uncivil war [with editorial comment by Lee Eisenberg] T. Branch. il *Esquire* 111:25, 89-90+ My '89
COLAS *See* Cost of living adjustments
COLBERT, JUDY
Spas that fit your fitness program. il *Women's Sports & Fitness* 11:54-6+ My '89
COLBURN, CAROL
about
Nursing gets a shot in the arm. D. E. Haupt. il pors *Life* 12:42-5+ O '89
COLBURN, DON
Elegy [poem] *Wilderness* 53:55 Wint '89
COLBURN, FORREST D.
Turning to the voters in Nicaragua [cover story] il pors *The New Leader* 72:5-7 N 13 '89
COLBURN, NANCY H.
(jt. auth) *See* Bernstein, Lori R., and Colburn, Nancy H.
COLD
See also
Low temperatures
Physiological effects
See also
Anti-freeze proteins
Fish, Effect of temperature on
Hibernation
Hypothermia
Insects, Effect of temperature on
Plants, Effect of temperature on
Raynaud's disease
Chill-chasing tips for winter workouts [walking] M. Spilner. il *Prevention (Emmaus, Pa.)* 41:87-9 Ja '89
Cold comfort. C. C. Johnson. il *Parents* 64:240+ D '89
The family guide to winter health [special section] B. Weinhouse. il *Ladies' Home Journal* 106:85-6+ Ja '89
I love winter running [cover story] H. Higdon. il *Runner's World* 24:52-7 D '89
Shiver no more. J. Mullich. il *Prevention (Emmaus, Pa.)* 41:54-5+ F '89
Six ways to avoid cold feet. R. Glenn. il *Field & Stream* 94:98 N '89
Snow season survivors. K. Fadiman. il *Sierra* 74:158-9 Ja/F '89
Surviving and thriving—plants and animals in winter. P. S. Busch. il *The Conservationist* 43:26-33 Ja/F '89
Winterize your workout. J. Rogoznica. il *Working Woman* 14:116-18 F '89
COLD (DISEASE)
See also
Rhinoviruses
Cold and flu update. J. Alper. *McCall's* 116:81-2+ Ja '89
A doctor's guide to staying well this winter; ed. by Maxine Abrams. A. Conill. il por *Good Housekeeping* 209:100+ N '89
Help! The stuffy nose, watery eyes, aches and pain, chills and fever, sore throat, colds and flu book; ed. by Seth Rolbein. L. Weinstein. il *Good Housekeeping* 208:56+ Ja '89
How colds affect your performance [improved concentration; research by Tami McGraw and others] J. Davidson. *Psychology Today* 23:20 D '89
COLD (DISEASE) REMEDIES
Blowing hot and cold over Viralizers. il *Newsweek* 113:62 Ja 16 '89
The chicken-soup solution. M. Castleman. il *New Choices for the Best Years* 29:46-7+ N '89
Cold remedies: which ones work best? [cover story] il *Consumer Reports* 54:8-11 Ja '89
A cold remedy not to be sneezed at [identification of ICAM-1, rhinovirus receptor site] il *U.S. News & World Report* 106:14 Mr 20 '89
The cold war heats up [identification of rhinovirus receptor site] R. Trubo. il *American Health* 8:12 N '89
Coming closer to a common-cold cure [rhinovirus receptor molecule ICAM-1] il *Newsweek* 113:60 Mr 20 '89
Hot air for sale [Viralizer] il *Consumer Reports* 54:12 Ja '89
Rhinovirus receptor found; colds carry on [identification of ICAM-1] R. Weiss. *Science News* 135:165 Mr 18 '89
Snuffed sniffles [discovery of ICAM-1 receptor site for rhinoviruses] *Time* 133:61 Mr 20 '89
Taming the wily rhinovirus [work of Michael Rossmann and Richard Colonno] P. Radetsky. il *Discover* 10:38-43 Ap '89
Think zinc, cure a cold. S. Levin. il *Mademoiselle* 95:64-6 Ja '89
COLD CAMERAS *See* Cameras
COLD DARK MATTER (ASTRONOMY) *See* Dark matter (Astronomy)
COLD FEET [film] *See* Motion picture reviews—Single works
COLD FRAMES
Mother's deluxe, four-season cold frame. F. Sides. il *The Mother Earth News* 120:74-5 N/D '89

COLD FUSION
Analysis of the published calorimetric evidence for electrochemical fusion of deuterium in palladium. G. M. Miskelly and others. bibl f il *Science* 246:793-6 N 10 '89
Big chill for cold fusion as energy source. I. Amato. *Science News* 135:341 Je 3 '89
Chilling out [views of Energy Research Advisory Board panel] T. Beardsley. *Scientific American* 261:20 S '89
Cold fusion: bait and switch? R. Pool. *Science* 244:774 My 19 '89
Cold fusion confusion. R. P. Crease and N. P. Samios. il pors *The New York Times Magazine* p34-6+ S 24 '89
Cold-fusion debunked? T. H. Cole. il *Popular Mechanics* 166:29 Jl '89
Cold fusion: end of Act I. R. Pool. il *Science* 244:1039-40 Je 2 '89
Cold fusion gets a bruisin' from DOE [preliminary report] *Science News* 136:78 Jl 29 '89
Cold fusion getting hotter. *Science News* 135:229 Ap 15 '89
Cold fusion keeps its head just above water. I. Amato. *Science News* 136:278 O 28 '89
'Cold fusion': more questions. S. Begley. *Newsweek* 113:6 Ap 24 '89
Cold fusion: not dead yet. il *World Press Review* 36:55 Jl '89
A cold-fusion pioneer who kept his cool [work of S. E. Jones] W. C. Symonds. il por *Business Week* Special Issue:92 Je 16 '89
Cold fusion: searching for hidden helium. I. Amato. *Science News* 135:311 My 20 '89
Cold fusion: smoke, little light. R. Pool. *Science* 246:879 N 17 '89
Cold fusion still in state of confusion. R. Pool. *Science* 245:256 Jl 21 '89
Cold fusion—or something. *Science News* 136:406 D 23-30 '89
Cold water from Caltech. M. M. Waldrop. *Science* 244:523 My 5 '89
Confirmations heat up cold fusion prospects [work of Stanley Pons and Martin Fleischmann] R. Pool. *Science* 244:143-4 Ap 14 '89
The confusion profusion. D. E. Koshland, Jr. *Science* 244:753 My 19 '89
Dif-fusion: beware the ideas of March. I. Amato. *Science News* 135:276 My 6 '89
Doubts grow as many attempts at cold fusion fail. B. G. Levi. bibl f il *Physics Today* 42:17-19 Je '89
Electrochemists fail to heat up cold fusion. R. Pool and T. A. Heppenheimer. il *Science* 244:647 My 12 '89
Energy from seawater? [work of Stanley Pons and Martin Fleischmann] *National Review* 41:11-12 My 19 '89
Ferment in a jar [work of Stanley Pons and Martin Fleischmann] A. Steacy. il *Maclean's* 102:54 Ap 24 '89
Following the bouncing fusion ball. *Science News* 136:31 Jl 8 '89
Frustration over cold fusion [MIT research] il *Technology Review* 92:79-80 Jl '89
Furor over fusion [work of Stanley Pons and Martin Fleischmann] A. Fisher. il *Popular Science* 234:9-10 Je '89
Fusion, afussin' and afightin' [discovery of Stanley Pons found to be product of experimental error] *U.S. News & World Report* 106:13 My 15 '89
Fusion breakthrough? [work of Stanley Pons and Martin Fleischmann] T. Beardsley. *Scientific American* 260:28 My '89
Fusion breakthrough? [work of Stanley Pons and Martin Fleischmann] R. Pool. *Science* 243:1661-2 Mr 31 '89
Fusion claim electrifies scientists [work of Stanley Pons and Martin Fleischmann] I. Amato. *Science News* 135:196 Ap 1 '89
Fusion claims multiply, strengthen. I. Amato. *Science News* 135:212 Ap 8 '89
Fusion fever cools down. S. Begley. *Newsweek* 113:65 My 15 '89
Fusion fever is on the rise. M. D. Lemonick. il *Time* 133:57 Ap 24 '89
Fusion fizzle? A. Fisher. il *Popular Science* 235:8-9+ Ag '89
A fusion flier [Lithium Corp. of America] M. Gianturco. il por *Forbes* 143:161 My 15 '89
Fusion followup: confusion abounds [work of S. Pons and M. Fleischmann] R. Pool. il por *Science* 244:27-9 Ap 7 '89
Fusion fury: experiments, theories grow. I. Amato. *Science News* 135:244 Ap 22 '89
Fusion illusion? [attempts to disprove work of S. Pons and M. Fleischmann; cover story] M. D. Lemonick. il pors *Time* 133:72-6+ My 8 '89
Fusion in a bottle: can it be that easy? [work of Stanley Pons and Martin Fleischmann] O. Port. il *Business Week* p86-7 Ap 10 '89
Fusion in a bottle: miracle or mistake? [cover story] J. Carey and W. D. Marbach. il pors *Business Week* p100-3+ My 8 '89

COLD FUSION—*cont.*

Fusion in a flask: expert DOE panel throws cold water on Utah 'discovery'. I. Goodwin. il *Physics Today* 42:43-5 D '89

Fusion's future: it ain't dead yet. G. Bylinsky. il *Fortune* 119:125-8 Je 5 '89

The great palladium rush [mining asteroids for metal used in cold fusion] H. K. Henson. il *Ad Astra* 1:34-5 N '89

Has the genie escaped from the fusion bottle? J. Carey. *Business Week* p32-3 My 15 '89

How cold fusion happened—twice! [work of S. Pons and M. Fleischmann] R. Pool. il pors *Science* 244:420-3 Ap 28 '89

Hype-energy physics [press reports of University of Utah fusion breakthrough] R. Bazell. *The New Republic* 200:7-8 Ap 24 '89

If there's a tulip craze, sell trowels [Isotec's sales of heavy water in wake of cold fusion breakthrough] R. Bailey. il *Forbes* 143:132 My 15 '89

In hot pursuit of cold fusion. S. Budiansky. il *U.S. News & World Report* 106:66-7 Ap 24 '89

In hot water over cold fusion [P. Hagelstein] R. Pool. *Science* 246:1384 D 15 '89

More on cold fusion. D. Lancaster. *Radio-Electronics* 60:64 N '89

Navy will explore potential of fusion at room temperature [work of Stanley Pons and Martin Fleischmann] *Aviation Week & Space Technology* 130:21 Ap 17 '89

Perplexing times for fusion [attempts to verify cold fusion] S. Begley and M. Rogers. il *Newsweek* 113:66 My 1 '89

Playing with fire [work of Martin Fleischmann and Stanley Pons] T. Beardsley. *Scientific American* 260:22+ Je '89

Putting the heat on cold fusion [scientists dismiss research by Stanley Pons and Martin Fleischmann] D. Thompson. il *Time* 133:63 My 15 '89

The race for fusion [cover story; special section] il *Newsweek* 113:48-54+ My 8 '89

Science by press conference. F. Jerome. il *Technology Review* 92:72-3 Jl '89

Skeptical reactions [work of Stanley Pons and Martin Fleischmann] A. Steacy. il *Maclean's* 102:49 My 22 '89

Skepticism grows over cold fusion [claims of Stanley Pons and Martin Fleischmann] R. Pool. il *Science* 244:284-5 Ap 21 '89

Stanley Pons lays claim to table top fusion—but don't sell your oil stocks just yet [research with M. Fleischmann] P. Chin. il pors *People Weekly* 31:59-60+ My 8 '89

A sun in a test tube? [work of Martin Fleischmann and Stanley Pons] S. Begley. il *Newsweek* 113:58-9 Ap 17 '89

Table-top fusion looks less like a parlor trick [verifying work of Stanley Pons and Martin Fleischmann] O. Port. il *Business Week* p132+ Ap 24 '89

Teller, Chu "boost" cold fusion. R. Pool. *Science* 246:449 O 27 '89

Try cold fusion for yourself! D. Lancaster. il *Radio-Electronics* 60:64-9+ Ag '89

Trying to tame H-bomb power [research by Stanley Pons and Martin Fleischmann] P. Elmer-DeWitt. il *Time* 133:72 Ap 17 '89

The ultimate power trip [work of Martin Fleischmann and Stanley Pons] *U.S. News & World Report* 106:14-15 Ap 3 '89

The uproar over bottled fusion [work of Stanley Pons and Martin Fleischmann] G. Bylinsky. il *Fortune* 119:8 My 8 '89

Utah looks to Congress for cold fusion cash. M. Crawford. il *Science* 244:522-3 My 5 '89

Utah pours megabucks into cold fusion. *Science News* 136:126 Ag 19 '89

Will new evidence support cold fusion? R. Pool. *Science* 246:206 O 13 '89

COLD SASSY TREE [television program] *See* Television program reviews—Single works

COLD STORAGE

Your four-season harvest garden. N. Bubel. il *Country Journal* 16:44-51 N/D '89

COLD WAR (U.S. AND SOVIET UNION) *See* United States—Foreign relations—Soviet Union

COLD WEATHER

Baby, how cold can it get outside? [Alaska] il *U.S. News & World Report* 106:12-13 F 13 '89

A cold blast of winter [western Canada] P. Kaihla. il *Maclean's* 102:14 F 13 '89

Even the Eskimos froze [Alaskan cold wave] J. Langone. il *Time* 133:65 F 13 '89

Weather report [cold front in Montana] *The New Yorker* 65:28-9 F 20 '89

COLD WEATHER AND CROPS *See* Plants, Effect of temperature on

COLD WEATHER CLOTHING *See* Clothing, Cold weather

COLD WEATHER PHOTOGRAPHY *See* Photography—Cold weather conditions

COLDFRAMES *See* Cold frames

COLDS *See* Cold (Disease)

COLE, BARBARA

about

John Cole's Bookshop. W. Brisick. il por *Publishers Weekly* 236:95+ S 15 '89

COLE, CHARLES J., AND OTHERS

A lizard foretold. map *Natural History* p12+ My '89

COLE, DAVID

Non-alien speech. *The Nation* 248:220-1 F 20 '89

COLE, DIANE

Drifting away. il *Ms.* 18:52+ S '89

The entrepreneurial self. il *Psychology Today* 23:60-3 Je '89

Getting your name on everyone's lips. il *Working Woman* 14:68-70 Ag '89

My father's autobiography. il *Psychology Today* 22:56-7 D '88

Stamping out performance stoppers. il *Working Woman* 14:90-2 Mr '89

COLE, EDDIE

about

Natalie Cole's cousin, Eddie, produces song on hit album. il pors *Jet* 76:65 S 25 '89

COLE, GARY

about

You never know when he's going to explode. B. Davidson. por *TV Guide* 37:16-17 Ja 28-F 3 '89

COLE, HENRI

The annulment [poem] *The Atlantic* 264:78 D '89

Boy's life [poem] *The New Yorker* 65:38 Jl 17 '89

COLE, HUNTER, AND SRINIVASAN, SEETHA

Eudora Welty, inquiring photographer [interview] il *The New York Times Book Review* 94:1+ O 22 '89

COLE, JAMES

The scholar in the hospital [poem] *Commonweal* 116:146 Mr 10 '89

COLE, JOANNA

Monster manners [story] il *Parents* 64:147-8+ Je '89

Who put the pepper in the pot? [story] il *Parents* 64:147-8+ O '89

COLE, JOHN P., AND DEBRES, KAREN

A new Channel crossing: light at the end of the tunnel? il maps *Focus (New York, N.Y.: 1950)* 38:1-9+ Wint '88

COLE, JOHNNETTA B.

about

The 1989 Essence Awards [with editorial comment by Susan L. Taylor] il pors *Essence* 20:57-60+, 69 O '89

A conversation with Spelman's 'sister president'. K. D. Thompson. il por *Black Enterprise* 19:28 F '89

The inspiring leader of scholars (and dollars). A. Edwards. il pors *Working Woman* 14:68-9+ Je '89

Spelman prexy marries childhood sweetheart during campus nuptials. il por *Jet* 75:29 Ja 9 '89

COLE, K. C.

Aging bull. il *Ms.* 17:44+ Ap '89

COLE, KATHLEEN

about

My mother, the writer: master of a thousand disguises. G. Godwin. il pors *The New York Times Book Review* 94:7+ Je 11 '89

COLE, LEWIS

Def or dumb? il *Rolling Stone* p47-8+ O 19 '89

Prisoners of crack. il *Rolling Stone* p61-4+ F 9 '89

COLE, NATALIE

about

Natalie Cole and Andre Fischer: singer talks about her marriage, son and career [cover story] il pors *Jet* 77:54-8 O 16 '89

Natalie Cole says career is on right track and it's so 'good to be back' [cover story] R. E. Johnson. il pors *Jet* 76:56-8 My 29 '89

Natalie Cole weds in L.A. church ceremony. il pors *Jet* 76:57 O 2 '89

Natalie Cole's cousin, Eddie, produces song on hit album. il pors *Jet* 76:65 S 25 '89

COLE, NIKILA

about

Dancing out of time [dance] Reviews

Dance Magazine il 63:57-8 Ag '89. D. Scott

COLE, RICHIE

about

Richie Cole. M. Handler. il por *Down Beat* 56:14 Ja '89

COLE, THOMAS, 1801-1848

about

The American canvas. L. Bertrand. il por *National Parks* 63:32-6+ S/O '89

COLE, THOMAS W.

about

Cole sworn in as first Clark Atlanta U. prexy. il pors *Jet* 77:16 O 16 '89

COLE, TIMOTHY H.

Science. See issues of Popular Mechanics beginning July 1987

COLE, VINSON

about

Accentuate the positive. H. E. Phillips. il pors *Opera News* 54:26+ D 9 '89

COLE, WILLIAM, 1919-
'No author is a man of genius to his publisher'. *The New York Times Book Review* 94:1+ S 3 '89

COLEMAN, BETH
How one family spends its money. il *Good Housekeeping* 208:68+ Ja '89

COLEMAN, BILL, 1925-
Amish odyssey [photographs; condensation] il *Reader's Digest* 135:88-94 Jl '89

COLEMAN, EDMONIA SUE
about
Gary Coleman and mother battle over control of his $6 million fortune, income. il pors *Jet* 77:22-4 D 25 '89-Ja 1 '90
Gary Coleman's parents tell their side about his suit against them [cover story] R. E. Johnson. il pors *Jet* 76:56-60 Ap 17 '89

COLEMAN, ELIOT
Fertilizer from the garden. il *The Mother Earth News* 119:112+ S/O '89
Living soil. il por *Organic Gardening* 36:67-8+ O '89

COLEMAN, ELLEN
Carbo-loading: the tool for extra fuel. il *Women's Sports & Fitness* 11:16+ Je '89
Feed zone. See issues of Bicycling beginning March 1989
The hazards of eating too little. il *Women's Sports & Fitness* 11:18 Mr '89
Sugar: a performance boost or sweet nothing? il *Women's Sports & Fitness* 11:20-1 Jl/Ag '89
Winning the "losing" battle—for good. il *Women's Sports & Fitness* 11:44-5+ Ja/F '89

COLEMAN, ERICA
(jt. auth) See Horn, Denise, and Coleman, Erica

COLEMAN, GARY
about
Fending off illness and family, Gary Coleman turns 21, an age he wasn't sure he would see. T. Allis. il pors *People Weekly* 31:49-50+ F 20 '89
Gary Coleman and mother battle over control of his $6 million fortune, income. il pors *Jet* 77:22-4 D 25 '89-Ja 1 '90
Gary Coleman celebrates 21st birthday in Hollywood. il pors *Jet* 75:32-3 Mr 27 '89
Gary Coleman, 'Diff'rent strokes' star, sues his parents over earnings. il por *Jet* 75:60 F 27 '89
Gary Coleman's parents tell their side about his suit against them [cover story] R. E. Johnson. il pors *Jet* 76:56-60 Ap 17 '89
Goodbye, cute child star—hello, troubled young man. S. Littwin. il pors *TV Guide* 37:18-19+ Ap 1-7 '89

COLEMAN, JACK
about
The man in green. J. Stone. il *Discover* 10:88-91 O '89

COLEMAN, JAMES SAMUEL, 1926-
about
Why Catholic schools outperform all others [interview] por *U.S. Catholic* 54:6-12 Jl '89

COLEMAN, JOHN A.
Who are the Catholic 'fundamentalists'? [cover story] il *Commonweal* 116:42-7 Ja 27 '89

COLEMAN, JOHN MARSHALL
about
The New Dominion. R. G. Holland. il *National Review* 41:25+ S 29 '89
The Wilder side. F. Barnes. *The New Republic* 201:9-10 N 13 '89

COLEMAN, JONATHAN
about
PW interviews. C. Goodrich. il por *Publishers Weekly* 236:52-3 S 8 '89

COLEMAN, JULES L.
Products liability reform. *Society* 27:57-66 N/D '89

COLEMAN, M. DONALD
How to save communism: a modest prospectus. *National Review* 41:36-7 Mr 24 '89

COLEMAN, MITCH, AND JAFFE, DAVE
Last word. il *Omni (New York, N.Y.)* 11:110 Ja '89

COLEMAN, ORNETTE
about
Ornette Coleman's time. D. Fricke. il pors *Rolling Stone* p88-9+ Mr 9 '89

COLEMAN, PETER, 1928-
The brief life of liberal anti-communism. il *National Review* 41:34-6 S 15 '89

COLEMAN, WILLIE
about
Gary Coleman's parents tell their side about his suit against them [cover story] R. E. Johnson. il pors *Jet* 76:56-60 Ap 17 '89

COLEMAN LANTERNS *See* Lanterns

COLEN, B. D.
The extraordinary case of the woman who couldn't die. il por *Redbook* 172:126-9+ Mr '89
Hot seat. See occasional issues of Health (New York, N.Y.) beginning July 1986

COLEN, BRUCE DAVID
A California collection: sleek spaces for art in Beverly Hills. il *Architectural Digest* 46:126-33 D '89

Château de La Lorie: Marquise de Saint-Genys in the Haut-Anjou. il *Architectural Digest* 46:154-8+ Ja '89
Quake cabin conversion: Chuck Williams' 1906 house in San Francisco. il por *Architectural Digest* 46:290-5 My '89
View from Wappo Hill: Robert and Margrit Mondavi's Napa Valley vineyard. il pors *Architectural Digest* 46:276-83 My '89

COLES, JOHN
The world's oldest road. il maps *Scientific American* 261:100-6 N '89

COLES, PRESTON
I know you [poem] *Essence* 19:120 Ja '89

COLES, ROBERT
Day by day. See issues of New Choices for the Best Years beginning March 1989
How television's stories help us. il *TV Guide* 37:18-20 Je 3-9 '89
Lost youth. il *Vogue* 179:186-9 Jl '89
No. *Utne Reader* p80 Mr/Ap '89
Teaching our children to see. il por *Art News* 88:246 Ap '89
about
Learning by doing through public service for students and professors alike [interview] A. Levine. il pors *Change* 21:18-21+ S/O '89

COLES, ROSALIND BRADLEY
The proud rooster [story] il *Ebony* 44:188+ F '89

COLESCOTT, ROBERT, 1925-
about
Art. A. C. Danto. *The Nation* 248:709-13 My 22 '89
Black satire and bleeding hearts. B. W. Bloch. il *The New Leader* 72:22-3 My 1 '89
Colescott on black & white. K. Johnson. il *Art in America* 77:148-53+ Je '89
Mocking black stereotypes, a black artist makes waves. R. Lacayo. il pors *People Weekly* 31:149+ My 22 '89
Robert Colescott: New Museum of Contemporary Art; Phyllis Kind. R. Bass. il *Art News* 88:157-8 My '89

COLESLAW
Cole's role [anticancer coleslaw] J. Duke and R. A. Barnett. il *American Health* 8:100+ O '89

COLFER, RANDY
about
The endless winter. P. Mehlman. il pors *Gentlemen's Quarterly* 59:336-9+ Mr '89

COLGATE-PALMOLIVE CO. (DELAWARE)
The Street's view of Colgate needs brushing up. G. G. Marcial. il *Business Week* p108 Mr 27 '89

COLGATE UNIVERSITY
In the bonds of fraternity [abusive behavior of the Delta Kappa Epsilon fraternity; cover story] R. Warshaw. il *The Nation* 249:189+ Ag 21-28 '89

COLIN, MOLLY
California urges teaching of evolution in science textbooks. il *Publishers Weekly* 235:14 F 3 '89
Children's books: flourishing. *Publishers Weekly* 235:30 My 19 '89

COLINO, STACEY
(jt. auth) See Fellner, Michael J., and Colino, Stacey

COLINVAUX, PAUL A., 1930-
The past and future Amazon. bibl il maps *Scientific American* 260:102-8 My '89

COLITIS
See also
Ulcerative colitis

Nutritional aspects
Allergy causes colitis. C. SerVaas. il *The Saturday Evening Post* 261:98+ Ja/F '89

COLL, ELIZABETH ESTEVE- *See* Esteve-Coll, Elizabeth

COLLABORATION, ARTISTIC *See* Art—Collaboration

COLLABORATION, LITERARY *See* Authorship—Collaboration

COLLABORATIVE LEARNING *See* Group work in education

COLLAGE
See also
Photomontage
Corporate art [artist E. King] D. C. Bacon. il por *Nation's Business* 77:20 N '89
Mrs. Delany's fabulous flowers. J. Boysen. il por *International Wildlife* 19:44-5 Jl/Ag '89
Pieces of Robin Chandler. E. Strickland. il por *American Visions* 4:40-3 D '89

Exhibitions
Julia Kidd at Anne Plumb. K. Johnson. *Art in America* 77:153 Mr '89
Leo Manso at Armstrong. L. Campbell. il *Art in America* 77:156-7 Ja '89
Material witness [A. Ryan] H. Cotter. bibl f il *Art in America* 77:176-83+ N '89

COLLAGEN
Asbestos fiber shape may trigger radicals [study by Andrij Holian] D. E. Loupe. *Science News* 136:167 S 9 '89
Identification of the molecular defect in a family with spondyloepiphyseal dysplasia. B. Lee and others. bibl f il *Science* 244:978-80 My 26 '89

COLLAGEN—*cont.*

Need new tissue?—Grow your own [replacing damaged tissue in the mouth; work of Stephen Feinberg] il *USA Today (Periodical)* 118:8 O '89

The provocative pout: hot lips. J. Logan. il *Harper's Bazaar* 122:178-9+ Ap '89

COLLAGENASE

Autocrine induction of collagenase by serum amyloid A-like and β_2-microglobulin-like proteins. C. E. Brinckerhoff and others. bibl f il *Science* 243:655-7 F 3 '89

COLLATERALIZED MORTGAGE OBLIGATIONS *See* Mortgage bonds and notes

COLLAVO, KIM

Dark-field illumination. il *Petersen's Photographic Magazine* 18:88-9 My '89

COLLECTING *See* Collectors and collecting

COLLECTING OF ACCOUNTS

See also

Payment of accounts

Bad debts are worth collecting. C. A. Jaffe. il *Nation's Business* 77:53-4+ My '89

The check is in the mail. L. Arden. il *Home Office Computing* 7:54-5 F '89

Student loan financing; Student loan default [Guaranteed Student Loan program] E. Ginsberg and S. Ginsberg. il *Phi Delta Kappan* 70:556-8 Mr '89

Laws and regulations

Black schools facing new student loan default plan. *Jet* 76:9 Je 19 '89

"Due diligence" enforcement: is there risk sharing in the student loan program? L. E. Gladieux. *Change* 21:38 My/Je '89

From boon to bust in the student-loan business [banks curtail lending to students at schools with high default rates] P. Sherrid. il *U.S. News & World Report* 106:55 My 22 '89

COLLECTING OF TAXES *See* Tax collection

COLLECTIVE BARGAINING

See also

Collective labor agreements

Labor unions—Corporate campaigns

Collective bargaining and labor-management relations, 1988. G. Ruben. *Monthly Labor Review* 112:25-39 Ja '89

Collective bargaining in 1989: negotiators will face diverse issues. W. M. Davis and F. Sleemi. bibl f il *Monthly Labor Review* 112:10-24 Ja '89

Keeping U.S. business competitive: employers' rights vs. the unions'. T. W. Thee and W. J. Peterson. il *USA Today (Periodical)* 118:38-40 Jl '89

Labor is slowly raising its fist. A. Bernstein. il *Business Week* p36 F 27 '89

Labor's new agenda. H. Banks. *Forbes* 143:33 Ap 3 '89

Major agreements expiring next month. See issues of Monthly Labor Review

Needed: a replacement for the bargaining table. J. P. Hoerr. il *Business Week* p38-9 Ja 9 '89

Air pilots

See Collective bargaining—Airlines

Airlines

Airline industry update. *Monthly Labor Review* 112:44-5 S '89

ALPA to seek elimination of two-tier wage scales. *Aviation Week & Space Technology* 130:93 F 13 '89

Collective bargaining at Eastern. *Aviation Week & Space Technology* 130:9 Ja 30 '89

Eastern's labor mess may land in Bush's lap. A. Bernstein. il *Business Week* p26 Mr 6 '89

Northwest asks pilots to cooperate in thwarting hostile takeover. *Aviation Week & Space Technology* 130:106 My 1 '89

Northwest pilots warn that talks on new contract near breakdown. *Aviation Week & Space Technology* 131:99 Jl 24 '89

Pilots union threatens to seek declaration of impasse in talks with Northwest Airlines. *Aviation Week & Space Technology* 131:97 Jl 17 '89

Pilots will press Eastern to deal or face shutdown. J. T. McKenna and E. H. Kolcum. *Aviation Week & Space Technology* 130:68-9 F 27 '89

United swallows hard—and goes for growth. J. E. Ellis. il *Business Week* p34 My 15 '89

Wolf's bane [United Air Lines negotiations with its pilots] J. Zweig. il por *Forbes* 143:324 My 29 '89

Australia

Australia's airlines lay off pilots in wage dispute, grounding domestic flights. P. Proctor. map *Aviation Week & Space Technology* 131:69 Ag 28 '89

New Zealand

Air New Zealand says it will sell or lease first 747-400 [contract dispute with pilots] *Aviation Week & Space Technology* 131:136 O 9 '89

Automobile industry

Suddenly, the UAW is raising its voice at GM. W. Zellner. il por *Business Week* p96+ N 6 '89

The UAW rebels teaming up against teamwork. W. Zellner. il *Business Week* p110+ Mr 27 '89

Baseball, Professional

Baseball's owners want to play softball [revenue sharing proposal] A. Bernstein. il *Business Week* p52 D 18 '89

A crucial inning for baseball. W. C. Symonds. il por *Business Week* p90 O 23 '89

The players' main man [D. Fehr, executive director of the Major League Baseball Players Association] D. A. Kaplan. il por *The New York Times Magazine* p46+ O 29 '89

Electric industries

A look back at "Boulwarism". P. Brimelow. il pors *Forbes* 143:246+ My 29 '89

Football, Professional

The NFL's union could win by committing suicide [gaining free agency by disbanding] A. Bernstein. il por *Business Week* p84 N 27 '89

Government employees

Can employee associations negotiate new growth? S. A. Levitan and F. Gallo. bibl f il *Monthly Labor Review* 112:5-14 Jl '89

Graduate teaching assistants

Graduate students make history [University of California-Berkeley recognizes Association of Graduate Student Employees] P. Selvin. *The Progressive* 53:19 O '89

Lumber industry

West Coast lumber bargaining completed. *Monthly Labor Review* 111:48-9 D '88

Nurses

Canada

Temperature rising. R. Laver. il *Maclean's* 102:17 Jl 17 '89

Professions

Collective bargaining and private sector professionals. S. A. Levitan and F. Gallo. bibl f il *Monthly Labor Review* 112:24-33 S '89

Steel industry

Both sides are girded for grueling steel talks. M. Schroeder. il *Business Week* p40-1 Mr 13 '89

Closing up bars and closing up shop on the Monongahela. D. Ignatius. *The Washington Monthly* 21:62 F '89

Has Weirton's ESOP worked too well? M. Schroeder. il *Business Week* p66-7 Ja 23 '89

Telephone workers

Almost everyone is listening in on the telephone talks. A. Bernstein and S. B. Garland. il *Business Week* p32 Ap 10 '89

Mexico

Salinas goes after another monster: the phone system. S. Baker. il *Business Week* p42 Mr 6 '89

Germany (West)

Is the German featherbed on its way out? G. E. Schares. il *Business Week* p62 Mr 13 '89

COLLECTIVE FARMS *See* Collective settlements

COLLECTIVE LABOR AGREEMENTS

See also

Collective bargaining

Major agreements expiring next month. See issues of Monthly Labor Review

Major collective bargaining settlements in private industry in 1988. W. M. Davis. *Monthly Labor Review* 112:34-43 My '89

Unions and management are in a family way [recent settlements hinge on nonwage benefits] R. A. Taylor. *U.S. News & World Report* 106:24 Je 12 '89

Aerospace industries

Striking machinists return to work at Boeing; restoring full production may take six weeks. R. G. O'Lone. *Aviation Week & Space Technology* 131:85 N 27 '89

Why Boeing's hard line didn't pay off [strike ends] A. Bernstein. il *Business Week* p33 D 4 '89

Air pilots

See Collective labor agreements—Airlines

Air traffic controllers (Persons)

Air traffic controllers, FAA reach tentative agreement on three-year pact. *Aviation Week & Space Technology* 130:66 Ja 23 '89

Airlines

Eastern asks court's permission to break contract with pilots. *Aviation Week & Space Technology* 130:92 Je 26 '89

Automobile industry

Constant improvement? Or speedup? [Mazda's emphasis on kaizen concept fosters union discontent at Michigan plant] J. Flint. il *Forbes* 143:92+ Ap 17 '89

College employees

A beachhead for the beleaguered labor movement [Harvard clerical workers ratify contract] R. Kuttner. il *Business Week* p14 Jl 17 '89

Electric industries

Westinghouse's settlement deviates from pattern. *Monthly Labor Review* 111:47 D '88

Hotel workers

Look for the union label [housing trust fund in contract of Local 26 of Hotel Workers Union in Boston] P. Dreier. il *The Progressive* 53:30 Ap '89

Meat industry

Meatpacking settlements [Farmstead Foods] il *Monthly Labor Review* 112:41 Ap '89

COLLECTIVE LABOR AGREEMENTS—*cont.*

Newspapers

Two Chicago newspapers complete negotiations [Sun-times and Tribune] *Monthly Labor Review* 112:52 F '89

Paper industry

United Paperworkers and 16-month work stoppage. *Monthly Labor Review* 111:47-8 D '88

Publishers and publishing

Harper & Row, Penguin sign new labor accords. C. Reid. *Publishers Weekly* 235:12 F 3 '89

Railroads

Employment cuts sought in rail transportation [CSX and the United Transportation Union] *Monthly Labor Review* 112:43 Mr '89

Retail trade

Retail trade contracts. *Monthly Labor Review* 112:51-2 F '89

Shipbuilding

Shipbuilding settlements. *Monthly Labor Review* 111:49-50 D '88

State employees

Public sector agreements. *Monthly Labor Review* 112:43-4 O '89

Steel industry

Bethlehem-Steelworkers contract. il *Monthly Labor Review* 112:43-4 Jl '89

Did union leaders sell out the steelworkers? [USX accused of conspiring with negotiators] J. P. Hoerr. il *Business Week* p48-50 D 25 '89-Ja 1 '90

A stunning blow to cooperation at National Steel [rejection of labor pact] G. L. Miles. *Business Week* p32 Jl 3 '89

Supermarkets

Retail trade settlements. *Monthly Labor Review* 112:40-1 Je '89

Telephone companies

AT&T: all in the family [dependent care package included in new contract] il *Newsweek* 113:45 Je 12 '89

AT&T settlement. *Monthly Labor Review* 112:49-50 Ag '89

Regional telephone accords. *Monthly Labor Review* 112:79-81 N '89

Who won what at AT&T? L. A. Winokur. il *The Progressive* 53:29-32 D '89

Transportation workers

Transit accords. *Monthly Labor Review* 112:42-3 O '89

COLLECTIVE SETTLEMENTS

See also

Shakers

Great Britain

History

Gerrard Winstanley: England's pioneer Green? I. C. Bradley. bibl il *History Today* 39:12-17 Ag '89

Israel

See also

Kibbutzim

Oregon

See also

Rajneeshpuram (Or.)

Tennessee

History

See also

Historic Rugby

United States

See Collective settlements

COLLECTIVISM

It is later than you think: 1989. M. Lerner. *Society* 26:83-6 S/O '89

COLLECTORS AND COLLECTING

See also

Americana

Black collectibles

Children as collectors

Display of antiques, art objects, etc.

See also subheads Collectibles; Collectors and collecting under various subjects

And now, a little fun for not-so-serious investors. L. J. Moore and M. Horn. il *U.S. News & World Report* 107:82-3+ D 4 '89

Catalogue your collection. M. J. Youngken. il *Americana* 16:16+ Ja/F '89

Childhood revisited. S. Kozden. il *Antiques & Collecting Hobbies* 94:27+ D '89

Contemporary collectibles. L. Rosenkrantz. See issues of Antiques & Collecting Hobbies beginning October 1988

In God we trust, in dealers we don't [investing in various collectibles] M. K. Evans. il *Gentlemen's Quarterly* 59:217-18+ O '89

In the marketplace. F. Donegan. See issues of Americana

The latest on precious metals and collectibles. il *Black Enterprise* 20:60 O '89

Objects of affection. D. V. Gast. il *New Choices for the Best Years* 29:79-81 Je '89

Rinker on collectibles. H. L. Rinker. See issues of Antiques & Collecting Hobbies beginning October 1988

These dealers pay cash for your clutter. il *Good Housekeeping* 208:247 My '89

Bibliography

The bookshelf. See issues of Antiques & Collecting Hobbies beginning March 1985

COLLEGE, CHOICE OF *See* College choice

COLLEGE ADMINISTRATION *See* Colleges and universities—Administration

COLLEGE ADMISSION *See* Colleges and universities—Admission

COLLEGE ALUMNI *See* College graduates

COLLEGE AND HIGH SCHOOL COOPERATION *See* Educational cooperation

COLLEGE AND PUBLIC SCHOOL COOPERATION *See* Educational cooperation

COLLEGE AND SCHOOL JOURNALISM

See also

Dartmouth review

Bad Astra: the other side of the Spectrum [court rules against predistribution review policy in case of high school underground newspaper in Renton, Wash.] P. A. Zirkel. bibl f il *Phi Delta Kappan* 70:734-5+ My '89

College papers do the right-wing thing. J. B. Meigs. il *Rolling Stone* p98-9+ O 5 '89

Helping give students a sense of audience [junior high school magazine in Clinton, Ill.] K. S. Carter. *The Education Digest* 55:43-6 O '89

The kids are fine [personals in alumni magazines] J. Atlas. *The New Republic* 201:13-14 S 4 '89

School paper's story on teen mother who's class valedictorian is barred [C. M. Dixon] il por *Jet* 76:31 My 8 '89

Student journalists fight for free expression [Supreme Court ruling permits censorship of student press in Hazelwood, Mo. case] L. Eskin. il *Scholastic Update (Teachers' edition)* 122:19-21 S 8 '89

COLLEGE AND THE COMMUNITY *See* Colleges and universities—Public relations

COLLEGE ANNUALS *See* College yearbooks

COLLEGE ARCHITECTURE

See also

Dormitories

A crazy building in Columbus [Wexner Center; work of P. Eisenman] K. Andersen. il por *Time* 134:84+ N 20 '89

Educational facilities [theater facilities] M. LaRue. il *Theatre Crafts* 23:44-9+ D '89

Eisenman's gridlocked mind game [Wexner Center for the Visual Arts at Ohio State] C. McGuigan. il por *Newsweek* 114:74-5 N 20 '89

Machine tools [William Davis Computer Research Center at Univ. of Waterloo] M. Gaskie. il *Architectural Record* 177:122-7 O '89

Maritime maneuvers [Marine technology facility of Seattle Central Community College designed by Miller/Hull Partnership] P. M. Sachner. il *Architectural Record* 177:118-19 F '89

A multiformity of college buildings. il *Architectural Record* 177:41 S '89

Opening doors [Denver's Auraria Higher Education Center] M. Gaskie. il *Architectural Record* 177:102-7 Ag '89

Solid geometry [Wexner Center for the Visual Arts at Ohio State University designed by P. Eisenman] M. Sorkin. il por *House & Garden* 161:62+ O '89

COLLEGE ART GALLERIES AND MUSEUMS

See also

Hood Museum of Art

Palm Beach Community College. Lannon Gallery

Wexner Center for the Visual Arts (Columbus, Ohio)

Yale University. Art Gallery

COLLEGE ATHLETES *See* Athletes

COLLEGE ATHLETES, BLACK *See* Black athletes

COLLEGE ATHLETES, WOMEN *See* Women athletes

COLLEGE ATHLETICS

See also

Baseball, College

Basketball, College

Central Intercollegiate Athletic Association

Football, College

Hockey, College

National Collegiate Athletic Association

Rowing

Soccer, College

Softball, College

Swimming

Tennis

Track and field athletics

Volleyball, College

Women athletic directors

Wrestling, College

A study in frustration [American Institutes for Research study] R. Sullivan. il por *Sports Illustrated* 70:94 Je 19 '89

Cheerleading

See Cheerleading

Ethical aspects

An American disgrace [lawlessness among college athletes; special section] il *Sports Illustrated* 70:16-26+ F 27 '89

Athletes are exploited, Ashe tells N.C. Central. por *Jet* 77:50 N 13 '89

Baptists back Thompson in Proposition 42 fight [National Baptist Convention] il por *Jet* 75:50 F 27 '89

Foul! [scandals surrounding big-time college sports; cover story] T. Gup. il *Time* 133:54-60 Ap 3 '89

COLLEGE ATHLETICS—Ethical aspects—*cont.*

Gambling, payoffs and drugs [Univ. of Florida] R. Sullivan. il *Sports Illustrated* 71:40-2+ O 30 '89

Is Proposition 42 racist? J. B. Johnson; A. Ashe. il *Ebony* 44:138-40 Je '89

Jan Kemp [professor's stand against college athletes' low academic standards at the University of Georgia] S. Kanfer. il por *People Weekly* 32 Special Issue:124 Fall '89

Jocks with books [Duke and Notre Dame] J. Adler. il *Newsweek* 113:60-1 Ja 9 '89

National Collegiate Athletic Association [address, January 9, 1989] C. B. Reed. *Vital Speeches of the Day* 55:372-3 Ap 1 '89

A national disgrace [lawlessness among college athletes] il *Reader's Digest* 135:136-42 Ag '89

A new Proposition [NCAA's Proposition 42 stiffens rules governing awarding of scholarships] W. F. Reed. il *Sports Illustrated* 70:16-19 Ja 23 '89

Out of bounds [questions regarding the NCAA's Proposition 42 to tighten restrictions on scholarships] *The New Republic* 200:10-11 F 20 '89

Race becomes the game [J. Thompson challenges NCAA's Proposition 42 which tightens restrictions on scholarships] J. Kroll. il por *Newsweek* 113:56-9 Ja 30 '89

Thompson's walkout spurs review of Proposition 42. il *Jet* 75:50 F 13 '89

Tightening the rules [NCAA's Proposition 42 tightens scholarship requirements] il *Newsweek* 113:58 Ja 23 '89

When is the playing field too level? [NCAA's Proposition 42 tightens restrictions on scholarships] A. P. Sanoff. il *U.S. News & World Report* 106:68-9 Ja 30 '89

"You do it until you get caught" [NCAA investigations] T. Callahan. il *Time* 133:43 Ja 9 '89

COLLEGE BANDS *See* Bands (Music)

COLLEGE BOOKSTORES

See also

National Association of College Stores (U.S.)

Routledge boosts its sales and image in Iowa [book week at University of Iowa bookstore] J. Mutter. il *Publishers Weekly* 235:112-13 Ja 20 '89

Laws and regulations

California court upholds limits on trade books in college stores [case of Marin County Community College bookstore managed by Barnes & Noble] C. Reid. *Publishers Weekly* 235:18 Ap 28 '89

COLLEGE BUILDINGS *See* College architecture

COLLEGE CHOICE

The agony of college admissions [cover story; special section] il *Money* 18:142-4+ My '89

College Explorer [college selection program] K. Sternberg. il *Compute!* 11:67-8 Je '89

College Explorer [college selection program] J. Zornberg. il *Home Office Computing* 7:87-8+ My '89

COLLEGE CLUBS AND SOCIETIES

See also

College fraternities

College sororities

Skull and Bones Society

COLLEGE COACHES *See* Coaches (Athletics)

COLLEGE CREDITS

How to cut the cost of college [courses taken in high school] R. E. Deck, Jr. il *USA Today (Periodical)* 118:58-9 Jl '89

How to get credit for what you know. il *Occupational Outlook Quarterly* 33:18-19 Summ '89

Informal routes to a formal degree. N. Henderson. bibl il *Changing Times* 43:77+ Ja '89

COLLEGE DISCIPLINE

See also

College student suspension

COLLEGE DORMITORIES *See* Dormitories

COLLEGE EDUCATION

See also

Adult education

College teaching

Colleges and universities

Community and junior colleges

Computers—Educational use

Experimental college education

Liberal education

Professional education

The ivory foxhole. J. P. Hart. See occasional issues of National Review beginning September 26, 1986

Aims and objectives

Higher education and a civilization in trouble [address, November 15, 1988] J. A. Howard. *Vital Speeches of the Day* 55:314-18 Mr 1 '89

What the future holds for American colleges and universities [address, April 4, 1989] A. W. Ostar. *Vital Speeches of the Day* 55:558-62 Jl 1 '89

Bibliography

Books. See issues of Change beginning November/December 1984

Costs

See also

Michigan Education Trust

Scholarships and fellowships

Student aid

$50,000-a-year tuition? A. G. Shilling. il *Forbes* 144:323 D 11 '89

Brain trusts [Justice Dept. investigation of price fixing by private colleges] il *Time* 134:24 Ag 21 '89

The college crunch. A. Armstrong. il *Ms.* 17:118 Ja/F '89

Colleges in collusion [price fixing of tuition and financial aid] I. Ayres. *The New Republic* 201:19-20 O 16 '89

Corporate takeover on campus [high tuition costs attributed to increased funding of corporate-sponsored research; cover story] L. Minsky and D. F. Noble. il *The Nation* 249:477+ O 30 '89

Custodial accounts: saving for college made easy. M. Rowland. *Working Woman* 14:57 O '89

A double-E break on tuition costs [tax-free education bonds] L. Wiener. il *U.S. News & World Report* 106:64 Je 12 '89

Financing options for your child's education. I. Ness. il *Black Enterprise* 20:43-4 D '89

Have the halls of ivy grown too green? [possible collusion in fee setting by private colleges] il *U.S. News & World Report* 107:18-19 Ag 21 '89

Higher (-priced) education. J. Amberg. *The American Scholar* 58:521-32 Aut '89

How to cut the cost of college [courses taken in high school] R. E. Deck, Jr. il *USA Today (Periodical)* 118:58-9 Jl '89

How to pay a $150,000 tuition bill. N. Henderson. il *Changing Times* 43:88-90+ O '89

How you gonna pay for baby's B.A.? D. R. Katz. il *Esquire* 112:57-8 Ag '89

If colleges are fixing prices, it's a job for antitrust. G. S. Becker. il *Business Week* p30 S 25 '89

Investing for baby's B.A. il *Fortune* 120 no10 Special Issue:44 Fall '89

Ivy at a bargain? A. Bernstein. *Change* 21:4 Mr/Ap '89

An Ivy League cartel [colleges accused of violating antitrust laws] C. Leslie. il *Newsweek* 114:65 Ag 21 '89

Little-known gems in higher education. N. Henderson. il *Changing Times* 43:74-8 D '89

Making those college nest eggs grow. T. Segal. il *Business Week* p146-7 D 11 '89

Must college cost so much? J. Hood. *Reader's Digest* 134:108-10 Ap '89

No to separate checks [discussion of March/April 1989 article, Price as a lever for reform] C. Karelis. *Change* 21:5 Jl/Ag '89

Paying for college. M. Daly. il *Better Homes and Gardens* 68:26+ F '89

Paying those college bills. L. J. Brown. il *Good Housekeeping* 208:210 Mr '89

Price as a lever for reform [differential tuitions] C. Karelis. il *Change* 21:20-8 Mr/Ap '89

Sticker shock at the ivory tower. S. Tifft. il *Time* 134:72-3 S 25 '89

Tuition savers for school [zero coupons] T. Tilling. il *Parents* 64:144 Ja '89

Tuition shock! [special section] il *Money* 18:60-6+ S '89

Evaluation

See Colleges and universities—Evaluation

Federal aid

See Colleges and universities—Federal aid; Student aid

Philosophy

Apocalypse now in U.S. higher education [cover story] F. Oakley. *America* 160:286-7+ Ap 1 '89

The economics of academia. T. Sowell. por *Conservative Digest* 15:14-15 My/Je '89

Learning by story [work of E. D. Hirsch and A. Bloom] N. Postman. il *The Atlantic* 264:119-24 D '89

The opening of American minds [adaptation of address, January 1989] R. Rorty. *Harper's* 279:18-20+ Jl '89

The trouble with being open-minded [address, July 18, 1989] D. B. Lockerbie. *Vital Speeches of the Day* 55:723-7 S 15 '89

Research

See Educational research

COLLEGE EDUCATION, EXPERIMENTAL *See* Experimental college education

COLLEGE EDUCATION, VALUE OF

Diamonds of hope [address, June 11, 1989] P. Henmueller. *Vital Speeches of the Day* 55:680-1 S 1 '89

Is an Ivy degree worth remortgaging the farm? W. Shapiro. *Time* 134:73 S 25 '89

COLLEGE EDUCATION AND STATE

See also

Michigan Education Trust

A legislator looks at academe. W. A. Sederburg. il *Change* 21:30-8 Ja/F '89

The real crisis. M. I. Sovern. il *The New York Times Magazine* p24-5+ Ja 22 '89

What the future holds for American colleges and universities [address, April 4, 1989] A. W. Ostar. *Vital Speeches of the Day* 55:558-62 Jl 1 '89

China

Professors Marx and Mao are back. il *U.S. News & World Report* 107:13 Ag 28-S 4 '89

COLLEGE EDUCATION AND STATE—cont.
France
France to raise faculty enticements. D. Dickson. *Science* 243:1660 Mr 31 '89

Great Britain
Scholar slip [Britain's brain drain] A. Ryan. *The New Republic* 201:14-16 D 4 '89
Thatcherism and British higher education [address, April 1989] M. Shattock. il pors *Change* 21:30-9 S/O '89
Thatcherism and higher education: California, here she comes. R. M. Rosenzweig. il *Change* 21:40-1 S/O '89
COLLEGE EXTENSION *See* University extension
COLLEGE FRATERNITIES
Fraternity members punished for role in student's death at Morehouse College. *Jet* 77:13 N 6 '89
In the bonds of fraternity [abusive behavior of the Delta Kappa Epsilon fraternity at Colgate University; cover story] R. Warshaw. il *The Nation* 249:189+ Ag 21-28 '89
It's time to put an end to fraternity hazing. E. P. Gunn. *Seventeen* 48:200 Mr '89
A legacy of leadership and service [Alpha Phi Alpha] il *Ebony* 45:128-30 N '89
With a campus legend in peril, members of a fraternity vow to save the endangered M.I.T. smoot [markings spanning the length of the Harvard Bridge created by Lambda Chi Alpha pledges] N. Geeslin. il pors *People Weekly* 31:93-5 Ap 24 '89
COLLEGE GRADUATES
See also
    Baccalaureate addresses
    Business schools—Graduates
    College education, Value of
    Colleges and universities—Graduate work
    Women college graduates
The kids are fine [personals in alumni magazines] J. Atlas. *The New Republic* 201:13-14 S 4 '89
Employment
Cut the fluff [companies recruiting on campus] D. Machan. il *Forbes* 143:166 Je 26 '89
The future of work. R. B. Reich. *Harper's* 278:26+ Ap '89
Good prospects for class of '89. il *USA Today (Periodical)* 117:15 Ap '89
Japan faces a brain drain [college grads opting out of manufacturing sector] Y. Hoshiai and J. Schwartz. il *Newsweek* 114:47-8 S 4 '89
The uncommitted class of 1989. T. Paré. il *Fortune* 119:199+ Je 5 '89
Work experience of 1983-84 bachelor's and master's degree graduates [chart] il *Occupational Outlook Quarterly* 32:40 Wint '88
Ethics
Run Richmond graduates, run [address, May 11, 1989] R. E. Leestamper. *Vital Speeches of the Day* 56:156-7 D 15 '89
Sports
That old college try [Alamo Alumni Run] M. Bloom. il *Runner's World* 24:36-8 S '89
COLLEGE LIBRARIES
See also
    Howard-Tilton Memorial Library
    Research libraries
Theft
Microfilm thieves hit university libraries [Patent Depository Library] J. Palca. *Science* 245:248 Jl 21 '89
COLLEGE MASCOTS *See* Mascots
COLLEGE MUSEUMS
See also
    Arizona State University. University Art Museum
    Hampton University Museum (Hampton, Va.)
    LSU Rural Life Museum and Burden Research Plantation
COLLEGE NEWSPAPERS *See* College and school journalism
COLLEGE OF DRAMATIC ARTS (BANGKOK, THAILAND)
Learning to dance in Thailand. K. Swenson. il *Dance Magazine* 63:10+ F '89
COLLEGE OF ENVIRONMENTAL SCIENCE AND FORESTRY. ADIRONDACK WILDLIFE PROGRAM
The Adirondack Wildlife Program. D. A. Saunders. il *The Conservationist* 43:18-23 Ja/F '89
COLLEGE OF WOOSTER
After 58 years, a round-robin letter keeps on delivering [women graduates maintain contact] W. Plummer. il *People Weekly* 31:99-100 Ja 16 '89
COLLEGE OFFICIALS
See also
    College presidents
    Women college officials
COLLEGE PRESIDENTS
See also
    Botstein, Leon, 1946-
    Carsey, Julian Nance
    Jordan, I. King
The impossible life of a college president. J. Rose. *The Washington Monthly* 21:18-22+ Mr '89
Selection and appointment
The shady side of sunshine [selection of new president of University of Florida] J. McLaughlin and D. Riesman. il *Change* 21:44-57 Ja/F '89

COLLEGE PROFESSORS AND INSTRUCTORS *See* College teachers
COLLEGE RADIO STATIONS
Magna cum loud [favorite rock bands of college radio programmers] il *Rolling Stone* p127-8+ Mr 23 '89
New waves. K. Miller. il *Seventeen* 48:114+ My '89
COLLEGE RETIREMENT EQUITIES FUND
The $70 billion man [C. Wharton] C. V. Clarke. il pors *Black Enterprise* 19:100-2+ Je '89
COLLEGE REUNIONS
North Hatley's old world charm [class of 1964 reunion at Bishop's University] A. Fotheringham. il *Maclean's* 102:76 O 9 '89
COLLEGE SCHOLARSHIPS *See* Scholarships and fellowships
COLLEGE SORORITIES
A day at U. Va. il *Seventeen* 48:316-21+ Ag '89
Recruiting
Behind closed doors at sorority rush. C. Hanauer. il *Seventeen* 48:170-1+ S '89
COLLEGE SPORTS *See* College athletics
COLLEGE STUDENT SUSPENSION
At Dartmouth the clash of '89. J. Casey. il *The New York Times Magazine* p28-30+ F 26 '89
Dartmouth vs. freedom of speech [Dartmouth review case] D. Stone. il *Conservative Digest* 15:24-7 My/Je '89
Dartmouth's wild Indians stopped by the court. W. F. Buckley. *National Review* 41:15-16 Ja 27 '89
Return of the Dartmouth Two [Dartmouth review editors Christopher Baldwin and John Sutter contest suspension] T. Jacoby. il *Newsweek* 113:50-1 Ja 16 '89
COLLEGE STUDENTS
See also
    Asian American college students
    Black college students
    College graduates
    Foreign students
    Physics students
    Socially handicapped college students
    Women college students
Enhancing the education of college commuters. B. Jacoby. *The Education Digest* 54:62-4 Ap '89
Rewriting the code of conduct on campus [Boston University] J. Rachlin. il *U.S. News & World Report* 106:56 Ja 9 '89
Rolling stone on campus [special section] il *Rolling Stone* p98-9+ O 5 '89
Rolling stone on campus '89 [special section] il *Rolling Stone* p116-18+ Mr 23 '89
Admission
See Colleges and universities—Admission
Awards
See also
    Student Humanitarian Service Award
Business enterprises
See Youth and business
Clothing and dress
See Clothing and dress—Students
Crimes against
Campus crime: living the college life safely. A. Atkins. il *Better Homes and Gardens* 67:40+ My '89
Rape on campus. A. Rule. il *Good Housekeeping* 209:189+ S '89
Who says college campuses are safe? M. Hodge and J. Blyskal. il *Reader's Digest* 135:141-2+ O '89
Dating
See Dating (Social customs)
Economic conditions
Student expenses? Get real! D. Gershfield. il *Money* 18:81 S '89
Federal aid
See Student aid
Financial aid
See Student aid
Grading
See Grading and marking (Education)
Health and hygiene
See also
    AIDS (Disease) and college students
Housing
See also
    Dormitories
Nutrition
Fight the freshman 15. T. A. Watkins. pors *Seventeen* 48:162 Ag '89
Political activities
See also
    Student movement
    Student protests, demonstrations, etc.
    Students for a Better Society
    Students for a Democratic Society
Academic jackboots [leftists; cover story] S. L. M. Huck. il *Conservative Digest* 15:16-21 My/Je '89
Arms race as sitcom plot [decline of nuclear awareness] P. S. Boyer. il *The Bulletin of the Atomic Scientists* 45:6-8 Je '89
At Dartmouth the clash of '89. J. Casey. il *The New York Times Magazine* p28-30+ F 26 '89

COLLEGE STUDENTS—Political activities—*cont.*
Big movement on campus [push for abortion rights] P.
Simpson. il *Ms.* 17:74 Je '89
College papers do the right-wing thing. J. B. Meigs. il *Rolling
Stone* p98-9+ O 5 '89
Dartmouth vs. freedom of speech [Dartmouth review case]
D. Stone. il *Conservative Digest* 15:24-7 My/Je '89
Dartmouth's wild Indians stopped by the court. W. F. Buckley.
National Review 41:15-16 Ja 27 '89
Return of the Dartmouth Two [Dartmouth review editors
Christopher Baldwin and John Sutter contest suspension]
T. Jacoby. il *Newsweek* 113:50-1 Ja 16 '89

Protests, demonstrations, etc.
See Student protests, demonstrations, etc.

Psychology
The freshman year: unkind, ungentle. A. P. Sanoff. il *U.S.
News & World Report* 106:56-8 Ap 17 '89
How to assure student success [views of E. Glenn Griffin]
USA Today (Periodical) 117:12 Ap '89
What price glory? [toll that high achievement takes on Chinese
American students; research by Stanley Sue] L. Troiano.
il *American Health* 8:119 Mr '89

Reading
Postmodern romance. A. DeCurtis. il *Rolling Stone* p145-6+
Mr 23 '89

Recreation
Miller guy life [spring break beer ads] T. Riordan. *The
New Republic* 200:16-17 Mr 27 '89
Spring break at Padre Island: a new kind of tourism. J.
Gerlach. bibl il map *Focus (New York, N.Y.: 1950)* 39:13-16+
Spr '89

Recruiting
See Colleges and universities—Student recruiting

Religious life
See also
Campus Crusade for Christ
Rattling the dry bones of the student Christian movement
[denominational conferences] D. G. Shockley. *The Christian
Century* 106:1087-9 N 22 '89

Sexual behavior
Abortion: common at Christian colleges? il *Christianity Today*
33:42-3 Jl 14 '89
Dancing gays [gay-lesbian dance at Columbia University]
D. K. Mano. *National Review* 41:56-9 F 24 '89
Sex (how about love?) on Catholic campuses [with discussion;
cover story] D. J. O'Brien. *Commonweal* 116:169-77 Mr
24 '89
Sexual abandon [condoms unpopular on Canadian campuses]
J. Hanna. il *Maclean's* 102:48 S 25 '89

Volunteer service
See Volunteer service

COLLEGE STUDENTS AND ALCOHOL *See* Alcohol and
youth
COLLEGE STUDENTS AND DRUGS *See* Drugs and youth
COLLEGE STUDENTS AND TEACHERS *See* College
teachers and students
COLLEGE TEACHERS
See also
Academic freedom
American Association of University Professors
Asian American college teachers
College teaching
Colleges and universities—Administration—Faculty par-
ticipation
Science teachers
Faculty development from the inside [holistic assessment
and placement project for composition classes at Long
Beach City College] K. Burne and others. pors *Change*
21:43-9 My/Je '89
Opening doors for women in academia [countering discrimina-
tion; address, 1988] B. D. Webster. bibl f *BioScience* 39:96-8
F '89
ProfScam [excerpt] C. J. Sykes. il *Conservative Digest* 15:87+
My/Je '89
Pros and cons: a separate piece for general education [separate
faculty] G. Irvin. il *Change* 21:6-9 Jl/Ag '89

Dismissal
Jan Kemp [professor's stand against college athletes' low
academic standards at the University of Georgia] S. Kanfer.
il por *People Weekly* 32 Special Issue:124 Fall '89

Political activities
See also
National Association of Scholars
'60s protesters, '80s professors. A. P. Sanoff. il *U.S. News
& World Report* 106:54-5 Ja 16 '89
Academic jackboots [leftists; cover story] S. L. M. Huck.
il *Conservative Digest* 15:16-21 My/Je '89
The Gramscists are coming [Marxist analysis] M. Novak.
il por *Forbes* 143:54 Mr 20 '89
The new left vigilantes. J. P. Roche. il *National Review*
41:34-5 D 8 '89
Pride and perjury [firing of teacher and scientist A. Novikoff
for Communist activities by the University of Vermont
during McCarthy era] D. M. Oshinsky. por *The New Leader*
72:14-17 S 4 '89
The professor and the L-word. M. Decter. *Commentary*
87:39-48 F '89

Professional ethics
Ethical and moral responsibilities as faculty [address, September 23, 1988] J. H. Zumberge. *Vital Speeches of the Day*
55:199-202 Ja 15 '89
Profscam. J. P. Hart. il *National Review* 41:39 Ap 21 '89

Psychology
Claiming ourselves as teachers [AAHE Forum on Extraordinary Teaching] D. Gillespie. il *Change* 21:56-9 Jl/Ag '89

Publications
The academy's contribution to textbook impoverishment.
H. Tyson-Bernstein. *The Education Digest* 54:25-8 F '89

Recruiting
The great British brain drain. D. Foote. il *Newsweek* 114:60
Jl 17 '89
Scholar slip [Britain's brain drain] A. Ryan. *The New Republic*
201:14-16 D 4 '89

Salaries, pensions, etc.
See also
Teachers Insurance and Annuity Association
France to raise faculty enticements. D. Dickson. *Science*
243:1660 Mr 31 '89
Million-dollar professors: should the ivory tower be a gold
mine? J. F. Siler. il *Business Week* p90-2 Ag 21 '89
A new approach to faculty salaries. D. E. Koshland, Jr.
Science 243:1533 Mr 24 '89
Two academics face new choices in their retirement plans
[Carmen and Robby Greenlee] H. Wheelwright. il *Money*
18:159-60 My '89

Sexual behavior
Arms and the man: a sex scandal rocks Princeton [English
professor T. McFarland forced to retire from Princeton]
D. Rabinowitz. il pors *New York* 22:30-6 Jl 17 '89
Here's looking at you, kid [sexual harassment case against
Prof. R. Hummel at Univ. of Toronto] B. Amiel. il
Maclean's 102:9 Ap 10 '89
Homophobiaphobia [feminist linguistic course taught by les-
bian at Kenyon College] T. Short. *National Review* 41:19-20
Ag 18 '89

Supply and demand
The real crisis. M. I. Sovern. il *The New York Times Magazine*
p24-5+ Ja 22 '89
Remember the Ph.D. glut? Colleges will go begging [shortage
of liberal arts professors] D. L. Boroughs. il *U.S. News
& World Report* 107:55 S 25 '89

Tenure
Is academic freedom bad for business? [denial of tenure
to MIT professor D. Noble] K. Hart. il por *The Bulletin
of the Atomic Scientists* 45:28-31+ Ap '89
Wake-up call [reaction to wife's denial of tenure] R. B.
Reich. il *Ms.* 18:32-3 O '89
COLLEGE TEACHERS AND PUBLISHERS
Kickbacks in university textbook adoptions. R. B. McKenzie.
BioScience 39:326-7 My '89
Textbook publishers and authors clash over comp copy
proposals. C. Reid. il *Publishers Weekly* 236:12 O 20
'89
COLLEGE TEACHERS AND STUDENTS
Down to size. M. Kiefer. il *The New York Times Magazine*
p18+ Ja 8 '89
Getting students to think. S. Pinsker. *Current (Washington,
D.C.)* 318:18-21 D '89
Messages from a madman [terrorized by former student]
P. Rose. il *Glamour* 87:270 Je '89
My teacher, my friend [B. Turner] E. Stone. il *New Choices
for the Best Years* 29:80+ D '89
Teaching in a litigious time. S. Pinsker. il *Change* 21:50-4
Jl/Ag '89
COLLEGE TEACHING
See also
College teachers
Discussion method teaching. W. M. Welty. bibl il *Change*
21:40-9 Jl/Ag '89
Finding the call to teach [Miami-Dade Community College
teacher spends year at Evergreen State] B. Hilbert. il *Change*
21:6+ Mr/Ap '89
COLLEGE TELEVISION STATIONS
Student television learns to network. T. Appelo. il *Rolling
Stone* p107-8+ O 5 '89
COLLEGE TRUSTEES
Howard students force Atwater's resignation, and push other
demands. il *Jet* 75:37 Mr 27 '89
Now Willie Horton stalks the GOP [L. Atwater forced to
resign from Howard University board after student protest]
il *U.S. News & World Report* 106:13 Mr 20 '89
Saying no to Lee Atwater [Howard University students protest
appointment to board of trustees] J. V. Lamar, Jr. il
por *Time* 133:27 Mr 20 '89
Students fight naming of Atwater to Howard board. *Jet*
75:11 Mr 20 '89
COLLEGE TUITION *See* College education—Costs
COLLEGE YEARBOOKS
Blacks get own yearbook at Univ. of Pa.; It's a 1st for
Ivy League schools. il *Jet* 76:22 Ag 21 '89
COLLEGES AND BUSINESS *See* Business and education
COLLEGES AND UNIVERSITIES
See also
Academic freedom
American Association for Higher Education

COLLEGES AND UNIVERSITIES—See also—*cont.*
  Black colleges and universities
  Business schools
  Catholic colleges and universities
  Church colleges and universities
  Community and junior colleges
  Foreign students
  International Space University
  Law schools
  Teachers colleges
  Theological seminaries
  Veterinary colleges
Technology in college: where is its impact? D. R. McNeil. *The Education Digest* 55:58-9 D '89

Administration

See also
College presidents
Japan's search for U.S. colleges [attempts to buy various colleges] S. Tifft. il *Time* 133:57 Ja 23 '89
On changing academic culture from the inside [interview with D. Shalala] A. Bernstein and S. Mow. il pors *Change* 21:20-9 Ja/F '89
Pros and cons: a separate piece for general education [separate faculty] G. Irvin. il *Change* 21:6-9 Jl/Ag '89

Anecdotes, facetiae, satire, etc.
Primer for academic administrators. W. E. Vandament. *Change* 21:43+ Ja/F '89

Faculty participation
Beyond affirmative action: empowering Asian American faculty. S. Chan. il *Change* 21:48-51 N/D '89

Admission

The agony of college admissions [cover story; special section] il *Money* 18:142-4+ My '89
The alma mater derby. C. Leslie. il *Newsweek* 113:62-4 F 6 '89
Berkeley's changing student population. R. Buderi. il *Science* 245:694-6 Ag 18 '89
The confessions of a gatekeeper. D. A. Williams. il *Newsweek* 113:62-3 My 1 '89
The heat is on [parental pressure and applying to college] P. Goldsmith. il *Seventeen* 48:152-3+ O '89
The new 'open door' at Berkeley [Asian Americans' charges of quotas] *U.S. News & World Report* 106:13-14 Je 5 '89
Prejudice against excellence [Asian American students] G. F. Will. por *Conservative Digest* 15:15 Jl/Ag '89
A quota on excellence? The Asian American admissions debate. D. T. Nakanishi. il *Change* 21:38-47 N/D '89
Quotas on campus: the new phase [Asian American students] D. Seligman. il *Fortune* 119:205+ Ja 30 '89

Anecdotes, facetiae, satire, etc.
Campus comedy. See occasional issues of Reader's Digest

Antitrust cases

Brain trusts [Justice Dept. investigation of price fixing by private colleges] il *Time* 134:24 Ag 21 '89
Colleges in collusion [price fixing of tuition and financial aid] I. Ayres. *The New Republic* 201:19-20 O 16 '89
Have the halls of ivy grown too green? [possible collusion in fee setting by private colleges] il *U.S. News & World Report* 107:18-19 Ag 21 '89
If colleges are fixing prices, it's a job for antitrust. G. S. Becker. il *Business Week* p30 S 25 '89
An Ivy League cartel [colleges accused of violating antitrust laws] C. Leslie. il *Newsweek* 114:65 Ag 21 '89

Budget

See Colleges and universities—Finance

Buildings

See College architecture

Business activities

See Business and education

Curriculum

See also
Arts—Study and teaching
Comedy—Study and teaching
Creative writing—Study and teaching
Discipline-based art education
Humanities—Study and teaching
Intercultural education
International education
Jazz music—Study and teaching
Language and languages—Study and teaching
Liberal education
Literature—Study and teaching
Moral education
Popular culture—Study and teaching
Theater—Study and teaching
Women's studies
Interdisciplinary studies in higher education. J. G. Gaff. *The Education Digest* 55:57-60 O '89
Of many things [Lynne V. Cheney's 50 hours: a core curriculum for college students] J. W. Donohue. *America* 161:414 D 9 '89
Our uneducated graduates. M. Novak. il *Forbes* 144:96 N 13 '89
Why higher education is neither [cover story] J. DeParle and L. Mundy. il *The Washington Monthly* 21:30-6+ O '89

Departments of biology

British biologists learn small is not beautiful. D. Dickson. *Science* 244:766-7 My 19 '89

Departments of chemistry

New life for small science [abandonment of proposal to abolish many departments in British universities] J. Cherfas. *Science* 246:573 N 3 '89

Departments of dance

New York University, Tisch School of the Arts, and the Second Avenue Dance Company: a dancer prepares [work of dept. chairman L. Rhodes] O. Stuart. il por *Dance Magazine* 63:60-1 Mr '89

Departments of physics

Discontent with PhD programs voiced at AAPT-APS conference. I. Goodwin. *Physics Today* 42:62-3 Jl '89
New life for small science [abandonment of proposal to abolish many departments in British universities] J. Cherfas. *Science* 246:573 N 3 '89
Rutgers builds particle theory, surface science and computation. W. Sweet. *Physics Today* 42:62-3 Je '89

Desegregation

Southern Univ. fighting fed. desegregation order. *Jet* 77:26 N 27 '89

Directories

College bound: a guide to the guides. M. Berkman. *Seventeen* 48:184+ Mr '89

Employees

See also
Collective labor agreements—College employees

Enrollment

New strategies keep enrollments growing [1976-1986] il *Change* 21:39-42 Ja/F '89
Private colleges beating the odds. M. O'Keefe. il *Change* 21:10-19 Mr/Ap '89
Student migration patterns: what they mean for states. il *Change* 21:29-34 My/Je '89

Bibliography
Opportunities for minorities: new focus on concern for higher education. G. Orfield. il *Change* 21:50-3 My/Je '89

Entrance examinations

See also
American College Testing Program
Colleges and universities—Admission
Scholastic Aptitude Test

Entrance requirements

See Colleges and universities—Admission

Evaluation

See also
Higher Education Research Program
America's best colleges [cover story; special section] il *U.S. News & World Report* 107:53-8+ O 16 '89
General education at decade's end. J. G. Gaff. il *Change* 21:10-19 Jl/Ag '89
Higher (-priced) education. J. Amberg. *The American Scholar* 58:521-32 Aut '89
Little-known gems in higher education. N. Henderson. il *Changing Times* 43:74-8 D '89
The Money college value exam. il *Money* 18:78-9 S '89
What the future holds for American colleges and universities [address, April 4, 1989] A. W. Ostar. *Vital Speeches of the Day* 55:558-62 Jl 1 '89

Extension

See University extension

Faculty

See College teachers

Federal aid

See also
Colleges and universities—Research—Federal aid
Where the boys are [effect of Title IX on women athletic directors and coaches] M. Goodman. *The Washington Monthly* 21:18-20 Ap '89

Finance

See also
College education—Costs
Colleges and universities—Gifts, legacies, etc.
Colleges and universities—Investments
Universities Funding Council (Great Britain)
Caught in the web: the agenda of enrollments, costs, and student aid. M. A. Kramer. il *Change* 21:8 Mr/Ap '89
The economics of academia. T. Sowell. por *Conservative Digest* 15:14-15 My/Je '89
No to separate checks [discussion of March/April 1989 article, Price as a lever for reform] C. Karelis. *Change* 21:5 Jl/Ag '89
Price as a lever for reform [differential tuitions] C. Karelis. il *Change* 21:20-8 Mr/Ap '89
The rising crisis [Canadian universities; special section] il *Maclean's* 102:54-6+ S 18 '89
Slouching toward solvency. G. Keller. *Change* 21:7 S/O '89

Gifts, legacies, etc.

The 1980s: a halcyon decade for voluntary support. il *Change* 21:29-31+ Mr/Ap '89
A Gothic tale [Oxford fund raising campaign] T. Beardsley. *Scientific American* 260:20-1 Mr '89
A model mission [fund-raising at Mount Allison] G. Allen. il *Maclean's* 102:59+ S 18 '89

COLLEGES AND UNIVERSITIES—*cont.*
Graduate work
Discontent with PhD programs voiced at AAPT-APS conference. I. Goodwin. *Physics Today* 42:62-3 Jl '89
The recruitment trail: my MFA design program's better than yours. J. Dolan. *Theatre Crafts* 23:22+ Ag/S '89
Investments
At Boston University, Biotech 101 is no breeze [investment in Seragen] L. Jereski. *Business Week* p30-1 Ap 10 '89
Big money manager on campus. G. G. Marcial. il por *Business Week* p88 Ag 21 '89
Letting the losses run [Boston University's investment in Seragen Inc.] D. Wechsler. il *Forbes* 143:116 Ap 17 '89
Nuclear research laboratories
See Nuclear research laboratories
Public relations
The sports stars of UCSF. M. Barinaga. il *Science* 245:1442 S 29 '89
Publications
See also
University presses
Race relations
Banning ethnic slurs on campus [University of Wisconsin] *Newsweek* 113:68 Ap 24 '89
Bigots in the ivory tower. S. Tifft. il *Time* 133:56 Ja 23 '89
Black and blue, class of '89 [Stanford University] M. Mabry. il *Newsweek* 114:50-1 S 25 '89
Black UA homecoming queen wins by write-in campaign; stirs a furor [K. Ashley] il por *Jet* 77:18 N 6 '89
The campus: "an island of repression in a sea of freedom". C. E. Finn. *Commentary* 88:17-23 S '89
The class that deserves cutting [mandatory ethnic studies class at Berkeley] J. Leo. il *U.S. News & World Report* 106:58 My 29 '89
Daphne Maxwell Reid still bitter over snub as beauty queen at Northwestern U. il pors *Jet* 77:25 N 13 '89
Good news from Dartmouth [administration backs student protesting teacher S. Sully's finding of racism in submitted essay] *National Review* 41:18 S 15 '89
Lessons from Bigotry 101. C. Leslie. il *Newsweek* 114:48-9 S 25 '89
The new racism on campus. T. Sowell. il por *Fortune* 119:115-16+ F 13 '89
Race, scholarship, and affirmative action [special section] *National Review* 41:36-40 My 5 '89
Racial hatred on campus. J. Wiener. il *The Nation* 248:260-2+ F 27 '89
Racist Bigotry 101 at Harvard [week-long program on racism] R. R. Detlefsen. il *Conservative Digest* 15:40-3 Jl/Ag '89
The recoloring of campus life. S. Steele. il *Harper's* 278:47-55 F '89
The sources of racial discrimination [disparity in achievement levels; views of Thomas Sowell] W. F. Buckley. *National Review* 41:70 S 29 '89
White like me [conference on campus racism at Harvard] R. R. Detlefsen. *The New Republic* 200:18-21 Ap 10 '89
Rating
See Colleges and universities—Evaluation
Recruiting
See Colleges and universities—Student recruiting
Relations with business
See Business and education
Research
The academic elite. il *Business Week* Special Issue:56-7+ Je 16 '89
Advanced bio class? That's over in Hitachi Hall [Japanese companies setting up labs at U.S. colleges] D. P. Oran. il *Business Week* p73-4 Ag 7 '89
Animal Activism 101 [scientists get advice on how to combat attacks by animal activists] M. Barinaga. il *Science* 246:756-7 N 10 '89
Business goes to college [backing university labs] N. J. Freundlich. il *Business Week* Special Issue:50+ Je 16 '89
Corporate takeover on campus [high tuition costs attributed to increased funding of corporate-sponsored research; cover story] L. Minsky and D. F. Noble. il *The Nation* 249:477+ O 30 '89
Harvard chases biotech bucks [Medical Science Partners to market biotechnology research of Harvard Medical School] J. Wiener. il *The Nation* 248:12-16 Ja 2 '89
Is academic freedom bad for business? [denial of tenure to MIT professor D. Noble] K. Hart. il por *The Bulletin of the Atomic Scientists* 45:28-31+ Ap '89
Mergermania. J. Bourke. *The Nation* 249:495 O 30 '89
Million-dollar professors: should the ivory tower be a gold mine? J. F. Siler. il *Business Week* p90-2 Ag 21 '89
A preemptive strike for animal research [work of New York University and others] C. Holden. il *Science* 244:415-16 Ap 28 '89
Shiseido grant: more than skin deep [Japanese funding of Massachusetts General Hospital-Harvard University's Cutaneous Biology Research Center] M. Sun. *Science* 245:810-11 Ag 25 '89
Universities fight animal activists. C. Holden. il *Science* 243:17-19 Ja 6 '89

Ethical aspects
Malaria researcher indicted [W. Siddiqui charged with embezzling research funds at the University of Hawaii] E. Marshall. *Science* 245:1326 S 22 '89
Federal aid
Centers for the Commercial Development of Space. il *Ad Astra* 1:12 D '89
Conflict over conflict of interest [research fund recipients; guidelines drafted by the National Institutes of Health] J. Palca. *Science* 245:1440 S 29 '89
Funding fight over facilities. M. Crawford. *Science* 245:465 Ag 4 '89
House trims off academic pork. C. Norman. *Science* 246:990 N 24 '89
Intellectual exports [M.I.T.'s Industrial Liaison Program] T. Beardsley. *Scientific American* 261:17+ S '89
Keep Pentagon out of civilian economy. V. Kistiakowsky. *The Bulletin of the Atomic Scientists* 45:5 Ap '89
MIT-industry links draw congressional attention. M. Crawford. il *Science* 244:1136 Je 9 '89
NASA commercial centers gain greater independence. il *Aviation Week & Space Technology* 131:41+ N 20 '89
NIH grapples with conflict of interest. J. Palca. il *Science* 245:23 Jl 7 '89
NSF selects 11 science centers as boon to US competitiveness. I. Goodwin. il *Physics Today* 42:57-8 Ja '89
Universities reach into pork barrel with help from friends in Congress. I. Goodwin. il *Physics Today* 42:43-5 Ap '89
Security measures
Who says college campuses are safe? M. Hodge and J. Blyskal. il *Reader's Digest* 135:141-2+ O '89
Segregation
Kansas City Call publisher gets honorary degree at U. of Mo.; locked out in '39 [L. Bluford] il por *Jet* 76:16 My 22 '89
Standards
How can "intellectual property" be "protected?" [cover story; special section; with editorial comment by Harlan Cleveland] il *Change* 21:10-28 My/Je '89
Policy of "bombast" [discussion of July/August 1988 article, Judgment time for higher education] C. E. Finn. *Change* 20:6-7 N/D '88
State aid
A legislator looks at academe. W. A. Sederburg. il *Change* 21:30-8 Ja/F '89
Statistics
See also
Colleges and universities—Enrollment
Student recruiting
The agony of college admissions [cover story; special section] il *Money* 18:142-4+ My '89
Colleges learn to sell their services. E. Schurenberg. il *Working Woman* 14:65-8 N '89
The recruitment trail: my MFA design program's better than yours. J. Dolan. *Theatre Crafts* 23:22+ Ag/S '89
The search for minorities. S. Tifft. il *Time* 134:64-5 Ag 21 '89
Trustees
See College trustees
Alabama
See also
University of Alabama
California
See also
Art Center College of Design (Pasadena, Calif.)
Long Beach City College
Mount Saint Mary's College (Md.)
Stanford University
University of California, Berkeley
University of California, San Francisco
University of California (System)
University of Southern California
Westmont College
California perspectives: three viewpoints. W. H. Pickens. bibl il *Change* 21:42-51 S/O '89
Canada
The rising crisis [funding squeeze; special section] il *Maclean's* 102:54-6+ S 18 '89
Sexual abandon [condoms unpopular] J. Hanna. il *Maclean's* 102:48 S 25 '89
Central America
Central America and the education president [scholarships bring students to U.S. universities] J. J. Mullaney. *America* 160:524-5 Je 3 '89
China
See also
College education and state—China
Hebei University
Quiet on campus. J. L. Tyson. il *Scholastic Update (Teachers' edition)* 121:12+ My 5 '89
Colorado
See also
Auraria Higher Education Center (Colo.)
University of Colorado at Boulder
Connecticut
See also
Wesleyan College

COLLEGES AND UNIVERSITIES—Connecticut—See also
—cont.
Yale University
Florida
See also
Bethune-Cookman College
Florida A & M University
Miami-Dade Community College
University of Florida
France
See also
College education and state—France
A voice from the broom closet: an interview on French
university life. B. Forkner. *America* 160:585-6+ Je 17-24
'89
Georgia
See also
Clark Atlanta University
Georgia Institute of Technology
Morehouse College
Morehouse School of Medicine
Spelman College
University of Georgia
Germany (West)
German universities bursting at the seams. D. Kirk. il *Science*
243:1427 Mr 17 '89
Great Britain
See also
College education and state—Great Britain
Open University
Richmond College (London, England)
Universities Funding Council (Great Britain)
University of Cambridge
University of East Anglia
University of Oxford
Hawaii
See also
University of Hawaii
Illinois
See also
Art Institute of Chicago. School
Eureka College
Northwestern University (Evanston, Ill.)
Parks College of Saint Louis University
University of Chicago
Indiana
See also
Indiana University, Bloomington
University of Notre Dame
Iowa
See also
Maharishi International University
Kentucky
See also
University of Kentucky
Louisiana
See also
Southern University
Southern Univ. fighting fed. desegregation order. *Jet* 77:26
N 27 '89
Maryland
See also
Johns Hopkins University
University of Maryland, College Park
Massachusetts
See also
Boston University
Brandeis University
Emerson College
Harvard University
Massachusetts Institute of Technology
Northeastern University
Tufts University
Michigan
See also
Michigan Education Trust
Nebraska
See also
Creighton University
Nevada
See also
University of Nevada, Las Vegas
New Brunswick
See also
Mount Allison University
New Hampshire
See also
Dartmouth College
New Jersey
See also
Princeton University
Rutgers University
Seton Hall University
William Paterson College of New Jersey
New York (State)
See also
Barnard College
Colgate University

Columbia University
Hunter College
Manhattan School of Music
Mannes College of Music
New York University
Rockefeller University
Syracuse University
North Carolina
See also
Duke University
North Carolina State University at Raleigh
Southeastern Baptist Theological Seminary
Northeastern States
See also
Ivy League colleges
Ohio
See also
Central State University (Ohio)
College of Wooster
Kenyon College
Medical College of Ohio
Oklahoma
See also
University of Oklahoma
Ontario
See also
University of Toronto
University of Waterloo
Oregon
See also
Lane Community College
University of Oregon
Willamette University
Pennsylvania
See also
Eastern College
Lincoln University (Pa.)
Philadelphia College of Bible
Swarthmore College
University of Pennsylvania
Québec (Province)
See also
Bishop's University
Switzerland
See also
Art Center College of Design (Pasadena, Calif.). European
campus
Tennessee
See also
East Tennessee State University
Meharry Medical College
Texas
See also
Lamar University
Texas A & M University
Texas Southern University
United States
See Colleges and universities
Utah
See also
Brigham Young University
University of Utah
Virginia
See also
Liberty University
University of Virginia
Washington (D.C.)
See also
Catholic University of America
Gallaudet University
Georgetown University
Howard University
University of the District of Columbia
Washington (State)
See also
Evergreen State College
Seattle Central Community College
Western Europe
European vs American higher education. E. M. White and
R. Ahrens. il *Change* 21:52-5 S/O '89
Wisconsin
See also
University of Wisconsin—Madison
COLLEGES AND UNIVERSITIES, CHOICE OF *See* College
choice
COLLEGES AND UNIVERSITIES, EXPERIMENTAL *See*
Experimental college education
COLLEGES FOR WOMEN
See also
Barnard College
Spelman College
University of Oxford. Somerville College
COLLEGIATE CHORALE
Musical events:
Concert version of Strauss' opera Friedenstag. A. Porter.
The New Yorker 65:134-5 D 11 '89

COLLETT, MERRILL
Debt deal stacked against Indians. *The Progressive* 53:17-18 Ag '89
The next liberator? il *The Atlantic* 263:29+ F '89
COLLETT, ROSEMARY K.
Hydroponic gardening. il *Flower and Garden* 33:70-2+ Mr/Ap '89
COLLIDING-BEAM ACCELERATORS See Accelerators (Electrons, etc.)
COLLIER, ELLEN MANSOOR
I am not a terrorist. il *Glamour* 87:135 Ag '89
Read this article immediately. il *Nation's Business* 77:68+ O '89
COLLIER, JAMES LINCOLN, 1928-
Royalties from the library. il *Publishers Weekly* 236:14-16 Jl 21 '89
The Satchmo few people knew. il pors *TV Guide* 37:16-18 Jl 29-Ag 4 '89
COLLIER, PETER
The prodigal son. il *Reader's Digest* 135:64-8 Ag '89
about
Radical transformations. S. Churcher. il pors *The New York Times Magazine* p30-1+ Jl 16 '89
COLLIER, PETER, AND HOROWITZ, DAVID, 1939-
Panthers, contras, and other wars. *The New Republic* 200:38-41 Je 26 '89
COLLINS, ACE
(ed) See Chapin, Lauren. "All I ever wanted was my mother's love": the sad life of a child star
COLLINS, AMY FINE
Civilized liberties. bibl f il *Art in America* 77:164-9+ N '89
The man from Valencia. il *Art in America* 77:71-3 Ap '89
COLLINS, B. T.
The courage of Sam Bird. il *Reader's Digest* 134:49-54 My '89
COLLINS, BRADLEY
Van Gogh and Gauguin on the couch. bibl f il *Art in America* 77:57+ D '89
COLLINS, BUD
The Bud Collins classic guide to Wimbledon. il *World Tennis* 37:45-6+ Jl '89
Open the Open. il *World Tennis* 37:84-5 S '89
Roman holiday. il *World Tennis* 36:81-3 My '89
COLLINS, CLARE
Diabetes—the hidden symptoms. *Redbook* 172:20 Ap '89
COLLINS, DEAN
Collins on basics. See occasional issues of Petersen's Photographic Magazine beginning July 1983
COLLINS, DOUG
about
Jordan denies any role in Bulls' coach firing. il pors *Jet* 76:46 Jl 24 '89
COLLINS, GAIL
Rap as a second language. il *Ms.* 17:56-8 Ja/F '89
COLLINS, GREG
Joe Magrane strikes back. il pors *Gentlemen's Quarterly* 59:260-3 Ap '89
Why I wear what I wear: Miller time. il pors *Gentlemen's Quarterly* 59:65+ Ag '89
COLLINS, JACKIE
Anecdotes, facetiae, satire, etc.
The sisters Brontë and the sisters Collins: a study in stunning literary parallels. R. Hacker and J. Kaufman. pors *The New York Times Book Review* 94:12-13 Ag 20 '89
COLLINS, JIM
about
Computers vs. cerebrums. M. Hulbert. il *Forbes* 143:184 Ap 3 '89
COLLINS, JOAN
about
'I'm no angel': Joan Collins' parting shots at Dynasty [cover story] M. Leahy. il pors *TV Guide* 37:2-4+ Ap 15-21 '89
Anecdotes, facetiae, satire, etc.
The sisters Brontë and the sisters Collins: a study in stunning literary parallels. R. Hacker and J. Kaufman. pors *The New York Times Book Review* 94:12-13 Ag 20 '89
COLLINS, JOSEPH J.
The meaning of achievement. por *Channels (New York, N.Y.: 1986)* 9:34 Jl/Ag '89
COLLINS, LARRY
Media mixing in the rep business. il *Channels (New York, N.Y.: 1986)* 9:90-1 N '89
COLLINS, LIZZETTA LEFALLE- See LeFalle-Collins, Lizzetta
COLLINS, MARY, 1935-
Where do we go from here? *Commonweal* 116:271+ My 5 '89
COLLINS, MONICA
Extra! Extra! Tabloid clones invade TV. il *TV Guide* 37:14-16 N 18-24 '89
Roseanne Barr: the funniest "housewife" in America. il pors *Redbook* 172:34+ F '89
COLLINS, PAT
15 best videos for kids. il *Good Housekeeping* 209:114 O '89
Children's videos. il *Good Housekeeping* 208:66 Ap '89

COLLINS, PAT LOWERY, 1932-
Molly's baby [story] il *American Health* 8:98+ Je '89
COLLINS, PAULINE
about
Perils of Pauline. R. Laermer. il por *New York* 22:28 F 13 '89
Shirley Valentine's day. D. DeNicolo. il por *Glamour* 87:192 O '89
COLLINS, PHIL
about
Phil Collins and the Genesis of 'Buster'. F. Lovece. il por *Video* 13:12-13 Ag '89
COLLINS (WILLIAM) PLC See William Collins plc
COLLINS AVIONICS GROUP See Rockwell International Corp. Avionics Group
COLLISION AVOIDANCE SYSTEMS See Airplanes—Collision avoidance systems
COLLISION INSURANCE See Insurance, Automobile
COLLISIONS (NUCLEAR PHYSICS)
See also
Channeling (Physics)
Scattering (Physics)
COLLISON, MICHELE N-K
Syllabus for success. il *Black Enterprise* 19:113-14+ F '89
COLLODION PROCESS (PHOTOGRAPHY)
Guncotton and ether. il *American History Illustrated* 24:36-7 S/O '89
COLLOIDS
See also
Foams
Micelles
Hot and cloudy [Cloud Gel] V. E. Gilmore. il *Popular Science* 235:24 Ag '89
COLLOR DE MELLO, FERNANDO
about
Beat the devil. A. Cockburn. *The Nation* 249:232-3 S 4-11 '89
Brazil's election is a watershed no matter who wins. J. Ryser. il pors *Business Week* p61 D 4 '89
Lula's in town. K. Silverstein. *The Nation* 249:776-7 D 25 '89
COLLOTYPES
Going back to the past, using collotype art [publication of G. Catlin's North American Indian portfolio] J. P. Frank. il *Publishers Weekly* 236:62-4 Ag 4 '89
COLLUM, DANNY
Doing the Lord's work: churches energize the left. il *The Progressive* 53:34-7 F '89
COLMAN, PENNY
When parents make mistakes. *Ladies' Home Journal* 106:106 O '89
COLODNY, EDWIN I.
about
A promising flight plan—if no raiders show. S. Payne. il *Business Week* p81-2 Ag 14 '89
COLOGNE See Perfumes
COLOGNE FOR MEN See Perfumes for men
COLOMBIA
See also
Amazon River
Bogotá (Colombia)
Cartagena (Colombia)
Church and narcotics trade—Colombia
Civil rights—Colombia
Colombians
Israelis—Colombia
Medellin (Colombia)
Military assistance, American—Colombia
Narcotics laws and regulations—Colombia
Narcotics trade—Colombia
Police—Colombia
Rich—Colombia
Serranía de la Macarena (Colombia)
Terrorism—Colombia
Commerce
United States
See United States—Commerce—Colombia
Foreign relations
United States
See United States—Foreign relations—Colombia
Industries
See also
Banco de Occidente SA
Coffee industry—Colombia
Politics and government
Colombia's search for peace. J. D. Martz. bibl f *Current History* 88:125-8+ Mr '89
Dangerous days in the Macarena. A. Weisman. il map *The New York Times Magazine* p40-2+ Ap 23 '89
Religious institutions and affairs
See also
Evangelical churches—Colombia
Missions—Colombia

COLOMBIAN COOKING *See* Cooking, Colombian
COLOMBIAN TERRORISTS *See* Terrorists, Colombian
COLOMBIANS

Canada

Crime

Drugs and guns: is a Colombian assassination team in Canada? G. W. Taylor. il *Maclean's* 102:14 S 25 '89

Shuttle to jail [two Colombian pilots sentenced for smuggling cocaine into Canada] P. Kopvillem. il *Maclean's* 102:14-15 N 27 '89

Panama

The gutsy Panama option [Colombian drug king P. Escobar seeks refuge] pors *U.S. News & World Report* 107:19 S 11 '89

COLOMBO, CRISTOFORO *See* Columbus, Christopher
COLON (ANATOMY)

Cancer

See also
Colorectal cancer

Nutritional aspects

Reducing risk of colon cancer [study by Theresa B. Young] il *USA Today (Periodical)* 117:6 F '89

Prevention

Cancer protection [physical activity may reduce risk] il *Prevention (Emmaus, Pa.)* 41:12+ Ap '89

Therapy

Death-defying drug therapy [use of 5-fluorouracil and levamisole] il *Time* 134:76+ O 16 '89

DNA topoisomerase I-targeted chemotherapy of human colon cancer in xenografts. B. C. Giovanella and others. bibl f il *Science* 246:1046-8 N 24 '89

Drug availability is an issue for cancer patients, too [levamisole-5-fluorouracil therapy] J. L. Marx. il *Science* 245:346-7 Jl 28 '89

Drug duo takes on deadly colon cancer [levamisole and 5-fluorouracil; research by Charles G. Moertel] K. Fackelmann. *Science News* 136:228-9 O 7 '89

COLONIAL COOKING *See* Cooking, American
COLONIAL HISTORY (U.S.) *See* United States—History—Colonial period, ca. 1600-1775
COLONIAL MANAGEMENT ASSOCIATES, INC.

Calculated risk [computer investing] J. Clements. il *Forbes* 143:248-9 Je 26 '89

COLONIAL WILLIAMSBURG *See* Williamsburg (Va.)
COLONIALISM *See* Colonies
COLONIE (N.Y.)

Crime

A devoted brother believes he's found little Billy Ruff's killer 31 years after the crime [C. Ruff links cousin R. Ruff to 1957 murder] K. Gross. il pors *People Weekly* 31:69-70+ Je 5 '89

COLONIES

See also
Space colonies
United Nations. Decolonization Committee
United Nations. Special Committee on the Situation with Regard to the Implementation of the Declaration on the Granting of Independence to Colonial Countries and Peoples
United Nations. Trusteeship Council

Exploitation or benefaction? P. Brimelow. il por *Forbes* 144:110+ N 27 '89

COLONIZATION

See also
Colonies

COLONY COMMUNICATIONS

Down-home cable TV. J. Stilson. il *Channels (New York, N.Y.: 1986)* 9:42-3+ N '89

COLONY-STIMULATING FACTORS

Cranking up cancer treatments. R. Weiss. *Science News* 135:380 Je 17 '89

COLOR

See also
Black
Dyes and dyeing
Iridescence
Sky—Color
Sports uniforms—Color
Stars—Color

Homework [shape and color games for children] H. E. H. Aycock. il *Compute!* 11:114 N '89

The risk of breaking rules [preservation of Color Field oil paintings] B. Keyser. il *American Artist* 53:20+ O '89

True colors [exhibit of monochrome paintings in Lyon, France] M. Hafif. bibl f il *Art in America* 77:128-39+ Je '89

Watercolor page: using harmonious color relationships. S. Quiller. il por *American Artist* 53:40-3 O '89

Watercolor page: winning color combinations. M. Lacki. il por *American Artist* 53:44-7+ N '89

Psychology

Color schemes. B. Kanner. il *New York* 22:22-3 Ap 3 '89

Color! Shades of you. A. G. Britton. il *American Health* 8:26-8+ Ja/F '89

Dark forces [impact of black uniforms on temper of a team; research by Tom Gilovich and Mark G. Frank] S. Boxer. il *Sports Illustrated* 70:52-4+ Ap 17 '89

COLOR ASSOCIATION OF THE UNITED STATES

Color council or conspiracy? N. Darnton. il *Newsweek* 114:48 Jl 17 '89

COLOR ASTROPHOTOGRAPHY *See* Astronomical photography

COLOR BLINDNESS

The genes for color vision. J. Nathans. bibl il *Scientific American* 260:42-9 F '89

Molecular genetics of human blue cone monochromacy. J. Nathans and others. bibl f il *Science* 245:831-8 Ag 25 '89

COLOR COMPUTER GRAPHICS *See* Computer graphics
COLOR COMPUTERS *See* Computers
COLOR FILMS *See* Photography—Films
COLOR FILTERS *See* Light filters
COLOR IN FASHION

See also
Color Association of the United States

Au naturel [makeup colors] L. Wells. il *The New York Times Magazine* p70 Mr 26 '89

Dressing thin: the real black magic. N. Malkin. il *Harper's Bazaar* 122:90-1 Ja '89

The face of the nineties [natural shades in makeup] L. George. il *American Health* 8:102-3 S '89

Inventing spring's colors. K. Beckett-Young. il *Health (New York, N.Y.)* 21:56-63 Mr '89

Noir has gone too far. L. Lague. il *People Weekly* 32 Special Issue:110-11 Fall '89

Shocking hues. il *'Teen* 33:18 Ja '89

COLOR IN FLOWER GARDENS *See* Flower gardens and gardening

COLOR IN HOUSE DECORATION

Colors for a happy home [excerpt from Alexandra Stoddard's book of color] A. Stoddard. il *McCall's* 117:34-6 N '89

Cozy country cottage [blue and white color scheme used in log cabin] il *McCall's* 116:62-4 Ag '89

Newlyweds Ian Irving and Carolina Estrada have transformed a small house at the shore with big-impact color. J. Etra. il pors *Vogue* 179:260-1+ Ag '89

A study in red [London residence designed by John Stefanidis] E. Lambert. il *Architectural Digest* 46:78-83 Jl '89

COLOR OF ANIMALS

All things bright & bitter [cover story] E. Pennisi. il *International Wildlife* 19:46-51 N/D '89

COLOR OF BIRDS

Rhapsody in red [scarlet ibises in Venezuela] C. S. Luthin. il *International Wildlife* 19:46-51 Jl/Ag '89

Tough little turncoat [ptarmigan] G. Turbak. il *National Wildlife* 28:14-19 D '89/Ja '90

COLOR OF FISH

Signs of the season [fish in autumn] J. Barsness. il *Field & Stream* 94:22 O '89

COLOR OF LEAVES

Call for fall color. il *Southern Living* 24:33 S '89

Looking for Sierra gold [fall color tour] il map *Sunset (Central West edition)* 183:22-5 S '89

Signs of the season. J. Barsness. il *Field & Stream* 94:22 O '89

Vintage leaves [grape leaves] C. Fenyvesi. por *Organic Gardening* 36:71 Jl/Ag '89

Watch out, New England! [colorful trees for the garden] il *Sunset (Central West edition)* 183:88-91 N '89

Welcome the golden fall. S. Bender. il *Southern Living* 24:68-71 O '89

Anecdotes, facetiae, satire, etc.

Color wars. W. Geist. il *New York* 22:29 O 9 '89

COLOR OF MINERALS

Giant radiation-induced color halos in quartz: solution to a riddle. A. L. Odom and W. J. Rink. bibl f il *Science* 246:107-9 O 6 '89

COLOR OF SNOW AND ICE

Strange footprints in snow. C. F. Bohren. il *Weatherwise* 42:168-70 Je '89

COLOR PERCEPTION *See* Color vision
COLOR PHOTOGRAPHY *See* Photography
COLOR PRINTING

Color by numbers [Tektronix Phaser CP] K. Quirk. il *Byte* 14:177-9 Jl '89

Color pages via electronic prepress save publishers time and money. J. P. Frank. il *Publishers Weekly* 236:33-4+ Ag 18 '89

Color printer quells price-tag blues [Tektronix ColorQuick] T. Thompson. il *Byte* 14:187-8 O '89

Crisis: the demand for color [Heath School Division getting early commitments for separation work] J. P. Frank. il *Publishers Weekly* 235:120-1 Ja 20 '89

TekColor lets you really see what you get [color-matching system for the Macintosh] J. Bertolucci and T. Thompson. il *Byte* 14:84+ N '89

The wait for color laser printers. P. Honan. il *Personal Computing* 13:113 Ap '89

What price color PostScript? [QMS Colorscript 100 Model 10] H. Eglowstein. il *Byte* 14:229-30+ D '89

What's new in color printers and plotters. P. Honan. il *Personal Computing* 13:107-11+ Ap '89

COLOR PROCESSING (PHOTOGRAPHY) *See* Photography—Processing

COLOR VISION
See also
Color blindness
Color science for imaging systems. L. E. DeMarsh and E. J. Giorgianni. bibl f il *Physics Today* 42:44-52 S '89
Colored segments of a grid can shed a diffuse glow like the light from a neon tube. J. Walker. bibl il *Scientific American* 261:116-19 N '89
Colorvision: seeing the true character of color. J. Marvullo. il *Petersen's Photographic Magazine* 18:40-3 O '89
Jeepers, creepers [mantis shrimp; research by Thomas W. Cronin and N. Justin Marshall] A. W. Epstein. il *Scientific American* 261:33-4 S '89
Orange you glad? Fido sees the blues [research by Gerald Jacobs] R. Weiss. *Science News* 136:215 S 30 '89
Space coloristics [cosmonauts' reporting concerning earth's surface] V. Vasyutin and A. A. Tishchenko. bibl il *Scientific American* 261:84-90 Jl '89
Genetic aspects
The genes for color vision. J. Nathans. bibl il *Scientific American* 260:42-9 F '89
Molecular genetics of human blue cone monochromacy. J. Nathans and others. bibl f il *Science* 245:831-8 Ag 25 '89

COLORADO
See also
Agriculture—Colorado
Air pollution—Colorado
Alamosa National Wildlife Refuge (Colo.)
Arts and crafts—Colorado
Birds—Colorado
Booksellers and bookselling—Colorado
Coal mines and mining—Colorado
Gardens and gardening—Colorado
Geology—Colorado
Groundwater pollution—Colorado
Gunnison National Forest (Colo.)
Hovenweep National Monument (Colo. and Utah)
Hunting—Colorado
Indian Peaks Wilderness (Colo.)
La Plata County (Colo.)
Manti-LaSal National Forest (Utah and Colo.)
Monte Vista National Wildlife Refuge (Colo.)
National parks and reserves—Colorado
Paleontology—Colorado
Public health—Colorado
Radioactive pollution—Colorado
Radioactive waste disposal—Laws and regulations—Colorado
Resorts—Colorado
Skiing—Colorado
Wilderness areas—Colorado
Antiquities
The dark side of the Anasazi [evidence of a cannibalistic ritual at Yellow Jacket, Colo. site; work of John Cater] il *Discover* 10:12 Ap '89
Climate
Whatever the real reasons, the hot, dry weather in Colorado this summer was blamed on the greenhouse effect. R. M. Adams. il *Smithsonian* 20:12 S '89
Description and travel
See also
Motorcycling—Colorado
Colorado aspen loop. il map *Sunset (Central West edition)* 183:26+ O '89
Colorado gold. il map *Sunset (Central West edition)* 182:80-3 Je '89
Summer events in Colorado's gold country. il *Sunset (Central West edition)* 182:24 Je '89

COLORADO BALLET
Dancescape [guest artists Peihui Guo and V. Johnson] H. Ostlere. por *Dance Magazine* 63:9 Ag '89

COLORADO RIVER (COLO.-MEXICO)
See also
Central Arizona Project
Grand Canyon (Ariz.)
Floating down from Hoover Dam. il *Sunset (Central West edition)* 182:66 Je '89
A raft of fun [white water rafting in Utah; with editorial comment by Donald J. Barr] J. McCallum. il pors *Sports Illustrated* 71:4, 34-7 Jl 10 '89

COLORADO SPRINGS (COLO.)
Historic houses, sites, etc.
Colorado Springs. J. Colihan. il *American Heritage* 40:26+ Jl/Ag '89

COLORADO TRAIL (COLO.)
Trail blazer [work of G. Gaskill] T. Jenkins. il por *Women's Sports & Fitness* 11:76-7 Ap '89

COLORATURA SOPRANOS See Opera singers

COLORECTAL CANCER
Genetic aspects
Allelotype of colorectal carcinomas. B. Vogelstein and others. bibl f il *Science* 244:207-11 Ap 14 '89
Chromosome 17 deletions and p53 gene mutations in colorectal carcinomas. S. J. Baker and others. bibl f il *Science* 244:217-21 Ap 14 '89

COLORED PENCIL DRAWING See Pencil drawing

COLORIMETRY
Color science for imaging systems. L. E. DeMarsh and E. J. Giorgianni. bibl f il *Physics Today* 42:44-52 S '89

COLORING MATTER IN COSMETICS, FOOD, ETC.
Good food, good health: food, colorful food! B. Goldman. il *Better Homes and Gardens* 67:23 Ag '89
Kitchen color [use of food coloring in photos] J. Van Horne. il *Petersen's Photographic Magazine* 17:46-7 Ap '89

COLORING OF MOTION PICTURES See Motion pictures—Coloring

COLORING OF PHOTOGRAPHS See Photographs—Coloring

COLOROCS CORP.
A rosy future in cheap color copies. G. G. Marcial. *Business Week* p100 S 4 '89

COLORS See Color

COLORS [film] See Motion picture reviews—Single works

COLSON, CHARLES W.
Living in the new Dark Ages [excerpt from Against the night]; ed. by Ellen Santilli Vaughn. il *Christianity Today* 33:30-3 O 20 '89

COLSON, GREG
about
Greg Colson at Angles. M. Anderson. il *Art in America* 77:144-5 Jl '89

COLSON, JANET
about
When the honeymoon's over: how to tell how you're really doing. J. Ciabattari. il pors *Working Woman* 14:82-6+ Je '89

COLSON, JEFF, 1956-
about
Jeff Colson at Angles. R. Channin. *Art in America* 77:184 Je '89

COLT, GEORGE HOWE
Teen sexuality. il *Life* 12:24-30 Jl '89

COLTER, CLEVELAND
about
Safeties first. A. Murphy. il pors *Sports Illustrated* 71:78-80 S 4 '89

COLTON (CALIF.)
Housing
Colton, California, competition for affordable senior housing. il *Architectural Record* 177:64-5 O '89

COLTRANE, ALICE
about
Living with the spirit and legacy of John Coltrane. D. Donloe. il pors *Ebony* 44:46+ Mr '89

COLTRANE, JOHN, 1926-1967
about
John Coltrane-Cecil Taylor-Art Blakey: Philharmonic Hall, Lincoln Center, New York City [reprint] I. A. Baraka. il *Down Beat* 56:62 S '89
Living with the spirit and legacy of John Coltrane. D. Donloe. il pors *Ebony* 44:46+ Mr '89
'Trane on the track [reprint] I. Gitler. il por *Down Beat* 56:48-9 S '89
"Tribute to John Coltrane". C. Albertson. il por *Stereo Review* 54:124+ S '89

COLUMBIA (MD.)
James Rouse set out to do the impossible—build a city that works. D. Moreau. il por *Changing Times* 43:132 O '89

COLUMBIA (MO.)
Race relations
Blacks demand probe in death of Missouri youth found hanging from tree [A. Roland] por *Jet* 76:52 Ap 24 '89

COLUMBIA (S.C.)
Crime
Beauty and the beast [case of serial murderer L. G. Bell] E. H. Methvin. il pors *Reader's Digest* 134:132-8 F '89

COLUMBIA (SPACE SHUTTLE VEHICLE) See Space vehicles

COLUMBIA BROADCASTING SYSTEM, INC. See CBS Inc.

COLUMBIA COUNTY (N.Y.)
Historic houses, sites, etc.
Making time for your other life [country home of designer B. Johnson] S. Nelson. il por *Working Woman* 14:102-5 Mr '89

COLUMBIA GAS SYSTEM, INC.
Coastal warning [rumor of takeover of Columbia Gas by Coastal Corp.] T. Jaffe. *Forbes* 144:140-1 Jl 10 '89
The uses of adversity. J. Cook. il por *Forbes* 144:60+ N 27 '89

COLUMBIA PICTURES ENTERTAINMENT INC.
Bright as Dawn, strong as Steel. J. Taylor. il pors *New York* 22:40-7 My 29 '89
Dynamic duos don't come cheap [Warner sues Sony over services of P. Guber and J. Peters] C. Gorman. il pors *Time* 134:71 N 6 '89
Even for Walter Yetnikoff, this will be a stretch: can Sony's ace juggle both Columbia and CBS Records? D. Lieberman. il por *Business Week* p144-5 O 30 '89
From Walkman to showman [Sony buys Columbia Pictures] J. Castro. il *Time* 134:70-1 O 9 '89
Japan goes Hollywood [Sony's deal for Columbia Pictures and the competitive challenge to the U.S.; cover story; special section] il *Newsweek* 114:62-9+ O 9 '89

COLUMBIA PICTURES ENTERTAINMENT INC.—*cont.*
Making up, Hollywood style [Warner and Sony settle lawsuit over services of P. Guber and J. Peters] il pors *Time* 134:74 N 27 '89

Sony's big-picture strategy [purchase of Columbia Pictures] J. Egan. il *U.S. News & World Report* 107:35-6+ O 9 '89

Through the looking glass. L. Gubernick. il *Forbes* 143:44 Ap 3 '89

Walter Yetnikoff's $300 million mistake [Sony's deal to put J. Peters and P. Guber at helm of Columbia Pictures] L. Gubernick. il pors *Forbes* 144:108+ D 11 '89

When Columbia met Sony . . . a love story. R. Grover. il *Business Week* p44-5 O 9 '89

Why Sony is plugging into Columbia. N. Gross and W. J. Holstein. il *Business Week* p56+ O 16 '89

COLUMBIA RIVER
The Columbia River basin [cover story] K. N. Lee. bibl f il map *Environment* 31:6-11+ Jl/Ag '89

What's ahead for salmon? Let's look at two vital rivers, the Columbia and the Sacramento. il *Sunset (Central West edition)* 182:96-7 Ap '89

COLUMBIA RIVER GORGE (OR. AND WASH.)
In search of nuclear winds [windsurfing] M. Beauchamp. il *Forbes* 144:214-15 S 18 '89

Mouth of the Columbia, still a discovery. il maps *Sunset (Central West edition)* 183:56-9 S '89

COLUMBIA SAVINGS & LOAN ASSOC.
He who lives by the junk bond . . . [T. Spiegel's fall] K. Kerwin. il por *Business Week* p46-7 D 25 '89-Ja 1 '90

COLUMBIA SPORTSWEAR COMPANY
Gert Boyle has a vested interest in George Bush's fishing fortunes. H. Shapiro. il pors *People Weekly* 32:143-4 S 18 '89

COLUMBIA UNIVERSITY
Dancing gays [gay-lesbian dance] D. K. Mano. *National Review* 41:56-9 F 24 '89

Move over, Demosthenes [banner citing female authors displayed] il *U.S. News & World Report* 107:12 O 9 '89

COLUMBIA UNIVERSITY. DEPT. OF PHYSICS
Junk [electromagnet involved in 1939 splitting of an atom] *The New Yorker* 65:28-9 My 29 '89

COLUMBIA UNIVERSITY. GRADUATE SCHOOL OF JOURNALISM
From here to here [address, September 6, 1988] J. Konner. *Vital Speeches of the Day* 55:238-41 F 1 '89

COLUMBIAN EXPOSITION (1893: CHICAGO, ILL.) *See* World's Columbian Exposition (1893: Chicago, Ill.)

COLUMBO (FICTIONAL CHARACTER)
Columbo returns! What you can expect from him now; ed. by Jeff Kaye. P. Falk. il por *TV Guide* 37:10-12 F 4-10 '89

COLUMBO [television program] *See* Television program reviews—Single works

COLUMBUS, CHRISTOPHER
about
Holy Columbus! P. C. Montgomery. il *Common Cause Magazine* 15:24-7 N/D '89

The Santa Maria's excess baggage. il *U.S. News & World Report* 107:14 O 2 '89

Shipshape. il por *Life* 12:26-30 Ap '89

The three sisters. B. Weber. il *The New York Times Magazine* p102 My 14 '89

Where did Columbus land? map *USA Today (Periodical)* 117:10 Ap '89

COLUMBUS (CHRISTOPHER) DOLLAR COINS *See* Coins

COLUMBUS (GA.)
Moral conditions
Bobby Brown's *Cruel* beguiles fans—but not the cop who nabbed him for dirty dancing [arrested during concert in Columbus, Ga.] S. Dougherty. il pors *People Weekly* 31:108-10 Ap 10 '89

COLUMBUS (OHIO)
Auditoriums, convention facilities, etc.
Buckeye competitions: one for Columbus . . . il *Architectural Record* 177:57 Jl '89

Crime
A mother's revenge [R. Baldridge catches man who raped her daughter] M. Cohen. il por *Ladies' Home Journal* 106:140-1+ S '89

Economic conditions
The gleam along the Rust Belt. F. Washington. il *Newsweek* 113:48-9 F 6 '89

Industries
What's the best city? W. E. Sheeline. il *Fortune* 119:11 Ja 2 '89

Moral conditions
Watergate figure preaches honesty [J. S. Magruder] *Christianity Today* 33:47 Ap 21 '89

COLUMBUS (SPACE STATION) *See* Space stations, European

COLUMBUS CENTER (NEW YORK, N.Y.)
Beware the design police. C. Wiseman. il *New York* 22:64-5 My 22 '89

Columbus Center: $57 million buys 500,000 square feet. J. S. Russell. il *Architectural Record* 177:81 Je '89

COLUMBUS CIRCLE (NEW YORK, N.Y.)
See also
Columbus Center (New York, N.Y.)

COLUMBUS ENERGY CORPORATION
Fool's gold? [recent investments by C. Seaman] S. Flack. il por *Forbes* 144:150+ D 25 '89

COLUMNS, ADVICE (NEWSPAPERS) *See* Newspapers—Advice columns

COLUMNS, GOSSIP *See* Gossip columns

COLVIN, RICHARD
about
Personal newsletter. P. Duggan. il por *Forbes* 143:254 Je 26 '89

COLVIN, SHAWN
about
Shawn Colvin. J. Matthews. por *Rolling Stone* p32 N 16 '89

COLWILL-MCGEHEE ANTIQUE DECORATIVE AND FINE ARTS (FIRM)
From folk to Federal. A. Cunningham. il *House & Garden* 161:106 S '89

COMA
See also
Diabetic coma
Awakening from a coma, a Washington woman meets her miraculous baby boy [B. Blodgett gives birth] M. Green. il pors *People Weekly* 31:38-40+ F 27 '89

Coma. M. K. Blakely. il por *Life* 12:80-4+ Ag '89

The extraordinary case of the woman who couldn't die [coma patient N. Jobes kept alive because she had no living will] B. D. Colen. il por *Redbook* 172:126-9+ Mr '89

Twilight zones. S. M. Halpern. il *Ms.* 18:26+ S '89

COMANECI, NADIA, 1962-
about
Gymnast Nadia Comaneci leaps for freedom—and lands in the arms of a married father of four. il pors *People Weekly* 32:116 D 18 '89

Leap to the West. W. O. Johnson and A. Verschoth. il pors *Sports Illustrated* 71:40-1 D 11 '89

COMBAT AND WOMEN *See* Women and war

COMBATIVENESS *See* Fighting (Psychology)

COMBES, SIMON, 1940-
about
Hair, dust and sky. H. Gibson. il por *International Wildlife* 19:52-9 S/O '89

COMBI DISC PLAYERS *See* Combination disc players

COMBINATION DISC PLAYERS
Laser sharp. F. Vizard. il *Popular Mechanics* 166:109-10 O '89

Laser's new populism. L. B. Johnson. il *Video* 13:79-80+ S '89

Pioneer's pioneering is finally paying off. N. Gross. il *Business Week* p89 D 18 '89

Testing
3 top combi-players. E. J. Foster. il *Stereo Review* 54:94-9 D '89

Philips CDV-488 CD video player. E. J. Foster. il *High Fidelity (New York, N.Y.)* 39:19+ Jl '89

Philips CDV488 combi-player. J. D. Hirsch. il *Stereo Review* 54:68+ O '89

Pioneer combi player with digital effects [CLD-3030] il *Video* 12:40+ Ja '89

Pioneer dual-side combi player [CLD-2070] il *Video* 13:44-5+ S '89

Pioneer Elite deluxe combi player [CLD-91] il *Video* 13:50+ D '89

Play a disc, any disc [Sony MDP-210] F. Vizard. il *Popular Mechanics* 166:50 D '89

Sony combi player with digital effects [MDP-590] il *Video* 13:52+ D '89

Sony MDP-700 CD-V combination player. D. Ranada. il *High Fidelity (New York, N.Y.)* 39:21+ Ap '89

Videodiscs: CDs for eyes. J. B. Meigs. il *Rolling Stone* p71+ Ja 12 '89

Yamaha combi player. il *Video* 13:34+ Ag '89

COMBINATORIAL ANALYSIS
How the Grinch stole mathematics [computer-generated combinatorial proof; work of Herb Wilf and Down Zeilberger] B. A. Cipra. *Science* 245:595 Ag 11 '89

COMBINES *See* Harvesting machinery

COMBUSTIBLE MATERIALS *See* Inflammable materials

COMBUSTION ENGINEERING INC.
An insider caper in Liechtenstein [ASEA Brown Boveri helps SEC uncover insider trading during ABB's friendly takeover bid for Combustion Engineering] J. Kapstein. *Business Week* p58-9 D 11 '89

COMBUSTION ENGINES *See* Automobile engines; Gas and oil engines; Motorcycle engines

COMDEX (TRADE SHOW)
Computers and casinos, bean counters and bookies mix it up at Las Vegas COMDEX. A. R. Levitan. il *Compute!* 11:86+ F '89

Neither snow, nor Chicago . . . W. Rash, Jr. il *Byte* 14:119-20+ Ag '89

Not quite Comdex/2 yet. M. Minasi. il *Byte* 14:149-50+ Mr '89

Ready line overload. J. Pournelle. il *Byte* 14:121-2+ F '89

COMDEX (TRADE SHOW)—cont.
Report from Comdex. J. Holtzman. il *Radio-Electronics* 60
ComputerDigest:75-7 Ag '89
Spring Comdex: glimmers of acceptance [OS/2] M. Minasi.
il *Byte* 14:129-30+ Ag '89
What hath Comdex wrought? W. Rash, Jr. il *Byte* 14:135-6+
Mr '89
COMDISCO, INC.
Arb no more [K. Pontikes] J. Zweig. il por *Forbes* 144:348
N 13 '89
COMEDIANS
See also
American Comedy Awards
Aviles, Rick
Burns, George, 1896-
Caesar, Sid
Carvey, Dana
Clay, Andrew Dice
Cleese, John
Crystal, Billy
Elliott, Chris
Freberg, Stan
Kinison, Sam
Leno, Jay
Mason, Jackie
Miller, Dennis
Morris, Jim
Nealon, Kevin
Physicians as comedians
Quinn, Colin
Rodriguez, Paul
Smothers, Dick
Smothers, Tom
Wright, Steven
Wuhl, Robert
The comedian gets the girl. L. Gubernick. il *Forbes* 144:64+
S 4 '89
Special comedy issue [with editorial comment by Art Cooper]
il *Gentlemen's Quarterly* 59:20, 65+ Ag '89
What's so funny? [cover story; special section] il *Rolling
Stone* p45-8+ N 2 '89
Professional ethics
Thievery, what a concept. J. Martel. il *Gentlemen's Quarterly*
59:216 Ag '89
Psychology
Comedy shrink [therapist A. Lefkowitz] P. Mehlman. il
Gentlemen's Quarterly 59:218 Ag '89
COMEDIANS' DRUG AND ALCOHOL ABUSE FOUNDA-
TION
Straight men. J. Queenan. il *Rolling Stone* p72-3+ N 2 '89
COMEDY
See also
Cable television—Comedy programs
Gross National Product (Comedy troupe)
Humor
Kids in the Hall (Comedy troupe)
Motion pictures—Comedy films
Radio broadcasting—Comedy programs
Television broadcasting—Comedy programs
Videotapes—Comedy
Willow Street Carnival (Comedy troupe)
The comedian gets the girl. L. Gubernick. il *Forbes* 144:64+
S 4 '89
Special comedy issue [with editorial comment by Art Cooper]
il *Gentlemen's Quarterly* 59:20, 65+ Ag '89
What's so funny? [cover story; special section] il *Rolling
Stone* p45-8+ N 2 '89
Awards
See also
American Comedy Awards
Benefit performances
See also
Comic Relief (Project)
Study and teaching
Yukking it up for credit [M. Helitzer's comedy course] B.
Barol. il *Newsweek* 114:83 D 4 '89
COMEDY CHANNEL
The 8000-hour joke. T. Minsky. il *Rolling Stone* p66-7+
N 2 '89
Get ready for a mighty battle of wits. H. Polskin. il *TV
Guide* 37:14-19 N 11-17 '89
No laughing matter. B. Carter. il pors *The New York Times
Magazine* p50+ N 5 '89
Round-the-clock yucks. R. Zoglin. il *Time* 134:95 N 20
'89
Smiley's people. V. Ziegel. il por *Gentlemen's Quarterly*
59:240-3+ Ag '89
Take my comedy programming, please. D. Lieberman. il
Business Week p73 D 18 '89
Talk about a running gag. H. F. Waters. il *Newsweek* 113:62
My 29 '89
What's so funny about a Comedy Channel? J. Anderson.
il *Rolling Stone* p35 Ag 10 '89
COMEDY NIGHTCLUBS
Comedy clubs can be knockouts. D. H. Dunn. il *Business
Week* p118-19 Mr 27 '89
Sounds and laughs [New York City] C. S. Smith. il *New
York* 22:42-4+ D 25 '89-Ja 1 '90

COMER, JAMES P.
As they grow/11 through 13. See issues of Parents
Teaching your kids values. il *Parents* 64:220 N '89
about
Help for no-hope kids. C. Leslie. il por *Newsweek* 114:50
O 2 '89
COMETS
See also
Halley's comet
Joint Observatory for Cometary Research
Space flight—Cometary missions
2060 Chiron = Comet Kowal? il *Sky and Telescope* 78:14
Jl '89
Bombardment of earth is constant [research by Thomas
M. Donahue and Tamas I. Gombosi] il *USA Today
(Periodical)* 117:13 Je '89
A bright new comet at dusk and dawn [Comet Okazaki-Levy-
Rudenko, 1989r] A. MacRobert. il *Sky and Telescope*
78:510-11 N '89
Chiron becomes a comet. il *Astronomy* 17:14 S '89
Chiron's brightening hints it's a comet. J. Eberhart. il *Science
News* 135:247 Ap 22 '89
A combination of impact and volcano is dismissed. *Science*
243:479 Ja 27 '89
Comet Brorsen-Metcalf at dawn. il *Sky and Telescope* 78:288
S '89
Comet commotion [theory of L. A. Frank] R. Kunzig. il
Discover 10:24-5 Ja '89
Comet digest. J. E. Bortle. See issues of Sky and Telescope
through April 1989
Comets and meteorites: harbingers of life on earth . . .
and destructors of Mars. il *Sky and Telescope* 78:242
S '89
Comets and the perversity of nature. D. K. Yeomans. il
Sky and Telescope 78:253-4 S '89
Comets may have supplied earth with chemicals of life.
Earth Science 42:6-7 Summ '89
Double exposures reveal mini-comets? [work of L. A. Frank
and Clayne Yeates] R. A. Kerr. *Science* 243:170-1 Ja 13
'89
Fractal-shaped dust [work of Edward L. Wright] il *Sky and
Telescope* 78:240 S '89
Giant meteor impacts and great eruptions: dinosaur killers?
G. S. Paul. bibl f il *BioScience* 39:162-72 Mr '89
The next doomsday impact. C. R. Chapman and D. Morrison.
Astronomy 17:8 N '89
The night of the comets [November 12, 1987] M. L. Clark.
il *Astronomy* 17:102-3 Je '89
Return of a bright comet [Comet Brorsen-Metcalf] C. E.
Spratt. il *Astronomy* 17:76-7 Jl '89
The return of Comet Brorsen-Metcalf. R. Shaffer. il *Astronomy*
17:61-2 S '89
Searching for Comet Brorsen-Metcalf. il *Sky and Telescope*
78:182 Ag '89
Sighting comets with radar. *Sky and Telescope* 77:239 Mr
'89
A snowball's chance [theory of Louis A. Frank] J. Horgan.
Scientific American 260:21+ Mr '89
StarTrails [Comet Levy 1988e] D. H. Levy. il *Sky and
Telescope* 78:532-3 N '89
Stop to consider the stones that fall from the sky. J. S.
Trefil. il map *Smithsonian* 20:80-8+ S '89
Sungrazing comets: big and small. J. E. Bortle. il *Sky and
Telescope* 77:564-6 My '89
Waiting for the year's best comet [Comet Brorsen-Metcalf]
J. E. Bortle. il *Sky and Telescope* 78:108-9 Jl '89
Orbits
Whence come comets? A. H. Delsemme. il *Sky and Telescope*
77:260-4 Mr '89
COMETS, ARTIFICIAL
Where did AMPTE's ions go? [research by John B. Cladis
and William E. Francis] R. Monastersky. *Science News*
135:319 My 20 '89
COMFORT, NATHANIEL C.
Can you love animals and kill them? il *Utne Reader* p46+
S/O '89
COMFORT
See also
Ergonomics
Comforting habits [toddlers] J. T. Gibson. il *Parents* 64:208
D '89
Rock-a-bye toddler. J. T. Gibson. il *Parents* 64:210 N '89
COMFORT STATIONS *See* Public comfort stations
COMFORTERS *See* Quilts and quilting
COMIC BOOK CONFIDENTIAL [film] *See* Motion picture
reviews—Single works
COMIC BOOKS, STRIPS, ETC.
See also
Batman (Fictional character)
Copyright—Comic books, strips, etc.
Doonesbury (Comic strip)
Graphic novels
Kudzu (Comic strip)
Life in hell (Comic strip)
Peanuts (Comic strip)
Pogo (Comic strip)
Sex in comic books, strips, etc.
Steve Canyon (Fictional character)

COMIC BOOKS, STRIPS, ETC.—See also—cont.
Violence in comic books, strips, etc.
Has this Opus drawn to an end? [B. Breathed ends Bloom County] il por *Newsweek* 113:65 My 15 '89
Heaven can wait. il *U.S. News & World Report* 106:14 Ap 17 '89
A hooligan who wields a pen [interview with B. Breathed] D. S. Levy. il por *Time* 134:10+ D 25 '89
Serious business. F. McCoy and A. Edmond, Jr. il por *Black Enterprise* 20:86-8+ S '89

Economics use
Japanese comics are all business. S. Solo. il *Fortune* 120:143-4+ O 9 '89

Exhibitions
The Far side of science [exhibition at the American Museum of Natural History] T. R. Miller. il *Natural History* p78 My '89

Political aspects
Art Spiegelman [interview] C. Dreifus. il *The Progressive* 53:34-7 N '89

Religious use
Discrimination isn't comic [Chicago tribune replaces Kudzu with Pogo] M. E. Marty. *The Christian Century* 106:215 F 22 '89

Japan
Japanese comics are all business. S. Solo. il *Fortune* 120:143-4+ O 9 '89

COMIC BOOKS, STRIPS, ETC. AND MOTION PICTURES
Stan Lee comic-book hero. A. Roth. il *American Film* 15:12 O '89
They shoot comic books, don't they? H. A. Rodman. il *American Film* 14:34-9 My '89

Anecdotes, facetiae, satire, etc.
Gag reflex. P. Rudnick. il *Rolling Stone* p57-9 N 2 '89

COMIC RELIEF (PROJECT)
Comic Relief's canny comedians trade yuks for bucks to help the nation's homeless. il *People Weekly* 31:134-5 Ap 3 '89

COMIC STRIPS *See* Comic books, strips, etc.

COMINES, PHILIPPE DE, SIEUR D'ARGENTON, 1445?-1511
about
Philippe de Commynes: a courtly middle-man. M. Jones. bibl il *History Today* 39:34-41 Mr '89

COMING TO AMERICA [film] *See* Motion picture reviews—Single works

COMMAND, CONTROL, COMMUNICATIONS AND INTELLIGENCE NETWORK *See* Communications, Military

COMMANDER AIRCRAFT (FIRM)
Commander lawsuit settled. il *Flying* 116:10 Ag '89

COMMANDER AIRPLANES *See* Airplanes, Business

COMMANDER'S PALACE (NEW ORLEANS, LA.: RESTAURANT) *See* New Orleans (La.)—Restaurants, nightclubs, bars, etc.

COMME DES GARÇONS SHIRT (FIRM)
Tailor made. K. D. Stein. il *Architectural Record* 177:92-3 Ja '89

COMMEMORATIVE COINS *See* Coins
COMMEMORATIVE MEDALS *See* Medals
COMMEMORATIVE POSTAGE STAMPS *See* Postage stamps
COMMENCEMENT ADDRESSES *See* Baccalaureate addresses

COMMERCE
See also
Balance of trade
Barter
Business
Competition
East-West trade
Embargo
Export-import trade
Free ports and zones
Smuggling
Tariff
Trade marks and trade names
Trade routes
Trading companies
World Trade Week

COMMERCE CITY (COLO.)
Recreation centers
Recreation serves and shapes a community [Commerce City Recreation Center] M. Gaskie. il *Architectural Record* 177:100-3 N '89

COMMERCE DEPT. (U.S.) *See* United States. Dept. of Commerce

COMMERCE, SCIENCE, AND TRANSPORTATION COMMITTEE *See* United States. Congress. Senate. Committee on Commerce, Science, and Transportation

COMMERCIAL ART *See* Art, Commercial
COMMERCIAL BLACKLISTING *See* Blacklisting
COMMERCIAL CATALOGS *See* Catalogs, Commercial
COMMERCIAL CATTLE FEEDERS OF IOWA
Iowa custom feeders claim 3-8¢ cost edge. *Successful Farming* 87:16 Je '89

COMMERCIAL CONFERENCES *See* Economic conferences
COMMERCIAL CORRESPONDENCE *See* Business writing
COMMERCIAL CREDIT COMPANY
Primerica adds another feather to its cap [BarclaysAmerican/Financial Inc.] J. Friedman. il *Business Week* p98 D 11 '89

COMMERCIAL CRIMES
See also
Bribery
Computer crimes
Embezzlement
Insider trading
Beware the boomerang [question of attorney-client privilege in confidential probes of corporate criminality] D. Fanning. il *Forbes* 143:66-7 F 6 '89
Business may have found a way to defang RICO. P. Dwyer. il *Business Week* p26 Ag 28 '89
Don't let them gut RICO. M. Waldman and P. Gilbert. il *USA Today (Periodical)* 118:50-1 N '89
In defense of RICO. *The New Republic* 201:4+ O 16 '89
Make the punishment fit the corporate crime. G. S. Becker. il *Business Week* p22 Mr 13 '89
RICO: a racketeering law run amok. R. Boucher. il *USA Today (Periodical)* 118:48-9 N '89
White-collar crime isn't news [research by Donna Randall and others] *USA Today (Periodical)* 118:4-5 D '89

COMMERCIAL FISHERIES *See* Fisheries
COMMERCIAL INTERTECH CORP.
Commercial Intertech. R. Abelson. il *Fortune* 120:108 Jl 31 '89

COMMERCIAL JOURNALISM *See* Journalism, Commercial
COMMERCIAL LAW
See also
Antitrust law
Arbitration, Commercial
Contracts
Corporation law
Landlord and tenant
Maritime law
Payment of accounts
Trade marks and trade names
On the docket. See issues of Forbes
A right turn, but no free ride for business [Supreme Court] P. Dwyer. il *Business Week* p27 Jl 10 '89
Will business get the bill? [business issues and the 101st Congress] D. Harbrecht. il *Business Week* p28-9 Ja 16 '89

COMMERCIAL PHOTOGRAPHY *See* Photography, Commercial
COMMERCIAL POLICY
See also
British Columbia—Commercial policy
Canada—Commercial policy
Chile—Commercial policy
China—Commercial policy
Commodity control
Competition
Free ports and zones
Free trade and protection
Germany (West)—Commercial policy
Hungary—Commercial policy
Japan—Commercial policy
Mexico—Commercial policy
Ontario—Commercial policy
Soviet Union—Commercial policy
United States—Commercial policy
Trading blocs and the evolving world economy. J. E. Garten. *Current History* 88:15-16+ Ja '89

COMMERCIAL PRODUCTS
See also
Luxuries
Private brands
Products, New
Quality of products
Endorsements
See Advertising—Testimonials
Recall
Product recalls. See issues of Consumer Reports
Recalls: an up-to-date list. J. Gillis. See issues of Good Housekeeping beginning May 1987
Safety devices and measures
See also
U.S. Consumer Product Safety Commission
Testing
See also
Consumers Union of United States

COMMERCIAL SHEARING, INC.
See also
Commercial Intertech Corp.

COMMERCIAL TREATIES AND AGREEMENTS
See also
General Agreement on Tariffs and Trade
International Coffee Agreement

COMMERCIAL VIDEO LIBRARY (FIRM)
Tools of the trade. C. Reece. il *Channels (New York, N.Y.: 1986)* 9:28 Ja '89

COMMERCIALS *See* Television advertising

COMMERZBANK AKTIENGESELLSCHAFT
Post-1992 Europe [address, January 12, 1989] W. Seipp. *Vital Speeches of the Day* 55:300-3 Mr 1 '89

COMMISSARIAT *See* United States—Armed Forces—Commissariat

COMMISSION OF FINE ARTS (U.S.) *See* United States. Commission of Fine Arts

COMMISSION ON SCIENCE AND RESOURCE MANAGEMENT POLICY *See* National Parks and Conservation Association. Commission on Science and Resource Management Policy

COMMISSIONER OF BASEBALL *See* Baseball, Professional—Organization and administration

COMMISSIONS, GOVERNMENT *See* Government commissions

COMMISSIONS, INDEPENDENT REGULATORY *See* Regulatory agencies

COMMISSIONS (COMPENSATION)
See also
Brokers—Commissions
Investment advisers—Commissions
Sales personnel—Salaries, commissions, pensions, etc.

COMMITMENT (PSYCHOLOGY)
The big pullback [women] D. Heyn. *Mademoiselle* 95:84 Jl '89
Making and keeping commitments. J. P. Comer. il *Parents* 64:183 F '89
The no-regrets ultimatum. C. Bushnell. il *Mademoiselle* 95:186+ Ap '89
Social commitment: beyond self-interest. R. H. Frank. *Current (Washington, D.C.)* 316:4-13 O '89

COMMITTEE ON FOREIGN INVESTMENT IN THE UNITED STATES *See* United States. Committee on Foreign Investment in the United States

COMMITTEES, CONGRESSIONAL *See* United States. Congress—Committees

COMMODITY BROKERS
See also
Elders Futures Inc.
Henning-Krajewski Trading Company
Norman Kern & Company
Refco Group Ltd.
Women commodity brokers
Commissions
Heads you lose, tails you lose even more [B. Pearson's tale of trading in oil futures] R. L. Stern. *Forbes* 144:90-1 O 2 '89
Ethical aspects
A bid to salvage a go-go legacy [L. Melamed suggests areas for reform in wake of FBI investigation] W. McWhirter. il por *Time* 133:52 F 6 '89
Big trouble in the pits [indictment of Chicago commodities traders] T. Padgett. il *Newsweek* 114:36 Ag 14 '89
The CFTC drops its kid gloves. D. Zigas. il *Business Week* p142 My 22 '89
Commodities sting [FBI investigation of Chicago exchanges] J. J. Curran. il *Fortune* 119:12 F 13 '89
Crackdown on the Chicago boys [FBI uncovers widespread fraud in commodity markets] C. Gorman. il *Time* 133:52 Ja 30 '89
Did Refco help take Uncle Sam to the cleaners? [dodging taxes through phony London trading] D. Greising. il *Business Week* p33-4 O 2 '89
The feds strike again [New York commodity exchanges] *Newsweek* 113:52 My 15 '89
Futures shock: fraud charges shake the Chicago exchanges. D. Greising. il *Business Week* p44-5 Ag 14 '89
How scandal may change Chicago. *Successful Farming* 87:16 mid-Mr '89
In the futures pits, life is no longer a bowl of cherries [FBI uncovers fraud in Chicago's commodity exchanges] C. P. Work and R. F. Black. il *U.S. News & World Report* 106:44-5 F 6 '89
Life in the pits will never be the same [FBI sting of Chicago's trading system] K. A. Behof. il *Business Week* p32-4 F 6 '89
Life is the pits in Chicago's pits [probe of futures markets] il *U.S. News & World Report* 107:11-12 Ag 14 '89
More shoes drop in the pits [probe of Chicago's futures markets] D. Pauly. il *Newsweek* 113:50 F 6 '89
Production. G. Johnston. il *Successful Farming* 87:39 O '89
Snakes in the pits [FBI busts traders in Chicago] C. Gorman. il *Time* 134:52+ Ag 14 '89
The sting in the pits [FBI probe uncovers fraud at Chicago Board of Trade and Chicago Mercantile Exchange] J. McCormick. il *Newsweek* 113:54 Ja 30 '89
Was George Soros sheared by Shearson? [futures loss] D. Greising. il por *Business Week* p45 N 6 '89
You can almost hear a sigh of relief in the pits [Chicago probe] K. A. Behof. il *Business Week* p33 F 20 '89
Great Britain
See also
London & Atlantic Metal Brokers

COMMODITY CONTROL
Negotiations toward a new International Coffee Agreement [address, November 14, 1988] W. A. Wallis. *Department of State Bulletin* 89:15-17 Mr '89

COMMODITY EXCHANGES
See also
Chicago Board of Trade
Chicago Board Options Exchange
Chicago Mercantile Exchange
Commodity brokers
United States. Commodity Futures Trading Commission
Laws and regulations
How the futures markets can climb back out of the pits. D. Greising. il *Business Week* p29 Ag 21 '89
Sweating in the pits. D. Foust. il *Business Week* p45-6 N 6 '89

COMMODITY FUNDS
Commodity funds: an investment for all seasons. J. Friedman. il *Business Week* p86 Jl 24 '89
Elusive quarry. M. K. Evans. il *Gentlemen's Quarterly* 59:176+ My '89

COMMODITY FUTURES
See also
Chicago Board of Trade
Commodity brokers
Commodity funds
Hedging (Finance)
Interest rate futures
Random access memory futures
Stock index futures
United States. Commodity Futures Trading Commission
As peace breaks out, the pits should keep hopping. D. Greising. il *Business Week* p136-7 D 25 '89-Ja 1 '90
The Beijing factor makes this the year of the slide. D. Greising. il *Business Week* p106+ Je 26 '89
Farmer/adviser puts his money where his advice is [W. De Young] *Successful Farming* 87:50E Ja '89
Ferruzzi trading "illogical" for many months. *Successful Farming* 87:48P N '89
Futuristic markets [proposed futures markets for dynamic random access memory chips] E. Corcoran. il *Scientific American* 261:62-3 Ag '89
Heads you lose, tails you lose even more [B. Pearson's tale of trading in oil futures] R. L. Stern. *Forbes* 144:90-1 O 2 '89
An Italian 'peasant' who would be soybean king [Ferruzzi chairman R. Gardini's attempt to corner U.S. soybean market] E. Pomice. il por *U.S. News & World Report* 107:44-5 Ag 7 '89
Look at the crack spreads [energy securities analyst B. Sahgal checks spread between gasoline and crude oil futures prices] S. N. Chakravarty. il por *Forbes* 143:86+ My 29 '89
Why the pits are sick over soybeans [Chicago Board of Trade directive, in response to Ferruzzi Group maneuvers, sends prices tumbling] D. Greising. il *Business Week* p76+ Jl 31 '89

COMMODITY FUTURES TRADING COMMISSION *See* United States. Commodity Futures Trading Commission

COMMODITY OPTIONS
See also
Chicago Board Options Exchange
Stock index options

COMMODITY PARTNERSHIP
Heads they win, tails you lose. D. N. Dreman. il *Forbes* 143:114 Ja 23 '89

COMMODITY PRICES *See* Prices

COMMODORE INTERNATIONAL LTD.
Lost opportunity? E. McGlinn. il por *Forbes* 144:288+ N 13 '89

COMMODORES (MUSICAL GROUP)
S. Africa tour furor basis for Milan Williams firing from 'Commodores' group. il por *Jet* 76:17 Ag 14 '89

COMMON CAUSE (U.S.)
Ethics watchdog Fred Wertheimer: when he barks, Congress listens. B. Hewitt. il pors *People Weekly* 32:163-4 D 18 '89
In Common. See issues of Common Cause Magazine

COMMON CAUSE PUBLIC SERVICE ACHIEVEMENT AWARDS
Common Cause Public Service Achievement Awards. il *Common Cause Magazine* 15:41-3 My/Je '89

COMMON FUND
Big money manager on campus [G. Keane] G. G. Marcial. il por *Business Week* p88 Ag 21 '89

COMMON LAW MARRIAGE
Houston jury decides Winfield already wed. il pors *Jet* 76:28-9 Jl 17 '89
Love, hurt and money [courtroom proceedings in case of actor W. Hurt vs. ex-lover S. Jennings; cover story] S. Schindehette. il pors *People Weekly* 32:72-4+ Jl 10 '89
Marriage by another name. G. Carroll. il *Newsweek* 114:46-7 Jl 24 '89
An uncommon marriage [D. Winfield and S. Renfro] il pors *People Weekly* 32:79 Ag 7 '89
Winfield must pay support, plans appeal of decision. pors *Jet* 76:50 Jl 31 '89

COMMON MARKET *See* European Economic Community
COMMON STOCKS *See* Stocks
COMMONS, JOHN R., 1862-1945
about
John R. Commons: pioneer of labor economics [cover story] J. Barbash. bibl f *Monthly Labor Review* 112:44-9 My '89
COMMONWEAL (PERIODICAL)
65 [special issue] il *Commonweal* 116:611-32+ N 17 '89
Of many things [editor M. O. Steinfels] G. W. Hunt. *America* 160:546 Je 10 '89
COMMONWEAL CANCER HELP PROGRAM
Daring to care [work of M. Lerner] V. Brower. il por *American Health* 8:62-4 Ap '89
COMMONWEALTH OF NATIONS
Conferences
Canada in a hot seat [business transactions with South Africa questioned] M. Nemeth. il por *Maclean's* 102:21 F 20 '89
Family quarrel [British opposition to sanctions against South Africa at summit in Kuala Lumpur, Malaysia] R. Laver. il *Maclean's* 102:40-1 O 30 '89
The Thatcher factor [banks reschedule South African debt] R. Laver. il *Maclean's* 102:42 O 30 '89
A thorny dispute [Britain refuses to endorse call for sanctions against South Africa at conference in Malaysia] R. Laver. il por *Maclean's* 102:36-7 N 6 '89
COMMUNAL LIVING *See* Housing, Cooperative
COMMUNAL SETTLEMENTS *See* Collective settlements
COMMUNE DE PARIS, 1871 *See* Paris (France)—History—Commune, 1871
COMMUNES *See* Collective settlements
COMMUNICABLE DISEASES
See also
Animals as carriers of infection
Centers for Disease Control (U.S.)
Cold (Disease)
Epidemiology
Malaria
Measles
Mumps
National Institute of Allergy and Infectious Diseases (U.S.)
Quarantine
Sexually transmitted diseases
Smallpox
Typhoid fever
Vaccines and vaccination
Waterborne infection
Communicable diseases [Eastern Mediterranean] M. H. Wahdan. il *World Health* p20-1 Jl '89
Coordinate regulation and sensory transduction in the control of bacterial virulence. J. F. Miller and others. bibl f il *Science* 243:916-22 F 17 '89
How did you catch that? M. Oppenheim. il *Better Homes and Gardens* 67:46+ O '89
Setting the stage for infection [lowered response rate of natural killer cells; research by Sandra M. Levy] B. Bower. *Science News* 136:141 Ag 26 '89
COMMUNICATION
See also
Aviation—Communication systems
Communications satellites
Conversation
Cybernetics
Infrared communications
Intercultural communication
Interstellar communication
Language and languages
Language arts
Lasers—Communication use
Light communication systems
Mass media
Neurolinguistics
Persuasion (Psychology)
Public relations
Space stations—Communication systems
Space vehicles—Communication systems
Speech
Telecommunication
International aspects
See also
World Association for Christian Communication
Social aspects
The 10 worst things you can say to your kids (and how to stop saying them). A. Van der Meer. il *Redbook* 174:32+ N '89
Helping kids communicate. L. Salk. il *McCall's* 116:63 Mr '89
How much should we tell our kids? L. Salk. il *McCall's* 116:53 Jl '89
How to deal with difficult people [condensed from The feeling good handbook] D. D. Burns. *Reader's Digest* 135:113-15 D '89
How to say the right thing. S. Horwitz. il *Reader's Digest* 134:161-4 Mr '89
How to talk to each other . . . without yelling and screaming [views of Bonnie Jacobson] il *Glamour* 87:115 Ap '89

How to talk to your teenager. M. S. Miller. il *Good Housekeeping* 209:251 O '89
"Let's not discuss it". C. L. Mithers. il *Glamour* 87:340 S '89
Let's talk. J. Segal and Z. Segal. il *Parents* 64:148 Ag '89
Love is never enough [problem of automatic thoughts] A. T. Beck. *Reader's Digest* 134:57-8+ Ap '89
Not alone—but lonely. J. Stone. il *Glamour* 87:148 My '89
Signing off. P. Theroux. il *Parents* 64:51-2 N '89
Stickum up, love! [family communication via Post-It Notes] J. G. Hubbell. *Reader's Digest* 135:123-5 O '89
Table talk: the family detective story [research by Elinor Ochs] il *USA Today (Periodical)* 118:9 Jl '89
Tell me about your day. il *Glamour* 87:183 Ap '89
Things my children never told me [mother and daughter talk over old wounds] P. Theroux. il *Parents* 64:59-60+ O '89
Study and teaching
See also
Annenberg School of Communications
COMMUNICATION, ANIMAL *See* Animal communication
COMMUNICATION, CHEMICAL *See* Pheromones
COMMUNICATION, FIBER OPTIC *See* Fiber optics
COMMUNICATION, NONVERBAL
See also
Facial expression
Gesture
Sign language
Smiles
Touch
The way you walk that walk . . . [clue to personality and mood] H. E. Fisher. il *Health (New York, N.Y.)* 21:53-5+ S '89
Photographs and photography
The eyes have it [eye contact with viewer as depicted in photo of R. Urich] G. Bernstein. il por *Petersen's Photographic Magazine* 18:10 Je '89
COMMUNICATION (THEOLOGY)
See also
Direct broadcast satellite services—Religious programs
Mass media in religion
Radio broadcasting—Religious programs
Television broadcasting—Religious programs
World Association for Christian Communication
COMMUNICATION IN EDUCATION
Parent-teacher communication techniques [preschool] E. L. Morgan. *The Education Digest* 55:32-5 O '89
COMMUNICATION IN GOVERNMENT
See also
Government publicity
Opening doors: making risk communication agency reality [environmental protection agencies] C. Chess and B. J. Hance. bibl f il *Environment* 31:10-15+ Je '89
COMMUNICATION IN MANAGEMENT
See also
Business presentations
Business writing
Employee handbooks, manuals, etc.
Telecommunication in business
Beyond whistleblowing. S. C. Florman. il *Technology Review* 92:20+ Jl '89
Do you keep too many secrets? B. Benson. il *Nation's Business* 77:42+ Ag '89
The fine art of giving instructions. E. J. Belzer. *Working Woman* 14:14 F '89
How managers should handle staff conflicts [excerpt from One-on-one with Andy Grove] A. S. Grove. il *Working Woman* 14:146-8 N '89
How to defuse employee outbursts. M. R. Feinberg. *Working Woman* 14:26 D '89
How to get good ideas out of quiet employees [corporate meetings] P. Amend. *Working Woman* 14:44+ S '89
How to give feedback your staff can use [excerpt from One-on-one with Andy Grove] A. S. Grove. il *Working Woman* 14:54+ S '89
Listen carefully. T. W. Harris. il *Nation's Business* 77:78 Je '89
Straight talk from key employees [family owned business] R. S. Rapoza and L. C. Lancaster. il *Nation's Business* 77:40 N '89
The trust gap [employer-employee relations; cover story] A. Farnham. il *Fortune* 120:56-8+ D 4 '89
Turning confrontations into calm conversations [excerpt from 88 mistakes interviewers make and how to avoid them] A. Uris. il *Working Woman* 14:140-1+ S '89
COMMUNICATION IN POLITICS
See also
Television and politics
Misreading the shorthand. M. Greenfield. il *Newsweek* 114:100 D 11 '89
COMMUNICATION IN SCIENCE
See also
Exchanges, Literary and scientific
Science news
Restraints to communication for ecologists in developing countries [survey results] J. H. Cooley and F. B. Golley. bibl f il *BioScience* 39:805-9 D '89

COMMUNICATION IN SCIENCE—*cont.*

Suckers for science [conflicting results of carcinogenic risk studies] E. Kunes. *Omni (New York, N.Y.)* 11:25 Jl '89

COMMUNICATION OF TECHNICAL INFORMATION

See also

Aviation—Communication systems

Science news

Bolstering your high-tech image. M. Spaeth. il *High Technology Business* 9:26+ Ja '89

Opening doors: making risk communication agency reality [environmental protection agencies] C. Chess and B. J. Hance. bibl f il *Environment* 31:10-15+ Je '89

COMMUNICATION SATELLITES *See* Communications satellites

COMMUNICATION WITH THE DEAD *See* Spiritualism

COMMUNICATIONS, MILITARY

See also

Communications satellites—Military use

Submarines—Communication systems

Telephone—Military use

Television and the military

Air Force pursues photonics research [special section] il *Aviation Week & Space Technology* 130:54-8+ Ja 30 '89

Air Force selects Computer Sciences Corp. to develop information processing system [tracking Military Airlift Command aircraft] *Aviation Week & Space Technology* 130:51-2 Ja 23 '89

America's Doomsday Project [preserving the government in the event of a first strike] S. Emerson. il *U.S. News & World Report* 107:26-31 Ag 7 '89

Boeing told to solve Peace Shield problems [system for Saudi Arabia] D. Hughes. *Aviation Week & Space Technology* 131:114 D 18-25 '89

Gains in satellite technology shape trends in C³ development. P. J. Klass. il *Aviation Week & Space Technology* 130:251+ Mr 20 '89

Grumman lab will support variety of systems efforts. S. W. Kandebo. il *Aviation Week & Space Technology* 130:59+ My 1 '89

Military systems use new communications technologies. il *Aviation Week & Space Technology* 131:50-1 O 30 '89

My life as a NATO collaborator [pacifist computer scientist attends NATO workshop on computer-human interaction in command and control; cover story] N. S. Borenstein. il *The Bulletin of the Atomic Scientists* 45:14-20 Ap '89

Pentagon uses new computer system to help action teams manage crises [crisis management automatic data processing system] B. D. Nordwall. il *Aviation Week & Space Technology* 131:43+ D 4 '89

The watershed decade [address, June 20, 1989] J. D. Cosgrove. *Vital Speeches of the Day* 55:744-7 O 1 '89

COMMUNICATIONS, PRIVILEGED *See* Confidential communications

COMMUNICATIONS EQUITY ASSOCIATES

CEA's entertaining mix. M. Brown. il por *Channels (New York, N.Y.: 1986)* 9:73 S '89

COMMUNICATIONS EXCELLENCE TO BLACK AUDIENCES AWARDS

Johnson Publishing wins top honors at CEBA Awards. il *Jet* 77:54-5 D 11 '89

COMMUNICATIONS MUSEUMS

See also

National Museum of Communications (Irving, Tex.)

COMMUNICATIONS SATELLITE CORP.

Beam me up, Comsat. T. Jaffe. *Forbes* 143:414-15 My 1 '89

Panamsat files antitrust lawsuit against Comsat. *Aviation Week & Space Technology* 131:28 Jl 31 '89

COMMUNICATIONS SATELLITES

See also

Communications Satellite Corp.

General Electric Co. Astro Space Division

Hughes Aircraft Co.

INSCOM (Firm)

Vitalink Communications Corporation

Spy satellites: entering a new era [Tracking and Data Relay Satellite] D. Charles. il *Science* 243:1541-3 Mr 24 '89

Accidents

Insat satellite damaged after hoist cable snaps. *Aviation Week & Space Technology* 130:33 Je 26 '89

Antitrust cases

Panamsat files antitrust lawsuit against Comsat. *Aviation Week & Space Technology* 131:28 Jl 31 '89

Aviation use

See also

Inmarsat satellites

Carriers, manufacturers assess aerosat communication systems. P. J. Klass. il map *Aviation Week & Space Technology* 130:54-5 Ja 9 '89

Satcom calling [air ambulance equipped with Aerosat communications system] il *Flying* 116:19 F '89

Tests demonstrate potential benefits of satellites in air-ground communications. P. J. Klass. il *Aviation Week & Space Technology* 130:57+ Jl 10 '89

Defects

Technical problems with Japanese satellite could disrupt Ariane's payload launch sequence [traveling wave tube amplifier on Superbird B telecommunications satellite] il *Aviation Week & Space Technology* 131:30 N 13 '89

Design

Advances to boost power, capability of commercial communications satellites. M. A. Dornheim. il *Aviation Week & Space Technology* 130:124-6 Mr 20 '89

Economic aspects

Advances to boost power, capability of commercial communications satellites. M. A. Dornheim. il *Aviation Week & Space Technology* 130:124-6 Mr 20 '89

Changing orbits [fiber optics vs. satellites] M. Beauchamp. il *Forbes* 143:273-5 My 29 '89

Comsat study shows satellites competing successfully with fiber-optic cables. M. Mecham. *Aviation Week & Space Technology* 130:131 F 20 '89

Pennies from heaven. M. R. Chartrand. *Ad Astra* 1:38 D '89

Ground stations

Doing the dishes: a TV bonanza is up there in orbit. D. Stewart. il *Smithsonian* 20:156-60+ O '89

The FCC sends DBS flying. S. Chase. il *Channels (New York, N.Y.: 1986)* 9:97 D '89

Satellite TV's new landscape. R. Angus. il *Video* 13:56-8+ Jl '89

These dishes serve up a TV smorgasbord. S. Woolley. il *Business Week* p117 O 2 '89

Launching

Ariane 4 vehicle to orbit Hughes payloads in 1990. *Aviation Week & Space Technology* 131:35 Jl 24 '89

Brazil, China form space launch venture [INSCOM] E. H. Kolcum. il *Aviation Week & Space Technology* 130:35 My 29 '89

China agrees to limit marketing of Long March booster in U.S. C. Covault. il *Aviation Week & Space Technology* 130:37 Ja 2 '89

Discovery crew deploys TDRS, tests space station system. C. Covault. il *Aviation Week & Space Technology* 130:264-5 Mr 20 '89

First commercial Titan prepared for September launch. il *Aviation Week & Space Technology* 130:97 My 1 '89

Joint Atlas Centaur mission orbits FltSatCom spacecraft [Fleet Satellite Communication] E. H. Kolcum. il *Aviation Week & Space Technology* 131:23 O 2 '89

Pegasus, Ball to launch communication satellites into geosynchronous orbit. il *Aviation Week & Space Technology* 130:64 Je 12 '89

Shuttle Mission 29 set to conduct space station test, deploy TDRS [Tracking and Data Relay Satellite system] C. Covault. il *Aviation Week & Space Technology* 129:48-9 Mr 6 '89

U.S., China initial agreement on communications satellites [State Dept. statement, December 19, 1988] *Department of State Bulletin* 89:26-7 F '89

USAF launches twin strategic communications satellites. E. H. Kolcum. il *Aviation Week & Space Technology* 130:24 My 15 '89

Maritime use

See also

Inmarsat satellites

International Maritime Satellite Organization

Military use

First Milstar satellite to undergo final integration tests in 1990. P. J. Klass. il *Aviation Week & Space Technology* 130:61-3 Ap 3 '89

Gains in satellite technology shape trends in C³ development. P. J. Klass. il *Aviation Week & Space Technology* 130:251+ Mr 20 '89

General Dynamics will launch first Navy UHF follow-on satellite [Atlas booster] *Aviation Week & Space Technology* 131:22 Ag 21 '89

Joint Atlas Centaur mission orbits FltSatCom spacecraft [Fleet Satellite Communication] E. H. Kolcum. il *Aviation Week & Space Technology* 131:23 O 2 '89

Laser-based communication system eyed. *High Technology Business* 9:35 F '89

Milstar terminal capability demonstrated as Congress debates program budget. D. Hughes. il *Aviation Week & Space Technology* 131:49-50 O 30 '89

Shuttle Columbia poised to retrieve LDEF satellite, deploy Navy Syncom [Long-Duration Exposure Facility] C. Covault. il *Aviation Week & Space Technology* 131:35-6 D 11 '89

USAF launches twin strategic communications satellites. E. H. Kolcum. il *Aviation Week & Space Technology* 130:24 My 15 '89

Radio broadcasting use

See also

Satellite Music Network

Radiotelephone use

Teleglobe Canada to team on mobile satellite service. *Aviation Week & Space Technology* 131:81 Ag 21 '89

Television broadcasting use

See also

American Business Network

Cable News Network

COMMUNICATIONS SATELLITES—Television broadcasting use—See also—*cont.*

Direct broadcast satellite services

Breaking through [satellite master antenna television] R. Katz. il *Channels (New York, N.Y.: 1986)* 9:92 D '89

Doing the dishes: a TV bonanza is up there in orbit. D. Stewart. il *Smithsonian* 20:156-60+ O '89

The FCC sends DBS flying. S. Chase. il *Channels (New York, N.Y.: 1986)* 9:97 D '89

Satellite TV's new landscape. R. Angus. il *Video* 13:56-8+ Jl '89

These dishes serve up a TV smorgasbord. S. Woolley. il *Business Week* p117 O 2 '89

Tracking and trailing use

Bureau of Land Management evaluates automated flight following system [Radio Determination Satellite System] il *Aviation Week & Space Technology* 130:32-3 Je 26 '89

Glavcosmos signs Energetics as first U.S. launch customer [Proton rockets] J. R. Asker. il *Aviation Week & Space Technology* 131:40 N 20 '89

Tracking trucks by satellite. R. Schneiderman. il *High Technology Business* 9:24-6+ My '89

COMMUNICATIONS SATELLITES, BRITISH

U.S. reenters commercial launch arena with private Delta mission [launch of television relay spacecraft Marcopolo] E. H. Kolcum. il *Aviation Week & Space Technology* 131:24-5 S 4 '89

COMMUNICATIONS SATELLITES, GERMAN

German, Japanese satellites launched by Ariane 4 version. il *Aviation Week & Space Technology* 130:67 Je 12 '89

COMMUNICATIONS SATELLITES, INDIAN (EAST INDIAN)

Insat satellite damaged after hoist cable snaps. *Aviation Week & Space Technology* 130:33 Je 26 '89

COMMUNICATIONS SATELLITES, JAPANESE

Arianespace launches JCSAT, Meteosat; nine Ariane missions planned for 1989. J. M. Lenorovitz. il *Aviation Week & Space Technology* 130:29-30 Mr 13 '89

German, Japanese satellites launched by Ariane 4 version. il *Aviation Week & Space Technology* 130:67 Je 12 '89

Technical problems with Japanese satellite could disrupt Ariane's payload launch sequence [traveling wave tube amplifier on Superbird B telecommunications satellite] il *Aviation Week & Space Technology* 131:30 N 13 '89

COMMUNICATIONS SATELLITES, LATIN AMERICAN

See also

Pan American Satellite Corporation

COMMUNICATIONS SATELLITES, SPANISH

France's Matra will cooperate with Spain to develop Hispasat satellite network. J. M. Lenorovitz. maps *Aviation Week & Space Technology* 131:93 Jl 17 '89

COMMUNICATIONS SECURITY ESTABLISHMENT (CANADA) *See* Canada. Communications Security Establishment

COMMUNICATIONS SOFTWARE

Coming together [special section] il *Compute!* 11:20-2+ Mr '89

Computer mating. L. Van Gelder. il *Ms.* 17:34-5 Je '89

Put your computer to work while you're away [private bulletin board system] A. Glossbrenner. il *Home Office Computing* 7:36 My '89

Testing

The Bentley of communications programs [Crosstalk Mk.4] H. F. Beechhold. il *Home Office Computing* 7:84+ N '89

Communications get Hyper [HyperAccess/5] S. Miastkowski. *Byte* 14:84 O '89

Dialing up 1990. B. N. Meeks. il *Byte* 14:273-4+ Ja '89

A guide to painless telecommunications. S. Morgenstern. il *Home Office Computing* 7:59-62 Je '89

ProComm+ and Smartcom III. il *Radio-Electronics* 60 ComputerDigest:89 Ja '89

Reasonably priced modem software [Mirror III] T. A. Summers. il *Home Office Computing* 7:83-4 N '89

Remote computing with Co/Session. R. Lockwood. *Personal Computing* 13:162 Ag '89

Telecommunications software. C. D. Hanlon. *Compute!* 11:48-51 Ap '89

COMMUNICATIONS WORKERS OF AMERICA

AT&T settlement. *Monthly Labor Review* 112:49-50 Ag '89

Who won what at AT&T? L. A. Winokur. il *The Progressive* 53:29-32 D '89

COMMUNION *See* Anglican Communion; Catholic Church—Eucharist; Lord's Supper

COMMUNION [film] See Motion picture reviews—Single works

COMMUNISM

See also

Anti-Communist movements

Motion picture industry—Communist activities

Atari Communists: from hardline to software [effects of *perestroika*; cover story; special section; with editorial comment by Nathan Gardels] il *New Perspectives Quarterly* 5:2-60 Wint '88/'89

Collapse of communism [cover story; special section; with editorial comment by David Gergen] il map *U.S. News & World Report* 106:18-23+, 76 Je 19 '89

Defiance [cover story; special section] S. Talbott. il *Time* 133:11-22+ Je 19 '89

Economics made easy. R. J. Samuelson. il *Newsweek* 114:64 N 27 '89

End of the Marxist epoch. D. P. Moynihan. il *The New Leader* 72:9-11 Ja 23 '89

The irony of capitalism. R. J. Samuelson. il *Newsweek* 113:44 Ja 9 '89

Is communism reversible? [cover story] J.-F. Revel. *Commentary* 87:17-24 Ja '89

Marx is not quite dead. D. Selbourne. *World Press Review* 36:20+ O '89

Minority report [discussion of A. Cockburn's Stalinist leanings] C. Hitchens. *The Nation* 249:375 O 9 '89

A murderous word [adaptation of address, November 1988] H. Zinn. il *The Progressive* 53:16-17 F '89

'Not the end of socialism'. A. Das Gupta. *World Press Review* 36:26 Ag '89

Notes and comment [U.S. should stay clear of moral superiority in rebuking communism] *The New Yorker* 65:25-6 Je 26 '89

On the Atari Communists [discussion of Winter 1988-89 special section, Atari Communists: from hardline to software] *New Perspectives Quarterly* 6:60-1 Spr '89

The roots of communism. S. Manning. il *Scholastic Update (Teachers' edition)* 121:3 My 5 '89

Testing time for both socialism and capitalism. A. Chambraud. il *World Press Review* 36:11-13 D '89

They said it. D. Seligman. il *Fortune* 120:231 D 18 '89

This is the way a world ends. *National Review* 41:11-12 Ag 4 '89

Totalitarianism, dead and alive. S. Miller. *Commentary* 88:28-32 Ag '89

Who killed communism? M. Kinsley. *The New Republic* 201:4 D 4 '89

Who's burying whom? A. Cockburn. *The Nation* 248:222 F 20 '89

The world war created [World War II] M. B. Zuckerman. il map *U.S. News & World Report* 107:68-9+ Ag 28-S 4 '89

History

Cracking the ice. G. F. Will. il *Newsweek* 113:72 Je 19 '89

Truth and consequences [struggle for historical truth in the Soviet bloc] R. Knight. il *U.S. News & World Report* 106:33-4 Je 26 '89

Terminology

No leading role. W. Safire. il *The New York Times Magazine* p16+ D 17 '89

China

China and the U.S.S.R.: the changing face of communism [cover story; special issue] il map *Scholastic Update (Teachers' edition)* 121:2-12+ My 5 '89

Communism in turmoil [cover story; special section] il map *Business Week* p34-41+ Je 5 '89

The words of Marx, the methods of Lenin. G. Jochnowitz. *National Review* 41:31-2 Ag 4 '89

Cuba

The Albania of the Caribbean. R. Grenier. il *National Review* 41:41-3 My 5 '89

Castro keeps the faith—but can he keep it alone? A. Fins. il *Business Week* p81 D 11 '89

Czechoslovakia

See also

Communist Party (Czechoslovakia)

Czechoslovakia: realistic socialism? O. Ulč. bibl f *Current History* 88:389-92+ N '89

Eastern Europe

Communism at the crossroads in Eastern Europe. R. F. Staar. il *USA Today (Periodical)* 117:46-7 My '89

Democrat of the breakfast table. J. O'Sullivan. *National Review* 41:7 D 8 '89

Eastern Europe: the Iron Curtain cracks [cover story; special issue] il map *Scholastic Update (Teachers' edition)* 122:1-23 O 20 '89

Europe's second Reformation. G. F. Will. il *Newsweek* 114:90 N 20 '89

In Eastern Europe, little things count [move from a Communist to a free economy] M. Novak. *The Christian Century* 106:1164-5 D 13 '89

Lech Walesa, superstar, now faces the music. S. V. Roberts. il por *U.S. News & World Report* 107:10-11 N 27 '89

Life under communism today. A. Puddington. *Commentary* 87:32-8 F '89

Some ironies of Communist history. D. Heim. *The Christian Century* 106:1107-8 N 29 '89

Soviet-East European relations. A. R. Rachwald. bibl f *Current History* 88:377-80+ N '89

Watching a failed order die [interview with Z. Brzezinski] L. Kramer. il por *People Weekly* 32:49 N 27 '89

What's behind the 'Sinatra Doctrine' [Soviet influence over East European reforms] *U.S. News & World Report* 107:22 N 20 '89

Workers of the world ignite. D. Stanglin. il *U.S. News & World Report* 107:48-9 O 30 '89

Hungary

See also

Communist Party (Hungary)

COMMUNISM—*cont.*

Soviet Union

China and the U.S.S.R.: the changing face of communism [cover story; special issue] il map *Scholastic Update (Teachers' edition)* 121:2-12+ My 5 '89

The coming crack-up of communism [cover story; special section] il *National Review* 41:28-32 Ja 27 '89

Communism in crisis [views of Z. Brzezinski] R. K. Bennett. por *Reader's Digest* 135:99-104 Jl '89

Communism in turmoil [cover story; special section] il map *Business Week* p34-41+ Je 5 '89

Don't die yet. D. R. Carlin, Jr. *Commonweal* 116:265 My 5 '89

End of the Marxist epoch. D. P. Moynihan. il *The New Leader* 72:9-11 Ja 23 '89

The future of communism. R. K. Dornan. il *Conservative Digest* 15:12-15 S/O '89

Hastening the death of communism. J.-F. Revel. *Commentary* 88:19-23 O '89

How to dismantle communism [interview with I. Birman] P. Lubin. il *National Review* 41:29-33 D 8 '89

I was a teenage Communist. A. P. Tobias. il *Time* 134:39 Jl 31 '89

The ideology crisis. M. Sieff. *National Review* 41:30 Ap 7 '89

Life under communism today. A. Puddington. *Commentary* 87:32-8 F '89

The perils of *perestroika*. B. Rumer and G. Schoenfeld. il *The New Leader* 72:7-9 Ag 7-21 '89

Plastics. L. Wieseltier. *The New Republic* 200:4 Ja 2 '89

The rebirth of history. B. Crozier. *National Review* 41:18 D 22 '89

Will the Soviet empire self-destruct? Z. Brzezinski. il *The New York Times Magazine* p38+ F 26 '89

Will the Soviet Union survive until 1994? [interview with B. Shragin; cover story] D. Evanier. *National Review* 41:24+ Ap 7 '89

Anecdotes, facetiae, satire, etc.

How to save communism: a modest prospectus [leveraged buyout of Soviet Union] M. D. Coleman. *National Review* 41:36-7 Mr 24 '89

United States

See also

Rosenberg (Julius and Ethel) case

The wounds of *glasnost* [apprehension of the American left over changes in Soviet Union] A. Puddington. il *National Review* 41:26-8 N 24 '89

COMMUNISM AND DEMOCRACY

The beginning of nonsense [F. Fukuyama's theory of the end of history] S. Talbott. il *Time* 134:39 S 11 '89

Communism, capitalism, and dissent. D. E. Koshland, Jr. *Science* 245:109 Jl 14 '89

The end of history—or of liberalism? [views of F. Fukuyama] J. Gray. *National Review* 41:33-5 O 27 '89

The end of what? [theory of F. Fukuyama] R. E. Tyrrell. *The American Spectator* 22:10 N '89

Endgames [essays by F. Fukuyama and B. McKibben predicting the end of history and the end of nature] L. H. Lapham. *Harper's* 279:10-13 N '89

Entering post-history. F. Fukuyama. il *New Perspectives Quarterly* 6:49-52 Fall '89

Europe's second Reformation. G. F. Will. il *Newsweek* 114:90 N 20 '89

Freedom gusts on. P. Yancey. il *Christianity Today* 33:80 O 20 '89

Has history come to an end? [views of F. Fukuyama] J. Elson. il por *Time* 134:57 S 4 '89

Hastening the death of communism. J.-F. Revel. *Commentary* 88:19-23 O '89

History's last word? [views of F. Fukuyama] G. F. Will. il *Newsweek* 114:66 Ag 14 '89

How China's chaos affects the West. R. I. Kirkland, Jr. il *Fortune* 119:77-8 Je 19 '89

If communism fails, do we win? C. W. Colson. il *Christianity Today* 33:64 O 6 '89

Images of '89: the year that changed the world [special section; with editorial comment by Kevin Doyle] il *Maclean's* 102:2, 30-2+ D 18 '89

The intellectual Hula Hoop [end of history theory by F. Fukuyama] J. Alter. il *Newsweek* 114:39 O 9 '89

Is history over? [views of F. Fukuyama] *National Review* 41:14-15 S 1 '89

Lessons in humility. K. Kolenda. *The Humanist* 49:47 Ja/F '89

Minority report [F. Fukuyama's theory of the end of history] C. Hitchens. *The Nation* 249:302 S 25 '89

Nothing inevitable about democracy. K. Burris. *The Christian Century* 106:807 S 13-20 '89

People of the year [cover story; special section] il *Newsweek* 114:18-26+ D 25 '89

Reflections on the cold war: end of the game, or end of an inning? P. Mann. il *Aviation Week & Space Technology* 131:18-19 D 18-25 '89

Some ironies of Communist history. D. Heim. *The Christian Century* 106:1107-8 N 29 '89

Stopping time [views of F. Fukuyama] R. Corelli. il *Maclean's* 102:56+ O 2 '89

Washington diarist: the end of everything [views of F. Fukuyama] T. Noah. *The New Republic* 201:54 O 16 '89

What is Fukuyama saying? And to whom is he saying it? [essay on the end of history] J. Atlas. il por *The New York Times Magazine* p38-40+ O 22 '89

COMMUNISM AND EDUCATION

The Gramscists are. coming [Marxist analysis] M. Novak. il por *Forbes* 143:54 Mr 20 '89

Pride and perjury [firing of teacher and scientist A. Novikoff for Communist activities by the University of Vermont during McCarthy era] D. M. Oshinsky. por *The New Leader* 72:14-17 S 4 '89

COMMUNISM AND JEWS

Anti-Semitism [discussion of August 1988 article, Communism, anti-Semitism & the Jews] J. Z. Muller. *Commentary* 87:11-12+ Ja '89

COMMUNISM AND RELIGION

See also

Catholic Church—China

Catholic Church—Czechoslovakia

Catholic Church—Eastern Europe

Catholic Church—Hungary

Catholic Church—Poland

Catholic Church—Vietnam

CAUSA (Organization)

Christians—China

Christians—Eastern Europe

Christians—Germany (East)

Christians—Soviet Union

Christians—Vietnam

Church and state—Czechoslovakia

Church and state—Soviet Union

Pentecostal churches—Soviet Union

Protestant churches—Germany (East)

Soviet Union—Religious institutions and affairs

No more bad guys? L. Cryderman. il *Christianity Today* 33:16 My 12 '89

Perestroika in the pulpit? M. Novak. il *Forbes* 144:98-9 Jl 24 '89

The Vatican and the Kremlin: full circle. W. Doino, Jr. *National Review* 41:30 Je 30 '89

COMMUNISM IN DRAMA

The shrillest Stalinist [B. Brecht] R. Grenier. il *National Review* 41:53-4 N 24 '89

COMMUNIST COUNTRIES

See also

Albania

China

Czechoslovakia

Eastern Europe

Freedom of information—Communist countries

Germany (East)

Poland

Romania

Soviet Union

Telecommunication—Communist countries

Vietnam

Yugoslavia

Communism confronts its children. R. Hornik. il *Time* 133:126 My 22 '89

Images of '89: the year that changed the world [special section; with editorial comment by Kevin Doyle] il *Maclean's* 102:2, 30-2+ D 18 '89

Commerce

United States

See United States—Commerce—Communist countries

Economic policy

Can Marxist economies make it to market? L. Lief. *U.S. News & World Report* 107:47 Ag 21 '89

What price freedom? J. Klein. il *New York* 22:12+ Je 19 '89

Foreign relations

Canada

See Canada—Foreign relations—Communist countries

United States

See United States—Foreign relations—Communist countries

Nationalism

Torn by nationalism [cover story; special section] il *World Press Review* 36:11-19 Je '89

COMMUNIST PARTY (CHINA)

China erupts . . . the reasons why [cover story] N. D. Kristof. il *The New York Times Magazine* p26-9+ Je 4 '89

China: the party wins. B. Crozier. *National Review* 41:39-40 Je 30 '89

'Order' is restored—for now [special section] il *World Press Review* 36:22-4+ Ag '89

Rise of a perfect apparatchik [Jiang Zemin] W. R. Doerner. il por *Time* 134:32 Jl 10 '89

COMMUNIST PARTY (CZECHOSLOVAKIA)

Czech-out time. J. Škvorecký. *The New Republic* 201:15-17 D 25 '89

COMMUNIST PARTY (GERMANY: EAST)

East Germany: coping with Gorbachev. D. Childs. bibl f *Current History* 88:385-8+ N '89

COMMUNIST PARTY (GERMANY: EAST)—cont.
Filling the void [leadership changes] J. Bierman. il Maclean's 102:24+ D 18 '89
COMMUNIST PARTY (HUNGARY)
'Feeling our way to the future'. R. Watson. il Newsweek 114:36-7 O 23 '89
Hungary on the way to democracy. R. L. Tőkés. il The New Leader 72:9-11 S 18 '89
Hungary's hazy future. R. L. Tőkés. il The New Leader 72:5-7 O 30 '89
Hungary's quiet revolution. J. Rupnik. The New Republic 201:18-20+ N 20 '89
Letter from Budapest [party congress] D. K. Shipler. The New Yorker 65:74+ N 20 '89
Now you see it . . . [rejection of communism; with interview with I. Pozsgay] J. Borrell. il por Time 134:46+ O 23 '89
COMMUNIST PARTY (ITALY)
Achille's gamble [General Secretary A. Occhetto] D. Singer. The Nation 248:545 Ap 24 '89
The end of communism in Italy. E. Van den Haag. il National Review 41:21-2 D 8 '89
COMMUNIST PARTY (PHILIPPINES)
See also
New People's Army (Philippines)
COMMUNIST PARTY (POLAND)
The defeated party plays for time. J. Baczynski and A. Krzeminski. World Press Review 36:29-30 Ag '89
COMMUNIST PARTY (SOVIET UNION)
And now for my next trick . . . [M. Gorbachev forces members of Central Committee to resign] J. Kohan. il Time 133:41-2 My 8 '89
Dead souls. The Nation 248:687-8 My 22 '89
Exorcising the 'dead souls' [purge at the Plenum] A. Platt. il por Newsweek 113:37 My 8 '89
From now on, the buck stops here [purge at the Politburo] J. Trimble. il U.S. News & World Report 107:40 O 2 '89
Gorbachev's 'coup' [purge of hardliners from Politburo] A. Wilson-Smith. il por Maclean's 102:28-30 O 2 '89
Gorbachev's new grip on the Kremlin [Politburo purge] F. Coleman. il por Newsweek 114:22-3 O 2 '89
Is the Soviet Union next to explode? J. F. O. McAllister. il Time 134:18+ D 18 '89
Nikita Gorbachev? F. Coleman. il pors Newsweek 114:39 S 11 '89
Pooped party [meeting of the Higher Party School] S. F. Starr. The New Republic 201:20-1 D 4 '89
The Soviet Union, 1989 [cover story; special issue] bibl f map (inside back cover) Current History 88:321-44+ O '89
Twilight of the dinosaurs [members of the Central Committee forced to resign] U.S. News & World Report 106:46 My 8 '89
COMMUNIST PARTY (U.S.)
In Loyalties, Carl Bernstein digs up a past best remembered [parents' party membership] S. Dougherty. il pors People Weekly 31:89-90+ Ap 10 '89
Loyalties [excerpt] C. Bernstein. il pors Rolling Stone p82-3+ Mr 9 '89
Outlasting the F.B.I., a determined widow restores her husband's reputation as a loyal Communist [L. Albertson wins lawsuit on behalf of B. Albertson, falsely accused of being an informer] J. S. Kunen. il People Weekly 32:171-2 N 20 '89
The party's shaky line. B. Turque. il Newsweek 114:48-9 N 13 '89
The Robeson record. B. Gewen. The New Leader 72:17-18 F 20 '89
Still taking the Fifth [C. Bernstein's book about his parents' membership] D. Horowitz. Commentary 88:53-5 Jl '89
This boy's life [C. Bernstein's book about his parents' membership] E. Pooley. il pors New York 22:38-43 F 13 '89
COMMUNITY
The futility of global thinking [adaptation of address, June 1989] W. Berry. Harper's 279:16-19+ S '89
Individual rights, community claims. J. M. Wall. The Christian Century 106:707-8 Ag 2-9 '89
True integration. W. Berry. il Mother Jones 14:16+ Je '89
Unity and community. P. J. Ryan. America 160:407 Ap 29 '89
COMMUNITY AND BUSINESS See Business—Social aspects
COMMUNITY AND JUNIOR COLLEGE TEACHERS See College teachers
COMMUNITY AND JUNIOR COLLEGE TEACHING See College teaching
COMMUNITY AND JUNIOR COLLEGES
See also
Lane Community College
Long Beach City College
Miami-Dade Community College
Seattle Central Community College
Academia's other half. il U.S. News & World Report 107:82-4 O 16 '89
Training the workforce of the future. J. E. Jacobs. il Technology Review 92:66-72 Ag/S '89

Curriculum
See also
English language—Composition
International education
COMMUNITY AND THE COLLEGE See Colleges and universities—Public relations
COMMUNITY AND THE SCHOOL See School and the community
COMMUNITY ASSOCIATIONS See Condominium associations
COMMUNITY CENTERS
See also
Senior centers
Architecture
Holding the center [Petaluma Community Center, Calif.] D. Canty. il Architectural Record 177:120-3 N '89
Perfect pitch [Bärenmatte Community Center in Switzerland designed by S. Calatrava] J. S. Russell. il Architectural Record 177:108-17 mid-S '89
COMMUNITY DEVELOPMENT
See also
Community Reinvestment Act of 1977
Rural development
TACOLCY Economic Development Corporation, Inc.
Communities, not carpetbaggers [need for government support of nonprofit housing movement] P. Dreier. il The Nation 249:198-200+ Ag 21-28 '89
Local success stories. P. Dreier. il The Progressive 53:28 Ap '89
Local success stories [federal government should support nonprofit housing movement] P. Dreier. il Commonweal 116:201-2 Ap 7 '89
International aspects
Grass-roots groups are our best hope for global prosperity and ecology. A. B. Durning. il Utne Reader p40-3+ Jl/Ag '89
Developing countries
People power and development. A. B. Durning. Foreign Policy 76:66-82 Fall '89
Saving the planet. A. B. Durning. il The Progressive 53:35-9 Ap '89
Sustainable success stories from the third world. A. B. Durning. il Utne Reader p44-5 Jl/Ag '89
COMMUNITY DEVELOPMENT BANKS
See also
Foundation for International Community Assistance
COMMUNITY DEVELOPMENT CORPORATIONS
See also
Shorebank Corporation (Chicago, Ill.)
COMMUNITY FOR CREATIVE NON-VIOLENCE
"The art case of the decade" [copyright case against J. E. Reid] S. Staggs. il Art News 88:49-50 Ap '89
Copyright ruling favors artists [Supreme Court decision] il Art in America 77:240 S '89
Court aids freelancers in work-for-hire ruling [case of Community for Creative Non-Violence vs. J. E. Reid] H. Fields. Publishers Weekly 235:11 Je 16 '89
Professional page [case brought by Community for Creative Non-Violence against J. E. Reid] D. Grant. American Artist 53:10+ Jl '89
Sculpture clash [suit brought against J. E. Reid] il Time 133:63 Ja 30 '89
Supreme Court hears work-for-hire arguments [case against J. E. Reid] H. Fields. Publishers Weekly 235:14 Ap 14 '89
COMMUNITY HEALTH PROJECTS INC.
A doctor and his critics [F. Tennant] R. Demak and J. Kirshenbaum. il Sports Illustrated 71:46-7 Jl 10 '89
COMMUNITY HEALTH WORKERS See Health workers
COMMUNITY LIFE
See also
Neighborhoods
COMMUNITY OF CELEBRATION
Aliquippa's star attraction. J. Duin. il Christianity Today 33:14+ Ja 13 '89
COMMUNITY ORGANIZATION
See also
Crime prevention—Citizen participation
Local Initiatives Support Corporation
Functioning communities. C. A. Murray. Current (Washington, D.C.) 311:24-31 Mr/Ap '89
Mother Jones' third annual Heroes and Heroines. il Mother Jones 14:27-35 Ja '89
People power transforms a St. Louis housing project [B. Gilkey organizes Cochran Gardens] H. C. Boyte. il por Utne Reader p46-7 Jl/Ag '89
Saul Alinsky: homo ludens for urban democracy. R. Luecke. il por The Christian Century 106:1050-3 N 15 '89
Women to be thankful for. T. Fields. il McCall's 117:117-18+ N '89
You can fight city hall. J. Blyskal. il Reader's Digest 134:103-7 Ja '89
COMMUNITY-POLICE RELATIONS See Police—Public relations
COMMUNITY POWER See Community organization
COMMUNITY PSYCHIATRIC CENTERS
"We don't advertise". E. Paris. il por Forbes 143:44 Je 12 '89

COMMUNITY REINVESTMENT ACT OF 1977
A housing program that really works. P. Glastris. il *U.S. News & World Report* 106:26-7 F 27 '89
Unlocking the potential of the CRA. D. M. Watts. il *Black Enterprise* 19:21 Jl '89
COMMUNITY SERVICE *See* Community organization; Volunteer service
COMMUTER AIRLINES *See* Airlines—Local service
COMMUTER AIRPLANE INDUSTRY *See* Airplane industry
COMMUTER AIRPLANES *See* Airplanes, Jet
COMMUTER PRODUCTS CORPORATION
Easing the pain of gridlock. il *Newsweek* 114:51 D 18 '89
COMMUTERS
Commuter marriage: does it work? E. C. Ray. il *Essence* 19:103+ F '89
Enhancing the education of college commuters. B. Jacoby. *The Education Digest* 54:62-4 Ap '89
Monday morning miracle [commuters communicate on Chicago bus]; ed. by Philip Yancey. P. Wigand. il *Reader's Digest* 134:9+ Mr '89
The new bicoastals: love on Tokyo time [couples who commute between the West Coast and Japan] J. Hammer. il *Newsweek* 113:50 F 13 '89
Equipment
See also
Commuter Products Corporation
COMMYNES, PHILIPPE DE *See* Comines, Philippe de, sieur d'Argenton, 1445?-1511
COMO, WILLIAM, 1925-1989
Back in the U.S.A.: big times for Basel [cover story] il *Dance Magazine* 63:40-5 F '89
about
Obituary
Dance Magazine il pors 63:32-5 Ap '89
Dance Magazine por 63:5 Mr '89. R. Philp
COMO (ITALY)
Industries
See also
Silk industry—Italy
COMOROS
Cultural policy
Rediscovering 'the Islands of the Moon'. A. Libioulle. il *The Courier (Unesco)* 42:31-2 Mr '89
COMPACT CAMERAS *See* Cameras
COMPACT DISC INDUSTRY
See also
Koss Classics (Firm)
Rykodisc Inc.
International aspects
Serious music, serious money. N. Lebrecht. *World Press Review* 36:51 Ag '89
Japan
Got a yen for CDs? J. James. il *High Fidelity (New York, N.Y.)* 39:46-50 Je '89
COMPACT DISC INTERACTIVE
Interactive CDs. J. Free. il *Popular Science* 235:92-4 N '89
Why multimedia is multiconfusing. W. M. Hawkins. por *Personal Computing* 13:220 O '89
COMPACT DISC PLAYERS
See also
Compact disc video
The CD bit wars. G. Brockhouse. il *High Fidelity (New York, N.Y.)* 39:41-5 Ap '89
Chipping in with 18-bit DACs. D. Ranada. il *High Fidelity (New York, N.Y.)* 39:18 F '89
Compact-disc players. il *Consumer Reports* 54:103-9 D '89
Compact disc players. il *Stereo Review* 54:96-103+ F '89
The making of a CD player [Philips] W. Wolfe. il *Stereo Review* 54:55-61 Ag '89
Update on CD players. D. Moreau. il *Changing Times* 43:63-6 Jl '89
What? Warm sound from a CD player? T. Smart. il *Business Week* p176 O 9 '89
When less is more [1-bit CD players] M. Riggs. il *High Fidelity (New York, N.Y.)* 39:5 Je '89
Changers
CD changers. I. Masters. il *Stereo Review* 54:58-62 Jl '89
Fisher DAC-Z1 compact disc changer. J. D. Hirsch. il *Stereo Review* 54:52+ S '89
Hitachi DA-C70 compact disc changer. J. D. Hirsch. il *Stereo Review* 54:52+ My '89
Marantz CDC-320 compact disc changer. J. D. Hirsch. il *Stereo Review* 54:42+ F '89
Realistic CD-6000 compact disc changer. R. Long. il *High Fidelity (New York, N.Y.)* 39:31+ Mr '89
Sound advice for the '90s [Sony Disc Jockey changer for cars] B. J. Hoffman. il *Motor Trend* 41:186 My '89
Maintenance and repair
How to repair CD players. B. Phelps. il *Radio-Electronics* 60:52-3+ N '89
Specifications
The numbers madness. K. C. Pohlmann. *Stereo Review* 54:24 Je '89
Testing
Adcom GCD-575 CD player. J. D. Hirsch. il *Stereo Review* 54:51-3 Ja '89
Are there sonic differences among CD players? L. Klein. il *Radio-Electronics* 60:67+ D '89

Blaupunkt New York SCD-08 car tuner/CD player. R. Long. il *High Fidelity (New York, N.Y.)* 39:30-3 Jl '89
Blaupunkt New York SCD 08 CD tuner [car stereo] K. C. Pohlmann. il *Stereo Review* 54:24-5 N '89
CD player soundoff. S. A. Booth and F. C. Barr. il *Popular Mechanics* 166:67-9+ Jl '89
CD players: the new music medium. il *Consumer Reports* 54:165 Mr '89
Compact-disc players. il *Consumer Reports* 54:27-32 Ja '89
Conrad-Johnson DF1 compact disc player. J. D. Hirsch. il *Stereo Review* 54:72+ D '89
Denon DCD-3520 compact disc player. R. Long. il *High Fidelity (New York, N.Y.)* 39:30-1 My '89
Eclipse ESD-230 CD player [car stereo] J. D. Hirsch and K. C. Pohlmann. il *Stereo Review* 54:30+ Ja '89
Harman Kardon HD7500 compact disc player. J. D. Hirsch. il *Stereo Review* 54:76-7+ N '89
NEC CD-830DS compact disc player. J. D. Hirsch. il *Stereo Review* 54:35-6 My '89
The new CD players. I. Masters. il *Stereo Review* 54:84-9 O '89
Onkyo DX-7500 compact disc player. J. D. Hirsch. il *Stereo Review* 54:37-9 Ap '89
Pioneer DEH-66 car stereo receiver/CD player. R. Long. il *High Fidelity (New York, N.Y.)* 39:46+ Ja '89
Pioneer PD-71 compact disc player. J. D. Hirsch. il *Stereo Review* 54:31-2 Ag '89
Revox B-226S compact disc player. R. Long. il *High Fidelity (New York, N.Y.)* 39:32-3 Ja '89
Sansui Vintage CD-X711 compact disc player. J. D. Hirsch. il *Stereo Review* 54:49-50+ O '89
Sherwood CD-1160R compact disc player. J. D. Hirsch. il *Stereo Review* 54:46+ Mr '89
Sight and sound: a bit more. H. Fantel. *Opera News* 53:41 Je '89
Sony CDP-608 ESD compact disc player. J. D. Hirsch. il *Stereo Review* 54:33+ Je '89
Sony CDX-R77 car tuner/CD player. R. Long. il *High Fidelity (New York, N.Y.)* 39:33-5 Jl '89
Technics SL-P1300 compact disc player. J. D. Hirsch. il *Stereo Review* 54:23-5 Jl '89
Yamaha CDX-1120 compact disc player. J. D. Hirsch. il *Stereo Review* 54:61+ N '89
COMPACT DISC RECORDERS AND RECORDING
Compact-disc recorder [Meridian Data's system] J. Free. il *Popular Science* 235:19-21 S '89
Direct-to-disc recording. S. A. Booth. il *Popular Mechanics* 166:32-3 Mr '89
The future of tape. M. Riggs. il *High Fidelity (New York, N.Y.)* 39:5 F '89
COMPACT DISC VIDEO
Laser's new populism. L. B. Johnson. il *Video* 13:79-80+ S '89
Opera
The King James version [Metropolitan Opera performances] P. G. Davis. il *New York* 22:80-1 O 2 '89
Rock music
The 5-inch CD-V. K. Richardson. il *High Fidelity (New York, N.Y.)* 39:72+ Ja '89
See 'em, hear 'em. K. Richardson. il *High Fidelity (New York, N.Y.)* 39:53-4 Ap '89
Testing
6-disc CD-video player. il *Radio-Electronics* 60:22 Ap '89
Philips CDV-488 CD video player. E. J. Foster. il *High Fidelity (New York, N.Y.)* 39:19+ Jl '89
Philips CDV488 combi-player. J. D. Hirsch. il *Stereo Review* 54:68+ O '89
Philips video player with digital effects [CDV488] il *Video* 13:30-1+ Ap '89
Pioneer combi player with digital effects [CLD-3030] il *Video* 12:40+ Ja '89
Pioneer dual-side combi player [CLD-2070] il *Video* 13:44-5+ S '89
Pioneer Elite deluxe combi player [CLD-91] il *Video* 13:50+ D '89
The relapse of chroma phobia [luminance resolution vs. chrominance resolution] D. Ranada. il *High Fidelity (New York, N.Y.)* 39:17 Jl '89
Videodiscs: CDs for eyes. J. B. Meigs. il *Rolling Stone* p71+ Ja 12 '89
Yamaha combi player. il *Video* 13:34+ Ag '89
COMPACT DISCS
See also
CD-ROM (Compact disc-Read only memory)
Compact disc interactive
Compact disc video
Compact discs. M. C. Lehrer. See issues of USA Today (Periodical) beginning January 1988
Sight and sound: the CD at five. H. Fantel. *Opera News* 53:41 Ja 7 '89
The sound of CD (I). L. Klein. il *Radio-Electronics* 60:74-5 N '89
Sound on disc. R. De Toledano. See occasional issues of National Review
The two-sided CD. T. W. Libbey, Jr. il *High Fidelity (New York, N.Y.)* 39:57 Ap '89

COMPACT DISCS—cont.

American music

A century, and more, of American song [J. DeGaetani and G. Kalish's Songs of America] K. R. Schwarz. *High Fidelity (New York, N.Y.)* 39:52 Mr '89

Arias

Wagner, Richard: Opera excerpts and arias [Jessye Norman recordings]; Lotte Lehmann: Opera and operetta arias. P. Moor. *High Fidelity (New York, N.Y.)* 39:60-1 Mr '89

Ballet music

A vivid "Firebird" from Rattle. D. Hall. por *Stereo Review* 54:73 Ag '89

Baroque music

Fasch, Johann Friedrich: Various works. P. Moor. por *High Fidelity (New York, N.Y.)* 39:68-9 Ja '89

Williams, John: Baroque album. C. Manion. il *High Fidelity (New York, N.Y.)* 39:70 Ap '89

Black music

Sweet Honey in the Rock: Breaths; Live at Carnegie Hall. D. Palmer. il *High Fidelity (New York, N.Y.)* 39:74 My '89

Blues music

The blues—yesterday & today. B. Sandmel. il *Down Beat* 56:45-8 D '89

Coltrane, John: Coltrane plays the blues. J. Ephland. il *Down Beat* 56:40-1 D '89

Restoring harmony [country and blues material for RCA's Heritage Series] B. Altman. il *High Fidelity (New York, N.Y.)* 39:54-6 My '89

Brass instrument music

Hot brass. E. Salzman. il *Stereo Review* 54:162 N '89

Brazilian music

Bachianas brasileiras [Villa-Lobos works] R. Freed. il *Stereo Review* 54:87 Ap '89

Cantatas

Bach, Johann Sebastian: Cantatas (various) [Joshua Rifkin recordings] T. Teachout. *High Fidelity (New York, N.Y.)* 39:52-3 Mr '89

Care

CDs forever? J. W. Merline. il *Consumers' Research Magazine* 72:38 My '89

How long is forever? T. Clark. *Theatre Crafts* 23:38+ Ag/S '89

Where's the rot? [longevity] R. Day. il *Stereo Review* 54:23-4 Ap '89

Cello music

Bach, Johann Sebastian: Suites for solo cello [Pablo Casals recordings] P. Moor. il *High Fidelity (New York, N.Y.)* 39:59 My '89

Barber, Samuel: Orchestral works; Concerto for cello and orchestra [Leonard Slatkin and Yo-Yo Ma recordings] K. R. Schwarz. il *High Fidelity (New York, N.Y.)* 39:62+ Je '89

Herbert, Victor: Concertos for cello and orchestra; Five pieces for cello and strings. J. Wierzbicki. il *High Fidelity (New York, N.Y.)* 39:70 Ja '89

Matt Haimovitz comes of age [Lalo Cello concerto; Bruch Kol Nidrei and Saint-Saëns Cello concerto no. 1] R. Freed. il por *Stereo Review* 54:152 O '89

The romantic cello [J. Starker's recording of music by D. Popper] R. Freed. il por *Stereo Review* 54:147 D '89

Chamber music

Morricone, Ennio: Chamber works; Film music, vol. II. J. Wierzbicki. *High Fidelity (New York, N.Y.)* 39:62 Jl '89

Clarinet music

Copland, Aaron: Concerto for clarinet and string orchestra; Music for the theatre; Quiet city; Dance panels [Gerard Schwarz recording] K. R. Schwarz. *High Fidelity (New York, N.Y.)* 39:64 Je '89

Stoltzman, Richard: Ebony. T. Teachout. *High Fidelity (New York, N.Y.)* 39:62 Mr '89

Classical music

Beethoven, Bach, Tallis, & others. R. De Toledano. il *National Review* 41:53+ Jl 14 '89

Brave new label [Virgin Classics] D. Hurwitz. il *High Fidelity (New York, N.Y.)* 39:56-9 Ja '89

Budget compact discs. W. Livingstone. il *Stereo Review* 54:122-3 Je '89

The CD spread. See issues of High Fidelity (New York, N.Y.) beginning February 1986 through July 1989

Encores [reissues of A. Boult, F. Reiner and C. Munch recordings] R. Freed. pors *Stereo Review* 54:162 D '89

Mozart, Mahler, and others. R. De Toledano. *National Review* 41:55-6 Ap 7 '89

New compact discs with a difference. P. E. McCorry, III. il *Horizon (Tuscaloosa, Ala.)* 32:33 Ja/F '89

Old masters. T. Teachout. See alternate issues of High Fidelity (New York, N.Y.) beginning April 1989 through July 1989

A requiem & other celebrations. R. De Toledano. *National Review* 41:56 N 24 '89

Salute to France [works by C. Saint-Saëns] W. Livingstone. il *Stereo Review* 54:164 N '89

Serious music, serious money. N. Lebrecht. *World Press Review* 36:51 Ag '89

Silver rush. N. Lebrecht. il *Opera News* 54:8-10 Ag '89

A small gamut of music. R. De Toledano. il *National Review* 41:50-1 S 1 '89

Cleaning

See Compact discs—Care

Concertos

See also

Compact discs—Cello music
Compact discs—Piano music
Compact discs—Violin music

Country music

Jerry Jeff Walker [Live at Gruene Hall] A. Nash. il por *Stereo Review* 54:136 S '89

Restoring harmony [country and blues material for RCA's Heritage Series] B. Altman. il *High Fidelity (New York, N.Y.)* 39:54-6 My '89

Electronic music

Roland: a sound approach. J. Simpson. il *Down Beat* 56:43-4 Jl '89

Experimental music

Machover, Tod: VALIS. J. Wierzbicki. il *High Fidelity (New York, N.Y.)* 39:62-3 F '89

Musique de notre temps: repères 1945-1975. P. Moor. il *High Fidelity (New York, N.Y.)* 39:71-2 Ap '89

Folk music

Woody Guthrie. J. Nesin. il por *High Fidelity (New York, N.Y.)* 39:77-8 Ap '89

French music

Janequin, Clément [recent recordings] P. Moor. *High Fidelity (New York, N.Y.)* 39:67-8 Ap '89

Salute to France [works by C. Saint-Saëns] W. Livingstone. il *Stereo Review* 54:164 N '89

Gospel music

Sweet Honey in the Rock: Breaths; Live at Carnegie Hall. D. Palmer. il *High Fidelity (New York, N.Y.)* 39:74 My '89

Guitar music

Williams, John: Baroque album. C. Manion. il *High Fidelity (New York, N.Y.)* 39:70 Ap '89

Incidental music

Spirited Strauss from Gerard Schwarz [music provided for Molière's Le bourgeois gentilhomme] D. Hall. il *Stereo Review* 54:123-4 D '89

Jazz music

ABCs of swing on BBC [classic reissues] J. Sohmer. *Down Beat* 56:40 Ag '89

Abercrombie, John/Johnson, Marc/Erskine, Peter: John Abercrombie/Marc Johnson/Peter Erskine. J. Ephland. *Down Beat* 56:30 O '89

Bailey, Victor: Bottom's up. B. Milkowski. *Down Beat* 56:34 Ag '89

Benny Carter All-Star Sax Ensemble: Over the rainbow. J. McDonough. il *Down Beat* 56:31 D '89

Big bang. K. Whitehead. il *Down Beat* 56:41-4 D '89

Brecker, Michael: Don't try this at home. K. Whitehead. il *Down Beat* 56:36-7 Ja '89

Bringing it all back home. J. Miller. il *Newsweek* 114:59+ Ag 28 '89

Candid on chromium [Candid label reissues] P. Kostakis. il *Down Beat* 56:34-7 F '89

Cherry, Don: Art deco. E. Guregian. il *Down Beat* 56:29 O '89

Chimes of Freedom [Freedom label reissues] P. Kostakis. *Down Beat* 56:40+ Ja '89

Classic jazz on CD [Jazz masters] il *Stereo Review* 54:35 O '89

Davis, Miles: Amandla. J. Roberts. il *Down Beat* 56:29-30 O '89

Duke everlasting [recordings by D. Ellington and others] K. Whitehead. il pors *Down Beat* 56:38-40 Je '89

Elias, Elaine: Cross currents. O. Cordle. il *Down Beat* 56:38-9 Ja '89

Erskine, Peter: Motion poet. B. Milkowski. il *Down Beat* 56:42-3 My '89

From Hoagy to Nancy. R. De Toledano. *National Review* 41:62-3 F 10 '89

Gillespie, Dizzy: Jazz portrait of Duke Ellington. J. Ephland. il *Down Beat* 56:32-3 N '89

Goodman, Benny: Yale library vol. 1; vol. 2: Live at Basin Street. J. McDonough. il *Down Beat* 56:36-7 Mr '89

Grusin, Dave: Collection. R. Tolleson. il *Down Beat* 56:42-3 Jl '89

Hamm, Stu: Kings of sleep. R. Tolleson. il *Down Beat* 56:35 D '89

Herb Robertson Brass Ensemble: Shades of Bud Powell. K. Whitehead. il *Down Beat* 56:37 Ap '89

How big is big? [large ensembles] A. Lange. *Down Beat* 56:37-40 Ap '89

Ibrahim, Abdullah: Voice of Africa; African Sun; Tintinyana; Blues for hip king. A. Lange. il *Down Beat* 56:34-6 N '89

Jarrett, Keith: Personal mountains; Dark intervals; Works by Lou Harrison. B. Shoemaker. il *Down Beat* 56:39 Ag '89

Jones, Thad/Lewis, Mel: Thad Jones/Mel Lewis Quartet; New life: dedicated to Max Gordon. J. McDonough. il *Down Beat* 56:37-8 O '89

Kuriokhin & Kaiser: Popular science. R. Tolleson. il *Down Beat* 56:31-2 N '89

The Liebman connection [saxophonist D. Liebman] J. Roberts. il por *Down Beat* 56:37 Ag '89

COMPACT DISCS—Jazz music—*cont.*

Marsalis, Wynton: Majesty of the blues. J. Roberts. il *Down Beat* 56:31+ O '89

Maxine Sullivan [release of Swingin' sweet] P. Garland. por *Stereo Review* 54:124 Ja '89

MCA/Impulse! Jazz. R. C. Walls. il *High Fidelity (New York, N.Y.)* 39:76-7 Ap '89

Mulligan, Gerry: California concerts, vol. 2. J. McDonough. il *Down Beat* 56:34+ Ag '89

Music. G. Santoro. *The Nation* 248:390-2 Mr 20 '89

Musical comedy, CD jazz. R. De Toledano. *National Review* 41:56-8 O 13 '89

New compact discs with a difference [Runnin' ragged, the classic hot jazz duets by Joe Venuti] P. E. McCorry, III. il *Horizon (Tuscaloosa, Ala.)* 32:33 Ja/F '89

New Orleans memories on compact discs. S. M. Stroff. il *Antiques & Collecting Hobbies* 94:68-70 Ap '89

Oregon: 45th Parallel. J. Ephland. *Down Beat* 56:32 Ag '89

Ornithology [C. Parker] K. Whitehead. il *Down Beat* 56:37-9 Mr '89

Out of the mouths of babes . . . sometimes [school bands] J. Sohmer. *Down Beat* 56:34 O '89

Parker's brood [C. Parker] R. C. Walls. il pors *High Fidelity (New York, N.Y.)* 39:52-5 F '89

Patitucci, John: On the corner. B. Milkowski. il *Down Beat* 56:34 Ag '89

Petrucciani, Michel: Michel plays Petrucciani. O. Cordle. *Down Beat* 56:38-9 Ja '89

Portrait Masters jazz. M. Ullman. il *High Fidelity (New York, N.Y.)* 39:80-1 Ap '89

Pullen, Don: New beginnings. K. Whitehead. il *Down Beat* 56:30 O '89

Roberts, Marcus: Truth is spoken here. O. Cordle. il *Down Beat* 56:38 Je '89

Rogers, Shorty: Complete Atlantic and EMI jazz recordings. J. McDonough. il *Down Beat* 56:32-3 Ag '89

Severinsen, Doc: Big band hit parade; Facets. J. McDonough. il *Down Beat* 56:38 F '89

Solo/duo impressions. A. Lange. il *Down Beat* 56:39-40+ F '89

Stoltzman, Richard: Ebony. T. Teachout. *High Fidelity (New York, N.Y.)* 39:62 Mr '89

Strata Institute: C-I-P-H-E-R S-Y-N-T-A-X. G. Santoro. il *Down Beat* 56:33 O '89

Sun Ra: Blue delight. F.-J. Hadley. il *Down Beat* 56:29 N '89

Terry, Clark: Portraits. F.-J. Hadley. il *Down Beat* 56:36 Je '89

Threadgill, Henry: Rag, bush and all. J. Ephland. il *Down Beat* 56:40 Jl '89

Toward a jazz CD library. R. De Toledano. *National Review* 41:59-60 My 19 '89

Towner, Ralph: City of eyes. J. Ephland. *Down Beat* 56:32 Ag '89

Webster, Ben: Soulville. K. Whitehead. il *Down Beat* 56:30-1 Ag '89

Wilson, Cassandra: Blue skies. K. Whitehead. il *Down Beat* 56:37-8 Ja '89

Wilson, Gerald: Orchestra of the 80's: Love you madly. F. Bouchard. il *Down Beat* 56:36 Je '89

Words of love [women singers] J. Sohmer. il *Down Beat* 56:35-6 Ag '89

Yellowjackets: Spin. F.-J. Hadley. il *Down Beat* 56:30 Ag '89

Zorn, John: Spy vs. spy. G. Santoro. il *Down Beat* 56:34-5 D '89

Mexican music

Mexico in music [E. Bátiz conducts; works by Carlos Chávez and Silvestre Revueltas] R. Freed. por *Stereo Review* 54:158 N '89

Modern music

CDs: the composer's forum. B. Shoemaker. il *Down Beat* 56:37-9 F '89

Fine, Irving: Various works [Nonesuch recording] R. R. Reilly. il *High Fidelity (New York, N.Y.)* 39:62-3 My '89

Motion picture music

Glass, Philip: Powaqqatsi. K. R. Schwarz. *High Fidelity (New York, N.Y.)* 39:69 Ja '89

Morricone, Ennio: Chamber works; Film music, vol. II. J. Wierzbicki. *High Fidelity (New York, N.Y.)* 39:62 Jl '89

Stay awake: various interpretations of music from vintage Disney films. H. Bordowitz. il *High Fidelity (New York, N.Y.)* 39:70+ Mr '89

Musicals, revues, etc.

American musical theater: shows, songs, and stars [Smithsonian Collection] P. J. Smith. *Opera News* 54:32-3 Ag '89

Bernstein, Leonard: Bernstein songbook. P. Kresh. *High Fidelity (New York, N.Y.)* 39:73 Je '89

Gershwin crazy [recently discovered scores] S. Elliott. il pors *Opera News* 54:12-14+ Ag '89

Lullabies of Broadway [Smithsonian's American musical theater] J. Miller. il *Newsweek* 113:67-8 Mr 27 '89

Musical comedy, CD jazz [Smithsonian Collection's American Musical Theater] R. De Toledano. *National Review* 41:56-8 O 13 '89

New course charted for Show boat. T. Teachout. il *High Fidelity (New York, N.Y.)* 39:57-8 F '89

Threepenny romance [music of K. Weill] P. Moor. il pors *High Fidelity (New York, N.Y.)* 39:50-3 My '89

The voices of Kurt Weill. L. Schwartz. il *The Atlantic* 264:115-18 D '89

New Age music

Oregon: 45th Parallel. J. Ephland. *Down Beat* 56:32 Ag '89

Noise

MASH to the rescue. R. Hodges. il *Stereo Review* 54:164 S '89

Sonic Solutions [NoNoise system] K. C. Pohlmann. *Stereo Review* 54:28 Ap '89

Work in progress [work of L. Fielder] R. Hodges. il *Stereo Review* 54:97 Ag '89

Opera

See also
  Compact discs—Arias

Bartók, Béla: Bluebeard's castle. P. Moor. il *High Fidelity (New York, N.Y.)* 39:64 Ja '89

Berg, Alban: Wozzeck. R. Ackart. *Stereo Review* 54:88 Jl '89

Berg, Alban: Wozzeck. J. W. Freeman. il *Opera News* 54:30 Ag '89

Bizet, Georges: Carmen. J. W. Freeman. il *Opera News* 54:58 D 9 '89

Carlos Kleiber. J. W. Freeman. il *Opera News* 54:31 Ag '89

Cimarosa, Domenico: Il pittor parigino. J. W. Freeman. il *Opera News* 53:42 F 4 '89

Debussy, Claude: Pelléas et Mélisande. J. W. Freeman. il *Opera News* 53:42 Mr 18 '89

Gershwin, George: Porgy and Bess. J. W. Freeman. il *Opera News* 54:50 S '89

He knew his Wagner [L. Melchior] W. H. Youngren. il *The Atlantic* 264:83-5 Jl '89

Hindemith, Paul: Cardillac. E. Salzman. il *Stereo Review* 54:118 Je '89

Kuhlau, Friedrich: Lulu. J. W. Freeman. *Opera News* 53:48 My '89

Lully, Jean Baptiste: Atys. P. Moor. *High Fidelity (New York, N.Y.)* 39:60-2 F '89

Machover, Tod: VALIS. J. Wierzbicki. il *High Fidelity (New York, N.Y.)* 39:62-3 F '89

Maria Callas. T. Eckert, Jr. il pors *High Fidelity (New York, N.Y.)* 39:46-50 F '89

Mascagni, Pietro: Nerone. J. W. Freeman. il *Opera News* 53:43 Mr 4 '89

A memorable "Figaro" [Arnold Östman recording on L'Oiseau-Lyre] S. Lincoln. il *Stereo Review* 54:119 My '89

A new "Ariadne" [Kurt Masur recording] R. Ackart. il *Stereo Review* 54:119 Mr '89

New from the studios. M. Sevilla-Gonzaga. il *Opera News* 54:28-9 Ag '89

Nyman, Michael: The man who mistook his wife for a hat. J. W. Freeman. il *Opera News* 54:32 Ag '89

Nyman, Michael: The man who mistook his wife for a hat. J. Wierzbicki. *High Fidelity (New York, N.Y.)* 39:63-4 F '89

Offenbach, Jacques: Tales of Hoffmann. R. Ackart. *Stereo Review* 54:120 Je '89

Prokofiev, Sergey: War and peace. E. Salzman. il *Stereo Review* 54:93 Ag '89

Respighi, Ottorino: Belfagor. J. W. Freeman. il *Opera News* 54:35 D 23 '89

Ring fever. P. G. Davis. il *New York* 22:74+ Ap 3 '89

The Ring in the CD era. J. W. Freeman. il *Opera News* 53:66-7 Ap 1 '89

Rossini, Gioacchino: Ermione. J. W. Freeman. il *Opera News* 53:42 F 18 '89

Schmidt, Franz: Notre Dame. J. W. Freeman. *Opera News* 53:42-3 Mr 4 '89

Strauss, Richard: Ariadne auf Naxos. J. W. Freeman. il *Opera News* 53:42 Mr 4 '89

Strauss, Richard: Elektra. R. Ackart. il *Stereo Review* 54:71-2 Ag '89

Strauss, Richard: Elektra. J. W. Freeman. il *Opera News* 54:31-2 Ag '89

Strauss, Richard: Die Frau ohne Schatten. J. W. Freeman. il *Opera News* 53:48 My '89

Strauss, Richard: Die Frau ohne Schatten [Wolfgang Sawallisch recording] R. E. Benson. il *High Fidelity (New York, N.Y.)* 39:58-9 My '89

Tchaikovsky, Peter Ilich: Eugene Onegin. R. Ackart. il *Stereo Review* 54:92 Ag '89

Threepenny romance [music of K. Weill] P. Moor. il pors *High Fidelity (New York, N.Y.)* 39:50-3 My '89

Tokyo gala for the Met [Kathleen Battle and Placido Domingo: Live in Tokyo 1988] R. Freed. il *Stereo Review* 54:141 O '89

Top of the line [R. Strauss operas] P. G. Davis. il *New York* 22:100+ Ap 24 '89

Verdi redivivus. C. J. Luten. il *Opera News* 54:46-9 S '89

The voices of Kurt Weill. L. Schwartz. il *The Atlantic* 264:115-18 D '89

Wagner, Richard: Die Walküre. J. W. Freeman. il *Opera News* 53:66 Ap 1 '89

COMPACT DISCS—Opera—*cont.*

Weill, Kurt: Rise and fall of the city of Mahagonny. J. W. Freeman. *Opera News* 53:42 Ja 21 '89

Operetta

Myth into music [Benjamin Britten's Paul Bunyan] P. E. McCorry. *Horizon (Tuscaloosa, Ala.)* 32:12 Mr/Ap '89

Recordings [reissues] J. W. Freeman. il *Opera News* 53:42 Ja 7 '89

Strauss, Johann: Gypsy baron. J. W. Freeman. *Opera News* 54:34 D 23 '89

Oratorio

Handel, George Frideric: Messiah [anthology of recordings made by Metropolitan Opera artists] A. Porter. *The New Yorker* 65:72 D 25 '89

Handel, George Frideric: Messiah [Trevor Pinnock conducting English Concert] C. Rothko. *High Fidelity (New York, N.Y.)* 39:56 Mr '89

Scarlatti, Alessandro: La Giuditta [Nicholas McGegan and Capella Savaria] C. Rothko. il *High Fidelity (New York, N.Y.)* 39:64-5 My '89

Orchestral music

Barber, Samuel: Orchestral works; Concerto for cello and orchestra [Leonard Slatkin and Yo-Yo Ma recordings] K. R. Schwarz. il *High Fidelity (New York, N.Y.)* 39:62+ Je '89

Copland, Aaron: Concerto for clarinet and string orchestra; Music for the theatre; Quiet city; Dance panels [Gerard Schwarz recording] K. R. Schwarz. *High Fidelity (New York, N.Y.)* 39:64 Je '89

Olympian games [work of H. von Karajan] P. G. Davis. il por *New York* 22:113-14 D 11 '89

Rorem, Ned: String symphony; Sunday morning; Eagles. T. Teachout. *High Fidelity (New York, N.Y.)* 39:70-1 Ja '89

Wuorinen, Charles: Concerto for piano and orchestra no. 3; The golden dance [Garrick Ohlsson and San Francisco Symphony] P. Moor. il *High Fidelity (New York, N.Y.)* 39:62-3 Jl '89

Passion music

Bach, Carl Philipp Emanuel: St. Mark passion. C. Rothko. *High Fidelity (New York, N.Y.)* 39:63-4 Ja '89

Pärt, Arvo: Passio domini nostri Jesu Christi secundum Joannem. J. Wierzbicki. il *High Fidelity (New York, N.Y.)* 39:68-9 Ap '89

Piano music

Abbado's Ravel: the piano concertos. R. Freed. il por *Stereo Review* 54:108 O '89

András Schiff's Mozart. R. Freed. il *Stereo Review* 54:127 Ja '89

Bartók, Béla: Concerto for orchestra; Dance suite; Petite suite [piano transcriptions] P. Moor. *High Fidelity (New York, N.Y.)* 39:64-5 Ja '89

Beethoven, Ludwig van: Concertos for piano and orchestra [Daniel Barenboim] P. Moor. il *High Fidelity (New York, N.Y.)* 39:53-4 Mr '89

Bolcom, William: Symphony no. 4; Session 1; Twelve new etudes; Wolpe, Stefan: Battle piece. T. Teachout. *High Fidelity (New York, N.Y.)* 39:59 F '89

Chopin, Frederic: Ballades; Barcarolle, in F sharp; Fantasie, in F minor; Liszt, Franz: Totentanz [Krystian Zimerman recordings] D. Hurwitz. *High Fidelity (New York, N.Y.)* 39:64 Je '89

Copland, Aaron: Piano fantasy; Piano sonata; Piano variations. P. Turok. *High Fidelity (New York, N.Y.)* 39:58 Jl '89

Firkušný plays Martinů. R. Freed. por *Stereo Review* 54:126 D '89

Harrison, Lou: Piano concerto; Suite for violin, piano, and small orchestra. K. R. Schwarz. por *High Fidelity (New York, N.Y.)* 39:56-7 Mr '89

Jarrett, Keith: Personal mountains; Dark intervals; Works by Lou Harrison. B. Shoemaker. il *Down Beat* 56:39 Ag '89

Michelangeli plays Debussy [Preludes, book II] R. Freed. il por *Stereo Review* 54:70 Jl '89

Mozart à la mode [piano concertos] J. Kerman. bibl f il *The New York Review of Books* 36:50-2 My 18 '89

Richter live [S. Richter's Diabelli variations] R. Freed. il por *Stereo Review* 54:89 Jl '89

Schiff's Bach [English suites] S. Lincoln. il por *Stereo Review* 54:87 Ag '89

Schnabel: stylish as ever on CD. T. Teachout. il *High Fidelity (New York, N.Y.)* 39:75 Ap '89

Wuorinen, Charles: Concerto for piano and orchestra no. 3; The golden dance [Garrick Ohlsson and San Francisco Symphony] P. Moor. il *High Fidelity (New York, N.Y.)* 39:62-3 Jl '89

Popular music

Astaire, Fred: Astaire story. K. Whitehead. il *Down Beat* 56:36 Mr '89

Carmichael, Hoagy: Hoagy sings Carmichael. K. Whitehead. *Down Beat* 56:36 Mr '89

Cypress artists. R. Price. il *High Fidelity (New York, N.Y.)* 39:82-3 Ap '89

In short order. See issues of High Fidelity (New York, N.Y.) through July 1989

Joplin, Scott: Piano works [William Bolcom]; Porter, Cole: Songs [Joan Morris] T. Teachout. il *High Fidelity (New York, N.Y.)* 39:60 Jl '89

Ragtime music

Joplin, Scott: Piano works [William Bolcom]; Porter, Cole: Songs [Joan Morris] T. Teachout. il *High Fidelity (New York, N.Y.)* 39:60 Jl '89

Religious music

See also
Compact discs—Passion music
Compact discs—Vespers (Music)

Requiems

Fauré, Gabriel: Requiem, Op. 48 [Charles Dutoit and André Cluytens recordings] P. Moor. il *High Fidelity (New York, N.Y.)* 39:61-2 My '89

Verdi, Giuseppe: Messa per Rossini. J. W. Freeman. *Opera News* 54:34-5 D 23 '89

Rock music

Alternative anthologies. D. Browne. il *High Fidelity (New York, N.Y.)* 39:81-2 Ap '89

Astronauts: Surf party. J. Ephland. il *Down Beat* 56:43+ My '89

Bangles: Everything. B. Altman. il *High Fidelity (New York, N.Y.)* 39:72 Mr '89

Bruce, Jack: Willpower. J. Roberts. il *Down Beat* 56:38-9 Ag '89

CD news [1989] P. Howard. il *Rolling Stone* p216 D 14-28 '89

Crosby, Stills, Nash & Young: American dream. D. Browne. il *High Fidelity (New York, N.Y.)* 39:65+ Mr '89

'Pet' project due on CD [Beach Boys] J. Ressner. il *Rolling Stone* p23 Mr 23 '89

Pylon: Hits. K. Richardson. il *High Fidelity (New York, N.Y.)* 39:79+ Je '89

Reed, Lou: New York. J. Nesin. il *High Fidelity (New York, N.Y.)* 39:73 My '89

Tales from the crypt [rock reissues for CD] J. Ressner. il *Rolling Stone* p13-14 F 23 '89

World Saxophone Quartet: Rhythm & blues. K. Whitehead. il *Down Beat* 56:36 O '89

XTC: Oranges & lemons. R. C. Walls. il *High Fidelity (New York, N.Y.)* 39:82 Je '89

Saxophone music

Benny Carter All-Star Sax Ensemble: Over the rainbow. J. McDonough. il *Down Beat* 56:31 D '89

World Saxophone Quartet: Rhythm & blues. K. Whitehead. il *Down Beat* 56:36 O '89

Shelves and racks

See Shelves and racks

Sonatas

See also
Compact discs—Violin music

Songs

Berg, Alban: Songs; Schoenberg, Arnold: Caberet songs; Webern, Anton: Seven early songs. J. Wierzbicki. *High Fidelity (New York, N.Y.)* 39:65 Ap '89

A century, and more, of American song [J. DeGaetani and G. Kalish's Songs of America] K. R. Schwarz. *High Fidelity (New York, N.Y.)* 39:52 Mr '89

Sound effects

CD libraries: sound effects on compact disc. T. Clark. *Theatre Crafts* 23:38+ Ag/S '89

South African music

Ibrahim, Abdullah: Voice of Africa; African Sun; Tintinyana; Blues for hip king. A. Lange. il *Down Beat* 56:34-6 N '89

String quartet music

Blazing away at Bartók [Emerson String Quartet] K. R. Schwarz. il *High Fidelity (New York, N.Y.)* 39:61-2 Je '89

Britten, Benjamin: String quartet no. 3; Tippett, Michael: String quartet no. 4. P. Moor. *High Fidelity (New York, N.Y.)* 39:56 Mr '89

The Emerson's Bartók. R. Freed. il *Stereo Review* 54:163 F '89

Suites (Music)

Bach, Johann Sebastian: Suites for solo cello [Pablo Casals recordings] P. Moor. il *High Fidelity (New York, N.Y.)* 39:59 My '89

Bachianas brasileiras [Villa-Lobos works] R. Freed. il *Stereo Review* 54:87 Ap '89

Harrison, Lou: Piano concerto; Suite for violin, piano, and small orchestra. K. R. Schwarz. por *High Fidelity (New York, N.Y.)* 39:56-7 Mr '89

Schiff's Bach [English suites] S. Lincoln. il por *Stereo Review* 54:87 Ag '89

Symphonic poems

Blomstedt's resplendent Strauss [Also sprach Zarathustra and Don Juan] D. Hall. por *Stereo Review* 54:103-4 Mr '89

Dvořák, Antonin: Symphonic poems [recordings by Czech Philharmonic and Slovak Philharmonic] D. Hurwitz. *High Fidelity (New York, N.Y.)* 39:68 Ja '89

Symphonies

The "authentic" Beethoven [Hanover Band recordings] E. Salzman. il *Stereo Review* 54:126 My '89

Beethoven, Ludwig van: Symphonies nos. 1 and 6 [Roger Norrington] K. R. Schwarz. *High Fidelity (New York, N.Y.)* 39:54-5 Mr '89

Beethoven's nine, times two [recordings conducted by R. Muti and B. Haitink] E. Salzman. il pors *Stereo Review* 54:128 Ja '89

COMPACT DISCS—Symphonies—*cont.*

Bolcom, William: Symphony no. 4; Session 1; Twelve new etudes; Wolpe, Stefan: Battle piece. T. Teachout. *High Fidelity (New York, N.Y.)* 39:59 F '89

Bruckner, Anton: Symphony no. 8, in C minor. D. Hurwitz. *High Fidelity (New York, N.Y.)* 39:65+ Ja '89

Elgar, Edward: Symphony no. 2, in E flat [Giuseppe Sinopoli recording] D. Hurwitz. il *High Fidelity (New York, N.Y.)* 39:64-5 Je '89

Haydn, Joseph: Symphonies nos. 94, 95, 100, 104 [performed by the Hanover Band] C. Rothko. *High Fidelity (New York, N.Y.)* 39:67 Ap '89

Howard Hanson, American romantic [Seattle Symphony led by Gerard Schwarz] D. Hall. por *Stereo Review* 54:126 S '89

Mahler from a master [Symphonies nos. 2, 4 and 5 conducted by L. Bernstein] D. Hurwitz. il por *High Fidelity (New York, N.Y.)* 39:62-3 Ja '89

Mahler, Gustav: Symphony no. 1, in D [Berlin Philharmonic and Concertgebouw recordings] D. Hurwitz. il *High Fidelity (New York, N.Y.)* 39:68-9 Je '89

Mahler, Gustav: Symphony no. 2, in C minor. D. Hall. il *Stereo Review* 54:124 Mr '89

Making Beethoven the old-fashioned way [period instrument performances] S. Cantrell. il *High Fidelity (New York, N.Y.)* 39:61+ Ap '89

Mendelssohn, Felix: Symphonies nos. 3, 4 and 5 [recordings by Semyon Bychkov and Arturo Toscanini] T. Hathaway. *High Fidelity (New York, N.Y.)* 39:57-8 Mr '89

Mozart, Wolfgang Amadeus: Symphonies: nos. 34, 35 and 39 [London Mozart Players] T. Hathaway. *High Fidelity (New York, N.Y.)* 39:64 My '89

New views on Bruckner [Symphonies nos. 4, 6 and 7 by Giuseppe Sinopoli, Riccardo Muti and Libor Pešek] D. Hurwitz. il *High Fidelity (New York, N.Y.)* 39:56-7 Jl '89

Norrington conducts Berlioz [Symphonie fantastique] R. Freed. por *Stereo Review* 54:68 Jl '89

Orpheus Chamber Orchestra [Prokofiev's Classical symphony, Britten's Simple symphony, and Bizet's Symphony in C major] D. Hall. il *Stereo Review* 54:104 My '89

Prokofiev, Sergey: Symphony no. 5, in B flat. D. Hurwitz. *High Fidelity (New York, N.Y.)* 39:64 F '89

Rachmaninoff, Sergei: Symphony no. 2, in E minor. P. Moor. il *High Fidelity (New York, N.Y.)* 39:58-9 Mr '89

Rachmaninoff, Sergei: Symphony no. 3, in A minor [Stockholm Philharmonic] D. Hurwitz. *High Fidelity (New York, N.Y.)* 39:69-70 Je '89

Rachmaninoff's Second from Rozhdestvensky. R. Freed. por *Stereo Review* 54:93-4 Je '89

Schmidt, Franz: Symphonies nos. 1 and 3. R. R. Reilly. *High Fidelity (New York, N.Y.)* 39:59 Mr '89

Shostakovich's Eleventh [James DePreist and the Helsinki Philharmonic] D. Hall. il *Stereo Review* 54:115 Je '89

Simpson, Robert: Symphonies: no. 6; no. 7 [Royal Liverpool Philharmonic recording] D. Hurwitz. *High Fidelity (New York, N.Y.)* 39:70 Je '89

Vespers (Music)

Handel, George Frideric: Carmelite vespers. K. R. Schwarz. *High Fidelity (New York, N.Y.)* 39:65-6+ Je '89

Violin music

Brahms, Johannes: Concerto for violin and orchestra, in D; Prokofiev, Sergey: Sonatas for violin and piano, no. 1, in F minor [Shlomo Mintz recordings] K. R. Schwarz. il *High Fidelity (New York, N.Y.)* 39:57-8 Jl '89

Lutoslawski, Witold: Chain 2; Partita; Stravinsky, Igor: Concerto for violin and orchestra, in D [Anne-Sophie Mutter recording] K. R. Schwarz. il *High Fidelity (New York, N.Y.)* 39:60-2 Jl '89

Mullova and Previn and Shostakovich [First violin concerto] R. Freed. il por *Stereo Review* 54:123-4 N '89

Sitkovetsky's dazzling Prokofiev [two concertos] D. Hall. il por *Stereo Review* 54:96 Je '89

Vocal music

See also
Compact discs—Arias
Compact discs—Passion music

Janequin, Clément [recent recordings] P. Moor. *High Fidelity (New York, N.Y.)* 39:67-8 Ap '89

COMPACTION OF SOILS *See* Soil compaction

COMPACTS (COSMETICS)

Collectors and collecting

Excuse me a minute while I powder my nose. H. L. Rinker. il *Antiques & Collecting Hobbies* 94:20+ D '89

COMPAGNIE MAGUY MARIN

Burning the flag [performance of Hey, what's all this to me!?] T. Tobias. il *New York* 22:114+ N 20 '89

COMPAÑÍA MINERA DE CANANEA SA

Salinas strikes before the miners can. S. Baker. il map *Business Week* p50 S 4 '89

COMPANIES *See* Corporations

COMPANY NAMES *See* Corporations—Names

COMPANY PUBLICATIONS *See* House organs

COMPAQ COMPUTER CORPORATION

A coming-out party for Compaq's super-PC. G. Lewis and M. Ivey. il *Business Week* p99 N 13 '89

Compaq: super numbers that investors ignore. S. Gannes. il *Fortune* 120:24 N 6 '89

Compaq, Tandy unveil notebook systems. P. Honan. il *Personal Computing* 13:25 D '89

Compaq vs. IBM: peace comes to shove. M. Ivey and G. Lewis. il *Business Week* p132 Mr 13 '89

A genius for sales [R. Canion] D. Pauly. il por *Newsweek* 114:43 O 2 '89

A heavyweight lightweight [Compaq's new laptop] G. Lewis. *Business Week* p152 O 30 '89

How Compaq gets there firstest with the mostest. M. Ivey. il por *Business Week* p146-7+ Je 26 '89

The power behind Compaq's European powerhouse [E. Pfeiffer] T. Peterson. il por *Business Week* p150 Je 26 '89

Soft dollars, hard choices. N. Alster. il por *Forbes* 144:106-7+ S 4 '89

Stepping out from IBM's shadow [R. Canion] P. Honan. por *Personal Computing* 13:79 Jl '89

Suddenly, the PC juggernaut is stuck in the mud. D. A. Depke and others. il *Business Week* p45 D 25 '89-Ja 1 '90

COMPARABLE WORTH WAGE CONCEPT *See* Equal pay for equal work

COMPARATIVE BIOMECHANICS

An engineer's eye helps biologists understand nature. B. Fellman. bibl f (p122) il *Smithsonian* 20:98-105 Jl '89

Mammalian terrestrial locomotion and size. A. A. Biewener. bibl f il *BioScience* 39:776-83 D '89

The mechanics of natural success [cover story] I. Wickelgren. il *Science News* 135:376-8 Je 17 '89

Scaling body support in mammals: limb posture and muscle mechanics. A. A. Biewener. bibl f il *Science* 245:45-8 Jl 7 '89

COMPARATIVE EDUCATION

American textbook reform: what can we learn from the Soviet experience? H. D. Mehlinger. bibl f il *Phi Delta Kappan* 71:29-35 S '89

European vs American higher education. E. M. White and R. Ahrens. il *Change* 21:52-5 S/O '89

International comparisons and U.S. school reform. P. S. Hlebowitsh. *The Education Digest* 55:23-7 N '89

Learning, Chinese-style [children] H. Gardner. il *Psychology Today* 23:54-6 D '89

A look inside a Japanese school. C. Rapoport. il *Fortune* 120:155+ D 4 '89

Needed: an international perspective [school reform] P. G. Altbach. il *Phi Delta Kappan* 71:243-5 N '89

Probing the "myths" about Japanese education. P. Lukens. *The Education Digest* 54:13-16 My '89

Reform in Soviet and American education: parallels and contrasts. S. T. Kerr. bibl f il *Phi Delta Kappan* 71:19-28 S '89

Restructuring leadership [West German model] A. Shanker. *The Education Digest* 54:3-5 F '89

U.S. students flunk math, science [study by the Educational Testing Service] G. Byrne. *Science* 243:729 F 10 '89

U.S. students trail Soviets [views of Marjorie Gardner] *USA Today (Periodical)* 118:14-15 Ag '89

COMPARATIVE GENETICS

A lizard foretold [search for Gymnophthalmus species by chromosome comparison] C. J. Cole and others. map *Natural History* p12+ My '89

Phylogeny and molecular data [discussion of February 12, 1988 article, Molecular phylogeny of the animal kingdom] K. G. Field and others. *Science* 243:548-51 Ja 27 '89

Time bomb [DNA clock; work of Charles G. Sibley and Jon E. Ahlquist] J. Horgan. *Scientific American* 260:24+ Mr '89

Two cultures find common ground [conference of specialists in mouse and fruit fly development] J. L. Marx. il *Science* 244:652-3 My 12 '89

COMPARATIVE PSYCHOLOGY

See also
Sociobiology

COMPASS

See also
North (Direction)
Orienteering (Sport)

Bearing toward true north [electronic fluxgate compass] S. Stapleton. il *Motor Boating & Sailing* 163:48-9 F '89

Digi-compass. T. E. Black. il *Radio-Electronics* 60:43-5+ N '89

Directions—earth and sky. G. Lovi. il *Sky and Telescope* 77:399-400 Ap '89

COMPASS INTERNATIONAL, INC.

Gambling expert hits a different kind of jackpot [S. Micco] A. Nadler. il pors *Home Office Computing* 7:50-1 Ag '89

COMPASSION *See* Sympathy

COMPATIBILITY (AUDIO SYSTEMS) *See* Audio systems—Compatibility

COMPATIBILITY (COMPUTERS) *See* Computers—Compatibility

COMPENSATION (LAW)

See also
Damages
Insurance, Workers' compensation
Iranian air disaster, 1988—Compensation

How to control liability costs. G. L. Priest. il por *Fortune* 119:323-4 Ap 24 '89

COMPENSATION (LAW)—*cont.*

Canada

Facing the future [thalidomide victims seek compensation] A. Steacy. il *Maclean's* 102:41 F 20 '89

COMPENSATION FOR VICTIMS OF CRIME *See* Reparation

COMPENSATORY EDUCATION

Improving education for the disadvantaged: do we know whom to help? J. H. Ralph. bibl f il *Phi Delta Kappan* 70:395-401 Ja '89

COMPETENCY (LAW) *See* Capacity and disability

COMPETENCY TESTS *See* Educational tests and measurements

COMPETENCY TESTS FOR TEACHERS *See* Teachers—Examinations

COMPETING CURRENCIES *See* Free banking

COMPETITION

See also

Business intelligence

President's Task Force on Competitiveness

Price cutting

Trade marks and trade names

America still reigns in services. S. Nasar. il *Fortune* 119:64-6+ Je 5 '89

America's economic security [address, May 8, 1989] R. Mosbacher. *Vital Speeches of the Day* 55:554-6 Jl 1 '89

America's place in world competition. B. O'Reilly. il *Fortune* 120:83-4+ N 6 '89

America's stake in the new global economy. G. Greenwald. il *USA Today (Periodical)* 118:26-8 N '89

Brady's long-term plans will collide with the deficit [N. Brady's competitiveness policy] H. Gleckman. por *Business Week* p33 Ja 23 '89

The captains see a tilted field [global competition; Fortune poll] B. O'Reilly. il *Fortune* 120:93+ N 6 '89

CEOs gird for global battle [Fortune poll] B. Dumaine. il *Fortune* 119:65-6 Ap 24 '89

Companies that compete best [cover story] B. Saporito. il *Fortune* 119:36-8+ My 22 '89

Competing by cooperating [address, May 9, 1989] A. H. Magazine. *Vital Speeches of the Day* 55:604-8 Jl 15 '89

Competitive climate: industry leaders look to the government for a new era. E. Corcoran. il *Scientific American* 260:70+ Mr '89

Competitiveness in the global marketplace [address, May 11, 1989] R. T. McCormack. *Department of State Bulletin* 89:49-53 Jl '89

Education: the competitor's key [views of Chamber of Commerce chairman J. L. Clendenin] R. T. Gray. il pors *Nation's Business* 77:60+ Je '89

The excuse industry [explanations for lack of American success in global competition] R. J. Samuelson. il *Newsweek* 114:74 D 11 '89

Harnessing the American marketplace [special section] bibl *Society* 27:41-71 N/D '89

Henry Kaufman: corporate debt erodes competition [interview] J. H. Dobrzynski. por *Business Week* p40 Mr 20 '89

How managers can succeed through speed [cover story] B. Dumaine. il *Fortune* 119:54-7+ F 13 '89

How the U.S. can compete globally [interview with R. Noyce] il por *Fortune* 119:248 Je 5 '89

How to get the scoop on your competition [excerpt from Monitoring the competition] L. M. Fuld. il *Working Woman* 14:39-42 Ja '89

How we can regain our competitive edge. S. Ramo. *Scientific American* 260:148 My '89

Human resources [address, January 19, 1989] A. H. Magazine. *Vital Speeches of the Day* 55:502-7 Je 1 '89

Information technology, global linkage, and U.S. competitiveness [address, June 14, 1989] E. M. Ehrlich. *Vital Speeches of the Day* 55:755-9 O 1 '89

Is our eye on the wrong ball? [preoccupation with deficit] D. A. Levy. il por *Forbes* 143:232 Ap 17 '89

It's gloves-off time [global competition] S. Nasar. il *U.S. News & World Report* 107:40-2 D 25 '89-Ja 1 '90

Maintaining competitiveness [address, January 19, 1989] R. D. Tuttle. *Vital Speeches of the Day* 55:598-600 Jl 15 '89

The message of the market [stock plunges reflect business' response to competition] R. J. Samuelson. il *Newsweek* 114:64-8 O 30 '89

One man's poison . . . [competitors take advantage of leveraged rivals] N. Alster. il *Forbes* 144:38-9 O 16 '89

A plan for competitiveness and continued economic growth [Keeping America on top policy statement by U.S. Chamber of Commerce] il *Nation's Business* 77:80 Ja '89

Shooting for the moon [role of chaos in business; address, April 27, 1989] R. A. Ferchat. *Vital Speeches of the Day* 55:727-31 S 15 '89

Technology, employment and U.S. competitiveness. R. M. Cyert and D. C. Mowery. il *Scientific American* 260:54-60+ My '89

Toward a new industrial America [views of the M.I.T. Commission on Industrial Productivity] S. Berger and others. il map *Scientific American* 260:39-47 Je '89

U.S. competition in emerging technology areas [address, August 8, 1989] H. D. Bentley. *Vital Speeches of the Day* 56:2-5 O 15 '89

U.S. credibility and viability in worldwide competition [address, May 25, 1989] N. R. Augustine. *Vital Speeches of the Day* 55:693-7 S 1 '89

The U.S. gets back in fighting shape. A. L. Taylor, III. il *Fortune* 119:42-5+ Ap 24 '89

Will America become #2? A. K. Selimuddin. il *USA Today (Periodical)* 118:14-16 S '89

The will to take leadership [increasing America's competitiveness; address, March 22, 1989] L. A. Iacocca. *Vital Speeches of the Day* 55:454-8 My 15 '89

COMPETITION (PSYCHOLOGY)

See also

Sports—Psychological aspects

Compulsive comparing. J. Stone. il *Glamour* 87:132 Ag '89

Taking the edge off competition. H. McCandless. il *Working Woman* 14:110 S '89

COMPETITION POLICY BUREAU (CANADA) *See* Canada. Bureau of Competition Policy

COMPETITIONS

See also

All-American Girl Contest

Beauty contests

Odyssey of the Mind

Prize contests

Tractor pulling

See also subhead Competitions under various subjects

A contest and a cake [Great New Delectations Contest and chocolate cake] N. Hazelton. *National Review* 41:48+ Je 16 '89

COMPETITIVENESS *See* Competition

COMPILERS (COMPUTERS)

See also

Silicon compilers (Computers)

Clash of the object-oriented Pascals [Quick Pascal and Turbo Pascal 5.5] J. Udell. il *Byte* 14:104-6 Jl '89

Clipper applications get SQL. M. Schnapp. *Byte* 14:211-12+ D '89

Configuring parallel programs (I) [Occam Transpiler] D. Pountain. il *Byte* 14:349-52 D '89

A FORTRAN for the Mac forces [Language Systems FORTRAN] D. Barker and L. H. Loeb. *Byte* 14:102 F '89

Input: keep it clean [data-entry TSR program] R. Grehan. il *Byte* 14:387-90+ D '89

IntegrAda [Ada programming support environment] K. Nyberg and J. Udell. il *Byte* 14:213-14+ Ja '89

Language sojourn [using QuickBasic] J. Pournelle. il *Byte* 14:111-12+ Ap '89

Lisp dialect taps Mac riches [MacScheme + Toolsmith] J. Udell. il *Byte* 14:204 S '89

Modula-2 and OS/2 join forces. A. Schulman. il *Byte* 14:171-4 Ag '89

Optimizing numeric coprocessing. S. S. Fried. il *Byte* 14 Special Issue:221-4 Fall '89

Power to the programmer [Watcom C 386] F. Hommel. il *Byte* 14:199-200+ D '89

QuickBASIC comes to the Macintosh [Macintosh QuickBASIC 1.0] N. C. Shammas. il *Byte* 14:223-4+ Ja '89

Smoothing out C [optimizing compilers] S. Apiki and J. Udell. il *Byte* 14:170-8+ F '89

Think C goes OOP. T. Thompson. il *Byte* 14:81-2 O '89

TopSpeed Modula-2. B. Nance. il *Byte* 14:211-14 My '89

Unix filenames for Turbo Pascal. J. Kerr. il *Byte* 14 Special Issue:185-6+ Fall '89

Unix tools for DOS [MKS Make and MKS Lex and Yacc] B. Smith. *Byte* 14:97-8 F '89

COMPLAINTS

Best ways to get your money back [consumer complaints] S. Nasar. il *Money* 18:149+ Ap '89

Chronic complaining. J. Stone. il *Glamour* 87:116 F '89

Consumer gripes: how to get results. K. Davis. il *Changing Times* 43:79-83 N '89

How to complain effectively [consumers] G. L. Beiswinger. il *McCall's* 116:42 Ja '89

How to handle your own complaint. *Consumers' Research Magazine* 72:36-8 Jl '89

Where to complain [New York City] J. Blyskal and M. Hodge. il *New York* 22:70-3 My 1 '89

COMPLEMENTATION (GENETICS)

Human cells lacking mtDNA: repopulation with exogenous mitochondria by complementation. M. P. King and G. Attardi. bibl f il *Science* 246:500-3 O 27 '89

COMPLEMENTS (IMMUNITY)

Adipsin and complement factor D activity: an immune-related defect in obesity. B. S. Rosen and others. bibl f il *Science* 244:1483-7 Je 23 '89

COMPLEXES (CHEMISTRY)

See also

Cavitands

Host-guest complexes (Chemistry)

COMPLEXION *See* Skin

COMPLEXITY (PHYSICAL SCIENCE)

Complexity made simpler [work of Seth Lloyd and Heinz Pagels] W. F. Allman. il *U.S. News & World Report* 106:61 Ap 3 '89

COMPLICATIONS (SURGERY) See Surgery—Complications
COMPLIMENTS See Praise
COMPOSERS, AMERICAN
See also
Arlen, Harold, 1905-1986
Barber, Samuel, 1910-1981
Berlin, Irving, 1888-1989
Bernstein, Leonard, 1918-
Cage, John
Carter, Elliott, 1908-
Chadwick, George W.
Copland, Aaron, 1900-
Davis, Anthony
Ellington, Duke, 1899-1974
Frazelle, Kenneth
Gershwin, George, 1898-1937
Getty, Gordon P.
Glass, Philip
Hanson, Howard, 1896-1981
Harrison, Lou
Martino, Donald, 1931-
Paine, John Knowles, 1839-1906
Rieti, Vittorio
Rorem, Ned, 1923-
Sessions, Roger
Sondheim, Stephen
Telson, Bob
Thomson, Virgil, 1896-1989
Music's new generation. il *U.S. News & World Report* 107:70 N 27 '89
Stages [tracing the progress of the American opera composer from commission to production] B. Kellow. il por *Opera News* 54:18-22 S '89
COMPOSERS, ARGENTINE
See also
Gardel, Carlos
COMPOSERS, AUSTRIAN
See also
Bruckner, Anton, 1824-1896
Mahler, Gustav, 1860-1911
Mozart, Wolfgang Amadeus, 1756-1791
Schoenberg, Arnold, 1874-1951
Schubert, Franz, 1797-1828
COMPOSERS, CZECH
See also
Martinu, Bohuslav, 1890-1959
Popper, David, 1843-1913
COMPOSERS, DUTCH
See also
Altena, Maarten
Obrecht, Jacob, d. 1505
COMPOSERS, ENGLISH
See also
Tippett, Sir Michael, 1905-
COMPOSERS, FRENCH
See also
Janequin, Clément
Messiaen, Olivier
Offenbach, Jacques, 1819-1880
Rameau, Jean Philippe
Saint-Saëns, Camille, 1835-1921
COMPOSERS, GERMAN
See also
Bach, Carl Philipp Emanuel, 1714-1788
Bach, Johann Sebastian, 1685-1750
Beethoven, Ludwig van, 1770-1827
Fasch, Johann Friedrich, 1688-1758
Gluck, Christoph Willibald, Ritter von, 1714-1787
Handel, George Frideric, 1685-1759
Strauss, Richard, 1864-1949
Wagner, Richard, 1813-1883
Weill, Kurt, 1900-1950
COMPOSERS, HUNGARIAN
See also
Bartók, Béla, 1881-1945
Liszt, Franz, 1811-1886
COMPOSERS, ITALIAN
See also
Monteverdi, Claudio, 1567-1643
Rossini, Gioacchino, 1792-1868
Verdi, Giuseppe, 1813-1901
Zipoli, Domenico, 1688-1726
COMPOSERS, POLISH
See also
Lutoslawski, Witold, 1913-
COMPOSERS, POLISH AMERICAN
See also
Litwinski, Mieczyslaw
COMPOSERS, RUSSIAN
See also
Prokofiev, Sergey, 1891-1953
Shostakovich, Dmitrii Dmitrievich, 1906-1975
Stravinsky, Igor, 1882-1971
COMPOSERS, SOUTH AFRICAN
See also
Volans, Kevin

COMPOSITE MATERIALS
See also
Airplanes, Home-built—Materials
Airplanes, Jet—Materials
Airplanes, Military—Materials
Bicycles—Materials
Dow-United Technologies Composite Products (Firm)
Ceramic matrix composites improve. *High Technology Business* 9:36 Ja '89
Plastics that leave no space unfilled [work of General Electric] *Science News* 136:222 S 30 '89
Pourable plastics. E. Corcoran. il *Scientific American* 261:102+ D '89
Smart materials. S. R. Tessler. il *Technology Review* 92:8-9 Ap '89
Strong polymer composites. M. Mandell. *High Technology Business* 9:10-11 Ap '89
COMPOSITE PHOTOGRAPHS See Photomontage
COMPOSITION, ENGLISH See English language—Composition
COMPOSITION (MUSIC)
See also
Computers—Musical use
Instrumentation and orchestration
Jazz music—Writing
Melody
Musicals, revues, etc.—Writing
COMPOSITION (PHOTOGRAPHY)
Designer landscapes. M. Van Hesemans. il *Petersen's Photographic Magazine* 18:24-9 O '89
A few new angles on home videomaking [importance of camera angle] E. Stecker. il *Video* 13:38+ D '89
Inspired seeing is rekindled in this domestic self-assignment. F. Patterson. il *Petersen's Photographic Magazine* 18:22-3 Jl '89
Stopping power. A. Ganahl. il *Petersen's Photographic Magazine* 18:34-8 Je '89
COMPOST
Making compost. *The Mother Earth News* 116:88-9 Mr/Ap '89
Simple compost systems. il *Sunset (Central West edition)* 183:200+ N '89
The trouble with leaves. N. Shute. il *National Wildlife* 27:18-19 O/N '89
COMPOTES See Cooking—Fruit
COMPOUND Q (DRUG) See GLQ223 (Drug)
COMPOUNDS, ORGANIC See Organic compounds
COMPREHENSION
See also
Chinese Room Thought Experiment
Memory
Reading comprehension
COMPREHENSIVE TEST BAN See Nuclear weapons—Testing—Suspension
COMPRESSED AIR
Storage
Compressed-air power. S. Ashley. il *Popular Science* 235:73 Ag '89
New ways to meet off-peak power demands [compressed air storage facilities flushed out of underground salt domes] il *Popular Mechanics* 166:15 Mr '89
COMPRESSION
Dreaming up crystals that outdo diamond [work of Marvin L. Cohen and Amy Y. Liu] I. Amato. il *Science News* 136:134 Ag 26 '89
Prediction of new low compressibility solids. A. Y. Liu and M. L. Cohen. bibl f il *Science* 245:841-2 Ag 25 '89
COMPRESSION OF DATA (COMPUTER SCIENCE) See Data compression (Computer science)
COMPRESSORS, AIR See Air compressors
COMPTON, JOAN CALLAHAN
Modern-day monsters. il *Psychology Today* 23:30-1 Mr '89
COMPTON (F.E.) AND COMPANY See F.E. Compton Company
COMPULSIVE-OBSESSIVE BEHAVIOR See Obsessive-compulsive behavior
COMPULSIVE SHOPPING
When the urge to spend strikes [views of Georgia Witkin and Nancy Good] M. B. Brinley. il *McCall's* 116:39-41 Jl '89
COMPULSORY EDUCATION
See also
School age
COMPULSORY LABOR See Forced labor
COMPULSORY MILITARY SERVICE See Draft
COMPUSERVE (DATA BANK) See Information systems
COMPUTATIONAL COMPLEXITY
Information-based complexity. B. A. Cipra. *Science* 243:1142-3 Mr 3 '89
COMPUTE! (PERIODICAL)
Editorial license. P. Scisco. il *Compute!* 11:4 O '89
We know who you are [survey of readers] G. Keizer. il *Compute!* 11:4 My '89
COMPUTER-AIDED DESIGN See Computer graphics
COMPUTER-AIDED SOFTWARE ENGINEERING
CASE [special section] il *Byte* 14:206-7+ Ap '89
Computers programming computers. E. Dyson. il *Forbes* 143:137 Mr 6 '89

COMPUTER-AIDED SOFTWARE ENGINEERING—*cont.*
A different kind of CASE tool [Logic Gem] A. Schulman. il *Byte* 14:217-20 My '89

Domesticating Microsoft Windows [CASE:W] A. Lane. il *Byte* 14:205-7 Je '89

Making a case for CASE. il *Byte* 14:154-8+ D '89

microExplorer in action! A. Lane. il *Byte* 14:247-8+ N '89

COMPUTER ANIMATION
The magic theater. F. Hapgood. il *Omni (New York, N.Y.)* 12:114-16+ D '89

Programming
Art & Film Director. D. McNeill. il *Compute!* 11:62-3 Ag '89

Cartooners. N. Rentschler. il *Compute!* 11:71-2 Je '89

Create your own computer 'toons. S. Anzovin. il *Compute!* 11:34-6+ Jl '89

DeluxePaint III. S. Anzovin. il *Compute!* 11:64+ S '89

Fantavision. S. Anzovin. il *Compute!* 11:64 F '89

Let the Mac entertain you [MacroMind Director] N. Baran. il *Byte* 14:84+ Ag '89

Mac modeling in 3-D [Swivel 3D] D. Barker and L. H. Loeb. il *Byte* 14 Mac Special Ed:MAC219-MAC220 Je '89

Special F/X on the Mac [Showcase F/X] D. Barker. *Byte* 14 Mac Special Supp:MAC191-MAC192 Ag '89

COMPUTER ARCHITECTURE
A bold move in mainframes [IBM; cover story] J. W. Verity. il *Business Week* p72-8 My 29 '89

The end of application software? [IBM's Systems Application Architecture] F. Langa. *Byte* 14:6 F '89

IBM: does it have the right connections? C. O'Malley. il *Personal Computing* 13:88-91+ D '89

COMPUTER-ASSISTED INSTRUCTION *See* Computers— Educational use
COMPUTER ASSOCIATES INTERNATIONAL INC.
Sometimes it doesn't pay to keep a secret [Computer Associates won't spell out its plans for Cullinet] D. A. Depke. il *Business Week* p30-1 Ag 28 '89

COMPUTER BULLETIN BOARDS
BBSing on the cheap—the phoneless electronic bulletin board. D. Stanton. *Compute!* 11:14 Ap '89

Computer bulletin board systems (BBS's) [astronomy] *Sky and Telescope* 78 Resource Guide:16-17 S '89

Government bulletin boards. M. Lent. il *Home Office Computing* 7:34 Ja '89

Keeping in touch via the Major BBS. B. Krasnoff. *Personal Computing* 13:202 D '89

Put your computer to work while you're away [private bulletin board system] A. Glossbrenner. il *Home Office Computing* 7:36 My '89

Very personal computing [alcoholics' use] D. L. Gonzalez. il *Newsweek* 114:64 Ag 28 '89

COMPUTER CABLES
Fiber vs. metal. J. Y. Bryce. il *Byte* 14:253-8 Ja '89

RS-232 debugging with SAM 2000. il *Radio-Electronics* 60:83-5 O '89

Testing
Build an intelligent cable tester for only $25! J. Barbarello. il *Radio-Electronics* 60 ComputerDigest:77+ Ap '89

COMPUTER CHESS
The chess machines [Deep Thought computer] B. Wickens. il *Maclean's* 102:57 O 23 '89

Chess prodigy [Deep Thought computer] *Time* 133:74 F 27 '89

Computer chess: a masterful lesson [Deep Thought vs. G. Kasparov] I. Peterson. *Science News* 136:276 O 28 '89

The human chess champion: endangered species. W. F. Allman. il *U.S. News & World Report* 106:64 Mr 13 '89

Humanity 2, computers 0 [Deep Thought vs. G. Kasparov] M. M. Waldrop. il por *Science* 246:572-3 N 3 '89

It's mind over matter, 2-0 [G. Kasparov vs. Deep Thought] F. Lidz. il por *Sports Illustrated* 71:97 O 30 '89

More computers—and humans—are saying 'checkmate'. M. Schroeder. il *Business Week* p50 N 6 '89

Pawn to king four [Deep Thought computer] T. Waters. il *Discover* 10:28+ My '89

COMPUTER CIRCUITS *See* Integrated circuits
COMPUTER CLUBS
See also
Computer users groups
COMPUTER CONSULTANTS
See also
Goodman & Hayle Information Systems, Inc.
Computer consultant [home business] D. Atkin. *Compute!* 11:20 Ag '89

Tips on hiring a computer consultant. C.-F. Perez. il *Home Office Computing* 7:14 Mr '89

What a LAN consultant will tell you. C. Strehlo. il *Personal Computing* 13:97-9+ Ap '89

COMPUTER CONTROL *See* Automation
COMPUTER CRIMES
See also
Computer programming—Unauthorized use
Computer viruses
Desktop forgery
Are ATMs easy targets for crooks? P. Cole. il *Business Week* p30 Mr 6 '89

Astronomer Cliff Stoll stars in the espionage game, but for him spying doesn't really compute [responsible for tracking down Hannover, Germany hacker who gained access to U.S. government network] J. S. Kunen. il pors *People Weekly* 32:118+ D 11 '89

Drop the phone [arrest of K. Mitnick] por *Time* 133:49 Ja 9 '89

Free the hacker two. E. Corley. *Harper's* 279:22+ S '89

German computer spy ring broken. E. Marshall. *Science* 243:1545 Mr 24 '89

Goodbye, Mr. Chips. P. Wayner. il *Byte* 14:364 O '89

COMPUTER DATING (SOCIAL CUSTOMS) *See* Computers—Social use
COMPUTER EXPRESS, INC.
Electronic retailer makes cash register ring. L. Arden. il por *Home Office Computing* 7:42 My '89

COMPUTER FURNITURE
Make yourself comfortable. P. Scisco. il *Compute!* 11:28-31 My '89

COMPUTER GAMES *See* Video games
COMPUTER GRAPHICS
See also
Association for Computing Machinery. Special Interest Group on Computer Graphics
CalComp Inc.
Computer animation
Computer visualization
Desktop video
Digitizers (Computers)
Digitizing tablets
Light pens
Prototyping (Computers)
Radius, Inc.
Stereolithography
TIGA (Texas Instruments' Graphics Architecture)
VGA (Video graphics array)
Weyerhaeuser DesignCenters
The brains behind the graphics [graphics coprocessor boards] S. Apiki and others. il *Byte* 14:178-82+ N '89

Byte graphics supplement [special section] il *Byte* 14:249+ Ap '89

The color of geometry [cover story] I. Peterson. il *Science News* 136:408-10+ D 23-30 '89

Graphic design in the age of computers. S. Gamliel. il *Occupational Outlook Quarterly* 32:34-6 Wint '88

How to put 16 million colors to work [NuBus boards for 32-Bit QuickDraw] T. Thompson. il *Byte* 14:189-94+ D '89

Images for the computer age. F. Ward. il *National Geographic* 175:718-51 Je '89

Impressive full-page display system [NEC MonoGraph System] S. Chen. il *Home Office Computing* 7:55-6 Jl '89

Mac color by SCSI [ScuzzyGraph II external graphics display] H. Eglowstein. *Byte* 14:235 D '89

A matter fabricator provides matter for thought [Banach-Tarski paradox] A. K. Dewdney. il *Scientific American* 260:116-19 Ap '89

New graphics tools let designers see the future [auto styling] il *Popular Mechanics* 166:15 D '89

PixC leaves windows overhead in the dust. B. Smith. il *Byte* 14:202 S '89

Pixels on the march [8514/A and Artist 10 MC graphics coprocessor boards] B. D. Kliewer. il *Byte* 14:201-2+ Ja '89

Through the 3-D looking glass. P. Elmer-Dewitt. il *Time* 133:65-6 My 1 '89

True colors, revisited [Spectrum/24 video board] T. Thompson. il *Byte* 14 Mac Special Supp:MAC191 Ag '89

Ultra graphics [Ultra Clipper UM1280, bus-mastering coprocessor] B. D. Kliewer. il *Byte* 14:167-9 Ag '89

UltraVision. J. Nimersheim. il *Compute!* 11:130+ N '89

Update: standout graphics board [Rendition II] S. Apiki. il *Byte* 14:234 D '89

Ethical aspects
Graphics that tell the truth. J. Meade. il *Personal Computing* 13:79-80+ Ja '89

Exhibitions
Art in the computer age [SIGGRAPH 1989 Art Show] R. F. Malina. il *Technology Review* 92:71-2+ O '89

Photographs and photography
Double-exposing two media. S. Lewis. il *Petersen's Photographic Magazine* 17:76-7 Mr '89

Programming
See also
Clip art software
DeskMate (Computer program)
Graphical user interfaces
Prograph (Computer program)
Apple's 32-bit QuickDraw covers the spectrum. T. Thompson. il *Byte* 14:99-102+ Jl '89

Art + 2 years = science [workstation graphics] P. R. Robinson. il *Byte* 14:255-64 F '89

Buyer's guide: CAD software. il *Personal Computing* 13:121-6+ My '89

Buyer's guide: presentation graphics [Draw Applause; 35mm Express; Graphics Gallery; Freelance Plus; Graph Plus; Harvard Graphics; Pixie] il *Personal Computing* 13:121-3+ F '89

COMPUTER GRAPHICS—Programming—*cont.*

CADD for the non-draftsperson [Generic CADD Level 2 Starter Kit] L. Wood. il *Home Office Computing* 7:74 O '89

CADD for the theatre designer: a comparison of low-cost programs. M. Stauffer. il *Theatre Crafts* 23:66+ Ja '89

Canvas [version 2.0] R. Hart. il *Home Office Computing* 7:77-8 My '89

Catch of the day: biomorphs of Truchet tiles, served with popcorn and snails. A. K. Dewdney. il *Scientific American* 261:110-13 Jl '89

Certificates and More. L. Frey. il *Compute!* 11:130+ D '89

Claris CAD. P. Tuten. il *Byte* 14:209-10 Je '89

Computers: roundtable tackles the difficult issues (I) [use of CAD by architects] C. K. Hoyt. il *Architectural Record* 177:159+ F '89

Computers: roundtable tackles the difficult issues (II) [use of CAD] C. K. Hoyt. il *Architectural Record* 177:133+ Ap '89

Corel Draw shows great promise. S. Rosenberg. il *Byte* 14:213-14+ Je '89

Costumes by computer [use of AutoCAD] P. Ellsworth. il *Theatre Crafts* 23:78+ N '89

Create inexpensive, yet high-quality presentations [Pinstripe Presenter and PFS: First Graphics] R. Geist and H. Geist. il *Home Office Computing* 7:34-5 Je '89

Create professional slides and presentations [Freelance Plus] R. Geist and H. Geist. il *Home Office Computing* 7:86-8 N '89

Dazzling artwork from dull numbers [presentation graphics software] D. P. Wiener. il *U.S. News & World Report* 106:63 Ja 9 '89

DeluxePaint III. S. Anzovin. il *Compute!* 11:64+ S '89

The desktop presentation star [Aldus Persuasion 1.0] M. Antonoff. il *Personal Computing* 13:188-9 Jl '89

Displaying strength of character [trend toward graphic and visual orientation] M. Liskin. il *Personal Computing* 13:57-8+ Ja '89

Dots and vectors [Designer] il *Radio-Electronics* 60 ComputerDigest:91-2 Mr '89

Drawing Table. B. Hunt. il *Home Office Computing* 7:70 Ag '89

Drawing with precision. L. Kleinman. il *Personal Computing* 13:61-3 My '89

Easygoing 2-D CAD on the Macintosh [Vellum] H. Eglowstein. il *Byte* 14:82+ D '89

Editing in shades of gray [Picture Publisher 1.0] C. O'Malley. il *Personal Computing* 13:194+ My '89

Electronic Arts decolorizes Studio/8 [Studio/1 monochrome paint package] D. Barker. il *Byte* 14:81 S '89

The electronic darkroom [Picture Publisher] J. Fiderio. il *Byte* 14:104-5 Mr '89

Emerging trends in architectural CAD software. K. Sanders. il *Architectural Record* 177:130-1+ Mr '89

Fun beyond your wildest games. O. S. Card. il *Compute!* 11:8 Jl '89

Graphics formats. G. L. Graef. il *Byte* 14:305-6+ S '89

Homework [shape and color games for children] H. E. H. Aycock. il *Compute!* 11:114 N '89

How to get picture-perfect graphics on your printed pages. S. Morgenstern. il *Home Office Computing* 7:28+ D '89

How to get your readers' attention [GEM Artline and LetraStudio] S. Morgenstern. il *Home Office Computing* 7:50-1 My '89

Illustrator: Adobe throws a curve [Adobe Illustrator for Windows] L. Kleinman. il *Personal Computing* 13:158-9 Ag '89

Industrial-strength graphics [SuperPaint 2.0] T. Thompson. il *Byte* 14 Mac Special Ed:MAC219 Je '89

The layman's guide to presentation design. R. Raskin. il *Home Office Computing* 7:37-9 Jl '89

Light reflection models for computer graphics. D. Greenberg. bibl f il *Science* 244:166-73 Ap 14 '89

Mac desktop presentation software [StandOut! 1.0, PowerPoint 2.00A, and Cricket Presents 1.0] L. Stevens. il *Byte* 14:203-5 Ap '89

MacDraw II. R. Mansfield. il *Home Office Computing* 7:72+ Ja '89

Manage it with pictures [Project Scheduler 4] L. Wood. il *Byte* 14:223-4+ D '89

Mastering the PCX format [PCX Programmer's Toolkit] B. Tyler. il *Byte* 14:183-4+ S '89

New 32-bit QuickDraw means better Mac color. *Byte* 14:16+ Je '89

New graphics program debuts in concert hall [acoustic design graphics program developed by Donald Greenberg and Adam Stettner] A. S. Moffat. il *Science* 245:1452 S 29 '89

Opus I [graphics oriented database management program] P. R. Robinson. il *Byte* 14:233-4+ Ja '89

Paint and draw with one versatile package [SuperPaint] J. Latimer. il *Home Office Computing* 7:90+ D '89

Paint programs. C. D. Hanlon. il *Compute!* 11:48-50+ Ja '89

Painting on the Mac takes a step forward [PixelPaint 2.0] T. Thompson. il *Byte* 14:90 Jl '89

PC Paintbrush IV. D. Atkin. il *Compute!* 11:119+ N '89

Perspective Junior [presentation graphics program] J. Nimersheim. il *Compute!* 11:114+ O '89

Pinstripe Presenter [chart producing program] S. Anzovin. il *Compute!* 11:71 My '89

Powerful portable 3-D graphics [HOOPS 2.03] B. D. Kliewer. il *Byte* 14:193-4+ Jl '89

PowerPoint. B. Hunt. *Home Office Computing* 7:71-3 Ap '89

Presentation-graphics software. R. Raskin. il *Home Office Computing* 7:40-3 Jl '89

Presentations with punch. C. O'Malley. il *Personal Computing* 13:108-11+ Ja '89

Prodigious presentation power from Xerox [Xerox Presents] L. Kleinman. il *Personal Computing* 13:184-5 Je '89

Quality CAD on a budget [DesignCAD] J. Devlin. il *Personal Computing* 13:200+ N '89

Save and annotate your Mac output [SuperGlue II utility] T. Thompson. il *Byte* 14:82+ S '89

Simple but elegant 3-D CAD [Generic 3D Drafting] J. Udell. il *Byte* 14:86+ D '89

A simplified project manager with advanced capabilities [Project Scheduler 4] C. Hlavaty. il *Personal Computing* 13:195 N '89

Slide Shop. N. Rentschler. il *Compute!* 11:68-9 Mr '89

Slide Shop. T. A. Summers. il *Home Office Computing* 7:88+ F '89

Software reviews for architects [Architrion II, Series 4, Release 1.0] S. S. Ross. il *Architectural Record* 177:117+ S '89

Software reviews for architects [Dreams 1.0 and DataCAD 3.6e with DC Modeler] S. S. Ross. il *Architectural Record* 177:123+ Ja '89

Software reviews for architects [Electronic Sweet's and Auto CAD release 10 with ADE 3] il *Architectural Record* 177:137+ Mr '89

Software reviews for architects [FastCAD 2.05 and Snap! 3.0] S. S. Ross. il *Architectural Record* 177:139+ Ap '89

Software reviews for architects [MacProject II, version 2.0 and GEOCAD, version 3.3] S. S. Ross. il *Architectural Record* 177:133+ Jl '89

Splash! [paint program] S. Anzovin. il *Compute!* 11:90 Ja '89

Stalking the 8-bit spectrum. T. Thompson. il *Byte* 14:333-4+ S '89

Studio/8: the best paint yet. D. Barker. il *Byte* 14 Mac Special Ed:MAC5 Mr '89

TekColor lets you really see what you get [color-matching system for the Macintosh] J. Bertolucci and T. Thompson. il *Byte* 14:84+ N '89

The third dimension [three-dimensional modeling CAD] B. Holtz and J. Udell. il *Byte* 14:178-80+ My '89

Twist & Shout [printer utility program] L. Frey. il *Compute!* 11:68 Ap '89

Two architectural programs for the Mac [Architrion II and MacBravo! Facilities] il *Byte* 14:70 S '89

VersaCAD/386 version 5.4; Proposal Manager 254/255. S. S. Ross. il *Architectural Record* 177:149+ N '89

Visual Edge sharpens laser output [printer enhancement] C. O'Malley. il *Personal Computing* 13:192-3 My '89

Xerox Graph gives data its due [presentation graphics software] L. Kleinman. il *Personal Computing* 13:196+ N '89

Standards

Clash of the graphics titans. R. Cook. il *Byte* 14 Special Issue:143-4+ Fall '89

The RenderMan interface. T. Apodaca. il *Byte* 14:267-8+ Ap '89

COMPUTER IMAGING CENTER *See* Fine Arts Museum of Long Island. Computer Imaging Center

COMPUTER INDUSTRY

See also

3Com Corp.

Advanced Products & Technologies (Firm)

American Telephone & Telegraph Co.

Apollo Computer, Inc.

Apple Computer Inc.

Ardent Computer Inc.

Atari Corp.

Comdisco, Inc.

Commodore International Ltd.

Compaq Computer Corporation

Computer service industries

Control Data Corp.

Convergent Technologies Inc.

Cray Computer Corporation

Cray Research, Inc.

Data General Corp.

Datapoint Corp.

Dataproducts Corp.

Dell Computer Corporation

Digital Equipment Corp.

Encore Computer Corporation

ETA Systems Inc.

Floating Point Systems, Inc.

FPS Computing (Firm)

Franklin Computer Corporation

Gould Inc.

Grid Systems Inc.

Gtech Corporation

COMPUTER INDUSTRY—See also—*cont.*
Hayes Microcomputer Products, Inc.
Hewlett-Packard Co.
Honeywell Inc.
Intel Corp.
International Business Machines Corp.
Magnesys Corporation
MAI Basic Four, Inc.
MIPS Computer Systems Inc.
National Semiconductor Corp.
NCR Corp.
Next Inc.
Nodal Systems Corporation
Prime Computer, Inc.
Seagate Technology
Sequent Computer Systems Inc.
Stardent (Firm)
Stellar Computer Inc.
Sun Microsystems Inc.
Tandem Computers Inc.
Tandy Corp.
Tektronix, Inc.
Telxon Corporation
Texas Instruments Incorporated
Thinking Machines Corporation
Unisys Corp.
Women in the computer industry
Wyse Technology
Zenith Electronics Corp.

Are computers still a growth industry? S. Nasar. il *U.S. News & World Report* 107:60 O 23 '89
How computing changes everything: computing in America [cover story; special issue; with editorial comment by Fred Abatemarco] il *Personal Computing* 13:9, 21+ O '89
Industry watch. R. A. Shaffer. See issues of Personal Computing beginning January 1985
Microbytes. See issues of Byte
Random access. E. Dyson. See issues of Forbes beginning May 18, 1987
View from the Valley. S. R. Reed. See issues of Personal Computing beginning June 1987 through November 1989

Acquisitions and mergers
Caveat raider [MAI Basic Four's battle for Prime Computer sours customer relations] K. K. Wiegner. il *Forbes* 143:160 Je 12 '89
The company they couldn't sell [Prime Computer] G. Slutsker. il *Forbes* 144:227-9 O 2 '89
Gould will use same market strategy under Encore ownership. E. H. Kolcum. *Aviation Week & Space Technology* 130:53 Ap 17 '89
HP: now no. 1 in workstations [deal for Apollo] J. B. Levine. il *Business Week* p30 Ap 24 '89
"I love the tumult" [career of A. Michels] J. Pitta. il pors *Forbes* 144:296-8 N 13 '89
Is AT&T laying the cable for a hookup with NCR? G. G. Marcial. il *Business Week* p92 Ap 3 '89
The Prime buyout is tough to compute [J. H. Whitney's leveraged buyout of Prime Computer Inc.] L. Helm. il *Business Week* p28 Jl 10 '89

International aspects
Is the U.S. selling its high-tech soul to Japan? J. B. Levine. il *Business Week* p117-18 Je 26 '89
A Silicon Valley plum may drop into Taiwan's lap [Wyse Technology] D. J. Yang and M. Shao. il *Business Week* p38 D 4 '89
Why Jerry Pearlman gave up his brainchild [selling Zenith's computer unit to Bull] L. Therrien. il por *Business Week* p35 O 16 '89

Western Europe
The hottest computer command in Europe: merge. T. Peterson. il *Business Week* p47 Je 19 '89

Advertising
Faces that can sell a thousand computers [celebrity spokespersons] G. Keizer. il *Compute!* 11:4 Mr '89

Anecdotes, facetiae, satire, etc.
To get my columns in on time, I'm going to start covering the news before it happens. A. R. Levitan. *Compute!* 11:112+ Ja '89

Antitrust cases
Why IBM is cramping its biggest customers' style [leasing companies and antitrusts] J. W. Verity. il *Business Week* p78 My 29 '89

Automation
Big Blue's big overhaul. Z. Schiller. il *Business Week* Special Issue:147 Je 16 '89

Cooperation
See also
Microelectronics and Computer Technology Corporation
U.S. Memories Inc.

Customer relations
Caveat raider [MAI Basic Four's battle for Prime Computer sours customer relations] K. K. Wiegner. il *Forbes* 143:160 Je 12 '89
Computers, customers and hand-holding. E. Dyson. il *Forbes* 144:128 Ag 7 '89

Anecdotes, facetiae, satire, etc.
Heard it through the help line. W. Lee. il *Byte* 14:448 D '89

Employees
See Computer personnel

Export-import trade
Chips for the Soviet bloc? Computers from Asia short-circuit America's export controls. S. Budiansky. il *U.S. News & World Report* 107:28-30 O 9 '89
Cray versus Japan Inc. [interview with J. A. Rollwagen] D. Churbuck. il por *Forbes* 144:118-19 S 4 '89
Europe goes wild for Yankee PCs. R. I. Kirkland, Jr. il *Fortune* 119:257+ Je 5 '89
Government agencies at odds over computer sales to Soviets and Warsaw Pact countries. *Byte* 14:26+ O '89
NAE: revamp export controls. M. Crawford. *Science* 243:21 Ja 6 '89
O.K. to log on, comrades [U.S. relaxes controls on computer sales to Soviets] il *Time* 134:39 Jl 31 '89
The power behind Compaq's European powerhouse [E. Pfeiffer] T. Peterson. il por *Business Week* p150 Je 26 '89
Removing controls on PCs revives worries on exports. I. Goodwin. *Physics Today* 42:67-9 S '89
Responding to the Japanese 'threat'. P. Saffo. il *Personal Computing* 13:222 O '89
Soviet attempts to buy U.S. computers continue despite Customs crackdown. D. Hughes. *Aviation Week & Space Technology* 130:279+ Je 12 '89
Why Sun is losing its heat in the East [Sun Microsystems] N. Gross. il *Business Week* p114 S 18 '89

Finance
Computer makers are blue—but not IBM. D. A. Depke. il *Business Week* p76 Jl 24 '89
Computers and electronics. M. Beauchamp. il *Forbes* 143:114-16 Ja 9 '89
Computers are getting more personal than ever. G. Lewis. il *Business Week* p92-3 Ja 9 '89
The crowd at the funeral [mainframe business] J. Pitta. il *Forbes* 144:122-3 D 25 '89
If it looks like a slump and crawls like a slump . . . J. W. Verity. il *Business Week* p27 My 1 '89
Is the computer business maturing? [cover story] G. Lewis. il *Business Week* p68-71+ Mr 6 '89
Just squeaking along. T. McCarroll. il *Time* 134:72-3 O 30 '89
Suddenly, the PC juggernaut is stuck in the mud. D. A. Depke and others. il *Business Week* p45 D 25 '89-Ja 1 '90

Information services
See also
Gartner Group Inc.

International aspects
Computer sales haven't lost their sizzle overseas. T. Peterson. il *Business Week* p74 Mr 6 '89
A global supercomputer race for high stakes. M. Sun. il *Science* 243:1004-6 F '89
Supercomputing. E. Corcoran. il *Scientific American* 260:70+ F '89

Licensing agreements
How Steve Jobs linked up with IBM [Next computer; cover story] B. R. Schlender. il pors *Fortune* 120:48-51+ O 9 '89
Is U.S. business giving away its technology—again? [workstations] B. R. Schlender. il *Fortune* 120:10 S 11 '89
Will Sun get burned by its new partner? [Toshiba] J. B. Levine. *Business Week* p26-7 Je 12 '89

Management
The power brokers [cover story; special section; with editorial comment by Fred Abatemarco] il *Personal Computing* 13:5, 69-77+ Jl '89
View from the top. il *Personal Computing* 13:245+ O '89
Where are the microchip billionaires? G. F. Gilder. il *Forbes* 144 Special Issue:378-80+ O 23 '89

Marketing
See also
Computer Express, Inc.
Computer industry—Licensing agreements
Computer stores
Inmac Corp.
286 Christmas winner [80286-based personal computers] P. Scisco. il *Compute!* 11:6 My '89
AT&T's computer business may even start making money. J. J. Keller. il *Business Week* p144 N 6 '89
Award-winning mail order strategies [computers; cover story; special section] R. Lockwood. il *Personal Computing* 13:78-81+ F '89
A coming-out party for Compaq's super-PC. G. Lewis and M. Ivey. il *Business Week* p99 N 13 '89
Compaq vs. IBM: peace comes to shove. M. Ivey and G. Lewis. il *Business Week* p132 Mr 13 '89
DEC has one little word for 30,000 employees: sell. L. Helm. il por *Business Week* p86+ Ag 14 '89
From boom boxes to bargain-basement PCs [Emerson Radio] L. Therrien. il *Business Week* p65-6 Je 26 '89
A genius for sales [R. Canion of Compaq] D. Pauly. il por *Newsweek* 114:43 O 2 '89
Harris plans commercial sales of Night Hawk microcomputer. E. H. Kolcum. il *Aviation Week & Space Technology* 130:59 Mr 13 '89
The hottest computer in a white-hot market? [DEC's new workstation] L. Helm. il *Business Week* p88-9 Ja 16 '89

COMPUTER INDUSTRY—Marketing—*cont.*

IBM goes to war. J. Daly. il *Maclean's* 102:46-8 N 27 '89

Is that a supercomputer in your pocket? [pocket computers] D. Churbuck. il *Forbes* 143:121+ My 15 '89

Is the computer business maturing? [cover story] G. Lewis. il *Business Week* p68-71+ Mr 6 '89

Low-cost 386-based computers [buying by mail] H. F. Beechhold. il *Home Office Computing* 7:61-5 O '89

The power surge at computer dealers. S. Gelfond. il *Business Week* p134-5 Jl 17 '89

Rising above the industry chaos [Micro Channel vs. EISA buses] F. Abatemarco. il *Personal Computing* 13:5 F '89

Selling look and feel [Apple Computer] J. Pitta. il *Forbes* 144:229 O 2 '89

Supercomputer market needs supersalesmen. M. Sun. il *Science* 245:596-7 Ag 11 '89

A teacher for Apple [B. R. Gifford] A. Edmond, Jr. il pors *Black Enterprise* 19:176-8 F '89

This Cyclone is out to rain on IBM's parade [Tandem's new mainframe] J. B. Levine. il *Business Week* p114 O 23 '89

What slump? F. Langa. il *Byte* 14:8 N '89

What's in a name? A lot, says Tandy [selling computers to corporations under the Grid logo] K. Kelly. il *Business Week* p109 F 27 '89

Will DEC's new workhorse haul profits out of a rut? [VAX 9000 series] K. H. Hammonds. il *Business Week* p41-2 O 30 '89

Securities

The coming sizzle in computer stocks. G. Lewis. il *Business Week* p110-11 O 16 '89

Computer stocks vintage 1989. R. A. Shaffer. il *Forbes* 143:180+ Ap 17 '89

A double whammy spooks high-tech investors [IBM and DEC] J. W. Verity. il *Business Week* p37 Ap 3 '89

The next waves [interview with M. Stahlman] G. F. Gilder. il por *Forbes* 143:186+ Ap 17 '89

An ominous divergence. M. Gianturco. il *Forbes* 144:208 S 18 '89

On the Street, Big Blue is big blah. G. Weiss. il *Business Week* p76 My 29 '89

Suits and claims

Using the law to rein in computer runaways [buyers taking suppliers to court] J. Rothfeder. il *Business Week* p70+ Ap 3 '89

Canada

Hi-tech disagreements [Canadian Senator M. Cogger named in Japanese businessman T. Tsuru's lawsuit against entrepreneur G. Montpetit over misspent loans] P. Kaihla. il por *Maclean's* 102:16-17 Je 26 '89

China

See also
Stone Group Corporation

France

See also
Groupe Bull

Germany (West)

See also
Nixdorf Computer AG

Hong Kong

See also
Semi-Tech Microelectronics (Far East) Ltd.

Italy

See also
Ing. C. Olivetti & Co., SpA

Japan

See also
Hitachi, Ltd.
Kubota, Ltd.
NEC Corp.
Seiko Group
Sony Corp.
VM Technologies

Computers: Japan comes on strong [cover story] G. Lewis. il *Business Week* p104-7+ O 23 '89

Cray versus Japan Inc. [interview with J. A. Rollwagen] D. Churbuck. il por *Forbes* 144:118-19 S 4 '89

IBM clones a strategy from the clonemakers [mimicking Japanese machines] N. Gross. il *Business Week* p42 Ag 21 '89

Japan & AI: $38.4 billion in 1995? *High Technology Business* 9:39 Mr '89

Machine dreams [Fifth Generation project] H. Ullman. il *The New Republic* 201:12-14 Jl 17-24 '89

Responding to the Japanese 'threat'. P. Saffo. il *Personal Computing* 13:222 O '89

Poland

See also
Promotor (Firm)

Soviet Union

In search of hackers. P. Elmer-Dewitt. il *Time* 133:95 Ap 10 '89

Soviets pursue computer literacy. il *USA Today (Periodical)* 117:14 Je '89

Three weeks that shook my world [cover story] E. Dyson. il *Forbes* 143:103-8 Je 12 '89

Taiwan

Taiwan isn't just for cloning anymore. D. J. Yang. il *Business Week* p208+ S 25 '89

United States

See Computer industry

COMPUTER INPUT-OUTPUT EQUIPMENT

See also
Analog-to-digital converters
Computer cables
Computer printers
Computer terminals
Computers—Buses
Digital-to-analog converters
Digitizers (Computers)
Digitizing tablets
Graphical user interfaces
Information display systems
Interactive computer systems
Joysticks
Keyboards
MIDI (Musical instrument digital interface)
Modems
Mouse (Computer equipment)
Pen-based computers
Speech processing systems
Trackballs (Computer equipment)
User interfaces
Video display terminals
Video monitors
Virtual reality

The BIOS challenge. R. Vishney. *Byte* 14 Special Issue:72 Fall '89

Digi-compass. T. E. Black. il *Radio-Electronics* 60:43-5+ N '89

DoubleCOM [combined serial port and A/B switch] il *Radio-Electronics* 60 ComputerDigest:88-9 Ja '89

The IBM PC BIOS. B. Glass. il *Byte* 14:303-10 Ap '89

The Mac makes connections. B. N. Meeks. il *Byte* 14:171-2+ My '89

RS-232 debugging with SAM 2000. il *Radio-Electronics* 60:83-5 O '89

Smart RS-232 Data Meter. il *Radio-Electronics* 60 ComputerDigest:90-1 Mr '89

COMPUTER INTEGRATED MANUFACTURING

See also
Cimflex Teknowledge Corporation

Manufacturing intelligence [smart factories] P. Wallich. il *Scientific American* 261:100+ D '89

Smart factories: America's turn? O. Port. il *Business Week* p142-5+ My 8 '89

COMPUTER JUNKYARDS

Japan

Hardware hill. B. Weber. il *The New York Times Magazine* p74 Je 25 '89

COMPUTER LANGUAGES

See also
Ada (Computer language)
Assembler language (Computer language)
Basic (Computer language)
C (Computer language)
CaPSL (Computer language)
Character sets (Computer science)
Compilers (Computers)
Fortran (Computer language)
HyperTalk (Computer language)
Lisp (Computer language)
Logo (Computer language)
Modula-2 (Computer language)
Natural language processing
Occam (Computer language)
Pascal (Computer language)
PCL (Computer language)
PostScript (Computer language)
Prolog (Computer language)
Scheme (Computer language)
Smalltalk (Computer language)
Structured Query Language (Computer language)

Learning the language [object-oriented languages] P. Wegner. bibl f il *Byte* 14:245-50+ Mr '89

COMPUTER LITERACY See Computers—Study and teaching

COMPUTER LITERATURE

See also
Booksellers and bookselling—Computer literature
Computers—Bibliography
Publishers and publishing—Computer literature

COMPUTER LOGIC CIRCUITS See Logic circuits

COMPUTER MAPS

Cars that know where they're going [cover story] R. L. French. il por *The Futurist* 23:29-36 My/Je '89

The electronic transformation of maps. D. Bjerklie. il *Technology Review* 92:54-63 Ap '89

Geographic information systems: what they are, and how they work. S. P. Jessup and E. Cary. bibl il *Focus (New York, N.Y.: 1950)* 39:10-12 Summ '89

Just what we need. Automatic roads [onboard navigation systems] B. W. Yates. il *Car and Driver* 34:19 F '89

Managing with electronic maps. G. Bylinsky. il *Fortune* 119:237-8+ Ap 24 '89

COMPUTER MAPS—*cont.*

These maps can find oil—or sell burgers. J. Rothfeder. il *Business Week* p134 Mr 13 '89

Visually map your data [MapInfo] S. Miastkowski. il *Byte* 14:211-12+ O '89

COMPUTER MATCHMAKING *See* Computers—Social use

COMPUTER MUSIC *See* Computers—Musical use

COMPUTER NETWORK PROTOCOLS

　　　See also

　　NetBIOS (Local area network)

　　Open systems (Computers)

The ABCs of X-, Y-, and ZMODEM [file transfer protocols] B. N. Meeks. il *Byte* 14:163-6 F '89

Building heterogeneous networks. B. Glass. il *Byte* 14:235-6+ S '89

The glue for internetworking [TCP/IP] W. Stallings. il *Byte* 14:221-4 S '89

A logical choice [LU 6.2] R. Davis. bibl il *Byte* 14:309-15 Ja '89

Making applications talk [Communicating Applications Specification file transfer protocols] B. Glass. il *Byte* 14:155-8 Ja '89

The protocol pack [XMODEM and its file transfer heirs] B. N. Meeks. il *Byte* 14:155-6+ Mr '89

Sending information from here to there [file transfer protocols] A. Glossbrenner. il *Home Office Computing* 7:34-5 Mr '89

When one LAN is not enough. W. Stallings. il *Byte* 14:293-8 Ja '89

COMPUTER NETWORKS

　　　See also

　　American Telephone & Telegraph Co.

　　BIX (Computer network)

　　Communications software

　　Computer bulletin boards

　　Distributed data processing

　　Document delivery

　　File servers (Computers)

　　Information systems

　　Local area networks

　　Netframe Systems Inc.

　　NSFnet

　　Packet switching (Data transmission)

Chaos study could affect computers, networks. *Byte* 14:16+ My '89

Electronic networking [sub-Saharan African scientists] B. Gold. il map *Science* 245:538-9 Ag 4 '89

The global village under siege—we've met the enemy and he is us [viruses] D. D. Thornburg. il *Compute!* 11:13 Mr '89

Hostile takeovers [computer network security] P. Wallich. *Scientific American* 260:22+ Ja '89

Networks. See issues of Byte beginning June 1989

The personal computer finds its missing link. R. Brandt and D. A. Depke. il *Business Week* p120-3+ Je 5 '89

Supercomputer policy under review [Office of Technology Assessment report] E. Marshall. *Science* 246:207 O 13 '89

The supernets are coming! M. Gianturco. il *Forbes* 143:112-13+ F 20 '89

The Unix connection. B. Smith. bibl il *Byte* 14:245-51 My '89

COMPUTER NOVELS

　　　See also

　　Infocom (Firm)

　　Loom (Video game)

Floppy fiction. C. Zimmer. il *Discover* 10:34+ N '89

Light-years and lasers: science fiction inside your computer [cover story; with editorial comment by Gregg Keizer] O. S. Card. il *Compute!* 11:4, 28-34 Je '89

Nightmare on game street [horror games] S. Addams. il *Compute!* 11:106-8+ O '89

COMPUTER OPERATING SYSTEMS

　　　See also

　　DOS operating systems

　　Mach operating system

　　Macintosh operating systems

　　MS-DOS operating system

　　MultiFinder operating system

　　Open Desktop operating system

　　OS/2 operating system

　　PC DOS operating system

　　System 7.0 operating system

　　TRON operating systems

　　UNIX operating system

Battle of the network stars [LAN operating systems] S. Apiki and others. il *Byte* 14:154-6+ Jl '89

Breaking down the barriers [linking PCs and Macs on a LAN] M. L. Van Name and B. Catchings. il *Byte* 14:155-6 O '89

Directory assistance (I). R. Grehan. bibl il *Byte* 14:291-4+ My '89

Directory assistance (II). R. Grehan. il *Byte* 14:327-8+ Je '89

Growing pains [choosing a LAN operating system] J. Y. Bryce. il *Byte* 14:135-6+ Ag '89

Inside Intel's 80386 (II). N. Margulis. il *Radio-Electronics* 60 ComputerDigest:103-8 F '89

A manager's cram sheet for choosing operating systems. S. Gelfond. il *Working Woman* 14:63+ O '89

The multiuser solution. H. Eglowstein and S. Diehl. il *Byte* 14:148-54+ S '89

Protected mode. B. Glass. bibl il *Byte* 14:377-84 D '89

Why master the dance of standards? J. Blackford. il *Personal Computing* 13:216-17 S '89

COMPUTER PERSONNEL

　　　See also

　　Women in the computer industry

Artificial intelligence. D. P. Wash. il *Occupational Outlook Quarterly* 33:2-7 Summ '89

A need for information professionals [health information] D. Protti. il *World Health* p26-7 Ag/S '89

Anecdotes, facetiae, satire, etc.

Pachydermic personnel prediction. P. C. Olsen. il *Byte* 14:404 S '89

You, too, can look like a programmer. A. R. Levitan. il *Compute!* 11:88+ My '89

Salaries, pensions, etc.

Pay in data processing services varies by occupation and area. bibl f il *Monthly Labor Review* 112:52-4 My '89

Supply and demand

Computers. il *U.S. News & World Report* 107:63-4 S 25 '89

Where will the jobs go? K. K. Wiegner. il *Forbes* 144:270-2 D 11 '89

COMPUTER PICTURE BOOKS FOR CHILDREN

AmandaStories, Vol.1 [Hypercard children's stories] G. Solomon. il *Home Office Computing* 7:88 F '89

Flodd, The Bad Guy. C. S. Holzberg. il *Compute!* 11:72+ Je '89

Flodd, The Bad Guy—The Reading Magic Library. J. Latimer. il *Home Office Computing* 7:92 Je '89

High-tech storytelling [Reading Magic Library] K. Kane. *Psychology Today* 23:72-3 Jl/Ag '89

The Puzzle Storybook. J. Zornberg. il *Home Office Computing* 7:87-8 O '89

Read to me, Dad [Reading Magic Library] G. Keizer. il *Compute!* 11:7 Ja '89

Super Story Tree. C. S. Holzberg. il *Compute!* 11:122-3 N '89

COMPUTER PRINTERS

　　　See also

　　Daisywheel printers

　　Dataproducts Corp.

　　Dot matrix printers

　　Ink-jet printers

　　Iris Graphics Inc.

　　Laser printers

　　Liquid crystal shutter printers

　　Plotters (Computer printers)

　　Thermal printers

　　Wax transfer printers

First-class printing for under $1,000. D. P. Wiener. il *U.S. News & World Report* 107:75-6 O 9 '89

How to pick the right printer. J. Pepper. il *Working Woman* 14:54+ D '89

Not for lasers only [desktop publishing] M. Antonoff. il *Personal Computing* 13:59-60+ Ag '89

The root to happiness [use of Unix with a dedicated printer] D. Fiedler. il *Byte* 14:131-3 O '89

TekColor lets you really see what you get [color-matching system for the Macintosh] J. Bertolucci and T. Thompson. il *Byte* 14:84+ N '89

Twist & Shout [printer utility program] L. Frey. il *Compute!* 11:68 Ap '89

What's new in color printers and plotters. P. Honan. il *Personal Computing* 13:107-11+ Ap '89

COMPUTER PROGRAM LANGUAGES *See* Computer languages

COMPUTER PROGRAMMING

　　　See also

　　Advertising mediums—Computer programming

　　AppleWorks (Computer program)

　　Character sets (Computer science)

　　Clip art software

　　Communications software

　　Compilers (Computers)

　　Computer-aided software engineering

　　Computer animation—Programming

　　Computer graphics—Programming

　　Computer operating systems

　　Computer service industries

　　Computer viruses

　　Computers—Accounting use—Programming

　　Computers—Architectural use—Programming

　　Computers—Art use—Programming

　　Computers—Astronomical use—Programming

　　Computers—Aviation use—Programming

　　Computers—Banking use—Programming

　　Computers—Biological use—Programming

　　Computers—Business use—Programming

　　Computers—Chemical use—Programming

　　Computers—Demographic use—Programming

　　Computers—Diet use—Programming

　　Computers—Educational use—Programming

　　Computers—Employment use—Programming

COMPUTER PROGRAMMING—See also—*cont.*

Computers—Financial services use—Programming
Computers—Government use—Programming
Computers—Health use—Programming
Computers—Indexing use—Programming
Computers—Investment use—Programming
Computers—Irrigation use—Programming
Computers—Literary use—Programming
Computers—Mailing list use—Programming
Computers—Mathematical use—Programming
Computers—Medical use—Programming
Computers—Meteorological use—Programming
Computers—Military use—Programming
Computers—Musical use—Programming
Computers—Nature study use—Programming
Computers—Photographic use—Programming
Computers—Poetry use—Programming
Computers—Police use—Programming
Computers—Printing use—Programming
Computers—Prospecting use—Programming
Computers—Psychological use—Programming
Computers—Psychotherapeutic use—Programming
Computers—Religious use—Programming
Computers—Scientific use—Programming
Computers—Space flight use—Programming
Computers—Sports use—Programming
Computers—Statistical use—Programming
Computers—Tax return use—Programming
Computers—Telephone rate information use—Programming
Computers—Theatrical use—Programming
Computers—Videotape use—Programming
Copyright—Computer programming
Data entry—Programming
Data structures (Computer science)
DeskMate (Computer program)
Desktop publishing—Programming
DESQview (Computer program)
Emulators (Computer programs)
File organization (Computers)
Floating-point arithmetic
Genetic algorithms
Groupware (Computer programs)
HyperCard (Computer program)
HyperStudio (Computer program)
Hypertext
Integrated software
LapLink (Computer program)
LinkWay (Computer program)
Machine translating
Macroprocessors
Menus (Computer programming)
MIDI (Musical instrument digital interface)—Programming
Natural language processing
Object-oriented programming
OfficeVision software
Outlining software
Personal information management software
Presentation Manager (Computer program)
Prototyper (Computer program)
Shareware (Computer programs)
Spawn (Computer program)
Spreadsheets (Computer programs)
SuperCard (Computer program)
Text editors (Computer programs)
VisiCalc (Computer program)
Windows (Computer programs)

Answers. See issues of Personal Computing
Ask Byte. See issues of Byte
Compute! Specific. See issues of Compute! beginning May 1988
Computer scan. G. Branwyn and G. Clabaugh. See issues of The Futurist beginning January/February 1989
Computing gets easier every day. D. Stanton. il *Compute!* 11:16 Je '89
Extending your Macintosh [programming start-up routines] P. Mercer and F. A. Huxham. bibl il *Byte* 14 Mac Special Ed:MAC9-MAC20 Mr '89
Hotware: software bestsellers from around the country. See issues of Compute! beginning October 1989
How computing changes everything: computing in America [cover story; special issue; with editorial comment by Fred Abatemarco] il *Personal Computing* 13:9, 21+ O '89
Loaded for action [combination boot/data disk] P. Scisco. il *Compute!* 11:82 O '89
Machine specifics. See issues of Home Office Computing beginning October 1988
Of worms, viruses and Core War. A. K. Dewdney. il *Scientific American* 260:110-13 Mr '89
Software shortcuts to save time. P. Honan. il *Personal Computing* 13:111-14 D '89
Some assembly required. R. Grehan. See issues of Byte beginning July 1988
What lies ahead [symposium] il *Byte* 14:343-6+ Ja '89
What's new? See issues of Byte

Anecdotes, facetiae, satire, etc.

Mice in the kitchen [Apple Computer] D. Gookin. *Compute!* 11:143 N '89
Moby Dick 2.1. K. Sheldon. *Byte* 14:344 Jl '89

Bibliography

Book reviews. See issues of Byte through June 1989
The compleat PC library. A. Kleiner. il *Personal Computing* 13:88-91+ Mr '89

Debugging

See Debugging in computer science

Development

Hard times for software. J. Schwartz. il *Newsweek* 113:42-3 Ap 3 '89
How to break the software logjam. B. R. Schlender. il *Fortune* 120:100-1+ S 25 '89
A new life for old PC's. J. Schwartz. il *Newsweek* 114:44-5 Ag 28 '89
The status of applications software: late. D. Allen. il *Byte* 14 Special Issue:269-74 Fall '89
Suddenly, software houses have a Big Blue buddy. D. A. Depke. il *Business Week* p68-9 Ag 7 '89
A surfeit of vaporware. E. Dyson. il *Forbes* 143:132 My 1 '89

Patents

Intellectual property. E. Dyson. il *Forbes* 144:202 S 18 '89
See you in court. S. R. Reed. il *Personal Computing* 13:179 Ag '89
Software: in for a patent pounding? M. Galen. *Business Week* p30-1 Ag 28 '89
Software patents: franchising the information infrastructure. B. Kahin. *Change* 21:24-5 My/Je '89

Prices

Cheapware [shareware and public domain software] D. Stanton. il *Compute!* 11:36-8+ S '89
Cheapware—instant relief for an empty pocket [public domain, freeware, and shareware] D. Stanton. *Compute!* 11:104 Ja '89
The loneliness of the low-budget user. N. Baran. *Byte* 14:344 Ag '89

Standards

See also
Open systems (Computers)
A standards dictionary. B. Glass. il *Byte* 14 Special Issue:209-12+ Fall '89
Why master the dance of standards? J. Blackford. il *Personal Computing* 13:216-17 S '89

Study and teaching

Learn how to program [cover story] D. Gookin. *Compute!* 11:20-4+ My '89
Models and learning to program [research by Piraye Bayman and Richard Mayer] G. W. Bracey. il *Phi Delta Kappan* 71:79 S '89

Aids and devices

Pascal on the Mac [Just Enough Pascal tutorial] A. F. Lent and L. H. Loeb. *Byte* 14 Mac Special Ed:MAC5-MAC6 Mr '89

Testing

See also
Debugging in computer science
The 1989 Compute! Choice Awards [cover story; special section; with editorial comment by Gregg Keizer] il *Compute!* 11:4, 24-6+ Ja '89
Applications plus. E. Shapiro. See issues of Byte beginning March 1986 through July 1989
The Byte Awards. il *Byte* 14:327-30+ Ja '89
Computing at Chaos Manor. J. Pournelle. See issues of Byte beginning June 1984
DOS Power Tools. P. Scisco. il *Compute!* 11:66-8 Ag '89
DOSTALK [natural language interface] S. Anzovin. *Compute!* 11:132+ D '89
Guard against disk errors and viruses with Disk Watcher. J. Holtzman. il *Radio-Electronics* 60 ComputerDigest:77-9 My '89
Home software sampler. C. D. Hanlon. il *Compute!* 11:44+ O '89
MultiBoot brings OS/2 back to earth. S. Miastkowski. *Byte* 14:100+ My '89
A new face on DOS. D. Gookin. il *Compute!* 11:76-8+ O '89
PC-Kwik Power Pak. D. English. il *Compute!* 11:134-5 D '89
PC Tools Deluxe integrated utilities encourage greater productivity. R. Bel Bruno. il *Personal Computing* 13:186 D '89
PC Tools Deluxe, version 5.0. J. B. Lambert. il *Compute!* 11:63-4 Je '89
PopDrop [TSR memory manager] D. English. il *Compute!* 11:62+ S '89
PRD+. S. Morgenstern. il *Home Office Computing* 7:80 Je '89
Programs that help you put information in its place. V. S. Sussman. il *U.S. News & World Report* 107:88-9 N 20 '89
Sanity-saving software [for personal computers] D. P. Wiener. il *U.S. News & World Report* 106:59-60 Je 12 '89
SideKick for PM: more than just a pretty face [SideKick for Presentation Manager] S. Miastkowski. il *Byte* 14:97 Ap '89

COMPUTER PROGRAMMING—Testing—*cont.*

Sidekick revs up for OS/2 [Sidekick for Presentation Manager] R. Lockwood. *Personal Computing* 13:162 Ag '89

Simulation software for the Macintosh [STELLA and Extend] D. K. Bogen. bibl f il *Science* 246:138-42 O 6 '89

Sleuthing your troubles away [System Sleuth] G. Hartwig. *Byte* 14:104 Je '89

Software for little computers [laptops] *U.S. News & World Report* 107:97 Ag 28-S 4 '89

Special Days [custom birthday card computer program] J. Zornberg. il *Home Office Computing* 7:90-1 Ja '89

Swapping DOS to Mac the convenient way [DOS Mounter] D. Barker. il *Byte* 14:84+ O '89

Talk to me, DOS, talk to me [DOSTALK natural language interface] K. Sheldon. *Byte* 14:104 Ap '89

TimeOut SpreadTools, MacroTools, and MacroTools II [AppleWorks enhancement software] V. D. O'Connor. il *Compute!* 11:64-5 Jl '89

Total phone management [Hot Line Two] J. Nimersheim. il *Home Office Computing* 7:77-8 O '89

Transferring your data PDQ [PDQ² 2.0] J. Bell. il *Personal Computing* 13:212+ Mr '89

Unix tools for DOS [MKS Make and MKS Lex and Yacc] B. Smith. *Byte* 14:97-8 F '89

Utility wars: Mace vs. Norton. il *Radio-Electronics* 60 ComputerDigest:75-7 Jl '89

Year-end special: editors' picks 1989: software that shines [cover story] il *Home Office Computing* 7:52-5 D '89

Unauthorized use

Are there software pirates lurking among your staff? H. McCandless. *Working Woman* 14:27 Ja '89

This could be the key to keeping computer intruders out [Rainbow Technologies Inc.] L. Armstrong. il *Business Week* p54 Jl 31 '89

COMPUTER SCIENCE *See* Computers

COMPUTER SCIENCES CORP.

Air Force selects Computer Sciences Corp. to develop information processing system [tracking Military Airlift Command aircraft] *Aviation Week & Space Technology* 130:51-2 Ja 23 '89

A software star's long-term bonus. G. G. Marcial. *Business Week* p180 N 6 '89

COMPUTER SECURITY *See* Computers—Security measures

COMPUTER SERVICE INDUSTRIES

See also

Adobe Systems Inc.
Anacomp, Inc.
Answer Corporation
Ashton-Tate, Inc.
Autodesk Inc.
Automatic Data Processing, Inc.
Cadence Design Systems Inc.
Cimflex Teknowledge Corporation
Claris Corporation
Computer Associates International Inc.
Computer Sciences Corp.
Control Data Corp.
Cullinet Software, Inc.
Digital Research, Inc.
Dragon Systems Inc.
Electronic Data Systems Corp.
Fox Software Inc.
Hewlett-Packard Co.
Infocom (Firm)
Integrated Microcomputer Systems
Intel Corp.
IntelliCorp Inc.
International Business Machines Corp.
John M. Cockerham and Associates, Inc.
Lotus Development Corporation
Lysis Corporation
MacroMind Inc.
ManageWare Inc.
Mead Data Central, Inc.
Micrografx, Inc.
Microsoft Corporation
Network General Corporation
Novell Inc.
On Demand Systems, Inc.
Oracle Systems Corp.
Paperback Software International Inc.
Phoenix Technologies Ltd.
Pilot Executive Software (Firm)
Quarterdeck Office Systems
Radius, Inc.
Retix (Firm)
Sage Federal Systems
Santa Cruz Operation Inc.
Shilstone Software Company
Software 2000 Inc.
Software Publishers Association
Software Publishing Corporation
Software Toolworks Inc.
Strategic Information Inc.
Symbolics Inc.
Tengen Inc.
Tom Snyder Productions
Traveling Software Inc.

VM Software Inc.
WordPerfect Corporation

Taking the headaches out of equipment maintenance [third-party service providers; cover story] G. Graff. il *High Technology Business* 9:18-21+ S/O '89

Where will the jobs go? K. K. Wiegner. il *Forbes* 144:270-2 D 11 '89

Accounting

Software's dirty little secret [On Demand Systems tries to bring just-in-time distribution to computer software] D. Churbuck. il *Forbes* 143:128 My 15 '89

Acquisitions and mergers

Growth by merger or acquisition. R. A. Shaffer. il *Personal Computing* 13:47-8 N '89

Mort Meyerson is raring to slip the leash. K. Kelly. il por *Business Week* p58 S 11 '89

Sometimes it doesn't pay to keep a secret [Computer Associates won't spell out its plans for Cullinet] D. A. Depke. il *Business Week* p30-1 Ag 28 '89

Customer relations

The cobbler's wife has no shoes. E. Dyson. il *Forbes* 144:305 N 13 '89

Software must work the way people do. J. P. Manzi. por *Personal Computing* 13:211 O '89

International aspects

Designing software to span the globe. P. Kahn. por *Personal Computing* 13:224 O '89

Management

Letters to a young software company. E. Dyson. il *Forbes* 143:147 Ap 3 '89

Marketing

Best-selling software. See issues of Home Office Computing beginning October 1988

dBase IV is a godsend—to the competition [glitches] P. Cole. il *Business Week* p102 N 13 '89

Hard times for software. J. Schwartz. il *Newsweek* 113:42-3 Ap 3 '89

Hotware: software bestsellers from around the country. See issues of Compute! beginning October 1989

Lotus at war [cover story; with editorial comment by Fred Abatemarco] J. Schwartz. il *Personal Computing* 13:5, 70-5+ Je '89

'Microsoft is like an elephant rolling around, squashing ants'. R. Brandt. il *Business Week* p148-9+ O 30 '89

The software market is downright mushy. D. A. Depke and P. Cole. il *Business Week* p98-9 O 2 '89

Software's big guns take aim at small business. D. A. Depke. il *Business Week* p216-18 S 25 '89

The spreadsheet that nearly wore Lotus out [Release 3] K. H. Hammonds. il por *Business Week* p62-4 Jl 3 '89

The status of applications software: late. D. Allen. il *Byte* 14 Special Issue:269-74 Fall '89

Suddenly, software houses have a Big Blue buddy. D. A. Depke. il *Business Week* p68-9 Ag 7 '89

What not doing Windows costs Lotus. K. H. Hammonds. il *Business Week* p152 O 30 '89

Securities

Soft dollars [software companies' cash flow] D. Churbuck. il *Forbes* 143:126-7 My 1 '89

Suits and claims

Breaking up is hard to do [G.M. vs. R. Perot] D. P. Levin. il pors *The New York Times Magazine* p36-7+ Mr 26 '89

United States

See Computer service industries

COMPUTER SIMULATION

See also

Computer visualization
Flight simulators
Prototyping (Computers)
Stereolithography
Virtual computer systems
Virtual reality

Extend [version 1.05] R. Valdés. il *Byte* 14:197-200 Ap '89

Get real. H. E. H. Aycock. il *Compute!* 11:92-4+ N '89

Is it real, or is it Cray? R. Pool. il *Science* 244:1438-40 Je 23 '89

Machine dreams [computer modeling] B. Hayes. il *Discover* 10:82-7 O '89

Modeling the physical world with blocks [Extend 1.05] N. Baran. il *Byte* 14:97 Ja '89

The Qsim simulation toolkit. R. E. Kimbrell and others. il *Byte* 14:259-66 Jl '89

Simulation software for the Macintosh [STELLA and Extend] D. K. Bogen. bibl f il *Science* 246:138-42 O 6 '89

Simulations make you wonder what's real anymore. D. D. Thornburg. *Compute!* 11:72 N '89

COMPUTER SOFTWARE *See* Computer programming

COMPUTER SOFTWARE INDUSTRY *See* Computer service industries

COMPUTER SOLITAIRE *See* Solitaire (Game)

COMPUTER STORAGE DEVICES *See* Computers—Memory systems

COMPUTER STORES

See also

Businessland, Inc.
Egghead Inc.
Intertan Inc.

COMPUTER STORES—See also—*cont.*
Tandy Corp.
More than just salesmen. R. A. Shaffer. il *Personal Computing* 13:45-6 D '89
The power surge at computer dealers. S. Gelfond. il *Business Week* p134-5 Jl 17 '89
Time to look at the retailers. R. A. Shaffer. il *Forbes* 144:128 D 25 '89

Inventories
Software's dirty little secret [On Demand Systems tries to bring just-in-time distribution to computer software] D. Churbuck. il *Forbes* 143:128 My 15 '89

COMPUTER TERMINALS
See also
Information display systems
Keyboards
Video display terminals
Video monitors
Communications get Hyper [HyperAccess/5] S. Miastkowski. *Byte* 14:84 O '89
Data on the go [portable data terminals; cover story] G. T. Pope. il *High Technology Business* 9:16-19+ My '89

COMPUTER TEXT PROCESSING See Text processing (Computer science)

COMPUTER USERS GROUPS
User groups: the key to better office computing. R. DeMaria. *Working Woman* 14:34+ Mr '89

COMPUTER VIRUSES
See also
Spawn (Computer program)
Avoid it like the plague: protecting yourself from computer virus attacks. S. Esters. *Black Enterprise* 19:55-6 F '89
Avoiding virus hysteria [cover story] P. Honan. il *Personal Computing* 13:84-7+ My '89
Business-minded professor [security system developed by M. Schwartz's Digital Pathways] M. Alpert. il por *Fortune* 119:319 Ap 24 '89
Disease of the year: illness as glitch. S. Vogel. il *Discover* 10:64-6 Ja '89
Fighting viruses that do in data. B. Politzer. il *Home Office Computing* 7:10 Ja '89
The global village under siege—we've met the enemy and he is us [viruses that infect major networks] D. D. Thornburg. il *Compute!* 11:13 Mr '89
Hackers: is a cure worse than the disease? [case of R. Morris] M. Lewyn. por *Business Week* p37-8 D 4 '89
If your computer catches a virus on Friday the 13th, who you gonna call? John McAfee [creator of disinfectant program] il por *People Weekly* 32:77 O 16 '89
Information (mis)management. T. Thompson. *Byte* 14 Mac Special Ed:MAC2 Mr '89
Know thy viral enemy. R. M. Greenberg. il *Byte* 14:275-80 Je '89
A new strain of electronic vandalism [AIDS information diskette containing a Trojan horse program] *Newsweek* 114:82 D 25 '89
Of worms, viruses and Core War. A. K. Dewdney. il *Scientific American* 260:110-13 Mr '89
Revenge of the nerds [virus planted by R. T. Morris points up need for tighter security] N. Martin. il *The Washington Monthly* 20:21-2+ Ja '89
Spying and sabotage by computer. J. Peterzell. il *Time* 133:25-6 Mr 20 '89
Virus hacker nailed [D. Burleson] P. Scisco. il *Compute!* 11:7 Ja '89
Viruses that infect computers. M. Pietrantoni. il *USA Today (Periodical)* 117:64-6 Ja '89
Viruses, worms, trojans, and bombs [cover story] D. Stover. il *Popular Science* 235:59-62+ S '89

COMPUTER VISION See Machine vision
COMPUTER VISUALIZATION
Interacting with the tiny and the immense. C. Mundie. il *Byte* 14:279-80+ Ap '89
COMPUTER WORKSTATIONS See Workstations
COMPUTER WORMS See Computer viruses
COMPUTERIZED AXIAL TOMOGRAPHY See Tomography
COMPUTERIZED MAIL SYSTEMS See Electronic mail systems
COMPUTERIZED SPEECH See Speech processing systems
COMPUTERIZED TOMOGRAPHY See Tomography
COMPUTERPHONES
See also
Call processing systems
Phone programs yield instant recall of any conversation. C. Bermant. il *Home Office Computing* 7:28+ Ja '89

COMPUTERS
See also
Artificial intelligence
Automation
Calculators
Hackers (Computer enthusiasts)
Hypermedia
Information systems
Instruction sets (Computers)
Interactive computer systems
Logging on (Computers)
Multimedia
Multiprocessors

Neural network computers
Optical computers
Pen-based computers
Reduced instruction set computers
Supercomputers
Turing machines
VAX computers
Very long instruction word computers
21st century computing. P. Freiberger and D. McNeill. il *Compute!* 11:20-2+ O '89
The 486 systems are coming. J. Blackford. il *Personal Computing* 13:231-2 D '89
The accidental tourist [S. A. Rondel's Voice computer] M. Barrier. il por *Nation's Business* 77:78 Ap '89
Answers. See issues of Personal Computing
Ask Byte. See issues of Byte
The best PC maker? Maybe it's you. O. Port. il *Business Week* p126-7 S 18 '89
Beyond the laptop: the incredible shrinking computer [notebook and pocket portable computers] M. Shao. il *Business Week* p134+ My 15 '89
Big power, tiny package [Compaq's LTE laptop] il *Time* 134:73 O 30 '89
Compute! Specific. See issues of Compute! beginning May 1988
Computer recreations. A. K. Dewdney. See issues of Scientific American
Computer scan. G. Branwyn and G. Clabaugh. See issues of The Futurist beginning January/February 1989
Consumer computers [Vendex HeadStart III] G. Keizer. il *Compute!* 11:6 Ap '89
Does everyone need an 80386-based computer? *High Technology Business* 9:31-2 Ja '89
Double birth announcement from Apple [Macintosh portable and Mac IIci] E. P. Stevenson. il *Home Office Computing* 7:12 N '89
Fixes. See issues of Byte
A heavyweight lightweight [Compaq's new laptop] G. Lewis. *Business Week* p152 O 30 '89
How computing changes everything: computing in America [cover story; special issue; with editorial comment by Fred Abatemarco] il *Personal Computing* 13:9, 21+ O '89
IBM special edition [cover story] il *Byte* 14 Special Issue:8+ Fall '89
The incredible shrinking PC [pocket computers] P. Dworkin and N. Magoun. il *U.S. News & World Report* 106:48-9 My 29 '89
Information processing. See issues of Business Week
Instant spoken translation [S. A. Rondel's Voice computer] W. J. Hawkins. il por *Popular Science* 234:78+ My '89
Is that a supercomputer in your pocket? [pocket computers] D. Churbuck. il *Forbes* 143:121+ My 15 '89
Laptop update. M. Mandell. il *High Technology Business* 9:48+ Ja '89
Lightweight heavyweights [portable computers] W. J. Hawkins. il *Popular Science* 235:71-2+ S '89
Machine specifics. See issues of Home Office Computing beginning October 1988
Macinations. D. E. Crabb. See issues of Byte beginning August 1988
Macintosh special edition. il *Byte* 14 Mac Special Ed:MAC217+ Je '89
Macintosh special edition. il *Byte* 14 Mac Special Ed:MAC1-MAC2+ Mr '89
Macintosh special supplement. il *Byte* 14 Mac Special Supp:MAC185+ Ag '89
A Macintosh who's who. T. Thompson. il *Byte* 14:146-7 Je '89
Meet MIT's Mr. Biochips [M. S. Wrighton's work on molecular computers] R. Duffy. il por *Business Week* Special Issue:80 Je 16 '89
New products. See issues of High Technology Business through November/December 1989
Now, portable means practical [cover story; special section] il *Personal Computing* 13:74-7+ N '89
The quest for the molecular computer. M. A. Clarkson. il *Byte* 14:268-73 My '89
Random access. E. Dyson. See issues of Forbes beginning May 18, 1987
Run MS-DOS on the PT-68K. M. Henry. il *Radio-Electronics* 60 ComputerDigest:96-102 Ja '89
Small is powerful [laptops] J. DeMont. il *Maclean's* 102:50+ N 27 '89
Star tech. P. Hoban. See occasional issues of New York beginning September 24, 1984
Technology. J. Blackford. See occasional issues of Personal Computing beginning July 1987
Technology forecast 1989 [cover story; special section; with editorial comment by Fred Abatemarco] il *Personal Computing* 13:5, 91-8+ Ja '89
Update. See issues of Personal Computing beginning January 1986
What lies ahead [symposium] il *Byte* 14:343-6+ Ja '89
What's new? See issues of Byte

COMPUTERS—*cont.*

Access control

See Computers—Security measures

Accounting use

Programming

Accounting help! [video and disk tutorials] S. Miller. il *Home Office Computing* 7:32 Mr '89

Accounting software set to take off. R. A. Shaffer. il *Personal Computing* 13:45-6 My '89

Back to Basics: Professional. J. F. Wasik. il *Home Office Computing* 7:72-3 Mr '89

Buyer's guide: accounting software [BusinessWorks, Harmony, Platinum, RealWorld, Solomon III; special section] il *Personal Computing* 13:153-5+ Ja '89

When time is money [Timeslips III] S. P. Andrus. il *Personal Computing* 13:208 N '89

Advertising

See Computer industry—Advertising

Agricultural use

See also

Data Transmission Network Corp.

High-tech animal husbandry. J. E. Bahls. il *High Technology Business* 9:22-4+ S/O '89

Air traffic control use

See Computers—Aviation use

Airline use

See Airlines—Automation; Airlines—Reservation systems—Automation

Airplane factory use

See Airplane factories—Automation

Anecdotes, facetiae, satire, etc.

Off line. D. Gookin. il *Compute!* 11:151 O '89

Architectural use

See also

Weyerhaeuser DesignCenters

A/E/C Systems '89 product roundup. S. S. Ross. il *Architectural Record* 177:120-7 Ag '89

A/E/C Systems '89: the changing face of computer use for architects and engineers. C. K. Hoyt. il *Architectural Record* 177:33+ Jl '89

A/E/C Systems: pre-meeting products preview. S. S. Ross. il *Architectural Record* 177:158-63 My '89

The architects of their own success [Page-Zebrowski Architects] A. M. Russell. il pors *Working Woman* 14:81-2+ O '89

Architectural team wins the Helping Hands for Small Business Contest [Page-Zebrowski Architects] il *Working Woman* 14:73 Ap '89

Computer products for architects: AEC Expo showcases PC software, hardware, and add-ons. S. S. Ross. il *Architectural Record* 177:148-51 F '89

Expert panel explores the pros and cons of computerized building specifications (I). C. K. Hoyt. il *Architectural Record* 177:159+ Je '89

An expert panel explores the pros and cons of computerized building specifications (II). C. K. Hoyt. il *Architectural Record* 177:131+ Ag '89

Hardware reviews for architects: digitizing tablets for the Mac [Kurta IS/ADB and Summagraphics Bit Pad Plus] S. S. Ross. il *Architectural Record* 177:153 F '89

Sweet's surveys reveal architects' changing patterns of computer use and its growth. C. K. Hoyt. *Architectural Record* 177:33 N '89

Programming

See also

Autodesk Inc.

AutoCAD 10 for the Macintosh; ei:IntelliFile. S. S. Ross. il *Architectural Record* 177:153+ Je '89

Claris CAD. S. S. Ross. il *Architectural Record* 177:167+ My '89

Computers: roundtable tackles the difficult issues (I) [use of CAD] C. K. Hoyt. il *Architectural Record* 177:159+ F '89

Computers: roundtable tackles the difficult issues (II) [use of CAD] C. K. Hoyt. il *Architectural Record* 177:133+ Ap '89

Emerging trends in architectural CAD software. K. Sanders. il *Architectural Record* 177:130-1+ Mr '89

Hometown, U.S.A. [model building design program] N. Rentschler. il *Compute!* 11:77-8 Je '89

New graphics program debuts in concert hall [acoustic design graphics program developed by Donald Greenberg and Adam Stettner] A. S. Moffat. il *Science* 245:1452 S 29 '89

RFP Version 4.0. S. S. Ross. il *Architectural Record* 177:149+ O '89

Software reviews for architects [Architrion II, Series 4, Release 1.0] S. S. Ross. il *Architectural Record* 177:117+ S '89

Software reviews for architects [Dreams 1.0 and DataCAD 3.6e with DC Modeler] S. S. Ross. il *Architectural Record* 177:123+ Ja '89

Software reviews for architects [Electronic Sweet's and Auto CAD release 10 with ADE 3] il *Architectural Record* 177:137+ Mr '89

Software reviews for architects [FastCAD 2.05 and Snap! 3.0] S. S. Ross. il *Architectural Record* 177:139+ Ap '89

Software reviews for architects [MacProject II, version 2.0 and GEOCAD, version 3.3] S. S. Ross. il *Architectural Record* 177:133+ Jl '89

The third dimension [three-dimensional modeling CAD] B. Holtz and J. Udell. il *Byte* 14:178-80+ My '89

Two architectural programs for the Mac [Architrion II and MacBravo! Facilities] il *Byte* 14:70 S '89

VersaCAD/386 version 5.4; Proposal Manager 254/255. S. S. Ross. il *Architectural Record* 177:149+ N '89

Art use

See also

Fine Arts Museum of Long Island. Computer Imaging Center

Art in the computer age [SIGGRAPH 1989 Art Show] R. F. Malina. il *Technology Review* 92:71-2+ O '89

Creating art with computers. P. D. Prince. il *Personal Computing* 13:129-31 O '89

Old masters, new tricks [computerized art restoration in Italy] P. Elmer-Dewitt. il *Time* 134:84+ D 18 '89

The PC as paintbrush. K. H. Hammonds. il *Business Week* p127 S 11 '89

Roscomural [computerized painting system that produces expanded images] M. S. Eddy. il *Theatre Crafts* 23:90-1 Ja '89

Programming

See also

Clip art software

Apple's 32-bit QuickDraw covers the spectrum. T. Thompson. il *Byte* 14:99-102+ Jl '89

Art & Film Director. D. McNeill. il *Compute!* 11:62-3 Ag '89

Canvas [version 2.0] R. Hart. il *Home Office Computing* 7:77-8 My '89

Corel Draw shows great promise. S. Rosenberg. il *Byte* 14:213-14+ Je '89

DeluxePaint III. S. Anzovin. il *Compute!* 11:64+ S '89

Drawing Table. B. Hunt. il *Home Office Computing* 7:70 Ag '89

Drawing with precision. L. Kleinman. il *Personal Computing* 13:61-3 My '89

Easygoing 2-D CAD on the Macintosh [Vellum] H. Eglowstein. il *Byte* 14:82+ D '89

Electronic Arts decolorizes Studio/8 [Studio/1 monochrome paint package] D. Barker. il *Byte* 14:81 S '89

Illustrator: Adobe throws a curve [Adobe Illustrator for Windows] L. Kleinman. il *Personal Computing* 13:158-9 Ag '89

Industrial-strength graphics [SuperPaint 2.0] T. Thompson. il *Byte* 14 Mac Special Ed:MAC219 Je '89

MacDraw II. R. Mansfield. il *Home Office Computing* 7:72+ Ja '89

New 32-bit QuickDraw means better Mac color. *Byte* 14:16+ Je '89

Paint and draw with one versatile package [SuperPaint] J. Latimer. il *Home Office Computing* 7:90+ D '89

Paint programs. C. D. Hanlon. il *Compute!* 11:48-50+ Ja '89

Painting on the Mac takes a step forward [PixelPaint 2.0] T. Thompson. il *Byte* 14:90 Jl '89

PC Paintbrush IV. D. Atkin. il *Compute!* 11:119+ N '89

Slide Shop. N. Rentschler. il *Compute!* 11:68-9 Mr '89

Slide Shop. T. A. Summers. il *Home Office Computing* 7:88+ F '89

Splash! [paint program] S. Anzovin. il *Compute!* 11:90 Ja '89

Studio/8: the best paint yet. D. Barker. il *Byte* 14 Mac Special Ed:MAC5 Mr '89

Astronomical use

Clumps in the machine [computer modeling of galaxy cluster; research by Adrian Melott and Sergei Shandarin] il *Discover* 10:12 S '89

Computer-age stargazing [eliminating distorting effects of atmosphere; work of Gerry Neugebauer] M. M. Waldrop. il *Science* 245:1191 S 15 '89

Cosmic collisions: computer simulations suggest how elliptical galaxies formed. J. Horgan. il *Scientific American* 261:14+ Jl '89

Does chaos permeate the solar system? R. A. Kerr. il *Science* 244:144-5 Ap 14 '89

The ever-vigilant GNAT [global network of automatic telescopes] D. L. Crawford. il *Sky and Telescope* 77:143 F '89

From dust to dust [supercomputer simulation called galaxy-in-a-box; cover story] I. Peterson. il *Science News* 135:24-5 Ja 14 '89

Maximize the entropy, minimize the seeing [views of Nigel Sharp] il *Sky and Telescope* 78:571-2 D '89

Mixing it up in space [cover story] K. Hartley. il *Science News* 135:218-19 Ap 8 '89

Modeling galaxy interactions. il *Sky and Telescope* 77:22-3 Ja '89

Pumping gas to fuel a galaxy's active core [computer simulation by Lars Hernquist] I. Peterson. *Science News* 136:150 S 2 '89

The sky's the limit [Celestron's computer-controlled Compustar telescope] J. Engle. il *Popular Science* 234:34 F '89

Supercomputing the universe. D. Johnson. il *Astronomy* 17:48-54 D '89

Witness to creation [computer modeling of star formation; research by Richard Durisen] il *Discover* 10:8+ D '89

COMPUTERS—Astronomical use—*cont.*
Programming
Astronomical computing. R. W. Sinnott. See issues of Sky and Telescope beginning April 1984
Dance of the Planets [computer orrery] J. E. Mosley. il *Sky and Telescope* 78:642 D '89
Deep-sky database [Deepsky 2000] B. Anderson and others. *Astronomy* 17:112 O '89
Desktop planetarium [Voyager] W. Harwood. il *High Technology Business* 9:48 Ap '89
Moon over Miami [planetarium software Solarsim and Sky Travel] J. L. Wilson. *Ad Astra* 1:38 F '89
Observers' software [Astropoint II] D. W. Rasmus. *Astronomy* 17:112 N '89
Sky Travel. R. G. Sheffield. il *Compute!* 11:96 Ja '89
The universe in your computer [The Visible Universe] R. C. McNeil. *Astronomy* 17:104-6 Ag '89
Voyager: excellent software. B. Bond. il *Astronomy* 17:104 Mr '89

Automobile factory use
See Automobile factories—Automation
Automobile service station use
See Automobile service stations—Automation
Automotive use
See also
Automobile service stations—Automation
Automobiles—Electronic equipment
New graphics tools let designers see the future. il *Popular Mechanics* 166:15 D '89
Will power [W. South, systems support manager for Saab-Scania of America] S. M. Williams. il por *Black Enterprise* 20:71-2 N '89

Aviation use
See also
Airlines—Automation
Airlines—Reservation systems—Automation
Airplane factories—Automation
Inertial guidance systems
Army pursues voice-controlled avionics to improve helicopter pilot performance. B. W. Henderson. il *Aviation Week & Space Technology* 130:43+ My 22 '89
Around the Mall and beyond [Beyond the limits: flight enters the computer age; permanent exhibit at National Air and Space Museum] E. Park. il *Smithsonian* 20:16+ Jl '89
Black gen. heads computer systems at Ohio air base [J. F. Phillips] il por *Jet* 75:36 Ja 30 '89
Britain's Rediffusion Simulation offers microcomputer-based ATC trainer. C. A. Shifrin. il *Aviation Week & Space Technology* 131:83+ Ag 21 '89
Computational aerodynamics for aircraft design [cover story] A. Jameson. bibl f il *Science* 245:361-71 Jl 28 '89
CTA develops new computer system to speed civil aircraft maintenance. B. D. Nordwall. *Aviation Week & Space Technology* 130:153+ Je 19 '89
Digital Equipment introduces new engineering workstations, personal computer series. *Aviation Week & Space Technology* 130:51 Ja 23 '89
Fastest supercomputer [Cray Y-MP at Ames Research Center] A. Fisher. il *Popular Science* 234:8+ F '89
Flying the electric skies [Airbus A320 with fly-by-wire] M. M. Waldrop. il *Science* 244:1532-4 Je 30 '89
Grade-A Primus [Honeywell Primus 2000] J. M. McClellan. il *Flying* 116:52-4+ O '89
Human factors are critical in computer-driven systems. D. Hughes. il *Aviation Week & Space Technology* 131:104-5 D 18-25 '89
JPL computer researchers develop hardware for neural networks. B. W. Henderson. il *Aviation Week & Space Technology* 131:129+ O 9 '89
McDonnell restructures mission planning efforts to gain greater market share. il *Aviation Week & Space Technology* 130:293-4 Je 12 '89
Mikoyan Design Group upgrading MiG-29 with fly-by-wire controls, new cockpit. il *Aviation Week & Space Technology* 130:81 Je 5 '89
NASA develops system to monitor aircraft performance on takeoff. J. T. McKenna. il *Aviation Week & Space Technology* 131:43+ N 13 '89
Nonvolatile memory advances reduce avionics weight, power requirements. W. B. Scott. il *Aviation Week & Space Technology* 131:79+ Jl 17 '89
One digital computer to replace six flight control units in F-111. W. B. Scott. il *Aviation Week & Space Technology* 129:51+ Mr 6 '89
Phantom of the cockpit [A320 electronics] R. Sandza. il *Newsweek* 114:61 Jl 17 '89
Pilots react to the automated cockpit [NASA study of Boeing 757 pilots; cover story; special section] il *Aviation Week & Space Technology* 131:32-6 Ag 7 '89
Will machines replace pilots, controllers? *High Technology Business* 9:30 Ja '89
Programming
Flight testing of new ILS display format to begin; enhanced B-1B software could fly in December. *Aviation Week & Space Technology* 130:21 Ap 3 '89

Flight tests of Gripen to resume this year [new control logic devised to correct flaw in flight control system software] *Aviation Week & Space Technology* 130:64 Je 26 '89
ITT Avionics emphasizes development of software, improves electronic system. B. D. Nordwall. il *Aviation Week & Space Technology* 131:83+ Jl 17 '89
PC flight planning [Aviators Datalog and CompuServe] J. M. McClellan. *Flying* 116:23 Mr '89
Preflight planning [RMS Technology's Flitesoft 2.1] A. Laboda. il *Flying* 116:36 Je '89
Banking use
See also
Automated teller machines
Debit cards
Home banking services
Programming
A Banker's Secret [figures amortization schedules] L. Kleinholz. il *Home Office Computing* 7:78-9 F '89
Bits in the bank [CheckFree] P. Scisco. il *Compute!* 11:7 Mr '89
CheckFree. G. McClure. il *Compute!* 11:72-3 Jl '89
Checkless checkwriting [CheckFree] R. Cullen. il *Home Office Computing* 7:32+ My '89
Quicken [checking account management program] S. Anzovin. il *Compute!* 11:72 Ap '89
Quicken vs. Checkwrite Plus. R. Cullen. il *Home Office Computing* 7:28-9 Ag '89
Stocking-stuffer software. K. Davis. *Changing Times* 43:122-3 D '89
Bibliography
Book reviews. See issues of Byte through June 1989
The compleat PC library. A. Kleiner. il *Personal Computing* 13:88-91+ Mr '89
Biological use
Biologist's toolbox. See issues of BioScience beginning February 1985
Computer revealing language of life [technology that speeds analysis of DNA sequences; work of Leroy E. Hood] *Science News* 135:284 My 6 '89
Microcomputer data collection: bacterial growth curves. J. D. Diehl, Jr. and R. B. Angstadt. il *BioScience* 39:173-5 Mr '89
Programming
See also
Genetic algorithms
Catch of the day: biomorphs of Truchet tiles, served with popcorn and snails. A. K. Dewdney. il *Scientific American* 261:110-13 Jl '89
Simulated Evolution: wherein bugs learn to hunt bacteria. A. K. Dewdney. il *Scientific American* 260:138-41 My '89
Book industries use
See also
Bookland EAN system
Bookselling use
See also
BookBase
Computers in bookstores: the effect on special ordering. A. Symons. il *Publishers Weekly* 236:19-22 O 13 '89
Computers in bookstores: the menu of possibilities. K. O. Fakih. il *Publishers Weekly* 236:15-16+ O 13 '89
Have laser gun, Ballantine reps will travel—faster and smarter [speeding inventory and ordering] J. Mutter. il *Publishers Weekly* 235:53-5 F 17 '89
On-line on the road: Harper & Row sales reps computerize [using laptops for ordering] J. Mutter. il *Publishers Weekly* 235:50-1 Ja 13 '89
Botanical use
Garden of unearthly delight. H. Smith. il *Technology Review* 92:16 N/D '89
Buses
See also
EISA (Computer bus)
Micro Channel (Computer bus)
SCSI (Computer bus)
Backplane bus up against the wall; designers looking to new architectures. *Byte* 14:11-12 My '89
Boosting your home's IQ [wiring standard called Consumer Electronics Bus] P. Elmer-Dewitt. il *Time* 133:70-1 Ja 23 '89
A bus tour. G. White. il *Byte* 14:296-300+ S '89
Inside Intel's 80386 (III). J. Kardach and N. Margulis. il *Radio-Electronics* 60 ComputerDigest:98-101 Mr '89
The opposite tack. M. L. Smith and G. White. il *Byte* 14:216-17 Jl '89
Serving many masters. B. T. Anderson and M. A. Puhnaty. il *Byte* 14 Special Issue:131-2+ Fall '89
Should you wait to catch the bus? *High Technology Business* 9:31 F '89
Ultra graphics [Ultra Clipper UM1280, bus-mastering coprocessor] B. D. Kliewer. il *Byte* 14:167-9 Ag '89
Business use
See also
Offices—Automation
Telecommuting
Are there software pirates lurking among your staff? H. McCandless. *Working Woman* 14:27 Ja '89

COMPUTERS—Business use—*cont.*

Bargain systems that mean business. P. Honan. il *Personal Computing* 13:99-103+ D '89

The buck starts here [making money with a home computer; cover story; special section] il *Compute!* 11:18-22+ Ag '89

CEOs: computing in high places [cover story; special section; with editorial comment by Fred Abatemarco] il *Personal Computing* 13:5, 70-7+ Ap '89

Computer-buying trends [interview with A. Wohl] N. Sullivan. por *Home Office Computing* 7:63 S '89

Conquering "computer phobia" can pay off for small and mid-size businesses [purchasing decisions] *Black Enterprise* 20:47 N '89

Corporate pacesetters: the top 100 companies with PCs [cover story; with editorial comment by Fred Abatemarco] S. R. Reed. il *Personal Computing* 13:5, 70-3+ S '89

Customized road machines. C. O'Malley. il *Personal Computing* 13:92-6 N '89

Data on the go [portable data terminals; cover story] G. T. Pope. il *High Technology Business* 9:16-19+ My '89

Down to business. W. Rash, Jr. See issues of Byte beginning August 1988

High-tech cures for the time crunch. R. Farmanfarmaian. il *Psychology Today* 23:46-8 Mr '89

How to make business travel more productive. J. Borchardt. il *Working Woman* 14:99-100+ S '89

How you can achieve the information advantage [special section] il *Working Woman* 14:55+ Ap '89

Human factors: the gap between humans and machines. E. Weiner and A. Brown. il pors *The Futurist* 23:9-11 My/Je '89

In a cellular state of mind [computers and business travel] N. Sullivan. il *Home Office Computing* 7:116 N '89

In business. See occasional issues of Personal Computing beginning June 1987

Is it a tool or a toy: do you really need a laptop computer? S. Esters. il *Black Enterprise* 20:45-6 O '89

Living with a laptop [B. Moeller of Booz Allen] M. Antonoff. il pors *Personal Computing* 13:94-5+ F '89

A manager's cram sheet for choosing operating systems. S. Gelfond. il *Working Woman* 14:63+ O '89

More companies are chucking their computers [opting for outsourcing] J. Rothfeder. il *Business Week* p72+ Je 19 '89

The pace of change in corporate America. J. V. Roach. por *Personal Computing* 13:240 O '89

The personal computer finds its missing link [networks] R. Brandt and D. A. Depke. il *Business Week* p120-3+ Je 5 '89

Personal computers: increasingly versatile. J. Pepper. il *Nation's Business* 77:32 F '89

Personal computing's executive gift guide. R. Bel Bruno and N. McFeeley. il *Personal Computing* 13:118-25+ D '89

Pocket computing comes of age [hand held computers] S. Gelfond. *Working Woman* 14:46+ S '89

The power of information access. C. O'Malley. il *Personal Computing* 13:71+ O '89

Redefining old jobs, creating new ones. M. Piturro. il *Personal Computing* 13:141+ O '89

Small-business computing. il *Nation's Business* 77:32+ Jl '89

Small-business computing. il *Nation's Business* 77:34-5 D '89

Small-business computing [special section] il *Nation's Business* 77:65-6 O '89

Technologizing office work. M. R. Smith. bibl *Society* 26:65-72 My/Je '89

There's a computer in your future. J. Pepper. il *Nation's Business* 77:56-8 S '89

Training: a key ingredient in office automation. S. Gelfond. *Working Woman* 14:19 Jl '89

The truth behind get-rich-quick ads [business opportunity classifieds] E. King. il *Home Office Computing* 7:61-2 N '89

User groups: the key to better office computing. R. DeMaria. *Working Woman* 14:34+ Mr '89

View from the top. il *Personal Computing* 13:245+ O '89

We've only just begun to compute. E. Esber, Jr. por *Personal Computing* 13:236 O '89

What's in a name? A lot, says Tandy [selling computers to corporations under the Grid logo] K. Kelly. il *Business Week* p109 F 27 '89

With a personal computer and some original thinking, you could be rolling in the dough. D. D. Thornburg. il *Compute!* 11:13 Ag '89

Your home office [cover story; special section] il *Compute!* 11:23-6+ N '89

Anecdotes, facetiae, satire, etc.

10 more ways to make money with your computer. P. Scisco. *Compute!* 11:24 Ag '89

Programming

See also
Executive information systems
Groupware (Computer programs)
OfficeVision software
Santa Cruz Operation Inc.

Business-plan software. il *Home Office Computing* 7:51-2 Ap '89

Buyer's guide: presentation graphics [Draw Applause; 35mm Express; Graphics Gallery; Freelance Plus; Graph Plus; Harvard Graphics; Pixie] il *Personal Computing* 13:121-3+ F '89

The cobbler's wife has no shoes. E. Dyson. il *Forbes* 144:305 N 13 '89

Compute! choice [Better Working Eight-in-One] D. Stanton. il *Compute!* 11:68-70 O '89

Consultant in a bind [business modeling program Compete!] D. Churbuck. il por *Forbes* 144:285-6 N 13 '89

Create inexpensive, yet high-quality presentations [Pinstripe Presenter and PFS: First Graphics] R. Geist and H. Geist. il *Home Office Computing* 7:34-5 Je '89

Create professional slides and presentations [Freelance Plus] R. Geist and H. Geist. il *Home Office Computing* 7:86-8 N '89

Dazzling artwork from dull numbers [presentation graphics software] D. P. Wiener. il *U.S. News & World Report* 106:63 Ja 9 '89

The desktop presentation star [Aldus Persuasion 1.0] M. Antonoff. il *Personal Computing* 13:188-9 Jl '89

Effortless forms at a fair price [Horizon] H. F. Beechhold. il *Home Office Computing* 7:84+ D '89

Finish what you start [project management] B. Hunt. il *Home Office Computing* 7:52-5 My '89

Fitting PCs to small business needs. F. Gibbons. por *Personal Computing* 13:232 O '89

Forms for every function. S. Rosenthal. il *Home Office Computing* 7:28+ My '89

Forms management strategies. C. O'Malley. il *Personal Computing* 13:74-7+ Ag '89

FormSet. B. Gingher. il *Compute!* 11:64-5 Ap '89

FormSet. B. Hunt. il *Home Office Computing* 7:62-3 Jl '89

FormWorx goes GUI. S. Miastkowski. il *Byte* 14:86+ N '89

Grow your business with a professional identity. L. Simons. il *Home Office Computing* 7:45-9 Ag '89

Home office software sampler. C. D. Hanlon and J. Sloan. il *Compute!* 11:50+ N '89

How to break the software logjam. B. R. Schlender. il *Fortune* 120:100-1+ S 25 '89

The layman's guide to presentation design. R. Raskin. il *Home Office Computing* 7:37-9 Jl '89

Mac desktop presentation software [StandOut! 1.0, PowerPoint 2.00A, and Cricket Presents 1.0] L. Stevens. il *Byte* 14:203-5 Ap '89

Manage it with pictures [Project Scheduler 4] L. Wood. il *Byte* 14:223-4+ D '89

Perspective Junior [presentation graphics program] J. Nimersheim. il *Compute!* 11:114+ O '89

Pinstripe Presenter [chart producing program] S. Anzovin. il *Compute!* 11:71 My '89

PowerPoint. B. Hunt. *Home Office Computing* 7:71-3 Ap '89

Presentation-graphics software. R. Raskin. il *Home Office Computing* 7:40-3 Jl '89

Presentations with punch. C. O'Malley. il *Personal Computing* 13:108-11+ Ja '89

Prodigious presentation power from Xerox [Xerox Presents] L. Kleinman. il *Personal Computing* 13:184-5 Je '89

Professional-quality forms design [PerForm] R. Geist and H. Geist. il *Home Office Computing* 7:86+ D '89

Project management software helps you take care of business. M. Scott. il *Black Enterprise* 19:37-9 Mr '89

The rewards of creative modeling [spreadsheet models] T. Berry. il *Personal Computing* 13:61-2 S '89

A simplified project manager with advanced capabilities [Project Scheduler 4] C. Hlavaty. il *Personal Computing* 13:195 N '89

Software. J. Pepper. il *Nation's Business* 77:59 S '89

Software must work the way people do. J. P. Manzi. por *Personal Computing* 13:211 O '89

The software that makes your computer useful. J. Pepper. il *Nation's Business* 77:34 F '89

Software's big guns take aim at small business. D. A. Depke. il *Business Week* p216-18 S 25 '89

Tool to end indecisiveness [Decision Pad] R. Gehorsam. *Home Office Computing* 7:72+ O '89

Uncommon commonality [compatible business software] W. Rash, Jr. il *Byte* 14:151-2+ My '89

What corporate America wants from PCs. A. Ashton. por *Personal Computing* 13:216 O '89

Who-What-When [project manager] H. F. Beechhold. il *Home Office Computing* 7:78+ Ja '89

Xerox Graph gives data its due [presentation graphics software] L. Kleinman. il *Personal Computing* 13:196+ N '89

Carnival use

See Carnivals—Automation

Cartographic use

See also
Geographic information systems

Chemical use

Neural networks predict reactions [research by David W. Elrod] J. Raloff. *Science News* 135:271 Ap 29 '89

COMPUTERS—Chemical use—*cont.*

Supercomputing the liquid state of carbon [work of Richard M. Martin] I. Peterson. *Science News* 136:166 S 9 '89

Programming

Sweet and sour [sweetness determined by shape of molecule; work of Murray Goodman] T. Beardsley. *Scientific American* 261:22+ N '89

Circuits

See Integrated circuits

Compatibility

Coming together [special section] il *Compute!* 11:20-2+ Mr '89

Computer mating. L. Van Gelder. il *Ms.* 17:34-5 Je '89

From PC to Mac and back [transferring word processing files] R. Blodgett. il *Personal Computing* 13:53-5 D '89

IBM clones a strategy from the clonemakers [mimicking Japanese machines] N. Gross. il *Business Week* p42 Ag 21 '89

Inventing the PC's future. G. Campbell. il *Byte* 14 Special Issue:229-30+ Fall '89

Matching needs to software is key to shopping for PC-compatibles. S. Esters. il *Black Enterprise* 20:35-6 Ag '89

New variations on compatibility. R. A. Shaffer. il *Personal Computing* 13:49-50 Je '89

Swapping DOS to Mac the convenient way [DOS Mounter] D. Barker. il *Byte* 14:84+ O '89

Uncommon commonality [compatible business software] W. Rash, Jr. il *Byte* 14:151-2+ My '89

The wages of sin. P. Wilson. il *Byte* 14 Special Issue:276 Fall '89

Conferences

NECC's multimedia demos [National Educational Computing Conference] D. Stanton. il *Compute!* 11:88 O '89

Construction industry use

See Construction industry—Automation

Control use

AC lighting controls. D. Lancaster. il *Radio-Electronics* 60:26-8+ Mr '89

Build REACTS: the Radio-Electronics Advanced Control System (XI) [battery-backup power supply] J. Bybee. il *Radio-Electronics* 60:65-8 Ja '89

Defects

Anecdotes, facetiae, satire, etc.

Six-legged saboteurs. P. Hoffman. il *Discover* 10:80-3 My '89

Demographic use

Programming

IPSS [Interactive Population Statistical System] J. Pournelle. il *Byte* 14:110+ D '89

Dental use

Tooth tech: the new dentistry. A. Biesada. il *High Technology Business* 9:28-31 Ap '89

Design

See also

Massachusetts Institute of Technology. Media Laboratory

Computer scientists warn of physical limits. *Byte* 14:17 N '89

Hitch up your horseless carriages [antiquated features on computers] P. Saffo. il *Personal Computing* 13:235-7 D '89

Interview: Alan Kay. D. Sobel. il por *Omni (New York, N.Y.)* 12:80-2+ N '89

Inventing the PC's future. G. Campbell. il *Byte* 14 Special Issue:229-30+ Fall '89

Laptop technology redux. B. Glass. il *Byte* 14:323-6+ S '89

A Tinkertoy computer that plays tic-tac-toe. A. K. Dewdney. il *Scientific American* 261:120-3 O '89

We'll carry the information age with us—in our pockets, purses, and briefcases. P. Scisco. il *Compute!* 11:4 S '89

Diet use

Programming

How healthy is your diet? Compute it! il *Good Housekeeping* 208:141 My '89

Drugstore use

See Drugstores—Automation

Economics use

PARC brings Adam Smith to computing. M. M. Waldrop. il *Science* 244:145-6 Ap 14 '89

Physics for economists [computer simulations of economic scenarios conducted at Santa Fe Institute] E. Dyson. il *Forbes* 144:266 O 16 '89

Strange bedfellows [physicists and economists at the Santa Fe Institute] R. Pool. il *Science* 245:700-3 Ag 18 '89

Educational use

See also

Open School (West Hollywood, Calif.)

Art and computers: is there room in the studio for both? C. H. Welter. bibl f *Design for Arts in Education* 91:18-22 N/D '89

Computers and preschoolers: Head Start/IBM Partnership. L. Tsantis and others. il *Children Today* 18:21-3 Ja/F '89

The computer's impact on education: progress or problem? J. DelFrate. il *USA Today (Periodical)* 117:68-9 Ja '89

Computers in school: a loser? Or a lost opportunity? M. Shao. il *Business Week* p108-9+ Jl 17 '89

Computers make slow progress in class. C. Holden. il *Science* 244:906-9 My 26 '89

Discoveries. D. Stanton. See issues of Compute! beginning May 1988

Evaluating research on school computer use. G. Marshall. *The Education Digest* 54:30-3 Ja '89

Higher education: beyond personal computers. D. Lewin. por *Personal Computing* 13:242 O '89

Is classroom computing making the grade? *Byte* 14:17 O '89

Making the grade [family computer for home learning; cover story] D. Stanton. il *Compute!* 11:18-23 S '89

More on children and computers [research by Nira Hativa] G. W. Bracey. *Phi Delta Kappan* 70:733-4 My '89

The new school [computer use at Quince Orchard High School, Gaithersburg, Md.] J. Sloan. il *Compute!* 11:78-80+ D '89

The power of ideas and information [address, February 2, 1989] J. Sculley. *Vital Speeches of the Day* 55:565-9 Jl 1 '89

The revolution is yet to come. C. O'Malley. il *Personal Computing* 13:115+ O '89

A teacher for Apple [B. R. Gifford] A. Edmond, Jr. il pors *Black Enterprise* 19:176-8 F '89

Training teachers in technology. il *The Futurist* 23:43 Ja/F '89

Using computers in teaching physics [cover story] J. M. Wilson and E. F. Redish. bibl f il *Physics Today* 42:34-41 Ja '89

Programming

See also

Tom Snyder Productions

All Star Drill. L. Eiser. *Compute!* 11:130+ O '89

Attn: young publishers [Children's Writing and Publishing Center] K. Kane. il *Psychology Today* 23:76 D '89

The best learning software. K. Kane. il *Psychology Today* 23:66+ S '89

Can you read this article in one minute or less? [speed-reading software] T. A. Summers. il *Home Office Computing* 7:73-4 Ag '89

Caveman Clockwork. S. Hudson. il *Compute!* 11:106+ D '89

The Children's Writing & Publishing Center. C. S. Holzberg. il *Home Office Computing* 7:84-5 Ap '89

The Children's Writing & Publishing Center. G. Keizer. il *Compute!* 11:70 Ap '89

College Explorer [college selection program] K. Sternberg. il *Compute!* 11:67-8 Je '89

College Explorer [college selection program] J. Zornberg. il *Home Office Computing* 7:87-8+ My '89

Curious George in Outer Space. M. Furst. il *Home Office Computing* 7:69-70 Jl '89

The Dinosaur Discovery Kit. J. Zornberg. il *Home Office Computing* 7:96 N '89

Dinosaur Discovery Kit. L. Eiser. il *Compute!* 11:118+ D '89

Dinosaurs galore! C. S. Holzberg. il *Home Office Computing* 7:86+ Je '89

Editors' picks. il *Home Office Computing* 7:83-4+ O '89

Finding the lost generation [geography programs] G. Solomon. il *Home Office Computing* 7:82+ My '89

Gadgets no more: computers take hold in education and research. D. Stanton. *Compute!* 11:106 N '89

Geometry [tutoring program] C. S. Holzberg. il *Compute!* 11:70-1 Je '89

Give your child's reading skills a big boost—turn on the computer. D. Stanton. il *Compute!* 11:15 Mr '89

Giving computers an ethnic edge [educational software for black children] K. Moses. il *American Visions* 4:12 D '89

Homework [shape and color games for children] H. E. H. Aycock. il *Compute!* 11:114 N '89

How to give your family's software of the year awards. D. Stanton. il *Compute!* 11:16 Ag '89

Learn on me [Macintosh engineering and scientific courseware] D. E. Crabb. il *Byte* 14:143-4+ Jl '89

Learning with LogoWriter, Home Edition. C. S. Holzberg. il *Home Office Computing* 7:86-7 My '89

Logo and geography teaching. M. Eichen. bibl *Focus (New York, N.Y.: 1950)* 39:25-6 Summ '89

Look what I did! [software for learning disabled children] M. Furst. il *Home Office Computing* 7:82+ F '89

Mind travelers: explore the world through your computer [World GeoGraph] D. Stanton. il *Compute!* 11:16 S '89

The New Talking Stickybear Alphabet. N. Rentschler. il *Compute!* 11:69-70 My '89

Pascal on the Mac [Just Enough Pascal tutorial] A. F. Lent and L. H. Loeb. *Byte* 14 Mac Special Ed:MAC5-MAC6 Mr '89

PC-Globe+. K. Sternberg. il *Compute!* 11:74 Ag '89

Science! [with editorial comment by Gregg Keizer] D. Stanton. il *Compute!* 11:4, 18-24 Je '89

Speaking in tongues [foreign language software] T. Netsel. *Compute!* 11:108-10+ N '89

To heck with hunt-and-peck [typing programs] L. Williams. il *Home Office Computing* 7:81-2+ Ap '89

Employment use

Programming

The Perfect Career. H. E. H. Aycock. il *Compute!* 11:72-3 Mr '89

COMPUTERS—cont.

Energy usage

Build REACTS: the Radio-Electronics Advanced Control System (XI) [battery-backup power supply] J. Bybee. il *Radio-Electronics* 60:65-8 Ja '89

Curing the brownout blues [uninterruptible power systems] S. Apiki and others. il *Byte* 14:162-6+ Ap '89

Current events [CarrierNET, carrier current system] R. L. Mitchell. il *Byte* 14:97 Mr '89

The great power spike. J. Pournelle. il *Byte* 14:99-100+ Ag '89

Engineering use

A/E/C Systems '89: the changing face of computer use for architects and engineers. C. K. Hoyt. il *Architectural Record* 177:33+ Jl '89

Workstations boost productivity of aerospace, defense engineers. D. Hughes. *Aviation Week & Space Technology* 130:255+ Mr 20 '89

Programming

See also
Silicon compilers (Computers)

Environmental use

Computerized canaries [British Trust for Ornithology monitoring system] T. Beardsley. *Scientific American* 260:34 Ap '89

Southeast waterways will face an acid test [research by M. Robbins Church] J. Raloff. *Science News* 136:151 S 2 '89

Equipment

See also
VGA (Video graphics array)

386 power on a 286 budget [All ChargeCard] il *Radio-Electronics* 60:83-5 N '89

The 1989 Compute! Choice Awards [cover story; special section; with editorial comment by Gregg Keizer] il *Compute!* 11:4, 24-6+ Ja '89

Adding fax power to your PC [Complete Fax/9600] J. Pepper. il *Personal Computing* 13:202 Mr '89

Advanced floppy disk drive controllers [CompatiCard I, Mux Card, Omni-Bridge] J. Holtzman. il *Byte* 14:191-5 Mr '89

The brains behind the graphics [graphics coprocessor boards] S. Apiki and others. il *Byte* 14:178-82+ N '89

Brother bundles fax, modem, and software [Brother IntelliFax board] C. Lee. il *Personal Computing* 13:186 Je '89

Build an 80386SX motherboard (I). B. A. McIlhany. il *Radio-Electronics* 60 ComputerDigest:79+ Je '89

Build an 80386SX motherboard (II). B. A. McIlhany. il *Radio-Electronics* 60 ComputerDigest:81 Jl '89

Build an 80386SX motherboard (III). B. A. McIlhany. il *Radio-Electronics* 60 ComputerDigest:75+ Ag '89

The Byte Awards. il *Byte* 14:327-30+ Ja '89

Computer scan. G. Branwyn and G. Clabaugh. See issues of The Futurist beginning January/February 1989

Customized road machines. C. O'Malley. il *Personal Computing* 13:92-6 N '89

Customizing your computer. R. Scibilia. il *Popular Mechanics* 166:118+ O '89

DoubleCOM [combined serial port and A/B switch] il *Radio-Electronics* 60 ComputerDigest:88-9 Ja '89

EMS with a cache [Elite 16 Plus HyperCache] J. Holtzman. il *Byte* 14:181-2+ Jl '89

Fax board has many problems [Ricoh ImageCard fax system] S. Miller. il *Home Office Computing* 7:56-7 Jl '89

Fax boards: do you need one? S. Miller. il *Home Office Computing* 7:62+ My '89

A fax for your computer [Complete Fax/9600] J. J. McGonagle, Jr. il *Home Office Computing* 7:65 Ap '89

Global Specialties BOA microcomputer applications workstation. il *Radio-Electronics* 60:17-18 Je '89

A great communicator [Connection CoProcessor PC facsimile board] N. Baran. il *Byte* 14:195-6+ Ja '89

Holiday gift guide. H. E. H. Aycock and J. Sloan. il *Compute!* 11:46-8 D '89

How to put 16 million colors to work [NuBus boards for 32-Bit QuickDraw] T. Thompson. il *Byte* 14:189-94+ D '89

Just a few fax [Fax-mail 96 and JT Fax 9600 cards] W. Rash, Jr. il *Byte* 14:143-4 Je '89

Mac color by SCSI [ScuzzyGraph II external graphics display] H. Eglowstein. *Byte* 14:235 D '89

The Mac makes connections. B. N. Meeks. il *Byte* 14:171-2+ My '89

Memory expansion boards [tables] C. D. Hanlon. il *Compute!* 11:42+ S '89

PixC leaves windows overhead in the dust. B. Smith. il *Byte* 14:202 S '89

Pixels on the march [8514/A and Artist 10 MC graphics coprocessor boards] B. D. Kliewer. il *Byte* 14:201-2+ Ja '89

Pocket memory cards: companies seek standards for tiny storage devices. *Byte* 14:17-18 O '89

Power home computing. H. E. H. Aycock and others. il *Compute!* 11:36-40 Je '89

Radiation monitor update [with editorial comment by Brian C. Fenton] J. Jaffe and D. Sythe. il *Radio-Electronics* 60:4, 51-5+ Je '89

Send a POSTcard to your PC [power-on self test monitor card] S. Miastkowski. il *Byte* 14:88 S '89

Speed-up board gives decent return for your money [Orchid TwinTurbo 12] H. F. Beechhold. il *Home Office Computing* 7:62 Ja '89

Teletek X-Bandit EMS 4.0 memory board. J. Holtzman. il *Radio-Electronics* 60 ComputerDigest:79-80 Je '89

Three ways to improve your memory [expanded memory boards for XTs and ATs] H. F. Beechhold and E. P. Stevenson. il *Home Office Computing* 7:74+ D '89

True colors, revisited [Spectrum/24 video board] T. Thompson. il *Byte* 14 Mac Special Supp:MAC191 Ag '89

The ultimate upgrade [standard IBM PC AT turned into a personal workstation] S. Diehl. il *Byte* 14:313-14+ Je '89

UltraVision. J. Nimersheim. il *Compute!* 11:130+ N '89

Update: standout graphics board [Rendition II] S. Apiki. il *Byte* 14:234 D '89

Upgrading your computer: Macintosh. C. H. Gajeway. il *Home Office Computing* 7:54-6 Ja '89

What's new in accelerator boards. R. Bel Bruno. il *Personal Computing* 13:103-5+ Ag '89

Where PC-fax pays off. C. O'Malley. il *Personal Computing* 13:91-3+ Je '89

Year-end special: editors' picks 1989: the best and brightest hardware of the year [cover story] il *Home Office Computing* 7:47-51 D '89

Espionage use

Spying and sabotage by computer. J. Peterzell. il *Time* 133:25-6 Mr 20 '89

Exhibitions

See also
Comdex (Trade show)

A/E/C Systems '89 product roundup. S. S. Ross. il *Architectural Record* 177:120-7 Ag '89

A/E/C Systems '89: the changing face of computer use for architects and engineers. C. K. Hoyt. il *Architectural Record* 177:33+ Jl '89

A/E/C Systems: pre-meeting products preview. S. S. Ross. il *Architectural Record* 177:158-63 My '89

CeBIT. J. Endrijonas. il *Radio-Electronics* 60 ComputerDigest:73-5 Jl '89

Computer products for architects: AEC Expo showcases PC software, hardware, and add-ons. S. S. Ross. il *Architectural Record* 177:148-51 F '89

A lot of company [CeBIT in West Germany] N. Baran. il *Byte* 14:6 My '89

Much ado about Mac [MacWorld Expo] K. Ferrell. il *Compute!* 11:8 Ap '89

Showing PCs in the Windy City [PC Expo] C. Karnes. il *Compute!* 11:106 Ja '89

Federal aid

Aid for supercomputers and networks weighed in capital. I. Goodwin. *Physics Today* 42:50-2 N '89

White House, Congress push computer plan. M. Sun. *Science* 245:1186 S 15 '89

Financial services use

See also
Computers—Tax return use

When PCs make dollars and sense. R. D. R. Hoffmann. il *Personal Computing* 13:85+ O '89

Programming

BankMate; MoneyMate. L. Kleinholz. il *Home Office Computing* 7:73-5 Mr '89

Financial planning made easy with Andrew Tobias's Financial Calculator. K. Dennard. il *Home Office Computing* 7:32 Ja '89

Money, money, money [personal finance software; cover story] N. Randall. il *Compute!* 11:30-2+ F '89

On Balance. G. McClure. il *Compute!* 11:122+ D '89

WealthBuilder by Money Magazine. H. E. H. Aycock. il *Compute!* 11:124+ N '89

What's new in personal finance software. M. Antonoff. il *Personal Computing* 13:129-34 Ja '89

Which is the best financial software for you? [cover story] L. Kleinholz. il *Home Office Computing* 7:49-55 O '89

Forestry use

Fighting fires bit by byte. S. Begley. il *Newsweek* 114:53 Ag 28 '89

Gambling use

See also
Lotteries—Automation

Geological use

Coming down in sheets [computer model of convection in the earth's mantle; work of Dave Bercovici and others] T. Appenzeller. il *Scientific American* 261:17-18 Ag '89

Three-dimensional spherical models of convection in the earth's mantle. D. Bercovici and others. bibl f il *Science* 244:950-5 My 26 '89

Government use

See also
Computers—Espionage use
Computers—Military use
Public Electronic Network (Santa Monica, Calif.: Database)

Competition in the information industry [address, October 31, 1988] J. W. Simpson. *Vital Speeches of the Day* 55:284-6 F 15 '89

COMPUTERS—Government use—*cont.*

Government bulletin boards. M. Lent. il *Home Office Computing* 7:34 Ja '89

Government information goes on-line. H. H. Perritt. il *Technology Review* 92:60-5+ N/D '89

Not so fast [debate over whether or not computerized government records are covered under the Freedom of Information Act] B. Maxwell. il *Common Cause Magazine* 15:24-5 S/O '89

Strip search [weak enforcement due to computer system malfunction at Office of Surface Mining Reclamation and Enforcement] T. Sherwood. il *Common Cause Magazine* 15:8-9 My/Je '89

Programming

Congress finds bugs in the software [federal procurement process leads to faulty software] M. M. Waldrop. il *Science* 246:753 N 10 '89

Grocery trade use

A laptop brigade that focuses on the customer [City Provisioners, Inc.] C. O'Malley. il *Personal Computing* 13:76-7+ O '89

What new services? J. Schlefer. *Technology Review* 92:4 N/D '89

Health use

Informatics and health [cover story; special issue] il *World Health* p2-29 Ag/S '89

Tele-Health. R. Perreault and M.-C. Laurendeau. il *World Health* p6-7 Mr '89

Programming

Understanding AIDS & Alcohol [computer programs] K. Sternberg. *Compute!* 11:122+ O '89

WellAware: Food Sensitivity [computer program] R. M. Gilpin. il *Home Office Computing* 7:76 Ag '89

History

15 years and counting. il *Byte* 14:397-8 S '89

Even his banker didn't know that Ed Roberts had spawned a huge industry [inventor of the personal computer] D. Moreau. il por *Changing Times* 43:128 Ap '89

A look backward and forward. J. Pournelle. *Byte* 14:107 D '89

Paper, magnets, and light. R. R. Gaskin. il *Byte* 14:391-2+ N '89

Home use

See also
Home banking services

1990 home tech guide [special section] il *U.S. News & World Report* 107:82-5+ N 20 '89

Boosting your home's IQ [wiring standard called Consumer Electronics Bus] P. Elmer-Dewitt. il *Time* 133:70-1 Ja 23 '89

The buck starts here [making money with a home computer; cover story; special section] il *Compute!* 11:18-22+ Ag '89

A dream come true: homes that care for themselves—and you. S. Esters. il *Black Enterprise* 19:29+ Ja '89

Home computing explosion [special section] bibl il *Compute!* 11:31-3+ O '89

Houses of the future today [smart houses] P. Carroll. il *Working Woman* 14:82+ N '89

If home computers are bicycles for the mind, I can't wait to board the plane. P. Scisco. il *Compute!* 11:4 Ag '89

Making the grade [family computer for home learning; cover story] D. Stanton. il *Compute!* 11:18-23 S '89

On the home front [smart houses] D. P. Wiener. il *U.S. News & World Report* 107:80 D 25 '89-Ja 1 '90

See your computer for what it's worth. P. Scisco. *Compute!* 11:4 N '89

With a personal computer and some original thinking, you could be rolling in the dough. D. D. Thornburg. il *Compute!* 11:13 Ag '89

Hotel use
See Hotels, motels, etc.—Automation

Hunting use
Programming

High-tech hunting [deer hunting] B. Clede. il *Outdoor Life* 184:93-4 D '89

Shoot with a computer [analyzing bullet trajectories] J. Carmichel. il *Outdoor Life* 183:42+ Ja '89

Image processing use
See Image processing

Indexing use
Programming

Make your documents professional looking and efficient to use [indexing with word processing and Proindex programs] H. F. Beechhold. il *Home Office Computing* 7:22+ Ja '89

Text retrieval with a twist [Folio Views] D. Allen. il *Byte* 14:201-2+ Jl '89

Industrial use
See also
Automation
Computer integrated manufacturing
Flexible manufacturing systems

Research targets machines that learn. *High Technology Business* 9:39 F '89

Input-output equipment
See Computer input-output equipment

Investment use
See also
Program trading (Securities)
Tactical asset allocation (Investments)

Calculated risk [computer investing at Colonial Management] J. Clements. il *Forbes* 143:248-9 Je 26 '89

Can you beat the Street? D. R. Katz. il *Esquire* 112:81-2 N '89

Future shock is rattling the futures pits. K. A. Behof. il *Business Week* p93-4 Ap 17 '89

The man behind the curtain [global exchanges] R. L. Stern. il *Forbes* 143:44-5 Ap 17 '89

A real Live Wire [Cablesoft's LiveWire board delivers quotes from Financial News Network] R. Bel Bruno. il *Personal Computing* 13:38 Ja '89

Turning your desktop into a personal Big Board [LiveWire board delivers stock quotes from Financial News Network] O. Port. il *Business Week* p119 Mr 27 '89

When PCs make dollars and sense. R. D. R. Hoffmann. il *Personal Computing* 13:85+ O '89

You just can't keep Ed Thorp down. E. Schine. il por *Business Week* p83 Ag 21 '89

Programming

Coincidence versus cause [too rigid computerized investment programs] D. N. Dreman. il *Forbes* 144:158 Ag 7 '89

The computer option [options markets] E. Sturza. il por *Forbes* 143:250 Je 26 '89

Computers vs. cerebrums [face off between OTC insight and MPT review] M. Hulbert. il *Forbes* 143:184 Ap 3 '89

Discount hunter [closed end fund strategy on a personal computer] D. Churbuck. il *Forbes* 143:252-3 Je 26 '89

The golden median [median price-earnings ratios overlooked by computers] M. Gianturco. il *Forbes* 144:342 Jl 24 '89

A margin for the electronic broker [R. Baird, futures broker] R. D. R. Hoffmann. il por *Personal Computing* 13:90-2 O '89

The optimizers are coming. M. Gianturco. il *Forbes* 144:270 O 16 '89

Stock information is just a keystroke away [Telescan Analyzer v2.5 and Telescan Edge v1.0] N. Maffei. il *Home Office Computing* 7:36 Je '89

Watching and buying stocks by computer. B. R. Schlender. il *Fortune* 120:38 D 4 '89

Irrigation use
Programming

The electronic goddess: computerizing Bali's ancient irrigation rites [work of Stephen Lansing and James Kremer] G. Cowley. il *Newsweek* 113:50 Mr 6 '89

Journalistic use

A power trip that's not state of the art. B. Hume. il *Personal Computing* 13:35-6 O '89

Leasing and renting
See also
Comdisco, Inc.

Leasing equipment can bring your home office up to date. S. Chen. il *Home Office Computing* 7:12 D '89

Why IBM is cramping its biggest customers' style [leasing companies and antitrusts] J. W. Verity. il *Business Week* p78 My 29 '89

Literary use
See also
Computers—Poetry use

Programming

A potpourri of programmed prose and prosody. A. K. Dewdney. il *Scientific American* 260:122-5 Je '89

Logic circuits
See Logic circuits

Mailing list use
Programming

Address Book Plus [mailing list manager] B. Gingher. il *Compute!* 11:76-7 My '89

Addressing a common problem [Address Book Plus version B.00; mailing list manager] B. Krasnoff. il *Personal Computing* 13:204+ Ap '89

Label printing made easy [LabelPro] B. Krasnoff. *Personal Computing* 13:206 N '89

Labels! V. D. O'Connor. *Compute!* 11:70 S '89

Power Desk. T. A. Summers. il *Home Office Computing* 7:75-6 Ja '89

Maintenance and repair

Choosing the right PC repair option. R. Lockwood. il *Personal Computing* 13:117-19+ N '89

Send a POSTcard to your PC [power-on self test monitor card] S. Miastkowski. il *Byte* 14:88 S '89

Taking the headaches out of equipment maintenance [third-party service providers; cover story] G. Graff. il *High Technology Business* 9:18-21+ S/O '89

Anecdotes, facetiae, satire, etc.

Computer follies. M. Sterling. il *New Choices for the Best Years* 29:104 S '89

Makeup use

On-line looks. il *'Teen* 33:90-3 N '89

COMPUTERS—*cont.*

Marketing use
See Electronic marketing

Mathematical use
See also
Computers—Statistical use

Another piece of 3.14159 . . .? [work of David and Gregory Chudnovsky] B. A. Cipra. *Science* 244:1260 Je 16 '89

As American as apple pi [work of David and Gregory Chudnovsky] S. Begley. il *Newsweek* 113:61 Je 26 '89

Beyond understanding? [finite projective plane of order 10; work of Clement Lam] P. Wallich. *Scientific American* 260:24 Mr '89

A billion digits of pi [work of Gregory and David Chudnovsky] I. Peterson. *Science News* 136:166 S 9 '89

Biting off a record-breaking piece of pi [work of David and Gregory Chudnovsky] I. Peterson. il *Science News* 135:372 Je 17 '89

The color of geometry [cover story] I. Peterson. il *Science News* 136:408-10+ D 23-30 '89

Computing a prime champion. *Science News* 136:191 S 16 '89

Do mathematicians still do math? [computer-assisted proofs] B. A. Cipra. il *Science* 244:769-70 My 19 '89

Floating-point revisited. R. Grehan. il *Byte* 14:311-16+ Ap '89

From real numbers to strings of zeros [special section] B. A. Cipra. *Science* 243:1142-3 Mr 3 '89

How the Grinch stole mathematics [computer-generated combinatorial proof; work of Herb Wilf and Down Zeilberger] B. A. Cipra. *Science* 245:595 Ag 11 '89

Math team vaults over prime record [work of scientists at Amdahl Corporation] B. A. Cipra. *Science* 245:815 Ag 25 '89

Optimizing numeric coprocessing. S. S. Fried. il *Byte* 14 Special Issue:221-4 Fall '89

Say it again in plain algebra [Susan Landau devises algorithm to denest radicals produced by computer algebra systems] B. A. Cipra. *Science* 245:1190-1 S 15 '89; Correction. 246:997 N 24 '89

Search me and know me [religious reflections on computer search into existence of finite projective plane of order 10] M. E. Marty. *The Christian Century* 106:247 Mr 1 '89

Weitek pushing its own math chip for Intel's 80486. *Byte* 14:26 Jl '89

Programming

Computer chaos at home [Verhulst equation] D. H. Smith. il *Sky and Telescope* 78:139 Ag '89

From formulas to Fortran to results: the AUTOMATED PROGRAMMER system. C. B. Engle, Jr. il *Science* 246:1169-72 D 1 '89

The sorcerer's apprentice [Graffiti program developed by Siemion Fajtlowicz] B. A. Cipra. il *Science* 244:770 My 19 '89

Symbolic manipulation programs for the personal computer. K. R. Foster and H. H. Bau. bibl f il *Science* 243:679-84 F 3 '89

Symbolic math on the Mac [Mathematica 1.0] P. Wayner. il *Byte* 14:239-42+ Ja '89

Medical use
See also
Tomography—Medical use

Adultproof cap [medication event monitoring system uses computer chips in medicine bottle caps] *Time* 133:70 Je '89

Informatics and health [cover story; special issue] il *World Health* p2-29 Ag/S '89

Medical Center lifeline [computer use at M.D. Anderson Cancer Center in Houston] C. Strehlo. il *Personal Computing* 13:97 Ja '89

A research tool in the war against AIDS [computers at National Institute of Allergies and Infectious Diseases] P. Honan. il por *Personal Computing* 13:182-4 O '89

Programming

Compute your heart risk [program used by Framingham Heart Study] A. Sprout. il *American Health* 8:14-15 N '89

Life & Death. J. Latimer. il *Compute!* 11:71-2 My '89

Safeguarding the supply [computer program designed to interpret blood test data; work of Jack Smith] *USA Today (Periodical)* 118:14 O '89

The way the whorls turn [computer reads Down syndrome in parents' handprints] M. R. Meyer. il *Newsweek* 113:73 F 13 '89

Memory systems
See also
Cache memory
Data tapes
Ferroelectric storage devices
Nashua Corporation
Optical storage devices
Random access memory
Read only memory

5 steps to taming a wild hard disk. P. Honan. il *Personal Computing* 13:121-3+ Ja '89

386 power on a 286 budget [All ChargeCard] il *Radio-Electronics* 60:83-5 N '89

Advanced floppy disk drive controllers [CompatiCard I, Mux Card, Omni-Bridge] J. Holtzman. il *Byte* 14:191-5 Mr '89

Answers to my Mac mess [preventing hard disk crashes and MouseStick] E. Shapiro. il *Byte* 14:129-30+ Ap '89

Back in the driver's seat in disk drives [IBM's 3390] J. W. Verity. il *Business Week* p79-80 N 27 '89

A backup drive with the memory of an elephant [Jumbo tape backup system] M. Bryan. il *Personal Computing* 13:204 Mr '89

Breaking the memory barrier with 386IVMM. M. Heller. il *Byte* 14:187-8+ Jl '89

Bubble memory's ruggedness revives interest for military use. il *Aviation Week & Space Technology* 130:52-3+ Ja 16 '89

Buying a hard-disk drive: five pointers. S. Chen and M. D. Espindle. *Home Office Computing* 7:20 O '89

Circumnavigating the disk with Magellan. A. Reinhardt. il *Byte* 14:97-8 My '89

Counterpart mirrors your drives [card backup device for hard disk drives] S. Miastkowski. il *Byte* 14:94+ Jl '89

DAT drive eases Mac backups [Gigapack-Mac] D. E. Crabb. il *Byte* 14:225-6+ N '89

Data to go [Plus Passport and Tandon Ad-PAC removable hard disk drives] S. Chen. il *Home Office Computing* 7:66+ My '89

Data to go [Sysgen Maxi RD45 removable hard disk cartridge system] D. E. Crabb. il *Byte* 14:177-8+ S '89

Diamond film has promise for tough hard disks. *Byte* 14:11 My '89

Disaster recovery [hard disk crashes] D. E. Crabb. il *Byte* 14:127-8 S '89

Exploring a hard disk [Magellan] L. Kleinman. il *Personal Computing* 13:29 F '89

Floppy frustration . . . think hard. D. Stanton. il *Compute!* 11:32-3+ Ag '89

Get organized with ViewLink. il *Radio-Electronics* 60 ComputerDigest:80+ Je '89

Hard disk interfaces. B. Glass. il *Byte* 14:293-7 F '89

Hip-deep and rising [making upgrade decisions] F. Langa. il *Byte* 14:8 O '89

How smart is your disk drive? K. K. Wiegner. il *Forbes* 144:219+ O 30 '89

How to install a tape backup unit [Streaming tape drive] B. C. Fenton. il *Radio-Electronics* 60 ComputerDigest:81+ Je '89

If memory serves . . . [memory management routines] R. Grehan. il *Byte* 14:279-80+ Ag '89

The incredible shrinking disk. D. English. il *Compute!* 11:9 F '89

An infinitely expandable hard disk? [Iomega Bernoulli Box II] H. F. Beechhold. il *Home Office Computing* 7:64 Ja '89

Jumbo works for peanuts [tape backup unit] S. Miastkowski. il *Byte* 14:98+ Ja '89

The little drive that could [MegaMate 3½-inch external drive] D. Barker. il *Byte* 14:97 F '89

Loaded for action [combination boot/data disk] P. Scisco. il *Compute!* 11:82 O '89

Magellan: intrepid hard-disk explorer. L. Kleinman. il *Personal Computing* 13:192 Jl '89

Master the data on your hard-disk drive with Lotus Magellan. S. Morgenstern. il *Home Office Computing* 7:36+ N '89

A new twist on an old technology [helical-scan recording] J. Bretzmann. il *Byte* 14:380-2+ N '89

A new world for DOS [ViewLink and Magellan] S. Miastkowski. il *Byte* 14:177-8+ Ag '89

OS/2 disk geography. M. Minasi. il *Byte* 14:151-2+ Je '89

Out, out, damn disk [tips on using diskettes] L. Van Gelder. il *Ms.* 17:30 Ja/F '89

Paper, magnets, and light. R. R. Gaskin. il *Byte* 14:391-2+ N '89

Pocket memory cards: companies seek standards for tiny storage devices. *Byte* 14:17-18 O '89

Power home computing. H. E. H. Aycock and others. il *Compute!* 11:36-40 Je '89

A question-and-answer guide to floppies. S. Miller. il *Home Office Computing* 7:52-4 Ag '89

Tandon's Ad-Pac: a movable hard drive [removable disk drive] E. Berk. il *Personal Computing* 13:198 My '89

Tape capacity jumps up a notch [QFA-500 backup system] J. Blackford. il *Personal Computing* 13:200 S '89

Tecmar sets a standard for backup [QT-150e] J. Blackford. *Personal Computing* 13:200 S '89

Turn your Compaq into a LAN server with gigabytes [fixed disk drive expansion unit] S. J. Wszola. il *Byte* 14:100 My '89

Upgrading your computer: Macintosh. C. H. Gajeway. il *Home Office Computing* 7:54-6 Ja '89

ViewLink. D. Stanton. il *Compute!* 11:66-7+ Jl '89

ViewLink: uniting data and applications. C. Bermant. il *Personal Computing* 13:101 My '89

What's new in backup hardware and software. P. Honan. il *Personal Computing* 13:103-5+ Je '89

With tape, backing up's not hard to do [Irwin Model 5080 tape system] D. Barker. il *Byte* 14:98 Ja '89

COMPUTERS—Memory systems—*cont.*
Care
Dawn of the dead disk. W. Rash, Jr. il *Byte* 14:137-40 Jl '89
Disk Technician Advanced keeps disks virile. S. Miastkowski. *Byte* 14:102+ My '89
Disk Technician: the power of prevention [Disk Technician Advanced version 5.23] J. Blackford. il *Personal Computing* 13:198 Ap '89
Guard against disk errors and viruses with Disk Watcher. J. Holtzman. il *Radio-Electronics* 60 ComputerDigest:77-9 My '89
Hard disk maintenance software. B. Glass. il *Byte* 14:265-8+ Ag '89
The hunt for bad sectors [hard disk drive] J. Pournelle. il *Byte* 14:119-20+ Je '89
Lynx 470 disk drive tester and exerciser. il *Radio-Electronics* 60:17+ My '89

Meteorological use
Beam it up, Scotty [Weathertrak and Airborne Flight Information System access for Lasertrak FP100 owners] A. Laboda. il *Flying* 116:115 Jl '89
Forecasting pushed too far [dynamical extended range forecasting] R. A. Kerr. il *Science* 244:1139 Je 9 '89
Getting a clearer view of smog [supercomputer pollution model developed by G. J. McRae] M. Schroeder. il por *Business Week* Special Issue:73 Je 16 '89
Hot spot [Pangaea; research by Thomas J. Crowley] J. Horgan. il *Scientific American* 261:20+ S '89
Scandinavian, Siberian, and Arctic Ocean glaciation: effect of Holocene atmospheric CO_2 variations. D. R. Lindstrom and D. R. MacAyeal. bibl f il *Science* 245:628-31 Ag 11 '89
Wherefore the world's wobble? [Chandler wobble; research by Sultan Hameed and Robert G. Currie] *Science News* 135:220 Ap 8 '89

Programming
Using your computer. A. Blackadar. See issues of Weatherwise beginning June 1984
Weather prediction in the classroom [Accu-Weather Forecaster] M. Eichen. *Focus (New York, N.Y.: 1950)* 39:27+ Spr '89

Military use
Bubble memory's ruggedness revives interest for military use. il *Aviation Week & Space Technology* 130:52-3+ Ja 16 '89
Expert system puts clamp on enemy subs. *High Technology Business* 9:34 S/O '89
Four in race for sub AI deal. *High Technology Business* 9:32 Je '89
High-tech weapons are coming under friendly fire. D. Griffiths. il *Business Week* p118 My 22 '89
Human factors are critical in computer-driven systems. D. Hughes. il *Aviation Week & Space Technology* 131:104-5 D 18-25 '89
Military computer awards stalled; Conyers asks probe. por *Jet* 75:9 Mr 6 '89
My life as a NATO collaborator [pacifist computer scientist attends NATO workshop on computer-human interaction in command and control; cover story] N. S. Borenstein. il *The Bulletin of the Atomic Scientists* 45:14-20 Ap '89
Powerful light computers hold key to sensor, smart weapon research. P. A. Gilmartin. il *Aviation Week & Space Technology* 130:57+ Mr 20 '89
Radar networks, computing advances seen as keys to counter Stealth technologies [views of Robert W. Selden] D. F. Bond. *Aviation Week & Space Technology* 131:41 D 4 '89
Raytheon adapts color workstations to meet requirements of military users. D. Hughes. il *Aviation Week & Space Technology* 130:104-5 Ap 24 '89
USAF will automate analysis system used to characterize Soviet weapons [Red Mission Analysis] *Aviation Week & Space Technology* 131:112-13 S 11 '89
War games [C. J. Johnson sues Defense Dept. over computerized control of nuclear weapons] S. Ditlea. il *Omni (New York, N.Y.)* 11:32+ Mr '89
Who will yell fire when the house is ablaze? [conviction of anti-nuclear activist S. Komisaruk for damaging computer at Vandenburg Air Force Base] R. E. Burns. *U.S. Catholic* 54:2 F '89

Programming
Air Logistics Center keeps EW systems capable of countering changing threats [electronic warfare activities at Warner Robins Air Logistics Center, Ga.] il *Aviation Week & Space Technology* 131:103-6 S 11 '89
Software delays NORAD upgrade, increases costs by $207 million. B. D. Nordwall. *Aviation Week & Space Technology* 130:24-5 My 22 '89

Multiuser systems
Interrupts aren't always best [Unix] G. E. Pajari. il *Byte* 14:261-4 My '89
The multiuser solution. H. Eglowstein and S. Diehl. il *Byte* 14:148-54+ S '89

Musical use
See also
MIDI (Musical instrument digital interface)

More sound for less [music for TV productions] F. Moore. il *Channels (New York, N.Y.: 1986)* 9:72 Jl/Ag '89
Musical talent. F. Vizard. il *Popular Mechanics* 166:116-17 O '89
Video whizzes and musical mavens: don't overlook your most useful money-making tool. D. D. Thornburg. il *Compute!* 11:14 S '89

Programming
Compute! choice: The Music Studio 3.0. J. Latimer. il *Compute!* 11:102-4 N '89
Music Studio for Apple IIGS. J. Free. il *Popular Science* 234:58 Je '89
Music writing programs for the Macintosh (I). J. Simpson. il *Down Beat* 56:54-6 Ap '89
Music writing programs for the Macintosh (II) [Music Publisher and Finale] J. Simpson. il *Down Beat* 56:53-6 Je '89

Nature study use
Programming
Audubon Wildlife Adventures: Grizzly Bears [computer program] T. A. Summers. il *Home Office Computing* 7:69 Jl '89
Wildlife Adventures: Grizzly Bears. K. Sternberg. il *Compute!* 11:66 Jl '89

Navigational use
See also
Boats and boating—Electronic equipment

Newspaper publishing use
The bloke buckled [Britain's union bashing publisher E. Shah] E. McGlinn. il por *Forbes* 143:10 F 6 '89

Operating systems
See Computer operating systems

Optical equipment
See also
Light pens
Optical scanners
Optical storage devices

Periodicals
See also
Byte (Periodical)
Compute! (Periodical)
Home office computing (Periodical)
Computing for dollars [selling articles to computer magazines] C. Walnum. il *The Writer* 102:20-2 Mr '89

Photographic use
Programming
Changing perceptions of reality. B. M. Dawson. il *Byte* 14:293-7+ D '89
Editing in shades of gray [Picture Publisher 1.0] C. O'Malley. il *Personal Computing* 13:194+ My '89
The electronic darkroom [Picture Publisher] J. Fiderio. il *Byte* 14:104-5 Mr '89
Images through gray glasses. M. Antonoff. il *Personal Computing* 13:61-2+ N '89
Industrial-strength color processing [PhotoMac] T. Thompson. il *Byte* 14:97-8 Ap '89
Visual Edge sharpens laser output [printer enhancement] C. O'Malley. il *Personal Computing* 13:192-3 My '89

Photographs and photography
A balancing act in three exposures. J. Bartsch. il *Petersen's Photographic Magazine* 18:94-5 D '89
Double-exposing two media. S. Lewis. il *Petersen's Photographic Magazine* 17:76-7 Mr '89

Physics use
Getting a grip on rubbing bodies. R. Pool. il *Science* 246:445 O 27 '89

Poetry use
Programming
Poetry Palette. G. Solomon. il *Home Office Computing* 7:91-2 Ja '89

Police use
After the fact [LoJack Retrieve] D. Kott. il *Road & Track* 41:133 N '89
The electronic cop [Custom Electronics Model DXT Mobile Data Terminal used by Mesa, Ariz. police] D. C. Ross. il *Motor Trend* 41:70 Je '89
The new crime stoppers. R. C. Larson. il *Technology Review* 92:26-31 N/D '89
To catch a thief [LoJack tracking equipment] C. Torcellini. il *Forbes* 143:202 Ap 17 '89

Programming
Hard-driving detectives. L. Kahaner. il *Omni (New York, N.Y.)* 12:24+ D '89

Political use
See also
Computers—Espionage use
Computers—Government use
Computing as a political force. K. A. Frenkel. il *Personal Computing* 13:99+ O '89
The new breed of campaign manager [J. Cowart deploys personal computers] K. A. Frenkel. il por *Personal Computing* 13:108-10 O '89

Programming
See also
Hidden Agenda (Video game)

COMPUTERS—*cont.*

Prices

Award-winning mail order strategies [computers; cover story; special section] R. Lockwood. il *Personal Computing* 13:78-81+ F '89

Bargain systems that mean business. P. Honan. il *Personal Computing* 13:99-103+ D '89

The chip of tomorrow—in yesterday's machine [IBM to retrofit PS/2 with 1486 microchip] G. Lewis. il *Business Week* p64 Jl 3 '89

The economics of performance. G. Sumrall. *Byte* 14 Special Issue:68-9 Fall '89

Hold onto your hat (and your wallet) [Apricot 80486-based machine] F. Langa. il *Byte* 14:8 Ag '89

How much should a system cost? *Nation's Business* 77:65-6 O '89

The loneliness of the low-budget user. N. Baran. *Byte* 14:344 Ag '89

Low-cost 386-based computers [buying by mail] H. F. Beechhold. il *Home Office Computing* 7:61-5 O '89

More bang for your bucks [80486-based systems from Cheetah and ALR] F. Langa. il *Byte* 14 Special Issue:8 Fall '89

"Pay less, get more" is our rallying cry [personal computers] G. Keizer. il *Compute!* 11:4 F '89

PC buyer's guide. S. Miller. il *Essence* 20:107-8+ D '89

Print-out equipment
See Computer printers

Printing use

The ABCs of digital type. J. Collins. il *Byte* 14:403-8 N '89

Programming

Save and annotate your Mac output [SuperGlue II utility] T. Thompson. il *Byte* 14:82+ S '89

Twist & Shout [printer utility program] L. Frey. il *Compute!* 11:68 Ap '89

Programs
See Computer programming

Prospecting use
Programming

Computer programs for mineral exploration. F. P. Agterberg. bibl f il maps *Science* 245:76-81 Jl 7 '89

Psychological aspects

Human factors are critical in computer-driven systems [aviation and military] D. Hughes. il *Aviation Week & Space Technology* 131:104-5 D 18-25 '89

Human factors: the gap between humans and machines. E. Weiner and A. Brown. il pors *The Futurist* 23:9-11 My/Je '89

When I work, I just want to have fun. P. Scisco. *Compute!* 11:4 D '89

Psychological use
Programming

Brainstorming by computer [IdeaFisher] M. Roberts. il *Psychology Today* 23:51 Jl/Ag '89

The Idea Bank [IdeaFisher] P. McCarthy. il *Omni (New York, N.Y.)* 11:24 S '89

Smart software. il *Health (New York, N.Y.)* 21:60 Ap '89

Psychotherapeutic use
Programming

Inputting Sigmund. J. Hooper. il *Omni (New York, N.Y.)* 11:20+ Jl '89

Publishing use
See also
Computers—Newspaper publishing use
Computers—Printing use
Desktop publishing

Color pages via electronic prepress save publishers time and money. J. P. Frank. il *Publishers Weekly* 236:33-4+ Ag 18 '89

Purchasing use
See Electronic shopping

Railroad use
See Railroads—Automation

Real estate use

Bringing real-estate profits home [cover story] P. G. Miller. il *Home Office Computing* 7:31-6 Jl '89

Religious use

High-tech Bible [Franklin Computer's Electronic Bible] R. N. Ostling. il *Time* 134:82 O 30 '89

Programming

QuickVerse Bible Concordance. S. Hudson. il *Compute!* 11:70-1 Jl '89

Scientific use
See also
Apollo Computer, Inc.
Computers—Biological use
Computers—Chemical use
Stellar Computer Inc.
Sun Microsystems Inc.

How we explore the universe. P. Honan. il *Personal Computing* 13:177+ O '89

Interacting with the tiny and the immense [scientific visualization] C. Mundie. il *Byte* 14:279-80+ Ap '89

Is it real, or is it Cray? R. Pool. il *Science* 244:1438-40 Je 23 '89

Machine dreams [computer modeling] B. Hayes. il *Discover* 10:82-7 O '89

Turn on your computer and throw open a window onto the wonders of science. D. D. Thornburg. il *Compute!* 11:88 Je '89

Programming

Chaos on computers [Chaos Demonstrations program] *Science* 246:1172 D 1 '89

From formulas to Fortran to results: the AUTOMATED PROGRAMMER system. C. B. Engle, Jr. il *Science* 246:1169-72 D 1 '89

Science! [with editorial comment by Gregg Keizer] D. Stanton. il *Compute!* 11:4, 18-24 Je '89

Your own universe [Rudy Rucker's Cellular Automata Laboratory computer program] T. Waters. il *Discover* 10:24 D '89

Security measures
See also
Cypher Communications Technology Inc.
Digital Pathways (Firm)
Rainbow Technologies Inc.

Avoiding virus hysteria [cover story] P. Honan. il *Personal Computing* 13:84-7+ My '89

Counterpart mirrors your drives [card backup device for hard disk drives] S. Miastkowski. il *Byte* 14:94+ Jl '89

Fighting viruses that do in data. B. Politzer. il *Home Office Computing* 7:10 Ja '89

Guard against disk errors and viruses with Disk Watcher. J. Holtzman. il *Radio-Electronics* 60 ComputerDigest:77-9 My '89

Hostile takeovers [computer network security] P. Wallich. *Scientific American* 260:22+ Ja '89

If your computer catches a virus on Friday the 13th, who you gonna call? John McAfee [creator of disinfectant program] il por *People Weekly* 32:77 O 16 '89

Noise-blocking wallcovering [Saf'n'Shielded] T. O. Bakke. il *Popular Science* 235:87 Jl '89

Put a positive lock on your data [DataSentry] S. Miastkowski. il *Byte* 14:100 F '89

Revenge of the nerds [virus planted by R. T. Morris points up need for tighter security] N. Martin. il *The Washington Monthly* 20:21-2+ Ja '89

Safe and secure? [Unix] P. Wood. bibl il *Byte* 14:253-4+ My '89

Security [special section; with editorial comment by Wayne Rash] il *Byte* 14:254-5+ Je '89

Viruses, worms, trojans, and bombs [cover story] D. Stover. il *Popular Science* 235:59-62+ S '89

Social aspects
See Computers and civilization

Social use

The data game [video and computer dating; cover story] J. Bennet. *The New Republic* 200:20-2 F 13 '89

Sound recording and reproducing use
See Sound—Recording and reproducing

Space flight use

Big bytes in NASA's budget [plans to substitute computers for retiring personnel] R. Fleming. il *Omni (New York, N.Y.)* 12:30+ O '89

Engine controller problem delays launch of Galileo mission to Jupiter. E. H. Kolcum and C. Covault. *Aviation Week & Space Technology* 131:20-1 O 16 '89

GAO says computer problems keep USAF satellite control system behind schedule. *Aviation Week & Space Technology* 131:23 Ag 21 '89

Milstar terminal capability demonstrated as Congress debates program budget. D. Hughes. il *Aviation Week & Space Technology* 131:49-50 O 30 '89

NASA flight controllers become AI pioneers. M. M. Waldrop. il *Science* 244:1044-5 Je 2 '89

Neural networking. C. S. Fuqua. il *Ad Astra* 1:8-13 Ap '89

Programming

Probing the solar system by PC [XonVu: Voyager and Giotto Space Mission Simulator] J. L. Wilson. *Ad Astra* 1:14 Je '89

Reprogramming capability proves key to extending Voyager 2's journey. il *Aviation Week & Space Technology* 131:72 Ag 7 '89

Satellite viewing [Space Birds program] J. L. Wilson. il *Ad Astra* 1:30 Ap '89

Simple Voyager simulator [XonVu] M. Krochmal. il *Astronomy* 17:112-13 My '89

Will the Hubble Space Telescope compute? [problems with operations software] M. M. Waldrop. il *Science* 243:1437-9 Mr 17 '89

Speech therapy use

Laura Meyers creates software that talks friendly to help disabled kids find their voices [Keytalk] S. Adelson. il por *People Weekly* 32:165-6 D 4 '89

Speed

32.5 MHz and climbing [SIA 386/32; cover story] S. Apiki. il *Byte* 14:106-9 Ap '89

386 speed (almost) in a 286 system [ME 286-20] P. Honan. il *Personal Computing* 13:155-6 Ag '89

Battle of the chips [Intel 80286, 80386, and 80386SX; cover story] F. Hayes. il *Byte* 14:274-7+ Mr '89

Better than cache in the bank? [Western Digital Speedkit caching controller] H. Eglowstein. il *Byte* 14:204+ S '89

COMPUTERS—Speed—*cont.*

The fastest 80386s ever? [cover story] R. Malloy. il *Byte* 14:109-12 Je '89

The fastest PCs in the world [ALR FlexCache 33/386, AST Premium 386/33, Compaq Deskpro 386/33, Everex Step 386/33, Zenith Z-386/33, Zeos 386/33] P. Honan. il *Personal Computing* 13:95-7+ S '89

Greased lightning [Zenith Z-386/33] J. Udell. il *Byte* 14:114-16 Je '89

How fast is fast? B. Kindel. il *Byte* 14:251-4 F '89

Megahertz madness [15 of the world's fastest PCs] il *Byte* 14 Special Issue:13-18+ Fall '89

Photonics will boost near-term computer processing speeds. B. D. Nordwall. il *Aviation Week & Space Technology* 130:57+ Ap 17 '89

Software shortcuts to save time. P. Honan. il *Personal Computing* 13:111-14 D '89

Speed-up board gives decent return for your money [Orchid TwinTurbo 12] H. F. Beechhold. il *Home Office Computing* 7:62 Ja '89

What's new in accelerator boards. R. Bel Bruno. il *Personal Computing* 13:103-5+ Ag '89

Sports use

See also

Cyclecomputers

The era of the enhanced athlete. L. Winner. il *Technology Review* 92:22 F/Mr '89

Touching base with the new push-button machines [high tech weight training] M. Greenwood-Robinson. il *Women's Sports & Fitness* 11:16 My '89

Video cycle race [CompuTrainer system] S. F. Brown. il *Popular Science* 234:73 My '89

What would happen if . . . 20 of the best-ever NFL teams played a "Dream season"? [NFL Films and ESPN's simulated games] S. Smith. il *Sports Illustrated* 71:159 S 11 '89

Programming

Fitness with a byte [cycling software] F. Zahradnik. il *Bicycling* 30:144+ Ap '89

Frame and fortune? [Racquet Selector developed by G. Welling] D. Rosenbaum. il *World Tennis* 37:22 N '89

Standards

See also

Open systems (Computers)

Redefining the standards. M. Heller. il *Byte* 14 Special Issue:56-8+ Fall '89

A standards dictionary. B. Glass. il *Byte* 14 Special Issue:209-12+ Fall '89

Why master the dance of standards? J. Blackford. il *Personal Computing* 13:216-17 S '89

Statistical use

Programming

Coping with uncertainty [Basic program for Gaussian distribution curve] A. Blackadar. *Weatherwise* 42:221-3 Ag '89

Stock exchange use

See Computers—Investment use

Study and teaching

See also

William Davis Computer Research Center

The computer's impact on education: progress or problem? J. DelFrate. il *USA Today (Periodical)* 117:68-9 Ja '89

Training: a key ingredient in office automation. S. Gelfond. *Working Woman* 14:19 Jl '89

Training teachers in technology. il *The Futurist* 23:43 Ja/F '89

Soviet Union

In search of hackers. P. Elmer-Dewitt. il *Time* 133:95 Ap 10 '89

Soviets pursue computer literacy. il *USA Today (Periodical)* 117:14 Je '89

Tax return use

Doing your taxes on the desktop—no computation without human interpretation. D. D. Thornburg. il *Compute!* 11:14 F '89

On-line to the IRS [electronic filing] M. Antonoff. *Personal Computing* 13:134 Ja '89

A plug-in, high-cost fast refund [electronic filing] L. Wiener. il *U.S. News & World Report* 106:65 Mr 6 '89

Taxes [home business] A. Starkweather. *Compute!* 11:21-2 Ag '89

Their computers probably know more about you than you think [IRS] R. Wool. il *Money* 18:177 N '89

Programming

Autotax. D. Churbuck. il *Forbes* 143:184-5 Mr 20 '89

Computers vs. taxes. J. Pournelle. il *Byte* 14:109-10+ Jl '89

A Macintosh retrospective [MacInTax] D. E. Crabb. il *Byte* 14:143-4+ Mr '89

Tax-preparation software. S. F. Edwards. il *Home Office Computing* 7:47-8 F '89

Taxpayer-friendly software that almost does it all. O. Port. il *Business Week* p170-1 Mr 20 '89

Telephone management systems

See Computerphones

Telephone rate information use

Programming

Phone bill detective. S. B. Weiner. il *Forbes* 144:263-4 O 16 '89

Phone programs yield instant recall of any conversation. C. Bermant. il *Home Office Computing* 7:28+ Ja '89

Testing

32.5 MHz and climbing [SIA 386/32; cover story] S. Apiki. il *Byte* 14:106-9 Ap '89

286-based laptop for a select few [Bondwell B300] C. Bermant. il *Home Office Computing* 7:70-1 O '89

286 computers [cover story] H. F. Beechhold. il *Home Office Computing* 7:39-44 Mr '89

386 speed (almost) in a 286 system [ME 286-20] P. Honan. il *Personal Computing* 13:155-6 Ag '89

The 486s are here! [Apricot VX FT Server; cover story] P. Lavin and M. E. Nadeau. il *Byte* 14:95-8 S '89

80386SX performance trials. R. Lockwood. il *Personal Computing* 13:87-9+ Ag '89

An alluring SX computer for the cost conscious [Swan 386SX] R. Lockwood. il *Personal Computing* 13:188+ N '89

ALR revs up MCA [MicroFlex 7000] B. Catchings and M. L. Van Name. il *Byte* 14:165-9 S '89

ALR's other 80486s: the PowerCache 4 duo. il *Byte* 14:112-13 N '89

Altos 386 series 1000: for Unix only. B. Smith. il *Byte* 14 Special Issue:30-1 Fall '89

Apple's new compact Mac IIx. N. Baran. il *Byte* 14:117-18 My '89

An AT clone in PS/2 clothing [IBM PS/2 Model 30 286] R. Lockwood. il *Personal Computing* 13:213-14 Ja '89

At the apex of Macintosh power [Macintosh IIcx] J. Pepper. il *Personal Computing* 13:160-1 Ag '89

The Atari ST. R. L. Yap, Jr. il *Radio-Electronics* 60 ComputerDigest:99-102 F '89

Battle of the SXs [Twinhead Superset 490 Model A and the NCR PC916sx] M. E. Nadeau. il *Byte* 14:278 Mr '89

Benchmarks at a glance: 1989. S. Diehl. il *Byte* 14 Special Issue:49-53 Fall '89

Big Mac power in a small Mac box [SE/30] T. Thompson. il *Byte* 14:175-8 Je '89

Build your own computer—we did! [Heathkit HS-2860] S. A. Booth. il *Popular Mechanics* 166:48+ Je '89

Buyer's guide: 20 MHz 386-based PCs [cover story; special section] il *Personal Computing* 13:113-19+ Mr '89

Buyer's guide: laptop computers. il *Personal Computing* 13:121-3+ Ap '89

Buying your first computer [Amiga 500, Macintosh Plus, and HeadStart III] N. Randall and J. Fuchs. il *Compute!* 11:26-9 S '89

Buying your first computer [IBM PS/2 Model 25, Apple IIc Plus, and Tandy 1000 SL] G. Keizer. il *Compute!* 11:38-40 Ap '89

The Byte Awards. il *Byte* 14:327-30+ Ja '89

Cheetah Gold 33: an economical powerhouse. M. E. Nadeau. il *Byte* 14:107-8+ N '89

Color's here—could be better [NEC's ProSpeed CSX] P. Honan. il *Personal Computing* 13:79 N '89

Compact Compaq laptop features groundbreaking display [SLT/286 Model 20] S. Chen. il *Home Office Computing* 7:68+ F '89

Compaq, Tandy unveil notebook systems. P. Honan. il *Personal Computing* 13:25 D '89

Competitive mail-order AT compatible [Micro Express ME 286-20] C. Bermant. il *Home Office Computing* 7:54-5 Jl '89

Computer ease. C. Roth. il *Rolling Stone* p189-90 N 16 '89

Computer stars [MS-DOS and Macintosh computers] S. Chen and N. Sullivan. il *Home Office Computing* 7:51-60 N '89

Computing at Chaos Manor. J. Pournelle. See issues of Byte beginning June 1984

Computing in hand [Sharp Wizard and Psion Organiser] W. Rash, Jr. il *Byte* 14:195-6+ My '89

Dead heat [Tandon 386/20 and FiveStar Model 320] J. Unger. il *Byte* 14:181-4 Je '89

Dell System, service hard to match [System 325] P. Honan. il *Personal Computing* 13:186+ My '89

Desktop power to go [80386 portables] S. Diehl and S. J. Wszola. il *Byte* 14:142-6+ Ag '89

Digital diaries [Sharp Wizard, Psion Organiser II, Casio Digital Diary] F. Vizard. il *Popular Mechanics* 166:73-5 Ap '89

Do you need a laptop computer? il *Consumer Reports* 54:564-9 S '89

Downsizing the desktop [ADC Powerlite 386 SX] S. Satchell. il *Byte* 14:179-82 D '89

EISA arrives [Vectra 486; cover story] N. Baran. il *Byte* 14:93-6+ N '89

Electronic books will organize your life, replace your library and fit your pocket. G. Hedberg. il *Money* 18:183-4 Je '89

Electronic organizer [Wizard] il *Radio-Electronics* 60:26 F '89

The ever-shrinking, ever-expanding laptops [Agilis System and Zenith MinisPort; cover story] N. Baran and M. E. Nadeau. il *Byte* 14:90-6 Ag '89

Everex launches a 25MHz desktop rocket [Step 386/25] R. Lockwood. il *Personal Computing* 13:190-1 My '89

COMPUTERS—Testing—*cont.*

Fast, AC-powered laptop [Lyte-Byte 3400 portable computer] A. Torres. il *Home Office Computing* 7:80 D '89

Fast, affordable 286 laptop needs a better screen [Packard Bell PB286LP] C. O'Malley. il *Personal Computing* 13:194+ D '89

The fastest 80386s ever? [cover story] R. Malloy. il *Byte* 14:109-12 Je '89

The fastest PCs in the world [ALR FlexCache 33/386, AST Premium 386/33, Compaq Deskpro 386/33, Everex Step 386/33, Zenith Z-386/33, Zeos 386/33] P. Honan. il *Personal Computing* 13:95-7+ S '89

Finally, the Mactop . . . [Macintosh Portable] S. R. Reed. il *Personal Computing* 13:87-8 N '89

Full-powered, notebook-size computer [NEC UltraLite] C. Bermant. il *Home Office Computing* 7:76+ N '89

A good luggable [Altima One] J. T. Barron. il *Byte* 14:82 Ag '89

A good thing in a small package? [Atari Portfolio hand held computer] F. Hayes. il *Byte* 14:81-2 Ag '89

Greased lightning [Zenith Z-386/33] J. Udell. il *Byte* 14:114-16 Je '89

Have laptop, will travel. D. P. Wiener. il *U.S. News & World Report* 107:95-7+ Ag 28-S 4 '89

Hertz 386/25 slow but steady performer. R. Lockwood. il *Personal Computing* 13:173-4 Je '89

High performance on a low budget [Zeos 386-25] C. O'Malley. il *Personal Computing* 13:188+ F '89

High-tech computing, cafeteria style [CompuStar 286] M. L. Van Name. il *Byte* 14:179-80+ Ap '89

Honey, they shrunk the laptop computer [notebook computers] B. Hager. il *Money* 18:21-2 N '89

Hot hand-held electronic organizers [Psion Organiser II Model LZ and the Sharp Wizard Model OZ-7000] P. M. Cirullo. il *Home Office Computing* 7:68-70 O '89

Hyundai Super-16T. H. E. H. Aycock. il *Compute!* 11:100-1 Ja '89

IBM PS/2 Model 30 286. G. Keizer. il *Compute!* 11:60-1 Jl '89

IBM's new speed king [PS/2 Model 70-A21] C. Halliday. il *Byte* 14:173-6 Jl '89

IBM's P70: better late than never. P. Honan. il *Personal Computing* 13:184-5 S '89

Lab report: three singular systems [AST Premium/386C, the Swan 386SX, and the Wedge Turbo 286] S. Diehl. il *Byte* 14:287-8 N '89

The LAN terminal alternative [Wyse WY-212 and TeleVideo TS2 TeleStation diskless PCs] B. Catchings and M. L. Van Name. il *Byte* 14:211-14 My '89

Laptop computers. il *Consumer Reports* 54:69-73 D '89

Laptop dilemma [Compaq SLT/286 and Ogivar 286] J. Holtzman. il *Byte* 14:177-80+ Mr '89

A laptop for all occasions [Compaq SLT/286] P. Honan. il *Personal Computing* 13:96 F '89

Laptops [special section] il *Home Office Computing* 7:56-61 My '89

Laptops forever [cover story] il *Byte* 14:93-6+ D '89

Laptops: two for the road [Zenith SupersPort 286 and Mitsubishi MP-286 L] S. A. Booth. il *Popular Mechanics* 166:46+ Je '89

The last word on the SX? F. Langa. il *Byte* 14:8 O '89

The latest 386-based computers. E. Rutsch. il *Home Office Computing* 7:54-8 Je '89

Lighter PCs that put more features on your lap. G. Lewis. il *Business Week* p202-3 N 6 '89

Lightweight, dependable laptop [Toshiba T1200 HB] C. Bermant. il *Home Office Computing* 7:71 O '89

Long live the low end [AST Bravo/286] R. C. Alford. il *Byte* 14:173-6 S '89

Low-cost 386-based computers [buying by mail] H. F. Beechhold. il *Home Office Computing* 7:61-5 O '89

The Mac SE takes off [SE/30; cover story] N. Baran. il *Byte* 14:113-16 F '89

A Macintosh-compatible laptop from Wallaby. A. F. Lent and L. H. Loeb. il *Byte* 14:81 D '89

MCA meets SX [IBM PS/2 Model 55 SX and the American Mitac MPS2386] M. L. Van Name and B. Catchings. il *Byte* 14:181-4 O '89

Megahertz madness [15 of the world's fastest PCs] il *Byte* 14 Special Issue:13-18+ Fall '89

Mitac Paragon 386E: less bang for your buck. J. Pepper. il *Personal Computing* 13:181-2 Ap '89

Mitsubishi's 386SX is sleek but sleepy. P. Honan. il *Personal Computing* 13:183-4 O '89

Mixed blessings [Macintosh] J. Pournelle. *Byte* 14 Mac Special Ed:MAC249-MAC250+ Je '89

An MS-DOS user eyes the Mac. N. Sullivan. il *Home Office Computing* 7:80 Jl '89

NEC Ultralite is ultra-portable. R. Lockwood. il *Personal Computing* 13:179-80 Jl '89

NEC's Powermate goes portable. J. Bell. il *Personal Computing* 13:220+ Ja '89

NEC's prospeed powerhouse isn't a true laptop [NEC ProSpeed 386] P. Honan. il *Personal Computing* 13:181-2 F '89

The new breed of 286 computers [cover story] H. F. Beechhold. il *Home Office Computing* 7:41-4 Ag '89

New 'mini-386' makes high-end power affordable [Compaq Deskpro 386s Model 40] S. Chen. il *Home Office Computing* 7:66 Mr '89

On-the-go computing [Z88, Toshiba T1000, Tandy 100 laptop] il *Radio-Electronics* 60 ComputerDigest:96-8 F '89

Packed with power [AST Premium/386C Model 390] H. F. Beechhold. il *Home Office Computing* 7:60 Ag '89

The painlessly portable PC [NEC UltraLite] M. L. Van Name and B. Catchings. il *Byte* 14:161-4 Ag '89

A pair of sophisticated laptops [Zenith SupersPort 286 and Mitsubishi MP-286L] J. Unger. il *Byte* 14:189-92+ F '89

A PC in your pocket [Poqet PC] N. Baran. il *Byte* 14:115-17 N '89

Picking a machine that can make your life easier [home computers] bibl il *U.S. News & World Report* 107:84-5+ N 20 '89

Pocket computer [Sharp's Wizard] D. Stover. il *Popular Science* 234:32 Ja '89

Pocket organizer plus [Atari hand held computer] F. Chesleigh. il *Home Office Computing* 7:81-2 D '89

Pocket power. R. Bel Bruno. il *Personal Computing* 13:101-4 N '89

Portable 25MHz power is a compromise [Dolch PAC 386-25] R. Lockwood. il *Personal Computing* 13:181-2 S '89

The portable and the powerful [Macintosh; cover story] T. Thompson and F. Hayes. il *Byte* 14:98-102+ O '89

A portable companion for the Macintosh [Cambridge Z88 laptop] L. H. Loeb. il *Byte* 14 Mac Special Ed:MAC241-MAC242+ Je '89

A portable with punch [Dolch P.A.C. 386-20C] M. L. Van Name. il *Byte* 14:189-92 Ja '89

The power of a Wizard. G. Hartwig. il *Byte* 14:98+ Ap '89

PowerFlex: a versatile, upgradable AT clone. F. Hayes. il *Byte* 14:110-11+ N '89

Powerlite 386 slights performance to trim size. P. Honan. il *Personal Computing* 13:181-2 N '89

Powermate SX stakes out the middle ground [NEC Powermate SX] J. Pepper. il *Personal Computing* 13:184+ Ap '89

A PS/2 in Channel only [Tandy 5000 MC] M. L. Van Name. il *Byte* 14:197-200+ F '89

A quality 80386 machine [Dell 325] S. J. Wszola. il *Byte* 14:97 Je '89

Research à la Mac [Mac Portable and IIci] D. E. Crabb. il *Byte* 14:153-4 N '89

Risking pushed-chip performance [Dyna 30MHz 386 Cache Tower System] J. Pepper. il *Personal Computing* 13:190-1 S '89

Small footprint SE/30 leaves big impression [Macintosh SE/30] J. Bell. il *Personal Computing* 13:181-2 My '89

Strengthening the lineup [IBM PS/2 Models 70-E61 and 70-121] C. Halliday. il *Byte* 14:179-84+ Ja '89

T1600 falls short of today's standards [laptop] P. Honan. il *Personal Computing* 13:180+ Je '89

Tandy 1000 SL. P. Scisco. il *Compute!* 11:67 Mr '89

Three weeks that did not reorganize my life [Sharp Wizard, Psion Organiser II, Casio Digital Diary] D. P. Wiener. il *U.S. News & World Report* 106:76+ F 13 '89

Trim Mac IIcx still packs power. T. Thompson. il *Byte* 14:203 S '89

Two new Macs [Macintosh SE/30 and IIcx] D. Hallerman and S. Chen. il *Home Office Computing* 7:48-50 Jl '89

Upscale Acer [1100/33] J. Holtzman. il *Byte* 14:185-7 D '89

Year-end special: editors' picks 1989: the best and brightest hardware of the year [cover story] il *Home Office Computing* 7:47-51 D '89

Z88 [laptop] D. Will-Harris. il *Compute!* 11:75-6 Mr '89

Zenith TurbosPort 386: power and portability [laptop] J. Devlin. il *Personal Computing* 13:198+ Mr '89

Anecdotes, facetiae, satire, etc.

This is only a test . . . no, really. A. R. Levitan. il *Compute!* 11:80+ Jl '89

Theatrical use

Programming

See also

ArtSoft (Firm)

CADD for the theatre designer: a comparison of low-cost programs. M. Stauffer. il *Theatre Crafts* 23:66+ Ja '89

Costumes by computer [use of AutoCAD] P. Ellsworth. il *Theatre Crafts* 23:78+ N '89

Lightwright for lighting designers. R. Chase. il *Theatre Crafts* 23:28-9 F '89

MIDI and the theatre: a guide to music software applications. J. Roper. *Theatre Crafts* 23:70+ O '89

Time sharing systems

See also

Outsourcing centers (Data processing)

Traffic control use

Brainy cars are on the way [views of Robert L. French] il *USA Today (Periodical)* 118:6 D '89

Just what we need. Automatic roads. B. W. Yates. il *Car and Driver* 34:19 F '89

Keeping an 'eye' on traffic [West Berlin] A. Wormnes. il *World Press Review* 36:57 Mr '89

Smart cars and smart policies [address, March 28, 1989] R. B. Smith. *Vital Speeches of the Day* 55:534-7 Je 15 '89

COMPUTERS—Traffic control use—*cont.*
Smart highways. D. McCosh. il *Popular Science* 235:76-9+ N '89
Street smarts [Ali-Scout navigation system] W. Baldwin. il *Forbes* 144:298+ N 13 '89
Taking the crush out of rush hour. T. A. Heppenheimer. il *High Technology Business* 9:26-30 Mr '89

Translating use
See Machine translating

Travel agents' use
See Travel agencies and agents—Automation

Typesetting use
See Computers—Printing use

Videotape use
Computer aided video [Amiga 2000] K. D. Morton and W. M. Scott, III. il *Radio-Electronics* 60 ComputerDigest:93-7+ Mr '89
Video whizzes and musical mavens: don't overlook your most useful money-making tool. D. D. Thornburg. il *Compute!* 11:14 S '89

Programming
Art & Film Director. D. McNeill. il *Compute!* 11:62-3 Ag '89
Let the Mac entertain you [MacroMind Director] N. Baran. il *Byte* 14:84+ Ag '89
Special F/X on the Mac [Showcase F/X] D. Barker. *Byte* 14 Mac Special Supp:MAC191-MAC192 Ag '89

Workstations
See Workstations

COMPUTERS, USED
A new life for old PC's. J. Schwartz. il *Newsweek* 114:44-5 Ag 28 '89
New money from old (computers). D. Gookin. il *Compute!* 11:22+ Ag '89
The smart way to shop for used computers. W. J. Meyeroff. *Working Woman* 14:36-7 N '89
Used but not abused. T. Netsel. il *Compute!* 11:19-20+ F '89
Used computers: the new bargain. S. Berkman. il *Good Housekeeping* 208:238 Ap '89

COMPUTERS AND AIR TRAVEL
How to make business travel more productive. J. Borchardt. il *Working Woman* 14:99-100+ S '89
If He'd meant them to fly . . . [laptops] G. Eichler. il *Esquire* 111:88 Ap '89
Living with a laptop [B. Moeller of Booz Allen] M. Antonoff. il por *Personal Computing* 13:94-5+ F '89

COMPUTERS AND ALCOHOLICS
Very personal computing. D. L. Gonzalez. il *Newsweek* 114:64 Ag 28 '89

COMPUTERS AND CIVILIZATION
The computer has triggered a paper explosion. M. S. Forbes. *Forbes* 143:19-21 My 29 '89
The computer's future [Knowledge navigator video produced by Apple Computer Corp.] R. Howard. il *Technology Review* 92:74-5 F/Mr '89
Future tense. P. Saffo. See issues of Personal Computing beginning April 1989
Impact. D. D. Thornburg. See issues of Compute! beginning May 1988
Information technology, global linkage, and U.S. competitiveness [address, June 14, 1989] E. M. Ehrlich. *Vital Speeches of the Day* 55:755-9 O 1 '89
Is nothing private? [cover story] J. Rothfeder. il *Business Week* p74-7+ S 4 '89
Mind over matter [G. Gilder's Microcosm] T. Bethell. *The American Spectator* 22:11-13 N '89
Perspective [special section] il *Personal Computing* 13:21+ O '89
The world's next source of wealth [excerpt from Microcosm] G. F. Gilder. il por *Fortune* 120:116-20 Ag 28 '89

COMPUTERS AND CRIME *See* Computer crimes
COMPUTERS AND LIBRARIES
See also
Libraries—Automation
Research libraries—Automation

COMPUTERS AND SOCIETY *See* Computers and civilization
COMPUTERS AND THE DEAF
A computer that helps [HandsOn] W. J. Hawkins. il *Popular Science* 234:50 Ap '89
Listening to an inner voice [J. Yeh of Integrated Microcomputer Systems] A. A. Knocke. il por *Nation's Business* 77:52 F '89

COMPUTERS AND THE HANDICAPPED
A helping hand [Prab Voice Command workstation] W. Rash, Jr. il *Byte* 14:129-30 D '89
High-tech help. A. M. Cunningham. il *Technology Review* 92:16-17 F/Mr '89
Laura Meyers creates software that talks friendly to help disabled kids find their voices [Keytalk] S. Adelson. il por *People Weekly* 32:165-6 D 4 '89
More than wheelchairs. M. Rogers. il *Newsweek* 113:66-7 Ap 24 '89
Waiting for the bionic man. R. Simon. il *Forbes* 144:204-5+ S 18 '89

COMPUTERS AND WOMEN
Anecdotes, facetiae, satire, etc.
Computer follies. M. Sterling. il *New Choices for the Best Years* 29:104 S '89

COMPUTERS AND YOUTH
See also
Hackers (Computer enthusiasts)
Open School (West Hollywood, Calif.)
Here's how to beat back the midsummer doldrums with some style. D. Stanton. il *Compute!* 11:12 Jl '89
Kids' time. L. Eiser. il *Compute!* 11:92-4+ O '89
"Must I buy a computer?". F. Roberts. il *Parents* 64:53 D '89
Putting parents in the loop with kids and computers [interview with T. Snyder] K. Kane. il por *Home Office Computing* 7:80+ Mr '89
Will junior follow in your entrepreneurial footsteps? G. Solomon. il *Home Office Computing* 7:73-4 S '89

COMSAT *See* Communications Satellite Corp.
COMSTOCK, ROBERT
about
Selling true grit. F. Rogers. il pors *The New York Times Magazine* p58-61 O 8 '89

COMTE, ELIZABETH
Chris Evert, Openly. il pors *Sport (New York, N.Y.)* 80:68-70 S '89

CON EDISON *See* Consolidated Edison Co. of New York, Inc.
CONAGHAN, CATHERINE M.
Ecuador swings toward social democracy. bibl f *Current History* 88:137-41+ Mr '89

CONAGRA, INC.
Flying feathers in the coop [Holly Farms makes lockup deal with ConAgra to prevent takeover by Tyson Foods] il *Time* 133:52 F 6 '89
Omaha held hostage [historic district demolished to keep ConAgra from moving] J. Schwab. il *The Progressive* 53:36-9 My '89

CONAL, ROBBIE
about
Cultural kamikaze. J. Diamond. il por *Vogue* 179:350+ Mr '89
Facing the nation. il *Mother Jones* 14:56 F/Mr '89

CONANT, DEBORAH HENSON- *See* Henson-Conant, Deborah
CONANT, JENNET
Star reporter. il pors *Harper's Bazaar* 122:146-7+ N '89

CONAWAY, JEFF, 1950-
about
Jeff Conaway took a wrong turn after Taxi, but now he's back on track as a soap stud. T. Cunneff. il pors *People Weekly* 32:97-8 D 11 '89

CONCENTRATION *See* Attention
CONCENTRATION CAMPS
China
China's forbidden subject. M. Hopkins. il *The New Leader* 72:7-9 F 20 '89

Germany
See also
Dachau (Germany: Concentration camp)

Poland
See also
Auschwitz (Poland: Concentration camp)

Soviet Union
Glasnost in Perm 35? K. A. Lawton. il *Christianity Today* 33:37-8 O 20 '89
In a haunting new memoir, poet Irina Ratushinskaya recalls the agonies of a Soviet labor camp. S. K. Reed. il pors *People Weekly* 31:87-8 Ja 16 '89
Into the heart of the gulag [Perm 35] A. M. Rosenthal. il *Reader's Digest* 134:71-5 Ap '89
The wasted years [labor camp survivor A. Sandler] A. Wilson-Smith. il por *Maclean's* 102:24 My 15 '89

CONCENTRATION CAMPS IN ART
Exhibitions
In the shadow of the tower: poignant portrayals of life in a Nazi prison camp [work of painter J. Nassy] M. C. Rothschild-Boros. il por *USA Today (Periodical)* 118:74-83 S '89

CONCEPTUAL ART
Hélio Oiticica: reverie and revolt [cover story] G. Brett. bibl f il pors *Art in America* 77:110-21+ Ja '89
Exhibitions
New shows of minimalism and conceptualism prove the power of ideas. il *Vogue* 179:534 S '89

CONCERNED WOMEN FOR AMERICA
The women of the CWA. C. Kocol. il *The Humanist* 49:33-4 Mr/Ap '89

CONCERT HALLS
Acoustics
See Acoustics, Architectural
Conservation and restoration
A bath every century, need it or not [cleaning exterior of Carnegie Hall] B. Weber. il *The New York Times Magazine* p94 Ag 20 '89

CONCERT HALLS—cont.

Alaska
See also
Alaska Center for the Performing Arts (Anchorage, Alaska)

California
See also
Walt Disney Concert Hall (Los Angeles, Calif.)

New York (State)
See also
Carnegie Hall (New York, N.Y.)

Spain
Barcelona beauty: the Palau de la Música Catalana. R. Hughes. il Architectural Digest 46:96-102+ Mr '89

Texas
See also
Eugene McDermott Concert Hall (Dallas, Tex.)
Morton H. Meyerson Symphony Center (Dallas, Tex.)

CONCERT PRODUCTIONS INTERNATIONAL
The music man [promoter of Rolling Stones tour M. Cohl] T. Powis. il por Maclean's 102:53+ S 11 '89

CONCERT ROYAL
Musical events:
Rameau's Hippolyte et Aricie performed at Merkin Hall. A. Porter. The New Yorker 65:71-2 D 25 '89
Rousseau's opera Le devin du village. A. Porter. The New Yorker 65:74-5 Jl 3 '89
A slight case of opera [performance of Le devin du village] P. G. Davis. il New York 22:62-3 Je 19 '89

CONCERTO AND CONCERTOS
See also
Cello music
Piano music

CONCERTS
See also
Dance concerts
Jazz concerts
Rock concerts
Rafting piano, floating opera . . . here are musical river trips. il Sunset (Central West edition) 183:50-1 Jl '89

CONCESSIONS (FOOD, ETC.)
See also
National parks and reserves—Concessions (Food, etc.)
Stadiums—Concessions (Food, etc.)

CONCHOLOGY See Shells (Conchology)

CONCIERGES
The concierge concept [full service buildings] D. Di Costanzo. il House & Garden 161:156-7 F '89

CONCORD PACIFIC DEVELOPMENTS LTD.
A bubbling urban battle [vacant Expo site in Vancouver] H. Quinn. il por Maclean's 102:26-8 Ja 16 '89

CONCORD RIVER (MASS.)
Another week on the Concord and Merrimack [H. D. Thoreau's trip] R. Crum. Wilderness 53:11-12+ Fall '89

CONCORDANCES
See also
Bible—Concordances

CONCORDE AIRPLANES See Airplanes, Supersonic

CONCOURS D'ELEGANCE See Automobiles—Exhibitions

CONCRETE
See also
Porous concrete
Concrete's a natural. J. T. Hannibal and F. A. Crease. il Earth Science 41:19-20 Wint '88
Making concrete smarter than it looks [work of Robert E. Shannon and William G. Clark Jr.] I. Amato. Science News 135:284 My 6 '89

Curing
Concrete that sleeps [Delvo] E. R. C. Capulong. il Popular Science 234:39 F '89

CONCRETE BLOCK RETAINING WALLS See Retaining walls

CONCRETE BLOCKS
Toxic gases can penetrate concrete blocks [research by Karina Garbesi and Richard G. Sextro] J. Raloff. Science News 136:391 D 16 '89

CONCRETE CONSTRUCTION
Ka-boom! [impact resistance test at Sandia National Laboratories using an F-4 Phantom jet] J. Kluger. il Discover 10:44-5 D '89
Portland Cement Association 1988 Concrete Building Awards. il Architectural Record 177:51+ Ja '89
Propelled jet [Sandia National Laboratories crash resistance tests of critical structures] A. Fisher. il Popular Science 235:14+ D '89
Taming béton brut. J. S. Russell. il Architectural Record 177:106-111 S '89

CONCRETE DRIVEWAYS See Driveways

CONCRETE GARDEN OF EDEN (LUCAS, KAN.)
Paradise for sale. J. Mobley. il Travel Holiday 171:118 Ap '89

CONCRETE HOUSES
No pipe dream, Jim Stewart's house is built of bric-a-brac and mortar [Indian Creek, Fla.] il por People Weekly 31:101 Ap 24 '89

CONCRETE INDUSTRY
Automation
Ma-and-pa engineering. E. Dyson. il Forbes 143:122 F 6 '89

CONCRETE SCULPTURE
Looks like wood [work of D. Rodriguez] T. Kazas. il pors Americana 17:54-8 S/O '89

CONCRETE WORK
See also
Concrete blocks
Classing up your concrete: pave the way for stamped-in style underfoot. N. A. Hedberg. il Better Homes and Gardens 67:117-18 Je '89
Concrete results. M. Chotiner. il Home Mechanix 85:52-4+ S '89
Patch concrete. il The Family Handyman 39:46-7 S '89
A trail of little hands and feet [concrete stepping pads] il Southern Living 24:78-9 My '89

CONDE NAST PUBLICATIONS INC.
S.I. Newhouse and Conde Nast: taking off the white gloves [cover story] G. Mahon. il pors The New York Times Magazine p46-51+ S 10 '89

CONDENSATION (METEOROLOGY)
Frost at edges. C. F. Bohren. il Weatherwise 42:281-2 O '89
How to cure condensation. P. McCafferty. il Workbench 45:10-12 Mr/Ap '89

CONDENSED MATTER See Matter

CONDENSERS (ELECTRICITY) See Electric capacitors

CONDIMENTS
See also
Capers
Pickles and relishes

CONDITIONED RESPONSES
See also
Biofeedback training
Reinforcement (Psychology)
Pavlovian conditioning of rat mucosal mast cells to secrete rat mast cell protease II. G. MacQueen and others. bibl f il Science 243:83-5 Ja 6 '89
Pavlov's rats [allergic reaction produced by Pavlovian conditioning] il Discover 10:14 My '89
People can't be programmed [research by Michael Dawson] USA Today (Periodical) 118:12-13 Ag '89

CONDITIONERS (HAIR) See Hair care products

CONDITIONERS (SOIL) See Soil conditioners

CONDOMINIUM ASSOCIATIONS
Buying into a community association. K. McManus and W. Giese. Changing Times 43:22-3 My '89

CONDOMINIUMS
Home rule [condominium refuses to permit daughter J. Swartz to live with father in Margate, Fla.] I. Nelson. il por New Choices for the Best Years 29:12-13 Ap '89
Vacation homes: it's a buyer's market. M. C. Paulson. il Changing Times 43:37-8+ Je '89
White sales [ski resort condominium investments] M. Lukens. il House & Garden 161:142+ Ja '89
Why condominiums are underappreciated. S. Luxenberg. Money 18:30-1 N '89

Fractional ownership
See Fractional ownership (Real estate)

Timesharing ownership
See Timesharing (Real estate)

CONDOMINIUMS (BOAT DOCKING)
Home ports. R. J. Adamson. il House & Garden 161:60 Je '89

CONDOMS
Condom alert: the rubber you're using may not be as safe as you think. L. Kleinmann. il Glamour 87:250-1 Ag '89
Condom conundrum [FDA approval of women's condoms] M. Suh. il Ms. 17:87 Mr '89
Condoms in the cells [Philadelphia prisons] A. Hornblum. The Progressive 53:12 F '89
Facing facts. K. McCoy. Seventeen 48:26 F '89
My year of loving dangerously: confessions of a non-condom-user. L. Allen. Mademoiselle 95:221+ Mr '89
Sexual abandon [condoms unpopular on Canadian campuses] J. Hanna. il Maclean's 102:48 S 25 '89
Teen boys get condom sense [survey] E. Stark. Psychology Today 23:62-3 O '89

Advertising
Talk about 'placements' . . . [Ramses condoms in Lethal weapon 2] il Newsweek 114:50 Jl 31 '89

Defects
Holey condoms [Korean shipment seized by FDA] il FDA Consumer 23:42 F '89

Testing
Can you rely on condoms? [cover story] il Consumer Reports 54:135-41 Mr '89
Condom mania! [FDA requiring retesting of the microcondom and women's condom] E. Franklin. il American Health 8:18 Je '89
Condoms. il Consumer Reports 54:18-22 D '89
Rubber stamp [FDA requires stricter tests of microcondoms] B. Baker. Common Cause Magazine 15:7-8 Jl/Ag '89

CONDOR, BOB
Bowling for dollars! il *Sport (New York, N.Y.)* 80:58-60 Ja '89

CONDOR SYSTEMS, INC.
Small, high-tech companies thrive despite cuts in defense spending. il *Aviation Week & Space Technology* 131:118+ S 18 '89

CONDORS
Comeback trail of the California condor [hatching of chick named Molloko] il *National Geographic World* 171:25-9 N '89
Nine months of the condor [endangered California condor] L. Oliwenstein. il *Discover* 10:62 Ja '89

CONDUCT OF LIFE
See also
Advice
Altruism
Ambition
Anger
Apologies
Avarice
Caring
Character
Charity
Christian ethics
Christian life
Comfort
Conscience
Counterculture
Courtesy
Encouragement
Ethics
Etiquette
Fairness
Faith
Forgiveness
Friendship
Habits
Honesty
Human relations
Humility
Individuality
Leisure
Love
Loyalty
New Year's resolutions
Organization
Patience
Patriotism
Pleasure
Procrastination
Reliability
Responsibility
Simplicity
Spiritual life
Time management
Values
Work
And the music tells of history [address, May 6, 1989] J. E. Sloan. *Vital Speeches of the Day* 55:649-51 Ag 15 '89
Child's play [using game Punchbuggy to change outlook on life] S. H. Hogan. il *Reader's Digest* 134:29-30+ Mr '89
A letter to my children. C. M. Crooker. il por *The Humanist* 49:29+ Mr/Ap '89
Live and relearn. J. Stone. il *Glamour* 87:134 O '89
Living beautifully. A. Stoddard. See issues of McCall's beginning March 1989
The tapestry of your life [address, May 7, 1989] S. G. Finesilver. *Vital Speeches of the Day* 56:82-4 N 15 '89

CONDUCTING (MUSIC)
See also
Conductors (Music)

CONDUCTING POLYMERS *See* Conductive polymers

CONDUCTIVE POLYMERS
Conductive polymers recharged. J. Alper. il *Science* 246:208-10 O 13 '89
Forging superstrong conducting polymers [work of Alan J. Heeger] I. Amato. *Science News* 136:356 D 2 '89
Future brightens for conducting polymers. I. Amato. *Science News* 135:230 Ap 15 '89
Putting a real charge into plastic. N. J. Freundlich. il *Business Week* p114+ D 11 '89

CONDUCTORS, SUPER *See* Superconductors and superconductivity

CONDUCTORS (MUSIC)
See also
Abbado, Claudio
Barenboim, Daniel
Bátiz, Enrique
Bernstein, Leonard, 1918-
Black conductors (Music)
Blomstedt, Herbert, 1927-
Boult, Sir Adrian Cedric, 1889-1983
Dohnanyi, Christoph von
Domingo, Placido
Gardiner, John Eliot

Haitink, Bernard
Karajan, Herbert von
Kleiber, Carlos
Marriner, Neville, 1924-
Mehta, Zubin
Munch, Charles, 1891-1968
Muti, Riccardo
Norrington, Roger, 1934-
Previn, André, 1929-
Rattle, Simon
Reiner, Fritz, 1888-1963
Rozhdestvenski, Gennadi
Solti, Sir Georg, 1912-
Tate, Jeffrey
At last, some fresh faces. M. Walsh. il *Time* 134:85 O 30 '89
Keep your eye on . . . [young American opera conductors; with editorial comment by Patrick J. Smith] M. Sevilla-Gonzaga. il *Opera News* 54:4, 8-9 Jl '89
Lenny's kids leap forward [American conductors] K. Ames. il *Newsweek* 113:60-1 F 20 '89
Passing the baton. K. Ames. il *Newsweek* 114:72-3 O 30 '89
Passing the baton [successor to Z. Mehta at New York Philharmonic] P. G. Davis. il *New York* 22:82-6+ My 15 '89
Searching for a maestro with magic. il *U.S. News & World Report* 106:15 F 13 '89
Religious life
The maestro's greatest loyalty [H. Blomstedt] D. Neff. il por *Christianity Today* 33:62 Mr 3 '89
Robert Shaw's ministry of music. H. Ziegenhals. il por *The Christian Century* 106:311-13 Mr 22-29 '89

CONE, DAVID
about
Beers with . . . David Cone [interview] J. W. Poses. il pors *Sport (New York, N.Y.)* 80:16+ My '89

CONE, MARCIA, AND SNYDER, THELMA
Microwave entertaining [excerpt] il *Ladies' Home Journal* 106:273+ N '89
Microwave snacks for kids. il *Working Woman* 14:224 S '89

CONE, MARLA
Blueprint for clear skies. il *Sierra* 74:16+ Jl/Ag '89

CONE CELLS *See* Rods and cones

CONEFLOWERS *See* Black-eyed Susans

CONES, PINE *See* Pine cones

CONFECTIONERY
See also
Candy
Exhibitions
How sweet it is! [The confectioner's art] J. Friedrich. il *American Craft* 49:38-45+ F/Mr '89

CONFEDERATE AIR FORCE
Ghost story. N. Moll. il *Flying* 116:68-72+ F '89

CONFEDERATE STATES OF AMERICA
See also
United States—History—Civil War, 1861-1865
The South's inner Civil War. E. Foner. il *American Heritage* 40:46-8+ Mr '89
This one spells o-o-p-s [Kellogg Co.'s presidents puzzle wrongly includes name of J. Davis] il *Newsweek* 113:50 My 1 '89

CONFEDERATE WHITE HOUSE *See* White House of the Confederacy

CONFEDERATION OF REGIONS PARTY (CANADA)
Linguistic backlash [wages anti-French campaign in New Brunswick] G. Allen. *Maclean's* 102:17 Ag 28 '89

CONFERENCE ON CONFIDENCE AND SECURITY-BUILDING MEASURES AND DISARMAMENT IN EUROPE
Military openness proposals tabled at CSBM talks [State Dept. statement, June 9, 1989] *Department of State Bulletin* 89:74 Ag '89

CONFERENCE ON SECURITY AND COOPERATION IN EUROPE
Advancing the Helsinki process. W. Korey. il *The New Leader* 72:7-9 F 6 '89
Crossing the European divide. C. Bogdan. bibl f *Foreign Policy* 75:56-75 Summ '89
CSCE Conference on the Human Dimension [statement, May 31, 1989] M. B. Abram. *Department of State Bulletin* 89:88-90 S '89
CSCE follow-up meeting held in Vienna [text of concluding document; special section] il *Department of State Bulletin* 89:21-54 Mr '89
CSCE Information Forum [statement, April 21, 1989] L. H. Marks. *Department of State Bulletin* 89:86-7 S '89
Gulag? What gulag? M. Kondracke. *The New Republic* 200:8-9+ F 13 '89
Helsinki in Paris. W. Korey. il *The New Leader* 72:12-14 Jl 10-24 '89
Human rights get their biggest boost in a decade. B. Javetski. il *Business Week* p55 Ja 30 '89
A Moscow conference on human rights? *America* 160:51 Ja 28 '89
Waltzing in Vienna [human rights agreement] D. Seligman. *Fortune* 119:133-4 F 27 '89

CONFERENCE ON SECURITY AND COOPERATION IN EUROPE—*cont.*

When will the Wall fall? H. Anderson. il *Newsweek* 113:43 Ja 30 '89

CONFERENCE TABLES

Power tables: buying for the boardroom. J. L. Krotz. il *Working Woman* 14:82-4 Ag '89

CONFERENCES

See also
Authors' conferences
Conventions
Economic conferences
Religious conferences
Teleconferencing

CONFERENCES, PARENT-TEACHER *See* School and the home

CONFERENCING, COMPUTER *See* Computer networks

CONFESSION (CATHOLIC CHURCH) *See* Penance

CONFESSION (LAW)

Japan

Forcing confessions in Japan. Y. Takagi. *World Press Review* 36:57 Je '89

CONFIDENCE *See* Trust

CONFIDENCE, SELF *See* Self confidence

CONFIDENCES, PROFESSIONAL *See* Confidential communications

CONFIDENTIAL COMMUNICATIONS

See also
Official secrets
Right of privacy

Accountants

The case of the singing CPA [J. Checksfield gives IRS details of his client's tax evasion] *Newsweek* 114:41 Jl 17 '89

Banking

The drug war—European style [money laundering crackdown] B. Riemer. *Business Week* p31-2 O 2 '89

Lawyers

Beware the boomerang [question of attorney-client privilege in confidential probes of corporate criminality] D. Fanning. il *Forbes* 143:66-7 F 6 '89

Press

Off the record. W. Safire. il *The New York Times Magazine* p16+ O 29 '89

CONFINEMENT FEEDING OF SWINE *See* Swine—Confinement methods

CONFIRMATION

Rites of passage. M. E. Marty. por *Christianity Today* 33:20 N 3 '89

Rites of passage I. M. E. Marty. il *The Christian Century* 106:671 Jl 5-12 '89

Rites of passage II. M. E. Marty. *The Christian Century* 106:703 Jl 19-26 '89

Rites of passage III [receiving lamb cake as Confirmation Day present] M. E. Marty. il *The Christian Century* 106:735 Ag 2-9 '89

CONFLICT (PSYCHOLOGY)

See also
Competition (Psychology)

CONFLICT OF GENERATIONS *See* Generation gap

CONFLICT OF INTERESTS (BUSINESS)

Are analysts putting their mouths where the money is? W. Konrad. il *Business Week* p118 D 18 '89

Brady, buyouts, and Purolator [Nicholas Brady's role in thwarted buyout bid] il *Fortune* 119:66 My 22 '89

Ingram forms publisher fulfillment service [other wholesalers fear conflict of interest] M. Reuter. *Publishers Weekly* 235:17-18 Ap 28 '89

Quid pro junk? [federal probe of junk bond fund managers' personal portfolios] R. L. Stern and P. Berman. il *Forbes* 144:39-40 Ag 7 '89

Who calls the tune? [financial planners who take commissions have a built-in conflict of interest] J. B. Quinn. il *Newsweek* 114:51 Jl 31 '89

CONFLICT OF INTERESTS (PUBLIC OFFICE)

$1 billion worth of influence [C. Keating's dealings with five senators in the Lincoln Savings & Loan affair] M. B. Carlson. il por *Time* 134:27-8 N 6 '89

Anatomy of a smear [how N. Gingrich brought down J. Wright] J. M. Barry. il pors *Esquire* 112:215-20+ O '89

Asleep at the S&L switch [M. D. Wall and the Lincoln Savings & Loan scandal] R. Thomas and E. Clift. il por *Newsweek* 114:71 D 11 '89

The banker plan [disclosure of J. Baker's Chemical Bank holdings clouds his policy on Latin American debt relief] *The New Republic* 200:7-8 Mr 6 '89

Bob Bennett: on the trail of the 'Keating Five' [Senate Ethics inquiry into Lincoln Savings & Loan scandal] T. Smart. il por *Business Week* p60 D 11 '89

Bombshell in the House [Ethics Committee finds reason to believe J. Wright violated rules] G. J. Church. il por *Time* 133:33-4 My 1 '89

A cancer grows on the Speakership [allegations against J. Wright] G. Borger. il por *U.S. News & World Report* 106:20+ My 22 '89

A case of Wright and wrong [alleged wrongdoing by the Speaker of the House] M. B. Carlson. il por *Time* 133:25 Ap 17 '89

CC calls for ethics inquiry of five senators [dealings with C. Keating in the Lincoln Savings & Loan affair] J. Denny. *Common Cause Magazine* 15:28 N/D '89

Cleaning House [Speaker J. Wright] *The New Republic* 200:5-6 My 8 '89

Coelho under fire [congressman given easy deal on hard-to-get junk bonds] *Newsweek* 112:41 My 22 '89

CRADAs raise conflict issues [scientists in government] B. J. Culliton. *Science* 245:1035 S 8 '89

The Democrats' meltdown on the Hill. D. Harbrecht. il *Business Week* p25 Je 12 '89

Dr. Sullivan to get $215,000 in severance pay; Senators see no conflict in HHS post. il por *Jet* 76:38 Ap 17 '89

Dual careers mean potential conflicts for state legislators. A. E. Young. *Common Cause Magazine* 15:40 S/O '89

An emotional farewell [House Speaker J. Wright] H. Mackenzie. il pors *Maclean's* 102:32 Je 12 '89

The end of the line [House Speaker J. Wright] H. Mackenzie. il por *Maclean's* 102:24 Je 5 '89

The ethics monster rages [ramifications of Congressman J. Wright case] H. Sidey. il por *Time* 133:32 My 29 '89

Everybody doesn't do it [case of Speaker of the House J. Wright] M. Greenfield. il *Newsweek* 113:84 My 1 '89

Exit stage Wright [House Speaker J. Wright] W. McGurn. *National Review* 41:23 Je 30 '89

Facing the music [Speaker of the House J. Wright] T. Morganthau. il por *Newsweek* 113:26-7 Ap 24 '89

Fallen angel [T. Coelho] M. B. Carlson. il *The New Republic* 200:18-21 Je 12 '89

Financier Charles Keating is the $2 billion man of the savings and loan crisis [Lincoln Savings & Loan scandal involving five senators] B. Hewitt. il pors *People Weekly* 32:78-80 D 4 '89

Fraudulence I [case of C. B. Gray] R. E. Tyrrell. il *The American Spectator* 22:10 Ap '89

Frenzy on the Hill [ethics battles] T. Morganthau. il pors *Newsweek* 113:14-18 Je 12 '89

Hi-tech disagreements [Canadian Senator M. Cogger named in Japanese businessman T. Tsuru's lawsuit against entrepreneur G. Montpetit over misspent loans] P. Kaihla. il por *Maclean's* 102:16-17 Je 26 '89

House Democrats begin to imagine life after Jim Wright. D. Harbrecht. por *Business Week* p51 Mr 13 '89

House Speaker Jim Wright resigns; blacks note loss and attack on Bill Gray. il pors *Jet* 76:4-5 Je 19 '89

How many will fall? [resignation of majority whip T. Coelho and anticipated resignation of J. Wright] M. B. Carlson. il pors *Time* 133:34-5 Je 5 '89

In 'hip-deep water' [Speaker of the House J. Wright] R. Thomas. il por *Newsweek* 113:25-6 My 1 '89

The incumbent party, the party of incumbents [N. Gingrich's ethics drive against the Democrats] *National Review* 41:14-15 Je 30 '89

Is Danny Wall on the way out? [tainted by Lincoln Savings & Loan scandal] C. Yang and P. Dwyer. *Business Week* p59 N 13 '89

Jim Baker's conflict-of-interest problems. W. Greider. il *Rolling Stone* p43-5 Ap 20 '89

Jim Wright isn't the only pol with a sugar daddy. D. Harbrecht. il *Business Week* p82-3+ My 29 '89

Jim Wright: on the ropes. L. Martz. il por *Newsweek* 113:22-3 Ap 3 '89

Jim Wright's lonely fight. H. Mackenzie. il por *Maclean's* 102:24-5 My 1 '89

Judging Jim Wright [allegations against the Speaker of the House] G. Borger. il por *U.S. News & World Report* 106:18-19 Ap 17 '89

Keating takes the Fifth [Lincoln Savings & Loan scandal] M. B. Carlson. il por *Time* 134:46 D 4 '89

The last stand of Speaker Jim Wright. G. Borger. il por *U.S. News & World Report* 106:27-8 Ap 24 '89

The least and the dullest [J. Wright] J. Klein. il por *New York* 22:16+ Mr 27 '89

"A legal bank robbery" [complicity of federal regulators in Lincoln Savings and Loan scandal] M. B. Carlson. il pors *Time* 134:29 N 27 '89

Lessons in quitting [congressmen J. Wright and T. Coelho] T. Eastland. por *Newsweek* 113:8 Je 12 '89

Letter from Washington [controversy surrounding Speaker of the House J. Wright] E. Drew. *The New Yorker* 65:99-104+ My 1 '89

Letter from Washington [events leading to resignation of House Speaker J. Wright] E. Drew. *The New Yorker* 65:97-102 Je 12 '89

Looking for an exit [House Speaker J. Wright] T. Morganthau. il por *Newsweek* 113:18-20 Je 5 '89

The man who tried to buy Washington [C. Keating's dealings with five senators in the Lincoln Savings & Loan affair] G. Borger and S. J. Hedges. il pors *U.S. News & World Report* 107:18-21+ N 27 '89

Mr. Wright's wrongs. W. McGurn. *National Review* 41:16 My 19 '89

Now it's broke [D. Regan's role in S&L scandal] J. R. Adams. *The New Republic* 201:16-18 N 13 '89

The painful political trial of Speaker Wright. G. Borger. il *U.S. News & World Report* 106:31 My 1 '89

CONFLICT OF INTERESTS (PUBLIC OFFICE)—*cont.*

Partisanship fuels 'ethics' investigation. J. M. Wall. *The Christian Century* 106:579-80 Je 7-14 '89

The pious posturing over Speaker Wright. W. Greider. il *Rolling Stone* p37-8 Je 15 '89

Questions of ethics [business activities of Canadian Senator M. Cogger] B. Wallace. il por *Maclean's* 102:18+ N 13 '89

Quis custodiet? [J. Wright's efforts on behalf of Texas thrifts] R. C. Kirkwood and T. P. Jeffrey. il *National Review* 41:35-6 Ap 21 '89

Ready for Wright: a GOP grudge match. E. Salholz. il por *Newsweek* 113:28 Mr 20 '89

The real sleaze [J. Wright's suspected misdeeds in efforts on behalf of Texas S&Ls] *The Nation* 248:615-16 My 8 '89

Reeling [House Speaker J. Wright] *National Review* 41:11 Je 16 '89

The revolving door. S. Waldman. il *Newsweek* 113:16-18 F 6 '89

Revolving door at the E.P.A. [former officials taking high ranking jobs with private Superfund contractors] J. Sibbison. il *The Nation* 249:524-8 N 6 '89

The rise and fall of Tony Coelho. H. Fineman. *Newsweek* 113:20 Je 5 '89

The S&L scandal's biggest blowout [C. H. Keating's Lincoln Savings & Loan scandal involves five senators] T. Morganthau. il por *Newsweek* 114:35-6 N 6 '89

Science advisers need advice [toxicologists who served on Environmental Protection Agency advisory panel charged with breaking conflict of interest laws] E. Marshall. il *Science* 245:20-2 Jl 7 '89

The seduction of Senator Alan Cranston [Lincoln Savings & Loan Assn. scandal] P. Dwyer. il pors *Business Week* p82-4 D 4 '89

Shilling in the Senate. D. Corn. il *The Nation* 249:84-7 Jl 17 '89

Shredding the Democrats' agenda [charges against J. Wright] D. Harbrecht and R. Fly. il por *Business Week* p26 My 1 '89

The skeletons in Jim Wright's closet keep rattling Congress. D. Harbrecht. por *Business Week* p39 Ap 24 '89

Smoking gun [C. Yeutter's efforts on behalf of cigarette industry while U.S. Trade Representative] S. Hornik. il *Common Cause Magazine* 15:9 Mr/Ap '89

Speaker Jim Wright's old pal George Mallick is rarin' for a fight with Congress. M. Green. il pors *People Weekly* 31:101-2 My 15 '89

The Speaker should step down [case of J. Wright] H. Sidey. il *Time* 133:18 Ap 24 '89

Top brass [congressional defense complex] J. Cobb. il *Common Cause Magazine* 15:23-7 My/Je '89

Top talent leaving NASA . . . new recruits hard to find [effect of revolving door rules] E. Marshall and M. M. Waldrop. il *Science* 245:251 Jl 21 '89

The tumbling of Danny Wall [Lincoln Savings & Loan scandal] S. J. Hedges. *U.S. News & World Report* 107:55 D 11 '89

An uphill battle [ethical considerations and congressional wives] A. McCarthy. il *Commonweal* 116:329-30 Je 2 '89

What the Wright hand's doing [House Speaker J. Wright] il *National Review* 41:9-10 My 19 '89

Why won't NASA talk to scientists [effect of new ethics law on discussions of Advanced X-ray Astrophysics Facility] M. M. Waldrop. il *Science* 245:699 Ag 18 '89

Wright, Coelho and the S&L fiasco. M. Barone. il pors *U.S. News & World Report* 106:21-2 Je 12 '89

Wright fights back [Speaker of the House] M. B. Carlson. il por *Time* 133:16-17 Ap 24 '89

Wright should quit. W. F. Buckley. *National Review* 41:54 Je 16 '89

Wright was not wronged [excerpt from report issued by House Ethics Committee] *Harper's* 279:18+ Ag '89

Anecdotes, facetiae, satire, etc.

How one family handles its finances [J. Wright] J. Queenan. *Forbes* 143:42-3 Je 12 '89

CONFLICT RESOLUTION

See also

Arbitration and award

How managers should handle staff conflicts [excerpt from One-on-one with Andy Grove] A. S. Grove. il *Working Woman* 14:146-8 N '89

Parishes should learn to fight fair [Catholic Church] T. Unsworth. *U.S. Catholic* 54:29-31 F '89

Turning confrontations into calm conversations [excerpt from 88 mistakes interviewers make and how to avoid them] A. Uris. il *Working Woman* 14:140-1+ S '89

Study and teaching

Teaching students cultural mediation [Amos Alonso Stagg High School in Stockton, Calif.] B. Huie. *The Education Digest* 55:50-2 O '89

CONFOCAL MICROSCOPES

Confocal scanning optical microscopy. G. S. Kino and T. R. Corle. bibl f il *Physics Today* 42:55-62 S '89

CONFORMATIONAL ANALYSIS

Specific recognition of cruciform DNA by nuclear protein HMG1. M. E. Bianchi and others. bibl f il *Science* 243:1056-9 F 24 '89

CONFORMITY

See also

Eccentrics and eccentricities

Following the crowd. D. F. Bjorklund and B. Bjorklund. il *Parents* 64:197 Mr '89

Anecdotes, facetiae, satire, etc.

Rebel without a preschool [nonconformist attitude of toddler] J. Hope. il *Parents* 64:222+ S '89

CONFORTI, MICHAEL, AND KOHLS, ANN

The American craftsman and the European tradition, 1620-1820. il *Antiques* 136:834-43 O '89

CONFUCIANISM AND ECONOMICS

The merchants of Huizhou: commerce and Confucianism [cover story] M. Dillon. bibl il map *History Today* 39:24-30 F '89

CONGENITAL MALFORMATIONS *See* Birth defects

CONGER, BEACH, 1941-

about

A jocular doc. S. Brewer. il por *New Choices for the Best Years* 29:8-9 Jl '89

CONGER, STEVEN

about

Inventing a new Colorado vernacular. G. Greene. il por *Architectural Digest* 46:330+ O '89

CONGLOMERATE CORPORATIONS

Conglomerates. L. Jereski. il *Forbes* 143:118-19 Ja 9 '89

CONGREGATE HOUSING

Housing: promise and problems. H. B. Deets. il *Modern Maturity* 32:11 Ag/S '89

CONGREGATION FOR CATHOLIC EDUCATION *See* Catholic Church. Congregation for Catholic Education

CONGREGATION FOR THE DOCTRINE OF THE FAITH *See* Catholic Church. Congregation for the Doctrine of the Faith

CONGRESS (U.S.) *See* United States. Congress

CONGRESS FOR CULTURAL FREEDOM

The brief life of liberal anti-communism. P. Coleman. il *National Review* 41:34-6 S 15 '89

The intellectuals & the cold war. G. Szamuely. *Commentary* 88:54-6 D '89

CONGRESS OF PEOPLE'S DEPUTIES (SOVIET UNION) *See* Soviet Union. Congress of People's Deputies

CONGRESS OF THE NEW WORLD

The Rockefeller Congress. E. A. Finn, Jr. il pors *Forbes* 144:74+ O 30 '89

CONGRESS PARTY (INDIA) *See* Indian National Congress

CONGRESSIONAL AIDES *See* Congressmen—Staff

CONGRESSIONAL BLACK CAUCUS

Black U.S. leaders join those in England to start Parliament's Black Caucus. D. M. Cheers. il *Jet* 76:28-31 Ap 24 '89

Bush conducts a historic meeting with Black Caucus. il por *Jet* 76:6-7 Je 12 '89

CONGRESSIONAL BLACK CAUCUS FOUNDATION

Caucus weekend centers on plight of youth, pays tribute to Mickey Leland. il *Jet* 77:24-5+ O 9 '89

CONGRESSIONAL BUDGET OFFICE *See* United States. Congressional Budget Office

CONGRESSIONAL CAMPAIGN FUNDS *See* Campaign funds

CONGRESSIONAL CAMPAIGNS *See* Political campaigns

CONGRESSIONAL CANDIDATES *See* Political candidates

CONGRESSIONAL CLEARINGHOUSE ON THE FUTURE

Helping Congress look ahead [interview with R. McCord] T. Willard and D. M. Fields. il pors *The Futurist* 23:23-7 My/Je '89

CONGRESSIONAL COMMITTEES *See* United States. Congress—Committees

CONGRESSIONAL ELECTIONS *See* Elections

CONGRESSIONAL IMMUNITY *See* United States. Congress—Privileges and immunities

CONGRESSIONAL SCIENCE FELLOWS *See* Scientists in government

CONGRESSMEN

See also

Black congressmen

Senators

See also names of congressmen

Congress [cover story; special issue] il *Scholastic Update (Teachers' edition)* 121:2-22 F 24 '89

The world of Congress [cover story] J. Alter. il *Newsweek* 113:28-32+ Ap 24 '89

Your guy in Washington [assisting constituents] M. Kiernan. il *U.S. News & World Report* 107:54-6 Ag 7 '89

Campaign funds

See Campaign funds

Charitable contributions

Sweet charity [donating surplus honoraria to charities] V. Novak. il *Common Cause Magazine* 15:20-3 Ja/F '89

CONGRESSMEN—*cont.*

Conflict of interests
See Conflict of interests (Public office)

Election
See Elections

Ethics
See Political ethics

Financial disclosure
Anecdotes, facetiae, satire, etc.

Uncivil liberties [royalties and J. Wright] C. Trillin. il *The Nation* 248:762 Je 5 '89

Health and hygiene
Fit for office. A. Mangum. il *Common Cause Magazine* 15:7 Ja/F '89

Photographs and photography
By George, it's me [photos of congressmen in the Lincoln Bedroom taken by G. Bush] il *Life* 12:84-5 Ap '89

Press relations
All the congressmen's men: how Capitol Hill controls the press. W. Karp. bibl il *Harper's* 279:55-63 Jl '89

House Foleys [rumor of homosexuality of House Speaker T. Foley spread by Republicans and Democrats] T. Eastland. il *The American Spectator* 22:32-3 Ag '89

The score on Claude [C. Pepper obituaries] D. Seligman. *Fortune* 120:117-18 Jl 17 '89

What TV news doesn't report about Congress—and should. N. J. Ornstein. il *TV Guide* 37:10-13 O 21-27 '89

Who decides what is news? (Hint: it's not journalists). W. Karp. il *Utne Reader* p60-8 N/D '89

Public relations
Congressional shell game [tricks for staying in office] P. Weyrich. il *Conservative Digest* 15:18-21+ Mr/Ap '89

Rating
A house divided [ideological categories] R. Doyle. il map *The Atlantic* 263:81 Je '89

Looking leftward [most liberal congressmen] D. Seligman. il *Fortune* 120:228+ S 11 '89

Religious life
Of many things [Catholics in Congress] G. W. Hunt. *America* 160:74 F 4 '89

Resignation
Anatomy of a smear [how N. Gingrich brought down J. Wright] J. M. Barry. il pors *Esquire* 112:215-20+ O '89

The Democrats' meltdown on the Hill. D. Harbrecht. il *Business Week* p25 Je 12 '89

An emotional farewell [House Speaker J. Wright] H. Mackenzie. il pors *Maclean's* 102:32 Je 12 '89

Exit stage Wright [House Speaker J. Wright] W. McGurn. *National Review* 41:23 Je 30 '89

Frenzy on the Hill [ethics battles] T. Morganthau. il pors *Newsweek* 113:14-18 Je 12 '89

House Speaker Jim Wright resigns; blacks note loss and attack on Bill Gray. il pors *Jet* 76:4-5 Je 19 '89

Lessons in quitting [J. Wright and T. Coelho] T. Eastland. por *Newsweek* 113:8 Je 12 '89

Musical chairs [Democratic leadership; cover story] F. Barnes. *The New Republic* 200:14-15 Je 12 '89

The rise and fall of Tony Coelho. H. Fineman. *Newsweek* 113:20 Je 5 '89

Salaries, allowances, etc.
Are they worth it? [pay raises recommended by salary review board] J. Carney. il *Time* 133:12-13 Ja 23 '89

Cashing in on ethics [congressional pay raise in exchange for reforms] *Time* 134:16 Jl 3 '89

Curb speaking fees? W. F. Buckley. *National Review* 41:61 Jl 14 '89

Down and out in Washington on $89,500 a year. J. Rowe. *The Washington Monthly* 21:12-14+ Jl/Ag '89

The games Congress plays. H. Gorey. il por *Time* 133:38 F 13 '89

Give a little, get a little [pay raise and revision of ethics rules] N. Traver. il *Time* 134:24 N 27 '89

Hard times. *The Nation* 248:112 Ja 30 '89

It's back! The return of the pay raise. E. Clift. il por *Newsweek* 114:22 Jl 3 '89

Jim Wright isn't the only pol with a sugar daddy. D. Harbrecht. il *Business Week* p82-3+ My 29 '89

Just say no. *The New Republic* 200:7-9 F 6 '89

Moonlighting [honoraria; cover story] J. Cobb. il *Common Cause Magazine* 15:21-7 Jl/Ag '89

One for the Gypper. F. Barnes. *The New Republic* 200:14-15 F 27 '89

The packaging of a pay raise [in exchange for ethics reforms] M. Barone. *U.S. News & World Report* 107:24 N 27 '89

Pay dirt [congressional pay raise in the guise of ethics reform] C. Hanson. *The New Republic* 201:10-11 D 25 '89

Pay raises via the back door. L. Reibstein. il *Newsweek* 113:34 Ja 30 '89

Profiles in courage. L. Martz. il por *Newsweek* 113:14-16 F 13 '89

A raise by any other name [pay raise in the guise of ethics reform] J. N. Baker. il *Newsweek* 114:43 N 27 '89

Raise their pay? W. F. Buckley. *National Review* 41:71 F 10 '89

Santa and his reindeer could fit through the holes in this ethics bill. P. Dwyer. *Business Week* p59 D 18 '89

Should Congress get a 51 percent raise? [interviews with L. Cutler and R. Nader] J. P. Shapiro. pors *U.S. News & World Report* 106:28 F 13 '89

Sweet charity [donating surplus honoraria to charities] V. Novak. il *Common Cause Magazine* 15:20-3 Ja/F '89

Talk politics [radio campaign against congressional pay raise] J. Klein. il *New York* 22:28+ F 27 '89

Tea bag party [defeat of pay increase] *The Nation* 248:291-2 Mr 6 '89

The tea-bag revolution [backlash over pay raise] E. Clift. il *Newsweek* 113:18 F 6 '89

The time is up for honoraria. A. McBride. il *Common Cause Magazine* 15:44-5 Ja/F '89

Top brass [congressional defense complex] J. Cobb. il *Common Cause Magazine* 15:23-7 My/Je '89

White House balks at honoraria ban while momentum builds in Congress; Campaign finance reform. J. Denny. *Common Cause Magazine* 15:38-9 My/Je '89

You get what you pay for. N. J. Ornstein. por *Newsweek* 113:10 Ja 16 '89

Sexual behavior
Another scandal on the Hill [Congressman B. Frank involved in male homosexual prostitution scandal] por *Newsweek* 114:24 S 4 '89

Barney Frank's story [relationship with male prostitute S. Gobie; cover story; special section; with interview] il pors *Newsweek* 114:14-20 S 25 '89

In defense of Barney [Congressman B. Frank involved in male homosexual prostitution scandal] M. Kondracke. *The New Republic* 201:10-11 O 9 '89

Letter from Washington [Congressman B. Frank's relationship with male prostitute S. Gobie] E. Drew. *The New Yorker* 65:106-8+ O 2 '89

Presswatch [Congressman B. Frank's involvement in male prostitution] T. Eastland. *The American Spectator* 22:31-2 N '89

A skeleton in Barney's closet [B. Frank's relationship with gay prostitute S. Gobie] M. B. Carlson. il pors *Time* 134:24 S 25 '89

Trials of Barney [B. Frank involved in male prostitution scandal] *The Nation* 249:371-2 O 9 '89

U.S. rep. convicted for having sex with a minor [D. Lukens] il pors *Jet* 76:8 Je 12 '89

U.S. Rep. Lukens gets 30-day jail term, fine in sex with minor case. il pors *Jet* 76:33 Jl 24 '89

Why Frank's case is different [congressman involved in male homosexual prostitution scandal] il por *U.S. News & World Report* 107:30 O 2 '89

Winners and sinners: the D'Amato and Frank dossiers. J. Klein. il por *New York* 22:23-4 O 9 '89

Staff
See also
Council of Black Administrative Assistants and Associates (U.S.)

Former Gray aide denies she's object of FBI probe [W. H. Gray staffer L. Baskerville] por *Jet* 76:6 Je 19 '89

The hill climbers. P. Osterlund. il *Rolling Stone* p116-18+ Mr 23 '89

The long, lonely road of rights hero James Meredith ends in a job with Jesse Helms. A. Gonzalez. il pors *People Weekly* 32:40-1 O 16 '89

Washington watch: will we follow the new leaders? [members of baby bust generation working as staffers] L. Romano. *Mademoiselle* 95:236 Ag '89

Crime

All the Wright moves [criminal past of J. Wright's aide J. P. Mack] J. H. Fund. il *National Review* 41:19-20 Je 16 '89

Capitol offense [J. P. Mack, aide to J. Wright, arrested for assault in 1974] por *Time* 133:38 My 15 '89

A guilty plea confirms the dark rumors about Capitol Hill aide Quentin Crommelin [convicted of aggravated sexual battery] L. Kramer. il pors *People Weekly* 32:49-50 Ag 21 '89

One of the boys [assault of P. Small by J. Wright's former aide J. P. Mack] M. B. Carlson. *The New Republic* 200:11-13 Je 5 '89

The protégé and the victim [criminal past of J. Wright's aide J. P. Mack exposed] E. Clift. il pors *Newsweek* 113:38 My 15 '89

A victim's story [P. Small attacked by J. P. Mack] K. Ringle. pors *Reader's Digest* 135:49-54 Ag '89

A Washington morality tale [resignation of J. P. Mack, aide to J. Wright] il por *U.S. News & World Report* 106:22 My 22 '89

Wright's aide: too little, too late [J. P. Mack resigns] E. Clift. il pors *Newsweek* 112:41 My 22 '89

Statues, portraits, etc.
Portraits of Congress past [The first federal Congress at the National Portrait Gallery] K. M. Burke. il *Smithsonian* 19:196 Mr '89

Term
The least responsive branch. L. G. Crovitz. *Commentary* 87:38-41 Mr '89

Lifers on Capitol Hill, R. E. Tyrrell. il *The American Spectator* 22:10 F '89

So you want to reform Congress? F. Barnes. il *The American Spectator* 22:14-16 S '89

CONGRESSMEN—cont.

Training

Capitol hillbilly [freshmen orientation] M. Newman. *The New Republic* 200:13-15 F 6 '89

Travel

Moonlighting [cover story] J. Cobb. il *Common Cause Magazine* 15:21-7 Jl/Ag '89

CONGRESSMEN'S WIVES

Congressional spouses feel the heat [ethics scandals] il *Newsweek* 113:26 My 1 '89

I'm nobody, who are you? M. B. Carlson. il *Time* 133:29-30 My 8 '89

An uphill battle [ethical considerations and congressional wives] A. McCarthy. il *Commonweal* 116:329-30 Je 2 '89

CONGRESSWOMEN

See also names of congresswomen

New congresswomen squeak into office. A. F. Lewis. il *Ms.* 17:140-1 Ja/F '89

CONIFERS

See also

Pine

CONIGLIARO, TONY

about

A brother's keeper. M. Lupica. il por *Esquire* 111:77-80 Mr '89

CONILL, ALICIA

A doctor's guide to staying well this winter; ed. by Maxine Abrams. il por *Good Housekeeping* 209:100+ N '89

CONISTON PARTNERS

The Cayman connection [foreign investments in Coniston Partners may endanger deal for control of UAL] S. Flack. il *Forbes* 144:42-3 D 11 '89

Still trying to land UAL [proxy fight] J. E. Ellis. il *Business Week* p28-9 N 20 '89

CONJOINED TWINS *See* Siamese twins

CONJUGATION (BIOLOGY)

Trans-kingdom sex [ability of Escherichia to conjugate with yeast] J. Horgan. *Scientific American* 261:34-5 O '89

CONJUNCTIONS (ASTRONOMY)

All in line. T. D. Nicholson. il *Natural History* p100-1 Ap '89

Saturn and Neptune in the same field: act two. R. Shaffer. il *Astronomy* 17:63 Je '89

Syzygies all around us. T. D. Nicholson. il *Natural History* p106 F '89

Toward a March rendezvous. T. D. Nicholson. il *Natural History* p72+ Ja '89

CONJURING

See also

Jugglers and juggling

Games [trick for opening a locked change purse invented by M. Weber] S. Morris. il *Omni (New York, N.Y.)* 12:118 N '89

Open-and-shut case [trick for opening a locked change purse invented by M. Weber] S. Morris. il *Omni (New York, N.Y.)* 12:164-5+ O '89

Bibliography

Paperback history. J. Henry. *History Today* 39:53 Je '89

CONKLIN SHOWS (FIRM)

This way to the egress [computer use] P. Scisco. il *Compute!* 11:107 Ja '89

CONLEY, CLARE

Editorial page. See issues of Outdoor Life

CONLEY, JOHN J.

The bicentennial of a political idea. *America* 160:574-5+ Je 17-24 '89

CONLEY, LAURA

AAP-PSP market-driven publishing strategies. *Publishers Weekly* 235:47-8 F 10 '89

CONLIN, JENNIFER

Abloom in the city. il por *House & Garden* 161:168-73+ My '89

Gonna dress you up. il *Rolling Stone* Fashion Collection:51-6+ Ap 20 '89

CONN, HENRY P.

(jt. auth) See Boyett, Joseph H., and Conn, Henry P.

CONN, HERB

about

Following the wind. M. R. Taylor. il pors *Audubon* 91:90-9 Ja '89

CONN, JAN

about

Following the wind. M. R. Taylor. il pors *Audubon* 91:90-9 Ja '89

CONN, RICHARD

The aesthetics of storm chasing [cover story] il *Weatherwise* 42:143-7 Je '89

CONNAUGHT BIOSCIENCES INC.

Connaught's foreign sale [to Institut Mérieux] A. Walmsley. il *Maclean's* 102:44-5 D 25 '89

Lament for a cherished asset [proposed sale to Institut Mérieux] P. C. Newman. il *Maclean's* 102:51 O 16 '89

Science and PR north of the border [sale of Institut Merieux] D. Powell. *Science* 246:1555-6 D 22 '89

Tempest in a test tube [bidders] G. W. Taylor. il *Maclean's* 102:42 S 25 '89

CONNAUGHT HOTEL (LONDON, ENGLAND) *See* London (England)—Hotels, motels, etc.

CONNECTICUT

See also

Architecture, Domestic—Connecticut

Historic houses, sites, etc.—Connecticut

Law—Connecticut

Wildlife—Connecticut

Windham County (Conn.)

Description and travel

See also

Cycling—Connecticut

CONNECTICUT IN ART

Exhibitions

The mature years of John Henry Twachtman [National Gallery show] A. E. Ledes. il *Antiques* 136:942+ N '89

CONNECTICUT SOCIETY OF ARCHITECTS

The Connecticut Society of Architects/AIA 1988 Design Awards. il *Architectural Record* 177:74-5 Je '89

CONNECTION MACHINE *See* Massively parallel supercomputers

CONNECTIVE TISSUES

See also

Collagen

Diseases

See also

Lupus erythematosus

Marfan syndrome

CONNELL, DAN

The economic underpinnings of the intifada. *Utne Reader* p40-1 S/O '89

CONNELLY, CHUCK, 1956?-

about

Moving pictures. K. Larson. il *New York* 22:86 Ap 24 '89

CONNELLY, NANCY A.

(jt. auth) See Decker, Daniel J., and Connelly, Nancy A.

CONNEMARA (IRELAND)

Description and travel

Rambling in the wild Connemara. G. D. Ford. il *Southern Living* 24:32+ My '89

CONNERS, ROSEANNE (FICTIONAL CHARACTER) *See* Roseanne Conners (Fictional character)

CONNERY, SEAN

about

All together, now: "Sean Connery is an icon!" [cover story] D. K. Shah. il pors *Gentlemen's Quarterly* 59:126-31+ Jl '89

Connery. Sean Connery [cover story] B. Fong-Torres. il pors *American Film* 14:28-33 My '89

A man called Connery [cover story] S. Schindehette. il pors *People Weekly* 32:122-4 D 18 '89

Sean Connery against the odds. J. Culhane. il pors *Reader's Digest* 135:92-7 Ag '89

CONNICK, HARRY

about

The Bourbon Street Kid hits his stride. C. McGuigan. il por *Newsweek* 113:67 F 20 '89

The entertainer. R. Tannenbaum. por *Rolling Stone* p34 Mr 23 '89

Hitting his stride. E. Pooley. il por *New York* 22:14 Ja 2 '89

Isn't it romantic? T. Hamilton. il pors *Rolling Stone* p181-6 N 16 '89

The next big thing. S. Fried. por *Gentlemen's Quarterly* 59:442-5+ S '89

Profile. L. Longshore. por *Seventeen* 48:57 Jl '89

CONNIFF, RICHARD

Antiques: country clocks. il *Architectural Digest* 46:178-81+ Je '89

Antiques: Pennsylvania German chests. il *Architectural Digest* 46:276-81+ O '89

Coasters used to be scary, now they're downright weird. bibl (p135) il *Smithsonian* 20:82-6+ Ag '89

Flashy new 'items' make a big splash in the aquarium world. il *Smithsonian* 20:90-4+ My '89

Why God created flies. il *Audubon* 91:82-5 Jl '89

Yellowstone's 'rebirth' amid the ashes is not neat or simple, but it's real. il *Smithsonian* 20:36-44+ S '89

CONNOLLY, INA

about

Trapped inside her own world. B. Kantrowitz. il pors *Newsweek* 114:56-8 D 18 '89

CONNOLLY, SYBIL

about

Eire apparent. D. Brenner. il por *House & Garden* 161:90+ S '89

CONNOR, ELIZABETH BARRETT- *See* Barrett-Connor, Elizabeth

CONNOR, RUSSELL

about

Art. A. C. Danto. *The Nation* 248:709-13 My 22 '89

CONNOR, SUSAN SCHOLLE, AND FUENZALIDA-PUELMA, HERNÁN L.

Health ethics and the law. il *World Health* p10-13 Ap '89

CONNOR, W. ROBERT (WALTER ROBERT), 1934-

After smashing the Wedgwood. *The American Scholar* 58:533-41 Aut '89

CONNOR, WALTER ROBERT *See* Connor, W. Robert (Walter Robert), 1934-

CONNORS, JIMMY, 1952-
about
Never say die [cover story] J. Feinstein. il pors *World Tennis* 36:30-2+ My '89

CONNORS, JOSEPH M.
Operation Rescue. il *America* 160:400-2+ Ap 29 '89

CONODONTS
A soft body of evidence. R. J. Aldridge and D. E. G. Briggs. il *Natural History* p6+ My '89

CONOTOXINS
Localization and mobility of ω-conotoxin-sensitive Ca^{2+} channels in hippocampal CA1 neurons. O. T. Jones and others. bibl f il *Science* 244:1189-93 Je 9 '89

CONOVER, CARL
The glover's son [poem] *The New Republic* 201:34 Jl 31 '89

CONQUEST, ROBERT
Back to the USSR. il *National Review* 41:24-7 Ag 18 '89
Coming to terms with the past. il *National Review* 41:14-16 Mr 10 '89

CONRAD, HAROLD
Lord of the ring. il pors *Rolling Stone* p64-5+ O 19 '89

CONRAD, KENT
Should the Congress adopt the "Financial Institutions Reform, Recovery, and Enforcement Act of 1989"? [excerpts from address, April 19, 1989] *Congressional Digest* 68:185+ Je/Jl '89
Should the Senate-passed Immigration Act of 1989 be approved? [excerpts from debate, July 13, 1989] *Congressional Digest* 68:253+ O '89

CONRAD, KIMBERLEY
about
Hef gains a bride, loses a reputation [cover story] S. Schindehette. il pors *People Weekly* 32:34-9 Jl 17 '89
Mrs. Bunny. J. Ash. il pors *Life* 12:102-6 S '89

CONRAD, PAUL
St Martin's, Gospel Oak. il *History Today* 39:59-60 Jl '89

CONRAD, PETER
Bardolator. il pors *Opera News* 53:18-20 F 4 '89

CONRAD, ROBIN S.
(jt. auth) *See* Krasnow, Erwin G., and Conrad, Robin S.

CONRADSON, S. D., AND RAISTRICK, I. D.
The axial oxygen atom and superconductivity in $YBa_2Cu_3O_7$. bibl f il *Science* 243:1340-3 Mr 10 '89

CONRAIL *See* Consolidated Rail Corporation

CONRAN, TERENCE
about
Broken by the bottom line. J. Ferry. il por *Forbes* 144:180+ N 27 '89
Object lessons. E. MacSweeney. il por *Harper's Bazaar* 122:110 S '89

CONRATH, B., AND OTHERS
Infrared observations of the Neptunian system. bibl f il *Science* 246:1454-9 D 15 '89

CONROW, JOAN
Tourist choppers roil islands. *The Progressive* 53:16 My '89

CONROY, MARY
Bad habits: master these little monsters. il *'Teen* 33:77-8 Je '89
Going along with the crowd: should you? il *'Teen* 33:46+ Ag '89

CONSANGUINITY
See also
Incest

CONSCIENCE
See also
Guilt
A matter of conscience. H. Fehren. *U.S. Catholic* 54:39-41 N '89

CONSCIENTIOUS OBJECTORS
Germany (West)
Germans reject the military. il *The Futurist* 23:48 S/O '89

CONSCIOUSNESS
See also
Self
Instant nirvana [altered states of consciousness] il *Health (New York, N.Y.)* 21:66-7 Ap '89
Life is but a dream [alert relaxation techniques for experiencing waking dreams; cover story] K. Harary and P. Weintraub. il *Omni (New York, N.Y.)* 12:42-4+ N '89
Quantum consciousness [views of R. Penrose] J. Horgan. il por *Scientific American* 261:30+ N '89

CONSCRIPTION *See* Draft

CONSENT (LAW)
See also
Informed consent (Medical law)

CONSERVATION AND RESEARCH CENTER *See* Smithsonian Institution. Conservation and Research Center

CONSERVATION AREAS *See* Wilderness areas

CONSERVATION ASSOCIATIONS *See* Environmental associations

CONSERVATION CORPS (CALIF.) *See* California Conservation Corps

CONSERVATION EASEMENTS
Taxation
Protect your view and get a tax break, too. G. Morgenson. il *Forbes* 144:276-7 O 16 '89

CONSERVATION FOUNDATION
Hazardous choice [W. Reilly's attempts to defang Superfund] V. Novak. *The Nation* 248:406-8 Mr 27 '89

CONSERVATION LAW *See* Conservation of resources—Laws and regulations

CONSERVATION MOVEMENT *See* Environmental movement

CONSERVATION OF BOOKS *See* Books—Conservation and restoration

CONSERVATION OF HISTORIC SITES *See* Historic houses, sites, etc.

CONSERVATION OF RESOURCES
See also
Energy conservation
Environmental movement
Environmental policy
Forest conservation
Holistic resource management
Landscape protection
Nature conservation
Plant conservation
Reclamation of land
Shore protection
Soil conservation
Stream conservation
United Nations. Committee on Natural Resources
Water conservation
Wilderness areas
Wildlife conservation
133 ways to save the earth. il *Utne Reader* p71+ N/D '89
Conservation. G. Reiger. See issues of *Field & Stream*
Conservation is dead. R. Rodale. il *Organic Gardening* 36:37-8 Mr '89
The great outdoors. J. Walter. See issues of *Successful Farming* beginning February 1987
It's not easy being Green. G. Garelik. il *Time* 134:65 D 18 '89
Awards
See also
Ansel Adams Awards
Olaus and Margaret Murie Award
Economic aspects
Death and taxes. G. Reiger. il *Field & Stream* 93:18+ Ap '89
The issue of our environment [address, August 19, 1989] F. X. Stankard. *Vital Speeches of the Day* 56:84-6 N 15 '89
International aspects
See also
Foundation for Environmental Conservation
Conservation up front. G. Nelson. *Wilderness* 53:2 Wint '89
Report on reports: World resources 1988-89. J. A. McNeely. bibl f *Environment* 31:25-8 Ap '89
Laws and regulations
See also
Endangered Species Act (1973)
Land and Water Conservation Fund Grant Assistance Program (U.S.)
United States. Dept. of the Interior
Wildlife conservation—Laws and regulations
Maintaining nature's delicate balance. L. R. Jahn. il *USA Today (Periodical)* 118:84-6 N '89
California
See also
California Conservation Corps
Caribbean region
Of buccaneers and biodiversity. D. R. Wallace. il maps *Wilderness* 53:38-51 Wint '89
Florida Keys (Fla.)
Of buccaneers and biodiversity. D. R. Wallace. il maps *Wilderness* 53:38-51 Wint '89
United States
See Conservation of resources

CONSERVATION OF WORKS OF ART *See* Art—Conservation and restoration

CONSERVATION RESERVE PROGRAM (U.S.) *See* United States. Dept. of Agriculture. Conservation Reserve Program

CONSERVATION TILLAGE *See* Tillage

CONSERVATIONISTS *See* Ecologists

CONSERVATISM
See also
Center on Religion & Society (New York, N.Y.)
Concerned Women for America
Democratic Leadership Council
Moral Majority
Philadelphia Society
At Dartmouth the clash of '89. J. Casey. il *The New York Times Magazine* p28-30+ F 26 '89
Backing into modernity. D. R. Carlin, Jr. *Commonweal* 116:204 Ap 7 '89
Being right in a post-postwar world. R. Brookhiser. *Time* 134:112 D 11 '89

CONSERVATIVE PARTY (GREAT BRITAIN)—*cont.*

Has the Iron Lady lost her golden touch? [M. Thatcher] R. A. Melcher. il por *Business Week* p67 N 13 '89

Mrs. Thatcher under siege again. C. W. Weinberger. il por *Forbes* 144:31 N 27 '89

A question of judgment [resignation of Chancellor of the Exchequer N. Lawson] A. Phillips. il por *Maclean's* 102:38-9 N 6 '89

Splatcher. M. Elliott. il *The New Republic* 201:14-16 D 11 '89

Thatcher: can an old Tory learn new tricks? R. A. Melcher. por *Business Week* p37 Jl 24 '89

CONSERVATORIES (GREENHOUSES)

See also

Brooklyn Botanic Garden. Steinhardt Conservatory

San Antonio Botanical Gardens. Lucile Halsell Conservatory

World Financial Center (New York, N.Y.). Winter Garden

Butterfly gardens are soaring [live butterfly exhibits] R. Snyder. il *Flower and Garden* 33:50+ Mr/Ap '89

Christmas under glass. il *Sunset (Central West edition)* 183:54-7 D '89

Architecture

Reclaiming Eden [Lucile Halsell Conservatory; work of E. Ambasz] E. Edelman. il por *Art News* 88:73-4 F '89

San Antonio gardens under glass [Lucile Halsell Conservatory] il *Southern Living* 24:30-1 N '89

CONSERVATORSHIPS

De Kooning's co-conservators [L. De Kooning and J. Eastman] A. Decker. il pors *Art News* 88:58 O '89

Gary Coleman and mother battle over control of his $6 million fortune, income. il pors *Jet* 77:22-4 D 25 '89-Ja 1 '90

Who will represent de Kooning? A. Decker. il pors *Art News* 88:136-41 Summ '89

CONSERVATORY GARDEN (NEW YORK, N.Y.) *See* Central Park (New York, N.Y.)—Conservatory Garden

CONSIDINE, SHAUN

Bette vs. Joan: Hollywood's hottest feud [excerpt from Bette and Joan] il pors *Ladies' Home Journal* 106:142-4+ O '89

CONSOLIDATED-BATHURST INC.

Merger wave rolls on [acquired by Stone Container Corp.] D. Jenish. il *Maclean's* 102:28-30 F 6 '89

CONSOLIDATED EDISON CO. OF NEW YORK, INC.

Ruptured lives: how the Gramercy Park steam-pipe blast spewed misery with the asbestos. E. Pooley. il *New York* 22:50-4+ O 30 '89

CONSOLIDATED FOODS CORP.

See also

Sara Lee Corp.

CONSOLIDATED FREIGHTWAYS, INC.

Consolidated Freightways to acquire Emery Air Freight for $230 million. R. G. O'Lone. *Aviation Week & Space Technology* 130:119 F 20 '89

Emery's failing finances spur approval of merger. il *Aviation Week & Space Technology* 130:97 Ap 10 '89

"This global thing is not a fad". M. Beauchamp. il *Forbes* 144:122+ D 11 '89

CONSOLIDATED GOLD FIELDS PLC

Apartheid and the Canada connection [Bank of Nova Scotia's involvement in financing Minorco's bid] P. C. Newman. il *Maclean's* 102:29 F 13 '89

Harry Oppenheimer's empire: going for the gold. P. Schmeisser. il por *The New York Times Magazine* p32-3+ Mr 19 '89

Is Consgold 'just an appetizer' for Hanson? M. Maremont. il *Business Week* p41-2 Jl 10 '89

CONSOLIDATED RAIL CORPORATION

Countdown [takeover target] T. Pouschine. il *Forbes* 144:95 D 25 '89

CONSORTIUM FOR EXCELLENCE IN TEACHER EDUCATION

Joining teacher education and the liberal arts in the undergraduate curriculum. E. F. Travers and S. R. Sacks. il *Phi Delta Kappan* 70:470-4 F '89

CONSORTIUM FOR SUPERCONDUCTING ELECTRONICS

Consorting on superconductors. C. Norman. *Science* 244:1037 Je 2 '89

IBM, AT&T and MIT establish superconductor consortium. W. Sweet. *Physics Today* 42:61-2 Jl '89

Love thy competitor as thyself. il *U.S. News & World Report* 106:12 Je 5 '89

CONSPIRACY

Christic Institute woes [ordered to pay legal fees to defendants in conspiracy suit] *The Christian Century* 106:224 Mr 1 '89

Media campaigns in the courts [Christic Institute ordered to pay defendants' costs in conspiracy suit] *National Review* 41:13-14 Mr 10 '89

Whodunit? [conspiracy theory belief in the Middle East] D. Pipes. il *The Atlantic* 263:18+ My '89

CONSTABLE, JOHN, 1776-1837

about

One summer in Constable country. C. D. Berg. il *American Artist* 53:38-43+ Jl '89

CONSTABLE, PAMELA

(jt. auth) See Valenzuela, Arturo, 1944-, and Constable, Pamela

CONSTABLE, PAMELA, AND VALENZUELA, ARTURO, 1944-

Chile's return to democracy. *Foreign Affairs* 68:169-86 Wint '89/'90

CONSTANCE, LAKE *See* Lake Constance

CONSTANTINOPOLITAN CREED *See* Nicene Creed

CONSTANTS, PHYSICAL *See* Physical constants

CONSTANZO, ADOLFO DE JESÚS

about

Magic and murder in Matamoros. J. Burnett. *The Christian Century* 106:815-16 S 13-20 '89

CONSTAR INTERNATIONAL, INC.

Pure plastics play. il *Forbes* 143:183 Ja 9 '89

CONSTELLATIONS

See also

Pleiades

Deep-sky wonders [Lynx] W. S. Houston. il *Sky and Telescope* 77:227-8 F '89

Galaxies found in cosmic void [Bootes Void; work of Greg D. Bothun and Greg Aldering] *Astronomy* 17:10 Ap '89

January—the Dog, the stars, the president [viewing Orion; excerpt from Wheel of seasons] R. Marsi. il *The Conservationist* 43:56 Ja/F '89

A look at Delphinus. G. Lovi. il *Sky and Telescope* 78:283-4 S '89

Populating an astronomical void [Boötes void] *Science News* 135:30 Ja 14 '89

Rambling through the skies. G. Lovi. See issues of Sky and Telescope

A star-hop in Cassiopeia. A. MacRobert. il *Sky and Telescope* 78:370-2 O '89

A star-hop through Ophiuchus. A. MacRobert. il *Sky and Telescope* 77:603-5 Je '89

Treasures of the winter Milky Way. D. J. Eicher. il *Astronomy* 17:76-83 N '89

A trio of Big Dipper variables. il *Sky and Telescope* 77:522-3 My '89

CONSTELLATIONS IN ART

Sidelights on constellation art. G. Lovi. il *Sky and Telescope* 78:391-2 O '89

CONSTITUTIONAL AMENDMENTS *See* United States. Constitution—Amendments

CONSTITUTIONAL CONVENTIONS

A constitutional convention: history repeats itself. *Utne Reader* p62-3 S/O '89

CONSTITUTIONAL LAW

See also

Civil rights

Separation of powers

Veto

CONSTITUTIONS

See also

Canada. Constitution

South Africa. Constitution

Soviet Union. Constitution

State constitutions

United States. Constitution

CONSTRUCCIONES AERONAUTICAS SA

Fairchild Aircraft, Spain's CASA to cooperate on C-212 marketing. *Aviation Week & Space Technology* 130:61 Je 26 '89

CONSTRUCTION CONTRACTS *See* Building—Contracts and specifications

CONSTRUCTION EQUIPMENT

See also

Conveying equipment

CONSTRUCTION EQUIPMENT INDUSTRY

See also

Caterpillar Inc.

Petroleum equipment industry

CONSTRUCTION INDUSTRY

See also

Building materials industry

Cardinal Industries Inc.

Contractors

Engineering construction companies

Kaufman & Broad Home Corp.

Lindal Cedar Homes, Inc.

Maguire Thomas Partners

Miglin-Beitler Development Inc.

National Association of Home Builders (U.S.)

Northern Timber Framing Inc.

PHM Corp.

Trammell Crow Company

Washington Corporation (Mont.)

Building's foundation could be full of termites. J. C. Cooper and K. Madigan. il *Business Week* p28 F 6 '89

Construction. J. Willoughby. il *Forbes* 143:120-1+ Ja 9 '89

Construction economy outlook: three roads to more volume. G. A. Christie. il por *Architectural Record* 177:37+ N '89

Construction economy update: a kind and gentle letdown in 1988 leads to the seeds of a possible turnaround in 1990 [with editorial comment by Mildred F. Schmertz] G. A. Christie. il *Architectural Record* 177:5, 25+ Ap '89

CONSTRUCTION INDUSTRY—cont.

Construction economy update: a smaller-than-expected step backward. G. A. Christie. il *Architectural Record* 177:33+ S '89

Construction finance: in search of that elusive comfort zone. P. E. Kidd. il *Architectural Record* 177:37 Mr '89

Cyclical calm [views of W. Lasko] R. T. Grieves. il por *Forbes* 143:322 Ja 9 '89

For homebuilders, the wolf is at the door . . . but an even bleaker future may be looming. G. Koretz. il *Business Week* p20 Jl 3 '89

The funk at the factory gums up the big picture. J. C. Cooper and K. Madigan. il *Business Week* p27-8 O 16 '89

Homebuilders and consumers can handle the high interest. M. F. Allyn. il *Fortune* 119:23-4+ Ap 24 '89

Housing developments: increasing competition pushes more technology into houses. E. Corcoran. *Scientific American* 260:100-1 My '89

Lower interest rates are a good omen for construction. P. E. Kidd. il *Architectural Record* 177:37 Ag '89

Real estate is girded for a so-so year. T. Mason. il *Business Week* p110 Ja 9 '89

We have to conquer inflationary pressures to get building moving again. P. E. Kidd. *Architectural Record* 177:45 Je '89

What's pulling the rug out from under housing. K. Madigan. il *Business Week* p104+ Ja 23 '89

Automation

Managing costs with Excel [home-based construction consultant R. West] K. J. Novak. il *Home Office Computing* 7:32+ N '89

Employees

See also
Construction workers
Women construction workers

Management

Construction managers. A. Gartaganis. il *Occupational Outlook Quarterly* 33:26-9 Summ '89

Marketing

"Hit the prospect at every emotional level" [fully decorated model houses] R. Simon. il *Forbes* 143:310-11 Ja 9 '89

Securities

How, and why, to play a housing rebound. C. E. Babin. il por *Forbes* 144:256 O 30 '89

New streets, paved with gold [investing in public works] J. M. Laderman. il *Business Week* p92-3 O 16 '89

Seeking a solid payoff in crumbling public works. J. Friedman. *Business Week* p116 S 4 '89

CONSTRUCTION MATERIALS See Building materials

CONSTRUCTION WORKERS

See also
Black construction workers
Women construction workers

Year of the blue-collar guy. S. Olson. por *Newsweek* 114:16 N 6 '89

CONSTRUCTIVISM

Rodchenko in Moscow: miraculous survival of the constructivist's historic studio. M. Ruthven. il pors *Architectural Digest* 46:53+ O '89

CONSULS

The honorary consuls [Canada's volunteer diplomats] G. Allen. il *Maclean's* 102:18-19 Ja 30 '89

CONSULTANTS

See also
Agricultural consultants
Business consultants
Computer consultants
Educational consultants
Engineering consultants
Executive search consultants
Franchise consultants
Image consultants
Marketing consultants
Political consultants
Public relations consultants
Sentencing consultants
Tax consultants
Theater consultants

The advice peddlers. A. Miller and D. Tsiantar. il *Newsweek* 112:60-1 My 22 '89

CONSULTATION ON CHURCH UNION

COCU conceives a covenant. J. C. Lyles. *The Christian Century* 106:39-40 Ja 18 '89

COCU consensus. *The Christian Century* 106:8 Ja 4-11 '89

COCU revamped. *The Christian Century* 106:1040-1 N 15 '89

CONSULTING ENGINEERS See Engineering consultants

CONSUMER COMPLAINTS See Complaints

CONSUMER EDUCATION See Consumer protection

CONSUMER ELECTRONICS SHOW

4 trends worth watching. A. Levis. *Video* 13:6 S '89

Bold new gear [cover story] M. Fleischmann. il *Video* 13:36-9+ Ap '89

CES adapts and delivers. S. Pinkwas. il *Video* 13:10 Ag '89

CES at a glance: HDTV, still video, DAT. il *Video* 12:11 Mr '89

CES' crystal ball. S. Pinkwas. *Video* 13:12 S '89

CES show stoppers. R. Day. il *Stereo Review* 54:95-9 S '89

Eclectic electronics. il *Home Mechanix* 85:75-8 Jl '89

A look into an electronic crystal ball [special section] il *Home Office Computing* 7:8+ Ag '89

Nothing revolutionary, but . . . [video] il *Popular Photography* 96:50-4 Mr '89

The old soft show [Consumer Electronics Show; special section] il *Compute!* 11:6+ S '89

Real time pie in the sky [video] il *Popular Photography* 96:65-8+ Ag '89

Scouting report for 1990. S. A. Booth. il *Popular Mechanics* 166:20+ S '89

Show stoppers. R. Day. *Stereo Review* 54:57-61 Ap '89

Suddenly this summer. M. Fleischmann. il *Video* 13:74-7+ S '89

The ultimate music boxes. M. Rogers. il *Newsweek* 113:48-9 Ja 23 '89

CONSUMER FRAUD See Fraud

CONSUMER GOODS See Commercial products

CONSUMER LOANS See Loans, Personal

CONSUMER NEWS & BUSINESS CHANNEL

NBC gets down to business. R. Zoglin. il *Time* 133:69 Ap 17 '89

CONSUMER PRICE INDEX See Price indexes

CONSUMER PRODUCT SAFETY COMMISSION (U.S.)

See U.S. Consumer Product Safety Commission

CONSUMER PROTECTION

See also
Consumers Union of United States
Quality of products
Warranty

Calling all consumers. J. W. Merline. See issues of Consumers' Research Magazine

Consumer tips. See issues of Consumers' Research Magazine

Ralph Nader reconsidered. J. Rowe. *The Washington Monthly* 21:65+ F '89

The resurrection of Ralph Nader. T. A. Stewart. il pors *Fortune* 119:106-8+ My 22 '89

The second coming of Ralph Nader. D. Harbrecht. il por *Business Week* p28 Mr 6 '89

Speaker for the house/The Heloise helpline. Heloise. See issues of Good Housekeeping beginning November 1988

What risk-free society? [interview with R. Nader] il *New Perspectives Quarterly* 6:32-4 Fall '89

Whatever happened to the consumer movement? J. Bodnar. il *Changing Times* 43:45-8+ Ag '89

Yuppies and microwaves. F. Powledge. il *The Progressive* 53:46 D '89

Bibliography

Consumer pamphlets. K. K. Gracey and A. W. Simpson. *Consumers' Research Magazine* 72:2 S '89

Publications for consumers. K. K. Gracey. *Consumers' Research Magazine* 72:2 F '89

History

Consumers' past. J. W. Merline. *Consumers' Research Magazine* 72:38 O '89

Laws and regulations

See also
U.S. Consumer Product Safety Commission
United States. Federal Trade Commission
United States. Food and Drug Administration

Dateline Washington. See issues of Consumers' Research Magazine

Open letter to George Bush. *Consumer Reports* 54:20-1 Ja '89

Soviet Union

Oh, no here comes Joe [consumer advocate V. Shinkaretsky] A. Blackman. il por *Time* 133:76 Ap 10 '89

CONSUMER RELATIONS See Customer relations

CONSUMER REPORTS (PERIODICAL)

Memo to members. R. H. Karpatkin. See issues of Consumer Reports

CONSUMER REPORTS BOOKS (FIRM)

Consumer Reports Books. R. A. Carter. il *Publishers Weekly* 236:19+ O 27 '89

CONSUMERS

See also
Aged market
Black consumers
Compulsive shopping
Consumer protection
Consumption (Economics)
Electronic shopping
Hispanic American market
Japanese American market
Middle age market
Shopping
Women consumers
Youth market

Consumers are tougher customers [views of L. Cutler] M. Magnet. il por *Fortune* 120:76 Jl 3 '89

Foreign exchange [imported goods owned by one Los Angeles family] D. Rawson. il *Life* 12:176-9 Fall '89

Power to the consumer. C. Warden. *Consumers' Research Magazine* 72:19 Je '89

CONSUMERS—*cont.*
Trade protection: the consumer pays. J. W. Merline. il *Consumers' Research Magazine* 72:16-17 Ag '89
CONSUMERS' RESEARCH MAGAZINE
Consumers' past. J. W. Merline. *Consumers' Research Magazine* 72:38 O '89
CONSUMERS UNION OF UNITED STATES
CU buys a new testing center. il *Consumer Reports* 54:144 Mr '89
CONSUMPTION (ECONOMICS)
See also
  Christmas business
  Cost and standard of living
  Supply and demand
All shopped out? [cover story; special section] il *Utne Reader* p65-89 S/O '89
Attention, Mr. Greenspan [lower interest rates] H. Banks. *Forbes* 143:33 F 6 '89
The binge is over. R. J. Samuelson. il *Newsweek* 114:35 Jl 10 '89
The consumer shopping spree is still driving growth. J. C. Cooper and K. Madigan. il *Business Week* p23-4 F 13 '89
Consumers are still tightfisted—and the economy is feeling the squeeze. J. C. Cooper and K. Madigan. il *Business Week* p21-2 Jl 10 '89
Consumers: what turns free-spenders into tightwads [real interest rates] K. Madigan. *Business Week* p27 D 11 '89
Consumers will help the economy stay in shape next year. V. Brownstein. il *Fortune* 120:31-2 O 23 '89
Employment looks weak. Will consumers ride to the rescue? J. C. Cooper and K. Madigan. il *Business Week* p51-2 O 23 '89
Families of working wives spending more on services and nondurables [Consumer Expenditure Survey] E. Jacobs and others. bibl f il *Monthly Labor Review* 112:15-23 F '89
Interest earnings don't really fatten consumers' wallets. G. Koretz. il *Business Week* p28 F 27 '89
More people are busy working—but they're not so busy spending. J. C. Cooper and K. Madigan. il *Business Week* p25-6 Mr 27 '89
Rising rates may finally curb the urge to splurge. G. Koretz. *Business Week* p20 Mr 20 '89
Shoppers will keep spending, but with a little less gusto. M. F. Allyn. il *Fortune* 119:25-6 F 27 '89
The slowdown in consumer spending may be only a breather. J. C. Cooper and K. Madigan. il *Business Week* p23-4 Ap 10 '89
Spending patterns and income of single and married parents. M. Boyle. bibl f il *Monthly Labor Review* 112:37-41 Mr '89
A storekeeper's caveat: let the seller beware. A. Dunkin. il *Business Week* p84 Ja 9 '89
Why the Fed can't seem to brake the buying binge. G. Koretz. il *Business Week* p26 Ja 23 '89
Will Americans keep buying less and saving more? [views of Robert S. Gay] G. Koretz. il *Business Week* p20 Jl 31 '89
Yuppie spending gets serious. F. Rice. il *Fortune* 119:147-9 Mr 27 '89

Anecdotes, facetiae, satire, etc.
Consumer report. G. Schwartz. il *New York* 22:38 Ap 10 '89

International aspects
The great global buying binge. J. Egan. il *U.S. News & World Report* 107:42-4 Jl 3 '89
Shopping makes the world go 'round. N. Janus. *Utne Reader* p83 S/O '89

Soviet Union
A taste of the luxe life. A. Blackman. il *Time* 133:82 Ap 10 '89
CONSUMPTION TAX
The 1 percent solution [tax for the rich] J. S. Henry and M. Pomer. *The New Republic* 200:12-13 F 6 '89
A luxury consumption tax could relieve our budget deficit. J. S. Henry and M. Pomer. *Utne Reader* p88 S/O '89
Wilson's hidden taxes [Canada] M. Clark. il *Maclean's* 102:20-1 My 8 '89
CONTACT DERMATITIS
Look-good, feel-good jewelry [AllerGuard process] A. Biesada. *High Technology Business* 9:47 Ja '89
CONTACT LENS SOLUTIONS
How to care for contacts. il *Consumer Reports* 54:416-20 Je '89
CONTACT LENSES
20/20 beauty. il *Teen* 33:58-9 Ja '89
Contact-lens wearers need to follow a certain set of rules and use a special kind of makeup. L. F. McCarthy. *Vogue* 179:224 N '89
Contact lenses: what to consider. il *Consumer Reports* 54:411-20 Je '89
Contacts: a closer look. *Vogue* 179:226 Ag '89
Darling . . . your contacts [danger of ulcerative keratitis] *Newsweek* 114:66 O 2 '89
An eye doctor says wearing contacts for weeks at a time can be blindingly shortsighted [danger of ulcerative keratitis; interview with O. Schein] D. Mathison. il por *People Weekly* 32:65-6 N 6 '89

Focus on bifocals. A. Biesada. il *High Technology Business* 9:48 My '89
Guide to contact lenses. L. Holland. il *Good Housekeeping* 208:239 Ap '89
Letting your eyes "breath" [rigid gas permeable contact lenses] il *USA Today (Periodical)* 117:4 F '89
Making contacts safe [risk of acanthamoeba keratitis] il *Prevention (Emmaus, Pa.)* 41:12+ F '89
A new look at glasses and contacts. N. A. Osborn. il *Current Health 2* 16:12-13 N '89
New look at throwaway contacts. C. Schaeffer. il *Changing Times* 43:76 Jl '89
Soft contacts: extended wear poses hazard [ulcerative keratitis; research by Oliver D. Schein] K. Fackelmann. *Science News* 136:197 S 23 '89

Labeling
New labeling for extended-wear lenses [risk of ulcerative keratitis] *FDA Consumer* 23:3-4 S '89
CONTACTS (EMPLOYMENT) See Networking
CONTAGIOUS DISEASES See Communicable diseases
CONTAINER GARDENS AND GARDENING
See also
  Bonsai
  Flower boxes, planters, etc.
  Hanging plants
  House plants
  Indoor gardens and gardening
  Plants, Potted
Living bouquets for the holidays . . . and afterward. il *Sunset (Central West edition)* 181:162-3 D '88
Living holiday arrangements [cover story] il *Flower and Garden* 33:38-40 N/D '89
Parterre in a pot. L. A. Weathers. il *Southern Living* 24:44-5 Ag '89
Porch orchard [cover story] M. Damsker. il *Organic Gardening* 36:24-8+ D '89
CONTAINER INDUSTRY
See also
  Ball Corporation
  Constar International, Inc.
  Gaylord Container Ltd.
  Silgan Corporation
  Stone Container Corp.
Acquisitions and mergers
Scrapping over a food packager [Envirodyne] G. G. Marcial. *Business Week* p146 Mr 20 '89
Finance
Packaging. R. T. Grieves. il *Forbes* 143:182-3 Ja 9 '89
CONTAINERIZATION (FREIGHT)
See also
  McLean Industries Inc.
CONTAINERS
See also
  Bags
  Barrels
  Beverage containers
  Boxes, cases, etc.
  Cans
  Cookie jars
  Porcelain containers
  Thermos containers
  Vases
CONTAINMENT BUILDINGS (NUCLEAR REACTORS) See Nuclear reactors—Containment
CONTAINMENT POLICY See United States—Foreign relations—Soviet Union
CONTAMINATION
See also
  Airplane engines—Fuel—Contamination
  Apples—Contamination
  Bread—Contamination
  Cashew nuts—Contamination
  Corn—Contamination
  Cosmetics—Contamination
  Cows—Contamination
  Crabs—Contamination
  Eggs—Contamination
  Fish contamination
  Food contamination
  Fuel—Contamination
  Grasses—Seed—Contamination
  Meat contamination
  Milk contamination
  Moose—Contamination
  Mushrooms, Canned—Contamination
  Paper products—Contamination
  Potatoes—Contamination
  Poultry contamination
  Sandwiches—Contamination
  Seafood—Contamination
  Sheep—Contamination
  Shellfish contamination
  Shrimp—Contamination
  Swine—Contamination
  Truffles—Contamination
  Vegetables—Contamination

CONTAMINATION (TECHNOLOGY)
See also
Clean rooms
CONTE, JAMES W.
about
"We don't advertise". E. Paris. il por *Forbes* 143:44 Je 12 '89
CONTEMPLATION See Meditation
CONTEMPORARY ARTS CENTER (CINCINNATI, OHIO)
Infinite pattern [museum store designed by T. Brown] D. Dietsch. il *Architectural Record* 177:94-7 mid-S '89
CONTEMPORARY BOOKS, INC.
Contemporary Books closes New York office; drops fiction. *Publishers Weekly* 236:17 D 22 '89
CONTEMPORARY MUSEUM (HONOLULU, HAWAII)
Hawaii's Contemporary Museum. J. D. Houston. il *Architectural Digest* 46:150+ O '89
CONTEMPT OF COURT
A courageous mother's first taste of freedom [E. Morgan released from jail after serving 25 months; cover story] J. S. Podesta and P. Chin. il pors *People Weekly* 32:78-80+ O 16 '89
Elizabeth Morgan. il pors *People Weekly* 32:97-8 D 25 '89-Ja 1 '90
Elizabeth Morgan's brother risks jail as he joins her in defying a Washington judge [R. Morgan faces civil contempt charges for refusing to disclose whereabouts of niece] D. Grogan. il pors *People Weekly* 32:38-40 Jl 3 '89
A hard case of contempt [E. Morgan remains imprisoned for refusing to disclose whereabouts of daughter] J. Elson. il por *Time* 134:66 S 18 '89
Morganatic marriage [E. Morgan jailed for refusing to allow ex-husband to visit daughter] *The New Republic* 201:4+ Jl 31 '89
A mother's 759 days of defiance [E. Morgan released from jail following congressional overrule of District of Columbia court] il por *U.S. News & World Report* 107:12-13 O 9 '89
Stalemate for high stakes [E. Morgan jailed for refusing to allow ex-husband to visit daughter] P. Chin and J. S. Podesta. il pors *People Weekly* 31:84-5 Ja 23 '89
Update on Elizabeth Morgan [jailed for refusing to disclose whereabouts of child] il por *Glamour* 87:116 S '89
Vowing to protect her child from rape, Elizabeth Morgan faces her 23rd month in jail. P. Chin. il pors *People Weekly* 31:113-15+ Je 12 '89
"We had to kidnap our son from the hospital" [D. Pagán jailed after husband takes leukemia-stricken son from Memorial Sloan-Kettering Cancer Center] J. L. Block. il pors *Good Housekeeping* 209:144-5+ O '89
Who's to judge? [E. Morgan jailed for refusing ex-husband visitation rights to daughter] M. Szegedy-Maszak. il pors *The New York Times Magazine* p28-9+ My 21 '89
CONTESTS See Competitions; Prize contests
CONTINENTAL AIR LINES, INC.
Coffee, tea, and the power of positive thinking: seminars teach Continental's workers that good service 'feels' better. C. Power. il *Business Week* p36 Jl 31 '89
Continental orders 20 Airbus A330, A340 aircraft. *Aviation Week & Space Technology* 131:46 N 20 '89
Joseph Corr. T. Vogel. il por *Business Week* Special Issue:138 Ap 14 '89
Lorenzo weighs selling stake in Continental. *Aviation Week & Space Technology* 131:69-70 S 4 '89
A Mr. Fix-It goes to work on Lorenzo's Continental [D. J. Corr] T. Vogel. il por *Business Week* p132-3+ My 22 '89
Teaching teamwork. N. Moll. il *Flying* 116:84-5 Ap '89
Texas Air: empire in jeopardy [strike at Eastern; special section] il por *Business Week* p28-31 Mr 27 '89
CONTINENTAL BANK, N.A.
Continental comes back. K. Ballen. il *Fortune* 119:147 Je 19 '89
CONTINENTAL BASKETBALL ASSOCIATION
The slam-dunk comes to small-town America. B. Bremner. il *Business Week* p82 Mr 6 '89
CONTINENTAL CABLEVISION INC.
New customers at $50 a head, not $2,500. J. A. Trachtenberg. il *Forbes* 143:144-5 Mr 6 '89
CONTINENTAL CRUST See Earth—Crust
CONTINENTAL DRIFT
See also
Polar wander
Another movement in the dance of the plates [work of Paul F. Hoffman] R. A. Kerr. il *Science* 244:529-30 My 5 '89
Did the roof of the world start an ice age? [research by William Ruddiman] R. A. Kerr. il *Science* 244:1441-2 Je 23 '89
Hot spot [Pangaea; research by Thomas J. Crowley] J. Horgan. il *Scientific American* 261:20+ S '89
Rise of Tibet and Rockies set ice-age stage [research by William F. Ruddiman] R. Monastersky. *Science News* 135:309 My 20 '89
Spinning the supercontinent cycle [research by P. F. Hoffman; cover story] R. Monastersky. il map *Science News* 135:344-6 Je 3 '89

What brought on the 'icebox effect' [ice ages caused by winds; research by William Ruddiman and John Kutzbach] *U.S. News & World Report* 106:11 My 22 '89
CONTINENTAL HOTEL (SAIGON, VIETNAM) See Saigon (Vietnam)—Hotels, motels, etc.
CONTINENTAL ILLINOIS NATIONAL BANK & TRUST CO. OF CHICAGO
See also
Continental Bank, N.A.
CONTINENTS
See also
Continental drift
CONTINGENT WORKERS
The cost of flexibility [Western Europe] U. Huws. *World Press Review* 36:48 Je '89
How human resource systems adjust to the shift toward contingent workers. R. S. Belous. bibl f il *Monthly Labor Review* 112:7-12 Mr '89
Taking stock of the flexible work force. G. Koretz. il *Business Week* p12 Jl 24 '89
CONTINUED FRACTIONS See Fractions, Continued
CONTINUING EDUCATION See Adult education; University extension
CONTINUOUSLY VARIABLE TRANSMISSION See Automobiles, Foreign—Transmission
CONTOU-CARRÈRE, ENRIQUE JORGE
Chau bandoneón [story] *Américas* 41 no1:48-9 '89
CONTOUR FARMING
Laying out contour lines; Laying out contour buffer strips; Getting into contour strip-cropping. il *Successful Farming* 87:23-5 D '89
CONTOURS (CARTOGRAPHY)
Computer map analysis: drawing contours [weather maps] A. Blackadar. *Weatherwise* 42:109-13 Ag '89
CONTRA AID See Military assistance, American—Nicaragua
CONTRA AID-IRAN ARMS CASE See Iran-contra affair
CONTRA-SANDINISTA CONFLICT See Nicaragua—Politics and government
CONTRABAND TRADE See Smuggling
CONTRACEPTION See Birth control
CONTRACEPTIVES
See also
Cervical caps
Condoms
Dalkon Shield (Contraceptive)
Intrauterine devices
Pill (Contraceptive)
Birth control? Don't mention it. W. D. Leight. *Mademoiselle* 95:120 My '89
Birth control goes skin deep [Norplant] D. Carr. il *Ms.* 18:77 Jl/Ag '89
The bitter pill [lack of contraceptive research in the U.S.] C. Djerassi. bibl f *Science* 245:356-61 Jl 28 '89
Female contraceptive update. *McCall's* 116:94 F '89
The five-year contraceptive [Norplant releases continuous dose of levonorgestrel] D. M. Podolsky. il *American Health* 8:16 S '89
The great American birth-control crisis. B. Harvey. *Mademoiselle* 95:218-21+ Mr '89
Love, sex and condoms. il *Glamour* 87:146+ O '89
Research in human reproduction [WHO's Special Programme of Research, Development and Research Training in Human Reproduction] J. Barzelatto. il *World Health* p18-21 Ap '89
Sperm stopper [vaccines] il *Discover* 10:10 F '89
Tough choices. E. Frank. *Vogue* 179:220-2+ Ag '89
Vaccination with a synthetic zona pellucida peptide produces long-term contraception in female mice. S. E. Millar and others. bibl f il *Science* 246:935-8 N 17 '89
Why I use what I use. il *Mademoiselle* 95:171+ D '89
Laws and regulations
See Birth control—Laws and regulations
CONTRACTION, MUSCULAR See Muscle contraction
CONTRACTORS
See also
Fischbach Corporation
Independent contractors
Slagle & Slagle
Sound contractors
Women contractors
Hiring a contractor: the rundown on getting bids [remodeling project] *Better Homes and Gardens* 67:85 Je '89
Home remodeling: getting it done right. il *Consumers' Research Magazine* 72:34-6 S '89
How to survive home remodeling. D. Garr. il *Reader's Digest* 135:181-2+ S '89
My contractor, my self (I). J. Folds. il *Modern Maturity* 32:62-4+ O/N '89
My contractor, my self (II). J. Folds. il *Modern Maturity* 32:76-8+ D '89/Ja '90
Working with a contractor [home improvement project] il *McCall's* 116:101+ Ap '89
Bibliography
Should you act as your own contractor? il *Sunset (Central West edition)* 182:124 Je '89
Licenses
Contractor licensing: who benefits? [interview with M. Stone] il *Home Mechanix* 85:22-3+ Je '89

CONTRACTS
See also
Breach of contract
Building—Contracts and specifications
Collective labor agreements
Labor contracts
Marriage contracts
Partnership
Public works—Contracts and specifications
Put and call transactions
Rescission (Law)
Service contracts
Contracts [special section] il *Black Enterprise* 19:154-6+ F '89
How to read the fine print in contracts. S. M. Pollan and M. Levine. il *Money* 18:111-12+ Je '89
CONTRACTS, AUTHORS' *See* Authors and publishers
CONTRACTS, GOVERNMENT
See also
Military-industrial complex
Municipal contracts
Munitions
Pentagon procurement scandal
Privatization
United States. Air Force—Procurement
United States. Army—Procurement
United States. Coast Guard—Procurement
United States. Dept. of Defense—Procurement
United States. Federal Aviation Administration—Appropriations and expenditures
United States. General Services Administration
United States. Marine Corps—Procurement
United States. National Aeronautics and Space Administration—Procurement
United States. Navy—Procurement
United States Postal Service—Procurement
Business' role in war on drugs [federal contractors required to establish antidrug programs] D. C. Bacon. *Nation's Business* 77:5 Ja '89
Contracts [special section] il *Black Enterprise* 19:154-6+ F '89
Just say nothing? [Drug-Free Workplace Act] D. Fanning. il *Forbes* 144:220 N 27 '89
Accounting
See also
United States. General Accounting Office
Japan
And now, another form of Japanese hardball: lowball pricing. R. Neff. il *Business Week* p50 N 20 '89
CONTRAN CORPORATION
The whistling billionaire. A. E. Serwer. il pors *Fortune* 119:102+ Ap 10 '89
CONTRARIAN INVESTMENTS
Catching the rebound [views of P. Greco] D. Kortrey. il *Forbes* 144:227 S 18 '89
The contrarian. D. N. Dreman. See alternate issues of Forbes
A contrarian case for buying certain junk bond funds now. M. Meyer. il *Money* 18:51-2+ N '89
A contrarian case for junk bonds. M. J. Williams. il *Fortune* 120:36 S 11 '89
Fighting the market [contrarian newsletters] M. Hulbert. il *Forbes* 143:342 My 29 '89
Hong Kong's contrarians [buying stocks] J. Mendes. il *Fortune* 120:30 Jl 17 '89
How mutual funds have battled back. J. M. Laderman. il *Business Week* p100-1 S 18 '89
This contrarian strategy works—week in, week out [views of Bruce N. Lehmann] G. Koretz. il *Business Week* p28 My 8 '89
This top-ranked contrarian predicts stocks will hit their pre-crash highs in '89 [Market mania publisher G. Cutler] J. Ellis. il por *Money* 18:163-4 Ja '89
CONTRAST IN PHOTOGRAPHY *See* Photography—Light and lighting
CONTROL DATA CORP.
And then there was one [pulls out of supercomputer market] M. Quinn. il *Time* 133:56 My 1 '89
Control Data may finally have the right stuff. R. Mitchell. *Business Week* p30 Ap 24 '89
Control Data struggles to get back in control. R. Mitchell. il por *Business Week* p130-1 My 1 '89
Fine job, Larry—but don't get too settled [L. Perlman] R. Mitchell. il por *Business Week* p34 O 16 '89
CONTROL MECHANISMS, CELLULAR *See* Cellular control mechanisms
CONTROLLED FOREST FIRES *See* Forest fires—Controlled fires
CONVECTION OF HEAT *See* Heat—Convection
CONVECTION OVENS
Microwave/convection ovens. il *Consumer Reports* 54:287-94 D '89
Microwave/convection ovens. il *Consumer Reports* 54:580-6 S '89
CONVENIENCE FOODS
See also
Cooking—Convenience foods
Frozen dinners
Refrigerated dinners

CONVENIENCE STORES
See also
Circle K Corp.
Convenient Food Mart, Inc.
Southland Corp.
Sunshine-Jr. Stores, Inc.
CONVENIENT FOOD MART, INC.
How not to run a franchise. R. Koselka. *Forbes* 144:244 N 27 '89
CONVENTION AGAINST ILLICIT TRAFFIC IN NARCOTIC DRUGS AND PSYCHOTROPIC SUBSTANCES (1988)
UN narcotics trafficking conference adopts convention [text of convention] *Department of State Bulletin* 89:49-59 Ap '89
Vienna conference adopts world-wide convention against illicit drug traffic. il *UN Chronicle* 26:83 Mr '89
CONVENTION DELEGATES, DEMOCRATIC *See* National conventions, Democratic
CONVENTION FACILITIES
See also
Columbus (Ohio)—Auditoriums, convention facilities, etc.
First rate conventions you can afford [airport hotels] L. Hazelton. *Black Enterprise* 19:76-7 Mr '89
CONVENTION FOR THE PROTECTION OF THE WORLD CULTURAL AND NATURAL HERITAGE *See* World Heritage Convention
CONVENTION ON INTERNATIONAL TRADE IN ENDANGERED SPECIES OF WILD FAUNA AND FLORA (1973)
A ban on ivory. M. Nichols. il *Maclean's* 102:86 O 30 '89
Decision time on African ivory trade. J. Cherfas. il *Science* 246:26-7 O 6 '89
International tusk politics. *Science News* 136:94 Ag 5 '89
Reprieve for the giant of beasts [efforts to save the elephant] T. Gup. il *Time* 134:77 O 30 '89
CONVENTION ON THE CONTROL OF TRANSBOUNDARY MOVEMENTS OF HAZARDOUS WASTE AND THEIR DISPOSAL (1989) *See* Basel Convention on the Control of Transboundary Movements of Hazardous Waste and Their Disposal (1989)
CONVENTION ON THE LAW OF THE SEA (1982)
States asked to join Sea Law Convention. *UN Chronicle* 26:72 Mr '89
CONVENTION ON THE RIGHTS OF THE CHILD
All our children. *The Nation* 249:740 D 18 '89
CONVENTIONAL ARMED FORCES IN EUROPE TALKS *See* Disarmament—Conferences
CONVENTIONAL WAR *See* War
CONVENTIONS
Cutting deals at conventions. M. M. McDowell. il *Black Enterprise* 20:114-16+ O '89
Going places. E. C. Ray. il *Essence* 19:19+ Mr '89
CONVENTS
Peru
Out of sight, out of time [convents Santa Catalina and Santa Rosa] M. R. Day. il *Américas* 41 no2:11-15 '89
Poland
Auschwitz and the nuns. W. F. Buckley. *National Review* 41:63 O 13 '89
The Auschwitz Carmel. *America* 161:179 S 30 '89
Auschwitz ire [controversial Carmelite convent] il *Time* 134:49 Ag 21 '89
Cardinal Glemp's memory lapse [Carmelite convent at Auschwitz] J. M. Wall. *The Christian Century* 106:867 O 4 '89
Close enough to step on toes: tensions between Jews & Catholics [Auschwitz convent controversy] L. Klenicki and E. D. Mallon. il *Commonweal* 116:521-6 O 6 '89
Détente at a death camp [dispute over Carmelite convent at Auschwitz] K. L. Woodward. il *Newsweek* 114:58 O 2 '89
The ghosts of an ancient plague [controversial Carmelite convent at Auschwitz] il *U.S. News & World Report* 107:10 S 11 '89
The Glemp controversy [Carmelite convent at Auschwitz] *The Christian Century* 106:808 S 13-20 '89
Harsh homily [J. Glemp's remarks concerning Carmelite convent at Auschwitz] *Time* 134:77 S 11 '89
Mea culpa, Auschwitz [agreement to move Carmelite convent] il *Time* 134:25 O 2 '89
Peace signals from the papal chimney [Pope John Paul II calls for removal of Carmelite convent at Auschwitz] il *U.S. News & World Report* 107:14 O 2 '89
Polish memories [Auschwitz convent controversy] J. Neusner. il *National Review* 41:27-8 O 27 '89
A sign of contradiction [Auschwitz convent controversy] J. T. Pawlikowski. il *Commonweal* 116:485-8 S 22 '89
The Vatican and the Jews [support for relocation of Carmelite convent from Auschwitz] il *The Christian Century* 106:873 O 4 '89
Whose Auschwitz? [dispute over Carmelite convent] il *National Review* 41:18+ S 29 '89
Whose Holocaust? [controversy over Carmelite convent at Auschwitz] R. Watson. il *Newsweek* 114:35-6 S 11 '89

CONVENTS—*cont.*

Tibet

Buddhist nuns. B. N. Aziz. il *Natural History* p40-9 Mr '89

CONVERGENT TECHNOLOGIES INC.

"I love the tumult" [career of A. Michels] J. Pitta. il pors *Forbes* 144:296-8 N 13 '89

CONVERSATION

Conversation piece. A. R. Gurney. por *Newsweek* 113:10-11 Je 26 '89

The geometry of conversation [dining table's impact on conversation at a party] J. Giovannini. il *House & Garden* 161:62+ F '89

Strangers can enrich your life. A. Whitman. il *Reader's Digest* 134:57-8+ Je '89

Table talk: the family detective story [research by Elinor Ochs] il *USA Today (Periodical)* 118:9 Jl '89

CONVERSATION PROGRAMS *See* Cable television—Conversation programs; Radio broadcasting—Conversation programs; Television broadcasting—Conversation programs

CONVERSI, MARCELLO, 1917-1988

about

Obituary

Physics Today il por 42:114 N '89. G. Salvini and V. L. Telegdi

CONVERSION

See also

Converts

CONVERSION, ECONOMIC *See* Economic conversion

CONVERTERS, ANALOG-TO-DIGITAL *See* Analog-to-digital converters

CONVERTERS, DIGITAL-TO-ANALOG *See* Digital-to-analog converters

CONVERTERS, FREQUENCY *See* Frequency changers

CONVERTERS, RADIO FREQUENCY *See* Frequency changers

CONVERTIBLE BONDS

Bond funds with an extra kick [closed-end convertible bond funds] L. Zinn. il *Business Week* p98 Ag 28 '89

Convertible bond funds: safety plus the sizzle of stocks. E. Schultz. il *Fortune* 120:29-30 Jl 17 '89

Convertible bonds don't soar in price like stocks or fall as fast, either. R. R. Roha. il *Changing Times* 43:80 Ag '89

CONVERTIBLE SECURITIES

The reliability of a bond, the allure of a stock. T. Thompson. il *U.S. News & World Report* 106:77 My 22 '89

CONVERTIBLES (AUTOMOBILES)

Owners reports [Ford Probe, Jaguar XJ6, Lincoln Continental and Cadillac Allanté] M. Lamm. il *Popular Mechanics* 166:74-7 Je '89

Romancing the roadster [Mazda Miata] S. C. Gwynne. il *Time* 134:39 Jl 24 '89

Topless tote board. B. Visnic. il *Car and Driver* 34:72-5 F '89

Design

Designer genes [Miata designer M. Jordan] M. Beauchamp. il por *Forbes* 144:248 O 2 '89

How Chrysler's $30,000 sports car got sideswiped [venture with Maserati] J. Rossant. il *Business Week* p68+ Ja 23 '89

Mazda rolls out a poor man's Maserati [Miata] L. Armstrong. il *Business Week* p66 Je 26 '89

Mercedes-Benz 300/500SL. D. C. Ross. il *Motor Trend* 41:74-6+ Je '89

Mercedes' bright shining star [new SLs] P. Frère. il *Road & Track* 40:96-7 Jl '89

Miata movers [Mazda] J. Lamm. il *Road & Track* 40:36-7 Jl '89

Polishing Cadillac's image [Allanté] M. Keller. il *Motor Trend* 41:136 F '89

The siren song of the open road and the open roof led Bob Hall to the amazing Miata. D. Grogan. il pors *People Weekly* 32:57+ S 4 '89

Two for the road [Mazda Miata] P. Viladas. il *House & Garden* 161:44 Ag '89

History

1951 Riley 2½ Litre Drophead Coupe. il *Road & Track* 40:134-40 Mr '89

Now dasher, now dancer [Lotus Elan] S. L. Thompson. il *Car and Driver* 35:99-101+ D '89

A peerless pedigree [Mercedes-Benz SL series] L. Paddock. il *Road & Track* 41:65 D '89

Remodeled automobiles

See Automobiles, Remodeled

Testing

All in the name [Chrysler's TC by Maserati] M. Thomas. il *Vogue* 179:278 My '89

Aston Martin Vantage Volante. P. Bingham. il *Motor Trend* 41:168-70+ My '89

Back to the mother lode [old vs. new Alfa Romeos, Corvettes and Porsches; cover story] P. Egan. il *Road & Track* 40:38-49 Ag '89

BMW Z1. N. Bissoon Dath. il *Car and Driver* 34:68-9 F '89

BMW Z1. J. Miller. il *Motor Trend* 41:74-6+ F '89

Buick Reatta Convertible. R. Ceppos. il *Car and Driver* 34:36-8 F '89

Buick Reatta Convertible. B. Nagy. il *Motor Trend* 41:61-2 O '89

Cadillac Allanté. J. Lamm. il *Road & Track* 40:138 My '89

Cadillac Allanté. D. C. Ross. il *Motor Trend* 41:88-9+ F '89

Cadillac Allanté versus Mercedes 560SL. P. Bedard. il *Car and Driver* 34:46-51 F '89

Chevrolet Corvette Convertible. R. Ceppos. il *Car and Driver* 34:74-6 Je '89

Chrysler LeBaron GTC. D. C. Ross. il *Motor Trend* 41:89-91+ D '89

Chrysler's TC by Maserati. il *Road & Track* 40:100-2+ Je '89

Chrysler's TC by Maserati. J. Karr. il *Motor Trend* 41:120-2+ Ap '89

A classy new ragtop [Mazda MX-5 Miata] E. Henry. il *Changing Times* 43:123 S '89

Fall firsts [1990 Lexus, Infiniti, and Mercedes-Benz SL] il *Popular Mechanics* 166:51-3+ S '89

Infiniti M30 convertible. W. Jeanes. il *Car and Driver* 34:41+ F '89

Jaguar XJ-S. B. Visnic. il *Car and Driver* 34:55 F '89

Jaguar XJ-S Convertible. R. Grable. il *Motor Trend* 41:129-31+ D '89

Jaguar XJ-S V-12 Convertible. il *Road & Track* 40:58-60 Ja '89

Long-term update [Mazda MX-5 Miata and Eagle Talon TSi AWD] il *Road & Track* 41:109 N '89

Mazda MX-5 Miata. il *Road & Track* 40:52-6+ Jl '89

Mazda MX-5 Miata. J. Miller. il *Motor Trend* 41:80-2 Mr '89

Mazda MX-5 Miata [cover story] P. Bedard. il *Car and Driver* 34:40-3 Mr '89

Mazda MX-5 Miata [cover story] J. Karr. il *Motor Trend* 41:38-42+ Jl '89

Mazda MX-5 Miata [cover story] A. St. Antoine. il *Car and Driver* 35:40-5 S '89

Mazda MX-5 Miata: grand prize [cover story] D. Simanaitis. il *Road & Track* 40:44-51 Mr '89

Mazda RX-7s [RX-7 Turbo II and RX-7 Convertible] J. R. Nerad. il *Motor Trend* 41:96-9+ Ag '89

Mercedes-Benz 300SL/500SL. P. Berg. il *Car and Driver* 35:83-5+ S '89

Mercedes-Benz 300SL & 500SL. B. Nagy. il *Motor Trend* 41:54-7+ D '89

Mercedes-Benz 500SL. il *Road & Track* 41:58-62 D '89

Mercedes-Benz 500SL. C. Csere. il *Car and Driver* 35:60-3+ D '89

Mercedes-Benz 500SL [cover story] J. R. Nerad. il *Motor Trend* 41:40-6+ Ag '89

Mercedes-Benz SL. J. Lamm. il *Road & Track* 41:58-9+ S '89

Miata mania [cover story] R. Homan. il *Road & Track* 41:52-9 N '89

Miatific bliss in five gears [Mazda Miata] J. Skow. il *Time* 134:91 O 2 '89

Munich's marvel [BMW Z1 Roadster] J. Dinkel. il *Road & Track* 40:72-3 Mr '89

Olds Cutlass Supreme Convertible. B. Nagy. il *Motor Trend* 41:104-5 O '89

Past and present [1964 Ford Mustang GT convertible vs. 1989 model] R. Taylor. il *Popular Mechanics* 166:64-6 Ag '89

Porsche 944 S2 Cabriolet. J. Miller. il *Motor Trend* 41:73-6 D '89

Porsche 944S2 Cabriolet. J. Phillips, III. il *Car and Driver* 35:93+ N '89

A ragtop time machine [Miata] J. B. Treece. il *Business Week* p130 S 18 '89

Saab 900 Turbo. A. Assenza. il *Car and Driver* 34:59 F '89

Safety in style [Mercedes-Benz SL] B. Nadel. il *Popular Science* 235:32-4 S '89

Two's company, three's a pedestrian [Mazda MX-5 Miata] P. Bedard. il *Esquire* 112:64 S '89

Volkswagen Cabriolet. J. Lamm. il *Road & Track* 40:68 Mr '89

Volkswagen Cabriolet. P. Lyons. il *Car and Driver* 34:67 F '89

World's best cars [Ferrari Testarossa, Mazda MX-5 Miata, Mercedes-Benz 300E, Corvette ZR-1, and Porsche 911 Carrera 4; cover story] il *Road & Track* 40:40-51 Jl '89

Traction

High roller [Cadillac Allanté with traction control] D. McCosh. il *Popular Science* 235:71-3+ N '89

CONVERTS

Kairos international: call to conversion. R. M. Brown. il *The Christian Century* 106:1091-3 N 22 '89

CONVERTS, CATHOLIC

Against R.C.I.A. [Rite of Christian Initiation for Adults; with reply by R. D. Duggan; cover story] A. M. Greeley. il *America* 161:231-7 O 14 '89

Confessions of an erstwhile evangelizer. R. E. Burns. *U.S. Catholic* 54:2 N '89

A good race. B. C. Johnson. *America* 160:217-18 Mr 11 '89

CONVERTS, CATHOLIC—*cont.*
Mistaking Rome for heaven. J. I. Packer. il *Christianity Today* 33:15 My 12 '89
Of many things [M. Dally's account of acceptance of married Episcopal priest into Catholic priesthood] J. W. Donohue. *America* 160:362 Ap 22 '89
State of the question [discussion of October 14, 1989 article, Against R.C.I.A.] A. M. Greeley. *America* 161:328-30 N 11 '89
CONVERTS FROM ISLAM
Believers in Turkey claim their legal rights. B. G. Baker. il *Christianity Today* 33:44 Ap 7 '89
CONVERTS FROM JUDAISM
Catholics and Jews: can we bridge the abyss? [Holocaust martyr E. Stein; adaptation of address, October 16, 1988] S. M. Batzdorff. *America* 160:223-4+ Mr 11 '89
Document angers Jewish community [Willowbank Declaration on the Christian Gospel and the Jewish People] P. P. Wong. il *Christianity Today* 33:48 S 22 '89
CONVERTS FROM MORMONISM
Cashing in on conversions [B. Dintino accused of conning churches by claiming to be a disenchanted Mormon missionary] por *Christianity Today* 33:51 Je 16 '89
CONVEYING EQUIPMENT
See also
Pneumatic conveying
Product reports 1990. il *Architectural Record* 177:153+ D '89
CONVICT LABOR
The costly business of warehousing violent criminals [study of U.S. Penitentiary at Lompoc, Calif.] M. S. Fleisher. il *USA Today (Periodical)* 117:60-2 Mr '89
CONVICTS *See* Prisoners
CONVITO ITALIANO (FIRM)
That's Italian in Illinois. D. Weil. il por *Working Woman* 14:58-60 Ag '89
CONVULSIONS
See also
Epilepsy
Limbic seizures increase neuronal production of messenger RNA for nerve growth factor. C. M. Gall and P. J. Isackson. bibl f il *Science* 245:758-61 Ag 18 '89
Wildfire in the brain [cocaine linked to seizures; research by Robert Post] S. Blakeslee. il *American Health* 8:19-20 Ja/F '89
CONWAY, AVIA
about
Cooking up profits in Europe. A. McKenzie. por *Black Enterprise* 20:79-80 N '89
CONWAY (S.C.)
Race relations
Choosing sides [town torn apart by racial dispute involving two high school quarterbacks] H. Hersch. il pors *Sports Illustrated* 71:42-4+ N 27 '89
CONWAY MORRIS, S.
Burgess Shale faunas and the Cambrian explosion [cover story] bibl f il map *Science* 246:339-46 O 20 '89
CONWAYS (BRUSSELS, BELGIUM: RESTAURANT) *See* Brussels (Belgium)—Restaurants, nightclubs, bars, etc.
CONWAYS (PARIS, FRANCE: RESTAURANT) *See* Paris (France)—Restaurants, nightclubs, bars, etc.
CONYERS, JOHN, 1929-
about
Military computer awards stalled; Conyers asks probe. por *Jet* 75:9 Mr 6 '89
Rep. Conyers slated for chair of House Committee. por *Jet* 75:8 Ja 23 '89
COODY, DALE
about
In Oklahoma, Dale Coody sees a day when ostrich wrangling will replace cattle herding. D. Chu. il pors *People Weekly* 32:84+ N 13 '89
COOK, ALISON
On the road with Miss America. il pors *Ladies' Home Journal* 106:38+ S '89
COOK, ANTHONY
Survival is the best revenge. il pors *Gentlemen's Quarterly* 59:286-9+ Ap '89
COOK, COLIN
"I found freedom". il *Christianity Today* 33:22-4 Ag 18 '89
COOK, FREDERICK ALBERT, 1865-1940
about
Frederick Albert Cook, M.D. [with editorial comment by Gilbert L. Voss] R. M. Myerson. il por map *Sea Frontiers* 35:3, 8-13 Ja/F '89
COOK, GERRY
about
Only a buck [film] Reviews
People Weekly il 31:107 Ap 10 '89
COOK, JACK
Hot potatoes. il *Organic Gardening* 36:30-2+ Je '89
Soil advice. il *Organic Gardening* 36:47-50 F '89
Visions of hydropower. il *Country Journal* 16:27-31 F '89
COOK, KEVIN
The Iowa girl stands tall. il *Sports Illustrated* 70:76-84+ F 13 '89

There's no place like home. il pors *Sports Illustrated* 70:90 Je 5 '89
COOK, LODWRICK M.
about
What worries Arco's chief the most [interview] il por *Fortune* 120:102 O 9 '89
COOK, LYNN CRAWFORD
Moisturizing the air. il *Health (New York, N.Y.)* 21:34-5+ D '89
The office visitor nobody wants. il *Health (New York, N.Y.)* 21:78-81 My '89
COOK, MARSHALL J.
Lay Catholics: are the silent partners finding their voice? il *U.S. Catholic* 54:34-9 Ja '89
Why some men still want to be priests. il *U.S. Catholic* 54:31-8 Ap '89
COOK, PAUL
about
Science artifacts on the block. D. Dickson. il por *Science* 244:649 My 12 '89
COOK, PAUL MAXWELL, 1924-
about
"We've heard that all before". J. Heins. il por *Forbes* 143:40-1 F 6 '89
COOK, ROBERT
The plight of Palestine refugees. il *World Health* p8-10 Jl '89
COOK, ROBIN, 1940-
about
Doctor fear [interview] M. Segell. il *American Health* 8:82-4+ S '89
COOK, STEPHANI, 1944-
What men want (I). il *Gentlemen's Quarterly* 59:294-301+ O '89
What men want (II). il *Gentlemen's Quarterly* 59:272-7+ N '89
COOK & PALMIOTTO INTERNATIONAL LTD.
Cook & Palmiotto help exporters get a good night's sleep. R. Neff. il *Business Week* p82 Ap 3 '89
COOK EXPEDITION (1908-1909)
Frederick Albert Cook, M.D. [with editorial comment by Gilbert L. Voss] R. M. Myerson. il por map *Sea Frontiers* 35:3, 8-13 Ja/F '89
COOK INLET COMMUNICATIONS INC.
Minority partners. P. Noglows. il *Channels (New York, N.Y.: 1986)* 9:51 My '89
COOK ISLANDS
Description and travel
Cook Islands [cover story] J. Leveque. il *Travel Holiday* 172:40-9 S '89
COOKBOOKS
See also
Booksellers and bookselling—Cookbooks
Publishers and publishing—Cookbooks
British days, Bulgarian nights [Digby Anderson's Book of imperative cooking] N. Hazelton. *National Review* 41:55-6 F 24 '89
Pocket extends an "Open Hand" in new cookbook to benefit AIDS organization. B. Levine. il *Publishers Weekly* 236:58 Ag 4 '89
Bibliography
Books for cooking up a stylish storm. L. Zinn. il *Business Week* p212 N 27 '89
Bring on the grilled radicchio and toasted Rice Krispies. M. Silver. il *U.S. News & World Report* 107:69-70 D 11 '89
The cookbook shelf. L. Lerman. il *Gourmet* 49:82+ F '89
The cookbook shelf. L. Lerman. il *Gourmet* 49:80+ N '89
Cookbooks. R. Flaste. il *The New York Times Book Review* 94:16+ Je 11 '89
Cooking. R. Flaste. il *The New York Times Book Review* 94:18+ D 3 '89
The cook's corner [pamphlets to send for] il *Southern Living* 24:174-5 O '89
Fall cookbooks 1989. K. Riippa. il *Publishers Weekly* 236:34-8 S 8 '89
Garden of delights. M. O'Neill. il *Harper's Bazaar* 122:84-5+ Je '89
I'm cooking as fast as I can. L. Shapiro. il *Newsweek* 114:63 S 4 '89
Collectors and collecting
'O poor cook!': The annotating M. F. K. Fisher. J. Ferrary. por *The New York Times Book Review* 94:1+ Je 4 '89
Marketing
Cookbook sales beyond the bookstore. J. Makos and L. Morse. il *Publishers Weekly* 236:30+ S 8 '89
COOKE, COLLEEN
about
"Don't let my father die!". P. O. D'Aulaire and E. D'Aulaire. il *Reader's Digest* 134:115-20 Je '89
COOKE, DAVID C.
about
The bailout general who rose from the ranks. C. Yang. il por *Business Week* p178 N 6 '89
COOKE, ELIZABETH
"Someone is watching me" [story] il *McCall's* 116:118+ Ag '89

COOKE, KIM

about

"Don't let my father die!". P. O. D'Aulaire and E. D'Aulaire. il *Reader's Digest* 134:115-20 Je '89

COOKE, PATRICK

Are accents out? Hey, dude, like neh-oh way! il *The New York Times Magazine* p50+ N 19 '89

COOKE, SYLVIA JETER

Rumbling rafters. il *Women's Sports & Fitness* 11:38-9 Je '89

COOKERS, PRESSURE *See* Pressure cookers

COOKERY *See* Cooking

COOKIE [film] *See* Motion picture reviews—Single works

COOKIE HOUSES, ORNAMENTS, ETC. *See* Cooking, Ornamental

COOKIE JARS

Collectors and collecting

Jars for smart cookies. J. Jurnovoy and D. Jenness. bibl il *New Choices for the Best Years* 29:101-3 S '89

COOKIES

See also

Champ Cookies (Firm)
Girl Scout cookies
Mrs. Fields Cookies
Shortbread

50 (count 'em, 50) holiday cookies [Christmas] il *Good Housekeeping* 209:190+ N '89

After-school treat [peanut butter apple bars] il *Better Homes and Gardens* 67:184 N '89

Chewy-gooey treats [chocolate chip squares] il *Southern Living* 24:164 Je '89

A Christmas cooky masterpiece [nut lace cookies] il *Sunset (Central West edition)* 181:66-7 D '88

Christmas meringues. il *The Mother Earth News* 120:42-4 N/D '89

Holiday cookies. il *Better Homes and Gardens* 67:141-2 D '89

LHJ's most-requested Christmas cookies. J. T. Hazard. il *Ladies' Home Journal* 106:187-8+ D '89

Moms and daughters bake cookies. il *Southern Living* 24:100+ D '89

The Mouseketeer cookie book [bar cookies] J. T. Hazard. il *Ladies' Home Journal* 106:191-2+ S '89

Oatmeal cookies. il *Gourmet* 49:178 F '89

Pepperidge Farm's doughboy [cookie developer H. Tolmich] D. Machan. il por *Forbes* 143:198-9 Mr 20 '89

Rainy-day treats [4th of July cookies] il *Better Homes and Gardens* 67:134+ Jl '89

Recipe of the week [graham toffee bars] il *Jet* 76:30 Je 5 '89

Shortcuts to 45 holiday favorites [Christmas cookies] il *Redbook* 174:141-4+ D '89

Small wonders [Christmas cookies] il *Redbook* 174:124-5+ D '89

Sweet treats to bake 'n eat! [Valentine's Day] C. Thomas and S. Young. il *Teen* 33:30-1 F '89

A world of Christmas cookies. il *McCall's* 117:78-80+ D '89

Patents

The cookie war and how it crumbled [settlement reached in Procter & Gamble's chewy cookie patent dispute] il *U.S. News & World Report* 107:18-19 S 25 '89

COOKING

See also

Appetizers
Automobile engines—Cooking use
Baking
Barbecue cooking
Breakfasts
Broiling
Brunches
Buffet meals
Candy
Canning and preserving
Carving (Meat, etc.)
Casserole cooking
Caterers and catering
Chowder
Christmas cooking
Clambakes
Confectionery
Cookbooks
Custards
Desserts
Diet
Dinners and dining
Dumplings
Easter cooking
Entertaining
Food as gifts
Food mixes
Fritters
Gastronomy
Halloween cooking
Ice cream, ices, etc.
Jelly, jam, etc.
Kitchen utensils and appliances
Low calorie cooking

Low sodium cooking
Luncheons
Lunches
Marinades
Mayonnaise
Meals
Menus
Meringue
Microwave cooking
Mincemeat
Oils and fats, Edible
Outdoor meals
Pancakes, waffles, etc.
Papillote cooking
Pâté
Pickles and relishes
Pressure cooking
Puddings
Purées
Quiche
Salads
Sandwiches
Sauces
Sautéing
Savories
Skillet cooking
Snacks
Soups
Spreads (Food)
Steaming (Cooking)
Stew
Stocks (Cooking)
Stuffing (Food)
Suppers
Tarts
Television broadcasting—Cooking programs

25 time-savers. il *Parents* 64:209-10+ O '89

30 best recipes from 60 years. B. Johnson. il *Better Homes and Gardens* 68:112-19+ F '89

All-time-favorite recipes. il *Good Housekeeping* 208:136-46+ Mr '89

Best of McCall's cookbook. il *McCall's* 116:117-21+ S '89

Best restaurants' best recipes. il *Ladies' Home Journal* 106:198-9+ S '89

Bites of spring. C. Idone. il *The New York Times Magazine* p53-4 Mr 26 '89

Chefs' cooking secrets. il *Ladies' Home Journal* 106:218-20+ My '89

Comfort food. il *Ladies' Home Journal* 106:181-2+ Mr '89

Coming home to roast. J. Pépin. il *The New York Times Magazine* p99-100 S 17 '89

Cook's tour. K. Haedrich. See issues of Country Journal beginning January 1987

Cool comfort [summer cooking] J. Pruess. il *The New York Times Magazine* p53-4 Je 18 '89

Date with a dish. C. Lyons. See issues of Ebony

Dining in. B. Shacochis. See issues of Gentlemen's Quarterly beginning December 1988

Fix food fast. J. Nash. See issues of Essence through May 1988

Food. See occasional issues of The New York Times Magazine

Food. See issues of Vogue beginning September 1983

Food editor's tips. M. Ying. See issues of Good Housekeeping

Food tips to clip. M. Langan. See issues of McCall's beginning May 1986

From our kitchen to yours. See issues of Southern Living

Gourmet's menus. See issues of Gourmet

Gourmet's pantry. See issues of Gourmet

Great dinners for small families [30 minute entrees] il *Redbook* 173:145-8+ My '89

Home cooking 90s style. B. Johnson. il *Better Homes and Gardens* 67:127-36+ S '89

In short order. See issues of Gourmet beginning June 1984

Inside the Journal kitchen. See issues of Ladies' Home Journal beginning February 1988

Kitchen express. See issues of Parents beginning July 1986

Lazy days cookbook. il *Good Housekeeping* 209:120-30+ Jl '89

A matter of taste. R. Sokolov. See issues of Natural History

[Month] menus. See issues of Sunset (Central West edition)

No more than six ingredients, mostly 30 minutes or less. il *Sunset (Central West edition)* 183:154 O '89

Now we're cooking [kitchen hints] il *The Mother Earth News* 119:22-3 S/O '89

Oprah invites you to dinner [dishes from Eccentric restaurant] E. Byron. il por *Redbook* 173:102-3+ Ag '89

The pleasures of weekend cooking. B. Goldman. il *Better Homes and Gardens* 67:124-30+ O '89

Recipes. J. Nash. See issues of Essence

Recipes from our great new cookbook [excerpts from The Good housekeeping illustrated cookbook] il *Good Housekeeping* 208:200-10+ My '89

Restaurants of the stars. il *Ladies' Home Journal* 106:184-6+ Ap '89

So there, Thomas Wolfe [cooking at home vs. dining out] B. Kafka. il *Gourmet* 49:60 S '89

Specialties of the house [recipes from celebrity hangouts] il *Redbook* 172:104-7+ Ja '89

COOKING—*cont.*

Stars in the kitchen. il *Redbook* 172:133-8 Mr '89
Summer fun [special section] L. Holderness. il *Better Homes and Gardens* 67:127-34+ Jl '89
Sunset's kitchen cabinet. See issues of Sunset (Central West edition)
TV dinners [recipes inspired by primetime shows] il *Ladies' Home Journal* 106:176-80 O '89
Updated classics. il *Gourmet* 49:78-80+ F '89
You asked for it. See issues of Gourmet

Anecdotes, facetiae, satire, etc.

Last word [excerpt from The eat a pet cookbook] R. Jones. por *Omni (New York, N.Y.)* 12:128 N '89

Beer

Brewing something different [beer in fish and game cookery] S. Bashline. il *Field & Stream* 94:54 N '89

Bibliography

See Cookbooks—Bibliography

Canned food

Just open a can of vegetables. il *Southern Living* 24:210 N '89
Quick! Start with soup. il *Southern Living* 24:172 S '89
Soup-er game recipes [canned soup] S. Bashline. il *Field & Stream* 93:24 Ja '89

Cereals

See Cooking—Grain

Cheese

See also
Cheesecake

Eichten's dairy is the big cheese. B. Freese. il *Successful Farming* 87:40-1 Je '89
Good old teleme: a classic western cheese comes around again. il *Sunset (Central West edition)* 182:164-6 Mr '89
Whey to go. C. Taylor. il *The Mother Earth News* 116:58-61 Mr/Ap '89

Chocolate

Chocolate [microwaving] A. Johnson. il *Parents* 64:159-60 F '89
Mystery ingredient? Cocoa. il *Sunset (Central West edition)* 183:178-9 N '89

Coconut

The coconut trail. R. Sokolov. il *Natural History* p82+ O '89

Coffee

Cooking with coffee. R. Sax. il *Gourmet* 49:84-5+ My '89

Competitions

Can America stomach it? [haggis competition] M. Starr. il *Newsweek* 114:86 O 30 '89

Convenience foods

See also
Cooking—Canned food
Cooking—Frozen food

Abby Mandel: pantry magic. il *Organic Gardening* 36:50 O '89
Come on over for take-out [serving chicken, Chinese, or Italian take-out food; special section] M. Krondl. il *McCall's* 116:81-2+ S '89
Instant dinners! [microwaving packaged foods] il *Good Housekeeping* 208:219-20 Je '89

Cornmeal

Cornmeal. J. Nash. il *Essence* 19:88 Ja '89
Good and polenta [David Burke's roast-garlic-and-sage polenta] B. Costikyan. il *New York* 22:56 Mr 13 '89

Dairy products

Fast dairy recipes. il *Successful Farming* 87:42-3 mid-Mr '89

Eggs

See also
Omelets

The egg-lover's guide to low-cholesterol breakfasts. J. B. Hurley. il *Prevention (Emmaus, Pa.)* 41:83-6+ Ap '89

Fish

See also
Chowder
Cooking—Shellfish
Stew

Brewing something different [beer in fish and game cookery] S. Bashline. il *Field & Stream* 94:54 N '89
Catfish: old favorite, new ways. S. Dosier. il *Southern Living* 24:92-3 Mr '89
Cod with broccoli sauce. il *Good Housekeeping* 208:168 Je '89
Cooking fish southern style. S. Bashline. il *Field & Stream* 93:50 Ap '89
Counter revolutionary [bluefish à la normande] B. Shacochis. il *Gentlemen's Quarterly* 59:482+ S '89
Farm ponds yield tasty meals. B. Freese. il *Successful Farming* 87:50-1 Ag '89
Farm-raised salmon is here. Try it with ginger, rosemary, mustard. il *Sunset (Central West edition)* 183:116 D '89
Fish casseroles. S. Bashline. il *Field & Stream* 94:40 My '89
Fish for the Fourth. S. Bashline. il *Field & Stream* 94:38 Jl '89
Fish in the microwave. S. Bashline. il *Field & Stream* 94:68 Ag '89
The fish market revolution continues. il *Sunset (Central West edition)* 182:84-9, 130+ F '89

Fresh and salt cod. il *Gourmet* 49:76-7+ F '89
Fresh fish dinners. il *Better Homes and Gardens* 67:166-7 My '89
Game and fish, Italian style. S. Bashline. il *Field & Stream* 94:36 S '89
Ginger bass, salsa trout . . . in the microwave. il *Sunset (Central West edition)* 183:90 Ag '89
The LHJ cooking school: poached salmon. il *Ladies' Home Journal* 106:196-7 O '89
Me and my fish fetish. N. Lemann. il *Esquire* 112:70+ S '89
Mild fish, pungent sauce [steamed fish with pork sauce] il *Sunset (Central West edition)* 183:174 N '89
North-country fish dinners. S. Bashline. il *Field & Stream* 94:24 Je '89
One-dish fish. C. Irwin. il *The Saturday Evening Post* 261:18-21 Ap '89
Salmon, simple and splendid. il *Glamour* 87:286 My '89
Sea pig on rye, please [charred raw tuna with wasabi and pickled onions] A. J. McClane. il *Esquire* 111:39-40 Je '89
Sole & salmon roulades. il *Good Housekeeping* 208:54 Mr '89
A sworded affair [swordfish steaks] A. J. McClane. il *Esquire* 111:50+ Ap '89
To cook a fish. N. Hauser. il *American Health* 8:114-17 Je '89
Tuna steaks that sizzle. il *Glamour* 87:332 S '89

Flowers

Delicious flowers. il *Redbook* 173:78-9+ Je '89
Edible complex. A. Viadero. il *Ms.* 18:66-7 Jl/Ag '89

Frozen food

Cold cuisine [frozen vegetables] N. Hauser. il *American Health* 8:94 N '89

Fruit

Apple polishing. M. Adams. il *The New York Times Magazine* p71-2 O 8 '89
Apple-time treats. il *Good Housekeeping* 209:172+ O '89
Apples [microwaving] C. Koury. il *Parents* 64:215-16+ O '89
Bring on the citrus! [grapefruit and oranges] il *Southern Living* 24:134 F '89
Celebrating the harvest . . . in Italy and the West [cover story] il *Sunset (Central West edition)* 183:73-82 S '89
Cherimoya: lumpy, costly, but the flavor turns some people rhapsodic. il *Sunset (Central West edition)* 182:186+ Ap '89
Cherry celebration. M. Gorman. il *Organic Gardening* 36:34-7 N '89
Diet dinners [tropical fruit] J. B. Hurley. il *Prevention (Emmaus, Pa.)* 41:76-8+ Ja '89
Entertaining from your garden: party recipes. il *Organic Gardening* 36:41-4 O '89
Farm-fresh means fantastic! B. Freese. il *Successful Farming* 87:50-1 My '89
For dessert or breakfast, hot or cold . . . fresh figs. il *Sunset (Central West edition)* 182:195 Je '89
Fruit cookbook. il *McCall's* 116:111-15+ Jl '89
Gastronomie sans argent [pears] il *Gourmet* 49:120-1+ O '89
Gastronomie sans argent [strawberries] il *Gourmet* 49:90-1+ My '89
Go wild! [blueberries] *Women's Sports & Fitness* 11:19 O '89
Grapefruit! It's not just for breakfast! il *Good Housekeeping* 209:134 Ag '89
It's the berries! S. La Rosa. il *McCall's* 116:79-80 Je '89
Liven the feast with these hearty treats [cranberry treats] il *National Geographic World* 171:15 N '89
Mad about melons! R. Haskell. il *Flower and Garden* 33:48-50+ My/Je '89
Marvelous mangoes. il *Good Housekeeping* 208:235 Je '89
Meet some exotic tropicals . . . canned or fresh. il *Sunset (Central West edition)* 182:152+ Mr '89
Melon ideas. il *Better Homes and Gardens* 67:117-18 Ag '89
Merry citrus. il *Sunset (Central West edition)* 183:128-30 D '89
Merry fruit compote. il *Good Housekeeping* 209:226 D '89
Microwave harvests. N. Hauser. il *American Health* 8:104 O '89
Not just desserts. il *Health (New York, N.Y.)* 21:80-3+ Ag '89
Plantains. il *Good Housekeeping* 208:161 Ap '89
Pomegranates. il *Gourmet* 49:122-3+ D '89
Raspberry treat. B. Rodriguez. il *Organic Gardening* 36:48 S '89
Something wondrous happens when you cook European plums. il *Sunset (Central West edition)* 183:112-15 S '89
Summer fruits [microwaving] C. Koury. il *Parents* 64:128+ Ag '89
Susan Feniger and Mary Sue Milliken: fruits to nuts [dried fruit] il *Organic Gardening* 36:50 O '89
Sweeten the season with blueberries. il *Southern Living* 24:150 Je '89
The thoroughly modern olive. R. Sokolov. il *Natural History* p102-4 Ap '89

COOKING—Fruit—*cont.*
Treat yourself to apples and pears [microwaved] il *Southern Living* 24:184 S '89

Game

An appetite for food and sport [privately owned hunting preserves] S. Dosier. il *Southern Living* 24:154+ O '89
Boise birds. il *Sunset (Central West edition)* 183:168+ O '89
Brewing something different [beer in fish and game cookery] S. Bashline. il *Field & Stream* 94:54 N '89
Game and fish, Italian style. S. Bashline. il *Field & Stream* 94:36 S '89
Hearty game stews. S. Bashline. il *Field & Stream* 93:52 F '89
High-tech game cookery [microwaving] S. Bashline. il *Field & Stream* 94:30 O '89
Pass the buck [venison] A. J. McClane. il *Esquire* 112:50+ D '89
Perfect venison. E. Cutlip. il *Outdoor Life* 184:68-9+ D '89
Pheasants are fantastic. B. Freese. il *Successful Farming* 87:58-9 N '89
Run, rabbit. A. J. McClane. il *Esquire* 111:40 F '89
She has kitchen in barn [chicken bake and venison stew] il *Successful Farming* 87:38 Ja '89
Soup-er game recipes [canned soup] S. Bashline. il *Field & Stream* 93:24 Ja '89
There's no meal like . . . game for the holidays. S. Bashline. il *Field & Stream* 94:38 D '89
Wild game under pressure. J. Weiss. il *Outdoor Life* 183:92-3+ Ap '89
"Wild" to traditional, beef to buffalo, boneless choices for a holiday roast. il *Sunset (Central West edition)* 181:128-9 D '88

Garnishes

From our kitchen to yours [vegetable garnishes] K. Adams. il *Southern Living* 24:191 Ap '89
Garnish with fresh flowers. il *Southern Living* 24:198 Mr '89

Grain

The birdseed that's good to eat [millet] il *Sunset (Central West edition)* 183:176-7 N '89
Eat oats; lower cholesterol. H. A. Dorrough. il *Southern Living* 24:160+ My '89
Healthy oat meals [bran] K. Haedrich. il *Country Journal* 16:85-8+ S/O '89
Oat bran cookbook. il *Ladies' Home Journal* 106:199-200+ Ap '89
Puttin' on the grits. B. Greene. il *Harper's Bazaar* 122:230+ Mr '89
Rice bran recipes to lower cholesterol. il *The Saturday Evening Post* 261:92-3 Jl/Ag '89
Toasting good health [bran muffins and breads] J. B. Hurley. il *Prevention (Emmaus, Pa.)* 41:67-70+ O '89
Wholegrains: old and new. B. T. Hunter. il *Consumers' Research Magazine* 72:8-9 O '89

Herbs and spices

See also
Curry
Chicken 'n' spice. M. Jaffrey. il *Gourmet* 49:64-5+ Mr '89
Farm girl taps ground beef with magic wand [using Spice 'n Slice] B. Freese. il *Successful Farming* 87:58-9 S '89
Five pounds of garlic, please [chicken with forty cloves of garlic] E. Sahatjian. il *Esquire* 112:56 O '89
For a yellow color [saffron] A. Arndt. il por *Americana* 17:34-7 S/O '89
Fresh ginger for pungent flavor. il *Southern Living* 24:127 Ja '89
From our kitchen to yours. K. Adams. il *Southern Living* 24:156 My '89
Herbs help transform turkey or pork roast. il *Sunset (Central West edition)* 182:174+ Mr '89
Seeding time. R. Schrambling. il *The New York Times Magazine* p63-4 O 22 '89
She has a crush on herbs. il *Southern Living* 24:110+ Ag '89
Spice up the New Year! S. C. Finn. il *New Choices for the Best Years* 29:62-5+ F '89
Winter warmth. S. H. Loomis. il *The New York Times Magazine* p35-6 Ja 15 '89

Honey

Honey, nature's sweetener. P. Y. Cordell. il *Southern Living* 24:74-6 O '89

Leftovers

Delicious for days: roasts and leftovers. C. Koury. il *Parents* 64:99-100+ Ja '89
Turkey transformed. il *Women's Sports & Fitness* 11:14 N/D '89
Turkey—the second time around. J. Nash. il *Essence* 20:81-7+ N '89

Liquors

More than a taste of alcohol [research by Evelyn A. Augustin] J. Raloff. *Science News* 136:318 N 11 '89
Sauced. B. Shacochis. il *Gentlemen's Quarterly* 59:95+ Jl '89
Spirited vegetables. S. Belsinger and C. Dille. il *Gourmet* 49:182+ Je '89

Meat

See also
Hamburgers
Hash
Stew
Butterflied leg of lamb. il *Good Housekeeping* 208:44 Ap '89
Crab-shell derivative retards rancidity [chitosan compound, NCMC, developed by John R. Vercellotti and Allen J. St. Angelo] J. Raloff. *Science News* 136:189 S 16 '89
Delicious for days: roasts and leftovers. C. Koury. il *Parents* 64:99-100+ Ja '89
Dining Miss F. [lamb] B. Shacochis. il *Gentlemen's Quarterly* 59:146+ My '89
Dress up ground beef. il *Southern Living* 24:154 My '89
Easy meals from your slow cooker [spiced beef brisket] il *Better Homes and Gardens* 67:136 Mr '89
Extra step takes fat from marbled beef [pot roast] il *Sunset (Central West edition)* 183:160 N '89
Farm girl taps ground beef with magic wand [using Spice 'n Slice] B. Freese. il *Successful Farming* 87:58-9 S '89
Fast! Delicious! Beef dinners [microwaving] *Good Housekeeping* 208:159-60 F '89
From our kitchen to yours [baked ham] K. Adams. *Southern Living* 24:118+ D '89
Gastronomie sans argent [pork tenderloin] il *Gourmet* 49:94-5+ Ap '89
Gastronomie sans argent: a ground roundup. il *Gourmet* 49:100-1+ S '89
Healthful beef and pork entrées. il *Better Homes and Gardens* 67:141-2 Jl '89
Here's the secret to tender pot roasts. il *Southern Living* 24:158-9 My '89
Lean pork on the barbecue . . . chops or tenderloin. il *Sunset (Central West edition)* 182:176 Ap '89
Marinated pork roast. il *Good Housekeeping* 209:226 S '89
Micro-cooking meat: five steps for success. *Better Homes and Gardens* 67:151 Ap '89
Perfect rack of lamb. il *Glamour* 87:288 O '89
Pork and beef: leaner than ever. il *Southern Living* 24:90-2 Ag '89
Quick cutlet cookbook. il *Redbook* 172:123-8 Ja '89
A regal rib-eye roast. il *Better Homes and Gardens* 67:134 Mr '89
Savvy ways with meat [microwaved] il *Southern Living* 24:206+ Mr '89
Special entrées for Easter. il *Southern Living* 24:196 Mr '89
Special veal entrées. il *Better Homes and Gardens* 67:145-6 Ap '89
Succulent, spicy grilled pork. il *Glamour* 87:272 Je '89
Veal chops supreme. il *Good Housekeeping* 209:144 N '89
"Wild" to traditional, beef to buffalo, boneless choices for a holiday roast. il *Sunset (Central West edition)* 181:128-9 D '88

Mushrooms

Mushroom mania [shiitake recipes] B. Freese. il *Successful Farming* 87:48-9 Ap '89
Stuffed mushrooms. il *Gourmet* 49:192 Mr '89
Wild about mushrooms. S. Payne. il *Southern Living* 24:188+ Mr '89

Nuts

Beyond nibbling: pistachios as appetizers, with fish, as tidbits. il *Sunset (Central West edition)* 183:118 Jl '89
Going nuts. M. Simmons. il *New Choices for the Best Years* 29:82-5 S '89
Nutted savories. il *Gourmet* 49:318 N '89
A passion for pine nuts. S. Sarvis. il *Gourmet* 49:118-19+ O '89
Susan Feniger and Mary Sue Milliken: fruits to nuts [dried fruit] il *Organic Gardening* 36:50 O '89

Pasta

Eat thin! [excerpts from Weight Watchers quick success program cookbook] il *Redbook* 172:63-9+ F '89
Entertain with a light pasta bar. H. A. Dorrough. il *Southern Living* 24:168+ O '89
Four-star fettuccine! il *Good Housekeeping* 208:136 F '89
Light & luscious [fruit salad and pasta stuffed tomatoes] J. Nash. il *Essence* 20:76 Jl '89
Pasta main dishes [microwaving] il *McCall's* 116:139-40 Mr '89
Pasta presto. A. Johnson. il *Parents* 64:175-7 Mr '89
Pasta pronto! il *Ladies' Home Journal* 106:150-2+ F '89
Primavera hints of spring. il *Southern Living* 24:155 My '89
Recipe of the week [cheesy meatball lasagne] il *Jet* 75:46 F 6 '89
Seafood and pasta in parchment is effortless? All it takes is a good sense of timing. il *Sunset (Central West edition)* 182:192-3 Ap '89

Potatoes

Cutting edge [tracing origin of seafood and crisped potatoes] B. Miller and P. Franey. il *The New York Times Magazine* p43-4 Jl 16 '89
Dig in! B. Rodriguez. il *Organic Gardening* 36:38-40 Je '89
Do the mash. J. Steingarten. il *House & Garden* 161:42+ Ja '89

COOKING—Potatoes—*cont.*

Eat thin! [excerpts from Weight Watchers quick success program cookbook] il *Redbook* 172:63-9+ F '89

For potato lovers only [microwaving] il *Good Housekeeping* 209:209-10 O '89

The potato queen [R. Gjelsness] D. Blank. il por *Successful Farming* 87:64-5 O '89

Potato slivers or potatoes with apples or pesto. il *Sunset (Central West edition)* 182:116 Ja '89

Well-dressed potatoes. il *The Saturday Evening Post* 261:18-21 Ja/F '89

Poultry

See also
Thanksgiving dinners

The 10 winners! America's all-time favorite chicken dinners. J. Stern and M. Stern. il *Redbook* 172:137-42+ Ap '89

Chicken à la zing. M. Simmons. il *New Choices for the Best Years* 29:76-9 O '89

Chicken chinoise. il *Good Housekeeping* 208:230 My '89

Chicken cutlets: quick and elegant. il *Ladies' Home Journal* 106:158-60+ Mr '89

Chicken en papillote. il *Good Housekeeping* 208:34 Je '89

Chicken: ever changing, always good. S. Dosier. il *Southern Living* 24:182-4 Ap '89

Chicken 'n' spice. M. Jaffrey. il *Gourmet* 49:64-5+ Mr '89

Christmas cookbook. il *Good Housekeeping* 209:199-200+ D '89

Cornmeal. J. Nash. il *Essence* 19:88 Ja '89

Dinner-party entrée [Cornish hens] il *Better Homes and Gardens* 67:174 N '89

Easy-does-it chicken [microwave] A. Johnson. il *Parents* 64:189-90+ My '89

Fancy turkey roll. il *Southern Living* 24:112 D '89

Festive chicken [low calorie] il *Good Housekeeping* 209:105 D '89

Five pounds of garlic, please [chicken with forty cloves of garlic] E. Sahatjian. il *Esquire* 112:56 O '89

Game hens, ablaze with flavor [Mexican cooking] il *Glamour* 87:190 Jl '89

Going to stuff a goose? Try this cabbage-apple stuffing. il *Sunset (Central West edition)* 182:150 F '89

Home-style chicken cookbook. il *McCall's* 116:119-24 Ap '89

The LHJ cooking school: roast chicken. J. T. Hazard. il *Ladies' Home Journal* 106:193 O '89

Martha Stewart's fabulous orange-flavored fried chicken [excerpt from Martha Stewart's Quick cook menus] M. Stewart. il *Redbook* 172:20 Ja '89

Micro-way: quick chicken suppers. il *McCall's* 117:179 O '89

Microwave poultry. il *Better Homes and Gardens* 67:153-4 Je '89

Munchable "drumsticks" or quick scaloppine . . . with turkey parts. il *Sunset (Central West edition)* 182:196 My '89

Quick & easy: light chicken 'n' rice dishes. il *McCall's* 116:133 S '89

Quick! Bake some chicken. il *Southern Living* 24:136 Ja '89

Quick cutlet cookbook. il *Redbook* 172:123-8 Ja '89

Roast chicken with tzimmes stuffing [Passover dish] il *Good Housekeeping* 208:32 Ap '89

Roasting your goose. il *Country Journal* 16:78 N/D '89

Serves one [chicken dish] R. Sax. *Working Woman* 14:109 Jl '89

She has kitchen in barn [chicken bake and venison stew] il *Successful Farming* 87:38 Ja '89

Simply superb roast chicken. il *Glamour* 87:358 Ap '89

Tribute to turkey. M. Evans. il *The Saturday Evening Post* 261:18-20 N/D '89

Turkey breast, fast and flavorful [microwaved] il *Southern Living* 24:200-1 N '89

Turkey cutlets. il *Good Housekeeping* 209:52 Ag '89

Turkey-roasting guide. il *Better Homes and Gardens* 67:164 N '89

Turkey topics. il *Parents* 64:180+ N '89

Turkey transformed. il *Women's Sports & Fitness* 11:14 N/D '89

Turkey—the second time around. J. Nash. il *Essence* 20:81-7+ N '89

What's cookin'? Chicken! C. Lyons. il *Ebony* 44:108-10+ Mr '89

Rhubarb

For lively salsa or tender coffee cake . . . it's rhubarb time. il *Sunset (Central West edition)* 182:168 Mr '89

Rice

Bean there [red beans and rice] B. Shacochis. il *Gentlemen's Quarterly* 59:316+ Ap '89

A family dinner with Alice Waters and Paul Bertolli [wild mushroom risotto] M. Damsker. il pors *Organic Gardening* 36:46-9 O '89

Nutty and nice! [rice pilaf supreme] J. Taylor. il *Better Homes and Gardens* 67:150 O '89

Prizewinning holiday dishes. J. Nash. il *Essence* 20:94+ D '89

Quick & easy: light chicken 'n' rice dishes. il *McCall's* 116:133 S '89

Risotto! il *Seventeen* 48:216+ Ap '89

Sausage

Sage, sausage, and spinach [pie] il *Sunset (Central West edition)* 181:126 D '88

Seafood

See also
Chowder
Clambakes
Cooking—Fish
Cooking—Shellfish

Beyond expectations [English dishes] R. Schrambling. il *The New York Times Magazine* p67-8 D 17 '89

Beyond the burrito [Mexican] S. H. Loomis. il *The New York Times Magazine* p47-8 S 3 '89

Cutting edge [tracing origin of seafood and crisped potatoes] B. Miller and P. Franey. il *The New York Times Magazine* p43-4 Jl 16 '89

Entrées from the deep. K. Haedrich. il *Country Journal* 16:91-3 My/Je '89

Fruits de mer [seafood preparation in France] F. Levy. il *Gourmet* 49:60-1+ Jl '89

His cioppino starts with the daily catch in Avila Beach. il *Sunset (Central West edition)* 182:102 Ja '89

On a visit to Venice, Jeffrey Steingarten learns the mysteries of the deep from an undisputed master of Adriatic seafood, Marcella Hazan. J. Steingarten. il por *Vogue* 179:250+ Ag '89

Prize catch [excerpts from The great American seafood cookbook] S. H. Loomis. il *Ladies' Home Journal* 106:166-8+ Ap '89

The scalloping gourmet. B. Shacochis. il *Gentlemen's Quarterly* 59:274+ Je '89

Seafood [microwaving] A. Johnson. il *Parents* 64:195+ Je '89

Seafood grill. il *Good Housekeeping* 209:100 Jl '89

Seeds

Seeding time. R. Schrambling. il *The New York Times Magazine* p63-4 O 22 '89

Small talk about poppy seeds. il *Good Housekeeping* 208:148 Ap '89

Shellfish

See also
Chowder
Clambakes

Chesapeake bounty [crab and clams] R. Coyle. il *The New York Times Magazine* p59-60 Je 25 '89

A Chesapeake seafood sampler. il *Southern Living* 24:96+ Ag '89

Crab cakes rémoulade. il *Good Housekeeping* 209:80 Ag '89

The LHJ cooking school: shrimp scampi. il *Ladies' Home Journal* 106:199 O '89

Minute shrimp [boiling time required to reduce risk of listeriosis] D. Blumenthal. il *FDA Consumer* 23:29-30 My '89

Oysters year-round. J. Taylor. il *Better Homes and Gardens* 67:138 Mr '89

Seafood and pasta in parchment is effortless? All it takes is a good sense of timing. il *Sunset (Central West edition)* 182:192-3 Ap '89

Shellfish spectacular [barbecuing] il *Sunset (Central West edition)* 183:70-1 Jl '89

Shellfish treasures from the sea. H. A. Dorrough. il *Southern Living* 24:186+ Ap '89

Shrimp and champagne supper. il *Glamour* 87:234 D '89

Sizzling shrimp. il *Sunset (Central West edition)* 183:159 S '89

Anecdotes, facetiae, satire, etc.

Mr. Egan and my drowned lobsters. R. K. Bryant. il *Gourmet* 49:196+ My '89

Sorghum syrup

Sweet sorghum! il *Successful Farming* 87:32 F '89

Soybean products

Great-tasting soybeans. il *Successful Farming* 87 no4:50-1 Mr '89

Spices

See Cooking—Herbs and spices

Study and teaching

See also
École de Gastronomie Française Ritz-Escoffier
New England Culinary Institute
Thai Cooking School (Bangkok, Thailand)

The cooks who can't be fired [restaurants at U.S. cooking schools] J. D. Reed. il *Time* 133:99-100 My 8 '89

A day at Cordon Bleu or two other Paris cooking schools. il *Sunset (Central West edition)* 182:89 Ap '89

Testing

Test cases [getting a family to eat what you cook] A. Ward. il *The New York Times Magazine* p49-50 Ag 13 '89

Vegetables

See also
Ratatouille
Vegetarianism

30-minute main dish [couscous- and shrimp-stuffed zucchini; low wattage microwaving] il *Better Homes and Gardens* 67:101 Ja '89

About beets. S. Pacher. il *The Mother Earth News* 117:32-4+ My/Je '89

COOKING—Vegetables—cont.

Accent vegetables with an easy sauce [asparagus and broccoli] il *Southern Living* 24:202 N '89

The age of asparagus [asparagus frittata] E. Sahatjian. il *Esquire* 111:36 My '89

Ah . . . fresh asparagus! il *Good Housekeeping* 208:164-5 Ap '89

Ah, vegetables! il *Good Housekeeping* 209:182+ O '89

All about eggplant. il *Good Housekeeping* 209:130 Ag '89

Amaizing corn. S. S. Lang. il *American Health* 8:94-6+ O '89

And so to bed [building dishes on beds of vegetables] L. Land. il *The New York Times Magazine* p59-60 Ap 23 '89

Artichokes. J. Del Valle. il *Gourmet* 49:92-3+ Ap '89

Asparagus ideas. il *Better Homes and Gardens* 67:145-6 Ap '89

Back to our roots. J. Nash. il *Essence* 19:85-7+ Ja '89

Bean there [red beans and rice] B. Shacochis. il *Gentlemen's Quarterly* 59:316+ Ap '89

Bottom of the barrel supper. R. Haskell. il *Flower and Garden* 33:98-100+ Ja/F '89

Bring on the beans. P. Perry. il *The Saturday Evening Post* 261:96+ Ap '89

Broccoli: a vegetable superstar [microwaving] J. B. Hurley. il *Prevention (Emmaus, Pa.)* 41:92-3 Ap '89

Broccoli rabe. J. Coppola. il *Gourmet* 49:156+ Je '89

Cabbage! il *Good Housekeeping* 208:168 Mr '89

Cabbage surprise. il *Good Housekeeping* 208:68 Ap '89

Celebrating the harvest . . . in Italy and the West [cover story] il *Sunset (Central West edition)* 183:73-82 S '89

Chilies. B. Karoff. il *Gourmet* 49:114-17+ O '89

Cold cuisine [frozen vegetables] N. Hauser. il *American Health* 8:94 N '89

The dooryard garden [cover story] il *Flower and Garden* 33:35-7+ S/O '89

Dried bean cookery. A. Hirsch. il *Organic Gardening* 36:35 F '89

Entertaining from your garden: party recipes. il *Organic Gardening* 36:41-4 O '89

Farm-fresh means fantastic! B. Freese. il *Successful Farming* 87:50-1 My '89

Fresh off the cob [corn] M. Gorman. il *Organic Gardening* 36:54-6+ Ap '89

Fresh vegetables, simple dining. S. Dosier. il *Southern Living* 24:88-9 My '89

Garden of vegetable delights. F. Fabricant. il *Modern Maturity* 32:66-8+ Ag/S '89

Gastronomie sans argent [tomatoes] il *Gourmet* 49:66-7+ Ag '89

Golden tomato fritters from an Amish kitchen [excerpt from Cooking from quilt country] M. Adams. il *Redbook* 173:36 Je '89

Good-for-you legumes. il *Southern Living* 24:132+ Ja '89

Great greens. C. Koury. il *Parents* 64:180-2+ My '89

Great side dishes. il *McCall's* 117:161-5+ O '89

Hot stuff. R. Schrambling. il *The New York Times Magazine* p39-40 Jl 23 '89

Hurry-up vegetables [microwaved] *Good Housekeeping* 209:238 N '89

It's corn-shucking time! D. G. Lowery. il *Southern Living* 24:148-9 Je '89

Just open a can of vegetables. il *Southern Living* 24:210 N '89

Leaves upon leaves [dishes using cabbage, lettuce, or mustard greens] il *Sunset (Central West edition)* 182:182 Ap '89

Light & luscious [fruit salad and pasta stuffed tomatoes] J. Nash. il *Essence* 20:76 Jl '89

Light ways with summer vegetables. H. A. Dorrough. il *Southern Living* 24:60-2 Jl '89

Looking for a vegetable dish? il *Sunset (Central West edition)* 183:142 D '89

Meatless main dishes. il *Better Homes and Gardens* 68:143-4 F '89

The microwave at Thanksgiving. il *Gourmet* 49:126-7+ N '89

Microwave cookbook for summer-fresh vegetables. B. Goldman. il *Better Homes and Gardens* 67:95-100+ Ag '89

Microwave harvests [winter squash] N. Hauser. il *American Health* 8:104 O '89

Microwave side dishes. il *Better Homes and Gardens* 67:141-2 Mr '89

New ideas for squash. il *Southern Living* 24:160 Je '89

Not Mom's beans [gigandes] R. Schrambling. il *Esquire* 112:20 Jl '89

The not-so-humble cabbage. R. Haskell. il *Flower and Garden* 33:34-6 N/D '89

Offbeat veggies. M. Simmons. il *New Choices for the Best Years* 29:68-72 Ja '89

Olive oil flatters vegetables. il *Southern Living* 24:130 Jl '89

Peppers pack a rainbow of colors. S. Payne. il *Southern Living* 24:102-3 My '89

Pick of the crop. il *Redbook* 173:73-6+ Ag '89

Pint-size pumpkins. il *Sunset (Central West edition)* 183:86-7 N '89

Pumpkin-a-go-go! il *Seventeen* 48:143 N '89

Ratatouille, casserole, salad . . . the secret is blending vegetables. il *Sunset (Central West edition)* 182:206 Je '89

Red-hot peppers. H. Hylton. il *New Choices for the Best Years* 29:76-8+ Mr '89

A rich fat-free puree [microwaving butternut squash] J. B. Hurley. *Prevention (Emmaus, Pa.)* 41:118 N '89

The right stuff. J. R. Nyenhuis. il *The Saturday Evening Post* 261:106+ Ja/F '89

Roasted sweet peppers. il *Better Homes and Gardens* 67:145 Mr '89

Savory grilled vegetables [low calorie] il *McCall's* 116:126 Jl '89

Side dishes. A. Johnson. il *Parents* 64:113-15 Ja '89

Side dishes to please. il *Southern Living* 24:104-5 D '89

The simple goodness of tomatoes. il *Southern Living* 24:176 S '89

A small squash, but big on flavor! [yellow squash] W. E. Wooldridge. il *Flower and Garden* 33:73 My/Je '89

Speedy side dishes [microwaved] J. Galton. il *Parents* 64:199+ D '89

Spirited vegetables. S. Belsinger and C. Dille. il *Gourmet* 49:182+ Je '89

Spring's best vegetables. il *Glamour* 87:288 My '89

Spruce up your menu with cabbage. il *Southern Living* 24:208 N '89

Square, gassed tomatoes and other modern myths. R. Sokolov. il *Natural History* p70-2 Jl '89

St. Pat's cabbage [mirowaving] J. B. Hurley. il *Prevention (Emmaus, Pa.)* 41:80 Mr '89

Taming the bitter greens [chicory family] il *Sunset (Central West edition)* 182:104-5 Mr '89

The tastiest new ways with summer vegetables. il *Redbook* 173:69-72 Ag '89

Tasty ideas for turnips. il *Southern Living* 24:177 O '89

These black-eyed peas are Californians and fresh. il *Sunset (Central West edition)* 183:124+ Jl '89

The tomato explosion. il *Sunset (Central West edition)* 183:56-7 Ag '89

Uppity beans [dried beans] J. Pruess. il *The New York Times Magazine* p107-8 N 19 '89

Variety showcase. J. B. Hurley. il *Organic Gardening* 36:54-6 Ja '89

Vegetable casseroles. il *Better Homes and Gardens* 67:159-60 S '89

Vegetable casseroles for wholesome summer meals. il *Sunset (Central West edition)* 183:114+ Jl '89

Vegetable cookbook. il *Good Housekeeping* 209:110-20+ Ag '89

Vegetable strudel. il *Good Housekeeping* 208:88 Mr '89

Vegetables [microwaving] C. Koury and A. Johnson. il *Parents* 64:144+ Jl '89

Vegetating [Italian cooking] J. Barrett. il *The New York Times Magazine* p65-6 Je 4 '89

The well-traveled tomato. R. Sokolov. il *Natural History* p84-8 Je '89

We're all ears [corn] C. Idone. il *The New York Times Magazine* p63-4 Jl 9 '89

Winter warmth. S. H. Loomis. il *The New York Times Magazine* p35-6 Ja 15 '89

Vinegar

Acid angles. B. Miller and P. Franey. il *The New York Times Magazine* p67-8 Ag 20 '89

Wine

Whetting the appetite [cooking with champagne] B. Miller and P. Franey. il *The New York Times Magazine* p53-4 Ap 16 '89

COOKING, AMERICAN
See also
Barbecue cooking
Cooking, Black
Cooking, Tex-Mex

The 10 winners! America's all-time favorite chicken dinners. J. Stern and M. Stern. il *Redbook* 172:137-42+ Ap '89

Better-than ever good home cooking. L. Holderness. il *Better Homes and Gardens* 67:115-22+ Ap '89

Block Island. G. Trotta. il map *Gourmet* 49:76-81+ My '89

Bluegrass flavor [Kentucky cooking] R. Schrambling. il *The New York Times Magazine* p39-40 My 28 '89

Charleston. M. Elder. il *Gourmet* 49:68-73+ Ap '89

Coastal legacy [South Carolina Low Country cuisine] N. H. Jenkins. il *The New York Times Magazine* p39-40 Ja 22 '89

Come 'n' get it [ranch cooking] R. Coyle. il *The New York Times Magazine* p53-4 Ag 6 '89

Concerning food and wine [southwestern cuisine] R. L. Balzer. il *Travel Holiday* 171:20+ Ap '89

Cooking fish southern style. S. Bashline. il *Field & Stream* 93:50 Ap '89

Coyote cuisine [southwestern cooking] J. Steingarten. il *Vogue* 179:196-7+ Jl '89

A day for Old Glories [Fourth of July] L. Wells. il *The New York Times Magazine* p30-2 Jl 2 '89

Dinner of the decade. D. C. Craig. il *Life* 12:107-8+ Fall '89

Down-home hospitality. il *Redbook* 174:104-7+ N '89

COOKING, AMERICAN—*cont.*

Extra Ordinary [B. and C. Clark's Randall's Ordinary in North Stonington, Conn.] P. Mandell. il pors map *Americana* 17:26-31+ Mr/Ap '89

Feast on grandma's cookin'. D. A. Campbell. il *Southern Living* 24:148-50 O '89

The fire's always burning at Randall's Ordinary, a Revolutionary inn in Connecticut [proprietors B. and C. Clark] N. Geeslin. il pors *People Weekly* 32:143-4 N 13 '89

Folk art, friends and good food [home of A. Julian; excerpt from Mary Emmerling's American country cooking] M. E. Emmerling. il *Working Woman* 14:100-2 Ja '89

Food journal: July [special section] il *Ladies' Home Journal* 106:135-8+ Jl '89

From the heartland [midwestern cooking] C. Bushnell. il *Health (New York, N.Y.)* 21:62-5+ Jl '89

Going haute in the heartland. J. F. Siler. il *Business Week* p80 Ag 7 '89

Gourmet holidays: Santa Fe [southwestern cooking] Z. E. Zakroff. il *Gourmet* 49:86-93+ D '89

Lost in America [regional cooking] L. Wells. il *The New York Times Magazine* p115-16 D 3 '89

Mackinac Island [Grand Hotel] M. Elder. il maps *Gourmet* 49:70-5+ Je '89

New England fancy. N. H. Jenkins. il *The New York Times Magazine* p65-6 Ap 2 '89

Pacific Provençal: a food pro at home [K. Malody] S. H. Loomis. il pors *Working Woman* 14:112-16 Mr '89

Point Reyes. L. Alexander. il *Gourmet* 49:100-7+ D '89

Seattle crew. B. H. Fussell. il *The New York Times Magazine* p57-8 Ap 9 '89

Sonoma County: fresh from the farm. C. Bates. il map *Gourmet* 49:86-91+ S '89

A southern tree-trimming party. il *Gourmet* 49:132-4+ D '89

Southwest tastes. J. F. Mariani. il *Motor Boating & Sailing* 164:34-5 O '89

Steve Langlois is out to prove that haute cuisine and oat cuisine are not the same in the Midwest [executive chef at Prairie in Chicago, Ill.] D. Chu. il pors *People Weekly* 32:143-4 N 27 '89

Tucson. S. Wilding. il *Gourmet* 49:44-51+ Ja '89

Vulgar recipes [excerpt from Simple cooking] J. Thorne. *Harper's* 279:32+ N '89

What's cooking on the Coast? B. Palling. il *Vogue* 179:416+ Mr '89

COOKING, AMISH

Country kitchen [blueberry custard and Amish sugar-cream pie] M. Adams. il por *McCall's* 116:104 Ag '89

Golden tomato fritters from an Amish kitchen [excerpt from Cooking from quilt country] M. Adams. il *Redbook* 173:36 Je '89

COOKING, ASIAN

Bright chefs, big City [recipes of M. Milliken and S. Feniger, owners of City] S. Carlton. il pors *Health (New York, N.Y.)* 21:78-81 F '89

China trade. E. Y.-F. Lo. il *The New York Times Magazine* p117-18 Je 11 '89

COOKING, AUSTRALIAN

Gourmet holidays: islands off the Great Barrier Reef. P. J. Wade and K. Wade. il map *Gourmet* 49:46-51+ Mr '89

COOKING, BASQUE

Basque in it. S. H. Loomis. il *The New York Times Magazine* p83-4 N 26 '89

COOKING, BELGIAN

Gourmet holidays: Brussels. A. M. Zwack. il map *Gourmet* 49:72-9+ S '89

COOKING, BLACK

Food with thought [chef E. Lewis] J. Gruder. il por *Harper's Bazaar* 122:116-17 O '89

The new soul food. C. Lyons. il *Ebony* 44:108-10+ F '89

COOKING, BRAZILIAN

Rio! From companheiros . . . to cariocas. F. Ferretti. il *Gourmet* 49:94+ N '89

The trail of oil [use of dende oil in Bahian cooking] R. Sokolov. il *Natural History* p82-5 My '89

COOKING, BURMESE

Ginger salad, noodle salad, spiced vegetable soup . . . these are Burmese surprises. il *Sunset (Central West edition)* 181:138+ D '88

COOKING, CAJUN

Quick Cajun from K-Paul's. il *Ladies' Home Journal* 106:140-2+ Jl '89

Anecdotes, facetiae, satire, etc.

How to stew swags Cajun style. E. Zern. il *Field & Stream* 93:193 Ap '89

COOKING, CARIBBEAN

Island hopping. M. Evans. il *The New York Times Magazine* p55-6 F 26 '89

COOKING, CAUCASUS

Cookery of the Caucasus. A. W. Salmon. il *Gourmet* 49:132+ O '89

COOKING, CHINESE

Beyond egg roll: great Chinese food [Chinese American restaurants] il *Glamour* 87:293 O '89

China trade. E. Y.-F. Lo. il *The New York Times Magazine* p117-18 Je 11 '89

Chinese lessons. N. Simonds. il *American Health* 8:114-16+ S '89

Chinese peanut-chicken & noodles. il *Redbook* 172:20 F '89

Everyday dinners with an Italian, Greek or Chinese twist [excerpt from The frugal gourmet cooks three ancient cuisines] J. Smith. il *Redbook* 173:144-9+ S '89

Golden gates [chef B. Tropp of San Francisco's China Moon Cafe] S. H. Loomis. il *The New York Times Magazine* p49-50 F 12 '89

In Sichuan, mild tofu meets aggressive seasoning [hot and sour tofu soup] il *Sunset (Central West edition)* 182:202+ Ap '89

Leaner-than-ever Chinese cuisine [recipes of D. Keh, owner of David K's] T. Ney. il por *Prevention (Emmaus, Pa.)* 41:75-8+ F '89

Taipei. F. Ferretti. il map *Gourmet* 49:80-5+ Ap '89

The world's healthiest diet [Chinese diet and disease patterns; research by T. C. Campbell] S. S. Lang. il map *American Health* 8:105-7+ S '89

Anecdotes, facetiae, satire, etc.

The Chinese syndrome. D. Blum. il *New York* 22:42 O 23 '89

COOKING, COLOMBIAN

The coconut trail. R. Sokolov. il *Natural History* p82+ O '89

COOKING, CREOLE

Mardi Gras style [dinner party] J. Nash. il *Essence* 19:89-92+ F '89

Summer brunch New Orleans style. R. F. Guste. il *New Choices for the Best Years* 29:64-7 Jl '89

COOKING, CRUCIAN

Seafood paradise. J. Nash. il *Essence* 19:92-3+ Ap '89

COOKING, DUTCH

Beyond tulips and windmills. R. L. Balzer. il *Travel Holiday* 171:22-5 Ja '89

Gourmet holidays: Amsterdam. I. Keown. il *Gourmet* 49:74-9+ Ap '89

COOKING, ENGLISH

See also
Savories
Yorkshire pudding

Beyond expectations [seafood dishes] R. Schrambling. il *The New York Times Magazine* p67-8 D 17 '89

British days, Bulgarian nights [Digby Anderson's Book of imperative cooking] N. Hazelton. *National Review* 41:55-6 F 24 '89

Anecdotes, facetiae, satire, etc.

Dead and breakfast. J. Queenan. *The New Republic* 200:12+ Mr 20 '89

COOKING, FINNISH

Queen's cake . . . treasured recipe from old Finland. il *Sunset (Central West edition)* 183:100 Ag '89

COOKING, FRENCH

See also
Cassoulet
Crêpes
École de Gastronomie Française Ritz-Escoffier
Ratatouille

Bastille Day dinners. il *Gourmet* 49:76-82+ Jl '89

Christmas in Provence. E. Jones. il *Gourmet* 49:108-9+ D '89

Fruits de mer [seafood preparation in France] F. Levy. il *Gourmet* 49:60-1+ Jl '89

Gastronomie sans argent [salades françaises] il *Gourmet* 49:62-3+ Jl '89

Gourmet holidays: a corner of Provence. D. Beal. il map *Gourmet* 49:44-9+ Jl '89

The incredible lightness of cooking [New England Culinary Institute] R. A. Barnett. il *American Health* 8:126-8+ Mr '89

The inns of Alsace. J. Lubarsky. il map *Travel Holiday* 171:48-54 Ja '89

Let them eat brie! Bastille Day picnic. il *Seventeen* 48:106-9 Jl '89

Moustiers. T. Weeks. il map *Gourmet* 49:96-101+ O '89

New French fare: vive la revolution. P. Farrell. il *Business Week* p110 Je 12 '89

Pie to cry for [Alsatian onion tart] E. Sahatjian. il *Esquire* 111:28 Ja '89

Un pique-nique sur mer [cover story] il *Gourmet* 49:64-6+ Jl '89

The quest for a true choucroute leads Jeffrey Steingarten from the inns of Alsace to the meat markets of Harlem. J. Steingarten. il *Vogue* 179:336+ N '89

Rising to the top [D. Ponzek's French cuisine at Montrachet] B. Miller and P. Franey. il *The New York Times Magazine* p69-70 F 19 '89

Steaming the French way. G. Usher. il *Gourmet* 49:142+ N '89

Sunday best [dinners in France] P. Wells. il *The New York Times Magazine* p87-8 D 10 '89

Vence. D. Beal. il map *Gourmet* 49:86-91+ Ap '89

Vermont French light [recipes from the New England Culinary Institute] R. Barral. il *American Health* 8:140+ Mr '89

Vive la France—and her cuisine. P. Wells. il *Travel Holiday* 172:48-57 Jl '89

COOKING, FRENCH—*cont.*
Workman storms the culinary Bastille [P. Well's Bistro cooking] M. Simson. *Publishers Weekly* 236:44 S 8 '89

COOKING, GEORGIAN
Georgia on my mind [hospitality of Tbilisi] M. Burros. il *The New York Times Magazine* p41-2 F 5 '89

COOKING, GERMAN
Germany's Fairy-tale Road. S. Wilding and A. Del Balso. il map *Gourmet* 49:52-5+ Mr '89
Gourmet holidays: Lake Constance. L. Langseth-Christensen. il map *Gourmet* 49:60-5+ Je '89
New Year's in Munich. L. Langseth-Christensen. il *Gourmet* 49:42-3+ Ja '89

COOKING, GREEK
Dinner with Demosthenes [research by A. Dalby] S. J. Evans. il *History Today* 39:3-4 Ja '89
Everyday dinners with an Italian, Greek or Chinese twist [excerpt from The frugal gourmet cooks three ancient cuisines] J. Smith. il *Redbook* 173:144-9+ S '89

COOKING, GUATEMALAN
Of false tongues and Sunday bread. M. L. Milici. il *Américas* 41 no1:58-9 '89

COOKING, HAWAIIAN
Pupu party. il *Sunset (Central West edition)* 183:62-4, 106 Ag '89

COOKING, INDIAN (EAST INDIAN)
Chats? il *Sunset (Central West edition)* 182:186+ My '89
Essence of India. il *Seventeen* 48:158-61+ O '89

COOKING, INDONESIAN
See also
Rijsttafel

COOKING, INTERNATIONAL
Eating ethnic and lean [tips for eating out; excerpt from International cuisines calorie counter] D. Webb. il *Health (New York, N.Y.)* 21:46+ N '89
Free-trade cuisine. B. Miller and P. Franey. il *The New York Times Magazine* p89-90 S 10 '89
Light food [views of M. R. Shulman] L. Troiano. il *American Health* 8:147-8 Ap '89

COOKING, ITALIAN
Americans' quest for la dolce vita continues. il *Vogue* 179:610 S '89
Backyard barbecue Italian style. J. W. Wilson. il *New Choices for the Best Years* 29:64-9 Ag '89
Battling Spaghetti O taste buds [M. Hazan] C. Booth. il por *Time* 133:88-9 My 29 '89
Best ever Italian cookbook. il *McCall's* 116:113-17+ Mr '89
Celebrating the harvest . . . in Italy and the West [cover story] il *Sunset (Central West edition)* 183:73-82 S '89
Cucina fresca. M. Simmons. il *Working Woman* 14:96-8 Jl '89
Culinary crossroads [recipes of M. Chiarello from Tra Vigne in Saint Helena, Calif.] D. Welch. il por *Health (New York, N.Y.)* 21:74-9+ Ap '89
Dinner Italian style. il *Gourmet* 49:102-4+ S '89
"Everybody likes Italian food". J. F. Mariani. il *American Heritage* 40:122-31 D '89
Everyday dinners with an Italian, Greek or Chinese twist [excerpt from The frugal gourmet cooks three ancient cuisines] J. Smith. il *Redbook* 173:144-9+ S '89
First things first [leak and rice soup and Tuscan vegetable soup] N. Hazelton. *National Review* 41:54-5 N 24 '89
Game and fish, Italian style. S. Bashline. il *Field & Stream* 94:36 S '89
Hail, Cesare! [chef and restaurant owner C. Giaccone of Dei Cacciatore] J. Steingarten. il por *Vogue* 179:600-1+ S '89
Holiday-spanning bread [panettone] C. Kummer. il *The Atlantic* 263:84+ Mr '89
Into the woods [hunting white truffles in the Piedmont, Italy] J. Steingarten. il *House & Garden* 161:50+ F '89
Let's eat Italian! il *Good Housekeeping* 209:206-16+ S '89
Liguria. J. M. Taylor. il *The New York Times Magazine* p41-2 Ag 27 '89
Medici culinary Renaissance comes to Fawcett. il *Publishers Weekly* 236:43-4 S 8 '89
On a visit to Venice, Jeffrey Steingarten learns the mysteries of the deep from an undisputed master of Adriatic seafood, Marcella Hazan. J. Steingarten. il por *Vogue* 179:250+ Ag '89
Pasta to chicken to apricot tart . . . it's a three-course dinner from the Italian Riviera. il *Sunset (Central West edition)* 182:138-40 F '89
Pure and simple. R. Schrambling. il *The New York Times Magazine* p65-6 Mr 19 '89
A taste of Sicily: the gardens of paradise. M. T. Simeti. il *Gourmet* 49:98-9+ S '89
Vegetating. J. Barrett. il *The New York Times Magazine* p65-6 Je 4 '89

COOKING, JAPANESE
See also
Benihana National Corporation
Surimi
Sushi
Fugu, taxis, and Tender Buttons. H. Bridges. il *Gourmet* 49:48+ S '89

COOKING, JEWISH
See also
Latkes
Roast chicken with tzimmes stuffing [Passover dish] il *Good Housekeeping* 208:32 Ap '89

COOKING, MAYA
Of false tongues and Sunday bread. M. L. Milici. il *Américas* 41 no1:58-9 '89

COOKING, MEDITERRANEAN
Cool cooking: Mediterranean-style. J. T. Hazard. il *Ladies' Home Journal* 106:152-4+ Ag '89
Our high-energy diet for busy bodies [Wise woman's diet] il *Redbook* 173:115-19+ O '89
Sunny summer salads a la heart. J. B. Hurley. il *Prevention (Emmaus, Pa.)* 41:68-72+ Je '89

COOKING, MEXICAN
See also
Chili
Cooking, Tex-Mex
Gorditas
Tacos
Tamales
Tortillas
Before the Conquest. R. Sokolov. il *Natural History* p76-9 Ag '89
Beyond combination plates [work of D. Kennedy] L. Shapiro. il por *Newsweek* 114:105 N 13 '89
Beyond the burrito [seafood] S. H. Loomis. il *The New York Times Magazine* p47-8 S 3 '89
A celebration of Mexican tastes. M. A. Loos. il *Gourmet* 49:124-5+ N '89
A Cinco de Mayo dinner. il *Gourmet* 49:126-32+ My '89
Cuernavaca and Taxco. P. J. Bell. il *Gourmet* 49:64-9+ F '89
Game hens, ablaze with flavor. il *Glamour* 87:190 Jl '89
How to eat like an Aztec. R. Sokolov. *Natural History* p110+ N '89
Insects, worms, and other tidbits. R. Sokolov. il *Natural History* p84+ S '89
Mexican jumping scenes. M. O'Neill. il *Harper's Bazaar* 122:222+ Ap '89
Ole mole: eating south of the border. S. Baker. il *Business Week* p160 F 20 '89
Quinta Diana [garden of D. Kennedy; cover story] S. O. Daniels. il pors map *Organic Gardening* 36:40-6 Jl/Ag '89
Recipe of the week [enchilada casserole] il *Jet* 75:38 Mr 13 '89
Yucatán breakfast . . . and other Mexican surprises. il *Sunset (Central West edition)* 182:142 Je '89

COOKING, MIDDLE EASTERN
A Middle Eastern-style dinner from the grill. il *Gourmet* 49:90-2+ Je '89
Tiny bites, mighty taste. P. Wolfert. il *Modern Maturity* 32:72-5 F/Mr '89

COOKING, NORTH AFRICAN
See also
Couscous

COOKING, ORNAMENTAL
See also
Cooking—Garnishes
Deck the halls with cookie houses. S. West. il *Ladies' Home Journal* 106:154-6+ D '89
Easter creations. il *McCall's* 116:47-9+ Mr '89
Easy-to-make toy soldier [gingerbread] il *Good Housekeeping* 209:215+ D '89
Gingerbread Land. il *Good Housekeeping* 209:152-7+ D '89
Gingerbread stockings. il *Good Housekeeping* 209:168-71+ D '89
Holiday centerpieces to savor. il *McCall's* 116:31-7 Ja '89
Make our thatched-roof cottage [gingerbread; cover story] il *Good Housekeeping* 209:10+ D '89
Over the river . . . [Christmas cookie houses] il *McCall's* 117:49-52+ D '89

COOKING, OUTDOOR
See also
Barbecue cooking
Clambakes
Outdoor meals
Campers' cuisine. il *Better Homes and Gardens* 67:132-3+ Jl '89
The gallivanting gourmet. J. Fleming. il *Sierra* 74:62-3 Jl/Ag '89
How to feed a hungry camp. S. Netherby. il *Field & Stream* 94:67-8 Je '89
The outdoor gourmet [special section] il *The Mother Earth News* 118:75-6+ Jl/Ag '89
The outdoor gourmet [special section] il *American Health* 8:99-102+ Jl/Ag '89

COOKING, PERUVIAN
Peruvian provisions. R. Sokolov. *Natural History* p80 D '89

COOKING, POLYNESIAN
Gourmet holidays: Society Islands. C. Bates. il map *Gourmet* 49:36-41+ Ja '89
Gourmet holidays: Society Islands. C. Bates. il map *Gourmet* 49:58-63+ F '89

COOKING, RUSSIAN
See also
Cooking, Caucasus
Cooking, Georgian
Borscht Belt [Russian restaurants in NYC] J. Freiman. il *Harper's Bazaar* 122:172+ F '89
COOKING, SCOTTISH
See also
Haggis
Scotland's Brodick Castle kitchen. L. Langseth-Christensen. il *Gourmet* 49:82-3+ My '89
COOKING, SPANISH
A poolside Spanish luncheon. il *Gourmet* 49:78-84 Ag '89
Sizzling Spain. G. Greene. il *New York* 22:34-41 Jl 24 '89
Spain in a stew. P. Casas. il *The New York Times Magazine* p69-70 O 15 '89
COOKING, SWISS
Gourmet holidays: a Swiss Alpine sojourn. S. Wilding. il map *Gourmet* 49:48-53+ Ag '89
COOKING, TEX-MEX
See also
Gorditas
Corn, cheese, chilies: Santa Fe brunch [cover story] il *Sunset (Central West edition)* 182:98-9 Ap '89
Hot stuff. R. Schrambling. il *The New York Times Magazine* p39-40 Jl 23 '89
Southwest tastes. J. F. Mariani. il *Motor Boating & Sailing* 164:34-5 O '89
Tex-Mex for two. il *Southern Living* 24:186-7 S '89
Tex-Mex microwave [excerpt from Kids cook microwave] il *National Geographic World* 169:10-11 S '89
Western Europe: the Tex-Mex invasion [Paris] A. Bogart. il *Harper's Bazaar* 122:48+ F '89
COOKING, THAI
See also
Thai Cooking School (Bangkok, Thailand)
Spicy Thai dishes. il *Better Homes and Gardens* 67:154 O '89
Tongue Thai'd in Bangkok. D. G. Gordon. il *Travel Holiday* 172:52-7 O '89
COOKING, WEST INDIAN
Hot stuff. R. Schrambling. il *The New York Times Magazine* p39-40 Jl 23 '89
Nevis. D. Beal. il map *Gourmet* 49:60-3+ Mr '89
COOKING, ZIMBABWEAN
Hearty stews and side dishes from Zimbabwe. J. Nash. *Essence* 20:112+ O '89
COOKING BY ARTISTS
Pleasing the palette. B. Kafka. il *Art News* 88:162-5 O '89
COOKING BY CHILDREN
Cookbook for kids: snack attack! il *Redbook* 173:70+ S '89
Fun foods for moms and kids to make [microwaving] *Good Housekeeping* 209:224 N '89
Healthful recipes children can cook. il *The Saturday Evening Post* 261:44-5 Ap '89
Holiday treats. C. Koury. il *Parents* 64:176-8+ D '89
Microwave snacks for kids. M. Cone and T. Snyder. il *Working Woman* 14:224 S '89
Moms and daughters bake cookies. il *Southern Living* 24:100+ D '89
Tex-Mex microwave [excerpt from Kids cook microwave] il *National Geographic World* 169:10-11 S '89
What's cooking? Fun for all! [Christmas tree cakes] il *Redbook* 174:26 D '89
COOKING BY COWBOYS
Come 'n' get it [ranch cooking] R. Coyle. il *The New York Times Magazine* p53-4 Ag 6 '89
COOKING BY MEN
Chefs of the West. See issues of Sunset (Central West edition)
Anecdotes, facetiae, satire, etc.
The don't-try-it diet. M. G. Stoddard. il *The Saturday Evening Post* 261:60-2 My/Je '89
COOKING BY SINGLE PEOPLE
Single servings. J. Nash. *Essence* 20:90+ Ag '89
COOKING CONTESTS *See* Cooking—Competitions
COOKING ERRORS
10 most common cooking mistakes. il *Good Housekeeping* 209:122 Ag '89
COOKING OILS *See* Oils and fats, Edible
COOKING PROGRAMS *See* Television broadcasting—Cooking programs
COOKING SCHOOLS *See* Cooking—Study and teaching
COOKING THERMOMETERS *See* Thermometers, Cooking
COOKING UTENSILS AND APPLIANCES *See* Kitchen utensils and appliances
COOKS
See also
Bertolli, Paul
Chiarello, Michael
Children of cooks
Escoffier, Auguste, d. 1935
Giaccone, Cesare
Girardet, Fredy, 1936-
Langlois, Steve
Mills, Kelly
O'Donnell, Cornelius
Panish, Larry
Puck, Wolfgang

Sturges, Arthur
Women cooks
Chefs' cooking secrets. il *Ladies' Home Journal* 106:218-20+ My '89
Eat light! [recipes from famous chefs] il *Redbook* 173:125-8+ Je '89
Seattle crew. B. H. Fussell. il *The New York Times Magazine* p57-8 Ap 9 '89
COOKTOPS
Hot new cooktop technologies. il *Home Mechanix* 86:60-4+ Ap '89
COOKWARE *See* Kitchen utensils and appliances
COOL STORAGE
Cool storage. P. Glouchevitch. il *Forbes* 144:230 O 2 '89
COOLER CHESTS
Coolers & jugs. il *Consumer Reports* 54:319-22 D '89
How to keep a picnic on ice. il *Consumer Reports* 54:402-7 Je '89
Large cooler chests. il *Consumer Reports* 54:322-4 D '89
COOLERS, WINE *See* Wine coolers
COOLEY, DENTON A., 1920-
about
Will Denton Cooley make medical history again? M. Ivey. il por *Business Week* p56+ Mr 27 '89
COOLEY, EDWARD H.
about
Smooth flying. M. Beauchamp. il por *Forbes* 144:94+ S 18 '89
COOLEY, JUNE H., AND GOLLEY, FRANK B.
Restraints to communication for ecologists in developing countries. bibl f il *BioScience* 39:805-9 D '89
COOLIDGE, CALVIN, 1872-1933
Press conferences
The Coolidgean press conference. V. Gold. *The American Spectator* 22:32-3 Ap '89
COOLING
See also
Air conditioning
Airplane engines—Cooling
Automobile engines—Cooling
Diesel engines, Marine—Cooling
Fans, Electric
Magnetic refrigeration
Solar air conditioning
Truck engines—Cooling
Ventilators
Cool aid [home cooling; cover story; special section] il *Consumer Reports* 54:431-40 Jl '89
Cool house for a hot climate [Mark and Jennifer Zegels' Merritt Island, Fla. home utilizes passive cooling] D. Stover. il *Popular Science* 235:74-5 Ag '89
Keep your cool this summer: ways to beat the heat without air conditioning. L. Lamb. il *Utne Reader* p10-11 Jl/Ag '89
Whistle up a breeze. P. Steinhart. il *Audubon* 91:24-7 Jl '89
COON HUNTING *See* Raccoon hunting
COONEY, JOAN GANZ
about
Joan Ganz Cooney created Sesame Street 20 years ago. Now it's an institution. D. Moreau. il por *Changing Times* 43:88 Jl '89
COONEY, RAY, 1932-
about
Run for your wife! [drama] Reviews
The New Yorker 65:88-9 Mr 20 '89. M. Kramer
COONS, CARRIE
about
Whose death is it, anyway? J. Seligmann. *Newsweek* 113:69 Ap 24 '89
COONS *See* Raccoons
COOP HIMMELBLAU (GROUP)
Over the edge [projects; cover story] K. D. Stein. il *Architectural Record* 177:82-91 Ag '89
Vienna vanguard. J. Giovannini. il *House & Garden* 161:48 S '89
COOPER, ALICE
about
Alice Cooper: healthy, wealthy and dry. D. Koen. por *Rolling Stone* p49 Jl 13-27 '89
COOPER, BARRY MICHAEL
Bobby Brown. pors *Essence* 20:70-2+ My '89
COOPER, BERNARD, 1951-
Dream house. *Harper's* 279:34-6 Jl '89
COOPER, CHRISTIN
Inside racing. See issues of Skiing beginning September 1985 through March 1989
My turn. See issues of Skiing beginning September 1989
about
Christin's homecoming. W. Grout. il por *Skiing* 42:8 D '89
COOPER, GLENN, 1953-
(jt. auth) See Cooper, Tessa, 1954-, and Cooper, Glenn, 1953-
COOPER, GUY
about
Air Time. T. Carlson. il pors *Sport (New York, N.Y.)* 80:53-6 Ja '89

COOPER, HENRY F.
Status of the defense and space talks [statement, August 3, 1989] *Department of State Bulletin* 89:20-2 O '89
about
Arms control official leading candidate to head National Space Council staff. *Aviation Week & Space Technology* 130:22 F 27 '89

COOPER, JAMES F.
". . . nothing will destroy our culture while people are free to create . . ." [interview with M. S. Forbes] il por *Forbes* 144:20+ O 2 '89

COOPER, JAMES H.
Should President Bush's minimum wage proposal be adopted? [excerpts from address, March 23, 1989] *Congressional Digest* 68:148 My '89

COOPER, JIM
about
The devil and Jim Cooper. M. Will-Weber. por *Runner's World* 24:109 Je '89

COOPER, KENNETH H.
The basics of bone [excerpt from Preventing osteoporosis] il *Health (New York, N.Y.)* 21:80-2 Ap '89
Osteoporosis: are you at risk? [excerpt from Preventing osteoporosis] il *Ladies' Home Journal* 106:56+ Mr '89
about
Beating heart disease [interview] C. SerVaas. il pors *The Saturday Evening Post* 261:20-1+ Mr '89
Ken Cooper made fitness a fad. But that wasn't good enough for him. D. Moreau. il por *Changing Times* 43:100 Je '89

COOPER, LEON N., 1930-
First word. il *Omni (New York, N.Y.)* 11:6 Mr '89

COOPER, MARK J., AND OTHERS
Attracting bright adolescents to teaching careers. il *Phi Delta Kappan* 70:566-7 Mr '89

COOPER, MATTHEW
A pension for trouble. il *The Washington Monthly* 21:24-9 Jl/Ag '89

COOPER, NANCY
For richer and richer. il *Ladies' Home Journal* 106:184-6+ My '89

COOPER, PAULA
about
Quite contrary [cover story] J. Howell. il pors *Art News* 88:152-7 Mr '89

COOPER, PHIL
Babes in Crib Land. il *Parents* 64:268 O '89

COOPER, TESSA, 1954-, AND COOPER, GLENN, 1953-
The amazing two-day diet. il *Redbook* 172:49-52 Mr '89

COOPER, THEODORE
about
Will this formula cure what ails Upjohn? D. Woodruff. il *Business Week* p65 S 18 '89

COOPER (PAULA) GALLERY *See* Paula Cooper Gallery

COOPER COMPANIES, INC.
Can Arthur Bass rouse Cooper from its sickbed? J. O. Hamilton. il por *Business Week* p33 Ap 10 '89

COOPER-HEWITT MUSEUM
Around the Mall and beyond. E. Park. il *Smithsonian* 20:24-6+ O '89
The painter's progress [American drawings from the Cooper-Hewitt Museum] A. E. Ledes. il *Antiques* 135:396 F '89
Pilgrim's progress [D. Pilgrim] K. Pryor. il por *Art News* 88:87-8 Ap '89

COOPER TIRE & RUBBER COMPANY
Cooper Tire & Rubber. R. Abelson. il *Fortune* 120:82 O 9 '89

COOPERATION
See also
Collective settlements
Educational cooperation
International cooperation
Religious cooperation
How the kinder, more cooperative corporation wins [excerpt from When giants learn to dance] R. M. Kanter. *Working Woman* 14:118-20 My '89
On surviving the day after tomorrow. H. M. Hodges, Jr. *The Humanist* 49:25-9+ My/Je '89
The sources of cooperation [study by James Beggan and David Messick] W. Herbert. il *Psychology Today* 23:72 Ja/F '89

COOPERATIVE AGRICULTURE *See* Agriculture, Cooperative

COOPERATIVE APARTMENT HOUSES *See* Apartment houses—Cooperative ownership

COOPERATIVE ASSOCIATIONS
See also
Baby sitters' cooperatives
Credit unions
Freedom Quilting Bee (Organization)
Soviet Union
And you think Western capitalists have problems. P. Galuszka. il *Business Week* p50 Ja 30 '89
The bad smell of success. C. Bogert. il *Newsweek* 114:50 O 9 '89
On the front line. J. Elson. il *Time* 133:81-2 Ap 10 '89
Russia's embryonic capitalists. P. Dragadze. il *Forbes* 144:90-4+ O 16 '89

Soviet profits. A. Wilson-Smith. il *Maclean's* 102:24-5 Jl 17 '89

COOPERATIVE ASSOCIATIONS, AGRICULTURAL *See* Agriculture, Cooperative

COOPERATIVE EDUCATION *See* Business and education

COOPERATIVE HOUSING *See* Housing, Cooperative

COOPERATIVE LEARNING *See* Group work in education

COOPERATIVE LIVING ESTABLISHMENTS *See* Collective settlements; Housing, Cooperative

COOPERMAN, ROBERT
Cut dead [poem] *Commonweal* 116:266 My 5 '89

COOPERMAN, SAUL
Must principals have teaching experience? *The Education Digest* 54:11-12 Mr '89

COOPERMAN, SAUL, AND NADEL, SYBIL
The Academy: New Jersey improves professional growth opportunities for teachers. il *Phi Delta Kappan* 70:619-23 Ap '89

COOPERSTOWN (N.Y.)
Description
Baseball and memories in Cooperstown. L. Griffin. il *Car and Driver* 35:187 N '89
Cooperstown. A. R. Gochman. il *Gourmet* 49:102-7+ O '89
Return to Cooperstown. J. Orsini. il *Travel Holiday* 171:76+ F '89
Galleries and museums
See also
Farmers' Museum
National Baseball Hall of Fame and Museum
Music
See also
Glimmerglass Opera Theater
Social history
The Clarks of Cooperstown. W. P. Barrett. il *Forbes* 144:76+ S 18 '89

COORDINATING COMMITTEE ON MULTILATERAL EXPORT CONTROLS
The allies: fools or tools? [U.S. raises objection to machine tool exports to the Soviets] *Newsweek* 114:54 O 30 '89
Are the old rules still relevant? [CoCom high tech export controls] C. P. Work. il *U.S. News & World Report* 107:38 D 18 '89

COORDINATION (CHEMISTRY)
Silicon coordination and speciation changes in a silicate liquid at high pressures. X. Xue and others. bibl f il *Science* 245:962-4 S 1 '89

COORDINATION (MUSCULAR) *See* Motor ability

COORS (ADOLPH) CO. *See* Adolph Coors Co.

COPÁN (ANCIENT CITY)
City of kings and commoners: Copán. G. E. Stuart. il map *National Geographic* 176:488-504 O '89
Copán: a royal Maya tomb discovered. R. A. Fasquelle and W. L. Fash. il map *National Geographic* 176:480-7 O '89
Maya mañana. A. Hills. il *History Today* 39:4-5 S '89

COPAPAYO (EL SALVADOR)
Salvadoran refugees come home. R. R. Ruether. il *The Christian Century* 106:851-3 S 27 '89

COPAS, CARRIE ELLEN
about
Children of poverty. P. Meyer. il *Life* 12:56-62+ S '89

COPE, ANTHONY
about
Bailout bulls. J. Zweig. il pors *Forbes* 143:167 Ap 3 '89

COPE, STEVEN R.
An allowance of sentiment [poem] *America* 160:222 Mr 11 '89

COPELAND, ALVIN
about
Chicken that packs a punch. M. Barrier. il pors *Nation's Business* 77:52+ Jl '89

COPELAND, ANGELA MARIE
We are not 'lost'. por *Essence* 19:128 Ja '89

COPELAND, MILES, III
about
If you can't beat 'em . . . P. Newcomb. il por *Forbes* 144:152 D 25 '89

COPELAND, STEWART
about
The God who cries: an opera on the Mideast. H. W. Eberts. *The Christian Century* 106:1174-8 D 13 '89
Holy blood and crescent moon [opera] Reviews
The Christian Century 106:1174-8 D 13 '89. H. W. Eberts
The New York Times Magazine il pors p40-1+ S 24 '89. A. Tommasini
Opera News il pors 54:18-20+ O '89. L. Rubinstein
Police report. S. Fried. il pors *Gentlemen's Quarterly* 59:151+ O '89
Risk taker. L. Rubinstein. il pors *Opera News* 54:18-20+ O '89
Roll over, Wagner. A. Tommasini. il pors *The New York Times Magazine* p40-1+ S 24 '89

COPELON, RHONDA, AND KOLBERT, KATHRYN
Imperfect justice. il *Ms.* 18:42-4 Jl/Ag '89
Roe v. Wade. il *Ms.* 17:89-92 Ap '89

COPLAND, AARON, 1900-
about
Family ties. P. G. Davis. il *New York* 22:129-30 N 6 '89
COPLON, JEFF
The skinhead reich. il *Utne Reader* p80-3+ My/Je '89
COPPER, JOHN FRANKLIN
Political reform in Taiwan [address, March 4, 1989] *Vital Speeches of the Day* 55:394-6 Ap 15 '89
Taiwan: a nation in transition. bibl f *Current History* 88:173-6+ Ap '89
COPPER INDUSTRY
See also
Cox Creek Refining Company
Phelps Dodge Corporation
Employees
See also
Strikes—Copper industry workers
Mexico
See also
Compañía Minera de Cananea SA
COPPER MINERS
See also
Labor unions—Copper miners
COPPER MINES AND MINING
Canada
See also
Noranda Inc.
COPPER OXIDES
Anomalous scattering study of the Bi distribution in the 2212 superconductor: implications for Cu valency. P. Lee and others. bibl f il *Science* 244:62-3 Ap 7 '89
Electron superconductors challenge theories, start a new race. A. Khurana. bibl f il *Physics Today* 42:17-19 Ap '89
Magnon-exchange pairing and superconductivity [discussion of February 19, 1988 article, The magnon pairing mechanism of superconductivity in cuprate ceramics] G. Chen and W. A. Goddard, III. *Science* 243:547-8 Ja 27 '89
More surprises from new superconductors. *Science News* 135:367 Je 10 '89
New superconductor uses electrons [research by Y. Tokura and others] R. Pool. *Science* 243:741 F 10 '89
Rearranging oxygen for superconductivity [yttrium-barium-copper oxide; work of Robert B. Beyers] I. Peterson. *Science News* 136:133 Ag 26 '89
Spatially resolved observation of supercurrents across grain boundaries in YBaCuO films. J. Mannhart and others. bibl f il *Science* 245:839-41 Ag 25 '89
Superconducting gap in Bi-Sr-Ca-Cu-O by high-resolution angle-resolved photoelectron spectroscopy. C. G. Olson and others. bibl f il *Science* 245:731-3 Ag 18 '89
COPPER ROOFS *See* Roofs and roofing
COPPOLA, AUGUST
Life and death and the arts. *Design for Arts in Education* 91:43-5 S/O '89
COPPOLA, FRANCIS, 1939-
about
New York stories [film] Reviews
America 160:353 Ap 15 '89. R. A. Blake
The American Spectator il 22:37-8 My '89. B. Bawer
Commonweal 116:212-13 Ap 7 '89. T. O'Brien
Maclean's il pors 102:62 Mr 13 '89. B. D. Johnson
The Nation 248:426-7 Mr 27 '89. S. Klawans
National Review 41:45+ Je 16 '89. J. Simon
The New Leader il 72:20-1 Mr 6 '89. J. Morrone
The New Republic 200:24-6 Mr 27 '89. S. Kauffmann
New York il 22:63-4 Mr 13 '89. D. Denby
The New Yorker 65:93-6 Mr 20 '89. P. Kael
Newsweek il 113:58 Mr 6 '89. D. Ansen
People Weekly il 31:15-16 Mr 13 '89. S. Haller
Time il 133:68 Mr 6 '89. R. Schickel
Tucker: the man and his dream [film] Reviews
Video il 13:76 My '89. J. Young
COPPOLA, GIAN CARLO, D. 1986
about
Making up for dues left unpaid, Griffin O'Neal goes to jail. il por *People Weekly* 31:117 F 6 '89
COPPOLA, JO
Broccoli rabe. il *Gourmet* 49:156+ Je '89
COPROCESSORS *See* Multiprocessors
COPRODUCTION OF AIRPLANES *See* Airplane industry—International aspects
COPRODUCTION OF ARMS *See* Munitions—International aspects
COPRODUCTION OF HELICOPTERS *See* Helicopter industry—International aspects
COPS [television program] *See* Television program reviews—Single works
COPULOS, MILTON
The environment: a North-South conflict. *Current (Washington, D.C.)* 317:35-9 N '89
COPY TONERS (PHOTOCOPYING) *See* Photographic chemistry
COPYING EQUIPMENT
See also
Photocopying equipment
Slides (Photography)—Copying

COPYRIGHT
See also
Public lending rights (of authors)
Royalties
The ABC's of copyright. E. Preston. *The Writer* 102:21-3 D '89
How to protect your bright idea. D. Moreau. il *Changing Times* 43:63-4+ Ag '89
How to protect your products and ideas. R. Gunnerson. il *Home Office Computing* 7:38+ D '89
Keeping up with copyright. J. F. Baker. il *Publishers Weekly* 235:18-19 Je 23 '89
Key senators frown on adding moral rights to Copyright Act. H. Fields. *Publishers Weekly* 236:11 N 17 '89
Lawyers see little impact from High Court's work-for-hire ruling [Community for Creative Non-Violence v. Reid] H. Fields. *Publishers Weekly* 235:10-11 Je 23 '89
Oman urges extension of authors' moral rights [Copyright Office's views] H. Fields. *Publishers Weekly* 235:35 Ap 7 '89
Panel opens hearings on copyright changes with moral rights issue. H. Fields. *Publishers Weekly* 236:11 Jl 7 '89
Rights. P. S. Nathan. See issues of Publishers Weekly
Work for hire: round two [authors fight for full copyright] A. Dubro. por *Publishers Weekly* 235:80 Je 30 '89
Architecture
Copyright Office study recommends more protection for works of architecture. P. Hoffmann. il *Architectural Record* 177:35 Ag '89
The pitfalls in protecting your designs from the clutches of others. S. A. Glazer. il *Architectural Record* 177:37+ My '89
Art
"The art case of the decade" [copyright case brought by the Community for Creative Non-Violence against J. E. Reid] S. Staggs. il *Art News* 88:49-50 Ap '89
Copyright ruling favors artists [Supreme Court decision] il *Art in America* 77:240 S '89
Copyrighting works of art. D. Grant. *American Artist* 53:8+ Ja '89
Court aids freelancers in work-for-hire ruling [case of Community for Creative Non-Violence vs. J. E. Reid] H. Fields. *Publishers Weekly* 235:11 Je 16 '89
Professional page [case brought by Community for Creative Non-Violence against J. E. Reid] D. Grant. *American Artist* 53:10+ Jl '89
Resale royalties for artists: the debate continues. D. Grant. *American Artist* 53:12+ Je '89
Sculpture clash [suit brought by Community for Creative Non-Violence against J. E. Reid] il *Time* 133:63 Ja 30 '89
Supreme Court hears work-for-hire arguments [case brought by Community for Creative Non-Violence against J. E. Reid] H. Fields. *Publishers Weekly* 235:14 Ap 14 '89
"A time of sharpened swords" [impact of Supreme Court decisions on artists] D. Waterman. il *Art News* 88:59+ N '89
Broadcasting rights
Court enjoins Dove's distribution of 'Lonesome dove' audio [adaptation of television miniseries] J. Tangorra. *Publishers Weekly* 236:12 S 22 '89
Dueling 'Doves': acrimony clouds copyright issue. P. Sweeting. il *Publishers Weekly* 235:54-6 Je 2 '89
Scandal? Tragedy? Violence? Here come the wheeler-dealers waving their checkbooks [made for TV real life dramas] J. Kaye. il *TV Guide* 37:23-4+ Ja 7-13 '89
Comic books, strips, etc.
Free Peanuts! Free Beetle Bailey! E. Schmuckler. il *Forbes* 144:159+ O 30 '89
Computer programming
See also
Computer programming—Unauthorized use
A battle over a user-friendly computer [Xerox sues Apple over software copyright] il *Newsweek* 114:59 D 25 '89
Can Las Vegas sue Atlantic City? [cover story] K. K. Wiegner and J. Heins. il *Forbes* 143:130-3+ Mr 6 '89
Don't bury software's promise in a legal bog. K. H. Hammonds. il *Business Week* p86 My 22 '89
Facts on File settles claims in software copyright suit. C. Reid. *Publishers Weekly* 235:9-10 Je 23 '89
Intellectual property. E. Dyson. il *Forbes* 144:202 S 18 '89
Litigating a standard [Ashton-Tate suit against Fox Software] C. Strehlo. *Personal Computing* 13:73 Mr '89
Look but don't touch. E. Corcoran. *Scientific American* 261:101-2 S '89
See you in court. S. R. Reed. il *Personal Computing* 13:179 Ag '89
Integrated circuits
The uncertain payoff from Intel's landmark case [microcode copyrights] R. Brandt. il *Business Week* p35 F 20 '89
International aspects
See also
Berne Convention for the Protection of Literary and Artistic Works
1992 and all that [round table discussion on the implications for American publishers of the European Economic Community] il *Publishers Weekly* 235:21-8 F 3 '89

COPYRIGHT—International aspects—*cont.*
An open market for Australia? L. Vardey. por *Publishers Weekly* 236:100 S 15 '89

Motion pictures
Palm Springs ploy [movie companies sue La Mancha Private Club & Villas over royalties from videotapes shown in hotel rooms] P. Newcomb. il *Forbes* 143:100 Mr 20 '89
Survival of the fittest. P. Arthur. il *USA Today (Periodical)* 117:67 Ja '89

Music
Fogerty wins unusual self-plagiarism suit. M. Goldberg. il por *Rolling Stone* p15 Ja 12 '89
They're playing whose song? [record companies buy independent publishers] D. Lieberman. il *Business Week* p42 Ja 23 '89

Tape recordings
Court enjoins Dove's distribution of 'Lonesome dove' audio [adaptation of television miniseries] J. Tangorra. *Publishers Weekly* 236:12 S 22 '89
Dueling 'Doves': acrimony clouds copyright issue. P. Sweeting. il *Publishers Weekly* 235:54-6 Je 2 '89

Television rights
See Copyright—Broadcasting rights

Unauthorized reprints
See Copyright infringement

United States
See Copyright

COPYRIGHT INFRINGEMENT
See also
Photocopying—Unauthorized use
11th Amendment redraft hailed by publishers [declaring a congressional intent that states are not exempt from copyright law] H. Fields. *Publishers Weekly* 236:125 Jl 28 '89
11th Amendment ruling by High Court is 'hopeful' for copyright [question of states' liability] H. Fields. *Publishers Weekly* 236:9 Jl 7 '89
Chaos, 1989. *The Nation* 248:759-60 Je 5 '89
Copyright owners press Congress for new laws on 11th Amendment [court decision that copyright holders could not take action against state-held entities] H. Fields. *Publishers Weekly* 235:14 F 10 '89
Court splits over fair use language in Hubbard case [New Era Publications vs. Henry Holt and Co.] M. Reuter. *Publishers Weekly* 236:10 S 22 '89
Educator group objects to proposed remedy of 11th Amendment [restraining state institutions from infringing copyrights] H. Fields. *Publishers Weekly* 235:30 Je 2 '89
The end of history? [quoting from unpublished sources] D. A. Kaplan. il *Newsweek* 114:80 D 25 '89
Harlequin sues Bantam on promotional materials. C. Reid. *Publishers Weekly* 235:14 Ap 14 '89
House gets bill fortifying intent on states vs. federal copyright. H. Fields. *Publishers Weekly* 235:14 Mr 24 '89
House to push 11th Amendment remedy; Oman voices support [right of individual states and their entities to ignore requirements of U.S. Copyright Act] H. Fields. *Publishers Weekly* 235:18 Ap 28 '89
How can "intellectual property" be "protected?" [academic world; cover story; special section; with editorial comment by Harlan Cleveland] il *Change* 21:10-28 My/Je '89
New Era wins pre-pub review of Hubbard bio [case involving Carol Publishing Group] *Publishers Weekly* 236:332 Ag 11 '89
'Salinger' haunts ruling on Hubbard biography. M. Reuter. *Publishers Weekly* 235:102 My 12 '89
Supreme Court rejects second 11th Amendment case in month [brought by copyright holders against a state entity] H. Fields. *Publishers Weekly* 235:36 Ap 7 '89
UNESCO drops attempt to suppress book about itself [case against University of Minnesota Press] C. Reid. *Publishers Weekly* 235:16 Je 16 '89

International aspects
Annenberg study offers 12 ways to stem international piracy. H. Fields. *Publishers Weekly* 236:16 O 27 '89
China improves copyright status; India, Brazil on piracy list. H. Fields. *Publishers Weekly* 236:12 N 17 '89
IIPA targets 12 pirate nations, including China. H. Fields. *Publishers Weekly* 235:106+ My 12 '89
Pirated textbooks come to U.S. shores [unauthorized medical texts at the L.A. Chiropractic College] *Publishers Weekly* 236:50-1 S 8 '89
Pirates of the print shop. E. Watkins. *World Press Review* 36:76 S '89
Pursuing the pirates [work of the U.S. government] E. Simon. *Publishers Weekly* 236:88-9 S 15 '89

China
Commerce Dept. seeks reports of copyright abuse in China. H. Fields. *Publishers Weekly* 236:13 O 13 '89

Korea (South)
Korean govt. probing continued piracy. S. A. Taylor. *Publishers Weekly* 235:56 F 17 '89

CORAL REEF ALGAE *See* Algae
CORAL REEF FAUNA
See also
Sponges

Food and feeding
Reef fish feedings: amusement or nuisance? D. Perrine. il *Sea Frontiers* 35:272-9 S/O '89

CORAL REEFS AND ISLANDS
See also
Coral reef fauna
Great Barrier Reef (Australia)
Palau
Caribbean coral reefs: are they becoming algal reefs? B. E. Lapointe. il *Sea Frontiers* 35:82-91 Mr/Ap '89
Critical depth for the survival of coral islands: effects on the Hawaiian archipelago. R. W. Grigg and D. Epp. bibl f il map *Science* 243:638-41 F 3 '89
Go down, Moses [exploring reefs near Ras Muhammed off tip of Sinai Peninsula] N. MacFarquhar. il *Esquire* 112:56 D '89
Starry blight [destruction of reefs by crown of thorns starfish] K. Brower. il *Omni (New York, N.Y.)* 11:22+ My '89
State of the reef. K. Brower. il *Audubon* 91:56-81 Mr '89
What is really killing the corals [cover story] E. A. Shinn. bibl il map *Sea Frontiers* 35:72-81 Mr/Ap '89

Photographs and photography
A world of coral harmonies [macrophotography] S. Rudavsky. il *Omni (New York, N.Y.)* 11:58-63 Je '89

CORAM, ROBERT
Ancient rights. *The New Yorker* 64:76-86+ F 6 '89

CORBEIL, CHRISTINE
(jt. auth) *See* Descarries, Francine, and Corbeil, Christine

CORBERÓ, ANA
about
Different strokes: a touch of splash. S. Nelson. il pors *Harper's Bazaar* 122:124-7+ F '89

CORBETT, LYNNE TAYLOR- *See* Taylor-Corbett, Lynne
CORBETT, MIKE
about
Grit and a granite will conquer El Capitan. M. Brower. il pors *People Weekly* 32:36-9 Ag 14 '89

CORBETT, PATRICIA
A nation's storehouse. il *House & Garden* 161:52+ Jl '89

CORBIAU, GERARD
about
The music teacher [film] Reviews
The New Republic 201:24-5 Jl 31 '89. S. Kauffmann

CORBIN, CHARLES B.
Exercise Rx for those little aches and pains. il *Better Homes and Gardens* 67:38+ O '89

CORCORAN GALLERY OF ART
Can crippled Corcoran survive? B. Wallis. il *Art in America* 77:41+ N '89
Corcoran showdown [aftermath of cancellation of R. Mapplethorpe show] C. McGuigan. il pors *Newsweek* 114:111+ O 9 '89
Exhibitionism [cancels R. Mapplethorpe exhibit] *The New Republic* 201:6 Jl 17-24 '89
Mad about Mapplethorpe [cancels exhibit] A. Ferguson. *National Review* 41:20-1 Ag 4 '89
Mapplethorpe of my eye [exhibit opens at WPA gallery after cancellation by the Corcoran] A. Heard. *The New Republic* 201:10-12 Ag 21 '89
Robert Mapplethorpe. il por *People Weekly* 32:100-1 D 25 '89-Ja 1 '90
A "sacrificial lamb"? [aftermath of cancellation of R. Mapplethorpe show] S. Hochfield. il por *Art News* 88:62 N '89
Whose art is it, anyway? [cancels R. Mapplethorpe exhibit] M. B. Carlson. il *Time* 134:21 Jl 3 '89

CORD, BARRY KIESELSTEIN- *See* Kieselstein-Cord, Barry
CORD, CECE KIESELSTEIN- *See* Kieselstein-Cord, Cece
CORDAY, BARBARA
Barbara Corday: on turning Newman & Redford into Cagney & Lacey. por *People Weekly* 31 Special Issue:152 Summ '89

CORDAY, CHARLOTTE, 1768-1793
about
First encounters. E. Sorel and N. C. Sorel. il *The Atlantic* 264:77 Jl '89

CORDERO, ANGEL
about
Beers with . . . Angel Cordero [interview] I. Cohen. il por *Sport (New York, N.Y.)* 80:41-2 Je '89

CORDERO, LEÓN FEBRES *See* Febres Cordero, León, 1931-
CORDIALS *See* Liqueurs
CORDIERITE
Cordierite-spinel troctolite, a new magnesium-rich lithology from the lunar highlands. U. B. Marvin and others. bibl f il map *Science* 243:925-8 F 17 '89
Moonrock tells of little-known lunar layer. *Science News* 135:126 F 25 '89

CORDIS CORPORATION
Firm pleads guilty to selling faulty pacemakers. D. Farley. il *FDA Consumer* 23:38-9 S '89

CORDLESS KITCHEN UTENSILS AND APPLIANCES *See* Kitchen utensils and appliances
CORDLESS POWER TOOLS *See* Tools
CORDLESS SCREWDRIVERS *See* Screwdrivers
CORDLESS TELEPHONE
Cordless phones—now they're cookin'. M. Levine. il *Popular Science* 234:112-13+ Ap '89

CORDLESS TELEPHONE—*cont.*

Testing

Cordless phone with 10-number memory [Sony SPP-110] S. Miller. il *Home Office Computing* 7:80 N '89

Cordless phones: what price freedom? il *Consumer Reports* 54:680-5 N '89

A new breed of cordless phones: worth a second look. S. Usdin. il *Home Office Computing* 7:52-4 Jl '89

Quality cordless: a cut above the rest [Southwestern Bell Freedom Phone FF-1700] J. D. Oehler. il *Home Office Computing* 7:72 F '89

Two worlds merge [Panasonic KX-T3880 two-line cordless speakerphone] S. Usdin. il *Home Office Computing* 7:71 My '89

Unique cordless phone [Cobra Intenna Model CP-480] S. Usdin. il *Home Office Computing* 7:62 Ag '89

CORDS, ELECTRIC *See* Electric cords

CORDTZ, DAN

Are Americans retiring too early? il *Reader's Digest* 135:103-5 N '89

CORE CURRICULUM *See* Colleges and universities—Curriculum

CORE STOCKHOLDERS

Enter the 'core' investor—to cheers and boos. L. Jereski. il *Business Week* p104 S 18 '89

COREA, CHICK

about

Chick Corea's "Folk song"—an exercise in arranging. A. Laverne. il *Down Beat* 56:56-7 Ag '89

COREA, GENA

Encounter on the West Bank. il *The Progressive* 53:46 S '89

CORELL, ROBERT

(jt. auth) See Malone, Thomas F., and Corell, Robert

CORELLI, RAE

Boom time for futurists. *World Press Review* 36:26+ D '89

COREN, ALAN, 1938-

Take cover, Mike Tyson—Frank Bruno's got a secret weapon. il *TV Guide* 37:8-9 F 25-Mr 3 '89

U.S. TV? It's been better for the Brits than our spareribs or cruise missiles. il *TV Guide* 37:22-3 My 27-Je 2 '89

COREN, STANLEY

about

Psychologist Stanley Coren's bad news comes out of left field—lefties lead riskier, shorter lives [interview] D. K. Bacon. il por *People Weekly* 32:115-16+ N 6 '89

COREY, ELIAS J.

about

"Chemzymes" mimic biology in miniature. M. M. Waldrop. por *Science* 245:354-5 Jl 28 '89

COREY, JEFF, 1914-

about

Corey-ography [interview] P. McGilligan. il pors *Film Comment* 25:38-9+ N/D '89

CORFU (GREECE)

Description and travel

Ski odyssey [skiing behind the Ski Challenger 208] L. Rudeen. il *Motor Boating & Sailing* 164:58-61+ Jl '89

CORIDEN, JAMES A.

Inflating the oath. il *Commonweal* 116:455-6 S 8 '89

CORIOLANUS [drama] See Shakespeare, William, 1564-1616

CORIOLIS FORCE

The curling crystal club [cover story] I. Amato. il *Science News* 135:124-5 F 25 '89

CORK FLOORING *See* Flooring, Cork

CORLE, TIMOTHY R.

(jt. auth) See Kino, Gordon S., and Corle, Timothy R.

CORLEY, ERIC

Free the hacker two. *Harper's* 279:22+ S '89

CORLISS, MARY

Riviera refuge. il *Film Comment* 25:66+ Jl/Ag '89

CORLISS, RICHARD

14-karat oomph. il *Film Comment* 25:40-6 Jl/Ag '89

Who cares? il *Film Comment* 25:64-70 Ja/F '89

CORMIE, DONALD MERCER

about

Day of reckoning [special section] J. DeMont. il por *Maclean's* 102:30-4 Jl 31 '89

CORN, ALFRED, 1943-

After Rilke [poem] *The Nation* 249:176 Ag 7-14 '89

A village walk under snow [poem] *The New Yorker* 64:28 Ja 9 '89

CORN, DAVID

Beltway bandits. See issues of The Nation beginning July 18-25, 1987

Bugs, beans and too many bucks. *The Nation* 248:236+ F 20 '89

Did it blow up Flight 103? il *The Nation* 248:153-4 F 6 '89

Foreign aid for the right. il *The Nation* 249:744-6 D 18 '89

Shilling in the Senate. il *The Nation* 249:84-7 Jl 17 '89

Sticking it to the taxpayers. il *The Nation* 249:238-40 S 4-11 '89

Struggling for union democracy. il *The Nation* 248:48-50+ Ja 9-16 '89

. . . write me a letter about it'. il *The Nation* 248:414-15 Mr 27 '89

CORN, JACK W.

about

Quaker State switches into a quick-change artist. M. Schroeder. il por *Business Week* p126-7 O 16 '89

CORN

See also

Cooking—Vegetables

Feeds—Corn

The corn. P. Westfall. il *Country Journal* 16:20-6 Jl/Ag '89

Corn and culture in central Andean prehistory. S. Johannessen and C. A. Hastorf. bibl f il *Science* 244:690-2 My 12 '89

Sweet ears. J. Poncavage. il *Organic Gardening* 36:44-8+ Ap '89

Visual detection of transposition of the maize element Activator (Ac) in tobacco seedlings. J. D. G. Jones and others. bibl f il *Science* 244:204-7 Ap 14 '89

Breeding

Seeds that fill a niche. M. Lane. il *Successful Farming* 87:12-13 S '89

Contamination

Aflatoxin in corn. *FDA Consumer* 23:2-3 My '89

Corn that glows can still be safe from aflatoxin. *Successful Farming* 87:43 Ja '89

A harvest of toxin. C. Wood. il *Maclean's* 102:49 Mr 6 '89

Mold on corn tough on dairies hit by drought. J. R. Borcherding. *Successful Farming* 87:54 F '89

A scare in the Corn Belt [aflatoxin] R. Givens. il *Newsweek* 113:70 Mr 6 '89

Cultivation

Growing sweet corn in the home garden. N. Bubel. il *Country Journal* 16:27-9 Jl/Ag '89

Hand pollinating corn. T. Leonard. il *Organic Gardening* 36:28-9 My '89

Photographs and photography

Corn: a photo-essay [cover story] J. F. Hart. bibl il *Focus (New York, N.Y.: 1950)* 39:4-9 Summ '89

Disease and pest resistance

Microbes to aid plants from within [corn field trials of genetically altered Clavibacter xyli] J. A. Miller. *BioScience* 39:227-8 Ap '89

Diseases and pests

See also

Corn rootworms

Two years in bin, no bugs [use of low-cost insecticide treatment] M. Lane. il *Successful Farming* 87:48G O '89

Field experiments

18-year tillage trial ends in a tie. R. Fee. *Successful Farming* 87:48K My '89

Anhydrous perks ridge-till corn in Ohio trials. R. Fee. *Successful Farming* 87:66AD F '89

Seed

Seeds that fill a niche. M. Lane. il *Successful Farming* 87:12-13 S '89

Prices

Seed prices up $2-$3 per acre. R. Fee. il *Successful Farming* 87:50AB Ja '89

Production

See Seed industry

Storage

Two years in bin, no bugs [use of low-cost insecticide treatment] M. Lane. il *Successful Farming* 87:48G O '89

Yield

1989 corn may top 8 billion bushels, beans 1.9 billion. *Successful Farming* 87:63 F '89

Heavy load crushes yields 7 years later. il *Successful Farming* 87:24 S '89

CORN BRAN *See* Bran

CORN BREAD *See* Cornbread

CORN CHIPS

Cracking the code of corn chip aroma [research by Thomas H. Parliment] *Science News* 136:78 Jl 29 '89

CORN MEAL *See* Cornmeal

CORN PRODUCTS

Corn [special section] il *Successful Farming* 87:17-19+ O '89

Corn hits a hot streak. R. Fee. il *Successful Farming* 87:50AL-50AM Ja '89

CORN ROOTWORMS

Control

New era for insecticides. B. Freese. il *Successful Farming* 87 no4:64S Mr '89

CORN SEED INDUSTRY *See* Seed industry

CORN STARCH *See* Cornstarch

CORN SYRUP

Corn sweeteners a sweet market for growers. R. Fee. il *Successful Farming* 87:22 O '89

CORNBREAD

Family recipe. C. Taylor. il *The Mother Earth News* 120:84-6+ N/D '89

Light cornbread and a moist, springy cake. il *Sunset (Central West edition)* 182:112-13 Ja '89

CORNCOBS

Cobs bring $80 an acre. C. Peterson, Jr. il *Successful Farming* 87:48W N '89

CORNEA

Transplantation

A family's legacy. L. Rivers. *Reader's Digest* 134:159-60 Mr '89

CORNELIA & MICHAEL BESSIE BOOKS

Cornelia & Michael Bessie Books. R. A. Carter. il pors *Publishers Weekly* 235:46-8 Ja 13 '89

CORNELISSEN, MICHAEL

about

Canada's growing economic outreach. P. C. Newman. il *Maclean's* 102:42 Ja 23 '89

CORNELL, JAMES

Cosmic correspondence. il *Sky and Telescope* 77:348 Ap '89

CORNELL, NANCY

Winter in the Texas tropics [cover story] il *New Choices for the Best Years* 29:22-6 N '89

CORNELL UNIVERSITY. CENTER FOR THEATRE ARTS

The sky line [work of architect J. Stirling] B. Gill. *The New Yorker* 65:80-4 Ag 14 '89

A Stirling performance [cover story] D. Dietsch. il *Architectural Record* 177:98-107 O '89

CORNER BOOKSTORE (NEW YORK, N.Y.) *See* Booksellers and bookselling—New York (State)

CORNER CABINETS *See* Cabinets (Furniture)

CORNET, ANTONIO GAUDÍ Y *See* Gaudí, Antoni, 1852-1926

CORNISH GAME HEN COOKING *See* Cooking—Poultry

CORNMEAL

See also

Cooking—Cornmeal

Homemade cornmeal. W. J. Weber. il *Country Journal* 16:44-7 S/O '89

Stalking the goodness of corn. R. Rodale. il *Prevention (Emmaus, Pa.)* 41:23+ Ja '89

CORNSTARCH

Biodegradable plastics fit a changing world. R. Fee. il *Successful Farming* 87:17-19 O '89

Missouri's capital using trash bags made from corn. il *Successful Farming* 87:30 Ja '89

Obstacles slow degradable uses for cornstarch. *Successful Farming* 87:48N mid-Mr '89

CORNWELL, DAVID JOHN MOORE *See* Le Carré, John, 1931-

CORNWELL, HAROLD

about

Good scouts indeed. P. W. Moser. il pors *Sports Illustrated* 70:46-9 F 6 '89

CORNWELL, JOHN

about

Death in Rome. il por *Time* 133:53 Je 19 '89

CORNWELL, RUPERT

Is Gorbachev's economy doomed to collapse? il *World Press Review* 36:20+ S '89

CORNWELL, T. J.

The applications of closure phase to astronomical imaging. bibl f il *Science* 245:263-9 Jl 21 '89

CORODIMAS, PETER

The most beautiful place [story] *The New Yorker* 65:53-8 O 23 '89

CORONA, SOLAR *See* Sun—Corona

CORONA BAR & GRILL (SAN FRANCISCO, CALIF.) *See* San Francisco (Calif.)—Restaurants, nightclubs, bars, etc.

CORONA CORP.

The Pez is golden [Canadian Supreme Court ruling favors Corona Corp. in claim dispute] J. DeMont. il por *Maclean's* 102:39 Ag 21 '89

The tenderfoot and the claim jumper [Corona Corp. wins claim dispute with LAC Minerals] J. Cook. il *Forbes* 144:170+ O 2 '89

CORONADO (CALIF.)

Architecture

Second growth [Leightner Houses] J. S. Russell. il *Architectural Record* 177:68-71 mid-Ap '89

CORONAGRAPH

Special report: optics clear air for astronomers. il *Popular Mechanics* 166:16 N '89

CORONARY ARTERY CATHETERIZATION *See* Cardiac catheterization

CORONARY ARTERY DISEASE *See* Arteriosclerosis

CORONARY BYPASS SURGERY *See* Heart—Surgery

CORONARY DISEASES *See* Heart—Diseases

CORONATIONS

Great Britain

See also

Elizabeth II, Queen of Great Britain, 1926——Coronation

CORONERS

See also

Medical examiners (Law)

CORPORAL PUNISHMENT

Banning corporal punishment in the classroom. B. Keeshan. *The Education Digest* 54:19-22 Ap '89

The National PTA's stand on corporal punishment. J. Ball. *The Education Digest* 54:23-5 Ap '89

Spanking in schools? [results of poll] I. Groller. il *Parents* 64:39 Mr '89

CORPORATE AIRPLANES *See* Airplanes, Business

CORPORATE ART COLLECTIONS *See* Art and industry

CORPORATE ASSET STRATEGIES (FIRM)

A buyout guru shares two takeover visions [views of L. Smith] G. G. Marcial. il por *Business Week* p146 Mr 20 '89

CORPORATE AVERAGE FUEL ECONOMY STANDARD *See* Automobile engines—Energy usage

CORPORATE BONDS *See* Bonds

CORPORATE CAMPAIGNS *See* Labor unions—Corporate campaigns

CORPORATE COMMUNITY SCHOOL (CHICAGO, ILL.)

A school for families. G. F. Will. il *Newsweek* 114:118 O 9 '89

"We decided to show how things can work". S. B. Weiner. il por *Forbes* 144:180-1+ S 18 '89

CORPORATE COUPLES *See* Married couples—Employment

CORPORATE CRIMES *See* Commercial crimes

CORPORATE CULTURE

Cultural changes in a family firm [Amot Controls Corp.] S. Nelton. il *Nation's Business* 77:62-3+ Ja '89

Employee rights: can you buck the company culture? M. M. Kennedy. il *Glamour* 87:127 S '89

Meetings that make sense [effects of corporate culture] D. Cole. il *Psychology Today* 23:14-15 My '89

CORPORATE DEBT *See* Corporations—Finance

CORPORATE DINING ROOMS *See* Executive dining rooms

CORPORATE ETHICS *See* Business ethics

CORPORATE EXECUTIVE FELLOWS PROGRAM

CEF fellowship program adds mentorship touch. B. Watson. il *Black Enterprise* 19:19 Ja '89

CORPORATE FLYING *See* Airplanes in business

CORPORATE GIVING *See* Corporations—Charitable contributions

CORPORATE HEADHUNTERS *See* Executive search consultants

CORPORATE INCOME TAX *See* Corporations—Taxation

CORPORATE LAW *See* Corporation law

CORPORATE LIQUIDATION *See* Liquidation

CORPORATE LOBBY *See* Lobbyists and lobbying

CORPORATE LOYALTY

Where did the gung-ho go? J. Castro. il *Time* 134:52-4+ S 11 '89

CORPORATE MANAGEMENT *See* Business management

CORPORATE NAMES *See* Corporations—Names

CORPORATE NEPOTISM *See* Nepotism

CORPORATE PARTNERS LP

Round two for Polaroid and Shamrock [stock buyback] K. H. Hammonds. il *Business Week* p32 F 13 '89

CORPORATE PATRONAGE OF ART *See* Art and industry

CORPORATE PATRONAGE OF THE ARTS *See* Arts and industry

CORPORATE PILOTS *See* Air pilots

CORPORATE PLANNERS & COORDINATORS

Penthouse properties, corporate style [office of C. Ugiss, vice president] L. Rosch. il por *Working Woman* 14:120-1 O '89

CORPORATE PLANNING *See* Business planning

CORPORATE POWER *See* Big business

CORPORATE PROFIT *See* Corporations—Finance

CORPORATE RECREATION PROGRAMS *See* Industry—Recreation programs

CORPORATE RECRUITING *See* Employees—Recruiting

CORPORATE REORGANIZATION *See* Corporations—Reorganization

CORPORATE RESPONSIBILITY *See* Business—Social aspects

CORPORATE SECRETS *See* Trade secrets

CORPORATE SPONSORSHIP OF SPORTS EVENTS *See* Business and sports

CORPORATE TRAINING FILMS *See* Motion pictures in industry

CORPORATE TURNAROUNDS

Back from the brink of bankruptcy [C. Hayle of Goodman & Hayle Information Systems, Inc.] L. Washer. il pors *Working Woman* 14:61-4 S '89

Buying on bad news [purchasing stock of companies in trouble] W. Giese. il *Changing Times* 43:41-2+ Ag '89

Scuffle in the boardroom [L. T. Sovey vs. J. Hamilton at Texfi Industries] A. A. Lappen. pors *Forbes* 144:112+ O 16 '89

Sifting ashes on Wall Street: turnaround artists prosper rescuing failed LBOs. D. Pauly. il *Newsweek* 114:42-3 S 4 '89

To jump or not to jump [job in an ailing company] D. Machan. il *Forbes* 144:136 Ag 7 '89

CORPORATION FOR PUBLIC BROADCASTING

Highbrow pork barrel. R. J. Samuelson. il *Newsweek* 114:44 Ag 21 '89

CORPORATION LAW

See also

Antitrust law

Corporations—Acquisitions and mergers—Laws and regulations

Incorporation

Liability (Law)

Small business—Laws and regulations

United States. Securities and Exchange Commission

CORPORATION LAW—*cont.*

Managing your lawyer. E. G. Krasnow and R. S. Conrad. il *Nation's Business* 77:70-2 Ap '89

On the docket. See issues of Forbes

CORPORATION REPORTS

See also

Financial statements

Annual reports: the SEC cracks the whip. T. Smart. il *Business Week* p74 Ap 10 '89

Cute tricks on the bottom line. G. Hector. il *Fortune* 119:193+ Ap 24 '89

'Hello, sweetheart, get me corporate public relations' [1988 annual reports] A. Rothman. il *Business Week* p34 Ap 24 '89

How to read financial reports. W. M. Woodard. il *Black Enterprise* 19:90-2+ My '89

Nasty surprises [requiring audited quarterly reports] P. Wang. il *Forbes* 143:72 Ja 23 '89

CORPORATIONS

See also

Big business

Black business enterprises

Black executives

Closely held corporations

Executives

Family corporations

Farm corporations

Hispanic American business enterprises

Minority business enterprises

Proxies

Small business

Stockholders

Stocks

Women executives

The 50 best places for blacks to work [cover story] il *Black Enterprise* 19:73-8+ F '89

America's most admired corporations [cover story] C. Davenport. il *Fortune* 119:68-71+ Ja 30 '89

Business should speak up. M. Novak. il *Forbes* 143:120 My 1 '89

The corporation. See issues of Business Week

Accounting

See also

Audit committees

Corporation reports

Depreciation—Accounting

Insurance companies—Accounting

Photographic industry—Accounting

Small business—Accounting

Numbers game. See issues of Forbes

Acquisitions and mergers

See also

Accounting firms—Acquisitions and mergers

Advertising agencies—Acquisitions and mergers

Aerospace industries—Acquisitions and mergers

Air freight service—Acquisitions and mergers

Airlines—Acquisitions and mergers

Airplane industry—Acquisitions and mergers

Automobile equipment industry—Acquisitions and mergers

Automobile industry—Acquisitions and mergers

Avionics industry—Acquisitions and mergers

Bank holding companies—Acquisitions and mergers

Banks and banking—Acquisitions and mergers

Boating industry—Acquisitions and mergers

Booksellers and bookselling—Acquisitions and mergers

Brewing industry—Acquisitions and mergers

Brokers—Acquisitions and mergers

Building materials industry—Acquisitions and mergers

Cable television—Acquisitions and mergers

Casinos—Acquisitions and mergers

Cellular radio—Acquisitions and mergers

Chemical industries—Acquisitions and mergers

Computer industry—Acquisitions and mergers

Computer service industries—Acquisitions and mergers

Container industry—Acquisitions and mergers

Cosmetics industry—Acquisitions and mergers

Department stores—Acquisitions and mergers

Drug industry—Acquisitions and mergers

Electric utilities—Acquisitions and mergers

Electronic industries—Acquisitions and mergers

Entertainment industry—Acquisitions and mergers

Eyewear stores—Acquisitions and mergers

Fast food restaurants—Acquisitions and mergers

Financial institutions—Acquisitions and mergers

Food industry—Acquisitions and mergers

Fruit industry—Acquisitions and mergers

Genetic research industry—Acquisitions and mergers

Greenmail

Grocery trade—Acquisitions and mergers

Hospital management industry—Acquisitions and mergers

Hotels, motels, etc.—Acquisitions and mergers

Household appliances industry—Acquisitions and mergers

Household furnishings industry—Acquisitions and mergers

Insurance companies—Acquisitions and mergers

Investment banking—Acquisitions and mergers

Investment trusts—Acquisitions and mergers

Law firms—Acquisitions and mergers

Leveraged buyouts

Liquor industry—Acquisitions and mergers

Lumber industry—Acquisitions and mergers

Marketing consultants—Acquisitions and mergers

Mass media industry—Acquisitions and mergers

Meat industry—Acquisitions and mergers

Mining industry—Acquisitions and mergers

Motion picture industry—Acquisitions and mergers

Munitions—Acquisitions and mergers

Newspaper publishers and publishing—Acquisitions and mergers

Paper industry—Acquisitions and mergers

Perfume industry—Acquisitions and mergers

Personal care products industry—Acquisitions and mergers

Petroleum equipment industry—Acquisitions and mergers

Petroleum industry—Acquisitions and mergers

Phonograph record industry—Acquisitions and mergers

Photographic industry—Acquisitions and mergers

Pipeline companies—Acquisitions and mergers

Poultry industry—Acquisitions and mergers

Printing industry—Acquisitions and mergers

Publishers and publishing—Acquisitions and mergers

Railroads—Acquisitions and mergers

Real estate business—Acquisitions and mergers

Restaurants—Acquisitions and mergers

Retail trade—Acquisitions and mergers

Shoe industry—Acquisitions and mergers

Supermarkets—Acquisitions and mergers

Tape recording industry—Acquisitions and mergers

Telecommunication—Acquisitions and mergers

Telephone companies—Acquisitions and mergers

Television industry—Acquisitions and mergers

Textile industry—Acquisitions and mergers

Tire industry—Acquisitions and mergers

Tobacco industry—Acquisitions and mergers

Truck industry—Acquisitions and mergers

The acquisition boom has lost a lot of its thunder . . . but takeover candidates still thrill Wall Street. G. Koretz. il *Business Week* p18 Je 12 '89

America pays the price. R. B. Reich. il *The New York Times Magazine* p32-3+ Ja 29 '89

The art of selling shares when a raider is buying. L. Zinn. il *Business Week* p236 S 25 '89

"Bid-'em-up Bruce"? [B. Wasserstein; cover story] D. Fanning. il pors *Forbes* 144:58-61 Ag 7 '89

The big comeuppance [corporate raiders suffer setbacks] J. Greenwald. il *Time* 134:74-6 D 11 '89

Black & Decker cuts a neat dovetail joint [merger with Emhart] J. Weber, Jr. il por *Business Week* p52-3 Jl 31 '89

The case for takeovers. C. C. Icahn. *The New York Times Magazine* p34 Ja 29 '89

Corporate takeovers [address, February 7, 1989] J. G. Smale. *Vital Speeches of the Day* 55:330-2 Mr 15 '89

Deals of the year. R. Henkoff. il *Fortune* 119:162-4+ Ja 30 '89

Deals that smell bad [toxic waste undoing takeovers] R. Simon. il *Forbes* 143:49+ My 15 '89

Deals, yes. Maniac deals, no [aftermath of Friday the 13, 1989 stock plunge] J. H. Dobrzynski. il *Business Week* p30-1 O 30 '89

Do takeovers make managers myopic? [impact on R&D spending] S. Nasar. il *U.S. News & World Report* 107:59 D 4 '89

Good idea [earnout deals] E. F. Cone. il por *Forbes* 143:10 F 6 '89

Harold Simmons is coming out to play again. T. Mason. il por *Business Week* p44+ Ja 9 '89

Honeywell and GE may be thinking of meshing gears. G. G. Marcial. il *Business Week* p130 Jl 17 '89

How to play the takeover game. J. Kosnett. il *Changing Times* 43:69-70+ Ap '89

I call them "takeaways". K. L. Fisher. il *Forbes* 143:180 Ap 3 '89

Icahn edges closer to taking USX. G. G. Marcial. *Business Week* p180 N 6 '89

Intermark keeps pressing its luck—and winning [buying Fuqua] S. Toy. il por *Business Week* p60+ F 6 '89

Investors are developing a taste for this poison [poison put insurance] L. Light. il *Business Week* p78 Jl 10 '89

Is Wasserstein's star tarnished? L. J. Nathans. il por *Business Week* p88-90 O 2 '89

Look what restructuring can do [views of T. B. Pickens] M. Magnet. por *Fortune* 120:72-3 Jl 3 '89

Looking for a few good takeover stocks? J. Friedman. il *Business Week* p108-9 D 25 '89-Ja 1 '90

The Marvin Davis mystique: less than meets the eye? R. Grover and C. Welles. il por *Business Week* p70-1 Ag 28 '89

The merger wars are turning downright friendly [stock swaps] L. J. Nathans. il *Business Week* p116-17 O 23 '89

Nelson Peltz: shopping to chase the blues. K. Deveny. il pors *Business Week* p143 Je 26 '89

CORPORATIONS—Acquisitions and mergers—*cont.*

A new era of rapid rise and ruin [past five years' departures from Fortune 500] J. P. Newport, Jr. il *Fortune* 119:77+ Ap 24 '89

The other Disney in the spotlight [R. Disney] F. Rice. il pors *Fortune* 119:161+ Je 5 '89

The price was right [Sara Lee acquires Champion Products] W. Heuslein. il *Forbes* 143:10 My 15 '89

Progress isn't drowning in debt—yet [impact of leveraged buyouts and merger mania on R&D] K. Deveny. il *Business Week* Special Issue:110 Je 16 '89

R&D suffers after corporate raids [National Science Foundation survey] M. Crawford. *Science* 243:882 F 17 '89

Ready, aim, fire: acquirers are hunting a new flock of targets. J. Edgerton and others. il *Money* 18:7 Mr '89

Sam, make way for Ron [R. Perelman's wealth] il por *Time* 133:87 My 22 '89

Secret agent [R. M. Bass] J. P. Newport, Jr. il por *Fortune* 119:50 Ja 2 '89

Surviving corporate cutbacks [black women] J. Malveaux. il *Essence* 19:107 Ap '89

Take the money and run [stock that becomes target] M. J. Williams. il *Fortune* 119:26 Ja 2 '89

Takeovers [address, February 23, 1989] J. R. Munro. *Vital Speeches of the Day* 55:470-3 My 15 '89

That's Sam Spade leafing through the ledgers [using private eyes in takeover battles] R. Grover. il *Business Week* p95+ My 29 '89

The top 200 deals. J. H. Dobrzynski. il *Business Week* Special Issue:35+ Ap 14 '89

USX: Icahn's back, and this time he has the cash. G. L. Miles. il por *Business Week* p40 Je 19 '89

USX: the next apple of Icahn's keen eye? G. G. Marcial. il *Business Week* p134 F 20 '89

Victor Posner may soon taste his own medicine [how the raider's DWG got put into play] G. DeGeorge. il pors *Business Week* p34+ Ap 10 '89

The whistling billionaire [H. C. Simmons] A. E. Serwer. il pors *Fortune* 119:102+ Ap 10 '89

The wolves of Wall Street. D. R. Katz. il *Esquire* 111:99-100 Mr '89

The word from the playwright of Wall Street [interview with J. Sterner] R. Eisenberg. il por *Money* 18:12 O '89

International aspects

The 100 largest foreign investments in the U.S. il *Forbes* 144:313-16+ Jl 24 '89

A burgeoning empire [Canada's Irving family in Maine] S. McKay. il *Maclean's* 102:42+ F 6 '89

Forging new links [Semi-Tech's bid for SSMC] T. Fennell. il pors *Maclean's* 102:26-8 F 20 '89

Meet Wall Street's new bugaboo: CFIUS [Committee on Foreign Investment in the U.S.] L. J. Nathans. il *Business Week* p90-1 Je 12 '89

A raider from the north blows into the Windy City [Canada's J. Pattison eyes Whitman Corp.] B. Bremner. il por *Business Week* p34-5 Ja 16 '89

Restrictions on foreign investment [address, September 19, 1989] S. W. Liebeler. *Vital Speeches of the Day* 56:122-4 D 1 '89

Takeover fever [special section] il *Maclean's* 102:34-41 Ag 28 '89

Victor Posner and the case of the mystery financier [plan to sell Fischbach to an English investor] G. DeGeorge and R. A. Melcher. il por *Business Week* p34 Ag 28 '89

What foreigners will buy next. J. J. Curran. il *Fortune* 119:94-8 F 13 '89

Who is James Ting and what will he buy next? [SSMC] C. Hawkins. il por *Business Week* p33 F 13 '89

Laws and regulations

See also

Antitrust law

United States. Committee on Foreign Investment in the United States

Corporate merger legislation. il *Congressional Digest* 68:67-96 Mr '89

Delaware's Chancery Court: charting corporate futures. B. Saporito. il *Fortune* 120:10-11 Jl 17 '89

The feds finger an upstart raider, too [P. Bilzerian] D. Pauly. il por *Newsweek* 113:48 Ja 2 '89

First it was poison pills—now it's 'people pills' [resignation pact for top managers] C. Farrell. *Business Week* p33-4 Ja 16 '89

Heading for D-Day in Delaware [court to decide whether Time Inc. up for sale] J. Castro. il *Time* 134:44 Jl 10 '89

How to drive off a raider [battle over Time Inc.] J. Schwartz. il *Newsweek* 114:43 Ag 7 '89

Is getting rich quick becoming a crime? [case of P. Bilzerian] C. Byron. il por *New York* 22:25-6 Je 12 '89

A legal battle that could kill off friendly mergers [court to decide if Time-Warner stock swap put Time in play] M. Galen. il *Business Week* p27 Jl 3 '89

A legal victory for the long term [Delaware court allows Time Inc. to buy Warner and repel Paramount's hostile bid] B. Saporito. il *Fortune* 120:56-9 Ag 14 '89

More states are telling raiders: not here, you don't. T. Smart. il *Business Week* p28 F 13 '89

A new way to keep raiders at bay [ESOP defense gets court O.K.] K. H. Hammonds. il *Business Week* p39 Ja 23 '89

One for the books [Delaware court rejects Paramount's challenge to Time-Warner deal] J. Greenwald. il *Time* 134:34-6 Jl 24 '89

The quiet crusader [Treasury Secretary N. Brady; cover story] H. Gleckman. il por *Business Week* p80-3+ S 18 '89

A raider's days of reckoning [SEC files suit against P. Bilzerian] il por *Time* 134:45 Jl 10 '89

Real victim of the takeover fever [address, April 7, 1989] J. A. Katarincic. *Vital Speeches of the Day* 55:540-4 Je 15 '89

Time Inc. gets a green light [Delaware judge OKs Warner bid] J. Schwartz and C. Friday. il *Newsweek* 114:50 Jl 24 '89

Time-Warner: this close to victory [Delaware court decision; special section] il *Business Week* p26-9 Jl 31 '89

Time's next battleground [Delaware Chancery Court] R. Sandza. *Newsweek* 114:31 Jl 10 '89

Uncle Sam won't defend against raiders. H. Banks. *Forbes* 143:33 Mr 6 '89

Wall Street is glued to the Bilzerian trial. M. Galen. il por *Business Week* p33 My 15 '89

Laws and regulations—Canada

A warning from Ottawa. B. Wallace. il por *Maclean's* 102:38 Ja 30 '89

Laws and regulations—France

The chevalier blanc heading the industry ministry [R. Fauroux] F. J. Comes. il por *Business Week* p64 Mr 13 '89

Laws and regulations—Switzerland

The three-percent solution. J. Marcom, Jr. il *Forbes* 143:68 My 29 '89

Laws and regulations—Western Europe

Writing the new rules for Europe's merger game. J. Kapstein. il *Business Week* p48-9 F 6 '89

Australia

The high rollers hit a losing streak. S. Hutcheon. il *Business Week* p90-1 S 4 '89

Canada

The dark side of merger mania. P. C. Newman. il *Maclean's* 102:31 F 6 '89

The invasion of the frenzy-feeders. D. Francis. il *Maclean's* 102:11 Mr 20 '89

The North American shakeout arrives ahead of schedule. C. Hawkins and W. J. Holstein. il *Business Week* p34-5 Ap 17 '89

Takeover fever [special section] il *Maclean's* 102:34-41 Ag 28 '89

Takeover fever hits Canada [cover story; special section; with editorial comment by Kevin Doyle] il *Maclean's* 102:4, 30-6+ Ja 30 '89

Great Britain

A British war—on Yankee soil [Goldsmith-BAT takeover fight] T. Smart and M. Maremont. il *Business Week* p33 S 11 '89

'Goldfinger' is back [Sir J. Goldsmith's bid for BAT Industries] L. Reibstein. il por *Newsweek* 114:48-9 Jl 24 '89

Jimmy Goldsmith, leading indicator [bid for BAT Industries] C. P. Work. il por *U.S. News & World Report* 107:43-4 Jl 24 '89

A raider returns [J. Goldsmith's bid for BAT Industries] J. DeMont. il por *Maclean's* 102:34 Jl 24 '89

Storming a British blue chip [J. Goldsmith's bid for BAT] R. A. Melcher. il por *Business Week* p18-19 Jl 24 '89

Take that, Jimmy Goldsmith [BAT Industries sell-off] R. A. Melcher. il *Business Week* p60-1 O 9 '89

That's a reach, Sir James [J. Goldsmith's bid for B.A.T.] J. Castro. il por *Time* 134:36-7 Jl 24 '89

Up to B.A.T.? [J. Coxon and Cigna Corp. to benefit in battle for BAT Industries] J. Zweig. il por *Forbes* 144:102 Ag 21 '89

Italy

How to build a $30 billion empire in five years [R. Gardini] J. Rossant. il por *Business Week* p58-9 Jl 3 '89

Japan

Japan learns the takeover game. G. Hector. il *Fortune* 120:121+ Jl 31 '89

The Japanese aren't flocking to this boutique—yet [Nomura Wasserella] T. Holden. il *Business Week* p39+ Ag 21 '89

Japanese dealmakers yearn to play QB [Japanese act as silent partners to American investment bankers] J. Friedman. il *Business Week* p82-3 Ja 16 '89

Western Europe

Europe's giants are hungrier than ever. B. Riemer. il *Business Week* p144 Jl 17 '89

From Balzac to Salvador Dali. D. Singer. il *The Nation* 248:333-4+ Mr 13 '89

'Nothing is sacred, and no one is too big'. R. A. Melcher. il *Business Week* p44-5 Jl 31 '89

Tough guys with a genteel manner [Lazard Frères & Cie] P. Berman. il por *Forbes* 144:75-80 Jl 10 '89

Where will merger mania strike next? C. Farrell. il *Business Week* p32 D 18 '89

CORPORATIONS—*cont.*

Advertising
See Advertising

Charitable contributions
Armenia: what U.S. companies did. F. H. Katayama. il *Fortune* 119:10-11 Ja 16 '89

The arts—and more [corporations support black charities] J. R. Barras. il *American Visions* 4:35 Je '89

A call to pig out for peace [Ben & Jerry's support for 1% for Peace] il *Newsweek* 113:45 My 8 '89

Charity begins abroad [Japanese corporations donate to American charities] A. Miller. il *Newsweek* 114:41 Ag 21 '89

An executive's guide to volunteering. P. Kruger. *Working Woman* 14:86-8 D '89

How big business bankrolls the left. W. T. Poole. il *National Review* 41:34-7 Mr 10 '89

Let's make a deal [corporations match employee contributions to PACs with donations to charities] W. Montague. *Common Cause Magazine* 15:9 S/O '89

Planned Parenthood didn't plan on this: abortion foes are attacking the agency's corporate sponsors. B. Tierney. il *Business Week* p34 Jl 3 '89

The thoughts that count. A. Matthews. il *Forbes* 143:126-8 F 20 '89

Crime
See Commercial crimes

Directories
America's 50 biggest exporters [with introd. by Edward Prewitt] il *Fortune* 120:50-1 Jl 17 '89

The corporate elite [cover story] il *Business Week* Special Issue:9-16+ O 20 '89

Corporate pacesetters: the top 100 companies with PCs [cover story; with editorial comment by Fred Abatemarco] S. R. Reed. il *Personal Computing* 13:5, 70-3+ S '89

The Forbes 500s annual directory [special section] il *Forbes* 143:173-5+ My 1 '89

The Forbes foreign rankings [special section] il *Forbes* 144:277-80+ Jl 24 '89

The Fortune 500: the largest U.S. industrial corporations [special issue] il *Fortune* 119:42-5+ Ap 24 '89

The Fortune international 500 [with introd. by Susan E. Kuhn and David J. Morrow] il *Fortune* 120:279-83+ Jl 31 '89

The service 500 [special section] il *Fortune* 119:351-5+ Je 5 '89

Directors
Courts clamp down on boards. S. C. Bahls and J. E. Bahls. il *Nation's Business* 77:52-3 D '89

Employee representation on U.S., German boards. E. M. Kassalow. bibl f *Monthly Labor Review* 112:39-42 S '89

The most influential corporate director [former Alberta premier P. Lougheed] P. C. Newman. il *Maclean's* 102:53 S 18 '89

Public pensions play tougher [California Public Employees' Retirement System nominee J. Brademas appointed Texaco director] F. H. Katayama. il por *Fortune* 119:16 F 27 '89

Shareholders have too much power. P. Róna. il *Fortune* 120:125-6 Ag 28 '89

Taking charge [cover story; special section] il *Business Week* p66-71+ Jl 3 '89

Divestiture
Chrysler heads back to earth [selling aerospace and defense operations] W. Zellner. il *Business Week* p46 D 18 '89

Did Hanson hide bad news? [Smith Corona spinoff] C. Tucher. *Business Week* p27-8 Ag 28 '89

Happy breakups. C. Palmeri. *Forbes* 144:110-11 Ag 21 '89

Making money in unmergers [spinoffs as investments] R. J. Maturi. il *Changing Times* 43:31-2+ Je '89

A new iron man recasts USX [C. A. Corry sells Texas Oil & Gas assets] G. L. Miles. il por *Business Week* p37 O 16 '89

Spinning gold out of spinoffs [M. Gabelli's interest in Household International spinoffs] G. G. Marcial. *Business Week* p80 Jl 31 '89

Employees
See Employees

Finance
See also
Bonds
Business failures
Corporations—Accounting
Corporations—Valuation
Corporations, International—Finance
Cost control
Dividends
Employee stock ownership plans
Securities
Small business—Finance
Swap financing

Be wise, equitize [deleveraging of U.S. business] P. Berman. il *Forbes* 144:38-40 N 27 '89

The bills are coming due [leverage binge winds down; cover story] C. Farrell. il *Business Week* p84-7+ S 11 '89

Corporate America wants out from under its junk pile. L. Light. il *Business Week* p80-1 Ag 21 '89

Corporate earnings cast a shadow on the Street. K. Madigan. il *Business Week* p32-3 O 30 '89

Corporate finance. See issues of Business Week

Corporate profits: the old expansion is paying new dividends. il *Business Week* p30-1 F 13 '89

The debt addiction. F. G. Rohatyn. il *The New York Review of Books* 36:39-42 Ap 13 '89

Debt on trial [special section] il *U.S. News & World Report* 106:60-3+ F 13 '89

Five steps to profits. C. Gottlieb. *Fortune* 119:14 Ja 30 '89

The Fortune 500: the largest U.S. industrial corporations [special issue] il *Fortune* 119:42-5+ Ap 24 '89

Henry Kaufman: corporate debt erodes competition [interview] J. H. Dobrzynski. por *Business Week* p40 Mr 20 '89

Higher profits lie ahead, but getting them will take work. M. F. Allyn. il *Fortune* 119:33-4 Ja 30 '89

Industry outlook: 1989 [cover story; special section] il *Business Week* p63-71+ Ja 9 '89

The landing may be soft, but it's still hammering profits. M. J. Mandel. il *Business Week* p22 O 2 '89

Michael Milken, meet Sewell Avery [debt] J. Grant. il *Forbes* 144 Special Issue:60-2+ O 23 '89

Pie-slicers vs. pie-enlargers. R. B. Reich. *The Washington Monthly* 21:60 F '89

This credit squeeze is quiet—but it still hurts. C. Farrell. il *Business Week* p104-5 N 13 '89

Up from bean counting [chief financial officers] il *Business Week* Special Issue:62-3+ O 20 '89

Where all the money comes from [cash for deals] V. Brownstein. il *Fortune* 119:75-6+ Ja 2 '89

Will corporate debt force the Fed to scrap zero inflation? K. Pennar. il *Business Week* p22 O 23 '89

Statistics
See also
Corporations, International—Finance—Statistics

41st annual report on American industry [cover story; special issue] il *Forbes* 143:77-9+ Ja 9 '89

The 400 largest private companies in the U.S. il *Forbes* 144:220-2+ D 11 '89

The Business week top 1000. il *Business Week* Special Issue:14-17+ Ap 14 '89

Corporate scoreboard. il *Business Week* p138-42+ N 13 '89

Corporate scoreboard. il *Business Week* p62-5+ Mr 20 '89

Corporate scoreboard. il *Business Week* p64-7+ My 15 '89

Corporate scoreboard. il *Business Week* p106-10+ Ag 14 '89

The Forbes 500s annual directory [special section] il *Forbes* 143:173-5+ My 1 '89

The Fortune 500 [special section; with introd. by Reed Abelson and Rahul Jacob] il *Fortune* 119:345-8+ Ap 24 '89

A sample of first-quarter profits. il *Business Week* p28-9 My 1 '89

A sample of second-quarter profits. il *Business Week* p30-1 Jl 31 '89

A scoreboard to help you play by the numbers. il *Business Week* p155-62+ D 25 '89-Ja 1 '90

Foreign subsidiaries
See Corporations, International

Laws and regulations
See Corporation law

Liquidation
See Liquidation

Location
See Location in business and industry

Mailrooms
See Mailrooms

Management
See Business management

Meetings
How to get good ideas out of quiet employees. P. Amend. *Working Woman* 14:44+ S '89

How to keep your meetings upbeat. E. J. Belzer. il *Working Woman* 14:32 N '89

Meetings count. D. Machan. il *Forbes* 144:136-7 Ag 7 '89

Meetings that make sense [effects of corporate culture] D. Cole. il *Psychology Today* 23:14-15 My '89

No detail too small. P. Dininny. il *Nation's Business* 77:62+ O '89

Seating
Seating for success [research by Donald C. Stone] B. Lawren. il *Psychology Today* 23:16+ S '89

Names
Giving bad puns the business. il *Newsweek* 114:71 D 11 '89

Naming your company. P. Edwards and S. Edwards. il *Home Office Computing* 7:28 Jl '89

Playing a game of 'name that company' [contest to rename Fluorocarbon Corp.] il *Newsweek* 114:37 Ag 14 '89

Price policies
See Price policies

Public relations
See Business—Public relations

Real estate operations
From backwater to blockbuster. L. Light and D. Zigas. il *Business Week* p96-7 S 11 '89

CORPORATIONS—*cont.*

Regulation

See Industry and state

Reorganization

See also

Recapitalization

Workout investments

Is restructuring good for you after all? H. Banks. *Forbes* 144:33 N 13 '89

Look what restructuring can do [views of T. B. Pickens] M. Magnet. por *Fortune* 120:72-3 Jl 3 '89

Now all Global Marine needs is a market. T. Vogel. il *Business Week* p44 Mr 13 '89

Why cowboy management is bad for American business [excerpt from When giants learn to dance] R. M. Kanter. il por *Working Woman* 14:134-6+ Ap '89

Security measures

See Industry—Security measures

Social aspects

See Business—Social aspects

Spinoffs

See Corporations—Divestiture

Statistics

See also

Corporations—Finance—Statistics

Subsidiaries

Accounting

Mishmash accounting [companies forced to fold subs' assets and liabilities into parent's consolidated balance sheet] D. Wechsler. il *Forbes* 144:192 N 27 '89

What's off, what's on? [off balance sheet financial subsidiaries] P. Wang. il *Forbes* 143:110 F 20 '89

Taxation

See also

Alternative minimum tax

Corporations, International—Taxation

Family corporations—Taxation

Gas industry—Taxation

Insurance companies—Taxation

Inventories—Taxation

Investment trusts—Taxation

Personal holding companies—Taxation

Real estate business—Taxation

S corporations

Small business—Taxation

Debt and taxes [taxing debt and equity payments equally] A. Gray, Jr. and A. B. Laffer. il *National Review* 41:38-9 S 1 '89

Dr. Brady's cure for corporate myopia [plan to cut corporate taxes in order to increase capital investment] S. Dentzer. il *U.S. News & World Report* 107:48+ S 25 '89

Give us a break on these tax breaks. H. Gleckman. il *Business Week* p30 N 20 '89

Holdup in the Windy City [tax incentives spur Sears' move to suburbs] P. Glastris. il *U.S. News & World Report* 107:40-1 Jl 17 '89

"It's the right thing to do" [interest rate swap tax treatment] L. Saunders. il *Forbes* 143:104 Ap 17 '89

Taxing matters. See issues of Forbes

Tinkering with tax reform: a bad idea that will just get worse. H. Gleckman. il *Business Week* p104+ N 6 '89

Where losses are assets [tax-loss carryforwards] C. Palmeri. il *Forbes* 144:154-5 Ag 7 '89

Who got reformed? L. Saunders. il *Forbes* 143:297-8 Ja 9 '89

Valuation

5 ways to find good stocks now. M. Schiffres. il *Changing Times* 43:64-6+ D '89

Basic training for value investors [interview with T. Rosenberg of Burney Co.] E. Schultz. il por *Fortune* 119:29-31 Ja 2 '89

Berkshire Hathaway II? [M. Gabelli] J. Clements. il por *Forbes* 144:40-1 Jl 24 '89

Better dead than alive [stock picker P. Cundill] J. Clements. il por *Forbes* 143:208-9 Mr 20 '89

The Business week top 1000. il *Business Week* Special Issue:14-17+ Ap 14 '89

Cash flow can be the investor's best guide to a stock's true worth. A. Rock. *Money* 18:161-2 Mr '89

Cashing in on cash-rich companies. J. Kosnett. il *Changing Times* 43:29-33 Jl '89

The Dinkins stock crash [D. Dinkins accused of undervaluation of Inner City Broadcasting stock] C. Byron. il *New York* 22:30+ N 6 '89

Down-and-out investing. J. B. Quinn. il *Newsweek* 114:46 Jl 3 '89

Earnings, schmernings—look at the cash. J. M. Laderman. il *Business Week* p56-7 Jl 24 '89

The guy who helped invent the IRA tells you how to make money in one now [views of R. Murray] J. Edgerton. il por *Money* 18:195-6 O '89

Knowing when to stick it out is all in the numbers. T. Thompson. il *U.S. News & World Report* 107:77-8+ O 23 '89

Look before you laugh at 'Chapter 11' investments. L. Zinn. il *Business Week* p100 Ap 10 '89

A peculiar beauty contest [concentration on cash flow vs. earnings in stock valuation as highlighted in Time Inc. merger] D. Wechsler. il *Forbes* 144:43-4+ Jl 10 '89

Searching for value in the stock market [cover story] F. N. Jelks. il *Consumers' Research Magazine* 72:10-13 Mr '89

This professor majors in finding stocks that double in value [M. Reinganum] B. Hager. il por *Money* 18:153-4 F '89

Two different animals: brand awareness & corporate image [interview with M. S. Forbes] *Forbes* 143:20 Mr 6 '89

Value is where you find it [Fireman's Fund's stock picker B. Bruce] J. Clements. il por *Forbes* 143:62+ Mr 20 '89

Waltzing with the wallflowers [interview with C. Browne of Tweedy Browne] S. Smith. il por *Fortune* 119:43+ Ap 10 '89

What looks good to Mario Gabelli [interview] J. Mendes. il por *Fortune* 119:32+ Mr 27 '89

What to do when the stock market drops 200 points [dividend discount model] E. Schultz. il *Fortune* 120:53+ N 20 '89

Where a contrarian finds value in today's blue chips [M. O'Higgins] il por *Money* 18:7-8 My '89

Will the real Ben Graham please stand up? [stock pickers E. Kiehne and W. H. Miller] J. Clements. il pors *Forbes* 144:310+ D 11 '89

CORPORATIONS, GOVERNMENT *See* Government corporations

CORPORATIONS, INTERNATIONAL

See also

Banks and banking, International

Business—International aspects

Iranian seizure of United States embassy, 1979-1981—Economic aspects

United Nations. Commission on Transnational Corporations

The Forbes foreign rankings [special section] il *Forbes* 144:277-80+ Jl 24 '89

Holding big businesses accountable. R. J. Barnet. *Utne Reader* p68-9 Ja/F '89

Your rivals can be your allies [joint ventures with foreign competitors] L. Kraar. il map *Fortune* 119:66-8+ Mr 27 '89

Finance

The action is abroad. W. J. Holstein. il *Business Week* p28-9 My 1 '89

Seeking growth in a smaller world [investing in global companies] S. Reed. il *Business Week* p94-5 O 16 '89

Statistics

The 100 largest U.S. multinationals. il *Forbes* 144:320+ Jl 24 '89

The 500 largest foreign companies. il *Forbes* 144:282-6+ Jl 24 '89

America's 50 biggest exporters [with introd. by Edward Prewitt] il *Fortune* 120:50-1 Jl 17 '89

The Fortune international 500 [with introd. by Susan E. Kuhn and David J. Morrow] il *Fortune* 120:279-83+ Jl 31 '89

The global 1000. il *Business Week* p139-41+ Jl 17 '89

Management

The global corporation [address, October 2, 1989] R. G. Holder. *Vital Speeches of the Day* 56:98-100 D 1 '89

Going global. il *Business Week* Special Issue:9-16+ O 20 '89

How to go global—and why. J. Main. il map *Fortune* 120:70-3+ Ag 28 '89

Taxation

Tax Americana. R. S. McIntyre. *The New Republic* 200:18-20 Mr 27 '89

CORPORATIONS AND ART *See* Art and industry

CORPORATIONS AND DAY CARE *See* Day care and industry

CORPORATIONS AND EDUCATION *See* Business and education

CORPORATIONS AND GOVERNMENT *See* Industry and state

CORPORATIONS AND MASS MEDIA *See* Business and mass media

CORPORATIONS AND STATE *See* Industry and state

CORPORATIONS AND THE ARTS *See* Arts and industry

CORPS OF ENGINEERS *See* United States. Army. Corps of Engineers

CORPULENCE *See* Obesity

CORPUS CHRISTI (TEX.)

City hall

Government writ large [designed by Taft Architects and Kipp, Richter & Associates] P. M. Sachner. il *Architectural Record* 177:110-13 Ja '89

CORR, D. JOSEPH

about

Joseph Corr. T. Vogel. il por *Business Week* Special Issue:138 Ap 14 '89

A Mr. Fix-It goes to work on Lorenzo's Continental. T. Vogel. il por *Business Week* p132-3+ My 22 '89

CORREA G., HELENA

Choice tasters. il *World Press Review* 36:52 Je '89

CORRECTIONAL INSTITUTIONS *See* Prisons

CORREIA-AFONSO, JOHN

'Christians and spices': the Portuguese in India. il map *The Courier (Unesco)* 42:33-4 Ap '89

CORRELATION (EDUCATION)
Interdisciplinary studies in higher education. J. G. Gaff. *The Education Digest* 55:57-60 O '89
CORRELATION (STATISTICS)
Mr. Correlation speaks. D. Seligman. il *Fortune* 120:252 S 25 '89
CORRESPONDENCE *See* Business writing; Letters
CORRESPONDENCE SCHOOLS AND COURSES
Spotlight on schools. il *'Teen* 33:73 Ja '89
Spotlight on schools. il *'Teen* 33:97 Mr '89
CORRESPONDENTS, FOREIGN *See* Foreign correspondents
CORROSION AND ANTICORROSIVES
See also
Airplanes, Jet—Corrosion and anticorrosives
Automobiles—Corrosion and anticorrosives
Space vehicles—Corrosion and anticorrosives
Space vehicles—Propulsion systems—Corrosion and anticorrosives
Window on the chemistry of cracking glass [research by Bruce Bunker and Terry Michalske] F. Flam. *Science News* 135:167 Mr 18 '89
CORRUPTION, POLITICAL *See* Politics, Corruption in
CORRY, CHARLES A.
about
Charles Corry. G. L. Miles. il por *Business Week* Special Issue:136 Ap 14 '89
A new iron man recasts USX. G. L. Miles. il por *Business Week* p37 O 16 '89
LE CORSAIRE [ballet] *See* Ballet reviews—Single works
CORSON, BEN
New developments in corporate responsibility. *Utne Reader* p62 Ja/F '89
CORTESE, JOHN JOSEPH
about
Moonwalking. *The New Yorker* 65:45-6 N 13 '89
CORTEZ, HERNÁN TORRES *See* Torres Cortez, Hernán
CORTEZ, JAYNE
Big fine woman from Ruleville (for Fannie Lou Hamer) [poem] *Essence* 19:150 F '89
CORTEZ, MAURO
about
Big scam on campus. F. Trippett. il por *Time* 134:25 S 25 '89
CORTICOSTEROIDS
1,25-dihydroxyvitamin D-responsive element and glucocorticoid repression in the osteocalcin gene. N. A. Morrison and others. bibl f il *Science* 246:1158-61 D 1 '89
Corticosteroid modulation of hippocampal potentials: increased effect with aging. D. S. Kerr and others. bibl f il *Science* 245:1505-9 S 29 '89
Effects of glucocorticoids and norepinephrine on the excitability in the hippocampus. M. Joëls and E. R. de Kloet. bibl f il *Science* 245:1502-5 S 29 '89
CORTRIGHT, DAVID
Shaping a peacetime economy. il *The Progressive* 53:20-2 Ja '89
CORVETTE (AUTOMOBILE) *See* Sports cars
CORWIN, ISIDORE
about
Brother Isidore covers 20 miles a day on his spiritual trek. B. Johnson. il pors *People Weekly* 32:63-4 Ag 7 '89
COS *See* Conscientious objectors
COSBY, BILL, 1937-
Exclusive! Bill Cosby's newest, funniest book [excerpt from Love and marriage] il pors *Good Housekeeping* 208:126+ Je '89
"Help! My wife drives me crazy!" [excerpt from Love and marriage] il por *Redbook* 173:114-15+ Jl '89
about
Bill and Camille Cosby discuss the secrets of living a better life [cover story] R. E. Johnson. il pors *Jet* 76:58-62 O 2 '89
Bill and Camille Cosby: first family of philanthropy [cover story] R. E. Johnson. il pors *Ebony* 44:25-6+ My '89
Bill and Camille Cosby give $1.5 million to Meharry and Bethune-Cookman colleges. il pors *Jet* 75:5-6 Ja 9 '89
Bill Cosby. il pors *People Weekly* 31 Special Issue:38-9 Summ '89
Bill Cosby. B. Darrach. por *People Weekly* 32 Special Issue:85 Fall '89
Bill Cosby and black leaders urge affluent blacks to give money. il por *Jet* 75:30-1 Ja 23 '89
Bill Cosby makes academic deal with Texas students. il pors *Jet* 77:33 N 20 '89
Bill Cosby responds to daughter's drug abuse with tough love. il pors *Jet* 77:64-5 O 16 '89
Bill Cosby's all-stars shock Eddie Murphy's all-stars team 30-18. il pors *Jet* 76:56-8 Jl 3 '89
Central State U. honors Cosby family generosity at Cleveland Classic. pors *Jet* 76:10 S 11 '89
Cosby does fund-raiser at Apollo for David Dinkins' N.Y.C. mayoral campaign. il pors *Jet* 77:38-9 O 9 '89
'Cosby show' no. 1 for fourth straight year, his 'A different world' no. 3. il por *Jet* 76:26 My 8 '89
Cosby's $20 million gift: a source of funds—and hope. K. D. Thompson. il por *Black Enterprise* 19:27 F '89
Cosbys backing race car driver Willy T. Ribbs in championship auto racing. il pors *Jet* 77:16-17 D 4 '89

Entertainer Bill Cosby is favorite celebrity endorser. il por *Jet* 77:22 N 6 '89
Funny valentine. B. D. Johnson. il pors *Maclean's* 102:60-1 My 1 '89
Philip Roth and Bill Cosby move houses for high stakes. pors *Publishers Weekly* 236:42-3 S 8 '89
Why Robert Culp's not happy with Bill Cosby. E. Kiersh. pors *TV Guide* 37:13-15 O 7-13 '89
COSBY, CAMILLE
about
Bill and Camille Cosby discuss the secrets of living a better life [cover story] R. E. Johnson. il pors *Jet* 76:58-62 O 2 '89
Bill and Camille Cosby: first family of philanthropy [cover story] R. E. Johnson. il pors *Ebony* 44:25-6+ My '89
Camille Cosby: an intimate portrait [cover story] S. S. Oliver. il pors *Essence* 20:62-4+ D '89
Camille Cosby warns Spelman grads about use of sex and money. il por *Jet* 76:4 Je 12 '89
Central State U. honors Cosby family generosity at Cleveland Classic. pors *Jet* 76:10 S 11 '89
COSBY, ERINN
about
Bill Cosby responds to daughter's drug abuse with tough love. il pors *Jet* 77:64-5 O 16 '89
THE COSBY SHOW [television program] *See* Television program reviews—Single works
COSELL, HOWARD, 1920-
about
Yearning for Howard. F. Lidz. por *Sports Illustrated* 70:86 My 29 '89
COSGROVE, JOHN D.
The watershed decade [address, June 20, 1989] *Vital Speeches of the Day* 55:744-7 O 1 '89
COSGROVE, RICHARD
Thirty thousand years of human colonization in Tasmania: new Pleistocene dates. bibl f il map *Science* 243:1706-8 Mr 31 '89
COSÌ FAN TUTTE [opera] *See* Mozart, Wolfgang Amadeus, 1756-1791
COSMAN, HUGH
about
Hugh's truck. *The New Yorker* 65:46-7 N 13 '89
COSMATOS, GEORGE P., 1941-
about
Leviathan [film] Reviews
People Weekly il 31:18 Ap 3 '89. N. Geeslin
COSMETIC ALLERGY *See* Allergy
COSMETIC BRUSHES
The subject is brushes. il *Mademoiselle* 95:42 O '89
With the right brushes, cosmetics go on better and stay on longer. C. Sullivan. il *Vogue* 179:376 S '89
COSMETIC DENTISTRY *See* Dentistry
COSMETIC SURGERY *See* Surgery, Plastic
COSMETICS
See also
Department stores—Cosmetics departments
Lipstick
Makeup
Mascaras
Powder (Face, toilet, etc.)
Suntan products
Active-duty skin care. S. Lord. il *Vogue* 179:166+ F '89
Basic foundation in beauty [for black women] il *Essence* 19:76-7 Ja '89
Botanical beauty [natural cosmetics] il *Harper's Bazaar* 122:152-3+ F '89
Cosmedics—makeup that's good to your skin. K. C. Engles. il *Redbook* 174:8+ N '89
Does skin really "work harder" at night? Here, an update on night creams: who should use them, how much can they really improve skin? L. F. McCarthy. *Vogue* 179:222 O '89
Dream creams [moisturizers] P. Lister. il *American Health* 8:82-3 Ja/F '89
Face it [foundations] il *'Teen* 33:88-9 N '89
Facial cleansers. il *Consumer Reports* 54:408-9 Je '89
Facial cleansers. il *Consumer Reports* 54:35-9 D '89
Food for thought [natural cosmetics] L. Wells. il *The New York Times Magazine* p28 Jl 30 '89
For fast, short-term skin firming and toning, there are now a multitude of interesting products to choose from. L. F. McCarthy. *Vogue* 179:154 Ag '89
Great skin: 27 new ways to fake it [foundations and powders] il *Glamour* 87:202-5 D '89
Images: best sellers. L. F. McCarthy. *Vogue* 179:108 Je '89
Keeping your cosmetics fresh. P. Boyer. il *Prevention (Emmaus, Pa.)* 41:94+ Ja '89
Makeup moves. L. Wells. il *The New York Times Magazine* p45 Ja 22 '89
Making a splash [waterproof cosmetics] L. Wells. il *The New York Times Magazine* p63 Je 4 '89
Moisturiffic! L. Lebowitz. il *Harper's Bazaar* 122:158-61+ My '89
Serious face-saving [anti-aging cosmetics and drugs] D. Sobel. il *Health (New York, N.Y.)* 21:64-5+ O '89
Skin futures. S. Lord. il *Vogue* 179:48 Ja '89

COSMETICS—*cont.*

Slough off! [facial masks] P. Boyer. il *Prevention (Emmaus, Pa.)* 41:90+ Mr '89

Summer looks. R. Wiest. il *American Health* 8:24-6+ Je '89

Sweet things. il *'Teen* 33:60-1 D '89

Water colors [waterproof cosmetics] S. Lord. il *Vogue* 179:198-9 Je '89

Wet! [waterproof cosmetics] il *Mademoiselle* 95:118-21 Jl '89

Winter wrap session. N. Malkin. il *Harper's Bazaar* 122:30+ F '89

The wrinkles in anti-aging cream claims [views of Fred Novice] il *USA Today (Periodical)* 117:9-10 Ja '89

Contamination

Safe makeup practices [laws require separate testers at cosmetic counters] L. A. Mark. il *American Health* 8:20 O '89

History

Exhibitions

Even pharaohs had facials [Perfumes and cosmetics in the ancient world at the Israel Museum] il *Newsweek* 114:79 D 11 '89

Labeling

Beauty language. J. Shields. *Vogue* 179:208 Mr '89

Skin-care labels: what do they really mean? L. F. McCarthy. *Vogue* 179:170+ My '89

Laws and regulations

Safe makeup practices [laws require separate testers at cosmetic counters] L. A. Mark. il *American Health* 8:20 O '89

Packaging

Bonfire on the vanity. E. Neier. il *Vogue* 179:147 My '89

Enjoy the gilt! [gold cosmetics packaging] il *Harper's Bazaar* 122:34 Ja '89

Prices

How different can a $17 lipstick be from $3 version? [cover story] G. Morgenson. il *Forbes* 144:128-30+ S 18 '89

Prices: out of sight. L. Wells. il *The New York Times Magazine* p58 Jl 16 '89

Storage

Images: beauty to go. S. Mitchell. il *Vogue* 179:62 Jl '89

Testing

Cosmetics firms drop Draize test. C. Holden. *Science* 245:125 Jl 14 '89

New test could spare rabbits [use of Tetrahymena] il *USA Today (Periodical)* 117:4-5 Je '89

COSMETICS FOR CHILDREN

Babes in makeup land. L. Wells. il *The New York Times Magazine* p46 Ag 13 '89

COSMETICS FOR MEN

See also

Perfumes for men

Flirting with men. L. Wells. il *The New York Times Magazine* p64 Ap 9 '89

Anecdotes, facetiae, satire, etc.

Images: men's grooming. W. Geist. il *Vogue* 179:94+ Je '89

COSMETICS INDUSTRY

See also

American Health and Beauty Aids Institute

Avon Products, Inc.

BeautiControl Cosmetics

Elizabeth Arden, Inc.

Estée Lauder, Inc.

Faberge Inc.

Fashion Fair Cosmetics, Inc.

Gazelle International

Johnson Products Company, Inc.

Juin Rachele Cosmetics Inc.

M&M Products Company

Madame C. J. Walker Company

Mary Kay Cosmetics, Inc.

Naomi Sims Beauty Products Ltd.

Perfume industry

Revlon Inc.

Soft Sheen Products Inc.

Inventing spring's colors. K. Beckett-Young. il *Health (New York, N.Y.)* 21:56-63 Mr '89

Acquisitions and mergers

Ding-dong, raider calling [I. Jacobs goes after Avon] K. Deveny. *Business Week* p51+ Ag 14 '89

International aspects

Unilever is all made up, with everywhere to go [acquisition of Fabergé and Elizabeth Arden] M. Maremont. il *Business Week* p33-4 Jl 31 '89

Advertising

Acceptably sexy [Estée Lauder] S. N. Chakravarty. il por *Forbes* 144:122+ N 13 '89

As time goes by [cosmetics ads and the middle age market] L. Wells. il *The New York Times Magazine* p86 Mr 19 '89

Do it yourself [D. Tarlow appointed executive vice president of advertising at Revlon] B. Kanner. il por *New York* 22:26+ Ag 21 '89

Putting their best face forward [hunting for images that will appeal to age and ethnic groups] E. Pomice. il *U.S. News & World Report* 106:45-6 Je 12 '89

Anecdotes, facetiae, satire, etc.

Paul Rudnick is addicted to television's beauty show-and-sell. P. Rudnick. il *Vogue* 179:364+ S '89

Customer relations

At your service. L. Wells. *The New York Times Magazine* p86 Ap 23 '89

Marketing

See also

Cosmetics stores

Barrio makeover [selling Avon products to Hispanic migrant women] R. Kirk. il *Ms.* 17:73-5 My '89

How different can a $17 lipstick be from $3 version? [cover story] G. Morgenson. il *Forbes* 144:128-30+ S 18 '89

France

See also

L'Oreal SA

Savoir flair. A. Bogart. il *Harper's Bazaar* 122:68+ Ap '89

Great Britain

See also

Body Shop International plc

Japan

See also

Shiseido Company Ltd.

COSMETICS STORES

Boutique chic. L. Wells. il *The New York Times Magazine* p60 F 19 '89

Inside scoop: good looks . . . good news. il *Harper's Bazaar* 122:26+ F '89

One-stop shopping. K. Bonn. il *Vogue* 179:50 Ja '89

COSMIC BACKGROUND EXPLORER (ARTIFICIAL SATELLITE)

COBE: seeking traces of the beginning. J. Eberhart. *Science News* 136:279 O 28 '89

Cosmic Background Explorer to observe Big Bang radiation [cover story] C. Covault. il *Aviation Week & Space Technology* 131:36-7+ N 6 '89

First light [validity of Big Bang theory] S. J. Nadis. il *Omni (New York, N.Y.)* 11:94 S '89

Looking into the Big Bang. D. H. Smith and A. MacRobert. il *Sky and Telescope* 77:593 Je '89

Muzak of the spheres. T. Waters. il *Discover* 10:26 Je '89

COSMIC BACKGROUND RADIATION

See also

Cosmic Background Explorer (Artificial satellite)

Cosmic fire, terrestrial ice [project at South Pole] D. H. Smith. il *Sky and Telescope* 78:471-4 N '89

The homing instinct. D. Lago. il *Astronomy* 17:98-9 Jl '89

A smooth transition to a lumpy universe [theory of David N. Schramm] *Astronomy* 17:14+ S '89

COSMIC DUST *See* Matter, Interstellar

COSMIC JETS

Active young stars in Orion [Herbig-Haro objects] il *Sky and Telescope* 78:7-8 Jl '89

The curious shapes of cosmic jets. J. Kanipe. il *Astronomy* 17:40-2 Mr '89

Gigantic gas jet points to newborn star [within Orion star-formation region; research by Bo Reipurth] I. Peterson. il *Science News* 136:55 Jl 22 '89

The Milky Way's jet. il *Sky and Telescope* 78:127-8 Ag '89

Reshaping views of how young stars evolve [AS431; research by Richard J. Davis] R. Cowen. *Science News* 136:102 Ag 12 '89

Windy setting for a big, young star. il *Science News* 136:20 Jl 8 '89

A young star's active jet. il *Sky and Telescope* 77:9-10 Ja '89

COSMIC RAYS

The case of cosmic rays [new Utah observatory to study muons from Cygnus X-3 and Hercules X-1; cover story] G. Taubes. il *Discover* 10:52-8+ S '89

COSMIC STRINGS

Cosmic strings: topological fossils of the hot Big Bang [cover story] W. H. Press and D. N. Spergel. bibl f il *Physics Today* 42:29-35 Mr '89

The not-so-Great Attractor? *Sky and Telescope* 77:12-13 Ja '89

COSMOCHEMISTRY *See* Astrochemistry

COSMOLOGY *See* Universe

COSMONAUTS *See* Astronauts

COSMOS MISSIONS *See* Artificial satellites—Cosmos missions

COSS, RICHARD G., AND OWINGS, DONALD H.

Rattler battlers. il *Natural History* p30-5 My '89

COST

See also

Labor costs

COST (LAW)

See also

Lawyers—Salaries, fees, etc.

Lawyers and lawyering [address, October 1, 1988] R. D. Lamm. *Vital Speeches of the Day* 55:206-9 Ja 15 '89

Litigation's cost is rocketing—its efficiency isn't. G. Koretz. il *Business Week* p34 N 6 '89

COST ACCOUNTING

See also

Management accounting

COST AND STANDARD OF LIVING
See also
Budget, Household
Children—Cost of raising
Finance, Personal
Food—Prices
Home economics
Income
Inflation (Finance)
Price indexes
Prices
Saving and savings

Adding it up: the life style factor. H. Wheelwright. il *Money* 18 Money Guide:14-18+ Fall '89

The American dream [cover story; special section] M. Dovel and T. J. Miller. il *Changing Times* 43:27-39+ Mr '89

Are you watching, Chairman Greenspan? [Forbes four hundred cost of living extremely well index] M. Kripalani. il *Forbes* 144 Special Issue:388-9 O 23 '89

Experimental cost-of-living indexes: a summary of current research. M. F. Kokoski. bibl f il *Monthly Labor Review* 112:34-9 Jl '89

The great boomer bust. K. Butler. il *Mother Jones* 14:32-8 Je '89

Growing old frugally. J. B. Quinn. il *Newsweek* 114 Special Issue:102-5 Wint '89/Spr '90

How to live above your means . . . and get away with it. A. Poinsett. il *Ebony* 45:46+ D '89

Income growth: are we better off? L. S. Richman. il *Current (Washington, D.C.)* 312:4-9 My '89

Living grandly on less. M. Phillips and others. il *Utne Reader* p85-6 S/O '89

Paté poverty: downwardly mobile baby boomers lust after luxury. K. Butler. il *Utne Reader* p72-80 S/O '89

The problem of money and time [cover story; with editorial comment by Byron Dobell] J. S. Gordon. il *American Heritage* 40:7, 56-8+ My/Je '89

Slipping living standards. A. Bladen. il *Forbes* 143:340 My 29 '89

When $2 million isn't enough. P. Moffitt. il *Esquire* 111:79+ My '89

Australia
My bicentenary message [address, December 2, 1988] A. H. Pollard. *Vital Speeches of the Day* 55:346-9 Mr 15 '89

Canada
Looking ahead [Maclean's/Decima poll] D. Jenish. il *Maclean's* 102:10-13 Ja 2 '89

Japan
The hard life. J. M. Fallows. il *The Atlantic* 263:16+ Mr '89

To have and have not in Japan. J. Impoco. il *U.S. News & World Report* 106:41-2 F 13 '89

Soviet Union
A family of three in 323 square feet [Taldikin family of Moscow] il *U.S. News & World Report* 107:29 N 20 '89

Why the Bear's cupboards are bare. W. R. Doerner. il *Time* 133:33+ Ja 16 '89

United States
See Cost and standard of living

COST BENEFIT ANALYSIS See Cost effectiveness

COST CONTROL
How to cut the cost of headquarters. T. Paré. il *Fortune* 120:189+ S 11 '89

Ten ways to take the pain out of cost cutting. J. D. Rutherford. il *Working Woman* 14:20+ F '89

COST EFFECTIVENESS
The criteria of net benefit. R. Paehlke. *Society* 27:13-14 N/D '89

How much is a sea otter worth [putting price on the environment] M. J. Mandel. il *Business Week* p59+ Ag 21 '89

Six-million-dollar man [accident prevention] J. Bennet. *The New Republic* 200:18 Ja 23 '89

COST OF LIVING ADJUSTMENTS
Bankers have the classic COLA. G. P. Brockway. il *The New Leader* 72:14-15 Ja 9 '89

COSTA-GAVRAS
about
America's underculture [interview] il *New Perspectives Quarterly* 5:53-6 Wint '88/'89

Betrayed [film] Reviews
Video il 13:60 Ap '89. R. Gehr

COSTA RICA
See also
Americans—Costa Rica
Cocos Island (Costa Rica)
Environment—Costa Rica
Environmental policy—Costa Rica
Fishing—Costa Rica
Forests and forestry—Costa Rica
Golfo Dulce (Costa Rica)
Guanacaste National Park (Costa Rica)
Insects—Costa Rica
Loans, Bank—Costa Rica
Military assistance, American—Costa Rica
National parks and reserves—Costa Rica
Rain forests—Costa Rica

Securities—Laws and regulations—Costa Rica
United States—Diplomatic and consular service—Costa Rica

Foreign relations
Cuba
You can run—but maybe you can't hide in Cuba [penny stock fraud scam by L. Zrnic of International Swiss Investments] G. DeGeorge. il por *Business Week* p27 Mr 6 '89

United States
See United States—Foreign relations—Costa Rica

Industries
See also
Banana industry—Costa Rica

Politics and government
Costa Rica diarist: democracia. H. Hertzberg. *The New Republic* 201:46 D 4 '89

COSTAS, BOB
about
Beers with . . . Bob Costas [interview] L. Schwartz. il pors *Sport (New York, N.Y.)* 80:19-20 Mr '89

COSTELLO, ELVIS
about
E.C. is here there and everywhere. R. C. Walls. por *High Fidelity (New York, N.Y.)* 39:71+ My '89

Elvis Costello and the SNL weenies. M. Laswell. *Rolling Stone* p69 O 5 '89

Elvis Costello deals with the real world. S. Simels. il por *Stereo Review* 54:103 My '89

The Rolling stone interview. D. Wild. il pors *Rolling Stone* p62-4+ Je 1 '89

What's so funny about peace, love and Elvis? D. Wild. il por *Rolling Stone* p103-4 Mr 9 '89

Wise guys. M. Moses. *The New Yorker* 65:84-7 Ap 24 '89

COSTELLO, GERALD M.
[Column] See issues of U.S. Catholic beginning January 1985

COSTELLO, JOHN
Mask of treachery [excerpt] il por *Conservative Digest* 15:59+ Ja/F '89

COSTELLO, JOSEPH B.
about
The hot box syndrome. K. K. Wiegner. il por *Forbes* 143:178+ Ap 17 '89

Sure, he's wild and crazy—like a fox. R. D. Hof. il por *Business Week* p132 O 30 '89

COSTELLO, MARJORIE
A poor man's high-def. il *Channels (New York, N.Y.: 1986)* 9:64 Ap '89

COSTEN, BILL
about
Up, up, & away. A. Reid-Dove. il *Black Enterprise* 20:73-4+ Ag '89

COSTIKYAN, BARBARA
Fast feasts: for the holidays, take it out—take it all out. il *New York* 22:66-8+ D 18 '89

Great new places to have a party (I) [cover story] il *New York* 22:58-68+ N 13 '89

Great new places to have a party (II). il *New York* 22:48-52+ N 20 '89

Park Avenue Gothic: a family feud turns into a fight to the death. il pors *New York* 22:46-50+ Mr 20 '89

COSTNER, KEVIN
about
Hollywood's maverick hero. J. Foote. il pors *Newsweek* 113:72-3 Ap 24 '89

Kevin Costner. N. Anderson. il pors *Good Housekeeping* 209:76+ Ag '89

Kevin Costner: major-league star. D. Lamanna. il pors *Ladies' Home Journal* 106:98+ F '89

The new Gary Cooper? Yup. P. Rainer. il pors *The New York Times Magazine* p38-9+ Ap 23 '89

Pursuing the dream [cover story] R. Corliss. il pors *Time* 133:76-80+ Je 26 '89

COSTNER, SUSAN
Down-to-earth . . . and delicious. il por *Working Woman* 14:153-6 N '89

The sandwich club. il *Working Woman* 14:122-4 My '89

COSTUME
See also
Fashion
Halloween costumes
Hats
Wearable art

Costumed cows and other critters [4-H Club of Maryland sponsors costume parade at State Fair] il *National Geographic World* 167:26-9 Jl '89

Collectors and collecting
From Callot Soeurs to Gaultier, Sandy Schreier has it all. A. Palmer. il por *Architectural Digest* 46:52+ S '89

The jewelry designer's crush on Schiaparelli—and Barbie [Billy Boy] E. White. il por *Architectural Digest* 46:94+ S '89

Exhibitions
See also
Metropolitan Museum of Art (New York, N.Y.). Costume Institute

COSTUME—Exhibitions—*cont.*

Feats with pleats [M. Fortuny show at Houston's Museum of Fine Arts] J. McLaughlin. il *Harper's Bazaar* 122:128+ O '89

Jocks and nerds [exhibition at Fashion Institute of Technology] *The New Yorker* 65:30-2 Ap 24 '89

A master showman imbues clothes with life [S. de Pietri, curator of costume exhibits at M. H. de Young Museum] C. R. Milbank. il por *Architectural Digest* 46:88+ S '89

Museums of modern garb. N. Darnton. il *Newsweek* 113:78 F 27 '89

A new Smithsonian exhibit looks at the opportunities and rewards for both genders in American life [Men and women: a history of costume, gender and power at the National Museum of American History] R. M. Adams. il *Smithsonian* 20:10 N '89

Powerwear!! [Men and women: a history of costume, gender, and power at National Museum of American History] A. L. Powers. il *Americana* 17:17-20 S/O '89

Sartorially suited [Jocks and nerds exhibit at Fashion Institute of Technology] J. Perl. il *Vogue* 179:274+ Ap '89

Tested by time [Jocks and nerds at Fashion Institute of Technology] R. La Ferla. il *The New York Times Magazine* p66-7 Mr 12 '89

France
Exhibitions

Between times [fall ready-to-wear shows and costume exhibitions in Paris] H. Brubach. *The New Yorker* 65:100-2+ Ap 24 '89

The emperor's old clothes [Age of Napoléon exhibit at the Metropolitan Museum] D. Lida. il por *Harper's Bazaar* 122:71 N '89

The Opulent era: Worth, Doucet and Pingat at the Brooklyn Museum. D. Harris. il *Architectural Digest* 46:66+ S '89

Great Britain
Exhibitions

Franco Moschino [designer visits exhibition of Victorian costumes at the Metropolitan Museum] *The New Yorker* 64:19-20 Ja 9 '89

Japan

See also
Kimonos

Soviet Union
Exhibitions

Between times [fall ready-to-wear shows and costume exhibitions in Paris] H. Brubach. *The New Yorker* 65:100-2+ Ap 24 '89

COSTUME, THEATRICAL

Around the world in 80 days—and 165 masks [work of C. H. Jones] L. Stevens. il *Theatre Crafts* 23:56-7+ Ap '89

'Can you imagine them making love?' [film costume designer E. Mirojnick] C. Troy. il por *American Film* 14:46-51+ Je '89

Centerline: Jeannie Davidson [resident designer for the Oregon Shakespearean Festival] M. Sommers. por *Theatre Crafts* 23:10 My '89

The clothes make the cowboy . . . and even the Indian [television adaptation of Lonesome dove; work of V. B. Ramsey] il *Theatre Crafts* 23:44-6+ F '89

Collaborating on the spirit of a new age [ballet costumes by C. Chanel for S. Diaghilev] D. Harris. il pors *Architectural Digest* 46:42+ S '89

Costume chief Patrick Norris elevates the look of this season's dressed-up thirtysomething yups. L. Feldon. il pors *People Weekly* 32:115-17 S 25 '89

Costumes by computer [use of AutoCAD] P. Ellsworth. il *Theatre Crafts* 23:78+ N '89

Deirdre Clancy. M. Sommers. il por *Theatre Crafts* 23:34-9+ F '89

Designer [B. Ringwood's and A. Furst's work on Batman] L. Nickson and N. Le Quesne. il pors *Life* 12:84-6 Spr '89

Dressed for excess [films of the 1980s] D. Edelstein. il *Vogue* 179:186-7+ D '89

Dressing the part [relationship between film industry and clothing stores on Rodeo Drive] C. Fleming. il *American Film* 14:48-51 S '89

Gorgeous liaisons [lingerie designs influenced by movie Dangerous liaisons] R. La Ferla. il *The New York Times Magazine* p72 F 19 '89

The Great Blues Way [costumes for Black and blue] W. Goodman. il *New York* 22:37-40 Ja 2 '89

Inside Cosby's closet [interview with S. Lemire] J. Marion. il *TV Guide* 37:9 Ap 1-7 '89

Sew red [clothes designer J. Duroché at Miss America Pageant] B. Weber. il por *The New York Times Magazine* p66 Ag 27 '89

Sewing down a dream [costumes for Metropolitan Opera Ring cycle by R. Langenfass] G. Schmidgall. il pors *Opera News* 53:30-2 Ap 1 '89

Willa Kim. B. Howard. il *Theatre Crafts* 23:28-33+ Mr '89

Collectors and collecting

A rare collection of classic Hollywood costume sketches [L. Stanley] J. Chatfield-Taylor. il por *Architectural Digest* 46:250+ S '89

COSTUME ACCESSORIES *See* Dress accessories

COSTUME DESIGNERS

See also
Clancy, Deirdre
Davidson, Jeannie
Fashion designers
Kim, Willa
Langenfass, Rolf
Norris, Patrick
Ramsey, Van Broughton
Rose, Jürgen, 1937-

COSTUME INSTITUTE (NEW YORK, N.Y.) *See* Metropolitan Museum of Art (New York, N.Y.). Costume Institute

COSTUME JEWELRY *See* Jewelry

COTA CATS (MUSICAL GROUP)

COTA Cats [high school jazz band featured yearly at Celebration of the Arts festival in the Poconos] J. Cunniff. il *Down Beat* 56:46 Je '89

COTE, NANCY THOMAS- *See* Thomas-Cote, Nancy

COTÉ, SUZY

about

Decisions! Decisions! Who should play the sexy teenager? H. Polskin. il pors *TV Guide* 37:12-15 Ja 28-F 3 '89

COTSEN, LLOYD E., 1929-

about

Neutrogena defends its turf. J. Heins. il por *Forbes* 143:80+ Je 26 '89

COTTAGE GARDENS AND GARDENING *See* Gardens and gardening

COTTAGE INDUSTRIES

See also
Home-based business

COTTAGES

See also
House decoration

An airy Florida cottage. L. Hallam. il *Southern Living* 24:82-3 Je '89

Our Folk Victorian Cottage. il *Southern Living* 24:116 Jl '89

COTTAGES, REMODELED *See* Houses, Remodeled

COTTER, HOLLAND

A bland Biennial. il *Art in America* 77:80-1+ S '89

Material witness. bibl f il *Art in America* 77:176-83+ N '89

Medardo Rosso: radical anti-classicist. bibl f il *Art in America* 77:182-7 My '89

COTTER, JAMES FINN

Hopkins the mythmaker. *America* 161:106-8 Ag 26-S 2 '89

COTTER, JAMES J.

about

What's wrong with a little greenmail? R. King. il por *Forbes* 143:64+ Mr 6 '89

COTTINGHAM, LAURA

Uncovered artifacts. il *Harper's Bazaar* 122:14+ Jl '89

COTTLE, THOMAS J.

A son dies of AIDS. il *The New Leader* 72:15-17 N 13 '89

COTTON, ANTHONY

Free-for-all! [cover story] il *Sport (New York, N.Y.)* 80:28-30 My '89

COTTON, CROSBIE

A Red-letter day. il por *Sports Illustrated* 70:38-9 Ap 10 '89

COTTON

Prices

The cotton crisis. A. S. Johnson. *The New Republic* 201 [Reprint v1]:17-18 N 6 '89 [N 7 '14]

THE COTTON CLUB [film] *See* Motion picture reviews—Single works

COTTON FABRICS

See also
Denim

If you get blisters, check your socks [acrylic fibers more effective in preventing foot blisters; views of Kirk M. Herring] il *Prevention (Emmaus, Pa.)* 41:12+ Jl '89

COTTON INDUSTRY

See also
J.G. Boswell Company

History

The cotton crisis. A. S. Johnson. *The New Republic* 201 [Reprint v1]:17-18 N 6 '89 [N 7 '14]

COTTON MILLS *See* Cotton industry

COTTONWOOD

Disease and pest resistance

Plant hybrid zones as sinks for pests [aphids on hybrid cottonwoods] T. G. Whitham. bibl f il *Science* 244:1490-3 Je 23 '89

COTTONWOOD RANCH (WELLS, NEV.) *See* Ranches—Nevada

COTTRELL, COMER J.

about

Breaking into the majors. J. Coleman and C. C. Williams. il por *Black Enterprise* 20:18 S '89

COTURNIX *See* Quails

COUCH POTATOES

Bookworms versus couch potatoes. M. J. Weiss. map *The Atlantic* 264:81 O '89

COUCH POTATOES—cont.

The couch potato. B. Darrach. il *People Weekly* 32 Special Issue:63 Fall '89

Couch potatoes don't dine out. R. Phalon. il *Forbes* 144:209+ O 30 '89

Health and hygiene

Couch potato physique [correlation between television watching and obesity; research by Larry Tucker] E. Stark. il *Psychology Today* 23:8 S '89

Couch potatoes' half-baked future [inactivity affects muscle adaptability; research by Gary C. Sieck] il *USA Today (Periodical)* 117:13 Ap '89

Heavy viewing [correlation between TV watching and obesity; research by Larry Tucker] il *Prevention (Emmaus, Pa.)* 41:18-19 S '89

Tubby tubers [correlation between obesity and television watching; research by Larry Tucker] E. Franklin. il *American Health* 8:88 N '89

COUCHES *See* Sofas

COUDART, LAURENCE

Liberty, equality, festivity! il *The Unesco Courier* 42:42-6 D '89

COUDERT, JO

Andy Goose steps out. il *Reader's Digest* 135:169-70+ Jl '89

From street kids to Royal Knights. il por *Reader's Digest* 134:141-6 Je '89

"Go for it, lady!". il *Reader's Digest* 134:121-3 Ja '89

How to be a patient person. il *Reader's Digest* 135:45-6+ N '89

COUGAR, JOHN *See* Mellencamp, John Cougar

COUGARS *See* Pumas

COUGH

See also

Whooping cough

COUGHLIN, CHARLES EDWARD, 1891-1979

about

Father Coughlin and the Jews: a broadcast remembered. R. Modras. *America* 160:219-22 Mr 11 '89

COUGHLIN, MAGDALEN

Minority and disadvantaged students [address, February 2, 1989] *Vital Speeches of the Day* 55:569-72 Jl 1 '89

COUGHLIN, SHAUN R., AND OTHERS

Role of phosphatidylinositol kinase in PDGF receptor signal transduction. bibl f il *Science* 243:1191-4 Mr 3 '89

COULOMB'S LAW

Coulomb explosion imaging of small molecules. Z. Vager and others. bibl f il *Science* 244:426-31 Ap 28 '89

Splat prints of floppy molecules [Coulomb explosion imaging] *Science News* 136:47 Jl 15 '89

COULTERS (CULTIVATORS) *See* Cultivators—Equipment

COUNCIL OF BLACK ADMINISTRATIVE ASSISTANTS AND ASSOCIATES (U.S.)

Democrats move to recruit members for jobs in Party. il *Jet* 76:27 Je 19 '89

COUNCIL OF ECONOMIC ADVISERS (U.S.)

Boskin: "I have a lot of strong principles". R. Hornik. il por *Time* 133:48 Ja 30 '89

Masterminding the U.S. economy [M. J. Boskin] A. R. Dowd. il por *Fortune* 119:46 Ja 2 '89

Michael Boskin isn't just another ignored economist. H. Gleckman. il por *Business Week* p128-9 Je 26 '89

COUNCIL OF MINISTERS OF EDUCATION (CANADA)

A provincial vision of Canadian education. T. McConaghy. il *Phi Delta Kappan* 70:648-9 Ap '89

COUNCIL ON ENVIRONMENTAL QUALITY (U.S.)

Revive NEPA, Mr. Bush [National Environmental Policy Act] P. A. A. Berle. *Audubon* 91:6 Ja '89

COUNCILS AND SYNODS

See also

Episcopal Synod of America

Synod of Bishops (1987)

Vatican Council (2nd: 1962-1965)

COUNSELING

See also

Crisis management (Psychology)

Drug counseling

Educational counseling

Employee counseling

Family counseling

Grief counseling

Marriage counseling

Peer counseling

Rape counseling

Vocational guidance

Youth counseling

COUNSELING, FINANCIAL *See* Investment advisers

COUNSELORS

See also

Educational counselors

Training

N.Y. trains refugees to be counselors in service agencies. il *Aging* no359:29 '89

COUNTER, S. ALLEN

(jt. auth) See Borg, Erik, and Counter, S. Allen

COUNTER CULTURE *See* Counterculture

COUNTERCULTURE

See also

Beat culture

Hip culture

Bibliography

Voices from the fringe. R. Mungo. il *Utne Reader* p106-7+ S/O '89

COUNTERFEITING *See* Counterfeits and counterfeiting

COUNTERFEITS AND COUNTERFEITING

See also

Credit card crimes

Holy bootlegger! What a lot of phony Batstuff! G. Jacobson. il *Business Week* p70 Jl 17 '89

Sting operation nabs Iranian counterfeit drug dealer [counterfeit Tagamet dealer J. Naghdi] W. Grigg. il *FDA Consumer* 23:37-8 Ap '89

Disposal

Crunch time [government disposal] B. Weber. il *The New York Times Magazine* p102 Ja 29 '89

COUNTERGLOW

Glow and counterglow. il *Sky and Telescope* 77:147 F '89

COUNTERS, KITCHEN *See* Kitchen furniture

COUNTERTERRORISM *See* Terrorism—Retaliation

COUNTING MACHINES AND DEVICES

Down-counter cookbook. R. Marston. il *Radio-Electronics* 60:71-7 F '89

Flashing LED's [CMOS 4017 device] il *Radio-Electronics* 60:12+ My '89

Working with counters. R. Marston. il *Radio-Electronics* 60:63-8 Ap '89

COUNTRIES *See* Nations

COUNTRY AND CITY *See* City and country

COUNTRY AND WESTERN MUSIC *See* Country music

COUNTRY CHURCHES *See* Rural churches

COUNTRY CLUBS

See also

Club Corp. of America

Segregation

Members only [Senator L. Bentsen's membership in three restricted clubs] V. Kemper. *Common Cause Magazine* 15:6-7 N/D '89

What would our children think of us? [segregation at Lansdowne Swim Club, Pa.] J. T. Ryan. il *Commonweal* 116:115-17 F 24 '89

A COUNTRY DOCTOR [drama] *See* Jenkin, Len

COUNTRY DOCTORS *See* Medical care, Rural

COUNTRY ESTATES

Argentina

Nelly Arrieta de Blaquier's South American silver [collection at La Biznaga] J. Gruen. il por *Architectural Digest* 46:102+ O '89

Capri Island (Italy)

Mona Bismarck on Capri [Il Fortino] W. Weaver. il por *Architectural Digest* 46:32+ F '89

Wanda Ferragamo: the design matriarch's villa on Capri. S. Stephens. il por *Architectural Digest* 46:198-203 S '89

France

Artist's dialogue: Cesar [studio in Paris and house in the south of France] M. Peppiatt. il por *Architectural Digest* 46:27+ F '89

Great Britain

Architecture: John Outram [Sussex country house] E. Lambert. il por *Architectural Digest* 46:162-7+ D '89

The best of manors [country house hotels] il *House & Garden* 161:84+ Mr '89

An education abroad: living and learning in English country houses. E. Lambert. il *Architectural Digest* 46:140-2+ My '89

The functional folly in eighteenth-century Britain. G. Jackson-Stops. bibl f il *Antiques* 135:1412-23 Je '89

Illinois

Equestrian inspiration [architecture by James L. Nagle] J. Neisser. il *Architectural Digest* 46:172-7 Ap '89

Italy

Gianfranco Ferré: architectural flair on Italy's Lago Maggiore. J. Thurman. il por *Architectural Digest* 46:104-11 S '89

Tuscan pastoral [G. Giammetti's La Vagnola estate decorated by Renzo Mongiardino; cover story] C. Maclean. il por *House & Garden* 161:146-59+ S '89

Kentucky

Architecture: Quinlan Terry: a Palladian country house in Kentucky [J. Abercrombie's Pin Oak] C. Aslet. il por *Architectural Digest* 46:282-7 O '89

Long Island (N.Y.)

Artist in residence: Count and Countess de Claviére d'Hust on Long Island. S. Stephens. il pors *Architectural Digest* 46:156-61+ D '89

Oregon

Daniel Solomon: a villa of classical proportions in Oregon. L. Whiteson. il por *Architectural Digest* 46:86-91+ Ap '89

Sweden

Swedish fantasies [F. von Celsing's Biby estate] C. Petkanas. il por *House & Garden* 161:126-33+ Ag '89

COUNTRY HOUSES

See also

Farmhouses

COUNTRY HOUSES—*cont.*
All work (and hardly any play) [country retreats of artists, authors and musicians] M. Bethany. il *New York* 22:46-51 Ag 28 '89
American country houses [cover story; special issue] il *Architectural Digest* 46:118-214+ Je '89
Vernacular on a budget [country house near Meridian, Miss.] L. Hallam. il *Southern Living* 24:160+ Ap '89
COUNTRY HOUSES IN ART
Estate of the art [work of English painter J. Warrender] M. Girouard. il *House & Garden* 161:58 Mr '89
Portraits of houses: contemporary masters of a venerable genre. J. Lees-Miline. il *Architectural Digest* 46:118+ Mr '89
COUNTRY INNS *See* Hotels, motels, etc.
COUNTRY JOURNAL
Country journal goes bimonthly. F. W. Finn. *Country Journal* 16:5 Mr/Ap '89
The discomfort of change. P. V. Fossel. *Country Journal* 16:10-11 F '89
COUNTRY LIFE
    See also
    City and country
    Farm life
    Ranch life
Country lore. See issues of The Mother Earth News
Reclaiming rural life [cover story; special section] il *Country Journal* 16:67-83 My/Je '89
Rural persuasion. See issues of Country Journal beginning June 1987
Sporting pleasures. G. Logsdon. il *Country Journal* 16:36-41 Jl/Ag '89
Successful country living. See issues of Successful Farming beginning January 1988 through January 1989
A tapestry of prairie life [Greenfield, Iowa] H. Sidey. il *Time* 134:30-2+ O 9 '89
    Bibliography
A holiday compendium. P. Crowley. il *Country Journal* 16:11-12 N/D '89
Readings. See issues of Country Journal beginning October 1988
    Periodicals
    See also
    Country journal
Articles for the rural and country market. R. Matthews. *The Writer* 102:28-9 N '89
    Photographs and photography
This country life. See issues of Country Journal beginning October 1986
    Terminology
Country matters. W. Safire. il *The New York Times Magazine* p16+ O 1 '89
COUNTRY MUSIC
    See also
    Compact discs—Country music
    Gospel music
    Phonograph records—Country music
    Ryman Auditorium (Nashville, Tenn.)
Another country. K. Tucker. il *Vogue* 179:328-31 F '89
Another country [women of country music] H. Gleason. il *Harper's Bazaar* 122:112+ O '89
Hooked on country [excerpt from Behind closed doors] A. Nash. il *Stereo Review* 54:86-8+ Ja '89
It's a musical marathon as rock meets country for a Motown hoedown [This country's rockin' concert at Detroit's Silverdome] il *People Weekly* 31:53-4 My 22 '89
Lookin' for science in all the wrong places [J. M. Schaefer's study of the relationship between drinking and country music] J. Stone. il *Discover* 10:96-9 Mr '89
They'll make you listen—and look [male singers] N. Hickey. il *TV Guide* 37:10-11 O 7-13 '89
An unbroken circle [book Country: the music and the musicians] J. Miller. *Newsweek* 113:60 Ja 2 '89
    Canada
Even cowgirls sing the blues [Toronto] N. Jennings. il *Maclean's* 102:59 Ap 17 '89
COUNTRY STORES *See* General stores
COUNTY EMPLOYEES
    See also
    Fairfax County (Va.)—Employees
COUNTY OFFICERS
Across the editor's desk [importance of participating in county government] L. J. Kruse. il *Successful Farming* 87:2 O '89
COUPLES, UNMARRIED *See* Unmarried couples
COUPON CONNECTION, INC.
Property? Or perk? [American Airlines charges Coupon Connection with conspiring to defraud American by buying and selling frequent flier awards] D. Fanning. il *Forbes* 143:136 Je 26 '89
COUPS D'ETAT
Building a better coup [CIA wants clarification on political assassinations] C. S. Manegold. il *Newsweek* 114:55 O 30 '89
Mr. Webster has it exactly wrong [CIA policy on assassinations] W. F. Buckley. *National Review* 41:62-3 N 24 '89

Reopening a deadly debate: the CIA wants to have a freer hand during coups. J. Peterzell. il *Time* 134:54 O 30 '89
COURAGE, PIERS
    about
The trinity. C. Fox. il pors *Car and Driver* 34:139-40+ Mr '89
COURAGE
    See also
    Encouragement
    Heroes and heroines
The courage of Sam Bird [example set by U.S. Army captain in Vietnam] B. T. Collins. il *Reader's Digest* 134:49-54 My '89
COURBET, GUSTAVE, 1819-1877
    about
An abiding passion for reality. R. Hughes. il *Time* 133:68-9 Ja 9 '89
Art. A. C. Danto. *The Nation* 248:97-100 Ja 23 '89
Courbet and salon politics. J. House. bibl f il *Art in America* 77:160-73+ My '89
COURIER, JIM
    about
Jim Courier: quietly coming of age [interview] M. Winters. il por *World Tennis* 36:80-1+ F '89
Special D from this Courier. C. Kirkpatrick. il pors *Sports Illustrated* 70:84+ Je 12 '89
COURIERS
Miss those frequent-flyer deals? Try carrying a pouch. P. Cole. il *Business Week* p156 Mr 13 '89
COURLANDER, HAROLD, 1908-
The emperor wore clothes: visiting Haile Selassie in 1943. *The American Scholar* 58:271-81 Spr '89
COURMAYEUR (ITALY)
At the foot of Mont Blanc. L. Tejada-Flores. il *Skiing* 42:168-72+ N '89
COURSES OF STUDY *See* Curriculum
COURSON, STEVE
    about
Was the X factor a factor? por *Sports Illustrated* 70:34 Ap 3 '89
COURT OF JUSTICE OF THE EUROPEAN COMMUNITIES
European Court ruling could ban bilateral air fare agreements. *Aviation Week & Space Technology* 130:32 Ap 17 '89
COURT ORDERS OF PROTECTION *See* Orders of protection
COURTESY
    See also
    Etiquette
    Rudeness
    Anecdotes, facetiae, satire, etc.
Uncivil liberties. C. Trillin. il *The Nation* 249:230 S 4-11 '89
COURTHOUSES
    See also
    Courtrooms
COURTIERS
The prince and his courtiers: at the White House, the Kremlin, and the Reichschancellery. R. Baker and C. Peters. *The Washington Monthly* 21:38+ F '89
COURTIN, PIERRE, 1921-
    about
Pierre Courtin: Claude Bernard. A. Silverman. il *Art News* 88:204-5 O '89
COURTROOMS
Have gavel, will travel. V. Warren. il *Common Cause Magazine* 15:9 N/D '89
COURTS
    See also
    Contempt of court
    Courtrooms
    Grand jury
    Judges
    Judicial power
    Jury
    Legal procedure
    Small claims courts
    Television broadcasting—Trials
    Translators and translating—Court use
    Trials
    United States. Supreme Court
The swing to the left in state courts. T. Gest. il *U.S. News & World Report* 107:32 O 23 '89
    Arkansas
3 blacks get judgeships in Arkansas from governor. il *Jet* 77:22 O 9 '89
    California
    See also
    Los Angeles (Calif.)—Courts
    Canada
    See also
    Canada. Supreme Court
Battle fatigue [drug cases overwhelm courts] P. Kaihla. il *Maclean's* 102:14-16 D 11 '89
Disorder in the court [Canadian provincial court judges under fire] N. Underwood. il *Maclean's* 102:55-6 Ap 24 '89
Rating the judiciary [list of best and worst judges in Canadian lawyer] N. Underwood. il *Maclean's* 102:56 My 22 '89

COURTS—cont.

Delaware

Delaware's Chancery Court: charting corporate futures. B. Saporito. il *Fortune* 120:10-11 Jl 17 '89

Time's next battleground [Chancery Court] R. Sandza. *Newsweek* 114:31 Jl 10 '89

Florida

See also
Miami (Fla.)—Courts

Crime & punishment: a view from a broad [woman judge known for tough sentencing]; ed. by Linda Marx. E. Morphonios. il pors *People Weekly* 32:79-80+ Jl 3 '89

Fla. judge Alcee Hastings is removed by U.S. Senate. il por *Jet* 77:12-13 N 6 '89

Hastings impeachment trial slated to begin next month. por *Jet* 75:12 F 27 '89

The leaden wings of Senate justice [vote to remove Judge A. L. Hastings] il por *U.S. News & World Report* 107:18 O 30 '89

New York (State)

Edwin Torres. L. Carcaterra. il pors *People Weekly* 32:155-6+ D 4 '89

Pennsylvania

A career of firsts [black woman Supreme Court justice J. K. Stout] il pors *Ebony* 44:76+ F '89

Juanita Stout forced off Philadelphia high court. il por *Jet* 76:12 Je 5 '89

Soviet Union

In Gorbachev's courts. G. P. Fletcher. bibl f il *The New York Review of Books* 36:13-14+ My 18 '89

Texas

Justice for sale. E. H. Methvin. *Reader's Digest* 134:131-6 My '89

United States

See Courts

Western Europe

See also
Court of Justice of the European Communities

COURTS (FOR GAMES)

See also
Tennis courts

COURTSHIP

See also
Dating (Social customs)

COURTYARDS

Bringing the Low Country home. *Southern Living* 24:76-7 My '89

Careful planning casts a spell. R. W. Strickland. il *Southern Living* 24:90-1 Mr '89

They created a courtyard by adding a master suite. il *Sunset (Central West edition)* 183:74-5 Ag '89

Think of it as a house with an outdoor and indoor courtyard [Redding, Calif.] il *Sunset (Central West edition)* 182:112-14 F '89

COUSCOUS

Couscous with chicken or shellfish. il *Sunset (Central West edition)* 182:200 My '89

COUSINS, NORMAN

Doctors and patients must talk [condensed from Head first] *Reader's Digest* 135:133-4+ O '89

First word. por *Omni (New York, N.Y.)* 12:6 D '89

Norman Cousins helps other patients as he once helped himself—by laughing [excerpt from Head first] il por *Good Housekeeping* 209:92 N '89

Proving the power of laughter. il *Psychology Today* 23:22-5 O '89

COUSINS

The dangerous uncle returns. J. D. Houston. il *Gentlemen's Quarterly* 59:235-8+ D '89

COUSINS [film] See Motion picture reviews—Single works

COUTURIER COLLECTIONS See Fashion shows

COUVELIER, MEL

about

A balancing act in Lotus Land. P. C. Newman. il *Maclean's* 102:43 Ap 3 '89

Strategic budgeting. J. Pifer. *Maclean's* 102:16 Ap 10 '89

COUVREUX FAMILY

about

Citizens of the world. G. Jaynes. il *Life* 12:15 O '89

COUZENS, MICHAEL

An aging watchdog. il *Channels (New York, N.Y.: 1986)* 9:12 Jl/Ag '89

Demos do the talking. il *Channels (New York, N.Y.: 1986)* 9:20 Mr '89

Denver does ScanAmerica. *Channels (New York, N.Y.: 1986)* 9:24 N '89

Down from the count. il *Channels (New York, N.Y.: 1986)* 9:16 My '89

Man the lifeboats. il *Channels (New York, N.Y.: 1986)* 9:22 Ap '89

Political quick-step. il *Channels (New York, N.Y.: 1986)* 9:26 F '89

Want a local meter? il *Channels (New York, N.Y.: 1986)* 9:26 Ja '89

COVARIANCE ANALYSIS

Covariance mapping: a correlation method applied to multiphoton multiple ionization. L. J. Frasinski and others. bibl f il *Science* 246:1029-31 N 24 '89

COVENANT HOUSE (NEW YORK, N.Y.)

Crisis at Covenant House [charges against Father B. Ritter] J. N. Baker. il por *Newsweek* 114:82 D 25 '89

Saving kids from the streets [Father B. Ritter] I. Nelson. il por *New Choices for the Best Years* 29:14+ Ag '89

COVENT GARDEN OPERA HOUSE See Royal Opera House (London, England)

COVER CROPS

See also
Green manuring

The great cover-up. J. Walter. il *Successful Farming* 87:20-1 S '89

Growing good soil. J. Poncavage. il *Organic Gardening* 36:42-4+ D '89

COVER DESIGN See Book covers; Periodical covers

COVER GIRLS See Models (Persons)

COVERED BRIDGES

Photographs and photography

Covering covered bridges. J. Drafahl and S. Drafahl. il *Petersen's Photographic Magazine* 18:30-3 S '89

COVERED WAGON TRAINS See Wagon trains

COVERLETS

Collectors and collecting

Sleepers awake [Jacquard coverlets] M. Guralnick. il *House & Garden* 161:46-7 Ja '89

COVERS, BOOK See Book covers

COVERS, PERIODICAL See Periodical covers

COVERS, PHONOGRAPH RECORD See Phonograph record covers

COVERT AMERICAN MILITARY ASSISTANCE See Military assistance, American

COVETOUSNESS See Avarice

COVINGTON, RICHARD

Editorial. See issues of Oceans beginning July/August 1986 through March/April 1989

COVINO, FRANK

Painting values accurately. il *American Artist* 53:64-7 Mr '89

COVINO, PAUL F. X.

Sex, gender, & love. *Commonweal* 116:171-2 Mr 24 '89

COW BARNS See Barns and stables

COW MANURE AS FUEL See Refuse as fuel

COWAN, CONNELL

(jt. auth) See Kinder, Melvyn, and Cowan, Connell

COWAN, DENYS

about

Serious business. F. McCoy and A. Edmond, Jr. il por *Black Enterprise* 20:86-8+ S '89

COWAN, R. GUY, 1884-1957

about

Mr. Cowan's pottery: how one man's vision shaped a generation of potters. E. Beal. il por *Antiques & Collecting Hobbies* 94:55-7+ O '89

COWAN, RALPH WOLFE

about

When society portrait artist Ralph Wolfe Cowan met a mugger, he captured him—on canvas. il por *People Weekly* 32:91-2 S 4 '89

COWAN, RICHARD

None dare call it lobbying! il *Common Cause Magazine* 15:13-16 Mr/Ap '89

COWAN, THOMAS DALE

(jt. auth) See Norman, Laura, and Cowan, Thomas Dale

COWARD, NOEL

about

Coward's Jamaica. D. Butwin. il pors *Oceans* 22:54-7 Mr/Ap '89

COWARD (SIR NOEL) FIREFLY HILL MUSEUM (JAMAICA) See Sir Noel Coward's Firefly Hill Museum (Jamaica)

COWART, JOSEPH L.

about

The new breed of campaign manager. K. A. Frenkel. il por *Personal Computing* 13:108-10 O '89

COWBOY ART See Western States in art

COWBOY BOOTS

See also
Tony Lama Company

Anecdotes, facetiae, satire, etc.

The origins of the cowboy boot. R. Sodowsky. il *The Atlantic* 264:46+ D '89

COWBOY HATS

See also
Kirkpatrick Custom Hatters (Firm)

COWBOY JUNKIES (MUSICAL GROUP)

The Cowboy Junkies, country music subversives shooting up—relax—the pop charts. il *People Weekly* 31:151 My 8 '89

Cowboy Junkies shoot for success. H. Gleason. il *Rolling Stone* p22 Mr 9 '89

Easy living with Cowboy Junkies [Toronto] il *Rolling Stone* p34 Jl 13-27 '89

Music [release of Trinity session] G. Santoro. *The Nation* 248:67-8 Ja 9-16 '89

COWBOY MUSEUMS

See also
Gene Autry Western Heritage Museum

COWBOY POETRY
Buckaroo poets: whoop-ee-ti-yi-yo, git along, little doggerel. E. Hoagland. il *The New York Times Book Review* 94:3+ Ja 8 '89
Cowboy poetry: ridin', ropin', and recitin'. il *Sunset (Central West edition)* 182:148 Ja '89
Cowboys, poets & gatherings. D. Swift. il *The Mother Earth News* 115:104+ Ja/F '89

COWBOYS
See also
Cooking by cowboys
Rodeos
Today's embattled cowboys. H. L. Lund. *National Review* 41:26 D 31 '89

COWBOYS IN MOTION PICTURES *See* Motion pictures— Westerns

COWIN, DANA B.
As the wheel turns. il por *House & Garden* 161:76 Je '89
Captain Hook. il por *House & Garden* 161:110 My '89
Hidden treasures. il *House & Garden* 161:70+ D '89
Tile file. il *House & Garden* 161:154 F '89

COWLEY, MALCOLM, 1898-1989
about
Obituary
National Review 41:14 My 5 '89
The New Republic 200:10 Ap 17 '89

COWPEAS
See also
Cooking—Vegetables

COWPOX VIRUS *See* Pox viruses

COWS
See also
Dairying
American classics: a guide to milk cows. il *The Mother Earth News* 119:64-5 S/O '89
Blossom comes home. J. Herriot. il *Good Housekeeping* 208:86 Ja '89
Anecdotes, facetiae, satire, etc.
Madame Vache. W. Hamilton. il *Gourmet* 49:68+ Mr '89
Contamination
Mold on corn tough on dairies hit by drought. J. R. Borcherding. *Successful Farming* 87:54 F '89
Diseases and pests
See Cattle—Diseases and pests
Feeding
Ammoniated 'junk' will feed cows. *Successful Farming* 87:33 Je '89
Gut-level control of aflatoxin [use of hydrated sodium calcium aluminosilicate in feeds; research by Roger B. Harvey] *Science News* 135:111 F 18 '89
Homegrown approach to least-cost rations. J. R. Borcherding. il *Successful Farming* 87:31 mid-Mr '89
How to pick and use silage additives. J. R. Borcherding. il *Successful Farming* 87:26+ Je '89
Rations for all cow seasons. J. R. Borcherding. il *Successful Farming* 87:46-7 S '89
Milk production
See Milk—Production
Prices
Buy cows, not heifers. L. Stalcup. il *Successful Farming* 87:30 mid-Mr '89
Anecdotes, facetiae, satire, etc.
Bill Eftink. B. Eftink. il *Successful Farming* 87:19 Ap '89

COWS IN ART
See also
Holy Cow, Inc.

COX, CHRISTOPHER
Tame the budget beast. il por *Conservative Digest* 15:6-7+ Jl/Ag '89

COX, COURTENEY
about
Courteney Cox: she's flying high in Judith Krantz's 'Till we meet again'. S. Littwin. il pors *TV Guide* 37:7+ N 18-24 '89

COX, ELIZABETH
Alaska on my mind. il *Ms.* 17:63-5 Je '89

COX, JANET
about
Prognosis: excellent following lumpectomy and radiation. C. SerVaas. por *The Saturday Evening Post* 261:46+ Jl/Ag '89

COX, JEFF
First season. See issues of Organic Gardening beginning April 1988 through November 1989

COX, KATHLEEN
Himalayan hideaways. il *Harper's Bazaar* 122:48+ O '89

COX, RICH
about
Cycle savvy! M. Stensvold. il *Petersen's Photographic Magazine* 17:14-17 Ap '89

COX, ROGER W.
Beauty and the beach. il map *Travel Holiday* 171:56-61 F '89
Under the Long Island Sound. il *Travel Holiday* 171:103-7 Mr '89

COX, SCOTT
about
One of our own: one man's struggle with AIDS [interview] *Christianity Today* 33:56 F 3 '89

COX CREEK REFINING COMPANY
Union victory in a copper refinery. K. Kleiner. il *The Progressive* 53:13 S '89

COXON, JAMES
about
Up to B.A.T.? J. Zweig. il por *Forbes* 144:102 Ag 21 '89

COY, PATRICK G.
Qaddafi's revolution. *Commonweal* 116:552-3 O 20 '89

COYLE, RENA
Chesapeake bounty. il *The New York Times Magazine* p59-60 Je 25 '89
Come 'n' get it. il *The New York Times Magazine* p53-4 Ag 6 '89
Memories are made of this. il *The New York Times Magazine* p85-6 Mr 5 '89

COYNE, JOHN R., JR.
Blowing in the wind. por *National Review* 41:19-21 N 24 '89
Henry Regnery: a public private man. il *National Review* 41:40-2 Je 16 '89
A wet mayor or what? *National Review* 41:20-1 Ap 21 '89

COYNE, PETAH
about
Petah Coyne: Jack Shainman. N. Grimes. il *Art News* 88:161-2 N '89

COYNE, WILLIAM J.
Should the House-passed wage proposal be enacted? [excerpts from address, March 23, 1989] *Congressional Digest* 68:154+ My '89

COYOTE HUNTING
Hunting the hunters [predators at night with varmint calls] B. Tarrant. il *Field & Stream* 94:95-6 Jl '89

COYOTES
God's dog [Connecticut] F. Graham. *Audubon* 91:24-5 S '89
A Yankee coat fits the coyote well [New England; cover story] R. Wolkomir and J. Wolkomir. il *National Wildlife* 27:34-8 Ap/My '89

COZUMEL ISLAND (MEXICO)
This is Mexico? R. J. Margolis. *The New Leader* 72:11-12 My 1 '89

COZZENS, BETTY
about
Clown around town. F. Greve. il por *New Choices for the Best Years* 29:11-12 Mr '89

COZZO, FRANCO
about
The king of hospitality. R. Levio. il por *Harper's Bazaar* 122:52 Ap '89

COZZONE, CAMILLE
Family ties. il pors *Harper's Bazaar* 122:114-17 Ag '89
Independent spirits. il pors *Harper's Bazaar* 122:44-9 Jl '89
A special effect. il por *Harper's Bazaar* 122:84+ N '89

CPI (CONSUMER PRICE INDEX) *See* Price indexes

CPI CORPORATION
CPI Corp. J. Slovak. il *Fortune* 119:73 Mr 13 '89

CPR (CARDIOPULMONARY RESUSCITATION) *See* Resuscitation

CRAANE, JANINE
about
Mom/mentor: keeping Wall Street in the family. A. L. Ball. il pors *Working Woman* 14:136-7 O '89

CRAANE, VALERY
about
Mom/mentor: keeping Wall Street in the family. A. L. Ball. il pors *Working Woman* 14:136-7 O '89

CRAB (NEBULA) *See* Nebulae

CRAB INDUSTRY *See* Shellfish industry

CRAB ORCHARD NATIONAL WILDLIFE REFUGE (ILL.)
Toxins on tap? [contaminated water supply at Marion Federal Penitentiary] L. Rocawich. il *The Progressive* 53:24-7 My '89

CRAB SUPERNOVA *See* Supernovas

CRABB, DONALD EVAN
Macinations. See issues of Byte beginning August 1988

CRABGRASS
Control
Crabgrass wars: my father's surrender. W. French. il *Commonweal* 116:421-2 Ag 11 '89

CRABS
See also
Cooking—Shellfish
Advance of the red army [red crabs on Christmas Island] J. W. Hicks. il *International Wildlife* 19:4-11 N/D '89
The arrow crab: a spindly crawler. il *Sea Frontiers* 35:303 S/O '89
Room without a view [rivulus living in land crab burrows] D. S. Taylor. il *Natural History* p26+ S '89
Contamination
E. coli clue to contamination [Louisiana seafood processing plant] il *FDA Consumer* 23:34-5 O '89

CRABS, HORSESHOE *See* Horseshoe crabs
CRABTREE, AUGUST F.
about
The August Crabtree ship model collection. il *Americana* 17:43 S/O '89
CRABTREE, GERALD R.
Contingent genetic regulatory events in T lymphocyte activation. bibl f il *Science* 243:355-61 Ja 20 '89
CRACIDS (BIRDS)
Saving the cracids. N. Angier. il *The Atlantic* 264:26+ Ag '89
CRACK (COCAINE)
1989: crack. T. Morganthau. il *Newsweek* 114:55 Jl 3 '89
Aftermath of a crack article [articles in New republic and Nation stir debate concerning government policy] J. Morley. il *The Nation* 249:592+ N 20 '89
Attitude problem [reactions to J. Morley's article on using crack] *The New Republic* 201:4+ O 9 '89
Children of the underclass [cover story] il *Newsweek* 114:16-20+ S 11 '89
Cocaine's youngest victims. C. García-Barrio. il *American Visions* 4:16 D '89
Counting trees as the forest burns: why the experts have been slow to respond to the crack epidemic. il *Newsweek* 114:26-8 S 11 '89
Crack. il *Life* 12:54-5+ Ja '89
Crack in the cradle. A. C. Revkin. il *Discover* 10:62-9 S '89
Crack invades the countryside [Martinsburg, W. Va.] M. McConnell. il *Reader's Digest* 134:73-8 F '89
The crack kid. W. Plummer. il *People Weekly* 32 Special Issue:73 Fall '89
Crack pushes dads to duty. J. Seligmann. il *Newsweek* 113:64-5 Ap 17 '89
Crackdown [cover story] J. Q. Wilson and J. J. DiIulio. *The New Republic* 201:21-5 Jl 10 '89
Crackmire. *The New Republic* 201:7+ S 11 '89
Crack's destructive sprint across America. M. Massing. il *The New York Times Magazine* p38-41+ O 1 '89
D.C. cracks down on drugs, evicts suspected dealers. il *Jet* 76:52 Je 5 '89
A deadly plague of drugs [cover story; special section; with editorial comment by Kevin Doyle] il *Maclean's* 102:4, 44-51 Ap 3 '89
The drug-violence nexus. P. Goldstein and H. Brownstein. *New Perspectives Quarterly* 6:24 Summ '89
Fighting back against crack [New York City; cover story] E. Pooley. il *New York* 22:30-9 Ja 23 '89
It's déjà vu all over again [drug-related crime wave in Washington, D.C.; views of D. P. Moynihan] *U.S. News & World Report* 106:15 Ap 3 '89
Just another night on crack street [drug dealers in East Harlem] P. Bourgois. il *The New York Times Magazine* p52-3+ N 12 '89
Kinsley does it again [defense of J. Morley's article] R. E. Tyrrell. *The American Spectator* 22:10-11 D '89
Murder wave in the capital [Washington, D.C.] T. Morganthau. il *Newsweek* 113:16-19 Mr 13 '89
The newest drug war [rural America] J. N. Baker. il *Newsweek* 113:20-2 Ap 3 '89
A night in a crack house. S. Minerbrook. il *U.S. News & World Report* 106:29 Ap 10 '89
A nightmare on 42nd Street [Port Authority Bus Terminal in New York] G. Hackett and P. McKillop. il *Newsweek* 113:22-4 F 27 '89
A plague without boundaries [upper middle class users] P. Elmer-Dewitt. il *Time* 134:95+ N 6 '89
Prisoners of crack. L. Cole. il *Rolling Stone* p61-4+ F 9 '89
Profits in a risky business [Harlem crack trade] R. Sandza. il *Newsweek* 113:37 My 29 '89
The sad tale of Sweet Pea [basketball player L. Daniels shot during reported drug dispute] il por *Sports Illustrated* 70:12 My 22 '89
Scar tissue [racism as cause of drug use debunked] L. Wieseltier. *The New Republic* 200:18-20+ Je 5 '89
Smokeless cigarettes under fire [can be used to smoke crack] *Science News* 135:30 Ja 14 '89
So little time, so many cases [Georgia] A. Murr. il *Newsweek* 114:59+ S 25 '89
Street-wise crack research. C. Holden. il *Science* 246:1376-81 D 15 '89
There's crack on my block [neighborhood patrols in New York City] C. Buffum. il *Glamour* 87:128 D '89
A tide of drug killing. L. Martz. il *Newsweek* 113:44-5 Ja 16 '89
Tracing the tracks of his tears in a new book, Smokey Robinson says crack nearly killed him. S. Dougherty. il pors *People Weekly* 31:79-80+ Ap 3 '89
What crack is like. J. Morley. *The New Republic* 201:12-13 O 2 '89
CRACK FORMATION (MECHANICS) *See* Fracture mechanics
CRACKER JACK
Collectibles
They're all Crackerjacks! [A. Jaramillo's collection] E. Hunt. il *Americana* 17:38-9 S/O '89

CRACKERS
Crackers and crisps. il *Gourmet* 49:226 S '89
How healthy are your crackers? M. Madsen. il *Women's Sports & Fitness* 11:12 Ja/F '89
CRADLE SONGS *See* Lullabies
CRAFT, ROBERT
An affair of the heart. il *The New York Review of Books* 36:37-8 Ap 13 '89
Jews and geniuses. il pors *The New York Review of Books* 36:35-7 F 16 '89
'Jews and geniuses': an exchange [discussion of February 16, 1989 article] il *The New York Review of Books* 36:57-8 Je 15 '89
Pipe dreams. bibl f il *The New York Review of Books* 36:6+ N 23 '89
CRAFT FAIRS *See* Arts and crafts—Exhibitions
CRAFTS *See* Arts and crafts
CRAFTSMANSHIP
See also
Arts and crafts
Made in the U.S.A. W. Hoffer. il por maps *Popular Mechanics* 166:58-60+ My '89
CRAFTSMEN *See* Artisans
CRAGG, TONY
about
Cragg's way. A. Graham-Dixon. il pors *Art News* 88:132-7 Mr '89
CRAIG, BERRY
What's right about humanism? por *The Humanist* 49:31-2 Jl/Ag '89
CRAIG, GEORGE
about
Craig to head all Murdoch book business; Chapman resigns from Collins; authors' reaction uncertain. por *Publishers Weekly* 235:10+ F 3 '89
Murdoch wins Collins, promises autonomy; Craig assesses Harper's new owner. V. Menkes. *Publishers Weekly* 235:16+ Ja 20 '89
CRAIG, GORDON ALEXANDER, 1913-
Dangerous liaisons. bibl f il *The New York Review of Books* 36:15-19 Mr 30 '89
Facing up to the Nazis. il *The New York Review of Books* 36:10-15 F 2 '89
The grand decider. il *The New York Review of Books* 36:31-6 Ag 17 '89
Making way for Hitler. bibl f il *The New York Review of Books* 36:11-12+ O 12 '89
The rising star of the German right. il *The New York Review of Books* 36:22-4 Je 15 '89
CRAIG, ROGER, 1960-
about
Double trouble. J. Brant. il pors *Runner's World* 24:30-2 O '89
CRAIG CORP.
What's wrong with a little greenmail? [deals by J. J. Cotter] R. King. il por *Forbes* 143:64+ Mr 6 '89
CRAM, DONALD J., 1919-
about
The man with a new breed of molecule. P. Cole. il por *Business Week* Special Issue:74 Je 16 '89
CRAM (GEORGE F.) CO. *See* George F. Cram Co.
CRAM COURSES *See* Tutors and tutoring
CRAMER, JAMES J.
Basket case. *The New Republic* 201:12-14 N 13 '89
CRAMPS, MENSTRUAL *See* Menstruation—Disorders
CRAMPTON, JUANITA
about
Lunch is being served at the world's smallest restaurant; reservations available in 1990. il pors *People Weekly* 32:150 N 20 '89
CRANBERRIES
See also
Cooking—Fruit
Harvesting
Pilgrim [Cambodian Savath Bon working in New Jersey fields] *The New Yorker* 65:47 N 20 '89
CRANDALL, DAVID P.
Ruminations on the end of a regime: a response to Chester Finn. il *Phi Delta Kappan* 70:816-18 Je '89
CRANDALL, ROBERT L.
about
American aims for the sky. K. Kelly and T. Mason. il por *Business Week* p54-5+ F 20 '89
The best and the brassiest. C. P. Work. il pors *U.S. News & World Report* 107:52-4 O 23 '89
Boxed in by Trump [special section] il por *Business Week* p54-6 O 23 '89
Commercial air transport: Robert L. Crandall. por *Aviation Week & Space Technology* 130:16 Ja 2 '89
An ego as big as American. L. Reibstein. il pors *Newsweek* 114:56-7 O 16 '89
How the new no. 1 got there. R. Woodbury. il por *Time* 133:57 My 15 '89
Interview: Robert Crandall. W. Garvey. il pors *Flying* 116:86-8+ Je '89

CRANDON (WIS.)
Social history
Crandon, 1969 [moon landing] K. Trainor. il map *Ad Astra* 1:16-26 Jl/Ag '89
CRANE, EDWARD H., 1944-
Reagan, Bush, and the liberal revolution [address, December 8, 1988] *Vital Speeches of the Day* 55:265-8 F 15 '89
CRANE, PETER R., AND LIDGARD, SCOTT
Angiosperm diversification and paleolatitudinal gradients in Cretaceous floristic diversity. bibl f il *Science* 246:675-8 N 3 '89
CRANE, PHILIP M., 1930-
Should the Congress adopt the "Textile and Apparel Trade Act of 1987"? [excerpts from address, September 16, 1987] *Congressional Digest* 68:25+ Ja '89
CRANE, ROBERT
Roseanne. il pors *Good Housekeeping* 209:60+ Jl '89
CRANE, STEPHEN, 1871-1900
about
The courage of Stephen Crane. C. E. G. Benfey. il *The New York Review of Books* 36:31-4 Mr 16 '89
CRANES (BIRDS)
Barges, boats and big birds [boat traffic on the Gulf Intracoastal Waterway eroding whooping crane habitat at Aransas National Wildlife Refuge] T. Turner. il *The Mother Earth News* 118:112 Jl/Ag '89
Migration
The ancient faith of cranes [sandhill crane gathering on the Platte River] P. Gruchow. il *Audubon* 91:40-55 My '89
Watching the sandhills in New Mexico and Arizona. il *Sunset (Central West edition)* 182:46 Ja '89
Where will the cranes go? [Two Forks dam planned by Denver may threaten sandhill crane habitat on Platte River] J. Adler. il map *Newsweek* 113:62-3 Ap 3 '89
CRANK (DRUG)
The newest drug war [rural America] J. N. Baker. il *Newsweek* 113:20-2 Ap 3 '89
Tales of the crank trade [southern California] J. Beaty. il *Time* 133:10+ Ap 24 '89
CRANKS AND CRANKSHAFTS
See also
   Motorcycle engines—Crankshafts
   Ohio Crankshaft (Firm)
CRANSTON, ALAN
Should the Senate-passed Immigration Act of 1989 be approved? [excerpts from debate, July 12-13, 1989] *Congressional Digest* 68:239+ O '89
about
Ansel Adams Awards. il pors *Wilderness* 52:9 Summ '89
Old softie. R. Kuttner. *The New Republic* 201:17-19 D 11 '89
The seduction of Senator Alan Cranston. P. Dwyer. il pors *Business Week* p82-4 D 4 '89
CRANSTON, MAURICE
Can government outlaw drugs? pors *National Review* 41:43-5 O 13 '89
Ideas and ideologies. bibl il *History Today* 39:10-14 My '89
Should we celebrate the French Revolution? il *The American Spectator* 22:15-17 Je '89
CRANSTON (R.I.)
Race relations
The town that said "No" to racism [case of C. Berkley and family] A. Cassidy. il pors *Good Housekeeping* 208:62+ F '89
CRAPPIE FISHING
The complete game plan for spring crappies. B. Ignizio. il *Field & Stream* 93:60-1+ F '89
Secrets to slab-size crappies. G. Nelson. il *Outdoor Life* 183:64-5+ F '89
Tactics for spring spawners. J. E. Phillips. il *Outdoor Life* 183:76-7+ My '89
To catch a crappie. B. Taylor and others. il *Field & Stream* 94:50-1+ Je '89
CRASEMANN, BERND
about
Bloembergen elected vice president; Crasemann to head nominating group. il pors *Physics Today* 42:93-4 Ja '89
CRASH TELEVISION
TV's new wisdom: the worse the show, the better the ratings. R. Grover. il *Business Week* p95 Ja 30 '89
CRASH TESTING OF AUTOMOBILES *See* Automobiles—Testing; Automobiles, Foreign—Testing
CRASSULA *See* Jade plants
CRATERS
See also
   Meteor Crater (Ariz.)
^{40}Ar-^{39}Ar dating of the Manson impact structure: a Cretaceous-Tertiary boundary crater candidate [north-central Iowa] M. J. Kunk and others. bibl f il *Science* 244:1565-8 Je 30 '89
Back to Bohemia [Praha Basin meteorite crater; theory of Michael Papagiannis] R. Kunzig. il *Discover* 10:22-3 Je '89
Good news for volcano watchers [study of Long Valley Caldera by Christopher Newhall and Daniel Dzurisin] R. A. Kerr. il *Science* 245:255 Jl 21 '89

Manson, Iowa: where the 'big one' struck? [research by M. J. Kunk] *Astronomy* 17:10-11 O '89
Planetary scientists focus on impact geology [Lunar and Planetary Science Conference] *Astronomy* 17:14+ Ag '89
Stop to consider the stones that fall from the sky. J. S. Trefil. il map *Smithsonian* 20:80-8+ S '89
World's largest impact crater? [Praha basin] il *Sky and Telescope* 77:351 Ap '89
CRATERS, MOON *See* Moon—Surface
CRAUGHWELL, THOMAS J.
Should I have let him in? il *Commonweal* 116:702-3 D 15 '89
CRAVEN, WES
about
After A nightmare on Elm Street, director Wes Craven dreams up Shocker's maniacal killer. M. H. J. Farrell. il pors *People Weekly* 32:159+ N 13 '89
Professor Gore. M. Mancini. il *Film Comment* 25:8 S/O '89
Shocker [film] Reviews
   People Weekly il 32:17-18 N 13 '89. R. Novak
CRAVENS, GWYNETH
Past present. *The Nation* 249:574-5 N 13 '89
CRAVINGS, FOOD *See* Food cravings
CRAWFISH *See* Crayfish
CRAWFISH CULTURE *See* Crayfish culture
CRAWFISH FISHERIES *See* Crayfish fisheries
CRAWFORD, ALAN PELL
Fast forward. *Vogue* 179:430-1 N '89
Reactionaries' reaction. il *The Nation* 248:231+ F 20 '89
CRAWFORD, ALAN PELL, AND LEVINE, ART
Planet stricken. il *Vogue* 179:710-15+ S '89
CRAWFORD, ANNE
about
Pretty poison: Anne Crawford skewers Hollywood. E. J. Carroll. il *Mademoiselle* 95:202-3+ O '89
CRAWFORD, CINDY
about
American beauty. B. Sherman. il pors *Harper's Bazaar* 122:58-63+ Jl '89
The face [cover story] M. Gross. il pors *New York* 22:32-9 O 30 '89
Model Cindy Crawford, the new Revlon girl, has little time for small talk. B. Bull. il por *Vogue* 179:378 Ag '89
Show and television. P. Sikowitz. il por *Harper's Bazaar* 122:43 N '89
CRAWFORD, DAVID LIVINGSTONE, 1931-
The ever-vigilant GNAT. il *Sky and Telescope* 77:143 F '89
Who will miss the night sky? *Astronomy* 17:8 Mr '89
CRAWFORD, GORDON
about
Gordon Crawford. N. Koch. por *Channels (New York, N.Y.: 1986)* 9:53-4 Jl/Ag '89
CRAWFORD, JOAN, 1908-1977
about
Bette vs. Joan: Hollywood's hottest feud [excerpt from Bette and Joan] S. Considine. il pors *Ladies' Home Journal* 106:142-4+ O '89
CRAWFORD, LISA
about
A living nightmare. B. Burgower. il pors *Ladies' Home Journal* 106:74+ Mr '89
CRAWFORD, TRISH
Home is where the office is. *World Press Review* 36:49 F '89
CRAWSHAW, SIMON R. A.
Anti-terrorism networks. il por *The Futurist* 23:12-13 Mr/Ap '89
CRAY, ROBERT
about
Asking for water. M. Moses. *The New Yorker* 64:83+ F 13 '89
Value for your roots-rock dollar. D. Browne. il pors *Rolling Stone* p28 Mr 23 '89
CRAY, SEYMOUR
about
Computer chip off the old block. P. Elmer-Dewitt. il por *Time* 133:70 My 29 '89
Now Cray faces life without Cray. R. Mitchell. il por *Business Week* p31 My 29 '89
CRAY COMPUTER CORPORATION
Computer chip off the old block. P. Elmer-Dewitt. il por *Time* 133:70 My 29 '89
Cray Research will create company to develop, market Cray-3 computers. D. Hughes. *Aviation Week & Space Technology* 130:33 My 22 '89
Divided we flourish. E. Dyson. il *Forbes* 144:102 Jl 10 '89
Now Cray faces life without Cray. R. Mitchell. il por *Business Week* p31 My 29 '89
CRAY RESEARCH, INC.
Computer chip off the old block [breakup into two rival entities] P. Elmer-Dewitt. il por *Time* 133:70 My 29 '89
Cray Research will create company to develop, market Cray-3 computers. D. Hughes. *Aviation Week & Space Technology* 130:33 My 22 '89

CRAY RESEARCH, INC.—*cont.*
Cray versus Japan Inc. [interview with J. A. Rollwagen] D. Churbuck. il por *Forbes* 144:118-19 S 4 '89
Divided we flourish. E. Dyson. il *Forbes* 144:102 Jl 10 '89
Now Cray faces life without Cray. R. Mitchell. il por *Business Week* p31 My 29 '89
Supercomputing. E. Corcoran. il *Scientific American* 260:70+ F '89

CRAYFISH
The best bass bait. K. Etling. il *Outdoor Life* 183:64-5+ Je '89
Live bait traps. B. Volkart. il *Field & Stream* 93:164 Ap '89
Summer smallmouth secrets [live crayfish bait] W. Ryan. il *Outdoor Life* 183:78-9+ My '89

Nervous system
See Nervous system—Crustaceans

CRAYFISH CULTURE
Crawfish as big as armadillos (almost) [Texas vs. Louisiana] il *Newsweek* 113:35 Mr 20 '89
Outraged by uppity Texans, Louisiana gears up for a great crawfish showdown. il *People Weekly* 31:82 My 15 '89

CRAYFISH FISHERIES

Bahamas
Crawfishing in the Bahamas. N. Popov. il *Sea Frontiers* 35:222-30 Jl/Ag '89

CRAZES *See* Fads

CRAZY EDDIE INC.
Stable Jerry [former Crazy Eddie pitchman J. Carroll] J. Queenan. il pors *Forbes* 144:350 N 13 '89

CRAZY HORSE, SIOUX CHIEF, CA. 1842-1877

Memorials
The Ziolkowskis are honoring Chief Crazy Horse, by blasting out a mountain of a sculpture [Thunderhead Mountain] D. Grogan. il pors *People Weekly* 32:105+ D 4 '89

CREAM PUFFS *See* Pastry

CREAMS, FACIAL *See* Cosmetics

CREAMWARE *See* Pottery, English

CREASE, FRAY A.
(jt. auth) *See* Hannibal, Joseph T., and Crease, Fray A.

CREASE, ROBERT P.
In praise of the polka. il *The Atlantic* 264:78-83 Ag '89

CREASE, ROBERT P., AND SAMIOS, NICHOLAS P.
Cold fusion confusion. il pors *The New York Times Magazine* p34-6+ S 24 '89

CREASY, ROSALIND
Tomato leather. il *Organic Gardening* 36:32-3 Jl/Ag '89
Your new yard. il *Organic Gardening* 36:60-5 Ap '89

CREATION
The creation myths of Cooperstown. S. J. Gould. il *Natural History* p14+ N '89
An essay on a pig roast [role of F. Osborn's erroneous Nebraska Man theory in the creationism debate] S. J. Gould. il *Natural History* p14+ Ja '89
Genesis 1 [discussion of November 1988 article, Evolution and the Bible] L. Kass. *Commentary* 87:2+ Ap '89
A new story of creation [theology of ecology] K. L. Woodward. il por *Newsweek* 113:70-2 Je 5 '89
Q: Who made me? J. Garvey. *U.S. Catholic* 54:25-7 Jl '89
Thomas Berry and a new creation story [eco-spiritual movement] M. Hope and J. Young. il por *The Christian Century* 106:750-3 Ag 16-23 '89

Study and teaching
Educators adopt evolution as 'theory' [California] K. H. Sidey. *Christianity Today* 33:57 D 15 '89

CREATION (LITERARY, ARTISTIC, ETC.) *See* Creativity

CREATION SPIRITUALITY
Original blessing, not original sin [interview with M. Fox] S. Keen. il pors *Psychology Today* 23:54-8 Je '89
The taming of a New Age prophet [M. Fox] R. Brow. il *Christianity Today* 33:28-30 Je 16 '89

CREATIVE ABILITY *See* Creativity

CREATIVE ARTISTS AGENCY
Hollywood's most secret agent [M. Ovitz; cover story] L. J. Davis. il pors *The New York Times Magazine* p24-7+ Jl 9 '89
Movie shogun [M. Ovitz] S. L. Kirsch. il por *Fortune* 119:50+ Ja 2 '89
Pocketful of stars. J. Castro. il por *Time* 133:58-9 F 13 '89
The scarlet letter [alleged threats made to J. Eszterhas by M. Ovitz] L. Klady. il pors *American Film* 15:15-16 D '89

CREATIVE ARTS (FIRM)
Not your typical family-business wife [M. Forthman] S. Nelton. il por *Nation's Business* 77:40 Ag '89

CREATIVE EDUCATION
See also
Dramatization in education

CREATIVE IMAGINATION *See* Imagination

CREATIVE THINKING *See* Creativity

CREATIVE WRITING
See also
English language—Composition

Study and teaching
For $2,400, Gordon Lish will tell you how to reach God. N. Karlen. il *Gentlemen's Quarterly* 59:240-3+ My '89
Ken Kesey's eclectic writing acid test [collaboration with University of Oregon students results in novel, Caverns] D. Weddle. il por *Rolling Stone* p119-20+ O 5 '89
Remember this: write what you don't know [University of Oregon students collaborate on novel] K. Kesey. *The New York Times Book Review* 94:1+ D 31 '89
Writing workshops: a publishers' clearinghouse [colleges] D. Weddle. *Rolling Stone* p120 O 5 '89

Aids and devices
KidWriter Gold. N. Rentschler. il *Compute!* 11:67 S '89
KidWriter Golden Edition. M. B. Eltgroth. il *Home Office Computing* 7:85 Ap '89

CREATIVITY
See also
Odyssey of the Mind
100 years of attitude [end-of-century effect in creative endeavors; excerpt from American renaissance] M. J. Cetron and O. Davies. il *Omni (New York, N.Y.)* 12:18+ O '89
The art of the mind: how I learned to draw [art teacher B. Edwards] T. Schwartz. il por *New York* 22:42-6+ D 11 '89
The case for creativity: encouraging our kids to think. A. Atkins. il *Better Homes and Gardens* 67:40+ Ap '89
Children and creativity. H. Horvath. por *The Humanist* 49:22-3+ Ja/F '89
The creative child. J. Segal and Z. Segal. il *Parents* 64:178 F '89
Creativity begins at home [children] *Harper's Bazaar* 122:165+ O '89
The creativity doctors [activities that stimulate the brain] il *Health (New York, N.Y.)* 21:61-3 Ap '89
Creativity in turbulent times. B. I. Page and R. Theobald. il pors *The Futurist* 23:25-8 S/O '89
Does teacher evaluation diminish creativity? M. T. Bryant. *The Education Digest* 54:20-1 Mr '89
Getting creative: birth of a notion. N. McAleer. il *Omni (New York, N.Y.)* 11:112-19 Ap '89
The innovators [special section; cover story] il *Newsweek* 114:34-5 O 2 '89
Learning, Chinese-style [children] H. Gardner. il *Psychology Today* 23:54-6 D '89
On creativity [cover story] N. McAleer. il *Omni (New York, N.Y.)* 11:42-4+ Ap '89
On the road to higher creativity [benefits of aerobic walking; excerpt from Maximum brain power] il *Prevention (Emmaus, Pa.)* 41:86+ O '89
Original spin. L. Dormen and P. Edidin. il *Psychology Today* 23:46-50+ Jl/Ag '89
The paradoxes of creativity. J. Barzun. *The American Scholar* 58:337-51 Summ '89
The special art of managing creative people. M. R. Feinberg. *Working Woman* 14:40 Ap '89
Ten ways to fire up your creativity [excerpt from Career tracking] J. Calano and J. Salzman. *Working Woman* 14:94-5 Jl '89
Turn group input into stellar output [brainstorming; excerpt from Innovation, Inc.] S. R. Grossman and others. il *Working Woman* 14:36+ D '89

CRÈCHES *See* Christmas cribs

CREDIT
See also
Agricultural credit
Collecting of accounts
Debit cards
Debt
Discount, Cash
Finance companies
Government lending
Instalment plan
Interest (Economics)
Letters of credit
Loans, Bank
Loans, Personal
Payment of accounts
Hey, big spenders. J. Crudele. il *New York* 22:19 F 20 '89
This credit squeeze is quiet—but it still hurts. C. Farrell. il *Business Week* p104-5 N 13 '89

Information services
See Credit bureaus

Rating
See also
Credit bureaus
"Credit doctors" can hurt you. P. Plawin. il *Changing Times* 43:78 Ag '89
Credit history scam. K. K. Gracey. *Consumers' Research Magazine* 72:2 Je '89
Fickle credit policies. T. Tilling. il *Parents* 64:199 F '89
How to check your credit rating. R. G. Ledesma. il *Consumers' Research Magazine* 72:30-3 S '89
When you don't get credit where credit is due. D. H. Dunn. il *Business Week* p116-17 O 2 '89

CREDIT ADVISORS INC.
Outrageous fortune? Two guys from D&B cash in. J. Rothfeder. il pors *Business Week* p190 N 27 '89

CREDIT BUREAUS
Is nothing private? [cover story] J. Rothfeder. il *Business Week* p74-7+ S 4 '89
Unwilling players in the name game [sale of credit and medical information to direct marketing companies] A. Mundy. il *U.S. News & World Report* 106:52+ My 1 '89
Who checks the checkers? [HUD's reliance on incomplete credit reports] M. Schifrin. il *Forbes* 144:64 Ag 7 '89

Ethical aspects
Damage control at Dun & Bradstreet. J. Rothfeder. il *Business Week* p187-8+ N 27 '89

CREDIT CARD CRIMES
Check fraud [problems with credit card numbers written on checks] J. W. Merline. il *Consumers' Research Magazine* 72:2 D '89
Newest credit-card scam [applying for credit card under an assumed name: yours] L. Weber. *Good Housekeeping* 208:169 Ja '89
Quick checks [point-of-sale systems that verify checks and credit cards] J. Wynn. il *Nation's Business* 77:45-6 D '89

CREDIT CARDS
See also
Affinity cards
American Express Co.
Certificates of credit card receivables
Diners Club International
Visa International Inc.
Accepting credit cards from your customers [home based business] P. Edwards and S. Edwards. il *Home Office Computing* 7:36 Mr '89
Can't get credit? [secured credit cards] B. G. Quint. il *Glamour* 87:131-2 O '89
Don't get swamped this holiday season [views of Elgie Holstein] *USA Today (Periodical)* 118:1-2 D '89
Free CDW insurance [credit card collision insurance on rentals] K. McCormally. il *Changing Times* 43:120 S '89
Guess how I became rich without working. G. Richardson. il *Utne Reader* p74-5 S/O '89
High-mileage credit cards [airline-affiliated cards] K. Davis. *Changing Times* 43:120+ O '89
Leave home without it [American Express; cover story] M. Lewis. il *The New Republic* 201:19-20+ S 4 '89
Leave the coverage to us [credit card collision insurance causes rental rates to rise] B. Rudolph. il *Time* 133:46 Ja 16 '89
A little plastic can help small companies, too [corporate travel and entertainment cards] S. Woolley. il *Business Week* p180 My 22 '89
New law makes credit-card shopping easier. *Consumer Reports* 54:550 S '89
Not guilty as charged [effect of eel skin wallets on credit card scrambling] il *Discover* 10:12 Mr '89
Plastic is as good as gold. W. Ecenbarger. il *Reader's Digest* 134:37-8+ My '89
Plastic surgery. E. Giltenan. il *Forbes* 143:318 Ja 9 '89
Playing your cards right. I. M. Diaz. il *Black Enterprise* 19:80+ Mr '89
The right credit card for the road. L. Wiener. il *U.S. News & World Report* 106:68 Je 26 '89
With credit cards, as ever, if you see bait, look for a trap. il *Money* 18:15 My '89

Accounting
Those $*&*!!# statements [bank credit cards] B. Hager. il *Money* 18:120-1 F '89

Collectors and collecting
You gotta give a card like Walter some credit [collector W. Cavanagh] il por *People Weekly* 31:69 Ja 30 '89

Fees
Get a cheaper card. P. Plawin. il *Changing Times* 43:111-12 Mr '89
The hidden costs of credit cards. E. Holstein. il *USA Today (Periodical)* 118:82-3 N '89
How to beat down credit-card issuers. E. M. MacDonald. il *Money* 18:22+ N '89
Preparing for higher credit card costs. P. Plawin. il *Changing Times* 43:90 F '89
Update: bargain credit [bank credit cards] K. Davis. il *Changing Times* 43:120 D '89

Interest (Economics)
The cheapest credit cards. *Consumers' Research Magazine* 72:18-19 Mr '89
Get a cheaper card. P. Plawin. il *Changing Times* 43:111-12 Mr '89
The hidden costs of credit cards. E. Holstein. il *USA Today (Periodical)* 118:82-3 N '89
Plastic explosives. M. K. Evans. il *Gentlemen's Quarterly* 59:188+ N '89
Plastic puzzle: why rates for credit cards don't go down. A. S. Blinder. il *Business Week* p14 Ag 7 '89
Preparing for higher credit card costs. P. Plawin. il *Changing Times* 43:90 F '89
Update: bargain credit [bank credit cards] K. Davis. il *Changing Times* 43:120 D '89

Laws and regulations
Ripped off? [right to withhold payment] B. G. Quint. *Glamour* 87:118+ Ag '89

Your credit muscle [right to withhold payment] P. Plawin. il *Changing Times* 43:90 Je '89

Marketing
Can AmEx win the masses—and keep its class? J. Friedman and J. Meehan. il *Business Week* p134-6+ O 9 '89
A credit card is not a commodity [American Express] S. N. Chakravarty. il *Forbes* 144:128-30 O 16 '89
The Discover Card is no longer a joker. D. Greising. il *Business Week* p138 O 9 '89
Easy to leave home without it? [Diners Club card] C. Siler. il *Forbes* 144:140 S 4 '89
Paramount's Card Trek [special credit card issued as part of promotional campaign for Star trek] N. Koch. il *Channels (New York, N.Y.: 1986)* 9:52 F '89

CREDIT PERSONNEL
Giving credit where it is due: loan and credit clerks, credit checkers, and credit authorizers. J. Fumanti. il *Occupational Outlook Quarterly* 33:29-32 Spr '89

CREDIT RATING See Credit—Rating
CREDIT REPORTING AGENCIES See Credit bureaus
CRÉDIT SUISSE
The Bulgarian connection [drugs and money laundering] P. Fuhrman. il map *Forbes* 143:40-4 Ap 17 '89

CREDIT UNIONS
See also
American Association of Retired Persons. Federal Credit Union
Credit unions: a primer. M. Mayer. il *Modern Maturity* 32:84-6+ D '89/Ja '90
Toward a more perfect union. F. McCoy. il *Black Enterprise* 20:86-8+ O '89
Why a credit union could be the best "bank" for you. B. G. Quint. *Glamour* 87:142 S '89

Finance
Credit unions may be tempting fate. C. Yang. il *Business Week* p112-13 D 18 '89

CREDITS, COLLEGE See College credits
CREDITS, HIGH SCHOOL See High school credits
CREE INDIANS
Canadian utility threatens Cree [Hydro-Québec's James Bay II] D. Schulze. il *The Progressive* 53:18 O '89
In search of pride [contrasting Indians of Canada and the United States] B. Came. il *Maclean's* 102:40-1 Jl 3 '89
Unhealed wounds [inquiry into circumstances surrounding 1971 murder and 1987 trial in H. B. Osborne case in Manitoba] N. Underwood. il *Maclean's* 102:41 Jl 10 '89

CREEDS
See also
Nicene Creed

CREEDY, KATHRYN B.
States, not Washington, must develop Essential Air Services. por *Aviation Week & Space Technology* 131:113-16 S 25 '89

CREEK WAR, 1813-1814
See also
Horse Shoe, Battle of the, 1814

CREEKS See Brooks, creeks, etc.
CREEL CREEK FISH CARVING (FIRM)
Fish carvings at Creel Creek [E. and F. Ralph] D. W. Hollis. il pors *The Conservationist* 43:36-9 My/Je '89

CREEP OF GLACIERS See Glaciers
CREF See College Retirement Equities Fund
CREIGHTON UNIVERSITY
Former basketball player sues Creighton University [K. Ross] por *Jet* 76:50 Ag 14 '89

CRENSHAW, BEN
about
Scholar of golf [interview] H. Quinn. il por *Maclean's* 102:73 Ap 10 '89

CRENSHAW, MARSHALL
about
Marshall Crenshaw's "Good evening". S. Simels. il por *Stereo Review* 54:123 S '89

CRENSHAW, THERESA LARSEN
A surgical patient's transfusion survival guide. il por *The Saturday Evening Post* 261:60+ Mr '89
Transfusions: it's a bloody shame. il por *The Humanist* 49:16-20+ My/Je '89

CRENSHAW CHRISTIAN CENTER
FaithDome: 'a grand-slam homer for Jesus' [work of F. Price] A. Collier. il pors *Ebony* 45:40-2+ D '89
TV's Rev. Fred Price opens $9 million FaithDome in L.A. il pors *Jet* 77:32-3 O 16 '89

CREOLE COOKING See Cooking, Creole
CREOSOTE
Controlling creosote. S. Benado. *Popular Science* 234:51 Mr '89

CRÊPES
Three-mushroom sauce in crêpes, on asparagus. il *Sunset (Central West edition)* 182:108-9 Ja '89

CRESTED BUTTE (COLO.)
Colorado nouveau [skiing] L. Tejada-Flores. il *Skiing* 42:238-46+ S '89
Head over wheels [mountain cycling] K. Castle. il *Travel Holiday* 171:18-21 Ja '89

CRESWELL (N.C.)

Historic houses, sites, etc.

See also

Somerset Place State Historic Site (Creswell, N.C.)

CRETACEOUS PERIOD *See* Geology, Stratigraphic—Cretaceous; Paleobotany—Cretaceous; Paleoclimatology—Cretaceous; Paleontology—Cretaceous

CRETE

Antiquities

The Thera theory [evidence against S. Marinatos' hypothesis that the disappearance of the Minoans was linked to volanic eruption on Thera] A. Chen. il maps *Discover* 10:76-80+ F '89

CREW RACING *See* Rowing

CREWS, ED

Of menhaden and watermen. il map *Americana* 17:40-3 S/O '89

CREWS, FREDERICK C.

The parting of the Twains. bibl f il *The New York Review of Books* 36:39-44 Jl 20 '89

CREWS, AIRPLANE *See* Airplane crews

CRIB DEATHS *See* Sudden infant death syndrome

CRIBB, JULIAN

How to stop the desert's march. *World Press Review* 36:32 Ap '89

CRIBBAGE BOARDS

Cribbage critters. il *Sunset (Central West edition)* 181:70-1 D '88

CRIBIER, PASCAL

about

Green geometry. M. K. Griswold. il por *House & Garden* 161:46+ Jl '89

CRIBS (BEDS)

Anecdotes, facetiae, satire, etc.

Babes in Crib Land. P. Cooper. il *Parents* 64:268 O '89

CRICENTI, A., AND OTHERS

Molecular structure of DNA by scanning tunneling microscopy. bibl f il *Science* 245:1226-7 S 15 '89

CRICHTON, CHARLES, 1910-

about

A fish called Wanda [film] Reviews

American Film il 14:16-18+ Ja/F '89

Video 13:59 Ap '89. J. Walker

CRICHTON, JEAN

The crowded world of travel books [special section] il *Publishers Weekly* 235:36-8+ Ja 20 '89

Easy on the eyes. il *Publishers Weekly* 236:14+ Jl 7 '89

In search of older readers. il por *Publishers Weekly* 236:20+ Jl 7 '89

CRICHTON, MICHAEL, 1942-

Spaceport America. il por maps *Popular Mechanics* 166:32-6+ My '89

about

Physical evidence [film] Reviews

People Weekly il 31:20 F 13 '89. R. Novak

CRICK, FRANCIS, 1916-

about

Two sides to every science story. G. Johnson. *The New York Times Book Review* 94:1+ Ap 9 '89

CRICKET (SPORT)

Ten things you never knew about cricket. K. Modesti. il *Sport (New York, N.Y.)* 80:83 Ap '89

Great Britain

History

Carry on cricket: the Duke of Dorset's 1789 tour [cover story] J. Goulstone and M. J. Swanton. bibl il *History Today* 39:18-23 Ag '89

CRICKETS

Live bait traps. B. Volkart. il *Field & Stream* 93:164 Ap '89

Sexual behavior

See Sexual behavior—Insects

CRIER, CATHERINE

about

Here comes the judge—Catherine Crier now presides at a news desk. J. Park. il pors *People Weekly* 32:59-60 N 6 '89

Vet Bernard Shaw, rookie newcomer, co-anchor CNN's 'The world today' newscast. pors *Jet* 77:23 O 30 '89

CRIME AND CRIMINALS

See also

Aged—Crime

Arson

Assassination

Assault and battery

Athletes—Crime

Black markets

Blacks—Crime

Blacks—Crimes against

Bribery

Burglary and burglars

Bus hijacking

Capital punishment

Children—Crimes against

Clergy—Crime

College students—Crimes against

Commercial crimes

Computer crimes

Congressmen—Staff—Crime

Convict labor

Counterfeits and counterfeiting

Credit card crimes

Crime and the press

Crime prevention

Criminal investigation

Criminal psychology

Cyclists—Crimes against

Day care workers—Crime

Drugs and crime

Embezzlement

Escapes

Fraud

Fugitives from justice

Gangs

Gas utility workers—Crime

Hate crimes

Helicopter hijacking

Insurance crimes

Jamaicans—United States—Crime

Juvenile delinquents and delinquency

Kidnapping

Mafia

Mentally handicapped—Crimes against

Mexicans—United States—Crime

Motorcycles—Theft

Murder

Narcotics trade

Nurses and nursing—Crime

Parole

Payola

Pillage

Pirates

Poaching

Priests—Crime

Prisoners

Prisons

Punishment

Rape

Recidivists

Romanians—United States—Crime

Rural crimes

Self defense for women

Sex crimes

Shoplifting

Single men—Crimes against

Smuggling

Stealing

Tax evasion

Teachers—Crime

Telephone crimes

Television broadcasting—Crime programs

Terrorism

Traffic ticket fixing

Trials

Urban crimes

Victims of crime

Women—Crimes against

Calling Lyndon Johnson. *National Review* 41:13-14 My 5 '89

A nation afraid. G. F. Kreyche. il *USA Today (Periodical)* 117:98 My '89

Biography

Out to make killings [true crime literature] S. Kanfer. il *Time* 133:98+ F 20 '89

Economic aspects

See also

Laundering of money

Reparation

For states and cities, the Bush drug plan is small consolation [high cost of law enforcement] G. Witkin. *U.S. News & World Report* 107:33 S 18 '89

Identification

See also

Computers—Police use

Did Billy really die a kid? G. Byrne. il por *Science* 243:610 F 3 '89

International aspects

See also

United Nations Congress on the Prevention of Crime and the Treatment of Offenders

Public opinion

Crime watch [results of survey] I. Groller. il *Parents* 64:30 Ja '89

Statistics

The states pay the price [increase in violent crimes] il *Time* 134:25 Ag 21 '89

Arizona

See also

Flagstaff (Ariz.)—Crime

Brazil

Rural workers face murder. W. Steif. il *The Progressive* 53:26 Je '89

California

See also

Arleta (Los Angeles, Calif.)—Crime

Hollywood (Calif.)—Crime

CRIME AND CRIMINALS—California—See also—*cont.*
    Los Angeles (Calif.)—Crime
    Manhattan Beach (Calif.)—Crime
    San Francisco (Calif.)—Crime
    Santa Cruz (Calif.)—Crime
    Stockton (Calif.)—Crime
Daughter of Manson victims finds forgiveness [S. LaBerge and inmate C. Watson] J. Shaver. il pors *Christianity Today* 33:50-1 S 22 '89
Manson. J. Adler. por *Newsweek* 114:54-5 Jl 3 '89

Canada
    See also
    Colombians—Canada—Crime
Fear on the streets [crimes against women] G. W. Taylor. il *Maclean's* 102:25-6 O 23 '89
The missing lists [series of break-ins at offices of environmental organizations] A. Steacy. il *Maclean's* 102:58 My 15 '89

Colombia
    See also
    Medellin (Colombia)—Crime

Colorado
    See also
    Denver (Colo.)—Crime

Connecticut
    See also
    Hartford (Conn.)—Crime

Delaware
    See also
    Hazlettville (Del.)—Crime

Egypt
Pyramid scheme [investment fraud perpetrated by A. Abdul-Fattah] W. P. Barrett. il *Forbes* 143:106+ Ap 17 '89

Florida
    See also
    Lighthouse Point (Fla.)—Crime
    Miami (Fla.)—Crime
    West Palm Beach (Fla.)—Crime

France
    See also
    Paris (France)—Crime

Georgia
    See also
    Atlanta (Ga.)—Crime
    Forsyth (Ga.)—Crime

Illinois
    See also
    Chicago (Ill.)—Crime
    Winnetka (Ill.)—Crime

Indiana
    See also
    Indianapolis (Ind.)—Crime

Italy
    See also
    Mafia
    Rome (Italy)—Crime

Japan
    See also
    Tokyo (Japan)—Crime

Jordan
    See also
    Bayan, Lauren—Kidnapping

Kansas
    See also
    Goessel (Kan.)—Crime
    Wichita (Kan.)—Crime

Kentucky
    See also
    Jackson County (Ky.)—Crime
    Lexington (Ky.)—Crime
    Louisville (Ky.)—Crime
    Marion County (Ky.)—Crime

Kenya
Death in the African bush [murder of lion enthusiast G. Adamson] C. S. Manegold. il *Newsweek* 114:32 S 4 '89
Murder in the game reserve [G. Adamson murdered] il *Time* 134:21 S 4 '89
The murder of innocence in Africa [death of lion enthusiast G. Adamson] M. Vollers. il *People Weekly* 32:46-51 S 11 '89

Lebanon
Of piracy and payoffs [ships diverted into Lebanese ports] J. Penycate. *World Press Review* 36:53 My '89

Maine
    See also
    Hermon (Me.)—Crime

Mexico
    See also
    Matamoros (Tamaulipas, Mexico)—Crime
    Tijuana (Mexico)—Crime

Michigan
    See also
    Detroit (Mich.)—Crime
    Wyandotte (Mich.)—Crime

Mississippi
    See also
    Biloxi (Miss.)—Crime

Two blacks face murder charges in voodoo scheme [charges against J. and L. Ivy in voodoo scheme against judge T. Gardner] il pors *Jet* 76:52-3 Jl 17 '89

Missouri
    See also
    Kansas City (Mo.)—Crime

New Brunswick
    See also
    Miramichi River region (N.B.)—Crime
    Newcastle (N.B.)—Crime

New Jersey
    See also
    Glen Ridge (N.J.)—Crime
    Montclair (N.J.)—Crime
    Sparta (N.J.)—Crime
    Toms River (N.J.)—Crime
    Westfield (N.J.)—Crime

New York (State)
    See also
    Bronx (New York, N.Y.)—Crime
    Colonie (N.Y.)—Crime
    Mount Marion (N.Y.)—Crime
    New York (N.Y.)—Crime
    Schenectady (N.Y.)—Crime
    Staten Island (New York, N.Y.)—Crime
    Yonkers (N.Y.)—Crime

Newfoundland
    See also
    Saint John's (Nfld.)—Crime
A breach of faith [sex charges against priests] G. Allen. il *Maclean's* 102:16-17 Mr 13 '89
Sins of the flesh [priests and sex crimes] G. W. Taylor. il *Maclean's* 102:10-12 Jl 17 '89

North Carolina
    See also
    Burlington (N.C.)—Crime

Northwest Territories
    See also
    Pond Inlet (N.W.T.)—Crime

Ohio
    See also
    Cleveland (Ohio)—Crime
    Columbus (Ohio)—Crime

Ontario
    See also
    Ottawa (Ont.)—Crime
    Toronto (Ont.)—Crime

Pennsylvania
    See also
    Pittsburgh (Pa.)—Crime

Québec (Province)
    See also
    Montreal (Québec)—Crime

Saint Croix (Virgin Islands of the U.S.)
Anarchy in paradise [violence and looting follow Hurricane Hugo] il *Time* 134:18 O 2 '89

Saskatchewan
    See also
    Regina (Sask.)—Crime

South Carolina
    See also
    Columbia (S.C.)—Crime

Texas
    See also
    Austin (Tex.)—Crime
    Bastrop County (Tex.)—Crime
    Dallas (Tex.)—Crime
    Malone (Tex.)—Crime

United States
    See Crime and criminals

Washington (D.C.)
    See Washington (D.C.)—Crime

Washington (State)
Stalking the Green River killer [suspect W. J. Stevens] A. Sachs. il por *Time* 134:57 Jl 31 '89

West Virginia
    See also
    Martinsburg (W. Va.)—Crime

CRIME AND THE PRESS
    See also
    Central Park wilding attack, 1989—Reporters and reporting
    Contempt of court
    Steinberg, Lisa, d. 1987—Child abuse case—Reporters and reporting
Clark Kent, please call your office [G. Bush asks press to do something about crime] il *Newsweek* 113:28 F 27 '89
Crime: that's entertainment [TV interview with T. Bundy] J. Leo. il por *U.S. News & World Report* 106:53 F 6 '89
Notes and comment [TV interview with T. Bundy] *The New Yorker* 65:23-4 F 27 '89
White-collar crime isn't news [research by Donna Randall and others] *USA Today (Periodical)* 118:4-5 D '89

CRIME DETECTION See Criminal investigation
CRIME FILMS See Motion pictures—Crime films
CRIME NOVELS See Detective and mystery stories
CRIME PREVENTION
See also
Electronics in criminal investigation, espionage, etc.
Mannequins (Figures) in crime prevention
Police
Taxicabs in crime prevention
United Nations Congress on the Prevention of Crime and the Treatment of Offenders
Campus crime: living the college life safely. A. Atkins. il *Better Homes and Gardens* 67:40+ My '89
Citizen participation
See also
Guardian Angels (Organization)
Youth Force (Organization)
Community [reclaiming the streets from drugs] J. P. Shapiro. il *U.S. News & World Report* 107:80-3 S 11 '89
Fighting back against crack [New York City; cover story] E. Pooley. il *New York* 22:30-9 Ja 23 '89
How to keep from getting ripped off. D. Fortune. il *Ebony* 44:62+ Mr '89
Making neighborhoods safe [community-oriented policing] J. Q. Wilson and G. L. Kelling. il *The Atlantic* 263:46-52 F '89
The Muslims to the rescue [anti-drug patrol in Washington, D.C.'s Mayfair Mansions housing project] il *Ebony* 44:136+ Ag '89
On the front lines [citizens rising up against drug dealers] R. Lacayo. il *Time* 134:14-18 S 11 '89
There's crack on my block [neighborhood patrols in New York City] C. Buffum. il *Glamour* 87:128 D '89
CRIME PROGRAMS See Television broadcasting—Crime programs
CRIMES AND MISDEMEANORS [film] See Motion picture reviews—Single works
CRIMINAL CODE See Criminal law
CRIMINAL INVESTIGATION
See also
Computers—Police use
Electronics in criminal investigation, espionage, etc.
Fingerprints
Forensic anthropology
Forensic dentistry
Forensic entomology
Forensic illustration
Forensic meteorology
Forensic pathology
Forensic psychiatry
Forensic sculpture
Fugitives from justice
Image processing in criminal investigation
Informers
Lie detectors and detection
Medical examiners (Law)
Medical jurisprudence
Missing persons
Parapsychology and criminal investigation
Police—Surveillance operations
Police questioning
Public prosecutors
United States. Federal Bureau of Investigation
United States. Marshals Service
Murder most puzzling: can you solve this case? L. Treat. il *The New York Times Book Review* 94:36 O 15 '89
The think tank murder [puzzle to solve] T. Chastain. il *Discover* 10:96+ O '89
CRIMINAL JURY See Jury
CRIMINAL JUSTICE, ADMINISTRATION OF
See also
Bail
Criminal investigation
Criminal law
Jury
Juvenile justice, Administration of
Medical examiners (Law)
Miscarriage of justice
Pardon
Parole
Political prisoners
Preventive detention
Public prosecutors
Punishment
Reparation
Searches and seizures
Sentencing consultants
United States. Dept. of Justice
Cops: we're losing the war. K. W. Perry. por *Newsweek* 113:6-7 Mr 13 '89
Criminals belong in jail. T. Bethell. *The Washington Monthly* 21:68-9 F '89
Doing the crime, not the time [lenient alternative sentences] A. Sachs. il *Time* 134:81 S 11 '89
An end to judicial roulette [sentencing guidelines upheld by Supreme Court] T. Jacoby. il *Newsweek* 113:76 Ja 30 '89

An eye for an eye in the courts [U.S. Sentencing Commission guidelines upheld by Supreme Court] *U.S. News & World Report* 106:11-12 Ja 30 '89
Future justice: from retribution to reconciliation. G. Stephens. il por *The Futurist* 23:21-4 S/O '89
A hard line on crime is no easy answer. R. E. Burns. *U.S. Catholic* 54:2 Mr '89
Hard time [alternative sentences] J. Klein. il *New York* 22:18+ My 8 '89
Let punishment fit the crime [Supreme Court upholds guidelines established by U.S. Sentencing Commission] R. N. Ostling. il *Time* 133:63 Ja 30 '89
Personalized penalties [alternative sentences arranged by consultants] T. Gest. il *U.S. News & World Report* 107:75-6 N 20 '89
Scandal in the courts [views of S. Brill] M. Greenfield. il *Newsweek* 114:68 Ag 21 '89
Sweatshirt justice: how the war on crime is expanding to crush some rights. C. Byron. il *New York* 22:42-4+ O 2 '89
Victims of crime [cover story; special section] il *U.S. News & World Report* 107:16-21+ Jl 31 '89
'We need drastic measures'. M. Beck. il *Newsweek* 113:21 Mr 13 '89
When criminal rights go wrong [cover story] P. Savoy. *The Washington Monthly* 21:36-41+ D '89
When the guilty go free [views of H. Rothwax] H. Evans. il *U.S. News & World Report* 106:84 My 22 '89
Why justice can't be done [drug cases] B. Turque. il *Newsweek* 113:36-7 My 29 '89
The wrath of "Maximum Bob" [J. Bakker's punishment raises questions over sentencing] A. L. Sanders. il por *Time* 134:62 N 6 '89
International aspects
See also
United Nations Congress on the Prevention of Crime and the Treatment of Offenders
Alabama
The execution of Ronnie Dunkins [electrocution] D. Aukerman. il *The Christian Century* 106:783-5 Ag 30-S 6 '89
California
See also
Butte County (Calif.)—Criminal justice, Administration of
A criminal lack of common sense [career criminal W. Bland finally sentenced to life imprisonment] J. Leo. il *U.S. News & World Report* 107:56 Ag 21 '89
Private mercy [execution of R. A. Lindsey; excerpt from Public justice, private mercy]; ed. by Dick Adler. E. G. Brown. il *Common Cause Magazine* 15:28-33 Jl/Ag '89
Vicious crime, double jeopardy [parole of A. R. Jackson, attacker of actress T. Saldana] D. Bacon. il pors *People Weekly* 31:44-9 Je 5 '89
Who will yell fire when the house is ablaze? [conviction of anti-nuclear activist S. Komisaruk for damaging computer at Vandenburg Air Force Base] R. E. Burns. *U.S. Catholic* 54:2 F '89
Colorado
See also
Denver (Colo.)—Criminal justice, Administration of
Florida
See also
Clearwater (Fla.)—Criminal justice, Administration of
The Bundy carnival [electrocution] D. Gelman. il por *Newsweek* 113:66 F 6 '89
Burning question [T. Bundy] *The New Republic* 200:4+ F 20 '89
A condemned man's last bequest [execution of T. Bundy] P. Axthelm and M. Ryan. il pors *People Weekly* 31:44-51 F 6 '89
Convicted of murdering one of his children, James Richardson hopes the truth will set him free [Florida man imprisoned for 1967 poisonings] P. Chin. il pors *People Weekly* 31:191-2+ Mr 6 '89
Crime & punishment: a view from a broad [woman judge known for tough sentencing]; ed. by Linda Marx. E. Morphonios. il pors *People Weekly* 32:79-80+ Jl 3 '89
From tragedy to travesty [questioning the guilt of J. Richardson who served 21 years for poisoning his children] J. N. Baker. il por *Newsweek* 113:68 Ap 24 '89
"I deserve punishment" [T. Bundy executed] J. V. Lamar, Jr. il por *Time* 133:34 F 6 '89
A killer's final hour [T. Bundy] M. Nichols. il por *Maclean's* 102:54 F 6 '89
Presumed guilty [half brothers E. L. Miller and W. R. Jent released from death row after new evidence uncovered concerning 1979 murder case] D. Finkel. il pors *Esquire* 111:178-80+ Mr '89
France
French court convicts Palestinian terrorist [A. A. al-Hamid Labid; State Dept. statement and fact sheet, October 31, 1988] *Department of State Bulletin* 89:64-5 F '89
Germany (West)
Selling security for deutschemarks [R. Mueller gets suspended sentence for selling military technology to the Soviets] R. N. Perle. il *U.S. News & World Report* 107:36 Jl 31 '89

CRIMINAL JUSTICE, ADMINISTRATION OF—*cont.*

Great Britain

British justice, Irish victims [release of Guildford Four who were wrongfully imprisoned in England for terrorist bombings] A. Cockburn. *The Nation* 249:554-5 N 13 '89

Cops above the law [release of Guildford Four who were wrongfully imprisoned in England for being IRA suspects] A. Phillips. il *Maclean's* 102:76+ N 6 '89

Illinois

See also

Chicago (Ill.)—Criminal justice, Administration of

Cecil A. Partee becomes Cook County state's atty.: first black to hold post. por *Jet* 76:14-15 My 8 '89

Louisiana

Execute Ronald Monroe? W. F. Buckley. *National Review* 41:63 S 15 '89

Only two weeks to live [impending execution of R. Monroe] G. Carroll and A. Press. il por *Newsweek* 114:62-4 Ag 21 '89

Ronald Monroe fights a Louisiana verdict of murder for a crime many think he did not commit. J. S. Kunen. il por *People Weekly* 32:95-6+ Ag 28 '89

Maine

Murder and the right to die [M. Weaver's right to die protested by criminal N. Pagan] il por *Newsweek* 113:33 Ap 10 '89

Massachusetts

See also

Lawrence (Mass.)—Criminal justice, Administration of

Mexico

When jailbirds are also fat cats [luxurious treatment of suspects in the E. Camarena Salazar murder case] *U.S. News & World Report* 107:13 Jl 31 '89

Minnesota

See also

Minneapolis (Minn.)—Criminal justice, Administration of

Hardening their hearts. T. Padgett. il *Newsweek* 113:28 Ap 3 '89

Missouri

. . . detention [conviction of anti-nuclear activists for trespassing at Whiteman Air Force Base] J. Munves. *The Nation* 248:509 Ap 17 '89

Sam Day's example [jailed for trespassing on missile silo site during protest] E. Knoll. *The Progressive* 53:4 Je '89

New York (State)

See also

Brawley, Tawana—Assault case

Bronx (New York, N.Y.)—Criminal justice, Administration of

The death penalty debate. *America* 160:443 My 13 '89

"I won't kill, I'll just maim" [career criminal W. Bosket] R. Behar. il por *Time* 133:30-1 My 29 '89

Pressure in New York for death penalty. R. F. Drinan. *The Christian Century* 106:582-3 Je 7-14 '89

Ontario

See also

Toronto (Ont.)—Criminal justice, Administration of

South Carolina

Jesse Jackson calls for release of James Brown. pors *Jet* 75:10 Mr 13 '89

Wife and fans outraged by 6-year prison term handed to James Brown. il pors *Jet* 75:18+ Ja 9 '89

Soviet Union

In Gorbachev's courts. G. P. Fletcher. bibl f il *The New York Review of Books* 36:13-14+ My 18 '89

Texas

See also

Dallas (Tex.)—Criminal justice, Administration of

Execute an 8-year-old? The Johnny Penry case [mentally retarded adult awaiting execution] R. F. Drinan. *The Christian Century* 106:199-200 F 22 '89

United States

See Criminal justice, Administration of

Washington (D.C.)

See Washington (D.C.)—Criminal justice, Administration of

CRIMINAL LAW

See also

Capital punishment

Conspiracy

Contempt of court

Criminal justice, Administration of

Entrapment (Law)

Liability (Law)

Libel and slander

Obscenity (Law)

Pardon

Racketeer Influenced and Corrupt Organizations Act of 1970

Rape

Tax evasion

The Bush anticrime plan that meowed. *U.S. News & World Report* 106:10 My 22 '89

Dial-a-porn, find-a-lawyer [Supreme Court rulings] A. L. Sanders. il *Time* 134:56 Jl 3 '89

The politics of hate [laws dealing with bias-related crime] J. Leo. il *U.S. News & World Report* 107:24 O 9 '89

Rebalancing justice's scales. D. Gergen. il *U.S. News & World Report* 106:96 Mr 27 '89

When criminal rights go wrong [cover story] P. Savoy. *The Washington Monthly* 21:36-41+ D '89

China

The law bends to party needs. L. D. Rosario. *World Press Review* 36:23-4 Ag '89

CRIMINAL LAW [film] See Motion picture reviews—Single works

CRIMINAL PSYCHOLOGY

See also

Forensic psychiatry

Prison psychology

Adding up violent vulnerabilities [research by Dorothy Otnow Lewis] B. Bower. *Science News* 135:318 My 20 '89

The arrogance of predicting dangerousness. R. E. Vatz and L. S. Weinberg. il *USA Today (Periodical)* 118:62-3 N '89

CRIMINAL RECORDS

The law criminals love [controversy over confidentiality] R. J. Bidinotto. *Reader's Digest* 135:57-62 S '89

CRIMINALLY INSANE

See also

Forensic psychiatry

Insanity defense

CRIMINALS See Crime and criminals

CRIMINOLOGY See Crime and criminals

CRINKLEY, RICHMOND, 1940-1989

about

Obituary

National Review il 41:17 Mr 10 '89. W. F. Buckley

CRISIS INTERVENTION

How the school responded [shooting spree aftermath in Winnetka, Ill.] J. Bultman. il *Parents* 64:108-9 My '89

CRISIS MANAGEMENT (PSYCHOLOGY)

Make hard times work for your marriage. C. Jabs. *Reader's Digest* 135:145-7 Ag '89

The secret of life at the limits: cogs become big wheels [research by Todd La Porte and others] J. E. Pfeiffer. il *Smithsonian* 20:38-46+ Jl '89

CRISIS MANAGEMENT IN BUSINESS

How Safeway coped with the quake [Bay Area] G. Hector. il map *Fortune* 120:101-2+ N 20 '89

How to expect the unexpected and handle it well. J. Ciabattari. il *Working Woman* 14:84-6+ F '89

CRISIS MANAGEMENT IN GOVERNMENT

Exercises in diplomacy: simulating future crises. M. Schofield. il *The Futurist* 23:8-11 Mr/Ap '89

Mock crisis, real players [U.S. and Soviet officials participate in televised crisis game] B. Van Voorst. il por *Time* 134:88 D 11 '89

Pentagon uses new computer system to help action teams manage crises [crisis management automatic data processing system] B. D. Nordwall. il *Aviation Week & Space Technology* 131:43+ D 4 '89

CRISP, D., AND OTHERS

The nature of the near-infrared features on the Venus night side. bibl f il *Science* 246:506-9 O 27 '89

CRISP, QUENTIN

Camping out. il por *House & Garden* 161:184-7 O '89

Taste be damned. il *House & Garden* 161:90-1 Ag '89

CRISSIER (SWITZERLAND)

Restaurants, nightclubs, bars, etc.

The best restaurant in the world [Girardet] D. Shaw. il pors *Gentlemen's Quarterly* 59:196-201 F '89

CRIST, JUDITH

Movies. il *TV Guide* 37:82-2+ S 9-15 '89

CRIST, STEVEN

Silent Shoe's last ride. il pors *The New York Times Magazine* p42-4+ Je 4 '89

about

The daily double. G. Norman. il pors *Sports Illustrated* 70:92-6+ Je 5 '89

CRISTI, JOHN

about

John Cristi, who sees 300 plays and concerts a year, may be the greatest show man on earth. S. Dougherty. il pors *People Weekly* 32:81+ O 2 '89

CRISTIANI, ALFREDO

about

Back to square one. W. R. Doerner. il pors *Time* 133:28-9 Ap 3 '89

Bush's Central American albatross. L. Lief. *U.S. News & World Report* 107:33 D 4 '89

Conversations with two foes. J. Smolowe. il pors *Time* 134:26 O 2 '89

A done deal and an undone deal in Central America. C. A. Robbins and others. il por *U.S. News & World Report* 106:29 Ap 3 '89

One dilemma after another. D. Waller. il por *Newsweek* 113:32 Ap 3 '89

Presidential election held in El Salvador. *Department of State Bulletin* 89:84 My '89

The return of the right. C. Lane. il por *Newsweek* 113:38+ Mr 20 '89

A shift to the right. A. Bilski. il por *Maclean's* 102:27+ Ap 3 '89

CRISTIANI, ALFREDO—cont.
Visit to the United States, 1989
President's meeting with El Salvador's president-elect [White House statement, April 7, 1989] *Department of State Bulletin* 89:66 Je '89

CRITERION GROUP INC.
Excitement we can live without. W. P. Barrett. il *Forbes* 143:112+ Je 12 '89

CRITICAL THINKING *See* Thought and thinking

CRITICALITY, SELF ORGANIZING *See* Self organizing systems

CRITICISM, PERSONAL
Criticizing your boss—tactfully. J. Weber, Jr. il *Business Week* p98 Ag 28 '89
"He expects me to be perfect" [husband constantly criticizing wife] C. L. Mithers. il *Ladies' Home Journal* 106:8+ D '89
How not to give criticism [excerpt from The critical edge] H. Weisinger. il *Glamour* 87:126+ Mr '89
How to criticize a man. J. Stone. il *Glamour* 87:146 Je '89
How tough critics may be mentors in disguise [excerpt from The critical edge] H. Weisinger. il *Working Woman* 14:102-4 Je '89
Take the sting out of criticism. R. Graber. il *Reader's Digest* 134:120-2 Ap '89

CRITICS AND CRITICISM
See also
Art critics and criticism
Book reviews and reviewing
Education critics and criticism
Food critics and criticism
Literary critics and criticism
Motion picture critics and criticism
Photography—Criticism, interpretation, etc.
Wine critics and criticism

CROCE, ARLENE
Dancing. See occasional issues of The New Yorker

CROCHETING
Exhibitions
Norma Minkowitz: shadow boxes [crocheted sculptures] M. Shermeta. il *American Craft* 49:38-41 D '89/Ja '90

CROCK POTS *See* Kitchen utensils and appliances

CROCKER, CHESTER A.
Southern Africa: eight years later. bibl f *Foreign Affairs* 68:144-64 Fall '89

CROCKER, GEORGE ALLEN
about
The West Point story [excerpt from The long gray line; cover story] R. Atkinson. il pors *U.S. News & World Report* 107:44-54 O 9 '89

CROCKETT, DAVY, 1786-1836
about
Davy Crockett—he was hardly king of the wild frontier. P. A. Hutton. il por *TV Guide* 36:24-5 F 4-10 '89
Whangdoodling. B. A. Weisberger. il *American Heritage* 40:24+ F '89

CROCKETT, GEORGE W., JR.
about
Rep. Crockett seeks one more term to help Detroit. por *Jet* 77:4 D 4 '89

CROCODILE SHOES *See* Footwear

CROCODILES
Crocodile attack! [V. Plumwood attacked in Kakadu National Park, Australia; condensation] H. Edwards. il *Reader's Digest* 135:70-5 O '89
Marine crocodiles [cover story] T. Ritchie. bibl il *Sea Frontiers* 35:212-19 Jl/Ag '89

CROCODILES, FOSSIL
Mammal-like dentition in a Mesozoic crocodylian. J. M. Clark and others. bibl f il *Science* 244:1064-6 Je 2 '89

CROCUSES
See also
Saffron
Spring crocus. B. B. Mackey. il *Flower and Garden* 33:30 S/O '89

CROFT, JOHN-ED
about
Chocolate Milk. *The New Yorker* 65:25-6 Ag 14 '89

CROLY, HERBERT DAVID, 1869-1930
about
Herbert Croly's promise. J. B. Judis. por *The New Republic* 201:84-7 N 6 '89

CROMARTIE, WARREN
about
The master of besaboru. R. Whiting. il por *Sports Illustrated* 71:68-9 Ag 21 '89

CROMMELIN, QUENTIN
about
A guilty plea confirms the dark rumors about Capitol Hill aide Quentin Crommelin. L. Kramer. il pors *People Weekly* 32:49-50 Ag 21 '89

CROMOLYN
A drug for the sneeze season. A. Dane. il *American Health* 8:15 My '89

CRONENBERG, DAVID
about
Dead ringers [film] Reviews
Video il 13:62+ Je '89. I. Robbins
Video il 13:17-18 Je '89. D. Schweiger

CRONENWORTH, BRIAN
He knew what he wanted. il pors *American Film* 14:46-52 Ja/F '89

CRONIN, MARTHA
Good times: summer of '89: where to go and what to do in the national parks. il *National Parks* 63:37-41 My/Je '89

CRONIN, THOMAS E.
Kennedy was America's best TV president—Johnson the worst. il *TV Guide* 37:22-3 O 14-20 '89

CRONISE, RAYMOND
The class of '88. il *Ad Astra* 1:19 Mr '89

CRONKITE, WALTER
about
Walter Cronkite. il pors *People Weekly* 31 Special Issue:26-7 Summ '89

CRONYN, MARGARET
Cardinal John F. Dearden: a remembrance. *America* 161:100-1 Ag 26-S 2 '89

CROOKER, BARBARA
Amusement park [poem] *America* 161:352 N 18 '89
Terrestrial navigation [poem] *Country Journal* 16:59 Jl/Ag '89

CROOKER, CHRISTINA M.
A letter to my children. il por *The Humanist* 49:29+ Mr/Ap '89

CROOKS, LOUISE
Older Americans in a changing society [address, March 22, 1989] *Vital Speeches of the Day* 55:556-8 Jl 1 '89
Our opinion. See issues of Modern Maturity beginning June/July 1988

CROOM, JOHN HENRY, 1932-
about
The uses of adversity. J. Cook. il por *Forbes* 144:60+ N 27 '89

CROP ART
Cultivating art in the heartland [S. Herd] L. Barash. il *National Wildlife* 27:30-3 Je/Jl '89
The grandest art on earth [art by farmer S. Herd] G. Sledge. il *Reader's Digest* 134:178-80 My '89

CROP CIRCLES
Around and around in circles [crop field rings in southern England] S. B. Donnelly. il *Time* 134:50 S 18 '89
The thumb prints of the gods? [unexplained circular patterns of wheat in England] il *U.S. News & World Report* 107:13 S 11 '89

CROP GENETICS *See* Plant genetics

CROP INSURANCE *See* Federal Crop Insurance Corporation

CROP PROTECTION *See* Plants—Protection

CROP RESEARCH *See* Agricultural research

CROP RESIDUES
Check residue in less than an hour. R. Fee. il *Successful Farming* 87:48H My '89
Crop residue—going, going, gone! R. Fee. il *Successful Farming* 87:24-7 N '89
Get to the point to save residue [chisel plowing] R. Fee. il *Successful Farming* 87 no4:18-21 Mr '89
Measuring and managing residue. il *Successful Farming* 87:22-3 D '89
Residue repositioned. R. Fee. il *Successful Farming* 87:36-7 D '89

CROP SPRAYING AND DUSTING, AERIAL *See* Airplanes in agriculture

CROP YIELDS
See also
Corn—Yield
Rice—Yield
Soybeans—Yield
Wheat—Yield

CROPS
See also
Alfalfa
Cover crops
Forage plants
Grain
Soybeans
Marketing
See Farm produce—Marketing; Produce trade
Prices
See Farm produce—Prices

CROPS, EFFECT OF AIR POLLUTION ON *See* Plants, Effect of air pollution on

CROPS AND CLIMATE *See* Plants, Effect of climate on

CROPS AND COLD WEATHER *See* Plants, Effect of temperature on

CROQUET
Study and teaching
School of hard knocks [instructional course at Newport Casino, R.I.] J. McCallum. il *Sports Illustrated* 71:85 Ag 28 '89

CROSBIE, JOHN CARNELL
about
Test of wills. M. Nemeth. il pors *Maclean's* 102:63-4 Jl 3 '89

CROSBY, DAVID
about
David Crosby. J. Ephland. il por *Down Beat* 56:14 S '89
CROSS, AMANDA, 1926-
about
PW interviews. M. Berkley. il por *Publishers Weekly* 235:47-8 Ap 14 '89
CROSS, AMY WILLARD- *See* Willard-Cross, Amy
CROSS, GEORGE A. M.
(jt. auth) *See* Bellofatto, Vivian, and Cross, George A. M.
CROSS, ROBERT
about
A death in Winnipeg. P. Kaihla. il por *Maclean's* 102:16 S 11 '89
CROSS, SHARON L., AND OTHERS
Functionally distinct NF-κB binding sites in the immunoglobulin κ and IL-2 receptor α chain genes. bibl f il *Science* 244:466-9 Ap 28 '89
CROSS, TARA
about
Calif. volleyball star aiming for NCAA crown. il por *Jet* 77:50 N 27 '89
CROSS, WILLIAM
China on my mind. il *New Choices for the Best Years* 29:36-42 My '89
CROSS COUNTRY RUNNING
Return of the crusher [P. Porter wins U.S. title] M. Noden. il pors *Sports Illustrated* 71:78-9 D 4 '89
Team theme [relays] J. Henderson. il *Runner's World* 24:14 S '89
Tracks of my fears [remembering a high school race] J. Summers. il *Runner's World* 24:104 N '89
Photographs and photography
World Series [World Cross Country Championships] il *Runner's World* 24:52-5 Je '89
CROSS COUNTRY SKI EXERCISERS *See* Exercising equipment
CROSS COUNTRY SKI RACING
Heading for an 'off' year [year without a nordic world championship] P. Robbins. il *Skiing* 42:42+ S '89
CROSS COUNTRY SKIING
A coast-to-coast guide for cross-country skiers. S. Woolley. il *Business Week* p147 D 11 '89
Cross-country skiing: the anywhere winter sport. N. K. Molitar. il *Current Health 2* 15:13-15 Ja '89
Hunting & fishing on skis. S. Netherby. il *Field & Stream* 93:30+ F '89
The sport that lets you laugh at winter. S. J. Henry. il *Women's Sports & Fitness* 11:54-5 N/D '89
Technique terrorists. B. Koch. il *Skiing* 42:40+ N '89
X country skiing. D. Petersen. il *The Mother Earth News* 115:88-90+ Ja/F '89
Equipment
A pull-along sled for baby. il *Sunset (Central West edition)* 183:29 D '89
International aspects
My favorite touring centers. B. Koch. il *Skiing* 42:28+ D '89
Study and teaching
Catwalk cross-country. J. Dostal and J. Tidd. il *Skiing* 41:100-1+ F '89
The double pole. B. Koch. il *Skiing* 41:30 Ja '89
The incredible rhythm of cross-country skiing. S. J. Henry. il por *Women's Sports & Fitness* 11:54 Ja/F '89
Alaska
Hot on the trail. M. Steere. il map *Travel Holiday* 171:55-9 Ja '89
Montana
Glide through a 'snow forest' [Lone Mountain Ranch] G. Lichtenstein. il *New Choices for the Best Years* 29:54-5 Ja '89
Western States
Cross-country getaways. il map *Sunset (Central West edition)* 182:54-9 Ja '89
CROSS COUNTRY SKIS
Up hill and down dale. R. Kimber. il *Country Journal* 16:72+ F '89
Testing
Nordic. J. Dostal. il *Skiing* 42:214+ S '89
Waxless winners. J. Dostal. il *Skiing* 41:50-4 F '89
CROSS CULTURAL STUDIES *See* Intercultural research
CROSS OF FIRE [television program] *See* Television program reviews—Single works
CROSS TRAINING
Break out of that fitness rut! D. Welch. il *Health (New York, N.Y.)* 21:66-71+ N '89
Commit to get fit [tennis players; special section]; ed. by Marc Bloom. D. Scott. il *World Tennis* 36:69-70+ My '89
Cross-training. L. F. McCarthy. il *Good Housekeeping* 208:91-2 My '89
Cross-training [cyclists] S. Johnson. il *Bicycling* 30:84+ D '89
Cross training: more than just the sum of its parts. J. M. Rippe and D. Groves. il *American Health* 8:92-4+ S '89
Fitness via cross-training! il *Essence* 19:82-3 Ja '89
Mixing it up—the cross-training alternative. R. McGuire. il *Women's Sports & Fitness* 11:26-8+ Jl/Ag '89

Total fitness '89 [triathlon training; cover story; special section] il *Runner's World* 24:45-50+ My '89
Triple your pleasure. G. Sheehan. il *Runner's World* 24:16 S '89
CROSSETTE, BARBARA
King Bhumibol's reign. il pors *The New York Times Magazine* p30-2+ My 21 '89
CROSSING DELANCEY [film] *See* Motion picture reviews—Single works
CROSSING OF RIVERS *See* River crossing
CROSSLAND, JOHN
The dockers who won. il *History Today* 39:9-10 O '89
CROSSON, PIERRE R., AND ROSENBERG, NORMAN J., 1930-
Strategies for agriculture. bibl il *Scientific American* 261:128-35 S '89
CROSSWAY BOOKS (FIRM)
Crossway's crossover novelist [S. Lawhead's Arthurian saga] B. Summer. il por *Publishers Weekly* 236:28+ O 6 '89
CROSSWORD PUZZLES
Crazy over crosswords. W. Ecenbarger. il *Reader's Digest* 134:93-6 Mr '89
CROSWELL, KEN
Target: Phobos. il *Ad Astra* 1:16-21 Ja '89
CROTEAU, JULIE
about
Innerviews [interview] il por *Women's Sports & Fitness* 11:64 S '89
Who's on first? E. Gibson. il por *Seventeen* 48:54 S '89
CROTTA, CAROL A.
'I set out to be the worst person I've ever met'. il por *TV Guide* 37:12-13+ Je 3-9 '89
CROUCH, LEONA G.
about
Meet Leona Crouch; Delphi, Indiana, antiques dealer and collector [cover story; interview] por *Antiques & Collecting Hobbies* 94:33+ Je '89
CROUCH, STANLEY
Bird land [cover story] il por *The New Republic* 200:25-31 F 27 '89
CROUSE, JAMES, AND TRUSHEIM, DALE
Five challenges for the Scholastic Aptitude Test. *The Education Digest* 54:26-8 Ap '89
CROVITZ, L. GORDON
The least responsive branch. *Commentary* 87:38-41 Mr '89
CROW, JAMES T.
about
Obituary
Road & Track il por 40:40 Mr '89. T. L. Bryant
CROW, JOHN WILLIAM
about
Marching bravely towards recession. D. Francis. il *Maclean's* 102:19 O 2 '89
CROWD CONTROL
See also
Art galleries and museums—Crowd control
Soccer, Professional—Crowd control
CROWDER, CHARLES L.
about
Charlie Crowder sees utopia, and it's a border town. S. Baker. il por map *Business Week* p35-6 Jl 31 '89
CROWDER, WILLIAM W.
Helping students use leisure time effectively. *The Education Digest* 55:54-6 N '89
CROWDS
See also
Riots
CROWE, CAMERON, 1957-
about
How to succeed in Hollywood by saying anything. S. Roman. por *Video* 13:21 N '89
Say anything [film] Reviews
The New Yorker 65:122-3 My 15 '89. P. Kael
Newsweek 113:72 Ap 17 '89. D. Ansen
People Weekly il 31:16 Ap 24 '89. S. Haller
Video il 13:88 D '89. I. Robbins
CROWE, CHRISTOPHER
about
Off limits [film] Reviews
Video 12:83 Ja '89. D. Schweiger
CROWE, PAT
Snow cover. il *Country Journal* 16:42-7 Ja '89
CROWE, WILLIAM J., 1925-
about
Crowe calls for review of military intelligence. *Aviation Week & Space Technology* 131:31 N 20 '89
From cold war to odd couple. J. Barry. il pors *Newsweek* 114:42 Jl 31 '89
The soldiers' summit. K. M. Campbell. bibl f *Foreign Policy* 75:76-91 Summ '89
'There is little question that real change is afoot' [interview] il por *U.S. News & World Report* 107:80 Ag 28-S 4 '89
A Yankee in Gorbachev's court. S. Talbott. il por *Time* 134:32 Jl 3 '89
CROWFOOT, JOHN
(tr) *See* Averintsev, Sergei S. The idea of Holy Russia

CROWLEY, CAROLYN HUGHES
Land of milk and maple syrup. il *The Saturday Evening Post* 261:68-9 Jl/Ag '89

CROWLEY, KATE
about
She's got to have it all now! S. Seixas. il pors *Money* 18:86-8+ O '89

CROWLEY, PATTY
about
Helping the homeless. C. Reeve. il por *New Choices for the Best Years* 29:16 F '89

CROWN, LESTER, 1925-
about
Maytag may be back in the takeover cycle. G. G. Marcial. il *Business Week* p78 Ag 28 '89

CROWN AMERICAN CORPORATION
Look who wants to try Bloomie's on for size. M. Schroeder. il por *Business Week* p30 O 2 '89

CROWN BOOKS CORPORATION
Auel signs major three-book deal with Crown, Bantam. G. Feldman. il por *Publishers Weekly* 236:34-5 D 22 '89

CROWN CENTRAL PETROLEUM CORP.
A gas marketer primes its pump with a makeover. J. M. Laderman. il *Business Week* p60 Ja 9 '89

CROWN COMMUNICATIONS GROUP PLC
Britain's biggest new radio star. R. A. Melcher. il por *Business Week* p114 My 22 '89

CROWN OF THORNS STARFISH *See* Starfish
CROWS
The bird with brains. H. Middleton. il *Southern Living* 24:41+ O '89
The crow man [interview with L. Kilham] B. Gilbert. il pors *Life* 12:25-7 Je '89
Let it pau out? [controversy surrounding efforts to save the Hawaiian crow] F. Graham. *Audubon* 91:14+ N '89
A new look at the uncommon common crow. J. P. Hoeschele. il *The Conservationist* 43:16-19 Mr/Ap '89
One fine crow. B. Gilbert. il *Reader's Digest* 134:149-52 Ap '89

CROZIER, BRIAN
The protracted conflict. See issues of National Review
CRT DISPLAY TERMINALS *See* Video display terminals
CRUCIAN COOKING *See* Cooking, Crucian
CRUCIFEROUS VEGETABLES
Good news from the garden. il *Better Homes and Gardens* 67:40+ Mr '89
CRUCIFIXION
See also
Jesus Christ—Crucifixion
CRUCIFIXION IN ART
Exhibitions
Eleanor Dickinson at Hatley Martin. P. Selz. il *Art in America* 77:219 S '89
CRUDE OIL *See* Petroleum
CRUDE OIL FUTURES *See* Commodity futures
CRUELTY
See also
Police cruelty
Sadomasochism
CRUICKSHANK, ALEXANDER M.
Gordon Research Conferences. il *Science* 246:264-9 O 13 '89
Gordon Research Conferences [cover story] *Science* 243:1201-17 Mr 3 '89
CRUIKSHANK, DALE P., AND OTHERS
Triton: do we see to the surface? bibl f il *Science* 245:283-6 Jl 21 '89
CRUISE, TOM
about
Tom Terrific [cover story] R. Corliss. il pors *Time* 134:74-9 D 25 '89
Who's on first? D. Ansen. il pors *Newsweek* 113:52-6 Ja 16 '89
CRUISE LINES *See* Steamship lines
CRUISE MISSILES *See* Guided missiles
CRUISE SHIPS *See* Ocean liners
CRUISERS (PLEASURE BOATS)
Speed
Magnificent 75 mph Magnum [63 Sport] P. A. Janssen. il *Motor Boating & Sailing* 163:23 My '89
Testing
Adventure in Wonderland [cruising to Disney World in a Cobia San Marino 278E] M. Benson. il *Motor Boating & Sailing* 163:52-5+ Je '89
All in the family. D. Fales. il *Motor Boating & Sailing* 163:58-63 Je '89
Bayliner 43. P. A. Janssen. il *Motor Boating & Sailing* 164:29 N '89
Bluewater 55. D. Fales. il *Motor Boating & Sailing* 163:38 My '89
Brand new golden oldie [Windsor 26] P. A. Janssen. il *Motor Boating & Sailing* 163:82-3+ F '89
Bristol 47.7. R. Marshall. il *Motor Boating & Sailing* 163:36 My '89
Carver 25. P. Whittell. il *Motor Boating & Sailing* 163:29 Je '89
Century 310XL. T. P. Banse. il *Motor Boating & Sailing* 164:27 Ag '89

Chris-Craft 37. D. Fales. il *Motor Boating & Sailing* 163:30 Ap '89
Cobalt Condurre 223. J. Skorupa. il *Popular Mechanics* 166:99-100 Ag '89
Cruising comfort [Sea Ray's 42-foot Sundancer] L. Rudeen. il *Motor Boating & Sailing* 163:64-7+ Je '89
Cuddy cruisers. T. P. Banse. il *Popular Mechanics* 166:75-8 Ag '89
Express lane [cruising the Florida Keys in a Trojan 12 Meter] M. Benson. il *Motor Boating & Sailing* 163:58-61+ F '89
Formula 29 PC. D. Fales. il *Motor Boating & Sailing* 164:21 Jl '89
Formula 34. D. Fales. il *Motor Boating & Sailing* 163:30 Mr '89
Formula 36 PC. J. Clemans. il *Motor Boating & Sailing* 164:29 O '89
Grand Banks 46. D. Fales. il *Motor Boating & Sailing* 163:96 Ja '89
Hatteras 40. D. Fales. il *Motor Boating & Sailing* 164:30 O '89
Heading south [Prestancia 300] L. Rudeen. il *Motor Boating & Sailing* 164:50-3+ D '89
High spirits [Cruisers 36 Esprit on run around Lake Michigan] D. Fales. il *Motor Boating & Sailing* 164:56-9+ D '89
Larson 30. T. P. Banse. il *Motor Boating & Sailing* 163:30 Je '89
Maximum Magnum [70 Sport] R. Friese. il *Motor Boating & Sailing* 164:44-5+ D '89
Moving up [cruising Florida's Gulf Coast in a Wellcraft St. Tropez] L. Rudeen. il *Motor Boating & Sailing* 164:56-9+ N '89
Overnight sensation [Cobalt Condúrre 263] M. Benson. il *Motor Boating & Sailing* 163:70-3+ My '89
Pearson 34. R. Marshall. il *Motor Boating & Sailing* 163:34 F '89
Pearson 34. R. Marshall. il *Motor Boating & Sailing* 164:25 Jl '89
Regal 26. P. A. Janssen. il *Motor Boating & Sailing* 163:38 F '89
Rinker 230. T. P. Banse. il *Motor Boating & Sailing* 164:24 Ag '89
Sun Runner 30. D. Fales. il *Motor Boating & Sailing* 163:33 Je '89
Sunbird 27. T. P. Banse. il *Motor Boating & Sailing* 164:21 D '89
Topnotch Tolly [Tollycraft 40 convertible] J. Clemans. il *Motor Boating & Sailing* 163:68-9+ Mr '89
Wellcraft's new port of call [37-foot Corsica] D. Fales. il *Motor Boating & Sailing* 163:56-7 Je '89
CRUISES *See* Cruising
CRUISING
See also
River trips
Voyages
Voyages around the world
Best buys on the high seas [repositioning cruises] H. Basch and S. Slater. il *Travel Holiday* 172:22-4 Ag '89
Christmas cruises. S. Birnbaum. il *Good Housekeeping* 209:32-3 D '89
Cross-country cruise [Miami to Los Angeles in Tempest powerboats] J. Catlett. il map *Motor Boating & Sailing* 163:72-5+ F '89
Cruising: a low-cost family vacation. C. Loomis. il *Parents* 64:233+ My '89
Cruising tips [family cruising] P. Whittell. il *Motor Boating & Sailing* 163:40+ Je '89
A cruising winterlude. H. Basch and S. Slater. il *Travel Holiday* 171:62-6 Ja '89
Cruising with a cause. B. Peurifoy-Green. il *Black Enterprise* 19:61-2 Jl '89
Family cruising. P. A. Janssen. il *Motor Boating & Sailing* 163:15 Je '89
Last-minute cruisers can be choosers. G. DeGeorge. il *Business Week* p106 F 13 '89
Setting sail with Mozart—or Steve Allen [theme cruises] T. Segal. il *Business Week* p206 N 6 '89
Ship-to-shore wildlife watching. H. Basch and S. Slater. il *Travel Holiday* 171:105 Ap '89
Shipshape: fitness at sea. S. Lord. *Vogue* 179:318 D '89
The shipshape way to cruise. E. E. Rosenbaum. il *New Choices for the Best Years* 29:23-5 Ag '89
Shore leave [land excursions] H. Basch and S. Slater. il *Travel Holiday* 172:10+ S '89
Theatre at sea [special section] il *Theatre Crafts* 23:40-5+ Mr '89
Weekend mini-cruises. H. Basch and S. Slater. il *Travel Holiday* 171:87 F '89
Winter cruises that won't sink your budget. P. Plawin. il *Changing Times* 43:85-9 F '89
Photographs and photography
Seascapes. M. Grimm and T. Grimm. il *Travel Holiday* 171:32-3 Ja '89
Terminology
Nautically speaking. H. Basch and S. Slater. il *Travel Holiday* 172:32-4 N '89

CRUISING—cont.

Aegean Islands

Islands in a dream. M. Benson. il *Motor Boating & Sailing* 164:62-5+ Ag '89

Alaska

Alaska cruise bargains. H. Basch and S. Slater. il *Travel Holiday* 171:117 Mr '89

Alaska in a Donzi 33 [cover story] P. A. Janssen. il *Motor Boating & Sailing* 164:40-5+ O '89

Alaska: morning of creation. C. Davidson. il *American Heritage* 40:26+ Mr '89

An Alaskan cruise. D. Z. Jackson. il *Essence* 20:31-2+ My '89

Alaska—Northwest passages [Inside Passage] M. T. O'Keefe. il *The Saturday Evening Post* 261:82-4 My/Je '89

Heading north [Seattle to Juneau in a Donzi F-33] P. A. Janssen. il *Motor Boating & Sailing* 164:15+ S '89

Ice sizzle & totem poles. P. L. Buckley. *National Review* 41:65-6 Ja 27 '89

A passage to Alaska [Inside Passage] L. Levinger. il map *New Choices for the Best Years* 29:40-5 O '89

Antarctic regions

Going down to the ice. C. N. Barnard. il map *Modern Maturity* 32:42-7+ O/N '89

The last continent. il *Women's Sports & Fitness* 11:11 O '89

Bahamas

Debut in paradise [maiden voyage of Donzi Z-65] J. Clemans. il *Motor Boating & Sailing* 164:36-41+ S '89

Dream from Down Under [Southern Cross 53 motor yacht] J. Clemans. il *Motor Boating & Sailing* 163:76-7+ F '89

British Virgin Islands

Carefree charter. D. Fales. il *Motor Boating & Sailing* 164:60-1+ Ag '89

Riding the wind. S. Moore. il *Black Enterprise* 19:119 My '89

Canada

Navigating New England and Canada. H. Basch and S. Slater. il *Travel Holiday* 171:81 Je '89

Caribbean region

12,000 mile dream cruise (III). B. Kessler. il *Motor Boating & Sailing* 163:68-9+ My '89

Amazing boon. L. Mosher. il *Américas* 41 no2:32-40 '89

Caribbean sales [bargains] H. Basch and S. Slater. il *Travel Holiday* 172:32-3+ O '89

Lust at sea [cruise conference for romance writers] S. Anthony. il *Ms.* 17:128-9 Ja/F '89

S.S. Norway jazz cruise. J. McDonough. il *Down Beat* 56:48+ F '89

Sail away on a cruise! R. S. Devine. il *Better Homes and Gardens* 68:163-6 F '89

East Asia

The occidental tourist. S. Slater and H. Basch. il *Travel Holiday* 172:28-9 Jl '89

Europe

Land-sea options in Europe. H. Basch and S. Slater. il *Travel Holiday* 171:93 My '89

Florida

Adventure in Wonderland [cruising to Disney World in a Cobia San Marino 278E] M. Benson. il *Motor Boating & Sailing* 163:52-5+ Je '89

Bon voyage for a day. il *Southern Living* 24:26+ Ap '89

Californian . . . here I come [three-day delivery of a Carver 48 from Sarasota to Miami] D. Fales. il *Motor Boating & Sailing* 163:58-61+ Ap '89

Moving up [cruising Florida's Gulf Coast in a Wellcraft St. Tropez] L. Rudeen. il *Motor Boating & Sailing* 164:56-9+ N '89

Florida Keys (Fla.)

Express lane [cruising in a Trojan 12 Meter] M. Benson. il *Motor Boating & Sailing* 163:58-61+ F '89

France

Floating through Europe [canal cruise on hotel barge from Strasbourg to Nancy] P. L. Buckley. il *National Review* 41:48-9 D 31 '89

Sexy expatriates [American-made yachts in St. Tropez] J. Clemans. il *Motor Boating & Sailing* 163:62-5+ Ja '89

Great Lakes

High spirits [Cruisers 36 Esprit on run around Lake Michigan] D. Fales. il *Motor Boating & Sailing* 164:56-9+ D '89

New England

Navigating New England and Canada. H. Basch and S. Slater. il *Travel Holiday* 171:81 Je '89

Pacific Northwest

Northwest passage [cruising from the Columbia River bar to the San Juan Islands in a Tollycraft 53] D. Fales. il *Motor Boating & Sailing* 164:44-7+ Ag '89

South Georgia Island

Wildlife quest to the icy seas of South Georgia. S. Poncet. il map *National Geographic* 175:340-75 Mr '89

Thailand

Boating's new magic kingdom: Thailand. P. B. Wright. il *Motor Boating & Sailing* 163:92-4+ Je '89

Washington (State)

Football flotilla [cruising to University of Washington's Husky Stadium] N. Rabinowitz. il *Motor Boating & Sailing* 163:76-7 Ja '89

CRUISING, AUTOMOBILE (SOCIAL CUSTOM) See Automobiles—Social aspects

CRUM, ROBERT

Another week on the Concord and Merrimack. *Wilderness* 53:11-12+ Fall '89

Calling the owls. il *Sierra* 74:73-4+ N/D '89

CRUMBLEY, D. LARRY

about

D. Larry Crumbley: laying bare the fleshpots of accounting. T. Vogel. il por *Business Week* p91 Je 26 '89

CRUMP, KATHY

How to do your best without driving yourself (and others) crazy. *McCall's* 116:58+ Je '89

CRUSADES

Mapping a Crusade [work of 14th century cartographer M. Sanudo] O. A. W. Dilke and M. Dilke. bibl il maps *History Today* 39:31-5 Ag '89

Retracing the First Crusade [cover story] T. Severin. il map *National Geographic* 176:326-65 S '89

CRUSHES (EMOTIONS)

Family crushes. P. R. Satran. il *Glamour* 87:274-5+ My '89

Handling an office crush. P. R. Satran. il *Working Woman* 14:103 N '89

Is a friend's crush off-limits? J. C. Johnson. *Mademoiselle* 95:140 S '89

A married woman's crush. D. Porretto. *Glamour* 87:114 F '89

My girlfriend dreams about other men [infatuation with B. Springsteen] B. Patrick. il por *Glamour* 87:230 D '89

Summer loves [women's crushes on male celebrities] il *Ladies' Home Journal* 106:48+ Ag '89

CRUSOE [film] See Motion picture reviews—Single works

CRUSSI, F. GONZALEZ- See Gonzalez-Crussi, F.

CRUST (EARTH) See Earth—Crust

CRUSTACEANS

See also

Anilocra

Crabs

Crayfish

Eye—Crustaceans

Krill

Nervous system—Crustaceans

Shrimp

Diseases and pests

Symbiotic marine bacteria chemically defend crustacean embryos from a pathogenic fungus. M. S. Gil-Turnes and others. bibl f il *Science* 246:116-18 O 6 '89

CRUTCHER, DIANE

about

An expert explains her daughter's disorder [interview] G. Breu. il por *People Weekly* 32:67 O 16 '89

CRUTZEN, PAUL J.

(jt. auth) See Graedel, T. E., and Crutzen, Paul J.

CRUVER, PHILIP C.

America is running out of power. *USA Today (Periodical)* 118:62-3 Jl '89

Hydrogen: tomorrow's limitless power source. il por *The Futurist* 23:24-6 N/D '89

Lighting the 21st century. il por *The Futurist* 23:29-34 Ja/F '89

CRUZ, ARTURO, JR.

Anatomy of an execution. *Commentary* 88:54-6 N '89

Mr. Yankee goes home. *Commentary* 88:47-8 Ag '89

CRUZ, HECTOR

about

Threading the needle. A. A. Knocke. il por *Nation's Business* 77:70 Mr '89

CRUZAN, JOE

about

Nancy Cruzan's parents want to let her die—and are taking the case to the Supreme Court. M. Brower. il pors *People Weekly* 32:135-6+ D 4 '89

CRUZAN, NANCY

about

The Cruzan decision: refusing treatment. J. M. Swomley. *The Christian Century* 106:1110-11 N 29 '89

Is there a right to die? T. Gest. il por *U.S. News & World Report* 107:35-7 D 11 '89

Last rights. M. G. Maudlin. *Christianity Today* 33:15 N 3 '89

Nancy Cruzan's parents want to let her die—and are taking the case to the Supreme Court. M. Brower. il pors *People Weekly* 32:135-6+ D 4 '89

To be or not to be. M. Kinsley. *The New Republic* 201:6+ N 27 '89

Whose right to die? A. L. Sanders. il *Time* 134:80 D 11 '89

CRUZAT, ROSCOE MODESTA, D. 1989

about

Obituary

Jet 76:53 Ap 24 '89

CRY-BABY [film] See Motion picture reviews—Single works

A CRY FOR HELP: THE TRACEY THURMAN STORY [television program] See Television program reviews—Single works

CRY FREEDOM [film] See Motion picture reviews—Single works

A CRY IN THE DARK [film] See Motion picture reviews—Single works
CRYER, JON
about
TV's best new sitcom: The famous Teddy Z. A. King. il por *Glamour* 87:194 O '89
CRYING
See also
Infants—Crying
Will you cry on the job? [excerpt from Working up a storm] J. M. Plas and K. V. Hoover-Dempsey. il *Glamour* 87:286-7+ Mr '89
CRYOBIOLOGY
See also
Cryonics
Frozen embryos
CRYOGENIC INTERMENT See Cryonics
CRYONICS
Putting death on ice. A. Ben-Abraham. il *The Saturday Evening Post* 261:60-2+ Ap '89
Reruns will keep sitcom writer Dick Clair on ice—indefinitely. J. S. Kunen. il pors *People Weekly* 32:57+ Jl 17 '89
Moral and religious aspects
An ethical approach to cryonics. D. J. Doherty. *USA Today (Periodical)* 117:73-4 Ja '89
CRYPTOGAMS
Supersoil [cryptogamic soils; research by Tyler Volk and David W. Schwartzman; cover story] R. Monastersky. il *Science News* 136:376-7 D 9 '89
CRYPTOGRAPHY
The Church cryptogram: to catch a Tory spy [message intercepted by Washington's forces during the American Revolution] M. L. Peterson. il *American History Illustrated* 24:36-43 N/D '89
Hostile takeovers [computer network security] P. Wallich. *Scientific American* 260:22+ Ja '89
Quantum cryptography [research by Charles H. Bennett] P. Wallich. *Scientific American* 260:28+ My '89
Secret codes [encryption] A. Dror. bibl f il *Byte* 14:267-70 Je '89
CRYPTOLOGY See Cryptography
CRYPTOSPORIDIUM INFECTION See Coccidiosis
CRYPTOZOOLOGY
Monster mania. il *National Geographic World* 168:22-5 Ag '89
CRYSTAL, BILLY
Red-faced in Moscow? Would Billy Crystal get his laughs? il por *TV Guide* 37:14-15+ O 21-27 '89
about
Billy Crystal. il por *People Weekly* 32:75 D 25 '89-Ja 1 '90
Billy Crystal. M. Beller. il pors *Life* 12:68-71 Jl '89
Crystal bawls [cover story] B. Buschel. il pors *Gentlemen's Quarterly* 59:198-203+ Ag '89
Men, women, sex, love and marriage—from the mouths of Billy Crystal and Meg Ryan [interview] D. DeNicolo. il pors *Glamour* 87:205 S '89
Pals. R. Lloyd. il pors *American Film* 14:28-33+ Jl/Ag '89
CRYSTAL, GRAEF S.
Seeking the sense in CEO pay. il *Fortune* 119:88-9+ Je 5 '89
CRYSTAL, GRAEF S., AND VINCENT, FRANCIS T., JR.
Take the mystery out of CEO pay. il *Fortune* 119:217+ Ap 24 '89
CRYSTAL (GLASS) See Glassware
CRYSTAL BRANDS INC.
Do Crystal's vibes say 'takeover'? G. G. Marcial. *Business Week* p100 S 4 '89
CRYSTAL METH (DRUG)
See also
Ice (Drug)
CRYSTAL NIGHT, 1938 See Kristallnacht, 1938
CRYSTAL OIL CO.
A clear shot at Crystal Oil. G. G. Marcial. *Business Week* p104 Ag 14 '89
CRYSTAL PALACE RESORT & CASINO (NASSAU, BAHAMAS)
Carnival tries sailing upstream. A. Fins. il *Business Week* p82-3+ S 25 '89
CRYSTAL-WERNER CORPORATION
Headhunters in reverse. D. Machan. il pors *Forbes* 144:238-9 O 30 '89
CRYSTALLINE LENS
See also
Cataracts (Eye defect)
CRYSTALLIZATION
Better crystals? It's a matter of space [research by Charles W. J. Scaife] J. Raloff. il *Science News* 136:206 S 23 '89
Crystal clear [Intospace protein crystallization experiment] W. H. Ganoe. *Ad Astra* 1:47 Ja '89
Crystals in zero-G [growing protein crystals in space] J. Kluger. il *Discover* 10:16 Ap '89
Dendrites, viscous fingers, and the theory of pattern formation. J. S. Langer. bibl f il *Science* 243:1150-6 Mr 3 '89

First U.S. commercial cargo for Mir set to lift off Dec. 20 [Payload Systems protein crystal growth experiments] J. M. Lenorovitz. *Aviation Week & Space Technology* 131:34 D 11 '89
Making bigger, better crystals . . . [work of Charles E. Bugg] *Science News* 136:349 N 25 '89
Payload's payload [protein crystal experiments on Mir space station] W. H. Ganoe. *Ad Astra* 1:38 Je '89
Protein crystal growth in microgravity. L. J. DeLucas and others. bibl f il *Science* 246:651-4 N 3 '89
U.S. firm's use of Mir faces probable delay [Payload Systems' protein crystal experiment] *Aviation Week & Space Technology* 130:21 Ap 17 '89
Zero gravity produces weighty improvement [protein crystals grown on the space shuttle] R. Pool. *Science* 246:580 N 3 '89
CRYSTALLOGRAPHY
See also
American Crystallographic Association
Channeling (Physics)
Liquid crystals
X ray crystallography
Chemists probe new crystalline vistas [work of Richard Robson and Bernard F. Hoskins] I. Amato. *Science News* 136:86 Ag 5 '89
Crystallography. bibl f *Physics Today* 42:S33-S35 Ja '89
Domain separation in the activation of glycogen phosphorylase α. E. J. Goldsmith and others. bibl f il *Science* 245:528-32 Ag 4 '89
Intermetallic compounds for high-temperature structural use. A. I. Taub and R. L. Fleischer. bibl f il *Science* 243:616-21 F 3 '89
The photosynthetic reaction center from the purple bacterium Rhodopseudomonas viridis. J. Deisenhofer and H. Michel. bibl f il *Science* 245:1463-73 S 29 '89
Reexamination of the three-dimensional structure of the small subunit of RuBisCo from higher plants. S. Knight and others. bibl f il *Science* 244:702-5 My 12 '89
Serum albumin seen in three dimensions [work of Daniel C. Carter] I. Amato. *Science News* 135:359 Je 10 '89
Three-dimensional structure of human serum albumin. D. C. Carter and others. bibl f il *Science* 244:1195-8 Je 9 '89
Turning cancer off [*ras* protein structure; work of Sung-Hou Kim] G. Montgomery. il *Discover* 10:66-7 Ja '89
Water-inserted α-helical segments implicate reverse turns as folding intermediates. M. Sundaralingam and Y. C. Sekharudu. bibl f il *Science* 244:1333-7 Je 16 '89
CRYSTALS
See also
Ice crystals
Liquid crystals
Quasicrystals
Snow crystals
Cold traps for ion crystals, solid plasmas [research by David J. Wineland] I. Peterson. *Science News* 135:279 My 6 '89
The curling crystal club [cover story] I. Amato. il *Science News* 135:124-5 F 25 '89
Dreaming up crystals that outdo diamond [work of Marvin L. Cohen and Amy Y. Liu] I. Amato. il *Science News* 136:134 Ag 26 '89
Explosive molecular ionic crystals. W. L. Faust. bibl f il *Science* 245:37-42 Jl 7 '89
Prediction of new low compressibility solids. A. Y. Liu and M. L. Cohen. bibl f il *Science* 245:841-2 Ag 25 '89
Defects
Long-range electronic perturbations caused by defects using scanning tunneling microscopy [graphite] H. A. Mizes and J. S. Foster. bibl f il *Science* 244:559-62 My 5 '89
Growth
See Crystallization
Lattices
Quantifying the information content of lattice images. A. Ourmazd and others. bibl f il *Science* 246:1571-7 D 22 '89
Therapeutic use
Let's skip the bit about shrunken heads [athletes' re-energizing therapy] T. Mulgannon. il *Sport (New York, N.Y.)* 80:83 My '89
CRYSTALS, HOLOGRAPHIC STORAGE See Optical storage devices
CSA See Czechoslovak Airlines
CSCE See Conference on Security and Cooperation in Europe
CSFS See Colony-stimulating factors
CSIS See Canadian Security Intelligence Service
CSONKA, LARRY
about
Oomph, oomph, oomph . . . Csonka! il por *Sports Illustrated* 70:60 Ja 9 '89
CSX CORPORATION
Employment cuts sought in rail transportation [CSX and the United Transportation Union] *Monthly Labor Review* 112:43 Mr '89

CT (COMPUTERIZED TOMOGRAPHY) *See* Tomography
CTA, INC.
CTA develops new computer system to speed civil aircraft maintenance. B. D. Nordwall. *Aviation Week & Space Technology* 130:153+ Je 19 '89
CTW *See* Children's Television Workshop
CUADRADO, JOHN A.
Antiques: garden ornament. il *Architectural Digest* 46:150-5+ Jl '89
Antiques: Napoleon III style. il *Architectural Digest* 46:290-5+ N '89
Art: trompe l'oeil painting. il *Architectural Digest* 46:168-73+ Mr '89
Inside the Drouot auctions. il *Architectural Digest* 46:180-6+ O '89
CUAU, YVES
Did Reagan betray the conservatives? *World Press Review* 36:28 Ja '89
The sad lesson for Moscow. il *World Press Review* 36:24 Ap '89
CUBA
See also
Americans—Cuba
Baseball—Cuba
Civil rights—Cuba
Cubans
Dance festivals—Cuba
Fishing—Cuba
Government and the press—Cuba
Havana (Cuba)
Meteorology—Cuba
Motion picture festivals—Cuba
Narcotics laws and regulations—Cuba
Political prisoners—Cuba
United Nations—Cuba
Commerce
Middle East
Off the record [Cuban-Palestinian arms smuggling network] *National Review* 41:18 F 24 '89
Economic policy
Castro: dilemmas of the last idealist. T. Szulc. *New Perspectives Quarterly* 5:50-1 Wint '88/'89
Foreign relations
Costa Rica
See Costa Rica—Foreign relations—Cuba
Soviet Union
See Soviet Union—Foreign relations—Cuba
United States
See United States—Foreign relations—Cuba
History
Invasion, 1961
A father's homecoming [J. Weininger's search for T. W. Ray, shot down during Bay of Pigs invasion] C. M. Turtle. il *Reader's Digest* 134:57-61 F '89
Missile Crisis, 1962
See Cuban Missile Crisis, 1962
Industries
See also
Cigar industry—Cuba
Tourist trade—Cuba
Politics and government
See also
Communism—Cuba
Politics, Corruption in—Cuba
After Castro [cover story] S. Landau. il por *Mother Jones* 14:20-6+ Jl/Ag '89
'Castro lives in a cloud'. C. S. Manegold. il por *Newsweek* 114:36 Ag 7 '89
The graying of a revolution. C. A. Robbins. il pors *U.S. News & World Report* 106:37-41 Ja 9 '89
The revolution at 30. S. McGuire. il por *Newsweek* 113:36-7 Ja 9 '89
Social policy
Cuba: freedom vs. equality. M. Vargas Llosa. il *World Press Review* 36:45 Mr '89
CUBAN, LARRY
The 'at-risk' label and the problem of urban school reform. bibl f il *Phi Delta Kappan* 70:780-4+ Je '89
What can be done for at-risk students. *The Education Digest* 54:3-6 My '89
CUBAN AMERICAN NATIONAL FOUNDATION (U.S.)
Art, intrigue and human rights [U.S. confiscation of paintings by Cuban artist N. Guillen Landrian] E. Shorris. il *The Nation* 249:14-18 Jl 3 '89
CUBAN AMERICANS
Political activities
See also
Cuban American National Foundation (U.S.)
Caught up in Miami's Cuban politics [deportation case of O. Bosch] B. Turque. il por *Newsweek* 114:24 S 4 '89
Miami advice [campaign of victorious congressional candidate I. Ros-Lehtinen] W. McGurn. *National Review* 41:39 N 24 '89
Off-key notes in an ethnic symphony [I. Ros-Lehtinen wins Florida's House seat] il por *U.S. News & World Report* 107:10 S 11 '89
The quiet rise of the 'yucas' in America. A. M. Arrarte. *U.S. News & World Report* 106:41 Ja 9 '89

Washington isn't mellowing on Cuba—but Miami is. A. Fins. il *Business Week* p41 Ap 17 '89
CUBAN DEFECTORS *See* Defectors
CUBAN MILITARY ASSISTANCE *See* Military assistance, Cuban
CUBAN MISSILE CRISIS, 1962
Commentary: the Cuban missile crisis. R. S. Cline. bibl f *Foreign Affairs* 68:190-6 Fall '89
Cuban Crisis. D. Schorr. *The New Leader* 72:4 F 6 '89
Cuban graffiti. J. S. Nye, Jr. *The New Republic* 200:16-18 Mr 13 '89
The Cuban Missile Crisis revisited. J. P. Roche. *The New Leader* 72:5 Mr 6 '89
The Cuban missiles [discussion of March 1989 article, Nuclear revisionism] P. Glynn. *Commentary* 88:9-12 Ag '89
"I'm staying right here" [statement by J. F. Kennedy] H. Sidey. il por *Time* 133:40 F 13 '89
A joint U.S.-Soviet reexamination of the Cuban Missile Crisis. J. G. Blight. il *USA Today (Periodical)* 117:70-2 Mr '89
The lessons of October. R. S. McNamara. il por *Newsweek* 113:47 F 13 '89
A near tragedy of errors [conference of alumni in Moscow] il *Time* 133:40 F 13 '89
Nuclear revisionism [views of M. Bundy] P. Glynn. *Commentary* 87:42-7 Mr '89
CUBANS
United States
See also
Cuban Americans
Midnight race for freedom [defection of Cuban violinist A. Ponce, Jr.] S. Kelly. il pors *Reader's Digest* 135:198-202+ S '89
With help from his wife and his lover, jazzman Paquito D'Rivera gets back the son he left in Cuba. P. Chin. il pors *People Weekly* 31:94-7 Ja 30 '89
CUBBLER, CAROLE A.
Encounters with great horned owls. il *The Conservationist* 43:8-9 Ja/F '89
CUBERLI, LELLA
about
A Texan for Tancredi. C. Battaglia. il pors *Opera News* 53:16-18 Ja 21 '89
CUBIC CORP.
Operation Ill Wind has Cubic fighting for air. E. Schine. il por *Business Week* p90 D 11 '89
CUBISM
Cube roots. D. Kazanjian. il *Vogue* 179:728-9+ S '89
The legacy of cubism [interview with W. S. Rubin] M. Horn. il pors *U.S. News & World Report* 107:68 O 23 '89
Exhibitions
The Adam and Eve of modernism [Picasso and Braque: pioneering cubism at the Museum of Modern Art] R. Hughes. il *Time* 134:93-4 O 2 '89
The art world [Picasso and Braque: pioneering cubism at the Museum of Modern Art] A. Gopnik. *The New Yorker* 65:132-6+ O 23 '89
Braque, Picasso and early cubism. A. C. Danto. *The Nation* 249:540-4 N 6 '89
Cubiquitous [Picasso and Braque: pioneering cubism at the Museum of Modern Art] J. D. Flam. il pors *Art News* 88:144-9 D '89
Cubism's odd couple [Picasso and Braque: pioneering cubism at the Museum of Modern Art] D. Solomon. il pors *House & Garden* 161:58+ S '89
Double vision [Picasso and Braque: pioneering cubism at the Museum of Modern Art] B. Adams. il pors *Harper's Bazaar* 122:142-3+ Ag '89
Married . . . with cubism [Picasso and Braque: pioneering cubism at the Museum of Modern Art] S. Schwartz. *The New Republic* 201:28-30 D 25 '89
Picasso, Braque, and an art revolution. J. Perl. il pors *Vogue* 179:722-7 S '89
Present at the creation [Picasso and Braque: pioneering cubism at Museum of Modern Art] P. Plagens. il *Newsweek* 114:73 O 2 '89
Rubin's cube [Picasso and Braque: pioneering cubism] K. Larson. il *New York* 22:77-8 O 9 '89
To find originality [Picasso and Braque: pioneering cubism] L. J. O'Donovan. *America* 161:299-300 N 4 '89
CUCCHI, ENZO, 1950-
about
Enzo Cucchi: Luigi Pecci Museum of Contemporary Art. J. Turner. il *Art News* 88:175-6 D '89
Enzo Cucchi: Marlborough. M. Moorman. il *Art News* 88:136 F '89
CUCKOOS
Tricks of the egg trade. M. Brooke. il *Natural History* p50-4 Ap '89
CUCUMBERS
Crossing cultures. B. Pleasant. il *Organic Gardening* 36:57-60 Ja '89
The cucumber scandal [Newfoundland minister C. Power resigns] C. White. *Maclean's* 102:16 Ja 23 '89
Year of the cucumber. il *Flower and Garden* 33:33-5+ Mr/Ap '89

CUCURBITS
See also
Melons
Squashes
CUELLAR, JAVIER PÉREZ DE See Pérez de Cuellar, Javier
CUENCA (SPAIN)
Galleries and museums
See also
Museo de Arte Abstracto Español (Cuenca, Spain)
CUERNAVACA (MEXICO)
Description
Cuernavaca and Taxco. P. J. Bell. il *Gourmet* 49:64-9+ F '89
CUES, POOL See Pool cues
CUFF LINKS
Up links [C. Baron's wares] E. G. Carter. il *Gentlemen's Quarterly* 59:31 Jl '89
CUFFARO, HARRIET
Blocks! Much more than a toy. il *Good Housekeeping* 209:156 S '89
CUISINARTS, INC.
Diced and sliced. K. Hannon. il por *Forbes* 144:68+ O 2 '89
CULHANE, JOHN
Oprah Winfrey: how truth changed her life. por *Reader's Digest* 134:101-5 F '89
Sean Connery against the odds. il pors *Reader's Digest* 135:92-7 Ag '89
Unforgettable Gone with the wind. il *Reader's Digest* 135:146-51 D '89
World's greatest showman. il pors *Reader's Digest* 135:90-5 N '89
CULLAR, MEG
Promoting religious books. il *Publishers Weekly* 235:31-3 Mr 3 '89
CULLATHER, JAMES L.
Cheap prints [poem] *America* 161:274 O 21 '89
CULLBERG BALLET
Swedish choreographer protests bureaucratic incompetence [M. Ek seeks permanent theater] L. Schubert. il *Dance Magazine* 63:18 S '89
CULLEN, JENNY
A triumph of love. il pors *Ladies' Home Journal* 106:34+ Ja '89
Whitney's big sound of success. il pors *Ladies' Home Journal* 106:120+ Mr '89
CULLEN, ROBERT B.
Compounding the problem. il *Common Cause Magazine* 15:10 Mr/Ap '89
Letter from Rostov-on-Don. *The New Yorker* 65:107-20 Je 12 '89
CULLINET SOFTWARE, INC.
Sometimes it doesn't pay to keep a secret [Computer Associates won't spell out its plans for Cullinet] D. A. Depke. il *Business Week* p30-1 Ag 28 '89
CULLMAN, BRIAN
The global beat. il *Vogue* 179:192-3+ My '89
Wynton Marsalis journeys to the heart of New Orleans. il por *Vogue* 179:206 Ag '89
CULP, ROBERT
about
Why Robert Culp's not happy with Bill Cosby. E. Kiersh. pors *TV Guide* 37:13-15 O 7-13 '89
CULT (MUSICAL GROUP)
Cult following. M. Goldberg. il *Rolling Stone* p57 Jl 13-27 '89
CULT SHOWS See Television broadcasting—Cult shows
CULTIVATION See Tillage
CULTIVATORS
The cultivator everyone wants [ridge till style cultivators] R. Fee. il *Successful Farming* 87:66AA F '89
Equipment
Coulters: the path makers. C. Finck. il *Successful Farming* 87:20-1 mid-Mr '89
Fertilizer 'feeders'. D. Mowitz and C. Finck. il *Successful Farming* 87:24-5 mid-Mr '89
Iron to run on ridges. C. Finck and D. Mowitz. il *Successful Farming* 87:34H-34I mid-F '89
Ridge tools in your toolbox. D. Mowitz. il *Successful Farming* 87:34AB mid-F '89
Testing
Electric garden tiller. B. Kitzmeyer. il *Popular Mechanics* 166:93 Mr '89
Mini-tiller roundup. S. Nesbitt. il *Flower and Garden* 33:89-93 Ja/F '89
Small tillers. M. Ferrara. il *Organic Gardening* 36:61-6 Ja '89
The state of tiller tech. il *Country Journal* 16:67 Mr/Ap '89
Tiller choices. M. Ferrara. il *Organic Gardening* 36:47-50 Je '89
CULTS
See also
Church Universal and Triumphant
Mithraism
MOVE (Organization)
Palo Mayombe (Cult)
Satanism

Sullivan Institute for Research in Psychoanalysis
Keeping an eye on the cults [Rockford Conference on Discernment and Evangelism] *Christianity Today* 33:50 N 17 '89
Salt substitutes. T. C. Muck. il *Christianity Today* 33:14-15 F 3 '89
Bibliography
Why cults? H. Yorkshire. il *Utne Reader* p134-5+ Mr/Ap '89
Brazil
See also
Candomblé
CULTURAL CENTERS See Centers for the performing arts
CULTURAL DIFFERENCES See Ethnopsychology
CULTURAL EDUCATION See Intercultural education
CULTURAL LITERACY
In pursuit of cultural literacy [challenging views of E. D. Hirsch as applied to teaching of contemporary American fiction] E. H. Schuster. il *Phi Delta Kappan* 70:539-42 Mr '89
Learning by story [work of E. D. Hirsch and A. Bloom] N. Postman. il *The Atlantic* 264:119-24 D '89
Of Billie Jean and 73-0 [E. D. Hirsch's book on cultural literacy slights the import of sport] F. Deford. il por *Sports Illustrated* 70:70 F 6 '89
The primal scene of education [curriculum of the elementary school] E. D. Hirsch. bibl f il *The New York Review of Books* 36:29-35 Mr 2 '89
'The primal scene of education': an exchange [discussion of March 2, 1989 article] E. D. Hirsch. il *The New York Review of Books* 36:50 Ap 13 '89
R U literate? Take this test. il *Utne Reader* p102 Mr/Ap '89
CULTURAL POLICY
See also
Cambodia—Cultural policy
China—Cultural policy
Comoros—Cultural policy
France—Cultural policy
Soviet Union—Cultural policy
United States—Cultural policy
International aspects
See also
World Decade for Cultural Development, 1988-1997
CULTURAL PROPERTY
Protection
See also
Art—Conservation and restoration
Heritage education
Anecdotes, facetiae, satire, etc.
The tithe. C. Murphy. il *The Atlantic* 264:20+ S '89
Conferences
See also
World Heritage Convention
International aspects
The antiquities boom: who pays the price? [cover story] W. Grimes. il pors *The New York Times Magazine* p16-19+ Jl 16 '89
Cyprus
Court orders return of looted art [Cypriot mosaics] *Art in America* 77:256 O '89
In Indiana, a battle over stolen mosaics [Cypriot mosaics] D. Tsiantar. il *Newsweek* 113:66-7 My 29 '89
Litigators of the lost art [Cypriot mosaics] S. Mannheimer. il *The Saturday Evening Post* 261:62-8 O '89
Raiders of the lost art, the nonmovie [Cypriot mosaics] il *U.S. News & World Report* 106:13 Je 12 '89
Rightful owners [court decisions involving Cypriot mosaics and Peruvian pre-Columbian art] R. W. Walker and L. Nilson. il *Art News* 88:51+ O '89
Egypt
Perilous times for the pyramids. M. D. Lemonick. il *Time* 133:60-2 My 15 '89
France
See also
Mobilier National (Paris, France)
Great Britain
To build or not to build [preservation of London's antiquities] A. Toufexis. il *Time* 133:64-5 My 29 '89
Greece
See also
Elgin marbles
Guatemala
Treasures of the Guatemala rain forest. A. Wade. il *The New Leader* 72:11-13 Ap 3-17 '89
India
Who owns the Nataraja? [British court rules that Siva bronze bought by Canadian collector belongs to India] S. E. Weil. il *Art News* 88:188 My '89
Italy
Italy's crumbling heritage [interview with G. Urbani] A. Mammi. il *World Press Review* 36:74 D '89
See Italy before it's too late. M. Piccolomini. il *Art News* 88:190 N '89
Peru
Rightful owners [court decisions involving Cypriot mosaics and Peruvian pre-Columbian art] R. W. Walker and L. Nilson. il *Art News* 88:51+ O '89

CULTURAL PROPERTY—Protection—*cont.*
Vietnam
The spirit of inventiveness. J. Turner. il *Art News* 88:75 O '89
Yemen Arab Republic
Helping Ham's hammams. A. Hills. il *History Today* 39:4-5 Ja '89
Yucatan (Mexico: State)
Walking on ancestral gods [Mayan ruins damaged by modern Mayas] T. Padgett. il *Newsweek* 114:83 O 9 '89
CULTURAL RELATIONS
See also
Brazil—Cultural relations
Canada—Cultural relations
Great Britain—Cultural relations
Soviet Union—Cultural relations
United States—Cultural relations
The global issue: a symposium [cover story] il *Art in America* 77:86-9+ Jl '89
CULTURAL REVOLUTION (CHINA) See China—History—Cultural Revolution, 1966-1969
CULTURALLY DEPRIVED CHILDREN See Socially handicapped children
CULTURE
See also
Acculturation
Civilization
Corporate culture
Intercultural communication
Intercultural research
Popular culture
United Nations. International Fund for the Promotion of Culture
CULTURE, AMERICAN See United States—Civilization; United States—Popular culture
CULTURE AND CHRISTIANITY See Christianity and culture
CULTURE OF CANCER CELLS See Cancer cells—Culture
CULTURE OF CELLS See Cells—Culture
CULTURE OF NERVE CELLS See Nerve cells—Culture
CULVER, JANET
A deadly struggle against the sea [cover story]; ed. by Ron Arias. il pors *People Weekly* 32:62-6+ Ag 21 '89
CUMBERLAND ASSOCIATES
Richard Reiss. P. Noglows. il por *Channels (New York, N.Y.: 1986)* 9:54 Jl/Ag '89
CUMBERLAND ISLAND (GA.)
Description and travel
The other Georgia [cover story] H. Leifermann. il map *New Choices for the Best Years* 29:46-52 Jl '89
CUMBERLAND MOUNTAINS REGION
Description and travel
New life, old dreams on the Cumberland Plateau. D. Young. il *Southern Living* 24:50-5 Ag '89
CUMMINGS, GORDON
about
Tangled nets. J. DeMont. il por *Maclean's* 102:54-5 S 4 '89
CUMMINGS, JOHN
Go ask Alice. *Omni (New York, N.Y.)* 11:42+ S '89
CUMMINGS, PETER
On the road again. *Bicycling* 30:180-1 Mr '89
CUMMINS, CYNTHIA
Sports bra round-up. il *Women's Sports & Fitness* 11:66-71 Ap '89
CUMMINS, DEBORAH BOLDA
Rural American artifact carries weight with collectors. il *Antiques & Collecting Hobbies* 93:32-4 F '89
CUMMINS, KENNETH W., AND OTHERS
Shredders and riparian vegetation. bibl f il *BioScience* 39:24-30 Ja '89
CUMMINS ENGINE COMPANY, INC.
Cummins Engine on the fast track. G. G. Marcial. *Business Week* p130 Ap 24 '89
The engine that couldn't. R. Henkoff. il *Fortune* 120:124 D 18 '89
Hanson, White and Cummins. T. Jaffe. *Forbes* 143:196-7 Je 12 '89
Why Henry Schacht is watching his rearview mirror [Britain's Hanson's stake in Cummins] J. E. Ellis. il por *Business Week* p43 Ja 9 '89
CUMMOCK, VICKY
about
Legacy of a grim Christmas past. B. Hewitt. il pors *People Weekly* 32:58-64 D 18 '89
CUNDILL, PETER
about
Better dead than alive. J. Clements. il por *Forbes* 143:208-9 Mr 20 '89
CUNDILL VALUE FUND
Better dead than alive [stock picker P. Cundill] J. Clements. il por *Forbes* 143:208-9 Mr 20 '89
CUNNIFF, JOE
Paul Shaffer and the World's Most Dangerous Band [cover story] il pors *Down Beat* 56:16-19 O '89
CUNNINGHAM, AMY
From folk to Federal. il *House & Garden* 161:106 S '89

CUNNINGHAM, ANN MARIE
Ten years after: cleaning up Three Mile Island. il *Technology Review* 92:18+ Ap '89
CUNNINGHAM, ANN PAMELA, 1816-1875
about
The Mount Vernon Ladies' Association of the Union. N. W. Horstman. il pors *Antiques* 135:454-61 F '89
CUNNINGHAM, BRADLEY, 1925-1988
about
Requiem for a saloonkeeper. R. Merkin. il *Gentlemen's Quarterly* 59:48+ Jl '89
CUNNINGHAM, BRIAN C., AND OTHERS
Receptor and antibody epitopes in human growth hormone identified by homolog-scanning mutagenesis. bibl f il *Science* 243:1330-6 Mr 10 '89
CUNNINGHAM, BRIAN C., AND WELLS, JAMES A.
High-resolution epitope mapping of hGH-receptor interactions by alanine-scanning mutagenesis. bibl f il *Science* 244:1081-5 Je 2 '89
CUNNINGHAM, DAVID S.
Structures of interest, structures of love: a response to Michael Novak. *America* 160:369-71 Ap 22 '89
CUNNINGHAM, DOUG
Civilians caught in Philippine 'total war'. *The Christian Century* 106:1036-7 N 15 '89
CUNNINGHAM, LAURA
My two uncles. il *The New York Times Magazine* p32+ D 3 '89
Sleeping arrangements [story] *The New Yorker* 65:30-40 Jl 17 '89
CUNNINGHAM, LAWRENCE
Experience & the claims of faith. *Commonweal* 116:379-80 Je 16 '89
An extraordinary woman in an ordinary world. il *U.S. Catholic* 54:7-8 F '89
The God that matters. il *Commonweal* 116:56-8 Ja 27 '89
Practicing ethics & spirituality. *Commonweal* 116:572-4 O 20 '89
The seers of Siena. il *Commonweal* 116:213-14 Ap 7 '89
Taking pains to see. il *Commonweal* 116:699+ D 15 '89
Theology, history, & transitions. *Commonweal* 116:539-41 O 6 '89
CUNNINGHAM, MARK
Socialists at work and play. *National Review* 41:19-21 My 5 '89
CUNNINGHAM, MARY
about
When people cared that Miss Liberty was Irish! E. Rochette. il *Antiques & Collecting Hobbies* 94:55+ Mr '89
CUNNINGHAM, MERCE
about
Dancing:
Performances of Five stone wind, Cargo X, and Field and figures. A. Croce. *The New Yorker* 65:106-8 Ap 3 '89
Five stone wind [dance] Reviews
New York il 22:84 Mr 20 '89. T. Tobias
Mature talents. L. A. Jacobs. il *The New Leader* 72:23 Ap 3-17 '89
Reviews:
Performances at City Center, New York City. N. V. Dalva. il por *Dance Magazine* 63:66+ Je '89
CUNNINGHAM, MICHAEL, 1952-
Ghost night [story] il *The New Yorker* 65:30-8+ Jl 24 '89
about
Real writing. T. Young. por *Vogue* 179:62 Ja '89
CUNNINGHAM, RANDALL
about
Superback!!! [cover story] R. Wiley. il pors *Sports Illustrated* 71:38-42+ S 11 '89
CUNNINGHAM, RANDY, 1941-
about
Lion heart. C. Furlong. il pors *Cycle* 40:78-80+ Je '89
CUNNINGHAM, SEAN
about
Deepstar six [film] Reviews
People Weekly 31:16 Ja 30 '89. P. Travers
CUOMO, MARIO
A governor responds. *America* 161:265 O 28 '89
about
All-star family feud. P. Blauner. il pors *New York* 22:34-7 F 13 '89
Gorilla warfare. J. Klein. il pors *New York* 22:24+ Ap 10 '89
Marry-o? Mahr-yo? W. Safire. il *The New York Times Magazine* p10+ Jl 23 '89
Will the poor always be with us? [interview] N. Gardels. il *New Perspectives Quarterly* 6:28-32 Fall '89
CUOMO, MATILDA
about
All-star family feud. P. Blauner. il pors *New York* 22:34-7 F 13 '89
CUPBOARDS
See also
Kitchen cabinets

CUPCAKES
Kid-pleasin' cupcakes: fun food for St. Pat's Day. il *Better Homes and Gardens* 67:135 Mr '89
CURATORS *See* Museum directors
CURE (MUSICAL GROUP)
Searching for the Cure. M. Lazerrad. il *Rolling Stone* p47+ S 7 '89
CURING OF CONCRETE *See* Concrete—Curing
CURIO CABINETS *See* Cabinets (Furniture)
CURIOUS GEORGE (FICTIONAL CHARACTER)
Curious George in Outer Space. M. Furst. il *Home Office Computing* 7:69-70 Jl '89
CURLEW (MUSICAL GROUP)
George Cartwright. B. Shoemaker. il por *Down Beat* 56:48+ N '89
CURLEY, JOHN J.
about
Al Neuharth is a tough act to follow. T. Smart. il por *Business Week* p119-20 My 8 '89
CURLING (SPORT)
Ten things your never knew about curling. T. Gallagher. il *Sport (New York, N.Y.)* 80:86 My '89
CURRAN, ANN
Why men don't take paternity leaves. *Health (New York, N.Y.)* 21:49+ Ja '89
CURRAN, CHARLES E.
about
Academic freedom and the Catholic University of America. F. R. McManus. *America* 160:506-9 My 27 '89
The Curran decision. *America* 160:259 Mr 25 '89
Curran loses—so does Catholic education. S. Maloney. *The Christian Century* 106:278-9 Mr 15 '89
In rejoinder: what next at Catholic U? [special section] il *Commonweal* 116:270-5+ My 5 '89
The Pope wins in court. R. N. Ostling. por *Time* 133:70 Mr 13 '89
Verdicts yet to come [with excerpts from court decision] *Commonweal* 116:163-5+ Mr 24 '89
CURRAN, DOLORES
How to find time for faith in a two-career marriage. il *U.S. Catholic* 54:19-24 O '89
CURRAN, KEITH
about
Dalton's back [drama] Reviews
New York 22:72-3 F 20 '89. J. Simon
The New Yorker 65:89 F 20 '89. M. Kramer
CURRAN, WALTER F.
about
Dean Witter braces for a backlash in Boston. K. H. Hammonds. il por *Business Week* p86 Mr 6 '89
CURRENCY *See* Money
CURRENCY (FIRM)
Doubleday launches business imprint. C. Goodrich. il *Publishers Weekly* 236:42 S 29 '89
CURRENCY CASH FUNDS *See* Foreign exchange cash funds
CURRENCY EXCHANGE WARRANTS
Lower-risk bets on a resurgent buck. A. Kupfer. il *Fortune* 119:40 Ap 10 '89
CURRENCY FUTURES *See* Foreign exchange futures
CURRENT EVENTS
Events and people. See issues of The Christian Century Intelligencer. J. Kasindorf. See issues of New York beginning August 19, 1985
The month in review. See issues of Current History
Oh, what a year! [news events of 1989] P. Jennings. il por *TV Guide* 37:20-1 D 30 '89-Ja 5 '90
One week. See issues of U.S. News & World Report beginning October 10, 1988
People of the year [cover story; special section] il *Newsweek* 114:18-26+ D 25 '89
Politics: winners and sinners of 1989. J. Klein. il *New York* 22:17-18 D 25 '89-Ja 1 '90
The top 10 news stories of 1988. B. Shelby. il *World Press Review* 36:4-5 F '89
What do you know: test your knowledge of current events [cover story; special issue] il *Scholastic Update (Teachers' edition)* 122:1-14 N 3 '89
Year of oat bran and ozone [1988] G. F. Will. il *Newsweek* 113:68 Ja 2 '89
The zeitgeist checklist. See occasional issues of The New Republic beginning September 8, 1986
Anecdotes, facetiae, satire, etc.
1989—slime time live. P. J. O'Rourke. il *Rolling Stone* p36-8+ D 14-28 '89
Small favors. M. Ivins. See issues of The Progressive beginning March 1986
Caricatures and cartoons
The world in cartoons. See issues of World Press Review
Photographs and photography
'88: the year in pictures [special issue] il *Life* 12:2-3+ Ja '89
Images '89. il *Time* 134:38-52+ D 25 '89
Snapshots. See issues of Life beginning July 1987
CURRENT EVENTS IN LITERATURE
Vampire agents at play [headline related books] J. Hammer. il *Newsweek* 114:64 S 11 '89

CURRENT EVENTS IN TELEVISION
Ripping off the headlines. H. F. Waters. il *Newsweek* 114:62-3+ S 11 '89
Scandal? Tragedy? Violence? Here come the wheeler-dealers waving their checkbooks [made for TV real life dramas] J. Kaye. il *TV Guide* 37:23-4+ Ja 7-13 '89
CURRENT HISTORY (PERIODICAL)
Toward the 21st century [special 75th anniversary issue; cover story] bibl f *Current History* 88:1-59+ Ja '89
CURRENTS, OCEAN *See* Ocean currents
CURREY, AGNETA
about
High style in Manhattan. J. Taylor. il *Architectural Digest* 46:134-41 D '89
CURREY, BROWNLEE
about
High style in Manhattan. J. Taylor. il *Architectural Digest* 46:134-41 D '89
CURREY, FREDERICK
about
Greyhound is bringing travelers down to earth again. K. Kelly. il *Business Week* p52-3 Je 19 '89
CURRICULUM
See also
Agricultural colleges—Curriculum
Asian American studies
Black studies
Colleges and universities—Curriculum
Correlation (Education)
Correspondence schools and courses
High schools—Curriculum
Peace studies
Theological seminaries—Curriculum
Vocational-technical education
Women's studies
See also subhead Study and teaching under various subjects
Assessing the curriculum experienced by children. V. R. Rogers. bibl f il *Phi Delta Kappan* 70:714-17 My '89
The irrelevant curriculum. A. C. Ornstein. *The Education Digest* 54:21-3 Ja '89
The primal scene of education [elementary school] E. D. Hirsch. bibl f il *The New York Review of Books* 36:29-35 Mr 2 '89
'The primal scene of education': an exchange [discussion of March 2, 1989 article] E. D. Hirsch. il *The New York Review of Books* 36:50 Ap 13 '89
Urban teachers: their new colleagues and curriculum. C. A. Grant. bibl f il *Phi Delta Kappan* 70:764-70 Je '89
CURRICULUM AUDITING
Formal curriculum audits. M.-L. Paddock. *The Education Digest* 54:35-6 F '89
CURRICULUM DEVELOPMENT *See* Curriculum planning
CURRICULUM PLANNING
Education by charter [restructuring school districts] R. Budde. il *Phi Delta Kappan* 70:518-20 Mr '89
University scientists as precollege science curriculum developers [discussion of September 1988 article, The role of universities in developing precollege science curricula] J. D. McInerney. bibl f *BioScience* 39:102-3 F '89
CURRIE, PHILIP J.
Dragons and dinosaurs. il *Earth Science* 42:10-13 Summ '89
Long-distance dinosaurs. il *Natural History* p60-5 Je '89
CURRY, DAVID PARK
Folk, or art? bibl f il *Antiques* 135:274-6 Ja '89
CURRY, GEORGE E.
A season in hell. il pors *Ms.* 18:58-60+ O '89
CURRY, TRAY *See* D.O.C.
CURRY
Curry, a seasoning with many spices. il *Southern Living* 24:182-3 S '89
CURSING *See* Swearing
CURTAIN WALLS
Curtainwalls—present trends and future prospects [roundtable] il *Architectural Record* 177:114-21 Ja '89
CURTAINS AND DRAPERIES
See also
Shower curtains
Curtain call [designs by M. Bright] H. S. MacIsaac. il por *House & Garden* 161:60+ N '89
Draped with canvas. il *Southern Living* 24:113 Jl '89
A little fabric, a lot of look. il *Southern Living* 24:134-5 My '89
Tied and true [swags] il *Southern Living* 24:178-9 Ap '89
CURTAINWALLS *See* Curtain walls
CURTIS, ANTHONY R.
E-Z listening. il *Omni (New York, N.Y.)* 11:22+ F '89
CURTIS, BRUCE
The wimp factor [cover story] il *American Heritage* 40:40-4+ N '89
CURTIS, CYNTHIA R.
(jt. auth) *See* Giles, Joe W., and Curtis, Cynthia R.
CURTIS, JAMIE LEE
about
Dragon Lady—or battler with a cause? [cover story] M. Leahy. il pors *TV Guide* 37:4-8 O 21-27 '89

CURTIS, JAMIE LEE—about—*cont.*
"It's hard being the child of movie stars" [cover story]
M. Morrison. il pors *Redbook* 173:98+ O '89
CURTIS, JEANNETTE
Native sons [poem] *Essence* 19:152 F '89
Old weary one [poem] *Essence* 19:123 Ap '89
CURTIS, MARGARET
Paradise found? Hot flash on the G-spot. il *Mademoiselle*
95:64 Ja '89
CURTIS, RICHARD
1988: everybody's going global. *Publishers Weekly* 235:41
Ja 6 '89
CURTIS, WILLIAM J. R.
Contemporary transformations of modern architecture. il
Architectural Record 177:108-19 Je '89
CURTIS'S BOTANICAL MAGAZINE
Blooming beauties from Britain [Flowers from the Royal
Gardens of Kew at the National Museum of Natural
History] K. M. Burke. il *Smithsonian* 19:176 F '89
CURVES
See also
Elliptic curves
Fractals
CURZIO, FRANCIS X.
about
Nice call, guys. J. Nocera. il pors *Esquire* 112:79+ O '89
CUSACK, JOAN
about
Joan Cusack can't take a joke. G. Sikes. por *Mademoiselle*
95:85+ Ag '89
CUSACK, JOHN
about
John Cusack's life after high school. G. Sikes. il por
Mademoiselle 95:86+ F '89
CUSHIONS
See also
Pillows
CUSP (TERM)
Ahead of the vanguard. W. Safire. il *The New York Times*
Magazine p10+ Ag 6 '89
CUSSON, MICHEL, AND MCNEIL, JEREMY N.
Involvement of juvenile hormone in the regulation of
pheromone release activities in a moth. bibl f il *Science*
243:210-12 Ja 13 '89
CUSTARD SAUCES *See* Sauces
CUSTARDS
Port wine foam over strawberries [zabaglione] il *Sunset*
(Central West edition) 183:131 Jl '89
CUSTER, GEORGE ARMSTRONG, 1839-1876
about
George Custer: nomad hunter of the Plains. J. McCafferty.
il *Outdoor Life* 184:60-1+ Jl '89
Here Custer died. J. Merritt. il por map *Americana* 16:30-5
Ja/F '89
CUSTER BATTLEFIELD NATIONAL MONUMENT
(MONT.)
Here Custer died. J. Merritt. il por map *Americana* 16:30-5
Ja/F '89
Park dig yields Custer artifacts [excavations] il *National Parks*
63:12-13 N/D '89
CUSTODY KIDNAPPING
See also
Bayan, Lauren—Kidnapping
Running for their lives [underground railroad for parents
fleeing with molested children] J. S. Podesta and D. Van
Biema. il *People Weekly* 31:70-8+ Ja 23 '89
CUSTODY OF CHILDREN
See also
Baby M case
Foretich, Hilary—Custody case
Guardian and ward
Visitation rights (Parents)
Crack pushes dads to duty. J. Seligmann. il *Newsweek* 113:64-5
Ap 17 '89
Does peer review have a place in child custody evaluations?
S. P. Herman and A. M. Levy. il *Children Today* 18:15-18
My/Je '89
I gave up custody of my children. il *Good Housekeeping*
209:30+ Ag '89
Interfaith divorce. D. Neff. il *Christianity Today* 33:14-15
F 17 '89
John Wayne's daughter Aissa is brutally beaten, and her
ex-husband is soon to stand trial. M. Green. il pors *People*
Weekly 31:106-8 My 29 '89
Joint custody: are the kids alright? M. Beckstrom. il *Utne*
Reader p11-12 My/Je '89
Joint custody, double trouble? [research by Janet Johnston]
E. Franklin. il *American Health* 8:113 Jl/Ag '89
"A judge split my children—body and soul" [ex-husband
gets spiritual custody of daughters]; ed. by John Duggleby.
D. Boeke. il por *Redbook* 173:26+ S '89
Little girl, big trouble [surrogate mother L. Stotski sues
for custody of Tessa] D. Grogan. il pors *People Weekly*
31:36-41 F 20 '89
The post-divorce family, legal practice, and the child's needs
for stability. A. P. Derdeyn. bibl il *Children Today* 18:12-14
My/Je '89

Psycho drama [P. Sprecher and M. Bray sue Sullivanians
for custody of their children] P. Hoban. il pors *New York*
22:40-2+ Je 19 '89
Solomon's choice [mishandling of child abuse cases by social
workers] D. Zegart. il *Ms.* 17:78-83 Je '89
CUSTOM FARMING
His own labor, custom work turns farm around. il *Successful*
Farming 87:66I F '89
CUSTOMER RELATIONS
See also
Automobile dealers—Customer relations
Banks and banking—Customer relations
Brokers—Customer relations
Computer industry—Customer relations
Computer service industries—Customer relations
Cosmetics industry—Customer relations
Customer service
Insurance companies—Customer relations
Investment trusts—Customer relations
Getting customers to love you [cover story] P. Sellers. il
Fortune 119:38-40+ Mr 13 '89
Happy customers boost profits [views of Jagdish Sheth] *USA*
Today (Periodical) 118:5-6 Ag '89
How to hire employees your customers will love. L. Touby.
il *Working Woman* 14:40+ D '89
The secret of your success. J. Iaconetti. il *Seventeen* 48:90+
Je '89
CUSTOMER SERVICE
See also
Quality Service Institute
Across the editor's desk. L. J. Kruse. il *Successful Farming*
87:1 Ag '89
I thought this was a service economy—so where's the service?
C. Cohl. il *Home Office Computing* 7:4 Ag '89
Learning from Millie. R. Brauer. por *Newsweek* 114:10 N
20 '89
Service = survival [cover story] J. C. Szabo. il *Nation's*
Business 77:16-19+ Mr '89
An urge to service. J. Flint. il *Forbes* 144:172+ S 18 '89
Automation
Computers, customers and hand-holding. E. Dyson. il *Forbes*
144:128 Ag 7 '89
CUSTOMS SERVICE
Border patrols. K. Cameron. il *Cycle* 40:8 S '89
Carnets and customs [theater equipment on international
tours] J. Calhoun. *Theatre Crafts* 23:79-80 My '89
CUSTOMS SERVICE (U.S.) *See* U.S. Customs Service
CUT *See* Church Universal and Triumphant
CUT GLASS *See* Glassware
CUTANEOUS BIOLOGY RESEARCH CENTER (BOSTON,
MASS.)
Shiseido grant: more than skin deep. M. Sun. *Science*
245:810-11 Ag 25 '89
CUTLER, BLAYNE
Are you an "average" person? *Reader's Digest* 135:189-90+
S '89
CUTLER, DAVID, 1956-
Bookstores from A to Z. il *Publishers Weekly* 235:125-7
My 12 '89
Hangouts and watering holes. il *Publishers Weekly* 235:121
My 12 '89
Literary lights on the Potomac. il *Publishers Weekly*
235:112-14 My 12 '89
CUTLER, GLENN
about
Is this a blow-off? M. Hulbert. il *Forbes* 143:191 Je 12
'89
The same . . . but different. M. Hulbert. il *Forbes* 143:408
My 1 '89
This top-ranked contrarian predicts stocks will hit their
pre-crash highs in '89. J. Ellis. il por *Money* 18:163-4
Ja '89
CUTLER, JAMES
about
All natural. P. M. Sachner. il *Architectural Record* 177:60-7
mid-Ap '89
CUTLER, JONATHAN C.
Minotaurs and mentors [address, October 4, 1988] *Vital*
Speeches of the Day 55:202-3 Ja 15 '89
A student's view of youth participation [address, July 20,
1987] *The Education Digest* 54:45-8 Ap '89
CUTLER, LAUREL
about
Consumers are tougher customers. M. Magnet. il por *Fortune*
120:76 Jl 3 '89
Shuttle consultancy. M. E. Kirk. il por *Forbes* 143:324 Ja
9 '89
CUTLER, LLOYD N.
about
Should Congress get a 51 percent raise? [interview] J. P.
Shapiro. pors *U.S. News & World Report* 106:28 F 13
'89
CUTTERS (SHIPS)
Ocean stations [work of Coast Guard cutters] R. L. Scheina.
il *Sea Frontiers* 35:53-5 Ja/F '89
CUTTING BOARDS
A rack and cleaning board. P. Butler and M. Butler. il
Outdoor Life 183:32+ Ap '89

CUTTING OF GLASS *See* Glass cutting
CUTTING TOOLS
See also
Knives
Saws and sawing
Confessions of a metal butcher. K. Collier. il *The Family Handyman* 39:7-8 S '89
True grit [structured carbide tools] P. McCafferty. il *Popular Science* 235:84-6 D '89
CUTTINGS, PLANT *See* Plant propagation
CVS *See* Chorionic villi sampling
CWA *See* Communications Workers of America
CYANIDE POISONING
Artificial nail remover poses poisoning risk [acetonitrile] D. Blumenthal. il *FDA Consumer* 23:22-3 Je '89
The cyanide scare: a tale of two grapes [Chilean fruit scare] W. Grigg and V. Modeland. il *FDA Consumer* 23:7-11 Jl/Ag '89
CYANIDES
See also
Hydrocyanic acid
CYANOBACTERIA *See* Algae
CYANOPHYTES *See* Algae
CYBERNETICS
See also
Computers

China
History
A cybernetic machine. R. K. G. Temple. il *The Courier (Unesco)* 41:14-15 O '88
CYBERPUNK CULTURE
Cyberpunk. E. Selbin. il *Utne Reader* p28+ Jl/Ag '89
Video scans [W. Gibson's novel Neuromancer made into a video game] B. Lindstrom. il *Omni (New York, N.Y.)* 12:166 O '89
CYCLE (PERIODICAL)
Editorial. S. Anderson. See issues of Cycle beginning March 1989
Editorial. P. Schilling. See issues of Cycle through February 1989
Target [Geico targets Cycle in anti-radar detector campaign] P. Schilling. il *Cycle* 40:9+ Ja '89
CYCLECOMPUTERS
Chips ahoy! Confessions of a cyclecomputing mileage maniac. E. Pavelka. il *Bicycling* 30:228 Je '89
CYCLES
See also
Biological rhythms
Business cycles
Hydrologic cycle
Life's cycles. J. Goldsmith. il por *Organic Gardening* 36:72 My '89
Pagan holidays mark earth's yearly cycles. T. Knepher. *Utne Reader* p74-5 N/D '89
CYCLIC ADENOSINE MONOPHOSPHATE *See* Adenosine monophosphate
CYCLIC COMPOUNDS
See also
Propellanes
CYCLIC GMP *See* Guanosine monophosphate
CYCLIN
The cell cycle coming under control. J. L. Marx. il *Science* 245:252-5 Jl 21 '89
CYCLING
See also
Bicycle racing
Century rides (Cycling)
Cyclists
Motorcycling
Mountain cycling
10 great weekend rides [special section] il maps *Bicycling* 30:100-4+ Ap '89
1989 cross-state ride directory. S. Sorensen and N. Pena. *Bicycling* 30:192-3 Mr '89
Are we having fun yet? [death rides] J. Kukoda. il *Bicycling* 30:110 S '89
Are we there yet? [maps for cycling] G. D. MacFadden. map *Bicycling* 30:152 Je '89
A beginner's guide to cycling [special section] il *Bicycling* 30:95-8+ Ja/F '89
Bicycle days. G. Lichtenstein. il *Harper's Bazaar* 122:36+ S '89
Bicycling. il *World Tennis* 36:79 My '89
Bikes & tykes [special section] il *Bicycling* 30:77+ Je '89
Breaking away [planning a bike tour] A. Solomon. bibl il *Women's Sports & Fitness* 11:28-32 Ja/F '89
Can bicycles save the world? J. Bosveld. *Omni (New York, N.Y.)* 11:33 F '89
Celebrity cyclists [cover story] D. Cuerdon. il *Bicycling* 30:56-8+ D '89
Keeping drivers friendly [traffic safety] J. Hargett. *Bicycling* 30:58 Ag '89
Mileage junkies [F. Hoffman, D. Tonelli, B. and N. Gerlich] S. Martin. il pors *Bicycling* 30:48-50+ Ap '89
The power of motion. J. Kita. il *Bicycling* 30:132 Ja/F '89

Pushing pedalers: bicycles may be the key to unlocking our traffic woes. M. D. Lowe. il *Utne Reader* p90-2 Mr/Ap '89
Safe cycling. il *Current Health 2* 15:20-1 Mr '89
Speed sports: the rush of getting fit—fast! il *Mademoiselle* 95:218-21 O '89
Wanted: touring companion [advertising for bicycle trip partners] S. Martin. il *Bicycling* 30:32-4+ Ag '89
A wheel good time [tandem cycling; cover story] G. Lichtenstein. il *New Choices for the Best Years* 29:39-42 Ap '89
Where the women are. J. C. McCullagh. il *Bicycling* 30:14+ Mr '89

Accidents and injuries
Not-so-hot seat [impotence; research by Harin Padma-Nathan] L. Schroepfer. il *American Health* 8:40 O '89
Road rash [abrasions] S. Johnson. *Bicycling* 30:134 Je '89
Saddle sores. S. Johnson. il *Bicycling* 30:74 O/N '89
Awards
Mileposts [T. G. Stevenson earns Golden Wheel] J. Kita. il por *Bicycling* 30:88 D '89
Clothing and dress
See Clothing and dress—Sports clothes
Directories
Where to go for more information. S. Sorensen. *Bicycling* 30:120 Ja/F '89
International aspects
See also
International Cycling Union
Luxury tours. J. Kita. il *Bicycling* 30:74-8+ Ja/F '89
Pedaling into the future. M. D. Lowe. il *The Futurist* 23:18 Mr/Ap '89
Lightning hazards
Lightning. N. J. Ney. il *Bicycling* 30:108 Jl '89
Physiological effects
Are your defenses down? [effect of cycling on immune system] N. Pena. il *Bicycling* 30:170-3 Mr '89
Bicycling's exclusive calorie counter [cover story]; ed. by Nelson Pena. J. Hagberg. il *Bicycling* 30:100-3 My '89
Biking & baby. M. Drake. il pors *Bicycling* 30:82+ My '89
Cycling's impact on your sex life [women] N. Pena. il *Bicycling* 30:32 S '89
How cycling makes you a better (or worse) lover [men] N. Pena. il *Bicycling* 30:30-1 S '89
Lactic acid [responsible for burning sensation] S. Johnson. *Bicycling* 30:60 Ag '89
Riding to lose (weight, that is). J. Barone. *Bicycling* 30:104+ My '89
Psychological aspects
Are RAAM riders crazy? M. Shermer. *Bicycling* 30:108+ Ag '89
Astound yourself! [setting goals] M. Shermer. il *Bicycling* 30:36-40 S '89
Be a big wheel. J. Kita. *Bicycling* 30:82 Jl '89
'Health centeredness'. J. Kita. il *Bicycling* 30:136 Je '89
How to make every ride a great one [cover story] N. Pena. il *Bicycling* 30:68-70+ Jl '89
Just for fun. G. L. Hopper. *Bicycling* 30:138-9 My '89
'Look at me!' How to reinforce and nourish a child's natural love for the bicycle. J. Kita. il *Bicycling* 30:80+ Je '89
On the road again. P. Cummings. *Bicycling* 30:180-1 Mr '89
Riding smart: Can intelligence hinder a cyclist? J. Kita. *Bicycling* 30:50 S '89
So long, Horse: sometimes losing a bicycle can be like losing a friend. M. Westerman. *Bicycling* 30:76 O/N '89
Storm hazards
Rain man. G. Drake. il *Bicycling* 30:72-3 O/N '89
Study and teaching
7 off-road tips. F. Zahradnik. il *Bicycling* 30:116 My '89
Better braking. J. Kukoda. il *Bicycling* 30:46-7 S '89
Cadence [pedaling speed] S. Johnson. il *Bicycling* 30:162 Ap '89
Dream camps [bicycle racing] K. Kendrick. *Bicycling* 30:164 Mr '89
Learn to love the hills. F. Zahradnik. il *Bicycling* 30:114-16 My '89
New racer (I). F. Matheny. il *Bicycling* 30:160-2+ Mr '89
New racer (II). F. Matheny. il *Bicycling* 30:120-2+ Je '89
New racer (III). F. Matheny. il *Bicycling* 30:62-4+ O/N '89
Pacelines. J. Kukoda. il *Bicycling* 30:130+ Je '89
The principles of pedaling. S. Sorensen. *Bicycling* 30:104+ Ja/F '89
A question that's gone round & round [best pedaling speed] O. Anderson. il *Women's Sports & Fitness* 11:58 Ja/F '89
Surviving on two wheels. S. J. Henry. il *Women's Sports & Fitness* 11:46-9 Je '89
Ten tips toward a better ride. J. Lehrer. il *Women's Sports & Fitness* 11:16 Mr '89
Your first riding lesson. S. Martin. il *Bicycling* 30:116+ Ja/F '89

Aids and devices
Screen test [videotaping yourself] B. Prichard. il *Bicycling* 30:136-8+ Ap '89
Australia
In the land of Oz. S. Sorensen. il *Bicycling* 30:44-6+ Je '89

CYCLING—cont.

California

Biking the Delta [Sacramento-San Joaquin Delta] il map *Sunset (Central West edition)* 182:18+ Mr '89

Joining in on a bike trek. il *Sunset (Central West edition)* 182:20-1 Ap '89

The pedal pusher [cycling enthusiast E. Fletcher] il por *New Choices for the Best Years* 29:12 O '89

A pedaler's paradise. J. Langley. il *Bicycling* 30:126 O/N '89

Rockin' in San Francisco. M. McCloy. il *Bicycling* 30:80-1 O/N '89

Sampling Livermore Valley by bike. il map *Sunset (Central West edition)* 183:18 O '89

Sunday outings into the Palm Springs mountains . . . join with fellow cyclists. il *Sunset (Central West edition)* 182:48 Ja '89

Anecdotes, facetiae, satire, etc.

Star trek [Hollywood bike tour] D. Cuerdon. il *Bicycling* 30:66-8 D '89

China

Bicycling the back roads of China [cover story] G. McTigue. il map *Travel Holiday* 171:40-5 My '89

Connecticut

. . . an offer we should have refused [ex-convict holds cyclists at gunpoint] R. M. Wallack. il *Bicycling* 30:38-40+ Jl '89

Connecticut: prepped for autumn. S. Martin. il *Bicycling* 30:54-6+ S '89

Denmark

In search of Denmark's bog people [cycling trip] G. Thomson. il map *Bicycling* 30:68-72+ Ag '89

France

Gîte d'étape [inexpensive accommodations] M. McCloy. *Bicycling* 30:158-9 My '89

Georgia

Something to 'BRAG' about [Bicycle Ride Across Georgia] R. Salzman. il *Bicycling* 30:190-1 Mr '89

Illinois

Chicago's badlands. F. Staub. il *Bicycling* 30:82 O/N '89

India

The tour of doom [cycling the length of the Ganges River] S. O'Grady. il map *Bicycling* 30:150-4+ My '89

Italy

Braking away [biking tour through Tuscany] J. Schneller. il *Gentlemen's Quarterly* 59:326-9+ O '89

Maui (Hawaii)

Downhill all the way [children's bicycling trip in Haleakala National Park] il map *National Geographic World* 170:20-5 O '89

Minnesota

Minnesota: no kidding. S. Sorensen. il *Bicycling* 30:60+ S '89

New Jersey

Escape from New York [cycling along the Palisades] F. Staub. il *Bicycling* 30:86 O/N '89

New Mexico

Exploring Taos by bike. il map *Sunset (Central West edition)* 183:44-5 Ag '89

North America

Hell on wheels: the 10 toughest one-day rides in North America. S. Martin. il *Bicycling* 30:70+ My '89

Oregon

From hell to highwater [Oregon Bicycle Ride] H. Esteve. il *Bicycling* 30:188-91 Mr '89

Pacific Northwest

Joining in on a bike trek. il *Sunset (Central West edition)* 182:20-1 Ap '89

United States

See Cycling

Utah

Zion's splendors by bike. il *Sunset (Central West edition)* 182:86+ My '89

Vermont

Tour de Vermont. J. Augustine. il *Petersen's Photographic Magazine* 18:4 O '89

Washington (State)

Taming Seattle's Tiger [cycling on Tiger Mountain] M. McCloy. il *Bicycling* 30:84 O/N '89

Wyoming

Yellowstone: after the fire. S. Kearin. il map *Bicycling* 30:96-100+ Jl '89

CYCLING HELMETS *See* Helmets

CYCLING IN ADVERTISING

Peddle power [mountain biking used in television ad for Mountain Dew] S. Martin. il *Bicycling* 30:41 O/N '89

CYCLING IN MOTION PICTURES

Why other cycling movies failed. T. Blumenthal. *Bicycling* 30:76+ Ap '89

CYCLING RECORDS

The daily record [P. Maass sets 24 hour distance record] G. Knuth and L. Rothlein. il por *Women's Sports & Fitness* 11:62+ My '89

CYCLING SHOES

Pedal power. il *Women's Sports & Fitness* 11:44-5 Mr '89

CYCLING TRIPS *See* Cycling

CYCLING WITH CHILDREN

Biking & baby. M. Drake. il pors *Bicycling* 30:82+ My '89

Safe cycling for tots [views of Michael Weitzman] R. Robinson. *American Health* 8:120 Mr '89

Towing your toddler. G. Drake. il *Bicycling* 30:94+ Je '89

CYCLISTS

Waiting for the black Merckx [lack of black bicycle racers] M. E. Mantell. il *Bicycling* 30:90-1+ My '89

Crimes against

. . . an offer we should have refused [ex-convict holds cyclists at gunpoint in Connecticut] R. M. Wallack. il *Bicycling* 30:38-40+ Jl '89

Health and hygiene

How to make every ride a great one [cover story] N. Pena. il *Bicycling* 30:68-70+ Jl '89

What ails you? E. Burke. il *Bicycling* 30:152-3 Ap '89

Your finest hour [effects of circadian rhythms] R. Eichner. il *Bicycling* 30:122-5 My '89

Nutrition

Bananas, bagels, & beer [survey results] N. Pena. il *Bicycling* 30:110+ My '89

Bonk [glucose depletion] S. Johnson. *Bicycling* 30:48 S '89

The facts about cycling nutrition. N. Pena. il *Bicycling* 30:112+ Ja/F '89

Feed zone. E. Coleman. See issues of Bicycling beginning March 1989

The human machine [energy efficiency of riders in Race Across America] C. Kyle. il *Bicycling* 30:196+ My '89

Sexual behavior

Cycling gets sexy [cover story; special section] N. Pena. il *Bicycling* 30:28-32 S '89

Not-so-hot seat [impotence; research by Harin Padma-Nathan] L. Schroepfer. il *American Health* 8:40 O '89

Training

9 coaching secrets [cover story] S. Martin. *Bicycling* 30:112+ Je '89

Anaerobic threshold. S. Johnson. *Bicycling* 30:178 Mr '89

Century training secrets. G. Drake. il *Bicycling* 30:48-51 Ag '89

Cross-training. S. Johnson. il *Bicycling* 30:84+ D '89

Enter the iron age [weight training] F. Matheny. il *Bicycling* 30:70-1+ D '89

Fitness with a byte [cycling software] F. Zahradnik. il *Bicycling* 30:144+ Ap '89

How not to waste time on your indoor trainer. S. Martin. il *Bicycling* 30:124-6 Ja/F '89

Interval training. S. Johnson. *Bicycling* 30:136-7 My '89

Logging the miles [keeping a journal] J. Kita. *Bicycling* 30:62 Ag '89

Master of my fate [maximizing potential] M. Shermer. il *Bicycling* 30:73-5 Je '89

More power to you with interval training [women cyclists] C. Patterson. il por *Women's Sports & Fitness* 11:18-19 S '89

New racer (I). F. Matheny. il *Bicycling* 30:160-2+ Mr '89

New racer (II). F. Matheny. il *Bicycling* 30:120-2+ Je '89

New racer (III). F. Matheny. il *Bicycling* 30:62-4+ O/N '89

Target heart rate [intensity] S. Johnson. il *Bicycling* 30:81 Jl '89

VO$_2$ max. S. Johnson. *Bicycling* 30:130 Ja/F '89

CYCLOCROSS RACING *See* Bicycle racing

CYCLODEXTRINS

Control of angiogenesis with synthetic heparin substitutes. J. Folkman and others. bibl f il *Science* 243:1490-3 Mr 17 '89

CYCLOMORPHOSIS

Predator-induced reaction norms. S. I. Dodson. bibl f il *BioScience* 39:447-52 Jl/Ag '89

CYCLONES

See also
Cyclonoscopes

CYCLONOSCOPES

The Antilles cyclonoscope [hurricane observation in the late 1800s]; tr. by Isabella Owen. B. Viñes. il por *Weatherwise* 42:258-61 O '89

CYCLORAMAS

Big sky [new cyclorama installed at the Metropolitan Opera] *The New Yorker* 65:30-1 S 4 '89

CYCLOSPORIN A

Cyclosporin A specifically inhibits function of nuclear proteins involved in T cell activation. E. A. Emmel and others. bibl f il *Science* 246:1617-20 D 22 '89

CYCLOSPORINE

Cyclosporin therapy heals colon ulcers [ulcerative colitis; research by Simon Lichtiger and Daniel H. Present] K. Fackelmann. *Science News* 135:310 My 20 '89

CYCLOTHYMIA

Ups and downs . . . and ups [research by Hagop Akiskal] J. Folkenberg. il *American Health* 8:46+ S '89

CYCLOTRONS *See* Accelerators (Electrons, etc.)

CYERT, RICHARD MICHAEL, 1921-, AND MOWERY, DAVID C.

Technology, employment and U.S. competitiveness. il *Scientific American* 260:54-60+ My '89

LE CYGNE (NEW YORK, N.Y.: RESTAURANT) *See* New York (N.Y.)—Restaurants, nightclubs, bars, etc.

CYGNUS X-3 (STAR) *See* Stars, Double

CYLINDERS (ENGINES, ETC.)

See also
Airplane engines—Cylinders

CYLINDERS (ENGINES, ETC.)—See also—*cont.*
Automobile engines—Cylinders
CYMBELINE [drama] See Shakespeare, William, 1564-1616
CYNICISM
See also
Irony
Who cares? [film Talk radio triggers reflections on the body politic] R. Corliss. il *Film Comment* 25:64-70 Ja/F '89
CYPHER COMMUNICATIONS TECHNOLOGY INC.
Outwitting the hackers. S. Kauffman. il por *Nation's Business* 77:17 S '89
CYPRESS SEMICONDUCTOR CORP.
A flood of chips from Cypress. G. G. Marcial. *Business Week* p94 Mr 6 '89
CYPRUS
See also
Americans—Cyprus
Cultural property—Protection—Cyprus
Saint Napa (Cyprus)
United Nations—Cyprus
Women—Cyprus
39th report on Cyprus [message to Congress, October 3, 1988] R. Reagan. *Department of State Bulletin* 88:37 D '88
40th report on Cyprus [message to Congress, December 7, 1988] R. Reagan. *Department of State Bulletin* 89:50 F '89
Draft outline of overall agreement on Cyprus to be prepared. il *UN Chronicle* 26:28 Je '89
First report on Cyprus [message to Congress, March 1, 1989] G. Bush. *Department of State Bulletin* 89:43 Ap '89
Second report on Cyprus [message to Congress, June 5, 1989] G. Bush. *Department of State Bulletin* 89:89 S '89
Secretary-General outlines ideas to bridge positions on Cyprus. il *UN Chronicle* 26:24-5 S '89
Defenses
See also
United Nations—Armed Forces—Forces in Cyprus
CYRANO DE BERGERAC [drama] See Rostand, Edmond, 1868-1918
CYRUS J. LAWRENCE INCORPORATED
Why you should own a 'slug' of Treasury bonds [interview with E. Hyman] J. Mendes. il por *Fortune* 119:36 F 27 '89
CYSTIC FIBROSIS
The basic defect in cystic fibrosis. I. B. Levitan. bibl f *Science* 244:1423 Je 23 '89
Blood cells yield cystic fibrosis clues [cyclic adenosine monophosphate-regulated chloride channel in lymphocytes; research by Jennifer H. Chen and others] *Science News* 135:110 F 18 '89
A cAMP-regulated chloride channel in lymphocytes that is affected in cystic fibrosis. J. H. Chen and others. bibl f il *Science* 243:657-60 F 3 '89
Cl⁻ channels in CF: lack of activation by protein kinase C and cAMP-dependent protein kinase. T.-C. Hwang and others. bibl f il *Science* 244:1351-3 Je 16 '89
Cystic fibrosis: cloning and genetics [cover story; special section; with editorial comment by Daniel E. Koshland] *Science* 245:1029, 1059-80 S 8 '89
Cystic fibrosis gene and protein identified [work of Francis S. Collins and Lap-Chee Tsui] K. Fackelmann. *Science News* 136:149 S 2 '89
The cystic fibrosis gene is found [work of Lap-Chee Tsui and Francis Collins] J. L. Marx. il *Science* 245:923-5 S 1 '89
Cystic fibrosis: hunting down a killer gene. J. Seligmann. il *Newsweek* 114:60-1 S 4 '89
Discoveries of hope at the heart of human life [work of L.-C. Tsui] D. Jenish. il por *Maclean's* 102:22-3 D 25 '89
Fighting heredity: doctors identify the cystic fibrosis gene. R. Corelli. il *Maclean's* 102:63 S 4 '89
Is regulation of a chloride channel in lymphocytes affected in cystic fibrosis? [discussion of February 3, 1989 article, A cAMP-regulated chloride channel in lymphocytes that is affected in cystic fibrosis] J. H. Chen and others. *Science* 246:1049-50 N 24 '89
A medical breakthrough gives new hope to David Reitz—and all kids with cystic fibrosis [research by Francis Collins and Lap-Chee Tsui] R. Arias. il *People Weekly* 32:83-4+ S 11 '89
Modifying Mendel one more time. P. Young. *Science News* 136:92 Ag 5 '89
Persistence of abnormal chloride conductance regulation in transformed cystic fibrosis epithelia. A. M. Jetten and others. bibl f il *Science* 244:1472-5 Je 23 '89
Regulation of chloride channels by protein kinase C in normal and cystic fibrosis airway epithelia. M. Li and others. bibl f il *Science* 244:1353-6 Je 16 '89
Winning candidate [identification of gene by Lap-Chee Tsui and John R. Riordan] T. Beardsley. *Scientific American* 261:28+ N '89
Diagnosis
CF screen: still too soon. R. Weiss. *Science News* 136:325 N 18 '89

Testing newborns for cystic fibrosis [measuring immunoreactive trypsinogen; work of Frank J. Accurso] S. Hart and A. McKenzie. *Science News* 136:233 O 7 '89
CYSTITIS
Bladder fire [interstitial cystitis] S. Greengard. il *American Health* 8:20 Je '89
CYSTS
Ovarian cysts [linked to oral contraceptives; research by James Caillouette] *Prevention (Emmaus, Pa.)* 41:16 Ja '89
Ovarian cysts: what they are, how they're treated. L. Holland. il *Good Housekeeping* 209:253 O '89
CYTIDINE MONOPHOSPHATE
Template-directed oligomerization catalyzed by a polynucleotide analog [polycytidylic acid] J. Visscher and others. bibl f il *Science* 244:329-31 Ap 21 '89
CYTIDYLIC ACID See Cytidine monophosphate
CYTOCHROMES
Identification by ENDOR of Trp¹⁹¹ as the free-radical site in cytochrome c peroxidase compound ES. M. Sivaraja and others. bibl f il *Science* 245:738-40 Ag 18 '89
Molecular custodians sweep away odorants [research by Doren Lancet] I. Amato. *Science News* 136:374 D 9 '89
Treatment with tin prevents the development of hypertension in spontaneously hypertensive rats. D. Sacerdoti and others. bibl f il *Science* 243:388-90 Ja 20 '89
CYTOGENETICS See Chromosomes
CYTOKINES
AIDS-Kaposi's sarcoma-derived cells express cytokines with autocrine and paracrine growth effects. B. Ensoli and others. bibl f il *Science* 243:223-6 Ja 13 '89
The cholinergic neuronal differentiation factor from heart cells is identical to leukemia inhibitory factor. T. Yamamori and others. bibl f il *Science* 246:1412-16 D 15 '89; Correction. 247:271 Ja 19 '90
Macrophage inflammatory protein-1: a prostaglandin-independent endogenous pyrogen. G. Davatelis and others. bibl f il *Science* 243:1066-8 F 24 '89
Translational blockade imposed by cytokine-derived UA-rich sequences [Xenopus oocytes] V. Kruys and others. bibl f il *Science* 245:852-5 Ag 25 '89
CYTOLOGY
See also
Cells
Methodology
Identifying cells' chemical personalities [open tubular liquid chromatography; work of James W. Jorgenson and Robert T. Kennedy] I. Amato. *Science News* 135:150 Mr 11 '89
Microcolumn separations and the analysis of single cells [capillary zone electrophoresis and open tubular liquid chromatography] R. T. Kennedy and others. bibl f il *Science* 246:57-63 O 6 '89
CYTOMEGALOVIRUS
CMV a risk in child care [research by Stuart Adler] J. Raloff. *Science News* 136:327 N 18 '89
An enigma named Gloria [woman with cytomegalovirus pneumonia] T. Dajer. il *Discover* 10:86-9 N '89
CYTOPLASM
See also
Cytosol
Mitochondria
CYTOSOL
Recombinant 47-kilodalton cytosol factor restores NADPH oxidase in chronic granulomatous disease. K. J. Lomax and others. bibl f il *Science* 245:409-12 Jl 28 '89; Correction. 246:987 N 24 '89
CYTOWIC, RICHARD E.
about
A mingling of the senses. E. E. Goode. il *U.S. News & World Report* 107:70-2 N 13 '89
CZARNECKI, JOSEPH P.
about
Auschwitz. il *Life* 12:79-80+ S '89
CZECH AMERICAN NOVELISTS See Novelists, Czech American
CZECH AUTHORS See Authors, Czech
CZECH DEFECTORS See Defectors
CZECH LANGUAGE
The typewriter made me do it. J. Novák. il por *The New York Times Book Review* 94:1+ Ap 2 '89
CZECHOSLOVAK AIRLINES
Changes at Czechoslovak Airlines to increase responsibility, freedom. J. M. Lenorovitz. il *Aviation Week & Space Technology* 130:121+ F 20 '89
CZECHOSLOVAKIA
See also
Civil rights—Czechoslovakia
Czechs
Dance festivals—Czechoslovakia
Geology—Czechoslovakia
Government and the press—Czechoslovakia
Literature and state—Czechoslovakia
Music and state—Czechoslovakia
Opera—Czechoslovakia
Political prisoners—Czechoslovakia
Prague (Czechoslovakia)
Rock music—Czechoslovakia

CZECHOSLOVAKIA—*cont.*

Antiquities

The origins of ceramic technology at Dolni Věstonice, Czechoslovakia. P. B. Vandiver and others. bibl f il *Science* 246:1002-8 N 24 '89

History

Intervention, 1968

Anniversary of Warsaw Pact invasion of Czechoslovakia [State Dept. statement, August 21, 1989] *Department of State Bulletin* 89:40 O '89

When the tanks rolled in. il *Time* 134:24 D 4 '89

Industries

See also

Czechoslovak Airlines

LET National Corporation

Motorlet (Firm)

Politics and government

See also

Civic Forum (Czechoslovakia)

Communism—Czechoslovakia

Communist Party (Czechoslovakia)

Anatomy of a purge [ouster of M. Jakes] K. W. Banta. il por *Time* 134:44 D 11 '89

Another domino falls. R. Z. Chesnoff. il *U.S. News & World Report* 107:34-5+ D 4 '89

Bittersweet days in Czechoslovakia. P. C. Newman. il *Maclean's* 102:53 N 27 '89

The changing of the guard. M. R. Meyer. il *Newsweek* 114:36-9 D 4 '89

Czech-out time. J. Škvorecký. *The New Republic* 201:15-17 D 25 '89

Czechoslovakia: realistic socialism? O. Ulč. bibl f *Current History* 88:389-92+ N '89

An early Czech spring. *The Nation* 249:737 D 18 '89

Filling the void [leadership changes] J. Bierman. il *Maclean's* 102:24+ D 18 '89

Havel: a playwright seizes center stage. M. R. Meyer. il por *Newsweek* 114:34 D 18 '89

"Our time has come". W. R. Doerner. il *Time* 134:20-4 D 4 '89

Out of control? J. Smolowe. il *Time* 134:14-17 D 18 '89

Perestroika's next domino just might be Czechoslovakia. G. E. Schares. il *Business Week* p69 O 9 '89

Prague sprung. *The New Republic* 201:7-8 D 18 '89

Prague: the next domino? S. Sullivan. il *Newsweek* 114:32-3 N 27 '89

Prague's autumn revolt [cover story; special section; with editorial comment by Kevin Doyle] il *Maclean's* 102:2, 28-32+ D 4 '89

The rebirth of a proud nation. R. Z. Chesnoff. il *U.S. News & World Report* 107:42-3 D 11 '89

Ringing in a new era. A. Phillips. il *Maclean's* 102:34+ D 11 '89

Ten-day wonder. T. Omestad. *The New Republic* 201:19-20+ D 25 '89

The three holdouts against change. J. Borrell. il *Time* 134:51 N 6 '89

Time is a gentleman [interview with A. Dubcek] il *New Perspectives Quarterly* 5:46-9 Wint '88/'89

Unleashing democracy. M. Nemeth. il *Maclean's* 102:54 N 20 '89

What have you done for us lately? [reform demands] J. Smolowe. il *Time* 134:41-2 D 11 '89

Will Prague be the next domino? R. Knight. il *U.S. News & World Report* 107:49-50 O 30 '89

Religious institutions and affairs

See also

Catholic Church—Czechoslovakia

Church and state—Czechoslovakia

CZECHS

Canada

Calgary power play [hockey player P. Nedved defects to Canada] J. Howse. il por *Maclean's* 102:17 Ja 16 '89

Watching from a distance. M. Nemeth. *Maclean's* 102:32 D 4 '89

CZEISLER, CHARLES A., AND OTHERS

Bright light induction of strong (type O) resetting of the human circadian pacemaker. bibl f il *Science* 244:1328-33 Je 16 '89

CZERKAS, STEPHEN

about

Skinning the dinosaur. D. Lessem. il pors *Discover* 10:4, 38-42+ Mr '89

CZETLI, NANCY

about

Psych out! The woman who catches killers with her mind. il por *Redbook* 173:140-2+ My '89

D

D.A. CAMPBELL COMPANY

Global phone plays. R. King. il por *Forbes* 144:192+ S 18 '89

D.A.D. (MUSICAL GROUP)

D.A.D. F. Goodman. il *Rolling Stone* p25 S 21 '89

D. C. HEATH AND COMPANY. SCHOOL DIVISION

Crisis: the demand for color [getting early commitments for separation work] J. P. Frank. il *Publishers Weekly* 235:120-1 Ja 20 '89

D-DAY INVASION, 1944, IN ART

Exhibitions

The Overlord Embroidery [272-foot-wide cloth tribute at D-Day Museum in Portsmouth, England] R. L. Burgis. il *American Heritage* 40:108-13 My/Je '89

D.J. JAZZY JEFF AND FRESH PRINCE (MUSICAL GROUP)

D.J. Jazzy Jeff & the Fresh Prince. R. Hoerburger. il *Seventeen* 48:97-8+ My '89

Rockers on a roll. K. Turman. il por *'Teen* 33:43 Ja '89

D. L. BLAIR INC.

Treasure hunters denounce concealment of book's solution [case against D. L. Blair, administrator of contest contained in book Treasure in search of the golden horse] C. Reid. *Publishers Weekly* 236:10-11 Ag 25 '89

D.O.C.

about

The D.O.C. J. Ressner. por *Rolling Stone* p30 N 2 '89

D W G CORPORATION

Lenny Pelullo's checkered past—and present. G. DeGeorge. il por *Business Week* p84+ O 23 '89

Victor Posner may soon taste his own medicine [how the raider's DWG got put into play] G. DeGeorge. il pors *Business Week* p34+ Ap 10 '89

DA CAMERA SOCIETY

Architecture and music in Los Angeles [Chamber Music in Historic Sites program] M. Webb. il *Architectural Digest* 46:116+ My '89

DA SILVA, LUIS INÁCIO See Silva, Luis Inácio da

DA VINCI, LEONARDO See Leonardo, da Vinci, 1452-1519

D'ABO, OLIVIA

about

Olivia d'Abo says: bras, yes—car phones, no. J. Marion. il por *TV Guide* 37:32 Jl 22-28 '89

DACHAU (GERMANY): CONCENTRATION CAMP)

Dachau—and a pastoral call. P. Yancey. il *Christianity Today* 33:80 Ja 13 '89

DAD [film] See Motion picture reviews—Single works

DADAISM

Exhibitions

Thinking pictures [The dada & surrealist word-image exhibition] B. W. Bloch. *The New Leader* 72:22-3 N 27 '89

DADDY TRACK

The daddy track. A. L. Ball. il *New York* 22:52-7+ O 23 '89

The daddy track. T. K. Jones. il *Christianity Today* 33:16 Je 16 '89

The daddy track. R. J. Samuelson. il *Newsweek* 113:47 Ap 3 '89

Forget the mommy track: make room for daddy. il *Glamour* 87:156 Je '89

Anecdotes, facetiae, satire, etc.

The daddy track. K. Fury. il *Working Woman* 14:114 Jl '89

DADE COUNTY (FLA.)

Education

A different business school [satellite learning centers] C. Leslie. *Newsweek* 113:77 Ja 30 '89

DAEDALUS PROJECT

Human-powered flight. J. Kluger. il *Discover* 10:70-1 Ja '89

Prize flight [physiologist E. Nadel] A. Burfoot. il pors *Runner's World* 24:28-30 F '89

DAEWOO CORPORATION

Daewoo expands machining base to increase production capacity [Aerospace Products Division] J. D. Morrocco. il *Aviation Week & Space Technology* 130:219-21+ Je 12 '89

Daewoo wins contract to assemble wing panels for Lockheed P-7A. M. A. Dornheim. *Aviation Week & Space Technology* 131:29 S 4 '89

DAFOE, WILLEM

about

Lords of the ring. M. Rochlin. il pors *Harper's Bazaar* 122:103 D '89

The next Brando. M. Kram. il pors *Esquire* 111:78-85 Ja '89

Willem tells. G. Sikes. por *Mademoiselle* 95:42+ Ja '89

DAGGET, DAN

An old foe with new tricks. il *Sierra* 74:30-2 Ja/F '89

DAGON, JANET

A step & a half [story] il *'Teen* 33:30+ Mr '89

DAGUERREOTYPES

Scenes of "exquisite perfection" [special section] il *American History Illustrated* 24:22-30+ S/O '89

Collectors and collecting

Daguerre's own. F. Donegan. il *Americana* 17:60-2 My/Je '89

DAHL, LARS

Safety in the air. *World Press Review* 36:78 O '89

DAHL, ROALD
about
Roald Dahl lambastes Booker for giving elitist awards. V. Menkes. *Publishers Weekly* 236:19 D 15 '89
DAHLBERG, JAMES E.
(jt. auth) See Htun, Han, and Dahlberg, James E.
DAHLEM KONFERENZEN
Dahlem conferences face ax. R. Lewin. *Science* 245:122 Jl 14 '89
DAHLIAS
Discover dahlias. C. Beck. il *Organic Gardening* 36:54-5 O '89
Sleeping beauties [storing dahlias] D. A. Jimerson. il *Better Homes and Gardens* 67:120 O '89
DAI-ICHI KANGYO BANK, LTD.
Dai-Ichi's move on CIT: it's bold—and about time. T. Holden. il *Business Week* p202 S 25 '89
DAI-ICHI TOKYO BAY HOTEL (JAPAN) See Tokyo (Japan)—Hotels, motels, etc.
DAIEI, INC.
Japan's master of retailing [I. Nakauchi] S. Wagstyl. por *World Press Review* 36:52 Ja '89
DAIGLE, CHANTAL
about
Abortion agony. B. Wallace and L. Van Dusen. il por *Maclean's* 102:12-14 Ag 21 '89
Abortion in the courts. B. Wallace. il por *Maclean's* 102:14-16 Ag 7 '89
Abortion on trial [cover story; special section; with editorial comment by Kevin Doyle] il pors *Maclean's* 102:2, 14-16+ Jl 31 '89
Court fails to block abortion. L. Mackey. *Christianity Today* 33:65 S 8 '89
The final appeal. L. Van Dusen. il por *Maclean's* 102:10-11 Ag 14 '89
A unanimous view. L. Van Dusen. il por *Maclean's* 102:16 N 27 '89
DAIGNEAULT, LORRAINE
The nail file [special section] il *Health (New York, N.Y.)* 21:64-9 Ag '89
DAIGRE, JEAN FRANÇOIS
about
A Parisian bijou: glittering prizes in a designer's Louis XVI pavilion [cover story] Suzy. il *Architectural Digest* 46:204-11+ O '89
DAIHATSU (AUTOMOBILE) See Automobiles, Foreign
DAILY, GLENN
about
This expert shares a secret: get your life insurance wholesale and save big bucks. L. Luciano. il por *Money* 18:189-90 D '89
DAILY GRILL (BRENTWOOD, CALIF.) See Brentwood (Los Angeles, Calif.)—Restaurants, nightclubs, bars, etc.
DAILY NEWS (NEW YORK, N.Y.)
Daily news case update [racial discrimination] T. Chapelle. il *Black Enterprise* 20:20 Ag '89
Street beat [columnist B. Herbert] E. Diamond. il por *New York* 22:16+ Ja 30 '89
DAILY TELEGRAPH (LONDON, ENGLAND)
Some sackings are more civil than others. G. Bain. il *Maclean's* 102:46 Ag 28 '89
DAIMIO See Daimyo
DAIMLER-BENZ AG
Daimler accepts German constraints on its buyout of MBB. *Aviation Week & Space Technology* 131:31 S 18 '89
The even-bigger shadow Daimler could cast [MBB takeover] J. Templeman. il por *Business Week* p54-5 My 22 '89
German Cartel Office raises antitrust issues in MBB takeover. *Aviation Week & Space Technology* 130:271 Mr 20 '89
Herr Reuter takes to the skies. P. Fuhrman. il por *Forbes* 143:88+ Mr 20 '89
Miscellaneous ramblings [reaction to introduction of Japanese luxury cars] T. L. Bryant. il *Road & Track* 41:37-8 S '89
Top British Aerospace, Daimler officials discuss collaboration in aerospace markets. *Aviation Week & Space Technology* 130:56 Ap 17 '89
DAIMYO
Exhibitions
The arts of war and peace [Japan: the shaping of daimyo culture 1185-1868] P. S. Prescott. il *Newsweek* 113:59 Ja 2 '89
DAIRY BARNS See Barns and stables
DAIRY COWS See Cows
DAIRY FARMING See Dairying
DAIRY INDUSTRY See Dairying
DAIRY PRICE SUPPORTS See Agricultural administration
DAIRY PRODUCTS
See also
Butter
Cheese
Cooking—Dairy products
Ice cream, ices, etc.
Kefir
Milk
Yogurt
Dairy products: milk does a body good [dancers] J. Scala. il *Dance Magazine* 63:74-5 F '89

Dairy tales [runners' diet] N. Clark. il *Runner's World* 24:44-8+ Je '89
DAIRYING
See also
All-Ways Best Dairy
Carnation Co.
Coach Farm
Cows
Fitz-Haven Dairy
Jackson-Mitchell (Firm)
Rodgers Dairy Farm
Condos where cows once grazed [Vermont] K. J. Kelley. il *The Progressive* 53:28 N '89
Immigrating dairies push into Idaho. J. R. Borcherding. il *Successful Farming* 87:22 S '89
Successful family farm: deep roots and dairy traditions [Skellie farm in New York State] J. R. Borcherding. il *Successful Farming* 87:46-8 Ag '89
DAIRYLAND INSURANCE CO.
State Farm and Dairyland abolish superbike blacklists. T. Van Hooydonk. *Cycle* 40:23 My '89
DAISIES, SHASTA See Shasta daisies
DAISYWHEEL PRINTERS
Silence is golden [Xerox's quiet printing mechanism] W. J. Hawkins. il *Popular Science* 235:20+ Ag '89
DAJANI-SHAKEEL, HADIA
A twisted history. il *Maclean's* 102:21-2 F 27 '89
DAJER, TONY
An enigma named Gloria. il *Discover* 10:86-9 N '89
Going by the book. il *Discover* 10:30-3 Ap '89
Medicine man. il *Discover* 10:47-8+ Jl '89
DAK INDUSTRIES, INC.
Geico versus the DAKonians [anti-radar detector campaign] B. Visnic. *Car and Driver* 35:32-3 N '89
DAKE, HELEN
about
Down-to-earth . . . and delicious. S. Costner. il por *Working Woman* 14:153-6 N '89
DAKOTA INDIANS
See also
Sicangu Elderly Concerns, Inc.
Disputed land [Black Hills] J. Naughton. il *Scholastic Update (Teachers' edition)* 121:8-10 My 26 '89
DALAI LAMA XIV, 1935-
about
A bow to Tibet. por *Time* 134:44 O 16 '89
China's Nobel rebuke. *Newsweek* 114:54 O 16 '89
Honoring a god-king. R. Corelli. il por *Maclean's* 102:58 O 16 '89
Tibet's agony. M. Moynihan. *The New Republic* 201:10-11 N 20 '89
Unrest in Tibet. J. T. Dreyer. bibl f *Current History* 88:281-4+ S '89
You don't have to be a Buddhist to dig the Dalai Lama. M. S. Forbes. por *Forbes* 144:19-20 S 4 '89
DALBY, ANDREW
about
Dinner with Demosthenes. S. J. Evans. il *History Today* 39:3-4 Ja '89
DALEY, RICHARD M.
about
Battling an old bugaboo. L. I. Barrett. il pors *Time* 133:26-7 Ap 17 '89
Chicago's sonny days. il *U.S. News & World Report* 107:30 Ag 21 '89
In Chicago, it's back to the future. J. McCormick. il por *Newsweek* 113:26 F 6 '89
Jackson strikes out. J. McCormick. il pors *Newsweek* 113:24 Mr 13 '89
The old man's Irish eyes are smiling. il por *U.S. News & World Report* 106:12-13 Mr 13 '89
Primogeniture in the Windy City. G. Scott. il por *Time* 133:24 Mr 13 '89
Racial politics—Chicago's raw nerve. D. Johnson. il pors *The New York Times Magazine* p34-8+ F 19 '89
Richard Daley wins Chicago mayoral race; blacks fail to unite behind Tim Evans. il pors *Jet* 76:8-9 Ap 24 '89
Richard M. Daley calls for racial 'harmony' at inaugural. il por *Jet* 76:12-13 My 8 '89
Skin deep. F. Barnes. *The New Republic* 200:10-11 Ap 10 '89
A wet mayor or what? J. R. Coyne, Jr. *National Review* 41:20-1 Ap 21 '89
DALGLISH, JAMIE, 1947-
about
Jamie Dalglish at Barbara Braathen. J. Ash. il *Art in America* 77:172-3 Je '89
DALí, SALVADOR, 1904-1989
about
Gaudí and Dalí, the art of excess. D. Giralt-Miracle. il por *The Courier (Unesco)* 42:32-4 My '89
Obituary
Art in America il por 77:21+ Mr '89. C. Ratcliff
Art News il por 88:69 Ap '89. W. Feaver
Maclean's il por 102:58 F 6 '89. P. Young
Newsweek por 113:77 F 6 '89. D. Gates and C. Dickey
People Weekly il pors 31:105-8 F 6 '89. R. Lacayo
Time il por 133:82 F 6 '89. R. Hughes

DALKEY ARCHIVE PRESS
Dalkey Archive: quarrying for a literary readership. J. Barbato. *Publishers Weekly* 235:38 F 10 '89
DALKON SHIELD (CONTRACEPTIVE)
Day of reckoning [Dalkon Shield case] C. Breslin. il *Ms.* 17:46-52 Je '89
Fatal contraption. M. Kort. il *Essence* 20:16+ Jl '89
How to reward the criminals [A. H. Robins' use of bankruptcy law to avoid Dalkon Shield suits] R. Shereff. *The Nation* 248:192-5 F 13 '89
DALLAS, GREGOR
An incense in terror? The Paris Commune, 1871. bibl il *History Today* 39:38-44 F '89
DALLAS (TEX.)
Dallas does it again. M. Ivins. il *The Progressive* 53:40 F '89

Banks
See also
Texop Bancshares
Buildings
See also
Cityplace (Dallas, Tex.)
Churches (Buildings)
To gather together [St. Rita Catholic Church, designed by Tapley/Lunow Architects] M. Gaskie. il *Architectural Record* 177:102-5 F '89
City planning
See also
Cityplace (Dallas, Tex.)
Crime
Attacking the real 'Jane Roe' [N. McCorvey] S. Waldman. il por *Newsweek* 113:22 Ap 17 '89
The victim of a savage attack, a minister's wife is condemned to a long death in life [P. Railey, severely brain damaged after being strangled in home] J. Young. il pors *People Weekly* 31:50-2+ Ja 16 '89
Criminal justice, Administration of
'Because I was a nobody' [wrongful jailing of R. D. Adams as depicted in The thin blue line] D. Hill. il pors *TV Guide* 37:20-2 My 20-26 '89
Crossing a line that is not thin at all, Randall Dale Adams wins release from a Texas prison. M. Brower. il pors *People Weekly* 31:155-6 Ap 10 '89
Crossing 'The thin blue line' [R. D. Adams sues filmmaker E. Morris] M. Lasswell. il por *Rolling Stone* p30 O 19 '89
Department of amplification [R. D. Adams, wrongly convicted for murder, released from Texas jail] M. Singer. *The New Yorker* 65:119-20 Ap 10 '89
A movie for the defense [R. D. Adams murder case and film The thin blue line] J. N. Baker. il por *Newsweek* 113:27 Mr 13 '89
No happy ending [R. Adams denied parole] J. E. Gallagher. il por *Time* 133:56 Mr 6 '89
Recrossing The thin blue line [R. Adams released from jail] M. B. Carlson. il por *Time* 133:23 Ap 3 '89
Why did Randall Adams almost die? F. Bruning. il *Maclean's* 102:9 Mr 27 '89
Description
Dallas. B. Wallach. il map *Focus (New York, N.Y.: 1950)* 39:22-6 Spr '89
McKinney Avenue: great street in the heart of Dallas. L. Thomas. il map *Southern Living* 24:62-7 O '89
Putting on the pigskin [annual Texas-Oklahoma game] S. Stevens. il *Esquire* 112:54 O '89
Galleries and museums
See also
Southwest Museum of Science and Technology, The Science Place
Gardens and gardening
Lush and green in Dallas. il *Southern Living* 24:60 S '89
Historic houses, sites, etc.
See also
Texas School Book Depository Building
Old world treasures in Dallas [home of E. Gertz decorated by Axel Vervoordt] M. Ennis. il por *Architectural Digest* 46:120-9+ Ag '89
Industries
Indie angst in teetering Texas [independent TV stations] D. Holder. il *Channels (New York, N.Y.: 1986)* 9:71-3 Ja '89
Music
See also
Dallas Opera
Politics and government
Texas time machine [blacks and Hispanics demand greater role in government] R. Woodbury. il *Time* 134:30 Ag 14 '89
Race relations
Texas time machine [blacks and Hispanics demand greater role in government] R. Woodbury. il *Time* 134:30 Ag 14 '89
Savings and loan associations
See also
American Federal Bank FSB (Dallas, Tex.)
Sports
Dallas. R. Galloway. il *Sport (New York, N.Y.)* 80:76-9 N '89

Stores
See also
Neiman Marcus
Streets
See also
McKinney Avenue (Dallas, Tex.)
DALLAS [television program] See Television program reviews—Single works
DALLAS OPERA
Dallas. P. Swank. *Opera News* 53:38 F 18 '89
DALLIN, ALEXANDER
(jt. auth) See Lapidus, Gail Warshofsky, and Dallin, Alexander
DALLY, MARY VINCENT
about
Of many things. J. W. Donohue. *America* 160:362 Ap 22 '89
DALTON, NEIL
Evolution, not revolution. il *History Today* 39:10-11 Ag '89
DALTON (B.) BOOKSELLERS See B. Dalton Booksellers
DALTON'S BACK [drama] See Curran, Keith
DALVA, NANCY VREELAND
Bill Irwin: dance clown [cover story] il pors *Dance Magazine* 63:40-4 S '89
A Metamorphosis indeed: Baryshnikov's bug bit. il por *Dance Magazine* 63:49 Je '89
Paul Taylor, Santo Loquasto and Speaking in tongues: the right mix. il *Dance Magazine* 63:36-8 Ap '89
DALY, CHUCK
about
A perfect fit. J. McCallum. il pors *Sports Illustrated* 71:52-4+ D 18 '89
DALY, HERMAN E.
First word. il *Omni (New York, N.Y.)* 11:8 Ja '89
DALY, JOHN, 1937-
about
Movies you'll never see. A. Hornaday. il *Mother Jones* 14:53-4 F/Mr '89
DALY, LES
The artistry of Auvers. il *The Atlantic* 264:78-82 Jl '89
DALY, MARGARET
Money. See issues of Better Homes and Gardens
DALY, MARTIN, 1944-, AND WILSON, MARGO
Evolution and family homicide [discussion of October 28, 1988 article, Evolutionary social psychology and family homicide] *Science* 243:462-4 Ja 27 '89
DALY, TYNE
about
From trooper to trouper, ex-TV cop Tyne Daly nabs a role as Gypsy's Mama Rose. il por *People Weekly* 32:88-9 Jl 3 '89
DALY, VICTORIA ZIMET
Bump/set/spike! il *Health (New York, N.Y.)* 21:62-3+ Je '89
Ray blockers. il *Health (New York, N.Y.)* 21:45-6 My '89
DAMAGES
See also
Bhopal poisonous gas disaster, India, 1984—Suits and claims
Liability (Law)
Libel and slander
Courting disaster [disaster attorney J. Coale] J. A. Jenkins. il pors *Gentlemen's Quarterly* 59:214-17+ F '89
High Court hears arguments on large punitive damage awards. H. Fields. *Publishers Weekly* 235:18 My 5 '89
Innovation on trial: punitive damages versus new products. R. J. Mahoney and S. E. Littlejohn. bibl f *Science* 246:1395-9 D 15 '89
No pleasure for lawyers [New York State rules against hedonic damages] *Newsweek* 113:48 Mr 6 '89
The pleasure principle [lawyers sue for hedonic damages] T. Jacoby. *Newsweek* 113:61 F 27 '89
Punitive damages: how much is too much? E. G. Olson. il *Business Week* p54+ Mr 27 '89
Supreme Court delivers blow to consumers [punitive damages decision] B. Keating-Edh. *Consumers' Research Magazine* 72:20-1 S '89
Supreme Court upholds public figure libel charge; High Court refuses to place limits on jury awards in civil suits. H. Fields. *Publishers Weekly* 236:12 Jl 14 '89
What is life worth? [hedonic damages] H. Smith. il *Christianity Today* 33:14-15 Mr 3 '89
DAMARISCOTTA (ME.)
Markets
To market, to market. R. F. Baldwin. il *Country Journal* 16:51-4 Jl/Ag '89
D'AMATO, ALFONSE
about
Al's pals. M. J. Green. il *The New Republic* 201:16-20 O 30 '89
Everybody's pal. il por *Time* 134:28 N 6 '89
Fonzie on the spot: the HUD revelations tarnish the 'new' D'Amato. P. Blauner. il pors *New York* 22:42-8 N 13 '89
Great-man theory. J. Klein. pors *New York* 22:16+ F 13 '89
Winners and sinners: the D'Amato and Frank dossiers. J. Klein. il por *New York* 22:23-4 O 9 '89

D'AMBOISE, CHARLOTTE
about
Dance. T. Tobias. il pors *New York* 22:114-15 S 11 '89
D'AMBOISE, CHRISTOPHER
about
Dance. T. Tobias. il pors *New York* 22:114-15 S 11 '89
DAMIAN, MICHAEL
about
He's young—and he's restless. J. Marion. por *TV Guide* 37:23 S 23-29 '89
Michael Damian: from soap star to singing sensation! [interview] K. Turman. por *'Teen* 33:44 Jl '89
TV alchemist Michael Damian turns pure soap into rock gold. S. Dougherty. il pors *People Weekly* 32:102-3 Jl 10 '89
DAMIANO, STEPHEN
NATPE '89: inside the money pit. il *Channels (New York, N.Y.: 1986)* 9:72+ F '89
DAMIEN, FATHER, 1840-1889
about
Father Damien, citizen of the world. por *The Unesco Courier* 42:47 D '89
DAMINOZIDE
The Alar debate [with reply by M. Stanton Evans] E. Groth, III. *Consumers' Research Magazine* 72:28-30 Jl '89
Alar in apples [discussion of April 7, 1989 article, Scare of the week] D. E. Koshland, Jr. *Science* 244:755 My 19 '89
Alar: not gone, not forgotten [use in apples; cover story] il *Consumer Reports* 54:288-92 My '89
Alar: the numbers game [risk assessment controversy between the Natural Resources Defense Council and the Environmental Protection Agency] L. Roberts. *Science* 243:1430 Mr 17 '89
Apples without Alar. il *Newsweek* 114:86 O 30 '89
Bad apples. R. Coorsh. il *Consumers' Research Magazine* 72:4 Ap '89
Bye-bye Alar [end of U.S. sales by Uniroyal Chemical] *Science News* 135:358 Je 10 '89
Daminozide: now you see it . . . *Science News* 135:155 Mr 11 '89
Does everything cause cancer? [Alar in apples and other carcinogens; cover story; special section] il *Consumers' Research Magazine* 72:11-18 My '89
The EPA is looking for a few bad apples. *Newsweek* 113:65 F 13 '89
NRDC on Alar. R. M. Whyatt. bibl f *Science* 245:910-11 S 1 '89
Risky business [Alar and cancer] T. Beardsley. *Scientific American* 260:35-6 My '89
Scare of the week [Alar-treated apples and cyanide in Chilean grapes] D. E. Koshland, Jr. *Science* 244:9 Ap 7 '89
DAMPERS
Balloon dampers [developed by Enerzone Systems] E. Powell. il *Popular Science* 235:74-5 O '89
DAMPIER, WILLIAM, 1652-1715
about
The pirate scientist. M. Cherrington. il por *Weatherwise* 42:205-7 Ag '89
DAMPIERRE, FLORENCE DE
Tole tales. il *House & Garden* 161:50 Ag '89
DAMPING (MECHANICS)
Amplifier damping factor: how important is it? L. Klein. il *Radio-Electronics* 60:78-9 Ja '89
DAMPNESS IN BUILDINGS
See also
Waterproofing
How to cure condensation. P. McCafferty. il *Workbench* 45:10-12 Mr/Ap '89
Sweaty walls and windows mean moisture problems. *Sunset (Central West edition)* 183:86 Jl '89
Why basements leak. D. Johnson. il *The Family Handyman* 39:12+ Je '89
DAMROSCH, BARBARA
How to think like a plant [cover story] bibl il *New Choices for the Best Years* 29:55-60 My '89
DAMS
See also
Dikes (Engineering)
Duking it out in the Carolinas [proposed hydroelectric dam to be built by Duke Power in the Jocassee Watershed] B. Fuller. il *Sierra* 74:96-7 My/Je '89
Fish and power in a riverine rivalry [call for the removal of Edwards Dam in Augusta, Me. in order to restore Kennebec River fisheries] B. Carpenter. il map *U.S. News & World Report* 107:90+ O 16 '89
The Platte pretzel [proposed water projects; with editorial comment by Peter A. A. Berle] S. Winckler. il map *Audubon* 91:8, 86-102+ My '89
Tap into tailwaters [fishing] J. Gibbs. il *Outdoor Life* 183:46+ My '89
Where will the cranes go? [Two Forks dam planned by Denver may threaten sandhill crane habitat on Platte River] J. Adler. il map *Newsweek* 113:62-3 Ap 3 '89

Failure
Impalpable dust [author explores father M. Montgomery's role in construction of Fort Peck Dam, Montana] M. R. Montgomery. il *The New Yorker* 65:94-111 Mr 27 '89
Africa
River basin projects in Africa [cover story] T. Scudder. bibl f il map *Environment* 31:4-9+ Mr '89
Brazil
Hegel and the Amazon Basin [environmental cost of hydroelectric dams] S. C. Florman. il *Technology Review* 92:19 O '89
Canada
Rafferty goes on hold. P. Kopvillem. il *Maclean's* 102:14 Ap 24 '89
France
That dammed Hercules [fresco painted on the face of the Tignes Dam for 1992 Olympics] B. Weber. il *The New York Times Magazine* p130 N 5 '89
United States
See Dams
DAN WAGONER AND DANCERS
Dance. T. Tobias. il *New York* 22:70-1 My 29 '89
Reviews:
Performances at the Joyce Theater, New York City. R. A. Thom. il *Dance Magazine* 63:88 S '89
Wagoner's Joyce dates may be his last in the U.S.A. il por *Dance Magazine* 63:17 My '89
DANA, BILL
Last word. il *Omni (New York, N.Y.)* 11:110 Jl '89
DANA, ROBERT, 1929-
The writer as starling: advice to a young poet. *The Writer* 102:14-16+ My '89
DANBURY (CONN.)
Stores
See also
Indian Trading Post (Danbury, Conn.)
DANCE, STANLEY
(ed) *See* Ellington, Duke, 1899-1974. The art is in the cooking
DANCE
See also
Alvin Ailey American Dance Theater
Angela Caponigro Dance Ensemble
Ballet
Ballet of the Dolls
Ballroom dancing
Barbara Feldman and Dancers
Bebe Miller and Company
Belly dancing
Bill T. Jones/Arnie Zane & Company
Catlin Cobb and Dancers
Clogging (Dance)
Dan Wagoner and Dancers
Dance Alloy (Dance company)
Dance music
Dance notation
Danceworks (Dance company)
Daniel West Dancers
David Gordon/Pick Up Company
David Puszh Dance Company
Diane Jacobowitz Dance Company
Douglas Dunn and Dancers
Erick Hawkins Dance Company
Ethnic Dance Theatre
Garth Fagan Bucket Dance
HARRY (Dance company)
J Fregalette Jansen Dance
Jamison Project
Jazzdance (Dance company)
Jennifer Muller/The Works
Joyce Trisler Danscompany
Lewitzky Dance Company
Lucinda Childs Dance Company
Martha Graham Dance Company
Merce Cunningham Dance Company
Motion pictures—Dance films
Nevada Dance Theatre
New Dance Ensemble
New York Baroque Dance Company
Nikolais and Louis Dance
North Carolina Dance Theater
Paul Taylor Dance Company
Pilobolus Dance Theatre
Polka
Repertory-West (Dance company)
Rockettes
Rose Polsky and Dancers
Sports and dance
Susan Marshall and Company
Synergic Theater
Tango (Dance)
Tap dance
Trisha Brown Dance Company
Videotapes—Dance
Vogueing
Zenon Dance Company
Dance. T. Tobias. See issues of New York

DANCE—*cont.*

Dance magazine special summer events calendar 1989. il *Dance Magazine* 63:SC1-SC4+ My '89

Neoromanticism, men, and the eighties: dancing the difference. P. Kelly and O. Stuart. il *Dance Magazine* 63:34-8 Ja '89

Performance calendar. See issues of Dance Magazine

Presstime news. See issues of Dance Magazine

Accidents and injuries

Feet first. M. Horosko. il *Dance Magazine* 63:56-7 N '89

New knee options [reconstructing dancers' anterior cruciate ligaments] M. Horosko. il *Dance Magazine* 63:96-7 Je '89

Pain. M. Horosko. il *Dance Magazine* 63:62-3 Ja '89

Auditions

A dancer's audition guide: building careers in Europe. V. Fell. il *Dance Magazine* 63:66-7 F '89

Awards

Grand Prix International Vidéo-Danse

Benefit performances

On the town [France-Danse benefit in New York City] J. Gruen. il *Dance Magazine* 63:68-71 Jl '89

Bibliography

Dancebooks. See issues of Dance Magazine

Choreography

See Choreography

Conferences

The artists' last resort: the Orcas Conference '88. E. Zimmer. il *Dance Magazine* 63:68-9 F '89

Directories

Dance directory. See issues of Dance Magazine

Finance

Kickoff. R. Philp. *Dance Magazine* 63:7 O '89

History

Stimulating the senses: going for baroque [reconstructing baroque dances] C. Turocy. il por *Dance Magazine* 63:30-4 Je '89

Study and teaching

Transforming dance history: the lost history of rehearsals. S. Hodes. bibl f *Design for Arts in Education* 91:10-17 N/D '89

Moral and religious aspects

Cleaning up the dance halls [early 1900s] E. I. Perry. bibl il *History Today* 39:20-6 O '89

Photographs and photography

Women at work: Lois Greenfield. J. Kirschenbaum. il pors *Ms.* 18:42-4 S '89

Production and direction

See Dance production

Research

Stimulating the senses: going for baroque [reconstructing baroque dances] C. Turocy. il por *Dance Magazine* 63:30-4 Je '89

Social aspects

She wants to dance with me . . . I'd rather die. M. Zussman. il *Seventeen* 48:137-8 Ap '89

Stage setting and scenery

Frontier of design: Isamu Noguchi 1904-1988 [work with M. Graham] M. U. West. il pors *Dance Magazine* 63:58-60 My '89

Paul Taylor, Santo Loquasto and Speaking in tongues: the right mix. N. V. Dalva. il *Dance Magazine* 63:36-8 Ap '89

Study and teaching

See also

Colleges and universities—Departments of dance

Dance schools

Johannesburg Dance Foundation

National Dance Association

Education. M. Horosko. See issues of Dance Magazine

Hoopla! Put on your boots and let's go! [folk, ethnic, and character dance] M. Horosko. il *Dance Magazine* 63:84-5 Je '89

Parents: what you can teach them (I) [children's dance education] M. Horosko. il *Dance Magazine* 63:70-1 F '89

Parents: what you can teach them (II) [children's dance education] M. Horosko. il *Dance Magazine* 63:64-5 Ap '89

Belgium

See also

Monnaie Dance Group/Mark Morris

California

See also

Los Angeles (Calif.)—Dance

The talking dance blues. E. Zimmer. il *Dance Magazine* 63:60-1 Ap '89

Canada

See also

La La La Human Steps (Dance company)

O Vertigo Danse

Toronto Dance Theatre

Denmark

See also

New Danish Dance Theater

Florida

Reviews:

Florida choreographers present their work at the New Music America Festival in Miami. L. Horn. il *Dance Magazine* 63:70+ Ap '89

France

See also

Compagnie Maguy Marin

France dance: le nouveau stuff. L. Kilman. il *Dance Magazine* 63:46-8 F '89

Photographs and photography

Paris a la Perazio. P. Perazio. il *Dance Magazine* 63:30-1 F '89

Germany (West)

See also

Tanztheater Reinhild Hoffmann

A dancer's audition guide: building careers in Europe. V. Fell. il *Dance Magazine* 63:66-7 F '89

The independent dance scene in West Germany. N. Servos. il *Dance Magazine* 63:60-1 O '89

Great Britain

See also

DV8 Physical Theatre

Illinois

See also

Chicago (Ill.)—Dance

New Jersey

Reviews:

Modern dance performances in Trenton. N. Plett. *Dance Magazine* 63:58 Ag '89

New York (State)

See also

New York (N.Y.)—Dance

Oregon

See also

Portland (Or.)—Dance

South Africa

See also

Johannesburg Dance Foundation

Soviet Union

Here and there [dance exchanges] M. Horosko. il *Dance Magazine* 63:62 D '89

United States

See Dance

DANCE, AEROBIC *See* Aerobics

DANCE, AFRICAN

Africa oye! M. Aloff. il *Art in America* 77:63 Jl '89

Reviews:

Africa oyé! at City Center, New York City. *Dance Magazine* 63:94-6 D '89

Soulful strut [Afrobics] M. Southgate. il *Essence* 20:13 D '89

DANCE, BALINESE

Bali high, ballet low [Dancers and musicians of Bali at City Center] T. Tobias. il *New York* 22:145 Ap 24 '89

Reviews:

Dancers and musicians of Bali at City Center. D. Hering. il *Dance Magazine* 63:59-60 Ag '89

DANCE, BLACK

Blacks enrich modern dance [cover story] L. A. Small. il *American Visions* 4:24-9 Je '89

'Martin' [classical ballet about M. L. King] D. Moore. il *American Visions* 4:34-9 D '89

DANCE, BRAZILIAN

See also

Capoeira (Dance)

DANCE, CAMBODIAN

Cambodia's royal dance [Khmer court ballet; cover story] E. Blumenthal. il *Natural History* p55-63 Ap '89

DANCE, CHINESE

See also

Chinese Folk Dance Company

Young People's Chinese Cultural Center

DANCE, INDIAN (EAST INDIAN)

See also

Kathakali

DANCE, JAPANESE

See also

Butoh

Reviews:

Japan's traditional dance—now at the Brooklyn Academy of Music. M. McQuade. *Dance Magazine* 63:113-14 My '89

DANCE, LATIN AMERICAN

Reviews:

Performances in New York City [Tour de Fuerza] R. A. Thom. il *Dance Magazine* 63:22+ F '89

DANCE, RELIGIOUS *See* Dance in religion, folklore, etc.

DANCE, RUSSIAN

See also

Moiseyev Dance Company

DANCE, SIBERIAN

Recalling art as a way of life: Siberian dancers debut in the U.S.A. [Music & dance of the Siberian-Asians at the Smithsonian] B. Gordon. il *Dance Magazine* 63:21 Mr '89

DANCE REVIEWS—Single works—Speaking in tongues—
cont.
　The New Leader il 72:22-3 Je 12-26 '89. L. A. Jacobs
　The New Yorker 65:78-80 My 1 '89. A. Croce
Thirst
　The New Leader 72:22 Ja 9 '89. L. A. Jacobs
Tree
　The New Leader 72:22 Ja 9 '89. L. A. Jacobs
United States
　Dance Magazine 63:94-5 Ap '89. C. Hardy
DANCE SCHOOLS
　See also
　Harid Conservatory
　School of American Ballet
Beyond the box step [learning ballroom dancing as a child
　in the sixties] W. B. Logan. il *House & Garden* 161:82+
　N '89
It's 10:00 a.m.—where are your classes now? [New York
　City] M. Horosko. il *Dance Magazine* 63:81 Je '89
Canada
　See also
　National Ballet School (Canada)
Soviet Union
　See also
　Vaganova Choreographic Institute (Leningrad, Soviet
　Union)
Thailand
　See also
　College of Dramatic Arts (Bangkok, Thailand)
DANCE SPACES *See* Dance theaters
DANCE STUDIOS
Leasing and renting
It's 10:00 a.m.—where are your classes now? [New York
　City] M. Horosko. il *Dance Magazine* 63:81 Je '89
DANCE TEACHERS
　See also
　Danilova, Alexandra
DANCE THEATER WORKSHOP
Points in space [S. Krieckhaus] T. Tobias. il *New York*
　22:84-5 Mr 20 '89
DANCE THEATERS
　See also
　R. A. Laidlaw Center/Betty Oliphant Theatre (Toronto,
　Ont.)
Space: the final frontier [unusual spaces for dance in New
　York City] R. Sandla. *Dance Magazine* 63:61 D '89
Air conditioning
Too darn hot. C. Barnes. *Dance Magazine* 63:82 Ag '89
DANCE THEATRE OF HARLEM
Company as community: DTH at 20 [cover story] E. Kendall.
　il por *Dance Magazine* 63:40-2 Je '89
Dance Theatre of Harlem launches twentieth anniversary
　tour. il *Dance Magazine* 63:6 Ja '89
Feathers [revival of works by B. Nijinska] T. Tobias. il
　New York 22:53 Jl 17 '89
Musical events:
　Les noces. A. Croce. *The New Yorker* 65:86-7 Jl 17
　'89
Reviews:
　Performances at City Center, New York City. C. Hardy.
　il *Dance Magazine* 63:69-70+ N '89
Stepping out with Arthur Mitchell. H. Sterne. il por
　Gentlemen's Quarterly 59:428-9 S '89
DANCE THERAPY
　See also
　STEPS Theater Company
DANCERS
　See also
　Clothing and dress—Dancers
　See also names of dancers
Dancescape. See issues of Dance Magazine
Presstime news. See issues of Dance Magazine
Where are all the men? [ballet] L. Shapiro. il *Newsweek*
　113:62-3 Ap 10 '89
Accidents and injuries
　See Dance—Accidents and injuries
Health and hygiene
New hips for a veteran dancer. M. Beddow. il pors *Dance*
　Magazine 63:46-50 S '89
The personal you. M. Horosko. See issues of Dance Magazine
When classes are not enough: body therapies. M. Myers
　and M. Horosko. il *Dance Magazine* 63:47-51 Jl '89
Nutrition
Nutrition. J. Scala. See issues of Dance Magazine beginning
　September 1988
Salaries, pensions, etc.
Making money talk (I). G. Byron. il *Dance Magazine* 63:44-7
　O '89
Making money talk (II). G. Byron. il *Dance Magazine* 63:40-3
　N '89
DANCES (BALLS) *See* Balls (Parties)
DANCES (STUDENT ACTIVITIES)
　See also
　Proms (Dances)
Dancing gays [gay-lesbian dance at Columbia University]
　D. K. Mano. *National Review* 41:56-9 F 24 '89

DANCEWORKS (DANCE COMPANY)
A big surprise in Boston: everything's coming up (Susan)
　Rose. I. M. Fanger. il pors *Dance Magazine* 63:42-3 My
　'89
DANCING OUT OF TIME [dance] *See* Dance reviews—Single
　works
DANCO, SUZANNE
　about
In harmony. M. Scott. il pors *Opera News* 53:30-2 Ap 15
　'89
DANDIES
Fine & dandy [B. Brummell] P. Kinmonth. il *Vogue* 179:334-9
　Ag '89
D'ANDRILLI, STEPHEN
　about
Protection. *The New Yorker* 64:22-3 Ja 9 '89
DANDYISM *See* Dandies
DANGEROUS GAMES [musical] *See* Musicals, revues, etc.—
　Reviews—Single works
DANGEROUS GOODS *See* Hazardous substances
DANGEROUS LIAISONS [film] *See* Motion picture reviews—
　Single works
DANI, AHMAD HASAN
A silken bond between East and West. il map *The Courier*
　(Unesco) 42:4-10 Mr '89
DANICA, ELLY
　about
The long road to recovery. N. Underwood. il por *Maclean's*
　102:64 N 27 '89
DANIEL, DAVID
Dance steppes. por *Vogue* 179:254 Ap '89
Freed by *glasnost*, the Kirov Ballet arrives in America this
　month with new prima ballerina Altynai Asylmuratova.
　por *Vogue* 179:84-5 Jl '89
Vitalized with fresh talent, the Met's new season heralds
　the return of opera mania. il *Vogue* 179:470+ S '89
DANIEL, JOHN
Some mortal speculations. *Wilderness* 52:14-15+ Summ '89
DANIEL, ROD
　about
K-9 [film] Reviews
　People Weekly il 31:13 My 22 '89. R. Novak
DANIEL WEST DANCERS
Daniel West Dancers. G. Jackson. il *Dance Magazine* 63:70-1
　S '89
DANIELL, ROBERT F.
　about
Where 1990s-style management is already hard at work.
　T. Vogel. il por *Business Week* p92-3+ O 23 '89
DANIELS, ANTHONY, 1949-
Curtain still down. por *National Review* 41:21-3 D 22 '89
In the shadows. *National Review* 41:24-5 Jl 14 '89
People's democratic revue. *National Review* 41:19-20 S 1
　'89
DANIELS, BILL
　about
'Wild Bill' Daniels tries one more comeback. W. C. Symonds.
　il por *Business Week* p85-6 Ja 30 '89
DANIELS, EDDIE
　about
Blindfold test. M. Bourne. il por *Down Beat* 56:41 Ap '89
DANIELS, ELIZABETH
The children of Gettysburg. il *American Heritage* 40:97-101+
　My/Je '89
DANIELS, JEFF
　about
No place like home. J. E. Fitch. il por *American Film*
　15:65 D '89
DANIELS, JUDITH
Where to find supporting characters. *The Writer* 102:27-8
　D '89
DANIELS, LASHANDA
　about
Lashanda Daniels's outstanding essay on the homeless was
　no academic exercise—she'd been there. W. Plummer.
　il pors *People Weekly* 32:39-40 Jl 31 '89
DANIELS, LLOYD
　about
The sad tale of Sweet Pea. il por *Sports Illustrated* 70:12
　My 22 '89
DANIELS, MITCHELL E.
The decline of central government [address, September 18,
　1989] *Vital Speeches of the Day* 56:34-7 N 1 '89
DANIELS, ROBERT E.
A Kipsigis parable. il *Natural History* p66+ Je '89
DANIELS, STEVIE O.
Openings. See issues of Organic Gardening beginning April
　1988
DANIELS, THEODORE R.
　about
HUD director hosts black finance show on network. por
　Jet 76:24 My 8 '89
DANIELS, THOMAS J., AND FALCO, RICHARD C.
The Lyme disease invasion. il *Natural History* p4+ Jl '89
DANIELS & ASSOCIATES INC.
'Wild Bill' Daniels tries one more comeback. W. C. Symonds.
　il por *Business Week* p85-6 Ja 30 '89

DANILOVA, ALEXANDRA
about
Ballerina leaves school to coach. R. Johnson. il pors *Dance Magazine* 63:16 S '89
DANILUK, AGNES
about
Out of the ashes, a family restored. M. Dougherty. il pors *People Weekly* 31:46-51 F 13 '89
DANILUK, PAUL
about
Out of the ashes, a family restored. M. Dougherty. il pors *People Weekly* 31:46-51 F 13 '89
DANN, LAURIE WASSERMAN, D. 1988
about
Diary of a tragedy. J. Bultman. il por *Parents* 64:105-10 My '89
DANNER, MARK
Beyond the mountains (I). maps *The New Yorker* 65:55-6+ N 27 '89
Beyond the mountains (II). maps *The New Yorker* 65:68+ D 4 '89
Beyond the mountains (III). map *The New Yorker* 65:100-2+ D 11 '89
DANNER, RAYMOND L.
about
Shoney's needs a recipe for succession. W. Konrad. il por *Business Week* p52 D 25 '89-Ja 1 '90
DANSES CONCERTANTES [ballet] See Ballet reviews—Single works
DANSON, TED
about
"I nearly lost my marriage". V. J. Radovsky. il pors *Redbook* 173:46+ Je '89
Ted Danson's crusade. T. Green. il por *Oceans* 22:18-20+ Mr/Ap '89
The word of mouth on Ted Danson's Hawaiian celeb bash: it was a ball. il por *People Weekly* 32:113-15 O 16 '89
DANTE, JOE
about
The 'burbs [film] Reviews
  Newsweek il 113:58 Mr 6 '89. D. Ansen
  People Weekly il 31:17 Mr 6 '89. R. Novak
  Time il 133:81-2 F 27 '89. R. Corliss
  Video il 13:91+ S '89. J. Young
DANTLEY, ADRIAN
about
And the winner is . . . J. McCallum. il pors *Sports Illustrated* 70:34-6 Mr 6 '89
DANTO, ARTHUR COLEMAN, 1924-
Art. See issues of The Nation beginning October 20, 1984
The art of darkness. il *Vogue* 179:186-91 Ja '89
The gorgeousness of life. il *Art News* 88:108-13 Ja '89
Growing up absurd. il por *Art News* 88:118-21 N '89
about
Art's off-the-wall critic. E. Frank. il pors *The New York Times Magazine* p46-7+ N 19 '89
DANTO, GINGER
France: let them have art. il *Art News* 88:136-9 N '89
DANTON'S DEATH [drama] See Büchner, Georg, 1813-1837
DANVERS STATE HOSPITAL (MASS.) See Hospitals, Psychiatric—Massachusetts
DANVILLE (CALIF.)
Education
Teaching character development [Child Development Project] W. Streshly and E. Schaps. *The Education Digest* 54:25-8 Mr '89
DANZA, TONY
about
Tony Danza: "I tried, but I wasn't a good father" [interview] V. J. Radovsky. il por *Redbook* 172:54+ Mr '89
Tony Danza, my husband, and me. V. Scott. il pors *Good Housekeeping* 208:86+ Ap '89
DANZIG (POLAND) See Gdańsk (Poland)
DANZIGER, RENÉE
Women and AIDS. il *World Health* p14-15 O '89
DAPPEN, ANDY
Zanzibar. il *Travel Holiday* 171:86-9 Ja '89
D'AQUINO, THOMAS
Deficits and the national debt [address, February 23, 1989] *Vital Speeches of the Day* 55:427-9 My 1 '89
Environment and economy [address, May 17, 1989] *Vital Speeches of the Day* 55:621-4 Ag 1 '89
DARA See Deutsche Agentur fur Raumfahrtangelegenheiten
D'ARBANVILLE, PATTI
about
Her roses are red and black and blue. Does Patti need a 7th tattoo? L. Eisenberg. il por *TV Guide* 37:15 Jl 8-14 '89
Meet the new Patti D'Arbanville, star of Wiseguy and Wired, no longer just Don Johnson's ex. M. Dougherty. il pors *People Weekly* 31:58-60 Ap 3 '89
Patty D'Arbanville, Wired for success. A. M. Schiffman. il por *Mademoiselle* 95:102 Mr '89
DARBAR (NEW YORK, N.Y.: RESTAURANT) See New York (N.Y.)—Restaurants, nightclubs, bars, etc.

D'ARBY, TERENCE TRENT
about
D'Arby's strange soul search. M. Coleman. il *Rolling Stone* p109-10 N 30 '89
DARCEY (FRANCE)
Description
Darcey: a village that refuses to die. W. S. Ellis. il *National Geographic* 176:138-45 Jl '89
D'ARCY-MACMANUS & MASIUS WORLDWIDE, INC.
See also
  D'Arcy Masius Benton & Bowles, Inc.
D'ARCY MASIUS BENTON & BOWLES, INC.
The 'bridesmaid' ad agency finally catches the bouquet. W. Konrad. il *Business Week* p27-8 Je 12 '89
Home of the whoppers. B. Kanner. il *New York* 22:19-20 Jl 31 '89
DARDER, JAMIE
about
"How did I know the guy was calling from jail?". R. L. Stern. il por *Forbes* 143:120+ My 29 '89
DARE, DIANE
Gifts of the Magi: precious resins. *Earth Science* 41:14 Wint '88
DARE AMERICA (PROGRAM)
A drug program that really works! M. O'Koon. il *Good Housekeeping* 208:165 F '89
Girl 13, raps death penalty at White House event for children's anti-drug group [views of C. Charles] il pors *Jet* 76:31 O 2 '89
DARGEMONT, CATHERINE, AND OTHERS
Thymotaxin, a chemotactic protein, is identical to β_2-microglobulin. bibl f il *Science* 246:803-6 N 10 '89
DARIEN (CONN.)
Gardens and gardening
Nature's aid [garden of R. A. Binns] K. Martin. il pors *Organic Gardening* 36:68-72+ Ja '89
DARK, SANDRA
Shape up your firm's image. il *Nation's Business* 77:42+ Jl '89
DARK GLASSES See Sunglasses
DARK MATTER (ASTRONOMY)
See also
  Charged massive particles
Giant gas ring "weighs" massive halo [elliptical galaxy IC 2006] *Sky and Telescope* 77:587-8 Je '89
Laboratory limits on dark matter. il *Sky and Telescope* 77:131-2 F '89
Pruning the thickets of cosmic speculation [Center for Particle Astrophysics] M. M. Waldrop. il *Science* 243:168-9 Ja 13 '89
Ringing in a new estimate for dark matter [research by Stephen E. Schneider] R. Cowen. il *Science News* 136:84 Ag 5 '89
Spiral arms and dark halos [research by Magnus Thomasson] il *Sky and Telescope* 78:134 Ag '89
DARK-RUMPED PETRELS See Petrels
DARK SHADOWS [television program] See Television program reviews—Single works
DARKNESS
See also
  Fear of the dark
DARKROOM EQUIPMENT See Photography—Processing—Equipment
DARKROOM TECHNIQUE IN PHOTOGRAPHY See Photography—Processing
DARKROOMS See Photography—Studios and darkrooms
DARLING, DARLENE DUFFY
A message from Brian. il por *Ladies' Home Journal* 106:22+ My '89
DARLING, RON
about
Simply Darling. M. Lupica. il *Esquire* 111:67+ Ap '89
Team spirit. il pors *Harper's Bazaar* 122:150-3 My '89
DARLING, TONI O'REILLY See O'Reilly, Toni
DARLING-DELAWARE CO., INC.
Fat city [Bass Brothers invest in Darling-Delaware] H. Rudnitsky. il *Forbes* 144:70 Jl 10 '89
DARLING-HAMMOND, LINDA, 1951-
The future of teaching. *The Education Digest* 54:7-10 Mr '89
Teacher professionalism and accountability. *The Education Digest* 55:15-19 S '89
DARLINGTON, DAVID
The pastures of Class-L heaven. il *Sierra* 74:70-3+ S/O '89
DARMAN, RICHARD
about
A bout of Fed-bashing. M. McNamee and H. Gleckman. il por *Business Week* p24-5 Ag 28 '89
Bush's audacious new czar of domestic policy. K. T. Walsh. il por *U.S. News & World Report* 106:25-6 Ja 16 '89
Darman: the collapse of a grand strategy. E. Clift. por *Newsweek* 114:54 N 20 '89
Darman's 'Maypo' pitch: how will it go down? por *Newsweek* 114:44 Ag 7 '89
Did Darman diddle while the deficit burned? H. Gleckman. il por *Business Week* p56-7 D 11 '89
Driven to beat the budget. L. I. Barrett. il por *Time* 133:58-60 F 27 '89

DARMAN, RICHARD—about—*cont.*

The Fed's hot seat at Darman's breakfast table. M. W. Karmin. il por *U.S. News & World Report* 107:90 Ag 28-S 4 '89

The Nick & Dick show: what next? C. Hutton. il pors *Fortune* 119:12 Ja 30 '89

Pinball wizard at the flippers. P. C. Roberts. il *National Review* 41:24+ F 24 '89

Say hello to charmin' Darman. T. M. DeFrank and A. McDaniel. por *Newsweek* 113:24 Je 5 '89

The trillion dollar man [cover story] H. Gleckman. il pors *Business Week* p100-3+ Mr 13 '89

What the smartest man in Washington doesn't understand. And why it will hurt you [cover story] J. DeParle. il por *The Washington Monthly* 21:24-6+ N '89

White House wonk [cover story] F. Barnes. *The New Republic* 200:19-21 Ja 2 '89

DARNELL, AUGUST

about

The renaissance kid. S. Fried. il pors *Gentlemen's Quarterly* 59:63-4+ Jl '89

DARNTON, ROBERT

Liberty, equality, absurdity. il *The New Republic* 200:29-32 Ap 3 '89

What was revolutionary about the French Revolution? il *The New York Review of Books* 35:3-4+ Ja 19 '89

DARNTON-HILL, IAN

Non-communicable diseases: no longer just diseases of affluence. il *World Health* p7-9 N '89

DARPA *See* United States. Defense Advanced Research Projects Agency

DARRACH, BRAD

Goodbye Today, hello tomorrow [cover story] il pors *Life* 12:46-8+ D '89

DARRELL'S (NEW YORK, N.Y.: RESTAURANT) *See* New York (N.Y.)—Restaurants, nightclubs, bars, etc.

DART, JUSTIN, JR.

Should the Senate approve the "Americans with Disabilities Act of 1989"? [excerpts from testimony, May 9, 1989] *Congressional Digest* 68:310+ D '89

about

An agency in trouble. C. A. Davis. il por *The Progressive* 53:13 Ja '89

DARTMOUTH COLLEGE

Science fiction: imaginary worlds and real-life questions. N. Perrin. il *The New York Times Book Review* 94:37-8 Ap 9 '89

DARTMOUTH COLLEGE. HOOD MUSEUM OF ART *See* Hood Museum of Art

DARTMOUTH REVIEW

At Dartmouth the clash of '89. J. Casey. il *The New York Times Magazine* p28-30+ F 26 '89

Dartmouth vs. freedom of speech. D. Stone. il *Conservative Digest* 15:24-7 My/Je '89

Dartmouth's wild Indians stopped by the court. W. F. Buckley. *National Review* 41:15-16 Ja 27 '89

Good news from Dartmouth [administration backs student protesting teacher S. Sully's finding of racism in submitted essay] *National Review* 41:18 S 15 '89

Return of the Dartmouth Two [editors Christopher Baldwin and John Sutter contest college suspension] T. Jacoby. il *Newsweek* 113:50-1 Ja 16 '89

DARTS (GAME)

Bulletin! Government takes only 18 years to ban lawn darts! il *Consumer Reports* 54:5 Ja '89

DARVES, BONNIE

(jt. auth) *See* Holtel, Bob, and Darves, Bonnie

DARVISHIAN, DAN

Mint julep memoirs. il *Travel Holiday* 171:14-18 Je '89

Sacramento's Railroad Museum. il *Travel Holiday* 172:64-6+ O '89

DARWIN, CHARLES, 1809-1882

about

Full of hot air. S. J. Gould. il *Natural History* p28+ O '89

George Canning's left buttock and the origin of species. S. J. Gould. *Natural History* p18+ My '89

The wheel of fortune and the wedge of progress. S. J. Gould. *Natural History* p14+ Mr '89

DARWIN, CHARLES ROBERT *See* Darwin, Charles, 1809-1882

DARWIN, CHRISTOPHER

about

Darwin's legacy: has evolution brought us to this? il por *People Weekly* 31:71 Je 26 '89

DARWINISM *See* Evolution; Natural selection

DARWISCH, TIFFANY *See* Tiffany

DAS GUPTA, AMALENDU

'Not the end of socialism'. *World Press Review* 36:26 Ag '89

DASH, J. G.

Thermomolecular pressure in surface melting: motivation for frost heave. bibl f il *Science* 246:1591-3 D 22 '89

DASH RIP ROCK (MUSICAL GROUP)

Dash Rip Rock builds up southern steam. P. Puterbaugh. il *Stereo Review* 54:123 N '89

DASS, RAM *See* Ram Dass

DASSAULT BREGUET AVIATION (AVIONS MARCEL)

Dassault-Breguet's 1988 aircraft orders valued at $2.6 billion. *Aviation Week & Space Technology* 130:30 Ja 23 '89

Dassault launches twin-engine, transcontinental business jet as signs of market recovery are seen [Falcon X] *Aviation Week & Space Technology* 130:34 Je 19 '89

Dassault nears end of production on two Mirage fighter versions. il *Aviation Week & Space Technology* 131:66 N 13 '89

Dassault seeks partner for Falcon 2000 production. il *Aviation Week & Space Technology* 131:30 O 30 '89

Future Falcon jet [views of Bernard Leroldier] *Flying* 116:26 Je '89

DASSER, VERENA, AND OTHERS

The perception of intention. bibl f *Science* 243:365-7 Ja 20 '89

DASSOULAS, MARK

about

Mark Dassoulas [cover story] M. S. Doherty. il *American Artist* 53:36-41 Je '89

DATA (STATISTICS) *See* Statistics

DATA BANKS *See* Information systems

DATA BUSES *See* Computers—Buses

DATA CENTER (OAKLAND, CALIF.)

Where to find the facts. F. Setterberg. il *The Progressive* 53:14 Jl '89

DATA COMPRESSION (COMPUTER SCIENCE)

Fractals in your future [work of Michael F. Barnsley] T. Waters. il *Discover* 10:26+ Mr '89

Image capture by computer [work of Michael F. Barnsley and Alan D. Sloan] B. A. Cipra. *Science* 243:1288-9 Mr 10 '89

Tape capacity jumps up a notch [QFA-500 backup system] J. Blackford. il *Personal Computing* 13:200 S '89

DATA ENTRY

Programming

Input: keep it clean [data-entry TSR program] R. Grehan. il *Byte* 14:387-90+ D '89

DATA GENERAL CORP.

Data General: RISC-ing most of its chips. G. McWilliams. il *Business Week* p195 N 27 '89

DATA METERS

RS-232 debugging with SAM 2000. il *Radio-Electronics* 60:83-5 O '89

Smart RS-232 Data Meter. il *Radio-Electronics* 60 ComputerDigest:90-1 Mr '89

DATA PROCESSING PERSONNEL *See* Computer personnel

DATA STRUCTURES (COMPUTER SCIENCE)

Directory assistance (I). R. Grehan. bibl il *Byte* 14:291-4+ My '89

Directory assistance (II). R. Grehan. il *Byte* 14:327-8+ Je '89

Handy DOS commands give directory assistance. T. Roberts. *Compute!* 11:82 N '89

Trees 'n keys (I). R. Grehan. il *Byte* 14:379-80+ Ja '89

Trees 'n keys (II). R. Grehan. il *Byte* 14:301-7 F '89

Trees 'n keys (III). R. Grehan. il *Byte* 14:287-8+ Mr '89

DATA TAPES

Answers to my Mac mess [preventing hard disk crashes and MouseStick] E. Shapiro. il *Byte* 14:129-30+ Ap '89

A backup drive with the memory of an elephant [Jumbo tape backup system] M. Bryan. il *Personal Computing* 13:204 Mr '89

DAT drive eases Mac backups [Gigapack-Mac] D. E. Crabb. il *Byte* 14:225-6+ N '89

Disaster recovery [hard disk crashes] D. E. Crabb. il *Byte* 14:127-8 S '89

How to install a tape backup unit [Streaming tape drive] B. C. Fenton. il *Radio-Electronics* 60 ComputerDigest:81+ Je '89

Jumbo works for peanuts [tape backup unit] S. Miastkowski. il *Byte* 14:98+ Ja '89

A new twist on an old technology [helical-scan recording] J. Bretzmann. il *Byte* 14:380-2+ N '89

Tape capacity jumps up a notch [QFA-500 backup system] J. Blackford. il *Personal Computing* 13:200 S '89

Tecmar sets a standard for backup [QT-150e] J. Blackford. *Personal Computing* 13:200 S '89

What's new in backup hardware and software. P. Honan. il *Personal Computing* 13:103-5+ Je '89

With tape, backing up's not hard to do [Irwin Model 5080 tape system] D. Barker. il *Byte* 14:98 Ja '89

DATA TRANSMISSION NETWORK CORP.

Keep it simple. R. Reiff. il *Forbes* 144:226-7 O 2 '89

DATA TRANSMISSION SYSTEMS

See also

American Telephone & Telegraph Co.
Communications software
Computer networks
Computerphones
Computers—Buses
Electronic mail systems
Fax machines
Integrated services digital network
Local area networks
MCI Communications Corp.
Offices—Automation

DATA TRANSMISSION SYSTEMS—See also—*cont.*
Packet switching (Data transmission)
T1 networks
Teleconferencing
Acquisitions and mergers
International aspects
British Telecom is getting less British all the time [buying McDonnell Douglas Corp.'s electronic data communications operations] M. Maremont. il *Business Week* p62 Ag 14 '89
DATABASE MANAGEMENT
See also
File servers (Computers)
HyperPad (Database)
LinkWay (Computer program)
Location transparency (Database management)
Personal information management software
Reflex (Computer program)
Relational databases
Transparency (Database management)
Data base management. M. Liskin. See issues of Personal Computing beginning June 1987
The database meets desktop publishing. R. Kendall. il *Home Office Computing* 7:36-7 O '89
Database trends [special section] il *Byte* 14:244-5+ S '89
Keys to the magic kingdom. D. McNeill. il *Compute!* 11:38-42 My '89
The metamorphosis of information management. D. Gelernter. bibl il *Scientific American* 261:66-73 Ag '89
Reflections on database design. A. Kleiner. il *Personal Computing* 13:108-12 N '89
Testing
Address Book Plus [mailing list manager] B. Gingher. il *Compute!* 11:76-7 My '89
Addressing a common problem [Address Book Plus version B.00; mailing list manager] B. Krasnoff. il *Personal Computing* 13:204+ Ap '89
AskSam: making order out of chaos [version 4.1] C. Strehlo. il *Personal Computing* 13:200 Ap '89
Clarion Personal Developer. B. Hunt. il *Home Office Computing* 7:61-2 Jl '89
Database of the dead [For the Record] D. Barker. *Byte* 14:104+ Ja '89
Eighty/20. H. F. Beechhold. il *Home Office Computing* 7:76+ Je '89
FileMaker II. R. Hart. il *Home Office Computing* 7:78+ Je '89
For the Record. J. Nimersheim. il *Compute!* 11:124-6 O '89
Get at information quickly with Reference File. J. Nimersheim. il *Home Office Computing* 7:24+ Ag '89
'Growing' a database without programming [Clarion Personal Developer] C. O'Malley. il *Personal Computing* 13:224+ Ja '89
Hold Everything! [preconfigured database program] B. Hunt. il *Home Office Computing* 7:74-5 Ja '89
IZE [text database program] L. Wood. il *Home Office Computing* 7:70+ Ag '89
Label printing made easy [LabelPro] B. Krasnoff. *Personal Computing* 13:206 N '89
Labels! V. D. O'Connor. *Compute!* 11:70 S '89
List Manager techniques. J. Eugenides. il *Byte* 14 Mac Special Supp:MAC199-MAC203 My '89
Meet Dr. Database [use of RapidFile by E. Gordy] K. J. Novak. il por *Home Office Computing* 7:24-5 Jl '89
MyBASE. C. Karnes. *Compute!* 11:99-100 Ja '89
Opus I [graphics oriented database management program] P. R. Robinson. il *Byte* 14:233-4+ Ja '89
Power Desk. T. A. Summers. il *Home Office Computing* 7:75-6 Ja '89
Text retrieval with a twist [Folio Views] D. Allen. il *Byte* 14:201-2+ Jl '89
When is flat OK? [Professional File 2.0 and Q&A] R. Hotch. il *Nation's Business* 77:66 O '89
DATABASE SYSTEMS *See* Information systems
DATAPOINT CORP.
A raider tries to beat Asher Edelman at his own game [M. Ackerman's proxy fight] G. Lewis. il pors *Business Week* p50 S 25 '89
DATAPRODUCTS CORP.
Dataproducts is in play, but where are the players? G. G. Marcial. *Business Week* p104 Ag 14 '89
DATE NAILS *See* Nails
DATE RAPE
Preventing date rape. D. Elkind. il *Parents* 64:198 Ap '89
DATEBOOKS
See also
Day-Timers (Firm)
Filofax
Computing in hand [Sharp Wizard and Psion Organiser] W. Rash, Jr. il *Byte* 14:195-6+ My '89
Digital diaries [Sharp Wizard, Psion Organiser II, Casio Digital Diary] F. Vizard. il *Popular Mechanics* 166:73-5 Ap '89
Electronic books will organize your life, replace your library and fit your pocket. G. Hedberg. il *Money* 18:183-4 Je '89

Electronic organizer [Wizard] il *Radio-Electronics* 60:26 F '89
Hot hand-held electronic organizers [Psion Organiser II Model LZ and the Sharp Wizard Model OZ-7000] P. M. Cirullo. il *Home Office Computing* 7:68-70 O '89
Let your computer be your date book. W. C. Symonds and M. Shao. il *Business Week* p81 Ag 7 '89
Pocket computer [Sharp's Wizard] D. Stover. il *Popular Science* 234:32 Ja '89
The power of a Wizard. G. Hartwig. il *Byte* 14:98+ Ap '89
Three weeks that did not reorganize my life [Sharp Wizard, Psion Organiser II, Casio Digital Diary] D. P. Wiener. il *U.S. News & World Report* 106:76+ F 13 '89
DATES (FRUIT)
Dates: deliciously different. *Good Housekeeping* 209:304 N '89
DATING (ARCHEOLOGY) *See* Archeology—Methodology
DATING (GEOLOGY) *See* Geological time
DATING (RADIOACTIVE) *See* Radioactive dating
DATING (SOCIAL CUSTOMS)
See also
Date rape
The agony and the ecstasy of first dates. L. Dormen. il *Seventeen* 48:258-9+ Mr '89
Asking him out: what the guys say, what do you say? A. Bell. il *'Teen* 33:28+ Je '89
Dates for dad [divorced father] L. Brown. por *Essence* 19:10 F '89
Dream Date Sweepstakes: meet the winner! [A. Yeager's date with J. H. Newton] J. Clay. il pors *'Teen* 33:46 Jl '89
"If you could read my mind . . . you'd probably go home": behind the lines of a first date [blind date] K. A. Samon. il *Mademoiselle* 95:142+ My '89
In love with the boy next dorm [college students] C. Parkhurst. il *Seventeen* 48:199 S '89
Night of the living dud and other . . . dates from hell. K. A. Samon. il *Mademoiselle* 95:162-3+ S '89
Rate your date. il *'Teen* 33:22+ F '89
Sixteen—the third time around. I. Davis. il *The New York Times Magazine* p22+ D 17 '89
Social studies: dating do's and don'ts. il *'Teen* 33:12+ D '89
Tall, dark first date [effect of height on perceptions of attractiveness; research by Alan Strathman and James Shepperd] V. Bozzi. il *Psychology Today* 23:67 Jl/Ag '89
The way we are [returning to dating after being widowed] L. Wyse. il *Good Housekeeping* 208:268 Je '89
When mom plays the dating game, do you lose? D. Dodds. il *'Teen* 33:68-9 D '89
Women: if you like heavy metal, don't tell your date [effect of musical preference on perceptions of attractiveness; research by Dolf Zillmann and Azra Bhatia] E. Stark. il *Psychology Today* 23:14 N '89
Anecdotes, facetiae, satire, etc.
The Coast. G. Stone. il *Gentlemen's Quarterly* 59:139 My '89
Dating at forty. N. Kelton. il *Parents* 64:126-8 S '89
The new dating game. L. Sunshine. *Harper's Bazaar* 122:177+ Mr '89
Women, pick up the phone! G. Nachman. por *Newsweek* 114:8 Jl 31 '89
DATING (SOCIAL CUSTOMS) BY COMPUTER *See* Computers—Social use
DATING (SOCIAL CUSTOMS) BY FAX MACHINE *See* Fax machines—Social use
DATING (SOCIAL CUSTOMS) BY VIDEOTAPE *See* Videotapes—Social aspects
DATING (SOCIAL CUSTOMS) IN RADIO
The magic mating-call letters for Desperate and dateless singles are WKRC in Cincinnati [phone in program hosted by deejay J. B. Miller] il por *People Weekly* 32:59 Jl 24 '89
DATING (SOCIAL CUSTOMS) IN TELEVISION
TV dating. G. Hirshey. il *Utne Reader* p54-5 Mr/Ap '89
DATING (SOCIAL CUSTOMS) SERVICES
The data game [cover story] J. Bennet. *The New Republic* 200:20-2 F 13 '89
DATS (DIGITAL AUDIO TAPE RECORDERS AND RECORDING) *See* Digital audio tape recorders and recording
DAUBERVAL, JEAN, 1742-1806
about
La fille mal gardée [ballet] Reviews
Dance Magazine il 63:9 Jl '89. R. C. Lamont
D'AUBUISSON, ROBERTO
about
Confessions of an assassin. D. Farah and T. Gibb. por *Mother Jones* 14:10+ Ja '89
Demonizing D'Aubuisson. J. Morley. il *The Nation* 248:624-6 My 8 '89
DAUGHTERS AND PARENTS *See* Parent-child relationship
DAUGHTERS OF DIVORCED PARENTS *See* Children of divorced parents
D'AULAIRE, EMILY
Animal stars. il *Good Housekeeping* 208:60+ My '89
(jt. auth) See D'Aulaire, Per Ola, and D'Aulaire, Emily

D'AULAIRE, PER OLA, AND D'AULAIRE, EMILY
"Don't let my father die!". il *Reader's Digest* 134:115-20 Je '89
Killer on the loose? il *Reader's Digest* 134:64-70 Ja '89
Too tough to die. il *Reader's Digest* 135:81-6 N '89
DAULTE, FRANÇOIS, 1928-
about
Scholarly sleuth. E. Beck. il por *Art News* 88:83-4 O '89
DAUM, RAYMOND
Garbo talks (a little). il pors *Life* 12:96-8+ Spr '89
DAUTRESME, BÉATRICE
about
Beauty at a fair price. il pors *Harper's Bazaar* 122:192-3+ Mr '89
DAVATELIS, GEORGE, AND OTHERS
Macrophage inflammatory protein-1: a prostaglandin-independent endogenous pyrogen. bibl f il *Science* 243:1066-8 F 24 '89
DAVENPORT, SUZANNE
(jt. auth) See Moore, Donald R., and Davenport, Suzanne
DAVEY, JOCELYN See Raphael, Chaim
DAVEY TREE EXPERT CO.
Men working in trees [tree surgeon R. Hill] J. Stuller. il por *Audubon* 91:86-91 Jl '89
DAVI, ROBERT
about
Don't get cute with Robert Davi. il pors *Gentlemen's Quarterly* 59:132-5 Jl '89
DAVID, C. DORMAN
about
Lone Star fakes. L. Belkin. il pors *The New York Times Magazine* p66+ D 10 '89
DAVID, IRENE
(jt. auth) See David, Lester, and David, Irene
DAVID, JAY See Adler, Bill, 1929-
DAVID, JO, AND FILE, KAREN
Saintly companies that make heavenly profits [special section] il *Working Woman* 14:122-4+ O '89
DAVID, LAUREN
AIDS testing: are you positive you're negative? il *Mademoiselle* 95:138+ N '89
"It's 3 a.m. . . . where can I get some sleep!". il *Mademoiselle* 95:130 O '89
DAVID, LESTER
The family's first year. il pors *McCall's* 116:12-14 Ag '89
DAVID, LESTER, AND DAVID, IRENE
Paul Newman: sexy, surprising and almost 65. il pors *McCall's* 116:50-2+ Mr '89
DAVID, MORTON E.
about
Top-down lexicography. R. D. Hylton. il por *Forbes* 144:98-9 Jl 10 '89
DAVID GORDON/PICK UP COMPANY
Reviews:
United States performed at the Brooklyn Academy of Music. C. Hardy. *Dance Magazine* 63:94-5 Ap '89
DAVID J. GREENE AND COMPANY
Stocks that pass tough tests [interview with A. Greene] S. Smith. il por *Fortune* 119:36+ Ap 24 '89
DAVID K'S (NEW YORK, N.Y.: RESTAURANT) See New York (N.Y.)—Restaurants, nightclubs, bars, etc.
DAVID LINLEY FURNITURE LTD.
The crafty Viscount. L. Distelheim. il pors *Life* 12:165-6 Mr '89
The Viscount Linley: at home with a royal entrepreneur. E. Lambert. il por *Architectural Digest* 46:50+ F '89
DAVID PUSZH DANCE COMPANY
Reviews:
Performances in Evanston, Illinois. C. Survant. *Dance Magazine* 63:21+ F '89
DAVID SARNOFF RESEARCH CENTER
Sarnoff Center girds loins for global competition in HDTV. W. Sweet. *Physics Today* 42:63-5 Je '89
DAVIDOFF, ZINO
about
Seeing red. M. Kripalani. il por *Forbes* 144 Special Issue:370+ O 23 '89
DAVIDOFF & CIE
Seeing red. M. Kripalani. il por *Forbes* 144 Special Issue:370+ O 23 '89
DAVIDOWITZ, ESTHER
"Die mother father brother". il por *Redbook* 172:132-4+ Ap '89
Scared to death! Terror and tragedy at America's amusement parks. il por *Redbook* 173:106-7+ Jl '89
DAVIDSON, JEANNIE
about
Centerline: Jeannie Davidson. M. Sommers. por *Theatre Crafts* 23:10 My '89
DAVIDSON, JENNIFER
Confessions of a bloodthirsty flower child. il *Seventeen* 48:180 Mr '89
DAVIDSON, JOE
An agenda for the 1990s. il *Black Enterprise* 19:152-4+ Je '89

DAVIDSON, LEN
about
When neon signs were art. J. O'Dwyer. il pors *Americana* 17:50-5 My/Je '89
DAVIDSON, NICHOLAS, 1955-
The myths of feminism. il *National Review* 41:44+ My 19 '89
DAVIDSON, OSHA
Doing home work down on the farm. il *The Nation* 249:87-8+ Jl 17 '89
DAVIDSON, ROBYN, 1950-
Rock dreams. il *Mother Jones* 14:39-40 O '89
DAVIES, CHRISTIE
Solving the Rumanian problem. *National Review* 41:37 D 31 '89
DAVIES, DEREK
about
Looking toward the new Pacific century [interview] A. Balk. por *World Press Review* 36:34+ S '89
DAVIES, GAIL, 1948-
about
Country's queen of attitude. D. Gates. il por *Newsweek* 112:86+ My 22 '89
DAVIES, GRAYHAM
about
Dance takes hold in South Africa: rewriting the present. R. Nelan. il por *Dance Magazine* 63:54-8 F '89
DAVIES, MICHAEL
(tr) See Debray, Régis. Gorbachev's crisis of faith
(tr) See Debray, Régis. When God fails, Russia remains
DAVIES, OWEN
(jt. auth) See Cetron, Marvin J., and Davies, Owen
DAVIES, PETE, 1959-
The shooting party. il *Gentlemen's Quarterly* 59:330-4+ O '89
DAVIES, ROBERTSON, 1913-
A giant of the stage. il *Maclean's* 102:48-9 Jl 24 '89
Signing away Canada's soul [adaptation of address, May 1988] il *Harper's* 278:43-7 Ja '89
about
The muse of the north [interview] A. P. Sanoff. por *U.S. News & World Report* 106:61 Ja 16 '89
DAVIES, S. N. G.
The capitalism/socialism debate in East Asia. bibl *Society* 26:29-37 Mr/Ap '89
DAVIES, TERENCE
about
Distant voices, still lives [film] Reviews
The Nation 249:252-3 S 4-11 '89. S. Klawans
The New Yorker il 65:88-9 S 4 '89. T. Rafferty
Time il 134:78-9 Ag 14 '89. R. Corliss
DAVIES, WILLIAM ROBERTSON See Davies, Robertson, 1913-
DAVIS, AL
about
As time goes by, the Raiders should go back to Oakland. K. Garrett. il *Sport (New York, N.Y.)* 80:38 Ag '89
A happy homecoming. P. King. por *Sports Illustrated* 71:76 Jl 31 '89
Lord of the rings. R. Hoffer. il pors *Sports Illustrated* 71:104-8+ D 11 '89
DAVIS, ALEXANDER JACKSON, 1803-1892
about
A. J. Davis and American classicism [cover story] C. S. Laise. bibl f il por *Antiques* 136:1320-33 D '89
DAVIS, ANDREA R.
Pinkney: illustrating the point. il por *American Visions* 4:46-9 Ap '89
Wheeling and dealing. il *Essence* 20:96-8+ N '89
DAVIS, ANDREW
about
Above the law [film] Reviews
Video 12:83-4 Ja '89. D. Schweiger
The package [film] Reviews
Newsweek 114:68 S 4 '89. D. Ansen
People Weekly il 32:13 S 4 '89. R. Novak
DAVIS, ANGELA YVONNE, 1944-
about
Word star. P. Giddings. por *Essence* 20:24 Je '89
DAVIS, ANTHONY
about
A change of pace. T. Page. il por *Opera News* 53:24+ Je '89
Under the double moon [opera] Reviews
The New Yorker 65:68-9 Jl 31 '89. A. Porter
Opera News por 53:24+ Je '89. T. Page
DAVIS, BARRY K.
about
The many incarnations of Barry Davis. L. J. Nathans and D. Zigas. il por *Business Week* p94 My 29 '89
DAVIS, BERNARD DAVID
Government and quality in science. *Science* 246:736 N 10 '89
DAVIS, BERNARD DAVID, AND ROCHE, LISSA
Genetic engineering: sorcerer's apprentice or handmaiden to humanity? il *USA Today (Periodical)* 118:68-70 N '89

DAVIS, BETTE, 1908-1989
about
Bette [cover story] R. Schickel. il pors *Film Comment* 25:20-2+ Mr/Ap '89
Bette vs. Joan: Hollywood's hottest feud [excerpt from Bette and Joan] S. Considine. il pors *Ladies' Home Journal* 106:142-4+ O '89
Obituary
America 161:250 O 21 '89. G. W. Hunt
The American Spectator il 22:44-6 D '89. B. Bawer
Newsweek il pors 114:69 O 16 '89. J. Hammer
People Weekly il pors 32:82-6+ O 23 '89. B. Darrach
Time por 134:49 O 16 '89
Streep vs. Davis. pors *Life* 12:114-15 Spr '89
DAVIS, BOB
about
The little rocket that could. J. Kluger. il pors *Discover* 10:30+ F '89
DAVIS, CHERYL A.
An agency in trouble. il por *The Progressive* 53:13 Ja '89
DAVIS, CLAUDIA
about
Girl, 5, 1st in U.S. to get artificial ear. il por *Jet* 75:24 Ja 16 '89
DAVIS, CLIFTON
about
Clifton Davis, 'Amen' TV star visits children at La Rabida Hospital. il pors *Jet* 76:24-5 My 15 '89
Clifton Davis and Tempestt Bledsoe star in TV movie. A. Collier. il pors *Jet* 77:22-3+ O 16 '89
Clifton Davis lives his fantasy of being pilot. il por *Jet* 75:33 Ja 9 '89
Clifton Davis of 'Amen' gets honorary degree at Lincoln U. commencement. il pors *Jet* 76:16 My 29 '89
DAVIS, DANA
(jt. auth) See Gumpert, David E., and Davis, Dana
DAVIS, DARREL See Davis, Mouse
DAVIS, DOROTHY
about
Ova to you, Dorothy Davis, egg fancier extraordinaire. il por *People Weekly* 31:94 Mr 27 '89
DAVIS, DOROTHY SALISBURY, 1916-
It's entertainment. *The Writer* 102:12-14 Jl '89
DAVIS, DOUGLAS, 1933-
Slaying the neo-modern dragon. il *Art in America* 77:43-5+ Ja '89
DAVIS, ERNIE, 1939-1963
about
A life cut short. W. Nack. il pors *Sports Illustrated* 71:136-46 S 4 '89
DAVIS, FRANCIS
An American in Paris. il por *The Atlantic* 264:120+ N '89
Blowing in from Chicago. il *The Atlantic* 263:71-3 F '89
DAVIS, GEENA
about
America's 10 most beautiful women. T. Johnson. il pors *Harper's Bazaar* 122:180+ S '89
The couple that stars together . . . R. Gehr. il por *Video* 13:14-15 N '89
Married . . . with chicken [cover story] J. Schneller. il pors *Gentlemen's Quarterly* 59:222-7+ Je '89
Unique star quality. Y. Z. McDonough. il pors *Harper's Bazaar* 122:208-15+ Ap '89
What's so strange about Geena Davis? B. Handy. por *Rolling Stone* p43-4 Mr 23 '89
DAVIS, GEORGE N.
Wilderness: New York sets a global stage. il pors *The Conservationist* 44:2-9+ N/D '89
DAVIS, GLENN
about
Glenn Davis. S. Kanfer. il por *People Weekly* 32 Special Issue:125 Fall '89
DAVIS, ISABEL
Sixteen—the third time around. il *The New York Times Magazine* p22+ D 17 '89
DAVIS, J. P.
What men love about the women of summer. il *Glamour* 87:170-1+ Jl '89
What men really want in bed. il *Glamour* 87:256-7+ Je '89
DAVIS, JAMES KOTSILIBAS- See Kotsilibas-Davis, James
DAVIS, JAMES WARREN, 1935-
Bring back the draft. il *USA Today (Periodical)* 118:12-13 S '89
DAVIS, JEFFERSON, 1808-1889
about
Jefferson Davis called them home. il por *Southern Living* 24:24 Ag '89
This one spells o-o-p-s. il *Newsweek* 113:50 My 1 '89
The White House of the Confederacy: restoring the historic residence of President Jefferson Davis. J. S. Wamsley. il *Architectural Digest* 46:262-9 O '89
DAVIS, JOHN D.
The Lowry Dale Kirby Collection of old Sheffield plate. il *Antiques* 136:848-59 O '89
DAVIS, JOSEPH A.
The grand plans of Congressman Udall. il por *Sierra* 74:86-8+ My/Je '89

DAVIS, JUNIOR
about
The eggs. B. McCollister. por *The Humanist* 49:39 N/D '89
Future shock. il *Time* 133:42 Mr 27 '89
Tempest in a test tube. J. Seligmann. il pors *Newsweek* 114:66-7 Ag 21 '89
Whose lives are these? A. L. Sanders. il pors *Time* 134:19 O 2 '89
DAVIS, K. E., AND OTHERS
Disorder-to-order transition in settling suspensions of colloidal silica: X-ray measurements. bibl f il *Science* 245:507-10 Ag 4 '89
DAVIS, KATHIE
Pregnant and fit. bibl il pors *Women's Sports & Fitness* 11:50-5 Je '89
DAVIS, KEITH F., 1952-
The Hallmark Photographic Collection: a commitment to fine photography. il *USA Today (Periodical)* 117:54-63 Ja '89
DAVIS, L. J. (LAWRENCE J.)
Hollywood's most secret agent [cover story] il pors *The New York Times Magazine* p24-7+ Jl 9 '89
Philip Morris's big bite [cover story] il por *The New York Times Magazine* p30-3+ Ap 9 '89
DAVIS, LAWRENCE J. See Davis, L. J. (Lawrence J.)
DAVIS, LEILA
Another medium for the message. il *Nation's Business* 77:54-6 Ag '89
Wider uses for bar codes. il *Nation's Business* 77:34+ Mr '89
DAVIS, LENNARD J., 1949-
Raising vegetarian kids. il *Parents* 64:190 Jl '89
DAVIS, LINDSAY
about
Sam Spade in ancient Rome. S. J. Evans. il *History Today* 39:4-5 Jl '89
DAVIS, MARTHA
about
One point of light. D. Finkel. il pors *Esquire* 112:123-8+ O '89
DAVIS, MARTIN S.
about
"Lead, follow, or get out of the way". il por *Time* 133:43 Je 19 '89
DAVIS, MARVIN
about
Davis' bid prompts UAL to weigh alternatives. C. Fotos. il *Aviation Week & Space Technology* 131:21-2 Ag 14 '89
Davis increases bid for UAL, threatens to oust board if offer is rejected. *Aviation Week & Space Technology* 131:95 Ag 21 '89
Davis ups buyout bid for United but pilot offer still stronger. J. Ott and C. A. Shifrin. il *Aviation Week & Space Technology* 131:126-7 S 11 '89
He's hungry to buy an airline. J. Castro. il por *Time* 134:42 Ag 21 '89
In hot pursuit of airlines. L. Reibstein. il por *Newsweek* 114:40 Ag 21 '89
The Marvin Davis mystique: less than meets the eye? R. Grover and C. Welles. il por *Business Week* p70-1 Ag 28 '89
Northwest asks pilots to cooperate in thwarting hostile takeover. *Aviation Week & Space Technology* 130:106 My 1 '89
NWA seeks strategy to block Davis' $3.1-billion takeover attempt. *Aviation Week & Space Technology* 130:107 Ap 24 '89
Pan Am Corp., Davis among Northwest bidders. C. Fotos. il *Aviation Week & Space Technology* 130:108-9 Je 5 '89
A squeeze play at Northwest. C. Power. il *Business Week* p30 My 1 '89
"This will be all-out war". J. Greenwald. il por *Time* 133:46 Ap 17 '89
UAL investigates alternatives to Davis' $6.19-billion takeover bid. C. Fotos. *Aviation Week & Space Technology* 131:70 Ag 28 '89
Unions, Minnesota officials vow to fight any break-up of Northwest. *Aviation Week & Space Technology* 130:90 Ap 10 '89
DAVIS, MARY SUE
about
The eggs. B. McCollister. por *The Humanist* 49:39 N/D '89
Future shock. il *Time* 133:42 Mr 27 '89
Tempest in a test tube. J. Seligmann. il pors *Newsweek* 114:66-7 Ag 21 '89
Whose lives are these? A. L. Sanders. il pors *Time* 134:19 O 2 '89
Anecdotes, facetiae, satire, etc.
People in Petri dishes. M. Ivins. il *The Progressive* 53:38 N '89
DAVIS, MILES
about
Jazz. W. Balliett. *The New Yorker* 65:153-5 D 4 '89

DAVIS, MILES—about—cont.
A master class in Times Square. F. Goodman. il por *Rolling Stone* p12 Ja 26 '89
Miles [interview; reprint] N. Hentoff. il por *Down Beat* 56:46-7 S '89
An open letter to Miles Davis [reprint] C. Mingus. il por *Down Beat* 56:48 S '89

DAVIS, MOUSE
about
Building a better Mousetrap. R. Telander. il por *Sports Illustrated* 71:66-70+ S 11 '89
Run 'n' Shoot. J. D. Miller. il por *Sport (New York, N.Y.)* 80:38-40+ Jl '89

DAVIS, NAN DOAK- See Doak-Davis, Nan
DAVIS, OSSIE, 1917-
Challenge for the year 2000. *The Nation* 249:144-8 Jl 24-31 '89

DAVIS, PETER
about
With a lineup like this, who needs charisma? M. Maremont. il por *Business Week* p59 My 22 '89

DAVIS, PETER G.
Music. See issues of New York
Passing the baton. il *New York* 22:82-6+ My 15 '89

DAVIS, ROBBIE
about
The longest ride. W. Nack. il pors *Sports Illustrated* 70:116-20+ Mr 20 '89

DAVIS, ROBERT
about
Coming of age. B. Dunlop. il map *Architectural Record* 177:96-103 Jl '89

DAVIS, ROBERT GORHAM
Back to the '60s: five post-mortems on years of campus violence. il *Change* 20:48-53 N/D '88

DAVIS, SAMMY, JR.
about
Given the chance to wish Sammy Davis well, no one in Hollywood stayed home. il pors *People Weekly* 32:50-1 N 27 '89
Hollywood honors Sammy Davis Jr.'s 60 years in show business [cover story] A. Collier. il pors *Jet* 77:52-9 D 4 '89
Sammy Davis, Jr. and Gregory Hines move to the beat in 'Tap' [cover story] il por *Jet* 75:58-61 F 13 '89
Sammy Davis Jr. treated for throat malignancy. il por *Jet* 76:54-5 S 25 '89

DAVIS, SAMMY, JR., AND OTHERS
Sammy Davis Jr. and . . . the trailblazing years [excerpt from Why me?] il por *TV Guide* 37:20-3 Mr 25-31 '89
Sammy Davis Jr. faces life, aging and cocaine [excerpt from Why me?] il pors *Ebony* 44:66+ Jl '89

DAVIS, SHELBY CULLOM
about
Three raging bulls and two restrained ones. R. King. il pors *Forbes* 144 Special Issue:362+ O 23 '89

DAVIS, SUSAN PEARSON- See Pearson-Davis, Susan
DAVIS, THULANI
Local hero. il pors *American Film* 14:26-7 Jl/Ag '89
DAVIS, VICTOR, D. 1989
about
An untimely end. B. Wickens. il por *Maclean's* 102:68 N 27 '89

DAVIS, WADE
about
Chemistry of voodoo. M. Kemp. il *Discover* 10:26-8 Ja '89

DAVIS (CALIF.)
City planning
Creative alternatives to urban sprawl: a tale of two cities. T. Oppenheimer. il *Utne Reader* p95-8 Mr/Ap '89

DAVIS (WILLIAM) COMPUTER RESEARCH CENTER See William Davis Computer Research Center
DAVIS WATER & WASTE INDUSTRIES, INC.
Waste not, want not. J. Cook. il por *Forbes* 144:191-2 O 16 '89

DAVISON, PETER
Autobiographer [poem] *The American Scholar* 58:188 Spr '89
Generations of swan [poem] il *The Atlantic* 264:59 Jl '89
The hub of the solar system. il map *American Heritage* 40:54-6+ Ap '89
The passing of Thistle [poem] il *The Atlantic* 264:71 S '89

DAWDLING See Procrastination
DAWES, JOSEPH
The business-education link. il por *Nation's Business* 77:27 Je '89

DAWES, ROBYN M., AND OTHERS
Clinical versus actuarial judgment. bibl f *Science* 243:1668-74 Mr 31 '89

DAWIDOFF, NICHOLAS
The best little ballpark in Texas (or anywhere else). il *Sports Illustrated* 71:58-64+ Jl 31 '89
Gold amid the coal. il por *Sports Illustrated* 70:44-6+ Ja 16 '89
Men: what do they expect from marriage today? il *Glamour* 87:236-9+ My '89

Too good to be left out. por *Sports Illustrated* 70:118 Je 12 '89
about
From the publisher. D. J. Barr. il por *Sports Illustrated* 70:4 Je 12 '89
DAWIDOWICZ, LUCY S.
Perversions of the Holocaust. *Commentary* 88:56-60 O '89
about
PW interviews. W. Gelles. por *Publishers Weekly* 235:264-5 My 12 '89

DAWN See Sunrise
DAWSON, DEBORAH L.
about
Get ready for life after motherhood. il por *Nation's Business* 77:52 O '89

DAWSON, GREG
Ted Turner [cover story; interview] il pors *American Film* 14:36-9+ Ja/F '89

DAWSON, JOHN MYRICK, 1930-
Plasma particle accelerators. bibl il *Scientific American* 260:54-61 Mr '89

DAWSON, KEITH, AND NIXON, LAURA
Looking it up. il *Publishers Weekly* 236:18+ Jl 14 '89

DAWSON, MARIE
"I can't have breast cancer—I'm only 35!". il *Ladies' Home Journal* 106:104+ N '89

DAWSON, TONY
A poisoned dart in Alaska's heart. il *Audubon* 91:90-1 S '89

DAWSON-MEDINA, LESLIE
Women at work: Holly Eissler. il pors *Ms.* 18:34-6 O '89

DAY, BURKE
Butterfly paradise. il *The Saturday Evening Post* 261:62-3 Jl/Ag '89

DAY, JEANNE PAULSON
Pour salt-free freshness on salads. il *The Saturday Evening Post* 261:18-21 O '89

DAY, KATHLEEN
When hell sleazes over [cover story] *The New Republic* 200:26-30 Mr 20 '89

DAY, MARK R.
Out of sight, out of time. il *Américas* 41 no2:11-15 '89

DAY, PAT, 1954?-
about
Day of reckoning. J. E. Vader. il pors *Sports Illustrated* 70:74-6+ My 1 '89

DAY, ROBERT, 1941-
Carry from Kansas became a Nation all unto herself. il pors *Smithsonian* 20:147-8+ Ap '89
'Sooners' or 'Goners,' they were hellbent on grabbing free land. bibl (p247) il map *Smithsonian* 20:192-4+ N '89

DAY, SAMUEL H.
about
Sam Day's example. E. Knoll. *The Progressive* 53:4 Je '89

DAY
Dem bones, dem bones [Chinese oracle bone shows evidence of shorter days; work of Kevin D. Pang] A. Fisher. *Popular Science* 235:12 S '89
Length-of-day variations caused by El Niño-Southern Oscillation and Quasi-Biennial Oscillation. B. F. Chao. bibl f il *Science* 243:923-5 F 17 '89
Oracle bone shows a once-shorter day [work of Kevin D. Pang] I. Peterson. *Science News* 135:374 Je 17 '89
Stratospheric winds alter day's length [research by B. Fong Chao] R. Monastersky. *Science News* 135:102 F 18 '89
Turtle logic [engraved tortoise shell shows rotation of earth is slowing; research by Kevin Pang] T. Waters. il *Discover* 10:16 D '89

DAY BUTTERFLY CENTER See Callaway Gardens. Day Butterfly Center

DAY CARE
See also
After school programs
Church and day care
Play groups
School of the 21st Century (Program)
America's child-care crisis: the first tiny steps toward solutions. S. B. Garland. il *Business Week* p64-5+ Jl 10 '89
Brighter afternoons for latchkey children [involving seniors in day care programs] il *Aging* no359:20-1 '89
Child care news. See issues of Parents beginning February 1989
The child-care patchwork. I. Nyborg-Andersen and P. G. O'Brien. il *Ladies' Home Journal* 106:199-200+ N '89
Choosing safe day care [views of Barbara Willer] S. Mahler. il *McCall's* 117:62 N '89
CMV a risk in child care [research by Stuart Adler] J. Raloff. *Science News* 136:327 N 18 '89
Day care: are we shortchanging our kids? [with editorial comment by David Jordan] P. Krantz. il *Better Homes and Gardens* 67:14, 20+ Je '89
Day care for sick kids. R. Levine. *American Health* 8:108 Ap '89
The day care generation. P. Wingert and B. Kantrowitz. il *Newsweek* 114 Special Issue:86-7+ Wint '89/Spr '90
Day care: the new surrogacy. G. F. Kreyche. il *USA Today (Periodical)* 118:91-3 S '89

DAY CARE—*cont.*

Designing programs for infant day care. W. F. Hignett. *The Education Digest* 54:62-3 F '89

Guide to infant day care research [Infants, families and child care] *Children Today* 18:3-4 Ja/F '89

Juggling jobs and child care [report titled One hundred working women] *Children Today* 18:3 Ja/F '89

Old baggage, new visions: shaping policy for early childhood programs [cover story; with editorial comment by Pauline B. Gough] A. W. Mitchell. bibl f il *Phi Delta Kappan* 70:658, 664-72 My '89

Old hands [senior citizens working at a day care center in Union City, N.J.] C. Dowling. il *Life* 12:102-4+ D '89

Quality counts in day care [research by Deborah Vandell and others] G. W. Bracey. il *Phi Delta Kappan* 70:409-10 Ja '89

Singing the child-care blues. A. P. Murphy. il *Parents* 64:6 F '89

Who's minding the children? il *Black Enterprise* 19:35 Jl '89

Who's watching the kids? C. Tevis. il *Successful Farming* 87:64+ S '89

The working mom's handbook [special section] il *Ladies' Home Journal* 106:55-6+ Ag '89

Chain and franchise operations

See also
Kinder-Care Learning Centers Inc.

Federal aid

The ABCs of child care [Senate passes the Act for Better Child Care] N. Traver. il *Time* 134:17 Jl 3 '89

Catching up on child care. M. B. Carlson. il *Time* 134:36 O 16 '89

Child care: as easy as ABC? D. Slingluff. *Christianity Today* 33:47 S 8 '89

A child care bill will pass as soon as the Democrats grow up. S. B. Garland. il *Business Week* p73 D 11 '89

Child care bills confront new Congress. E. J. Larson. il *Christianity Today* 33:53-4 F 3 '89

Congress delivers new child care bill. L. Brown. il *Black Enterprise* 20:27 S '89

The day-care deadline. S. Mernit. *Harper's Bazaar* 122:65+ Jl '89

The day-care reform juggernaut. R. Haskins and H. Brown. il *National Review* 41:40-1 Mr 10 '89

Do congressmen have mothers? M. Gallagher. *National Review* 41:38-9+ O 27 '89

Letter from the president. G. Bush. il por *Parents* 64:45 Mr '89

Options for child care. il *Nation's Business* 77:79 Mr '89

Politicians discover children. K. A. Lawton. il *Christianity Today* 33:34-6 Mr 17 '89

A really spooky security blanket [day care center opens at CIA headquarters] il *Newsweek* 114:100 N 27 '89

Suffer the little children [Act for Better Child Care] S. T. Mandel. il *National Review* 41:20-1 S 1 '89

Sure, spend more on child care. But spend wisely. G. S. Becker. il *Business Week* p24 My 8 '89

Laws and regulations

An "accommodating" Court [Supreme Court lets stand a licensing law that allows child care centers run by religious organizations to seek an exempt status] D. Neff. *Christianity Today* 33:15 Mr 3 '89

Sanitation

In day-care centers, cleanliness is a must. F. E. Young. il *FDA Consumer* 23:5-6 Jl/Ag '89

Canada

The high cost of child care. A. Walmsley. *Maclean's* 102:60 N 6 '89

China

Children and child care in China: some observations. E. S. Galvin. il *Children Today* 18:19-23 My/Je '89

DAY CARE AND INDUSTRY

See also
Dependent care (Employee benefits)

A center of quality. il *Nation's Business* 77:8 O '89

Corporate nannies for a new decade [businesses coping with family issues] B. Brophy. il *U.S. News & World Report* 107:70+ D 25 '89-Ja 1 '90

The corporation vs. the family: can the conflict be resolved? [special section] il *Working Woman* 14:125-7+ N '89

Make room for the children. N. Thomas-Cote. por *Nation's Business* 77:13 O '89

DAY CARE FOR EMOTIONALLY DISTURBED CHILDREN

Intensive day treatment provides an alternative to residential care [Phoenix program in Moline, Ill.] J. Hamm. il *Children Today* 18:11-15 S/O '89

DAY CARE WORKERS

Attitudes

What do they really think of us? Child-care workers talk candidly to moms. D. Sobel. il *Ladies' Home Journal* 106:70 Ag '89

Crime

Making history—of a dubious sort [McMartin Preschool trial] *U.S. News & World Report* 106:20 My 1 '89

Salaries, pensions, etc.

Staff turnover may be day care's biggest problem. J. P. Shapiro. *U.S. News & World Report* 107:33 O 23 '89

DAY-LEWIS, DANIEL

about
My left foot. A. Insdorf. *American Film* 15:64-5 D '89

A special effect. C. Cozzone. il por *Harper's Bazaar* 122:84+ N '89

DAY LILIES *See* Daylilies

DAY OF JUDGMENT *See* Judgment Day

DAY OF THE DEAD *See* All Souls' Day

DAY OF THE DEAD (SAN FRANCISCO, CALIF.: FESTIVAL) *See* San Francisco (Calif.)—Festivals

DAY ONE [television program] *See* Television program reviews—Single works

DAY-TIMERS (FIRM)

To sell in Japan, meet the Japanese. R. C. Dorney. il *Nation's Business* 77:10 F '89

DAYBREAK *See* Sunrise

DAYDREAMS *See* Fantasy

DAYLIGHT

Living on borrowed light [architectural use of daylight] J. S. Russell. il *Architectural Record* 177:150-3 My '89

DAYLIGHT SAVING

Washington diarist. H. Fairlie. *The New Republic* 200:43 Ap 24 '89

DAYLILIES

Consider the daylilies. A. Lovejoy. il *House & Garden* 161:68+ Je '89

DAYS

See also
Birthdays

DAYS INNS CORP.

Cultivating the gray [managing seniors] D. Machan. il pors *Forbes* 144:126+ S 4 '89

DAYS OF RAGE [television program] *See* Television program reviews—Single works

DAYTON, ELAHE T., AND OTHERS

Functional analysis of CAR, the target sequence for the Rev protein of HIV-1. bibl f il *Science* 246:1625-9 D 22 '89

DAYTON, PAUL K.

Interdecadal variation in an Antarctic sponge and its predators from oceanographic climate shifts. bibl f il *Science* 245:1484-6 S 29 '89

DAYTON (OHIO)

Religious institutions and affairs

A Catholic taste in clothes [dress code at Sacred Heart Church] il por *Newsweek* 114:27 S 18 '89

DAYTON-HUDSON CORP.

From punching bag to retailing black belt. R. Mitchell. il por *Business Week* p62+ N 20 '89

Rounding out with lateral moves [vice president of human resources S. Boren] L. Dusky. il por *Working Woman* 14:112 O '89

DAYTONA 500 *See* Automobile racing

DAYTONA SPEED WEEK *See* Motorcycle racing

DBASE (DATABASE MANAGEMENT SYSTEM) *See* Relational databases

DBCP *See* Dibromochloropropane

DC-10 AIRPLANES *See* Airplanes, Jet

DC3 (SANTA MONICA, CALIF.: RESTAURANT) *See* Santa Monica (Calif.)—Restaurants, nightclubs, bars, etc.

DDI (DRUG) *See* Dideoxyinosine

DE ALBUQUERQUE, LUIS *See* Albuquerque, Luis de

DE ANDRADE, JOAQUIM PEDRO *See* Andrade, Joaquim Pedro de

DE ANGELIS, BARBARA

Try a little tenderness. *Redbook* 173:98-9+ Je '89

DE ARAUJO, CARLOS A. PAZ *See* Paz de Araujo, Carlos A.

DE BELLEVAL, DENIS

about
Via's rocky future. M. Clark. il por *Maclean's* 102:17 My 15 '89

DE BENEDETTI, CARLO

about
A firestorm scorches De Benedetti's media empire. J. Rossant. il pors *Business Week* p68 D 25 '89-Ja 1 '90

DE BLAQUIER, NELLY ARRIETA *See* Blaquier, Nelly Arrieta de

DE BLIJ, HARM J.

Greenhouse effect? *Focus (New York, N.Y.: 1950)* 39:37 Spr '89

Rise of the lowly blenders. *Focus (New York, N.Y.: 1950)* 39:37 Fall '89

Wine list geography. *Focus (New York, N.Y.: 1950)* 39:37 Summ '89

DE CAMÕES, LUÍS *See* Camões, Luís de, 1524?-1580

DE CAMP, L. SPRAGUE (LYON SPRAGUE), 1907-

Brachiating in the family tree. il por *The Humanist* 49:9-12+ Mr/Ap '89

DE CAMP, LYON SPRAGUE *See* De Camp, L. Sprague (Lyon Sprague), 1907-

DE CANSON, SUZANNE *See* Canson, Suzanne de, d. 1986

DE CASTELBAJAC, JEAN-CHARLES *See* Castelbajac, Jean-Charles de

DE CASTELBAJAC, KATE *See* Castelbajac, Kate de
DE CHABRIS, FELICIA
    about
Timely obsessions. M. Guralnick. il pors *House & Garden* 161:94+ S '89
DE CHAMORRO, VIOLETA BARRIOS *See* Chamorro, Violeta Barrios de
DE CLAVIÈRE D'HUST, ANNE-MARIE *See* Clavière d'Hust, Anne-Marie de, comtesse
DE CLAVIÈRE D'HUST, BERNARD *See* Clavière d'Hust, Bernard de, comte
DE COMINES, PHILLIPE *See* Comines, Philippe de, sieur d'Argenton, 1445?-1511
DE DAMPIERRE, FLORENCE *See* Dampierre, Florence de
DE DUBOVAY, DIANE
    A triumph of spirit. il pors *Ladies' Home Journal* 106:62+ S '89
DE FELS, LAURE
    about
Gallic aristocrat. N. Frey. il pors *Harper's Bazaar* 122:114-19 Jl '89
DE FOREST, CALVERT *See* Melman, Larry Bud
DE FORTABAT, AMALIA *See* Fortabat, Amalia de
DE FOUCHECOUR, CHARLES-HENRI *See* Fouchecour, Charles-Henri de
DE GANAY, BIRGITTE *See* Ganay, Birgitte de
DE GANAY, CHARLES *See* Ganay, Charles, comte de
DE GAULLE, CHARLES *See* Gaulle, Charles de, 1890-1970
DE GREIFF, MÓNICA
    about
A minister under fire. A. Bilski. *Maclean's* 102:20 S 11 '89
DE GRUCHY, JOHN W.
A new phase in the antiapartheid struggle? *The Christian Century* 106:1078-9 N 22 '89
DE HAMEL, CHRISTOPHER, 1950-
    about
Profiles. I. Shenker. il por *The New Yorker* 65:48+ My 29 '89
DE HARTOG, JAN *See* Hartog, Jan de, 1914-
DE HAVILLAND AIRCRAFT OF CANADA, LIMITED *See* DeHavilland Aircraft of Canada, Limited
DE HOFFMANN, FREDERIC, 1924-1989
    about
The race to build the bomb. D. O. Relin. il *Scholastic Update (Teachers' edition)* 122:11-13 O 6 '89
DE JONGE, PETER
A Soviet hoopster in the Promised Land. il pors *The New York Times Magazine* p64+ N 5 '89
DE KLERK, FREDERIK WILLEM
    about
The beginning of the end of apartheid? S. V. Roberts. il *U.S. News & World Report* 107:55 O 30 '89
Botha vs. De Klerk: same song, different singer? F. D. Brown. il *Black Enterprise* 20:26 N '89
Brother against brother. S. MacLeod. il pors *Time* 134:49 O 9 '89
The divisions in South Africa get even deeper. J. Kapstein. il por *Business Week* p55 S 18 '89
The end of an era: President Botha bids a resentful goodbye. A. Bilski. il por *Maclean's* 102:22 Ag 28 '89
'F.W.' brings cautious hope for reform. B. Schiller. *World Press Review* 36:30-1 N '89
Falling apartheid. M. R. Hoffenberg. *The New Republic* 201:16-17 Jl 31 '89
The great white hope. B. W. Nelan. il por *Time* 134:42 S 11 '89
An heir apparent in the march to Pretoria. por *Newsweek* 113:35 F 13 '89
How far will De Klerk go? C. S. Wren. il por *The New York Times Magazine* p42-3+ N 19 '89
In the teeth of the 'Great Crocodile'. S. Reiss. il pors *Newsweek* 113:39 Mr 27 '89
Meeting of different minds. S. MacLeod. il pors *Time* 134:28 D 25 '89
Moving to the next stage. M. Gevisser. il *The Nation* 249:674+ D 4 '89
The need to break the stalemate. M. Swilling. il por *World Press Review* 36:32 N '89
New steps in a freedom walk. il *U.S. News & World Report* 107:17 O 23 '89
Peace at the mouth of the water cannon. il por *U.S. News & World Report* 107:14 S 25 '89
Pretoriastroika? *The New Republic* 201:9 O 23 '89
Return of the Great Crocodile. B. W. Nelan. il por *Time* 133:56 Mr 27 '89
Showdown in Cape Town. M. Nemeth. por *Maclean's* 102:30 Mr 27 '89
South Africa: a step forward on Namibia, a step backward at home? A. Fine. il *Business Week* p66 Mr 13 '89
South Africa: the squeeze is on. J. Kapstein. il por *Business Week* p44-5+ S 11 '89
South Africa's violent rage [cover story; special section; with editorial comment by Kevin Doyle] il pors *Maclean's* 102:4, 32-6+ S 18 '89
Squeezed left, squeezed right. B. W. Nelan. il por *Time* 134:46-7 S 18 '89

Stopping apartheid on the beach. il *U.S. News & World Report* 107:14+ N 27 '89
'We're committed to reform, and we really mean business' [interview] S. Reiss and W. Claiborne. il por *Newsweek* 114:70 D 4 '89
DE KLERK, WILLEM, 1928-
    about
Brother against brother. S. MacLeod. il pors *Time* 134:49 O 9 '89
DE KLOET, E. R. *See* Kloet, E. R. de
DE KOENIGSWARTER, PANNONICA *See* Koenigswarter, Pannonica de, Baroness, 1913-1988
DE KOONING, LISA
    about
De Kooning's co-conservators. A. Decker. il pors *Art News* 88:58 O '89
Who will represent de Kooning? A. Decker. il pors *Art News* 88:136-41 Summ '89
DE KOONING, WILLEM, 1904-
    about
De Kooning's co-conservators. A. Decker. il pors *Art News* 88:58 O '89
Who will represent de Kooning? A. Decker. il pors *Art News* 88:136-41 Summ '89
DE KOSTER, OTILIA *See* Koster, Otilia de
DE LA FALAISE, LUCIE *See* La Falaise, Lucie de
DE LA FRESSANGE, INÈS *See* La Fressange, Inès de
DE LA FUENTE, PAT
Beyond Baby M: the controversy over surrogate motherhood. il *Utne Reader* p118-21+ My/Je '89
DE LA GUARDIA FONT, ANTONIO *See* Guardia Font, Antonio de la
DE LA RENTA, OSCAR
    about
Charmed circles. G. Howell. il pors *Vogue* 179:730-7 S '89
DE LA SOUL (MUSICAL GROUP)
De la Soul's hippie-hop. M. Azerrad. il *Rolling Stone* p22 My 4 '89
DE LACY, JUSTINE
SoHo-sur-Seine. il *House & Garden* 161:36+ Jl '89
DE LARA CASTRO, CARMEN *See* Lara Castro, Carmen de
DE L'ISLE, WILLIAM PHILIP SIDNEY, VISCOUNT
    about
'Not built to envious show'. F. Barker. il por *History Today* 39:3-4 Ap '89
DE LOREAN, CRISTINA *See* Ferrare, Cristina
DE MAN, PAUL
    about
The strange case of Paul de Man. D. Donoghue. il *The New York Review of Books* 36:32-7 Je 29 '89
DE MARGERIE, EMMANUEL *See* Margerie, Emmanuel de
DE MARIA, WALTER, 1935-
    about
Permutations in steel. K. Johnson. il *Art in America* 77:198-9 S '89
Walter De Maria: Moderna Museet. I. Lind. il *Art News* 88:188 Summ '89
DE MARIS, RON
In the Tetons [poem] *The Nation* 249:286 S 18 '89
DE MITA, CIRIACO
    about
Finding gold in the rubble. *Newsweek* 113:35 Ja 9 '89
Italy's DC recycles Forlani. S. F. Senigallia. il *The New Leader* 72:9-10 Mr 6 '89
DE MITA, LUIGI CIRIACO *See* De Mita, Ciriaco
DE MOLA, YOLANDA T.
The language of power. *America* 160:364-5 Ap 22 '89
DE MONVILLE, FRANCOIS-NICOLAS-HENRI RACINE *See* Monville, Francois-Nicolas-Henri Racine, baron de, 1737-1794
DE MORGAN, WILLIAM
    about
The drawings of William De Morgan. H. Young. bibl f il *Antiques* 135:1432-43 Je '89
DE MOUBRAY, AMICIA
Found objects. il *Vogue* 179:267-9+ D '89
DE NIRO, ROBERT, 1945?-
    about
If he can make it here . . . por *Time* 134:52 S 4 '89
Maximum expression [cover story] B. Paris. il pors *American Film* 15:30-7+ O '89
DE ONIS, JUAN
Brazil on the tightrope toward democracy. *Foreign Affairs* 68:127-43 Fall '89
DE PALMA, BRIAN
    about
Body count. G. Smith. il *Film Comment* 25:49-52 Jl/Ag '89
Casualties of war [film] Reviews
    The Christian Century 106:925-6 O 18 '89. S. Henderson
    Commonweal 116:502-3 S 22 '89. P. D. Baumann
    Gentlemen's Quarterly il 59:211+ S '89. K. Turan
    Maclean's il 102:46 Ag 21 '89. P. Hluchy
    The Nation 249:252 S 4-11 '89. S. Klawans
    National Review il 41:63-4 S 29 '89. J. Simon
    The New Republic 201:26-8 O 2 '89. S. Kauffmann
    New York il 22:53+ Ag 28 '89. D. Denby

DE PALMA, BRIAN—about—Casualties of war—*cont.*
The New Yorker 65:76-9 Ag 21 '89. P. Kael
Newsweek il 114:58 Ag 21 '89. D. Ansen
People Weekly il 32:17 Ag 28 '89. R. Novak
People Weekly il 32:47+ Ag 28 '89. M. H. J. Farrell
Rolling Stone il p31 S 7 '89. P. Travers
Time il 134:54 Ag 21 '89. R. Schickel
Cool head, hot images. B. Weber. il pors *The New York Times Magazine* p24-7+ My 21 '89
DE PASSE, SUZANNE
about
The 1989 Essence Awards [with editorial comment by Susan L. Taylor] il pors *Essence* 20:57-60+, 69 O '89
The golden dove. G. Button. il por *Forbes* 143:58-9 Ja 23 '89
Hitsville goes Hollywood. J. Castro. il por *Time* 133:51 Ja 30 '89
Motown soars with "Dove". S. Herbert. il por *Black Enterprise* 19:40 My '89
DE PIETRI, STEPHEN
about
A master showman imbues clothes with life. C. R. Milbank. il por *Architectural Digest* 46:88+ S '89
DE PREE, MAX
about
Advice to bosses: try a little kindness. J. Greenwald. il por *Time* 134:56 S 11 '89
DE PRÉMONVILLE, MYRÈNE
about
Nouvelle couture. A. LeClerc. il por *Harper's Bazaar* 122:46 N '89
DE RIBES, JACQUELINE *See* Ribes, Jacqueline de
DE ROSE, ROSE
about
By any other name. W. P. Rayner. il *House & Garden* 161:70+ My '89
DE ROY, TUI
March of the feathered thugs: Johnny Rook birds in the Falklands wreak havoc on an albatross colony. il *International Wildlife* 19:52-9 Mr/Ap '89
DE SAINT-BLANQUAT, HENRI *See* Saint-Blanquat, Henri de
DE SAUVAGE, FRÉDÉRIC, AND OCTAVE, JEAN-NOËL
A novel mRNA of the A4 amyloid precursor gene coding for a possibly secreted protein. bibl f il *Science* 245:651-3 Ag 11 '89
DE SERIGNY, EUGENIA *See* Serigny, Eugenia de
DE SILVA, NEVILLE
The thaw brings hope to Indochina. *World Press Review* 36:17-18 My '89
DE SOTO, HERNANDO *See* Soto, Hernando de
DE SOUSA, MARIA JOÃO LEAL *See* Sousa, Maria João Leal de
DE STAEBLER, STEPHEN *See* DeStaebler, Stephen, 1933-
DE TOCQUEVILLE, ALEXIS *See* Tocqueville, Alexis de
DE TOLEDANO, RALPH
Sound on disc. See occasional issues of National Review
DE TOMASO, ALEJANDRO, 1928-
about
De Tomaso fires back. *Motor Trend* 41:35 Ag '89
DE TOMASO INDUSTRIES, INC.
De Tomaso fires back. *Motor Trend* 41:35 Ag '89
DE VAUCOULEURS, GERARD HENRI *See* Vaucouleurs, Gerard Henri de
DE VEAUX, ALEXIS, 1948-
Alice Walker [cover story] il pors *Essence* 20:56-8+ S '89
DE VELASCO, ANAMELI MONROY *See* Monroy de Velasco, Anameli
DE VILLALPANDO, CRISTÓBAL *See* Villalpando, Cristóbal de
DE VINCK, CHRISTOPHER, 1951-
Acceptance [poem] *America* 161:314 N 11 '89
A neighbor's gift. il *Reader's Digest* 135:9 N '89
DE VITO, DANNY
about
Funny as hell [cover story] R. Seidenberg. il pors *American Film* 14:42-7+ S '89
Little boss man. J. Ressner. por *Rolling Stone* p40 N 16 '89
The War of the Roses [film] Reviews
Maclean's il por 102:62-4 D 11 '89. B. D. Johnson
Newsweek il 114:88 D 11 '89. D. Ansen
People Weekly il 32:15 D 18 '89. R. Novak
Time il 134:93 D 11 '89. R. Schickel
DE VITO, E. B.
Chrysanthemums [poem] *America* 161:267 O 28 '89
Graduates [poem] *The American Scholar* 58:282 Spr '89
Shadow picture [poem] *America* 160:63 Ja 28 '89
DE WERTH, GORDON
about
Headhunters in reverse. D. Machan. il pors *Forbes* 144:238-9 O 30 '89
DE YOUNG, WAYNE
about
Farmer/adviser puts his money where his advice is. *Successful Farming* 87:50E Ja '89

DE YOUNG (M. H.) MEMORIAL MUSEUM *See* M. H. De Young Memorial Museum
DE YTURBE, JEAN *See* Yturbe, Jean de
DE YTURBE, SANDY *See* Yturbe, Sandy de
DEACCESSIONING *See* Art galleries and museums—Deaccessioning
DEACIDIFICATION OF BOOKS *See* Books—Conservation and restoration
DEACON BLUE (MUSICAL GROUP)
Deacon Blue. D. Wild. il *Rolling Stone* p32 N 16 '89
THE DEAD [film] *See* Motion picture reviews—Single works
DEAD-BANG [film] *See* Motion picture reviews—Single works
DEAD BODIES
See also
Autopsies
DEAD CALM [film] *See* Motion picture reviews—Single works
DEAD MAN OUT [television program] *See* Television program reviews—Single works
DEAD POETS SOCIETY [film] *See* Motion picture reviews—Single works
DEAD RINGERS [film] *See* Motion picture reviews—Single works
DEAD SEA SCROLLS
The Dead Sea scrolls: a new perspective. N. Golb. *The American Scholar* 58:177-207 Spr '89
The Dead Sea scrolls—an exchange [discussion of Spring 1989 article] N. Golb. *The American Scholar* 58:626-32 Aut '89
The mystery of the Dead Sea scrolls. M. Nichols. il *Maclean's* 102:52+ D 11 '89
Scrolls scandal. *The Christian Century* 106:746 Ag 16-23 '89
Secrets of the Dead Sea scrolls. R. N. Ostling. il *Time* 134:71-2 Ag 14 '89
DEAF
Oliver Sacks journeys into the world of the deaf for title from California. por *Publishers Weekly* 235:28-9 My 26 '89
A strange and marvelous culture [O. Sacks' book Seeing voices] *U.S. News & World Report* 107:88 O 16 '89
Civil rights
The revolution at Gallaudet [students demand a deaf president] H. Orlans. il pors *Change* 21:8-18 Ja/F '89
Education
See also
Gallaudet University
Rachel remembers [poetry written by deaf student for teacher] R. McCord. *Reader's Digest* 135:170-2 D '89
Sink or swim in the mainstream [placement of hearing-impaired students R. and J. Visco in Pittsburgh] P. A. Zirkel. bibl f il *Phi Delta Kappan* 70:411-13 Ja '89
Equipment
See also
Computers and the deaf
Ear, Artificial
Hearing aids
High-tech aids offer new options to deaf, blind. il *The Futurist* 23:50-1 S/O '89
Means of communication
See also
Lipreading
Sign language
Recreation
See also
Deaf-Blind Trailblazers (Organization)
Sports
Enjoying a quiet success [Fordham woman basketball player C. Cass] W. F. Reed. il por *Sports Illustrated* 70:108 Ja 9 '89
Developing countries
Deafness and poverty in third-world countries. G. M. Anderson. il *America* 160:531-4 Je 3 '89
DEAF ACTORS AND ACTRESSES
Actress Marlee Matlin builds A bridge to silence to star in her first speaking role. P. Freeman. il pors *People Weekly* 31:158-60 Ap 10 '89
Marlee Matlin: breaking the silence. L. A. Walker. il pors *Ladies' Home Journal* 106:42+ Ap '89
DEAF-BLIND TRAILBLAZERS (ORGANIZATION)
The sights and smells of the mountains come vividly alive for the Deaf-Blind Trailblazers [horseback trip into the Pasayten Wilderness, Wash.] H. Shapiro. il *People Weekly* 32:99+ O 23 '89
DEAF CHILDREN
Language
A computer that helps [HandsOn] W. J. Hawkins. il *Popular Science* 234:50 Ap '89
The signs of silence [ability to learn English after mastering American Sign Language] S. Brownlee. il *U.S. News & World Report* 107:86+ O 16 '89
DEAFNESS
See also
Deaf
Hearing Education and Awareness for Rockers (Organization)
Noise—Physiological effects
Hold on to your hearing. D. Benzaia. il *The Saturday Evening Post* 261:40+ Ja/F '89

DEAFNESS—*cont.*
"I can't hear you". M. Callahan. il *Parents* 64:249-50+ N '89
Into the plug zone [effects of noise on rock musicians] T. Imbimbo. il *Seventeen* 48:65 F '89
My toughest campaign: hearing loss. C. H. Percy. il por *Modern Maturity* 32:88-91 Ap/My '89
We are helping—have you heard? [AARP actions] il *Modern Maturity* 32:96 Ap/My '89

DEÁK, GLORIA-GILDA, 1930-
Banished by Napoleon: the American exile of Baron and Baroness Hyde de Neuville. bibl f il pors *Antiques* 136:1148-57 N '89

DEAK, ISTVAN
The incomprehensible Holocaust [cover story] il *The New York Review of Books* 36:63-72 S 28 '89
The incomprehensible Holocaust: an exchange [discussion of September 28, 1989 article] il *The New York Review of Books* 36:62-5 D 21 '89

DEALERS, AUTOMOBILE *See* Automobile dealers; Black automobile dealers
DEALERS [film] *See* Motion picture reviews—Single works
DEALERSHIPS
A franchise? Or a dealership? M. I. Finney. il *Nation's Business* 77:63-4 Mr '89

DEAN, BILLY
about
Locked in bloodless combat, Billy Dean's foxy boxers show more jiggle than punch. il pors *People Weekly* 31:116-17 Mr 13 '89

DEAN, DAVID H.
(jt. auth) *See* Berkowitz, Edward D., and Dean, David H.

DEAN, DEBORAH GORE
about
Deborah Gore Dean. il por *People Weekly* 32:84-5 D 25 '89-Ja 1 '90

DEAN, JAMES, 1931-1955
Collectibles
Collecting James Dean memorabilia. R. J. Headrick, Jr. il pors *Antiques & Collecting Hobbies* 94:33-6+ Ap '89
Statues, portraits, etc.
Obsessed by James Dean, Japan's Seita Onishi makes a monument to that fallen rebel his cause. il por *People Weekly* 32:66-7 Ag 7 '89

DEAN, JONATHAN
Can NATO agree on arms control? il *Technology Review* 92:58-62+ O '89
Conventional talks: a good first round. il *The Bulletin of the Atomic Scientists* 45:26-31 O '89

DEAN, SIDNEY W., JR., AND SHAYON, ROBERT LEWIS
Grabbing an electronic bonanza [cover story] il *The Nation* 249:369+ O 9 '89

DEAN FOODS CO.
Ripe for the picking. C. Siler. il *Forbes* 143:110+ Ap 3 '89

DEAN WITTER REYNOLDS INC.
Dean Witter braces for a backlash in Boston [arrest of broker W. F. Curran] K. H. Hammonds. il por *Business Week* p86 Mr 6 '89

DEANDREA, JOHN, 1941-
about
John DeAndrea at Carlo Lamagna. K. Johnson. *Art in America* 77:203 S '89

DEANE (T.) INC. *See* T. Deane Inc.
DEANGELIS, DICK
The hurricane priest. il por *Weatherwise* 42:256-7 O '89

DEAR, JOHN, 1959-
The legacy of Horace McKenna. il *America* 160:170-2 F 25 '89

DEAR JOHN [television program] *See* Television program reviews—Single works

DEARDEN, JOHN, CARDINAL
about
Cardinal John F. Dearden: a remembrance. M. Cronyn. *America* 161:100-1 Ag 26-S 2 '89

DEARING, JAMES W.
(jt. auth) *See* Rogers, Everett M., and Dearing, James W.

DEATH
See also
Euthanasia
Funeral rites and ceremonies
Longevity
Near-death experiences
Resurrection
Right to die
Suicide
Wrongful death
Confronting the death of a parent. M. Silver. bibl il *U.S. News & World Report* 106:74-5 My 22 '89
Death of a secular humanist. M. Rosenbaum. *The Christian Century* 106:167-8 F 15 '89
"I wish I could hold you more" [cancer victim B. Wagner videotapes messages for his children before his death] B. Remsberg. il *Reader's Digest* 134:147-52 Je '89
Phenomena, comment and notes [nature walks taken with mother] J. P. Wiley, Jr. il *Smithsonian* 20:26+ Ag '89
Some mortal speculations. J. Daniel. *Wilderness* 52:14-15+ Summ '89

Causes
See also
Autopsies
Medical examiners (Law)
Mortality
Life's little gambles. B. Bryson. il *Reader's Digest* 135:61-2+ D '89

Psychology
See also
Children and death
Fear of death lawsuits
Grief
"All these things were loved by me" [excerpt from It was on fire when I lay down on it] R. Fulghum. il por *Good Housekeeping* 209:36 O '89
A death in the family 1989 [cover story] H. Epstein. il pors *New York* 22:34-43 N 27 '89
A letter to Fred [letter to dead husband] L. Clifton. il pors *Essence* 20:65-6 N '89
The lost art of dying. G. Turner. *World Press Review* 36:37-8 Je '89
My mother died too soon. J. Kaufman. il por *Glamour* 87:144+ N '89
A sense of direction [reflections on father's death] T. Brookes. il *The New York Times Magazine* p18+ Ap 30 '89
Turning loss into gain. R. Coles. il *New Choices for the Best Years* 29:85+ Jl '89
When old men went out of my life [father's death; excerpt from Sweet summer] B. M. Campbell. il pors *Essence* 20:58-60+ Je '89

Religious aspects
See also
Church work with the dying
Figuring out how to die well. W. H. Willimon. *The Christian Century* 106:838-9 S 27 '89
Health: the great escape. J. Garvey. il *Commonweal* 116:294-5 My 19 '89
How do we live with dying? P. Perkins. il *The Christian Century* 106:979 N 1 '89
On the triumph of memories. J. M. Wall. *The Christian Century* 106:899-900 O 11 '89

Terminology
The Man with the pictures. W. Safire. il *The New York Times Magazine* p14+ Je 18 '89

DEATH (BIOLOGY)
See also
Cell death

DEATH AND CHILDREN *See* Children and death
DEATH BENEFITS *See* Survivors' benefits
DEATH IN ART
Exhibitions
In the beginning was the word [J. Holzer's Laments] K. Larson. il *New York* 22:71 Ap 3 '89

DEATH NOTICES *See* Obituaries
DEATH OF GOD THEOLOGY
The dangerous God: a profile of William Hamilton [cover story] L. H. Steffen. *The Christian Century* 106:844-7 S 27 '89

DEATH PENALTY *See* Capital punishment
DEATH RATE *See* Mortality
DEATH ROW PRISONERS *See* Prisoners
DEATHERAGE, JIM
about
Reading, 'riting & running. R. Blount. il pors *Runner's World* 24:26-8 Ja '89

DEATS, RICHARD L.
Agony and hope in Armenia. *The Christian Century* 106:81-2 Ja 25 '89

DEAUVILLE FILM FESTIVAL *See* Motion picture festivals—France
DEBELLO, JOHN
about
Return of the killer tomatoes: the sequel [film] Reviews *Video* 12:86+ Ja '89. M. Pierson

DEBIT CARDS
The coming joys and possible jolts of shopping with a cash card. R. J. Klein. il *Money* 18:191-2 O '89
The era of debit cards. J. B. Quinn. il *Newsweek* 113:51 Ja 2 '89

DEBORD, GUY, 1931-
about
The invisible films of Guy Debord. C. Phillips. il por *Art in America* 77:190 O '89

DEBRAY, RÉGIS
Gorbachev's crisis of faith; tr. by Michael Davies. *Harper's* 278:22+ Ap '89
When God fails, Russia remains [tr. by Michael Davies] il *New Perspectives Quarterly* 5:30-3 Wint '88/'89

DEBRES, KAREN
(jt. auth) *See* Cole, John P., and DeBres, Karen
DEBRIS, SPACE *See* Space debris
DEBT
See also
Bankruptcy
Trade claims (Debt)
After euphoria, reality. F. E. Rowe. il *Forbes* 144:372 N 13 '89

DEBT—*cont.*

Are we over our heads in debt? il *Changing Times* 43:36-7 Mr '89

Caught in the eighties: the new debtors. M. Stone. il *New York* 22:40-6 Ap 24 '89

In debt? Help is available [views of Robert W. Johnson] il *USA Today (Periodical)* 117:5 Ap '89

Michael Milken, meet Sewell Avery. J. Grant. il *Forbes* 144 Special Issue:60-2+ O 23 '89

Money hell. D. R. Katz. il *Esquire* 112:89-90 O '89

This credit report might come as a shock [views of Alison A. Deans on consumer debt] C. Farrell. il *Business Week* p18 O 30 '89

This credit squeeze is quiet—but it still hurts. C. Farrell. il *Business Week* p104-5 N 13 '89

Walking the tightrope of serious debt. D. LaMaute. il *Black Enterprise* 19:25 Ja '89

Canada

The new debt crisis. P. Chisholm. il *Maclean's* 102:26-7 Ap 10 '89

DEBTOR AND CREDITOR

See also
Collecting of accounts
Payment of accounts
Trade claims (Debt)

A stacked deck? [trading in bankruptcy claims discriminates against small creditors] D. Fanning. il *Forbes* 143:126-7 Je 12 '89

DEBTS, CORPORATE *See* Corporations—Finance

DEBTS, EXTERNAL

An African view of the debt [interview with J. Ki-Zerbo] H. Ziady. il por *World Press Review* 36:50 Ag '89

The alarming truth about the World Bank. J. Bovard. *Reader's Digest* 134:108-12 Je '89

America's economic dependence. F. G. Rohatyn. *Foreign Affairs* 68 Special Issue:53-65 ['89]

And now, back to the issues: budget, trade, banking and debtors [address, November 10, 1988] W. C. Butcher. *Vital Speeches of the Day* 55:241-3 F 1 '89

At debt's door [effect of loan repayment on women in developing countries] J. Steinberg. il *Ms.* 18:74-9 N '89

Attack on problem of external debt urged by Assembly. il *UN Chronicle* 26:75 Mr '89

The banker plan [disclosure of J. Baker's Chemical Bank holdings clouds his policy on Latin American debt relief] *The New Republic* 200:7-8 Mr 6 '89

Banking on African conservation [debt-for-nature swaps] *Science News* 135:62 Ja 28 '89

Banks are getting those third world jitters again [push for higher reserves] J. Meehan and W. Glasgall. il *Business Week* p200+ S 25 '89

Big bank stocks rise on hopes of a third world deal. J. Mendes. il *Fortune* 120:39+ Jl 31 '89

Brady bailout II. *National Review* 41:10 My 5 '89

Can this flight be grounded? [exodus of capital from Latin debtor nations] M. McNamee. il *Business Week* p74 Ap 10 '89

Capital conservation [Costa Rica's debt for nature swaps] J. Zweig. por *Forbes* 143:208 Ap 17 '89

Children are paying the third world debt with their lives. *Utne Reader* p62 S/O '89

Comrade, can you spare a dime? [Soviet Union] E. Van den Haag. *National Review* 41:35-7 Mr 24 '89

Danger in a 'dormant' crisis [third world debt] N. M. Healey. il *World Press Review* 36:30-2 Ja '89

Dealing with the international debt crisis [remarks, March 10, 1989] N. F. Brady. *Department of State Bulletin* 89:53-6 My '89

Debt and forgiveness [Brady plan] S. Talbott. *Time* 134:25 Jl 31 '89

Debt and politics in Venezuela. J. Ewell. bibl f *Current History* 88:121-4+ Mr '89

Debt and the Brady plan. il *World Press Review* 36:9 My '89

Debt deal stacked against Indians [debt for nature swap in Bolivia] M. Collett. *The Progressive* 53:17-18 Ag '89

Debt: killer of third world children. il *UN Chronicle* 26:48 S '89

The debt plan Brady floated is still, well, floating. M. McNamee. por *Business Week* p51 My 8 '89

The debt presidency. I. M. Stelzer. il *The American Spectator* 22:26-7 Ja '89

The dilemma of third world debt. C. W. Weinberger. il *Forbes* 143:31 My 15 '89

The dirty little debt secret [Latin capital flight] D. Pauly. il *Newsweek* 113:46 Ap 17 '89

Easing third world debt [exit bonds] J. Williamson. il *USA Today (Periodical)* 117:28-9 Mr '89

Enter the Brady plan [Latin debt] B. Rudolph. il por *Time* 133:54 Mr 20 '89

Favor debt cancellation [U.S. Catholic bishops' statement on third world debt] *The Christian Century* 106:976-7 N 1 '89

The Fed lifts the Brady plan out of its sickbed [relaxing reserve accounting rules] M. McNamee and W. Glasgall. il *Business Week* p43 O 9 '89

Forgive us our debts . . . [third world] P. Henriot. *America* 161:420-2+ D 9 '89

Giving a little to save a lot [Mexican debt] E. A. Finn, Jr. il *Forbes* 143:38-9 Mr 6 '89

A global Chapter 11. B. J. Cohen. *Foreign Policy* 75:109-27 Summ '89

The great experiment [Living Bridges International arranges debt exchange with Catholic priest E. Gonzalez Torres in Mexico] R. Bautch. *America* 160:316-17 Ap 8 '89

Half a loaf for third world debtors. M. W. Karmin. *U.S. News & World Report* 107:48 Ag 7 '89

The Harvard debt doctor's controversial cure [views of J. Sachs] J. Greenwald. il por *Time* 134:66 N 6 '89

Hogwash [debtor status of U.S.] M. S. Forbes, Jr. il *Forbes* 144 Special Issue:29 O 23 '89

How bad will China's debt crunch get? D. Lee. il *Business Week* p62 S 25 '89

How do we solve the global debt crisis? [statement by Interfaith Action for Economic Justice] J. W. Skillen. *The Christian Century* 106:1004-6 N 8 '89

International Bank for Ruination and Destruction [World Bank] M. S. Tammen. il *Conservative Digest* 15:45+ Mr/Ap '89

IOU's and third world blues. S. Dentzer. il *U.S. News & World Report* 107:51 O 2 '89

It's not all that complicated [Relieving third world debt; a statement released by the U.S. bishops] *America* 161:263-4 O 28 '89

Jim Baker's conflict-of-interest problems. W. Greider. il *Rolling Stone* p43-5 Ap 20 '89

A Latin debt plan that might work [Brady plan] J. Main. il *Fortune* 119:205+ Ap 24 '89

A little easing [Mexican debt] R. Koselka. il *Forbes* 144:10 Ag 21 '89

Loan sharks [Brady plan to ease Latin debt] B. D. Nossiter. *The Nation* 248:652-3 My 15 '89

Making the Brady plan work. J. D. Sachs. bibl f il *Foreign Affairs* 68:87-104 Summ '89

The Mexican kleptocracy. T. Bethell. il *The American Spectator* 22:11-13 Jl '89

Moscow's debt crisis. P. Fuhrman. il *Forbes* 143:40-1 My 29 '89

Nature reaps a cash bonanza [debt-for-nature swaps] T. A. Lewis. il *International Wildlife* 19:37 Ja/F '89

A new plan for debt [Canadian banks wary of Brady plan for Latin America] J. DeMont. il *Maclean's* 102:32-3 Mr 27 '89

The new spelling of relief [Brady plan to ease Latin debt] D. Pauly. il por *Newsweek* 113:32 Mr 20 '89

The next liberator? [C. A. Perez's approach to debt crisis in Venezuela] M. Collett. il *The Atlantic* 263:29+ F '89

No relief on Latin debt—without World Bank reform. P. C. Roberts. il *Business Week* p15 Mr 6 '89

An offer they can't refuse [IRS ruling limits tax advantages banks get for writing off foreign loan losses] L. Saunders. il *Forbes* 143:144 My 29 '89

On drugs, debt and poverty [interview with C. A. Perez] J. Moody and S. Talbott. il por *Time* 134:12-14 N 27 '89

The onset of big-debt blues [Paris summit] J. Egan. il maps *U.S. News & World Report* 107:20-2 Jl 24 '89

Rhodes to Latin America [Citibank loan negotiator] J. Zweig. il por *Forbes* 144:142+ S 4 '89

Robbin' hoods [big banks and debt relief; cover story] J. D. Sachs. il *The New Republic* 200:19-20+ Mr 13 '89

Salinas' flashy new step in the Mexican debt dance [relaxing foreign ownership rules] A. Bard. il *Business Week* p28 My 29 '89

Saving forests—with debt [less money for environmentally destructive projects in third world] P. Adams. il *World Press Review* 36:47 O '89

Scenes from the inferno [third world] A. Cockburn. *The Nation* 248:510-11 Ap 17 '89

Self-made crisis [debt crisis in Latin America] M. S. Forbes, Jr. il *Forbes* 143:27 F 20 '89

A small sigh of relief [Mexico's debt] W. Glasgall. il *Business Week* p33 Jl 24 '89

So what took them so long? [agreement reached with creditor banks] C. Gorman. il *Time* 134:38 Ag 7 '89

Sounding the alarm [Latin American countries] G. D. Garcia. il *Time* 133:32-3 Ja 9 '89

The Thatcher factor [banks reschedule South African debt] R. Laver. il *Maclean's* 102:42 O 30 '89

Third world deadbeats. I. M. Stelzer. il *The American Spectator* 22:34-5 Ap '89

Third world hydraulics. T. Bethell. il *The American Spectator* 22:9-11 Je '89

Triple play [U.S. Catholic bishops' statement on third world debt] *Commonweal* 116:581-2 N 3 '89

The U.S. role in a changing world economy. P. D. Nigro. il *USA Today (Periodical)* 117:21-2 My '89

Using red ink to keep tropical forests green [debt-for-nature swaps in Brazil] C. P. Work and G. Smith. il map *U.S. News & World Report* 106:48-9 Mr 6 '89

A vote of confidence [U.S. loan to Mexico] L. Meyer. il *World Press Review* 36:64 Ja '89

Washington's new, softer line on Latin debt [Brady plan] M. McNamee. il por *Business Week* p58 Mr 20 '89

DEBTS, EXTERNAL—*cont.*

What are they waiting for? [reserve boosts by banks with third world loans] P. Duggan. il *Forbes* 144:45-6 O 2 '89

What Bush owes [Latin debt] M. Nadle. *The Nation* 248:400-1 Mr 27 '89

Who swallows the debt? [third world] L. Stoléru. *World Press Review* 36:80 S '89

Will the U.S. be left holding the bag on third world debt? P. C. Roberts. il *Business Week* p22 O 16 '89

The world puts the heat on Brazil [forgiving part of debt in exchange for help in protecting nature] *World Press Review* 36:38 My '89

DEBTS, PUBLIC

See also

Debts, External

Treasury bills and notes

All rich nations need their debt. R. L. Heilbroner. *The Nation* 248:81-2 Ja 23 '89

By adding up how much Uncle Sam owes, Susan Williams gives us each day our daily debt. il por *People Weekly* 31:76 My 1 '89

The debt presidency. I. M. Stelzer. il *The American Spectator* 22:26-7 Ja '89

Fiscal legerdemain. E. Rubenstein. *National Review* 41:17 Jl 14 '89

Is the U.S. national debt a problem? E. Corcoran and P. Wallich. il *Scientific American* 260:84-5 Je '89

The party's getting rough. A. Bladen. il *Forbes* 144:160 Ag 7 '89

Canada

Back to a chilling financial future. D. Francis. il *Maclean's* 102:9 Ap 17 '89

Deficits and the national debt [address, February 23, 1989] T. D'Aquino. *Vital Speeches of the Day* 55:427-9 My 1 '89

The growing debt. D. Jenish. il *Maclean's* 102:50-1 My 1 '89

United States

See Debts, Public

DEBUGGING IN COMPUTER SCIENCE

See also

Disassemblers (Computer programs)

Four debuggers in one [MultiScope] M. Heller. il *Byte* 14:195-6 O '89

The hunt for bad sectors [hard disk drive] J. Pournelle. il *Byte* 14:119-20+ Je '89

Is there a doctor in the house? [software to diagnose failures in local area networks from Network General] J. Pitta. il *Forbes* 144:254+ N 27 '89

RS-232 debugging with SAM 2000. il *Radio-Electronics* 60:83-5 O '89

Sleuthing your troubles away [System Sleuth] G. Hartwig. *Byte* 14:104 Je '89

DEBUTANTES

The deb of the minute [S. Borden] M. Gross. il pors *New York* 22:42-5 Ag 28 '89

Anecdotes, facetiae, satire, etc.

Good ol debs [Texas] M. Ivins. il *Ms.* 18:22 Jl/Ag '89

DEC See Digital Equipment Corp.; New York (State). Dept. of Environmental Conservation

DEC-TAM CORPORATION

Dec-Tam corporation: selling peace of mind. J. David and K. File. il por *Working Woman* 14:124+ O '89

DECADE FOR CULTURAL DEVELOPMENT, 1988-1997 See World Decade for Cultural Development, 1988-1997

DECAFFEINATED COFFEE See Coffee

DECARBOXYLASES

Prevention of rapid intracellular degradation of ODC by a carboxyl-terminal truncation. L. Ghoda and others. bibl f il *Science* 243:1493-5 Mr 17 '89

DECARLO, TESSA

Big white wedding? Bad idea. il *Glamour* 87:186 S '89

DECATUR, STEPHEN, 1779-1820

about

Stephen Decatur. J. B. Graves. il por *Conservative Digest* 15:31-5 My/Je '89

DECATUR (GA.)

Gardens and gardening

The private domain of Ryan Gainey. A. C. Sinnes. il *Flower and Garden* 33:34-8+ Ja/F '89

DECAY (BIOLOGY) See Biodegradation

DECAY (DENTAL) See Dental caries

DECEDENTS' ESTATES See Estates, Decedents'

DECEIT See Deception

DECEMBER

The December almanac. il *The Atlantic* 264:18 D '89

DECENTRALIZATION IN BUSINESS MANAGEMENT See Business management

DECENTRALIZATION IN GOVERNMENT

The decline of central government [address, September 18, 1989] M. E. Daniels. *Vital Speeches of the Day* 56:34-7 N 1 '89

DECENTRALIZATION IN SCHOOL ADMINISTRATION See School management and organization

DECEPTION

See also

Fraud

Lying

Deceptive successes in young children [research by Michael Lewis] B. Bower. *Science News* 135:343 Je 3 '89

Animals

Nature's knaves and tricksters. E. E. Goode. il *U.S. News & World Report* 107:61-3 O 23 '89

DECISION MAKING

See also

Choice (Psychology)

Risk taking (Psychology)

Clinical versus actuarial judgment [diagnosing and predicting human behavior] R. M. Dawes and others. bibl f *Science* 243:1668-74 Mr 31 '89

Experimental research on jury decision-making. R. J. MacCoun. bibl f *Science* 244:1046-50 Je 2 '89

Intuition & strategic planning. W. H. Agor. il por *The Futurist* 23:20-3 N/D '89

Mr. Consensus [G. Bush; cover story] M. Duffy. il pors *Time* 134:16-22 Ag 21 '89

Tool to end indecisiveness [Decision Pad] R. Gehorsam. *Home Office Computing* 7:72+ O '89

Understanding behavior in escalation situations. B. M. Staw and J. Ross. bibl f il *Science* 246:216-20 O 13 '89

Why smart managers make bad decisions. E. Tanouye. il *Working Woman* 14:55-7+ Ag '89

DECK, ALLAN FIGUEROA

Books on Catholicism and inter-American affairs. *America* 161:279-81 O 28 '89

DECK, ROBERT E., JR.

How to cut the cost of college. il *USA Today (Periodical)* 118:58-9 Jl '89

DECKER, ANDREW

The price of fame. il pors *Art News* 88:96-101 Ja '89

DECKER, DANIEL J., AND CONNELLY, NANCY A.

Deer in suburbia—pleasures and pests. il *The Conservationist* 43:46-9 Mr/Ap '89

DECKER, DANIEL J., AND LOCONTI, KATHLENE M.

When two worlds collide. il *The Conservationist* 44:44-7 N/D '89

DECKER, MARY See Slaney, Mary Decker

DECKER, ROBERT H.

Can schools eliminate sexual harassment? *The Education Digest* 54:59-62 Ja '89

DECKS, PATIOS, TERRACES, ETC.

See also

Porches

Boardwalk connects house to deck on garage roof. il *Sunset (Central West edition)* 182:148-9 My '89

Build yourself a patio. D. Johnson. il *The Family Handyman* 39:56-9 Je '89

Computer design center [Weyerhaeuser system] R. Berendsohn. il *Popular Mechanics* 166:92 S '89

A deck for the decades [cover story] R. Freudenberger. il *The Mother Earth News* 117:86-91 My/Je '89

Deck in the forest? Forest in the deck? il *Sunset (Central West edition)* 183:82 Ag '89

Deck out some summer space [home of Kathy and Larry Zimpleman] W. L. Nolan. il *Better Homes and Gardens* 67:55+ My '89

Decked out [using Weyerhaeuser DesignCenter computer] T. O. Bakke. il *Popular Science* 235:28 Jl '89

The decks came first. il *Southern Living* 24:144 Je '89

Deckscaping. M. Chotiner. il *Home Mechanix* 85:37-40+ Jl '89

Full deck. E. Thompson and E. Thompson. il *Popular Mechanics* 166:84-7 Je '89

A little privacy, please. S. Sheetz. il *Better Homes and Gardens* 67:99-100+ Je '89

Long-legged decks . . . they're steep site solutions. il *Sunset (Central West edition)* 182:100-1 Mr '89

Modules set off his deck and gazebo. il *Sunset (Central West edition)* 182:138 Je '89

Now this garden's on the level. il *Southern Living* 24:80-1 Ap '89

The outdoor living room. F. Greenberg. il *Working Woman* 14:108-11 Je '89

Outdoor living space [patios and gazebos] B. Vila. il *Popular Mechanics* 166:44+ Jl '89

Private retreat in the sliver of space between houses. il *Sunset (Central West edition)* 182:152 My '89

Showcase deck [cover story] A. Rooze. il *The Family Handyman* 39:29-40 Ap '89

Solution for a steep slope: big deck with built-in planters. il *Sunset (Central West edition)* 183:92-3 Jl '89

This spa-deck is leafy-private . . . and 10 feet off the ground. il *Sunset (Central West edition)* 183:92-3 S '89

Why waste sun on a driveway? Make it into a patio. il *Sunset (Central West edition)* 182:252-3 My '89

Maintenance and repair

Deck defense. M. Phair. il *Home Mechanix* 85:61-2+ Je '89

How you can bring an old deck back to life. il *Sunset (Central West edition)* 183:102+ S '89

Rescue an old deck. K. Collier. il *The Family Handyman* 39:71-2+ Ap '89

DECKS, PATIOS, TERRACES, ETC.—cont.
Railings
See Hand railings
DECLARATION OF PRINCIPLES CONCERNING ACTIVITIES FOLLOWING THE DETECTION OF EXTRATERRESTRIAL INTELLIGENCE
Intergalactic diplomacy. S. Strauss. il *Technology Review* 92:17-18 My/Je '89
Interstellar diplomacy. M. A. G. Michaud. *Ad Astra* 1:22 S '89
Listening for ET. J. Eberhart. il *Science News* 135:296-8 My 13 '89
UFO update. P. McCarthy. il *Omni (New York, N.Y.)* 11:89 Je '89
DECLARATION OF THE RIGHTS OF MAN AND OF THE CITIZEN *See* France. Declaration of the Rights of Man and of the Citizen
DECLARATION OF THE RIGHTS OF THE CHILD
Children in combat. E. Egan. il *Commonweal* 116:104-5 F 24 '89
So they may have a happy childhood . . . il *UN Chronicle* 26:51 S '89
DECO ART *See* Art deco
DECODING OF CIPHERS *See* Cryptography
DECOLONIZATION COMMITTEE (UNITED NATIONS) *See* United Nations. Decolonization Committee
DECOLONIZATION SPECIAL COMMITTEE (UNITED NATIONS) *See* United Nations. Special Committee on the Situation with Regard to the Implementation of the Declaration on the Granting of Independence to Colonial Countries and Peoples
DECOMMISSIONING OF NUCLEAR POWER PLANTS *See* Nuclear power plants—Decommissioning
DECOMPOSITION (BIOLOGY) *See* Biodegradation
DECOMPOSITION (CHEMISTRY)
See also
Spinodal decomposition
Explosive molecular ionic crystals. W. L. Faust. bibl f il *Science* 245:37-42 Jl 7 '89
DECOMPRESSION (PHYSIOLOGY)
Fighting the bends in the Indian Ocean [joint Soviet-U.S. effort to rescue Soviet researchers] M. Sun. il *Science* 244:1134 Je 9 '89
Heart defect may lie behind 'bends' [patent foramen ovale; research by Richard E. Moon] *Science News* 135:188 Mr 25 '89
Too much pressure? [research by Richard E. Moon] K. Wright. *Scientific American* 261:36+ S '89
DECOMPRESSION SICKNESS *See* Decompression (Physiology)
DECONSTRUCTION
A dictionary for deconstructors. A. Lurie. il *The New York Review of Books* 36:49-50 N 23 '89
The strange case of Paul de Man. D. Donoghue. il *The New York Review of Books* 36:32-7 Je 29 '89
DECONSTRUCTIVIST ARCHITECTURE
Exhibitions
Slaying the neo-modern dragon. D. Davis. il *Art in America* 77:43-5+ Ja '89
DECONTROL OF NATURAL GAS PRICES *See* Natural gas—Prices
DECORATED EGGS *See* Eggs, Decorated
DECORATION AND ORNAMENT
See also
Antiques
Art deco
Arts and crafts
Baskets
Beadwork
Buttons
Candles and candleholders
Christmas decorations
Church decoration and ornament
Cooking, Ornamental
Decoupage
Design
Eggs, Decorated
Faux (Style)
Flower arrangement
Food, Artificial
Fraktur
Frescoes
Fruit, Artificial
Fruits, vegetables, etc. in decoration
Furniture, Decorated
Garden ornaments
Glassware
House decoration
Inlay
Mosaics
Needlework
Paneling
Pottery—Decoration
Stencil work
Table decoration
Tassels
Textile design
Tiles

Tole painting
French decorative arts in America [cover story] W. Garrett. bibl f il *Antiques* 135:696-707 Mr '89
Paper chase [Victorian papier-mâché pieces] M. Guralnick. il *House & Garden* 161:62+ Mr '89
Exhibitions
See also
Metropolitan Museum of Art (New York, N.Y.). American Wing
Musée des Arts Décoratifs (Strasbourg, France)
Musée Nissim de Camondo (Paris, France)
Royal Ontario Museum. Samuel European Galleries
The American craftsman and the European tradition, 1620-1820 [show at the Minneapolis Institute of Arts] M. Conforti and A. Kohls. il *Antiques* 136:834-43 O '89
Civilized liberties [L'art de vivre: decorative arts and design in France, 1789-1989 at the Cooper-Hewitt Museum] A. F. Collins. bibl f il *Art in America* 77:164-9+ N '89
Two centuries of French decorative arts [L'art de vivre: decorative arts and design in France, 1789-1989] A. E. Ledes. il *Antiques* 135:590+ Mr '89
DECORATION AND ORNAMENT, ARCHITECTURAL
See also
Finials
Floor painting and decoration
Latticework
Moldings (Architecture)
Mural painting and decoration
Mural painting and decoration, Exterior
Stone carving
Weather vanes
DECORATION AND ORNAMENT, ROCOCO
The legacy of Ireland's stuccodores. N. F. Weber. il *Architectural Digest* 46:42+ Ag '89
DECORATION DAY *See* Memorial Day
DECORATION OF FOOD *See* Cooking—Garnishes
DECORATIONS OF HONOR
See also
Medals of honor
DECORATIVE ARTS *See* Decoration and ornament
DECOUPAGE
Antiques: lacca povera furniture. J. Simpson. il *Architectural Digest* 46:168-73 F '89
DECOYS (HUNTING)
Decoys [ducks] *Field & Stream* 93:154 Ap '89
Dove hunting with a difference [dove farming] G. Reiger. il *Field & Stream* 94:50-1+ S '89
Anecdotes, facetiae, satire, etc.
Whittlin' [making duck decoys] A. Liere. il *Field & Stream* 94:18+ Je '89
Exhibitions
Massachusetts waterfowl decoys [cover story] R. Moir and J. Parker. bibl f il *Antiques* 136:516-27 S '89
DECRANE, ALFRED C.
The greening of the energy world [address, September 8, 1989] *Vital Speeches of the Day* 56:117-21 D 1 '89
DECTER, MIDGE
The professor and the L-word. *Commentary* 87:39-48 F '89
The Rushdiad. *Commentary* 87:18-23 Je '89
DEDICATIONS (IN BOOKS)
'To my husband, Donald, without whom . . .'. M. Woolfolk. il *Smithsonian* 19:200 Mr '89
DEDUCTIONS, INCOME TAX *See* Income tax—Deductions
DEE, JOEY
about
Joey Dee, past master of twist, plans a refuge for those caught between rock and a hard place. P. Freeman. il pors *People Weekly* 32:131-2+ N 20 '89
DEE, JOHN, 1527-1608
about
The political magic of John Dee. I. Seymour. bibl il por *History Today* 39:29-35 Ja '89
DEE, WILLIAM V.
Defense contractors must change to survive competition in 1990s. por *Aviation Week & Space Technology* 131:99+ Jl 17 '89
DEEDS
A coal-field victory [broad-form deed that allows coal companies to strip mine land; Kentucky case] D. Giardina. il *The Progressive* 53:14-15 Mr '89
This land is my land . . . or is it? D. Fanning. il *Forbes* 143:62 Ja 23 '89
DEEDY, JOHN
Challenges facing U.S. Catholics. *Commonweal* 116:622-3 N 17 '89
Do Catholics let the Spirit move them? il *U.S. Catholic* 54:21-7 Mr '89
How holy days can catch the holiday spirit. il *U.S. Catholic* 54:18-25 Ja '89
How to get through to a lapsed Catholic [cover story] il *U.S. Catholic* 54:6-13 Ap '89
Why Catholics can't get enough of the Bible. il *U.S. Catholic* 54:6-11 S '89
DEEN, ROSEMARY
Infant and martyrs [poem] *Commonweal* 116:700 D 15 '89

DEEP ECOLOGY

Ecology wars. R. Hill. *Omni (New York, N.Y.)* 11:25 Ag '89

John Seed and the Council of All Beings [interview] P. Stone. il por *The Mother Earth News* 117:58-63 My/Je '89

Planet stricken. A. P. Crawford and A. Levine. il *Vogue* 179:710-15+ S '89

Thinking like a mountain. A. Leopold. il *The Mother Earth News* 117:10 My/Je '89

DEEP SEA DEPOSITS *See* Marine sediments

DEEP SEA DIVING *See* Diving, Submarine

DEEP SEA FISHING *See* Salt water fishing

DEEPSTAR SIX [film] See Motion picture reviews—Single works

DEER

See also
Antlers
Caribou
Elk
Whitetail Institute of North America

Deer in suburbia—pleasures and pests. D. J. Decker and N. A. Connelly. il *The Conservationist* 43:46-9 Mr/Ap '89

Unwelcome whitetails. H. Willis. il *Field & Stream* 93:58-9+ F '89

Accidents and hazards

Not tonight, deer [cars hitting deer] P. Bedard. il *Car and Driver* 34:22 F '89

When two worlds collide [cars hitting deer in New York State] D. J. Decker and K. M. Loconti. il *The Conservationist* 44:44-7 N/D '89

Food and feeding

Irresistible edibles [whitetails] S. Curtis. il *Field & Stream* 94:52-4 Je '89

Migration

Bottleneck your buck [whitetails] J. O. Cartier. il *Outdoor Life* 184:84-5+ N '89

Photographs and photography

Oh deer [fallow deer] il *National Geographic World* 166:14-15 Je '89

DEER, DRESSING OF *See* Game, Dressing of

DEER, FOSSIL

Evolution's rapid shrinkage [dwarf fossil deer on the island of Jersey; research by Adrian M. Lister] R. Monastersky. *Science News* 136:357 D 2 '89

DEER BAITS

Hunting downwind [scent driving deer] W. L. Prothero. il *Field & Stream* 94:42-3+ Jl '89

DEER CALLING *See* Animal calling

DEER DRIVES

Small party deer drives. N. Nelson. il *Field & Stream* 94:48-9+ O '89

DEER FARMING

Bambi and the baron [J. Kerckerinck's efforts to persuade Americans to eat venison] D. Machan. il por *Forbes* 144:298+ D 11 '89

DEER HUNTING

1988 Big Buck Club winners. il *The Conservationist* 44:47 S/O '89

The art of solo deer hunting. J. Weiss. il *Field & Stream* 94:48-9+ S '89

Back of beyond bucks [hunting whitetails in the wilderness] G. Miller. il *Outdoor Life* 183:69+ Ja '89

Banking for big bucks [mule deer] J. Weiss. il *Outdoor Life* 184:68-9+ Ag '89

A beginner's guide to deer hunting. B. Woods. il *The Mother Earth News* 120:98-103+ N/D '89

Blueprinting big bucks [study on hunting trophy whitetails; cover story]; ed. by Kathy Etling. S. Demarais and B. Zaiglin. il *Outdoor Life* 184:61-3+ O '89

Bottleneck your buck [whitetails] J. O. Cartier. il *Outdoor Life* 184:84-5+ N '89

Bowhunting's moment of truth [whitetail deer] T. L. Torget. il *Field & Stream* 94:52-3+ Ag '89

Bucks in the 'burbs. M. Pearce. il *Outdoor Life* 184:56-7+ Jl '89

Bucks of the big bogs. N. Nelson. il *Field & Stream* 94:42-3+ S '89

Bucks where you least expect them [sleep habits] G. Miller. il *Outdoor Life* 184:92-3+ N '89

The cold and the bold. N. Nelson. il *Field & Stream* 94:52-3 D '89

Cold-weather whitetails . . . minus the misery [tree stand hunting] P. Nelson. il *Field & Stream* 94:72-3+ N '89

Deer chase prevention [breaking hunting dogs from running deer] L. Mueller. il *Outdoor Life* 184:29+ Ag '89

Deer forecast 1989. S. R. Boyle. il *Outdoor Life* 184:69-71 S '89

Don't shoot a wet doe [myths of shooting lactating mule deer] S. Curtis. il *Field & Stream* 94:88 O '89

Floating for river-bottom bucks [mule deer] W. L. Prothero. il *Field & Stream* 93:52-3+ Mr '89

Grandpa and the kid [grandfather gets lost] D. Sisson. il *Field & Stream* 94:37+ O '89

The hated season [New York] S. Lewis. il *The New York Times Magazine* p24+ N 26 '89

High-tech hunting [computer program] B. Clede. il *Outdoor Life* 184:93-4 D '89

How to tickle a whitetail [antlers used as deer calls] J. Weiss. il *Outdoor Life* 184:74-5+ S '89

Hunting downwind [scent driving deer] W. L. Prothero. il *Field & Stream* 94:42-3+ Jl '89

Hunting mule deer—and related thoughts. D. Petersen. il *The Mother Earth News* 120:104-7 N/D '89

Hunting spooked mule deer. S. Curtis. il *Field & Stream* 94:44-5+ S '89

Irresistible edibles [whitetails] S. Curtis. il *Field & Stream* 94:52-4 Je '89

Lifestyles of the old and wary [whitetailed deer] N. Nelson. il *Outdoor Life* 184:82-3+ S '89

A matter of faith [mule deer hunting] J. Barsness. il *Field & Stream* 94:38-9+ O '89

Mountain muleys. N. Strung. il *Field & Stream* 94:27+ O '89

The mourning after [pursuing a deer by canoe leads to near tragedy during Lake Erie storm] G. Laycock. il *Outdoor Life* 183:68-9+ Je '89

Murphy's pride. P. Johnson. il *Outdoor Life* 183:84-5+ My '89

On the margin [mule deer habitat] S. Curtis. il *Field & Stream* 94:42-3+ Ag '89

On the right track for muleys. W. L. Prothero. il *Outdoor Life* 184:78-9+ S '89

Rainy-day deer. H. Buck. il *Field & Stream* 94:46-7 S '89

Return for a trophy [mule deer] W. L. Prothero. il *Field & Stream* 94:66-7+ N '89

A second chance. J. Spencer. il *Outdoor Life* 183:76-7+ Mr '89

Small party deer drives. N. Nelson. il *Field & Stream* 94:48-9+ O '89

Stone cold muleys. B. Journey. il *Outdoor Life* 184:70-1+ O '89

Stop, pause, and start for bucks [mule deer hunting methods] W. L. Prothero. il *Field & Stream* 94:44-5+ D '89

Strategies for stumping deer. J. Bashline. il *Field & Stream* 94:28-9 Ag '89

Whitetail fingers. S. Curtis. il *Field & Stream* 94:59+ N '89

Whitetails west. J. Barsness. il map *Field & Stream* 93:38-9+ Ja '89

Words to the whitetail [cover story] P. Fiduccia. il *Outdoor Life* 184:63+ Ag '89

DEER LODGE (MONT.)

Historic houses, sites, etc.

See also
Grant-Kohrs Ranch National Historic Site (Mont.)

DEER MEAT *See* Venison

DEER MEAT COOKING *See* Cooking—Game

DEER PARK (WASH.)

Crime

See also
Weflen, Julie—Kidnapping

DEER REPELLENTS

Deer don't help your garden. il *Southern Living* 24:67 My '89

DEER VALLEY (UTAH: RESORT) *See* Resorts—Utah

DEERE & COMPANY

But will they ever know Zytel from Lycra? [Du Pont and Deere & Co. introduce new mail order catalogs] S. B. Weiner. il *Forbes* 143:150+ Je 26 '89

Deere pleased with stocking parts on farms. *Successful Farming* 87:44 Ag '89

Deere's new Maximizer combines roll off the line. C. Finck. il *Successful Farming* 87:26-7 F '89

Is Deere looking at bumper profits? G. G. Marcial. *Business Week* p136 N 20 '89

Mighty mower [200 Series garden tractors] T. O. Bakke. il *Popular Science* 234:165 Je '89

DEERFIELD (MASS.)

See also
Historic Deerfield, Inc.

Education

See also
Deerfield Academy (Mass.)

DEERFIELD ACADEMY (MASS.)

Boys and girls at Deerfield. K. Ames. il *Newsweek* 114:77 O 16 '89

DEET

A tick buster's guide to bug repellents [preventing Lyme disease] J. Silberner. il *U.S. News & World Report* 107:57 Ag 7 '89

DEETS, HORACE B.

Health care for a caring America [address, May 23, 1989] *Vital Speeches of the Day* 55:636-7 Ag 1 '89

Our opinion. See issues of Modern Maturity beginning April/ May 1988

DEFAMATION *See* Libel and slander

DEFAULT (FINANCE)

See also
Bonds—Default
Mortgages—Default
Municipal bonds—Default

Abandon ship! [Integrated Resources] H. Rudnitsky. il *Forbes* 144:68-9 Jl 10 '89

DEFAULT (FINANCE)—cont.

Day of reckoning [report on Principal Group collapse; special section] J. DeMont. il por *Maclean's* 102:30-4 Jl 31 '89

Desperate hours at Integrated Resources. M. D. Oneal. il *Business Week* p44 O 30 '89

Drexel rushes in to save a fallen disciple [bailout of Integrated Resources] L. Light. il *Business Week* p65 Jl 17 '89

How much bad luck can one Texan take? [J. Hay's plan to remake Lomas Financial] T. Mason. il *Business Week* p33 S 18 '89

Integrated Resources: the rise and fall of a debt addict. M. D. Oneal and J. H. Dobrzynski. il *Business Week* p182-4+ N 6 '89

A Principal toll [Alberta agrees to compensate investors in failed company] J. DeMont. il por *Maclean's* 102:28-9 Ag 7 '89

The Principal vote [Principal Group scandal at center of Alberta election campaign] J. Howse. il *Maclean's* 102:12-13 Mr 20 '89

DEFEAT (PSYCHOLOGY) *See* Failure (Psychology)

DEFECTORS

> *See also*
> Asylum, Right of

Calgary power play [Czech hockey player P. Nedved defects to Canada] J. Howse. il por *Maclean's* 102:17 Ja 16 '89

Dissident diplomats [Chinese envoys defect to Canada following Tiananmen Square massacre] T. Tedesco. il *Maclean's* 102:21 Je 26 '89

Gymnast Nadia Comaneci leaps for freedom—and lands in the arms of a married father of four [defection from Romania] il por *People Weekly* 32:116 D 18 '89

K.G.B. defector Gundarev: it's cold coming out [cover story] D. Wise. il *The New York Times Magazine* p36-9+ S 17 '89

Leap to the West [Romanian gymnast N. Comaneci] W. O. Johnson and A. Verschoth. il pors *Sports Illustrated* 71:40-1 D 11 '89

Midnight race for freedom [defection of Cuban violinist A. Ponce, Jr.] S. Kelly. il pors *Reader's Digest* 135:198-202+ S '89

A Moscow suicide reveals Glenn Souther's double life as a U.S. sailor spying for the K.G.B. W. Plummer. il *People Weekly* 32:105-6 Jl 17 '89

The odd case of M. Orlov [suicide of American defector G. M. Souther in the Soviet Union] il *Time* 134:40 Jl 10 '89

With help from his wife and his lover, jazzman Paquito D'Rivera gets back the son he left in Cuba. P. Chin. il pors *People Weekly* 31:94-7 Ja 30 '89

DEFECTORS, POLITICAL *See* Defectors
DEFECTS, CRYSTAL *See* Crystals—Defects
DEFELICE, LOUISE

The bibbidibobbidiboo factor in teaching. il *Phi Delta Kappan* 70:639-41 Ap '89

DEFENSE, CIVIL *See* Civil defense
DEFENSE ADVANCED RESEARCH PROJECTS AGENCY (U.S.) *See* United States. Defense Advanced Research Projects Agency

DEFENSE APPROPRIATIONS *See* United States. Dept. of Defense—Appropriations and expenditures

DEFENSE APPROPRIATIONS SUBCOMMITTEE (SENATE) *See* United States. Congress. Senate. Committee on Appropriations. Subcommittee on Dept. of Defense

DEFENSE DEPT. (U.S.) *See* United States. Dept. of Defense

DEFENSE INDUSTRIAL SECURITY PROGRAM (U.S.) *See* United States. Defense Investigative Service. Defense Industrial Security Program

DEFENSE INDUSTRIES *See* Military-industrial complex; Munitions

DEFENSE INFORMATION, CLASSIFIED *See* Classified information

DEFENSE MECHANISMS (BIOLOGY)

> *See also*
> Cyclomorphosis
> Mimicry (Biology)

All things bright & bitter [cover story] E. Pennisi. il *International Wildlife* 19:46-51 N/D '89

Arms race on the grass flats [mollusks and their predators] E. S. Iversen and D. E. Jory. il *Sea Frontiers* 35:304-11 S/O '89

Defensive behaviors in infant rhesus monkeys: environmental cues and neurochemical regulation. N. H. Kalin and S. E. Shelton. bibl f il *Science* 243:1718-21 Mr 31 '89

Pa-tooey! [spitting by animals] N. Vietmeyer. il *International Wildlife* 19:20-3 Ja/F '89

Rattler battlers [California ground squirrels] R. G. Coss and D. H. Owings. il *Natural History* p30-5 My '89

Samurai aphids: survival under siege [Japan] M. W. Moffett. il *National Geographic* 176:406-22 S '89

Spanish fly's lure: ardor or armor? [aphrodisiac for pyrochroid beetles; research by Jerrold Meinwald] J. Raloff. *Science News* 136:189 S 16 '89

Starlight on the reef [brittle stars glow with displeasure when touched; cover story] M. S. Grober. il *Natural History* p72-6+ O '89

Symbiotic marine bacteria chemically defend crustacean embryos from a pathogenic fungus. M. S. Gil-Turnes and others. bibl f il *Science* 246:116-18 O 6 '89

DEFENSE MECHANISMS (PSYCHOLOGY)

> *See also*
> Repression (Psychology)

DEFENSE PROCUREMENT SCANDAL *See* Pentagon procurement scandal

DEFENSE SPENDING, AMERICAN *See* United States. Dept. of Defense—Appropriations and expenditures

DEFENSE SPENDING, INTERNATIONAL *See* Armed Forces—Appropriations and expenditures

DEFENSE STOCKS *See* Munitions—Securities

DEFERENCE *See* Respect

DEFERRED COMPENSATION

> *See also*
> 401(k) plan
> 403(b) plan

DEFIBRILLATORS

The defibrillator question [use in air travel] *Prevention (Emmaus, Pa.)* 41:64 Ap '89

Delay can be dangerous! C. SerVaas. il *The Saturday Evening Post* 261:98 Jl/Ag '89

Heart starter [automatic implantable defibrillators; work of David Newman] il *Prevention (Emmaus, Pa.)* 41:14+ Ag '89

DEFICIENCY *See* Scarcity

DEFICIENCY DISEASES

> *See also*
> Malnutrition
> Scurvy

DEFICITS, BUDGET *See* Budget

DEFICITS, TRADE *See* Balance of trade

DEFINED CONTRIBUTION PENSION PLANS

The new breed of pensions that may leave retirees poorer. L. J. Nathans. il *Business Week* p164+ N 6 '89

DEFLATION (FINANCE)

The next best thing to bond market nirvana. C. Farrell. il *Business Week* p102+ Je 26 '89

DEFOLIANTS *See* Herbicides

DEFORD, FRANK

The ageless warrior. il pors *Sports Illustrated* 70:102-6+ My 8 '89

A gentleman and a scholar. il pors *Sports Illustrated* 70:86-90+ Ap 17 '89

How it all began. il *Sports Illustrated* 70 Special Issue:38-40+ F '89

Let the words wobble. por *Sports Illustrated* 70:120 My 8 '89

Lights, camera, action! il pors *Sports Illustrated* 70 Special Issue:51-2+ F '89

Of Billie Jean and 73-0. il por *Sports Illustrated* 70:70 F 6 '89

> *about*

A fan's notes. E. Diamond. il pors *New York* 22:22-3 Ag 14 '89

Make room in the press box. M. Beck. il pors *Newsweek* 113:53 Je 12 '89

DEFORESTATION

> *See also*
> Clearcutting

Air pollution and forest decline in a spruce (Picea abies) forest [West Germany] E.-D. Schulze. bibl f il map *Science* 244:776-83 My 19 '89

Are the Swiss forests in peril? C. Mehr. il map *National Geographic* 175:636-51 My '89

As trees fall in the tropics, songbirds fall silent. il *U.S. News & World Report* 107:52 Ag 7 '89

Bear of the clouds [effects of deforestation on the Latin American spectacled bear] P. Steinhart. il map *Audubon* 91:92-4+ Jl '89

Bungle in the jungle. C. Spencer. *Omni (New York, N.Y.)* 11:48-9 S '89

Can't see China's forests—or its trees. K. Forestier. *World Press Review* 36:42 S '89

Capital conservation [Costa Rica's debt for nature swaps] J. Zweig. por *Forbes* 143:208 Ap 17 '89

A catbird's seat on Amazon destruction [monitoring of illegal agricultural burning by remote sensing satellites] F. Golden. il *Science* 246:201-2 O 13 '89

Chronicle of a death foretold [murder of environmentalist C. Mendes Filho in Brazil] M. Beck. il por *Newsweek* 113:62 Ja 9 '89

Debt deal stacked against Indians [debt for nature swap in Bolivia] M. Collett. *The Progressive* 53:17-18 Ag '89

Defenders of the Amazon [Brazil's rubber tappers; cover story] S. Hecht and A. Cockburn. il *The Nation* 248:695-6+ My 22 '89

Deforestation and the greenhouse effect. M. Morain. *The Humanist* 49:31 Ja/F '89

Deforestation in Amazonia. P. M. Fearnside. bibl f il map *Environment* 31:16-20+ My '89

Deforestation in the Amazon [discussion of May 1989 article, Deforestation in Amazonia] P. M. Fearnside. *Environment* 31:4-5 S '89

A dubious plan for the Amazon [Brazil] M. S. Serrill. il *Time* 133:67 Ap 17 '89

Extractive reserves in Brazilian Amazonia [rubber workers' proposal to fight deforestation] P. M. Fearnside. bibl f il map *BioScience* 39:387-93 Je '89

DEFORESTATION—*cont.*

Fall of the rain forest [Brazil] T. Waters. il *Discover* 10:40 Ja '89

The fate of the earth depends on the fate of the trees. M. N. Mead and others. il *Utne Reader* p49-57 My/Je '89

Fire at the equator [tropical deforestation] R. Wild. il por map *Organic Gardening* 36:54-9 My '89

A forest dies in Guatemala [rain forest conservation initiatives] V. Perera. *The Nation* 249:521-2+ N 6 '89

The fragile forest [special section] S. Postel and L. Heise. il *The Courier (Unesco)* 42:12-23 Ja '89

Here a parcel, there a parcel—fragmented forests [New York State] M. Greason. il *The Conservationist* 44:46-9 Jl/Ag '89

'Hug a tree' kiss an herb [making money saving Brazil's forests] S. Seibert. il *Newsweek* 113:50 My 1 '89

In memory of Chico Mendes [union leader and ecologist slain in Brazil] J. D. Hair. il *International Wildlife* 19:30 Mr/Ap '89

John Seed and the Council of All Beings [interview] P. Stone. il por *The Mother Earth News* 117:58-63 My/Je '89

Making a noise over falling trees. M. Dregni. il *Utne Reader* p28+ Ja/F '89

Monitoring the fate of the forests from space. W. Booth. il *Science* 243:1428-9 Mr 17 '89

Murder in the Amazon [union leader and ecologist C. Mendes Filho slain] J. Bierman. il por *Maclean's* 102:21 Ja 9 '89

Notes and comment [murder of environmentalist C. Mendes Filho in Brazil] il *The New Yorker* 65:27-8 F 20 '89

Our vanishing forests. A. Proulx. il *Organic Gardening* 36:60-4+ Mr '89

Our vanishing forests [special section] il *World Press Review* 36:40-1+ O '89

Our vanishing rain forests. S. McCabe. il *Scholastic Update (Teachers' edition)* 121:13-14 Ap 21 '89

The past and future Amazon. P. A. Colinvaux. bibl il maps *Scientific American* 260:102-8 My '89

Playing with fire [destruction of Brazilian rain forest; cover story] E. Linden. il map *Time* 134:76-80+ S 18 '89

Rain forest politics [discussion of May 22, 1989 article, Defenders of the Amazon] S. Hecht and A. Cockburn. *The Nation* 249:262+ S 18 '89

Saving the rain forests. il *Scholastic Update (Teachers' edition)* 122:11 N 3 '89

The scorched earth [Brazilian rain forests] A. DeCurtis. il *Rolling Stone* p40-9 F 23 '89

A tale of two forests [Amazon] *World Press Review* 36:40+ S '89

Threats to biodiversity. E. O. Wilson. bibl il *Scientific American* 261:108-12+ S '89

Tropical chic [saving the rain forests] P. Swire. *The New Republic* 200:18+ Ja 30 '89

Tropical forests: an endangered species. il *World Press Review* 36:36-8 My '89

Trouble on the wind [research by Robert I. Bruck] H. Middleton. il *Southern Living* 24:42+ Je '89

Using red ink to keep tropical forests green [debt-for-nature swaps in Brazil] C. P. Work and G. Smith. il map *U.S. News & World Report* 106:48-9 Mr 6 '89

Where acids reign: do dying stands of Bavarian timber portend the future of polluted U.S. forests? [research by Ernst-Detlef Schulze; cover story] J. Raloff. il *Science News* 136:56-8 Jl 22 '89

Whose hands will shape the future of the Amazon's green mansions? [plight of the rubber tappers; cover story] M. Parfit. bibl (p245) il maps *Smithsonian* 20:58-68+ N '89

A world in crisis. P. H. Raven. il *USA Today (Periodical)* 117:48-50 My '89

Worldwide weather threatens millions [views of Philip Johnston] il *USA Today (Periodical)* 117:1-3 Ap '89

DEFORESTATION IN LITERATURE

A boy sides with Dr. Seuss's Lorax, and puts a town at loggerheads [parents of S. Bailey call for removal of title from school reading list in Laytonville, Calif.] R. Arias. il pors *People Weekly* 32:67-8 O 23 '89

DEFORMATION (MECHANICS)

See also

　Crystals—Defects
　Fracture mechanics
　Rock deformation

DEFORMATION (TECTONICS) *See* Geology

DEGAETANI, JAN, 1933-1989

about

A century, and more, of American song. K. R. Schwarz. *High Fidelity (New York, N.Y.)* 39:52 Mr '89

Obituary

New York 22:152+ O 23 '89. P. G. Davis

DEGAS, EDGAR, 1834-1917

about

"Please have your tickets ready for 'Degas'". M. Esterow. il *Art News* 88:198 Mr '89

DEGAS, HILAIRE GERMAIN EDGAR *See* Degas, Edgar, 1834-1917

DEGNAN, DANIEL A.

When (if) 'Roe' falls [cover story] *Commonweal* 116:267-9 My 5 '89

DEGRADABLE PLASTICS *See* Plastics—Degradability

DEGRADATION (BIOLOGY) *See* Biodegradation

DEGRADO, WILLIAM F., AND OTHERS

Protein design, a minimalist approach. bibl f il *Science* 243:622-8 F 3 '89

DEGRAFF, ROBIN

about

A gamble that paid off. B. D. Gibson. il por *Nation's Business* 77:30 Ja '89

DEGRASSI JUNIOR HIGH [television program] *See* Television program reviews—Single works

DEGREES, ACADEMIC

Detroit minister and wife send 8 daughters through college; 2 M.D.s, 3 Ph.D.s [H. and J. Green] W. Wofford, Jr. il pors *Jet* 75:22-3 F 13 '89

Foreign language studies making slight rebound [degree programs] il *Change* 20:27-31 N/D '88

Is an astronomy degree useful? R. Lopes. il *Sky and Telescope* 78:236 S '89

DEGREES, HONORARY

Central St. fetes Tyson with honorary doctorate [M. Tyson] il pors *Jet* 76:14 My 15 '89

Clifton Davis of 'Amen' gets honorary degree at Lincoln U. commencement. il pors *Jet* 76:16 My 29 '89

Kansas City Call publisher gets honorary degree at U. of Mo.; locked out in '39 [L. Bluford] il por *Jet* 76:16 My 22 '89

Toni Morrison, Kenneth Clark get honorary degrees during Harvard University graduation. il pors *Jet* 76:13 Je 26 '89

DEHAVILLAND AIRCRAFT OF CANADA, LIMITED

GPA Jetprop prepares for 1990s with orders for ATRs, Dash 8s. J. M. Lenorovitz. il *Aviation Week & Space Technology* 130:90 Mr 27 '89

DEHMELT, HANS

about

Basic measurements lead to Physics Nobel. R. Pool. il pors *Science* 246:327-8 O 20 '89

Physics. il pors *Time* 134:74 O 23 '89

Physics Nobel: traps, clocks, quantum leaps. E. Peterson. *Science News* 136:262 O 21 '89

Ramsey, Dehmelt, Paul win Nobel for helping to set high standards. B. G. Levi. il pors *Physics Today* 42:17-19 D '89

DEHUMIDIFIERS

Dehumidifier buying guide. il *Consumers' Research Magazine* 72:34-7 Ag '89

DEHYDRATION (PHYSIOLOGY)

High and dry [skiers] M. Bloom. *Skiing* 41:16-17 Mr '89

DEHYDROEPIANDROSTERONE

Flab-to-muscle pill? [use to burn body fat] A. Dane. *American Health* 8:18 Jl/Ag '89

Ommm . . . please pass the DHEAS [effects of transcendental meditation] J. Hooper. il *Health (New York, N.Y.)* 21:34 O '89

DEI CACCIATORE (ALBARETTO DELLA TORRE, ITALY: RESTAURANT) *See* Albaretto della Torre (Italy)—Restaurants, nightclubs, bars, etc.

DEIBEL, TERRY L.

Reagan foreign policy: a mixed legacy. *Current (Washington, D.C.)* 317:16-24 N '89

Reagan's mixed legacy. *Foreign Policy* 75:34-55 Summ '89

DEIGNER, PETER S., AND OTHERS

Membranes as the energy source in the endergonic transformation of vitamin A to 11-*cis*-retinol. bibl f il *Science* 244:968-71 My 26 '89

DEISENHOFER, JOHANN, 1943-

about

Nobel chemists shed light on key structure in photosynthesis. B. G. Levi. il por *Physics Today* 42:17-18 F '89

DEISENHOFER, JOHANN, 1943-, AND MICHEL, HARTMUT, 1948-

The photosynthetic reaction center from the purple bacterium Rhodopseudomonas viridis. bibl f il *Science* 245:1463-73 S 29 '89

DEITIES *See* Gods and goddesses

DEITZ, PAULA

The Désert de Retz, near Paris. bibl f il *Antiques* 135:718-31 Mr '89

Mediterranean light. il *House & Garden* 161:124-31+ D '89

DEJARNATT, STEVE

about

Miracle mile [film] Reviews

People Weekly 31:15-16 Je 5 '89. R. Novak

DEJOHNETTE, JACK

about

Jack DeJohnette: multidirectional musician [interview; cover story] J. Levenson. il pors *Down Beat* 56:16-19 D '89

DEKALB CORP.

The ultimate crossbred [Chinese and American pigs] B. Freese. il *Successful Farming* 87:28-9 Ag '89

DEKTOR, LESLIE

about

Soft focus. B. Kanner. il *New York* 22:20+ My 22 '89

DEL BALSO, ANTHONY
(jt. auth) See Wilding, Suzanne, and Del Balso, Anthony
DEL DOTTO, DAVE
about
Real-estate revivalist. C. Byron. il por *New York* 22:22-3 S 18 '89
DEL E. WEBB CORP.
The playboy and the 'teddy bear' taking aim at Del Webb [U. Sheinbaum and D. Brumlik] T. Carson. *Business Week* p43-4 Ja 9 '89
DEL MONTE CORP.
Meet Asil Nadir, the billion-dollar fruit king [Polly Peck to buy Del Monte fresh fruit operations] M. Maremont. il por *Business Week* p32 S 18 '89
DEL PINO, EUGENIA M. *See* Pino, Eugenia M. del
DEL VALLE, JOHN
Artichokes. il *Gourmet* 49:92-3+ Ap '89
DELACORTE PRESS
Delacorte's Dutch treat [return of E. Leonard] M. Simson. il *Publishers Weekly* 236:24 O 20 '89
DELAMINATION
Firm develops new method to test for delamination [National Technical Systems] *Aviation Week & Space Technology* 130:52 Ap 17 '89
DELAMOIR, JEANNETTE
(jt. auth) See Romer, Grant B., and Delamoir, Jeannette
DELANCEY STREET FOUNDATION
Delancey Street's road to success [work of J. Maher and M. Silbert] C. Males and J. Raskin. il por *Reader's Digest* 134:108-12 Mr '89
DELANY, MARY GRANVILLE PENDARVES, 1700-1788
about
Mrs. Delany's fabulous flowers. J. Boysen. il por *International Wildlife* 19:44-5 Jl/Ag '89
DELATINER, BARBARA
Upgrading education in local public schools. *The Education Digest* 55:28-30 S '89
DELATTRE, PIERRE
Beauty and the aesthetics of survival. il *Utne Reader* p64-7+ Jl/Ag '89
DELAWARE
See also
Courts—Delaware
DELAWARE BAY (DEL. AND N.J.)
Doing their primal thing [horseshoe crabs mating on the N.J. shore] M. Riley. il *Time* 134:10-11+ Ag 21 '89
DELAWARE BAY COMPANY
Yes, Virginia, there is a way to make money in troubled junk. L. Jereski. il pors *Business Week* p87 S 11 '89
DELAWARE MANAGEMENT COMPANY, INC.
What goes up must come down [nuclear plant decommissioning trust funds managed by J. Meehan and R. Bernstein] J. Zweig. pors *Forbes* 143:200 Mr 20 '89
DELAWARE RIVER (N.Y.-DEL. AND N.J.)
See also
Delaware River Basin Commission
DELAWARE RIVER BASIN COMMISSION
Restoration along the Delaware. C. M. Roberts. il *The Conservationist* 43:2-9 My/Je '89
DELAY OF GRATIFICATION
Delay of gratification in children. W. Mischel and others. bibl f il *Science* 244:933-8 My 26 '89
Preschool self-control and pretzel logic [research by Walter Mischel] B. Bower. *Science News* 135:325 My 27 '89
DELBANCO, ANDREW, 1952-
Lyrical Dreiser. bibl f il *The New York Review of Books* 36:32-7 N 23 '89
The seer of Lafayette Square. il *The New Republic* 201:32-8 O 16 '89
To the Gettysburg station. il *The New Republic* 201:31-6+ N 20 '89
DELEGATES, DEMOCRATIC CONVENTION *See* National conventions, Democratic
DELEGATION OF AUTHORITY IN BUSINESS *See* Personnel management
DELFIN SYSTEMS, INC.
Small, high-tech companies thrive despite cuts in defense spending. il *Aviation Week & Space Technology* 131:118+ S 18 '89
DELFRATE, JUDITH
The computer's impact on education: progress or problem? il *USA Today (Periodical)* 117:68-9 Ja '89
DELFT WARE
Collectors and collecting
John Philip Kassebaum's unparalleled ceramics in Charleston [Branford-Horry House] J. S. Wamsley. il pors *Architectural Digest* 46:86+ D '89
DELFTWARE *See* Delft ware
DELGADO, DANIEL
about
Boning up leads to sloth as a student makes a rare find. il por *People Weekly* 32:61 Jl 3 '89
DELHAGEN, KATE
Health watch. See issues of Runner's World
The runner's companion [cover story; special section] il *Women's Sports & Fitness* 11:31+ S '89
The self-coached runner. il *Women's Sports & Fitness* 11:14-15 Je '89

Total fitness. See issues of Runner's World
DELHAGEN, KATE, AND WILL-WEBER, MARK
Medical & training advice. See issues of Runner's World
DELIA'S (NEW YORK, N.Y.: RESTAURANT) *See* New York (N.Y.)—Restaurants, nightclubs, bars, etc.
DELICATESSENS
Ronald Reagan is full of bologna [deli sandwiches named for celebrities] J. Queenan. il *Gentlemen's Quarterly* 59:161-2 Ag '89
DELINQUENTS *See* Juvenile delinquents and delinquency
DELISLE, LAWRENCE
about
A father lifts his "burdens". E. Magnuson. il *Time* 134:13 Ag 28 '89
DELIVERANCE IN OPERA
How true it Rings [R. Wagner's works] M. Gurewitsch. il *Opera News* 53:12-15 Ap 1 '89
DELIVERY OF GOODS
See also
Food delivery service
Home delivery service
United Parcel Service of America, Inc.
DELL, MICHAEL
about
Dell Computer hits the drawing board. K. Kelly. il por *Business Week* p138 Ap 24 '89
DELL, PAMELA
Debbie: the modern day Gibson girl talks . . . [interview] por *'Teen* 33:49 O '89
More than One life to live. il pors *'Teen* 33:45-6 D '89
Pop-pourri. il *'Teen* 33:68-9 Ag '89
DELL COMPUTER CORPORATION
Dell Computer hits the drawing board. K. Kelly. il por *Business Week* p138 Ap 24 '89
DELL PUBLISHING CO., INC.
A new series from Dell for "armchair verbalists". M. Simson. il *Publishers Weekly* 236:29 D 8 '89
DELLA CASA, NICHOLAS
Kidnapping
Rescue in Mozambique [English journalist N. della Casa freed from Renamo through efforts of Freedom Inc.; with editorial comment by James R. Whelan] R. MacKenzie. il pors map *Conservative Digest* 15:39+, 70 Mr/Ap '89
DELLA FEMINA, JERRY, 1936-
Jerry Della Femina: on the ad game, shiny kitchen floors and a choking cat. il por *People Weekly* 31 Special Issue:124-5 Summ '89
about
The Madman of Mad Ave prepares for takeoff. W. Konrad. il por *Business Week* p124 F 20 '89
DELLA FEMINA, MCNAMEE WCRS
The image of creative control [office of L. R. McNamee] L. Rosch. il por *Working Woman* 14:132-3 S '89
The Madman of Mad Ave prepares for takeoff [Pan Am account goes to Della Femina] W. Konrad. il por *Business Week* p124 F 20 '89
DELLA FEMINA, TRAVISANO & PARTNERS
See also
Della Femina, McNamee WCRS
DELLINGER, WALTER
Case closed. *The New Republic* 200:14-16 Ja 9-16 '89
Day in court. *The New Republic* 200:11-12 My 8 '89
Should a constitutional amendment to prevent flag desecration be approved? [excerpts from testimony, July 18, 1989] *Congressional Digest* 68:209+ Ag/S '89
DELLUMS, RONALD V., 1935-
about
Dellums urges support for Chinese freedom struggle. il por *Jet* 76:15 Je 26 '89
DELONG, EDWARD F., AND OTHERS
Phylogenetic stains: ribosomal RNA-based probes for the identification of single cells. bibl f il *Science* 243:1360-3 Mr 10 '89
DELORME, MARY
A watery paradise: Rowland Vaughan and Hereford's 'Golden Vale'. bibl il *History Today* 39:38-43 Jl '89
DELORS, JACQUES
Secretary meets with EC ministers [text of joint conference, December 9, 1988] *Department of State Bulletin* 89:27-30 F '89
about
Creating 1992. S. Tully. il por *Fortune* 119:41-2 Ja 2 '89
The Czar of Brussels. S. Sullivan. il pors *Newsweek* 113:32-3 F 6 '89
"Mr. Europe" leads the way. il por *Time* 134:43 S 18 '89
President's meeting with EC Commission president [White House statement, June 14, 1989] il por *Department of State Bulletin* 89:83 Ag '89
Who is going to govern Europe? [interview] Y. de L'Ecotais and J. Leclerc du Sablon. il por *World Press Review* 36:28+ S '89
DELPHINIUMS
Delphiniums move south. il *Southern Living* 24:101 Ap '89
DELPHINUS (CONSTELLATION) *See* Constellations
DELSEMME, ARMAND H.
Whence come comets? il *Sky and Telescope* 77:260-4 Mr '89

DELSOHN, STEVE
Beers with . . . Jack McKeon [interview] il pors *Sport (New York, N.Y.)* 80:19+ Jl '89
(ed) See Getty, Estelle. If I knew then what I know now . . . so what?
DELTA (LAUNCH VEHICLE) *See* Space vehicles—Propulsion systems
DELTA AIR LINES, INC.
American, Delta computer reservations deal may intensify global competition. C. A. Shifrin. il *Aviation Week & Space Technology* 130:94-5 F 13 '89
American, Delta lower price for shares of joint CRS venture [computer reservations system] *Aviation Week & Space Technology* 130:108 Ap 24 '89
Douglas launches MD90 transport with Delta order. B. A. Smith. il *Aviation Week & Space Technology* 131:34-5 N 20 '89
Making a little look like a lot [Delta Air Lines Reservations and Training Center, Salt Lake City, Utah] G. Anderson. il *Architectural Record* 177:128-31 My '89
MD90, 737 transport orders set stage for Delta's increased share of U.S. market. il *Aviation Week & Space Technology* 131:35+ N 20 '89
Safety Board blames lax crew behavior but also faults Delta, FAA for Dallas crash [August 1988] J. Ott. *Aviation Week & Space Technology* 131:103-4 O 2 '89
DELTA WOODSIDE INDUSTRIES, INC.
Chink in the armor [Stroud family sells small stake in Milliken & Co. to Delta Woodside Industries] A. A. Lappen. il *Forbes* 144:84+ N 13 '89
Iconoclasts. R. Addis. il pors *Forbes* 143:49+ Ap 17 '89
DELTAS
See also
Nile River—Delta
Sacramento-San Joaquin Delta (Calif.)
Yazoo River (Miss.)—Delta
DELUCAS, LAWRENCE J., AND OTHERS
Protein crystal growth in microgravity. bibl f il *Science* 246:651-4 N 3 '89
DELUISE, PETER
about
Dom's son Peter Deluise juggles a job on 21 Jump Street and life with a wife 1,078 miles away. M. Dougherty. il pors *People Weekly* 31:159-60 My 15 '89
DELWICHE, CHARLES F., AND OTHERS
Lignin-like compounds and sporopollenin in Coleochaete, an algal model for land plant ancestry. bibl f il *Science* 245:399-401 Jl 28 '89
DEMAK, RICHARD
Was it worth the risk? il pors *Sports Illustrated* 71:76-81+ D 18 '89
(jt. auth) See Wulf, Steve, and Demak, Richard
DEMAK, RICHARD, AND KIRSHENBAUM, JERRY
The NFL fails its drug test. il *Sports Illustrated* 71:38-41+ Jl 10 '89
DEMAND AND SUPPLY *See* Supply and demand
DEMARAIS, STEVE, AND ZAIGLIN, BOB
Blueprinting big bucks [cover story]; ed. by Kathy Etling. il *Outdoor Life* 184:61-3+ O '89
DEMARCO, DONALD
There's no such thing as a right to bear children [with readers' comments] *U.S. Catholic* 54:13-19 Ag '89
DEMARCO, SUSAN
A fresh crop of ideas. il *The Progressive* 53:26-31 Ja '89
DEMARCO FAMILY
about
Wagon, roll! Like pioneers of old, the DeMarco family heads west with hope. D. Chu. il *People Weekly* 32:123-4+ N 6 '89
DEMAREST, JEFFERY R., AND OTHERS
Activation of apical chloride channels in the gastric oxyntic cell. bibl f il *Science* 245:402-4 Jl 28 '89
DEMARINIS, RICK, 1934-
Insulation [story] il *Harper's* 279:51-4 Jl '89
DEMARS, STANFORD E.
Worship by-the-sea; camp-meetings and seaside resorts in 19th century America. bibl il maps *Focus (New York, N.Y.: 1950)* 38:15-20 Wint '88
DEMARSH, LEROY E., AND GIORGIANNI, EDWARD J.
Color science for imaging systems. bibl f il *Physics Today* 42:44-52 S '89
DEMBLING, SOPHIA
Coming up: new heads and tails. il *The Saturday Evening Post* 261:32+ O '89
DE'MEDICI, LORENZA
about
Medici culinary Renaissance comes to Fawcett. il *Publishers Weekly* 236:43-4 S 8 '89
DEMENTIA
See also
AIDS (Disease)
Alzheimer's disease
DEMENY, PAUL
World population trends. bibl f *Current History* 88:17-19+ Ja '89
DEMERATH, N. J., AND WILLIAMS, RHYS H.
Religion and power in the American experience. bibl il *Society* 26:29-38 Ja/F '89

DEMERLE, RICHARD C.
Imagine a river: understanding the balance between power and morality. por *The Humanist* 49:27-8 Mr/Ap '89
DEMETRACOPOULOS, ELIAS
about
Minority report. C. Hitchens. *The Nation* 248:764 Je 5 '89
DEMICHEAL, DON
Father and son: an interview with Muddy Waters and Paul Butterfield [reprint] pors *Down Beat* 56:68-71 S '89
DEMILITARIZED ZONE, KOREAN (KOREA) *See* Korean Demilitarized Zone (Korea)
DEMING, W. EDWARDS
about
W. Edwards Deming is the American who taught the Japanese how to compete. D. Moreau. il por *Changing Times* 43:132 S '89
DEMKO, GEORGE J., 1933-, AND HEZLEP, W.
USSR: mapping the blank spots [cover story] maps *Focus (New York, N.Y.: 1950)* 39:20-1 Spr '89
DEMME, JONATHAN
about
Married to the Mob [film] Reviews
Video il 12:62 Mr '89. S. L. Siegel
Mob boss is Mr. Nice Guy. M. Fleischmann. il por *Video* 12:12 Mr '89
Something wilder. J. Farber. il *Rolling Stone* p23 N 2 '89
DEMOCRACY
See also
Black suffrage
Christianity and democracy
Communism and democracy
Education and democracy
Liberty
National Endowment for Democracy
The battle for democracy [cover story] S. V. Roberts. il *U.S. News & World Report* 106:35-8 My 22 '89
Boredom, virtue, and democratic capitalism. M. Novak. *Commentary* 88:34-7 S '89
The Chinese massacres underscore the timeliness of a new book, The democratic imperative. M. S. Forbes, Jr. il *Forbes* 144:27 Ag 7 '89
Democracy and tyranny: dealing with friendly tyrants. R. N. Haass. *Current (Washington, D.C.)* 316:34-40 O '89
Democracy as the wave of the future. C. Gershman. *Current (Washington, D.C.)* 312:18-25 My '89
The democracy boosters. C. G. Ryn. *National Review* 41:30-2+ Mr 24 '89
The democracy gang. M. Kondracke. il *The New Republic* 201:18+ N 6 '89
Exchanging a prison for a maze [East German refugees and A. de Tocqueville's views on democracy] R. Rosenblatt. il *U.S. News & World Report* 107:10-11 S 25 '89
Hook on democracy [discussion of March 24, 1989 article, The democracy boosters] C. G. Ryn. *National Review* 41:4+ Je 2 '89
Is democratic theory for export? J. Barzun. *Society* 26:16-23 Mr/Ap '89
It is later than you think: 1989. M. Lerner. *Society* 26:83-6 S/O '89
Notes and comment [democracy and world politics] *The New Yorker* 65:29 S 4 '89
People power. R. A. Falk. *The Nation* 248:801 Je 12 '89
The politics of cold blood. R. J. Rummel. bibl *Society* 27:32-40 N/D '89
The rapidly changing world [address, June 14, 1989] M. M. Kampelman. *Vital Speeches of the Day* 55:731-4 S 15 '89
Robbing the future. R. W. Wilkins. il *Mother Jones* 14:6+ S '89
Rules of the game. J. Garvey. *Commonweal* 116:697-8 D 15 '89
The tentative triumph of the ballot. F. Ajami. il *U.S. News & World Report* 107:40+ D 4 '89
Welcome to democracy. M. Greenfield. il *Newsweek* 113:70 My 29 '89
Will democracy in Latin America simply mean plunder? P. C. Roberts. il *Business Week* p18 S 18 '89
DEMOCRACY IN TELEVISION
Making 'Democracy' [Canadian series The struggle for democracy; cover story; with editorial comment by Kevin Doyle] B. D. Johnson. il pors *Maclean's* 102:4, 38-40+ Ja 16 '89
DEMOCRATIC CAPITALISM *See* Capitalism
DEMOCRATIC CAUCUS (U.S.) *See* House Democratic Caucus (U.S.)
DEMOCRATIC CONVENTIONS *See* National conventions, Democratic
DEMOCRATIC LEADERSHIP COUNCIL
Warm spit. R. Kuttner. *The New Republic* 200:43 Ap 3 '89
DEMOCRATIC NATIONAL COMMITTEE
Brown seeks DNC chair. K. D. Thompson. il por *Black Enterprise* 19:30 F '89
Democrat Brown. *The Nation* 248:219-20 F 20 '89
The Democrats' next dilemma [R. Brown seeks chairmanship] P. R. Range. il por *U.S. News & World Report* 106:23 F 6 '89

DEMOCRATIC NATIONAL COMMITTEE—*cont.*
'Democrats should pick Ron Brown,' state some powerful white backers. il por *Jet* 75:8 Ja 30 '89
Donkey serenade [R. Brown campaigns for chairman] J. Klein. il por *New York* 22:10-11 Ja 30 '89
From two new party chairmen: plans to woo and keep the black vote. R. Brown; L. Atwater. il *American Visions* 4:16-18 Je '89
Meet Ron Brown, pillar of the establishment. R. Fly. il por *Business Week* p54 F 13 '89
A move to 'Stop Ron' [keeping R. Brown from being elected chairman] il por *Newsweek* 113:4 Ja 23 '89
A new act in the Democratic Party [R. Brown] K. D. Thompson. por *Black Enterprise* 19:29 Ap '89
Party games [costs of R. Brown's campaign to become chairman] V. Novak. por *Common Cause Magazine* 15:7 My/Je '89
Playing the politics of race [R. Brown to be Democratic Party chairman while Republicans woo blacks] H. Fineman. il por *Newsweek* 113:20 F 6 '89
Ron Brown: chairman of the Democratic National Committee. il pors *Ebony* 44:36+ My '89
Ron Brown is voted first black to chair Dem. Party. il por *Jet* 75:4+ F 27 '89
Ron Brown sets priorities, names his senior staff. il por *Jet* 76:5 My 1 '89
Ron Brown's first test [presidential nomination rules] il por *Newsweek* 113:7 F 20 '89
Ron Brown's party line. R. Kuttner. il pors *The New York Times Magazine* p44+ D 3 '89
Running as his own man [R. Brown] W. Isaacson. il por *Time* 133:56-8 Ja 30 '89
Solomon with a computer [chairman R. Brown] M. B. Zuckerman. il *U.S. News & World Report* 106:84 F 20 '89
"Ten steps, then we shoot," says Ron Brown. "I've got my AK-47," replies Lee Atwater. "What've you got?". M. Kelly. il pors *Gentlemen's Quarterly* 59:142-7+ Jl '89
DEMOCRATIC PARTY (U.S.)
Act II, winning an election. N. Lemann. *The Washington Monthly* 21:30+ Mr '89
. . . and on Capitol Hill [Democrats lack agenda] H. Gorey. il *Time* 134:23 S 25 '89
The Atwater flag sting. N. Hentoff. il *The Progressive* 53:12-14 N '89
Bring back big spending. il *The New Republic* 200:7-8 Mr 27 '89
Capital gained [House Democrats support cut in capital gains tax] *The Nation* 249:443-4 O 23 '89
Capital gains: as the Democrats squabble, Bush may score. D. Harbrecht and R. Fly. il *Business Week* p58 S 25 '89
The Capitol gains of the well-to-do [Democratic Congress addresses tax cuts] M. Barone. il *U.S. News & World Report* 107:26-7+ O 2 '89
A child care bill will pass as soon as the Democrats grow up. S. B. Garland. il *Business Week* p73 D 11 '89
Choosing presidential candidates: why the best man doesn't necessarily win. D. G. Stephenson, Jr. il *USA Today (Periodical)* 117:15-18 Mr '89
The Democratic Party and foreign policy: a proposed manifesto. A. Tonelson. *Current (Washington, D.C.)* 317:25-34 N '89
The Democrats [discussion of February 1989 article, Why the Democrats lost again] J. Muravchik. *Commentary* 87:2-5 Je '89
Democrats after Dukakis. il *National Review* 41:16-17 F 10 '89
The Democrats' meltdown on the Hill. D. Harbrecht. il *Business Week* p25 Je 12 '89
Democrats move to recruit members for jobs in Party [Council of Black Administrative Assistants and Associates] il *Jet* 76:27 Je 19 '89
The Democrats' state-takeover strategy. P. Glastris. *U.S. News & World Report* 107:38 N 27 '89
The Democrats' success formula: they repeatedly win in conservative places by playing all the local angles [congressmen] M. Barone. il *U.S. News & World Report* 106:23-4 Je 26 '89
Democrats try therapy again. G. Borger and D. Baer. il *U.S. News & World Report* 107:28 S 18 '89
Dems win Congress but will they lose blacks? il *Black Enterprise* 19:13 Ja '89
Drugs, Democrats and priorities [call for blacks to fight drug plague] M. Waters. *The Nation* 249:141-4 Jl 24-31 '89
End of the rainbow [voting patterns of poor and minorities] R. A. Teixeira. il *The New Republic* 200:11-12+ Ap 3 '89
Flix mix in politix [Hollywood activism; cover story] F. Barnes. *The New Republic* 201:20+ O 30 '89
Grabbing the creative initiative: a new Democratic opportunity. E. M. Kennedy. por *USA Today (Periodical)* 118:35-7 Jl '89
How far can the Democrats ride this wave? D. Harbrecht and R. Fly. il *Business Week* p45 N 20 '89
How the Democrats can win in '92. D. R. Mayhew and B. Russett. *The New Leader* 72:13 Ja 9 '89

How the Democrats hold on to Congress. S. T. Mandel and W. McGurn. *National Review* 41:37-40 N 24 '89
The HUD party, the party of patronage. *National Review* 41:10 S 1 '89
The incumbent party, the party of incumbents [N. Gingrich's ethics drive against the Democrats] *National Review* 41:14-15 Je 30 '89
Is liberalism still possible? R. H. Bates. *National Review* 41:17 D 31 '89
Jackson action [Democrats hope that J. Jackson will run for mayor of Washington, D.C.] J. Klein. il por *New York* 22:20+ My 15 '89
Jackson rules [presidential nomination rules] F. Barnes. *The New Republic* 200:14+ My 1 '89
Jerry Brown: a California comeback [interview with state chairman] L. Wright. il por *Newsweek* 113:6 F 27 '89
Jerry Brown rises from the ashrams. R. D. Hof. il por *Business Week* p36 F 13 '89
JFK's children: the class of '74 [neoliberal Democrats; cover story] W. Schneider. il por *The Atlantic* 263:35-40+ Mr '89
Less government, more activism. R. J. Dennis. *New Perspectives Quarterly* 6:63 Spr '89
Lessons of campaign '88. F. Barnes. il *The American Spectator* 22:14-16 Ja '89
Let the great gerrymander war begin [effects of reapportionment after 1990 census] P. R. Range. il map *U.S. News & World Report* 106:29-30 F 20 '89
Missing mandate. *National Review* 41:12-13 Mr 10 '89
Musical chairs [leadership in the House; cover story] F. Barnes. *The New Republic* 200:14-15 Je 12 '89
A narrow escape for the Democrats [1914 congressional elections] *The New Republic* 201 [Reprint v1]:8-9 N 6 '89 [N 7 '14]
On the Hill, class war over taxes [Democratic plan to raise top rate] E. Clift and R. Thomas. il *Newsweek* 114:24 O 2 '89
Parting shot: a labor leader blasts the Democrats. W. W. Winpisinger. il *The Progressive* 53:28-30 Jl '89
'A party within a party': Jim Hightower proposes a populist alliance. D. A. Denison. il *The Progressive* 53:22-3 Mr '89
The players to watch [Democratic leadership shakeup in the House] *Newsweek* 113:21 Je 5 '89
Profiles [House majority leader T. S. Foley] J. Newhouse. il por *The New Yorker* 65:48-50+ Ap 10 '89
Progressive values for America [cover story] M. J. Green. il *The Nation* 248:109+ Ja 30 '89
Putting their House in order [R. Gephardt becomes majority leader and W. Gray becomes party whip] E. Salholz. il pors *Newsweek* 113:18 Je 26 '89
Raising issues, hope and hell. J. Hightower. il *The Nation* 248:160+ F 6 '89
The shifty Richard Gephardt [cover story] R. D. Novak. il *The American Spectator* 22:14-16 Ag '89
Shredding the Democrats' agenda [charges against J. Wright] D. Harbrecht and R. Fly. il por *Business Week* p26 My 1 '89
Talking chop [Democratic support of capital gains tax cut] *The New Republic* 201:4+ O 23 '89
Tanned, rested, and ready [J. Brown running for state Democratic Party chairman in California] R. Brownstein. il *The New Republic* 200:23+ Ja 30 '89
That was Zen, this is now [J. Brown elected chairman of state Democrats] R. Lacayo. por *Time* 133:20 F 27 '89
To Congress, Bush looked like a pushover. D. Harbrecht and R. Fly. il *Business Week* p27-8 Ag 21 '89
Tough talk. R. E. Tyrrell. *The American Spectator* 22:10-11 N '89
Tough talk for Democrats. J. A. Califano. il *The New York Times Magazine* p28-9+ Ja 8 '89
What liberals haven't learned & why [presidential election] F. F. Siegel. il *Commonweal* 116:16-20 Ja 13 '89
Where are the Democrats? *The New Republic* 201:4 S 18-25 '89
Why the catastrophic-care fight will change generational politics. G. Borger. il *U.S. News & World Report* 107:18 O 9 '89
Why the Democrats lost again [presidential election] J. Muravchik. *Commentary* 87:13-22 F '89
The wonder year. *The Nation* 249:551-2 N 13 '89
DEMOGRAPHY
See also
Computers—Demographic use
Population forecasting
United States—Population
DEMOLITION OF BUILDINGS *See* Wrecking
DEMONOLOGY
See also
Satanism
DEMONSTRATIONS *See* Protests, demonstrations, etc.
DEMOPOLIS (ALA.)
Education
A star shines from Alabama [successful integration] A. Waldron. il *The Nation* 248:664-6 My 15 '89
DEMOTT, BENJAMIN
An education emperor: teachings from the life of K'ang-hsi. *Change* 21:62 Mr/Ap '89

DEMOTT, BENJAMIN—*cont.*
Knowing and not knowing. *Change* 21:62 S/O '89
Resurrecting liberalism. *Current (Washington, D.C.)* 309:14-22 Ja '89

DEMPEWOLFF, RITA
A strange ailment left me speechless for 27 years. il *Good Housekeeping* 209:74+ O '89

DEMPSEY, JUDY
A minor revolution in Austria. il *World Press Review* 36:60 Ja '89

DEMPSEY, KATHLEEN V. HOOVER- *See* Hoover-Dempsey, Kathleen V.

DEMPSEY, PATRICK
about
Patrick Dempsey. E. Miller. il pors *Seventeen* 48:53-4+ Ja '89
Patrick Dempsey: an East Coast kid conquers Hollywood. por *'Teen* 33:51 O '89

DEN HAAG, ERNEST VAN *See* Van den Haag, Ernest

DENALI NATIONAL PARK AND PRESERVE (ALASKA)
Stubborn hunter in a harsh land [tracking caribou herds and wolf packs] L. D. Mech. il map *National Wildlife* 27:20-4 Ag/S '89

DENATONIUM SACCHARIDE
In bad taste [use of saccharin to increase potency of foul tasting repellent; work of Gary Hollander and Mel Blum] il *Discover* 10:14 S '89

DENBY, DAVID
Movies. See issues of New York

DENDE OIL *See* Palm oil

DENDROBATES *See* Frogs

DENEUVE, CATHERINE
about
Catherine Deneuve. C. Aillaud. il por *Architectural Digest* 46:36+ Ja '89

DENG XIAOPING, 1904-
about
Another little red book. S. Burton. il por *Time* 134:47 S 18 '89
Bad days in Beijing. M. Liu. il *Newsweek* 114:34-5 Jl 31 '89
Behind China's anger [cover story] J. Wallace. il *U.S. News & World Report* 106:20-3 Je 5 '89
Beijing's bad-times bash. E. MacFarquhar. il *U.S. News & World Report* 107:33-5 O 2 '89
China. *Business Week* p56 O 2 '89
China: what price peace? J. Wallace. il map *U.S. News & World Report* 106:20-3+ Je 19 '89
China's next great leap could be backward. D. Lee. il *Business Week* p54-5 My 8 '89
Deng strikes back [special section] il pors *Newsweek* 113:30-6 Je 5 '89
Deng's hard-liners and their enemies list. E. MacFarquhar. il pors *U.S. News & World Report* 106:24-6 Je 5 '89
Deng's 'pact with the devil'. C. S. Manegold. il por *Newsweek* 114:33 S 18 '89
Deng's pyrrhic victory [cover story] Liu Binyan. *The New Republic* 201:21-4 O 2 '89
The making of Deng's successor. S. Burton. il por *Time* 134:44 O 9 '89
Marriage of convenience. D. Doder. il pors *U.S. News & World Report* 106:30-2 My 15 '89
Reinventing China: what began as another hapless student protest has become a revolution. D. Doder and H. Trewhitt. il por *U.S. News & World Report* 106:30-4+ My 29 '89
A reunion of comrades [special section] il pors map *Newsweek* 112:46-9+ My 22 '89
An unlikely 'emperor'. M. Nemeth. il por *Maclean's* 102:36 My 29 '89
The view from the Forbidden City. W. Lord. il por *Newsweek* 114:36 D 18 '89
The wrath of Deng. H. G. Chua-Eoan. il por map *Time* 133:18-21 Je 19 '89

DENHART, GUN
about
The new entrepreneurial establishment: 1989 Harriet Alger Award. il pors *Working Woman* 14:53-6+ N '89

DENICOLO, DAVID
Barbara Hershey—a serious star talks about Beaches, Bette, Temptation, friends . . . and Oscars. il por *Glamour* 87:138 F '89

DENIM
Done-up denim. il *'Teen* 33:48-51 Ja '89

DENIM JEANS *See* Jeans (Clothing)

DENIS, CLAIRE
about
Chocolat [film] Reviews
America 161:124-5 Ag 26-S 2 '89. R. A. Blake
The New Republic 200:28-9 Ap 17 '89. S. Kauffmann
Newsweek il 113:68 Mr 27 '89. J. Kroll
Vogue il 179:268 Mr '89. K. Bishop

DENIS, CORINNE
'The sea has its limits'. il *World Press Review* 36:55 Je '89

DENISON, DAVE A.
'A party within a party': Jim Hightower proposes a populist alliance. il *The Progressive* 53:22-3 Mr '89

DENISON (TEX.)
Historic houses, sites, etc.
See also
Eisenhower Birthplace State Historic Site (Denison, Tex.)

DENMARK
See also
Dance festivals—Denmark
Geology—Denmark
Housing—Denmark
Iron Age—Denmark
Motion pictures—Denmark
Public welfare—Denmark
Romo (Denmark)
Description and travel
See also
Cycling—Denmark

DENNEHY, BRIAN
about
They call him Captain Blood. M. Long. il por *Gentlemen's Quarterly* 59:244-5 My '89

DENNER, BARBARA W., AND KIRCHHOFF, SUSAN
The Gahanna-Jefferson City internship program. *Phi Delta Kappan* 71:166-7 O '89

DENNING, ROBERT
about
Victorian revival. B. Adams. il *House & Garden* 161:102-9 D '89

DENNIS, CARL
My congressman [poem] *America* 161:78 Ag 12-19 '89

DENNIS, ED
Diesels. See issues of Motor Boating & Sailing

DENNIS, JERRY
Bridges. il *Audubon* 91:46-7 Jl '89

DENNIS, LISL
Traveler's camera. See issues of Popular Photography beginning June 1988

DENNIS, RICHARD J.
Less government, more activism. *New Perspectives Quarterly* 6:63 Spr '89

DENNIS, SANDY
about
Sandy Dennis. D. Hutchings. il pors *People Weekly* 31:64-6+ Mr 13 '89

DENNIS GREEN DESIGN GROUP LTD.
Got those smelly gym clothes blues? Try Dennis Green's Sneaker Balls and it's arrivederci, aroma [small space deodorizers] il por *People Weekly* 32:58 Jl 3 '89

DENNISON, JOE
Bill Frisell's solo on "Evidence"—a guitar transcription. il *Down Beat* 56:56-7 My '89

DENNY, ALMA
The day the tears came [poem] *Good Housekeeping* 209:184 Jl '89

DENOON, DAVID B. H.
Japan and the U.S.—the security agenda [reprint from November 1983 issue] bibl f *Current History* 88:37-8+ Ja '89

DENS (ROOMS)
A classic garage conversion. il *Southern Living* 24:110 Ja '89

DENT, DAVID J.
Readin', ritin' & rage: how schools are destroying black boys. il *Essence* 20:54-6+ N '89

DENT, RICHARD
about
Dent's $6.25 million highest pact for Bears. por *Jet* 77:50 N 20 '89

DENTAL CARIES
Cavity risk [food chart] R. Asa. il *American Health* 8:58 Mr '89
Chewing pays off [reduced with use of xylitol gum; research by Kauko Makinen] il *Prevention (Emmaus, Pa.)* 41:22 Mr '89
Flap over fluoride. L. Oliwenstein. il *Discover* 10:34-5 Jl '89
Fluoridation: friends and foes. C. Sears. il map *American Health* 8:36+ O '89
Koop speaks out [support of fluoridated drinking water] C. Sears. il *American Health* 8:51 Ja/F '89
Seal of approval [dentists' endorsements for snacks safe for teeth] C. Sears. il *American Health* 8:55 Mr '89
Genetic aspects
The genetics factor. il *Prevention (Emmaus, Pa.)* 41:19-20 O '89
Prevention
See Teeth—Care and hygiene

DENTAL ENAMEL *See* Tooth enamel

DENTAL EQUIPMENT
See also
Dental floss
Dental materials
Lasers—Dental use
Toothbrushes

DENTAL FEES
Down and out—in the mouth [prohibitive cost of dental care] C. Sears. il *American Health* 8:40 D '89
Anecdotes, facetiae, satire, etc.
Uncivil liberties. C. Trillin. il *The Nation* 249:670 D 4 '89

DENTAL FLOSS
Dental flosses & tapes. il *Consumer Reports* 54:46-8 D '89
Which flosses are best? il *Consumer Reports* 54:508-9 Ag '89
DENTAL HYGIENE *See* Teeth—Care and hygiene
DENTAL INSURANCE *See* Insurance, Dental
DENTAL MATERIALS
Dentist's device [Amalgameter to measure mercury vapor emitted from fillings] il *FDA Consumer* 23:35-6 O '89
Scared of the dentist's chair? [hazards of filling cavities with silver-mercury amalgams] C. Fahey. il *Utne Reader* p16+ N/D '89
Sealing cavities [dental sealants] il *Prevention (Emmaus, Pa.)* 41:16+ Ja '89
Sealing out decay [use of dental sealants] J. P. Cohn. il *FDA Consumer* 23:18-21 N '89
Smile! You may need new fillings [composite resin fillings] C. Schaeffer. il *Changing Times* 43:118-19 Ap '89
DENTAL OFFICES
Strong medicine [dentists' offices designed by Burr & McCallum in Bennington, Vt.] P. M. Sachner. il *Architectural Record* 177:94-7 O '89
DENTAL PHOBIA
Fear of fillings. S. Chollar. il *Psychology Today* 23:74 Ja/F '89
Good news for dental phobics. P. Avery. il *American Health* 8:46+ My '89
Scared of the dentist's chair? C. Fahey. il *Utne Reader* p16+ N/D '89
DENTAL PLAQUE
New ways to save your teeth? [cover story; special section] il *Consumer Reports* 54:504-9 Ag '89
Tailoring plaque control. C. Sears. il *American Health* 8:48 Ap '89
DENTAL SCHOOLS AND COLLEGES
Enrollment
Enrollment ups and downs in dental and veterinary fields. il *Change* 21:27-9 S/O '89
DENTAL WORKERS
Health and hygiene
She who laughs gas conceives last [research by Gerard Kugel and Carlos Letelier] F. Flam. *Science News* 135:182 Mr 25 '89
DENTAL X RAYS *See* Radiography, Medical
DENTATE GYRUS *See* Brain
DENTISTRY
See also
AIDS patients—Dental care
American Dental Association
Cancer patients—Dental care
Cardiacs—Dental care
Computers—Dental use
Dentures
Forensic dentistry
Holistic dentistry
Lasers—Dental use
Orthodontics
Root canal therapy
Teeth
Veterinary dentistry
Bright future for cosmetic dentistry. il *USA Today (Periodical)* 118:3 O '89
A certain smile [cosmetic dentistry] H. Hansen. il *Vogue* 179:432-3+ N '89
Chiclet choppers [dental bleaching; views of Jacqueline Dzierzak] I. Springer. il *American Health* 8:36 N '89
Cosmetic breakthroughs that can save your teeth. S. Williams. il *Prevention (Emmaus, Pa.)* 41:107-8+ Je '89
The drill is gone [painless dentistry] M. Kaplan. il *Gentlemen's Quarterly* 59:170+ N '89
The high-tech mouth [cosmetic dentistry] C. Sears. il *American Health* 8:42 Jl/Ag '89
Informed choices [cosmetic dentistry; views of Jan Linhart] E. Franklin. il *American Health* 8:44 Jl/Ag '89
Smile power. il *Glamour* 87:220-3 D '89
Tooth truths. N. Gallo. il *Better Homes and Gardens* 68:41-3 F '89
Fees
See Dental fees
Psychological aspects
See also
Dental phobia
DENTISTS
See also
American Dental Association
Fees
See Dental fees
DENTISTS AND PATIENTS
See also
Dental phobia
DENTISTS' OFFICES *See* Dental offices
DENTON, HERBERT H., 1943-1989
about
Obituary
The New Republic 200:4 My 29 '89. H. Hertzberg
DENTSU INC.
Number one. E. F. Cone. il *Forbes* 143:10 Je 26 '89

DENTURES
'Permanent' dentures [tooth implants; views of Max Listgarten] *Prevention (Emmaus, Pa.)* 41:18-19 Ja '89
Tooth tech: the new dentistry. A. Biesada. il *High Technology Business* 9:28-31 Ap '89
History
George Washington's false teeth. J. Gustaitis. il *American History Illustrated* 23:22-3 F '89
DENVER, JOHN
about
Seeking higher ground. C. Charles and B. Samples. il por *National Wildlife* 27:29 Je/Jl '89
DENVER (COLO.)
Airports
Congressional pledge of $500 million for Denver airport seen as key victory. *Aviation Week & Space Technology* 131:71 O 23 '89
Denver voters to decide fate of proposed airport. *Aviation Week & Space Technology* 130:73 My 15 '89
Escape from jaws of microburst [alert system at Stapleton International Airport] *Science News* 136:159 S 2 '89
Microburst radar may spur review of tower's role in aborting landings [Doppler radar tested] P. J. Klass. il *Aviation Week & Space Technology* 130:79+ My 1 '89
Proposed Denver International passes environmental test, but funding slips. M. Mecham. *Aviation Week & Space Technology* 131:94-5 Ag 21 '89
Urban growing pains [Denver approves new airport] G. J. Church. il *Time* 133:33 My 29 '89
Voters approve Denver airport, but project faces more hurdles. *Aviation Week & Space Technology* 130:104 My 22 '89
Why new airports are backed up on the runway [politics and corporate self-interest stall construction] W. C. Symonds and S. Payne. il *Business Week* p36-7 My 22 '89
Bookstores
See Booksellers and bookselling—Colorado
Crime
Killer on the loose? [news reporters in helicopter help capture gunman P. Hutchinson] P. O. D'Aulaire and E. D'Aulaire. il *Reader's Digest* 134:64-70 Ja '89
Pushing his luck—and his blood pressure—an aged bank robber is caught red-handed [J. Kelm] il por *People Weekly* 31:108 Ap 17 '89
Criminal justice, Administration of
Sentence for trespassing [religious pacifist J. Haines given nine months for trespassing at Rocky Flats Plant] *The Christian Century* 106:256 Mr 8 '89
Description
First impressions. D. Shiflett. il *The American Spectator* 22:55 D '89
Education
See also
Auraria Higher Education Center (Colo.)
Galleries and museums
See also
Black American West Museum
Denver Art Museum
Gardens and gardening
Expanding their Denver garden gave them more space for outdoor living. il *Sunset (Central West edition)* 182:220-1 Je '89
Industries
Crash course in Denver [TV newsrooms cover Sioux City air crash, July 1989] J. M. Robins. il *Channels (New York, N.Y.: 1986)* 9:16 O '89
Denver does ScanAmerica [Arbitron's single-source media research] M. Couzens. *Channels (New York, N.Y.: 1986)* 9:24 N '89
Music
See also
Opera Colorado
Race relations
Birth certificate says she's white, but woman gets a judge to declare her black [M. C. Walker] por *Jet* 76:36 S 18 '89
Water supply
Where will the cranes go? [Two Forks dam planned by Denver may threaten sandhill crane habitat on Platte River] J. Adler. il map *Newsweek* 113:62-3 Ap 3 '89
DENVER ART MUSEUM
Indian art in Denver . . . the best work of 300 tribes. il *Sunset (Central West edition)* 182:54+ F '89
DENVER INTERNATIONAL AIRPORT *See* Denver (Colo.)—Airports
DENWORTH, LYDIA
(jt. auth) *See* Suh, Mary, and Denworth, Lydia
DENZAU, ARTHUR T.
Trade protection comes to Silicon Valley. *Society* 26:38-42 Mr/Ap '89
DEODORANTS
See also
Dennis Green Design Group Ltd.
Marketing
Sweating it out [Mennen's Real deodorant] C. Poole. il *Forbes* 144:274 O 16 '89

DEOXYGUANOSINE
Template-directed oligomerization catalyzed by a polynucleotide analog [polycytidylic acid] J. Visscher and others. bibl f il *Science* 244:329-31 Ap 21 '89
DEOXYRIBONUCLEIC ACID *See* DNA
DEPALMA, ANTHONY
The lessons of St. Joe's. il por *The New York Times Magazine* p34-7 F 5 '89
DEPARLE, JASON
Beyond the legal right: why liberals and feminists don't like to talk about the morality of abortion [cover story] *The Washington Monthly* 21:28-9+ Ap '89
The juice ain't no use: why the death penalty won't work in D.C. *The Washington Monthly* 21:32-3 My '89
Spy anxiety. il *Utne Reader* p38-9 My/Je '89
Spy anxiety [cover story] il *The Washington Monthly* 21:10-14+ F '89
Warning: sports stars may be hazardous to your health [cover story] il *The Washington Monthly* 21:34-44+ S '89
What the smartest man in Washington doesn't understand. And why it will hurt you [cover story] il por *The Washington Monthly* 21:24-6+ N '89
Why America loves letter carriers and hates postal clerks [cover story] il *The Washington Monthly* 21:40-6+ Jl/Ag '89
The worst city government in America [cover story] *The Washington Monthly* 20:33-8+ Ja '89
DEPARLE, JASON, AND MUNDY, LIZA
Why higher education is neither [cover story] il *The Washington Monthly* 21:30-6+ O '89
DEPARLE, JIM
My banker wouldn't back my building. il *The Washington Monthly* 20:30-1 Ja '89
DEPARTMENT OF STATE BULLETIN
50th anniversary of the Bulletin [reprint of July 1, 1939 issue; cover story] il *Department of State Bulletin* 89:1-15 Jl '89
DEPARTMENT STORES
See also
Abraham & Straus
Allied Stores Corp.
Ames Department Stores, Inc.
B. Altman & Co.
Bloomingdale's
Carson Pirie Scott & Co.
Dayton-Hudson Corp.
Dillard Department Stores, Inc.
Eyewear stores
F. W. Woolworth Co.
Federated Department Stores, Inc.
Goldblatt's Department Stores
J. C. Penney Company, Inc.
May Department Stores Co.
Neiman Marcus
Nordstrom, Inc.
R. H. Macy & Co., Inc.
Sears, Roebuck and Co.
Shopping centers
Elevate or escalate? J. Herron. *Harper's* 278:27 My '89
Acquisitions and mergers
The big deal at Bloomingdale's: Marvin Traub makes a run at the top. M. Gross. il pors *New York* 22:56-60+ O 16 '89
Bloomie's may be on JMB's Christmas list. D. Greising. il *Business Week* p54 D 25 '89-Ja 1 '90
The great chain-store massacre [effects of debt-laden takeovers] E. Pomice. il *U.S. News & World Report* 107:39 O 9 '89
Look who wants to try Bloomie's on for size [Crown American] M. Schroeder. il por *Business Week* p30 O 2 '89
A wholesale makeover of retail? A. Dunkin and L. J. Nathans. il *Business Week* p134+ O 23 '89
International aspects
Banned in Britain: a new chapter in the Harrods saga [government outlaws publication of secret report] M. Maremont. pors *Business Week* p36 Ap 17 '89
Brawling over Harrods [T. Rowland vs. M. Al-Fayed] S. Lohr. il pors *The New York Times Magazine* p32-3+ O 8 '89
Campeau's big sell-off [proposed sale of Bloomingdale's] P. Chisholm. il por *Maclean's* 102:48 S 18 '89
Campeau's day of reckoning [loan from Olympia & York] A. Walmsley. il pors *Maclean's* 102:38-40 S 25 '89
Debacle on 34th Street: how takeover debt helped kill off the venerable B. Altman chain. B. Rudolph. il por *Time* 134:77 D 11 '89
A desperate Campeau grabs a Canadian lifeline [capital infusion by Olympia & York] C. Hawkins. il por *Business Week* p44 S 25 '89
The empire shrinks back [Campeau Corp.] J. Castro. il *Time* 134:54 S 25 '89
Low marks, few sparks [Marks & Spencer] S. B. Weiner. il *Forbes* 144:146-7 S 18 '89
Sorry, these don't fit [foreign investors overreaching in department store acquisitions] il *Time* 134:77 O 9 '89
Tiny Rowland versus Mohamed Al-Fayed (cont.) [House of Fraser takeover] E. F. Cone. il pors *Forbes* 143:10 My 1 '89

Tit for tat on London's High Street [M. Al-Fayed's takeover of Harrods] J. Barnes. il pors *U.S. News & World Report* 106:63 Ja 30 '89
Cosmetics departments
Safe makeup practices [laws require separate testers at cosmetic counters] L. A. Mark. il *American Health* 8:20 O '89
Employees
See also
Buyers (Retail trade)
Salaries, commissions, pensions, etc.
Now salespeople really must sell for their supper. A. Dunkin. il *Business Week* p50+ Jl 31 '89
Finance
Breathing easier [fallout from Campeau's teetering operations] A. Dunkin and C. Hawkins. il *Business Week* p28-9 O 2 '89
The great chain-store massacre [effects of debt-laden takeovers] E. Pomice. il *U.S. News & World Report* 107:39 O 9 '89
A season of hope for Sears. P. Glastris. il *U.S. News & World Report* 107:52+ D 11 '89
Shop till they drop. N. Darnton. il *Newsweek* 114:76-8 D 11 '89
Management
The changing retail scene [address, April 25, 1989] E. C. Hambrecht. *Vital Speeches of the Day* 55:629-32 Ag 1 '89
What ails retailing. S. Caminiti. il *Fortune* 119:61+ Ja 30 '89
Why big-name stores are losing out. S. J. Winkelman. il por *Fortune* 119:131-2 Ja 16 '89
Spa services
Spa-in-store [Nordstrom's in San Francisco] P. Orenstein. il *Vogue* 179:145-6+ My '89
Great Britain
See also
Harrods, Ltd.
Marks & Spencer plc
Japan
See also
Mitsukoshi Ltd.
Seibu Group
Yaohan Department Store Co. Ltd.
Western Europe
The changing retail scene [address, April 25, 1989] E. C. Hambrecht. *Vital Speeches of the Day* 55:629-32 Ag 1 '89
DEPAUL, TONY
When cruise missiles zoom across Maine. *The Progressive* 53:12-13 Ja '89
DEPAULO, LISA
The indomitable Donna Shalala. il por *New Choices for the Best Years* 29:26-30 Ag '89
Miss America—was last year's voting suspect? il pors *TV Guide* 37:4-7 S 2-8 '89
Oprah's private life: the inside story. il pors *TV Guide* 37:2-6 Je 3-9 '89
DEPECHE MODE 101 [film] *See* Motion picture reviews—Single works
DEPENDABILITY *See* Reliability
DEPENDENCY (PSYCHOLOGY)
See also
Addictive behavior
Return to babyhood. L. G. Katz. il *Parents* 64:231 O '89
DEPENDENT CARE (EMPLOYEE BENEFITS)
An appealing employee benefit: tax savings for child and elder care. M. Rowland. *Working Woman* 14:92 O '89
AT&T: all in the family [new contract] il *Newsweek* 113:45 Je 12 '89
DEPENDENT CARE TAX CREDITS *See* Tax credits
DEPILATION *See* Hair—Removal
DEPORTATION
See also
Asylum, Right of
Extradition
Author wins citizenship battle [case of M. Randall] L. Stapleton. il por *Ms.* 18:71 N '89
The bloody war in Belfast spills into the U.S. courts [IRA member J. Doherty in U.S. prison] T. Clifton. il por *Newsweek* 114:96+ D 11 '89
Caught up in Miami's Cuban politics [deportation case of O. Bosch] B. Turque. il por *Newsweek* 114:24 S 4 '89
Judge orders INS to stop the delays [failure to abide by Freedom of Information Act in deportation cases] E. Pell. il *The Progressive* 53:13-14 S '89
Non-alien speech [decision striking down alien deportation provisions of McCarren-Walter Act] D. Cole. *The Nation* 248:220-1 F 20 '89
Texas pitches a 'tent city' [Port Isabel detention center holds refugees for deportation] E. Salholz. il *Newsweek* 113:27 Mr 6 '89
Canada
A race against time [Nazi collaborators V. Sokolov and J. Luitjens face possible deportation] N. Underwood. pors *Maclean's* 102:44 Ja 23 '89

DEPORTATION—cont.

El Salvador

Unwelcome in El Salvador [treatment of volunteers assisting refugees] J. Lindsay-Poland. il *The Progressive* 53:32-5 My '89

Israel

Security Council regrets deportations by Israel of Palestinians. il *UN Chronicle* 26:24 D '89

United States

See Deportation

DEPOSITS, BANK *See* Bank accounts

DEPP, JOHNNY

about

Johnny Depp: a quiet cool. B. Baker. il pors *Seventeen* 48:66-7+ N '89

DEPRECIATION

Accounting

Earnings helper. D. Wechsler. il *Forbes* 143:150+ Je 12 '89

The sliding investment myth [views of Frank de Leeuw] T. May, Jr. il *Fortune* 119:18 My 22 '89

DEPRENYL *See* Selegiline

DEPRESSION, BUSINESS *See* Business depression

DEPRESSION, MENTAL

See also

Cyclothymia

Postpartum depression

Seasonal affective disorder

The black dog blues [holiday depression] G. Jaynes. il *Life* 12:24 D '89

Caring for the caregiver [depression caused by caring for chronically ill family member] D. Burden. il *Psychology Today* 23:22 Jl/Ag '89

Dealing with the holiday blues. R. Coles. il *New Choices for the Best Years* 29:74-5 D '89

Demonstrating the disability of depression [research by Kenneth B. Wells] B. Bower. *Science News* 136:132 Ag 26 '89

Depressed youngsters. J. P. Comer. il *Parents* 64:237 O '89

Depression and cancer: no clear connection [disease causation; research by Alan B. Zonderman] S. Hart. *Science News* 136:150 S 2 '89

Depression and drinking [interview with E. Stutzman] B. K. Mills. il por *People Weekly* 32:118 N 27 '89

Depression can be conquered [aged] L. Crooks. il *Modern Maturity* 32:10-11 O/N '89

Drug abuse tied to 'fatal despondency' [research by Charles L. Rich] B. Bower. *Science News* 135:332 My 27 '89

Growing up sad. B. Bower. il *Science News* 136:90-1 Ag 5 '89

Happy hearts [linked with coronary artery disease; research by Robert M. Carney] *Prevention (Emmaus, Pa.)* 41:10-12 F '89

The heart of depression [link with coronary artery disease; research by Robert M. Carney] *Science News* 135:13 Ja 7 '89

In the dumps? 10 easy picker-uppers. il *Teen* 33:52+ N '89

Memories of Frank [manic-depressive brother who committed suicide] M. K. Blakely. il *Psychology Today* 23:48-50+ O '89

The (meno)pause that refreshes [depression aspect; research by Sonja and John McKinlay] P. King. il *Psychology Today* 22:11 D '88

Post-divorce blues [views of Ed Beckham] il *USA Today (Periodical)* 118:9 S '89

Post-vacation blues. O. S. Nordberg. il *Parents* 64:112-14 S '89

A sad state of mind [mood disorders] M.-L. Kamberg. il *Current Health 2* 16:17-19 D '89

Surviving family blues [ability of teens to cope with depressed parents; research by William R. Beardslee and Dona Podorefsky] J. Folkenberg. *American Health* 8:119 Mr '89

Taking the high road out of depression. M. Spilner. il *Prevention (Emmaus, Pa.)* 41:82-4 Mr '89

Weep and you weep alone [nurses unsympathetic to depressed patients; study by Timothy Elliott and Robert Umlaut] H. Hall. *Psychology Today* 23:18 Je '89

When sadness turns to childhood depression. L. M. Smelser. *The Education Digest* 55:52-3 S '89

Diagnosis

How to tell if you're depressed. L. Holland. il *Good Housekeeping* 208:209 Mr '89

Sleep problems send psychiatric signals [research by Daniel E. Ford and Douglas B. Kamerow] B. Bower. *Science News* 136:180 S 16 '89

Genetic aspects

Manic depression gene put in limbo [follow-up on Amish study by John Kelsoe] M. Barinaga. il *Science* 246:886-7 N 17 '89

Manic depression: suspect gene acquitted [follow-up on Amish study] A. McKenzie. *Science News* 136:327 N 18 '89

Immunological aspects

Is your body bringing you down? L. Jack. il *Mademoiselle* 95:154 S '89

Therapy

See also

Cognitive therapy

"Accentuate the positive" [research by Richard M. Wenzlaff] V. Adler. *American Health* 8:50 My '89

Don't just sit there—do something [exercise may prevent symptoms; research by Mary E. Farmer] il *Prevention (Emmaus, Pa.)* 41:10+ My '89

Kind ears help some depressed patients [comparison of interpersonal psychotherapy with cognitive behavior therapy; work of Irene Elkin] *Science News* 136:365 D 2 '89

DEPRIEST, DARRYL

about

Darryl DePriest: lawyers' lawyer. R. Brown. il pors *Ebony* 44:27-8 Je '89

DEPRIEST FAMILY

about

Successful family farm. J. Patrick. il *Successful Farming* 87:54-6 N '89

DEPRIVATION, MATERNAL *See* Maternal deprivation

DEPRIVATION, SLEEP *See* Sleep deprivation

DEPROGRAMMING

Brainwashed or converted? [suit against Unification Church by former members] L. D. Streiker. *The Christian Century* 106:721-3 Ag 2-9 '89

DEPTH INDICATORS

Current finder. J. D. Lusk. il *Field & Stream* 93:78 F '89

Riding radio waves to your fish. J. Gibbs. il *Outdoor Life* 184:66-7+ Ag '89

Tips on reading the bottom. S. Stapleton. il *Motor Boating & Sailing* 164:30 Jl '89

DEPTH OF FIELD (PHOTOGRAPHY) *See* Photography—Focusing

DEPTH PERCEPTION *See* Space perception

DEPTH SOUNDERS *See* Depth indicators

DER HOVANESSIAN, DIANA

Fractals [poem] *The American Scholar* 58:382 Summ '89

(tr) *See* Haroutunian, Saghatel. Age

DERBY FIGURINES *See* Figurines

DERBYSHIRE (ENGLAND)

Description and travel

Britain's Derbyshire: heather and hedgerows. L. Griffin. il *Car and Driver* 34:196 My '89

DERDEYN, ANDRE P.

The post-divorce family, legal practice, and the child's needs for stability. bibl il *Children Today* 18:12-14 My/Je '89

DEREGULATION OF AIRLINES *See* Aviation—Laws and regulations

DEREGULATION OF BANKING *See* Banks and banking—Laws and regulations

DEREGULATION OF FINANCIAL INSTITUTIONS *See* Financial institutions—Laws and regulations

DEREGULATION OF INDUSTRY *See* Industry and state

DEREGULATION OF TELEVISION BROADCASTING *See* Television laws and regulations

DEREVLANY, JOHN, 1964-

Anatomy of a racial murder. il pors *Seventeen* 48:108-11+ D '89

DEREVO (THEATER COMPANY)

Freedom and skepticism: snapshots of the *glasnost* era. N. Marcus. il por *Scholastic Update (Teachers' edition)* 121:18-20 My 5 '89

DERIVATION OF WORDS *See* English language—Etymology

DERMAN-SPARKS, LOUISE, AND OTHERS

"Mommy, why is she different?". il *Parents* 64:120-3 D '89

DERMATOLOGISTS

World-class skin care. il *Harper's Bazaar* 122:182-5 Ap '89

DERMATOLOGY *See* Skin

DERN, LAURA

about

Behind her blue eyes. L. Ochoa. il pors *American Film* 15:46-7 O '89

Laura Dern. E. Ormand. il pors *Seventeen* 48:62 N '89

This is Laura Dern? L. Morice. il por *Mademoiselle* 95:90+ N '89

DERON, FRANCIS

A pocket of reform. *World Press Review* 36:60 D '89

DERR, KENNETH T.

about

Can Ken Derr turn Chevron around? T. Mack. il por *Forbes* 144:49+ N 27 '89

DERRON, P. S.

Do you have the working-girl flu? il *Mademoiselle* 95:120 D '89

Do you know enough about herpes? *Mademoiselle* 95:88+ Je '89

Hips hooray! Heartening news for the pear shaped. il *Mademoiselle* 95:136 Ag '89

DERRY (NORTHERN IRELAND) *See* Londonderry (Northern Ireland)

DERSHOWITZ, ALAN M.

Shouting "Fire!". il pors *The Atlantic* 263:72-4 Ja '89

about

Beat the devil. A. Cockburn. il *The Nation* 249:42-3 Jl 10 '89

The left and Tiananmen Square [discussion of July 10, 1989 column] A. Cockburn. *The Nation* 249:370+ O 9 '89

DERVAN, PETER B.
(jt. auth) See Griffin, Linda C., and Dervan, Peter B.
DES JARLAIS, DON, 1945-, AND FRIEDMAN, SAMUEL R., 1942-
AIDS and IV drug use. *Science* 245:578 Ag 11 '89
DES MOINES (IOWA)

Historic houses, sites, etc.
See also
Living History Farms (Des Moines, Iowa)

Stores
See also
Lagniappe (Firm)
DES MOINES BALLET
A streamlined Des Moines Ballet focuses on success. J. Williams. il *Dance Magazine* 63:18-19 Ag '89)
DES PLAINES (ILL.)

Galleries and museums
See also
Jimi Hendrix Information Management Institute
DESALINATION OF WATER *See* Saline water conversion
DESALTING OF WATER *See* Saline water conversion
DESAULNIERS, JANET
The good fight [story] *The New Yorker* 65:38-42 D 18 '89
Where we all should have been [story] *The New Yorker* 65:35-44 Ag 7 '89
DESCARRIES, FRANCINE, AND CORBEIL, CHRISTINE
New family structures. il *The Unesco Courier* 42:42-5 Jl '89
DESCENT *See* Genealogy
DESCHANEL, CALEB, 1941-
about
Crusoe [film] Reviews
The New Yorker 65:114-15 Ap 17 '89. P. Kael
People Weekly 31:13 Mr 15 '89. S. Haller
DESEGREGATION *See* Blacks—Segregation
DESEGREGATION IN EDUCATION *See* Colleges and universities—Desegregation; Public schools—Desegregation
DESERT ARCHITECTURE
21st century pyramid [energy-efficient home of B. Rutan in the Mojave Desert; cover story] J. L. Schefter. il por *Popular Science* 235:65-9 N '89
Desert flamboyance and practicality. il *Sunset (Central West edition)* 183:90-1 O '89
Owner-built, an eight-year labor of love [Arizona] il *Sunset (Central West edition)* 183:134 O '89
Project: Marc Appleton: plans for a producer's dream estate. il por *Architectural Digest* 46:82-3 Ag '89
DESERT DE RETZ (FRANCE: HISTORIC HOUSE) *See* Historic houses, sites, etc.—France
DESERT ECOLOGY
See also
Desertification
DESERT FAUNA
See also
Kangaroo rats
Scorpions
Living in a land of extremes [work of biologist P. Holm in Organ Pipe Cactus National Monument] E. Pennisi. il por *National Wildlife* 27:14-21 Ap/My '89
DESERT FLORA
See also
Agave
Cactus
DESERT RUNNING
Desert son [Marathon Des Sables] K. McKinney. il *Omni (New York, N.Y.)* 12:16+ N '89
Sahara marathoners: they're hot to trot [Marathon Des Sables] D. Van Biema. il *People Weekly* 31:56-61 Ap 10 '89
Sand dudes [Marathon Des Sables] J. Loeschhorn. il *Runner's World* 24:58-9 S '89
Some like it hot [Marathon Des Sables] S. Brummell. il *Women's Sports & Fitness* 11:58 N/D '89
DESERTIFICATION
See also
Holistic resource management
Environment [special section] *World Press Review* 36:32-5 Ap '89
Halting land degradation. S. Postel. il *Focus (New York, N.Y.: 1950)* 39:5-12 Spr '89
Regaining land productivity. S. Postel. il *Focus (New York, N.Y.: 1950)* 39:13-18 Summ '89
DESERTION BY HUSBANDS *See* Runaway husbands
DESERTS
See also
Mojave Desert (Calif.)
Sonoran Desert

Botswana
See also
Kalahari Desert

Israel
See also
Negev (Israel)

North Africa
See also
Sahara

DESERTS IN ART
Mel Pekarsky. L. K. Petrich. il pors *American Artist* 53:50-5 Ap '89
DESHANEY, JOSHUA
about
The battered child. *The New Republic* 200:7-8 Mr 20 '89
"Poor Joshua!". il por *Time* 133:56 Mr 6 '89
Poor Joshua. P. A. Zirkel. bibl f il *Phi Delta Kappan* 70:828-9 Je '89
DESHINGKAR, GIRI
China's hard line in Tibet. *World Press Review* 36:18-19 Je '89
DESIDERIO, ROBERT
about
Tony Danza, my husband, and me. V. Scott. il pors *Good Housekeeping* 208:86+ Ap '89
DESIGN
See also
Book design
Designer's Saturday
Fins (Design)
Textile design
A compelling new modernism: best of '88. K. Andersen. il *Time* 133:92-3 Ja 2 '89
Innovations. See issues of Essence beginning August 1987 through January 1989
Living. See issues of Vogue
Nile style [use of Egyptian motifs in contemporary design] A. Foxley. il *House & Garden* 161:86 Ap '89

Exhibitions
See also
Cooper-Hewitt Museum
Design Museum (London, England)
Miller high style [shows by design curator R. C. Miller] M. Filler. il por *House & Garden* 161:48 Ja '89
Who will bury whom, Nikita? [USIA exhibit Design USA in Soviet Union] il *U.S. News & World Report* 107:12-13 S 18 '89

Study and teaching
See also
Art Center College of Design (Pasadena, Calif.)
Art Center College of Design (Pasadena, Calif.). European campus
DESIGN, DECORATIVE
See also
Book covers
Decoupage
Pattern books
Pottery—Decoration
Stencil work
Textile design
DESIGN, INDUSTRIAL
See also
Computers—Design
Design for manufacturability and assembly
Ergonomics
Designed in America. B. Nussbaum. il *Business Week* Special Issue:138-41+ Je 16 '89
Does good design pay off? R. Farmanfarmaian. il *Working Woman* 14:47+ Jl '89
So you're still having trouble making those Christmas toys work? Don't worry, it's not your fault [interview with D. A. Norman] K. MacMurran. il pors *People Weekly* 31:91-2+ Ja 9 '89

History
The shaping of things to come [work of N. Bel Geddes] L. W. Speck. il por *Omni (New York, N.Y.)* 12:86-95 O '89

Japan
The man behind the O [N. Sakai] H. Gaffin. il pors *Popular Photography* 96:34 D '89
DESIGN FIRMS
See also
Burdick Group (Firm)
Canetti Inc.
Donovan & Green
Duffy Design Group
Memphis (Firm)

Italy
See also
Alessi SpA
DESIGN FOR ASSEMBLY *See* Design for manufacturability and assembly
DESIGN FOR MANUFACTURABILITY AND ASSEMBLY
The best-engineered part is no part at all [NCR's new cash register] O. Port. il *Business Week* p150 My 8 '89
Pssst! Want a secret for making superproducts? O. Port. il pors *Business Week* p106+ O 2 '89
DESIGN MUSEUM (LONDON, ENGLAND)
Object lessons. E. MacSweeney. il por *Harper's Bazaar* 122:110 S '89
DESIGNER DRUGS
See also
Ice (Drug)
MDMA (Drug)
DESIGNERS
See also
Arad, Ron, 1951-

DESIGNERS—See also—*cont.*
Benson, W. A. S. (William Arthur Smith), 1854-1924
Binazzi, Lapo, 1943-
Bonetti, Mattia
Bugatti, Carlo, 1855 or 6-1940
Burdick, Bruce, 1933-
Fashion designers
Ferren, Bran, 1954-
Gagnère, Olivier
Garouste, Elizabeth
Iosa Ghini, Massimo
Lighting designers
Locadia, Alex
Mackintosh, Charles Rennie, 1868-1928
McConnico, Hilton
Mollino, Carlo, 1905-1973
Morris, William, 1834-1896
Rice, Matthew
Sakai, Naoki
Seguso, Archimede
Set designers
Space planners
Starck, Philippe, 1950?-
Villa, Mario

DESIGNERS' COLLECTIVE
This cat's pajamas. R. Merkin. il *Gentlemen's Quarterly* 59:102+ Je '89

DESIGNER'S SATURDAY
New products: Designer's Saturday. il *Architectural Record* 177:132-5+ mid-S '89

DESIGNS, INC.
All in the family. E. Schmuckler. il *Forbes* 143:14 Ja 23 '89

DESIRE
See also
Sexual desire
The ten great wants of 1989 [survey of readers] N. Perrin. il *Country Journal* 16:17-19 Jl/Ag '89

DESIRE UNDER THE ELMS [opera] See Thomas, Edward

DESK DIARIES *See* Datebooks

DESK FURNISHINGS
See also
Memo pads
Paper holders, etc.
Personalizing "organizers" with colorful fabric. il *Sunset (Central West edition)* 182:166+ Ap '89
Teen desk set [cover story; special section] il *Workbench* 45:53-61 Mr/Ap '89

DESK ORGANIZERS See Desk furnishings

DESKMATE (COMPUTER PROGRAM)
Hot software adopts DeskMate standard. S. Miller. il *Home Office Computing* 7:12 D '89

DESKS
See also
Computer furniture
Hand work [special section] il *Popular Mechanics* 166:71-6+ N '89
Secretary shop. H. Wyssen. il *Popular Science* 234:88-9 Ja '89
Tilt-top desk. L. M. Dalsgaard. il *Workbench* 45:48-52 Mr/Ap '89
Walnut lap desk. A. Weaver. il *Workbench* 45:44-7 N/D '89

Prices
The greatest [1760 mahogany secretary built by J. Goddard sold at auction for over twelve million dollars] *The New Yorker* 65:39-40 O 9 '89

DESKTOP FORGERY
Desktop forgery [cover story] D. Churbuck. il *Forbes* 144:246-9+ N 27 '89

DESKTOP PUBLISHING
Boost your bottom line with the dazzle of desktop publishing. M. Scott. il *Black Enterprise* 19:89+ Je '89
A copy writer's journey into the age of PCs [J. Lane, manager of electronic publishing at MONY] M. Piturro. il por *Personal Computing* 13:146-7 O '89
Desktop publishing. M. Antonoff. See issues of Personal Computing beginning April 1989
Desktop publishing. P. Saffo. See issues of Personal Computing beginning May 1987 through December 1988
From Telstar to typefaces, computers bring the information age home. D. D. Thornburg. *Compute!* 11:12 Ap '89
A panoramic view of publishing [Venture Lifestyles Publishing] S. Harvey. il por *Home Office Computing* 7:56-7 O '89
Print your publications the professional way. S. Morgenstern. il *Home Office Computing* 7:30+ Je '89
Sell yourself—with a newsletter! [cover story; with editorial comment by Claudia Cohl] R. Raskin. il *Home Office Computing* 7:6, 37-41 Ap '89
What the new and affordable desktop publishing tools can do to help you. G. Hedberg. *Money* 18:167-8 S '89

Handbooks, manuals, etc.
Help! (I). S. Morgenstern. il *Home Office Computing* 7:30+ O '89
Help! (II). S. Morgenstern. il *Home Office Computing* 7:28+ N '89

Programming
See also
Clip art software
PostScript (Computer language)
The $89 page [MaxPage 1.2] M. Hicks. il *Byte* 14 Mac Special Supp:MAC192-MAC193 Ag '89
Attn: young publishers [Children's Writing and Publishing Center] K. Kane. il *Psychology Today* 23:76 D '89
Buyer's guide: desktop publishing [special section] il *Personal Computing* 13:115-20+ Je '89
The Children's Writing & Publishing Center. C. S. Holzberg. il *Home Office Computing* 7:84-5 Ap '89
The Children's Writing & Publishing Center. G. Keizer. il *Compute!* 11:70 Ap '89
Color Extension for Macintosh Pagemaker. M. Antonoff. il *Personal Computing* 13:25 My '89
The database meets desktop publishing. R. Kendall. il *Home Office Computing* 7:36-7 O '89
Designed on a desktop [newsletter design using WordPerfect] J. Latimer. il *Compute!* 11:64-6+ D '89
Desktop publishing. M. McLean. il *Compute!* 11:43-4+ Jl '89
Desktop publishing software. L. Simons. il *Home Office Computing* 7:42-5 Ap '89
Displaying strength of character [trend toward graphic and visual orientation] M. Liskin. il *Personal Computing* 13:57-8+ Ja '89
DTP under Presentation Manager. M. Antonoff. il *Personal Computing* 13:63-4+ Je '89
Entry-level desktop publishing [PFS:First Publisher version 2.0] B. Sillery. *Personal Computing* 13:228+ Ja '89
Entry-level DTP via Windows [Springboard Publisher] L. P. Lefkowitz. il *Personal Computing* 13:194 S '89
Grow your business with a professional identity. L. Simons. il *Home Office Computing* 7:45-9 Ag '89
Hot new features of Ventura Publisher 2.0. S. Morgenstern. il *Home Office Computing* 7:26-7 Ja '89
How to get picture-perfect graphics on your printed pages. S. Morgenstern. il *Home Office Computing* 7:28+ D '89
How to get your readers' attention [GEM Artline and LetraStudio] S. Morgenstern. il *Home Office Computing* 7:50-1 My '89
Logitech brings Finesse to low-cost desktop publishing. D. Barker. *Byte* 14:82+ Ag '89
Macintosh vs. MS-DOS: which system is better for page layout? S. Morgenstern. il *Home Office Computing* 7:32+ F '89
A man of characters [J. Warnock of Adobe Systems] M. Antonoff. por *Personal Computing* 13:86 Jl '89
Move over, PageMaker [Publish It for the Mac] D. Gabaldon. il *Byte* 14:217-18+ D '89
MS-DOS word processors for desktop publishing [Microsoft Word, WordPerfect, and WordStar Plus 2000] J. Latimer. il *Home Office Computing* 7:24+ Mr '89
Not for lasers only. M. Antonoff. il *Personal Computing* 13:59-60+ Ag '89
OS/2 puts desktop publishing in the fast lane [PageMaker for OS/2 Presentation Manager] H. Eglowstein. il *Byte* 14:81 O '89
Pages. D. Will-Harris. il *Compute!* 11:75-6 My '89
The power of the press [Interleaf's Technical Publishing Software] J. Udell. il *Byte* 14:271-2+ N '89
Powerful publisher now easier to use [Ventura Publisher 2.0] M. Antonoff. il *Personal Computing* 13:216+ Ja '89
Publish-It! Lite! D. Will-Harris. il *Compute!* 11:74+ Je '89
QuarkStyle. L. Simons. il *Home Office Computing* 7:66+ Ag '89
Springboard Publisher. D. Kovacs. il *Home Office Computing* 7:76+ Ja '89
Total Word [word processor with desktop publishing features] J. Nimersheim. il *Home Office Computing* 7:68+ Ag '89
VersaCAD/386 version 5.4; Proposal Manager 254/255. S. S. Ross. il *Architectural Record* 177:149+ N '89
Word publishing for OS/2 [DeScribe word publisher] S. Miastkowski. il *Byte* 14:82 S '89

DESKTOP VIDEO
Compute! Choice: VGA-TV. D. Stanton. il *Compute!* 11:68-70 N '89

Home use
Couch potatoes! Now it's smart TV. B. R. Schlender. il *Fortune* 120:111-12+ N 20 '89

DESPAIN, DON G.
(jt. auth) See Romme, William H., and Despain, Don G.

DESPARD, LUCY EDWARDS
Recent books on international relations. See issues of Foreign Affairs

DESPERATE AND DATELESS [radio program] See Radio program reviews—Single works

DESPOTISM
See also
Dictators
For a new humanist militancy. M. Maneli. il por *The Humanist* 49:14-16+ S/O '89

DESQVIEW (COMPUTER PROGRAM)
DESQview pains. J. Pournelle. *Byte* 14:114+ D '89
Desqview's different drummer [T. Meyers] E. S. Ely. por *Personal Computing* 13:76 Jl '89

DESQVIEW (COMPUTER PROGRAM)—*cont.*

Multitasking with DOS now. M. Antonoff. il *Personal Computing* 13:192 S '89

Patents

Little Quarterdeck throws its weight around. P. Cole. il por *Business Week* p76 Je 19 '89

DESSERTS

See also

Cake
Cookies
Custards
Ice cream, ices, etc.
Meringue
Pastry
Petits fours
Pie
Puddings
Tarts

Berry sweet. il *Redbook* 173:80-3+ Je '89

Blackberrying. K. Stewart. il *Gourmet* 49:62-3+ Ag '89

Can-do desserts. C. Koury. il *Parents* 64:191-5 N '89

Cherry desserts. il *Better Homes and Gardens* 67:141-2 Jl '89

Chocolate fit for a queen [black-bottom goodies] il *Southern Living* 24:161 O '89

"Come for a dessert tasting party". il *Sunset (Central West edition)* 182:76-7, 142+ F '89

A cool Yule dessert [microwaved apple filling] J. B. Hurley. il *Prevention (Emmaus, Pa.)* 41:76 D '89

Dazzling desserts. J. T. Hazard. il *Ladies' Home Journal* 106:174-6+ Mr '89

Deluxe holiday desserts. il *McCall's* 117:153 N '89

Dessert lovers' cookbook. il *McCall's* 116:115-20+ F '89

Desserts for the galley. J. F. Mariani. il *Motor Boating & Sailing* 163:46+ Ap '89

Fabulous desserts from America's best restaurants. il *Good Housekeeping* 208:156-66+ Je '89

Famous Amos' dynamite double-chocolate desserts. il *Redbook* 172:111-14 F '89

Fruit taco? il *Sunset (Central West edition)* 183:64-5 Jl '89

The fruits of summer. il *Ladies' Home Journal* 106:146-8+ Ag '89

Holiday sweets [recipes of Winnifred Jardine] B. Goldman. il *Better Homes and Gardens* 67:122-6+ D '89

It's the berries! il *Ladies' Home Journal* 106:166-8+ Je '89

Julia Child's sweet indulgences. J. Child. il *Ladies' Home Journal* 106:282-4+ N '89

Just desserts. K. Anderson. il *Runner's World* 24:40-4 S '89

Lace eggs [white chocolate with mousse filling] il *Sunset (Central West edition)* 182:158 Mr '89

The LHJ cooking school [layer cake, raspberry soufflé, and apple pie] il *Ladies' Home Journal* 106:179-80+ S '89

Light chocolate desserts. H. A. Dorrough. il *Southern Living* 24:108+ D '89

Lite eating: summery desserts. M. Langan. il *McCall's* 116:107 Ag '89

Memories are made of this. R. Coyle. il *The New York Times Magazine* p85-6 Mr 5 '89

Micro-way: deluxe chocolate desserts. il *McCall's* 117:181 O '89

A passion for pralines. S. Payne. il *Southern Living* 24:76-7 N '89

Peach treats. M. Gorman. il *Organic Gardening* 36:46-50 Mr '89

Peaches and pralines. il *Sunset (Central West edition)* 182:151 Je '89

Pear desserts. il *Better Homes and Gardens* 67:161-2 O '89

Perfect endings. C. Koury. il *Parents* 64:134-6+ Jl '89

Prime-time strawberries. P. Y. Cordell. il *Southern Living* 24:142-4+ My '89

Quick country desserts [microwaving] il *Good Housekeeping* 208:101-2 Ap '89

Say it with chocolate. E. Gonzáles. il *Ladies' Home Journal* 106:156-8 F '89

Serve mom dessert. il *Southern Living* 24:166 My '89

Summer-winter desserts. il *Sunset (Central West edition)* 182:60-1 Ja '89

Summer's golden fruit [peaches] il *Southern Living* 24:124-6 Jl '89

Surprise-ingredient desserts! il *Redbook* 172:35-6 Ap '89

Sweet cheats. il *Ladies' Home Journal* 106:128-9 Ja '89

Sweet entertaining. C. Lyons. il *Ebony* 45:108-10+ N '89

Sweet temptation: why you can't say no. il *Glamour* 87:258-9 N '89

Trimming Christmas. N. Hauser. il *American Health* 8:92 D '89

Ways with rhubarb. il *Better Homes and Gardens* 67:166-7 My '89

Yummy chocolate desserts. il *Good Housekeeping* 208:123-6+ F '89

DESTAEBLER, STEPHEN, 1933-

about

Time pieces. D. Ketcham. il pors *Art News* 88:152-7 O '89

DESTRUCTION OF BUILDINGS *See* Wrecking

DETAILING (AUTOMOBILE CLEANING) *See* Automobiles—Cleaning

DETAILS (TERM)

Who's in those details? W. Safire. il *The New York Times Magazine* p8+ Jl 30 '89

DETASSELERS (FARM LABOR)

Detasselers wooed for big seed harvest [seed corn] il *Successful Farming* 87:57 Ap '89

DETECTION OF CRIME *See* Criminal investigation

DETECTIVE AND MYSTERY STORIES

See also

Motion pictures—Crime films
Publishers and publishing—Detective and mystery stories

Economic intrigue. E. Corcoran. *Scientific American* 261:104 D '89

A gastronome, a magician and a First Lady: detectives and their day jobs [professions of moonlighting detectives] M. Stasio. *The New York Times Book Review* 94:49 O 15 '89

The homicidal maniac: a novelist's best friend [serial murder mysteries] M. Stasio. il *The New York Times Book Review* 94:1+ O 15 '89

Out to make killings [true crime literature] S. Kanfer. il *Time* 133:98+ F 20 '89

Authorship

Make no bones about it, Sue Grafton's detective heroine is a real pistol. A. Chambers. il por *People Weekly* 32:81-2 Jl 10 '89

Mistress of fright [P. Highsmith] J. Pearlman. il por *Harper's Bazaar* 122:52+ F '89

Murderous secrets [R. Rendell] D. Turbide. por *Maclean's* 102:94+ N 6 '89

Navajo cops on the case [T. Hillerman] A. Ward. il pors *The New York Times Magazine* p38-9+ My 14 '89

Police story [W. J. Caunitz] C. S. Smith. il por *New York* 22:30 Mr 13 '89

PW interviews [M. H. Clark] E. H. O'Neill. por *Publishers Weekly* 235:64-5 My 19 '89

PW interviews [R. Rendell] M. Field. por *Publishers Weekly* 235:46+ My 26 '89

PW interviews [W. Bayer] M. Harris. il por *Publishers Weekly* 235:45-6 Je 9 '89

Sam Spade in ancient Rome [work of L. Davis] S. J. Evans. il *History Today* 39:4-5 Jl '89

Shedunnit [M. H. Clark] R. Hoopes. il por *Modern Maturity* 32:52-7 Ag/S '89

Bibliography

Crime. M. Stasio. See occasional issues of The New York Times Book Review beginning September 18, 1988

Going beyond brand names [new mysteries from lesser-known writers] W. A. Henry. il *Time* 133:81-3 Ap 3 '89

Single works

See name of author for full entry

The Anastasia syndrome. Clark, Mary Higgins
Cold feet. Swansick, Robin
Housebound. Swick, Marly
Mama was right. McCafferty, Taylor
The mystery of the mall. Lester, DeeGee
The quick one. Chesterton, G. K. (Gilbert Keith), 1874-1936

Technique

The birth of a series character. G. C. Chesbro. *The Writer* 102:14-16 Mr '89

Free-form plotting the mystery novel. M. Muller. *The Writer* 102:12-15 S '89

Grilling Ed McBain. E. Hunter. *The Writer* 102:11-14+ N '89

I could have died laughing [humorous crime fiction] R. Barnard. il *The Writer* 102:15-18 F '89

It's entertainment. D. S. Davis. *The Writer* 102:12-14 Jl '89

Plot and character in suspense fiction. J. Aiken. *The Writer* 102:9-13 My '89

What if . . . ? W. G. Tapply. *The Writer* 102:17-19 Ja '89

Which viewpoint—and why. M. Byrd. *The Writer* 102:12-14 O '89

DETECTIVES

See also

Clothing and dress—Detectives
Jackson Lynn Travers (Firm)
Sahlen & Associates Inc.
United Intelligence Inc.
Youth as detectives

Sex, spies and videotape [private detectives investigate for AIDS] C. Leerhsen. il *Newsweek* 114:66 O 2 '89

That's Sam Spade leafing through the ledgers [using private eyes in takeover battles] R. Grover. il *Business Week* p95+ My 29 '89

Using 'spies to win a war': corporations turn to detectives to catch workers with drug problems. J. Schwartz. il *Newsweek* 114:56-7 N 6 '89

DETECTORS

See also

Biosensors
Bomb detectors
Draft detectors (Air infiltration measurement)
Fire detectors
Life detectors
Light detectors
Microwave detectors

DETECTORS—See also—*cont.*
    Moisture meters
    Motion detectors
    Position sensors
    Radar detectors
    Radio detectors
    Radon detectors
    Ultraviolet detectors
    Viscosity detectors
    Wind shear detectors
Digital peak detector. R. D. Secura. il *Radio-Electronics* 60:59-62 Ap '89
Mass appeal [neutrino detectors] S. J. Nadis. il *Omni (New York, N.Y.)* 11:28 Ap '89
Tiny sensors pay off big. G. T. Pope. il *High Technology Business* 9:28-31 S/O '89

DETECTORS, INFRARED
Airborne infrared system provides advance warning of turbulence. il *Aviation Week & Space Technology* 130:130-1 Je 19 '89
Airborne Optical Adjunct program threatened with cancellation. P. A. Gilmartin. *Aviation Week & Space Technology* 131:24 Ag 21 '89
Coast Guard uses Hu-25 Flir, radar to detect smugglers. il *Aviation Week & Space Technology* 130:42+ Ja 30 '89
Falcon Eye Flir, GEC helmet aid F-16 mission flexibility [cover story] W. B. Scott. il *Aviation Week & Space Technology* 130:34-6+ Ap 17 '89
Flight restrictions prompt U.S. Air Force to reassess Lantirn training in Germany. J. D. Morrocco. map *Aviation Week & Space Technology* 131:26-7 O 16 '89
Infrared detector technology [platinum silicide detectors; special section] il *Aviation Week & Space Technology* 130:51+ Mr 27 '89
Marine OV-10Ds with Flir systems detect, track aircraft smuggling narcotics into southeast U.S. [forward-looking infrared systems] *Aviation Week & Space Technology* 130:49 Jl 10 '89
More capable IR-guided weapons prompting improved jammers, decoys. il *Aviation Week & Space Technology* 131:50+ S 11 '89
Sanders upgrades IR countermeasures, explores techniques for future systems [coverage against infrared guided missiles] il *Aviation Week & Space Technology* 131:118-19+ S 11 '89
SDIO begins measuring booster plumes with Delta Star sensors. E. H. Kolcum. il *Aviation Week & Space Technology* 130:26-7 Ap 3 '89
U.S. developing survivable warning/antimissile satellites [Boost Surveillance Tracking System; cover story] T. M. Foley. il *Aviation Week & Space Technology* 130:34-5+ Ja 23 '89

DÉTENTE POLICY See United States—Foreign relations—Soviet Union

DETERGENTS
Dishwasher detergents. il *Consumer Reports* 54:268-9 D '89
Dishwashing liquids. il *Consumer Reports* 54:270-2 D '89
Hand-laundry detergents. il *Consumer Reports* 54:308-10 D '89
Who needs special detergents? il *Consumer Reports* 54:297-8 My '89

DETERIORATION OF PLASTICS See Plastics—Degradability

DETLEFSEN, ROBERT R.
Racist Bigotry 101 at Harvard. il *Conservative Digest* 15:40-3 Jl/Ag '89
White like me. *The New Republic* 200:18-21 Ap 10 '89

DETONOGRAPHY See Explosives in art

DETRICH, TAMAS
    about
Tamas Detrich: an American prince in Europe. M. Hunt. il pors *Dance Magazine* 63:50-3 F '89

DETRITUS
Magnification of secondary production by kelp detritus in coastal marine ecosystems. D. O. Duggins and others. bibl f il *Science* 245:170-3 Jl 14 '89

DETROIT (MICH.)
    Crime
Halloween fright night [arson] il *Newsweek* 114:49 N 13 '89
A sanctuary no more [summer basketball program at St. Cecilia church shut down] R. Sullivan. il *Sports Illustrated* 71:12 Ag 28 '89
    Description
Out in left field with Was (Not Was). il *Rolling Stone* p23 Jl 13-27 '89
    Education
Bing saves school sports [D. Bing's work] V. Lynn. por *Black Enterprise* 20:34 O '89
Robberies push Detroit's school board to propose district-wide dress code. *Jet* 77:29 D 25 '89-Ja 1 '90
    Historic houses, sites, etc.
Aretha Franklin's former Detroit neighbors want to her to show a little R-E-S-P-E-C-T [refuses to maintain vacant home and grounds] P. Axthelm. il por *People Weekly* 31:36-7 Je 26 '89
    Municipal improvement
Junk magic [work of artist T. Guyton] S. Yolles. il *Art News* 88:27 O '89

    Newspapers
    See also
    Detroit free press
    Detroit news
    Police
A Detroit police corruption probe. *Newsweek* 114:30 D 18 '89
    Politics and government
Detroit only major city with two blacks battling to win the mayor's race. il por *Jet* 76:8 O 2 '89
Detroit's biggest survivor [Mayor C. Young] M. Barone. il por *U.S. News & World Report* 107:27 S 25 '89
Giving birth to a scandal [A. Calvert investigated by police after winning paternity suit against mayor C. Young] por *Time* 133:23 Je 26 '89
Mom of Detroit mayor's son wants FBI probe of police [A. Calvert vs. C. Young] por *Jet* 76:8 Jl 10 '89
Rep. Crockett seeks one more term to help Detroit. por *Jet* 77:4 D 4 '89
A salty mayor seeks no. 5 [C. Young] F. Washington. il por *Newsweek* 114:32 Jl 31 '89
    Religious institutions and affairs
Black Catholics vs. the Church. R. N. Ostling. il por *Time* 134:57 Jl 10 '89
    Sports
Detroit. J. Lapointe. il *Sport (New York, N.Y.)* 80:56-61 My '89

DETROIT DIESEL CORPORATION
Roger Penske: Detroit Diesel's dynamo [new marine engines] E. Dennis. il por *Motor Boating & Sailing* 164:78-80 Jl '89

DETROIT FREE PRESS
Preserving newspapers or monopoly? [proposed joint operating agreement between Detroit free press and Detroit news; cover story] S. Barnett. *The Nation* 249:513+ N 6 '89

DETROIT NEWS
Preserving newspapers or monopoly? [proposed joint operating agreement between Detroit free press and Detroit news; cover story] S. Barnett. *The Nation* 249:513+ N 6 '89

DETROIT SYMPHONY ORCHESTRA
False note [agrees to hire more blacks] *The New Republic* 200:9 Mr 27 '89
A limit to affirmative action? [black bassist R. Robinson] J. Blanton. *Commentary* 87:28-32 Je '89

DETWEILER, SUSAN GRAY
The ceramics. il *Antiques* 135:496-501 F '89

DEUTCH, JOHN M.
The decision to modernize U.S. intercontinental ballistic missiles. bibl f *Science* 244:1445-50 Je 23 '89
ICBM modernization [discussion of June 23, 1989 article, The decision to modernize U.S. intercontinental ballistic missiles] *Science* 246:192-4 O 13 '89

DEUTERIUM OXIDE
Analysis of the published calorimetric evidence for electrochemical fusion of deuterium in palladium. G. M. Miskelly and others. bibl f il *Science* 246:793-6 N 10 '89
If there's a tulip craze, sell trowels [Isotec's sales of heavy water in wake of cold fusion breakthrough] R. Bailey. il *Forbes* 143:132 My 15 '89

DEUTSCH, CYNTHIA
Love and marriage. See issues of Parents

DEUTSCH, DAVIDA TENENBAUM
The polite lady: portraits of American schoolgirls and their accomplishments, 1725-1830. bibl f il *Antiques* 135:742-53 Mr '89

DEUTSCHE AEROSPACE AG
European aerospace industry enters period of restructuring. J. M. Lenorovitz. il *Aviation Week & Space Technology* 131:34-5 Jl 3 '89

DEUTSCHE AGENTUR FUR RAUMFAHRTANGELEGENHEITEN
Germany sets up new space agency. D. Dickson and D. Kirk. *Science* 244:648 My 12 '89

DEUTSCHE BANK AG
Deutsche Bank nabs a plum—but it didn't come cheap [Morgan Grenfell] J. Templeman. il *Business Week* p102 D 11 '89

DEUTSCHE GRAMMOPHON GMBH
Watch on the Elbe [G. Breest leaves Deutsche Grammophon to head CBS Masterworks] T. W. Libbey, Jr. il *High Fidelity (New York, N.Y.)* 39:55 Ja '89

DEUTSCHE OPER BERLIN
Musical events:
    Wagner's Ring presented at the Kennedy Center. A. Porter. *The New Yorker* 65:68-70 Jl 10 '89
Next stop: Kennedy Center [Wagner's Ring directed by G. Friedrich] M. Swed. il por *Opera News* 53:18-20+ Je '89
A resounding Ring [Der Ring des Nibelungen at Kennedy Center] M. Gurewitsch. il *Harper's Bazaar* 122:58 Je '89
The Ring: the Deutsche Oper Berlin at Kennedy Center. B. Howard. il *Theatre Crafts* 23:45+ My '89
West Berlin [premiere of Los Alamos] J. H. Sutcliffe. il *Opera News* 53:40 Mr 4 '89

DEVALUATION OF MONEY See Money

DEVELOPING (PHOTOGRAPHY) See Photography—Developing and developers

DEVELOPING COUNTRIES
See also
Agricultural administration—Developing countries
Agricultural research—Developing countries
Air pollution—Developing countries
Birth control—Developing countries
Birth rate—Developing countries
Children—Developing countries
Church and social problems—Developing countries
Cities and towns—Developing countries
Community development—Developing countries
Deaf—Developing countries
Ecology—Developing countries
Economic assistance—Developing countries
Economic assistance, American—Developing countries
Economic assistance, German—Developing countries
Economic assistance, Japanese—Developing countries
Environmental movement—Developing countries
Environmental policy—Developing countries
Food supply—Developing countries
Genetic research—Developing countries
Handicapped—Developing countries
Indoor air pollution—Developing countries
Investments, American—Developing countries
Loans, Bank—Developing countries
Loans, East European—Developing countries
Loans, Russian—Developing countries
Local transit—Developing countries
Medical care—Developing countries
Military assistance, American—Developing countries
Military assistance, Russian—Developing countries
Missions, Medical—Developing countries
Munitions—Developing countries
Nutrition problems—Developing countries
Power resources—Developing countries
Public health—Developing countries
Recycling (Waste, etc.)—Developing countries
Relief work—Developing countries
Science—Developing countries
Technical assistance—Developing countries
Technology—Developing countries
Telecommunication—Developing countries
Television broadcasting—Developing countries
Trade waste—Disposal—Developing countries
Videotapes—Developing countries
Water supply—Developing countries
Wilderness areas—Developing countries
Women—Developing countries

Civilization
Cultures in transition: what the West can learn from developing countries [cover story] W. N. Ellis and M. M. Ellis. il pors The Futurist 23:22-5 Mr/Ap '89

Commerce
See also
United Nations Conference on Trade and Development
Germany (West)
See Germany (West)—Commerce—Developing countries
United States
See United States—Commerce—Developing countries

Cultural policy
See also
World Decade for Cultural Development, 1988-1997

Defenses
See also
Guided missiles, Developing countries

Description and travel
Take an ounce of prevention to the third world [health aspects] D. H. Dunn. il Business Week p142 My 1 '89
Anecdotes, facetiae, satire, etc.
A banana republic Baedeker. W. McGurn. il The American Spectator 22:16-18 Mr '89

Economic conditions
See also
Underground economy—Developing countries
Give them their daily bread [improvements in health result in economic growth; views of Robert Fogel] S. Nasar. U.S. News & World Report 107:64 O 30 '89
Rich country, poor country [cover story] D. S. Landes. il The New Republic 201:23-7 N 20 '89
Scenes from the inferno. A. Cockburn. The Nation 248:510-11 Ap 17 '89
Strategies for sustainable economic development. J. MacNeill. bibl il Scientific American 261:154-9+ S '89

Economic relations
See also
United Nations. Committee for Development Planning
United Nations Conference on Trade and Development
Foreign relations
Notes on the new political culture. F. Halliday. il The Nation 249:234-6+ S 4-11 '89
South-North dangers. I. L. Head. Foreign Affairs 68:71-86 Summ '89
Soviet Union
See Soviet Union—Foreign relations—Developing countries

United States
See United States—Foreign relations—Developing countries

Industries
See also
Aluminum industry—Developing countries
Investment trusts—Developing countries
Tourist trade—Developing countries
Politics and government
Democracy as the wave of the future. C. Gershman. Current (Washington, D.C.) 312:18-25 My '89
Thesis disPeruvian [third world conflicts] T. Rosenberg. The New Republic 201:15-17 O 9 '89
Religious institutions and affairs
See also
Christians—Developing countries
Vital statistics
See also
Mortality—Developing countries

DEVELOPMENT, BIOLOGICAL See Developmental biology; Morphogenesis
DEVELOPMENT, ECONOMIC See Economic development
DEVELOPMENT, NEUROLOGICAL See Developmental neurology
DEVELOPMENT, ORGANIZATIONAL See Organizational change
DEVELOPMENT, REAL ESTATE See Real estate business
DEVELOPMENT, RURAL See Rural development
DEVELOPMENT BANKS
See also
African Development Bank
World Bank
Request for U.S. contributions to multilateral development banks [statement, April 17, 1989] N. F. Brady. Department of State Bulletin 89:21-30 Je '89
DEVELOPMENT OF CHILDREN See Children—Growth and development
DEVELOPMENT OF INFANTS See Infants—Growth and development
DEVELOPMENT PROGRAMME (UNITED NATIONS) See United Nations Development Programme
DEVELOPMENT SPECIALISTS INC.
William Brandt: putting small businesses back in the black. L. Therrien. il por Business Week p99 Ag 21 '89
DEVELOPMENTAL BIOLOGY
See also
Homeoboxes
Insects—Development
Pattern (Biology)
Developmental biology in outer space [effects of microgravity] G. M. Malacinski and others. bibl f il BioScience 39:314-20 My '89
Developmental biology of T cell receptors. J. L. Strominger. bibl f il Science 244:943-50 My 26 '89
A different kind of inheritance [DNA methylation as an epigenetic mechanism] R. Holliday. bibl il Scientific American 260:60-5+ Je '89
The science of metamorphoses [J. Loeb] R. C. Lewontin. bibl f il The New York Review of Books 36:18-22 Ap 27 '89
Two cultures find common ground [conference of specialists in mouse and fruit fly development] J. L. Marx. il Science 244:652-3 My 12 '89
DEVELOPMENTAL NEUROLOGY
See also
Brain—Growth
A biochemical correlate of the critical period for synaptic modification in the visual cortex. S. M. Dudek and M. F. Bear. bibl f il Science 246:673-5 N 3 '89
Glial cell diversification in the rat optic nerve. M. C. Raff. bibl f il Science 243:1450-5 Mr 17 '89
Neuroscientists track nerve development [reports at annual meeting of Society for Neuroscience] M. Barinaga. Science 246:756-7 N 10 '89
Plasticity and differentiation of embryonic retinal cells after terminal mitosis [chick eye] R. Adler and M. Hatlee. bibl f il Science 243:391-3 Ja 20 '89
Purification, cloning, and expression of ciliary neurotrophic factor (CNTF). L.-F. H. Lin and others. bibl f il Science 246:1023-5 N 24 '89
Subplate neurons pioneer the first axon pathway from the cerebral cortex. S. K. McConnell and others. bibl f il Science 245:978-82 S 1 '89
Transient pioneer neurons are essential for formation of an embryonic peripheral nerve [grasshoppers; cover story] M. Klose and D. R. Bentley. bibl f il Science 245:982-4 S 1 '89
DEVELOPMENTAL SCIENCES (FIRM)
Egypt begins using unmanned aircraft for reconnaissance. M. A. Dornheim. il Aviation Week & Space Technology 130:56-7 Ja 23 '89
DEVELOPMENTALLY DISABLED See Mentally handicapped
DEVELOPMENTALLY DISABLED CHILDREN See Mentally handicapped children

DEVERE, ASHER
about
Victor Posner and the case of the mystery financier. G. DeGeorge and R. A. Melcher. il por *Business Week* p34 Ag 28 '89

DEVEREAUX, KATHRYN
Calcium tablets: bone up on the basics. il *Women's Sports & Fitness* 11:22 My '89

DEVIL
See also
Satanism
Satan. J. Furth and M. Murphy. il *Life* 12:48-51+ Je '89
Should parents speak of the devil? L. Jacquet. il *U.S. Catholic* 54:31-7 Mr '89

Anecdotes, facetiae, satire, etc.
They're back [personal demons] C. Murphy. il *The Atlantic* 264:20+ O '89

THE DEVIL AND BILLY MARKHAM [drama] See Silverstein, Shel

DEVIL WORSHIP *See* Satanism

DEVILLE, MICHEL
about
La lectrice [film] Reviews
Commonweal 116:278-9 My 5 '89. T. O'Brien
The New Leader 72:21 Ap 3-17 '89. J. Morrone

DEVIN, JUDI
about
When bigger doesn't mean better. K. J. Novak. il por *Home Office Computing* 7:60-1 D '89

DEVIN, RICHARD
about
Centerline: Richard Devin. M. Sommers. il por *Theatre Crafts* 23:16-17 O '89

LE DEVIN DU VILLAGE [opera] See Rousseau, Jean-Jacques, 1712-1778

DEVINCENZO, JOSEPH
about
Upstairs, downstairs. A. Logan. *The New Yorker* 65:80-6 Ag 21 '89

DEVINE, BOB
Getting a second pet. il *Better Homes and Gardens* 67:206+ N '89

DEVINE, DONALD J.
A free market in government. *National Review* 41:40-1 O 27 '89

DEVINE, ELIZABETH, 1938-, AND BRAGANTI, NANCY, 1941-
A matter of custom. *Travel Holiday* 172:82 S '89

DEVINE, GRANT
about
Privatizing the symbols. T. Fennell. il por *Maclean's* 102:28-9 Mr 6 '89

DEVINE, RICHARD J.
The amicus curiae brief: public policy versus personal freedom. *America* 160:323-6+ Ap 8 '89

DEVINE, ROBERT S.
Sail away on a cruise! il *Better Homes and Gardens* 68:163-6 F '89

DEVONIAN PERIOD *See* Paleontology—Devonian

DEVONSHIRE, ANDREW ROBERT BUXTON CAVENDISH, 11TH DUKE OF, 1920-
Chiswick House—polishing a family jewel. il *Architectural Digest* 46:28+ Ag '89

DEVONSHIRE, DEBORAH VIVIEN FREEMAN-MITFORD CAVENDISH, DUCHESS OF, 1920-
about
Brand name nobility. J. Marcom, Jr. il por *Forbes* 144:318+ N 13 '89

DEVORE, SHERYL
Arts therapy: creativity that heals. il *Current Health 2* 15:20-2 Ap '89
The facts of life with epilepsy. il *Current Health 2* 15:10-12 Ja '89
Reshaping lives. il *Current Health 2* 16:20-1 D '89

DEVORKIN, DAVID H., 1944-
Henry Norris Russell. bibl il por *Scientific American* 260:126-33 My '89

DEVOTIONS, CATHOLIC *See* Catholic Church—Prayer books and devotions

DEVREOTES, PETER
Dictyostelium discoideum: a model system for cell-cell interactions in development. bibl f il *Science* 245:1054-8 S 8 '89

DEVRIES, ARTHUR L.
(jt. auth) See Knight, C. A., and DeVries, Arthur L.

DEVYATKIN, DIMITRI
An interview with a leader of the Green Movement. il *Environment* 30:13-15 D '88

DEW
Dew vs. fog. T. Schlatter. il *Weatherwise* 42:283-4 O '89
Frost at edges. C. F. Bohren. il *Weatherwise* 42:281-2 O '89

DEWDNEY, A. K.
Computer recreations. See issues of Scientific American

DEWHURST, COLLEEN
about
Taking the stage. pors *Harper's Bazaar* 122:150-3+ Ag '89

DEWHURST, PETER
about
Pssst! Want a secret for making superproducts? O. Port. il pors *Business Week* p106+ O 2 '89

DEWITT, HUGH E.
At peace with the bomb. il *The Progressive* 53:26-7 S '89

DEWKIST PLANTS, INC.
Gentleman scamster [G. Bissell's fraudulent DewKist Plants] R. L. Stern. il por *Forbes* 143:104+ F 20 '89

DEWOODY, JAMES
about
Pochoir printing. R. Williams. il pors *American Artist* 53:70-5 S '89

DEXTER CORP.
A chemical maker's secret admirer? [Sherwin-Williams' interest in Dexter Corp.] G. G. Marcial. *Business Week* p76 Ja 30 '89

DEXTRAN SULFATE
FDA broadens use of unproven AIDS drug [DDI in; dextran sulfate out] D. E. Loupe. *Science News* 136:231 O 7 '89

DEY, SUSAN
about
'I love you perfect': a show that could save your life. D. Hudson. il por *TV Guide* 37:30-1 O 7-13 '89
"I'm trying to save women's lives" [interview] V. J. Radovsky. il pors *Redbook* 174:18+ N '89

DEYNEKA, ANITA, AND DEYNEKA, PETER
Russian revolution? il *Christianity Today* 33:22-5 O 20 '89

DEYNEKA, PETER
(jt. auth) See Deyneka, Anita, and Deyneka, Peter

DEYO, RICHARD A., AND OTHERS
Nimodipine facilitates associative learning in aging rabbits. bibl f il *Science* 243:809-11 F 10 '89

DEZELL, MAUREEN
What happens when the acceleration syndrome backfires? Welcome to the dawning age of sloth. *Utne Reader* p42-3 Ja/F '89

DI BIASE, ANGELO
about
Ellen Barkin and the man behind her new look. C. Krupp. pors *Glamour* 87:192 O '89

DI CICCO, DENNIS
Observer's page. See issues of Sky and Telescope

DI COSTANZO, DIANE
The concierge concept. il *House & Garden* 161:156-7 F '89
Remembering tomorrow. il *House & Garden* 161:56+ My '89
Southern exposure. il *House & Garden* 161:52+ Ap '89

DI GIORGIO CORP.
"It's frightening". R. King. *Forbes* 143:152-3 F 20 '89

DI PIERO, W. S.
Thrasher [poem] *The New Yorker* 65:76 My 8 '89

DI SILVESTRO, ROGER L.
Nature stories. See issues of Audubon beginning July 1987 through January 1989

DIABETES
See also
Diabetic coma
Diabetic retinopathy
Diabetes peril for developing children [deficits in spatial or verbal skills; research by Joanne F. Rovet] K. Fackelmann. *Science News* 135:383 Je 17 '89
Diabetes: the silent partner. C. Pesmen. il *Seventeen* 48:86-7+ Ja '89
Exercise could be dangerous [hypoglycemia in diabetics; views of Michael MacDonald] *USA Today (Periodical)* 117:5 F '89
Minority health: an enigma to solve. J. Wood. *Modern Maturity* 32:22+ F/Mr '89
Transgenic mice with I-A on islet cells are normoglycemic but immunologically intolerant. J. Böhme and others. bibl f il *Science* 244:1179-83 Je 9 '89

Causes
Bad news bellies [paunchiness linked to diabetes and heart disease in men] D. Grady. il *American Health* 8:20 My '89
Pregnancy raises risk of type II diabetes [research by Donna Kritz-Silverstein] K. Fackelmann. *Science News* 136:294-5 N 4 '89

Diagnosis
Diabetes—know the symptoms [juvenile diabetes] C. SerVaas. il *The Saturday Evening Post* 261:98-9 N/D '89
Diabetes—the hidden symptoms. C. Collins. *Redbook* 172:20 Ap '89

Genetic aspects
Gene test foretells type I diabetes risk [work of Massimo Trucco] K. Fackelmann. *Science News* 135:357 Je 10 '89
Human diabetes associated with a deletion of the tyrosine kinase domain of the insulin receptor. M. Taira and others. bibl f il *Science* 245:63-6 Jl 7 '89
Human diabetes associated with a mutation in the tyrosine kinase domain of the insulin receptor. M. Odawara and others. bibl f il *Science* 245:66-8 Jl 7 '89
Molecular defects in insulin action. C. R. Kahn and B. J. Goldstein. bibl f *Science* 245:13 Jl 7 '89
Pretranslational suppression of an insulin-responsive glucose transporter in rats with diabetes mellitus. W. T. Garvey and others. bibl f il *Science* 245:60-3 Jl 7 '89

DIABETES—cont.
Nutritional aspects
Diabetes and vitamin C. I. Nelson. *New Choices for the Best Years* 29:15 My '89
Diabetic diet [use of olive oil to lower cholesterol; research by Abhimanyu Garg] il *Prevention (Emmaus, Pa.)* 41:10 Ja '89
Top tips for diabetes self-care [weight loss] G. Maleskey. il *Prevention (Emmaus, Pa.)* 41:73-80 S '89
Therapy
See also
Insulin
Beta-cell break benefits diabetics [research by Shirish C. Shah] *Science News* 135:156 Mr 11 '89
Diabetes? Relax! [after meals] il *Prevention (Emmaus, Pa.)* 41:10+ N '89
A medical messiah? [R. Bernstein] S. S. Hall. il pors *New Choices for the Best Years* 29:31-6 Ap '89
A ray of hope for diabetics [transplanting insulin-producing cells] *Maclean's* 102:62 S 18 '89
The revolution in diabetes care. D. Benzaia. *McCall's* 117:151-2 O '89
What doctors aren't telling diabetics. J. Carey. il *U.S. News & World Report* 107:60 Jl 3 '89

DIABETES IN ANIMALS
How sweet it's not [pets] M. Rosenfeld. il *American Health* 8:80 D '89

DIABETIC COMA
Halfway to heaven! [excerpt from Wake me when it's over] M. K. Blakely. il por *Redbook* 173:126-7+ Jl '89

DIABETIC RETINOPATHY
Help for diabetic eyes? [high blood pressure link] il *Prevention (Emmaus, Pa.)* 41:18 O '89
Hypertension predicts diabetic eye-disease risk [work of Ronald Klein] K. Fackelmann. *Science News* 135:383 Je 17 '89

DIAGANA, WALDÉ
A husband of one's own. il *World Health* p10 Mr '89

DIAGHILEV, SERGE, 1872-1929
about
Collaborating on the spirit of a new age. D. Harris. il pors *Architectural Digest* 46:42+ S '89
Diaghilev sits out WWI in Spain: Iberian idyll. J. R. Acocella. il pors *Dance Magazine* 63:45-8 Je '89
Diaghilev tantalizes the ballet world. R. Johnson. il *Dance Magazine* 63:17 N '89

DIAGNOSIS
See also
Computers—Medical use
Gene probes
Genetic screening
Image processing—Medical use
Radiography, Medical
Second opinion (Medical consultation)
Tomography—Medical use
Ultrasonic waves—Medical use
Urine—Analysis
See also subhead Diagnosis under names of diseases
A beauty checkup [at-home assessment tests] il *Mademoiselle* 95:94-7 Ja '89
Listen to your body: little aches and pains that signal trouble. E. Stukane. il *Redbook* 172:104-5+ Ap '89
Medical tests for healthy women only. L. Holland. il *Good Housekeeping* 209:269-70 S '89
The mouth as body's mirror [clue to illness] J. Folkenberg. il *FDA Consumer* 23:22-4 D '89/Ja '90
Mystery on arrival [difficulties of emergency room diagnosis] E. Rosenthal. il *Discover* 10:78+ D '89
The one-two-threes of a complete blood count. D. Farley. il *FDA Consumer* 23:28-31 S '89
Skin symptoms you must not ignore [clues to internal illness] W. Korn. il *Ladies' Home Journal* 106:66+ S '89
The stories nails can tell [excerpt from Symptoms] I. Rosenfeld. il *Health (New York, N.Y.)* 21:68-9+ Ag '89
Top 10 laboratory tests: blood will tell [cover story] D. Farley. *FDA Consumer* 23:22-7 Jl/Ag '89
What your tongue tells about your health [views of Stephen A. Mitchell] L. C. Ragan. *Good Housekeeping* 209:255 O '89
Why doctors mistreat women: special medical report. R. Baron-Faust. *Redbook* 173:114-15+ My '89

DIAGNOSTIC EQUIPMENT *See* Medical equipment

DIAL, GARRY
about
Dial & Oatts. B. Milkowski. il pors *Down Beat* 56:46-7 N '89

DIAL-A-PORN *See* Telephone pornography
DIAL-A-SHUTTLE *See* Telephone information service
DIALECTS
See also
English language—Dialects
DIALECTS, BLACK *See* Black-English dialects
DIALING SYSTEMS, TELEPHONE *See* Telephone dialing systems
DIALLO, SIRADIOU
Get rid of the dictators. *World Press Review* 36:64 My '89

DIALOGUE
Talk of the times [excerpts from plays by D. Hare, D. Mamet and H. Pinter demonstrate the art of dialogue] *Harper's* 278:37-9+ F '89

DIALYSIS
See also
Hemodialysis

DIAMANDIS, PETER G.
Living out every manager's dream. il por *Fortune* 120:109+ O 9 '89

DIAMANDIS, PETER H., AND HAWLEY, TODD B.
Educating tomorrow's leaders in space. il *Sky and Telescope* 78:4 Jl '89

DIAMOND, BOBBY
about
Bobby Diamond's grown-up and a lawyer, but the kid from Fury hasn't stopped horsing around. T. Allis. il pors *People Weekly* 31:141-2 My 8 '89

DIAMOND, DEBRA JOSEPH
about
Searching for small gems. R. Simon. il por *Forbes* 143:214-15 Je 26 '89

DIAMOND, EDWIN
Anatomy of a horror. il *New York* 22:41-5 My 15 '89
Media. See issues of New York beginning January 28, 1985
The new (land)lords of the press. il *New York* 22:44-50 F 27 '89
Trump vs. Stern: the unmaking of a documentary [cover story] il pors *New York* 22:30-7 S 4 '89

DIAMOND, EDWIN, AND MAROE, JIM
Will TV give Dan Quayle a fair chance? What he can do to improve his image. por *TV Guide* 37:16-19 F 11-17 '89

DIAMOND, EDWIN, AND MEAD, REBECCA
Is TV news getting all the dirt? il *TV Guide* 37:20-2 Je 24-30 '89

DIAMOND, EDWIN, AND O'NEIL, KATRYNA
Is TV news guilty of Japan bashing? il *TV Guide* 37:24-7 My 20-26 '89

DIAMOND, JAMIE
Film school confidential. il *American Film* 14:34-9+ Jl/Ag '89
Victoria's British wit and polish. il pors *Harper's Bazaar* 122:114-17+ F '89

DIAMOND, JARED M.
The accidental conqueror. il *Discover* 10:70-6 D '89
Bittersweet dreams of glory. il pors *Natural History* p28-30+ N '89
Blood, genes, and malaria. il maps *Natural History* p8+ F '89
The cruel logic of our genes. il *Discover* 10:72-8 N '89
The ethnobiologist's dilemma. *Natural History* p26+ Je '89
The great leap forward [cover story; with editorial comment by Paul Hoffman] il map *Discover* 10:4, 50-60 My '89
The price of human folly. il *Discover* 10:72-7 Ap '89
Publish or perish. il *Discover* 10:96-101 Jl '89
Sexual deception. il *Discover* 10:70-4 Ag '89
This-fellow frog, name belong-him dakwo. *Natural History* p16+ Ap '89

DIAMOND, JOHN
Redrawing the map. maps *World Press Review* 36:61 Je '89

DIAMOND, JOHN NATHAN
Mr. Smith goes to Augusta. *The Washington Monthly* 21:36-8 Jl/Ag '89

DIAMOND, NEIL
about
Neil Diamond. D. Browne. por *High Fidelity (New York, N.Y.)* 39:74-5 Jl '89

DIAMOND, S. L., AND OTHERS
Fluid flow stimulates tissue plasminogen activator secretion by cultured human endothelial cells. bibl f il *Science* 243:1483-5 Mr 17 '89

DIAMOND, SHIFRA
Red-hot and blue: the new summer depression. il *Mademoiselle* 95:134 My '89

DIAMOND, WILLIAM
about
Custom of the country. G. Harrell. il *House & Garden* 161:116-21+ Ag '89
Manhattan country. D. Sacks. il *House & Garden* 161:132-43 Ap '89

DIAMOND SHAMROCK R&M INC.
Nothing rough about this Diamond. G. G. Marcial. *Business Week* p76 Ap 17 '89

DIAMOND-STAR MOTORS CORPORATION
Looking forward to the '90s. J. R. Nerad. il *Motor Trend* 41:8 D '89

DIAMOND THIN FILMS
Diamond chips [semiconductor production and doping through carbon in bombardment of silicon; work of Wayne Rabalais] *Discover* 10:12 Jl '89
Diamond film has promise for tough hard disks. *Byte* 14:11 My '89
Diamond films are the new gems. *High Technology Business* 9:39-40 N/D '89
Don't try Tiffany's. E. Corcoran. il *Scientific American* 261:60+ Ag '89

DIAMOND THIN FILMS—*cont.*
Epitaxial growth of diamond films on Si(111) at room temperature by mass-selected low-energy C⁺ beams. J. L. Robertson and others. bibl f il *Science* 243:1047-50 F 24 '89
Scientists form-fit diamond-like cloak [research by John A. Woollam] I. Amato. *Science News* 135:261 Ap 29 '89

DIAMONDS
Diamonds are for boardrooms. P. Baldwin and L. Calvacca. *Working Woman* 14:44 Ag '89
Diamonds from heaven and earth. *Sky and Telescope* 77:244-5 Mr '89
If only this diamond truly lasted forever [study of Beni Bousera by Peter H. Nixon] F. Flam. *Science News* 135:133 Mr 4 '89

DIANA, PRINCESS OF WALES, 1961-
about
Charles and Diana: portrait of a marriage [excerpt from King Charles III] A. Holden. il pors *Ladies' Home Journal* 106:115-17+ F '89
Diana comes of age. P. Junor. il pors *McCall's* 117:38-41 O '89
Diana makes a splash. il pors *Time* 133:71 F 13 '89
Diana's double life [cover story] S. Pearson. il pors *Ladies' Home Journal* 106:115-17+ Ag '89
Do good friends dress alike? (Di & Fergie do). il pors *Redbook* 173:18+ O '89
Dressing for success in New York, Diana cuts the frills and froufrou. il pors *People Weekly* 31:42-3 F 20 '89
Fashion fit for a Princess. N. Darnton. il pors *Newsweek* 113:75 Mr 27 '89
Hair to the throne. C. Sullivan. il pors *Vogue* 179:160 My '89
A new peek at two princesses provides royal watchers some relief from the blahs. S. Schindehette. il pors *People Weekly* 31:64-6 Ap 10 '89
A Princess by profession. N. Cooper. il pors *Newsweek* 113:41 F 6 '89
Princess Di visits infant AIDS victims in Harlem. il pors *Jet* 75:10 F 20 '89
Princess Diana. J. Kaufman. il por *People Weekly* 32 Special Issue:60-1 Fall '89
Princess Diana: the secrets of her style [excerpt from The Princess and the Duchess] J. Fairley. il pors *McCall's* 116:14-16+ Je '89
A Princess makes perfect. K. Ames. il pors *Newsweek* 113:81+ F 13 '89
The rush-rush routine of Charles and Diana [cover story] I. Seward. il pors *The Saturday Evening Post* 261:42-7 S '89
Signs of poise and polish. A. Phillips. il por *Maclean's* 102:42 Jl 24 '89
Di takes a walk. il pors *People Weekly* 32:172 D 25 '89-Ja 1 '90

Photographs and photography
Crown jewel. il pors *Life* 12:130-2 Fall '89

DIANA CORPORATION
The beauty beneath the beast. R. Koselka. il por *Forbes* 144:240+ N 27 '89

DIANE JACOBOWITZ DANCE COMPANY
Modern dancers reach out to prisoners and to homeless men. R. Johnson. il *Dance Magazine* 63:15 S '89

DIANETICS
See also
Scientology

DIAPAUSE
Alien influence [wasp larvae manipulation of potato aphid behavior; research by Jacques Brodeur and Jeremy N. McNeil] T. Beardsley. *Scientific American* 261:26 Jl '89
Dying aphids obey wasp's commands [research by Jacques Brodeur and Jeremy N. McNeil] R. Weiss. *Science News* 135:231 Ap 15 '89
Seasonal microhabitat selection by an endoparasitoid through adaptive modification of host behavior. J. Brodeur and J. N. McNeil. bibl f il *Science* 244:226-8 Ap 14 '89

DIAPERS
Environmental aspects
The continuing diaper debate [disposables are a serious solid waste problem] J. Brooks. il *Utne Reader* p24-5 Jl/Ag '89
Environmental costs of keeping baby dry [disposable diapers] *Science News* 135:141 Mr 4 '89
Export-import trade
Cautionary wail from the nursery [import quotas on Chinese cloth diapers] il *U.S. News & World Report* 106:44 Je 12 '89
Marketing
A pitched battle for baby's bottom. A. Miller. il *Newsweek* 113:44 Mr 6 '89
Recycling
It's diaper city at the landfill [recycling disposable diapers] *U.S. News & World Report* 107:12 Jl 3 '89

DIARIES
See also
Datebooks
All's well that's Boswell. T. Mallon. il *Gentlemen's Quarterly* 59:75+ D '89

Diaries are a girl's best friend. B. Israel. il *Seventeen* 48:84-5+ Ja '89
A diary for living. A. Lindstrom. il *Reader's Digest* 134:158-60 F '89
In progress [diarist E. R. Ellis] *The New Yorker* 65:30-1 Mr 6 '89
Logging the miles [keeping a cycling journal] J. Kita. *Bicycling* 30:62 Ag '89
"Read the 'me' book!". T. Wood. il *Parents* 64:230-1 My '89
Save your life: notes on the value of keeping a diary. J. Moore. il *Utne Reader* p90-3 My/Je '89
She reaches for her pen, not her plate. J. Case. il pors *Prevention (Emmaus, Pa.)* 41:107-8+ O '89

DIARRHEA
Therapy
Pinpointing the culprits [combating infant diarrhea in Mexico] H. Nelson. il *World Health* p12-15 Je '89
A simple cure for diarrhoea [oral rehydration program in the Western Pacific region] A. Borra. il *World Health* p14-15 N '89

DIATRYMA *See* Birds, Fossil

DÍAZ, ADA MARÍA ISASI- *See* Isasi-Díaz, Ada María

DIAZ, ANN THOMPSON
Rust protection. il *Better Homes and Gardens* 67:102-3 Ja '89

DIAZ, IDRIS M.
Playing your cards right. il *Black Enterprise* 19:80+ Mr '89

DIAZ, JAIME
Different strokes for different folks. il *Money* 18:112-15+ Ap '89
Find the golf here? il *Sports Illustrated* 70:58-60+ F 13 '89
Giving out high marks. il pors *Sports Illustrated* 70:20-1 Mr 6 '89
No keeping up with Jones. il por *Sports Illustrated* 70:34-5 Ja 16 '89
No prima donna. il pors *Sports Illustrated* 70 Special Issue:115-17 F '89
Perils of putting. il *Sports Illustrated* 70:76-8+ Ap 3 '89

DIAZ VILAR, J. JUAN
The success of the sects among Hispanics in the United States. il *America* 160:174-5+ F 25 '89

DIBNER, MARK D. (MARK DOUGLAS)
Factories of our future. il *Consumers' Research Magazine* 72:15-18 Ap '89
(jt. auth) See Stoddard, Alan G., and Dibner, Mark D. (Mark Douglas)

DIBOLL, NEIL
Wildflowers: the case for native plants [cover story] il *Flower and Garden* 33:22-8+ Mr/Ap '89

DIBROMOCHLOROPROPANE
Will the circle be unbroken? [infertility in Costa Rican banana workers] D. Weir and C. Matthiessen. il *Mother Jones* 14:20-7 Je '89

DICICCO, RICHARD
Absorbing Japanese technology. il *High Technology Business* 9:9 N/D '89

DICK GIDRON CADILLAC & FORD INC.
Driven by excellence. K. D. Thompson. il pors *Black Enterprise* 19:236-40 Je '89

DICK GREGORY HEALTH ENTERPRISES, INC.
Gregory buys hotel and fattens his diet empire. H. Manly. il por *Black Enterprise* 19:22 Mr '89

DICKENS, CHARLES, 1812-1870
Ralph Nickelby's tell-tale guise [fiction] il *Gentlemen's Quarterly* 59:254 F '89
about
Dickens on stage and screen [cover story] R. Samuel. il por *History Today* 39:44-51 D '89
Love in the lower depths. G. Wills. bibl f il *The New York Review of Books* 36:60-7 O 26 '89
The second greatest Christmas story ever told. T. J. Burns. il *Reader's Digest* 135:65-70 D '89
What the Dickens a la Tuck [postcards] S. S. Carver. il *Antiques & Collecting Hobbies* 94:64-7 My '89

DICKERSON, ERIC
about
Dog days. R. Reilly. il pors *Sports Illustrated* 71:58-60+ D 4 '89

DICKEY, GLENN
Beers with . . . Jerry Rice [interview] il pors *Sport (New York, N.Y.)* 80:19-20 N '89
Tell a friend: Joe Montana may be the best ever. il por *Sport (New York, N.Y.)* 80:55 Ag '89

DICKIN, GEORGE
Eyewitness report from the right seat of the Wright Flyer. il *Flying* 116:82-6 O '89

DICKINSON, ELEANOR, 1931-
about
Eleanor Dickinson at Hatley Martin. P. Selz. il *Art in America* 77:219 S '89

DICKINSON, EMILY, 1830-1886
about
A certain slant of light: drawings by Will Barnet, poems by Emily Dickinson. S. Marcus. il *American Artist* 53:56-61 N '89

DICKINSON, WARREN W.
Plankton to petroleum. il *Earth Science* 41:21-3 Wint '88

DICKSON, PAUL
about
A new guide to baseball slang is a dinger of a read. J. Friedman. il pors *People Weekly* 31:93+ My 1 '89
Paul Dickson talks about language for his baseball dictionary. G. Corcoran. il por *Publishers Weekly* 235:42 F 17 '89
DICKSON, TOM
Home is where the fish are. il *National Wildlife* 27:24-8 F/Mr '89
DICKSON CONCEPTS LTD.
Keep the calculators out of sight. A. Tanzer. il *Forbes* 143:96+ Mr 20 '89
DICTATORS
Democracy and tyranny: dealing with friendly tyrants. R. N. Haass. *Current (Washington, D.C.)* 316:34-40 O '89
Get rid of the dictators [Africa] S. Diallo. *World Press Review* 36:64 My '89
DICTIONARIES
See also
Baseball—Dictionaries
CD-ROM (Compact disc-Read only memory)—Dictionaries
English language—Dictionaries
Information systems—Dictionaries
Publishers and publishing—Dictionaries
DIDDLEBOCK, BOB
Beers with . . . Doug Moe. il pors *Sport (New York, N.Y.)* 80:21-2 F '89
Digestive disorders: a treatment update. il *McCall's* 116:77-9+ Ag '89
DIDEOXYINOSINE
AIDS drug DDI under treatment IND. il *FDA Consumer* 23:2-3 D '89/Ja '90
AIDS drug shows promise [research by Robert Yarchoan] *Science News* 136:69 Jl 29 '89
AIDS drug trials enter new age. J. Palca. il *Science* 246:19-21 O 6 '89
FDA broadens use of unproven AIDS drug [DDI in; dextran sulfate out] D. E. Loupe. *Science News* 136:231 O 7 '89
Fighting AIDS all the way. L. Josephs. il *The New York Times Magazine* p42+ O 8 '89
Government DDI trials on trial. J. Palca. *Science* 246:1244 D 8 '89
In vivo activity against HIV and favorable toxicity profile of 2', 3'-dideoxyinosine. R. Yarchoan and others. bibl f il *Science* 245:412-15 Jl 28 '89
A new AIDS drug gets the go-ahead. *Newsweek* 114:40 O 9 '89
New AIDS drug passes first clinical test [DDI] J. L. Marx. il *Science* 245:353 Jl 28 '89
A new AIDS finding. G. W. Taylor. il *Maclean's* 102:47 Ag 7 '89
A new antiviral drug: promising or problematic? J. Palca. *Science* 246:20 O 6 '89
A risky lifeline for AIDS victims [Bristol-Myers distributes unproven drug] *U.S. News & World Report* 107:14 Jl 24 '89
Testing, testing [FDA and new AIDS drug] D. Ellen. *The New Republic* 201:14-15 Ag 28 '89
DIDION, JOAN
Letter from Los Angeles. *The New Yorker* 65:88+ Ap 24 '89
Letter from Los Angeles. *The New Yorker* 65:92-9 S 4 '89
Life at court. il *The New York Review of Books* 36:3-4+ D 21 '89
Some women [cover story] il por *Esquire* 112:214-23 S '89
DIDN'T (TERM)
Breakout [didn't pronounced as dit'n] C. Murphy. il *The Atlantic* 264:14+ Jl '89
DIDO AND AENEAS [dance] See Dance reviews—Single works
DIDO AND AENEAS [opera] See Purcell, Henry, 1659-1695
DIDRIKSON (BABE) MEMORIAL MUSEUM (BEAUMONT, TEX.) See Babe Didrikson Zaharias Memorial Museum (Beaumont, Tex.)
DIE HARD [film] See Motion picture reviews—Single works
DIEBENKORN, RICHARD, 1922-
about
Richard Diebenkorn: Museum of Modern Art. R. B. Woodward. il *Art News* 88:168 Mr '89
DIEBOLD, JIM
about
Marcia Anderson and Jim Diebold marry for money—the dollars their guests gave to charity. P. Freeman. il pors *People Weekly* 31:139+ Je 19 '89
DIECKMANN, KATHERINE
Elitist kitsch. *Utne Reader* p36 My/Je '89
Tim Robbins comes to off-Broadway, via Hollywood. por *Vogue* 179:258 O '89
DIEDERICH, FRANÇOIS, AND OTHERS
All-carbon molecules: evidence for the generation of cyclo[18]carbon from a stable organic precursor. bibl f il *Science* 245:1088-90 S 8 '89
DIEGMUELLER, KAREN S.
Middle America: priced out of house and home. *Current (Washington, D.C.)* 314:16-21 Jl/Ag '89

DIEHL, CHUCK
about
Appliance lover Chuck Diehl takes a spin-dry on memory lane. M. Neill. il pors *People Weekly* 31:277-8 Mr 6 '89
DIEHL, JACK D., JR., AND ANGSTADT, ROBERT B.
Microcomputer data collection: bacterial growth curves. il *BioScience* 39:173-5 Mr '89
DIELECTRICS
Surface discharges on natural dielectrics in the solar system. H. Campins and E. P. Krider. bibl f il *Science* 245:622-4 Ag 11 '89
DIERDORF, DAN
about
Beers with . . . Dan Dierdorf [interview] J. Schuster. il pors *Sport (New York, N.Y.)* 80:17-19 D '89
DIESEL ENGINES
See also
Stewart & Stevenson Services, Inc.
Fuel
See Diesel fuels
DIESEL ENGINES, AIRCRAFT
West German firm developing diesel engines for general aviation aircraft [Michael Zoche] *Aviation Week & Space Technology* 131:57+ Ag 28 '89
DIESEL ENGINES, AUTOMOTIVE
Fuel
See Diesel fuels
Noise
The quiet diesel [design from Steyr-Daimler-Puch] D. Scott. il *Popular Science* 234:111+ Ap '89
Superchargers
Super Suburban [GMC Suburban with turbocharged diesel engine designed by Gale Banks] L. Frank. il *Popular Mechanics* 166:104+ Ag '89
A winner fit for the Gipper [Newell motorhomes] L. Griffin. il *Car and Driver* 34:107-9+ My '89
DIESEL ENGINES, MARINE
Diesels. E. Dennis. See issues of Motor Boating & Sailing
Next: diesel stern drives. J. A. Fishman. *Motor Boating & Sailing* 164:28-9+ Jl '89
Cooling
None like it hot. E. Dennis. il *Motor Boating & Sailing* 164:73-4 S '89
Superchargers
SR-84. L. Rudeen. il *Motor Boating & Sailing* 163:32 Mr '89
DIESEL FUELS
Ethanol and diesel fuel do mix. C. Peterson, Jr. *Successful Farming* 87 no4:64F Mr '89
DIET
See also
Aged—Nutrition
Aging—Nutritional aspects
Athletes—Nutrition
Blacks—Nutrition
Boron in the body
Calcium in the body
Carbohydrates
Celebrities—Nutrition
Children—Nutrition
College students—Nutrition
Computers—Diet use
Cyclists—Nutrition
Dancers—Nutrition
Digestion
Duke University. Diet and Fitness Center
Executives—Nutrition
Fiber in diet
Hispanic Americans—Nutrition
Infants—Nutrition
Infants, Premature—Nutrition
Iron in the body
Liquid diets
Low calorie cooking
Low sodium cooking
Magnesium in the body
Minerals in the body
Nutri/System, Inc.
Nutrition
Nutrition education
Pregnancy—Nutritional aspects
Pritikin Longevity Centers
Project LEAN
Proteins
Runners—Nutrition
Skiers—Nutrition
Vegetarianism
Vitamins
Weight loss clinics
Weight Watchers International Inc.
Women—Nutrition
Women athletes—Nutrition
Yolanda Enterprises, Inc.
Youth—Nutrition
Zinc in the body
10 tactical weight-loss tips. M. Bricklin. il *Prevention (Emmaus, Pa.)* 41:144+ My '89
32 little diet changes. L. Gordon. il *Glamour* 87:74 F '89

DIET—*cont.*

100 pounds lighter—and loving it [J. Carter] il pors *Ebony* 45:104+ D '89

The amazing two-day diet. T. Cooper and G. Cooper. il *Redbook* 172:49-52 Mr '89

Attention dieters . . . L. Lindner and G. Zyla. il *Redbook* 173:14 S '89

The battle of the bulge: how to budge that extra pudge! il *'Teen* 33:81 D '89

"Believe us it works!" 8 total makeovers [Wise woman's diet] il *Redbook* 173:120-5 O '89

The big makeover—you can do it, too! M. Bricklin. il *Prevention (Emmaus, Pa.)* 41:144+ Ja '89

Crying the weight-loss blues [national diet programs] N. Henderson. il *Changing Times* 43:75-8 Ap '89

The dangers of dieting [cover story; special section; with editorial comment by Kevin Doyle] il *Maclean's* 102:2, 48-52+ O 9 '89

Diet centers are really in fat city. B. O'Reilly. il *Fortune* 119:137+ Je 5 '89

Diet news. See issues of Mademoiselle

Diet Q & A. See issues of Mademoiselle

Diet the T-factor way [condensed from The T-factor diet] M. Katahn. *Reader's Digest* 135:119-22 O '89

Diets Incorporated. A. Miller. il *Newsweek* 114:56-60+ S 11 '89

The diets that keep stars looking trim. B. Goodwin. il *TV Guide* 37:26-8 Je 10-16 '89

Don't rotate—ambulate! [effectiveness of rotation diet when combined with exercise; research by James Hill] R. A. Barnett. *American Health* 8:85-6+ D '89

Drop 30-plus pounds. J. Whitlock. il *Prevention (Emmaus, Pa.)* 41:66-73+ Ja '89

Eating ethnic and lean [tips for eating out; excerpt from International cuisines calorie counter] D. Webb. il *Health (New York, N.Y.)* 21:46+ N '89

Gobble, gobble [eating sensibly during the holidays] E. Coleman. il *Bicycling* 30:78 D '89

Holiday weight watching. il *Seventeen* 48:78-9 D '89

Holiday willpower [dancers] J. Scala. il *Dance Magazine* 63:64-5 D '89

How to avoid holiday overindulgence. il *USA Today (Periodical)* 118:10 N '89

The 'I love to nibble' diet. S. Lally. il *Prevention (Emmaus, Pa.)* 41:66-8+ Mr '89

I'll always be fat . . . and six other overweight myths. C. Hacinli. il *Mademoiselle* 95:110 D '89

The latest on weight loss. G. L. Blackburn. il *Prevention (Emmaus, Pa.)* 41:34-6 My '89

Long-term weight loss. il *Prevention (Emmaus, Pa.)* 41:8-9 D '89

Lose 15 pounds fast! Play tic-tac-low [Wise woman's diet] il *Redbook* 173:95-101+ My '89

Losing 100 pounds the old-fashioned way [B. Wiggins] il pors *Ebony* 44:98+ S '89

Melvin Hazer: a thinner, happier man. il pors *Ebony* 44:88+ Ja '89

The new diet mindset [cover story; special section] il *Psychology Today* 23:31-4+ Je '89

The new Hilton Head diet [excerpt from The Hilton Head over 35 diet] P. M. Miller. il *Ladies' Home Journal* 106:88+ F '89

New rules for a better body. il *Glamour* 87:146-7 Ja '89

New weight-loss discovery: common sense. E. E. Rosenbaum. il *New Choices for the Best Years* 29:26+ Ap '89

The oldest diet ever—but it works. J. Wood. *Modern Maturity* 32:30-1 Ap/My '89

The one-day quick-fix diet. il *Glamour* 87:236 D '89

Oprah reveals her battle to stay slim on dieting segment of her TV show. il por *Jet* 77:14 D 4 '89

Our high-energy diet for busy bodies [Wise woman's diet] il *Redbook* 173:115-19+ O '89

"The Paris restaurant diet" [developed by Pierre Azam] il *Glamour* 87:265 Ag '89

The Pritikin plan for better health. R. Pritikin and J. J. Kenney. il pors *The Humanist* 49:14-16+ Ja/F '89

Psyche yourself slim. M. Golin. il *Prevention (Emmaus, Pa.)* 41:108+ My '89

Quick tips from diet doctors. D. R. Hales. *Reader's Digest* 135:160-2 D '89

Rethinking eating out. C. A. Sweet. il *FDA Consumer* 23:8-13 N '89

Richard Simmons' New Year's revolution [holiday season dieting] P. Perry. il por *The Saturday Evening Post* 261:58-9+ Ja/F '89

Riding the crest of victory; ed. by Deborah Grandinetti. L. B. Teets. il pors *Prevention (Emmaus, Pa.)* 41:113-14+ Jl '89

Riding to lose (weight, that is). J. Barone. *Bicycling* 30:104+ My '89

Say good-bye to feast-and-famine! J. Laughridge. il *Good Housekeeping* 208:124-5 My '89

Secrets of the sleek chic [France] A. Bogart. il *Harper's Bazaar* 122:36+ Ap '89

She reaches for her pen, not her plate. J. Case. il pors *Prevention (Emmaus, Pa.)* 41:107-8+ O '89

Take shape. il *'Teen* 33:65-72 O '89

Taking it off: the diet explosion. il *Ebony* 44:136+ Mr '89

Thin thighs, heavy heart. D. Kent. il *Mademoiselle* 95:166+ S '89

Tipping the scales for vibrant health; ed. by Deborah Grandinetti. G. Kostka. il pors *Prevention (Emmaus, Pa.)* 41:102-4 Ag '89

Top tips for diabetes self-care [weight loss] G. Maleskey. il *Prevention (Emmaus, Pa.)* 41:73-80 S '89

Tuning up & trimming down [singer B. Lipscomb] il pors *Ebony* 44:68+ Ap '89

Turning a 'dark day' into triumph. M. Mullaly. il pors *Prevention (Emmaus, Pa.)* 41:100+ D '89

Two years and 216 pounds lighter; ed. by Cathy Perlmutter. M. Parzych. il pors *Prevention (Emmaus, Pa.)* 41:74+ Ja '89

Type A diet traps. L. Lindner. il *Health (New York, N.Y.)* 21:36-7 Ag '89

We kept it off! ['Body makeovers' alumni] il *Prevention (Emmaus, Pa.)* 41:92-4+ My '89

Weigh-ins made easy: diet dilemma data. il *'Teen* 33:90+ Mr '89

Weigh to go! [K. Beyer loses sixty pounds] N. Amdur. il pors *World Tennis* 37:42-3 O '89

The weight-loss perk [effect of caffeine on metabolism] K. Hamilton. il *Health (New York, N.Y.)* 21:32+ Jl '89

Weight-loss success stories. il *McCall's* 116:23+ Mr '89

The Weight Watchers New Year's diet. S. Berkman. *Ladies' Home Journal* 106:49-50+ Ja '89

Why your last diet flopped. il *Glamour* 87:238-41 Je '89

Winning the "losing" battle—for good. E. Coleman. il *Women's Sports & Fitness* 11:44-5+ Ja/F '89

Winning the war against sugar cravings. G. L. Blackburn. il *Prevention (Emmaus, Pa.)* 41:103+ N '89

Anecdotes, facetiae, satire, etc.

The don't-try-it diet. M. G. Stoddard. il *The Saturday Evening Post* 261:60-2 My/Je '89

Bibliography

Rating the diet books. M. Gee and L. Cheung. *McCall's* 116:102 Jl '89

Moral and religious aspects

Confessions of a glutton [cover story] M. L. Bringle. *The Christian Century* 106:955-8 O 25 '89

The newer, thinner me. P. Yancey. il *Christianity Today* 33:56 Ag 18 '89

DIET COOKING *See* Low calorie cooking

DIET IN DISEASE

See also
>
> Anorexia nervosa
> Antinutrients
> Arthritis—Nutritional aspects
> Breast—Cancer—Nutritional aspects
> Bulimia
> Cancer—Nutritional aspects
> Cataracts (Eye defect)—Nutritional aspects
> Celiac disease—Nutritional aspects
> Cerebrovascular disease—Nutritional aspects
> Colitis—Nutritional aspects
> Colon (Anatomy)—Cancer—Nutritional aspects
> Diabetes—Nutritional aspects
> Gallstones—Nutritional aspects
> Heart—Diseases—Nutritional aspects
> Hypertension—Nutritional aspects
> Liver—Diseases—Nutritional aspects
> Lungs—Cancer—Nutritional aspects
> Lungs—Diseases—Nutritional aspects

100 best diet and healing foods. S. Lally. il *Prevention (Emmaus, Pa.)* 41:42-4+ S '89

As evidence mounts of the strong link between nutrition and immunity, Lori Miller Kase asks: can the use of supplements help in the fight against disease? L. M. Kase. *Vogue* 179:288+ N '89

The best nutrition discoveries of 1989. M. Bricklin. il *Prevention (Emmaus, Pa.)* 41:144+ D '89

Diet and immunity: the new frontier. C. Perlmutter. il *Prevention (Emmaus, Pa.)* 41:46-52+ O '89

Eating for whole health [benefits of oat bran and whole foods] R. Rodale. il *Prevention (Emmaus, Pa.)* 41:28+ Ap '89

The fish nobody knows [beneficial effects of fish oil in treatment of disease] R. A. Barnett and J. Barone. il *American Health* 8:104-6+ Je '89

The great American health pitch [cover story; special section] il *Business Week* p114-17+ O 9 '89

The health-diet link: charting a rising awareness. D. Blumenthal. il *FDA Consumer* 23:22-7 O '89

Junk food monkeys [olive baboons in Masai Mara Game Reserve feeding on humans' garbage] R. M. Sapolsky. il *Discover* 10:48-51 S '89

The Pritikin plan for better health. R. Pritikin and J. J. Kenney. il pors *The Humanist* 49:14-16+ Ja/F '89

The world's healthiest diet [Chinese diet and disease patterns; research by T. C. Campbell] S. S. Lang. il map *American Health* 8:105-7+ S '89

DIET IN TELEVISION

Anecdotes, facetiae, satire, etc.

Watch and grow thin. D. Virtue. il *TV Guide* 37:17-19 Je 24-30 '89

DIET PILLS *See* Weight reducing products
DIETARY LAWS, JEWISH *See* Jews—Dietary laws
DIETARY SUPPLEMENTS
Shortcuts. J. Carey. il *U.S. News & World Report* 106:70 My 29 '89
You lead, I'll swallow [runners' use] H. Higdon. il *Runner's World* 24:82-5 Ap '89
DIETARY SUPPLEMENTS INDUSTRY
See also
Shaklee Corp.
DIETHYL TOLUAMIDE *See* Deet
DIETRICH, MARLENE, 1904-
The mystique of Marlene [excerpt from Marlene] il por *Harper's Bazaar* 122:202-3 Ap '89
DIETRICH, RICHARD V.
Rock music. il *Earth Science* 42:24-5 Summ '89
DIETS *See* Diet
DIETZEL, JESSICA
The drift of oil. il *World Press Review* 36:66 S '89
DIFFERENCES, INDIVIDUAL *See* Individual differences
DIFFERENCES, RACE *See* Race differences
DIFFERENT LIGHT (FIRM)
A Different Light: bookselling beacon. J. Mutter. il *Publishers Weekly* 236:26-8 D 8 '89
A DIFFERENT WORLD [television program] *See* Television program reviews—Single works
DIFFERENTIAL EQUATIONS
Computer chaos at home [Verhulst equation] D. H. Smith. il *Sky and Telescope* 78:139 Ag '89
DIFFERENTIALS, WAGE *See* Wage differentials
DIFFERENTIATION (BIOLOGY)
See also
Morphogenesis
5-bromo-2'-deoxyuridine blocks myogenesis by extinguishing expression of MyoD1. S. J. Tapscott and others. bibl f il *Science* 245:532-6 Ag 4 '89
Commitment of mouse fibroblasts to adipocyte differentiation by DNA transfection. S. Chen and others. bibl f il *Science* 244:582-5 My 5 '89
Commitment of neural crest cells to the sensory neuron lineage [quail] M. Sieber-Blum. bibl f il *Science* 243:1608-11 Mr 24 '89
Diffusible factors essential for epidermal cell redifferentiation in Catharanthus roseus. B. A. Siegel and J. A. Verbeke. bibl f il *Science* 244:580-2 My 5 '89
Genetic control of differentiation of the Caenorhabditis elegans touch receptor neurons. M. Chalfie and M. Au. bibl f il *Science* 243:1027-33 F 24 '89
Glial cell diversification in the rat optic nerve. M. C. Raff. bibl f il *Science* 243:1450-5 Mr 17 '89
DIFFICULT CHILDREN *See* Problem children
DIFFLEY, JOHN F. X., AND STILLMAN, BRUCE
Similarity between the transcriptional silencer binding proteins ABF1 and RAP1. bibl f il *Science* 246:1034-8 N 24 '89
DIFFRACTION
See also
X ray diffraction
DIFFUSION
See also
Biological transport
Light—Scattering
An empirical model for predicting diffusion coefficients in silicate minerals. S. M. Fortier and B. J. Giletti. bibl f il *Science* 245:1481-4 S 29 '89
Time and spatial dependence of the concentration of less than 10^5 microelectrode-generated molecules. S. Licht and others. bibl f il *Science* 243:1176-8 Mr 3 '89
Unexpected leakage through landfill liners [diffusion of chemicals through clay] J. Raloff. *Science News* 135:164 Mr 18 '89
DIFRANCESCO, DARIO, AND OTHERS
Muscarinic modulation of cardiac rate at low acetylcholine concentrations. bibl f il *Science* 243:669-71 F 3 '89
DIFRANZA, AMERICO, 1919-
about
Americo DiFranza. E. Agar. il por *American Artist* 53:48-53 Ag '89
DIGESTION
Eat and run. L. Applegate. il *Runner's World* 24:22-3 S '89
The relaxed tummy [effects of stress upon digestion; research by Donald R. Morse] W. Cole. il *American Health* 8:126-8 Je '89
DIGESTIVE SYSTEM
See also
Colon (Anatomy)
Intestines
Pancreas
Stomach
Alimentary, my dear hoatzin [research by Stuart D. Strahl] R. Cowen. il *Science News* 136:269-70 O 21 '89
Foregut fermentation in the hoatzin, a neotropical leaf-eating bird [cover story] A. Grajal and others. bibl f il *Science* 245:1236-8 S 15 '89
The gastrointestinal tract in growth and reproduction. K. Uvnäs-Moberg. bibl il *Scientific American* 261:78-83 Jl '89

What's a hoatzin? [only bird with foregut fermentation; research by Stuart D. Strahl] J. Horgan. il *Scientific American* 261:30 D '89
Diseases
See also
Celiac disease
Inflammatory bowel disease
Irritable bowel syndrome
Digestive disorders: a treatment update. B. Diddlebock. il *McCall's* 116:77-9+ Ag '89
Holiday ailments: causes and cures. L. Holland. il *Good Housekeeping* 208:167 Ja '89
DIGGERS (POLITICAL MOVEMENT) *See* Levellers (Political movement)
DIGGES, DEBORAH
The flower thief [poem] *The New Yorker* 65:48-9 My 15 '89
The Rockettes [poem] *The New Yorker* 65:34 Mr 13 '89
DIGIORGIO, JOSEPH, 1931-
about
Get a consultant. il *American Artist* 53:51 D '89
DIGITAL AMPLIFIERS *See* Amplifiers
DIGITAL AUDIO TAPE RECORDERS AND RECORDING
DAT: cons and pros. R. Hodges. il *Stereo Review* 54:171 N '89
DAT drive eases Mac backups [Gigapack-Mac] D. E. Crabb. il *Byte* 14:225-6+ N '89
Digital audio tape gets a green light. il *Newsweek* 114:68 Ag 7 '89
The future of tape. M. Riggs. il *High Fidelity (New York, N.Y.)* 39:5 F '89
Get ready for DATs. J. Donnelly. il *Popular Science* 235:100+ N '89
Is there a DAT in your future? *Consumer Reports* 54:32 Ja '89
It's a deal. L. G. Boundas. il *Stereo Review* 54:4 O '89
A new twist on an old technology [helical-scan recording] J. Bretzmann. il *Byte* 14:380-2+ N '89
The sound of music, Japanese style. il *U.S. News & World Report* 107:10-11 Ag 7 '89
Sweet harmony [dispute is settled] il *Time* 134:43 Ag 7 '89
Still video format
DAT goes video. B. Harrell. il *Stereo Review* 54:36 S '89
Testing
From Nakamichi: DAT at last? [Model 1000] M. Riggs. il *High Fidelity (New York, N.Y.)* 39:5 Mr '89
Pursuing DAT [Nakamichi 1000] K. C. Pohlmann. il *Stereo Review* 54:32 Mr '89
Unauthorized recording
Calling the RIAA's bluff [threat to sue any company trying to sell a DAT recorder] R. Long. il *High Fidelity (New York, N.Y.)* 39:18 Ap '89
Copy-protected DAT [Solocopy] il *Radio-Electronics* 60:4 O '89
The DAT controversy. *Byte* 14:384 N '89
Labels back down on DAT. M. Goldberg. *Rolling Stone* p26 S 21 '89
DIGITAL COMPACT DISC PLAYERS *See* Compact disc players
DIGITAL COMPACT DISCS *See* Compact discs
DIGITAL COMPUTERS *See* Computers
DIGITAL COUNTERS *See* Counting machines and devices
DIGITAL ELECTRONICS
See also
Analog-to-digital converters
Digital-to-analog converters
Integrated circuits
Digital update. K. C. Pohlmann. il *Stereo Review* 54:95-9 O '89
Digital's future: bits and pieces. S. A. Booth. il *Popular Mechanics* 166:44 Ap '89
High-definition TV is rallying a digital revolution. O. Port. il *Business Week* p64-6 Ja 30 '89
DIGITAL EQUIPMENT CORP.
DEC has one little word for 30,000 employees: sell. L. Helm. il por *Business Week* p86+ Ag 14 '89
Digital Equipment introduces improved data storage system [RV64 jukebox] *Aviation Week & Space Technology* 130:61 Mr 13 '89
Digital Equipment introduces new engineering workstations, personal computer series. *Aviation Week & Space Technology* 130:51 Ja 23 '89
A double whammy spooks high-tech investors. J. W. Verity. il *Business Week* p37 Ap 3 '89
The hottest computer in a white-hot market? [new workstation] L. Helm. il *Business Week* p88-9 Ja 16 '89
Will DEC's new workhorse haul profits out of a rut? [VAX 9000 series] K. H. Hammonds. il *Business Week* p41-2 O 30 '89
DIGITAL LOUDSPEAKERS *See* Loudspeakers
DIGITAL MICROWAVE RECEIVERS *See* Microwave receivers
DIGITAL MULTIMETERS *See* Multimeters
DIGITAL PAPER
Digital paper. D. Pountain. il *Byte* 14:274-6+ F '89
Optical film. D. Scott. il *Popular Science* 234:49 Ap '89

DIGITAL PATHWAYS (FIRM)
Business-minded professor [computer virus security system] M. Alpert. il por *Fortune* 119:319 Ap 24 '89
DIGITAL RESEARCH, INC.
Coulda been a contender. J. Pitta. il *Forbes* 144:99-100 Jl 10 '89
Digital Research still lives. R. A. Shaffer. il *Personal Computing* 13:45-6 Ag '89
DIGITAL SOUND RECORDING AND REPRODUCING *See* Sound—Recording and reproducing
DIGITAL SYNTHESIZERS *See* Musical instruments, Electronic
DIGITAL TELEVISION CIRCUITS *See* Television circuits
DIGITAL-TO-ANALOG CONVERTERS
Build a digital to analog converter. D. Weber. il *Radio-Electronics* 60 ComputerDigest:77+ My '89
The CD bit wars. G. Brockhouse. il *High Fidelity (New York, N.Y.)* 39:41-5 Ap '89
Chipping in with 18-bit DACs. D. Ranada. il *High Fidelity (New York, N.Y.)* 39:18 F '89
MASH to the rescue. R. Hodges. il *Stereo Review* 54:164 S '89
RGB-to-NTSC converter. R. Bek. il *Radio-Electronics* 60:81+ D '89
When less is more [1-bit CD players] M. Riggs. il *High Fidelity (New York, N.Y.)* 39:5 Je '89
Work in progress [work of L. Fielder] R. Hodges. il *Stereo Review* 54:97 Ag '89
DIGITAL VIDEODISC PLAYERS *See* Videodisc players
DIGITAL VIDEODISCS *See* Videodiscs
DIGITAL VIDEOTAPE RECORDERS AND RECORDING *See* Videotape recorders and recording
DIGITALIS (PLANT) *See* Foxgloves
DIGITIZER TABLETS *See* Digitizing tablets
DIGITIZERS (COMPUTERS)
Chips ahoy. K. C. Pohlmann. *Stereo Review* 54:22 My '89
Compute! choice [Sound Blaster card] R. C. Leinecker. il *Compute!* 11:88-90 D '89
Dealing with a digital world [DSP chips] D. A. Mindell. il *Byte* 14:246-8+ Ag '89
Digi-View Gold. S. Anzovin. il *Compute!* 11:80 My '89
Digital signal-processing news [DSP chips] D. Ranada. il *High Fidelity (New York, N.Y.)* 39:22 Mr '89
Innovation Sound Standard. J. Latimer. *Compute!* 11:68 Ag '89
Low-cost digitizing on the Mac [ComputerEyes] L. H. Loeb and A. F. Lent. il *Byte* 14:98+ Je '89
Putting DSPs to work. B. Saffari. il *Byte* 14:259-60+ D '89
DIGITIZING TABLETS
Graphic details. S. Diehl and S. Apiki. il *Byte* 14:162-6+ Ja '89
Hardware reviews for architects: digitizing tablets for the Mac [Kurta IS/ADB and Summagraphics Bit Pad Plus] S. S. Ross. il *Architectural Record* 177:153 F '89
Pencil me in [Wang Laboratories' Freestyle] P. Scisco. il *Compute!* 11:9 F '89
DIHYDROPYRIDINES
Primary structure of the β subunit of the DHP-sensitive calcium channel from skeletal muscle. P. Ruth and others. bibl f il *Science* 245:1115-18 S 8 '89
Specific block of calcium channel expression by a fragment of dihydropyridine receptor cDNA. I. Lotan and others. bibl f il *Science* 243:666-9 F 3 '89
DIHYDROXYVITAMIN D_3 *See* Vitamin D_3
DIIANNI, ALBERT
Faith and justice: a delicate balance. il *America* 161:32-4+ Jl 15-22 '89
DIIULIO, JOHN J.
Managing constitutionally. *Society* 26:81-3 Jl/Ag '89
(jt. auth) See Wilson, James Q., and DiIulio, John J.
DIJOSEPH, JASON
about
Di-talent of DiJoseph. M. Will-Weber. il por *Runner's World* 24:101 My '89
DIKES (ENGINEERING)
Netherlands
The reclamation of Holland. P. Canova. il map *Sea Frontiers* 35:154-64 My/Je '89
DILEO, FRANK
about
Michael Jackson and his manager Frank Dileo go their separate ways. il pors *Jet* 75:57 Mr 6 '89
DILIBERTO, JOHN
Bill Frisell: guitars & scatterations [cover story] il pors *Down Beat* 56:16-19 My '89
DILIP HIRO *See* Hiro, Dilip
DILKE, MARGARET
(jt. auth) See Dilke, Oswald Ashton Wentworth, and Dilke, Margaret
DILKE, OSWALD ASHTON WENTWORTH, AND DILKE, MARGARET
Mapping a Crusade. bibl il maps *History Today* 39:31-5 Ag '89
DILKS, CAROL
Alzheimer's disease: the search for a cure. il *Nation's Business* 77:86 O '89

DILLARD, ANNIE
Ship in a bottle [story] il *Harper's* 279:68-71 S '89
The stunt pilot. il *Esquire* 111:118-23 Ja '89
Write till you drop. il *The New York Times Book Review* 94:1+ My 28 '89
Writing back [correspondence from fans] *Harper's* 278:28-9 Je '89
The writing life [excerpt] *The Writer* 102:9-10 N '89
about
Annie Dillard: pilgrim at midstream. P. S. Hawkins. *The Christian Century* 106:592-5 Je 7-14 '89
Of many things. G. W. Hunt. *America* 161:366 N 25 '89
PW interviews. K. Weber. il por *Publishers Weekly* 236:67-8 S 1 '89
DILLARD, WILLIAM, 1914-
about
A quiet superstar rises in retailing. S. Caminiti. il por *Fortune* 120:167+ O 23 '89
DILLARD DEPARTMENT STORES, INC.
A quiet superstar rises in retailing. S. Caminiti. il por *Fortune* 120:167+ O 23 '89
DILLARD SCHOOL OF PERFORMING ARTS
Dillard School of Performing Arts. P. Booth. *Down Beat* 56:23-4 Je '89
DILLE, CAROLYN
(jt. auth) See Belsinger, Susan, and Dille, Carolyn
DILLENBERGER, JOHN
about
Stalking the spiritual in the visual arts [cover story] D. Morgan. il *The Christian Century* 106:1152-5 D 6 '89
DILLER, BARRY
about
Fox elbows into the networks' big picture. R. Grover. il por *Business Week* p74+ F 20 '89
Ready for prime time. J. Hammer. il por *Newsweek* 114:68-70 D 25 '89
DILLER, PHYLLIS, 1917-
about
Phyllis Diller. L. Eisenberg. por *TV Guide* 37:16 N 4-10 '89
Phyllis Diller's about-face. J. McCollister. il pors *The Saturday Evening Post* 261:30-2 Ap '89
DILLON, MATT
about
Matt's back (and badder than ever). A. Elliot. por *Mademoiselle* 95:62 Jl '89
Mighty Matt. C. Arrington. por *Rolling Stone* p50 N 30 '89
DILLON, MICHAEL
The merchants of Huizhou: commerce and Confucianism [cover story] bibl il map *History Today* 39:24-30 F '89
DILLON, NANCY
A celluloid charm [cover story] il pors *Modern Maturity* 32:38-43 D '89/Ja '90
DILLON, RODERICK H., JR.
Age 50: rich, with three teenagers. il por *Fortune* 120 no10 Special Issue:136 Fall '89
DILLON READ & CO. INC.
Brady, buyouts, and Purolator [Nicholas Brady's role in thwarted buyout bid] il *Fortune* 119:66 My 22 '89
DILLOW, GORDON
The cop who cared too much. il por *TV Guide* 37:26-7 Ap 1-7 '89
Do you know this actress? . . . She thinks you don't. il pors *TV Guide* 37:25-6+ N 25-D 1 '89
Hollywood's drug scene—how bad is it now? [cover story] il *TV Guide* 37:4-8 Ag 19-25 '89
DILORENZO, THOMAS J.
Antitrust policy and competitiveness. bibl *Society* 27:67-71 N/D '89
Why free trade works. *Reader's Digest* 134:119-23 F '89
DIMAGGIO, JOE
about
The great Joe D. [excerpt from Summer of '49] D. Halberstam. il pors *New York* 22:42-52 My 8 '89
A restless legend. T. Brewster. il por *Life* 12:102 O '89
Where have you gone, Joe DiMaggio? W. Sheed. il pors *Life* 12:94-8+ O '89
DIMARINO, ANTHONY J.
Gallstones: new treatments offer relief. il por *McCall's* 116:112 My '89
DIMARIO, J., AND OTHERS
Fibroblast growth factor in the extracellular matrix of dystrophic (mdx) mouse muscle. bibl f il *Science* 244:688-90 My 12 '89
DIME SAVINGS BANK OF NEW YORK
Short-doc woes [bad mortgage loans] C. Byron. *New York* 22:23 Je 5 '89
Turning on a Dime [interview with R. D. Parsons] K. D. Thompson. il pors *Black Enterprise* 19:144-6+ F '89
DIMIJIAN, GREGORY G.
Curiosity killed the hat. il *Natural History* p62-5 N '89
Serious necking [photograph] il *Natural History* p92-3 S '89
DIMORPHISM (BIOLOGY)
Cost accounting for lizards [size differences among lizards of the Galapagos Islands; research by Howard L. Snell] J. A. Miller. il *BioScience* 39:674-5 N '89

DINAMATION INTERNATIONAL CORPORATION
Dinosaurs in 3-D [work of C. Mays] J. Schwartz. il por *Newsweek* 114:51 O 2 '89
Say 'ah' [Real sea monsters exhibit] B. Weber. il *The New York Times Magazine* p102 O 29 '89
They move, they roar: dinosaurs are here once more. W. H. Jordan, Jr. il *Smithsonian* 20:46-52+ Ag '89
DINAND, PIERRE
about
Message in a bottle. E. Stern. il por *Gentlemen's Quarterly* 59:329-32 D '89
DINERS (RESTAURANTS)
See also
Rock Store (Calif.)
Down home at the diner [low calorie cooking] R. A. Barnett. il *American Health* 8:104-6+ Ja/F '89
DINERS CLUB INTERNATIONAL
Easy to leave home without it? C. Siler. il *Forbes* 144:140 S 4 '89
DINERSTEIN, ERIC
Around the Mall and beyond. il *Smithsonian* 20:24+ Ap '89
King of the marsh [cover story] il *International Wildlife* 19:4-11 Mr/Ap '89
DING, K. H. *See* Ting, K. H.
DING GUANGXUN *See* Ting, K. H.
DINGELL, JOHN D.
about
Bad cop. F. Barnes. il *The New Republic* 201:10-12 O 23 '89
The baddest overseer on the Hill. il por *U.S. News & World Report* 107:26 S 11 '89
Conduct unbecoming? P. Weiss. il pors *The New York Times Magazine* p40-1+ O 29 '89
The Dingell probe finally goes public. B. J. Culliton. *Science* 244:643-6+ My 12 '89
Dingell v. Baltimore. B. J. Culliton. pors *Science* 244:412-14 Ap 28 '89
The Kings of the Hills. il pors *Maclean's* 102:60-1 Jl 3 '89
New round in Dingell v. NIH? J. Palca. *Science* 245:349 Jl 28 '89
Teflon John and Jim. T. Eastland. il *The American Spectator* 22:40-1 Je '89
DINGHIES *See* Boats and boating
DINGS, FRED
Redwing blackbirds [poem] *The New Republic* 201:31 Jl 10 '89
Sycamores [poem] *The New Republic* 200:34 My 15 '89
DINI, MASSIMO, 1946-
A Wall Street in Budapest. il *World Press Review* 36:49 Ap '89
DINING *See* Dinners and dining
DINING ALCOVES, ETC.
3 eat-in kitchens. W. L. Nolan. il *Better Homes and Gardens* 67:58-62 Ag '89
DINING ESTABLISHMENTS *See* Restaurants
DINING MUSIC
Lean listening cuisine. K. Ames. il por *Newsweek* 114:62 Ag 7 '89
DINING ROOM CHAIRS *See* Chairs
DINING ROOMS
See also
Executive dining rooms
Opening up without adding on. il *Southern Living* 24:115 Ja '89
DINING TABLES *See* Tables
DININNY, PAULETTE
No detail too small. il *Nation's Business* 77:62+ O '89
DINKINS, DAVID, 1927-
about
A breakthrough. H. Mackenzie. il por *Maclean's* 102:38-40 N 20 '89
Brotherhood week. J. Klein. il por *New York* 22:36+ S 11 '89
California dreaming. J. Klein. il por *New York* 22:24+ O 23 '89
A call for racial harmony. E. Salholz. il pors *Newsweek* 114:21-2 S 25 '89
Can Dinkins do it? [cover story] J. Klein. il pors *New York* 22:30-7 Jl 31 '89
Cosby does fund-raiser at Apollo for David Dinkins' N.Y.C. mayoral campaign. il pors *Jet* 77:38-9 O 9 '89
David Dinkins seeks New York mayor's seat. il por *Jet* 75:28 Mr 6 '89
David N. Dinkins: 'I'll bring New York City together' [cover story] D. M. Cheers. il pors *Jet* 77:4-7 N 27 '89
Dinkins readies for N.Y.C. mayoral race after major primary election victory. il pors *Jet* 76:4+ O 2 '89
The Dinkins stock crash. C. Byron. il *New York* 22:30+ N 6 '89
The friends of David Dinkins. J. Klein. il por *New York* 22:14+ O 30 '89
Gandhi vs. Gumby. J. Klein. il pors *New York* 22:42-5 N 6 '89
Gotham rainbow. *The Nation* 249:335-6 O 2 '89

The "healer" takes New York: Dinkins wins primary. F. McCoy. il por *Black Enterprise* 20:21-2 N '89
Hope, not fear: New York may be the next city to elect a black mayor. R. Lacayo. il por *Time* 134:20-1 S 25 '89
How'd I do? E. Koch. il pors *The New York Times Magazine* p26-7+ D 31 '89
Inexakte. A. Logan. *The New Yorker* 65:138-44+ N 6 '89
Jackie Mason tries to talk himself out of trouble [cover story] J. Kasindorf. il pors *New York* 22:36-42 O 16 '89
Jackie Mason's racial remarks about Dinkins, Jews' relations with blacks bring backlash. pors *Jet* 77:5 O 16 '89
Mason bombs in New York. B. Turque. il pors *Newsweek* 114:42 O 9 '89
Mayor-elect David Dinkins. D. Baer. il pors *U.S. News & World Report* 107:54+ N 20 '89
The mayor's race: Dinkins vs. Giuliani. F. Barnes. *The New Republic* 201:9-10 O 9 '89
Mr. Softy. J. Klein. il por *New York* 22:20-1 Ja 16 '89
The new mayor and the crisis of New York [cover story] J. Klein. il pors *New York* 22:36-40 N 20 '89
New York's first and last hurrahs. D. Baer. il pors *U.S. News & World Report* 107:26-7 S 25 '89
A nice guy finishes first. J. Attinger. il por *Time* 134:60 N 20 '89
Now, the showdown: Dinkins vs. Giuliani in the void left by Koch. J. Klein. il pors *New York* 22:50-3 S 25 '89
The race for New York: Edward Koch loses a bid for a new term. H. Mackenzie. il pors *Maclean's* 102:32-3 S 25 '89
The real thing. J. Klein. il por *New York* 22:16+ N 13 '89
Sorry. A. Logan. *The New Yorker* 65:126-31 O 9 '89
Spike Lee replies: "Say it ain't so, Joe" [discussion of June 26, 1989 article, Spiked?] J. Klein. il por *New York* 22:6 Jl 17 '89
Spiked? J. Klein. il pors *New York* 22:14-15 Je 26 '89
That's life. A. Logan. *The New Yorker* 65:97-102 D 25 '89
DINKS
The rewards of being a dink: freedom and lots of cash. J. Reid. il *Money* 18:64+ Mr '89
DINNER AT EIGHT [television program] See Television program reviews—Single works
DINNER PARTIES *See* Dinners and dining
DINNER THEATERS
See also
Chanhassen Dinner Theatre
DINNERS AND DINING
See also
Buffet meals
Christmas dinners
Frozen dinners
Gastronomy
Outdoor meals
Refrigerated dinners
Table setting
Thanksgiving dinners
Valentine's Day dinners
20-minute dinners [microwaving] A. Johnson. il *Parents* 64:179-81 Mr '89
20-minute meals. C. Koury. il *Parents* 64:193-4+ D '89
30-minute meals. A. Johnson. il *Parents* 64:169-73 Ap '89
30-menu menu cookbook. M. Langan. il *McCall's* 116:159-64+ My '89
Bastille Day dinners. il *Gourmet* 49:76-82+ Jl '89
Busy-day dinners. il *Good Housekeeping* 208:134-44+ Ap '89
A candlelight New Year's Eve. C. Rossant. il *McCall's* 116:131 Ja '89
A Cinco de Mayo dinner. il *Gourmet* 49:126-32+ My '89
Come on over for take-out [serving chicken, Chinese, or Italian take-out food; special section] M. Krondl. il *McCall's* 116:81-2+ S '89
A day for Old Glories. L. Wells. il *The New York Times Magazine* p30-2 Jl 2 '89
Dinner for a special occasion. il *Gourmet* 49:152-8+ O '89
Dinner Italian style. il *Gourmet* 49:102-4+ S '89
Dinner of the decade. D. C. Craig. il *Life* 12:107-8+ Fall '89
A family dinner with Alice Waters and Paul Bertolli [wild mushroom risotto] M. Damsker. il pors *Organic Gardening* 36:46-9 O '89
For Mom with love. il *Ebony* 44:140-2+ My '89
The geometry of conversation [dining table's impact on conversation at a party] J. Giovannini. il *House & Garden* 161:62+ F '89
An ice-skating party. il *Gourmet* 49:54-6+ Ja '89
Love at first bite [Valentine's Day dinner] B. Shacochis. il *Gentlemen's Quarterly* 59:240+ F '89
Love bites: dinners that spark desire. il *Glamour* 87:228-31 F '89
Mardi Gras style [dinner party] J. Nash. il *Essence* 19:89-92+ F '89
A month of slimming dinners. J. Nash. il *Essence* 19:83-6+ Mr '89
No cook dinners. A. Johnson. il *Parents* 64:128+ Jl '89

DINNERS AND DINING—*cont.*

Our dinner table university [father's use of dinner time to teach children; condensed from Papa, my father] L. F. Buscaglia. il *Reader's Digest* 135:78-80 S '89

Pacific Provençal: a food pro at home [K. Malody] S. H. Loomis. il pors *Working Woman* 14:112-16 Mr '89

Rio with love [S. Monacella's dinner parties] M. Matousek. il por *Harper's Bazaar* 122:390+ S '89

A romantic meal for two. J. Nash. il *Essence* 19:98 F '89

Soirées on the Seine [S. and J. Yturbe] A. Bogart. il pors *Harper's Bazaar* 122:199+ D '89

Sunday best [dinners in France] P. Wells. il *The New York Times Magazine* p87-8 D 10 '89

Table talk: the family detective story [research by Elinor Ochs] il *USA Today (Periodical)* 118:9 Jl '89

Tête à tête dining. B. Gibbons. il *Modern Maturity* 32:72-4+ Ap/My '89

Anecdotes, facetiae, satire, etc.

Why I haven't invited Martha Stewart to dinner. K. Fury. il *Working Woman* 14:152 Je '89

DINNERWARE *See* Tableware

DINOFLAGELLATES

See also

Red tide

DINOSAUR MODELS *See* Paleontological models and exhibits

DINOSAURS

See also

Dinamation International Corporation

Birth of the dinosaurs [Petrified Forest National Park; cover story] S. Nash. il *National Parks* 63:16-23 N/D '89

Could a cold heart stand a cold winter? [Australian dinosaurs; research by Thomas H. Rich and Patricia V. Rich] R. Monastersky. *Science News* 136:38 Jl 15 '89

The cycle of fate. J. S. Trefil. bibl il por *Modern Maturity* 32:60-4 D '89/Ja '90

The Dinosaur Discovery Kit. J. Zornberg. il *Home Office Computing* 7:96 N '89

Dinosaur Discovery Kit [computer program] L. Eiser. il *Compute!* 11:118+ D '89

The dinosaur rip-off. S. J. Gould. *Natural History* p14+ Ag '89

Dinosaur tracks found, on exhibit in Virginia [Culpeper quarry; research by Robert Weems] il *Earth Science* 42:8 Fall '89

Dinosaur tragedy yields birth clues [research by Karl F. Hirsch] *Science News* 135:220 Ap 8 '89

Dinosaurs galore! [educational software] C. S. Holzberg. il *Home Office Computing* 7:86+ Je '89

Dinosaurs used their heads to beat the heat [work of J. Keith Rigby] R. Monastersky. il *Science News* 136:309 N 11 '89

Dragons and dinosaurs [Dinosaur Project findings in China and Alberta] P. J. Currie. il *Earth Science* 42:10-13 Summ '89

'Earth-shaker' found: seeing is believing this 50-ton monster [Seismosaurus] N. Hickey. il *TV Guide* 36:27-8 F 4-10 '89

A fleet-footed Montana monster [Tyrannosaurus skeleton uncovered] il *U.S. News & World Report* 107:18 N 13 '89

Giant meteor impacts and great eruptions: dinosaur killers? G. S. Paul. bibl f il *BioScience* 39:162-72 Mr '89

Homing in on the longest animal [use of seismic tomography to find Seismosaurus fossils; work of David D. Gillette] R. Monastersky. *Science News* 136:413 D 23-30 '89

Huge dinosaur bones discovered hollow [pelvis of Supersaurus; research by Wade E. Miller] R. Monastersky. il *Science News* 135:261 Ap 29 '89

Oldest dinosaur [Herrerasaurus discovered in Argentina] il *Time* 134:75 N 13 '89

Return of the Dinosaurs [video game] L. Eiser. il *Compute!* 11:126+ O '89

Skinning the dinosaur [work of S. Czerkas; with editorial comment by Paul Hoffman] D. Lessem. il pors *Discover* 10:4, 38-42+ Mr '89

Supersaurus [hollow pelvis bone; research by Wade E. Miller] il *Discover* 10:8 S '89

Tracking the early Permian [fossil footprints in Las Cruces, New Mexico discovered by J. P. MacDonald] L. S. Bowlds. il pors *Earth Science* 42:16-19 Summ '89

Uncovering the mystery of the dinosaur [theories of R. T. Bakker and J. R. Horner] E. Ziegler. il *Reader's Digest* 135:163-8 D '89

Upper Jurassic dinosaur egg from Utah. K. F. Hirsch and others. bibl f il *Science* 243:1711-13 Mr 31 '89

A walk along the lakeshore, dinosaur-style [footprints in Culpeper, Va. quarry; research by Robert E. Weems] R. Monastersky. il *Science News* 136:21 Jl 8 '89

Migration

Long-distance dinosaurs. P. J. Currie. il *Natural History* p60-5 Je '89

Secrets of the Gobi Desert [evidence of migration from Asia to North America; work of Philip Currie and others] D. Lessem. il map *Discover* 10:40-6 Je '89

Nests

Dinosaur eggs: the inside story [cover story] J. R. Horner and D. B. Weishampel. il *Natural History* p60-7 D '89

Interview: Jack Horner. J. Gorman. il por *Omni (New York, N.Y.)* 11:72-4+ Mr '89

DINOSAURS IN ART

Prehistoric mailbag [children's drawings] il *National Geographic World* 161:10-11 Ja '89

With an instinct for the extinct, John Kearney brings back the dinosaurs—bumper-to-bumper. il por *People Weekly* 32:94 O 16 '89

DINOTO, ANDREA

Jewelry American style. il *American Craft* 49:46-53 Je/Jl '89

DINSMOOR, SAMUEL PERRY

about

Paradise for sale. J. Mobley. il *Travel Holiday* 171:118 Ap '89

DINTER, HEINZ

about

A panoramic view of publishing. S. Harvey. il por *Home Office Computing* 7:56-7 O '89

DINTER, PAUL E.

Standing in the way of worship. il *Commonweal* 116:367-70 Je 16 '89

Standing in the way of worship [discussion of June 16, 1989 article] *Commonweal* 116:495+ S 22 '89

DINTINO, BOBBIE

about

Cashing in on conversions. por *Christianity Today* 33:51 Je 16 '89

DIODES

A complete circuit [character generator] R. Grossblatt. il *Radio-Electronics* 60:28-9+ Jl '89

A custom-character generator [EPROM character sets for LED displays] R. Grossblatt. il *Radio-Electronics* 60:80-2+ Mr '89

Diagnosing the state of an unruly plasma [research by Yitzhak Maron on pulsed-power diodes] I. Peterson. *Science News* 136:247 O 14 '89

Fishing for current with an STM rod [tunnel diodes; work of Peter J. Bedrossian] *Science News* 136:351 N 25 '89

Flashing LED's [CMOS 4017 device] il *Radio-Electronics* 60:12+ My '89

Games [B. Bell's LED sculptures] S. Morris. il *Omni (New York, N.Y.)* 11:128 F '89

Let's start programming! [EPROM character sets for LED displays] R. Grossblatt. il *Radio-Electronics* 60:72-3+ My '89

Negative differential resistance on the atomic scale: implications for atomic scale devices. I.-W. Lyo and P. Avouris. bibl f il *Science* 245:1369-71 S 22 '89

A small, small, very small diode [tunnel diode] R. Pool. il *Science* 246:1251 D 8 '89

DIOMEDE ISLANDS IN ART

Exhibitions

Art [G. Weiss organizes exhibit of proposals to link the Diomede Islands] N. Princenthal. il por *Vogue* 179:140+ Je '89

Fall into the gap [Exhibition Diomede at the Clocktower] K. Larson. il *New York* 22:99 Je 5 '89

DIONIS, KIM

The other side of innocence [story] il *Mademoiselle* 95:170+ S '89

DIONNE, J. ROBERT (JAMES ROBERT), 1929-

about

An interview with the author of The papacy and the Church. il *America* 160:12-13+ Ja 7-14 '89

DIONNE, JAMES ROBERT *See* Dionne, J. Robert (James Robert), 1929-

DIOR, CHRISTIAN, 1905-1957

about

Couture report: the four schools of design. J. J. Buck. il *Vogue* 179:324-5+ O '89

DIOR (CHRISTIAN) (FIRM) *See* Christian Dior (Firm)

DIOXIN

See also

Agent Orange

Dioxin-in-paper update. *Science News* 136:94 Ag 5 '89

Dioxin: paper's trace. J. Raloff. il *Science News* 135:104-6 F 18 '89

Dioxin via skin: a hazard at low doses? [research by Linda S. Birnbaum] *Science News* 135:141 Mr 4 '89

FDA finds dioxin in milk. *Science News* 136:165 S 9 '89

DIPHTHERIA TOXIN

Second cytotoxic pathway of diphtheria toxin suggested by nuclease activity. M. P. Chang and others. bibl f il *Science* 246:1165-8 D 1 '89

DIPLOMACY

See also

Diplomatic gifts

World War, 1939-1945—Diplomatic history

DIPLOMATIC AND CONSULAR SERVICE

See also

Ambassadors

Canada—Diplomatic and consular service

Cape Verde—Diplomatic and consular service

Consuls

Diplomats

United States—Diplomatic and consular service

DIPLOMATIC DOCUMENTS, CLASSIFIED *See* Classified information
DIPLOMATIC GIFTS
Arctic treasures: what ruler could resist the allure of white falcons, giant moles, and unicorns? F. Bruemmer. il *Natural History* p38-47 Je '89
DIPLOMATIC RECEPTIONS *See* Government entertaining
DIPLOMATS
See also
Ambassadors
Consuls
Language
Diplomatese. A. de Soto. il *The New York Times Magazine* p34+ S 10 '89
DIPS *See* Appetizers
DIR BROADCASTING CORPORATION
Dig in, Robert [R. Meyrowitz] P. Newcomb. il por *Forbes* 143:328 My 29 '89
DIRECT BROADCAST SATELLITE SERVICES
Doing the dishes: a TV bonanza is up there in orbit. D. Stewart. il *Smithsonian* 20:156-60+ O '89
The FCC sends DBS flying. S. Chase. il *Channels (New York, N.Y.: 1986)* 9:97 D '89
Satellite TV's new landscape. R. Angus. il *Video* 13:56-8+ Jl '89
Educational programs
Beam me up, students. S. Tifft. il *Time* 133:107 My 22 '89
Motion pictures
Hollywood reaps a windfall from television's richest endeavor [British services] K. Pearce. il *Channels (New York, N.Y.: 1986)* 9:9 Mr '89
Religious programs
Soft sell and satellites deliver biggest audience [B. Graham] il por *Christianity Today* 33:48-9 Ag 18 '89
Great Britain
See also
British Satellite Broadcasting (Firm)
The Sky-watchers [Sky TV] A. Phillips. il *Maclean's* 102:51 F 27 '89
Latin America
Residuals woes plague ESPN, CNN [advertisements beamed into Latin America] J. Loftus. il *Channels (New York, N.Y.: 1986)* 9:8 Jl/Ag '89
Spain
France's Matra will cooperate with Spain to develop Hispasat satellite network. J. M. Lenorovitz. maps *Aviation Week & Space Technology* 131:93 Jl 17 '89
DIRECT ENERGY CONVERSION
See also
Biomass energy
Ocean thermal power plants
Solar cells
DIRECT MAIL ADVERTISING *See* Advertising, Direct mail
DIRECT MAIL ADVERTISING, POLITICAL *See* Advertising, Political
DIRECT MARKETING *See* Direct selling
DIRECT SELLING
See also
Advertising, Direct mail
Mail order business
Mary Kay Cosmetics, Inc.
Stanhome Inc.
Telephone selling
Direct marketing [home computer business] J. B. Lambert. *Compute!* 11:25 Ag '89
Direct-response selling for the 1990s [strategies for publishers] P. Hodges. il *Publishers Weekly* 235:260+ My 12 '89
Sell some, recruit some [S. Hutton of Mary Kay Cosmetics] L. Washer. il por *Working Woman* 14:95 My '89
Ethical aspects
Unwilling players in the name game [sale of credit and medical information to direct marketing companies] A. Mundy. il *U.S. News & World Report* 106:52+ My 1 '89
DIRECT USER ACCESS TERMINAL SYSTEM (DATABASE)
DUAT is on the line. *Flying* 116:20 My '89
DUAT: weather beaten. F. George. il *Flying* 116:112-14 Jl '89
DIRECTION, SENSE OF *See* Orientation
DIRECTION, THEATRICAL *See* Musicals, revues, etc.—Production and direction; Theater—Production and direction
DIRECTION FINDING EQUIPMENT
See also
Compass
DIRECTORIES
See also
Telephone directories
DIRECTORS, CORPORATION *See* Corporations—Directors
DIRECTORS, MOTION PICTURE *See* Motion picture directors
DIRT
See also
Soils

DIRT TRACK RACING *See* Motorcycle racing
DIRTY ROTTEN SCOUNDRELS [film] See Motion picture reviews—Single works
DISABILITY, READING *See* Reading disability
DISABILITY INSURANCE *See* Insurance, Disability
DISABLED *See* Handicapped
DISADVANTAGED CHILDREN *See* Socially handicapped children
DISALVO, CHARLES R.
What's wrong with Operation Rescue? *Commonweal* 116:664-7 D 1 '89
DISARMAMENT
See also
Anti-nuclear movement
Church and disarmament
MEND (Organization)
Nuclear weapons—Testing—Suspension
Parliamentarians Global Action for Disarmament, Development, and World Reform (Organization)
Pugwash movement
Seabed Treaty (1972)
United Nations. Disarmament Commission
The abolitionist [arms control efforts during R. Reagan's first term] J. Newhouse. *The New Yorker* 64:37-52 Ja 2 '89
About face: how the Soviets stopped planning for world war. M. K. MccGwire. il *Technology Review* 92:32-6+ N/D '89
After the cold war: new tasks for arms controllers. K. Tsipis. *The Bulletin of the Atomic Scientists* 45:7-8 Jl/Ag '89
Agreement to disagree [new Soviet proposals during J. Baker visit] A. Wilson-Smith. il pors *Maclean's* 102:25-6 My 22 '89
Allies in dispute [West Germany calls for reducing short-range nuclear weapons] J. Bierman. il *Maclean's* 102:22 My 15 '89
And now it's George's turn [seeking dramatic arms proposal to counter M. Gorbachev's initiatives] H. Anderson. il pors *Newsweek* 113:30-2 Ap 17 '89
Arms at sea [discussion of January 1989 article, Troubled waters] W. M. Arkin. il *Technology Review* 92:6-7+ Ag/S '89
Arms control [special section] *World Press Review* 36:22-4 F '89
Arms control after the cold war. J. S. Nye, Jr. bibl f *Foreign Affairs* 68:42-64 Wint '89/'90
Arms control and Soviet relations [address, March 1, 1989] M. M. Kampelman. *Vital Speeches of the Day* 55:386-90 Ap 15 '89
Arms negotiations in Europe. J. Erickson. *Current History* 88:369-72+ N '89
Back in business. S. Talbott. il *Time* 133:34 Je 12 '89
The battle inside NATO. S. Head. bibl f il *The New York Review of Books* 36:41-6 My 18 '89
Biological weapons proliferation [statement, May 17, 1989] H. A. Holmes. *Department of State Bulletin* 89:43-5 Jl '89
A blind eye to nuclear proliferation. G. C. Smith and H. Cobban. bibl f *Foreign Affairs* 68:53-70 Summ '89
Bush and NATO [Brussels summit] il *World Press Review* 36:8 Jl '89
Bush includes combat aircraft cuts in NATO arms proposal [Brussels summit; special section] il map *Aviation Week & Space Technology* 130:16-21 Je 5 '89
Bush makes his mark [peace initiative at NATO summit] J. Bierman. il por *Maclean's* 102:24-5+ Je 12 '89
Bush: 'moving beyond containment' [excerpts from address, May 12, 1989] G. Bush. *Aviation Week & Space Technology* 130:9 My 22 '89
Bush pulls one out of a hat [arms proposal at NATO summit] B. Javetski. il por *Business Week* p22-3 Je 12 '89
Bush's bold bid to rescue NATO [U.S. troop cuts] H. Trewhitt. il por *U.S. News & World Report* 106:26-9 Je 12 '89
Bush's first foreign crisis [disagreement with West Germany over disarmament] il por *Newsweek* 113:16-18 My 8 '89
Bush's folly [treaty banning chemical weapons] *National Review* 41:20-1 O 27 '89
Bush's new look for the NATO alliance [troop reduction proposal] H. Anderson. il por *Newsweek* 113:34-5 Je 12 '89
By the numbers [Bush's arms proposals at NATO summit] *The Nation* 248:835-6 Je 19 '89
Calm down [West Germany and NATO] M. S. Forbes, Jr. il *Forbes* 143:27 My 29 '89
Can NATO agree on arms control? J. Dean. il *Technology Review* 92:58-62+ O '89
Can we trust this nice Mr. Gorbachev? C. W. Weinberger. il *Forbes* 143:37 Ja 9 '89
The case for the third zero. H. Beach. *The Bulletin of the Atomic Scientists* 45:14-15 D '89
Challenges to NATO in the 1990s [address, September 4, 1989] S. Nunn. *Vital Speeches of the Day* 56:135-40 D 15 '89
Changing times: Sakharov in the US on human rights and arms control. I. Goodwin. il *Physics Today* 42:91-5 F '89
Chemical disarmament: the superpowers propose a major arms cutback. J. Bierman. il *Maclean's* 102:26 O 9 '89

DISARMAMENT—cont.

China's "new thinking" on nuclear arms. J. Prados. bibl f il *The Bulletin of the Atomic Scientists* 45:32-5 Je '89

Clearing the air [proposed global ban on chemical weapons] T. Beardsley. il *Scientific American* 260:17-18 Mr '89

Converging on peace? Sir S. Zuckerman. bibl f il *The New York Review of Books* 36:26+ S 28 '89

Counterpunching Gorbachev [Bush's policies overshadowed by Soviet arms proposals on eve of NATO summit] S. V. Roberts. il por *U.S. News & World Report* 106:16-17 My 29 '89

Crowing before sunrise [G. Bush at NATO summit] *Commonweal* 116:355-6 Je 16 '89

The dangers beyond containment [cover story] P. Glynn. *Commentary* 88:15-22 Ag '89

Daniel Ellsberg [interview; cover story] B. Blanchard and S. Watrous. il por *The Progressive* 53:17-21 S '89

Dead souls. *The Nation* 248:687-8 My 22 '89

Decade of decision. J. B. Hehir. *Commonweal* 116:362-3 Je 16 '89

A decision not to decide [NATO response to Soviet arms initiatives] B. Van Voorst. il *Time* 133:46-7 My 1 '89

Disarmament at sea. M. Ross. *Foreign Policy* 77:94-112 Wint '89/90

Divided over defense. T. Bethell. *The American Spectator* 22:11-13 O '89

Divorce, alliance-style. A. Tonelson and C. Layne. *The New Republic* 200:23-5 Je 12 '89

Effective NATO defenses or none at all. *National Review* 41:11-12 Je 2 '89

Ending a common danger. M. Bundy. *The New York Times Magazine* p54-6+ Ag 20 '89

Europe's short-range missiles nail their first victim [H. D. Genscher] J. Templeman and G. E. Schares. il por *Business Week* p50 Je 12 '89

Federal Republic of Germany [address, April 27, 1989] H. Kohl. *Vital Speeches of the Day* 55:482-6 Je 1 '89

First anniversary of INF treaty [White House statement, December 8, 1988] *Department of State Bulletin* 89:24-5 F '89

First word. A. C. Clarke. por *Omni (New York, N.Y.)* 12:8 O '89

Foreign policy implications of biological weapons [statement, July 26, 1989] H. A. Holmes. *Department of State Bulletin* 89:22-4 O '89

The future agenda in arms control [address, October 31, 1988] G. P. Shultz. *Department of State Bulletin* 89:1-4 Ja '89

George Bush moves in. J. D. Isaacs. il *The Bulletin of the Atomic Scientists* 45:3-4 Ja/F '89

Germany and the alliance [short range nuclear missiles] il *World Press Review* 36:6 Je '89

Gorba Claus [effects of Soviet troop reduction proposal] *The New Republic* 200:5-7 Ja 2 '89

Gorbachev speaks to the Council of Europe [excerpts from address, July 6, 1989] M. Gorbachev. *Current History* 88:347 O '89

Gorbachev strikes again [plan to reduce short-range nuclear weapons in Europe] H. Anderson. il por *Newsweek* 112:57 My 22 '89

Gorbachev talks but who listens? W. M. Arkin. il por *The Bulletin of the Atomic Scientists* 45:5-6 Mr '89

Gorbachev's initiatives. *World Press Review* 36:12 F '89

Gorbachev's new thinking. D. Holloway. bibl f *Foreign Affairs* 68 Special Issue:66-81 ['89]

"Here we go, on the offensive" [G. Bush offers troop reduction initiative at NATO meeting] G. J. Church. il por *Time* 133:28-31+ Je 12 '89

Hot rock, cold war [Soviet initiatives] *The Nation* 249:225 S 4-11 '89

The international community and change [address, July 6, 1989] M. Gorbachev. *Vital Speeches of the Day* 55:706-11 S 15 '89

Is Bush bold enough to answer Gorbachev? W. Greider. il *Rolling Stone* p48+ F 9 '89

Is Bush losing the struggle for Europe's hearts and minds? B. Javetski and D. Griffiths. il *Business Week* p61 My 8 '89

It takes two not to tango. J. Tirman. il *The Nation* 248:520-2 Ap 17 '89

Joint statement on chemical weapons, Sept. 23, 1989 [U.S. and Soviet Union] il *Department of State Bulletin* 89:8-9 N '89

Keep the powder dry [interview with J. Galvin] M. Kramer. il por *Time* 133:78-9 My 29 '89

The key to the alliance [West Germany] M. B. Zuckerman. il *U.S. News & World Report* 106:83 Ja 30 '89

The Kohl war [West German opposition to NATO disarmament strategy] *The New Republic* 200:7-8 My 22 '89

Let's ban nuclear reactors from orbit. J. R. Primack. il *Technology Review* 92:27-8 My/Je '89

Madison Avenue, Moscow [M. Gorbachev's proposal to J. Baker] G. J. Church. il pors *Time* 133:33-4 My 22 '89

A nasty spat among friends [U.S. opposition to West German demand for talks on reduction of short-range nuclear weapons] D. Brand. il *Time* 133:42 My 8 '89

A NATO balancing act [G. Bush's proposals] D. Goodgame. il por *Time* 133:39 Je 5 '89

The NATO compromise: dangerous [G. Bush's proposals] *National Review* 41:12-13 Je 30 '89

NATO disputes Warsaw Pact claim of conventional parity. K. F. Mordoff. *Aviation Week & Space Technology* 130:21-2 F 6 '89

NATO in disarray? This time, reality. D. Gergen. il map *U.S. News & World Report* 106:24-6 Ja 23 '89

NATO's mid-life crisis. R. K. Betts. bibl f *Foreign Affairs* 68:37-52 Spr '89

Navy shuns credit for cuts [retirement of three types of missiles from nuclear arsenal] M. Flournoy. il *The Bulletin of the Atomic Scientists* 45:3-4 Jl/Ag '89

The naysayer and new détente [J. A. Baker's Soviet visit yields new arms proposals] H. Trewhitt. il pors *U.S. News & World Report* 106:18-19 My 22 '89

Negotiate now, but carefully [West Germany's call for short-range missile negotiations] *America* 160:499 My 27 '89

A new age of world peace . . . breaking the wall of suspicion . . . [R. Reagan and M. Gorbachev address the United Nations] pors *UN Chronicle* 26:31-3 Mr '89

A new Concert of Europe. J. E. Mueller. *Foreign Policy* 77:3-16 Wint '89/90

Notes and comment. *The New Yorker* 65:25-6 Mr 13 '89

Nuclear abolition: would cheaters count? [discussion of July/August 1989 article, Why not now?] T. B. Taylor and S. D. Drell. il *The Bulletin of the Atomic Scientists* 45:16-17 D '89

Nuclear cooperation with EURATOM [letter to Congress, March 9, 1989] G. Bush. *Department of State Bulletin* 89:44 Je '89

One for the Gipper [G. Bush's proposals at NATO summit] il *The New Republic* 200:7-8 Je 19 '89

Out of the cold [excerpt] R. S. McNamara. il por *Newsweek* 114:35-6+ S 4 '89

An overview of U.S. arms control objectives [statement, October 18, 1988] W. F. Burns. *Department of State Bulletin* 89:41-4 Ja '89

Perception of declining Soviet threat erodes support for NATO modernization. K. F. Mordoff. il *Aviation Week & Space Technology* 130:84-5 Mr 20 '89

The pistol on the mantel [nuclear deterrence] M. B. Zuckerman. il *U.S. News & World Report* 106:78 Je 26 '89

Plutonium—no supply, no demand? W. J. Lanouette. il *The Bulletin of the Atomic Scientists* 45:42-5 D '89

President visits Europe; attends North Atlantic Council meeting [cover story; special section] G. Bush. il pors *Department of State Bulletin* 89:11-45 Ag '89

Reading the fine print. B. Van Voorst. il *Time* 134:24 O 9 '89

Reagan's security legacy [cover story; special issue; with editorial comment by Len Ackland] bibl f il pors *The Bulletin of the Atomic Scientists* 45:2, 5-32+ Ja/F '89

Record number of resolutions on disarmament adopted by consensus [United Nations] il *UN Chronicle* 26:68-71 Mr '89

Reviving the U.S.-Soviet dialogue. D. Schorr. *The New Leader* 72:3-4 O 2-16 '89

Ronald Reagan & Mikhail Gorbachev. B. Darrach. il pors *People Weekly* 32 Special Issue:44-6 Fall '89

The Russians are still there. W. F. Buckley. *National Review* 41:54-5 D 31 '89

The Russians aren't coming. S. Budiansky. il *U.S. News & World Report* 107:47+ N 27 '89

Secretary's news conference [May 23, 1989] J. A. Baker, III. *Department of State Bulletin* 89:21-4 Jl '89

Secretary's trip to Moscow and NATO [remarks, news conferences, etc., May 10-12, 1989] J. A. Baker, III. *Department of State Bulletin* 89:29-36 Jl '89

Security challenges facing NATO in the 1990s [address, February 6, 1989] P. H. Nitze. *Department of State Bulletin* 89:44-8 Ap '89

Seize the day. M. Dönhoff. *World Press Review* 36:64 F '89

Soviet military adviser addresses House panel [S. Akhromeyev] *Aviation Week & Space Technology* 131:26 Jl 31 '89

Soviets building naval strength while pursuing maritime arms control. B. M. Greeley. il *Aviation Week & Space Technology* 130:63 Mr 13 '89

Space reactors and arms control. C. Norman. il *Science* 243:476 Ja 27 '89

Taking apart the doomsday machine [adaptation of address, December 1988] F. Von Hippel. il *The Bulletin of the Atomic Scientists* 45:10-12 My '89

Testing weapons in space [problems of Anti-Ballistic Missile Treaty compliance] A. B. Carter. bibl il *Scientific American* 261:33-40 Jl '89

Third world missile proliferation emerges as key arms control issue. il *Aviation Week & Space Technology* 131:31 Jl 3 '89

Times full of promise [excerpts from address, October 23, 1989] J. A. Baker, III. *Aviation Week & Space Technology* 131:7 O 30 '89

Tower says administration to link arms control stance, strategic goals. P. A. Gilmartin. *Aviation Week & Space Technology* 129:23 Mr 6 '89

Troubled waters: the Navy's aggressive war strategy. W. M. Arkin. il *Technology Review* 92:54-63 Ja '89

DISARMAMENT—*cont.*

U.S. efforts against the spread of chemical weapons [statement, June 22, 1989] R. Bartholomew. *Department of State Bulletin* 89:74-7 S '89

U.S.S.R. arms reduction [address, December 7, 1988] M. Gorbachev. *Vital Speeches of the Day* 55:229-36 F 1 '89

U.S. senators threaten troop cutback if West Germany blocks Lance upgrade [with editorial comment] P. A. Gilmartin. *Aviation Week & Space Technology* 130:7, 29 My 8 '89

Unilateral disarmament—Labor's lost love [British Labor Party] N. Moss. il por *The Bulletin of the Atomic Scientists* 45:9-11 O '89

United States and NATO [address, May 31, 1989] G. Bush. *Vital Speeches of the Day* 55:546-9 Jl 1 '89

The untaming of the bomb. S. Budiansky. il *U.S. News & World Report* 106:8-9 Je 12 '89

The uphill fight to contain chemical weapons. L. Lief. il *U.S. News & World Report* 106:42 Ja 9 '89

US-Soviet research in arms control [cover story; special section; with editorial comment by William Sweet] il *Physics Today* 42:31-6+ N '89

The war inside NATO [U.S.-German conflict over proposed introduction of new nuclear missiles] D. Johnstone. il *The Progressive* 53:16-18 Ap '89

When Johnny comes marching home: the pressure for U.S. troops to leave Europe. D. White. map *World Press Review* 36:25-7 S '89

Why Kohl is right [call for U.S. and Soviet Union to negotiate on short-range nuclear weapons] S. Talbott. il por *Time* 133:26 My 15 '89

Why not now? Debating a nuclear-free millennium [excerpts from debate, March 11, 1989] T. B. Taylor and S. D. Drell. il *The Bulletin of the Atomic Scientists* 45:25-31 Jl/Ag '89

Will NATO settle for Kohl cuts? T. Risse-Kappen. il *The Bulletin of the Atomic Scientists* 45:9-12 Je '89

Will the allies leave Bush behind? B. Javetski and D. Griffiths. il pors *Business Week* p30-1 My 15 '89

Wither NATO. H. Hertzberg. *The New Republic* 200:4 My 22 '89

Your move again, George [Warsaw Pact proposal on conventional arms] H. Anderson. il *Newsweek* 114:24 Jl 10 '89

Anecdotes, facetiae, satire, etc.

The finer points of *perestroika* [imaginary meeting among Gorbachev and his advisers following the Baker mini-summit] R. N. Perle. *U.S. News & World Report* 107:41 O 2 '89

Now, something completely different. R. N. Perle. il *U.S. News & World Report* 106:31 Je 12 '89

Conferences

See also
Bush-Gorbachev summit conference, 1989
Conference on Confidence and Security-Building Measures and Disarmament in Europe
Strategic Arms Limitation Talks
Strategic Arms Reduction Talks
United Nations. Conference on Disarmament

The abolitionist [Reagan-Gorbachev summits] J. Newhouse. *The New Yorker* 64:51-62+ Ja 9 '89

Arms control: games Soviets play. K. L. Adelman. *Reader's Digest* 134:65-9 Mr '89

Bad chemical reactions [meeting to convene in Paris] J. L. Galloway. il *U.S. News & World Report* 106:30-1 Ja 16 '89

Bush's chintzy offer at Vienna [conventional arms reductions] R. Leavitt. *The Bulletin of the Atomic Scientists* 45:13 O '89

Can Moscow play defense? [concerns of NATO negotiators as they begin conventional arms talks with Warsaw Pact] M. B. Zuckerman. il *U.S. News & World Report* 106:76 Mr 13 '89

CFE talks end round two [statement, July 13, 1989] S. J. Ledogar. *Department of State Bulletin* 89:75 S '89

Chemical arms ban still uncertain [Paris conference] D. Dickson. il *Science* 243:301-2 Ja 20 '89

A cold war retreat [conventional arms talks in Vienna] J. Bierman. il *Maclean's* 102:39 Mr 20 '89

Conference against chemical weapons [government-industry conference in Canberra, Australia; statement, September 19, 1989] R. A. Clarke. *Department of State Bulletin* 89:45-7 N '89

Conference on chemical weapons use [White House statement, October 21, 1988] *Department of State Bulletin* 89:16 Ja '89

The conventional balance: a TKO for NATO? [cover story] J. Mendelsohn and T. Halverson. ibibl f il *The Bulletin of the Atomic Scientists* 45:30-4+ Mr '89

Conventional talks: a good first round. J. Dean. il *The Bulletin of the Atomic Scientists* 45:26-31 O '89

Cut the numbers game [conventional force reduction talks] *Aviation Week & Space Technology* 131:9 Ag 14 '89

European security negotiations open in Vienna [conventional armed forces; statements and text of Western position paper, March 9, 1989] G. Bush; S. J. Ledogar; J. J. Maresca. *Department of State Bulletin* 89:33-6 My '89

From East Germany: it's NATO's move now [reductions in troops and conventional weapons] M. Schmidt and W. Schwarz. il *The Bulletin of the Atomic Scientists* 45:5-6 S '89

Government/military: Lord Carrington, Paul H. Nitze, Marshal Sergei Fedorovich Akhromeyev [breakthroughs in nuclear arms reduction negotiations; aerospace laureate] il pors *Aviation Week & Space Technology* 130:18 Ja 2 '89

Krasnoyarsk radar discussions [element of ABM Treaty; State Dept. statement, November 2, 1988] *Department of State Bulletin* 89:16 Ja '89

Let's count down [Negotiations on Conventional Armed Forces in Europe] J. Smolowe. il *Time* 133:32-4 Mr 20 '89

NATO Secretary General stresses West's lead in arms negotiations [conventional arms talks; views of M. Woerner] K. F. Mordoff. *Aviation Week & Space Technology* 130:105 F 20 '89

NATO weighs air force modernization in light of conventional arms cuts. J. D. Morrocco. il *Aviation Week & Space Technology* 131:29-30 Jl 24 '89

NATO's conventional force reduction proposal [White House fact sheet, July 12, 1989] *Department of State Bulletin* 89:76 S '89

The new face of war [chemical warfare; cover story; special section] il *World Press Review* 36:11-14+ Mr '89

New horizons in Europe [address, March 6, 1989] J. A. Baker, III. *Department of State Bulletin* 89:56-9 My '89

North Atlantic Council session held in Brussels [texts of statement on conventional arms control, final communique, extracts from minutes of meeting, and news conference, December 8-9, 1988] G. P. Shultz. *Department of State Bulletin* 89:43-50 F '89

Nuclear and space arms talks conclude round 10 [statement, November 16, 1988] R. Reagan. *Department of State Bulletin* 89:10 Mr '89

Nuclear and space talks open round 11 [statements, June 19-20, 1989] G. Bush; R. Burt. *Department of State Bulletin* 89:73-4 Ag '89

Paris conference calls for complete ban on chemical weapons. *UN Chronicle* 26:58-9 Je '89

A poisonous threat [chemical weapons conference in Paris] A. Phillips. il *Maclean's* 102:20-2 Ja 23 '89

Prohibition of chemical weapons conference held in Paris [address, news conference, text of final declaration and statement, January 7-11, 1989] G. P. Shultz; W. F. Burns. *Department of State Bulletin* 89:4-10 Mr '89

Real weapons, high hopes [Negotiations on Conventional Armed Forces in Europe] S. Talbott. il *Time* 133:34 Mr 20 '89

The search for a poison antidote [convening Paris meeting to stop proliferation of chemical weapons] J. Smolowe. il *Time* 133:22 Ja 16 '89

The Silver Fox [P. Nitze; cover story] Sir S. Zuckerman. bibl f il *The New York Review of Books* 35:21-5 Ja 19 '89

Status of the defense and space talks [statement, August 3, 1989] H. F. Cooper. *Department of State Bulletin* 89:20-2 O '89

Superpowers advance disarmament talks despite clash over tactical nuclear arms. P. Mann. il *Aviation Week & Space Technology* 130:26-7 My 22 '89

U.S., U.S.S.R. hold nonproliferation talks [U.S. statement, December 15, 1988] *Department of State Bulletin* 89:59 F '89

Vienna talks trigger NATO air force review [cover story; special section] J. D. Morrocco. il map *Aviation Week & Space Technology* 131:34-7+ O 30 '89

What did the swallows learn in Geneva? [CIA investigation of social activities and female Soviet spies during 1985 arms talks] L. Galtney and C. Fenyvesi. il por *U.S. News & World Report* 106:27 F 20 '89

Will test ban conference self-destruct? K. P. Clements. bibl f il *The Bulletin of the Atomic Scientists* 45:16-18 Jl/Ag '89

The 'winds of death' [chemical warfare conference in Paris] R. Watson. il *Newsweek* 113:22-5 Ja 16 '89

Economic aspects

Converts to conversion. D. Johnstone. il *The Progressive* 53:14-15 O '89

Cost reduction dubious. B. M. Blechman. il *The Bulletin of the Atomic Scientists* 45:38-9 My '89

Fewer guns could mean a whole lot more butter. K. Pennar. il *Business Week* p66-7 Je 12 '89

How to end the cold war [proposal that U.S. purchase and then destroy Soviet military equipment] W. F. Buckley. *National Review* 41:44 N 10 '89

The peace dividend. R. J. Samuelson. il *Newsweek* 113:56 Je 26 '89

The peace economy [cover story] K. Pennar and M. J. Mandel. il *Business Week* p50-5 D 11 '89

Preparing for a different world [views of F. Rohatyn] P. Mann. il *Aviation Week & Space Technology* 130:17 Mr 20 '89

Shaping a peacetime economy. D. Cortright. il *The Progressive* 53:20-2 Ja '89

DISARMAMENT—cont.

History

Has arms control worked? [criteria proposed by T. Schelling and M. Halperin in 1961 book; cover story; special section; with introd. by Michael Krepon] bibl f il *The Bulletin of the Atomic Scientists* 45:26-45 My '89

A history of cutoff proposals [fissile materials production] W. J. Lanouette. *The Bulletin of the Atomic Scientists* 45:43 D '89

How to kill arms control [INF and test ban talks] Sir S. Zuckerman. bibl f il *The New York Review of Books* 36:35-9 O 12 '89

Three men and the bomb [1946 deliberations of UN Atomic Energy Commission] M. Oliphant. il pors *The Bulletin of the Atomic Scientists* 45:41-2 Mr '89

Inspection

Arms and the woman [Soviet admission that Krasnoyarsk radar violates ABM Treaty] J. O'Sullivan. *National Review* 41:9 N 24 '89

Black Sea experiment only a start [joint Soviet-American nuclear sea-launched cruise missile verification exercise aboard Soviet cruiser] T. B. Cochran. il *The Bulletin of the Atomic Scientists* 45:12-16 N '89

The costs of secrecy [Krasnoyarsk radar] M. Bundy. il *The New York Times Magazine* p71 Ag 20 '89

Dispelling myths about verification of sea-launched cruise missiles. G. N. Lewis and others. bibl f il *Science* 246:765-70 N 10 '89

An exercise in trust [Soviets accelerating acceptance of verification procedures] B. Van Voorst. il *Time* 134:24 Jl 31 '89

Getting out of the STARTing block [verification issues] S. N. Graybeal and P. B. McFate. il *Scientific American* 261:61-7 D '89

INF: the Soviets cheat. D. J. Trachtenberg. *National Review* 41:17 My 19 '89

Measurements of radiation from a Soviet warhead [cruise missile] S. Fetter and F. Von Hippel. il *Physics Today* 42:45 N '89

Merchants of peace. T. Beardsley. *Scientific American* 260:98+ Ja '89

Missile check [U.S. arms-control verification team] A. Sabirov. *World Press Review* 36:40 Mr '89

Monitoring Soviet space weapons adds to demand for U.S. intelligence. T. M. Foley. *Aviation Week & Space Technology* 130:22-3 F 27 '89

The new nuclear technology. T. H. Cole. il *Popular Mechanics* 166:34 Ja '89

Nuclear abolition: would cheaters count? R. K. Perkins. *The Bulletin of the Atomic Scientists* 45:16-17 D '89

A plea for scientific help [chemical weapons] D. Dickson. *Science* 243:302 Ja 20 '89

Safeguards controversy, continued [discussion of December 1988 article, Plutonium for all: leaks in global safeguards] R. Bolt. il *The Bulletin of the Atomic Scientists* 45:38-40 Je '89

Trust, but verify—and verify first. il *U.S. News & World Report* 107:54 Jl 3 '89

Turning off the gas [global, comprehensive, and verifiable ban on chemical weapons] *Commonweal* 116:548-9 O 20 '89

U.S., Soviet scientists propose system to monitor laser ASATs. T. M. Foley. *Aviation Week & Space Technology* 130:31 My 15 '89

Weapons scientists retool [verifying limits on sea-launched cruise missiles] V. Kiernan. il *Technology Review* 92:10-11 Ag/S '89

What GLCMs? [Soviets protest announced plan to convert ground-launched cruise missiles to sea-launched ones in violation of INF Treaty] M. Flournoy. il *The Bulletin of the Atomic Scientists* 45:5 My '89

Public opinion

Changing cold war attitudes: America's "new thinking". D. Yankelovich and R. Smoke. il *Current (Washington, D.C.)* 309:32-40 Ja '89

DISARMAMENT COMMISSION (UNITED NATIONS) *See* United Nations. Disarmament Commission

DISASSEMBLERS (COMPUTER PROGRAMS)

Testing

Sourcer magic disassembles machine code [Sourcer] B. Smith. *Byte* 14:104 F '89

DISASTER INSURANCE *See* Insurance, Disaster

DISASTER RELIEF *See* Relief work

DISASTERS

See also
Avalanches
Brush fires
Earthquakes
Environmental refugees
Floods
Forest fires
Hurricanes
Nuclear power plants—Accidents and explosions
Tornadoes

Africa better prepared to deal with catastrophes [WHO opens Regional Centre for Emergency Preparedness and Response] il *World Health* p30-1 Mr '89

Courting disaster [disaster attorney J. Coale] J. A. Jenkins. il pors *Gentlemen's Quarterly* 59:214-17+ F '89

Hurricane Hugo and the Bay Area earthquake: America responds to disaster [cover story; special issue] il maps *Scholastic Update (Teachers' edition)* 122:1-15 D 15 '89

Low probability—high consequence accidents. D. E. Koshland, Jr. *Science* 244:405 Ap 28 '89

Anecdotes, facetiae, satire, etc.

Interview with a disaster expert. D. E. Koshland, Jr. *Science* 246:1221 D 8 '89

Photographs and photography

The earth . . . strikes back [natural disasters] il *Life* 12:8-15+ Ja '89

Psychological aspects

Dealing with a distant disaster [study of Armenian American adolescents by Viken V. Yacoubian] *Science News* 136:92 Ag 5 '89

A disaster brings out the best in people. Why? G. Cowley. il *Newsweek* 114:40+ N 6 '89

DISC JOCKEYS

See also
Bonaduce, Danny
Children as disc jockeys
Kasem, Casey, 1932-
Miller, J. B.
Payola
Stevens, Shadoe

DISC SANDERS *See* Sanding and sanding equipment

DISCARDING OF BOOKS *See* Book discarding

DISCH, THOMAS M.

Egg and chips [fiction] *Omni (New York, N.Y.)* 12:56-7 N '89

DISCHARGE OF EMPLOYEES *See* Employees—Dismissal

DISCHARGES, ELECTRIC *See* Electric discharges

DISCIPLESHIP *See* Christian life

DISCIPLINE

See also
Children—Management and training
Corporal punishment
Labor discipline
School discipline

DISCIPLINE-BASED ART EDUCATION

Discipline-based art education. R. H. Silverman. *The Education Digest* 55:53-6 O '89

Discipline-based art education neglects learning theory: an affirmation of studio art. J. A. Stinespring and L. Kennedy. bibl f *Design for Arts in Education* 90:33-40 N/D '88

The great art education debate. M. Moorman. il *Art News* 88:124-31 Summ '89

Metamorphosis to individual responsibility: a search for curriculum. L. Ball. bibl f *Design for Arts in Education* 91:36-42 S/O '89

University art programs and the discipline-based art education movement: what prospects? C. Stroh. *Design for Arts in Education* 91:38-47 N/D '89

DISCLOSURE OF PERSONAL FINANCES *See* Bush, George, 1924—Financial disclosure; Congressmen—Financial disclosure

DISCOTHEQUES

See also
New York (N.Y.)—Restaurants, nightclubs, bars, etc.

DISCOUNT, CASH

Discounts: yours for the asking [elderly] M. C. Paulson. *Changing Times* 43:124+ O '89

DISCOUNT, TRADE

H & R to offer free freight, new discount schedule. *Publishers Weekly* 236:9 Ag 25 '89

Pocket and Warner announce retail incentive plans [end of antitrust campaign by independent bookstores] J. Mutter. *Publishers Weekly* 235:19-20 Ja 6 '89

DISCOUNT AIRLINE FARES *See* Airlines—Fares

DISCOUNT BROKERS *See* Brokers—Commissions

DISCOUNT COMMODITY BROKERS *See* Commodity brokers—Commissions

DISCOUNT HOUSES (RETAIL TRADE)

See also
Crazy Eddie Inc.
Jamesway Corp.
K Mart Corp.
One Price Clothing Stores, Inc.
Outlet stores
Pic 'n' Save Corp.
Rose's Stores, Inc.
Wal-Mart Stores, Inc.
Warehouse clubs
Zayre Corp.

Japan

See also
Mr. Max Corporation

DISCOURTESY *See* Rudeness

DISCOVER (CREDIT CARD) *See* Credit cards

DISCOVER (PERIODICAL)

From the editor. P. Hoffman. See issues of Discover beginning September 1987

DISCOVERIES IN SCIENCE *See* Science

DISCOVERY (SPACE SHUTTLE VEHICLE) *See* Space vehicles

DISCOVERY AIRWAYS INC.
It's not even flying yet, and already there's a flap [Japanese financing] J. B. Levine and S. Payne. il *Business Week* p36-7 D 4 '89
DISCOVERY CHANNEL
John Hendricks' big adventure [cover story] P. Pagano. il pors *Channels (New York, N.Y.: 1986)* 9:20-3 O '89
DISCOVERY SYSTEMS (COMPUTERS)
"Discovery" opens new path for computer applications. *Radio-Electronics* 60:4 Mr '89
DISCOVERY TOYS
Spot a problem? Make it your business [L. Nemeth] L. Washer. il por *Working Woman* 14:100 My '89
DISCRIMINATION
    See also
    Anti-Semitism
    Race discrimination
    Sex discrimination
    Toleration
    United Nations. Sub-commission on Prevention of Discrimination and Protection of Minorities
"Affirmative action": a worldwide disaster [cover story] T. Sowell. *Commentary* 88:21-41 D '89
Civil rights: a presidential agenda. T. Eastland. *Current (Washington, D.C.)* 310:36-8 F '89
The complexities of affirmative action. R. J. Bresler. il *USA Today (Periodical)* 118:7 S '89
Is affirmative action fair? P. M. Jones. il *Scholastic Update (Teachers' edition)* 121:22 Ap 7 '89
Let's try discriminating for once. J. Leo. il *U.S. News & World Report* 107:53 Ag 7 '89
Permaffirm action [affirmative action] A. M. Thernstrom. *The New Republic* 201:17-19 Jl 31 '89
DISCRIMINATION IN EDUCATION
    See also
    Asian Americans—Education
    Blacks—Education
    Colleges and universities—Desegregation
    Colleges and universities—Segregation
    Public schools—Desegregation
    Public schools—Segregation
    Sex discrimination in education
Race, scholarship, and affirmative action [special section] *National Review* 41:36-40 My 5 '89
    Bibliography
Affirmative action: an exchange [discussion of October 12, 1989 article] A. Hacker. *The New York Review of Books* 36:52-3 D 7 '89
Affirmative action: the new look. A. Hacker. il *The New York Review of Books* 36:63-8 O 12 '89
DISCRIMINATION IN EMPLOYMENT
    See also
    Aged—Employment
    Black women—Employment
    Blacks—Employment
    Cancer patients—Employment
    Equal pay for equal work
    Minorities—Employment
    United States. Equal Employment Opportunity Commission
    Women—Employment
Academy panel joins the fray over job testing [question of reinterpreting scores of blacks and Hispanics on General Aptitude Test Battery] C. Holden. il *Science* 244:1036-7 Je 2 '89
Affirmative action. D. T. Dingle. il *Black Enterprise* 20:42-6+ S '89
Are you smiling, Robert Bork? [Justice A. M. Kennedy's decisions] il por *U.S. News & World Report* 106:10 Je 26 '89
Bias in the casino [charges of bias in job tests developed by U.S. Employment Service] D. Seligman. il *Fortune* 119:153-4 Ap 10 '89
The blow to affirmative action may not hurt that much [Supreme Court] P. Dwyer. il *Business Week* p61-2 Jl 3 '89
Chambers warns of dire impact of recent rulings by U.S. Supreme Court [affirmative action] por *Jet* 76:38 Ag 21 '89
Changes ahead for Section 89. D. C. Bacon. il *Nation's Business* 77:6 Je '89
Chipping away at civil rights [recent Supreme Court decisions] A. L. Sanders. il *Time* 133:63+ Je 26 '89
Choreographer charges AIDS discrimination at Legs Diamond [case of M. Shawn] R. Sandla. por *Dance Magazine* 63:18 Je '89
Civil rights cases [Supreme Court] *Monthly Labor Review* 112:50-1 Ag '89
Constitutional crisis [Supreme Court rulings on employment discrimination] P. Simpson. il *Ms.* 18:90+ S '89
The Court spins right [affirmative action decisions and Justice A. M. Kennedy] A. McDaniel. il por *Newsweek* 113:16-18 Je 26 '89
Deaffirmation [Supreme Court decisions deal blow to affirmative action] M. E. Dyson. *The Nation* 249:4-5 Jl 3 '89
Doubts multiply on Section 89 [federal benefits law] R. Thompson. il *Nation's Business* 77:17-18+ My '89

Fairness in employment testing [discussion of June 2, 1989 article, Academy panel joins the fray over job testing] C. Holden. *Science* 245:14 Jl 7 '89
Giving workers the boss's benefits [Section 89 of tax code] D. L. Boroughs. il *U.S. News & World Report* 106:BC1 Ap 10 '89
"Government gone crazy" [Section 89 of tax code on employee benefits discrimination; cover story] R. Thompson. il *Nation's Business* 77:20-4+ F '89
Health insurance: a tax-reform footnote trips up small business. S. B. Garland. il *Business Week* p45 Ja 30 '89
Holding firm on affirmative action [Fortune poll] A. Farnham. il *Fortune* 119:87-8 Mr 13 '89
How the good guys won the battle of Section 89. il *Nation's Business* 77:101 N '89
Illogical force [affirmative action and civil rights Supreme Court decisions] H. Schwartz. *The Nation* 249:40-1 Jl 10 '89
More normal nonsense [National Research Council report on General Aptitude Test Battery] D. Seligman. il *Fortune* 120:118 Jl 17 '89
Predisposition and prejudice [genetic discrimination; cover story] R. Weiss. il *Science News* 135:40-2 Ja 21 '89
A push to repeal Section 89 [strictures on employee benefits] R. Thompson. il *Nation's Business* 77:6 Mr '89
Real rights [Supreme Court rulings on employment discrimination] *National Review* 41:15-16 Jl 14 '89
Section 89: beyond repair. R. Thompson. il *Nation's Business* 77:65-7 Ap '89
The slippery slope in Foggy Bottom [Foreign Service and employment bias] D. Seligman. *Fortune* 119:167 My 8 '89
The Supreme Court expands religious freedom [unemployment benefits for individual who refused to work on Sundays] R. F. Drinan. *America* 160:388-9 Ap 29 '89
Supreme Court press [reporting of affirmative action cases] T. Eastland. *The American Spectator* 22:32-4 O '89
Supreme Court splits on two landmark bias cases. il *Jet* 76:4-5 Jl 3 '89
There's only one way to clear up this misunderstanding [repeal of Section 89] *Nation's Business* 77:80 Ag '89
Toward a real restoration of civil rights [Supreme Court rulings] T. Eastland. *Commentary* 88:25-9 N '89
'White people, black people' not wanted here? [Japanese employment agencies in U.S. charged with discrimination] M. Galen and L. J. Nathans. il *Business Week* p31 Jl 10 '89
Working late: the railroad to retirement. R. Hoopes. il *Modern Maturity* 32:34-7+ F/Mr '89
Wounds of race [Supreme Court affirmative action decisions] H. Hertzberg. *The New Republic* 201:4+ Jl 10 '89
    Alaska
A question of statistics [Supreme Court decision on racial discrimination at Alaskan fish canneries] T. Jacoby. il *Newsweek* 113:58 Je 19 '89
    United States
    See Discrimination in employment
DISCRIMINATION IN HOUSING
    See also
    Black women—Housing
    Children—Housing
    Fair Housing Act
    Unmarried couples—Housing
Beverly Hills HUD [subsidized housing for the elderly] T. Noah. *The New Republic* 201:14-16 Ag 21 '89
DISCRIMINATION IN MORTGAGES
Mortgage mumbo jumbo. D. Seligman. *Fortune* 120:185 D 4 '89
New Kennedy, old solutions [proposals authored by J. P. Kennedy] S. T. Mandel. *National Review* 41:22-3 Jl 14 '89
DISCRIMINATION IN SPORTS
    See also
    Sex discrimination in sports
Arthur Ashe remembers the forgotten men of sport—America's early black athletes [interview] S. K. Reed. il pors *People Weekly* 31:243-4+ Mr 6 '89
Ashe applauds ATP move to avoid South Africa. por *Jet* 76:48 S 18 '89
Black named NFL coach after 7 decades [A. Shell] L. Ransom. il pors *Jet* 77:48-50 O 23 '89
Choosing sides [Conway, S.C. torn apart by racial dispute involving two high school quarterbacks] H. Hersch. il pors *Sports Illustrated* 71:42-4+ N 27 '89
Color commentary [lack of black distance runners] J. Henderson. il *Runner's World* 24:12 F '89
Fighting from the inside [interview with H. Edwards] D. Wyss. il por *Time* 133:62-3 Mr 6 '89
The Greek in purgatory [Jimmy the Greek] M. Lupica. il *Esquire* 111:43-4+ Ja '89
Parker: double standard in his, Pete Rose cases. il pors *Jet* 76:48 Jl 24 '89
Top blacks qualified to replace Pete Rozelle. il por *Jet* 76:51 Ap 10 '89
Toronto hires Cito Gaston as fourth black manager. il por *Jet* 76:46+ Je 19 '89
Waiting for the black Merckx [lack of black bicycle racers] M. E. Mantell. il *Bicycling* 30:90-1+ My '89

DISCRIMINATION IN SPORTS—*cont.*

The Wayne and Lenny show [Cleveland's black general manager W. Embry and coach L. Wilkens] M. Lupica. pors *Esquire* 111:61-3+ Je '89

Why the obsession with race? [NBC special Black athletes—fact & fiction] S. Smith. il por *Sports Illustrated* 70:12 My 8 '89

DISCRIMINATION IN THE THEATER

John Amos raps critics of interracial cast in Shakespeare's '12th night'. il por *Jet* 76:63 Jl 17 '89

DISCS, COMPACT *See* Compact discs

DISCS, VIDEO *See* Videodiscs

DISCUSSION

See also
Negotiation

DISEASE CONTROL CENTERS *See* Centers for Disease Control (U.S.)

DISEASE MODELS, ANIMAL *See* Diseases—Animal models

DISEASE PREVENTION *See* Medicine, Preventive

DISEASE RESISTANCE *See* Immunity

DISEASE RESISTANCE OF PLANTS *See* Plants—Disease and pest resistance

DISEASES

See also
Animals as carriers of infection
Arteries—Diseases
Brain—Diseases
Breast—Diseases
Cardiovascular system—Diseases
Cerebrovascular disease
Children—Diseases
Diagnosis
Digestive system—Diseases
Ear—Diseases
Epidemics
Eye—Diseases and defects
Fetus—Diseases
Gums—Diseases
Heart—Diseases
Heredity of disease
Immunologic diseases
Infants, Newborn—Diseases
Infection
Kidneys—Diseases
Liver—Diseases
Lungs—Diseases
Muscle—Diseases
Nervous system—Diseases
Neural tube—Diseases
Reproductive organs—Diseases
Respiratory organs—Diseases
Skin—Diseases
Thyroid gland—Diseases
Urinary organs—Diseases
Virus diseases
Women—Diseases
See also names of diseases; also subhead Diseases and pests under names of plants and animals

The changing patterns of disease. il *Current Health 2* 16:18-19 S '89

Comeback diseases. *The Mother Earth News* 116:22 Mr/Ap '89

The family guide to winter health [special section] B. Weinhouse. il *Ladies' Home Journal* 106:85-6+ Ja '89

Fostering more orphan-disease research [report of National Commission on Orphan Diseases] *Science News* 135:255 Ap 22 '89

Just ask us . . . [questions and answers] See issues of Current Health 2

Non-communicable diseases: no longer just diseases of affluence [Western Pacific region] I. Darnton-Hill. il *World Health* p7-9 N '89

Animal models

See also
AIDS (Disease)—Animal models

Almost human? Marine animal models. M. Root. il *BioScience* 39:520-1 S '89

Beyond the lab rat [unusual mammals] J. P. Cohn. il *BioScience* 39:518-22 S '89

A model of human acute lymphoblastic leukemia in immune-deficient SCID mice. S. Kamel-Reid and others. bibl f il *Science* 246:1597-600 D 22 '89

Recombinant rodents, human hemoglobin [work of R. R. Behringer] R. Weiss. *Science News* 136:149 S 2 '89

Synthesis of functional human hemoglobin in transgenic mice. R. R. Behringer and others. bibl f il *Science* 245:971-3 S 1 '89

Causes

See also
Medicine, Psychosomatic
Stress

Nutritional aspects

See Diet in disease

Spontaneous remission

See Spontaneous remission

Therapy

See Therapeutics

Transmission by water

See Waterborne infection

DISEASES, INDUSTRIAL *See* Occupational health and safety

DISEASES, MENTAL *See* Mental illness

DISEASES, PREHISTORIC *See* Paleopathology

DISH TOWELS *See* Towels

DISHES *See* Pottery

DISHNO, RICHARD

America's Lutherans: who they are. il *Christianity Today* 33:18-21 N 3 '89

DISHWASHERS

Hoses

Replacing dishwasher hoses [WP600 Maytag portable] C. Maxwell. il *The Family Handyman* 39:100+ My '89

Installation

Install a dishwasher. A. Rooze. il *The Family Handyman* 39:42+ F '89

Maintenance and repair

Fixing a nonfilling dishwasher. C. Maxwell. il *The Family Handyman* 39:102 Ap '89

How to repair a dishwasher. M. J. Schultz. il *Popular Mechanics* 166:91-4 Ag '89

DISHWASHING DETERGENTS *See* Detergents

DISINFLATION (FINANCE) *See* Deflation (Finance)

DISINFORMATION *See* Propaganda

DISK DRIVE MEMORY SYSTEMS (COMPUTERS) *See* Computers—Memory systems

DISLOCATIONS

Look before you leap. P. G. Gill. il *Outdoor Life* 183:61-3 Mr '89

DISMISSAL OF EMPLOYEES *See* Employees—Dismissal

DISMISSAL OF TEACHERS *See* Teachers—Dismissal

DISMORE, MARGARET

Forever Adele. il por *Opera News* 53:34-5 Ja 7 '89

DISNEY, ROY E.

about

The other Disney in the spotlight. F. Rice. il pors *Fortune* 119:161+ Je 5 '89

DISNEY (WALT) COMPANY *See* Walt Disney Company

DISNEY (WALT) CONCERT HALL (LOS ANGELES, CALIF.) *See* Walt Disney Concert Hall (Los Angeles, Calif.)

DISNEY (WALT) HOME VIDEO *See* Walt Disney Home Video

DISNEY-MGM STUDIOS THEME PARK (FLA.)

How Disney does it [cover story] C. Leerhsen. il por *Newsweek* 113:48-54 Ap 3 '89

Movie studio tours—the new, fun vacation! S. Birnbaum. il *Good Housekeeping* 208:36+ Je '89

The tight-budget, no-hassle way to see Disney World. M. Kiernan. il *U.S. News & World Report* 106:62-3+ Je 5 '89

Walt Disney World chooses Ebony to boost its new MGM Theme Park. il *Jet* 76:62 Je 12 '89

You're under arrest! R. Corliss. il *Time* 133:102-3 My 8 '89

DISNEYANA *See* Walt Disney Company—Collectibles

DISNEYWORLD (FLA.) *See* Walt Disney World (Fla.)

DISORDERLINESS *See* Messiness

DISORGANIZED CRIME [film] See Motion picture reviews—Single works

DISPLAY OF ANTIQUES, ART OBJECTS, ETC.

Beans to baskets to books . . . on display. il *Sunset (Central West edition)* 182:110 Mr '89

Building a sidewalk art booth. E. V. Cohen. il *American Artist* 53:68-72+ My '89

DISPLAY OF MERCHANDISE

See also
Show windows

DISPLAY SYSTEMS, AIRPLANE *See* Airplanes, Military—Electronic equipment

DISPLAY SYSTEMS, HELICOPTER *See* Helicopters—Electronic equipment

DISPLAY SYSTEMS, INFORMATION *See* Information display systems

DISPLAY TERMINALS, VIDEO *See* Video display terminals

DISPOSABLE CAMERAS

Cameras for forgetful snapshooters. F. L. Kritz. il *U.S. News & World Report* 107:58-9 Jl 10 '89

Playing leapfrog in disposable cameras [Kodak vs Fuji] L. Helm. il *Business Week* p34 My 1 '89

What's new? M. Grimm and T. Grimm. il *Travel Holiday* 171:16-19 Mr '89

Testing

Cameras away! [Kodak's waterproof and panoramic disposable cameras] A. Fisher. il *Popular Science* 235:80-1 N '89

Kodak's wild disposables are wide and wet; Fuji's is a tele! D. Richards. il *Popular Photography* 96:26+ Jl '89

DISPOSABLE DIAPERS *See* Diapers

DISPOSABLE WORKERS *See* Contingent workers

DISPOSAL OF RADIOACTIVE WASTE *See* Radioactive waste disposal

DISPOSAL OF REFUSE See Refuse and refuse disposal
DISSENTERS
See also
Political prisoners
Protests, demonstrations, etc.
745 Boylston Street [Fang Lizhi] il por *The Atlantic* 264:4 S '89
An act of defiance [Chinese dissenter Fang Lizhi barred from state dinner; cover story] O. Schell. il pors *The New York Times Magazine* p26-7+ Ap 16 '89
Chinese bar physicist from Bush dinner [dissident Fang Lizhi] M. Sun. il por *Science* 243:1282 Mr 10 '89
Fang Lizhi: speaking out for human rights. M. Sun. il por *Science* 244:417-18 Ap 28 '89
Fang loses post, gains award. por *Science* 246:1252 D 8 '89
The fate of Fang Lizhi. il por *Sky and Telescope* 78:240-1 S '89
From Big Bang to big trouble [Fang Lizhi seeks refuge at U.S. embassy] il por *U.S. News & World Report* 106:38 Je 26 '89
The furious flap over Fang Lizhi [Washington and Beijing clash over Chinese dissident] S. MacLeod. por *Time* 133:38 Mr 13 '89
Gorbie's choice [influence of dissident literature on Soviet reforms] S. Anderson. *The New Republic* 200:11-12 Ap 17 '89
A journey of conscience [China] R. Bernstein. il *The New York Times Magazine* p22-5+ Ap 16 '89
Letters from the other China [letters written to dissident Fang Lizhi in 1987]; tr. by Orville Schell. bibl f il por *The New York Review of Books* 36:32-3 Jl 20 '89
Notes and comment [exclusion of Fang Lizhi from G. Bush's banquet in Beijing] *The New Yorker* 65:34-5 Mr 20 '89
Pantheon to publish autobiography of Chinese dissident next spring [Liu Binyan] por *Publishers Weekly* 235:29-30 My 26 '89
Physicists protest treatment by PRC of Fang Lizhi. W. Sweet. *Physics Today* 42:59 Ap '89
Quotations from dissident Fang. il por *Newsweek* 113:26-7 Je 26 '89
Would I move back? [Soviet dissident now living in Paris] A. Sinyavsky. il pors *Time* 133:129-30+ Ap 10 '89
DISSOCIATION (PSYCHOLOGY)
The long nightmare of Ruth Finley [dissociative reaction victim] P. Michelmore. il por *Reader's Digest* 134:97-104 Mr '89
DISTANCES
Measurement
Do you speak metric? [measuring race distances] J. Henderson. il *Runner's World* 24:12 Ja '89
DISTANCES, ASTRONOMICAL See Astronomical distances
DISTANT VOICES, STILL LIVES [film] See Motion picture reviews—Single works
DISTEFANO, BENNY
about
He won't be left out. S. Rushin. il por *Sports Illustrated* 70:99 My 8 '89
DISTELHEIM, ROCHELLE
The betrayal of Fernald, Ohio. il *Good Housekeeping* 209:176+ S '89
Rape: a woman's worst nightmare. *McCall's* 116:60+ S '89
DISTEMPER VIRUS
Vaccines and vaccination
Vaccination success convicts seal killer [canine distemper virus in harbor seals; research by Alfred D. M. E. Osterhaus] I. Wickelgren. *Science News* 135:39 Ja 21 '89
DISTILLERS COMPANY PLC
The House of Guinness. J. Marcom, Jr. il por *Forbes* 143:85+ Je 12 '89
DISTILLING INDUSTRIES See Liquor industry
DISTORTION, AUDIO See Amplifiers—Noise; Audio systems—Noise
DISTRACTION
The best way to tough it out [comparison of distraction methods while running; research by Vernon Padgett and Angela Hill] J. C. Horn. *Psychology Today* 23:72-3 N '89
DISTRIBUTED DATA PROCESSING
Distributed processing [special section; with editorial comment by Jane Morrill Tazelaar] il *Byte* 14:212-13, 215-18+ Jl '89
"Location transparency" next hurdle for database technology. *Byte* 14:12+ Ap '89
A logical choice [LU 6.2] R. Davis. bibl il *Byte* 14:309-15 Ja '89
PARC brings Adam Smith to computing. M. M. Waldrop. il *Science* 244:145-6 Ap 14 '89
Sharing the wealth [distributed database technology] R. Davis. bibl il *Byte* 14:267-70+ S '89
Terminal chaos. il *Discover* 10:12 F '89
DISTRIBUTION (PROBABILITY THEORY)
Coping with uncertainty [Basic program for Gaussian distribution curve] A. Blackadar. *Weatherwise* 42:221-3 Ag '89
DISTRIBUTION OF FOOD See Food industry—Marketing
DISTRIBUTION OF GOODS
See also
Marketing channels

Wholesale trade
Japan
Japan's master of retailing [I. Nakauchi] S. Wagstyl. por *World Press Review* 36:52 Ja '89
A land of papa-mama shops [complex marketing regulations deter foreign retailers] J. Impoco. il *U.S. News & World Report* 106:47-8 Ap 24 '89
DISTRIBUTION OF INCOME See Income
DISTRIBUTION OF WEALTH See Wealth
DISTRIBUTORS, BOOK See Book wholesalers and distributors
DISTRICT OF COLUMBIA See Washington (D.C.)
DISTRICT OF COLUMBIA ART ASSOCIATION
Across generations, a creative legacy [Anacostia Museum retrospective Inspiration: 1961-1989] K. M. Burke. il *Smithsonian* 19:151 Ja '89
DISULFIDES See Sulfides
DITH, PRAN
Return to the killing fields [cover story] il pors *The New York Times Magazine* p30-3+ S 24 '89
DITLEA, STEVE
War games. il *Omni (New York, N.Y.)* 11:32+ Mr '89
DITTMER, THOMAS H.
about
Did Refco help take Uncle Sam to the cleaners? D. Greising. il *Business Week* p33-4 O 2 '89
DITZ, NANCY
On top of the world. il por *Runner's World* 24:50 Ja '89
DIURETICS
Diuretic dilemma [increased danger of heart attacks; Swedish study] *Time* 134:103 O 9 '89
Hypertension, heart disease and diuretics. R. Weiss. *Science News* 136:254 O 14 '89
DIVERS See Diving; Diving, Submarine
DIVERSIFICATION IN AGRICULTURE
Farms with many 'baskets' [low-input, sustainable farming] J. Walter. il *Successful Farming* 87:16-17 Ap '89
Successful family farm [Frank Farms, Inc.] C. Tevis. il *Successful Farming* 87 no4:46-8 Mr '89
DIVERSIFICATION IN INDUSTRY
The corporation. See issues of Business Week
Surviving the slowdown: diversity is key. K. Madigan. il *Business Week* p57-8 Jl 3 '89
Utility stocks can deliver a nasty shock. S. Woolley. *Business Week* p96 Jl 3 '89
Japan
Back to basics in Japan. il *World Press Review* 36:54-5 N '89
DIVERSITY (BIOLOGY)
Angiosperm diversification and paleolatitudinal gradients in Cretaceous floristic diversity. P. R. Crane and S. Lidgard. bibl f il *Science* 246:675-8 N 3 '89
Asymmetries of clade shape and the direction of evolutionary time [discussion of May 27, 1988 article, Macroevolutionary interpretations of symmetry and synchroneity in the fossil record] J. A. Kitchell and N. S. MacLeod. *Science* 243:1613-15 Mr 24 '89
Biodiversity bill update. D. E. Blockstein. *BioScience* 39:677 N '89
Biodiversity loss faces the Southern Appalachians. *Wilderness* 52:iii Spr '89
Blueprint for conserving plant diversity. C. Mlot. il *BioScience* 39:364-8 Je '89
A center of crop genetic diversity in western Amazonia. C. R. Clement. bibl f il maps *BioScience* 39:624-31 O '89
The death of birth. E. Linden. il *Time* 133:32-4+ Ja 2 '89
Gauging the biological impacts of the greenhouse effect. J. P. Cohn. il *BioScience* 39:142-6 Mr '89
Nature under glass [greenhouse effect] J. R. Udall. il map *Sierra* 74:34-40 Jl/Ag '89
Of buccaneers and biodiversity [Caribbean Islands and Florida Keys] D. R. Wallace. il maps *Wilderness* 53:38-51 Wint '89
Our biological heritage under siege [address, August 6, 1989] N. Brown. *BioScience* 39:725-8 N '89
The role of somatic hypermutation in the generation of antibody diversity. D. L. French and others. bibl f il *Science* 244:1152-7 Je 9 '89
Threats to biodiversity. E. O. Wilson. bibl il *Scientific American* 261:108-12+ S '89
Using nature as a model [biological diversity in the national parks] D. Hunter. il *National Parks* 63:40-1 S/O '89
DIVESTITURE BY CORPORATIONS See Corporations—Divestiture
DIVIDEND REINVESTMENT
Dividend plans that deserve a critical look [fees charged for dividend reinvestment] M. Meyer. *Money* 18:61 Ap '89
DIVIDENDS
See also
Primes (Securities)
Cannibal bond funds [bond funds that pay lavish dividends but eat up principal] W. Baldwin. il *Forbes* 144:166+ S 4 '89
Dividend days. J. Lieblich. il *Fortune* 119:9 Mr 13 '89
Dividends and interest matter a lot more than you think. R. E. Norton. il *Fortune* 120:19+ N 6 '89
Growth yields. E. Sturza. il *Forbes* 143:222 Ap 17 '89

DIVIDENDS—cont.

More money, less yield. K. Deveny. il *Business Week* p30 F 13 '89

The party's over, but there's still fun to be had. J. Friedman. il *Business Week* p110+ D 25 '89-Ja 1 '90

What to do when the stock market drops 200 points [dividend discount model] E. Schultz. il *Fortune* 120:53+ N 20 '89

When do 'dividend plays' really pay off? J. Friedman. il *Business Week* p150 N 20 '89

Taxation

Debt and taxes [taxing debt and equity payments equally] A. Gray, Jr. and A. B. Laffer. il *National Review* 41:38-9 S 1 '89

A sexy new tax shelter from across the Atlantic [British preferred stock] L. Jereski. *Business Week* p108 Je 12 '89

DIVIDERS, ROOM See Room dividers

DIVIGALPITIYA, W. M. R., AND OTHERS

Inclusion systems of organic molecules in restacked single-layer molybdenum disulfide. bibl f il *Science* 246:369-71 O 20 '89

DIVINATION

See also
    Astrology
    Oracle bones

DIVINE GLORY See Glory of God
DIVINE HEALING See Faith cure
DIVINE LOVE See Love (Theology)
DIVING

Competitions

Wendy flew high in Indy [W. Williams in World Cup] M. Noden. il pors *Sports Illustrated* 70:68+ My 15 '89

DIVING, SUBMARINE

See also
    Decompression (Physiology)
    Skin diving

Working underwater [professional divers on an offshore oil rig in the Gulf of Mexico] J. S. McKinna. il *Sea Frontiers* 35:348-55 N/D '89

DIVING BY ANIMALS See Animal locomotion
DIVING EQUIPMENT

See also
    Gills, Artificial

DIVING EQUIPMENT IN MOTION PICTURES

Deep-sea cinema [making of The abyss] A. Maurer. il *Omni (New York, N.Y.)* 11:14+ Ag '89

Wave of the future [making of The abyss] J. Calhoun. il *Theatre Crafts* 23:46-7+ Ag/S '89

DIVING MASKS See Skin diving—Equipment
DIVINING ROD See Dowsing
DIVINITY SCHOOLS See Theological seminaries
DIVISION OF POWERS See Separation of powers
DIVOKY, DIANE

Ritalin: education's fix-it drug? bibl f il *Phi Delta Kappan* 70:599-605 Ap '89

DIVORCE

See also
    Alimony
    Children of divorced parents
    Custody of children
    Palimony
    Support (Domestic relations)

After the loving, counting the cost [celebrity breakups; cover story; special section] S. Schindehette. il *People Weekly* 32:68-70+ Ag 7 '89

Ed McMahon, late-night TV's favorite foil, decides it's time to wrap up his 13-year marriage. J. Kaufman. il pors *People Weekly* 32:87-8 Ag 14 '89

Family affairs [celebrity divorces] il *Rolling Stone* p135 D 14-28 '89

'Free at last,' Tyson says of divorce from actress Robin Givens. il pors *Jet* 76:12-13 Je 19 '89

Future shock [J. and M. S. Davis' custody fight over fertilized eggs] il *Time* 133:42 Mr 27 '89

How her painful divorce helped her on Knots Landing [M. Lee] J. Hicks. il pors *TV Guide* 37:18-20 Ag 5-11 '89

Jane Fonda enters a new era. A. Sachs. il pors *McCall's* 116:32-4+ S '89

September spells severance for Harry Hamlin and other soon-to-be single celebs. il *People Weekly* 32:93-4+ S 18 '89

Steven Spielberg finally suffers a big-budget flop—his marriage. il pors *People Weekly* 31:67 My 8 '89

The trouble with divorce [condensed from The case against divorce] D. Medved. *Reader's Digest* 134:96-9 My '89

Tyson-Givens split final, $125 million suit ended. il pors *Jet* 75:52 Mr 6 '89

When a marriage ends: how men, women and children cope. J. S. Wallerstein and S. Blakeslee. *McCall's* 116:78+ Mr '89

History

The road to polygamy [views of R. Phillips] L. Stone. bibl f il *The New York Review of Books* 36:12-15 Mr 2 '89

Religious aspects

Churches unite, take a stand to prevent divorce [Modesto, Calif.] J. Williams. il *Christianity Today* 33:65-6 S 8 '89

United States

See Divorce

DIVORCE LAWYERS

A struggle for splitsville's bucks [R. Felder and M. M. Mitchelson] J. D. Reed. il pors *Time* 133:53 Ja 9 '89

DIVORCED FATHERS

See also
    Support (Domestic relations)

Dates for dad. L. Brown. por *Essence* 19:10 F '89

Weekend dads. J. T. Gibson. il *Parents* 64:188 Mr '89

DIVORCED FATHERS IN TELEVISION

Dear John—look for the lady buying small tins of caviar. H. Gold. il *TV Guide* 37:16-17 Ap 8-14 '89

DIVORCEES

See also
    Parents of divorcees

Diary of an ex. L. Michaels. *Harper's* 279:31-2 D '89

Post-divorce blues [views of Ed Beckham] il *USA Today (Periodical)* 118:9 S '89

Economic conditions

Court limits sharing of Army pension in divorce; Marshall pens decision [Supreme Court] por *Jet* 76:8 Je 19 '89

Divvying up before you split [postnuptial agreements] N. Santelmann. il *Forbes* 144:276+ N 27 '89

Learning the rules on divorce. M. Rowland. il *Working Woman* 14:69-70+ S '89

When trouble strikes twice: at home, at work. M. Rowland. il *Working Woman* 14:61-2+ Je '89

DIXIE BELLES (MUSICAL GROUP)

Struttin' their stuff, the Dixie Belles are having a ball. il *People Weekly* 32:98-9 Jl 3 '89

DIXON, ALAN J.

about

Mortgage mumbo jumbo. D. Seligman. *Fortune* 120:185 D 4 '89

DIXON, ANDREW GRAHAM- See Graham-Dixon, Andrew
DIXON, CAROL

After the beep [story] il *Essence* 20:85-6 O '89

DIXON, CARRIE MAE

about

School paper's story on teen mother who's class valedictorian is barred. il por *Jet* 76:31 My 8 '89

Teen mom tells of 'beating odds' to be valedictorian. il pors *Jet* 76:12 Je 26 '89

Teen mother with straight A's tells how education is changing her life. D. M. Cheers. il pors *Jet* 76:28-30 My 22 '89

Valedictorian Carrie Dixon gets top grades in high school—even with a second child on the way. il por *People Weekly* 31:62 My 29 '89

DIXON, DON

about

The big fix [cover story] J. R. Adams. il *The American Spectator* 22:21-4 Mr '89

DIXON, HERBERT

about

Elizabeth Morgan's brother risks jail as he joins her in defying a Washington judge. D. Grogan. il pors *People Weekly* 32:38-40 Jl 3 '89

DIXON, HUGO

A mobile phone in every home. il *World Press Review* 36:36+ O '89

DIXON, PHILLIP

The sensate body [photographs] il *Esquire* 111:145-50 My '89

DIXON, WILLIE

about

Two Chess mates at their very best. D. Fricke. il pors *Rolling Stone* p40-1 Ja 26 '89

Willie Dixon. R. Wolmuth. il pors *People Weekly* 32:120-1+ S 11 '89

Willie Dixon and the wisdom of the blues. A. DeCurtis. il pors *Rolling Stone* p109+ Mr 23 '89

DIXON TICONDEROGA CO.

Better than an M.B.A. F. Meeks. il por *Forbes* 143:88+ Je 26 '89

DIZZINESS

When the world turns [vertigo] B. H. Dobkin. il *The New York Times Magazine* p51-2 Ap 9 '89

DJEBAR, ASSIA, 1936-

Behind the veil. il *The Unesco Courier* 42:34-7 O '89

DJERASSI, CARL

The bitter pill. bibl f *Science* 245:356-61 Jl 28 '89

DLAMINI, ZENANI MANDELA, PRINCESS

about

Word from South Africa [interview] S. L. Taylor and E. B. Washington. il por *Essence* 20:42-4+ Jl '89

DMZ (KOREA) See Korean Demilitarized Zone (Korea)
DNA

See also
    Genetic code
    Genetic research
    Mitochondrial DNA
    Polymerase chain reaction
    Restriction fragment length polymorphisms
    Transposons

Calicheamicin γ_1^1 and DNA: molecular recognition process responsible for site-specificity. N. Zein and others. bibl f il *Science* 244:697-9 My 12 '89

DNA—cont.

Checkpoints: controls that ensure the order of cell cycle events. L. H. Hartwell and T. A. Weinert. bibl f il *Science* 246:629-34 N 3 '89

Chemically fingerprinting DNA damage [work of Miral Dizdaroglu] J. Raloff. *Science News* 135:199 Ap 1 '89

Cloning and sequencing of porcine LH-hCG receptor cDNA: variants lacking transmembrane domain. H. Loosfelt and others. bibl f il *Science* 245:525-8 Ag 4 '89

Cognate DNA binding specificity retained after leucine zipper exchange between GCN4 and C/EBP. P. Agre and others. bibl f il *Science* 246:922-6 N 17 '89

Construction of large DNA segments in Escherichia coli. M. O'Connor and others. bibl f il *Science* 244:1307-12 Je 16 '89

The DNA binding domain of the rat liver nuclear protein C/EBP is bipartite [support for leucine zipper hypothesis] W. H. Landschulz and others. bibl f il *Science* 243:1681-8 Mr 31 '89

DNA looping generated by DNA bending protein IHF and the two domains of lambda integrase. L. Moitoso De Vargas and others. bibl f il *Science* 244:1457-61 Je 23 '89

DNA mismatch correction in a defined system. R. S. Lahue and others. bibl f il *Science* 245:160-4 Jl 14 '89

DNA's extended domain [cover story] I. Wickelgren. il *Science News* 136:234-7 O 7 '89

Evidence that the leucine zipper is a coiled coil. E. K. O'Shea and others. bibl f il *Science* 243:538-42 Ja 27 '89

Eyeing the ingrained origins of DNA [research by Ronald Berezney] I. Wickelgren. *Science News* 135:5 Ja 7 '89

Generalized tube model of biased reptation for gel electrophoresis of DNA. J. Noolandi and others. bibl f il *Science* 243:1456-8 Mr 17 '89

Identification of the cystic fibrosis gene: cloning and characterization of complementary DNA. J. R. Riordan and others. bibl f il *Science* 245:1066-73 S 8 '89

Increased expression of DNA cointroduced with nuclear protein in adult rat liver. Y. Kaneda and others. bibl f il *Science* 243:375-8 Ja 20 '89

Inhibition of DNA binding proteins by oligonucleotide-directed triple helix formation. L. J. Maher, III and others. bibl f il *Science* 245:725-30 Ag 18 '89

Introduction of human DNA into mouse eggs by injection of dissected chromosome fragments. J. Richa and C. W. Lo. bibl f il *Science* 245:175-7 Jl 14 '89

Isolation and expression of functional high-affinity Fc receptor complementary DNAs. J. M. Allen and B. Seed. bibl f il *Science* 243:378-81 Ja 20 '89

Isolation of a cDNA clone derived from a blood-borne non-A, non-B viral hepatitis genome. Q.-L. Choo and others. bibl f il *Science* 244:359-62 Ap 21 '89

Isolation of a novel receptor cDNA establishes the existence of two PDGF receptor genes. T. Matsui and others. bibl f il *Science* 243:800-4 F 10 '89

Kappa B-specific DNA binding proteins: role in the regulation of human interleukin-2 gene expression. B. Hoyos and others. bibl f il *Science* 244:457-60 Ap 28 '89

Leucine repeats and an adjacent DNA binding domain mediate the formation of functional cFos-cJun heterodimers [proposed function of the leucine zipper] R. Turner and R. Tjian. bibl f il *Science* 243:1689-94 Mr 31 '89

The location of DNA in RecA-DNA helical filaments. E. H. Egelman and X. Yu. bibl f il *Science* 245:404-7 Jl 28 '89

The mechanism of DNA transfer in the mating system of an archaebacterium. I. Rosenshine and others. bibl f il *Science* 245:1387-9 S 22 '89

Observation of individual DNA molecules undergoing gel electrophoresis. S. B. Smith and others. bibl f il *Science* 243:203-6 Ja 13 '89

Parallel association of Fos and Jun leucine zippers juxtaposes DNA binding domains. R. Gentz and others. bibl f il *Science* 243:1695-9 Mr 31 '89

Pictures show smoking's ill effects on DNA [research by Kurt and Erika Randerath] J. Raloff. il *Science News* 135:151 Mr 11 '89

Policy forum:
Are radiation-induced effects hormetic? [low-dose ionizing radiation] S. Wolff. bibl f *Science* 245:575+ Ag 11 '89

On radiation, paradigms, and hormesis [low-dose ionizing radiation] L. A. Sagan. bibl f *Science* 245:574+ Ag 11 '89

Preferential heterodimer formation by isolated leucine zippers from Fos and Jun. E. K. O'Shea and others. bibl f il *Science* 245:646-8 Ag 11 '89

Purification and complementary DNA cloning of a receptor for basic fibroblast growth factor. P. L. Lee and others. bibl f il *Science* 245:57-60 Jl 7 '89

Reverse transcriptase in a clinical strain of Escherichia coli: production of branched RNA-linked msDNA. B. C. Lampson and others. bibl f il *Science* 243:1033-8 F 24 '89

S phase of the cell cycle. R. A. Laskey and others. bibl f il *Science* 246:609-14 N 3 '89

Scissors-grip model for DNA recognition by a family of leucine zipper proteins. C. R. Vinson and others. bibl f il *Science* 246:911-16 N 17 '89

Sequence-specific isotope effects on the cleavage of DNA by bleomycin. J. W. Kozarich and others. bibl f il *Science* 245:1396-9 S 22 '89

Similarity between the transcriptional silencer binding proteins ABF1 and RAP1 [Saccharomyces] J. F. X. Diffley and B. Stillman. bibl f il *Science* 246:1034-8 N 24 '89

Specific block of calcium channel expression by a fragment of dihydropyridine receptor cDNA. I. Lotan and others. bibl f il *Science* 243:666-9 F 3 '89

Specific recognition of cruciform DNA by nuclear protein HMG1. M. E. Bianchi and others. bibl f il *Science* 243:1056-9 F 24 '89

Stabilization of Z DNA in vivo by localized supercoiling. A. R. Rahmouni and R. D. Wells. bibl f il *Science* 246:358-63 O 20 '89

Three-dimensional solution structure of a single zinc finger DNA-binding domain [cover story] M. S. Lee and others. bibl f il *Science* 245:635-7 Ag 11 '89

Time bomb [DNA clock; work of Charles G. Sibley and Jon E. Ahlquist] J. Horgan. *Scientific American* 260:24+ Mr '89

Topology and formation of triple-stranded H-DNA. H. Htun and J. E. Dahlberg. bibl f il *Science* 243:1571-6 Mr 24 '89

Transcriptional regulation in mammalian cells by sequence-specific DNA binding proteins [RNA polymerase II transcription initiation] P. J. Mitchell and R. Tjian. bibl f il *Science* 245:371-8 Jl 28 '89

Understanding the anomalous electrophoresis of bent DNA molecules: a reptation model. S. D. Levene and B. H. Zimm. bibl f il *Science* 245:396-9 Jl 28 '89

Volatilization of high molecular weight DNA by pulsed laser ablation of frozen aqueous solutions [mass spectrometry] R. W. Nelson and others. bibl f il *Science* 246:1585-7 D 22 '89

Photographs and photography

The coil of life [structure viewed with scanning tunneling microscope] A. Fisher. il *Popular Science* 234:10+ Je '89

Direct observation of native DNA structures with the scanning tunneling microscope. T. P. Beebe, Jr. and others. bibl f il *Science* 243:370-2 Ja 20 '89

Direct view of DNA [use of scanning tunneling microscope] J. A. Miller. il *BioScience* 39:225-6 Ap '89

Images of the DNA double helix in water [cover story] S. M. Lindsay and others. bibl f il *Science* 244:1063-4 Je 2 '89

A kinky new look for DNA [use of scanning tunneling microscope; work of Stuart Lindsay] il *Discover* 10:18 O '89

Molecular structure of DNA by scanning tunneling microscopy. A. Cricenti and others. bibl f il *Science* 245:1226-7 S 15 '89

The picture of life [use of scanning tunneling microscope] il *Newsweek* 113:67 F 6 '89

Scanning the winding coils of naked DNA [use of scanning tunneling microscope; research by Miquel B. Salmeron] I. Peterson. il *Science News* 135:53 Ja 28 '89

Scanning tunneling microscopy of uncoated recA-DNA complexes. M. Amrein and others. bibl f il *Science* 243:1708-11 Mr 31 '89

Sequencing DNA using remote Braille [work of David D. Dunlap and Carlos Bustamante] *Science News* 136:351 N 25 '89

Synthesis

Histone H5 in the control of DNA synthesis and cell proliferation. J.-M. Sun and others. bibl f il *Science* 245:68-71 Jl 7 '89

DNA BANKS *See* Gene banks

DNA FINGERPRINTS

Big-game forensics [use of DNA fingerprinting to discourage elephant poaching] J. Horgan. il *Scientific American* 261:27+ D '89

Caution urged on DNA fingerprinting [ruling in J. Castro case] C. Norman. *Science* 245:699 Ag 18 '89

DNA analysis in forensic science. M. D. Moody. bibl f il *BioScience* 39:31-6 Ja '89

DNA on trial. il *Time* 134:63 Ag 28 '89

DNA takes the stand. R. Weiss. il *Science News* 136:74-6 Jl 29 '89

DNA test says Ali isn't father of Houston girl [B. Mensah's suit] il pors *Jet* 75:52 F 20 '89

DNA typing and parentage. L. Levine and L. Kobilinsky. *BioScience* 39:588-9 O '89

DNA typing is called flawed [J. Castro case] R. Lewin. il *Science* 245:355 Jl 28 '89

DNA typing on the witness stand [challenging reliability of forensic DNA fingerprinting; case of J. Castro] R. Lewin. il *Science* 244:1033-5 Je 2 '89

Doling out DNA [captive breeding programs; cover story] R. Weiss. il *Science News* 135:72-4 F 4 '89

Genetic fingerprints [used in convicting Ottawa rapist P. J. McNally] R. Laver. il *Maclean's* 102:54 Ap 17 '89

Genetics meets forensics. R. Lewis. il *BioScience* 39:6-9 Ja '89

DNA FINGERPRINTS—*cont.*

Judging paternity in the hedge sparrow's world [research by Nicholas Davies] R. Lewin. il *Science* 243:1663-4 Mr 31 '89

Limits to DNA fingerprinting [use in animal population biology] R. Lewin. il *Science* 243:1549-51 Mr 24 '89

Maine case deals blow to DNA fingerprinting. C. Norman. il *Science* 246:1556-8 D 22 '89

Misprint [reliability] M. Thompson. *The New Republic* 200:14-15 Ap 3 '89

Misprints [problems with forensic DNA typing; case of J. Castro] J. Kinoshita. *Scientific American* 261:12+ Ag '89

Science gives ivory a sense of identity [DNA fingerprinting and isotope analyses] J. Cherfas. il *Science* 246:1120-1 D 1 '89

The startling Shelly Prine case [use to convict O. Smith of murder in Goessel, Kan.] P. Michelmore. *Reader's Digest* 135:179-80+ Jl '89

A trial of high-tech detectives [challenge to reliability of DNA analysis; case of J. Castro] D. Thompson. il por *Time* 133:63 Je 5 '89

DNA GENE PROBES *See* Gene probes
DNA METHYLATION *See* Methylation
DNA POLYMERASE *See* Polymerases
DNC *See* Democratic National Committee
DO-IT-YOURSELF DIAGNOSIS *See* Diagnosis
DO-IT-YOURSELF HOUSE BUILDING *See* House construction
DO-IT-YOURSELF HOUSEHOLD REPAIRING *See* Houses—Maintenance and repair
DO-IT-YOURSELF MEDICAL KITS *See* Medical equipment
DO-IT-YOURSELF WORK

100 ideas under $100 [cover story; with editorial comment by David Jordan] J. Williams and J. Severson. il *Better Homes and Gardens* 67:10, 19-24+ Jl '89

Anecdotes, facetiae, satire, etc.

We, the handy. T. Leeson. il *Field & Stream* 93:18+ F '89

Bibliography

Book reviews. See issues of Workbench

Competitions

D-I-Y Landscaping Contest: the winners. D. Colby. il *Home Mechanix* 86:47-58+ Mr '89

Study and teaching
Aids and devices

See also
Videotapes—Do-it-yourself work

DO ROSARIO, LOUISE *See* Rosario, Louise do
DO THE RIGHT THING [film] *See* Motion picture reviews—Single works
DO YOU KNOW THE MUFFIN MAN? [television program] *See* Television program reviews—Single works
DOAK-DAVIS, NAN

about

Super Nan. M. Will-Weber. il por *Runner's World* 24:93 Mr '89

DOBBS FERRY (N.Y.)

Education

First days in first grade. P. La Farge. il pors *Parents* 64:104-8+ S '89

DOBELL, BYRON

Letter from the editor. See issues of American Heritage

DOBIE, KATHY

Yolanda Serrano. il pors *Ms.* 17:79-83 Ja/F '89

DOBKIN, BRUCE H.

Challenge of gravity. il *The New York Times Magazine* p36-7 Ag 27 '89

Ill, or just the blahs? il *The New York Times Magazine* p36-7 Jl 16 '89

Shooing elephants. il *The New York Times Magazine* p54-5 My 14 '89

Sleeping pills. il *The New York Times Magazine* p39-40 F 5 '89

When the world turns. il *The New York Times Magazine* p51-2 Ap 9 '89

D'O'BRIAN, JOSEPH

Roughing it. il *New York* 22:42-7 Jl 24 '89

DOBRIANSKY, PAULA J.

The Baltic States in an era of Soviet reform [address, March 11, 1989] *Department of State Bulletin* 89:35-9 Je '89

Human rights and policy: the American tradition. *Current (Washington, D.C.)* 314:28-37 Jl/Ag '89

DOBSON, JAMES C., 1936-

about

Bundy told Dobson, "It was pornography". *Christianity Today* 33:43 F 17 '89

James Dobson sued by former employees. K. A. Lawton. il pors *Christianity Today* 33:42 F 3 '89

The rising voice of a family crusader. P. Ellis-Simons. il por *U.S. News & World Report* 106:27 F 6 '89

DOBSON, JOHN

about

John Dobson: a man with a mission [interview] S. J. O'Meara. por *Sky and Telescope* 78:530-2 N '89

A salesman for the heavens wants to rope you in. D. Moser. bibl (p174) il pors *Smithsonian* 20:102-6+ Ap '89

DOBSONIAN TELESCOPES *See* Telescopes
DOBYNS, HENRY F.

about

Large numbers, big assumptions. L. Roberts. por *Science* 246:1246 D 8 '89

DOCK WORKERS *See* Longshore workers
DOCKING IN SPACE *See* Orbital rendezvous (Space flight)
DOCKING OF BOATS *See* Boats and boating—Handling
DOCKOMINIUMS *See* Condominiums (Boat docking)
DOCKS, WHARVES, ETC.

See also
Condominiums (Boat docking)
Marinas

The dock side of bassing. N. Ward. il *Outdoor Life* 183:66-7+ Je '89

Grand Cayman (Cayman Islands)

Don't leave the dock [exotic marine life off Cayman Kai dock] F. J. Viola. il *Sea Frontiers* 35:336-41 N/D '89

DOCTOROW, E. L., 1931-

E.L. Doctorow [address, May 21, 1989] il *The Nation* 249:349+ O 2 '89

about

Attentive to mysteries. il por *Time* 133:76 F 27 '89

The audacious lure of evil [interview] A. P. Sanoff. il por *U.S. News & World Report* 106:56 Mr 6 '89

Comedy of errors? [discussion of October 2, 1989 article, 'A gangsterdom of the spirit'] *The Nation* 249:406 O 16 '89

'A gangsterdom of the spirit'. *The Nation* 249:348 O 2 '89

DOCTORS *See* Physicians
DOCTORS, WOMEN *See* Women physicians
DOCTRINAL HERESY *See* Heresy
DOCTRINE, RELIGIOUS *See* Theology
DOCUDRAMAS (TELEVISION) *See* Television broadcasting—Docudramas
DOCUMENT DELIVERY

Pepperoni and paperwork. I. Scherr. il *Byte* 14:309-10+ D '89

DOCUMENTARY MOTION PICTURES *See* Motion pictures—Documentary films
DOCUMENTARY PHOTOGRAPHY *See* Photography, Documentary
DOCUMENTARY TELEVISION PROGRAMS *See* Television broadcasting—Documentary programs
DOCUMENTS

See also
Government publications

DOCUMENTS, HOUSEHOLD *See* Household records
DOD *See* United States. Dept. of Defense
DODANI, MAHESH H., AND OTHERS

Separation of powers. bibl f il *Byte* 14:255-6+ Mr '89

DODD, BARBARA

about

Abortion on trial [cover story; special section; with editorial comment by Kevin Doyle] il pors *Maclean's* 102:2, 14-16+ Jl 31 '89

Bittersweet victory. G. W. Taylor. il por *Maclean's* 102:18 Jl 24 '89

DODD, MEAD & CO.

Authors concerned about Dodd, Mead liquidation. *Publishers Weekly* 235:20 Ja 6 '89

Dodd, Mead operations suspended over arbitration [dispute with authors] C. Reid. *Publishers Weekly* 235:11 Mr 31 '89

DODDS, BILL

Faith lift: how to navigate midlife's mysteries. il *U.S. Catholic* 54:31-5 O '89

DODDS, DARCIE

When mom plays the dating game, do you lose? il *'Teen* 33:68-9 D '89

DODGE, PRYOR

about

Re-cycling the past. E. Siff. il por *Gentlemen's Quarterly* 59:83 O '89

DODGE & COX STOCK FUND

Be stodgy and make money. J. Clements. il *Forbes* 144:154-5 S 4 '89

DODGE FAMILY

about

"Where's Mommy?". C. Latham. il *Forbes* 144 Special Issue:86-8+ O 23 '89

DODGING (PHOTOGRAPHY) *See* Photography—Processing
DODSON, JEROME

about

Clean vs. dirty. R. O'Connor. il *Mother Jones* 14:56-7 Je '89

DODSON, STANLEY I.

Predator-induced reaction norms. bibl f il *BioScience* 39:447-52 Jl/Ag '89

DOE *See* United States. Dept. of Energy
DOE HUNTING *See* Deer hunting
DOELP, ALAN

Emergency treatment! True cases from the files of an extraordinary children's hospital [excerpt from In the blink of an eye] il *Redbook* 172:82-3+ F '89

Race against death [condensed from In the blink of an eye] il *Reader's Digest* 135:221-4+ N '89

DOERFLINGER, THOMAS M.
about
Lessons in the ledgers. J. Willoughby. il por *Forbes* 143:104+ My 15 '89
DOERR, EDD
Abortion: right or wrong? il *USA Today (Periodical)* 117:51-3 Ja '89
Church and state. See issues of The Humanist
DOERR, JOHN
about
Making money the new-fashioned way. E. S. Ely. por *Personal Computing* 13:74 Jl '89
DOG BITES
Tuffy go home! [fending off a threatening dog] D. Halpern. *American Health* 8:102 My '89
DOG FOOD *See* Dogs—Food and feeding
DOG HOUSES *See* Kennels
DOG RACING
See also
Greyhound racing
Sled dog racing
DOG SLEDDING
The 4,000-mile marathon [W. Steger and sled dogs prepare for Antarctic expedition] L. Troiano. il por *American Health* 8:95-7 Jl/Ag '89
At last, the South Pole [W. Steger's expedition] R. Sullivan. il *Sports Illustrated* 71:14 D 18 '89
The iceman cometh [W. Steger plans to cross Antarctica by dogsled and on foot] R. Sullivan. il pors map *Sports Illustrated* 71:40-5+ Jl 31 '89
The last treasure [W. Steger and J.-L. Etienne plan to cross Antarctica by dogsled and on foot] *The New Yorker* 65:27-8 Jl 17 '89
To the South Pole by sled [Trans-Antarctica Expedition] A. Toufexis. il map *Time* 134:73 D 25 '89
DOG STUNTS
Rad dog! Rad dog! When it comes to skateboarding, Sidney the bulldog is a wheelie big star. il *People Weekly* 31:80 Je 12 '89
DOG TRACKS
Economic aspects
The Bear trap [P. W. Bryant, son of late Alabama coach] W. M. Adler. il por *Esquire* 112:204-6+ S '89
Paws [greyhound racing] J. E. Vader. il *Sports Illustrated* 70:46-8+ Je 26 '89
The puppies get plush [greyhound tracks] C. Leerhsen. il *Newsweek* 113:64 Ja 16 '89
DOG TRICKS *See* Dog stunts
DOG WALKING
Walking the dog [services in New York City] C. Hainer. il *New York* 22:75 My 1 '89
DOGGETT, LEROY E., AND SCHAEFER, BRADLEY E.
Results of the July Moonwatch. il map *Sky and Telescope* 77:373+ Ap '89
DOGGETT, RON E.
about
"The chance of a lifetime". P. Duggan. il por *Forbes* 143:140+ Ap 17 '89
DOGMA, CATHOLIC *See* Theology
DOGS
See also
Airedale terriers
Beagles (Dogs)
Boxers (Dogs)
Bulldogs
Golden retrievers
Gordon setters
Great Pyrenees (Dogs)
Guide dogs
Hounds
Hunting dogs
Labrador retrievers
Pit bull terriers
Pointers (Dogs)
Police dogs
Retrievers
Sled dogs
Spaniels
Another dog? G. Hill. il *Field & Stream* 94:11 S '89
Cheryl Tevis: family [farm dogs] C. Tevis. il *Successful Farming* 87:53 S '89
Choosing the right puppy. S. L. Gerstenfeld. il *Parents* 64:244 Je '89
Dog hide-and-seek [word search puzzle] il *National Geographic World* 171:10-11 N '89
The little dog nobody wanted [excerpt from The market square dog] J. Herriot. il *Good Housekeeping* 209:112+ D '89
Picking the perfect pooch. B. Devine. il *Better Homes and Gardens* 67:169-70 Mr '89
A shaggy dog story. D. Petersen. il *The Mother Earth News* 115:37-8+ Ja/F '89
Woman's best friend [excerpts from Dogs and their women] B. E. Cohen and L. Taylor. il *Good Housekeeping* 208:106 Mr '89
Care
See also
Dog walking

The aging pet. R. Kidd. *The Mother Earth News* 118:34-6 Jl/Ag '89
Care for pregnant dogs. M. W. Fox. il *McCall's* 117:158 O '89
Exercising your cat and dog. S. L. Gerstenfeld. il *Parents* 64:202 F '89
Diseases and pests
See also
Rabies
Brain fire [epilepsy] D. Calkins. il *American Health* 8:122+ Mr '89
Hip dysplasia. R. Kidd. il *The Mother Earth News* 116:42+ Mr/Ap '89
Equipment
Behind the Invisible Fence [electronic boundary for dogs] L. Jenson. il *Home Mechanix* 85:52-3 Ag '89
Food and feeding
'Frosty Paws' ice cream can teach an old dog new licks [developed by W. Tyznik] il *People Weekly* 31:132-3 Je 5 '89
The pet food dilemma. G. Hoeppner. il *The Saturday Evening Post* 261:26+ O '89
Quaker Oats' pet peeve [Gaines dog food line slips] L. Therrien. *Business Week* p32-3 Jl 31 '89
Kennels
See Kennels
Photographs and photography
Best friends [excerpt] P. Rattazzi. il *Good Housekeeping* 209:48 Ag '89
Candid canines. il *Seventeen* 48:96 Je '89
Training
Behind the Invisible Fence [electronic boundary for dogs] L. Jenson. il *Home Mechanix* 85:72-3 Ag '89
For women only. J. S. Shadlich. il *Ladies' Home Journal* 106:198 D '89
Vision
See Vision—Animals
DOGS, EFFECT OF TEMPERATURE ON
Hot car caveat [views of Michael Garvey] M. Behen. *American Health* 8:118 Je '89
DOGS, WILD
See also
African hunting dogs
DOGS AND THE HANDICAPPED *See* Handicapped and animals
DOGS IN ART
Design unleashed [dog motifs on fabric] E. A. Berthold. il *House & Garden* 161:200 N '89
Goin' to the dogs [crafts projects] J. Williams and J. Severson. il *Better Homes and Gardens* 67:75-8+ Ag '89
A stamp for Staehle. M. G. Stoddard. il por *The Saturday Evening Post* 261:28 Ap '89
DOGS IN CRIME PREVENTION
See also
Project Safe Run
DOGS IN MOTION PICTURES
Get used to it, Cybill—there's a new Shepherd in Hollywood [Rando, dog in film K-9] M. Neill. il *People Weekly* 31:121-2 My 22 '89
DOGS IN NARCOTICS REGULATION
Searching and researching [use of sniffer dogs in detecting suspicious student automobiles in Joshua, Tex.] P. A. Zirkel. bibl f *Phi Delta Kappan* 71:330-2 D '89
DOGS IN POLICE WORK *See* Police dogs
DOGWOOD
Dogwoods from scratch. il *Southern Living* 24:59 S '89
Diseases and pests
Dogwood's day [anthracnose fungus] B. Pleasant. il *Organic Gardening* 36:34-8 Jl/Ag '89
Dogwoods fight fungus; fungus wins [research by Frank S. Santamour] *Science News* 135:110 F 18 '89
DOHENY, KATHLEEN
House calls—or bad calls? il *Modern Maturity* 32:92-4 D '89/Ja '90
DOHERTY, BILL
Human race. *The New Republic* 200:12+ My 1 '89
DOHERTY, DENNIS J.
An ethical approach to cryonics. *USA Today (Periodical)* 117:73-4 Ja '89
DOHERTY, JIM
A barn is more than a building, it is a shrine to our agrarian past [cover story] il *Smithsonian* 20:30-43 Ag '89
DOHERTY, JOE
about
The bloody war in Belfast spills into the U.S. courts. T. Clifton. il por *Newsweek* 114:96+ D 11 '89
DOHNANYI, CHRISTOPH VON
about
Festive spirits. P. G. Davis. il por *New York* 22:73-4 F 13 '89
DOI, TAKAKO, 1928-
about
A pinball empire greased by graft? il por *U.S. News & World Report* 107:18 O 30 '89
Sex, taxes and 'the Madonna factor'. J. Impoco. il por *U.S. News & World Report* 107:36 Ag 7 '89
Takako Doi: an unmarried woman. *Time* 134:26 Ag 7 '89

DOI, TAKAKO, 1928----about—*cont.*

Upset in Japan. H. Jensen. il pors *Maclean's* 102:22-3 Ag 7 '89

DOIG, DAVID

The man who found Christmas [story] il *Good Housekeeping* 209:54+ D '89

DÖINGHAUS, ULI SCHULTE- *See* Schulte-Döinghaus, Uli

DOINO, WILLIAM, JR.

The Vatican and the Kremlin: full circle. *National Review* 41:30 Je 30 '89

DOKES, MICHAEL

about

You're next, Tyson. P. Putnam. il pors *Sports Illustrated* 70:34-5 Mr 20 '89

DOKOUPIL, GEORG JIŘI, 1954-

about

Jiri Georg Dokoupil: Robert Miller. L. Holst. il *Art News* 88:159 D '89

DOLAN, ANTHONY R.

Reagan revisited. por *National Review* 41:45+ N 24 '89

DOLAN, BEVERLY FRANKLIN

about

Being a conglomerate is not all bad. H. Banks. il por *Forbes* 144:40-1 D 11 '89

DOLAN, CHARLES F.

about

A cable mogul's daring dance on the high wire. D. Lieberman. il por *Business Week* p133-4+ Je 5 '89

Can a maverick run a giant? C. Reece. il por *Channels (New York, N.Y.: 1986)* 9:49-50+ Je '89

DOLBY NOISE REDUCTION SYSTEM

Are you ready for Dolby S? R. Long. il *High Fidelity (New York, N.Y.)* 39:16 Jl '89

Dolby S. K. C. Pohlmann. *Stereo Review* 54:20 Ag '89

HX-Pro: a "new" and improved cassette-deck circuit. L. Klein. il *Radio-Electronics* 60:84-5 Mr '89

New Dolby system? D. Ranada. *High Fidelity (New York, N.Y.)* 39:13 F '89

Revisiting a rubber ruler. R. Long. il *High Fidelity (New York, N.Y.)* 39:15 Je '89

Save that Studer, continued [Dolby SR] R. Hodges. il *Stereo Review* 54:176 F '89

DOLD, GAYLORD

about

An honored tradition: the bookstore as publisher. J. Barbato. *Publishers Weekly* 236:431 Ag 11 '89

DOLE, ELIZABETH HANFORD, 1936-

about

As labor and Dole warm up, business is feeling a chill. S. B. Garland. il *Business Week* p35 Mr 6 '89

DOLENGA, JULIE

The Civic Achievement Award Program. *The Education Digest* 55:47-9 O '89

DOLENZ, AMI

about

Ami Dolenz. il pors *Seventeen* 48:46 F '89

Raised on Monkee business, Micky Dolenz's daughter Ami takes her swing at film acting. J. Kaufman. il pors *People Weekly* 31:59-60 My 1 '89

DOLENZ, MICKY

about

Raised on Monkee business, Micky Dolenz's daughter Ami takes her swing at film acting. J. Kaufman. il pors *People Weekly* 31:59-60 My 1 '89

DOLL HOUSES

A very different dollhouse. il *The Mother Earth News* 120:68-71 N/D '89

DOLLAR *See* Money

DOLLAR BRAND *See* Abdullah Ibrahim

DOLLAR COINS *See* Coins

DOLLAR COST AVERAGING *See* Investment trusts—Dollar cost averaging

DOLLAR DEVALUATION *See* Money

DOLLHOUSES *See* Doll houses

DOLLS

See also

Barbie dolls

G.I. Joe dolls

GI Joe dolls

Kewpie dolls

Mommy dolls

Oopsie-Daisy dolls

Paper dolls

Is this kid for real? Artist Anne Mitrani's dolls can fool you even in the, er, flesh. G. Oliver. il por *People Weekly* 32:157-9 N 27 '89

The last doll [baby dolls] E. Berg. il *Parents* 64:126-8 Je '89

Collectors and collecting

The doll in the doll in the doll in the doll [nesting dolls] L. Rosenkrantz. *Antiques & Collecting Hobbies* 94:58 O '89

Dolls of the East. M. Jailer. il *Antiques & Collecting Hobbies* 94:39+ Mr '89

Happy birthday, Shirley! [S. Temple Black's collection] M. Forrest. il pors *Antiques & Collecting Hobbies* 94:30-2 Ap '89

Jumeau: maker of beautiful dolls. M. Jailer. il *Antiques & Collecting Hobbies* 94:36-8 N '89

Made in the U.S.A. [L. Greiner's dolls] M. Jailer. il *Antiques & Collecting Hobbies* 94:36-7 Jl '89

DOLNICK, EDWARD

Panda paradox. il map *Discover* 10:70-4+ S '89

DOLPHINS

See also

Killer whales

Close encounters of the dolphin kind. G. DeGeorge. il *Business Week* p101 Ap 10 '89

The day of the dolphins. J. Kaplan. il *Omni (New York, N.Y.)* 11:42-4+ Je '89

Dolphins [diver aids wounded baby dolphin] W. Grover. il *Sea Frontiers* 35:28-30 Ja/F '89

Incident at Ossabaw [boaters witness bottlenose dolphin giving birth to stillborn calf] N. McIntosh. il *Reader's Digest* 135:112-14 N '89

The joys of a big brain [social behavior of dolphins] W. Booth. il *Psychology Today* 23:57 Ap '89

Secrets of a high society [social behavior of bottlenose dolphins; cover story] R. S. Wells. il por *National Wildlife* 27:38-44 Ag/S '89

Taking the plunge with Flipper. il *Travel Holiday* 172:82-3 Jl '89

Mortality

The destruction of dolphins [trapped in tuna nets; cover story] K. Brower. il *The Atlantic* 264:35-8+ Jl '89

Why the dolphins died [effects of red tide] S. Hersh. il *Sea Frontiers* 35:246-7 Jl/Ag '89

Photographs and photography

Dolphins: your most willing and joyous subjects ever! [work of D. McCulloch] F. Cameron. il por *Petersen's Photographic Magazine* 18:32-4 O '89

Training

Conversations with the dolphins [work of L. M. Herman] S. Chollar. il pors *Psychology Today* 23:52-6 Ap '89

Interview: Louis Herman [dolphin communication] J. Kaplan. il pors *Omni (New York, N.Y.)* 11:76-8+ Je '89

These guards just love fish [dolphins used by Navy] E. Linden. il *Time* 133:77 Ap 24 '89

Treatment

Flipper's ex-trainer wants his favorite mammals free to swim with the fishes [R. O'Barry wants swim centers closed] B. Hewitt. il por *People Weekly* 32:40-1 S 4 '89

An uneasy dip with the dolphins [objections to swim-with-the-dolphins programs] E. Linden. il *Time* 134:80-1 N 27 '89

DOLPHINS, FOSSIL

Whales, dolphins, porpoises. il *Earth Science* 42:20-3 Summ '89

DOLPHINS IN TELEVISION

Anecdotes, facetiae, satire, etc.

Last word [Flipper] T. Runté. il *Omni (New York, N.Y.)* 11:132 F '89

DOMAN INDUSTRIES LTD.

The Crown's case [former B.C. premier W. Bennett goes on trial in insider trading case] H. Quinn. il por *Maclean's* 102:36-7 My 1 '89

A victory for Bennett [former B.C. premier and codefendants acquitted of insider trading charges] J. DeMont. il por *Maclean's* 102:28-9 My 22 '89

DOME STADIUMS *See* Stadiums

DOMES

See also

Geodesic domes

Geotangent domes

The domes of Paris. C. Marriott. il map *Gourmet* 49:52-9+ Jl '89

DOMES (GEOLOGY)

See also

Salt domes

DOMESTIC ANIMALS

See also

Cats

Dogs

Horses

Pets

DOMESTIC APPLIANCES *See* Household appliances

DOMESTIC ARCHITECTURE *See* Architecture, Domestic

DOMESTIC ECONOMY *See* Home economics

DOMESTIC EMPLOYEES *See* Household employees

DOMESTIC FINANCE *See* Finance, Personal

DOMESTIC PHOTOGRAPHY

Inspired seeing is rekindled in this domestic self-assignment. F. Patterson. il *Petersen's Photographic Magazine* 18:22-3 Jl '89

DOMESTIC QUARRELS *See* Quarrels

DOMESTIC RELATIONS

See also

Divorce

Family

Marriage

Marriage counseling

Married couples

Support (Domestic relations)

Unmarried couples

Wife abuse

DOMESTIC VIOLENCE *See* Family violence
DOMESTICATION
The accidental conqueror [importance of animal and plant domestication in the European colonization of the New World] J. M. Diamond. il *Discover* 10:70-6 D '89
The ancient contract [evidence suggesting domestication of animals was a result of coevolution; cover story] S. Budiansky. il *U.S. News & World Report* 106:74-9 Mr 20 '89
DOMICILE IN PUBLIC WELFARE
Welfare migrants: getting a cold shoulder in Wisconsin. J. N. Baker. il *Newsweek* 114:23 Ag 14 '89
DOMICILE IN TAXATION
Neighbors, not friends [tax feud between Maine and New Hampshire] M. Starr. il *Newsweek* 113:28 Je 5 '89
Rules for the relocation-minded. B. Hager. il *Money* 18:132 Ag '89
DOMINANCE, LATERAL *See* Laterality
DOMINANCE IN ANIMALS *See* Animals—Habits and behavior
DOMINGO, PLACIDO
about
Placido. il por *Life* 12:72-3 O '89
DOMINICA
Description and travel
Dominica: the wild isle. A. Weller. il *Vogue* 179:310+ N '89
DOMINICAN REPUBLIC
See also
Baseball—Dominican Republic
San Pedro de Macoris (Dominican Republic)
Politics and government
In the land of the blind caudillo. M. Kurlansky. il pors *The New York Times Magazine* p24-6+ Ag 6 '89
DOMINICANS (RELIGIOUS ORDER)
Savonarola—preacher and patriot? D. Weinstein. bibl il por *History Today* 39:30-6 N '89
DOMINION TEXTILE INC.
Spreading the net widely [Dominion Textile and Telenet Communications map strategy for U.S.-Canada free trade agreement] J. DeMont. il *Maclean's* 102:76-7 Jl 3 '89
DOMINO'S PIZZA INC.
Domino's [after-school job at Domino's Pizza in Ann Arbor, Mich.] *The New Yorker* 65:37 Mr 27 '89
Domino's delivery pledge: danger to go? [traffic accidents while delivering pizza] il *Newsweek* 114:32 Jl 10 '89
Just say no: boycotts at the barricades [prochoice boycott of Domino's Pizza and prolife boycott of Maxwell House coffee] *Newsweek* 114:21 Ag 14 '89
Pie in the sky [president T. Monaghan's devotion to running] K. Shyne. il pors *Runner's World* 24:34-6 N '89
Tom Monaghan. P. Alson and J. Greenwalt. il pors *People Weekly* 32:102-3+ S 25 '89
Tom Monaghan kneads the dough. E. Stern. il pors *Gentlemen's Quarterly* 59:136-41+ Jl '89
Why the pizza king may abdicate the throne [T. Monaghan] W. Zellner. il por *Business Week* p46 S 25 '89
Youth Opportunity: a private sector investment in prevention [summer work at Domino's Pizza Inc.'s Whatley Farm in Ann Arbor, Mich.] C. H. Tice. il *Children Today* 18:20-3 Mr/Ap '89
DOMNARSKI, WILLIAM
The country lawyer remembered. *The American Scholar* 58:283-8 Spr '89
DON CARLOS [opera] *See* Verdi, Giuseppe, 1813-1901
DON GIOVANNI [opera] *See* Mozart, Wolfgang Amadeus, 1756-1791
DON QUIXOTE (FICTIONAL CHARACTER) IN ART
Exhibitions
Izhar Patkin at Holly Solomon. N. Princenthal. il *Art in America* 77:169-70 D '89
DON QUIXOTE [ballet] *See* Ballet reviews—Single works
DONAHUE, ELINOR
about
After Father knows best, it was drugs, jail, depression. M. Littwin. il pors *TV Guide* 37:6-8 Je 17-23 '89
DONAHUE, HUGH CARTER
Choosing the TV of the future. il *Technology Review* 92:30-4+ Ap '89
DONAHUE, RICHARD
'Dear Scrooge . .'. il *Publishers Weekly* 236:34-7 O 27 '89
Frightening books for a frightful holiday. il *Publishers Weekly* 236:36 S 29 '89
DONAHUE, THOMAS R.
Worker dignity on the job [address, March 3, 1989] *Vital Speeches of the Day* 55:423-6 My 1 '89
DONALD, BEULAH MAE
about
Woman awarded $7 million against KKK dies without will; daughters administer. pors *Jet* 76:12 Ap 24 '89
DONALD, JOHN A.
(jt. auth) *See* Lillywhite, Harvey B., and Donald, John A.
DONALD, MARK
The natural. il *Gentlemen's Quarterly* 59:151+ My '89
DONALD, MICHAEL
about
Woman awarded $7 million against KKK dies without will; daughters administer. pors *Jet* 76:12 Ap 24 '89

DONALD I. FINE, INC.
The irrepressible Don Fine. R. A. Carter. il por *Publishers Weekly* 236:16+ D 1 '89
DONALD T. STERLING CORPORATION
Poor little rich man [D. T. Sterling] D. Wechsler. il por *Forbes* 144:196+ N 27 '89
DONALDSON, JOAN
about
A committed news junkie. R. Corelli. il por *Maclean's* 102:36 Ag 7 '89
DONALDSON, ROGER
about
Cocktail [film] Reviews
Video il 13:61 Je '89. J. Young
DONALDSON, SAM
Loud and clear (as ever) . . . Sam Donaldson's parting shot: how TV can cover the White House a whole lot better. il pors *TV Guide* 37:36-8 Ja 28-F 3 '89
about
Let's go to the videotape. E. Diamond. il por *New York* 22:24+ D 4 '89
On the roller coaster with Diane and Sam. E. Diamond. pors *New York* 22:10-12 Jl 24 '89
DONATI, ENRICO, 1909-
about
Enrico Donati: Manhattan transfer. C. Ratcliff. bibl f il pors *Art in America* 77:174-81 My '89
DONATION OF ORGANS, TISSUES, ETC.
Death-row murderers could be lifesavers [proposal by J. Kevorkian to harvest organs from executed prisoners] *Newsweek* 113:49 Ja 9 '89
Desperate measures. B. D. Colen. il *Health (New York, N.Y.)* 21:84-5 Ap '89
A family's legacy. L. Rivers. *Reader's Digest* 134:159-60 Mr '89
Marrow donors: reaching beyond family [chronic myelogenous leukemia] R. Weiss. *Science News* 135:348 Je 3 '89
So many patients, so few donors. J. Rothfeder. *Business Week* p94-5 Ag 28 '89
There just aren't 'enough hearts to go around'. J. Carey. il *Business Week* p94+ N 27 '89
Transplants in demand. J. Rothfeder. il *The Saturday Evening Post* 261:12-13 N/D '89
Laws and regulations
Whose spleen is it? D. Andrews. il por *Technology Review* 92:14 N/D '89
DONAVEL, DAVID F.
Needles and pins. il *Sea Frontiers* 35:18-25 Ja/F '89
DONDERS, JOSEPH G.
about
Good news from missionaries: God was already there [interview] por *U.S. Catholic* 54:26-33 Ja '89
DONEGAN, FRANK
In the marketplace. See issues of Americana
about
Note from the editor. S. Wilmot. il por *Americana* 17:2 S/O '89
DONELIAN, ARMEN
about
Armen Donelian. L. Birnbaum. il por *Down Beat* 56:51-2 Ag '89
DONELSON, TOM
(jt. auth) *See* Nadler, Richard, and Donelson, Tom
DONEN, STANLEY
about
Singin' in the rain [film] Reviews
Video il 12:63-4 Mr '89. M. Fleischmann
DONER, COLONEL V., 1948-
about
A crusader's regrets. R. Digitale. por *Christianity Today* 33:39 F 17 '89
DONETSK BALLET
The customs of the country [performances at City Center] T. Tobias. il *New York* 22:81-2 Mr 13 '89
Reviews:
Performances in Baltimore. G. Jackson. *Dance Magazine* 63:60-1 Je '89
Stranded Soviets pull tour out of a capitalist hat. il *Dance Magazine* 63:20 My '89
DÖNHOFF, MARION, GRÄFIN, 1909-
Seize the day. *World Press Review* 36:64 F '89
DONIZETTI, GAETANO, 1797-1848
about
L'elisir d'amore [opera] Reviews
Opera News il 53:24-7 Ap 15 '89
Opera News il 53:28-9 Ap 15 '89. F. Merkling
Lucia di Lammermoor [opera] Reviews
Opera News il 53:24-7 F 18 '89
Opera News il 53:8-11+ F 18 '89. J. Kestner
Maria Stuarda [opera] Reviews
The New Yorker 65:117-18 N 13 '89. A. Porter
Rita [opera] Reviews
The New Yorker 65:118-19 Ap 17 '89. A. Porter
DONKEYS
See also
Mules

DONKEYS—*cont.*

Anecdotes, facetiae, satire, etc.

Charly's loss, Bardot's gain [actress orders castration of neighbor's donkey] A. Fotheringham. il *Maclean's* 102:56 Ag 7 '89

DONLOE, DARLENE

Living with the spirit and legacy of John Coltrane. il pors *Ebony* 44:46+ Mr '89

DONLOU, JOHN

about

Injured in a climbing accident, a doctor tests his will in the mountains again. D. Chu. il pors *People Weekly* 31:93-4+ Mr 20 '89

DONNA KARAN COMPANY

Prima Donna. S. Mansfield. il pors *Vogue* 179:290-7+ Ag '89

Turning rags into riches. N. Darnton. il por *Newsweek* 113:84 Ap 24 '89

DONNE, JOHN, 1572-1631

about

A wrestling match with the Almighty. P. Yancey. il *Christianity Today* 33:22-6 S 8 '89

DONNELLY, DOROTHY

The face of God. *America* 160:212 Mr 11 '89

DONNER, HANS

about

New dimensions in creativity [cover story] G. Smith. il por *Américas* 41 no1:24-31 '89

DONNER, RICHARD

about

Lethal weapon 2 [film] Reviews
Commonweal 116:530 O 6 '89. P. D. Baumann
Newsweek il 114:53 Jl 17 '89. D. Ansen
People Weekly il 32:12 Jl 24 '89. R. Novak
Time il 134:53 Jl 24 '89. R. Corliss
Scrooged [film] Reviews
Video il 13:89 D '89. R. Gehr

DONNEY, GENE

about

A new tune. il por *Forbes* 144:287 N 27 '89

DONOGHUE, DENIS

Haggling presences. il *The New York Review of Books* 36:39-43 S 28 '89

The strange case of Paul de Man. il *The New York Review of Books* 36:32-7 Je 29 '89

DONOGHUE, WILLIAM E.

about

Don't worry about interest rates [interview] E. Schultz. il por *Fortune* 119:46+ Je 5 '89

DONOHUE, JOHN J.

An inside view of Lebanon. *America* 161:378-81 N 25 '89

DONOHUE, JOHN W.

Those were the days. il *America* 161:258-61 O 21 '89

DONOHUE, THOMAS J.

The congestion-pollution connection [address, July 7, 1989] *Vital Speeches of the Day* 55:763-6 O 1 '89

DONORS, ORGAN *See* Donation of organs, tissues, etc.

DONORS, SPERM *See* Artificial insemination, Human

DONOVAN, CARRIE

Fashion. See occasional issues of The New York Times Magazine

DONOVAN, CHRISTINE S.

about

Get ready for life after motherhood. il por *Nation's Business* 77:52 O '89

DONOVAN, HEDLEY

Managing your intellectuals [excerpt from Right places, right times] il pors *Fortune* 120:177-8+ O 23 '89

DONOVAN, MARY ELLEN

Shame: the secret emotion. *Ladies' Home Journal* 106:70+ My '89

DONOVAN, PRISCILLA

(jt. auth) See Wonder, Jacquelyn, and Donovan, Priscilla

DONOVAN & GREEN

Logic plus magic [office of designer N. Green] L. Rosch. il por *Working Woman* 14:142-4 N '89

DON'T WORRY 'BOUT ME (SONG)

Don't worry 'bout me [sung by B. Holiday] J. Berendt. por *Esquire* 112:50 O '89

DOOBIE BROTHERS (MUSICAL GROUP)

Relighting the Doobies. J. Ressner. *Rolling Stone* p20 Je 1 '89

DOODLES

Breaking the code of doodles. J. Torrey. il *Omni (New York, N.Y.)* 11:64-6+ Ap '89

DOODY, ALISON

about

Doody calls: life as Indiana Jones's girlfriend. S. Edelson. por *Mademoiselle* 95:54 Je '89

For Alison Doody in Indiana Jones, the price of stardom was a swim through fire and rats. J. Kaufman. il pors *People Weekly* 31:66-7 Je 26 '89

Paris: inside couture. il pors *Harper's Bazaar* 122:151-61 Ap '89

DOOGIE HOWSER, M.D. [television program] See Television program reviews—Single works

DOOLEY, DAVID

Applying colored pencil over an acrylic wash. il *American Artist* 53:66-9 D '89

DOOLEY, SUSAN

Popping your cork. il *Harper's Bazaar* 122:36+ Ja '89
Spirit of '89. il *Harper's Bazaar* 122:230+ Mr '89
Vintage celebrations. il *Harper's Bazaar* 122:131+ Je '89

DOOMSDAY See End of the world; Judgment Day

DOONESBURY (COMIC STRIP)

Doonesbury comes home to Andrews & McMeel [G. Trudeau] por *Publishers Weekly* 235:61 Ja 13 '89

Smoke signals [Doonesbury mocks cigarette ads that entice teens to smoke] P. Theiler. il *Common Cause Magazine* 15:8 S/O '89

DOOR COUNTY (WIS.)

Description and travel

All-weather Door County. W. Mueller. il *The Saturday Evening Post* 261:82-3 O '89

DOOR PORTERS See Dummy board figures

DOORKNOBS, PULLS, ETC.

Making hardware choices. il *Southern Living* 24:140-1 My '89

DOORS

See also

Airplanes, Jet—Doors
Automobiles—Doors
Garage doors
Revolving doors

Dress-up details [special section] K. Collier. il *The Family Handyman* 39:30-7 Ja '89

How to install French doors [cover story] D. Johnson. il *The Family Handyman* 39:28-33 Je '89

Install your own bifold doors. K. Childers and D. Stoffel. il *The Family Handyman* 39:49-50+ O '89

Making an entrance. D. B. Cowin. il *House & Garden* 161:160+ Je '89

Product reports 1990. il *Architectural Record* 177:85-9+ D '89

Splashes belong inside the tub [Kinkead Showerfold] J. Wicks. il *Workbench* 45:34-5 Mr/Ap '89

Working with oversized fixtures [showers] il *Popular Mechanics* 166:112-13 Ap '89

Maintenance and repair

Drafty doors [weatherstripping] J. Barrett. il *Home Mechanix* 85:18-19 N '89

Restore a cracked door jamb. il *The Family Handyman* 39:44+ S '89

Warm-weather door problem. il *The Family Handyman* 39:12 Ap '89

DOORS, MECHANICALLY OPERATED

See also

Garage doors—Control

DOORWAYS

Energy-efficient entry: add-on brings welcoming bonus. il *Better Homes and Gardens* 67:118 My '89

DOPAMINE

The search for cocaine's methadone [link to dopamine pathways in the brain] D. Hurley. il *Psychology Today* 23:59-60 Jl/Ag '89

DOPAMINE RECEPTORS See Chemoreceptors

DOPAMINERGIC NEURONS See Nerve cells

DOPE TRADE See Narcotics trade

DOPP, SUSAN MARIE

about

Susan Marie Dopp at the San Francisco MOMA. D. L. Strauss. il *Art in America* 77:185 Je '89

DOPPLER EFFECT

The radial-velocity revolution. R. Griffin. il *Sky and Telescope* 78:263+ S '89

DOPPLER RADAR IN METEOROLOGY See Radar meteorology

DORAN, DIANE

about

The gorillas in the mist have a new champion: Diane Doran. B. Johnson. il pors *People Weekly* 32:151-2 D 4 '89

DORCHESTER (SHIP)

Legend of the four chaplains [courage displayed by Lieutenants Fox, Goode, Poling, and Washington during sinking in World War II] L. Elliott. il *Reader's Digest* 134:65-70 Je '89

DORDEVIC, DEAN M.

(jt. auth) See Masi, Thomas A., and Dordevic, Dean M.

DORDRECHTS MUSEUM (NETHERLANDS)

Dutch disaster [vandalism of paintings] M. K. Talley, Jr. il *Art News* 88:60-1 Summ '89

DORFMAN, ARIEL

Adiós, General: saying good-bye to Pinochet. il *Harper's* 279:72-6 D '89

DORFMAN, DAN

about

America's no. 1 tipster. J. Egan. il por *U.S. News & World Report* 107:59-60 Ag 21 '89

The little guy's little guy. J. Nocera. il *Esquire* 112:109+ S '89

DORFMAN, ELSA, 1937-

about

Indecent exposure? C. Giuliano. il pors *Art News* 88:31 F '89

DORIN, JULIA R., AND OTHERS
Selection for precise chromosomal targeting of a dominant marker by homologous recombination. bibl f il *Science* 243:1357-60 Mr 10 '89

DORITY, BARBARA
Feminist moralism, "pornography", and censorship. il *The Humanist* 49:8-9+ N/D '89

DORMANCY (BIOLOGY)
See also
Diapause

DORMEN, LESLEY
The agony and the ecstasy of first dates. il *Seventeen* 48:258-9+ Mr '89
Can you trust each other? il *Glamour* 87:236-7+ N '89
Is your relationship going anywhere? il *Glamour* 87:252-5+ Mr '89
Sexual lies: his and yours. il *Glamour* 87:262-3+ O '89
Will there be bad fairies at your wedding? il *Glamour* 87:236-7+ Je '89

DORMEN, LESLEY, AND EDIDIN, PETER
Original spin. il *Psychology Today* 23:46-50+ Jl/Ag '89

DORMERS
Doing dormers right. il *Southern Living* 24:110+ F '89

DORMITORIES
In love with the boy next dorm [college students] C. Parkhurst. il *Seventeen* 48:199 S '89
School ways [special section] C. Pearson. il *Architectural Record* 177:108-21 O '89
Up against the wall [swimsuit photos on dorm walls] B. Newman. il *Sports Illustrated* 70 Special Issue:222+ F '89

DORN, CHARLES M.
The Florida state initial teacher certification test: a case study. bibl f *Design for Arts in Education* 90:37-42 Mr/Ap '89

DORNAN, ROBERT K., 1933-
The future of communism. il *Conservative Digest* 15:12-15 S/O '89

D'ORNANO, HUBERT *See* Ornano, Hubert d'
D'ORNANO, ISABELLE *See* Ornano, Isabelle d'

DORNBERG, JOHN
Chancellor Kohl on "heirless" art [discussion of September 1988 article, The mounting embarrassment of Germany's Nazi treasures] il por *Art News* 88:17 Summ '89
The powerful and playful forms of Magdalena Jetelova. bibl (p164) il pors *Smithsonian* 20:106-12+ My '89

DORNEY, ROBERT C.
To sell in Japan, meet the Japanese. il *Nation's Business* 77:10 F '89

DORNHELM, ROBERT
about
Cold feet [film] Reviews
People Weekly il 31:13 Je 19 '89. R. Novak

DORNIER GMBH
Dornier, Aeritalia to use twin-engine design for advanced amphibian concept. il *Aviation Week & Space Technology* 130:64 Je 19 '89
Dornier freezes DO. 328 design; joint certification effort planned [regional turboprop transport] il *Aviation Week & Space Technology* 131:36 Jl 3 '89
Dornier Seastar begins certification tests of CD. 2 amphibious aircraft. K. F. Mordoff. il *Aviation Week & Space Technology* 129:31 Mr 6 '89

DORRANCE, JOHN T., JR.
about
'Deathwatch' investments. D. Pauly. il por *Newsweek* 113:62 Ap 24 '89
From soup to sèvres. S. Greenspan. il *House & Garden* 161:244+ O '89

DORRIS, MICHAEL
The broken cord [excerpt] il *Ladies' Home Journal* 106:104+ Ag '89
Rite of passage. il *Parents* 64:246+ Je '89
Severing the cord [excerpt from The broken cord] il *Mother Jones* 14:47-8 S '89
about
Pregnancy + alcohol = problems. C. Leerhsen. il por *Newsweek* 114:57 Jl 31 '89
PW interviews. D. Brainard. por *Publishers Weekly* 236:73-4 Ag 4 '89

DORROS, KAREN, AND DORSEY, PATRICIA
Whose rights are we protecting, anyway? [with discussion] il *Children Today* 18:6-11+ My/Je '89

DORSET, JOHN FREDERICK SACKVILLE, 3RD DUKE OF, 1745-1799
about
Carry on cricket: the Duke of Dorset's 1789 tour [cover story] J. Goulstone and M. J. Swanton. bibl il *History Today* 39:18-23 Ag '89

DORSETT, LYLE W.
Unscrambling the C. S. Lewis 'hoax'. *The Christian Century* 106:208-9 F 22 '89

DORSETT, TONY
My wars with teammates, Dallas—and myself [excerpt from Running tough] il pors *TV Guide* 37:14-17 Ag 19-25 '89

DORSEY, GAIL ANN
about
Star quality. M. Southgate. por *Essence* 20:29 Ag '89

DORSEY, PATRICIA
(jt. auth) See Dorros, Karen, and Dorsey, Patricia

DORWART, NANCY
about
Garden swap party. C. A. Rossell. il pors *Organic Gardening* 36:34-7 O '89

DOS OPERATING SYSTEMS
See also
MS-DOS operating system
PC DOS operating system
DOS at RISC. C. B. Hunter and J. Banning. il *Byte* 14:361-2+ N '89
Handy DOS commands give directory assistance. T. Roberts. *Compute!* 11:82 N '89
If memory serves . . . [memory management routines] R. Grehan. il *Byte* 14:279-80+ Ag '89
LAN-aware DOS programs. B. Nance. il *Byte* 14:227-8+ S '89
Looking beyond the DOS prompt. S. Miastkowski. il *Byte* 14 Special Issue:105-6+ Fall '89
Multitasking with DOS now [Desqview 386] M. Antonoff. il *Personal Computing* 13:192 S '89
Stretching DOS to the limit [Virtual Control Program Interface] F. Hayes. il *Byte* 14 Special Issue:79-80+ Fall '89
Swapping DOS to Mac the convenient way [DOS Mounter] D. Barker. il *Byte* 14:84+ O '89
Unix tools for DOS. C. Herring. *Byte* 14:318-19 S '89

DOS SANTOS, JOSÉ EDUARDO *See* Santos, José Eduardo dos, 1942-

DOSAGE FORMS OF DRUGS *See* Drugs—Dosage forms
DOSAGE OF DRUGS *See* Drugs—Dosage

DOSS, BOB
about
Making a fast break out of the ghetto. J. Tabor. il pors *Time* 133:14-15+ F 6 '89

DOT *See* United States. Dept. of Transportation

DOT MATRIX PRINTERS
24-pin dot-matrix printers [special section] il *Home Office Computing* 7:56-60 F '89
Adequate 24-pin output for a low price [Panasonic KX-P1124] R. Bel Bruno. il *Personal Computing* 13:216+ Mr '89
An affordable printer with a bundle of fonts [Star Micronics XB-2410 multi-font] H. F. Beechhold. il *Home Office Computing* 7:78+ N '89
Brother's M-2518: practical paper handling. T. Hazen. il *Home Office Computing* 7:64-5 Ap '89
Epson's medium-carriage alternative [Epson LQ950] R. Bel Bruno. il *Personal Computing* 13:232+ Ja '89
IBM's Proprinter: a modest upgrade [XL24E] R. Bel Bruno. il *Personal Computing* 13:188 Je '89
Inexpensive, high-decibel printing [Epson LQ510] R. Bel Bruno. il *Personal Computing* 13:184 N '89
Multiple fonts and options [Star NX-2400 multi-font] R. Bel Bruno. il *Personal Computing* 13:198+ F '89
Near-laser quality for about $500 [Star Micronics NX-2400 Multi-Font] C. Bermant. il *Home Office Computing* 7:71 My '89

DOTSON, GARY
about
Jailed for a rape that never happened, Gary Dotson has his name cleared at last. M. Brower. il pors *People Weekly* 32:80-1 Ag 28 '89

D'OTTAVIO, TONY
She goes round in circles. il por *American Health* 8:86 My '89

DOTY, ROY, 1922-
Wordless workshop. See issues of Popular Science

DOUB, JACK
The little yellow airplane. il *Reader's Digest* 135:197-8+ O '89

DOUBILET, DAVID
Ballet with stingrays. il map *National Geographic* 175:84-95 Ja '89
New Zealand's magic waters. il map *National Geographic* 176:506-29 O '89

DOUBLE BASS MUSIC
See also
Phonograph records—Double bass music

DOUBLE BASS PLAYERS
See also
Altena, Maarten
Carter, Ron, 1937-
Friesen, David
Holland, Dave
McBride, Christian
Mingus, Charles, 1922-1979
Moore, Michael
Robinson, Richard
Sharpe, Avery

DOUBLE-BETA DECAY
Double-beta decay. M. K. Moe and S. P. Rosen. bibl il *Scientific American* 261:48-52+ N '89

DOUBLE INCOME, NO KIDS COUPLES *See* Dinks
DOUBLE MUSKY INN (GIRDWOOD, ALASKA: RESTAURANT) *See* Girdwood (Alaska)—Restaurants, nightclubs, bars, etc.

DOUBLE REFRACTION See Refraction, Double
DOUBLE STARS See Stars, Double
DOUBLE YOUR PLEASURE [television program] See Television program reviews—Single works
DOUBLEDAY & COMPANY, INC.
Court removes ban on 'Spy notes' parody. il *Publishers Weekly* 236:10 O 6 '89
Doubleday fights block of 'Spy notes' parody. *Publishers Weekly* 236:9 Ag 18 '89
DOUBLEDAY BOOK & MUSIC CLUBS
BOMC's Riger is president of Doubleday Clubs. M. Reuter. por *Publishers Weekly* 235:34-5 Ap 7 '89
DOUBLEDAY U.K. (FIRM)
Doubleday U.K. launches imprint with champagne and a bestseller. V. Menkes. *Publishers Weekly* 235:15 My 5 '89
DOUG WILLIAMS FOUNDATION
Doug Williams Foundation annual benefit awards $100,000 in scholarships. il pors *Jet* 76:28-9 Je 26 '89
DOUGHERTY, SHANNON
The undertow [story] il por *Redbook* 172:76+ Mr '89
DOUGHNUTS
See also
Dunkin' Donuts Incorporated
DOUGLAS, A. VIBERT
about
Obituary
Physics Today por 42:88-9 Jl '89. H. S. Hogg
DOUGLAS, ALAN
about
The curator of solid gold. S. Fried. il por *Gentlemen's Quarterly* 59:78+ Ja '89
DOUGLAS, BARRY
about
Barry Douglas has the range and technique of a classic virtuoso. D. Daniel. por *Vogue* 179:264 O '89
DOUGLAS, CHARLOTTE, 1936-
Behind the suprematist mirror. bibl f il *Art in America* 77:164-77 S '89
DOUGLAS, GAIL
about
A nurse's battle with burnout. S. Seixas. il pors *Money* 18:104-6+ S '89
DOUGLAS, MARJORY STONEMAN
about
Marjory Stoneman Douglas. V. Gladstone. il pors *Ms.* 17:68-71 Ja/F '89
DOUGLAS, MICHAEL
about
A prince of Hollywood. L. Blandford. il pors *The New York Times Magazine* p56-7+ D 3 '89
Tough guise. J. Truman. il por *Vogue* 179:436-7+ O '89
DOUGLAS, PAUL W., 1926-
about
Miscalculated risk? R. Phalon. il por *Forbes* 143:41-2 Je 12 '89
DOUGLAS, SALLY L.
Should the Senate approve the "Americans with Disabilities Act of 1989"? [excerpts from testimony, May 10, 1989] *Congressional Digest* 68:305+ D '89
DOUGLAS, SUZZANNE
about
Star quality. R. Torres. por *Essence* 19:39 Ap '89
DOUGLAS, WILLIAM LAKE
Vintage New Orleans: contemporary renovation in the Pontalba Buildings. il *Architectural Digest* 46:158-63+ F '89
DOUGLAS DUNN AND DANCERS
Reviews:
Performances of Sky eye at St. Mark's Church, New York City. D. Hering. *Dance Magazine* 63:55+ Jl '89
DOUGLAS ELLIMAN GIBBONS & IVES INC.
When the honeymoon's over: how to tell how you're really doing [J. Colson and J. Simon] J. Ciabattari. il pors *Working Woman* 14:82-6+ Je '89
DOUGLAS-HOME, ALEC See Home of the Hirsel, Alec Douglas-Home, Baron, 1903-
DOUGLAS-SCOTT-MONTAGU, EDWARD JOHN BARRINGTON See Montagu of Beaulieu, Edward John Barrington Douglas-Scott-Montagu, Baron, 1926-
DOUGLASS, FREDERICK, 1817?-1895
Statues, portraits, etc.
Frederick Douglass statue unveiled at Lincoln Univ. il *Jet* 77:36-7 N 20 '89
DOUGLIS, CAROLE A.
A corridor in peril. il map *Wilderness* 53:32-7 Wint '89
DOULTON POTTERY See Pottery, English
DOURIF, BRAD
about
Wonder Brad [interview] M. Clicksman. il pors *Film Comment* 25:44-5 N/D '89
DOURISH, COLIN T., AND OTHERS
Postponement of satiety by blockade of brain cholecystokinin (CCK-B) receptors. bibl f il *Science* 245:1509-11 S 29 '89
DOURLEN-ROLLIER, ANNE-MARIE
Family planning and the law. il *World Health* p7-9 Ap '89

DOUTHIT, WILLIAM L.
about
Global warfare. J. Harris. il por *Forbes* 144:120 O 16 '89
DOVE, GRANT A.
Advancing U.S. technology [address, December 6, 1988] *Vital Speeches of the Day* 55:268-70 F 15 '89
DOVE, RITA
Used [poem] il *The Atlantic* 264:61 Jl '89
DOVE BOOKS ON TAPE, INC.
Court enjoins Dove's distribution of 'Lonesome dove' audio. J. Tangorra. *Publishers Weekly* 236:12 S 22 '89
Dueling 'Doves': acrimony clouds copyright issue. P. Sweeting. il *Publishers Weekly* 235:54-6 Je 2 '89
DOVE DECOYS See Decoys (Hunting)
DOVE SHOOTING See Mourning dove shooting
DOVETAIL JOINTS See Joints (Carpentry)
DOVLATOV, SERGEÏ
Driving gloves [story]; tr. by Antonina W. Bouis. *The New Yorker* 65:36-40 My 8 '89
Grandpa Isaak [excerpt from Ours]; tr. by Anne Frydman. *Harper's* 278:24-6 My '89
The photo album [story]; tr. by Antonina W. Bouis. *The New Yorker* 65:43-7 Mr 27 '89
DOW CHEMICAL CO.
Adding some spice to an old formula. D. Woodruff. il *Business Week* Special Issue:134 Je 16 '89
Has Dow Chemical found the right formula? D. Woodruff. il *Business Week* p62+ Ag 7 '89
Let's call them bundle bonds. B. Weberman. il *Forbes* 143:333 Ja 9 '89
DOW JONES & CO., INC.
Dow Jones: still sluggish, still optimistic. D. Lieberman. il *Business Week* p114+ My 1 '89
A tale Dow Jones won't tell [woes of Wall Street journal] A. L. Taylor, III. il *Fortune* 120:100-2+ Jl 3 '89
DOW JONES AVERAGES See Stocks—Price indexes and averages
DOW JONES NEWS/RETRIEVAL (INFORMATION SYSTEM)
Dow Jones makes a young dog do new tricks [revamped online system] J. Rothfeder. il por *Business Week* p89+ Ja 16 '89
A new and easy way to get business information. A. Glossbrenner. il *Home Office Computing* 7:32 D '89
DOW-UNITED TECHNOLOGIES COMPOSITE PRODUCTS (FIRM)
New Dow/United Technologies joint venture to focus on advanced composite products. *Aviation Week & Space Technology* 131:22 S 18 '89
DOWD, MAUREEN
Addiction chic: are we hooked on being hooked? *Mademoiselle* 95:216-17+ O '89
The education of Dan Quayle [cover story] il pors *The New York Times Magazine* p18-21+ Je 25 '89
DOWDESWELL, JOHN
about
Miscellaneous ramblings. T. L. Bryant. il pors *Road & Track* 40:35-6 Jl '89
DOWDLE, JAMES C.
about
In the eye of the storm [interview] K. Haley. il pors *Channels (New York, N.Y.: 1986)* 9:62-3 Ja 16 '89
DOWEL JOINTS See Joints (Carpentry)
DOWER, JOHN W.
Japan's new military edge [cover story] il *The Nation* 249:1+ Jl 3 '89
DOWIE, MARK
Maverick surgeon. il pors *American Health* 8:86-9+ Je '89
Organ masters. il *Omni (New York, N.Y.)* 11:26+ F '89
Transplant fever. il *Mother Jones* 14:19-20 Ap '89
DOWIS, DEE
about
On top of the world. D. S. Looney. il pors *Sports Illustrated* 71:54-6+ O 16 '89
DOWN, GOLDIE M.
Ten tips for writing humor. *The Writer* 102:21-3 Jl '89
DOWN BEAT (PERIODICAL)
The 54th annual Down Beat Readers Poll. il *Down Beat* 56:20-2 D '89
55th anniversary issue [cover story; special issue; with editorial comment by John Ephland] il *Down Beat* 56:6, 16-19+ S '89
For the records [Readers Poll] J. Ephland. *Down Beat* 56:6 Ja '89
On the beat. See issues of Down Beat
DOWN BEAT INTERNATIONAL JAZZ CRITICS POLL See Jazz music—Awards
DOWN BEAT STUDENT MUSIC AWARDS
The 12th annual Down Beat Student Music Awards. D. Helland. il *Down Beat* 56:25-7 Je '89
DOWN CLOTHING See Clothing, Cold weather
DOWN SYNDROME
An expert explains her daughter's disorder [interview with D. Crutcher] G. Breu. il por *People Weekly* 32:67 O 16 '89
"My amazing Lisa" [teenager L. Grossman's Bat mitzvah]; ed. by Susan Lapinski. A. S. Grossman. il por *Redbook* 172:56+ Ap '89

DOWN SYNDROME—*cont.*
"My son will always amaze me" [C. Burke]; ed. by Sara Nelson. M. Burke. il pors *Redbook* 174:48+ N '89
Diagnosis
The way the whorls turn [computer reads Down syndrome in parents' handprints] M. R. Meyer. il *Newsweek* 113:73 F 13 '89

DOWN SYNDROME IN TELEVISION
For Chris Burke, the first actor with Down syndrome to star on TV, Life goes on in a big way. K. McMurran. il pors *People Weekly* 32:61-2+ O 16 '89
Reflections of a real grouch [unrealistic depiction in Life goes on] R. Zoglin. il *Time* 134:79 O 16 '89
Takes guts [C. Burke, actor with Down syndrome, on TV show Life goes on; cover story] J. B. McDaniel. il pors *Life* 12:70-2+ N '89

DOWNE, SUE
The reluctant prime minister. *World Press Review* 36:36 D '89

DOWNER, GREGORY
What's in a gnome? il pors *Opera News* 53:34-5 Ap 1 '89

DOWNES, LAWRENCE
Pictures of the year. il *Petersen's Photographic Magazine* 18:14-16 S '89

DOWNEY, EDWARD M.
about
Targeting the military market. L. Williams. il pors *Nation's Business* 77:66+ My '89

DOWNEY, LORETTA M.
about
Targeting the military market. L. Williams. il pors *Nation's Business* 77:66+ My '89

DOWNEY, MARY JO
On my own. *The Humanist* 49:26+ Ja/F '89

DOWNEY, MORTON, JR.
about
Morton Downey Jr. faces a terrible fate: silence. il por *People Weekly* 32:42-3 Ag 7 '89
On the air with Downey. M. Brown. il *Channels (New York, N.Y.: 1986)* 9:24 Ap '89

DOWNEY, ROBERT, JR.
about
Arresting appeal. B. Borns. pors *Harper's Bazaar* 122:50+ F '89
Robert Downey Jr.—a natural tease. D. Denicolo. il pors *Glamour* 87:184 Mr '89

DOWNS, ANTHONY
about
After Tokyo, all the world's a bargain [interview] J. Egan. il *U.S. News & World Report* 106:58-9 Ja 30 '89

DOWNS, PETER
Union blues. il *The Progressive* 53:32-5 Ja '89

DOWN'S SYNDROME *See* Down syndrome

DOWNSBROUGH, PETER
about
Peter Downsbrough at Julian Pretto. N. Princenthal. il *Art in America* 77:154-5 Mr '89

DOWNTOWN AREAS *See* Business districts

DOWSING
Water witching. C. Kraus. *The New Yorker* 65:97+ O 9 '89

DOWSON, KENNETH
about
A final act of despair. B. Bergman. *Maclean's* 102:22 N 13 '89
An unfolding tragedy. P. Kopvillem. il por *Maclean's* 102:23 O 2 '89

DOXYCYCLINE
PMS pill. il *Prevention (Emmaus, Pa.)* 41:14+ F '89

DOYLE, BRIAN
Baby on board. il *U.S. Catholic* 54:20-7 Je '89
Do the Gospels put words in Jesus' mouth? il *U.S. Catholic* 54:32-5 S '89
Who owns the sacraments? [cover story] il *U.S. Catholic* 54:6-12 O '89

DOYLE, JIM
A recipe for humble pie. il *U.S. Catholic* 54:14-15 F '89

DOYLE, KATHLEEN
Madam C. J. Walker: first black woman millionaire. por *American History Illustrated* 24:24-5 Mr '89
"Stamping" out tuberculosis: the story of Christmas seals. il por *American History Illustrated* 24:66-8 N/D '89

DOYLE, KEVIN
From the editor's desk. See issues of Maclean's beginning March 14, 1983

DOYLE, MICHAEL
about
Living on the edge. J. Nielsen. il pors *National Wildlife* 27:20-3 O/N '89

DOYLE, RICHARD A.
about
Building a brewery is no small beer. il pors *Business Week* p40-1 Jl 24 '89

DOYLE, RICK
You are there! il *Petersen's Photographic Magazine* 18:14-16 Ag '89

DOYLE, RODGER
A house divided. il map *The Atlantic* 263:81 Je '89

DOYLE, ROY P.
The resistance of conventional wisdom to research evidence: the case of retention in grade. bibl f il *Phi Delta Kappan* 71:215-20 N '89

DOZOIS, GARDNER R.
Solace [story] il *Omni (New York, N.Y.)* 11:48-50+ F '89

DRABBLE, MARGARET, 1939-
The dinner party [fiction] *Harper's* 279:36+ S '89
Killing time. il *Harper's* 278:69-72 Ap '89

DRABELLE, DENNIS
Exporting park know-how. il *National Parks* 63:32-8 Mr/Ap '89
A wilderness commonplace book. *Wilderness* 52:xi-xvii+ Spr '89

DRABINSKY, GARTH, 1948-
about
Closing credits. J. Daly. *Maclean's* 102:34 Ap 24 '89
Every trick in the books. D. Wechsler. il por *Forbes* 143:46+ My 29 '89
Fast fade for a cinema king. J. Hammer. il por *Newsweek* 114:61 N 6 '89
A melodrama's final scene. J. DeMont and P. Chisholm. il por *Maclean's* 102:42-3 D 11 '89
Mogul in distress. B. Bremner. *Business Week* p45 O 9 '89
An Olympian extravaganza. D. Francis. il *Maclean's* 102:11 F 6 '89
The screen wars. J. Daly. il pors *Maclean's* 102:40-1 My 29 '89
Showdown at Cineplex. J. DeMont. il por *Maclean's* 102:46-7 My 8 '89

DRACUNCULIASIS *See* Guinea worm disease

DRAFT
See also
Conscientious objectors
Bring back the draft. J. W. Davis. il *USA Today (Periodical)* 118:12-13 S '89
Can patriotism be legislated? D. J. Boorstin. il *U.S. News & World Report* 106:26 F 13 '89
The rich don't serve—so what? M. Kinsley. il *The Washington Monthly* 21:26-7 Mr '89

DRAFT DETECTORS (AIR INFILTRATION MEASUREMENT)
The fresh air contest [backdraft problems] D. Johnson. il *The Family Handyman* 39:10+ S '89

DRAFT HORSES
See also
Horse ferries
Four-legged tractors in action late August into November. il *Sunset (Central West edition)* 183:52-3 S '89
A quiet revolution—the horse in agriculture, 1100-1500. J. Langdon. bibl il map *History Today* 39:32-7 Jl '89

DRAFT RESISTERS
Learning to love draft-dodgers. J. D. Isaacs. *The Bulletin of the Atomic Scientists* 45:4 Je '89

DRAFTING OF BASKETBALL PLAYERS *See* Basketball, Professional—Draft

DRAFTING OF FOOTBALL PLAYERS *See* Football, Professional—Draft

DRAG (AERODYNAMICS)
See also
Large eddy breakup devices
Burnelli's lifting fuselage. P. Garrison. il por *Flying* 116:80+ Ap '89
Drag eraser [Piaggio Avanti; cover story] J. M. McClellan. il *Flying* 116:28-32+ Ja '89
Once upon a winglet. P. Garrison. il *Flying* 116:108+ Ag '89

DRAG (HYDRODYNAMICS)
The reel stuff [fishing reel drag] P. B. Wright. il *Motor Boating & Sailing* 163:52+ F '89

DRAG IMPERSONATORS *See* Impersonators, Female

DRAG RACING
The big Thrill [driver E. Hill] D. Wallace. il por *Sport (New York, N.Y.)* 80:66-8 Jl '89
The first lady of funny cars [D. Woods] T. Swan. il por *Popular Mechanics* 166:36 Ap '89
Anecdotes, facetiae, satire, etc.
Things that go fast in the night. M. Anson. il *Motor Trend* 41:8 F '89

DRAGADZE, PETER
"Let your readers be reassured there will be no military coup" [interview with N. Ryzhkov; with reply by Paul Klebnikov] il por *Forbes* 144:82+ O 16 '89
Russia's embryonic capitalists. il *Forbes* 144:90-4+ O 16 '89

DRAGON SYSTEMS INC.
Talking to your typewriter [DragonDictate system] *Science News* 135:351 Je 3 '89

DRAGONFLIES
Photographs and photography
Mite riders. R. Noonan. il *Natural History* p80-1 My '89

DRAGOTI, STAN
about
She's out of control [film] Reviews
People Weekly il 31:19 My 8 '89. T. Cunneff

DRAIN CLEANING See Plumbing—Maintenance and repair

DRAINAGE
See also
Runoff

DRAIZE TEST
Cosmetics firms drop Draize test. C. Holden. *Science* 245:125 Jl 14 '89
New test could spare rabbits [use of Tetrahymena] il *USA Today (Periodical)* 117:4-5 Je '89

DRAKE, B., AND OTHERS
Imaging crystals, polymers, and processes in water with the atomic force microscope. bibl f il *Science* 243:1586-9 Mr 24 '89

DRAKE, JAMES, 1946-
about
James Drake at Barbara Fendrick. G. Henry. il *Art in America* 77:264-5 Ap '89

DRAKE, MEREDITH
Biking & baby. il pors *Bicycling* 30:82+ My '89

DRAKE, ROBERT, 1930-
Robert Penn Warren's enormous spider web. por *The Christian Century* 106:1089-91 N 22 '89

DRAKULIĆ, SLAVENKA
Glasnostradamus. *The New Republic* 200:18-20 Ap 24 '89
Yugoslavia's new political truth. il *The Nation* 248:297-8+ Mr 6 '89

DRAM (DYNAMIC RANDOM ACCESS MEMORY) See Random access memory

DRAMA
See also
Black drama
Opera
Rushdie, Salman—Satanic verses case—Drama
Theater
Theatrical adaptations
Study and teaching
How do you spell "wound," as in gunshot? [teacher helps inner city child write a play] J. Murphy. il *U.S. Catholic* 54:36-9 O '89
Technique
An object lesson for playwrights. J. Sweet. *The Writer* 102:18-20 D '89
Talk of the times [excerpts from plays by D. Hare, D. Mamet and H. Pinter demonstrate the art of dialogue] *Harper's* 278:37-9+ F '89
Themes
See also
Baseball fans in drama
Business in drama
Communism in drama
France—History—Revolution, 1789-1799—Drama
Holocaust, Jewish (1939-1945), in drama
Indians (American) in drama
Iran-contra affair in drama

DRAMA, FILMED See Motion picture adaptations

DRAMA CRITICS AND CRITICISM
See also
Theater reviews

DRAMA FESTIVALS
See also
Shakespeare festivals
Student competition: plague or pestilence? [high school] D. Finney. *Design for Arts in Education* 90:38-41 Ja/F '89
Kentucky
Some vigor and vinegar [Humana Festival] W. A. Henry. il *Time* 133:70-1 Ap 17 '89
New York (State)
See also
New York Shakespeare Festival
The theatre [Young Playwrights Festival] E. Oliver. *The New Yorker* 65:97 O 2 '89
Ontario
See also
Shaw Festival (Niagara-on-the-Lake, Ont.)
Stratford Festival (Ont.)
Country comforts [Blyth Festival] J. Bemrose. il *Maclean's* 102:54 Ag 28 '89
Oregon
See also
Oregon Shakespearean Festival

DRAMA IN EDUCATION See Dramatization in education

DRAMA PRODUCTION AND DIRECTION See Theater—Production and direction

DRAMA REVIEWS See Theater reviews

DRAMATISTS, AMERICAN
See also
Gelbart, Larry
Greenberg, Richard
Gurney, A. R. (Albert Ramsdell), 1930-
Hansberry, Lorraine, 1930-1965
Harling, Robert, 1951-
Henley, Beth
Miller, Arthur, 1915-
O'Neill, Eugene, 1888-1953
Sorkin, Aaron
Sterner, Jerry
Wasserstein, Wendy
Williams, Tennessee, 1911-1983

Wilson, August

DRAMATISTS, CANADIAN
See also
Gray, John, 1946-
Rose, Richard
Walker, George F.

DRAMATISTS, CZECH
See also
Havel, Václav

DRAMATISTS, ENGLISH
See also
Shakespeare, William, 1564-1616
Stoppard, Tom
The charge of the Angry Brigade [left-wing playwrights] C. Tookey. il *National Review* 41:41-4 N 24 '89

DRAMATISTS, FRENCH
See also
Hervieu, Paul

DRAMATISTS, GERMAN
See also
Brecht, Bertolt, 1898-1956

DRAMATISTS, IRISH
See also
Wilde, Oscar, 1854-1900

DRAMATISTS, ISRAELI
See also
Sobol, Joshua

DRAMATIZATION IN EDUCATION
Drama in the curriculum for troubled young people: is it worth the fight? S. Pearson-Davis. bibl f *Design for Arts in Education* 90:25-32 N/D '88
A high school play helps suicidal teenagers [Empty chairs written and performed by students in Roanoke, Va.] P. Feinour. *The Education Digest* 54:50-1 My '89

DRANOV, PAULA
"Am I sick or am I tired?". *Ladies' Home Journal* 106:120+ S '89
Exercising their options. il *Harper's Bazaar* 122:186-7+ Mr '89
Go with a pro. il *Harper's Bazaar* 122:74+ My '89
How do you know if it's PMS? il *American Health* 8:54-8 D '89
Slow forward. il *American Health* 8:62-4+ Jl/Ag '89

DRAPER, E. LINN
about
Fast answers make for timely decisions. C. O'Malley. il por *Personal Computing* 13:83 Ap '89

DRAPER, POLLY
about
Single again, thirtysomething's Polly Draper brushes up on becoming a sexy working girl. S. Schindehette. il pors *People Weekly* 31:157-9 My 8 '89

DRAPER, THEODORE, 1912-
Revelations of the North trial. bibl f il *The New York Review of Books* 36:54-9 Ag 17 '89
Rewriting the Iran-contra story. il *The New York Review of Books* 35:38-45 Ja 19 '89
'Rewriting the Iran-contra story': an exchange [discussion of January 19, 1989 article] il *The New York Review of Books* 36:38-9 Mr 2 '89

DRAPER PRIZE
Ignored by the Nobels, engineering and technology are at last being honored by a significant new prize [R. Noyce and J. S. Kilby win] R. M. Adams. il *Smithsonian* 20:12 D '89
Kilby and Noyce win Draper Prize for developing microchips. I. Goodwin. il *Physics Today* 42:52 N '89

DRAPERIES See Curtains and draperies

DRAVECKY, DAVE
After a courageous comeback, a star pitcher breaks his arm but keeps his faith intact; ed. by Liz McNeil. il pors *People Weekly* 32:69-70+ S 11 '89
about
Armed with a miracle. il pors *Sports Illustrated* 71:18 Ag 21 '89
Giant comeback cut short. J. Carvalho. il por *Christianity Today* 33:54+ O 20 '89
'It felt like I lost my arm'. il por *Newsweek* 114:65 Ag 28 '89

DRAWERS
Drawer making. R. Capotosto. il *Popular Mechanics* 166:93-4 N '89

DRAWING
See also
Architectural drawing
Doodles
Fashion drawing
Illustration
Pastel drawing
Pen drawing
Pencil drawing
Portrait drawing
Scientific illustration
Still life drawing

DRAWING—*cont.*

Conservation and restoration

Picking up the pieces [restoration of damage to L. da Vinci's The Virgin and child with St. Anne and John the Baptist at the National Gallery in London] B. Taylor. il *Art News* 88:43+ F '89

Study and teaching

The art of the mind: how I learned to draw [art teacher B. Edwards] T. Schwartz. il por *New York* 22:42-6+ D 11 '89

No need to be a Rembrandt [drawing from nature] A. Zwinger. il *Reader's Digest* 134:136-8 Ap '89

DRAWING, AMERICAN

Collectors and collecting

Chacun à son pocketbook [I. R. Koger's collection of paintings and H. Adler's collection of drawings from 1870 to 1930] C. Brown. il pors *Forbes* 144:144-5 D 25 '89

Exhibitions

An act of salvation [work of P. Guston] P. Brach. il *Art in America* 77:130-5 Ja '89

Ann McCoy at ACA Contemporary. B. Adams. il *Art in America* 77:144-5 Ja '89

Jan C. Baltzell at Giannetta. W. P. Scott. il *Art in America* 77:269 Ap '89

Mike Glier at Barbara Gladstone and Wave Hill. H. Cotter. il *Art in America* 77:193 N '89

The painter's progress [American drawings from the Cooper-Hewitt Museum] A. E. Ledes. il *Antiques* 135:396 F '89

Susan Chrysler White at Janet Fleisher. D. S. Rubin. il *Art in America* 77:181-2 Je '89

The work of Roy Lichtenstein in the age of Walter Benjamin's and Jean Baudrillard's popularity [cover story] C. Ratcliff. il *Art in America* 77:110-23+ F '89

DRAWING, CHILDREN'S *See* Children's art

DRAWING, ENGLISH

Exhibitions

The drawings of William De Morgan. H. Young. bibl f il *Antiques* 135:1432-43 Je '89

DRAWING, GERMAN

Exhibitions

The romantic spirit: Pierpont Morgan Library. M. Moorman. il *Art News* 88:153 F '89

Tracing God's fingerprint [The romantic spirit: German drawings, 1780-1850] R. Hughes. il *Time* 133:62 Ja 23 '89

DRAWINGS *See* Drawing

DRAY, PHILIP

Back on the bus. il pors *Mother Jones* 14:37-9+ N '89

DREAM DATE [television program] *See* Television program reviews—Single works

DREAM STREET [television program] *See* Television program reviews—Single works

THE DREAM TEAM [film] *See* Motion picture reviews—Single works

DREAMS

See also

Nightmares

Do your dreams have any meaning? [views of Hans von Brauchitsch] *USA Today (Periodical)* 118:10 Jl '89

Dreamchasers. S. Chollar. il *Psychology Today* 23:60-1 Ap '89

Dreams on the couch. D. Gelman. il *Newsweek* 114:45-7 Ag 14 '89

Inside our sleeping minds. S. Boxer. bibl il *Modern Maturity* 32:48-54 O/N '89

Making a prophet [precognitive dreams; interview with U. Montague] N. Guccione. il *Omni (New York, N.Y.)* 12:12 N '89

Midnight dreams [lucid dreams] J. Bosveld. il *Harper's Bazaar* 122:188-93+ O '89

The Omni book of dreams. il *Omni (New York, N.Y.)* 12 Book of Dreams:1-8 N '89

The repressed road to trauma recovery [lack of dream recall in Holocaust survivors; research by Peretz Lavie] B. Bower. *Science News* 136:4 Jl 1 '89

The stuff of dreams [views of J. Maguire] C. B. Fleming. il *Health (New York, N.Y.)* 21:28+ D '89

The stuff that dreams are made of [cover story] S. Begley. il *Newsweek* 114:40-4 Ag 14 '89

Take control of your dreams [lucid dreams; excerpt from Control your dreams; cover story] J. Gackenbach and J. Bosveld. il *Psychology Today* 23:27-32 O '89

Twilight zones [lucid dreams; excerpt from Control your dreams] J. Gackenbach and J. Bosveld. il *Omni (New York, N.Y.)* 12:74-6+ N '89

Anecdotes, facetiae, satire, etc.

Are you a midnight genius? H. A. Smith. il *The Saturday Evening Post* 261:54-7+ Mr '89

DREAMS IN THE BIBLE

Dreams and letting God be God. L. O. Sanneh. *The Christian Century* 106:1195 D 20-27 '89

DREIER, DAVID

Should the House-passed wage proposal be enacted? [excerpts from address, March 23, 1989] *Congressional Digest* 68:155+ My '89

DREIER, PETER

Communities, not carpetbaggers. il *The Nation* 249:198-200+ Ag 21-28 '89

Local success stories. il *Commonweal* 116:201-2 Ap 7 '89

(jt. auth) See Atlas, John, and Dreier, Peter

DREIFUS, CLAUDIA

Alice Walker [interview] il *The Progressive* 53:29-31 Ag '89

Art Spiegelman [interview] il *The Progressive* 53:34-7 N '89

Susan Sarandon [interview] il *The Progressive* 53:33-6 O '89

Yehoshafat Harkabi [interview] il *The Progressive* 53:36-9 Je '89

DREISER, THEODORE, 1871-1945

about

First encounters. E. Sorel and N. C. Sorel. il *The Atlantic* 264:101 N '89

Lyrical Dreiser. A. Delbanco. bibl f il *The New York Review of Books* 36:32-7 N 23 '89

DRELL, SIDNEY D. (SIDNEY DAVID), 1926-

Celebrating Sakharov [excerpts from address, November 1988] *Physics Today* 42:92-3 F '89

Prevention first. *The Bulletin of the Atomic Scientists* 45:39 My '89

(jt. auth) See Taylor, Theodore B., and Drell, Sidney D. (Sidney David), 1926-

DREMAN, DAVID N.

The contrarian. See alternate issues of Forbes

DRESCHER, FRAN

about

In movies you can't remember, you don't forget Fran Drescher. J. Wadler. il pors *People Weekly* 32:127-8+ N 27 '89

DRESDEN, MAX, 1918-

The long chain from Kramers's polymer work [discussion of September 1988 article, Kramers's contributions to statistical mechanics] bibl *Physics Today* 42:13+ O '89

DRESDEN FESTIVAL *See* Music festivals—Germany (East)

DRESNER, HAL

Those Beverly Hills kids. por *Newsweek* 114:10 D 25 '89

DRESNER, SUSAN

Shopping smart. il *Essence* 20:42 O '89

A working wardrobe. il *New Choices for the Best Years* 29:37-44 Ja '89

DRESS *See* Clothing and dress

DRESS ACCESSORIES

See also

Belts (Clothing)

Night for day. J. Shields. il *Vogue* 179:280-9 Ag '89

Only Isabel Canovas could convince women to slip on a banana peel or put a snail on their wrist. V. Woods. il por *Vogue* 179:86+ Ag '89

The power of accessories. C. Donovan. il *The New York Times Magazine* p88-93 Mr 19 '89

Shrunken treasures. il *Vogue* 179:134 F '89

Straw bargains. S. Clark. il *Glamour* 87:186 Ag '89

True craftiness [work of H. Hodge] il por *Vogue* 179:112+ My '89

DRESS CODES (CATHOLICS) *See* Clothing and dress—Catholics

DRESS CODES (STUDENTS) *See* Clothing and dress—Students

DRESS DESIGNERS *See* Fashion designers

DRESSER, ROBERT A.

When to fight, when to switch. por *Nation's Business* 77:13 S '89

DRESSER INDUSTRIES, INC.

Better all the time. il *Forbes* 143:179 Ja 9 '89

Murphy's law. T. Mack. il por *Forbes* 143:174+ Mr 20 '89

DRESSES *See* Clothing and dress

DRESSING (STUFFING) *See* Stuffing (Food)

DRESSING OF FISH *See* Fish, Dressing of

DRESSING OF GAME *See* Game, Dressing of

DRESSING ROOMS

See also

Powder rooms

Reflections in a mass eye [women in a communal dressing room at Loehmann's] S. A. Feeney. il *Ms.* 18:30+ N '89

Suite retreat. C. Poole. il *Home Mechanix* 86:78-80+ Mr '89

THE DRESSMAKER [film] *See* Motion picture reviews—Single works

DREW, ELIZABETH

Letter from Washington. il *The New Yorker* 65:81-92 Ag 28 '89

Letter from Washington. *The New Yorker* 65:74-81 Jl 31 '89

Letter from Washington. *The New Yorker* 65:77-85 F 27 '89

Letter from Washington. *The New Yorker* 65:87-93 My 15 '89

Letter from Washington. *The New Yorker* 65:102-8+ O 2 '89

Letter from Washington. *The New Yorker* 65:121-4+ N 27 '89

Letter from Washington. *The New Yorker* 65:97-100+ Mr 20 '89

Letter from Washington. *The New Yorker* 65:99-104+ My 1 '89

Letter from Washington. *The New Yorker* 65:97-102 Je 12 '89

DREW, ELIZABETH—cont.
Letter from Washington. *The New Yorker* 65:100-4+ O 30 '89
Letter from Washington. *The New Yorker* 65:72-82 Je 26 '89

DREWERY, CORINNE
about
The effortless style of Swing Out Sister's Corinne Drewery. J. Powell. il por *Glamour* 87:206 S '89

DREXEL BURNHAM LAMBERT INCORPORATED
And the next test will be Giuliani vs. Milken. C. Welles. por *Business Week* p37 Ja 9 '89
Can Fred Joseph save Drexel? M. J. Williams. il por *Fortune* 119:89-90+ My 8 '89
Checkmate for the King of Junk Bonds [Drexel Burnham agrees to fire M. Milken] por *U.S. News & World Report* 106:44-5 F 6 '89
Coelho under fire [congressman given easy deal on hard-to-get junk bonds] *Newsweek* 112:41 My 22 '89
The deal Drexel could not resist [settlement of fraud case] P. Sherrid. il *U.S. News & World Report* 106:46-8 Ja 9 '89
Drexel is in the doghouse with cities and states. L. J. Nathans. il *Business Week* p81-2 F 13 '89
Drexel pays the piper. D. Pauly. il *Newsweek* 113:40 Ja 16 '89
Drexel rushes in to save a fallen disciple [bailout of Integrated Resources] L. Light. il *Business Week* p65 Jl 17 '89
Drexel's deal with the feds: how much will it hurt? C. Welles. il por *Business Week* p36 F 6 '89
Drexel's profit and potential loss. M. J. Williams. il *Fortune* 119:8+ F 27 '89
The friends of Michael Milken [public relations campaign] M. Hosenball. il por *The New Republic* 201:23-5 Ag 28 '89
G. Robert Blakey versus Michael Milken [author of RICO statute] J. Queenan. il por *Forbes* 143:57+ My 1 '89
Got big deals, big problems, big bucks? Get Arthur Liman [defending M. Milken] M. Galen. il por *Business Week* p112+ My 15 '89
Hitting Milken where it hurts. C. Friday and D. Pauly. il por *Newsweek* 113:49 Ap 10 '89
'I woke up with my stomach churning' [views of F. Joseph] C. Leinster. il por *Fortune* 120:120-2 Jl 3 '89
John Kissick. E. Schine. il por *Business Week* Special Issue:95 Ap 14 '89
The junk bond plague moves north. P. C. Newman. il *Maclean's* 102:32 Ja 16 '89
The Junk King starts anew [M. Milken resigns from Drexel Burnham to start new firm] por *Newsweek* 113:55 Je 26 '89
The junk market's black hole. L. J. Nathans. il *Business Week* p156-7 N 27 '89
Just how corrupt is Wall Street? [agreement to plead guilty] C. Welles. il *Business Week* p34-6 Ja 9 '89
Let's make a deal [Drexel pleads guilty to fraud] J. Greenwald. il *Time* 133:84-6 Ja 2 '89
A lion of the Texas bar snarls at KKR and Drexel [S. Susman builds asbestos case stemming from Jim Walter Corp. LBO] M. Ivey. il por *Business Week* p73+ O 9 '89
Liquid assets [backing of Publicker Industries] M. Schifrin. il *Forbes* 143:48 F 20 '89
Michael Milken. por *People Weekly* 32:72-3 D 25 '89-Ja 1 '90
Michael Milken. B. Darrach. por *People Weekly* 32 Special Issue:48-9 Fall '89
Milken's shadow hovers over Fred Carr [First Executive Corp.] K. Kerwin. il por *Business Week* p24 Ap 17 '89
Nailing the junk kings [admits securities fraud] L. Reibstein. il por *Newsweek* 113:44-5+ Ja 2 '89
No dice for Drexel? [possibly barred from doing business with Bally in N.J.] J. Crudele. il *New York* 22:22 Ja 23 '89
The phantom of Wall Street: how Ivan Boesky's bitter legacy haunts Mike Milken and his former firm. C. Byron. il pors *New York* 22:52-6 D 4 '89
Predators' fall [M. Milken indicted] *National Review* 41:10-11 My 5 '89
Quid pro junk? [federal probe of junk bond fund managers' personal portfolios] R. L. Stern and P. Berman. il *Forbes* 144:39-40 Ag 7 '89
Securities exchange [J. Shad to head Drexel Burnham] *The Nation* 248:613 My 8 '89
Shackling a Wall Street giant. C. Friday and L. Reibstein. il *Newsweek* 114:49 Jl 31 '89
Taking it all back, plus interest [criminal charges against M. Milken] C. Gorman. il por *Time* 133:42 Ap 10 '89
The U.S. vs. Milken: now the last act begins. C. Welles. il por *Business Week* p29 Ap 10 '89
A verdict that Mike Milken hopes is no warm-up [conviction of five officials of Princeton/Newport Partners and former Drexel Burnham trader] M. Galen. por *Business Week* p46 Ag 14 '89
Wall Street runs scared. J. Friedman. il *Business Week* p24-5 My 1 '89
Wanted: a Mr. Clean for Drexel Burnham [J. Shad] il por *Newsweek* 113:42 Ja 23 '89

Welcome to the world of sleaze. il *Time* 134:52 Ag 14 '89
What hath Drexel wrought? [guilty plea] M. J. Williams. il *Fortune* 119:10 Ja 16 '89
What Milken means; Will Mike fight? A. Farnham. il por *Fortune* 119:16-17 Ap 24 '89
Why blacks like Mike Milken [support of black business enterprises] J. Lieblich. il por *Fortune* 119:10 My 22 '89
Why Mike Milken was so eager to help Peter Ueberroth [Eastern Air Lines takeover] A. Bernstein. *Business Week* p30 My 1 '89
Will Michael Milken go to jail? P. Sherrid. il por *U.S. News & World Report* 106:49-50 Ap 10 '89
Will Mike Milken sue? L. Howard. il por *Newsweek* 113:7 F 6 '89
Without Milken, can Drexel still be Drexel? E. Schine. il pors *Business Week* p34 Mr 27 '89

DREXLER, HENRY J., 1947-
An unusual approach to acrylics. il por *American Artist* 53:44-9 F '89

DREXLER, K. ERIC
about
Interview: Eric Drexler. E. Regis. por *Omni (New York, N.Y.)* 11:66-8+ Ja '89

DREXLER, MICHAEL
The blind high. *Utne Reader* p99-100 S/O '89

DREYER, CARL THEODOR, 1889-1968
about
Dreyer. A. White. il por *Film Comment* 25:24-6 My/Je '89
Films. S. Klawans. *The Nation* 248:353 Mr 13 '89

DREYER, JUNE TEUFEL
Unrest in Tibet. bibl f *Current History* 88:281-4+ S '89

DREYFUS, ALFRED, 1859-1935
about
A shifty-eyed spy who was likely the nastiest man ever. R. Wernick. il pors *Smithsonian* 20:114-16+ Ag '89

DREYFUS, ROBERT LOUIS- *See* Louis-Dreyfus, Robert

DREYFUS CORP.
Miracle of the fee-free fund. D. P. Wiener. *U.S. News & World Report* 107:80 O 9 '89

DREYFUS WORLDWIDE DOLLAR MONEY MARKET FUND
Money market funds that pack a real punch. L. J. Nathans. il *Business Week* p104 Ag 21 '89

DRG FUNDING (FIRM)
The next big housing scandal [excessively high mortgage loans] il *U.S. News & World Report* 107:27 Jl 3 '89

DRG PLC
Jimmy Goldsmith's gun bearer goes gunning [R. A. E. Franklin's hostile bid] P. Finch. il por *Business Week* p63+ O 16 '89

DRIBBLING (BASKETBALL)
Bob Nickerson, the round man of roundball, shows off his degree as the Doctor of Dribble. il pors *People Weekly* 31:102-3 Ja 9 '89

DRIED MEAT *See* Meat, Dried
DRIED TOMATOES *See* Tomatoes, Dried
DRIFTING OF CONTINENTS *See* Continental drift
DRILLING AND BORING (EARTH AND ROCKS)
Deep holes yielding geoscience surprises. R. A. Kerr. il *Science* 245:468-70 Ag 4 '89
Drilling begins in search of molten energy [Long Valley Caldera] R. Monastersky. il *Science News* 136:101 Ag 12 '89
European deep drilling leaves Americans behind. R. A. Kerr. il *Science* 245:816-17 Ag 25 '89
The furnace beneath us [drilling to the magma in California] G. Carroll. il *Newsweek* 114:55 Ag 28 '89
Inner space [deep drilling programs by Soviet Union and West Germany; cover story] R. Monastersky. il *Science News* 136:266-8 O 21 '89

DRILLING AND BORING MACHINERY
See also
Jigs (Tools)
Anywhere drills. T. Klenck. il *Popular Mechanics* 166:89-92+ Mr '89
Computer-controlled drill designed to meet unique B-2 fabrication needs. il *Aviation Week & Space Technology* 130:51-2 Ap 17 '89

Equipment
See also
Bits (Drilling and boring)

DRILLING FUNDS (OIL WELLS) *See* Petroleum investment trusts
DRILLING RIGS, OIL WELL *See* Oil well drilling rigs
DRILLS (MACHINERY) *See* Drilling and boring machinery
DRILLS (SURGICAL) *See* Surgical drills
DRINAN, ROBERT F.
Execute an 8-year-old? The Johnny Penry case. *The Christian Century* 106:199-200 F 22 '89
The flowering of legal ethics in America [cover story] il *America* 161:76-8 Ag 12-19 '89
International human rights and the Bush administration. *America* 160:242-4 Mr 18 '89
Is the NRA being shot down? *The Christian Century* 106:372-3 Ap 12 '89

DRINAN, ROBERT F.—*cont.*
Pressure in New York for death penalty. *The Christian Century* 106:582-3 Je 7-14 '89
Protection against racial discrimination. *America* 160:52 Ja 28 '89
The Supreme Court expands religious freedom. *America* 160:388-9 Ap 29 '89
DRINK MIXERS (APPLIANCES)
Blenders & milkshake makers. il *Consumer Reports* 54:261-4 D '89
DRINKING AND DRIVING *See* Alcohol and automobile drivers
DRINKING AND EMPLOYMENT *See* Alcohol and employment
DRINKING AND THE AGED *See* Alcohol and the aged
DRINKING CUSTOMS
Anecdotes, facetiae, satire, etc.
Whiskey codes [men's drinking preferences] K. MacNeil. il *Ms.* 18:35 N '89
Soviet Union
Straight shots [drinking vodka] K. Eldredge. il *Harper's Bazaar* 122:170+ F '89
DRINKING PROBLEM *See* Alcoholics and alcoholism
DRINKING VESSELS
The quest for Blackbeard's cup [C. Whedbee's search for silver-plated skull] L. Fleischer. *Publishers Weekly* 235:74 F 3 '89
DRINKING WATER
See also
Bottled water
Risky waters. P. Jaret. il *Health (New York, N.Y.)* 21:70-3+ Ag '89
Pollution
See Water pollution
Purification
See Water purification
DRINKS *See* Alcoholic beverages; Beverages
DRIP IRRIGATION *See* Watering of gardens, lawns, etc.
DRIP IRRIGATION EQUIPMENT *See* Irrigation equipment
DRISCOLL, HOLLY
about
Holly Driscoll had a fine idea, but it left her in the soup. il por *People Weekly* 31:97 My 22 '89
DRISCOLL, SYLVIA
about
The case of the missing mineral. A. Roblin. il *Prevention (Emmaus, Pa.)* 41:120+ F '89
DRIVE-IN RESTAURANTS
Anecdotes, facetiae, satire, etc.
Drive-in etiquette. M. Anson. il *Motor Trend* 41:8 Mr '89
DRIVE-IN THEATERS
Sneakin' in. M. Anson. il *Motor Trend* 41:8 Ja '89
DRIVER, SENTA
about
Wishful thinking. T. Tobias. il *New York* 22:86+ N 27 '89
DRIVER EDUCATION *See* Automobile driving—Study and teaching
D'RIVERA, PAQUITO
about
With help from his wife and his lover, jazzman Paquito D'Rivera gets back the son he left in Cuba. P. Chin. il pors *People Weekly* 31:94-7 Ja 30 '89
DRIVERS, STUNT *See* Automobile driving—Stunt driving
DRIVEWAYS
Driveway surfaces: concrete vs. asphalt [interview with J. Christo and T. Buss] il pors *Home Mechanix* 85:16-21+ Jl '89
Path to glory [Tom Hasman's prize-winning brick walkway; cover story] C. Weese. il *Home Mechanix* 85:34-6+ My '89
Why waste sun on a driveway? Make it into a patio. il *Sunset (Central West edition)* 182:252-3 My '89
Maintenance and repair
Asphalt driveway. D. Prestly. il *The Family Handyman* 39:58+ S '89
Driveway damage. M. J. Schultz. il *Home Mechanix* 85:24+ Ag '89
DRIVING, AUTOMOBILE *See* Automobile driving
DRIVING, MOTOR VEHICLE *See* Motor vehicle driving
DRIVING MISS DAISY [film] *See* Motion picture reviews—Single works
DRIVING SIMULATORS *See* Automobile driving simulators
DROHOJOWSKA, HUNTER
The '80s: stop making sense [cover story] il *Art News* 88:146-51 O '89
Above Beverly Hills. il *Architectural Digest* 46:230-7 My '89
Helen the Great. il *Harper's Bazaar* 122:102-3+ Je '89
LACMA revisited. il por *Architectural Digest* 46:172+ My '89
Pop provocateur. il *Harper's Bazaar* 122:222 S '89
Strength of vision. il *Harper's Bazaar* 122:204-7+ Ap '89
DRONE AIRCRAFT *See* Remotely piloted vehicles
DRONZEK, ANNA
Now I think I might almost understand [story] il *Seventeen* 48:120-1+ N '89
DROOD [musical] *See* Musicals, revues, etc.—Reviews—Single works

DROP LEAF TABLES *See* Tables
DROPOUTS
See also
Youth Employment Skills Canada Inc.
Can business throw a net under Hispanic dropouts? T. Mason. il *Business Week* p151+ F 20 '89
Can the school drop-out problem be solved? L. Ransom. il *Jet* 77:12-13+ O 9 '89
Early action can prevent dropouts. *USA Today (Periodical)* 117:12 Ap '89
Keeping kids in school—should we try? [research by Sandra Miller and others and by Edwin Farrell] G. W. Bracey. il *Phi Delta Kappan* 71:77-9 S '89
Moving around and dropping out [research by Ridge Hammons and Miles Olson] G. W. Bracey. il *Phi Delta Kappan* 70:407 Ja '89
A new approach to the dropout problem. P. Woodring. *Phi Delta Kappan* 70:468-9 F '89
"No one's born a loser!" [work of J. Williams in Enterprise High program for dropouts in Utica, Mich.] P. Skalka. *Reader's Digest* 134:21-2+ F '89
No pass, no drive [requiring school attendance for driver's license] J. Rachlin and J. P. Shapiro. il *U.S. News & World Report* 106:49-51 Je 5 '89
The quick fix or a lasting solution? [requiring school attendance for obtaining driver's license] C. Pipho. il *Phi Delta Kappan* 70:502-3 Mr '89
School dropouts: dead-end ahead. E. Karlsberg. il *'Teen* 33:24-5+ Ja '89
Some data on dropouts [research by Byron Barrington and Bryan Hendricks] G. W. Bracey. il *Phi Delta Kappan* 71:247-8 N '89
Tuning in to the needs of high school dropouts. G. S. Becker. il *Business Week* p18 Jl 3 '89
Why kids drop out. B. B. Remmes. por *Newsweek* 113:10-11 Mr 6 '89
DROPS
A drop of water becomes a gateway into the world of catastrophe optics. J. Walker. il *Scientific American* 261:176-9 S '89
DROSOPHILA
Developmental and physiological aspects of reaction norms. W. Scharloo. bibl f il *BioScience* 39:465-71 Jl/Ag '89
Drosophila nuclear proteins bind to regions of alternating C and T residues in gene promoters. D. S. Gilmour and others. bibl f il *Science* 245:1487-90 S 29 '89
A family of putative potassium channel genes in Drosophila. A. Butler and others. bibl f il *Science* 243:943-7 F 17 '89
Growing old together: fruit flies and you [effects of catalase production on cell aging in Drosophila; research by Glenn Bewley] il *Discover* 10:8 Ap '89
Mapping the Drosophila genome with yeast artificial chromosomes. D. Garza and others. bibl f il *Science* 246:641-6 N 3 '89
Reciprocal effects of hyper- and hypoactivity mutations in the Drosophila pattern gene *torso*. T. R. Strecker and others. bibl f il *Science* 243:1062-6 F 24 '89
Two cultures find common ground [conference of specialists in mouse and fruit fly development] J. L. Marx. il *Science* 244:652-3 My 12 '89
Development
See Insects—Development
Eye
See Eye—Insects
DROTTNINGHOLM (SWEDEN)
Music
See also
Opera—Sweden
DROUGHT-RESISTANT GARDENING *See* Xeriscaping
DROUGHTS
See also
Plants, Effect of drought on
An Amish drought journal [Ohio] D. Kline. il *The Mother Earth News* 118:60-1 Jl/Ag '89
Cattleman's nightmare. V. Ehmke. il *Successful Farming* 87:38 Ag '89
A climate for death [effect on wildlife] P. W. Moser. il *Sports Illustrated* 70:48-50+ Mr 13 '89
Drought, fires, and large mammals [Yellowstone National Park] F. J. Singer and others. bibl f il maps *BioScience* 39:716-22 N '89
Far-off clues to nearby weather [research by Kevin Trenberth] B. Carpenter. il map *U.S. News & World Report* 106:56 Ja 16 '89
Farm wife shares drought journal of despair, hope. M. Wilcox. il *Successful Farming* 87:66AI F '89
The long, hot summer of '88 [special section] il maps *Natural History* p42-5+ Ja '89
The real deficit is water. H. Sidey. il *Time* 133:19 F 27 '89
The summer of '88 [research by Kevin E. Trenberth] L. Burnham. *Scientific American* 260:21 Mr '89
A sun-baked summer in the U.S. D. LeComte. il *Weatherwise* 42:13-16 F '89
Weathering the drought [duck hunting curtailed] L. Williamson. il *Outdoor Life* 183:48+ Ja '89

DROUGHTS—*cont.*

Written in the winds: the great drought of '88. J. Namias. maps *Weatherwise* 42:85-7 Ap '89

Anecdotes, facetiae, satire, etc.

Dry humor. R. L. Welsch. il *Natural History* p70-1 Ja '89

I know who caused drought. D. Allen. il *Successful Farming* 87:38 Ja '89

Rain, man! W. Geist. il *New York* 22:30 Je 12 '89

History

The Dust Bowl [Cimarron County, Okla.; cover story] M. Parfit. bibl (p174) il *Smithsonian* 20:44-54+ Je '89

International aspects

Water rules the world. E. M. Wieckowski. il *Discover* 10:36 Ja '89

North Africa

Seasonal dust [airborne global dust] map *Sea Frontiers* 35:197 Jl/Ag '89

United States

See Droughts

DROWNING

Drowning myths & facts. A. C. Mallozzi. *Good Housekeeping* 209:175 Jl '89

The luckiest little girl in the world [hypothermia patient M. Funk saved by extracorporeal rewarming] A. Sunshine-Genova. il pors *Ladies' Home Journal* 106:140-1+ Mr '89

My dream house and my boy [near drowning of son causes author to realize what is important in life]; ed. by Linda Lawrence. F. E. Baird. il *Reader's Digest* 135:9-10+ O '89

"My son is under the ice—find him!" [rescue and revival of drowning victim]; ed. by Elaine Fein. M. H. Garza. il por *Redbook* 172:44+ Mr '89

DROWNING BY NUMBERS [film] See Motion picture reviews—Single works

DROWNING RESCUES *See* Rescue work

DRUAR, JOSEPH

(jt. auth) See Wynne, Susan, and Druar, Joseph

DRUCKER, PETER FERDINAND, 1909-

How schools must change. il *Psychology Today* 23:18-20 My '89

about

Managing the post-business society. M. Magnet. *Fortune* 120:70-1 Jl 3 '89

The post-business society [interview] il *New Perspectives Quarterly* 6:21-5 Fall '89

DRUG ABUSE

See also

Alcoholics and alcoholism
Cocaine
Crack (Cocaine)
Drug education
Drugs and air pilots
Drugs and airplane accidents
Drugs and artists
Drugs and automobile drivers
Drugs and blacks
Drugs and bus drivers
Drugs and celebrities
Drugs and crime
Drugs and employment
Drugs and Eskimos
Drugs and infants
Drugs and journalists
Drugs and musicians
Drugs and nobility
Drugs and physicians
Drugs and politicians
Drugs and sports
Drugs and the aged
Drugs and the handicapped
Drugs and the mentally ill
Drugs and the press
Drugs and women
Drugs and youth
Heroin
Inhalant abuse
Marijuana
National Institute on Drug Abuse (U.S.)
PCP

Addicted to life [AIDS and drugs] M. B. Zuckerman. il *U.S. News & World Report* 106:84 Ap 24 '89

AIDS and IV drug use. D. Des Jarlais and S. R. Friedman. *Science* 245:578 Ag 11 '89

Alice in Drugland [scenario by Dennis Thompson] il *USA Today (Periodical)* 118:18-19 O '89

America's domestic quagmire [cover story; special section; with editorial comments by Nathan Gardels and Stanley K. Sheinbaum] il *New Perspectives Quarterly* 6:2-51, 64 Summ '89

Andean strategy [Bush antidrug plan] H. Jensen. il por *Maclean's* 102:26-8 S 18 '89

Apocalypse now: drugs [parallels between drug war and Vietnam war] E. Barnes. il *Life* 12:18-25 S '89

Attitude problem [reactions to J. Morley's article on using crack] *The New Republic* 201:4+ O 9 '89

Bennett the drug czar: an agenda. F. Barnes. il *The American Spectator* 22:14-15 Ap '89

Bennett's drug war. T. Morganthau. il por *Newsweek* 114:16-18 Ag 21 '89

The big drug bust [Bush program] *America* 161:155 S 23 '89

Cowboy in the capital: drug czar Bill Bennett. H. Kohn. il *Rolling Stone* p41-2+ N 2 '89

Cycles of craving. D. Hurley. il *Psychology Today* 23:54-8 Jl/Ag '89

Do humans need to get high? [views of R. K. Siegel] J. Beaty. il *Time* 134:58 Ag 21 '89

Drug abuse: gambling with infection [needle use] K. M. Porterfield. il *Current Health 2* 15:17-19 My '89

Drug abuse tied to 'fatal despondency' [research by Charles L. Rich] B. Bower. *Science News* 135:332 My 27 '89

Drug czar in search of a throne [W. Bennett; cover story] W. McGurn. il por *National Review* 41:22-4 Je 16 '89

The drug czar: no "Walter Wallflower". E. Marshall. por *Science* 243:1287 Mr 10 '89

Drug dealings. R. E. Tyrrell. il *The American Spectator* 22:8 Je '89

Drug frenzy: why the war on drugs misses the real target. B. Ehrenreich. il *Utne Reader* p76-9+ Mr/Ap '89

The drug trap. *Esquire* 111:138 My '89

Drugs and white America. D. Gergen. il *U.S. News & World Report* 107:79 S 18 '89

Drugs, lies & TV [G. Bush's televised war on drugs speech] R. Clark. *The Nation* 249:408-9 O 16 '89

Drugs of choice [non-addicted drug users; cover story] B. Bower. il *Science News* 136:392-3 D 16 '89

Feeling low over old highs. W. Shapiro. il *Time* 134:104 S 18 '89

Fighting on two fronts [W. J. Bennett targets dealers and users] il *Time* 134:29 Ag 14 '89

The 'fourth drive' [views of R. K. Siegel] N. Underwood. por *Maclean's* 102:45 Ag 28 '89

General Bennett. F. Barnes. *The New Republic* 201:14+ S 18-25 '89

Go ask Alice. J. Cummings. *Omni (New York, N.Y.)* 11:42+ S '89

High rate of HTLV-II infection in seropositive IV drug abusers in New Orleans. H. Lee and others. bibl f il *Science* 244:471-5 Ap 28 '89

HIV and IV drug abuse. K. Fackelmann. il *Science News* 135:168-9+ Mr 18 '89

How to beat drugs [cover story; special section] il *U.S. News & World Report* 107:69-72+ S 11 '89

How to win the war on drugs: target the users. J. A. Eisenach. il *USA Today (Periodical)* 117:46-8 Ja '89

HTLV-II common among drug abusers [study by Irvin S. Y. Chen] *Science News* 135:284 My 6 '89

Is your medicine an Rx for disaster? [prescription drug abuse] C. Marks. il *Mademoiselle* 95:130+ My '89

Kleber offers expert and blunt opinions on addiction. C. Holden. por *Science* 246:1381 D 15 '89

Let's get tough with drug users! C. T. Rowan. *Reader's Digest* 135:107-10 Jl '89

Letter from Washington [G. Bush's televised address on war on drugs] E. Drew. *The New Yorker* 65:102-4 O 2 '89

A lost cause is a lost cause. W. F. Buckley. *National Review* 41:70-1 S 29 '89

Moral propaganda [curbing spread of AIDS through needle exchange programs] K. McAuliffe. *Omni (New York, N.Y.)* 12:41 O '89

Mr. Bennett's war. *National Review* 41:13-14 S 15 '89

National drug control strategy [address, September 5, 1989] G. Bush. *Vital Speeches of the Day* 55:738-40 O 1 '89

Notes and comment [G. Bush's address on the drug problem] *The New Yorker* 65:33-4 S 18 '89

Now it's Bush's war [televised address] T. Morganthau. il pors *Newsweek* 114:22-4 S 18 '89

On the drug war [discussion of Summer 1989 special section, America's domestic quagmire] *New Perspectives Quarterly* 6:62-3 Fall '89

Over-the-counter addictions. J. E. Laird. *Better Homes and Gardens* 67:40+ S '89

The phony war [Bush administration war on drugs] *Commonweal* 116:515-16 O 6 '89

Phony war on drugs. il *The Progressive* 53:8-9 O '89

Plain talk about drugs: users are bums. H. Williams. il *Reader's Digest* 134:129-30 Je '89

A political opiate [war on drugs; cover story] L. H. Lapham. bibl f il *Harper's* 279:43-8 D '89

The president's drug war: is it enough? S. Manning. il *Scholastic Update (Teachers' edition)* 122:15-16 N 17 '89

Reading the signs of a drug-plagued time [Bush drug program] J. M. Wall. *The Christian Century* 106:803-4 S 13-20 '89

Reps hit Bush plan to fund drug war with money cut from domestic programs. il *Jet* 76:4-5 S 25 '89

Roots of addiction [cover story] D. Gelman. il *Newsweek* 113:52-7 F 20 '89

Some things you do because they're right [interview with W. J. Bennett] J. Cook. il por *Forbes* 144:118+ N 13 '89

The struggle with ourselves [G. Bush's speech] H. Sidey. il por *Time* 134:32 S 18 '89

DRUG ABUSE—*cont.*

Taking drugs—seriously. P. J. O'Rourke. il *Rolling Stone* p57-8+ N 30 '89

Trading good needles for bad [D. Purchase tries to fight AIDS in Tacoma] R. Givens. il por *Newsweek* 113:49 Ja 9 '89

Users, like me. G. Regier. il *Harper's* 278:51-4 My '89

Waging war without weapons. F. Bruning. il *Maclean's* 102:15 O 9 '89

A walk on the demand side [address, May 14, 1989] W. J. Byron. *Vital Speeches of the Day* 55:627-9 Ag 1 '89

War on what? [Bush proposals] *National Review* 41:14 S 29 '89

The war? program? experiment? on drugs. D. E. Koshland, Jr. *Science* 245:1309 S 22 '89

Why we're losing the war on drugs. R. Flick. *Reader's Digest* 135:83-8 O '89

Will fear make Americans kick the drug habit? [Bush administration plan] R. Stodghill, II. il *Business Week* p30 S 11 '89

Animal models

Factors that predict individual vulnerability to amphetamine self-administration. P. V. Piazza and others. bibl f il *Science* 245:1511-13 S 29 '89

Rats yield active clues to drug addiction [research by Pier Vincenzo Piazza] B. Bower. *Science News* 136:215 S 30 '89

Bibliography

Desperate over drugs [cover story] M. Massing. il *The New York Review of Books* 36:22-6 Mr 30 '89

History

Drug frenzy is nothing new in the U.S. Kalamu ya Salaam. *Utne Reader* p78 Mr/Ap '89

From Coca-Cola to the cartels: battling drugs in America. L. Tarshis. il *Scholastic Update (Teachers' edition)* 122:10-11 N 17 '89

Insurance

Just say, it's covered. il *Esquire* 112:60 Jl '89

Legal aspects

One toke over the line [drug abuse as legal defense] M. Graham. *The New Republic* 200:20-1 Ap 17 '89

Rehabilitation

See also

Addiction Research and Treatment Corporation
Association for Drug Abuse Prevention and Treatment
Church work with drug addicts
Comedians' Drug and Alcohol Abuse Foundation
Delancey Street Foundation
Drug counseling
Hazelden Foundation
Mandela House (Oakland, Calif.)
Save America's Future (Organization)
Straight, Inc.

Addicted to tough talk. C. W. Colson. il *Christianity Today* 33:88 N 3 '89

Breaking the patterns that lead to relapse. E. Chiauzzi. il *Psychology Today* 23:18-19 D '89

Buprenorphine suppresses cocaine self-administration by rhesus monkeys [possible use in treatment of cocaine addiction] N. K. Mello and others. bibl f il *Science* 245:859-62 Ag 25 '89

Can drugs cure drug addiction? A. Purvis. il *Time* 134:104 D 11 '89

Coming clean, staying sober: how good girls kick bad drugs. J. Neimark. *Mademoiselle* 95:172-3+ F '89

Getting clean [cover story] P. Hoban. il *New York* 22:38-45 F 20 '89

Lukewarm turkey [drug firms balk at pursuing buprenorphine, a heroin addiction treatment] J. Horgan. *Scientific American* 260:32 Mr '89

NIDA aims to fight drugs with drugs. M. M. Waldrop. *Science* 245:1443-4 S 29 '89

Running from drugs. R. Rodale. il por *Runner's World* 24:24 F '89

The search for cocaine's methadone [link to dopamine pathways in the brain] D. Hurley. il *Psychology Today* 23:59-60 Jl/Ag '89

Some winning maneuvers in the war on drugs. E. Ehrlich. il *Business Week* p120-2+ N 27 '89

A technical fix for cocaine addiction. J. Silberner. il *U.S. News & World Report* 106:61 Ap 17 '89

Teen drug rehab: the inside story [Adolescent Addiction Recovery Unit at St. Luke's Hospital in Denver] K. M. Porterfield. il *Current Health 2* 15:19-21 F '89

Treatment. S. Findlay. il *U.S. News & World Report* 107:74-6+ S 11 '89

What to do when the drug problem strikes home. il *Ebony* 44:152+ Ag '89

Testing

A boost for drug testing [Supreme Court rulings] A. L. Sanders. il *Time* 133:62 Ap 3 '89

Business moves against drugs. D. C. Bacon. il *Nation's Business* 77:82+ N '89

Drug testing is here to stay. *USA Today (Periodical)* 118:8-9 D '89

Drug testing on the job. J. Malveaux. il *Essence* 19:122 F '89

Employee drug testing. bibl f il *Monthly Labor Review* 112:75-6 N '89

The High Court weighs drug tests [testing of federal employees] il *Newsweek* 113:8 Ap 3 '89

Industry slow to comply with FAA drug testing rule [airlines] M. Mecham. il *Aviation Week & Space Technology* 131:20-3 S 18 '89

Jar wars [politicians taking drug tests] W. Saletan. *The New Republic* 201:13-14 O 2 '89

The NFL fails its drug test. R. Demak and J. Kirshenbaum. il *Sports Illustrated* 71:38-41+ Jl 10 '89

On the job against drugs. il *Nation's Business* 77:29-31 Jl '89

Supreme Court decisions set precedent for pilot drug testing [with editorial comment] P. Proctor. *Aviation Week & Space Technology* 130:9, 30 Mr 27 '89

Supreme Court drug test rulings. *Monthly Labor Review* 112:43 Je '89

The war on drugs: saying 'yes' to getting involved [address, December 1, 1988] J. W. Johnstone, Jr. *Vital Speeches of the Day* 55:325-7 Mr 15 '89

Bolivia

Choking off the supply [cocaine] J. Madeley. il *World Health* p28-9 Je '89

Canada

A deadly plague of drugs [cover story; special section; with editorial comment by Kevin Doyle] il *Maclean's* 102:4, 44-51 Ap 3 '89

Great Britain

No quick drug fix. A. Lejeune. *National Review* 41:21-3 Mr 24 '89

Hawaii

The fire of 'ice'. M. A. Lerner. il *Newsweek* 114:37-8+ N 27 '89

Latin America

Victims of the drug trade. il *Christianity Today* 33:42 S 8 '89

United States

See Drug abuse

DRUG ABUSE IN MOTION PICTURES

Dead men don't act [J. Belushi biography Wired] M. Rochlin. por *American Film* 14:72 Jl/Ag '89

Finally, the Belushi story [release of Wired] R. Zoglin. il por *Time* 133:90-1 Ap 24 '89

DRUG ABUSE IN TELEVISION

Drugs on TV. J. Kalter. il *TV Guide* 37:14-16 Ap 1-7 '89

DRUG ABUSE RESISTANCE EDUCATION (PROGRAM)

See DARE America (Program)

DRUG ADDICTS *See* Drug abuse

DRUG CONTROL *See* Narcotics laws and regulations

DRUG COUNSELING

Treating addictions. M. Stanton. il *Occupational Outlook Quarterly* 32:18-26 Wint '88

DRUG DELIVERY SYSTEMS IN THE BODY *See* Drugs—Dosage forms

DRUG EDUCATION

See also

Celebrities for a Drug-Free America
DARE America (Program)

Alcohol and drug education in elementary schools. D. F. Bradley. *The Education Digest* 54:61-3 Mr '89

Don't let drug programs send deadly messages. L. Horton. *The Education Digest* 54:38-9 My '89

Schooling children about drugs. G. Witkin. *U.S. News & World Report* 107:80-1 S 11 '89

Some winning maneuvers in the war on drugs. E. Ehrlich. il *Business Week* p120-2+ N 27 '89

Teaching kids to say no. M. Miller. il *Newsweek* 113:77 Je 5 '89

Aids and devices

Drug Alert! [computer game] C. S. Holzberg. il *Compute!* 11:96-8 Ja '89

DRUG ENFORCEMENT ADMINISTRATION (U.S.) *See* United States. Drug Enforcement Administration

DRUG INDUSTRY

See also

A. H. Robins Company, Inc.
Abbott Laboratories
Alza Corp.
Bergen Brunswig Corp.
Block Drug Co.
Bristol-Myers Co.
Burroughs Wellcome Co.
Clinical Technologies Associates
Enzon, Inc.
Hoffmann-La Roche Inc.
Johnson & Johnson
Kanasco, Ltd.
LyphoMed Inc.
Magainin Sciences Inc.
Marion Laboratories, Inc.
McKesson Corp.
Merck & Co., Inc.
Monsanto Company
Mylan Laboratories Inc.
Nova Pharmaceutical Corp.
Ortho Pharmaceutical Corporation
Pfizer Inc.

DRUG INDUSTRY—See also—*cont.*
Procter & Gamble Co.
Rorer Group Inc.
Schering-Plough Corp.
SmithKline Beckman Corp.
Squibb Corp.
Sterling Drug Inc.
Upjohn Co.
AIDS: bioscience attacks a killer [cover story] F. Lunzer. il *High Technology Business* 9:18-21+ F '89
The bitter pill [lack of contraceptive research in the U.S.] C. Djerassi. bibl f *Science* 245:356-61 Jl 28 '89

Acquisitions and mergers
Filling Bristol-Myers' prescription [Squibb merger] J. Weber, Jr. and S. Benway. il pors *Business Week* p80-1 Ag 14 '89
Friendly medicine [merger of Bristol-Myers and Squibb] *Time* 134:39 Ag 7 '89
Kodak may wish it never went to the drugstore [Sterling Drug acquisition] K. H. Hammonds. il *Business Week* p72+ D 4 '89

International aspects
The Rx for Japan's drug companies: America. A. Borrus. il *Business Week* p49-50 N 20 '89
SmithKline thinks Beecham can cure what ails it. J. Weber, Jr. and M. Maremont. il *Business Week* p22 Ap 17 '89

Advertising
Pitching to patients [prescription drugs] A. Miller and T. Barrett. il *Newsweek* 113:40-1 My 8 '89

Cooperation
Merck wants to be alone—but with lots of friends. J. Weber, Jr. il *Business Week* p62 O 23 '89

Ethical aspects
Drug abuse [Mylan Laboratories' suspicions of FDA corruption bear fruit] J. Novack. il *Forbes* 143:42-3 Je 26 '89
Ensuring the safety of generic drugs. F. E. Young. il *FDA Consumer* 23:5-7 D '89/Ja '90
FDA monitoring generics. *FDA Consumer* 23:2 N '89
Generic concern. R. Coorsh. *Consumers' Research Magazine* 72:4 O '89
How far has the cancer spread at the FDA? [generic drug scandal] J. Carey. il *Business Week* p30-1 S 18 '89
Not what the doctor ordered [FDA accused of carelessness about generic drugs] J. N. Baker. il *Newsweek* 114:32 Ag 28 '89
The other drug war here at home [generic drug scandal] *U.S. News & World Report* 107:11 S 11 '89
A prescription for scandal [generic drug industry] C. Gorman. il *Time* 134:56 Ag 28 '89
A shaggy drug tale [Kanasco Ltd.] il *FDA Consumer* 23:39-40 Ap '89
Watchdogs overdose on generic drugs [FDA investigation of fraudulent activities] S. Dentzer. il *U.S. News & World Report* 107:26 Ag 28-S 4 '89

Export-import trade
When the corner drugstore falls short [importing drugs not approved by FDA] F. Lunzer. il *U.S. News & World Report* 106:82 F 13 '89

Finance
Drug profits seem to be on steroids. J. H. Cutaia. il *Business Week* p97 Ja 9 '89
Health. M. Fritz. il *Forbes* 143:150-1 Ja 9 '89

Laws and regulations
See Drug laws and regulations

Licensing agreements
Drug extender [Alza Corp.] I. Chithelen. il por *Forbes* 144:95-6 Jl 10 '89

Marketing
See also
Drug industry—Licensing agreements
Orphan drugs
Can P&G commandeer more shelves in the medicine chest? [prescription drug marketing] Z. Schiller. il *Business Week* p64+ Ap 10 '89
The heart attack business. C. Messina. il *High Technology Business* 9:22-5 Mr '89
Pitching doctors. M. S. Wilkes and M. Shuchman. il *The New York Times Magazine* p88+ N 5 '89
What's wrong with generic drugs? [cover story] J. W. Merline. il *Consumers' Research Magazine* 72:11-17 D '89

Public relations
Romantics, radicals and realists [address, April 10, 1989] D. C. Jones. *Vital Speeches of the Day* 55:750-5 O 1 '89

Securities
Drug deals. T. Jaffe. il *Forbes* 143:124 Ja 23 '89
Wrong medicine. E. Sturza and D. Kortrey. il *Forbes* 143:334 My 29 '89

Suits and claims
Day of reckoning [Dalkon Shield case] C. Breslin. il *Ms.* 17:46-52 Je '89
A drug that could replace transfusions—if it ever reaches the market [Ortho vs. Amgen in battle over erythropoietin] J. O. Hamilton and J. Weber, Jr. il *Business Week* p60+ Mr 27 '89
Fatal contraption [Dalkon Shield] M. Kort. il *Essence* 20:16+ Jl '89

How to reward the criminals [A. H. Robins' use of bankruptcy law to avoid Dalkon Shield suits] R. Shereff. *The Nation* 248:192-5 F 13 '89
Suspect vaccine [K. Fox files suit against Merck & Co. after developing rubella vaccine side effects] H. S. Miller. il por *Ms.* 17:81-2 Ap '89

France
See also
Institut Merieux SA
Roussel-Uclaf SA

Great Britain
See also
Beecham Group plc
Glaxo Holdings plc

Japan
Rising pharmaceutical force. C. Messina. il *High Technology Business* 9:14 Ap '89
The Rx for Japan's drug companies: America. A. Borrus. il *Business Week* p49-50 N 20 '89

Switzerland
See also
Ciba-Geigy AG

United States
See Drug industry

Western Europe
Are U.S. multi-nationals ready for the U.S. of Europe? [address, May 16, 1989] R. E. Cawthorn. *Vital Speeches of the Day* 55:654-7 Ag 15 '89
DRUG INTERACTIONS IN THE BODY See Drugs—Physiological effects
DRUG LAWS AND REGULATIONS
See also
Drugs—Labeling
Narcotics laws and regulations
United States. Food and Drug Administration
1988 product approvals: an FDA annual report. F. E. Young. il *FDA Consumer* 23:6-7 Ap '89
At last, quicker access to AIDS drugs. J. Seligmann. *Newsweek* 114:76 Jl 10 '89
Conflicting prescriptions. *The New Republic* 201:4 Ag 28 '89
Desperation drugs [AIDS drugs] S. Begley. il *Newsweek* 114:48-51 Ag 7 '89
Drugs from the underground [FDA allows wider use of experimental AIDS drugs] D. Thompson. il *Time* 134:49 Jl 10 '89
The facts of life [need for faster drug approval and information on side effects] H. Evans. il *U.S. News & World Report* 106:79 F 27 '89
FDA—hazardous to our health? M. S. Forbes, Jr. il *Forbes* 144:27 Ag 21 '89
Proposal seeks wider access to AIDS drugs [views of Anthony S. Fauci] K. Fackelmann. *Science News* 136:6 Jl 1 '89
Putting pressure on illegal steroid traffic [anabolic steroids] V. Modeland. il *FDA Consumer* 23:33-4 O '89
Quick release of AIDS drugs. E. Marshall. il *Science* 245:345+ Jl 28 '89
A risky lifeline for AIDS victims [Bristol-Myers distributes unproven drug] *U.S. News & World Report* 107:14 Jl 24 '89
Rx for the FDA [pressure to speed up approval process] J. E. Groopman. *The New Republic* 200:17-18+ F 13 '89
Scientific necessity, patients' rights [pressuring FDA to speed up approval process] J. Carey. il *U.S. News & World Report* 106:50-1 Ja 23 '89
Speeding help and hope to the desperately ill. F. E. Young. il *FDA Consumer* 23:8-9 F '89
Why can't we get the medicine we need? R. Flick. *Reader's Digest* 135:101-6 Ag '89

International aspects
When the corner drugstore falls short [importing drugs not approved by FDA] F. Lunzer. il *U.S. News & World Report* 106:82 F 13 '89

Brazil
U.S. import duties increase for certain Brazilian products [response to failure to provide patent protection for U.S. pharmaceuticals; proclamation, October 20, 1988] R. Reagan. *Department of State Bulletin* 89:49 Ja '89

Canada
An abrupt reversal [making available unapproved AIDS drugs] M. Nichols. il *Maclean's* 102:49+ Mr 13 '89

Great Britain
Sting operation nabs Iranian counterfeit drug dealer [counterfeit Tagamet dealer J. Naghdi] W. Grigg. il *FDA Consumer* 23:37-8 Ap '89

North America
A new war on AIDS [access to experimental drugs] N. Underwood. il *Maclean's* 102:62 S 18 '89

Southeast Asia
ASEAN togetherness in pharmaceuticals. T. Yoshida. il *World Health* p29 N '89

DRUG LAWS AND REGULATIONS—*cont.*
United States
See Drug laws and regulations
DRUG PARAPHERNALIA
Laws and regulations
In Chicago, two angry priests declare a holy war on drugs [M. Pfleger and G. Clements put pressure on stores to stop selling drug paraphernalia] W. Plummer. il pors *People Weekly* 32:102-3 S 4 '89
DRUG PLANTS *See* Botany, Medical
DRUG RECEPTORS
The chemistry of reefer madness [THC receptor; research by Allyn Howlett] L. Wallach. il *Omni (New York, N.Y.)* 11:18+ Ag '89
Flipping the main switch in the central reward system? [cocaine and the brain] C. Holden. il *Science* 246:1378-9 D 15 '89
The search for cocaine's methadone [link to dopamine pathways in the brain] D. Hurley. il *Psychology Today* 23:59-60 Jl/Ag '89
Type I and type II GABA_A-benzodiazepine receptors produced in transfected cells. D. B. Pritchett and others. bibl f il *Science* 245:1389-92 S 22 '89
DRUG RESEARCH *See* Pharmaceutical research
DRUG RESISTANCE
Multidrug resistance in cancer. N. Kartner and V. Ling. bibl il *Scientific American* 260:44-51 Mr '89
Tumor resistance: weakening the pulse [research by Thomas P. Miller] R. Weiss. *Science News* 135:348 Je 3 '89
DRUG STORES *See* Drugstores
DRUG TESTING *See* Drug abuse—Testing; Pharmaceutical research
DRUG TOLERANCE *See* Drugs—Physiological effects
DRUG TRADE *See* Drug industry
DRUG TRAFFIC *See* Narcotics trade
DRUG WARS: THE CAMARENA STORY [television program]
See Television program reviews—Single works
DRUGGISTS *See* Pharmacists
DRUGS
See also
Abortifacients
Adrenergic blocking agents
Alcohol antagonists
Amphetamines
Anti-inflammatory agents
Antibiotics
Antihypertensive agents
Botany, Medical
Cancer inhibiting substances
Generic drugs
Hypnotics
Medicines, Nonprescription
Narcotics
Orphan drugs
Placebos
Tranquilizing drugs
Veterinary drugs
See also names of drugs
10 questions to ask your pharmacist [taking medications correctly] C. Slom. *McCall's* 116:96 F '89
Advertising
See Drug industry—Advertising
Dosage
See also
Microdoses
Doing more good than harm with children's medications. S. J. Ackerman. il *FDA Consumer* 23:28-31 Mr '89
Getting to the heart of the Chinese [Chinese men more sensitive than Caucasian men to propranolol] *Science News* 135:156 Mr 11 '89
It's time to talk about children's medications. F. E. Young. il *FDA Consumer* 23:6-7 O '89
Dosage forms
See also
Nasal sprays
Oral medication
Pills
Transdermal patches
Candy-coated cholesterol cutter [cholestyramine in candy bar form] M. Behen. il *American Health* 8:18+ Jl/Ag '89
Drug extender [Alza Corp.] I. Chithelen. il por *Forbes* 144:95-6 Jl 10 '89
Getting kids to take their medicine [views of Barton D. Schmitt] S. Mahler. il *McCall's* 117:62 N '89
Lollipop draws consumer group's ire [presurgical sedative laced with fentanyl] *Science News* 135:156 Mr 11 '89
Labeling
Drug label mix-ups lead to recalls, lawsuits [cases involving My-K and Humco Laboratories] C. Carey. il *FDA Consumer* 23:33-4 Mr '89
Mixed messages [need for warning labels on over-the-counter ibuprofen] A. E. Young. *Common Cause Magazine* 15:11-12 S/O '89
Product labels: first-line protection from harm. F. E. Young. il *FDA Consumer* 23:5-6 Je '89

Laws and regulations
See Drug laws and regulations
Names
Alliterative prescriptions pose problems [drugs related to the antibiotic cephalosporin] *Science News* 135:237 Ap 15 '89
Packaging
See also
Medicine bottles
Patents
U.S. import duties increase for certain Brazilian products [response to failure to provide patent protection for U.S. pharmaceuticals; proclamation, October 20, 1988] R. Reagan. *Department of State Bulletin* 89:49 Ja '89
Physiological effects
See also
Fetus, Effect of drugs on the
Drugs and alcohol: a dangerous mix. il *McCall's* 116:90 Ja '89
Drugs with summertime side effects [views of James W. Long] L. Holland. il *Good Housekeeping* 209:173 Jl '89
The facts of life [need for faster drug approval and information on side effects] H. Evans. il *U.S. News & World Report* 106:79 F 27 '89
High-risk pain pills. L. Morgenroth. il *The Atlantic* 264:36+ D '89
Sex offenders [prescription drugs can inhibit sexual desire] C. Platt. *Harper's Bazaar* 122:135+ Ag '89
There are no perfect drugs. E. E. Rosenbaum. il *New Choices for the Best Years* 29:24+ Mr '89
Prices
Drug price bust. J. Novack. il *Forbes* 144:39-40 O 30 '89
Psychological effects
See Psychopharmacology
Research
See Pharmaceutical research
Side effects
See Drugs—Physiological effects
Testing
See Drug abuse—Testing; Pharmaceutical research
DRUGS AND AIR PILOTS
Have one for the runway: how Transportation Department policies add new meaning to the word "red-eye" [FAA policies] D. Nather. *The Washington Monthly* 21:12-14+ Ap '89
Supreme Court decisions set precedent for pilot drug testing [with editorial comment] P. Proctor. *Aviation Week & Space Technology* 130:9, 30 Mr 27 '89
DRUGS AND AIRPLANE ACCIDENTS
Autopsy on Trans-Colorado captain reveals evidence of cocaine use [crash in January 1988] il *Aviation Week & Space Technology* 131:71+ Jl 3 '89
Board urges closer review of special approach procedures, pilots' skills [Trans-Colorado Airlines crash in January 1988] *Aviation Week & Space Technology* 131:111+ Jl 31 '89
Industry slow to comply with FAA drug testing rule. M. Mecham. il *Aviation Week & Space Technology* 131:20-3 S 18 '89
Metro 3 crashed during special approach to airport in Colorado [January 1988] *Aviation Week & Space Technology* 130:75+ Jl 10 '89
NTSB asserts captain's cocaine use contributed to crash of Continental Express Metro 3 [Capt. S. Silver; January 1988 crash near Durango, Colo.] C. Fotos. *Aviation Week & Space Technology* 130:59 F 6 '89
Safety Board cites captain's failure to monitor approach as key in crash [Trans-Colorado Airlines crash in January 1988] *Aviation Week & Space Technology* 131:103+ Jl 17 '89
Safety Board cites copilot's flying, captain's drug use in Metro 3 crash [Trans-Colorado Airlines crash in January 1988] *Aviation Week & Space Technology* 130:103-4 Je 26 '89
Snow storm [cocaine and lack of skill blamed for crash of commuter airliner on approach to Durango, Colo.] P. Garrison. *Flying* 116:30-2 N '89
DRUGS AND ARTISTS
The price of fame [J.-M. Basquiat] A. Decker. il pors *Art News* 88:96-101 Ja '89
DRUGS AND AUTOMOBILE DRIVERS
The hot pursuit of drugged drivers. il *U.S. News & World Report* 107:8 D 25 '89-Ja 1 '90
"I thought I could make it home". K. Barrett and R. Greene. il *Reader's Digest* 134:148-50 Mr '89
DRUGS AND BLACKS
The blind high [narcotics trade not just a black problem in Cleveland] M. Drexler. *Utne Reader* p99-100 S/O '89
Can the drug crisis be solved? il *Jet* 76:12-14 S 18 '89
Drugs, Democrats and priorities [call for blacks to fight drug plague] M. Waters. *The Nation* 249:141-4 Jl 24-31 '89
Ebony special issue examines drug crisis in black America. *Jet* 76:57 Ag 7 '89
Far beyond indifference. M. Greenfield. il *Newsweek* 114:88 S 18 '89

DRUGS AND BLACKS—*cont.*

Just say no [excerpts from The autobiography of Malcolm X] Malcolm X. il *New Perspectives Quarterly* 6:26-32 Summ '89

Muslim dopebusters: the brightest point of light [work of the Nation of Islam; interview with A. Muhammed] il *New Perspectives Quarterly* 6:32-6 Summ '89

Opportunity foreclosure zones. J. D. Kasarda. il *New Perspectives Quarterly* 6:16-21 Summ '89

Prisoners of crack. L. Cole. il *Rolling Stone* p61-4+ F 9 '89

Scar tissue [racism as cause of drug use debunked] L. Wieseltier. *The New Republic* 200:18-20+ Je 5 '89

War! The drug crisis [cover story; special section] il *Ebony* 44:97-100+ Ag '89

Will new drug 'ice' freeze hope in black communities? A. Carthane. il *Jet* 77:12-15 D 18 '89

DRUGS AND BUS DRIVERS

Bus drivers: dealing while driving [school bus drivers arrested in Chicago] *Newsweek* 114:50 D 11 '89

DRUGS AND CELEBRITIES

See also

Celebrities for a Drug-Free America

Apollonia arrested for marijuana; claims buy was research for movie. il por *Jet* 77:31 O 23 '89

Bail is set at $2 mil. for Bridges; faces more charges [T. Bridges] por *Jet* 75:12 Mr 20 '89

Bill Cosby responds to daughter's drug abuse with tough love [E. Cosby] il pors *Jet* 77:64-5 O 16 '89

Bridges' mother blames son's problems on drugs [T. Bridges] il por *Jet* 75:52 F 27 '89

Celebs speak out on addiction [C. Haim, D. Barrymore and G. O'Neal] L. E. Brooks. pors *'Teen* 33:30+ S '89

Dead men don't act [J. Belushi biography Wired] M. Rochlin. por *American Film* 14:72 Jl/Ag '89

The devil and John Holmes: drugs, porn and the murders on Wonderland Avenue. M. Sager. il pors *Rolling Stone* p50-2+ Je 15 '89

Finally, the Belushi story [release of Wired] R. Zoglin. il por *Time* 133:90-1 Ap 24 '89

Healthy, wealthy and a Wiseguy no longer, rehabbed Ray Sharkey is looking at a bright future. S. Schindehette. il pors *People Weekly* 31:50-2 F 27 '89

Hollywood's drug scene—how bad is it now? [cover story] G. Dillow. il *TV Guide* 37:4-8 Ag 19-25 '89

'I thought there was something emotionally wrong with me' [J. Walton] E. Warren. por *TV Guide* 37:26 Ap 15-21 '89

'I wanted people to know I had a problem' [D. Barrymore] E. Warren. il pors *TV Guide* 37:16-18 Mr 25-31 '89

Sammy Davis Jr. faces life, aging and cocaine [excerpt from Why me?] S. Davis, Jr. and others. il pors *Ebony* 44:66+ Jl '89

The secret Drew Barrymore [cover story]; ed. by Todd Gold. D. Barrymore. il pors *People Weekly* 31:70-2+ Ja 16 '89

Todd Bridges tells how Hollywood destroyed his life and how God is rebuilding it. il pors *Jet* 76:28-30 Ap 10 '89

DRUGS AND CHILDREN *See* Drugs and youth

DRUGS AND COMEDIANS

See also

Comedians' Drug and Alcohol Abuse Foundation

DRUGS AND CRIME

Bring back the Mafia. R. Moran. por *Newsweek* 114:8 Ag 7 '89

Crackdown [cover story] J. Q. Wilson and J. J. DiIulio. *The New Republic* 201:21-5 Jl 10 '89

Dead zones [urban crime areas; cover story; special section] T. Moore. il *U.S. News & World Report* 106:20-5+ Ap 10 '89

The drug-violence nexus [crack-related violence] P. Goldstein and H. Brownstein. *New Perspectives Quarterly* 6:24 Summ '89

Fighting back: America wages war on drugs and crime [cover story; special issue] il map *Scholastic Update (Teachers' edition)* 122:2-22 N 17 '89

It's déjà vu all over again [drug-related crime wave in Washington, D.C.; views of D. P. Moynihan] *U.S. News & World Report* 106:15 Ap 3 '89

Murder capital [Washington, D.C.] M. Tidwell. il *The Progressive* 53:46 Jl '89

Murder wave in the capital [Washington, D.C.] T. Morganthau. il *Newsweek* 113:16-19 Mr 13 '89

The newest drug war [crack and crank in rural America] J. N. Baker. il *Newsweek* 113:20-2 Ap 3 '89

No safe place. A. McCarthy. il *Commonweal* 116:72 F 10 '89

Notes and comment [drug murders in Washington, D.C.] *The New Yorker* 65:29-30 Ap 17 '89

On the firing line [police and war on drugs] G. Hackett. il *Newsweek* 113:32-4+ My 29 '89

One toke over the line [drug abuse as legal defense] M. Graham. *The New Republic* 200:20-1 Ap 17 '89

A slaughter of innocents [bystanders caught in narcotics trade crossfire] *U.S. News & World Report* 107:12 Jl 10 '89

An ugly epidemic [Washington D.C. at war with crack] W. Lowther. il *Maclean's* 102:50 Ap 3 '89

'We need drastic measures'. M. Beck. il *Newsweek* 113:21 Mr 13 '89

When drug gangs move to nice places. S. J. Hedges. *U.S. News & World Report* 106:42 Je 5 '89

DRUGS AND EMPLOYMENT

A boost for drug testing [Supreme Court rulings] A. L. Sanders. il *Time* 133:62 Ap 3 '89

Business moves against drugs. D. C. Bacon. il *Nation's Business* 77:82+ N '89

Business' role in war on drugs [federal contractors required to establish antidrug programs] D. C. Bacon. *Nation's Business* 77:5 Ja '89

Drug testing is here to stay. *USA Today (Periodical)* 118:8-9 D '89

Drug testing on the job. J. Malveaux. il *Essence* 19:122 F '89

Employee drug testing. bibl f il *Monthly Labor Review* 112:75-6 N '89

The High Court weighs drug tests [testing of federal employees] il *Newsweek* 113:8 Ap 3 '89

Just say nothing? [Drug-Free Workplace Act] D. Fanning. il *Forbes* 144:220 N 27 '89

The most effective weapon in the war against drugs: the paycheck. il *Nation's Business* 77:99 O '89

On the job against drugs. il *Nation's Business* 77:29-31 Jl '89

Supreme Court drug test rulings. *Monthly Labor Review* 112:43 Je '89

Using 'spies to win a war': corporations turn to detectives to catch workers with drug problems. J. Schwartz. il *Newsweek* 114:56-7 N 6 '89

The war on drugs: saying 'yes' to getting involved [address, December 1, 1988] J. W. Johnstone, Jr. *Vital Speeches of the Day* 55:325-7 Mr 15 '89

DRUGS AND ESKIMOS

Off with their heads [walrus heads traded for illicit drugs by Eskimos in Alaska] M. Beck. il *Newsweek* 113:78 Je 5 '89

DRUGS AND INFANTS

Cocaine babies: the littlest victims [penalties to mothers] il *Newsweek* 114:55 O 2 '89

Cocaine mothers imperil babies' brains [reports by Ira J. Chasnoff and Barry Zuckerman] K. Fackelmann. *Science News* 135:198 Ap 1 '89

Cocaine's youngest victims. C. García-Barrio. il *American Visions* 4:16 D '89

Crack in the cradle. A. C. Revkin. il *Discover* 10:62-9 S '89

Here come the pregnancy police [legal action against mothers of infants exposed to drugs] A. Sachs. il *Time* 133:104-5 My 22 '89

Jailing mothers for drug abuse [screening newborns in Butte County, Calif.] S. LaCroix. il *The Nation* 248:585-6+ My 1 '89

DRUGS AND JOURNALISTS

'Drugs almost destroyed my career' [black TV anchorman W. Bell] L. Norment. il pors *Ebony* 44:124-5 Ag '89

A real bad trip [substance abuse by TV newspeople] J. M. Robins. il *Channels (New York, N.Y.: 1986)* 9:19 Jl/Ag '89

A veteran TV anchorman's toughest story was his own—he had to beat drugs and depression; ed. by Jeannie Park. J. Jensen. il pors *People Weekly* 32:67-8+ S 4 '89

DRUGS AND MUSICIANS

Clean & sober [J. Hiatt] D. Wild. il pors *Rolling Stone* p56-7+ Ja 12 '89

Motown sues Rick James. S. Assael. *Rolling Stone* p30 My 18 '89

Prodigal son: after the drug bust, Eugene Fodor tries a comeback. P. Hoban. il pors *New York* 22:100-2+ D 4 '89

Smokey Robinson reveals: how infidelity and drugs destroyed his marriage. S. Robinson. il pors *Ebony* 44:148+ My '89

Tracing the tracks of his tears in a new book, Smokey Robinson says crack nearly killed him. S. Dougherty. il pors *People Weekly* 31:79-80+ Ap 3 '89

DRUGS AND NOBILITY

Death turns out the lights at a noble couple's last soirée [Ludwig Rudolph of Hanover and wife I. von Thurn-Valsassina] M. Brower. il *People Weekly* 31:51-2 Ja 9 '89

DRUGS AND PHYSICIANS

Docs in need of detox. D. Gelman. il *Newsweek* 113:61-2 My 29 '89

Pharmacists, doctors, and drug abuse [views of Robert Holt] il *USA Today (Periodical)* 117:8 Ja '89

DRUGS AND POLITICIANS

Jar wars [taking drug tests] W. Saletan. *The New Republic* 201:13-14 O 2 '89

The mayor's new drug crisis [Washington's M. Barry] L. Martz. por *Newsweek* 113:25 Ja 9 '89

Scandal at the top [revelations about Washington mayor M. Barry] W. Lowther. il por *Maclean's* 102:36 Ja 16 '89

Washington's mayor with nine lives, Marion Barry, risks another amid rumors of scandal [alleged cocaine use] M. Brower. il por *People Weekly* 31:48-9 Ja 16 '89

DRUGS AND RELIGION
See also
Church work with drug addicts
Peyotism

DRUGS AND SPORTS
Aaron Henry's dangerous journey [high school football player who used anabolic steroids] S. J. Smith. il *Reader's Digest* 135:116-20 D '89

Brown's Mack a free man, returns to football team [use of cocaine] il por *Jet* 77:48 N 27 '89

A day of reckoning [B. Johnson admits he took steroids] il pors *Maclean's* 102:32-3 Je 26 '89

The death of an athlete [high school steroid user B. Ramirez of Ashtabula, Ohio] R. Telander and M. Noden. il pors *Sports Illustrated* 70:68-72+ F 20 '89

A deepening scandal [physician J. Astaphan testifies on steroid use by B. Johnson] B. Wickens. pors *Maclean's* 102:49-50 Je 5 '89

Did Ria or didn't she? [disqualification of woman marathon runner R. van Landeghem for failing Olympic drug test] *Runner's World* 24:42-3 Ja '89

A dirty coach comes clean [C. Francis testifies on steroid use by B. Johnson and other Canadian athletes] M. Noden. il pors *Sports Illustrated* 70:22-3 Mr 13 '89

Doping for the competitive edge. S. Bressan. il *World Press Review* 36:59 Je '89

Drugs and track [D. Robinson charges F. Griffith Joyner and C. Lewis with taking of illicit drugs] C. Neff. il pors *Sports Illustrated* 71:25-6 O 2 '89

A dubious call to arms [call for athletes to become role models in war against drugs] R. Telander. il por *Sports Illustrated* 70:116 Je 5 '89

The era of the enhanced athlete. L. Winner. il *Technology Review* 92:22 F/Mr '89

Flo Jo confronts accuser on drug use allegations [D. Robinson] il por *Jet* 77:46 O 9 '89

From dream to nightmare [testimony by track coach C. Francis during Canadian government inquiry into steroid use by B. Johnson] A. Burfoot and B. Wischnia. il pors *Runner's World* 24:12 Je '89

He has suffered enough [B. Johnson facing lifetime ban and possible loss of 100 meter world record over steroid use] M. Noden. por *Sports Illustrated* 70:98 Je 26 '89

It gives athletes a boost—maybe too much [erythropoietin] L. Jereski. il *Business Week* p123 D 11 '89

Look back in anger [drug rumors hurt Florida safety L. Oliver's pick in draft] D. Scheiber. il pors *Sports Illustrated* 70:42-4+ My 8 '89

Moses blasts edict to strip Johnson's records. por *Jet* 76:46 O+2 '89

The NFL fails its drug test. R. Demak and J. Kirshenbaum. il *Sports Illustrated* 71:38-41+ Jl 10 '89

Olympic images [Maclean's/Decima poll] H. Quinn. il *Maclean's* 102:33 Ja 2 '89

On ice for keeps [NHL bans B. Probert after arrest for importing cocaine] B. Newman. il por *Sports Illustrated* 70:26 Mr 13 '89

Putting pressure on illegal steroid traffic [anabolic steroids] V. Modeland. il *FDA Consumer* 23:33-4 O '89

Racing's cocaine mystery [race horses test positive] il *Sports Illustrated* 70:14 F 27 '89

Redskins' Manley aims for NFL reinstatement. por *Jet* 77:48 D 11 '89

A revealing inquiry [testimony of J. Astaphan on runner B. Johnson's steroid use] M. Noden. il por *Sports Illustrated* 70:19 Je 5 '89

Sabotage at Seoul? [testimony on steroid use by B. Johnson] R. Dolphin. il por *Maclean's* 102:47 Mr 20 '89

The sad tale of Sweet Pea [basketball player L. Daniels shot during reported drug dispute] il por *Sports Illustrated* 70:12 My 22 '89

The saga behind the shame [J. Scott describes J. Astaphan's role in B. Johnson's steroid use] J. Brant. il pors *Runner's World* 24:78-80 Ap '89

A sanctuary no more [summer basketball program at St. Cecilia church in Detroit shut down] R. Sullivan. il *Sports Illustrated* 71:12 Ag 28 '89

The sportswriters' big drug coverup [government push to improve Canada's Olympics performance] A. Fotheringham. il *Maclean's* 102:68 Ap 24 '89

Starting over [B. Johnson to lose world records in drug use ruling] N. Underwood. il por *Maclean's* 102:66 S 18 '89

The steroid scandal [Canadian weight lifters testify at government inquiry] D. Burke. il *Maclean's* 102:40 F 20 '89

The steroid scandal [testimony of track coach C. Francis at Canadian inquiry; cover story; special section; with editorial comment by Kevin Doyle] il pors *Maclean's* 102:2, 36-42 Mr 13 '89

Steroids: the power drugs. P. Pfotenhauer. il *USA Today (Periodical)* 117:88-90 Mr '89

Up to speed [drug taking charges against P. Rose] R. Wright. *The New Republic* 201:42 Jl 31 '89

Users and losers [drug use by runners] J. Henderson. il *Runner's World* 24:14 Mr '89

Was the X factor a factor? [former football player and steroid user S. Courson suffering from cardiomyopathy] por *Sports Illustrated* 70:34 Ap 3 '89

Whistle blower [track coach C. Francis, testifying during Canadian government inquiry, confirms B. Johnson's steroid use] por *Time* 133:50 Mr 13 '89

DRUGS AND THE AGED
At 90, the zombie shuffle. H. Willard. por *Newsweek* 113:10 F 20 '89

Is grandma drowsy, or is she drugged? [nursing home care] S. Findlay. il *U.S. News & World Report* 106:68 Je 12 '89

Medication concerns in rest homes. *Science News* 135:88 F 11 '89

On medication: a call for caution. M. Masterson. *New Choices for the Best Years* 29:12-13 Jl '89

A poor rest home remedy: drugs in place of care. L. Drew. *Newsweek* 113:56 F 6 '89

Rx for rising costs [computer network coordinating Medicare prescriptions] S. Dentzer. il *U.S. News & World Report* 107:50-1+ S 11 '89

A sobering story. G. Rosenblum. il *New Choices for the Best Years* 29:62-9 My '89

There are no perfect drugs. E. E. Rosenbaum. il *New Choices for the Best Years* 29:24+ Mr '89

DRUGS AND THE HANDICAPPED
Substance abuse among the disabled . . . [wheelchair-bound college students; study by Dennis Moore and Harvey Siegal] *Science News* 136:239 O 7 '89

DRUGS AND THE MENTALLY ILL
. . . and among young schizophrenics [drug abuse; study by Mary Ann Test] *Science News* 136:239 O 7 '89

DRUGS AND THE PRESS
Aftermath of a crack article [articles in New republic and Nation stir debate concerning government policy] J. Morley. il *The Nation* 249:592+ N 20 '89

The deadliest beat [Colombian journalists covering the drug story] W. A. Henry. il *Time* 134:76 N 13 '89

Reporters as targets [Colombia] J. Contreras. il *Newsweek* 114:59 O 2 '89

DRUGS AND WOMEN
See also
Mandela House (Oakland, Calif.)
Coming clean, staying sober: how good girls kick bad drugs. J. Neimark. il *Mademoiselle* 95:172-3+ F '89

Girls and substance use. il *Children Today* 18:5-6 Mr/Ap '89

White lies: cocaine—the dirty little secret in the age of clean. A. L. Ball. il *Mademoiselle* 95:266-9+ Ap '89

DRUGS AND YOUTH
See also
Drug education
Save America's Future (Organization)
Straight, Inc.
Youth Force (Organization)
Aaron Henry's dangerous journey [high school football player who used anabolic steroids] S. J. Smith. il *Reader's Digest* 135:116-20 D '89

An all-American teen's descent into a life of drugs and crime. L. Eskin. il *Scholastic Update (Teachers' edition)* 122:7 N 17 '89

. . . and among young schizophrenics [drug abuse; study by Mary Ann Test] *Science News* 136:239 O 7 '89

The billionaire and the students [Kansas City, Mo., students helped to stay drug free by E. M. Kauffman] D. Narine. il pors *Ebony* 44:146+ Ag '89

Bright kids; bad business [T. Williams' study of young cocaine dealers in New York's Washington Heights] E. Magnuson. il por *Time* 134:18 S 11 '89

Busted [college student arrested for drug trafficking] R. Hamilton. il pors *Seventeen* 48:122+ O '89

"But you promised" [Indian legend recounted for youths tempted by drugs] I. E. Cody. il *Reader's Digest* 134:130-1 Je '89

Children of the underclass [cover story] il *Newsweek* 114:16-20+ S 11 '89

Cocaine kids: the underground American dream [teenage drug dealers in New York City's Washington Heights] T. M. Williams. il *New Perspectives Quarterly* 6:21-5 Summ '89

Dangerous new drugs [speed and Ecstasy] M. O'Koon. il *Good Housekeeping* 208:235-6 Ap '89

Dealing death [teenage drug dealers in Hartford, Conn. housing projects] il *Scholastic Update (Teachers' edition)* 122:4-6 N 17 '89

The death of an athlete [high school steroid user B. Ramirez of Ashtabula, Ohio] R. Telander and M. Noden. il pors *Sports Illustrated* 70:68-72+ F 20 '89

Doing more good than harm with children's medications. S. J. Ackerman. il *FDA Consumer* 23:28-31 Mr '89

Drinking, drugs, & children. G. Youcha and J. S. Seixas. il *Parents* 64:142-4+ Mr '89

Drug talk: what your friends don't tell you. V. S. Brown. il *Teen* 33:22+ Je '89

Drugs and youth [cover story] J. Adelson. *Commentary* 87:24-8 My '89

Drugs: no exit. R. B. Millman. il *American Health* 8:68 O '89

Drugs: not for adults only. *UN Chronicle* 26:50 S '89

DRUGS AND YOUTH—*cont.*

A dubious call to arms [call for athletes to become role models in war against drugs] R. Telander. il por *Sports Illustrated* 70:116 Je 5 '89

Fighting for her own life, Jill Ireland now must mourn the loss of her son Jason. J. Park. il pors *People Weekly* 32:59+ N 27 '89

Girls and substance use. il *Children Today* 18:5-6 Mr/Ap '89

It's time to talk about children's medications. F. E. Young. il *FDA Consumer* 23:6-7 O '89

Latchkey kids risk substance use [study by Jean L. Richardson] *Science News* 136:188 S 16 '89

Marijuana and learning: grass gets an F. K. M. Porterfield. il *Current Health 2* 15:20-2 Ja '89

Marijuana mangles memory [research by Richard H. Schwartz] *Science News* 136:332 N 18 '89

Midnight rescue [Midnight Basketball League founded in Md. to combat youth drug abuse] B. A. McKee. il por *Nation's Business* 77:86 N '89

Narcotics: a primer. J. E. Cohn. il *Current Health 2* 15:11-13 Mr '89

An outbreak of teen alcoholism [interview with D. Miller] G. Breu. il por *People Weekly* 31:81 Ja 16 '89

Prevention. V. S. Sussman. il *U.S. News & World Report* 107:70-2 S 11 '89

Saying no nicely. il *Current Health 2* 16:14-16 S '89

Shattered for the second time [J. Ireland fights cancer and son's drug addiction] B. Kantrowitz. pors *Newsweek* 113:66 My 8 '89

Shortcut to the Rambo look [steroid use by teenage boys] A. Toufexis. il *Time* 133:78 Ja 30 '89

Steroids built Mike Keys up; then they tore him down [teen's suicide linked to use of anabolic steroids] M. Brower. il pors *People Weekly* 31:107-8 Mr 20 '89

Substance abuse among the disabled . . . [wheelchair-bound college students; study by Dennis Moore and Harvey Siegal] *Science News* 136:239 O 7 '89

Teen drug rehab: the inside story [Adolescent Addiction Recovery Unit at St. Luke's Hospital in Denver] K. M. Porterfield. il *Current Health 2* 15:19-21 F '89

Teenager in trouble: 'I lied. I stole. I cheated' [S. McCollum] il pors *Ebony* 44:120+ Ag '89

Teens and steroids. D. Sobel. il *Ladies' Home Journal* 106:110 O '89

The trouble with steroids. G. Legwold. il *Better Homes and Gardens* 67:42 N '89

"We have a problem". J. Marks. il *Parents* 64:67-71 Je '89

Who says 'no' to drugs? [study by Denise B. Kandel and Victoria H. Raveis] *Science News* 135:141 Mr 4 '89

Youth and drug abuse. S. Greenbaum. il *USA Today (Periodical)* 118:45-7 N '89

DRUGS FROM THE SEA *See* Marine pharmacology

DRUGSTORE COWBOY [film] *See* Motion picture reviews— Single works

DRUGSTORES

See also
Albertson's Inc.
American Stores Co.
Arbor Drugs, Inc.
Nekos Pharmacy
Revco D.S., Inc.
Rite Aid Corp.
Wall Drug Store (Wall, S.D.)

Automation

Rx for rising costs [computer network coordinating Medicare prescriptions] S. Dentzer. il *U.S. News & World Report* 107:50-1+ S 11 '89

DRUM, CHARLES S.

Prairie Lights Books: a beacon in the Midwest. il *Publishers Weekly* 235:95-6+ Ap 7 '89

DRUM

Different drum uses computer, radio waves [M. Mathews's Radio Drum] *Byte* 14:14+ Mr '89

Remo Belli: an industry innovator reflects [synthetic drum head] H. Nolan. il *Down Beat* 56:62 D '89

DRUM MUSIC

See also
Phonograph records—Drum music

Remo bash for cash [Drums in Concert fundraiser at UCLA] L. J. Scheuerell. *Down Beat* 56:11 D '89

DRUM SANDERS *See* Sanding and sanding equipment

DRUMLINS

After the deluge [Ice Age floods; research by John Shaw] T. Appenzeller. il *Scientific American* 261:22+ D '89

Hills point to catastrophic Ice Age floods [work of John Shaw] R. Monastersky. *Science News* 136:213 S 30 '89

DRUMMERS

See also
Armen, Jacob
Baker, Ginger
Bellson, Louis, 1924-
Blackman, Cindy
Blakey, Art
Carrington, Terri Lyne
Chambers, Dennis
Copeland, Stewart

DeJohnette, Jack
Hakim, Omar
Hemingway, Gerry
Morello, Joe
Moses, Bob
Phillips, Simon
Previte, Bobby
Reyes, Walfredo, Jr.
Roach, Max
Smith, Steve
Thigpen, Ed
Williams, Tony

And the beat goes on . . . [special section] il *Down Beat* 56:27-9 D '89

Just say yes to rhythms [path to altered consciousness and spiritual exploration] J. Tibbetts. il *Utne Reader* p32+ N/D '89

DRUMMOND, KAY

about

Florida pioneer: a woodland house on the Gulf Coast. B. Dunlop. il *Architectural Digest* 46:174-7+ Je '89

DRUMMOND, LUTHER

about

Florida pioneer: a woodland house on the Gulf Coast. B. Dunlop. il *Architectural Digest* 46:174-7+ Je '89

DRUMMOND, SARAH

Antiques: topographical porcelains. il *Architectural Digest* 46:228-33+ Ap '89

DRUMS *See* Drum

DRUNK DRIVING *See* Alcohol and automobile drivers

DRUNKENNESS *See* Alcoholics and alcoholism

DRURY, CHRIS

about

Boy, oh boy, what a year! D. S. Looney. il pors *Sports Illustrated* 71:76-80+ D 25 '89-Ja 1 '90

DRURY, JOHN

Postmodern love [poem] *The New Republic* 201:36 D 4 '89

DRURY, MICHAEL

Painted faces [poem] *McCall's* 116:64 Ja '89

DRY BARS

Dry times at Slick's Bar [Minneapolis] M. A. Kuharski. il pors *Christianity Today* 33:14-15 Mr 17 '89

DRY BEER *See* Beer

DRY CELL ELECTRIC BATTERIES *See* Electric batteries

DRY CLEANING

Study and teaching

See also
New York School of Drycleaning

DRY EYES *See* Eye—Diseases and defects

DRY FARMING

Food, not dust [work of B. A. Stewart] A. Farnham. il *Fortune* 119:37 Ja 2 '89

DRY FLIES *See* Fishing lures, flies, etc.

DRY ICE

A dry-ice fogger: how to make the moodiest prop of all. A. B. Smith. il *Petersen's Photographic Magazine* 17:46-8 F '89

DRY LIPS OUGHTA MOVE TO KAPUSKASING [drama] *See* Highway, Tomson

DRY TROPICAL FORESTS *See* Forests and forestry

A DRY WHITE SEASON [film] *See* Motion picture reviews— Single works

DRYANSKY, G. Y.

Royal lineage. il por *House & Garden* 161:148-55+ Jl '89

Seaworthy style. il pors *House & Garden* 161:122-5 Ag '89

DRYER, FRED, 1946-

about

Can 800 million Chinese be wrong? F. Schruers. por *Rolling Stone* p52-4 My 4 '89

DRYERS, CLOTHES *See* Clothes dryers

DRYING

See also
Wood—Dryers and drying

DRYING (CROPS)

See also
Grain—Drying

DRYING EQUIPMENT

See also
Clothes dryers
Wood—Dryers and drying

DRYLAND FARMING *See* Dry farming

DRYWALL MATERIALS *See* Wallboard

D'SOUZA, DINESH, 1961-

What ever happened to neoliberalism? *National Review* 41:34-6 Je 2 '89

DTMF *See* Dual-tone multifrequency signalling

DU BOIS, FELIX PÈNE *See* Pène du Bois, Felix, 1957-

DU BOIS, GUY PÈNE, 1884-1958

about

Guy Pène du Bois. J. D. Flam. il por *American Heritage* 40:72-82 F '89

DU GUESCLIN, BERTRAND, COMTE DE LONGUEVILLE, CA. 1320-1380

about

Bertrand Du Guesclin—careerist in arms? K. Fowler. bibl il pors *History Today* 39:37-43 Je '89

DU MAURIER VANCOUVER JAZZ FESTIVAL *See* Music festivals—British Columbia
DU PONT, PETER
Who needs a water tank? il *Consumers' Research Magazine* 72:18-21 Ag '89
DU PONT DE NEMOURS (E. I.) & CO. *See* E. I. Du Pont de Nemours & Co.
DU RHÔNE CHOCOLATIER
Geneva's Du Rhône Chocolatier. G. Trotta. il *Gourmet* 49:128+ D '89
DU SABLON, JEAN LECLERC
The limits of mercy. *World Press Review* 36:17-18 N '89
Two dissidents challenge 'feudal communism' [interview with Liu Binyan and Bai Hua] il pors *World Press Review* 36:26-7 F '89
DU SAILLANT, COUNTESS
Coup de maître in the Dordogne: a flourish of classical traditions at Eyrignac. il por *Architectural Digest* 46:132-5 Ja '89
Meditative explorations in a French manor house. il por *Architectural Digest* 46:116+ O '89
DUAL-TONE MULTIFREQUENCY SIGNALLING
Phonlink II (I). J. McNabb and G. Roseth. il *Radio-Electronics* 60:44-9 F '89
Phonlink II (II). J. McNabb and G. Roseth. il *Radio-Electronics* 60:46-9 Mr '89
DUALISM
See also
Mind and body
DUANY, ANDRES, 1950?-
Granny flats: another idea for creating affordable housing and strengthening community ties [excerpt from address] *Utne Reader* p72 My/Je '89
DUAT *See* Direct User Access Terminal System (Database)
DUBAI (UNITED ARAB EMIRATES: EMIRATE)
Industries
See also
Aerospace industries—Dubai (United Arab Emirates: Emirate)
DUBBING OF MOTION PICTURES
The rub in the dubbing [films and serials meant for TV screening to be dubbed in Argentina] I. Pardal. *Américas* 41 no2:64 '89
DUBČEK, ALEXANDER
about
A historic encounter. il pors *Time* 133:48 My 29 '89
The return of Alexander Dubcek. M. R. Meyer. il por *Newsweek* 114:39 D 4 '89
Time is a gentleman [interview] il *New Perspectives Quarterly* 5:46-9 Wint '88/'89
DUBERMAN, MARTIN B.
about
PW interviews. S. Staggs. por *Publishers Weekly* 235:72-3 Ja 13 '89
DUBINSKII, ROSTISLAV
The night Stalin died. il *The New York Times Magazine* p42-3+ Mr 5 '89
DUBLER, NANCY N.
about
Tough cases, hard choices. A. Rosenfeld. il pors *New York* 22:32-7 Ja 9 '89
DUBLIN (IRELAND)
Historic houses, sites, etc.
The legacy of Ireland's stuccodores. N. F. Weber. il *Architectural Digest* 46:42+ Ag '89
DUBOS, RENÉ JULES, 1901-1982
about
Righting the antibiotic record. R. P. Crease. il pors *Science* 246:883-4 N 17 '89
DUBREUIL, ANDRE
about
Forging ahead. C. Maclean. il por *House & Garden* 161:150-5+ N '89
DUBRO, ALEC
G.O.P. formula. *The Nation* 248:329-30 Mr 13 '89
Work for hire: round two. por *Publishers Weekly* 235:80 Je 30 '89
DUBUS, ELIZABETH NELL
When two hearts meet [story] il *Good Housekeeping* 209:171-2+ S '89
DUCHENNE DYSTROPHY *See* Muscular dystrophy
DUCHESNE, LUC C., AND LARSON, D. W.
Cellulose and the evolution of plant life. bibl f il *BioScience* 39:238-41 Ap '89
DUCHIN, PETER
about
The Duchin Touch. M. Bethany. il por *New York* 22:24 My 29 '89
DUCHIN TOUCH (FIRM)
The Duchin Touch. M. Bethany. il por *New York* 22:24 My 29 '89
DUCK CALLING *See* Bird calling
DUCK DECOYS *See* Decoys (Hunting)
DUCK SHOOTING
Changing times [locally reared ducks] N. Strung. il *Field & Stream* 94:29+ S '89
Grandpa and the kid. D. Sisson. il *Field & Stream* 93:55+ F '89

Hunting with the Cossacks [southern Soviet Union] G. Reiger. il *Field & Stream* 93:72-3+ Ap '89
The Louisiana story. G. Reiger. il *Field & Stream* 94:50-1+ O '89
Weathering the drought [duck hunting curtailed] L. Williamson. il *Outdoor Life* 183:48+ Ja '89
Where duck management went wrong [adaptation of address, June 10, 1989] G. Reiger. il *Field & Stream* 94:13-14 S '89
Wildfowling: here and abroad. G. Reiger. il map *Field & Stream* 93:34-5+ Ja '89
Wildfowling: my favorite four. G. Reiger. il *Field & Stream* 94:54-5+ D '89
DUCKS
American classics. il *The Mother Earth News* 116:56-7 Mr/Ap '89
Treatment
Murder most fowl: the Florida duck war [Muscovy ducks in St. Augustine Beach] il *Newsweek* 113:32 Ja 2 '89
DUCKS, WILD
Weathering the drought [duck hunting curtailed] L. Williamson. il *Outdoor Life* 183:48+ Ja '89
Control
Dimples on a black desert [wetland conservation efforts hampered by North Dakota farmers] T. Williams. il *Audubon* 91:36-8+ S '89
Increasing ducks in New York. D. Carroll. il *The Conservationist* 43:12-15 Mr/Ap '89
Portrait of a deepening crisis [loss of wetlands endangers water birds] P. Steinhart. il *National Wildlife* 27:4-13 O/N '89
Where duck management went wrong [adaptation of address, June 10, 1989] G. Reiger. il *Field & Stream* 94:13-14 S '89
Migration
Changing times [locally reared ducks] N. Strung. il *Field & Stream* 94:29+ S '89
Shooting
See Duck shooting
DUCKS ON REVENUE STAMPS *See* Revenue stamps
DUCKS UNLIMITED
Where duck management went wrong [adaptation of address, June 10, 1989] G. Reiger. il *Field & Stream* 94:13-14 S '89
DUCKSWORTH, MARILYN
about
Taking charge [cover story] K. D. Thompson and others. il pors *Black Enterprise* 20:42-4+ Ag '89
DUCKWEEDS
Pipes Lake, Mississippi. R. H. Mohlenbrock. il map *Natural History* p74-6 My '89
DUCKWORTH, KEVIN
about
Big men, big problems. P. Korn. il pors *Sport (New York, N.Y.)* 80:71-3+ Ap '89
DUCLOS-LASSALLE, GILBERT
Tour de France. il map *National Geographic* 176:132-7 Jl '89
DUCOMMUN, RICK
about
The 'burbs' big guy, Rick Ducommun, is half the man he used to be. M. Dougherty. il pors *People Weekly* 31:103-5+ Ap 3 '89
DUDEK, SERENA M., AND BEAR, MARK F.
A biochemical correlate of the critical period for synaptic modification in the visual cortex. bibl f il *Science* 246:673-5 N 3 '89
DUDLEY, GUILFORD, JR.
about
A Republican heritage in the South: Ambassador and Mrs. Guilford Dudley, Jr., in Nashville and Palm Beach. C. T. Buckley. il pors *Architectural Digest* 46:200-9 Ap '89
DUDLEY, JANE
about
A Republican heritage in the South: Ambassador and Mrs. Guilford Dudley, Jr., in Nashville and Palm Beach. C. T. Buckley. il pors *Architectural Digest* 46:200-9 Ap '89
DUE PROCESS OF LAW
See also
Jury
Right to counsel
DUES, LABOR UNION *See* Labor unions—Dues, fees, etc.
DUESBERG, PETER H.
about
AIDS paper raises red flag at PNAS. W. Booth. *Science* 243:733 F 10 '89
DUFAULT, PETER KANE
Reductio [poem] *The New Yorker* 65:34 F 27 '89
DUFFEL BAGS
What's your bag? T. Morrison. il *Field & Stream* 93:34 F '89
DUFFEY, JOSEPH
Reconstituting America through national service [address, July 19, 1989] *Vital Speeches of the Day* 56:26-9 O 15 '89
DUFFY, BRUCE
Catching a westbound freight [cover story] il map *Harper's* 278:49-55+ Je '89

DUFFY, GILLIAN
Holiday entertaining [cover story] il *New York* 22:63-73+ O 23 '89
Summer entertaining: the best and the lightest [cover story] il *New York* 22:46-56+ My 15 '89

DUFFY, GLEN
His father's the short, bald one, right? Or is it the large, round one? il pors *Gentlemen's Quarterly* 59:246-9+ My '89

DUFFY, JOE
about
The Duffy Group. L. S. Hurwitz. il *American Artist* 53:72-4 O '89

DUFFY, JULIA
about
Baby boom! [cover story] A. Meisler. il pors *TV Guide* 37:4-7+ D 30 '89-Ja 5 '90
Julia Duffy. S. Rubin. il pors *McCall's* 116:14-16 My '89

DUFFY, STEPHEN
about
Folklure. J. Leland. por *Vogue* 179:280 Mr '89

DUFFY DESIGN GROUP
The Duffy Group. L. S. Hurwitz. il *American Artist* 53:72-4 O '89

DUFOUR, PAUL
about
Paul Dufour: line and lucidity. J. McMullan. il por *American Craft* 49:40-5 Je/Jl '89

DUGAN, JOHN V., JR.
about
Washington ins & outs: moves from House Science Panel; new positions at NSF and SSC. I. Goodwin. *Physics Today* 42:50-1 My '89

DUGAN, LAWRENCE
Schuylkill navy [poem] *America* 161:292 N 4 '89

DUGGAN, ROBERT D.
A response to Andrew M. Greeley. *America* 161:235-7 O 14 '89

DUGGAN, T. K.
about
Yes, Virginia, there is a way to make money in troubled junk. L. Jereski. il pors *Business Week* p87 S 11 '89

DUGGINS, D. O., AND OTHERS
Magnification of secondary production by kelp detritus in coastal marine ecosystems. bibl f il *Science* 245:170-3 Jl 14 '89

DUGGLEBY, JOHN
(ed) See Boeke, Duffy. "A judge split my children—body and soul"

DUHÉ, CAMILLE
De-tangling tactics. il *Health (New York, N.Y.)* 21:78-80+ S '89

DUIGAN, JOHN
about
Romero [film] Reviews
America 161:167+ S 23 '89. R. A. Blake
The Christian Century il 106:870-2 O 4 '89. D. G. Peerman
Christianity Today il 33:77-8 N 3 '89. S. Ulstein
Commonweal 116:471 S 8 '89. T. O'Brien
The New Republic 201:26 S 11 '89. S. Kauffmann

DUIGNAN, PETER
What should President Bush do in Africa [address, January 27, 1988] *Vital Speeches of the Day* 55:328-9 Mr 15 '89

DUIKER, WILLIAM J.
Vietnam: the challenge of reform. bibl f *Current History* 88:177-80+ Ap '89

DUILLO, ELAINE
about
When Elaine Duillo paints it, a romance novel's cover is worth a thousand steamy words. M. Neill. il pors *People Weekly* 31:141+ My 15 '89

DUIN, JULIA
Aliquippa's star attraction. il *Christianity Today* 33:14+ Ja 13 '89

DUKA, JOHN, 1949-1989
about
Obituary
Vogue por 179:84 Mr '89. L. Bennetts

DUKAKIS, KITTY
about
Free advice. por *Time* 134:71 D 4 '89
From Kitty Dukakis, a cry of despair [cover story] J. S. Kunen. il pors *People Weekly* 32:114-19 N 27 '89
The losses keep mounting. R. Ajemian. il pors *Time* 134:66 N 20 '89
'She clearly recognizes she has a sickness'. B. Kantrowitz and M. Starr. il por *Newsweek* 113:54-5 F 20 '89
The struggle of Kitty Dukakis. A. Toufexis. il por *Time* 133:79 F 20 '89
'Trying to ease the pain'. B. Turque. il por *Newsweek* 114:55 N 20 '89
What did happen to Kitty Dukakis? M. Jacobbi. il pors *Good Housekeeping* 208:52+ Je '89

DUKAKIS, MICHAEL
about
The 1988 election. N. J. Ornstein and M. Schmitt. *Foreign Affairs* 68 Special Issue:39-52 ['89]

The Democrats [discussion of February 1989 article, Why the Democrats lost again] J. Muravchik. *Commentary* 87:2-5 Je '89
The Duke did his best. R. E. Tyrrell. *The American Spectator* 22:10 Ja '89
The iceman goeth. H. Hertzberg. *The New Republic* 200:6 Ja 30 '89
Illegal money and the '88 campaign. F. Wertheimer. il *Common Cause Magazine* 15:44 Mr/Ap '89
JFK's children: the class of '74 [cover story] W. Schneider. il por *The Atlantic* 263:35-40+ Mr '89
Lessons of campaign '88. F. Barnes. il *The American Spectator* 22:14-16 Ja '89
The losses keep mounting. R. Ajemian. il pors *Time* 134:66 N 20 '89
Manipulating the media and America: the negative 1988 presidential campaign. R. L. Fischer. il *USA Today (Periodical)* 117:20-2 Mr '89
The 'Massachusetts mess'. M. Starr. il por *Newsweek* 113:28 Ja 2 '89
A season in hell. G. E. Curry. il pors *Ms.* 18:58-60+ O '89
A tale of two candidates. M. A. Kramer. *Change* 20:9+ N/D '88
Verities. R. Kuttner. *The New Republic* 200:46 Ja 30 '89
What liberals haven't learned & why. F. F. Siegel. il *Commonweal* 116:16-20 Ja 13 '89
Why the Democrats lost again. J. Muravchik. *Commentary* 87:13-22 F '89

DUKE, DAVID
about
Duke election symptomatic of U.S. racism: Jackson. *Jet* 75:7 Mr 6 '89
Duke shows his true colors. B. Turque. il por *Newsweek* 114:53 D 25 '89
An ex-Klansman trades his robes for a cloak of respectability in the Louisiana legislature. D. Grogan. il pors *People Weekly* 31:215-16 Mr 6 '89
The GOP's cross to bear. il pors *U.S. News & World Report* 106:14-15 Mr 6 '89
Hate gets a haircut. L. K. Truscott. il pors map *Esquire* 112:174-6+ N '89
Kluck! Kluck! Kluck! E. Magnuson. il por *Time* 133:29 Mr 6 '89
Louisiana's blow-dried Grand Wizard. il por *Newsweek* 113:27 Ja 23 '89
Republican racist. L. Cohler. *The New Republic* 201:11-14 S 18-25 '89
A seat for the Klansman. J. Hammer. il por *Newsweek* 113:6 Mr 6 '89

DUKE POWER CO.
Duking it out in the Carolinas [proposed hydroelectric dam to be built by Duke Power in the Jocassee Watershed] B. Fuller. il *Sierra* 74:96-7 My/Je '89

DUKE UNIVERSITY
Big scam on campus [M. Cortez masquerades as member of Rothschild family] F. Trippett. il por *Time* 134:25 S 25 '89
Jocks with books. J. Adler. il *Newsweek* 113:60-1 Ja 9 '89

DUKE UNIVERSITY. DIET AND FITNESS CENTER
Tales from the diet trenches. T. M. DeFrank. il *Newsweek* 114:58 S 11 '89

DUKE UNIVERSITY. THELONIOUS MONK INSTITUTE OF JAZZ See Thelonious Monk Institute of Jazz

DUKES, PAUL, 1934-
Black and white houses? il *History Today* 39:9-11 Ap '89

DULANEY, ROBERT
about
Living proof that walking changes walkers. M. Spilner. il pors *Prevention (Emmaus, Pa.)* 41:84+ Jl '89

DULCE GULF (COSTA RICA) See Golfo Dulce (Costa Rica)

DULL, RALPH
about
Planting some new ideas. W. Sloane. il por *Time* 134:14-15 O 2 '89

DULUTH (MINN.)
Protests, demonstrations, etc.
Marines hit the beaches in Minnesota [recruitment drive meets with antiwar protest] M. Helmberger. il *The Progressive* 53:17 O '89

DUMARS, DENISE
Poet to poet. *The Writer* 102:24-6+ D '89
Poet to poet. il *The Writer* 102:23-6 Mr '89
Poet to poet. *The Writer* 102:26-30 Je '89
Poet to poet. *The Writer* 102:21-4 S '89

DUMARS, JOE
about
The 1989 Sport NBA Finals MVP: Joe Dumars. il pors *Sport (New York, N.Y.)* 80:82 S '89
Man in the slow lane. B. Newman. il pors *Sports Illustrated* 70:28-30+ Je 26 '89

DUMAS, DICK
about
In the light of Provence [cover story] D. Kazanjian. il por *House & Garden* 161:98-107+ Ja '89

DUMAS, HENRY, 1934-1968
Black star line [poem] *Essence* 20:138-9 O '89
If I were earth [poem] *Essence* 20:126 N '89

DUMAS, HENRY, 1934-1968—*cont.*
"Love song" [poem] *Essence* 19:149 F '89
Mississippi song [poem] *Essence* 20:141 O '89
DUMAS, KITTY
Stand & deliver. il por *Black Enterprise* 19:276-8+ Je '89
DUMMY BOARD FIGURES
Collectors and collecting
Dummy boards [cover story] C. Graham. bibl f il *Antiques* 135:1424-31 Je '89
DUMPLINGS
Country kitchen [rolled apple dumplings] M. Adams. il por *McCall's* 117:120 D '89
DUN & BRADSTREET CORP.
Damage control at Dun & Bradstreet. J. Rothfeder. il *Business Week* p187-8+ N 27 '89
DUN HOUSE (MONTROSE, SCOTLAND) *See* House of Dun (Montrose, Scotland)
DUNAWAY, FAYE
about
America's 10 most beautiful women. T. Johnson. il pors *Harper's Bazaar* 122:160+ S '89
'I've been through . . . several layers of hell'. F. Ashley. il pors *TV Guide* 37:16-20 O 14-20 '89
DUNBAR, CYNTHIA E., AND OTHERS
COOH-terminal-modified interleukin-3 is retained intracellularly and stimulates autocrine growth. bibl f il *Science* 245:1493-6 S 29 '89
DUNBAR, PAUL LAURENCE, 1872-1906
Speakin' o' Christmas [poem] il *Ebony* 45:38 D '89
DUNCAN, ALASTAIR, 1942-
Master of Murano. il *House & Garden* 161:118 My '89
The silver of Carlo Bugatti. bibl f il por *Antiques* 136:1344-55 D '89
DUNCAN, JEFF, 1930-1989
about
Obituary
Dance Magazine por 63:28 N '89. D. Jowitt
DUNCAN, JOHN ALASTAIR *See* Duncan, Alastair, 1942-
DUNCAN, MICHAEL A., AND ROUVRAY, D. H.
Microclusters. bibl il *Scientific American* 261:110-15 D '89
DUNCAN, PATRICK
about
84 Charlie MoPic [film] Reviews
Commonweal 116:278 My 5 '89. T. O'Brien
The New Republic 200:24-5 Ap 24 '89. S. Kauffmann
Newsweek 113:67+ Ap 3 '89. D. Ansen
People Weekly il 31:12 My 1 '89. R. Novak
Rolling Stone il p32 My 4 '89. J. Marchese
Time il 133:83 Ap 17 '89. R. Schickel
Company man. K. Jaehne. il por *Film Comment* 25:11-15 Mr/Ap '89
DUNDON, SUSAN
Turning loss into growth. il por *Working Woman* 14:92-4 Ag '89
DUNGEONS & DRAGONS (GAME)
Hillsfar. B. Guerra. il *Compute!* 11:67+ S '89
Pool of Radiance [computer game] S. Addams. il *Compute!* 11:62 F '89
DUNHAM, BOB
Aloe: the healing plant. il *Flower and Garden* 33:37 N/D '89
DUNHAM, CARROLL, 1949-
about
Carroll Dunham at Sonnabend. K. Johnson. il *Art in America* 77:167-8 Je '89
DUNHAM, CHRISTINE
about
ABT's Christine Dunham: finding the nuance. L. Horn. *Dance Magazine* 63:48 My '89
DUNHAM, KATHERINE
about
President Bush praises Gillespie and Dunham at White House fete. il pors *Jet* 77:27 D 11 '89
DUNKEL, TOM
Big bucks, tough tactics. il pors *The New York Times Magazine* p56-7+ S 17 '89
DUNKIN' DONUTS INCORPORATED
Why Dunkin' Donuts looks so yummy. K. H. Hammonds. il *Business Week* p42 My 8 '89
Win one, lose one. S. Flack. il *Forbes* 144:67 Ag 21 '89
DUNKINS, RONNIE, D. 1989
about
The execution of Ronnie Dunkins. D. Aukerman. il *The Christian Century* 106:783-5 Ag 30-S 6 '89
DUNKLE, TERRY
The big glass [cover story] il *Discover* 10:68-81 Jl '89
Catch these falling stars! il *Reader's Digest* 135:41-2+ Ag '89
DUNLAP, CARLA
about
Carla Dunlap: more than muscle. M. Greenwood-Robinson. il por *Women's Sports & Fitness* 11:62 Je '89
DUNLAP, JOHN R.
Kiddie litter. il *The American Spectator* 22:19-21 D '89
DUNLAP (TENN.)
Parks and playgrounds
See also
Dunlap Coke Ovens Park (Tenn.)

DUNLAP COKE OVENS PARK (TENN.)
Preserving the South's past, city to town [work of C. Camp] D. Young. il pors *Southern Living* 24:90-1+ F '89
DUNLEAVY, ROSEMARY
about
Follow the leader. A. Bespaloff. il por *New York* 22:28 F 6 '89
DUNLOP, BETH, 1947-
Coconut Grove Tudor: the Miami residence of Maurice and Mercedes Ferré. il *Architectural Digest* 46:108-13+ F '89
Coming of age. il map *Architectural Record* 177:96-103 Jl '89
Florida pioneer: a woodland house on the Gulf Coast. il *Architectural Digest* 46:174-7+ Je '89
DUNLOP, CINDY
about
"I have to save my baby!". J. Stuller. il *Reader's Digest* 134:65-70 Ap '89
DUNLOP, DAVID J.
(jt. auth) *See* Özdemir, Özden, and Dunlop, David J.
DUNMORE, ALBERT J., D. 1989
about
Obituary
Jet 75:18 F 20 '89
DUNN, ARLAND D.
about
The facts behind the figures. R. L. Stern and M. Beauchamp. il por *Forbes* 144:41-2 Ag 21 '89
DUNN, DOUGLAS
about
Sky eye [dance] Reviews
Dance Magazine 63:55+ Jl '89. D. Hering
DUNN, J. R.
The gates of Babel [fiction] il *Omni (New York, N.Y.)* 11:50-2+ My '89
DUNN, KATHERINE
about
Novelist Katherine Dunn admits her Geek love is stranger than most fiction—but aren't we all. G. Stone. il pors *People Weekly* 31:127-8 Ap 17 '89
PW interviews. S. Bolle. por *Publishers Weekly* 235:66-7 Mr 10 '89
DUNN, SAMUEL L.
Christianity's future. il por *The Futurist* 23:34-7 Mr/Ap '89
DUNN, STEPHEN, 1939-
On the death of a colleague [poem] *The American Scholar* 58:352-3 Summ '89
DUNN, WILLIAM L.
about
Dow Jones makes a young dog do new tricks. J. Rothfeder. il por *Business Week* p89+ Ja 16 '89
DUNN (DOUGLAS) AND DANCERS *See* Douglas Dunn and Dancers
DUNNAN, NANCY
Borrowing money: smart moves in today's money market. *Better Homes and Gardens* 67:90+ Je '89
DUNNAVANT, KEITH
To follow greatness. il *Sport (New York, N.Y.)* 80:33-5+ O '89
The ultimate poll. il *Sport (New York, N.Y.)* 80:28-32+ D '89
DUNNE, DOMINICK
about
Writer's turf. M. Cantwell. il por *House & Garden* 161:108+ O '89
DUNNE, DONNALEE
Resurrect old linens. il *Americana* 17:14-16 Mr/Ap '89
DUNNE, JIM, 1931-
Inside Detroit. See issues of Popular Mechanics beginning January 1986 through September 1989
DUNNE, JOHN GREGORY, 1932-
Goldwynism. il *The New York Review of Books* 36:28-33 My 18 '89
DUNNING, JOHN S., 1905-
about
Watch the birdie! A. Meadows. il por *Américas* 41 no2:61-3 '89
DUNNOCKS
Sexual behavior
See Sexual behavior—Birds
DUNST, HILARY
Eyewitness video. il *Video* 13:48-50+ Ap '89
DUNTOV, ZORA ARKUS- *See* Arkus-Duntov, Zora
DUODENAL ULCERS *See* Peptic ulcers
DUPITON, SANDRA
about
Sandra Dupiton, who came out of her shell to dazzle the dance world. por *People Weekly* 32:69 Jl 24 '89
DUPLEX APARTMENTS *See* Apartments
DUPLEX HOUSES *See* Two family houses
DUPLICATING PROCESSES *See* Photocopying
DUPONT, JOAN
An American in Brussels. il pors *The New York Times Magazine* p22-3+ Ja 22 '89
DUQUESNE, JACQUES, 1930-
The Pope's critics. il por *World Press Review* 36:56 Je '89

DUQUETTE, TONY
Fantasies by the Bay: Tony Duquette's San Francisco residence and sculpture pavilion. il por *Architectural Digest* 46:262-9+ My '89

DUQUETTE PAVILION
Fantasies by the Bay: Tony Duquette's San Francisco residence and sculpture pavilion. T. Duquette. il por *Architectural Digest* 46:262-9+ My '89

DUQUIN, LORENE HANLEY
Learning in style. il *Seventeen* 48:92+ S '89

DURABLE GOODS, INDUSTRIAL
Are U.S. companies dangerously addicted to foreign equipment? G. Koretz. il *Business Week* p22 Mr 27 '89
Capital idea [capital goods stocks] T. Jaffe. il *Forbes* 144:326 D 11 '89
Why capital goods stocks look strong for 1989—and beyond. A. E. Serwer. il *Fortune* 119:25-6 Ja 16 '89

DURAN, JUNE C.
Plant rescue operation. *Flower and Garden* 33:30 Mr/Ap '89

DURAN, ROBERTO
about
Leonard dances to win as Duran has 'no mas'. il pors *Jet* 77:51-2 D 25 '89-Ja 1 '90
One for the ages. P. Putnam. il pors *Sports Illustrated* 71:24-5 D 18 '89
One more time! J. Torres. pors *TV Guide* 37:34-6 D 2-8 '89
Stonehands rules again. B. Newman. il pors *Sports Illustrated* 70:18-19 Mr 6 '89

DURAN DURAN (MUSICAL GROUP)
Duran Duran: 'notorious' boys are back! il *'Teen* 33:51 Mr '89

DURAND, RICARDO
The Peruvian Church and liberation theology. *America* 161:84-5+ Ag 12-19 '89

DURANG, CHRISTOPHER, 1949-
about
Theater [Chris Durang & Dawne] J. Simon. *New York* 22:166 O 23 '89

DURANGO (COLO.)
Description
La Plata County, Colorado [cover story] D. Petersen. il map *The Mother Earth News* 119:56-63 S/O '89
"DURANTE" THE MUSICAL COMEDY [musical] See Musicals, revues, etc.—Reviews—Single works
DURATION OF LIFE See Longevity
DURENBERGER, DAVID
Should the Congress adopt the "High Risk Occupational Disease Notification and Prevention Act of 1987"? [excerpts from address, March 29, 1988] *Congressional Digest* 68:118+ Ap '89

DÜRER, ALBRECHT, 1471-1528
about
Extracting art from nature. J. Kastner. il *Natural History* p76+ S '89

DÜRER, MICHAEL
about
Flight to freedom. M. Ryan. il pors *People Weekly* 32:36-9 O 2 '89

DURHAM (N.C.)
Education
N.C. students get state to outlaw its poll tax. *Jet* 76:8 Je 19 '89

DURHAM FAMILY
about
The Durhams' fight to save themselves [interview with Miami family scarred by drugs and alcohol] A. M. Arrarte. il *U.S. News & World Report* 107:86 S 11 '89

DURKIN, JOHN F.
Stressful situation. il *Runner's World* 24:28 O '89

DURNING, ALAN B.
Grass-roots groups are our best hope for global prosperity and ecology. il *Utne Reader* p40-3+ Jl/Ag '89
People power and development. *Foreign Policy* 76:66-82 Fall '89
Saving the planet. il *The Progressive* 53:35-9 Ap '89

DUROCHÉ, JULIE
about
Sew red. B. Weber. il por *The New York Times Magazine* p66 Ag 27 '89

DURONIO, ROBERT J., AND OTHERS
Disruption of the yeast N-myristoyl transferase gene causes recessive lethality. bibl f il *Science* 243:796-800 F 10 '89

DURRETT, CHARLES, 1955-
(jt. auth) See McCamant, Kathryn, 1959-, and Durrett, Charles, 1955-

D'URSO, JOE, 1943-
about
Gandee at large. C. K. Gandee. il por *House & Garden* 161:194 Ap '89

DURST, G. MICHAEL
The manager as a developer [address, November 5, 1988] *Vital Speeches of the Day* 55:309-14 Mr 1 '89

DURST, SEYMOUR B., 1913-
about
From bad to Durst. E. Schmuckler. il por *Forbes* 144:120 Jl 10 '89

DUSENBERRY, PHIL
Media whizzes and washouts: my advice for them all. il *TV Guide* 37:12-15 Je 17-23 '89

DUSENBURY, SUSAN
about
Rerun: 1929 Women's Air Derby. *Flying* 116:20 Ag '89

DUSKIN CO. LTD.
American knowhow, Japan style. H. Katayama. il *Forbes* 144:76+ O 2 '89

DUSKY, LORRAINE
Hard work (alone) gets you . . . nowhere: the awful truth about office politics. il *Mademoiselle* 95:138+ F '89
Will this be the year we lose abortion? il *Mademoiselle* 95:214-15+ My '89

DUSKY SEASIDE SPARROW See Sparrows
DUST
Seasonal dust [airborne global dust] map *Sea Frontiers* 35:197 Jl/Ag '89
DUST, INTERSTELLAR See Matter, Interstellar
DUST, VOLCANIC See Volcanic ash, tuff, etc.
DUST BOWL (U.S.) See Great Plains
DUST COLLECTORS
Lost suction [discussion of September/October, 1986 article, Furnace blower powers shop dust collector system] A. Kruger. *Workbench* 45:52 Ja/F '89
The Workbench guide to dust collection systems. P. McCafferty. il *Workbench* 45:70-4+ Ja/F '89
DUST DISEASES See Lungs—Dust diseases
DUST JACKETS See Book covers
DUST MASKS
Selecting a respirator. D. Lane. il *Workbench* 45:68-9 Ja/F '89
DUST REMOVAL
See also
Vacuum cleaning
DUST STORMS
Signs of old Mars: written in the dust [evidence for warmer period, complete with water; research by Ted L. Roush] J. Eberhart. *Science News* 135:173 Mr 18 '89
DUSTIN, VIRGINIA SHEELEY
Just as you are. il *Good Housekeeping* 208:66+ Mr '89
DUTCH, PENNSYLVANIA See Pennsylvania Germans
DUTCH ART See Art, Dutch
DUTCH COOKING See Cooking, Dutch
DUTCH DELTA DIKES See Dikes (Engineering)—Netherlands
DUTCH-ENGLISH WARS, 1652-1784 See Anglo-Dutch Wars, 1652-1784
DUTCH FURNITURE See Furniture, Dutch
DUTCH NATIONAL BALLET
Reviews:
Performance of works by T. van Schayk in Amsterdam. H. Klooss. *Dance Magazine* 63:75-6 Ap '89
DUTCH PAINTING See Painting, Dutch
DUTIES (TARIFF) See Tariff
DUTTON (E. P.) & COMPANY, INC. See E. P. Dutton & Company, Inc.
DUTY FREE IMPORTATION
How Europe 1992 could cost its airports $2 billion. B. Baudoin and others. il *Business Week* p55 Mr 6 '89
Soaring sales at duty-free shops. H. Weil. il *Fortune* 119:225+ Ap 24 '89
Taking the Tigers off the dole [U.S. discontinues duty free status for Taiwan, Hong Kong, South Korea and Singapore] E. A. Finn, Jr. il *Forbes* 143:70 Ja 23 '89
DUTY-FREE ZONES See Free ports and zones
DUVA, LOU
about
We've grown accustomed to his face. B. Newman. il pors *Sports Illustrated* 70:84-8+ Ap 10 '89
DUVALIER, FRANÇOIS, 1907-1971
about
Beyond the mountains (II). M. Danner. maps *The New Yorker* 65:68+ D 4 '89
DUVALIER, JEAN-CLAUDE
about
Beyond the mountains (III). M. Danner. map *The New Yorker* 65:100-2+ D 11 '89
DUVALL, ROBERT
about
Star Robert Duvall says: it's going to be like a western Godfather. L. D. Estleman. il pors *TV Guide* 36:14-16+ F 4-10 '89
DUVALL, SHELLEY
about
Nightmare classics. A. Klein. il por *American Film* 14:56-7 Jl/Ag '89
DUVE, FREIMUT
Khomeini's declaration of war [excerpts from address] il *New Perspectives Quarterly* 6:52-3 Spr '89
DUVERGER, MAURICE, 1917-
The evolving European Parliament. *World Press Review* 36:32 S '89
DUVIGNAUD, JEAN
The festive spirit. il *The Unesco Courier* 42:10-15 D '89
DUYFF, ROBERTA L.
The nutri-ditionalist. il *Ladies' Home Journal* 106:262-4+ N '89

DV8 PHYSICAL THEATRE
Reviews:
Performances at the Brooklyn Academy of Music. R. A. Thom. il *Dance Magazine* 63:69+ Ap '89
DWARF FRUIT TREES *See* Fruit trees, Dwarf
DWARF GALAXIES *See* Galaxies
DWARF STARS *See* Stars, Dwarf
DWARFS AND DWARFISM
"God made you little and special" [adoption of dwarfs Davina and Matt Wilson]; ed. by Rebecca Nappi. B. Wilson. il *Redbook* 173:84+ O '89
DWARFS AND DWARFISM IN MOTION PICTURES
Now a half century down the yellow brick road, six Munchkins remember Oz. M. Neill. il *People Weekly* 31:38-40 Je 26 '89
DWELLINGS *See* Architecture, Domestic
DWIGHT D. EISENHOWER (AIRCRAFT CARRIER)
Dame at sea [four day Navy tour] J. M. Stapleton. *The New Republic* 200:42 My 22 '89
DWORETZKY, TOM
Lucky [fiction] *Omni (New York, N.Y.)* 12:106+ N '89
DWORKIN, RONALD MYLES, 1931-
The future of abortion. bibl f il *The New York Review of Books* 36:47-51 S 28 '89
The great abortion case. bibl f il *The New York Review of Books* 36:49-53 Je 29 '89
DWORKIN, SUSAN
Straight from the heart [cover story] pors *Redbook* 174:20+ D '89
DWYER, NANCY
about
Nancy Dwyer: Josh Baer. E. Heartney. il *Art News* 88:177-8 Mr '89
THE DYBBUK [drama] *See* Ansky, S., 1863-1920
DYCE, BYRON
about
Roll with the Dyce. M. Will-Weber. il por *Runner's World* 24:117 Ap '89
DYCHTWALD, KEN, 1950-
about
A ride on the age wave. S. Walton. il *Health (New York, N.Y.)* 21:40+ Jl '89
The senior boom: how it will change America. F. S. Chapman. il por *Fortune* 119:62 Mr 27 '89
DYCK, SIR ANTHONIE VAN, 1599-1641
about
A Duke fit for a King. G. Barker. il por *Art News* 88:87+ D '89
DYE, PHIL
about
Worm and remembrance. W. J. Elvin. il *The American Spectator* 22:30-1 Ja '89
DYER, ALAN
Genesis of a legend. il *Astronomy* 17:86-91 O '89
In defense of casual astronomy. il *Sky and Telescope* 77:580 Je '89
Why isn't there a good $200 scope? *Astronomy* 17:8 Jl '89
DYER, GWYNNE
The odds of saving the planet. il *World Press Review* 36:96 O '89
DYER, WAYNE W.
Are you a forgiving person? [excerpt from You'll see it when you believe it] *Redbook* 173:96-7+ Ag '89
How to get lucky in life [excerpt from You'll see it when you believe it] *Redbook* 173:120-1+ Jl '89
DYES AND DYEING
See also
Coloring matter in cosmetics, food, etc.
Hair—Dyeing and bleaching
Textile painting
Do or dye! [tie-dying] il *'Teen* 33:16 Je '89
DYETT, LINDA
Adults: so much time, so much to do. il *New York* 22:93-4+ Jl 3-10 '89
DYETT, WALTER HENRI
about
Alumni tribute to Walter Dyett: Jazz Showcase, Dusable High School/Chicago. J. Cunniff. il *Down Beat* 56:51-2 Je '89
DYING *See* Death
DYKE MARSH (VA.)
Dyke Marsh. F. Graham. *Audubon* 91:17-8 My '89
DYLAN, BOB, 1941-
about
Dylan and the Stones: the shock of the old. A. DeCurtis. il *Rolling Stone* p115-16 S 21 '89
Getting back on track. D. Gates. por *Newsweek* 113:67 Mr 13 '89
Legend. *The New Yorker* 65:26-7 Ag 28 '89
Oh, Bob, 'Oh mercy' [concert] J. D. Considine. il por *Rolling Stone* p32 N 30 '89
Trotsky, whose lively street art became an off-the-wall album cover for Bob Dylan. il por *People Weekly* 32:112 O 23 '89
DYNAMIC GRAPHIC FINISHING INC.
New engraving process debuts at Dynamic Graphic [Dyna-Etch] J. P. Frank. il *Publishers Weekly* 235:44 Je 16 '89

DYNAMIC RANDOM ACCESS MEMORY *See* Random access memory
DYNAMICS
See also
Fluid dynamics
Molecular dynamics
Thermodynamics
DYNASTY [television program] *See* Television program reviews—Single works
DYSCHONDROPLASIA *See* Chondrodysplasia
DYSENTERY, AMEBIC *See* Amebiasis
DYSGRAPHIA
Unreadable handwriting. F. Roberts. il *Parents* 64:47 N '89
DYSLEXIA
Living and learning with dyslexia [story of Harvard graduate] S. L. Levine and S. Osbourne. bibl il *Phi Delta Kappan* 70:594-8 Ap '89
DYSMENORRHEA *See* Menstruation—Disorders
DYSON, BRIAN
about
Bottling is hardly a classic for Coke. W. Konrad. il por *Business Week* p130+ D 11 '89
DYSON, ESTHER
Random access. See issues of Forbes beginning May 18, 1987
DYSON, FREEMAN J., 1923-
Feynman at Cornell. il por *Physics Today* 42:32-8 F '89
DYSON, MICHAEL ERIC
Deaffirmation. *The Nation* 249:4-5 Jl 3 '89
The two racisms. *The Nation* 249:300-1 S 25 '89
DYSON, NICHOLAS, AND OTHERS
The human papilloma virus-16 E7 oncoprotein is able to bind to the retinoblastoma gene product. bibl f il *Science* 243:934-7 F 17 '89
DYSPLASIA, HIP *See* Hip dysplasia
DYSTEL, JANE
about
Acton and Dystel form partnership. il pors *Publishers Weekly* 235:16 Ap 21 '89
DYSTROPHIN
Biochemical clues to muscular dystrophy [role of brain dystrophin in Duchenne dystrophy; research by U. Nudel] *Science News* 135:30 Ja 14 '89
DYSTROPHY, MUSCULAR *See* Muscular dystrophy

E

E. & J. GALLO WINERY
Pride goeth before a fall? [E. & J. Gallo refuses to call its fancier wines anything but Gallo] J. Levine. il *Forbes* 143:306+ My 29 '89
E-6A AIRPLANES *See* Airplanes, Military
E. COLI *See* Escherichia coli
E. I. DU PONT DE NEMOURS & CO.
But will they ever know Zytel from Lycra? [Du Pont and Deere & Co. introduce new mail order catalogs] S. B. Weiner. il *Forbes* 143:150+ Je 26 '89
Du Pont's 'drug hunter' stalks his next big trophy [P. B. Timmermans] J. Weber, Jr. il por *Business Week* p174+ N 27 '89
Du Pont's version of a maverick [E. S. Woolard] J. Weber, Jr. il pors *Business Week* p80-1 Ap 3 '89
Edgar Woolard. J. Weber, Jr. il por *Business Week* Special Issue:140 Ap 14 '89
Hitting the roof [corrupt management practices at Savannah River nuclear complex] N. Roland. il *Common Cause Magazine* 15:8-9 Jl/Ag '89
The new organization man [E. Woolard and others] J. Buckley. il pors *U.S. News & World Report* 106:40-51 Ja 16 '89
Potential replacement for ozone killer [development of chemical blend] *Science News* 135:94 F 11 '89
Step aside, Superman [Kevlar vs. Spectra Shield] A. A. Lappen. il *Forbes* 143:124+ F 6 '89
US superconductivity effort shapes up, with Du Pont emerging a big player. W. Sweet. *Physics Today* 42 pt1:55-8 Ag '89
E-II HOLDINGS INC.
Riklis' fancy footwork may be tripping him up. A. Rothman. il por *Business Week* p86-8 Je 19 '89
E. P. DUTTON & COMPANY, INC.
Dutton becomes Penguin imprint; 20 of adult trade staff are fired. *Publishers Weekly* 236:10 N 10 '89
Dutton hopes to make a killing with Spillane's latest Mike Hammer. il *Publishers Weekly* 236:59 O 6 '89
E-PRIME AEROSPACE CORPORATION
The little rocket that could [launch of E-Prime's Loft-1 rocket] J. Kluger. il pors *Discover* 10:30+ F '89
E STREET BAND
The Boss announces a layoff on E Street, but is it a halt or a hiatus? il por *People Weekly* 32:207-8 D 4 '89
E.T. (FICTIONAL CHARACTER)
E.T. B. Darrach. il *People Weekly* 32 Special Issue:91 Fall '89

E.T. THE EXTRA-TERRESTRIAL [film] See Motion picture reviews—Single works
E.U. (MUSICAL GROUP)
Star quality. M. Southgate. il *Essence* 20:19 Jl '89
EADIE, WILLIAM F.
Hearing what we ought to hear [address, May 8, 1989] *Vital Speeches of the Day* 55:587-8 Jl 15 '89
EAGAN, ANDREA BOROFF, 1943-
The estrogen fix. il *Ms.* 17:38-41+ Ap '89
EAGLE CAP WILDERNESS (OR.)
The woman in the yellow hat [encounter with a stranger] P. G. Quinnett. il *Audubon* 91:46-8 S '89
EAGLE-PICHER INDUSTRIES INC.
Eagle-Picher is stronger than it looks. J. M. Laderman. il *Business Week* p128 N 13 '89
EAGLEBURGER, LAWRENCE S.
The challenge of the European landscape in the 1990s [statement, June 22, 1989] *Department of State Bulletin* 89:37-8 O '89

Indochinese refugees conference held in Geneva [statement, June 18, 1989; texts of draft declaration and comprehensive plan of action, June 14, 1989] *Department of State Bulletin* 89:69-73 O '89

The OAS and the Panama crisis [statements, August 24 and 31, 1989] *Department of State Bulletin* 89:67-75 N '89

U.S., Japan agree to codevelop FSX aircraft [statement, May 3, 1989] *Department of State Bulletin* 89:49 Jl '89
about
Deputy Secretary Eagleburger's interview, "Good morning, America," May 11, 1989 [transcript of program] *Department of State Bulletin* 89:69-70 Jl '89
EAGLES
America's other eagle [golden eagle] G. Turbak. il *National Wildlife* 27:34-41 O/N '89
Gunning for bald eagles [Alaska Chilkat Bald Eagle Preserve] il *Newsweek* 113:33 F 27 '89
Rebirth of the American eagle [bald eagles] M. J. Walters. il *Reader's Digest* 135:95-100 S '89
A soiled symbol [bald eagles affected by Exxon Valdez oil spill] J. R. Luoma. il *Audubon* 91:101 S '89
EAKIN, JULIE SINCLAIR
Avant-garde in the desert. il *New Choices for the Best Years* 29:36-8 Je '89
Trading places. il *New Choices for the Best Years* 29:28-32 D '89
EALEY, LANCE A.
Continental drift. il *House & Garden* 161:184-5 Ap '89
EAPS (EMPLOYEE ASSISTANCE PROGRAMS) See Employee counseling
EAR
See also
Deafness
The middle-ear muscles. E. Borg and S. A. Counter. bibl il *Scientific American* 261:74-80 Ag '89
Diseases
See also
Tinnitus
Beware of swimmer's ear. S. Mahler. *McCall's* 116:88 Jl '89
Vestibular disorders: causes and effects of a hidden problem. J. Blomgren. il *Children Today* 18:14-17 Jl/Ag '89
Therapy
Corporate-funded research may be hazardous to your health [case of E. Cantekin, Univ. of Pittsburgh Medical School professor who questioned effectiveness of antibiotic amoxicillin] K. Hart. *The Bulletin of the Atomic Scientists* 45:32 Ap '89
Protection
Choosing hearing protection. *The Saturday Evening Post* 261:18 Mr '89
Surgery
A no-tears trip to the hospital [six-year-old prepares for a myringotomy] L. Kotrosits. il *Parents* 64:85-6+ Je '89
EAR, ARTIFICIAL
Girl, 5, 1st in U.S. to get artificial ear [C. Davis] il por *Jet* 75:24 Ja 16 '89
EAR PIERCING
Rite of passage [adolescent son] M. Dorris. il *Parents* 64:246+ Je '89
EARLE, BRENT NICHOLSON
Running for our lives; ed. by Gary Smith. il pors *People Weekly* 32 Special Issue:134-5+ Fall '89
EARLE, SHANE
about
Sex and scandal. N. Underwood. il por *Maclean's* 102:84 O 30 '89
EARLE, STEVE
about
Steve Earle: a bad boy settles down. H. Gleason. il por *Rolling Stone* p13 Ja 26 '89
EARLE, SYLVIA A., 1935-
about
Profiles. W. White. il *The New Yorker* 65:41-2+ Jl 3 '89
EARLY ADOLESCENT HELPER PROGRAM
Adolescents help themselves by helping others. J. G. Schine. il *Children Today* 18:10-15 Ja/F '89

EARLY CHILDHOOD EDUCATION See Preschool education
EARLY ONE EVENING AT THE RAINBOW BAR AND GRILLE [drama] See Graham, Bruce
EARLY RETIREMENT See Retirement
EARLY STARS
See also
B stars
EARLY WARNING AIRPLANES See Airplanes, Military
EARNED RUN AVERAGE See Baseball, Professional—Statistics
EARNINGS, CORPORATE See Corporations—Finance
EARRINGS
Do your earrings hang low, do they wobble to and fro? At big name shows, the style's jumbo [dangling clip-on earrings] il *People Weekly* 32:175 N 20 '89
The earring thing [black men] D. C. Lyons. il *Ebony* 44:98-100 Ja '89
EARTH
See also
Atmosphere
Biosphere
Creation
Geophysics
Longitude
Magnetism, Terrestrial
Ocean
How the environmental crisis can improve our lives [cover story; special section; with editorial comment by Eric Utne] il *Utne Reader* p2, 69-97 N/D '89
Planet of the year: what on earth are we doing? [cover story; special section] il *Time* 133:24-30+ Ja 2 '89
Save the planet [cover story; special section] il *Omni (New York, N.Y.)* 11:34-6+ S '89
Age
The age-of-the-earth debate. L. Badash. il *Scientific American* 261:90-4+ Ag '89
New record for world's oldest rocks [work of Samuel Bowring] R. Monastersky. il *Science News* 136:228 O 7 '89
Core
See Earth—Internal structure
Crust
See also
Faults (Geology)
Folds (Geology)
Ocean bottom
Deep holes yielding geoscience surprises. R. A. Kerr. il *Science* 245:468-70 Ag 4 '89
European deep drilling leaves Americans behind. R. A. Kerr. il *Science* 245:816-17 Ag 25 '89
Global Positioning System measurements for crustal deformation: precision and accuracy [California] W. H. Prescott and others. bibl f il *Science* 244:1337-40 Je 16 '89
Inner space [deep drilling programs by Soviet Union and West Germany; cover story] R. Monastersky. il *Science News* 136:266-8 O 21 '89
Just a veneer [study of strike-slip faults by B. Clark Burchfiel and Peter Molnar] T. Appenzeller. *Scientific American* 261:26+ N '89
Origin of granulite terranes and the formation of the lowermost continental crust. S. R. Bohlen and K. Mezger. bibl f il *Science* 244:326-9 Ap 21 '89
Origins and movement of fluids during deformation and metamorphism in the Canadian Cordillera [gold deposits] B. E. Nesbitt and K. Muehlenbachs. bibl f il map *Science* 245:733-6 Ag 18 '89
Underplating and partial melting: implications for melt generation and extraction. G. W. Bergantz. bibl f il *Science* 245:1093-5 S 8 '89
Where on earth is the crust? D. L. Anderson. bibl f il *Physics Today* 42:38-46 Mr '89
Evolution
It's about time. R. Pestrong. il *Earth Science* 42:14-15 Summ '89
Making the moon, remaking earth [giant impact theory] R. A. Kerr. il *Science* 243:1433-5 Mr 17 '89
Piecing together earth's early history. W. K. Hartmann. il *Astronomy* 17:24-34 Je '89
Internal structure
See also
Hot spots (Geology)
Another movement in the dance of the plates [work of Paul F. Hoffman] R. A. Kerr. il *Science* 244:529-30 My 5 '89
Coming down in sheets [computer model of convection in the earth's mantle; work of Dave Bercovici and others] T. Appenzeller. il *Scientific American* 261:17-18 Ag '89
Composition of the earth. D. L. Anderson. bibl f il *Science* 243:367-70 Ja 20 '89
Deep water: "phase B" is decoded. R. Pool. *Science* 246:887 N 17 '89
Elasticity of $MgSiO_3$ in the perovskite structure. A. Yeganeh-Haeri and others. bibl f il *Science* 243:787-9 F 10 '89
Evidence for a heterogeneous upper mantle in the Cabo Ortegal Complex, Spain. J. Girardeau and others. bibl f il map *Science* 245:1231-3 S 15 '89
The evolution of the earth's magnetic field. J. Bloxham and D. Gubbins. bibl il maps *Scientific American* 261:68-75 D '89

EARTH—Internal structure—*cont.*

Hidden chemistry [core-mantle boundary; research by Raymond Jeanloz] T. Appenzeller. *Scientific American* 260:17-18 F '89

Is our view of the core obscured by "clouds"? [core-mantle boundary] R. A. Kerr. *Science* 243:739 F 10 '89

Spinning the supercontinent cycle [research by P. F. Hoffman; cover story] R. Monastersky. il map *Science News* 135:344-6 Je 3 '89

Three-dimensional spherical models of convection in the earth's mantle. D. Bercovici and others. bibl f il *Science* 244:950-5 My 26 '89

When the earth rumbles. W. F. Allman. il map *U.S. News & World Report* 107:38-40+ O 30 '89

Where on earth is the crust? D. L. Anderson. bibl f il *Physics Today* 42:38-46 Mr '89

A wizard of middle earth under fire [R. Jeanloz] R. A. Kerr. por *Science* 246:758-60 N 10 '89

Mantle

See Earth—Internal structure

Observations from space

See also

Artificial satellites—Earth sciences use
Earth—Photographs and photography
Earth Observing System
Mission to Planet Earth (Project)

The Great Wall of China: shattering a myth [visibility from space] il *Sky and Telescope* 78:457 N '89

Space coloristics [cosmonauts' reporting concerning earth's surface] V. Vasyutin and A. A. Tishchenko. bibl il *Scientific American* 261:84-90 Jl '89

Photographs and photography

Earthscapes [cover story] J. Zuckerman. il *Petersen's Photographic Magazine* 17:12-15 Ja '89

Open skies tested. D. F. Robertson. il *Ad Astra* 1:7 Je '89

Rotation

See also

Coriolis force
Planetesimal hypothesis
Polar wander

Earth as egg: hard-boiled or raw? [research by Richard Muller and Donald Morris] R. Monastersky. *Science News* 135:319 My 20 '89

Turtle logic [engraved tortoise shell shows rotation of earth is slowing; research by Kevin Pang] T. Waters. il *Discover* 10:16 D '89

Surface

See Earth—Crust

Temperature

See Earth temperature

EARTH, EFFECT OF MAN ON *See* Man—Influence on nature

EARTH ART *See* Environment (Art)

EARTH DAY

Let earth have its day. J. McDowell. il *Time* 134:71 D 18 '89

EARTH FIRST! (ORGANIZATION)

Earth last! [D. Foreman and others of Earth First! charged with attempted sabotage of the Central Arizona Project] D. Russell. *The Nation* 249:77 Jl 17 '89

Monkey-wrenching for planet earth [infiltrated by FBI] T. Vanderpool. il por *The Progressive* 53:15 S '89

EARTH GIRLS ARE EASY [film] See Motion picture reviews—Single works

EARTH OBSERVING SYSTEM

Bringing NASA down to earth. E. Marshall. il *Science* 244:1248-51 Je 16 '89

Earth observations from space. P. H. Abelson. *Science* 244:901 My 26 '89

The next giant leap for mankind may be saving planet earth. J. Carey. il *Business Week* p90-2 Jl 31 '89

Water-cycle watch [Penn State experiment] J. A. Yeaple. *Popular Science* 235:93 D '89

EARTH RADIATION BUDGET SATELLITE *See* Artificial satellites—Meteorological use

EARTH SCIENCES

See also

Artificial satellites—Earth sciences use
Climate
Geochemistry
Geology
Geophysics
Image processing—Earth sciences use
Meteorology

Talking about earth. See issues of Earth Science

Bibliography

Books & maps. See issues of Earth Science

Study and teaching

Earth plays to full house at Johns Hopkins University. *Earth Science* 42:7-8 Fall '89

EARTH SHELTERED HOUSES *See* Houses, Earth sheltered

EARTH STATIONS (COMMUNICATIONS SATELLITES) *See* Communications satellites—Ground stations

EARTH TEMPERATURE

Chemico-viscous remanent magnetization in the Fe_3O_4-γFe_2O_3 system. Ö. Özdemir and D. J. Dunlop. bibl f il *Science* 243:1043-7 F 24 '89

EARTH TREMORS *See* Earthquakes

EARTHQUAKE INSURANCE *See* Insurance, Earthquake

EARTHQUAKE PREDICTION

Bracing for a quake [Canada's West coast] J. Hanna. il *Maclean's* 102:59 My 1 '89

Earthquake hazard after a mainshock in California. P. A. Reasenberg and L. M. Jones. bibl f il *Science* 243:1173-6 Mr 3 '89

East of the Rockies: a lot of shaking going on. *Newsweek* 114:41 O 30 '89

Estimating earthquake losses. il *The Futurist* 23:50 Jl/Ag '89

Loma Prieta quake unsettles geophysicists. R. A. Kerr. il *Science* 246:1562-3 D 22 '89

Magnetic signal preceded October quake. R. Monastersky. *Science News* 136:390 D 16 '89

New fault picture points toward Bay Area quakes [Calaveras fault; research by David Oppenheimer] R. A. Kerr. map *Science* 244:286-7 Ap 21 '89

Not yet accurate to a fault [San Andreas fault] B. Carpenter and S. Brownlee. il *U.S. News & World Report* 107:44-5 O 30 '89

The origins of killer quakes. H. Jensen. il *Maclean's* 102:66-7 O 30 '89

Predicting earthquakes [strainmeter developed by Michael Gladwin] S. F. Brown. il *Popular Science* 234:124-5 Je '89

'Preshock' pattern may foretell quakes [research by Karen C. McNally] R. Monastersky. *Science News* 136:374-5 D 9 '89

Reading the future in Loma Prieta. R. A. Kerr. il map *Science* 246:436-9 O 27 '89

Shaky ground. A. Meyer. il *The Mother Earth News* 116:36+ Mr/Ap '89

Signal warns of impending quakes [Advanced Warning System installed in Calif.] il *High Technology Business* 9:11 N/D '89

Smashing plates, broken ground [future California quakes] S. Begley. il map *Newsweek* 114:37-8+ O 30 '89

Still waiting for the big one. J. M. Nash. il map *Time* 134:44-5 O 30 '89

Swimming is Oscar's only real skill—but he predicts earthquakes on the side [tropical fish at Corona Del Mar High School in California] il *People Weekly* 32:77 S 11 '89

Taking the pulse of the San Andreas fault [research by Kerry Sieh] *Science* 243:479-80 Ja 27 '89

U.S., Soviets share seismic posts [joint network to collect earthquake and bomb test data] R. J. Smith. il map *Science* 245:807-8 Ag 25 '89

Unstudied California fault poses hazard [Rodgers Creek fault] R. Monastersky. *Science News* 136:388 D 16 '89

EARTHQUAKE PROTECTION

The benefits of being prepared [San Francisco Bay Area] J. Castro. il *Time* 134:42-3 O 30 '89

Bracing for the big one. E. Salholz. il map *Newsweek* 114:28-32 O 30 '89

The high cost of poor planning [lack of preparedness in Armenia] L. Tarshis. il *Scholastic Update (Teachers' edition)* 122:14-15 D 15 '89

Is Los Angeles next? F. Trippett. il map *Time* 134:24 N 6 '89

EARTHQUAKE RELIEF CONCERT, 1989

Earthquake Relief concert raises more than $2 million. il *Jet* 77:6 D 18 '89

EARTHQUAKES

See also

Seismic waves

Deep earthquakes. C. Frohlich. bibl il maps *Scientific American* 260:48-55 Ja '89

Deep-rooted disturbance [link between earthquakes and El Niño; research by Daniel Walker] S. Vogel. il *Discover* 10:26+ Jl '89

Geologic events. See issues of Earth Science

Hidden earthquakes [cover story] R. S. Stein and R. S. Yeats. bibl il maps *Scientific American* 260:48-57 Je '89

How earthquakes happen. G. H. Colt. il map *Life* 12:40-1+ F '89

Oil wells cause earthquakes [research by Paul Segall] A. McKenzie. *Science News* 136:279 O 28 '89

Shaking down deep [hidden faults] J. M. Nash. *Time* 134:108 O 23 '89

The sound of silent earthquakes [research by Gregory C. Beroza and Thomas H. Jordan] R. Monastersky. *Science News* 135:335 My 27 '89

When the earth cracks open. L. Morrow. *Time* 134:100 O 30 '89

Measurement

See Seismometers and seismometry

Prediction

See Earthquake prediction

Protection

See Earthquake protection

Armenia (Soviet Union)

Anguish in Armenia. il *Reader's Digest* 134:140-6 Mr '89

Armenia: what U.S. companies did. F. H. Katayama. il *Fortune* 119:10-11 Ja 16 '89

Armenian earthquakes and Soviet tremors. G. J. Libaridian. *Society* 26:59-63 Mr/Ap '89

EARTHQUAKES—Armenia (Soviet Union)—*cont.*
Christians send aid to Armenian quake victims. *Christianity Today* 33:62-3 Ja 13 '89
Dealing with a distant disaster [study of Armenian American adolescents by Viken V. Yacoubian] *Science News* 136:92 Ag 5 '89
Earthquake in the Soviet Union [White House statement, December 8, 1988] *Department of State Bulletin* 89:39 F '89
Faucet sales and crush syndrome [cover story] M. J. Arlen. il *The Nation* 248:548-50+ Ap 24 '89
From the ground up, warily [extent of damage; views of John Filson] B. Weber. il *The New York Times Magazine* p66 Jl 23 '89
From the rubble. J. Lloyd. il *National Review* 41:31-2 Ja 27 '89
Gorbachev in Armenia. M. Kempton. il *The New York Review of Books* 35:58 Ja 19 '89
The high cost of poor planning. L. Tarshis. il *Scholastic Update (Teachers' edition)* 122:14-15 D 15 '89
How the Armenian quake became a killer. R. A. Kerr. il *Science* 243:170 Ja 13 '89
Jackson visits earthquake victims in Soviet Union. D. M. Cheers. il pors *Jet* 75:4-6+ F 20 '89
Lessons and questions emerge from Armenian quake. R. Monastersky. map *Science News* 135:43 Ja 21 '89
Life in a weary land. J. Kohan. il *Time* 133:83 Ja 2 '89
The mystery of a 'miracle' [Aikaz Akopyan claims he survived 35 day burial] *Newsweek* 113:38 Ja 23 '89
Shaky ground. A. Meyer. il *The Mother Earth News* 116:36+ Mr/Ap '89
A shattered land. il *Life* 12:34-9 F '89
A struggle for new life. A. Wilson-Smith. il *Maclean's* 102:20-2 Ap 24 '89
A year later, Armenia is still at ground zero. il *U.S. News & World Report* 107:10-11 D 18 '89
British Columbia
Bracing for a quake. J. Hanna. il *Maclean's* 102:59 My 1 '89
California
See also
San Francisco Bay Area (Calif.)—Earthquake, 1989
Another California seismic hot spot [southern Santa Cruz segment of San Andreas fault] R. A. Kerr. map *Science* 245:704 Ag 18 '89
Bay Area shock may foreshadow strong quake [San Andreas fault in southern Santa Cruz mountains] R. Monastersky. *Science News* 136:119 Ag 19 '89
Dynamics of liquefaction during the 1987 Superstition Hills, California, earthquake [cover story] T. L. Holzer and others. bibl f il map *Science* 244:56-9 Ap 7 '89
Earthquake hazard after a mainshock in California. P. A. Reasenberg and L. M. Jones. bibl f il *Science* 243:1173-6 Mr 3 '89
Flurry of quakes in L.A. R. A. Kerr. il map *Science* 244:1542 Je 30 '89
Is California worth the risk? R. Lacayo. il *Time* 134:18-20 N 6 '89
Is Los Angeles next? F. Trippett. il map *Time* 134:24 N 6 '89
Microearthquake imaging of the Parkfield asperity [San Andreas fault] P. E. Malin and others. bibl f il *Science* 244:557-9 My 5 '89
New fault picture points toward Bay Area quakes [Calaveras fault; research by David Oppenheimer] R. A. Kerr. map *Science* 244:286-7 Ap 21 '89
Not yet accurate to a fault [San Andreas fault] B. Carpenter and S. Brownlee. il *U.S. News & World Report* 107:44-5 O 30 '89
Signal warns of impending quakes [Advanced Warning System installed in Calif.] il *High Technology Business* 9:11 N/D '89
Smashing plates, broken ground [future quakes] S. Begley. il map *Newsweek* 114:37-8+ O 30 '89
Swimming is Oscar's only real skill—but he predicts earthquakes on the side [tropical fish at Corona Del Mar High School in California] il *People Weekly* 32:77 S 11 '89
Taking the pulse of the San Andreas fault [research by Kerry Sieh] *Science* 243:479-80 Ja 27 '89
Unstudied California fault poses hazard [Rodgers Creek fault] R. Monastersky. *Science News* 136:388 D 16 '89
History
See also
San Francisco (Calif.)—Earthquake and fire, 1906
Italy
Finding gold in the rubble [allegations that Irpinia officials misused 1980 earthquake relief funds] *Newsweek* 113:35 Ja 9 '89
Japan
When the big one hits Tokyo . . . E. B. Terry. *World Press Review* 36:42+ D '89
Ohio
Wastequakes [injection wells implicated in Ohio earthquake near Perry Nuclear Power Plant] il *Discover* 10:8+ Ap '89
Pacific Northwest
New quake forecast: north by northwest. R. A. Kerr. *Science* 246:1562 D 22 '89

Pacific region
Birth of a subduction zone [along the Macquarie Ridge; research by Susan L. Beck] R. Monastersky. *Science News* 136:396 D 16 '89
Powerful quake shakes South Pacific. R. Monastersky. map *Science News* 135:340 Je 3 '89
EARTHQUAKES AND BRIDGES
A blessing in disguise [partial collapse of Oakland Bay Bridge] M. Barinaga. map *Science* 246:1391 D 15 '89
EARTHQUAKES AND BUILDING
Designed for survival. G. Cowley. il *Newsweek* 114:34-5+ O 30 '89
From the ground up, warily [extent of damage caused by Armenian earthquake; views of John Filson] B. Weber. il *The New York Times Magazine* p66 Jl 23 '89
How the Armenian quake became a killer. R. A. Kerr. il *Science* 243:170 Ja 13 '89
Learning from the big quake, getting ready for the future. il *Sunset (Central West edition)* 183:106-7 D '89
Loma Prieta: saved by a short, sharp shock. M. Barinaga. il map *Science* 246:1390-1 D 15 '89
Resonance implicated in Nimitz tragedy [collapse of Oakland freeway] *Science News* 136:367 D 2 '89
"We have built our houses on sand" [San Francisco Bay Area] M. Barinaga. il *Science* 246:437 O 27 '89
EARTHWORK
See also
Dams
Underground structures
EARTHWORKS (ART) *See* Environment (Art)
EARTHWORMS
Grandpa and the kid [brown trout fishing] D. Sisson. il *Field & Stream* 94:39+ Je '89
Mother nature's plow. M. Holmberg. il *Successful Farming* 87:52 O '89
The wood turtle stomp. J. H. Kaufmann. il *Natural History* p8+ Ag '89
Worm and remembrance [Consumer Product Safety Commission's recall of Worm Gett'r, an electronic worm probe for fishermen] W. J. Elvin. il *The American Spectator* 22:30-1 Ja '89
Worm mornings. N. Strung. il *Field & Stream* 93:44-5+ Mr '89
Worm warfare [running on a track with an earthworm] R. M. Owens. il *Runner's World* 24:120 O '89
Anecdotes, facetiae, satire, etc.
As the worm squirms. P. F. McManus. il *Outdoor Life* 183:142+ Mr '89
EASELS
Child's easel for paint, crayon, chalk. A. Rooze. il *The Family Handyman* 39:66-7 O '89
EASELS, ENLARGER (PHOTOGRAPHY) *See* Photography—Enlargers and enlarging
EASEMENTS
See also
Conservation easements
EAST AFRICA
See also
Ethiopia
Kenya
Lakes—East Africa
Mozambique
Zanzibar
Native peoples
See also
Kipsigis (African people)
Masai (African people)
Politics and government
Doing it the army way in Africa's Horn. E. Ransdell. il map *U.S. News & World Report* 107:32+ Jl 24 '89
EAST AND WEST
See also
East-West trade
A big wet kiss. *The Nation* 248:4-5 Ja 2 '89
Declaration on East-West Relations, July 15, 1989 [text of Paris economic summit declaration] *Department of State Bulletin* 89:2 S '89
East-West, North-South [papal letter] J. B. Hehir. il *Commonweal* 116:614-15 N 17 '89
East-West relation [escorting a Communist visitor around New York City] R. Stone. il *Harper's* 279:63-7 N '89
East-West relations. V. Giscard d'Estaing and others. *Foreign Affairs* 68:1-21 Summ '89
Eastern cultures experts on "self". R. Williams. *The Humanist* 49:40 N/D '89
How should the West respond? *America* 161:203 O 7 '89
The last socialist? [John Paul II; cover story] J. Gray. il *National Review* 41:27-9+ Je 30 '89
Notes and comment. *The New Yorker* 65:37-8 O 2 '89
Problems in paradigm. G. Flynn. *Foreign Policy* 74:63-84 Spr '89
A third encounter of the close kind [cover story] A. S. Ahmed. il *History Today* 39:4-9 N '89
A Western response [Islam] W. M. Watt. il *History Today* 39:5-8 D '89
Who's afraid of tearing down the Iron Curtain? T. Moore. il *U.S. News & World Report* 106:10-11 My 15 '89

EAST AND WEST—*cont.*
'Why the West distrusted us'. A. Novikov. *World Press Review* 36:28-30 Je '89
EAST ASIA
See also
Airlines—East Asia
Airports—East Asia
Americans—East Asia
Banks and banking—East Asia
Economic assistance, American—East Asia
Investments, American—East Asia
Labor costs—East Asia
Pacific region
Paleontology—East Asia
Securities—East Asia
Bibliography
Book reviews. *Current History* 88:189+ Ap '89
Commerce
Asia's 'Tigers' will pounce. K. Kuwabara. *World Press Review* 36:22 D '89
Taking the Tigers off the dole [U.S. discontinues duty free status for Taiwan, Hong Kong, South Korea and Singapore] E. A. Finn, Jr. il *Forbes* 143:70 Ja 23 '89
Canada
See Canada—Commerce—East Asia
Soviet Union
See Soviet Union—Commerce—East Asia
United States
See United States—Commerce—East Asia
Description and travel
See also
Cruising—East Asia
Economic conditions
The challenge of Asia in the 1990s [cover story] il *Fortune* 120 no13 Special Issue:10-11 Fall '89
East Asia, the Pacific, and the U.S.: an economic partnership. il map *Department of State Bulletin* 89:33-7 Ap '89
Japan builds a new power base. D. J. Yang and N. Gross. il *Business Week* p42-5 Ap 10 '89
Economic policy
The capitalism/socialism debate in East Asia. S. N. G. Davies. bibl *Society* 26:29-37 Mr/Ap '89
Challenges and issues for Asia and the Pacific [address, June 7, 1989] W.-C. Kim. *Vital Speeches of the Day* 55:642-4 Ag 15 '89
Why Asian countries blossomed while Latin America wilted [income inequality] G. Koretz. il *Business Week* p16 Ag 28 '89
Economic relations
Japan
See Japan—Economic relations—East Asia
Soviet Union
See Soviet Union—Economic relations—East Asia
United States
See United States—Economic relations—East Asia
Foreign relations
Soviet Union
See Soviet Union—Foreign relations—East Asia
United States
See United States—Foreign relations—East Asia
Industries
See also
Audio equipment industry—East Asia
Black business enterprises—East Asia
Printing industry—East Asia
Publishers and publishing—East Asia
Politics and government
See also
Socialism—East Asia
East Asia [cover story; special issue] bibl f map (inside back cover) *Current History* 88:161-202 Ap '89
Looking toward the new Pacific century [interview with D. Davies] A. Balk. por *World Press Review* 36:34+ S '89
Recent developments in East Asia [address, July 20, 1989] R. H. Myers. *Vital Speeches of the Day* 55:716-18 S 15 '89
EAST BERLIN *See* Berlin (Germany: East)
EAST CHICAGO (IND.)
Politics and government
The last city machine in America [Mayor R. A. Pastrick] P. Glastris. il por *U.S. News & World Report* 107:29-30 Ag 21 '89
EAST COAST MEDIA (FIRM)
Stable Jerry [former Crazy Eddie pitchman J. Carroll] J. Queenan. il pors *Forbes* 144:350 N 13 '89
EAST EUROPEAN REFUGEES *See* Refugees, East European
EAST EUROPEAN STUDIES
Periodicals
The third way: publications bridging the East-West gap. M. Specktor. *Utne Reader* p116-19 Ja/F '89
EAST GERMAN ATHLETES *See* Athletes
EAST GERMAN REFUGEES *See* Refugees, East German
EAST GERMANY *See* Germany (East)
EAST HAMPTON (N.Y.)
Architecture
Cottage classic [shingle style house designed by J. T. Robertson] M. Filler. il *House & Garden* 161:192-9+ My '89

Art
Two American artists' colonies [En plein air: the art colonies at East Hampton and Old Lyme, 1880-1930] A. E. Ledes. *Antiques* 136:42+ Jl '89
EAST SAINT LOUIS (ILL.)
Economic conditions
A city without bootstraps. L. Griggs. il *Time* 133:10+ Je 12 '89
Education
Award-winning director faces layoff [band director R. Carter] D. Helland. il *Down Beat* 56:12 Ag '89
Poor
Santa's special helper [donating and distributing gifts for needy families] R. Swiener. il por *Ladies' Home Journal* 106:18+ D '89
EAST SIDE HOUSE SETTLEMENT WINTER ANTIQUES SHOW *See* Antiques—Exhibitions
EAST TENNESSEE STATE UNIVERSITY. CENTER FOR APPALACHIAN STUDIES AND SERVICES
From offices of excellence [work of R. Blaustein] D. Young. il pors *Southern Living* 24:142+ Ap '89
EAST TIMOR (INDONESIA)
Politics and government
Visiting a forgotten war [Pope John Paul II] R. Nordland. il map *Newsweek* 114:38 O 23 '89
Religious institutions and affairs
See also
John Paul II, Pope, 1920——Visit to East Timor (Indonesia), 1989
EAST VILLAGE (NEW YORK, N.Y.) *See* Greenwich Village (New York, N.Y.)
EAST-WEST TRADE
See also
Coordinating Committee on Multilateral Export Controls
A silken bond between East and West [silk roads] A. H. Dani. il map *The Courier (Unesco)* 42:4-10 Mr '89
EASTER
See also
Jesus Christ—Resurrection and Ascension
Christ's Resurrection and Ascension. G. O'Collins. *America* 160:262-3 Mr 25 '89
Easter meditation:
The resurrection of the body. J. P. Baumgaertner. *The Christian Century* 106:302-3 Mr 22-29 '89
A fixed date for Easter? P. H. Pfatteicher. *The Christian Century* 106:300-1 Mr 22-29 '89
The great reversal [cover story; special section] il *Christianity Today* 33:19-27 Mr 17 '89
Spring holiday helper. P. Schiller. il *McCall's* 116:37+ Mr '89
Ways of looking. P. J. Ryan. il *America* 160:255 Mr 18 '89
EASTER CAKE *See* Cake
EASTER CANDY *See* Candy
EASTER COOKING
See also
Cooking, Ornamental
Easter luncheon. il *Gourmet* 49:96-102+ Mr '89
A Russian Easter zakuska party. il *Gourmet* 49:98-100+ Ap '89
Special entrées for Easter. il *Southern Living* 24:196 Mr '89
EASTER EGGS *See* Eggs, Decorated
EASTER ISLAND
Antiquities
Amazing mysteries: giants on Easter Island [cover story] il map *National Geographic World* 162:4-7 F '89
EASTERBROOK, GREGG
All aboard Air Oblivion. *The Washington Monthly* 21:53+ F '89
The sky is always falling [cover story] il *The New Republic* 201:21-5 Ag 21 '89
What Charlie Peters can learn from Henry Kravis. *The Washington Monthly* 21:32-3 Mr '89
What is the Air Force really worried about: national security or job security? *The Washington Monthly* 21:18-20+ S '89
Who says the sky is falling? *Reader's Digest* 135:103-5 D '89
EASTERN AIR LINES, INC.
Advantage, Lorenzo [Chapter 11 strategy] G. DeGeorge and S. Payne. il por *Business Week* p24-6 Jl 10 '89
Air sickness [F. Lorenzo] H. Fairlie. *The New Republic* 200:14-16+ Je 5 '89
Back to you, Frank [F. Lorenzo's deal with P. Ueberroth collapses] A. Bernstein and C. Power. il pors *Business Week* p24-6 Ap 24 '89
Beat the devil [coverage of the strike against Eastern and of the struggle in El Salvador] A. Cockburn. *The Nation* 248:438-9 Ap 3 '89
A boss they love to hate [F. Lorenzo and Eastern Air Lines strike] J. Schwartz. il por *Newsweek* 113:20-4 Mr 20 '89
Can Eastern Air Lines survive? D. Pauly. il *Newsweek* 113:42 Mr 13 '89
Caught in Eastern's slipstream [airlines raise fares as a result of strike] il *U.S. News & World Report* 106:10+ Mr 27 '89

EASTERN AIR LINES, INC.—cont.

Collective bargaining at Eastern. *Aviation Week & Space Technology* 130:9 Ja 30 '89

Court approves proposed sale of Eastern air-shuttle. J. T. McKenna. *Aviation Week & Space Technology* 130:102-3 My 22 '89

Court frees $75 million from escrow after talks between Eastern, creditors. C. Fotos. *Aviation Week & Space Technology* 131:98 Jl 24 '89

Crashing Eastern [unions urging re-regulation of airlines] il *National Review* 41:12 Ap 7 '89

Creditors pose key threat to Eastern revival effort. J. T. McKenna. *Aviation Week & Space Technology* 130:106-7 Ap 24 '89

The crowded skies [bidders] A. Walmsley. *Maclean's* 102:32 Ap 10 '89

The designated hero [P. Ueberroth's plan to buy Eastern] J. Castro. il por *Time* 133:44-6 Ap 17 '89

Eastern adds flights, signs $210-million Midway pact. C. Fotos. *Aviation Week & Space Technology* 131:74-5 Ag 7 '89

Eastern Air Lines. *Monthly Labor Review* 112:44 S '89

Eastern asks court's permission to break contract with pilots. *Aviation Week & Space Technology* 130:92 Je 26 '89

Eastern building pilot corps amid strike, bankruptcy battles. C. Fotos. il *Aviation Week & Space Technology* 131:101-2 Jl 31 '89

Eastern, creditors divided on new reorganization plan. J. T. McKenna. *Aviation Week & Space Technology* 131:68-9 O 23 '89

Eastern: does anybody win? W. Woods. il por *Fortune* 119:14 Ap 10 '89

Eastern expands systemwide flight operations; bankruptcy court to hear arguments on trustee. *Aviation Week & Space Technology* 130:62 Jl 10 '89

Eastern goes bust. J. Castro. il por *Time* 133:52-3 Mr 20 '89

Eastern reopens bidding for shuttle as Trump balks at $365 million price. P. Proctor and J. T. McKenna. *Aviation Week & Space Technology* 130:31 Mr 27 '89

Eastern resumes efforts to sell South American route network [to American Airlines] *Aviation Week & Space Technology* 131:83 N 27 '89

Eastern seeks creditors' approval of recovery plan. J. T. McKenna. *Aviation Week & Space Technology* 130:104-5 My 1 '89

Eastern struggles to expand service, fend off lawsuits. E. H. Kolcum. *Aviation Week & Space Technology* 130:268-9 Mr 20 '89

Eastern trains replacement pilots, weighs buyout offers. *Aviation Week & Space Technology* 130:33 Ap 3 '89

Eastern unions losing bid to unseat Lorenzo. J. T. McKenna. il *Aviation Week & Space Technology* 130:108-9 My 29 '89

Eastern's labor mess may land in Bush's lap. A. Bernstein. il *Business Week* p26 Mr 6 '89

Eastern's merry-go-round [collapse of P. Ueberroth deal] *Newsweek* 113:62 Ap 24 '89

Eastern's shuttlers vote with their seats [impact of strike] il *Newsweek* 113:46 Mr 27 '89

FAA cites recurring failures in maintenance at Eastern. J. T. McKenna. *Aviation Week & Space Technology* 131:7, 64-5 Jl 3 '89

FAA officials say Eastern safety matches that of other airlines. C. Fotos. *Aviation Week & Space Technology* 131:80-1 Ag 7 '89

A fight for the friendly skies: takeover artists go after Eastern and Northwest. L. Reibstein. il *Newsweek* 113:50 Ap 10 '89

A fight to the death? [strike] *The Nation* 248:397 Mr 27 '89

GAO will review Ritchie, Lorenzo plans for Eastern. J. T. McKenna. *Aviation Week & Space Technology* 131:100-1 Jl 31 '89

Going for broke at Eastern [strike] J. Castro. il *Time* 133:42 Mr 13 '89

Judge set to rule on shuttle sale, Eastern business plan. *Aviation Week & Space Technology* 130:72 My 15 '89

Judge threatens to auction Eastern after buyout fails [bid by P. Ueberroth] J. T. McKenna and E. H. Kolcum. *Aviation Week & Space Technology* 130:60-1 Ap 17 '89

Lorenzo is running out of choices—and time. P. Engardio and G. DeGeorge. il *Business Week* p37-8 Mr 20 '89

Lorenzo's magnificent airline [offers to purchase Eastern] il *U.S. News & World Report* 106:14+ Ap 10 '89

Pilot supply may be key issue in talks on Eastern recovery. J. T. McKenna. *Aviation Week & Space Technology* 130:315 Je 12 '89

A pilot with a golden record [P. Ueberroth wants to purchase Eastern Airlines] il por *U.S. News & World Report* 106:14-15 Ap 17 '89

Pilots, flight attendants end walkout at Eastern. *Aviation Week & Space Technology* 131:33 D 4 '89

Pilots vote to continue Eastern strike, but many decide to cross picket lines. *Aviation Week & Space Technology* 131:59 Ag 14 '89

Pilots will press Eastern to deal or face shutdown. J. T. McKenna and E. H. Kolcum. *Aviation Week & Space Technology* 130:68-9 F 27 '89

Recovery strategy poses major risks for Eastern. J. T. McKenna. *Aviation Week & Space Technology* 130:103 My 8 '89

Skinner calls USAir bid for more Philadelphia gates anticompetitive [Eastern gates] *Aviation Week & Space Technology* 130:110 Je 5 '89

The story at Eastern Airlines [strike] W. F. Buckley. *National Review* 41:54 Ap 21 '89

Strike forces Eastern into bankruptcy court [special section; with editorial comment] il *Aviation Week & Space Technology* 130:7, 16-23 Mr 13 '89

Suicide pact at Eastern Air Lines [filing for bankruptcy during strike; with interview with F. A. Lorenzo] T. Moore and C. P. Work. il por *U.S. News & World Report* 106:18-21 Mr 20 '89

Texas Air: empire in jeopardy [strike at Eastern; special section] il por *Business Week* p28-31 Mr 27 '89

U.S. airline industry braces for Eastern machinists' strike. J. Ott. *Aviation Week & Space Technology* 130:92-3 F 13 '89

The Ueberroth touch. L. Reibstein. il por *Newsweek* 113:44-5 Ap 17 '89

Ueberroth woos unions in bid to take over Eastern, resume flight operations. J. T. McKenna and E. H. Kolcum. *Aviation Week & Space Technology* 130:89 Ap 10 '89

Unions, investor plead for time to negotiate pact to buy Eastern. *Aviation Week & Space Technology* 130:113 Je 5 '89

Where's my escape hatch? [P. Ueberroth's deal with Eastern stalls] il *Time* 133:51 Ap 24 '89

Why Mike Milken was so eager to help Peter Ueberroth [takeover] A. Bernstein. *Business Week* p30 My 1 '89

EASTERN COLLEGE

Roberta Hestenes: taking charge [cover story] T. Stafford. il pors *Christianity Today* 33:16-22 Mr 3 '89

EASTERN ENTERPRISES

From coal to water. J. Cook. il por *Forbes* 144:62 Ag 7 '89

EASTERN EUROPE

See also
    Airlines—Routes—Eastern Europe
    Americans—Eastern Europe
    Anti-Semitism—Eastern Europe
    Civil rights—Eastern Europe
    Economic assistance—Eastern Europe
    Economic assistance, American—Eastern Europe
    Food supply—Eastern Europe
    Freedom of information—Eastern Europe
    Investments, American—Eastern Europe
    Investments, Foreign—Eastern Europe
    Loans, East European
    Money—Eastern Europe
    Peace movement—Eastern Europe
    Poland
    Pollution—Eastern Europe
    Romania
    Telephone—Eastern Europe
    Terrorism—Eastern Europe
    United Nations—Eastern Europe
    Yugoslavia

Bibliography

Book reviews. *Current History* 88:397+ N '89

Commerce

See also
    Coordinating Committee on Multilateral Export Controls
    East-West trade

Eastern bloc nations seek Western-built transports to meet growing demand. il *Aviation Week & Space Technology* 131:102+ N 20 '89

United States

See United States—Commerce—Eastern Europe

Defenses

See also
    Soviet Union—Armed Forces—Forces in Eastern Europe
    Warsaw Treaty Organization

Economic conditions

Go east, young man? R. Ball. il *Time* 134:65 D 4 '89

A new economic miracle? [cover story; special section] il *Business Week* p58-66+ N 27 '89

Who gains from the new Europe. R. I. Kirkland, Jr. il map *Fortune* 120:83-5+ D 18 '89

Economic policy

Communism's capitalists. H. Jensen. il *Maclean's* 102:50+ N 13 '89

Free-market economics: antidote for war and poverty. il *Nation's Business* 77:71 D '89

In Eastern Europe, little things count [move from a Communist to a free economy] M. Novak. *The Christian Century* 106:1164-5 D 13 '89

Perestroika may be both good and bad for Eastern Europe's severe ecological crisis. A. Hittle and D. Malakoff. il *Utne Reader* p86-7 Ja/F '89

Perestroika shakes Eastern Europe. F. S. Larrabee. il por *The Bulletin of the Atomic Scientists* 45:25-9 Mr '89

EASTERN EUROPE—*cont.*
Economic relations
Germany (West)
See Germany (West)—Economic relations—Eastern Europe

Korea (South)
See Korea (South)—Economic relations—Eastern Europe

United States
See United States—Economic relations—Eastern Europe

Foreign relations
Crossing the European divide. C. Bogdan. bibl f *Foreign Policy* 75:56-75 Summ '89
What do we do next? S. Sullivan. il *Newsweek* 114:41+ N 20 '89

Germany (West)
See Germany (West)—Foreign relations—Eastern Europe

Israel
See Israel—Foreign relations—Eastern Europe
Italy
See Italy—Foreign relations—Eastern Europe
Soviet Union
See Soviet Union—Foreign relations—Eastern Europe
United States
See United States—Foreign relations—Eastern Europe
History
.1945-
Reforms and crackdowns. S. Flack. il *Scholastic Update (Teachers' edition)* 122:14-15 O 20 '89
Industries
See also
Airlines—Eastern Europe
Nationalism
New hopes, old grudges, great dangers. R. Knight. il *U.S. News & World Report* 107:30-2 Jl 31 '89
Post-Communist nationalism. Z. Brzezinski. il map *Foreign Affairs* 68:1-25 Wint '89/'90
Politics and government
See also
Communism—Eastern Europe
Socialism—Eastern Europe
1848, 1948, 1989 . . . *National Review* 41:11-12 N 24 '89
After the party's over [Solidarity's influence on reform movements] D. Stanglin. il *U.S. News & World Report* 107:76-7 Ag 28-S 4 '89
After the Wall [special section] il *Newsweek* 114:30-5 N 27 '89
Behind the masks of Eastern Europe. S. Smith and M. R. Meyer. il *Newsweek* 114:46 O 16 '89
Bloc busters [cover story] J. Rupnik. *The New Republic* 200:18+ My 22 '89
A bloc turned upside down. H. Anderson. il por map *Newsweek* 114:30-3 Jl 17 '89
Chips off the old bloc. C. Ogden. il *Time* 133:46-8+ Mr 27 '89
Communism at the crossroads in Eastern Europe. R. F. Staar. il *USA Today (Periodical)* 117:46-7 My '89
Days of the whirlwind. M. Meyer. il *Newsweek* 114:26+ D 25 '89
East bloc political changes add to West's budget battles [with editorial comment by Paul Mann] M. Mecham. il *Aviation Week & Space Technology* 131:19, 28-31 N 20 '89
East Europe [cover story; special issue] bibl f il map (inside back cover) *Current History* 88:369-410 N '89
East European divides. M. Svec. *Foreign Policy* 77:41-63 Wint '89/'90
Eastern Europe: now the hard part. R. Knight. il *U.S. News & World Report* 107:42-4 D 11 '89
Eastern Europe on its own. C. Gati. bibl f *Foreign Affairs* 68 Special Issue:99-119 ['89]
Eastern Europe: the Iron Curtain cracks [cover story; special issue] il map *Scholastic Update (Teachers' edition)* 122:1-23 O 20 '89
Europe's second Reformation. G. F. Will. il *Newsweek* 114:90 N 20 '89
The events in Eastern Europe [address, November 22, 1989] G. Bush. *Vital Speeches of the Day* 56:130-2 D 15 '89
Fighting off hasty change. M. Nemeth. il *Maclean's* 102:42-3 D 25 '89
Free at last! [cover story; special section] il map *Maclean's* 102:44-8+ N 20 '89
The freedom they need. *National Review* 41:11 D 8 '89
Glasnost as a verb: to open a Wall. *America* 161:367-8 N 25 '89
How Kissinger sees it. H. Kissinger. il *Newsweek* 114:45 O 16 '89
I didn't tell you so. M. Greenfield. il *Newsweek* 114:104 N 27 '89
Images of '89: the year that changed the world [special section; with editorial comment by Kevin Doyle] il *Maclean's* 102:2, 30-2+ D 18 '89
An irresistible tide. H. G. Chua-Eoan. il map *Time* 134:36-8 N 27 '89
Is Stalin dead? Yes—at last. M. B. Zuckerman. il *U.S. News & World Report* 107:88+ D 4 '89

Lech Walesa, superstar, now faces the music. S. V. Roberts. il por *U.S. News & World Report* 107:10-11 N 27 '89
Lifelines of freedom. D. Gergen. il *U.S. News & World Report* 107:95 N 27 '89
The mould breaks. J. Bierman. il *Maclean's* 102:16-17 S 4 '89
New days that shake the world [cover story] D. Singer. il *The Nation* 248:577+ My 1 '89
Notes and comment. *The New Yorker* 65:41-3 D 4 '89
Perestroika shakes Eastern Europe. F. S. Larrabee. il por *The Bulletin of the Atomic Scientists* 45:25-9 Mr '89
Political quakes and storms. *America* 161:311 N 11 '89
Problems in paradigm. G. Flynn. *Foreign Policy* 74:63-84 Spr '89
The rebirth of history. B. Crozier. *National Review* 41:18 D 22 '89
Rules of the game. J. Garvey. *Commonweal* 116:697-8 D 15 '89
Satellites do it their way. M. R. Meyer. il *Newsweek* 114:48 N 6 '89
The 'Sinatra Doctrine' [Kremlin's hands-off attitude] J. Bierman. il *Maclean's* 102:40+ N 6 '89
The Soviet empire: Eastern Europe [special section] il *U.S. News & World Report* 106:35-6+ Mr 27 '89
Trying to control a runaway train. D. Stanglin. il *U.S. News & World Report* 107:24-6 D 18 '89
Turning visions into reality [cover story; special section] il *Time* 134:34-42+ D 11 '89
Uncharted waters. J. Smolowe. il *Time* 134:18-20 S 4 '89
Vic Damone in Eastern Europe. J. Klein. il por map *New York* 22:24-5 N 27 '89
Vindication of a hard-liner [interview with Z. Brzezinski] S. Talbott and R. T. Zintl. il por *Time* 134:10+ D 18 '89
Watching a failed order die [interview with Z. Brzezinski] L. Kramer. il por *People Weekly* 32:49 N 27 '89
What the future holds. F. Painton. il *Time* 134:23+ D 18 '89
The winds of change. S. Manning. il *Scholastic Update (Teachers' edition)* 121:26 My 5 '89
The winds of change. M. Nemeth. il *Maclean's* 102:28 Ag 28 '89
Workers of the world ignite. D. Stanglin. il *U.S. News & World Report* 107:48-9 O 30 '89
Yes, he's for real [M. Gorbachev; cover story; special section] il por *Time* 134:40-2+ N 6 '89
Religious institutions and affairs
See also
Catholic Church—Eastern Europe
Christians—Eastern Europe
Study and teaching
See East European studies
EASTERN GAS & FUEL ASSOCIATES
See also
Eastern Enterprises
EASTERN ORTHODOX CHURCH *See* Orthodox Eastern Church
EASTERN STANDARD [drama] See Greenberg, Richard
EASTLAKE, CHARLES L. (CHARLES LOCKE), 1836-1906
about
American Eastlake furniture. K. M. McClinton. il *Antiques & Collecting Hobbies* 94:28-30+ My '89
EASTLAND, TERRY
The 80-percenters. *The New Republic* 200:14-15 Ja 2 '89
Civil rights: a presidential agenda. *Current (Washington, D.C.)* 310:36-8 F '89
Impeachment by other means. *Commentary* 88:40-4 Ag '89
Lessons in quitting. por *Newsweek* 113:8 Je 12 '89
Nurturing faith in the nation's capital. il por *Christianity Today* 33:27-8 Ja 13 '89
Presswatch. See issues of The American Spectator beginning February 1989
Racial preference in court (again). *Commentary* 87:32-8 Ja '89
Toward a real restoration of civil rights. *Commentary* 88:25-9 N '89
While justice sleeps [cover story] il *National Review* 41:24-6 Ap 21 '89
EASTMAN, GEORGE, 1854-1932
about
Photography for everyman. il *American History Illustrated* 24:64-5 S/O '89
EASTMAN, JOHN
about
De Kooning's co-conservators. A. Decker. il pors *Art News* 88:58 O '89
EASTMAN, MARY-JEAN
about
The woman-managed firm: how big a deal? R. L. Miller. il pors *Architectural Record* 177:47+ Je '89
EASTMAN, REBECCA
Fluid action [excerpt from Full circle fitness] il *Health (New York, N.Y.)* 21:66-9 My '89
EASTMAN KODAK CO.
Kodak and Polaroid? Or GE? How about Disney? G. G. Marcial. il *Business Week* p84 Je 19 '89

EASTMAN KODAK CO.—cont.
Kodak may wish it never went to the drugstore [Sterling Drug acquisition] K. H. Hammonds. il *Business Week* p72+ D 4 '89
Kodak prepares to make larger, cheaper optics for aerospace use. B. D. Nordwall. il *Aviation Week & Space Technology* 131:44-6 Ag 14 '89
Playing leapfrog in disposable cameras [Kodak vs Fuji] L. Helm. il *Business Week* p34 My 1 '89

EASTMAN KODAK CO. PHOTOGRAPHIC PRODUCTS GROUPS
Those little yellow boxes are looking a little paler. K. H. Hammonds. il *Business Week* p26 Ag 7 '89

EASTWOOD, CLINT
about
Bird [film] Reviews
 Down Beat il 56:6 F '89. K. Whitehead
 The New Republic il 200:25-31 F 27 '89. S. Crouch
Not-so-tough talk from Clint Eastwood. P. Leigh. il pors *Ladies' Home Journal* 106:38+ Je '89
Suing Clint Eastwood, Sondra Locke strikes with Magnum force. J. Kaufman. il pors *People Weekly* 31:58-60 My 15 '89
When Harry left Sondra. il pors *People Weekly* 32:68-9 Ag 7 '89

EAT A BOWL OF TEA [film] See Motion picture reviews—Single works

EAT THE RICH [film] See Motion picture reviews—Single works

EATING
  See also
  Appetite
  Diet
  Gastronomy
  Gluttony
  Nutrition
Crumbs in the covers [eating in bed] L. Wells. il *The New York Times Magazine* p99-100 N 12 '89
Does chocolate give you a headache? A sip of wine make you woozy? Explaining food quirks, hang-ups and glitches. J. L. Lippert. il *Health (New York, N.Y.)* 21:84+ Je '89
Dueling palates. J. Gerard. il *Health (New York, N.Y.)* 21:85-6 Mr '89
Eating habits [21st century] L. Shapiro. il *Newsweek* 114 Special Issue:78-9 Wint '89/Spr '90
Eight hot trends of the '90s. P. Edidin. *Psychology Today* 23:44 D '89
It's all right to eat. B. Kafka. il *Gourmet* 49:92 N '89
Sin, you eaters! B. Kanner. il *New York* 22:28+ Ap 10 '89
The two taste cultures [diet dichotomy of Americans] W. Belasco. il *Psychology Today* 23:29+ D '89
  Anecdotes, facetiae, satire, etc.
Radicchio ad absurdum! il *People Weekly* 32 Special Issue:130-3 Fall '89
  International aspects
Foreign secrets for eating well, staying slim. il *Glamour* 87:276-9 My '89
  Psychological aspects
  See also
  Food cravings
  Overeaters Anonymous
Do you know why you eat? S. D. Gilbert. il *Glamour* 87:81+ Ap '89
Eating cues. S. R. Arbetter. il *Current Health 2* 16:25-7 O '89
How to prevent eating binges [views of Kay Stanfill] il *USA Today (Periodical)* 118:3-4 D '89
The irrational connection between diet and demeanor [research by Paul Rozin and Carol Nemeroff] E. Stark. il *Psychology Today* 23:14 O '89
The meaning of meals [special section] il *Psychology Today* 23:29+ D '89
Real women do eat food. W. D. Leight. *Mademoiselle* 95:120 Ag '89
Sweet temptation: why you can't say no. il *Glamour* 87:258-9 N '89
TV bingers [effects of food commercials; research by Carol Raupp] J. Fischman. il *Psychology Today* 23:24 N '89
Unsweetened stress [link between stress and desire for sweets; research by Neil Grunberg] B. Fischman. il *Psychology Today* 23:72 Mr '89
  Anecdotes, facetiae, satire, etc.
Eat this! J. Steingarten. il *Vogue* 179:354-5+ My '89
  Social aspects
The joys of eating alone [research by John and Elizabeth de Castro] J. Newman. il *American Health* 8:82 D '89

EATING AND MUSIC See Dining music
EATING AREAS See Dining alcoves, etc.
EATING DISORDERS
  See also
  Anorexia nervosa
  Bulimia
  Food cravings
Carbohydrates and depression. R. J. Wurtman and J. J. Wurtman. il map *Scientific American* 260:68-75 Ja '89
Eating disorders: emotional food fights [cover story] S. R. Arbetter. bibl il *Current Health 2* 15:4-10 Mr '89

Fat is a black women's issue [overeating] R. Powers. il *Essence* 20:75+ O '89
Overeating remedy [use of pectin] il *Prevention (Emmaus, Pa.)* 41:10 My '89
"We have a problem". J. Marks. il *Parents* 64:67+ Ap '89
When you eat too much [overeating during the holiday season] M. Lodge. il *Ladies' Home Journal* 106:42+ D '89

EATON, CYRUS, 1918-
about
Forging a really big deal. J. DeMont. il pors *Maclean's* 102:46-7 N 13 '89

EATON, MARK
about
Big man on the block. H. Hersch. il pors *Sports Illustrated* 70:32-5 My 1 '89

EATON CORPORATION
Eaton to propose $600 million modification to ALQ-161 system [B-1B] *Aviation Week & Space Technology* 130:75+ Je 26 '89
Rockwell declines AIL deal due to plan's complexity [plan to acquire AIL subsidiary of Eaton Corp. to expedite fixes to B-1B bomber's ALQ-161 system] *Aviation Week & Space Technology* 130:67 F 6 '89
Rockwell working with AIL to develop B-1B avionics fix. *Aviation Week & Space Technology* 130:101+ Ja 2 '89
USAF will use stand-alone radar warning system to shore up B-1B's EW capabilities. *Aviation Week & Space Technology* 130:101 Ja 2 '89

EAVESDROPPING, ELECTRONIC See Electronics in criminal investigation, espionage, etc.
EAVESDROPPING, LASER See Lasers in criminal investigation, espionage, etc.

EBER, DOROTHY
Eskimo memories. bibl il map *History Today* 39:45-50 N '89
about
Grandmother as lawbreaker. M. Ervin. il por *The Progressive* 53:11 Ja '89

EBERHARDT, THOM
about
Without a clue [film] Reviews
 Video il 13:63 Je '89. M. Pierson

EBERLE, NANCY
How not to turn into your mother: for your child to grow up free, you have to remember all the ways in which you didn't. il *Glamour* 87:160+ My '89

EBERLY, DONALD J.
National service and the high school. *The Education Digest* 55:54-7 S '89
What President Bush should do about national youth service [address, February 23, 1989] *Vital Speeches of the Day* 55:651-3 Ag 15 '89

EBERSOL, DICK
about
Boy wonder gets the boot at NBC. S. Smith. il por *Sports Illustrated* 70:82 My 22 '89

EBERT, ALAN
We talk to Larry King. il por *Good Housekeeping* 209:131+ O '89

EBERTS, HARRY W., 1926-
The God who cries: an opera on the Mideast. *The Christian Century* 106:1174-8 D 13 '89

EBEY'S LANDING NATIONAL HISTORICAL RESERVE (WASH.)
Kindly meeting of land and sea . . . and a new kind of park. il maps *Sunset (Central West edition)* 182:30-1+ Je '89

EBIHARA, L., AND OTHERS
Cloning and expression of a Xenopus embryonic gap junction protein. bibl f il *Science* 243:1194-5 Mr 3 '89

EBONY (PERIODICAL)
Walt Disney World chooses Ebony to boost its new MGM Theme Park. il *Jet* 76:62 Je 12 '89

EBONY FLYERS (GYMNASTICS TROUPE)
Flying high. H. E. Charles. il *American Visions* 4:8+ Ap '89

EBV See Epstein-Barr virus

ECCENTRIC (CHICAGO, ILL.: RESTAURANT) See Chicago (Ill.)—Restaurants, nightclubs, bars, etc.

ECCENTRICS AND ECCENTRICITIES
Free spirits. P. Chance. il *Psychology Today* 23:16 Ap '89

ECCLESIASTICAL ARCHITECTURE See Churches (Buildings)
ECCLESIASTICAL ART See Christian art and symbolism
ECCLESIASTICAL LAW
  See also
  Blasphemy
  Canon law

ECCLESTONE, BERNIE
about
Bernie's "dog and pony show". R. Behar. il por *Forbes* 143:64 F 20 '89

ECDYSIS See Molting

ECENBARGER, WILLIAM
Crazy over crosswords. il *Reader's Digest* 134:93-6 Mr '89
Plastic is as good as gold. il *Reader's Digest* 134:37-8+ My '89

ECENBARGER, WILLIAM—cont.
When is a ladybug a matter of state? il *Reader's Digest* 135:134-6 D '89
ECG See Electrocardiography
ECHAURREN, ROBERTO SEBASTIÁN ANTONIO MATTA See Matta, 1911-
ECHINODERMS
    See also
    Brittle stars
    Embryology—Echinoderms
    Sea urchins
    Starfish
ECHIUM See Viper's bugloss
ECHO [ballet] See Ballet reviews—Single works
ECHO [drama] See Lepage, Robert
ECHO-HAWK, WALTER
    about
Walter Echo-Hawk fights for his people's right to rest in peace—not in museums. M. Brower. il pors *People Weekly* 32:42-4 S 4 '89
ECHO SOUNDERS See Depth indicators
ECKERD COLLEGE. ACADEMY OF SENIOR PROFESSIONALS
A new class of seniors. T. C. Tobin. il *New Choices for the Best Years* 29:13-14 F '89
ECKERT, THOR, JR., AND PHILLIPS, HARVEY E.
Videocassettes. See occasional issues of Opera News beginning January 17, 1987
ECKHARDT, LINDA WEST
Soulful salads. il *Organic Gardening* 36:37-42 My '89
ECKHOLM, ERIK P.
Conquering an ancient scourge [cover story] il map *The New York Times Magazine* p20-7+ Ja 8 '89
ECKMAN, FERN MARJA
Women in the Armed Forces. il *McCall's* 116:63-4+ Ap '89
ECL (EMITTER COUPLED LOGIC) CIRCUITS See Logic circuits
ECLECTICISM IN ART
Consistency is no longer a concern, finds Richard B. Woodward. Not confined to a signature style, many artists are exploring diversity. R. B. Woodward. il *Vogue* 179:98+ Jl '89
ECLIPSES
    See also
    Occultations
Pluto at perihelion: mutual events continue [Charon] il *Sky and Telescope* 78:347 O '89
ECLIPSES, LUNAR
The August 16th eclipse of the moon. il map *Sky and Telescope* 78:182-5+ Ag '89
August's eclipsed moon. D. Di Cicco. il *Sky and Telescope* 78:548-50 N '89
Copper moon. T. D. Nicholson. il *Natural History* p62-3 Ag '89
A dawn lunar eclipse. il *Sky and Telescope* 77:184 F '89
An 'eyeball in the sky'. il *Astronomy* 17:105 D '89
Observing this month's lunar eclipse. R. Shaffer. il *Astronomy* 17:61-2 Ag '89
A picture-perfect lunar eclipse. D. J. Eicher. il *Astronomy* 17:78-9 F '89
    Photographs and photography
February's lunar eclipse. il *Sky and Telescope* 77:567 My '89
Gallery. il *Sky and Telescope* 78:551-3 N '89
The summer eclipse of the moon. D. J. Eicher. il *Astronomy* 17:80-3 D '89
ECLIPSES, SOLAR
Astrology faces the Gemini Challenge. D. Di Cicco. il *Sky and Telescope* 78:149 Ag '89
The big one is coming! il maps *Sky and Telescope* 77:134-9 F '89
Eclipse prospects for the 1990s. J. Anderson. il maps *Astronomy* 17:71-6 F '89
March 7's partial solar eclipse. D. J. Eicher. il *Astronomy* 17:98+ Je '89
The March 7th partial solar eclipse. il maps *Sky and Telescope* 77:292-3 Mr '89
Moon shadow. T. D. Nicholson. il *Natural History* p94-5 Mr '89
Solar eclipse '91: an update. L. J. Robinson. il maps *Sky and Telescope* 78:479 N '89
    History
Dem bones, dem bones [Chinese oracle bone shows evidence of shorter days; work of Kevin D. Pang] A. Fisher. *Popular Science* 235:12 S '89
A life devoted to astronomy [C. Burckhalter] K. Bracher. il por *Astronomy* 17:50-4 O '89
Oppolzer's great canon of eclipses. W. H. C. Carton. il por *Sky and Telescope* 78:475-8 N '89
Oracle bone shows a once-shorter day [work of Kevin D. Pang] I. Peterson. *Science News* 135:374 Je 17 '89
Turtle logic [engraved tortoise shell shows rotation of earth is slowing; research by Kevin Pang] T. Waters. il *Discover* 10:16 D '89
ECLIPSING BINARIES See Stars, Eclipsing binary
L'ECLUSE (NEW YORK, N.Y.: RESTAURANT) See New York (N.Y.)—Restaurants, nightclubs, bars, etc.

ECM (ELECTRONIC COUNTERMEASURES) ON MILITARY AIRPLANES See Airplanes, Military—Electronic equipment
ECO, UMBERTO
Umberto Eco: a memo to Roone [excerpt from The open work]; tr. by Anna Cancogni. *Harper's* 278:31-3 Je '89
    about
Ecco Ecomania! E. Helping. il por *Harper's Bazaar* 122:108+ N '89
A literary high-wire act. M. Blonsky. il por *The New York Times Magazine* p42-3+ D 10 '89
The master of semiotic thrillers [interview] E. E. Goode. il por *U.S. News & World Report* 107:78-9 N 20 '89
PW interviews. W. Smith. por *Publishers Weekly* 236:50-1 O 27 '89
Return of Ecomania. O. Friedrich. il por *Time* 133:71 Mr 6 '89
A talk with Eco. F. Saunders. *Newsweek* 114:96 N 13 '89
ECOFEMINISM
Ecofeminists draw the connections between sexism and environmental degradation. C. Merchant. il *Utne Reader* p76 N/D '89
It's not nice to mess with Mother Nature. L. Van Gelder. il *Ms.* 17:60-3 Ja/F '89
ÉCOLE DE CAVALERIE
For honour alone [teenage cadets defend French Cavalry School, June 1940] R. Macnab. il *History Today* 39:5-7 Ja '89
ÉCOLE DE GASTRONOMIE FRANÇAISE RITZ-ESCOFFIER
Making petits fours at Ritz-Escoffier. A. Touchet. il *Gourmet* 49:102-5+ N '89
ECOLOGICAL ART See Environment (Art)
ECOLOGICAL FIBERS (FIRM)
Toward the totally acid-free book. J. P. Frank. il *Publishers Weekly* 236:28-9 Jl 21 '89
ECOLOGICAL MODELS
Inferring process from pattern in natural communities. W. G. Cale and others. bibl f il *BioScience* 39:600-5 O '89
ECOLOGICAL MOVEMENT See Environmental movement
ECOLOGISTS
    See also
    Carson, Rachel, 1907-1964
    Attitudes
Restraints to communication for ecologists in developing countries [survey results] J. H. Cooley and F. B. Golley. bibl f il *BioScience* 39:805-9 D '89
ECOLOGY
    See also
    Adaptation (Biology)
    Agricultural ecology
    Biogeography
    Birds—Ecology
    Botany—Ecology
    Clinical ecology
    Deep ecology
    Environment
    Fire ecology
    Food chains (Ecology)
    Forest ecology
    Human ecology
    Indians of North America—Influence on nature
    Island ecology
    Lake ecology
    Landscape ecology
    Man and the Biosphere Programme
    Marine ecology
    Microbial ecology
    Paleoecology
    Pond ecology
    Population biology
    Predation (Biology)
    Productivity, Biological
    Religion and the environment
    Restoration ecology
    Sagebrush ecology
    Seashore ecology
    Snow ecology
    Soil ecology
    Stream ecology
Apocalypse now? Ecology and the peril of doomsday visions. E. Zencey. il *Utne Reader* p90-3 Ja/F '89
Bootstrapping in ecosystems [reciprocal interactions between plants and soils] D. A. Perry and others. bibl f il *BioScience* 39:230-7 Ap '89
Earth diary. T. Turner. See issues of The Mother Earth News beginning January/February 1987
Fads in ecology. W. G. Abrahamson and others. bibl f il *BioScience* 39:321-5 My '89
In defense of species [emphasis on ecology in soil research] N. L. Stanton and J. D. Lattin. *BioScience* 39:67 F '89
Input management of production systems. E. P. Odum. bibl f il *Science* 243:177-82 Ja 13 '89
Lack of data is frustrating [incomplete ecosystem knowledge hampers ability to deal with atmosphere and climate; views of Hal Mooney and Peter Vitousek] *USA Today (Periodical)* 117:6 Je '89

ECOLOGY—*cont.*
Sources and sinks complicate ecology. R. Lewin. il *Science* 243:477-8 Ja 27 '89
Taxonomic differences in the scaling of brain on body weight among mammals. M. D. Pagel and P. H. Harvey. bibl f il *Science* 244:1589-93 Je 30 '89
The United States needs an ecological survey. J. Roughgarden. *BioScience* 39:5 Ja '89
What makes bigger brains? [research by Paul Harvey and Mark Pagel] R. Lewin. *Science* 244:1544 Je 30 '89

Models
See Ecological models

Study and teaching
See Environmental education

Developing countries
Restraints to communication for ecologists in developing countries [survey results] J. H. Cooley and F. B. Golley. bibl f il *BioScience* 39:805-9 D '89

Hawaii
Losing paradise. K. Brower. il map *Wilderness* 53:20-8 Wint '89

ECOLOGY PARTY (GREAT BRITAIN)
See also
Green Party (Great Britain)

ECOMAR (FIRM)
Mussel man Bob Meek runs a seafood farm built on mutual shellfishness [harvesting mussels attached to legs of offshore drilling platforms] N. Geeslin. il pors *People Weekly* 31:135-6 My 1 '89

ECONOMETRICS
Physics for economists [computer simulations of economic scenarios conducted at Santa Fe Institute] E. Dyson. il *Forbes* 144:266 O 16 '89
Strange bedfellows [physicists and economists at the Santa Fe Institute] R. Pool. il *Science* 245:700-3 Ag 18 '89

ECONOMIC ADVISERS *See* Economists

ECONOMIC AND FINANCIAL COMMITTEE (UNITED NATIONS) *See* United Nations. Economic and Financial Committee

ECONOMIC AND SOCIAL COUNCIL (UNITED NATIONS) *See* United Nations. Economic and Social Council

ECONOMIC ASSISTANCE
See also
Relief work
World Bank

Africa
Does foreign aid really help? L. Eskin. il *Scholastic Update (Teachers' edition)* 121:11 Ja 27 '89

China
The outside world puts China on hold. D. J. Yang and B. Javetski. il *Business Week* p40-1 Jl 10 '89

Developing countries
Playing the aid game. *World Press Review* 36:51 F '89

Eastern Europe
Aiding Eastern Europe. il *World Press Review* 36:8 S '89
The freedom they need. *National Review* 41:11 D 8 '89
A golden opportunity. K. Doyle. il *Maclean's* 102:2 N 20 '89
A new economic miracle? [cover story; special section] il *Business Week* p58-66+ N 27 '89

Hungary
Breaking ranks: the West aids Poland and Hungary. P. Lewis. il *Maclean's* 102:43 O 16 '89
Helping the East without busting the budget. G. E. Schares. il *Business Week* p44-5 O 2 '89

Poland
Breaking ranks: the West aids Poland and Hungary. P. Lewis. il *Maclean's* 102:43 O 16 '89
First aid. P. Lemaître. il *World Press Review* 36:16 O '89
Helping the East without busting the budget. G. E. Schares. il *Business Week* p44-5 O 2 '89
More help is on the way [with interview with T. Mazowiecki] H. Anderson. il *Newsweek* 114:46-7 O 9 '89

Soviet Union
Vladimir Bukovsky. V. Bukovsky. il *National Review* 41:22-3 F 10 '89
The Western economic response [address, March 14, 1989] J. Shelton. *Vital Speeches of the Day* 55:429-33 My 1 '89

ECONOMIC ASSISTANCE, AMERICAN
See also
National Endowment for Democracy
A capitalist requiem for old Karl Marx [American advisers aiding foreign governments] E. Pomice. il *U.S. News & World Report* 107:44-5 D 25 '89-Ja 1 '90

Africa
FY 1990 assistance request for Sub-Saharan Africa [statement, April 14, 1989] A. Rosenberg. *Department of State Bulletin* 89:39-42 Jl '89

Caribbean region
See also
Caribbean Basin Initiative
FY 1990 assistance request for Latin America and the Caribbean [statement, March 2, 1989] M. G. Kozak. il *Department of State Bulletin* 89:59-66 Je '89

Central America
Developing solutions for Central American refugee problems [address, May 30, 1989] J. Moore. *Department of State Bulletin* 89:87-8 Ag '89

Developing countries
Disconnections and anomalies [restrictions on aid for family planning] M. Morain. *The Humanist* 49:31 S/O '89
Request for U.S. contributions to multilateral development banks [statement, April 17, 1989] N. F. Brady. *Department of State Bulletin* 89:21-30 Je '89
U.S. contributions to communications development. il *Department of State Bulletin* 89:62-5 Jl '89

East Asia
FY 1990 assistance request for East Asia and the Pacific [statement, February 27, 1989] W. Clark, Jr. il *Department of State Bulletin* 89:49-53 My '89

Eastern Europe
Lifelines of freedom. D. Gergen. il *U.S. News & World Report* 107:95 N 27 '89

Egypt
The money pit. W. P. Barrett. il *Forbes* 143:100+ My 15 '89

El Salvador
The colony of El Salvador. T. Bethell. il *The American Spectator* 22:11-13 My '89

Honduras
Classes for the contras [U.S.-backed operation in Honduras preparing contras for civilian life] il *Newsweek* 113:5 F 27 '89

Hungary
To help or not to help? S. Manning. il *Scholastic Update (Teachers' edition)* 122:18-19 O 20 '89
U.S. program in support of Hungarian reform [White House fact sheet, July 12, 1989] il *Department of State Bulletin* 89:41-3 S '89

Israel
A frosty response [U.S. refuses to provide loan guarantees to Israel for housing emigrating Soviet Jews] *Time* 134:45 O 16 '89

Latin America
See also
Katalysis Foundation
FY 1990 assistance request for Latin America and the Caribbean [statement, March 2, 1989] M. G. Kozak. il *Department of State Bulletin* 89:59-66 Je '89

Liberia
Treasure for pleasure [American money managers leave Liberia] B. Martin. il *Newsweek* 113:39 F 13 '89

Middle East
FY 1990 assistance request for the Middle East [statements, March 1-9, 1989] E. S. Walker; A. P. Burleigh. *Department of State Bulletin* 89:61-8 My '89

Nicaragua
All together now. *The Nation* 248:507-8 Ap 17 '89
Back burner, front burner. il *The Progressive* 53:8-9 My '89
Back to square one [humanitarian aid to contras] W. R. Doerner. il pors *Time* 133:28-9 Ap 3 '89
Classes for the contras [U.S.-backed operation in Honduras preparing contras for civilian life] il *Newsweek* 113:5 F 27 '89
Copping out on the contras. *National Review* 41:10-11 Je 16 '89
Crimping the accords [latest U.S. aid package for Nicaragua contradicts U.S. support for regional peace plan] *Commonweal* 116:227-8 Ap 21 '89
A done deal. *The New Republic* 200:5-6 Ap 24 '89
A done deal and an undone deal in Central America [Congress agrees to humanitarian aid for contras] C. A. Robbins and others. il por *U.S. News & World Report* 106:29 Ap 3 '89
The limits of bipartisanship. *National Review* 41:12 Ap 21 '89
Minority report [U.S. funding of Nicaraguan elections] C. Hitchens. *The Nation* 249:590 N 20 '89
Money isn't everything [U.S. funding of V. Chamorro's campaign] R. Watson. il por *Newsweek* 114:47 O 9 '89
One dilemma after another [Congress agrees to humanitarian aid for contras] D. Waller. il por *Newsweek* 113:32 Ap 3 '89
Overt meddling [U.S. plans to fund Nicaraguan elections] *The Nation* 249:407-8 O 16 '89
The pragmeologues [J. A. Baker's pragmatism] D. Seligman. il *Fortune* 119:165 My 8 '89
Secretary's interview on "MacNeil/Lehrer newshour" [J. A. Baker; transcript of program, March 24, 1989] *Department of State Bulletin* 89:23-5 My '89
Secretary's interview on "This week with David Brinkley" [deal over contra aid; interview with J. A. Baker; transcript of program, March 26, 1989] *Department of State Bulletin* 89:25-7 My '89
U.S. embassy aids pastors [conservative evangelical pastors] *The Christian Century* 106:808-9 S 13-20 '89

ECONOMIC ASSISTANCE, AMERICAN — Nicaragua — cont.

U.S. support for democracy and peace in Central America [bipartisan accord; statements and text of accord, March 24, 1989; texts of joint declarations of Central American presidents, January 16, 1988 and February 14, 1989; cover story] G. Bush. il por map *Department of State Bulletin* 89:55-9 Je '89

A vote of confidence. *Commonweal* 116:516-17 O 6 '89

Pacific region

FY 1990 assistance request for East Asia and the Pacific [statement, February 27, 1989] W. Clark, Jr. il *Department of State Bulletin* 89:49-53 My '89

Philippines

Future prospects for the Philippines [statement, March 7, 1989] D. F. Lambertson. *Department of State Bulletin* 89:43-9 My '89

MAI pledging conference, Tokyo, July 4, 1989 [address] J. A. Baker, III. *Department of State Bulletin* 89:56-8 S '89

Poland

Action plan for Poland [White House fact sheet, July 10, 1989] il *Department of State Bulletin* 89:27-9 S '89

As the world turns, where's George? J. Alter. il *Newsweek* 114:30 S 4 '89

Bush's politics of evasion. A. J. Glass. il *The New Leader* 72:3-4 S 18 '89

Economy tour. *The Nation* 249:155-6 Ag 7-14 '89

Encouraging political and economic reforms in Poland [address, April 17, 1989] G. Bush. *Department of State Bulletin* 89:3-5 Je '89

Getting to know you, part 2 [U.S. support for reform] G. D. Garcia. il *Time* 133:46 My 1 '89

The high price of reforms [L. Walesa's visit] *Maclean's* 102:30 N 27 '89

A July surprise for Gorby? [G. Bush's trip] B. Javetski and R. Fly. il por *Business Week* p60-2 Jl 17 '89

Lack of Solidarity [cover story] J. D. Sachs. *The New Republic* 201:20-1 Ag 7-14 '89

The last mile. *The New Republic* 201:7-8 O 9 '89

Liberalization in Poland has put Bush in a bind over aid. B. Javetski and others. il *Business Week* p47 Ap 24 '89

Nobody here but us Democrats. R. Sikorski. il *National Review* 41:40-2 S 29 '89

Poland [address, November 15, 1989] L. Wałęsa. *Vital Speeches of the Day* 56:132-5 D 15 '89

To help or not to help? S. Manning. il *Scholastic Update (Teachers' edition)* 122:18-19 O 20 '89

Washington shows Solidarity. W. McGurn. *National Review* 41:24-5 O 27 '89

Where are the Democrats? *The New Republic* 201:4 S 18-25 '89

Soviet Union

Comrade, can you spare a dime? E. Van den Haag. *National Review* 41:35-7 Mr 24 '89

Endgame: pressuring Gorbo. M. Ledeen. il *The American Spectator* 22:29-31 My '89

Is the Soviet economy too sick for *perestroika?* R. Brady and M. McNamee. *Business Week* p33 O 16 '89

Zaire

'Peacemaker' Mobutu is under fire. S. Askin and B. Javetski. il por *Business Week* p42 Jl 10 '89

ECONOMIC ASSISTANCE, DOMESTIC

See also

Community development
Government lending
Old age assistance
Public welfare
United States. Office of Economic Opportunity

How much poverty is reduced by state income transfers? R. D. Plotnick. bibl f il *Monthly Labor Review* 112:21-6 Jl '89

Reps hit Bush plan to fund drug war with money cut from domestic programs. il *Jet* 76:4-5 S 25 '89

Welfare for the rich. A. Etzioni. il *The New Leader* 72:13-14 My 1 '89

Canada

A zestful protector of Canadian values [views of A. W. Johnson] P. C. Newman. il *Maclean's* 102:34 Ap 10 '89

United States

See Economic assistance, Domestic

ECONOMIC ASSISTANCE, GERMAN

Developing countries

Playing the aid game. *World Press Review* 36:51 F '89

ECONOMIC ASSISTANCE, JAPANESE

The cop and the benefactor [U.S. and Japan] R. Watson. il *Newsweek* 113:36+ F 6 '89

Japan's growing global reach. C. Rapoport. il *Fortune* 119:48-50+ My 22 '89

Developing countries

Charging Japan with crimes against the earth. N. Gross. il *Business Week* p108+ O 9 '89

ECONOMIC CONDITIONS

See also

Business conditions
Business cycles
Business depression
Cost and standard of living
Inflation (Finance)

See also subhead Economic conditions under names of continents, countries, states, cities, etc.

The great global buying binge. J. Egan. il *U.S. News & World Report* 107:42-4 Jl 3 '89

International business. See issues of Business Week

The post-business society [interview with P. F. Drucker] il *New Perspectives Quarterly* 6:21-5 Fall '89

Where global growth is going [economy in charts and tables; special section] il *Fortune* 120:71-3+ Jl 31 '89

ECONOMIC CONFERENCES

See also

European Economic Community—Conferences

Canada's fictional role at summits. A. Fotheringham. il *Maclean's* 102:52 Jl 24 '89

Economic summits 1981-88. *Department of State Bulletin* 88:34-5 D '88

George Bush: what I did on my summer vacation [call for European unity] *National Review* 41:10-11 Ag 18 '89

The green summit [Paris] L. Martz. il *Newsweek* 114:12-15 Jl 24 '89

Greening the summit [Paris economic summit] T. Beardsley. *Scientific American* 261:17 S '89

The Group of Seven won't be singing harmony [Paris summit] B. Riemer. il *Business Week* p63 Jl 17 '89

A high-level fete [Paris summit] M. Clark. il *Maclean's* 102:20 Jl 17 '89

The industrial nations make a start [Paris economic summit] J. D. Hair. il *International Wildlife* 19:26 N/D '89

Mellow George and the don't worry, be happy summit [Paris economic summit] R. Fly and B. Riemer. por *Business Week* p32 Jl 31 '89

New issues for the economic summit [address, May 18-19, 1989] R. T. McNamar. *Vital Speeches of the Day* 56:60-4 N 1 '89

News conference of June 29 [upcoming Paris summit] J. A. Baker, III. *Department of State Bulletin* 89:63-5 S '89

The onset of big-debt blues [Paris summit] J. Egan. il maps *U.S. News & World Report* 107:20-2 Jl 24 '89

Summit of the Arch [Paris summit; cover story; special section] il pors *Department of State Bulletin* 89:1-21 S '89

Summit surprises [Paris] M. Clark. il *Maclean's* 102:24 Jl 24 '89

Upward from a foothills summit [environmental issues at the Paris economic summit] T. O'Riordan. *Environment* 31:inside front cover Jl/Ag '89

What you won't hear in Paris. R. Thomas. il *Newsweek* 114:38-40 Jl 17 '89

ECONOMIC CONSULTANTS

See also

Polyconomics (Firm)

ECONOMIC CONVERSION

Closing a base opens doors [Mineral Wells, Tex.] D. C. Bacon. il map *Nation's Business* 77:9+ My '89

Converts to conversion. D. Johnstone. il *The Progressive* 53:14-15 O '89

Preparing for a different world [views of F. Rohatyn] P. Mann. il *Aviation Week & Space Technology* 130:17 Mr 20 '89

Shaping a peacetime economy. D. Cortright. il *The Progressive* 53:20-2 Ja '89

China

China seeks aid from West in shift military to commercial manufacture. il *Aviation Week & Space Technology* 131:53 D 11 '89

Soviet Union

Missile check [U.S. arms-control verification team] A. Sabirov. *World Press Review* 36:40 Mr '89

ECONOMIC COOPERATION *See* Economic relations

ECONOMIC CYCLES *See* Business cycles

ECONOMIC DEVELOPMENT

See also

Developing countries
Development banks
Organisation for Economic Co-operation and Development
Rural development
United Nations. Committee for Development Planning
United Nations. Intergovernmental Committee on Science and Technology for Development
United Nations Conference on Trade and Development
World Bank
World Commission on Environment and Development

See also subhead Economic conditions under names of countries

Death of a small planet [cover story] M. Bookchin. il *The Progressive* 53:19-23 Ag '89

The environment: a North-South conflict. M. Copulos. *Current (Washington, D.C.)* 317:35-9 N '89

First word [steady-state economics] H. E. Daly. il *Omni (New York, N.Y.)* 11:8 Ja '89

Making the world work for people [sustainable development] N. Myers. il *International Wildlife* 19:12-14 N/D '89

Rich country, poor country [cover story] D. S. Landes. il *The New Republic* 201:23-7 N 20 '89

Strategies for sustainable economic development. J. MacNeill. bibl il *Scientific American* 261:154-9+ S '89

ECONOMIC DEVELOPMENT—cont.

Sustainable development: lessons from success [cover story] W. V. C. Reid. bibl f il *Environment* 31:6-9+ My '89

We can't heal the environment without remaking our society. M. Bookchin. il *Utne Reader* p80-2 N/D '89

What Charlie Peters can learn from Jerry Brown. A. Levine. *The Washington Monthly* 21:34-5 Mr '89

Environmental aspects

See Environment—Economic aspects

ECONOMIC EDUCATION *See* Economics—Study and teaching

ECONOMIC FORECASTING

See also

Business forecasting

Econometrics

Economic indicators

Stocks—Price forecasting

1989 should be a good year. M. S. Forbes, Jr. il *Forbes* 143:33 Ja 9 '89

2010: a new great powers lineup? *Society* 27:3 N/D '89

Adrift in the doldrums [weakening economy] B. Rudolph. il *Time* 134:32-4 Jl 31 '89

Advising the new administration [Black enterprise Board of Economists report] C. C. Williams. il *Black Enterprise* 19:48-53 Ja '89

The aggregate structure of the economy. N. C. Saunders. bibl f il *Monthly Labor Review* 112:13-24 N '89

American mirage: a post-industrial economy? L. C. Thurow. *Current History* 88:13-14+ Ja '89

America's bright global future [excerpt from America in the global '90s] A. H. Kiplinger and K. Kiplinger. il *Changing Times* 43:111-12+ O '89

Apocalypse revisited. *National Review* 41:16+ S 29 '89

Chugging along. C. Byron. il *New York* 22:22+ Ag 21 '89

The coming global boom [cover story; with editorial comment] C. R. Morris. il *The Atlantic* 264:6, 51-8+ O '89

Dr. Doom [views of J. Forrester] R. Bailey. il por *Forbes* 144:44+ O 16 '89

The economic outlook is perfect—or lousy. How do you tell? C. Farrell. il *Business Week* p84-5 O 2 '89

Economic predictions: personal future seems brightest [Gallup poll] B. Fischman. il *Psychology Today* 23:16 O '89

Economic prospects for the year 2000. K. Pennar. il *Business Week* p158-9+ S 25 '89

Economics for the '90s. D. Pauly. il *Newsweek* 114:58-60 N 27 '89

The economy/18-month forecast [special section] il *Fortune* 120:62-70+ Jl 17 '89

Eight forecasts for U.S. banking. B. P. Beckwith. il por *The Futurist* 23:27-33 Mr/Ap '89

The fairy-tale economy. D. Pauly. il *Newsweek* 114:44 S 11 '89

Fortune forecast. See issues of Fortune

Hoping for a 'soft landing'. R. Thomas and D. Pauly. il *Newsweek* 113:54 Je 19 '89

The international economic outlook for 1989 [address, January 19, 1989] R. P. Forrestal. *Vital Speeches of the Day* 55:367-9 Ap 1 '89

Issues shaping the U.S. economic outlook in 1989 [address, December 6, 1988] R. T. Parry. *Vital Speeches of the Day* 55:197-9 Ja 15 '89

It's gloves-off time [global competition] S. Nasar. il *U.S. News & World Report* 107:40-2 D 25 '89-Ja 1 '90

A new world order? T. D. Kane. il *USA Today (Periodical)* 117:23 My '89

Nine years ago we offered you $10,000 [Forbes readers' forecasts] M. S. Forbes. il *Forbes* 143:20 F 20 '89

No joyride in 1989 [results of Time's survey of economists] B. Rudolph. il *Time* 133:44-6 Ja 9 '89

Observations. A. Bladen. See occasional issues of Forbes

Outlook 2000. bibl f il *Monthly Labor Review* 112:2-74 N '89

The outlook for the U.S. economy: complacency is unwarranted. E. A. Treichel. *USA Today (Periodical)* 117:19-20 My '89

"Panic in Wall Street, good times coming" [views of L. Kimbell] R. Bailey. il por *Forbes* 144:68+ N 27 '89

Parting predictions from Exxon's Jack Bennett [interview] W. Glasgall. por *Business Week* p73 Ja 30 '89

The peace economy [cover story] K. Pennar and M. J. Mandel. il *Business Week* p50-5 D 11 '89

A perilous walk on the mild side. T. May, Jr. il *Fortune* 119:52-4+ Ja 16 '89

The sky is rising? [J. Rutledge and D. Allen's views in Rust to riches] P. Brimelow. il pors *Forbes* 144:156+ N 13 '89

A soft landing will send the market soaring. J. M. Laderman. il *Business Week* p92-3 My 29 '89

Some bold forecasts for 1990 [Money's roundtable of experts] J. Edgerton. il *Money* 18:116-17+ D '89

Thumbs up for the '90s [cover story; special section] il maps *Changing Times* 43:31-6+ Ja '89

Tomorrow? Who cares? T. Oberhofer. *The Futurist* 23:59 My/Je '89

Trouble in the engine. il *Time* 134:70 N 20 '89

What's ahead for business. H. Banks. See issues of Forbes beginning January 16, 1984

Where to invest [midyear investment outlook; cover story; special section] il *Business Week* p92-102+ Je 26 '89

Where to invest in 1990 [cover story; special section] il *Business Week* p73-7+ D 25 '89-Ja 1 '90

Anecdotes, facetiae, satire, etc.

A midwinter's nightmare: looking back on the Bush years. A. S. Blinder. il *Business Week* p22 Ja 23 '89

ECONOMIC GROWTH *See* Economic development

ECONOMIC HISTORY

See also

Africa—Economic history

Business depression, 1901

Business depression, 1929-1939

Great Britain—Economic history

Huizhou (China)—Economic history

Hungary—Economic history

Latin America—Economic history

London (England)—Economic history

Medieval & Early Modern Data Bank

Puerto Rico—Economic history

United States—Economic history

Doomsday again. E. Rubenstein. il *National Review* 41:16 Ag 4 '89

ECONOMIC INDICATORS

See also

Price indexes

The economic outlook is perfect—or lousy. How do you tell? C. Farrell. il *Business Week* p84-5 O 2 '89

A new, improved index says recession isn't a threat. G. Koretz. il *Business Week* p24 Je 19 '89

Seasoning leading economic indicators with salt. P. Wallich and E. Corcoran. *Scientific American* 261:104-5 S '89

A statistic that seeks to divine the future—and what it says will happen next. J. S. DeMott. il *Changing Times* 43:24 Ja '89

ECONOMIC MODELS *See* Econometrics

ECONOMIC NEWS

See also

Stock market crash, 1987—Reporters and reporting

Television broadcasting—Economic news

The case against Ted Koppel [ignorance concerning economics among reporters; cover story] M. Miller. il *The Washington Monthly* 21:34-6+ My '89

The JFJ will get you if you don't watch out [media coverage of Forbes four hundred] il *Forbes* 144 Special Issue:390-1 O 23 '89

Money update. See issues of Money beginning January 1988

News/Trends. See issues of Fortune beginning March 5, 1984

Off the record [views on the economy in the Washington post] Cato. il *National Review* 41:72 N 10 '89

$$$-saver: money-gram. See issues of Good Housekeeping

The sky is always falling [cover story] G. Easterbrook. il *The New Republic* 201:21-5 Ag 21 '89

A vintage year for greed and stupidity [1989] P. C. Newman. il *Maclean's* 102:46 D 25 '89

Wall St.: winners and sinners of 1989. C. Byron. il *New York* 22:31-2 D 25 '89-Ja 1 '90

What Charlie Peters can learn from Henry Kravis [views of Washington monthly] G. Easterbrook. *The Washington Monthly* 21:32-3 Mr '89

Who says the sky is falling? G. Easterbrook. *Reader's Digest* 135:103-5 D '89

Yellow-peril journalism: is latent racism coloring business coverage of Japan? E. Cose. il *Time* 134:79 N 27 '89

ECONOMIC PLANNING *See* Economic policy

ECONOMIC POLICY

See also

Commercial policy

Deflation (Finance)

Economic development

Group of Seven

Inflation (Finance)

Resource allocation

Sanctions (International law)

United Nations. Economic and Financial Committee

United Nations. Economic and Social Council

See also subhead Economic policy under names of countries and states

A capitalist requiem for old Karl Marx [American advisers aiding foreign governments] E. Pomice. il *U.S. News & World Report* 107:44-5 D 25 '89-Ja 1 '90

A global compact. D. Gergen. il *U.S. News & World Report* 106:87 My 8 '89

Hope for the world economy. P. Norman. *World Press Review* 36:22 D '89

Markets unbound? P. Wallich. map *Scientific American* 261:80 N '89

Preventing economic anemia. *World Press Review* 36:47 F '89

ECONOMIC RELATIONS

See also

Balance of payments

European Economic Community

General Agreement on Tariffs and Trade

Organisation for Economic Co-operation and Development

ECONOMIC RELATIONS—*cont.*
   See also subhead Economic relations under names of countries
Global economic integration [address, September 20, 1988] J. C. Whitehead. *Department of State Bulletin* 89:18-20 Ja '89
A new world order? T. D. Kane. il *USA Today (Periodical)* 117:23 My '89
Trading blocs and the evolving world economy. J. E. Garten. *Current History* 88:15-16+ Ja '89

ECONOMIC RESEARCH
   See also
   Claremont Economics Institute
   Econometrics
An economic animal [use of rats to test economic theories; work of John H. Kagel and Raymond C. Battalio] E. Corcoran. *Scientific American* 260:73 Mr '89

ECONOMIC RESOURCES CORPORATION
Black theater gets new run [Baldwin Entertainment Complex, Los Angeles] S. Herbert. *Black Enterprise* 20:18 Ag '89

ECONOMIC STATISTICS
   See also
   Economic indicators
   Employment—Statistics
   Gross national product
   Unemployment—Statistics
   United States—Economic statistics

ECONOMIC STATUS *See* Social status
ECONOMIC THEORY *See* Economics
ECONOMIC VALUE OF CHILDREN *See* Children—Economic value
ECONOMIC VALUE OF HUMANS *See* Human capital
ECONOMIC VALUE OF WOMEN *See* Women—Economic value

ECONOMICS
   See also
   American Economic Association
   Business
   Business cycles
   Capitalism
   Claremont Economics Institute
   Comic books, strips, etc.—Economics use
   Competition
   Computers—Economics use
   Confucianism and economics
   Consumption (Economics)
   Cost and standard of living
   Debt
   Deflation (Finance)
   Employment
   Experimental economics
   Finance
   Income
   Inflation (Finance)
   Judaism and economics
   Labor
   Liquidity (Economics)
   Money
   Physics and economics
   Prices
   Resource allocation
   Saving and savings
   Socialism
   Socioeconomics
   Stock exchanges
   Supply and demand
   Supply-side economics
   Surplus (Budget)
   Value (Economics)
   Wealth
At long last, laurels [Nobel Prize in Economics won by T. Haavelmo] M. J. Mandel. por *Business Week* p66 O 23 '89
The dismal science. G. P. Brockway. See issues of The New Leader
Early work rewarded [Nobel Prize in Economics to T. Haavelmo] J. Cherfas. por *Science* 246:328 O 20 '89
Economics [Nobel Prize awarded to T. Haavelmo] il por *Time* 134:74 O 23 '89
Economics made easy. R. J. Samuelson. il *Newsweek* 114:64 N 27 '89
It's dismal, all right—but is it a science? R. Kuttner. il *Business Week* p16 Ja 30 '89
Keynes the able. R. Kuttner. por *The New Republic* 201:62+ N 6 '89
Knitting new notions. J. Greenwald. il *Time* 133:46-8 Ja 30 '89
"No water" economics [theories of M. Rothbard] P. Brimelow. por *Forbes* 143:86+ Mr 6 '89
   Bibliography
Book reviews. See issues of Monthly Labor Review
Books I didn't read. R. J. Samuelson. il *Newsweek* 114:62 D 25 '89
Economics: reading your way out of chaos. P. Passell. il *The New York Times Book Review* 94:1+ O 29 '89

   History
   See Economic history
   Mathematical models
   See Econometrics
   Study and teaching
Adam Smith? Never heard of the guy [survey by the Joint Council on Economic Education] *U.S. News & World Report* 106:14 Ja 9 '89
Economic literacy in the schools [address, December 28, 1988] W. B. Walstad. *Vital Speeches of the Day* 55:327-8 Mr 15 '89
Test your economic I.Q. il *Changing Times* 43:89+ Mr '89
   Terminology
Happy soft landings. W. Safire. il *The New York Times Magazine* p6 D 24 '89
   Textbooks
Socialism by the textbook. T. Bethell. il *National Review* 41:36-8 O 13 '89

ECONOMICS AND CHRISTIANITY *See* Christianity and economics
ECONOMICS AND CONFUCIANISM *See* Confucianism and economics
ECONOMICS AND EDUCATION
   See also
   School children—Social and economic status
Education reform and economic competition [address, August 15, 1989] W. Wilkinson. *Vital Speeches of the Day* 56:40-3 N 1 '89
ECONOMICS AND JUDAISM *See* Judaism and economics
ECONOMICS AND POLITICS
Don't hand out prizes for historical ax-grinding [books critical of Reaganomics and tax reform] P. C. Roberts. il *Business Week* p18 My 1 '89
My life as a Dee-Cline. H. Stein. il *The American Spectator* 22:23-6 Ap '89
ECONOMICS IN LITERATURE
Economic intrigue [murder mysteries] E. Corcoran. *Scientific American* 261:104 D '89
ECONOMICS LITERATURE
Don't hand out prizes for historical ax-grinding [books critical of Reaganomics and tax reform] P. C. Roberts. il *Business Week* p18 My 1 '89
ECONOMISTS
   See also
   American Economic Association
   Commons, John R., 1862-1945
   Haavelmo, Trygve
   Hayek, Friedrich A. von (Friedrich August von), 1899-
   Hufbauer, Gary Clyde
   Hymans, Saul H.
   Jensen, Michael C.
   Kaufman, Henry
   Keynes, John Maynard, 1883-1946
   Kimbell, Larry
   Robinson, Joan, 1903-1983
   Rothbard, Murray Newton, 1926-
   Rutledge, John
   Smith, Adam, 1723-1790
   Smith, Vernon L.
   Solow, Robert M.
A capitalist requiem for old Karl Marx [American advisers aiding foreign governments] E. Pomice. il *U.S. News & World Report* 107:44-5 D 25 '89-Ja 1 '90
ECONOMY *See* Thrift
ECOSOC *See* United Nations. Economic and Social Council
ECOSYSTEMS *See* Ecology
ECPA *See* Evangelical Christian Publishers Association
ECRU (FIRM)
Muse of Melrose [owner E. Kim] L. Berger. il por *Harper's Bazaar* 122:72 N '89
ECSTASY (DRUG) *See* MDMA (Drug)
ECT (ELECTROCONVULSIVE THERAPY) *See* Shock therapy
ECTOPIC PREGNANCY *See* Pregnancy—Complications
ECU *See* European Currency Unit
ECUADOR
   Politics and government
Ecuador swings toward social democracy. C. M. Conaghan. bibl f *Current History* 88:137-41+ Mr '89
ECUMENICAL COUNCIL (2ND: 1962-1965) *See* Vatican Council (2nd: 1962-1965)
ECUMENICAL MOVEMENT
   See also
   Catholic Church—Relations—Church of England
   Catholic Church—Relations—Episcopal Church
   Catholic Church—Relations—Orthodox Eastern Church
   Catholic Church—Relations—Protestant churches
   Consultation on Church Union
   Interfaith Action for Economic Justice
   Week of Prayer for Christian Unity
   World Council of Churches
American ecumenism: separatism, separation and schism [adaptation of address] M. E. Marty. *The Christian Century* 106:958-61 O 25 '89
Christian unity amid diversity. *America* 160:27-8 Ja 21 '89
Four new faces of Europe. A. F. Geyer. *The Christian Century* 106:711-13 Ag 2-9 '89
THE ED SULLIVAN SHOW [television program] *See* Television program reviews—Single works

EDDIE BAUER INC.
Pig sweaters versus sleeping bags. C. Siler. il por *Forbes* 144:211-12 S 18 '89
EDDIES
See also
Vortex motion
EDDOWES, E. ANNE, AND HRANITZ, JOHN R.
Educating children of the homeless. *The Education Digest* 55:15-17 O '89
EDDY BREAKUP DEVICES *See* Large eddy breakup devices
EDDY CURRENTS (ELECTRIC)
Device simplifies skin crack detection [Physical Research's magneto-optic imager] il *Aviation Week & Space Technology* 131:137 O 9 '89
EDE, JIM
about
Ede's corner. C. Rose. il por *Art News* 88:103-4 N '89
EDELIN, KENNETH C.
about
Kenneth Edelin named chair of Planned Parenthood bd. por *Jet* 77:8 N 13 '89
EDELMAN, ASHER B.
about
Another bloody nose for Asher? J. Ferry. il por *Forbes* 144:184+ N 27 '89
Cash cows, so where's the cash? J. Clements. il por *Forbes* 144:246-7 O 30 '89
A golden boy's woe: "I'm virtually a slave". R. Behar. il por *Time* 134:76 D 11 '89
A raider tries to beat Asher Edelman at his own game. G. Lewis. il pors *Business Week* p50 S 25 '89
EDELMAN, GERALD M., 1929-
Topobiology. bibl il *Scientific American* 260:76-8+ My '89
EDELMAN, MARIAN WRIGHT
about
Profiles. C. Tomkins. il por *The New Yorker* 65:48-50+ Mr 27 '89
Who's behind the ABC? [interview] il por *Christianity Today* 33:35 Mr 17 '89
EDELSKY, CAROLE
(jt. auth) See Harman, Susan, and Edelsky, Carole
EDELSTEIN, DAVID
Dressed for excess. il *Vogue* 179:186-7+ D '89
EDELSTEIN, JEFFREY, AND WREN, LEE
Easton meets Midwest. il *House & Garden* 161:112-19 F '89
EDELSTEIN, VICTOR
about
Victor Edelstein: period clarity for the couturier's London flat. E. Lambert. il por *Architectural Digest* 46:184-7+ S '89
EDEN, ALVIN N.
Kenny, Emmo & the Newk. il pors *World Tennis* 37:31-3+ N '89
EDEN, BARBARA
about
Barbara Eden. il pors *Redbook* 172:86 Ja '89
EDEN, DIANE BURN *See* Burn, Diane
EDEN (N.C.)
Education
Blah Na Na! For the blahs [rock and roll band formed by teachers] J. M. Carter. il *Phi Delta Kappan* 71:84-5 S '89
EDER, BRUCE
Betting on Batman. il *Video* 13:80-1+ D '89
EDEY, ANNA
about
Greenhouse gold. C. Perlmutter. il pors *Organic Gardening* 36:56-60 O '89
EDGAR ALLAN POE MUSEUM (RICHMOND, VA.)
Poe forevermore. il *Southern Living* 24:40 S '89
EDGERLY, WILLIAM S.
Developing healthy state economies: innovation, vision, and strategy. *USA Today (Periodical)* 118:18-19 S '89
EDGEWATER (N.J.)
Restaurants, nightclubs, bars, etc.
Jersey's Japanese gem [Chinzan-So] G. Greene. il *New York* 22:60+ S 18 '89
Stores
A Japanese mall in—New Jersey? [Yaohan Plaza] L. J. Nathans. il *Business Week* p100 Ja 30 '89
EDGEWORTH, ANTHONY
Semper finery [photographs] il *Esquire* 111:135-9 F '89
EDGINGTON, BYRON H.
In praise of Mister Rogers. il *Parents* 64:120 Mr '89
EDH, BARBARA KEATING- *See* Keating-Edh, Barbara
EDIACARAN FOSSILS *See* Paleontology—Precambrian
EDIBLE GREENS *See* Greens, Edible
EDIBLE PLANTS *See* Plants, Edible
EDIDIN, PETER
Drowning in wealth. il *Psychology Today* 23:32-5+ Ap '89
(jt. auth) See Dormen, Lesley, and Edidin, Peter
EDIE BRICKELL AND THE NEW BOHEMIANS (MUSICAL GROUP)
Bohemian rhapsody. H. Gleason. il *Rolling Stone* p24 F 9 '89
Edie Brickell & New Bohemians. B. Stepko. il pors *Seventeen* 48:105-6 Ap '89

Edie Brickell stands by her band. B. Balfour. il por *Mademoiselle* 95:92 Ag '89
Who she is is who she is. S. Pond. il pors *Rolling Stone* p44-6+ My 4 '89
EDINBURGH INTERNATIONAL FESTIVAL
Edinburgh. N. Goodwin. *Opera News* 53:37-9 Mr 18 '89
Edinburgh. N. Goodwin. *Opera News* 54:42 D 23 '89
Nixon in China, via Edinburgh [opera performance] M. S. Eddy. il *Theatre Crafts* 23:42-4+ My '89
EDISON, HARRY, 1915-
about
Harry "Sweets" Edison. G. Kalbacher. il por *Down Beat* 56:44-6 Mr '89
EDISON, SWEETS *See* Edison, Harry, 1915-
EDISON, THOMAS A. (THOMAS ALVA), 1847-1931
about
Interview: Reese Jenkins. J. Briggs. il por *Omni (New York, N.Y.)* 11:82-4+ Ap '89
Technological turkeys. J. S. Gordon. il *American Heritage* 40:18+ My/Je '89
EDISON BROTHERS STORES, INC.
Edison Brothers Stores. R. Abelson. il *Fortune* 120:116 N 6 '89
EDISON INSTITUTE *See* Henry Ford Museum and Greenfield Village
EDITING *See* Editors and editing
EDITING ROOMS
How suite it is [self-service editing rooms] S. Sweetow. il *Video* 13:51-2+ O '89
EDITIONS PIERRE BELFOND
French trade publisher Belfond joins Masson medical group. H. R. Lottman. *Publishers Weekly* 236:11 N 17 '89
EDITORIAL CARTOONS *See* Political cartoons
EDITORS, VIDEOTAPE (MACHINES) *See* Videotape recorders and recording—Equipment
EDITORS AND EDITING
See also
Authors and editors
Hayes, Harold
Motion pictures—Editing
Proofreading
Sterling, John
Television editing
Videotapes—Editing
Dog days, cat nights and pogonips [editing the Old farmer's almanac] M. White. il por *The New York Times Magazine* p38+ Ap 2 '89
Dog days, cat nights and pogonips [editing the Old farmer's almanac] M. White. il *Reader's Digest* 135:5-6 Jl '89
Mistah Perkins—he dead: publishing today. G. Howard. *The American Scholar* 58:355-69 Summ '89
See Spot write. S. Salerno. *The Writer* 102:9-10 Ja '89
Awards
Crown's Jane von Mehren wins Tony Godwin Award. por *Publishers Weekly* 235:11 Je 23 '89
International Editor of the Year [V. Korotich, editor of Soviet weekly Ogonyok; with interview] il por *World Press Review* 36:22-6 My '89
EDMOND, RAYFUL, III
about
A family business. R. Sandza. il *Newsweek* 113:20 Je 26 '89
EDMONDS, KENNY
about
Black music's new hit doctors. S. Bloom. il pors *Rolling Stone* p32 My 18 '89
L.A. & Babyface. il pors *Ebony* 44:134+ Je '89
EDMONDSON, JOLEE
Mexico's Oaxaca coast. il *Harper's Bazaar* 122:58+ Mr '89
EDMONDSON, SIMON, 1955?-
about
Simon Edmondson at David Beitzel. J. Ash. il *Art in America* 77:198-9 N '89
EDMONTON (ALTA.)
Anecdotes, facetiae, satire, etc.
Oy, Canada [J. Queenan's views] M. Richler. il *Gentlemen's Quarterly* 59:181+ Mr '89
Education
The quiet revolution: school-based budgeting. T. McConaghy. il *Phi Delta Kappan* 70:486-7 F '89
Stores
See also
West Edmonton Mall (Alta.)
Theater
See also
Citadel Theatre (Edmonton, Alta.)
EDMUNDSON, MARK
Prophet of a new postmodernism: the greater challenge of Salman Rushdie. il *Harper's* 279:62-6+ D '89
EDO PAINTING *See* Painting, Japanese
EDPER ENTERPRISES
Reshaping an empire [Bronfmans to sell portion of Edper Enterprises to public] D. Jenish. *Maclean's* 102:43 My 29 '89
EDSALL, THOMAS BYRNE
Black vs. white in Chicago. il *The New York Review of Books* 36:21-3 Ap 13 '89

EDTA *See* Ethylenediamine tetraacetic acid
EDTV *See* Extended definition television
EDUCATION
> *See also*
>> Ability grouping in education
>> Accountability (Education)
>> Adult education
>> Aged—Education
>> Aged refugees—Education
>> Alcohol education
>> Amish—Education
>> Arts teachers—Education
>> Asian Americans—Education
>> Athletes—Education
>> Bilingual education
>> Black athletes—Education
>> Black women—Education
>> Blacks—Education
>> Business and education
>> Cable television in education
>> Case method
>> Catholic schools
>> Children—Education
>> Children, Gifted—Education
>> Children as actors and actresses—Education
>> Children of missionaries—Education
>> Chinese Americans—Education
>> Citizenship education
>> Coeducation
>> College education
>> Colleges and universities
>> Communication in education
>> Communism and education
>> Community and junior colleges
>> Comparative education
>> Compensatory education
>> Computers—Educational use
>> Correlation (Education)
>> Curriculum
>> Deaf—Education
>> Direct broadcast satellite services—Educational programs
>> Dramatization in education
>> Drug education
>> Economics and education
>> Elementary education
>> Environmental education
>> Experimental education
>> Family education
>> Foreign students
>> Foreign study
>> Grade repetition (Education)
>> Grading and marking (Education)
>> Grandparent education
>> Group work in education
>> Handicapped—Education
>> Health education
>> Heritage education
>> Hispanic Americans—Education
>> Home education
>> Homeless children—Education
>> Humor in education
>> Hypermedia—Educational use
>> Hypnotism—Educational use
>> Indians of North America—Education
>> Information systems—Educational use
>> Intercultural education
>> International education
>> Japanese—United States—Education
>> Knowledge
>> Labor—Education
>> Language and education
>> Learning, Psychology of
>> Liberal education
>> Literacy education
>> Mentally handicapped children—Education
>> Mexican Americans—Education
>> Middle schools
>> Military education
>> Minorities—Education
>> Moral education
>> Motion pictures in education
>> Motivation (Education)
>> Multimedia—Educational use
>> National parks and reserves—Educational use
>> Nature study
>> Nutrition education
>> Oceanographic education
>> Palestinian Arabs—Education
>> Parent education
>> Photocopying—Educational use
>> Physical education and training
>> Politics and education
>> Preschool education
>> Private schools
>> Problem children—Education
>> Professional education
>> Psychology, Educational
>> Public schools
>> Refugee children—Education
>> Refugees—Education
>> Religious education
>> Rural education
>> Safety education
>> Secondary education
>> Self improvement
>> Sex discrimination in education
>> Single mothers—Education
>> Social education
>> Socialism and education
>> Socially handicapped children—Education
>> Special education
>> Steel workers—Education
>> Study
>> Summer schools
>> Teachers
>> Teaching
>> Television in education
>> Textbooks
>> Tibetans—India—Education
>> Urban education
>> Veterans—Education
>> Videotapes—Educational use
>> Vocational-technical education
>> Women—Education
>> Word processors and processing—Educational use

Can educational research keep pace with education reform? [need for teachers to participate in research] J. M. Atkin. bibl f il *Phi Delta Kappan* 71:200-5 N '89
Conservatives can turn the tide [education reform] P. Weyrich. il *Conservative Digest* 15:77-80 My/Je '89
A conversation with Mary Hatwood Futrell. M. E. Howard. por *Black Enterprise* 20:30 O '89
Demilitarizing public education: school reform in the era of George Bush. T. R. McDaniel. bibl f il *Phi Delta Kappan* 71:15-18 S '89
Education. See occasional issues of Better Homes and Gardens
Education isn't a problem. D. R. Carlin, Jr. il *Commonweal* 116:584-5 N 3 '89
Education reform in the 1980s: lessons from the states [cover story] T. Timar and D. L. Kirp. bibl f il *Phi Delta Kappan* 70:504-11 Mr '89
Fourth-wave education reform: are we ready? M. H. Futrell. *The Education Digest* 55:3-6 N '89
How to help America's schools [Fortune's second education summit] N. J. Perry. il *Fortune* 120:137-40+ D 4 '89
The illiteracy epidemic [need for reform] M. B. Zuckerman. il *U.S. News & World Report* 106:72 Je 12 '89
In the wake of the waves [reform] C. Pipho. il *Phi Delta Kappan* 71:102-3 O '89
Lessons from the states about education reform. T. Timar and D. L. Kirp. *The Education Digest* 55:11-14 S '89
Mission not accomplished: education reform in retrospect [cover story] M. H. Futrell. bibl f il *Phi Delta Kappan* 71:8-14 S '89
Of robins' eggs, teachers, and education reform. R. C. Nelson. bibl f il *Phi Delta Kappan* 70:632-8 Ap '89
Reeducating America [interview with R. Ornstein] K. Emmons. il *Omni (New York, N.Y.)* 11:16+ My '89
The role of business in educational reform [address, December 8, 1988] V. R. Ruggiero. *Vital Speeches of the Day* 55:286-8 F 15 '89
Saving the schools: how business can help. N. J. Perry. *Current (Washington, D.C.)* 310:20-6 F '89
School reform: a proposal for change. A. Shanker. il *USA Today (Periodical)* 117:71-3 My '89
The simplest and hardest of education reforms. N. King. *Design for Arts in Education* 91:2-9 N/D '89
The superintendent's role in reform. N. Paulu. *The Education Digest* 55:31-3 S '89
When outsiders try to change schools from the inside. J. P. McDonald. bibl f il *Phi Delta Kappan* 71:206-12 N '89

Aims and objectives
> *See also*
>> College education—Aims and objectives
>> Educational sociology

A box full of tools but no blueprint [national goals for schools] A. C. Lewis. *Phi Delta Kappan* 71:180-1 N '89
Can the states agree to national performance goals? C. Pipho. *Phi Delta Kappan* 71:182-3 N '89
Fly again, mourning cloak. Y. B. Estes. il *Phi Delta Kappan* 70:440-5 F '89
How can a student 'fail' to be educated? P. Rogers. *Phi Delta Kappan* 70:478-9 F '89
Knowledge and education reform in a democratic republic. M. Hartoonian. *The Education Digest* 55:11-14 D '89
The old school. L. H. Lapham. *Harper's* 278:10+ Ap '89
The true purpose of education [cultivation of wisdom and virtue] H. B. Gow. il *Phi Delta Kappan* 70:545-6 Mr '89

Awards
> *See also*
>> Teachers—Awards

Bibliography
Books. L. D. Brown. See issues of Phi Delta Kappan beginning September 1985

EDUCATION—Bibliography—*cont.*
New materials. See issues of The Education Digest beginning September 1986

Conferences
Calendar. See issues of The Education Digest beginning September 1986

Evaluation
See also
Accountability (Education)
Curriculum auditing
National Assessment of Educational Progress

The 21st annual Gallup poll of the public's attitudes toward the public schools. S. M. Elam and A. Gallup. il *Phi Delta Kappan* 71:41-54 S '89
American education is stagnant [address, May 16, 1989] J. B. Wyatt. *Vital Speeches of the Day* 56:12-14 O 15 '89
Are schools flunking out? [LHJ Roper poll of mothers] il *Ladies' Home Journal* 106:72+ S '89
Century 21 education [address, October 11, 1988] J. F. Alibrandi. *Vital Speeches of the Day* 55:247-50 F 1 '89
Education reforms: mistakes, misconceptions, miscues. D. C. Orlich. bibl f il *Phi Delta Kappan* 70:512-17 Mr '89
The horse is dead [brain-compatible approach to restructuring schools] L. A. Hart. bibl f il *Phi Delta Kappan* 71:237-42 N '89
Is education as bad as ever? B. J. Wattenberg. il *U.S. News & World Report* 106:50-1 Mr 20 '89
The ivory tower triggerman [views of J. Silber] S. Allis. il por *Time* 134:69 Ag 28 '89
Multiple choice. L. H. Lapham. *Harper's* 278:12-15 Mr '89
A nation still at risk [cover story] C. E. Finn. *Commentary* 87:17-23 My '89
The politics of school restructuring [cover story] T. Timar. bibl f il *Phi Delta Kappan* 71:264-75 D '89
Readers comment on education [results of survey] A. H. Jones and M. D. Kolar. *The Education Digest* 55:40-1 S '89
A report card on schools after 20 years. J. Kozol. *The Education Digest* 54:7-9 Ja '89
Sizing up your local school. N. Henderson. il *Changing Times* 43:101-2+ N '89
Targeting education for the 1990s [special section] *Society* 26:32-63 My/Je '89
What they learn in school. J. Stern. *Harper's* 279:22 Ag '89
What to do about the schools [discussion of May 1989 article, A nation still at risk] C. E. Finn. *Commentary* 88:4-6+ O '89

Federal aid
See also
Catholic schools—Federal aid
Colleges and universities—Federal aid
Environmental education—Federal aid
Literacy education—Federal aid
Science—Study and teaching—Federal aid
Student aid
Vocational-technical education—Federal aid
Voucher plan in education

Budget aids education, hampers libraries. H. Fields. *Publishers Weekly* 235:330 Ja 27 '89
Bush budget proposes new educational aid. H. Fields. *Publishers Weekly* 235:123-4 F 24 '89
Education doldrums [Educational Excellence Act of 1989] *National Review* 41:11 My 19 '89
Knitting a new sweater [proposals of Southern Education Foundation's Continuing Conference] A. C. Lewis. il *Phi Delta Kappan* 70:348-9 Ja '89
Title IX is back in action! [effect on women athletes] K. M. Reith. il *Women's Sports & Fitness* 11:74 Mr '89

Finance
See also
Church schools—Finance
Colleges and universities—Finance
Education—State aid
Voucher plan in education

The big shift in school finance [Texas Supreme Court rules tax-based financing method unconstitutional] S. Tifft. il *Time* 134:48 O 16 '89
How courts are trying to make schools equal [modifying tax-based school financing systems] M. Cooper. *U.S. News & World Report* 107:36 O 16 '89
The quiet revolution: school-based budgeting [Edmonton, Alta.] T. McConaghy. il *Phi Delta Kappan* 70:486-7 F '89
Rich schools, poor schools [issue of local control] A. E. Wise and T. Gendler. *The Education Digest* 55:3-7 D '89

History
Going to school with Mr. Jefferson. il *U.S. News & World Report* 107:13 O 9 '89
In a schoolroom. R. S. Bourne. *The New Republic* 201 [Reprint v1]:23-4 N 6 '89 [N 7 '14]

International aspects
See also
Student exchange programs
Needed: an international perspective [school reform] P. G. Altbach. il *Phi Delta Kappan* 71:243-5 N '89

Laws and regulations
See Educational laws and regulations

Periodicals
See also
Change (Periodical)
Education digest

Philosophy
See also
College education—Philosophy

Civilizing the dialogue in the forgetting society. I. J. Winn. *Phi Delta Kappan* 70:630-1 Ap '89
Developmentally appropriate practice: philosophical and practical implications [contrasted with psychometric educational psychology] D. Elkind. bibl f il *Phi Delta Kappan* 71:113-17 O '89
Educational misconceptions of a democratic public [views of A. Bloom and E. D. Hirsch] W. Feinberg. *The Education Digest* 55:7-10 O '89
Some thoughts on treasure-keeping. T. C. O'Brien. bibl f il *Phi Delta Kappan* 70:360-4 Ja '89

Research
See Educational research

Social aspects
See Educational sociology

Standards
See also
Colleges and universities—Standards
Honor system (Education)

Quality is the key to the disciplines. W. Glasser. *The Education Digest* 55:24-7 S '89

State aid
See also
Church schools—State aid
Colleges and universities—State aid
Vocational-technical education—State aid

Education and the state budget squeeze. C. Pipho. il *Phi Delta Kappan* 70:582-3 Ap '89
Full agenda, empty pockets. C. Pipho. il *Phi Delta Kappan* 70:750-1 Je '89

Study and teaching
See also
Teachers—Education
Teachers colleges

Taxation for
See Education—Finance

Terminology
Communicating with teachers—honestly. L. A. Bader. bibl f il *Phi Delta Kappan* 70:626-9 Ap '89

Alabama
See also
Demopolis (Ala.)—Education
Sumiton (Ala.)—Education

Alaska
See also
Alaska Sister Schools Network

Alberta
See also
Edmonton (Alta.)—Education

Arkansas
See also
Little Rock (Ark.)—Education

Australia
Long-range learning. M. Skilbeck. il *The Courier (Unesco)* 41:32-4 D '88

Bois Blanc Island (Mich.)
Second grader Brandon Schlund is a standout student in his school—he's also the only one. M. Neill. il pors *People Weekly* 32:111-12 N 6 '89

British Columbia
See also
Educational laws and regulations—British Columbia

California
See also
Berkeley (Calif.)—Education
Colleges and universities—California
Danville (Calif.)—Education
Hollywood (Calif.)—Education
Laytonville (Calif.)—Education
Lemon Grove (Calif.)—Education
Los Angeles (Calif.)—Education
Oakland (Calif.)—Education
Oroville (Calif.)—Education
San Diego (Calif.)—Education
San Jose (Calif.)—Education
Stockton (Calif.)—Education
Union City (Calif.)—Education

Teaching history the way it happened. J. Leo. il *U.S. News & World Report* 107:73 N 27 '89

Canada
See also
Colleges and universities—Canada

China
See also
Colleges and universities—China

Learning, Chinese-style [children] H. Gardner. il *Psychology Today* 23:54-6 D '89
'People's education' in the People's Republic of China. Z. Su. bibl f il *Phi Delta Kappan* 70:614-18 Ap '89

EDUCATION—China—*cont.*

History

An education emperor: teachings from the life of K'ang-hsi. B. DeMott. *Change* 21:62 Mr/Ap '89

Connecticut

See also
West Haven (Conn.)—Education

Florida

See also
Dade County (Fla.)—Education
Educational laws and regulations—Florida
Pinellas County (Fla.)—Education
Tampa (Fla.)—Education

France

See also
Colleges and universities—France
Education in France: renewal in the secondary schools; tr. by John L. Farrand. D. Salin. *America* 160:587-90 Je 17-24 '89

Georgia

See also
Ocilla (Ga.)—Education

Germany (West)

See also
Colleges and universities—Germany (West)
Restructuring leadership. A. Shanker. *The Education Digest* 54:3-5 F '89

Great Britain

See also
Educational laws and regulations—Great Britain
History tomorrow [teaching of history in new national curriculum; special section; with editorial comment] il *History Today* 39:6-15 Je '89

History

See also
Workers' Educational Association (Great Britain)

Hawaii

Hawaii's school system is one of a kind [centralized system] J. Zulich. bibl f il *Phi Delta Kappan* 70:546-9 Mr '89

Illinois

See also
Chicago (Ill.)—Education
Clinton (Ill.)—Education
East Saint Louis (Ill.)—Education
Lombard (Ill.)—Education
Pekin (Ill.)—Education
Winnetka (Ill.)—Education

India

See also
Education and state—India

Jammu and Kashmir (India)

Journey to knowledge [Tibetan children travel 100 miles on frozen Zanskar River to go to school] O. Föllmi. il *Life* 12:108-16 D '89

Japan

See also
Tokyo (Japan)—Education
How Japan hits the books. P. Sudo. il *Scholastic Update (Teachers' edition)* 122:11-12 D 8 '89
In Japan, first grade isn't a boot camp. B. Kantrowitz. il *Newsweek* 113:54 Ap 17 '89
Probing the "myths" about Japanese education. P. Lukens. *The Education Digest* 54:13-16 My '89

Kentucky

See also
Educational laws and regulations—Kentucky

Louisiana

See also
Colleges and universities—Louisiana
New Orleans (La.)—Education

Maine

The arts in education program: a state's perspective. E. M. Bither and S. J. Kestenbaum. *Design for Arts in Education* 90:35-7 Ja/F '89

Maryland

See also
Baltimore (Md.)—Education
Gaithersburg (Md.)—Education

Massachusetts

See also
Boston (Mass.)—Education
Cambridge (Mass.)—Education
Chelsea (Mass.)—Education
Holyoke (Mass.)—Education
Lawrence (Mass.)—Education
Lowell (Mass.)—Education
Equality and excellence education in arts. E. Lazarus. bibl f *Design for Arts in Education* 90:30-2 Jl/Ag '89

Michigan

See also
Ann Arbor (Mich.)—Education
Detroit (Mich.)—Education
Utica (Mich.)—Education

Minnesota

See also
Educational laws and regulations—Minnesota

Missouri

See also
Hazelwood (Mo.)—Education
Kansas City (Mo.)—Education
Saint Louis (Mo.)—Education
Missouri Youth 2000 Conference [address, November 30, 1988] M. Barnett. *Vital Speeches of the Day* 55:349-52 Mr 15 '89
No easy answers [business ethics] R. Thompson. il *Nation's Business* 77:38-9 Jl '89
Small children learn to identify fossils [program developed by Terry Berkland and James M. Cocke] il *Earth Science* 41:8 Wint '88

New Jersey

See also
Academy for the Advancement of Teaching and Management
Educational laws and regulations—New Jersey
Jersey City (N.J.)—Education
Paterson (N.J.)—Education
West New York (N.J.)—Education
New Jersey's battle for better schools [efforts of T. Kean] T. Armbrister. *Reader's Digest* 135:159-64 N '89
New Jersey's plan for improving education. F. R. Hobbie. *The Education Digest* 54:10-12 Ja '89

New York (State)

See also
Brooklyn (New York, N.Y.)—Education
Dobbs Ferry (N.Y.)—Education
Educational laws and regulations—New York (State)
New York (N.Y.)—Education
Penfield (N.Y.)—Education
Rochester (N.Y.)—Education
Teaching history the way it happened. J. Leo. il *U.S. News & World Report* 107:73 N 27 '89

North Carolina

See also
Durham (N.C.)—Education
Eden (N.C.)—Education

Nova Scotia

See also
Halifax County (N.S.)—Education
A smouldering race issue [blacks seek school reform] G. Allen. il *Maclean's* 102:14 F 27 '89

Ohio

See also
Gahanna (Ohio)—Education
Shaker Heights (Ohio)—Education

Ontario

See also
Educational laws and regulations—Ontario
Teacher education in Ontario: a case for tuning the whole instrument [report by Michael Fullan and F. M. Connelly] T. McConaghy. bibl f il *Phi Delta Kappan* 70:830-1 Je '89

Oregon

See also
Eugene (Or.)—Education

Pacific region

See also
Alaska Sister Schools Network

Pennsylvania

See also
Montgomery County (Pa.)—Education
Philadelphia (Pa.)—Education
Pittsburgh (Pa.)—Education
High school students study Hurricane Gilbert [use of GOES satellite] R. J. Summers. il *Weatherwise* 42:95-6 Ap '89

Québec (Province)

See also
Montreal (Québec)—Education

South Carolina

See also
Greenville County (S.C.)—Education
An administrator training program for minorities [internship program] A. B. Pigford. *Phi Delta Kappan* 70:650-1 Ap '89

Southern States

How to tackle school reform [Arkansas, South Carolina, and West Virginia] S. Tifft. il *Time* 134:46-7 Ag 14 '89

Soviet Union

See also
Computers—Study and teaching—Soviet Union
Science—Study and teaching—Soviet Union
Education in the Soviet Union: has *perestroika* met its match? G. H. Read. bibl f il *Phi Delta Kappan* 70:606-13 Ap '89
Reform in Soviet and American education: parallels and contrasts. S. T. Kerr. bibl f il *Phi Delta Kappan* 71:19-28 S '89
Restructuring the 3 R's. N. Traver. il *Time* 133:96-7 Ap 10 '89

Tennessee

See also
Campbell County (Tenn.)—Education
Educational laws and regulations—Tennessee
Sweetwater (Tenn.)—Education

EDUCATION—Tennessee—cont.

A state strategy for teacher training: the Tennessee Arts Academy. J. W. Giles and C. R. Curtis. *Design for Arts in Education* 90:39-42 Jl/Ag '89

Texas

See also

Amarillo (Tex.)—Education
Beaumont (Tex.)—Education
Educational laws and regulations—Texas
Houston (Tex.)—Education

United States

See Education

Utah

See also

Salt Lake City (Utah)—Education

Virginia

See also

McLean (Va.)—Education
Prince Edward County (Va.)—Education
Roanoke (Va.)—Education

Washington (D.C.)

See Washington (D.C.)—Education

Washington (State)

See also

Renton (Wash.)—Education
Richland (Wash.)—Education
Seattle (Wash.)—Education
Spokane (Wash.)—Education

Western Europe

See also

Colleges and universities—Western Europe

Power to parents. M. G. Bruce. il *Phi Delta Kappan* 70:413-14 Ja '89

Practicing 'international education'. M. G. Bruce. *Phi Delta Kappan* 70:738-9 My '89

Primary education [Council of Europe report] M. G. Bruce. il *Phi Delta Kappan* 71:82-3 S '89

Wisconsin

See also

Milwaukee (Wis.)—Education
Washburn (Wis.)—Education

EDUCATION, BOARDS OF *See* School boards

EDUCATION, VALUE OF

See also

College education, Value of

EDUCATION AND DEMOCRACY

Educational misconceptions of a democratic public [views of A. Bloom and E. D. Hirsch] W. Feinberg. *The Education Digest* 55:7-10 O '89

Institutional democracy in the public schools. M. A. Raywid. *The Education Digest* 55:8-10 D '89

Knowledge and education reform in a democratic republic. M. Hartoonian. *The Education Digest* 55:11-14 D '89

EDUCATION AND ECONOMIC PROBLEMS *See* School and social and economic problems

EDUCATION AND MANPOWER *See* Labor—Education

EDUCATION AND SOCIAL PROBLEMS *See* School and social and economic problems

EDUCATION AND SOCIETY *See* Educational sociology

EDUCATION AND SOCIOLOGY *See* Educational sociology

EDUCATION AND STATE

See also

College education and state
Colleges and universities—Federal aid
Colleges and universities—Research—Federal aid
Education—Federal aid
Education—State aid
Educational laws and regulations
United States. Dept. of Education
Voucher plan in education

Are school boards on the way out? A. Shanker. *The Education Digest* 55:34-6 S '89

Calling for an overhaul [George Bush meets with governors] D. Goodgame. il *Time* 134:60+ O 9 '89

A case of academic bankruptcy [state-appointed superintendent E. J. Scambio to run Jersey City, N.J. school system] *Newsweek* 114:74 O 16 '89

Children, teachers, national goals: ideas for an education president [roundtable discussion; cover story] T. J. Machese. *Change* 20:10-19 N/D '88

The debate at home [education summit] D. Schorr. *The New Leader* 72:4 O 2-16 '89

Demilitarizing public education: school reform in the era of George Bush. T. R. McDaniel. bibl f il *Phi Delta Kappan* 71:15-18 S '89

Education reform and economic competition [address, August 15, 1989] W. Wilkinson. *Vital Speeches of the Day* 56:40-3 N 1 '89

Education reform in the 1980s: lessons from the states [cover story] T. Timar and D. L. Kirp. bibl f il *Phi Delta Kappan* 70:504-11 Mr '89

Education reform in the age of George Bush. H. A. Giroux. *The Education Digest* 55:3-6 O '89

Excellence in education: President Bush's strategy. G. Bush. *The Education Digest* 54:3-6 Ja '89

Federal education policy: playing catch-up. F. Newman. *Change* 20:4-5 N/D '88

Forum: the new administration and arts education. *Design for Arts in Education* 90:16-23 Ja/F '89

A high-performance system: five federal education initiatives. M. S. Tucker and J. Wills. il *Change* 20:8+ N/D '88

How to tackle school reform [Arkansas, South Carolina, and West Virginia] S. Tifft. il *Time* 134:46-7 Ag 14 '89

Lessons from the states about education reform. T. Timar and D. L. Kirp. *The Education Digest* 55:11-14 S '89

Life is imitation [education summit] R. E. Tyrrell. il *The American Spectator* 22:10 D '89

National conditions and policy imperatives. S. Hope. bibl f *Design for Arts in Education* 91:15-35 S/O '89

Pap talk [meeting of George Bush and governors] *National Review* 41:19 O 27 '89

The politics of school restructuring [cover story] T. Timar. bibl f il *Phi Delta Kappan* 71:264-75 D '89

Reagan's final report card. D. L. Clark and T. A. Astuto. *Society* 26:32-9 My/Je '89

Reformation and responsibilities: a memo to members of the arts education establishment. B. Wilson. bibl f *Design for Arts in Education* 90:27-35 My/Je '89

Rethinking education reform in the age of George Bush. H. A. Giroux. *Phi Delta Kappan* 70:728-30 My '89

School reform [address, June 5, 1989] E. L. Boyer. *Vital Speeches of the Day* 55:741-4 O 1 '89

Seizing control of school disasters [state takeovers of public schools] T. Toch. il *U.S. News & World Report* 107:69 O 23 '89

Silber bullet [J. Silber's plans] D. P. Hamilton. *The New Republic* 201:18-19 D 4 '89

Sorry summit [education summit] M. Kondracke. *The New Republic* 201:12-14 O 23 '89

State takeover [Jersey City, N.J.] *Time* 134:48 O 16 '89

Stateline. C. Pipho. See issues of *Phi Delta Kappan*

A summit for schools [meeting of George Bush and state governors] J. Alter. il *Newsweek* 114:56+ O 2 '89

Toward civilization: next responsibilities [report issued by National Endowment for the Arts] F. Hodsoll. *Design for Arts in Education* 90:10-15 Ja/F '89

Very hostile takeovers: states may step in when local schools fail. C. Leslie. il *Newsweek* 113:63+ Mr 13 '89

Washington commentary. A. C. Lewis. See issues of *Phi Delta Kappan*

Washington news. A. C. Lewis. See issues of *The Education Digest* beginning September 1986

Canada

See also

Council of Ministers of Education (Canada)

Great Britain

Lessons from the British schoolmarm [reforms] O. Scott. il por *Conservative Digest* 15:47-9 My/Je '89

India

A new policy for education. A. Bordia. il *The Courier (Unesco)* 42:16-21 F '89

EDUCATION AND TECHNOLOGY *See* Educational technology

EDUCATION CRITICS AND CRITICISM

Let's again talk sense about our schools. J. Georgeoff. bibl f il *Phi Delta Kappan* 71:72-3 S '89

Pavlov lives: who's to blame for educational failures? G. Keller. il *Change* 21:54 My/Je '89

EDUCATION DEPT. (U.S.) *See* United States. Dept. of Education

EDUCATION DIGEST

Readers comment on education [results of survey] A. H. Jones and M. D. Kolar. *The Education Digest* 55:40-1 S '89

EDUCATION IN ART

The polite lady: portraits of American schoolgirls and their accomplishments, 1725-1830. D. T. Deutsch. bibl f il *Antiques* 135:742-53 Mr '89

EDUCATION IN LITERATURE

Tales from "the author of" an education best-seller [excerpt from preface to the 25th anniversary edition of Up the down staircase] B. Kaufman. *The Education Digest* 54:41-4 Ap '89

EDUCATIONAL ACHIEVEMENTS *See* Student achievements

EDUCATIONAL ADMINISTRATION *See* School management and organization

EDUCATIONAL ASSISTANCE LIMITED

The business of making dreams come true. C. Lutes. il por *Christianity Today* 33:12-13 Ag 18 '89

EDUCATIONAL ASSOCIATIONS

See also

American Association for Higher Education
American Association of University Professors
National Education Association of the United States
Parents' and teachers' associations

EDUCATIONAL ATTAINMENT *See* Student achievements

EDUCATIONAL CENSORSHIP *See* Censorship

EDUCATIONAL CONFERENCES *See* Education—Conferences

EDUCATIONAL CONSULTANTS

When outsiders try to change schools from the inside. J. P. McDonald. bibl f il *Phi Delta Kappan* 71:206-12 N '89

EDUCATIONAL COOPERATION

Attracting bright adolescents to teaching careers [program developed by Lamar University and Beaumont School District, Tex.] M. J. Cooper and others. il *Phi Delta Kappan* 70:566-7 Mr '89

Children's booksellers and teachers: partners in literacy. S. Wilensky-Lanford. il *Publishers Weekly* 235:101-3 Ja 20 '89

The Gahanna-Jefferson City internship program [Ohio] B. W. Denner and S. Kirchhoff. *Phi Delta Kappan* 71:166-7 O '89

How to cut the cost of college [courses taken in high school] R. E. Deck, Jr. il *USA Today (Periodical)* 118:58-9 Jl '89

Mentorships and the perceived educational payoffs [Houston program pairing secondary teachers with mathematicians and scientists] L. M. Miller and others. il *Phi Delta Kappan* 70:465-7 F '89

Science, technology, and public knowledge [having high school teachers spend time in university and industrial research laboratories] G. Pallrand. bibl f il *Phi Delta Kappan* 70:460-4 F '89

University scientists as precollege science curriculum developers [discussion of September 1988 article, The role of universities in developing precollege science curricula] J. D. McInerney. bibl f *BioScience* 39:102-3 F '89

EDUCATIONAL COUNSELING

See also
   Peer counseling
Child abuse hysteria: a warning for educators. L. D. Spiegel. *The Education Digest* 54:55-8 Ja '89

Giving students reasons for wanting to live [advising programs in secondary schools] T. K. Edwards. *The Education Digest* 54:22-4 Mr '89

The mentor as an expert coach: a model for rural school districts [program in Oroville, Calif.] B. Benoit and J. A. Braun. il *Phi Delta Kappan* 70:488-9 F '89

The mentor chase [many Science Talent Search winners worked with professional scientists] il *U.S. News & World Report* 106:14 Mr 20 '89

Mentorships and the perceived educational payoffs [Houston program pairing secondary teachers with mathematicians and scientists] L. M. Miller and others. il *Phi Delta Kappan* 70:465-7 F '89

Western Europe

Guiding our paths. M. G. Bruce. *Phi Delta Kappan* 71:252-4 N '89

EDUCATIONAL COUNSELORS

The counselor in effective schools. M. D. Thomas. *The Education Digest* 55:18-20 D '89

EDUCATIONAL CRITICISM *See* Education critics and criticism

EDUCATIONAL DISCRIMINATION *See* Discrimination in education

EDUCATIONAL EVALUATION *See* Education—Evaluation

EDUCATIONAL EXCHANGES

See also
   Alaska Sister Schools Network
   Foreign students
   Student exchange programs
Sino-American academic exchanges. P. J. Glassman. il *Change* 21:36-43 Mr/Ap '89

EDUCATIONAL EXTENSION *See* University extension
EDUCATIONAL FILMS *See* Motion pictures in education

EDUCATIONAL FORECASTING

The future of teaching. L. Darling-Hammond. *The Education Digest* 54:7-10 Mr '89

How schools must change [preparing knowledge workers for the post-business society] P. F. Drucker. il *Psychology Today* 23:18-20 My '89

Missouri Youth 2000 Conference [address, November 30, 1988] M. Barnett. *Vital Speeches of the Day* 55:349-52 Mr 15 '89

The next century: the impact of social and economic trends on the arts in education. J. K. Urice. bibl f *Design for Arts in Education* 90:36-43 My/Je '89

Preparing education for the year 2000. M. J. Cetron. *The Education Digest* 54:3-6 Ap '89

Preparing the 21st-century superintendent [adaptation of address, February 1988] J. Hoyle. bibl f il *Phi Delta Kappan* 70:376-9 Ja '89

Targeting education for the 1990s [special section] *Society* 26:32-63 My/Je '89

EDUCATIONAL GAMES

See also
   Video games—Educational use
Toys and games to learn by. H. Boehm. il *Psychology Today* 23:62-4 S '89

EDUCATIONAL INNOVATIONS

See also
   Educational technology
Opening a new book on school reform [innovative projects] il *U.S. News & World Report* 107:13 S 18 '89

PET and the pendulum: faddism in education and how to stop it [cover story] R. E. Slavin. bibl f il *Phi Delta Kappan* 70:752-8 Je '89

EDUCATIONAL LAWS AND REGULATIONS

See also
   Education—Federal aid
   United States. Dept. of Education
The impact of policies for handicapped children on future early education policy. J. J. Gallagher. bibl f il *Phi Delta Kappan* 71:121-4 O '89

The Minor Suit Award returns [petty cases of education litigation] P. A. Zirkel. bibl f il *Phi Delta Kappan* 70:484-5 F '89

Stateline. C. Pipho. See issues of Phi Delta Kappan

Washington commentary. A. C. Lewis. See issues of Phi Delta Kappan

Washington news. A. C. Lewis. See issues of The Education Digest beginning September 1986

British Columbia

An ungraded approach. H. Quinn. *Maclean's* 102:42 F 20 '89

California

California backs evolution education. M. Barinaga. il *Science* 246:881 N 17 '89

California urges teaching of evolution in science textbooks. M. Colin. il *Publishers Weekly* 235:14 F 3 '89

Educators adopt evolution as 'theory'. K. H. Sidey. *Christianity Today* 33:57 D 15 '89

Facts of life [science textbooks support evolution] R. N. Ostling. il *Time* 134:118 N 20 '89

Florida

The Florida state initial teacher certification test: a case study [art teachers] C. M. Dorn. bibl f *Design for Arts in Education* 90:37-42 Mr/Ap '89

Great Britain

Is there a crisis in British secondary schools? H. G. Judge. bibl f *Phi Delta Kappan* 70:813-16 Je '89

Kentucky

Entire Kentucky education system unconstitutional! C. Pipho. il *Phi Delta Kappan* 71:6-7 S '89

Minnesota

Choice: claims of success, predictions of failure. L. W. Finch. *The Education Digest* 55:12-15 N '89

Helping all children, empowering all educators: another view of school choice [with reply by J. Pearson] J. Nathan. bibl f il *Phi Delta Kappan* 71:304-11 D '89

Myths of choice: the governor's new clothes? [open enrollment plan] J. Pearson. *Phi Delta Kappan* 70:821-3 Je '89

Should parents choose their child's school? M. C. Rist. *The Education Digest* 55:3-6 S '89

The uncertain benefits of school choice [open enrollment policy] P. Glastris and T. Toch. il *U.S. News & World Report* 107:79-80+ N 6 '89

New Jersey

Must principals have teaching experience? [requirement eliminated] S. Cooperman. *The Education Digest* 54:11-12 Mr '89

Why principals should first be teachers [critique of decision to remove teaching experience as a qualification] J. W. Guthrie. *The Education Digest* 54:13-15 Mr '89

New York (State)

The Regents' Round Table [report calling for greater multicultural inclusion in curricula] L. Auster. il *National Review* 41:18+ D 8 '89

Yes, but where are your credits in Recess Management 101? S. Ohanian. *The Washington Monthly* 21:46-7 F '89

Ontario

Media literacy mandated in Ontario English curriculum. T. McConaghy. *Phi Delta Kappan* 71:332-3 D '89

Tennessee

See also
   Tennessee evolution controversy
Lamar Alexander on schools and business [interview] D. C. Bacon. il por *Nation's Business* 77:24 Ap '89

Texas

The big shift in school finance [Texas Supreme Court rules tax-based financing method unconstitutional] S. Tifft. il *Time* 134:48 O 16 '89

How courts are trying to make schools equal [modifying tax-based school financing systems] M. Cooper. *U.S. News & World Report* 107:36 O 16 '89

NCATE and Texas eyeball to eyeball: who will blink? [interview with C. Parker and H. Gideonse] D. Watts. il *Phi Delta Kappan* 71:311-18 D '89

United States

See Educational laws and regulations
EDUCATIONAL LEADERSHIP *See* Leadership
EDUCATIONAL LITERATURE
See also
   Self help literature

Authorship

Contributing to Change. T. J. Marchese. *Change* 21:4 Ja/F '89

Learning to love bibliospeak [articles and books about higher education] G. Keller. *Change* 21:19 Ja/F '89

EDUCATIONAL MEASUREMENTS *See* Educational tests and measurements

EDUCATIONAL NEWS

Education briefs. See issues of The Education Digest

EDUCATIONAL NEWS—*cont.*

The rising tide of mediocre education coverage [newspaper coverage] E. P. McQuaid. *The Education Digest* 54:7-10 Ap '89

A story at risk: the rising tide of mediocre education coverage. E. P. McQuaid. il *Phi Delta Kappan* 70:K1-K8 Ja '89

EDUCATIONAL ORGANIZATION *See* School management and organization

EDUCATIONAL PHILOSOPHY *See* Education—Philosophy

EDUCATIONAL PLANNING

See also
Curriculum planning
International Institute for Educational Planning

Features of effective school improvement plans. L. W. Lezotte. *The Education Digest* 55:15-17 D '89

Using research data to shape our schools [interview with R. Carriedo] D. B. Strother. il por *Phi Delta Kappan* 70:480-3 F '89

EDUCATIONAL POLICY *See* College education and state; Education and state

EDUCATIONAL PSYCHOLOGY *See* Psychology, Educational

EDUCATIONAL RECORDS *See* School reports and records

EDUCATIONAL REFORM *See* Education

EDUCATIONAL RESEARCH

See also
Reading research
Teachers colleges—Research
United States. Office of Educational Research and Improvement

Can educational research keep pace with education reform? [need for teachers to participate in research] J. M. Atkin. bibl f il *Phi Delta Kappan* 71:200-5 N '89

Communicating with teachers—honestly. L. A. Bader. bibl f il *Phi Delta Kappan* 70:626-9 Ap '89

Evaluating research on school computer use. G. Marshall. *The Education Digest* 54:30-3 Ja '89

General education: in search of facts. L. F. Locke. il *Change* 21:20-3 Jl/Ag '89

K-12 drama/theatre research for the 1990s: an agenda for dramatic action. J. Klein. bibl f *Design for Arts in Education* 91:27-34 N/D '89

Nurturing the critical, practical, and artistic thinking of teachers. N. L. Gage and D. C. Berliner. il *Phi Delta Kappan* 71:212-14 N '89

Policies, agendas, and arts education research. D. B. Pankratz. bibl f *Design for Arts in Education* 90:2-13 My/Je '89

Research. G. W. Bracey. See alternate issues of Phi Delta Kappan beginning March 1984

Research in review. T. N. Tice. See issues of The Education Digest beginning May 1988

The resistance of conventional wisdom to research evidence: the case of retention in grade. R. P. Doyle. bibl f il *Phi Delta Kappan* 71:215-20 N '89

Simultaneous replication: a technique for large-scale research. J. R. Frymier and others. bibl f il *Phi Delta Kappan* 71:228-31 N '89

The unscientific character of educational research. R. A. Gibboney. bibl f il *Phi Delta Kappan* 71:225-7 N '89

EDUCATIONAL SOCIOLOGY

See also
School and social and economic problems
Social education
Socially handicapped children—Education

Reflections on education and our society [address, April 16, 1989] B. H. Alexander. *Vital Speeches of the Day* 55:563-5 Jl 1 '89

EDUCATIONAL SOFTWARE *See* Computers—Educational use—Programming

EDUCATIONAL STANDARDS *See* Education—Standards

EDUCATIONAL TECHNOLOGY

See also
Computers—Educational use
Information systems—Educational use
Video games—Educational use
Word processors and processing—Educational use

Technology in college: where is its impact? D. R. McNeil. *The Education Digest* 55:58-9 D '89

EDUCATIONAL TELEVISION *See* Television in education

EDUCATIONAL TELEVISION STATIONS *See* Television stations, Public

EDUCATIONAL TESTS AND MEASUREMENTS

See also
American College Testing Program
Aptitude tests
General educational development tests
Intelligence tests
Law School Admissions Test
Medical College Admissions Test
Reading—Testing
Scholastic Aptitude Test

Faculty development from the inside [holistic assessment and placement project for composition classes at Long Beach City College] K. Burne and others. pors *Change* 21:43-9 My/Je '89

The first test of childhood [kindergarten screenings] P. Wilkes. por *Newsweek* 114:8 Ag 14 '89

High-stakes testing in kindergarten. S. J. Meisels. *The Education Digest* 55:25-8 O '89

How to improve your child's test scores [standardized tests] E. Kiester and S. V. Kiester. il *Reader's Digest* 134:84-8 My '89

In-school breakfasts improve test scores [Lawrence, Mass. study] J. Raloff. *Science News* 136:247 O 14 '89

New ways of thinking about testing [interview with G. Madaus] M. C. McClellan. por *Phi Delta Kappan* 70:642-5 Ap '89

Reflections on measuring thinking, while listening to Mozart's Jupiter symphony. S. Wassermann. bibl f il *Phi Delta Kappan* 70:365-70 Ja '89

[Special section on testing] bibl f il *Phi Delta Kappan* 70:683-722 My '89

Testing and retention of young children: moving from controversy to reform. T. Schultz. bibl f il *Phi Delta Kappan* 71:125-9 O '89

The testing paradox. T. Gendler. *The Education Digest* 54:27-9 Ja '89

Tracked to fail. S. Tobias. il *Psychology Today* 23:54-8+ S '89

EDUCATIONAL THEORY *See* Education—Philosophy

EDUCATIONAL TOYS

Toys and games to learn by. H. Boehm. il *Psychology Today* 23:62-4 S '89

Toys that teach can be fun, too. M. Silver. il *U.S. News & World Report* 107:64-6 O 2 '89

EDUCATORS

See also
College presidents
College teachers
Teachers

EDWARD VIII, KING OF GREAT BRITAIN *See* Windsor, Edward, Duke of, 1894-1972

EDWARD, DUKE OF WINDSOR *See* Windsor, Edward, Duke of, 1894-1972

EDWARD ALBERT, PRINCE OF WALES *See* Windsor, Edward, Duke of, 1894-1972

EDWARD C. MAZIQUE PARENT-CHILD CENTER (WASHINGTON, D.C.)

D.C. ground-breaking for Edward Mazique Center. il *Jet* 76:6 Ap 10 '89

EDWARD F. CALDWELL & COMPANY

Luster of the past. M. B. Caldwell. il *House & Garden* 161:96+ N '89

EDWARD O. THORP & ASSOCIATES

You just can't keep Ed Thorp down. E. Schine. il por *Business Week* p83 Ag 21 '89

EDWARD THOMAS COMPANIES

Two guys sitting around with $100 million [E. and T. Slatkin] E. Schine. il pors *Business Week* p76+ O 9 '89

EDWARDIAN HOUSE DECORATION *See* House decoration, Edwardian

EDWARDS, AUDREY, 1947-

The inspiring leader of scholars (and dollars). il pors *Working Woman* 14:68-9+ Je '89

The plateau payoff. il *Working Woman* 14:114-16+ O '89

You, men and money. *Essence* 20:55-6+ Ag '89

EDWARDS, BEN

about

Ben Edwards. M. Sommers. il *Theatre Crafts* 23:48-55+ Ag/S '89

EDWARDS, BETTY

about

The art of the mind: how I learned to draw. T. Schwartz. il por *New York* 22:42-6+ D 11 '89

EDWARDS, BLAKE, 1922-

about

Skin deep [film] Reviews
  Maclean's 102:59 Mr 20 '89. B. D. Johnson
  Newsweek 113:69 Mr 13 '89. J. Kroll
  People Weekly il 31:20-1 Mr 20 '89. S. Haller
  Video il 13:76+ N '89. I. Robbins

Survival is the best revenge. A. Cook. il pors *Gentlemen's Quarterly* 59:286-9+ Ap '89

EDWARDS, FRANK J.

See you in court! [excerpt] il por *Health (New York, N.Y.)* 21:52+ N '89

EDWARDS, HARRY

about

Fighting from the inside [interview] D. Wyss. il por *Time* 133:62-3 Mr 6 '89

EDWARDS, HENRY, AND RAINER, PETER

Sex-rated. il *Vogue* 179:236-7+ Ap '89

EDWARDS, HUGH

Crocodile attack! [condensation] il *Reader's Digest* 135:70-5 O '89

EDWARDS, JAMES R.

When bad things happen. il *Christianity Today* 33:30-2 Ag 18 '89

EDWARDS, JULIE *See* Andrews, Julie

EDWARDS, KAREN S.

A great ship. il por *Americana* 17:63-5 N/D '89

EDWARDS, KAREN S., AND ANTLE, SHARON

"Just clogging". il *Americana* 17:17-20 N/D '89

EDWARDS, MARISETTE L.

Fighting for two lives. il por *Ladies' Home Journal* 106:18+ S '89

EDWARDS, MIKE
Washington State, riding the Pacific tide. il map *National Geographic* 176:782-815 D '89
EDWARDS, OWEN
Office politics. See alternate issues of Gentlemen's Quarterly beginning February 1988
EDWARDS, PAUL, AND EDWARDS, SARAH (SARAH A.)
Working smarter. See issues of Home Office Computing beginning September 1988
EDWARDS, SALLY, 1947-
about
Innerviews [interview] L. Rothlein. il por *Women's Sports & Fitness* 11:77 Ap '89
EDWARDS, SARAH (SARAH A.)
(jt. auth) See Edwards, Paul, and Edwards, Sarah (Sarah A.)
EDWARDS, THOMAS K.
Giving students reasons for wanting to live. *The Education Digest* 54:22-4 Mr '89
EDWARDS, TRACY
about
Woman to watch: sailor Tracy Edwards. C. Flanagan. il *Women's Sports & Fitness* 11:76 Ap '89
EDWARDS (A. G.) & SONS, INC. See A. G. Edwards & Sons, Inc.
EDWARDS DAM (ME.) See Dams
EDWORDS, FREDERICK
Rushdie versus the sword of Islam. il por *The Humanist* 49:5-6+ My/Je '89
EDZARD, CHRISTINE, 1945-
about
Little Dorrit [film] Reviews
Maclean's il 102:47 Ja 16 '89. J. Bemrose
The New York Review of Books il 36:16-18 F 2 '89. G. Wills
EEC See European Economic Community
EEG See Electroencephalography
EELS
See also
Electric eels
Much ado about eels. E. Pennisi. il map *BioScience* 39:594-8 O '89
EEOC See United States. Equal Employment Opportunity Commission
EFE (AFRICAN PEOPLE)
The Efe: archers of the African rain forest. R. C. Bailey. il maps *National Geographic* 176:664-86 N '89
EFFICIENCY, ADMINISTRATIVE
See also
President's Private Sector Survey on Cost Control (U.S.)
EFFICIENCY, HOUSEHOLD See Home economics
EFFICIENCY, INDUSTRIAL
See also
Factory management
Office management
Productivity, Industrial
Team work in industry
How managers can succeed through speed [cover story] B. Dumaine. il *Fortune* 119:54-7+ F 13 '89
Shaping up your suppliers. J. Dreyfuss. il *Fortune* 119:116+ Ap 10 '89
EFFICIENT MARKET HYPOTHESIS
Dangerously inefficient [views of A. Arbel] M. Schifrin. il por *Forbes* 144:60-1 Jl 10 '89
The efficient market hypothesis [discussion of March 10, 1989 article, Is the stock market efficient?] B. G. Malkiel. *Science* 244:1424-5 Je 23 '89
Is the stock market efficient? B. G. Malkiel. bibl f il *Science* 243:1313-18 Mr 10 '89
EFFROS, EDWARD G.
When "everybody counts," perhaps no one will. *The Education Digest* 55:18-20 O '89
EFIS (ELECTRONIC FLIGHT INSTRUMENT SYSTEM) DISPLAY See Airplanes, Military—Electronic equipment
EFRON, EDITH, 1922-
Nature's carcinogens are everywhere [excerpt from The apocalyptics] *Consumers' Research Magazine* 72:16-18 My '89
EFTA See European Free Trade Association
EFTINK, BILL
Bill Eftink. See issues of Successful Farming beginning March 1989
EGAN, EILEEN
Children in combat. il *Commonweal* 116:104-5 F 24 '89
EGAN, JENNIFER
The stylist [story] *The New Yorker* 65:32-7 Mr 13 '89
EGAN, JOHN
For sale: commercial space. il *Ad Astra* 1:8-11+ D '89
EGAN, KEITH J.
Letters from a lady in love. il *U.S. Catholic* 54:12-13 F '89
EGAN, KIERAN
Memory, imagination, and learning: connected by the story. bibl f il *Phi Delta Kappan* 70:455-9 F '89
Understanding the USSR. *The Education Digest* 54:40-2 Mr '89

EGAN, PETER
Side glances. See issues of Road & Track beginning November 1983
EGAN, WILLIAM C.
about
Mr. Egan and my drowned lobsters. R. K. Bryant. il *Gourmet* 49:196+ My '89
EGELMAN, E. H., AND YU, X.
The location of DNA in RecA-DNA helical filaments. bibl f il *Science* 245:404-7 Jl 28 '89
EGG CREAMS
The egg cream [formula holder S. Auster] J. Berendt. il por *Esquire* 112:48 D '89
The secret of life [expert egg cream maker S. Auster] *The New Yorker* 65:37-8 My 15 '89
EGG DECORATION See Eggs, Decorated
EGG INDUSTRY
Finance
Eggshells everywhere. J. Willoughby. il *Forbes* 143:254+ My 29 '89
EGG TEMPERA PAINTING See Tempera painting
EGGHEAD INC.
CDs come to consumers [CD-ROM] P. Scisco. *Compute!* 11:10 Ja '89
Soft in the head? L. Jereski. il *Forbes* 143:54 Mr 6 '89
EGGINTON, JOYCE
The bad mother. il pors *Good Housekeeping* 208:119+ Ap '89
Menace of Whispering Hills. il *Audubon* 91:28+ Ja '89
The radon menace: and update. il *Reader's Digest* 134:141-4+ My '89
EGGLESTON, NILES
Sweet sugar maple memories. il *The Conservationist* 43:2-5 Mr/Ap '89
EGGNOG
Leaner eggnogs? il *Sunset (Central West edition)* 183:118-19 D '89
EGGPLANT
See also
Cooking—Vegetables
Purple reign. B. Pleasant. il *Organic Gardening* 36:47-50 Jl/Ag '89
EGGS
See also
Amphibia—Eggs
Cooking—Eggs
Incubation
Insects—Eggs
The egg news is scrambled [cholesterol] J. Seligmann. il *Newsweek* 113:60 My 29 '89
The egg scramble [lowered cholesterol eggs] S. McKee. il *American Health* 8:132 S '89
Egging on cholesterol-wary diners [research by Gary R. Beecher] *Science News* 135:349 Je 3 '89
An egg's an egg, but slightly less so [cholesterol levels] J. Silberner. il *U.S. News & World Report* 106:61 Je 5 '89
Eggs naturally rich in 'fish oils' [omega-3 fatty acids from purslane] *Science News* 136:351 N 25 '89
Eggs . . . reconsidered [cholesterol levels] il *Glamour* 87:360 Ap '89
Fear of eggs [cholesterol and salmonellosis] il *Consumer Reports* 54:650-2 O '89
Good food, good health: unscrambling the facts about eggs. B. Goldman. il *Better Homes and Gardens* 67:45-6 Ap '89
Low-cholesterol eggs are coming. *USA Today (Periodical)* 117:13-14 Ap '89
Skinny eggs and other dream foods [low-cholesterol products] C. Hudson. il *Health (New York, N.Y.)* 21:30+ S '89
Contamination
From our kitchen to yours [handling eggs safely] K. Adams. il *Southern Living* 24:126 Ja '89
Trojan eggs [eggs and salmonella] A. A. Hanson and W. I. Bennett. il *The New York Times Magazine* p25-6 Jl 30 '89
Photographs and photography
Eggs to see. F. Lanting. il *Omni (New York, N.Y.)* 11:58-63 My '89
EGGS, DECORATED
They're gift-wrapped Easter eggs. il *Sunset (Central West edition)* 182:98-9 Mr '89
Collectors and collecting
Ova to you, Dorothy Davis, egg fancier extraordinaire. il por *People Weekly* 31:94 Mr 27 '89
The ultimate Easter eggs [Malcolm Forbes' collection of Fabergé Easter eggs; cover story] M. Forrest. il *Antiques & Collecting Hobbies* 94:44-5+ Mr '89
EGGS, FOSSIL
Dinosaur eggs: the inside story [cover story] J. R. Horner and D. B. Weishampel. il *Natural History* p60-7 D '89
Dinosaur tragedy yields birth clues [research by Karl F. Hirsch] *Science News* 135:220 Ap 8 '89
Upper Jurassic dinosaur egg from Utah. K. F. Hirsch and others. bibl f il *Science* 243:1711-13 Mr 31 '89

EGGS (OVA) See Ova
EGO See Self
EGOISM
See also
Boastfulness
Narcissism
EGOYAN, ATOM
about
Up and Atom. A. Taubin. il por Film Comment 25:27-9
N/D '89
EGUCHI, TEIJI
about
Why Bridgestone's chairman is making tracks to Akron.
Z. Schiller. il por Business Week p32-3 N 20 '89
EGYPT
See also
Alexandria (Egypt)
Americans—Egypt
Cairo (Egypt)
Crime and criminals—Egypt
Cultural property—Protection—Egypt
Economic assistance, American—Egypt
Geology—Egypt
Investments, Egyptian
Nile River
Opera—Egypt
Rivers—Egypt
Shore protection—Egypt
Sinai (Peninsula)
Stone Age—Egypt
Taxation—Egypt
Antiquities
See also
Mummies
Pyramids—Egypt
Rosetta Stone
Temple of Luxor
Rivers in the sand [interpretation of shuttle radar imaging
in the Sahara] B. Bower. map Science News 136:138-9
Ag 26 '89
Civilization
Interview with Najib Mahfouz. V. Massuh. il por The Unesco
Courier 42:4-6 D '89
Climate
Weather of the pharaohs. R. S. Cerveny. il Weatherwise
42:307-14 D '89
Defenses
See also
Remotely piloted vehicles—Egypt
Description and travel
Blazing sandals. T. Young. il Vogue 179:250+ F '89
Foreign relations
Israel
See also
Israel-Arab Wars, 1967-
Middle East
A defeated compromise [Israel turns down Mubarak plan]
J. Bierman. il por Maclean's 102:31 O 16 '89
Mubarak moves to the front lines of the Mideast crisis.
B. Slavin and others. il Business Week p59 Ja 9 '89
Mubarak's peace plan. il World Press Review 36:8 N '89
The politics of peace in the Mideast [cover story] E. Salpeter.
il The New Leader 72:5-7 O 2-16 '89
Sowing dragons' teeth or talking. America 161:228 O 14
'89
Waiting for Godot [Israeli opposition to H. Mubarak's peace
plan] B. W. Nelan. il por Time 134:45 O 16 '89
United States
See United States—Foreign relations—Egypt
History
To 332 B.C.
Weather of the pharaohs. R. S. Cerveny. il Weatherwise
42:307-14 D '89
Greco-Roman period, 332 B.C.-640 A.D.
Think that taxes take a big bite today? L. Casson. il
Smithsonian 19:122-7 Mr '89
1250-1517
See also
Mamelukes
French occupation, 1798-1801
The eagle and the sphinx. M. Hussein. il The Unesco Courier
42:24-9 Je '89
Industries
See also
Al-Rayyan (Firm)
Kings and rulers
See also
Pharaohs
Maps
First geological map may have been Egyptian scroll [Turin
Papyrus; research by James A. Harrell and V. Max Brown]
il Earth Science 41:5-6 Wint '88
Politics and government
Islam and democracy in Egypt. R. Bianchi. bibl f Current
History 88:93-5+ F '89
Religious institutions and affairs
See also
Muslims—Egypt

Study and teaching
See Egyptian studies
EGYPT IN ART
Nile style [use of Egyptian motifs in contemporary design]
A. Foxley. il House & Garden 161:86 Ap '89
EGYPTIAN ART See Art, Egyptian
EGYPTIAN MATHEMATICS See Mathematics, Egyptian
EGYPTIAN MUSEUM
Mummy under glass [preservation with nitrogen] il Discover
10:18 Ag '89
EGYPTIAN POETRY
See also
Epic poetry, Egyptian
EGYPTIAN STUDIES
Champollion, a hero of the Enlightenment [interview with
J. Lacouture] il por The Unesco Courier 42:4-9 O '89
EHRENREICH, BARBARA
Bad attitude. See issues of Mother Jones
Clothes klutz. il Ms. 17:24-5 Je '89
Drug frenzy: why the war on drugs misses the real target.
il Utne Reader p76-9+ Mr/Ap '89
Public freaking. por Ms. 18:40-1 S '89
Sick chic. il Ms. 17:28-9 Ja/F '89
Single jeopardy. il Ms. 17:24-5 My '89
Someone you know? il Ms. 17:35-6 Mr '89
Stop ironing the diapers. il Ms. 17:30-1 Ap '89
Two steps back. il Ms. 18:24-5 O '89
Working-class heroes no more. Harper's 279:22+ D '89
EHRENREICH, BARBARA, AND ENGLISH, DEIRDRE
Blowing the whistle on the "mommy track". il Ms. 18:56-8
Jl/Ag '89
EHRHARDT, WALTER
about
Bearing fruit. K. Martin. il pors Organic Gardening 36:68-72
Mr '89
EHRLICH, ANNE H.
(jt. auth) See Ehrlich, Paul R., and Ehrlich, Anne H.
EHRLICH, EVERETT M.
Information technology, global linkage, and U.S. competitive-
ness [address, June 14, 1989] Vital Speeches of the Day
55:755-9 O 1 '89
EHRLICH, GRETEL
A season of portents: the long summer of '88: a Wyoming
diary. il Harper's 279:50-7 Ag '89
EHRLICH, PAUL R.
Facing the habitability crisis [adaptation of address, February
16, 1989] BioScience 39:480-2 Jl/Ag '89
The mission of AIBS. BioScience 39:810-11 D '89
EHRLICH, PAUL R., AND EHRLICH, ANNE H.
Intelligent planning for safety. Society 27:15-16 N/D '89
EHRLICH, PAUL R., AND ORNSTEIN, ROBERT E.
(ROBERT EVAN), 1942-
New world, new mind [excerpt] il New Perspectives Quarterly
6:26-33 Spr '89
EHRMANN, ERIC
Peron's latest hurrah. National Review 41:20-1 Je 16 '89
EI See Environmental illness
EICHELBERGER, ETHYL
about
Ethyl Eichelberger. R. Smith. il pors Theatre Crafts 23:28-33+
Ja '89
EICHEN, MARC
Bringing maps home. il Parents 64:143-6 S '89
Logo and geography teaching. bibl Focus (New York, N.Y.:
1950) 39:25-6 Summ '89
Weather prediction in the classroom. Focus (New York, N.Y.:
1950) 39:27+ Spr '89
EICHLER, GLENN
The business traveler. See issues of Esquire beginning July
1986
EICHMANN, ADOLF, 1906-1962
about
Triumph and tragedy. S. Shields. il por American Heritage
40:82-6+ D '89
EICHNER, RANDY
Your finest hour. il Bicycling 30:122-5 My '89
EICOSAPENTAENOIC ACID
Fish oil slows some developing cancers [research by T. Colin
Campbell] J. Raloff. Science News 135:390 Je 24 '89
EIDETICS INTERNATIONAL (FIRM)
U.S. firm claims modified F-16 could match Su-27 'Cobra'
maneuver. M. A. Dornheim. il Aviation Week & Space
Technology 131:54-5 Ag 14 '89
EIE INTERNATIONAL CORPORATION
Meet the world's busiest man—oops, you missed him [H.
Takahashi] A. Borrus. il por Business Week p64+ Ap
17 '89
EIFFEL, ALEXANDRE GUSTAVE, 1832-1923
about
Eiffel's Tower. J.-P. Navailles. bibl il por History Today
39:38-43 D '89
A Parisian love affair. J. A. Harriss. il Reader's Digest
134:57-8+ Mr '89
EIFFEL TOWER (PARIS, FRANCE)
1789's echo in steel. G. F. Will. il Newsweek 114:62 Jl
17 '89
The birthday tower. J. Njor. il World Press Review 36:62
Mr '89

EIFFEL TOWER (PARIS, FRANCE)—*cont.*
Eiffel's Tower. J.-P. Navailles. bibl il por *History Today* 39:38-43 D '89
A Parisian love affair. J. A. Harriss. il *Reader's Digest* 134:57-8+ Mr '89
EIFMAN, BORIS
about
The master and Margarita [ballet] Reviews
Dance Magazine 63:53+ Jl '89. V. Vanslov
EIGEN, M. (MANFRED), 1927-, AND OTHERS
How old is the genetic code? Statistical geometry of tRNA provides an answer. bibl f il *Science* 244:673-9 My 12 '89
AN EIGHT IS ENOUGH WEDDING [television program]
See Television program reviews—Single works
EIGHTEENTH CENTURY
See also
Enlightenment
EIGHTIES (DECADE) *See* Nineteen hundred and eighties
EIGSTI, KARL
about
Centerline: Karl Eigsti. M. LaRue. il por *Theatre Crafts* 23:12-13 Mr '89
EIKENBERRY, JILL
Jill Eikenberry: role model [excerpts from address] il por *Ladies' Home Journal* 106:68 N '89
about
King and queen of torts [cover story] H. G. Miller. il pors *The Saturday Evening Post* 261:50-3+ Ap '89
A triumph of love. J. Cullen. il pors *Ladies' Home Journal* 106:34+ Ja '89
EIKO
about
Thirst [dance] Reviews
The New Leader 72:22 Ja 9 '89. L. A. Jacobs
Tree [dance] Reviews
The New Leader 72:22 Ja 9 '89. L. A. Jacobs
EINHORN, STEVEN G.
about
The top bear. R. Henkoff. il por *Fortune* 119:47+ Ja 2 '89
EINIGER, CAROL B.
about
Carol Einiger: one-of-a-kind at Wasserella. R. Conniff. il por *Business Week* p99 Ag 21 '89
EINSTEIN, ALBERT, 1879-1955
about
Besso. J. Bernstein. *The New Yorker* 65:86-92 F 27 '89
Bumbling toward the bomb. W. J. Lanouette. bibl f il por *The Bulletin of the Atomic Scientists* 45:7-11 S '89
Did Einstein espouse his spouse's ideas? [discussion of May 1987 article, Einstein and ether drift experiments] J. Stachel. il *Physics Today* 42:9+ F '89
Jews and geniuses. R. Craft. il pors *The New York Review of Books* 36:35-7 F 16 '89
EINSTEIN, CLIFF
about
"The big hit". P. Clothier. il pors *Art News* 88:113-14+ D '89
EINSTEIN, MANDY
about
"The big hit". P. Clothier. il pors *Art News* 88:113-14+ D '89
EINSTEIN ON THE BEACH [opera] See Glass, Philip
EISA (COMPUTER BUS)
EISA arrives [Vectra 486; cover story] N. Baran. il *Byte* 14:93-6+ N '89
EISA sets the stage for open standards. J. Blackford. il *Personal Computing* 13:301-2 Ja '89
EISA under the glass. P. Honan. il *Personal Computing* 13:66-70 Ag '89
Inside EISA. B. Glass. il *Byte* 14:417-20+ N '89
Rising above the industry chaos [Micro Channel vs. EISA buses] F. Abatemarco. il *Personal Computing* 13:5 F '89
EISELE (SHIP)
Calling all shipmates [F. Krawczyk arranges reunion of crew] S. Brewer. il por *New Choices for the Best Years* 29:12-13 My '89
EISELEY, LOREN C., 1907-1977
The flow of the river [excerpt from The immense journey] il *Audubon* 91:82-5 My '89
about
A boy, a bird, and a book. B. Wisner. il por *Audubon* 91:78-81 My '89
EISEN, MARK
about
New talents: Mark Eisen. il por *Harper's Bazaar* 122:88 Mr '89
EISENACH, JEFFREY A.
How to win the war on drugs: target the users. il *USA Today (Periodical)* 117:46-8 Ja '89
EISENBERG, DEBORAH
Under the 82nd Airborne [story] *The New Yorker* 64:28-40+ F 13 '89
EISENBERG, EVAN
Back to Eden [cover story; with editorial comment] il por *The Atlantic* 264:6, 57-9+ N '89

EISENBERG, LAWRENCE
Drink to me only with thy $23,000 goblet. il por *TV Guide* 37:24-5 Ap 22-28 '89
EISENBERG, SUSAN
Women hard hats speak out. *The Nation* 249:272-4+ S 18 '89
EISENDRATH, JOHN
Have Mac, will publish. *The Washington Monthly* 21:28-34+ Je '89
EISENHOWER, DWIGHT D. (DWIGHT DAVID), 1890-1969
about
Did Eisenhower oppose A-bomb? il por *USA Today (Periodical)* 118:15 Ag '89
He didn't like Ike [excerpt from Where the buck stops]; ed. by Margaret Truman. H. S. Truman. il pors *The New York Times Magazine* p40-2+ S 17 '89
Ike's revenge? por *Time* 134:19 O 2 '89
Homes
They liked Ike first in Denison. il por *Southern Living* 24:24 Ja '89
EISENHOWER (DWIGHT D.) (AIRCRAFT CARRIER) *See* Dwight D. Eisenhower (Aircraft carrier)
EISENHOWER BIRTHPLACE STATE HISTORIC SITE (DENISON, TEX.)
They liked Ike first in Denison. il por *Southern Living* 24:24 Ja '89
EISENMAN, PETER, 1932-
about
A crazy building in Columbus. K. Andersen. il por *Time* 134:84+ N 20 '89
Eisenman's gridlocked mind game. C. McGuigan. il por *Newsweek* 114:74-5 N 20 '89
Solid geometry. M. Sorkin. il por *House & Garden* 161:62+ O '89
With the opening of the first major public building by Peter Eisenman, theory and reality collide. H. Muschamp. il por *Vogue* 179:272+ O '89
EISENSTADT, JILL
about
New working class. il pors *Harper's Bazaar* 122:160-75+ Mr '89
EISENSTEIN, SAM
Too far from Texas [story] il *Seventeen* 48:88-9+ Ja '89
EISENSTEIN, ZILLAH R.
Fetal position. *The Nation* 249:588-9 N 20 '89
EISNER, MICHAEL
about
How Disney does it [cover story] C. Leerhsen. il por *Newsweek* 113:48-54 Ap 3 '89
How Disney keeps the magic going. C. Knowlton. il por *Fortune* 120:111-12+ D 4 '89
EISNER, ROBERT, 1922-
Liberal Keynesian. *National Review* 41:47 Ja 27 '89
EISNER, THOMAS
If looks could kill . . . Florida jumping spider [photographs] il *Natural History* p76-7 Jl '89
EISSLER, HOLLY
about
Women at work: Holly Eissler. L. Dawson-Medina. il pors *Ms.* 18:34-6 O '89
EJECTION DEVICES (AIRPLANES) *See* Airplanes, Military—Escape devices
EK, MATS
about
Swedish choreographer protests bureaucratic incompetence. L. Schubert. il *Dance Magazine* 63:18 S '89
EKMAN, PAUL
Would a child lie? il *Psychology Today* 23:62-5 Jl/Ag '89
about
The figments of childhood. *U.S. News & World Report* 107:62-3 O 23 '89
Understanding kids' lies. N. Darnton. il *Newsweek* 114:62-3 O 2 '89
EKSTEINS, MODRIS
A yearning for change. il *Maclean's* 102:20-1 S 4 '89
EL AL ISRAEL AIRLINES LTD.
Buy me, I'm El Al. H. Kestin. il *Forbes* 144:42-3 N 27 '89
EL-ASHRY, MOHAMED T.
(jt. auth) See MacKenzie, James J., 1939-, and El-Ashry, Mohamed T.
EL CAPITAN (CALIF.)
Grit and a granite will conquer El Capitan [paraplegic M. Wellman makes climb assisted by M. Corbett] M. Brower. il pors *People Weekly* 32:36-9 Ag 14 '89
EL-HAKAWATI (THEATER COMPANY)
Notes and comment. il *The New Yorker* 65:23-4 Ag 28 '89
EL MAHDI, SADIQ, 1936-
about
An early-morning coup. *Time* 134:33 Jl 10 '89
EL NIÑO (OCEAN CURRENT)
Amazon River discharge and climate variability: 1903 to 1985. J. E. Richey and others. bibl f il map *Science* 246:101-3 O 6 '89
The big picture of the Pacific's undulations [Geosat data] R. A. Kerr. *Science* 243:739-40 F 10 '89

EL NIÑO (OCEAN CURRENT)—*cont.*

Deep-rooted disturbance [link between earthquakes and El Niño; research by Daniel Walker] S. Vogel. il *Discover* 10:26+ Jl '89

Ghosts of Christmas [effects on Christmas Island bird populations; study by Ralph and Elizabeth Schreiber] L. Oliwenstein. il *Discover* 10:22 Ag '89

Length-of-day variations caused by El Niño-Southern Oscillation and Quasi-Biennial Oscillation. B. F. Chao. bibl f il *Science* 243:923-5 F 17 '89

Stratospheric winds alter day's length [research by B. Fong Chao] R. Monastersky. *Science News* 135:102 F 18 '89

EL RUKN (GANG)

A snitch's tale: the killer gang [informer A. Sumner] P. King. il por *Newsweek* 114:45 N 6 '89

EL SALVADOR

See also

   Americans—El Salvador

   Canadians—El Salvador

   Civil rights—El Salvador

   Copapayo (El Salvador)

   Deportation—El Salvador

   Economic assistance, American—El Salvador

   Land reform—El Salvador

   Military assistance, American—El Salvador

   Military assistance, Nicaraguan—El Salvador

   Military assistance, Russian—El Salvador

   Political prisoners—El Salvador

   Relief work—El Salvador

   Repatriation—El Salvador

   San Salvador (El Salvador)

   Trifinio (Central America)

Army

El Salvador's Army: a force unto itself. J. Millman. il *The New York Times Magazine* p46-7+ D 10 '89

Civil War, 1980-

'Absolute, diabolical terror'. S. Miles and B. Ostertag. il *Mother Jones* 14:22-7+ Ap '89

Adolf's heirs [electoral victory by Arena] A. Cockburn. *The Nation* 248:655 My 15 '89

The battle for San Salvador [FMLN offensive] J. Smolowe. il *Time* 134:42-4 N 27 '89

A bloody misfire on the streets of El Salvador [FMLN offensive] il *U.S. News & World Report* 107:12-13 N 27 '89

Bombs in El Salvador. *The Christian Century* 106:1042-3 N 15 '89

Bush's Central American albatross [A. Cristiani rejects rebel cease-fire offer] L. Lief. *U.S. News & World Report* 107:33 D 4 '89

Can benign neglect solve El Salvador's problems? D. Farah. il *U.S. News & World Report* 107:59-60 N 6 '89

Confessions of an assassin [H. Torres Cortez, former member of a death squad] D. Farah and T. Gibb. por *Mother Jones* 14:10+ Ja '89

Conversations with two foes [J. Villalobos and A. Cristiani] J. Smolowe. il pors *Time* 134:26 O 2 '89

Death's democracy. C. Lane. il *The Atlantic* 263:18+ Ja '89

A democratic revolution for El Salvador. J. Villalobos. *Foreign Policy* 74:103-22 Spr '89

A dirty war gets dirtier. C. Lane. il *Newsweek* 113:43 Ja 2 '89

Eichmann with a smile [G. Bush's comments on U.S. aid] *The Nation* 249:701 D 11 '89

El Salvador: behind the lines with the rebels. F. Smyth. il *The Progressive* 53:26-9 F '89

El Salvador: keep your eye on the ball. *National Review* 41:13-14 D 22 '89

El Salvador's Army: a force unto itself. J. Millman. il *The New York Times Magazine* p46-7+ D 10 '89

El Salvador's forgotten war. J. LeMoyne. *Foreign Affairs* 68:105-25 Summ '89

The evidence in the bean field: Nicaragua's fingerprints in El Salvador's war. C. S. Manegold. il *Newsweek* 114:67-8 D 4 '89

Fighting in the streets [special section] il maps *Maclean's* 102:42-6+ D 4 '89

The guns of Salvador [cover story] J. LeMoyne. il *The New York Times Magazine* p18-21+ F 5 '89

Hanging in the balance: El Salvador's future & the limits of U.S. power. L. S. Robinson. il *Commonweal* 116:242-5 Ap 21 '89

In freedom's name. A. Cockburn. *The Nation* 249:706-7 D 11 '89

In Salvador time waits for no one [cover story] R. Zamora. *The Nation* 248:253+ F 27 '89

Losing gamble [U.S. military aid continues despite human rights abuses] *The Nation* 249:704 D 11 '89

A murderous cross-fire [FMLN offensive] C. Lane. il map *Newsweek* 114:48-50+ N 27 '89

No place to hide. J. F. O. McAllister. il *Time* 134:53-4 D 11 '89

Notes and comment [plight of Green Berets and American church worker J. J. Casolo] *The New Yorker* 65:42-4 D 11 '89

An offer they couldn't refuse [FMLN offensive] J. Moody. il *Time* 133:40 Ja 30 '89

The return of the right. C. Lane. il por *Newsweek* 113:38+ Mr 20 '89

Revolt under the coconut palms [FMLN rebels] R. Chavira. il *Time* 133:38 Mr 20 '89

Rubén Zamora [interview] M. Shaffer. pors *The Progressive* 53:32-5 Jl '89

Sad new El Salvador. M. Massing. il *The New York Review of Books* 36:53-60 My 18 '89

Salvadoran death threats: a dialogue. *Harper's* 278:19-20 Ap '89

Save El Salvador. *Commonweal* 116:660-1 D 1 '89

The Sheraton siege. D. Brand. il *Time* 134:50-1 D 4 '89

A slow dying in El Salvador. D. France. il *Rolling Stone* p63-4+ Mr 23 '89

Tet in Salvador. *The Nation* 249:667-8 D 4 '89

Unwelcome in El Salvador [treatment of volunteers assisting refugees] J. Lindsay-Poland. il *The Progressive* 53:32-5 My '89

The war continues. P. Lacefield. il *Commonweal* 116:197-9 Ap 7 '89

War for those who want it. C. Lane. il *Newsweek* 114:57 N 13 '89

The war that will not end [cover story] C. Lane. *The New Republic* 201:23-7 O 16 '89

Wave of terror. A. Bilski. il *Maclean's* 102:26-7 N 27 '89

Aerial operations

A Soviet missile mystery [plane crash reveals arms flow through Nicaragua] D. Waller. il *Newsweek* 114:35 D 11 '89

Moral and religious aspects

Barbarity in El Salvador [Jesuits murdered] *The Christian Century* 106:1112-13 N 29 '89

Celluloid evangelism [motion picture Romero] S. Ulstein. il por *Christianity Today* 33:77-8 N 3 '89

A community of remembrance. S. Hutchinson. *The Christian Century* 106:853-6 S 27 '89

Death in El Salvador [murder of six Jesuit priests] J. Sobrino. il *Commonweal* 116:693-5 D 15 '89

Demonizing D'Aubuisson [role in assassination of Archbishop O. Romero] J. Morley. il *The Nation* 248:624-6 My 8 '89

The El Salvador horror [need for papal intervention] *The New Republic* 201:7-9 D 11 '89

Fear in the midst of war [army detains church workers] M. Nemeth. il *Maclean's* 102:48 D 4 '89

Grave thoughts [conversation with Jesuit priest I. Ellacuria nine months before his murder] M. Massing. *The New Republic* 201:12-14 D 11 '89

Home for the holidays—from El Salvador [church worker J. J. Casolo] por *Newsweek* 114:52 D 25 '89

In cold blood [murder of six Jesuit priests] *Time* 134:44 N 27 '89

In solidarity with the slain Jesuits of El Salvador [address, November 22, 1989] J. A. O'Hare. *America* 161:443-6 D 16 '89

In the name of God, stop the killing [Jesuit priests] R. A. Hyde. *The Christian Century* 106:1144 D 6 '89

'Now you be quiet, Oscar' [death squad killings] *America* 161:415 D 9 '89

Of many things [murder of Jesuits] T. H. Stahel. *America* 161:390 D 2 '89

Romero: evolution of a martyr [motion picture] D. G. Peerman. il *The Christian Century* 106:870-2 O 4 '89

Salvadoran refugees come home [village of Copapayo] R. R. Ruether. il *The Christian Century* 106:851-3 S 27 '89

Peace and mediation

Bush wades into his first quagmire. il *U.S. News & World Report* 106:12 F 6 '89

Compromise or lose. R. E. White. *Commonweal* 116:390-1 Jl 14 '89

Guerrilla tactics. S. MacLeod. il *Time* 133:47 F 6 '89

Negotiations or total war [possible FMLN compromise settlement] F. Smyth. il *The Nation* 249:164-6 Ag 7-14 '89

A Salvadoran peace 'trap'? C. Lane. il *Newsweek* 113:40 F 6 '89

Salvador's silver lining. M. Kondracke. *The New Republic* 200:23-5 Mr 13 '89

Reporters and reporting

Beat the devil [coverage of the strike against Eastern and of the struggle in El Salvador] A. Cockburn. *The Nation* 248:438-9 Ap 3 '89

Hazardous duty [detained by security forces] J. Gannon. il *Maclean's* 102:45-6 D 4 '89

Notes and comment [death of cameraman Dutch C. Lagrouw while covering presidential election] *The New Yorker* 65:29-31 Ap 3 '89

'The very worst and the very best'. J. Carlin. *World Press Review* 36:26-7 Mr '89

Foreign relations

United States

See United States—Foreign relations—El Salvador

Politics and government

See also

   El Salvador—Civil War, 1980-

   Elections—El Salvador

   Political campaigns—El Salvador

Death's democracy. C. Lane. il *The Atlantic* 263:18+ Ja '89

EL SALVADOR—Politics and government—*cont.*
A democratic revolution for El Salvador. J. Villalobos. *Foreign Policy* 74:103-22 Spr '89
El Salvador: the battle for democracy. *Department of State Bulletin* 89:44-9 Ja '89
The guns of Salvador [cover story] J. LeMoyne. il *The New York Times Magazine* p18-21+ F 5 '89
Rubén Zamora [interview] M. Shaffer. pors *The Progressive* 53:32-5 Jl '89
Secretary's news conference [November 14, 1988] G. P. Shultz. *Department of State Bulletin* 89:13 Ja '89

Religious institutions and affairs
See also
Catholic Church—El Salvador
Church and social problems—El Salvador
Missions—El Salvador
EL SALVADOR IN MOTION PICTURES
Celluloid evangelism [Romero] S. Ulstein. il por *Christianity Today* 33:77-8 N 3 '89
Romero: evolution of a martyr. D. G. Peerman. il *The Christian Century* 106:870-2 O 4 '89
ELAM, STANLEY M.
The second Gallup/Phi Delta Kappa poll of teachers' attitudes toward the public schools [with editorial comment by Pauline B. Gough] il *Phi Delta Kappan* 70:746, 785-98 Je '89
ELAM, STANLEY M., AND GALLUP, ALEC
The 21st annual Gallup poll of the public's attitudes toward the public schools. il *Phi Delta Kappan* 71:41-54 S '89
ELBOW
Wounds and injuries
See also
Tennis elbow
ELDER, JAMES T., AND OTHERS
Overexpression of transforming growth factor α in psoriatic epidermis. bibl f il *Science* 243:811-14 F 10 '89
ELDER, JIM
Family vacation videos: how to make them really fun to watch. il *Better Homes and Gardens* 67:162 Ap '89
ELDER, MIMI
Charleston. il *Gourmet* 49:68-73+ Ap '89
Mackinac Island. il maps *Gourmet* 49:70-5+ Je '89
A young person's guide to London. il *Gourmet* 49:108-13+ O '89
ELDER, SEAN
High school confidential. il *American Health* 8:62-3+ O '89
ELDERCARE *See* Aged—Care and hygiene; Industry—Elderly services programs
ELDERHOSTEL
Elderhostel: travel-study programs for seniors. il *Sunset (Central West edition)* 183:26 S '89
ELDERLY *See* Aged
ELDERLY SERVICES PROGRAMS *See* Industry—Elderly services programs
ELDERS, JOYCELYN
about
The crusade of Dr. Elders. S. Barnes. il pors *The New York Times Magazine* p38-41+ O 15 '89
ELDERS FUTURES INC.
A new tune [broker G. Donney] il por *Forbes* 144:287 N 27 '89
ELDON INDUSTRIES, INC.
Pedestrian products, powerhouse profits. A. E. Serwer. il *Fortune* 119:38+ Ja 30 '89
ELDRED, DALE, 1934-
about
Glass, steel and sunlight. B. Kantrowitz. il *Newsweek* 113:69 My 15 '89
ELDRED, KENNETH A., 1943-
about
Shakeout. F. Meeks. il por *Forbes* 143:120+ Mr 6 '89
ELDREDGE, KAY
The Alpes-Maritimes: Riviera refuge. il *Harper's Bazaar* 122:91-2 My '89
Straight shots. il *Harper's Bazaar* 122:170+ F '89
Wine before its time. il *Esquire* 112:53 N '89
ELDRIDGE, JOSEPH
Honduras left to push contra pram. il *The Nation* 248:734-6+ My 29 '89
ELDRIDGE, ROY, 1911-1989
about
Buck Clayton, Roy Eldridge. C. Deffaa. il pors *Down Beat* 56:48 F '89
Jazz. W. Balliett. *The New Yorker* 65:106-7 S 11 '89
Obituary
Down Beat por 56:11 My '89. J. McDonough
Jet il por 75:53 Mr 13 '89
ELECTION DISTRICTS
See also
Apportionment (Election law)
Gerrymander
The return of segregation [black election districts] M. Cooper. il *U.S. News & World Report* 107:24 N 6 '89
ELECTION EXPENSES *See* Campaign funds
ELECTION LAWS
See also
Black suffrage
Campaign funds—Laws and regulations

Electoral College
Voter registration
ELECTIONS
See also
Black suffrage
Labor unions—Elections
Political campaigns
Political candidates
Presidential candidates
Presidents—Election
Public opinion polls
Referendum
Vice-presidential candidates
Voting
See also subhead Politics and government under names of states and cities
Congressional shell game [tricks for staying in office] P. Weyrich. il *Conservative Digest* 15:18-21+ Mr/Ap '89
Dems win Congress but will they lose blacks? il *Black Enterprise* 19:13 Ja '89
Elections and efficiency [results affecting education] C. Pipho. il *Phi Delta Kappan* 70:350-1 Ja '89
The end of the Civil War. M. Barone. il *U.S. News & World Report* 107:45-6+ N 20 '89
How coalition politics put blacks in power as mayors across nation. W. Wofford, Jr. il *Jet* 77:14-16+ N 27 '89
How far can the Democrats ride this wave? D. Harbrecht and R. Fly. il *Business Week* p45 N 20 '89
Jesse: election exposes growth of white voters. por *Jet* 77:18+ N 27 '89
The lessons of the elections of 1989. M. Barone. il *U.S. News & World Report* 107:41 N 13 '89
Losing well is the best revenge [Republicans] W. McGurn. *National Review* 41:16 D 8 '89
Moderates' day? [blacks win state and city elections] *The Nation* 249:668-9 D 4 '89
The new black politics [winning candidates] H. Fineman. il *Newsweek* 114:52-3 N 20 '89
New congresswomen squeak into office. A. F. Lewis. il *Ms.* 17:140-1 Ja/F '89
Spacepac's election results. D. Brandt. *Ad Astra* 1:15 Ap '89
There were other elections in November '88. *American Visions* 4:22+ F '89
Voters decide to strike a balance. J. M. Wall. *The Christian Century* 106:1075-6 N 22 '89
What the people said. D. Schorr. *The New Leader* 72:3 N 13 '89
History
A narrow escape for the Democrats [1914 congressional elections] *The New Republic* 201 [Reprint v1]:8-9 N 6 '89 [N 7 '14]
Argentina
Argentina's return to Peronism [C. Menem] R. Graham and G. Mead. *World Press Review* 36:23-4 Jl '89
A Peronist triumph [C. Menem wins] M. Nemeth. il por *Maclean's* 102:24 My 29 '89
Perón's latest hurrah [election of C. S. Menem] E. Ehrmann. *National Review* 41:20-1 Je 16 '89
Brazil
Brazil's election is a watershed no matter who wins. J. Ryser. il pors *Business Week* p61 D 4 '89
Lula's in town [L. da Silva vs. F. Collor de Mello] K. Silverstein. *The Nation* 249:776-7 D 25 '89
A return to democracy. M. Nemeth. il *Maclean's* 102:45 N 27 '89
Canada
See also subhead Politics and government under names of provinces and cities
The book on the backroom boys [book by Hugh Segal, Gerald Caplan and Michael Kirby] A. Fotheringham. il *Maclean's* 102:52 Ja 30 '89
Canadian conundrums: nationalism, socialism, and free trade. A. Stark. il *The American Spectator* 22:20-2 Ap '89
The Canadian election. *World Press Review* 36:12 Ja '89
Contest in Canada. L. K. Tarr. *Christianity Today* 33:48 Ja 13 '89
Fickle voters, new loyalties [Maclean's/Decima poll] R. Laver. il *Maclean's* 102:14-17 Ja 2 '89
Chile
The Chilean plebiscite: defeat of a dictator. A. Valenzuela and P. Constable. bibl f *Current History* 88:129-32+ Mr '89
A clown—and an anchorman—take on a dictator [TV ads] D. Marash. il *TV Guide* 37:28 F 25-Mr 3 '89
El Salvador
Adolf's heirs [electoral victory by Arena] A. Cockburn. *The Nation* 248:655 My 15 '89
Back burner, front burner. il *The Progressive* 53:8-9 My '89
Back to square one [ARENA party candidate A. Cristiani elected president] W. R. Doerner. il pors *Time* 133:28-9 Ap 3 '89
A done deal and an undone deal in Central America [right wing victory of A. Cristiani] C. A. Robbins and others. il por *U.S. News & World Report* 106:29 Ap 3 '89

ELECTIONS—El Salvador—*cont.*

Hanging in the balance: El Salvador's future & the limits of U.S. power. L. S. Robinson. il *Commonweal* 116:242-5 Ap 21 '89

Listening to the voices from El Salvador. *America* 160:315-16 Ap 8 '89

Notes and comment [death of cameraman Dutch C. Lagrouw while covering presidential election] *The New Yorker* 65:29-31 Ap 3 '89

One dilemma after another [right wing victory of A. Cristiani] D. Waller. il por *Newsweek* 113:32 Ap 3 '89

Presidential election held in El Salvador [White House statement, March 22, 1989] *Department of State Bulletin* 89:84 My '89

Sad new El Salvador. M. Massing. il *The New York Review of Books* 36:53-60 My 18 '89

A shift to the right. A. Bilski. il por *Maclean's* 102:27+ Ap 3 '89

The war continues. P. Lacefield. il *Commonweal* 116:197-9 Ap 7 '89

Great Britain

More than ever, Thatcher is odd woman out [defeat in the Europarliament vote] R. A. Melcher. il por *Business Week* p40 Jl 3 '89

Notes on Italy and England [elections to the European Parliament] W. Goodman. *The New Leader* 72:7-8 Je 12-26 '89

Greece

Caught in the labyrinth [A. Papandreou] il por *Time* 134:29 Jl 3 '89

Greece adrift. R. C. Carpenter. il *National Review* 41:17-18 D 8 '89

Scandal and stalemate. J. Bierman. por *Maclean's* 102:17 Jl 3 '89

Haiti

Beyond the mountains (I). M. Danner. maps *The New Yorker* 65:55-6+ N 27 '89

India

The end of a dynasty [R. Gandhi defeated] R. Moreau and S. Mazumdar. il pors *Newsweek* 114:60 D 11 '89

The end of a dynasty: voters reject Prime Minister Rajiv Gandhi. A. Bilski. il pors *Maclean's* 102:40-1 D 11 '89

The fall of the House of Nehru [V. P. Singh elected prime minister] L. Beyer. il pors *Time* 134:57 D 11 '89

No rerun for the Gandhi-dynasty show [V. P. Singh elected prime minister] E. MacFarquhar. il pors *U.S. News & World Report* 107:47-8 D 11 '89

Israel

Knesset comedown: Israeli women lose reps in fall election, but make points at polls. E. Burkett. *Ms.* 17:141 Ja/F '89

Letter from Israel. A. Elon. *The New Yorker* 64:74-80 F 13 '89

Shamir gets set for Washington [cover story] E. Salpeter. il *The New Leader* 72:6-8 Mr 6 '89

Italy

How the Italians see Europe. S. F. Senigallia. *The New Leader* 72:8 Je 12-26 '89

Notes on Italy and England [elections to the European Parliament] W. Goodman. *The New Leader* 72:7-8 Je 12-26 '89

Jamaica

After the storm [victory of M. Manley] P. Jordan. il *Commonweal* 116:261-3 My 5 '89

A comeback in Jamaica [with interview with M. Manley] E. Calonius. il por *Newsweek* 113:29 F 20 '89

Courting capitalism, Manley takes over in Jamaica. M. A. Fortune. il por *Black Enterprise* 19:38 My '89

Manley returns. M. Kaufman. *The Nation* 248:293 Mr 6 '89

Manley wins national election in Jamaica. il por *Jet* 75:14 F 27 '89

Once more, with moderation [M. Manley returned to power] G. D. Garcia. il por *Time* 133:48 F 20 '89

A sweet victory [M. Manley] A. Bilski. il por *Maclean's* 102:22 F 20 '89

Japan

Japan's new political activism [vote for upper house of parliament] M. Kanezashi. *World Press Review* 36:52-3 S '89

A mountain moves [results of vote for the upper house of parliament] J. Smolowe. il *Time* 134:24-6 Ag 7 '89

Sex, taxes and 'the Madonna factor' [T. Doi's Socialist Party wins parliamentary elections] J. Impoco. il por *U.S. News & World Report* 107:36 Ag 7 '89

The Socialists' stunning win. B. Powell and others. il *Newsweek* 114:33 Ag 7 '89

Upset in Japan [vote for upper house of parliament] H. Jensen. il pors *Maclean's* 102:22-3 Ag 7 '89

Jordan

Bye-bye moderates. por *Time* 134:50 N 20 '89

Jordan votes the Islamic ticket. S. Hubbell. il *The Nation* 249:786+ D 25 '89

Lebanon

Celebrations and bombs [R. Moawad elected president] A. Bilski. il por *Maclean's* 102:42-3 N 20 '89

Namibia

Bush names three blacks to observe Namibia elections; Shortage of ballots halts voting for some Namibians. il *Jet* 77:22 N 27 '89

The doves win. il *Time* 134:53 N 27 '89

A rebel victory. M. Nemeth. *Maclean's* 102:35 N 27 '89

Pakistan

Benazir Bhutto's victory. il *World Press Review* 36:11 Ja '89

Panama

Brute politics [U.S. dispatches additional troops following disputed election] A. Bilski. il por *Maclean's* 102:22-4 My 22 '89

A defiant dictator. B. Levin. il *Maclean's* 102:25 My 29 '89

Lead-pipe politics [U.S. sends troops to Panama in wake of election fraud; cover story; special section] il por map *Time* 133:40-4+ My 22 '89

A man, a plan, an election. K. E. Schuette. il *National Review* 41:18-19 Je 16 '89

Mr. Ex-President [J. Carter's visit] H. Hertzberg. *The New Republic* 200:4 Je 5 '89

Panama elections [statements, April 27-May 18, 1989] G. Bush. *Department of State Bulletin* 89:66-72 Jl '89

Panama, through Latin eyes. V. A. Palacios. il *World Press Review* 36:24+ Jl '89

Panama, United States swap charges before Security Council. il *UN Chronicle* 26:15 S '89

The perils of Panama. *Commonweal* 116:323-5 Je 2 '89

Standoff in Panama [M. A. Noriega vs U.S. after fraudulent election] J. L. Galloway. il por *U.S. News & World Report* 106:28-32 My 22 '89

T.R.'s invention [M. A. Noriega's election fraud] G. Black. *The Nation* 248:760-1 Je 5 '89

A test of wills [U.S. vs. Noriega government] L. Martz. il por map *Newsweek* 112:34-9 My 22 '89

U.S. severs diplomatic contact with Noriega regime [statement, September 1, 1989] G. Bush. *Department of State Bulletin* 89:69 N '89

Poland

Between issues [Solidarity's victory] A. Husarska. *The New Leader* 72:2 Je 12-26 '89

The defeated party plays for time. J. Baczynski and A. Krzeminski. *World Press Review* 36:29-30 Ag '89

A humiliation for the party [victory for Solidarity candidates] T. A. Sancton. il *Time* 133:24-6 Je 19 '89

I'm a Pole watcher. T. R. Swick. il *The American Spectator* 22:24-5 S '89

In Poland, if you can't beat them, ask them to join you [victory for Solidarity candidates] D. Stanglin. il *U.S. News & World Report* 106:30 Je 19 '89

Look who popped up on the firing line [W. Jaruzelski wins presidency] il por *U.S. News & World Report* 107:11 Jl 31 '89

Partnership for Poland? [Solidarity's victory] D. Singer. il *The Nation* 248:878-80 Je 26 '89

Poland's elections. *World Press Review* 36:10 Jl '89

Refolution in Hungary and Poland. T. Garton Ash. bibl f il *The New York Review of Books* 36:9-15 Ag 17 '89

Solidarity has no time to celebrate. G. E. Schares. il *Business Week* p46-7 Je 19 '89

Solidarity's many faces. K. Moore. il *Commonweal* 116:391-2 Jl 14 '89

Solidarity's stunning win. M. R. Meyer. il *Newsweek* 113:42-3 Je 19 '89

Something happened. C. Kiechel. *National Review* 41:23-4 Jl 14 '89

A stunning victory. A. Wilson-Smith. il *Maclean's* 102:18-19 Je 19 '89

'This farewell to communism'. E. Clemente. il *World Press Review* 36:28-9 Ag '89

South Africa

Botha vs. De Klerk: same song, different singer? F. D. Brown. il *Black Enterprise* 20:26 N '89

The divisions in South Africa get even deeper. J. Kapstein. il por *Business Week* p55 S 18 '89

'F.W.' brings cautious hope for reform [F. W. De Klerk] B. Schiller. *World Press Review* 36:30-1 N '89

The need to break the stalemate. M. Swilling. il por *World Press Review* 36:32 N '89

South Africa's violent rage [cover story; special section; with editorial comment by Kevin Doyle] il pors *Maclean's* 102:4, 32-6+ S 18 '89

Squeezed left, squeezed right [results of parliamentary elections] B. W. Nelan. il por *Time* 134:46-7 S 18 '89

Two cheers for moderation. S. Reiss. il *Newsweek* 114:31 S 18 '89

Soviet Union

Comrade Gorbachev's leap in the dark. *National Review* 41:13-14 Ap 21 '89

Counting the votes and the dead [cover story] K. Vanden Heuvel. il *The Nation* 248:505+ Ap 17 '89

Freedom of no choice. *The Nation* 248:505 Ap 17 '89

Late returns. H. Hertzberg. *The New Republic* 200:4+ Ap 17 '89

Let the joy be unconfined. W. F. Buckley. *National Review* 41:62-3 My 5 '89

ELECTIONS—Soviet Union—*cont.*

A message to Moscow. H. Anderson. il *Newsweek* 113:34-6 Ap 10 '89

New days that shake the world [cover story] D. Singer. il *The Nation* 248:577+ My 1 '89

People's choice. A. Wilson-Smith. il *Maclean's* 102:18-20 Ap 10 '89

Power to the people? J. Trimble. il *U.S. News & World Report* 106:41-3 Ap 10 '89

The Soviet election. il *World Press Review* 36:8 My '89

Soviet scientists rebel, Sakharov and Sagdeev elected to new Congress. W. Sweet. il *Physics Today* 42:65-6 My '89

The vote heard round the world. P. Galuszka. il por *Business Week* p26-7 Ap 10 '89

Spain

Shifting politics in Spain. J. Valls-Russell. il *The New Leader* 72:9-10 N 27 '89

Sri Lanka

Voting for peace. M. Nemeth. il por *Maclean's* 102:44-5 Ja 2 '89

United States

See Elections

Western Europe

Gains and losses [European Parliament election results] D. Singer. *The Nation* 249:41+ Jl 10 '89

ELECTIVE MUTISM

"We have a problem". J. Marks. il *Parents* 64:63-6 F '89

ELECTORAL COLLEGE

Helpful, useful antique. M. S. Forbes, Jr. *Forbes* 143:27 F 6 '89

ELECTRAMOTIVE INC.

Electramotive Nissan GTP. D. Fuller. il *Motor Trend* 41:128-32 Mr '89

ELECTRIC AUTOMOBILES *See* Automobiles, Electric

ELECTRIC BATTERIES

See also

Nuclear batteries

Storage batteries

Nicad batteries: important questions and some surprising answers [cameras] J. Bailey. il *Popular Photography* 96:42+ S '89

Portable power. J. Asher. il *Home Mechanix* 85:58-60+ D '89

Renewing bonds to recharge batteries [work of Lutgard C. De Jonghe] *Science News* 136:342 N 25 '89

Tales of a rewind crank, or Powerless in New Jersey. J. Schneider. il *Popular Photography* 96:35 My '89

Charging

How to recharge your gel-cell drive. M. Harner. il *Sky and Telescope* 78:97-9 Jl '89

Solar power supply. D. Becker. il *Radio-Electronics* 60:47-51 Ag '89

Patents

A costly lesson in patent law [case of A. M. Hermann] R. Pool. por *Science* 245:932 S 1 '89

Testing

Running on batteries [Company Seven battery pack for telescopes] D. Di Cicco. il *Sky and Telescope* 77:266-7 Mr '89

Speedotron accelerator [rechargeable battery pack for portable flash systems] il *Petersen's Photographic Magazine* 18:66 My '89

ELECTRIC BATTERY INDUSTRY

Canada

See also

Battery Technologies Inc.

China

China's headlong rush to capitalism [Battery Technologies of Canada] P. C. Newman. il *Maclean's* 102:38 Je 12 '89

ELECTRIC BLANKETS *See* Blankets, Electric

ELECTRIC CABLES

See also

Computer cables

Electric lines

Storage batteries—Booster cables

Television cables

Testing

American Reliance AR-6400P cable tester. il *Radio-Electronics* 60:22+ F '89

Cable tester. C. L. Rowe. il *Radio-Electronics* 60:73 Mr '89

ELECTRIC CAPACITORS

Capacitors (I). J. Bernard. il *Radio-Electronics* 60:49-53 My '89

Capacitors (II). J. Bernard. il *Radio-Electronics* 60:56-9 Ag '89

Condensers and tubes [for antique radios] R. D. Fitch. il *Radio-Electronics* 60:84-5 Ja '89

Picking filter capacitors. D. Lancaster. il *Radio-Electronics* 60:65-8 O '89

R-C decade box. M. Lashansky. il *Radio-Electronics* 60:39-42+ N '89

ELECTRIC CHAIR *See* Electrocution

ELECTRIC CHARGES

Forcing the details of contact charging [research by Bruce D. Terris] I. Peterson. *Science News* 136:406 D 23-30 '89

Optimum chemical sites and techniques for searches for negatively charged rare particles. R. N. Boyd and others. bibl f il *Science* 244:1450-7 Je 23 '89

ELECTRIC CIRCUIT BREAKERS

See also

Ground fault circuit interrupters

ELECTRIC CONDUCTORS AND CONDUCTIVITY

See also

Conductive polymers

Semiconductors

Superconductors and superconductivity

ELECTRIC CONTROL

See also

Electric switches

ELECTRIC CONTROL, REMOTE *See* Remote control

ELECTRIC CORDS

Now: an extension cord that can save your life [Guardian] R. Day. il *Popular Science* 234:36 My '89

ELECTRIC CURRENT CONVERTERS

See also

Electric current inverters

Frequency changers

Inside track. K. Best. *Travel Holiday* 171:86 F '89

ELECTRIC CURRENT INVERTERS

A.C. power without a generator [boats] B. Gladstone. il *Motor Boating & Sailing* 163:83-5 Je '89

ELECTRIC CURRENTS

See also

Eddy currents (Electric)

Hall effect

Transients (Electricity)

ELECTRIC DISCHARGES

The shocking surface of Io. *Science News* 136:143 Ag 26 '89

Surface discharges on natural dielectrics in the solar system. H. Campins and E. P. Krider. bibl f il *Science* 245:622-4 Ag 11 '89

ELECTRIC DISHWASHERS *See* Dishwashers

ELECTRIC DRILLS *See* Drilling and boring machinery

ELECTRIC EELS

Not guilty as charged [effect of eel skin wallets on credit card scrambling] il *Discover* 10:12 Mr '89

ELECTRIC ENGINEERING

See also

Frequency response (Electric engineering)

ELECTRIC EQUIPMENT

See also

Automobiles—Electric equipment

Boats and boating—Electric equipment

Electric generators

Remote control

Transducers

ELECTRIC FANS *See* Fans, Electric

ELECTRIC FENCES *See* Fences, Electric

ELECTRIC FIELDS

Physiological effects

See Electricity—Physiological effects

ELECTRIC FILTERS

Picking filter capacitors. D. Lancaster. il *Radio-Electronics* 60:65-8 O '89

ELECTRIC GENERATORS

See also

Airplanes, Light—Electric generators

Boats and boating—Electric generators

Portable generators. R. Freudenberger. il *The Mother Earth News* 119:88-91 S/O '89

ELECTRIC HEATERS *See* Heaters

ELECTRIC HOUSEHOLD APPLIANCES *See* Household appliances

ELECTRIC INDUSTRIES

See also

Baldor Electric Co.

Collective bargaining—Electric industries

Collective labor agreements—Electric industries

Electric utilities

Electronic industries

Emerson Electric Co.

General Electric Co.

General Signal Corp.

GTE Corp.

Kuhlman Corporation

Reliance Electric Co.

Square D Co.

Sundstrand Corporation

Telecom Electrical Supply Company

Westinghouse Electric Corp.

Great Britain

See also

General Electric Company plc

Japan

See also

Hitachi, Ltd.

Matsushita Electric Industrial Co. Ltd.

Toshiba Corporation

Netherlands

See also

Philips Industries, NV

ELECTRIC LAMPS
See also
Lighting fixtures

The artist and the businessman [arts and crafts lighting fixtures made by M. Adams] B. E. Johnson. il *Antiques & Collecting Hobbies* 94:44-5+ O '89

Boost your lighting IQ. N. Wing. il *Parents* 64:168-70 Je '89

Japanese glow lamps [made with rice paper] il *Sunset (Central West edition)* 182:74-5 F '89

No, it isn't a Tizio. P. Patton. il *Esquire* 111:30 F '89

Versatile swing-arm lamps. il *Southern Living* 24:174 Ap '89

Collectors and collecting
Pairpoint lamps. G. Michael. il *Antiques & Collecting Hobbies* 94:26 D '89

ELECTRIC LIGHT FIXTURES *See* Lighting fixtures
ELECTRIC LIGHTING *See* Lighting
ELECTRIC LINES
Environmental aspects
The hazards of electromagnetic fields (I). P. Brodeur. *The New Yorker* 65:51-2+ Je 12 '89

The hazards of electromagnetic fields (II). P. Brodeur. *The New Yorker* 65:47-9+ Je 19 '89

Power play [link between ELF fields and cancer; with editorial comment by Paul Hoffman] D. Noland. il *Discover* 10:4, 62-8 D '89

Rising tension over high-tension lines. P. Black. il *Business Week* p158-60 O 30 '89

Poles and towers
The knock on woodpeckers [efforts of electric companies to halt destruction] R. Wolkomir and J. Wolkomir. il *National Wildlife* 27:22-3 F/Mr '89

ELECTRIC MATTRESS PADS *See* Mattress pads
ELECTRIC MEASUREMENTS
See also
Electric meters
Strain gages

ELECTRIC METERS
See also
Multimeters
Spectrum analyzers

Digital capacitance meter. M. Lashansky. il *Radio-Electronics* 60:38-43 Jl '89

Sencore LC102 capacitance/inductance meter. il *Radio-Electronics* 60:17-18 Ap '89

ELECTRIC MOTORS
See also
Electric generators
Stepping motors

Control
See also
Frequency changers

ELECTRIC OUTBOARDS *See* Motor boat engines
ELECTRIC OUTLETS *See* Electric wire and wiring
ELECTRIC PLANTS
See also
Electric utilities
Hydroelectric plants
Nuclear power plants
Ocean thermal power plants

Energy usage
Compressed-air power. S. Ashley. il *Popular Science* 235:73 Ag '89

New ways to meet off-peak power demands [compressed air storage facilities flushed out of underground salt domes] il *Popular Mechanics* 166:15 Mr '89

Environmental aspects
All fired up [substituting natural gas for coal in a power plant] T. Mack. il *Forbes* 144:266 N 27 '89

Difficult days ahead [impact of Bush Clean Air proposals] D. Jenish. il *Maclean's* 102:42-3 Je 26 '89

Greenhouse gas. P. W. Huber. il por *Forbes* 144:226 O 30 '89

Membranes could remove coal pollutants. *High Technology Business* 9:38 Mr '89

Pollutant recovery techniques ready for use. il *Popular Mechanics* 166:14 S '89

Polluting rights [coal-fired electric power plants] E. Corcoran. il *Scientific American* 261:76+ N '89

Striving for balanced growth [address, May 16, 1989] T. R. Kuhn. *Vital Speeches of the Day* 55:637-40 Ag 1 '89

Study finds source of canyon haze [Navajo Generating Station near Grand Canyon] il *National Parks* 63:10 Jl/Ag '89

Interconnection
See Interconnected electric power systems
ELECTRIC PLUGS *See* Electric wire and wiring
ELECTRIC POWER
See also
Electric plants
Electric utilities
Hydroelectric power

Pacific Northwest
See also
Northwest Power Planning Council

ELECTRIC POWER, SOLAR *See* Solar energy
ELECTRIC POWER DISTRIBUTION
See also
Interconnected electric power systems
ELECTRIC POWER FAILURES
Get ready for power brownouts. P. Nulty. il map *Fortune* 119:116-18+ Je 5 '89

How brownouts could brighten funds that buy utilities. M. Meyer. il *Money* 18:47 Jl '89

Reliability of electric service. P. H. Abelson. *Science* 245:689 Ag 18 '89

ELECTRIC POWER LINES *See* Electric lines
ELECTRIC POWER PLANTS *See* Electric plants
ELECTRIC POWER PRODUCTION
See also
Electric plants
Energy cogeneration
Hydroelectric plants
Nuclear power plants
Ocean thermal power plants

ELECTRIC POWER SUPPLY *See* Electricity supply
ELECTRIC RELAYS
All about relays (I). H. L. Trietley. il *Radio-Electronics* 60:59-63+ N '89

All about relays (II). H. L. Trietley. il *Radio-Electronics* 60:59-62+ D '89

ELECTRIC RESISTORS
R-C decade box. M. Lashansky. il *Radio-Electronics* 60:39-42+ N '89

ELECTRIC SHAVERS *See* Razors
ELECTRIC SHOCK
See also
Electrocution

Behind the Invisible Fence [electronic boundary for dogs] L. Jenson. il *Home Mechanix* 85:72-3 Ag '89

Inescapable versus escapable shock modulates long-term potentiation in the rat hippocampus [evidence that controllability modulates plasticity] T. J. Shors and others. bibl f il *Science* 244:224-6 Ap 14 '89

Prevention
See also
Ground fault circuit interrupters

What's dangerous about electricity? D. Johnson. il *The Family Handyman* 39:22-5 F '89

ELECTRIC SHOCK TREATMENT *See* Shock therapy
ELECTRIC SIGNS
See also
Neon signs

ELECTRIC STANDARDS
New measurement standards for 1990 [cover story] B. N. Taylor. bibl f il *Physics Today* 42 pt1:23-6 Ag '89

ELECTRIC STOVES *See* Stoves
ELECTRIC SWITCHES
See also
Electric relays
Packet switching (Data transmission)
Telephone switching systems

Bilateral switches [CMOS switches] R. Marston. il *Radio-Electronics* 60:54-8 N '89

JVC audio/video selector [JX-S900U] il *Video* 13:30+ My '89

Remote A/B switch. R. A. Heil. il *Radio-Electronics* 60:37+ O '89

Replace a faulty switch. il *The Family Handyman* 39:50-1 S '89

Replacing a mixer switch. C. Maxwell. il *The Family Handyman* 39:76 Mr '89

Sony video/audio selector [SB-V1000] il *Video* 12:32+ F '89

ELECTRIC TOOLS *See* Tools
ELECTRIC TOOTHBRUSHES *See* Toothbrushes
ELECTRIC TRAINS *See* Railroad models
ELECTRIC TRANSMISSION
See also
Carrier current transmission
Electric lines

ELECTRIC UTILITIES
See also
Consolidated Edison Co. of New York, Inc.
Duke Power Co.
Gulf States Utilities Co.
Minnesota Power
Nevada Power Co.
Nuclear industry
Pacific Gas & Electric Co.
PacifiCorp
Pinnacle West Capital Corporation
Public Service Co. of N. H.
Texas Utilities Electric Company
Tucson Electric Power Co.
Utah Power & Light Co.
Washington Public Power Supply System

Acquisitions and mergers
Power goals [merger of Pacificorp and Utah Power & Light] J. Cook. il map *Forbes* 143:116-17 Ap 3 '89

PSNH: down to the last lines in Chapter 11. L. Jereski. il *Business Week* p36 O 2 '89

ELECTRIC UTILITIES—*cont.*

Energy usage

See Electric plants—Energy usage

Environmental aspects

See Electric plants—Environmental aspects

Finance

Demand-side economics [utilities promote conservation] P. Klebnikov. il *Forbes* 143:148+ Ap 3 '89

Electric utilities. E. F. Cone. il *Forbes* 143:132+ Ja 9 '89

Utilities are making more by selling less. C. Brown. il *Business Week* p90 Ja 9 '89

Laws and regulations

Adequate supply of electricity [address, May 22, 1989] D. Reed. *Vital Speeches of the Day* 55:687-90 S 1 '89

Regulation

See Electric utilities—Laws and regulations

Securities

How brownouts could brighten funds that buy utilities. M. Meyer. il *Money* 18:47 Jl '89

The new surge in power company stocks. S. Nasar. il *Fortune* 120:32 Jl 17 '89

Utility stocks can deliver a nasty shock. S. Woolley. *Business Week* p96 Jl 3 '89

Hawaii

See also

Hawaiian Electric Industries Inc.

ELECTRIC VEHICLES

See also

Automobiles, Electric

ELECTRIC WAVES

See also

Electromagnetic waves

Microwaves

ELECTRIC WIRE AND WIRING

See also

Automobile trailers—Electric wiring

Electric cords

Electric switches

Damaged electrical plugs. il *The Family Handyman* 39:69-70+ My '89

Electric service panel. M. Henkenius. il *Popular Mechanics* 166:82-3 D '89

Electricity: is your home office safe? il *Home Office Computing* 7:10 S '89

How to add electrical outlets. D. Prestly and A. Hildenbrand. il *The Family Handyman* 39:44-8 O '89

Install a recessed outdoor outlet. K. Childers and A. Hildenbrand. il *The Family Handyman* 39:82-3 Je '89

Power an outbuilding. M. Henkenius. il *Workbench* 45:42-4 My/Je '89

Run a new electrical outlet. A. Rooze. il *The Family Handyman* 39:78+ Ap '89

Testing

Circuit checker [SureTest] D. Petraglia. il *Popular Science* 234:32 Je '89

ELECTRIC WORKERS

See also

International Brotherhood of Electrical Workers

United Electrical, Radio and Machine Workers of America

ELECTRICAL MUSCLE STIMULATION

Charged-up muscles [electrical stimulation used in rehabilitation of fractures; research by Joseph Kahn] il *Prevention (Emmaus, Pa.)* 41:16-17 Ap '89

Martin Ergas: helping paraplegics keep fit [Therapeutic Technologies Inc.] I. Recio. il por *Business Week* p68 S 18 '89

Stimulating athletes [use by weight lifter Derrick Crass] il *Discover* 10:14 Mr '89

Waiting for the bionic man. R. Simon. il *Forbes* 144:204-5+ S 18 '89

ELECTRICITY

See also

Hall effect

Lightning

Transients (Electricity)

Keeping cool is hot work [use of electrical power contributes to global warming; views of Russell Valentine] il *USA Today (Periodical)* 117:12 Je '89

Art use

Current affairs [work of D. Archer] A. McDonald. il por *Omni (New York, N.Y.)* 11:66-71 S '89

Conservation

See Energy conservation

Physiological effects

See also

Electric shock

Electrotherapy

Ants get a transforming charge [affinity for electric fields; research by William P. MacKay] R. Weiss. *Science News* 136:412 D 23-30 '89

ELECTRICITY IN MEDICINE *See* Electrotherapy

ELECTRICITY IN THE HOME

See also

Electric wire and wiring

Electric service panel. M. Henkenius. il *Popular Mechanics* 166:82-3 D '89

Electrical system. D. Prestly. il *The Family Handyman* 39:62+ N/D '89

Conservation

See Energy conservation

ELECTRICITY SUPPLY

See also

Computers—Energy usage

Electronic equipment—Energy usage

Lasers—Energy usage

Adequate supply of electricity [address, May 22, 1989] D. Reed. *Vital Speeches of the Day* 55:687-90 S 1 '89

America is running out of power. P. C. Cruver. *USA Today (Periodical)* 118:62-3 Jl '89

The coming power crunch. K. R. Sheets. il map *U.S. News & World Report* 106:49-50 Je 19 '89

Compressed-air power. S. Ashley. il *Popular Science* 235:73 Ag '89

Demand-side economics [utilities promote conservation] P. Klebnikov. il *Forbes* 143:148+ Ap 3 '89

Get ready for power brownouts. P. Nulty. il map *Fortune* 119:116-18+ Je 5 '89

Improving the efficiency of electricity use in manufacturing. M. H. Ross. bibl f il *Science* 244:311-17 Ap 21 '89

Lighting the 21st century. P. C. Cruver. il por *The Futurist* 23:29-34 Ja/F '89

New ways to meet off-peak power demands [compressed air storage facilities flushed out of underground salt domes] il *Popular Mechanics* 166:15 Mr '89

Utilities are making more by selling less. C. Brown. il *Business Week* p90 Ja 9 '89

ELECTROBIOLOGY *See* Electrophysiology

ELECTROCARDIOGRAPHY

Computer analysis of the ECG. J. L. Willems. il *World Health* p21-3 Ag/S '89

ELECTROCHEMISTRY

An X-ray peek into electrochemistry [work of Owen R. Melroy] I. Peterson. *Science News* 135:77 F 4 '89

ELECTROCONVULSIVE THERAPY *See* Shock therapy

ELECTROCOPYING

Two views of electrocopying: the American experience. C. Risher and J. A. Baumgarten. por *Publishers Weekly* 236:52 Jl 14 '89

Two views of electrocopying: the international view. C. Clark. il por *Publishers Weekly* 236:53 Jl 14 '89

ELECTROCUTION

The Bundy carnival [electrocution in Florida] D. Gelman. il por *Newsweek* 113:66 F 6 '89

Burning question [T. Bundy] *The New Republic* 200:4+ F 20 '89

A condemned man's last bequest [execution of T. Bundy in Florida] P. Axthelm and M. Ryan. il pors *People Weekly* 31:44-51 F 6 '89

The execution of Ronnie Dunkins [electrocution in Alabama] D. Aukerman. il *The Christian Century* 106:783-5 Ag 30-S 6 '89

"I deserve punishment" [T. Bundy executed in Fla.] J. V. Lamar, Jr. il por *Time* 133:34 F 6 '89

A killer's final hour [T. Bundy] M. Nichols. il por *Maclean's* 102:54 F 6 '89

'This man has expired': witness to an execution [cover story] R. Johnson. il *Commonweal* 116:9-15 Ja 13 '89

ELECTRODEPOSITION OF METALS

Fashioning see-through metal [work of Charles R. Martin and Michael J. Tierney] *Science News* 136:31 Jl 8 '89

ELECTRODES

See also

Microelectrodes

Regenerated nerves send first messages. R. Weiss. il *Science News* 136:244 O 14 '89

ELECTRODES, BIOMEDICAL *See* Biosensors

ELECTRODYNAMICS

See also

Quantum electrodynamics

André-Marie Ampère. L. P. Williams. il por *Scientific American* 260:90-7 Ja '89

ELECTROENCEPHALOGRAMS *See* Electroencephalography

ELECTROENCEPHALOGRAPHY

See also

Brain waves

Is it healthy to be chaotic? R. Pool. bibl il *Science* 243:604-7 F 3 '89

Model of the origin of rhythmic population oscillations in the hippocampal slice. R. D. Traub and others. bibl f il *Science* 243:1319-25 Mr 10 '89

ELECTROLUX CORPORATION

Cleaning up. J. Zweig. il por *Forbes* 144:302 D 11 '89

ELECTROLYSIS (HAIR REMOVAL)

Electrolysis update. A. C. Mallozzi. *Good Housekeeping* 208:251 My '89

ELECTROLYTES

See also

Ionophores

ELECTROMAGNETIC INTERFERENCE *See* Electromagnetic waves

ELECTROMAGNETIC LAUNCHERS *See* Electromagnetic propulsion

ELECTROMAGNETIC PROPULSION
See also
Railguns
Railway to heaven [space train; research by Alvin Marks and Peter H. Diamandis] S. J. Nadis. il *Omni (New York, N.Y.)* 12:30+ N '89

ELECTROMAGNETIC THEORY
See also
Field theory (Physics)

ELECTROMAGNETIC WAVES
See also
Microwaves
Effects of the large June 1975 meteoroid storm on earth's ionosphere [very low frequency radio wave propagation anomalies] P. Kaufmann and others. bibl f il map *Science* 246:787-90 N 10 '89
HERF: a new hurdle for new aircraft. *Flying* 116:16 S '89
High-energy radiation field testing delays full certification of Starship 1. *Aviation Week & Space Technology* 131:91 Jl 17 '89
Noise-blocking wallcovering [Saf'n'Shielded] T. O. Bakke. il *Popular Science* 235:87 Jl '89
Noisy cosmic neighbors [interference from Soviet Glonass satellite] S. Vogel. il *Discover* 10:28 Ap '89
Nonlinear mixing of electromagnetic waves in plasmas. V. Stefan and others. bibl f il *Science* 243:494-500 Ja 27 '89
Sunrise and sunset affect frequency propagation. S. Leinwoll. il *Radio-Electronics* 60:87-8 F '89
Telescopes observe earth's atmosphere [research by Paul A. Bernhardt] il *Sky and Telescope* 78:129 Ag '89

Physiological effects
Are electric blankets safe? il *Consumer Reports* 54:715-16 N '89
The danger of ignoring non-ionizing radiation. L. Slesin. il *Technology Review* 92:22-3 Ja '89
Effects of electric and magnetic fields. P. H. Abelson. *Science* 245:241 Jl 21 '89
An electromagnetic storm [views of P. Brodeur] G. Cowley. il por *Newsweek* 114:77 Jl 10 '89
Electrophobia. P. W. Huber. por *Forbes* 144:313 S 4 '89
Feeling fatigued and forgetful? The power line next door may be the source of your burnout [interview with P. Brodeur] D. Mathison. il pors *People Weekly* 32:137-8+ N 27 '89
The hazards of electromagnetic fields (I). P. Brodeur. *The New Yorker* 65:51-2+ Je 12 '89
The hazards of electromagnetic fields (II). P. Brodeur. *The New Yorker* 65:47-9+ Je 19 '89
The hazards of electromagnetic fields (III). P. Brodeur. *The New Yorker* 65:39-42+ Je 26 '89
Panic over power lines. A. Toufexis. il *Time* 134:71 Jl 17 '89
Power play [link between ELF fields and cancer; with editorial comment by Paul Hoffman] D. Noland. il *Discover* 10:4, 62-8 D '89
Rising tension over high-tension lines. P. Black. il *Business Week* p158-60 O 30 '89
UFO update [Michael Persinger's theory that UFO investigation causes brain tumors] P. Huyghe. il *Omni (New York, N.Y.)* 11:73 F '89

ELECTROMAGNETISM
Heinrich Hertz and the development of physics. J. F. Mulligan. bibl f il por *Physics Today* 42:50-7 Mr '89

ELECTROMETALLURGY
See also
Electrodeposition of metals
High-voltage metallurgy [research team at North Carolina State University led by Hans Conrad] *High Technology Business* 9:12-13 N/D '89

ELECTRON BEAMS
See also
Aharonov-Bohm effect

Photographs and photography
Seeing is believing! [Echo 7 sounding rocket experiment photographs electrons spiraling around earth's magnetic field lines] il *Sky and Telescope* 77:130-1 F '89

ELECTRON MICROSCOPES
See also
Scanning electron microscopes
Scanning tunneling microscopes
Seeing cracks in three dimensions [work of David Carter] R. Pool. il *Science* 243:1293 Mr 10 '89

ELECTRON MOBILITY
HEMT devices could speed work on next-generation radar systems [high electron mobility transistors] B. D. Nordwall. il *Aviation Week & Space Technology* 130:65+ My 15 '89

ELECTRON OPTICS
See also
Image intensifiers

ELECTRON-POSITRON COLLIDERS See Accelerators (Electrons, etc.)
ELECTRON SPECTROSCOPY See Spectrum analysis
ELECTRON SPIN
George Uhlenbeck and the discovery of electron spin. A. Pais. bibl f il pors *Physics Today* 42:34-40 D '89

ELECTRON SPIN RESONANCE DATING (ARCHEOLOGY)
See Archeology—Methodology
ELECTRON TRANSFER REACTIONS
Dispersed polaron simulations of electron transfer in photosynthetic reaction centers. A. Warshel and others. bibl f il *Science* 246:112-16 O 6 '89
Mimicking photosynthesis. D. Gust and T. A. Moore. bibl f il *Science* 244:35-41 Ap 7 '89
Polar solvent dynamics and electron-transfer reactions. M. Maroncelli and others. bibl f il *Science* 243:1674-81 Mr 31 '89

ELECTRONEGATIVITY
Mapping the periodic landscape of elements [3-D periodic table proposed by Leland C. Allen] I. Amato. il *Science News* 136:390 D 16 '89
ELECTRONIC ALARMS See Alarms
ELECTRONIC BANKING See Computers—Banking use
ELECTRONIC BULLETIN BOARDS See Computer bulletin boards
ELECTRONIC CASH REGISTERS See Point-of-sale systems
ELECTRONIC CIRCUITS
See also
Integrated circuits
Printed circuits
Television circuits
Transistors

Design
The drawing board. R. Grossblatt. See issues of Radio-Electronics
ELECTRONIC COMMUNICATION See Telecommunication
ELECTRONIC COMPASS See Compass
ELECTRONIC COMPONENTS See Electronic equipment
ELECTRONIC CONTROL
See also
Camera shutters—Control
Household appliances—Control
Microcontrollers
Remote control
Television receivers—Control
Video games—Control
ELECTRONIC COUNTERMEASURES ON MILITARY AIRPLANES See Airplanes, Military—Electronic equipment
ELECTRONIC COUNTERS See Counting machines and devices
ELECTRONIC DATA PROCESSING
See also
Computers
Data entry
Data transmission systems
Distributed data processing
File organization (Computers)
Information systems
Online searching
Optical data processing
Parallel processing (Computers)
Data on the go [portable data terminals; cover story] G. T. Pope. il *High Technology Business* 9:16-19+ My '89
ELECTRONIC DATA PROCESSING DEPARTMENTS
See also
Offshore offices
ELECTRONIC DATA PROCESSING PERSONNEL See Computer personnel
ELECTRONIC DATA SYSTEMS CORP.
Breaking up is hard to do [G.M. vs. R. Perot] D. P. Levin. il pors *The New York Times Magazine* p36-7+ Mr 26 '89
EDS: how sweet it is to have a sugar daddy. K. Kelly. il *Business Week* p110-11 S 18 '89
Mort Meyerson is raring to slip the leash. K. Kelly. il por *Business Week* p58 S 11 '89
The Ross Perot riddle. L. Reibstein. il por *Newsweek* 113:38-9 Ja 9 '89
ELECTRONIC DETECTORS See Detectors
ELECTRONIC DISPLAY SYSTEMS See Information display systems
ELECTRONIC EQUIPMENT
See also
Automobiles—Electronic equipment
Automobiles, Police—Electronic equipment
Boats and boating—Electronic equipment
Computers
Home electronics
Intercom systems
Transducers
Hardware hacker. D. Lancaster. See issues of Radio-Electronics beginning January 1988
Minimum-order hassles [electronics parts] D. Lancaster. *Radio-Electronics* 60:26-7 Ap '89
New products. See issues of Radio-Electronics
Product reports 1990. il *Architectural Record* 177:163-6+ D '89
What's new in electronics. W. J. Hawkins. See issues of Popular Science

Anecdotes, facetiae, satire, etc.
Electronics 101, or Why you are so tired. K. Fury. il *Working Woman* 14:168 Mr '89

Energy usage
Power-supply woes. *Radio-Electronics* 60:12 Ja '89

ELECTRONIC EQUIPMENT—*cont.*
Prices
Panasonic gets zapped, too [price fixing case] *Newsweek* 113:54 Ja 30 '89
Testing
See also
Automatic test equipment
Equipment reports. See issues of Radio-Electronics
ELECTRONIC EQUIPMENT INDUSTRY *See* Electronic industries
ELECTRONIC FILING OF TAX RETURNS *See* Computers—Tax return use
ELECTRONIC FLIGHT INSTRUMENT SYSTEM DISPLAY *See* Airplanes, Military—Electronic equipment
ELECTRONIC FUNDS TRANSFER SYSTEMS *See* Computers—Banking use
ELECTRONIC GAMES
See also
Video games
ELECTRONIC IGNITION SYSTEMS *See* Gas and oil engines—Ignition
ELECTRONIC INDUSTRIES
See also
Allen-Bradley Co.
American Science & Engineering, Inc.
Analog Devices, Inc.
Anaren Microwave, Inc.
Audio equipment industry
Avantek, Inc.
Avionics industry
AVX Corp.
Bally Manufacturing Corp.
Bendix Corp.
Bipolar Integrated Technology (Firm)
Cartwright Electronics, Inc.
Chips and Technologies, Inc.
Cincinnati Microwave, Inc.
Cirrus Logic (Firm)
Commodore International Ltd.
Computer industry
Condor Systems, Inc.
Cubic Corp.
Cypress Semiconductor Corp.
Delfin Systems, Inc.
Eaton Corporation
Emerson Electric Co.
Emerson Radio Corp.
ESSI (Firm)
Fairchild Semiconductor Corporation
General Electric Co.
General Instrument Corp.
Genus Inc.
GM-Hughes Electronics Corporation
Gould Inc.
GTE Corp.
Harris Corp.
Hazeltine Corp.
Hercules Defense Electronics Systems (Firm)
Hewlett-Packard Co.
Honeywell Inc.
Hughes Aircraft Co.
Hypres Inc.
IEC Electronics Corp.
II Morrow Inc.
Intel Corp.
Kaiser Aerospace & Electronics Corp.
Kollmorgen Corp.
Loral Corp.
M/A-COM Inc.
Motorola, Inc.
National Semiconductor Corp.
Optex Corporation
Ovonic Imaging Systems Inc.
Physical Acoustics Corp.
RCA Corp.
Rockwell International Corp.
Sanders Associates, Inc.
Sedco Systems, Inc.
Sequential Information Systems Inc.
Silicon Systems, Inc.
Sundstrand Corporation
Tandy Corp.
Teledyne, Inc.
Television equipment industry
Texas Instruments Incorporated
Tracor, Inc.
United Silicon Structures (Firm)
Varian Associates, Inc.
Vitelic Corporation
Watkins-Johnson Co.
Western Digital Corp.
Westinghouse Electric Corp.
Westmark Systems, Inc.
Zenith Electronics Corp.
The chip makers call, but no cavalry rides to the rescue. M. Sun. il *Science* 246:1240-1 D 8 '89
Electronic intelligence. See issues of Aviation Week & Space Technology beginning June 6, 1988

So long, silicon [end of U.S. silicon wafer manufacturing] E. Corcoran. *Scientific American* 260:84 Je '89
View from the Valley. S. R. Reed. See issues of Personal Computing beginning June 1987 through November 1989
Who's afraid of the Japanese? [semiconductor industry; views of G. Gilder] P. Elmer-Dewitt. il por *Time* 134:102+ O 23 '89
Will corporate myopia mean goodbye, U.S. chips? [semiconductor industry] P. Dworkin. il *U.S. News & World Report* 107:36+ D 18 '89

Acquisitions and mergers
International aspects
A case of culture shock along the Wabash [aftermath of GE's sale of consumer electronics division to Thomson SA] L. Therrien. il *Business Week* p102 My 15 '89
Investors' yen for U.S. technology. M. Sun. il *Science* 246:1238-41 D 8 '89
Matsushita may tune in to cable [possible bid for General Instrument] G. G. Marcial. *Business Week* p76 Ja 30 '89
Possible Japanese buyout of U.S. chip equipment manufacturer draws fire [Perkin-Elmer Corp. unit; with editorial comment] B. D. Nordwall. il *Aviation Week & Space Technology* 131:9, 26-7 D 4 '89
Sprechen sie high tech? [foreign buyers love U.S. technology companies] N. Alster. il *Forbes* 143:172-4+ Ap 17 '89
Great Britain
British-French bid to buy GEC fails after AT&T refuses to join. *Aviation Week & Space Technology* 130:30 Ja 23 '89
British Monopolies panel approves GEC/Siemens offer for Plessey. *Aviation Week & Space Technology* 130:39 My 1 '89
Electronics firms maneuver to gain from GEC, Plessey takeover bids. D. A. Brown. *Aviation Week & Space Technology* 130:25+ Ja 16 '89
For Plessey, a gutsy offense may be its best defense [bid for predator GEC] M. Maremont. *Business Week* p52+ Ja 23 '89
GEC, Siemens renew their bid to buy Plessey. *Aviation Week & Space Technology* 131:34 Ag 14 '89
GEC, Siemens win bid to take over Plessey. *Aviation Week & Space Technology* 131:31 S 18 '89
Western Europe
British Aerospace, Thomson-CSF consider making joint bid for Ferranti International Signal. *Aviation Week & Space Technology* 131:32 O 16 '89
Antitrust cases
Panasonic gets zapped, too [price fixing case] *Newsweek* 113:54 Ja 30 '89
Cooperation
See also
JESSI Project
Sematech
U.S. Memories Inc.
Can consortiums defeat Japan? L. Smith. il *Fortune* 119:245-6+ Je 5 '89
High tech's united front [consortiums] A. Gabor. il *U.S. News & World Report* 107:43-5 Jl 10 '89
A transatlantic Mexican standoff [exclusion of foreign-owned firms from research consortiums] D. Dickson. il *Science* 245:245-6 Jl 21 '89
Environmental aspects
Highest disregard [use of CFCs by the electronics industry] D. Hayes. il *Mother Jones* 14:32-6+ D '89
Ethical aspects
Ferranti defends health of primary business, despite contract irregularities at subsidiary [ISC Technologies] *Aviation Week & Space Technology* 131:30 S 25 '89
The sad saga of a penny-stock company [Sequential Information Systems Inc.] G. Weiss. il por *Business Week* p124-6+ My 15 '89
Export-import trade
The EC just says no to Japan's cheap chips. T. Peterson. il *Business Week* p46-7 Ja 30 '89
Has the Orient totally conquered U.S. electronics? Seven companies say no [cover story] M. C. Lehrer. il *USA Today (Periodical)* 117:16-22 Ja '89
Honest, Japan would love to buy American chips . . . N. Gross. il *Business Week* p92 Jl 10 '89
Let's make a deal, comrade [Fairchild Semiconductor's trade negotiations with Hungary] *High Technology Business* 9:17 Jl/Ag '89
The rival Japan respects [Motorola; cover story] L. Therrien. il pors *Business Week* p108-10+ N 13 '89
Silicon Valley is watching its worst nightmare unfold [losing competitiveness in chips and chipmaking equipment] R. D. Hof and N. Gross. il *Business Week* p63+ S 4 '89
Trade protection comes to Silicon Valley. A. T. Denzau. *Society* 26:38-42 Mr/Ap '89
U.S. chips are down [dynamic random access memory] M. Mandell. il *High Technology Business* 9:12 Mr '89
Federal aid
See also
Sematech
Study says federal commitment needed to save U.S. chip industry. B. D. Nordwall. il *Aviation Week & Space Technology* 131:24+ N 27 '89

ELECTRONIC INDUSTRIES—*cont.*

Finance

Computers and electronics. M. Beauchamp. il *Forbes* 143:114-16 Ja 9 '89

Electrical equipment. A. A. Lappen. il *Forbes* 143:128-9 Ja 9 '89

The graying of Silicon Valley. P. Dworkin. il *U.S. News & World Report* 107:44-6 O 2 '89

This time, the cycle won't be quite so vicious for chipmakers. R. Brandt. il *Business Week* p95 Ja 9 '89

International aspects

A transatlantic Mexican exclusion [exclusion of foreign-owned firms from research consortiums] D. Dickson. il *Science* 245:245-6 Jl 21 '89

What's behind the Texas Instruments-Hitachi deal. O. Port and T. Mason. il *Business Week* p93+ Ja 16 '89

Management

Has the Orient totally conquered U.S. electronics? Seven companies say no [cover story] M. C. Lehrer. il *USA Today (Periodical)* 117:16-22 Ja '89

Where are the microchip billionaires? G. F. Gilder. il *Forbes* 144 Special Issue:378-80+ O 23 '89

Marketing

Intel to Motorola: race ya [new 860 chip] O. Port. il *Business Week* p42 Mr 13 '89

Minimum-order hassles [electronics parts] D. Lancaster. *Radio-Electronics* 60:26-7 Ap '89

Quality control

Westinghouse gets respect at last. T. A. Stewart. il *Fortune* 120:92-4+ Jl 3 '89

What Motorola learns from Japan. R. Henkoff. il *Fortune* 119:157+ Ap 24 '89

Securities

Modernizing your defense portfolio. A. Ramirez. il *Fortune* 119:32 F 27 '89

France

See also
Thomson-C S F

French electro-optic, IR firms to bid on U.S. aircraft carrier systems. B. D. Nordwall. il *Aviation Week & Space Technology* 130:89+ My 8 '89

Germany (West)

See also
Siemens AG

Great Britain

See also
Ferranti plc
General Electric Company plc
Marconi Co. Ltd.
Plessey Co. plc
Thorn E M I plc

Ireland

Why Irish eyes are smiling [attracting American electronics firms] J. Ames. *U.S. News & World Report* 107:47 Jl 10 '89

Israel

Israel has everything it needs—except peace. J. Rossant. il *Business Week* p54+ D 4 '89

Japan

See also
Hitachi, Ltd.
Matsushita Electric Industrial Co. Ltd.
NEC Corp.
Panasonic Company
Pioneer Electronic Corp.
Sony Corp.

Can consortiums defeat Japan? L. Smith. il *Fortune* 119:245-6+ Je 5 '89

Silicon Valley is watching its worst nightmare unfold [losing competitiveness in chips and chipmaking equipment] R. D. Hof and N. Gross. il *Business Week* p63+ S 4 '89

U.S. chips are down [dynamic random access memory] M. Mandell. il *High Technology Business* 9:12 Mr '89

What Motorola learns from Japan. R. Henkoff. il *Fortune* 119:157+ Ap 24 '89

Korea (South)

Outshining the Rising Sun. M. Brien. il *High Technology Business* 9:13 F '89

Netherlands

See also
Philips Industries, NV

Taiwan

Brain drain in reverse [Taiwan's U.S.-trained returnees] A. Tanzer. il *Forbes* 143:114-15 Ap 17 '89

Taiwan goes for broke on semiconductors. D. J. Yang. il *Business Week* p90+ Ag 14 '89

United States

See Electronic industries

Western Europe

See also
European Silicon Structures (Firm)
JESSI Project

ELECTRONIC LEVELS (TOOLS) *See* Levels (Tools)

ELECTRONIC LOCKS *See* Locks and keys

ELECTRONIC MAIL SYSTEMS

See also
Computer bulletin boards
United States Postal Service—Automation

Voice mail systems

E-mail for LANs: redefining corporate networking. E. Kay. il *Personal Computing* 13:127-31 N '89

Electronic mail: neither rain, nor sleet, nor software . . . F. Seghers. il *Business Week* p36 F 20 '89

Fax it by modem. A. Glossbrenner. il *Home Office Computing* 7:38 O '89

The mailman cometh. M. L. Van Name and B. Catchings. il *Byte* 14:143-4+ S '89

Neither rain, nor sleet, nor computer glitches . . . J. Rothfeder. il *Business Week* p135+ My 8 '89

Prepare for E-mail attack [cover story] D. Churbuck. il *Forbes* 143:82-3+ Ja 23 '89

Sending information from here to there. A. Glossbrenner. il *Home Office Computing* 7:34-5 Mr '89

Rates

E-mail economics. B. N. Meeks. il *Byte* 14:151-2+ Ap '89

Standards

Let your modem do the walking. D. Churbuck. il *Forbes* 143:280 My 29 '89

ELECTRONIC MARKETING

See also
Computer Express, Inc.
Hot Net (Firm)
Interactive marketing
Marketel International Inc.

Computers may turn the world into one big commodities pit. R. Kuttner. il *Business Week* p17 S 11 '89

Direct marketing [home computer business] J. B. Lambert. *Compute!* 11:25 Ag '89

Doing business with videotex [Artec Inc.'s use of Prodigy network in video cassette marketing] M. Antonoff. il *Personal Computing* 13:77 My '89

Sales aid for cold callers [Maximizer] L. Wood. il *Home Office Computing* 7:88+ D '89

Stealing the right shoppers [expanding market share] J. Levine. *Forbes* 144:104-5 Jl 10 '89

Sweet success in sales automation [Godiva Chocolatier] J. Pepper. il *Working Woman* 14:59-60+ Ap '89

Technology and direct marketing [address, June 8, 1989] W. B. Wriston. *Vital Speeches of the Day* 55:678-80 S 1 '89

ELECTRONIC MEASUREMENTS

See also
Biotelemetry

ELECTRONIC MEDIA RATING COUNCIL

An aging watchdog. M. Couzens. il *Channels (New York, N.Y.: 1986)* 9:12 Jl/Ag '89

ELECTRONIC MUSIC *See* Music, Electronic

ELECTRONIC MUSIC SYNTHESIZERS *See* Musical instruments, Electronic

ELECTRONIC MUSICAL INSTRUMENTS *See* Musical instruments, Electronic

ELECTRONIC NOISE

See also
Amplifiers—Noise
Audio systems—Noise
Compact discs—Noise
Tape recorders and recording—Noise
Videotape recorders and recording—Noise

ELECTRONIC NOVELS *See* Computer novels

ELECTRONIC OVENS *See* Microwave ovens

ELECTRONIC PARTS *See* Electronic equipment

ELECTRONIC PICTURE BOOKS FOR CHILDREN *See* Computer picture books for children

ELECTRONIC PISTOLS *See* Pistols

ELECTRONIC PUBLISHING

See also
Computers—Publishing use
Desktop publishing
Information systems

ELECTRONIC SHOPPING

See also
Home Shopping Network Inc.
QVC Network Inc.

Closing up shop, setting up shop. M. Couzens. il *Channels (New York, N.Y.: 1986)* 9:80-1 D '89

Penney isn't the only casualty in high-tech home shopping. B. Bremner. il *Business Week* p90 Ap 17 '89

Shop around. H. E. H. Aycock. il *Compute!* 11:41-2 Ap '89

Splurge through the tube [cable television shows] S. McKee. il *American Health* 8:60 Mr '89

ELECTRONIC SIRENS *See* Sirens

ELECTRONIC SURVEILLANCE *See* Electronics in criminal investigation, espionage, etc.

ELECTRONIC TYPEWRITERS *See* Typewriters, Electronic

ELECTRONIC WARFARE *See* Electronics—Military use; Superconductors and superconductivity—Military use

ELECTRONICS

See also
Cybernetics
Digital electronics
Home electronics
Microelectronics
Molecular electronics
Optoelectronics
Pulse techniques (Electronics)

ELECTRONICS—See also—*cont.*
Semiconductors
Transistors
Electronics. See issues of *Popular Mechanics* beginning June 1984
Electronics newsfront. W. J. Hawkins. See issues of *Popular Science* beginning February 1986

Military use
See also
Aircraft carriers—Electronic equipment
Airplanes, Military—Electronic equipment
Cartwright Electronics, Inc.
Communications satellites—Military use
Computers—Military use
Condor Systems, Inc.
Delfin Systems, Inc.
ESSI (Firm)
Ferranti plc
Hercules Defense Electronics Systems (Firm)
Loral Corp.
Sanders Associates, Inc.
Sedco Systems, Inc.
Watkins-Johnson Co.
Westmark Systems, Inc.
Defense Dept. contracts to spur use of digital GaAs microcircuits. P. J. Klass. *Aviation Week & Space Technology* 130:283-4 Je 12 '89
Defense electronic industry expects little sales growth. D. Hughes. il *Aviation Week & Space Technology* 130:66+ My 29 '89
Electronic intelligence. See issues of *Aviation Week & Space Technology* beginning June 6, 1988
Electronic warfare (I) [cover story; special section; with editorial comment] il *Aviation Week & Space Technology* 131:19, 44-7+ S 11 '89
Electronic warfare (II) [cover story; special section] il *Aviation Week & Space Technology* 131:84-5+ S 18 '89
Harris unit develops advanced GaAs facility to supply MMICs to military [gallium arsenide monolithic microwave integrated circuits] B. W. Henderson. il *Aviation Week & Space Technology* 130:101+ Ap 24 '89
High-tech weapons are coming under friendly fire. D. Griffiths. il *Business Week* p118 My 22 '89
Military systems use new communications technologies. il *Aviation Week & Space Technology* 131:50-1 O 30 '89
Modernizing your defense portfolio. A. Ramirez. il *Fortune* 119:32 F 27 '89
A new generation of 'smart' weapons. il *Newsweek* 113:14-15 Ja 23 '89
Powerful light computers hold key to sensor, smart weapon research. P. A. Gilmartin. il *Aviation Week & Space Technology* 130:57+ Mr 20 '89

ELECTRONICS, AUTOMOTIVE *See* Automobiles—Electronic equipment

ELECTRONICS IN AGRICULTURE
High-tech animal husbandry. J. E. Bahls. il *High Technology Business* 9:22-4+ S/O '89

ELECTRONICS IN CRIMINAL INVESTIGATION, ESPIONAGE, ETC.
See also
Computers—Espionage use
Lasers in criminal investigation, espionage, etc.
Wiretapping
Anti-terrorism networks. S. R. A. Crawshaw. il por *The Futurist* 23:12-13 Mr/Ap '89

ELECTRONICS IN FISHING
See also
Depth indicators
Worm and remembrance [Consumer Product Safety Commission's recall of Worm Gett'r, an electronic worm probe for fishermen] W. J. Elvin. il *The American Spectator* 22:30-1 Ja '89

ELECTRONICS IN MEDICINE *See* Medical electronics
ELECTRONICS IN PHOTOGRAPHY *See* Photography—Electronic equipment
ELECTRONICS INDUSTRY *See* Electronic industries
ELECTRONICS RESEARCH
See also
Microelectronics and Computer Technology Corporation
Sematech
Can consortiums defeat Japan? L. Smith. il *Fortune* 119:245-6+ Je 5 '89
High tech's united front [consortiums] A. Gabor. il *U.S. News & World Report* 107:43-5 Jl 10 '89
A transatlantic Mexican standoff [exclusion of foreign-owned firms from research consortiums] D. Dickson. il *Science* 245:245-6 Jl 21 '89

ELECTRONICS STORES
See also
Crazy Eddie Inc.
Good Guys Inc.

Ethical aspects
Cat 'n mouse tips for dealing with audio/video salespeople [cover story] G. Brockhouse. il *High Fidelity (New York, N.Y.)* 39:40-3+ Mr '89

ELECTRONICS WORKERS
See also
Labor unions—Electronics workers

Women electronics workers
ELECTRONS
See also
Free electron lasers
Positrons
Electron superconductors challenge theories, start a new race. A. Khurana. bibl f il *Physics Today* 42:17-19 Ap '89
Electrons may shed light for X-ray lasers [research by David B. Chang and James C. McDaniel] R. Cowen. *Science News* 136:183 S 16 '89
Energetic electrons and ozone loss. R. Monastersky. *Science News* 135:335 My 27 '89
New superconductor uses electrons [research by Y. Tokura and others] R. Pool. *Science* 243:741 F 10 '89
Superconductors with electrons in charge [discovered by Yoshi Tokura] *Science News* 135:143 Mr 4 '89
Update on electron superconductors. R. Pool. *Science* 243:1436 Mr 17 '89

Beams
See Electron beams
Energy levels
See Energy levels (Quantum mechanics)
Mobility
See Electron mobility
Scattering
See also
Aharonov-Bohm effect
Spin
See Electron spin

ELECTROOSMOSIS
Plug-in pollution control. J. Free. il *Popular Science* 234:31 My '89

ELECTROPHORESIS
Generalized tube model of biased reptation for gel electrophoresis of DNA. J. Noolandi and others. bibl f il *Science* 243:1456-8 Mr 17 '89
Microcolumn separations and the analysis of single cells [capillary zone electrophoresis and open tubular liquid chromatography] R. T. Kennedy and others. bibl f il *Science* 246:57-63 O 6 '89
Observation of individual DNA molecules undergoing gel electrophoresis. S. B. Smith and others. bibl f il *Science* 243:203-6 Ja 13 '89
Understanding the anomalous electrophoresis of bent DNA molecules: a reptation model [polyacrylamide gel electrophoresis] S. D. Levene and B. H. Zimm. bibl f il *Science* 245:396-9 Jl 28 '89

ELECTROPHYSIOLOGY
See also
Biomuse system
Electricity—Physiological effects
Electrocardiography
Electroencephalography
Activity-dependent enhancement of presynaptic inhibition in Aplysia sensory neurons. S. A. Small and others. bibl f il *Science* 243:1603-6 Mr 24 '89
Central synaptic inputs to identified leech neurons determined by peripheral targets. C. M. Loer and W. B. Kristan, Jr. bibl f il *Science* 244:64-6 Ap 7 '89
Clot-busters bring bioelectrical benefits [research by Eli S. Gang and others] R. Weiss. *Science News* 136:182 S 16 '89
Corticosteroid modulation of hippocampal potentials: increased effect with aging. D. S. Kerr and others. bibl f il *Science* 245:1505-9 S 29 '89
Does voltage affect excitation-contraction coupling in the heart? [discussion of May 19, 1989 article, Regulation of calcium release is gated by calcium current, not gating charge, in cardiac myocytes] M. Näbauer and others. bibl f *Science* 246:1640 D 22 '89
Effect of serotonergic afferents on quantal release at central inhibitory synapses. I. Mintz and others. bibl f il *Science* 245:190-2 Jl 14 '89
Electrophysiologic responses in hamster superior colliculus evoked by regenerating retinal axons. S. A. Keirstead and others. bibl f il *Science* 246:255-7 O 13 '89
Ethanol inhibits NMDA-activated ion current in hippocampal neurons. D. M. Lovinger and others. bibl f il *Science* 243:1721-4 Mr 31 '89
Gating of retinal transmission by afferent eye position and movement signals [cats] R. Lal and M. J. Friedlander. bibl f il *Science* 243:93-6 Ja 6 '89
Indole-2-carboxylic acid: a competitive antagonist of potentiation by glycine at the NMDA receptor. J. E. Huettner. bibl f il *Science* 243:1611-13 Mr 24 '89
Inescapable versus escapable shock modulates long-term potentiation in the rat hippocampus [evidence that controllability modulates plasticity] T. J. Shors and others. bibl f il *Science* 244:224-6 Ap 14 '89
Inhibition of postsynaptic PKC or CaMKII blocks induction but not expression of LTP. R. Malinow and others. bibl f il *Science* 245:862-6 Ag 25 '89
Long-term potentiation in the motor cortex. A. Iriki and others. bibl f il *Science* 245:1385-7 S 22 '89
Memory in a neuron [associative learning in Hermissenda; work of Daniel L. Alkon] J. Kinoshita. *Scientific American* 260:28+ Ja '89

ELECTROPHYSIOLOGY—*cont.*

Mental rotation of the neuronal population vector [motor cortex of monkeys] A. P. Georgopoulos and others. bibl f il *Science* 243:234-6 Ja 13 '89

Modulation of calcium channels in cardiac and neuronal cells by an endogenous peptide. G. Callewaert and others. bibl f il *Science* 243:663-6 F 3 '89

Modulation of rod-cone coupling by light. X.-L. Yang and S. M. Wu. bibl f il *Science* 244:352-4 Ap 21 '89

Molecules of memory [neurobiologist E. R. Kandel's work with Aplysia; cover story] G. Montgomery. il por *Discover* 10:46-50+ D '89

Monkey think, monkey do [mental rotation of neuronal population vector in motor cortex; work of Apostolos Georgopoulos] L. Oliwenstein. il *Discover* 10:20 Je '89

Odor-induced membrane currents in vertebrate-olfactory receptor neurons. S. Firestein and F. Werblin. bibl f il *Science* 244:79-82 Ap 7 '89

A pertussis toxin-sensitive G protein in hippocampal long-term potentiation. J. W. Goh and P. S. Pennefather. bibl f il *Science* 244:980-3 My 26 '89

Protection of dentate hilar cells from prolonged stimulation by intracellular calcium chelation. H. E. Scharfman and P. A. Schwartzkroin. bibl f il *Science* 246:257-60 O 13 '89

Receptor encounters: untangling the threads of the serotonin system. R. Cowen. il *Science News* 136:248-50+ O 14 '89

Regenerated nerves send first messages. R. Weiss. il *Science News* 136:244 O 14 '89

Regulation of calcium concentration in voltage-clamped smooth muscle cells. P. L. Becker and others. bibl f il *Science* 244:211-14 Ap 14 '89

Regulation of calcium release is gated by calcium current, not gating charge, in cardiac myocytes. M. Näbauer and others. bibl f il *Science* 244:800-3 My 19 '89

Spatial buffering of light-evoked potassium increases by retinal Müller (Glial) cells. C. J. Karwoski and others. bibl f il *Science* 244:578-80 My 5 '89

Spatial selectivity of rat hippocampal neurons: dependence on preparedness for movement. T. C. Foster and others. bibl f il *Science* 244:1580-2 Je 30 '89

Switching of a neuron from one network to another by sensory-induced changes in membrane properties [lobsters] S. L. Hooper and M. Moulins. bibl f il *Science* 244:1587-9 Je 30 '89

Synapse formation in the developing brain. R. E. Kalil. bibl il *Scientific American* 261:76-9+ D '89

Synaptic connections in vitro: modulation of number and efficacy by electrical activity. P. G. Nelson and others. bibl f il *Science* 244:585-7 My 5 '89

Thinking in circles [mental rotation of neuronal population vector in monkey motor cortex; work of Apostolos Georgopoulos] T. Appenzeller. *Scientific American* 260:26-7 Mr '89

Tonic activation of NMDA receptors by ambient glutamate enhances excitability of neurons. P. Sah and others. bibl f il *Science* 246:815-18 N 10 '89

Two molecular transitions influence cardiac sodium channel gating. D. T. Yue and others. bibl f il *Science* 244:349-52 Ap 21 '89

ELECTROPLATING
> *See also*
> Electrodeposition of metals

ELECTRORHEOLOGICAL FLUIDS

"Smart fluids" control hydraulic equipment. *Radio-Electronics* 60:4 S '89

"Smart fluids": wavelet of the future? M. Mandell. il *High Technology Business* 9:20-3 Jl/Ag '89

Smart materials. S. R. Tessler. il *Technology Review* 92:8-9 Ap '89

ELECTROSTATICS
> *See also*
> Electric charges
> Electric discharges

ELECTROTHERAPY
> *See also*
> Electrical muscle stimulation
> Shock therapy

Precious metals: sutures with silver . . . [work of Chih-Chang Chu] *Science News* 136:223 S 30 '89

ELECTROWEAK INTERACTIONS

The unification of electromagnetism with the weak force. P. Langacker and A. K. Mann. bibl f il *Physics Today* 42:22-31 D '89

ELEEMOSYNARY [drama] *See* Blessing, Lee

ELEKTRA/ASYLUM RECORDS

Elektra comes on strong. F. Goodman. il *Rolling Stone* p37 F 9 '89

ELEMENTARY EDUCATION
> *See also*
> Alcohol education
> Arts—Study and teaching
> Citizenship education
> Drug education
> English language—Composition
> Language arts—Study and teaching
> Moral education

> Reading—Study and teaching
> Satellite learning centers
> Science—Study and teaching
> Social sciences—Study and teaching
> Theater—Study and teaching

Adjusting to changing families [survey by the National Association of Elementary School Principals] il *USA Today (Periodical)* 118:11 D '89

After a year as a fifth-grade Gulliver, author Tracy Kidder speaks up for teachers [writes book about C. Zajac's class in Holyoke, Mass.] K. Hubbard. il pors *People Weekly* 32:77+ O 9 '89

First days in first grade. P. La Farge. il pors *Parents* 64:104-8+ S '89

From 'House' to schoolhouse [T. Kidder's study of C. Zajac, fifth grade teacher in Holyoke, Mass.] C. Leslie. il por *Newsweek* 114:67 S 11 '89

How kids learn [cover story; special section] B. Kantrowitz and P. Wingert. il *Newsweek* 113:50-7 Ap 17 '89

The primal scene of education [curriculum] E. D. Hirsch. bibl f il *The New York Review of Books* 36:29-35 Mr 2 '89

'The primal scene of education': an exchange [discussion of March 2, 1989 article] E. D. Hirsch. il *The New York Review of Books* 36:50 Ap 13 '89

Primary education [Council of Europe report] M. G. Bruce. il *Phi Delta Kappan* 71:82-3 S '89

PW interviews [T. Kidder, author of book about fifth grade class in Holyoke, Mass.] A. Smith. por *Publishers Weekly* 236:101-2 S 15 '89

ELEMENTARY PARTICLES *See* Particles (Nuclear physics)
ELEMENTARY SCHOOL TEACHERS *See* Teachers
ELEPHANT HUNTING
> **Anecdotes, facetiae, satire, etc.**

Pachydermic personnel prediction. P. C. Olsen. il *Byte* 14:404 S '89

ELEPHANT POACHING *See* Poaching
ELEPHANT SEALS *See* Seals (Animals)
ELEPHANT TOKENS *See* Tokens
ELEPHANTS

Africa is becoming an elephant graveyard. W. Booth. il *Science* 243:732 F 10 '89

A ban on ivory. M. Nichols. il *Maclean's* 102:86 O 30 '89

Big-game forensics [use of DNA fingerprinting to discourage elephant poaching] J. Horgan. il *Scientific American* 261:27+ D '89

Decision time on African ivory trade. J. Cherfas. il *Science* 246:26-7 O 6 '89

Elephant talk [cover story] K. Payne. il maps *National Geographic* 176:264-77 Ag '89

Elephants in Alaska [handicrafts made from poached African ivory] F. Graham. *Audubon* 91:27-9 S '89

Elephants look best in ivory [ban on imports] L. Troiano. il *American Health* 8:92 O '89

Endangered species: can they be saved? [African elephants; cover story] W. F. Allman. il map *U.S. News & World Report* 107:52-8 O 2 '89

Global ban sought on ivory trade [to save elephants] R. Lewin. il *Science* 244:1135 Je 9 '89

Heavy artillery for horns of plenty [Kenya's war on ivory poachers] E. Ransdell. il *U.S. News & World Report* 106:61+ F 20 '89

How to save the African elephant [economic incentives] M. S. Forbes, Jr. *Forbes* 144:29 N 13 '89

In the African interior, the ivory trade and the slave trade helped each other become paying propositions. R. M. Adams. il *Smithsonian* 19:14 Mr '89

International tusk politics. *Science News* 136:94 Ag 5 '89

The ivory dispute [African countries in opposition to trade ban] F. Bridgland. *World Press Review* 36:69 S '89

Kenya burns $3 mil. in ivory to stop its trade. il *Jet* 76:18 Ag 7 '89

Last stand for Africa's elephants [ivory poaching] E. Linden. il *Time* 133:76-7 F 20 '89

Outlawing ivory [U.S. ban in order to save elephants] il *Time* 133:62 Je 19 '89

Pachyderm policy [herds growing in African countries that permit ivory trading] D. Seligman. il *Fortune* 120:235+ N 20 '89

Reprieve for the giant of beasts [efforts to save the elephant] T. Gup. il *Time* 134:77 O 30 '89

Saving the African elephant. il *The Futurist* 23:49 S/O '89

Science gives ivory a sense of identity [DNA fingerprinting and isotope analyses] J. Cherfas. il *Science* 246:1120-1 D 1 '89

The shrinking roots of heaven [efforts to stop illegal poaching of elephants by restricting ivory trade] *U.S. News & World Report* 106:11-12 My 22 '89

Symbolic flames [proposed ban on ivory sales] A. Steacy. il *Maclean's* 102:37 Jl 31 '89

Trail of shame [elephants endangered by ivory poachers; cover story] T. Gup. il map *Time* 134:66-9+ O 16 '89

Tusk, tusk [Sotheby's removes elephant tusks from market to alleviate poaching] il *Time* 133:56 My 1 '89

A tussle over tusks [African nations debate ban on ivory trade] J. Bartholet. il *Newsweek* 114:25 Jl 24 '89

ELEPHANTS—*cont.*
Breeding
The only harmless great thing [Asian elephant breeding research at Washington Park Zoo] S. Tisdale. il *The New Yorker* 64:38-40+ Ja 23 '89
ELEPHANTS, FOSSIL
See also
Mastodons
ELEPHANTS AS ARTISTS
At Chicago's Lincoln Park Zoo, artistic elephants and chimps are living the easel life. il *People Weekly* 32:108-9 Ag 28 '89
ELEVATORS
See also
Otis Elevator Co., Ltd.
Elevate or escalate? J. Herron. *Harper's* 278:27 My '89
History
Elevating thoughts from Elisha Otis and fellow uplifters. D. D. Jackson. bibl (p247) il por *Smithsonian* 20:210-12+ N '89
THE ELEVENTH HOUR [television program] See Television program reviews—Single works
ELF (EXTREMELY LOW FREQUENCY) WAVES *See* Electromagnetic waves
ELFRING, CHRIS
Preserving land through local land trusts. il *BioScience* 39:71-4 F '89
Yellowstone: fire storm over fire management. il map *BioScience* 39:667-72 N '89
ELGIN MARBLES
On losing one's marbles [C. Hitchens's Imperial spoils] J. Gardner. *National Review* 41:53-5 O 27 '89
ELI BRIDGE COMPANY
Big wheel [cover story] K. Horan. il *Modern Maturity* 32:78-82 Je/Jl '89
ELIADES, PETER
about
Music of the spheres? P. Brimelow. il por *Forbes* 144:192+ O 2 '89
ELIAS *See* Elijah (Biblical figure)
ELIJAH (BIBLICAL FIGURE)
about
The prophetic touch. P. J. Ryan. il *America* 160:543 Je 3 '89
Understanding faith and miracle. P. Perkins. *The Christian Century* 106:555 My 24-31 '89
ELING TIDE MILL
Eling Tide Mill. T. Holloway. bibl il map *Sea Frontiers* 35:114-19 Mr/Ap '89
ELION, GERTRUDE BELLE, 1918-
The purine path of chemotherapy [Nobel Prize lecture, December 8, 1988] bibl f il *Science* 244:41-7 Ap 7 '89
about
The Nobel pair. K. Bouton. il pors *The New York Times Magazine* p28-9+ Ja 29 '89
ELIOT, T. S. (THOMAS STEARNS), 1888-1965
about
My shirt tale. S. Elkin. il *Harper's* 278:73-6 Ap '89
Of time and poetry. D. Jacobson. *Commentary* 88:48-53 N '89
T. S. Eliot at 101. C. Ozick. *The New Yorker* 65:119-28+ N 20 '89
Two cheers for heterogeneity. M. E. Marty. *The Christian Century* 106:837 S 27 '89
What was T. S. Eliot? R. Alter. *Commentary* 87:31-7 Mr '89
Anecdotes, facetiae, satire, etc.
Mr. Eliot's guide to quantum theory. J. Lowell. il *Physics Today* 42:46-7 Ap '89
ELIOT, THOMAS STEARNS *See* Eliot, T. S. (Thomas Stearns), 1888-1965
ELIOT FELD BALLET *See* Feld Ballet
ELISION *See* English language—Elision
L'ELISIR D'AMORE [opera] See Donizetti, Gaetano, 1797-1848
ELISSA (SHIP)
Now "Elissa" hauls history. il *Southern Living* 24:44 My '89
ELITE (SOCIAL SCIENCES)
Blue-blood blues [Bush presidency] E. D. Baltzell. *The New Republic* 200:15-16 Ap 3 '89
In defense of elitism. O. Edwards. il *Gentlemen's Quarterly* 59:147+ F '89
Soviet Union
Caviar wishes and vodka dreams [children of the elite in Zhukovka] T. Johnson. il *Rolling Stone* p47+ Ap 6 '89
ELIZABETH II, QUEEN OF GREAT BRITAIN, 1926-
Coronation
Brown-bagging it to Buckingham. R. Baker. il pors *The New York Times Magazine* p16-19+ Ja 1 '89
ELIZABETH, QUEEN, CONSORT OF GEORGE VI, KING OF GREAT BRITAIN, 1900-
about
Queen Mum turns 89 as Baby Bea hits the big one. M. H. J. Farrell. il pors *People Weekly* 32:40-2 Ag 21 '89
ELIZABETH ARDEN, INC.
Unilever is all made up, with everywhere to go [acquisition of Fabergé and Elizabeth Arden] M. Maremont. il *Business Week* p33-4 Jl 31 '89

ELIZABETH PARK (HARTFORD, CONN.)
New Elizabeth Park [rose garden restored] G. Morris. il *Americana* 17:61-3 Mr/Ap '89
ELIZABETHAN PERIOD *See* Great Britain—History— Elizabethan period, 1558-1603
ELJER INDUSTRIES
Spinning gold out of spinoffs [M. Gabelli's interest in Household International spinoffs] G. G. Marcial. *Business Week* p80 Jl 31 '89
ELK
See also
Antlers
Bison, elk deaths high in Yellowstone. il *National Parks* 63:11 My/Je '89
Drought, fires, and large mammals [Yellowstone National Park] F. J. Singer and others. bibl f il maps *BioScience* 39:716-22 N '89
Sifting ashes in Yellowstone [management of bison and elk in wake of forest fires] T. Williams. il *Audubon* 91:30-2+ N '89
Food and feeding
Elk in the full moon [night feeding myths] H. Buck. il *Field & Stream* 94:40 D '89
Photographs and photography
Rivers of life. E. A. Bauer and P. Bauer. il *Natural History* p90-1 Ja '89
ELK, IRISH *See* Irish elk
ELK CALLING *See* Animal calling
ELK HUNTING
Beyond the bugle. J. Byers. il *Outdoor Life* 184:64-5+ Ag '89
Buck 'n bull bow. R. Hinton. il *Outdoor Life* 184:86-7+ N '89
Elk dreams. G. Hill. il *Field & Stream* 93:12 F '89
Elk holes. W. L. Prothero. il maps *Field & Stream* 94:52-3+ O '89
Elk in all seasons. D. C. Mace. il *Outdoor Life* 184:64-5+ O '89
Elk in the full moon [night feeding myths] H. Buck. il *Field & Stream* 94:40 D '89
Empty-niche elk. S. M. Weaver. il *Outdoor Life* 184:64-5+ D '89
Getting close to elk. N. Strung. il *Field & Stream* 94:22-3 Ag '89
Know your limits. G. Hill. il *Field & Stream* 94:12 O '89
Quest for a dream bull. K. Etling. il *Outdoor Life* 183:70-1+ Ja '89
The serious elk rifle. J. Carmichel. il *Outdoor Life* 184:28+ S '89
Solitude. K. McCafferty. il *Field & Stream* 94:48-9+ D '89
Success—and elk—come to . . . he who waits. H. Buck. il *Field & Stream* 94:64-5+ N '89
Un-called-for elk. B. Journey. il *Outdoor Life* 184:72-3+ S '89
The voices of wilderness. K. McCafferty. il *Field & Stream* 93:66-7+ F '89
ELKIN, STANLEY, 1930-
In darkest Hollywood. il *Harper's* 279:51-61 D '89
My shirt tale. il *Harper's* 278:73-6 Ap '89
ELKIND, DAVID, 1931-
As they grow/14 through 18. See issues of Parents beginning January 1987
Developmentally appropriate practice: philosophical and practical implications. bibl f il *Phi Delta Kappan* 71:113-17 O '89
Handle with care: educating young children. il *USA Today (Periodical)* 117:66-8 Mr '89
What happens when markers of maturity disappear? *The Education Digest* 54:34-6 Ja '89
ELKINS, MIKE
about
Maximum exposure. J. Lieber. il pors *Sports Illustrated* 70:38-40+ My 1 '89
ELLACURIA BEAS COECHEA, IGNACIO, D. 1989
about
Grave thoughts. M. Massing. *The New Republic* 201:12-14 D 11 '89
ELLEN, DAVID
Payback time. *The New Republic* 201:10-11 Jl 31 '89
The phone flushaway. *The New Republic* 201:13-15 O 9 '89
ELLEN, LEONARD
about
Canadian imperialism. J. Willoughby. il por *Forbes* 143:52 Ja 9 '89
ELLER, KARL
about
Troubled Circle K is turning this way and that. K. Kerwin. il por *Business Week* p78+ N 20 '89
ELLERBE BECKET INC.
Against all odds. K. D. Stein. il *Architectural Record* 177:90-5 Ap '89
ELLERBEE, LINDA
about
Women on the verge of a nervy breakthrough [interview] P. Orenstein. il pors *Mother Jones* 14:28-31+ Je '89

ELLERMAN, A. DENNY
Should the Congress adopt the "Acid Deposition Control Act of 1987"? [excerpts from statement, July 9, 1987] *Congressional Digest* 68:57+ F '89
ELLESMERE ISLAND (N.W.T.)
   See also
   Wildlife—Ellesmere Island (N.W.T.)
ELLINGTON, DUKE, 1899-1974
The art is in the cooking [reprint]; ed. by Stanley Dance. il por *Down Beat* 56:60 S '89
   about
'Duke Ellington Month' celebrates 90th natal day of famous composer. il pors *Jet* 76:56-7 My 22 '89
Duke everlasting. K. Whitehead. il pors *Down Beat* 56:38-40 Je '89
Paramount's publishing arm purchases Ellington catalog. pors *Jet* 76:62 My 29 '89
ELLINGTON, MERCER
   about
Paramount's publishing arm purchases Ellington catalog. pors *Jet* 76:62 My 29 '89
ELLIOT, ANN
Places in the heart: the most romantic thing a girl's ever done: boys' true tales. il *Seventeen* 48:90-1 F '89
ELLIOTT, BILL
   about
Birdman of Dawsonville. L. Griffin. il pors *Car and Driver* 34:175-7+ Ap '89
Wheels of fortune. K. Hannon. il pors *Sport (New York, N.Y.)* 80:72-4+ Mr '89
ELLIOTT, CHRIS
   about
His father's the short, bald one, right? Or is it the large, round one? G. Duffy. il pors *Gentlemen's Quarterly* 59:246-9+ My '89
ELLIOTT, DEIDRE
The marvelous hunt. il *Field & Stream* 94:29+ N '89
ELLIOTT, GEORGE P., 1918-1980
   about
George P. Elliott and the common reader. L. C. Tisdale. *The American Scholar* 58:421-8 Summ '89
ELLIOTT, JOCK
Man at his best. *Reader's Digest* 135:95-6 Jl '89
The perfect Christmas card. il *The New York Times Magazine* p10+ D 24 '89
ELLIOTT, JOHN
Fear and trembling in Hong Kong. *World Press Review* 36:18 Jl '89
ELLIOTT, KIM ANDREW
Too many Voices of America. *Foreign Policy* 77:113-31 Wint '89/'90
ELLIOTT, LAWRENCE
Legend of the four chaplains. il *Reader's Digest* 134:65-70 Je '89
Steve Kerr: comeback kid. il por *Reader's Digest* 134:37-8+ Ap '89
ELLIOTT, MICHAEL
Britain's shame. *The New Republic* 201:15-16 Ag 7-14 '89
EC, phone home. *The New Republic* 200:20+ Mr 27 '89
My girl. *The New Republic* 200:15-16 My 29 '89
Splatcher. il *The New Republic* 201:14-16 D 11 '89
ELLIOTT, SUSAN
Gershwin crazy. il pors *Opera News* 54:12-14+ Ag '89
ELLIPTIC CURVES
Getting a grip on elliptic curves. B. A. Cipra. *Science* 243:30-1 Ja 6 '89
ELLIPTICAL GALAXIES *See* Galaxies
ELLIS, ABBY
Sing a song of self-esteem. il *American Visions* 4:54+ D '89
ELLIS, EDWARD ROBB
   about
In progress. *The New Yorker* 65:30-1 Mr 6 '89
ELLIS, ERIC
The economic root of the problem. il *World Press Review* 36:16-17 Jl '89
ELLIS, HAROLD A.
   about
But where's the dessert? E. Paris. il por *Forbes* 144:60+ O 2 '89
ELLIS, JOE
Between a sock and a hard place. il *Runner's World* 24:28 Ag '89
Heavy duty. il *Runner's World* 24:50-4 O '89
ELLIS, LAKEAL
   about
D.C. girls first to play on boys' football team. D. M. Cheers. il pors *Jet* 77:28-30 N 13 '89
ELLIS, MARGARET MCMAHON
(jt. auth) See Ellis, William N., and Ellis, Margaret McMahon
ELLIS, PATRICK
Teaching orders and the efficacy of school. *America* 161:262-5 O 21 '89
ELLIS, PERRY
   about
Life after Perry Ellis. N. Darnton. il por *Newsweek* 113:67 Ja 2 '89

ELLIS, ROSEMARY
Sexual chemistry. il *Glamour* 87:322-3+ Ap '89
ELLIS, WILLIAM N., AND ELLIS, MARGARET MCMAHON
Cultures in transition: what the West can learn from developing countries [cover story] il pors *The Futurist* 23:22-5 Mr/Ap '89
ELLIS, WILLIAM S.
Darcey: a village that refuses to die. il *National Geographic* 176:138-45 Jl '89
Malta. il maps *National Geographic* 175:700-17 Je '89
Skyscrapers. il *National Geographic* 175:140-73 F '89
ELLIS (PERRY) SPORTSWEAR INC. *See* Perry Ellis Sportswear Inc.
ELLIS AG
Just smart stock pickers? R. L. Stern. *Forbes* 144:40-1 S 18 '89
ELLISON, JASON
   about
'Who I really am'. J. Mason. il pors *Life* 12:74-8 O '89
ELLSBERG, DANIEL, 1931-
   about
Daniel Ellsberg [interview; cover story] B. Blanchard and S. Watrous. il por *The Progressive* 53:17-21 S '89
ELLSBERG, MARGARET R.
The lost child [poem] *America* 161:244 O 14 '89
ELLSTRAND, NORMAN C.
Coming attractions. *Omni (New York, N.Y.)* 11:33 My '89
Gene rustlers. *Omni (New York, N.Y.)* 11:33 Ap '89
ELLSWORTH, PAMELA
Costumes by computer. il *Theatre Crafts* 23:78+ N '89
ELLWOOD, DAVID T.
(jt. auth) See Bane, Mary Jo, and Ellwood, David T.
ELMAN, RICHARD M.
Some Scribners memories. por *Publishers Weekly* 235:439 Ja 27 '89
ELMANDJRA, MAHDI
Informatics and telematics: the future. il *World Health* p28-9 Ag/S '89
ELMWOOD (WIS.)
UFO update [proposed landing site] S. Baker. il *Omni (New York, N.Y.)* 11:81 Ag '89
   Festivals
E.T. come home [Elmwood UFO Days] S. Kaplan. il *Travel Holiday* 171:104 My '89
ELOCUTION
   See also
   Public speaking
ELOISE (FICTIONAL CHARACTER)
Hilary of the Plaza [illustrator H. Knight] E. Newhall. il por *New York* 22:22 Ja 16 '89
ELON, AMOS
Jerusalem: the future of the past. il *The New York Review of Books* 36:37-9 Ag 17 '89
Letter from Israel. *The New Yorker* 64:74-80 F 13 '89
ELSEN, ALBERT EDWARD, 1927-
Nothing to hide [discussion of Summer 1989 article, An outrageous anomaly] il *Art News* 88:190 D '89
An outrageous anomaly. il *Art News* 88:196 Summ '89
Public rights and critics' failures. il *Art News* 88:174 F '89
ELSHTAIN, JEAN BETHKE, 1941-
Technology as destiny: the new eugenics challenges feminism [cover story] il *The Progressive* 53:19-23 Je '89
ELTON, ORVILLE
   about
Connoisseur Orville Elton is definitely small-minded: he has amassed 40,000 tiny treasures. D. Chu. il por *People Weekly* 32:197-8 D 4 '89
ELVIN, W. J.
Worm and remembrance. il *The American Spectator* 22:30-1 Ja '89
ELVIS IMPERSONATORS
A Sikh singer who gives Elvis fans a Singh-King feeling [impersonator P. Singh] il por *People Weekly* 31:87 My 1 '89
ELWAY, JOHN
   about
'I'm about to suffocate'. R. Reilly. il pors *Sports Illustrated* 71:34-6+ N 6 '89
EMBALMING
   See also
   Mummies
EMBARGO
The coffee connection [nonviolent opposition to U.S. embargo against Nicaraguan imports] L. Cizewski. il *The Progressive* 53:46 N '89
EMBASSIES (BUILDINGS)
   See also
   Art in Embassies (Program)
   Iranian seizure of United States embassy, 1979-1981
A fiery reception [Canadian embassy in Washington] C. Wood. il por *Maclean's* 102:52-3 Mr 6 '89
   Security measures
Bugs, beans and too many bucks [security at the U.S. embassy in Moscow] D. Corn. *The Nation* 248:236+ F 20 '89
Compounding the problem [security at the U.S. embassy in Moscow] R. B. Cullen. il *Common Cause Magazine* 15:10 Mr/Ap '89

EMBASSIES (BUILDINGS)—Security measures—*cont.*
Our Moscow embassy mess. J. Barron. *Reader's Digest* 134:193-6+ F '89
EMBEZZLEMENT
Malaria researcher indicted [W. Siddiqui charged with embezzling research funds at the University of Hawaii] E. Marshall. *Science* 245:1326 S 22 '89
EMBLEMS
Fleur de bees [French emblems in fabric design] E. A. Berthold. il *House & Garden* 161:162 Jl '89
EMBOLISM
See also
Pulmonary embolism
Thrombosis
EMBRACING
See also
National Hugging Day
From hugs to happiness: the affection connection. A. Bell. il *Teen* 33:20-1+ O '89
To hug or not to hug [teachers and students] K. Paterson. *The Education Digest* 54:58-60 Mr '89
EMBRAER EMPRESA BRASILEIRA DE AERONAUTICA SA
Brazilian aerospace [special section] il *Aviation Week & Space Technology* 131:65-7 S 4 '89
Brazilian Air Force to accept first production AMX in August. E. H. Kolcum. il *Aviation Week & Space Technology* 130:87 Mr 20 '89
Embraer developing stretched Brasilia for regional market. C. A. Shifrin. il *Aviation Week & Space Technology* 130:158 Je 19 '89
Flying in the fast lane. M. A. Rocha and M. Rodrigues Alves. il *Américas* 41 no2:16-21 '89
EMBROIDERY
See also
Samplers
Exhibitions
The Overlord Embroidery [272-foot-wide cloth tribute at D-Day Museum in Portsmouth, England] R. L. Burgis. il *American Heritage* 40:108-13 My/Je '89
EMBRY, WAYNE
about
The Wayne and Lenny show. M. Lupica. pors *Esquire* 111:61-3+ Je '89
EMBRYO TRANSPLANTATION See Ova—Transplantation
EMBRYOLOGY
See also
Developmental biology
Developmental neurology
Fetus
Morphogenesis
Neural plate
Neural tube
Ova
Ovaries
Umbilical cord
Zygotes
Directing cell division during development. P. H. O'Farrell and others. bibl f il *Science* 246:635-40 N 3 '89
Topobiology [role of cell adhesion molecules in molecular embryology] G. M. Edelman. bibl il *Scientific American* 260:76-8+ My '89

Amphibia
Cloning and expression of a Xenopus embryonic gap junction protein. L. Ebihara and others. bibl f il *Science* 243:1194-5 Mr 3 '89
Induction of mesoderm by a viral oncogene in early Xenopus embryos. M. Whitman and D. A. Melton. bibl f il *Science* 244:803-6 My 19 '89

Birds
Germline transmission of exogenous genes in the chicken. R. A. Bosselman and others. bibl f il *Science* 243:533-5 Ja 27 '89

Echinoderms
Unusual pattern of accumulation of mRNA encoding EGF-related protein in sea urchin embryos. Q. Yang and others. bibl f il *Science* 246:806-8 N 10 '89

Insects
Transient pioneer neurons are essential for formation of an embryonic peripheral nerve [grasshoppers; cover story] M. Klose and D. R. Bentley. bibl f il *Science* 245:982-4 S 1 '89

Rodents
The EGF receptor kinase substrate p35 in the floor plate of the embryonic rat CNS. J. A. McKanna and S. Cohen. bibl f il *Science* 243:1477-9 Mr 17 '89
Germ-line transmission of a *c-abl* mutation produced by targeted gene disruption in ES cells [cover story] P. L. Schwartzberg and others. bibl f il *Science* 246:799-803 N 10 '89
Mouse embryonic stem cells and reporter constructs to detect developmentally regulated genes. A. Gossler and others. bibl f il *Science* 244:463-5 Ap 28 '89
Novel sites of expression of functional angiotensin II receptors in the late gestation fetus. M. A. Millan and others. bibl f il *Science* 244:1340-2 Je 16 '89

Targeting of nonexpressed genes in embryonic stem cells via homologous recombination. R. S. Johnson and others. bibl f il *Science* 245:1234-6 S 15 '89
EMBRYOLOGY, EXPERIMENTAL
See also
Clones (Biology)
Fertilization in vitro
Frozen embryos
Gamete intrafallopian transfer
Ova—Transplantation
Zygote intrafallopian transfer
Britain's Lords debate embryo research. J. Cherfas. il *Science* 246:1554-5 D 22 '89
Germany to ban embryo use. D. Kirk. *Science* 245:464 Ag 4 '89
Playing demigod [limits to tinkering with reproduction] K. Wright. *Scientific American* 260:30-1 My '89
Test screens live 'test tube' embryos. R. Weiss. *Science News* 135:132 Mr 4 '89
EMERGENCIES See Accidents
EMERGENCIES, ASSISTANCE IN See Assistance in emergencies
EMERGENCY FIRST AID See First aid in illness and injury
EMERGENCY MEDICAL CENTERS See Health facilities
EMERGENCY POWERS See War and emergency powers
EMERGENCY SERVICES, HOSPITAL See Hospitals—Emergency services
EMERGING MARKETS GROWTH FUND
Ooops, a success. E. F. Cone. il *Forbes* 143:10 Je 26 '89
EMERICH, JIM
Speed up VCR troubleshooting. il *Radio-Electronics* 60:65-7 Mr '89
EMERSON, STEVEN
Film flam. *The New Republic* 201:29-30+ S 18-25 '89
To catch a terrorist. il por *Reader's Digest* 135:107-11 O '89
EMERSON, SYLVIA
about
The tragedy of teenage smoking. il pors *The Saturday Evening Post* 261:52 My/Je '89
EMERSON COLLEGE
Emerson College [theater design training program] il *Theatre Crafts* 23:52+ N '89
EMERSON ELECTRIC CO.
Shades of Geneen at Emerson Electric. il por *Fortune* 119:39 My 22 '89
EMERSON RADIO CORP.
From boom boxes to bargain-basement PCs. L. Therrien. il *Business Week* p65-6 Je 26 '89
EMERSON STRING QUARTET
Blazing away at Bartók. K. R. Schwarz. il *High Fidelity (New York, N.Y.)* 39:61-2 Je '89
The Emerson's Bartók. R. Freed. il *Stereo Review* 54:163 F '89
Musical events:
Members solo in twentieth century concertos with the Hartt Wind Symphony. A. Porter. *The New Yorker* 65:96-7 My 1 '89
Recent recitals. A. Porter. *The New Yorker* 64:95-7 Ja 23 '89
EMERY AIR FREIGHT CORP.
Consolidated Freightways to acquire Emery Air Freight for $230 million. R. G. O'Lone. *Aviation Week & Space Technology* 130:119 F 20 '89
Emery's failing finances spur approval of merger [purchase by Consolidated Freightways] il *Aviation Week & Space Technology* 130:97 Ap 10 '89
"This global thing is not a fad" [Consolidated Freightways takeover] M. Beauchamp. il *Forbes* 144:122+ D 11 '89
EMH See Efficient market hypothesis
EMHART CORP.
Black & Decker cuts a neat dovetail joint [merger with Emhart] J. Weber, Jr. il por *Business Week* p52-3 Jl 31 '89
Great, Scott [CEO P. Scott] K. Hannon. il por *Forbes* 143:172 Mr 6 '89
Makeover by invitation. il *Forbes* 143:119 Ja 9 '89
EMI (ELECTROMAGNETIC INTERFERENCE) See Electromagnetic waves
EMIGRATION See Immigration and emigration
EMILIA-ROMAGNA (ITALY)
Description and travel
Italian provincial. C. Males. il map *Travel Holiday* 172:60-71 N '89
EMINASE (DRUG)
Genentech: a David that comes on like Goliath [fighting SmithKline Beecham's Eminase] J. Carey and J. O. Hamilton. il *Business Week* p165 O 30 '89
EMINESCU, MIHAI, 1850-1889
about
Mihai Eminescu, Romania's national poet. por *The Courier (Unesco)* 42:11 Mr '89
EMISSION REDUCTION CREDITS
Grime and punishment. *The New Republic* 200:7-8 F 20 '89
Pollution—going once, going twice . . . G. P. Brockway. *The New Leader* 72:14-15 O 30 '89

EMISSION STANDARDS, AUTOMOBILE *See* Automobiles—Environmental aspects

EMISSIONS, ACOUSTIC *See* Acoustic emissions

EMITTER COUPLED LOGIC CIRCUITS *See* Logic circuits

EMLEN PHYSICK HOUSE (CAPE MAY, N.J.) *See* Cape May (N.J.)—Historic houses, sites, etc.

EMMAUS HOUSE, INC.
Annie Troy Clark. S. Kanfer. il por *People Weekly* 32 Special Issue:23 Fall '89

EMMEL, ELIZABETH A., AND OTHERS
Cyclosporin A specifically inhibits function of nuclear proteins involved in T cell activation. bibl f il *Science* 246:1617-20 D 22 '89

EMMERLING, JOHN
Wind socked. il *Flying* 116:102 Ap '89

EMMERLING, MARY ELLISOR
Folk art, friends and good food [excerpt from Mary Emmerling's American country cooking] il *Working Woman* 14:100-2 Ja '89
Hearts [excerpt from Mary Emmerling's American country hearts] il *Good Housekeeping* 208:40+ F '89
Southern country [excerpt from Mary Emmerling's American country South] il *Redbook* 174:97-103 N '89

EMMERLING, MARY ELLISOR, AND MEAD, CHRIS
American country Christmas [excerpt] il *Good Housekeeping* 209:139-47 D '89

EMMERMAN, MICHAEL N.
about
Air travail. J. Poppy. il *Esquire* 112:141-2+ S '89

EMMERSON, MICHAEL
about
New regime at RCA. T. W. Libbey, Jr. il *High Fidelity (New York, N.Y.)* 39:60 Je '89

EMMETT, MARTIN F. C., 1934-
about
They're more single-minded at Tambrands. A. Dunkin. il *Business Week* p28 Ag 28 '89

EMMETT-ARTHUR, ARIELLE
Genetic counseling. *Parents* 64:126-9+ My '89

EMMONS, KAREN
Hire education. il *Omni (New York, N.Y.)* 11:18+ Je '89
Reeducating America [interview with R. Ornstein] il *Omni (New York, N.Y.)* 11:16+ My '89

EMMRICH, STUART
Foreign intrigue. il *American Film* 14:38-41+ S '89

EMMY AWARDS
Emmys '89. S. King. il *American Film* 14:46-7 Jl/Ag '89
Motown Production of 'Lonesome dove' gets 18 Emmy nominations. il *Jet* 76:64 Ag 21 '89
On their night of honors, TV's top stars prove that they're Emmy-nently presentable. il *People Weekly* 32:102-3 O 2 '89

EMORINE, LAURENT J., AND OTHERS
Molecular characterization of the human B₃-adrenergic receptor. bibl f il *Science* 245:1118-21 S 8 '89

EMORY, JERRY
Where the sky was born. il *Wilderness* 52:55-7 Summ '89

EMOTIONAL ABUSE OF CHILDREN *See* Child abuse

EMOTIONAL ILLNESS *See* Mental illness

EMOTIONALLY DISTURBED CHILDREN
Care and treatment
See also
Day care for emotionally disturbed children

EMOTIONS
See also
Alexithymia
Ambivalence
Anger
Anxiety
Bashfulness
Crying
Desire
Empathy
Envy
Facial expression
Fear
Grief
Guilt
Hate
Hostility (Psychology)
Innocence (Psychology)
Love
Mind and body
Moods
Peeves
Security and insecurity (Psychology)
Shame
Smiles
Surprise
Temper
Temperament
Wonder
Worry
Baby faces show the right side of emotion. B. Bower. il *Science News* 135:149 Mr 11 '89

The nature and nurture of emotions [cross cultural study of relationship between facial expression and the physiology of emotion; research by Paul Ekman and Robert W. Levenson] P. Young. *Science News* 135:59 Ja 28 '89
No fooling [relationship between facial expressions and emotion; excerpt from About faces; cover story] T. Landau. il *Health (New York, N.Y.)* 21:49-51+ My '89
Seeking the source of emotions [amygdala research by Nathan A. Fox] *Science News* 136:175 S 9 '89
Skin and emotion. J. J. Buck. *Vogue* 179:204-5 Ja '89
Underneath, we're all the same [cross cultural study of relationship between facial expression and the physiology of emotion; research by Paul Ekman] C. Raymond. il *Psychology Today* 23:17 Je '89

EMOTIONS IN LITERATURE
Emotion in fiction. R. Pilcher. il *The Writer* 102:9-11 S '89

EMPATHY
Man in the pink shirt [comparison of Kennedy assassination with witnessing shooting of two security guards] J. Glaeg. *America* 161:370-1 N 25 '89
Trying on a different perspective. J. M. Wall. *The Christian Century* 106:339-40 Ap 5 '89

EMPEROR WORSHIP, JAPANESE
After Hirohito: what remains sacred. I. Buruma. il por *The New York Times Magazine* p28-9+ My 28 '89
Do non-Japanese fear the flame? [death of Hirohito reopens issues of imperialism and nationalism] C. S. Inouye. il *The Nation* 248:120-2 Ja 30 '89
Hirohito and the fate of the emperor system. Y. Suzuki. *The Christian Century* 106:5-7 Ja 4-11 '89

EMPHYSEMA
Therapy
A genetic shield to prevent emphysema? [work of Ronald G. Crystal with antitrypsin gene-carrying retrovirus] B. J. Culliton. il *Science* 246:750-1 N 10 '89
New treatment found for hereditary emphysema [research by Ronald Crystal] J. L. Marx. il *Science* 243:315-16 Ja 20 '89
Two new approaches to genetic emphysema [antitrypsin gene-carrying retrovirus; work of Ronald G. Crystal] S. Hart and A. McKenzie. *Science News* 136:233 O 7 '89

EMPIRE *See* Imperialism

EMPIRE (VIDEO GAME)
Empire. J. Delson. il *Home Office Computing* 7:96 Ja '89

EMPIRE OF CAROLINA, INC.
Child's play. K. Hannon. il *Forbes* 143:101 Ap 3 '89

EMPIRE SAVINGS AND LOAN ASSOCIATION
Fast money and fraud. A. Pusey. il pors *The New York Times Magazine* p30-2+ Ap 23 '89

EMPLOYEE ASSISTANCE PROGRAMS *See* Employee counseling

EMPLOYEE ASSOCIATIONS
Can employee associations negotiate new growth? S. A. Levitan and F. Gallo. bibl f il *Monthly Labor Review* 112:5-14 Jl '89

EMPLOYEE BENEFITS *See* Fringe benefits

EMPLOYEE COUNSELING
When an employee's performance slumps [employee assistance programs] J. Greiff. il *Nation's Business* 77:44-5 Ja '89

EMPLOYEE DISABILITY INSURANCE *See* Insurance, Disability

EMPLOYEE-EMPLOYER RELATIONS *See* Industrial relations; Personnel management; Psychology, Industrial

EMPLOYEE HANDBOOKS, MANUALS, ETC.
Writing the book on employees. R. G. Hesser. il *Nation's Business* 77:50-1 D '89

EMPLOYEE HEALTH INSURANCE *See* Insurance, Health

EMPLOYEE INCENTIVES *See* Incentives in industry

EMPLOYEE LEASING
Give your employees a break—by leasing them. S. Woolley. il *Business Week* p135 Ag 14 '89
How leasing employees saves time and money. M. Olivero. *Working Woman* 14:32+ Mr '89

EMPLOYEE LIFE INSURANCE *See* Insurance, Life

EMPLOYEE MORALE
See also
Incentives in industry
Job satisfaction
How important is morale, really? [effect on productivity] W. Kiechel. il *Fortune* 119:121-2 F 13 '89
Managing survivors in the wake of cutbacks [views of Lynn Isabella] J. A. Werman. *Working Woman* 14:22+ D '89

EMPLOYEE MOTIVATION *See* Motivation (Psychology)

EMPLOYEE OWNERSHIP
See also
Employee stock ownership plans
Leveraged buyouts
Has Weirton's ESOP worked too well? M. Schroeder. il *Business Week* p66-7 Ja 23 '89
Union plan for Eastern takeover released at congressional hearing. il *Aviation Week & Space Technology* 130:22 Mr 13 '89
When workers become entrepreneurs [Monongahela Valley steel mills] B. Harrison. il *Technology Review* 92:19+ Jl '89

Ukraine
First GASP. Q. Peel. *World Press Review* 36:53 Jl '89

EMPLOYEE PHYSICAL FITNESS PROGRAMS *See* Industry—Physical fitness programs

EMPLOYEE RECREATION PROGRAMS *See* Industry—Recreation programs

EMPLOYEE REPRESENTATION IN MANAGEMENT *See* Participative management

EMPLOYEE RIGHTS *See* Employees—Civil rights

EMPLOYEE SENIORITY *See* Seniority, Employee

EMPLOYEE STOCK OWNERSHIP PLANS

ALPA begins drive to win pilots' support for United buyout. *Aviation Week & Space Technology* 131:124 S 18 '89

Buying out the boss [ESOPs in leveraged buyouts] M. Berss. il *Forbes* 143:41-2 Ap 3 '89

A crazy deal? [Hospital Corp. of America to sell its psychiatric hospitals] S. Flack. il *Forbes* 144:58 Jl 24 '89

Davis ups buyout bid for United but pilot offer still stronger. J. Ott and C. A. Shifrin. il *Aviation Week & Space Technology* 131:126-7 S 11 '89

ESOPs: are they good for you? [cover story] C. Farrell and J. P. Hoerr. il *Business Week* p116-19+ My 15 '89

ESOPs aren't the magic key to anything. G. S. Becker. il *Business Week* p20 O 23 '89

The foolish rush to ESOPs. S. Nasar. il *Fortune* 120:141-2+ S 25 '89

Giving 'United' a new meaning [pilot buyout] J. Schwartz. il *Newsweek* 114:34 S 25 '89

Giving workers a piece of the action. J. Schwartz. il *Newsweek* 113:45 Ap 17 '89

Louis Kelso's baby is making daddy proud [ESOPs] J. B. Levine. il por *Business Week* p130 My 8 '89

Pilots' buyout of United swaps concessions for company control [with editorial comment] C. Fotos. *Aviation Week & Space Technology* 131:9, 109 S 25 '89

Stuffing nest eggs with ESOPs [use as catalyst for improving productivity] C. Farrell. il *Business Week* p124-5 Ap 24 '89

Suddenly, blue chips are red-hot for ESOPs. C. Farrell. il *Business Week* p144 Mr 20 '89

They own the place. F. Ungeheuer. il *Time* 133:50-1 F 6 '89

U.S. asks United buyout group for details on debt, foreign stake. C. Fotos. *Aviation Week & Space Technology* 131:105 O 2 '89

UAL sets aside buyout effort, but pilots still pursue takeover. C. Fotos. *Aviation Week & Space Technology* 131:54 O 30 '89

United: why labor needs some parachutes on board [pilots plan buyout of United Air Lines] J. E. Ellis. il *Business Week* p28 S 18 '89

Why the United buyout is no great deal for workers. R. Kuttner. il *Business Week* p26 O 9 '89

Will everybody get on board? [UAL buyout bid by executives and pilots] J. Greenwald. il *Time* 134:63 S 18 '89

Workable firm-ownership transitions through ESOPs [architectural firms] C. M. Sapers. por *Architectural Record* 177:37+ Ja '89

Laws and regulations

A new way to keep raiders at bay [ESOP defense gets court O.K.] K. H. Hammonds. il *Business Week* p39 Ja 23 '89

Taxation

ESOP fable [Joseph Littlejohn & Levy's deal using ESOPs to buy carryforwards] T. Pouschine. il *Forbes* 143:98+ Je 26 '89

EMPLOYEE VACATIONS

Variations in holidays, vacations, and area pay levels. J. E. Buckley. bibl f il *Monthly Labor Review* 112:24-30 F '89

EMPLOYEES

See also
Executives
Government employees
Household employees
Job satisfaction
Labor turnover
Personnel management

Attitudes

How to keep your finger on the pulse of productivity [attitude surveys] E. Flax. il *Working Woman* 14:44 S '89

The trust gap [relations; cover story] A. Farnham. il *Fortune* 120:56-8+ D 4 '89

Civil rights

See you in court [cover story] D. C. Bacon. il *Nation's Business* 77:16-18+ Jl '89

Discipline

See Labor discipline

Dismissal

See also
Layoffs
Outplacement consultant services

The courts shouldn't become pink-slip police. G. S. Becker. il *Business Week* p14 Ag 28 '89

Firing: there's (almost) always a better way. A. Jaffe. il *Psychology Today* 23:68-9 Jl/Ag '89

A manager's toughest job. J. Homer. il *Working Woman* 14:67 Ja '89

Why courts are always making law [employment-at-will issue] G. E. Frug. il por *Fortune* 120:245+ S 25 '89

You've just fired someone: how to handle the aftermath. P. Amend. il *Working Woman* 14:20 Ja '89

Education

See Labor—Education

Health and hygiene

See Occupational health and safety

Monitoring

See also
Telephone call accounting systems

Learn your firm's inside story. M. Stevens. il *Nation's Business* 77:59-60 Ag '89

Promotion

See Promotions

Psychology

See Psychology, Industrial

Rating

See also
Employment tests

Catch a falling star system [eliminating yearly performance appraisals] A. Gabor. il *U.S. News & World Report* 106:43-4 Je 5 '89

How does your staff measure up? [excerpt from Maximum performance management] J. H. Boyett and H. P. Conn. il *Working Woman* 14:26+ Je '89

How to give feedback your staff can use [excerpt from One-on-one with Andy Grove] A. S. Grove. il *Working Woman* 14:54+ S '89

A win-win approach to performance appraisals. C. McIntosh. il *Working Woman* 14:22 D '89

Recruiting

See also
Employment agencies
Employment interviewing

Cut the fluff [companies recruiting on campus] D. Machan. il *Forbes* 143:166 Je 26 '89

Finding the right employee (I). B. Stein. il *Home Office Computing* 7:44-5 O '89

Finding the right employee (II). B. Stein. il *Home Office Computing* 7:40+ N '89

The hiring crisis of the '90s. R. Sandroff. il *Working Woman* 14:92-4 F '89

How to hire employees your customers will love. L. Touby. il *Working Woman* 14:40+ D '89

M.B.A.s with blue collars [manufacturers should recruit best and brightest young managers] A. G. Shilling. il por *Forbes* 144:300 O 16 '89

Relocation

See Labor mobility

Resignation

The hidden cost of golden handshakes [voluntary termination programs] D. Machan. il *Forbes* 143:130+ F 20 '89

Knowing when to leave your job. B. Nivens. il *Essence* 20:110+ D '89

Should you quit if you're not getting respect? [results of survey on tactics of television character Roseanne] il *Glamour* 87:123 N '89

Seniority

See Seniority, Employee

Tenure

See Labor turnover

Testing

See Employment tests

Training

See also
Apprentices
Motion pictures in industry
Multiskilling

American workers lack training [report by the American Society for Training and Development] *USA Today (Periodical)* 118:6-7 D '89

The demand for more training. il *Black Enterprise* 20:41 Ag '89

A good start for new hires. G. Geromel. il *Nation's Business* 77:21+ Ja '89

The need for training. *Monthly Labor Review* 112:2 Je '89

Tailor-made work forces [customized training targeted to individual companies offered in states' development packages] H. Bacas. il *Nation's Business* 77:33-6 N '89

Training: a key ingredient in office automation. S. Gelfond. *Working Woman* 14:19 Jl '89

Training the workforce of the future. J. E. Jacobs. il *Technology Review* 92:66-72 Ag/S '89

EMPLOYEES AS STOCKHOLDERS *See* Employee stock ownership plans

EMPLOYER-EMPLOYEE RELATIONS *See* Industrial relations; Personnel management; Psychology, Industrial

EMPLOYMENT

See also
Aged—Employment
Aged refugees—Employment
AIDS (Disease) and employment
Americans—Foreign countries—Employment
Blacks—Employment
Cancer patients—Employment
Cardiacs—Employment
Computers—Employment use
Contingent workers
Discrimination in employment

EMPLOYMENT—See also—*cont.*
> Drugs and employment
> Farm women—Employment
> Hispanic Americans—Employment
> Hours of labor
> Job sharing
> Married couples—Employment
> Mothers—Employment
> Networking
> Nobility—Employment
> Part time employment
> Poor—Employment
> Retirement
> Smoking and employment
> Supplementary employment
> Temporary employment
> Unemployment
> Women—Employment
> Youth—Employment

The American job machine is hitting on all cylinders. J. C. Cooper and K. Madigan. il *Business Week* p27-8 F 20 '89

Are we becoming a nation of burger flippers? il *Changing Times* 43:32-3 Mr '89

Employment looks weak. Will consumers ride to the rescue? J. C. Cooper and K. Madigan. il *Business Week* p51-2 O 23 '89

Favorite cities for tomorrow's workers. il *The Futurist* 23:52 Jl/Ag '89

A great American job machine? W. Serrin. il *The Nation* 249:269-70+ S 18 '89

The job juggernaut is squelching fears of recession. J. C. Cooper and K. Madigan. il *Business Week* p29-30 Ja 23 '89

The little chill blowing through the job market [employment growth slows] J. C. Cooper and K. Madigan. il *Business Week* p31-2 My 22 '89

Technology, employment and U.S. competitiveness. R. M. Cyert and D. C. Mowery. il *Scientific American* 260:54-60+ My '89

Statistics
> *See also*
> Wage differentials

Characteristics of occupational entrants. M. L. Carey. il *Occupational Outlook Quarterly* 33:8-17 Summ '89

Economic impact study [increase in minimum wage; study by the Congressional Budget Office] *Congressional Digest* 68:135+ My '89

Employment gains slow in the first half of 1989. S. E. Haugen. il *Monthly Labor Review* 112:3-9 Ag '89

How many new jobs since 1982? Data from two surveys differ. P. O. Flaim. bibl f il *Monthly Labor Review* 112:10-15 Ag '89

Industry output and employment: a slower trend for the nineties. V. A. Personick. bibl f il *Monthly Labor Review* 112:25-41 N '89

Labor market completes sixth year of expansion in 1988. W. J. Howe and W. Parks, II. il *Monthly Labor Review* 112:3-14 F '89

The payroll numbers may be hiding economic trouble . . . G. Koretz. il *Business Week* p22 N 20 '89

Projections of occupational employment, 1988-2000. G. T. Silvestri and J. M. Lukasiewicz. bibl f il *Monthly Labor Review* 112:42-65 N '89

Japan
Japan faces a brain drain [college grads opting out of manufacturing sector] Y. Hoshiai and J. Schwartz. il *Newsweek* 114:47-8 S 4 '89

Western Europe
'Help wanted' signs are springing up across Europe. B. Riemer. il *Business Week* p46-7 Ja 16 '89

EMPLOYMENT AGENCIES
> *See also*
> Executive search consultants
> Interplace/Transworld Recruit (Firm)
> Manpower, Inc.
> Norrell Corporation
> Recruit USA
> Theatrical agencies and agents
> United States Employment Service

The agency route—is it better? [temporary help agencies] S. McHenry. *Ms.* 17:94 Mr '89

Temporary solutions. M. Whittemore. il *Nation's Business* 77:48-9 Jl '89

Ethical aspects
Employment-agency scams. L. Reibstein. il *Newsweek* 113:40 F 20 '89

Finance
Temp agencies are praying the slump is just temporary. D. Greising. il *Business Week* p62 D 11 '89

Great Britain
> *See also*
> Blue Arrow plc

EMPLOYMENT AND ALCOHOLISM *See* Alcohol and employment

EMPLOYMENT AND DRUGS *See* Drugs and employment

EMPLOYMENT AND SMOKING *See* Smoking and employment

EMPLOYMENT CONTRACTS *See* Labor contracts

EMPLOYMENT COUNSELING *See* Vocational guidance

EMPLOYMENT DISCRIMINATION *See* Discrimination in employment

EMPLOYMENT INTERVIEWING

4 danger signals: how to spot a job that looks right but is wrong. M. M. Kennedy. il *Glamour* 87:121 O '89

Answers that get you hired. D. Moreau. il *Changing Times* 43:53-5 Ap '89

Bad job interview? Here's how to recoup. M. M. Kennedy. *Glamour* 87:114 Ag '89

Dear Betty Harragan. B. L. Harragan. il *Working Woman* 14:42+ Mr '89

Finding the right employee (II). B. Stein. il *Home Office Computing* 7:40+ N '89

Hire smart, hire right [special section] *Working Woman* 14:71-4+ Mr '89

How to hire the right person for the job [excerpt from Strategies and skills for managerial women] J. Hunsaker and P. L. Hunsaker. il *Working Woman* 14:28+ Ja '89

Interviewing for the nineties: answering—and asking—questions like a winner. M. M. Kennedy. il *Glamour* 87:73-4 Ja '89

Job interview update: navy suit not required. il *Glamour* 87:217-20 Mr '89

Mastering the meeting [older applicants] *Modern Maturity* 32:38 Je/Jl '89

Ethical aspects
The untruthful interviewee. *Working Woman* 14:162 Mr '89

EMPLOYMENT REFERENCES

Reference checks: how to get the information you need. M. Olivero. *Working Woman* 14:25 My '89

Anecdotes, facetiae, satire, etc.
Of many things [Robert Thornton's Lexicon of intentionally ambiguous recommendations] G. W. Hunt. *America* 160:314 Ap 8 '89

EMPLOYMENT SENIORITY *See* Seniority, Employee

EMPLOYMENT TESTS

Academy panel joins the fray over job testing [question of reinterpreting scores of blacks and Hispanics on General Aptitude Test Battery] C. Holden. il *Science* 244:1036-7 Je 2 '89

Bias in the casino [charges of bias in job tests developed by U.S. Employment Service] D. Seligman. il *Fortune* 119:153-4 Ap 10 '89

Fairness in employment testing [discussion of June 2, 1989 article, Academy panel joins the fray over job testing] C. Holden. *Science* 245:14 Jl 7 '89

Honestly, can we trust you? [pencil-and-paper tests] C. Gorman. il *Time* 133:44 Ja 23 '89

How to comply with the polygraph law. il *Nation's Business* 77:36-7 D '89

Job applicants come clean [integrity test; research by Reid Psychological Systems] *USA Today (Periodical)* 118:7-8 Ag '89

More normal nonsense [National Research Council report on General Aptitude Test Battery] D. Seligman. il *Fortune* 120:118 Jl 17 '89

Putting honesty in the office—the old-fashioned way. W. Cole. *Working Woman* 14:14+ Jl '89

The slippery slope in Foggy Bottom [Foreign Service and employment bias] D. Seligman. *Fortune* 119:167 My 8 '89

Tests to target dependability. T. J. Burns. il *Nation's Business* 77:26+ Mr '89

This is your life [psychological evaluation test administered by Target Stores] *Harper's* 279:19-20+ D '89

A true test of skill for your employees [psychological assessment] M.-P. Royer. *Working Woman* 14:32+ N '89

EMPORIO ARMANI (FIRM)

Armani takes Fifth. M. Gross. il por *New York* 22:20 Mr 20 '89

EMPRESS (VICTORIA, B.C.: RESTAURANT) *See* Victoria (B.C.)—Restaurants, nightclubs, bars, etc.

EMPTY NEST [television program] *See* Television program reviews—Single works

EMPTY SUIT (TERM)

How to spot an empty suit. W. Kiechel. il *Fortune* 120:227-8+ N 20 '89

EMS *See* Electrical muscle stimulation; European Monetary System

EMULATORS (COMPUTER PROGRAMS)

Almost-magic EMS emulation [Turbo EMS] S. Miastkowski. il *Byte* 14:97-8 Mr '89

Communications get Hyper [HyperAccess/5] S. Miastkowski. *Byte* 14:84 O '89

Emulation—who needs it? *Compute!* 11:32 Mr '89

Plug and play PostScript [PacificPage PostScript emulation cartridge] M. Antonoff. il *Personal Computing* 13:206 D '89

The sincerest form of flattery. D. Churbuck. il *Forbes* 143:116+ F 20 '89

Turbo EMS. J. B. Lambert. il *Compute!* 11:116+ D '89

ENAMEL, TOOTH *See* Tooth enamel

ENAMELS AND ENAMELING
> *See also*
> Cloisonné

ENBERG, DICK
Looking for Mr. Goodwill. il por *World Tennis* 36:106 Mr '89
ENCEPHALOGRAPHY
See also
Electroencephalography
Magnetoencephalography
ENCEPHALOMYELITIS
Control of experimental autoimmune encephalomyelitis by T cells responding to activated T cells. A. W. Lohse and others. bibl f il *Science* 244:820-2 My 19 '89
Vaccination against experimental allergic encephalomyelitis with T cell receptor peptides. M. D. Howell and others. bibl f il *Science* 246:668-70 N 3 '89
ENCHANTED ROCK STATE NATURAL AREA (TEX.)
Texas mountain of stone. il *Southern Living* 24:40 Ap '89
ENCORE COMPUTER CORPORATION
Gould will use same market strategy under Encore ownership. E. H. Kolcum. *Aviation Week & Space Technology* 130:53 Ap 17 '89
ENCOURAGEMENT
The fine art of encouragement. M. R. Littleton. *Reader's Digest* 135:141-3 N '89
ENCRYPTION *See* Cryptography
ENCYCLOPEDIAS
See also
CD-ROM (Compact disc-Read only memory)—Encyclopedias
Religion—Encyclopedias
Southern States—Civilization—Encyclopedias
END (TERM)
The end is not near. S. Budiansky. il *U.S. News & World Report* 107:26-7 O 30 '89
END OF THE WORLD
See also
Antichrist
Judgment Day
Why some Christians believe the end of the world is near. W. J. Whalen. il *U.S. Catholic* 54:32-8 F '89
The year 1000 [excerpt from AD 1000] R. Erdoes. il *Psychology Today* 23:44-5 My '89
END TABLES *See* Tables
ENDANGERED SPECIES *See* Rare animals; Rare plants
ENDANGERED SPECIES ACT (1973)
Endangered species need more help. *Science News* 135:79 F 4 '89
ENDARTERECTOMY *See* Blood vessels—Surgery
ENDEN, AAD VAN DEN, AND SPEKREIJSE, H.
Binocular depth reversals despite familiarity cues. bibl f il *Science* 244:959-61 My 26 '89
ENDER, CLARA ADAMS- *See* Adams-Ender, Clara
ENDINGS, LITERARY
Calling it quits. L. Lowry. *The Writer* 102:13-14+ Ap '89
The living end. R. Makoul. il *The Writer* 102:7-8 F '89
The shape that satisfies. R. Twohy. *The Writer* 102:16-17 D '89
ENDŌ, SHŪSAKU, 1923-
about
The message the Japanese have missed. P. Yancey. il *Christianity Today* 33:56 Mr 17 '89
A silence that is not hollow. E. Beverly. il por *Commonweal* 116:491-4 S 22 '89
ENDOCARDITIS *See* Heart—Diseases
ENDOCRINE GLANDS
See also
Adrenal glands
Pancreas
Pituitary body
Thyroid gland
ENDOCRINOLOGY
See also
Hormone receptors
Hormones
Neuroendocrinology
ENDOCYTOSIS
Regulatory role for GTP-binding proteins in endocytosis. L. S. Mayorga and others. bibl f il *Science* 244:1475-7 Je 23 '89
ENDOD
Africa's 'wonder weed' [to control schistosomiasis] il *The Unesco Courier* 42:48-9 Jl '89
ENDOGENOUS PYROGENS *See* Pyrogens
ENDOMETRIOSIS
Surgery
Escape from pain [work of David Redwine] S. D. Driedger. il *Maclean's* 102:61 N 13 '89
Therapy
Hope for endometriosis sufferers [use of gonadotropin releasing hormone analogs] *McCall's* 116:90-1 F '89
ENDOPHYTES
Trespassers will be poisoned [endophyte-infected tall fescue] K. Clay. il *Natural History* p8+ S '89
ENDORSEMENTS IN ADVERTISING *See* Advertising—Testimonials
ENDOTHELIAL GROWTH FACTOR, VASCULAR *See* Vascular endothelial growth factor

ENDOTHELIUM *See* Epithelium
ENDOVASCULAR EMBOLIZATION *See* Blood vessels—Surgery
ENDOWMENTS
See also
Black colleges and universities—Gifts, legacies, etc.
Colleges and universities—Gifts, legacies, etc.
ENDURANCE
E for elevation [research on vitamin E and free radicals in high altitude athletics] il *Women's Sports & Fitness* 11:11 O '89
Stamina smart [special section] il *Health (New York, N.Y.)* 21:41-53 F '89
ENDURANCE SWIMMING *See* Marathon swimming
ENEMIES, A LOVE STORY [film] *See* Motion picture reviews—Single works
ENEMY IN THE BIBLE
Did Jesus really mean it when he said "Love your enemies"? J. H. Forest. il *U.S. Catholic* 54:35-8 Je '89
ENERGETICS, BIOLOGICAL *See* Bioenergetics
ENERGETICS SATELLITE CORPORATION
Glavcosmos signs Energetics as first U.S. launch customer [Proton rockets] J. R. Asker. il *Aviation Week & Space Technology* 131:40 N 20 '89
ENERGY, VITAL *See* Vitality
ENERGY AND COMMERCE COMMITTEE *See* United States. Congress. House. Committee on Energy and Commerce
ENERGY COGENERATION
Home-size cogenerator [work of F. Wicks] V. E. Gilmore. il *Popular Science* 234:82+ Mr '89
ENERGY CONSERVATION
See also
Automobile engines—Energy usage
Cool storage
Cooling
Electric plants—Energy usage
Energy cogeneration
Energy policy
Environmental engineering
Environmental engineering (Buildings)
Heating
Industry—Energy usage
Insulation (Heat)
Motor vehicle engines—Energy usage
Weatherproofing
Windbreaks
Burning the candle at neither end [restoring cars as a way to save gasoline] P. Egan. il *Road & Track* 40:16+ Ja '89
Conserving energy in the home. J. Seisler. *Consumers' Research Magazine* 72:18-21 D '89
Demand-side economics [utilities promote conservation] P. Klebnikov. il *Forbes* 143:148+ Ap 3 '89
Energy [Environmental Quality Index] il *National Wildlife* 27:37 F/Mr '89
Mortgages to warm your home and wallet [energy efficient mortgages] I. Hellman. il *Money* 18:24+ N '89
S.O.S. [implications of the Alaska oil spill] *The Nation* 248:543-4 Ap 24 '89
Strategies for energy use. J. H. Gibbons and others. bibl il *Scientific American* 261:136-43 S '89
Utilities are making more by selling less. C. Brown. il *Business Week* p90 Ja 9 '89
Psychological aspects
Energy: psyched to save [views of Elliot Aronson] *Psychology Today* 23:10 Ja/F '89
ENERGY COSTS *See* Fuel—Prices; Heating—Costs
ENERGY CRISIS *See* Petroleum supply; Power resources
ENERGY DEPT. (U.S.) *See* United States. Dept. of Energy
ENERGY EFFICIENT BUILDINGS *See* Environmental engineering (Buildings)
ENERGY INDUSTRIES
See also
Archer-Daniels-Midland Co.
Coal industry
Coastal Corporation
Columbus Energy Corporation
Combustion Engineering Inc.
Exxon Corporation
Gas industry
Mapco Inc.
National Energy Associates
O'Brien Energy Systems Inc.
Pennzoil Company
Petroleum industry
Phibro Energy, Inc.
Phillips Petroleum Company
Solar energy industry
USX Corporation
Valero Energy Corp.
W.R. Grace & Co.
Canada
See also
American Barrick Resources Corp.

ENERGY LEVELS (QUANTUM MECHANICS)
Keeping a quantum kettle from boiling [study by Wayne M. Itano] I. Peterson. il *Science News* 136:292-3 N 4 '89

Quantum chaos: enigma wrapped in a mystery. R. Pool. *Science* 243:893-5 F 17 '89

Quantum pot watching [research by Wayne Itano] R. Pool. il *Science* 246:888 N 17 '89

ENERGY POLICY
See also
United States. Dept. of Energy

America is running out of power. P. C. Cruver. *USA Today (Periodical)* 118:62-3 Jl '89

Can the government govern? [address, November 17, 1988] J. E. Chubb. *Vital Speeches of the Day* 55:363-7 Ap 1 '89

Energy priorities outlined for Bush. D. C. Bacon. il *Nation's Business* 77:8 Mr '89

Hydrocarbon energy revisited. P. H. Abelson. *Science* 245:1433 S 29 '89

Our energy future: time horizons and instability. R. S. Berry. *Environment* 31:5+ Jl/Ag '89

Running on empty. M. Kondracke. *The New Republic* 201:13-15 N 27 '89

Environmental aspects

Energy technology for survival. J. G. Speth. il *The Bulletin of the Atomic Scientists* 45:9-10 Mr '89

Environmental delusions. R. J. Samuelson. il *Newsweek* 113:45 My 29 '89

Government policies that hurt the environment [views of James J. Mackenzie] *The Futurist* 23:51-2 Jl/Ag '89

The greenhouse. C. P. Gilmore. *Popular Science* 235:4+ Ag '89

The growing strain on Asia's muscular economies [energy shortages] K. R. Sheets. il *U.S. News & World Report* 107:69-70 N 6 '89

Strategies for energy use. J. H. Gibbons and others. bibl il *Scientific American* 261:136-43 S '89

Striving for balanced growth [address, May 16, 1989] T. R. Kuhn. *Vital Speeches of the Day* 55:637-40 Ag 1 '89

Will changing your light bulb save the world? C. A. Moore. il *International Wildlife* 19:18-23 My/Je '89

International aspects
See also
International Energy Agency

Renewable energy: power for tomorrow. R. L. San Martin. il por *The Futurist* 23:37-40 My/Je '89

Solar power and priorities. D. E. Koshland, Jr. *Science* 245:805 Ag 25 '89

California
See also
Palm Springs (Calif.)—Energy policy

Canada
See also
National Energy Board (Canada)

A call for action. B. Wickens. il *Maclean's* 102:38-9 Jl 17 '89

Canada, carbon dioxide, and the greenhouse effect. L. Hughes and S. Scott. bibl f il *Environment* 31:4-5+ N '89

Controlling energy. J. Howse. il *Maclean's* 102:37 Ag 28 '89

Hibernia postponed [oilfields off Newfoundland] J. Daly. il *Maclean's* 102:31+ Jl 24 '89

A spectacular hand in a high-stakes game [Kierans report] D. Francis. il *Maclean's* 102:9 My 15 '89

China

Assessing the benefits of biogas. R. Hamburg. bibl f il *Environment* 30:31-2 D '88

Iowa
See also
Osage (Iowa)—Energy policy

Japan

World's worst oil policy? A. Tanzer. il *Forbes* 144:245+ Jl 24 '89

United States
See Energy policy

ENERGY RESEARCH *See* Power resources—Research
ENERGY RESOURCES *See* Power resources
ENERGY SERVICE COMPANY, INC.
Diamonds in his own backyard [deals made by R. E. Rainwater] J. H. Taylor. il *Forbes* 143:49-50+ Mr 6 '89

ENERGY STORAGE
See also
Compressed air—Storage
Cool storage

ENERGY SUPPLY *See* Power resources
ENGA, RICHARD J.
about
On deck. il por *Sport (New York, N.Y.)* 80:12 D '89

ENGAGEMENT RINGS
Anecdotes, facetiae, satire, etc.
The ring cycle. R. Bacher. il *The New York Times Magazine* p20+ Ag 13 '89

ENGEL, ELIOT L., 1947-
Should the House-passed wage proposal be enacted? [excerpts from address, March 23, 1989] *Congressional Digest* 68:158 My '89

ENGEL, JOANNE B.
Preserving quality: teacher training from a liberal arts perspective. il *Phi Delta Kappan* 70:475-7 F '89

ENGEL, THOM
Night flyers. il *The Conservationist* 43:32-5 My/Je '89

ENGELBERGER, JOSEPH F.
about
Homebody. E. Corcoran. il por *Scientific American* 261:77-8 O '89

ENGELEITER, SUSAN
about
SBA's woman in charge. D. C. Bacon. il por *Nation's Business* 77:66 Je '89

ENGELER, AMY
For women golfers, life in the rough. il *The New York Times Magazine* p42+ O 1 '89

ENGELHARDT, TOM
Star Wars won't die. il *The Progressive* 53:22-3 S '89

ENGELSMAN, EDDY
The Dutch model. *New Perspectives Quarterly* 6:44-5 Summ '89

ENGINE COMPONENTS, INC.
Engine Components uses coating to increase life of piston cylinder [Cermicrome process] E. H. Phillips. il *Aviation Week & Space Technology* 131:40-2 S 18 '89

ENGINE KNOCK *See* Automobile engines—Detonation
ENGINE PING *See* Automobile engines—Detonation
ENGINEERING
See also
Audio engineering
Automobile engineering
Aviation engineering
Building materials
Chemical engineering
Computers—Engineering use
Environmental engineering
Motorcycle engineering
Petroleum engineering
Structural engineering

Awards
See also
Draper Prize

Study and teaching
Teaching statistics to engineers. A. A. Penzias. *Science* 244:1025 Je 2 '89

Universities incorporate TQM in engineering curriculum [total quality management] *Aviation Week & Space Technology* 131:67 D 4 '89

Aids and devices
Learn on me [Macintosh engineering and scientific courseware] D. E. Crabb. il *Byte* 14:143-4+ Jl '89

Great Britain
Fail Britannia? B. Harrison. il *Technology Review* 92:17 O '89

Canada
Shaping a new industrial Canada [address, September 11, 1989] B. M. McGourty. *Vital Speeches of the Day* 56:104-8 D 1 '89

ENGINEERING AS A PROFESSION
Things they never teach you in engineering school. S. C. Florman. il *Technology Review* 92:16+ Ap '89

ENGINEERING CONSTRUCTION COMPANIES
See also
Dresser Industries, Inc.
Fluor Corp.
Osborn Engineering Company

Export-import trade
U.S. contractors finally break ground in Tokyo. N. Usui and N. Gross. il *Business Week* p56 Ap 3 '89

Securities
New streets, paved with gold [investing in public works] J. M. Laderman. il *Business Week* p92-3 O 16 '89

Seeking a solid payoff in crumbling public works. J. Friedman. *Business Week* p116 S 4 '89

Japan
Reconstructing construction. R. C. Wood. il *High Technology Business* 9:11 Ja '89

ENGINEERING CONSULTANTS
How to get the best from your consulting engineers. R. B. McMichael. por *Architectural Record* 177:35 N '89

ENGINEERING DESIGN
See also
Design for manufacturability and assembly

ENGINEERING FLIGHT SIMULATORS *See* Flight simulators
ENGINEERING RESEARCH
See also
Aviation research

ENGINEERING RESEARCH, GENETIC *See* Genetic research
ENGINEERING SOCIETIES
See also
Audio Engineering Society
National Academy of Engineering

ENGINEERS
See also
Black engineers
Engineering as a profession
Women engineers

ENGINEERS—*cont.*

Legal status, laws, etc.

Architects, engineers, and the "practice overlap". M. F. Schmertz. *Architectural Record* 177:11 Jl '89

Who will design buildings for human habitation? (I) [interview with M. Lunch] C. M. Sapers. pors *Architectural Record* 177:41+ Je '89

Who will design buildings for human habitation? (II) [interview with M. Lunch] C. M. Sapers. il por *Architectural Record* 177:41-2 Jl '89

Supply and demand

Engineering. il *U.S. News & World Report* 107:64+ S 25 '89

The hot demand for new scientists. P. Nulty. il *Fortune* 120:155+ Jl 31 '89

Research Council cites flaws in NSF employment statistics. C. S. Powell. *Physics Today* 42:49 Jl '89

Scientist shortage. E. Stark. il *Psychology Today* 23:12 My '89

Wanted: 675,000 future scientists and engineers. C. Holden. il *Science* 244:1536-7 Je 30 '89

ENGINEERS CORPS *See* United States. Army. Corps of Engineers

ENGINES

See also

Airplane engines
Automobile engines
Automobiles, Racing—Engines
Cummins Engine Company, Inc.
Gas and oil engines
Locomotives
Marine engines
Motor boat engines
Motorcycle engines
Pistons
Rotary engines
Spaceplane engines
Stirling engines
Tractor engines

ENGLAND, CATHERINE

(jt. auth) *See* Niskanen, William, 1933-, and England, Catherine

ENGLAND, ROBERT

Coming to terms with campaign reform. il *The American Spectator* 22:22-5 N '89

ENGLAND

See also

Barnsley (England)
Bradford (England)
Bristol (England)
Burgh Island (England)
Derbyshire (England)
Great Britain
Hull (England)
Lancashire (England)
Lincoln (England)
London (England)
Plymouth (England)
Stoke-on-Trent (England)
West Country (England)

ENGLE, CHARLES B., JR.

From formulas to Fortran to results: the AUTOMATED PROGRAMMER system. il *Science* 246:1169-72 D 1 '89

ENGLE, CLYDE WILLIAM

about

Acton in action. T. Jaffe. *Forbes* 144:164-5 Ag 7 '89

ENGLE, JAMES A.

Age 30: single, just getting under way. il por *Fortune* 120 no10 Special Issue:128 Fall '89

ENGLEBARDT, STANLEY L.

Are you over-exercising? il *Reader's Digest* 134:135-9 Mr '89

The disease women fear most. il *Reader's Digest* 134:61-3 Ja '89

Matt's biggest race. il pors *Reader's Digest* 135:53-8 Jl '89

ENGLER, ROBERT

Exxon's one-act. *The Nation* 248:836-7 Je 19 '89

ENGLES, KATHLEEN C.

5 beautiful moms say, "Go for it all!". il por *Redbook* 173:123-7 My '89

ENGLEWOOD (COLO.)

Churches (Buildings)

A city upon a hill [Bethany Lutheran Church, designed by Tapley/Lunow Architects] M. Gaskie. il *Architectural Record* 177:106-9 F '89

ENGLISH, DEIRDRE

(jt. auth) *See* Ehrenreich, Barbara, and English, Deirdre

ENGLISH, RAYMOND

Trials of a textbook writer. *National Review* 41:36 F 24 '89

ENGLISH AS A SECOND LANGUAGE *See* English language—Study and teaching

ENGLISH BACH FESTIVAL *See* Music festivals—Great Britain

ENGLISH CHANNEL TUNNEL

Chunnel vision. M. Ciriello. il *World Press Review* 36:54 Je '89

Eurotunnel of love? [stock price] M. Maremont. il *Business Week* p56 F 27 '89

Full throttle toward a new era. S. Tully. il maps *Fortune* 120:131-2+ N 20 '89

A new Channel crossing: light at the end of the tunnel? J. P. Cole and K. DeBres. il maps *Focus (New York, N.Y.: 1950)* 38:1-9+ Wint '88

Trouble in the tunnel. A. Phillips. il *Maclean's* 102:40+ O 9 '89

ENGLISH COMPOSITION *See* English language—Composition

ENGLISH COOKING *See* Cooking, English

ENGLISH DECORATIVE ARTS *See* Decoration and ornament

ENGLISH DICTIONARIES *See* English language—Dictionaries

ENGLISH DRAMATISTS *See* Dramatists, English

ENGLISH DRAWING *See* Drawing, English

ENGLISH FICTION

See also

Booker Prize

The decline of the English novel. D. J. Taylor. *World Press Review* 36:59 F '89

The English novel unsheathes its claws [W. Baldwin's Beware the cat] A. Broyard. il *The New York Times Book Review* 94:12 F 5 '89

ENGLISH FURNITURE *See* Furniture, English

ENGLISH HISTORY *See* Great Britain—History

ENGLISH HOUSE DECORATION *See* House decoration, English

ENGLISH LANGUAGE

See also

Sex discrimination in language

Bilingualism in America: English should be the only language. S. I. Hayakawa. il *USA Today (Periodical)* 118:32-4 Jl '89

English: the language of liberty [English as official language] J. R. Joelson. *The Humanist* 49:35-6 Jl/Ag '89

Legislating assimilation: the English-only movement. M. R. Halton. il *The Christian Century* 106:1119-21 N 29 '89

Say it in English. E. Salholz. il *Newsweek* 113:22-3 F 20 '89

Unbreakable language barriers [English and French processed differently in the brain; research by Anne Cutler and others] *Discover* 10:10+ D '89

Accents

Are accents out? Hey, dude, like neh-oh way! P. Cooke. il *The New York Times Magazine* p50+ N 19 '89

Acronyms

See Acronyms

Anecdotes, facetiae, satire, etc.

Drawing the line [English-only crusade] B. Ehrenreich. il *Mother Jones* 14:7-8 Je '89

Bibliography

O little town of Plugsville. W. Safire. il *The New York Times Magazine* p24+ D 3 '89

Composition

See also

Creative writing

English and journalism: reaching the same goal [high school instruction] C. Witt. *The Education Digest* 55:51-3 N '89

Faculty development from the inside [holistic assessment and placement project for composition classes at Long Beach City College] K. Burne and others. pors *Change* 21:43-9 My/Je '89

Helping give students a sense of audience [junior high school magazine in Clinton, Ill.] K. S. Carter. *The Education Digest* 55:43-6 O '89

In defense of "vague" assignments [stimulating creative thinking in high school students] D. Wolfe. *The Education Digest* 55:40-2 O '89

Whole-language instruction: teaching authorship [elementary students] L. L. Lamme. *The Education Digest* 55:46-50 N '89

Aids and devices

Homework Writer [computer program] C. S. Holzberg. il *Home Office Computing* 7:75-6 S '89

Homework Writer [computer program] C. S. Holzberg. il *Compute!* 11:70 Ag '89

Revising: the fourth R? [effect of access to word processing on students' attitudes toward writing; research by Vicki Baer] G. W. Bracey. il *Phi Delta Kappan* 70:561-2 Mr '89

Dialects

See also

Black-English dialects

Don't ax the mayor [letter to R. Green on New Yorkese spoken by New York City students] E. Koch. *Harper's* 278:21-2 Mr '89

Dictionaries

See also

Information systems—Dictionaries
Oxford English dictionary
Publishers and publishing—Dictionaries

Profiles [A. W. Read] M. Stacey. por *The New Yorker* 65:51-3+ S 4 '89

Shades of gray/grey [Webster's dictionary of English usage] W. Safire. il *The New York Times Magazine* p8+ Jl 16 '89

ENGLISH LANGUAGE—*cont.*
Elision
The elision fields. W. Safire. il *The New York Times Magazine*
p16+ Ag 13 '89
Errors in speech
See Speech errors
Etymology
Haunted words. R. Lederer. il *The New York Times Magazine*
p14+ S 3 '89
Profiles [A. W. Read] M. Stacey. por *The New Yorker* 65:51-3+
S 4 '89
Saved by what bell? [condensed from Everyday phrases]
N. Ewart. il *Reader's Digest* 134:165-6+ My '89
Who said it first? [origins of expressions] M. Vanoni. *Good
Housekeeping* 208:247 Je '89
Word histories. C. M. Carver. See alternate issues of The
Atlantic beginning October 1988
Foreign words and phrases
Succinctly spoken. H. Rheingold. *The New York Times
Magazine* p18+ Ag 27 '89
Gender
See also
Sex discrimination in language
Grammar
See also
English language—Usage
Pronouns
Gender benders. D. Seligman. il *Fortune* 119:154 Ap 10
'89
Pronunciation
Breakout [didn't pronounced as dit'n] C. Murphy. il *The
Atlantic* 264:14+ Jl '89
Spelling
See Spelling
Study and teaching
See also
English language—Composition
English teachers
Project LEIF
"Broadcast English" for nonstandard dialect speakers [black
high school students] J. F. Robbins. *The Education Digest*
54:52-3 F '89
Chicago law maker tells grocers to learn English [W. Henry]
por *Jet* 77:15 D 25 '89-Ja 1 '90
Don't ax the mayor [letter to R. Green on New Yorkese
spoken by New York City students] E. Koch. *Harper's*
278:21-2 Mr '89
Elderly refugees and language learning. A. G. Grognet. il
Aging no359:8-11 '89
English classes open up new opportunities for Hispanic New
Yorkers. il *Aging* no359:23 '89
Leadership through language training [English as a second
language at the WHO Learning Centre] E. N. Francisco.
il *World Health* p6 N '89
A "mastery curriculum" for English, grades 5-12. A. A.
Glatthorn. *The Education Digest* 54:40-3 Ja '89
On alienation and the ESL student [English teacher's year
in Spain] L. Carey. il *Phi Delta Kappan* 71:74-5 S '89
Reading, 'riting & running [J. Deatherage incorporates running
into his high school English class in Richland, Wash.]
R. Blount. il pors *Runner's World* 24:26-8 Ja '89
Aids and devices
Homework [Mad Libs program] H. E. H. Aycock. il *Compute!*
11:98 O '89
Video technology: its effects on teaching English and film.
B. Gallagher. *The Education Digest* 54:29-32 Mr '89
Great Britain
See English language in Great Britain
Terms and phrases
See also
Clichés
Slogans
On language. W. Safire. See issues of The New York Times
Magazine
Saved by what bell? [condensed from Everyday phrases]
N. Ewart. il *Reader's Digest* 134:165-6+ My '89
Who said it first? [origins of expressions] M. Vanoni. *Good
Housekeeping* 208:247 Je '89
A word edgewise. P. Lubin. See issues of National Review
beginning October 13, 1989
Word watch. A. H. Soukhanov. See alternate issues of The
Atlantic beginning January 1987
Wordwise. See issues of National Geographic World beginning
August 1987
Anecdotes, facetiae, satire, etc.
Of many things [Richard Lederer's Crazy English] G. W.
Hunt. *America* 161:438 D 16 '89
Usage
English, anyone? S. Agnew. por *Conservative Digest* 15:44-5
My/Je '89
Lederer's "linguistic ludicrousness" lands at Pocket Books.
G. Corcoran. il *Publishers Weekly* 235:34 Je 9 '89
On language. W. Safire. See issues of The New York Times
Magazine
A word edgewise. P. Lubin. See issues of National Review
beginning October 13, 1989

Anecdotes, facetiae, satire, etc.
I still remember English. R. Schoenstein. il *New Choices
for the Best Years* 29:96 Mr '89
ENGLISH LANGUAGE ARTS *See* Language arts
ENGLISH LANGUAGE IN FOREIGN COUNTRIES
The medium is the message [use of English signs by
demonstrators around the world] il *Time* 133:64-5 Je 5
'89
ENGLISH LANGUAGE IN FRANCE
"L'affaire Pasteur" prompts Canadian outcry [decision to
publish journals in English] D. Dickson. il *Science* 244:280-1
Ap 21 '89
ENGLISH LANGUAGE IN GREAT BRITAIN
Speaking the prince's English. M. Bradbury. il *The New
York Times Magazine* p46+ S 24 '89
Accents
You are what you speak. il *U.S. News & World Report*
106:14 F 13 '89
ENGLISH LANGUAGE IN JAPAN
See also
Janglish
ENGLISH LANGUAGE IN THE UNITED STATES *See*
English language
ENGLISH LITERATURE
The duty of harsh criticism. Dame R. West. *The New Republic*
201 [Reprint v1]:18-20 N 6 '89 [N 7 '14]
Study and teaching
See also
English teachers
ENGLISH NATIONAL BALLET
Another language [New York City performances] T. Tobias.
il *New York* 22:136+ Ag 21 '89
Bad boy makes good [artistic director P. Schaufuss] T. Tobias.
il por *New York* 22:16 Jl 24 '89
Trinidad Sevillano's special promise: straight from the heart.
J. Mackrell. il pors *Dance Magazine* 63:24-7 Jl '89
ENGLISH NATIONAL OPERA
London. N. Goodwin. il *Opera News* 53:36-7 Mr 18 '89
London. N. Goodwin. *Opera News* 54:43 Jl '89
ENGLISH PAINTING *See* Painting, English
ENGLISH PEOPLE *See* British
ENGLISH POTTERY *See* Pottery, English
ENGLISH SILVERWARE *See* Silverware
ENGLISH SPRINGER SPANIELS *See* Spaniels
ENGLISH TEACHERS
Education in service
Knowing and not knowing [serving as evaluator at American
literature seminar for master teachers of high school English]
B. DeMott. *Change* 21:62 S/O '89
ENGLUND, ROBERT
about
Not another pretty face. B. Weber. il pors *The New York
Times Magazine* p66 Jl 16 '89
ENGLUND, SORELLA
about
Witchcraft. T. Tobias. il *New York* 22:121-2 S 25 '89
ENGLUND, STEVEN
Christians and the French Revolution. *The Christian Century*
106:679-80 Jl 19-26 '89
ENGRAILED (GENE)
Old gene, new trick [research by Nipam H. Patel] J. Rennie.
Scientific American 261:30-1 D '89
ENGRAVING
See also
Etching
ENGRAVINGS, ROCK *See* Petroglyphs
ENGVER, NIKOLAI NIKOLAYEVICH
about
Comrade Engver goes to Moscow [cover story] B. Keller.
il pors *The New York Times Magazine* p24-7+ Ag 27
'89
ENHANCEMENT, IMAGE *See* Image intensifiers
ENID A. HAUPT GARDEN (WASHINGTON, D.C.)
Around the Mall and beyond [death of hundred year old
linden tree] E. Park. il *Smithsonian* 20:26+ Je '89
ENKEPHALINS
See also
Proenkephalin
ENLARGER EASELS (PHOTOGRAPHY) *See* Photography—
Enlargers and enlarging
ENLARGERS (PHOTOGRAPHY) *See* Photography—Enlargers
and enlarging
ENLARGING LENSES *See* Lenses, Photographic
ENLIGHTENMENT
The dark legacy of the Enlightenment [image of blacks]
G. Wills. il *The New York Review of Books* 36:9-11 Mr
30 '89
Ideas and ideologies [philosophers of the French Enlighten-
ment and the French Revolution] M. Cranston. bibl il
History Today 39:10-14 My '89
ENNIS, MICHAEL
Artful independence: up-to-date backdrop for a contemporary
collection in Dallas. il *Architectural Digest* 46:212-19 O
'89
Old world treasures in Dallas. il por *Architectural Digest*
46:120-9+ Ag '89

ENNIS BUSINESS FORMS, INC.
Limited options. K. Wandycz. il por *Forbes* 144:166 N 27 '89

ENNOSUKE, ICHIKAWA, 1939-
about
Ennosuke III and his "Super Kabuki": Kabuki's revolutionary traditionalist. P. Grilli. il pors *Dance Magazine* 63:30-5 S '89
Exquisitely oriented. L. A. Jacobs. *The New Leader* 72:23 S 18 '89
Witchcraft. T. Tobias. il *New York* 22:121-2 S 25 '89

ENOLA GAY (AIRPLANE)
Silver Hill [restoration work] P. Scott. il *Flying* 116:66-8+ N '89

ENOS, CLIVE, AND ENOS, SONDRA FORSYTH
How we live now. il *Ladies' Home Journal* 106:140-1+ Ap '89

ENOS, SONDRA FORSYTH
How to have a second honeymoon (without leaving home). il *Redbook* 174:118-19+ N '89
"My husband wanted the perfect housewife". il *Ladies' Home Journal* 106:12+ Ja '89
"Our dream house made our marriage a nightmare". il *Ladies' Home Journal* 106:14+ Je '89
(jt. auth) See Enos, Clive, and Enos, Sondra Forsyth

ENQUIRER *See* National enquirer

ENRICO FERMI AWARD
DOE honors Setlow and Weisskopf with Fermi Award. pors *Physics Today* 42:89-90 Ap '89

ENRICO IV [drama] See Pirandello, Luigi, 1867-1936

ENRICO LEONE [opera] See Steffani, Agostino

ENROLLMENT, COLLEGE See Colleges and universities—Enrollment

ENROLLMENT, DENTAL SCHOOL AND COLLEGE See Dental schools and colleges—Enrollment

ENROLLMENT, SCHOOL *See* School enrollment

ENROLLMENT, VETERINARY COLLEGE See Veterinary colleges—Enrollment

ENRON CORP.
The hour before the dawn. J. Cook. il por *Forbes* 143:52+ My 15 '89

ENSEMBLES (MUSIC) *See* Instrumental ensembles

ENSOLI, BARBARA, AND OTHERS
AIDS-Kaposi's sarcoma-derived cells express cytokines with autocrine and paracrine growth effects. bibl f il *Science* 243:223-6 Ja 13 '89

ENSRUD, BARBARA
The fighting varietals. il *Ms.* 17:62+ My '89

ENSTAR GROUP INC.
Ring around the rosie at Kinder-Care. C. Hawkins. il *Business Week* p45-6 D 18 '89

ENSTROM HELICOPTER CORP.
Schweizer, Enstrom join teams to bid for Army trainer work. il *Aviation Week & Space Technology* 130:18-19 Ja 23 '89

ENTAMOEBA *See* Amebas

ENTERITIS, COCCIDIAL *See* Coccidiosis

ENTEROTOXINS *See* Toxins and antitoxins

ENTERPRISE FOUNDATION
A new Enterprise. F. B. Harvey. il por *The Humanist* 49:14-15+ My/Je '89

ENTERPRISE ZONES
Enterprise zones—or twilight zones? R. Stodghill, II. il *Business Week* p113 F 27 '89
Inside an 'enterprise zone' [Miami] M. Miller. il *Newsweek* 113:43 Mr 6 '89
The Kemp cure-all. D. Osborne. *The New Republic* 200:21+ Ap 3 '89
The Kemp plan for rebuilding the city. C. Oglesbee. *The Christian Century* 106:340-1 Ap 5 '89

ENTERS, ANGNA, 1907-1989
about
Obituary
Dance Magazine por 63:28+ My '89

ENTERTAINERS
See also
Actors and actresses
Black entertainers
Children as entertainers
Clowns
Comedians
Geishas
Vaudeville

ENTERTAINERS, HANDICAPPED
First since illness: Lola performs onstage with Wayne Newton. il pors *Jet* 76:55-6 Je 26 '89
Lola Falana: 'I'm back! I'm not cured. But I'm healed!' [cover story] R. E. Johnson. il pors *Jet* 76:54-7 Ag 14 '89

ENTERTAINING
See also
Balls (Parties)
Birthday parties
Buffet meals
Business entertaining
Caterers and catering
Children's parties
Christmas entertaining
Dinners and dining
Duchin Touch (Firm)
Etiquette
Government entertaining
Guests
Halloween parties
Luncheons
Slumber parties
Table decoration
Table setting
Teas
Tricks
America entertains. C. Rossant. See issues of McCall's beginning February 1987
America entertains [special section] il *McCall's* 116:43-6+ Ap '89
. . . and bring the kids [entertaining at the home of K. Beckwith and S. Barrow] L. Rosch. il pors *Working Woman* 14:118-21+ Je '89
Down-to-earth . . . and delicious [entertaining at the home of H. Dake] S. Costner. il por *Working Woman* 14:153-6 N '89
Easy entertaining [summer] C. Koury. il *Parents* 64:106-8+ Ag '89
Entertaining from your garden [special section; with editorial comment by Stevie O. Daniels] il *Organic Gardening* 36:5, 33-52 O '89
Entertaining with cheese. S. La Rosa. il *McCall's* 116:57-8+ My '89
Folk art, friends and good food [home of A. Julian; excerpt from Mary Emmerling's American country cooking] M. E. Emmerling. il *Working Woman* 14:100-2 Ja '89
Great new places to have a party (I) [New York City; cover story] B. Costikyan. il *New York* 22:58-68+ N 13 '89
Great new places to have a party (II) [New York City] B. Costikyan. il *New York* 22:48-52+ N 20 '89
Holiday entertaining [cover story] G. Duffy. il *New York* 22:63-73+ O 23 '89
How to host the perfect poker party. S. Wyler. il *New Choices for the Best Years* 29:70-5 Ap '89
Last-minute parties: the best kind! il *Glamour* 87:164-7 Ja '89
Let's get together. C. Koury. il *Parents* 64:156-8+ Ap '89
Lucky breaks [New Year's open house] R. Schrambling. il *The New York Times Magazine* p25-6 D 24 '89
Parties with flair [Monique and Leslie Bond's tips] B. Goldman. il *Better Homes and Gardens* 67:79-86+ Ja '89
Patio party. C. Lyons. il *Ebony* 44:108-10+ S '89
Safari [theme party staged by Chéz-zam] *The New Yorker* 65:35-6 Mr 20 '89
Summer entertaining [casual and elegant] J. T. Hazard. il *Ladies' Home Journal* 106:146-8+ Je '89
Summer entertaining: the best and the lightest [cover story] G. Duffy. il *New York* 22:46-56+ My 15 '89
Welcome to party paradise [teenage party] il *Seventeen* 48:194-8+ My '89
Anecdotes, facetiae, satire, etc.
Party strategies. S. Parriott. il *Mademoiselle* 95:128+ D '89
Photographs and photography
Point, shoot, hob, nob. E. Nemy. il *Popular Photography* 96:30-1 Ja '89

ENTERTAINMENT AND SPORTS PROGRAMMING NETWORK
ESPN is playing in an international arena now. R. W. King. *Business Week* p71 Ag 14 '89
Late-night score wars [SportsCenter] A. Wolff. il *Sports Illustrated* 70:74 Je 26 '89
Residuals woes plague ESPN, CNN [advertisements beamed into Latin America] J. Loftus. il *Channels (New York, N.Y.: 1986)* 9:8 Jl/Ag '89
What would happen if . . . 20 of the best-ever NFL teams played a "Dream season"? S. Smith. il *Sports Illustrated* 71:159 S 11 '89

ENTERTAINMENT INDUSTRY
See also
Chéz-zam (Firm)
Geffen Company
Jeremy's Place (Firm)
Jerry Kravat Entertainment Services (Firm)
Management Company Entertainment Group Inc.
MCA Inc.
Radio City Music Hall Productions
SBK Entertainment World Inc.
Spectacor (Firm)
Walt Disney Company
Leisure and recreation. D. Fanning. il *Forbes* 143:168-9 Ja 9 '89
Most of '88. il *Time* 133:103 Ja 2 '89
Acquisitions and mergers
Are MCA and Disney ready to co-star? G. G. Marcial. il *Business Week* p97 Je 26 '89
International aspects
Invasion of the studio snatchers. R. Grover. il *Business Week* p52-4 O 16 '89
History
What was hot [entertainment in the eighties] L. Jay. il *Ladies' Home Journal* 106:148+ N '89

ENTERTAINMENT INDUSTRY—cont.

Periodicals

See also
Entertainment weekly

Securities

See also
Fidelity Select Leisure & Entertainment Fund

Suits and claims

All my children [lawyer L. Marks] P. Newcomb. il por *Forbes* 144:287 N 27 '89
Big bad Bert [interview with B. Fields] C. Stauth. il por *American Film* 15:46-50 D '89

Canada

See also
BCL Entertainment Corporation

Japan

See also
PIA Company

ENTERTAINMENT WEEKLY

News that you can choose. il *Time* 134:49 Jl 24 '89
Time Inc.'s coming attraction. E. Diamond. il *New York* 22:16+ N 20 '89

ENTOMOLOGY

See also
Forensic entomology
Entomologists wane as insects wax. C. Holden. il *Science* 246:754-6 N 10 '89

History

Garden of earthy delights. J. Bosveld. il *Omni (New York, N.Y.)* 11:60-3 Ja '89

ENTOMOPHAGA

An Aussie fungus among us [Entomophaga grylli kills grasshoppers; research by Ray Carruthers] *Science News* 136:46 Jl 15 '89
The moth killers [fungus kills gypsy moths] il *Discover* 10:8 N '89

ENTRANCE REQUIREMENTS, COLLEGE See Colleges and universities—Admission
ENTRANCE REQUIREMENTS, HIGH SCHOOL See High schools—Admission
ENTRANCE STAIRWAYS See Stairways
ENTRANCES (DOORWAYS) See Doorways
ENTRANCEWAY LANDSCAPE ARCHITECTURE See Landscape architecture
ENTRANCEWAY LANDSCAPE GARDENING See Landscape gardening
ENTRAPMENT (LAW)

DEA Don Juan [women set up and arrested for cocaine dealing by undercover agent M. R. Portell] J. Carney. il por *Time* 133:24 Ap 3 '89

ENTREPRENEURS

See also
Aged and business
Black entrepreneurs
Business enterprises
Women entrepreneurs
Youth and business
The 1990 guide to small business [special section] bibl il *U.S. News & World Report* 107:72-3+ O 23 '89
America on the rise: a new breed of innovators. G. F. Gilder. il *Reader's Digest* 135:126-8 Ag '89
Britain's fallen idols of free enterprise. R. Knight. il *U.S. News & World Report* 107:55+ D 4 '89
Building your own portfolio. M. O'Brien. il *Nation's Business* 77:30+ Ap '89
Enterprise. See issues of Business Week beginning July 27, 1987
Entrepreneurial couples [views of Frank and Sharan Barnett] il *The Futurist* 23:50 My/Je '89
An entrepreneurial tree sprouts in Europe [high tech companies] D. Dickson. il *Science* 245:1038-40 S 8 '89
Entrepreneurs: how to streamline your business. P. Edwards and S. Edwards. il *Home Office Computing* 7:38 My '89
Entrepreneurs: the real cultural revolutionaries [excerpts from address, October 23, 1987] P. Hawken. *Utne Reader* p72-3 Ja/F '89
For Italy's entrepreneurs, the figures are bella. C. Haberman. il *The New York Times Magazine* p32-4+ Jl 16 '89
High-tech guru Steven Burrill [interview] M. Mandell. il por *High Technology Business* 9:20-3 N/D '89
How entrepreneurial couples work together. F. Barnett and S. Barnett. il pors *Working Woman* 14:77-80 Ap '89
How we can regain our competitive edge. S. Ramo. *Scientific American* 260:148 My '89
Maine millionaire David Franklin goes for broke by giving big bucks to people who need it. D. Mathison. il pors *People Weekly* 32:83-4+ D 18 '89
Making it. See issues of Nation's Business beginning September 1985
Partners in entrepreneurship [married couples; research by Frank and Sharan Barnett] S. Nelton. il *Nation's Business* 77:38-9 Mr '89
Putting yourself on the line. C. Peters. *The Washington Monthly* 21:64-5 F '89
Russia's embryonic capitalists. P. Dragadze. il *Forbes* 144:90-4+ O 16 '89
Should you be in business for yourself? [quiz] P. Lohr. il *Reader's Digest* 135:49-52 Jl '89

The start-up blues. J. Schlosberg. *The Washington Monthly* 20:25-30 Ja '89
State funds for start-ups. J. C. Szabo. il *Nation's Business* 77:42+ Je '89
Success by surprise. C. A. Jaffe. il *Nation's Business* 77:30+ S '89
A team approach from the start. W. J. Stolze. por *Nation's Business* 77:9 N '89
The up & comers. See issues of Forbes
Wedded to their work [entreprenurial couples; views of Frank and Sharan Barnett] S. Brewer. il *New Choices for the Best Years* 29:13 Jl '89
A well-grounded plan can launch your business. S. Woolley. il *Business Week* p124-5 D 4 '89

History

Enterprise past and present [working class entrepreneurs in late 19th and early 20th century Britain] J. Benson. il *History Today* 39:5-7 Ag '89

Psychology

The entrepreneurial self. D. Cole. il *Psychology Today* 23:60-3 Je '89
How to get rid of an MBA (marginal business attitude). P. Edwards and S. Edwards. il *Home Office Computing* 7:42+ D '89

Training

To make the grade, just go do it. C. Grant. por *Nation's Business* 77:12 D '89
What B-school doesn't teach you about startups. il *Business Week* p40-1 Jl 24 '89

ENTROPY

Cosmic quarrel [Huw Price questions S. W. Hawking's arrow of time explanation] T. Beardsley. *Scientific American* 261:22+ O '89

ENUFF Z'NUFF (MUSICAL GROUP)

Enuff Z'Nuff. K. Neely. il *Rolling Stone* p17 O 19 '89

ENVIRODYNE INDUSTRIES, INC.

Scrapping over a food packager. G. G. Marcial. *Business Week* p146 Mr 20 '89

ENVIRONMENT

See also
Adaptation (Biology)
Aged and the environment
All terrain vehicles—Environmental aspects
Amusement parks—Environmental aspects
Antarctic research—Environmental aspects
Arts and the environment
Automobiles—Environmental aspects
Bicycles—Environmental aspects
Celebrities and the environment
Children and the environment
Computers—Environmental use
Council on Environmental Quality (U.S.)
Diapers—Environmental aspects
Ecology
Electric lines—Environmental aspects
Energy policy—Environmental aspects
Environmental refugees
Express highways—Environmental aspects
Genetic research—Environmental aspects
Guided missiles—Deactivation—Environmental aspects
Helicopters—Environmental aspects
Herbicides—Environmental aspects
Heredity and environment
Human ecology
Indians of North America—Influence on nature
Indians of North America—Reservations—Environmental aspects
Industry and the environment
Laboratories—Environmental aspects
Man—Influence of environment
Man—Influence on nature
Military and the environment
Nuclear energy—Environmental aspects
Pesticides—Environmental aspects
Religion and the environment
Rock musicians and the environment
Shopping centers—Environmental aspects
Snowmobiles and snowmobiling—Environmental aspects
Television and the environment
Tourist trade—Environmental aspects
Trucks—Environmental aspects
War—Environmental aspects
Women and the environment
The earth . . . strikes back. il *Life* 12:8-15+ Ja '89
Enduring earth. B. Gilbert. il *Life* 12:82-4+ F '89
Heaven on earth: the race for renewal [special section] il *Harper's Bazaar* 122:58-67+ Ja '89
How the environmental crisis can improve our lives [cover story; special section; with editorial comment by Eric Utne] il *Utne Reader* p2, 69-97 N/D '89
Managing planet earth [cover story; special section] il *Scientific American* 261:46-54+ S '89
Now wait just a minute [scientists dispute gloomy environmental outlook] E. Linden. il *Time* 134:68 D 18 '89
Our fragile earth. J. Schell. il *Discover* 10:44-7+ O '89
Save the planet [cover story; special section] il *Omni (New York, N.Y.)* 11:34-6+ S '89

ENVIRONMENT—*cont.*

Save the whales, screw the shrimp. J. Williams. il *Esquire* 111:89-95 F '89

Sign of the times. P. C. Pritchard. *National Parks* 63:5 Jl/Ag '89

Synergistic interactions and environment. N. Myers. *BioScience* 39:506 S '89

Warning: planet in peril [cover story; special issue] il maps *Scholastic Update (Teachers' edition)* 121:2-8+ Ap 21 '89

Bibliography

Books of note. See issues of Environment

Conferences

See also

International Conference on the Changing Atmosphere: Implications for Global Security

A failed initiative [conference at The Hague] B. Wallace. *Maclean's* 102:14 Mr 20 '89

Global risk assessment [Washington, D.C. forum] C. Mlot. il *BioScience* 39:428-30 Jl/Ag '89

Global warming becomes hot issue for Bromley. M. Sun. il por *Science* 246:569 N 3 '89

Economic aspects

See also

World Commission on Environment and Development

A bankers' world [environmental assessment program at the World Bank] D. Henwood. *The Nation* 249:481 O 30 '89

Bankrolling debacles? [World Bank] A. Levine. il map *U.S. News & World Report* 107:43-4+ S 25 '89

Big dividends from pollution cleanup. *Science News* 136:191 S 16 '89

The boiling pot [development vs. conservation] D. Gergen. il *U.S. News & World Report* 106:76 My 15 '89

Conservation woes at the World Bank. B. Rich. il *The Nation* 248:73+ Ja 23 '89

Death of a small planet [cover story] M. Bookchin. il *The Progressive* 53:19-23 Ag '89

Ecopolitics in the global greenhouse. W. B. Wood and others. bibl f il *Environment* 31:12-17+ S '89

The environment: a North-South conflict. M. Copulos. *Current (Washington, D.C.)* 317:35-9 N '89

Environment and economy [address, May 17, 1989] T. D'Aquino. *Vital Speeches of the Day* 55:621-4 Ag 1 '89

Environment, poverty and growth [address, February 9, 1989] A. Karaosmanoglu. *Vital Speeches of the Day* 55:396-400 Ap 15 '89

First word. B. E. Babbitt. por *Omni (New York, N.Y.)* 11:6 S '89

First word [steady-state economics] H. E. Daly. il *Omni (New York, N.Y.)* 11:8 Ja '89

Global change and our common future [address, May 2, 1989; with editorial comment by Timothy O'Riordan] G. H. Brundtland. bibl f il por *Environment* 31:inside cover, 16-20+ Je '89

Greening the summit [Paris economic summit] T. Beardsley. *Scientific American* 261:17 S '89

Harnessing market forces to protect the environment [Project 88 report; cover story] R. N. Stavins. bibl f il *Environment* 31:4-7+ Ja/F '89

Health over money: the new environmental consciousness [Harris poll] B. Fischman. il *Psychology Today* 23:10 N '89

How much is a sea otter worth [putting price on the environment] M. J. Mandel. il *Business Week* p59+ Ag 21 '89

How to secure our common future. G. H. Brundtland. *Scientific American* 261:190 S '89

The industrial nations make a start [Paris economic summit] J. D. Hair. il *International Wildlife* 19:26 N/D '89

Making the world work for people [sustainable development] N. Myers. il *International Wildlife* 19:12-14 N/D '89

The materials we need to create a sustainable society lie close to home. D. J. Morris. il *Utne Reader* p84-5+ N/D '89

Protecting the environment. M. L. Weidenbaum. *Society* 27:49-56 N/D '89

Risk, safety and capitalism [special section] bibl *Society* 27:4-31 N/D '89

Sustainable development: lessons from success [cover story] W. V. C. Reid. bibl f il *Environment* 31:6-9+ My '89

A sustainable society. G. W. Barrett. *BioScience* 39:754 D '89

The test of our civilization [interview] N. Gardels. il *New Perspectives Quarterly* 6:4-8 Spr '89

Upward from a foothills summit [Paris economic summit] T. O'Riordan. *Environment* 31:inside front cover Jl/Ag '89

The virtue of enoughness. W. Sachs. il *New Perspectives Quarterly* 6:16-19 Spr '89

We can't heal the environment without remaking our society. M. Bookchin. il *Utne Reader* p80-2 N/D '89

Who bears the burden of sustainability? K. Piddington. il *New Perspectives Quarterly* 6:8-11 Spr '89

Wildlands: balancing conversion with conservation in World Bank projects [cover story] R. Goodland and G. Ledec. bibl f il *Environment* 31:6-11+ N '89

Influence on man

See Environmental psychology

Laws and regulations

See Environmental policy

Research

See Environmental research

Statistics

21st Environmental Quality Index: the planet strikes back! il *National Wildlife* 27:33-40 F/Mr '89

Study and teaching

See Environmental education

China

China's environmental morass. V. Smil. bibl f *Current History* 88:277-80+ S '89

Costa Rica

Death of a small country [U.S. military presence and the environment] M. I. Niman. il *The Progressive* 53:24-5 Ag '89

Madagascar

No nation an island. M. L. Knox. il *Sierra* 74:78-84 My/Je '89

ENVIRONMENT (ART)

Four by four [Boyle Family] il *Esquire* 111:120-3 My '89

Opus 40: a sculptor's obsession in upstate New York [work of H. Fite] B. Gill. il por *Architectural Digest* 46:46+ Mr '89

ENVIRONMENT (HUMAN) *See* Human ecology

ENVIRONMENT AND PUBLIC WORKS COMMITTEE *See* United States. Congress. Senate. Committee on Environment and Public Works

ENVIRONMENT AND STATE *See* Environmental policy

ENVIRONMENT IN MUSIC

Troubadours for Mother Nature [B. Oliver and G. Waldeck] C. P. Alexander. il pors *Time* 134:76 N 6 '89

ENVIRONMENTAL ASSOCIATIONS

See also

Anti-nuclear movement

Coalition to Cease Ocean Dumping

Conservation Foundation

Earth First! (Organization)

Foundation for Environmental Conservation

Friends of the Earth

Greenpeace Foundation

Land trusts

National Audubon Society

National Parks and Conservation Association

National Wildlife Federation

Natural Resources Defense Council

Oceanic Society

Sierra Club

TreePeople (Organization)

Wilderness Society

Windstar Foundation

A selective guide to environmental groups. H. Goldstein and J. Walljasper. *Utne Reader* p96-7 N/D '89

Canada

See also

Pollution Probe Foundation

The missing lists [series of break-ins at offices of environmental organizations] A. Steacy. il *Maclean's* 102:58 My 15 '89

ENVIRONMENTAL CONSERVATION DEPT. (N.Y.) *See* New York (State). Dept. of Environmental Conservation

ENVIRONMENTAL DESIGN

See also

City planning

ENVIRONMENTAL EDUCATION

See also

Alliance for Environmental Education

AuSable Institute of Environmental Studies

Oceanographic education

Vanderbilt University. Student Environmental Health Project

Environmental Trojan horse [Learning Alliance courses] D. K. Mano. *National Review* 41:50-1 Ag 4 '89

Reaching out from the inner city [Inner City Outings leader M. Pyeatt] B. Fuller. il por *Sierra* 74:50-4 Jl/Ag '89

Scaring our children. M. Novak. il *Forbes* 144:167 O 30 '89

Federal aid

Personnel and research shortages: policy recommendations for the environmental professions. R. G. Luthy. bibl f *Environment* 31:4-5+ Ap '89

ENVIRONMENTAL ENGINEERING

See also

Environmental impact statements

Personnel and research shortages: policy recommendations for the environmental professions. R. G. Luthy. bibl f *Environment* 31:4-5+ Ap '89

ENVIRONMENTAL ENGINEERING (BUILDINGS)

See also

Baubiologie

Solar houses

21st century pyramid [energy-efficient home of B. Rutan in the Mojave Desert; cover story] J. L. Schefter. il por *Popular Science* 235:65-9 N '89

The case for natural schools. M. Wells. il *Country Journal* 16:34-9 Mr/Ap '89

ENVIRONMENTAL ENGINEERING (BUILDINGS)—*cont.*
The environmental kitchen. H. Huber. il *Country Journal* 16:39 F '89
Suppressing the office energy appetite [new headquarters for National Resources Defense Council] J. S. Russell. il *Architectural Record* 177:128-33 O '89

ENVIRONMENTAL FIELD SERVICES INC.
Once burned, twice the CEO? [S. M. Mecum] S. Ticer. il por *Business Week* Special Issue:169 Je 16 '89

ENVIRONMENTAL HEALTH
See also
Allergy
Clinical ecology
Occupational health and safety
United States. Occupational Safety and Health Administration
Acid rain—one of America's worst killers. il *Utne Reader* p61-2 S/O '89
Cleaning up our act [special section] il *Health (New York, N.Y.)* 21:41-7+ Mr '89
From heresy to conventional wisdom. L. Winner. il *Technology Review* 92:18 Ag/S '89
Health is development. P. Ponrattanawanarom. il *World Health* p21 Mr '89
Opening doors: making risk communication agency reality [environmental protection agencies] C. Chess and B. J. Hance. bibl f il *Environment* 31:10-15+ Je '89
Our planet, our health [cover story] G. Scott. bibl il *Current Health 2* 16:4-7+ D '89
Promoting a healthy environment [Western Pacific region] P. H. Guo. il *World Health* p10-11 N '89
Reducing the incidence of disease: clues from the environment [esophageal cancer] H. D. Foster. bibl f il maps *Environment* 31:12-17+ Ap '89
Risk, safety and capitalism [special section] bibl *Society* 27:4-31 N/D '89
A world fit to live in. M. T. Morgan. il *World Health* p25-7 My '89

ENVIRONMENTAL ILLNESS
Environmental illness: the new plague. L. Lamb. il *Utne Reader* p14-15 S/O '89

ENVIRONMENTAL IMPACT STATEMENTS
As for the impact on the environment . . . [mass mailing of impact statements on super collider sites] J. Tully. il *Common Cause Magazine* 15:8 N/D '89
Bill calls for wolf recovery EIS [reintroduction of grey wolves to Yellowstone] il *National Parks* 63:9 S/O '89
Environmental impact statements and climate change. G. T. Prickett and D. A. Wirth. bibl f *Environment* 31:44-inside back cover Mr '89

ENVIRONMENTAL INDEXES *See* Environment—Statistics
ENVIRONMENTAL LAW *See* Environmental policy
ENVIRONMENTAL LAW INSTITUTE
Environmental Law Institute. J. W. Futrell. *Environment* 31:45 S '89
ENVIRONMENTAL LOBBY *See* Environmental movement
ENVIRONMENTAL MARKETING
A new sales pitch: the environment. B. Bremner. il *Business Week* p50 Jl 24 '89

Canada
A divisive alliance [Pollution Probe and Friends of the Earth endorse Loblaw's environmentally friendly line of products] *Maclean's* 102:40 Jl 17 '89

ENVIRONMENTAL MOVEMENT
See also
Aged and the environment
Anti-nuclear movement
Arts and the environment
Bioregionalism
Celebrities and the environment
Cleaning of lakes, rivers, etc.
Conservation of resources
Earth Day
Ecofeminism
Energy conservation
Environmental associations
Industry and the environment
Religion and the environment
Rock musicians and the environment
Women and the environment
21st Environmental Quality Index: the planet strikes back! il *National Wildlife* 27:33-40 F/Mr '89
Animal activists: get green! P. Greanville. il *Utne Reader* p52 S/O '89
Apocalypse now? Ecology and the peril of doomsday visions. E. Zencey. il *Utne Reader* p90-3 Ja/F '89
Back-yard conservationists. *Reader's Digest* 135:159-60+ O '89
The daily planet [cover story; special section; with editorial comment by Joel Gurin] il *American Health* 8:51-4+, 148 S '89
Environmental activism: here we go again. B. J. Wattenberg. il *U.S. News & World Report* 106:29+ Ap 17 '89
Environmental politics [Alaskan oil spill reinvigorates environmentalists] G. Hackett. il *Newsweek* 113:18-19 Ap 17 '89
Help wanted: an activist's guide to a better earth [special section] C. Spencer. il *Omni (New York, N.Y.)* 11:109+ S '89

Home, sweet planet [special section] il *American Health* 8:85-90+ Mr '89
Moving to greener pastures [ecological consciousness infusing social movements] B. Ahlberg. il *Utne Reader* p10-11 Mr/Ap '89
Neo-modern ecology. A. Touraine. il *New Perspectives Quarterly* 6:33-6 Spr '89
On environmentalism. D. K. Mano. *National Review* 41:63+ F 10 '89
Organic living. R. Rodale. il *Organic Gardening* 36:23-4 F '89
Our environment: realistic solutions for a growing problem. T. Jackson. il *Better Homes and Gardens* 67:32 S '89
People who make a difference. il *National Wildlife* 27:4-11 Ag/S '89
Planet stricken. A. P. Crawford and A. Levine. il *Vogue* 179:710-15+ S '89
Putting the earth first. il *Business Week* p154+ S 25 '89
Seeing Green: how we can create a more satisfying society. J. Porritt. il *Utne Reader* p70-5+ N/D '89
A spill destined to grease wheels [Alaskan oil spill expected to increase environmental activism] il *U.S. News & World Report* 106:13-14 Ap 17 '89
The toxic avenger strikes at corporate polluters [work of M. Kaltofen] M. Satchell. il por *U.S. News & World Report* 106:28 Je 26 '89
'We are all losing the war'. D. Russell. il *The Nation* 248:403-8 Mr 27 '89

Anecdotes, facetiae, satire, etc.
Last word. T. Runté. por *Omni (New York, N.Y.)* 11:116 S '89

History
From heresy to conventional wisdom. L. Winner. il *Technology Review* 92:18 Ag/S '89
Phenomena, comment and notes [A. Leopold] J. P. Wiley, Jr. il por *Smithsonian* 20:38+ N '89

International aspects
See also
World Environment Day
Going local goes global [grass roots environmentalism] R. Sullivan. il *Sports Illustrated* 71:98 Jl 24 '89
Grass-roots groups are our best hope for global prosperity and ecology. A. B. Durning. il *Utne Reader* p40-3+ Jl/Ag '89

Alaska
The two Alaskas [conflict between conservation ethic and industrial development reinforced by Exxon oil spill; cover story] M. D. Lemonick. il map *Time* 133:56-9+ Ap 17 '89

Alberta
See also
Alberta Wilderness Association

Arizona
Biology versus astronomy: the battle for Mount Graham [impact of proposed observatory on red squirrels] E. Pennisi. il *BioScience* 39:10-13 Ja '89
Mount Graham telescopes get the green light. il *Sky and Telescope* 77:130 F '89

Brazil
Chronicle of a death foretold [murder of environmentalist C. Mendes Filho] M. Beck. il por *Newsweek* 113:62 Ja 9 '89
Defenders of the Amazon [rubber tappers; cover story] S. Hecht and A. Cockburn. il *The Nation* 248:695-6+ My 22 '89
Extractive reserves in Brazilian Amazonia [rubber workers' proposal to fight deforestation] P. M. Fearnside. bibl f il map *BioScience* 39:387-93 Je '89
In memory of Chico Mendes [union leader and ecologist slain] J. D. Hair. il *International Wildlife* 19:30 Mr/Ap '89
Murder in the Amazon [union leader and ecologist C. Mendes Filho slain] J. Bierman. il por *Maclean's* 102:21 Ja 9 '89
Notes and comment [murder of environmentalist C. Mendes Filho] il *The New Yorker* 65:27-8 F 20 '89
Rain forest politics [discussion of May 22, 1989 article, Defenders of the Amazon] S. Hecht and A. Cockburn. *The Nation* 249:262+ S 18 '89
Whose hands will shape the future of the Amazon's green mansions? [plight of the rubber tappers; cover story] M. Parfit. bibl (p245) il maps *Smithsonian* 20:58-68+ N '89

Canada
Greening the provinces. H. Quinn. il *Maclean's* 102:44-6 Je 26 '89
Unpopular packaging [Canadians protest chlorofluorocarbons] M. Nichols. *Maclean's* 102:51 D 25 '89

Developing countries
People power and development. A. B. Durning. *Foreign Policy* 76:66-82 Fall '89
Saving the planet. A. B. Durning. il *The Progressive* 53:35-9 Ap '89
Sustainable success stories from the third world. A. B. Durning. il *Utne Reader* p44-5 Jl/Ag '89

Estonia
An interview with a leader of the Green Movement [J. Aare] D. Devyatkin. il *Environment* 30:13-15 D '88

ENVIRONMENTAL MOVEMENT—*cont.*

Florida

Marjory Stoneman Douglas. V. Gladstone. il pors *Ms.* 17:68-71 Ja/F '89

Great Britain

The year of the Greens. T. Burke. bibl f il *Environment* 31:18-20+ N '89

Hungary

Will the sun ever shine on Budapest? D. Hinrichsen. il *International Wildlife* 19:18-23 S/O '89

Maine

Fish and power in a riverine rivalry [call for the removal of Edwards Dam in Augusta, Me. in order to restore Kennebec River fisheries] B. Carpenter. il map *U.S. News & World Report* 107:90+ O 16 '89

Massachusetts

On once-wild Walden Pond. J. H. Houvouras. il *Sierra* 74:94-6 My/Je '89

Oregon

Still at loggerheads [timber industry vs. conservationists] il *Time* 134:24 Jl 10 '89

Pacific Northwest

Showdown in the treetops [confrontations over old-growth forests] M. D. Lemonick. il *Time* 134:58-9 Ag 28 '89

South Carolina

See also

Citizens Asking for a Safe Environment

Soviet Union

Excerpts from a roundtable at Moscow State University. I. I. Altshuler and R. A. Mnatsakanyan. il *Environment* 30:10-12 D '88

United States

See Environmental movement

Western Europe

Europe's Green light. D. Johnstone. il *The Progressive* 53:12-13 Jl '89

Western States

Sunset and the environment: working with you to help conserve and improve the West. B. Lane. il *Sunset (Central West edition)* 183:230-1 N '89

ENVIRONMENTAL NEWS

Afield. See issues of Sierra beginning March/April 1986

Briefings. C. Wille. See issues of Audubon beginning September 1987

Circus whales [reporting the rescue of trapped gray whales in Alaska] T. Williams. il *Audubon* 91:16-18+ Mr '89

Covering the world, ignoring the earth. M. Hertsgaard. il *Rolling Stone* p47-9 N 16 '89

Effective communication: there is much to learn. A. McGowan. *Environment* 31:inside cover Mr '89

Environmental journalism: guardian of the Asian commons [cover story] S. M. Friedman and K. A. Friedman. bibl f il *Environment* 31:6-9+ Je '89

How the EPA pollutes the news. il *Utne Reader* p60 S/O '89

An industry's mania for nightmares [press inflames concerns over storage of PCBs in Canada] G. Bain. il *Maclean's* 102:60 O 23 '89

Is TV news getting all the dirt? E. Diamond and R. Mead. il *TV Guide* 37:20-2 Je 24-30 '89

Media coverage [discussion of March 1989 article, Network television news coverage of environmental risks] M. R. Greenberg and others. il *Environment* 31:2-3 Je '89

Network television news coverage of environmental risks. M. R. Greenberg and others. bibl f il *Environment* 31:16-20+ Mr '89

The ozone's shot, the oceans stink—so what has the Monthly had to say? [Washington monthly] P. Keisling. *The Washington Monthly* 21:36-7 Mr '89

Spectrum. See issues of Environment beginning January/February 1987

Wildlife digest. See issues of International Wildlife

Wildlife digest. See issues of National Wildlife

ENVIRONMENTAL POLICY

See also

Acid rain—Laws and regulations

Conservation of resources—Laws and regulations

Energy policy—Environmental aspects

Environmental impact statements

Genetic research—Environmental aspects

Industry and the environment

Land utilization—Laws and regulations

Man—Influence on nature

Military and the environment

Pollution

Radioactive waste disposal—Laws and regulations

Strip mining—Laws and regulations

Trade waste—Disposal—Laws and regulations

United States. Congress. House. Committee on Interior and Insular Affairs

United States. Congress. Senate. Committee on Environment and Public Works

United States. Dept. of the Interior

United States. Environmental Protection Agency

Water pollution—Laws and regulations

Wilderness areas

The 101st Congress can make history. J. D. Hair. il *International Wildlife* 19:26 Ja/F '89

Battle for a safe environment gains ground. L. Brown. il *Black Enterprise* 19:39-40 F '89

Biodiversity bill update. D. E. Blockstein. *BioScience* 39:677 N '89

A Blueprint for the environment. S. McKee. *American Health* 8:88-9 Mr '89

Changing the guards [Bush administration] T. Turner. il *The Mother Earth News* 117:56 My/Je '89

Cleaning up [cover story; special section] G. Easterbrook. il *Newsweek* 114:26-9+ Jl 24 '89

E pluribus, plures [states set environmental agenda] S. Begley. il *Newsweek* 114:70-2 N 13 '89

An environmental agenda for Bush. il *USA Today (Periodical)* 118:1-2 Ag '89

Environmental priorities for the new president. W. C. Clark. *Environment* 31:inside cover Ja/F '89

Fishing for leadership [G. Bush] D. Thompson. il por *Time* 133:91-2 My 22 '89

George Bush & environmental leadership. J. D. Hair. il *National Wildlife* 27:30 F/Mr '89

Get going, Mr. Bush. E. Linden. il *Time* 134:62-3 D 18 '89

Global change begins at home. W. C. Clark. *Environment* 31:inside cover+ My '89

The grand plans of Congressman Udall. J. A. Davis. il por *Sierra* 74:86-8+ My/Je '89

The great outdoors. J. Walter. See issues of Successful Farming beginning February 1987

A green Blueprint for Bush. M. J. McCloskey. il *Sierra* 74:36-8 Ja/F '89

Harnessing market forces to protect the environment [Project 88 report; cover story] R. N. Stavins. bibl f il *Environment* 31:4-7+ Ja/F '89

How the U.S. can take the lead in the third world. E. Linden. il *Time* 134:63 O 23 '89

Law. See occasional issues of Environment

Maintaining nature's delicate balance. L. R. Jahn. il *USA Today (Periodical)* 118:84-6 N '89

Open letter to President Bush. P. C. Pritchard. il *National Parks* 63:16-17 S/O '89

A plan to help the planet [bill sponsored by A. Gore] *Time* 133:57 F 6 '89

Political science. P. A. A. Berle. *Audubon* 91:8 Jl '89

Political update. T. Turner. il *The Mother Earth News* 119:24 S/O '89

Presidential challenges. S. Manning. il map *Scholastic Update (Teachers' edition)* 121:15-17 Ap 21 '89

Protecting the environment. M. L. Weidenbaum. *Society* 27:49-56 N/D '89

Protecting the environment: where your state stands. S. Nielsen. *Good Housekeeping* 209:175 Jl '89

Revive NEPA, Mr. Bush [National Environmental Policy Act] P. A. A. Berle. *Audubon* 91:6 Ja '89

Running on empty [federal positions not being filled] L. Williamson. il *Outdoor Life* 184:16-18 O '89

Setting a tone [Bush administration] P. C. Pritchard. *National Parks* 63:4 S/O '89

States seek pollution solution. il *USA Today (Periodical)* 117:16+ Je '89

Thoughts. F. Graham. il *Audubon* 91:12 My '89

U.S. global change research: who's in charge here? R. Monastersky. *Science News* 135:235 Ap 15 '89

The United States needs an ecological survey. J. Roughgarden. *BioScience* 39:5 Ja '89

'We are all losing the war'. D. Russell. il *The Nation* 248:403-8 Mr 27 '89

What can Americans do? [preserving the rain forests] M. D. Lemonick. il *Time* 134:85 S 18 '89

What the U.S. should do. *Time* 133:65 Ja 2 '89

Who are those guys? il *Sierra* 74:18-19 S/O '89

Why Bush should sweat. S. Talbott. il *Time* 134:59 N 6 '89

Will the world be here for our kids? [roundtable on the environment] M. Mohler and M. D. Rosen. il *Ladies' Home Journal* 106:122-3+ Je '89

International aspects

See also

Man and the Biosphere Programme

United Nations Environment Programme

World Commission on Environment and Development

An agenda for global environmental change [white papers issued by National Academies of Science and Engineering and the Institute of Medicine] *Environment* 31:30-1 Ja/F '89

Can the world cooperate? P. M. Jones. il *Scholastic Update (Teachers' edition)* 121:18 Ap 21 '89

Carrot and stick. il *Time* 134:85 O 9 '89

The ecology of survival. A. Gore, Jr. il *The New Republic* 201:26+ N 6 '89

Ecopolitics in the global greenhouse. W. B. Wood and others. bibl f il *Environment* 31:12-17+ S '89

Facing the habitability crisis [adaptation of address, February 16, 1989] P. R. Ehrlich. *BioScience* 39:480-2 Jl/Ag '89

The fight to save the planet [special section] il *Time* 134:60-4+ D 18 '89

First word. B. E. Babbitt. por *Omni (New York, N.Y.)* 11:6 S '89

ENVIRONMENTAL POLICY—International aspects—*cont.*

Getting serious about the environment threat. J. M. Wall. il *The Christian Century* 106:371-2 Ap 12 '89

Global change and our common future [address, May 2, 1989; with editorial comment by Timothy O'Riordan] G. H. Brundtland. bibl f il por *Environment* 31:inside cover, 16-20+ Je '89

Global change is key political topic for 1989. K. E. Hoagland. *BioScience* 39:151 Mr '89

Governments warm to greenhouse action. J. Raloff. il *Science News* 136:394-5+ D 16 '89

A Green Peace Corps. T. Turner. il *The Mother Earth News* 116:48-50 Mr/Ap '89

Greening the summit [Paris economic summit] T. Beardsley. *Scientific American* 261:17 S '89

How to secure our common future. G. H. Brundtland. *Scientific American* 261:190 S '89

Independence Day blues. I. M. Stelzer. il *The American Spectator* 22:28-9 S '89

The industrial nations make a start [Paris economic summit] J. D. Hair. il *International Wildlife* 19:26 N/D '89

The mote & the beam. *Commonweal* 116:260-1 My 5 '89

A new ecological ethos [cover story; special section; with editorial comment by Nathan Gardels] il *New Perspectives Quarterly* 6:2-47 Spr '89

A new item on the agenda. G. Garelik. il *Time* 134:60-2 O 23 '89

The odds of saving the planet. G. Dyer. il *World Press Review* 36:96 O '89

On the ecological ethos [discussion of Spring 1989 special section, A new ecological ethos] il *New Perspectives Quarterly* 6:59-63 Summ '89

Our biological heritage under siege [address, August 6, 1989] N. Brown. *BioScience* 39:725-8 N '89

Our changing environment. V. Smil. bibl f *Current History* 88:9-12+ Ja '89

Planet of the year: what on earth are we doing? [cover story; special section] il *Time* 133:24-30+ Ja 2 '89

Planning for our common future. M. W. Holdgate. bibl f *Environment* 31:14-17+ O '89

The politics of planetary management. W. C. Clark. *Environment* 31:inside cover S '89

Redefining security. J. T. Mathews. *Foreign Affairs* 68:162-77 Spr '89

Sovereignty and the environment. K. Piddington. il *Environment* 31:18-20+ S '89

A sustainable society. G. W. Barrett. *BioScience* 39:754 D '89

Tough carbon budget could slow warming [Energy policy in the greenhouse report] J. Raloff. *Science News* 136:359 D 2 '89

Toward a sustainable world. W. D. Ruckelshaus. il map *Scientific American* 261:166-70+ S '89

Upward from a foothills summit [Paris economic summit] T. O'Riordan. *Environment* 31:inside front cover Jl/Ag '89

US and Soviet academies reach global ecology agreement. W. Sweet. *Physics Today* 42:101-2 F '89

"What is wrong with us?" [excerpts from address, November 1988] A. Gore, Jr. il por *Time* 133:66 Ja 2 '89

White House global climate plan calls for research by 7 agencies. I. Goodwin. il *Physics Today* 42:52-4 O '89

The whole earth agenda. M. Satchell. il *U.S. News & World Report* 107:50-2 D 25 '89-Ja 1 '90

A world at risk. L. R. Brown and others. il pors *Country Journal* 16:44-8 My/Je '89

Public opinion

Health over money: the new environmental consciousness [Harris poll] B. Fischman. il *Psychology Today* 23:10 N '89

Africa

Banking on African conservation [debt-for-nature swaps] *Science News* 135:62 Ja 28 '89

Asia

Environment, poverty and growth [address, February 9, 1989] A. Karaosmanoglu. *Vital Speeches of the Day* 55:396-400 Ap 15 '89

Environmental journalism: guardian of the Asian commons [cover story] S. M. Friedman and K. A. Friedman. bibl f il *Environment* 31:6-9+ Je '89

Australia

The natural legacy. R. Slatyer. il *The Courier (Unesco)* 41:16-22 D '88

Brazil

Conservation woes at the World Bank. B. Rich. il *The Nation* 248:73+ Ja 23 '89

A dubious plan for the Amazon. M. S. Serrill. il *Time* 133:67 Ap 17 '89

Fall of the rain forest. T. Waters. il *Discover* 10:40 Ja '89

California

A corrosive fight over California's toxics law [Safe Drinking Water and Toxic Enforcement Act] L. Roberts. il *Science* 243:306-9 Ja 20 '89

Forewarned is fairly warned [Safe Drinking Water and Toxic Enforcement Act] C. Russell. il *Sierra* 74:36-8+ N/D '89

Canada

See also

Canada. Centre for Sustainable Economic Development

The ball sits in Ottawa's court. C. Gordon. il *Maclean's* 102:15 O 16 '89

Environmental politics. B. Wallace. il *Maclean's* 102:14+ Ap 17 '89

Greening the provinces. H. Quinn. il *Maclean's* 102:44-6 Je 26 '89

A keener earth watch [Maclean's/Decima poll] P. Kopvillem. il *Maclean's* 102:18-20 Ja 2 '89

Risky business. B. Wallace. il *Maclean's* 102:12-13 S 11 '89

China

China's environmental morass. V. Smil. bibl f *Current History* 88:277-80+ S '89

Costa Rica

The good news: Costa Rica guards its forests. *Time* 133:35 Ja 2 '89

Developing countries

A bankers' world [environmental assessment program at the World Bank] D. Henwood. *The Nation* 249:481 O 30 '89

Bankrolling debacles? [World Bank] A. Levine. il map *U.S. News & World Report* 107:43-4+ S 25 '89

The boiling pot [development vs. conservation] D. Gergen. il *U.S. News & World Report* 106:76 My 15 '89

Charging Japan with crimes against the earth. N. Gross. il *Business Week* p108+ O 9 '89

Conservation woes at the World Bank. B. Rich. il *The Nation* 248:73+ Ja 23 '89

The environment: a North-South conflict. M. Copulos. *Current (Washington, D.C.)* 317:35-9 N '89

Environment and security. N. Myers. *Foreign Policy* 74:23-41 Spr '89

How the U.S. can take the lead in the third world. E. Linden. il *Time* 134:63 O 23 '89

Making the world work for people [sustainable development] N. Myers. il *International Wildlife* 19:12-14 N/D '89

Putting our houses in order. T. O'Riordan. *Environment* 31:inside cover Je '89

Saving forests—with debt [less money for environmentally destructive projects] P. Adams. il *World Press Review* 36:47 O '89

Sovereignty and the environment. K. Piddington. il *Environment* 31:18-20+ S '89

Strategies for sustainable economic development. J. MacNeill. bibl il *Scientific American* 261:154-9+ S '89

Sustainable development: lessons from success [cover story] W. V. C. Reid. bibl f il *Environment* 31:6-9+ My '89

Florida

Last gasp for the Everglades [U.S. Attorney D. Lehtinen sues Florida for polluting federal lands] J. Carney. il por map *Time* 134:26-7 S 25 '89

Saving America's swamp of swamps [Everglades National Park] il *U.S. News & World Report* 107:8-9 D 25 '89-Ja 1 '90

Japan

About-face [Japanese curtail use of drift nets and ban import of ivory] il *Time* 134:86 O 2 '89

Charging Japan with crimes against the earth. N. Gross. il *Business Week* p108+ O 9 '89

Japan: new voices cite solutions for pollution. H. Cordes. *Utne Reader* p30 Mr/Ap '89

Putting the heat on Japan. E. Linden. il *Time* 134:50-2 Jl 10 '89

Report on reports: three reports on Japan and the global environment. A. S. Miller. bibl f *Environment* 31:25-9 Jl/Ag '89

Wasteful Japan [tropical timber trade] *World Press Review* 36:43+ O '89

The world's eco-outlaw? S. Begley. il *Newsweek* 113:70 My 1 '89

Lake Tahoe region (Calif. and Nev.)

Lake Tahoe: preserving a fragile ecosystem [cover story] C. R. Goldman. bibl f il map *Environment* 31:6-11+ S '89

Netherlands

Cleaning up the West's dirtiest nation. D. Lawday. map *U.S. News & World Report* 107:68 S 11 '89

Is it time to build another ark? [concern over greenhouse-induced sea level changes] il *U.S. News & World Report* 107:12 N 20 '89

New York (State)

See also

New York (State). Dept. of Environmental Conservation

New Zealand

See also

New Zealand. Dept. of Conservation

Nicaragua

A casualty of war: the Nicaraguan environment. R. A. Rice. il map *Technology Review* 92:62-71 My/Je '89

Pacific Northwest

The Columbia River basin [cover story] K. N. Lee. bibl f il map *Environment* 31:6-11+ Jl/Ag '89

Québec (Province)

A campaign setback [uproar over disposal of PCBs] M. Rose. il *Maclean's* 102:12-13 S 4 '89

Environmental setbacks. G. W. Taylor. *Maclean's* 102:13 S 11 '89

ENVIRONMENTAL POLICY—*cont.*

Soviet Union

An environmental thaw? A. McGowan. *Environment* 31:inside cover N '89

Glasnost and ecology [cover story; special section; with introduction by Gilbert F. White] il *Environment* 30:4-15 D '88

The greening of the Soviet Union. *USA Today (Periodical)* 118:11-12 D '89

The greening of the U.S.S.R. D. Thompson. il *Time* 133:68-9 Ja 2 '89

United States

See Environmental policy

Vermont

Try convertibles [ban on auto air conditioners that use CFCs] *Time* 133:92 My 22 '89

Western Europe

- Europe recognizes the ozone threat [banning of chlorofluorocarbons] D. Dickson and E. Marshall. *Science* 243:1279 Mr 10 '89

Europe to ban CFCs by 2000. *Science News* 135:148 Mr 11 '89

First aid for the ozone layer [European Community agrees to ban CFCs] M. D. Lemonick. il *Time* 133:50 Mr 13 '89

ENVIRONMENTAL POLLUTION *See* Pollution

ENVIRONMENTAL PROTECTION AGENCY (U.S.) *See* United States. Environmental Protection Agency

ENVIRONMENTAL PSYCHOLOGY

See also

Color—Psychology

A room with a view [seeing photos of outdoor scenes helps reduce stress; study by Richard G. Coss] il *Harper's Bazaar* 122:62-3 Ja '89

ENVIRONMENTAL REFUGEES

Environmental refugees. *The Futurist* 23:54 My/Je '89

Environmental refugees [research by Jodi L. Jacobson] il *USA Today (Periodical)* 117:6-7 Ap '89

ENVIRONMENTAL REGULATIONS *See* Environmental policy

ENVIRONMENTAL RESEARCH

Federal aid

How do you spell relief? C. Peterson. il *National Wildlife* 27:40-3 Ap/My '89

Personnel and research shortages: policy recommendations for the environmental professions. R. G. Luthy. bibl f *Environment* 31:4-5+ Ap '89

ENVIRONMENTAL RESEARCH LABORATORIES

Lab for the environment. R. Kerson. il *Technology Review* 92:11-12 Ja '89

ENVIRONMENTAL TREATMENT & TECHNOLOGIES CORPORATION

See also

OHM Corporation

ENVIRONMENTALISTS *See* Ecologists

ENVY

Envy, the writer's disease. B. Friedman. il *The New York Times Book Review* 94:1+ N 26 '89

The executive Joneses. M. Novak. il *Forbes* 143:94-5 My 29 '89

A few kind words for envy. J. Epstein. *The American Scholar* 58:487-8+ Aut '89

Will the '90s be the age of envy? [cover story] J. Ciabattari. il *Psychology Today* 23:46-50 D '89

ENYA

about

Enya, the Irish troubador, whose heavenly tones set 'Orinoco flow' surging up the U.S. charts. il por *People Weekly* 31:113 Mr 27 '89

ENZON, INC.

Also worth noting [development of polyethylene glycol that attaches to enzymes and some biopharmaceuticals] *High Technology Business* 9:6 Jl/Ag '89

ENZYMES

See also

Adenosine triphosphatase

Adenylate cyclase

Allosterism

Amylases

Catalase

Catalytic antibodies

Collagenase

Decarboxylases

Galactosidases

Guanosine triphosphatase

Guanylate cyclase

Hydrolases

Isomerases

Kinases

Lactamases

Lipases

Luciferase

Lysosomes

Lysozymes

Nucleases

Pectinases

Peroxidases

Phosphorylases

Plasminogen

Polymerases

Proteases

Ribonucleases

Ribozymes

Superoxide dismutase

Synthases

Synthetases

Thrombin

Transaminases

Transcriptases

Transferases

Trypsinogen

DNA mismatch correction in a defined system. R. S. Lahue and others. bibl f il *Science* 245:160-4 Jl 14 '89

Hydrogen tunneling in enzyme reactions. Y. Cha and others. bibl f il *Science* 243:1325-30 Mr 10 '89

Major enhancement of the affinity of an enzyme for a transition-state analog by a single hydroxyl group. W. M. Kati and R. Wolfenden. bibl f il *Science* 243:1591-3 Mr 24 '89

Quantum biology [hydrogen tunneling in enzyme reactions; research by Yuan Cha] J. Kinoshita. *Scientific American* 260:31-2 My '89

Therapeutic use

See also

Streptokinase

Also worth noting [Enzon's development of polyethylene glycol that attaches to enzymes and some biopharmaceuticals] *High Technology Business* 9:6 Jl/Ag '89

. . . and toxic chemicals from the blood [enzyme filters] J. Raloff. *Science News* 135:271 Ap 29 '89

Inhibitors of angiotensin-converting enzyme prevent myointimal proliferation after vascular injury [use of cilazapril after balloon catheterization] J. S. Powell and others. bibl f il *Science* 245:186-8 Jl 14 '89

ENZYMES, CHEMICAL *See* Chemzymes

ENZYMES, FUNGAL

Disruption of the yeast *N*-myristoyl transferase gene causes recessive lethality. R. J. Duronio and others. bibl f il *Science* 243:796-800 F 10 '89

Intracellular targeting and structural conservation of a prohormone-processing endoprotease [*Saccharomyces*] R. S. Fuller and others. bibl f il *Science* 246:482-6 O 27 '89

Put a cassava in your tank [genetically altered yeast cells produce ethanol] il *Discover* 10:10 F '89

ENZYMES, PLANT

The manganese site of the photosynthetic water-splitting enzyme. G. N. George and others. bibl f il *Science* 243:789-91 F 10 '89

Reexamination of the three-dimensional structure of the small subunit of RuBisCo from higher plants. S. Knight and others. bibl f il *Science* 244:702-5 My 12 '89

EOCENE PERIOD *See* Paleobotany—Eocene

EOS *See* Earth Observing System

EOSAT (FIRM)

Eosat urges U.S. to fund Landsat 7 to capture minor share of data market. T. M. Foley. *Aviation Week & Space Technology* 130:89+ My 1 '89

Landsat/Spot merger talks spark debate on commercial space venture [with editorial comment] C. Covault. il *Aviation Week & Space Technology* 130:7, 20-1 Ja 23 '89

Remotely incensed: the search for profits [Landsat; cover story] C. E. Knox. il *Ad Astra* 1:22-4+ Ap '89

EOSINOPHILS *See* Leukocytes

EPA *See* United States. Environmental Protection Agency

EPCOT (FLA.)

The bloodstream express [special effects in film to be part of Body Wars exhibit] B. Weber. il *The New York Times Magazine* p142 Je 11 '89

EPENDYMA

Another fish tale [ependymal cells in knifefish spinal cord responsible for tissue regeneration; research by Marilyn Anderson] il *Discover* 10:15 Ag '89

EPHEMERA

Collectors and collecting

Print pursuit. C. E. Rinzler. il *House & Garden* 161:68+ Ap '89

EPHLAND, JOHN

On the beat. See issues of Down Beat beginning January 1988

Tony Williams: still, the rhythm magician [interview] il pors *Down Beat* 56:20-3 My '89

EPHRON, DELIA

The private Bette Midler—a big surprise! il pors *Redbook* 172:28+ Mr '89

"Yuk! Gross! I won't eat that turkey!" [excerpt from Do I have to say hello?] il *Redbook* 174:30 N '89

EPHRON, LARRY

The next Ice Age. *The Futurist* 23:38-9 S/O '89

EPHRON, NORA

Famous first words. *Esquire* 111:103-4+ Je '89

EPI PRODUCTS INC.

Bye-bye razors, so long wax—if you want a clean shave, the Krok Sisters are at the EPIcenter. K. S. Schneider. il *People Weekly* 32:89-90 D 11 '89

EPIC POETRY
Great epics: heroic tales of man and superman [cover story; special issue] il *The Unesco Courier* 42:10-47 S '89

EPIC POETRY, EGYPTIAN
The poet's tale [Hilaliyya] M. Hussein. il *The Unesco Courier* 42:12-17 S '89

EPIC POETRY, GERMAN
See also
Nibelungenlied

EPIC POETRY, GREEK
See also
Iliad

EPIC POETRY, MONGOLIAN
The secret history of the Mongols. S. Bira. il *The Unesco Courier* 42:36-9 S '89

EPIC POETRY, PERSIAN
The Epic of the Kings. N. Tadjadod. il *The Unesco Courier* 42:28-31 S '89

EPIC POETRY, PORTUGUESE
The Lusiads: from national epic to universal myth. E. Lourenço. il *The Courier (Unesco)* 42:26-7 Ap '89

EPIC POETRY, ROMAN
See also
Aeneid

EPIC POETRY, RUSSIAN
Ilya the invincible. H. Yvert-Jalu. il *The Unesco Courier* 42:32-5 S '89

EPIC POETRY, SRI LANKAN
See also
Mahāvamsa

EPIC POETRY, ZULU
Shaka Zulu, a living legend. K. I. Bosco. il *The Unesco Courier* 42:44-7 S '89

EPICONDYLITIS See Tennis elbow

EPIDEMICS
See also
AIDS (Disease)
Cholera
Influenza
Quarantine
Syphilis
Comeback diseases. *The Mother Earth News* 116:22 Mr/Ap '89

History
Disease and death in the New World [debate over the size of pre-Columbian populations] L. Roberts. il *Science* 246:1245-7 D 8 '89

EPIDEMIOLOGY
See also
AIDS (Disease)—Epidemiology
Centers for Disease Control (U.S.)
Diseases for our future: global ecology and emerging viruses. J. A. Miller. il *BioScience* 39:509-17 S '89
Epidemiologic investigation [discussion of December 2, 1988 article, Scientific standards in epidemiologic studies of the menace of daily life] A. R. Feinstein. *Science* 243:1255-6 Mr 10 '89
Epidemiology: essential tool for health [special issue] il *World Health* p3-27 Je '89
Hand-held computers. K. C. Lun. il *World Health* p9-11 Ag/S '89
Is it chaos, or is it just noise? [patterns in epidemics] R. Pool. bibl il *Science* 243:25-8 Ja 6 '89
The viral advantage [cover story] R. Weiss. il *Science News* 136:200-3 S 23 '89

Ethical aspects
Ethics and epidemiology. J. M. Last. il *World Health* p22-4 Je '89

EPIDERMAL GROWTH FACTOR
Skin deep [wound healing; research by Gregory L. Brown and Lillian B. Nanney] R. Rusting. *Scientific American* 261:38 S '89
Speeding up wound healing the EGF way [research by Gregory L. Brown] R. Cowen. *Science News* 136:39 Jl 15 '89
Structure and function of human amphiregulin: a member of the epidermal growth factor family. M. Shoyab and others. bibl f il *Science* 243:1074-6 F 24 '89
Unusual pattern of accumulation of mRNA encoding EGF-related protein in sea urchin embryos. Q. Yang and others. bibl f il *Science* 246:806-8 N 10 '89

EPIDERMAL GROWTH FACTOR RECEPTORS See Hormone receptors

EPIDERMIS See Skin

EPILEPSY
Brain fire [canine epilepsy] D. Calkins. il *American Health* 8:122+ Mr '89
The facts of life with epilepsy. S. DeVore. il *Current Health 2* 15:10-12 Ja '89
Just happy to be here [G. Walker back with White Sox after suffering brain seizure] B. Newman. il pors *Sports Illustrated* 70:34-6+ Ap 17 '89
Matt's biggest race [epileptic M. Margules wins the All-American Soap Box Derby] S. L. Englebardt. il pors *Reader's Digest* 135:53-8 Jl '89
NMDA antagonists differentiate epileptogenesis from seizure expression in an in vitro model. S. F. Stasheff and others. bibl f il *Science* 245:648-51 Ag 11 '89

Genetic aspects
A genetic link to epilepsy [juvenile myoclonic epilepsy; research by Antonio Delgado] *USA Today (Periodical)* 118:12-13 O '89

Therapy
Electric brain waves: acid test [use of magnet oencephalography] J. Partridge. il *Omni (New York, N.Y.)* 12:34+ D '89
The epilepsy "cure": bold claims, weak data [controversy over peer-reviewed article by Phodios A. Anninos and N. Tsagas in International journal of neuroscience] R. P. Crease. il *Science* 245:1444-5 S 29 '89
Vitamin E and epilepsy [children] il *Prevention (Emmaus, Pa.)* 41:16 N '89

EPIPHANY
Celebration. P. J. Ryan. *America* 160:22 Ja 7-14 '89

EPISCOPAL CHURCH
See also
Catholic Church—Relations—Episcopal Church

United States
See also
Episcopal Synod of America
Aliquippa's star attraction [Community of Celebration] J. Duin. il *Christianity Today* 33:14+ Ja 13 '89
A bishop who won't be one of the boys [woman Episcopal bishop B. Harris] por *Newsweek* 113:60 F 13 '89
Bishops reach accord on women clergy. R. Walker. *Christianity Today* 33:57 N 3 '89
Consecration of bishop stirs Episcopal dissent [B. Harris] R. Walker. il por *Christianity Today* 33:41+ Mr 17 '89
Episcopal Church ordains its first female bishop [B. C. Harris] il pors *Jet* 75:13 F 27 '89
Episcopalian accord [women bishops] il *The Christian Century* 106:977 N 1 '89
The first of the 'mitered mamas' [black bishop B. C. Harris] L. Rosellini. por *U.S. News & World Report* 106:56-7 Je 19 '89
The first woman Episcopal bishop [B. C. Harris] R. D. Turner. il pors *Ebony* 44:40+ My '89
Harris approved [woman bishop B. C. Harris] *The Christian Century* 106:104-5 F 1-8 '89
That new time religion [ordination of woman bishop B. C. Harris] *National Review* 41:16-17 Mr 10 '89
When the Spirit leads [consecration of woman bishop B. C. Harris] J. Redmont. il por *Commonweal* 116:133-5 Mr 10 '89

EPISCOPAL CHURCH AND LABOR See Church and labor
EPISCOPAL SYNOD OF AMERICA
A denominational gender gap [movement against women priests] J. Carey. il *U.S. News & World Report* 106:56-7 Je 19 '89
Episcopal conservatives form new synod. J. Duin. il *Christianity Today* 33:52-3 Jl 14 '89
Episcopal family feud. *The Christian Century* 106:615-16 Je 21-28 '89
The Episcopal Synod: reinforcing boundaries. W. L. Sachs. *The Christian Century* 106:710-11 Ag 2-9 '89
Episcopalians' semi-schism. R. N. Ostling. il *Time* 133:53 Je 19 '89

EPISTEMOLOGY See Knowledge, Theory of
EPISTLES OF PAUL See Bible. N.T. Epistles of Paul
EPITHELIUM
See also
Ependyma
Mucous membranes
Cl⁻ channels in CF: lack of activation by protein kinase C and cAMP-dependent protein kinase. T.-C. Hwang and others. bibl f il *Science* 244:1351-3 Je 16 '89
Endothelial cell gene expression of a neutrophil chemotactic factor by TNF-α, LPS, and IL-1β. R. M. Strieter and others. bibl f il *Science* 243:1467-9 Mr 17 '89
Endothelial cells to the rescue. B. J. Culliton. il *Science* 246:749 N 10 '89
Endothelial interleukin-8: a novel inhibitor of leukocyte-endothelial interactions. M. A. Gimbrone and others. bibl f il *Science* 246:1601-3 D 22 '89
Epithelial cell surfaces induce Salmonella proteins required for bacterial adherence and invasion. B. B. Finlay and others. bibl f il *Science* 243:940-3 F 17 '89
Fluid flow stimulates tissue plasminogen activator secretion by cultured human endothelial cells. S. L. Diamond and others. bibl f il *Science* 243:1483-5 Mr 17 '89
High-level recombinant gene expression in rabbit endothelial cells transduced by retroviral vectors. J. A. Zwiebel and others. bibl f il *Science* 243:220-2 Ja 13 '89
Human KGF is FGF-related with properties of a paracrine effector of epithelial cell growth. P. W. Finch and others. bibl f il *Science* 245:752-5 Ag 18 '89
Implantation of vascular grafts lined with genetically modified endothelial cells. J. M. Wilson and others. bibl f il *Science* 244:1344-6 Je 16 '89
An inducible endothelial cell surface glycoprotein mediates melanoma adhesion. G. E. Rice and M. P. Bevilacqua. bibl f il *Science* 246:1303-6 D 8 '89
Mechanism of membrane anchoring affects polarized expression of two proteins in MDCK cells. D. A. Brown and others. bibl f il *Science* 245:1499-501 S 29 '89

EPITHELIUM—*cont.*

Molecular custodians sweep away odorants [research by Doren Lancet] I. Amato. *Science News* 136:374 D 9 '89

Morphogenesis of the polarized epithelial cell phenotype. E. Rodriguez-Boulan and W. J. Nelson. bibl f il *Science* 245:718-25 Ag 18 '89

Now in vivo: altering endothelial cells. R. Cowen. *Science News* 135:373 Je 17 '89

Persistence of abnormal chloride conductance regulation in transformed cystic fibrosis epithelia. A. M. Jetten and others. bibl f il *Science* 244:1472-5 Je 23 '89

Recombinant gene expression in vivo within endothelial cells of the arterial wall. E. G. Nabel and others. bibl f il *Science* 244:1342-4 Je 16 '89

Regulation of chloride channels by protein kinase C in normal and cystic fibrosis airway epithelia. M. Li and others. bibl f il *Science* 244:1353-6 Je 16 '89

EPITHETS, RACIAL *See* Racial slurs

EPO *See* Erythropoietin

LA EPOCA (GUATEMALA: NEWSPAPER)

War of words [firebombing of S. Godoy's newspaper] V. Perera. il por *Mother Jones* 14:19-21 F/Mr '89

EPP, DAVID

(jt. auth) See Grigg, Richard W., and Epp, David

EPP, GEORGE

A mixed welcome for returning Germans. *The Christian Century* 106:902-3 O 11 '89

EPPINGER, JOSH

Life on the Nile. bibl il map *New Choices for the Best Years* 29:32-9 Ag '89

EPPLEY, MARK

about

Hey, who is this guy? C. Bermant. il pors *Personal Computing* 13:96-9+ My '89

EPROM (ERASABLE PROGRAMMABLE READ-ONLY MEMORY) *See* Read only memory

EPSTEIN, DANIEL MARK

Recent poetry. *America* 160:592-4 Je 17-24 '89

EPSTEIN, DIANA

about

Fugu, taxis, and Tender Buttons. H. Bridges. il *Gourmet* 49:48+ S '89

EPSTEIN, EDWARD Z.

(jt. auth) See Morella, Joe, and Epstein, Edward Z.

EPSTEIN, FRANCES, D. 1989

about

A death in the family 1989 [cover story] H. Epstein. il pors *New York* 22:34-43 N 27 '89

EPSTEIN, HELEN, 1947-

Crusader on the Charles [cover story] il pors *The New York Times Magazine* p26-9+ Ap 23 '89

A death in the family 1989 [cover story] il pors *New York* 22:34-43 N 27 '89

EPSTEIN, JASON

about

The book of Jason. D. Smith. il pors *New York* 22:26-31 Ag 7 '89

Empire building. J. J. Buck. il por *Vogue* 179:350-1+ N '89

EPSTEIN, JOSEPH

Educated by novels. *Commentary* 88:33-9 Ag '89

A few kind words for envy. *The American Scholar* 58:487-8+ Aut '89

The Goldin boys [story] *Commentary* 88:46-55 O '89

The joys of victimhood. il *The New York Times Magazine* p20-1+ Jl 2 '89

Kaplan's big deal [story] *Commentary* 87:42-53 Je '89

Low anxiety [story] *Commentary* 87:47-54 Ja '89

The man in the green hat. *The American Scholar* 58:167-8+ Spr '89

Novels [discussion of August 1989 article, Educated by novels] *Commentary* 88:8-9 N '89

Smoke gets in your eyes. *The American Scholar* 58:7-10+ Wint '89

Waiter, there's a paragraph in my soup! *The American Scholar* 58:327-9+ Summ '89

EPSTEIN, NADINE

From a remote jungle site, a trail of striking clues. bibl (p183) il pors map *Smithsonian* 20:98-104+ D '89

EPSTEIN, ROBERT

The lost art of letter writing. il *Utne Reader* p92 My/Je '89

EPSTEIN, STEVEN

(jt. auth) See Kirp, David L., and Epstein, Steven

EPSTEIN, WILLIAM, 1912-, AND SEABORG, GLENN THEODORE, 1912-

Non-nuclear states move to end testing. il *The Bulletin of the Atomic Scientists* 45:36-7 Je '89

EPSTEIN-BARR VIRUS

The baffling case of chronic fatigue [research by Stephen E. Straus] K. Fackelmann. *Science News* 135:4 Ja 7 '89

Just the facts please. C. A. Reese. il *Current Health 2* 15:12-13 F '89

Transformation and plasmacytoid differentiation of EBV-infected human B lymphoblast by *ras* oncogenes. S. Seremetis and others. bibl f il *Science* 243:660-3 F 3 '89

EQUAL EMPLOYMENT OPPORTUNITY COMMISSION (U.S.) *See* United States. Equal Employment Opportunity Commission

EQUAL PAY FOR EQUAL WORK

Comparable worth. S. Saetre. il *Utne Reader* p14-15 Ja/F '89

Dear Betty Harragan. B. L. Harragan. il *Working Woman* 14:40+ My '89

Pay-equity update: will it up your salary? S. Chan. il *Working Woman* 14:73 Ja '89

R.N.s get pay fix: nurses lead way for pay equity in state jobs [Illinois] C. Kleiman. *Ms.* 17:73-4 My '89

EQUAL RIGHTS FOR WOMEN *See* Women—Equal rights

EQUAL TIME DOCTRINE *See* Fairness Doctrine (Broadcasting)

EQUALITY

See also

Democracy

EQUALIZERS, AUDIO *See* Audio systems—Equipment

EQUATIONS

See also

Differential equations

Elliptic curves

EQUESTRIANISM *See* Horsemanship

EQUIBANK

Alan Fellheimer wears combat boots. M. Schroeder. il por *Business Week* p119-20 Mr 20 '89

EQUILIBRIUM (PHYSIOLOGY)

Lead effects show in child's balance [research by Amit Bhattacharya] J. Raloff. il *Science News* 135:54 Ja 28 '89

EQUILIBRIUM (THERMAL) *See* Thermodynamics

EQUIMARK CORP.

Alan Fellheimer wears combat boots. M. Schroeder. il por *Business Week* p119-20 Mr 20 '89

EQUIPMENT INDUSTRY, INDUSTRIAL *See* Industrial equipment industry

EQUITABLE CAPITAL MANAGEMENT CORPORATION

On the prowl in big-growth country [interview with A. Stewart] A. E. Serwer. il por *Fortune* 120:48+ D 18 '89

EQUITY CONVERSION, HOME *See* Home equity conversion

EQUITY INCOME FUNDS *See* Investment trusts

EQUITY INVESTMENT CORPORATION

Companies should "create capital" [interview with J. Barksdale] E. Schultz. il por *Fortune* 120:48+ Jl 31 '89

EQUITY PROGRAMS INVESTMENT CORPORATION

Epic task [Skyline Financial sells off properties] J. Novack. il por *Forbes* 143:142+ F 6 '89

EQUITY SHARING MORTGAGES

Unreal estate. M. K. Evans. il *Gentlemen's Quarterly* 59:183-4 D '89

ER FLUIDS *See* Electrorheological fluids

ERA (EARNED RUN AVERAGE) *See* Baseball, Professional—Statistics

ERASABLE OPTICAL STORAGE DEVICES *See* Optical storage devices

ERCS *See* Emission reduction credits

ERDOES, RICHARD

The year 1000 [excerpt from AD 1000] il *Psychology Today* 23:44-5 My '89

ERDRICH, LOUISE

A wedge of shade [story] *The New Yorker* 65:35-40 Mr 6 '89

ERENS, PAMELA

Anti-abortion, pro-feminism? *Mother Jones* 14:31+ My '89

ERGAS, MARTIN

about

Martin Ergas: helping paraplegics keep fit. I. Recio. il por *Business Week* p68 S 18 '89

ERGODIC THEORY

Ergodic theory, randomness, and "chaos". D. S. Ornstein. bibl f il *Science* 243:182-7 Ja 13 '89

ERGONOMICS

So you're still having trouble making those Christmas toys work? Don't worry, it's not your fault [interview with D. A. Norman] K. MacMurran. il pors *People Weekly* 31:91-2+ Ja 9 '89

ERGOT

An LSD trip in France, 1789 [Mary Matossian's theory that the peasant revolt was caused by fungus in rye bread] il *U.S. News & World Report* 107:14 D 4 '89

ERICK HAWKINS DANCE COMPANY

Reviews:

Performances at the Joyce Theater, New York City. D. Hering. *Dance Magazine* 63:88-90 Ap '89

ERICKSON, ARTHUR, 1924-

about

A fiery reception. C. Wood. il por *Maclean's* 102:52-3 Mr 6 '89

ERICKSON, CRAIG

about

Just call it Erickson U. B. Newman. il por *Sports Illustrated* 70:82-3 My 1 '89

On deck. il por *Sport (New York, N.Y.)* 80:16 F '89

ERICKSON, DENNIS

about

Arrivals and departures. H. Hersch. il por *Sports Illustrated* 70:24-5 Mr 13 '89

ERICKSON, DENNIS—about—*cont.*
Just call it Erickson U. B. Newman. il por *Sports Illustrated* 70:82-3 My 1 '89
ERICKSON, JIM
The regeneration gap. il *National Parks* 63:30-3 Jl/Ag '89
ERICKSON, JOHN
Arms negotiations in Europe. *Current History* 88:369-72+ N '89
ERICKSON, LORI
Cinderella city. il *Travel Holiday* 172:83-5 S '89
Pitching a shoe or two. il *Travel Holiday* 171:130 Mr '89
ERICSON, KATE
about
"Signature piece". R. Cembalest. il *Art News* 88:15 F '89
ERICSSON (L.M.) TELEPHONE CO. See L.M. Ericsson Telephone Co.
ERIE, LAKE See Lake Erie
ERIE WILDLIFE RESCUE (ORGANIZATION)
House calls in the wild. T. Pawlick. il *International Wildlife* 19:12-17 Mr/Ap '89
ERIK BRUHN PRIZE See Bruhn Prize
ERIK THE VIKING [film] See Motion picture reviews—Single works
ERIM, KENAN T.
about
A white marble city that an emperor chose for his own. D. J. Hamblin. il *Smithsonian* 19:142-8+ Mr '89
ERKERT, JAN
about
Reviews:
Work of J. Erkert and A. Osgood at MoMing Dance and Arts Center. C. Survant. il *Dance Magazine* 63:82-3 D '89
ERLANGER, STEVEN
The return of the Khmer Rouge [cover story] il map *The New York Times Magazine* p24-7+ Mr 5 '89
ERLICK, JUNE CAROLYN
Questions for the East German church. *The Christian Century* 106:791-5 Ag 30-S 6 '89
ERNA'S ELDERBERRY HOUSE (OAKHURST, CALIF.: RESTAURANT) See Oakhurst (Calif.)—Restaurants, nightclubs, bars, etc.
ERNST, DENNIS J.
A timely schedule of '89 Civil War events. il *Petersen's Photographic Magazine* 18:28 Ag '89
ERNST, MAX, 1891-1976
about
Max Ernst: collages: Kunstsammlung Nordhrhein-Westfalen. D. Galloway. il *Art News* 88:180 My '89
ERNST & WHINNEY
How Barry Minkow fooled the auditors. D. Akst. il pors *Forbes* 144:126-7+ O 2 '89
When one plus one equals no. 1 [merger with Arthur Young] J. M. Laderman. *Business Week* p92+ Je 5 '89
EROSION
See also
Coast changes
Contour farming
Dust storms
Filter strips (Soil conservation)
Potholes
Sedimentation and deposition
Terraces (Agriculture)
Weathering
Soil [Environmental Quality Index] il *National Wildlife* 27:39 F/Mr '89
Spotting erosion from space [research by Jerry C. Ritchie] R. Monastersky. *Science News* 136:61 Jl 22 '89
EROTIC ART
See also
Pinup art
EROTIC PHOTOGRAPHY
See also
Photography of the nude
Boudoir photography for fun and profit. R. Hurth and S. Hurth. il *Petersen's Photographic Magazine* 18:12-15+ N '89
EROTICA
The value of erotica. D. E. Olson. il por *The Humanist* 49:12-13+ S/O '89
Anecdotes, facetiae, satire, etc.
The sex life. D. Cale. *Harper's* 278:36 F '89
EROTOMANIA
The delusions of love. D. Gelman. il *Newsweek* 114:82 D 4 '89
ERP, DIRK VAN, 1859-1933
about
Dirk van Erp: artistry in metal. B. E. Johnson. bibl f il *Antiques & Collecting Hobbies* 94:32-3+ O '89
ERRICO, CHARLES J., AND WALKER, J. SAMUEL
The New Deal and the guru. il pors *American Heritage* 40:92-5+ Mr '89
ERRORS
See also
Cooking errors
Human error
Literary errors
Scientific errors

Speech errors
Television broadcasting—Errors
Typographical errors
ERSHAD, HUSSAIN MOHAMMAD
about
The struggle for development in Bangladesh. C. Baxter. bibl f *Current History* 88:437-40+ D '89
ERTEGUN, NESUHI
about
Obituary
Rolling Stone il pors p22-3 S 7 '89. F. Goodman
ERVIN, JOHN, JR.
Graywolf: a literary press ponders its problems. il *Publishers Weekly* 235:30-1 Ap 14 '89
ERVIN, MICHAEL
Grandmother as lawbreaker. il por *The Progressive* 53:11 Ja '89
Unfriendly skies. il *The Progressive* 53:28-31 Je '89
A watchdog guards the public schools. por *The Progressive* 53:16-17 N '89
ERVIN, P. R., JR., AND OTHERS
Production of mammastatin, a tissue-specific growth inhibitor, by normal human mammary cells. bibl f il *Science* 244:1585-7 Je 30 '89
ERVIN, SUSAN
The cottage garden. il *The Mother Earth News* 120:76-81 N/D '89
ERWARTUNG [opera] See Schoenberg, Arnold, 1874-1951
ERWITT, ELLIOTT, 1928-
about
Erwitt gets personal. il *Newsweek* 113:67 Ja 23 '89
ERYTHROCYTES
See also
Blood boosting
Erythropoietin
Hemoglobin
Identification of a platelet membrane glycoprotein as a falciparum malaria sequestration receptor. C. F. Ockenhouse and others. bibl f il *Science* 243:1469-71 Mr 17 '89
Malaria red cell cytoadherence [discussion of March 17, 1989 article, Identification of a platelet membrane glycoprotein as a falciparum malaria sequestration receptor] C. F. Ockenhouse and others. *Science* 246:1051 N 24 '89
Postponing red-cell retirement. R. Weiss. il *Science News* 136:424-5 D 23-30 '89
ERYTHROPOIETIN
Anemia drug approved. *FDA Consumer* 23:2 S '89
A biotech bonanza [Amgen gets FDA approval] L. Armstrong. il *Business Week* p30 Jl 31 '89
A drug that could replace transfusions—if it ever reaches the market [Ortho vs. Amgen] J. O. Hamilton and J. Weber, Jr. il *Business Week* p60+ Mr 27 '89
EPO is not the way to go [too risky for use by athletes] R. Goldingay. il *Women's Sports & Fitness* 11:10 Jl/Ag '89
An 'insulin' for anemia sufferers [Epogen replaces erythropoietin in kidney dialysis patients] *U.S. News & World Report* 106:13 Je 12 '89
It gives athletes a boost—maybe too much. L. Jereski. il *Business Week* p123 D 11 '89
Patents
Amgen is hot—and bothered. J. O. Hamilton and C. Brown. il *Business Week* p40+ Ja 23 '89
ESA See European Space Agency
ESALEN INSTITUTE
Rolfing with Yeltsin [B. Yeltsin's U.S. visit] A. Heard. *The New Republic* 201:11-13 O 9 '89
ESBER, ED, JR.
We've only just begun to compute. por *Personal Computing* 13:236 O '89
ESCADA AG
Art of the spiel. J. McLaughlin. il por *Harper's Bazaar* 122:54 N '89
ESCALANTE, JAIME
about
Miracle worker at Garfield High [condensed from Escalante] J. Mathews. il pors *Reader's Digest* 134:165-70+ Ja '89
ESCALATION (PSYCHOLOGY)
Understanding behavior in escalation situations. B. M. Staw and J. Ross. bibl f il *Science* 246:216-20 O 13 '89
ESCALATORS
Elevate or escalate? J. Herron. *Harper's* 278:27 My '89
L'ESCALE (NEW YORK, N.Y.: RESTAURANT) See New York (N.Y.)—Restaurants, nightclubs, bars, etc.
ESCAPE CLUB (MUSICAL GROUP)
The Escape Club. il *'Teen* 33:65 My '89
The Escape Club. E. Miller. il *Seventeen* 48:69-70+ F '89
ESCAPE DEVICES (AIRPLANES) See Airplanes, Military—Escape devices
ESCAPE DEVICES (SPACE STATIONS) See Space stations—Escape devices
ESCAPE DEVICES (SPACEPLANE) See Spaceplane—Escape devices
ESCAPES
A last mile to freedom [East German refugee A. Rudolf's escape route to Austria] R. Nordland. il por map *Newsweek* 114:34 S 18 '89

ESCAPES—*cont.*
With a hijacked copter, she rescued her boyfriend from jail [case of J. Mattox] L. Murray. il por *TV Guide* 37:38 F 11-17 '89

ESCH, MARTHA
about
Have goggles, will travel. G. Baxter. il por *Flying* 116:86+ My '89

ESCHATOLOGY
See also
Antichrist
End of the world
Millennium
Second Advent
Apocalypse now? Ecology and the peril of doomsday visions. E. Zencey. il *Utne Reader* p90-3 Ja/F '89

ESCHERICHIA COLI
Activation of bacterial porin gene expression by a chimeric signal transducer in response to aspartate. R. Utsumi and others. bibl f il *Science* 245:1246-9 S 15 '89
The anticodon contains a major element of the identity of arginine transfer RNAs. L. H. Schulman and H. Pelka. bibl f il *Science* 246:1595-7 D 22 '89
Construction of large DNA segments in Escherichia coli. M. O'Connor and others. bibl f il *Science* 244:1307-12 Je 16 '89
Correct folding of circularly permuted variants of a βα barrel enzyme in vivo. K. Luger and others. bibl f il *Science* 243:206-10 Ja 13 '89
DNA mismatch correction in a defined system. R. S. Lahue and others. bibl f il *Science* 245:160-4 Jl 14 '89
E. coli clue to contamination [crab meat in Louisiana seafood processing plant] il *FDA Consumer* 23:34-5 O '89
Generation of a catalytic antibody by site-directed mutagenesis. E. Baldwin and P. G. Schultz. bibl f il *Science* 245:1104-7 S 8 '89
Generation of a large combinatorial library of the immunoglobulin repertoire in phage lambda. W. D. Huse and others. bibl f il *Science* 246:1275-81 D 8 '89
Hungry to evolve? [controversy over John Cairns' work] J. P. Rennie. *Scientific American* 261:20+ N '89
The location of DNA in RecA-DNA helical filaments. E. H. Egelman and X. Yu. bibl f il *Science* 245:404-7 Jl 28 '89
Reverse transcriptase in a clinical strain of Escherichia coli: production of branched RNA-linked msDNA. B. C. Lampson and others. bibl f il *Science* 243:1033-8 F 24 '89
Specific interactions in RNA enzyme-substrate complexes. C. Guerrier-Takada and others. bibl f il *Science* 246:1578-84 D 22 '89
Stabilization of Z DNA in vivo by localized supercoiling. A. R. Rahmouni and R. D. Wells. bibl f il *Science* 246:358-63 O 20 '89
Structural basis for misaminoacylation by mutant E. coli glutaminyl-tRNA synthetase enzymes. J. J. Perona and others. bibl f il *Science* 246:1152-41 D 1 '89
Structure of E. coli glutaminyl-tRNA synthetase complexed with tRNA^{Gln} and ATP at 2.8 Å resolution. M. A. Rould and others. bibl f il *Science* 246:1135-42 D 1 '89
Trans-kingdom sex [ability of Escherichia to conjugate with yeast] J. Horgan. *Scientific American* 261:34-5 O '89
Triggering of allostery in an enzyme by a point mutation: ornithine transcarbamoylase. L. C. Kuo and others. bibl f il *Science* 245:522-4 Ag 4 '89

ESCOBAR, MARISOL *See* Marisol, 1930-
ESCOBAR, PABLO
about
The gutsy Panama option. pors *U.S. News & World Report* 107:19 S 11 '89
Most wanted in Medelin. J. Contreras. il pors *Newsweek* 114:30 S 25 '89
Pablo Escobar. por *People Weekly* 32:88 D 25 '89-Ja 1 '90

ESCOFFIER, AUGUSTE, D. 1935
about
Escoffier. N. Barry. il por *Gourmet* 49:124+ O '89
ESCONDIDO (CALIF.)
City hall
The turning point [designed by Pacific Associates Planners] P. M. Sachner. il *Architectural Record* 177:104-7 Ja '89
ESCRIVÁ DE BALAGUER Y ALBÁS, JOSÉ MARIA, 1902-1975
about
My Opus [discussion of April 10, 1989 article, Opus Dei and the 'perfect society'] P. Lernoux. *The Nation* 249:74+ Jl 17 '89
Opus Dei and the 'perfect society' [cover story] P. Lernoux. il *The Nation* 248:469+ Ap 10 '89
ESCROW ACCOUNTS
Do you know where your mortgage is? Or whether your property taxes and insurance premiums have been paid? il *Consumer Reports* 54:441 Jl '89
ESIASON, BOOMER
about
Back to basics [cover story] P. King. il pors *Sports Illustrated* 71:14-18+ Ag 7 '89

Once reviled, now revered, Top Cat Boomer Esiason sharpens his claws for the Super Bowl. P. Axthelm. il pors *People Weekly* 31:42-3 Ja 23 '89
ESKIMO CHILDREN *See* Eskimos—Children
ESKIMOS
See also
Drugs and Eskimos
Art
Collectors and collecting
Spirits in the gallery [work of native Canadians] P. Young. il *Maclean's* 102:78+ N 13 '89
Children
Eskimo spring [Pond Inlet, N.W.T.] il map *National Geographic World* 166:26-31 Je '89
Government relations
Project Chariot: how Alaska escaped nuclear excavation [1958 plan to create a harbor by detonating thermonuclear bombs; cover story] D. O'Neill. bibl f il maps *The Bulletin of the Atomic Scientists* 45:28-37 D '89
Hunting
The Arctic hunters [pursuit of narwhals by Inuits in Greenland] C. Dowling. il *Life* 12:140-5 Mr '89
Eskimo memories [whaling in Canadian eastern Arctic at turn of century] D. Eber. bibl il map *History Today* 39:45-50 N '89
Off with their heads [walrus heads traded for illicit drugs by Eskimos in Alaska] M. Beck. il *Newsweek* 113:78 Je 5 '89
Social conditions
Isolated in the 'refrigerator' [Thule Eskimos of Greenland] L. Tonstad. *World Press Review* 36:58 Jl '89
ESOPHAGEAL PAIN
Esophageal pain: another price of success. P. McKeown. il *Nation's Business* 77:89 N '89
ESOPHAGUS
Cancer
Mortality
Reducing the incidence of disease: clues from the environment. H. D. Foster. bibl f il maps *Environment* 31:12-17+ Ap '89
ESOPS *See* Employee stock ownership plans
ESP *See* Extrasensory perception
ESPAILLAT, RHINA P.
Framing the view [poem] *America* 160:145 F 18 '89
ESPARZA, JOSÉ
Prospects for a vaccine. il *World Health* p10-11 O '89
ESPERIAN, KALLEN
about
Kallen Esperian steps in after a raucous night at the opera, and critics sing her praises. il por *People Weekly* 32:65 Jl 17 '89
ESPINAL, LUIS
about
Tribute to a Latin American martyr. M. O'Sullivan. *America* 160:8-11+ Ja 7-14 '89
ESPIONAGE
See also
Computers—Espionage use
Cryptography
Electronics in criminal investigation, espionage, etc.
Intelligence service
Lasers in criminal investigation, espionage, etc.
Police—Surveillance operations
Trials (Espionage)
United States—History—Revolution, 1775-1783—Secret service
ESPIONAGE, AMERICAN
Can America adjust to the new world of spying? D. L. Wheeler. il *USA Today (Periodical)* 118:16-18 N '89
Where spies really matter [efforts to improve U.S. intelligence] P. Cary. il *U.S. News & World Report* 107:24-5 Ag 28-S 4 '89
Lebanon
The failure of American intelligence. C. S. Manegold. il *Newsweek* 114:16-17 Ag 14 '89
Middle East
Relying on RUMINT [U.S. Mideast intelligence based on rumor] E. Salholz. il *Newsweek* 113:27 F 27 '89
ESPIONAGE, BRITISH
United States
How we got an Official Secrets Act [Supreme Court declines to review S. L. Morison case] N. Hentoff. il *The Progressive* 53:10-11 Mr '89
The quiet coup [case against S. Morison] P. Weiss. il *Harper's* 279:54-65 S '89
ESPIONAGE, CHINESE
United States
Tracking China's master spy [L. W.-T. Chin] J. Barron. il *Reader's Digest* 135:97-102 D '89
ESPIONAGE, GERMAN
France
History
A shifty-eyed spy who was likely the nastiest man ever [C. F. W. Esterhazy responsible for the Dreyfus Affair] R. Wernick. il pors *Smithsonian* 20:114-16+ Ag '89

ESPIONAGE, INDUSTRIAL *See* Business intelligence
ESPIONAGE, ISRAELI
United States
Cruel and unusual punishment [imprisonment of A. Pollard, wife of convicted spy J. Pollard] L. C. Pogrebin. por *Ms.* 18:36-7 N '89
ESPIONAGE, RUSSIAN
Canada
Catching a spy [trial of S. J. Ratkai in Newfoundland] G. Allen. il por *Maclean's* 102:13 F 20 '89
Great Britain
Cold war on ice. J. Reed. *National Review* 41:18-19 Ag 18 '89
Mask of treachery [K. Philby; excerpt] J. Costello. il por *Conservative Digest* 15:59+ Ja/F '89
Bibliography
The upper class and the underworld. N. G. A. Annan, Baron. il *The New York Review of Books* 36:24-9 Ap 13 '89
United States
See also
Rosenberg (Julius and Ethel) case
Another spy scandal [case of Air Force Capt. J. V. Hirsch] *Newsweek* 114:28 Ag 14 '89
The Bloch case. *World Press Review* 36:8-9 S '89
Bugs, beans and too many bucks [security at the U.S. embassy in Moscow] D. Corn. *The Nation* 248:236+ F 20 '89
A case of espionage [diplomat F. Bloch] H. Mackenzie. il por *Maclean's* 102:27 Ag 7 '89
Compounding the problem [security at the U.S. embassy in Moscow] R. B. Cullen. il *Common Cause Magazine* 15:10 Mr/Ap '89
First the verdict, then the trial [FBI's investigation of F. S. Bloch] B. Van Voorst. il pors *Time* 134:16 Ag 7 '89
High spy at State? [career diplomat F. S. Bloch suspected of spying for Soviets] *Time* 134:16 Jl 31 '89
K.G.B. defector Gundarev: it's cold coming out [cover story] D. Wise. il *The New York Times Magazine* p36-9+ S 17 '89
Loose lips in Hawaii. il *Newsweek* 113:4 Ja 2 '89
Making a case against Bloch [alleged Soviet spy F. S. Bloch] R. Moreau. il por *Newsweek* 114:32 Ag 7 '89
More secrets from the life of Felix Bloch [revelations by Austrian prostitute] il *Newsweek* 114:40 O 23 '89
The Moscow bug hunt [no evidence that Marines C. Lonetree and A. Bracy allowed Soviets into the U.S. embassy] J. Peterzell. il pors *Time* 134:26-8 Jl 10 '89
Moscow station: how the KGB penetrated the American embassy [Marine guard spy case; excerpts; cover story] R. Kessler. il *Time* 133:50-2+ F 20 '89
A Moscow suicide reveals Glenn Souther's double life as a U.S. sailor spying for the K.G.B. W. Plummer. il *People Weekly* 32:105-6 Jl 17 '89
My lunch with Felix [suspected spy F. Bloch] B. Van Voorst. il por *Time* 134:16 S 4 '89
The odd case of M. Orlov [suicide of American defector G. M. Souther] il *Time* 134:40 Jl 10 '89
One Gundarev revelation: the strange case of officer Bothwell. D. Wise. il por *The New York Times Magazine* p82 S 17 '89
Our Moscow embassy mess. J. Barron. *Reader's Digest* 134:193-6+ F '89
A spy in high places? [diplomat F. S. Bloch] H. Anderson. il por *Newsweek* 114:36 Jl 31 '89
'The spy war is heating up'. D. Waller and R. Sandza. il *Newsweek* 114:28 Ag 21 '89
Stategate [F. Bloch spy case] *National Review* 41:10-12 S 1 '89
Summer spy scoops [F. Bloch and J. V. Hirsch spy cases] D. Schorr. *The New Leader* 72:3-4 Ag 7-21 '89
Suspected spy Felix Bloch leads G-men and the press on a wild spook chase [Chappaqua, N.Y.] B. Hewitt. il por *People Weekly* 32:42-3 Ag 14 '89
Tinker, tailor, soldier, deputy chief of mission [F. Bloch suspected of spying for the Soviets] B. Duffy. il por *U.S. News & World Report* 107:21 Ag 7 '89
Top secrets for sale? [case of J. Hall] R. Parry. il por *Newsweek* 113:27 Ja 2 '89
Vienna waltz [alleged Soviet spy F. S. Bloch] *The Nation* 249:228-9 S 4-11 '89
What did the swallows learn in Geneva? [CIA investigation of social activities and female Soviet spies during 1985 arms talks] L. Galtney and C. Fenyvesi. il por *U.S. News & World Report* 106:27 F 20 '89
Who says A must say B. W. F. Buckley. *National Review* 41:62 S 15 '89
ESPIONAGE IN LITERATURE *See* Spy stories
ESPN *See* Entertainment and Sports Programming Network
ESPY, MICHAEL
about
Espy to probe rural Miss. water crisis. *Jet* 76:27 S 11 '89
Miss. Rep. Espy, Gov. Mabus blaze new political trail to push progress in state. S. Booker. il pors *Jet* 75:26-7 Ja 16 '89
ESQUIRE (PERIODICAL)
Dubious Achievement Awards of 1988 [cover story] il *Esquire* 111:87-90+ Ja '89

ESREY, WILLIAM TODD
about
People aren't laughing at U.S. Sprint anymore. W. C. Symonds. il por *Business Week* p82-3+ Jl 31 '89
ESSAOUIRA (MOROCCO)
Historic houses, sites, etc.
The Moroccan moods of Laise Adzer. I. Borger. il por *Architectural Digest* 46:168-73 S '89
ESSAYS
Competitions
See also
Mott's Apple Awards
Foxglove laughter, hard listening, and the cut: the winners of *Sierra*'s annual nature writing contest [special section] il *Sierra* 74:68-74+ N/D '89
Lashanda Daniels's outstanding essay on the homeless was no academic exercise—she'd been there [Boston, Mass.] W. Plummer. il pors *People Weekly* 32:39-40 Jl 31 '89
North American Essay Contest [special section] il por *The Humanist* 49:21-9+ Mr/Ap '89
North American Essay Contest [special section] il *The Humanist* 49:20-30+ Ja/F '89
'The president of the United States speaks to the United Nations' [winners of essay contest for high school students] il *UN Chronicle* 26:78 S '89
Toward a more perfect union of black and white Americans [Cardinal Joseph Ritter Award Essay Contest; cover story; special section; with editorial comment by George W. Hunt] il *America* 160:130, 134-49+ F 18 '89
ESSENCE (PERIODICAL)
The 1989 Essence Awards [with editorial comment by Susan L. Taylor] il pors *Essence* 20:57-60+, 69 O '89
ESSENCES, FLAVORING *See* Flavoring essences
ESSENCES AND ESSENTIAL OILS
The search for "living" spices [work of Braja D. Mookherjee] il *USA Today (Periodical)* 117:14 F '89
ESSENTIAL OILS *See* Essences and essential oils
ESSEX INSTITUTE
Restoring the restored [Gardner-Pingree House] K. Korieth. il por map *Americana* 17:44-9 S/O '89
ESSI (FIRM)
Small, high-tech companies thrive despite cuts in defense spending. il *Aviation Week & Space Technology* 131:118+ S 18 '89
ESSMAN, JANET
Seep, drip, dribble. il *The Conservationist* 43:24-31 My/Je '89
ESTATE AUCTIONS *See* Auctions
ESTATE PLANNING
See also
Executors and administrators
Information systems—Estate planning use
Inheritance tax
Joint ownership
Living trusts
Trusts and trustees
Wills
Confronting the death of a parent. M. Silver. bibl il *U.S. News & World Report* 106:74-5 My 22 '89
How to keep it all in the family. D. M. Topolnicki. il *Money* 18 Money Guide:104-8 Fall '89
Less than half confident farm will pass to kids. B. Freese. *Successful Farming* 87:8 D '89
Passing down the dream [passing the family farm to the next generation] B. Freese. il *Successful Farming* 87:26-9 O '89
Passing wealth on intact takes a will and a way. L. Wiener. bibl il *U.S. News & World Report* 107:60-4 Jl 17 '89
Protecting your estate. D. N. Dreman. il *Forbes* 144 Special Issue:396 O 23 '89
Securing your future financially. M. Rowland. il *Working Woman* 14:95-6+ N '89
See a lawyer now to save your heirs time and taxes. J. Reid. il *Money* 18:84+ F '89
ESTATE TAX *See* Inheritance tax
ESTATES, COUNTRY *See* Country estates
ESTATES, DECEDENTS'
See also
Survivors' benefits
All-star family feud [M. Cuomo's feud with her brother, S. Raffa, over their father's estate] P. Blauner. il pors *New York* 22:34-7 F 13 '89
The art of the feud: sculptor Louise Nevelson's tangled legal legacy. D. Rabinowitz. il pors *New York* 22:82-8+ S 25 '89
A battle over a legacy pits sculptor Louise Nevelson's son against her loyal aide. P. Freeman. il pors *People Weekly* 32:42-4 Jl 17 '89
The cross fire over Jack Ruby's gun. il por *U.S. News & World Report* 107:10 D 25 '89-Ja 1 '90
Dealing with a death in the family. M. Rowland. il *Working Woman* 14:47-8+ Ag '89
Famed civil rights lawyer Wiley Branton leaves entire estate to his widow. il por *Jet* 76:5 My 29 '89
Fray erupts when white woman wills estate worth $476,000 to black man [Giuffre Medical Center makes claim on M. Barnett's estate] *Jet* 76:4 My 22 '89

ESTATES, DECEDENTS'—*cont.*

Frederick D. Patterson, founder of UNCF leaves entire estate to widow. il por *Jet* 76:5 Ag 14 '89

Jack Ruby's family and lawyer battle for possession of the gun that killed Lee Harvey Oswald. W. Plummer. il por *People Weekly* 31:42-3 My 22 '89

Lovers, liars and other strangers [M. Christian's claim against R. Hudson estate] pors *Newsweek* 113:61 F 27 '89

Lutcher Stark's third wife. W. P. Barrett. il por *Forbes* 144:216+ N 27 '89

Making money from the grave [black entertainers] D. Narine. il *Ebony* 44:142+ Je '89

Marley's estate sparks bitter court battle. il por *Jet* 75:16 Mr 6 '89

The Midas curse [family feud over S. Goldman's estate; cover story] D. Smith. il pors *New York* 22:32-40 Ap 3 '89

Old collectors never die . . . H. L. Rinker. il *Antiques & Collecting Hobbies* 94:26+ Mr '89

The price of betrayal [M. Christian awarded $21.75 million in lawsuit against estate of R. Hudson] P. Chin. il pors *People Weekly* 31:180-3 Mr 6 '89

They are hip, hot—and dead [late celebrities used in advertising] J. Hammer and K. Springen. il *Newsweek* 114:34 Jl 10 '89

Woman awarded $7 million against KKK dies without will; daughters administer [B. M. Donald] pors *Jet* 76:12 Ap 24 '89

Taxation

See Inheritance tax

ESTATES, UNCLAIMED

Billions in unclaimed funds sit in state treasures—this is how to retrieve what's there for you. C. J. Ferris. il *Money* 18:133 F '89

Unclaimed cash: could some be yours? M. C. Paulson. il *Reader's Digest* 134:37-8+ Mr '89

ESTÉE LAUDER, INC.

Acceptably sexy. S. N. Chakravarty. il por *Forbes* 144:122+ N 13 '89

How Leonard Lauder is making his mom proud. K. Deveny. il pors *Business Week* p68-9+ S 4 '89

ESTEFAN, GLORIA

about

Gloria Estefan. G. Flowers and J. Nash. il por *Seventeen* 48:70+ D '89

Gloria Estefan is a very nautical girl. il por *Rolling Stone* p36 Jl 13-27 '89

ESTELLER, EDUARD CARBONELL I *See* Carbonell i Esteller, Eduard

ESTEP, K. W., AND OTHERS

Linnaeus: interactive taxonomy using the Macintosh computer and HyperCard. bibl f il *BioScience* 39:635-8 O '89

ESTERHAZY, FERDINAND WALSIN, 1857-1923

about

A shifty-eyed spy who was likely the nastiest man ever. R. Wernick. il pors *Smithsonian* 20:114-16+ Ag '89

ESTERLY, GLENN

Can't sing. Can't cook. But she thinks she can make you laugh. il pors *TV Guide* 37:30-1+ N 18-24 '89

Carroll O'Connor calls it luck. il pors *The Saturday Evening Post* 261:58-9+ O '89

Gil Gerard: my weight cost me $1 million in TV roles. il pors *TV Guide* 37:8-10 N 25-D 1 '89

The ultimate prime-time love story [cover story] il pors *TV Guide* 37:4-5+ O 7-13 '89

Woody Harrelson was out of control. il pors *TV Guide* 37:20-2+ Ag 12-18 '89

ESTERS, STEPHANIE

What to get for the car that has everything. il *Black Enterprise* 20:95-6 N '89

ESTERS

See also

Phorbol esters

Attraction of the parasitic mite Varroa to the drone larvae of honey bees by simple aliphatic esters. Y. Le Conte and others. bibl f il *Science* 245:638-9 Ag 11 '89

Baby bee odor lures cradle-robbing mites [research by Guy Ourisson] S. Hart. *Science News* 136:103 Ag 12 '89

Inhibition of a class C β-lactamase by a specific phosphonate monoester. R. F. Pratt. bibl f il *Science* 246:917-19 N 17 '89

ESTES, CARROLL LYNN, 1938-

(jt. auth) See Wallace, Steven P., and Estes, Carroll Lynn, 1938-

ESTES, YVONNE BARON

Abandon in biology class [poem] *Phi Delta Kappan* 70:631 Ap '89

Fly again, mourning cloak. il *Phi Delta Kappan* 70:440-5 F '89

ESTEVE-COLL, ELIZABETH

about

Brouhaha at the V & A. M. Alexander. *Art in America* 77:29+ Jl '89

The fall of a great museum [cover story] Sir J. Pope-Hennessy. il *The New York Review of Books* 36:10-14 Ap 27 '89

Uproar at the V & A. G. Barker. il *Art News* 88:59 Summ '89

ESTEVEZ, EMILIO, 1963-

about

Fame in the family. il pors *'Teen* 33:51 Ap '89

ESTEY, WILLARD ZEBEDEE

about

Canadian justice rules out new effort to find cause of DC-8 crash at Gander. D. Hughes. *Aviation Week & Space Technology* 131:29 Jl 31 '89

ESTHETICS *See* Aesthetics

ESTIMATED TAX

Estimate carefully to avoid penalties; Penalty proliferation. G. W. Padwe. il *Nation's Business* 77:72 My '89

ESTIMATES, BUILDING *See* Building—Costs

ESTLEMAN, LOREN D.

Star Robert Duvall says: it's going to be like a western Godfather. il pors *TV Guide* 36:14-16+ F 4-10 '89

ESTONIA

See also

Environmental movement—Estonia
Television broadcasting—Estonia

History

Historiography

Lifting the veil on Estonia's past. C. Thomson. il *History Today* 39:9-11 S '89

Nationalism

See also

Estonian Popular Front

Candles in the wind. L. Hasse. *The New Republic* 200:24-5 F 20 '89

Rising demands in the Baltics. Y. Preston. *World Press Review* 36:13-16 Je '89

Symbols of sovereignty. D. K. Shipler. *The New Yorker* 65:52+ S 18 '89

ESTONIAN POPULAR FRONT

Pushing forward [views of M. Lauristin] J. Kohan. il por *Time* 133:66+ Ap 10 '89

ESTRADA, CAROLINA

about

Newlyweds Ian Irving and Carolina Estrada have transformed a small house at the shore with big-impact color. J. Etra. il pors *Vogue* 179:260-1+ Ag '89

ESTROGEN

The anti-aging patch for women [use of transdermal patch during menopause] S. Fields and L. Holland. il *Good Housekeeping* 208:163-4 F '89

Don't believe everything you read . . . [inaccurate newspaper accounts of sex hormone research by Doreen Kimura and Elizabeth Hampson] B. L. Benderly. il *Psychology Today* 23:67-9 N '89

Estrogen effects assessed [risk of breast cancer in postmenopausal women] *Science News* 136:86 Ag 5 '89

The estrogen fix. A. B. Eagan. il *Ms.* 17:38-41+ Ap '89

Estrogen use linked to breast cancer. J. L. Marx. *Science* 245:593 Ag 11 '89

Hard looks at hormones [estrogen and progestin may increase risk of breast cancer] J. Langone. il *Time* 134:56 Ag 14 '89

Hormone replacement therapy: is it for you? S. Mahler. *McCall's* 117:149 O '89

How sex hormones boost—or cut—intellectual ability. D. Kimura. il *Psychology Today* 23:62-6 N '89

The miracles and misfires of medicine [progestin and estrogen increase risk of breast cancer in postmenopausal women] *U.S. News & World Report* 107:16+ Ag 14 '89

Should you take estrogen? [hormone replacement therapy] C. Perlmutter. il *Prevention (Emmaus, Pa.)* 41:42-51 N '89

An update on estrogen-replacement therapy. N. Simon. il *Working Woman* 14:148+ My '89

ESTRUS

Availability of metabolic fuels controls estrous cyclicity of Syrian hamsters. J. E. Schneider and G. N. Wade. bibl f il *Science* 244:1326-8 Je 16 '89

ESTUARIES

See also

South Slough National Estuarine Research Reserve (Or.)

ESZTERHAS, JOE

about

The scarlet letter. L. Klady. il pors *American Film* 15:15-16 D '89

ETA CARINAE (STAR) *See* Stars, Variable

ETA SYSTEMS INC.

Control Data struggles to get back in control. R. Mitchell. il por *Business Week* p130-1 My 1 '89

ETCH A SKETCH

An Etch A Sketch revival: is it an adult art form for baby boomers? S. Morris. il *Omni (New York, N.Y.)* 11:100-1 Ag '89

ETCHING

Giving the etch to superior optics [work of Wilfrid B. Veldkamp] I. Peterson. *Science News* 135:287 My 6 '89

ETCHINGS *See* Etching

ETHANOL *See* Alcohol

ETHANOL AS FUEL *See* Alcohol as fuel

ETHERIDGE, MELISSA

about

Rocker Melissa Etheridge, who is both acoustic and electrifying. il por *People Weekly* 31:163 My 15 '89

ETHICAL EDUCATION See Moral education
ETHICS
> See also
> Accounting ethics
> Advertising ethics
> Altruism
> Apologies
> Art and morals
> Bioethics
> Business ethics
> Character
> Charity
> Christian ethics
> Conscience
> Courage
> Crime and criminals
> Deception
> Honesty
> Integrity
> Journalistic ethics
> Judgment (Ethics)
> Judicial ethics
> Justice
> Legal ethics
> Literary ethics
> Loyalty
> Lying
> Medical ethics
> Mercy
> Moral education
> Natural law
> Patience
> Political ethics
> Prison ethics
> Professional ethics
> Puritans and puritanism
> Responsibility
> Righteousness
> Science and ethics
> Secularism
> Sexual ethics
> Sin
> > See also subhead Ethical aspects under various subjects

The business of being ethical [address, December 14, 1988] R. D. Garton. *Vital Speeches of the Day* 55:435-7 My 1 '89
Faith, values & morals [results of survey] S. Jacoby. *McCall's* 116:69-71+ My '89
Imagine a river: understanding the balance between power and morality. R. C. Demerle. por *The Humanist* 49:27-8 Mr/Ap '89
Inspectors general. L. H. Lapham. *Harper's* 279:12-15 Jl '89
Is society morally bankrupt? [results of poll] I. Groller. il *Parents* 64:35 Je '89
Moral obtuseness in America [TV series Ethics in America] H. Arkes. il *National Review* 41:33-6 Je 16 '89
Of many things [TV series Ethics in America] J. W. Donohue. *America* 160:2 Ja 7-14 '89
A question of scruples [address, March 6, 1989] C. J. Silas. *Vital Speeches of the Day* 55:473-6 My 15 '89
Recoiling from reason [views of A. MacIntyre] M. C. Nussbaum. bibl f il *The New York Review of Books* 36:36-41 D 7 '89

Anecdotes, facetiae, satire, etc.
Your permanent record [condensed from Cheeseburgers] B. Greene. il *Reader's Digest* 134:147-8 Ap '89
ETHICS COMMITTEE (HOUSE) See United States. Congress. House. Committee on Standards of Official Conduct
ETHICS COMMITTEE (SENATE) See United States. Congress. Senate. Select Committee on Ethics
ETHICS IN AMERICA [television program] See Television program reviews—Single works
ETHICS IN GOVERNMENT ACT
Impeachment by other means [special prosecutor law] T. Eastland. *Commentary* 88:40-4 Ag '89
ETHIOPIA
> See also
> Americans—Ethiopia
> Famines—Ethiopia
> Medical care—Ethiopia
> Missing children—Ethiopia
> Relief work—Ethiopia

History
1889-1974
> See also
> World War, 1939-1945—Ethiopia

Industries
> See also
> Ethiopian Airlines

Kings and rulers
> See also
> Haile Selassie I, Emperor of Ethiopia, 1891-1975

Native peoples
> See also
> Oromo (African people)

Politics and government
Fizzled coup [attempt to topple Mengistu] *Time* 133:61 My 29 '89

Religious institutions and affairs
> See also
> Christians—Ethiopia
ETHIOPIAN AIRLINES
An Ethiopian success story. J. Ozanne. *World Press Review* 36:63 S '89
ETHIOPIAN REFUGEES See Refugees, Ethiopian
ETHNIC DANCE FESTIVAL (SAN FRANCISCO, CALIF.)
See Dance festivals—California
ETHNIC DANCE THEATRE
Reviews:
> Spring performances in St. Paul, Minn. J. Timmis. il *Dance Magazine* 63:78-80 S '89
ETHNIC JEWELRY See Jewelry
ETHNIC JOKES See Humor
ETHNIC MINORITIES See Minorities
ETHNIC NATIONALISM See Nationalism
ETHNIC STUDIES See Intercultural education
ETHNOBIOLOGY
The ethnobiologist's dilemma. J. M. Diamond. *Natural History* p26+ Je '89
ETHNOBOTANY
Just another day in paradise [M. Plotkin's work with the Tirió Indians of Suriname] D. D. Jackson. il *Reader's Digest* 134:166-8+ Ap '89
Searching for medicinal wealth in Amazonia [M. Plotkin's work with Tirió Indians of Suriname] D. D. Jackson. bibl (p171) il pors *Smithsonian* 19:94-103 F '89
ETHNOCENTRISM
Why we all love to hate. D. Gelman. il *Newsweek* 114:62-4 Ag 28 '89
ETHNOGRAPHY See Anthropological literature—Authorship
ETHNOLOGY
> See also
> Acculturation
> Anthropology
> Cannibalism
> Ethnobiology
> Ethnobotany
> Headhunters

Japan
Samurai anthropologist [evidence that samurai were descendants of the Ainu people; research by C. Loring Brace] *Discover* 10:12-13 S '89
ETHNOPSYCHOLOGY
> See also
> Blacks—Psychology
> Blacks—Race identity
Black and white houses? [contrasting cultures of United States and Soviet Union] P. Dukes. il *History Today* 39:9-11 Ap '89
Hidden messages [gestures in different countries] E. Ferrieux. il *World Press Review* 36:39 Jl '89
The irrational connection between diet and demeanor [research by Paul Rozin and Carol Nemeroff] E. Stark. il *Psychology Today* 23:14 O '89
The screw-you spirit. J. M. Fallows. *The Washington Monthly* 21:42-3 Mr '89
ETHOLOGY See Animals—Habits and behavior
ETHYL ALCOHOL See Alcohol
ETHYL ALCOHOL AS FUEL See Alcohol as fuel
ETHYLENE
> See also
> Polyethylene
Ethylene gene control: research ripens [gene for ACC synthase cloned; work of Takahide Sato and Athanasios Theologis] *Science News* 136:188 S 16 '89
ETHYLENEDIAMINE TETRAACETIC ACID
Defining the inside and outside of a catalytic RNA molecule [structure of Tetrahymena ribozyme] J. A. Latham and T. R. Cech. bibl f il *Science* 245:276-82 Jl 21 '89
ETIENNE, JEAN-LOUIS
> about
The last treasure. *The New Yorker* 65:27-8 Jl 17 '89
ETIQUETTE
> See also
> Business etiquette
> Courtesy
> Salutations
> Thank-you notes
Courtesy afloat. B. Stearns. il *Field & Stream* 94:72+ My '89
Entertaining etiquette. L. Baldrige. il *McCall's* 116:57 Ap '89
Etiquette: doing it right. C. Ford. See issues of McCall's beginning January 1987
Etiquette for every day. E. L. Post. See issues of Good Housekeeping
Etiquette for the '90s. E. L. Post. il *Good Housekeeping* 209:70+ Jl '89
Miss Manners lets her hair down. R. Hills. il *Esquire* 111:194-9 Je '89
Please, thank you, I love you. C. L. Mithers. *Glamour* 87:234 F '89

ETIQUETTE—*cont.*
Anecdotes, facetiae, satire, etc.
Serving up Emily Post with a wicked twist, P. J. O'Rourke takes aim at Modern manners. K. Hubbard. il pors *People Weekly* 32:47-8+ Jl 3 '89
"Yuk! Gross! I won't eat that turkey!" [excerpt from Do I have to say hello?] D. Ephron. il *Redbook* 174:30 N '89

ETIQUETTE OF THE UNDERCASTE [drama] See Hardman, Chris

ETLING, KATHY
(ed) See Demarais, Steve, and Zaiglin, Bob. Blueprinting big bucks

ETON COLLEGE
Days at Eton. J. Bainbridge. il *Gourmet* 49:48+ F '89

ETRA, JON
Back to the garden. il *Harper's Bazaar* 122:93+ Ag '89
Chelsea collector. il *House & Garden* 161:140-5 Mr '89
Comic relief. il *Harper's Bazaar* 122:31-2 Jl '89
The joy of risk. *Harper's Bazaar* 122:162-3+ My '89
Vass horizons. il por *House & Garden* 161:60-9+ Ja '89

ETTEDGUI, JOSEPH
about
The merchant of style. C. K. Gandee. il por *House & Garden* 161:46 Ap '89

ETTINGER, AUSTEN A.
The retiring kind. il *The New York Times Magazine* p18+ My 28 '89

ETTINGER, LINDA F., AND HUTCHENS, JAMES
Preparing arts administrators of the future: the need for interprofessional education. bibl f *Design for Arts in Education* 90:32-6 Mr/Ap '89

ETYMOLOGY See English language—Etymology

ETZIONI, AMITAI
Money, power and fame. por *Newsweek* 114:10 S 18 '89
Recession is not a solution. il *The New Leader* 72:15-16 Mr 20 '89
Welfare for the rich. il *The New Leader* 72:13-14 My 1 '89

EUBANK, HORACE WREN
Intuitive renaissance man [poem] il *Mother Jones* 14:19 Jl/Ag '89

EUBANKS, ROBIN
Wayne Shorter's solo on On Green Dolphin St.—a trombonist's analysis. il *Down Beat* 56:58-9 Ja '89
about
Robin Eubanks: a true sense of perspective. D. Helland. il pors *Down Beat* 56:26-8 Ja '89

EUBANKS, TONY
about
Tony Eubanks. P. Van Gelder. il por *American Artist* 53:58-63+ Ja '89

EUCALYPTUS MARGINATA See Jarrah
EUCHARIST See Catholic Church—Eucharist; Lord's Supper
EUGENE (OR.)
Education
Building an atmosphere of success in a middle school [Roosevelt Middle School] R. E. Rubinstein. *Phi Delta Kappan* 71:328-9 D '89
Sports
Trail blazers [running] J. Henderson. il *Runner's World* 24:14 Jl '89

EUGENE MCDERMOTT CONCERT HALL (DALLAS, TEX.)
But . . . how does it play? K. Ames. il *Newsweek* 114:64 S 25 '89

EUGENE ONEGIN [opera] See Tchaikovsky, Peter Ilich, 1840-1893

EUGENICS
Technology as destiny: the new eugenics challenges feminism [cover story] J. B. Elshtain. il *The Progressive* 53:19-23 Je '89

EUGSTER, O.
History of meteorites from the moon collected in Antarctica. bibl f il *Science* 245:1197-1202 S 15 '89

EURASIA
See also
Nomads—Eurasia

EURATOM
Nuclear cooperation with EURATOM [letter to Congress, March 9, 1989] G. Bush. *Department of State Bulletin* 89:44 Je '89

EUREKA COLLEGE
A shrine to the Gipper [R. Reagan memorabilia] B. Turque. il *Newsweek* 113:28 My 8 '89

EUREKA SOUTHERN RAILROAD
Along the Eel and through the redwoods [North Coast Daylight train] il map *Sunset (Central West edition)* 182:28+ My '89

EURIDICE [opera] See Peri, Jacopo, 1561-1633
EUROCONTROL See Air traffic control—Western Europe
EUROJET TURBO GMBH
Assembly of second, third EJ200 test engines nears end. K. F. Mordoff. *Aviation Week & Space Technology* 130:26 Ja 30 '89

EUROPE
See also
Alps
Anti-Semitism—Europe

Central Europe
Civil rights—Europe
Eastern Europe
Family—Europe
Jews—Europe
Motorcycle racing—Europe
Nutrition policy—Europe
Poor—Europe
Preschool education—Europe
Stone Age—Europe
Theater—Europe
Western Europe
Civilization
One (forgetful) Europe [address, 1985] T. Garton Ash. *Harper's* 279:30-1 S '89
Cultural relations
United States
See United States—Cultural relations—Europe
Defenses
See also
Conference on Confidence and Security-Building Measures and Disarmament in Europe
Conference on Security and Cooperation in Europe
Guided missiles, European
Now, 'lite' warfare? [conventional warfare] P. Cary and D. Stanglin. il *U.S. News & World Report* 106:28 Je 12 '89
Problems in paradigm. G. Flynn. *Foreign Policy* 74:63-84 Spr '89
The Russians aren't coming. S. Budiansky. il *U.S. News & World Report* 107:47+ N 27 '89
Description and travel
See also
Cruising—Europe
Motor scooter touring—Europe
The wonderful husband [F. and E. Roosevelt's European honeymoon in 1905] G. C. Ward. il pors *American Heritage* 40:57-8+ S/O '89
Economic conditions
A new economic miracle? [cover story; special section] il *Business Week* p58-66+ N 27 '89
Economic relations
One big European economy seems less like a dream. B. Riemer and others. il map *Business Week* p43-5 N 13 '89
Reinventing Europe. D. Stanglin and others. il maps *U.S. News & World Report* 107:39-43 N 27 '89
Foreign relations
Soviet Union
See Soviet Union—Foreign relations—Europe
United States
See United States—Foreign relations—Europe
History
1815-1848
In Europe, history repeats itself [parallels between 1989 and 1848] M. Mandelbaum. il *Time* 134:80 D 25 '89
1871-1918
See also
World War, 1914-1918
20th century
Turbulent era. il maps *Maclean's* 102:30+ S 4 '89
1918-1945
See also
Munich Four-Power Agreement (1938)
World War, 1939-1945
The last wise man [excerpts from Sketches from a life; cover story] G. F. Kennan. il pors *The Atlantic* 263:39-47+ Ap '89
1945-
The last wise man [excerpts from Sketches from a life; cover story] G. F. Kennan. il pors *The Atlantic* 263:39-47+ Ap '89
Politics and government
See also
Socialism—Europe
After the Wall. *The New Republic* 201:7-8 D 4 '89
The common house of Europe. F. R. Stern. bibl f il *The New York Review of Books* 36:6+ D 7 '89
A design after all. J. Barry. il *Newsweek* 114:33-4 D 11 '89
Designing 'a new era' [with interview with G. Bush] T. M. DeFrank and A. McDaniel. il *Newsweek* 114:22-4 D 18 '89
An embarrassment of riches. J. O'Sullivan. *National Review* 41:8 D 31 '89
Europe in the post-Yalta era [cover story] D. Singer. il *The Nation* 249:701+ D 11 '89
Four new faces of Europe. A. F. Geyer. *The Christian Century* 106:711-13 Ag 2-9 '89
Gorbachev speaks to the Council of Europe [excerpts from address, July 6, 1989] M. Gorbachev. *Current History* 88:347 O '89
The international community and change [address, July 6, 1989] M. Gorbachev. *Vital Speeches of the Day* 55:706-11 S 15 '89
The legacy of World War II. A. Phillips. il *Maclean's* 102:22-4+ S 4 '89
NATO's last mission. R. Steel. *Foreign Policy* 76:83-95 Fall '89

EUROPE—Politics and government—*cont.*

A new Concert of Europe. J. E. Mueller. *Foreign Policy* 77:3-16 Wint '89/'90

New horizons in Europe [address, March 6, 1989] J. A. Baker, III. *Department of State Bulletin* 89:56-9 My '89

The next few years will be the most momentous. M. S. Forbes, Jr. il *Forbes* 144:27 S 18 '89

Pax Bush. B. Javetski and D. Harbrecht. il *Business Week* p40-1 D 18 '89

Proceed with caution. *National Review* 41:11-13 D 31 '89

Religious institutions and affairs

See also
Reformation

Four new faces of Europe. A. F. Geyer. *The Christian Century* 106:711-13 Ag 2-9 '89

EUROPE AND THE UNITED STATES

See also
United States—Foreign opinion—European

EUROPEAN ART *See* Art, European

EUROPEAN ARTIFICIAL SATELLITES *See* Artificial satellites, European

EUROPEAN ATOMIC ENERGY COMMUNITY *See* Euratom

EUROPEAN CIVIL AVIATION CONFERENCE

European Aviation Conference, U.S. fail to agree on extending fare pact. il *Aviation Week & Space Technology* 131:66 Ag 14 '89

EUROPEAN COURT OF JUSTICE *See* Court of Justice of the European Communities

EUROPEAN CURRENCY UNIT

Post-1992 Europe [address, January 12, 1989] W. Seipp. *Vital Speeches of the Day* 55:300-3 Mr 1 '89

EUROPEAN DECORATIVE ARTS *See* Decoration and ornament

EUROPEAN ECONOMIC COMMUNITY

See also
European Parliament

1992 and all that [round table discussion on the implications for American publishers] il *Publishers Weekly* 235:21-8 F 3 '89

"1992" is closer than we think. C. W. Weinberger. il *Forbes* 143:33 Ap 17 '89

1992: unifying Europe's markets [effects on aerospace industry; special section; with editorial comment by Donald E. Fink] il map *Aviation Week & Space Technology* 130:51, 78-9+ Je 12 '89

The agricultural swamp [subsidies] J. Bovard. il *National Review* 41:46-8 F 10 '89

An alliance for progress? E. Corcoran. il *Scientific American* 260:78-9 Ap '89

Are U.S. multi-nationals ready for the U.S. of Europe? [pharmaceutical industry; address, May 16, 1989] R. E. Cawthorn. *Vital Speeches of the Day* 55:654-7 Ag 15 '89

As Spain rushes toward '92. E. Ontiveros. il *The New Leader* 72:10-11 O 2-16 '89

Bill Eftink [EEC hormone ban on U.S. beef imports] B. Eftink. il *Successful Farming* 87:19 mid-Mr '89

The birth of a new continental power. P. C. Newman. il *Maclean's* 102:38 My 1 '89

Breaking ranks: the West aids Poland and Hungary. P. Lewis. il *Maclean's* 102:43 O 16 '89

Britain's vexing ties with Europe. B. Amiel. il *Maclean's* 102:13 D 18 '89

Champagne diplomacy [Ontario Premier D. Peterson leads business delegation to France] J. Daly. *Maclean's* 102:39+ Ap 17 '89

Charging ahead. C. Redman. il *Time* 134:40-3+ S 18 '89

Come together [aviation under 1992 integration] N. Moll. il map *Flying* 116:86-90+ Jl '89

The coming boom in Europe. S. Tully. il *Fortune* 119:108+ Ap 10 '89

The coming revival of Europe. M. K. Evans. il *Gentlemen's Quarterly* 59:131-2+ F '89

Commission approves subsidies for Airbus. *Aviation Week & Space Technology* 130:67 Mr 13 '89

The Common Market—friend or foe? C. W. Weinberger. il map *Forbes* 143:31 Mr 6 '89

Creating 1992 [J. Delors] S. Tully. il por *Fortune* 119:41-2 Ja 2 '89

The curtain that still divides Europe. D. Lawday. il maps *U.S. News & World Report* 107:36+ Jl 17 '89

The Czar of Brussels [J. Delors] S. Sullivan. il pors *Newsweek* 113:32-3 F 6 '89

Don't tread on us—please [Ford and GM poised to be winners in European car market] J. Flint. il *Forbes* 143:92 Je 12 '89

"A dream that may soon come true". M. S. Forbes. *Forbes* 143:22 Ap 17 '89

The EC just says no to Japan's cheap chips. T. Peterson. il *Business Week* p46-7 Ja 30 '89

EC, phone home [British view on 1992 unification plan] M. Elliott. *The New Republic* 200:20+ Mr 27 '89

EC project 1992: the dynamics of change [address, September 9, 1988] D. Lamb. *Department of State Bulletin* 89:31-5 F '89

EC92 [cover story] R. Thompson. il map *Nation's Business* 77:18-24+ Je '89

EEC delays action on aircraft that fail to meet noise limits. E. H. Phillips. il *Aviation Week & Space Technology* 130:30 F 13 '89

Empty threat? [measures against U.S. TV programming] J. Marcom, Jr. il *Forbes* 144:43 N 13 '89

Europe. *Business Week* p47 Jl 10 '89

Europe '92 [address, April 19, 1989] W. F. Ryan. *Vital Speeches of the Day* 55:492-4 Je 1 '89

Europe bans boeuf's à l'estradiol. E. Marshall. *Science* 243:161-2 Ja 13 '89

Europe may exempt business jets from Stage 2 nonaddition rule. il *Aviation Week & Space Technology* 131:53+ O 2 '89

Europe may slap a quota on General Hospital [limiting American TV imports] B. Riemer and K. Wolman. il *Business Week* p46-7 Mr 27 '89

The Europe of 1992. G. Agnelli. *Foreign Affairs* 68:61-70 Fall '89

Europe recognizes the ozone threat [banning of chlorofluorocarbons] D. Dickson and E. Marshall. *Science* 243:1279 Mr 10 '89

Europe to ban CFCs by 2000. *Science News* 135:148 Mr 11 '89

Europe without frontiers [British view] N. Gelb. il *The New Leader* 72:7-8 Ja 9 '89

The European Community and 1992. S. Hoffmann. *Foreign Affairs* 68:27-47 Fall '89

The European Community's program for a single market in 1992. il map *Department of State Bulletin* 89:23-8 Ja '89

European engine makers fear social issues may impede sales. *Aviation Week & Space Technology* 130:134 Je 19 '89

European genome program delayed? D. Dickson. *Science* 243:1548 Mr 24 '89

Europe's bumpy road to '92. J. Valls-Russell. il *The New Leader* 72:8-9 S 4 '89

Europe's economic integration in 1992 [address, May 3, 1989] R. P. Forrestal. *Vital Speeches of the Day* 55:633-5 Ag 1 '89

First aid [Poland] P. Lemaître. il *World Press Review* 36:16 O '89

First aid for the ozone layer [banning CFCs] M. D. Lemonick. il *Time* 133:50 Mr 13 '89

Flying in formation. D. Lawday. il *U.S. News & World Report* 106:37-9 My 8 '89

A food fight as big as the Atlantic [EEC threatens ban on U.S. meat] *Newsweek* 113:41 Ja 9 '89

Fortress Europe for 1992. A. Rosenbaum. il *The Nation* 249:748-50 D 18 '89

The future of the European stock exchange system approaching 1992 [address, April 29, 1989] R. V. Rosen. *Vital Speeches of the Day* 56:49-53 N 1 '89

Genome project gets rough ride in Europe. D. Dickson. *Science* 243:599 F 3 '89

A 'grenade' aimed at Hollywood: Europe votes to slap a quota on U.S. TV imports. D. Pedersen. il *Newsweek* 114:58 O 16 '89

Holding pep rallies for 1992 [states help U.S. firms with export strategy] J. McCormick. il *Newsweek* 114:60 N 6 '89

How Europe 1992 could cost its airports $2 billion [loss of duty free business] B. Baudoin and others. il *Business Week* p55 Mr 6 '89

How the Italians see Europe. S. F. Senigallia. *The New Leader* 72:8 Je 12-26 '89

The international economic outlook for 1989 [address, January 19, 1989] R. P. Forrestal. *Vital Speeches of the Day* 55:367-9 Ap 1 '89

Is the beef flap a taste of trade wars to come? [U.S. vs. European Community] F. J. Comes and P. Magnusson. il *Business Week* p47 Ja 16 '89

Japanese carmakers flash their cash at the EC. T. Peterson and A. Borrus. il *Business Week* p43+ F 13 '89

The Japanese invade Europe. B. Powell. il map *Newsweek* 114:28-9 O 2 '89

Joint ventures with the EC. S. Y. Chow. il *High Technology Business* 9:10 Jl/Ag '89

Jumping into the Euromarket: is it cheaper by the dozen? C. P. Work. il *U.S. News & World Report* 107:44-5+ Jl 3 '89

Keeping up with EC92. A. Holzinger. il *Nation's Business* 77:38-40 D '89

Lack of centralized European ATC could hinder trade reforms in 1992 [air traffic control] E. H. Phillips. il *Aviation Week & Space Technology* 131:73 S 4 '89

Lille gets ready for '92. J. Ardagh. il map *The New York Times Magazine* p58-60+ D 3 '89

Losing on both fronts [U.S. commerce] I. M. Stelzer. il *The American Spectator* 22:37-8 Je '89

More than ever, Thatcher is odd woman out [defeat in the Europarliament vote] R. A. Melcher. il por *Business Week* p40 Jl 3 '89

A new boomtown sprouts as Western Europe unites [Brussels] D. Lawday. il *U.S. News & World Report* 107:32-3 O 9 '89

One big European economy seems less like a dream. B. Riemer and others. il map *Business Week* p43-5 N 13 '89

EUROPEAN ECONOMIC COMMUNITY—cont.

One Europe . . . [cover story; special section] il *World Press Review* 36:13-16+ Ja '89
One Europe indivisible? [Italy's role] S. F. Senigallia. il *The New Leader* 72:5-6 Ja 23 '89
Paradox for Switzerland. M. Legris and J.-M. Gonin. *World Press Review* 36:63 D '89
The politics of 1992. G. Szamuely. *Commentary* 88:42-5 O '89
Post-1992 Europe [address, January 12, 1989] W. Seipp. *Vital Speeches of the Day* 55:300-3 Mr 1 '89
President's meeting with EC Commission president [J. Delors; White House statement, June 14, 1989] il por *Department of State Bulletin* 89:83 Ag '89
The race to stock Europe's common supermarket [BSN buys European operations of RJR Nabisco with more food deals to follow] S. Toy and R. A. Melcher. il *Business Week* p80+ Je 26 '89
Redefining Europe and the Atlantic link. R. D. Hormats. *Foreign Affairs* 68:71-91 Fall '89
Reinventing Europe. D. Stanglin and others. il maps *U.S. News & World Report* 107:39-43 N 27 '89
S & S, H & R publishing titles on 1992 and all that. C. Goodrich. *Publishers Weekly* 235:46+ My 19 '89
A social charter for the E.C.? H. Wainwright. il *The Nation* 249:80-2+ Jl 17 '89
Spain tightens its European ties. J. Valls-Russell. il *The New Leader* 72:7-8 My 1 '89
The spark for a new Mediterranean miracle [Spain] R. J. Gwyn. il *World Press Review* 36:22-4 Mr '89
'Subsidy' becomes a dirty word. J. Kapstein. il *Business Week* p48 Je 19 '89
Talking about 1992 [implications of the consolidation for publishers] H. R. Lottman. *Publishers Weekly* 235:58 Je 30 '89
Tasteless Dutch tomatoes and waiters named Terry [homogenization of European culture] D. C. Anderson. *The New York Times Magazine* p60+ D 3 '89
Thatcher at odds with Europe. N. Gelb. por *The New Leader* 72:12-13 O 30 '89
Thatcherism across the Channel [Bruges group meeting in Paris] J.-M. Benoist. map *National Review* 41:23-5 N 10 '89
Transporting waste in the European Community: a free market? D. Laurence and B. Wynne. bibl f il *Environment* 31:12-17+ Jl/Ag '89
Two cheers for the new Europe [investments] J. Reid. il *Money* 18:93-4+ Jl '89
U.S. airlines establish new European flights before 1992 market restructuring. J. T. McKenna. il *Aviation Week & Space Technology* 131:79+ N 20 '89
U.S. criticizes E.C. plan to shield MBB from fluctuations in exchange rate. M. Mecham. *Aviation Week & Space Technology* 130:91 Mr 27 '89
The United States of Europe [1992 merger] C. Peacock. il *Utne Reader* p17-18 Mr/Ap '89
United we fall? [British view] J. Biffen. *National Review* 41:25-6 Je 30 '89
What's the beef? [ban on imports of beef injected with growth hormones] W. E. Sheeline. il *Fortune* 119:8 Ja 30 '89
Who is going to govern Europe? [interview with J. Delors] Y. de L'Ecotais and J. Leclerc du Sablon. il por *World Press Review* 36:28+ S '89
Why the beef over hormones? [European Community bans import of U.S. meat from animals treated with hormones] J. Castro. il *Time* 133:44 Ja 16 '89
Writing the new rules for Europe's merger game. J. Kapstein. il *Business Week* p48-9 F 6 '89

Conferences

Secretary meets with EC ministers [text of joint press conference, December 9, 1988] J. Delors; G. P. Shultz. *Department of State Bulletin* 89:27-30 F '89
Thatcher's compromise. A. Phillips. il por *Maclean's* 102:28 Jl 10 '89

EUROPEAN FREE TRADE ASSOCIATION

One big European economy seems less like a dream. B. Riemer and others. il map *Business Week* p43-5 N 13 '89

EUROPEAN HELICOPTER INDUSTRIES

EH101 antisubmarine version begins flight test program. il *Aviation Week & Space Technology* 131:68 N 13 '89
EUROPEAN HINGES *See* Hinges
EUROPEAN HOUSE DECORATION *See* House decoration, European

EUROPEAN MONETARY SYSTEM

Europe. *Business Week* p47 Jl 10 '89

EUROPEAN ORGANIZATION FOR NUCLEAR RESEARCH

Britain will remain in CERN; management reforms adopted. *Physics Today* 42:65 Ja '89
A colossal collision course [CERN's large electron-positron collider] M. D. Lemonick. il *Time* 134:72 Jl 17 '89
New machine sparks rivalries at CERN [large electron-proton collider] D. Dickson. il *Science* 244:1257-60 Je 16 '89
New physics, old rivalries [SLAC vs. CERN] J. Cherfas. il *Science* 246:323-4 O 20 '89
Smashing atom dust. S. O'Dy. *World Press Review* 36:67 S '89

EUROPEAN PAINTING *See* Painting, European

EUROPEAN PARLIAMENT

The European Parliament gets its act together. B. Riemer. il *Business Week* p44+ Je 12 '89
The evolving European Parliament. M. Duverger. *World Press Review* 36:32 S '89
Gains and losses [election results] D. Singer. *The Nation* 249:41+ Jl 10 '89
How the Italians see Europe. S. F. Senigallia. *The New Leader* 72:8 Je 12-26 '89\
More than ever, Thatcher is odd woman out [defeat in the Europarliament vote] R. A. Melcher. il por *Business Week* p40 Jl 3 '89
New times [recent elections] *Time* 134:29 Jl 3 '89
Notes on Italy and England [elections] W. Goodman. *The New Leader* 72:7-8 Je 12-26 '89

EUROPEAN PATENT OFFICE

Europe says no to animal patents. D. Dickson. *Science* 245:25 Jl 7 '89
No patent for Harvard's mouse? D. Dickson. *Science* 243:1003 F 24 '89
EUROPEAN POTTERY *See* Pottery, European
EUROPEAN PROPULSION SOCIETY *See* Société Européenne de Propulsion
EUROPEAN SECURITY CONFERENCE *See* Conference on Security and Cooperation in Europe

EUROPEAN SILICON STRUCTURES (FIRM)

Custom chips for sale, no job too small. O. Port. il *Business Week* p99+ Mr 6 '89

EUROPEAN SOUTHERN OBSERVATORY (ORGANIZATION)

A sharp, new eye scans the southern sky [New Technology Telescope] il *Science News* 135:324 My 27 '89
A telescope for tomorrow [New Technology Telescope; cover story] D. Fischer. il *Sky and Telescope* 78:248-52 S '89

EUROPEAN SPACE AGENCY

Britain reconsiders limited role with France on Ariane 5 program. *Aviation Week & Space Technology* 130:28 Ja 30 '89
ESA council endorses French Matra design for polar platform [Columbus space station] *Aviation Week & Space Technology* 131:24 O 30 '89
ESA director general selects Matra polar platform design. il *Aviation Week & Space Technology* 130:26 F 27 '89
ESA's next decade. I. Pryke. il *Ad Astra* 1:16-19+ My '89
Europe delays Soho spacecraft work until U.S. approves joint project MOU [solar and heliospheric satellite] J. M. Lenorovitz. il *Aviation Week & Space Technology* 131:31-2 N 13 '89
European industry submits proposal for space station design/development [Columbus] J. M. Lenorovitz. il *Aviation Week & Space Technology* 131:22 O 16 '89
Hipparcos failure stuns Europeans. S. Mitton. il *Astronomy* 17:14 N '89
Ulysses spacecraft prepared for long-delayed mission to sun. il *Aviation Week & Space Technology* 131:25 N 6 '89
EUROPEAN SPACE STATIONS *See* Space stations, European
EUROPEAN WAR, 1914-1918 *See* World War, 1914-1918

EUROTUNNEL (FIRM)

Eurotunnel of love? [stock price] M. Maremont. il *Business Week* p56 F 27 '89
Trouble in the tunnel [rising costs] A. Phillips. il *Maclean's* 102:40+ O 9 '89

EUTHANASIA

See also
Right to die
Euthanasia: a bedside view [cover story] H. Goetz. *The Christian Century* 106:619-22 Je 21-28 '89
Feeling no pain. *The New Republic* 201:9-10 N 27 '89
"It's over, Debbie" [account of mercy killing in the Journal of the American Medical Association] L. Oliwenstein. il *Discover* 10:80-1 Ja '89
Should a doctor help his patient commit suicide? il *Jet* 76:14-16 Ap 24 '89
Tiring of life without freedom, quadriplegic David Rivlin chooses to die among friends [wins right to refuse treatment] M. Dougherty. il pors *People Weekly* 32:56-8 Ag 7 '89
A White House promise [Health and Human Services nominee R. Fulton's stand on spina bifida and euthanasia] *National Review* 41:15-16 Ap 7 '89

Animals

Farewell to Foxy. D. D. Zentay. il *The Saturday Evening Post* 261:22 Ja/F '89

Netherlands

Euthanasia: how it works: the Dutch experience. R. Fenigsen. *Current (Washington, D.C.)* 313:4-14 Je '89

EUTROPHICATION

See also
Water bloom
EVA (EXTRAVEHICULAR ACTIVITY) *See* Space flight—Extravehicular activity

EVACUATION OF CIVILIANS

Nuclear sneak attack [executive order on evacuation of civilian nuclear power plants] *The Progressive* 53:7 Ja '89
EVALUATION (EDUCATION) *See* Colleges and universities—Evaluation; Education—Evaluation

EVANGELICAL CHRISTIAN PUBLISHERS ASSOCIATION
Religious bestsellers. L. Sibley. *Publishers Weekly* 235:39
Mr 3 '89
EVANGELICAL CHURCHES
See also
Assemblies of God
National Association of Evangelicals
Conferences
See Religious conferences
Africa
The church in Africa [interview with T. Adeyemo] il por
Christianity Today 33:52-3 O 20 '89
Canada
Contest in Canada. L. K. Tarr. *Christianity Today* 33:48
Ja 13 '89
Central America
Ambassadors of Zion [International Christian Embassy Jerusa-
lem] T. Barry and D. Preusch. *The Christian Century*
106:79-81 Ja 25 '89
Colombia
Violence in Colombia unites evangelicals. J. Maust.
Christianity Today 33:49 S 22 '89
Guatemala
Evangelicals may become a majority in Guatemala. S. Sy-
wulka. il map *Christianity Today* 33:46 Ap 21 '89
Latin America
Speaking in Latin tongues [cover story] D. Martin. il *National
Review* 41:30-5 S 29 '89
Nicaragua
U.S. embassy aids pastors. *The Christian Century* 106:808-9
S 13-20 '89
Singapore
Faith at the top [interview with D. Howard] por map
Christianity Today 33:58-9 Jl 14 '89
EVANGELICAL COLLEGES *See* Church colleges and univer-
sities
**EVANGELICAL COMMITTEE FOR AID AND DEVELOP-
MENT IN NICARAGUA**
One Nicaraguan Christian's perspective [interview with G.
Parajón] por *Christianity Today* 33:48 Mr 3 '89
EVANGELICAL CONFERENCES *See* Religious conferences
**EVANGELICAL COUNCIL FOR FINANCIAL ACCOUNT-
ABILITY**
ECFA celebrates ten years. *Christianity Today* 33:44 O 20
'89
EVANGELICAL LUTHERAN CHURCH IN AMERICA *See*
Lutheran Church—United States
EVANGELICAL PRESS ASSOCIATION
Focus bids farewell to EPA. il *Christianity Today* 33:40
Mr 17 '89
EVANGELICAL RADIO PROGRAMS *See* Radio broadcast-
ing—Religious programs
EVANGELICAL TELEVISION PROGRAMS *See* Television
broadcasting—Religious programs
EVANGELICALISM
See also
Fundamentalism
International Christian Embassy Jerusalem (Organization)
Moral Majority
Presbyterians for Renewal
Signs and wonders movement
World Evangelical Fellowship
The 90s [cover story; special section] il *Christianity Today*
33:18-28 N 17 '89
Evangelical voice heard at World Council meeting [conference
on Mission and Evangelism] R. Frame. il *Christianity
Today* 33:45-6 Jl 14 '89
Gender, education and the new Christian right. S. D. Rose.
bibl *Society* 26:59-66 Ja/F '89
Leaders disagree on future of the church. A. L. Sherman.
il *Christianity Today* 33:42 Ap 21 '89
A tour among the evangelicals [Randall Balmer's Mine eyes
have seen the glory] J. G. Stackhouse, Jr. *The Christian
Century* 106:529-30+ My 17 '89
What does it mean to be evangelical? [conference at Trinity
Evangelical Divinity School] il *Christianity Today* 33:60+
Je 16 '89
Will history be repeated in New England? [surge of evangelical
piety] T. K. Jones. il *Christianity Today* 33:72+ N 17
'89
The years of the evangelicals [cover story] M. E. Marty.
il *The Christian Century* 106:171-4 F 15 '89
History
Epitaph for the eighties. il *Christianity Today* 33:18 D 15
'89
EVANGELICALISM AND POLITICS *See* Religion and politics
EVANGELICALS AND JEWS *See* Christianity and other
religions
EVANGELISTIC CONFERENCES *See* Religious conferences
EVANGELISTIC WORK
See also
Campus Crusade for Christ
Child Evangelism Fellowship Inc.
Child Evangelism Ministries, Inc.
Church growth
Missions
National Association of Evangelicals
Revivals

Confessions of an erstwhile evangelizer [Catholic Church]
R. E. Burns. *U.S. Catholic* 54:2 N '89
Finance
See also
Evangelical Council for Financial Accountability
National Religious Broadcasters. Ethics and Financial
Integrity Commission
The day of reckoning delayed [J. Bakker's bizarre behavior
forces suspension of fraud trial] R. N. Ostling. il por
Time 134:76-7 S 11 '89
A guilty evangelist [J. Bakker] B. Wickens. il por *Maclean's*
102:55-6 O 16 '89
Having a devil of a time [J. Bakker's trial] il por *Newsweek*
114:61 S 11 '89
Healing the church—after Bakker. T. C. Muck. il *Christianity
Today* 33:16 N 17 '89
How the others are faring [O. Roberts, J. Swaggart, and
P. Robertson] pors *Time* 134:76 S 11 '89
Jim & Tammy Faye Bakker. D. Barry. il pors *People Weekly*
32 Special Issue:70-1 Fall '89
Jim Bakker and the Eternal Revenue Service. G. Wacker.
il pors *The Christian Century* 106:1053-5 N 15 '89
Judgment day [J. Bakker convicted of fraud] il por *Time*
134:65 O 16 '89
The living legacy of Jim Bakker [effects of PTL scandal
on TV ministries] il por *U.S. News & World Report* 107:14
N 6 '89
Questions raised about Bob Larson campaign [evangelical
radio programs] L. Cryderman. il *Christianity Today* 33:47-8
Mr 3 '89
Surviving the slump [evangelical broadcasters; cover story;
special section] il *Christianity Today* 33:32-4+ F 3 '89
Trial and tribulation [J. Bakker] N. Underwood. il por
Maclean's 102:63 S 11 '89
Unholy roller coaster [J. Bakker trial; cover story] M. Brower.
il pors *People Weekly* 32:98-100+ S 18 '89
The wrath of "Maximum Bob" [J. Bakker's punishment
raises questions over sentencing] A. L. Sanders. il por
Time 134:62 N 6 '89
International aspects
See also
Lausanne Committee for World Evangelization
AD 2000: eleven years to reach the world [Global Consultation
on World Evangelization by AD 2000 and beyond] A.
Toalston. il *Christianity Today* 33:48+ F 3 '89
Beyond the maintenance mentality. D. A. McGavran. il
Christianity Today 33:28-9 F 3 '89
Evangelical voice heard at World Council meeting [conference
on Mission and Evangelism] R. Frame. il *Christianity
Today* 33:45-6 Jl 14 '89
Evangelism: the best form of social action [interview with
L. Palau] il por *Christianity Today* 33:51-2 F 17 '89
A new era for black missionaries. V. Becker. il *Christianity
Today* 33:38+ O 20 '89
'Solidarity' meets 'evangelism' in WCC [World Conference
on Mission and Evangelism at Trinity University] J. C.
Lyles. *The Christian Century* 106:613-15 Je 21-28 '89
Great Britain
Billy brings 'em in [use of B. Graham's crusades to stimulate
clerical vocations in the Church of England] A. McCarthy.
il *Commonweal* 116:456-7 S 8 '89
Soft sell and satellites deliver biggest audience [B. Graham]
il por *Christianity Today* 33:48-9 Ag 18 '89
Greece
Orthodox Greeks clash with evangelicals. B. G. Baker. il
Christianity Today 33:41 O 6 '89
Hungary
Glasnost opens way for Graham. E. E. Plowman. il por
Christianity Today 33:61 S 8 '89
Nicaragua
See also
Evangelical Committee for Aid and Development in
Nicaragua
Evangelist offers advice to Nicaraguan president [interview
with A. Mottesi] R. Frame. il pors *Christianity Today*
33:41-2 N 3 '89
Soviet Union
Believers push forward despite legal limbo. K. A. Lawton.
il *Christianity Today* 33:63-4+ N 17 '89
An open-air crusade in the Soviet Union? Believe it! [L.
Palau crusade] T. C. Muck. il por *Christianity Today*
33:36-7 O 20 '89
Under the eye of the big, red machine [L. Palau crusade;
cover story] T. C. Muck. il por *Christianity Today* 33:20-5
D 15 '89
EVANGELISTS
See also
Bakker, Jim
Falwell, Jerry
Graham, Billy, 1918-
Larson, Bob
Palau, Luis, 1934-
Price, Frederick
Robertson, Pat
Roever, Dave
Sumrall, Lester Frank, 1913-
Swaggart, Jimmy Lee
Wilkerson, David

EVANGELIZATION See Evangelistic work

EVANIER, DAVID
Will the Soviet Union survive until 1994? [interview with B. Shragin; cover story] *National Review* 41:24+ Ap 7 '89

EVANIER, DAVID, AND KLEHR, HARVEY
Anticommunism and mental health. il *The American Spectator* 22:28-30 F '89

EVANS, BETSY, AND NELSON, TODD
The power of old flames. *Glamour* 87:156 Mr '89

EVANS, BILL, 1929-1980
about
Natural flow: the Bill Evans Trio [reprint] J. A. Tynan. il por *Down Beat* 56:61 S '89

EVANS, BILL, 1958-
about
Bill Evans: the art of the fisherman. L. Birnbaum. il pors *Down Beat* 56:20-2 Ja '89

EVANS, BOB, 1930-
about
The 'Cotton Club' murder: cocaine and hit men in Hollywood—a 1980s film noir [cover story] J. Kasindorf. il pors *New York* 22:24-33 Jl 24 '89
Letter from Los Angeles. J. Didion. *The New Yorker* 65:92-9 S 4 '89

EVANS, COOPER
about
Bush's farmer in the White House. G. Vincent. il por *Successful Farming* 87:34AF mid-F '89

EVANS, DAVID
about
National policies to encourage service [interview; cover story; with editorial comment by Susan Stroud] F. Newman. il *Change* 21:4, 8-17 S/O '89

EVANS, GAYNELLE
Good reads for black kids. il *American Visions* 4:50-2 D '89

EVANS, GIL
about
Gil Evans: the lone arranger [reprint from April 1984 issue] H. Mandel. por *Down Beat* 56:92 S '89

EVANS, JANET
about
The golden girl makes a splash. J. E. Vader. il por *Sports Illustrated* 70:86 Ap 3 '89
Janet Evans: good as gold. K. Carlisle. il pors *Women's Sports & Fitness* 11:28-33 Ap '89

EVANS, JONI
Joy riding. il *Vogue* 179:340 Ap '89
about
Well-read women. D. Lida. il pors *House & Garden* 161:228-31 O '89

EVANS, LARRY
Blue-collar scholar: a former steelworker hits the books. il *The Progressive* 53:22-5 Ap '89

EVANS, LINDA, 1942-
about
Linda Evans: good-bye to Hollywood. C. Jahr. il pors *Ladies' Home Journal* 106:44+ Ag '89
Linda Evans: her second blooming. N. Gittelson. il pors *McCall's* 116:66-7+ Mr '89

EVANS, MARA
Tribute to turkey. il *The Saturday Evening Post* 261:18-20 N/D '89

EVANS, MARK
Andy Razaf, the word man of Broadway. il pors *American Visions* 4:32-6 O '89

EVANS, MICHAEL K.
Money. See issues of Gentlemen's Quarterly

EVANS, MICHELE
Island hopping. il *The New York Times Magazine* p55-6 F 26 '89

EVANS, NANCY, 1950-
about
Well-read women. D. Lida. il pors *House & Garden* 161:228-31 O '89

EVANS, RICHARD, 1939-
Mind games in Melbourne. il *World Tennis* 36:127+ Ap '89

EVANS, RICHARD L.
about
A Dow theorist sees stocks falling 400 points only to soar again to beyond 3000. C. E. Cohen. il por *Money* 18:177-8 S '89

EVANS, ROBERT O.
Supernova hunter; ed. by Robert Reeves. il *Astronomy* 17:94-7 N '89
about
StarTrails. D. H. Levy. il por *Sky and Telescope* 78:85 Jl '89

EVANS, ROWLAND, AND NOVAK, ROBERT D.
Congressmen for life: the incumbency scandal. *Reader's Digest* 134:79-83 Je '89
James Baker: pragmatist at State. il pors *Reader's Digest* 135:213-14+ N '89

EVANS, TIMOTHY
about
Chicago alderman Evans to run for mayor after Sawyer's primary defeat. il pors *Jet* 75:4-5 Mr 20 '89
Chicago blacks back Tim Evans, Harold Washington Party candidate for mayor. R. E. Johnson. il pors *Jet* 75:4+ Ap 3 '89
Race after Washington. P. Greene. il *Commonweal* 116:199-201 Ap 7 '89
Richard Daley wins Chicago mayoral race; blacks fail to unite behind Tim Evans. il pors *Jet* 76:8-9 Ap 24 '89
Skin deep. F. Barnes. *The New Republic* 200:10-11 Ap 10 '89

EVANS, WALKER, 1903-1975
about
Walker Evans: American photographs. L. Kirstein. il *USA Today (Periodical)* 117:54-9 Mr '89
Walker Evans: Museum of Modern Art. R. B. Woodward. il *Art News* 88:206 Ap '89

EVANS (BILL) TRIO See Bill Evans Trio

EVANS-PRITCHARD, AMBROSE
Argentina drifts toward disaster [cover story] il *The American Spectator* 22:19-21+ S '89
Voodoo deficits. il *The American Spectator* 22:14-15 F '89

EVANSTON (ILL.)
Hospitals
Code blue [nursing shortage; case of Evanston Hospital] L. Kleinmann. il *Health (New York, N.Y.)* 21:68-71+ F '89

EVANSTON HOSPITAL (EVANSTON, ILL.) See Evanston (Ill.)—Hospitals

EVAPORATION
See also
Vaporization

EVAPORITES
Origin of ancient potash evaporites: clues from the modern nonmarine Qaidam basin of western China. T. K. Lowenstein and others. bibl f il map *Science* 245:1090-2 S 8 '89

EVATT, HERBERT VERE, 1894-1965
about
Three men and the bomb. M. Oliphant. il pors *The Bulletin of the Atomic Scientists* 45:41-2 Mr '89

EVENARI, MICHAEL, 1904-
about
Desert bloom. D. Starr. il *Omni (New York, N.Y.)* 11:28+ Mr '89

EVENING AND CONTINUATION SCHOOLS
See also
Adult education
University extension

EVENING PRIMROSES See Sundrops

EVENTIDE AVIONICS (FIRM)
Motion pictures [Argus 5000 moving map] N. Moll. il *Flying* 116:66-7 Ja '89

EVERAERT, PIERRE
about
Shopping for bargains. J. Zweig. il por *Forbes* 144:274 Jl 24 '89

EVERDING, AUGUST
about
The sleeping Prince. G. M. Loney. il *Opera News* 53:14+ My '89

EVEREST, MOUNT (CHINA AND NEPAL) See Mount Everest (China and Nepal)

EVERETT, MARJORIE L.
about
Is Hollywood Park on the way to the glue factory? K. Kerwin. il *Business Week* p36 My 29 '89

EVERETT, RALPH
about
First and only black to head U.S. Senate committee staff joins 400-lawyer firm. il pors *Jet* 77:37 O 16 '89

EVERETT, WILLIAM JOHNSON
Sunday monarchists and Monday citizens? *The Christian Century* 106:503-5 My 10 '89

EVERGLADES (FLA.)
Marjory Stoneman Douglas. V. Gladstone. il pors *Ms.* 17:68-71 Ja/F '89

EVERGLADES NATIONAL PARK (FLA.)
Amazing Glades [canoe trip] S. Lechner. il *Sierra* 74:134-40 Ja/F '89
Everglades. G. S. Bush. il *Better Homes and Gardens* 67:178 Ap '89
Last gasp for the Everglades [U.S. Attorney D. Lehtinen sues Florida for polluting federal lands] J. Carney. il por map *Time* 134:26-7 S 25 '89
New areas likely for Everglades. il *National Parks* 63:8-9 Jl/Ag '89
Saving America's swamp of swamps. il *U.S. News & World Report* 107:8-9 D 25 '89-Ja 1 '90
Photographs and photography
The nature photographer's guide to shooting in the Everglades. J. Shaw. il map *Popular Photography* 96:22-3 F '89

EVERGREEN STATE COLLEGE
Finding the call to teach [Miami-Dade Community College teacher spends year at Evergreen State] B. Hilbert. il *Change* 21:6+ Mr/Ap '89

EVERGREENS
See also
Christmas trees
Pine
Spruce
EVERLAST [ballet] *See* Ballet reviews—Single works
EVERLASTING WREATHS *See* Wreaths
EVERT, CHRIS
Down memory lane. il por *World Tennis* 37:66+ S '89
The final chapter. il pors *World Tennis* 37:31-2+ D '89
Giving it my best shot. il pors *World Tennis* 36:34-6 F '89
Peaking after 30 [cover story] il pors *World Tennis* 37:28-30 Je '89
Taking it to the limit. il por *World Tennis* 36:58-9 Ap '89
'Tennis was my showcase' [cover story]; ed. by Curry Kirkpatrick. il pors *Sports Illustrated* 71:72-8+ Ag 28 '89
A view from above. il pors *World Tennis* 37:26-8 N '89
about
An American original [cover story] N. Amdur. il pors *World Tennis* 37:20-2 D '89
Behind closed doors. D. B. Krass. il por *World Tennis* 37:96 D '89
Chris Evert believes there is life after tennis. P. Axthelm. il pors *People Weekly* 32:26-9 Jl 24 '89
Chris Evert, Openly. E. Comte. il pors *Sport (New York, N.Y.)* 80:68-70 S '89
The end of a fairy tale. C. Leerhsen. il *Newsweek* 114:47 Jl 17 '89
Garrison ruins Evert's U.S. Open goodbye party. il pors *Jet* 76:46+ S 25 '89
A great friend and foe. M. Navratilova. por *Sports Illustrated* 71:88 Ag 28 '89
"I can see how tough I was". W. A. Henry. il por *Time* 134:85 S 11 '89
The net results. il por *U.S. News & World Report* 107:11 S 11 '89
The way she was. S. Flink. il pors *World Tennis* 37:24-30 D '89
EVERTS, PHILIP P.
Where the peace movement goes when it disappears. bibl f il *The Bulletin of the Atomic Scientists* 45:26-30 N '89
EVIATAR, DAPHNE
Bard of the airwaves [interview] il por *Gentlemen's Quarterly* 59:41-2 Ja '89
EVICTION
D.C. cracks down on drugs, evicts suspected dealers. il *Jet* 76:52 Je 5 '89
EVIDENCE, EXPERT *See* Expert evidence (Law)
EVIDENCE (LAW)
See also
Confession (Law)
Evidence Store (Firm)
Expert evidence (Law)
Police questioning
Searches and seizures
Wiretapping
Witnesses
Child-abuse evidence debated [variations in girls' genitals] D. Nathan. *Ms.* 17:81-2 Mr '89
EVIDENCE STORE (FIRM)
Stephen Appelbaum gives lawyers a hand, a leg, or any other body part for their day in court. A. Abrahams. il pors *People Weekly* 31:143-4+ My 22 '89
EVIGAN, GREG
about
Why Greg Evigan wouldn't come out of the bathroom. B. Goodwin. il pors *TV Guide* 37:16-18 Ap 15-21 '89
EVIKAR INTERNATIONAL
A Kenyan tycoon [businesswoman E. K. Mungai] W. Machua. il por *World Press Review* 36:52 Jl '89
EVIL *See* Good and evil
EVINS (JOE L.) APPALACHIAN CENTER FOR CRAFTS *See* Joe L. Evins Appalachian Center for Crafts
EVOKED POTENTIALS (ELECTROPHYSIOLOGY) *See* Electrophysiology
EVOLUTION
See also
Adaptation (Biology)
Biology
Creation
Earth—Evolution
Galaxies—Evolution
Homology (Biology)
Kin selection
Life (Biology)—Origin
Man, Prehistoric
Moon—Evolution
Natural selection
Phylogeny
Plants—Evolution
Sociobiology
Species
Stars—Evolution
Tennessee evolution controversy
Variation (Biology)

The ancient contract [evidence suggesting domestication of animals was a result of coevolution; cover story] S. Budiansky. il *U.S. News & World Report* 106:74-9 Mr 20 '89
An asteroid to die for. S. J. Gould. il *Discover* 10:60-5 O '89
Asymmetries of clade shape and the direction of evolutionary time [discussion of May 27, 1988 article, Macroevolutionary interpretations of symmetry and synchroneity in the fossil record] J. A. Kitchell and N. S. MacLeod. *Science* 243:1613-15 Mr 24 '89
Bamboo and human evolution. G. G. Pope. il map *Natural History* p48-57 O '89
A biologist whose heresy redraws earth's tree of life [L. Margulis' symbiotic theory of cell evolution] J. McDermott. bibl (p135) il pors *Smithsonian* 20:72-6+ Ag '89
Chromosomal location and evolutionary rate variation in enterobacterial genes. P. M. Sharp and others. bibl f il *Science* 246:808-10 N 10 '89
Coming attractions. N. C. Ellstrand. *Omni (New York, N.Y.)* 11:33 My '89
Evolution and extinction [species preservers trying to stop the clock; with reply by N. Meyers] N. D. Levine. *BioScience* 39:38-40 Ja '89
Evolution set fast-forward [viral genetics] *BioScience* 39:512-13 S '89
Evolution's rapid shrinkage [dwarf fossil deer on the island of Jersey; research by Adrian M. Lister] R. Monastersky. *Science News* 136:357 D 2 '89
Genesis 1 [discussion of November 1988 article, Evolution and the Bible] L. Kass. *Commentary* 87:2+ Ap '89
The great leap forward [human evolution; cover story; with editorial comment by Paul Hoffman] J. M. Diamond. il map *Discover* 10:4, 50-60 My '89
How do you read from the palimpsest of life? M. M. Waldrop. il *Science* 246:578-9 N 3 '89
New world, new mind [excerpt] P. R. Ehrlich and R. E. Ornstein. il *New Perspectives Quarterly* 6:26-33 Spr '89
Phenomena, comment and notes [P. Sheldon's work with trilobites] J. S. Trefil. il por *Smithsonian* 20:34+ Je '89
Rethinking evolution [work of L. Margulis on symbiotic origin of cells] G. Cowley. il por *Newsweek* 114:38 O 2 '89
Simulated Evolution: wherein bugs learn to hunt bacteria. A. K. Dewdney. il *Scientific American* 260:138-41 My '89
Stages of evolution and their messengers. E. Rubenstein. il *Scientific American* 260:132 Je '89
Taxonomic differences in the scaling of brain on body weight among mammals. M. D. Pagel and P. H. Harvey. bibl f il *Science* 244:1589-93 Je 30 '89
This view of life. S. J. Gould. *See* issues of Natural History
Tracing living signs of ancient life forms [research by Andrew D. Ellington] I. Amato. *Science News* 136:229 O 7 '89
Vision optics and evolution [cover story] D.-E. Nilsson. bibl f il *BioScience* 39:298-307 My '89
We're all lucky to be here [S. J. Gould's evolutionary theory and Burgess Shale fossils] J. Adler. il por *Newsweek* 114:68 N 20 '89
What makes bigger brains? [research by Paul Harvey and Mark Pagel] R. Lewin. *Science* 244:1544 Je 30 '89
Study and teaching
California backs evolution education. M. Barinaga. il *Science* 246:881 N 17 '89
California urges teaching of evolution in science textbooks. M. Colin. il *Publishers Weekly* 235:14 F 3 '89
Educators adopt evolution as 'theory' [California] K. H. Sidey. *Christianity Today* 33:57 D 15 '89
Facts of life [science textbooks support evolution in California] R. N. Ostling. il *Time* 134:118 N 20 '89
EVOLUTION, SOCIAL *See* Social change
EWART, NEIL
Saved by what bell? [condensed from Everyday phrases] il *Reader's Digest* 134:165-6+ My '89
EWELL, JUDITH, 1943-
Debt and politics in Venezuela. bibl f *Current History* 88:121-4+ Mr '89
EWEN, HAROLD I.
about
Ewen and Purcell win Tinsley Prize. P. H. Andersen. *Physics Today* 42:92+ Ap '89
EWEN, STUART
Waste a lot, want a lot: our all-consuming quest for style. il *Utne Reader* p81-4 S/O '89
EWENS, THOMAS
Discipline: science and art as reflective activities. bibl f *Design for Arts in Education* 90:2-14 Mr/Ap '89
EWING, J.R. (FICTIONAL CHARACTER) *See* J.R. Ewing (Fictional character)
EX-CONVICTS
See also
Children of ex-convicts
EX-IM BANK *See* Export-Import Bank of the United States
EX-PRESIDENTS OF THE UNITED STATES *See* Presidents
EXAGGERATION
See also
Hyperbole

EXAMINATION TUTORS *See* Tutors and tutoring
EXAMINATIONS
See also
Air pilots—Examinations
Educational tests and measurements
Physical examinations
Teachers—Examinations
A midterm night's dream [exam nightmares] il *New Choices for the Best Years* 29:13 Ap '89
Which tests teach most? [research by Ronald P. Fisher and Paul W. Foos] C. Potera. *Psychology Today* 23:28 Mr '89
EXCEL (COMPUTER PROGRAM) *See* Spreadsheets (Computer programs)
EXCESS GOVERNMENT PROPERTY *See* Surplus government property
EXCHANGE, FOREIGN *See* Foreign exchange
EXCHANGE (BARTER) *See* Barter
EXCHANGE OF PERSONS PROGRAMS
See also
Project Self-Help and Awareness
EXCHANGE RATES *See* Foreign exchange
EXCHANGES, COMMODITY *See* Commodity exchanges
EXCHANGES, EDUCATIONAL *See* Educational exchanges
EXCHANGES, LITERARY AND SCIENTIFIC
Arms control physics: the new Soviet connection. F. Von Hippel. bibl f il *Physics Today* 42:39-42+ N '89
Black Russian. Y. Khanga. il pors *Essence* 20:59-60+ Ag '89
China's turmoil touches U.S. science; U.S.-Chinese scientists see dreams imperiled. M. Sun and E. Marshall. il *Science* 244:1130-2 Je 9 '89
Comrades in rocketry [Soviet and U.S. amateur rocketeers compete at Wallops Station, Va.] A. Jackson. il *Ad Astra* 1:29-31 F '89
Far from Beijing, Chinese students in US fear for future of science and nation. I. Goodwin. il *Physics Today* 42:45-7 Jl '89
Into Africa [American Association for the Advancement of Science programs] L. A. Levey; B. Gold. il map *Science* 245:538-9 Ag 4 '89
Japan lays out welcome mat for U.S. scientists. M. Sun. *Science* 243:1546-7 Mr 24 '89
Krumhansl protests China situation, urges support for scholars in USA. *Physics Today* 42 pt1:79 Ag '89
NAS suspends collaboration with China. *Science News* 135:383 Je 17 '89
An open door the U.S. isn't using [few American researchers in Japan's labs] A. Borrus. il *Business Week* p59+ My 15 '89
Rolfing with Yeltsin [B. Yeltsin's U.S. visit sponsored by the Esalen Institute] A. Heard. *The New Republic* 201:11-13 O 9 '89
Soul-searching after China crackdown [U.S. scientists debate maintaining scientific cooperation with China] M. Sun. *Science* 245:461-2 Ag 4 '89
Soviet sociology makes a comeback [exchanges with U.S.] C. Holden. il *Science* 246:991-2 N 24 '89
To Russia, with books [USIA exhibit titled Many-booked America] Y. Richmond. por *Publishers Weekly* 235:76 F 3 '89
U.S. and Soviets sign 'unique' accord [scientists may initiate joint ventures] *Science News* 135:62 Ja 28 '89
U.S. international activities in science and technology [message to Congress, April 5, 1989] G. Bush. *Department of State Bulletin* 89:51-2 Je '89
Uncertain of future, Chinese students find helpful friends in high places. I. Goodwin. *Physics Today* 42 pt1:39-41 Ag '89
A week in Beijing. D. J. Gross. il pors *Physics Today* 42 pt1:9+ Ag '89
EXCHANGES, REAL ESTATE *See* Real estate exchanges
EXCIMER LASERS *See* Lasers
EXCISE TAX
See also
Alcoholic beverages—Taxation
The OMB octopus [wildlife programs] L. Williamson. il *Outdoor Life* 183:62+ My '89
EXCITED STATES *See* Energy levels (Quantum mechanics)
EXCLUSIVE ECONOMIC ZONE
Mapping a wet frontier [Sea Beam sonar maps declassified] A. C. Revkin. il *Discover* 10:30 S '89
Navy relents in battle over mapping sea floor. C. Norman. *Science* 244:25 Ap 7 '89
Seafloor maps no longer secret. *Science News* 135:255 Ap 22 '89
EXCOMMUNICATION
Apologizing to Anne Hutchinson [United Church of Christ members burn 1638 writ of excommunication] M. P. Nugent. *The Christian Century* 106:304-5 Mr 22-29 '89
EXCRETION
See also
Feces
Urine
EXCUSES
Excuses, excuses: here's why they're healthy [views of C. R. Snyder] il *Glamour* 87:95 N '89
No-fault psychology. C. Tavris. *Vogue* 179:116 Ja '89

When to lie to yourself [research by C. R. Snyder and Raymond Higgins] N. Jordan. il *Psychology Today* 23:24 Je '89
EXECUTIONS AND EXECUTIONERS
See also
Capital punishment
Electrocution
Guillotine
Hanging
Anatomy of an execution [A. Ochoa Sanchez found guilty in drug trafficking case in Cuba] A. Cruz, Jr. *Commentary* 88:54-6 N '89
Death in Havana [execution of Gen. A. Ochoa Sánchez in drug trafficking case] *Newsweek* 114:24 Jl 24 '89
Death-row murderers could be lifesavers [proposal by J. Kevorkian to harvest organs from executed prisoners] *Newsweek* 113:49 Ja 9 '89
Execution in China [prodemocracy demonstrators] B. Came. il *Maclean's* 102:14-15 Jl 3 '89
The face of repression [execution of demonstrators in China] W. R. Doerner. il *Time* 134:27 Jl 3 '89
Small carrot, big stick [China executes pro-democracy demonstrators] R. Watson. il *Newsweek* 114:28-30 Jl 3 '89
'This man has expired': witness to an execution [cover story] R. Johnson. il *Commonweal* 116:9-15 Ja 13 '89
The trial that shook Cuba [drug trafficking case involving A. Ochoa Sanchez and A. de la Guardia; cover story] J. Preston. il pors *The New York Review of Books* 36:24-31 D 7 '89
EXECUTIVE DEPARTMENTS (U.S.) *See* United States—Executive departments
EXECUTIVE DINING ROOMS
Company dining deluxe. K. MacNeil. il *Working Woman* 14:72 F '89
EXECUTIVE INFORMATION SYSTEMS
At last, software CEOs can use. J. Main. il *Fortune* 119:77-8+ Mr 13 '89
Next time, think big. D. Churbuck. il *Forbes* 143:155-6 Je 12 '89
EXECUTIVE ORDERS
The backbone of hidden government [National Security Decision Directives; cover story] E. Pell. *The Nation* 248:833+ Je 19 '89
EXECUTIVE POWER
See also
Executive orders
Executive privilege (Government information)
Pardon
Presidents—Powers and duties
Veto
War and emergency powers
EXECUTIVE PRIVILEGE (GOVERNMENT INFORMATION)
Minority report. C. Hitchens. *The Nation* 248:764 Je 5 '89
Ollie North's eleventh-hour stratagem [subpoenas to R. Reagan and G. Bush challenge executive privilege] T. Morganthau. il pors *Newsweek* 113:24 Ja 9 '89
EXECUTIVE SEARCH CONSULTANTS
See also
Black executive search consultants
Spencer Stuart & Associates
The new headhunters [cover story] J. A. Byrne. il pors *Business Week* p64-7+ F 6 '89
When a headhunter calls. W. Kiechel. il *Fortune* 119:161-2 My 8 '89
Why hiring through a headhunter makes psychological sense. D. Cole. il *Psychology Today* 23:14+ D '89
Fees
The clients are restless [cover story] D. Machan. il *Forbes* 144:114-18 Jl 10 '89
EXECUTIVES
See also
Bankers
Black executives
Business Hall of Fame
Clothing and dress—Businessmen
Corporations—Directors
Daddy track
Entrepreneurs
Pension fund managers
Women executives
25 executives to watch. il *Business Week* Special Issue:90-1+ Ap 14 '89
The corporate elite [cover story] il *Business Week* Special Issue:9-16+ O 20 '89
Faces behind the figures. See issues of Forbes
For the tidy sum of $250 an hour, Jeffrey Mayer does top-drawer desk cleaning. il por *People Weekly* 32:49 Jl 31 '89
Fortune people. See issues of Fortune beginning May 9, 1988
How to get more done in fewer hours [excerpt from One-on-one with Andy Grove] A. S. Grove. il *Working Woman* 14:20+ Jl '89
Lessons of leadership. See issues of Nation's Business
News/Trends. See issues of Fortune beginning March 5, 1984

EXECUTIVES—*cont.*

The year's 25 most fascinating business people [cover story; special section] il *Fortune* 119:32-7+ Ja 2 '89

Age

The Pepsi Generation heads for the corner office. J. Carey. il *Business Week* p170 S 25 '89

Anecdotes, facetiae, satire, etc.

Where I'm at right now. S. Bing. il *Esquire* 111:84 Je '89

Attitudes

1990s key ideas [cover story; special section] il *Fortune* 120:48-51+ Jl 3 '89

America's most admired corporations [cover story] C. Davenport. il *Fortune* 119:68-71+ Ja 30 '89

Business week/Harris poll. See occasional issues of Business Week

The captains see a tilted field [global competition; Fortune poll] B. O'Reilly. il *Fortune* 120:93+ N 6 '89

CEOs: computing in high places [cover story; special section; with editorial comment by Fred Abatemarco] il *Personal Computing* 13:5, 70-7+ Ap '89

CEOs gird for global battle [Fortune poll] B. Dumaine. il *Fortune* 119:65-6 Ap 24 '89

CEOs see clout shifting [Fortune poll] T. A. Stewart. il *Fortune* 120:66 N 6 '89

CEOs think the seven-year boom has at least another year to run [Fortune poll] F. Rice. il *Fortune* 120:17+ S 25 '89

CEOs to Bush: raise taxes now. D. Kirkpatrick. il *Fortune* 119:95-6 Ja 16 '89

Holding firm on affirmative action [Fortune poll] A. Farnham. il *Fortune* 119:87-8 Mr 13 '89

How the next CEO will be different [results of international survey] L. B. Korn. il *Fortune* 119:157-8+ My 22 '89

How to spread Potomac fever [government service; Fortune poll] A. Deutschman. il *Fortune* 120:84-5 Ag 14 '89

Industry and technology leaders in 2003. *The Futurist* 23:54-5 Jl/Ag '89

The new organization man [poll of middle level executives; cover story; special section] J. Buckley. il pors *U.S. News & World Report* 106:40-51 Ja 16 '89

No more health care on the house [Fortune poll] A. Farnham. il *Fortune* 119:71-2 F 27 '89

Ready to ride out China's turmoil [Fortune poll] A. Farnham. il *Fortune* 120:117-18 Jl 3 '89

So what is the best way to pay? [CEO pay; Fortune poll] C. Gottlieb. il *Fortune* 119:109+ Je 5 '89

Who business bosses hate most. T. Paré. il *Fortune* 120:107-9 D 4 '89

Biography

Remedial reading. J. Queenan. il por *Forbes* 144:48 S 18 '89

Compensation

See Executives—Salaries, pensions, etc.

Dismissal

See also

Outplacement consultant services

You got the ax. Now what should you do? W. C. Symonds. il *Business Week* p110-11 Ja 23 '89

Health and hygiene

CEO fitness: the performance plus [exercise and job performance; excerpt from Dr. James M. Rippe's Fit for success] J. M. Rippe. il *Psychology Today* 23:50-3 My '89

New truths about staying healthy. B. O'Reilly. il *Fortune* 120:57-8+ S 25 '89

To your health. See issues of Nation's Business beginning May 1983

Mortality

'Deathwatch' investments. D. Pauly. il por *Newsweek* 113:62 Ap 24 '89

Nutrition

Sure, you're busy. That's no reason not to eat right. R. Mitchell. il *Business Week* p122 O 9 '89

Promotion

The get-ahead guy (will he leave you behind?). D. Heyn. *Mademoiselle* 95:116 My '89

When the honeymoon's over: how to tell how you're really doing [J. Colson and J. Simon] J. Ciabattari. il pors *Working Woman* 14:82-6+ Je '89

Anecdotes, facetiae, satire, etc.

High plains drifter. S. Bing. il *Esquire* 111:108 Mr '89

Psychology

The charisma merchants. D. Machan. il *Forbes* 143:100-1 Ja 23 '89

A hard look at executive vision. W. Kiechel. il *Fortune* 120:207+ O 23 '89

How to spot an empty suit. W. Kiechel. il *Fortune* 120:227-8+ N 20 '89

The Inc.ed man. S. Keen. il *American Health* 8:70-1 Ja/F '89

A kinder, gentler job: descending the ladder without leaving your company. A. Saltzman. il *U.S. News & World Report* 106:74-6 F 13 '89

Making over middle managers. K. Labich. il *Fortune* 119:58-61+ My 8 '89

The manager as a developer [address, November 5, 1988] G. M. Durst. *Vital Speeches of the Day* 55:309-14 Mr 1 '89

New ways to exercise power. T. A. Stewart. il *Fortune* 120:52-4+ N 6 '89

Revolving door jobs: how to beat the odds. K. Locitzer. *Psychology Today* 23:16 D '89

An SOB's guide to the top [reactions to A. Neuharth's autobiography] V. S. Sussman. il *U.S. News & World Report* 107:71-2 O 9 '89

The workaholic generation [cover story] W. Kiechel. il *Fortune* 119:50-4+ Ap 10 '89

Anecdotes, facetiae, satire, etc.

Having a nice day. S. Bing. il *Esquire* 111:94 Ap '89

Rating

America's toughest bosses [cover story] P. Nulty. il *Fortune* 119:40-3+ F 27 '89

The best of managers [1988] il *Business Week* p122-3 Ja 9 '89

When subordinates evaluate the boss. W. Kiechel. il *Fortune* 119:201-2 Je 19 '89

Reading

Which books CEOs are reading now. R. Jacob. il *Fortune* 120:14 Jl 17 '89

Recreation

How CEOs relax. J. Lieblich. il *Fortune* 119:12 F 27 '89

Recruiting

See also

Executive search consultants

Relocation

Easing the moving blues. K. Springen and A. Miller. il *Newsweek* 114:40-1 Jl 3 '89

How to sell top staffers on a relocation. *Working Woman* 14:20+ Ja '89

Resignation

First it was poison pills—now it's 'people pills' [resignation pact for top managers] C. Farrell. *Business Week* p33-4 Ja 16 '89

The hidden cost of golden handshakes [voluntary termination programs] D. Machan. il *Forbes* 143:130+ F 20 '89

Just when you thought you had the perfect job lined up [counteroffers] T. Segal. il *Business Week* p234 S 25 '89

Life after the corporation: building a business of your own [cover story; with editorial comment by Claudia Cohl] N. Sullivan and W. C. Banks. il *Home Office Computing* 7:6, 43-8 Ja '89

Retirement

Retired dads: a real resource. J. L. Ward and L. Sorenson. il *Nation's Business* 77:72-3 Je '89

Tapping the talent of retired execs. D. H. Dunn. il *Business Week* p154-5 D 18 '89

Will you be able to retire? [cover story] D. Kirkpatrick. il *Fortune* 120:56-9+ Jl 31 '89

Salaries, pensions, etc.

See also

Restricted stock grants

The executive Joneses. M. Novak. il *Forbes* 143:94-5 My 29 '89

"Finch, my boy, here are the keys to your Porsche" [perks] O. Edwards. il *Gentlemen's Quarterly* 59:143+ Ag '89

Good idea [earnout deals] E. F. Cone. il por *Forbes* 143:10 F 6 '89

Is the boss getting paid too much? [cover story; special section] il *Business Week* p46-53+ My 1 '89

Just when you thought you had the perfect job lined up [counteroffers] T. Segal. il *Business Week* p234 S 25 '89

Lower pay, lots of stock [small companies' CEOs] il *Forbes* 144:244+ N 13 '89

The power and the pay: the 800 best paid executives in America [cover story; special section] il *Forbes* 143:159-65+ My 29 '89

Seeking the sense in CEO pay. G. S. Crystal. il *Fortune* 119:88-9+ Je 5 '89

So what is the best way to pay? [CEO pay; Fortune poll] C. Gottlieb. il *Fortune* 119:109+ Je 5 '89

Take the mystery out of CEO pay [dollars concealed in proxy statements] G. S. Crystal and F. T. Vincent, Jr. il *Fortune* 119:217+ Ap 24 '89

Supply and demand

Business. L. J. Moore and M. Silver. il *U.S. News & World Report* 107:70+ S 25 '89

Hire an executive—by the hour. M. Stevens. il *Working Woman* 14:29-30 Ag '89

Training

See also

Corporate Executive Fellows Program

Higher Commercial Management School (Moscow, Soviet Union)

International Management Center (Budapest, Hungary)

Give your business skills a B-school brush-up. L. Helm. il *Business Week* p88 Jl 24 '89

An honorable retreat [IBM Palisades Advanced Business Institute, Palisades, N.Y.] C. Pearson. il *Architectural Record* 177:84-91 S '89

How 21 men got global in 35 days [Noel Tichy's Global Leadership Program] J. Main. il *Fortune* 120:71+ N 6 '89

In praise of followers. L. Touby. *Working Woman* 14:34+ Ap '89

Take charge of your job [views of P. Nickerson] R. Thompson. il por *Nation's Business* 77:36-7 Ap '89

EXECUTIVES—Training—*cont.*

'We need yuppies in Moscow' [Soviet managers attend business course in U.S.] C. Leinster. il *Fortune* 120:153+ N 20 '89

Transfer

Approaching a better job sideways. P. Bernstein. il *New Choices for the Best Years* 29:48-50 D '89

Job-hopping: a mixed bag, for employers and employees. P. N. Strassels. il *Nation's Business* 77:70 Ja '89

The smart way to handle relocations. D. Burden. *Psychology Today* 23:20 O '89

To jump or not to jump [job in an ailing company] D. Machan. il *Forbes* 144:136 Ag 7 '89

Travel

See Business travel

EXECUTIVES AS ARCHEOLOGISTS

Archeology for fun and profit [B. Heafitz] R. Koselka. il pors *Forbes* 144:146+ D 25 '89

EXECUTIVES AS AUTHORS

Madison Avenue's mystery guy [J. Patterson of J. Walter Thompson] S. J. Madden. il por *Fortune* 119:192 Ja 30 '89

Remedial reading. J. Queenan. il por *Forbes* 144:48 S 18 '89

EXECUTIVES AS PUBLIC OFFICERS

How to spread Potomac fever [Fortune poll] A. Deutschman. il *Fortune* 120:84-5 Ag 14 '89

Public service. il *Business Week* Special Issue:33+ O 20 '89

Who wants to work in Washington? R. E. Norton. il *Fortune* 120:77-80+ Ag 14 '89

EXECUTIVES' FAMILIES

See also

Children of executives

EXECUTIVES IN ADVERTISING

Wendy's burger king [founder R. D. Thomas stars in commercials] J. Nocera. il por *Esquire* 112:69-71 N '89

Anecdotes, facetiae, satire, etc.

Okay, you scared me! S. Bing. il *Esquire* 111:58 Ja '89

EXECUTIVES' WIVES

The CEO's second wife [cover story] J. Connelly. il *Fortune* 120:52-7+ Ag 28 '89

EXECUTORS AND ADMINISTRATORS

See also

Trusts and trustees

When you're asked to be an executor. R. R. Roha. il *Changing Times* 43:87-8+ Ap '89

Widow of 'Sam & Dave' star, Dave Prater, to administer his estate. por *Jet* 75:17 Mr 27 '89

EXEMPTION, PERSONAL (TAX DEDUCTIONS) *See* Income tax—Deductions

EXEMPTION FROM TAXATION *See* Taxation, Exemption from

EXERCISE

See also

Aerobics
Ankle exercises
Bodybuilding
Boxercise
Breathing exercises
Cross training
Exercising equipment
Eye exercises
Gymnasiums
Gymnastics
Health clubs
Interval training
Muscle strength
Plyometrics
Pregnancy exercises
Rope jumping
Running
Sports
Squatting (Exercise)
Stress reducing exercises
Stretching exercises
Videotapes—Exercise use
Walking
Water exercises
Weight lifting
Winter sports
Yoga

7 fast firm-ups for bigger bodies [used by Women at Large exercise studio] il *Redbook* 173:92-5 Ag '89

10 minute total body tone-up. il *Good Housekeeping* 209:116-19 Jl '89

100 pounds lighter—and loving it [J. Carter] il pors *Ebony* 45:104+ D '89

Are you a sloucher? [excerpt from Workouts that work for women who work] B. Pearlman. il *Redbook* 172:18 Mr '89

Are you workout wise? E. Walzer. il *Seventeen* 48:166+ Ag '89

Are your exercising right for your body? il *Glamour* 87:278-81 Mr '89

Be your own personal trainer! il *Glamour* 87:292-7 S '89

Beach station workout [cover story] il *Seventeen* 48:146-51 Je '89

Beauty workshop. See issues of Mademoiselle

Body [presummer exercises] il *Seventeen* 48:188-9 Ap '89

The busy woman's guide to a better shape. il *Redbook* 172:106-9 Ap '89

Can exercise make you sexier? P. Whitten and E. J. Whiteside. il *Psychology Today* 23:42-4 Ap '89

CEO fitness: the performance plus [exercise and job performance; excerpt from Dr. James M. Rippe's Fit for success] J. M. Rippe. il *Psychology Today* 23:50-3 My '89

Don't fight it, firm it [stomach exercises] il *Mademoiselle* 95:190-3 Je '89

Don't rotate—ambulate! [effectiveness of rotation diet when combined with exercise; research by James Hill] R. A. Barnett. *American Health* 8:85-6+ D '89

Exercise and your breasts. A. P. Lynn. il *Glamour* 87:50 O '89

Exercise lite: lazier moves to a great body. il *Glamour* 87:134-7 Ja '89

Exercises to give you the body you want. il *Glamour* 87:214-17 F '89

Exercising their options. P. Dranov. il *Harper's Bazaar* 122:186-7+ Mr '89

Fanny firmers. C. Staley. il *Parents* 64:31 Je '89

The fat firmers [workout demonstrated by L. Kent] P. Nicoll. pors *Harper's Bazaar* 122:34+ Ag '89

Fitness matters. G. Legwold. See issues of Better Homes and Gardens beginning October 1987

Flab attack! il *Glamour* 87:264-7 My '89

Flex your pecs to shape your chest [weight training to tone breasts] M. Greenwood-Robinson. il *Women's Sports & Fitness* 11:20 S '89

Fluid action [lower body exercises; excerpt from Full circle fitness] R. Eastman. il *Health (New York, N.Y.)* 21:66-9 My '89

Get in the slim [use of Bodyball] il *Teen* 33:94-5 My '89

Give your bust a boost! C. Straley. il *Parents* 64:37 Mr '89

Hans and Franz get pumped [D. Carvey and K. Nealon] P. Serrani. il pors *Gentlemen's Quarterly* 59:230-5 Ag '89

Have fun with fitness. C. Straley. il *Parents* 64:32 Ap '89

It's easy to get fit. A. Finkelstein. il *Parents* 64:170+ Jl '89

Jane Fonda's 3 best potbelly exercises. il *Redbook* 173:102-5 My '89

A leggier look is in fashion for fall, and, luckily, heredity is not destiny: with a focused workout, legs can be reshaped. J. Scandura. il *Vogue* 179:402+ S '89

Legs—a long story. il *Mademoiselle* 95:48 S '89

A million-dollar body for $47.95—one pair of fleet sneaks gets you fit . . . fast. il *Mademoiselle* 95:124-7 Ja '89

New rules for a better body. il *Glamour* 87:146-7 Ja '89

No-sweat exercise. S. Berkman. il *Ladies' Home Journal* 106:94+ Ag '89

The optimal abdominal workout. il *Ladies' Home Journal* 106:40 N '89

Our super shapeup for every part of you. il *Good Housekeeping* 208:94+ My '89

Physically fit families. D. F. Bjorklund and B. Bjorklund. il *Parents* 64:215 Je '89

Relief for sore joints [special section] il *New Choices for the Best Years* 29:58-60+ S '89

Say good-bye to feast-and-famine! J. Laughridge. il *Good Housekeeping* 208:124-5 My '89

Scent-sible workout [wearing fragrance] L. A. Mark. il *American Health* 8:22 N '89

Shaping up. S. Findlay. il *U.S. News & World Report* 106:60-2+ My 29 '89

Six ways to a better bottom [thigh and buttocks exercises for teens] il *Seventeen* 48:70 O '89

Spry energy [81 year old W. Stack] J. Brant. il pors *Runner's World* 24:30-2 My '89

Stomach crunches. il *Seventeen* 48:88 N '89

Super savvy shape-ups. il *Teen* 33:54-7 Ja '89

Super shape-up [routine designed by Denise Austin] il *Ladies' Home Journal* 106:124+ Ap '89

Supertoning your hips and thighs [weight training] M. Greenwood-Robinson. il *Women's Sports & Fitness* 11:18-19 Ja/F '89

Take shape. il *Teen* 33:65-72 O '89

Tap snaps back. D. Groves. il *American Health* 8:34 S '89

Tennis body by Jake [J. Steinfeld] S. Stevenson. il pors *World Tennis* 37:33-6 Je '89

To New Yorkers, exercise is a no-frills business. H. Sweet. *Vogue* 179:170+ Ag '89

The totally hip workout [hip exercises] il *Mademoiselle* 95:36+ Ap '89

Turning into strength. J. Nelson. il *Women's Sports & Fitness* 11:31-3 N/D '89

The twice-a-day workout. il *Mademoiselle* 95:216-19 N '89

Ultimate tummy flatteners. il *Ladies' Home Journal* 106:38+ F '89

Walk it off! [excerpt from Thin thighs in 30 days] W. Stehling. il *Redbook* 173:118-19 Je '89

What is the best exercise for you? R. D. Turner. il *Ebony* 44:102+ Jl '89

Why are you exercising? L. Gordon. il *Glamour* 87:65 Je '89

EXERCISE—*cont.*

Wind-down workout. M. Rhodes. il *Health (New York, N.Y.)* 21:50-1 F '89

Winning the "losing" battle—for good. E. Coleman. il *Women's Sports & Fitness* 11:44-5+ Ja/F '89

Accidents and injuries

Basic training [incidence of exercise-related injuries linked to fitness level in Army recruits; research by Bruce H. Jones] R. Flippen. il *American Health* 8:36 S '89

Be injury-free: eliminate the terrible ten. T. Thompson. il *Women's Sports & Fitness* 11:24-5 My '89

Anecdotes, facetiae, satire, etc.

Let's not get physical. S. Bing. il *Esquire* 112:87-8+ D '89

Physiological effects

Antifitness medication [propranolol takes the good out of exercise] il *Prevention (Emmaus, Pa.)* 41:20 Mr '89

Are you over-exercising? S. L. Englebardt. il *Reader's Digest* 134:135-9 Mr '89

Built to last [retarding the effects of physical decline] J. Bailey. il *Health (New York, N.Y.)* 21:60-3+ O '89

Can running lower metabolism? [views of Kelly Brownell] A. M. Fletcher. *American Health* 8:152-3 Mr '89

Cancer protection [may reduce risk of colon cancer] il *Prevention (Emmaus, Pa.)* 41:12+ Ap '89

Climbs of the heart [rate increase] C. L. Otis. il *Women's Sports & Fitness* 11:8 Je '89

Exercise could be dangerous [hypoglycemia in diabetics; views of Michael MacDonald] *USA Today (Periodical)* 117:5 F '89

Exercise: how much is enough; how much is too much? D. C. Nieman. il *Women's Sports & Fitness* 11:30-4 Je '89

An exercise in longevity [cardiovascular benefits of playing tennis] P. Stites. il *World Tennis* 36:16+ My '89

Exercise Rx for those little aches and pains. C. B. Corbin. il *Better Homes and Gardens* 67:38+ O '89

Exercise: some routines burn fat better than others. il *Psychology Today* 23:34 Je '89

Exercise the right way. L. E. Koszuta. il *Current Health 2* 15:12-13 Ap '89

Exercising bones. J. Kaplan. il *Vogue* 179:246+ Mr '89

Exercising choice [prevention of cardiovascular disease; research by Lars-Göran Ekelund] T. Beardsley. *Scientific American* 260:24 F '89

A fitter formula [more precise way to figure training heart rate zone] il *Women's Sports & Fitness* 11:14 My '89

How fast does your heart beat? [Tecumseh Step Test] C. SerVaas. il *The Saturday Evening Post* 261:96+ My/Je '89

Play it cool. C. Straley. il *Parents* 64:26 Jl '89

Putting fat in its place. L. E. Koszuta. il *Current Health 2* 16:14-16 N '89

Real-life experiments [monitoring Ironman triathletes] K. Delhagen. il *Runner's World* 24:62-4+ My '89

Save your skin: skin care during hot-weather workouts [views of Rodney Basler] A. R. New. *Better Homes and Gardens* 67:33 Ag '89

Survivors' exercise guide (revised ed.) [effects on longevity; study by the Institute for Aerobics Research] il *U.S. News & World Report* 107:18+ N 13 '89

Take a walk—and live [mild exercise can postpone death; research by the Institute for Aerobics Research] M. D. Lemonick. il *Time* 134:90 N 13 '89

Thirty years of fortitude [staying active to offset physical decline] J. Poppy. il *Esquire* 112:83-5 D '89

To live longer, take a walk [benefits of moderate exercise; study by the Institute of Aerobics Research] C. Leerhsen. il *Newsweek* 114:77 N 13 '89

Top tips for diabetes self-care. G. Maleskey. il *Prevention (Emmaus, Pa.)* 41:73-80 S '89

Vitamin vigor [deficiency in B and C vitamins linked to fatigue; research by Erik van der Beek] V. Brower. *American Health* 8:36 Jl/Ag '89

Warm-up exercises for young and old. il *The Saturday Evening Post* 261:55-8 My/Je '89

Which exercise is best depends on one's fitness goals. L. M. Kase. il *Vogue* 179:116-17 Je '89

Winterize your workout. J. Rogoznica. il *Working Woman* 14:116-18 F '89

Psychological aspects

10 ways to psych up to work out. C. Straley. il *Parents* 64:30 F '89

Climb every mountain. G. Sheehan. il *Runner's World* 24:16 My '89

Don't just sit there—do something [may prevent symptoms of depression; research by Mary E. Farmer] il *Prevention (Emmaus, Pa.)* 41:10+ My '89

Exercise and the mind. D. C. Nieman. il *Women's Sports & Fitness* 11:54-7 S '89

Finding the exerciser in you. D. V. Morgan. il *Health (New York, N.Y.)* 21:38-9 Mr '89

Five good reasons to laugh it up when you exercise. L. Gordon. il *Glamour* 87:40 Jl '89

Is it chemistry or body heat? [fitness high] B. Livermore. il *Health (New York, N.Y.)* 21:52-7 D '89

Managing your mileage—are you feeling groovy or burning out? R. Flippin; K. Cobb. il *American Health* 8:78-84 O '89

Who stays fit [lifelong link between personality and exercise habits; research by Paula Schnurr and others] E. Stark. *Psychology Today* 23:73 N '89

Workout for one. M. Bloom. il *Health (New York, N.Y.)* 21:42-3 Ap '89

Safety devices and measures

Defensive moves [safety while exercising] R. Mayer. il *Health (New York, N.Y.)* 21:90-1 S '89

EXERCISE CLOTHES *See* Clothing and dress—Sports clothes

EXERCISE CLUBS *See* Health clubs

EXERCISE FOR CATS *See* Cats—Care

EXERCISE FOR DOGS *See* Dogs—Care

EXERCISE-INDUCED ASTHMA *See* Asthma

EXERCISE TEACHERS

See also

Personal trainers

EXERCISE TESTING *See* Physical fitness—Testing

EXERCISE VIDEOTAPES *See* Videotapes—Exercise use

EXERCISES, MILITARY *See* Military maneuvers

EXERCISING EQUIPMENT

See also

Rubber bands (Exercising equipment)

America goes stair crazy [stair climbers] L. Williams. il *Time* 134:83 D 18 '89

Be your own personal trainer! il *Glamour* 87:292-7 S '89

Fitness-to-go [easy-to-pack workout gear] il *Parents* 64:26 Ag '89

Gliding and climbing to fitness [cross-country ski machines and stair climbers] G. McVeigh. il *Prevention (Emmaus, Pa.)* 41:92+ N '89

Home body [exercise bicycles] F. Zahradnik. il *Bicycling* 30:104-7 D '89

A home fitness center. V. S. Sussman. il *U.S. News & World Report* 106:67-9 My 29 '89

Home sweat home [special section] K. Delhagen. il *Runner's World* 24:41-6+ D '89

Home sweat home: the new exercise machines. T. Segal. il *Business Week* p132-3 Ja 9 '89

The homebodies. C. Vogel. il *The New York Times Magazine* p83 My 7 '89

Homestyle fitness. L. E. Koszuta. il *Current Health 2* 15:28-9 F '89

Inside information: our annual home workout equipment guide. P. Netter and K. Casady. il *Women's Sports & Fitness* 11:34-6+ N/D '89

No-frills fitness. il *Vogue* 179:180 F '89

The precision workout: girl meets machine, gets better body. il *Mademoiselle* 95:234-7 Mr '89

Pump it up [walking with weights; research by James E. Graves] L. Warner. il *American Health* 8:38 S '89

Row, row, row your boat. C. Schaeffer. *Changing Times* 43:95 Ja '89

Serious fun [fitness programs and equipment for children] il *American Health* 8:30 N '89

Shortcuts. J. Carey. il *U.S. News & World Report* 106:70 My 29 '89

Sit down & shape up! [rowing machines and stationary bikes] il *Prevention (Emmaus, Pa.)* 41:94+ O '89

Six gifts that are sure to work out. P. Netter. il *Gentlemen's Quarterly* 59:173-4 D '89

Ski-specific exercise gear. J. Chase. il *Skiing* 42:30+ N '89

Step to it [climbing machines] D. Groves. il *Health (New York, N.Y.)* 21:28+ F '89

Step up to fitness [stair machines] C. Schaeffer. il *Changing Times* 43:114+ Mr '89

There's no place like the home gym [weight training] M. Greenwood-Robinson. il *Women's Sports & Fitness* 11:62-5 Mr '89

Touching base with the new push-button machines [high tech weight training] M. Greenwood-Robinson. il *Women's Sports & Fitness* 11:16 My '89

Video cycle race [CompuTrainer system] S. F. Brown. il *Popular Science* 234:73 My '89

Working out while staying home. il *Good Housekeeping* 208:112+ My '89

EXHAUSTION *See* Fatigue

EXHIBITION BUILDINGS

See also

Harlem International Trade Center

EXHIBITIONS

See also

Book exhibits

EPCOT (Fla.)

Trade fairs

World's fairs

EXHIBITIONS, TRAVELING

See also

Art—Exhibitions

EXILES

Banished by Napoleon: the American exile of Baron and Baroness Hyde de Neuville. G.-G. Deák. bibl f il pors *Antiques* 136:1148-57 N '89

From Russia with love [reunion of I. Yershov and exiled son-in-law E. D. Lozansky] il pors *U.S. News & World Report* 107:16 O 2 '89

The man who would be Shah [Reza Pahlavi] P. Axthelm. il pors *People Weekly* 31:46-51 Ap 3 '89

EXILES—*cont.*
'Mother Russia' and her exiles. L. Pochivalov. il *World Press Review* 36:30-2 Mr '89
True confessions of an exiled Afrikaner [B. Breytenbach] G. Marzorati. il pors *The New York Times Magazine* p32-3+ Ag 27 '89

EXISTENTIALISM
Exploring psychic interiors [interview with I. D. Yalom] E. E. Goode. por *U.S. News & World Report* 107:67 O 30 '89

EXLEY, CHARLES E., JR.
about
NCR is finding out that no strategy works forever. S. Phillips and J. W. Verity. il por *Business Week* p80-1 Ja 30 '89

EXLEY, FREDERICK
If Nixon could possess the soul of this woman, why the hell can't I? il *Esquire* 112:208-10+ D '89

EXODUS YOUTH SERVICES (WASHINGTON, D.C.)
"Are you going to cry, Father Jackson?". K. Menehan. il por *Christianity Today* 33:12-13 S 22 '89

THE EXORCIST 1990 [film] See Motion picture reviews—Single works

EXOTIC PETS *See* Pets
EXPANSION, BUSINESS *See* Business expansion
EXPANSION, HOUSE *See* Houses, Remodeled
EXPECTATION OF LIFE *See* Longevity
EXPEDITIONS, SCIENTIFIC *See* Scientific expeditions
EXPENDITURE COMMITTEES, INDEPENDENT (POLITICAL CAMPAIGNS) *See* Campaign funds
EXPENDITURES, GOVERNMENT *See* United States—Appropriations and expenditures
EXPENDITURES, MUNICIPAL *See* Municipal finance
EXPERIENCE, COLLEGE CREDITS FOR *See* College credits
EXPERIENCE UNLIMITED (MUSICAL GROUP) *See* E.U. (Musical group)
EXPERIMENTAL AIRCRAFT ASSOCIATION
From antiques to Antonovs [Soviet cargo plane highlight of Oshkosh '89] G. Baxter. il *Flying* 116:86-8+ N '89
Oshkosh: a day in the life. N. Moll. il *Flying* 116:62-4+ Jl '89
Poberezny and son [interview with P. and T. Poberezny] W. Garvey. il pors *Flying* 116:40-5 Ap '89
Soviet displays, kit-built aircraft highlight EAA show at Oshkosh [with editorial comment] E. H. Phillips. il *Aviation Week & Space Technology* 131:7, 24-5 Ag 7 '89

EXPERIMENTAL AIRPLANES *See* Airplanes, Experimental
EXPERIMENTAL AUTOMOBILES *See* Automobiles, Experimental
EXPERIMENTAL COLLEGE EDUCATION
Requiem for the Hutchins College. F. C. Ward. il por *Change* 21:24-33 Jl/Ag '89
EXPERIMENTAL DRUG REGULATIONS *See* Drug laws and regulations
EXPERIMENTAL ECONOMICS
The economists' new guinea pigs. R. Bailey. il pors *Forbes* 144:148+ N 13 '89
EXPERIMENTAL EDUCATION
See also
Coalition of Essential Schools
Educational innovations
Experimental college education
Open School (West Hollywood, Calif.)
An ungraded approach [British Columbia] H. Quinn. *Maclean's* 102:42 F 20 '89
EXPERIMENTAL FILMS *See* Motion pictures—Experimental films
EXPERIMENTAL PROTOTYPE COMMUNITY OF TOMORROW *See* EPCOT (Fla.)
EXPERIMENTATION ON ANIMALS *See* Animal experimentation
EXPERIMENTATION ON HUMANS *See* Genetic research—Human experimentation; Medical research—Human experimentation; Pharmaceutical research—Human experimentation
EXPERIMENTS, FIELD *See* Field experiments (Agriculture)
EXPERT EVIDENCE (LAW)
See also
Evidence Store (Firm)
Medical jurisprudence
The case against expert witnesses. W. Olson. il *Fortune* 120:133+ S 25 '89
The invasion of the expert witnesses. T. Gest. il *U.S. News & World Report* 107:58 S 25 '89
Science in court. C. Holden. *Science* 243:1658-9 Mr 31 '89
EXPERT SYSTEMS (COMPUTERS)
See also
Discovery systems (Computers)
Expert system puts clamp on enemy subs. *High Technology Business* 9:34 S/O '89
Expert systems in medicine. R. Salamon. il *World Health* p12-13 Ag/S '89
Machine dreams [Japan's Fifth Generation project] H. Ullman. il *The New Republic* 201:12-14 Jl 17-24 '89
microExplorer in action! A. Lane. il *Byte* 14:247-8+ N '89
NASA flight controllers become AI pioneers. M. M. Waldrop. il *Science* 244:1044-5 Je 2 '89

New-product blues for expert systems. H. I. Blank. *High Technology Business* 9:20 Ja '89
Repairman in a box. E. Dyson. il *Forbes* 143:306 Ja 9 '89
EXPERTISING OF ART *See* Art—Expertising
EXPERTS
Being an expert about expert advice. *Glamour* 87:116 N '89
You may be an expert and not know it. C. A. Smith. *The Writer* 102:26-7 Ja '89
EXPLORATION
See also
America—Discovery and exploration
Antarctic exploration
Arctic exploration
Botanical exploration
Namibia—Exploring expeditions
New Guinea—Exploring expeditions
Economic aspects
The sugar daddies of high adventure [need for corporate sponsorship] il *U.S. News & World Report* 107:10-11 Ag 14 '89
EXPLORERS
See also
Explorers Club
Women explorers
EXPLORERS, AMERICAN
See also
Byrd, Richard Evelyn, 1888-1957
Cook, Frederick Albert, 1865-1940
Lewis, Meriwether, 1774-1809
Peary, Robert Edwin, 1856-1920
EXPLORERS, ENGLISH
See also
Dampier, William, 1652-1715
EXPLORERS, PORTUGUESE
Camões and the Portuguese voyages of discovery [cover story; special issue] il maps *The Courier (Unesco)* 42:3-38 Ap '89
EXPLORERS CLUB
Great explorations [admission of women explorers] J. Mills. bibl il *Ms.* 17:58-62 Je '89
EXPLOSIONS, ATOMIC WEAPON *See* Nuclear weapons—Testing
EXPLOSIVES
See also
New Mexico Institute of Mining and Technology. Center for Explosives Technology Research
Plastic explosives
Bacteria that eat TNT [research by Pat Unkefer] M. M. Soviero. *Popular Science* 235:116 N '89
Explosive bacteria [biodegradation of explosive wastes; research by Pat Unkefer] *Discover* 10:18 O '89
Explosive molecular ionic crystals. W. L. Faust. bibl f il *Science* 245:37-42 Jl 7 '89
EXPLOSIVES DETECTORS *See* Bomb detectors
EXPLOSIVES IN ART
First impressions [work of E. Rosenberg] R. Ruthen. il *Scientific American* 260:18+ F '89
EXPO 92 (SEVILLE, SPAIN)
Andalusia's age of the Expo. H. Gordon. il *World Press Review* 36:76 N '89
EXPORT CONTROLS, AMERICAN *See* United States—Commercial policy
EXPORT-IMPORT BANK OF THE UNITED STATES
Europe '92 [address, April 19, 1989] W. F. Ryan. *Vital Speeches of the Day* 55:492-4 Je 1 '89
How Eximbank works in today's global environment [address, December 6, 1988] H. Sundstrom. *Vital Speeches of the Day* 55:262-5 F 15 '89
EXPORT-IMPORT TRADE
See also
Aerospace industries—Export-import trade
Agricultural industries—Export-import trade
Airplane industry—Export-import trade
Animal products—Export-import trade
Architectural firms—Export-import trade
Automobile equipment industry—Export-import trade
Automobiles—Export-import trade
Avocado industry—Export-import trade
Balance of trade
Books—Export-import trade
Cable television—Export-import trade
Cellular radio—Export-import trade
Chemical and biological weapons—Export-import trade
Chemical industries—Export-import trade
Cigarette industry—Export-import trade
Clothing industry—Export-import trade
Coffee industry—Export-import trade
Computer industry—Export-import trade
Diapers—Export-import trade
Drug industry—Export-import trade
Electronic industries—Export-import trade
Engineering construction companies—Export-import trade
Fish industry—Export-import trade
Food industry—Export-import trade
Free trade and protection

EXPORT-IMPORT TRADE—See also—*cont.*
Fruit industry—Export-import trade
Gas industry—Export-import trade
Grain trade
Guided missile industries—Export-import trade
Helicopter industry—Export-import trade
Hides and skins—Export-import trade
Hydroelectric power—Export-import trade
Industrial equipment industry—Export-import trade
Ivory industry—Export-import trade
Jeep automobiles—Export-import trade
Lumber industry—Export-import trade
Machine tool industry—Export-import trade
Meat industry—Export-import trade
Motion picture industry—Export-import trade
Motor vehicles, Military—Export-import trade
Munitions—Export-import trade
Nuclear industry—Export-import trade
Pesticides—Export-import trade
Petroleum industry—Export-import trade
Produce trade
Rotor aircraft—Export-import trade
Service industries—Export-import trade
Shoe industry—Export-import trade
Small business—Export-import trade
Soybean industry—Export-import trade
Steel industry—Export-import trade
Sugar industry—Export-import trade
Telecommunication—Export-import trade
Telephone equipment industry—Export-import trade
Television industry—Export-import trade
Textile industry—Export-import trade
Trade waste—Export-import trade
Trading companies
Truck industry—Export-import trade
United States—Commercial policy
Wheat trade
See also subhead Commerce under names of countries
America's 50 biggest exporters [with introd. by Edward Prewitt] il *Fortune* 120:50-1 Jl 17 '89
BLS to produce monthly indexes of export and import prices. W. Alterman. bibl f il *Monthly Labor Review* 111:36-40 D '88
Exports have the vapors. M. J. Mandel. il *Business Week* p37-8 My 22 '89
Foreign exchange [imported goods owned by one Los Angeles family] D. Rawson. il *Life* 12:176-9 Fall '89
U.S. companies lack trade aggressiveness. W. T. Brookes. por *Nation's Business* 77:13 F '89
U.S. import and export prices continued to register sizable gains in 1988. L. A. Livingston and S. Richards. bibl f il *Monthly Labor Review* 112:11-33 My '89
Why have import and export prices marched in lockstep? K. Pennar. il *Business Week* p24 O 16 '89
EXPOSÉ (MUSICAL GROUP)
Stop the presses! Stunning Exposé reveals a talent for delivering pop-candy hits. il *People Weekly* 32:185 D 4 '89
EXPOSITION UNIVERSELLE DE 1889 (PARIS, FRANCE)
American artists at the 1889 Exposition Universelle in Paris. A. Blaugrund. bibl f il *Antiques* 136:1158-69 N '89
EXPOSURE (PHOTOGRAPHY) *See* Photography—Exposure
EXPOSURE METERS
Gossen Luna-Pro F & Pilot 2 meters. il *Petersen's Photographic Magazine* 18:72 My '89
Gossen Ultra-Spot. D. Brooks. il *Petersen's Photographic Magazine* 17:52-3 Ja '89
Matrix metering: simple solution or dire delusion??? H. Keppler. il *Popular Photography* 96:20-1+ Mr '89
Minolta flash meter IV. il *Petersen's Photographic Magazine* 18:54 My '89
Overriding your exposure meter for precise results. F. Patterson. il *Petersen's Photographic Magazine* 17:26-7 Ap '89
Sekonic L-328 Digi Lite F meter. il *Petersen's Photographic Magazine* 18:60 My '89
Why flash in the dark? Get the right exposure with a top-flight flashmeter. B. Schwalberg. il *Popular Photography* 96:28+ Ap '89
EXPRESS AIRLINES 1, INC
Northwest commuter boosts Saab sales with orders for 340B, 2000 aircraft. C. A. Shifrin. il *Aviation Week & Space Technology* 131:62 N 6 '89
EXPRESS HIGHWAYS
How to analyze the shock waves that sweep through expressway traffic. J. Walker. il *Scientific American* 261:98-100+ Ag '89
I-80. K. Emmons. il *Life* 12:96-102+ Fall '89
Environmental aspects
Charles, Cromwell and Channon [highway threatens Naseby battlefield in England] *History Today* 39:4-5 Ap '89
Striped bass [effects of Westway decision and PCBs on New York's commercial fisheries] S. D. Garber. il *Focus (New York, N.Y.: 1950)* 39:34-6 Summ '89
Fees
Another Panamanian headache [to duck highway fees, U.S. truckers are registering and insuring their rigs in Panama] D. Fanning. il *Forbes* 144:80 N 13 '89

Finance
Fifteen miles—that'll be $1.50 [for-profit roads] R. Stodghill, II. il *Business Week* p54 Ag 14 '89
McHighways [private toll roads] H. Ullman. *The New Republic* 201:18-19 S 4 '89
The private path to new highways. D. J. Ward. il *Nation's Business* 77:19 Ag '89
Maintenance and repair
Crumbling highways and congested byways: can you steer clear? H. Gieseking. il *Travel Holiday* 172:12-13 Jl '89
Diagnosing ailing highways [CAT scans] il *USA Today (Periodical)* 118:12 D '89
Getting money to fix the roads will take more than an earthquake. P. Dworkin. *U.S. News & World Report* 107:44 N 6 '89
Brazil
Jungle road to Tokyo [U.S. soybean growers concern over Brazilian highway's impact on trade with Japan] P. Duggan. il map *Forbes* 143:96 My 29 '89
California
Resonance implicated in Nimitz tragedy [collapse of Oakland freeway] *Science News* 136:367 D 2 '89
"We have built our houses on sand" [San Francisco Bay Area earthquake] M. Barinaga. il *Science* 246:437 O 27 '89
Massachusetts
The rats are coming [effect of Central Artery project in Boston] S. Allis. il *Time* 133:63 F 27 '89
New York (State)
Striped bass [effects of Westway decision and PCBs on commercial fisheries] S. D. Garber. il *Focus (New York, N.Y.: 1950)* 39:34-6 Summ '89
Weekend getaways [getting out of New York City on summer weekends] J. Blyskal and M. Hodge. il *New York* 22:148-9 My 1 '89
Texas
Highways in the city [Houston] B. Ouvry-Vial. il *The Unesco Courier* 42:34-7 Ag '89
EXPRESS MAIL SERVICE *See* Air freight service
EXPRESSION
See also
Communication, Nonverbal
Rhetoric
EXPRESSION, FACIAL *See* Facial expression
EXPRESSION, GENETIC *See* Genetic regulation
EXPRESSION UNLIMITED
A magnet for gourmets. V. Bohigian. il por *Nation's Business* 77:66 Ja '89
EXPRESSIONISM (ART)
See also
Abstract expressionism
Brücke (Group)
Exhibitions
German expressionism: Los Angeles County Museum of Art. P. Clothier. il *Art News* 88:154 F '89
Some like it hot! [German expressionism in Washington, D.C. and Atlanta, Ga.] G. Sikes. il *Harper's Bazaar* 122:88+ N '89
EXTEMPORIZATION (MUSIC) *See* Improvisation (Music)
EXTENDED DEFINITION TELEVISION
A poor man's high-def. M. Costello. il *Channels (New York, N.Y.: 1986)* 9:64 Ap '89
EXTENDED INDUSTRY STANDARD ARCHITECTURE BUS *See* EISA (Computer bus)
EXTENDED WARRANTY *See* Warranty
EXTENDED WEAR CONTACT LENSES *See* Contact lenses
EXTENSION CORDS *See* Electric cords
EXTENSION EDUCATION
See also
University extension
EXTERIOR HOUSE DECORATION *See* House decoration, Exterior
EXTERMINATION OF TERMITES *See* Termites—Control
EXTERNAL DEGREE PROGRAMS *See* University extension
EXTINCT ANIMALS
See also
Dinosaurs
Irish elk
Mass extinction of species
Mastodons
Passenger pigeons
Blood from a stone [analysis of hemoglobin residue on tools leads to identification of prehistoric species; work of Thomas Loy] il *Discover* 10:18 N '89
Extinctions [cover story] R. Gore. il supp (folded chart) *National Geographic* 175:662-99 Je '89
EXTINCTION OF SPECIES, MASS *See* Mass extinction of species
EXTOL OF OHIO (FIRM)
A gamble that paid off. B. D. Gibson. il por *Nation's Business* 77:30 Ja '89
EXTON, PETER
D.C. sites to see. il *Publishers Weekly* 235:116-17 My 12 '89

EXTRACTION (DENTISTRY) *See* Teeth—Extraction
EXTRACTS, FLAVORING *See* Flavoring essences
EXTRACURRICULAR ACTIVITIES *See* Student activities
EXTRADITION

Bring them back to justice. A. L. Sanders. il *Time* 133:42 My 1 '89

The cocaine war: Washington and Bogotá battle the drug lords. M. Nemeth. il *Maclean's* 102:18-19 S 4 '89

From jet set to jail cell [U.S. asks for extradition of A. Khashoggi, jailed in Switzerland in connection with alleged looting of Philippine treasure by F. Marcos] C. Dickey. il por *Newsweek* 113:10 My 1 '89

'Now the fight is with blood' [drug wars in Colombia] T. Morganthau. il *Newsweek* 114:37 Ag 28 '89

Passing the extradition test [Colombian drug lord E. Martínez Romero shipped to the U.S.] M. S. Serrill. il por *Time* 134:48 S 18 '89

EXTRAMARITAL RELATIONSHIPS *See* Adultery
EXTRAS (ACTORS AND ACTRESSES) *See* Motion picture actors and actresses
EXTRASENSORY PERCEPTION

Making a prophet [precognitive dreams; interview with U. Montague] N. Guccione. il *Omni (New York, N.Y.)* 12:12 N '89

Parents and kids: the ESP connection: C. Jones. *McCall's* 116:64+ My '89

EXTRATERRESTRIAL LIFE *See* Life on other planets
EXTRATERRESTRIAL MATERIAL *See* Matter, Interstellar
EXTRATERRESTRIAL SIGHTINGS *See* UFOs
EXTRAVEHICULAR ACTIVITY *See* Space flight—Extravehicular activity
EXTREMELY LOW FREQUENCY WAVES *See* Electromagnetic waves
EXURBS

Moving out to the city. il *Business Week* p148+ S 25 '89

EXXON CORPORATION

See also

Exxon Valdez (Ship) oil spill, 1989

Exxon's one-act [shareholders' meeting] R. Engler. *The Nation* 248:836-7 Je 19 '89

In ten years you'll see 'nothing' [Alaskan oil spill; interview with chief L. Rawl] il por *Fortune* 119:50-1+ My 8 '89

Not mad about Manhattan [Exxon moves headquarters to Texas] il *Time* 134:69 N 6 '89

Nowhere to run or to hide [L. Rawl confronted at shareholders' meeting] B. Rudolph. il *Time* 133:69 My 29 '89

An oil slick trips up Exxon. B. Rudolph. il *Time* 133:46 Ap 24 '89

Parting predictions from Exxon's Jack Bennett [interview] W. Glasgall. por *Business Week* p73 Ja 30 '89

Who's that screaming at Exxon? Not the environmentalists [Alaska oil spill] A. Rothman. il *Business Week* p31 My 1 '89

EXXON VALDEZ (SHIP) OIL SPILL, 1989

America's oil tanker mess [cover story] A. Dane. il *Popular Mechanics* 166:51-4 N '89

The big spill. G. J. Church. il *Time* 133:38-41 Ap 10 '89

The biggest spill in U.S. history. S. MacLeod. il *Time* 133:63 Ap 3 '89

Captain Hazelwood: what Exxon knew. B. Amero. *Harper's* 279:42-4 Jl '89

Dead otters, silent ducks. G. Cowley. il *Newsweek* 113:70 Ap 24 '89

Disturbing numbers. il map *U.S. News & World Report* 106:14 My 15 '89

Environmental politics [Alaskan oil spill reinvigorates environmentalists] G. Hackett. il *Newsweek* 113:18-19 Ap 17 '89

Exxon befouled. J. Lieblich. il *Fortune* 119:16 Ap 24 '89

Grave waters. J. Kenney. il map *National Parks* 63:18-23+ Jl/Ag '89

He devastated Alaska, but Capt. Jeff Hazelwood, friends say, is an environmentalist [captain of ship whose negligence led to oil spill] K. Gross. il por *People Weekly* 31:48-50 Ap 24 '89

In ten years you'll see 'nothing' [interview with Exxon chief L. Rawl] il por *Fortune* 119:50-1+ My 8 '89

Joe's bad trip [cover story] R. Behar. il pors map *Time* 134:42-7 Jl 24 '89

Letter from Prince William Sound. J. D. Hair. il *National Wildlife* 27:25-6 Je/Jl '89

Low probability—high consequence accidents. D. E. Koshland, Jr. *Science* 244:405 Ap 28 '89

A marriage gone wrong. T. Carr. por *Newsweek* 113:6 My 8 '89

Matters of measure. G. Reiger. il *Field & Stream* 94:13-14 Je '89

The mote & the beam. *Commonweal* 116:260-1 My 5 '89

Oil on troubled water. T. Turner. il *The Mother Earth News* 118:112 Jl/Ag '89

An oil slick trips up Exxon. B. Rudolph. il *Time* 133:46 Ap 24 '89

Oil spills. P. H. Abelson. *Science* 244:629 My 12 '89

Paradise lost. T. Horton. il *Rolling Stone* p150-1+ D 14-28 '89

Questions that keep surfacing after the spill. W. Glasgall and V. Cahan. il *Business Week* p18 Ap 17 '89

S.O.S. *The Nation* 248:543-4 Ap 24 '89

Smothering the waters. S. Begley. il map *Newsweek* 113:54-7 Ap 10 '89

The Sound and our fury. M. L. Fischer. *Sierra* 74:6 Jl/Ag '89

A spill destined to grease wheels [expected to increase environmental activism] il *U.S. News & World Report* 106:13-14 Ap 17 '89

The spills and spoils of big oil [cover story] J. Greely. il *The Nation* 248:721+ My 29 '89

Spillwatch [Center for Marine Conservation report] T. H. Watkins. il *Wilderness* 53:66+ Wint '89

A stitch, but not in time [repairing damage to ship] B. Weber. il *The New York Times Magazine* p86 O 22 '89

Tests for Bush. D. Schorr. *The New Leader* 72:3 Ap 3-17 '89

That's oil, folks. H. Hertzberg. *The New Republic* 200:4 Ap 24 '89

Tragedy in Alaska. T. A. Lewis. il map *National Wildlife* 27:4-9 Je/Jl '89

Tragedy in Alaska waters. D. Lee. il map *National Geographic* 176:260-3 Ag '89

Tragedy on a reef. B. Came. il *Maclean's* 102:76-7 Ap 10 '89

Tug of war over oil drilling. M. Satchell. il map *U.S. News & World Report* 106:47-8 Ap 10 '89

The two Alaskas [conflict between conservation ethic and industrial development reinforced by Exxon oil spill; cover story] M. D. Lemonick. il map *Time* 133:56-9+ Ap 17 '89

The Valdez finally leaves Alaska. *Newsweek* 114:24 Jl 3 '89

Valdez: the predicted oil spill. E. Marshall. il *Science* 244:20-1 Ap 7 '89

Waiting game: the Gulf of Alaska will recover, but not quickly. T. Beardsley. *Scientific American* 260:24+ Je '89

Wake of the Valdez. B. Wickens. il *Maclean's* 102:49 Ap 17 '89

Wreck of the Exxon Valdez [cover story; special section; with editorial comment by Les Line and Peter A. A. Berle] il map *Audubon* 91:4, 6, 10, 73-111 S '89

Cleanup

Alaska after Exxon [cover story] il maps *Newsweek* 114:50-5+ S 18 '89

Alaska: how clean is clean? *Newsweek* 114:52 Ag 7 '89

Alaska still needs your help. A. C. Mallozzi. il *Good Housekeeping* 209:166 Ag '89

Alaskan housekeeping. A. F. Lewis. il *Ms.* 17:76 Je '89

Alaskan oil spill flight operations [special section] il *Aviation Week & Space Technology* 130:16-18 Ap 10 '89

Alaskan oil spill: health risks uncovered. M. Barinaga. il *Science* 245:463 Ag 4 '89

CH-54, C-5 aircraft play key roles in cleanup of Alaskan oil spill. il *Aviation Week & Space Technology* 130:73-4 My 1 '89

Cleaning up after the big cleanup. J. R. Luoma. il *Audubon* 91:107 S '89

A disaster that wasn't. M. Satchell and B. Carpenter. il map *U.S. News & World Report* 107:60-4+ S 18 '89

Exxon bets on bugs in Alaska cleanup. M. Crawford. *Science* 245:704 Ag 18 '89

Exxon oil slick. *The Nation* 249:299-300 S 25 '89

The high cost of catastrophe. il *Time* 134:40 Ag 7 '89

Long, slow recovery predicted for Alaska. L. Roberts. il *Science* 244:22-4 Ap 7 '89

A losing battle. B. Came. il *Maclean's* 102:52-3 My 8 '89

Microbes recruited in Valdez cleanup. *Science News* 135:383 Je 17 '89

Muckrakers of the far north. il *U.S. News & World Report* 107:8-9 Ag 7 '89

Nature aids the Alaska cleanup. J. Bonfante. il *Time* 133:84 My 8 '89

Oil, water, and wilderness. G. Frampton. il *Wilderness* 52:3-6+ Summ '89

Potemkin cleanup. R. Bazell. *The New Republic* 201:22 S 18-25 '89

Profiles [work of S. A. Earle] W. White. il *The New Yorker* 65:41-2+ Jl 3 '89

Revealing the tricks of Raven's child. J. D. Hair. il *National Wildlife* 28:30 D '89/Ja '90

Special report: Alaskan oil-spill tests technology. il *Popular Mechanics* 166:14 Jl '89

Spillwatch. K. Heacox. il *Wilderness* 53:15+ Fall '89

The stain will remain on Alaska. P. A. Witteman. il *Time* 134:58-9 S 25 '89

Terror and triage at the laundry [caring for oil-soaked animals] J. R. Luoma. il *Audubon* 91:92-101 S '89

'They'll never get it all'. G. Hackett. il *Newsweek* 113:25-6 My 8 '89

Valdez 'bugs' chomp away. *Science News* 136:38 Jl 15 '89

Would you believe $16.67 an hour to scrub rocks? K. R. Sheets. il *U.S. News & World Report* 106:48 Ap 17 '89

Economic aspects

The big spill's big chill. T. Vogel and M. Ivey. il *Business Week* p102-3 My 1 '89

Black gold [positive effects on Alaskan economy] C. P. Wohlforth. *The New Republic* 201:20+ S 18-25 '89

Coping with the big spill [Alaska couple Jeff and Claire Bailey] S. Seixas. il *Money* 18:76-80+ Jl '89

EXXON VALDEZ (SHIP) OIL SPILL, 1989—Economic aspects—*cont.*

Exxon and squatter economics. G. P. Brockway. *The New Leader* 72:13-14 Ag 7-21 '89

The future of big oil [drilling in Arctic National Wildlife Refuge after Exxon oil spill; cover story] P. Nulty. il map *Fortune* 119:46-9 My 8 '89

Tanker from hell. J. Edgerton. il *Money* 18:66-7 Je '89

Government investigations

'One way to end a career'. J. Adler. il *Newsweek* 113:52 My 29 '89

Public opinion

Exxon's one-act [shareholders' meeting] R. Engler. *The Nation* 248:836-7 Je 19 '89

Nowhere to run or to hide [L. Rawl confronted at shareholders' meeting] B. Rudolph. il *Time* 133:69 My 29 '89

Who's that screaming at Exxon? Not the environmentalists. A. Rothman. il *Business Week* p31 My 1 '89

Suits and claims

Getting ready for Exxon vs. practically everybody. M. Galen and V. Cahan. il *Business Week* p190+ S 25 '89

EYE

See also
Cornea
Eyelids
Photoreceptors
Retina
Rods and cones
Vision
Visual purple

Accommodation and refraction

Light adaptation in cat retinal rods. T. Tamura and others. bibl f il *Science* 245:755-8 Ag 18 '89

Animals

Gating of retinal transmission by afferent eye position and movement signals [cats] R. Lal and M. J. Friedlander. bibl f il *Science* 243:93-6 Ja 6 '89

Arachnids

If looks could kill . . . Florida jumping spider. T. Eisner. il *Natural History* p76-7 Jl '89

Birds

Plasticity and differentiation of embryonic retinal cells after terminal mitosis [chick eye] R. Adler and M. Hatlee. bibl f il *Science* 243:391-3 Ja 20 '89

Cancer

Genetic aspects

Cell cycle-dependent regulation of phosphorylation of the human retinoblastoma gene product. K. Mihara and others. bibl f il *Science* 246:1300-3 D 8 '89

The human papilloma virus-16 E7 oncoprotein is able to bind to the retinoblastoma gene product. N. Dyson and others. bibl f il *Science* 243:934-7 F 17 '89

Point mutational inactivation of the retinoblastoma antioncogene. J. M. Horowitz and others. bibl f il *Science* 243:937-40 F 17 '89

Care and hygiene

See also
Eye exercises
Project Orbis

Ex-sight-ing eye contact. il *Harper's Bazaar* 122:204-7+ Mr '89

It's never too late to keep an eye on your eyes. L. George. il *American Health* 8:26-8+ Mr '89

The save-your-sight eye book; ed. by Florence Isaacs. R. S. Koplin. il *Good Housekeeping* 208:69-72 F '89

Visionary facts, visible differences [cover story] C. Bushnell. il *Health (New York, N.Y.)* 21:66-73 D '89

Crustaceans

Deep-see shrimp [from hydrothermal vents; cover story] R. Monastersky. il *Science News* 135:90-3 F 11 '89

Jeepers, creepers [mantis shrimp; research by Thomas W. Cronin and N. Justin Marshall] A. W. Epstein. il *Scientific American* 261:33-4 S '89

Diseases and defects

See also
Blindness
Cataracts (Eye defect)
Color blindness
Leber's hereditary optic neuropathy
Macular degeneration
Myopia
Onchocerciasis
Presbyopia
Retinopathy of prematurity

The aging eye. R. M. Henig. il *The New York Times Magazine* p47-8 Mr 26 '89

Cloning of breakpoints of a chromosome translocation identifies the AN2 locus [aniridia] M. Gessler and others. bibl f il *Science* 244:1575-8 Je 30 '89

Darling . . . your contacts [danger of ulcerative keratitis] *Newsweek* 114:66 O 2 '89

An eye doctor says wearing contacts for weeks at a time can be blindingly shortsighted [danger of ulcerative keratitis; interview with O. Schein] D. Mathison. il por *People Weekly* 32:65-6 N 6 '89

Hospital faulted for dry eye study [Harvard-affiliated Massachusetts Eye and Ear Infirmary] W. Booth. *Science* 243:1000 F 24 '89

Making contacts safe [risk of acanthamoeba keratitis] il *Prevention (Emmaus, Pa.)* 41:12+ F '89

New help for dry eyes. S. Lally. *Prevention (Emmaus, Pa.)* 41:60-4+ Ag '89

New labeling for extended-wear lenses [risk of ulcerative keratitis] *FDA Consumer* 23:3-4 S '89

The sight of your life. N. Brown. il *Nation's Business* 77:55 F '89

Soft contacts: extended wear poses hazard [ulcerative keratitis; research by Oliver D. Schein] K. Fackelmann. *Science News* 136:197 S 23 '89

Examination

See also
Eye charts

Detecting infants' eye problems [Teller Acuity Card test] il *USA Today (Periodical)* 118:17-18 O '89

Fish

The eyes have it! il *National Geographic World* 167:10-13 Jl '89

Innervation

See also
Optic nerve

Insects

See also
Moth-eye technology

Ubiquitous expression of *sevenless*: position-dependent specification of cell fate. K. Basler and E. Hafen. bibl f il *Science* 243:931-4 F 17 '89

Invertebrates

Vision optics and evolution [cover story] D.-E. Nilsson. bibl f il *BioScience* 39:298-307 My '89

Movements

Gating of retinal transmission by afferent eye position and movement signals [cats] R. Lal and M. J. Friedlander. bibl f il *Science* 243:93-6 Ja 6 '89

In the blink of an eye [blink rate relates to mental processes] J. A. Stern. il *Reader's Digest* 134:99-101 Ap '89

In the blink of an eye [blink rate relates to mental processes; research by John A. Stern] S. Vogel. il *Discover* 10:62-4 F '89

Ocular responses to linear motion are inversely proportional to viewing distance. U. Schwarz and others. bibl f il *Science* 245:1394-6 S 22 '89

Protection

See also
Goggles

Surgery

See also
Cataracts (Eye defect)—Surgery

Bankruptcy snarls device seizure [unsterile eye surgery devices manufactured by Trueline Instruments] il *FDA Consumer* 23:35-6 Mr '89

Excimer laser surgery. A. Biesada. il *High Technology Business* 9:9 F '89

How to get rich off *perestroika* [eye surgeon and entrepreneur S. Fyodorov] P. Péan. il pors *Fortune* 119:145-6 My 8 '89

A tale of two eyes [cost of laser eye surgery in France compared to that in U.S.] L. Malkin. *The New Republic* 201:15-16 S 4 '89

Wounds and injuries

Burns, eye injuries from tanning devices. il *FDA Consumer* 23:3-4 O '89

The specs on eye care [injuries in the outdoors] P. G. Gill, Jr. il *Outdoor Life* 184:44-5 Jl '89

EYE CHARTS

A new eye test. L. Holland. il *Good Housekeeping* 209:275 N '89

EYE CONTACT *See* Communication, Nonverbal

EYE EXERCISES

Eye workouts that don't work [views of Maria-Therese Wegner-Aiello] C. Marks. il *Mademoiselle* 95:142 N '89

Eyes on the prize [sports vision] D. Wise. il *Gentlemen's Quarterly* 59:168-75 Jl '89

Eyes right [vision exercises for athletes] B. Hasselbring. il *Women's Sports & Fitness* 11:12 My '89

Workouts for the eyes [vision therapy] A. Toufexis. il *Time* 133:86 F 13 '89

EYE MAKEUP *See* Makeup

EYE MOVEMENTS *See* Eye—Movements

EYE ON CRIME [television program] *See* Television program reviews—Single works

EYEBROWS

Brows now! il *Essence* 20:40 D '89

Just browsing. il *'Teen* 33:58-9 Jl '89

The language of brows. C. Bushnell. il *Health (New York, N.Y.)* 21:62-7 F '89

EYEGLASSES

See also
Contact lenses
Goggles
Sunglasses

20/20 beauty. il *'Teen* 33:58-9 Ja '89

Assertiveness framing. K. A. Samon. il *Working Woman* 14:98 O '89

A new look at glasses and contacts. N. A. Osborn. il *Current Health 2* 16:12-13 N '89

EYEGLASSES—cont.
Sex and specs [mock tortoiseshells] D. Wise. il *Gentlemen's Quarterly* 59:59 S '89
Specs appeal. il *'Teen* 33:94-5 N '89
The vision thing. J. Miller. il *Ms.* 17:30+ Je '89
Prices
Court blocks FTC vision-care ruling. *Modern Maturity* 32:13 D '89/Ja '90
EYELASH MAKEUP *See* Makeup
EYELIDS
Surgery
Surgery gives sight to infant born with rare case of inverted eyelids [J. Turner] il *Jet* 76:31 Ag 28 '89
EYES *See* Eye
EYESIGHT *See* Vision
EYESTONE, ED
about
Ed Eyestone. M. Will-Weber. il por *Runner's World* 24:50 F '89
Man with a mission. C. Negron. il por *Runner's World* 24:101 N '89
EYEWEAR STORES
See also
International Sun Shade Inc.
Oliver Peoples (Firm)
Royal International Optical Corporation
Visionaries [sunglasses] H. Brubach. il *The New Yorker* 65:64+ Ag 28 '89
Acquisitions and mergers
This raider may have beaten 'em by joining 'em [E. Buchanan may sell Royal International Optical] G. G. Marcial. il *Business Week* p88 F 13 '89
EYEWITNESSES *See* Witnesses
EYRIGNAC (FRANCE: HISTORIC HOUSE)
Coup de maître in the Dordogne: a flourish of classical traditions at Eyrignac. Countess Du Saillant. il por *Architectural Digest* 46:132-5 Ja '89
EYSENCK, H. J. (HANS JURGEN), 1916-
Health's character. il pors *Psychology Today* 22:28-32+ D '88
EYSENCK, HANS JURGEN *See* Eysenck, H. J. (Hans Jurgen), 1916-
EYTON, TREVOR
about
Contributions from the elite. B. Wickens. il por *Maclean's* 102:48 Je 12 '89
EZE (NEW YORK, N.Y.: RESTAURANT) *See* New York (N.Y.)—Restaurants, nightclubs, bars, etc.
EZRA (BIBLICAL FIGURE)
about
When the semi-saints come marching in. P. Yancey. il *Christianity Today* 33:64 S 22 '89

F

F-5 AIRPLANES *See* Airplanes, Military
F-14 AIRPLANES *See* Airplanes, Military
F-15 AIRPLANES *See* Airplanes, Military
F-16 AIRPLANES *See* Airplanes, Military
F-111 AIRPLANES *See* Airplanes, Military
F.E. COMPTON COMPANY
Compton's debuts CD-ROM encyclopedia. J. Zinsser. il *Publishers Weekly* 236:56 N 3 '89
F. SCHUMACHER & CO.
A century of opulent textiles: the Schumacher Collection [cover story] il *Horizon (Tuscaloosa, Ala.)* 32:57-72 Mr/Ap '89
F. Schumacher and Company and the art moderne style. R. E. Slavin, III. il *Antiques* 135:964-73 Ap '89
F. W. WOOLWORTH CO.
This five-&-dime may go for big bucks. G. G. Marcial. il *Business Week* p100 S 4 '89
Woolworth to rule the malls. B. Saporito. il *Fortune* 119:145+ Je 5 '89
FA *See* Fanconi anemia
FAA *See* United States. Federal Aviation Administration
FABER, ADELE, AND MAZLISH, ELAINE
Wouldn't you like your kids to be closer? il *Redbook* 172:98-9+ F '89
FABER & FABER INC.
Faber & Faber restructures to safeguard its independence. V. Menkes. *Publishers Weekly* 236:10 D 8 '89
Thunder's Mouth, Faber both profiling filmmaker Martin Scorsese. M. Simson. il por *Publishers Weekly* 236:28 S 22 '89
FABERGÉ, PETER CARL, 1846-1920
about
The ultimate Easter eggs [cover story] M. Forrest. il *Antiques & Collecting Hobbies* 94:44-5+ Mr '89
FABERGE INC.
Riklis' fancy footwork may be tripping him up. A. Rothman. il por *Business Week* p86-8 Je 19 '89

Unilever is all made up, with everywhere to go [acquisition of Fabergé and Elizabeth Arden] M. Maremont. il *Business Week* p33-4 Jl 31 '89
FABIAN, BOBBY JOE
about
The murder—and the mayor. J. N. Baker. il por *Newsweek* 114:32 O 23 '89
FABRIC CABANAS *See* Cabanas
FABRIC CRAFTS *See* Textile crafts
FABRIC WALL COVERINGS *See* Wall coverings
FABRICA ARGENTINA DE MATERIAL AEROSPACIAL
IA-63 trainer offers smooth handling, expanded envelope [Pampa jet; cover story] B. M. Greeley, Jr. il *Aviation Week & Space Technology* 129:36-9+ Mr 6 '89
FABRICA MILITAR DE AVIONES
See also
Fabrica Argentina de Material Aerospacial
FABRICANT, FLORENCE
Garden of vegetable delights. il *Modern Maturity* 32:66-8+ Ag/S '89
FABRICATED FOODS *See* Food substitutes
FABRICS *See* Textile fabrics
FABRICS, SYNTHETIC *See* Textile fabrics, Synthetic
THE FABULOUS BAKER BOYS [film] *See* Motion picture reviews—Single works
FABULOUS THUNDERBIRDS (MUSICAL GROUP)
Powerful fun in T-bird Town [Austin] il *Rolling Stone* p24 Jl 13-27 '89
FACE
See also
Facial expression
Face it! [false faces that appear in plants, animals, and landscapes] il *National Geographic World* 168:11-14 Ag '89
Care and hygiene
See Skin—Care and hygiene
FACE MASKS *See* Masks
FACE RECOGNITION *See* Recognition (Psychology)
FACIAL CREAMS *See* Cosmetics
FACIAL EXPRESSION
See also
Smiles
Baby faces show the right side of emotion. B. Bower. il *Science News* 135:149 Mr 11 '89
Facial clues to deceptive behavior [study by Brian Mullen and Martin Skinner] il *USA Today (Periodical)* 118:8 S '89
The nature and nurture of emotions [cross cultural study of relationship between facial expression and the physiology of emotion; research by Paul Ekman and Robert W. Levenson] P. Young. *Science News* 135:59 Ja 28 '89
No fooling [relationship between facial expressions and emotion; excerpt from About faces; cover story] T. Landau. il *Health (New York, N.Y.)* 21:49-51+ My '89
Recognizing faces and expressions [research by Michael Hasselmo] J. Rubin. *Psychology Today* 23:22 My '89
Underneath, we're all the same [cross cultural study of relationship between facial expression and the physiology of emotion; research by Paul Ekman] C. Raymond. il *Psychology Today* 23:17 Je '89
FACIAL MASKS *See* Cosmetics
FACIAL MASSAGE *See* Massage
FACIAL PARALYSIS
See also
Bell's palsy
FACIAL TISSUES
Facial tissues. il *Consumer Reports* 54:332-4 My '89
Facial tissues. il *Consumer Reports* 54:39-41 D '89
FACSIMILE TRANSMISSION *See* Fax machines
FACT CHECKING
Dog-bites-dog journalism. L. I. Barrett. il *Time* 134:87 O 30 '89
FACTIONS (SPECIAL INTEREST GROUPS) *See* Special interest groups
FACTORIES
See also
Airplane factories
Automobile factories
Chemical plants
Factory management
Mills
Potteries
Automation
See Automation
Clean rooms
See Clean rooms
Location
See Location in business and industry
Photographs and photography
Factories that shine. A. Ramirez. il *Fortune* 119:92-3+ Ap 24 '89
Shutdowns
Industrial America's suicide pact. P. Keisling. *The Washington Monthly* 21:59-60 F '89
Surviving organizational death [study by Robert Sutton] E. Stark. *Psychology Today* 23:15 Je '89

FACTORIES—Shutdowns—*cont.*
Laws and regulations
Closing law's key provisions. *Nation's Business* 77:58+ Ja '89

Does the plant-closing law apply to brokerages? M. Galen. il *Business Week* p146 My 22 '89

FACTORIES IN SPACE *See* Space processing

FACTORY AND TRADE WASTE *See* Trade waste

FACTORY MANAGEMENT
See also
Industrial revolution
Quality control
Team work in industry
M.B.A.s with blue collars [manufacturers should recruit best and brightest young managers] A. G. Shilling. il por *Forbes* 144:300 O 16 '89

Soviet Union
At factories, it's do-it-or-die time. *Business Week* p56-7 Je 5 '89

Why there is no soap. C. Bogert. il *Newsweek* 114:46-7 D 4 '89

FACTORY OUTLETS *See* Outlet stores

FACTORY TOURS *See* Industrial tours

FACTS
See also
Fact checking
Far-out facts. See issues of National Geographic World
Of many things [David Feldman's When do fish sleep?] G. W. Hunt. *America* 161:334 N 18 '89

FACTS ON FILE, INC.
Facts on File settles claims in software copyright suit. C. Reid. *Publishers Weekly* 235:9-10 Je 23 '89

FACULTY, COLLEGE *See* College teachers

FADEN, ALAN I., AND OTHERS
The role of excitatory amino acids and NMDA receptors in traumatic brain injury. bibl f il *Science* 244:798-800 My 19 '89

FADER, KIM BROWN
Sex during pregnancy. il *Glamour* 87:64+ F '89

FADIMAN, KIM
Snow season survivors. il *Sierra* 74:158-9 Ja/F '89

FADLALLAH, MOHAMMED HUSSEIN
about
A voice of the Hizballah. W. Dowell. por *Time* 134:58-9 O 9 '89

FADS
See also
Food fads
Business week's 1989 hip parade. il *Business Week* p37 Ja 16 '89

Fads in ecology. W. G. Abrahamson and others. bibl f il *BioScience* 39:321-5 My '89

The hot list. D. Handelman and L. Hirschberg. il *Rolling Stone* p133-4+ My 18 '89

The way it was, the way it is! J. Romberger and J. K. Davis. il *Teen* 33:22+ Jl '89

FAESY, A. ROBERT
about
A. Robert Faesy, Jr.: structural drama for a New Canaan poolhouse. il *Architectural Digest* 46:78-81 Ag '89

FAGAN, ELEANORA *See* Holiday, Billie, 1915-1959

FAGAN (GARTH) BUCKET DANCE *See* Garth Fagan Bucket Dance

FAGEN, DONALD, 1948-
All that jazz. il *Harper's Bazaar* 122:178+ Ag '89
about
Fagen flies again. R. Laermer. il por *New York* 22:30 N 20 '89

FAGEROS, KAROL, D. 1988
Memoirs of the golden goddess [excerpt from Heaven will have to wait]; ed. by Julie Murphy. il pors *World Tennis* 36:48-50+ Mr '89

FAHDEL, ABBAS
An Orient of myth and mystery. il *The Unesco Courier* 42:24-9 O '89

FAHY, EVERETT
about
Maestro at the Met. C. McGee. il por *House & Garden* 161:50+ S '89

FAID, ROBERT W.
Gorby the Antichrist [excerpt from Gorbachev! Has the real Antichrist come?] *Harper's* 278:24+ Ja '89

FAIDLEY, WARREN E., AND KRIDER, E. PHILIP
A lucky strike. bibl f il *Weatherwise* 42:136-9 Je '89

FAILING, PATRICIA
Black artists today: a case of exclusion. il *Art News* 88:124-31 Mr '89

FAILURE (PSYCHOLOGY)
See also
Fear of success
How can a student 'fail' to be educated? P. Rogers. *Phi Delta Kappan* 70:478-9 F '89

The tapestry of your life [address, May 7, 1989] S. G. Finesilver. *Vital Speeches of the Day* 56:82-4 N 15 '89

FAILURES, BUSINESS *See* Business failures

FAINLIGHT, RUTH
Flower feet [poem] *The New Yorker* 65:36 Jl 10 '89

FAINTING
Me and my phobia [fear of blood leads to fainting] L. C. Pogrebin. por *Ms.* 18:16 O '89

FAIR HOUSING ACT
Opening the door to kids [amendment combats discrimination against children] A. L. Sanders. il *Time* 134:75 S 18 '89

A welcome mat for kids. W. Giese. il *Changing Times* 43:22 F '89

FAIRBANK, JOHN KING, 1907-
Keeping up with the new China. il *The New York Review of Books* 36:17-20 Mr 16 '89

Why China's rulers fear democracy. il *The New York Review of Books* 36:32-3 S 28 '89

FAIRBANKS, CHARLES H., JR.
Gorbachev & the U.S. [discussion of August 1989 article, Gorbachev's cultural revolution] *Commentary* 88:2+ N '89

Gorbachev's cultural revolution. *Commentary* 88:23-7 Ag '89

FAIRCHILD, JOHN
Chic savages [excerpt] il por *New York* 22:44-54 O 16 '89

FAIRCHILD AIRCRAFT CORPORATION
Development of Metro 5 commuter aircraft delayed. *Aviation Week & Space Technology* 130:39 Ap 24 '89

Fairchild Aircraft, Spain's CASA to cooperate on C-212 marketing. *Aviation Week & Space Technology* 130:61 Je 26 '89

Fairchild delivers first two C-26As to Air National Guard [cover story] C. A. Shifrin. il *Aviation Week & Space Technology* 130:36-7+ Ap 24 '89

Fairchild prepares for Metro 25 commuter production decision [twin turboprop] D. A. Brown. il *Aviation Week & Space Technology* 131:31-2 O 16 '89

FAIRCHILD SEMICONDUCTOR CORPORATION
Let's make a deal, comrade [trade negotiations with Hungary] *High Technology Business* 9:17 Jl/Ag '89

FAIRFAX COUNTY (VA.)
Employees
Fed. probe of job bias in Fairfax, Va., government. il *Jet* 76:38 Jl 17 '89

FAIRGROUND ATTRACTION (MUSICAL GROUP)
Fairground Attraction [release of First of a million kisses] R. Givens. il *Stereo Review* 54:107 Mr '89

FAIRLEY, JOSEPHINE
Princess Diana: the secrets of her style [excerpt from The Princess and the Duchess] il pors *McCall's* 116:14-16+ Je '89

FAIRLIE, HENRY
Pen ultimate. il *Vogue* 179:268+ Ap '89

FAIRNESS
The "no fair" solution. C. Hyde. il *Parents* 64:78+ D '89

FAIRNESS DOCTRINE (BROADCASTING)
Why the FCC can't get its signal across. F. Seghers. *Business Week* p49 Ja 23 '89

FAIRS
See also
Book fairs
Gift fairs
World's fairs

Maryland
Costumed cows and other critters [4-H Club of Maryland sponsors costume parade at State Fair] il *National Geographic World* 167:26-9 Jl '89

THE FAIRY QUEEN [opera] *See* Purcell, Henry, 1659-1695

FAIRY TALE ROAD (GERMANY: WEST) *See* Roads—Germany (West)

FAIRY TALES
Past present [W. Grimm's Dear Mili] L. Metzger. *The Nation* 249:801-2 D 25 '89

Anecdotes, facetiae, satire, etc.
Fairy two tales. J. Spelman. il *The Mother Earth News* 116:135 Mr/Ap '89

Bibliography
Stories for the once-upon-a-time crowd. M. Silver. il *U.S. News & World Report* 107:81 D 18 '89

FAITH
See also
Justification
Truth
Faith lift: how to navigate midlife's mysteries. B. Dodds. il *U.S. Catholic* 54:31-5 O '89

A faith that trembles and dances [S. Kierkegaard] V. S. Owens. il *Christianity Today* 33:19-22 Jl 14 '89

Feeling saved. R. A. Fowler. il *Christianity Today* 33:26-7 Ap 7 '89

How faith works [Lordship Salvation debate] S. L. Johnson, Jr. il *Christianity Today* 33:21-5 S 22 '89

I wondered if I would pass the test. S. H. Johnson. il *Commonweal* 116:208-10 Ap 7 '89

Integrating faith and functionality [address, January 18, 1989] S. Muto. *Vital Speeches of the Day* 55:370-1 Ap 1 '89

Meeting God in others. K. P. Cecala. il *Commonweal* 116:400-2 Jl 14 '89

Naming and the act of faith. L. O. Sanneh. *The Christian Century* 106:875 O 4 '89

Night watch. P. J. Ryan. *America* 161:71 Jl 29-Ag 5 '89

On troubled belief. M. Garvey. *America* 160:164 F 25 '89

Priority. P. J. Ryan. il *America* 161:199 S 30 '89

FAITH—*cont.*
The reconstruction of faith [excerpt from Faith on earth] H. R. Niebuhr. *The Christian Century* 106:780-3 Ag 30-S 6 '89
Surviving. P. J. Ryan. *America* 161:331 N 11 '89
Understanding faith and miracle. P. Perkins. *The Christian Century* 106:555 My 24-31 '89
When bad things happen. J. R. Edwards. il *Christianity Today* 33:30-2 Ag 18 '89
When risk analysis confronts faith. J. M. Wall. *The Christian Century* 106:1139-40 D 6 '89
A wrestling match with the Almighty. P. Yancey. il *Christianity Today* 33:22-6 S 8 '89

FAITH AND REASON
A leap in the light: faith, science, & the imagination. W. J. O'Malley. il *Commonweal* 116:141-3+ Mr 10 '89

FAITH CURE
See also
Mental healing
Miracles
Signs and wonders movement
Crimes of faith? [denial of medical care to children] D. Neff. *Christianity Today* 33:17 Je 16 '89
The prayer war [relaxation response theories of H. Benson] S. Kiesling and T. G. Harris. *Psychology Today* 23:65-6 O '89
Tales of miraculous healing. L. O. Sanneh. *The Christian Century* 106:906 O 11 '89
What I was doing at the hospital. R. Brow. il *Christianity Today* 33:31-2 Ap 21 '89

FAITH HEALING *See* Faith cure

FAITH MOUNTAIN COMPANY
The catalog concept grows a cottage industry. D. Weil. il por *Working Woman* 14:64+ Ag '89

FAITHDOME (LOS ANGELES, CALIF.)
FaithDome: 'a grand-slam homer for Jesus' [work of F. Price] A. Collier. il pors *Ebony* 45:40-2+ D '89
TV's Rev. Fred Price opens $9 million FaithDome in L.A. il pors *Jet* 77:32-3 O 16 '89

FAJER, ERIC D., AND OTHERS
The effects of enriched carbon dioxide atmospheres on plant-insect herbivore interactions. bibl f il *Science* 243:1198-200 Mr 3 '89

FAKE FUR *See* Fur, Artificial

FAKERS *See* Quacks and quackery

FAKHRO, ALI MOHAMED
Truth and tolerance in Islam. il *New Perspectives Quarterly* 6:51-2 Spr '89

FALANA, LOLA
about
Celebs pay tribute to Lola Falana at recent Filmmakers Hall gala. il por *Jet* 75:24-5+ Mr 20 '89
First since illness: Lola performs onstage with Wayne Newton. il pors *Jet* 76:55-6 Je 26 '89
Lola Falana: 'I'm back! I'm not cured. But I'm healed!' [cover story] R. E. Johnson. il pors *Jet* 76:54-7 Ag 14 '89

FALCO, RICHARD C.
(jt. auth) See Daniels, Thomas J., and Falco, Richard C.

FALCO, RICK
Life and death: scenes from a hospital emergency ward [cover story] il *USA Today (Periodical)* 118:41-53 Jl '89

FALCOFF, MARK, 1941-
The only hope for Latin America. *Commentary* 87:34-8 Ap '89

FALCON AIRPLANES *See* Airplanes, Business

FALCON COMMUNICATIONS
Falcon's eye on classic kind of service [interview with M. Nathanson] il pors *Channels (New York, N.Y.: 1986)* 9:74-5 Jl/Ag '89

FALCONBRIDGE LIMITED
The final victory [Noranda's takeover] J. Daly. il pors *Maclean's* 102:40-1 O 2 '89
Getting the best price [Falconbridge Ltd. favoring AMAX over Noranda in takeover battle; special section] il *Maclean's* 102:34-7 Ag 14 '89
This mining buy is on solid ground. G. G. Marcial. *Business Week* p108 Mr 27 '89

FALCONS
Arctic treasures: what ruler could resist the allure of white falcons, giant moles, and unicorns? F. Bruemmer. il *Natural History* p38-47 Je '89
A case of urban renewal [peregrine falcons adapt to city life] M. Wexler. il *National Wildlife* 27:10-13 Je/Jl '89

FALDO, NICK
about
Britannia rules again. S. Ballard. il pors *Sports Illustrated* 71:60-4+ Jl 10 '89
A British victory in British weather. H. W. Wind. *The New Yorker* 65:97-103+ My 15 '89
Jolly good show [cover story] E. M. Swift. il pors *Sports Illustrated* 70:18-25 Ap 17 '89

FALES, MARTHA GANDY
The jewelry. il *Antiques* 135:512-7 F '89
The silver. bibl f il *Antiques* 135:518-23 F '89

FALES, SUSAN
about
'Different world' producer featured in June Ebony. il por *Jet* 76:58 Je 12 '89
Susan Fales: in A different world. il pors *Ebony* 44:160+ Je '89

FALK, PETER
Columbo returns! What you can expect from him now; ed. by Jeff Kaye. il por *TV Guide* 37:10-12 F 4-10 '89
about
Back in the raincoat again. P. Simms. il por *Rolling Stone* p34 Mr 9 '89

FALK, RICHARD A.
The damaged U.S. image. il *The Bulletin of the Atomic Scientists* 45:59-61 Ja/F '89
People power. *The Nation* 248:801 Je 12 '89
Preventive . . . *The Nation* 248:508-9 Ap 17 '89

FALKLAND ISLANDS
See also
Birds—Falkland Islands
History
Whose island story? P. J. Beck. il map *History Today* 39:8-11 F '89

FALL *See* Autumn

FALL OF MAN
Original sin: a new look at the oldest sin in the book [cover story] L. Jacquet. il *U.S. Catholic* 54:6-12 Je '89
Original sin: when sex was clean [views of Elaine Pagels] W. Herbert. il *Psychology Today* 22:67 D '88

THE FALL OF THE HOUSE OF USHER [opera] See Glass, Philip

FALL RIVER (MASS.)
Historic houses, sites, etc.
The 200-year-old house that moved [house transported to New York] il *Good Housekeeping* 208:140-3 Je '89

FALLING BODIES
How cats survive falls from New York skyscrapers [research by Wayne Whitney and Cheryl Mehlhaff] J. M. Diamond. il *Natural History* p20-6 Ag '89

FALLON, TOM
about
Gentleman's quarters. M. Cantwell. il por *House & Garden* 161:78-81+ Ja '89

FALLON MCELLIGOTT (FIRM)
Bouncing back. B. Kanner. il *New York* 22:16+ Je 26 '89

FALLOPIAN TUBES
Surgery
Balloon angioplasty finds other applications. il *Popular Mechanics* 166:16 Ap '89

FALLOUT, RADIOACTIVE *See* Radioactive pollution

FALLOUT SHELTERS *See* Atomic bomb shelters

FALLOW DEER *See* Deer

FALLOWELL, DUNCAN
Letter from Sicily: Mr. Sciascia explains [excerpt from To noto, or Through Europe in a Ford] *The American Scholar* 58:581-5 Aut '89

FALLOWS, JAMES M.
America helps itself by helping others. il *U.S. News & World Report* 107:47 O 23 '89
Containing Japan [cover story] il *The Atlantic* 263:40-8+ My '89
A few pointers. il *The Atlantic* 264:24+ N '89
Getting along with Japan. il *The Atlantic* 264:53-6+ D '89
The hard life. il *The Atlantic* 263:16+ Mr '89
IQ and intelligence: what's wrong with testing? [excerpt from More like us] *Current (Washington, D.C.)* 315:4-10 S '89
The Japan-handlers. il *The Atlantic* 264:14+ Ag '89
Japan's secret weapon. il *U.S. News & World Report* 107:46 D 25 '89-Ja 1 '90
Land of plenty. il *The Atlantic* 263:29-31 Je '89
Let them defend themselves. il *The Atlantic* 263:17-18+ Ap '89
Rediscovering the American spirit. il *U.S. News & World Report* 106:60-1 Ap 10 '89
The screw-you spirit. *The Washington Monthly* 21:42-3 Mr '89
So you'll be moving to Asia. il *Fortune* 120 no13 Special Issue:91+ Fall '89
South Korea only wants a little respect. il *U.S. News & World Report* 107:38+ Ag 14 '89
What's wrong with testing? [excerpt from More like us] *The Washington Monthly* 21:12-14+ My '89
Who's a snob and who's not. *The Washington Monthly* 21:34+ F '89
about
745 Boylston Street. il por *The Atlantic* 264:4 Ag '89
Crazy but harmless. M. Kinsley. *The New Republic* 201:4 D 11 '89
Rewriting the book on how to deal with Japan. R. Neff. il pors *Business Week* p49 Ag 7 '89
To our own selves be true. B. Powell. il *Newsweek* 113:45 Ap 3 '89

FALLS (ACCIDENTS)
Challenge of gravity [falls and the elderly] B. H. Dobkin. il *The New York Times Magazine* p36-7 Ag 27 '89
A "Fallsafe" against broken hips [tethering system] il *High Technology Business* 9:13-14 N/D '89

FALSE ARREST See Miscarriage of justice

FALSE WITNESS [television program] See Television program reviews—Single works

FALSEHOOD See Lying

FALSTAFF [opera] See Verdi, Giuseppe, 1813-1901

FALÚ, EDUARDO

about

Taut strings. C. Bach. il pors *Américas* 41 no1:20-3 '89

FALUDI, SUSAN

"Diary of a mad supermom". il *Mother Jones* 14:39-41 Je '89

Where did Randy go wrong? [cover story] il pors *Mother Jones* 14:22-8+ N '89

FALWELL, JERRY

about

Exit right. L. Cryderman. *Christianity Today* 33:15 Ag 18 '89

Falwell claims victory, dissolves Moral Majority. R. Walker. por *Christianity Today* 33:58-9 Jl 14 '89

The last temptation of price. J. D. Miller. il *Sport (New York, N.Y.)* 80:12 Jl '89

Scrapping the Moral Majority. *Time* 133:26 Je 26 '89

FALZO, ANTHONY

about

Faster than a speeding bullet, Anthony Falzo saved two tots from a powerful locomotive. il por *People Weekly* 31:159 My 22 '89

FAMA See Fabrica Argentina de Material Aerospacial

FAME

See also

Black celebrities

Celebrities

Attitudes [posthumous fame for choreographers] C. Barnes. il *Dance Magazine* 63:98 Je '89

Celebrity victims: crime casualties are turning into stars on tabloid TV. F. Rose. il *New York* 22:38-44 Jl 31 '89

The end of celebrity. D. Hurley. il *Psychology Today* 22:50-3+ D '88

Farewell, my unlovelies. R. Merkin. il *Gentlemen's Quarterly* 59:112+ Ap '89

Nymphs and satyrs [worship of celebrity] L. H. Lapham. *Harper's* 279:8-10 Ag '89

Private lives [special issue; with editorial comment by Lee Eisenberg] *Esquire* 111:35, 103-4+ Je '89

Anecdotes, facetiae, satire, etc.

16 reasons I'm glad I'm not famous. S. Bing. il *Esquire* 111:220 Je '89

Celebrity dirt, but not in the usual sense. R. Wolkomir. il *Smithsonian* 20:172 My '89

FAMILY

See also

Aged—Family relationships

AIDS patients—Family relationships

Alternative family

Alzheimer's disease patients—Family relationships

Ancestor worship

Authors' families

Birth order

Black family

Cancer patients—Family relationships

Celebrities' families

Children

Church work with families

Cousins

Divorce

Fathers

Focus on the Family (Organization)

Foster home care

Grandparents

Handicapped—Family relationships

Home

Home education

Homeless families

Households

Husbands

Marriage

Marriage counseling

Married couples

Mentally handicapped—Family relationships

Mentally ill—Family relationships

Mothers

Mothers-in-law

Only child

Parent-child relationship

Parents

Police families

Servicemen's families

Siblings

Sick—Family relationships

Single parent families

Sons

Stepparents and stepchildren

Uncles

Wives

The 21st century family [cover story] il *Newsweek* 114 Special Issue:14-18+ Wint '89/Spr '90

Adjusting to changing families [survey by the National Association of Elementary School Principals] il *USA Today (Periodical)* 118:11 D '89

All in the family [running; cover story; special section] il *Runner's World* 24:59-66+ Je '89

Bring home the joy! [traditions] E. Byron. il *Redbook* 174:118-19+ D '89

Christmas in July. T. Peters. il *The Mother Earth News* 120:10 N/D '89

The evening rush hour [family stress at day's end] K. Levine. il *Parents* 64:58+ Ag '89

Family crushes. P. R. Satran. il *Glamour* 87:274-5+ My '89

Family network. See issues of Better Homes and Gardens beginning May 1986

Family rituals [with editorial comment by Ann Pleshette Murphy] N. Rubin. il *Parents* 64:6, 105-9 Mr '89

First word [growing up in a troubled family] C. L. Whitfield. por *Omni (New York, N.Y.)* 11:6 Je '89

Habits of the hearth [interview with R. Bellah] R. Clapp. il pors *Christianity Today* 33:20-4 F 3 '89

Helping children: income tax reform. A. C. Carlson. *Current (Washington, D.C.)* 314:12-15 Jl/Ag '89

Looking to Harriet. D. Seligman. il *Fortune* 120:117 Jl 17 '89

Make the most of your weekends. M. Hodge and J. Blyskal. il *Reader's Digest* 134:9-10+ Ap '89

Meeting her family. V. Klinkenborg. il *Glamour* 87:232 F '89

Our summer retreat [sharing a summer house with husband's parents] R. Israeloff. *Glamour* 87:256 Ag '89

Rebel without a Claus [college freshman returns home for Christmas] B. Stepko. il *Seventeen* 48:44+ D '89

Stickum up, love! [family communication via Post-It Notes] J. G. Hubbell. *Reader's Digest* 135:123-5 O '89

This is what you thought: 93% say strong family ties bring happiness [results of survey] il *Glamour* 87:129 F '89

Tips for closer family ties. N. M. Lobsenz. *Reader's Digest* 134:139-42 F '89

Caricatures and cartoons

It's all in the family. S. Berenstain and J. Berenstain. See occasional issues of Good Housekeeping

History

The heroes we know. D. F. Bjorklund and B. Bjorklund. il *Parents* 64:203 S '89

"Read the 'me' book!". T. Wood. il *Parents* 64:230-1 My '89

Stories worth retelling. E. Stone. il *New Choices for the Best Years* 29:89-90 F '89

International aspects

Families of the world. H. Tremblay. il *The Unesco Courier* 42:46-7 Ag '89

The family: past and present [cover story; special issue] il *The Unesco Courier* 42:8-47 Jl '89

Photographs and photography

Families of the world [work of H. Tremblay] F. Cameron. il *Petersen's Photographic Magazine* 17:20-3 Mr '89

Public opinion

Dear President Bush . . . [results of survey] K. Greer. il *Better Homes and Gardens* 67:19-20 Ag '89

Religious life

The begats. M. E. Marty. *The Christian Century* 106:399 Ap 12 '89

A child shall lead us. L. O. Sanneh. *The Christian Century* 106:1146 D 6 '89

The daddy track. T. K. Jones. il *Christianity Today* 33:16 Je 16 '89

Do Catholic couples view having kids as a given? D. Morris. il *U.S. Catholic* 54:32-7 My '89

Does simple living have to be so complicated? L. Jacquet. il *U.S. Catholic* 54:28-35 Jl '89

Don't skip family meals [with readers' comments] J. Breig. *U.S. Catholic* 54:13-19 Jl '89

Mom liked you best: how Christians outgrow sibling rivalry [cover story] D. Morris. il *U.S. Catholic* 54:6-12 Ja '89

A mother's manner of looking to the sky [instilling awareness of mystery of life] J. M. Wall. *The Christian Century* 106:99-100 F 1-8 '89

Revive home remedies for listless faith. R. E. Burns. *U.S. Catholic* 54:2 Ap '89

Should parents speak of the devil? L. Jacquet. il *U.S. Catholic* 54:31-7 Mr '89

Statistics

All kinds of families [data collected by the National Survey of Families and Households] J. A. Miller. *BioScience* 39:227 Ap '89

Africa

Lines of descent. M. B. Priso. il *The Unesco Courier* 42:22-7 Jl '89

Brazil

The women of Arembepe. M. de A. Figueiredo and D. Prado. il *The Unesco Courier* 42:38-41 Jl '89

Canada

A retreat from ideals [Maclean's/Decima poll] C. Wood. il *Maclean's* 102:36-7 Ja 2 '89

China

The empire of the ancestors. Qi Yanfen. il *The Unesco Courier* 42:16-21 Jl '89

FAMILY—*cont.*

Europe

Marina, Sarah, Michel and Jean [new forms of family life] A. Michel. il *The Unesco Courier* 42:34-7 Jl '89

Great Britain

Younger sons in Tudor and Stuart England. L. A. Pollock. bibl il *History Today* 39:23-9 Je '89

Japan

Under new management. K. Kazuo. il *The Unesco Courier* 42:28-33 Jl '89

Québec (Province)

New family structures. F. Descarries and C. Corbeil. il *The Unesco Courier* 42:42-5 Jl '89

Soviet Union

Hearth, home and rural community [nineteenth century] H. Yvert-Jalu. il *The Unesco Courier* 42:10-15 Jl '89

United States

See Family

Uzbekistan (Soviet Union)

A visit to an Uzbek family. C. Fournier. il *The Unesco Courier* 42:46-7 Jl '89

FAMILY BUDGET *See* Budget, Household

FAMILY BUSINESS *See* Family corporations

FAMILY CORPORATIONS

Blood and money. E. Calonius. il *Newsweek* 114 Special Issue:82-4 Wint '89/Spr '90

Can their problem be solved? See issues of Successful Farming beginning January 1988

The coming of the next generation [black business] E. G. Graves. il *Black Enterprise* 19:7 Ap '89

Cultural changes in a family firm [Amot Controls Corp.] S. Nelton. il *Nation's Business* 77:62-3+ Ja '89

Do you keep too many secrets? B. Benson. il *Nation's Business* 77:42+ Ag '89

Fair pay in family firms. S. Nelton. il *Nation's Business* 77:72-3 O '89

Family affairs [cover story] R. Koselka and others. il *Forbes* 144:212-14+ D 11 '89

Fathers and sons: no easy business. S. Nelton. il *Nation's Business* 77:16 F '89

The feuding families of fine goods [Gucci and Rémy Martin] C. Dickey. il *Newsweek* 114:42 Ag 7 '89

Fun and games—and ethics. S. Nelton. il *Nation's Business* 77:38 N '89

Give your daughter a chance. S. Nelton. il *Nation's Business* 77:72 Je '89

Marrying into a family business. S. Nelton. il *Nation's Business* 77:42-3+ Ap '89

The next generation takes over at the B.E. 100s [Black enterprise] A. Edmond, Jr. *Black Enterprise* 19:54 Ap '89

Professionalizing: a necessary hurdle. J. L. Ward. il por *Nation's Business* 77:38-9 N '89

Retired dads: a real resource. J. L. Ward and L. Sorenson. il *Nation's Business* 77:72-3 Je '89

The role of "mom". J. L. Ward and L. Sorenson. il *Nation's Business* 77:40-1 Ag '89

Staying aboard after the sale. S. Nelton. il *Nation's Business* 77:34-5 S '89

Straight talk from key employees. R. S. Rapoza and L. C. Lancaster. il *Nation's Business* 77:40 N '89

Turning arguments into agreements. A. L. Matz and M. Matz. *Nation's Business* 77:74 Je '89

Advertising

Promote, celebrate your family ties. J. L. Ward and L. Sorenson. il *Nation's Business* 77:16-17 F '89

Taxation

All in the family [family businesses and estate taxes] J. C. Szabo. il *Nation's Business* 77:73-4 Ap '89

Congress warms to estate freeze. J. C. Szabo. il *Nation's Business* 77:48+ Je '89

FAMILY COUNSELING

See also

Homebuilders (Program)

Families in trouble: how to know when to get help. D. Morris. il *U.S. Catholic* 54:30-6 Ag '89

In it together. M. Blau. il *New York* 22:44-8+ S 4 '89

FAMILY CRUISES *See* Cruising

FAMILY DINNERS *See* Dinners and dining

FAMILY EDUCATION

See also

Grandparent education

Parent education

Teaching teens to marry smart. D. Hurley. *McCall's* 116:77 My '89

FAMILY FARM MANAGEMENT *See* Farm management

FAMILY FINANCE *See* Finance, Personal

FAMILY IN LITERATURE

See also

Parent-child relationship in literature

FAMILY IN MOTION PICTURES

Back to the family. T. K. Jones. *Christianity Today* 33:15 O 20 '89

FAMILY IN TELEVISION

Family a la Roseanne. C. Valentino. il *American Health* 8:112-13 Mr '89

FAMILY INCOME *See* Income

FAMILY MATTERS [television program] See Television program reviews—Single works

FAMILY MEALS *See* Meals

FAMILY PLANNING *See* Birth control

FAMILY PSYCHOTHERAPY

"We have a problem". J. Marks. See issues of Parents beginning February 1987

FAMILY QUARRELS *See* Quarrels

FAMILY RESORTS *See* Resorts

FAMILY REUNIONS

Come together in joyous reunion. S. Seixas. il *Money* 18:130-4+ D '89

The family gathering. B. Lindeman. il *New Choices for the Best Years* 29:78-9 Ag '89

Family reunion vacations. B. Murphy. il *Better Homes and Gardens* 67:123-4+ Ag '89

Gathering together in their name [black families] F. Brown, Jr. il *American Visions* 4:12-13 Ag '89

The Jacksons return to their Gary roots after 18 years away. il *Jet* 76:24-6 S 25 '89

Jet goes to the Jackson family reunion. il *Jet* 76:14-17 Ag 21 '89

A love of family affairs. M. A. Kuharski. por *Newsweek* 114:8 Ag 21 '89

One big, happy family has a grand reunion [Smith family of Atlantic Highlands, N.J.] J. Ralston. il *McCall's* 116:62+ Jl '89

FAMILY ROOMS

A big, cozy family room. il *Southern Living* 24:176 Ap '89

Exposed for architectural detailing. il *Southern Living* 24:135 Je '89

Finishing a family room/office. il *Workbench* 45:48-9 S/O '89

The new family room [home of Russell and Alexis Dow] W. L. Nolan and R. E. Dittmer. il *Better Homes and Gardens* 67:60-8+ S '89

New family room also cleans up entry confusion. il *Sunset (Central West edition)* 182:158 Ap '89

Planned for family living. il *Southern Living* 24:180 Mr '89

Retreat to Santa Fe. il *Southern Living* 24:112-13 Ja '89

The southern home [special section] il *Southern Living* 24:95+ O '89

The ultimate family room [work of Andy Pressman] A. W. Lees. il *Popular Science* 234:117-18+ Mr '89

FAMILY SAVINGS & LOAN ASSOCIATION (LOS ANGELES, CALIF.)

CEOs shift at S&Ls: one moves over, other moves out. S. Herbert. il *Black Enterprise* 19:13 Jl '89

FAMILY SIZE

See also

Only child

Considering a second baby? K. Karlsrud and D. Schultz. il *Parents* 64:208 N '89

Number of siblings and educational attainment. J. Blake. bibl f il *Science* 245:32-6 Jl 7 '89

Spaces in the heart. A. P. Murphy. il *Parents* 64:6 Ag '89

Spacing children [cover story] J. Gaylin. il *Parents* 64:71-4 Ag '89

Success and the second child. K. Levine. il *Parents* 64:57-8+ Jl '89

FAMILY SOUVENIRS *See* Souvenirs (Keepsakes)

FAMILY THERAPY *See* Family psychotherapy

FAMILY TIES [television program] See Television program reviews—Single works

FAMILY TRUSTS *See* Trusts and trustees

FAMILY VACATIONS *See* Vacations

FAMILY VIOLENCE

See also

Wife abuse

Evolution and family homicide [discussion of October 28, 1988 article, Evolutionary social psychology and family homicide] M. Daly and M. Wilson. *Science* 243:462-4 Ja 27 '89

The Hansel and Gretel syndrome [evolutionary significance of family homicide; research by Martin Daly and Margo Wilson] H. Pringle. il *Omni (New York, N.Y.)* 12:38+ D '89

FAMINE RELIEF *See* Relief work

FAMINES

Africa

Before death, Leland wrote in Ebony about starvation in Africa. il pors *Jet* 76:16-18+ Ag 28 '89

Hunger in Africa: why it persists, why we must care [cover story; special section] il map *Scholastic Update (Teachers' edition)* 121:2-15 Ja 27 '89

What African-Americans can do about starvation in Africa. M. Leland. il *Ebony* 44:80-2+ O '89

Ethiopia

Five years after the famine. R. Wilson. il *Christianity Today* 33:50-1 O 6 '89

Sudan

The collapse born of civil war. K. Soyinka. il *World Press Review* 36:28-9 Mr '89

Desperate hunger. D. Jones. il *Maclean's* 102:29+ Je 12 '89

Famine. R. Bonner. map *The New Yorker* 65:85-96+ Mr 13 '89

FAMINES—Sudan—*cont.*

One teen's bout with hunger [A. Chol] E. Whitford. il por *Scholastic Update (Teachers' edition)* 121:3 Ja 27 '89

'Operation Lifeline Sudan' launched; 100,000 lives at stake. il *UN Chronicle* 26:35 Je '89

Peace and relief in Sudan. *Department of State Bulletin* 89:24-6 Ap '89

Politics block relief efforts to Sudan. K. Blomquist. il map *Christianity Today* 33:40-1 Ap 7 '89

Starvation as a political weapon. L. Lief. il map *U.S. News & World Report* 106:34-5+ F 6 '89

Photographs and photography

Death zone. J. Nachtwey. il *Life* 12:28-34 Mr '89

FAMOUS MEN AND WOMEN *See* Celebrities

FAMOUS MUSIC PUBLISHING *See* Paramount Pictures Corp. Famous Music Publishing

FAMOUS PLAYERS LTD.

The screen wars [Famous Players vs. Cineplex Odeon] J. Daly. il *Maclean's* 102:40-1 My 29 '89

THE FAMOUS TEDDY Z [television program] *See* Television program reviews—Single works

THE FAN [opera] *See* Goldstein, Lee Scott

FAN BELTS (AUTOMOBILE) *See* Automobile engines—Fan belts

FAN CLUBS

See also

Helper's Network (Fan club)

Stephen Hawking Fan Club

FAN MAIL

How to write the perfect fan letter. Zoro. por *'Teen* 33:84 My '89

Writing back [correspondence from fans] A. Dillard. *Harper's* 278:28-9 Je '89

FANATICISM

For a new humanist militancy. M. Maneli. il por *The Humanist* 49:14-16+ S/O '89

FANCONI ANEMIA

Therapy

Marrow rebuilt with umbilical-cord blood [work of Arleen D. Auerbach] A. McKenzie. *Science News* 136:293 N 4 '89

FANCY THAT ANTIQUES & UNIQUES (FIRM)

The collecting life [interview with R. and J. McAuliffe] il pors *Antiques & Collecting Hobbies* 94:54-6+ Ag '89

FANG, LI-CHIH *See* Fang Lizhi

FANG LIZHI

China's despair and China's hope; tr. by Perry Link. il *The New York Review of Books* 36:3-4 F 2 '89

Keeping the faith [address, November 15, 1989]; tr. by James H. Williams and Orville Schell. il por *The New York Review of Books* 36:43-4 D 21 '89

about

745 Boylston Street. il por *The Atlantic* 264:4 S '89

An act of defiance [cover story] O. Schell. il pors *The New York Times Magazine* p26-7+ Ap 16 '89

Chinese bar physicist from Bush dinner. M. Sun. il por *Science* 243:1282 Mr 10 '89

Fang Lizhi: speaking out for human rights. M. Sun. il por *Science* 244:417-18 Ap 28 '89

Fang loses post, gains award. por *Science* 246:1252 D 8 '89

The fate of Fang Lizhi. il por *Sky and Telescope* 78:240-1 S '89

From Big Bang to big trouble. il por *U.S. News & World Report* 106:38 Je 26 '89

The furious flap over Fang Lizhi. S. MacLeod. por *Time* 133:38 Mr 13 '89

Letters from the other China; tr. by Orville Schell. bibl f il por *The New York Review of Books* 36:32-3 Jl 20 '89

Notes and comment. *The New Yorker* 65:34-5 Mr 20 '89

Physicists protest treatment by PRC of Fang Lizhi. W. Sweet. *Physics Today* 42:59 Ap '89

Quotations from dissident Fang. il por *Newsweek* 113:26-7 Je 26 '89

FANGER, DONALD

The two *perestroikas*. *The New Republic* 201:26-30 O 23 '89

FANGER, IRIS M.

A big surprise in Boston: everything's coming up (Susan) Rose. il pors *Dance Magazine* 63:42-3 My '89

The new Lucinda Childs. il pors *Dance Magazine* 63:48-53 O '89

FANNIE MAE *See* Federal National Mortgage Association

FANNIN, MINXIE J.

(jt. auth) *See* Lehner, Monique B., and Fannin, Minxie J.

FANNING, KATHERINE

about

A conscientious objector. R. Loth. il por *New Choices for the Best Years* 29:16+ S '89

FANNY EXERCISES *See* Exercise

FANS, ELECTRIC

See also

Modern Supply Company

Ventilators

Easy hanger [ceiling fan installation] R. Stepler. il *Popular Science* 235:102 Jl '89

Other ways to cool your house. il *Consumer Reports* 54:437-40 Jl '89

FANS, VENTILATING *See* Ventilators

FANS (PERSONS)

See also

Baseball fans

Basketball fans

Football fans

Groupies

Hockey fans

Horse racing fans

Sports fans

Tennis fans

Psychology

A fatal obsession with the stars [murder of actress R. Schaeffer and other incidents] A. Toufexis. il por *Time* 134:43-4 Jl 31 '89

An innocent life, a heartbreaking death [actress R. Schaeffer killed by obsessive fan and other celebrities who have been threatened] P. Axthelm. il por *People Weekly* 32:60-2+ Jl 31 '89

Justine Bateman becomes the latest celebrity to be menaced by an obsessive fan [J. Smetek apprehended by police] B. Hewitt. il por *People Weekly* 32:112-13 S 25 '89

FANSHAWE, JOHN HEW

Serengeti's painted wolves [cover story] il *Natural History* p56-67 Mr '89

FANTASIES, LITERARY

Fantasy for young readers. S. R. Murphy. *The Writer* 102:19-20+ S '89

Think of the reader. P. Anthony. *The Writer* 102:11-13+ Ag '89

FANTASTIC ARCHITECTURE *See* Architecture, Fantastic

FANTASTIC ART *See* Art, Fantastic

FANTASTIC FURNITURE *See* Furniture, Fantastic

FANTASY

See also

Fairy tales

Sexual fantasy

Daydreaming: was Walter Mitty right? [views of Ed Beckham and Povl Toussieng] *USA Today (Periodical)* 118:9-10 Jl '89

Daydreams: what they tell us about ourselves. E. Glicksman. *McCall's* 116:77-8 Jl '89

Island fantasies [who or what Canadians would take along to a desert island; Maclean's/Decima poll] il *Maclean's* 102:32 Ja 2 '89

One boy's daydream. G. Schwartz. *Seventeen* 48:56 N '89

Who would you like to be tomorrow? [women's fantasies] il *Glamour* 87:144 Mr '89

FANTASY FURNITURE *See* Furniture, Fantastic

FANTASY VACATIONS *See* Vacations

FANTE, JOHN, 1909-1983

about

The hottest dead man in Hollywood. F. Spotnitz. il pors *American Film* 14:40-4+ Jl/Ag '89

FANTEL, HANS

Sight and sound: a bit more. *Opera News* 53:41 Je '89

Sight and sound: best buys '89. il *Opera News* 54:56 N '89

Sight and sound: complete packages. *Opera News* 53:41 Mr 18 '89

Sight and sound: is LP obsolete? il *Opera News* 54:26 Ag '89

Sight and sound: maverick speakers. il *Opera News* 54:36-7 D 23 '89

Sight and sound: the CD at five. *Opera News* 53:41 Ja 7 '89

FANZINES

See also

Motion pictures—Periodicals

FAPA *See* Future Aviation Professionals of America (Firm)

FAR EAST *See* East Asia

FAR EAST NATIONAL BANK

Bradley: down and nearly out? [L.A. mayor T. Bradley] E. Schine. *Business Week* p29 Ag 7 '89

FAR EASTERN AIR TRANSPORT

Far Eastern Air Transport of Taiwan reduces flying hours of older 737s. J. Ott. il *Aviation Week & Space Technology* 130:68 My 8 '89

FAR EASTERN ECONOMIC REVIEW

Looking toward the new Pacific century [interview with D. Davies] A. Balk. por *World Press Review* 36:34+ S '89

FAR NORTH [film] *See* Motion picture reviews—Single works

FAR NORTH RECREATION (FIRM)

Fishing the bush on a budget. N. Strung. il *Field & Stream* 93:42+ Ap '89

FAR SIDE (COMIC STRIP) *See* Comic books, strips, etc.

FARABUNDO MARTÍ NATIONAL LIBERATION FRONT

The battle for San Salvador. J. Smolowe. il *Time* 134:42-4 N 27 '89

Beat the devil [coverage of the strike against Eastern and of the struggle in El Salvador] A. Cockburn. *The Nation* 248:438-9 Ap 3 '89

A bloody misfire on the streets of El Salvador. il *U.S. News & World Report* 107:12-13 N 27 '89

FARABUNDO MARTÍ NATIONAL LIBERATION FRONT—*cont.*

Bush wades into his first quagmire [election proposal from Marxist rebels] il *U.S. News & World Report* 106:12 F 6 '89

Conversations with two foes [J. Villalobos and A. Cristiani] J. Smolowe. il pors *Time* 134:26 O 2 '89

A democratic revolution for El Salvador. J. Villalobos. *Foreign Policy* 74:103-22 Spr '89

El Salvador: behind the lines with the rebels. F. Smyth. il *The Progressive* 53:26-9 F '89

The El Salvador horror [need for papal intervention] *The New Republic* 201:7-9 D 11 '89

Grave thoughts [conversation with Jesuit priest I. Ellacuria nine months before his murder] M. Massing. *The New Republic* 201:12-14 D 11 '89

Guerrilla tactics [FMLN offers to participate in electoral process] S. MacLeod. il *Time* 133:47 F 6 '89

A murderous cross-fire. C. Lane. il map *Newsweek* 114:48-50+ N 27 '89

Negotiations or total war [possible compromise settlement] F. Smyth. il *The Nation* 249:164-6 Ag 7-14 '89

No place to hide. J. F. O. McAllister. il *Time* 134:53-4 D 11 '89

An offer they couldn't refuse [FMLN offensive] J. Moody. il *Time* 133:40 Ja 30 '89

Revolt under the coconut palms. R. Chavira. il *Time* 133:38 Mr 20 '89

A Salvadoran peace 'trap'? [offer to support elections] C. Lane. il *Newsweek* 113:40 F 6 '89

Salvador's silver lining [offer to participate in electoral process] M. Kondracke. *The New Republic* 200:23-5 Mr 13 '89

The Sheraton siege. D. Brand. il *Time* 134:50-1 D 4 '89

FARAH, DOUGLAS, AND GIBB, TOM

Confessions of an assassin. por *Mother Jones* 14:10+ Ja '89

FARAH, JOSEPH

The real blacklist. *National Review* 41:42-3 O 27 '89

FARBER, DANIEL A.

You little tort. *The Washington Monthly* 20:49-50+ Ja '89

FARBER, JIM

The Woodstock (re)generation. il *Seventeen* 48:148+ Ag '89

FARBER, SHARON N., AND KILLUS, JAMES

Last word. il *Omni (New York, N.Y.)* 11:128 Je '89

FARBER, STEPHEN

They watch what we watch. il *The New York Times Magazine* p42+ My 7 '89

FARENTINO, JAMES

about

How her painful divorce helped her on Knots Landing. J. Hicks. il pors *TV Guide* 37:18-20 Ag 5-11 '89

FARES, AIRLINE *See* Airlines—Fares

FAREWELL, KELLY

about

Two faces in a crowd of graduates. J. R. Hacala. *America* 161:190-1 S 30 '89

FARGANIS, SONDRA

(jt. auth) *See* Clifford, Catherine, and Farganis, Sondra

FARHANG, MANSOUR

Rafsanjani's no moderate. il *The Nation* 249:560+ N 13 '89

FARK, WILLIAM E.

California Ballet at twenty: staking a claim. il por *Dance Magazine* 63:52-5 Ja '89

FARLEY, FRANK H.

Taking risks and seeking stimulation: the Type T personality. il *USA Today (Periodical)* 118:60-1 Jl '89

FARLEY, LAURENCE J.

about

Last chance for Love? G. L. Miles. *Business Week* p31-2 Ap 24 '89

FARLEY, WILLIAM F.

about

Bill Farley is on pins and needles. D. Greising. il por *Business Week* p58+ S 18 '89

Billion-dollar mind. C. Bruck. *The New Yorker* 65:76-88 Ag 7 '89

FARLEY INDUSTRIES INC.

Bill Farley is on pins and needles [West Point-Pepperell takeover] D. Greising. il por *Business Week* p58+ S 18 '89

Billion-dollar mind [W. Farley's acquisition of West Point-Pepperell] C. Bruck. *The New Yorker* 65:76-88 Ag 7 '89

FARM ACCIDENTS *See* Agriculture—Accidents

FARM ANIMALS *See* Livestock

FARM ANIMALS, TREATMENT OF *See* Animals—Treatment

FARM BEAUTIFUL! (PROJECT)

Farm Beautiful! D. Mowitz and B. Freese. il *Successful Farming* 87:51-5 mid-Mr '89

FARM BUILDINGS

See also

Barns and stables

Swine houses

FARM CHILDREN

Courage on wheels. D. Gosch. il por *The Mother Earth News* 119:38-9 S/O '89

How to help your children farm. G. Johnston. *Successful Farming* 87:6 Ap '89

Less than half confident farm will pass to kids. B. Freese. *Successful Farming* 87:8 D '89

Passing down the dream [passing the family farm to the next generation] B. Freese. il *Successful Farming* 87:26-9 O '89

Sharing the farm with kids in need. B. Freese. il *Successful Farming* 87:56 D '89

We kill too many farm kids [special section] C. Tevis and C. Finck. il *Successful Farming* 87:18A-18B+ mid-F '89

FARM COOPERATIVES *See* Agriculture, Cooperative

FARM CORPORATIONS

Can their problem be solved? See issues of Successful Farming beginning January 1988

Laws and regulations

Group wants laws tightened on 'big' farm. *Successful Farming* 87:64C Ap '89

FARM CREDIT *See* Agricultural credit

FARM DOGS *See* Dogs

FARM EQUIPMENT *See* Agricultural equipment

FARM EQUIPMENT INDUSTRY *See* Agricultural equipment industry

FARM FINANCE *See* Agriculture—Economic aspects

FARM HOUSE FOODS CORP.

The beauty beneath the beast. R. Koselka. il por *Forbes* 144:240+ N 27 '89

FARM HOUSES *See* Farmhouses

FARM LABOR

See also

Detasselers (Farm labor)

Migrant labor

Peasantry

Sugar workers

Youth Opportunity: a private sector investment in prevention [summer work at Domino's Pizza Inc.'s Whatley Farm in Ann Arbor, Mich.] C. H. Tice. il *Children Today* 18:20-3 Mr/Ap '89

FARM LEGISLATION *See* Agricultural administration

FARM LIFE

Farm wife shares drought journal of despair, hope. M. Wilcox. il *Successful Farming* 87:66AI F '89

Long road home to an upland farm. M. Kumin. il *Country Journal* 16:75-9 My/Je '89

Anecdotes, facetiae, satire, etc.

To hell with farming! [reprint of 1940 essay in the American Mercury] il *The Mother Earth News* 119:144+ S/O '89

FARM MACHINERY *See* Agricultural equipment

FARM MANAGEMENT

See also

Cattle farm management

Custom farming

Farm corporations

Farms—Size

Swine farm management

Can their problem be solved? See issues of Successful Farming beginning January 1988

Gene Johnston [risk management in farming] G. Johnston. il *Successful Farming* 87:7 mid-Mr '89

His own labor, custom work turns farm around. il *Successful Farming* 87:66I F '89

How to help your children farm. G. Johnston. *Successful Farming* 87:6 Ap '89

The perfect 600-acre farm. G. Johnston and D. Allen. il *Successful Farming* 87:8-9 mid-F '89

Successful family farm [Koskan family of Wood, S.D.] J. Walter. il *Successful Farming* 87:46-8 D '89

Successful family farm [Milligan family of Dana, Ind.] M. Holmberg. il pors *Successful Farming* 87:60-2 O '89

FARM MARRIAGE

Can their problem be solved? D. J. Jonovic and W. D. Messick. *Successful Farming* 87:60 N '89

For better, for worse. B. Freese. il *Successful Farming* 87:46-8+ Je '89

FARM MECHANIZATION

See also

Harvesting machinery

FARM OWNERSHIP

Less than half confident farm will pass to kids. B. Freese. *Successful Farming* 87:8 D '89

Passing down the dream [passing the family farm to the next generation] B. Freese. il *Successful Farming* 87:26-9 O '89

FARM POLICY *See* Agricultural administration

FARM PONDS *See* Ponds

FARM PRICE SUPPORTS *See* Agricultural administration

FARM PRICES *See* Farm produce—Prices

FARM PRODUCE

See also

Surplus products, Agricultural

Going for the great-taste health diet. R. Rodale. il *Prevention (Emmaus, Pa.)* 41:30+ F '89

Marketing

See also

Farmers' markets

Produce trade

Farmer/adviser puts his money where his advice is [W. De Young] *Successful Farming* 87:50E Ja '89

FARM PRODUCE—Marketing—*cont.*
Gene Johnston production. G. Johnston. il *Successful Farming* 87:15 S '89
'I'm in the dark' [views of R. Allen] G. Johnston. il por *Successful Farming* 87:34X mid-F '89
Market advisers get a report card. il *Successful Farming* 87:15 mid-Mr '89
Marketing. See issues of Successful Farming

Prices
See also
Agricultural administration
There will be no silent spring for these farmers [trend towards organic farming in wake of pesticide scare] il *U.S. News & World Report* 106:13 Ap 3 '89
Why $2.60 corn should be worth at least $5.50! il *Successful Farming* 87:40H Ag '89

FARM RENTS
Cash rents volatile, risky. R. Fee. *Successful Farming* 87:12 Ja '89
Share risk with owners, and keep 'em smiling. J. Carlson. il *Successful Farming* 87:8-9 mid-Mr '89

FARM SHOPS *See* Workshops
FARM SIZE *See* Farms—Size
FARM TAXATION *See* Farmers—Taxation
FARM TEAMS (BASEBALL) *See* Baseball, Professional—Minor leagues
FARM TENANCY
See also
Farm rents
Sharecropping
Nobody loves their lease. R. Fee. *Successful Farming* 87:16 F '89

FARM WASTE

Disposal
See also
Swine houses—Sanitation
Anatomy of a fish kill [Spruce Creek, Pa.] J. Bashline. il *Field & Stream* 93:38+ F '89
Rural America laid to waste. C. Tevis. il *Successful Farming* 87:32-4 O '89

FARM WOMEN
Cheryl Tevis. C. Tevis. See issues of Successful Farming beginning March 1989
Joint venture. C. Tevis. See issues of Successful Farming beginning September 1984 through January 1989
Lobbyist in the winter/farmer in the summer [K. Kelley] il por *Successful Farming* 87:39 Ja '89

Employment
What farmers are saying. C. Tevis. il *Successful Farming* 87:56 mid-Mr '89

FARM WORKERS *See* Farm labor
FARMAN FARMAIAN, ROXANE
High-tech cures for the time crunch. il *Psychology Today* 23:46-8 Mr '89
Worksteading. il *Psychology Today* 23:37-8+ N '89

FARMER, FOREST J.
about
Forest Farmer: Chrysler's component parts president. C. Whitaker. il pors *Ebony* 44:90-2+ Mr '89

FARMER, GARY
about
Highway of dreams. B. D. Johnson. il por *Maclean's* 102:62-3 Ap 24 '89

FARMER-HUNTER RELATIONS
Dove hunting with a difference [dove farming] G. Reiger. il *Field & Stream* 94:50-1+ S '89
Hunter etiquette. J. Bashline. il *Field & Stream* 94:24+ S '89

Anecdotes, facetiae, satire, etc.
Social skills. P. F. McManus. il *Outdoor Life* 184:144+ S '89

FARMER MAC *See* Federal Agricultural Mortgage Corporation
FARMER-PATRICK, SANDRA
about
A pair of aces. M. Noden. il pors *Sports Illustrated* 71:64-6+ O 16 '89
World-class speed, family style. il pors *Ebony* 45:116+ D '89

FARMERS
See also
Agriculture
Black farmers
Farm children
Farm women
Farmer-hunter relations
Nuns as farmers
The last farmer [condensation] H. Kohn. il *Reader's Digest* 134:115-20 Mr '89

Attitudes
Across the editor's desk. L. J. Kruse. il *Successful Farming* 87:1 Je '89
What farmers are saying. See issues of Successful Farming beginning March 1989

Economic conditions
See Agriculture—Economic aspects

Health and hygiene
See also
National Coalition for Agricultural Safety and Health

Rural health. C. Tevis. See issues of Successful Farming beginning March 1989
These rural hospitals want to lose their patients [Iowa] C. Tevis. il *Successful Farming* 87:50AR Ja '89

Political activities
Across the editor's desk [importance of participating in county government] L. J. Kruse. il *Successful Farming* 87:2 O '89
Agriculture's hell-raising nun [Sister Thomas More Bertels] J. Midgett. il por *Successful Farming* 87:33 F '89
PACs: farmers' $8-million muscle man. P. Smith. il *Successful Farming* 87:8-9 Ap '89

Psychology
What farmers are saying. C. Tevis. il *Successful Farming* 87:49 My '89

Public relations
Cheryl Tevis. C. Tevis. il *Successful Farming* 87:35 Je '89

Retirement
Can their problem be solved? *Successful Farming* 87:52 D '89
'Can we afford dad's retirement?'. *Successful Farming* 87 no4:54 Mr '89

Taxation
A tax cut! What it'll mean to you. *Successful Farming* 87:14 N '89

FARMER'S ALMANAC *See* Almanacs
FARMERS AS ARTISTS
Cultivating art in the heartland [crop art by S. Herd] L. Barash. il *National Wildlife* 27:30-3 Je/Jl '89
The grandest art on earth [crop art by S. Herd] G. Sledge. il *Reader's Digest* 134:178-80 My '89

FARMERS HOME ADMINISTRATION (U.S.) *See* United States. Farmers Home Administration
FARMERS' MARKETS
To market, to market [Damariscotta, Me.] R. F. Baldwin. il *Country Journal* 16:51-4 Jl/Ag '89

FARMERS' MUSEUM
A winter day in the life of a 19th century farmstead. E. Pilcher. il *The Conservationist* 43:34-9 Ja/F '89

FARMERS' WIVES *See* Farm women
FARMHOUSES
See also
House decoration
Art of Eastover: Clare and Eugene Thaw in upstate New York. S. M. Alsop. il por *Architectural Digest* 46:118-25+ Je '89
Escape to Normandy [P. Mathieu's and M. Ray's farmhouse; cover story] C. K. Gandee. il pors *House & Garden* 161:96-105+ F '89
The essence of Provence [home of J. and I. Amic] C. Carter. il por *House & Garden* 161:126-31+ Jl '89
Farm-fresh style [home of Liz and Peter Robinson] S. S. Soria and D. A. Jimerson. il *Better Homes and Gardens* 67:75-89 Ap '89
Hunt country [master of the hunt R. Smith-Ryland's 16th century farmhouse in Warwickshire] G. Nevill. il pors *House & Garden* 161:132-9 Mr '89
Killearn Farm: F. William Free's Hudson Valley horse farm. J. Gruen. il por *Architectural Digest* 46:182-7+ Je '89
A minka revival: Japanese farmhouse traditions reinterpreted in Hawaii. M. Webb. il *Architectural Digest* 46:198-204 Ag '89
Norman retreat [N. Worms' 1823 timbered farmhouse] R. Koenig. il *House & Garden* 161:142-7+ Jl '89
A Philadelphia story: Edgar and Hope Scott at Ardrossan Farms. M. Tree. il por *Architectural Digest* 46:164-9 Je '89
Rustic frame for a modern collection: the Connecticut house of Katharine and Nicholas Fox Weber [18th century farmhouse and converted barn] R. W. B. Lewis. il *Architectural Digest* 46:200-5+ Je '89
Sympathetic, but separate [addition to 200 year old farmhouse in West Virginia] il *Southern Living* 24:120-1 O '89
The Vermont farmhouse. il *Esquire* 112:98 O '89

FARMHOUSES, REMODELED *See* Houses, Remodeled
FARMING *See* Agriculture
FARMING, ORGANIC *See* Organic farming
FARMING, TRUCK *See* Truck farming
FARMING COOPERATIVES *See* Agriculture, Cooperative
FARMING IN THE FLYWAYS (PROGRAM)
The farmer's secret. J. Walter. il *Successful Farming* 87:52 Je '89
Farming in the Flyways. J. Walter. il *Successful Farming* 87:60 My '89
Farming in the Flyways. J. Walter. il maps *Successful Farming* 87:59-61 Ap '89

FARMLAND VALUES *See* Land values
FARMS
See also
Agriculture
Plantations

Size
See also
Farms, Small
The 400 largest farms in the U.S. [with editorial comment by Loren Kruse] G. Johnston and D. Ohrtman. il *Successful Farming* 87:1, 8-15 My '89

FARMS, SMALL
Family farms forever! [Tuttle farm in New Hampshire named oldest in America] J. Walter. il map *Successful Farming* 87:22-4 Ja '89
A fighter for family farming [M. Strange] il por *Successful Farming* 87:24-5 Ja '89
Helping farms caught in the middle [farm policy] W. Meyers. il *Successful Farming* 87:48U mid-Mr '89
Saving the family farm can benefit all of us. F. M. Lappé. il *Utne Reader* p86 Jl/Ag '89
Who says the family farm is dead? Welcome to future farming's best bet [specialty farms] G. Logsdon. il *Utne Reader* p82-8 Jl/Ag '89

FARMSTEAD FOODS (FIRM)
Meatpacking settlements. il *Monthly Labor Review* 112:41 Ap '89

FARNAN, IAN
(jt. auth) See Stebbins, Jonathan F., and Farnan, Ian

FARNBOROUGH AIR SHOW *See* Aviation—Exhibitions

FARNER, MARK
about
Mark Farner. M. Azerrad. *Rolling Stone* p52+ Ag 10 '89

FARNSWORTH, ELIZABETH
Privatizing Peru [interview with M. Vargas Llosa] il *New Perspectives Quarterly* 6:38-41 Fall '89
The temptation of Mario. il por *Mother Jones* 14:22-6+ Ja '89

FARNSWORTH, ELMA
Mrs. Philo T. Farnsworth: on a potato field and the farm boy inventor of television. il por *People Weekly* 31 Special Issue:155 Summ '89

FARNSWORTH, PHILO T., 1906-1971
about
Mrs. Philo T. Farnsworth: on a potato field and the farm boy inventor of television. E. Farnsworth. il por *People Weekly* 31 Special Issue:155 Summ '89

FAROCKI, HARUN
about
In the eye of the beholder: poetic documentaries about technology. K. Rosenberg. il *Technology Review* 92:62-8 F/Mr '89

FARR, MICHAEL K.
Tips on finding an investment advisor. il *Consumers' Research Magazine* 72:35-7 N '89

FARRAND, JOHN L.
(tr) See Salin, Dominique. Education in France: renewal in the secondary schools

FARRAND, ROBERT W.
Human rights issues in Africa [statement, February 8, 1989] *Department of State Bulletin* 89:32 My '89

FARRAND, WILLIAM R.
Lunar prospecting [cover story] il *Ad Astra* 1:8-12 F '89

FARRAR STRAUS & GIROUX, INC.
FSG signs second novel from Scott Turow. G. Feldman. por *Publishers Weekly* 236:92 S 15 '89

FARRELL, DAVID
about
As the wheel turns. D. B. Cowin. il por *House & Garden* 161:76 Je '89

FARRELL, JANE
Memories of Mary Jo. il pors *Ladies' Home Journal* 106:108-10+ Jl '89

FARRELL, JANE, AND GRAY, BARBARA BRONSON
Marilyn Quayle: the woman nobody knows. il pors *Ladies' Home Journal* 106:84+ O '89

FARRELL, KATHY
Hearty one-dish suppers. il *McCall's* 117:49+ N '89

FARRELL, M. J. *See* Keane, Molly

FARRELL, MARY
about
As the wheel turns. D. B. Cowin. il por *House & Garden* 161:76 Je '89

FARRELL, SUZANNE, 1945-
about
Notes and comment. *The New Yorker* 65:44-6 D 11 '89

FARRELLY, PETER
Falling out of love with L.A. por *Newsweek* 114:8 S 25 '89

FARRÈRE, MICHEL
Secular Turkey. *World Press Review* 36:34 Jl '89

FARSIGHTEDNESS *See* Presbyopia

FARUQUI, AKHTAR MAHMUD
An Academy of Sciences for the third world. il *The Unesco Courier* 42:50 N '89

FAS *See* Fetal alcohol syndrome

FASANELLA, RALPH, 1914-
about
Ideal union. N. Gill. il por *Mother Jones* 14:16 N '89

FASB *See* Financial Accounting Standards Board

FASCH, JOHANN FRIEDRICH, 1688-1758
about
Fasch, Johann Friedrich: Various works. P. Moor. por *High Fidelity (New York, N.Y.)* 39:68-9 Ja '89

FASCISM
See also
National socialism

Italy
History
Fiddling in fascist Italy. H. Sachs. il *Opera News* 53:28-30 Mr 4 '89

FASCISM AND MUSIC
Fiddling in fascist Italy. H. Sachs. il *Opera News* 53:28-30 Mr 4 '89

FASEL, IDA
Playing the parts [poem] *The Christian Century* 106:956 O 25 '89
Worshipfully [poem] *The Christian Century* 106:350 Ap 5 '89

FASH, WILLIAM L.
(jt. auth) See Fasquelle, Ricardo Agurcia, and Fash, William L.

FASHION
See also
Circle in fashion
Clothing and dress
Color in fashion
Costume
Dress accessories
Hairstyling
Sex and fashion
Tailoring
Trash (Style)
American style! The Palm Beach story. A. Stanley. il *Vogue* 179:274-93 F '89
Blast from the past [1960s and current fashion] il *'Teen* 33:8 F '89
Chic savages [excerpt] J. Fairchild. il por *New York* 22:44-54 O 16 '89
Close fit [influence of athletic clothes] D. Schefer. il *Vogue* 179:408-15 Ap '89
Couture report: the four schools of design. J. J. Buck. il *Vogue* 179:324-5+ O '89
The cutting edge. M. Gross. See issues of New York beginning February 22, 1988
Fashion. C. Donovan. See occasional issues of The New York Times Magazine
Fashion workshop. See issues of Glamour
Images: French style. J. J. Buck. il *Vogue* 179:57-8+ Jl '89
Is everybody ready for Star trek chic? il *U.S. News & World Report* 106:16 Mr 13 '89
Joan Juliet Buck unravels the complex structure of Italian style and makes some astonishing discoveries. J. J. Buck. il *Vogue* 179:143-4+ D '89
L.A. international. B. Bull. il *Vogue* 179:332-5 F '89
Modernism outmoded. H. Brubach. *The New Yorker* 65:102-9 N 20 '89
An old look is new again [black street fashions] N. Darnton. il *Newsweek* 114:78-9 O 16 '89
On the prowl with vulgar chic [animal prints] J. D. Reed. il *Time* 134:92 O 16 '89
Potpourri. C. Donovan. il *The New York Times Magazine* p30-1 Ja 1 '89
School of Chanel [continuing influence of C. Chanel] H. Brubach. *The New Yorker* 65:71-6 F 27 '89
View. See issues of Vogue
The Vogue 100. C. Heimel. il *Vogue* 179:262-9 Je '89
What do you want from fashion right now! [survey results] A. Kleiner. il *Glamour* 87:207+ Mr '89
Anecdotes, facetiae, satire, etc.
From my lips to your hips. C. Faux. il *Ms.* 18:18+ S '89
History
Spines like us. J. Shields. il *Vogue* 179:228-9 Ja '89
Timeless style. il *Glamour* 87:290-9 Ap '89
Periodicals
See also
Glamour (Periodical)
Mirabella (Periodical)
Vogue (Periodical)

FASHION AND ART
See also
Wearable art
Museums of modern garb. N. Darnton. il *Newsweek* 113:78 F 27 '89

FASHION AND SEX *See* Sex and fashion

FASHION DESIGNERS
See also
Abboud, Joseph, 1950-
Adolfo, 1933-
Adzer, Laise
Agrusa, Lisa
Amies, Hardy
Armani, Giorgio
B., Agnes
Balenciaga
Banks, Jeffrey, 1954-
Beene, Geoffrey
Bikkembergs, Dirk
Blair, Alistair
Bruce, Liza
Canovas, Isabel
Carven, Madame
Castelbajac, Jean-Charles de
Chanel, Coco, 1883-1971
Charles, Caroline

FASHION DESIGNERS—See also—*cont.*
    Choron, Gaston
    Claiborne, Liz
    Comstock, Robert
    Connolly, Sybil
    De la Renta, Oscar
    De Prémonville, Myrène
    Dior, Christian, 1905-1957
    Duroché, Julie
    Edelstein, Victor
    Eisen, Mark
    Ellis, Perry
    Ferré, Gianfranco
    Fezza, Andrew
    Flusser, Alan (Alan J.)
    Fortuny y Madrazo, Mariano
    Galliano, John
    Gertz, Geoffry
    Gigli, Romeo
    Halston
    Harcourt, Michel
    Hayes, David
    Heller, Nancy
    Hempel, Anouska
    Henderson, Gordon
    Herrera, Carolina
    Jacobs, Marc, 1963-
    Johnson, Betsey
    Karan, Donna
    Karesh, Lance
    Kawakubo, Rei
    Kelly, Patrick
    Kors, Michael
    Lacroix, Christian
    Lagerfeld, Karl
    Lamy, Michele
    Lauren, Ralph
    Leva, Michael
    London, Rachel
    Mackie, Bob
    Max, Leon
    McFadden, Mary
    Mizrahi, Isaac
    Monacella, Suzana
    Montana, Claude
    Morgan, Donna
    Mori, Hanae
    Moschino, Franco
    Moses, Rebecca
    Neuville, Charlotte
    Ozbek, Rifat
    Ribes, Jacqueline de
    Ricci, Robert, 1905-1988
    Robinson, Bill, 1949-
    Roehm, Carolyne
    Rogers, Jackie
    Roth, Christian Francis
    Russo, Janet
    Saint Laurent, Yves
    Sanchez, Fernando
    Sant' Angelo, Giorgio
    Scaasi, Arnold, 1932?-
    Shamask, Ronaldus
    Sitbon, Martine
    Smith, Paul
    Smith, Willi
    Soprani, Luciano
    Stavropoulos, George, 1920-
    Steffe, Cynthia
    Sybilla, 1963-
    Tiel, Vicky
    Trigère, Pauline
    Valentino
    Vass, Joan
American independents. C. R. Milbank. il *Vogue* 179:106-7+ D '89
The attitude sell. G. Howell. il *Vogue* 179:370+ Mr '89
The business of chic [Paris fashion industry] N. Hyde. il *National Geographic* 176:146-57 Jl '89
Chic savages [excerpt] J. Fairchild. il por *New York* 22:44-54 O 16 '89
Couture for the comrades [Soviet designers] N. Traver. il *Time* 133:128 Ap 10 '89
A cute number for the taxman [IRS investigates N. Reagan's borrowing of designer clothes] il por *Time* 134:42 D 18 '89
Fashion fidelity. N. Malkin. il *Vogue* 179:104-5+ My '89
French impressions [Paris] il *Harper's Bazaar* 122:108-17 Ja '89
Gonna dress you up [rock couturiers] J. Conlin. il *Rolling Stone* Fashion Collection:51-6+ Ap 20 '89
The new rack pack [American fashion] D. Michals. il *Harper's Bazaar* 122:82+ O '89
Rare flair. il *Harper's Bazaar* 122:110-21 My '89
Sometimes a designer's inspiration comes from a snip of fringe, an old photo, a string of beads. P. Green. il *Vogue* 179:36-8 Jl '89

Special fashion issue [cover story] il *Architectural Digest* 46:29+ S '89
Upward bound. C. Donovan. il *The New York Times Magazine* p108-11 S 10 '89
What they're wearing in bed. C. Donovan. il *The New York Times Magazine* p96-7 N 12 '89
The wild bunch. M. Gross. il *New York* 22:30+ D 4 '89
                   Nutrition
A fashionable love affair with food [favorite restaurants of fashion designers in Milan] C. Petkanas. il *Harper's Bazaar* 122:81+ Ja '89
                   Travel
Great escapes. D. Michals. il *Harper's Bazaar* 122:106+ D '89
FASHION DRAWING
          Collectors and collecting
A rare collection of classic Hollywood costume sketches [L. Stanley] J. Chatfield-Taylor. il por *Architectural Digest* 46:250+ S '89
FASHION FAIR COSMETICS, INC.
Fashion Fair maintains poise. il *Black Enterprise* 19:50-1 Mr '89
FASHION INDUSTRY *See* Clothing industry
FASHION PHOTOGRAPHY *See* Photography, Fashion
FASHION PROGRAMS (CABLE TELEVISION) *See* Cable television—Fashion programs
FASHION SHOWS
      See also
      Ground Crew (Firm)
The allure of Milan and London [fall collections] R. La Ferla. il *The New York Times Magazine* p82-4 Je 4 '89
Between times [fall ready-to-wear shows and costume exhibitions in Paris] H. Brubach. *The New Yorker* 65:100-2+ Ap 24 '89
The big surprise on Seventh Ave. C. Donovan. il *The New York Times Magazine* p86-90 My 14 '89
The business of chic [Paris fashion industry] N. Hyde. il *National Geographic* 176:146-57 Jl '89
Class notes. N. Scovell. il *Vogue* 179:400 F '89
Do your earrings hang low, do they wobble to and fro? At big name shows, the style's jumbo [dangling clip-on earrings] il *People Weekly* 32:175 N 20 '89
Everyone cheers the couture, says André Leon Talley, but only a special woman puts her money where her mouth is [Paris] A. L. Talley. il *Vogue* 179:480 O '89
Fashion without frontiers [Valentino and R. Gigli show in Paris rather than Milan] J. Cocks. il pors *Time* 133:94 Mr 20 '89
French fashion goes global. N. Darnton. il *Newsweek* 114:75-6 N 6 '89
Halting the slump [Canada] B. Wickens. il *Maclean's* 102:36+ Ap 10 '89
Influence peddlers [New York collections] M. Gross. il *New York* 22:22+ My 8 '89
Lace at $300 a yard [Paris' haute couture industry] R. Morais. il *Forbes* 144 Special Issue:76-8+ O 23 '89
Landing front-row seats at fashion shows is a socioeconomic coup. B. Handy. il *Vogue* 179:218-20 Jl '89
Lookahead: Fall. il *Harper's Bazaar* 122:15-17 Je '89
The looks from Milan. P. McColl. il *The New York Times Magazine* p100-4 Mr 5 '89
Major moves in Paris [fall collections] C. Donovan. il *The New York Times Magazine* p70-4 Je 4 '89
Milan, London and Madrid. R. La Ferla. il *The New York Times Magazine* p48-52 F 5 '89
Modernism outmoded [Milan ready-to-wear collections] H. Brubach. *The New Yorker* 65:102-9 N 20 '89
The 'New' new look [Paris fall collections] M. Gross. il *New York* 22:33-4+ Ap 10 '89
New York. C. Donovan. il *The New York Times Magazine* p84-90 O 29 '89
New York. C. Donovan. il *The New York Times Magazine* p84-90 Ap 2 '89
Paris. C. Donovan. il *The New York Times Magazine* p44-6 F 5 '89
Paris. P. McColl. il *The New York Times Magazine* p90-6 Mr 12 '89
Paris. P. McColl. il *The New York Times Magazine* p56-60 O 15 '89
The Paris couture: shaping up. C. Donovan. il *The New York Times Magazine* p44-8 Ag 27 '89
Paris couture today. C. Donovan. il *The New York Times Magazine* p42-5 Jl 23 '89
Paris: inside couture. il pors *Harper's Bazaar* 122:151-61 Ap '89
The Paris revue. il *Vogue* 179:368-79 Ap '89
Return of the native: Europe's spring collections. M. Gross. il *New York* 22:26+ N 13 '89
A season that can't make up its mind [fall 1989 lines] N. Darnton. il *Newsweek* 113:56-7 Ap 3 '89
Sexy chic [Paris fashions] C. Donovan. il *The New York Times Magazine* p82-5 F 19 '89
Think beige? [New York's collections] M. Gross. il *New York* 22:28-9 N 20 '89
Will bare be beautiful? [spring 1990 collections] C. Donovan. il *The New York Times Magazine* p130-4 D 3 '89

FASHION SHOWS—*cont.*
With crosses, cloaks, and long satin skirts, designers bring the women of Sicily down the runway. il *Vogue* 179:108 O '89
FASHION VIDEOS *See* Videotapes—Fashion
FASMAN, ZACHARY D.
Should the Senate approve the "Americans with Disabilities Act of 1989"? [excerpts from testimony, May 9, 1989] *Congressional Digest* 68:299+ D '89
FASQUELLE, RICARDO AGURCIA, AND FASH, WILLIAM L.
Copán: a royal Maya tomb discovered. il map *National Geographic* 176:480-7 O '89
FAST, HOWARD, 1914-
about
Mr. Fast explains. W. F. Buckley. *National Review* 41:62-3 F 24 '89
FAST FOOD RESTAURANT EMPLOYEES
Luring youth to fast-food jobs [research by Bonnie M. Farber] il *USA Today (Periodical)* 118:7 Ag '89
Training
Tuition payments cut job turnover [Burger King in downtown Detroit] S. D. Rinella and R. J. Kopecky. il por *Nation's Business* 77:25-6 Ag '89
FAST FOOD RESTAURANTS
See also
Arby's Inc.
Burger King Corporation
Church's Fried Chicken, Inc.
Drive-in restaurants
Hardee's Food Systems, Inc.
In-N-Out Burger (Firm)
McDonald's Corp.
PepsiCo, Inc.
Popeyes Famous Fried Chicken & Biscuits Inc.
Wendy's International Inc.
Among restaurateurs, it's dog eat dog. B. Bremner. il *Business Week* p86 Ja 9 '89
Fast food fare and nutrition. C. Roberts. il *Consumers' Research Magazine* 72:30-3 D '89
This fast food won't slow down your diet. E. Kunes. il *Mademoiselle* 95:260 S '89
Acquisitions and mergers
International aspects
Trying to get Burger King out of the flames [Grand Met executive B. J. Gibbons] M. Maremont. il por *Business Week* p29-30 Ja 30 '89
Advertising
Wendy's burger king [founder R. D. Thomas stars in commercials] J. Nocera. il por *Esquire* 112:69-71 N '89
Collectibles
Hamburger heaven: a burger blitz [collection of J. Tennyson] T. Mewborne. il por *Antiques & Collecting Hobbies* 94:22-5 D '89
International aspects
Anecdotes, facetiae, satire, etc.
Uncivil liberties. C. Trillin. il *The Nation* 248:473 Ap 10 '89
Canada
See also
McDonald's Restaurants of Canada Ltd.
United States
See Fast food restaurants
FAST LANE *See* Time pressure
FASTENERS
See also
Nails
Rivets and riveting
Screws
Staples and stapling machines
Zippers
Hardware for fast assembly [KD hardware] T. H. Jones. il *Home Mechanix* 85:25-9 Jl '89
Wood to concrete. D. Stoffel and D. Johnson. il *The Family Handyman* 39:53-6 Ap '89
FASTING
See also
Hunger strikes
FASTS AND FEASTS
See also
Advent
All Souls' Day
Ash Wednesday
Carnival (Pre-Lenten festival)
Christmas
Easter
Epiphany
Lent
High days and holidays [cover story; special issue] il *The Unesco Courier* 42:8-46 D '89
Buddhism
The Pavilion of the Second Moon [festival celebrated at Buddhist monastery, Nara, Japan] L. Caillet. il *The Unesco Courier* 42:24-31 D '89
Catholic Church
See also
Jesus Christ the King, Feast of

How holy days can catch the holiday spirit. J. Deedy. il *U.S. Catholic* 54:18-25 Ja '89
Judaism
See also
Hanukkah
Passover
Rosh Hashanah
Seder
FAT
See also
Lean body mass
Lipids
Obesity
Bad news bellies [paunchiness linked to diabetes and heart disease in men] D. Grady. il *American Health* 8:20 My '89
The fats of life [body fat percentage and tennis players] M. Bloom. il *World Tennis* 37:92-5 S '89
Hips hooray! Heartening news for the pear shaped [waist-to-hip ratio; research by C. Wayne Callaway] P. S. Derron. il *Mademoiselle* 95:136 Ag '89
The paunch line [link between waist-to-hip girth ratio and health; research by Richard Terry] J. Poppy. il *Esquire* 111:59-60 F '89
The paunch line [link between waist-to-hip girth ratio and health; research by Richard Terry] J. Poppy. il *Reader's Digest* 135:133-5 Ag '89
FAT CONTENT OF FOODS *See* Food—Fat content
FAT FARMS *See* Health resorts, watering places, etc.
FAT MAN AND LITTLE BOY [film] *See* Motion picture reviews—Single works
FAT SUBSTITUTES
See also
Sucrose polyesters
FAT VACUUMING (COSMETIC SURGERY) *See* Liposuction
FATE, TOM MONTGOMERY- *See* Montgomery-Fate, Tom
FATHER DOWLING MYSTERIES [television program] *See* Television program reviews—Single works
FATHER KNOWS BEST [television program] *See* Television program reviews—Single works
FATHER-SON CORPORATIONS *See* Family corporations
FATHERHOOD OF GOD *See* God
FATHERS
See also
Daddy track
Divorced fathers
Overprotective parents
Parent education
Paternity
Paternity leaves
Single fathers
Stepparents and stepchildren
Support (Domestic relations)
About fathers. See issues of Parents beginning July 1985
Are dads doing more? K. Levine. il *Parents* 64:73-6 Je '89
The benefits of fatherhood [research by John Snarey and others] M. Roberts. il *Psychology Today* 23:76 Mr '89
Bittersweet victory [Ontario court decides abortion case in favor of woman B. Dodd] G. W. Taylor. il por *Maclean's* 102:18 Jl 24 '89
Bringing up daddy [cover story; with editorial comment by Lisa Grunwald] bibl il *Esquire* 112:35, 116-20+ N '89
The changing role of fathers. R. M. Barkin. il *USA Today (Periodical)* 118:56-7 Jl '89
Dads' big role. B. Weissbourd. il *Parents* 64:158 Jl '89
Does father know best? [fathers' rights and abortion] P. Orenstein. *Vogue* 179:314+ Ap '89
Equal rights: not for women only [fathers' rights and abortion] M. J. Weiss. il *Glamour* 87:276-7+ Mr '89
Father's rights case declined by High Court. *Christianity Today* 33:53 Ja 13 '89
Flex-time fathers. H. Herman. il *Health (New York, N.Y.)* 21:44-9 Ja '89
Gay and lesbian couples. J. Seligmann. il *Newsweek* 114 Special Issue:38-40 Wint '89/Spr '90
Help your husband be a great dad. J. Marzollo. il *Parents* 64:98-102 S '89
Hollywood's proud new papas. D. Lamanna. il *Ladies' Home Journal* 106:46-7 Mr '89
"I'm still doing everything" [sharing child care responsibilities] M. D. Rosen. il *Ladies' Home Journal* 106:20+ N '89
My husband was afraid to be a father. il *Good Housekeeping* 209:34+ S '89
The "new father": no real role reversal [views of Michael Lamb] il *USA Today (Periodical)* 118:11 Jl '89
Second generation: children tell why they follow in their parents' footsteps. il *Jet* 76:58-60 Je 19 '89
What makes a good dad? E. Greer. il *Good Housekeeping* 208:40 Je '89
Without office. A. Gelb. il *Parents* 64:204 F '89
Yes, you can work at home. R. Cohen. il *Parents* 64:64+ Jl '89
Photographs and photography
Capturing a love he missed out on, a photographer pays homage to dads and sons [work of S. Begleiter] il por *People Weekly* 31:123-6 Je 19 '89

FATHERS—Photographs and photography—*cont.*
Fathers & sons [excerpt] S. Begleiter. il *Parents* 64:143-5 Je '89
FATHERS, UNMARRIED *See* Single fathers
FATHERS AND CHILDREN *See* Parent-child relationship
FATHERS AND CHILDREN IN LITERATURE *See* Parent-child relationship in literature
FATHER'S DAY BRUNCHES *See* Brunches
FATIGUE
See also
Chronic fatigue syndrome
Relaxation
Countering the chemistry of fatigue. M. Rhodes. il *Health (New York, N.Y.)* 21:48-9 F '89
Ill, or just the blahs? B. H. Dobkin. il *The New York Times Magazine* p36-7 Jl 16 '89
Too tired too often? Vitamins can work wonders. R. N. Podell. il *Redbook* 172:108-9+ Ja '89
Vitamin vigor [deficiency in B and C vitamins linked to fatigue after exercising; research by Erik van der Beek] V. Brower. *American Health* 8:36 Jl/Ag '89
FATIGUE OF METALS *See* Metals—Fatigue
FATS *See* Oils and fats, Edible
FATT, AMELIA
about
Amelia's island. S. Nelson. il pors *Working Woman* 14:198-202 S '89
FAUBUS, ORVAL
about
Former Arkansas gov. Orval Faubus honors Daisy Bates. pors *Jet* 76:30 Ag 21 '89
FAUCETS *See* Plumbing
FAUCI, ANTHONY S.
about
Bush goes 0 for 2 with Anthony Fauci. B. J. Culliton. por *Science* 246:880 N 17 '89
FAULKNER, D. L.
about
Fast money and fraud. A. Pusey. il pors *The New York Times Magazine* p30-2+ Ap 23 '89
FAULKNER, WILLIAM, 1897-1962
about
Answering Faulkner. L. Phillips. il *America* 160:452-3 My 13 '89
Faulkner's Mississippi [cover story] W. Morris. il por *National Geographic* 175:312-39 Mr '89
FAULTS (GEOLOGY)
See also
Project PROBE
Another California seismic hot spot [southern Santa Cruz segment of San Andreas fault] R. A. Kerr. map *Science* 245:704 Ag 18 '89
Bay Area shock may foreshadow strong quake [San Andreas fault in southern Santa Cruz mountains] R. Monastersky. *Science News* 136:119 Ag 19 '89
Hidden earthquakes [cover story] R. S. Stein and R. S. Yeats. bibl il maps *Scientific American* 260:48-57 Je '89
Just a veneer [study of strike-slip faults by B. Clark Burchfiel and Peter Molnar] T. Appenzeller. *Scientific American* 261:26+ N '89
Magnitude of late Quaternary left-lateral displacements along the north edge of Tibet [SPOT images of the Altyn Tagh fault] G. Peltzer and others. bibl f il maps *Science* 246:1285-9 D 8 '89
Microearthquake imaging of the Parkfield asperity [San Andreas fault] P. E. Malin and others. bibl f il *Science* 244:557-9 My 5 '89
New fault picture points toward Bay Area quakes [Calaveras fault; research by David Oppenheimer] R. A. Kerr. map *Science* 244:286-7 Ap 21 '89
Not yet accurate to a fault [San Andreas fault] B. Carpenter and S. Brownlee. il *U.S. News & World Report* 107:44-5 O 30 '89
The origins of killer quakes. H. Jensen. il *Maclean's* 102:66-7 O 30 '89
Shaking down deep [hidden faults] J. M. Nash. *Time* 134:108 O 23 '89
Smashing plates, broken ground [future California quakes] S. Begley. il map *Newsweek* 114:37-8+ O 30 '89
Taking the pulse of the San Andreas fault [research by Kerry Sieh] *Science* 243:479-80 Ja 27 '89
Unstudied California fault poses hazard [Rodgers Creek fault] R. Monastersky. *Science News* 136:388 D 16 '89
Volcanism at rifts [mid-ocean ridges] R. S. White and D. P. McKenzie. bibl il maps *Scientific American* 261:62-71 Jl '89
FAUROUX, ROGER
about
The chevalier blanc heading the industry ministry. F. J. Comes. il por *Business Week* p64 Mr 13 '89
FAUST, RITA BARON- *See* Baron-Faust, Rita
FAUST, W. L.
Explosive molecular ionic crystals. bibl f il *Science* 245:37-42 Jl 7 '89
FAUTIN, DAPHNE GAIL
Sexual stunts of clownfish [cover story] il *Natural History* p42-7 S '89

FAUX, CAMILLE
From my lips to your hips. il *Ms.* 18:18+ S '89
FAUX (STYLE)
Mimicking marble [kit from Plaid Enterprises] N. J. Freundlich. il *Popular Science* 235:88-9 Jl '89
Painting. il *The Family Handyman* 39:58-66 My '89
FAVRE, WILLIAM
about
The strange case of William Favre. B. W. Yates. il pors *Car and Driver* 35:77+ D '89
FAVRET, RÉMI
Inside Mecca. il *Mother Jones* 14:16+ Jl/Ag '89
FAWCETT, FARRAH
about
Farrah Fawcett. il pors *People Weekly* 31 Special Issue:60-1 Summ '89
Farrah is 42 . . . and a little out of sync. M. Leahy. il pors *TV Guide* 37:16-18+ Ap 22-28 '89
FAX MACHINE INDUSTRY
Marketing
Who's fueling the fax frenzy. F. H. Katayama. il *Fortune* 120:151-2+ O 23 '89
FAX MACHINES
Adding fax power to your PC [Complete Fax/9600] J. Pepper. il *Personal Computing* 13:202 Mr '89
Brother bundles fax, modem, and software [Brother IntelliFax board] C. Lee. il *Personal Computing* 13:186 Je '89
Canon FAX-L920 laser facsimile. il *Radio-Electronics* 60:22-3 F '89
The facts about FAX. F. Vizard. il *Popular Mechanics* 166:65-7 Mr '89
The facts on facsimile machines. J. Pepper. il *Nation's Business* 77:31 F '89
Facts on faxes [guide for small business] D. Moreau. il *Changing Times* 43:55-6+ O '89
Fax. P. H. Abelson. *Science* 243:1121 Mr 3 '89
Fax and a whole lot more [Connection coprocessor] C. O'Malley. il *Personal Computing* 13:194-5 Jl '89
Fax board has many problems [Ricoh ImageCard fax system] S. Miller. il *Home Office Computing* 7:56-7 Jl '89
Fax boards: do you need one? S. Miller. il *Home Office Computing* 7:62+ My '89
A fax for high volume [Toshiba 3700] N. Sullivan. il *Home Office Computing* 7:70+ F '89
A fax for your computer [Complete Fax/9600] J. J. McGonagle, Jr. il *Home Office Computing* 7:65 Ap '89
Fax it by modem. A. Glossbrenner. il *Home Office Computing* 7:38 O '89
Fax machines. F. Chesleigh. il *Home Office Computing* 7:69-72 D '89
Fax Mate [cover story] D. F. Plant. il *Radio-Electronics* 60:33-6 O '89
The fax phenomenon. A. M. Russell. il *Working Woman* 14:70-1 Ap '89
Fax + scanner [Relisys Tefax Model RA2110P] S. Miller. il *Home Office Computing* 7:62 Ag '89
Fax to the max. R. Gunnerson. il *Working Woman* 14:76 O '89
"Fax unto others as you would have them fax unto you" [junk fax] S. Harvey. il *Home Office Computing* 7:14 My '89
First TandyFax makes good impression [TandyFax 1000] S. Miller. il *Home Office Computing* 7:65-6 Ap '89
Getting the facts on buying a fax. A. Miller and E. William. il *Newsweek* 113:60 Ap 24 '89
A great communicator [Connection CoProcessor PC facsimile board] N. Baran. il *Byte* 14:195-6+ Ja '89
How to choose—and live with—the ultimate paper pusher. G. Hedberg. il *Money* 18:163-4 My '89
How to get on the fax track. S. Gelfond. *Working Woman* 14:27 My '89
Initial preparation can help you get the most from fax technology. il *Black Enterprise* 20:35-6 S '89
I've seen the future and it's the fax. A. Sampson. *World Press Review* 36:28+ D '89
Just a few fax [Fax-mail 96 and JT Fax 9600 cards] W. Rash, Jr. il *Byte* 14:143-4 Je '89
Life in the fax lane. N. Wartik. il *Ms.* 18:42+ N '89
Mac goes fax [InterFax, AppleFax, FaxSTF modems] D. E. Crabb. il *Byte* 14:208C-208D+ My '89
Olyfax 100: not worth the trouble. S. Usdin. il *Home Office Computing* 7:66 Ja '89
Olympia builds a better fax machine [Olympia OlyFax 200] S. Usdin. il *Home Office Computing* 7:68 Je '89
Panasonic puts it all together [Panasonic KX-F120 fax + telephone answering system with facsimile] S. Miller. il *Home Office Computing* 7:68-9 Je '89
The squeaky fax gets the grease. N. Sullivan. il *Home Office Computing* 7:96 Ap '89
The squeaky fax gets the grease. N. Sullivan. il *Home Office Computing* 7:112 D '89
Take this fax with you [Cobra Print Phone Portable PP-110] S. Miller. il *Home Office Computing* 7:70 F '89
The truth about fax. J. Cohen. il *Consumers' Research Magazine* 72:22-5 Ag '89
Where PC-fax pays off. C. O'Malley. il *Personal Computing* 13:91-3+ Je '89

FAX MACHINES—*cont.*
Anecdotes, facetiae, satire, etc.
Neighborhood fax and dime. N. Sullivan. il *Home Office Computing* 7:88 Ag '89
Laws and regulations
The technological fax of life [junk fax mail legislation] il *U.S. News & World Report* 106:14 Je 5 '89
Political use
Fax against fictions [use by Chinese students in the U.S. to send news home] il *Time* 133:32 Je 19 '89
Fax for freedom. J. Saltzman. il *USA Today (Periodical)* 118:67 S '89
Social use
Before he goes out on a date, Paul Hohendorf has a simple request: 'Just the fax, Ma'am'. il por *People Weekly* 31:107 F 20 '89
FAX PAPER
Cashing in on the fax frenzy [fax paper by Stuart Hall] G. G. Marcial. *Business Week* p80 Jl 10 '89
In search of a fax-paper standard. S. Chen and M. D. Espindle. *Home Office Computing* 7:22 N '89
FAY, ROBERT E., AND OTHERS
Prevalence and patterns of same-gender sexual contact among men. bibl f il *Science* 243:338-48 Ja 20 '89
FAY, SIDNEY B.
The Marshall Plan [reprint from September 1947 issue] *Current History* 88:30-1+ Ja '89
FAYED, MOHAMED AL- *See* Al-Fayed, Mohamed, 1933-
FAYETTEVILLE (N.C.)
Description
Fayetteville. D. Baer. il *U.S. News & World Report* 107:66-7 D 18 '89
FBD (FIBROCYSTIC BREAST DISEASE) *See* Breast—Diseases
FBI *See* United States. Federal Bureau of Investigation
FBI INFORMERS *See* Informers
FCC *See* United States. Federal Communications Commission
FCIC *See* Federal Crop Insurance Corporation
FDA *See* United States. Food and Drug Administration
FDIC *See* Federal Deposit Insurance Corporation
FEAGLEY, NATHALIE
about
"That car is going to explode!". S. Kelly. il pors *Reader's Digest* 134:96-100 Ja '89
FEAR
See also
Anxiety
Bashfulness
Dental phobia
NIMBY syndrome
Phobias
Stage fright
Fear shifts, trouble floats as the cold war ends. J. M. Wall. *The Christian Century* 106:1190-1 D 20-27 '89
FEAR IN CHILDREN
"Mommy, Mommy, I'm scared!". J. A. Oppenheim. il *Good Housekeeping* 209:108+ S '89
"We have a problem" [child's fear of going to sleep] J. Marks. il *Parents* 64:65-9 S '89
FEAR OF AUTOMOBILE DRIVING
Sy Cohn steers phobic drivers around mental roadblocks. il por *People Weekly* 32:72 N 6 '89
FEAR OF BLOOD
Me and my phobia [fear of blood leads to fainting] L. C. Pogrebin. por *Ms.* 18:16 O '89
FEAR OF DEATH LAWSUITS
The 'fear of death' lawsuits [legal action after Flight 232 crash at Sioux City, Iowa] K. Springen. il *Newsweek* 114:27 Ag 7 '89
FEAR OF FLYING
Help for fearful flyers. S. Richmond. il *Changing Times* 43:118-19 D '89
FEAR OF HEIGHTS *See* Acrophobia
FEAR OF SUCCESS
Dear Betty Harragan. B. L. Harragan. il *Working Woman* 14:32+ Ja '89
FEAR OF THE DARK
Fear of the dark. J. T. Gibson. il *Parents* 64:202 My '89
FEARNSIDE, PHILIP M. (PHILIP MARTIN)
Deforestation in Amazonia. bibl f il map *Environment* 31:16-20+ My '89
Deforestation in the Amazon [discussion of May 1989 article, Deforestation in Amazonia] *Environment* 31:4-5 S '89
Extractive reserves in Brazilian Amazonia. bibl f il map *BioScience* 39:387-93 Je '89
FEARRINGTON, FLORENCE
about
Old-fashioned and proud of it [interview] A. E. Serwer. il por *Fortune* 119:32 My 22 '89
FEARS, LINDA
Hollywood garden tour. il *Ladies' Home Journal* 106:126-30 Jl '89
FEATHERBEDDING (INDUSTRIAL RELATIONS)
Germany (West)
Is the German featherbed on its way out? G. E. Schares. il *Business Week* p62 Mr 13 '89

FEATHERS
Women are gobbling up the Massullo sisters' turkey-feather coats. il *People Weekly* 32:154-5 N 27 '89
Photographs and photography
Down and out: feathered victims in living color. F. Lanting. il *Omni (New York, N.Y.)* 11:58-63 Ag '89
FEAZEL, CHARLES T.
Inner space. il *Sea Frontiers* 35:49-52 Ja/F '89
FEBRES CORDERO, LEÓN, 1931-
about
Ecuador swings toward social democracy. C. M. Conaghan. bibl f *Current History* 88:137-41+ Mr '89
FEBRUARY
The February almanac. il *The Atlantic* 263:14 F '89
February folklore. D. M. Ludlum. il *Country Journal* 16:6 F '89
FEBRUARY REVOLUTION, 1848 *See* France—History—February Revolution, 1848
FECES
Muck and its entanglements. J. Berger. *Harper's* 278:60-1 My '89
FECHER, CHARLES A.
(ed) *See* Mencken, H. L. (Henry Louis), 1880-1956. Mencken's diaries: sustained by scorn and beer
FECHTNER, LEOPOLD
about
Leopold Fechtner has collected 2¼ million jokes, but his wife says his humor is no laughing matter. il por *People Weekly* 31:123 F 13 '89
FECKNER, ARTHUR
about
Fury over an unholy alliance. B. Turque. il por *Newsweek* 113:26 My 8 '89
FEDDERS CORP.
Fedders Corp. R. Abelson. il *Fortune* 120:152 S 11 '89
FEDER, BARNABY
Pressuring Perdue. il por *The New York Times Magazine* p32+ N 26 '89
FEDER, MIKE
McFreud's. *Harper's* 279:32 Ag '89
FEDERAL AGENCIES *See* United States—Executive departments
FEDERAL AGRICULTURAL MORTGAGE CORPORATION
Farmer Mac alive, loaning this year. G. Johnston. *Successful Farming* 87:10 F '89
FEDERAL AID
See also
Economic assistance, Domestic
Government lending
Public works—Federal aid
FEDERAL AND MUNICIPAL RELATIONS
See also
Decentralization in government
FEDERAL AND PROVINCIAL RELATIONS (CANADA)
See also
Canada. Constitution
Québec (Province)—Nationalism
An assault on Meech [interview with Newfoundland's premier C. Wells] G. Allen. il por *Maclean's* 102:26 O 16 '89
A battle joined [P. Trudeau enters debate over constitutional accord; cover story; special section] il pors *Maclean's* 102:20-2+ N 6 '89
By popular demand [S. Waters' Alberta nomination election victory part of drive to reform Senate; special section] il por *Maclean's* 102:24-5+ O 30 '89
Dissension in 'the Club' [premiers discuss Meech Lake constitutional accord] B. Wallace. il *Maclean's* 102:14 Mr 13 '89
The divided nation [Meech Lake constitutional accord; cover story; special section; with editorial comment by Kevin Doyle] il *Maclean's* 102:4, 18-23+ Mr 20 '89
Feuding Tories [Winnipeg-Ottawa relations] P. Kopvillem. il por *Maclean's* 102:20 My 29 '89
Hibernia postponed [oilfields off Newfoundland] J. Daly. il *Maclean's* 102:31+ Jl 24 '89
A mover and shaker [Quebec finance minister P. Fortier] P. Chisholm. por *Maclean's* 102:32 Mr 13 '89
The nation's agenda [premiers attack federal policies] B. Wallace. il *Maclean's* 102:14 S 4 '89
A parallel accord [Manitoba politicians near agreement on Meech Lake constitutional accord] G. W. Taylor. il *Maclean's* 102:15+ Jl 24 '89
Revisiting Meech Lake. T. Tedesco. il *Maclean's* 102:16 Jl 17 '89
Stepping back from the brink [debate over constitutional accord at First Ministers' conference; special section] il *Maclean's* 102:22-6+ N 20 '89
Storm clouds over Quebec [separatism issue in provincial election campaign; cover story; special section; with editorial comment by Kevin Doyle] il pors *Maclean's* 102:2, 16-22+ S 25 '89
Stormy weather [Manitoba premier G. Filmon withdraws support for Meech Lake constitutional accord] B. Wallace. il por *Maclean's* 102:12-14 Ja 16 '89
Test in the West [public hearings on Meech Lake constitutional accord in Manitoba] R. Laver. il por *Maclean's* 102:12-14 Ap 24 '89

FEDERAL AND PROVINCIAL RELATIONS (CANADA)
—cont.

Trouble on the Quebec front [R. Bourassa vs. J. Chrétien on constitutional accord] B. Wallace. *Maclean's* 102:12 Je 26 '89

Troubled waters [Meech Lake constitutional accord] B. Wallace. il *Maclean's* 102:18-19 O 9 '89

Under the gun [pressure on New Brunswick and Manitoba to support Meech Lake constitutional accord; with interview with F. McKenna] il por *Maclean's* 102:10-13 F 27 '89

War over words [Quebec's move to restrict use of English signs; special section] il por *Maclean's* 102:38-42 Ja 2 '89

Words of conciliation [interview with Ontario premier D. Peterson] T. Tedesco. il por *Maclean's* 102:16 Ja 30 '89

Anecdotes, facetiae, satire, etc.

A community of small communities [demands of Quebec and New Brunswick for own teams at Francophone Games] S. MacLeod. por *Maclean's* 102:64 Je 5 '89

FEDERAL AND STATE RELATIONS
See also
Decentralization in government
Intergovernmental tax relations

11th Amendment redraft hailed by publishers [declaring a congressional intent that states are not exempt from copyright law] H. Fields. *Publishers Weekly* 236:125 Jl 28 '89

11th Amendment ruling by High Court is 'hopeful' for copyright [question of states' liability in copyright infringement] H. Fields. *Publishers Weekly* 236:9 Jl 7 '89

Copyright owners press Congress for new laws on 11th Amendment [court decision that copyright holders could not take action against state-held entities] H. Fields. *Publishers Weekly* 235:14 F 10 '89

Educator group objects to proposed remedy of 11th Amendment [restraining state institutions from infringing copyrights] H. Fields. *Publishers Weekly* 235:30 Je 2 '89

House gets bill fortifying intent on states vs. federal copyright. H. Fields. *Publishers Weekly* 235:14 Mr 24 '89

House to push 11th Amendment remedy; Oman voices support [right of individual states and their entities to ignore requirements of U.S. Copyright Act] H. Fields. *Publishers Weekly* 235:18 Ap 28 '89

Last gasp for the Everglades [U.S. Attorney D. Lehtinen sues Florida for polluting federal lands] J. Carney. il por map *Time* 134:26-7 S 25 '89

Should states regulate biotechnology? M. Crawford. il *Science* 245:466 Ag 4 '89

Supreme Court rejects second 11th Amendment case in month [brought by copyright holders against a state entity] H. Fields. *Publishers Weekly* 235:36 Ap 7 '89

FEDERAL ARCHITECTURE *See* Architecture, Federal

FEDERAL ASSET DISPOSITION ASSOCIATION

Bankrupt policies. V. Novak. il *Common Cause Magazine* 15:9-10 Ja/F '89

An odd sort of takeover play [proposed buyout by J. Robert] J. R. Hayes. il por *Forbes* 143:142 F 6 '89

FEDERAL AVIATION ADMINISTRATION (U.S.) *See* United States. Federal Aviation Administration

FEDERAL BUILDINGS *See* Public buildings

FEDERAL BUREAU OF INVESTIGATION (U.S.) *See* United States. Federal Bureau of Investigation

FEDERAL COMMUNICATIONS COMMISSION (U.S.) *See* United States. Federal Communications Commission

FEDERAL CROP INSURANCE CORPORATION

Congress told to change Federal Crop Insurance. B. Black. il *Successful Farming* 87:11 S '89

Farmers want changes in crop insurance. R. Fee. *Successful Farming* 87:4 Ag '89

How to get more of you interested in crop insurance. *Successful Farming* 87:30 Je '89

What's wrong with crop insurance. R. Fee. il *Successful Farming* 87:64AJ Ap '89

FEDERAL DEBT *See* Debts, Public

FEDERAL DEPOSIT INSURANCE CORPORATION

Bowery follies [1985 federal bailout of Bowery Savings arranged by R. Ravitch] C. Byron. il por *New York* 22:14+ My 29 '89

Congress and the banking community [proposed merger of FDIC and FSLIC; address, October 10, 1988] R. L. Clarke. *Vital Speeches of the Day* 55:203-6 Ja 15 '89

KKR tiptoes into Texas [Kohlberg Kravis Roberts pumps capital into MCorp] T. Mason. il *Business Week* p33 Ja 16 '89

Moral hazard. J. K. Glassman. *The New Republic* 200:28-9 Mr 20 '89

'This is a dirty business' [interview with chairman L. W. Seidman] G. Hector. il pors *Fortune* 119:133-4+ My 22 '89

FEDERAL EMERGENCY MANAGEMENT AGENCY (U.S.)
See United States. Federal Emergency Management Agency

FEDERAL EMPLOYEES *See* Government employees

FEDERAL EMPLOYERS' LIABILITY ACT

Is this liability law a gravy train? R. Stodghill, II. il *Business Week* p93+ N 6 '89

FEDERAL EXPRESS CORP.

Federal Express/Tigers merger would reshape cargo industry. J. T. McKenna. *Aviation Week & Space Technology* 130:106 Ja 2 '89

The Federal Express connection [drug trafficking] *Newsweek* 114:18 Ag 21 '89

The flying-package trade takes off [expansion of Federal Express and UPS] C. P. Work. il *U.S. News & World Report* 107:47+ O 2 '89

Fred Smith [Federal Express buys Flying Tiger] D. Foust. il por *Business Week* Special Issue:102 Ap 14 '89

Mr. Smith goes global [merger with Tiger International; cover story] D. Foust. il pors map *Business Week* p66-8+ F 13 '89

FEDERAL GOVERNMENT
See also
Decentralization in government

FEDERAL HOME LOAN BANK BOARD *See* United States. Federal Home Loan Bank Board

FEDERAL HOME LOAN MORTGAGE CORPORATION

Freddie and Fannie clean up after the S&L mess. C. Yang. il *Business Week* p112-13 Je 5 '89

FEDERAL HOUSING ADMINISTRATION (U.S.) *See* United States. Federal Housing Administration

FEDERAL INSECTICIDE, FUNGICIDE AND RODENTICIDE ACT *See* Pesticides—Laws and regulations

FEDERAL JUDGES *See* Judges

FEDERAL LANDS *See* Public lands

FEDERAL NATIONAL MORTGAGE ASSOCIATION

Fannie Mae helps put a roof over the nation's poor. C. Yang. il por *Business Week* p113 Je 5 '89

Freddie and Fannie clean up after the S&L mess. C. Yang. il *Business Week* p112-13 Je 5 '89

FEDERAL PAPER BOARD CO., INC.

Finding plays without fancy footwork. G. G. Marcial. il *Business Week* p124 My 1 '89

FEDERAL REGULATORY AGENCIES *See* Regulatory agencies

FEDERAL RESERVE BANK OF N. Y.

Gold [main vault] *The New Yorker* 64:20-1 Ja 2 '89

FEDERAL RESERVE BANKS

How to skip the middleman when buying a T-bill. L. J. Nathans. *Business Week* p112 Ja 23 '89

Now the inflation battle is inside the Fed [Washington-based Board of Governors vs regional Fed banks] M. McNamee. il *Business Week* p124+ Mr 13 '89

FEDERAL RESERVE SYSTEM (U.S.)

Attention, Mr. Greenspan [lower interest rates] H. Banks. *Forbes* 143:33 F 6 '89

A bout of Fed-bashing. M. McNamee and H. Gleckman. il por *Business Week* p24-5 Ag 28 '89

Caution at the Fed [A. Greenspan; cover story] L. Uchitelle. il pors *The New York Times Magazine* p18-21+ Ja 15 '89

Collision course: Bush and the Fed. M. McNamee and H. Gleckman. il *Business Week* p34-6 F 27 '89

Curves in the right places? A. C. Brown. il *Forbes* 143:215 Mr 20 '89

The deep, dark secret of our government [views of W. Greider] B. Edmondson. il *Utne Reader* p14-15 Mr/Ap '89

Don't compromise the Fed. T. May, Jr. *Fortune* 120:32 O 23 '89

False dilemma [need to lower interest rates] M. S. Forbes, Jr. il *Forbes* 143:27 Je 12 '89

The Fed can't count [raising interest rates] *National Review* 41:13-14 Mr 24 '89

The Fed gets one of Brady's boys [D. W. Mullins] M. McNamee. por *Business Week* p102 D 11 '89

The Fed is firming up the odds on a 'soft landing'. J. C. Cooper and K. Madigan. il *Business Week* p25-6 Je 19 '89

The Fed is still loosening credit—notch by careful notch. J. C. Cooper and K. Madigan. il *Business Week* p15-16 Jl 24 '89

The Fed lifts the Brady plan out of its sickbed [relaxing reserve accounting rules] M. McNamee and W. Glasgall. il *Business Week* p43 O 9 '89

The Fed may stop tinkering for a while. J. C. Cooper and K. Madigan. il *Business Week* p21-2 Ag 28 '89

The Fed seems to be wrestling inflation into submission. J. C. Cooper and K. Madigan. il *Business Week* p31-2 Je 5 '89

The Fed walks against the wind [pressure for lower interest rates] M. McNamee. il *Business Week* p40-1 N 6 '89

The Fed will be the economy's skipper. M. McNamee. il *Business Week* p84-5+ D 25 '89-Ja 1 '90

The Federal Reserve's dilemma: reduce inflation and keep construction growing. P. E. Kidd. il *Architectural Record* 177:37 O '89

The Fed's brakes aren't slowing capital spending. M. J. Mandel. il *Business Week* p74 Mr 27 '89

The Fed's hot seat at Darman's breakfast table [push to lower interest rates] M. W. Karmin. il por *U.S. News & World Report* 107:90 Ag 28-S 4 '89

The Fed's yo-yo. B. D. Nossiter. *The Nation* 249:76-7 Jl 17 '89

Feeling the heat [attempt to halt inflation trend] J. Greenwald. il *Time* 133:50-1 Mr 6 '89

FEDERAL RESERVE SYSTEM (U.S.)—*cont.*

A Greenspan recession? M. S. Forbes, Jr. il *Forbes* 143:27 Ap 3 '89

Greenspan vs. inflation. R. E. Norton. il *U.S. News & World Report* 106:45-6 F 27 '89

Greenspan's moment of truth: can he manage a soft landing without skidding into a recession? [cover story] M. McNamee. il pors *Business Week* p58-62+ Jl 31 '89

Hands off the Fed. D. Gergen. il *U.S. News & World Report* 107:84 O 30 '89

How the fed-watchers pulled the wool over their own eyes [quick reversal in interest rates] M. McNamee. il *Business Week* p57 D 11 '89

Inflation II: the sequel [possiblity of a recession] R. E. Norton. il *U.S. News & World Report* 106:18-20+ Ap 3 '89

Inflation is lurking—but Greenspan is on the case. J. C. Cooper and K. Madigan. il *Business Week* p27-8 F 6 '89

Interest rates will rebound in the next year as the Fed tightens. T. May, Jr. il *Fortune* 120:20-1 Ag 14 '89

Issues shaping the U.S. economic outlook in 1989 [address, December 6, 1988] R. T. Parry. *Vital Speeches of the Day* 55:197-9 Ja 15 '89

It's wait-and-seesaw time at the Fed [debating interest hikes] M. McNamee. il *Business Week* p34 Ap 3 '89

Keeping the cow, selling the milk [Air Products' ten year plan contrasted with Federal Reserve anxiety about tight industrial capacity] H. Banks. il por *Forbes* 143:40-1 Mr 20 '89

A matter of interest [new members of the Open Market Committee] J. Crudele. il *New York* 22:24 Mr 20 '89

Memo to Bush: don't take your economic luck for granted. M. McNamee. il *Business Week* p27 Ja 30 '89

Monetary democracy. M. Kinsley. *The New Republic* 201:4+ O 30 '89

Now the inflation battle is inside the Fed [Washington-based Board of Governors vs regional Fed banks] M. McNamee. il *Business Week* p124+ Mr 13 '89

The ominous warning signs of recession. W. Greider. il *Rolling Stone* p37+ Mr 9 '89

The P-star factor. P. Chisholm. il *Maclean's* 102:28 Je 26 '89

The peek-a-boo recession. R. Thomas. il *Newsweek* 114:60 N 20 '89

Putting 'Keynes's head on Milton Friedman's body' [P-star index] M. McNamee. il *Business Week* p66 Jl 31 '89

A rare glimpse inside the Fed [interview with R. Heller] R. E. Norton. il por *Fortune* 120:155-6 S 11 '89

The real world, and the Fed's world. H. Banks. *Forbes* 143:35 Ap 17 '89

The Reserve's silly new equation [P-star index] G. P. Brockway. il *The New Leader* 72:15-16 Je 12-26 '89

Second thoughts on soft landings. M. W. Karmin. *U.S. News & World Report* 107:44 Jl 17 '89

Soaring dollar, easier money. M. W. Karmin and P. Sherrid. *U.S. News & World Report* 106:51 My 29 '89

Stop panicking over inflation. P. C. Roberts. *The Washington Monthly* 21:26-30 My '89

Summertime, and the Fed may keep easing. J. C. Cooper and K. Madigan. il *Business Week* p55-6 Je 26 '89

There's nothing fickle about the Fed's war on inflation . . . and if rates rise, capital spending will take the biggest hit. G. Koretz. il *Business Week* p22 S 18 '89

The tide turns for lower interest rates. M. W. Karmin. il *U.S. News & World Report* 107:55-6 O 23 '89

Why is the Fed still trying to kill the expansion? P. C. Roberts. il *Business Week* p20 Je 26 '89

Why the Fed can't seem to brake the buying binge. G. Koretz. il *Business Week* p26 Ja 23 '89

Will corporate debt force the Fed to scrap zero inflation? K. Pennar. il *Business Week* p22 O 23 '89

Will the Fed's tighter grip on credit choke off the expansion? J. C. Cooper and K. Madigan. il *Business Week* p31-2 Mr 13 '89

Zero inflation. *National Review* 41:12 D 8 '89

FEDERAL SAVINGS AND LOAN INSURANCE CORPORATION

Congress and the banking community [proposed merger of FDIC and FSLIC; address, October 10, 1988] R. L. Clarke. *Vital Speeches of the Day* 55:203-6 Ja 15 '89

Feds: 40 taxpayers: love [inherits control of International Tennis Center of Delray Beach, Fla. from failed thrift] R. L. Stern. il *Forbes* 144:43-4 S 4 '89

FSLIC fizzles. *National Review* Ja 18 Ja 27 '89

FSLIC insurance: are we covered? A. Winter. *Modern Maturity* 32:16 Je/Jl '89

Moral hazard. J. K. Glassman. *The New Republic* 200:28-9 Mr 20 '89

The thrift police [FSLIC files malpractice suit against law firm Jenkens & Gilchrist over its dealings with State Savings & Loan Association of Lubbock] D. Fanning. il *Forbes* 143:74 Ja 9 '89

The unending deposit insurance mess. E. J. Kane. bibl f il *Science* 246:451-6 O 27 '89

FEDERAL SPENDING POLICY *See* United States—Appropriations and expenditures

FEDERAL-STATE TAX RELATIONS *See* Intergovernmental tax relations

FEDERAL TRADE COMMISSION (U.S.) *See* United States. Federal Trade Commission

FEDERALISM *See* Federal and state relations

FEDERATED DEPARTMENT STORES, INC.

Campeau is up on that high wire again. C. Hawkins and S. Phillips. il por *Business Week* p108-10 My 15 '89

Walking a fine line [R. Campeau] P. Chisholm. il por *Maclean's* 102:50-1 Ja 2 '89

FEDERATION OF AMERICAN SCIENTISTS

FAS and Brazilian physicists discuss improved nuclear safeguards. W. Sweet. *Physics Today* 42:57-8 Ap '89

FEDORA [opera] *See* Giordano, Umberto, 1867-1948

FEED ADDITIVES *See* Feed supplements

FEED MIXERS AND MIXING

Grinder-mixers. F. Buckingham. il *Successful Farming* 87:18-19 S '89

FEED SUPPLEMENTS

Ammoniated 'junk' will feed cows. *Successful Farming* 87:33 Je '89

How to pick and use silage additives. J. R. Borcherding. il *Successful Farming* 87:26+ Je '89

Spike forage to beat meal prices [anhydrous ammonia] V. Ehmke. il *Successful Farming* 87:40 My '89

FEED SUPPLEMENTS, ANTIBIOTIC *See* Antibiotic feed supplements

FEEDBACK (PSYCHOLOGY)

See also

Biofeedback training

How to give feedback your staff can use [excerpt from One-on-one with Andy Grove] A. S. Grove. il *Working Woman* 14:54+ S '89

Rx for cholesterol: frequent feedback [research by Tony Burkett] B. Py-Lieberman. il *Psychology Today* 23:26 S '89

FEEDERS (BIRDS) *See* Bird feeders

FEEDING, TUBE *See* Tube feeding

FEEDING OF PLANTS *See* Plants—Nutrition

FEEDLOTS

See also

Cattle feedlots

FEEDS

See also

Forage plants

Silage

Corn

Combine grain, steal the stalks! il *Successful Farming* 87:48X N '89

Lysine content

PST-treated hogs need lysine—lots of lysine [porcine somatotropin] il *Successful Farming* 87:50 F '89

Magnesium content

Magnesium for farm animals [interview with J. Hollifield] C. SerVaas. il *The Saturday Evening Post* 261:102 Jl/Ag '89

Medicated feed

See also

Antibiotic feed supplements

Milo

All milo is not created equal. *Successful Farming* 87 no4:38 Mr '89

Protein content

See also

Feeds—Lysine content

FEELINGS *See* Emotions

FEENEY, JOSEPH J.

'Earth is the fairer': the centennial of Gerard Manley Hopkins. *America* 161:102-5 Ag 26-S 2 '89

FEENEY, SHEILA ANNE

Dirty rotten scalpers. il *Ms.* 17:26+ Ap '89

Hedda's secret: what no one understands about abused women [with introduction by Jennifer Farbar] por *Mademoiselle* 95:242-5+ Mr '89

Reflections in a mass eye. il *Ms.* 18:30+ N '89

FEES, BANK *See* Banks and banking—Service charges

FEES, DENTAL *See* Dental fees

FEES, IMMIGRATION *See* Immigration and emigration—Right of entry fees

FEES, LABOR UNION *See* Labor unions—Dues, fees, etc.

FEES, LEGAL *See* Cost (Law); Lawyers—Salaries, fees, etc.

FEET *See* Foot

FEHLAU, FRED

about

Fred Fehlau at Newport Harbor Art Museum. F. Colpitt. il *Art in America* 77:203+ N '89

FEHR, DONALD

about

The players' main man. D. A. Kaplan. il por *The New York Times Magazine* p46+ O 29 '89

FEHREN, HENRY

[Column] *See* issues of U.S. Catholic

FEIFFER, JULES

about

Anthony Rose [drama] Reviews

Commonweal 116:676 D 1 '89. G. C. Weales

Feiffer at sixty. D. K. Mano. por *National Review* 41:58-60 S 15 '89

FEIGEL, WILLIAM

Hell on heels. il *Runner's World* 24:30 N '89

FEIGENBAUM, EDWARD A.
about
Machine dreams. H. Ullman. il *The New Republic* 201:12-14
Jl 17-24 '89
FEIL, DINA
about
All-American Girl-talk. il pors *Teen* 33:92 Ag '89
FEIN, BRUCE
A court that obeys the law. *National Review* 41:50-1 S 29
'89
FEIN, ELAINE
(ed) See Garza, Mary Helen. "My son is under the ice—find
him!"
(ed) See Lazarchick, Susan. "Please save my leg!"
(ed) See Mohr, Jane. Love multiplied by three
FEIN, ESTHER B.
Moscow yuppies? Nyet quite! il *Mademoiselle* 95:222-3+ O
'89
A raised *glasnost*. il *Gentlemen's Quarterly* 59:106+ O '89
FEIN, NAOMI
It pays to get clipped. il *Ms.* 18:28-30 N '89
FEINBERG, ANDREW
Collectors' items: artful investments. *Harper's Bazaar* 122:42+
Ja '89
The richest woman on TV? Oprah! [cover story] il pors
TV Guide 37:2-7 Ag 26-S 1 '89
FEINBERG, WALTER, 1937-
Educational misconceptions of a democratic public. *The
Education Digest* 55:7-10 O '89
FEINBLUM, BARNET M.
about
Why Celestial Seasonings wasn't Kraft's cup of tea. S. D.
Atchison. il por *Business Week* p76 My 8 '89
FEINERMAN, JAMES V.
Human rights in China. bibl f *Current History* 88:273-6+
S '89
FEINOUR, PAM
A high school play helps suicidal teenagers. *The Education
Digest* 54:50-1 My '89
FEINSTEIN, ALVAN R.
Epidemiologic investigation [discussion of December 2, 1988
article, Scientific standards in epidemiologic studies of
the menace of daily life] *Science* 243:1255-6 Mr 10 '89
FEINSTEIN, HAROLD
Proud, proud beauties [photographs] il *Life* 12:84-7 Jl '89
FEINSTEIN, JOHN
Better way for Barcelona. il *World Tennis* 36:20+ Mr '89
Coaches, ad nauseam. por *Sports Illustrated* 70:102 Ap 10
'89
Heeling process. il *Sports Illustrated* 70:18-21 Mr 20 '89
Mac's last stand. il pors *World Tennis* 37:58-60+ S '89
Never say die [cover story] il pors *World Tennis* 36:30-2+
My '89
The ordeal of Jim Valvano. il por *Sports Illustrated* 70:34-6
Ja 30 '89
Q. What makes better TV than the World Series or Super
Bowl? A. This week's NCAA finals. il *TV Guide* 37:10-12
Ap 1-7 '89
Semi-tough. il *World Tennis* 37:57-8+ Jl '89
FEINSTEIN, LEE
Heard on the Street. il *Common Cause Magazine* 15:12-15
Jl/Ag '89
FEINSTEIN, MARTIN
about
A capital enterprise. M. Mayer. il pors *Opera News* 54:24-9+
N '89
FEIRSTEIN, BRUCE
Funny money. *Harper's Bazaar* 122:177+ Mr '89
We're sorry to inform you. *Harper's Bazaar* 122:103+ Ja
'89
FEIT, EDWARD
George Van Hook [cover story] il por *American Artist*
53:38-43+ Mr '89
Linden Frederick. il por *American Artist* 53:48-53+ Jl '89
Nature as teacher: the art of Jim McVicker. il *American
Artist* 53:38-43+ D '89
Painting with oil sticks [cover story] il *American Artist* 53:44-9
Ap '89
Richard Taicher. il por *American Artist* 53:56-9 F '89
Securing gallery representation. il *American Artist* 53:69-73
Je '89
FEIZ, REZA
Love sacred and profane. il *The Courier (Unesco)* 42:12
Mr '89
FELA *See* Federal Employers' Liability Act
FELD, ELIOT
about
Love song waltzes [ballet] Reviews
New York il 22:81-2 Mr 13 '89. T. Tobias
Reviews:
Performances at the Joyce Theater, New York City.
D. Hering. il *Dance Magazine* 63:56-7+ Je '89
FELD BALLET
The customs of the country [performance of Love song
waltzes] T. Tobias. il *New York* 22:81-2 Mr 13 '89
Reviews:
Performances at the Joyce Theater, New York City.
D. Hering. il *Dance Magazine* 63:56-7+ Je '89

FELDER, RAOUL
about
A struggle for splitsville's bucks. J. D. Reed. il pors *Time*
133:53 Ja 9 '89
FELDMAN, BARBARA
about
Reviews:
Performances in New Haven, Conn. D. Scott. il *Dance
Magazine* 63:56-8 Ag '89
FELDMAN, BEVERLY NEUER
Preparing your child to enjoy work [excerpt from Kids who
succeed] il *Working Woman* 14:155-6 My '89
FELDMAN, BRUCE
Inside the Kestrel MX-Z. il *Bicycling* 30:204+ Mr '89
FELDMAN, IRVING, 1928-
Immortality [poem] *The New Yorker* 64:32 Ja 2 '89
The life and letters [poem] *The New Yorker* 65:52
S 25 '89
West Street [poem] *The New Republic* 201:32 N 27
'89
FELDMAN, JAY
Parents keep out! por *Newsweek* 112:8 My 22 '89
FELDMAN, LEN
Beyond stereo. il *Radio-Electronics* 60:51-4 S '89
FMX: is it good for FM? il *Radio-Electronics* 60:52-5+ O
'89
Video tapes: choosing the one that's right for you. il
Radio-Electronics 60:45-8 My '89
FELDMAN, LOREN
The keys to this season? Jack Clark's bat and Jesse Orosco's
pranks. il *TV Guide* 37:10-12+ Ap 8-14 '89
The yessss! man can play rough. il por *TV Guide* 37:16-18
Jl 1-7 '89
FELDMAN, SHERYL
(jt. auth) See Armstrong, Penny, and Feldman, Sheryl
FELDMAN (BARBARA) AND DANCERS *See* Barbara Feld-
man and Dancers
FELDMAN (RONALD) FINE ARTS, INC. *See* Ronald Feld-
man Fine Arts, Inc.
FELDMANN, EDWARD S.
Winter rabbit hunting. il *The Conservationist* 43:14-17 Ja/F
'89
FELDMANN, KENNETH A., AND OTHERS
A dwarf mutant of Arabidopsis generated by T-DNA insertion
mutagenesis [cover story] bibl f il *Science* 243:1351-4 Mr
10 '89
FELINE LEUKEMIA *See* Cats—Diseases and pests
FELIX *See* Pène du Bois, Felix, 1957-
FELIX NECK WILDLIFE SANCTUARY (MASS.)
Awesome ospreys. il *National Geographic World* 165:8-11
My '89
FELL, VERONICA
A dancer's audition guide: building careers in Europe. il
Dance Magazine 63:66-7 F '89
FELLER, MICHAEL J.
(jt. auth) See Nadareski, Christopher A., and Feller, Michael
J.
FELLHEIMER, ALAN
about
Alan Fellheimer wears combat boots. M. Schroeder. il por
Business Week p119-20 Mr 20 '89
FELLING OF TREES *See* Tree felling
FELLINI, FEDERICO
about
Fellini's magical '8½'. F. Pierson. il por *American Film* 14:16-17
Je '89
FELLMAN, BRUCE
An engineer's eye helps biologists understand nature. bibl
f (p122) il *Smithsonian* 20:98-105 Jl '89
FELLNER, MICHAEL J., AND COLINO, STACEY
Block that burn! il *Travel Holiday* 172:28-9 D '89
FELLOUS, MARILYNE
Tristan and Pavlova through the looking glass. il *The Unesco
Courier* 42:30-3 O '89
FELLOWSHIPS *See* Scholarships and fellowships
FELNER, BOB
Best bids. See occassional issues of New York beginning
November 14, 1988
Imperial standard. il *House & Garden* 161:204-13 O '89
FEMALE IMPERSONATORS *See* Impersonators, Female
FEMININE BEAUTY *See* Beauty, Personal
FEMININE HYGIENE PRODUCTS
See also
Kimberly-Clark Corp.
Tambrands Inc.
Go with the flow [choosing the right tampon to avoid toxic
shock syndrome] *Prevention (Emmaus, Pa.)* 41:14 S '89
FEMININITY (PSYCHOLOGY)
Women in sports: what's changed? [negative perception of
female high school athletes; research by Mary Jo Kane]
V. Bozzi. *Psychology Today* 23:70 O '89
FEMINISM
See also
Ecofeminism
International Jewish Feminist Network
National Organization for Women
Abortion as insurrection. W. M. Hern. por *The Humanist*
49:18-20+ Mr/Ap '89

FEMINISM—*cont.*

Anti-abortion, pro-feminism? P. Erens. *Mother Jones* 14:31+ My '89

Beyond the legal right: why liberals and feminists don't like to talk about the morality of abortion [cover story] J. DeParle. *The Washington Monthly* 21:28-9+ Ap '89

Black feminists. C. Kocol. *The Humanist* 49:35-6 S/O '89

Feminism hits middle age [cover story] B. Amiel. il *National Review* 41:23-5+ N 24 '89

Feminist moralism, "pornography", and censorship. B. Dority. il *The Humanist* 49:8-9+ N/D '89

Feminist update. C. Kocol. See issues of The Humanist beginning September/October 1986

Goals for the future [views of G. Steinem] por *USA Today (Periodical)* 118:3 Ag '89

The myths of feminism. N. Davidson. il *National Review* 41:44+ My 19 '89

Not for women only. B. Friedan. il pors *Modern Maturity* 32:66-8+ Ap/My '89

Onward, women! [cover story] C. Wallis. il *Time* 134:80-2+ D 4 '89

The Rushdie riddle. L. C. Pogrebin. il *Ms.* 18:28 Jl/Ag '89

Technology as destiny: the new eugenics challenges feminism [cover story] J. B. Elshtain. il *The Progressive* 53:19-23 Je '89

Who needs NOW? [women's attitudes] D. Seligman. *Fortune* 120:251-2 S 25 '89

The woman warrior [former model A. Simonton] J. Lieber. il pors *Sports Illustrated* 70 Special Issue:131-4 F '89

History

Abortion: the usable past. L. Flanders. *The Nation* 249:175-7 Ag 7-14 '89

Father knows best [discussion of May 8, 1989 article, March to a crossroads on abortion] M. Tax. *The Nation* 249:110+ Jl 24-31 '89

It started with a lunch. L. C. Pogrebin. il *Ms.* 17:50 Ja/F '89

March to a crossroads on abortion [cover story] M. Tax. *The Nation* 248:613+ My 8 '89

Language question

See Sex discrimination in language

Periodicals

Feminist publications. S. E. Searing. il *Utne Reader* p134+ N/D '89

FEMINISM AND RELIGION *See* Women and religion

FEMINIST ART

Exhibitions

Two lives: ordinary/extraordinary [photomontages of R. Luxemburg and artist M. Stevens' mother, Alice] C. Jacobsen. bibl f il pors *Art in America* 77:152-7+ F '89

FEMINIST LAW

Now for a woman's point of view. A. Toufexis. il *Time* 133:51-2 Ap 17 '89

FEMINIST LITERARY CRITICISM

Feminist literary criticism [discussion of Autumn 1988 article] P. Shaw. *The American Scholar* 58:317-19 Spr '89

Report from a phallocrat. J. P. Hart. *National Review* 41:45 F 24 '89

FEMINIST LITERATURE

See also

Booksellers and bookselling—Feminist literature

FEMINIST STUDIES *See* Women's studies

FEMINISTS FOR LIFE OF AMERICA

Anti-abortion, pro-feminism? P. Erens. *Mother Jones* 14:31+ My '89

FENCE POSTS

Fenceposts. J. Vara. il *Country Journal* 16:84-6 My/Je '89

FENCES

See also

Barbed wire fences

Fence posts

Snow fences

Bamboo fences, light but strong. il *Sunset (Central West edition)* 181:168 D '88

A little privacy, please. S. Sheetz. il *Better Homes and Gardens* 67:99-100+ Je '89

Privacy screen is also a picture screen. il *Sunset (Central West edition)* 183:142-3 O '89

Privacy with style. T. O. Bakke. il *Popular Science* 234:145 Je '89

Private domain [lattice fence] E. Thompson and E. Thompson. il *Popular Mechanics* 166:88-9 Je '89

Maintenance and repair

Iron fences. B. Vila. il *Popular Mechanics* 166:50+ Mr '89

FENCES, ELECTRIC

Polywire fences. M. Holmberg. il *Successful Farming* 87:30-2 D '89

FENCES (RECEIVERS OF STOLEN GOODS) *See* Receiving stolen goods

FENCING

Fencing [San Francisco Bay Area] il *Sunset (Central West edition)* 181:58+ D '88

Touché! C. Moekle. il *American Health* 8:41 Ja/F '89

FENDERS (BICYCLES) *See* Bicycles—Fenders

FENFLURAMINE

The feel-full pill [used to suppress carbohydrate cravings] W. T. Buckley. il *Health (New York, N.Y.)* 21:28-9+ Ja '89

Neurotoxicity creates regulatory dilemma. D. M. Barnes. *Science* 243:29-30 Ja 6 '89

FENICHEL, MARILYN

Women's health handbook [special section] *McCall's* 116:89-92+ F '89

FENIGER, SUSAN

about

Bright chefs, big City. S. Carlton. il pors *Health (New York, N.Y.)* 21:78-81 F '89

FENIGSEN, RICHARD

Euthanasia: how it works: the Dutch experience. *Current (Washington, D.C.)* 313:4-14 Je '89

FENN, JOHN B., 1917-, AND OTHERS

Electrospray ionization for mass spectrometry of large biomolecules. bibl f il *Science* 246:64-71 O 6 '89

FENN, KAY LYNN HARRIS

Hitting the wall. il *The Futurist* 23:60 Ja/F '89

FENNEL

The French and Italians consider it a delicacy [finocchio] il *Sunset (Central West edition)* 183:124 Ag '89

FENNEL (SANTA MONICA, CALIF.: RESTAURANT) *See* Santa Monica (Calif.)—Restaurants, nightclubs, bars, etc.

FENNER, DERRICK

about

The comeback chronicles. H. Hersch. il pors *Sports Illustrated* 71:38-44+ Jl 24 '89

FENNIMORE, DONALD L., AND TRUMP, ROBERT T.

Joseph B. Barry, Philadelphia cabinetmaker. bibl f il *Antiques* 135:1212-25 My '89

FENS

See also

Grasshopper Hollow (Mo.)

FENSTER MUSEUM OF JEWISH ART (TULSA, OKLA.)

Jewish history preserved in Tulsa. il *Southern Living* 24:34 Ja '89

FENTANYL

Lollipop draws consumer group's ire [presurgical sedative laced with fentanyl] *Science News* 135:156 Mr 11 '89

FENTON, BRIAN C.

(jt. auth) See Friedman, Herbert, 1931-1988, and Fenton, Brian C.

FENYVESI, CHARLES

Genetic design. il *Organic Gardening* 36:76-8+ Ja '89

Returning home. por *Organic Gardening* 36:99 Ap '89

Vintage leaves. por *Organic Gardening* 36:71 Jl/Ag '89

Why a tree. il *Organic Gardening* 36:80 N '89

FERAL HOGS *See* Wild boars

FERCHAT, ROBERT A.

Shooting for the moon [address, April 27, 1989] *Vital Speeches of the Day* 55:727-31 S 15 '89

FERENCI, LUANNE

Field hockey will stick with you for life. il por *Women's Sports & Fitness* 11:60-1 S '89

FERGUS, CHARLES

Camping overnight. il *Country Journal* 16:50-2 My/Je '89

Hunting for giants. il pors *Country Journal* 16:56-61 Ja '89

FERGUSON, ANDREW

Mad about Mapplethorpe. *National Review* 41:20-1 Ag 4 '89

A sea of stars. il *National Review* 41:26 N 10 '89

FERGUSON, CHARLES H.

America's high-tech decline. *Foreign Policy* 74:123-44 Spr '89

FERGUSON, EDWARD W., AND OTHERS

Tornadoes: slow start, fast finish. il maps *Weatherwise* 42:28-35 F '89

FERGUSON, HERMAN

about

The fugitive. P. Blauner. il pors *New York* 22:32-7 Ag 7 '89

FERGUSON, JANE

AIDS and young people. il *World Health* p12-13 O '89

FERGUSON, SARAH *See* Sarah, Duchess of York, 1959-

FERGUSON, THOMAS, 1949-

F.D.R., anyone? il *The Nation* 248:689 My 22 '89

FERGUSON, TOM, 1943-

The guilt-free guide to a smoke-free life. il *Modern Maturity* 32:76-7+ F/Mr '89

FERIA, MONICA

Aquino's new economic agenda. *World Press Review* 36:54 My '89

FERIA INTERNACIONAL DE LIBRO (MEXICO) *See* Book fairs

FERLING, JOHN E.

The evolving presidency. il *American History Illustrated* 24:12-18+ Ap '89

"An office of unprofitable dignity". il pors *American History Illustrated* 24:12-23+ Mr '89

FERMAT'S THEOREM

Fermat still has the last laugh. P. Hoffman. il *Discover* 10:48-50 Ja '89

FERMENTATION
Alimentary, my dear hoatzin [research by Stuart D. Strahl] R. Cowen. il *Science News* 136:269-70 O 21 '89
Foregut fermentation in the hoatzin, a neotropical leaf-eating bird [cover story] A. Grajal and others. bibl f il *Science* 245:1236-8 S 15 '89
What's a hoatzin? [only bird with foregut fermentation; research by Stuart D. Strahl] J. Horgan. il *Scientific American* 261:30 D '89
FERMI (ENRICO) AWARD See Enrico Fermi Award
FERMI NATIONAL ACCELERATOR LABORATORY
The site contest for Fermilab [Illinois site chosen in 1966] C. L. Westfall. bibl f il *Physics Today* 42:44-52 Ja '89
Zs for two: a critical mass [Fermilab vs. SLAC] M. M. Waldrop. *Science* 245:350 Jl 28 '89
FERMILAB See Fermi National Accelerator Laboratory
FERMIONS See Particles (Nuclear physics)
FERNALD (OHIO)

Radioactive pollution

The betrayal of Fernald, Ohio [residents tell their story] R. Distelheim. il *Good Housekeeping* 209:176+ S '89
Bomb makers' secrets. S. J. Hedges. il maps *U.S. News & World Report* 107:22-3+ O 23 '89
Dropping a bomb on 'radioactive junkyards' [jury decision against National Lead in pollution case] M. Mallory. il *Business Week* p29-30 Jl 3 '89
A living nightmare [L. Crawford turns activist over radioactive pollution from nuclear weapons plant] B. Burgower. il pors *Ladies' Home Journal* 106:74+ Mr '89
Uranium, in moderation [National Lead of Ohio defends radioactive leakage] *Harper's* 278:18+ Ja '89
Workers welfare [address, March 22, 1989] R. F. Celeste. *Vital Speeches of the Day* 55:490-2 Je 1 '89
FERNANDES LOPES, JOSE LUIS
about
Lopes in line to lead elite corps of envoys. por *Jet* 76:9 Jl 24 '89
FERNANDEZ, ANNA MARIA
about
Innerviews [interview] il por *Women's Sports & Fitness* 11:62 My '89
FERNÁNDEZ, BECKY
about
The Great Model Search 1989 [special section] il pors *'Teen* 33:76-85 O '89
FERNANDEZ, JOSEPH
about
Iran-contra: a CIA win. *Newsweek* 114:62 D 4 '89
FERNANDEZ, LOUIS
about
All they can eat. S. J. Madden. il *Fortune* 119:191-2 Ja 30 '89
FERNANDEZ, WALDO
about
Gandee at large. C. K. Gandee. il por *House & Garden* 161:218 N '89
Wall-to-wall Waldo means California cool to the likes of Merv and Liz. H. Shapiro. il pors *People Weekly* 31:131-2 My 1 '89
FERNANDO, RAMANI
A mix of extremes. il *World Health* p14-15 Mr '89
FERNAU & HARTMAN ARCHITECTS
Rational moves [Fernau & Hartman design offices for SBG Partners] K. D. Stein. il *Architectural Record* 177:68-75 mid-S '89
FERNDALE (MICH.)

Moral conditions

'Porndale' sings the red-light blues [zoning for red light district] il *Newsweek* 113:28 Ap 3 '89
FERNS
Stunning staghorn ferns. il *Southern Living* 24:61 Je '89
FERRAGAMO, WANDA
about
Wanda Ferragamo: the design matriarch's villa on Capri. S. Stephens. il por *Architectural Digest* 46:198-203 S '89
FERRANTI PLC
British Aerospace, Thomson-CSF consider making joint bid for Ferranti International Signal. *Aviation Week & Space Technology* 131:32 O 16 '89
Ferranti defends health of primary business, despite contract irregularities at subsidiary [ISC Technologies] *Aviation Week & Space Technology* 131:30 S 25 '89
FERRAR, ANN
The facts about bowel disease. *Ladies' Home Journal* 106:195 Mr '89
FERRARA, JERRY L.
Starting over. il *National Wildlife* 27:18-21 F/Mr '89
FERRARA, MIKE
Tools of the trade. See issues of Organic Gardening beginning February 1989
FERRARA, PETER J.
Catastrophic health benefits translate into catastrophic taxes [cover story] *Consumers' Research Magazine* 72:11-14 Ap '89

FERRARE, CRISTINA
about
Cristina Ferrare [cover story] V. Scott. il pors *Good Housekeeping* 209:16+ S '89

FERRARI, DEBORAH A. GLOCKNER- *See* Glockner-Ferrari, Deborah A.
FERRARI, MARK J.
about
O rare leviathan. K. Moore. il pors *Sports Illustrated* 70:66-72+ My 29 '89
FERRARI (AUTOMOBILE) See Sports cars
FERRARY, JEANNETTE
'O poor cook!': The annotating M. F. K. Fisher. por *The New York Times Book Review* 94:1+ Je 4 '89
FERRÉ, GIANFRANCO
about
Couture's future. C. Donovan. il pors *The New York Times Magazine* p48 Ag 27 '89
Gianfranco Ferré: architectural flair on Italy's Lago Maggiore. J. Thurman. il por *Architectural Digest* 46:104-11 S '89
The nonconformist. G. Howell. il por *Vogue* 179:198-203+ Jl '89
FERRÉ, MAURICE
about
Coconut Grove Tudor: the Miami residence of Maurice and Mercedes Ferré. B. Dunlop. il *Architectural Digest* 46:108-13+ F '89
FERRÉ, MERCEDES
about
Coconut Grove Tudor: the Miami residence of Maurice and Mercedes Ferré. B. Dunlop. il *Architectural Digest* 46:108-13+ F '89
FERRELL, TREVOR
about
One teen's campaign for the homeless. P. W. Cohen. il pors *Scholastic Update (Teachers' edition)* 121:20-2 F 10 '89
FERREN, BRAN, 1954-
about
Funny [film] Reviews
The New Republic 201:25 Jl 17-24 '89. S. Kauffmann
Theatre Crafts il 23:12-13 Ja '89. J. Calhoun
Truly special effects. J. Adler. il por *Newsweek* 114:45 O 2 '89
FERRER, GABRIEL
(jt. auth) See Boone, Debby, and Ferrer, Gabriel
FERRETTI, FRED
A gourmet at large. See issues of Gourmet beginning January 1985
Taipei. il map *Gourmet* 49:80-5+ Ap '89
FERRI, ROGER C., 1949-
about
The recovery of ornament. R. Kimball. il *Architectural Record* 177:132-7 My '89
FERRIER (NEW YORK, N.Y.: RESTAURANT) *See* New York (N.Y.)—Restaurants, nightclubs, bars, etc.
FERRIES
See also
Horse ferries
Ferry tales [southeast Alaska] M. Steere. il map *Travel Holiday* 172:58-67 Ag '89
The Washington State ferries. J. Stiak. il *Travel Holiday* 172:72-9 N '89
FERRIEUX, EMMANUELLE
Hidden messages. il *World Press Review* 36:39 Jl '89
FERRIOLA, JOSEPH, D. 1989
about
A change of command for the Chicago Mob. *Newsweek* 113:34 Mr 27 '89
FERRIS, MARY C.
Moonlight sonata [poem] *America* 161:381 N 25 '89
FERRIS WHEELS
Big wheel [Eli Bridge Company; cover story] K. Horan. il *Modern Maturity* 32:78-82 Je/Jl '89
FERRISS, LUCY, 1954-
And the babies had fun, too. il *The New York Times Magazine* p16+ My 21 '89
FERRITIN
Oxidation-reduction and the molecular mechanism of a regulatory RNA-protein interaction. M. W. Hentze and others. bibl f il *Science* 244:357-9 Ap 21 '89
FERROELECTRIC STORAGE DEVICES
Ferroelectric memories. J. F. Scott and C. A. Paz de Araujo. bibl f il *Science* 246:1400-5 D 15 '89
Nonvolatile memory advances reduce avionics weight, power requirements. W. B. Scott. il *Aviation Week & Space Technology* 131:79+ Jl 17 '89
FERROMAGNETISM See Magnetism
FERROTYPES See Tintypes
FERRUZZI GROUP
Ferruzzi trading "illogical" for many months. *Successful Farming* 87:48P N '89
How to build a $30 billion empire in five years [R. Gardini] J. Rossant. il por *Business Week* p58-9 Jl 3 '89
An Italian 'peasant' who would be soybean king [chairman R. Gardini's attempt to corner U.S. soybean market] E. Pomice. il por *U.S. News & World Report* 107:44-5 Ag 7 '89
Why the pits are sick over soybeans [Chicago Board of Trade directive, in response to Ferruzzi Group maneuvers, sends prices tumbling] D. Greising. il *Business Week* p76+ Jl 31 '89

FERRY, BRYAN
about
Bryan Ferry: the original art rocker. J. Powell. il pors *Glamour* 87:224 Ap '89
FERRY, DANNY
about
How do you say 'slam dunk' in Italian? J. Rossant. il *Business Week* p48 Ag 28 '89
Sitting pretty in Rome. C. Kirkpatrick. il pors *Sports Illustrated* 71:26-8+ O 9 '89
FERSH, SEYMOUR H.
(jt. auth) See King, Maxwell C., and Fersh, Seymour H.
FERTILITY (BIOLOGY)
See also
Artificial insemination, Human
Infertility
The blessings of fertility. M. Shivanandan. *America* 161:474-7 D 23-30 '89
Insuring a later pregnancy [views of Gilbert Haas] il *Prevention (Emmaus, Pa.)* 41:14 N '89
Make love now, babies later [fertility protection] J. Nash. il *Mademoiselle* 95:168-9+ D '89
Safeguarding future fertility [views of Gilbert Haas] *USA Today (Periodical)* 118:6 O '89
FERTILITY CONTROL See Birth control
FERTILIZATION (ARTIFICIAL INSEMINATION) See Artificial insemination, Human
FERTILIZATION (BIOLOGY)
See also
Conjugation (Biology)
Ova
Spermatozoa
Zygotes
FERTILIZATION IN VITRO
See also
Zygote intrafallopian transfer
Domestic cat bears exotic kitten [endangered Indian desert cat born at Cincinnati Zoo] il *Science News* 135:172 Mr 18 '89
Drilling for fertility [hole made in zona pellucida allows easier passage of sperm; work of Jacques Cohen] M. L. Fuerst. il *Discover* 10:22 O '89
An early-warning system [testing for genetic defects in the human egg] A. Purvis. il *Time* 134:56 N 27 '89
The facts of life for infertile couples [survey providing success rates of IVF clinics; work of Ron Wyden] S. McKee. il *American Health* 8:11-12 O '89
Genetic testing possible before conception [testing unfertilized egg; work of Yury Verlinsky] R. Weiss. *Science News* 136:326 N 18 '89
Infertility: a search for solutions. S. M. Halpern. *Reader's Digest* 135:129-30+ Jl '89
Infertility: playing the odds. S. M. Halpern. il *Ms.* 17:146-51+ Ja/F '89
Love multiplied by three [Mohr triplets born 21 months apart]; ed. by Elaine Fein. J. Mohr. il pors *Redbook* 173:100-1+ Ag '89
A technique originally developed for overcoming human infertility may also help endangered species. R. M. Adams. *Smithsonian* 19:12 Ja '89
Test screens live 'test tube' embryos. R. Weiss. *Science News* 135:132 Mr 4 '89
The test-tube generation celebrates its first decade [anniversary of the opening of Bourn Hall Clinic] il *People Weekly* 31:77 Je 5 '89
Wild child [Indian desert cat born to surrogate domestic mother at Cincinnati Zoo] il *Discover* 10:12 Jl '89
Ethical aspects
A piece of yourself in the world [human embryos frozen for later implantation] J. Lieber. il *The Atlantic* 263:76-80 Je '89
The rights of frozen embryos. J. Elson. il *Time* 134:63 Jl 24 '89
Test-tube tangle. D. Neff. *Christianity Today* 33:15 O 20 '89
There's no such thing as a right to bear children [with readers' comments] D. DeMarco. *U.S. Catholic* 54:13-19 Ag '89
Trying to fool the infertile [IVF clinics misrepresent success rates] M. D. Lemonick. il *Time* 133:53 Mr 13 '89
What do infertility clinics really deliver? [misrepresentation of success rates] S. Findlay. il *U.S. News & World Report* 106:74-5 Ap 3 '89
Laws and regulations
The case of the frozen embryos. J. Lieber. il *The Saturday Evening Post* 261:50-3 O '89
The eggs [J. and M. S. Davis' custody fight over fertilized eggs] B. McCollister. por *The Humanist* 49:39 N/D '89
Future shock [J. and M. S. Davis' custody fight over fertilized eggs] il *Time* 133:42 Mr 27 '89
Tempest in a test tube [J. and M. S. Davis' legal fight over frozen embryos] J. Seligmann. il pors *Newsweek* 114:66-7 Ag 21 '89
A tragic side effect [casualty of the administration's prolife offensive] *Time* 134:44 D 4 '89
The trial of an embryonic issue [debate over ownership of frozen embryos] il *U.S. News & World Report* 107:13 Ag 21 '89

Whose lives are these? [decision in custody battle between J. and M. S. Davis over frozen embryos] A. L. Sanders. il pors *Time* 134:19 O 2 '89
Anecdotes, facetiae, satire, etc.
People in Petri dishes. M. Ivins. il *The Progressive* 53:38 N '89
Great Britain
Britain's Lords debate embryo research. J. Cherfas. il *Science* 246:1554-5 D 22 '89
FERTILIZATION OF PLANTS
See also
Pollen
Directed movement of latex particles in the gynoecia of three species of flowering plants. L. C. Sanders and E. M. Lord. bibl f il *Science* 243:1606-8 Mr 24 '89
Hand pollinating corn. T. Leonard. il *Organic Gardening* 36:28-9 My '89
FERTILIZER INDUSTRY
See also
Nu-West Industries Inc.
FERTILIZERS AND MANURES
See also
Compost
Green manuring
Mulching
Potash
Sewage as fertilizer
Nitrogen fertilizer saps veggies' vitamin C [research by Sharon B. Hornick] *Science News* 136:255 O 14 '89
What about the new liquid lawn fertilizers? il *Sunset (Central West edition)* 183:204-5 N '89
Handling
20-year study vindicates anhydrous. *Successful Farming* 87:64A Ap '89
Anhydrous perks ridge-till corn in Ohio trials. R. Fee. *Successful Farming* 87:66AD F '89
Beyond starter to full-feed planters. D. Mowitz. il *Successful Farming* 87:20-3 F '89
Fall fertilizing. D. Mowitz. il *Successful Farming* 87:38-9 S '89
Fertilizer 'feeders'. D. Mowitz and C. Finck. il *Successful Farming* 87:24-5 mid-Mr '89
No-sweat sidedress. D. Mowitz. il *Successful Farming* 87:20-1 My '89
Old pits gets recharged [using water for manure disposal in swine houses] K. Coble and A. Muehling. il *Successful Farming* 87:56-7 Ja '89
Pull a plug to flush away hog manure. il *Successful Farming* 87:66 F '89
FESCUE
Trespassers will be poisoned [endophyte-infected tall fescue] K. Clay. il *Natural History* p8+ S '89
FESTA, SUSAN
The mechanics of motion. il *Health (New York, N.Y.)* 21:56-8 S '89
Yuppie flu or overtraining? *Runner's World* 24:56 Ja '89
FESTIVAL OF FESTIVALS (TORONTO, ONT.) See Motion picture festivals—Ontario
FESTIVAL OF NEW LATIN AMERICAN CINEMA (HAVANA, CUBA) See Motion picture festivals—Cuba
FESTIVAL OF TREES (ATLANTA, GA.) See Atlanta (Ga.)—Festivals
FESTIVALS
See also
Carnival (Pre-Lenten festival)
Dance festivals
Drama festivals
Motion picture festivals
Music festivals
Shakespeare festivals
Television festivals
World Festival of Youth and Students for Peace and Friendship
Healthy hearts across America [American Heart Association Food Festival] M. Roberts. *Psychology Today* 23:33 S '89
Sell your photos at festivals. K. Geller-Shinn. il *Petersen's Photographic Magazine* 17:28 Ja '89
Summer spirit: 20 travel money savers and the best of the cultural festivals. M. Burns. il *Essence* 19:27+ Ap '89
International aspects
High days and holidays [cover story; special issue] il *The Unesco Courier* 42:8-46 D '89
California
See also
Oakland (Calif.)—Festivals
San Francisco (Calif.)—Festivals
Caribbean region
Around the Mall and beyond [Caribbean festival arts at the S. Dillon Ripley Center] E. Park. il *Smithsonian* 20:18+ Ag '89
Art à la carte [Caribbean festival arts at the Saint Louis Art Museum] K. Best. il *Travel Holiday* 171:78 Ja '89
China
See also
Harbin (China)—Festivals

FESTIVALS—cont.

France

Liberty, equality, festivity! [French Revolution] L. Coudart. il *The Unesco Courier* 42:42-6 D '89

Georgia

See also

Atlanta (Ga.)—Festivals

Germany (West)

See also

Munich (Germany)—Festivals

India

See also

Pushkar (India)—Festivals

High days and holidays. V. S. Naravane. il *The Courier (Unesco)* 42:31-2 F '89

Italy

See also

Palio di Siena (Italy)

Japan

See also

Nara (Japan)—Festivals

Louisiana

Putting up the Christmas lights, Louisiana-style [bonfires] M. A. Sternberg. il *Smithsonian* 20:146-51 D '89

Massachusetts

See also

Westwood (Mass.)—Festivals

Mexico

See also

Guadalajara (Mexico)—Festivals

Skeletons at the feast [Feast of the Dead] J. Pérez Siller. il *The Unesco Courier* 42:19-24 D '89

Minnesota

See also

Hastings (Minn.)—Festivals

Minneapolis (Minn.)—Festivals

New York (State)

See also

PepsiCo Summerfare

Ohio

See also

Twinsburg (Ohio)—Festivals

Scotland

See also

Edinburgh International Festival

Senegal

Mock lion and real heroes [Simb] M. Seck. il *The Unesco Courier* 42:16-18 D '89

South Carolina

See also

Spoleto Festival U.S.A.

Southern States

Fairly good ways to see the South. *The Saturday Evening Post* 261:85-7+ My/Je '89

United States

See Festivals

Western Europe

Festive days, festive nights! [cover story] M. McHugh. il map *Travel Holiday* 172:36-47 D '89

Western States

Join the Portuguese for a festa. il *Sunset (Central West edition)* 182:20+ My '89

Wisconsin

See also

Elmwood (Wis.)—Festivals

Milwaukee (Wis.)—Festivals

FETAL AIDS SYNDROME

Fetal AIDS mimicked in brain-cell culture [research by William D. Lyman] I. Wickelgren. *Science News* 135:199 Ap 1 '89

The infant brain [cell culture pinpoints onset of infection; research by Arye Rubenstein and William Lyman] G. Montgomery. il *Discover* 10:30+ Ag '89

FETAL ALCOHOL SYNDROME

Alcohol abuse grows among pregnant poor [study by Bertis B. Little] B. Bower. *Science News* 136:230 O 7 '89

Alcohol's youngest victims. A. Dorfman. il *Time* 134:60 Ag 28 '89

The broken cord [excerpt] M. Dorris. il *Ladies' Home Journal* 106:104+ Ag '89

Bruised before birth. A. Steacy. il *Maclean's* 102:48 Ag 14 '89

Drinking while pregnant risks child's IQ [research by Ann P. Streissguth] B. Bower. *Science News* 135:68 F 4 '89

Pregnancy + alcohol = problems [views of M. Dorris] C. Leerhsen. il por *Newsweek* 114:57 Jl 31 '89

PW interviews [M. Dorris] D. Brainard. por *Publishers Weekly* 236:73-4 Ag 4 '89

Saving the children. B. L. Benderly. il *Health (New York, N.Y.)* 21:74-5 D '89

Severing the cord [son with fetal alcohol syndrome; excerpt from The broken cord] M. Dorris. il *Mother Jones* 14:47-8 S '89

FETAL REDUCTION

Selective abortion of twin [work of Usha Chitkara and Richard L. Berkowitz] *Science News* 135:278 My 6 '89

FETAL RESEARCH *See* Fetus

FETAL TISSUE

Transplantation

Bypassing the ban [neuroscientists seek alternatives to research on human fetal cells] R. Weiss. il *Science News* 136:378-9 D 9 '89

Fetal research. J. T. Hansen and J. R. Sladek. bibl f il *Science* 246:775-9 N 10 '89

Fetal tissue transplants win U.K. approval. D. Dickson. il *Science* 245:464-5 Ag 4 '89

The human mouse [infection of SCID-hu mouse by HIV; work of M. McCune; cover story; with editorial comment by Paul Hoffman] G. Montgomery. il por *Discover* 10:4, 48-55 Ag '89

One womb to another [fetal cell transplant] J. Langone. il *Time* 133:71 Ap 3 '89

Ethical aspects

Federal fetal transplant ban continues. *Science News* 136:310 N 11 '89

Fetal attraction [National Institutes of Health panel report recommending use of fetal tissue in medical research] R. J. Neuhaus. *National Review* 41:12-13 D 8 '89

Fetal research: the underlying issue. R. J. Levine. *Scientific American* 261:112 Ag '89

Fetal tissue transplants remain off limits. J. Palca. il *Science* 246:752 N 10 '89

This is what you thought: 69% favor using fetal tissue for medical research. il *Glamour* 87:153 Je '89

The use of aborted fetal tissue in medical research is as controversial as abortion itself. P. Orenstein. *Vogue* 179:298+ O '89

FETISOV, VIACHESLAV

about

Is it nyet or not yet? E. M. Swift. il pors *Sports Illustrated* 70:30-3 Ja 16 '89

FETOPROTEIN

Hypertension in pregnancy cuts cancer risk [role of alpha fetoprotein; research by Herbert I. Jacobson] J. Raloff. *Science News* 136:263 O 21 '89

FETTINGIS, JOSEPH

The watercolor page [cover story] il por *American Artist* 53:40-3 My '89

FETTUCINE COOKING *See* Cooking—Pasta

FETUS

See also

Fetoprotein

Maternally acquired immunity

Prenatal influences

Umbilical cord

The debate about life. R. Laver. il *Maclean's* 102:20 Jl 31 '89

The fascinating world of the unborn. H. Goer. *Reader's Digest* 135:150-4 N '89

Fetal research. J. T. Hansen and J. R. Sladek. bibl f il *Science* 246:775-9 N 10 '89

When does life begin? [interview with C. Grobstein] E. Hall. il pors *Psychology Today* 23:42-6 S '89

Diseases

See also

Fetal AIDS syndrome

Fetal alcohol syndrome

Diagnosis

See also

Amniocentesis

Chorionic villi sampling

Made to order babies. G. Cowley. il *Newsweek* 114 Special Issue:94-5+ Wint '89/Spr '90

The perfect baby? P. Klass. il *The New York Times Magazine* p45-6 Ja 29 '89

When prenatal tests bring bad news [lack of support groups available for couples choosing to abort pregnancies] M. Krance. bibl il *American Health* 8:11-12 Jl/Ag '89

Legal status, laws, etc.

If fetuses are people . . . [Missouri] W. Saletan. *The New Republic* 201:18-20 S 18-25 '89

Is an embryo a person? C. A. Gardner. il *The Nation* 249:557-9 N 13 '89

The politics of pregnancy. C. Tavris. *Vogue* 179:572-3+ S '89

The pregnancy police, on patrol [enforcing fetal rights by jailing negligent mothers] T. Gest. il *U.S. News & World Report* 106:50 F 6 '89

Prenatal development and the law [Webster v. Reproductive Health Services] J. Kagan. *Psychology Today* 23:46 S '89

When the law and medicine collide [conflict over age of fetal viability] J. Silberner. il *U.S. News & World Report* 107:23 Jl 17 '89

Surgery

One womb to another [fetal cell transplant] J. Langone. il *Time* 133:71 Ap 3 '89

Operating on the unborn. G. Kolata. il *The New York Times Magazine* p34-5+ My 14 '89

FETUS, DEATH OF

See also

Abortion

Miscarriage

FETUS, EFFECT OF DRUGS ON THE
See also
Fetal alcohol syndrome
Cocaine babies: the littlest victims [penalties to mothers] il *Newsweek* 114:55 O 2 '89
Cocaine mothers imperil babies' brains [reports by Ira J. Chasnoff and Barry Zuckerman] K. Fackelmann. *Science News* 135:198 Ap 1 '89
Cocaine's youngest victims. C. García-Barrio. il *American Visions* 4:16 D '89
Crack in the cradle. A. C. Revkin. il *Discover* 10:62-9 S '89
Drugs and pregnancy: often the two don't mix. E. Zamula. il *FDA Consumer* 23:7-10 Je '89
Here come the pregnancy police [legal action against mothers of infants exposed to drugs] A. Sachs. il *Time* 133:104-5 My 22 '89
Jailing mothers for drug abuse [screening newborns in Butte County, Calif.] S. LaCroix. il *The Nation* 248:585-6+ My 1 '89
Saving the children. B. L. Benderly. il *Health (New York, N.Y.)* 21:74-5 D '89

FEUDALISM
Japan
See also
Daimyo

FEUER, LEWIS SAMUEL, 1912-
The inventor of 'pluralism'. por *The New Leader* 72:12-13 S 4 '89

FEUERSTEIN, PHYLLIS A.
Periodontal disease: nothing to smile about. il *Current Health 2* 15:28-9 Ja '89
Yes, there's help. il *Current Health 2* 15:10-11 F '89

FEULNER, EDWIN J.
Experienced conservatives for Bush. il *The American Spectator* 22:28-9 Ja '89

FEVER
See also
Pyrogens
Typhoid fever
Macrophage inflammatory protein-1: a prostaglandin-independent endogenous pyrogen. G. Davatelis and others. bibl f il *Science* 243:1066-8 F 24 '89
Treating a fever [infants] K. Karlsrud and D. Schultz. il *Parents* 64:205 Je '89
When baby has a fever. P. Klass. il *The New York Times Magazine* p57-8 Ag 20 '89

A FEW GOOD MEN [drama] See Sorkin, Aaron

FEYNMAN, RICHARD PHILLIPS
about
Richard Feynman [cover story; special issue; with editorial comment by Gloria B. Lubkin] bibl f pors *Physics Today* 42:22-8+ F '89

FEZZA, ANDREW
about
Fezza's new point of hue. H. Sterne. il por *Gentlemen's Quarterly* 59:378 S '89

FGF See Fibroblast growth factor

FHA See United States. Farmers Home Administration; United States. Federal Housing Administration

FIAT SPA
Agnelli on cars, greens, and Japan. R. I. Kirkland, Jr. il pors *Fortune* 120:133+ Jl 31 '89

FIBER CRAFTS See Textile crafts

FIBER GLASS See Fiberglass

FIBER IN DIET
See also
Bran
Cooking—Grain
100 top fiber foods. S. Stocker-Ferguson. il *Prevention (Emmaus, Pa.)* 41:73+ N '89
Another dietary advantage to fiber [research by Allen S. Levine] *Science News* 136:412 D 23-30 '89
The facts on fiber. *McCall's* 117:89 O '89
Fiber fills the bill. il *Ebony* 45:139+ D '89
Fill up on complex carbohydrates [excerpt from Good fat/bad fat] G. C. Griffin and W. P. Castelli. il *The Saturday Evening Post* 261:12-13+ O '89
Healthful high-fiber, low-fat recipes. il *The Saturday Evening Post* 261:32 N/D '89
Our thresh-hold to health [psyllium] M. G. Stoddard. il *The Saturday Evening Post* 261:28-9 N/D '89
The right way to fiber up. G. L. Blackburn. il *Prevention (Emmaus, Pa.)* 41:25+ D '89
Taking oat bran to heart [lowering cholesterol] J. W. Anderson. il *The Saturday Evening Post* 261:18+ Jl/Ag '89
A tangle of fibers [cover story] A. McKenzie. il *Science News* 136:344-5 N 25 '89
Tough to swallow. O. Anderson. il *Women's Sports & Fitness* 11:13 Je '89

FIBER OPTIC TECHNOLOGY CENTER (U.S.)
USAF center solves communications, avionics problems with fiber optics. B. W. Henderson. il *Aviation Week & Space Technology* 130:103+ Je 5 '89

FIBER OPTIC TELEVISION
Charge of the 'telcos' [fiber optic TV vs. cable] B. Brewin. il *Video* 12:142 Ja '89

The coming battle over your TV set [telephone companies vs. cable operators] J. Dreyfuss. il *Fortune* 119:104-7 F 13 '89
End run [phone companies] G. Slutsker. il *Forbes* 144:124-5 Ag 7 '89
A fiber-optics future? T. Wetmore. il *Channels (New York, N.Y.: 1986)* 9:93 Ja '89
Grabbing an electronic bonanza [telephone companies enter cable business; cover story] S. W. Dean, Jr. and R. L. Shayon. il *The Nation* 249:369+ O 9 '89
Here come the RBOCs [phone companies seek cable TV acquisitions] il *Channels (New York, N.Y.: 1986)* 9:72-7 Je '89
The latest telco debate [telephone companies entering cable business] M. Brown. il *Channels (New York, N.Y.: 1986)* 9:28 Mr '89
Telecom apartheid. P. W. Huber. il *Forbes* 144:268 N 27 '89

Patents
Severed heads and wasted resources [Fibermedia charged with stealing trade secrets from Advance Display Technologies Inc.] G. F. Gilder. il *Forbes* 143:45-6+ Je 26 '89

FIBER OPTICS
See also
Fiber Optic Technology Center (U.S.)
Guided missiles—Optical equipment
Integrated services digital network
Changing orbits [fiber optics vs. satellites] M. Beauchamp. il *Forbes* 143:273-5 My 29 '89
Comsat study shows satellites competing successfully with fiber-optic cables. M. Mecham. *Aviation Week & Space Technology* 130:131 F 20 '89
Fiber-optic periscope could alter sub design. *High Technology Business* 9:35 Je '89
Fiber optics for astronomy. il *Sky and Telescope* 78:569-70 D '89
Fiber vs. metal [computer cables] J. Y. Bryce. il *Byte* 14:253-8 Ja '89
Fiberoptic gyros promise new inertial guidance. il *Popular Mechanics* 166:15 Je '89
Firms research fiber-optic gyros as successors to ring-laser systems. P. J. Klass. il *Aviation Week & Space Technology* 130:79+ F 13 '89
Land of the midnight melons? [fiber optic transmission of rays to Arctic crops in indoor gardens; work of Dennis R. St. George] *Science News* 136:412 D 23-30 '89
The light at the end of the LAN [Fiber Distributed Data Interface standard] B. Glass. il *Byte* 14:269-72+ Jl '89
The natural roots of fiber optics [gray hair] I. Amato. il *Science News* 136:414-15 D 23-30 '89
Optical fibers in medicine. A. Katzir. bibl il *Scientific American* 260:120-5 My '89
Photonics shed light on diverse uses. il *Popular Mechanics* 166:17 F '89
USAF studies linking phased array radar with fiber-optic cable. *Aviation Week & Space Technology* 130:61+ Ja 30 '89
What goes around comes around [optical solitons; work of Linn Mollenauer] il *Discover* 10:14+ F '89

FIBER OPTICS INDUSTRY
See also
Advance Display Technologies Inc.
FiberMedia Corporation
US Sprint Communications Inc.
Fiber optics: getting cheap enough to start rewiring America. L. Therrien. il *Business Week* p86 Jl 31 '89
Light talk [goal of putting optical fibers in the home] E. Corcoran. il *Scientific American* 261:74+ O '89
The U.S. electronics industry can be reinvigorated. B. D. Nordwall. il *Aviation Week & Space Technology* 131:40-1 D 18-25 '89

FIBERGLASS
High-fiber connectors [Thermomass Foam Sandwich Foundation System] C. M. Fiorillo. il *Popular Science* 235:44+ N '89

FIBERGLASS BOATS See Boats and boating—Materials

FIBERGLASS WALL COVERINGS See Wall coverings

FIBERMEDIA CORPORATION
Severed heads and wasted resources [Fibermedia charged with stealing trade secrets from Advance Display Technologies Inc.] G. F. Gilder. il *Forbes* 143:45-6+ Je 26 '89

FIBERVIEW CORPORATION
See also
FiberMedia Corporation

FIBRILLATION, HEART See Arrhythmia

FIBRINOLYSIS
See also
Plasminogen
Plasminogen activators

FIBROBLAST GROWTH FACTOR
Fibroblast growth factor in the extracellular matrix of dystrophic (mdx) mouse muscle. J. DiMario and others. bibl f il *Science* 244:688-90 My 12 '89
Purification and complementary DNA cloning of a receptor for basic fibroblast growth factor. P. L. Lee and others. bibl f il *Science* 245:57-60 Jl 7 '89

FIBROBLASTS
Autocrine induction of collagenase by serum amyloid A-like and β_2-microgobulin-like proteins. C. E. Brinckerhoff and others. bibl f il *Science* 243:655-7 F 3 '89

Commitment of mouse fibroblasts to adipocyte differentiation by DNA transfection. S. Chen and others. bibl f il *Science* 244:582-5 My 5 '89

Ectopic expression of the serotonin 1c receptor and the triggering of malignant transformation. D. Julius and others. bibl f il *Science* 244:1057-62 Je 2 '89

Fibroblasts transformed with v-*src* show enhanced formation of an inositol tetrakisphosphate. R. M. Johnson and others. bibl f il *Science* 246:121-4 O 6 '89

G_1 events and regulations of cell proliferation. A. B. Pardee. bibl f il *Science* 246:603-8 N 3 '89

Interleukin-1 mitogenic activity of fibroblasts and smooth muscle cells is due to PDGF-AA. E. W. Raines and others. bibl f il *Science* 243:393-6 Ja 20 '89

Normal expression of a rearranged and mutated c-*myc* oncogene after transfection into fibroblasts [Burkitt's lymphoma] A. Richman and A. Hayday. bibl f il *Science* 246:494-7 O 27 '89

Perineurium originates from fibroblasts: demonstration in vitro with a retroviral marker. M. B. Bunge and others. bibl f il *Science* 243:229-31 Ja 13 '89

FIBROCYSTIC BREAST DISEASE *See* Breast—Diseases
FIBROID TUMORS
What are uterine fibroids? P. A. Hillard. il *Parents* 64:183-4 Mr '89

FIBROMYALGIA *See* Fibrositis
FIBROSIS, CYSTIC *See* Cystic fibrosis
FIBROSITIS
"Am I sick or am I tired?". P. Dranov. *Ladies' Home Journal* 106:120+ S '89

FICHTENBAUM, PAUL
Another Hull's apoppin'. il pors *Sports Illustrated* 71:144+ D 25 '89-Ja 1 '90

Beers with . . . Evander Holyfield [interview] il pors *Sport (New York, N.Y.)* 80:19-20 Ag '89

Joe Walton: the coach everyone loves to hate. por *Sport (New York, N.Y.)* 80:50 Ag '89

FICHTER, JOSEPH HENRY, 1908-
The Church: looking to the future [cover story] *America* 160:189-92 Mr 4 '89

FICHTER, NANCY SMITH
Stalking [the] deep coherence: curricular design in the arts. bibl f *Design for Arts in Education* 91:2-10 S/O '89

FICTION
See also
American fiction
Best sellers
Bolívar, Simón, 1783-1830—Fiction
Characters in literature
Chinese fiction
Computer novels
Detective and mystery stories
English fiction
Fantasies, Literary
Ghost stories
Graphic novels
Historical fiction
Homosexuality in literature
Horror tales
Israeli fiction
Realism in literature
Religion in literature
Romance fiction
Science fiction
Western stories
Women in literature
Young adults' literature

Educated by novels. J. Epstein. *Commentary* 88:33-9 Ag '89

Gee, I kind of like fiction. J. Nocera. *The Washington Monthly* 21:28-9 Mr '89

Novels [discussion of August 1989 article, Educated by novels] J. Epstein. *Commentary* 88:8-9 N '89

The novel's next step. M. H. Kingston. il *Mother Jones* 14:37-41 D '89

Authorship
Creative lying [lying as a child helpful to adult fiction writers] J. VanOosting. *The Writer* 102:7-8 O '89

Opus in a drawer: on having written an unpublished novel. M. Mitcham. il *Commonweal* 116:296-7 My 19 '89

The professional response. S. Sheldon. *The Writer* 102:9-10 Mr '89

The professional response. S. Sheldon. *The Writer* 102:7-8 Jl '89

The professional response. S. Sheldon. *The Writer* 102:11 D '89

Write the story you want to tell. S. Isaacs. *The Writer* 102:11-13 Je '89

Writing a first novel (I). *The Writer* 102:24-7 Jl '89
Writing a first novel (II). *The Writer* 102:27-31 Ag '89
Writing a first novel (III). *The Writer* 102:25-9 S '89
Writing a first novel (IV). *The Writer* 102:23-6 O '89

Collaboration
See Authorship—Collaboration
Bibliography
Summer reading. L. Yelin. il *Parents* 64:176+ Jl '89
Competitions
Anecdotes, facetiae, satire, etc.
Across the river and into Harry's Bar [International Imitation Hemingway Competition; excerpt from The best of bad Hemingway] G. Plimpton. *The New York Times Book Review* 94:1+ Ap 16 '89

Narration
Which viewpoint—and why. M. Byrd. *The Writer* 102:12-14 O '89

Single works
See also
Short stories
See name of author for full entry
Abo's wine. Widener, S. L.
Anger of the sea-goddess. Pillai, Thakazhi S.
Birth. Walker, Alice, 1944-
The captive. Holt, Victoria, 1906-
Catch-and-release. Richler, Mordecai, 1931-
Cat's eye. Atwood, Margaret, 1939-
The charmed circle. Gaskin, Catherine, 1929-
Claude imagines himself a colonel. West, Nathanael, 1903-1940
The dinner party. Drabble, Margaret, 1939-
East is east. Boyle, T. Coraghessan
Erogenous South Africa. Breytenbach, Breyten
Hayduke lives! Abbey, Edward, 1927-1989
In transit. Mukherjee, Bharati
Informed risk. Carr, Robyn
The Joy Luck Club. Tan, Amy
The lost language of love. Kingsolver, Barbara
Lucy and Ricky and the Mambo Kings. Hijuelos, Oscar
Marriage vs freedom. Walker, Alice, 1944-
A master of the universe. Wolfe, Tom
Mere mortals. Ravin, Neil
My brother. Atwood, Margaret, 1939-
'Personal for Mr. Bartholomew Scott Blair, urgent'. Le Carré, John, 1931-
Piano fingers. Mason, Bobbie Ann
The place of the skull. Aĭtmatov, Chingiz
Ralph Nickelby's tell-tale guise. Dickens, Charles, 1812-1870
Rightfully mine. Mortman, Doris
The sands of time. Sheldon, Sidney, 1917-
Sockless in Singapore. Theroux, Paul
St. Valentine's night. Greeley, Andrew M., 1928-
Star. Steel, Danielle
Stood up. Christopherson, Teri
The storyteller speaks. Vargas Llosa, Mario, 1936-
A taste of heaven. Simon, Laura
The temple of my familiar. Walker, Alice, 1944-
A time to sing. Mandel, Sally
Under this very mall. Gurganus, Allan
Waverly Place. Brownmiller, Susan
Zora and Franklin. McMillan, Terry

Style
See Style, Literary
Technique
See also
Characterization
Dialogue
Short story
Effective transitions. G. R. Hemingway. *The Writer* 102:21-3 Ag '89

Great storytelling. L. Barlow. *The Writer* 102:14-17 Ag '89

The lax habits of the free imagination [excerpt from The Houghton Mifflin anthology of short fiction] P. Hampl. il *The New York Times Book Review* 94:1+ Mr 5 '89

Rewriting your novel. S. L. Stebel. *The Writer* 102:17-19 Je '89

FICTION AND MOTION PICTURES *See* Motion picture adaptations
FICTION IN PERIODICALS AND NEWSPAPERS
When truth isn't stranger than fiction. M. L. Johnson. *The Writer* 102:26-7 F '89

FIDDLE MUSIC *See* Violin music
FIDELITY CAPITAL APPRECIATION FUND
Fidelity's newest wunderkind runs the fund that may be the next Magellan [T. Sweeney] G. Anrig, Jr. il por *Money* 18:201-2 Ap '89

FIDELITY MAGELLAN FUND
Can Lynch live up to his reputation? J. Clements. il por *Forbes* 143:174+ Ap 3 '89

Inside traitor [views of P. Lynch] M. K. Evans. il *Gentlemen's Quarterly* 59:153-4 Je '89

Investing: how to beat the pros [interview with P. Lynch; cover story] il pors *Changing Times* 43:32-4+ My '89

Johnson and Lynch: an odd couple with a hit formula. J. Friedman. il por *Business Week* p73 Ap 17 '89

Lynch's law? [record of P. Lynch] M. Hulbert. il *Forbes* 143:230 Ap 17 '89

One up on Wall Street [excerpt]; ed. by J. Rothchild. P. Lynch. il pors *Money* 18:128-9+ Ja '89

Peter Lynch's seven rules for making money. il por *Money* 18:74-5 D '89

FIDELITY MAGELLAN FUND—*cont.*
What Magellan's man at the top is buying [views of P. Lynch] G. G. Marcial. por *Business Week* p142 O 9 '89

FIDELITY MANAGEMENT & RESEARCH CO.
Fidelity fights back [cover story] L. Helm. il pors *Business Week* p68-72 Ap 17 '89

FIDELITY SELECT LEISURE & ENTERTAINMENT FUND
A boomer plays the leisure boom [interview with K. Firestone] K. Nickel. il por *Fortune* 120:63+ N 20 '89

FIDELITY SPARTAN MONEY MARKET FUND
Money market funds that pack a real punch. L. J. Nathans. il *Business Week* p104 Ag 21 '89

FIEDLER, DAVID
The UNIX/bin. See issues of Byte beginning August 1989

FIEL, MAXINE LUCILLE
Starcast. See issues of Mademoiselle

FIELD, BENJAMIN P.
U.S. history in a box. il *National Geographic* 175:652-60 My '89

FIELD, FRANK
Could your family survive a fire? il *Reader's Digest* 135:137-40 N '89

FIELD, KATHERINE G., AND OTHERS
Phylogeny and molecular data [discussion of February 12, 1988 article, Molecular phylogeny of the animal kingdom] *Science* 243:548-51 Ja 27 '89

FIELD, SALLY
about
Spunky Sally Field. A. Sachs. il pors *McCall's* 117:10-13+ N '89
Straight from the heart [cover story] S. Dworkin. pors *Redbook* 174:20+ D '89

FIELD, THOMAS WALTER, JR.
about
McKesson dumps another asset: the boss. R. D. Hof. il pors *Business Week* p47 S 25 '89

FIELD ATHLETICS *See* Track and field athletics
FIELD CAMERAS *See* Cameras
FIELD EXPERIMENTS (AGRICULTURE)
See also
Corn—Field experiments
Farmers cutting costs in own on-farm research. J. Walter. *Successful Farming* 87:33 mid-F '89
The fruits of summer testing. G. Vincent. il *Successful Farming* 87:50X-50Y Ja '89

FIELD GLASSES *See* Binoculars
FIELD HOCKEY
Field hockey will stick with you for life. L. Ferenci. il por *Women's Sports & Fitness* 11:60-1 S '89

FIELD MUSEUM OF NATURAL HISTORY
Art à la carte [permanent exhibit inside ancient Egypt] K. Best. il *Travel Holiday* 171:86 F '89

FIELD OF DREAMS [film] See Motion picture reviews—Single works

FIELD THEORY (PHYSICS)
See also
Electroweak interactions
Can we scale the Planck scale? D. J. Gross. il por *Physics Today* 42:9+ Je '89

FIELDER, FLORIAN
about
A secret cache. B. Grauman. il *Art News* 88:59-60 Summ '89

FIELDER, LOUIS
about
Work in progress. R. Hodges. il *Stereo Review* 54:97 Ag '89

FIELDS, ADAM
about
'Nothin' but weddings and funerals'. R. Palmer. il por *American Film* 14:32 Je '89

FIELDS, BERT, 1929-
about
Big bad Bert [interview] C. Stauth. il por *American Film* 15:46-50 D '89

FIELDS, CRAIG I.
about
Knapp resigns from URA leadership; Truly to pilot NASA, Fields at DARPA. I. Goodwin. *Physics Today* 42:42-4 Je '89

FIELDS, DIANE
Caution: your stress style may be hazardous to your health. il *Mademoiselle* 95:158 Ap '89

FIELDS, KIM
about
Kim Fields: what happened to child stars after TV fame? [cover story] il pors *Jet* 75:56-9 Ja 23 '89

FIELDS, PATRICIA I., AND OTHERS
A Salmonella locus that controls resistance to microbicidal proteins from phagocytic cells. bibl f il *Science* 243:1059-62 F 24 '89

FIELDS, RICK
about
Buddhist editor leaves amid controversy. J. Walljasper. il *Utne Reader* p36-7 Jl/Ag '89

FIELDS, TERRI, 1948-
Women to be thankful for. il *McCall's* 117:117-18+ N '89

FIELDS, WAYNE
A wonderful place to live. il *American Heritage* 40:114-17 Ap '89

FIELDS, MAGNETIC *See* Magnetic fields
FIENBERG, STEPHEN E., AND TANUR, JUDITH M.
Combining cognitive and statistical approaches to survey design. bibl f il *Science* 243:1017-22 F 24 '89

FIERO (AUTOMOBILE) *See* Sports cars
FIERSTEIN, HARVEY
about
Dignity in drag [cover story] J. Scott. il pors *Film Comment* 25:9-12+ Ja/F '89
Fierstein's Torch song saga. T. Soter. il por *Video* 13:15 Jl '89

FIFTH FORCE (PHYSICS)
Faith in fifth force fades. M. M. Waldrop. *Science* 246:760 N 10 '89
Gravity under siege [testing Newton's law] T. Waters. il *Discover* 10:18+ Ap '89
Searching for the secrets of gravity. J. Boslough. il *National Geographic* 175:562-83 My '89

FIFTIES (DECADE) *See* Nineteen hundred and fifties
FIFTY-PLUS RUNNERS ASSOCIATION
Fifty something. J. Brant. il *Runner's World* 24:58-61 Ag '89

FIG, ANTON
about
The World's Most Dangerous sidemen. il pors *Down Beat* 56:18 O '89

FIGARSKY, B. B.
"Worthless" stock. il *Antiques & Collecting Hobbies* 94:46-8+ Jl '89

FIGHTER PILOTS *See* Air pilots
FIGHTER PLANES *See* Airplanes, Military
FIGHTING *See* Boxing
FIGHTING (PSYCHOLOGY)
See also
Quarrels
Fighting the good fight. M. M. Hunt. il *New Choices for the Best Years* 29:71-3 Ag '89

FIGHTING AMONG ARACHNIDS *See* Arachnids—Habits and behavior
FIGS
See also
Cooking—Fruit
FIGUEIREDO, MARIZA DE ATHAYDE, AND PRADO, DANDA
The women of Arembepe. il *The Unesco Courier* 42:38-41 Jl '89

FIGUEROA, JOHN
When laity lead. *Commonweal* 116:470-1 S 8 '89

FIGURATIVE ART
Exhibitions
A new exhibition proves that even when abstraction dominates, the figure remains irresistible [Bay Area figurative art, 1950-1965] J. Tarshis. il *Vogue* 179:210+ D '89

FIGURE, HUMAN *See* Human body
FIGURE SKATING
See also
Ice dancing
Next Ice Age (Skating company)
Conquering the elements: choreography on ice. S. C. Turner and R. Harris. il *Dance Magazine* 63:34-9 F '89
A skating star's long fall from grace [cover story]; ed. by Lois Armstrong. T. Babilonia. il pors *People Weekly* 31:86-8+ Ap 17 '89

Competitions
Beauty on ice [skater J. Mills] il pors *'Teen* 33:86-7 N '89
A dazzling gold [K. Browning wins men's World Figure Skating Championships] A. Steacy. il por *Maclean's* 102:53 Mr 27 '89
Innerviews [interview with E. Manley] por *Women's Sports & Fitness* 11:58 Je '89
Mite makes right [M. Ito at World Figure Skating finals] D. S. Looney. il pors *Sports Illustrated* 70:38-9 Mr 27 '89
New girl in town [K. Yamaguchi at U.S. Figure Skating Championships] E. M. Swift. il por *Sports Illustrated* 70:22-3 F 20 '89
A skating sprite with a towering talent, Kristi Yamaguchi wants to ice the world title. il por *People Weekly* 31:71 Mr 20 '89
The split-second skill of a figure skating prodigy [Canadian K. Browning] D. Jenish. il por *Maclean's* 102:38-9 D 25 '89

FIGURES OF SPEECH
See also
Metaphor
FIGURINES
The Derby animal band [porcelain] S. Bagdade and A. Bagdade. il *Antiques & Collecting Hobbies* 94:19 My '89

FIJI
See also
Americans—Fiji
Laucala (Fiji)
Sunday—Laws and regulations—Fiji
Women—Fiji

FIJI—*cont.*

Description and travel

Where the world's day begins. R. Ariyoshi. il map *Travel Holiday* 171:40-7 Ja '89

Foreign relations

United States

See United States—Foreign relations—Fiji

Industries

See also

Fisheries—Fiji

Politics and government

Fiji: a second Grenada? M. Stevenson. il *The American Spectator* 22:21-5 Jl '89

Religious institutions and affairs

See also

Methodist Church—Fiji

FILA PASTRY *See* Pastry

FILALI, FOUAD

about

"My father-in-law is very demanding". P. Gupte. il por *Forbes* 143:44-5 My 1 '89

FILARIASIS

See also

Onchocerciasis

FILE, KAREN

(jt. auth) *See* David, Jo, and File, Karen

FILE ORGANIZATION (COMPUTERS)

See also

Data structures (Computer science)

LapLink (Computer program)

Personal information management software

The ABCs of X-, Y-, and ZMODEM [file transfer protocols] B. N. Meeks. il *Byte* 14:163-6 F '89

Circumnavigating the disk with Magellan. A. Reinhardt. il *Byte* 14:97-8 My '89

Coming together [special section] il *Compute!* 11:20-2+ Mr '89

Directory assistance (I). R. Grehan. bibl il *Byte* 14:291-4+ My '89

Directory assistance (II). R. Grehan. il *Byte* 14:327-8+ Je '89

Exploring a hard disk [Magellan] L. Kleinman. il *Personal Computing* 13:29 F '89

Fast and flexible data transfer program [FastLynx] C. Lee. il *Personal Computing* 13:204 N '89

FileMaker II. R. Hart. il *Home Office Computing* 7:78+ Je '89

From PC to Mac and back [transferring word processing files] R. Blodgett. il *Personal Computing* 13:53-5 D '89

Get organized with ViewLink. il *Radio-Electronics* 60 ComputerDigest:80+ Je '89

Graphics formats. G. L. Graef. il *Byte* 14:305-6+ S '89

Handy DOS commands give directory assistance. T. Roberts. *Compute!* 11:82 N '89

If memory serves . . . [memory management routines] R. Grehan. il *Byte* 14:279-80+ Ag '89

Magellan: intrepid hard-disk explorer. L. Kleinman. il *Personal Computing* 13:192 Jl '89

Making applications talk [Communicating Applications Specification file transfer protocols] B. Glass. il *Byte* 14:155-8 Ja '89

Master the data on your hard-disk drive with Lotus Magellan. S. Morgenstern. il *Home Office Computing* 7:36+ N '89

Mastering the PCX format [PCX Programmer's Toolkit] B. Tyler. il *Byte* 14:183-4+ S '89

Meet Dr. Database [use of RapidFile by E. Gordy] K. J. Novak. il por *Home Office Computing* 7:24-5 Jl '89

A new world for DOS [ViewLink and Magellan] S. Miastkowski. il *Byte* 14:177-8+ Ag '89

A pair of Paradox helpers [DataFinder and ScriptView] S. Miastkowski. il *Byte* 14:100 Je '89

PC Tools Deluxe integrated utilities encourage greater productivity. R. Bel Bruno. il *Personal Computing* 13:186 D '89

PC Tools Deluxe, version 5.0. J. B. Lambert. il *Compute!* 11:63-4 Je '89

The protocol pack [XMODEM and its file transfer heirs] B. N. Meeks. il *Byte* 14:155-6+ Mr '89

Pushing Standard File to the limit. J. Eugenides. il *Byte* 14 Mac Special Ed:MAC225-MAC228+ Je '89

Reports [file management program for Hypercard] H. E. H. Aycock. il *Compute!* 11:94-5 Ja '89

Sending information from here to there [file transfer protocols] A. Glossbrenner. il *Home Office Computing* 7:34-5 Mr '89

Swapping DOS to Mac the convenient way [DOS Mounter] D. Barker. il *Byte* 14:84+ O '89

Transferring your data PDQ [PDQ² 2.0] J. Bell. il *Personal Computing* 13:212+ Mr '89

Trees 'n keys (I). R. Grehan. il *Byte* 14:379-80+ Ja '89

Trees 'n keys (II). R. Grehan. il *Byte* 14:301-7 F '89

Trees 'n keys (III). R. Grehan. il *Byte* 14:287-8+ Mr '89

Two tin cans and some string. R. Grehan. il *Byte* 14:303-4+ O '89

Unix filenames for Turbo Pascal. J. Kerr. il *Byte* 14 Special Issue:185-6+ Fall '89

ViewLink. D. Stanton. il *Compute!* 11:66-7+ Jl '89

ViewLink: uniting data and applications. C. Bermant. il *Personal Computing* 13:101 My '89

Whose data is it anyhow? [file structure for shared databases] M. Liskin. il *Personal Computing* 13:55-6+ Je '89

Windows made clearer [ClearView and PubTech File Organizer] S. Miastkowski. il *Byte* 14:290 N '89

FILE SERVERS (COMPUTERS)

The 486s are here! [Apricot VX FT Server; cover story] P. Lavin and M. E. Nadeau. il *Byte* 14:95-8 S '89

High-fashion UNIX on a PC [Hewlett-Packard Accelerated X Window Display Server] B. Smith. il *Byte* 14:205-6+ D '89

Serving business [SQL database server products] W. Rash, Jr. il *Byte* 14:147-8+ N '89

Serving up data. M. L. Van Name and B. Catchings. il *Byte* 14:259-60+ S '89

The spotlight turns to database servers. M. Liskin. il *Personal Computing* 13:53-6 N '89

Turn your Compaq into a LAN server with gigabytes. S. J. Wszola. il *Byte* 14:100 My '89

Will you be my server? E. Dyson. il *Forbes* 144:272 D 11 '89

FILES AND RASPS

Files in the workshop. H. Wicks. il *Home Mechanix* 85:26-9 Je '89

FILHO, CHICO MENDES *See* Mendes Filho, Chico

FILIBUSTER WAR *See* Nicaragua—History—Filibuster War, 1855-1860

FILING SYSTEMS

See also

Filofax

Household records

LA FILLE MAL GARDÉE [ballet] *See* Ballet reviews—Single works

FILLER, MARTIN, 1948-

Artists' assemblage. il *House & Garden* 161:198-205 S '89

Bring me no flowers. il *House & Garden* 161:68+ F '89

Caro. il por *House & Garden* 161:174-5 Mr '89

Charles: England's designing prince. il pors *House & Garden* 161:158-61+ Mr '89

Cottage classic. il *House & Garden* 161:192-9+ My '89

George Washington's garden. il *House & Garden* 161:140-9 My '89

Gothic getaway. il *House & Garden* 161:104-9 Je '89

Kyoto comforts. il *House & Garden* 161:74+ D '89

Legacy of splendor. il *House & Garden* 161:86-91 Jl '89

Master of cabinetry. il por *House & Garden* 161:146-9+ Mr '89

Merchant of Memphis. il por *House & Garden* 161:64+ S '89

Schloss Charlottenhof in Potsdam: a Karl Friedrich Schinkel masterpiece restored. il *Antiques* 135:930-41 Ap '89

Society's café. il pors *House & Garden* 161:100+ O '89

SoHo salon. il pors *House & Garden* 161:170-3 O '89

Terry: keeper of the faith. il por *House & Garden* 161:162-3+ Mr '89

What price glory. il *House & Garden* 161:118-25+ Jl '89

FILLING (EARTHWORK)

See also

Sanitary landfills

FILLING MATERIALS

Matching patches [wood fillers] L. Okrend. *Workbench* 45:12 Jl/Ag '89

FILLINGS, DENTAL *See* Dental materials

FILLMORE, MILLARD, 1800-1874

Anecdotes, facetiae, satire, etc.

'Millard Fillmore was my kind of guy'. B. Holland. il *Smithsonian* 20:238 O '89

FILM *See* Motion pictures

FILM ADAPTATIONS *See* Motion picture adaptations

FILM AND TELEVISION PRODUCER'S PROGRAM *See* University of California, Los Angeles. Independent Film and Television Producer's Program

FILM ARCHIVES *See* Motion picture collections

FILM AUDIENCES *See* Motion picture audiences

FILM COMMENT (PERIODICAL)

Anecdotes, facetiae, satire, etc.

This decade in review. J. Barth. il *Film Comment* 25:50-1 Ja/F '89

FILM EDITING *See* Motion pictures—Editing

FILM FESTIVALS *See* Motion picture festivals

FILM MAGAZINES *See* Motion pictures—Periodicals

FILM SCRIPTS *See* Motion picture scripts

FILM SPEEDS *See* Photography—Exposure

FILM-TO-VIDEO TRANSFER SYSTEM

Betting on Batman. B. Eder. il *Video* 13:80-1+ D '89

Improving your memories. *Home Mechanix* 86:10 Ap '89

The letterbox advantage [scanned and letterboxed versions of wide screen films] M. Fleischmann. il *Video* 13:21-3 Jl '89

Make your own still videos [Spiratone Sharpshooter Video-Dupliscope] K. Geller-Shinn. il *Petersen's Photographic Magazine* 17:14 F '89

FILMON, GARY

about

Feuding Tories. P. Kopvillem. il por *Maclean's* 102:20 My 29 '89

FILMON, GARY—about—*cont.*
Stormy weather. B. Wallace. il por *Maclean's* 102:12-14 Ja 16 '89
Test in the West. R. Laver. il por *Maclean's* 102:12-14 Ap 24 '89
FILMS
See also
Photography—Films
Soap bubbles and films
Thin films
FILMWRITING See Motion picture authorship
FILOFAX
Anecdotes, facetiae, satire, etc.
Filofaxed to the max [women executives] S. Johnson and C. Marcil. *Mademoiselle* 95:133+ Jl '89
FILOLI (WOODSIDE, CALIF.)
The flowering of Filoli. J. Chatfield-Taylor. il *Architectural Digest* 46:222-9+ My '89
FILOPODIA See Cells—Motility
FILTER STRIPS (SOIL CONSERVATION)
Filter strips: a little land with a big bang. J. Walter. il *Successful Farming* 87:36-7 F '89
FILTERS AND FILTRATION
See also
Air filters
Automobile engines—Filters
Ceramic membranes (Technology)
Electric filters
Light filters
Pall Corp.
Water filters and filtration
Water reuse
. . . and toxic chemicals from the blood [enzyme filters] J. Raloff. *Science News* 135:271 Ap 29 '89
FILUTZE, BARBARA
about
Life in the Filutze lane. M. Bloom. il pors *Runner's World* 24:68-72 Je '89
FIMRITE, RON
1954. il *Sports Illustrated* 71 Special Issue:24-8+ N 15 '89
'A modest little sporting event'. il *Sports Illustrated* 71:22-7 O 30 '89
Big George. il pors *Sports Illustrated* 71:128-34+ N 6 '89
The day we blasted Moscow. il *Sports Illustrated* 70:46-8+ Je 19 '89
A fan's view of Bay's ball. il *Sports Illustrated* 71:40-1 O 23 '89
Gloves across the water: put the world in World Series. por *Sports Illustrated* 70 Special Issue:120 Ap '89
Growing up with Trux. por *Sports Illustrated* 71:72 Jl 3 '89
The hero as huckster. por *Sports Illustrated* 70:92 F 13 '89
On the stick [cover story] il pors *Sports Illustrated* 71:18-23 Jl 10 '89
One Giant step. il *Sports Illustrated* 71:38-40+ O 16 '89
The second time around. il pors *Sports Illustrated* 70:110-14+ Ja 9 '89
The selling of spring. il *Sports Illustrated* 70:58-60+ Mr 27 '89
Sir Walter. il pors *Sports Illustrated* 70:74-8+ Je 19 '89
Sticking it to the Stick. por *Sports Illustrated* 71:102 Ag 21 '89
A wallflower blossomed. il pors *Sports Illustrated* 70 Special Issue:77-9 F '89
A wanted man. il pors *Sports Illustrated* 70:34-6 Ap 24 '89
THE FINAL DAYS [television program] See Television program reviews—Single works
THE FINAL SEASON [film] See Motion picture reviews—Single works
FINANCE
See also
Asset-backed financing
Banks and banking
Bonds
Cash management
Church finance
Credit
Debt
Debts, Public
Default (Finance)
Deflation (Finance)
Depreciation
Federal Reserve System (U.S.)
Financial institutions
Government securities
Hedging (Finance)
Inflation (Finance)
Interest (Economics)
Investment trusts
Investments
Leverage (Finance)
Liquidity (Economics)
Local finance
Money
Municipal finance
Securities

Speculation
Stock exchanges
Stocks
Surplus (Budget)
Swap financing
Taxation
Television broadcasting—Financial programs
United States—Appropriations and expenditures
United States—Economic conditions
United States. Dept. of the Treasury
See also subhead Finance under various subjects
Finance. See issues of Business Week
Observations. A. Bladen. See occasional issues of Forbes
Raise money, not taxes. E. Rubenstein. *National Review* 41:15 Ap 7 '89
British Columbia
A balancing act in Lotus Land. P. C. Newman. il *Maclean's* 102:43 Ap 3 '89
Strategic budgeting [balanced budget] J. Pifer. *Maclean's* 102:16 Ap 10 '89
Canada
See also
Bank of Canada
Banks and banking—Canada
Budget—Canada
Debts, Public—Canada
Securities—Canada
Developing countries
See also
Loans, Bank—Developing countries
East Asia
See also
Securities—East Asia
Great Britain
See also
Budget—Great Britain
Italy
See also
Budget—Italy
Japan
See also
Securities—Japan
Massachusetts
The 'Massachusetts mess'. M. Starr. il por *Newsweek* 113:28 Ja 2 '89
Michigan
New deal. J. A. Barnes and J. Hadden. *The New Republic* 200:20+ My 1 '89
Montana
A new way to charge it—on your state [Montana sponsors an affinity card] *Newsweek* 113:20 Je 26 '89
Northeastern States
Dukakis, Cuomo, and other egg-splattered faces. R. Kuttner. il *Business Week* p20 D 4 '89
Nova Scotia
Barking about a budget [charges that Sobeys supermarket chain obtained advance information on budget] G. Allen. il *Maclean's* 102:21 My 22 '89
Ontario
A tale of two budgets. P. Kaihla. il *Maclean's* 102:18 My 29 '89
Oregon
Shot in the foot. M. Beauchamp. il *Forbes* 143:104+ F 6 '89
Québec (Province)
See also
Caisse de dépôt et placement du Québec
A mover and shaker [Quebec finance minister P. Fortier] P. Chisholm. por *Maclean's* 102:32 Mr 13 '89
A tale of two budgets. P. Kaihla. il *Maclean's* 102:18 My 29 '89
Soviet Union
The coming Soviet crash [excerpt] J. Shelton. il *Conservative Digest* 15:63+ Mr/Ap '89
Financing Gorbachev's economic program: a bad investment for the West? S. Symms. il *USA Today (Periodical)* 118:25-7 Jl '89
The Western economic response [address, March 14, 1989] J. Shelton. *Vital Speeches of the Day* 55:429-33 My 1 '89
Switzerland
See also
Securities—Switzerland
United States
See Finance
West Virginia
A mountainous loss in West Virginia [investment fund fraud] G. L. Miles. il *Business Week* p42 Ap 3 '89
Western Europe
See also
European Currency Unit
Securities—Western Europe
FINANCE, INTERNATIONAL
See also
Balance of payments
Banks and banking, International
Capital movements
Debts, External

FINANCE, INTERNATIONAL—See also—*cont.*
    Development banks
    Foreign exchange
    Inflation (Finance)—International aspects
    International Finance Corporation
    International Monetary Fund
    Iranian seizure of United States embassy, 1979-1981—
        Economic aspects
    Money—International aspects
    World Bank

FINANCE, PERSONAL
    See also
    Aged—Economic conditions
    Bankruptcy
    Black children—Economic conditions
    Black women—Economic conditions
    Blacks—Economic conditions
    Budget, Household
    Children—Cost of raising
    Children's allowances
    College students—Economic conditions
    Debt
    Divorcees—Economic conditions
    Estate planning
    Home economics
    Investments
    Loans, Personal
    Money—Psychological aspects
    Parents of the handicapped—Economic conditions
    Purchasing, Household
    Saving and savings
    Single men—Economic conditions
    Single people—Economic conditions
    Single women—Economic conditions
    Thrift
    Unmarried couples—Economic conditions
    Wealth
    Widows—Economic conditions
    Women—Economic conditions
    Youth—Economic conditions
10 quick money savers. K. McManus. il *Changing Times*
    43:74 Ja '89
10 tough money tasks made easy. W. Giese. il *Changing
    Times* 43:24-30 My '89
33 great ways to simplify your life [cutting time spent on
    financial matters; cover story] J. Bodnar. il *Changing Times*
    43:22-8 Je '89
1989 money guide [cover story; special section] il *U.S. News
    & World Report* 107:50-2+ Jl 17 '89
Can you trust a rule of thumb? Only with a grain of salt
    [financial maxims] B. Kobliner. il *Money* 18:187-8 Ap
    '89
[Column] J. B. Quinn. See occasional issues of Newsweek
Economic predictions: personal future seems brightest [Gallup
    poll] B. Fischman. il *Psychology Today* 23:16 O '89
Family finance. T. Tilling. See issues of Parents beginning
    July 1986
Get your act together!!! [cover story; special section] il *Money*
    18:66-72+ F '89
How one family spends its money [Christina and Kevin
    Sherrod] B. Coleman. il *Good Housekeeping* 208:68+ Ja
    '89
How one family spends its money [Debbie and Dean Sartain]
    J. Wechsler. il *Good Housekeeping* 208:58+ Mr '89
How one family spends its money [Donald and Dianne
    Schwarz] D. M. Topolnicki. il *Good Housekeeping* 208:36+
    My '89
How one family spends its money [Guy and Leanne Sommers]
    L. Stern. il *Good Housekeeping* 209:58+ S '89
How one family spends its money [Jeff and Nancy Dickerson]
    A. Warren. il *Good Housekeeping* 209:50+ Jl '89
How one family spends its money [Kenneth and Linda
    Feusse] G. W. Weinstein. il *Good Housekeeping* 209:104+
    O '89
How one family spends its money [Lisa and Wells Eckhardt]
    D. Gage. il *Good Housekeeping* 208:34-5 Ap '89
It's your money. P. N. Strassels. See issues of Nation's
    Business beginning September 1988
Money. M. Daly. See issues of Better Homes and Gardens
Money helps. See issues of Money
Money news. K. Barrett and R. Greene. See issues of Ladies'
    Home Journal beginning March 1983 through April 1989
Money scorecard. See issues of Money beginning August
    1989
More for your money. B. G. Quint. See issues of Glamour
The new gospel of financial planning [cover story; special
    section] il *Money* 18:54-8+ Mr '89
One family's finances. See issues of Money
Out with dad—and guess who's paying for dinner? [adult
    children and parents] S. Mansfield. *Mademoiselle* 95:122
    My '89
Personal affairs. W. G. Flanagan. See issues of Forbes
Personal business. See issues of Business Week
A question of money. M. Rowland. See issues of New Choices
    for the Best Years beginning January 1989
Questions you're asking about your money. W. Giese. il
    Changing Times 43:84-8+ S '89
$$$$-saver: money-gram. See issues of Good Housekeeping

Thumbs up for the '90s [cover story; special section] il
    maps *Changing Times* 43:31-6+ Ja '89
Two go-getters skip the basics in their rush toward riches
    [Mark and Toya Evans] L. Luciano. il *Money* 18:177-8
    Ap '89
What to do with a windfall. M. C. Paulson. il *Changing
    Times* 43:93-4+ N '89
When a spender marries a saver [Joe and Brenda Neal]
    S. Seixas. il *Money* 18:114-16+ N '89
Working parents: how to get the most from 2 incomes
    [cover story] K. McManus. il *Changing Times* 43:22-8
    Jl '89
Your money. G. W. Weinstein. See issues of Good
    Housekeeping
        Bibliography
Money selects the nine best personal-finance books of 1989.
    D. W. Englander. il *Money* 18:18+ D '89

FINANCE COMPANIES
    See also
    AT&T Credit Corp.
    Commercial Credit Company
    Ford Motor Credit Co.
    General Electric Capital Corporation
    Household International, Inc.
        Accounting
What's off, what's on? [off balance sheet financial subsidiaries]
    P. Wang. il *Forbes* 143:110 F 20 '89

FINANCIAL ACCOUNTING FOUNDATION
The great GASB. D. Wechsler. il *Forbes* 144:60 D 11 '89

FINANCIAL ACCOUNTING STANDARDS BOARD
Retiree benefits: this footnote doesn't have to become a
    nightmare. J. R. Norman. il *Business Week* p39 F 27
    '89

FINANCIAL ANALYSTS See Investment advisers
FINANCIAL CONSULTANTS See Investment advisers
FINANCIAL GUARANTIES See Securities—Guaranty
FINANCIAL INSTITUTIONS
    See also
    Banks and banking
    Brokers
    Credit unions
    Finance companies
    Insurance companies
    Investment trusts
    Savings and loan associations
    Savings banks
    Thrift institutions
        Acquisitions and mergers
Eli Broad's revenge [buying core financial services assets
    of Integrated Resources] K. Kerwin. il *Business Week*
    p35 N 20 '89
        International aspects
Canadian imperialism [R. Cohen and L. Ellen buy into
    U.S. Trust Co.] J. Willoughby. il por *Forbes* 143:52 Ja
    9 '89
Dai-Ichi's move on CIT: it's bold—and about time. T. Holden.
    il *Business Week* p202 S 25 '89
Primerica adds another feather to its cap [BarclaysAmerican/
    Financial Inc.] J. Friedman. il *Business Week* p98 D 11
    '89
        Canada
Into the hands of the powerful. D. Francis. il *Maclean's*
    102:9 Mr 6 '89
        France
A marriage of giants to defend French finance [joining Union
    des Assurances de Paris with Banque Nationale de Paris]
    B. Riemer. il por *Business Week* p46 Ap 10 '89
        Investments
    See Institutional investments
        Laws and regulations
Does deregulation make sense? J. J. Curran. il *Fortune*
    119:181+ Je 5 '89
Financial reform [address, August 29, 1989] W. L. Hoskins.
    Vital Speeches of the Day 56:111-14 D 1 '89
        Canada
Bankers against Tories [American Express bids for bank
    status] M. Clark. il *Maclean's* 102:16 F 6 '89
Breaking barriers. P. Chisholm. il *Maclean's* 102:24-5 F 13
    '89
Into the hands of the powerful. D. Francis. il *Maclean's*
    102:9 Mr 6 '89
A mover and shaker [Quebec finance minister P. Fortier]
    P. Chisholm. por *Maclean's* 102:32 Mr 13 '89
        Canada
    See also
    American Express Canada, Inc.
    Central Capital Corporation
    First City Financial Corporation
    Principal Group Ltd.

FINANCIAL INSTITUTIONS, INTERNATIONAL
    See also
    Banks and banking, International
    Development banks
    International Monetary Fund
    World Bank

FINANCIAL JOURNALISM See Journalism, Commercial
FINANCIAL NEWS NETWORK INC.
HUD director hosts black finance show on network [T. R. Daniels] por *Jet* 76:24 My 8 '89
A real Live Wire [Cablesoft's LiveWire board delivers quotes from Financial News Network] R. Bel Bruno. il *Personal Computing* 13:38 Ja '89
Turning your desktop into a personal Big Board [LiveWire board delivers stock quotes] O. Port. il *Business Week* p119 Mr 27 '89
FINANCIAL PLANNERS See Investment advisers
FINANCIAL PLANNING (PERIODICAL)
Prophet without honor [H. W. Gourgue's theory that ads in Financial planning portend investment disaster] J. Queenan. il por *Forbes* 143:129+ Ap 17 '89
FINANCIAL SERVICES
See also
American Express Co.
Boston Company, Inc.
Broad, Inc.
Brokers
Calculators—Financial services use
Computers—Financial services use
Dean Witter Reynolds Inc.
Dow Jones & Co., Inc.
Dreyfus Corp.
Dun & Bradstreet Corp.
First City Financial Corporation
Goldman, Sachs & Co.
Gulf & Western, Inc.
Investment advisers
Lomas Financial Corp.
McNay Financial Services
Merrill Lynch & Co., Inc.
Moody's Investors Service, Inc.
Primerica Corp.
Sears, Roebuck and Co.
Skyline Financial Services Corporation
· Standard & Poor's Corp.
Tax consultants
Transamerica Corp.
Videotapes—Financial services use
Visa International Inc.
Does deregulation make sense? J. J. Curran. il *Fortune* 119:181+ Je 5 '89
Financial services. M. Schifrin. il *Forbes* 143:136+ Ja 9 '89
FINANCIAL STATEMENTS
See also
Bush, George, 1924——Financial disclosure
Congressmen—Financial disclosure
Corporation reports
Securities—Prospectuses
Vice-presidential candidates—Financial disclosure
Brokers' statements: close, but no cigar. W. Giese. il *Changing Times* 43:47-9+ Mr '89
How to read financial reports. W. M. Woodard. il *Black Enterprise* 19:90-2+ My '89
Mishmash accounting [companies forced to fold subs' assets and liabilities into parent's consolidated balance sheet] D. Wechsler. il *Forbes* 144:192 N 27 '89
Time is money [time value of money as reflected in financial statements] P. Wang. il *Forbes* 143:300 Ja 9 '89
What's off, what's on? [off balance sheet financial subsidiaries] P. Wang. il *Forbes* 143:110 F 20 '89
FINANCIAL TELECOMMUNICATIONS INC.
Unwelcome Recruit [Japan's Recruit Co. forces out G. Chichilnisky from management of Financial Telecommunications Inc.] J. Zweig. il por *Forbes* 143:149 My 15 '89
FINANCIAL TIMES OF CANADA
Buying the Times [Globe and mail] D. Todd. il *Maclean's* 102:47-8 D 25 '89
Yellow and red all over. J. Daly. *Maclean's* 102:53 N 6 '89
FINCH, CHRISTOPHER, 1939-
Color Close-ups. il *Art in America* 77:112-19+ Mr '89
FINCH, LEWIS W.
Choice: claims of success, predictions of failure. *The Education Digest* 55:12-15 N '89
FINCH, PAUL W., AND OTHERS
Human KGF is FGF-related with properties of a paracrine effector of epithelial cell growth. bibl f il *Science* 245:752-5 Ag 18 '89
FINCHER, JACK, 1930-
America's deadly rendezvous with the 'Spanish Lady'. bibl (p147) il *Smithsonian* 19:130-2+ Ja '89
The 'Belles of the Ball Game' were a hit with their fans. il *Smithsonian* 20:88-94+ Jl '89
Lifting 'latents' is now very much a high-tech matter. bibl (p230) il *Smithsonian* 20:201-2+ O '89
On wings of forgiveness. il *Reader's Digest* 134:85-90 Mr '89
Transplant emergency! il *Reader's Digest* 135:43-8 Jl '89
FINCHER, JOHN H.
Zhao's fall, China's loss. *Foreign Policy* 76:3-25 Fall '89
FINDER, ALAN
Don't look back. il *Gentlemen's Quarterly* 59:45+ My '89
FINDERSCOPES FOR TELESCOPES See Telescopes—Equipment

FINDLEY, DANIELLE
about
Annie. C. Dowling. il pors *Life* 12:42-9 N '89
FINDLEY, ROWE
The life and times of William Henry Jackson. il pors map *National Geographic* 175:216-51 F '89
FINE, DONALD I.
The boy in the photograph. il por *The New York Times Magazine* p28+ Ap 2 '89
about
The irrepressible Don Fine. R. A. Carter. il por *Publishers Weekly* 236:16+ D 1 '89
FINE (DONALD I.), INC. See Donald I. Fine, Inc.
FINE ARTS MUSEUM OF LONG ISLAND. COMPUTER IMAGING CENTER
A showcase for computer art. P. D. Prince. il *Personal Computing* 13:132-4 O '89
FINE BLANCHE
Wine before its time. K. Eldredge. il *Esquire* 112:53 N '89
FINE-QUALITY EDITION PUBLISHING See Publishers and publishing—Limited editions
FINE STRUCTURE CONSTANT
On the calculation of the fine-structure constant. D. J. Gross. il por *Physics Today* 42:9+ D '89
FINE YOUNG CANNIBALS (MUSICAL GROUP)
Chewing the fat with Fine Young Cannibals. R. Tannenbaum. il *Rolling Stone* p59-60+ Ap 20 '89
Fine Young Cannibal Roland Gift has it all: great voice, good looks and a juicy Scandal. S. Dougherty. il pors *People Weekly* 31:145-6 My 1 '89
Gift wrapped for a ruckus. J. Cocks. il por *Time* 133:87 My 29 '89
Looking a Gift horse in the mouth [cover story] S. Pond. il pors *Rolling Stone* p44-5+ O 5 '89
Soul kiss. J. Leland. por *Vogue* 179:256 Ap '89
FINES, JOHN
History tomorrow. il *History Today* 39:9-11 Je '89
FINES (PENALTIES)
See also
Tax penalties
Traffic tickets
Make the punishment fit the corporate crime. G. S. Becker. il *Business Week* p22 Mr 13 '89
FINESILVER, SHERMAN G.
The tapestry of your life [address, May 7, 1989] *Vital Speeches of the Day* 56:82-4 N 15 '89
FINEVEST FOODS
Boy wonder grows up [W. Berkley] E. F. Cone. il por *Forbes* 143:49+ F 20 '89
FINGER LAKES REGION (N.Y.)
Wine industry
See Wine industry
FINGERNAIL BITING See Nail biting
FINGERNAIL MANICURING See Manicuring
FINGERNAILS See Nails (Anatomy)
FINGERPRINT NEWS (NEWSLETTER) See Genetic newsletters
FINGERPRINTS
Lifting 'latents' is now very much a high-tech matter. J. Fincher. bibl (p230) il *Smithsonian* 20:201-2+ O '89
FINGERPRINTS, DNA See DNA fingerprints
FINIAL TECHNOLOGY (FIRM)
The optical turntable. R. Hodges. il *Stereo Review* 54:136 Mr '89
FINIALS
Finish with finials. il *Southern Living* 24:112 Jl '89
FINISHES AND FINISHING
See also
Furniture—Finishes and finishing
Wood—Finishes and finishing
FINISHING SANDERS See Sanding and sanding equipment
FINITE GEOMETRY
Beyond understanding? [finite projective plane of order 10; work of Clement Lam] P. Wallich. *Scientific American* 260:24 Mr '89
Search me and know me [religious reflections on computer search into existence of finite projective plane of order 10] M. E. Marty. *The Christian Century* 106:247 Mr 1 '89
FINK, DONALD E.
Editorial. See issues of Aviation Week & Space Technology beginning October 28, 1985
FINK, MICHAEL
Rose of Sharon. il por *Organic Gardening* 36:72 D '89
FINKE, JAMES
about
The making of a consultant. il por *Home Office Computing* 7:46 Ja '89
FINKEL, DAVID
One point of light. il pors *Esquire* 112:123-8+ O '89
Presumed guilty. il pors *Esquire* 111:178-80+ Mr '89
FINKELMAN, PAUL, 1949-
The Union Army's fighting 54th [cover story] il *American Visions* 4:20-3+ D '89

FINKELSON, ALLEN
about
Shingle style revival: new life for a rambling Connecticut residence. C. D. B. Bryan. il pors *Architectural Digest* 46:152-7+ Je '89
FINKELSON, SUSAN WEXLER
about
Shingle style revival: new life for a rambling Connecticut residence. C. D. B. Bryan. il pors *Architectural Digest* 46:152-7+ Je '89
FINKELSTEIN, EDWARD S., 1925-
about
The benefits of leverage. S. N. Chakravarty. il por *Forbes* 143:42 My 1 '89
FINKIELKRAUT, ALAIN
Universality and national identity. bibl f il pors *The Unesco Courier* 42:30-3 Je '89
FINLAND
See also
Television broadcasting—Finland
Description and travel
Those wacky Finns. D. A. Rose. il *Esquire* 111:47-8 Mr '89
FINLAY, B. BRETT, AND OTHERS
Epithelial cell surfaces induce Salmonella proteins required for bacterial adherence and invasion. bibl f il *Science* 243:940-3 F 17 '89
FINLAY, IAN HAMILTON, 1925-
about
Gardens: politics of Little Sparta: Ian Hamilton Finlay's statements in stone. M. Ruthven. il por *Architectural Digest* 46:104-11+ Jl '89
FINLEY, CHARLES
about
Another bright idea. R. O'Brien. il por *Sports Illustrated* 71:30 O 23 '89
FINLEY, MITCH
The Church and family life: more than avoiding contraceptives. *America* 161:205 O 7 '89
Confessions of a modern Catholic layman [cover story] *America* 160:366-8 Ap 22 '89
Of thee (and thy, and thou) I sing. *America* 160:76 F 4 '89
Parents should teach the joy of sex. *U.S. Catholic* 54:16-21 F '89
FINLEY, RUTH
about
The long nightmare of Ruth Finley. P. Michelmore. il por *Reader's Digest* 134:97-104 Mr '89
FINN, CHESTER E., 1944-
The campus: "an island of repression in a sea of freedom". *Commentary* 88:17-23 S '89
The choice backlash. il *National Review* 41:30-2 N 10 '89
Education as funny business. il *National Review* 41:34-5+ F 24 '89
A nation still at risk [cover story] *Commentary* 87:17-23 My '89
Policy of "bombast" [discussion of July/August 1988 article, Judgment time for higher education] *Change* 20:6-7 N/D '88
Ruminations on the end of a regime: a response to Chester Finn [discussion of October 1988 article, Lessons learned: federal policy making and the education research community] il *Phi Delta Kappan* 70:816-20 Je '89
The science of bad science. il *The American Spectator* 22:34-5 Ag '89
What to do about the schools [discussion of May 1989 article, A nation still at risk] *Commentary* 88:4-6+ O '89
FINN, TIM
about
Tim Finn: all's well that Enz well. M. Azerrad. por *Rolling Stone* p28 Je 15 '89
FINNBOGADÓTTIR, VIGDIS See Vigidis Finnbogadóttir, 1930-
FINNEGAN, WILLIAM
The emergency (I). map *The New Yorker* 65:43-4+ My 22 '89
The emergency (II). map *The New Yorker* 65:69-96 My 29 '89
Irish missed. il *Mother Jones* 14:41-2 My '89
FINNEY, DOUG
Student competition: plague or pestilence? *Design for Arts in Education* 90:38-41 Ja/F '89
FINNEY, MARTHA I.
A franchise? Or a dealership? il *Nation's Business* 77:63-4 Mr '89
TMJ: when teeth bite back. il *Nation's Business* 77:65 Mr '89
FINNISH COOKING See Cooking, Finnish
FINNISH GLASS See Glassware
FINNISH NATIONAL BALLET
Reviews:
Performance of Lady of the camellias. R. Libermann. il *Dance Magazine* 63:26 Mr '89

FINNISH SCULPTURE See Sculpture, Finnish
FINOCCHIO See Fennel
FINS (DESIGN)
Winging it. C. Vogel. il *The New York Times Magazine* p46-7 Ja 22 '89
FINSTER, HOWARD
about
Divinely inspired: the folk art of Howard Finster. il *Americana* 17:26 N/D '89
Holy art! D. Handelman. il por *Rolling Stone* p64-6+ Ap 20 '89
FINTA, IMRE
about
The case of Imre Finta. B. Wickens. *Maclean's* 102:70 N 27 '89
FIONDELLA, JAY
about
Abandon ship! A galleon runs aground in a highway wreck. il por *People Weekly* 32:206 D 4 '89
FIORE, MARY
26 years of famous weddings. il *Good Housekeeping* 208:46+ Je '89
FIORE, NEIL A.
How to get procrastinators up to speed [excerpt from The now habit] il *Working Woman* 14:38+ Mr '89
FIORENZA, JOSEPH A.
Racism, fear and reconciliation [cover story] *America* 160:444-6 My 13 '89
FIORI, PAMELA
about
AMEX goes for the glossies. A. Rothman. il por *Business Week* p66 O 23 '89
FIORINI, FLORIO
about
Puzzle in Movieland: the case of the mystery moguls. J. Rossant. il pors *Business Week* p80-1+ Mr 13 '89
FIRDAWSI
about
The Epic of the Kings. N. Tadjadod. il *The Unesco Courier* 42:28-31 S '89
FIRE ACADEMY (NEW YORK, N.Y.)
A lot to learn. *The New Yorker* 65:37-8 Je 12 '89
FIRE ALARMS
See also
Fire detectors
FIRE ANTS
March of the fire ants. A. C. Revkin. il maps *Discover* 10:70-6 Mr '89
Control
Ants get a transforming charge [affinity for electric fields; research by William P. MacKay] R. Weiss. *Science News* 136:412 D 23-30 '89
FIRE DEPARTMENTS
See also
Birmingham (Ala.)—Firefighters
Brooklyn (New York, N.Y.)—Firefighters
Firefighters
FIRE DETECTORS
Home fire protection. D. Schoonmaker. il *The Mother Earth News* 120:64-7 N/D '89
FIRE ECOLOGY
See also
Forest fires—Controlled fires
Combustible grass winning the West [cheat grass; research by Dwight Billings] J. Raloff. *Science News* 136:127 Ag 19 '89
Fire: a blessing in disguise. G. H. Harrison. il *National Wildlife* 27:36-7 Ag/S '89
These woods are made for burning [fire studies of giant sequoia groves] R. Kunzig. il map *Discover* 10:86-7+ Mr '89
The Yellowstone fires. W. H. Romme and D. G. Despain. bibl il map *Scientific American* 261:36-44+ N '89
The Yellowstone fires: issues in landscape ecology. D. H. Knight and L. L. Wallace. bibl f il *BioScience* 39:700-6 N '89
FIRE ENGINES
Collectors and collecting
Unabashed fire buffs. M. Beauchamp. il *Forbes* 144:266-8 Jl 24 '89
Testing
Pumping iron [driving fire engines from Fla. to Calif.] D. Kott. il *Road & Track* 40:60+ Jl '89
FIRE ESCAPES
Build a better fire escape. il *The Mother Earth News* 120:66-7 N/D '89
FIRE EXTINCTION
See also
Firefighters
Equipment
See also
Fire engines
Fire extinguishers
FIRE EXTINGUISHERS
Boeing: new dents in a sterling record [flaws in fire extinguisher systems] *Newsweek* 113:51 F 13 '89
Boeing takes steps to prevent fire extinguisher malfunctions. *Aviation Week & Space Technology* 130:71 F 27 '89

FIRE EXTINGUISHERS—cont.

FAA probes Boeing's reporting of faulty wiring in 757 extinguisher systems. C. Fotos. *Aviation Week & Space Technology* 130:66 Ja 23 '89

The right fire extinguisher and how to use it. il *Sunset (Central West edition)* 182:120+ Mr '89

FIRE ISLAND NATIONAL SEASHORE (N.Y.)

Living legacies [R. Stavdal continues box turtle research started by J. T. Nichols] M. Lipske. il por *National Wildlife* 27:14-16 Je/Jl '89

FIRE MAKING

See also

Campfires

Cold water on the fire [doubtful research by Steven R. James] J. Benditt. *Scientific American* 260:21-2 My '89

Prehistoric barbecue [evidence of fire use at Swartkrans; research by C. K. Brain and Andrew Sillen] *Discover* 10:14-15 Mr '89

FIRE PITS *See* Fireplaces, Outdoor

FIRE PREVENTION

See also

Airplanes, Jet—Fires and fire prevention

Airports—Fires and fire prevention

Chimneys—Fires and fire prevention

Fireproofing

Forest fires—Prevention and control

Hazardous substances—Fires and fire prevention

Houses—Fires and fire prevention

Lightning protection

Space vehicles—Fires and fire prevention

FIRE RESCUES *See* Rescue work

FIRE RESEARCH

See also

Boise Interagency Fire Center

FIRE RESISTANT CIGARETTES *See* Cigarettes—Fire resistance

FIRE SAFETY

Could your family survive a fire? F. Field. il *Reader's Digest* 135:137-40 N '89

Home fire protection. D. Schoonmaker. il *The Mother Earth News* 120:64-7 N/D '89

Save your family from a fire. J. H. Sousa. il *Parents* 64:82+ O '89

FIRE TRUCKS *See* Fire engines

FIREARMS

See also

Air guns

Cartridges

Children and firearms

Gunshot wounds

Gunsmiths and gunsmithing

Machine guns

Pistols

Revolvers

Rifles

Shotguns

7 deadly days [deaths by gunfire in the U.S.; cover story] il *Time* 134:30-52+ Jl 17 '89

Arsenal [guns used in assassination attempts] D. C. Craig. il *Life* 12:156-7+ Fall '89

Do guns save lives? E. Magnuson. il *Time* 134:25-6 Ag 21 '89

Giving up guns [Vietnam vet] D. Graham. il *The New York Times Magazine* p34+ Ag 20 '89

Gun buffs risk loading lungs with lead [handgun hobbyists using indoor firing ranges] *Science News* 136:126 Ag 19 '89

Guns à la mode [designer handguns for women] B. G. Harrison. *Mademoiselle* 95:140 Mr '89

The other arms race [police, criminals, and terrified citizens wielding guns; cover story] G. J. Church. il *Time* 133:20-6 F 6 '89

Protection [use of firearms in self defense; views of S. D'Andrilli] *The New Yorker* 64:22-3 Ja 9 '89

Should you own a gun for protection? [interviews with D. B. Kates and G. Napper] il *U.S. News & World Report* 106:28 My 8 '89

Suicides: the gun factor. E. Magnuson. il *Time* 134:61 Jl 17 '89

Women and crime: is this the answer? [handgun ownership; excerpt from Armed and female] P. Quigley. il *Glamour* 87:344-5+ Ap '89

Accidents

A message from Brian [ten year old son accidentally killed by handgun] D. D. Darling. il por *Ladies' Home Journal* 106:22+ My '89

Tiny fingers on the trigger [Florida proposal authorizing prison terms for parents whose children misuse guns] il *U.S. News & World Report* 107:11-12 Jl 3 '89

With a new law, Florida heeds a child's plaintive cry to 911: 'I shot her—I didn't mean to'. M. Green. il *People Weekly* 32:56-8+ Jl 10 '89

Clubs and societies

Loss of habitat. G. Hill. il *Field & Stream* 93:11 Ja '89

Exhibitions

New guns for 1989 [Shooting, Hunting and Outdoor Trade Show] J. Carmichel. il *Outdoor Life* 184:62-3+ Jl '89

What's new? Plenty! [Shooting, Hunting and Outdoor Trade Show] B. Brister. il *Field & Stream* 94:65-6+ My '89

Laws and regulations

See also

Press and gun control

Arms and the states. A. Bilski. il *Maclean's* 102:36-7 Jl 3 '89

Ban the guns? [assault rifles] W. F. Buckley. *National Review* 41:54-5 Ap 21 '89

Bang, bang! [weekend war games vs. ownership of handguns] B. D. Colen. il *Health (New York, N.Y.)* 21:90-1 Mr '89

Carnage control [assault weapons] il *Commonweal* 116:195-6 Ap 7 '89

Clark Kent, please call your office [G. Bush asks press to do something about crime] il *Newsweek* 113:28 F 27 '89

Endangered tradition. D. E. Petzal. See issues of Field & Stream beginning March 1985

Gub control [assault rifle ban] H. Hertzberg. *The New Republic* 200:4+ Ap 10 '89

Gunning for assault rifles [import ban] J. V. Lamar, Jr. il *Time* 133:39 Mr 27 '89

Guns [cover story] D. Baer. il *U.S. News & World Report* 106:20-2+ My 8 '89

Guns 'R' Us. M. Maranz. *The New Republic* 200:12+ Ja 23 '89

Guns: should they be in Christian homes? il *Christianity Today* 33:42-3+ Ag 18 '89

Have weapons, will shoot. L. I. Barrett. il *Time* 133:22 F 27 '89

His object a gentler L.A., a councilman buys up AK-47s [N. Holden's cash-for-guns scheme to combat crime] il por *People Weekly* 31:120 F 13 '89

How citizens can beat the gun lobby [National Rifle Association; cover story] R. W. Bruner. il *The Nation* 248:433+ Ap 3 '89

The impact of Stockton [schoolyard murders gives momentum to gun control] J. Hammer. il *Newsweek* 113:8 F 20 '89

Is the NRA being shot down? R. F. Drinan. *The Christian Century* 106:372-3 Ap 12 '89

Lock and load for the gunfight of '89 [ban on imports of AK-47 assault rifles] il *U.S. News & World Report* 106:9 Mr 27 '89

Mad about guns [New York City's proposed ban on assault rifles] M. Kempton. *The New York Review of Books* 36:62 D 21 '89

The N.R.A. in a hunter's sights. R. Hughes. il *Time* 133:86 Ap 3 '89

A nation of certified killers [murderer P. Purdy's firearms transaction record] J. D. McNamara. il *Harper's* 278:58-9 My '89

Nibbling the bullet on gun control [congressional hearings on bill requiring one week waiting period for handgun buyers] il *U.S. News & World Report* 107:14 D 4 '89

The NRA comes under the gun [on the defensive as opposition to assault weapons grows] R. Sandza. il *Newsweek* 113:28-30 Mr 27 '89

Playing with guns [G. Bush vacillates on assault rifle ban] G. F. Will. il *Newsweek* 113:78 Mr 27 '89

The right to bear AK-47s. il *Scholastic Update (Teachers' edition)* 122:14 N 3 '89

The right to bear (and die by) arms. F. Bruning. il *Maclean's* 102:13 Je 19 '89

Sarah Brady [crusader for handgun control] S. Weller. il pors *Ms.* 17:84-7 Ja/F '89

Secrets behind the gun lobby's staying power. D. Gergen and T. Gest. il *U.S. News & World Report* 106:26 My 8 '89

The shots heard 'round the Congress [J. T. Wesbecker's Louisville murder spree with AK-47] il *U.S. News & World Report* 107:15 S 25 '89

Should more limits be placed on guns? [interviews with D. Stokes and W. LaPierre] il *U.S. News & World Report* 106:32 Ap 10 '89

Tiny fingers on the trigger [Florida proposal authorizing prison terms for parents whose children misuse guns] il *U.S. News & World Report* 107:11-12 Jl 3 '89

Top Gun [NRA president J. Foss] G. Smith. il pors *Sports Illustrated* 71:56-62+ Ag 7 '89

Up in arms [women and gun control] J. Torrey. *Harper's Bazaar* 122:64+ Jl '89

We the geeks [comparing auto regulations with gun laws] P. Bedard. il *Car and Driver* 35:17 S '89

With a new law, Florida heeds a child's plaintive cry to 911: 'I shot her—I didn't mean to'. M. Green. il *People Weekly* 32:56-8+ Jl 10 '89

Canada

Arms and the states. A. Bilski. il *Maclean's* 102:36-7 Jl 3 '89

Sights

High-class glass. D. E. Petzal. il *Field & Stream* 94:80+ N '89

Mounting worries [installing a scope] D. E. Petzal. il *Field & Stream* 93:74+ F '89

FIREARMS INDUSTRY

See also

Gunsmiths and gunsmithing

Smith & Wesson

FIREARMS INDUSTRY—*cont.*

Advertising

For the ladies, a .38 caliber [Smith & Wesson's gun ads targeted at women] il *Newsweek* 113:48 F 27 '89

Pistols for the women of America [Smith & Wesson's Lady Smith revolver targeted at women; cover story] L. C. Pogrebin. *The Nation* 248:649+ My 15 '89

Marketing

Death by mail. J. Sugarmann. *The Nation* 248:450 Ap 3 '89

FIREBALLS *See* Meteors

FIREBOARDS *See* Dummy board figures

FIREFIGHTERS

See also

Bath County (Va.)—Firefighters
Birmingham (Ala.)—Firefighters
Black firefighters
Brooklyn (New York, N.Y.)—Firefighters
International Association of Fire Fighters

Living my childhood dream [volunteer fireman] R. P. Smith. il por *Reader's Digest* 134:163-4 Ja '89

Rural firemen [volunteers] D. McCaig. il *Country Journal* 16:79-83 Mr/Ap '89

Promotion

Birmingham firehouse [Supreme Court decision permitting white firemen to bring suit against the city for job discrimination] *Commonweal* 116:387-8 Jl 14 '89

Training

See also

Fire Academy (New York, N.Y.)

FIREFLY HILL MUSEUM (JAMAICA) *See* Sir Noel Coward's Firefly Hill Museum (Jamaica)

FIREMAN, PAUL

about

Paul Fireman pulls on his old running shoes. L. Jereski. il por *Business Week* p46-7 N 6 '89

FIREMAN'S FUND INSURANCE COMPANY

Value is where you find it [stock picker B. Bruce] J. Clements. il por *Forbes* 143:62+ Mr 20 '89

FIREPLACES

See also

Chimneys
Mantels

How to install a woodburning fireplace and build the hearth and mantle too. D. Johnson. il *The Family Handyman* 39:48-55 Jl/Ag '89

Shelves, steel, and black paint worked wonders on the fireplace. il *Sunset (Central West edition)* 182:134 Ap '89

Storage, display, and still a fireplace. il *Sunset (Central West edition)* 182:122 F '89

You gotta have hearth? Try a prefab fireplace. T. Segal. il *Business Week* p135 F 27 '89

Equipment

Efficient heater [Mendota Gas Insert] M. DiChristina. il *Popular Science* 235:47+ N '89

Maintenance and repair

What to do about fireplace problems. J. Seisler. il *Consumers' Research Magazine* 72:25-8 O '89

FIREPLACES, OUTDOOR

Seating and eating space around firepit. il *Sunset (Central West edition)* 182:150 My '89

FIREPROOFING

Fire-resistant shingles: treatments for cedar. *Better Homes and Gardens* 67:63 Ap '89

FIRES

See also

Airplanes, Jet—Fires and fire prevention
Airplanes, Military—Fires and fire prevention
Airports—Fires and fire prevention
Arson
Art galleries and museums—Fires and fire prevention
Bonfires
Brush fires
Burning of land
Chimneys—Fires and fire prevention
Forest fires
Gas fires
Hazardous substances—Fires and fire prevention
Houses—Fires and fire prevention
Inflammable materials
Laboratories—Fires and fire prevention
Nuclear submarines, Russian—Fires and fire prevention
Space vehicles—Fires and fire prevention
Warehouses—Fires and fire prevention

Rescue work

See Rescue work

FIRESTEIN, STUART, AND WERBLIN, FRANK

Odor-induced membrane currents in vertebrate-olfactory receptor neurons. bibl f il *Science* 244:79-82 Ap 7 '89

FIRESTONE, KAREN

about

A boomer plays the leisure boom [interview] K. Nickel. il por *Fortune* 120:63+ N 20 '89

FIRESTONE TIRE & RUBBER CO.

Can Bridgestone make the climb? [acquisition of Firestone] Z. Schiller. il *Business Week* p78-9 F 27 '89

Why Bridgestone's chairman is making tracks to Akron [T. Eguchi transferred to Firestone] Z. Schiller. il por *Business Week* p32-3 N 20 '89

FIREWOOD SHEDS *See* Sheds

FIREWOOD STORAGE *See* Woodbins, racks, etc.

FIREWORKS

Photographs and photography

July 4th: first there's the big bang then you make that fire work [cover story] J. Zuckerman. il *Petersen's Photographic Magazine* 18:14-17 Je '89

FIRING OF EMPLOYEES *See* Employees—Dismissal

FIRING OF EXECUTIVES *See* Executives—Dismissal

FIRING OF NEWSPAPER EMPLOYEES *See* Newspapers—Employees—Dismissal

FIRING OF TEACHERS *See* Teachers—Dismissal

FIRING OF WOMEN EXECUTIVES *See* Women executives—Dismissal

FIRING RANGES *See* Shooting ranges

FIRKUŠNÝ, RUDOLF

about

Firkušný plays Martinů. R. Freed. por *Stereo Review* 54:126 D '89

FIRMENICH, MÁRIO EDUARDO

about

Dirty secrets of the 'dirty war'. M. Andersen. *The Nation* 248:339-40+ Mr 13 '89

FIRST AFRICAN BAPTIST CHURCH

In Savannah, First African Baptist Church means first. W. Yancey. il *American Visions* 4:42-3 Ag '89

FIRST AID FOR ANIMALS

Help for a four-legged friend [pets] il *Current Health 2* 15:18-19 Ap '89

FIRST AID IN ILLNESS AND INJURY

See also

Burns and scalds
Heimlich maneuver
Resuscitation

10 mistakes not to make in a medical emergency. P. G. Gill. *McCall's* 116:110 Ap '89

An alert response to head injury. il *Current Health 2* 16:28-9 D '89

Farm group focuses on first aid. N. Stannard. il *Successful Farming* 87:54 Ag '89

First aid tips [National Safety Council] K. K. Gracey and C. Brumback. *Consumers' Research Magazine* 72:2 Ag '89

Is your child ever alone at home? [first aid poster] il *Redbook* 173:105-8 O '89

Just say don't [outdoor emergency] P. G. Gill. il *Outdoor Life* 184:58+ O '89

Press on: to reduce swelling, ice is nice but compressed is best. O. Anderson. il *Women's Sports & Fitness* 11:11 Ja/F '89

Save a Life [emergency first aid TV shows in Britain] P. Riding. il *World Health* p29 Ja/F '89

Sudden illness: there is something you can do. il *Current Health 2* 16:28-9 O '89

Summer first aid. S. Squires. *Ladies' Home Journal* 106:54 Jl '89

Think before you (baby)sit. C. Purdy. il *Current Health 2* 16:22-3 N '89

When accidents happen to kids. P. E. King. *McCall's* 116:51 Jl '89

Wounds: treat them seriously. il *Current Health 2* 16:26-7 S '89

FIRST AID KITS *See* Medical equipment

FIRST BANK SYSTEM INC.

Bad news bank. T. Jaffe. *Forbes* 144:327 D 11 '89

Pete's problem. J. Zweig. il por *Forbes* 143:134-5 F 20 '89

FIRST BASEMEN (BASEBALL PLAYERS) *See* Baseball players

FIRST BOSTON CORP.

First Boston: trying to shake off the junk-bond jitters. J. Friedman. il *Business Week* p90 O 2 '89

FIRST BRANDS CORP.

First Brands: anatomy of an LBO that worked. T. Vogel. il *Business Week* p104 D 4 '89

FIRST CAPITAL PARTNERS

Count the cash and go home early [strategies of G. Angulo] T. Pouschine. il por *Forbes* 143:124+ My 29 '89

FIRST CHILDREN'S BANK

Amassing a small fortune, Neale Godfrey teaches thrift at the First Children's Bank. R. Arias. il por *People Weekly* 32:127-8 S 18 '89

FIRST CITY BANCORPORATION OF TEXAS, INC.

Why Robert Abboud wants MCorp in his corral. T. Vogel. il por *Business Week* p31 Ap 10 '89

FIRST CITY FINANCIAL CORPORATION

The Belzberg brats. S. Flack. il *Forbes* 144:41-2 N 13 '89

FIRST-CLASS AIRLINE SERVICE *See* Airlines—Passenger service

FIRST COMMITTEE (UNITED NATIONS) *See* United Nations. Political and Security Committee

THE FIRST EMPEROR OF CHINA [film] *See* Motion picture reviews—Single works

FIRST EXECUTIVE CORP.
Milken's shadow hovers over Fred Carr. K. Kerwin. il por *Business Week* p24 Ap 17 '89
Staying in the kitchen. J. Heins. il *Forbes* 143:108+ Ap 17 '89
This could be the end of a beautiful friendship [ICH stake in First Executive Corp.] K. Kerwin and Z. Schiller. il pors *Business Week* p33-4 S 4 '89
When the safety net is frayed [takeover of Pacific Lumber by Charles E. Hurwitz causes pension plan termination] J. B. Levine. il *Business Week* p158 N 6 '89
FIRST FINANCIAL FUND
Bailout bulls [A. Cope and N. Adams] J. Zweig. il pors *Forbes* 143:167 Ap 3 '89
FIRST GRADE *See* Elementary education
FIRST LADIES *See* Presidents—Wives
FIRST LINES, LITERARY *See* Beginnings, Literary
FIRST MISSISSIPPI CORP.
First Mississippi may reroute. G. G. Marcial. *Business Week* p120 D 18 '89
FIRST TEXAS GIBRALTAR (FIRM)
The screwiest S&L bailout ever. B. D. Fromson. il por *Fortune* 119:114-15+ Je 19 '89
FIRSTENBERG, JEAN PICKER
AFI calendar. See issues of American Film
FIRTH, COLIN
about
Going Firth class. J. Szabo. il por *Mademoiselle* 95:102 N '89
FISCHBACH CORPORATION
Reading Posner the riot act. G. DeGeorge. il por *Business Week* p48 D 18 '89
Victor Posner and the case of the mystery financier [plan to sell Fischbach to an English investor] G. DeGeorge and R. A. Melcher. il por *Business Week* p34 Ag 28 '89
FISCHER, ANDRE
about
Natalie Cole and Andre Fischer: singer talks about her marriage, son and career [cover story] il pors *Jet* 77:54-8 O 16 '89
Natalie Cole weds in L.A. church ceremony. il pors *Jet* 76:57 O 2 '89
FISCHER, ARLENE
Danger! A short fuse can kill you. il *Redbook* 173:162-3+ S '89
Don't let it happen to you! *Redbook* 174:20+ N '89
The foods that are poisoning your child. *Redbook* 173:116-18+ My '89
A little love goes a long way. il *Redbook* 173:134-5+ My '89
Working moms gripe. *Redbook* 173:126-7+ O '89
(jt. auth) See Podell, Richard N., and Fischer, Arlene
FISCHER, D. A. V.
Safeguards controversy, continued. il *The Bulletin of the Atomic Scientists* 45:38-40 Je '89
FISCHER, DANIEL
A telescope for tomorrow [cover story] il *Sky and Telescope* 78:248-52 S '89
FISCHER, DAVID HACKETT
about
Remapping American culture. A. P. Sanoff. il maps *U.S. News & World Report* 107:60-4 D 4 '89
FISCHER, RAYMOND L.
Manipulating the media and America: the negative 1988 presidential campaign. il *USA Today (Periodical)* 117:20-2 Mr '89
FISCHER, RUTH
People. See issues of World Press Review beginning August 1987 through February 1989
FISCHETTI, VINCENT A., AND OTHERS
Protection against streptococcal pharyngeal colonization with a vaccinia: M protein recombinant. bibl f il *Science* 244:1487-90 Je 23 '89
FISCHL, ERIC
about
Portrait of the artists: Eric Fischl and April Gornik on Long Island. S. M. L. Aronson. il pors *Architectural Digest* 46:234-9+ Ap '89
FISH, ALLAN *See* Marioni, Tom, 1937-
FISH, JOHN H., AND KRETZMANN, JOHN
Reviving Mexico City neighborhood by neighborhood. il *The Christian Century* 106:1116-18 N 29 '89
FISH
See also
Aquariums
Eye—Fish
Fisheries
Hearing—Fish
Skin—Fish
Snappers
Tropical fish
See also names of fish
Fish as model systems. D. A. Powers. bibl f il *Science* 246:352-8 O 20 '89
Anatomy
See also
Swim bladders (Fish)

Anecdotes, facetiae, satire, etc.
Fishy fables!! E. Zern. il *Field & Stream* 93:123 F '89
Breeding
See also
Fish culture
Care
Fantailed fantasies and other fauna for the pond [ornamental fish] D. Hufford. il *Flower and Garden* 33:26-30 Jl/Ag '89
In the age of aquariums, Wu Li-Hsia finds acupuncture is not a tankless job [treating fish] il por *People Weekly* 31:268 Mr 6 '89
Coloration
See Color of fish
Contamination
See Fish contamination
Ecology
See also
Fish populations
Food and feeding
Reef fish feedings: amusement or nuisance? D. Perrine. il *Sea Frontiers* 35:272-9 S/O '89
A truly fresh fish [snorkeling off Santa Catalina Island] N. Vander Velde. il *Sea Frontiers* 35:320 S/O '89
When they bite [feeding frenzy] B. Yaeger. il *Field & Stream* 94:30+ My '89
Habits and behavior
See also
Mimicry (Biology)
Sexual behavior—Fish
Room without a view [rivulus living in land crab burrows] D. S. Taylor. il *Natural History* p26+ S '89
School days. K. Schultz. il *Field & Stream* 94:40-1+ O '89
Shooing fish with sound [schools of fish] R. Friedman. il *Sea Frontiers* 35:136-41 My/Je '89
Swimming is Oscar's only real skill—but he predicts earthquakes on the side [tropical fish at Corona Del Mar High School in California] il *People Weekly* 32:77 S 11 '89
Inspection
See Fish inspection
Larvae
See Larvae
Migration
See also
Salmon
Photographs and photography
Fish faces in the kelp forest. N. Wu. il *Sea Frontiers* 35:366-9 N/D '89
Reproduction
See also
Spawning
Respiration
See Respiration
Antarctic regions
Melting inhibition and superheating of ice by an antifreeze glycopeptide. C. A. Knight and A. L. DeVries. bibl f il *Science* 245:505-7 Ag 4 '89
Arizona
Fitness differences among remnant populations of the endangered Sonoran topminnow. J. M. Quattro and R. C. Vrijenhoek. bibl f il *Science* 245:976-8 S 1 '89
Belize
Grouper sex in Belize. J. Carter. il *Natural History* p60-9 O '89
Great Lakes region
Great Lakes fish and the greenhouse effect. C. Mlot. *BioScience* 39:145 Mr '89
New York (State)
The pike of New York. E. Stegemann. il *The Conservationist* 44:26-33 N/D '89
Some catfishes of New York. E. Stegemann. il *The Conservationist* 44:38-45 Jl/Ag '89
Santa Catalina Island (Calif.)
A truly fresh fish [snorkeling off Santa Catalina Island] N. Vander Velde. il *Sea Frontiers* 35:320 S/O '89
FISH, CANNED
Hold the tuna [risk of mercury poisoning from cat food] V. Adler. *American Health* 8:110 Jl/Ag '89
A tuna a day makes the cat slow to play [research by Katherine A. Houpt] *Science News* 135:111 F 18 '89
FISH, DEEP SEA
See also
Tuna fish
FISH, DRESSING OF
After you land that salmon . . . il *Sunset (Central West edition)* 182:196 Ap '89
FISH, EFFECT OF TEMPERATURE ON
Antifreezes in fish work quite similarly [research by Arthur L. DeVries] F. Flam. *Science News* 135:102 F 18 '89
Beat the heat bass. J. Gibbs. il *Outdoor Life* 184:24+ Jl '89
Cold-water surface bass [night fishing] J. Potts. il *Outdoor Life* 183:60-1+ F '89
Fish on ice [antifreeze proteins; research by Arthur DeVries] *Discover* 10:19 Jl '89
Great Lakes fish and the greenhouse effect. C. Mlot. *BioScience* 39:145 Mr '89

FISH, EFFECT OF TEMPERATURE ON—cont.

Is it too hot to fish? [bass] C. Hauptman. il *Field & Stream* 94:44-5+ Ag '89

Keep the heat on fall bass [largemouth] J. Dean. il *Outdoor Life* 184:68-9+ O '89

A matter of degrees. B. Yaeger. il *Field & Stream* 93:23+ F '89

Melting inhibition and superheating of ice by an antifreeze glycopeptide. C. A. Knight and A. L. DeVries. bibl f il *Science* 245:505-7 Ag 4 '89

Tricks that take other fish in hot weather. J. Bashline. il *Field & Stream* 94:90 Jl '89

Water temperature cycle. B. Volkart. il *Field & Stream* 94:34+ D '89

FISH, PICKLED See Pickles and relishes

FISH, RAW

See also

Sushi

Sushi, sashimi, and sickness: raw fish and parasites. E. S. Iversen. bibl il por *Sea Frontiers* 35:176-83 My/Je '89

FISH, SMOKED

Oven-smoked fish. R. Kutas. il *Outdoor Life* 184:72 Jl '89

FISH AND WILDLIFE SERVICE (U.S.) See U.S. Fish and Wildlife Service

FISH AS FOOD

See also

Caviar

Ciguatera

Cooking—Fish

Fish, Canned

Scombroid poisoning

Surimi

The fish market revolution continues. il *Sunset (Central West edition)* 182:84-9, 130+ F '89

Contamination

See Fish contamination

Prices

Fishy arguments [Seattle bottom fishermen blame Japanese poaching in Alaskan waters for lower prices] M. Beauchamp. il *Forbes* 143:130+ Mr 20 '89

A FISH CALLED WANDA [film] See Motion picture reviews—Single works

FISH CAMOUFLAGE See Mimicry (Biology)

FISH CONTAMINATION

See also

Ciguatera

Scombroid poisoning

11 ways to eat safer fish. J. Barone. *American Health* 8:112-13 Je '89

Anatomy of a fish kill [Spruce Creek, Pa.] J. Bashline. il *Field & Stream* 93:38+ F '89

Are Great Lakes fish safe to eat? [polychlorinated biphenyls] W. A. Schmidt. il map *National Wildlife* 27:16-19 Ag/S '89

Are Lake Michigan fish dangerous to your health? J. Gibbs. il *Outdoor Life* 184:72-4+ D '89

Don't blame the messenger [poisoning of Lake Michigan fish] J. D. Hair. il *National Wildlife* 27:30 O/N '89

Fishing for facts on fish safety [cover story] V. Modeland. il *FDA Consumer* 23:16-21+ F '89

Hold the tuna [risk of mercury poisoning from cat food] V. Adler. *American Health* 8:110 Jl/Ag '89

Is fish safe to eat? [cover story] F. E. Young. il *Consumers' Research Magazine* 72:10-12 Ag '89

Something fishy. P. G. Gill. il *Outdoor Life* 183:50+ Je '89

Striped bass [effects of Westway decision and PCBs on New York's commercial fisheries] S. D. Garber. il *Focus (New York, N.Y.: 1950)* 39:34-6 Summ '89

Sushi, sashimi, and sickness: raw fish and parasites. E. S. Iversen. bibl il por *Sea Frontiers* 35:176-83 My/Je '89

Tolerance and stress in a polluted environment [killifish in New Jersey waters] J. S. Weis and P. Weis. bibl f il *BioScience* 39:89-95 F '89

A tuna a day makes the cat slow to play [research by Katherine A. Houpt] *Science News* 135:111 F 18 '89

Warning: if you eat Great Lakes fish . . . [cancer risk] *Science News* 135:300 My 13 '89

What's that wiggling in my sushi? [worms] *Science News* 135:300 My 13 '89

FISH COOKING See Cooking—Fish

FISH CULTURE

Farm ponds yield tasty meals. B. Freese. il *Successful Farming* 87:50-1 Ag '89

The men's club [synthetic male hormones induce feminization in catfish] *Discover* 10:18 Ag '89

Environmental aspects

Down on the fish farm. S. Cline. il *Sierra* 74:30+ Mr/Ap '89

FISH FARMING See Fish culture

FISH HATCHERIES See Fish culture

FISH HOOKS See Fishhooks

FISH IN ART

See also

Creel Creek Fish Carving (Firm)

Gyotaku on your sweatshirt. il *Sunset (Central West edition)* 183:98+ Jl '89

Collectors and collecting

Catch of the day [A. Helou's London house decorated with fishing tackle and art] R. Koenig. il por *House & Garden* 161:54-5 Ja '89

FISH INDUSTRY

See also

Alaska Gourmet Seafood (Firm)

Arctic Alaska Fisheries (Firm)

Shellfish industry

Silver Lining Seafood (Firm)

Export-import trade

An ambiguous victory [trade panel ruling on salmon and herring caught off British Columbia] B. Bergman. il *Maclean's* 102:38 O 30 '89

Marketing

To market, to market [P. Schilling of Alaska Gourmet Seafood and B. Woldrop of Silver Lining Seafood] N. C. Baker. il por *Nation's Business* 77:61 Ja '89

Alaska

See also

Wards Cove Packing Co.

Canada

See also

National Sea Products Ltd.

An ambiguous victory [trade panel ruling on salmon and herring caught off British Columbia] B. Bergman. il *Maclean's* 102:38 O 30 '89

Stormy waters [Atlantic fishery] G. Allen. il *Maclean's* 102:40-1 D 25 '89

Tangled nets [troubled Atlantic fishery] J. DeMont. il por *Maclean's* 102:54-5 S 4 '89

FISH INSPECTION

Improving the fish inspection program. B. T. Hunter. il *Consumers' Research Magazine* 72:13-15 Ag '89

FISH LOCOMOTION

How fast are fish? P. B. Wright. il *Motor Boating & Sailing* 164:64 N '89

Tunas [swimming adaptations] P. G. Bushnell and K. N. Holland. il *Sea Frontiers* 35:42-8 Ja/F '89

FISH MARKETS

See also

Fulton Fish Market

FISH NETS See Fishing nets

FISH OIL

See also

Eicosapentaenoic acid

The anti-arthritis diet. G. L. Blackburn. il *Prevention (Emmaus, Pa.)* 41:34-5+ F '89

Breathing easier [use of fish oil to relieve asthma] il *Prevention (Emmaus, Pa.)* 41:10 Ap '89

Can fish oil drop B.P.? il *Prevention (Emmaus, Pa.)* 41:8-9 Ag '89

The fish nobody knows [beneficial effects in treatment of disease] R. A. Barnett and J. Barone. il *American Health* 8:104-6+ Je '89

Fish-oil capsules: good for the heart? S. Mahler. *McCall's* 116:108 S '89

Fish oil lowers even normal blood pressure [research by Constance Kies] J. Raloff. *Science News* 136:181 S 16 '89

Fish oil: new hope in fighting malaria [research by Orville A. Levander and Arba L. Ager] *Science News* 135:237 Ap 15 '89

Fish oil slows some developing cancers [research by T. Colin Campbell] J. Raloff. *Science News* 135:390 Je 24 '89

A mackerel a day . . . [may reduce risk of heart disease] *Health (New York, N.Y.)* 21:75 My '89

New hope from the fish-oil factor [use in prevention of heart disease and cancer] G. L. Blackburn. il *Prevention (Emmaus, Pa.)* 41:29-30+ Je '89

Prairie dogs and gallstone information [research by Thomas H. Magnuson] K. Fackelmann. *Science News* 135:332 My 27 '89

Revealing the finicky functions of fish oil. I. Wickelgren. *Science News* 135:183 Mr 25 '89

FISH PACKING INDUSTRY See Fish industry

FISH PONDS See Ponds

FISH POPULATIONS

See also

Population genetics—Fish

Meanderings of larval fish. il *Sea Frontiers* 35:199 Jl/Ag '89

FISH PROCESSING INDUSTRY See Fish industry

FISH PROTECTION

The trout of winter [catch and release] J. Barsness. il *Field & Stream* 93:56-7+ F '89

FISH SCHOOLS See Fish—Habits and behavior

FISH SOUPS See Chowder; Soups

FISH STEW See Stew

FISH TRAPS

Live bait traps [crickets and crayfish] B. Volkart. il *Field & Stream* 93:164 Ap '89

FISHER, ANDREW, 1935-

A patriot for whom? Wallace & Bruce: Scotland's uneasy heroes. bibl il *History Today* 39:18-23 F '89

FISHER, ARTHUR

Science newsfront. See issues of Popular Science

FISHER, ARTHUR—cont.
What's new: photography. See alternate issues of Popular Science beginning January 1986
FISHER, FRANCIS DUMMER
The electronic lumberyard and builders' rights. il *Change* 21:12-21 My/Je '89
FISHER, GEORGE M. C.
about
The rival Japan respects [cover story] L. Therrien. il pors *Business Week* p108-10+ N 13 '89
FISHER, HELEN E.
The way you walk that walk . . . il *Health (New York, N.Y.)* 21:53-5+ S '89
FISHER, KENNETH L.
Portfolio strategy. See issues of Forbes beginning July 16, 1984
FISHER, M. F. K. (MARY FRANCES KENNEDY), 1908-
Native truths. il por *Architectural Digest* 46:78+ My '89
Some other picnics. il por *Architectural Digest* 46:34+ Jl '89
Travel notes: cafe olives. il *Architectural Digest* 46:70+ Mr '89
about
'O poor cook!': The annotating M. F. K. Fisher. J. Ferrary. por *The New York Times Book Review* 94:1+ Je 4 '89
Bibliography
The art of M. F. K. Fisher. P. Storace. il *The New York Review of Books* 36:42-5 D 7 '89
FISHER, MARC
Pacifica's next wave. il *Mother Jones* 14:50-2 My '89
FISHER, MARY FRANCES KENNEDY See Fisher, M. F. K. (Mary Frances Kennedy), 1908-
FISHER, MATTHEW
The children who come alone. *World Press Review* 36:14+ N '89
FISHER, RICHARD YALE
about
The beauty beneath the beast. R. Koselka. il por *Forbes* 144:240+ N 27 '89
FISHER, STEVE
about
The right man for the job. A. Wolff. il pors *Sports Illustrated* 70:58-60+ Ap 17 '89
FISHER, WILLIAM
Occupational hazards. il por *Harper's Bazaar* 122:98 N '89
FISHER, WILLIAM, AND SCHAPIRO, MARK
Four titans carve up European TV [cover story] il *The Nation* 248:37+ Ja 9-16 '89
FISHER (JULES) & PAUL MARANTZ, INC. See Jules Fisher & Paul Marantz, Inc.
FISHERIES
See also
Crayfish fisheries
Fish culture
Fish traps
Fishermen
Poaching
Shellfish fisheries
Squid fisheries
Turtle fisheries
United States. National Marine Fisheries Service
Fish and power in a riverine rivalry [call for the removal of Edwards Dam in Augusta, Me. in order to restore Kennebec River fisheries] B. Carpenter. il map *U.S. News & World Report* 107:90+ O 16 '89
Monsters of the deep—delights for the palate [New York's offshore ocean fisheries; cover story] J. M. Mason and J. G. Casey. il *The Conservationist* 44:2-9+ S/O '89
Striped bass [effects of Westway decision and PCBs on New York's commercial fisheries] S. D. Garber. il *Focus (New York, N.Y.: 1950)* 39:34-6 Summ '89
The striper tug of war [sport and commercial fishermen on Chesapeake Bay] L. Williamson. il *Outdoor Life* 184:56-7 Ag '89
Equipment
See also
Fishing nets
International aspects
The destruction of dolphins [trapped in tuna nets; cover story] K. Brower. il *The Atlantic* 264:35-8+ Jl '89
A domestic squabble [Canada and France at odds over fishing rights off Newfoundland] G. Allen. il *Maclean's* 102:16 Ja 16 '89
A troubled cod truce [Ottawa's Atlantic fish accord with France] A. Walmsley. il *Maclean's* 102:36-8 Ap 17 '89
U.S. responsibilities in international fisheries matters [reauthorization of Magnuson Fisheries Conservation and Management Act; statement, May 2, 1989] E. E. Wolfe. *Department of State Bulletin* 89:56-8 Jl '89
Laws and regulations
See Fishery laws and regulations
Management
Managing the oceans. T. M. Hawley. il *Technology Review* 92:18 F/Mr '89
Alaska
Fishy arguments [Seattle bottom fishermen blame Japanese poaching in Alaskan waters for lower prices] M. Beauchamp. il *Forbes* 143:130+ Mr 20 '89

Canada
An ambiguous victory [trade panel ruling on salmon and herring caught off British Columbia] B. Bergman. il *Maclean's* 102:38 O 30 '89
Atlantic chill. G. Allen. il *Maclean's* 102:14-16 My 29 '89
A domestic squabble [Canada and France at odds over fishing rights off Newfoundland] G. Allen. il *Maclean's* 102:16 Ja 16 '89
Stormy waters [Atlantic fishery] G. Allen. il *Maclean's* 102:40-1 D 25 '89
Tangled nets [troubled Atlantic fishery] J. DeMont. il por *Maclean's* 102:54-5 S 4 '89
A troubled cod truce [Ottawa's Atlantic fish accord with France] A. Walmsley. il *Maclean's* 102:36-8 Ap 17 '89
Fiji
A Fijian way of fishing. M. Timmons. il *Sea Frontiers* 35:64 Ja/F '89
Georges Bank
Predation on ocean krill [discussion of July 15, 1988 article, Acoustical detection of high-density krill demersal layers in the submarine canyons off Georges Bank] C. H. Greene and others. *Science* 243:237-8 Ja 13 '89
Great Lakes region
Are Great Lakes fish safe to eat? [polychlorinated biphenyls] W. A. Schmidt. il map *National Wildlife* 27:16-19 Ag/S '89
Is Lake Michigan dying again? [salmon] T. Huggler. il *Outdoor Life* 183:80-1+ My '89
Japan
An alarming catch [critics condemn use of drift nets] M. Nichols. il *Maclean's* 102:49 Je 12 '89
Fish mining on the open seas [U.S. attempt to curb Japanese use of drift nets that ensnare various types of marine life] il *Time* 133:70 Je 5 '89
Fishy arguments [Seattle bottom fishermen blame Japanese poaching in Alaskan waters for lower prices] M. Beauchamp. il *Forbes* 143:130+ Mr 20 '89
Spain
Photographs and photography
In the rhythms of the tides fishing [work of S. Salgado] il *Life* 12:70-4+ Je '89
Tahiti (French Polynesia)
Can overboard! [throwing beer cans into ocean from tuna fishing boat] C. Safina. il *Sea Frontiers* 35:384 N/D '89
FISHERMAN'S WHARF (SAN FRANCISCO, CALIF.)
Dickens to Dungeness: Fisherman's Wharf holiday doings. il *Sunset (Central West edition)* 181:16-18 D '88
FISHERMEN
Fishers, trappers, and hunters [commercial fishing industry] A. Gartaganis. il *Occupational Outlook Quarterly* 33:20-5 Summ '89
In defense of outdoorsmen. W. G. Tapply. por *Newsweek* 113:10-11 Ap 10 '89
The real environmentalist. R. E. Tyrrell. il *The American Spectator* 22:10 S '89
Age
A fisherman is old . . . L. B. Webb. il *Field & Stream* 94:20+ My '89
Anecdotes, facetiae, satire, etc.
Angling English. W. Burton. il *Field & Stream* 93:22 Ja '89
On becoming a bassman. B. R. Hooten. il *Field & Stream* 93:30+ Mr '89
Health and hygiene
Anecdotes, facetiae, satire, etc.
Shaping up. T. Leeson. il *Field & Stream* 94:22 S '89
Psychology
New eyes. G. Hill. il *Field & Stream* 94:12 Jl '89
Northern lights [steelhead] K. McCafferty. il *Field & Stream* 94:60-1+ My '89
Patience. T. Leeson. il *Field & Stream* 93:26+ Mr '89
FISHERMEN'S TERMINAL (SEATTLE, WASH.)
New home for Seattle fishermen. il *Sunset (Central West edition)* 183:54 N '89
FISHERS ISLAND (N.Y.)
See also
Architecture, Domestic—Fishers Island (N.Y.)
FISHERY LAWS AND REGULATIONS
See also
Poaching
Shellfish fisheries—Laws and regulations
United States. National Marine Fisheries Service
Through the slot [slot regulations for bass and trout] J. Bashline. il *Field & Stream* 93:18 Ja '89
U.S. responsibilities in international fisheries matters [reauthorization of Magnuson Fisheries Conservation and Management Act; statement, May 2, 1989] E. E. Wolfe. *Department of State Bulletin* 89:56-8 Jl '89
FISHES See Fish
FISHFINDERS (DEPTH INDICATORS) See Depth indicators
FISHHOOKS
The book on hooks. P. B. Wright. il *Motor Boating & Sailing* 163:80 Ap '89
A case in point. B. Stearns. il *Field & Stream* 94:110+ S '89
Midge magic. W. G. Tapply. il *Field & Stream* 94:36+ Ag '89

FISHHOOKS—cont.

A new look at fly-fishing hooks. J. Bashline. il *Field & Stream* 93:32-3 Mr '89

A new twist to an old hook. D. Mermon. il *Outdoor Life* 183:126 Mr '89

FISHING

See also

    Bait

    Barracuda fishing

    Bass fishing

    Billfish fishing

    Bluefish fishing

    Bluegill fishing

    Bullhead fishing

    Casting (Fishing)

    Catfish fishing

    Crappie fishing

    Fisheries

    Fishermen

    Grayling fishing

    Halibut fishing

    Indians of North America—Fishing

    Marlin fishing

    Muskellunge fishing

    Panfish fishing

    Pike fishing

    Pompano fishing

    Redfish fishing

    Sailfish fishing

    Salmon fishing

    Salt water fishing

    Shad fishing

    Shark fishing

    Spear fishing

    Tarpon fishing

    Trawls and trawling

    Trout fishing

    Walleye fishing

    Weakfish fishing

    Women in fishing

Fishing. P. Barrett. See issues of Field & Stream beginning February 1984

Fishing. J. Gibbs. See issues of Outdoor Life

Fishing by phases. N. Rothery. il map *Outdoor Life* 184:76-8+ Ag '89

Fishing holes U.S.A. T. Williams. il pors maps *Popular Mechanics* 166:74-5+ My '89

Fishing the tides. P. B. Wright. il *Motor Boating & Sailing* 164:30 S '89

Footloose on vacation lakes. P. Barrett. il *Field & Stream* 94:56-7+ Ag '89

Luck! [reprint from February 1965 issue] T. Trueblood. il *Field & Stream* 93:34+ Mr '89

Moon talk. P. B. Wright. il *Motor Boating & Sailing* 164:84 Ag '89

Simple pleasures. R. C. Murray. *Outdoor Life* 183:4 Ja '89

Solunar tables. See issues of Field & Stream

Time to change. T. Syron. il *Field & Stream* 93:68+ F '89

Accidents and injuries

Outdoor medicine [D. T. McCrady supplies medical kit after author slips on rock] H. Middleton. il *Southern Living* 24:26+ Ag '89

Anecdotes, facetiae, satire, etc.

How to cook a sea bass. E. Zern. il *Field & Stream* 93:108 Ja '89

Reel life. W. Geist. il *New York* 22:26 My 8 '89

Bibliography

Books & comments. See occasional issues of Field & Stream beginning April 1985

Competitions

Battleground [Bertram-Hatteras Shootout at Walker's Cay] M. Benson. il *Motor Boating & Sailing* 164:50-3+ Jl '89

Calendar. See issues of Motor Boating & Sailing beginning October 1988

Light and lively [Hawaii's Light Tackle Tournament] J. Foster. il *Motor Boating & Sailing* 164:52-5+ N '89

Pacifica shootout [West Coast Marlin Shootout] B. Duke. il *Motor Boating & Sailing* 163:134+ Mr '89

Anecdotes, facetiae, satire, etc.

Bassin' for bucks. W. McLoughlin. il *Field & Stream* 94:18 Ag '89

Equipment

See also

    Depth indicators

    Electronics in fishing

    Fishing lights

    Fishing nets

    Fishing tackle

What's new. See issues of Outdoor Life

Ethical aspects

Catch of a lifetime [son learns about ethics from fishing with father] J. P. Lenfestey. il *Reader's Digest* 134:111-12 F '89

Grandpa and the kid. D. Sisson. il *Field & Stream* 93:61+ Ap '89

A report from salmon run [controversial fishing practices in Pulaski, N.Y.] C. Robohm. il *Country Journal* 16:72-3 S/O '89

The snag in Pulaski [controversial salmon fishing practices] D. W. Hollis. il map *Country Journal* 16:68-71+ S/O '89

Laws and regulations

See Fishery laws and regulations

Noise

Good vibrations [sound waves created by fishing boats] P. B. Wright. il *Motor Boating & Sailing* 163:74+ Je '89

Photographs and photography

Keep and release fishing. J. Gibbs. il *Outdoor Life* 183:74-5+ Je '89

Storm conditions

Grandpa and the kid [snowstorm] D. Sisson. il *Field & Stream* 93:61+ Ap '89

The pitter-patter principle. N. Strung. il *Field & Stream* 94:42-3 Je '89

Wind. K. Schultz. il *Field & Stream* 94:20+ Je '89

Study and teaching

Father to daughter. B. Journey. il *Outdoor Life* 184:94-5+ N '89

Lessons for a lifetime [raising a daughter to hunt and fish] K. Etling. il *Outdoor Life* 183:76-8+ Je '89

Aids and devices

Reel Fish'n & Rich Tauber's Bass Champ [video games] K. Ferrell and P. Scisco. il *Compute!* 11:136+ O '89

Television broadcasting

See Television broadcasting—Sports

Terminology

Anecdotes, facetiae, satire, etc.

Toads in the scumline [trout fishing lingo in the West] W. G. Tapply. il *Field & Stream* 94:32+ O '89

Alaska

Not just for the halibut [southeast Alaska] B. Stearns. il *Field & Stream* 94:84+ N '89

Arkansas

The gentleman from Kentucky [spotted bass fishing] P. Barrett. il *Field & Stream* 94:69-70 My '89

The Ozarks: where the big trout run. H. Middleton. il *Southern Living* 24:84-7 Je '89

Azores

Oh Magnifica! [giant marlin hooked off the Azores] E. M. Swift. il *Sports Illustrated* 71:154-8+ S 4 '89

Bahamas

Battleground [Bertram-Hatteras Shootout at Walker's Cay] M. Benson. il *Motor Boating & Sailing* 164:50-3+ Jl '89

Best of the Bahamas. A. J. McClane. il map *Field & Stream* 93:42+ Ja '89

Baja California (Mexico: Peninsula)

Before Cabo [marlin fishing] R. R. Holster, Jr. il *Sport (New York, N.Y.)* 80:62-5 Ja '89

Numero Uno [marlin fishing off Cabo San Lucas in a Barattucci 82-foot sportsfisher] N. Rabinowitz. il *Motor Boating & Sailing* 163:52-7+ Ap '89

British Columbia

Lodges on the run [floating lodges for salmon fishing] J. Gibbs. il *Outdoor Life* 183:86-7+ My '89

Northern lights [steelhead] K. McCafferty. il *Field & Stream* 94:60-1+ My '89

Canada

Fishing across Canada. il *Field & Stream* 93:54-5+ Mr '89

Gone fishing [oilless gasoline causes boat engine failure] D. Sprockett. *Flower and Garden* 33:104-7 Ja/F '89

Chesapeake Bay (Md. and Va.)

The striper tug of war [sport and commercial fishermen on Chesapeake Bay] L. Williamson. il *Outdoor Life* 184:56-7 Ag '89

Costa Rica

Debunking Hemingway's marlin theories. J. Skorupa. il *Popular Mechanics* 166:44 O '89

The sweet gulf [billfish fishing] B. Stearns. il *Field & Stream* 94:64-6 Ag '89

Cuba

Fishing Cuba's forbidden waters. S. Stapleton. il *Motor Boating & Sailing* 164:42-4+ S '89

Florida

Chased out of the sea [catching barracuda while swimming off Fort Lauderdale] B. Masselink. il *Sea Frontiers* 35:256 Jl/Ag '89

Go fishing, young man [sailfish fishing off Palm Beach, Fla. in a 32-foot Marlin 28] J. Skorupa. il *Popular Mechanics* 166:28+ Je '89

Florida Keys (Fla.)

Permit me this. H. Middleton. il *Southern Living* 24:36+ S '89

Playing in the bonefish league [T. Williams] J. Skorupa. il pors *Popular Mechanics* 166:28-9 Mr '89

The ugly, inedible fish that hooked a president [bonefish] P. Engardio. il *Business Week* p108 Mr 6 '89

Great Lakes region

Lake Michigan fishing: no shore thing. J. White. il *The Saturday Evening Post* 261:86-7 S '89

Hawaii

Light and lively [Hawaii's Light Tackle Tournament] J. Foster. il *Motor Boating & Sailing* 164:52-5+ N '89

FISHING—*cont.*

Labrador (Nfld.)

The land of legendary brook trout. T. Huggler. il *Outdoor Life* 184:58-9+ Jl '89

Manitoba

Cat with a million friends [channel catfish] P. Barrett. il *Field & Stream* 94:58-9+ Jl '89

Manitoba's new pike and walleye hotspot. K. Schultz. il *Field & Stream* 93:56+ Mr '89

Middle Western States

Black earth, spring creeks. P. Kaminsky. il *Field & Stream* 94:50-1+ D '89

Minnesota

Home is where the fish are [ice fishing for walleyes] T. Dickson. il *National Wildlife* 27:24-8 F/Mr '89

Lake of the Woods. E. L. Rogers. il *Outdoor Life* 183:94-6+ Ap '89

Missouri

Out of bed bass [views of D. Brauer] K. Etling. il *Outdoor Life* 183:71-3+ My '89

Montana

Bighorn of plenty. W. G. Tapply. il map *Field & Stream* 93:32-3+ Ja '89

New Brunswick

Canada's "secret" smallmouths. K. Schultz. il map *Field & Stream* 93:27+ Ja '89

New Jersey

Cold-water surface bass [night fishing] J. Potts. il *Outdoor Life* 183:60-1+ F '89

New York (State)

Big lakers on Seneca [trout] T. P. Maguire. il *The Conservationist* 43:10-13 My/Je '89

Bluefish—a great marine resource. A. Ristori. il *The Conservationist* 44:18-21 Jl/Ag '89

Just a bullhead. W. Ryan. il *The Conservationist* 44:34-7 Jl/Ag '89

Monsters of the deep—delights for the palate [New York's offshore ocean fisheries; cover story] J. M. Mason and J. G. Casey. il *The Conservationist* 44:2-9+ S/O '89

New York's great angling secret [fall trout fishing] J. Rowen. il *The Conservationist* 44:34-9 S/O '89

A report from salmon run [controversial fishing practices in Pulaski] C. Robohm. il *Country Journal* 16:72-3 S/O '89

The snag in Pulaski [controversial salmon fishing practices] D. W. Hollis. il map *Country Journal* 16:68-71+ S/O '89

Welcome, world, to Trout Town U.S.A., where all the flies are fit to be tied [flyfishing the Beaverkill River] J. Friedman. il *People Weekly* 32:92-4+ Jl 3 '89

Ontario

The ultimate excuse [muskellunge fishing] K. Schultz. il *Field & Stream* 94:30+ Ag '89

Pacific Northwest

Salmon. il map *Sunset (Central West edition)* 182:90-7 Ap '89

Québec (Province)

Helen's Falls [Atlantic salmon fishing on George River] D. Barnes. il *Field & Stream* 94:90+ Je '89

Saskatchewan

Fishing the bush on a budget [Far North Recreation] N. Strung. il *Field & Stream* 93:42+ Ap '89

Southern States

Snowbird bass. S. Price. il map *Field & Stream* 93:40-1+ Ja '89

Texas

The fertile crescent [lower Texas coast] J. Doggett. il *Field & Stream* 93:36-7+ Ja '89

Thailand

Boating's new magic kingdom: Thailand. P. B. Wright. il *Motor Boating & Sailing* 163:92-4+ Je '89

United States

See Fishing

Western States

The other West [trout fishing] D. Hughes. il *Field & Stream* 94:40-1+ S '89

Anecdotes, facetiae, satire, etc.

Toads in the scumline [trout fishing lingo in the West] W. G. Tapply. il *Field & Stream* 94:32+ O '89

Wisconsin

Mississippi of the North [protests over Chippewa fishing rights] D. Parmentier. il por *The Humanist* 49:17-19+ S/O '89

Nate Berg, 12, approaches 500 fishing days—the mind reels. il por *People Weekly* 32:65 Ag 14 '89

Spearing fish, playing 'chicken' [confrontation over Chippewa Indian fishing rights] J. Oberly. il *The Nation* 248:844-5+ Je 19 '89

The Wisconsin fishing war [spearfishing by Chippewa Indians] il *Sports Illustrated* 70:16 My 15 '89

FISHING, WINTER

Cold-current smallmouths. K. Etling. il *Outdoor Life* 184:88-9+ N '89

Cold weather walleyes. P. M. Liikala. il *Outdoor Life* 183:76-7+ Ja '89

Home is where the fish are [ice fishing for walleyes at Mille Lacs Lake, Minn.] T. Dickson. il *National Wildlife* 27:24-8 F/Mr '89

Hunting & fishing on skis. S. Netherby. il *Field & Stream* 93:30+ F '89

Icefisherman's sled. P. Butler and M. Butler. il *Outdoor Life* 184:66+ N '89

The trout of winter [catch and release] J. Barsness. il *Field & Stream* 93:56-7+ F '89

Winterfest. N. Strung. il *Field & Stream* 94:58+ D '89

FISHING BOATS

The great escapes. J. Gibbs. il *Outdoor Life* 184:32+ Ag '89

Chartering

See Fishing boats—Leasing and renting

Engines

See Motor boat engines

Handling

Tips on reading the bottom. S. Stapleton. il *Motor Boating & Sailing* 164:30 Jl '89

Leasing and renting

Lake Michigan fishing: no shore thing. J. White. il *The Saturday Evening Post* 261:86-7 S '89

Licenses

In the jaws of the law [F. Mundus, inspiration for Jaws shark hunter] il por *Sports Illustrated* 71:10 Ag 7 '89

Noise

Good vibrations [sound waves created by fishing boats] P. B. Wright. il *Motor Boating & Sailing* 163:74+ Je '89

Speed

55 mph [Monterey 80] P. B. Wright. il *Motor Boating & Sailing* 163:52-5+ My '89

Testing

Alaska in a Donzi 33 [cover story] P. A. Janssen. il *Motor Boating & Sailing* 164:40-5+ O '89

Bass blitzers. J. Skorupa. il *Popular Mechanics* 166:81-4 Jl '89

Battleground [Bertram-Hatteras Shootout at Walker's Cay] M. Benson. il *Motor Boating & Sailing* 164:50-3+ Jl '89

Debut in paradise [maiden voyage of Donzi Z-65 in the Bahamas] J. Clemans. il *Motor Boating & Sailing* 164:36-41+ S '89

Donzi Z-54. J. Clemans. il *Motor Boating & Sailing* 163:34 Ap '89

Express sportfishermen: all aboard. J. Clemans. il *Motor Boating & Sailing* 163:56-61+ My '89

Go fishing, young man [sailfish fishing off Palm Beach, Fla. in a 32-foot Marlin 28] J. Skorupa. il *Popular Mechanics* 166:28+ Je '89

Grady-white 231. T. P. Banse. il *Motor Boating & Sailing* 164:23 Ag '89

Grady-white 28. T. P. Banse. il *Motor Boating & Sailing* 163:28 Ap '89

Heading north [Seattle to Juneau in a Donzi F-33] P. A. Janssen. il *Motor Boating & Sailing* 164:15+ S '89

High-tech Hydrasport [3300] R. Marshall. il *Motor Boating & Sailing* 163:62-3+ My '89

Numero Uno [marlin fishing off Cabo San Lucas in a Barattucci 82-foot sportsfisher] N. Rabinowitz. il *Motor Boating & Sailing* 163:52-7+ Ap '89

Ocean Yachts 32. D. Fales. il *Motor Boating & Sailing* 163:34 Mr '89

Offshore showdown. J. Skorupa. il *Popular Mechanics* 166:76-9 Ap '89

PT 36. P. A. Janssen. il *Motor Boating & Sailing* 163:40 F '89

Pursuit 32. D. Fales. il *Motor Boating & Sailing* 164:23 D '89

Tiara 43. D. Fales. il *Motor Boating & Sailing* 163:34 My '89

Tiara nova [4300 Convertible] M. Benson. il *Motor Boating & Sailing* 164:46-9+ O '89

Topnotch Tolly [Tollycraft 40 convertible] J. Clemans. il *Motor Boating & Sailing* 163:68-9+ Mr '89

Whaler's new macho machine [Boston Whaler 25] P. Whittell. il *Motor Boating & Sailing* 164:52-3+ S '89

Wilbur 34. D. Fales. il *Motor Boating & Sailing* 164:22 Jl '89

Towing

Need a tow? B. Stearns. il *Field & Stream* 94:78+ D '89

FISHING CLOTHES *See* Clothing and dress—Sports clothes

FISHING FLIES *See* Fishing lures, flies, etc.

FISHING GUIDES *See* Guides

FISHING INDUSTRY *See* Fisheries

FISHING LICENSES

Anecdotes, facetiae, satire, etc.

Fishing license application test. C. Hauptman. il *Field & Stream* 94:24-5 Jl '89

FISHING LIGHTS

Black light trolling. J. Gibbs. il *Outdoor Life* 183:34+ Je '89

Night fishing light. L. Witman. il *Field & Stream* 94:36 Je '89

FISHING LINES *See* Fishing tackle

FISHING LODGES *See* Lodges

FISHING LURES, FLIES, ETC.

See also

Casting (Fishing)

The all-day beetle. W. G. Tapply. il *Field & Stream* 94:46-7+ Jl '89

FISHING LURES, FLIES, ETC.—*cont.*

Bass between a rock and a hard place [light lines and small baits] K. Jackson. il *Outdoor Life* 184:74-5+ Ag '89

Bass on a fly. J. Bashline. il *Field & Stream* 94:34+ Je '89

Bottom bouncing walleyes. M. Pearce. il *Outdoor Life* 184:72-3+ O '89

Bugging summer smallmouths. T. Davis. il *Field & Stream* 94:46-7+ Ag '89

Butter tub fur blender. R. Drew. il *Field & Stream* 94:14 Je '89

Buzzing for white bass. K. Schultz. il *Field & Stream* 94:32-3 S '89

Down-under panfish. J. Dean. il *Outdoor Life* 183:78-9+ Mr '89

Fine-tune your lures. D. A. Ecker. il *Outdoor Life* 183:96+ Mr '89

Fly bum. G. Hill. il *Field & Stream* 93:14 Ap '89

Fly fishing slow currents. J. Gierach. il *Field & Stream* 94:56-7+ My '89

Froggin' for largemouths. B. Volkart. *Field & Stream* 94:72 Ag '89

Getting down to bassness. C. Hauptman. il *Field & Stream* 94:74+ N '89

The glass key [bass] C. Hauptman. il *Field & Stream* 93:64-5+ Ap '89

Grandpa and the kid [brown trout fishing] D. Sisson. il *Field & Stream* 94:39+ Je '89

Hidden-jig lures. M. Hicks. il *Field & Stream* 94:70 Ag '89

Jousting with river kings [backtrolling for chinook salmon] P. Barrett. il *Field & Stream* 94:57-8+ O '89

Lifting weights [nymphs] D. Hughes. il *Field & Stream* 93:50-1+ Mr '89

Midge magic. W. G. Tapply. il *Field & Stream* 94:36+ Ag '89

A midsummer night's dream fly. L. M. Wright. il *Field & Stream* 94:48-9+ Jl '89

Mono bucktails. N. Strung. il *Field & Stream* 94:78 Ag '89

Open-water icefishing [spring] D. Zutz. il *Outdoor Life* 183:88-9+ Ap '89

Plastic worms for summer bass. K. Schultz. il *Field & Stream* 94:41+ Jl '89

Pumping iron [jigging spoons] J. Weiss. il *Outdoor Life* 183:88-90+ My '89

Pumping lead for walleyes [jigs] N. Strung. il *Field & Stream* 94:50-1+ My '89

Rising to the occasion [catching smallmouth and largemouth bass with topwater lures] J. Bashline. il *Field & Stream* 94:20-1 O '89

Serpents on the surface [snake lures] C. Hauptman. il *Field & Stream* 93:43+ Mr '89

Shake, rattle & reel. C. Hauptman. il *Field & Stream* 94:52-3+ My '89

Small bait, big fish. P. B. Wright. il *Motor Boating & Sailing* 163:102 My '89

Spinning for trout. E. Cutlip. il *Field & Stream* 94:44 My '89

Stringers with streamers. J. Gibbs. il *Outdoor Life* 184:20+ O '89

Tie your own flies. P. Barrett. il *Field & Stream* 93:46+ Ja '89

Top lures for shallow bass [spinner baits] K. Schultz. il *Field & Stream* 94:82+ My '89

Trout in the spring runoff [fishing with nymphs] J. Gierach. il *Field & Stream* 93:70-1+ Ap '89

The two-fly cast. K. McCafferty. il *Field & Stream* 94:26+ Je '89

Walleye systems for bass. J. Gibbs. il *Outdoor Life* 183:20+ Ja '89

Walleyes on slip-sinker rigs. B. Volkart. il *Field & Stream* 94:25 Ag '89

When less is best. J. Gibbs. il *Outdoor Life* 184:42+ S '89

Why fish bite. P. B. Wright. il *Motor Boating & Sailing* 164:37 O '89

Wing it [dry flies] J. Bashline. il *Field & Stream* 94:34 My '89

Collectors and collecting

Getting hooked on antique fishing lures. H. Wheelwright. il *Money* 18:23 Ap '89

FISHING NETS

See also

Fish traps

About-face [Japanese curtail use of drift nets] il *Time* 134:86 O 2 '89

An alarming catch [critics condemn use of drift nets] M. Nichols. il *Maclean's* 102:49 Je 12 '89

The destruction of dolphins [trapped in tuna nets; cover story] K. Brower. il *The Atlantic* 264:35-8+ Jl '89

Dropping the net on Gulf shrimpers [requiring trapdoor devices on nets to prevent ridley turtle drownings in Gulf of Mexico] il *Newsweek* 114:28 Ag 7 '89

An expert warns of the dangers of driftnets, lethal curtains that reap fish—and controversy—by the ton [interview with J. Coe] J. H. Blackman. il pors *People Weekly* 31:145-6+ My 15 '89

Fish mining on the open seas [U.S. attempt to curb Japanese use of drift nets that ensnare various types of marine life] il *Time* 133:70 Je 5 '89

Shrimpers and lawmakers collide over a move to save the sea turtles [Turtle Excluder Devices] J. Rudloe and A. Rudloe. il *Smithsonian* 20:44-55 D '89

FISHING POLES *See* Fishing tackle

FISHING REELS *See* Fishing tackle

FISHING ROD CASES *See* Fishing tackle—Storage

FISHING RODS *See* Fishing tackle

FISHING TACKLE

See also

Fishhooks

Fishing lures, flies, etc.

Bass between a rock and a hard place [light lines and small baits] K. Jackson. il *Outdoor Life* 184:74-5+ Ag '89

Bass on a fly. J. Bashline. il *Field & Stream* 94:34+ Je '89

Choosing the right rod. P. Barrett. il *Field & Stream* 93:58+ Mr '89

Fall's finer side [bass fishing gear] J. Doggett. il *Field & Stream* 94:54+ O '89

First-class fly rod bargains. P. Barrett. il *Field & Stream* 94:72+ D '89

First rod. P. Smith. il *Field & Stream* 93:16-17 Ja '89

Hook line and sinker. B. Woods. il *The Mother Earth News* 117:110+ My/Je '89

Hooking the perfect fly rod. J. O. Hamilton. il *Business Week* p156 My 8 '89

The incomplete angler. R. Kimber. il *Country Journal* 16:78-80 Jl/Ag '89

Innovative new fishing tackle '89. K. Schultz. il *Field & Stream* 93:44+ F '89

Mano a mono [leaders] P. B. Wright. il *Motor Boating & Sailing* 163:146+ Ja '89

Modern pole fishing. J. Gibbs. il *Outdoor Life* 183:66+ Ap '89

A new cast to lines. J. Gibbs. il *Outdoor Life* 183:18+ F '89

Newest tackle for '89. J. Gibbs. il *Outdoor Life* 183:84-7 Mr '89

The newest way to take fish [float trotting] J. Gibbs. il *Outdoor Life* 184:84-5+ S '89

The reel stuff [fishing reel drag] P. B. Wright. il *Motor Boating & Sailing* 163:52+ F '89

The reel things [casting reels] J. Gibbs. il *Outdoor Life* 184:62+ N '89

The reel world. P. B. Wright. il *Motor Boating & Sailing* 164:54-5+ O '89

Strip-tease trouting. G. A. Borger. il *Field & Stream* 94:46-7+ Je '89

Ultralight largemouths. J. Dean. il *Outdoor Life* 183:84-5+ Ap '89

What's light and what's right? [lines] P. B. Wright. il *Motor Boating & Sailing* 164:34 Jl '89

Anecdotes, facetiae, satire, etc.

Reel of the future. W. McLoughlin. il *Field & Stream* 94:18 O '89

Collectors and collecting

Catch of the day [A. Helou's London house decorated with fishing tackle and art] R. Koenig. il por *House & Garden* 161:54-5 Ja '89

Up front. D. Barnes. il *Field & Stream* 94:7 O '89

Photographs and photography

Creating a nostalgic theme assembly. M. Hammarlund. il *Petersen's Photographic Magazine* 17:84-5 Ap '89

Storage

A case for travel. T. Clauss. il *Outdoor Life* 183:46 F '89

A rack and cleaning board. P. Butler and M. Butler. il *Outdoor Life* 183:32+ Ap '89

FISHING TOURNAMENTS *See* Fishing—Competitions

FISHING TROPHIES

Three ploys for trophy-bass [largemouth] C. Hauptmann; A. H. Putnam; E. J. Mendus. il *Field & Stream* 94:56-7 D '89

Where to hook a hawg next year [best places in America to fish for trophy largemouth bass] L. Larsen. il *Outdoor Life* 184:70-1+ D '89

Anecdotes, facetiae, satire, etc.

A shrimp cocktale. P. F. McManus. il *Outdoor Life* 184:112+ D '89

FISHKIND, BETH C.

The autophile. See issues of High Fidelity (New York, N.Y.) beginning March 1989 through July 1989

FISHMAN, KEITH

about

"Merchandise that motivates". M. Barrier. il pors *Nation's Business* 77:64 My '89

FISHMAN, STANLEY

about

"Merchandise that motivates". M. Barrier. il pors *Nation's Business* 77:64 My '89

FISHMAN, STEVE

Cancer comes for dinner. il *The New York Times Magazine* p70-1 Je 11 '89

Questions for the cosmos. il por *The New York Times Magazine* p50+ N 26 '89

FISHWORMS See Earthworms
FISK, CARLTON, 1947-
about
Old catchers never die . . . P. Korn. il pors *Sport (New York, N.Y.)* 80:44-9 Jl '89
FISK, ROBERT
Hands off by the superpowers. il *World Press Review* 36:26-7 O '89
FISSION, NUCLEAR See Nuclear fission
FITCH, RICHARD D.
Antique radios. See issues of Radio-Electronics beginning February 1985 through May 1989
FITCH, ROBERT
Making New York City safe for plutocracy. il *The Nation* 249:709-12+ D 11 '89
FITCH, VAL LOGSDON, 1923-
An APS president reflects on his two-year term. il por *Physics Today* 42:49-53 D '89
FITCH INVESTORS SERVICE INC.
A new itch at Fitch. J. Zweig. il por *Forbes* 143:326 My 29 '89
FITE, HARVEY, 1903-1976
about
Opus 40: a sculptor's obsession in upstate New York. B. Gill. il por *Architectural Digest* 46:46+ Mr '89
FITEL See Financial Telecommunications Inc.
FITNESS See Physical fitness
FITTIPALDI, EMERSON
about
A bumper-car Indy. S. Moses. il *Sports Illustrated* 70:32-4+ Je 5 '89
A fast comeback. P. Lerner. il pors *The New York Times Magazine* p42+ O 15 '89
One bright day in May. T. West. il por *Road & Track* 41:96-7+ S '89
FITTS, C. AUSTIN, 1950-
about
Austin Fitts better be good with hammer and nails. R. Stodghill, II. il por *Business Week* p152-3 N 27 '89
FITZ-HAVEN DAIRY
Successful family farm. J. R. Borcherding. il *Successful Farming* 87:44-6 Ap '89
FITZGERALD, ELLA
about
As singers sang to help their own, the sweet tones and high notes were all for Ella. il por *People Weekly* 31:56-7 My 15 '89
FITZGERALD, FRANCES, 1940-
Iran-contra. *The New Yorker* 65:51-4+ O 16 '89
Maine stay. il *Vogue* 179:236-8+ Ag '89
Memoirs of the Reagan era. il *The New Yorker* 64:71-83+ Ja 16 '89
The North case. *The Nation* 248:149 F 6 '89
FITZGERALD, GERALD, 1932-
about
Details! Details! A. Porter; F. Merkling. il pors *Opera News* 54:18-20+ N '89
FITZGERALD, KAREN
(jt. auth) See Watson, Rita Esposito, and FitzGerald, Karen
FITZGERALD, RANDY
America's amazing treasure chest. il *Reader's Digest* 134:47-8+ Je '89
Comeback in Indian country. *Reader's Digest* 135:29-30+ O '89
This congressman beat the system. il por *Reader's Digest* 134:125-8 Ap '89
FITZGIBBON, ANN
A view from the back porch. il *Southern Living* 24:146 Mr '89
FITZPATRICK, JEAN GRASSO
How to slow down. il *Parents* 64:97-102 Ap '89
"Mommy, are homeless people bad?". il *Parents* 64:95-8+ F '89
FITZROY, ROBERT, 1805-1865
about
George Canning's left buttock and the origin of species. S. J. Gould. *Natural History* p18+ My '89
FITZWATER, MARLIN
about
Who's a 'drugstore cowboy'? il *Newsweek* 113:48 My 29 '89
FITZWILLIAM MUSEUM
Britain's treasure house of art: the Fitzwilliam Collection. B. L. Brown. il *USA Today (Periodical)* 118:68-83 Jl '89
A British university collection travels. A. E. Ledes. il *Antiques* 135:818 Ap '89
FIVE EASY PIECES [film] See Motion picture reviews—Single works
FIVE STONE WIND [dance] See Dance reviews—Single works
FIXED BASE OPERATORS (AVIATION) See Airplane service stations
FIXED RATE MORTGAGES See Mortgages
FIXTURES, BATHROOM See Bathroom fixtures
FIXX (MUSICAL GROUP)
The Fixx: five wild men become calm animals. il *'Teen* 33:56 S '89

FJ'S (FIRM)
A luxury supermarket woos its upscale clients with a yuppie credo—you are what you eat! [owned by F. Straface] il por *People Weekly* 32:135-6 D 11 '89
FK-506 (DRUG)
Lifesaver [FK-506 used to prevent organ rejection] *Time* 134:77 O 30 '89
A wonder drug in the transplant ward [FK-506 prevents organ rejection] il *U.S. News & World Report* 107:17 O 30 '89
FLACH, KEN, AND SEGUSO, ROBERT
The Flach/Seguso guide to championship doubles. il pors *World Tennis* 37:47+ Je '89
FLACK, ROBERTA
about
An intimate talk with Roberta. S. L. Taylor. il *Essence* 19:52-4+ F '89
FLAG BURNING
The Atwater flag sting. N. Hentoff. il *The Progressive* 53:12-14 N '89
Behind the flag-burning firestorm [Supreme Court decision] M. Barone. il *U.S. News & World Report* 107:28 Jl 3 '89
Blast! [constitutional amendment] W. F. Buckley. *National Review* 41:63 N 24 '89
Burn, baby, burn! [Supreme Court ruling] *National Review* 41:13-14 Ag 4 '89
Bushwaterism [L. Atwater's role in persuading Bush to call for flag burning amendment] *The New Republic* 201:5-6 Jl 17-24 '89
Congress rallies around the flag [constitutional amendment proposed to overrule Supreme Court] T. Jacoby. il *Newsweek* 114:19 Jl 10 '89
The Court and the flag decision. W. F. Buckley. *National Review* 41:54 Ag 4 '89
The 'crime' of flag burning [Supreme Court to review case] M. Garbus. il *The Nation* 248:369-70 Mr 20 '89
The dynamics of flag-burning [Supreme Court decision] J. M. Wall. *The Christian Century* 106:643-4 Jl 5-12 '89
Faith and flag-burning [discussion of July 5-12, 1989 article, The dynamics of flag-burning] J. M. Wall. il *The Christian Century* 106:757-9 Ag 16-23 '89
A few symbol-minded questions. F. Trippett. il *Time* 134:72 Ag 28 '89
A fiery furor over the flag. il *Life* 12:106-8+ Ag '89
A fight for Old Glory [Supreme Court rules flag burning is not a crime] T. Jacoby. il *Newsweek* 114:18-20 Jl 3 '89
The flag and freedom of speech [Supreme Court decision] *America* 161:3 Jl 1-8 '89
Flag-burning & other modes of expression. W. Berns. *Commentary* 88:37-41 O '89
Flag-burning attempt in Little Rock incites a race riot at the capitol. il *Jet* 76:6-7 Jl 24 '89
Flag desecration legislation. *Congressional Digest* 68:193-224 Ag/S '89
Flag flap. V. Gold. il *The American Spectator* 22:9 S '89
Flag-saving [Supreme Court ruling] *The Nation* 249:229-30 S 4-11 '89
Flagellation [constitutional amendment proposed] H. Hertzberg. *The New Republic* 201:4 Jl 17-24 '89
Guarding Old Glory. J. Garvey. il *Commonweal* 116:423-4 Ag 11 '89
The High Court stands 5-4 on a burning issue. il *U.S. News & World Report* 107:8 Jl 3 '89
Hooray for the amendment. W. F. Buckley. *National Review* 41:54-5 Ag 4 '89
The humanist. L. L. Morain. *The Humanist* 49:2 S/O '89
Loophole patriotism. *The New Republic* 201:4 Ag 7-14 '89
O'er the land of the free [Supreme Court upholds right to burn the flag] W. Isaacson. il *Time* 134:14-15 Jl 3 '89
Oh say, can you see an amendment? G. Borger. il *U.S. News & World Report* 107:20 Jl 10 '89
Our flag is not sacred. R. McKinniss. por *Christianity Today* 33:8 S 8 '89
A shift in the winds swirling around Old Glory [Senate rejects flag burning amendment] il *U.S. News & World Report* 107:14 O 30 '89
Should Congress pass laws to protect flag and gains of blacks? W. Wofford, Jr. il *Jet* 76:6-9 Jl 17 '89
The speech market [Supreme Court ruling] D. Seligman. *Fortune* 120:135 Ag 28 '89
Star-spangled clamor [Supreme Court ruling] T. C. Muck. il *Christianity Today* 33:11 S 22 '89
Symbol—or substance? [drive for flag burning amendment vs. addressing needs of poor children] P. B. Gough. *Phi Delta Kappan* 71:99 O '89
"A time of sharpened swords" [impact of Supreme Court decisions on artists] D. Waterman. il *Art News* 88:59+ N '89
Unimpressed by the freedom to burn Old Glory, Joey Johnson still wants a revolution. D. Grogan. il pors *People Weekly* 32:98-100 Jl 10 '89
Waiving the flag [Supreme Court to review flag burning issue] *The New Republic* 200:7-8 Ja 23 '89
What price Old Glory? [call for constitutional amendment] *Time* 134:23 Jl 10 '89

FLAG BURNING—*cont.*
Where is the Rehnquist Court headed? [oral arguments in flag burning case heard March 21, 1989] il *Harper's* 278:35-9+ Je '89
FLAGELLA
Direct measurements of sliding between outer doublet microtubules in swimming sperm flagella [sea urchins] C. J. Brokaw. bibl f il *Science* 243:1593-6 Mr 24 '89
FLAGELLIN
Immune response to cholera toxin epitope inserted in Salmonella flagellin. S. M. C. Newton and others. bibl f il *Science* 244:70-2 Ap 7 '89
FLAGS
See also
American flag
Banners
Passions that stir in the breeze. M. Horn. il *U.S. News & World Report* 106:54+ My 29 '89
FLAGS IN ART
See also
American flag in art
FLAGSTAFF (ARIZ.)

Crime
Blood circle [author J. E. Wideman haunted by murder convictions of son and brother] C. Brown. il *Esquire* 112:122-8+ Ag '89

Lighting
Lights out in Flagstaff. *Astronomy* 17:12+ Jl '89
FLAHERTY, LIZ
Good-bye, June Cleaver. il *Ladies' Home Journal* 106:62+ Jl '89
FLAHERTY, PAUL
about
Who's Harry Crumb? [film] Reviews
The American Spectator 22:38-9 Ap '89. B. Bawer
People Weekly il 31:17 F 20 '89. R. Novak
FLAIG, DICK
about
Life on a small but fast track. J. McCallum. il pors *Sports Illustrated* 71:58+ Ag 14 '89
FLAM, JACK D.
Cubiquitous. il pors *Art News* 88:144-9 D '89
Fleeting impressionism. bibl f il *The New York Review of Books* 36:20-5 S 28 '89
Guy Pène du Bois. il por *American Heritage* 40:72-82 F '89
In a different light. il *Art News* 88:112-17 Summ '89
FLAMENCO
Reviews:
Olé! Shabash! at the American Theatre of Actors, New York City. C. Hardy. *Dance Magazine* 63:115-16 My '89
FLAMINGO EAST (NEW YORK, N.Y.: RESTAURANT)
See New York (N.Y.)—Restaurants, nightclubs, bars, etc.
FLAMM, MATTHEW
Movie muses. il *Harper's Bazaar* 122:86-91+ Je '89
FLAMMABLE MATERIALS See Inflammable materials
FLAMMIA, HAROLD
about
The .44-caliber mouthpiece. W. P. Barrett. il *Forbes* 144:166 S 18 '89
FLAMSTEED, SAM
Birth of a pulsar. il *Discover* 10:26 My '89
FLANAGAN, TOMMY
about
Blindfold test. F. Bouchard. il por *Down Beat* 56:41 Mr '89
FLANAGAN, WILLIAM G.
Personal affairs. See issues of Forbes
FLANDERS, JANE, 1940-
Family ground [poem] *The New Yorker* 65:50 N 13 '89
FLANDERS, LAURA
Abortion: the usable past. *The Nation* 249:175-7 Ag 7-14 '89
Northern Ireland hit-squad scandal. il *The Nation* 249:491-4 O 30 '89
FLANNER, JANET, 1892-1978
about
Legendary as Genêt, the New Yorker's Paris correspondent, Janet Flanner exuded both wit and style. C. R. Stimpson. il pors *Vogue* 179:204+ D '89
FLANNERY, GREGORY
Eavesdropping left and right. il *The Nation* 248:516-18+ Ap 17 '89
FLANNERY, TIM
about
The great glove shark. J. E. Vader. il por *Sports Illustrated* 70:89 Je 5 '89
FLANSBURGH, JOHN
about
Giant steps. P. Tyre. il pors *New York* 22:52-5 F 6 '89
FLANTZ, RICHARD
(tr) See Kenan, Amos. Four decades of blood vengeance
FLAPS (AIRPLANE) See Airplanes, Jet—Flaps; Airplanes, Military—Flaps

FLAPS (SPACE VEHICLE) See Space vehicles—Flaps
FLARES, SOLAR See Solar flares
FLASHLIGHT PHOTOGRAPHY See Photography, Flashlight
FLASTE, RICHARD
Cookbooks. il *The New York Times Book Review* 94:16+ Je 11 '89
Cooking. il *The New York Times Book Review* 94:18+ D 3 '89
FLAT-SCREEN TELEVISION RECEIVERS See Television receivers
FLATHEAD NATIONAL FOREST (MONT.)
Run! [fighting forest fire] J. D. Vickery. il *Audubon* 91:86-9 Ja '89
War in the woods: Swan song [confrontations over destruction of old-growth timber] J. G. Mitchell. il map *Audubon* 91:92-102+ N '89
FLATHERS, MARJORIE
Creating articles for the crafts market. *The Writer* 102:24-6 Ag '89
FLATOW, SHERYL
Impressions vs. effects. il pors *Theatre Crafts* 23:56-60+ N '89
FLATS (FOOTWEAR) See Footwear
FLATTERY See Praise
FLATWARE, SILVER See Silverware
FLAUBERT, GUSTAVE, 1821-1880
about
Through dooms of love. S. Willier. por *Opera News* 53:12-14+ F 18 '89
FLAVORING ESSENCES
See also
International Flavors & Fragrances Inc.
Cracking the code of corn chip aroma [research by Thomas H. Parliment] *Science News* 136:78 Jl 29 '89
FLAX, LARRY S.
about
Flax and Rosenfield: taking pizza way past pepperoni. P. Cole. il pors *Business Week* p98 My 8 '89
FLAX, NEW ZEALAND See New Zealand flax
FLEA MARKETS
The joy of kitsch. T. Hine. il *Gentlemen's Quarterly* 59:61+ O '89
Treasure Island [New York City] J. Molloy. il *New York* 22:84+ My 1 '89
"We take a bite out of everybody". R. King. il *Forbes* 143:136+ My 15 '89
FLEAS

Control
What's bugging your pet? *The Saturday Evening Post* 261:17 Jl/Ag '89
DIE FLEDERMAUS [operetta] See Strauss, Johann, 1825-1899
FLEETWOOD ENTERPRISES, INC.
Getting the lowdown. K. L. Fisher. il *Forbes* 143:334 Ja 9 '89
Security analysis updated. K. L. Fisher. il *Forbes* 143:166 F 6 '89
Survival of the fittest. E. F. Cone. il *Forbes* 143:10 Ja 23 '89
FLEISCHER, ERNEST
about
Ernest Fleischer finally tastes humble pie. D. Zigas. il por *Business Week* p67 Jl 17 '89
FLEISCHER, LEONORE
Sales & bargains. See issues of New York
Talk of the trade. See issues of Publishers Weekly
FLEISCHER, R. L.
(jt. auth) See Taub, A. I. (Alan I.), and Fleischer, R. L.
FLEISCHMAN, JANET
A journey to 'Absurdistan'. *The Nation* 249:276+ S 18 '89
FLEISCHMANN, MARTIN
about
Cold fusion confusion. R. P. Crease and N. P. Samios. il pors *The New York Times Magazine* p34-6+ S 24 '89
Fusion followup: confusion abounds. R. Pool. il por *Science* 244:27-9 Ap 7 '89
Fusion illusion? [cover story] M. D. Lemonick. il pors *Time* 133:72-6+ My 8 '89
Fusion in a bottle: miracle or mistake? [cover story] J. Carey and W. D. Marbach. il pors *Business Week* p100-3+ My 8 '89
How cold fusion happened—twice! R. Pool. il pors *Science* 244:420-3 Ap 28 '89
Stanley Pons lays claim to table top fusion—but don't sell your oil stocks just yet. P. Chin. il pors *People Weekly* 31:59-60+ My 8 '89
FLEISHCHMAN, JOHN
Of Buckeyes and buckeyes. il map *Audubon* 91:112-14+ S '89
FLEISHER, MARK S.
The costly business of warehousing violent criminals. il *USA Today (Periodical)* 117:60-2 Mr '89
FLEISHMAN, DIANA
(jt. auth) See Fleishman, Norman, and Fleishman, Diana
FLEISHMAN, NORMAN, AND FLEISHMAN, DIANA
Beer ads: fuel for the drug bonfire. il pors *The Humanist* 49:18-19+ N/D '89

FLEMING, CARROL B.
The stuff of dreams. il *Health (New York, N.Y.)* 21:28+
D '89
FLEMING, CHARLES
Dressing the part. il *American Film* 14:48-51 S '89
FLEMING, GENE
about
Andy Goose steps out. J. Coudert. il *Reader's Digest*
135:169-70+ Jl '89
A footless goose becomes a footloose goose—in sneaks. il
People Weekly 31:66 Ja 30 '89
FLEMING, IAN, 1908-1964
about
Bird, James Bird. *Discover* 10:13 Jl '89
FLEMING, JUNE
The gallivanting gourmet. il *Sierra* 74:62-3 Jl/Ag '89
FLEMING, LINDA
about
Linda Fleming at Esprit Park. G. Morris. il *Art in America*
77:221 S '89
FLEMING, ROBERT
Big bytes in NASA's budget. il *Omni (New York, N.Y.)*
12:30+ O '89
Teach your children. il *Omni (New York, N.Y.)* 11:36+ S
'89
FLEMING, THOMAS, 1945-
Lincoln's tragic heroism. por *National Review* 41:38-40 D
8 '89
FLEMING, THOMAS J., 1927-
Truth? It's in TV's fiction . . . not the reality shows. il
TV Guide 37:24-6 F 25-Mr 3 '89
FLEMING, VICTOR, 1883-1949
about
The Wizard of Oz [film] Reviews
Video il 12:63-4 Mr '89. M. Fleischmann
FLEMING COMPANIES, INC.
Unsung giant. il *Forbes* 143:142 Ja 9 '89
FLETCH LIVES [film] See Motion picture reviews—Single
works
FLETCHER, ANNE M.
Food and your health [special section] il *McCall's* 117:89+
O '89
FLETCHER, ARTHUR ALLEN, 1924-
about
Fletcher loses Labor bid; others await appointments. il por
Jet 75:4 Ja 16 '89
Garrett, Fletcher named to key positions by Bush. il pors
Jet 76:4-5 Ap 10 '89
FLETCHER, COLIN
A bend in the road. *Wilderness* 52:12+ Wint '88
FLETCHER, ELLEN
about
The pedal pusher. il por *New Choices for the Best Years*
29:12 O '89
FLETCHER, GEORGE P.
In Gorbachev's courts. bibl f il *The New York Review of
Books* 36:13-14+ My 18 '89
FLETCHER, JAMES C.
U.S. space leadership in danger [address, January 17, 1989]
Vital Speeches of the Day 55:298-300 Mr 1 '89
about
Fletcher supports moon outpost by 2004. il *Ad Astra* 1:46
Ja '89
FLETCHER, JOHN C.
(jt. auth) See Wertz, Dorothy C., and Fletcher, John C.
FLETCHER, PAM
about
After the fall. S. Nelson. il por *Health (New York, N.Y.)*
21:28-9 Mr '89
FLETCHER, SCOTT
about
Great Scott! E. M. Swift. il pors *Sports Illustrated* 70 Special
Issue:78-81+ Ap '89
FLEXIBLE MANUFACTURING SYSTEMS
Can Caterpillar inch its way back to heftier profits? B.
Bremner. il *Business Week* p75+ S 25 '89
A dozen motor factories—under one roof [Ford's flexible
manufacturing plant in Romeo, Mich.] D. Woodruff. il
Business Week p90+ N 20 '89
A new vision for the factory. O. Port. il *Business Week*
Special Issue:146 Je 16 '89
Ultrasonics used for factory measurements. *High Technology
Business* 9:33 Je '89
FLEXIBLE SPENDING ACCOUNTS
Attention: All employees; From: Your benefits dept.; Re:
The tax break you shouldn't ignore. L. Luciano. il *Money*
18:127-8+ N '89
The next best thing to a 401(k). L. Luciano. il *Money* 18:132-3
Ag '89
FLEXTIME
Commuters hate staggered hours [Honolulu study reveals
objection to mandatory changes] *USA Today (Periodical)*
118:8-9 Ag '89
FLICK, RACHEL
Blacks and Jews. *National Review* 41:14 Ja 27 '89
Why can't we get the medicine we need? *Reader's Digest*
135:101-6 Ag '89

Why we're losing the war on drugs. *Reader's Digest* 135:83-8
O '89
FLICKERS (PICTURES) See Winkies (Pictures)
FLIEGER, KEN
It's spring again and allergies are in bloom [cover story]
il *FDA Consumer* 23:16-20 My '89
Memories are made of this [cover story] il *FDA Consumer*
23:14-19 S '89
FLIERMANS, CARL B., AND BALKWILL, DAVID L.
Microbial life in deep terrestrial subsurfaces. bibl f il
BioScience 39:370-7 Je '89
FLIES
See also
Dragonflies
Drosophila
Fruit flies
Moth flies
Why God created flies. R. Conniff. il *Audubon* 91:82-5 Jl
'89
Anecdotes, facetiae, satire, etc.
Lord of the flies. P. F. McManus. il *Outdoor Life* 183:124+
Ja '89
FLIES, ARTIFICIAL See Fishing lures, flies, etc.
FLIES AS CARRIERS OF INFECTION
See also
Onchocerciasis
FLIGHT
See also
Hang gliding
Physiological aspects
See Aviation—Physiological aspects
FLIGHT, INTERPLANETARY See Space flight
FLIGHT ATTENDANTS
See also
Independent Federation of Flight Attendants
Strikes—Airline employees
Beauty and the beasts [feminism and standards of beauty]
R. E. Tyrrell. il *The American Spectator* 22:10 O '89
Wings of desire. P. Rudnick. il *Vogue* 179:384-5 My '89
Health and hygiene
Flying blind [Pan Am's weight standards for female flight
attendants ruled illegal] D. Seligman. il *Fortune* 120:204
O 9 '89
A future up in the air: flight attendants contest weight rules
[suit against American Airlines] M. Suh. il *Ms.* 18:83-4
S '89
Salaries, pensions, etc.
Just living together [Bob Elsken and Karen Cramer] S. Seixas.
il *Money* 18:107-12 Ja '89
FLIGHT CONTROL SYSTEMS (COMPUTER SYSTEMS)
See Computers—Aviation use
FLIGHT CREWS See Airplane crews
FLIGHT DATA CENTER (DATABASE)
Flight-planning automat. J. M. McClellan. il *Flying* 116:116-17
Jl '89
FLIGHT INSTRUCTORS See Aviation—Study and teaching
FLIGHT PLANNING (COMPUTER SYSTEMS) See Com-
puters—Aviation use
FLIGHT RECORDERS
See also
Space flight recorders
ALPA claims Gander probe relied on some faulty, fabricated
data [1985 crash] D. Hughes. *Aviation Week & Space
Technology* 131:66-7 Jl 3 '89
Capt. Al Haynes [recording of conversation between control
tower and Flight 232 before crash in Sioux City, Iowa]
il por *People Weekly* 32:102-3 D 25 '89-Ja 1 '90
Flight safety advances hinge on pilot-management teamwork.
C. Fotos. il *Aviation Week & Space Technology* 131:31-2
O 9 '89
'I had to turn away' [tapes of conversations between crew
and controllers of UAL flight 232 in Sioux City, Iowa]
Newsweek 114:37 Ag 28 '89
FLIGHT SIMULATORS
See also
FlightSafety International, Inc.
Singer Company. Link Flight Simulation Division
Space flight simulators
Threat simulators
The Airplane Factory [video game] R. G. Sheffield. il
Compute! 11:74-5 Ag '89
Battlehawks 1942. B. Guerra. il *Compute!* 11:63 Ap '89
Britain's Rediffusion Simulation offers microcomputer-based
ATC trainer. C. A. Shifrin. il *Aviation Week & Space
Technology* 131:83+ Ag 21 '89
Chuck Yeager's Advanced Flight Trainer 2.0. R. G. Sheffield.
Compute! 11:116+ O '89
F-19 Stealth Fighter. B. Guerra. il *Compute!* 11:70-1 Ap
'89
F-19 Stealth Fighter. S. Williams. il *Home Office Computing*
7:87-8 Mr '89
Falcon A.T. S. Williams. il *Home Office Computing* 7:91-2
F '89
Flight Simulator 3.0. R. G. Sheffield. il *Compute!* 11:68-70
Ap '89
Gamescope [flying a flight simulator] D. Atkin. il *Compute!*
11:112 O '89

FLIGHT SIMULATORS—*cont.*
GE simulator image generator offers 3D resolution, fast data base updates [Compu-Scene 5 for use in military mission rehearsal simulation] E. H. Kolcum. il *Aviation Week & Space Technology* 130:286-7+ Je 12 '89
Gould will use same market strategy under Encore ownership. E. H. Kolcum. *Aviation Week & Space Technology* 130:53 Ap 17 '89
Growing flight, maintenance simulator market attracts many competitors. E. H. Kolcum. *Aviation Week & Space Technology* 130:91+ Ja 2 '89
Hover act [Sikorsky S-76 simulator] J. M. McClellan. il *Flying* 116:58-61 F '89
JetFighter: The Adventure. R. Gehorsam. il *Home Office Computing* 7:90+ My '89
Pressure group: it's your altitude [altitude chamber flight at Andrews Air Force Base] P. Scott. il *Flying* 116:36+ Ag '89
Rockwell's simulator emulates NASP flight characteristics [National Aero-Space Plane] W. B. Scott. il *Aviation Week & Space Technology* 131:50-1+ O 23 '89
Simulated lights. J. M. McClellan. il *Flying* 116:44-5 S '89
Simulator, flight tests validate integrated pictorial cockpit display. W. B. Scott. il *Aviation Week & Space Technology* 130:51+ Ja 9 '89
Simulators aid LHX design [Army helicopter; cover story; special section] il *Aviation Week & Space Technology* 131:34-5+ N 27 '89
USAF controllers, F-15 pilots train for combat using multiship simulation. S. W. Kandebo. il *Aviation Week & Space Technology* 130:71+ Mr 27 '89
FLIGHT TRAINING *See* Aviation—Study and teaching
FLIGHTSAFETY INTERNATIONAL, INC.
Airline training's missing link. A. Laboda. il *Flying* 116:34-5 S '89
FlightSafety rides boom in airline, military training to record earnings. N. C. Kernstock. il *Aviation Week & Space Technology* 131:89-91 N 27 '89
Hover act [Sikorsky S-76 simulator] J. M. McClellan. il *Flying* 116:58-61 F '89
The pilots' pilot. F. Meeks. il por *Forbes* 144:198+ N 13 '89
Simulated lights. J. M. McClellan. il *Flying* 116:44-5 S '89
TWA, FlightSafety to launch low-time pilot training program. *Aviation Week & Space Technology* 130:72-3 F 27 '89
FLINT HILLS (KAN. AND OKLA.)
A prairie park? [Spring Hill Ranch offered for national park status] F. Graham. il *Audubon* 91:20+ S '89
FLIPPEN, ROYCE
Can do. il por *American Health* 8:70 S '89
FLIPPER (DOLPHIN) *See* Dolphins in television
FLIPPIN, ROYCE
Lionhearted. il *Runner's World* 24:36-9+ Ap '89
Managing your mileage—are you feeling groovy or burning out? il *American Health* 8:78+ O '89
FLIPPO, CHET, 1943-
John Lennon: good guy—or as bad as his critics say? il pors *TV Guide* 37:16-19 Mr 4-10 '89
FLIR (FORWARD-LOOKING INFRARED) SENSORS *See* Detectors, Infrared
FLIRTING
Blocking the uninvited pass. S. Mansfield. *Mademoiselle* 95:134 Mr '89
Have you ever shared a look, a touch, a moment of flirtation with a stranger? S. Nelson. il *Glamour* 87:222-3+ N '89
The sexual tease. C. L. Mithers. il *Glamour* 87:268 Ag '89

Anecdotes, facetiae, satire, etc.
I was a flirtatious backwalker for the CIA. J. Harkison. il *Smithsonian* 20:128 Jl '89
FLOAT (BANKING) *See* Banks and banking—Float
FLOAT HUNTING *See* Hunting
FLOAT TRIPS *See* River trips
FLOAT TROTTING TACKLE *See* Fishing tackle
FLOATING HOUSES *See* Houseboats
FLOATING-POINT ARITHMETIC
Floating-point revisited. R. Grehan. il *Byte* 14:311-16+ Ap '89
Optimizing numeric coprocessing. S. S. Fried. il *Byte* 14 Special Issue:221-4 Fall '89
FLOATING POINT SYSTEMS, INC.
"We won't make that mistake again". K. K. Wiegner. il *Forbes* 144:257-8 Jl 24 '89
FLOATS, PARADE *See* Parade floats
FLODEN, ANNE
Tiospaye Teca: working with young Native American families in the Dakotas. il *Children Today* 18:28-32 S/O '89
FLOOD PREVENTION AND CONTROL
See also
Dams
Dikes (Engineering)
Rivers—Regulation
Yahoos in the Yazoo [U.S. Army Corps of Engineers] L. Williamson. il *Outdoor Life* 183:42+ Ap '89
Bangladesh
Bailing out Bangladesh. B. Powell and H. Shahriar. il map *Newsweek* 114:42 Ag 28 '89

FLOODS
See also
Dams—Failure
Trees, Effect of floods on
Flash floods. R. A. Wood. il *Weatherwise* 42:93-4 Ap '89
History
After the deluge [Ice Age floods; research by John Shaw] T. Appenzeller. il *Scientific American* 261:22+ D '89
Hills point to catastrophic Ice Age floods [drumlins; work of John Shaw] R. Monastersky. *Science News* 136:213 S 30 '89
International aspects
Water rules the world. E. M. Wieckowski. il *Discover* 10:36 Ja '89
Pennsylvania
History
See also
Johnstown (Pa.)—Flood, 1889
United States
See Floods
FLOOR CLEANING APPLIANCES
See also
Vacuum cleaners
FLOOR COVERINGS
See also
Floorcloths
Flooring
Rugs and carpets
FLOOR PAINTING AND DECORATION
Bordering on beautiful [cover story] il *Home Mechanix* 85:32-6 Je '89
Floor show [rout-and-stain method] J. Truini. il *Home Mechanix* 85:74-6 D '89
Transform a wood floor [stenciled border] il *McCall's* 116:96 Ap '89
FLOOR SHOWS
Locked in bloodless combat, Billy Dean's foxy boxers show more jiggle than punch [Knockout Foxy Fighting Revue] il pors *People Weekly* 31:116-17 Mr 13 '89
FLOORCLOTHS
Comfortable, colorful floorcloths. il *Southern Living* 24:170-1 Ap '89
FLOORING
Install a hardwood floor. J. A. Hufnagel. il *Better Homes and Gardens* 67:120 My '89
Surface materials. J. Vara. il *Country Journal* 16:47-9 F '89
Wood flooring, on walls and ceilings. il *Popular Mechanics* 166:124+ Ap '89
FLOORING, CORK
Floors like Ike liked [Cork-o-Plast] P. Patton. il *Esquire* 111:39-40 Ap '89
FLOORING, PLASTIC
Goof-proof flooring [Armstrong's Trim and Fit Kit] M. DiChristina. il *Popular Science* 234:164 My '89
How to install sheet flooring. D. Prestly. il *The Family Handyman* 39:40-4 Jl/Ag '89
How to install vinyl sheet flooring. P. Barrett. il *Popular Mechanics* 166:107-10 Je '89
FLOORING, RUBBER
New products: rubber flooring. il *Architectural Record* 177:128 Jl '89
Soft pavers. il *Popular Science* 235:67-8 Ag '89
FLOORS
See also
Dance floors
Care
See Floors—Maintenance and repair
Maintenance and repair
Stop squeaky floors. G. Branson. il *Workbench* 45:11 N/D '89
FLOPPY DISK MEMORY (COMPUTERS) *See* Computers—Memory systems
FLORA, FOREST *See* Forest vegetation
FLORAL DECORATION *See* Flower arrangement
FLORENCE (ITALY)
See also
Piazza della Signoria (Florence, Italy)
Antiquities
Uncommon glimpses of Florence [archeological excavation of Piazza della Signoria] C. Booth. il *Time* 133:63 Ja 23 '89
Festivals
See also
Calcio Storico (Florence, Italy)
Religious institutions and affairs
History
Savonarola—preacher and patriot? D. Weinstein. bibl il por *History Today* 39:30-6 N '89
Sports
See also
Calcio Storico (Florence, Italy)
FLORENCE FENNEL *See* Fennel
FLORENTINE OPERA COMPANY
Accessible opera. J. McAdams. il *Horizon (Tuscaloosa, Ala.)* 32:25 Mr/Ap '89

FLORES, EDITH
Battle of the heirs: son of Ayatollah vs. son of Shah. il pors *World Press Review* 36:16 Ag '89
FLORICULTURE *See* Flower gardens and gardening
FLORIDA
See also
Abortion clinics—Florida
Architecture—Florida
Architecture, Domestic—Florida
Automobile touring—Florida
Beaches—Florida
Big Cypress National Preserve (Fla.)
Birds—Florida
Broward County (Fla.)
Courts—Florida
Criminal justice, Administration of—Florida
Dade County (Fla.)
Dance—Florida
Educational laws and regulations—Florida
Environmental movement—Florida
Environmental policy—Florida
Everglades (Fla.)
Everglades National Park (Fla.)
Fishing—Florida
Fort Jefferson National Monument (Fla.)
Health resorts, watering places, etc.—Florida
Historic houses, sites, etc.—Florida
Hobe Sound National Wildlife Refuge (Fla.)
Hunting—Florida
Insurance law—Florida
Islands—Florida
Land utilization—Laws and regulations—Florida
Law—Florida
Music festivals—Florida
Organic gardens and gardening—Florida
Paleontology—Florida
Palm Beach County (Fla.)
Pinellas County (Fla.)
Resorts—Florida
Sanibel Island (Fla.)
Space centers—Florida
Sports—Florida
Theater—Florida
Wildlife—Florida
Wildlife conservation—Florida
Description and travel
See also
Cruising—Florida
The second hundred years [visiting spring training sites] P. Oliver. il map *Travel Holiday* 171:62-7 F '89
Touching base with the boys of spring. R. Hoffman. il *Business Week* p174 Mr 20 '89
Industries
See also
Sugar industry
Politics and government
With friends like Bob Martinez, the GOP doesn't need . . . G. DeGeorge and R. Fly. il por *Business Week* p47 O 30 '89
Sanitary affairs
Amtrak's Florida wasteland [dumping human sewage on the tracks] B. Turque. il *Newsweek* 114:50 D 11 '89
FLORIDA. UNIVERSITY, GAINESVILLE *See* University of Florida
FLORIDA A & M UNIVERSITY
The funkiest half-time show [Marching 100 band] D. Winbush. il *Time* 134:14-15 S 18 '89
FLORIDA A & M UNIVERSITY. SCHOOL OF BUSINESS AND INDUSTRY
Giving students a taste of the executive life. S. M. Williams. *Black Enterprise* 19:181-2 F '89
FLORIDA AGRICULTURAL AND MECHANICAL UNIVERSITY *See* Florida A & M University
FLORIDA DERBY *See* Horse racing
FLORIDA EAST COAST INDUSTRIES INC.
Land bank. J. Drummond. il *Forbes* 144:266 O 2 '89
FLORIDA KEYS (FLA.)
See also
Conservation of resources—Florida Keys (Fla.)
Fishing—Florida Keys (Fla.)
Key West (Fla.)
Description and travel
See also
Automobile touring—Florida Keys (Fla.)
Cruising—Florida Keys (Fla.)
FLORIDA PANTHERS *See* Pumas
FLORIO, DONNA
Field of fish [special section] il *Health (New York, N.Y.)* 21:71-7+, 94 My '89
FLORIS (J.) LTD. *See* J. Floris Ltd.
FLORISTS
Flower brokers [work of Manhattan florists Anita Widder, VSF, and Zezé] M. K. Griswold. il *House & Garden* 161:80+ O '89
FLORMAN, SAMUEL C.
[Column] See occasional issues of Technology Review

FLOSS, DENTAL *See* Dental floss
FLOUD, RODERICK
Words, not numbers: John Harold Clapham. bibl il pors *History Today* 39:42-7 Ap '89
FLOUR MILLS
History
See also
Eling Tide Mill
FLOW OF FLUIDS *See* Fluid dynamics
FLOWER AND GARDEN (PERIODICAL)
Flower & garden's own garden. R. Snyder. il *Flower and Garden* 33:84-8 Ja/F '89
FLOWER ARRANGEMENT
See also
Bouquets
Florists
The beautiful bloom. S. La Rosa. il *McCall's* 116:45-7 My '89
Bloom service deluxe [work of R. Reynolds] E. Louie. il por *Harper's Bazaar* 122:134+ Je '89
Flowers for your table. J. Williams and J. Severson. il *Better Homes and Gardens* 67:128+ My '89
Living holiday arrangements [cover story] il *Flower and Garden* 33:38-40 N/D '89
Matching flowers to art. T. A. Steadman. il *Southern Living* 24:58-60 Ja '89
Two classic spring arrangements. D. Temple. il *Flower and Garden* 33:82-3 Mr/Ap '89
FLOWER AUTOMAT GALLERY (BERLIN, GERMANY: WEST)
Put another nickel in. D. Galloway. il *Art News* 88:21 D '89
FLOWER BORDERS *See* Garden borders
FLOWER BOXES, PLANTERS, ETC.
Handsome planters you can make [cover story] il *Sunset (Central West edition)* 182:94-6 Je '89
Make a mighty mouse planter. il *National Geographic World* 165:17 My '89
Pots that water themselves? il *Sunset (Central West edition)* 182:183 F '89
Water and flower boxes. il *Sunset (Central West edition)* 183:144-5 Jl '89
Window box beauties. T. Martin. il *Country Journal* 16:32-5 Jl/Ag '89
FLOWER EXHIBITS
Calendar. See issues of Flower and Garden
Garden events [title varies] See issues of Sunset (Central West edition)
Major flower shows for '89. il *Flower and Garden* 33:42-3 Ja/F '89
Southern garden events. See issues of Southern Living
FLOWER GARDENS AND GARDENING
See also
Annuals (Plants)
Butterfly gardens
Perennials (Plants)
Shade gardens and gardening
Wildflower gardens and gardening
See also names of flowers
Color in a dry year. il *Sunset (Central West edition)* 182:234-5 My '89
In praise of yellow. P. Thorpe. il *House & Garden* 161:40+ Ag '89
Living bouquets for the holidays . . . and afterward. il *Sunset (Central West edition)* 181:162-3 D '88
Bainbridge Island (Wash.)
Farm-fresh style [home of Liz and Peter Robinson] S. S. Soria and D. A. Jimerson. il *Better Homes and Gardens* 67:75-89 Ap '89
France
Floral decorum. J. Kramer. il *House & Garden* 161:112+ S '89
Germany (West)
Our real roots. A. Lacy. il *Organic Gardening* 36:73-6+ F '89
Great Britain
Garden party [All England Lawn Tennis Club] il *World Tennis* 37:38-9 Jl '89
Long Island (N.Y.)
Hampton classic [L. Mezzacappa's Southampton garden designed by D. Nevins] K. Whiteside. il *House & Garden* 161:82-9 Ja '89
Netherlands
Dutch treats [tulips] E. Henke. il *The Saturday Evening Post* 261:64-6 My/Je '89
Switzerland
Our real roots. A. Lacy. il *Organic Gardening* 36:73-6+ F '89
FLOWER SHOWS *See* Flower exhibits
FLOWERING PLANTS *See* Angiosperms
FLOWERING TREES
See also
Cherry trees
Dogwood
Golden rain trees

FLOWERLESS PLANTS See Cryptogams

FLOWERS, CHARLES

Images of a brief moment. il *The New York Times Magazine* p20+ Jl 9 '89

Searching for the one true cat. il *National Wildlife* 27:24-8 O/N '89

FLOWERS, RICHMOND, SR.

about

Outcast to hero. J. Wooten. il pors *TV Guide* 37:36-8 Ja 14-20 '89

FLOWERS, RICHMOND, JR.

about

Outcast to hero. J. Wooten. il pors *TV Guide* 37:36-8 Ja 14-20 '89

FLOWERS

See also

Annuals (Plants)

Bouquets

Boutonnieres

Bulbs

Flower gardens and gardening

Perennials (Plants)

Wildflowers

See also names of flowers

All-America Selections

See Plants—All-America Selections

Fertilization

See Fertilization of plants

Marketing

Mexico's flower children [flower sellers in New York City] R. Miller. il *New York* 22:31 O 16 '89

Photographs and photography

Proud, proud beauties. H. Feinstein. il *Life* 12:84-7 Jl '89

Rare beauty: fashion & fantasy [work of F. Scavullo at the Brooklyn Museum] il *Harper's Bazaar* 122:132-7 D '89

Spring has sprung, the flowers are abloom; I wonder where's my macro zoom? G. Schaub. il *Popular Photography* 96:28+ My '89

Varieties

1989 gardeners' choice [cover story] V. Mattern. *Organic Gardening* 36:34-53 Ja '89

New plants '89. il *Flower and Garden* 33:51-66+ Ja/F '89

FLOWERS, DRIED

See also

Potpourri

FLOWERS, FORCING OF See Forcing (Plants)

FLOWERS, MECHANICAL

See also

Rock'n Flowers

FLOWERS AS FOOD

See also

Cooking—Flowers

Edible bouquet. B. Pleasant. il *Organic Gardening* 36:79-80+ Ja '89

Edible flowers. J. Taylor and D. A. Jimerson. il *Better Homes and Gardens* 67:142 Ap '89

Step into our edible garden. J. Rapp. il *Redbook* 173:75-7+ Je '89

FLOWERS IN ART

See also

Roses in art

Mrs. Delany's fabulous flowers. J. Boysen. il por *International Wildlife* 19:44-5 Jl/Ag '89

Out of Amazonia [botanical illustrator M. Mee] B. Maddox. il por *Ms.* 18:54-7 O '89

Exhibitions

Blooming beauties from Britain [Flowers from the Royal Gardens of Kew at the National Museum of Natural History] K. M. Burke. il *Smithsonian* 19:176 F '89

Eloquent bouquets [A prosperous past: the sumptuous still life in the Netherlands, 1600-1700 at the Kimbell Art Museum] R. Bernier. il *House & Garden* 161:96-101+ D '89

Patronage and the publication of botanical illustration [Nature's mirror exhibit; cover story] B. G. Callery. il *Antiques* 136:268-81 Ag '89

FLOWERS IN HOUSE DECORATION See Plants in house decoration

FLOYD, SAMUEL A.

about

Dr. Samuel A. Floyd Jr.: man with a mission. il pors *Ebony* 44:194-5 My '89

FLU See Influenza

FLUDARABINE

Hopes heighten for new leukemia drug [use in chronic lymphocytic leukemia; research by Michael J. Keating] R. Weiss. *Science News* 135:348 Je 3 '89

FLUID DYNAMICS

See also

Cavitation

Laminar flow

Computational aerodynamics for aircraft design [cover story] A. Jameson. bibl f il *Science* 245:361-71 Jl 28 '89

Dendrites, viscous fingers, and the theory of pattern formation. J. S. Langer. bibl f il *Science* 243:1150-6 Mr 3 '89

Fluid dynamics. bibl f il *Physics Today* 42:S40-S42 Ja '89

The mixing of fluids [cover story] J. M. Ottino. il *Scientific American* 260:56-7+ Ja '89

NASA adds to understanding of high angle of attack regime [cover story] W. B. Scott. il *Aviation Week & Space Technology* 130:36-8+ My 22 '89

A tight squeeze for mobile water [research by William P. Halperin] *Science News* 136:47 Jl 15 '89

FLUID JET CUTTING See Jet cutting

FLUIDS

See also

Electrorheological fluids

Fluid dynamics

Liquids

Solvents

How to build a Hele-Shaw cell and watch bubbles playing tag in a viscous fluid [air bubbles] J. Walker. bibl il *Scientific American* 261:116-19 O '89

FLUOR CORP.

Flush times for Fluor. N. J. Perry. il *Fortune* 120:113 N 6 '89

Trade in the Pacific Rim [address, October 28, 1988] D. S. Tappan, Jr. *Vital Speeches of the Day* 55:217-20 Ja 15 '89

FLUORESCENCE SPECTROSCOPY See Spectrum analysis

FLUORESCENT INDICATORS IN BIOLOGICAL RESEARCH

Phylogenetic stains: ribosomal RNA-based probes for the identification of single cells. E. F. DeLong and others. bibl f il *Science* 243:1360-3 Mr 10 '89

FLUORIDATION See Water supply—Fluoridation

FLUORIDES

See also

Sodium fluoride

Fluoride-calcium combo builds better bones [research by Charles Y. C. Pak] K. Fackelmann. *Science News* 135:36 Ja 21 '89

FLUORINE COMPOUNDS

See also

Perfluoro compounds

FLUOROCARBON COMPANY

A case of mistaken identity. M. Beauchamp. il por *Forbes* 144:103 Jl 24 '89

Playing a game of 'name that company' [contest to rename Fluorocarbon Corp.] il *Newsweek* 114:37 Ag 14 '89

FLUOROCARBONS

See also

Chlorofluorocarbons

Polyvinylidene fluoride

FLUOROURACIL

Death-defying drug therapy [use of 5-fluorouracil and levamisole to treat colon cancer] il *Time* 134:76+ O 16 '89

Drug availability is an issue for cancer patients, too [levamisole-5-fluorouracil therapy for colon cancer] J. L. Marx. il *Science* 245:346-7 Jl 28 '89

Drug duo takes on deadly colon cancer [levamisole and 5-fluorouracil; research by Charles G. Moertel] K. Fackelmann. *Science News* 136:228-9 O 7 '89

FLUOXETINE

Bye-bye, blues: a new wonder drug for depression [Prozac; cover story] F. Schumer. il *New York* 22:46-50+ D 18 '89

FLUSSER, ALAN (ALAN J.)

about

Alan Flusser upstate: an offbeat cabin designed with humor in New York. S. M. L. Aronson. il pors *Architectural Digest* 46:192-7+ S '89

FLUTIE, DOUG

about

Remembrance of flings past. M. Lupica. il *Esquire* 112:97-8 S '89

FLUXGATE COMPASS See Compass

FLUXUS (ART MOVEMENT)

A Fluxus funeral [memorial for R. Watts] J. Johnston. il pors *Art in America* 77:42-3+ Mr '89

Exhibitions

The Flux stops here [work of Y. Ono] K. Larson. il *New York* 22:149 F 27 '89

FLY-BY-WIRE SYSTEMS See Computers—Aviation use

FLY CASTING See Casting (Fishing)

FLY FISHING See Casting (Fishing)

THE FLY II [film] See Motion picture reviews—Single works

FLY RODS See Fishing tackle

FLY TYING See Fishing lures, flies, etc.

FLYCATCHERS

Sexual behavior

See Sexual behavior—Birds

FLYING, FEAR OF See Fear of flying

FLYING (PERIODICAL)

Course correction. W. Garvey. il *Flying* 116:12-13 Ap '89

FLYING AND POPULAR AVIATION (PERIODICAL)

Looking backward [January 1941 issue] G. Baxter. il *Flying* 116:116+ O '89

FLYING BOATS See Seaplanes

FLYING CARS See Aerocars

THE FLYING DUTCHMAN [opera] See Wagner, Richard, 1813-1883

FLYING MACHINES
See also
Autogiros
Gliders (Aviation)
Ornithopters
FLYING OBSERVATORIES See Airplanes in astronomy
FLYING REPTILES See Pterosaurs
FLYING SAUCERS See UFOs
FLYING SCHOOLS See Aviation—Study and teaching
FLYING TIGER LINE INC.
Federal Express/Tigers merger would reshape cargo industry. J. T. McKenna. *Aviation Week & Space Technology* 130:106 Ja 2 '89
Fred Smith [Federal Express buys Flying Tiger] D. Foust. il por *Business Week* Special Issue:102 Ap 14 '89
Mr. Smith goes global [Federal Express merger with Tiger International; cover story] D. Foust. il pors map *Business Week* p66-8+ F 13 '89
FLYNN, DANA
about
Personalities plus. J. Gruder. il pors *Harper's Bazaar* 122:173-4 Ag '89
FLYNN, GEORGE WILLIAM, 1938-
Chemical cartography: finding the keys to the kinetic labyrinth. bibl f il *Science* 246:1009-15 N 24 '89
FLYNN, GREGORY
Problems in paradigm. *Foreign Policy* 74:63-84 Spr '89
FLYNN, GREGORY C., AND OTHERS
Peptide binding and release by proteins implicated as catalysts of protein assembly. bibl f il *Science* 245:385-90 Jl 28 '89
FLYNN, TIMOTHY
about
WestAir flies high. M. Berss. il pors *Forbes* 143:147 Je 12 '89
FLYNT, HENRY
about
Henry Flynt at Emily Harvey. E. Heartney. *Art in America* 77:197-8 My '89
FM See Radio frequency modulation
FM ANTENNAS See Radio antennas
FM RECEIVERS See Radio receivers
FM TRANSMITTERS See Radio transmitters
FM TUNERS See Radio receivers—Tuning
FMC CORPORATION
Competing GE, FMC armored turrets offer different weapons configurations [Marine Corps Light Armored Vehicle-Air Defense system] D. F. Bond. il *Aviation Week & Space Technology* 131:45+ S 25 '89
A lemon? Don't tell the Saudis [Bradley Fighting Vehicle] B. Bremner. il *Business Week* p40 Ja 23 '89
FMLN See Farabundo Martí National Liberation Front
FNMA See Federal National Mortgage Association
FNN See Financial News Network Inc.
FOAM BOARDS (PHOTOGRAPHY)
Those fabulous foams. K. Geller-Shinn. il *Petersen's Photographic Magazine* 17:8 Ap '89
FOAM INSULATION See Insulation (Heat)
FOAMS
Frothy physics [cover story] F. Flam. il *Science News* 136:72-3+ Jl 29 '89
FOCUS ON THE FAMILY (ORGANIZATION)
Focus bids farewell to EPA [Evangelical Press Association] il *Christianity Today* 33:40 Mr 17 '89
James Dobson sued by former employees. K. A. Lawton. il pors *Christianity Today* 33:42 F 3 '89
FOCUSING See Photography—Focusing
FOCUSING ATTACHMENT FOR TELESCOPES See Telescopes—Equipment
FODOR, EUGENE, 1950-
about
Prodigal son: after the drug bust, Eugene Fodor tries a comeback. P. Hoban. il pors *New York* 22:100-2+ D 4 '89
FOG
See also
Aviation—Fog hazards
Dew vs. fog. T. Schlatter. il *Weatherwise* 42:283-4 O '89
The game was lost in the fog [Chicago defeats Philadelphia in NFC playoff game] P. Zimmerman. il *Sports Illustrated* 70:22-6+ Ja 9 '89
FOG, ARTIFICIAL
Cutting through the fog; Safely navigating the haze [fog and smoke machines] M. S. Eddy. il *Theatre Crafts* 23:26+ O '89
A dry-ice fogger: how to make the moodiest prop of all. A. B. Smith. il *Petersen's Photographic Magazine* 17:46-8 F '89
FOG-M (FIBER OPTIC GUIDED MISSILES) See Guided missiles—Optical equipment
FOGAL AG
Pantyhose at $249 the pair. D. Fong. il *Forbes* 143:76 Mr 20 '89
FOGARI, ROBERT A.
about
Biggest drug research fraud case in FDA history. J. Folkenberg. il *FDA Consumer* 23:25-6 Je '89

FOGDEN, MICHAEL
From eggs to legs [photograph] il *Natural History* p112-13 F '89
FOGDEN, MICHAEL, AND FOGDEN, PATRICIA
Don't hurry, be happy [photograph] il *Natural History* p92-3 Je '89
FOGDEN, PATRICIA
(jt. auth) See Fogden, Michael, and Fogden, Patricia
FOGEL, SEYMOUR, 1911-1984
about
Seymour Fogel at Graham Modern. E. Heartney. il *Art in America* 77:190-1 N '89
FOGELMAN, EVA
Moral heroes of our time: Christian rescuers. *America* 161:426-8+ D 9 '89
FOGELMAN, ILANA, AND CHAVES, EDUARDO O. C.
User-friendly videotex. il *World Health* p14-15 Ag/S '89
FOGELMAN, MARLA
50 reasons to stay home with your children. il *Parents* 64:127-9 Ap '89
FOGERTY, JOHN
about
Fogerty wins unusual self-plagiarism suit. M. Goldberg. il por *Rolling Stone* p15 Ja 12 '89
FOGLE, JAMES
about
Despite 35 years in the big house, real-life Drugstore cowboy James Fogle steals the big screen. C. Sanz. il pors *People Weekly* 32:87+ N 20 '89
FOGLINO, HANK, AND FOGLINO, RUTH
Some Long Island seashells. il *The Conservationist* 44:22-5 Jl/Ag '89
FOGLINO, RUTH
(jt. auth) See Foglino, Hank, and Foglino, Ruth
FOIA (FREEDOM OF INFORMATION ACT) See Freedom of information
FOIL, ALUMINUM See Aluminum foil
FOKKER BV
American Fokker 100 order caps carrier's growth plan. J. T. McKenna. il *Aviation Week & Space Technology* 130:88-9 Mr 27 '89
Bombardier, GEC-Fokker team lead field of suitors for Northern Ireland's Short Brothers. *Aviation Week & Space Technology* 130:31 Mr 13 '89
Fokker initiates North American service with Inter-Canadian. C. Fotos. il *Aviation Week & Space Technology* 130:98 F 13 '89
The quiet little Dutch invader [Fokker 100 airliner] il *Time* 133:42 Ap 3 '89
FOLBRE, NANCY
Those welfare bankers. por *Newsweek* 114:17 O 16 '89
FOLDING BICYCLES See Bicycles
FOLDING BOATS See Boats and boating
FOLDING CAMERAS See Cameras
FOLDING DOORS See Doors
FOLDING TABLES See Tables
FOLDS, JOHN
My contractor, my self (I). il *Modern Maturity* 32:62-4+ O/N '89
My contractor, my self (II). il *Modern Maturity* 32:76-8+ D '89/Ja '90
FOLDS (GEOLOGY)
Hidden earthquakes [cover story] R. S. Stein and R. S. Yeats. bibl il maps *Scientific American* 260:48-57 Je '89
Whaleback anticline [geological structure evident at Bear Valley Strip Mine, Pa.] C. Blue. il *Earth Science* 42:19-21 Fall '89
FOLEY, MICHAEL W.
Church behind the scenes. *Commonweal* 116:549-50 O 20 '89
FOLEY, R. A., AND LEE, P. C.
Finite social space, evolutionary pathways, and reconstructing hominid behavior. bibl f il *Science* 243:901-6 F 17 '89
FOLEY, ROBERT M.
Hiring foreign experts. *High Technology Business* 9:12-13 Ja '89
FOLEY, THOMAS S., 1929-
about
After Wright's fall. S. V. Roberts. il pors *U.S. News & World Report* 106:34-5 Je 5 '89
Anatomy of a smear. G. Borger. il pors *U.S. News & World Report* 106:40-1 Je 19 '89
Atwatergate. H. Hertzberg. *The New Republic* 201:4 Jl 3 '89
Dirtball politics. T. Morganthau. il pors *Newsweek* 113:32-3 Je 19 '89
The GOP feeding frenzy is far from over. D. Harbrecht. il por *Business Week* p36-7 Je 19 '89
House Democrats begin to imagine life after Jim Wright. D. Harbrecht. por *Business Week* p51 Mr 13 '89
House Foleys. T. Eastland. il *The American Spectator* 22:32-3 Ag '89
How to spread a smear. M. B. Carlson. il pors *Time* 133:33 Je 19 '89
It's back! The return of the pay raise. E. Clift. il por *Newsweek* 114:22 Jl 3 '89
Mission accomplished. F. Barnes. il *The New Republic* 201:8-10 Jl 3 '89

FOLEY, THOMAS S., 1929----about----*cont.*

A nasty job for a nice guy. E. Clift. il por *Newsweek* 113:16-17 Je 12 '89

The nation's closets. *Commonweal* 116:388-9 Jl 14 '89

Profiles. J. Newhouse. il por *The New Yorker* 65:48-50+ Ap 10 '89

The rise of the accidental Speaker. G. Borger. por *U.S. News & World Report* 106:38-9 Je 5 '89

That memo. W. McGurn. por *National Review* 41:22-3 N 10 '89

Waiting for opportunity to knock. H. Gorey. il por *Time* 133:36 Je 5 '89

FOLK ART

See also

Fraktur

Whirligigs

Folk, or art? A symposium [American folk art; with introduction by Frank J. Miele] bibl f il *Antiques* 135:272-87 Ja '89

Hearts [excerpt from Mary Emmerling's American country hearts] M. E. Emmerling. il *Good Housekeeping* 208:40+ F '89

Collectors and collecting

Art: primitive landscapes [American folk artists] J. R. Mellow. il *Architectural Digest* 46:186-91 D '89

Colonial collectibles. K. Lineberger. il *Harper's Bazaar* 122:92 O '89

Frank J. Miele's urban folklore. J. Simpson. il por *Architectural Digest* 46:88+ Je '89

Hooked [B. Johnson's collection] C. Brown. il por *Forbes* 143:158+ Ap 3 '89

Juliana Force and folk art. A. Berman. il *Antiques* 136:542-53 S '89

A Manhattan sampler [remodeled brownstone owned by M. Malcé and J. Kelter] S. M. L. Aronson. il pors *Architectural Digest* 46:158-63+ Je '89

The outsiders are in [American art] J. Kroll. il *Newsweek* 114:72-3 D 25 '89

Exhibitions

See also

Abby Aldrich Rockefeller Folk Art Center

Hirschl & Adler Folk

Metropolitan Museum of Art (New York, N.Y.). American Wing

Museum of American Folk Art

Museum of International Folk Art (Santa Fe, N.M.)

Abby's folk art [Treasures of American folk art from the Abby Aldrich Rockefeller Folk Art Center] A. L. Powers. il *Americana* 16:62-5 Ja/F '89

Folk art? Or not? [By good hands: New Hampshire folk art] A. E. Ledes. il *Antiques* 136:42 Jl '89

The Grand generation: memory, mastery, legacy. P. Jones. il *Aging* no359:44-5 '89

Please touch the art works [Bringing folk art closer, exhibit geared to visually handicapped] J. Seligmann. il por *Newsweek* 114:77+ N 6 '89

A pre-eminent folk art collection on tour [Treasures of American folk art from the Abby Aldrich Rockefeller Folk Art Center] A. E. Ledes. il *Antiques* 135:46+ Ja '89

FOLK ART IN THE HOME *See* Art in the home

FOLK DANCE *See* Dance

FOLK MEDICINE

See also

Medicine men

A cure that's worse than the ailment [folk remedies containing lead; research by Robert T. Trotter] *Science News* 135:60 Ja 28 '89

FOLK MUSIC

See also

Compact discs—Folk music

Phonograph records—Folk music

Polka

Tape recordings—Folk music

Talkin' 'bout a revolution. P. Krassner. il *Vogue* 179:84+ Ja '89

FOLK MUSIC, AMERICAN

See also

Country music

Brave new folksingers. J. Walljasper. il *Utne Reader* p10-11 Ja/F '89

FOLK MUSIC, BULGARIAN

See also

Phonograph records—Bulgarian folk music

FOLK MUSIC, SIBERIAN

Recalling art as a way of life: Siberian dancers debut in the U.S.A. [Music & dance of the Siberian-Asians at the Smithsonian] B. Gordon. il *Dance Magazine* 63:21 Mr '89

FOLKENBERG, JUDY

The big chill: how safe are "sous-vide" refrigerated foods? il *FDA Consumer* 23:32-3+ S '89

Biggest drug research fraud case in FDA history. il *FDA Consumer* 23:25-6 Je '89

'High-tech' comes to 'vet med'. il *FDA Consumer* 23:18-23 Ap '89

The mouth as body's mirror. il *FDA Consumer* 23:22-4 D '89/Ja '90

FOLKLORE

See also

Moon in religion, folklore, etc.

Plant lore

Superstition

Weather lore

FOLKLORE, INDIAN (AMERICAN) *See* Indians of North America—Legends

FOLKLORE AND CHILDREN

See also

Fairy tales

FOLKMAN, JUDAH, AND OTHERS

Control of angiogenesis with synthetic heparin substitutes. bibl f il *Science* 243:1490-3 Mr 17 '89

FOLLETT, KEN, 1949-

about

The 'pillars' of a new success from Ken Follett and Morrow. S. S. Steinberg. il por *Publishers Weekly* 236:38-9 Jl 21 '89

FOLLIES (ARCHITECTURE)

Caro. M. Filler. il por *House & Garden* 161:174-5 Mr '89

The Désert de Retz, near Paris. P. Deitz. bibl f il *Antiques* 135:718-31 Mr '89

The functional folly in eighteenth-century Britain. G. Jackson-Stops. bibl f il *Antiques* 135:1412-23 Je '89

A Russian folly: visiting Catherine the Great's baroque roller coaster near Leningrad. P. Lauritzen. il por *Architectural Digest* 46:146-9+ My '89

FOLLINI, STEFANIA

about

Ace in the hole Stefania Follini never caved in. T. Allis. il por *People Weekly* 31:52-3 Je 12 '89

A cave dweller's chronicle: fifty-six days and counting [interview] A. R. Oberg. il *Omni (New York, N.Y.)* 11:50-2+ Je '89

Notes from the underground. S. Begley. il pors *Newsweek* 113:64 Je 5 '89

Stefania Follini goes down under. L. Morgan. il *Seventeen* 48:34 D '89

The times of your life. A. Toufexis. il por *Time* 133:66-7 Je 5 '89

Voluntary solitary. M. Heenan. il por *Ad Astra* 1:35 O '89

FOLLOWERSHIP

In praise of followers. L. Touby. *Working Woman* 14:34+ Ap '89

FOLTZ, SHAWN

about

Wristy business. J. E. Loehr. il pors *World Tennis* 37:24-5 N '89

FOLWELL, SAMUEL, 1764?-1813

about

A follow-up on our man Folwell. E. H. Gustafson. bibl f il por *Antiques* 135:616+ Mr '89

FONDA, BRIDGET

about

Bridget Fonda has a family problem. L. Morice. il por *Mademoiselle* 95:108+ Mr '89

Dressed to kill. L. J. Nonkin. il pors *Vogue* 179:716-21 S '89

The new Fonda 'Scandal'. J. Kaplan. por *Rolling Stone* p40 Ap 20 '89

FONDA, JANE, 1937-

about

An all-star cast turns out to toast Jane Fonda, queen of workouts, for good works. il pors *People Weekly* 31:49-50 Je 26 '89

The great divide. B. D. Johnson. il por *Maclean's* 102:60-1 O 16 '89

Jane Fonda enters a new era. A. Sachs. il pors *McCall's* 116:32-4+ S '89

Jane Fonda: "I'm stronger than ever" [cover story] C. P. Andersen. il pors *Ladies' Home Journal* 106:112+ O '89

Jane Fonda's 3 best potbelly exercises. il *Redbook* 173:102-5 My '89

Jane Fonda's daughter, Vanessa Vadim, is jailed for mouthing off at a drug bust. J. S. Kunen. il pors *People Weekly* 32:44-5 O 23 '89

Jane Fonda's spa. P. Viladas. il por *House & Garden* 161:92-7 Je '89

Will Jane share her wealth? il pors *People Weekly* 32:81 Ag 7 '89

FONER, ERIC

The South's inner Civil War. il *American Heritage* 40:46-8+ Mr '89

FONG-TORRES, BEN

Connery. Sean Connery [cover story] il pors *American Film* 14:28-33 My '89

Golden Gate late spots. il *Harper's Bazaar* 122:178+ My '89

FONT, ANTONIO DE LA GUARDIA *See* Guardia Font, Antonio de la

FONTAINE, PIERRE FRANÇOIS LÉONARD, 1762-1853

about

Building an empire. O. Bernier. il *House & Garden* 161:40+ D '89

FONTANA, LUCIO, 1899-1968
about
Fontana's base materialism. Y.-A. Bois. bibl f il *Art in America* 77:238-49+ Ap '89
Lucio Fontana: Panicali Fine Art. H. Cotter. il *Art News* 88:144 F '89
FONTE, MORRIS
about
Nice psychic. *The New Yorker* 65:27-8 Mr 13 '89
FOOD
See also
Appetite
Breakfasts
Cooking
Diet
Digestion
Dinners and dining
Eating
Fish as food
Flowers as food
Frankfurters
Gastronomy
Indians of North America—Food
Insects as food
Irradiated food
Larvae as food
Menus
Nutrition
Paleo-Indians—Food
Proteins
Salads
Sandwiches
Space flight—Food problems
Spreads (Food)
Vitamins
1990's fashions in drinks and food. J. F. Mariani. il *Motor Boating & Sailing* 164:26+ S '89
Cavity risk [food chart] R. Asa. il *American Health* 8:58 Mr '89
Eating habits [21st century] L. Shapiro. il *Newsweek* 114 Special Issue:78-9 Wint '89/Spr '90
Ever so humble. L. Wells. il *The New York Times Magazine* p35-6 Ja 1 '89
Food. See issues of Vogue beginning September 1983
Food for thought. B. T. Hunter. See issues of Consumers' Research Magazine
Good taste. L. Wells. il *The New York Times Magazine* p53-4 D 31 '89
What's in store for you [new products] M. Friedman. See issues of Good Housekeeping beginning December 1989
Analysis and chemistry
See also
Food additives
Anecdotes, facetiae, satire, etc.
Flour children [trendy food] B. Shacochis. il *Gentlemen's Quarterly* 59:262+ Ag '89
Caloric content
See Calories, Food
Canning and preserving
See Canning and preserving
Coatings
See also
Fruit—Coatings
Coloring matter
See Coloring matter in cosmetics, food, etc.
Contamination
See Food contamination
Fat content
See also
Project LEAN
Animal protein and breast cancer. *Prevention (Emmaus, Pa.)* 41:9-10 Ag '89
Are you up on your facts about fat? [quiz] K. Levine. il *Reader's Digest* 134:87-90 F '89
Building a low-fat kid. J. Poppy. il *Esquire* 112:93-5 N '89
Face the fats. L. Applegate. il *Runner's World* 24:22+ Ag '89
The fat-fighter's bible (I). il *Prevention (Emmaus, Pa.)* 41:83-5+ My '89
The fat-fighter's bible (II). il *Prevention (Emmaus, Pa.)* 41:77-8+ Je '89
The fat-fighter's bible (III). il *Prevention (Emmaus, Pa.)* 41:65-8+ Jl '89
The fat-fighter's bible (IV). il *Prevention (Emmaus, Pa.)* 41:83-8 Ag '89
Fat: where it's at. R. A. Barnett. il *American Health* 8:84-5+ Ja/F '89
Fats and figures. *World Tennis* 37:44-5 O '89
Fats and sodium in your diet. T. Mendoza. il *Current Health 2* 16:18-21 O '89
Fight fat by forgoing fats [views of Olivia B. Wood] il *USA Today (Periodical)* 118:18-19 O '89
Good food, good health: low-fat strategies. B. Goldman. il *Better Homes and Gardens* 67:33+ Ja '89
"Hidden fats": key to weight control. L. Green. il *Reader's Digest* 134:85-7 F '89

High-fat diets that lower cholesterol [study by Jean T. Snook] J. Raloff. *Science News* 136:318 N 11 '89
Low-fat foods with a high-fat pleasure quotient. M. A. Gilman. il *Psychology Today* 23:50 Je '89
Putting tropical oils in their place [emphasis should be on reducing total dietary fat] G. L. Blackburn. il *Prevention (Emmaus, Pa.)* 41:30+ Ag '89
Rev up [reducing fat calories] L. Moll. il *Health (New York, N.Y.)* 21:45-6 Je '89
Skinny eggs and other dream foods [low-cholesterol products] C. Hudson. il *Health (New York, N.Y.)* 21:30+ S '89
Strategies to reduce dietary fat. B. T. Hunter. il *Consumers' Research Magazine* 72:29-31 Ap '89
Twinkie power. E. Coleman. il *Bicycling* 30:56-7 Ag '89
History
See also
Aztecs—Food
Dinner with Demosthenes [research by A. Dalby] S. J. Evans. il *History Today* 39:3-4 Ja '89
Labeling
Battle of the food blurbs [health claims] A. Toufexis. il *Time* 134:66 S 11 '89
Do you know light from lite? [excerpt from The Canyon Ranch health and fitness program] K. Moloney. il *Health (New York, N.Y.)* 21:32+ F '89
Food health claims: what should you believe? il *Glamour* 87:328-30 S '89
Food labeling chaos must end [report by the Center for Science in the Public Interest] il *USA Today (Periodical)* 118:14 D '89
Food labels: the hype behind the type. C. Schaeffer. il *Changing Times* 43:34-8 Jl '89
A Good Heartkeeping seal of approval [American Heart Association labeling of approved processed foods] C. Jennings-Sauer. il *American Health* 8:16 Je '89
The great American health pitch [cover story; special section] il *Business Week* p114-17+ O 9 '89
The high price of health approval [HeartGuide seal program] C. Sugarman. il *Consumers' Research Magazine* 72:33-4 N '89
How to read a food label. N. Goldbeck and D. Goldbeck. il map *The Mother Earth News* 116:72-5 Mr/Ap '89
Label ease [FDA proposals] L. Giuca. il *Organic Gardening* 36:53-6+ N '89
A lite portion of truth in labeling [health claims] il *U.S. News & World Report* 107:14+ S 18 '89
The lowdown on nutrition labels. il *Ladies' Home Journal* 106:290 N '89
Making sense of food labels [condensed from The Canyon Ranch health and fitness program] K. Moloney. *Reader's Digest* 135:117-20 Jl '89
Mandatory labeling of food products [address, March 2-3, 1989] H. M. Baum. *Vital Speeches of the Day* 55:458-61 My 15 '89
A new look at food labeling. D. Blumenthal. il *FDA Consumer* 23:14-17 N '89
Seeing through advertisers' health claims. J. Storm. il *Women's Sports & Fitness* 11:82 Ap '89
Snap, crackle, stop [misleading food claims] J. Carey. il *Business Week* p42-3 S 25 '89
Marketing
See Food industry—Marketing
New sources
See Food supply—New sources
Packaging
See also
Food, Canned
Food pouches
Food wraps
Beyond the tin can. J. Folkenberg. il *FDA Consumer* 23:34 S '89
Photographs and photography
Conceptual Cibachromes: techniques inspired by a menu [work of J. Pallone] F. Cameron. il *Petersen's Photographic Magazine* 18:34-7+ Ag '89
Prices
All that rain has been good for most farmers—and every shopper. T. Young. il *Fortune* 120:25+ S 11 '89
Crisis in Poland. M. Nemeth. il por *Maclean's* 102:16-17 Ag 14 '89
High cost vs. low risk [pesticide ban will increase prices] J. W. Merline. il *Consumers' Research Magazine* 72:38 Je '89
Poland pays the price. H. Anderson. il *Newsweek* 114:26-7 Ag 14 '89
A springtime drought with a silver lining [low wheat yield] L. W. Adkins. il *U.S. News & World Report* 106:48 My 15 '89
Social aspects
The meaning of meals [special section] il *Psychology Today* 23:29+ D '89
Storage
See also
Cold storage
Vegetables—Storage
FOOD, ARTIFICIAL
See also
Fruit, Artificial

FOOD, ARTIFICIAL—See also—*cont.*
Vegetables, Artificial
Fake food [theater props] B. Burns. il *Theatre Crafts* 23:30+ Ap '89

Photographs and photography

The synthetic kitchen [work of T. Trengove] B. Lobron. il *Popular Photography* 96:63+ O '89

FOOD, CANNED
See also
Beans, Canned
Cooking—Canned food
Fish, Canned
Soups, Canned
Tomatoes, Canned
Canned produce: mush no more [work of Malcolm Bourne] J. Raloff. *Science News* 136:206 S 23 '89

FOOD, CHOKING ON See Choking

FOOD, DRIED
See also
Meat, Dried

FOOD, EFFECT OF RADIATION ON See Irradiated food

FOOD, FERMENTED
See also
Tempeh

FOOD, FROZEN
See also
Cooking—Frozen food
Frozen dinners
Ice cream, ices, etc.

FOOD, IRRADIATED See Irradiated food

FOOD, ORGANIC See Organic food

FOOD, RAW
Raw, raw, raw! [uncooked fruits and vegetables may offer greater protection against cancer; research by Blossom Patterson] R. A. Barnett. il *American Health* 8:130+ S '89
To stymie cancer, eat broccoli raw [study by Lloyd D. Campbell and Bogdan A. Slominski] *Science News* 136:351 N 25 '89
Uncooked? Unsafe! B. Hayton. il *Current Health 2* 15:13-15 My '89

FOOD, SMOKED
Campfire cachet. R. Schrambling. il *The New York Times Magazine* p69-70 O 1 '89

FOOD, SYNTHETIC See Food substitutes

FOOD ADDITIVES
See also
Coloring matter in cosmetics, food, etc.
'Consumer-friendly' food additives. B. T. Hunter. il *Consumers' Research Magazine* 72:8-9 My '89

FOOD ADULTERATION See Food contamination

FOOD ALLERGY
See also
Lactose intolerance
Does chocolate give you a headache? A sip of wine make you woozy? Explaining food quirks, hang-ups and glitches. J. L. Lippert. il *Health (New York, N.Y.)* 21:84+ Je '89
Eating can make you ill: understanding food allergies. J. H. Wells. il *USA Today (Periodical)* 118:54-5 Jl '89
Hives at first bite. M. Callahan. il *Parents* 64:210+ Mr '89
Stop the bed-wetting blues. M. Kelly. *American Health* 8:124 S '89
WellAware: Food Sensitivity [computer program] R. M. Gilpin. il *Home Office Computing* 7:76 Ag '89
What to do when your dinner bites you back. S. Findlay. il *U.S. News & World Report* 106:77-8 F 20 '89

FOOD AND DRUG ADMINISTRATION (U.S.) See United States. Food and Drug Administration

FOOD AS GIFTS
Cakes for giving. il *Southern Living* 24:106-7 D '89
Foods for holiday giving: culinary postcards. il *Gourmet* 49:120-1+ D '89
From the Sugarplum Fairy: wonderful things to eat [mail order products] il *Glamour* 87:232-3 D '89
Gift breads [Christmas] B. Ojakangas. il *Ladies' Home Journal* 106:178-80+ D '89
Gifts of food by phone. il *Gourmet* 49:112-14 D '89
Holiday treats. C. Koury. il *Parents* 64:176-8+ D '89
Last-minute gifts. M. Langan. il *McCall's* 116:124 Ja '89
Mixes to make and give. il *Southern Living* 24:113 D '89
Present the best: 25 quick & easy gifts from your kitchen [Christmas] il *Redbook* 174:135-8+ N '89
Say it with food. J. Steingarten. il *Vogue* 179:252-3+ D '89
Special deliveries [excerpt from The gift-giver's cookbook] J. Choate and J. Green. il *Health (New York, N.Y.)* 21:80-3+ N '89
Tasteful presents to give [Christmas] il *McCall's* 117:45 D '89
Tokens of love [Valentine's Day gifts] il *Seventeen* 48:106-7+ F '89

FOOD BANKS
A place at the table. C. Taylor. il *The Mother Earth News* 120:60-3 N/D '89

FOOD CALORIES See Calories, Food

FOOD CHAINS (ECOLOGY)
See also
Detritus
Food chains: the carbon link [cover story] S. Hart. il map *Science News* 136:168-70 S 9 '89
Habitat compartmentation and environmental correlates of food chain length [discussion of November 13, 1987 article, Environmental correlates of food chain length] F. Briand and J. E. Cohen. il *Science* 243:238-40 Ja 13 '89
Macroecology: the division of food and space among species on continents. J. H. Brown and B. A. Maurer. bibl f il *Science* 243:1145-50 Mr 3 '89
Scale invariance in food web properties. G. Sugihara and others. bibl f il *Science* 245:48-52 Jl 7 '89
Shredders and riparian vegetation [relationship between plant litter and aquatic invertebrate growth] K. W. Cummins and others. bibl f il *BioScience* 39:24-30 Ja '89

FOOD COLORING MATTER See Coloring matter in cosmetics, food, etc.

FOOD CONTAINERS, PORCELAIN See Porcelain containers

FOOD CONTAMINATION
See also
Apples—Contamination
Bread—Contamination
Cashew nuts—Contamination
Eggs—Contamination
Fish contamination
Food inspection
Fruit—Contamination
Meat contamination
Milk contamination
Mushrooms, Canned—Contamination
Pesticide residues in food
Potatoes—Contamination
Poultry contamination
Sandwiches—Contamination
Seafood—Contamination
Shellfish contamination
Truffles—Contamination
Vegetables—Contamination
The big chill: how safe are "sous-vide" refrigerated foods? J. Folkenberg. il *FDA Consumer* 23:32-3+ S '89
Concern shifts to the food [microwaving] *Consumer Reports* 54:693 N '89
Food safety is no fad! N. Byal. il *Successful Farming* 87:12-13 D '89
How much dioxin did you consume today? J. Raloff. il *Science News* 135:105 F 18 '89
Mycotoxins: a significant public health problem. B. T. Hunter. il *Consumers' Research Magazine* 72:8-9 Je '89
Uncooked? Unsafe! B. Hayton. il *Current Health 2* 15:13-15 My '89
Warning! Your food, nutritious and delicious, may be hazardous to your health [cover story; special section] il *Newsweek* 113:16-20+ Mr 27 '89
Weighing food safety risks. F. E. Young. il *FDA Consumer* 23:8-13 S '89
What about pesticides and other chemicals? *Consumers' Research Magazine* 72:34 Jl '89

FOOD CRAVINGS
The feel-full pill [fenfluramine used to suppress carbohydrate cravings] W. T. Buckley. il *Health (New York, N.Y.)* 21:28-9+ Ja '89
Winning the war against sugar cravings. G. L. Blackburn. il *Prevention (Emmaus, Pa.)* 41:103+ N '89

FOOD CRITICS AND CRITICISM
Palate polls [Zagat restaurant surveys] J. Elson. il por *Time* 134:65-6 Ag 28 '89

FOOD DECORATION See Cooking—Garnishes; Cooking, Ornamental

FOOD DELIVERY SERVICE
See also
Domino's Pizza Inc.
Critics charge that Domino's is making pizza to die for [accidents involving delivery drivers] il *People Weekly* 32:105 S 25 '89
A dashing way to dine [home-delivered gourmet meals] D. Brand. il *Time* 134:96 S 18 '89
Dial-a-dinner party [New York City] J. Miller. il *Harper's Bazaar* 122:221+ Mr '89
Domino's delivery pledge: danger to go? [traffic accidents while delivering pizza] il *Newsweek* 114:32 Jl 10 '89
Feasts to go [New York City restaurants] B. Costikyan. il *New York* 22:109+ My 1 '89
Move over, moo shu pork [gourmet foods] J. Schwartz. il *Newsweek* 113:42 F 20 '89

FOOD DISTRIBUTION See Food industry—Marketing

FOOD FADS
Food fads. B. Kafka. il *Gourmet* 49:72 O '89
Food for thought: what's out, what's in. *Ladies' Home Journal* 106:292 N '89

FOOD FESTIVALS See Festivals

FOOD FOR CHILDREN See Children—Nutrition

FOOD FOR INFANTS See Infants—Nutrition

FOOD FOR THE POOR (ORGANIZATION)
Blessings from and for the poor [work in Kingston, Jamaica] M. G. Harter. il *America* 161:395-8 D 2 '89

FOOD HABITS *See* Eating
FOOD HANDLING
   See also
   Seafood handling
Bacteria love summer heat. *USA Today (Periodical)* 118:13
   Ag '89
Foodborne viral illness. B. T. Hunter. il *Consumers' Research
   Magazine* 72:8-9 Ag '89
From kitchen to table. il *Time* 133:35+ Mr 27 '89
Protecting against one bad apple [pesticide residues] J. Silber-
   ner. il *U.S. News & World Report* 106:59 Mr 27 '89
Salmonella and food safety. il *Consumers' Research Magazine*
   72:29-31 Mr '89
The WHO Golden Rules for safe food preparation. il *World
   Health* p30 Je '89
FOOD IN ADVERTISING
The synthetic kitchen [work of T. Trengove] B. Lobron.
   il *Popular Photography* 96:63+ O '89
FOOD IN ART
Pleasing the palette. B. Kafka. il *Art News* 88:162-5 O '89
   Exhibitions
From a Rijksmuseum buffet. F. Ferretti. il *Gourmet* 49:82+
   O '89
FOOD INDUSTRY
   See also
   Agricultural industries
   B. Manischewitz Co.
   Beech-Nut Nutrition Corp.
   Blacks in the food industry
   Borden, Inc.
   Campbell Soup Company
   Carnation Co.
   Castle & Cooke, Inc.
   Celestial Seasonings Inc.
   City Provisioners, Inc.
   ConAgra, Inc.
   Dean Foods Co.
   Del Monte Corp.
   Di Giorgio Corp.
   Farm House Foods Corp.
   Finevest Foods
   Fish industry
   Frito-Lay, Inc.
   Fruit industry
   General Foods Corp.
   General Mills, Inc.
   Gerber Products Co.
   Golden Valley Microwave Foods Inc.
   GoodMark Foods Inc.
   H. J. Heinz Co.
   Hershey Foods Corp.
   J. M. Smucker Co.
   Jays Foods, Inc.
   K. T.'s Kitchens Inc.
   Kellogg Co.
   Kraft General Foods Group
   Kraft Inc.
   McIlhenny Co.
   Michael Foods Inc.
   Natural Food Products (Firm)
   Pepperidge Farm, Inc.
   PepsiCo, Inc.
   Pillsbury Co.
   Poultry industry
   Procter & Gamble Co.
   Quaker Oats Co.
   Ralston Purina Co.
   Rich Products Corporation
   Sara Lee Corp.
   Schwan's Sales Enterprises
   Shellfish industry
   Smartfoods, Inc.
   Sorrell Ridge (Firm)
   Stokely USA, Inc.
   Tyson Foods, Inc.
   Universal Foods Corp.
   Weight Watchers International Inc.
   Women in the food industry
Eight hot trends of the '90s. P. Edidin. *Psychology Today*
   23:44 D '89
   Acquisitions and mergers
The food companies haven't finished eating. L. Therrien.
   il *Business Week* p70 Ja 9 '89
How Philip Morris diversified right [acquiring Kraft] S. P.
   Sherman. il por *Fortune* 120:120-2+ O 23 '89
Is bigger better for Philip Morris? [interview with H. Maxwell]
   C. Leinster. il por *Fortune* 119:66-71 My 8 '89
Michael Miles. L. Therrien. il por *Business Week* Special
   Issue:126 Ap 14 '89
Philip Morris's big bite [cover story] L. J. Davis. il por
   The New York Times Magazine p30-3+ Ap 9 '89
Ripe for the picking [Dean Foods] C. Siler. il *Forbes* 143:110+
   Ap 3 '89
   International aspects
Grand Met's recipe for Pillsbury. R. I. Kirkland, Jr. il *Fortune*
   119:61+ Mr 13 '89

A little cash and a lot of moxie [Hyde Park Holdings'
   bid for Universal Foods Corp.] L. J. Nathans. il pors
   Business Week p74 Ja 30 '89
   Western Europe
Is BSN's stomach as big as its eyes? F. J. Comes. il por
   Business Week p55+ Ja 9 '89
The race to stock Europe's common supermarket [BSN buys
   European operations of RJR Nabisco with more food
   deals to follow] S. Toy and R. A. Melcher. il *Business
   Week* p80+ Je 26 '89
   Advertising
Battle of the food blurbs [health claims] A. Toufexis. il
   Time 134:66 S 11 '89
The great American health pitch [cover story; special section]
   il *Business Week* p114-17+ O 9 '89
Hot potatoes. B. Kanner. il *New York* 22:22+ F 6 '89
A lite portion of truth in labeling [health claims] il *U.S.
   News & World Report* 107:14+ S 18 '89
Seeing through advertisers' health claims. J. Storm. il *Women's
   Sports & Fitness* 11:82 Ap '89
Snap, crackle, stop [misleading food claims] J. Carey. il
   Business Week p42-3 S 25 '89
Splitting up the eats [TV expenditures] il *Channels (New
   York, N.Y.: 1986)* 9:48 O '89
TV bingers [effects of food commercials; research by Carol
   Raupp] J. Fischman. il *Psychology Today* 23:24 N '89
   Export-import trade
The great global food fright. C. P. Work and R. E. Norton.
   il *U.S. News & World Report* 106:56-7+ Mr 27 '89
How effective are controls on imported food? B. T. Hunter.
   il *Consumers' Research Magazine* 72:36 Je '89
   Finance
The food companies haven't finished eating. L. Therrien.
   il *Business Week* p70 Ja 9 '89
Food processors. J. Novack. il *Forbes* 143:144+ Ja 9 '89
   Marketing
Sin, you eaters! B. Kanner. il *New York* 22:28+ Ap 10
   '89
   Securities
Green groceries [stocks for ethical investors] S. S. Ross.
   il *Mother Jones* 14:48-52 F/Mr '89
How to buy safe food stocks without paying gourmet prices.
   P. Sellers. il *Fortune* 120:31+ D 4 '89
   France
   See also
   BSN SA
   Great Britain
   See also
   Chatsworth Foods Ltd.
   Japan
   See also
   Ajinomoto Co., Inc.
   Switzerland
   See also
   Nestle SA
   United States
   See Food industry
FOOD INSPECTION
   See also
   Fish inspection
   Meat inspection
On the road to market. il *Time* 133:30+ Mr 27 '89
FOOD LAWS AND REGULATIONS
   See also
   Food inspection
   United States. Food and Drug Administration
FOOD LITERATURE
Eat these words. B. Shacochis. il *Gentlemen's Quarterly*
   59:206+ D '89
FOOD MAIL ORDER BUSINESS *See* Mail order business
FOOD MIXERS (APPLIANCES) *See* Mixers (Appliances)
FOOD MIXES
   See also
   Grain mixes
   Meat mixes
Mixes to make and give. il *Southern Living* 24:113 D '89
FOOD PLANTS *See* Plants, Edible
FOOD POISONING
   See also
   Botulism
   Ciguatera
   Salmonellosis
   Scombroid poisoning
Bacteria love summer heat. *USA Today (Periodical)* 118:13
   Ag '89
Foodborne viral illness. B. T. Hunter. il *Consumers' Research
   Magazine* 72:8-9 Ag '89
FOOD POLICY *See* Nutrition policy
FOOD POUCHES
The big chill: how safe are "sous-vide" refrigerated foods?
   J. Folkenberg. il *FDA Consumer* 23:32-3+ S '89
FOOD PRESERVATION AND PRESERVATIVES
   See also
   Canning and preserving
FOOD PROCESSING INDUSTRY *See* Food industry
FOOD PROCESSORS (APPLIANCES)
   See also
   Cuisinarts, Inc.

FOOD PROCESSORS (APPLIANCES)—cont.
Prices
Diced and sliced [Cuisinarts in Chapter 11] K. Hannon. il por *Forbes* 144:68+ O 2 '89

FOOD RELIEF *See* Relief work

FOOD RESEARCH
See also
Food supply—New sources
Anecdotes, facetiae, satire, etc.
Cream of science soup. J. Stone. il *Discover* 10:82-4 Ag '89

FOOD SAFETY INSPECTION *See* Food inspection
FOOD SANITATION *See* Food handling
FOOD SENSITIVENESS *See* Food allergy
FOOD SERVICE
See also
Airlines—Food service
Caterers and catering
Clubs—Food service
Restaurants
Schwan's Sales Enterprises
Shopping centers—Food service
Speedways—Food service

FOOD SERVICE, GOVERNMENT
See also
United States—Armed Forces—Commissariat

FOOD SPOILAGE
See also
Food contamination
Food inspection
Rancidity

FOOD STORES
See also
Convito Italiano (Firm)
Delicatessens
Expression Unlimited
National Convenience Stores Inc.
Soup Kitchen International (Firm)
Southland Corp.
Supermarkets
. . . and cheese [New York City] R. D. Story. il *New York* 22:67+ My 1 '89
The Christmas table [New York City] *The New Yorker* 65:89-94 D 18 '89
Fast feasts: for the holidays, take it out—take it all out [New York City] B. Costikyan. il *New York* 22:66-8+ D 18 '89
A food lover's tour of East Bay "gourmet gulches" [shops in Oakland, Berkeley, Albany] il map *Sunset (Central West edition)* 183:168+ S '89
Minding the family store [Korean greengrocers in New York City] C. Koehl. il *Newsweek* 114 Special Issue:4 Wint '89/Spr '90
Takeout [New York City] B. Costikyan. il *New York* 22:60-2+ Jl 3-10 '89

FOOD STYLING
Why our Christmas dinner looks better than yours [work of food stylist Karen Gillingham] il *Esquire* 112:166-9 D '89
Competitions
Salon [Garden State Culinary Salon's presentation food competition] *The New Yorker* 65:28-9 My 1 '89

FOOD SUBSTITUTES
See also
Butter substitutes
Faux better or worse? L. Applegate. il *Runner's World* 24:20-1 Ap '89

FOOD SUPPLY
See also
Famines
Grain supply
Production, Agricultural
World Food Day
International aspects
The grain drain: the waning of food security [excerpt from State of the world: 1989] L. R. Brown. il por *The Futurist* 23:9-16 Jl/Ag '89
The world food crisis. L. R. Brown. il *USA Today (Periodical)* 117:51-3 Mr '89
World food research. P. H. Abelson. *Science* 244:125 Ap 14 '89
The world's cupboard is emptying out. E. T. Smith. il *Business Week* p106-9 Ap 3 '89
New sources
Food variety in the marketplace. B. T. Hunter. il *Consumers' Research Magazine* 72:27-9 S '89
A taste of things to come. J. Steingarten. il *Vogue* 179:410-11+ O '89
Africa
Hunger in Africa: why it persists, why we must care [cover story; special section] il map *Scholastic Update (Teachers' edition)* 121:2-15 Ja 27 '89
Developing countries
Frances Moore Lappé's diet for a better world. P. Carroll. il pors *Utne Reader* p42-8 My/Je '89
Hunger threat looming over poor countries. il *UN Chronicle* 26:66-7 S '89

World hunger amidst plenty. J. W. Helmuth. il *USA Today (Periodical)* 117:48-50 Mr '89
Eastern Europe
Why the long food lines? P. Sudo. il *Scholastic Update (Teachers' edition)* 122:16-17 O 20 '89
Poland
Crisis in Poland. M. Nemeth. il por *Maclean's* 102:16-17 Ag 14 '89
Poland pays the price. H. Anderson. il *Newsweek* 114:26-7 Ag 14 '89
Soviet Union
Can Gorbachev feed Russia? M. Kramer. il *The New York Times Magazine* p42-3+ Ap 9 '89
Why Russia can't feed itself. D. Satter. *Reader's Digest* 135:61-6 O '89
Tropics
Iguana conservation and economic development [captive breeding project in Panama; work of D. Werner; cover story] J. P. Cohn. il *BioScience* 39:359-63 Je '89
Iguana mama [work of D. Werner] N. Vietmeyer. il por *International Wildlife* 19:24-7 S/O '89

FOOD WRAPS
The best ways to keep food fresh. il *Consumer Reports* 54:120-3 F '89
Food wraps & bags. il *Consumer Reports* 54:277-82 D '89

A FOOL FOR YOU [ballet] *See* Ballet reviews—Single works

FOOS, RICHARD
about
The gold in oldies. F. Meeks. il pors *Forbes* 143:68+ My 1 '89

FOOT
Toe-to-toe with Paranthropus [foot bone gives evidence of bipedality at Swartkrans site; research by Randall Susman] il *Discover* 10:16 Ag '89
Abnormalities
See also
Bunions
Care and hygiene
See also
Pedicure
A guide to common foot problems. P. G. Gill. *McCall's* 116:92+ Je '89
Help yourself to happy feet. M. A. Brenner. il *Women's Sports & Fitness* 11:58 S '89
"Oh, my aching feet". il *Ladies' Home Journal* 106:40+ D '89
Six ways to avoid cold feet. R. Glenn. il *Field & Stream* 94:98 N '89
The sportsman's guide to foot care. P. G. Gill. il *Field & Stream* 93:54 Ap '89
Treat your feet. H. E. Lee. il *Vogue* 179:152 My '89
Walk away from aches and pains [views of Alan Kalker] il *USA Today (Periodical)* 117:8-9 F '89
Wounds and injuries
See also
Blisters
Plantar fasciitis
Feet first [dancers] M. Horosko. il *Dance Magazine* 63:56-7 N '89
See Larry run [L. Bird plays in exhibition game seven months after foot surgery] L. Montville. il pors *Sports Illustrated* 71:26-9 Jl 3 '89

FOOT, ARTIFICIAL
What every mother fears [riding mower severs the foot of 17 month old daughter] B. Phelps. il por *Ladies' Home Journal* 106:20+ Jl '89

FOOT-AND-MOUTH DISEASE VIRUS
Portrait of a virus [research by David Stuart and others] il *Discover* 10:10 Je '89

FOOT REFLEXOLOGY *See* Reflexology
FOOT TENNIS
A leg up. B. Weber. il *The New York Times Magazine* p66 My 28 '89

FOOTBALL
See also
Australian rules football
Football players
Passing (Football)
Rugby
Soccer
Touch football
Another bright idea [C. Finley's fluorescent football] R. O'Brien. il por *Sports Illustrated* 71:30 O 23 '89
Bibliography
In short/football. il *The New York Times Book Review* 94:44-5 N 19 '89
Equipment
See also
Footballs

FOOTBALL, COLLEGE
See also
Football coaches
Football players
Football records
All South '89 [special section] il *Southern Living* 24:81+ S '89

FOOTBALL, COLLEGE—*cont.*

Arrivals and departures [coach D. Erickson leaves Washington State for Miami] H. Hersch. il por *Sports Illustrated* 70:24-5 Mr 13 '89

'Bama roars back [victory over Tennessee] W. F. Reed. il *Sports Illustrated* 71:46-8+ O 30 '89

Beast from Down East [Univ. of Maine] P. Putnam. il *Sports Illustrated* 71:54-5 O 30 '89

Boffo Buffs! [Colorado defeats Nebraska] A. Murphy. il *Sports Illustrated* 71:20-7 N 13 '89

College football. See issues of Sports Illustrated published during the college football season beginning September 15, 1986

College football preview '89 [cover story; special issue] il *Sports Illustrated* 71:38-44+ S 4 '89

The fella expects to win [Notre Dame coach L. Holtz] P. A. Witteman. il por *Time* 134:90-2 N 27 '89

High times [Tennessee upsets Auburn] A. Murphy. il *Sports Illustrated* 71:18-21 O 9 '89

Home at last [Auburn defeats Alabama] H. Hersch. il *Sports Illustrated* 71:50-3 D 11 '89

Just call it Erickson U. [Miami coach D. Erickson and quarterback C. Erickson] B. Newman. il por *Sports Illustrated* 70:82-3 My 1 '89

A lid-lifter in Texas [Texas A & M upsets Houston] A. Murphy. il pors *Sports Illustrated* 71:56-8+ O 23 '89

The luck of the Irish [Notre Dame vs. Southern Cal] D. S. Looney. il *Sports Illustrated* 71:36-9 O 30 '89

The man who said no to $1 million [condensed from Paterno]; ed. by Bernard Asbell. J. Paterno. il por *Reader's Digest* 135:19-22+ D '89

No. 1 no more [Miami ends Notre Dame's winning streak; cover story] A. Murphy. il *Sports Illustrated* 71:24-31 D 4 '89

The one-two punch [Notre Dame beats Michigan; cover story] A. Murphy. il *Sports Illustrated* 71:32-6 S 25 '89

Paws! [Clemson] C. Kirkpatrick. il pors *Sports Illustrated* 71:98-102+ O 23 '89

Pocket acquires book by Notre Dame football coach Lou Holtz. *Publishers Weekly* 235:61 Ja 13 '89

A run for the Roses [Michigan defeats Illinois] D. S. Looney. il *Sports Illustrated* 71:34-5 N 20 '89

Say goodbye to fallball [Louisville vs. West Virginia] A. Murphy. il *Sports Illustrated* 71:38-40+ O 2 '89

Shaking down the thunder [L. Holtz] G. Kingdom. il pors *The Saturday Evening Post* 261:52-3+ S '89

The Sport 1989 college football preview [cover story; special section] M. Francesa. il *Sport (New York, N.Y.)* 80:22-6+ S '89

SWAC conference aiming at changing small image. *Jet* 77:46 D 4 '89

This coach did it right [retiring Kentucky coach J. Claiborne] W. F. Reed. il por *Sports Illustrated* 71:126 D 11 '89

This is for you, Sal [Colorado routs Washington a week after death of quarterback S. Aunese] B. Newman. il *Sports Illustrated* 71:22-5 O 9 '89

A very sorry State [Penn State upset by Virginia] A. Murphy. il *Sports Illustrated* 71:48-50+ S 18 '89

Accidents and injuries

Was it worth the risk? [Arizona State player M. Tingstad injured after continuing to play despite being warned of paralysis risk] R. Demak. il pors *Sports Illustrated* 71:76-81+ D 18 '89

Awards

See also

Heisman Trophy

Central State Marauders, 'Tank' Younger feted in L.A. il por *Jet* 76:49 My 22 '89

Betting

See Football betting

Bowl games

No. 1 with a bullet [Notre Dame defeats West Virginia in Fiesta Bowl; cover story] R. Telander. il *Sports Illustrated* 70:16-21 Ja 9 '89

Economic aspects

Bowling for dollars! [bowls scramble for sponsors, position, and survival] B. Condor. il *Sport (New York, N.Y.)* 80:58-60 Ja '89

New Year's run for the money [Fiesta and other bowls] T. Barrett. il *Newsweek* 113:62-3 Ja 2 '89

So many bowls, so little to cheer about. R. Grover and A. Fins. il *Business Week* p56 D 25 '89-Ja 1 '90

These players are really going long. G. L. Miles. il *Business Week* p138 D 11 '89

What's next—the Mazda Fed-Ex Big Mac Pine-Sol Bowl? M. Durslag. il *TV Guide* 37:12-14 D 30 '89-Ja 5 '90

Economic aspects

Pass the gravy, please [Georgia Tech's solicitation of corporate sponsors for home games] D. Kindred. il por *Sports Illustrated* 70:96 My 15 '89

Ethical aspects

Hazard to your health [columnist excoriated after criticizing Georgia Tech's handling of violent incident involving players] R. S. Johnson. por *Sports Illustrated* 70:77 F 27 '89

Oklahoma gridders nabbed for drugs, rape, shooting. *Jet* 75:50 Mr 20 '89

Oklahoma is not OK. R. Givens. il por *Newsweek* 113:80 F 27 '89

An open letter to Alex [Northwestern coach A. Agase] R. Telander. il por *Sports Illustrated* 71:106 N 27 '89

A question of fairness [conviction of agents N. Walters and L. Bloom] R. Telander. por *Sports Illustrated* 70:114 My 1 '89

Something must be done [excerpt from The hundred yard lie] R. Telander. il *Sports Illustrated* 71:92-8+ O 2 '89

Tough message [sports agents N. Walters and L. Bloom found guilty of racketeering, conspiracy, and mail fraud] il pors *Time* 133:78 Ap 24 '89

What price glory? [criminal behavior among Univ. of Colorado players] R. Reilly. il *Sports Illustrated* 70:32-4 F 27 '89

You reap what you sow [Oklahoma; cover story] R. Telander and R. Sullivan. il por *Sports Illustrated* 70:20-6+ F 27 '89

History

20 years ago the Ohio State Buckeyes won the Big Ten's last national championship. K. W. Kessler. il *Sport (New York, N.Y.)* 80:74-5 Ja '89

'80s football. J. D. Miller. il *Sport (New York, N.Y.)* 80:48-50+ O '89

The Bear trap [P. W. Bryant, son of late Alabama coach] W. M. Adler. il por *Esquire* 112:204-6+ S '89

A life cut short [Syracuse running back E. Davis] W. Nack. il pors *Sports Illustrated* 71:136-46 S 4 '89

Of many things [book titled College football's 25 greatest teams] G. W. Hunt. *America* 161:202 O 7 '89

International aspects

These players are really going long. G. L. Miles. il *Business Week* p138 D 11 '89

Organization and administration

Football playoff: they just said no. R. Hurley. *Sport (New York, N.Y.)* 80:60 Ja '89

Polls

The ultimate poll [top college football teams of all time] K. Dunnavant. il *Sport (New York, N.Y.)* 80:28-32+ D '89

Recruiting

Here today, gone today [Miami University recruit D. Krein wants out of letter of intent after coach J. Johnson goes back on word about not leaving] R. Reilly. por *Sports Illustrated* 70:102 Mr 27 '89

On the road again [Univ. of Texas recruiter B. J. Wright] D. S. Looney. il pors *Sports Illustrated* 70:52-6+ F 20 '89

Religious aspects

Thou shalt not lose [Jerry Falwell's Liberty University] L. Montville. il *Sports Illustrated* 71:82-6+ N 13 '89

Social aspects

Football flotilla [cruising to University of Washington's Husky Stadium] N. Rabinowitz. il *Motor Boating & Sailing* 163:76-7 Ja '89

Murder in broad daylight [Ivy League football] J. P. Hart. *National Review* 41:52 F 10 '89

Putting on the pigskin [annual Texas-Oklahoma game in Dallas] S. Stevens. il *Esquire* 112:54 O '89

Canada

A jewel waiting to be discovered. T. Frayne. il *Maclean's* 102:69 D 4 '89

FOOTBALL, HIGH SCHOOL

The boys on the varsity get a real kick out of homecoming queen Tamara Browder [Woodward High School in Toledo, Ohio] il por *People Weekly* 32:113 N 13 '89

D.C. girls first to play on boys' football team [S. Wells and L. Ellis] D. M. Cheers. il pors *Jet* 77:28-30 N 13 '89

A high school football record gets smashed in the name of Law [running back in Sheridan, Ind.] J. Friedman. il pors *People Weekly* 32:61-2 O 23 '89

Out of the blue [Animas, N.M. high school team on longest winning streak in the country] G. Smith. il *Life* 12:82-4+ N '89

Ethical aspects

Aaron Henry's dangerous journey [player who used anabolic steroids] S. J. Smith. il *Reader's Digest* 135:116-20 D '89

Choosing sides [Conway, S.C. torn apart by racial dispute involving two quarterbacks] H. Hersch. il pors *Sports Illustrated* 71:42-4+ N 27 '89

The death of an athlete [steroid user B. Ramirez of Ashtabula, Ohio] R. Telander and M. Noden. il pors *Sports Illustrated* 70:68-72+ F 20 '89

Religious aspects

Prayers ignore court ban. B. Wilburn. il *Christianity Today* 33:38 N 3 '89

Throwing God for a loss [prayer ban] F. Trippett. il *Time* 134:34 S 18 '89

Television broadcasting

See Cable television—Sports

FOOTBALL, PROFESSIONAL

See also

Arena football

Collective bargaining—Football, Professional

Football coaches

Football fans

Football players

FOOTBALL, PROFESSIONAL—See also—*cont.*

Pro Football Hall of Fame

Armed and ready [Chicago defeats Cincinnati] P. Zimmerman. il *Sports Illustrated* 71:30-2+ S 18 '89

Back in the groove [49ers beat Minnesota in NFC playoffs] R. Reilly. il *Sports Illustrated* 70:36-9 Ja 9 '89

Back to basics [ailing quarterbacks and other preseason concerns; cover story] P. King. il pors *Sports Illustrated* 71:14-18+ Ag 7 '89

The big, bad blue bullies [New York Giants vs. Phoenix] P. Zimmerman. il *Sports Illustrated* 71:42-4 N 13 '89

Big Buddy is watching [Philadelphia coach B. Ryan] M. Lupica. il *Esquire* 112:49-50 Ag '89

Big changes in Big D [Dallas under new coach J. Johnson; cover story] P. Zimmerman. il pors *Sports Illustrated* 70:26-8+ Mr 20 '89

The Bucs don't stop here [Tampa Bay vs. New Orleans] R. Telander. il *Sports Illustrated* 71:56-8+ O 2 '89

Ditka's Bad News Bears: what's next? [cover story] K. Lamb. il *Sport (New York, N.Y.)* 80:66-73 Ja '89

Down and dirty [Philadelphia defeats New York Giants] P. Zimmerman. il *Sports Illustrated* 71:46-50 O 16 '89

A duel in the sun: quarterbacks Troy Aikman and Steve Walsh compete to be the Cowboys' starter [cover story] A. Murphy. il pors *Sports Illustrated* 71:30-2+ Ag 21 '89

Fight to the finish [push into final week of regular season] P. King. il *Sports Illustrated* 71:26-31 D 25 '89-Ja 1 '90

The game was lost in the fog [Chicago defeats Philadelphia in NFC playoff game] P. Zimmerman. il *Sports Illustrated* 70:22-6+ Ja 9 '89

Inside the NFL. P. King. See issues of Sports Illustrated published during the football season beginning September 11, 1989

The Majik show [Green Bay] P. Zimmerman. il por *Sports Illustrated* 71:34-9 D 11 '89

NFL preview '89 [special issue] il *Sports Illustrated* 71:28-32+ S 11 '89

Nipped in the Bud [Cleveland defeats Denver] P. Zimmerman. il por *Sports Illustrated* 71:36-8+ O 9 '89

No trick, just treat [Cincinnati defeats Buffalo in AFC championship game; cover story] R. Reilly. il *Sports Illustrated* 70:14-17 Ja 16 '89

Now it gets grisly [Redskins rout Chicago Bears] P. King. il *Sports Illustrated* 71:40+ D 4 '89

Putting the clamps on [Buffalo beats Houston in AFC playoff game] R. Wiley. il *Sports Illustrated* 70:42-4+ Ja 9 '89

Rocky flight into first [Minnesota Vikings] J. Lieber. il por *Sports Illustrated* 71:36-8+ N 20 '89

Run 'n' Shoot [offense devised by M. Davis, currently with the Detroit Lions] J. D. Miller. il por *Sport (New York, N.Y.)* 80:38-40+ Jl '89

The Sport 1989 pro football preview [cover story; special section] J. D. Miller. il *Sport (New York, N.Y.)* 80:30-2+ Ag '89

Taking care of business [Cincinnati defeats Seattle in AFC playoffs] J. Lieber. il *Sports Illustrated* 70:49-50 Ja 9 '89

That man again [J. Montana rallies 49ers to victory over Philadelphia; cover story] P. King. il por *Sports Illustrated* 71:52-4 O 2 '89

"This is where it starts" [Houston Oilers coach J. Glanville prepares team to take on Minnesota Vikings] J. D. Miller. il por *Sport (New York, N.Y.)* 80:85-8 D '89

Those Rice Capades [San Francisco beats Chicago for NFC championship] P. Zimmerman. il *Sports Illustrated* 70:18-21 Ja 16 '89

Where Eagles dare [Philadelphia vs. Washington] P. Zimmerman. il *Sports Illustrated* 71:16-21 S 25 '89

Wimps they aren't [Denver vs. New York Giants] P. Zimmerman. il *Sports Illustrated* 71:26-8+ D 18 '89

Wiseguy [Houston Oiler coach J. Glanville] F. Lidz. il pors *Sports Illustrated* 71:58-60+ O 30 '89

Ye shall pass. A. Barra. il *Sport (New York, N.Y.)* 80:58-60+ S '89

Accidents and injuries

The boys of fall [quarterback injuries] J. Czarnecki. il *Sport (New York, N.Y.)* 80:9 Ja '89

Broken but unbowed [Cincinnati's T. Krumrie recuperates from leg fracture suffered in Super Bowl] J. Lieber. il pors *Sports Illustrated* 70:104-7 Mr 20 '89

Joe says it's so: New York Giants star Joe Morris reconditions for the long road back. A. Tardio. il pors *Gentlemen's Quarterly* 59:314-18+ N '89

Betting

See Football betting

Cheerleading

See Cheerleading

Draft

15 black college stars hope to crack NFL lists. il *Jet* 76:46 My 15 '89

Barry breaks away [Heisman winner B. Sanders seeks admission to draft] W. Nack. il pors *Sports Illustrated* 70:24-6+ Ap 10 '89

Dr. Z's magnificent seven. P. Zimmerman. il *Sports Illustrated* 70:50-1 Ap 24 '89

Filling the Bills. J. D. Miller. il *Sport (New York, N.Y.)* 80:38-43 My '89

Look back in anger [drug rumors hurt Florida safety L. Oliver's pick in draft] D. Scheiber. il pors *Sports Illustrated* 70:42-4+ My 8 '89

Maximum exposure [Wake Forest quarterback M. Elkins' four-month odyssey to NFL draft] J. Lieber. il pors *Sports Illustrated* 70:38-40+ My 1 '89

Rookie roulette. P. King. il *Sports Illustrated* 71:68 D 4 '89

Supplemental signal caller [S. Walsh picked by Dallas Cowboys] P. King. il por *Sports Illustrated* 71:10 Jl 17 '89

Economic aspects

All those big, bad Raiders want is a home sweet home [deal to play in Irwindale, Calif. stalled] P. Cole. il *Business Week* p44 My 22 '89

Bum Bright goes for the long bomb [selling Dallas Cowboys] K. Kelly. il por *Business Week* p98+ F 6 '89

'A chapter closed' [new Dallas Cowboys owner J. Jones replaces coach T. Landry with J. Johnson] W. O. Johnson. il pors *Sports Illustrated* 70:22-4+ Mr 6 '89

Jerry Jones: the man who fired Tom Landry. K. Kelly. il por *Business Week* p148 Ap 24 '89

That head-banging you hear is the NFL owners. B. Bremner. il *Business Week* p36 S 4 '89

Ethical aspects

Brown's Mack a free man, returns to football team [use of cocaine] il por *Jet* 77:48 N 27 '89

Look back in anger [drug rumors hurt Florida safety L. Oliver's pick in draft] D. Scheiber. il pors *Sports Illustrated* 70:42-4+ My 8 '89

The NFL fails its drug test. R. Demak and J. Kirshenbaum. il *Sports Illustrated* 71:38-41+ Jl 10 '89

Redskins' Manley aims for NFL reinstatement. por *Jet* 77:48 D 11 '89

Remorse? Not in the NFL [Jet running back F. McNeil's regret over injuring Colt linebacker O'Brien Alston] B. Newman. il por *Sports Illustrated* 71:112 O 16 '89

Was the X factor a factor? [former player and steroid user S. Courson suffering from cardiomyopathy] por *Sports Illustrated* 70:34 Ap 3 '89

History

'80s football. J. D. Miller. il *Sport (New York, N.Y.)* 80:48-50+ O '89

The Bronk and the gazelle [B. Nagurski and D. Hutson, dominating players of 1930s] P. Zimmerman. il pors *Sports Illustrated* 71:128-32+ S 11 '89

A gathering of Eagles [reunion of 1948 championship team] H. Nuwer. il *Sport (New York, N.Y.)* 80:50-2 Jl '89

A reunion in friendship [former Giants quarterback Y. A. Tittle to make campaign appearance for Wake County, N.C. sheriff J. Baker, whose hit in 1964 helped end Tittle's career] il pors *Sports Illustrated* 71:12+ N 27 '89

International aspects

See also

World League of American Football

Officiating

Replay replay. P. King. il *Sports Illustrated* 71:84 N 27 '89

Organization and administration

See also

National Football League

World League of American Football

As time goes by, the Raiders should go back to Oakland. K. Garrett. il *Sport (New York, N.Y.)* 80:38 Ag '89

Even Cowboys lovers get the blues [new owner J. Jerral and coach J. Johnson] L. Rosellini. il pors *U.S. News & World Report* 107:65-6 S 11 '89

A happy homecoming [Raiders owner A. Davis now an NFL peacemaker] P. King. por *Sports Illustrated* 71:76 Jl 31 '89

Hold the tortillas! The Cowboys are in good hands [new owner J. Jones] R. Galloway. il *Sport (New York, N.Y.)* 80:63 Ag '89

Lord of the rings [Raiders owner A. Davis] R. Hoffer. il pors *Sports Illustrated* 71:104-8+ D 11 '89

Payton seeks ownership of St. Louis NFL team. il por *Jet* 77:46 D 11 '89

Throwing a curve ball at city hall [relocation threats] il *U.S. News & World Report* 107:20 O 23 '89

Top blacks qualified to replace Pete Rozelle. il por *Jet* 76:51 Ap 10 '89

Unforgettable Art Rooney [owner of the Pittsburgh Steelers] R. Bleier. il por *Reader's Digest* 135:15-16+ N '89

Player trades

Jilted Jim's big McLove-in [Charger J. McMahon faces former teammates in preseason game in Chicago] P. King. il pors *Sports Illustrated* 71:20-1 Ag 28 '89

Sudden impact [megadeal sends Dallas' H. Walker to Minnesota; cover story] P. King. il pors *Sports Illustrated* 71:42-4+ O 23 '89

Records

See Football records

Rules

It's time for a tune-up. R. Reilly. il *Sports Illustrated* 70:80 Ja 16 '89

Super Bowl

The 1989 Sport Super Bowl MVP [J. Rice of the 49ers] il pors *Sport (New York, N.Y.)* 80:46 My '89

FOOTBALL, PROFESSIONAL—Super Bowl—*cont.*
. . . and your Super game plan [watching the game] J. Schuster. il *Sport (New York, N.Y.)* 80:37-9 F '89
The big fourth down [preview of 49ers-Bengals matchup] W. Lowther. il *Maclean's* 102:19 Ja 23 '89
Bulls, bears and bowls [Super Bowl games and stock market] T. Jaffe. il *Forbes* 143:172 F 6 '89
The hero as huckster [MVP J. Rice complains of being slighted by press] R. Fimrite. por *Sports Illustrated* 70:92 F 13 '89
Joe Cool [49ers beat Cincinnati; cover story] P. Zimmerman. il *Sports Illustrated* 70:14-24+ Ja 30 '89
Just a Super Bowl of crescendos [San Francisco 49ers vs. Cincinnati Bengals] T. Callahan. il *Time* 133:52-3 Ja 23 '89
Rice, 49ers top Bengals to win Super Bowl XXIII. il *Jet* 75:52 F 6 '89
Super Bowl preview [special section] il *Sports Illustrated* 70:36-8+ Ja 23 '89
You may not need a great quarterback—or the best talent—to make the Super Bowl. D. Friedman. il *TV Guide* 37:28-9 Ja 7-13 '89
Caricatures and cartoons
Heard at the Super Bowl. S. Mack. il por *Sports Illustrated* 70:86 Ja 30 '89
Economic aspects
A Super Sunday victory for Joe Robbie. A. Fins. il por *Business Week* p62 Ja 23 '89
Halftime
Halftime spectacles [telecast in 3-D] il *Time* 133:53 Ja 23 '89
History
Replaying Super Bowl III, Namath and the '69 Jets meet and beat the Colts again [Legends Bowl] T. Nugent. il pors *People Weekly* 32:56-7 N 13 '89
Super Bowl game plan. J. D. Miller. il *Sport (New York, N.Y.)* 80:25-6+ F '89
Super Bowl: the quarterly report [decisive quarters] W. Bingham. il *Sports Illustrated* 70:51+ Ja 9 '89
Scouting
Spying at the Super Bowl: the inside story. V. Carucci. il *TV Guide* 37:14-17 Ja 21-27 '89
Taxation
Court cancels a Super Bowl bid [denial of tax deduction for corporate entertainment expenses] G. W. Padwe. il *Nation's Business* 77:60 Jl '89
Television broadcasting
See Cable television—Sports; Television broadcasting—Sports
Training camps
The comeback chronicles. H. Hersch. il pors *Sports Illustrated* 71:38-44+ Jl 24 '89
Canada
See also
Canadian Football League
FOOTBALL BETTING
Autumn madness [professional football] D. Sheridan. il *Sport (New York, N.Y.)* 80:109-10 O '89
College education. D. Sheridan. il *Sport (New York, N.Y.)* 80:79-80 S '89
A touchdown for sports gambling [Oregon lottery to offer pro football betting] *U.S. News & World Report* 107:11+ Jl 31 '89
Turkey weekend wagering [college and pro betting on Thanksgiving weekend] D. Sheridan. il *Sport (New York, N.Y.)* 80:80 D '89
FOOTBALL COACHES
See also
Agase, Alex
Bryant, Bear
Carson, Bud
Claiborne, Jerry
Davis, Mouse
Erickson, Dennis
Glanville, Jerry
Holtz, Lou
Hout, Morgan
Howard, Frank
Johnson, Jimmy
Jordan, Chuck
Landry, Tom
Ortmayer, Roland
Rutigliano, Sam, 1932-
Ryan, Buddy
Shell, Art
Simrell, Dan
Switzer, Barry
Walton, Joe
Wyche, Sam
Black named NFL coach after 7 decades [A. Shell] L. Ransom. il pors *Jet* 77:48-50 O 23 '89
Dreams do come true [A. Shell of Raiders becomes first black NFL head coach in 64 years] J. Lieber. il pors *Sports Illustrated* 71:74-8 O 23 '89
The fall of the genius coach. T. Callahan. il *Newsweek* 114:82 O 9 '89

Wins, not race, are the issue for new Raiders coach Art Shell [first black NFL head coach in modern era] J. Park. il pors *People Weekly* 32:95-6 D 4 '89
Dismissal
The ax falls at Toledo [firing of coach D. Simrell] D. S. Looney. il por *Sports Illustrated* 71:32-3 D 25 '89-Ja 1 '90
'A chapter closed' [new Dallas Cowboys owner J. Jones replaces T. Landry with J. Johnson] W. O. Johnson. il pors *Sports Illustrated* 70:22-4+ Mr 6 '89
Fired after 29 years as coach of the Cowboys, Tom Landry drops his bland, stoic mask. P. Axthelm. por *People Weekly* 31:44-5 Mr 13 '89
The last temptation of price [J. Falwell fires Liberty University football coach M. Hout] J. D. Miller. il *Sport (New York, N.Y.)* 80:12 Jl '89
FOOTBALL FANS
But let's leave those backstops up [National Fan Alliance campaigns for removal of nets behind goalposts in order to keep footballs that go into the stands] S. Rosenbloom. il *Sport (New York, N.Y.)* 80:80 Ja '89
FOOTBALL HUDDLES
Are these huddles? Or muddles? G. Morgenstein. il *TV Guide* 37:37-8 N 18-24 '89
FOOTBALL IN MOTION PICTURES
See also
NFL Films, Inc.
FOOTBALL PLAYERS
See also
Aikman, Troy
Aunese, Sal
Bailey, Johnny
Baker, John
Baur, Frank
Blount, Mel
Brister, Bubby
Carrier, Mark
Carter, Anthony
Colter, Cleveland
Courson, Steve
Craig, Roger, 1960-
Csonka, Larry
Cunningham, Randall
Davis, Ernie, 1939-1963
Dent, Richard
Dickerson, Eric
Dierdorf, Dan
Dowis, Dee
Elkins, Mike
Elway, John
Erickson, Craig
Esiason, Boomer
Fenner, Derrick
Flutie, Doug
Francis, James
Frank, John
Friesz, John
Gilbert, Sean
Griffin, Archie, 1954-
Hagan, Darian
Hampton, Dan
Harris, Tim
Hunt, Carlos
Hutson, Don, 1913-
Ismail, Raghib
Jackson, Bo
Johnson, Vance
Krein, Darren
Krumrie, Tim
Law, Brett
Lott, Ronnie, 1959-
Mack, Kevin
Majkowski, Don
Mandarich, Tony
Manley, Dexter
McCallum, Napoleon
McColl, Bill
McMahon, Jim
McNeil, Freeman
Mitchell, Scott
Montana, Joe
Morris, Joe
Nagurski, Bronko, 1908-1990
Namath, Joe
National Football League Players Association
Okoye, Christian
Oliver, Louis
Payton, Walter, 1954-
Rice, Jerry
Rice, Tony
Ridlon, Jim
Sanders, Barry
Sanders, Deion
Schroeder, Jay, 1961-
Shell, Art
Simms, Phil, 1955-
Simpson, O. J.
Stallworth, John

FOOTBALL PLAYERS—See also—*cont.*
Thurston, Fuzzy, 1933-
Tingstad, Mark
Tittle, Y. A. (Yelberton Abraham), 1926-
Toran, Stacy, 1961-1989
Waldrep, Kent
Walker, Herschel
Walsh, Steve
Ware, Andre
White, Reggie
Williams, Doug
Wilson, Otis
Wood, Willie
Woods, Ickey
Wyatt, Greg
Younger, Paul
15 black college stars hope to crack NFL lists. il *Jet* 76:46 My 15 '89
The 1989 Sport pre-season All-America team [college football] M. Francesa. il *Sport (New York, N.Y.)* 80:36 S '89
1995 All-pro team. P. Zimmerman. il *Sports Illustrated* 71:62-3 S 11 '89
The All-America team turns 100 [college football] K. Lawless. il *Sport (New York, N.Y.)* 80:14 S '89
The boys of fall [quarterback injuries] J. Czarnecki. il *Sport (New York, N.Y.)* 80:9 Ja '89
College football's bumper crop of black quarterbacks. D. C. Lyons. il *Ebony* 45:60+ N '89
The dirty dozen [linebacker ratings] J. D. Miller. il *Sport (New York, N.Y.)* 80:45-50 N '89
Our changing football heroes. B. Barnett. il *The Saturday Evening Post* 261:36+ Ja/F '89
To follow greatness [college football players] K. Dunnavant. il *Sport (New York, N.Y.)* 80:33-5+ O '89
The ultimate poll [top college football teams of all time] K. Dunnavant. il *Sport (New York, N.Y.)* 80:28-32+ D '89

Accidents and injuries
See Football, College—Accidents and injuries; Football, Professional—Accidents and injuries

Awards
See Football, College—Awards

Health and hygiene
Back to basics [ailing quarterbacks and other NFL preseason concerns; cover story] P. King. il pors *Sports Illustrated* 71:14-18+ Ag 7 '89
This is for you, Sal [Colorado routs Washington a week after death of quarterback S. Aunese] B. Newman. il *Sports Illustrated* 71:22-5 O 9 '89

Photographs and photography
Hit men [college linebackers] il *Sports Illustrated* 71:50-5 S 4 '89
Soaring into the '90s [future NFL stars] il *Sports Illustrated* 71:48-61 S 11 '89

Press relations
The hero as huckster [Super Bowl MVP J. Rice complains of being slighted by press] R. Fimrite. por *Sports Illustrated* 70:92 F 13 '89

Religious life
Sanders gives his church $1/4 million in tithes [gifts to Paradise Baptist Church, Wichita, Kan.] il por *Jet* 76:51 S 25 '89

Retirement
No bones about it [49er tight end J. Frank retires to study medicine] J. Lieber. il pors *Sports Illustrated* 71:54-8+ Ag 28 '89

Salaries, pensions, etc.
See also
Collective bargaining—Football, Professional
Dent's $6.25 million highest pact for Bears. por *Jet* 77:50 N 20 '89
The free-agency follies. P. Zimmerman. il por *Sports Illustrated* 70:82 Mr 13 '89
He's dialing for dollars [football agent L. Steinberg] il por *Sports Illustrated* 71:18-19 Ag 7 '89
Look who's paying big bucks to football players [Vikings' M. Lynn] T. Kennedy. il por *Business Week* p54 O 30 '89
The NFL's union could win by committing suicide [gaining free agency by disbanding] A. Bernstein. il por *Business Week* p84 N 27 '89
Rocky flight into first [Minnesota Vikings] J. Lieber. il por *Sports Illustrated* 71:36-8+ N 20 '89
Shake-up in Title Town [Green Bay invests heavily in free-agent market] D. S. Looney. il *Sports Illustrated* 71:34-7 Ag 28 '89
Weather or not [money, not weather, greatest factor in free agents deciding where to play] G. Castle. il *Sport (New York, N.Y.)* 80:13 O '89

Trades
See Football, Professional—Player trades

Training
See also
Football, Professional—Training camps
Double trouble [running as part of R. Craig's training] J. Brant. il pors *Runner's World* 24:30-2 O '89

Joe says it's so: New York Giants star Joe Morris reconditions for the long road back. A. Tardio. il pors *Gentlemen's Quarterly* 59:314-18+ N '89

FOOTBALL RECORDS
A high school football record gets smashed in the name of Law [running back in Sheridan, Ind.] J. Friedman. il pors *People Weekly* 32:61-2 O 23 '89
New standard for yardage [J. Bailey of Texas A&I breaks Tony Dorsett's NCAA career rushing mark] M. McKenzie. il por *Sports Illustrated* 71:96 O 23 '89
Out of the blue [Animas, N.M. high school team on longest winning streak in the country] G. Smith. il *Life* 12:82-4+ N '89

FOOTBALL SCOUTING *See* Football, Professional—Super Bowl—Scouting

FOOTBALL VIDEO GAMES *See* Video games

FOOTBALLS
A dry idea that won't soak a budget [Chuck Grant has developed a chemical product that dries wet balls] P. Fichtenbaum. il *Sport (New York, N.Y.)* 80:16 Jl '89

FOOTE, TIMOTHY, 1926-
A tale of some tails, and the story of their shy creator. bibl (p146-7) il pors *Smithsonian* 19:80-4+ Ja '89

FOOTE, CONE & BELDING COMMUNICATIONS, INC.
Foote Cone can't afford not to gamble. B. Bremner. il *Business Week* p119 Mr 13 '89

FOOTPRINTS, FOSSIL
Dinosaur tracks found, on exhibit in Virginia [Culpeper quarry; research by Robert Weems] il *Earth Science* 42:8 Fall '89
Tracking the early Permian [fossil footprints in Las Cruces, New Mexico discovered by J. P. MacDonald] L. S. Bowlds. il pors *Earth Science* 42:16-19 Summ '89
A walk along the lakeshore, dinosaur-style [footprints in Culpeper, Va. quarry; research by Robert E. Weems] R. Monastersky. il *Science News* 136:21 Jl 8 '89
A walk back through evolution [study of gaits and footprints of modern people who walk barefooted indicates Laetoli prints are not Australopithecus afarensis; work of Russell H. Tuttle] B. Bower. *Science News* 135:251 Ap 22 '89

FOOTT, JEFF
Leap of faith [photograph] il *Natural History* p112-13 O '89

FOOTWEAR
See also
Aerobics shoes
Boots
Cleated shoes
Cycling shoes
Insoles
Running shoes
Tennis shoes
Volleyball shoes
Walking shoes
Wet socks
Andy Goose steps out [G. Fleming fits footless goose with sneakers] J. Coudert. il *Reader's Digest* 135:169-70+ Jl '89
Back to basics [women's sports shoes] D. Sparrow. il *Health (New York, N.Y.)* 21:30-1+ Ag '89
Fancy footwork [beaded sneakers by M. Lightfeather] J. O'Dwyer. il por *Americana* 16:6 Ja/F '89
Feet first! il *'Teen* 33:66-7 F '89
Flatwear. J. Shields. il *Vogue* 179:100+ Ap '89
A footless goose becomes a footloose goose—in sneaks [G. Fleming fits gander with sneakers] il *People Weekly* 31:66 Ja 30 '89
Foot's paradise [athletic shoes] B. Rudolph. il *Time* 134:54-5 Ag 28 '89
For real haute dogs, these shoes are made for stalking [animal flats by E. Albanese] il *People Weekly* 32:102-3 Ag 14 '89
Get your money's worth from summer shoes [women's shoes] S. Clark. il *Glamour* 87:126 Jl '89
Gloves for the feet [Belgian Shoes] S. Dinkel. il *Gentlemen's Quarterly* 59:70 D '89
Hell on heels [effects of wearing high heeled shoes] W. Feigel. il *Runner's World* 24:30 N '89
Keeping pace [athletic shoes] R. La Ferla. il *The New York Times Magazine* p60 My 14 '89
Loafer with the fringe on top [tasseled shoes] J. Morgan. il *Gentlemen's Quarterly* 59:39 Je '89
A million-dollar body for $47.95—one pair of fleet sneaks gets you fit . . . fast. il *Mademoiselle* 95:124-7 Ja '89
My magnificent obsession [crocodile shoes] O. Edwards. il *Gentlemen's Quarterly* 59:41 Ag '89
New talents: Vanessa Noel. N. Malkin. il por *Harper's Bazaar* 122:123 Mr '89
Sneak attacks [athletic shoes] J. Kaplan. il *Vogue* 179:178+ My '89
Super shoes '89 [sports shoes for women; special section] il *Women's Sports & Fitness* 11:25+ Mr '89
An unbridled passion [saddle shoes] B. Berinsky. il *Gentlemen's Quarterly* 59:47 Ap '89
Ups and downs [effects of wearing high heeled shoes] L. Wells. il *The New York Times Magazine* p68 O 8 '89

FOOTWEAR—*cont.*

Care

See also
Dennis Green Design Group Ltd.
Shoeshine business

History

Footnotes from history: Ann Magnuson. A. Magnuson. il *Vogue* 179:122+ O '89
Stepping out in style. il *National Geographic World* 168:16-19 Ag '89

Manufacture

See Shoe industry

Prices

Has sneaker madness gone too far? [industry accused of exploiting youth] T. Barrett. il *Newsweek* 114:51 D 18 '89

FOR DEAR LIFE [drama] See Miller, Susan
FOR QUEEN AND COUNTRY [film] See Motion picture reviews—Single works
FOR SALE BY OWNER TRANSACTIONS See House selling
FORAGE PLANTS

See also
Alfalfa

Ammoniated 'junk' will feed cows. *Successful Farming* 87:33 Je '89
Late grazing for low-input cows [stockpiling forage] J. Walter. il *Successful Farming* 87:54+ O '89
FORAGING FOR EDIBLE PLANTS See Plants, Edible
FORAGING FOR SEAFOOD See Seafood gathering
FORBES, GEORGE

about

Forbes, White battle to become Cleveland mayor. il pors *Jet* 77:12 O 23 '89
FORBES, GREGORY S.

A storm chaser's dreamscape. il *Weatherwise* 42:304-6 D '89
FORBES, JAMES, JR.

about

Riverside Church in N.Y. gets 1st black sr. pastor. por *Jet* 75:23 F 20 '89
FORBES, MALCOLM S., JR.

Fact and comment II. See issues of Forbes through March 5, 1990
FORBES, MALCOLM STEVENSON

Fact and comment. See issues of Forbes through March 5, 1990
They went that-a-way [excerpt] il *The Saturday Evening Post* 261:12+ My/Je '89

about

Ali-Dada's Arabian night. M. Dougherty. il pors *People Weekly* 32:34-9 S 4 '89
Armand Hammer, 90, who doesn't have time to retire or die. A. Hammer. il por *Forbes* 143:20 Ja 23 '89
Celebrity homes. M. Fiore. il por *Good Housekeeping* 208:118-21 Mr '89
Forbes's publicity machine. J. Alter. il por *Newsweek* 114:50-1 Ag 28 '89
In defence of the freedom to spend. B. Amiel. il *Maclean's* 102:17 O 23 '89
It's your party. *The New Republic* 201:4+ S 11 '89
Malcolm Forbes, a very good pal, arrives at Liz's house bearing gifts. il pors *People Weekly* 31:152-3 Je 19 '89
Malcolm Forbes in Fiji: the publisher's private island in the South Seas. J. Taylor. il por *Architectural Digest* 46:180-8+ F '89
New standards of wretched excess. F. Bruning. il *Maclean's* 102:9 S 11 '89
". . . nothing will destroy our culture while people are free to create . . ." [interview] J. F. Cooper. il por *Forbes* 144:20+ O 2 '89
Selling with style, wit and class [interview] il por *Forbes* 144:20+ Jl 24 '89
Tapas, bulls and kings. R. Morais. il pors map *Forbes* 144:140-6+ Ag 7 '89
That party [cover story] J. Baumgold. il pors *New York* 22:30-41 O 2 '89
Tooling down the Mississippi. B. Sipchen. il pors map *Forbes* 144:22-3 O 30 '89
Two different animals: brand awareness & corporate image [interview] *Forbes* 143:20 Mr 6 '89
The ultimate Easter eggs [cover story] M. Forrest. il *Antiques & Collecting Hobbies* 94:44-5+ Mr '89
FORBES, STEVE

about

To the rescue. R. MacInnis. il pors *Runner's World* 24:36-8 Ag '89
FORBES (PERIODICAL)

Flashbacks. D. A. Saunders. See issues of Forbes
Forbes's publicity machine. J. Alter. il por *Newsweek* 114:50-1 Ag 28 '89
Selling with style, wit and class [interview with M. S. Forbes] il por *Forbes* 144:20+ Jl 24 '89
FORBES FOUR HUNDRED See Rich
FORBES MAGAZINE FABERGÉ COLLECTION See Eggs, Decorated—Collectors and collecting
THE FORBIDDEN CITY [drama] See Gunn, Bill, d. 1989
FORBIS, STEVEN J.

Reinventing the VCR. il *Video* 13:70-3+ S '89

FORCE, JULIANA

about

The Force behind the Whitney. A. Berman. il pors *American Heritage* 40:102-13 S/O '89
Juliana Force and folk art. A. Berman. il *Antiques* 136:542-53 S '89
FORCE AND ENERGY

See also
Coriolis force
Fifth force (Physics)
Quantum theory
FORCED LABOR

Namibia

'Worse than Robben Island' [Zinc and Lead Company (Namibia) Ltd.] J. Apter. *The Progressive* 53:15-16 Jl '89
FORCED MARCH [film] See Motion picture reviews—Single works
FORCING (PLANTS)

Blooming bulbs this winter? il *Sunset (Central West edition)* 183:82-4 O '89
FORD, CHARLOTTE

Etiquette: doing it right. See issues of McCall's beginning January 1987
FORD, EDSEL BRYANT, II

about

Edsel Ford. J. B. Treece. por *Business Week* Special Issue:134 Ap 14 '89
FORD, FAITH

about

Ford's flaw? Don't make her laugh. J. Marion. il por *TV Guide* 37:17 Mr 11-17 '89
Murphy Brown's Faith Ford loves puttin' on the ditz. J. Stark. il pors *People Weekly* 31:239-40 Mr 6 '89
FORD, HARRISON

about

"I've finally learned how to be happy". J. Wolf. il pors *Redbook* 173:20+ Ag '89
FORD, HENRY, 1863-1947

about

1914. A. Nielsen. il *American Heritage* 40:38-40 F '89
FORD, JOHNNY LAWRENCE, 1942-

about

Attacked by pit bulls! A. Rankin. il *Reader's Digest* 135:105-10 S '89
FORD, JUDITH E.

Educating New York's hunters. il *The Conservationist* 44:34-7 N/D '89
FORD, LOUIS HENRY

about

COGIC bishop Louis Ford lauded during 54th anniv. of his church in Chicago. il pors *Jet* 76:18 Jl 31 '89
FORD, MAURICE DEG.

Rocking the Roe boat. *Commonweal* 116:326-8 Je 2 '89
FORD, MICHAEL P., AND OHLHAUSEN, MARILYN M.

Helping disabled readers in the regular classroom. *The Education Digest* 54:48-51 Ja '89
FORD, RICHARD, 1944-

Heartbreak motels. il *Harper's* 279:12-15 Ag '89
So little time, so many rooms. il pors *Money* 18:102-4+ My '89

about

America's moral landscape in the fiction of Richard Ford. R. A. Schroth. por *The Christian Century* 106:227-30 Mr 1 '89
FORD (HENRY) MUSEUM AND GREENFIELD VILLAGE See Henry Ford Museum and Greenfield Village
FORD FAMILY

about

The Ford family wants to take the wheel again. J. B. Treece. il pors *Business Week* p32 Ja 16 '89
Ford: the family strikes back. B. Powell. il *Newsweek* 113:42 Ja 16 '89
Fords for the future [cover story] A. L. Taylor, III. il *Fortune* 119:36-40+ Ja 16 '89
FORD FOUNDATION

Not just a Tin Lizzie [effect of grants to American ballet companies in the 1960s] C. Barnes. *Dance Magazine* 63:106 O '89
FORD MODEL AGENCY

Follow that girl [Click Agency brings suit against Ford Agency over defection of R. Williams] A. Keteyian. il pors *New York* 22:38-43 Mr 6 '89
FORD MOTOR CO.

1914 [H. Ford initiates five-dollar day for employees] A. Nielsen. il *American Heritage* 40:38-40 F '89
A bid for upward mobility [Ford bids on Jaguar and Saab] A. Gabor. il *U.S. News & World Report* 107:46 O 2 '89
Caution: bumps ahead at Ford. A. L. Taylor, III. il pors *Fortune* 120:93+ D 18 '89
A dozen motor factories—under one roof [flexible manufacturing plant in Romeo, Mich.] D. Woodruff. il *Business Week* p90+ N 20 '89
Edsel Ford. J. B. Treece. por *Business Week* Special Issue:134 Ap 14 '89
Ford and PUSH sign $2.5 billion deal. H. Manly. il *Black Enterprise* 19:18 Mr '89

FORD MOTOR CO.—*cont.*

Ford and PUSH sign affirmative action pact. il *Jet* 75:8+ Ja 9 '89

The Ford family wants to take the wheel again. J. B. Treece. il pors *Business Week* p32 Ja 16 '89

Ford is kicking Saab's tires. R. A. Melcher. il *Business Week* p52 S 18 '89

Ford: the family strikes back. B. Powell. il *Newsweek* 113:42 Ja 16 '89

Ford will need someone to share the driving [A. D. Gilmour] J. B. Treece. il por *Business Week* p28 Ap 24 '89

Fords for the future [Ford family; cover story] A. L. Taylor, III. il *Fortune* 119:36-40+ Ja 16 '89

Ford's sporty new number [acquisition of Jaguar] il *Time* 134:83 N 13 '89

Have you driven a Jag, lately? [Ford buys Jaguar] D. Pauly. il *Newsweek* 114:64 N 13 '89

The hole in Ford's doughnut [pursuit of Jaguar and luxury model market] J. Flint. il *Forbes* 144:50+ N 13 '89

How to teach old plants new tricks. J. B. Treece. il *Business Week* Special Issue:130 Je 16 '89

Is Ford a blue-chip bargain? G. G. Marcial. *Business Week* p94 O 2 '89

A Jaguar buyer may be in for a long, slow drive [GM or Ford] M. Maremont. il *Business Week* p48-9 N 13 '89

The law of the jungle catches up with Jaguar. R. A. Melcher. il *Business Week* p54 O 2 '89

Red Poling sure won't have it easy. J. B. Treece. il por *Business Week* p132-3+ N 27 '89

The rise of black auto dealers. F. Rice. il *Fortune* 120:68-71 Ag 14 '89

Would you pay $2 billion for a sick cat? [GM and Ford go after Jaguar] M. Maremont. il *Business Week* p58 O 23 '89

FORD MOTOR CO. LINCOLN-MERCURY DIVISION

50 years of Mercury [cover story] F. M. H. Gregory. il *Motor Trend* 41:40-5 Ja 9 '89

FORD MOTOR CREDIT CO.

Ford Credit is learning to say 'no'. D. Woodruff. il *Business Week* p131 My 8 '89

FORD OF EUROPE INC.

Detroit's Euro-boom. J. Marcom, Jr. il *Forbes* 143:38-9 Mr 20 '89

Don't tread on us—please [Ford and GM poised to be winners in European car market] J. Flint. il *Forbes* 143:92 Je 12 '89

Why Ford's European cash cow is giving less. R. A. Melcher. il *Business Week* p136 N 27 '89

FORE (PAPUA NEW GUINEA PEOPLE)

This-fellow frog, name belong-him dakwo. J. M. Diamond. *Natural History* p16+ Ap '89

FORECASTING

See also

Architectural forecasting
Business forecasting
Congressional Clearinghouse on the Future
Economic forecasting
Educational forecasting
Franklin Institute (Philadelphia, Pa.). Science Museum and Planetarium. Futures Center
Institute for 21st Century Studies
Nineteen hundred and nineties
Political forecasting
Population forecasting
Social forecasting
Stocks—Price forecasting
Technological forecasting
Twenty-first century
Twenty-second century
Two thousand (Year)
Two thousand eighty-nine (Year)
Two thousand nine (Year)
Two thousand seventy-three (Year)
Two thousand six (Year)
Two thousand sixty (Year)
Two thousand ten (Year)
Two thousand three (Year)
Weather forecasting
World Future Society

Boom time for futurists. R. Corelli. *World Press Review* 36:26+ D '89

Early warning. See issues of World Press Review

Eight visions of our ecological future [symposium] il *Utne Reader* p92-5 N/D '89

The futures of the past. D. Macdonald. il *Maclean's* 102:44+ S 11 '89

Is everybody ready for Star trek chic? il *U.S. News & World Report* 106:16 Mr 13 '89

Now wait just a minute [scientists dispute gloomy environmental outlook] E. Linden. il *Time* 134:68 D 18 '89

Outlook '90 and beyond. il *The Futurist* 23:53-60 N/D '89

Tomorrow in brief. See issues of The Futurist

Tomorrow: newsletter. See issues of U.S. News & World Report

What lies ahead? [survey by the World Future Society] *USA Today (Periodical)* 118:3-4 Ag '89

Anecdotes, facetiae, satire, etc.

2054: a sports odyssey. R. Reilly. il *Sports Illustrated* 71 Special Issue:226-8+ N 15 '89

Interview with a disaster expert. D. E. Koshland, Jr. *Science* 246:1221 D 8 '89

Tomorrow doesn't wait. R. Blount. il *The Atlantic* 264:50+ N '89

Study and teaching

Hitting the wall. K. L. H. Fenn. il *The Futurist* 23:60 Ja/F '89

Sri Lanka

Futures studies in Sri Lanka [views of J. E. Jayasuriya] map *The Futurist* 23:35-6 Ja/F '89

FORECLOSURE

Let's make a deal [FHA and Veterans Administration loan guaranty funds] J. Novack. il *Forbes* 143:48 Ja 23 '89

Mitchell family home in Baltimore up for auction due to default on loan. *Jet* 76:9 Jl 3 '89

FOREIGN ADOPTION *See* Adoption and adopted children

FOREIGN AID *See* Economic assistance

FOREIGN AUTOMOBILES *See* Automobiles, Foreign

FOREIGN CORRESPONDENTS

Afghanistan

See also

Afghanistan—Russian invasion, 1979-1989—Reporters and reporting

Africa

Africa up close. S. Rule. il *The New York Times Magazine* p36+ Ap 30 '89

China

Thrust onto center stage [U.S. reporters covering demonstrations] L. Zuckerman. il *Time* 133:64-5 Je 5 '89

El Salvador

See also

El Salvador—Civil War, 1980- —Reporters and reporting

Great Britain

Brown-bagging it to Buckingham [reporting on Queen Elizabeth's coronation] R. Baker. il pors *The New York Times Magazine* p16-19+ Ja 1 '89

Israel

See also

Israel-Arab Wars, 1967- —Reporters and reporting

Pakistan

Bizarre bazaar. P. J. O'Rourke. il *Rolling Stone* p87-8+ Ap 20 '89

Sri Lanka

My half year of living dangerously. W. McGowan. il *Gentlemen's Quarterly* 59:152-7+ Ja '89

FOREIGN CURRENCY CASH FUNDS *See* Foreign exchange cash funds

FOREIGN DEBTS *See* Debts, External

FOREIGN EXCHANGE

See also

Balance of payments
Capital movements
International Monetary Fund

A fair exchange [handling money abroad] D. Wishik. il *Travel Holiday* 172:58-63 D '89

The Group of Seven is acting more like the Seven Dwarfs [dollar runup] M. McNamee. il *Business Week* p90 Je 5 '89

What your bucks will buy abroad this summer. K. McManus and B. Stauffer. il *Changing Times* 43:72-4+ My '89

Laws and regulations

Soviet Union

Farming for dollars: Gorbachev's latest gamble. P. Galuszka. il *Business Week* p44 Ag 28 '89

Now it's more like real money. R. Hornik. il *Time* 134:52 N 6 '89

Soviet T-bonds? They're only the beginning. R. Brady. il *Business Week* p46 N 13 '89

Soviet Union. *Business Week* p70 N 6 '89

Venezuela

A crackdown in Caracas sends foreign executives fleeing [currency scheme] G. DeGeorge. il *Business Week* p46 Jl 31 '89

FOREIGN EXCHANGE BROKERS

See also

Women foreign exchange brokers

The shadow bankers [currency brokers control dollar's fate] B. Powell. il *Newsweek* 114:47-8 O 23 '89

FOREIGN EXCHANGE CASH FUNDS

Foreign currency plays for faint hearts. E. Schultz. il *Fortune* 120:34+ O 9 '89

Like the yen? The mark? Here's an easy way to play. L. Zinn. il *Business Week* p160-1 O 23 '89

FOREIGN EXCHANGE FUTURES

Currency strategies that will pay off big if the dollar drops. S. Nasar. il *Fortune* 120:29+ Jl 3 '89

FOREIGN EXCHANGE OPTIONS

Currency strategies that will pay off big if the dollar drops. S. Nasar. il *Fortune* 120:29+ Jl 3 '89

FOREIGN LANGUAGE FILMS *See* Motion pictures—Foreign language films

FOREIGN LANGUAGES *See* Language and languages
FOREIGN MISSIONS *See* Missions
FOREIGN NEWS
See also
Bush, George, 1924—Visit to Poland, 1989—Reporters and reporting
El Salvador—Civil War, 1980- —Reporters and reporting
Gorbachev, Mikhail—Visit to Cuba, 1989—Reporters and reporting
Lebanon hostage cases, 1984- —Reporters and reporting
Tiananmen Square (China) student occupation, 1989—Reporters and reporting
The threat to foreign news. D. Rather. por *Newsweek* 114:9 Jl 17 '89
Who cares about foreigners? W. A. Henry. il *Time* 134:106 O 9 '89
FOREIGN OPINION OF THE UNITED STATES *See* United States—Foreign opinion
FOREIGN POPULATION *See* Immigrants
FOREIGN RELATIONS *See* International relations
FOREIGN RELATIONS COMMITTEE *See* United States. Congress. Senate. Committee on Foreign Relations
FOREIGN RIGHTS (BOOKS) *See* Copyright—International aspects
FOREIGN SERVICE (U.S.) *See* United States. Dept. of State. Foreign Service
FOREIGN STATION WAGONS *See* Station wagons, Foreign
FOREIGN STOCK FUNDS *See* Investment trusts
FOREIGN STOCKS *See* Stocks
FOREIGN STUDENTS

Canada
Fear—and opportunity: talented Chinese choose to stay in Canada. P. Kaihla. il *Maclean's* 102:12-13 S 25 '89
China
"Beat the black devils!" [Chinese students march against African students in Nanjing] S. Burton. il *Time* 133:37 Ja 9 '89
China: 'Kill the black devils' [Chinese college students protest against African students in Nanjing] M. Beck. il *Newsweek* 113:35 Ja 9 '89
The fallout from Nanjing [continued anti-African demonstrations by Chinese students] M. S. Serrill. il *Time* 133:38 Ja 16 '89
More than just Chinese racism [anti-African demonstrations by Chinese students] R. Seidelman. il *The Nation* 248:195-6 F 13 '89
The roots of racism are rubbed raw [Chinese college students protest against African students in Nanjing] il *U.S. News & World Report* 106:10-11 Ja 9 '89
Great Britain
'The dark forces of lust': Plath at Cambridge [excerpt from *Bitter fame*] A. Stevenson. il pors *The New York Times Book Review* 94:1+ Ag 13 '89
Spotlight on schools [summer study at Homerton College] il *Teen* 33:89 Je '89
United States
See also
Bishop Desmond Tutu Southern African Refugee Scholarship Fund
Black female student from Russia to attend U. of D.C. [A. Mensah] il por *Jet* 76:24 Ag 21 '89
China's new Long March [students keep the spirit] J. Bartholet. il *Newsweek* 114:37 Ag 7 '89
China's turmoil touches U.S. science; U.S.-Chinese scientists see dreams imperiled. M. Sun and E. Marshall. il *Science* 244:1130-2 Je 9 '89
The Chinese intelligentsia: training the new elite. F. Strebeigh. il *Current (Washington, D.C.)* 318:32-40 D '89
The Chinese student movement moves to America. A. Riles. il *The Progressive* 53:28-30 S '89
Chinese students: alone in America. *Christianity Today* 33:56 S 8 '89
Far from Beijing, Chinese students in US fear for future of science and nation. I. Goodwin. il *Physics Today* 42:45-7 Jl '89
Fax against fictions [use by Chinese students in the U.S. to send news home] il *Time* 133:32 Je 19 '89
For now, the Chinese students can stay [G. Bush vetoes legislation to extend visas of Chinese students] P. Wingert and D. Waller. il *Newsweek* 114:98 D 11 '89
Honk if you care [Chinese students in Washington, D.C. demonstrate in favor of Tiananmen Square uprising] A. McCarthy. *Commonweal* 116:393-4 Jl 14 '89
Krumhansl protests China situation, urges support for scholars in USA. *Physics Today* 42 pt1:79 Ag '89
Life after "exam hell" [Japanese student N. Hirata] P. Sudo. il por *Scholastic Update (Teachers' edition)* 122:13 D 8 '89
Notes and comment [Chinese students' views on Tiananmen massacre] *The New Yorker* 65:26-7 Je 19 '89
Outside agitators for democracy [Chinese students in U.S. keeping up protest movement] E. MacFarquhar. il *U.S. News & World Report* 107:34-5 Ag 7 '89
Stories of repression from China [problems for students in the U.S.] M. Sun. il *Science* 245:462 Ag 4 '89
Three-quarters of foreign students take postdocs [physics graduate students] P. Janowski. *Physics Today* 42:66 Ja '89

Training China's new elite. F. Strebeigh. il *The Atlantic* 263:72-80 Ap '89
U.S. response to changes in China [statements, July 13 and 20, 1989] R. L. Williams. *Department of State Bulletin* 89:27-30 O '89
Uncertain future for Chinese students. M. Sun. *Science* 246:1114 D 1 '89
Uncertain of future, Chinese students find helpful friends in high places. I. Goodwin. *Physics Today* 42 pt1:39-41 Ag '89
'Why should they die and we live?' [Chinese students react to Tiananmen Square] F. Turner. il *The Progressive* 53:15-16 Ag '89
FOREIGN STUDY
See also
Student exchange programs
The pause that refreshes. L. Tarshis. *Harper's Bazaar* 122:32+ Je '89
FOREIGN SUBSIDIARIES *See* Corporations, International
FOREIGN TRADE *See* Export-import trade
FOREIGN TRADE REGULATION
See also
General Agreement on Tariffs and Trade
FOREIGN TRADE ZONES *See* Free ports and zones
FOREIGN TRAVEL *See* Travel
FOREIGN TRUCKS *See* Trucks, Foreign
FOREIGN WORKERS *See* Alien labor
FOREIGNER (MUSICAL GROUP)
A Foreigner takes his solo sojourn [M. Jones] S. Rogers. por *Rolling Stone* p32 S 21 '89
FOREMAN, DAVE
about
Earth last! D. Russell. *The Nation* 249:77 Jl 17 '89
Monkey-wrenching for planet earth. T. Vanderpool. il por *The Progressive* 53:15 S '89
FOREMAN, GEORGE
about
Former champ Foreman turns 40, says he is ready to take on Tyson. il por *Jet* 75:46 Ja 30 '89
A slugger and a dream. R. Woodbury. il por map *Time* 134:8+ Jl 24 '89
Still hungry after all these years [cover story] R. Hoffer. il pors *Sports Illustrated* 71:60-6+ Jl 17 '89
FOREMAN, LAURA
about
Laura Foreman's houses have something to say; no longer are they just for the birds. B. Johnson. il pors *People Weekly* 31:143-4 Je 19 '89
FOREMOST-MCKESSON, INC. *See* McKesson Corp.
FORENSIC ANTHROPOLOGY
Modern technology meets Billy the Kid. il por *Newsweek* 113:28 Je 5 '89
Ningún nombre: identifying Argentina's desaparecidos. T. Beardsley. il *Scientific American* 261:18+ N '89
Old bones solve new problems [work of Douglas Owsley] E. Marshall. il *Science* 245:1185 S 15 '89
Scientists as detectives: investigating human rights. C. Snow and others. il *Technology Review* 92:42-9+ F/Mr '89
FORENSIC DENTISTRY
Tooth of the crime [dentist J. Burkes] N. Hirschfeld. il por *New York* 22:22 Je 19 '89
FORENSIC ENTOMOLOGY
The witness was a maggot. A. Underwood. il *International Wildlife* 19:34-7 My/Je '89
FORENSIC ILLUSTRATION
Faces from the future [Scott Barrows and Lewis Sadler use computer system to age photographs of missing children] G. Cowley. il *Newsweek* 113:62 F 13 '89
When society portrait artist Ralph Wolfe Cowan met a mugger, he captured him—on canvas [West Palm Beach, Fla.] il por *People Weekly* 32:91-2 S 4 '89
FORENSIC MEDICINE *See* Medical jurisprudence
FORENSIC METEOROLOGY
Forensic meteorology. S. Salamone. il *Technology Review* 92:7-8 Ap '89
FORENSIC PATHOLOGY
Coroners who miss all the clues. A. Toufexis. il *Time* 134:61 Ag 14 '89
FORENSIC PSYCHIATRY
Marcus Welby, J.D. [mental illness diagnosis and legal defense; cover story] W. Saletan and N. Watzman. *The New Republic* 200:19-22+ Ap 17 '89
FORENSIC SCULPTURE
The three faces of John List [fugitive apprehended through use of bust created from computer-aged photograph] il pors *U.S. News & World Report* 106:13 Je 12 '89
FOREST, JAMES H.
Did Jesus really mean it when he said "Love your enemies"? il *U.S. Catholic* 54:35-8 Je '89
Religious openings in the U.S.S.R. *The Christian Century* 106:848-50 S 27 '89
Russia's tenacious Old Believers. il *The Christian Century* 106:1121-3 N 29 '89
THE FOREST [drama] *See* Wilson, Robert, 1941-
FOREST CLEARCUTTING *See* Clearcutting
FOREST CONSERVATION
See also
Forest fires—Prevention and control

FOREST CONSERVATION—*cont.*
Forests [Environmental Quality Index] il *National Wildlife* 27:38 F/Mr '89
FOREST CROWN CANOPY
Photogenic science [studying the tropical forest canopy by hot air balloon; work of Francis Hallé] J. Horgan. il *Scientific American* 261:20+ D '89
Treed [exploring the tropical forest canopy by hot air balloon; work of Francis Halle and others] B. Weber. il *The New York Times Magazine* p86 D 17 '89
FOREST ECOLOGY
See also
Deforestation
Forest crown canopy
Forest fires—Controlled fires
Daniel Janzen's dry idea [dry forest re-creation in Costa Rica's Guanacaste National Park] T. A. Lewis. il pors map *International Wildlife* 19:30-6 Ja/F '89
The fragile forest [cover story; special section] il *The Courier (Unesco)* 42:3-33 Ja '89
Interdependence [work of M. Leighton in Borneo's Gunung Palung Nature Reserve] F. Graham. il *Audubon* 91:14+ My '89
Lovely cheetahs, meter-saved [California zoos use old parking meters to raise money to fund Guanacaste National Park project in Costa Rica] J. Howard. il *Sierra* 74:26 Mr/Ap '89
The past and future Amazon. P. A. Colinvaux. bibl il maps *Scientific American* 260:102-8 My '89
Slime time [reduced numbers of slime molds in Central African rain forests; research by James Cavender] il *Discover* 10:10 O '89
Tom Lovejoy and the last crusade [battle to save the Brazilian rain forest] R. Migler. il pors *Gentlemen's Quarterly* 59:286-9+ O '89
FOREST FALLOW CULTIVATION *See* Shifting cultivation
FOREST FAUNA
See also
Cracids (Birds)
Forest insects
Owls
Woodcocks
Photographs and photography
On a camera walkabout across the forest floor [work of K. Givens] P. Skinner. il *Petersen's Photographic Magazine* 17:56-8 Ja '89
FOREST FIRE ECOLOGY *See* Fire ecology
FOREST FIRE FIGHTING *See* Forest fires—Prevention and control
FOREST FIRES
See also
Fire ecology
Beyond the burn [National Park Service's handling of forest fires in Yellowstone National Park] G. O'Gara. il map *Sierra* 74:40-51 Ja/F '89
Born again [Yellowstone's recovery] T. Cahill. il *Life* 12:32-4+ Je '89
The cremation of Yellowstone Park. A. Harris. il *Field & Stream* 94:54-5+ Jl '89
Debate on forest fire policy. *Science News* 135:94 F 11 '89
Fire [Yellowstone National Park] T. Hackett. maps *The New Yorker* 65:50-4+ O 2 '89
Fire and glory [horseback trip in Yellowstone National Park] R. Rudner. il *Ms.* 18:34 S '89
Fire, then ice [D. Sholly, head ranger at Yellowstone National Park] M. Brower. il pors *People Weekly* 31:42-7 Ja 16 '89
Firestorm! [P. Hedges and children survive forest fire in the Greater Yellowstone region] J. L. Moore. il *Reader's Digest* 134:77-82 Mr '89
The flames of '88 [Yellowstone fires] G. Wuerthner. il *Wilderness* 52:40-54 Summ '89
The forest is for burning [influence of climate on Minnesota forest fires] J. S. Clark. il *Natural History* p50-3 Ja '89
The great Hinckley fire of 1894 [excerpt from Memorials of the Minnesota forest fires in the year 1894] W. Wilkinson. il *Natural History* p54-5 Ja '89
The great Yellowstone fire [cover story; special section] il *Natural History* p34-51 Ag '89
Hellroaring: fighting last summer's fires. P. M. Leschak. il *Harper's* 279:70-3 Jl '89
Incineration of Yellowstone [cover story; with editorial comment by Les Line] T. Williams. il map *Audubon* 91:4, 38-85 Ja '89
Interpreting the Yellowstone fires of 1988 [cover story; special section] bibl f il maps *BioScience* 39:678-722 N '89
Out of the ashes [Yellowstone National Park] M. McCoy. il *Bicycling* 30:100+ Jl '89
Run! [fighting forest fire in Flathead National Forest] J. D. Vickery. il *Audubon* 91:86-9 Ja '89
A season of infernos [Canada] G. W. Taylor. il *Maclean's* 102:17-18 Ag 7 '89
A season of portents: the long summer of '88: a Wyoming diary. G. Ehrlich. il *Harper's* 279:50-7 Ag '89
Senate holds hearings on NPS fire policy. il *National Parks* 63:10-11 Ja/F '89

Sifting ashes in Yellowstone [management of bison and elk in wake of forest fires] T. Williams. il *Audubon* 91:30-2+ N '89
Springtime in the Rockies [Yellowstone National Park] P. A. Witteman. il *Time* 133:94-5 My 29 '89
Terrorists torch Israeli forests. il *Audubon* 91:16 Ja '89
These woods are made for burning [fire studies of giant sequoia groves] R. Kunzig. il map *Discover* 10:86-7+ Mr '89
They nibbled while the forests burned [forest insects attack trees] R. A. Haack and W. J. Mattson. il *Natural History* p56-7 Ja '89
Yellowstone a year later [cover story] il maps *Sunset (Central West edition)* 182:108-20+ My '89
Yellowstone: better than before? E. McGowan. il *Travel Holiday* 172:22-3 Jl '89
Yellowstone: fire storm over fire management. C. Elfring. il map *BioScience* 39:667-72 N '89
The Yellowstone fires. W. H. Romme and D. G. Despain. bibl il map *Scientific American* 261:36-44+ N '89
Yellowstone lives! [recovery from forest fires] M. Satchell. il *U.S. News & World Report* 106:24-6 My 15 '89
The Yellowstone scam. M. Morrison. il *The American Spectator* 22:17-20 Ag '89
Yellowstone: the great fires of 1988 [cover story] D. Jeffery. il supp (folded map) map *National Geographic* 175:252-73 F '89
Yellowstone: the smoke clears. R. Barbee and P. Schullery. il *National Parks* 63:18-21 Mr/Ap '89
Yellowstone's 'rebirth' amid the ashes is not neat or simple, but it's real. R. Conniff. il *Smithsonian* 20:36-44+ S '89
Controlled fires
Fight fire with fire. L. Williamson. il *Outdoor Life* 183:48+ Mr '89
Political fires still smolder. W. Wood. il *The Nation* 249:162-4 Ag 7-14 '89
Wildfire in the West's woods: fire policy in the wake of the fires of 1988. G. Matzke and D. Key. il *Focus (New York, N.Y.: 1950)* 39:1-2+ Summ '89
Wildfire: it's a hot topic [Yellowstone Park] il map *National Geographic World* 169:26-31 S '89
History
Historical perspective on the Yellowstone fires of 1988. W. H. Romme and D. G. Despain. bibl f il map *BioScience* 39:695-9 N '89
Maps
Airborne surveillance will give Forest Service real-time fire maps. B. D. Nordwall. il *Aviation Week & Space Technology* 130:105+ My 29 '89
Prevention and control
See also
Airplanes in forest fire control
Image processing—Forest fire control use
Fighting fires bit by byte. S. Begley. il *Newsweek* 114:53 Ag 28 '89
Forest fire strikes home [New York State] E. Jacoby. il *The Conservationist* 44:40-3 S/O '89
FOREST FLORA *See* Forest vegetation
FOREST GENETICS *See* Tree genetics
FOREST INSECTS
Genetic engineering of trees to enhance resistance to insects [cover story] K. F. Raffa. bibl f il *BioScience* 39:524-34 S '89
They nibbled while the forests burned [forest insects attack trees] R. A. Haack and W. J. Mattson. il *Natural History* p56-7 Ja '89
FOREST MANAGEMENT
See also
Clearcutting
Fire ecology
Forest conservation
Forest fires—Controlled fires
Tree farms
United States. Forest Service
FOREST PLANTING
See also
Reforestation
FOREST PRODUCTS
See also
Timber
FOREST PRODUCTS INDUSTRY
See also
Champion International Corp.
Gregory Forest Products Inc.
International Paper Co.
Louisiana-Pacific Corp.
Lumber industry
Pope & Talbot, Inc.
Potlatch Corp.
Temple-Inland Inc.
Weyerhaeuser Company
Environmental aspects
Greenhouse gases, climate change, and U.S. forest markets. J. L. Regens and others. bibl f il *Environment* 31:4-5+ My '89
Finance
Papermakers will be as busy as beavers. J. B. Levine. il *Business Week* p101 Ja 9 '89

FOREST PRODUCTS INDUSTRY—cont.

Brazil

'Hug a tree' kiss an herb [making money saving Brazil's forests] S. Seibert. il *Newsweek* 113:50 My 1 '89

Canada

See also

Alberta-Pacific Forest Industries Inc.

MacMillan Bloedel Limited

FOREST REPRODUCTION, ARTIFICIAL *See* Reforestation

FOREST SERVICE (U.S.) *See* United States. Forest Service

FOREST SUCCESSION *See* Plant succession

FOREST VEGETATION

Surveys slash away at forest estimates. J. Raloff. *Science News* 136:124 Ag 19 '89

FORESTER SISTERS (MUSICAL GROUP)

Sitting pretty. il *Redbook* 174:114-17 N '89

FORESTIER, KATHARINE

Can't see China's forests—or its trees. *World Press Review* 36:42 S '89

FORESTRY *See* Forests and forestry

FORESTRY, URBAN *See* Urban forestry

FORESTS, NATIONAL *See* National forests

FORESTS AND FORESTRY

See also

Computers—Forestry use

Forest conservation

Forest fires

Hardwoods

Lumber industry

Lumbering

National forests

Rain forests

Reforestation

Timber

Tree farms

Trees

United States. Forest Service

Urban forestry

How fast can trees migrate? [climate models predict greenhouse warming doom for forests; research by Margaret Davis] L. Roberts. il maps *Science* 243:735-7 F 10 '89

International aspects

The fragile forest [cover story; special section] il *The Courier (Unesco)* 42:3-33 Ja '89

Alaska

Coming into clearcut [excerpt from The island within] R. K. Nelson. *Harper's* 279:28+ D '89

Alberta

The forest fight. R. Corelli. il *Maclean's* 102:60 N 13 '89

How do you say 'tim-ber' in Japanese? [investment in Alberta-Pacific Forest Industries] T. Mason. il *Business Week* p52 D 4 '89

China

Can't see China's forests—or its trees. K. Forestier. *World Press Review* 36:42 S '89

Costa Rica

Daniel Janzen's dry idea [dry forest re-creation in Guanacaste National Park] T. A. Lewis. il pors map *International Wildlife* 19:30-6 Ja/F '89

The good news: Costa Rica guards its forests. *Time* 133:35 Ja 2 '89

Lovely cheetahs, meter-saved [California zoos use old parking meters to raise money to fund Guanacaste National Park project] J. Howard. il *Sierra* 74:26 Mr/Ap '89

Germany (West)

Air pollution and forest decline in a spruce (Picea abies) forest. E.-D. Schulze. bibl f il map *Science* 244:776-83 My 19 '89

Where acids reign: do dying stands of Bavarian timber portend the future of polluted U.S. forests? [research by Ernst-Detlef Schulze; cover story] J. Raloff. il *Science News* 136:56-8 Jl 22 '89

Israel

Terrorists torch Israeli forests. il *Audubon* 91:16 Ja '89

Manchuria (China)

Shaking gold from China's treetops [harvesting pine nuts] T. B. Allen. il *International Wildlife* 19:34-6 Jl/Ag '89

New England

New England forests sought by developers [Northern Forest Lands Study] map *National Parks* 63:13-14 Mr/Ap '89

Studying the big woods. P. Byrnes. *Wilderness* 53:6+ Wint '89

Whose woods these are [cover story; with editorial comment by T. H. Watkins] N. Boucher. il map *Wilderness* 53:16-41 Fall '89

New York (State)

See also

New York Botanical Garden. Forest

Here a parcel, there a parcel—fragmented forests. M. Greason. il *The Conservationist* 44:46-9 Jl/Ag '89

North Carolina

Trouble on the wind [research by Robert I. Bruck] H. Middleton. il *Southern Living* 24:42+ Je '89

Oregon

Oregon's not-so-Sweet Home [decline in logging and mill jobs] S. Doherty. il *Newsweek* 114:55 D 11 '89

Still at loggerheads [timber industry vs. conservationists] il *Time* 134:24 Jl 10 '89

Pacific Northwest

Ancient forests agreement. P. Byrnes. il *Wilderness* 53:3-4 Wint '89

A council of trees [excerpt from The island within] R. K. Nelson. il *Life* 12:21-2+ My '89

Enough is enough [destruction of old growth forest] J. D. Hair. il *International Wildlife* 19:30 S/O '89

How the owl drove a wedge between Stroh and Audubon [beer company pulls ads from TV show on Pacific Northwest old growth forests] V. Cahan. *Business Week* p99 S 18 '89

Intimidation [advertisers cancel sponsorship of Audubon television program] L. Line. il *Audubon* 91:4 N '89

The last stand for old growth? J. Watson. il *National Wildlife* 28:24-5 D '89/Ja '90

Please don't eat the trees [damage caused by black bears] B. J. Bashin. il *Sierra* 74:22-4 Jl/Ag '89

Showdown in the treetops [confrontations over old-growth forests] M. D. Lemonick. il *Time* 134:58-9 Ag 28 '89

'The spotted owl could wipe us out'. J. B. Levine. il *Business Week* p94+ S 18 '89

Succession. J. Metzler. il *Sierra* 74:71-2+ N/D '89

Switzerland

See also

Sihlwald Forest (Switzerland)

Are the Swiss forests in peril? C. Mehr. il map *National Geographic* 175:636-51 My '89

Vancouver Island (B.C.)

A towering fight [proposed logging of Sitka spruce] H. Quinn. il *Maclean's* 102:46 Je 5 '89

Western States

Climate change: boon to western trees? [research by Steven W. Running] J. Raloff. *Science News* 136:127 Ag 19 '89

Wyoming

Hunting for an elusive hunter [field studies of American martens] S. Buskirk and H. Harlow. il *National Wildlife* 28:20-3 D '89/Ja '90

FORETICH, ERIC A.

about

A courageous mother's first taste of freedom [cover story] J. S. Podesta and P. Chin. il pors *People Weekly* 32:78-80+ O 16 '89

A hard case of contempt. J. Elson. il por *Time* 134:66 S 18 '89

Morganatic marriage. *The New Republic* 201:4+ Jl 31 '89

Stalemate for high stakes. P. Chin and J. S. Podesta. il pors *People Weekly* 31:84-5 Ja 23 '89

Vowing to protect her child from rape, Elizabeth Morgan faces her 23rd month in jail. P. Chin. il pors *People Weekly* 31:113-15+ Je 12 '89

Who's to ¶udge? M. Szegedy-Maszak. il pors *The New York Times Magazine* p28-9+ My 21 '89

FORETICH, HILARY

Custody case

A courageous mother's first taste of freedom [cover story] J. S. Podesta and P. Chin. il pors *People Weekly* 32:78-80+ O 16 '89

Elizabeth Morgan. il pors *People Weekly* 32:97-8 D 25 '89-Ja 1 '90

Elizabeth Morgan's brother risks jail as he joins her in defying a Washington judge. D. Grogan. il pors *People Weekly* 32:38-40 Jl 3 '89

A hard case of contempt. J. Elson. il por *Time* 134:66 S 18 '89

Morganatic marriage. *The New Republic* 201:4+ Jl 31 '89

A mother's 759 days of defiance. il por *U.S. News & World Report* 107:12-13 O 9 '89

Stalemate for high stakes. P. Chin and J. S. Podesta. il pors *People Weekly* 31:84-5 Ja 23 '89

Update on Elizabeth Morgan. il por *Glamour* 87:116 S '89

Vowing to protect her child from rape, Elizabeth Morgan faces her 23rd month in jail. P. Chin. il pors *People Weekly* 31:113-15+ Je 12 '89

Who's to judge? M. Szegedy-Maszak. il pors *The New York Times Magazine* p28-9+ My 21 '89

FOREVER, LULU [film] *See* Motion picture reviews—Single works

FORGERY

See also

Art—Forgeries

Bronzes—Forgeries

Checks—Forgeries

Counterfeits and counterfeiting

Desktop forgery

Manuscripts, American—Forgeries

A "hoax" observed [panel finds charges against executor of C. S. Lewis' literary estate unsubstantiated] R. Frame. il pors *Christianity Today* 33:64-5 Je 16 '89

Unscrambling the C. S. Lewis 'hoax' [book by K. Lindskoog] L. W. Dorsett. *The Christian Century* 106:208-9 F 22 '89

FORGETFULNESS *See* Memory

FORGING AND FORGINGS

See also

Blacksmiths and blacksmithing

Wyman-Gordon Co.

FORGIONE, LARRY
about
Larry's home cooking. G. Greene. il por *New York* 22:72+ Mr 27 '89

FORGIVENESS
Are you a fool to forgive a cheat? D. Heyn. *Mademoiselle* 95:138 S '89
Are you a forgiving person? [excerpt from You'll see it when you believe it] W. W. Dyer. *Redbook* 173:96-7+ Ag '89
Forgiveness [Mary Magdalene] P. J. Ryan. il *America* 160:567 Je 10 '89

A FORGOTTEN TUNE FOR THE FLUTE [film] See Motion picture reviews—Single works

FORKNER, BEN
A voice from the broom closet: an interview on French university life. *America* 160:585-6+ Je 17-24 '89

FORLANI, ARNALDO
about
Italy's DC recycles Forlani. S. F. Senigallia. il *The New Leader* 72:9-10 Mr 6 '89

FORM (AESTHETICS)
See also
Natural forms

FORM IN BIOLOGY See Morphology

FORM PERCEPTION
Homework [shape and color games for children] H. E. H. Aycock. il *Compute!* 11:114 N '89

FORMALDEHYDE
Formaldehyde caution [nail hardeners] *Health (New York, N.Y.)* 21:66 Ag '89
Was adenine the first purine? A. W. Schwartz and C. G. Bakker. bibl f il *Science* 245:1102-4 S 8 '89

FORMAN, BRENDA
Are we serious about a commercial launch industry? *Ad Astra* 1:3 Je '89
How politics killed Landsat. il *Omni (New York, N.Y.)* 11:22+ Ap '89
Lunar labors lost. il *Omni (New York, N.Y.)* 11:16+ Jl '89

FORMAN, MICHAEL ROBERT
about
"Forman's folly". R. King. il *Forbes* 143:72 Mr 6 '89

FORMAN, MILOŠ
about
Valmont [film] Reviews
  Commonweal 116:670-1 D 1 '89. T. O'Brien
  Life il 12:70-5 Spr '89. T. Skari
  Maclean's il 102:82-3 N 20 '89. B. D. Johnson
  The Nation 249:727-8 D 11 '89. S. Klawans
  The New Republic 201:24-5+ D 11 '89. S. Kauffmann
  New York 22:122 N 20 '89. D. Denby
  The New Yorker 65:105-7 N 27 '89. P. Kael
  Newsweek il 114:77 N 20 '89. J. Kroll
  Rolling Stone il p48 N 30 '89. P. Travers
  Time il 134:92 N 20 '89. R. Schickel
  Vogue il 179:252-3 N 1 '89. J. Morgenstern

FORMOSA PLASTICS CORP.
Taiwan's U.S. strategy. R. Simon. il *Forbes* 143:43-4 My 29 '89

FORMS, BLANKS, ETC.
See also
Ennis Business Forms, Inc.
Tax returns
Effortless forms at a fair price [Horizon] H. F. Beechhold. il *Home Office Computing* 7:84+ D '89
Forms for every function [computer programs] S. Rosenthal. il *Home Office Computing* 7:28+ My '89
Forms management strategies. C. O'Malley. il *Personal Computing* 13:74-7+ Ag '89
FormSet [computer program] B. Gingher. il *Compute!* 11:64-5 Ap '89
FormSet [computer program] B. Hunt. il *Home Office Computing* 7:62-3 Jl '89
FormWorx goes GUI. S. Miastkowski. il *Byte* 14:86+ N '89
How to format documents quickly and accurately [using templates with any word processor] H. F. Beechhold. il *Home Office Computing* 7:30-1 F '89
Professional-quality forms design [PerForm] R. Geist and H. Geist. il *Home Office Computing* 7:86+ D '89

FORMS OF ADDRESS
See also
Catholic Church—Clergy—Titles
Nuns—Titles

FORMULA, INFANTS' See Infant formula

FORMULA ONE CONSTRUCTOR'S ASSOCIATION
Bernie's "dog and pony show". R. Behar. il por *Forbes* 143:64 F 20 '89

IL FORNAIO (SAN FRANCISCO, CALIF.: RESTAURANT)
See San Francisco (Calif.)—Restaurants, nightclubs, bars, etc.

FORNARA, PETER
Home sharing as a housing alternative. *Utne Reader* p71 My/Je '89

FORNASETTI, PIERO, 1913-1988
about
Classic lines. P. Kinmonth. il *Vogue* 179:344-6 Ap '89

IL FORNO (SANTA MONICA, CALIF.: RESTAURANT)
See Santa Monica (Calif.)—Restaurants, nightclubs, bars, etc.

FORQUET, FEDERICO
about
Noble Roman. M. Mewshaw. il por *House & Garden* 161:128-39+ My '89

FORREST, MICHAEL
Happy birthday, Shirley! il pors *Antiques & Collecting Hobbies* 94:30-2 Ap '89
Remarkable Sèvres [cover story] il *Antiques & Collecting Hobbies* 94:31-4+ D '89
The ultimate Easter eggs [cover story] il *Antiques & Collecting Hobbies* 94:44-5+ Mr '89
Wow! Barbie is thirty! il *Antiques & Collecting Hobbies* 94:22-5 S '89

FORRESTAL, ROBERT PATRICK, 1931-
Europe's economic integration in 1992 [address, May 3, 1989] *Vital Speeches of the Day* 55:633-5 Ag 1 '89
The international economic outlook for 1989 [address, January 19, 1989] *Vital Speeches of the Day* 55:367-9 Ap 1 '89

FORRESTER, JAY WRIGHT, 1918-
about
Dr. Doom. R. Bailey. il por *Forbes* 144:44+ O 16 '89

FORSE, BILL
. . . or is the desert really moving? *World Press Review* 36:33-5 Ap '89

FORSHEE, RON
about
With Ron Forshee's Granny Fannies, suburban gardeners can exhibit some early bloomers. il por *People Weekly* 31:105 My 15 '89

FORSKOLIN
Autonomic regulation of a chloride current in heart. R. D. Harvey and J. R. Hume. bibl f il *Science* 244:983-5 My 26 '89

FÖRSTER, THERESE HERBERT- See Herbert-Förster, Therese

FORSTNER BITS See Bits (Drilling and boring)

FORSYTH, BILL
about
Breaking in [film] Reviews
  The New Republic 201:24-5 O 23 '89. S. Kauffmann
  The New Yorker 65:109-10 O 16 '89. P. Kael
  People Weekly 32:14 O 16 '89. R. Novak

FORSYTH (GA.)
Crime
Death of a bard [F. Fowle stabbed to death] T. Moore. il pors *U.S. News & World Report* 107:20-1+ Jl 31 '89

FORSYTH COUNTY (GA.)
Race relations
A turn in Atlanta [protest march against racism] V. S. Naipaul. il *The New York Review of Books* 35:52-7 Ja 19 '89

FORSYTHE, WILLIAM
about
Dancing:
  Comparison of W. Forsythe and M. Morris. A. Croce. *The New Yorker* 65:70-2 Jl 31 '89
Impressing the czar [ballet] Reviews
  The New Leader il 72:20 N 27 '89. L. A. Jacobs

FORT COLLINS (COLO.)
Gardens and gardening
Water-saving ideas in Fort Collins [xeriscape demonstration garden] il *Sunset (Central West edition)* 182:242 My '89

FORT JEFFERSON NATIONAL MONUMENT (FLA.)
Military sonic booms shake Fort Jefferson. il *National Parks* 63:10-11 Mr/Ap '89

FORT LAUDERDALE (FLA.)
Historic houses, sites, etc.
See also
Stranahan House (Fort Lauderdale, Fla.)
Housing
Working for our cities [B. Lindsey, executive director of the Housing Authority] D. Young. il pors *Southern Living* 24:141-2+ S '89

FORT MITCHELL (KY.)
Galleries and museums
See also
Vent Haven Museum

FORT MOJAVE TELECOMMUNICATIONS, INC.
Smoke on the line [D. Segress wins cellular licenses for American Indian-owned companies] F. Meeks. il *Forbes* 144:114+ S 4 '89

FORT MYERS (FLA.)
Description
Fort Myers, Fla. il map *New Choices for the Best Years* 29:12 Mr '89

FORT NELSON (PORTSMOUTH, ENGLAND)
A folly no more. D. Gregory. il *History Today* 39:3-4 Je '89

FORT PECK DAM (MONT.) See Dams

FORT TRYON PARK (NEW YORK, N.Y.)
Altimeter man [W. Peet demonstrates efficacy of hand-held altimeter in exploring Fort Tryon Park] *The New Yorker* 65:48-50 S 25 '89

FORT WAYNE (IND.)
Social history
Where I grew up: Shelley Long [interview] L. Konner. il pors map *Glamour* 87:155 My '89
FORT WORTH (TEX.)
Airports
Airport '89 [H. R. Perot's Alliance Airport receives federal funding] E. Buckberg. *The New Republic* 201:12-13 Ag 21 '89
Arts
See also
Caravan of Dreams
Economic conditions
Still where the real West begins. D. Pedersen. il *Newsweek* 113:45 F 6 '89
Galleries and museums
See also
Kimbell Art Museum
Gardens and gardening
The flowering of Fort Worth [garden designed for A. Bass by R. Page] C. Burden. il por *House & Garden* 161:84-91+ F '89
Restaurants, nightclubs, bars, etc.
Also on the menu—tradition [Joe T. Garcia's Mexican Dishes] D. Young. il *Southern Living* 24:110-12+ My '89
FORT WORTH ZOOLOGICAL PARK
Rounding up Texas critters. il *Southern Living* 24:45 N '89
FORTABAT, AMALIA DE
about
Argentine elan: Amalia Lacroze de Fortabat in Buenos Aires. J. Gruen. il por *Architectural Digest* 46:202-7+ Mr '89
FORTE, CHARLES FORTE, BARON
about
Diana slept here. J. Marcom, Jr. il *Forbes* 143:116+ My 15 '89
FORTEY, RICHARD A.
(jt. auth) See Briggs, Derek E. G., and Fortey, Richard A.
FORTHMAN, MARY
about
Not your typical family-business wife. S. Nelton. il por *Nation's Business* 77:40 Ag '89
FORTIER, PIERRE
about
A mover and shaker. P. Chisholm. por *Maclean's* 102:32 Mr 13 '89
FORTIER, STEVEN M., AND GILETTI, BRUNO J.
An empirical model for predicting diffusion coefficients in silicate minerals. bibl f il *Science* 245:1481-4 S 29 '89
FORTIFICATION
Great Britain
See also
Hull (England)—Fortification
FORTIN, LOUIS P.
Adventures of a reluctant Forty-sixer. il *The Conservationist* 44:10-15 N/D '89
IL FORTINO (CAPRI ISLAND, ITALY: COUNTRY ESTATE) *See* Country estates—Capri Island (Italy)
FORTRAN (COMPUTER LANGUAGE)
A FORTRAN for the Mac forces [Language Systems FORTRAN] D. Barker and L. H. Loeb. *Byte* 14:102 F '89
FORTUNE, DARRYLL
How to keep from getting ripped off. il *Ebony* 44:62+ Mr '89
FORTUNE, MARK A.
Food, glorious food. il *Black Enterprise* 19:74-6+ My '89
Vaulting into new ventures. il *Black Enterprise* 19:245-6+ Je '89
FORTUNE, ROBERTA
about
Mail-order success only looks easy . . . D. E. Gumpert. il pors *Working Woman* 14:37-8+ Jl '89
FORTUNE TELLING
See also
Astrology
Tarot
FORTUNY Y MADRAZO, MARIANO
about
Feats with pleats. J. McLaughlin. il *Harper's Bazaar* 122:128+ O '89
FORTY HOURS' DEVOTION
Forty hours [devotions for end to AIDS at Most Holy Redeemer Catholic Church in San Francisco] T. McGrath. il *U.S. Catholic* 54:20-7 N '89
FORWARD-LOOKING INFRARED SENSORS *See* Detectors, Infrared
FOSHAY, WILBUR B.
about
Minneapolis, D.C. il *American Heritage* 40:106-7 Jl/Ag '89
FOSKETT, J. KEVIN, AND MELVIN, JAMES E.
Activation of salivary secretion: coupling of cell volume and [Ca^{2+}], in single cells. bibl f il *Science* 244:1582-5 Je 30 '89
FOSLER, R. SCOTT
Demographics of the 90s [address, April 12, 1989] *Vital Speeches of the Day* 55:572-6 Jl 1 '89

FOSS, JOE
about
Top Gun. G. Smith. il pors *Sports Illustrated* 71:56-62+ Ag 7 '89
FOSSEL, PETER V.
Rural persuasion. See issues of Country Journal beginning April 1988
FOSSIL MAN *See* Man, Prehistoric
FOSSIL MICROORGANISMS *See* Micropaleontology
FOSSIL PLANTS *See* Paleobotany
FOSSILS *See* Paleontology
FOSSILS, LIVING *See* Living fossils
FOSTER, DOUGLAS
Yuppie activists: not an oxymoron. *Utne Reader* p96 Jl/Ag '89
FOSTER, EDWARD J.
3 top combi-players. il *Stereo Review* 54:94-9 D '89
FOSTER, GREG
about
Greg Foster marries, returns to competition. il por *Jet* 77:36 D 18 '89
FOSTER, HAROLD D.
Reducing the incidence of disease: clues from the environment. bibl f il maps *Environment* 31:12-17+ Ap '89
FOSTER, J. S.
(jt. auth) See Mizes, H. A., and Foster, J. S.
FOSTER, JODIE
about
America's 10 most beautiful women. T. Gold. il pors *Harper's Bazaar* 122:158+ S '89
Jodie Foster takes a stand in 'The accused'. S. Roman. il pors *Video* 13:14 My '89
FOSTER, KENNETH R., AND BAU, HAIM H.
Symbolic manipulation programs for the personal computer. bibl f il *Science* 243:679-84 F 3 '89
FOSTER, KIMBERLY
about
Kimberly Foster. K. Turan. por *TV Guide* 37:8 S 23-29 '89
FOSTER, MIKE
A battle of words with the IRS. il *Nation's Business* 77:42+ Mr '89
FOSTER, NORMAN, 1935-
about
Heroic transformations. D. Dietsch. il *Architectural Record* 177:72-83 S '89
FOSTER, PETER
about
Australian convicted in 'Cho Low' fraud. il por *FDA Consumer* 23:35 D '89/Ja '90
FOSTER, TOM C., AND OTHERS
Spatial selectivity of rat hippocampal neurons: dependence on preparedness for movement. bibl f il *Science* 244:1580-2 Je 30 '89
FOSTER HOME CARE
See also
LIFE Program
"Are you going to love me?" Children with AIDS. E. Steinbaum. il *McCall's* 116:57-9 Jl '89
Foster home recruitment and retention: a success story [Prince Georges County, Md.] D. Phelps. il *Children Today* 18:7-9+ Mr/Ap '89
Sharing the farm with kids in need. B. Freese. il *Successful Farming* 87:56 D '89
Specialized foster family care: a community-based program for children with special needs [Charles County, Md.] M. Luginbill and A. Spiegler. il *Children Today* 18:5-9 Ja/F '89
Youth in transition [need for more services for those moving from foster care to independent living] il *Children Today* 18:2-3 Mr/Ap '89
FOSTLE, D. W.
The roaring twenties [excerpt from Speedboat] il *Motor Boating & Sailing* 163:78-81+ Ja '89
FOTHERINGHAM, ALLAN, 1932-
Canadians cope, Americans conquer. *World Press Review* 36:36 Ap '89
Column. See issues of Maclean's
FOUCAULT, MICHEL, 1926-1984
about
On not understanding Michel Foucault. J. Weightman. *The American Scholar* 58:383-406 Summ '89
FOUCHECOUR, CHARLES-HENRI DE
Hafez: the golden age of Persian literature. il *The Courier (Unesco)* 42:13-16 Mr '89
FOUL SHOOTING (BASKETBALL) *See* Free throw shooting (Basketball)
FOUND MONEY
In good faith [out-of-work Chicagoan J. Loveras returns contents of missing briefcase to Japanese owner] B. Greene. il pors *Esquire* 111:67-8 Mr '89
The stolen briefcase [J. Loveras returns contents to Japanese owner] B. Greene. il *Reader's Digest* 134:23-4+ Je '89
FOUNDATION FOR ENVIRONMENTAL CONSERVATION
Foundation for Environmental Conservation. N. Polunin. *Environment* 31:44-5 My '89

FOUNDATION FOR INTERNATIONAL COMMUNITY AS-SISTANCE
Foundation for International Community Assistance. M. Kelly. il *Utne Reader* p77 Ja/F '89
Villagers get capital ideas [assistance to women in developing countries] J. Jenner. il *Ms.* 17:73 Je '89

FOUNDATION GARMENTS
See also
Brassieres

FOUNDATION PLANTING *See* Landscape gardening

FOUNDATIONS, CHARITABLE AND EDUCATIONAL
See also
Albert Hofmann Foundation
Americares Foundation
Andrew W. Mellon Foundation
Bagby Foundation for the Musical Arts
Barbara Bush Foundation for Family Literacy
Barnes Foundation (Merion, Pa.)
Better Homes Foundation
Business Council for Effective Literacy
Chi Chi Rodriguez Youth Foundation
Congressional Black Caucus Foundation
Delancey Street Foundation
Doug Williams Foundation
Ford Foundation
Giraffe Project
I Have a Dream Foundation
International Foundation for the Survival and Development of Humanity
International Oceanographic Foundation
John D. and Catherine T. MacArthur Foundation
Katalysis Foundation
Lilly Endowment, Inc.
Mark Rothko Foundation
Pediatric AIDS Foundation
Pew Charitable Trusts
Pollock-Krasner Foundation
Sister Thea Bowman Black Catholic Educational Foundation
Starlight Foundation
Windstar Foundation
Winthrop Rockefeller Foundation
Women's Sports Foundation
World Research Foundation

Canada
See also
Young Naturalist Foundation

Communist countries
See also
Soros Foundation

Eastern Europe
See also
Soros Foundation

Spain
See also
Fundación Casa Ducal de Medinaceli

FOUNDATIONS (BUILDING)
A close look at wood foundations. D. Johnson. il *The Family Handyman* 39:10+ N/D '89

Insulation
See Insulation (Heat)

Maintenance and repair
Dealing with an old foundation. B. Vila. il *Popular Mechanics* 166:32+ Ap '89

FOUNDATIONS (COSMETICS) *See* Cosmetics

FOUNDERS SAVINGS & LOAN ASSOCIATION
CEOs shift at S&Ls: one moves over, other moves out. S. Herbert. il *Black Enterprise* 19:13 Jl '89

FOUNTAIN, JANE W., AND OTHERS
Physical mapping of a translocation breakpoint in neurofibromatosis. bibl f il *Science* 244:1085-7 Je 2 '89

FOUNTAIN COFFEE ROOM (BEVERLY HILLS, CALIF.)
See Beverly Hills (Calif.)—Restaurants, nightclubs, bars, etc.

FOUNTAIN OF YOUTH STAKES *See* Horse racing

FOUNTAIN PENS *See* Pens

FOUNTAINS
Water music [gardens] D. Hufford. il *Flower and Garden* 33:20-3 S/O '89

Switzerland
See also
Bern (Switzerland)—Fountains

FOUR ADVENTURES OF REINETTE AND MIRABELLE [film] See Motion picture reviews—Single works

FOUR SEASONS (NEW YORK, N.Y.: RESTAURANT) *See* New York (N.Y.)—Restaurants, nightclubs, bars, etc.

FOUR SEASONS HOTELS LIMITED
Four Seasons heads for the beach. C. Hawkins. il por *Business Week* p111 Ap 24 '89
Sharp's luxury empire [cover story; special section] il por *Maclean's* 102:30-4+ Je 5 '89

FOUR WALLS EIGHT WINDOWS (FIRM)
Four Walls, Eight Windows, lots of ideas. J. Barbato. *Publishers Weekly* 235:58 Mr 10 '89

FOUR WHEEL DRIVE VEHICLES
See also
Automobiles—Four wheel drive
Automobiles, Foreign—Four wheel drive

Automobiles, Racing—Four wheel drive
Sports cars—Four wheel drive
Station wagons, Foreign—Four wheel drive
Tractors—Four wheel drive
Trucks—Four wheel drive
Trucks, Foreign—Four wheel drive
Vans—Four wheel drive
Driving 4 fun. J. Voelcker. il *Essence* 20:110 My '89
Four-wheel-drive vehicles aren't just for outdoorsmen anymore. M. Thomas. il *Vogue* 179:248 Ag '89
Off-road in style [Vehma International's Torrero] D. McCosh. il *Popular Science* 234:18 Je '89
Power truckin'. T. Swan and J. Dunne. il *Popular Mechanics* 166:67-70 N '89
Sport/utility [special section] il *Popular Mechanics* 166:109+ Mr '89

Maintenance and repair
Pounds of prevention. B. W. Smith. il *Popular Mechanics* 166:128-9 Mr '89

Testing
4-doors for all seasons. T. Swan. il *New Choices for the Best Years* 29:84+ D '89
4Runner. J. Miller. il *Motor Trend* 41:105-7 Jl '89
Anytime . . . anywhere [Lamborghini LM002] D. Chaikin. il *Home Mechanix* 85:68 Jl '89
Back-country brute [Lamborghini LM002] T. Swan. il *Popular Mechanics* 166:42-3 S '89
Dirt rods. R. Taylor and R. Millen. il *Popular Mechanics* 166:113-16+ Mr '89
Dustbusters! [Geo Tracker, Isuzu Amigo XS, Jeep Wrangler Islander, and Suzuki Samurai JL in the Mojave Desert] A. Assenza. il *Car and Driver* 35:136-40+ N '89
Fighting instinct. S. L. White. il *Field & Stream* 94:78+ My '89
Goodness gracious, it's the Greenbrier [testing the Range Rover] W. Jeanes. il *Car and Driver* 34:143 F '89
Great Lakes and ghosts [touring in a Ford Bronco II] M. B. Lewis. il *Car and Driver* 34:187 Ja '89
How safe is the Ford Bronco II? [Geo Tracker, Dodge Raider, Chevrolet S-10] il *Consumer Reports* 54:393-402 Je '89
Isuzu Amigo XS 4WD. A. Assenza. il *Car and Driver* 34:165-7+ Je '89
Keeping pace [Toyota 4Runner] S. L. White. il *Field & Stream* 94:84-6 D '89
Laforza. B. J. Hoffman. il *Motor Trend* 41:127-8+ Je '89
Laforza. R. Homan. il *Road & Track* 40:142 Je '89
Laforza. P. Lyons. il *Car and Driver* 34:175-6+ Je '89
Laforza: beauty and the beast. B. Brazier. il *Popular Mechanics* 166:70 N '89
Life with Range Rover [long-term test] N. Bissoon Dath. il *Car and Driver* 34:156+ Je '89
New four-door 4x4 [Mitsubishi Montero] T. Opre. il *Outdoor Life* 183:42+ Mr '89
Nissan Pathfinder SE. P. Bedard. il *Car and Driver* 35:147-9 O '89
Personal pick. T. Opre. il *Outdoor Life* 183:20+ Je '89
Range Rover. M. Anson. il *Motor Trend* 41:152-3+ My '89
Range Rover. J. Dinkel. il *Road & Track* 40:54+ F '89
The Range Rover: a British brute with good manners. R. Mitchell. il *Business Week* p116 S 4 '89
Smooth operator [Mitsubishi Montero] S. L. White. il *Field & Stream* 93:72+ Mr '89
Toyota 4Runner. L. Griffin. il *Car and Driver* 35:111-13 Ag '89
Trendy Toyota 4Runner. T. Opre. il *Outdoor Life* 184:32+ Jl '89
Trooper II to go [Isuzu] T. Opre. il *Outdoor Life* 184:50+ D '89
User friendly 4x4 [Isuzu Amigo] T. Opre. il *Outdoor Life* 184:36+ S '89

Vibration
Hope for hop [1987 Ford Bronco II] P. Brand. il *The Family Handyman* 39:96 My '89

FOUR WHEEL DRIVE VEHICLES, REMODELED
A Bronco with a stretch [Magnum Motor Coach] T. Opre. il *Outdoor Life* 183:28+ F '89

FOUR WHEEL STEERING (AUTOMOBILES) *See* Automobiles, Foreign—Steering gear

FOURIER TRANSFORMATION
The Fourier transform. R. N. Bracewell. bibl il *Scientific American* 260:86-9+ Je '89

FOURNIER, BILL
about
On the trail of a shot. R. Kokernak. il por *Country Journal* 16:37-41 Ja '89

FOURNIER, CLAIRE
A visit to an Uzbek family. il *The Unesco Courier* 42:46-7 Jl '89

FOURTH COMMITTEE (UNITED NATIONS) *See* United Nations. Decolonization Committee

FOURTH DIMENSION *See* Hyperspace

FOURTH OF JULY
A prayer for July Fourth [mother's hope for son] E. Harrington. il *Reader's Digest* 135:121-2 Jl '89
Remembering the first Fourth [Old Salem] il *Southern Living* 24:41 Jl '89
Star-spangled summer picnic. il *Redbook* 173:101-5+ Jl '89

FOURTH OF JULY COOKIES *See* Cookies
FOURTOU, JEAN-RENÉ
about
On the prowl in America. J. Zweig. il por *Forbes* 143:154 My 1 '89
FOWL SHOOTING *See* Game bird shooting; Water bird shooting
FOWLE, FRANK FULLER
about
Death of a bard. T. Moore. il pors *U.S. News & World Report* 107:20-1+ Jl 31 '89
FOWLER, CHARLES B.
Conditioning artists for teaching. *Design for Arts in Education* 90:30-4 Ja/F '89
Making the grade. il *Opera News* 54:35-6+ N '89
FOWLER, JACK
The war within the states. *National Review* 41:35-6 Ag 4 '89
FOWLER, JOHN, 1906-1977
about
The House of Lancaster [excerpt from Colefax & Fowler] C. Jones. il pors *House & Garden* 161:188-95+ N '89
FOWLER, KAREN JOY
Faded roses [fiction] *Omni (New York, N.Y.)* 12:108-10 N '89
FOWLER, KENNETH
Bertrand Du Guesclin—careerist in arms? bibl il pors *History Today* 39:37-43 Je '89
FOWLER, RAYMOND D.
Vive la différence. il por *Psychology Today* 22:78 D '88
FOWLER, RICHARD A., 1948-
Feeling saved. il *Christianity Today* 33:26-7 Ap 7 '89
FOWLER BROTHERS (LOS ANGELES, CALIF.: BOOKSTORE) *See* Booksellers and bookselling—California
FOWLIE, WALLACE, 1908-
Remembering Renan. *The American Scholar* 58:245-56 Spr '89
FOX, BILL
Shooting soccer strategies. il *Petersen's Photographic Magazine* 18:38-40+ S '89
FOX, CHAPPIE
about
The parade that's making Milwaukee famous. L. A. Goth. il *Reader's Digest* 134:154-60 Je '89
FOX, KAY
about
Suspect vaccine. H. S. Miller. il por *Ms.* 17:81-2 Ap '89
FOX, MARGARET
about
The taste of Mendocino. M. Barrier. il por *Nation's Business* 77:11-12 Je '89
FOX, MATTHEW, 1940-
about
Original blessing, not original sin [interview] S. Keen. il pors *Psychology Today* 23:54-8 Je '89
The taming of a New Age prophet. R. Brow. il *Christianity Today* 33:28-30 Je 16 '89
FOX, MEGAN
The influence of the pictorialists on the art of photography. il *Antiques* 136:120-31 Jl '89
FOX, MICHAEL J.
about
Facing the future [cover story] S. Pond. il pors *Gentlemen's Quarterly* 59:266-71+ N '89
Getting back to his future [cover story] M. Alexander. il pors *People Weekly* 32:142-4+ D 4 '89
Michael J. Fox: what's next? A. Sachs. il pors *McCall's* 116:71+ Jl '89
FOX, MICHAEL J., AND POLLAN, MICHAEL
Michael J. Fox's nuptials in hell! il pors map *Esquire* 111:136-8+ Je '89
FOX, MICHAEL W., 1937-
Pet life. See issues of McCall's beginning March 1986
FOX, NICOLS
What are our real values? por *Newsweek* 113:8 F 13 '89
FOX, NILES, AND OTHERS
Metastatic hibernomas in transgenic mice expressing an α-amylase-SV40 T antigen hybrid gene. bibl f il *Science* 244:460-3 Ap 28 '89
FOX, SAMANTHA
about
Music makers: lend an ear! pors *Teen* 33:50 Je '89
FOX, TERRY, 1943-
about
The Anchorage. *The New Yorker* 65:35-6 S 18 '89
FOX BROADCASTING COMPANY
Demos do the talking [targets under 34 age group] M. Couzens. il *Channels (New York, N.Y.: 1986)* 9:20 Mr '89
Fox elbows into the networks' big picture. R. Grover. il por *Business Week* p74+ F 20 '89
The great Fox chase. T. Carson. il *American Film* 14:14 Je '89
Ready for prime time. J. Hammer. il por *Newsweek* 114:68-70 D 25 '89
With a little help from my TV [health-oriented campaign called Life: be in it] M. Edelston. il *American Health* 8:38 Je '89

FOX HUNTING
Hunt country [master of the hunt R. Smith-Ryland's 16th century farmhouse in Warwickshire] G. Nevill. il pors *House & Garden* 161:132-9 Mr '89
FOX INC.
Fox elbows into the networks' big picture. R. Grover. il por *Business Week* p74+ F 20 '89
FOX SOFTWARE INC.
Litigating a standard [Ashton-Tate suit against Fox Software] C. Strehlo. *Personal Computing* 13:73 Mr '89
FOXES
See also
Fox hunting
Photographs and photography
The invisible world of Alaska's Arctic fox. J. Zuckerman. il *Petersen's Photographic Magazine* 18:86-7 N '89
FOXGLOVES
Foxgloves' new faces. il *Sunset (Central West edition)* 183:60-1 S '89
FOXX, REDD
about
After the IRS comes to collect, an angry Redd Foxx starts playing to an empty house. il por *People Weekly* 32:68 D 18 '89
Redd Foxx faces homeless holidays; IRS seizes property. A. Collier. il pors *Jet* 77:52-8 D 18 '89
FOY, DENNIS
about
New Foy in town. il por *Harper's Bazaar* 122:228 Mr '89
FPS COMPUTING (FIRM)
"We won't make that mistake again". K. K. Wiegner. il *Forbes* 144:257-8 Jl 24 '89
FRACHON, ALAIN
Reconquering Palestine. *World Press Review* 36:32+ Jl '89 (jt. auth) *See* Amalric, Jacques, and Frachon, Alain
FRACTALS
Dancing to fractal time. J. McDermott. il *Technology Review* 92:6+ Ja '89
Digging into sand [sandpile avalanches and self-organized criticality; cover story] I. Peterson. il *Science News* 136:40-2 Jl 15 '89
Fractal-shaped dust [work of Edward L. Wright] il *Sky and Telescope* 78:240 S '89
Fractals in your future [work of Michael F. Barnsley] T. Waters. il *Discover* 10:26+ Mr '89
Image capture by computer [work of Michael F. Barnsley and Alan D. Sloan] B. A. Cipra. *Science* 243:1288-9 Mr 10 '89
Polymers, fractals, and ceramic materials. D. W. Schaefer. bibl f il *Science* 243:1023-7 F 24 '89
Time to relax [fractal time; cover story] I. Peterson. il *Science News* 135:157-9 Mr 11 '89
A tour of the Mandelbrot set aboard the Mandelbus. A. K. Dewdney. il *Scientific American* 260:108-11 F '89
FRACTIONAL OWNERSHIP (REAL ESTATE)
Why a quarter of a vacation home may be worse than none. *Money* 18:22 Je '89
FRACTIONS
Fraction Munchers [computer program] C. S. Holzberg. il *Home Office Computing* 7:70 Jl '89
FRACTIONS, CONTINUED
Continued fractions and the sky [Basic astronomical computer program] R. W. Sinnott. il *Sky and Telescope* 77:80-2 Ja '89
FRACTURE MECHANICS
See also
Glass—Fracture
Seeing cracks in three dimensions [work of David Carter] R. Pool. il *Science* 243:1293 Mr 10 '89
FRACTURES
After a courageous comeback, a star pitcher breaks his arm but keeps his faith intact; ed. by Liz McNeil. D. Dravecky. il pors *People Weekly* 32:69-70+ S 11 '89
After the fall [skier P. Fletcher recovers from leg fracture] S. Nelson. il por *Health (New York, N.Y.)* 21:28-9 Mr '89
Broken but unbowed [Cincinnati's T. Krumrie recuperates from leg fracture suffered in Super Bowl] J. Lieber. il pors *Sports Illustrated* 70:104-7 Mr 20 '89
By the skin of his neck [fractured vertebra ends season for Ohio State basketball player J. Burson] H. Hersch. il pors *Sports Illustrated* 70:46-9 Mr 6 '89
Charged-up muscles [electrical stimulation used in rehabilitation; research by Joseph Kahn] il *Prevention (Emmaus, Pa.)* 41:16-17 Ap '89
Dual demons [use of painkillers to treat pain from wrist fracture] B. D. Colen. il *Health (New York, N.Y.)* 21:34-5 Ap '89
A "Fallsafe" against broken hips [tethering system] il *High Technology Business* 9:13-14 N/D '89
Giant comeback cut short [pitcher D. Dravecky] J. Carvalho. il por *Christianity Today* 33:54+ O 20 '89
'It felt like I lost my arm' [baseball player D. Dravecky breaks arm during comeback from cancer surgery] il por *Newsweek* 114:65 Ag 28 '89
Look before you leap. P. G. Gill. il *Outdoor Life* 183:61-3 Mr '89

FRACTURES—*cont.*
Stressful situation [stress fractures] J. F. Durkin. il *Runner's World* 24:28 O '89
FRACTURES (GEOLOGY) *See* Rock deformation
FRAENKEL, JEFFREY
about
Perfect exposure. B. Lifson. il por *House & Garden* 161:40+ F '89
FRAENKEL GALLERY
Perfect exposure. B. Lifson. il por *House & Garden* 161:40+ F '89
FRAGILE X SYNDROME
"Fragile X" syndrome and its puzzling genetics. D. M. Barnes. il *Science* 243:171-2 Ja 13 '89
A new DNA marker tightly linked to the fragile X locus (FRAXA). G. K. Suthers and others. bibl f il *Science* 246:1298-1300 D 8 '89
FRAGRANCE *See* Perfumes
FRAGRANT GARDENS
Fragrant delights. il *Southern Living* 24:54 Ja '89
Scents and sensibility. S. Lacey. il *House & Garden* 161:80+ Ap '89
Uncommon scents [herbs] S. Gilbertie. il *Organic Gardening* 36:43-6 F '89
FRAKNOI, ANDREW
Your astrology defense kit. il *Sky and Telescope* 78:146-50 Ag '89
FRAKTUR
The fraktur. A. Berman. *American Heritage* 40:28 F '89
FRALEY, ROBERT T.
(jt. auth) See Gasser, Charles S., and Fraley, Robert T.
FRAME, J. DAVIDSON
(jt. auth) See Narin, Francis, 1934-, and Frame, J. Davidson
FRAME-ROUSE, MEREDITH
A future for colonial waterbirds in New York State. il *The Conservationist* 43:2-7 Ja/F '89
FRAMES FOR MIRRORS *See* Mirror frames and framing
FRAMES FOR PICTURES *See* Picture frames and framing
FRAMES OF MOTORCYCLES *See* Motorcycles—Frames
FRAMING (BUILDING)
See also
Northern Timber Framing Inc.
FRAMINGHAM (MASS.)
Public health
Compute your heart risk [computer program used by Framingham Heart Study] A. Sprout. il *American Health* 8:14-15 N '89
FRAMPTON, KENNETH, 1930-
Architecture: Walter Gropius. il por *Architectural Digest* 46:82+ F '89
FRANCE, DAVID
A slow dying in El Salvador. il *Rolling Stone* p63-4+ Mr 23 '89
FRANCE
See also
Airports—France
Aix-les-Bains (France)
Albi (France)
Alpes-Maritimes (France)
Alps
Alsace (France)
Americans—France
Anti-Semitism—France
Architecture—France
Arles (France)
Art—France
Astronomy—France
Auctions—France
Autheil (France)
Automobile racing—France
Auvers-sur-Oise (France)
Aviation—France
Aviation and state—France
Booksellers and bookselling—France
Cap d'Antibes (France)
Cap Martin (France)
Castles—France
Cathedrals—France
Chamonix (France)
Chinese—France
Christmas—France
College education and state—France
Colleges and universities—France
Corporations—Acquisitions and mergers—Laws and regulations—France
Costume—France
Country estates—France
Criminal justice, Administration of—France
Dams—France
Dance—France
Dance festivals—France
Darcey (France)
Education—France
Espionage, German—France
Festivals—France
Flower gardens and gardening—France
French
Gardens and gardening—France

Giverny (France)
Great Britain—Diplomatic and consular service—France
Historic houses, sites, etc.—France
Homeopathy—France
Île-de-France (France)
Industry and state—France
Information systems—France
Insider trading—France
Insurance, Health—France
Investments, French
Lille (France)
Loire River Valley (France)
Lot (France)
Marseilles (France)
Medical policy—France
Mesmerism—France
Military assistance, American—France
Motion picture festivals—France
Motion pictures—France
Moustiers-Sainte-Marie (France)
Museums—France
Music festivals—France
Muslims—France
Nice (France)
Nîmes (France)
Nobility—France
Normandy (France)
Opera—France
Oppède-le-Vieux (France)
Palaces—France
Paleobotany—France
Paris (France)
Passports—France
Peasantry—France
Provence (France)
Reims (France)
Resorts—France
Restaurants—France
Saint-Tropez (France)
Science and state—France
Sculpture gardens and parks—France
Seine River (France)
Social security—France
Sologne (France)
South Africans—France
Strasbourg (France)
Strikes—Automobile industry workers—France
Strikes—France
Technology—France
Television broadcasting—France
Television festivals—France
Vence (France)
Vietnamese—France
Weight loss clinics—France
Wildlife—France
Wildlife conservation—France
Women—France
The global zeitgeist checklist: France. M. Lilla. *The New Republic* 200:21 Ap 10 '89
Antiquities
See also
Megalithic monuments—France
Commerce
Canada
Champagne diplomacy [Ontario Premier D. Peterson leads business delegation to France] J. Daly. *Maclean's* 102:39+ Ap 17 '89
China
China uses Trinidad TB-20s to replace aging Y-5 biplanes in pilot training. il *Aviation Week & Space Technology* 131:97 Ag 21 '89
Great Britain
See Great Britain—Commerce—France
Israel
Snecma to deliver Atar 9K50 powerplants for use in prototypes of upgraded Kfir. il *Aviation Week & Space Technology* 131:19 O 30 '89
Spain
France's Matra will cooperate with Spain to develop Hispasat satellite network. J. M. Lenorovitz. maps *Aviation Week & Space Technology* 131:93 Jl 17 '89
United States
See United States—Commerce—France
Cultural policy
An exclusive interview with the president of the French Republic: François Mitterrand. pors *The Unesco Courier* 42:4-9 Je '89
Cultural relations
Canada
Remembering a motherland. P. Young. il *Maclean's* 102:41 My 15 '89
United States
See United States—Cultural relations—France
Defenses
See also
Airplanes, Military—France
Guided missiles, French

FRANCE—Defenses—cont.

A bad rap for the force de frappe? [views of Richard H. Ullman] C. Dickey. il *Newsweek* 113:35 Je 12 '89

The covert French connection [nuclear collaboration with U.S.] R. H. Ullman. *Foreign Policy* 75:3-33 Summ '89

Plutonium in paradise [weapons testing on Mururoa Atoll] A. C. Revkin. il *Discover* 10:38-42 My '89

Description and travel

See also

Automobile touring—France

Cruising—France

Cycling—France

France celebrates its bicentennial [special issue; with editorial comment by Wilbur E. Garrett] il supp (folded map) maps *National Geographic* 176:1-174 Jl '89

The houses of a French summer. J. Salter. il *Esquire* 111:145-53 Ap '89

Travel journal. P. J. Bell. il *Gourmet* 49:134 Jl '89

Economic policy

See also

Price regulation by government—France

Foreign relations

Canada

A domestic squabble [Canada and France at odds over fishing rights off Newfoundland] G. Allen. il *Maclean's* 102:16 Ja 16 '89

A troubled cod truce [Ottawa's Atlantic fish accord with France] A. Walmsley. il *Maclean's* 102:36-8 Ap 17 '89

Czechoslovakia

See also

Mitterrand, François, 1916—Visit to Czechoslovakia, 1988

Egypt—History

See also

Egypt—History—French occupation, 1798-1801

United States

See United States—Foreign relations—France

History

Vive la France. M. B. Zuckerman. il *U.S. News & World Report* 107:68 Jl 24 '89

To 987

See also

Carolingians

Medieval period, 987-1515

See also

Hundred Years' War, 1339-1453

House of Valois, 1328-1589—Historiography

Philippe de Commynes: a courtly middle-man. M. Jones. bibl il *History Today* 39:34-41 Mr '89

18th century

When radical chic courted the guillotine [influence of French intellectuals] J. H. Huizinga. il *The New York Times Book Review* 94:1+ F 5 '89

Revolution, 1789-1799

Astronomy in the French Revolution. R. Barthalot. il *Sky and Telescope* 78:21-3 Jl '89

Celebrating the Bastille: fact and fable. C. P. Reynolds. il *Gourmet* 49:28+ Jl '89

The costs of the French Revolution. C. P. Issawi. *The American Scholar* 58:371-81 Summ '89

Editorial. W. Garrett. *Antiques* 135:259 Ja '89

First encounters [J. P. Marat and C. Corday] E. Sorel and N. C. Sorel. il *The Atlantic* 264:77 Jl '89

Gory means, righteous ends. S. Dentzer. il *U.S. News & World Report* 107:45 Jl 17 '89

The great Revolution. M. Severy. il map *National Geographic* 176:18-49 Jl '89

The heirs of Madame Guillotine [P. Brunet, descendant of executioner C.-H. Sanson] D. Lawday. il por *U.S. News & World Report* 107:46-8 Jl 17 '89

Let them eat hot dogs [cover story] H. Fairlie. il *The New Republic* 201:19-20+ Jl 31 '89

Liberty, equality, festivity! [festivals] L. Coudart. il *The Unesco Courier* 42:42-6 D '89

The liberty tree [comparison of French and Nicaraguan revolutions] A. Cockburn. *The Nation* 249:160 Ag 7-14 '89

The once and future Revolution. M. Agulhon. il *The Courier (Unesco)* 42:17-22 Mr '89

The Palais-Royal, garden of the Revolution. C. P. Reynolds. il *Gourmet* 49:62+ Ap '89

The passion of Antoine Lavoisier. S. J. Gould. *Natural History* p16+ Je '89

Patrick Brunet, whose ancestor guillotined Louis XVI, swears he's no chip off the old block [executioner C.-H. Sanson] T. Allis. il pors *People Weekly* 31:128+ Je 5 '89

Radical and chic, a duke who courted revolt and doom [Duc d'Orléans] R. Wernick. bibl (p122) il *Smithsonian* 20:66-75 Jl '89

Reappraising the French Revolution. C. P. Issawi. il *Current (Washington, D.C.)* 317:4-9 N '89

Reflections on the Revolution. N. Gash. il *National Review* 41:35-8 Jl 14 '89

Reflections on the Terror. E. von Kuehnelt-Leddihn. il *National Review* 41:38+ Jl 14 '89

The Revolution, warts and all. S. Sullivan. il *Newsweek* 114:35-6 Jl 3 '89

Should we celebrate the French Revolution? M. Cranston. il *The American Spectator* 22:15-17 Je '89

A tale of two revolutions. O. Scott. il *Conservative Digest* 15:48-51 S/O '89

What was revolutionary about the French Revolution? R. Darnton. il *The New York Review of Books* 35:3-4+ Ja 19 '89

Revolution, 1789-1799—Art

À la mode. E. White. il *Vogue* 179:236+ My '89

Fragments of a Revolution [exhibition at the Grand Palais] L. Nochlin. bibl f il *Art in America* 77:156-67+ O '89

Musée Carnavalet [French Revolution collection] C. P. Reynolds. il *Gourmet* 49:50+ O '89

Representing the Revolution. T. Gretton. bibl f il *History Today* 39:39-44 My '89

Revolution, 1789-1799—Bibliography

Getting ahead. *History Today* 39:57 My '89

Views from the barricades. il *The New York Times Book Review* 94:13 Jl 9 '89

Revolution, 1789-1799—Catholic Church

Turbulent priests? The Church and the Revolution. N. Aston. bibl il *History Today* 39:20-5 My '89

Revolution, 1789-1799—Centennial celebrations, etc.

La bicentenaire II [photographs] T. L. Cafaro and D. Neumaier. il *Art in America* 77:55-9 O '89

Bicentennial of the French Revolution and the Musée de l'Histoire de France. C. P. Reynolds. il *Gourmet* 49:24+ Ja '89

A bicentennial party. M. Nemeth. il *Maclean's* 102:25 Jl 24 '89

Celebrate Paris. S. Birnbaum. il *Good Housekeeping* 209:64+ Ag '89

Celebrating Revolution [cover story; special section] il *Maclean's* 102:28-34+ My 15 '89

France celebrates its bicentennial [special issue; with editorial comment by Wilbur E. Garrett] il supp (folded map) maps *National Geographic* 176:1-174 Jl '89

The French Revolution, 1789-1989 [special issue] bibl il *History Today* 39:3-57+ My '89

A Gallic gala comes to America. G. Lee. il *Harper's Bazaar* 122:26+ Ap '89

Homage with some distinctions [cover story; special section] *America* 160:571-5+ Je 17-24 '89

Les jours de gloire. J. Adler. il *Newsweek* 114:20-3 Jl 24 '89

Liberté, egalité, fraternité? M. Hornblower. il *Time* 133:48-50 My 1 '89

Liberté, egalité, have a nice day. D. A. Bell. *The New Republic* 200:22-5 Ja 23 '89

Liberte, egalite—and one hell of a party. P. Farrell. il *Business Week* p162-3 Je 26 '89

Long live the Revolution! D. Lawday. il *U.S. News & World Report* 106:67-8+ My 22 '89

Mlle. Liberty at 200. G. Leduc. il *World Press Review* 36:26 Je '89

Moonwalk on the Champs-Elysées [parade to celebrate bicentennial] B. Weber. il *The New York Times Magazine* p130 My 21 '89

Once more, the barricades! [public safety plan announced in Paris to cope with bicentennial festivities] il *Newsweek* 113:45 Je 26 '89

Over here [events in U.S.] C. Davidson. il *American Heritage* 40:72 Jl/Ag '89

Paris: remembering the Revolution [cover story; special issue] il *Travel Holiday* 172:36-73 Jl '89

Revolutionary Fêtes '89. H. Lipstadt. il *Art in America* 77:198-203+ O '89

Vive la Révolution! il *Time* 134:30-1 Jl 24 '89

Revolution, 1789-1799—Drama

Caesar at the Bastille [comparison of W. Shakespeare's Julius Caesar and G. Buchner's Danton's death]; tr. by Jadwiga Kosicka. J. Kott. il *The New York Review of Books* 36:40-2 O 12 '89

Revolution, 1789-1799—Exhibitions

À la mode. E. White. il *Vogue* 179:236+ My '89

Central Park's Conservatory Garden and a revolutionary exhibition [Words of blood, images of fire: the French Revolution at the Pierpont Morgan Library] H. Bridges. il *Gourmet* 49:48+ Je '89

Fragments of a Revolution [exhibition at the Grand Palais] L. Nochlin. bibl f il *Art in America* 77:156-67+ O '89

A tale of two cities [British exhibition] D. Byrne. il *History Today* 39:62 My '89

Revolution, 1789-1799—Foreign opinion

Liberté, egalité, animosité. G. Wills. il *American Heritage* 40:36-45 Jl/Ag '89

Revolution, 1789-1799—Historiography

Dancing on the grave of revolution [views of F. Furet; cover story] D. Singer. *The Nation* 248:145+ F 6 '89

Demystifying the French Revolution. D. Gress. bibl f *Commentary* 88:42-9 Jl '89

The nightmares of reason. S. Schama. il *The New Republic* 201:26-33 Jl '89

Reflections on Revolution [Simon Schama's Citizens] J. P. Hart. il *National Review* 41:45-7 D 31 '89

Winds of change. D. W. J. Johnson. bibl il *History Today* 39:3-9 My '89

FRANCE—History—*cont.*
Revolution, 1789-1799—Influence
1789: an idea that changed the world [cover story; special issue] il *The Unesco Courier* 42:4-58 Je '89
The abortive crusade. T. C. W. Blanning. bibl il *History Today* 39:33-8 My '89
Bolsheviks of the Bastille. L. Steinmetz. *National Review* 41:39 Jl 14 '89
The Revolution is finally over. R. W. Johnson. il *World Press Review* 36:22-3 Je '89
Revolution, 1789-1799—Literature
Words as weapons: romantic literature and the Revolution. J. Bloch. bibl il *History Today* 39:45-50 My '89
Revolution, 1789-1799—Medical and sanitary affairs
An LSD trip in France, 1789 [Mary Matossian's theory that the peasant revolt was caused by ergot fungus in rye bread] il *U.S. News & World Report* 107:14 D 4 '89
Revolution, 1789-1799—Meteorological aspects
Bad weather and the Bastille. D. M. Ludlum. il *Weatherwise* 42:141-2 Je '89
Bastille Day weather. D. M. Ludlum. il *Country Journal* 16:10 Jl/Ag '89
Revolution, 1789-1799—Motion pictures
A farrago of nonsense? The French Revolution in the cinema. P. Burley. bibl il *History Today* 39:51-6 My '89
Lights, action, Revolution. N. Mills. il *American Film* 15:12-13 O '89
Revolution, 1789-1799—Music
From gods to citizens [changes in opera] J. Keates. il *Opera News* 54:27-9 Jl '89
Revolution, 1789-1799—Religious aspects
Christians and the French Revolution. S. Englund. *The Christian Century* 106:679-80 Jl 19-26 '89
A tale of two countries [French and American revolutions] M. A. Noll. il *Christianity Today* 33:24-5 Jl 14 '89
Revolution, 1789-1799—Terminology
Glossary. *The Unesco Courier* 42:58 Je '89
Revolution, 1789-1799—Women
Voilà la citoyenne. O. Hufton. bibl il *History Today* 39:26-32 My '89
Consulate and Empire, 1799-1815
Building an empire [work of architects C. Percier and P. F. L. Fontaine] O. Bernier. il *House & Garden* 161:40+ D '89
February Revolution, 1848—Historiography
Alexis de Tocqueville's Recollections. F. Braudel. *Society* 26:67-72 Mr/Ap '89
Commune, 1871
See Paris (France)—History—Commune, 1871
20th century
See also
World War, 1939-1945—Campaigns and battles—France
German occupation, 1940-1945
L'affaire Touvier: opening old wounds. T. Morgan. il pors *The New York Times Magazine* p32-3+ O 1 '89
For honour alone [teenage cadets defend French Cavalry School, June 1940] R. Macnab. il *History Today* 39:5-7 Ja '89
Scandalous sanctuary [P. Touvier, French war criminal arrested] R. Marshall. il por *Newsweek* 113:44 Je 5 '89
Industries
See also
Aerospace industries—France
Air France
Art trade—France
Automobile industry—France
Avionics industry—Acquisitions and mergers—France
Bakers and bakeries—France
Banque Nationale de Paris
Bénéteau (Firm)
BSN SA
Canal Plus (Firm)
Carrefour (Firm)
Cartier (Firm)
Chanel (Firm)
Chloé (Firm)
Christian Dior (Firm)
Clothing industry—France
Cosmetics industry—France
Dassault Breguet Aviation (Avions Marcel)
Editions Pierre Belfond
Electronic industries—France
Financial institutions—Acquisitions and mergers—France
Groupe Bull
Groupe de la Cité
Guerlain SA
House of Hermès (Firm)
Lazard Frères et Cie
LVMH Moët Hennessy Louis Vuitton
Masson Editeur
Matra SA
Michelin et Cie
Pechiney (Firm)
Peugeot SA
Publishers and publishing—Acquisitions and mergers—France
Rémy Martin et Compagnie SA

Renault (Regie Nationale des Usines Renault)
Rhone-Poulenc SA
Roussel-Uclaf SA
Salomon et Fils François
Sextant Avionique (Firm)
Silk industry—France
SNECMA
SOCATA
Société Européenne de Propulsion
Source Perrier SA
Tailors—France
Taittingers (Firm)
Thomson-C S F
Thomson SA
L'Union des Assurances de Paris
Wine industry—France
Yves Saint Laurent (Firm)
Intellectual life
In Paris—miniskirts of the mind. R. A. Shweder. il *The New York Times Book Review* 94:1+ Ja 8 '89
Kings and rulers
See also
Louis XVI, King of France, 1754-1793
Napoleon I, Emperor of the French, 1769-1821
A royal pain in La France [movement to reinstitute monarchy] S. O'Shea. il *Mother Jones* 14:39-41+ Jl/Ag '89
Languages
See also
English language in France
French language in France
Photographs and photography
Letters from France. D. Belt and others. il *National Geographic* 176:56-91 Jl '89
Politics and government
See also
Conservatism—France
Political attitudes—France
Politics, Corruption in—France
Socialist Party (France)
L'édifice, c'est moi [F. Mitterrand] A. J. Blinken. *The New Republic* 200:16+ My 15 '89
The end of French exceptionalism. C. Imbert. *Foreign Affairs* 68:48-60 Fall '89
France's Mitterrand: a study in ambition. R. Chelminski. il pors *Reader's Digest* 134:141-6 Ap '89
Population
See also
Algerians—France
Immigrants—France
Religious institutions and affairs
See also
Catholic Church—France
Protestants—France
Social conditions
See also
Women—France

FRANCE. BIBLIOTHÈQUE NATIONALE *See* Bibliothèque Nationale (France)
FRANCE. DECLARATION OF THE RIGHTS OF MAN AND OF THE CITIZEN
1789: an idea that changed the world [cover story; special issue] il *The Unesco Courier* 42:4-58 Je '89
Bicentennial events worth commemorating; tr. by Patrick H. Samway. E. de Margerie. *America* 160:572-3 Je 17-24 '89
The bicentennial of a political idea. J. J. Conley. *America* 160:574-5+ Je 17-24 '89
FRANCE AND GERMANY (WEST)
A meeting of motherlands. W. Jäger. *World Press Review* 36:24+ Je '89
FRANCE AND THE UNITED STATES
See also
United States—History—Revolution, 1775-1783—French participation
France & America: 1789-1989 [cover story; special section; with editorial comment by Byron Dobell] il *American Heritage* 40:5, 36-54+ Jl/Ag '89
FRANCESA, MIKE
The Sport 1989 college football preview [cover story; special section] il *Sport (New York, N.Y.)* 80:22-6+ S '89
FRANCESCHINI, ENRICO
Someone who will listen. il *World Press Review* 36:12+ S '89
FRANCHISE CONSULTANTS
Making the most of consultants. M. Whittemore. *Nation's Business* 77:36-8 Je '89
FRANCHISE SYSTEM
See also
Booksellers and bookselling—Chain and franchise operations
Cable television—Franchise operations
Office equipment industry—Chain and franchise operations
Restaurants—Chain and franchise operations
The elusive affordable franchise. R. R. Roha. il *Changing Times* 43:60-4+ O '89

FRANCHISE SYSTEM—*cont.*

Exploring new frontiers [Black Enterprise Franchise 50; cover story; special section; with editorial comment by Earl G. Graves] W. M. Woodard. il *Black Enterprise* 20:9, 53-4+ S '89

Fed-up franchisees: they're mad as hell and . . . G. DeGeorge. il por *Business Week* p83+ N 13 '89

Five traps to avoid when buying a franchise. G. Brackett. il *Working Woman* 14:42 D '89

Four paths to franchising. M. Whittemore. il *Nation's Business* 77:75-6+ O '89

A franchise? Or a dealership? M. I. Finney. il *Nation's Business* 77:63-4 Mr '89

Franchising draws minorities. M. Whittemore. il *Nation's Business* 77:68 Ap '89

Franchising's appeal to women. M. Whittemore. il *Nation's Business* 77:63-4 N '89

Franchising's pathfinders [capitalizing on lifestyle trends] N. C. Baker and M. Whittemore. il *Nation's Business* 77:61-3+ F '89

A hot decade for franchising [black franchisors] il *Black Enterprise* 20:39 S '89

The hottest franchises for the home-based [cover story; special section] L. Arden. il *Home Office Computing* 7:41-50 Je '89

How to expand by franchising. L. Rager. *Nation's Business* 77:33-6 Je '89

Independents try franchising. N. C. Baker. il *Nation's Business* 77:31-3 Je '89

Investing in franchising. M. Whittemore. il *Nation's Business* 77:61+ Ag '89

You can own your own business [condensed from Franchising]; ed. by John Phillip Hayes. J. E. Kinch. il *Reader's Digest* 134:187-90+ F '89

Laws and regulations

The disclosure document. *Nation's Business* 77:78 O '89

Japan

See also

Duskin Co. Ltd.

Who says you can't break into Japan? [American franchises] T. Holden. il *Business Week* p49 O 16 '89

FRANCIS, DE SALES, SAINT, 1567-1622

about

A recipe for humble pie. J. Doyle. il *U.S. Catholic* 54:14-15 F '89

FRANCIS, OF ASSISI, SAINT, 1182-1226

Art

Lost and found [C. de Villalpando's St. Francis before the Pope] R. J. Stroessner and T. Dewalt. il *Américas* 41 no1:60-2 '89

FRANCIS, CHARLIE

about

A dirty coach comes clean. M. Noden. il pors *Sports Illustrated* 70:22-3 Mr 13 '89

From dream to nightmare. A. Burfoot and B. Wischnia. il pors *Runner's World* 24:12 Je '89

Sabotage at Seoul? R. Dolphin. il por *Maclean's* 102:47 Mr 20 '89

The steroid scandal [cover story; special section; with editorial comment by Kevin Doyle] il pors *Maclean's* 102:2, 36-42 Mr 13 '89

Whistle blower. por *Time* 133:50 Mr 13 '89

FRANCIS, DIANE

Column. See alternate issues of Maclean's beginning May 4, 1987

Trouble on Canada's farms. *World Press Review* 36:61 N '89

FRANCIS, JAMES

about

Big bad Bear. A. Murphy. il pors *Sports Illustrated* 71:56-8+ S 4 '89

FRANCIS, SAMUEL T.

Imperial conservatives? *National Review* 41:37-8 Ag 4 '89

Inhospitable neos. *National Review* 41:43-4+ Ap 7 '89

FRANCIS BEIDLER FOREST (S.C.)

South Carolina's sublime swamp. il *Southern Living* 24:26 Ja '89

FRANCISCANS

Brother Isidore covers 20 miles a day on his spiritual trek [Claymont, Del.] B. Johnson. il pors *People Weekly* 32:63-4 Ag 7 '89

FRANCISCO, ELOISA N.

Leadership through language training. il *World Health* p6 N '89

FRANCK, JAN

One dandy doghouse packed with style, storage, and fun. il *Better Homes and Gardens* 67:124 Jl '89

FRANCK, LOUIS

'80s racing. il *Sport (New York, N.Y.)* 80:85 O '89

FRANCO, FRANCISCO, 1892-1975

about

The Spanish Civil War [cover story; special section] bibl il pors map *History Today* 39:13-33 Mr '89

FRANCO, JOHN, 1960-

about

A hometown hero. H. Hersch. il pors *Sports Illustrated* 70:48-50+ My 15 '89

FRANCO, MARJORIE

Chance of a lifetime [story] il *Redbook* 172:66+ Mr '89

Making room for baby [story] il *Redbook* 173:38+ Ag '89

FRANCOPHONE GAMES

Anecdotes, facetiae, satire, etc.

A community of small communities [demands of Quebec and New Brunswick for own teams] S. MacLeod. por *Maclean's* 102:64 Je 5 '89

FRANCOPHONIE (ORGANIZATION)

Canada at the summit. B. Wallace. il *Maclean's* 102:17 My 29 '89

Facing French power [Senegal summit] B. Wallace. il *Maclean's* 102:15 Je 5 '89

FRANK, ALFRED

about

Doing well by sitting tight. M. Hulbert. il *Forbes* 144:161 Ag 7 '89

Marty Zweig? Or Al Frank? M. Hulbert. il *Forbes* 144:368 N 13 '89

"Star" funds: three hits, three misses. M. Schiffres. il pors *Changing Times* 43:59-63 My '89

FRANK, ANNE, 1929-1945

about

The complete Anne Frank. A. Pons. *World Press Review* 36:73 D '89

Doubleday, St. Martin's mark Anne Frank's 60th birthday. B. Levine. il por *Publishers Weekly* 235:34-5 F 10 '89

War and remembrance: a new entry from Anne Frank. J. Hendel. il por *Seventeen* 48:112-13 Je '89

FRANK, ANTHONY M.

about

Can this man really deliver? [interview] C. Leinster. il por *Fortune* 120:87-8 Ag 14 '89

Postal Frank. E. Hardy. il por *Forbes* 144:139 Ag 7 '89

FRANK, BARNEY

Should the "balanced budget constitutional amendment" be adopted? [excerpts from statement, November 17, 1987] *Congressional Digest* 68:267+ N '89

about

Another scandal on the Hill. por *Newsweek* 114:24 S 4 '89

Barney Frank's story [cover story; special section; with interview] il pors *Newsweek* 114:14-20 S 25 '89

In defense of Barney. M. Kondracke. *The New Republic* 201:10-11 O 9 '89

Letter from Washington. E. Drew. *The New Yorker* 65:106-8+ O 2 '89

The nation's closets. *Commonweal* 116:388-9 Jl 14 '89

Presswatch. T. Eastland. *The American Spectator* 22:31-2 N '89

A skeleton in Barney's closet. M. B. Carlson. il pors *Time* 134:24 S 25 '89

Trials of Barney. *The Nation* 249:371-2 O 9 '89

Why Frank's case is different. il por *U.S. News & World Report* 107:30 O 2 '89

Winners and sinners: the D'Amato and Frank dossiers. J. Klein. il por *New York* 22:23-4 O 9 '89

FRANK, ELIZABETH, 1945-

Art's off-the-wall critic. il pors *The New York Times Magazine* p46-7+ N 19 '89

FRANK, ERICA

Tough choices. *Vogue* 179:220-2+ Ag '89

Women & smoking. *Vogue* 179:412-13 O '89

FRANK, JEROME P.

Book design & manufacturing. See alternate issues of Publishers Weekly

FRANK, JOHN

about

No bones about it. J. Lieber. il pors *Sports Illustrated* 71:54-8+ Ag 28 '89

FRANK, LOUIS A.

about

Comet commotion. R. Kunzig. il *Discover* 10:24-5 Ja '89

Double exposures reveal mini-comets? R. A. Kerr. *Science* 243:170-1 Ja 13 '89

FRANK, LUCY

When they hate the one you love. il *Seventeen* 48:96+ N '89

FRANK, MICHAEL

An agile aesthetic: dancer Barrie Chase's country cottage in Los Angeles. il por *Architectural Digest* 46:248-55+ O '89

A creative collaboration: softening a modern house in Los Angeles. il pors *Architectural Digest* 46:130-7 Ag '89

Gardens: subtropical artistry: Jack Baker's exuberant creation near Santa Barbara. il pors *Architectural Digest* 46:284-9+ My '89

No longer my brother's keeper. il *The New York Times Magazine* p30+ S 17 '89

FRANK, ROBERT H.

Social commitment: beyond self-interest. *Current (Washington, D.C.)* 316:4-13 O '89

FRANK, RUTH S.

(jt. auth) See Wollheim, William, and Frank, Ruth S.

FRANK, THOMAS E.
On making it in the pros. *The Christian Century* 106:103-4
F 1-8 '89
FRANK BOLLING ADAPTIVE BASEBALL LEAGUE
Going to bat for special children. D. Young. il pors *Southern
Living* 24:100+ Jl '89
**FRANK CHURCH-RIVER OF NO RETURN WILDERNESS
(IDAHO)**
Lone ranger of the Rockies [boreal owls] P. H. Hayward
and G. D. Hayward. il *Natural History* p78-85 N '89
FRANK FARMS, INC.
Successful family farm. C. Tevis. il *Successful Farming* 87
no4:46-8 Mr '89
FRANKEL, STANLEY A.
The story behind Rudolph the Red-Nosed Reindeer. il *Good
Housekeeping* 209:126+ D '89
FRANKEL, TRACY
about
Tracy Frankel: keeping an eye on the action. C. R. Wolpert.
il por *Women's Sports & Fitness* 11:59 Jl/Ag '89
FRANKEN, ROSE, 1895-1988
The third child [story] il por *Redbook* 172:66+ Ap
'89
FRANKENHEIMER, JOHN
about
Dead-bang [film] Reviews
People Weekly il 31:17-18 Ap 10 '89. R. Novak
John Frankenheimer [interview] il por *American Film* 14:20-2+
Mr '89
FRANKENTHALER, HELEN, 1928-
about
Artful survivor [cover story] D. Solomon. il pors *The New
York Times Magazine* p30-3+ My 14 '89
Arts and craftiness. A. Wallach. il por *Ms.* 18:24-6 Jl/Ag
'89
Helen Frankenthaler. A. C. Danto. *The Nation* 249:217-20
Ag 21-28 '89
Helen Frankenthaler: Museum of Modern Art. R. Bass. il
Art News 88:169 S '89
Helen the Great. H. Drohojowska. il *Harper's Bazaar*
122:102-3+ Je '89
In pursuit of beauty. C. McGuigan. il por *Newsweek* 113:62-3
Je 12 '89
A landmark painting. M. S. Doherty. il *American Artist*
53:5 O '89
Living color. C. Ratcliff. il pors *Vogue* 179:242-9 Je '89
A love of spontaneous gesture. R. Hughes. il *Time* 133:74-5
Je 12 '89
News from nowhere. K. Larson. il *New York* 22:58 Je 26
'89
Pigments of the imagination. B. W. Bloch. il *The New Leader*
72:22-3 S 4 '89
With her greatest works on display, Helen Frankenthaler
paints a quirky portrait of the artist. S. K. Reed. il pors
People Weekly 32:117+ D 4 '89
FRANKFURT AM MAIN (GERMANY)
Airports
Security levels increased at Frankfurt, Heathrow [following
Pan Am Flight 103 bombing] K. F. Mordoff. il *Aviation
Week & Space Technology* 130:28-9 Ja 9 '89
Buildings
Frankfurt builds upward [boom in high-rise buildings] H.
Uniewski. il *World Press Review* 36:59 N '89
FRANKFURT AUTOMOBILE SHOW *See* Automobiles—Ex-
hibitions
FRANKFURT BOOK FAIR *See* Book fairs
FRANKFURT STOCK EXCHANGE *See* Frankfurt Wertpapier-
borse
FRANKFURT WERTPAPIERBORSE
The shudder heard round the world [consequences of Friday
the 13th drop] M. Tharp. il *U.S. News & World Report*
107:62 O 30 '89
FRANKFURTERS
American classics: the hamburger and hot-dog cookbook.
il *Ladies' Home Journal* 106:139-40+ Ag '89
Perros caliente. P. Edidin. il *Psychology Today* 23:36 D
'89
FRANKINCENSE
Gifts of the Magi: precious resins. D. Dare. *Earth Science*
41:14 Wint '88
FRANKING PRIVILEGE
Congress's $113 million junk-mail habit [target of reform
by Republicans] G. Borger. il *U.S. News & World Report*
107:17-18 Ag 7 '89
Stamp out Congress's "franking" privilege. W. Safire. *Reader's
Digest* 135:131-2 O '89
FRANKLET, DUANE
Lobstermen [story] *Américas* 41 no2:41 '89
FRANKLIN, ARETHA
about
Aretha. M. Jacobson. por *Esquire* 111:102-3 Ja '89
Aretha Franklin holds a gala birthday in Detroit. il pors
Jet 76:14-16 Ap 17 '89
Aretha Franklin's former Detroit neighbors want to her to
show a little R-E-S-P-E-C-T. P. Axthelm. il por *People
Weekly* 31:36-7 Je 26 '89
Senate honors Franklin for her work in fighting drunken
driving problem. il por *Jet* 76:59 Ag 7 '89

FRANKLIN, BENJAMIN, 1706-1790
Ben's bird. G. Reiger. il *Field & Stream* 94:48-9 My '89
FRANKLIN, DAVID
about
Maine millionaire David Franklin goes for broke by giving
big bucks to people who need it. D. Mathison. il pors
People Weekly 32:83-4+ D 18 '89
FRANKLIN, DEBORAH
What a child is given. il *The New York Times Magazine*
p36-41+ S 3 '89
FRANKLIN, H. BRUCE (HOWARD BRUCE), 1934-
Fatal fiction: a weapon to end all wars [cover story] bibl
f il *The Bulletin of the Atomic Scientists* 45:18-25 N '89
FRANKLIN, HOWARD BRUCE *See* Franklin, H. Bruce
(Howard Bruce), 1934-
FRANKLIN, JERRY F.
about
Olaus and Margaret Murie Award. *Wilderness* 52:6 Wint
'88
FRANKLIN, JOHN HOPE, 1915-
Stalking George W. Williams. il por *American Visions* 4:28-31
Ap '89
FRANKLIN, KAREN E.
Deforestation hits home: U.S. Forest Service levels our
landscape. il *Utne Reader* p52 My/Je '89
Fields of dreams. il *Sport (New York, N.Y.)* 80:64-6 S '89
Timber! *The New Republic* 200:12-14 Ja 2 '89
FRANKLIN, ROLAND A. E.
about
Jimmy Goldsmith's gun bearer goes gunning. P. Finch. il
por *Business Week* p63+ O 16 '89
FRANKLIN, ROMAIN
China's slipping economy. *World Press Review* 36:56 N '89
FRANKLIN, WILLIAM E.
Japan and the United States [address, May 17, 1989] *Vital
Speeches of the Day* 55:647-9 Ag 15 '89
FRANKLIN COMPUTER CORPORATION
Top-down lexicography. R. D. Hylton. il por *Forbes* 144:98-9
Jl 10 '89
FRANKLIN D. ROOSEVELT LIBRARY
'Future historians will curse as well as praise me'. G. C.
Ward. il *Smithsonian* 20:58-66+ D '89
FRANKLIN INSTITUTE (PHILADELPHIA, PA.)
Franklin Institute honors Lorenz, Oatley and Madey. M.
Siegel. pors *Physics Today* 42:113 S '89
**FRANKLIN INSTITUTE (PHILADELPHIA, PA.). SCIENCE
MUSEUM AND PLANETARIUM. FUTURES CENTER**
The Futures Center: tomorrow's science and technology. A.
E. Mintz. il por *The Futurist* 23:19-24 Ja/F '89
FRANKLIN SAVINGS ASSOCIATION
Ernest Fleischer finally tastes humble pie [filing for bankruptcy
for L.F. Rothschild Holdings] D. Zigas. il por *Business
Week* p67 Jl 17 '89
FRANKLIN SPIER INC.
Spier sold to senior management and investors. *Publishers
Weekly* 236:16 D 15 '89
FRANKLIN-TROUT, JO
about
Film flam. S. Emerson. *The New Republic* 201:29-30+ S
18-25 '89
FRANKOLA, KAREN
Pain behind the camera. por *Newsweek* 113:9 F 6 '89
FRANKS, LUCINDA
The little red chair. il *The New York Times Magazine* p28+
Mr 12 '89
FRANKS, NANCI B.
about
The rocky road to launching a business. M. Bekey. il por
Working Woman 14:41-2+ Je '89
FRANKSTON, BOB
about
Birthing the visible calculator [interview] il pors *Byte* 14:326-8
D '89
FRANN, MARY
about
Newhart's Mary Frann takes a holiday from the inn to
advise single women about married men. J. Kaufman.
il pors *People Weekly* 32:109-10+ O 30 '89
FRANTZ, CHRIS
about
Tom Tom Club. R. Givens. il pors *Stereo Review* 54:100-1
D '89
FRANZÉN, ANDERS
Kronan: remnants of a warship's past. il map *National
Geographic* 175:438-65 Ap '89
FRANZESE, MICHAEL
about
Tour shakedowns alleged. J. Capeci. il por *Rolling Stone*
p20 My 4 '89
FRAPPIER, JUDY
about
Jon Bon Jovi gives his home to non-Jovi Judy Frappier.
il pors *People Weekly* 31:135 Ap 17 '89
FRASCA, MICHAEL A.
Don't blame the moon. il *Sky and Telescope* 78:340 O
'89

FRASER, C. GERALD
Cry freedom [interview with M. Tutu] por *Essence* 20:34 S '89
FRASER, CAROLINE
Immature technology [poem] *The New Yorker* 65:60 S 25 '89
FRASER, DOUGLAS ANDREW, 1916-
about
From the top. il pors *Car and Driver* 35:93-6+ O '89
FRASER, H. RUSSELL
about
A new itch at Fitch. J. Zweig. il por *Forbes* 143:326 My 29 '89
FRASER, JOHN, 1944-
about
The Saturday night wars. G. Bain. il *Maclean's* 102:72 N 27 '89
FRASER, JOYCE
about
Top middleweight Marcus learned ropes from mom. pors *Jet* 76:50 Ag 21 '89
FRASINSKI, L. J., AND OTHERS
Covariance mapping: a correlation method applied to multiphoton multiple ionization. bibl f il *Science* 246:1029-31 N 24 '89
FRATERNITIES *See* College fraternities
FRATKIN, ELLIOT M.
Two lives for the Ariaal. il map *Natural History* p38-49 My '89
DIE FRAU OHNE SCHATTEN [opera] *See* Strauss, Richard, 1864-1949
FRAUD
See also
Advertising ethics
Appraisers—Ethical aspects
Audio equipment stores—Ethical aspects
Automobile industry—Ethical aspects
Automobiles—Leasing and renting—Ethical aspects
Avionics industry—Ethical aspects
Banks and banking—Ethical aspects
Brokers—Ethical aspects
Cancer research—Ethical aspects
Checks, Fraudulent
Cleaning services—Ethical aspects
Commercial crimes
Commodity brokers—Ethical aspects
Computer crimes
Counterfeits and counterfeiting
Credit card crimes
Digital audio tape recorders and recording—Unauthorized recording
Drug industry—Ethical aspects
Electronics stores—Ethical aspects
Employment agencies—Ethical aspects
Employment interviewing—Ethical aspects
Fund raising—Ethical aspects
Guides—Ethical aspects
Heart research—Ethical aspects
Hoaxes
Hydrology research—Ethical aspects
Impostors
Insurance companies—Ethical aspects
Insurance crimes
Investment fraud
Job applications—Ethical aspects
Mail fraud
Medical laboratories—Ethical aspects
Nursing homes—Ethical aspects
Paleontology—Ethical aspects
Pharmaceutical research—Ethical aspects
Phonograph record industry—Ethical aspects
Phonograph records—Unauthorized recording
Politics, Corruption in
Ponzi schemes
Psychiatric research—Ethical aspects
Quacks and quackery
Real estate investment fraud
Religious investment fraud
Research—Ethical aspects
Tax evasion
Telephone crimes
Television industry—Ethical aspects
Ticket selling—Ethical aspects
Timesharing (Real estate)—Ethical aspects
Tourist trade—Ethical aspects
Videotapes—Unauthorized use
Vision research—Ethical aspects
Comedian Bob McDonald gets jail term for scam. il pors *Jet* 77:25 D 25 '89-Ja 1 '90
"Credit doctors" can hurt you. P. Plawin. il *Changing Times* 43:78 Ag '89
Credit history scam. K. K. Gracey. *Consumers' Research Magazine* 72:2 Je '89
"Credit repair" companies. *Consumers' Research Magazine* 72:32 S '89
"Dad would make a deal with the devil" [financier H. K. Beebe, Sr.] R. Woodbury. il por *Time* 133:71 F 20 '89

Do only the suckers pay? [Medicaid fraud perpetrated by elderly seeking shelter from nursing home costs] J. B. Quinn. il *Newsweek* 114:52 D 18 '89
From grand slams to grand scams [baseball collectibles] il *U.S. News & World Report* 107:17 O 30 '89
Latest scams [New York City] P. Blauner. il *New York* 22:54-5 My 1 '89
Reach out and rob someone [telemarketing scams] J. Castro. il *Time* 133:38-9 Ap 3 '89
Scam alert! How to avoid a rip-off. J. Hamburg. il *Ladies' Home Journal* 106:44+ Jl '89
The sticks, the slides, and the shaker [shell game con in New York City] J. P. Zane. il *New York* 22:36-9 Je 19 '89
To catch a thief [man attempts to get books from publishers by posing as a reviewer for Business week] L. Fleischer. *Publishers Weekly* 235:76 Ja 6 '89
The top ten scams. il *Consumers' Research Magazine* 72:32-3 Je '89
"You have definitely won a fabulous prize!". M. C. Paulson. il *Changing Times* 43:34-6+ Ag '89
You may already be a victim of fraud. M. J. Harris. il *Money* 18:74-80+ Ag '89
FRAYN, MICHAEL
The trick of it [story] il *The New Yorker* 65:29-40+ Ag 14 '89
FRAYNE, TRENT
Sports watch. See occasional issues of Maclean's beginning November 6, 1989
FRAZEE, WILLIAM
about
The Supreme Court expands religious freedom. R. F. Drinan. *America* 160:388-9 Ap 29 '89
FRAZELLE, KENNETH
about
Naturalissimo. B. Weber. il por *The New York Times Magazine* p66 Ja 8 '89
FRAZER, LANCE
Go forth & multiply? il *Ad Astra* 1:24-9 Je '89
Listening for life. il *Ad Astra* 1:16-19+ S '89
Opportunity knocking, no one home: educating space entrepreneurs. map *Ad Astra* 1:36-7 D '89
FRAZER, PHILLIP
Gimme shelter. il *Mother Jones* 14:48+ N '89
FRAZIER, CLAUDE A.
Five grains of corn. il *The Saturday Evening Post* 261:62-3 N/D '89
FRAZIER, IAN
Great Plains (I). *The New Yorker* 65:49-50+ F 20 '89
Great Plains (II). il *The New Yorker* 65:35-40+ F 27 '89
Great Plains (III). il *The New Yorker* 65:41-4+ Mr 6 '89
Thanks for the memory. *The New Yorker* 65:36-7 D 18 '89
about
History with a human face. L. Shapiro. il por *Newsweek* 113:64 Je 12 '89
Ian Frazier's search for paradise on Flathead Lake. il *U.S. News & World Report* 107:52 S 25 '89
What's so great about the Great Plains? Ian Frazier took the time to find out. M. Neill. il pors *People Weekly* 32:104-6 Ag 7 '89
FRAZIER, JOHN M.
(jt. auth) *See* Goldberg, Alan M., and Frazier, John M.
FRAZIER, PAULA NEWBY- *See* Newby-Frazier, Paula
FRAZIER, SHERVERT, 1921-
about
Did the penalty fit the crime? M. M. Hunt. il por *The New York Times Magazine* p36-7+ My 14 '89
FRAZIER, WALT, III
about
Belatedly learning that father knows best, Walt Frazier III tries to be a Clyde off the old block. J. Friedman. il pors *People Weekly* 31:73-4+ F 27 '89
FRAZIER, WALT, 1945-
about
Belatedly learning that father knows best, Walt Frazier III tries to be a Clyde off the old block. J. Friedman. il pors *People Weekly* 31:73-4+ F 27 '89
FREARS, STEPHEN, 1941-
about
Dangerous liaisons [film] Reviews
America 160:88 F 4 '89. R. A. Blake
American Film il 14:64 Jl/Ag '89. P. Rainer
The American Spectator 22:38 My '89. B. Bawer
Commonweal 116:147 Mr 10 '89. T. O'Brien
Glamour il 87:186+ Mr '89. J. G. Boyum
The Humanist il 49:45-6 My/Je '89. H. M. Geduld
Mademoiselle 95:92 F '89. R. Rosenbaum
The Nation 248:173-4 F 6 '89. S. Klawans
National Review 41:54-5 F 24 '89. J. Simon
The New Republic 200:24-5 Ja 2 '89. S. Kauffmann
New York il 22:52+ Ja 9 '89. D. Denby
The New Yorker 64:78-80 Ja 9 '89. P. Kael
Time il 133:64 Ja 16 '89. R. Corliss
Video il 13:59 Ag '89. J. Bernard

FREBERG, STAN
about
Stan Freberg pens a memoir about his strange career move—from comedy to commercials. M. Frankel. il pors *People Weekly* 31:153-4 My 8 '89
FRECHETTE, PETER
about
Double play. D. Shaw. il por *New York* 22:14 Ja 9 '89
FRECKLES *See* Skin
FRECKMAN, DIANA W.
The scientist shortage and the gender gap. *BioScience* 39:523 S '89
FRED SILVERMAN COMPANY
"I'm not rumpled anymore" [F. Silverman] L. Gubernick. il por *Forbes* 143:84-5 Mr 6 '89
FRED THE FURRIER *See* Schwartz, Fred
FREDDIE MAC *See* Federal Home Loan Mortgage Corporation
FREDDY KRUEGER (FICTIONAL CHARACTER)
"It's great for a date". L. Gubernick. il por *Forbes* 143:110+ F 6 '89
Not another pretty face [creating makeup for R. England's Freddy Krueger character] B. Weber. il pors *The New York Times Magazine* p66 Jl 16 '89
FREDERICK, JOHN E., AND SNELL, HILARY E.
Ultraviolet levels under sea ice during the Antarctic spring [discussion of July 22, 1988 article, Ultraviolet radiation levels during the Antarctic spring] *Science* 245:194-5 Jl 14 '89
FREDERICK, LINDEN
about
Linden Frederick. E. Feit. il por *American Artist* 53:48-53+ Jl '89
FREDERICK'S OF HOLLYWOOD, INC.
Frederick's of Hollywood trades its X rating for an R. K. Kerwin. il *Business Week* p64 D 11 '89
FREDKIN, EDWARD
about
The soul of a new machine. G. Cowley. il por *Newsweek* 113:53 My 29 '89
FREDRICKSON, GEORGE M., 1934-
Can South Africa change? [cover story] il *The New York Review of Books* 36:48-55 O 26 '89
FREE, F. WILLIAM
about
Killearn Farm: F. William Free's Hudson Valley horse farm. J. Gruen. il por *Architectural Digest* 46:182-7+ Je '89
FREE AGENTS (BASEBALL PLAYERS) *See* Baseball players—Salaries, pensions, etc.
FREE AGENTS (FOOTBALL PLAYERS) *See* Football players—Salaries, pensions, etc.
FREE BANKING
An end to monetary instability? [privatizing money] P. Brimelow. il *Forbes* 143:120+ Ap 3 '89
FREE ELECTRON LASERS
Free-electron lasers [cover story] H. P. Freund and R. K. Parker. bibl il *Scientific American* 260:84-9 Ap '89
Military use
Advances in induction-type FEL add to its antimissile potential. B. W. Henderson. il *Aviation Week & Space Technology* 130:81+ My 8 '89
Boeing Aerospace wins SDI contract for RF-driven free electron laser. P. A. Gilmartin. il *Aviation Week & Space Technology* 131:21 O 23 '89
Los Alamos free electron laser altered for higher-power tests. T. M. Foley. il *Aviation Week & Space Technology* 130:88-9 F 13 '89
SDI free electron laser faces cut in power, delay. il *Aviation Week & Space Technology* 130:22 My 22 '89
FREE ENTERPRISE
See also
Center for International Private Enterprise
Competition
Free ports and zones
Doomsday again. E. Rubenstein. il *National Review* 41:16 Ag 4 '89
Enterprise and meaning: sponsored film, 1939-1949. W. L. Bird. bibl il *History Today* 39:24-30 D '89
Free enterprise and the insurance agency [address, June 9, 1989] E. J. Noha. *Vital Speeches of the Day* 56:45-9 N 1 '89
Free-market economics: antidote for war and poverty. il *Nation's Business* 77:71 D '89
"No water" economics [theories of M. Rothbard] P. Brimelow. por *Forbes* 143:86+ Mr 6 '89
What is business? [address, March 17, 1989] E. A. Opitz. *Vital Speeches of the Day* 55:497-500 Je 1 '89
The world turns [views of F. A. Hayek] R. Bailey. il por *Forbes* 143:43-4 My 15 '89
FREE PORTS AND ZONES
Beyond GATT. G. C. Hufbauer. *Foreign Policy* 77:64-76 Wint '89/'90
The lure of the Gold Coast [China] L. Doder. il *Maclean's* 102:38 My 29 '89
Oases of opportunity. S. Golob. il *Nation's Business* 77:45-6 Jl '89

FREE PRESS *See* Freedom of the press
FREE PRESS (DETROIT, MICH.) *See* Detroit free press
FREE RADICALS (CHEMISTRY)
See also
Superoxides
E for elevation [research on vitamin E and free radicals in high altitude athletics] il *Women's Sports & Fitness* 11:11 O '89
Identification by ENDOR of Trp[191] as the free-radical site in cytochrome c peroxidase compound ES. M. Sivaraja and others. bibl f il *Science* 245:738-40 Ag 18 '89
Mouse study suggests a cure for influenza [research by Hiroshi Maeda] I. Wickelgren. *Science News* 135:325 My 27 '89
Vitamin C protects blood from radicals [research by Balz Frei] J. Raloff. *Science News* 136:133 Ag 26 '89
Vitamin E fights radicals—again and again [research by Lester Packer on mitochondrial membranes] J. Raloff. *Science News* 135:327 My 27 '89
Wanted: 40 more years. D. Teresi. il *Health (New York, N.Y.)* 21:58-9+ O '89
FREE SPEECH *See* Freedom of speech
FREE SPIRIT [television program] *See* Television program reviews—Single works
FREE-STANDING EMERGENCY MEDICAL CENTERS *See* Health facilities
FREE THOUGHT
Enlarging your child's horizons. J. Van Dam. *The Humanist* 49:37-8 S/O '89
FREE THROW SHOOTING (BASKETBALL)
Failure most foul [NBA's worst free throw shooters] J. McCallum. il *Sports Illustrated* 70:96-8+ Mr 20 '89
FREE TRADE AND PROTECTION
See also
Balance of trade
General Agreement on Tariffs and Trade
Tariff
United States—Commercial policy
Bloc that trade. R. Kuttner. *The New Republic* 200:16-19 Ap 17 '89
Creating a global constituency for free trade [address, September 13-15, 1989] D. E. Moore. *Vital Speeches of the Day* 56:108-10 D 1 '89
Export barriers the U.S. hates most. R. Jacob. il *Fortune* 119:88-9 F 27 '89
Free trade's double-header. M. W. Karmin. *U.S. News & World Report* 107:48 Jl 10 '89
A new cold war? [rise of protectionism] E. A. Finn, Jr. il *Forbes* 143:56+ Mr 6 '89
"Pressure has its uses" [views of J. Bhagwati] L. Minard. il por *Forbes* 143:96+ Je 12 '89
Sons of Smoot-Hawley [protectionism making a comeback] E. A. Finn, Jr. il *Forbes* 143:38-40 F 6 '89
Why free trade works. T. J. DiLorenzo. *Reader's Digest* 134:119-23 F '89
World without borders [views of G. Hufbauer] E. A. Finn, Jr. il por *Forbes* 143:118+ Ap 17 '89
FREE WILL AND DETERMINISM
See also
Freedom (Theology)
FREED, JAMES INGO, 1930-
about
How buildings remember. H. Muschamp. *The New Republic* 201:27-33 Ag 28 '89
FREEDMAN, DAVID, 1938-
Beyond Einstein [cover story; with editorial comment by Paul Hoffman] il pors *Discover* 10:4, 56-61 F '89
Cosmic time travel [cover story] il *Discover* 10:58-64 Je '89
Fission in the fusion camp. il *Discover* 10:32-4+ D '89
FREEDMAN, JONATHAN
Pop culture, auto-canonized. *Harper's* 278:31-2+ Ja '89
FREEDMAN, LEONARD P., AND OTHERS
In vitro transcription enhancement by purified derivatives of the glucocorticoid receptor. bibl f il *Science* 245:298-301 Jl 21 '89
FREEDMAN, MARC
Fostering intergenerational relationships for at-risk youth. il *Children Today* 18:10-15 Mr/Ap '89
FREEDMAN, RITA JACKAWAY
Life at large [excerpt from Bodylove] il *Health (New York, N.Y.)* 21:40+ Ap '89
about
Body image, body love. C. Valentino. il *American Health* 8:60-2 Je '89
FREEDMAN, ROBERT O.
A talk with Arafat [cover story] il *The New York Review of Books* 36:8+ Ap 13 '89
FREEDMAN, SAMUEL G.
Inside a New York City high school: snapshots of hope and hopelessness. il *The New York Times Magazine* p58-9+ S 17 '89
FREEDOM *See* Liberty
FREEDOM (THEOLOGY)
The love of randomness. D. K. Mano. *National Review* 41:58-9 O 13 '89
True freedom. P. J. Ryan. il *America* 160:599 Je 17-24 '89

FREEDOM INC.

Rescue in Mozambique [English journalist N. della Casa freed from Renamo through efforts of Freedom Inc.; with editorial comment by James R. Whelan] R. MacKenzie. il pors map *Conservative Digest* 15:39+, 70 Mr/Ap '89

FREEDOM OF INFORMATION

See also

Classified information

Executive privilege (Government information)

Government and the press

Journalistic ethics

Science, Freedom of

Sunshine laws

At war with the First Amendment [Reagan administration] J. Kalven. *The Bulletin of the Atomic Scientists* 45:56-9 Ja/F '89

Ballantine releases updated edition of 'Dangerous dossiers' [H. Mitgang book on FBI surveillance of authors and Freedom of Information Act] B. Levine. il *Publishers Weekly* 235:27 Mr 17 '89

Government information goes on-line. H. H. Perritt. il *Technology Review* 92:60-5+ N/D '89

Judge orders INS to stop the delays [failure to abide by Freedom of Information Act in deportation cases] E. Pell. il *The Progressive* 53:13-14 S '89

Needed: a free flow of information and ideas. J. H. F. Shattuck and M. M. Spence. *Scientific American* 260:114 Ja '89

Not so fast [debate over whether or not computerized government records are covered under the Freedom of Information Act] B. Maxwell. il *Common Cause Magazine* 15:24-5 S/O '89

Use of the original records of the Department of State [reprint from July 1, 1939 issue] *Department of State Bulletin* 89:9-11 Jl '89

Conferences

See also

Information Forums

China

Revolution by information. L. Martz. il *Newsweek* 113:28-9 Je 19 '89

Communist countries

Our chip has come in. *The New Republic* 200:7-8 Je 12 '89

Eastern Europe

CSCE Information Forum [statement, April 21, 1989] L. H. Marks. *Department of State Bulletin* 89:86-7 S '89

Latin America

The open society and its friends [address, October 11, 1988] G. P. Shultz. *Department of State Bulletin* 88:13-16 D '88

Soviet Union

Is *glasnost* genuine? [address, November 6, 1988] M. Warder. *Vital Speeches of the Day* 55:341-4 Mr 15 '89

FREEDOM OF INFORMATION ACT *See* Freedom of information

FREEDOM OF RELIGION *See* Religious liberty

FREEDOM OF SCIENCE *See* Science, Freedom of

FREEDOM OF SPEECH

See also

Blasphemy

Freedom of the press

Libel and slander

The Atwater flag sting. N. Hentoff. il *The Progressive* 53:12-14 N '89

Behind the flag-burning firestorm [Supreme Court decision] M. Barone. il *U.S. News & World Report* 107:28 Jl 3 '89

Burn, baby, burn! [Supreme Court ruling on flag burning] *National Review* 41:13-14 Ag 4 '89

The campus: "an island of repression in a sea of freedom". C. E. Finn. *Commentary* 88:17-23 S '89

The Court and the flag decision. W. F. Buckley. *National Review* 41:54 Ag 4 '89

The 'crime' of flag burning [Supreme Court to review case] M. Garbus. il *The Nation* 248:369-70 Mr 20 '89

Dial-a-porn, find-a-lawyer [Supreme Court rulings] A. L. Sanders. il *Time* 134:56 Jl 3 '89

Don't ban the banners [stadiums] R. Telander. por *Sports Illustrated* 71:100 O 30 '89

The dynamics of flag-burning [Supreme Court decision] J. M. Wall. *The Christian Century* 106:643-4 Jl 5-12 '89

Faith and flag-burning [discussion of July 5-12, 1989 article, The dynamics of flag-burning] J. M. Wall. il *The Christian Century* 106:757-9 Ag 16-23 '89

A fight for Old Glory [Supreme Court rules flag burning is not a crime] T. Jacoby. il *Newsweek* 114:18-20 Jl 3 '89

The flag and freedom of speech [Supreme Court decision] *America* 161:3 Jl 1-8 '89

Flag-burning & other modes of expression. W. Berns. *Commentary* 88:37-41 O '89

Flag desecration legislation. *Congressional Digest* 68:193-224 Ag/S '89

Flag-saving [Supreme Court ruling] *The Nation* 249:229-30 S 4-11 '89

Free speech on the campus. N. Hentoff. il *The Progressive* 53:12-13 My '89

Guarding Old Glory. J. Garvey. il *Commonweal* 116:423-4 Ag 11 '89

The High Court stands 5-4 on a burning issue [flag burning] il *U.S. News & World Report* 107:8 Jl 3 '89

In praise of censure. G. Wills. il *Time* 134:71-2 Jl 31 '89

McMurtry and others decry continuing use of McCarran Act. H. Fields. *Publishers Weekly* 235:15 My 26 '89

Non-alien speech [decision striking down alien deportation provisions of McCarren-Walter Act] D. Cole. *The Nation* 248:220-1 F 20 '89

O'er the land of the free [Supreme Court upholds right to burn the flag] W. Isaacson. il *Time* 134:14-15 Jl 3 '89

Shouting "Fire!" [O. W. Holmes' analogy] A. M. Dershowitz. il pors *The Atlantic* 263:72-4 Ja '89

The speech market [Supreme Court ruling on flag burning] D. Seligman. *Fortune* 120:135 Ag 28 '89

The speech supression movement [universities] D. Seligman. il *Fortune* 119:195-6 Je 19 '89

Taxation of advertising: a violation of free speech? W. Murray. il *USA Today (Periodical)* 117:23-4 Mr '89

Unimpressed by the freedom to burn Old Glory, Joey Johnson still wants a revolution. D. Grogan. il pors *People Weekly* 32:98-100 Jl 10 '89

Waiving the flag [Supreme Court to review flag burning issue] *The New Republic* 200:7-8 Ja 23 '89

Great Britain

Britain: under the iron (high) heel? J. O'Sullivan. *Commentary* 88:47-52 S '89

FREEDOM OF TEACHING *See* Academic freedom

FREEDOM OF THE PRESS

See also

Government and the press

Libel and slander

The Hill case [impact of 1967 Time Inc. v. Hill privacy case, argued by R. Nixon, on freedom of the press] L. Garment. *The New Yorker* 65:90-110 Ap 17 '89

The honeymoon will never last. J. R. Joelson. por *The Humanist* 49:33-4 S/O '89

New threats in the democracies. *World Press Review* 36:52-7 F '89

International aspects

Pressing for a free press. S. J. Ungar. *Foreign Policy* 77:132-53 Wint '89/'90

FREEDOM QUILTING BEE (ORGANIZATION)

Hard times for Freedom Quilters [Freedom Quilting Bee in Alabama] N. Callahan. *The Christian Century* 106:317-18 Mr 22-29 '89

FREEDOM REGIONAL BANK FUND

Banking on regionals. C. Poole. il *Forbes* 144:190 S 4 '89

FREEDOM RIDERS *See* Civil rights demonstrations—History

FREELANCE WRITING

The four P's for free lancers. V. Buchan. *The Writer* 102:30 S '89

Freelance writers claim nonpayment by 'Inside books'. C. Reid. *Publishers Weekly* 235:25 Je 30 '89

A specialist in many fields. G. Stern. *The Writer* 102:17-19 My '89

Spring training for writers. J. McCollister. *The Writer* 102:7-8 Ap '89

Three surefire ways to write and sell nonfiction. S. S. Baker. *The Writer* 102:11-13 Mr '89

You may be an expert and not know it. C. A. Smith. *The Writer* 102:26-7 Ja '89

FREEMAN, ARTHUR M.

"Woulda/coulda/shoulda": how to avoid no-win thinking [excerpt] il *Ladies' Home Journal* 106:124+ O '89

FREEMAN, BRIAN M.

about

The workingman's man at the takeover table. C. Tucher. il por *Business Week* p62 S 4 '89

FREEMAN, CAROLYN

about

23 years of outrageous water bills spur two sisters to fight city hall. (P.S.: they won!). S. Percy. il pors *Good Housekeeping* 209:52+ O '89

FREEMAN, CHARLES W.

The Angola/Namibia accords. *Foreign Affairs* 68:126-41 Summ '89

FREEMAN, CLAIRE

about

Claire Freeman takes oath as asst. secretary of HUD. il por *Jet* 77:8 D 4 '89

FREEMAN, DAVID, 1941-

High on Kauai. il *Vogue* 179:396+ Mr '89

FREEMAN, HAROLD P.

about

Dr. Harold P. Freeman. D. C. Lyons. il pors *Ebony* 44:60+ Ag '89

FREEMAN, JOHN W.

The good life [cover story] il pors *Opera News* 54:8-12 D 23 '89

Records. See issues of Opera News

The subject is Rose [cover story] il pors *Opera News* 53:8-13 Mr 18 '89

FREEMAN, MORGAN
about
Johnny Handsome. R. Seidenberg. il por *American Film* 15:96-7 O '89
Morgan Freeman stars as tough principal Joe Clark in hit movie, 'Lean on me'. T. S. Moore. il pors *Jet* 75:24-6 Mr 6 '89

FREEMAN, ROBERT M.
about
Conspiracy of strangers. C. Byron. il pors *New York* 22:16+ S 4 '89
The debris in Rudolph Giuliani's wake. C. Welles. pors *Business Week* p36-7 Ja 23 '89

FREEMAN, STEVEN
about
Pulling the plug on a real estate data base. por *Business Week* p41 Jl 24 '89

FREEPORT-MCMORAN INC.
"When preparation meets opportunity". K. Hannon. il por *Forbes* 143:266+ My 29 '89

FREESTYLE SKIING
Competitions
Nelson Carmichael: the bumpy road to the top [mogul champion] L. Tejada-Flores. il pors *Skiing* 42:72-6+ D '89

FREEZE-DRYING
See also
Jeff's Preservation Specialties, Inc.

FREEZING
See also
Ice
Water pipes—Freezing

FREEZING OF HUMAN BODIES *See* Cryonics

FREI, HANS W. (HANS WILHELM), 1922-1988
about
Hans Frei and the meaning of biblical narrative [cover story] W. C. Placher. *The Christian Century* 106:556-9 My 24-31 '89

FREIGHT AIRPLANES *See* Airplanes, Freight

FREIGHT AND FREIGHTAGE
See also
Air freight service
Trucking

FREIGHT RATES
See also
Railroads—Rates

FREIGHTERS
See also
Tankers

FREIMAN, JANE
Affairs to remember. il *Harper's Bazaar* 122:132+ Je '89
At home on the range. il pors *Harper's Bazaar* 122:216+ Ap '89
Borscht Belt. il *Harper's Bazaar* 122:172+ F '89
Deals on meals. il *New York* 22:48-52 Ja 23 '89
The underground gourmet. See occasional issues of New York

FREIWALD, TANI
about
The great talk-show hoax. B. G. Harrison. *Mademoiselle* 95:62 Ja '89

FRELINGHUYSEN, ALICE COONEY
American stoneware in the collection of Arthur and Esther Goldberg. bibl f il *Antiques* 136:568-81 S '89
Tucker porcelain, Philadelphia, 1826-1838 [cover story] il *Antiques* 135:918-29 Ap '89

FRELK, JAMES J.
Defense cubed. *National Review* 41:34-5 My 5 '89

FRENCH, A. P. (ANTHONY PHILIP), 1920-
about
AAPT top honors awarded to French and Birgeneau. pors *Physics Today* 42:126-8 Mr '89

FRENCH, ANTHONY PHILIP *See* French, A. P. (Anthony Philip), 1920-

FRENCH, DANIEL CHESTER, 1850-1931
about
Chesterwood: a sculptor's studio. D. Sherwood. il *Gourmet* 49:76-9+ Je '89

FRENCH, DANIEL W.
Spilled milk. il por *Parents* 64:232 Mr '89

FRENCH, DEBORAH L., AND OTHERS
The role of somatic hypermutation in the generation of antibody diversity. bibl f il *Science* 244:1152-7 Je 9 '89

FRENCH, MARILYN, 1929-
A Gothic romance. il *Ms.* 17:60 Ap '89

FRENCH, ROBERT L.
Cars that know where they're going [cover story] il por *The Futurist* 23:29-36 My/Je '89

FRENCH, WILLIAM
Crabgrass wars: my father's surrender. il *Commonweal* 116:421-2 Ag 11 '89

FRENCH
Prisoners of taste. J. Kramer. il *House & Garden* 161:106-7 Jl '89

United States
History
Banished by Napoleon: the American exile of Baron and Baroness Hyde de Neuville. G.-G. Deák. bibl f il pors *Antiques* 136:1148-57 N '89
Bernhardt in America. J. Kobler. il pors *American Heritage* 40:52-4+ Jl/Ag '89

FRENCH ART *See* Art, French

FRENCH ARTIFICIAL SATELLITES *See* Artificial satellites, French

FRENCH BREAD *See* Bread

FRENCH CANADA *See* Québec (Province)

FRENCH CANADIAN BUSINESS ENTERPRISES
The color of money [francophone business community in Quebec] G. W. Taylor. il *Maclean's* 102:25-6 S 25 '89

FRENCH CANADIANS
See also
Acadians
Remembering a motherland. P. Young. il *Maclean's* 102:41 My 15 '89

FRENCH CAVALRY SCHOOL *See* École de Cavalerie

FRENCH CHEESE *See* Cheese

FRENCH CLOCKS *See* Clocks

FRENCH COOKING *See* Cooking, French

FRENCH DECORATIVE ARTS *See* Decoration and ornament

FRENCH DOORS *See* Doors

FRENCH EMBLEMS *See* Emblems

FRENCH FASHION *See* Fashion

FRENCH FASHION DESIGNERS *See* Fashion designers

FRENCH FURNITURE *See* Furniture, French

FRENCH GRAND PRIX *See* Automobile racing—France

FRENCH GUIANA
See also
Rain forests—French Guiana
Space centers—French Guiana

FRENCH HOUSE DECORATION *See* House decoration, French

FRENCH JEWELRY *See* Jewelry, French

FRENCH LANGUAGE
See also
Francophonie (Organization)
"L'affaire Pasteur" prompts Canadian outcry [decision to publish journals in English] D. Dickson. il *Science* 244:280-1 Ap 21 '89
Unbreakable language barriers [English and French processed differently in the brain; research by Anne Cutler and others] *Discover* 10:10+ D '89

FRENCH LANGUAGE IN FRANCE
Spelling
Changing the rules. P. Lewis. il *Maclean's* 102:56+ Ja 2 '89
A gizmo for the president. W. F. Buckley. *National Review* 41:70-1 F 10 '89
Simplifying French. P. Lewis. il *World Press Review* 36:56 Mr '89

FRENCH LANGUAGE QUESTION IN CANADA *See* Canada—Languages

FRENCH LANGUAGE QUESTION IN NEW BRUNSWICK *See* New Brunswick—Languages

FRENCH LANGUAGE QUESTION IN ONTARIO *See* Ontario—Languages

FRENCH LANGUAGE QUESTION IN QUÉBEC (PROV-INCE) *See* Québec (Province)—Languages

FRENCH LITERATURE
'Slaves of one man' [portrayal of American Indians] C. de Grandpré. il *The Unesco Courier* 42:44-7 O '89

FRENCH MARKET (NEW ORLEANS, LA.)
Mornings at the French Market. C. Maddox. il *Southern Living* 24:20+ Ap '89

FRENCH PAINTING *See* Painting, French

FRENCH PHILOSOPHY *See* Philosophy, French

FRENCH PHOTOGRAPHERS *See* Photographers, French

FRENCH POLYNESIA
See also
Bora Bora (French Polynesia)
Huahine (French Polynesia)
Moorea (French Polynesia)
Raiatea (French Polynesia)
Tahiti (French Polynesia)

FRENCH POTTERY *See* Pottery, French

FRENCH REVOLUTION *See* France—History—Revolution, 1789-1799

THE FRENCH REVOLUTION [film] *See* Motion picture reviews—Single works

FRENCH REVOLUTION OF 1848 *See* France—History—February Revolution, 1848

FRENCH ROOM (SAN FRANCISCO, CALIF.: RESTAURANT) *See* San Francisco (Calif.)—Restaurants, nightclubs, bars, etc.

FRENCH SCULPTURE *See* Sculpture, French
FRENCH SPACEPLANE *See* Spaceplane, French
FRENCH TWIST *See* Hairstyling
FRENCH VASES *See* Vases, French
FRENTE POPULAR PARA LA LIBERACION DE SAGUIA EL HAMRA Y RIO DE ORO *See* Polisario Front
FRENZEL, BILL
Should the House-passed wage proposal be enacted? [excerpts from address, March 23, 1989] *Congressional Digest* 68:151+ My '89
FREON *See* Fluorocarbons
FREQUENCY ALLOCATION, TELEVISION *See* Television frequency allocation
FREQUENCY CHANGERS
B + K Model 1201SR television frequency converter/modulator. il *Radio-Electronics* 60:22 O '89
Low frequency converter. W. Sheets and R. F. Graf. il *Radio-Electronics* 60:47-50+ S '89
One-band shortwave converter. R. F. Graf and W. Sheets. il *Radio-Electronics* 60:49-51 O '89
FREQUENCY MODULATION, RADIO *See* Radio frequency modulation
FREQUENCY MODULATION RECEIVERS *See* Radio receivers
FREQUENCY RESPONSE (ELECTRIC ENGINEERING)
Frequency response: what do the numbers really mean? L. Klein. il *Radio-Electronics* 60:71-2 Ag '89
FREQUENCY STANDARDS
10-MHz frequency standard. A. Palmer. il *Radio-Electronics* 60:63-9 F '89
FREQUENT FLIER PROGRAMS
High-mileage credit cards. K. Davis. *Changing Times* 43:120+ O '89
I'm flying as fast as I can [elite programs] G. Eichler. il *Esquire* 112:78 D '89
Miss those frequent-flyer deals? Try carrying a pouch. P. Cole. il *Business Week* p156 Mr 13 '89
What's good for the boss . . . G. Eichler. il *Esquire* 111:52 Ja '89
Ethical aspects
Flying the shadow market [frequent flier ticket brokers] J. Popkin. il *U.S. News & World Report* 107:77-80+ N 13 '89
Property? Or perk? [American Airlines charges Coupon Connection with conspiring to defraud American by buying and selling frequent flier awards] D. Fanning. il *Forbes* 143:136 Je 26 '89
FRESCOES
Born to paint [work of A. Romano] *The New Yorker* 64:24-6 F 6 '89
Orozco's American epic [acquisition of fresco cycle by Hood Museum of Art] C. Giuliano. il por *Art News* 88:53+ N '89
Palladio and Veronese at the Villa Barbaro in Maser, Italy. B. L. Brown. bibl f il *Antiques* 135:298-309 Ja '89
That dammed Hercules [painted on the face of the Tignes Dam in France for 1992 Olympics] B. Weber. il *The New York Times Magazine* p130 N 5 '89
Conservation and restoration
A renaissance for Michelangelo [cover story] D. Jeffery. il *National Geographic* 176:688-713 D '89
FRESHMEN, COLLEGE *See* College students
FRESHWATER ECOLOGY
See also
Lake ecology
Pond ecology
Stream ecology
FRESNO (CALIF.)
Historic houses, sites, etc.
Fresno as 19th-century farm town. il map *Sunset (Central West edition)* 183:76-7 N '89
Restaurants, nightclubs, bars, etc.
Spécialités de la maison:
Harlands. C. Bates. il *Gourmet* 49:24+ My '89
FRESNO ZOO
Rain forest in Fresno? il *Sunset (Central West edition)* 182:58 F '89
FRESTON, TOM
about
Into the groove [cover story] J. M. Robins. il pors *Channels (New York, N.Y.: 1986)* 9:22-3+ My '89
FREUD, SIGMUND, 1856-1939
about
David Riesman's Freud. S. Weiland. *Society* 26:73-7 My/Je '89
Encountering Freud. P. Roazen. *Society* 26:77-82 My/Je '89
Free associations. M. Jones. *Society* 27:81-6 N/D '89
Freud, efficiency and pragmatism. P. M. Shields. bibl *Society* 26:67-72 Ja/F '89
Re-examining Freud. il *Psychology Today* 23:48-50+ S '89
Sigmund and Minna? The biographer as voyeur. P. Gay. por *The New York Times Book Review* 94:1+ Ja 29 '89
FREUDENBERGER, GLENN
about
Freud's greatest adventure: full moon over Bonneville. K. Vreeke. il pors *Cycle* 40:65-7+ F '89

FREUDENHEIM, BETTY
An ambiguous art: the jewelry of J. Fred Woell. il *American Craft* 49:32-5 Ap/My '89
FREUDIANISM *See* Psychoanalysis
FREUND, HENRY P., AND PARKER, ROBERT K.
Free-electron lasers [cover story] bibl il *Scientific American* 260:84-9 Ap '89
FREUNDLICH, PETER
Confessions of a head case. il *Esquire* 112:231-4+ S '89
A pretty girl is like a malady. il *Esquire* 111:122-6 F '89
FREWER, MATT
about
With Max Headroom behind him, Matt Frewer mad-libs through Doctor, doctor and a smash film. M. Dougherty. il pors *People Weekly* 32:111-12 Jl 17 '89
FREY, NADINE
Hautes Boîtes. il *Harper's Bazaar* 122:202+ D '89
Tailored perfection. il por *Harper's Bazaar* 122:70 Ap '89
FRICK, THOMAS
Song and set. il por *Art in America* 77:67+ D '89
FRICTION
See also
Tribology
FRIDAY, CAROLYN
(jt. auth) See Reibstein, Larry, and Friday, Carolyn
FRIDAY THE 13TH, PART VIII: JASON TAKES MANHATTAN [film] See Motion picture reviews—Single works
FRIED, EUNICE, 1933-
Wine & spirits. See issues of Black Enterprise
FRIED, NANCY
about
The art of healing. C. Langer. il *Ms.* 17:132-3 Ja/F '89
FRIED, STEPHEN
Music. See issues of Gentlemen's Quarterly
FRIED CHICKEN *See* Cooking—Poultry
FRIEDAN, BETTY
Not for women only. il pors *Modern Maturity* 32:66-8+ Ap/My '89
FRIEDENSTAG [opera] See Strauss, Richard, 1864-1949
FRIEDERSDORF, MAX L.
Chemical weapons disposal program [statement, April 4, 1989] *Department of State Bulletin* 89:19-21 Je '89
FRIEDLAND, HOWARD
about
Howard Friedland. M. C. Nelson. il *American Artist* 53:60-5 Jl '89
FRIEDLANDER, LEE, 1934-
about
American monument. R. B. Woodward. il por *Art News* 88:140-5 N '89
FRIEDLANDER, MICHAEL J.
(jt. auth) See Lal, Ratneshwar, and Friedlander, Michael J.
FRIEDLANDER, SHELDON K.
Pollution prevention. bibl f il maps *Environment* 31:10-15+ My '89
FRIEDMAN, AMY
Peddero. il *Country Journal* 16:50-5 F '89
FRIEDMAN, BENJAMIN M.
The deficit: an exchange [discussion of June 1, 1989 article, A deficit of civic courage] *The New York Review of Books* 36:73-4 S 28 '89
A deficit of civic courage. il *The New York Review of Books* 36:23-6 Je 1 '89
What is the 'right' amount of saving? *National Review* 41:31-2 Je 16 '89
FRIEDMAN, BONITA
Envy, the writer's disease. il *The New York Times Book Review* 94:1+ N 26 '89
FRIEDMAN, BRUCE JAY, 1930-
about
The funny guy's book of life. J. Taylor. il pors *New York* 22:46-50 O 9 '89
FRIEDMAN, DAVID
You may not need a great quarterback—or the best talent—to make the Super Bowl. il *TV Guide* 37:28-9 Ja 7-13 '89
FRIEDMAN, HERBERT
Youth of today. il *World Health* p3 Mr '89
FRIEDMAN, HERBERT, 1931-1988
Communications corner. See issues of Radio-Electronics through January 1989
High-tech home security [cover story] il *Radio-Electronics* 60:33-7+ Ap '89
about
Obituary
Radio-Electronics il 60:4 Ja '89. B. C. Fenton
FRIEDMAN, HERBERT, 1931-1988, AND FENTON, BRIAN C.
Install a home security system. il *Radio-Electronics* 60:42-6+ Ap '89
FRIEDMAN, INA
(tr) See Ya'ari, Ehud. Israel's prison academies
FRIEDMAN, JENNY
Helping your learning-disabled child. il *Parents* 64:106-8+ D '89

FRIEDMAN, KAREN
about
From rags to riches in the tough world of retail. D. E. Gumpert. il por *Working Woman* 14:45-6+ O '89

FRIEDMAN, KEN
about
Movies you'll never see. A. Hornaday. il *Mother Jones* 14:53-4 F/Mr '89

FRIEDMAN, KENNETH A.
(jt. auth) See Friedman, Sharon M., and Friedman, Kenneth A.

FRIEDMAN, LOUIS, AND LYNCH, TIMOTHY B.
Science as a national priority. il *USA Today (Periodical)* 118:47-8 S '89

FRIEDMAN, MARTIN
What's in store for you. See issues of Good Housekeeping beginning December 1989

FRIEDMAN, MARTIN L., 1925-
about
The director's director. M. A. Martin. il pors *Art News* 88:132-7 My '89

FRIEDMAN, MEL
Her majesty's censors. il *The Progressive* 53:30-3 F '89

FRIEDMAN, MEYER, 1910-
about
Type A: healing the spirit. J. P. Rodgers. il *Psychology Today* 23:22 Ap '89

FRIEDMAN, MILTON, 1912-
Straight talk about deficits. *Reader's Digest* 134:105-7 Mr '89
What is the 'right' amount of saving? [with discussion] il *National Review* 41:25-32 Je 16 '89
about
Forget those phony problems. M. Magnet. *Fortune* 120:68-9 Jl 3 '89

FRIEDMAN, ROBERT I.
Israel's fateful hour [interview with Y. Harkabi] *Harper's* 279:28+ Jl '89
The settlers. bibl f il *The New York Review of Books* 36:49-56 Je 15 '89
West Bank story [discussion of June 15, 1989 article, The settlers] *The New York Review of Books* 36:59 N 23 '89

FRIEDMAN, ROBERTA
Shooing fish with sound. il *Sea Frontiers* 35:136-41 My/Je '89

FRIEDMAN, SAMUEL R., 1942-
(jt. auth) See Des Jarlais, Don, 1945-, and Friedman, Samuel R., 1942-

FRIEDMAN, SHARON M., AND FRIEDMAN, KENNETH A.
Environmental journalism: guardian of the Asian commons [cover story] bibl f il *Environment* 31:6-9+ Je '89

FRIEDMAN, STEVE
Confessions of a high school big shot: maybe what you think about the jock/brain/heartthrob is all wrong. por *Seventeen* 48:100-1+ Jl '89

FRIEDMAN, STEVE, 1946-
about
TV's big turnoff [cover story] J. Morgenstern. il por *The New York Times Magazine* p12-15+ Ja 1 '89

FRIEDMAN, THOMAS L.
The politicians: avoiding decisions [cover story] il map *The New York Times Magazine* p34-6+ My 7 '89
about
PW interviews. S. Staggs. por *Publishers Weekly* 236:54-5 Jl 14 '89

FRIEDMAN, WARNER, 1934-
about
Warner Friedman. E. Agar. il por *American Artist* 53:44-7+ Ja '89

FRIEDMAN, WILLIAM S.
about
Old dog, old tricks. J. Zweig. il por *Forbes* 144:246+ O 2 '89

FRIEDMANN, THEODORE, 1935-
Progress toward human gene therapy. bibl f il *Science* 244:1275-81 Je 16 '89

FRIEDRICH, GÖTZ
about
Next stop: Kennedy Center. M. Swed. il por *Opera News* 53:18-20+ Je '89

FRIEDRICH, JACQUELINE
How sweet it is! il *American Craft* 49:38-45+ F/Mr '89

FRIEDRICH, OTTO, 1929-
The enigma variations [excerpts from Glenn Gould: a life and variations] il pors *Maclean's* 102:50-4 My 15 '89
Gone blind. il *Harper's* 278:73-80 Mr '89

FRIEDRICHS, MARK S., AND WOLYNES, PETER G.
Toward protein tertiary structure recognition by means of associative memory Hamiltonians. bibl f il *Science* 246:371-3 O 20 '89

FRIEDRICHSTRASSE (BERLIN, GERMANY)
The Friedrichstrasse, a link in the chain of history. C. Mengin. il map *The Unesco Courier* 42:10-14 Ag '89

FRIEDSON, DAVID M.
about
Windmere tries to comb out the kinks. G. DeGeorge. il por *Business Week* p44 Jl 24 '89

FRIEL, BRIAN
about
Aristocrats [drama] Reviews
Commonweal 116:437 Ag 11 '89. G. C. Weales
New York 22:88+ My 8 '89. J. Simon
The New Yorker 65:104 My 8 '89. E. Oliver
Time il 133:87 My 15 '89. W. A. Henry

FRIEND, TAD
G'day, wimp. il *Esquire* 112:61-2 S '89
Travel. il *Vogue* 179:164+ Je '89
The verdict on Arthur Liman. il por *Esquire* 111:66-75 Ja '89
Waikiki confidential. il *Vogue* 179:406+ Mr '89
The waning (and careful waxing) of a dynasty. il *Harper's* 279:68-71 Ag '89

FRIENDS OF THE EARTH
A divisive alliance [Pollution Probe and Friends of the Earth endorse Loblaw's environmentally friendly line of products] *Maclean's* 102:40 Jl 17 '89

FRIENDSHIP
See also
Pen pals
7 stars say what makes a good friend [women] il *Redbook* 173:22+ O '89
Advice for advice-givers: don't! E. Kaye. *Mademoiselle* 95:124 Ag '89
After 58 years, a round-robin letter keeps on delivering [women graduates of the College of Wooster maintain contact] W. Plummer. il *People Weekly* 31:99-100 Ja 16 '89
Are you a good friend? [quiz] il *'Teen* 33:81-2 Je '89
As super as 1-2-3 ['Teen magazine contest alumni Alison, Angi and Michelle] il *'Teen* 33:62-3 Ja '89
Best friends, all the way [celebrities] L. Stover. il *Mademoiselle* 95:212-17 S '89
Cherishing our friends. A. Stoddard. il *McCall's* 116:146 Mr '89
Creative chemistry. A. Tapert. il *Working Woman* 14:106-8+ Mr '89
Death of a friendship. S. Mansfield. *Mademoiselle* 95:146 Ap '89
A delicate balance [strain of miscarriage on women's friendship] K. W. Wiley. il *Health (New York, N.Y.)* 21:30+ My '89
Drifting away [women's friendships] D. Cole. il *Ms.* 18:52+ S '89
Every woman needs a champion. C. G. Vogel. il pors *Good Housekeeping* 208:158+ My '89
The evolution of women's friendships. P. R. Satran. il *Working Woman* 14:158-60+ N '89
Flip-flop friendships: turn them right-side up. W. Woodward. il *'Teen* 33:24+ N '89
The gains and pains of friendship [children] J. P. Comer. il *Parents* 64:197 Ap '89
How kids make friends [with editorial comment by Ann Pleshette Murphy] L. Yarrow. il *Parents* 64:9, 95-100+ O '89
How to have a boyfriend without losing your friends. D. Kent. il *Seventeen* 48:155-6+ My '89
How to keep a close friend close [women] J. Viorst. il *Redbook* 174:84+ D '89
In the company of friends [children] L. G. Katz. il *Parents* 64:193 Mr '89
Is a friend's crush off-limits? J. C. Johnson. *Mademoiselle* 95:140 S '89
It's never too early to make a friend [children] B. Brenner. il *Good Housekeeping* 209:81+ S '89
Just friends [black woman's friendship with lesbian] R. Weems. il *Essence* 20:60-2+ My '89
Kids without friends. P. Chance. il *Psychology Today* 23:28-31 Ja/F '89
Living with choices. F. Prose. il *Parents* 64:130-3 My '89
Lonely teardrops: when kids have trouble making friends. J. K. Rosemond. il *Better Homes and Gardens* 67:27 Mr '89
Loose lips sink friendships. S. Mansfield. *Mademoiselle* 95:56 Ja '89
Love's losses: must losing a lover mean you can't keep his friends? C. L. Mithers. *Glamour* 87:294 My '89
Marriage's unfulfilled promise [importance of women's friendships with other women; research by Stacey Oliker] P. King. il *Psychology Today* 23:71-2 D '89
My best friend's girlfriend. B. Weber. il *The New York Times Magazine* p18+ Ap 16 '89
My teacher, my friend [B. Turner] E. Stone. il *New Choices for the Best Years* 29:80+ D '89
No ties to bind [friendships between single men and married men] C. Yearwood. por *Essence* 20:10 S '89
One's single, one's married: can these women still be friends? S. Jacoby. il *Glamour* 87:162-3+ Ja '89
Single women, married women: can we be friends? B. M. Campbell. il *Essence* 20:47-8+ Jl '89
Social butterflies. P. Theroux. il *Parents* 64:47-9 Jl '89
Straight from the heart [women's friendships; cover story] S. Dworkin. pors *Redbook* 174:20+ D '89
Surprising key to the happiest couples [condensed from Husbands and wives] M. Kinder and C. Cowan. il *Reader's Digest* 135:149-52 Jl '89

FRIENDSHIP—cont.

That perfect blendship. B. W. Wright. il *New Choices for the Best Years* 29:51-3+ Mr '89

Toward a new definition of singleness: building a life with close friends [female friends] R. Kranz. il *Utne Reader* p56-7+ Mr/Ap '89

Two friends with one dream: "She gave me my baby" [donation of ova] J. Liebmann-Smith. *Redbook* 172:122-3+ Mr '89

"We have a problem" [developing child's social skills] J. Marks. il *Parents* 64:63-6 D '89

What do you owe a friend? [women's friendships] J. Stone. il *Glamour* 87:74 Jl '89

What friendship means to teens. D. Elkind. il *Parents* 64:223 D '89

What male friends can & can't teach you about love. C. L. Mithers. il *Glamour* 87:338-9+ Ap '89

When all the stars are gone [homeless best friend] F. Waitzkin. il *The New York Times Magazine* p20-3+ Jl 16 '89

When she's sad and you're happy . . . shut up! E. Kaye. *Mademoiselle* 95:78 Je '89

When you and your best friend grow apart [teenagers] S. Nelson. il *Seventeen* 48:308-9+ Ag '89

When your best friend's parents get divorced. J. Schneller. il *Seventeen* 48:113-14+ Mr '89

When your friend picks the wrong man. C. L. Mithers. il *Glamour* 87:268 N '89

Where have you gone, Billy boy? M. Milton. il *The New York Times Magazine* p32+ D 10 '89

Why breaking plans is bad to do. S. Mansfield. *Mademoiselle* 95:104 F '89

Writers beware writers. A. Broyard. il *The New York Times Book Review* 94:14 My 21 '89

Anecdotes, facetiae, satire, etc.

No man is an isthmus [male friendships] S. Bing. il *Esquire* 112:53-4 Ag '89

Pale bonding [men's friendships] K. A. Samon. il *Gentlemen's Quarterly* 59:183-4+ N '89

FRIENDSHIP'S DEATH [film] See Motion picture reviews—Single works

FRIESEN, DAVID

about

David Friesen. W. Minor. il pors *Down Beat* 56:44-5 Ap '89

FRIESEN, DOROTHY

Human rights abuses shrouded in Philippines. *The Christian Century* 106:678-9 Jl 19-26 '89

FRIESS, FOSTER

about

Will the pendulum swing again? J. Clements. il por *Forbes* 144:360+ N 13 '89

FRIESZ, JOHN

about

Big guns in the Big Sky. D. S. Looney. il pors *Sports Illustrated* 71:83-4 O 16 '89

FRIMAN, ALICE

Sunday drive [poem] *America* 161:318 N 11 '89

FRINGE BENEFITS

See also

Bonus system

Dependent care (Employee benefits)

Employee vacations

Executives—Salaries, pensions, etc.

Flexible spending accounts

Industry—Elderly services programs

Insurance, Health

Profit sharing

Retirement benefits

Comparing employee benefits in the public and private sectors. W. J. Wiatrowski. bibl f il *Monthly Labor Review* 111:3-8 D '88

Make the most of your fringe benefits. J. Bodnar. il *Changing Times* 43:93-8 S '89

Six ways to be "family-friendly". S. Nelton. il *Nation's Business* 77:12-13 Mr '89

Unions and management are in a family way [recent settlements hinge on nonwage benefits] R. A. Taylor. *U.S. News & World Report* 106:24 Je 12 '89

What attracts the best workers. P. Kruger. *Working Woman* 14:76+ Mr '89

Laws and regulations

"Antibusiness bills" reappear. D. C. Bacon. il *Nation's Business* 77:6 Ap '89

The ever-tightening federal grip on employee benefits. *Nation's Business* 77:26 F '89

Labor targets the states on benefits. J. C. Szabo. *Nation's Business* 77:16 Ja '89

Taxation

Changes ahead for Section 89. D. C. Bacon. il *Nation's Business* 77:6 Je '89

Doubts multiply on Section 89 [federal benefits law] R. Thompson. il *Nation's Business* 77:17-18+ My '89

Giving workers the boss's benefits [Section 89 of tax code] D. L. Boroughs. il *U.S. News & World Report* 106:BC1 Ap 10 '89

"Government gone crazy" [Section 89 of tax code on employee benefits discrimination; cover story] R. Thompson. il *Nation's Business* 77:20-4+ F '89

How the good guys won the battle of Section 89. il *Nation's Business* 77:101 N '89

Is it time to bust the postwar benefits boom? G. Koretz. il *Business Week* p34 N 13 '89

Looking beyond Section 89. R. Thompson. il *Nation's Business* 77:27-8 D '89

A push to repeal Section 89 [strictures on employee benefits] R. Thompson. il *Nation's Business* 77:6 Mr '89

Section 89 among House GOP targets. D. C. Bacon. por *Nation's Business* 77:6 Jl '89

Section 89: beyond repair. R. Thompson. il *Nation's Business* 77:65-7 Ap '89

There's only one way to clear up this misunderstanding [repeal of Section 89] *Nation's Business* 77:80 Ag '89

FRINGE MOVEMENTS See Counterculture

FRINK, STEPHEN

Snaps under the sea. il *Travel Holiday* 172:18-21 Jl '89

FRISBEE (GAME)

Frisbee whizzes [World Junior Frisbee Disc Championships] il *National Geographic World* 169:32-5 S '89

FRISELL, BILL

about

Bill Frisell: guitars & scatterations [cover story] J. Diliberto. il pors *Down Beat* 56:16-19 My '89

Bill Frisell's solo on "Evidence"—a guitar transcription. J. Dennison. il *Down Beat* 56:56-7 My '89

FRISELL, SONJA

about

Private lives. B. Paolucci. il por *Opera News* 53:14-15 Ja 7 '89

FRISHBERG, DAVE, 1933-

about

Isn't it ironic? D. Okrent. il por *Esquire* 112:54 D '89

FRISHMAN, ELYSE D.

Hanukkah [excerpt from These lights are holy] il *Good Housekeeping* 209:74 D '89

FRIST, WILLIAM H.

The doctor with the heart of gold [excerpt from Transplant] il *Redbook* 173:134-6+ Jl '89

FRITILLARIAS

Fritillarias. J. Glattstein. il *Flower and Garden* 33:28-9+ S/O '89

FRITO-LAY, INC.

Frito-Lay's cooking again, and profits are starting to pop. A. Dunkin. il *Business Week* p66+ My 22 '89

FRITTATA See Omelets

FRITTERS

Golden tomato fritters from an Amish kitchen [excerpt from Cooking from quilt country] M. Adams. il *Redbook* 173:36 Je '89

FRITZ, SANDY

Bon Voyager. il *Omni (New York, N.Y.)* 12:67-71 N '89

FROG RIGS (FISHING LURES) See Fishing lures, flies, etc.

FROGFISH

The frogfish: disappearing angler. il *Sea Frontiers* 35:231 Jl/Ag '89

FROGS

Frogs that sweat—not bullets, but a poison for darts [dendrobates and phyllobates] J. S. Bainbridge, Jr. il *Smithsonian* 19:70-4+ Ja '89

Nature's way [snake eating a frog] M. Gadomski. il *The Conservationist* 43:56 My/Je '89

Eggs

See Amphibia—Eggs

Embryology

See Embryology—Amphibia

Hearing

See Hearing—Amphibia

Reproduction

See Amphibia—Reproduction

FROHLICH, CLIFF

Deep earthquakes. bibl il maps *Scientific American* 260:48-55 Ja '89

FROHNMAYER, JOHN E., 1942-

about

Testing the new arts rules. *Newsweek* 114:43 N 27 '89

FROIS, JEANNE

The mulberry tree. il *Southern Living* 24:108 Je '89

FROLIC, B. MICHAEL

China's need for leadership. *World Press Review* 36:17-18+ Jl '89

FROMARTZ, S. J.

Coping with the OPEC oil glut. il *The Nation* 248:692-5 My 22 '89

FROME, MICHAEL

Wilderness. bibl il *National Parks* 63:34-41 Jl/Ag '89

FROMER, YEHIEL

about

The man who would be magnate. M. Schifrin. il por *Forbes* 144:41-4 S 18 '89

FROMMER, ARTHUR

about

Beyond the Eiffel Tower [interview] J. Popkin. il por *U.S. News & World Report* 107:63 O 2 '89

FROMMER, HARVEY

(ed) See Dorsett, Tony. My wars with teammates, Dallas—and myself

FROMSTEIN, MITCHELL S.
about
For Mitchell Fromstein, how sweet it is. R. A. Melcher and J. E. Ellis. il por *Business Week* p32 Ja 30 '89
FRONSAC (FRANCE)
Wine industry
See Wine industry—France
FRONSAC WINES *See* Wine
FRONT, MARSHALL B.
Age 70: a duo comfortably retired. il por *Fortune* 120 no10 Special Issue:142 Fall '89
FRONT WHEEL DRIVE VEHICLES
See also
Automobiles—Front wheel drive
Automobiles, Racing—Front wheel drive
FRONT YARDS *See* Home grounds
FRONTAL LOBES *See* Brain
FRONTERO, VINCENT
What's free, what's cheap [cover story] il *New York* 22:38-47 Mr 27 '89
Window on the city. il maps *New York* 22:88-9 My 1 '89
FRONTIER AND PIONEER LIFE
See also
Oregon Trail
Wagon trains
Nebraska
On the seacoast of Nebraska [Oregon Trail] J. G. Mitchell. il map *Audubon* 91:56-77 My '89
Western States
Photographs and photography
Exploring the frontier. il *American History Illustrated* 24:50-1 S/O '89
The life and times of William Henry Jackson. R. Findley. il pors map *National Geographic* 175:216-51 F '89
FROSCH, ROBERT A., AND GALLOPOULOS, NICHOLAS E.
Strategies for manufacturing. bibl il *Scientific American* 261:144-52 S '89
FROSETH, DAN
The sun also sets. il *Flying* 116:138-9 N '89
FROST
See also
Ice crystals
Frost at edges. C. F. Bohren. il *Weatherwise* 42:281-2 O '89
Photographs and photography
One lens, one film, one frosty morning. L. Mann. il *Petersen's Photographic Magazine* 18:30-3 N '89
FROST BOILS *See* Frost heaving
FROST HEAVING
Explaining and exploiting a winter worry [work of J. G. Dash] A. McKenzie. *Science News* 136:407 D 23-30 '89
Thermomolecular pressure in surface melting: motivation for frost heave. J. G. Dash. bibl f il *Science* 246:1591-3 D 22 '89
FROST PROTECTION OF PLANTS *See* Plants—Protection
FROTHS *See* Foams
FROWICK, ROY HALSTON *See* Halston
FROZEN DESSERTS *See* Ice cream, ices, etc.
FROZEN DINNERS
How to choose (and use) a frozen dinner; ed. by Cathy Perlmutter. G. L. Blackburn. il *Prevention (Emmaus, Pa.)* 41:30-1 Ja '89
FROZEN EMBRYOS
The case of the frozen embryos. J. Lieber. il *The Saturday Evening Post* 261:50-3 O '89
The eggs [J. and M. S. Davis' custody fight over fertilized eggs] B. McCollister. por *The Humanist* 49:39 N/D '89
Future shock [J. and M. S. Davis' custody fight over fertilized eggs] il *Time* 133:42 Mr 27 '89
Love multiplied by three [Mohr triplets born 21 months apart]; ed. by Elaine Fein. J. Mohr. il pors *Redbook* 173:100-1+ Ag '89
A piece of yourself in the world [human embryos frozen for later implantation] J. Lieber. il *The Atlantic* 263:76-80 Je '89
The rights of frozen embryos. J. Elson. il *Time* 134:63 Jl 24 '89
Tempest in a test tube [J. and M. S. Davis' legal fight over frozen embryos] J. Seligmann. il pors *Newsweek* 114:66-7 Ag 21 '89
The trial of an embryonic issue. il *U.S. News & World Report* 107:13 Ag 21 '89
Whose lives are these? [decision in custody battle between J. and M. S. Davis] A. L. Sanders. il pors *Time* 134:19 O 2 '89
Anecdotes, facetiae, satire, etc.
People in Petri dishes. M. Ivins. il *The Progressive* 53:38 N '89
Animals
Glass menageries [use of cryopreservation in captive breeding] T. Beardsley. il *Scientific American* 261:36+ O '89
FROZEN FOOD COOKING *See* Cooking—Frozen food
FROZEN GROUND
See also
Frost heaving

FRUEHAUF CORP.
Parlaying the winnings [Terex to buy Fruehauf's trailer business] R. Reiff. il por *Forbes* 144:45-6 Jl 24 '89
FRUG, GERALD E., 1939-
Why courts are always making law. il por *Fortune* 120:245+ S 25 '89
FRUGALITY *See* Thrift
FRUIT
See also
Cooking—Fruit
See also names of fruit
Good food, good health: pass the fruits and vegetables, please! B. Goldman. il *Better Homes and Gardens* 67:16 Jl '89
Raw, raw, raw! [uncooked fruits and vegetables may offer greater protection against cancer; research by Blossom Patterson] R. A. Barnett. il *American Health* 8:130+ S '89
Coatings
Putting fruit to sleep. J. A. Yeaple. *Popular Science* 234:167 My '89
Contamination
Alar in apples [discussion of April 7, 1989 article, Scare of the week] D. E. Koshland, Jr. *Science* 244:755 My 19 '89
Chilean fruit exports to the U.S. [poisoned fruit; statements, March 16 and 29, 1989] *Department of State Bulletin* 89:85 My '89
The cyanide scare: a tale of two grapes [Chilean fruit scare] W. Grigg and V. Modeland. il *FDA Consumer* 23:7-11 Jl/Ag '89
Do you dare to eat a peach? [contaminated Chilean grapes and Alar-treated apples; cover story] M. B. Carlson. il *Time* 133:24-7 Mr 27 '89
Fear of fruits (or, Waiter, there's a pesticide in my salad). J. Nash. il *Mademoiselle* 95:134 Ag '89
Forbidden fruit [Chilean fruit banned] N. Underwood. il *Maclean's* 102:10-12 Mr 27 '89
The great global food fright [U.S. bans imports of Chilean fruit] C. P. Work and R. E. Norton. il *U.S. News & World Report* 106:56-7+ Mr 27 '89
Pesticides & fruit: ways to lower your risks. S. Nielsen. il *Good Housekeeping* 208:241-2 Je '89
Please don't pass the pesticides. S. Squires. *Ladies' Home Journal* 106:56 Jl '89
Scare of the week [Alar-treated apples and cyanide in Chilean grapes] D. E. Koshland, Jr. *Science* 244:9 Ap 7 '89
Diseases and pests
See also
Codling moths
Fruit flies
Ripening
Ethylene gene control: research ripens [gene for ACC synthase cloned; work of Takahide Sato and Athanasios Theologis] *Science News* 136:188 S 16 '89
Thinning
Thinning. il *Sunset (Central West edition)* 182:220 Ap '89
FRUIT, ARTIFICIAL
A harvest of ceramics [work of A. Gordon and C. Potter] C. Petkanas. il pors *House & Garden* 161:28+ Ag '89
FRUIT, DRIED
See also
Cooking—Fruit
FRUIT BRANDY *See* Brandy
FRUIT CULTURE
See also
Grafting
Orchards
Bearing fruit [W. Ehrhardt's Maryland garden] K. Martin. il pors *Organic Gardening* 36:68-72 Mr '89
Planning a home fruit garden. B. Olcott-Reid. il *Flower and Garden* 33:24-9 N/D '89
FRUIT DESSERTS *See* Desserts
FRUIT DRINKS *See* Beverages
FRUIT DRINKS, ALCOHOLIC *See* Alcoholic beverages
FRUIT FLIES
See also
Drosophila
A breed apart [sympatric speciation in apple fruit flies; study by Guy L. Bush] K. Wright. il *Scientific American* 260:22+ F '89
FRUIT IN ART
Fruits of the loom. E. A. Berthold. il *House & Garden* 161:164 Je '89
Noble riddles and surrealist fruits [riddles by G. García Márquez accompany Matta paintings] I. Stavans. il *Art News* 88:29 N '89
FRUIT INDUSTRY
See also
Avocado industry
Banana industry
Blueberry industry
Southern California's new subtropical fruit belt. il *Sunset (Central West edition)* 183:208 S '89

FRUIT INDUSTRY—cont.
Acquisitions and mergers
International aspects
Meet Asil Nadir, the billion-dollar fruit king [Polly Peck to buy Del Monte fresh fruit operations] M. Maremont. il por *Business Week* p32 S 18 '89
Export-import trade
Chilean fruit exports to the U.S. [poisoned fruit; statements, March 16 and 29, 1989] *Department of State Bulletin* 89:85 My '89
The cyanide scare: a tale of two grapes [Chilean fruit scare] W. Grigg and V. Modeland. il *FDA Consumer* 23:7-11 Jl/Ag '89
Chile
Chilean fruit exports to the U.S. [poisoned fruit; statements, March 16 and 29, 1989] *Department of State Bulletin* 89:85 My '89
The cyanide scare: a tale of two grapes [Chilean fruit scare] W. Grigg and V. Modeland. il *FDA Consumer* 23:7-11 Jl/Ag '89
Do you dare to eat a peach? [contaminated grapes; cover story] M. B. Carlson. il *Time* 133:24-7 Mr 27 '89
Forbidden fruit [Chilean fruit banned] N. Underwood. il *Maclean's* 102:10-12 Mr 27 '89
The great global food fright [U.S. bans imports of Chilean fruit] C. P. Work and R. E. Norton. il *U.S. News & World Report* 106:56-7+ Mr 27 '89

FRUIT JUICES
See also
Apple juice
Lemonade
Orange juice

FRUIT OF THE LOOM, INC.
Bill Farley is on pins and needles. D. Greising. il por *Business Week* p58+ S 18 '89
Three easy steps. K. L. Fisher. il *Forbes* 144:253 O 30 '89

FRUIT PUNCH *See* Punch (Beverage)
FRUIT SALADS *See* Salads
FRUIT SAUCES *See* Sauces
FRUIT SOUPS *See* Soups
FRUIT TREES
See also
Apple trees
Cherry trees
Peach trees
Pear trees
Bringing in the harvest . . . and working toward next year's. il *Sunset (Central West edition)* 183:138+ Jl '89
Grafting
See Grafting
Protection
If this doesn't keep the birds away from the cherries . . . il *Sunset (Central West edition)* 182:234-5 Je '89
Thinning
See Fruit—Thinning

FRUIT TREES, DWARF
Porch orchard [cover story] M. Damsker. il *Organic Gardening* 36:24-8+ D '89

FRUITCAKE
Christmas giving. N. Hazelton. *National Review* 41:49-50 D 22 '89
Fabulous fruitcake finale. il *McCall's* 117:47 D '89
Anecdotes, facetiae, satire, etc.
Uncivil liberties. C. Trillin. *The Nation* 248:618 My 8 '89

FRUITS *See* Fruit
FRUITS, VEGETABLES, ETC. IN DECORATION
Citrus rings and apple wreaths. il *Sunset (Central West edition)* 183:62-3 D '89

FRUM, ELSIE
about
Elsie Frum remembers a train's desperate whistle 100 years ago—and the great Johnstown flood. B. Johnson. il pors *People Weekly* 31:85-8 Je 5 '89
A voice from the flood. por *American History Illustrated* 24:25 My '89

FRUMKIN, PETER
(jt. auth) *See* Lenkowsky, Leslie, 1946-, and Frumkin, Peter
FRUNCHTMAN, JERRY
Pure light. il *Petersen's Photographic Magazine* 17:58-9 Mr '89

FRUSTRATION
See also
Repression (Psychology)

FRY, ALICIA M., AND OTHERS
Thymic requirement for clonal deletion during T cell development. bibl f il *Science* 246:1044-6 N 24 '89
FRY, TONY, AND WILLIS, ANNE-MARIE
Aboriginal art: symptom or success? bibl f il *Art in America* 77:108-17+ Jl '89
FRYDMAN, ANNE
(tr) *See* Dovlatov, Sergeï. Grandpa Isaak
FRYE, ALTON
(jt. auth) *See* Stevenson, Adlai, 1930-, and Frye, Alton
FRYE, BARBARA
What Lloyd Cutler could learn from Acme Widget: target pay increases to jobs that are hard to fill. *The Washington Monthly* 21:18-22 Jl/Ag '89

FRYING
See also
Fritters
Stir-frying
FRYMIER, JACK RIMMEL, 1925-, AND GANSNEDER, BRUCE
The Phi Delta Kappa study of students at risk. il *Phi Delta Kappan* 71:142-6 O '89
FRYMIER, JACK RIMMEL, 1925-, AND OTHERS
Simultaneous replication: a technique for large-scale research. bibl f il *Phi Delta Kappan* 71:228-31 N '89
FSLIC *See* Federal Savings and Loan Insurance Corporation
FSX AIRPLANES *See* Airplanes, Military—Japan
FTC *See* United States. Federal Trade Commission
FU XIN-YUAN
about
Biologist monitors human rights. M. Sun. por *Science* 245:592 Ag 11 '89
FUCCI, ELIZABETH
about
Northeast Rat and Mouse Club. *The New Yorker* 65:35-6 Ap 10 '89
FUCHS, DANIEL, 1909-
Strictly movie. *Commentary* 88:38-46 S '89
FUCHS, MICHAEL JOSEPH
about
No laughing matter. B. Carter. il pors *The New York Times Magazine* p50+ N 5 '89
FUCHS, RUDOLF HERMAN, 1942-
about
Picassos for sale? J. Turner. il *Art News* 88:84-5+ D '89
FUDGE (CANDY)
Fudge fudgery. L. Langseth-Christensen. il *Gourmet* 49:110-11+ D '89
FUDGE FACTORY (FIRM)
From real-estate broker to chocolate maker [D. Anas] D. E. Gumpert and D. Davis. il por *New Choices for the Best Years* 29:52-3 O '89
FUEL
See also
Airplane engines—Energy usage
Airplane engines—Fuel
Airplane engines, Jet—Energy usage
Alcohol as fuel
Automobile engines—Energy usage
Automobile engines—Fuel
Biomass energy
Coal
Diesel fuels
Furnaces—Energy usage
Gasoline
Heating
Helicopter engines—Fuel
Hydrogen as fuel
Motor vehicle engines—Energy usage
Natural gas
Nuclear fuels
Peat
Petroleum
Refuse as fuel
Wood as fuel
Conservation
See Energy conservation
Contamination
Toxic fuel [illegally mixing hazardous waste with fuel] A. Porterfield. il *Common Cause Magazine* 15:6-7 Jl/Ag '89
Toxins by truckload [illicit waste-laden fuels enter Canada] B. Wickens. il *Maclean's* 102:17 My 22 '89
Prices
Comparing various heating fuel costs. P. L. Spencer. il *Consumers' Research Magazine* 72:26-8 D '89
FUEL, SYNTHETIC
See also
Alcohol as fuel
Hydrogen as fuel
Oil sands
FUEL CONSERVATION *See* Energy conservation
FUEL FILTERS
See also
Automobile engines—Filters
FUEL INJECTION SYSTEMS *See* Automobile engines—Fuel feeding; Motorcycle engines—Fuel feeding
FUEL REFINERIES IN SPACE *See* Space fuel refineries
FUEL SUPPLY
See also
Electric plants—Energy usage
Gas supply
Gasoline supply
Industry—Energy usage
Petroleum supply
FUEL SYSTEMS, AIRPLANE *See* Airplane engines—Fuel feeding
FUEL SYSTEMS, AUTOMOBILE *See* Automobile engines—Fuel feeding
FUEL SYSTEMS, MOTORCYCLE *See* Motorcycle engines—Fuel feeding

FUEL TANKS
See also
Space vehicles—Fuel tanks
FUENTES, CARLOS
Asphyxiation by progress [excerpts from Christopher unborn; with introd. by Nathan Gardels and Marilyn Berlin Snell] il *New Perspectives Quarterly* 6:43-7 Spr '89
Goya and the spirit of revolution. il por *Art News* 88:90-5 Ja '89
Sacred truth, novelistic truths. *Harper's* 278:17-18 My '89
Uncle Sam, stay home [adaptation of address, May 1988] *Harper's* 278:14-17 Ja '89
FUENTES, JULIO
Next year in Jerusalem? [interview with Y. Arafat] il por *World Press Review* 36:29 Ap '89
FUENZALIDA-PUELMA, HERNÁN L.
(jt. auth) See Connor, Susan Scholle, and Fuenzalida-Puelma, Hernán L.
FUERST, MARK L.
Drilling for fertility. il *Discover* 10:22 O '89
FUGITIVE SLAVES *See* Slavery—Fugitive slaves
FUGITIVES FROM JUSTICE
See also
Escapes
Freeze! You're on TV [America's most wanted] F. J. Prial. il *Reader's Digest* 134:189-92 Mr '89
The fugitive [former black militant H. Ferguson] P. Blauner. il pors *New York* 22:32-7 Ag 7 '89
'I am still devastated' [J. Walsh, host of America's most wanted] J. Marion. il pors *TV Guide* 37:22-4 Mr 18-24 '89
In hiding for 18 years, a wanted man is caught by the FBI and a TV posse [J. List, alleged murderer, featured on America's most wanted] K. Gross. il pors *People Weekly* 31:69-70+ Je 19 '89
Masters of deception [Heilbrunn family, accused of operating Indianapolis drug ring, now living in Austria] B. Shaw and D. Van Biema. il *People Weekly* 31:46-51 Je 19 '89
Murder, they broadcast [viewers of America's most wanted identify murderer J. List] T. Jacoby. pors *Newsweek* 113:58 Je 12 '89
Wanted: lowlifes and high ratings [America's most wanted] D. Friedman. il *Rolling Stone* p34-5 Ja 12 '89
Photographs and photography
The three faces of John List [fugitive apprehended through use of bust created from computer-aged photograph] il pors *U.S. News & World Report* 106:13 Je 12 '89
FUGLESANG, ANDREAS
Folk-wisdom and pseudo-information. il *World Health* p4-7 Ja/F '89
FUGU *See* Puffers (Fish)
FUHRER, DAVID
about
Nac uoy daer siht ecnetnes? David Fuhrer can—dna woh! il por *People Weekly* 31:253 Mr 6 '89
FUJI PHOTO FILM CO., LTD.
Playing leapfrog in disposable cameras [Kodak vs Fuji] L. Helm. il *Business Week* p34 My 1 '89
FUJISANKEI COMMUNICATIONS GROUP
'A big fuss of a visit' [sponsors of R. Reagan visit] il por *Newsweek* 114:54 N 6 '89
One hand clapping. D. Sneider. il *The New Republic* 201:16-17 N 20 '89
FUJITA, KENJI
about
Kenji Fujita at Luhring, Augustine & Hodes. B. Adams. il *Art in America* 77:147-8 Ja '89
FUKUYAMA, FRANCIS
Entering post-history. il *New Perspectives Quarterly* 6:49-52 Fall '89
about
The beginning of nonsense. S. Talbott. il *Time* 134:39 S 11 '89
The end of history—or of liberalism? J. Gray. *National Review* 41:33-5 O 27 '89
The end of what? R. E. Tyrrell. *The American Spectator* 22:10 N '89
Endgames. L. H. Lapham. *Harper's* 279:10-13 N '89
Has history come to an end? J. Elson. il por *Time* 134:57 S 4 '89
History's last word? G. F. Will. il *Newsweek* 114:66 Ag 14 '89
The intellectual Hula Hoop. J. Alter. il *Newsweek* 114:39 O 9 '89
Is history over? *National Review* 41:14-15 S 1 '89
Minority report. C. Hitchens. *The Nation* 249:302 S 25 '89
Stopping time. R. Corelli. il *Maclean's* 102:56+ O 2 '89
Washington diarist: the end of everything. T. Noah. *The New Republic* 201:54 O 16 '89
What is Fukuyama saying? And to whom is he saying it? J. Atlas. il por *The New York Times Magazine* p38-40+ O 22 '89
FULCHER, SARAH
about
The longest run ever. B. Kevles. il por *Women's Sports & Fitness* 11:67 Mr '89

FULD, LEONARD M.
How to get the scoop on your competition [excerpt from Monitoring the competition] il *Working Woman* 14:39-42 Ja '89
FULFILLMENT (PSYCHOLOGY) *See* Self realization
FULGHUM, ROBERT
"All these things were loved by me" [excerpt from It was on fire when I lay down on it] il por *Good Housekeeping* 209:36 O '89
All you really need to know about marriage you learn at the wedding. *Redbook* 173:84+ Je '89
The Daddy Prize [condensed from It was on fire when I lay down on it] il *Reader's Digest* 135:67-9 O '89
I believe in Mother Teresa [excerpt from All I really need to know I learned in kindergarten] por *The Saturday Evening Post* 261:63 Ap '89
My secret valentine [condensed from All I really need to know I learned in kindergarten] il *Reader's Digest* 134:9 F '89
The pageant [excerpt from It was on fire when I lay down on it] il *Good Housekeeping* 209:78+ D '89
Small miracles [condensed from All I really need to know I learned in kindergarten] il *Reader's Digest* 134:67-9 My '89
about
Lessons from the sandbox. P. L. Brown. il pors *The New York Times Magazine* p26-30+ Jl 23 '89
Robert Fulghum. il por *People Weekly* 32:52 D 25 '89-Ja 1 '90
Robert Fulghum proves the rules of kindergarten, even for grown-ups, aren't just kid stuff. A. Chambers. il pors *People Weekly* 31:91-2 F 27 '89
FULKERSON, ALLAN W.
about
Portfolio insurance. J. Clements. il por *Forbes* 144:160 D 25 '89
FULKERSON, WILLIAM, AND OTHERS
Global warming: an energy technology R&D challenge. bibl f il *Science* 246:868-9 N 17 '89
FULL EXPOSURE: THE SEX TAPES SCANDAL [television program] *See* Television program reviews—Single works
FULL HOUSE [television program] *See* Television program reviews—Single works
FULLER, BARBARA
Lewis & Nathan Clark: friends and brothers. il pors *Sierra* 74:148-50+ Ja/F '89
Reaching out from the inner city. il por *Sierra* 74:50-4 Jl/Ag '89
FULLER, BUCKMINSTER *See* Fuller, R. Buckminster, 1895-1983
FULLER, CHARLES
about
Prince [drama] Reviews
New York 22:57 Ja 9 '89. J. Simon
The New Yorker 64:82 Ja 9 '89. E. Oliver
Sally [drama] Reviews
New York 22:57 Ja 9 '89. J. Simon
The New Yorker 64:82 Ja 9 '89. E. Oliver
FULLER, CURTIS, 1934-
about
Curtis Fuller's solo on "Blues after all"—a trombone transcription. L. McClellan, Jr. il *Down Beat* 56:56 Jl '89
FULLER, GOGO
about
Gogo Fuller's sassy skeletal jewelry is not for the spineless. M. Dougherty. il pors *People Weekly* 32:101+ O 16 '89
FULLER, GRAHAM
Cine Sandino. il *Film Comment* 25:2+ Ja/F '89
Dennis Potter. il por *American Film* 14:31-3+ Mr '89
Kenneth. il pors *Film Comment* 25:2+ N/D '89
Undercovers. il por *Film Comment* 25:56-8+ Mr/Ap '89
War and revolution in Iran. bibl f *Current History* 88:81-4+ F '89
FULLER, JIM, D. 1988
about
Obituary
Motor Trend por 41:10 Mr '89
FULLER, JOHN FREDERICK CHARLES, 1878-1966
about
Theory from practice—Major General J.F.C. Fuller. B. H. Reid. bibl il pors *History Today* 39:44-9 Je '89
FULLER, MILLARD
about
A bootstrap approach to low-cost housing. D. Winbush. il pors *Time* 133:12-13 Ja 16 '89
FULLER, PETER, 1947-
Art: Victorian landscapes. il *Architectural Digest* 46:160-5+ Ag '89
FULLER, R. BUCKMINSTER, 1895-1983
about
The birth of the geodesic dome. L. S. Sieden. il pors *The Futurist* 23:14-19 N/D '89
FULLER, ROBERT S., AND OTHERS
Intracellular targeting and structural conservation of a prohormone-processing endoprotease. bibl f il *Science* 246:482-6 O 27 '89

FULLER, WILLIAM P.
Recent trends in U.S. refugee policy. *America* 161:238-40 O 14 '89
FULLER (H.B.) COMPANY *See* H.B. Fuller Company
FULLER BRUSH CO.
Never say quit to Charlie Tucker or he's likely to give you the brush [door-to-door salesman] il por *People Weekly* 32:106-7 Jl 10 '89
FULLERENES
Making chicken wire of molecular size [work of Orville L. Chapman] I. Amato. il *Science News* 136:406 D 23-30 '89
Soccer-ball molecules in space. il *Sky and Telescope* 77:358 Ap '89
Tracking an elusive carbon [cover story] C. Vaughan. il *Science News* 135:56-7 Ja 28 '89
FULLWRITE PROFESSIONAL (WORD PROCESSOR PROGRAM) *See* Word processors and processing—Programming
FULTON, ALICE, 1952-
The orthodox waltz [poem] *The New Republic* 200:35 Mr 13 '89
FULTON, ROBERT
about
A White House promise. *National Review* 41:15-16 Ap 7 '89
FULTON FISH MARKET
Fulton Fish Market and Urban Archaeology Ltd. H. Bridges. il *Gourmet* 49:36+ Mr '89
FUMENTO, MICHAEL
The asbestos rip-off [cover story] il *The American Spectator* 22:21-6 O '89
The incredible shrinking AIDS epidemic. il *The American Spectator* 22:21-6 My '89
about
Straight talk about AIDS. J. Queenan. il por *Forbes* 143:41-2 Je 26 '89
Why did Forbes run Fumento's fulminations on AIDS? [discussion of June 26, 1989 article, Straight talk about AIDS] J. Queenan. *Forbes* 144:20-1 Jl 10 '89
FUMES
Control
Smog-curbing limits on gas volatility [EPA regulations] *Science News* 135:191 Mr 25 '89
FUMIHITO, PRINCE OF JAPAN, 1965-
about
The Emperor's second son falls in love with a commoner—and so does the rest of Japan. il pors *People Weekly* 32:54-5 S 18 '89
FUN
All work and no play . . . isn't even good for work. il *Psychology Today* 23:34-6 Mr '89
Better health through the fun factor [concept of civic health] R. Rodale. il *Prevention (Emmaus, Pa.)* 41:25-7 Jl '89
Finding the fun at work. D. J. Abramis. *Psychology Today* 23:36+ Mr '89
Unguarded moments [cover story] R. Laliberte. il *Health (New York, N.Y.)* 21:52-7 Ag '89
When I work, I just want to have fun. P. Scisco. *Compute!* 11:4 D '89
FUNCTION GENERATORS *See* Signal generators
FUNCTIONS
See also
Hamiltonian function
FUND, JOHN H.
All the Wright moves. il *National Review* 41:19-20 Je 16 '89
Beware the gerrymander, my son. il *National Review* 41:34-6 Ap 7 '89
FUND RAISING
See also
AIDS (Disease)—Fund raising
Basketball, Professional—Benefit games
Campaign funds
Charitable gift annuities
Dance—Benefit performances
Evangelical Council for Financial Accountability
Homeless—Fund raising
Telethons
Brother, can you spare a grand? [opera companies] K. Mauney. *Opera News* 53:12 Ap 15 '89
Freedom Fund gala in Detroit raises $1 million for NAACP. il *Jet* 76:16-17 My 15 '89
I gave at the supermarket [cause related marketing] J. Levine. il *Forbes* 144:138+ D 25 '89
Let's have fun, too. R. R. Roha. il *Changing Times* 43:80 Jl '89
USArts: strategies for the 80's. See issues of Horizon (Tuscaloosa, Ala.)
Ethical aspects
Fed up with charity. J. Bourque. por *Newsweek* 114:10 S 4 '89
How worthy are these causes? [charity sweepstakes] *Modern Maturity* 32:12 F/Mr '89
New guidelines for giving. M. T. Smith. il *Money* 18:141-4+ D '89

NIH probes researcher's fundraising [case of leukemia researcher R. I. Glazer] C. Holden. *Science* 243:1000 F 24 '89
The thrift-shop connection [contracts with charities] R. R. Roha. il *Changing Times* 43:126 Mr '89
FUND RAISING AUCTIONS *See* Auctions
FUNDACIÓN CASA DUCAL DE MEDINACELI
A Spanish heritage: the Duke of Segorbe's crusade to preserve the family estates. Prince Michael. il por *Architectural Digest* 46:198-207+ D '89
FUNDAMENTALISM
See also
Moral Majority
Fundamentalism revisited. F. J. Lechner. bibl *Society* 26:51-9 Ja/F '89
Growing up fundamentalist. P. Yancey. il *Christianity Today* 33:56 F 17 '89
Religious fanatics and censorship. J. R. Joelson. il *The Humanist* 49:33 My/Je '89
A reverence for fundamentalism [Catholic Church] P. Lernoux. il *The Nation* 248:513-16 Ap 17 '89
SBC fundamentalists aim to defuse debate [Southern Baptist Convention in Las Vegas] S. Hastey. *The Christian Century* 106:548-50 My 24-31 '89
There's no such thing as a Catholic fundamentalist. E. LaVerdiere. il *U.S. Catholic* 54:36-8 S '89
Unflinching faith: what fires up the world's fundamentalists? [interview with R. S. Appleby; cover story] il por *U.S. Catholic* 54:6-13 D '89
Who are the Catholic 'fundamentalists'? [cover story] J. A. Coleman. il *Commonweal* 116:42-7 Ja 27 '89
FUNDAMENTALISM AND POLITICS *See* Religion and politics
FUNDS, INVESTMENT *See* Investment trusts
FUNDS, PENSION *See* Pensions
FUNERAL RITES AND CEREMONIES
See also
Indians of North America—Mortuary customs
A Fluxus funeral [memorial for R. Watts] J. Johnston. il pors *Art in America* 77:42-3+ Mr '89
Hot tombs [purchasing desirable burial plots; cover story] M. Specter. *The New Republic* 201:22-5 S 11 '89
History
Grave misunderstandings [changing mortuary customs; research by Aubrey Cannon] B. Bower. il *Science News* 136:330-1 N 18 '89
Austria
A Hapsburg goes home [burial of Zita] N. Darnton. il *Newsweek* 113:41 Ap 10 '89
Japan
A delicate burial [selection of Hirohito funeral delegations] W. R. Doerner. il *Time* 133:34 Ja 23 '89
An imperial farewell [Hirohito] il *Maclean's* 102:24-5 Mr 6 '89
A rite of passage [Hirohito's funeral] B. Martin. il por *Newsweek* 113:24-5 F 20 '89
"With grief, we bid you farewell" [interment of Hirohito] il *Time* 133:46-7 Mr 6 '89
Madagascar
Ways of the ancestors. J. Mack. il *Natural History* p24+ Ap '89
Philippines
Habeas corpse [efforts of citizens in Ilocos Norte to have F. Marcos's body returned to the Philippines] A. Berlow. *The New Republic* 201:12+ O 30 '89
The waning (and careful waxing) of a dynasty [Marcos family] T. Friend. il *Harper's* 279:68-71 Ag '89
FUNGAL ENZYMES *See* Enzymes, Fungal
FUNGAL GENETICS
Field in ferment. S. J. Nadis. *Technology Review* 92:12-13 My/Je '89
Fungal duo teaches evolutionary lesson [research by Jeffrey D. Palmer] B. Bower. *Science News* 135:318 My 20 '89
Genetic engineering of filamentous fungi. W. E. Timberlake and M. A. Marshall. bibl f il *Science* 244:1313-17 Je 16 '89
Put a cassava in your tank [genetically altered yeast cells produce ethanol] il *Discover* 10:10 F '89
FUNGAL TOXINS *See* Mycotoxins
FUNGI
See also
Basidiomycetes
Mushrooms
Mutation—Fungi
Neurospora
Slime molds
Truffles
Yeasts
Development
Dictyostelium discoideum: a model system for cell-cell interactions in development. P. Devreotes. bibl f il *Science* 245:1054-8 S 8 '89
FUNGI, PATHOGENIC
See also
Anthracnose
Entomophaga
Poisonous mushrooms

FUNGI, PATHOGENIC—*cont.*
One enzyme makes a fungal pathogen, but not a saprophyte, virulent on a new host plant. W. Schäfer and others. bibl f il *Science* 246:247-9 O 13 '89
Symbiotic marine bacteria chemically defend crustacean embryos from a pathogenic fungus. M. S. Gil-Turnes and others. bibl f il *Science* 246:116-18 O 6 '89

FUNGICIDES
See also
Antifungal agents

FUNK, DAVID H.
The mating of tree crickets. bibl il *Scientific American* 261:50-5+ Ag '89

FUNK, MICHELLE
about
The luckiest little girl in the world. A. Sunshine-Genova. il pors *Ladies' Home Journal* 106:140-1+ Mr '89

FUNK, PETER, 1921-
It pays to enrich your word power. See issues of Reader's Digest

FUNNIES *See* Comic books, strips, etc.

FUNNY [film] *See* Motion picture reviews—Single works

FUNNY FARM [film] *See* Motion picture reviews—Single works

FUNSTON, FREDERICK, 1865-1917
about
Manifest Destiny's man of the hour: Frederick Funston. D. H. Bain. bibl (p164) il pors *Smithsonian* 20:134-6+ My '89

FUNSTON, LANCE T.
about
Don't blame me. A. A. Lappen. il por *Forbes* 144:102-3+ S 4 '89

FUQUA, C. S.
Neural networking. il *Ad Astra* 1:8-13 Ap '89

FUQUA, J. B.
about
Russia as fourth leg. D. Lataniotis. il por *Forbes* 144 Special Issue:370 O 23 '89

FUQUA, JOHN BROOKS *See* Fuqua, J. B.

FUQUA INDUSTRIES, INC.
Intermark keeps pressing its luck—and winning [buying Fuqua] S. Toy. il por *Business Week* p60+ F 6 '89
Under new management. A. A. Lappen. il por *Forbes* 144:164 S 18 '89

FUR
See also
Antifur movement
Hides and skins

FUR, ARTIFICIAL
Faking it! il *Glamour* 87:220 O '89
Grand illusions. C. Bushnell. il *Health (New York, N.Y.)* 21:72-7+ S '89
Why not slip into a genuine fake? il *Newsweek* 114:82 D 18 '89
Will fur fanciers buy a bum wrap? il *Newsweek* 113:67 Je 5 '89

FUR BEARING ANIMALS
See also
Bobcats
Foxes
Martens
Otters
Seals (Animals)
Trapping

FUR COATS, WRAPS, ETC.
See also
Antifur movement
Sable-trimmed anoraks, spotted swings are but two of fall's fur options, as designers rethink the mink. P. H. Starzinger. il *Vogue* 179:240+ S '89
Stoles could be a steal this year, if you're thinking mink. il *Money* 18:18+ Ja '89

Care
Skin care. R. J. Katz. il *New York* 22:118+ My 15 '89

FUR INDUSTRY
See also
Fur Vault Inc.

History
See also
Fur traders

Marketing
R.I.P. Fred the Furrier. J. A. Trachtenberg. il por *Forbes* 143:122-3 F 20 '89

Public relations
The furriers fight back. il *Newsweek* 114:82 D 18 '89

Alaska
History
Russia's American adventure. L. Black. il map *Natural History* p46-57 D '89

Korea (South)
See also
Jindo Industries Ltd.

United States
See Fur industry

FUR SEALS *See* Seals (Animals)

FUR TRADE *See* Fur industry

FUR TRADERS
Portages into the past. J. Kulpa. il *Field & Stream* 93:48-9 Mr '89

FUR VAULT INC.
R.I.P. Fred the Furrier. J. A. Trachtenberg. il por *Forbes* 143:122-3 F 20 '89
Sans Fred, the fur vault may be ready to fly. J. M. Laderman. il *Business Week* p80 Jl 3 '89

FURANS
Dioxin via skin: a hazard at low doses? [research by Linda S. Birnbaum] *Science News* 135:141 Mr 4 '89

FURET, FRANÇOIS, 1927-
An idea and its destiny. il *The Unesco Courier* 42:50-7 Je '89

about
Dancing on the grave of revolution [cover story] D. Singer. *The Nation* 248:145+ F 6 '89

FUREY, JOSEPH E., 1907-
about
In memory of his wife, Joe Furey created an unusual artwork that may not survive. R. Arias. il pors *People Weekly* 32:104-5 S 4 '89

FURLAUD, ALICE, 1929-
Who said ignorance is bliss? *The New York Times Magazine* p20+ O 8 '89

FURLAUD, RICHARD M., 1923-
about
Filling Bristol-Myers' prescription. J. Weber, Jr. and S. Benway. il pors *Business Week* p80-1 Ag 14 '89

FURMAN, ASHRITA
about
Not explainable. *The New Yorker* 65:25-7 F 27 '89

FURNACES
Energy usage
The most efficient heating systems. il *Consumers' Research Magazine* 72:25-8 Ja '89

FURNESS, FRANK, 1839-1912
about
A stick style curiosity on the Jersey coast. V. J. Scully. il por *Architectural Digest* 46:34+ Mr '89
Two masterworks of American architecture. A. Berman. il por *Architectural Digest* 46:314+ O '89

FURNESS, R. W. (ROBERT WILLIAM)
Not by grass alone. il *Natural History* p8+ D '89

FURNESS, ROBERT WILLIAM *See* Furness, R. W. (Robert William)

FURNESS BUILDING
Two masterworks of American architecture [work of F. Furness] A. Berman. il por *Architectural Digest* 46:314+ O '89

FURNIER, VINCENT *See* Cooper, Alice

FURNISHINGS, HOUSEHOLD *See* Household furnishings

FURNITURE
See also
Beds
Benches
Bookcases
Buffets, sideboards, etc. (Furniture)
Cabinets (Furniture)
Chairs
Chests
Computer furniture
Desks
Drawers
Kitchen cabinets
Kitchen furniture
Office furniture
Ottomans (Furniture)
Settees
Shelves and racks
Sofas
Stools
Tables
Upholstery
Veneers and veneering
Wicker furniture
100 ideas under $100 [cover story; with editorial comment by David Jordan] J. Williams and J. Severson. il *Better Homes and Gardens* 67:10, 19-24+ Jl '89
The best of the worst: one man's pick of history's most unfortunate furniture styles. S. Greenspan. il *House & Garden* 161:66+ My '89
Check it out: use storage modules to build stylish furniture. L. M. Dalsgaard. il *Home Mechanix* 85:54-7+ F '89
Five great looks from five great galleries. D. L. Caringer and others. il *Better Homes and Gardens* 67:71-81 N '89

Anecdotes, facetiae, satire, etc.
Last word. M. Coleman and D. Jaffe. il *Omni (New York, N.Y.)* 11:110 Ja '89

FURNITURE—*cont.*

Care

See Furniture—Maintenance and repair

Decorating

See Furniture, Decorated

Design

See also

Pattern books

Barbarians at play [work of M. Bonetti and E. Garouste] C. K. Gandee. il pors *House & Garden* 161:132-5 Jl '89

Grand designs [work of C. Riley, A. Locadia, and T. Miller] D. Sapolin. il pors *Essence* 20:80-1+ Jl '89

Parlors with a pedigree [decorators making furniture] M. Malone. il *Newsweek* 113:72 Ap 10 '89

Something of a Druid [work of G. Nakashima] J. D. Reed. il por *Time* 133:75 Je 26 '89

Wild things [horn and antler furniture] A. De Moubray. il *House & Garden* 161:28-9 Ja '89

Woodwork. il *Vogue* 179:129-31 Ja '89

Exhibitions

Easy comfort [Southern Furniture Market] C. Vogel. il *The New York Times Magazine* p72 Ap 2 '89

High Point: new reliables [International Home Furnishings Market] C. Vogel. il *The New York Times Magazine* p62 O 15 '89

Finishes and finishing

See also

Furniture stripping

Comb-painted cabinet. il *Better Homes and Gardens* 67:52+ Ja '89

Fast finishes. T. Sweeney. il *Home Mechanix* 85:56-9 Ja '89

Finished for effect. il *Southern Living* 24:72-3 O '89

Finishing. R. Capotosto. il *Popular Mechanics* 166:95-6+ N '89

First aid for furniture [Craftsman's Wood Medic] R. Capotosto. il *Popular Mechanics* 166:103 Je '89

Repair furniture surface blemishes. M. Varese. il *Workbench* 45:14 Mr/Ap '89

Repairing wood finishes: fast, easy fixes for damaged furniture. *Better Homes and Gardens* 67:49 Ag '89

Restoring an oak table. K. Collier. il *The Family Handyman* 39:54-7 F '89

Super stripper [3M wood refinishing products] A. W. Lees. il *Popular Science* 234:152 Ap '89

Maintenance and repair

First aid for furniture [Craftsman's Wood Medic] R. Capotosto. il *Popular Mechanics* 166:103 Je '89

Repair furniture surface blemishes. M. Varese. il *Workbench* 45:14 Mr/Ap '89

Repairing pegged furniture. M. Varese. il *Workbench* 45:10-11 S/O '89

Repairing wood finishes: fast, easy fixes for damaged furniture. *Better Homes and Gardens* 67:49 Ag '89

Painting

See Furniture, Painted

Refinishing

See Furniture—Finishes and finishing

Reproductions

Period furniture. B. Vila. il *Popular Mechanics* 166:46+ O '89

A really big show. D. B. Cowin. il *House & Garden* 161:134-7 Ag '89

FURNITURE, AMERICAN

See also

House decoration, American

Mission furniture

Shaker furniture

Collectors and collecting

American Eastlake furniture. K. M. McClinton. il *Antiques & Collecting Hobbies* 94:28-30+ My '89

The bombé furniture of Boston and Salem, Massachusetts. H. Sack. bibl f il *Antiques* 135:1178-89 My '89

Joseph B. Barry, Philadelphia cabinetmaker. D. L. Fennimore and R. T. Trump. bibl f il *Antiques* 135:1212-25 My '89

The line-and-berry inlaid furniture of eighteenth-century Chester County, Pennsylvania. L. E. Griffith. bibl f il *Antiques* 135:1202-11 My '89

Exhibitions

The Boston Athenaeum and its furnishings. R. Armstrong. il *Antiques* 136:302-15 Ag '89

The furniture [Mount Vernon] C. Meadows. bibl f il *Antiques* 135:480-9 F '89

Pattern books [Furniture in print: pattern books from the Redwood Library at the Rhode Island School of Design] A. E. Ledes. il *Antiques* 136:662+ O '89

Prices

Old glories [auction prices for American furniture] S. Pennington. il *House & Garden* 161:140-1 Ja '89

Reproductions

Henry Ford slept here [constructing reproduction wicker bed for Ford Estate] K. P. Crombie. il *Workbench* 45:42-6 Mr/Ap '89

Out of the past, made for today [cover story] C. Engle. il *Southern Living* 24:68-75 N '89

FURNITURE, BUILT IN

Wardrobes and seats . . . built-ins were the answer. il *Sunset (Central West edition)* 182:156 My '89

FURNITURE, CANADIAN

Collectors and collecting

Cabinetmakers of St. John, New Brunswick. D. B. Webster. bibl il *Antiques* 135:942-9 Ap '89

FURNITURE, CHILDREN'S

See also

Beds

Cabinets (Furniture)

Chairs

Cribs (Beds)

Tables

Sitting zoo. N. Wing. il *Parents* 64:158-60+ Mr '89

That chair has arms! M. Malone. il *Newsweek* 114:46-7 Jl 17 '89

FURNITURE, DECORATED

Perfect penmanship [penwork on 18th and 19th century furniture] G. Harrell. il *House & Garden* 161:68 D '89

FURNITURE, DUTCH

Exhibitions

Rietveld's geometry. E. Silberman. il *Vogue* 179:100 Ja '89

FURNITURE, ENGLISH

Collectors and collecting

Forever English [odd furniture] G. Harrell. il *House & Garden* 161:76 Mr '89

Master of cabinetry [G. Bullock] M. Filler. il por *House & Garden* 161:146-9+ Mr '89

A penthouse with period grace [Manhattan apartment decorated by Mark Hampton] P. T. Buckley. il *Architectural Digest* 46:250-7 N '89

Reproductions

Heirloom curio cabinet [Queen Anne] G. E. Derzinski. il *Workbench* 45:30-6 S/O '89

Queen Anne gate-leg table. G. E. Derzinski. il *Workbench* 45:46-50 Jl/Ag '89

FURNITURE, FANTASTIC

Furniture that provokes fantasy. C. Vogel. il *The New York Times Magazine* p58-61 Ag 27 '89

Gandee at large [B. Newman, dealer in Fantasy Furniture] C. K. Gandee. il por *House & Garden* 161:246 S '89

FURNITURE, FRENCH

Collectors and collecting

Antiques: Napoleon III style. J. A. Cuadrado. il *Architectural Digest* 46:290-5+ N '89

Exhibitions

Claude and François-Xavier Lalanne at Marisa del Re [animal-shaped furniture] L. Campbell. il *Art in America* 77:166-7 F '89

FURNITURE, GERMAN

See also

Biedermeier furniture

FURNITURE, ITALIAN

Merchant of Memphis [American distributor K. Johnson] M. Filler. il por *House & Garden* 161:64+ S '89

Collectors and collecting

Antiques: lacca povera furniture. J. Simpson. il *Architectural Digest* 46:168-73 F '89

Local color [painted Italian furniture] M. Guralnick. il *House & Garden* 161:58+ F '89

Exhibitions

The 1988 Salone del Mobile: making it in Milan. K. D. Stein. il *Architectural Record* 177:45 Ja '89

Fifties flyer. J. Turner. il por *Art News* 88:117-18 O '89

Gandee at large [Salone del Mobile di Milano] C. K. Gandee. il *House & Garden* 161:154 Ja '89

Milano nuovo [Salone del Mobile di Milano] C. Vogel. il *The New York Times Magazine* p68 S 17 '89

Report from Milan: as usual, anything goes [Salone del Mobile] K. D. Stein. il *Architectural Record* 177:53 N '89

FURNITURE, OUTDOOR

See also

Benches

Chairs

Garden benches

Tables

Casual classics return. il *Southern Living* 24:136-7 My '89

Maintenance and repair

How to care for outdoor furniture. M. Varese. il *Workbench* 45:16 My/Je '89

FURNITURE, PAINTED

See also

Tole painting

Bargain lover's decorating guide. il *Glamour* 87:180-3 Jl '89

Fanciful furniture. D. L. Caringer. il *Better Homes and Gardens* 68:109-11 F '89

Playful painted pieces. il *Better Homes and Gardens* 67:123 O '89

With paint and imagination . . . new look for an old treasure. il *Sunset (Central West edition)* 183:74-6+ D '89

Collectors and collecting

Local color [painted Italian furniture] M. Guralnick. il *House & Garden* 161:58+ F '89

FURNITURE, ROCOCO
Collectors and collecting
The Belter chair. D. Bourdon. il *American Heritage* 40:24-5 Mr '89
FURNITURE, SHAKER *See* Shaker furniture
FURNITURE, SPANISH COLONIAL
Collectors and collecting
Antiques: Spanish colonial furniture. R. J. Stroessner. il *Architectural Digest* 46:256-61+ My '89
Hispanic cabinetmakers and the Anglo-American aesthetic. L. Taylor. bibl f il *Antiques* 136:554-67 S '89
FURNITURE, USED
Bargain lover's decorating guide. il *Glamour* 87:180-3 Jl '89
FURNITURE ARRANGEMENT
Small is beautiful. M. Walsh. il *Better Homes and Gardens* 68:50 F '89
FURNITURE FINISHING *See* Furniture—Finishes and finishing
FURNITURE INDUSTRY
See also
La-Z-Boy Chair Co.
Ladd Furniture Inc.
Murphy Door Bed Co., Inc.
History
The bombé furniture of Boston and Salem, Massachusetts. H. Sack. bibl f il *Antiques* 135:1178-89 My '89
Canada
History
Cabinetmakers of St. John, New Brunswick. D. B. Webster. bibl il *Antiques* 135:942-9 Ap '89
Great Britain
See also
David Linley Furniture Ltd.
FURNITURE MAKERS *See* Cabinetmakers
FURNITURE STORES
See also
IKEA Svenska Forsaljnings AB
OMO Home (Firm)
SCP Ltd.
Seaman Furniture Co., Inc.
Why competitors shop for ideas at IKEA. J. Bamford. il *Business Week* p88 O 9 '89
FURNITURE STRIPPING
The art of removing unwanted finishes. M. Varese. il *Workbench* 45:10 Jl/Ag '89
FURRH, CHRIS
about
Lord of the flies: two new teen stars take on a challenging movie. pors *Teen* 33:54 S '89
FURRIERS *See* Fur industry
FURST, ALAN
A love affair with water. il map *New Choices for the Best Years* 29:56-61 F '89
Surprising Strasbourg. il *New Choices for the Best Years* 29:54-7 Je '89
FURST, ANTON
about
Designer. L. Nickson and N. Le Quesne. il pors *Life* 12:84-6 Spr '89
FURST, AUSTIN
about
The crash of a moviemaker. J. Hammer. il por *Newsweek* 114:46 S 4 '89
FURST, STEPHEN
about
For cherubic Stephen Furst, Have faith could be a motto, not just his parish sitcom. M. Alexander. il pors *People Weekly* 31:95-6 Je 5 '89
FURY, KATHLEEN
This working life. See issues of Working Woman
FURY TO FREEDOM [film] *See* Motion picture reviews—Single works
FUSCO, COCO
Border Art Workshop/Taller de Arte Fronterizo. *The Nation* 248:602-4 My 1 '89
FUSCO, MARY ANN CASTRONOVO
What's new? What's wise to buy? *Redbook* 173:141 S '89
FUSELAGE, AIRPLANE *See* Airplanes—Fuselage; Airplanes, Jet—Fuselage
FUSION, COLD *See* Cold fusion
FUSION, LASER *See* Laser fusion
FUSION, MAGNETIC *See* Magnetic fusion
FUSION, NUCLEAR *See* Nuclear fusion
FUSION REACTORS
See also
Tokamaks
Fusion's future. J. Horgan. il *Scientific American* 260:25-8 F '89
Harnessing fusion energy. D. Burke. il *Maclean's* 102:51 Mr 27 '89
Moon power [helium-3] M. J. Mackowski. il por *Ad Astra* 1:34-9 Jl/Ag '89
FÜSS, ADAM, 1961-
about
Adam Füss at Massimo Audiello. H. Cotter. *Art in America* 77:175-6 Je '89

FUSSELL, BETTY HARPER
Reading food: there's a mythological construct in my soup. il *The New York Times Book Review* 94:36 S 24 '89
Seattle crew. il *The New York Times Magazine* p57-8 Ap 9 '89
FUSSELL, PAUL, 1924-
The real war 1939-1945 [cover story] il *The Atlantic* 264:32-40+ Ag '89
about
Books from Oxford and Algonquin question idea of a 'good' war. C. Goodrich. il pors *Publishers Weekly* 235:31-2 Je 23 '89
The real war [interview] R. J. Spiller. il por *American Heritage* 40:126-7+ N '89
FUTCH, EDDIE
about
Dear Mike . . . G. Smith. il pors *Sports Illustrated* 70:58-64+ F 27 '89
FUTRELL, J. WILLIAM
Environmental Law Institute. *Environment* 31:45 S '89
FUTRELL, MARY HATWOOD
Fourth-wave education reform: are we ready? *The Education Digest* 55:3-6 N '89
Mama and Miss Jordan. il *Reader's Digest* 135:75-80 Jl '89
Mission not accomplished: education reform in retrospect [cover story] bibl f il *Phi Delta Kappan* 71:8-14 S '89
about
A conversation with Mary Hatwood Futrell. M. E. Howard. por *Black Enterprise* 20:30 O '89
FUTURE
See also
Congressional Clearinghouse on the Future
Forecasting
Franklin Institute (Philadelphia, Pa.). Science Museum and Planetarium. Futures Center
Nineteen hundred and nineties
Twenty-first century
Twenty-second century
Two thousand (Year)
Two thousand eighty-nine (Year)
Two thousand nine (Year)
Two thousand seventy-three (Year)
Two thousand six (Year)
Two thousand sixty (Year)
Two thousand ten (Year)
Two thousand three (Year)
World Future Society
Future view. See issues of The Futurist beginning October 1984
FUTURE AVIATION PROFESSIONALS OF AMERICA (FIRM)
Hire education. A. Laboda. il *Flying* 116:70-2 Mr '89
FUTURE LIFE
See also
Eschatology
Heaven
Resurrection
FUTURES *See* Commodity futures; Foreign exchange futures; Hedging (Finance); Interest rate futures
FUTURES STUDIES *See* Forecasting—Study and teaching
FUTURIST (PERIODICAL)
Who writes for the Futurist? T. Willard. *The Futurist* 23:3 Jl/Ag '89
FUTUROLOGY *See* Forecasting
FUZZY SYSTEMS (COMPUTER SCIENCE)
Time for some fuzzy thinking. P. Elmer-Dewitt. il *Time* 134:79 S 25 '89
FYODOROV, ANDREI
about
A raised *glasnost*. E. B. Fein. il *Gentlemen's Quarterly* 59:106+ O '89
FYODOROV, SVYATOSLAV
about
How to get rich off *perestroika*. P. Péan. il pors *Fortune* 119:145-6 My 8 '89

G

G.I. JOE DOLLS
Hot date: Barbie and G.I. Joe. B. Kantrowitz. il *Newsweek* 113:59 F 20 '89
G PROTEINS
β-adrenergic inhibition of cardiac sodium channels by dual G-protein pathways. B. Schubert and others. bibl f il *Science* 245:516-19 Ag 4 '89
A G protein gamma subunit shares homology with *ras* proteins. N. Gautam and others. bibl f il *Science* 244:971-4 My 26 '89
G_{olf}: an olfactory neuron specific-G protein involved in odorant signal transduction. D. T. Jones and R. R. Reed. bibl f il *Science* 244:790-5 My 19 '89

G PROTEINS—cont.

Lutropin-choriogonadotropin receptor: an unusual member of the G protein-coupled receptor family. K. C. McFarland and others. bibl f il *Science* 245:494-9 Ag 4 '89

A pertussis toxin-sensitive G protein in hippocampal long-term potentiation. J. W. Goh and P. S. Pennefather. bibl f il *Science* 244:980-3 My 26 '89

Rapid β-adrenergic modulation of cardiac calcium channel currents by a fast G protein pathway. A. Yatani and A. M. Brown. bibl f il *Science* 245:71-4 Jl 7 '89

Selective amplification and cloning of four new members of the G protein-coupled receptor family. F. Libert and others. bibl f il *Science* 244:569-72 My 5 '89

Splice variants of the α subunit of the G protein G$_s$ activate both adenylyl cyclase and calcium channels. R. Mattera and others. bibl f il *Science* 243:804-7 F 10 '89

Tracing hormone action in the cell [work of A. G. Gilman] J. L. Marx. il por *Science* 245:1446-7 S 29 '89

G SPOT

Paradise found? Hot flash on the G-spot. M. Curtis. il *Mademoiselle* 95:64 Ja '89

G. T. EUROPE GROWTH FUND

A European expedition. E. Giltenan. il *Forbes* 144:172 S 4 '89

GABA (GAMMA-AMINOBUTYRIC ACID) *See* Aminobutyric acid

GABELLI, MARIO

about

Berkshire Hathaway II? J. Clements. il por *Forbes* 144:40-1 Jl 24 '89

In the boss' shadow. G. Button. il por *Forbes* 144:238+ N 27 '89

Mario Gabelli. P. Noglows. il por *Channels (New York, N.Y.: 1986)* 9:53 Jl/Ag '89

Spinning gold out of spinoffs. G. G. Marcial. *Business Week* p80 Jl 31 '89

"Star" funds: three hits, three misses. M. Schiffres. il pors *Changing Times* 43:59-63 My '89

What looks good to Mario Gabelli [interview] J. Mendes. il por *Fortune* 119:32+ Mr 27 '89

GABELLI GROWTH FUND

In the boss' shadow [E. Bramwell] G. Button. il por *Forbes* 144:238+ N 27 '89

GABLE, CLARK, 1901-1960

about

The making of Billy Gable. J. Wolfe. il pors *Life* 12:53-4 Spr '89

GABLER, HANS WALTER, 1938-

about

Miami J'yce: love walks right out of a 'Ulysses' symposium. B. Maddox. il *The New York Times Book Review* 94:7 F 26 '89

The new 'Ulysses': grave matters [discussion of December 8, 1988 article, The new 'Ulysses': the hidden controversy] C. Rossman. il *The New York Review of Books* 36:43-5 Mr 30 '89

The new 'Ulysses': unanswered questions [discussion of December 8, 1988 article, The new 'Ulysses': the hidden controversy] C. Rossman. *The New York Review of Books* 35:58-9 Ja 19 '89

'The scandal of Ulysses': yet another exchange [discussion of June 30, 1988 article] J. Kidd. il *The New York Review of Books* 36:40-1 Je 1 '89

GÁBOR, EVA, 1921-

Photographs and photography

Direction for the individual. G. Bernstein. por *Petersen's Photographic Magazine* 17:12 Ap '89

GÁBOR, ZSA ZSA

about

Amid tears and jeers, justice makes prison pen pals out of Zsa Zsa Gabor and Jim Bakker. R. Micheli and L. Marx. il pors *People Weekly* 32:129-30 N 6 '89

Witness for the persecution. S. Schindehette. il pors *People Weekly* 32:36-9 O 16 '89

Zsa Zsa Gabor has been courted before, but this time it's a trial. M. Dougherty. il pors *People Weekly* 32:128-9+ S 11 '89

GABRIEL, TRIP

Call my agent! il pors *The New York Times Magazine* p44-5+ F 19 '89

Cliffhanger [cover story] il pors *The New York Times Magazine* p20-5+ D 31 '89

Greening the White House [cover story] il pors *The New York Times Magazine* p24-7+ Ag 13 '89

GACHA, JOSÉ GONZALO RODRÍGUEZ *See* Rodríguez Gacha, José Gonzalo

GACKENBACH, JAYNE, 1946-, AND BOSVELD, JANE

Take control of your dreams [excerpt from Control your dreams; cover story] il *Psychology Today* 23:27-32 O '89

Twilight zones [excerpt from Control your dreams] il *Omni (New York, N.Y.)* 12:74-6+ N '89

GADDAFI, MUAMMAR *See* Qaddafi, Muammar al-, 1942-

GADDIS, JOHN LEWIS

Hanging tough paid off. bibl f il *The Bulletin of the Atomic Scientists* 45:11-14 Ja/F '89

GADESSA, HAILE MARIAM

about

African tribe rears white siblings found after 20 yrs. pors *Jet* 76:25 Ag 21 '89

GADESSA, TEGEST

about

African tribe rears white siblings found after 20 yrs. pors *Jet* 76:25 Ag 21 '89

GADGETS

Anecdotes, facetiae, satire, etc.

The art of inventing the unnecessary. V. S. Sussman. il *U.S. News & World Report* 106:70 Je 26 '89

What else is new? M. G. Stoddard. il *The Saturday Evening Post* 261:50-1+ Mr '89

GADOLINIUM IN THE BODY

Block of stretch-activated ion channels in Xenopus oocytes by gadolinium and calcium ions. X.-C. Yang and F. Sachs. bibl f il *Science* 243:1068-71 F 24 '89

GAEBELEIN, FRANK ELY, 1899-1983

about

A father's legacy. P. E. Alsdurf. il pors *Christianity Today* 33:58 O 20 '89

GAETTI, GARY

about

The Gospel and Gaetti. H. Hersch. il por *Sports Illustrated* 71:42-4+ Ag 21 '89

GAFF, JERRY G.

General education at decade's end. il *Change* 21:10-19 Jl/Ag '89

Interdisciplinary studies in higher education. *The Education Digest* 55:57-60 O '89

GAFFEY, MICHAEL J.

(jt. auth) See Vilas, Faith, and Gaffey, Michael J.

GAFFIN, HARRIS

The man behind the O. il pors *Popular Photography* 96:34 D '89

GAFFNEY, EDWARD MCGLYNN, JR.

O'Connor fumbles 'Christian nation' case. *The Christian Century* 106:373-5 Ap 12 '89

GAFFNEY, MO

about

Two good pals laughed together, then shared the joke in a smash comedy, The Kathy & Mo show. J. Cagle. il pors *People Weekly* 31:123-4 My 1 '89

GAGE, DIANE

How one family spends its money. il *Good Housekeeping* 208:34-5 Ap '89

A new year, a new life, a new love. il pors *Good Housekeeping* 208:95+ Ja '89

Thank you, Melissa. il pors *Good Housekeeping* 209:84+ O '89

GAGE, JOAN PAULSON

Greek visions. il *House & Garden* 161:72 F '89

GAGE, N. L. (NATHANIEL LEES), 1917-, AND BERLINER, DAVID C.

Nurturing the critical, practical, and artistic thinking of teachers. il *Phi Delta Kappan* 71:212-14 N '89

GAGE, THOMAS, 1721-1787

about

Benjamin Church: Son of Liberty, Tory spy. M. G. Stoler. il pors *American History Illustrated* 24:28-35 N/D '89

GAGE & TOLLNER (BROOKLYN, N.Y.: RESTAURANT) *See* Brooklyn (New York, N.Y.)—Restaurants, nightclubs, bars, etc.

GAGES

See also
Strain gages
Tire pressure gages

The mark of craftsmanship. il *Workbench* 45:96 N/D '89

GAGNÈRE, OLIVIER

about

New talents: Olivier Gagnère. il por *Harper's Bazaar* 122:78 Mr '89

GAGNON, RIA

"Doctor, please help me!". il por *Ladies' Home Journal* 106:26+ Ap '89

GAGOSIAN, LARRY

about

Going places. D. Kazanjian. il pors *Vogue* 179:412-17+ N '89

GAGOSIAN GALLERY

Going places. D. Kazanjian. il pors *Vogue* 179:412-17+ N '89

GAHANNA (OHIO)

Education

The Gahanna-Jefferson City internship program. B. W. Denner and S. Kirchhoff. *Phi Delta Kappan* 71:166-7 O '89

GAIA HYPOTHESIS

A biologist whose heresy redraws earth's tree of life [L. Margulis] J. McDermott. bibl (p135) il pors *Smithsonian* 20:72-6+ Ag '89

Gaia. T. Beardsley. il *Scientific American* 261:35-6 D '89

Gaia [theory proposed by J. Lovelock] il por *People Weekly* 32:63-4 D 25 '89-Ja 1 '90

The Gaia (guý-uh) hypothesis. il *Current Health 2* 16:8 D '89

How the earth maintains life. E. Linden. il *Time* 134:114 N 13 '89

GAIA HYPOTHESIS—*cont.*

James Lovelock: toward a new planetary perspective [interview] S. Pacher. il por *The Mother Earth News* 119:44-6+ S/O '89

Planetary medicine. J. Lovelock. il por *American Health* 8:86-8 Mr '89

What Gaia hath wrought: the story of a scientific controversy. F. Lyman. il *Technology Review* 92:54-61 Jl '89

GAILLOT, JACQUES
about
The French Church in crisis [interview]; tr. by James P. Jurich. P. H. Samway. *America* 160:576-8+ Je 17-24 '89

GAINERS INC.
Fighting new battles. J. DeMont. il por *Maclean's* 102:40+ Ag 14 '89

GAINES, VALERIE
about
Homeless couple given $50 tickets to attend a coveted inaugural ball. il pors *Jet* 75:14 F 13 '89

GAINSLEY, PHILLIP
Transformations. il *Opera News* 53:24-7 F 4 '89

GAITHERSBURG (MD.)
Education
The new school [computer use at Quince Orchard High School] J. Sloan. il *Compute!* 11:78-80+ D '89

GAITSKILL, MARY, 1954-
Modern romance: a lesson in appetite control. il por *Ms.* 17:55-6 My '89

GALA [musical] See Musicals, revues, etc.—Reviews—Single works

GALABERT, MICHEL
about
He knows what he likes. P. Viladas. il pors *House & Garden* 161:26+ F '89

GALACTIC HALOS See Halos (Astronomy)

GALACTOSE
Dairy sugar linked to ovarian cancer [research by Daniel W. Cramer] K. Fackelmann. *Science News* 136:52 Jl 22 '89

GALACTOSIDASES
A multiubiquitin chain is confined to specific lysine in a targeted short-lived protein. V. Chau and others. bibl f il *Science* 243:1576-83 Mr 24 '89

Now in vivo: altering endothelial cells. R. Cowen. *Science News* 135:373 Je 17 '89

Recombinant gene expression in vivo within endothelial cells of the arterial wall. E. G. Nabel and others. bibl f il *Science* 244:1342-4 Je 16 '89

GALAPAGOS ISLANDS
See also
Wildlife—Galapagos Islands

GALASSI, PETER, 1951-
about
Indelible images. R. Cembalest. il pors *Art News* 88:174-9 Ap '89

GALAXIES
See also
Milky Way
Nebulae
Radio sources (Astronomy)

Autumn's galaxies: the best and the brightest. M. Radloff. il *Astronomy* 17:78-84 S '89

Beyond the Andromeda "nebula". G. Lovi. il *Sky and Telescope* 78:503-4 N '89

A bowl full of galaxies. P. Harrington. il *Sky and Telescope* 77:444-5 Ap '89

Bright supernova found in galaxy M66. il *Astronomy* 17:98 My '89

Cloud links quasars to Seyfert galaxies [hydrogen cloud; work of Kimiaki Kawara] A. McKenzie. *Science News* 136:215 S 30 '89

Collision and cannibalism shape the galaxies. M. M. Waldrop. il *Science* 243:607-8 F 3 '89

Crashing galaxies, cosmic fireworks [cover story] W. C. Keel. il *Sky and Telescope* 77:18-21+ Ja '89

Deep-sky wonders. W. S. Houston. See issues of Sky and Telescope

The dregs of the universe [dim galaxy Malin 1] I. Peterson. il *Science News* 136:60 Jl 22 '89

Einstein's ring and a galaxy's mass [MG 1654 + 1346] il *Sky and Telescope* 77:465-6 My '89

Galaxies. J. S. Trefil. bibl (p146) il *Smithsonian* 19:36-46+ Ja '89

Galaxies found in cosmic void [Bootes Void; work of Greg D. Bothun and Greg Aldering] *Astronomy* 17:10 Ap '89

Galaxy hunting around the Big Dipper. A. Goldstein. il *Astronomy* 17:78-84 Mr '89

How far to the galaxies? [cover story] V. Kiernan. il *Astronomy* 17:48-54 Je '89

Invisible galaxies? [dwarf galaxy DDO 154] il *Sky and Telescope* 77:13 Ja '89

Legendary faint galaxies. S. Lucas. il *Astronomy* 17:80-2 F '89

M31 and its forgotten Roman poet [Andromeda galaxy in poems of R. F. Avienus] il *Sky and Telescope* 78:243-4 S '89

Populating an astronomical void [Boötes void] *Science News* 135:30 Ja 14 '89

Radio noise from colliding galaxies [Markarian 266; research by Joseph M. Mazzarella] il *Sky and Telescope* 77:241-2 Mr '89

Spiral arms and dark halos [research by Magnus Thomasson] il *Sky and Telescope* 78:134 Ag '89

Star formation in irregular galaxies. D. A. Hunter and J. S. Gallagher. bibl f il *Science* 243:1557-63 Mr 24 '89

Clusters
See also
Great Attractor (Astronomy)

Astronomers go up against the Great Wall [research by Margaret J. Geller and John P. Huchra] M. M. Waldrop. il *Science* 246:885 N 17 '89

The challenge of Abell 539. R. J. Morales. il *Sky and Telescope* 78:670-1 D '89

Clumps in the machine [computer modeling of galaxy cluster; research by Adrian Melott and Sergei Shandarin] il *Discover* 10:12 S '89

Cosmic cartographers find 'Great Wall' [work of Margaret J. Geller and John P. Huchra] A. McKenzie. il *Science News* 136:340 N 25 '89

A cross section of the universe. J. Kanipe. il *Astronomy* 17:44-6 N '89

Great bubbles in the cosmos [work of Margaret Geller and John Huchra] M. D. Lemonick. il *Time* 134:57-8 N 27 '89

Looking well beyond the Great Attractor [work of R. Scaramella] I. Peterson. *Science News* 135:230-1 Ap 15 '89

Mapping the universe [cover story] M. J. Geller and J. Huchra. bibl f il *Science* 246:897-903 N 17 '89

Virgo Cluster distance refined. il *Astronomy* 17:10 O '89

Evolution
Astronomers find evidence of galaxies still forming [interstellar hydrogen cloud found by Riccardo Giovanelli and Martha Haynes] *Earth Science* 42:9-10 Fall '89

The celestial Cartwheel [ring galaxy; research by Marshall Joy] il *Sky and Telescope* 78:570 D '89

Cosmic collisions: computer simulations suggest how elliptical galaxies formed. J. Horgan. il *Scientific American* 261:14+ Jl '89

Deep space [observation of extremely faint, bluish galaxies by J. Anthony Tyson] il *Sky and Telescope* 78:455-6 N '89

Elliptical galaxies forged by collision. K. Hartley. il *Astronomy* 17:42-5 My '89

From dust to dust [supercomputer simulation called galaxy-in-a-box; cover story] I. Peterson. il *Science News* 135:24-5 Ja 14 '89

Galactic birth? [intergalactic hydrogen cloud discovered by Riccardo Giovanelli and Martha Haynes] *Time* 134:66 S 11 '89

Galactic cannonballs [research by Jane C. Charlton and Edwin E. Salpeter] *Sky and Telescope* 78:246 S '89

In the beginning was a cloud [intergalactic hydrogen cloud discovered by Riccardo Giovanelli and Martha Haynes] S. Begley. *Newsweek* 114:66 S 11 '89

Island gas cloud may be protogalaxy [intergalactic hydrogen cloud discovered by Martha P. Haynes and Riccardo Giovanelli] il *Astronomy* 17:10 D '89

Mixing it up in space [cover story] K. Hartley. il *Science News* 135:218-19 Ap 8 '89

A new galaxy vs. old theories. F. Capone. *World Press Review* 36:67 D '89

Pumping gas to fuel a galaxy's active core [computer simulation by Lars Hernquist] I. Peterson. *Science News* 136:150 S 2 '89

Starlight shadows protogalaxy finding [intergalactic hydrogen cloud discovered by Martha P. Haynes and Riccardo Giovanelli] R. Cowen. il *Science News* 136:164 S 9 '89

Stillborn [interstellar hydrogen cloud found by Riccardo Giovanelli and Martha P. Haynes] J. Horgan. *Scientific American* 261:28 N '89

Supernova burps rid galaxies of hot gas [work of Jane C. Charlton and Edwin E. Salpeter] I. Peterson. *Science News* 136:310 N 11 '89

A surprise near Virgo [intergalactic hydrogen cloud discovered by Riccardo Giovanelli and Martha Haynes] J. Palca. *Science* 245:933 S 1 '89

Halos
See Halos (Astronomy)
Motion in line of sight
See also
Great Attractor (Astronomy)

No go for slow flow [work of R. Brent Tully and J. Richard Fisher] il *Sky and Telescope* 77:10-11 Ja '89

The not-so-Great Attractor? *Sky and Telescope* 77:12-13 Ja '89

Photographs and photography
'Exposing' a comet. T. Hallas and D. Mount. *Astronomy* 17:96-7 Mr '89

Now, that's far out! il *National Geographic World* 172:20-1 D '89

Radial velocity
See Galaxies—Motion in line of sight
Spectra and spectroscopy
Hint of a burst of supernova activity in a superluminous galaxy [NGC 6240; research by Bruce T. Draine] I. Peterson. *Science News* 136:252 O 14 '89

GALAXIES—Spectra and spectroscopy—*cont.*
Quasar-galaxy bridge? [work of Christopher L. Carilli] il *Sky and Telescope* 78:349 O '89
GALBRAITH, EVAN
What is the 'right' amount of saving? *National Review* 41:29-30 Je 16 '89
GALBRAITH, JAMES K.
Recession? *The Nation* 248:364-5 Mr 20 '89
GALBRAITH, JOHN KENNETH, 1908-
Have capitalism and socialism converged? il *New Perspectives Quarterly* 6:46-9 Fall '89
about
Dan, you're no Strunk or White [exchange of letters] D. Quayle. *Harper's* 278:24-6 Je '89
GALDIKAS, BIRUTÉ
about
Braving the hellish jungles of Borneo, Birute Galdikas probes the secrets of one of our oldest relations. J. Friedman. il pors *People Weekly* 31:102-6 Ja 16 '89
GALE, AUGUSTA
How I fought the no. 1 cancer killer of black women. il pors *Ebony* 44:58+ Je '89
GALE, ERIC
about
Eric Gale. S. Yanow. il por *Down Beat* 56:25 My '89
GALE, ROBERT PETER
about
West meets East. il pors *Esquire* 111:62-5 Ja '89
GALEANO, EDUARDO H., 1940-
Sign on the invisible line; tr. by Tracey Hill. *The Nation* 248:411-12 Mr 27 '89
GALEF, ANDREW GEOFFREY
about
The last fundamentalist? R. King. il por *Forbes* 144:132+ N 27 '89
GALERIE ST. ETIENNE
Keeping the flame. A. Decker. il *Art News* 88:28+ O '89
GALIANO, HENRY
about
All that's left. *The New Yorker* 65:35-6 O 30 '89
GALICH, ALEKSANDR, 1919-1977
about
My big land [drama] Reviews
New York il 22:56 Ag 28 '89. J. Simon
GALICIA, JOAQUÍN HERNANDEZ See Hernandez Galicia, Joaquín
GALICIA (POLAND AND UKRAINE)
Nationalism
The mermaid of the Dniester. O. Petrash. il *The Courier (Unesco)* 42:23 Mr '89
GALICO, SALVADOR
Three scenarios for Mexico's future. il por *The Futurist* 23:17-19 Jl/Ag '89
GALILEE, SEA OF (ISRAEL) See Sea of Galilee (Israel)
GALILEO FLIGHTS TO JUPITER See Space flight to Jupiter
GALILEO PROBE See Space vehicles
GALIMBERTI, CARLO
Luciano Soprani: quiet style for his Milan apartment. il pors *Architectural Digest* 46:162-7+ S '89
GALL, CHRISTINE M., AND ISACKSON, PAUL J.
Limbic seizures increase neuronal production of messenger RNA for nerve growth factor. bibl f il *Science* 245:758-61 Ag 18 '89
GALL, JIM
about
The man with the hammer. D. C. Bacon. il por *Nation's Business* 77:16 D '89
GALLAGHER, BRIAN
Video technology: its effects on teaching English and film. *The Education Digest* 54:29-32 Mr '89
GALLAGHER, DAVE
about
Playing ball and chain. N. Dawidoff. il por *Sports Illustrated* 70:81 My 22 '89
GALLAGHER, JAMES JOHN, 1926-
The impact of policies for handicapped children on future early education policy. bibl f il *Phi Delta Kappan* 71:121-4 O '89
GALLAGHER, JOHN SILL, 1947-
(jt. auth) See Hunter, D. A., and Gallagher, John Sill, 1947-
GALLAGHER, KIM, 1964?-
about
Kim Gallagher. L. Villarosa. il por *Runner's World* 24:50 F '89
GALLAGHER, MAGGIE
Do congressmen have mothers? *National Review* 41:38-9+ O 27 '89
GALLAGHER, MAURICE
about
WestAir flies high. M. Berss. il pors *Forbes* 143:147 Je 12 '89
GALLAGHER, NANCY LEE
about
In the Blue Chips. M. Barrier. il pors *Nation's Business* 77:54 F '89

GALLAGHER, PATRICIA C.
about
Savvy marketer learns about publishing . . . and vice versa? M. Reuter. il por *Publishers Weekly* 236:13 Ag 4 '89
GALLAGHER, TESS
Red poppy [poem]   *The New Yorker*   65:52 O 2 '89
GALLANT, MAVIS
In a war [story]   *The New Yorker*   65:38-48 O 30 '89
GALLARDO, MIGUEL ANGEL FÉLIX
about
A 'godfather' behind bars in the nick of time. M. Miller. il por *Newsweek* 113:55 Ap 24 '89
GALLATIN NATIONAL FOREST (MONT. AND WYO.)
Tom Miner Basin, Montana. R. H. Mohlenbrock. il maps *Natural History* p14-16 D '89
GALLAUDET UNIVERSITY
Louder than words. N. Karlen. il *Rolling Stone* p133-4+ Mr 23 '89
The revolution at Gallaudet [students demand a deaf president] H. Orlans. il pors *Change* 21:8-18 Ja/F '89
GALLAY, MADELEINE
about
New talents: Madeleine Gallay. N. Malkin. il por *Harper's Bazaar* 122:134 Mr '89
GALLAY (MADELEINE) (FIRM) See Madeleine Gallay (Firm)
GALLBLADDER
Diseases
See also
Gallstones
GALLEONS See Sailing vessels
GALLERIES AND MUSEUMS, ART See Art galleries and museums
GALLETTI, PIERRE M.
Artificial organs: living with risk. *Current (Washington, D.C.)* 311:16-19 Mr/Ap '89
GALLEYS (SHIPS)
See also
Triremes
GALLIANO, JOHN
about
British accents. K. Flett. il por *Harper's Bazaar* 122:356-7+ S '89
GALLIUM ARSENIDE SEMICONDUCTORS
Advances in integrated circuits. T. Kiely. il *Technology Review* 92:13-14 F/Mr '89
Defense Dept. contracts to spur use of digital GaAs microcircuits. P. J. Klass. *Aviation Week & Space Technology* 130:283-4 Je 12 '89
Electronic warfare (II) [cover story; special section] il *Aviation Week & Space Technology* 131:84-5+ S 18 '89
GaAs clusters in the quantum size regime: growth on high surface area silica by molecular beam epitaxy. C. J. Sandroff and others. bibl f il *Science* 245:391-3 Jl 28 '89
Harris unit develops advanced GaAs facility to supply MMICs to military [gallium arsenide monolithic microwave integrated circuits] B. W. Henderson. il *Aviation Week & Space Technology* 130:101+ Ap 24 '89
HEMT devices could speed work on next-generation radar systems [high electron mobility transistors] B. D. Nordwall. il *Aviation Week & Space Technology* 130:65+ My 15 '89
Laying-on of atoms: quantum-well wires [research by Pierre M. Petroff] I. Amato. il *Science News* 135:69 F 4 '89
Lift-off laser: GaAs on glass. R. Pool. il *Science* 243:1009-10 F 24 '89
Quantifying the information content of lattice images. A. Ourmazd and others. bibl f il *Science* 246:1571-7 D 22 '89
Sanders develops MMIC for phased array systems [monolithic microwave integrated circuit device] *Aviation Week & Space Technology* 130:291 Je 12 '89
Semiconductor devices transfer like decals [epitaxial liftoff] I. Amato. *Science News* 135:101 F 18 '89
GALLIUM PHOSPHIDE
Little lenses for little lasers. *Science News* 136:62 Jl 22 '89
GALLO, FRANK
(jt. auth) See Levitan, Sar A., and Gallo, Frank
GALLO, NICK
Lighten up: laugh your way to good health. *Better Homes and Gardens* 67:31-2 Ag '89
Tooth truths. il *Better Homes and Gardens* 68:41-3 F '89
GALLO, ROBERT C.
My life stalking AIDS. il por *Discover* 10:30-3+ O '89
GALLO, ROBERT C., AND MONTAGNIER, LUC
Letters [discussion of October 1988 article, AIDS in 1988] *Scientific American* 260:10-11 Je '89
GALLO (E. & J.) WINERY See E. & J. Gallo Winery
GALLOPOULOS, NICHOLAS E.
(jt. auth) See Frosch, Robert A., and Gallopoulos, Nicholas E.
GALLOWAY, DAVID
Elephant-walk follies. il *Art in America* 77:68-73+ S '89
Report from East Berlin. il *Art in America* 77:45-7+ Jl '89
GALLOWAY, JEFF, 1945-
Great workouts. il *Runner's World* 24:42-6+ Jl '89
Short strides: a short cut to the finish line. il *Women's Sports & Fitness* 11:12-13 Mr '89

GALLOWAY, RANDY
Dallas. il *Sport (New York, N.Y.)* 80:76-9 N '89
Hold the tortillas! The Cowboys are in good hands. il *Sport (New York, N.Y.)* 80:63 Ag '89

GALLSTONES
Are you stone prone? L. Holland. *Good Housekeeping* 209:275 S '89
Get rid of gallstones. J. Mullich. il *Prevention (Emmaus, Pa.)* 41:66-72 My '89

Nutritional aspects
Prairie dogs and gallstone information [research by Thomas H. Magnuson] K. Fackelmann. *Science News* 135:332 My 27 '89

Therapy
Gallstone quick-fix [percutaneous lithotripsy] *Prevention (Emmaus, Pa.)* 41:18 N '89
Gallstones: new treatments offer relief. A. J. DiMarino. il por *McCall's* 116:112 My '89
The good news on stones. A. J. Sheinman. il *New Choices for the Best Years* 29:55-7 Ag '89
Great options for gallstones. C. SerVaas. il *The Saturday Evening Post* 261:100 My/Je '89

GALLUP, ALEC
(jt. auth) See Elam, Stanley M., and Gallup, Alec

GALLUP, GEORGE, 1930-
about
Tracking America's soul [interview] T. K. Jones. il pors *Christianity Today* 33:22-5 N 17 '89

GALSTER, STEVEN R.
What will follow the pullout? il *The Nation* 248:9-10+ Ja 2 '89

GALSWORTHY, JOHN, 1867-1933
about
The mob [drama] Reviews
The New Republic 201 [Reprint v1]:27-8 N 6 '89 [N 7 '14]

GALVESTON (TEX.)
Galleries and museums
See also
Elissa (Ship)
Gardens and gardening
See also
Moody Gardens (Galveston, Tex.)
Historic houses, sites, etc.
Preserving the South's past, city to town [work of P. Brink] D. Young. il pors *Southern Living* 24:90-1+ F '89

GALVIN, EMILY S.
Children and child care in China: some observations. il *Children Today* 18:19-23 My/Je '89

GALVIN, JOHN
about
Keep the powder dry [interview] M. Kramer. il por *Time* 133:78-9 My 29 '89

GALVIN, ROBERT W.
about
The rival Japan respects [cover story] L. Therrien. il pors *Business Week* p108-10+ N 13 '89

GALWAY (IRELAND)
Description
In Galway's fair city. C. Murphy. il *The Atlantic* 263:81-3 My '89

GAMBACCINI, PETER
Burning bright. il por *Runner's World* 24:56-7 N '89

GAMBLING
See also
Baseball betting
Basketball betting
Bingo
Boxing betting
Casinos
Football betting
Horse race betting
Lotteries
Off-track betting
Poker (Game)
Sports betting
America's gambling fever [cover story] C. Welles. il *Business Week* p112-15+ Ap 24 '89
Why pick on Pete? [P. Rose case emblematic of American obsession with gambling; cover story] G. J. Church. il por *Time* 134:16-21 Jl 10 '89

Laws and regulations
Gambling and guns [St. Regis reserve] M. Clark. il *Maclean's* 102:21+ S 18 '89
Gary, Ind., voters back casino gambling in city. il *Jet* 77:56 N 27 '89

Moral and religious aspects
The lottery plague. G. K. Brushaber. *Christianity Today* 33:15 S 8 '89
Playing the lottery is idolatry. T. Watson. por *Christianity Today* 33:8 N 3 '89

Canada
Prairie high rollers. P. Kopvillem. *Maclean's* 102:17 Mr 6 '89

United States
See Gambling

GAMBLING MACHINES INDUSTRY
See also
Bally Manufacturing Corp.

GAMBON, MICHAEL
about
The mighty Gambon. S. Callow. por *Vogue* 179:352-3+ My '89

GAMBRELL, JAMEY
Perestroika shock. il *Art in America* 77:124-31+ F '89

GAMCO INVESTORS (FIRM)
What looks good to Mario Gabelli [interview] J. Mendes. il por *Fortune* 119:32+ Mr 27 '89

GAME
See also
Cooking—Game
Hunting
Venison
The game is up! [U.S. restaurants serving more game] N. S. Mehta. il *Time* 134:63 N 6 '89

Diseases and pests
More than you bargained for. T. Thomas. il *Field & Stream* 94:62-3+ N '89

GAME, DRESSING OF
After the shot. K. McCafferty. il *Field & Stream* 94:46+ N '89
The Montana method of field dressing [deer] J. Barsness. il *Field & Stream* 94:34 S '89
Save that venison! N. Strung. il *Field & Stream* 94:59 Je '89

GAME BIRD SHOOTING
See also
Duck shooting
Goose shooting
Grouse shooting
Mourning dove shooting
Partridge shooting
Pheasant shooting
Quail shooting
Water bird shooting
Woodcock shooting
A bird in hand. B. Tarrant. il *Field & Stream* 94:95-6 Ag '89
Wildfowling: here and abroad. G. Reiger. il map *Field & Stream* 93:34-5+ Ja '89
Wildfowling: my favorite four. G. Reiger. il *Field & Stream* 94:54-5+ D '89

GAME BIRDS
See also
Cooking—Game
Water birds
Woodcocks

GAME BOARDS
Antiques: American game boards. N. F. Weber. il *Architectural Digest* 46:168-73+ D '89

GAME CALLS *See* Animal calling
GAME GUNS *See* Shotguns
GAME HEN COOKING *See* Cooking—Poultry
GAME KEEPERS *See* Gamekeepers
GAME LAWS
See also
Game wardens
Poaching
Wildlife Legislative Fund of America
Game laws weren't writ for fat cats. T. Williams. il *Audubon* 91:104-6+ Jl '89
Weathering the drought [duck hunting curtailed] L. Williamson. il *Outdoor Life* 183:48+ Ja '89

Italy
Civilizing the hunt. D. Starr. il *International Wildlife* 19:16-19 N/D '89

Louisiana
Game agents foil a gross gros bec feast [night heron massacre] il *Audubon* 91:14 Ja '89
The Louisiana story. G. Reiger. il *Field & Stream* 94:50-1+ O '89

Maine
Deer season [female warden D. Palman] F. Graham. *Audubon* 91:18+ N '89

Texas
Up front [waterfowl sting operation] D. Barnes. il *Field & Stream* 93:7 Mr '89
Wildlife cops on a bust [Fish and Wildlife Service's Texas Waterfowl Operation] E. Linden. il *Time* 133:18 F 20 '89

GAME PRESERVES
See also
Shooting preserves

Georgia
See also
Little Saint Simons Island (Ga.)

Kenya
See also
Masai Mara Game Reserve (Kenya)
Kenya and Tanzania. P. Skinner. il map *Petersen's Photographic Magazine* 18:16-17+ My '89

GAME PRESERVES—*cont.*

Tanzania

Kenya and Tanzania. P. Skinner. il map *Petersen's Photographic Magazine* 18:16-17+ My '89

Texas

Oh, give me a home where wild rhinos roam [C. Bentsen's breeding farm for black rhinos in McAllen] M. Vollers. il por *Time* 133:12+ Je 26 '89

Texas rancher Calvin Bentsen, a former big-game hunter, takes his best shot at saving the rhinos [breeding farm for black rhinos in McAllen] K. Demaret. il pors *People Weekly* 32:103-4 D 11 '89

GAME PROTECTION *See* Wildlife conservation

GAME, SET & MATCH [television program] See Television program reviews—Single works

GAME SHOWS *See* Cable television—Game shows; Television broadcasting—Game shows

GAME THEORY

Games spiders play [use of game theory to predict fighting among woodland spiders; research by Susan E. Riechert] J. A. Miller. *BioScience* 39:225 Ap '89

GAME WARDENS

See also

Women game wardens

Training

Training our environmental conservation officers [New York State] D. Thomas. il *The Conservationist* 43:44-9 Ja/F '89

GAMEKEEPERS

Keepers of the game [shooting preserves in Great Britain] B. Alexander. il *International Wildlife* 19:34-40 S/O '89

GAMEL, THOMAS W.

about

Is Hollywood Park on the way to the glue factory? K. Kerwin. il *Business Week* p36 My 29 '89

GAMES

See also

Bingo

CD-ROM (Compact disc-Read only memory)—Games

Checkers (Game)

Chess

Croquet

Darts (Game)

Dungeons & Dragons (Game)

Educational games

Frisbee (Game)

Geographical recreations

Go (Game)

Information systems—Games

Marbles (Game)

Name games

Pool (Game)

Psychological games

Puzzles

Rotisserie League Baseball

Scruples (Game)

Table hockey

Tic-tac-toe (Game)

Toy and game industry

Tricks

Video games

War games

Word games

Child's play [using game Punchbuggy to change outlook on life] S. H. Hogan. il *Reader's Digest* 134:29-30+ Mr '89

Cooperative games. G. Cerny and A. Cerny. pors *The Humanist* 49:35+ Mr/Ap '89

The endless pursuit of all things trivial [adult board games] M. Silver. il *U.S. News & World Report* 107:102 N 6 '89

Fun with the market [investment games] D. P. Wiener. il *U.S. News & World Report* 106:68 Ap 3 '89

The game is afoot [adult board games] il *USA Today (Periodical)* 118:94 N '89

Games [board games testing session at Games magazine] *The New Yorker* 65:44-5 D 4 '89

Games for growing. J. Canary. il *Parents* 64:120-4 My '89

Play it safe [adult board games] B. Livermore. il *Health (New York, N.Y.)* 21:69 Je '89

GAMES, MATHEMATICAL *See* Mathematical recreations

GAMES, THEORY OF *See* Game theory

GAMETE INTRAFALLOPIAN TRANSFER

Two friends with one dream: "She gave me my baby" [donation of ova] J. Liebmann-Smith. *Redbook* 172:122-3+ Mr '89

Ethical aspects

What do infertility clinics really deliver? [misrepresentation of success rates] S. Findlay. il *U.S. News & World Report* 106:74-5 Ap 3 '89

GAMETES

See also

Spermatozoa

GAMM, GORDON

Abortion, Catholicism, and the Constitution. por *The Humanist* 49:24-5+ Jl/Ag '89

GAMM, RICHARD

Ice lander. il *Flying* 116:112 D '89

GAMMA RAY ASTRONOMY

Detailing Soviet gamma-ray 'garbage'. F. Flam. *Science News* 135:260 Ap 29 '89

Gamma-ray bursts. J. Horgan. *Scientific American* 260:26 My '89

Gamma-ray confusion at the galactic center. il *Sky and Telescope* 77:584-5 Je '89

Gamma-ray observations of orbiting nuclear reactors [cover story] J. R. Primack. bibl f *Science* 244:407-8 Ap 28 '89

High-energy summer for astrophysics [gamma ray source at center of Milky Way flickers out] M. M. Waldrop. *Science* 245:129 Jl 14 '89

Man-made transients observed by the gamma-ray spectrometer on the Solar Maximum Mission satellite. E. Rieger and others. bibl f il *Science* 244:441-4 Ap 28 '89

Missing by more than a mile [Milky Way gamma ray source; research by Thomas A. Prince] I. Peterson. *Science News* 135:44 Ja 21 '89

Observations of nuclear reactors on satellites with a balloon-borne gamma-ray telescope. T. J. O'Neill and others. bibl f il *Science* 244:451-4 Ap 28 '89

Out of the center: gamma-ray redux [research by Marvin Leventhal and Jeffrey E. McClintock] I. Peterson. *Science News* 135:303 My 13 '89

Seeking gamma rays from Supernova 1987A. il *Sky and Telescope* 78:455 N '89

Soviet heavyweight astronomy satellite to be launched with international payload [Granat satellite with French Sigma telescope] J. M. Lenorovitz. il *Aviation Week & Space Technology* 131:31 N 27 '89

Splotchy supernova shakes assumptions [1987A; research by Scott Barthelmy] I. Peterson. *Science News* 135:303 My 13 '89

GAMMA RAY OBSERVATORY (ARTIFICIAL SATELLITE)

NASA to modify GRO satellite operations to cut interference from Soviet reactors. *Aviation Week & Space Technology* 130:52 My 15 '89

GAMMON, CLIVE

America's teen. il pors *Sports Illustrated* 70:68-9+ Je 12 '89

Huge move, Hugo. il por *Sports Illustrated* 71:22-3 S 25 '89

It's a real kick. il *Sports Illustrated* 70:64+ Ap 17 '89

The last Olympian. il pors *Sports Illustrated* 70:42-4+ My 15 '89

Not just for kicks. il *Sports Illustrated* 71:96 D 11 '89

Safe at home on a close call. il *Sports Illustrated* 70:89+ My 8 '89

A way was found. il *Sports Illustrated* 71:22-3 N 27 '89

GAMMONS, PETER

The A's have it. il *Sports Illustrated* 70 Special Issue:84-6+ Ap '89

Baseball at midseason. il *Sports Illustrated* 71:30-2+ Jl 17 '89

The big stick [cover story] il pors *Sports Illustrated* 70:22-7 Je 12 '89

End of an era. il *Sports Illustrated* 71:16-23 Jl 24 '89

A flight to the finish. il *Sports Illustrated* 71:48-50 O 2 '89

For the love of the game: an open letter to new baseball commissioner Fay Vincent. il por *Sports Illustrated* 71:92 S 25 '89

A hero lives here. il pors *Sports Illustrated* 71:28-31 N 6 '89

He's an Angel now. il pors *Sports Illustrated* 71:34-9 Ag 7 '89

The hit man hits back. il pors *Sports Illustrated* 70:54-8+ F 6 '89

Inside baseball. See issues of Sports Illustrated published during the baseball season beginning April 14, 1986 through October 9, 1989

Morals and immortals. il por *Sports Illustrated* 70:78 Ja 23 '89

Oh happy Jays. il *Sports Illustrated* 70 Special Issue:98-100+ Ap '89

Oh, what a relief it is. il *Sports Illustrated* 71:106-7 O 9 '89

Oh, what a show! [cover story] il pors *Sports Illustrated* 71:30-3+ O 16 '89

¡Plei bol! il *Sports Illustrated* 70:16-21 F 20 '89

Rich man's game. il *Sports Illustrated* 71:60-2 D 11 '89

A series to shout about. il *Sports Illustrated* 71:42-4+ S 18 '89

Street smarts. il pors *Sports Illustrated* 70 Special Issue:92-6 Ap '89

The summer of his discontent. il pors *Sports Illustrated* 71:72-4+ O 2 '89

A team that's hard to top. il *Sports Illustrated* 71:28-31 Jl 31 '89

Their ride of terror. il por *Sports Illustrated* 71:28-9 O 30 '89

They don't make 'em like they used to [cover story] il *Sports Illustrated* 70 Special Issue:26-30+ Ap '89

Too much, too soon. il *Sports Illustrated* 71:22-7 Ag 21 '89

(ed) See Scioscia, Mike. Calling a game

GANACHAUD, BERNARD
about
The fall and rise of French bread. N. Barry. il por *Gourmet* 49:56-9+ Mr '89
GANADOS DEL VALLE (ORGANIZATION)
A land battle in New Mexico [sheep war] J. N. Baker. il *Newsweek* 114:27 S 18 '89
GANAHL, ANNA
Stopping power. il *Petersen's Photographic Magazine* 18:34-8 Je '89
GANAY, BIRGITTE DE
about
French independent. C. Petkanas. il pors *Harper's Bazaar* 122:106-9+ Ag '89
In her own fashion. J. Burstall. il pors *House & Garden* 161:114-17 Jl '89
GANAY, CHARLES, COMTE DE
about
Three faces of the 16th-century Château de Fleury. S. M. Alsop. il por *Architectural Digest* 46:106+ D '89
GANDEE, CHARLES K.
60 minutes in the garden. il pors *House & Garden* 161:110-17 Je '89
Barbarians at play. il pors *House & Garden* 161:132-5 Jl '89
Bright light in the big city. il pors *House & Garden* 161:190-5 O '89
Escape to Normandy [cover story] il pors *House & Garden* 161:96-105+ F '89
On the Rue de Rivoli. il por *House & Garden* 161:68-77 Jl '89
Once upon a time. il *House & Garden* 161:110-15+ Ag '89
The Palm Beach story. il pors *House & Garden* 161:110-19+ D '89
Parlor game. il *House & Garden* 161:92-7 Ag '89
Peter the Great. il pors *House & Garden* 161:174-83+ O '89
Prime time. il por *House & Garden* 161:182-7+ Mr '89
The Royalton treatment. il por *House & Garden* 161:70-7 Ja '89
Starck modern. il por *House & Garden* 161:78-85+ Jl '89
The well-appointed decorator [cover story] il pors *House & Garden* 161:108-15+ Mr '89
GANDHI, ARUN
about
In Gandhi's footsteps. G. Cowley. il por *Newsweek* 113:48 Mr 6 '89
Inspired by his famous forebear, Mahatma Gandhi's grandson takes a close look at racism in America. H. Shapiro. il pors *People Weekly* 31:257-8 Mr 6 '89
GANDHI, MAHATMA, 1869-1948
about
India's march to freedom. P. E. Rogers. il por *Scholastic Update (Teachers' edition)* 121:18-20 Mr 10 '89
GANDHI, MOHANDAS KARAMCHAND *See* Gandhi, Mahatma, 1869-1948
GANDHI, RAJIV, 1944-
about
A dynasty in doubt. A. Phillips. il por *Maclean's* 102:36-8+ N 27 '89
The end of a dynasty. R. Moreau and S. Mazumdar. il pors *Newsweek* 114:60 D 11 '89
The end of a dynasty: voters reject Prime Minister Rajiv Gandhi. A. Bilski. il pors *Maclean's* 102:40-1 D 11 '89
The fall of the House of Nehru. L. Beyer. il pors *Time* 134:57 D 11 '89
Gandhi's Watergate? *Newsweek* 114:42 O 23 '89
India: state and society diverge. J. Manor. bibl f *Current History* 88:429-32+ D '89
The Indian subcontinent [cover story; special issue] il maps *Scholastic Update (Teachers' edition)* 121:3-26 Mr 10 '89
No rerun for the Gandhi-dynasty show. E. MacFarquhar. il pors *U.S. News & World Report* 107:47-8 D 11 '89
Pilot error. J. C. Hollick. *The New Republic* 201:13-14 D 4 '89
A referendum on Rajiv. C. S. Manegold. por *Newsweek* 114:56 N 27 '89
GANESAN, INDIRA
The wedding [story] il *Seventeen* 48:110-11+ F '89
GANGES RIVER (INDIA AND BANGLADESH)
The tour of doom [cycling the length] S. O'Grady. il map *Bicycling* 30:150-4+ My '89
GANGLIOSIDOSIS
Mutation revealed for adult Tay-Sachs [work of Ruth Navon and Richard L. Proia] I. Wickelgren. *Science News* 135:167 Mr 18 '89
The mutations in Ashkenazi Jews with adult G_{M2} gangliosidosis, the adult form of Tay-Sachs disease. R. Navon and R. L. Proia. bibl f il *Science* 243:1471-4 Mr 17 '89
GANGS
See also
El Rukn (Gang)
Mothers Against Gangs (Organization)
Renkers Posse (Gang)
Wilding (Group violence)

Death among the innocent [gang related murders in Los Angeles] A. Gregor. il *Maclean's* 102:38 My 22 '89
The priest who loves gangsters [Los Angeles mission for gang members run by G. J. Boyle; cover story] E. Shorris. il *The Nation* 249:737+ D 18 '89
Turf wars [drug gangs] P. Sudo. il *Scholastic Update (Teachers' edition)* 122:6 N 17 '89
When drug gangs move to nice places. S. J. Hedges. *U.S. News & World Report* 106:42 Je 5 '89
When you're a Crip (or a Blood) [discussion with L.A. gang members] *Harper's* 278:51-9 Mr '89
Canada
Gang terror [cover story; special section; with editorial comment by Kevin Doyle] il *Maclean's* 102:2, 36-42+ My 22 '89
Soviet Union
Gang warfare, Soviet-style. A. Wilson-Smith. il *Maclean's* 102:44 My 22 '89
GANGSTERS *See* Mafia
GANN, LEWIS H., 1924-
Kristallnacht reflections. il *The American Spectator* 22:25-6 Ja '89
about
Exploitation or benefaction? P. Brimelow. il por *Forbes* 144:110+ N 27 '89
GANNAWAY, GARY
about
Gannaway's Genesis. A. B. Block. il pors *Channels (New York, N.Y.: 1986)* 9:36-7+ S '89
GANNETT CO., INC.
Al Neuharth is a tough act to follow [J. J. Curley] T. Smart. il por *Business Week* p119-20 My 8 '89
The Machiavelli of 'McPaper' [A. Neuharth's autobiography] J. Hammer. il por *Newsweek* 114:38 S 25 '89
Mainstreaming minorities [inclusion of minorities in news stories that are not specifically concerned with minority issues] *Harper's* 279:16 Ag '89
The manager who never says never [N. Woodhull] R. Sandroff. il pors *Working Woman* 14:90-2+ D '89
McProfitability. T. Smart. il *Business Week* p30-1 Jl 31 '89
GANNON, FRANK
Mmm, mmm, simulacrum. il *Harper's* 278:55-7 My '89
GANNON, ROBERT
Caught in an abyssal storm. il map *Earth Science* 42:18-20 Spr '89
GANOE, WILLIAM H.
The debris collector. il *Ad Astra* 1:35-7 Je '89
Enterprises. See issues of Ad Astra beginning January 1989
GANS, CARL, 1923-
The once and future museum. il *Natural History* p48-55 Jl '89
GANS, CURTIS B.
Why young people don't vote. *The Education Digest* 54:40-3 F '89
GANSNEDER, BRUCE
(jt. auth) See Frymier, Jack Rimmel, 1925-, and Gansneder, Bruce
GANTENBEIN, DOUGLAS
David Rockwood: a steel-and-glass bay-front house in Portland. il por *Architectural Digest* 46:72-7 Ag '89
Seattle CAPs downtown growth. il *Architectural Record* 177:51 Jl '89
GANTT, DIANA, 1986-
about
Twins: 1 black, 1 white, born to interracial pair. il pors *Jet* 76:16-17 Jl 31 '89
GANTT, TAMARA, 1986-
about
Twins: 1 black, 1 white, born to interracial pair. il pors *Jet* 76:16-17 Jl 31 '89
GAO, JIALI, AND OTHERS
Hidden thermodynamics of mutant proteins: a molecular dynamics analysis. bibl f il *Science* 244:1069-72 Je 2 '89
GAO *See* United States. General Accounting Office
GAP, INC.
From schlock to chic. N. Darnton. il *Newsweek* 113:73 My 15 '89
The Gap snaps back. il *Forbes* 143:190 Ja 9 '89
GAP JUNCTIONS *See* Junctions (Physiology)
GAPPA, ALLISON M.
A test of courage. il pors *Ladies' Home Journal* 106:22+ Ja '89
GARAFOLA, LYNN
Ann Hutchinson Guest goes back to the source: finding Faune. il pors *Dance Magazine* 63:32-4 O '89
Choreographer Bronislava Nijinska in revival: the exemplary daughterhood of Irina Nijinska. il pors *Dance Magazine* 63:43-4 Je '89
Variations on a theme of butoh. il *Dance Magazine* 63:66-8 Ap '89
GARAGE DOORS
Garage door screens. S. Kingman and P. Kingman. il *The Family Handyman* 39:82-3 Ap '89
Control
How to install a garage door opener. il *Popular Mechanics* 166:95-8 O '89

GARAGE DOORS—cont.

Maintenance and repair

Repairing your overhead garage door. D. Prestly. il *The Family Handyman* 39:58-61 F '89

Replacing a garage door section. M. Phair. il *Home Mechanix* 85:31-2+ Jl '89

GARAGES

The humble garage. M. T. Marsden. il *Motor Trend* 41:130-1 F '89

Storage strategies. J. Truini. il *Home Mechanix* 85:88+ O '89

GARAGES, REMODELED

Artful garage conversion: new studio shares space with storage. T. Jackson. il *Better Homes and Gardens* 67:64 My '89

A classic garage conversion [made into a den] il *Southern Living* 24:110 Ja '89

Forging ahead [converted garage apartment of A. Dubreuil in London] C. Maclean. il por *House & Garden* 161:150-5+ N '89

Garage getaway. W. Winans and D. Winans. il *Popular Mechanics* 166:84-5 Ag '89

Master bedroom over the garage. il *Sunset (Central West edition)* 182:144 Mr '89

Systems [Wayne Mackey's garage becomes media room] R. Day. il *Stereo Review* 54:82-3 Je '89

GARAVANI, VALENTINO *See* Valentino

GARBA, JOSEPH

about

A soldier-diplomat at the helm. il por *UN Chronicle* 26:42-3 D '89

GARBAGE *See* Refuse and refuse disposal

GARBAGE AS FUEL *See* Refuse as fuel

GARBAGE BAGS *See* Trash bags

GARBER, STEVEN D.

Bradford callery pear. il *Focus (New York, N.Y.: 1950)* 39:33-6 Fall '89

Cherry. il *Focus (New York, N.Y.: 1950)* 39:28-9 Spr '89

Maple: the biogeography of popular species. *Focus (New York, N.Y.: 1950)* 38:32-3+ Wint '88

Striped bass. il *Focus (New York, N.Y.: 1950)* 39:34-6 Summ '89

GARBER (PAUL E.) PRESERVATION, RESTORATION AND STORAGE FACILITY *See* Paul E. Garber Preservation, Restoration and Storage Facility

GARBERS, DAVID L.

(jt. auth) See Chinkers, Michael, and Garbers, David L.

GARBO, GRETA, 1905-1990

about

Garbo talks (a little). R. Daum. il pors *Life* 12:96-8+ Spr '89

GARBUS, MARTIN, 1934-

The 'crime' of flag burning. il *The Nation* 248:369-70 Mr 20 '89

The F.B.I. man who cried libel. il *The Nation* 249:564+ N 13 '89

Limiting our rights. *Publishers Weekly* 236:21 Ag 18 '89

McGinniss: a travesty of libel. *Publishers Weekly* 235:69 Ap 21 '89

GARCIA, GUY D.

The believers. il *Rolling Stone* p46-9+ Je 29 '89

GARCIA, JACQUES

about

Royal lineage. G. Y. Dryansky. il por *House & Garden* 161:148-55+ Jl '89

GARCIA, JERRY

about

Jerry Garcia [interview; cover story] F. Goodman. il pors *Rolling Stone* p66-8+ N 30 '89

GARCIA, JUAN

Barcelona's Olympic buildup. *World Press Review* 36:55 Ap '89

GARCIA, JUAN

about

Miracle on Hoe Avenue. P. M. Coan. il pors *World Tennis* 37:36-41+ O '89

GARCIA, MARCELO, AND PARKER, GARY

Experiments on hydraulic jumps in turbidity currents near a canyon-fan transition. bibl f il *Science* 245:393-6 Jl 28 '89

GARCIA, ROBERT

Should the House-passed wage proposal be enacted? [excerpts from address, March 23, 1989] *Congressional Digest* 68:152+ My '89

GARCÍA-BARRIO, CONSTANCE

Cocaine's youngest victims. il *American Visions* 4:16 D '89

GARCÍA MÁRQUEZ, GABRIEL, 1928-

about

New from García Márquez. S. Cato. il por *World Press Review* 36:60 Je '89

Noble riddles and surrealist fruits. I. Stavans. il *Art News* 88:29 N '89

GARCÍA PÉREZ, ALAN

about

Cocaine, communism and crisis in Peru. C. A. Robbins. il *U.S. News & World Report* 107:45-9 S 18 '89

Peru fights to overcome its past. A. Riding. il por *The New York Times Magazine* p40+ My 14 '89

GARD, JUDY RICHARDSON

The watercolor page. il por *American Artist* 53:56-9+ Ap '89

GARDEL, CARLOS

about

Gardel. *The New Yorker* 65:26-7 Ag 21 '89

GARDELS, NATHAN

Comment. See issues of New Perspectives Quarterly

The price China has paid: an interview with Liu Binyan [with introduction by Merle Goldman] il *The New York Review of Books* 35:31+ Ja 19 '89

GARDEN ARCHITECTURE *See* Landscape architecture

GARDEN BENCHES

Garden seat. M. Ferrara. il *Organic Gardening* 36:77-9 Mr '89

Kneeling bench. M. Ferrara. il *Organic Gardening* 36:62-3 Je '89

Rolling garden bench. D. Stewart. il *Flower and Garden* 33:90-1 Mr/Ap '89

Rolling redwood seat. il *Workbench* 45:54-7 My/Je '89

Sit-a-spell garden settee. W. L. Nolan. il *Better Homes and Gardens* 67:128 Ag '89

GARDEN BORDERS

Easygoing borders. il *Sunset (Central West edition)* 183:202-4 O '89

Keys to a classic perennial garden [flower borders; excerpt from The perennial gardener] F. McGourty. il *Country Journal* 16:32-8 S/O '89

Mixed borders [planting vegetables among flowers] V. Mattern. il *Organic Gardening* 36:51-2+ F '89

Spire plants [tall perennials] J. Glattstein. il *Flower and Garden* 33:34-9 My/Je '89

GARDEN CATALOGS *See* Catalogs, Seed and plant

GARDEN DESIGN

See also

Landscape gardening

The flowering of Fort Worth [garden designed for A. Bass by R. Page] C. Burden. il por *House & Garden* 161:84-91+ F '89

Painting with plants. S. Sides. il *The Mother Earth News* 117:92-4 My/Je '89

GARDEN EQUIPMENT

See also

Cultivators
Garden hose
Lawn equipment
Leaf balers
Lexington Gardens (Firm)
Plant labels
Plant supports
Potting benches
Pruning equipment
Toro Company
Tractors
Wheelbarrows

The best of lawn and garden equipment in 1989. H. E. Gibson. il *Flower and Garden* 33:51-2 N/D '89

Drilling for bulbs? A brighter idea than you'd think [planting tool] il *Sunset (Central West edition)* 183:194-5 O '89

Garden giftables. il *Flower and Garden* 33:8-9 N/D '89

Gifts for gardeners. L. A. Weathers. il *Southern Living* 24:46 D '89

The rake that's a saw [combination tools] il *Sunset (Central West edition)* 183:161 D '89

Tools for gardening. K. K. Gracey. *Consumers' Research Magazine* 72:2 Mr '89

Tools of the trade. M. Ferrara. See issues of Organic Gardening beginning February 1989

Maintenance and repair

How to maintain garden tools. R. Capotosto. il *Popular Mechanics* 166:101-4 Mr '89

Storage

See also

Sheds

Testing

9 best new yard and garden tools. B. Markovich. il *Home Mechanix* 85:48+ Je '89

Chipper/shredder review. H. E. Gibson. il *Flower and Garden* 33:52+ S/O '89

Yard-sized shredders. M. Ferrara. il *Organic Gardening* 36:49-53 My '89

GARDEN EXHIBITS

Calendar. See issues of Flower and Garden

Garden events [title varies] See issues of Sunset (Central West edition)

Southern garden events. See issues of Southern Living

GARDEN FOLLIES (ARCHITECTURE) *See* Follies (Architecture)

GARDEN FOUNTAINS *See* Fountains

GARDEN GATES *See* Gates

GARDEN HOSE

What's new in hoses and nozzles. S. Nesbitt. il *Flower and Garden* 33:56-8 My/Je '89

Maintenance and repair

How to repair a garden hose. R. Capotosto. il *Popular Mechanics* 166:105 Mr '89

GARDEN HOUSES, SHELTERS, ETC.
See also
Arbors
Sheds
The gazebo. C. Vogel. il *The New York Times Magazine* p56-7 Jl 23 '89
Gazebos to go. B. Nadel. il *Popular Science* 234:146-7 My '89
Outdoor living space [patios and gazebos] B. Vila. il *Popular Mechanics* 166:44+ Jl '89
Outer spaces [gazebo and screen house] J. Truini. il *Home Mechanix* 85:44-51 Ag '89

GARDEN LABELS See Plant labels
GARDEN LITERATURE
See also
Booksellers and bookselling—Garden literature
Gardens and gardening—Bibliography
Publishers and publishing—Garden literature

GARDEN MARKETS See Farmers' markets
GARDEN OF EDEN (LUCAS, KAN.) See Concrete Garden of Eden (Lucas, Kan.)
GARDEN ORNAMENTS
Outside in [used in interior decoration] C. Vogel. il *The New York Times Magazine* p56-9 Mr 26 '89
There's an art to art in the garden. il *Sunset (Central West edition)* 183:112-13 Ag '89
Tucked-away treasures. R. W. Strickland. il *Southern Living* 24:58-9 Jl '89
With Ron Forshee's Granny Fannies, suburban gardeners can exhibit some early bloomers. il por *People Weekly* 31:105 My 15 '89
Collectors and collecting
Antiques: garden ornament. J. A. Cuadrado. il *Architectural Digest* 46:150-5+ Jl '89
Theft
Heigh-ho, heigh-ho, it's far, far off we go; or, Grumpynappers give a cement dwarf a joyride [pranksters steal lawn ornament from the home of C. Horne in Mount Marion, N.Y.] il *People Weekly* 31:100-1 Je 26 '89

GARDEN PESTICIDES See Pesticides
GARDEN POOLS
See also
Water gardens and gardening
A garden pool. V. Strong. il *Organic Gardening* 36:27-9 S '89
In a small garden, the koi swim above the ground. il *Sunset (Central West edition)* 183:106-7 Jl '89
On the waterfront. D. Hufford. il *Flower and Garden* 33:30-2 N/D '89
Ponds or spas? il *Sunset (Central West edition)* 183:52-3 Ag '89
Practical reflections on garden pools. D. Hufford. il *Flower and Garden* 33:54-8, 60 Mr/Ap '89
A streetside retreat [New Orleans] R. W. Strickland. il *Southern Living* 24:62-3 Ag '89
Water music. D. Hufford. il *Flower and Garden* 33:20-3 S/O '89

GARDEN ROOMS
Jungle room brightens the house. il *Sunset (Central West edition)* 183:110 N '89

GARDEN SHEDS See Sheds
GARDEN STAKES AND STAKING See Plant supports
GARDEN STEPS
Scent and sound underfoot. il *Sunset (Central West edition)* 182:170 My '89

GARDEN THERAPY See Gardens and gardening—Therapeutic use
GARDEN TOURS
Gardens of delight [touring Roman palaces and their gardens] R. Koenig. il *House & Garden* 161:46+ F '89

GARDEN TRACTORS See Tractors
GARDEN WALKS (PATHS)
Garden path. E. Thompson and E. Thompson. il *Popular Mechanics* 166:90-2 Je '89
A trail of little hands and feet [concrete stepping pads] il *Southern Living* 24:78-9 My '89

GARDEN WALLS
Why not ask a garden wall also to work as a garden seat? il *Sunset (Central West edition)* 183:188-91 S '89

GARDENERS
See also
Authors as gardeners
Would you like to see my motherworts? [men gardeners] J. H. Kunstler. il *Gentlemen's Quarterly* 59:54+ Ap '89
Health and hygiene
Easing into spring. F. McGourty. il *Flower and Garden* 33:120 Mr/Ap '89

GARDENING See Gardens and gardening
GARDENS (LOS ANGELES, CALIF.: RESTAURANT) See Los Angeles (Calif.)—Restaurants, nightclubs, bars, etc.
GARDENS AND GARDENING
See also
Aged—Gardens and gardening
Artificial light gardening
Botanical gardens
Bulbs
Butterfly gardens
Catalogs, Seed and plant

Children's gardens and gardening
Cold frames
Container gardens and gardening
Flower gardens and gardening
Fragrant gardens
Grafting
Greenhouses
Herbs
Hillside gardens and gardening
Hydroponics
Indoor gardens and gardening
Landscape gardening
Lawns
Mulching
Native plant gardens and gardening
Nurseries (Horticulture)
Organic gardens and gardening
Pinching (Plant pruning)
Plant propagation
Plants—Protection
Pruning
Rock gardens and gardening
Sculpture gardens and parks
Seeding
Seeds
Shade gardens and gardening
Shrubs
Vegetable gardens and gardening
Water gardens and gardening
Watering of gardens, lawns, etc.
Weeds
Wildflower gardens and gardening
Window gardens and gardening
The cottage garden. S. Ervin. il *The Mother Earth News* 120:76-81 N/D '89
Easing into spring. F. McGourty. il *Flower and Garden* 33:120 Mr/Ap '89
Garden tips to try and treasure. il *The Mother Earth News* 117:16+ My/Je '89
Gardener's log. See issues of Better Homes and Gardens
The grass is always greener on Jerry Baker's lawn because he feeds it beer, soap and ammonia [interview] J. Greenwalt. il pors *People Weekly* 31:85+ Je 19 '89
How should your garden grow? L. Werner. il *Ladies' Home Journal* 106:158+ My '89
Letters to our garden editors [questions and answers] See issues of Southern Living
Life's cycles. J. Goldsmith. il por *Organic Gardening* 36:72 My '89
[Month] in your garden. See issues of Sunset (Central West edition)
My secret garden. A. Raver. il *Reader's Digest* 135:39-40 Jl '89
Our own garden. D. McCorkindale. See issues of Flower and Garden beginning January/February 1989
Pocketful of spring. A. Raver. il *Reader's Digest* 134:83-4 Mr '89
The rites (and wrongs) of spring. G. Williams and L. Williams. il *Home Mechanix* 86:70-2+ Ap '89
The seasons of the garden. G. Williams and P. Williams. See issues of The Mother Earth News beginning July/August 1985
Share your garden with a few chickens? W. D. Adams. il *Flower and Garden* 33:62-4+ Mr/Ap '89
Thoughts for the new year. F. McGourty. il *Flower and Garden* 33:112 Ja/F '89
Bibliography
Armchair gardener. See issues of Organic Gardening beginning April 1988
Books for the gardener. N. Bubel. il *Country Journal* 16:93-5 N/D '89
Garden plots. P. Thorpe; S. Mortimer. il *House & Garden* 161:90-1+ My '89
Gardening. L. Yang. il *The New York Times Book Review* 94:74-5 D 3 '89
Gardening books. A. Lacy. il *The New York Times Book Review* 94:30 Je 11 '89
Regional digest: the best regional garden books for gift giving. il *Flower and Garden* 33:14-18 N/D '89
Equipment
See Garden equipment
Exhibitions
See Garden exhibits
History
Editorial [England] W. Garrett. il *Antiques* 135:1410-11 Je '89
Insect control
See Insect control
International aspects
Seeds of diplomacy. R. Halaby. il *Organic Gardening* 36:95 F '89
Soil preparation
Soil sense. C. Shirley. il *Organic Gardening* 36:59-61 Je '89
Tilling the earth. J. Burland. il *Country Journal* 16:64-8 Mr/Ap '89

GARDENS AND GARDENING—*cont.*
Terminology
Oh, the buzzing of the words. F. McGourty. il *Flower and Garden* 33:64 N/D '89
Therapeutic use
Breathing space [labored breathing, brought on by anxiety, cured by visiting garden] S. Safransky. il por *Organic Gardening* 36:83-4 O '89
Weed control
See Weed control
Arctic regions
Land of the midnight melons? [fiber optic transmission of rays to Arctic crops in indoor gardens; work of Dennis R. St. George] *Science News* 136:412 D 23-30 '89
Australia
Out back in Australia [G. Geddes' garden] D. B. Pitt. il por *House & Garden* 161:126-31+ Ja '89
Bermuda
Bermuda in bloom. S. Mortimer. il *House & Garden* 161:144-9+ N '89
California
See also
Hollywood (Calif.)—Gardens and gardening
Montecito (Calif.)—Gardens and gardening
Palos Verdes Estates (Calif.)—Gardens and gardening
Saint Helena (Calif.)—Gardens and gardening
Santa Barbara (Calif.)—Gardens and gardening
Gardens: subtropical artistry: Jack Baker's exuberant creation near Santa Barbara. M. Frank. il pors *Architectural Digest* 46:284-9+ My '89
Cape Cod (Mass.)
A writer's garden. M. Piercy. il por *Organic Gardening* 36:72 Je '89
Colorado
See also
Denver (Colo.)—Gardens and gardening
Fort Collins (Colo.)—Gardens and gardening
The high ground. L. Caruso. il *Ms.* 17:52-3 Ja/F '89
Connecticut
See also
Darien (Conn.)—Gardens and gardening
France
See also
Giverny (France)—Gardens and gardening
Paris (France)—Gardens and gardening
The Désert de Retz, near Paris. P. Deitz. bibl f il *Antiques* 135:718-31 Mr '89
Gardens: a philosophy of fragrance: Robert Ricci's floral domain in the Ile-de-France. C. Styles-McLeod. il por *Architectural Digest* 46:142-7 Ja '89
Princess in the garden [G. Sturdza's La Vasterival in Normandy] M. K. Griswold. il por *House & Garden* 161:108-13+ Jl '89
Georgia
See also
Atlanta (Ga.)—Gardens and gardening
Decatur (Ga.)—Gardens and gardening
Great Britain
See also
Somerset (England)—Gardens and gardening
A budding genius [designer G. Jekyll] P. Weideger. il por *Ms.* 17:48-9 Mr '89
Editorial. W. Garrett. il *Antiques* 135:1410-11 Je '89
Gardens: High Beeches: preserving a woodland heritage in Sussex. E. Lambert. il *Architectural Digest* 46:150-3+ Ag '89
A homegrown view [designer D. Hicks' garden in Oxfordshire] C. Vogel. il *The New York Times Magazine* p68-71 Je 18 '89
Small wonders [cottage gardens] R. Verey. il *House & Garden* 161:102+ Mr '89
The vicar's walk [home of M. Keen; excerpt from Private landscape] C. Seebohm. il *House & Garden* 161:174-8 S '89

Photographs and photography
Miss Jekyll's garden [traveling exhibition] E. P. Williams. il *House & Garden* 161:166 F '89
Hawaii
See also
Waikiki Beach (Honolulu, Hawaii)—Gardens and gardening
Illinois
Woody and Ed [animal occupants] R. M. Lerner. il *Organic Gardening* 36:104 Ja '89
Italy
See also
Bellagio (Italy)—Gardens and gardening
Rome (Italy)—Gardens and gardening
Venice (Italy)—Gardens and gardening
Japan
In a Japanese garden. B. A. Coats. il map *National Geographic* 176:638-63 N '89
Long Island (N.Y.)
60 minutes in the garden [Hamptons garden of D. Hewitt and M. Berger] C. K. Gandee. il pors *House & Garden* 161:110-17 Je '89
Far afield [garden of N. M. Zohn] M. K. Griswold. il por *House & Garden* 161:108-15 Ap '89

Louisiana
See also
New Orleans (La.)—Gardens and gardening
Maryland
See also
Knoxville (Md.)—Gardens and gardening
Missouri
See also
Kansas City (Mo.)—Gardens and gardening
New Mexico
See also
Santa Fe (N.M.)—Gardens and gardening
New York (State)
See also
Southampton (N.Y.)—Gardens and gardening
Oregon
See also
Portland (Or.)—Gardens and gardening
Scotland
Tropical Scotland [gardens in Argyll] C. Maclean. il *House & Garden* 161:136-41+ F '89
South Carolina
See also
Charleston (S.C.)—Gardens and gardening
Southern States
The southern garden. See issues of Southern Living
Texas
See also
Dallas (Tex.)—Gardens and gardening
Fort Worth (Tex.)—Gardens and gardening
Virginia
See also
Monticello (Va.: Estate)—Gardens
Mount Vernon (Va.: Estate)—Gardens
Tori Thomas: agricultural abstractions in a Virginia landscape. il por *Architectural Digest* 46:100-1 Ap '89
GARDENS AND GARDENING, JAPANESE
See also
Bonsai
A jewel in the Japanese style [New Orleans garden] R. W. Strickland. il *Southern Living* 24:68-9 F '89
GARDENS AND GARDENING IN ART
Exhibitions
Painting with oil sticks [Giverny paintings by J. Chesley; cover story] E. Feit. il *American Artist* 53:44-9 Ap '89
GARDINER, JOHN ELIOT
about
Rooted, but not in the past. S. Cantrell. il pors *High Fidelity (New York, N.Y.)* 39:48-50 Jl '89
GARDINER, JULIET, 1945-
History tomorrow. il *History Today* 39:11-13 Je '89
GARDINER, ROBERT
about
Day tour. *The New Yorker* 65:26-8 Je 26 '89
Lord of ospreys. F. Graham. il *Audubon* 91:10+ S '89
Wasps' nest [cover story] D. Smith. il pors *New York* 22:30-9 Je 5 '89
GARDINERS ISLAND (N.Y.)
See also
Birds—Gardiners Island (N.Y.)
Natural history—Gardiners Island (N.Y.)
Wasps' nest [cover story] D. Smith. il pors *New York* 22:30-9 Je 5 '89
GARDINI, RAUL
about
How to build a $30 billion empire in five years. J. Rossant. il por *Business Week* p58-9 Jl 3 '89
An Italian 'peasant' who would be soybean king. E. Pomice. il por *U.S. News & World Report* 107:44-5 Ag 7 '89
Why Wall Street is furioso at Raul Gardini. J. Rossant and W. Glasgall. il por *Business Week* p48 F 20 '89
GARDINIER, SUZANNE
The stones [poem] *The New Yorker* 64:30 F 13 '89
GARDNER, CHARLES A.
Is an embryo a person? il *The Nation* 249:557-9 N 13 '89
GARDNER, CHARLES F.
about
Operation Ill Wind may have scared up a canary. P. Dwyer. il pors *Business Week* p37 F 6 '89
GARDNER, FRANK WEBB, JR.
about
Meanwhile, on the links, an Everyman scratches out a living. G. Waggoner. il pors *Sport (New York, N.Y.)* 80:89+ Je '89
GARDNER, HOWARD
Learning, Chinese-style. il *Psychology Today* 23:54-6 D '89
GARDNER, ISABELLA STEWART, 1840-1924
about
Mrs. Gardner's mistakes. C. Giuliano. il por *Art News* 88:47-8 My '89
Where there's a will . . . A. Higonnet. bibl f il *Art in America* 77:65-7+ My '89
GARDNER, JAMES
Having it all: uncritical critics in today's art world. il *National Review* 41:47-50 My 19 '89
Postmodernism [discussion of January 1989 article, Postmodernist blues] *Commentary* 87:11-12 My '89

GARDNER, JAMES—*cont.*
Postmodernist blues. *Commentary* 87:55-61 Ja '89
GARDNER, JOHN WILLIAM, 1912-
about
John Gardner: the serious optimist. D. Baldwin. por *Common Cause Magazine* 15:34-8 S/O '89
GARDNER, RANDY
about
A skating star's long fall from grace [cover story]; ed. by Lois Armstrong. T. Babilonia. il pors *People Weekly* 31:86-8+ Ap 17 '89
GARDNER, THOMAS, III
about
Two blacks face murder charges in voodoo scheme. il pors *Jet* 76:52-3 Jl 17 '89
GARDNER, WAYNE
about
Gardner tops Rainey at Australian GP. il *Cycle* 40:24 Jl '89
GARDNER (ISABELLA STEWART) MUSEUM *See* Isabella Stewart Gardner Museum
GARDNER-PINGREE HOUSE (SALEM, MASS.) *See* Salem (Mass.)—Historic houses, sites, etc.
GARFINKLE, ADAM M., 1951-
The world has changed. *The Bulletin of the Atomic Scientists* 45:44 My '89
(jt. auth) See Pipes, Daniel, 1949-, and Garfinkle, Adam M., 1951-
GARFUNKEL, E., AND OTHERS
Scanning tunneling microscopy and nanolithography on a conducting oxide, $Rb_{0.3}MoO_3$. bibl f il *Science* 246:99-100 O 6 '89
GARGIULO'S RESTAURANT (BROOKLYN, N.Y.) *See* Brooklyn (New York, N.Y.)—Restaurants, nightclubs, bars, etc.
GARLAND, NICHOLAS
Cartoonist's-eye view. il *National Review* 41:32-3 S 1 '89
GARLAND (TEX.)
Libraries
Spreading some good words [librarian P. Goodwin's program for foreign users of Walnut Creek Branch Library] D. Young. il por *Southern Living* 24:64 Ag '89
GARLIC
See also
Cooking—Herbs and spices
GARLIC WORLD (FIRM)
Out of this world. M. Barrier. il por *Nation's Business* 77:13 Ag '89
GARMENT, LEONARD
The Hill case. *The New Yorker* 65:90-110 Ap 17 '89
GARMENT, SUZANNE
The Tower precedent. *Commentary* 87:42-8 My '89
GARMENT DISTRICT (FIRM)
From rags to riches in the tough world of retail [K. Friedman] D. E. Gumpert. il por *Working Woman* 14:45-6+ O '89
GARMENT INDUSTRY *See* Clothing industry
GARN, JAKE
Should the Congress adopt the "Financial Institutions Reform, Recovery, and Enforcement Act of 1989"? [excerpts from address, April 17, 1989] *Congressional Digest* 68:170+ Je/Jl '89
Should the Congress adopt the "Tender Offer Disclosure and Fairness Act of 1987"? [excerpts from address, June 17, 1988] *Congressional Digest* 68:75+ Mr '89
GARNER, CHRIS
about
Picture this. J. E. Loehr. il por *World Tennis* 36:22-3 Ap '89
GARNER, JAMES, 1928-
about
James Garner. il por *People Weekly* 31 Special Issue:62 Summ '89
GARNETS
Rates of tectonometamorphic processes from rubidium and strontium isotopes in garnet [southeast Vermont] J. N. Christensen and others. bibl f il *Science* 244:1465-9 Je 23 '89
GARNISHES IN COOKING *See* Cooking—Garnishes
GARON, LEN, 1945-
An approach to success. il *American Artist* 53:66-71 Jl '89
GAROUSTE, ELIZABETH
about
Barbarians at play. C. K. Gandee. il pors *House & Garden* 161:132-5 Jl '89
GAROUSTE, GÉRARD
about
Gerard Garouste: Centre Pompidou; Fondation Cartier. C. Mosley. il *Art News* 88:161 Ja '89
GARR, DOUG
How to survive home remodeling. il *Reader's Digest* 135:181-2+ S '89
Scene three. il pors *Harper's Bazaar* 122:162-5+ F '89
GARR, TERI
about
Hollywood homestead. P. Viladas. il pors *House & Garden* 161:98-103 Ag '89
GARRARD, ALICE
"Queen of Hell Gate". il pors *Ms.* 18:52-5 Jl/Ag '89

GARRETS
The way we are. L. Wyse. il *Good Housekeeping* 208:254 Ap '89
GARRETT, JOYCE
about
Choir director Joyce Garrett battles D.C.'s mean streets with the power of positive singing. R. Arias. il por *People Weekly* 31:99-100 Je 12 '89
Song of Eastern High. K. McCabe. il *Reader's Digest* 135:51-6 S '89
GARRETT, THAD
about
Garrett, Fletcher named to key positions by Bush. il pors *Jet* 76:4-5 Ap 10 '89
GARRETT, WENDELL
Editorial. See issues of Antiques
GARRETT, WILBUR E.
La Ruta Maya. il supp (folded map) maps *National Geographic* 176:424-78 O '89
GARRETT, WILLIAM R.
Religion in China [cover story] il *The Christian Century* 106:748-9 Ag 16-23 '89
'Science and democracy' in Tiananmen Square. il *The Christian Century* 106:646-7 Jl 5-12 '89
GARRETT CANADA LTD.
Pilots sense attitude with peripheral vision using new Garrett display. B. D. Nordwall. il *Aviation Week & Space Technology* 130:97+ My 8 '89
GARRETT CORPORATION
Garrett's APU market dominance challenged by new competitors [special section] il *Aviation Week & Space Technology* 130:69+ Ap 10 '89
GARRIOTT, RICHARD
about
Conversations: Dungeon delving with Richard Garriott. K. Ferrell. il pors *Compute!* 11:16-17 Ja '89
GARRISON, PETER
Aftermath. See issues of Flying
Martian misgivings. il *Omni (New York, N.Y.)* 12:22 D '89
Technicalities. See alternate issues of Flying beginning March 1985
GARRISON, ZINA
about
Garrison ruins Evert's U.S. Open goodbye party. il pors *Jet* 76:46+ S 25 '89
Living a dream. K. Moore and J. E. Vader. il pors *Sports Illustrated* 71:70+ N 27 '89
Newlywed Zina Garrison captures Chicago Slims. il por *Jet* 77:51 N 27 '89
Tennis ace Zina Garrison ties Houston love match. il pors *Jet* 77:52-3 O 23 '89
GARRISON (N.Y.)
Historic houses, sites, etc.
See also
Boscobel Restoration
GARRITY, JOHN
Another Cup runneth overseas. il *Sports Illustrated* 71:64-5 Ag 28 '89
The College of Cardinals. il pors *Sports Illustrated* 71:64-8+ Ag 14 '89
High, wide and handsome. il por *Sports Illustrated* 71:169 S 4 '89
A King is crowned queen. il por *Sports Illustrated* 71:71-2 Jl 24 '89
The Midas touch. il por *Sports Illustrated* 71:42-3 N 6 '89
Old Sarge takes charge. il *Sports Illustrated* 71:56+ Jl 10 '89
Tennessee waltzes in Tacoma. il *Sports Illustrated* 70:80 Ap 10 '89
(ed) See Alford, Steve. The Knight I knew
GARRY, VINCENT F., AND OTHERS
Human genotoxicity: pesticide applicators and phosphine. bibl f il *Science* 246:251-5 O 13 '89
GARTEN, JEFFREY E.
Japan and Germany: American concerns. il *Foreign Affairs* 68:84-101 Wint '89/'90
Trading blocs and the evolving world economy. *Current History* 88:15-16+ Ja '89
GARTER SNAKES *See* Snakes
GARTH FAGAN BUCKET DANCE
Reviews:
Performances at the Joyce Theater New York City. J. Lewis. *Dance Magazine* 63:80-1 Mr '89
GARTNER, GIDEON
about
Gideon Gartner wants his baby back. T. Vogel. il por *Business Week* p108+ D 4 '89
GARTNER, MICHAEL G.
about
Behind the Peacock throne. E. Diamond. il por *New York* 22:21-2 F 13 '89
Power failure. E. Diamond. il por *New York* 22:24-5 N 6 '89
GARTNER GROUP INC.
Gideon Gartner wants his baby back. T. Vogel. il por *Business Week* p108+ D 4 '89

GARTON, ROBERT D.
The business of being ethical [address, December 14, 1988] *Vital Speeches of the Day* 55:435-7 My 1 '89

GARTON ASH, TIMOTHY
The German revolution. il *The New York Review of Books* 36:14+ D 21 '89
Moving on double tracks: deterrence and détente. il *World Press Review* 36:28-9 My '89
One (forgetful) Europe [address, 1985] *Harper's* 279:30-1 S '89
Refolution in Hungary and Poland. bibl f il *The New York Review of Books* 36:9-15 Ag 17 '89
Refolution: the springtime of two nations [cover story] bibl f il *The New York Review of Books* 36:3-4+ Je 15 '89
A two-speed Europe? il *World Press Review* 36:16+ Ja '89

GARVEY, CYNDY
about
Playing rough in a custody fight, Steve Garvey has Cyndy, his ex, tossed into jail. il pors *People Weekly* 32:93 O 16 '89

GARVEY, ED
It's money that matters [cover story] il *The Progressive* 53:17-21 Mr '89

GARVEY, JOHN
All I want is a cave somewhere. il *U.S. Catholic* 54:8-10 F '89
Eastern Orthodoxy. il *The Atlantic* 263:30+ My '89
Of several minds. See alternate issues of Commonweal
Q: Who made me? *U.S. Catholic* 54:25-7 Jl '89
Rules of the game. *Commonweal* 116:697-8 D 15 '89
Why the Orthodox Church has been such a mystery to Roman Catholics. il *U.S. Catholic* 54:26-30 D '89

GARVEY, MICHAEL
On troubled belief. *America* 160:164 F 25 '89
The scary fidelity of Jesus. il *Commonweal* 116:173-4 Mr 24 '89

GARVEY, MICHAEL S.
Now! High-tech help for sick pets. il *Good Housekeeping* 208:104+ Ap '89

GARVEY, STEVE
about
America's sweetheart. R. Reilly. il pors *Sports Illustrated* 71:92-6+ N 27 '89
The fallen Padre. R. Sullivan. il pors *Sports Illustrated* 70:12 Mr 6 '89
Garvey scores! M. Lupica. il *Esquire* 112:37-8+ Jl '89
In the game of love, Steve Garvey plays the Artful Dodger. P. Chin. il pors *People Weekly* 31:46-8+ Mr 13 '89
Playing rough in a custody fight, Steve Garvey has Cyndy, his ex, tossed into jail. il pors *People Weekly* 32:93 O 16 '89

GARVEY, W. TIMOTHY, AND OTHERS
Pretranslational suppression of an insulin-responsive glucose transporter in rats with diabetes mellitus. bibl f il *Science* 245:60-3 Jl 7 '89

GARVEY, WILLIAM
From the tower. See issues of Flying beginning October 1988

GARY (IND.)
Economic conditions
Steel's hollow comeback. P. Glastris. il *U.S. News & World Report* 106:49-50+ My 8 '89
Ordinances
Gary, Ind., voters back casino gambling in city. il *Jet* 77:56 N 27 '89
Social life and customs
The Jacksons return to their Gary roots after 18 years away. il *Jet* 76:24-6 S 25 '89

GARZA, DAN, AND OTHERS
Mapping the Drosophila genome with yeast artificial chromosomes. bibl f il *Science* 246:641-6 N 3 '89

GARZA, MARY HELEN
"My son is under the ice—find him!"; ed. by Elaine Fein. il por *Redbook* 172:44+ Mr '89

GARZARELLI, ELAINE
about
Nice call, guys. J. Nocera. il pors *Esquire* 112:79+ O '89
"Star" funds: three hits, three misses. M. Schiffres. il pors *Changing Times* 43:59-63 My '89

GAS *See* Glass Art Society
GAS, NATURAL *See* Natural gas
GAS AND OIL ENGINES
See also
Automobile engines
Motor boat engines
Motorcycle engines
Stewart & Stevenson Services, Inc.
Tractor engines
Truck engines
Test: ethanol works fine in small engines. G. Vincent. il *Successful Farming* 87:10-11 mid-F '89
Ignition
How to install an electronic ignition. M. J. Schultz. il *Popular Mechanics* 166:149-50 My '89
Maintenance and repair
"Won't start!". P. Stone. il *The Mother Earth News* 117:96+ My/Je '89

GAS BARBECUE GRILLS *See* Barbecue grills
GAS COMPANIES *See* Gas utilities
GAS FIREPLACES *See* Fireplaces
GAS FIRES
A deadly explosion [pipeline leak causes train disaster in Soviet Union] B. Wickens. il *Maclean's* 102:46-7 Je 19 '89

GAS HYPERSENSITIZED FILM *See* Photography—Films
GAS INDUSTRY
See also
Coastal Corporation
Columbia Gas System, Inc.
Gas utilities
Panhandle Eastern Corporation
Environmental aspects
All fired up [substituting natural gas for coal in a power plant] T. Mack. il *Forbes* 144:266 N 27 '89
Export-import trade
The great gas sellout [Canadian Arctic] J. DeMont. il *Maclean's* 102:36-7 Ap 3 '89
An old favorite returns [Canadian natural gas producers court U.S. market] J. DeMont. il *Maclean's* 102:26 Ja 9 '89
The value of gas [hearings on proposed export of Canadian Arctic gas] B. Wickens. il *Maclean's* 102:54-5 My 1 '89
Finance
Natural gas. W. P. Barrett. il *Forbes* 143:174-6 Ja 9 '89
Unrealistic expectations. J. Cook. il *Forbes* 143:72+ Je 12 '89
Why natural gas is burning brighter. M. Ivey. il *Business Week* p68-9 Ag 28 '89
The wonder fuel for the 1990s [natural gas] K. R. Sheets. il *U.S. News & World Report* 107:38-9 Jl 31 '89
Securities
All fired up about natural gas [views of C. Clough] J. Friedman. il por *Business Week* p110 D 25 '89-Ja 1 '90
Cashing in on a golden pipeline. *U.S. News & World Report* 107:39 Jl 31 '89
Taxation
Maybe we'll need it someday—maybe [tax credits for coalbed methane development] T. Mack. il *Forbes* 143:42-3 Ja 23 '89
Canada
The great gas sellout [Canadian Arctic] J. DeMont. il *Maclean's* 102:36-7 Ap 3 '89
An old favorite returns [natural gas producers court U.S. market] J. DeMont. il *Maclean's* 102:26 Ja 9 '89
The value of gas [hearings on proposed export of Canadian Arctic gas] B. Wickens. il *Maclean's* 102:54-5 My 1 '89

GAS LAWS AND REGULATIONS
See also
Pipeline companies—Laws and regulations
GAS LEASES *See* Oil and gas leases
GAS MASKS
Casualties of peace [Navy investigates faulty smoke protection gear from Scott Aviation] *Time* 134:30 N 27 '89
GAS METERS
Theft
A sour scam in Chicago [Peoples Gas Light & Coke Co. employees accused in stolen gas meter scam] T. Padgett. il *Newsweek* 114:84 N 6 '89
GAS MILEAGE, AUTOMOBILE *See* Automobile engines—Energy usage
GAS MILEAGE, MOTOR VEHICLE *See* Motor vehicle engines—Energy usage
GAS PIPELINE FIRES *See* Gas fires
GAS PIPELINES
Canada
The great gas sellout [Canadian Arctic] J. DeMont. il *Maclean's* 102:36-7 Ap 3 '89
Soviet Union
A deadly explosion [pipeline leak causes train disaster] B. Wickens. il *Maclean's* 102:46-7 Je 19 '89
GAS PRICES *See* Natural gas—Prices
GAS RATES *See* Natural gas—Prices
GAS ROYALTIES *See* Oil and gas leases—Royalties
GAS STATIONS *See* Airplane service stations; Automobile service stations
GAS STOVES *See* Stoves
GAS SUPPLY
Oil and gas estimates plummet. R. A. Kerr. *Science* 245:1330-1 S 22 '89
GAS TURBINES
See also
Stewart & Stevenson Services, Inc.
GAS TURBINES, AIRCRAFT *See* Airplane engines, Jet
GAS TURBINES, AUTOMOTIVE
Chrysler Turbine Car [1963 car] P. Bedard. il *Car and Driver* 34:147-9+ My '89
GAS UTILITIES
See also
Brooklyn Union Gas Co.
Peoples Gas Light & Coke Co.
Natural gas. W. P. Barrett. il *Forbes* 143:174-6 Ja 9 '89

GAS UTILITIES—cont.
Employees
See Gas utility workers
GAS UTILITY WORKERS
Crime
A sour scam in Chicago [Peoples Gas Light & Coke Co. employees accused in stolen gas meter scam] T. Padgett. il *Newsweek* 114:84 N 6 '89
GAS WARFARE See Chemical and biological weapons
GAS WATER HEATERS See Water heaters
GAS WELL DRILLING
After oil [excerpt from Oil notes] R. Bass. *Harper's* 278:27-8+ My '89
Environmental aspects
See Gas industry—Environmental aspects
GASB See Government Accounting Standards Board
GASES
See also
Atmosphere
Hydrogen
Methane
Plasma (Ionized gases)
See also
Air Products and Chemicals, Inc.
Industrial use
Physiological effects
See also
Decompression (Physiology)
GASES, ASPHYXIATING AND POISONOUS See Poisonous gases
GASH, NORMAN
Reflections on the Revolution. il *National Review* 41:35-8 Jl 14 '89
GASHBOW, ARTHUR
State of the Band, January 14, 1989 [address] *Vital Speeches of the Day* 55:409-13 Ap 15 '89
GASKILL, GUDRUN
about
Trail blazer. T. Jenkins. il por *Women's Sports & Fitness* 11:76-7 Ap '89
GASKIN, CATHERINE, 1929-
The charmed circle [fiction] il por *Good Housekeeping* 208:167-70+ Ap '89
GASKINS, RICHARD H.
Extending the search for safety. *Society* 27:19-21 N/D '89
GASOHOL See Alcohol as fuel
GASOLINE
Cleaner gasoline comes on line [Arco's EC-1] A. Dane. il *Popular Mechanics* 166:38 N '89
Fill 'er up with gas lite [Arco's Emission Control-1] il *Time* 134:56 Ag 28 '89
Lead content
Leaded fuel update '89 [marine engines] T. P. Banse. il *Motor Boating & Sailing* 164:97 Ag '89
Octane rating
Fuel for your car. K. Zino. il *Better Homes and Gardens* 68:161 F '89
Octane enhancers. D. Simanaitis and D. Kott. il *Road & Track* 40:82-3+ Ap '89
Save valuable money [unnecessary use of premium gas] P. Bedard. il *Car and Driver* 34:33 Je '89
Prices
What's pumping up gasoline prices? M. Ivey. il *Business Week* p38-9 My 8 '89
Taxation
Fill 'er up with no-fault, please [automatic auto insurance via gasoline tax] A. P. Tobias. il *Time* 133:52-3 F 27 '89
Fueling up a brawl [proposal to increase gas tax to reduce the deficit] J. Greenwald. il *Time* 133:42-3 Ja 23 '89
The hazards of a gas tax hike. il *Consumers' Research Magazine* 72:21-4 Ja '89
Is it time to raise the gasoline tax? K. Kelly. *Utne Reader* p88 Mr/Ap '89
Tapping the wells. *Commonweal* 116:100-1 F 24 '89
A tax hike on gas? The idea is picking up speed. G. Koretz. il *Business Week* p20 Ja 30 '89
GASOLINE-ALCOHOL FUELS See Alcohol as fuel
GASOLINE CONSUMPTION, AUTOMOBILE See Automobile engines—Energy usage
GASOLINE CONSUMPTION, MOTOR VEHICLE See Motor vehicle engines—Energy usage
GASOLINE FUMES See Fumes
GASOLINE FUTURES See Commodity futures
GASOLINE INDUSTRY See Petroleum industry
GASOLINE LANTERNS See Lanterns
GASOLINE STATIONS See Airplane service stations; Automobile service stations
GASOLINE SUPPLY
Burning the candle at neither end [restoring cars as a way to save gasoline] P. Egan. il *Road & Track* 40:16+ Ja '89
Fill 'er up. H. Rudnitsky. il *Forbes* 143:64+ Ja 9 '89
GASPERINI, WILLIAM
Roots of Tibet's clash with China. *Utne Reader* p35 Mr/Ap '89
GASQUE, LAUREL
(jt. auth) See Gasque, W. Ward, and Gasque, Laurel

GASQUE, W. WARD, AND GASQUE, LAUREL
F. F. Bruce: a mind for what matters [interview] il por *Christianity Today* 33:22-5 Ap 7 '89
GASS, WILLIAM H., 1924-
Johns [cover story] bibl f il por *The New York Review of Books* 36:22-7 F 2 '89
GASSÉE, JEAN-LOUIS
about
Seeking Buddha in the details. J. Littman. por *Personal Computing* 13:77 Jl '89
GASSER, CHARLES S., AND FRALEY, ROBERT T.
Genetically engineering plants for crop improvement. bibl f il *Science* 244:1293-9 Je 16 '89
GAST, DWIGHT V.
Brazil. il map *New Choices for the Best Years* 29:53-6 Ap '89
Courting the carnivalesque. il *Art in America* 77:66-7+ Ja '89
Objects of affection. il *New Choices for the Best Years* 29:79-81 Je '89
The paperweight chase. il *New Choices for the Best Years* 29:72+ Jl '89
Yours, truly. il *New Choices for the Best Years* 29:82+ N '89
GASTINEAU, ERIN
about
Model stats. il pors *'Teen* 33:14 Ag '89
GASTON, CITO
about
Birdland. F. Lidz. il pors *Sports Illustrated* 71:22-5 S 11 '89
Orioles, Blue Jays, put black managers on spot. il pors *Jet* 77:51 O 16 '89
Toronto, Baltimore game pits two black managers. il pors *Jet* 76:46 Jl 17 '89
Toronto hires Cito Gaston as fourth black manager. il por *Jet* 76:46+ Je 19 '89
GASTRIC BYPASS SURGERY See Stomach—Surgery
GASTRIC MUCOSA See Mucous membranes
GASTRIC ULCERS See Peptic ulcers
GASTROINTESTINAL DISEASES See Digestive system—Diseases
GASTROINTESTINAL TRACT See Digestive system
GASTRONOMY
See also
American Institute of Wine and Food
Food critics and criticism
A gourmet at large. F. Ferretti. See issues of Gourmet beginning January 1985
The marriage of wine and food. D. Scoblionkov. il *American Health* 8:74 N '89
Mix and match [food and wine] A. Bespaloff. il *New York* 22:170+ D 4 '89
An opinionated palate. B. Kafka. See issues of Gourmet beginning August 1989
Peachy keen [marrying food and wine] F. J. Prial. il *The New York Times Magazine* p44 S 3 '89
Recipe of the year: eat and be well: most of '88. M. Sheraton. il *Time* 133:98 Ja 2 '89
GASTROPODS
See also
Abalones
Slugs
Snails
GATES, ANITA
Born to run the show? The management test. il *Mademoiselle* 95:166+ Mr '89
GATES, HENRY LOUIS
Whose canon is it, anyway? *The New York Times Book Review* 94:1+ F 26 '89
GATES, ROBERT M.
about
Distrust, but verify. F. Barnes. *The New Republic* 200:12-13 Mr 6 '89
GATES, WILLIAM H.
Tomorrow's vision builds on today's reality. por *Personal Computing* 13:212 O '89
about
Meanwhile, back among the fir trees at Microsoft . . . il *Fortune* 120:61 O 9 '89
The once and future evangelist. S. R. Reed. por *Personal Computing* 13:75 Jl '89
Windows on the world. D. Churbuck. il pors *Forbes* 144:123+ D 25 '89
GATES
Plain or fancy, gates make the garden. R. W. Strickland. il *Southern Living* 24:114-17 Ap '89
GATEWAY ARCH (SAINT LOUIS, MO.)
Gateway to a new detente [architect Y. Platonov's visit to the U.S.] M. F. Schmertz. *Architectural Record* 177:9 Je '89
GATEWAY EDUCATION CENTER (GREENSBORO, N.C.)
Going to bat for special children. D. Young. il pors *Southern Living* 24:100+ Jl '89
GATEWAY FOODMARKETS LTD.
See also
Isosceles plc

GATEWAY FOODMARKETS LTD.—cont.
Has LBO fever struck Europe? [A&P's bid for Gateway] M. Maremont. il *Business Week* p28 Jl 3 '89
GATEWAY NATIONAL RECREATION AREA (N.J. AND N.Y.)
Gateway theme park plans dropped. J. Weinberg. *National Parks* 63:13 N/D '89
Where the sidewalk ends. A. Lachman. il map *National Parks* 63:30-6 N/D '89
GATEWAYS (INFORMATION SYSTEMS)
Everyone into the pool [asynchronous gateways] B. Nance. il *Byte* 14:167-8+ N '89
GATHERERS AND HUNTERS See Hunters and gatherers
GATHERS, HANK
about
Gathers 'round the rim. H. Hersch. il pors *Sports Illustrated* 70:68-9 F 13 '89
GATI, CHARLES
Eastern Europe on its own. bibl f *Foreign Affairs* 68 Special Issue:99-119 ['89]
GATORADE See Sports drinks
GATT See General Agreement on Tariffs and Trade
GATTON, DANNY
about
Hot guitarist. D. Fricke. il por *Rolling Stone* p63-4+ My 18 '89
GATWARD, JAMES
about
Why MTM isn't the cat's meow. R. A. Melcher and R. Grover. il por *Business Week* p49 S 25 '89
GAUCHER'S DISEASE
New insights into Gaucher's tricky course [research by Ari Zimran] R. Weiss. *Science News* 136:135 Ag 26 '89
GAUDENS, AUGUSTUS SAINT- See Saint-Gaudens, Augustus, 1848-1907
GAUDÍ, ANTONI, 1852-1926
about
Gaudí and Dalí, the art of excess. D. Giralt-Miracle. il por *The Courier (Unesco)* 42:32-4 My '89
GAUERKE, MARY
about
Obituary
National Review il 41:16-17 Ag 4 '89. P. L. Buckley
GAUGES See Gages
GAUGUIN, PAUL, 1848-1903
about
Going native. A. Solomon-Godeau. bibl f il *Art in America* 77:118-29+ Jl '89
Van Gogh and Gauguin on the couch. B. Collins. bibl f il *Art in America* 77:57+ D '89
GAULEY RIVER (W. VA.)
Shoot-out at Gauley Gorge. D. Harbrecht. il *Business Week* p142 O 16 '89
GAULLE, CHARLES DE, 1890-1970
about
First encounters. E. Sorel and N. C. Sorel. il *The Atlantic* 263:67 Mr '89
GAULTIER, JEAN-PAUL
about
Gaultier. J. Duka. il por *Vogue* 179:162-3+ Ja '89
GAUNT, JEREMY
GATT's influence for freer trade. il *Nation's Business* 77:54-6 D '89
GAUTAM, NARASIMHAN, AND OTHERS
A G protein gamma subunit shares homology with *ras* proteins. bibl f il *Science* 244:971-4 My 26 '89
GAUTHIER, DANIEL JAMES
A blueprint for the '90s—. il *Ad Astra* 1:24-5 My '89
Steps toward a real international space station. il *Ad Astra* 1:28-9 O '89
GAUTHIER, ISABELLE
about
Canadian women at arms. M. Suh. il *Ms.* 17:71-2 Je '89
GAVIN, JAMES
Your brand of sweat. il *Psychology Today* 23:50-3+ Mr '89
GAVISH, DOV, AND OTHERS
Heritable allele-specific differences in amounts of apoB and low-density lipoproteins in plasma. bibl f il *Science* 244:72-6 Ap 7 '89
GAY, PETER, 1923-
Sigmund and Minna? The biographer as voyeur. por *The New York Times Book Review* 94:1+ Ja 29 '89
GAY, RUTH
Danke schön, Herr Doktor: German Jews in Palestine. *The American Scholar* 58:567-77 Aut '89
GAY/LESBIAN PRIDE PARADE (NEW YORK, N.Y.) See New York (N.Y.)—Parades
GAY RIGHTS See Homosexuality
GAYE, MARVIN
about
Gaye's loyal fans clamor for Hollywood Walk star. il *Jet* 76:36 Ag 28 '89
Marvin Gaye: what's going on with his family five years later. A. Collier. il pors *Jet* 76:56-9 My 15 '89
GAYLE, CRYSTAL, 1951-
about
So close . . . and yet so far apart. N. Hickey. il pors *TV Guide* 37:10-12 Ag 19-25 '89

GAYLORD CONTAINER LTD.
The Marvin and Warren act. R. Reiff. il por *Forbes* 144:52+ S 18 '89
GAYNOR, JOHN
Home Q&A. See issues of Home Mechanix beginning January 1985
GAZA STRIP TERRITORIAL QUESTION See Israel-Arab Wars, 1967- —Territorial questions
GAZARIAN, JEAN
about
'A living reflection of the world . . .' [interview] il por *UN Chronicle* 26:48-55 D '89
GAZDAG, GYULA
about
A Hungarian fairy tale [film] Reviews
The Nation 248:175 F 6 '89. S. Klawans
Shelf life [interview] J. Hoberman. il por *Film Comment* 25:50-4+ My/Je '89
GAZEBOS See Garden houses, shelters, etc.
GAZELLE INTERNATIONAL
Battle of the vanities [cover story] A. Edmond, Jr. il por *Black Enterprise* 19:42-3+ Mr '89
GAZZANIGA, MARIN
Artistry in makeup. il pors *Harper's Bazaar* 122:26+ D '89
GAZZANIGA, MICHAEL S.
Organization of the human brain. bibl f il *Science* 245:947-52 S 1 '89
GAZZARA, BEN, 1930-
about
Fun with Ben & John [interview] G. Smith. il pors *Film Comment* 25:46-7 My/Je '89
GBC BANCORP
Mr. Wu knows his customer. G. Morgenson. il por *Forbes* 143:49+ Ja 23 '89
GDANSK (POLAND)
History
Is it our Danzig—or your Gdansk? *Newsweek* 113:34 Mr 6 '89
GDAŃSK SHIPYARD COMPANY See Barbara Piasecka Johnson-Gdańsk Shipyard Company
GE See General Electric Co.
GEAR (L.A.) INC. See L.A. Gear Inc.
GEARING
See also
Bicycles—Gearing
GEARRING, JOEL K.
about
Joel K. Gearring named vice pres./agency head at Supreme Life Insurance. por *Jet* 75:14 Ap 3 '89
GEARY, DEREK
about
Derek Geary hopes to play piano like Keith Jarrett; Boston hopes he plays hockey like Gretzky. G. Verner. il pors *People Weekly* 31:112-13 Ap 24 '89
GEARY, RILEY R.
Nevada Test Site's dirty little secrets. il *The Bulletin of the Atomic Scientists* 45:35-6+ Ap '89
GEBEL-WILLIAMS, GUNTHER
There's a customer born every minute. il por *U.S. News & World Report* 106:15 F 20 '89
World's greatest showman. J. Culhane. il pors *Reader's Digest* 135:90-5 N '89
GEBHART, FRED
Borneo. il *Travel Holiday* 172:72-9 S '89
Etched in stone. il *Travel Holiday* 172:44-51 O '89
GEBRÜDER BING (FIRM)
The many toys of Gebrüder Bing. M. Jailer. il *Antiques & Collecting Hobbies* 94:63-6 Ag '89
GEBRÜDER MÄRKLIN (FIRM)
Toymakers Gebrüder Märklin. M. Jailer. il *Antiques & Collecting Hobbies* 94:30-3 Mr '89
GECKOS See Lizards
GED TESTS See General educational development tests
GEDDES, GRAHAM
about
Out back in Australia. D. B. Pitt. il por *House & Garden* 161:126-31+ Ja '89
GEDDIS, BARBARA
about
The woman-managed firm: how big a deal? R. L. Miller. il pors *Architectural Record* 177:47+ Je '89
GEDRICK, JASON
about
Jason Gedrick. il por *'Teen* 33:53 Je '89
GEDULD, HARRY M.
Film review. See issues of The Humanist
GEDZELMAN, STANLEY DAVID
Dr. Stan, the TV weatherman. il pors *Weatherwise* 42:151-4 Je '89
GEE, MOLLY, AND CHEUNG, LILIAN
Rating the diet books. *McCall's* 116:102 Jl '89
GEERTZ, CLIFFORD
about
Ethnography as art. J. Horgan. *Scientific American* 261:28+ Jl '89

GEESAMAN, LYNN
about
Lynn Geesaman: Thomas Barry Fine Arts. M. A. Martin. il *Art News* 88:161 F '89

GEESE
See also
Cooking—Poultry
American classics. il *The Mother Earth News* 116:56-7 Mr/Ap '89
Andy Goose steps out [G. Fleming fits footless goose with sneakers] J. Coudert. il *Reader's Digest* 135:169-70+ Jl '89
A footless goose becomes a footloose goose—in sneaks [G. Fleming fits gander with sneakers] il *People Weekly* 31:66 Ja 30 '89
Starting with geese. G. Luttmann. il *Country Journal* 16:77-81 N/D '89

GEESE, WILD
Migration
Goose prelude to global warming [destruction of wetland vegetation due to delayed migration of snow geese; research by Robert Jefferies] J. A. Miller. *BioScience* 39:673 N '89
A small Christmas miracle: the great snow goose migration [Klamath Basin National Wildlife Refuges] il *Sunset (Central West edition)* 181:188 D '88
Photographs and photography
In every crowd. B. Millar. il *Field & Stream* 94:58-9 My '89
Shooting
See Goose shooting

GEESLIN, BAILEY M.
Funding the future infrastructure. bibl *Society* 26:16-21 Jl/Ag '89

GEFFEN, ALICE M., AND BERGLIE, CAROLE
A most favored food. il *Americana* 17:40-2 My/Je '89

GEFFEN, DAVID
about
Geffen's coming of age. J. Ressner. il por *Rolling Stone* p73 Jl 13-27 '89

GEFFEN COMPANY
Geffen's coming of age. J. Ressner. il por *Rolling Stone* p73 Jl 13-27 '89

GEGENSCHEIN *See* Counterglow

GEHRIG'S DISEASE *See* Amyotrophic lateral sclerosis

GEHRY, FRANK
about
Castles in the air? P. D. Slatin. il por *Forbes* 144:241 O 30 '89
Main Street. K. D. Stein. il *Architectural Record* 177:104-9 Jl '89
Of detritus and denial [interview] W. Meis and M. B. Snell. il *New Perspectives Quarterly* 5:57-60 Wint '88/'89
A renegade takes the prize. C. McGuigan. il por *Newsweek* 112:84-6 My 22 '89

GEIBEL, VICTORIA
Illusion and reality. il *Architectural Record* 177:58-63 mid-S '89

GEIBERGER, AL
about
Building a new life. S. Ballard. il pors *Sports Illustrated* 70:57-8+ My 15 '89

GEICO CORP.
Geico versus the DAKonians [anti-radar detector campaign] B. Visnic. *Car and Driver* 35:32-3 N '89
Target [Geico targets Cycle in anti-radar detector campaign] P. Schilling. il *Cycle* 40:9+ Ja '89

GEIGER, HENRY, D. 1989
about
Obituary
Utne Reader il p32 My/Je '89. R. Grossman

GEIGER, MARION
about
Artistry in makeup. M. Gazzaniga. il pors *Harper's Bazaar* 122:26+ D '89

GEIGER COUNTERS
Radiation monitor update [with editorial comment by Brian C. Fenton] J. Jaffe and D. Sythe. il *Radio-Electronics* 60:4, 51-5+ Je '89

GEISEL, THEODOR SEUSS, 1904- *See* Seuss, Dr.

GEISHAS
An affair to remember [S. Uno's affair with geisha] B. Hillenbrand. il por *Time* 134:33 Jl 10 '89
The dirt on 'Mr. Clean' [S. Uno] M. Nemeth. il por *Maclean's* 102:32 Jl 10 '89
The end of the affair? [S. Uno's affair with geisha triggers women's opposition] B. Powell. il por *Newsweek* 114:22-3 Jl 10 '89
The geisha who knew too much [charges against Prime Minister S. Uno] il *U.S. News & World Report* 106:15-16 Je 19 '89
Japan's geisha scandal [concerning Prime Minister S. Uno] *World Press Review* 36:6+ Ag '89
The premier and the geisha [S. Uno] *Newsweek* 113:46 Je 19 '89

GEIST, SIDNEY, 1914-
In the thick of it. il *Vogue* 179:226+ F '89

GEIST, WILLIAM
Images: men's grooming. il *Vogue* 179:94+ Je '89

GEL CELL BATTERIES *See* Electric batteries
GEL ELECTROPHORESIS *See* Electrophoresis
GELATIN LIGHT FILTERS *See* Light filters

GELB, ALAN (ALAN LLOYD)
Out in left field. il *Parents* 64:218 Ap '89
Without office. il *Parents* 64:204 F '89

GELB, BRUCE
about
G.O.P. formula. A. Dubro. *The Nation* 248:329-30 Mr 13 '89

GELB, NORMAN
Britons worry about civil rights. il *The New Leader* 72:5-6 F 20 '89
Europe without frontiers. il *The New Leader* 72:7-8 Ja 9 '89
London loses its luster. il *The New Leader* 72:12-13 S 18 '89
Thatcher at odds with Europe. por *The New Leader* 72:12-13 O 30 '89
Thatcherism isn't working. il *The New Leader* 72:8-9 Jl 10-24 '89
Trouble in Thatcherland. il *The New Leader* 72:6-7 Mr 20 '89
Turkey's identity problem. il *The New Leader* 72:9-10 My 1 '89

GELB, RICHARD L.
about
Filling Bristol-Myers' prescription. J. Weber, Jr. and S. Benway. il pors *Business Week* p80-1 Ag 14 '89

GELBART, LARRY
Mastergate—the scandal continues [excerpts from drama] il *The Nation* 249:528-30 N 6 '89
about
Is there life after 'M*A*S*H'? M. Rothstein. il por *The New York Times Magazine* p53-6+ O 8 '89
Mastergate [drama] Reviews
America 161:321 N 11 '89. T. P. O'Malley
New York il 22:165-6 O 23 '89. J. Simon
The New Yorker 65:131 O 23 '89. E. Oliver
Newsweek il 114:74 O 30 '89. J. Kroll

GELDZAHLER, HENRY
Indispensable Andy. *Vogue* 179:322+ F '89

GELERNTER, DAVID
The metamorphosis of information management. bibl il *Scientific American* 261:66-73 Ag '89

GELFAND, JENNIFER
about
Reviews:
J. Gelfand debuts in Don Quixote. I. M. Fanger. *Dance Magazine* 63:88-9 N '89

GELFOND, SUSAN
A manager's cram sheet for choosing operating systems. il *Working Woman* 14:63+ O '89

GÉLINAS, GRATIEN
about
The passion of Narcisse Mondoux [drama] Reviews
Commonweal 116:436-7 Ag 11 '89. G. C. Weales

GELL-MANN, MURRAY, 1929-
Dick Feynman—the guy in the office down the hall. il por *Physics Today* 42:50-4 F '89

GELLER, HENRY
Looking not far into the future. *Society* 26:21-6 Jl/Ag '89

GELLER, LARRY, 1937-, AND SPECTOR, JOEL
The secret Elvis diary [excerpt from If I can dream]; ed. by Patricia Romanowski. il pors *Good Housekeeping* 208:100-1+ F '89

GELLER, MARGARET J., AND HUCHRA, JOHN
Mapping the universe [cover story] bibl f il *Science* 246:897-903 N 17 '89

GELLER-SHINN, KAREN
Tools of the trade. See issues of Petersen's Photographic Magazine

GELLNER, ERNEST
Stalin takes the stand. *The New Republic* 200:20+ Mr 20 '89

GELMAN, DAVID
"Not tonight, dear". il *Reader's Digest* 134:33-4+ Je '89

GELS *See* Colloids

GEMEENTEMUSEUM (HAGUE, NETHERLANDS) *See* Haags Gemeentemuseum (Netherlands)

GEMINIDS (METEORS) *See* Meteors

GEMS *See* United Nations Environment Programme. Global Environmental Monitoring System

GEMS
See also
Diamonds
Jewelry
Gems: be on your guard. G. V. Axon. il *Consumers' Research Magazine* 72:24-8 Je '89
A guide to gemstones [excerpt from The right jewelry for you]; ed. by Karen Jackson. J. Avery. il *Good Housekeeping* 208:167 F '89

GENDER CHROMOSOMES *See* Chromosomes
GENDER DETERMINATION *See* Sex determination and control

GENDER DIFFERENCES *See* Sex differences
GENDER GENE *See* Testis determining factor
GENDLER, TAMAR
The testing paradox. *The Education Digest* 54:27-9 Ja '89 (jt. auth) See Wise, Arthur E., and Gendler, Tamar
GENE AMPLIFICATION
See also
Polymerase chain reaction
Amplification of a gene related to mammalian mdr genes in drug-resistant Plasmodium falciparum. C. M. Wilson and others. bibl f il *Science* 244:1184-6 Je 9 '89
Gene signals relapse of breast, ovarian cancers [research by Dennis Slamon] J. L. Marx. il *Science* 244:654-5 My 12 '89
Studies of the HER-2/*neu* proto-oncogene in human breast and ovarian cancer. D. J. Slamon and others. bibl f il *Science* 244:707-12 My 12 '89
GENE AUTRY WESTERN HERITAGE MUSEUM
The Old West, for real and for fun. il *Sunset (Central West edition)* 182:88-9 Je '89
GENE BANKS
See also
Germplasm resources
Banking on your DNA [waiting for discovery of gene probes for cancer] S. Begley. il *Newsweek* 114:64 Ag 21 '89
GENE CLONING *See* Clones (Biology)
GENE EXPRESSION *See* Genetic regulation
GENE MAPPING *See* Genetic mapping
GENE POSITION IN CHROMOSOMES *See* Locus (Genes)
GENE PROBES
Phylogenetic stains: ribosomal RNA-based probes for the identification of single cells. E. F. DeLong and others. bibl f il *Science* 243:1360-3 Mr 10 '89
GENE THERAPY
Altering the genome by homologous recombination [gene targeting] M. R. Capecchi. bibl f il *Science* 244:1288-92 Je 16 '89
Brain man [somatic cell therapy; work of E. A. Neuwelt] M. S. Glucksman. il *Omni (New York, N.Y.)* 11:28 My '89
Fighting cancer with designer cells [immunotherapy using tumor-infiltrating lymphocytes; work of S. A. Rosenberg] B. J. Culliton. il por *Science* 244:1430-3 Je 23 '89
Gene implants [battling HIV; research by Steven L. McKnight] G. Montgomery. il *Discover* 10:24 Mr '89
Gene test begins [patient with advanced melanoma receives infusion of his own white blood cells containing a foreign gene] B. J. Culliton. il *Science* 244:913 My 26 '89
Gene transfer test: so far, so good [treatment of advanced melanoma with tumor-infiltrating lymphocytes; work of Steven A. Rosenberg] B. J. Culliton. *Science* 245:1325 S 22 '89
Gene-transfer trial begins in humans [work of Steven A. Rosenberg] K. Fackelmann. *Science News* 135:324 My 27 '89
Genes in medicine [special section] B. J. Culliton. il *Science* 246:746-51 N 10 '89
A genetic road map [work of W. F. Anderson] D. Glick. il por *Newsweek* 114:46 O 2 '89
Human gene therapy: after a lot of looking, now the leap. J. Carey. il *Business Week* p133+ My 1 '89
Immunology's designer genes [tumor-infiltrating lymphocytes; work of S. A. Rosenberg] S. Brownlee. il por *U.S. News & World Report* 107:65-6 O 30 '89
Implantation of vascular grafts lined with genetically modified endothelial cells. J. M. Wilson and others. bibl f il *Science* 244:1344-6 Je 16 '89
An ingenious way to fix genes. il *U.S. News & World Report* 106:12-13 Je 5 '89
Labeled therapy [gene transfer experiment may improve a cancer treatment] T. Beardsley. *Scientific American* 260:24-5 F '89
Now in vivo: altering endothelial cells. R. Cowen. *Science News* 135:373 Je 17 '89
Progress toward human gene therapy. T. Friedmann. bibl f il *Science* 244:1275-81 Je 16 '89
Recombinant gene expression in vivo within endothelial cells of the arterial wall. E. G. Nabel and others. bibl f il *Science* 244:1342-4 Je 16 '89
Selection for precise chromosomal targeting of a dominant marker by homologous recombination. J. R. Dorin and others. bibl f il *Science* 243:1357-60 Mr 10 '89
Two new approaches to genetic emphysema [antitrypsin gene-carrying retrovirus; work of Ronald G. Crystal] S. Hart and A. McKenzie. *Science News* 136:233 O 7 '89
Ethical aspects
Brave new gene therapy [Steven Rosenberg's cancer experiments] S. Begley. il *Newsweek* 113:65 F 13 '89
Coming: a historic experiment [human gene transplant cancer therapy planned by National Institutes of Health] D. Thompson. il *Time* 133:64 F 13 '89
Ethical questions haunt new genetic technologies [battle between activist J. Rifkin and National Institutes of Health] L. Roberts. il por *Science* 243:1134-6 Mr 3 '89
Groups seek human gene-transfer delay [opposition to cancer experiment] R. Weiss. *Science News* 135:68 F 4 '89
Rifkin battles gene transfer experiment. L. Roberts. *Science* 243:734 F 10 '89

Scrambling for biotech bucks [human gene transplants] J. W. Anderson. il *The Nation* 248:476-8 Ap 10 '89
GENE TRANSFECTION
Commitment of mouse fibroblasts to adipocyte differentiation by DNA transfection. S. Chen and others. bibl f il *Science* 244:582-5 My 5 '89
Normal expression of a rearranged and mutated c-*myc* oncogene after transfection into fibroblasts [Burkitt's lymphoma] A. Richman and A. Hayday. bibl f il *Science* 246:494-7 O 27 '89
Transfer of a protein encoded by a single nucleus to nearby nuclei in multinucleated myotubes. E. Ralston and Z. W. Hall. bibl f il *Science* 244:1066-9 Je 2 '89
Type I and type II GABA$_A$-benzodiazepine receptors produced in transfected cells. D. B. Pritchett and others. bibl f il *Science* 245:1389-92 S 22 '89
GENE TRANSFER
See also
Gene therapy
Gene transfection
"Dangerous" liaisons in cell biology [controversy over work of C. Spadafora] D. Dickson. il por *Science* 244:1539-40 Je 30 '89; Correction. 245:252 Jl 21 '89
A dwarf mutant of Arabidopsis generated by T-DNA insertion mutagenesis [cover story] K. A. Feldmann and others. bibl f il *Science* 243:1351-4 Mr 10 '89
Expression of functional nerve growth factor receptors after gene transfer. B. L. Hempstead and others. bibl f il *Science* 243:373-5 Ja 20 '89
Fibroblasts transformed with v-*src* show enhanced formation of an inositol tetrakisphosphate. R. M. Johnson and others. bibl f il *Science* 246:121-4 O 6 '89
Gene-splicing revolution? [use of sperm cells] *Time* 133:59 Je 12 '89
Gene-transfer method fails test [trying to replicate; work of Corrado Spadafora] M. Barinaga. *Science* 246:446 O 27 '89
Genetic engineering of trees to enhance resistance to insects [cover story] K. F. Raffa. bibl f il *BioScience* 39:524-34 S '89
Genetically engineering plants for crop improvement. C. S. Gasser and R. T. Fraley. bibl f il *Science* 244:1293-9 Je 16 '89
Germline transmission of exogenous genes in the chicken. R. A. Bosselman and others. bibl f il *Science* 243:533-5 Ja 27 '89
Hope and hype in transgenics. il *High Technology Business* 9:6-8 My '89
Introduction of human DNA into mouse eggs by injection of dissected chromosome fragments. J. Richa and C. W. Lo. bibl f il *Science* 245:175-7 Jl 14 '89
Making transgenic mice: is it really that easy? [trying to replicate work of Corrado Spadafora] M. Barinaga. il *Science* 245:590-1 Ag 11 '89
The mechanism of DNA transfer in the mating system of an archaebacterium. I. Rosenshine and others. bibl f il *Science* 245:1387-9 S 22 '89
New genes for complete-protein beans [research by Samuel Sun] I. Wickelgren. *Science News* 135:300 My 13 '89
Please pass the genes [cover story] I. Wickelgren. il *Science News* 136:120-2+ Ag 19 '89
Regulated genes in transgenic plants. P. N. Benfey and N.-H. Chua. bibl f il *Science* 244:174-81 Ap 14 '89
Retrovirus vectors: promise and reality. H. M. Temin. bibl f *Science* 246:983 N 24 '89
Sperm capture genes to create new life [research by Corrado Spadafora] I. Wickelgren. *Science News* 135:356 Je 10 '89
Transformation by v-sis occurs by an internal autoactivation mechanism. B. E. Bejcek and others. bibl f il *Science* 245:1496-9 S 29 '89
Transgenic mice as probes into complex systems. D. Hanahan. bibl f il *Science* 246:1265-75 D 8 '89
Turning plants into antibody factories [work of Andrew Hiatt] *Science News* 136:334 N 18 '89
GENEALOGY
See also
Registers of births, etc.
Dot Redford found her roots at Somerset [plantation slave descendants] D. Young. il pors *Southern Living* 24:92+ Ja '89
I read it in the paper [use of newspapers as genealogical resource] C. E. Kraft. il *Antiques & Collecting Hobbies* 94:74-7 Mr '89
Looking into a shared past [K. W. Sakaris and C. O. Hervey trace Arkansas roots] D. Young. il pors *Southern Living* 24:79+ D '89
Plantation home [D. Redford traces descendants of slaves from Somerset Place, N.C.] R. Mashburn. il pors map *Americana* 16:50-4 Ja/F '89
Researching your roots. B. Bell. il *New Choices for the Best Years* 29:15 S '89
GENENTECH, INC.
Genentech: a David that comes on like Goliath [fighting SmithKline Beecham's Eminase] J. Carey and J. O. Hamilton. il *Business Week* p165 O 30 '89
Robert Swanson. J. O. Hamilton. il por *Business Week* Special Issue:104 Ap 14 '89

GENERAL ACCOUNTING OFFICE (U.S.) *See* United States. General Accounting Office

GENERAL AGREEMENT ON TARIFFS AND TRADE
Beyond GATT. G. C. Hufbauer. *Foreign Policy* 77:64-76 Wint '89/'90
Economist tells danger of totally free markets [views of Daryll Ray] *Successful Farming* 87:48E N '89
GATT—almost back on track. H. Banks. *Forbes* 143:33 Mr 20 '89
GATT's influence for freer trade. J. Gaunt. il *Nation's Business* 77:54-6 D '89
How GATT will affect the 1990 farm bill. *Successful Farming* 87:32A Je '89
The near collapse. M. S. Forbes, Jr. il *Forbes* 143:27 F 6 '89
Status of multilateral trade negotiations [statement, April 11, 1989] C. A. Hills. *Department of State Bulletin* 89:30-2 Je '89
U.S. trade objectives in the Uruguay Round. il *Department of State Bulletin* 89:35-7 F '89
Uruguay Round and U.S. trade policy: a foundation for the future [address, September 14, 1989] C. A. Hills. *Department of State Bulletin* 89:53-5 N '89

GENERAL APTITUDE TEST BATTERY
Academy panel joins the fray over job testing [question of reinterpreting scores of blacks and Hispanics] C. Holden. il *Science* 244:1036-7 Je 2 '89
Fairness in employment testing [discussion of June 2, 1989 article, Academy panel joins the fray over job testing] C. Holden. *Science* 245:14 Jl 7 '89
More normal nonsense [National Research Council report] D. Seligman. il *Fortune* 120:118 Jl 17 '89

GENERAL AVIATION *See* Aviation

GENERAL AVIATION INDUSTRY *See* Airplane industry

GENERAL AVIATION MANUFACTURERS ASSOCIATION
Guide to stepping up [Transition training master syllabus] il *Flying* 116:113-14 N '89
Shipment of general aviation aircraft: first-half 1989 GAMA shipments/billings. il *Aviation Week & Space Technology* 131:59 Ag 28 '89

GENERAL BINDING CORP.
High hopes for a home-office helper. G. G. Marcial. *Business Week* p130 Ap 24 '89

GENERAL DEVELOPMENT CORP.
Homebuilder for sale. Needs work. G. G. Marcial. *Business Week* p88 F 6 '89

GENERAL DYNAMICS CORP.
"Are we in the wrong business? No". M. Berss. il *Forbes* 144:38-9 D 25 '89
Belgium will use equipment provided under offset pact to expand industry [F-16 deal] il *Aviation Week & Space Technology* 130:57 F 13 '89
Bush approves FS-X codevelopment, but Japan must accept new terms. M. Mecham. *Aviation Week & Space Technology* 130:22 Mr 27 '89
A critical weakness [questions raised about Phalanx warship defense system for Canadian frigates] W. Lowther. il *Maclean's* 102:13 F 13 '89
General Dynamics alters marketing as Europeans focus on F-16 upgrades. il *Aviation Week & Space Technology* 130:57+ F 13 '89
General Dynamics expects to receive 75% of U.S. share of FS-X development work. C. A. Shifrin. *Aviation Week & Space Technology* 130:16-17 My 8 '89
General Dynamics offers four Atlas-Centaur versions. il *Aviation Week & Space Technology* 130:24 Ap 10 '89
General Dynamics will launch first Navy UHF follow-on satellite [Atlas booster] *Aviation Week & Space Technology* 131:22 Ag 21 '89
A 'little old agreement' on the F-16 [FSX deal with Mitsubishi Heavy Industries] *Newsweek* 113:34 Ja 30 '89
Technology concerns delay approval of FS-X agreement [sharing F-16 technology with Japan] M. Mecham. il *Aviation Week & Space Technology* 130:16-17 F 20 '89

GENERAL EDUCATION *See* Liberal education

GENERAL EDUCATIONAL DEVELOPMENT TESTS
The GED: a growing alternative route to higher education. il *Change* 21:35-9 Jl/Ag '89

GENERAL ELECTRIC CAPITAL CORPORATION
Why GE is firming up its cable connection. D. Lieberman. *Business Week* p134 Je 5 '89

GENERAL ELECTRIC CO.
After the crash, cash [offering rewards for scattered engine parts from Sioux City, Iowa plane crash] il *Newsweek* 114:32 O 23 '89
American signs long-term CF6 pricing pact with GE. S. W. Kandebo. il *Aviation Week & Space Technology* 130:20 F 13 '89
Big changes are galvanizing General Electric. T. Vogel. il por *Business Week* p100+ D 18 '89
The body count keeps growing at Kidder Peabody. J. R. Norman and J. Friedman. il *Business Week* p128-9 F 20 '89
A case of culture shock along the Wabash [aftermath of GE's sale of consumer electronics division to Thomson SA] L. Therrien. il *Business Week* p102 My 15 '89

Competing GE, FMC armored turrets offer different weapons configurations [Marine Corps Light Armored Vehicle-Air Defense system] D. F. Bond. il *Aviation Week & Space Technology* 131:45+ S 25 '89
GE and GEC. F. H. Katayama. il *Fortune* 119:8 F 13 '89
GE completes proof-of-concept ground tests of engine candidate for ATF [advanced tactical fighter] il *Aviation Week & Space Technology* 130:73 Je 12 '89
GE offers F110-GE-100 engine as alternative to Pratt & Whitney powerplant in new F-16A/Bs. *Aviation Week & Space Technology* 131:23 N 27 '89
GE simulator image generator offers 3D resolution, fast data base updates [Compu-Scene 5 for use in military mission rehearsal simulation] E. H. Kolcum. il *Aviation Week & Space Technology* 130:286-7+ Je 12 '89
GE whiz [woman executive T. M. LeGrand] M. Alpert. il por *Fortune* 119:151 Mr 27 '89
General Eclectic. C. Poole. il *Forbes* 143:10 Mr 20 '89
HEMT devices could speed work on next-generation radar systems [high electron mobility transistors] B. D. Nordwall. il *Aviation Week & Space Technology* 130:65+ My 15 '89
Honeywell and GE may be thinking of meshing gears. G. G. Marcial. il *Business Week* p130 Jl 17 '89
Inside the mind of Jack Welch [cover story] S. P. Sherman. il pors *Fortune* 119:38-42+ Mr 27 '89
A look back at "Boulwarism". P. Brimelow. il pors *Forbes* 143:246+ My 29 '89
Navy selects GE for future F404 turbofan orders, drops Pratt as second source. *Aviation Week & Space Technology* 131:26 Ag 28 '89
Pratt, General Electric to deliver ATF engines to Air Force by year-end [advanced tactical fighter] il *Aviation Week & Space Technology* 131:21 D 4 '89
This bright idea could make GE a billion [high intensity discharge headlights] M. Mallory. il *Business Week* p120 D 4 '89
This 'glitch' may cost GE $350 million [rotary compressor refrigerators] Z. Schiller. *Business Week* p28-9 Ja 30 '89
Why GE took a European bride [deal with Britain's General Electric Co. plc] J. R. Norman. il *Business Week* p28-9 Ja 30 '89

GENERAL ELECTRIC CO. ASTRO SPACE DIVISION
GE Astro-Space, Marconi will team to bid for Inmarsat 3 contract. *Aviation Week & Space Technology* 131:79 Ag 21 '89

GENERAL ELECTRIC COMPANY PLC
Bombardier, GEC-Fokker team lead field of suitors for Northern Ireland's Short Brothers. *Aviation Week & Space Technology* 130:31 Mr 13 '89
British-French bid to buy GEC fails after AT&T refuses to join. *Aviation Week & Space Technology* 130:30 Ja 23 '89
British Monopolies panel approves GEC/Siemens offer for Plessey. *Aviation Week & Space Technology* 130:39 My 1 '89
Electronics firms maneuver to gain from GEC, Plessey takeover bids. D. A. Brown. *Aviation Week & Space Technology* 130:25+ Ja 16 '89
For Plessey, a gutsy offense may be its best defense [bid for predator GEC] M. Maremont. *Business Week* p52+ Ja 23 '89
GE and GEC. F. H. Katayama. il *Fortune* 119:8 F 13 '89
GEC, Siemens renew their bid to buy Plessey. *Aviation Week & Space Technology* 131:34 Ag 14 '89
GEC, Siemens win bid to take over Plessey. *Aviation Week & Space Technology* 131:31 S 18 '89
Why GE took a European bride. J. R. Norman. il *Business Week* p28-9 Ja 30 '89

GENERAL ELECTRIC CREDIT CORP.
See also
General Electric Capital Corporation

GENERAL FOODS CORP.
The advertiser that didn't balk [National Right to Life Committee pressures General Foods to pull advertising for TV movie Roe vs. Wade] M. Suh. il *Ms.* 18:75 Jl/Ag '89

GENERAL INSTRUMENT CORP.
The company that can't keep up the pace. J. Cook. il *Forbes* 144:116-17 Ag 7 '89
General Instrument expands EW line following acquisition of Dalmo Victor [electronic warfare] il *Aviation Week & Space Technology* 131:94+ S 11 '89
Matsushita may tune in to cable [possible bid for General Instrument] G. G. Marcial. *Business Week* p76 Ja 30 '89

GENERAL MILLS, INC.
Big G is growing fat on oat cuisine [General Mills' cereals gain on Kellogg's] R. Mitchell. il *Business Week* p29 S 18 '89
Does this cereal belong in the medicine cabinet? [P&G claims that General Mills' cholesterol-reducing Benefit is a drug; Metamucil also contains psyllium] R. Mitchell and others. il *Business Week* p22-3 Jl 24 '89
General Mills a go-go. P. Sellers. il *Fortune* 119:173 Je 5 '89

GENERAL MINING ACT See Mining law
GENERAL MOTORS CORP.
"1990 will be the year of the General". J. Flint. il por *Forbes* 144:40-1 N 27 '89
Breaking up is hard to do [G.M. vs. R. Perot] D. P. Levin. il pors *The New York Times Magazine* p36-7+ Mr 26 '89
A car that's just the way its designers wanted it [GM200 minivan] D. Woodruff. il *Business Week* p103-4 Je 5 '89
EDS: how sweet it is to have a sugar daddy. K. Kelly. il *Business Week* p110-11 S 18 '89
Evolutionary, not revolutionary [GM-10 line] J. Flint. il *Forbes* 143:43 My 1 '89
General Motors reinvents the wheel. A. Gabor. il por *U.S. News & World Report* 107:40-1 Ag 21 '89
GM and UAW: together again for the first time. M. Keller. il *Motor Trend* 41:146 Ap '89
GM gets back in high gear. D. Pauly. il *Newsweek* 113:39 F 20 '89
GM, Hughes settle stock fight. B. J. Culliton. *Science* 243:1283 Mr 10 '89
GM settles six-year suit [employment opportunities for blacks] G. Huskisson. il *Black Enterprise* 19:36 My '89
GM's alphabet stocks spelled trouble [deal with Hughes] J. B. Treece. il *Business Week* p41 Mr 13 '89
GM's bumpy ride on the long road back. J. B. Treece. il *Business Week* p74-5+ F 13 '89
A Jaguar buyer may be in for a long, slow drive [GM or Ford] M. Maremont. il *Business Week* p48-9 N 13 '89
Lethal Lordstown: workers fight poison at a GM plant. J. Slaughter. il *The Progressive* 53:28-9+ Mr '89
Motor City madness. J. B. Treece. il *Business Week* p22-3 Mr 6 '89
One company's taxes. L. Saunders. *Forbes* 143:298 Ja 9 '89
Smart cars and smart policies [address, March 28, 1989] R. B. Smith. *Vital Speeches of the Day* 55:534-7 Je 15 '89
Suddenly, the UAW is raising its voice at GM. W. Zellner. il por *Business Week* p96+ N 6 '89
The tasks facing General Motors. A. L. Taylor. il *Fortune* 119:52-3+ Mr 13 '89
Teaming up in Detroit [GM and Chrysler teamup] *Newsweek* 114:59 O 16 '89
The turn signal is on. il *Forbes* 143:90 Ja 9 '89
'The U.S. must do as GM has done' [interview with R. Smith] C. Leinster. il por *Fortune* 119:70-3 F 13 '89
Would you pay $2 billion for a sick cat? [GM and Ford go after Jaguar] M. Maremont. il *Business Week* p58 O 23 '89
GENERAL MOTORS CORP. BUICK MOTOR DIVISION See Buick Motor Division
GENERAL MOTORS CORP. CADILLAC MOTOR CAR DIVISION See Cadillac Motor Car Division
GENERAL MOTORS CORP. CHEVROLET MOTOR DIVISION See Chevrolet Motor Division
GENERAL MOTORS CORP. OLDSMOBILE DIVISION See Oldsmobile Division
GENERAL MOTORS CORP. SATURN CORPORATION See Saturn Corporation
GENERAL MOTORS EUROPE AG
Detroit's Euro-boom. J. Marcom, Jr. il *Forbes* 143:38-9 Mr 20 '89
Don't tread on us—please [Ford and GM poised to be winners in European car market] J. Flint. il *Forbes* 143:92 Je 12 '89
GENERAL MOTORS HUGHES ELECTRONICS CORPORATION See GM-Hughes Electronics Corporation
GENERAL SERVICES ADMINISTRATION See United States. General Services Administration
GENERAL SIGNAL CORP.
Never look back. il *Forbes* 143:129 Ja 9 '89
GENERAL STORES
See also
Casey's General Stores Inc.
Learning from Millie. R. Brauer. por *Newsweek* 114:10 N 20 '89
GENERAL TELEPHONE & ELECTRONICS CORPORATION
See also
GTE Corp.
GENERALS
See also
Groves, Leslie R., 1896-1970
Patton, George S. (George Smith), 1885-1945
Phillips, John F.
Powell, Colin L.
First in 200 years: black generals head military at Bush's inaugural ceremony. il por *Jet* 75:24-5 Ja 23 '89
GENERATION GAP
Explaining today to yesterday [cover story] W. J. O'Malley. il *America* 161:254-7 O 21 '89
Who said ignorance is bliss? A. Furlaud. *The New York Times Magazine* p20+ O 8 '89
The young and the old are not enemies. W. R. Hutton. il *USA Today (Periodical)* 117:63-5 Mr '89

GENERATIONS [television program] See Television program reviews—Single works
GENERATIVE ORGANS See Reproductive organs
GENERATORS, AIRPLANE See Airplanes, Light—Electric generators
GENERATORS, BOAT See Boats and boating—Electric generators
GENERATORS, ELECTRIC See Electric generators
GENERATORS, RANDOM NUMBER See Random number generators
GENERATORS, SIGNAL See Signal generators
GENERATORS, WIND See Wind power
GENERIC DRUG INDUSTRY See Drug industry
GENERIC DRUGS
Brand-name or generic: what your body does—and doesn't—know. C. Marks. il *Mademoiselle* 95:128+ O '89
Drug abuse [Mylan Laboratories' suspicions of FDA corruption bear fruit] J. Novack. il *Forbes* 143:42-3 Je 26 '89
Ensuring the safety of generic drugs. F. E. Young. il *FDA Consumer* 23:5-7 D '89/Ja '90
FDA monitoring generics. *FDA Consumer* 23:2 N '89
Generic concern. R. Coorsh. *Consumers' Research Magazine* 72:4 O '89
How far has the cancer spread at the FDA? [generic drug scandal] J. Carey. il *Business Week* p30-1 S 18 '89
Not what the doctor ordered [FDA accused of carelessness about generic drugs] J. N. Baker. il *Newsweek* 114:32 Ag 28 '89
The other drug war here at home [generic drug scandal] *U.S. News & World Report* 107:11 S 11 '89
A prescription for scandal. C. Gorman. il *Time* 134:56 Ag 28 '89
Watchdogs overdose on generic drugs [FDA investigation of fraudulent activities] S. Dentzer. il *U.S. News & World Report* 107:26 Ag 28-S 4 '89
What's wrong with generic drugs? [cover story] J. W. Merline. il *Consumers' Research Magazine* 72:11-17 D '89
Why generic drugs are O.K. J. Silberner. il *U.S. News & World Report* 107:70-2 S 18 '89
Prices
The price of no-name drugs may soon be hard to swallow. J. Weber, Jr. il *Business Week* p87 O 2 '89
GENES
See also
Engrailed (Gene)
Linkage (Genetics)
Testis determining factor
Transposons
Tumor suppressor genes
GENESIS, BOOK OF See Bible. O.T. Genesis
GENESIS ENTERTAINMENT
Gannaway's Genesis. A. B. Block. il pors *Channels (New York, N.Y.: 1986)* 9:36-7+ S '89
Unlikely bedfellows [helping stations sell ads] C. Reece. il *Channels (New York, N.Y.: 1986)* 9:18 My '89
GENESIS HOUSE
Loving a prostitute [cover story] J. Hahn. il *The Christian Century* 106:415-16 Ap 19 '89
GENESSE, BRYAN
about
Bryan Genesse: from soaps to the silver screen! il por *'Teen* 33:68 My '89
GENET See Flanner, Janet, 1892-1978
GENET, JEAN, 1910-1986
about
The screens [drama] Reviews
Newsweek il 114:76 N 20 '89. J. Kroll
GENETIC ALGORITHMS
Genetic algorithms: what computers can learn from Darwin [cover story] C. T. Walbridge. il *Technology Review* 92:46-8+ Ja '89
Natural selection for computers. I. Peterson. il *Science News* 136:346-8 N 25 '89
On finding all suboptimal foldings of an RNA molecule. M. Zuker. bibl f il *Science* 244:48-52 Ap 7 '89
GENETIC CODE
See also
Amino acid sequence
Genetic transcription
Polymerase chain reaction
The anticodon contains a major element of the identity of arginine transfer RNAs. L. H. Schulman and H. Pelka. bibl f il *Science* 246:1595-7 D 22 '89
β-adrenergic receptor kinase: primary structure delineates a multigene family. J. L. Benovic and others. bibl f il *Science* 246:235-40 O 13 '89
Circumsporozoite protein heterogeneity in the human malaria parasite Plasmodium vivax. R. Rosenberg and others. bibl f il *Science* 245:973-6 S 1 '89
Computer revealing language of life [technology that speeds analysis of DNA sequences; work of Leroy E. Hood] *Science News* 135:284 My 6 '89
Control of gene expression by artificial introns in Saccharomyces cerevisiae. T. Yoshimatsu and F. Nagawa. bibl f il *Science* 244:1346-8 Je 16 '89
How old is the genetic code? Statistical geometry of tRNA provides an answer. M. Eigen and others. bibl f il *Science* 244:673-9 My 12 '89

GENETIC CODE—*cont.*

Isolation of human transcribed sequences from human-rodent somatic cell hybrids. P. Liu and others. bibl f il *Science* 246:813-15 N 10 '89

Mobile introns and intron-encoded proteins. P. S. Perlman and R. A. Butow. bibl f il *Science* 246:1106-9 D 1 '89

Repeat-induced G-C to A-T mutations in Neurospora. E. B. Cambareri and others. bibl f il *Science* 244:1571-5 Je 30 '89

Structure of E. coli glutaminyl-tRNA synthetase complexed with tRNA^{Gln} and ATP at 2.8 Å resolution. M. A. Rould and others. bibl f il *Science* 246:1135-42 D 1 '89

The structure of the "second genetic code" [work of T. A. Steitz] M. M. Waldrop. il por *Science* 246:1122 D 1 '89

An ultraviolet-sensitive RNA structural element in a viroid-like domain of the hepatitis delta virus. A. D. Branch and others. bibl f il *Science* 243:649-52 F 3 '89

GENETIC COUNSELING

Genetic counseling. A. Emmett-Arthur. *Parents* 64:126-9+ My '89

GENETIC DISEASES *See* Heredity of disease

GENETIC ENGINEERING (PLANTS) *See* Plant genetics

GENETIC ENGINEERING INDUSTRY *See* Genetic research industry

GENETIC ENGINEERING RESEARCH *See* Genetic research

GENETIC FINGERPRINTS *See* DNA fingerprints

GENETIC MAPPING

See also

> Genome mapping
> Linkage (Genetics)
> Locus (Genes)
> Restriction fragment length polymorphisms

Chromosome mapping and expression of a putative testis-determining gene in mouse. C. M. Nagamine and others. bibl f il *Science* 243:80-3 Ja 6 '89

Duplication, deletion, and polymorphism in the sex-determining region of the mouse Y chromosome. G. Mardon and others. bibl f il *Science* 243:78-80 Ja 6 '89

Identification of the cystic fibrosis gene: chromosome walking and jumping. J. M. Rommens and others. bibl f il *Science* 245:1059-65 S 8 '89

A new cluster of genes within the human major histocompatibility complex. T. Spies and others. bibl f il *Science* 243:214-17 Ja 13 '89

Physical mapping of a translocation breakpoint in neurofibromatosis. J. W. Fountain and others. bibl f il *Science* 244:1085-7 Je 2 '89

Two NF1 translocations map within a 600-kilobase segment of 17q11.2. P. O'Connell and others. bibl f il *Science* 244:1087-8 Je 2 '89

Yeutter backs plan to map crop genes. M. Crawford. *Science* 243:1137 Mr 3 '89

GENETIC NEWSLETTERS

Check on Fingerprint news. R. Lewin. *Science* 243:1550 Mr 24 '89

GENETIC POLYMORPHISM *See* Polymorphism (Biology)

GENETIC REGULATION

See also

> Antisense genetics
> Homeoboxes
> Imprinting (Genetics)
> Tumor suppressor genes

5-bromo-2'-deoxyuridine blocks myogenesis by extinguishing expression of MyoD1. S. J. Tapscott and others. bibl f il *Science* 245:532-6 Ag 4 '89

Anticancer tobacco? [transient gene expression system developed by Biosource Genetics] J. E. Rodgers. il *American Health* 8:16 S '89

Bacterial blight of soybean: regulation of a pathogen gene determining host cultivar specificity. T. V. Huynh and others. bibl f il *Science* 245:1374-7 S 22 '89

Beetlejuice genes now in biotechnicolor [click beetles; research by Keith V. Wood and William D. McElroy] R. Weiss. il *Science News* 135:308 My 20 '89

Brain region and gene specificity of neuropeptide gene expression in cultured astrocytes. H. Shinoda and others. bibl f il *Science* 245:415-17 Jl 28 '89

Cancer-fighting tobacco plants? [transient gene expression system developed at Biosource Genetics Corp.] K. Fackelmann. *Science News* 135:238 Ap 15 '89

Cell cycle-dependent regulation of phosphorylation of the human retinoblastoma gene product. K. Mihara and others. bibl f il *Science* 246:1300-3 D 8 '89

Cis-trans models for post-transcriptional gene regulation. R. D. Klausner and J. B. Harford. bibl f il *Science* 246:870-2 N 17 '89

Contingent genetic regulatory events in T lymphocyte activation. G. R. Crabtree. bibl f il *Science* 243:355-61 Ja 20 '89

Control of gene expression by artificial introns in Saccharomyces cerevisiae. T. Yoshimatsu and F. Nagawa. bibl f il *Science* 244:1346-8 Je 16 '89

A different kind of inheritance [DNA methylation as an epigenetic mechanism] R. Holliday. bibl il *Scientific American* 260:60-5+ Je '89

Directing cell division during development. P. H. O'Farrell and others. bibl f il *Science* 246:635-40 N 3 '89

Dominoes and clocks: the union of two views of the cell cycle. A. W. Murray and M. W. Kirschner. bibl f il *Science* 246:614-21 N 3 '89

Dynamic expression pattern of the *myc* protooncogene in midgestation mouse embryos. P. Schmid and others. bibl f il *Science* 243:226-9 Ja 13 '89

Endothelial cell gene expression of a neutrophil chemotactic factor by TNF-α, LPS, and IL-1β. R. M. Strieter and others. bibl f il *Science* 243:1467-9 Mr 17 '89

Expression of a bacterial gene in a trypanosomatid protozoan [Leptomonas] V. Bellofatto and G. A. M. Cross. bibl f il *Science* 244:1167-9 Je 9 '89

Expression of a cloned rat brain potassium channel in Xenopus oocytes. M. J. Christie and others. bibl f il *Science* 244:221-4 Ap 14 '89

Expression of functional nerve growth factor receptors after gene transfer. B. L. Hempstead and others. bibl f il *Science* 243:373-5 Ja 20 '89

Gene control research gets a boost [TATA protein gene cloned; work of Leonard Guarente] J. L. Marx. il *Science* 245:1329-30 S 22 '89

Genetic control of differentiation of the Caenorhabditis elegans touch receptor neurons. M. Chalfie and M. Au. bibl f il *Science* 243:1027-33 F 24 '89

High-level recombinant gene expression in rabbit endothelial cells transduced by retroviral vectors. J. A. Zwiebel and others. bibl f il *Science* 243:220-2 Ja 13 '89

Hormonal and genetic control of behavioral integration in honey bee colonies. G. E. Robinson and others. bibl f il *Science* 246:109-12 O 6 '89

How gene activators work. M. Ptashne. bibl il *Scientific American* 260:40-7 Ja '89

Human chromosome 12 is required for elevated HIV-1 expression in human-hamster hybrid cells. C. E. Hart and others. bibl f il *Science* 246:488-91 O 27 '89

Identification of an AUUUA-specific messenger RNA binding protein. J. S. Malter. bibl f il *Science* 246:664-6 N 3 '89

In vivo footprinting of a muscle specific enhancer by ligation mediated PCR. P. R. Mueller and B. Wold. bibl f il *Science* 246:780-6 N 10 '89

Increased expression of DNA cointroduced with nuclear protein in adult rat liver. Y. Kaneda and others. bibl f il *Science* 243:375-8 Ja 20 '89

Inhibition of DNA binding proteins by oligonucleotide-directed triple helix formation. L. J. Maher, III and others. bibl f il *Science* 245:725-30 Ag 18 '89

Kappa B-specific DNA binding proteins: role in the regulation of human interleukin-2 gene expression. B. Hoyos and others. bibl f il *Science* 244:457-60 Ap 28 '89

Kittyboo colors [gene tagging with luciferase from click beetles; research by Keith Wood and others] il *Discover* 10:12 N '89

Mechanisms for regulating expression of membrane isoforms of FcγRIII (CD16). M. L. Hibbs and others. bibl f il *Science* 246:1608-11 D 22 '89

Molecular monkeywrench [blocking gene expression with synthetic nucleic acids] T. Beardsley. *Scientific American* 260:34-5 Je '89

Mouse embryonic stem cells and reporter constructs to detect developmentally regulated genes. A. Gossler and others. bibl f il *Science* 244:463-5 Ap 28 '89

Neutrophil Mac-1 and MEL-14 adhesion proteins inversely regulated by chemotactic factors. T. K. Kishimoto and others. bibl f il *Science* 245:1238-41 S 15 '89

Reciprocal effects of hyper- and hypoactivity mutations in the Drosophila pattern gene *torso*. T. R. Strecker and others. bibl f il *Science* 243:1062-6 F 24 '89

Recombinant gene expression in vivo within endothelial cells of the arterial wall. E. G. Nabel and others. bibl f il *Science* 244:1342-4 Je 16 '89

Regulated genes in transgenic plants. P. N. Benfey and N.-H. Chua. bibl f il *Science* 244:174-81 Ap 14 '89

Retrovirus vectors: promise and reality. H. M. Temin. bibl f *Science* 246:983 N 24 '89

The role of cis-acting promoter elements in tissue-specific albumin gene expression. P. Maire and others. bibl f il *Science* 244:343-6 Ap 21 '89

Role of Na⁺/H⁺ exchange by interferon-γ in enhanced expression of JE and I-Aβ genes. V. Prpic and others. bibl f il *Science* 244:469-71 Ap 28 '89

Sindbis virus: an efficient, broad host range vector for gene expression in animal cells. C. Xiong and others. bibl f il *Science* 243:1188-91 Mr 3 '89

Targeting of nonexpressed genes in embryonic stem cells via homologous recombination. R. S. Johnson and others. bibl f il *Science* 245:1234-6 S 15 '89

Translational blockade imposed by cytokine-derived UA-rich sequences [Xenopus oocytes] V. Kruys and others. bibl f il *Science* 245:852-5 Ag 25 '89

Ubiquitous expression of *sevenless*: position-dependent specification of cell fate. K. Basler and E. Hafen. bibl f il *Science* 243:931-4 F 17 '89

GENETIC RESEARCH

See also

> Information systems—Genetic research use
> Jackson Laboratory (Bar Harbor, Me.)

GENETIC RESEARCH—*cont.*

Baculovirus for biocontrol and biotech. R. Lewis. il *BioScience* 39:431-4 Jl/Ag '89

The body's master controls: unraveling proteins to tackle disease at its roots. B. Carpenter. il *U.S. News & World Report* 106:57-9 My 8 '89

Costs and cures. S. Findlay and J. Silberner. il *U.S. News & World Report* 107:68-9 D 25 '89-Ja 1 '90

Design of life. J. Merritt. bibl il *Modern Maturity* 32:42-7 Je/Jl '89

Factories of our future. M. D. Dibner. il *Consumers' Research Magazine* 72:15-18 Ap '89

The new harvest: genetically engineered species [cover story; special section; with editorial comment by Daniel E. Koshland] bibl f il *Science* 244:1233, 1275-1317 Je 16 '89

Targeting of nonexpressed genes in embryonic stem cells via homologous recombination. R. S. Johnson and others. bibl f il *Science* 245:1234-6 S 15 '89

Environmental aspects

Benefits and risks of genetic engineering in agriculture. D. Pimentel and others. bibl f il *BioScience* 39:606-14 O '89

Biotech's bust and bloom. R. Rodale. il *Organic Gardening* 36:31-2 Ja '89

Controlling risk in biotech. S. Krimsky and others. il *Technology Review* 92:62-8+ Jl '89

Ecologists wary about environmental releases. L. Roberts. *Science* 243:1141 Mr 3 '89

Field tests: a weightier message [National Research Council report] M. Sun. il *Science* 245:1326 S 22 '89

First field test of engineered virus [weakened baculoviruses to be sprayed onto cabbages] *Science News* 136:46 Jl 15 '89

Genetic design. C. Fenyvesi. il *Organic Gardening* 36:76-8+ Ja '89

Genetic engineering: sorcerer's apprentice or handmaiden to humanity? B. D. Davis and L. Roche. il *USA Today (Periodical)* 118:68-70 N '89

Microbes to aid plants from within [corn field trials of genetically altered Clavibacter xyli] J. A. Miller. *BioScience* 39:227-8 Ap '89

Microbial census hints at biotech hurdles [study of pseudomonas by Michael H. Smith] R. Weiss. *Science News* 135:4 Ja 7 '89

Risk, regulation, and biotechnology. M. Gladwell. il *The American Spectator* 22:21-4 Ja '89

South Carolina blocks test of rabies vaccine [proposed use of genetically engineered virus on wild raccoons] M. Sun. il *Science* 244:1535 Je 30 '89

Super weeds. R. Twombly. il *Technology Review* 92:15-16 Ag/S '89

Thank you, Jeremy Rifkin. M. Fritz. il *Forbes* 144:268-9 O 16 '89

Toward a science-based policy on the release of genetically engineered organisms [report by the Ecological Society of America] Y. Grossman. *BioScience* 39:229 Ap '89

Virginia OKs rabies vaccine test [use of genetically engineered virus on raccoons] M. Sun. *Science* 245:126 Jl 14 '89

Ethical aspects

Baltimore case reopened. *Science News* 135:278 My 6 '89

Baltimore cleared of all fraud charges [disputed Cell paper] B. J. Culliton. il por *Science* 243:727 F 10 '89

Conduct unbecoming? [D. Baltimore case] P. Weiss. il pors *The New York Times Magazine* p40-1+ O 29 '89

"Dangerous" liaisons in cell biology [controversy over work of C. Spadafora] D. Dickson. il por *Science* 244:1539-40 Je 30 '89; Correction. 245:252 Jl 21 '89

The Dingell probe finally goes public [D. Baltimore case] B. J. Culliton. *Science* 244:643-6+ My 12 '89

Dingell v. Baltimore. B. J. Culliton. pors *Science* 244:412-14 Ap 28 '89

Fraud debate aired on Capitol Hill [D. Baltimore case] K. Fackelmann. *Science News* 135:294-5 My 13 '89

Gene rustlers. N. C. Ellstrand. *Omni (New York, N.Y.)* 11:33 Ap '89

Genes 'R' Us. W. Saletan. *The New Republic* 201:18-20 Jl 17-24 '89

Genetic advances, ethical risks. J. Leo. il *U.S. News & World Report* 107:59 S 25 '89

Genetics, medicine and ethics [cover story] Z. Bankowski. il *World Health* p3-5 D '88

High-tech fortunetelling. R. M. Henig. il *The New York Times Magazine* p20+ D 24 '89

Human genome program [discussion of October 13, 1989 article, Sequences and consequences of the human genome] D. E. Koshland, Jr. *Science* 246:873-4 N 17 '89

Looking for Mr. Good Genes? L. Mosedale. *Glamour* 87:152 O '89

The most hated man in science [J. Rifkin] D. Thompson. il por *Time* 134:102-4 D 4 '89

NIH finds scientific errors but no fraud [D. Baltimore case] K. Fackelmann. *Science News* 135:85 F 11 '89

The perils of treading on heredity [cover story] P. Elmer-Dewitt. il *Time* 133:70-1 Mr 20 '89

Self-regulation of science: reflections on a day spent testifying at a congressional hearing. D. Baltimore. il por *Technology Review* 92:20+ Ag/S '89

Sequences and consequences of the human genome. D. E. Koshland, Jr. *Science* 246:189 O 13 '89

Whose notes are they? [proposal to open scientists' personal data books to general scrutiny; Dingell hearings on D. Baltimore case] B. J. Culliton. il *Science* 244:765 My 19 '89

Experimentation on man
See Genetic research—Human experimentation

Human experimentation

Brave new gene therapy [Steven Rosenberg's cancer experiments] S. Begley. il *Newsweek* 113:65 F 13 '89

Coming: a historic experiment [human gene transplant cancer therapy planned by National Institutes of Health] D. Thompson. il *Time* 133:64 F 13 '89

Ethical questions haunt new genetic technologies [battle between activist J. Rifkin and National Institutes of Health] L. Roberts. il por *Science* 243:1134-6 Mr 3 '89

Gene test begins [patient with advanced melanoma receives infusion of his own white blood cells containing a foreign gene] B. J. Culliton. il *Science* 244:913 My 26 '89

Gene transfer test: so far, so good [treatment of advanced melanoma with tumor-infiltrating lymphocytes; work of Steven A. Rosenberg] B. J. Culliton. *Science* 245:1325 S 22 '89

Gene-transfer trial begins in humans [work of Steven A. Rosenberg] K. Fackelmann. *Science News* 135:324 My 27 '89

Groups seek human gene-transfer delay [opposition to cancer experiment] R. Weiss. *Science News* 135:68 F 4 '89

Human gene therapy: after a lot of looking, now the leap. J. Carey. il *Business Week* p133+ My 1 '89

An ingenious way to fix genes [cancer patient receives genetically engineered cells; work of Steven Rosenberg] il *U.S. News & World Report* 106:12-13 Je 5 '89

Labeled therapy [gene transfer experiment may improve a cancer treatment] T. Beardsley. *Scientific American* 260:24-5 F '89

Rifkin battles gene transfer experiment. L. Roberts. *Science* 243:734 F 10 '89

Scrambling for biotech bucks [human gene transplants] J. W. Anderson. il *The Nation* 248:476-8 Ap 10 '89

Laws and regulations

Biotechnology and agriculture [address, November 3, 1989] R. McGuire. *Vital Speeches of the Day* 56:147-50 D 15 '89

Biotechnology rules wither in OMB. M. Crawford. *Science* 243:602 F 3 '89

Controlling risk in biotech. S. Krimsky and others. il *Technology Review* 92:62-8+ Jl '89

NIH limits gene experiments done abroad. *Science News* 135:237 Ap 15 '89

Risk, regulation, and biotechnology. M. Gladwell. il *The American Spectator* 22:21-4 Ja '89

Should states regulate biotechnology? M. Crawford. il *Science* 245:466 Ag 4 '89

Toward a science-based policy on the release of genetically engineered organisms [report by the Ecological Society of America] Y. Grossman. *BioScience* 39:229 Ap '89

Unshackle scientists from stifling government regulations. D. Ritter. il *USA Today (Periodical)* 118:66-7 N '89

Germany (West)

Brain drain [biotech companies being chased out of Germany] R. Bailey. il *Forbes* 144:261-2 N 27 '89

Court blocks German biotech plant [Hoechst AG] B. Bachtler. *Science* 246:881 N 17 '89

German biotech firms flee regulatory climate. D. Dickson. il *Science* 244:1251-2 Je 16 '89

Patents

Brave new mouse [first animal patent for cancer-prone mouse] A. Kozlov. il *Discover* 10:78 Ja '89

Patenting genetic 'inventions'. J. E. Bahls. il *High Technology Business* 9:10 Je '89

Public responses to genetic engineering. B. Hanson and D. Nelkin. *Society* 27:76-80 N/D '89

A tiny mouse came forth [patented oncomouse] E. Corcoran. *Scientific American* 260:73 F '89

Whose spleen is it? [J. Moore case] D. Andrews. il por *Technology Review* 92:14 N/D '89

Western Europe

Europe says no to animal patents. D. Dickson. *Science* 245:25 Jl 7 '89

Europe tries to untangle laws on patenting life. D. Dickson. *Science* 243:1002-3 F 24 '89

No patent for Harvard's mouse? [rejection by European Patent Office] D. Dickson. *Science* 243:1003 F 24 '89

Plants
See Plant genetics

Public opinion

Public responses to genetic engineering. B. Hanson and D. Nelkin. *Society* 27:76-80 N/D '89

Developing countries

Appropriate biotech. T. Kiely. il *Technology Review* 92:11-12 Ag/S '89

Great Britain

Britain launches genome program. D. Dickson. *Science* 243:1657 Mr 31 '89

GENETIC RESEARCH—*cont.*

Japan

Consensus elusive on Japan's genome plans. M. Sun. il *Science* 243:1656-7 Mr 31 '89

Japan boosts genome research. L. Roberts. *Science* 246:439-40 O 27 '89

Watson versus Japan. L. Roberts. il *Science* 246:576+ N 3 '89

Western Europe

European genome program delayed? D. Dickson. *Science* 243:1548 Mr 24 '89

Genome project gets rough ride in Europe. D. Dickson. *Science* 243:599 F 3 '89

GENETIC RESEARCH INDUSTRY

See also

Agracetus Inc.
Amgen Inc.
Applied Microbiology Inc.
Biogen Incorporated
Blacks in the genetic research industry
Celgene Corporation
Cetus Corporation
Genentech, Inc.
Medical Science Partners
Monsanto Company
Seragen Inc.
SRA Life Sciences (Firm)
Thermedics Inc.

AIDS: bioscience attacks a killer [cover story] F. Lunzer. il *High Technology Business* 9:18-21+ F '89

Acquisitions and mergers
International aspects

Connaught's foreign sale [to Institut Mérieux] A. Walmsley. il *Maclean's* 102:44-5 D 25 '89

Lament for a cherished asset [proposed sale of Connaught Biosciences to Institut Mérieux] P. C. Newman. il *Maclean's* 102:51 O 16 '89

Next stop: U.S. biotechnology, a 'targeted industry' [Japanese investors] M. Sun. *Science* 246:1239 D 8 '89

Science and PR north of the border [sale of Connaught Biosciences to Institut Merieux] D. Powell. *Science* 246:1555-6 D 22 '89

Tempest in a test tube [bidders for Connaught Biosciences] G. W. Taylor. il *Maclean's* 102:42 S 25 '89

Finance

Biotech ventures in academia—have they paid off? L. Rothstein. *The Bulletin of the Atomic Scientists* 45:34 Ap '89

Cloning profits. G. Slutsker. il *Forbes* 143:152 Ja 9 '89

Laws and regulations
See Genetic research—Laws and regulations

Securities

The biotechnology crisscross. M. Gianturco. il *Forbes* 144:280 D 11 '89

Biotechnology isn't dead. M. Gianturco. il por *Forbes* 143:410 My 1 '89

Canada

See also
Connaught Biosciences Inc.

Germany (West)

Brain drain [biotech companies being chased out of Germany] R. Bailey. il *Forbes* 144:261-2 N 27 '89

Court blocks German biotech plant [Hoechst AG] B. Bachtler. *Science* 246:881 N 17 '89

German biotech firms flee regulatory climate. D. Dickson. il *Science* 244:1251-2 Je 16 '89

GENETIC SCREENING

The baby shoppers. R. Sandroff. *Vogue* 179:246+ My '89

CF screen: still too soon. R. Weiss. *Science News* 136:325 N 18 '89

Disclosing genetic information: who should know? D. C. Wertz and J. C. Fletcher. il *Technology Review* 92:22-3 Jl '89

An early-warning system [testing for genetic defects in the human egg] A. Purvis. il *Time* 134:56 N 27 '89

Genetic testing possible before conception [testing unfertilized egg; work of Yury Verlinsky] R. Weiss. *Science News* 136:326 N 18 '89

High-tech fortunetelling. R. M. Henig. il *The New York Times Magazine* p20+ D 24 '89

Made to order babies. G. Cowley. il *Newsweek* 114 Special Issue:94-5+ Wint '89/Spr '90

Mean gene tests [insurance discrimination because of inherited conditions] J. H. Tanne. il *American Health* 8:8-9 D '89

Predisposition and prejudice [genetic discrimination; cover story] R. Weiss. il *Science News* 135:40-2 Ja 21 '89

GENETIC TOXICOLOGY

Bias or safety? [appeals court upholds Johnson Controls ban excluding women of childbearing age from hazardous jobs] *Time* 134:61 O 16 '89

GENETIC TRANSCRIPTION

See also
Transcription factors

BAS1 has a myb motif and activates HIS4 transcription only in combination with BAS2 [Saccharomyces] K. Tice-Baldwin and others. bibl f il *Science* 246:931-5 N 17 '89

Drosophila nuclear proteins bind to regions of alternating C and T residues in gene promoters. D. S. Gilmour and others. bibl f il *Science* 245:1487-90 S 29 '89

Enhancement of bacteriophage T4 late transcription by components of the T4 DNA replication apparatus. D. R. Herendeen and others. bibl f il *Science* 245:952-8 S 1 '89

Function of a bacterial activator protein that binds to transcriptional enhancers. D. L. Popham and others. bibl f il *Science* 243:629-35 F 3 '89

Initiation by yeast RNA polymerase II at the adenoviral major late promoter in vitro. N. F. Lue and others. bibl f il *Science* 246:661-4 N 3 '89

Repression of the IgH enhancer in teratocarcinoma cells associated with a novel octamer factor. M. J. Lenardo and others. bibl f il *Science* 243:544-6 Ja 27 '89

Similarity between the transcriptional silencer binding proteins ABF1 and RAP1 [Saccharomyces] J. F. X. Diffley and B. Stillman. bibl f il *Science* 246:1034-8 N 24 '89

GENETIC TRANSFORMATION *See* Gene transfer

GENETIC VARIATION *See* Variation (Biology)

GENETICS

See also

Adaptation (Biology)
Alcoholics and alcoholism—Genetic aspects
Alzheimer's disease—Genetic aspects
Animal genetics
Antisense genetics
Autism—Genetic aspects
Behavioral genetics
Cancer—Genetic aspects
Chromosomes
Clones (Biology)
Color vision—Genetic aspects
Comparative genetics
Complementation (Genetics)
Dental caries—Genetic aspects
Depression, Mental—Genetic aspects
Diabetes—Genetic aspects
Epilepsy—Genetic aspects
Fungal genetics
Germplasm resources
Heredity and environment
Heredity of disease
Immunogenetics
Imprinting (Genetics)
Insect genetics
Intelligence
Linkage (Genetics)
Mental illness—Genetic aspects
Microbial genetics
Molecular genetics
Monoclonal antibodies
Mosaics (Biology)
Multiple sclerosis—Genetic aspects
Muscular dystrophy—Genetic aspects
Mutation
Natural selection
Obesity—Genetic aspects
Personality—Genetic aspects
Plant genetics
Population genetics
Schizophrenia—Genetic aspects
Tree genetics
Variation (Biology)

Research
See Genetic research

Social aspects

See also
Sociobiology

Study and teaching

Mendel to Monctezuma: the end-of-term review in genetics. T. Haffie. il *BioScience* 39:246-7+ Ap '89

GENETICS, COMPARATIVE *See* Comparative genetics

GENETICS AND ENVIRONMENT *See* Heredity and environment

GENEVA (N.Y.)

Historic houses, sites, etc.

See also
Rose Hill Mansion (Geneva, N.Y.)

GENEVA (SWITZERLAND)

Galleries and museums

See also
International Museum of the Red Cross

Music

See also
Opera—Switzerland

GENEVA AUTO SHOW *See* Automobiles—Exhibitions

GENGHIS KHAN, 1162-1227

about

The secret history of the Mongols. S. Bira. il *The Unesco Courier* 42:36-9 S '89

GENICULATE NUCLEUS *See* Brain

GENITAL WARTS *See* Warts

GENITALS *See* Reproductive organs

GENIUS

See also
Children, Gifted

GENIUS—*cont.*
The paradoxes of creativity. J. Barzun. *The American Scholar* 58:337-51 Summ '89
What produces scientific genius? [views of Dean Keith Simonton] il *USA Today (Periodical)* 117:11 Je '89
GENMAR INDUSTRIES INC.
Did Irv Jacobs sandbag Outboard Marine? [auction for assets of Murray Chris-Craft] G. DeGeorge. *Business Week* p38+ F 20 '89
GENNETT RECORD DIVISION *See* Starr Piano Company. Gennett Record Division
GENOA (ITALY)
City planning
See also
Il Porto Vecchio (Genoa, Italy)
Docks, wharves, etc.
See also
Il Porto Vecchio (Genoa, Italy)
GENOCIDE
Genocide in our time: 200,000 indigenous people killed last year. J. W. Clay. *Utne Reader* p112-13 N/D '89
GENOCIDE TREATY *See* International Convention on the Prevention and Punishment of the Crime of Genocide
GENOME MAPPING
Accounting made easy for gene mappers [sequence tagged sites] R. Weiss. *Science News* 136:230 O 7 '89
Back to the bases [J. D. Watson to head NIH project] T. Beardsley. *Scientific American* 260:16-17 Ja '89
Britain launches genome program. D. Dickson. *Science* 243:1657 Mr 31 '89
Budding plant genome projects. C. Strange. *BioScience* 39:760-2 D '89
A common language for physical mapping of the human genome [sequence-tagged sites] M. V. Olson and others. bibl f *Science* 245:1434-5 S 29 '89
Computer revealing language of life [technology that speeds analysis of DNA sequences; work of Leroy E. Hood] *Science News* 135:284 My 6 '89
Consensus elusive on Japan's genome plans. M. Sun. il *Science* 243:1656-7 Mr 31 '89
European genome program delayed? D. Dickson. *Science* 243:1548 Mr 24 '89
The gene dream [Human Genome Initiative] N. Angier. il *American Health* 8:102-6+ Mr '89
The gene hunt [cover story] L. Jaroff. il *Time* 133:62-7 Mr 20 '89
Gene mappers meet on strategy. J. Palca. *Science* 245:1036 S 8 '89
Genetic advances, ethical risks. J. Leo. il *U.S. News & World Report* 107:59 S 25 '89
Genetics, medicine and ethics [cover story] Z. Bankowski. il *World Health* p3-5 D '88
Genome mapping goal now in reach. L. Roberts. il *Science* 244:424-5 Ap 28 '89
Genome planners fear avalanche of red tape. R. Lewin. il *Science* 244:1543 Je 30 '89
Genome project gets rough ride in Europe. D. Dickson. *Science* 243:599 F 3 '89
Genome project under way, at last. L. Roberts. *Science* 243:167-8 Ja 13 '89
Genome projects are growing like weeds. J. Palca. il *Science* 245:131 Jl 14 '89
Genomic sequencing and methylation analysis by ligation mediated PCR. G. P. Pfeifer and others. bibl f il *Science* 246:810-13 N 10 '89
Human genome program [discussion of October 13, 1989 article, Sequences and consequences of the human genome] D. E. Koshland, Jr. *Science* 246:873-4 N 17 '89
Japan boosts genome research. L. Roberts. *Science* 246:439-40 O 27 '89
Many faces of a gene-mapping project. R. Weiss. *Science News* 136:254 O 14 '89
Mapping the Drosophila genome with yeast artificial chromosomes. D. Garza and others. bibl f il *Science* 246:641-6 N 3 '89
Mapping the genetic wilderness [Human Genome Initiative] D. Baltimore. il por *Technology Review* 92:20 N/D '89
Mapping the human genome. J. Richardson. il *The Unesco Courier* 42:54-5 S '89
New chip may speed genome analysis. L. Roberts. il *Science* 244:655-6 My 12 '89
New game plan for genome mapping [sequence tagged site approach proposed by Maynard V. Olson] L. Roberts. il *Science* 245:1438-40 S 29 '89
Plan for genome centers sparks a controversy. L. Roberts. il *Science* 246:204-5 O 13 '89
Sequences and consequences of the human genome. D. E. Koshland, Jr. *Science* 246:189 O 13 '89
Unesco seeks role in genome projects. D. Dickson. *Science* 243:1431-2 Mr 17 '89
Watson floats a plan to carve up the genome. D. Dickson. il por *Science* 244:521-2 My 5 '89
Watson versus Japan. L. Roberts. il *Science* 246:576+ N 3 '89
Anecdotes, facetiae, satire, etc.
A surge of phallic science. B. Ehrenreich. il *Mother Jones* 14:8 Ja '89

GENOMIC IMPRINTING *See* Imprinting (Genetics)
GENOTYPE AND PHENOTYPE
Developmental and physiological aspects of reaction norms [Drosophila] W. Scharloo. bibl f il *BioScience* 39:465-71 Jl/Ag '89
The evolutionary significance of phenotypic plasticity [cover story] S. C. Stearns. bibl f il *BioScience* 39:436-45 Jl/Ag '89
Morphogenesis of the polarized epithelial cell phenotype. E. Rodriguez-Boulan and W. J. Nelson. bibl f il *Science* 245:718-25 Ag 18 '89
Phenotypic integration and environmental change [plasticity] C. D. Schlichting. bibl f il *BioScience* 39:460-4 Jl/Ag '89
GENOVA, AMY SUNSHINE- *See* Sunshine-Genova, Amy
GENSCHER, HANS DIETRICH
about
Appeasement in our time [cover story] H. Walter. il por *National Review* 41:26-8+ Je 2 '89
Europe's short-range missiles nail their first victim. J. Templeman and G. E. Schares. il por *Business Week* p50 Je 12 '89
GENTAMICIN
Legal dance over vet drug [unapproved manufacture leads to injunction against Tri-Bio] il *FDA Consumer* 23:42-3 F '89
GENTILES IN THE BIBLE
Righteous Gentiles. P. J. Ryan. il *America* 160:519 My 27 '89
GENTILESCHI, ARTEMISIA, 1597-1651
about
A star is reborn. J. Gardner. il *National Review* 41:44-5 Ag 4 '89
GENTLEMEN'S QUARTERLY
Joe Magrane strikes back [St. Louis Cardinals have baseball player pose for phony GQ fashion layout] G. Collins. il pors *Gentlemen's Quarterly* 59:260-3 Ap '89
GENTRY, JERRY
The NAMES project: a catharsis of grief. *The Christian Century* 106:550-1 My 24-31 '89
GENTRY, THOMAS H.
about
Landed Gentry. D. Wallace. il por *Motor Boating & Sailing* 164:54-7+ O '89
GENTZ, REINER, AND OTHERS
Parallel association of Fos and Jun leucine zippers juxtaposes DNA binding domains. bibl f il *Science* 243:1695-9 Mr 31 '89
GENUS INC.
A semiconductor secret is out. G. G. Marcial. *Business Week* p134 My 8 '89
GEO. A. HORMEL & CO.
A company town decays [effect of strike against Hormel on Austin, Minn.] B. Koeppel. il *The Progressive* 53:12-13 F '89
GEOCAPITAL CORPORATION
Ballast. R. Phalon. il por *Forbes* 144:138 N 13 '89
GEOCHEMISTRY
Deep water: "phase B" is decoded. R. Pool. *Science* 246:887 N 17 '89
GEOCHRONOLOGY *See* Geological time
GEODESIC DOMES
The birth of the geodesic dome [work of R. B. Fuller] L. S. Sieden. il pors *The Futurist* 23:14-19 N/D '89
GEODUCK CLAM FISHERIES *See* Clam fisheries
GEOGHAN, JIM
about
Only kidding [drama] Reviews
Commonweal 116:503-4 S 22 '89. G. C. Weales
The New Yorker 65:97 My 29 '89. E. Oliver
GEOGHEGAN, THOMAS
Glory days [cover story] *The New Republic* 200:18-23 My 29 '89
GEOGLYPHS
Amazing mysteries. il maps *National Geographic World* 164:10-13 Ap '89
GEOGRAPHIC INFORMATION SYSTEMS
The electronic transformation of maps. D. Bjerklie. il *Technology Review* 92:54-63 Ap '89
Geographic information systems: what they are, and how they work. S. P. Jessup and E. Cary. bibl il *Focus (New York, N.Y.: 1950)* 39:10-12 Summ '89
Managing with electronic maps. G. Bylinsky. il *Fortune* 119:237-8+ Ap 24 '89
These maps can find oil—or sell burgers. J. Rothfeder. il *Business Week* p134 Mr 13 '89
GEOGRAPHICAL DISTRIBUTION OF ANIMALS AND PLANTS *See* Biogeography
GEOGRAPHICAL NAMES *See* Names, Geographical
GEOGRAPHICAL RECREATIONS
Bringing maps home. M. Eichen. il *Parents* 64:143-6 S '89
Finding the lost generation [geography programs] G. Solomon. il *Home Office Computing* 7:82+ My '89
Mind travelers: explore the world through your computer [World GeoGraph] D. Stanton. il *Compute!* 11:16 S '89
PC-Globe+. K. Sternberg. il *Compute!* 11:74 Ag '89
GEOGRAPHY
See also
Atlases

GEOGRAPHY—See also—*cont.*
Maps
Medical geography
National Geographic Society (U.S.)
Sports and geography
Destination unknown. R. S. Weber. il *Focus (New York, N.Y.: 1950)* 39:23-4 Summ '89
Test your Geo-Q [quiz] il map *National Geographic World* 170:18-19 O '89

Competitions
These kids really did it! [first annual National Geography Bee] il *National Geographic World* 169:24-5 S '89
World's 1988 Scholarship Contest [Geo-Whiz Quiz Scholarship Contest] il *National Geographic World* 163:10-13 Mr '89

Philosophy
Mapping the real geography. B. H. Lopez. *Harper's* 279:19-21+ N '89

Study and teaching
See also
Geographical recreations
Bring back geography. C. W. Weinberger. il *Forbes* 144:31 D 25 '89
The geography crisis. F. Roberts. il *Parents* 64:64+ Mr '89
Superpowers not so super in geography [National Geographic Society's 1989 projects] G. M. Grosvenor. il map *National Geographic* 176:816-21 D '89
Whereabouts [entering students given free atlases at Tufts University] *The New Yorker* 65:29-30 F 20 '89
The world affairs annual 1989-90 [cover story; special issue] il maps *Scholastic Update (Teachers' edition)* 122:3-32 S 22 '89

Aids and devices
Logo and geography teaching. M. Eichen. bibl *Focus (New York, N.Y.: 1950)* 39:25-6 Summ '89
GEOGRAPHY BEES *See* Geography—Competitions
GEOLOGICAL CLIMATE *See* Paleoclimatology
GEOLOGICAL MODELS
Coming down in sheets [computer model of convection in the earth's mantle; work of Dave Bercovici and others] T. Appenzeller. il *Scientific American* 261:17-18 Ag '89
An empirical model for predicting diffusion coefficients in silicate minerals. S. M. Fortier and B. J. Giletti. bibl f il *Science* 245:1481-4 S 29 '89
Three-dimensional spherical models of convection in the earth's mantle. D. Bercovici and others. bibl f il *Science* 244:950-5 My 26 '89
GEOLOGICAL PHYSICS *See* Geophysics
GEOLOGICAL RESEARCH
Deep holes yielding geoscience surprises. R. A. Kerr. il *Science* 245:468-70 Ag 4 '89
European deep drilling leaves Americans behind. R. A. Kerr. il *Science* 245:816-17 Ag 25 '89
Inner space [deep drilling programs by Soviet Union and West Germany; cover story] R. Monastersky. il *Science News* 136:266-8 O 21 '89
GEOLOGICAL SURVEY (U.S.)
Ethics and USGS [discussion of November 3, 1989 article, Ethics debate sends tremors through USGS] E. Marshall. *Science* 246:1548-9 D 22 '89
Ethics debate sends tremors through USGS [case of H. G. Wilshire] E. Marshall. il por *Science* 246:570-1 N 3 '89
USGS reports a fraud [case of R. L. Houghton] E. Marshall. *Science* 244:1436 Je 23 '89
GEOLOGICAL SURVEYS
See also
Geological Survey (U.S.)
GEOLOGICAL TIME
See also
Earth—Age
Radioactive dating
It's about time. R. Pestrong. il *Earth Science* 42:14-15 Summ '89
GEOLOGISTS
See also
Sheldon, Peter
GEOLOGY
See also
Caves
Computers—Geological use
Continental drift
Drilling and boring (Earth and rocks)
Earthquakes
Erosion
Faults (Geology)
Folds (Geology)
Geological research
Geological Survey (U.S.)
Geological time
Hot spots (Geology)
Landslides
Lunar geology
Magnetic resonance imaging—Geological use
Mars (Planet)—Geology
Metamorphism (Geology)
Mountains
Ocean bottom
Ore deposits
Paleogeography

Petroleum—Geology
Rock deformation
Rocks
Sand
Sedimentation and deposition
Subduction (Geology)
Submarine geology
Tomography—Geological use
Venus (Planet)—Geology
Volcanoes
Weathering
Geoquiz. J. V. O'Connor. See issues of Earth Science beginning Summer 1985 through Winter 1988
Origin of granulite terranes and the formation of the lowermost continental crust. S. R. Bohlen and K. Mezger. bibl f il *Science* 244:326-9 Ap 21 '89

Conferences
See also
International Geological Congress
Calendar. See issues of Earth Science

Maps
Books & maps. See issues of Earth Science
First geological map may have been Egyptian scroll [Turin Papyrus; research by James A. Harrell and V. Max Brown] il *Earth Science* 41:5-6 Wint '88

Methodology
The age-of-the-earth debate. L. Badash. il *Scientific American* 261:90-4+ Ag '89

Aegean Sea region
Eyes on the Africa-Eurasia vise [research by Kim A. Kastens using Global Positioning System] R. Monastersky. *Science News* 135:335 My 27 '89

Arizona
See also
Grand Canyon (Ariz.)

Australia
Blame it on the moon [Elatina sediment striations tidally induced; George E. Williams overturns his hypothesis] J. Horgan. *Scientific American* 260:18 F '89
It's not the sun, but the moon [tidally induced Australian rock laminations; research by George E. Williams] il *Sky and Telescope* 77:469 My '89

California
Global Positioning System measurements for crustal deformation: precision and accuracy. W. H. Prescott and others. bibl f il *Science* 244:1337-40 Je 16 '89

Chile
Where east meets west [ocean floor subduction zone caused by plate movement off southern Chile; research by Steven Cande and Stephen Lewis] il *Discover* 10:21 F '89

China
Ancient ocean upheaval marks the spot [Precambrian-Cambrian boundary in Yunnan Province; research by Martin Brasier] R. Monastersky. *Science News* 136:61 Jl 22 '89
Origin of ancient potash evaporites: clues from the modern nonmarine Qaidam basin of western China. T. K. Lowenstein and others. bibl f il map *Science* 245:1090-2 S 8 '89

Colorado
Slumgullion Slide, Colorado. R. H. Mohlenbrock. il map *Natural History* p34-7 Ap '89

Czechoslovakia
Back to Bohemia [Praha Basin meteorite crater; theory of Michael Papagiannis] R. Kunzig. il *Discover* 10:22-3 Je '89
World's largest impact crater? [Praha basin] il *Sky and Telescope* 77:351 Ap '89

Denmark
The impact giveth . . . [amino acids found in Cretaceous-Tertiary boundary clay; research by Meixun Zhao and Jeffrey L. Bada] J. Horgan. *Scientific American* 261:24+ S '89
New impact evidence: amino acids from space [Cretaceous-Tertiary boundary clay; research by Meixun Zhao and Jeffrey L. Bada] *Astronomy* 17:11+ O '89
Rare amino acids support impact theory [Cretaceous-Tertiary boundary clays; research by Jeffrey L. Bada] R. Monastersky. *Science News* 135:356 Je 10 '89

East Africa
See also
Project PROBE

Egypt
First geological map may have been Egyptian scroll [Turin Papyrus; research by James A. Harrell and V. Max Brown] il *Earth Science* 41:5-6 Wint '88
Large-scale, low-amplitude bedforms (chevrons) in the Selima sand sheet, Egypt [Landsat images] T. A. Maxwell and C. V. Haynes. bibl f il map *Science* 243:1179-82 Mr 3 '89

Great Basin
Pre-Mesozoic palinspastic reconstruction of the eastern Great Basin (western United States) [cover story] M. Levy and N. Christie-Blick. bibl f il maps *Science* 245:1454-62 S 29 '89

GEOLOGY—cont.

India

Earliest evidence for plate tectonics [Kolar schist belt; research by Eirik J. Krogstad] F. Flam. *Science News* 135:159 Mr 11 '89

Horizontal history [evidence of plate tectonics at Kolar schist belt; research by Eirik Krogstad] R. Kunzig. il *Discover* 10:16+ S '89

Plate tectonics 2.5 billion years ago: evidence at Kolar, South India. E. J. Krogstad and others. bibl f il map *Science* 243:1337-40 Mr 10 '89

Iowa

^{40}Ar-^{39}Ar dating of the Manson impact structure: a Cretaceous-Tertiary boundary crater candidate [north-central Iowa] M. J. Kunk and others. bibl f il *Science* 244:1565-8 Je 30 '89

Manson, Iowa: where the 'big one' struck? [crater; research by M. J. Kunk] *Astronomy* 17:10-11 O '89

Louisiana

Kisatchie Hills, Louisiana. R. H. Mohlenbrock. il map *Natural History* p30-2 F '89

Montana

Rhenium-osmium and samarium-neodymium isotopic systematics of the Stillwater Complex. D. D. Lambert and others. bibl f il *Science* 244:1169-74 Je 9 '89

Morocco

If only this diamond truly lasted forever [study of Beni Bousera by Peter H. Nixon] F. Flam. *Science News* 135:133 Mr 4 '89

New Mexico

Signs of an ancient worldwide wallop [stishovite discovery in New Mexico; research by John McHone] R. Monastersky. *Science News* 135:132 Mr 4 '89

Stishovite at the Cretaceous-Tertiary boundary, Raton, New Mexico. J. F. McHone and others. bibl f il *Science* 243:1182-4 Mr 3 '89

North America

Another movement in the dance of the plates [work of Paul F. Hoffman] R. A. Kerr. il *Science* 244:529-30 My 5 '89

Spinning the supercontinent cycle [research by P. F. Hoffman; cover story] R. Monastersky. il map *Science News* 135:344-6 Je 3 '89

Northwest Territories

New record for world's oldest rocks [work of Samuel A. Bowring] R. Monastersky. il *Science News* 136:228 O 7 '89

Where mountains once stood [research by Frederick A. Cook] R. Monastersky. *Science News* 135:319 My 20 '89

Ohio

Ohio natural bridges. M. C. Hansen. il map *Earth Science* 41:10-12 Wint '88

Pennsylvania

Whaleback anticline [geological structure evident at Bear Valley Strip Mine] C. Blue. il *Earth Science* 42:19-21 Fall '89

Sahara

Rivers in the sand [interpretation of shuttle radar imaging] B. Bower. map *Science News* 136:138-9 Ag 26 '89

South Africa

Geological and geochemical record of 3400-million-year-old terrestrial meteorite impacts. D. R. Lowe and others. bibl f il *Science* 245:959-62 S 1 '89

South Carolina

Microbial life in deep terrestrial subsurfaces [sediments from Savannah River Plant] C. B. Fliermans and D. L. Balkwill. bibl f il *BioScience* 39:370-7 Je '89

Spain

Evidence for a heterogeneous upper mantle in the Cabo Ortegal Complex, Spain. J. Girardeau and others. bibl f il map *Science* 245:1231-3 S 15 '89

Tibet

Magnitude of late Quaternary left-lateral displacements along the north edge of Tibet [SPOT images of the Altyn Tagh fault] G. Peltzer and others. bibl f il maps *Science* 246:1285-9 D 8 '89

Vermont

Rates of tectonometamorphic processes from rubidium and strontium isotopes in garnet [southeast Vermont] J. N. Christensen and others. bibl f il *Science* 244:1465-9 Je 23 '89

GEOLOGY, ECONOMIC

See also
Mines and mineral resources

GEOLOGY, STRATIGRAPHIC

See also
Paleontology

Cretaceous

^{40}Ar-^{39}Ar dating of the Manson impact structure: a Cretaceous-Tertiary boundary crater candidate [north-central Iowa] M. J. Kunk and others. bibl f il *Science* 244:1565-8 Je 30 '89

A combination of impact and volcano is dismissed. *Science* 243:479 Ja 27 '89

The impact giveth . . . [amino acids found in Cretaceous-Tertiary boundary clay; research by Meixun Zhao and Jeffrey L. Bada] J. Horgan. *Scientific American* 261:24+ S '89

Manson, Iowa: where the 'big one' struck? [crater; research by M. J. Kunk] *Astronomy* 17:10-11 O '89

Microbes complicate the K-T mystery [research by Betsey D. Dyer] R. Monastersky. *Science News* 136:341 N 25 '89

New impact evidence: amino acids from space [Cretaceous-Tertiary boundary clay; research by Meixun Zhao and Jeffrey L. Bada] *Astronomy* 17:11+ O '89

Rare amino acids support impact theory [Cretaceous-Tertiary boundary clays; research by Jeffrey L. Bada] R. Monastersky. *Science News* 135:356 Je 10 '89

Signs of an ancient worldwide wallop [stishovite discovery in New Mexico; research by John McHone] R. Monastersky. *Science News* 135:132 Mr 4 '89

Stishovite at the Cretaceous-Tertiary boundary, Raton, New Mexico. J. F. McHone and others. bibl f il *Science* 243:1182-4 Mr 3 '89

Precambrian

Ancient ocean upheaval marks the spot [Precambrian-Cambrian boundary in Yunnan Province, China; research by Martin Brasier] R. Monastersky. *Science News* 136:61 Jl 22 '89

Blame it on the moon [Elatina sediment striations tidally induced; George E. Williams overturns his hypothesis] J. Horgan. *Scientific American* 260:18 F '89

Earliest evidence for plate tectonics [Kolar schist belt; research by Eirik J. Krogstad] F. Flam. *Science News* 135:159 Mr 11 '89

Horizontal history [evidence of plate tectonics at Kolar schist belt; research by Eirik Krogstad] R. Kunzig. il *Discover* 10:16+ S '89

It's not the sun, but the moon [tidally induced Australian rock laminations; research by George E. Williams] il *Sky and Telescope* 77:469 My '89

Plate tectonics 2.5 billion years ago: evidence at Kolar, South India. E. J. Krogstad and others. bibl f il map *Science* 243:1337-40 Mr 10 '89

Quaternary

Magnitude of late Quaternary left-lateral displacements along the north edge of Tibet [SPOT images of the Altyn Tagh fault] G. Peltzer and others. bibl f il maps *Science* 246:1285-9 D 8 '89

GEOLOGY, STRUCTURAL *See* Geology

GEOMAGNETISM *See* Magnetism, Terrestrial

GEOMETRY

See also
Angles
Circle-squaring
Finite geometry
Fractals
Sphere packing
Spheres
Topology

The color of geometry [cover story] I. Peterson. il *Science News* 136:408-10+ D 23-30 '89

Study and teaching
Aids and devices

Geometry [tutoring program] C. S. Holzberg. il *Compute!* 11:70-1 Je '89

GEOPHYSICS

See also
American Geophysical Union
Earth—Internal structure
Magnetism, Terrestrial
Seismometers and seismometry

Geophysics. bibl f il *Physics Today* 42:S42-S49 Ja '89

Awards

Geophysical Union salutes excellent work in the field. pors *Physics Today* 42:87-91 D '89

GEOPOLITICS

It's a small world after all. *The New Republic* 201:7-8+ S 18-25 '89

GEORGE, GRAHAM N., AND OTHERS

The manganese site of the photosynthetic water-splitting enzyme. bibl f il *Science* 243:789-91 F 10 '89

GEORGE, HENRY, 1839-1897

about
George on my mind. M. Kinsley. *The New Republic* 201:8+ N 6 '89

GEORGE, KATHLEEN

Too much women [story] il *Mademoiselle* 95:175-6+ Mr '89

GEORGE, LESLIE

Head trips. il *American Health* 8:92+ Ap '89

The loneliness of motherhood. il *American Health* 8:114+ Mr '89

Playing hide and seek with the sun—safely. il *American Health* 8:26-8+ My '89

GEORGE, LINDA

"I was radioactive". il por *Ladies' Home Journal* 106:22+ O '89

GEORGE, NORMAN

about
A Poe man's Edgar Allan, actor Norman George evermore plays a haunting, telltale part. il por *People Weekly* 31:66 F 6 '89

GEORGE, PAUL S.
Which way the middle school? *The Education Digest* 54:13-16 Ja '89
GEORGE, PHYLLIS
about
The comeback of Phyllis George. J. Ralston. il pors *McCall's* 116:12-14+ S '89
GEORGE, UWE
Venezuela's islands in time. il maps *National Geographic* 175:526-61 My '89
GEORGE EASTMAN HOUSE INTERNATIONAL MUSEUM OF PHOTOGRAPHY *See* International Museum of Photography at George Eastman House
GEORGE F. CRAM CO.
Global warfare. J. Harris. il por *Forbes* 144:120 O 16 '89
GEORGE RIVER (QUÉBEC)
Helen's Falls [Atlantic salmon fishing] D. Barnes. il *Field & Stream* 94:90+ Je '89
GEORGEOFF, JOHN
Let's again talk sense about our schools. bibl f il *Phi Delta Kappan* 71:72-3 S '89
GEORGES BANK
See also
Fisheries—Georges Bank
GEORGETOWN (S.C.)
Historic houses, sites, etc.
Southern spirits [haunted dwellings] S. Baker. il *Omni (New York, N.Y.)* 12:28+ D '89
GEORGETOWN (TEX.)
Description
All around Georgetown. il *Southern Living* 24:33-4 D '89
GEORGETOWN (WASHINGTON, D.C.)
Capital ideas [antique shops] N. McKeon. il *House & Garden* 161:180+ Ap '89
GEORGETOWN UNIVERSITY
Golden cup and silver bag [address, September 24, 1989] W. J. Richardson. *America* 161:315-16+ N 11 '89
GEORGIA
See also
Architecture, Domestic—Georgia
Carroll County (Ga.)
Chattooga River
Cumberland Island (Ga.)
Forsyth County (Ga.)
Little Saint Simons Island (Ga.)
Public health—Georgia
Rabun County (Ga.)
Resorts—Georgia
Sapelo Island (Ga.)
Description and travel
See also
Cycling—Georgia
West central Georgia. S. Pacher. il map *The Mother Earth News* 115:70-4 Ja/F '89
Parks and reserves
See also
Okefenokee Swamp Park (Ga.)
Politics and government
Andrew Young taking fund-raising nationally [campaign to become first black governor] *Jet* 77:15 N 13 '89
Mr. Jones goes to D.C. [B. Jones] G. Jaynes. il *Life* 12:19 My '89
En route to Congress, actor Ben Jones first beat the bottle, then the incumbent. M. Brower. il pors *People Weekly* 31:38-40 Ja 30 '89
Race relations
Black fear: law and justice in rural Georgia. T. Branch. *The Washington Monthly* 21:70-2 F '89
GEORGIA (SOVIET UNION)
See also
Tbilisi (Soviet Union)
Nationalism
Communism's restless tribes. S. Jones. *World Press Review* 36:12-13 Je '89
The fires of discontent. J. Bierman. *Maclean's* 102:22 Ap 24 '89
'People feel no restraint'. C. Bogert. il *Newsweek* 114:28 Ag 14 '89
Summer of discontent. A. Wilson-Smith. il *Maclean's* 102:29 Jl 31 '89
U.S. physicians probe deaths in Soviet Georgia [use of riot control agent chloropicrin by Soviet troops] C. Norman. il *Science* 244:1133 Je 9 '89
With Georgia on his mind. N. Traver. il map *Time* 133:33 Ap 24 '89
GEORGIA GULF CORPORATION
Georgia Gulf may be ready to say 'I do'. G. G. Marcial. il *Business Week* p136 N 20 '89
GEORGIA INSTITUTE OF TECHNOLOGY
Hazard to your health [columnist excoriated after criticizing Georgia Tech's handling of violent incident involving football players] R. S. Johnson. por *Sports Illustrated* 70:77 F 27 '89
Pass the gravy, please [solicitation of corporate sponsors for home football games] D. Kindred. il por *Sports Illustrated* 70:96 My 15 '89

GEORGIAN ARCHITECTURE *See* Architecture, Georgian
GEORGIAN COOKING *See* Cooking, Georgian
GEORGIAN HOUSE DECORATION *See* House decoration, Georgian
GEORGOPOULOS, APOSTOLOS P., AND GRILLNER, STEN, 1941-
Visuomotor coordination in reaching and locomotion. bibl f *Science* 245:1209-10 S 15 '89
GEORGOPOULOS, APOSTOLOS P., AND OTHERS
Mental rotation of the neuronal population vector. bibl f il *Science* 243:234-6 Ja 13 '89
GEOSTATIONARY OPERATIONAL ENVIRONMENTAL SATELLITES *See* Artificial satellites—Meteorological use
GEOTANGENT DOMES
Surpassing the Buck [designed by J. Craig Yacoe] E. Corcoran. il *Scientific American* 261:102+ S '89
GEOTHERMAL ENERGY *See* Geothermal resources
GEOTHERMAL MEASUREMENTS *See* Earth temperature
GEOTHERMAL RESOURCES
See also
Hot springs
California
Drilling begins in search of molten energy [Long Valley Caldera] R. Monastersky. il *Science News* 136:101 Ag 12 '89
The furnace beneath us [drilling to the magma] G. Carroll. il *Newsweek* 114:55 Ag 28 '89
GEOTROPISM
See also
Plants, Effect of weightlessness on
Rapid redistribution of auxin-regulated RNAs during gravitropism. B. A. McClure and T. Guilfoyle. bibl f il *Science* 243:91-3 Ja 6 '89
GEPHARDT, RICHARD A.
U.S.-Japanese trade relations [address, March 20, 1989] *Vital Speeches of the Day* 55:450-4 My 15 '89
about
Man for all seasons. M. Kondracke. *The New Republic* 201:12-14 Jl 3 '89
Putting their House in order. E. Salholz. il pors *Newsweek* 113:18 Je 26 '89
The shifty Richard Gephardt [cover story] R. D. Novak. il *The American Spectator* 22:14-16 Ag '89
Trade hawk Gephardt pulls in his claws—a bit. P. Magnusson and D. Harbrecht. por *Business Week* p39 Ag 28 '89
GEPPI, STEVE
about
A business that outgrew nostalgia. M. Barrier. il por *Nation's Business* 77:22 D '89
GEPPI'S COMIC WORLD (FIRM)
A business that outgrew nostalgia. M. Barrier. il por *Nation's Business* 77:22 D '89
GERALDO [television program] *See* Television program reviews—Single works
GERARD, GIL
about
Gil Gerard: my weight cost me $1 million in TV roles. G. Esterly. il pors *TV Guide* 37:8-10 N 25-D 1 '89
GERARD, JIM
Dueling palates. il *Health (New York, N.Y.)* 21:85-6 Mr '89
GERASCHENKO, IGOR
about
In solitary cells on winter nights [interview] E. S. Vaughn. il pors *Christianity Today* 33:26-9 D 15 '89
GERBER, MERRILL JOAN
The adopted baby [story] il *Redbook* 173:66+ S '89
Ma's moving in! [story] *Redbook* 173:46+ Jl '89
Split ends [story] il *Seventeen* 48:128-9+ Ap '89
Staying with it. il *The Writer* 102:9-11 O '89
GERBER PRODUCTS CO.
Heating up the bottle battle [controversy over TV ads for Carnation and Gerber infant formulas; cover story] F. A. Oski. *The Nation* 249:665+ D 4 '89
GERBERAS
Gerberas are worth the price [cover story] S. P. Bender. il *Southern Living* 24:50-1 S '89
GERBERICH, STEPHEN J.
about
Windows. *The New Yorker* 65:40-1 O 2 '89
GERFEN, CHARLES R.
The neostriatal mosaic: striatal patch-matrix organization is related to cortical lamination. bibl f il *Science* 246:385-8 O 20 '89
GERGEN, KENNETH J., AND GERGEN, MARY M.
It's a love story. *Psychology Today* 22:48-9 D '88
GERGEN, MARY M.
(jt. auth) *See* Gergen, Kenneth J., and Gergen, Mary M.
GERHARDT, GARY
Land of death . . . and life. il map *National Wildlife* 28:34-40 D '89/Ja '90
GERIATRIC PSYCHIATRY *See* Aged—Psychiatric care
GERIATRICS *See* Aged—Care and hygiene; Aged—Medical care
GERLACH, JERRY
Spring break at Padre Island: a new kind of tourism. bibl il map *Focus (New York, N.Y.: 1950)* 39:13-16+ Spr '89

GERLACH, LUTHER P., AND WHITAKER, ELIZABETH D.
When the Land of Lakes went dry. il *Natural History* p62-4 Ja '89

GERLICH, BECKY
about
Mileage junkies. S. Martin. il pors *Bicycling* 30:48-50+ Ap '89

GERLICH, NICK
about
Mileage junkies. S. Martin. il pors *Bicycling* 30:48-50+ Ap '89

GERMAN, LINDA LOU
about
Babies were Linda German's obsession—was she crazy or just made in love? G. Stone. il pors *People Weekly* 31:84-8 Mr 20 '89

GERMAN ART *See* Art, German
GERMAN COMMUNICATIONS SATELLITES *See* Communications satellites, German
GERMAN COOKING *See* Cooking, German
GERMAN DRAWING *See* Drawing, German
GERMAN ESPIONAGE *See* Espionage, German
GERMAN GRAND PRIX *See* Automobile racing—Germany (West)
GERMAN HISTORIANS *See* Historians, German
GERMAN MEASLES *See* Rubella
GERMAN PAINTING *See* Painting, German
GERMAN REFUGEES *See* Refugees, German
GERMAN RESISTANCE MOVEMENT *See* Anti-Nazi movement—Germany
GERMAN REUNIFICATION QUESTION
Answering 'the German question'. J. Chace. *The New Republic* 201:19-20+ D 11 '89
Braking the juggernaut. S. Talbott. il *Time* 134:20 D 18 '89
Breaching the wall [exodus from East Germany] W. R. Doerner. il maps *Time* 134:32-4 S 11 '89
A chance to redraw the map. J. Barry. il *Newsweek* 114:49 N 20 '89
The death of the old order [opening of the Berlin Wall; cover story; with editorial comment by Stephen Budiansky] D. Stanglin and P. R. Range. il *U.S. News & World Report* 107:9, 20-2+ N 20 '89
A dog that doesn't bark. T. Sommer. il *Newsweek* 114:39 N 20 '89
East Germany: out of control. R. Watson. il *Newsweek* 114:32-4 D 18 '89
Facing up to the German question. R. Watson. il *Newsweek* 114:51-2 O 16 '89
The German question—again. M. B. Zuckerman. il *U.S. News & World Report* 107:92 O 23 '89
German questions. *The Nation* 249:587-8 N 20 '89
The German revolution. T. Garton Ash. il *The New York Review of Books* 36:14+ D 21 '89
How one fig leaf covered two Germanys. H. Trewhitt. map *U.S. News & World Report* 107:40 O 16 '89
In search of union. B. Came. il *Maclean's* 102:52 N 20 '89
The inescapable question. A. Nagorski. il *Newsweek* 114:32 O 2 '89
Is one Germany better than two? W. Isaacson. il maps *Time* 134:36+ N 20 '89
Kohl takes on topic A. D. Benjamin. il *Time* 134:45 D 11 '89
Lebensraum all over again [German claims on Polish territory] map *Newsweek* 114:25 Jl 24 '89
Living with the inevitable. H. Kissinger. il *Newsweek* 114:51-2+ D 4 '89
Minority report. C. Hitchens. *The Nation* 249:520 N 6 '89
No longer if but when. J. Borrell. il por *Time* 134:42-4 N 13 '89
The once and future German question. A.-M. Burley. bibl f *Foreign Affairs* 68:65-83 Wint '89/'90
One people, one country: a scenario [H. Kohl's speech] K. Breslau. il por *Newsweek* 114:34 D 11 '89
The quadrille of nations. G. F. Will. il *Newsweek* 114:84 D 18 '89
Recentralizing Europe. T. S. Molnar. *National Review* 41:34+ N 24 '89
The resurrection of the greater Reich? S. Sullivan. il *Newsweek* 114:56 N 13 '89
Return of the German question. C. Krauthammer. il *Time* 134:88 S 25 '89
Reunification? East German industry says 'not so fast'. G. E. Schares. il *Business Week* p66-7 D 25 '89-Ja 1 '90
Second thoughts on a unified Germany. J. Joffe. il *U.S. News & World Report* 107:46 N 27 '89
A state, not a nation. K. Prager. il *Time* 134:39-41 N 27 '89
Superpower disengagement. C. Layne. *Foreign Policy* 77:17-40 Wint '89/'90
Tearing down the Wall. S. Manning. il *Scholastic Update (Teachers' edition)* 122:13 O 20 '89
There goes the bloc. J. Smolowe. il map *Time* 134:48-51 N 6 '89
Uber alles? *National Review* 41:16+ O 13 '89

Ein Volk, ein Reich, ein Furor. B. Crozier. il *National Review* 41:26-7 O 27 '89
What if Germany . . . *World Press Review* 36:64 Ag '89
What the future holds. F. Painton. il *Time* 134:23+ D 18 '89
Whither Germany? J. H. Wolfe. il *USA Today (Periodical)* 118:73 S '89

GERMAN SHORT-HAIRED POINTERS
Anecdotes, facetiae, satire, etc.
The chase at pheasants. D. C. Proper. il *Field & Stream* 93:28-9 F '89
GERMAN SPACE VEHICLES *See* Space vehicles, German
GERMAN SPACEPLANE *See* Spaceplane, German
GERMAN TENNIS PLAYERS *See* Tennis players
GERMAN WINE ACADEMY
School days on the Rhine. G. Asher. il *Gourmet* 49:38+ Je '89
GERMANIUM IN THE BODY
Stopping toxic tablets. *FDA Consumer* 23:34-5 D '89/Ja '90

GERMANS
Great Britain
History
City freeman? [Hanseatic League's German enclave in medieval London] D. Keys. il *History Today* 39:4-5 D '89
Hungary
Where vacations can last forever [East German refugees reaching Austria via Hungary] map *U.S. News & World Report* 107:16 Ag 14 '89
United States
See also
Pennsylvania Germans
GERMANS IN MOTION PICTURES
Germans screened through French eyes. R. Prédal. il *The Unesco Courier* 42:18-23 O '89
GERMANY
See also
Berlin (Germany)
Germans
Jews—Germany
Romanticism—Germany
World War, 1939-1945—Campaigns and battles—Germany

Commerce
United States
See United States—Commerce—Germany
Foreign opinion
American
The conversion of Paul [P. H. Nitze's pro-Nazi sentiments] Z. Citron. *The New Republic* 200:33 Ja 30 '89
Foreign relations
Great Britain
See Great Britain—Foreign relations—Germany
Soviet Union
See Soviet Union—Foreign relations—Germany
History
1871-1918
See also
World War, 1914-1918—Germany
1918-1933
Correction [A. Hitler in Weimar Republic] N. Birnbaum. *The Nation* 248:617-18 My 8 '89
Stresemann and Weimar. J. Wright. bibl il pors *History Today* 39:35-41 O '89
1918-1933—Bibliography
No man's land. J. Joll. il *The New York Review of Books* 36:53-6 Ap 27 '89
1933-1945
See also
Anti-Nazi movement—Germany
Kristallnacht, 1938
National socialism
World War, 1939-1945—Germany
Minority report [Y. Shamir's involvement with Nazi Germany] C. Hitchens. *The Nation* 249:159 Ag 7-14 '89
What can England do about Hitler? [reprint from October 1938 issue] Sir W. Churchill. *Current History* 88:24-5+ Ja '89
1933-1945—Historiography
From Hirohito to Heimat. I. Buruma. *The New York Review of Books* 36:31-2+ O 26 '89
German historians at war. J. Z. Muller. bibl f *Commentary* 87:33-41 My '89
Industries
See also
Gebrüder Bing (Firm)
Nationalism
Universality and national identity. A. Finkielkraut. bibl f il pors *The Unesco Courier* 42:30-3 Je '89
Religious institutions and affairs
See also
Christians—Germany
Protestant churches—Germany
GERMANY (DEMOCRATIC REPUBLIC) *See* Germany (East)
GERMANY (EAST)
See also
Americans—Germany (East)

GERMANY (EAST)—See also—*cont.*
  Art and state—Germany (East)
  Berlin (Germany: East)
  Civil rights—Germany (East)
  Leipzig (Germany)
  Music festivals—Germany (East)
  Opera—Germany (East)
  Peace movement—Germany (East)
  Protests, demonstrations, etc.—Germany (East)
  Sports and state—Germany (East)
  Television and politics—Germany (East)

Economic conditions
The economic Wall. E. Rubenstein. il *National Review* 41:22 D 22 '89

Foreign relations
  See also
  Berlin question, 1945-
Honecker and the 'lesson of history'. M. R. Meyer and S. Sullivan. por *Newsweek* 113:45 Je 19 '89
      Germany (West)
  See Germany (West)—Foreign relations—Germany (East)
      Hungary
The great escape [Hungary grants East Germans passage across Austrian border] J. Smolowe. il map *Time* 134:30-2 S 25 '89

Industries
Reunification? East German industry says 'not so fast'. G. E. Schares. il *Business Week* p66-7 D 25 '89-Ja 1 '90

Politics and government
  See also
  Communist Party (Germany: East)
  New Forum (Germany: East)
  Politics, Corruption in—Germany (East)
Adjusting to change. J. Bierman. il *Maclean's* 102:28+ N 27 '89
As the Wall came tumbling down. J. Agee. il *The New York Times Magazine* p42-3+ N 26 '89
The choice for East Germany. D. R. Shanor. il por *The New Leader* 72:3-4 O 30 '89
Dateline East Germany: the wall behind the Wall. D. Hamilton. *Foreign Policy* 76:176-97 Fall '89
The death of the old order [opening of the Berlin Wall; cover story; with editorial comment by Stephen Budiansky] D. Stanglin and P. R. Range. il *U.S. News & World Report* 107:9, 20-2+ N 20 '89
East Berlin diary; tr. by Phillip Boehm. C. Hein. il *The New York Times Magazine* p34-7+ D 17 '89
East Germans go west. *Commonweal* 116:580-1 N 3 '89
East Germany: clinging to the hard line—and taking a hard fall. G. E. Schares and J. Templeman. il por *Business Week* p28-9 S 4 '89
East Germany: coping with Gorbachev. D. Childs. bibl f *Current History* 88:385-8+ N '89
East Germany: out of control. R. Watson. il *Newsweek* 114:32-4 D 18 '89
East Germany: the more things change . . . B. W. Nelan. il *Time* 134:33 S 25 '89
East Germany's winds of change. J. Bierman. *Maclean's* 102:34 D 4 '89
'Egon, here we come'. M. R. Meyer. il *Newsweek* 114:52 N 13 '89
'Feeling our way to the future'. R. Watson. il *Newsweek* 114:36-7 O 23 '89
The flight to freedom. H. Anderson. il por *Newsweek* 114:40-3+ O 16 '89
Freedom! [opening of Berlin Wall; cover story; special section] il *Time* 134:24-30+ N 20 '89
Freedom train. W. R. Doerner. il *Time* 134:38-41+ O 16 '89
The German revolution. T. Garton Ash. il *The New York Review of Books* 36:14+ D 21 '89
The great escape [cover story; special section; with editorial comment by Kevin Doyle] il *Maclean's* 102:8, 32-6+ O 16 '89
He stopped the shooting [interview with E. Krenz] J. O. Jackson and F. Ungeheuer. por *Time* 134:46-7 D 11 '89
In East Germany, 'order' crumbles and danger grows [E. Krenz ousted] P. R. Range. il *U.S. News & World Report* 107:24-5 D 18 '89
Krenz is cast from Honecker's mold. Now, can he break it? J. Templeman. il por *Business Week* p49 O 30 '89
Krenz takes charge. A. Phillips. il pors *Maclean's* 102:50+ O 30 '89
Lending an ear. J. Smolowe. il *Time* 134:44-5 O 23 '89
A model apparatchik [E. Krenz succeeds E. Honecker] R. Watson. il pors *Newsweek* 114:52-3 O 30 '89
No longer if but when. J. Borrell. il por *Time* 134:42-4 N 13 '89
Of turncoats and scapegoats. F. Painton. il *Time* 134:29 D 4 '89
One people still divided [ramifications of East Germans' flight into West Germany] H. Anderson. il *Newsweek* 114:27 S 25 '89
Opening up a new Europe? G. Minnerup. il *The Nation* 249:672-4 D 4 '89
Out of control? J. Smolowe. il *Time* 134:14-17 D 18 '89

A Politburo gives ground. J. Bierman. il *Maclean's* 102:28-30 O 23 '89
A purge of hard-liners. J. Bierman. *Maclean's* 102:37 N 13 '89
Rigid but prosperous. *Time* 133:48 Mr 27 '89
Rusting Iron Curtain. E. von Kuehnelt-Leddihn. il *National Review* 41:25 N 10 '89
A society deep in crisis. R. Watson. il maps *Newsweek* 114:31-2+ N 20 '89
They came, they saw, they went back to work [East Germans return home after seeing the West] R. Z. Chesnoff and R. Knight. il *U.S. News & World Report* 107:42-3 N 27 '89
Trading places [E. Krenz succeeds E. Honecker] J. Smolowe. il por *Time* 134:60-2 O 30 '89
Turmoil behind the wall. J. Altman. il *U.S. News & World Report* 107:38-9 O 16 '89
Up against the Wall in East Berlin. G. E. Schares. il *Business Week* p48-9 N 20 '89

Religious institutions and affairs
  See also
  Christians—Germany (East)
  Church and social problems—Germany (East)
  Protestant churches—Germany (East)
GERMANY (FEDERAL REPUBLIC) *See* Germany (West)
GERMANY (WEST)
  See also
  Acid rain—Germany (West)
  Airplanes, Training—Germany (West)
  Americans—Germany (West)
  Anti-nuclear movement—Germany (West)
  Anti-Semitism—Germany (West)
  Art—Germany (West)
  Art and state—Germany (West)
  Art galleries and museums—Germany (West)
  Automobile racing—Germany (West)
  Aviation and state—Germany (West)
  Baden-Baden (Germany)
  Berlin (Germany: West)
  Business management—Germany (West)
  Collective bargaining—Germany (West)
  Colleges and universities—Germany (West)
  Conscientious objectors—Germany (West)
  Criminal justice, Administration of—Germany (West)
  Dance—Germany (West)
  Education—Germany (West)
  Featherbedding (Industrial relations)—Germany (West)
  Flower gardens and gardening—Germany (West)
  Forests and forestry—Germany (West)
  Frankfurt am Main (Germany)
  Genetic research—Laws and regulations—Germany (West)
  Hackers (Computer enthusiasts)—Germany (West)
  Hamburg (Germany)
  Hours of labor—Germany (West)
  Immigration and emigration—Germany (West)
  Intelligence service—Germany (West)
  Interest (Economics)—Germany (West)
  Investments, West German
  Jews—Germany (West)
  Kelheim (Germany)
  Labor supply—Germany (West)
  Lake Constance
  Leveraged buyouts—Germany (West)
  Medical research—Germany (West)
  Money—Germany (West)
  Morale, National—Germany (West)
  Motion picture festivals—Germany (West)
  Motion pictures—Germany (West)
  Munich (Germany)
  Music festivals—Germany (West)
  Neo-Nazis—Germany (West)
  Opera—Germany (West)
  Paleontology—Germany (West)
  Participative management—Germany (West)
  Poles—Germany (West)
  Public health—Germany (West)
  Radioactive waste disposal—Laws and regulations—Germany (West)
  Rhine River
  Roads—Germany (West)
  Self help groups—Germany (West)
  Soccer—Germany (West)
  Television and politics—Germany (West)
  Tennis—Germany (West)
  Transplantation of organs, tissues, etc.—Germany (West)
  Video games—Germany (West)
  Vocational-technical education—Germany (West)

Air Force
West Germany eyes larger Air Force role in ground support. J. D. Morrocco. il *Aviation Week & Space Technology* 131:39+ O 30 '89

Commerce
  Developing countries
At your service [munitions trade] M. Brzoska. bibl f *The Bulletin of the Atomic Scientists* 45:34 Jl/Ag '89

GERMANY (WEST)—Commerce—cont.
Iran
More German dealing in the poison trade [selling chemical weapons to Iran] *Newsweek* 114:28 Jl 10 '89
Japan
Infiniti and Lexus: characters in a German nightmare. J. Templeman. il *Business Week* p64 O 9 '89
Libya
Anger and recrimination [government knowledge of West German firms' participation in construction of Libyan gas plant] J. O. Jackson. il *Time* 133:34 Ja 30 '89
Bonn finally comes clean [Imhausen-Chemie implicated in Libya's chemical weapons plant] M. G. Warner and T. Waldrop. il *Newsweek* 113:32 Ja 23 '89
Libya's chemical weapons plant [State Dept. statement, January 1, 1989] *Department of State Bulletin* 89:71 Mr '89
The new merchants of death [West German link to manufacture of chemical weapons by Libya] il *World Press Review* 36:13-14 Mr '89
On second thought [Imhausen-Chemie's role in building Libyan gas plant] W. R. Doerner. il *Time* 133:30-1 Ja 23 '89
A self-inflicted wound [West Germany's role in Libyan poison gas scandal] M. R. Meyer. il *Newsweek* 113:42 Ja 30 '89
Middle East
The curious case of chemical warfare. M. Ledeen. *Commentary* 88:37-41 Jl '89
Soviet Union
See Soviet Union—Commerce—Germany (West)
United States
See United States—Commerce—Germany (West)
Commercial policy
Behind the German export scandals [weapons trade] M. Brzoska. bibl f il *The Bulletin of the Atomic Scientists* 45:32-5 Jl/Ag '89
Learning to live with export controls [U.S. upset with lax attitude toward technology exports] L. Lief. il *U.S. News & World Report* 106:28 Ja 23 '89
Selling security for deutschemarks [R. Mueller gets suspended sentence for selling military technology to the Soviets] R. N. Perle. il *U.S. News & World Report* 107:36 Jl 31 '89
Cultural relations
Soviet Union
See Soviet Union—Cultural relations—Germany (West)
Defenses
See also
Airplanes, Military—Germany (West)
Germany (West)—Air Force
Guided missiles, German
North Atlantic Treaty Organization
United States. Air Force—Forces in Germany (West)
United States. Army—Forces in Germany (West)
Germany's attention wanders. *National Review* 41:14 Mr 24 '89
Economic conditions
See also
Inflation (Finance)—Germany (West)
The economic Wall. E. Rubenstein. il *National Review* 41:22 D 22 '89
Robust growth abroad will help keep the U.S. economy on track. R. E. Norton. il *Fortune* 120:15-16 N 6 '89
Economic relations
See also
Economic assistance, German
Japan and Germany: American concerns. J. E. Garten. il *Foreign Affairs* 68:84-101 Wint '89/'90
Eastern Europe
'We have an interest in the East'. H. Anderson. il *Newsweek* 114:55-6 N 13 '89
The West German mark may soon rule the East. B. Riemer and J. Kapstein. il *Business Week* p65 N 27 '89
Japan
Japan and Germany: American concerns. J. E. Garten. il *Foreign Affairs* 68:84-101 Wint '89/'90
Soviet Union
See Soviet Union—Economic relations—Germany (West)
United States
See United States—Economic relations—Germany (West)
Western Europe
In the eye of the storm. D. Lawday. il *U.S. News & World Report* 107:46-8 N 6 '89
Why should Europe dance to Germany's economic tune? B. Riemer. il *Business Week* p76 O 23 '89
Foreign relations
Appeasement in our time [Foreign Minister H. D. Genscher; cover story] H. Walter. il por *National Review* 41:26-8+ Je 2 '89
West Germany [special section] il *World Press Review* 36:28-31 My '89
Eastern Europe
Bonn's ostpolitik for the '90s. M. R. Meyer. il *Newsweek* 113:24 My 15 '89

In the eye of the storm. D. Lawday. il *U.S. News & World Report* 107:46-8 N 6 '89
Moving on double tracks: deterrence and détente. T. Garton Ash. il *World Press Review* 36:28-9 My '89
Recentralizing Europe. T. S. Molnar. *National Review* 41:34+ N 24 '89
The resurrection of the greater Reich? S. Sullivan. il *Newsweek* 114:56 N 13 '89
Germany (East)
See also
Berlin question, 1945-
Berlin Wall, 1961-1989
German reunification question
Bring down the Wall. E. Mortimer. *World Press Review* 36:31 My '89
The once and future German question. A.-M. Burley. bibl f *Foreign Affairs* 68:65-83 Wint '89/'90
Poland
Is it our Danzig—or your Gdansk? *Newsweek* 113:34 Mr 6 '89
Lebensraum all over again [German claims on Polish territory] map *Newsweek* 114:25 Jl 24 '89
Soviet Union
See Soviet Union—Foreign relations—Germany (West)
United States
See United States—Foreign relations—Germany (West)
Industries
See also
Aerospace industries—Acquisitions and mergers—Germany (West)
Aerospace industries—Germany (West)
Audi AG
Automobile factories—Germany (West)
Bayer AG
Bayerische Motoren Werke AG
Bertelsmann AG
Daimler-Benz AG
Deutsche Aerospace AG
Dornier GmbH
Escada AG
Gebrüder Märklin (Firm)
Genetic research industry—Germany (West)
Hoechst AG
Hoogovens Aluminium GmbH
Imhausen-Chemie (Firm)
Kayser-Threde GmbH
LTU Lufttransport Unt GmbH & Co. KG
Lufthansa
Melitta-Werke Bentz & Sohn
Messerschmitt-Bölkow-Blohm GmbH
Michael Zoche (Firm)
MPC Aircraft GmbH
Munitions—Germany (West)
Nixdorf Computer AG
Nuclear industry—Germany (West)
Porsche AG
Real estate business—Germany (West)
Rheineisen Chemical Products
Siemens AG
Springer-Verlag GmbH & Co. KG
Tengelmann Group
Transnuklear GmbH
Politics and government
See also
Green Party (Germany: West)
Political attitudes—Germany (West)
Politics, Corruption in—Germany (West)
Anger and recrimination [government knowledge of firms' participation in construction of Libyan gas plant] J. O. Jackson. il *Time* 133:34 Ja 30 '89
Federal Republic of Germany [address, April 27, 1989] H. Kohl. *Vital Speeches of the Day* 55:482-6 Je 1 '89
Fighting off the beer-hall boys. N. Birnbaum. il *The Nation* 248:588-9+ My 1 '89
The perilous trek of Helmut Kohl. R. Knight. il *U.S. News & World Report* 106:28-9 Je 5 '89
West Germany [special section] il *World Press Review* 36:28-31 My '89
Western Europe's man in the middle [H. Kohl] D. Lawday. il por *U.S. News & World Report* 107:45 D 11 '89
Population
See also
Immigrants—Germany (West)
Religious institutions and affairs
See also
Christians—Germany (West)
Protestant churches—Germany (West)
GERMANY (WEST) AND FRANCE *See* France and Germany (West)
GERMANY (WEST) AND THE UNITED STATES
See also
United States—Foreign opinion—German
GERMPLASM RESOURCES
Plants
See also
Seed Savers Exchange
Bad seeds in Nicaragua. B. Weinberg. *The Nation* 249:50+ Jl 10 '89

GERMPLASM RESOURCES—Plants—cont.

Blueprint for conserving plant diversity. C. Mlot. il *BioScience* 39:364-8 Je '89

A center of crop genetic diversity in western Amazonia. C. R. Clement. bibl f il maps *BioScience* 39:624-31 O '89

Quarantine and the exchange of crop genetic resources. D. L. Plucknett and N. J. H. Smith. bibl f il *BioScience* 39:16-23 Ja '89

GEROMEL, GENE

A good start for new hires. il *Nation's Business* 77:21+ Ja '89

GERONTOLOGY

Slowing down the march of time. T. Prentice. *World Press Review* 36:31-2 F '89

GERRYMANDER

Avoiding the Burtonmander [Republicans must win state elections so as to avoid gerrymandering] S. T. Mandel. *National Review* 41:17 D 22 '89

Beware the gerrymander, my son. J. H. Fund. il *National Review* 41:34-6 Ap 7 '89

Divide & conquer. F. Kuznik. il *Common Cause Magazine* 15:13-16 My/Je '89

Let the great gerrymander war begin [effects of reapportionment after 1990 census] P. R. Range. il map *U.S. News & World Report* 106:29-30 F 20 '89

One-man/one-vote Gingrich. W. F. Buckley. *National Review* 41:62 My 5 '89

GERSHMAN, CARL

Democracy as the wave of the future. *Current (Washington, D.C.)* 312:18-25 My '89

GERSHWIN, GEORGE, 1898-1937

about

Gershwin crazy. S. Elliott. il pors *Opera News* 54:12-14+ Ag '89

Porgy and Bess [opera] Reviews

New York il 22:105 O 16 '89. P. G. Davis

GERSHWIN, IRA, 1896-1983

about

Gershwin crazy. S. Elliott. il pors *Opera News* 54:12-14+ Ag '89

GERSI, MAROUSSIA

about

Out of Africa. M. J. Wilcove. il *Omni (New York, N.Y.)* 12:32+ O '89

GERSTENFELD, SHELDON L.

Pet set. See occasional issues of Parents

GERSTNER, LOUIS V., JR.

about

Lou Gerstner is girding for a long, hard campaign. S. Ticer. il por *Business Week* p32-3 Mr 27 '89

Louis Gerstner. S. Ticer. il por *Business Week* Special Issue:96 Ap 14 '89

RJR's gain could mean pain for Amex. F. A. Miller. il *Business Week* p33 Mr 27 '89

Running the biggest LBO [cover story] J. H. Dobrzynski. il pors *Business Week* p72-5+ O 2 '89

GERTZ, ALISON

about

Alison Gertz: Woman of the Year. il por *Esquire* 112:102-3 Ag '89

Alison's fight for life. M. Jacobbi. il pors *Good Housekeeping* 209:196-7+ S '89

GERTZ, ELIZABETH

about

Old world treasures in Dallas. M. Ennis. il por *Architectural Digest* 46:120-9+ Ag '89

GERTZ, GEOFFRY

about

New talents: Geoffry Gertz. N. Malkin. il por *Harper's Bazaar* 122:88 Mr '89

GERTZ, JAMI

about

Catch a rising star. pors *'Teen* 33:67 Ag '89

GERVASI, FRANK HENRY, 1908-1990

about

More fascinating lives. L. Fleischer. *Publishers Weekly* 235:72 Je 30 '89

GESELL, GERHARD

about

Gesell: Solomon with a chain saw. B. Turque. il por *Newsweek* 113:36 My 15 '89

A silver head and a steady gavel. il por *U.S. News & World Report* 106:13-14 F 27 '89

GESSLER, MANFRED, AND OTHERS

Cloning of breakpoints of a chromosome translocation identifies the AN2 locus. bibl f il *Science* 244:1575-8 Je 30 '89

GESTATION See Pregnancy

GESTATION IN ANIMALS See Pregnancy in animals

GESTURE

See also

Sign language

Hidden messages [gestures in different countries] E. Ferrieux. il *World Press Review* 36:39 Jl '89

GETLIN, JOSH

Mr. Clean's Air Act [interview with H. Waxman] il pors *Sierra* 74:76-81 N/D '89

GETTING IT RIGHT [film] See Motion picture reviews—Single works

GETTY, ANN

about

Ann Getty: publish and perish? A. Begley. il pors *The New York Times Magazine* p36-7+ O 22 '89

GETTY, DON

about

Post-election realities. P. Kopvillem. il por *Maclean's* 102:18+ Je 12 '89

A quarterback sack. J. Howse. il por *Maclean's* 102:14 Ap 3 '89

GETTY, ESTELLE

If I knew then what I know now . . . so what? [excerpt]; ed. by Steve Delsohn. il pors *Redbook* 172:60+ Ja '89

GETTY, GORDON P.

about

The Gettys. G. Jaynes. il pors *Life* 12:168-72 Mr '89

GETTY, PAUL BALTHAZAR

about

Lord of the flies: two new teen stars take on a challenging movie. pors *'Teen* 33:54 S '89

GETTY (J. PAUL) MUSEUM See J. Paul Getty Museum

GETTY CENTER FOR EDUCATION IN THE ARTS

The great art education debate [discipline-based art education] M. Moorman. il *Art News* 88:124-31 Summ '89

GETTYSBURG, BATTLE OF, 1863

The children of Gettysburg. E. Daniels. il *American Heritage* 40:97-101+ My/Je '89

Civil War photo diary: re-creating Gettysburg: summer of 1863. J. Marvullo. il *Petersen's Photographic Magazine* 18:24-6+ Ag '89

Collectibles

America's Memorial Day coin! [half-dollar commemorating 75th anniversary of the Battle of Gettysburg] E. Rochette. il *Antiques & Collecting Hobbies* 94:68-9 My '89

GETTYSBURG (PA.)

Description

This hallowed ground. V. Frontero. il map *New York* 22:74-6 O 9 '89

GETTYSBURG NATIONAL MILITARY PARK (PA.)

This hallowed ground. V. Frontero. il map *New York* 22:74-6 O 9 '89

Photographs and photography

Civil War photo diary: re-creating Gettysburg: summer of 1863. J. Marvullo. il *Petersen's Photographic Magazine* 18:24-6+ Ag '89

GETZ, STAN, 1927-

about

Meet Dr. Getz [reprint] J. A. Tynan. il por *Down Beat* 56:43-4 S '89

GEVA, TAMARA

about

Golden girl. *The New Yorker* 65:39-41 O 16 '89

GEVISSER, MARK

Moving to the next stage. il *The Nation* 249:674+ D 4 '89

Time stands still. *The Nation* 249:390-3 O 9 '89

GEWEN, BARRY

Writers & writing. See occasional issues of The New Leader

GEWIRTZ, ALAN M., AND OTHERS

G_1/S transition in normal human T-lymphocytes requires the nuclear protein encoded by c-*myb*. bibl f il *Science* 245:180-3 Jl 14 '89

GEYER, GEORGIE ANNE

Joy in our times [address, May 7, 1989] *Vital Speeches of the Day* 55:666-8 Ag 15 '89

GEZAIRY, HUSSEIN A.

Health is a human right. il *World Health* p2-3 Jl '89

GFCIS See Ground fault circuit interrupters

GHANA

Politics and government

See also

Populism—Ghana

GHAREKHAN, C. R.

Super power detente [address, June 16, 1989] *Vital Speeches of the Day* 55:644-7 Ag 15 '89

GHENT (BELGIUM)

Art

Artists in residences [installations in private houses] K. Baker. il *House & Garden* 161:38+ Ja '89

GHERMEZIAN FAMILY

about

Blue-sky planning. J. Daly. il *Maclean's* 102:38 Ag 21 '89

Will wonders never cease? J. Queenan. il *Forbes* 144:72-3+ S 4 '89

GHETTO [drama] See Sobol, Joshua

GHETTOS See Slums

GHIGNA, CHARLES

The price of perspiration [poem] il *Good Housekeeping* 209:293 S '89

GHINI, MASSIMO IOSA See Iosa Ghini, Massimo

GHIZ, JOE

about

The Island campaign. B. MacAndrew. il por *Maclean's* 102:20 My 22 '89

A Liberal landslide. G. Allen. il por *Maclean's* 102:17 Je 12 '89

GHODA, L., AND OTHERS
Prevention of rapid intracellular degradation of ODC by a carboxyl-terminal truncation. bibl f il *Science* 243:1493-5 Mr 17 '89
GHOST STORIES
See also
Horror tales
Tales from the basement. J. Garvey. il *Commonweal* 116:553-4 O 20 '89
Things that go bump in the mind. R. Nalley. *Omni (New York, N.Y.)* 12:33 N '89
GHOST TOWNS
See also
Cisco (Utah)
GHOSTBUSTERS (FICTIONAL CHARACTERS)
Who you gonna call if you want your kid's party to gel? Try faux Ghostbuster Peter Mosen. il por *People Weekly* 32:115 Jl 17 '89
GHOSTBUSTERS II [film] See Motion picture reviews—Single works
GHOSTS
Families who believe their houses are haunted—do you? J. Kelman. il *Redbook* 173:40+ O '89
Ghost busters at work. J. Wolkomir and R. Wolkomir. il *McCall's* 116:104+ Jl '89
Hosts of ghosts [haunted historic houses] G. Turim. il *Americana* 17:21-4 S/O '89
Southern spirits [haunted dwellings in Georgetown, S.C.] S. Baker. il *Omni (New York, N.Y.)* 12:28+ D '89
GHOSTWRITING See Authorship—Collaboration
GI JOE DOLLS
The story of GI Joe. L. Rosenkrantz. il *Antiques & Collecting Hobbies* 94:21 D '89
GIACCO, ALEXANDER F.
about
Defying the law of gravity. A. A. Lappen. il por *Forbes* 143:76-7 Ap 3 '89
GIACCONE, CESARE
about
Hail, Cesare! J. Steingarten. il por *Vogue* 179:600-1+ S '89
GIACCONI, RICCARDO
Heaven's scope. il *Omni (New York, N.Y.)* 11:20 Ag '89
GIACOMETTI, ALBERTO, 1901-1966
about
Alberto Giacometti: Hirshhorn Museum and Sculpture Garden. V. H. Winner. il *Art News* 88:149 Ja '89
Giacometti without tears. P. Brach. il *Art in America* 77:61+ Je '89
Giacometti's code. A. Arikha. il pors *The New York Review of Books* 36:20+ My 18 '89
GIAMATTI, A. BARTLETT, 1938-1989
Giamatti: talking baseball [excerpts from Take time for paradise] il por *Newsweek* 114:87-8 N 6 '89
about
A gentleman and a scholar. F. Deford. il pors *Sports Illustrated* 70:86-90+ Ap 17 '89
Obituary
America 161:130 S 9-16 '89. G. W. Hunt
National Review 41:20 S 29 '89. W. F. Buckley
Newsweek il por 114:49 S 11 '89. G. Hackett
People Weekly il por 32:56-7 S 18 '89. K. Gross
Sports Illustrated por 71:17 S 11 '89. S. Wulf
Of many things. G. W. Hunt. *America* 160:338 Ap 15 '89
Professor Hardball [cover story] B. Welling and W. C. Symonds. il pors *Business Week* p84-8 Ap 3 '89
Undying words from the front office. il por *U.S. News & World Report* 107:12 D 18 '89
Anecdotes, facetiae, satire, etc.
Baseball: not the movie. J. Leo. il *U.S. News & World Report* 107:54 Jl 10 '89
GIAMMETTI, GIANCARLO
about
Tuscan pastoral [cover story] C. Maclean. il por *House & Garden* 161:146-59+ S '89
GIANT FOOD INC.
Why Giant Foods is a gargantuan success. D. Foust. il por *Business Week* p80 D 4 '89
GIANT PANDAS See Pandas
GIANT STARS See Stars, Giant
GIANTURCO, MICHAEL
Insights. See issues of Forbes beginning May 1, 1989
GIAQUINTO, EUGENE F.
about
MCA suspends video head for allegedly funneling funds to Mafia. P. Sweeting. *Publishers Weekly* 235:27 Ja 13 '89
GIARDIA See Protozoa, Pathogenic
GIARDIASIS
"Don't drink the water". C. Slom. *McCall's* 116:86+ Jl '89
Don't go near the water. P. G. Gill. il *Outdoor Life* 183:58-9+ Ja '89
GIARDINA, DENISE, 1951-
A coal-field victory. il *The Progressive* 53:14-15 Mr '89
Solidarity in Appalachia. il *The Nation* 249:12-14 Jl 3 '89
GIARELLI, ANDREW
Regional report: Asia/Pacific. See issues of World Press Review beginning October 1986

GIBB, TOM
(jt. auth) See Farah, Douglas, and Gibb, Tom
GIBBONEY, RICHARD A.
The unscientific character of educational research. bibl f il *Phi Delta Kappan* 71:225-7 N '89
GIBBONS, ANN
Making plastics that biodegrade. il *Technology Review* 92:69-73 F/Mr '89
GIBBONS, BARBARA
Tête à tête dining. il *Modern Maturity* 32:72-4+ Ap/My '89
GIBBONS, BARRY J.
about
Can a new CEO pull Burger King out of the fire? P. Engardio. il *Business Week* p40 My 22 '89
The publican at Burger King. P. Sellers. il por *Fortune* 119:68 Mr 13 '89
Trying to get Burger King out of the flames. M. Maremont. il por *Business Week* p29-30 Ja 30 '89
GIBBONS, FRED
Fitting PCs to small business needs. por *Personal Computing* 13:232 O '89
about
Driving a company from the back seat. R. Brandt. il por *Business Week* p96 Ag 21 '89
GIBBONS, GRINLING, 1648-1721
about
Grinling Gibbons. G. W. Beard. bibl f il por *Antiques* 135:1444-55 Je '89
GIBBONS, JOHN H., 1929-, AND OTHERS
Strategies for energy use. bibl il *Scientific American* 261:136-43 S '89
GIBBS, JERRY
Fishing. See issues of Outdoor Life
GIBBS, TERESA L.
Call me the hunter. *Harper's* 278:20 Mr '89
GIBBS, TONY
Semper paratus. il *The New Yorker* 65:45-6+ Ag 7 '89
GIBLIN, JAMES, 1933-
Common failings in juvenile fiction—and how to correct them. *The Writer* 102:15-18 Jl '89
Picture books from A to Z. *The Writer* 102:18-21 N '89
GIBSON, BILL
about
Raise the Rio! J. Grissim. il map *Oceans* 22:30-7+ Mr/Ap '89
GIBSON, BOB D.
A gamble that paid off. il por *Nation's Business* 77:30 Ja '89
SETI: putting an ear to the universe [cover story] il *Ad Astra* 1:8-9+ S '89
GIBSON, C. B.
Parenting my parents. il *Glamour* 87:296 Mr '89
GIBSON, DANIEL
Land of disenchantment. il *Sierra* 74:38+ Mr/Ap '89
GIBSON, DEBBIE
about
Debbie: the modern day Gibson girl talks . . . [interview] P. Dell. por *Teen* 33:49 O '89
Good times for that Gibson girl. M. Hammer. il pors *Ladies' Home Journal* 106:124 Mr '89
Island hopping with Debbie Gibson. il por *Rolling Stone* p17 Jl 13-27 '89
She's the boss. B. Stepko. il pors *Seventeen* 48:92-3 Jl '89
GIBSON, EDIE
The sisterhood of sleuths. il *Publishers Weekly* 235:37-9 My 5 '89
GIBSON, HARVEY
about
The Hannes Schneider story. N. Howe. il pors *Skiing* 41:126-9+ Mr '89
GIBSON, HELEN
Hair, dust and sky. il por *International Wildlife* 19:52-9 S/O '89
GIBSON, HOOT
about
Old postcards featuring famous people: Hoot Gibson. C. Thompson. por *Antiques & Collecting Hobbies* 94:68 Mr '89
GIBSON, JANICE T.
As they grow/1-year-olds. See issues of Parents beginning January 1984
GIBSON, MATTHEW
Kidnapping
Deaths in the name of life [R. and J. Lynch accused of murder and kidnapping in Delaware] G. Cerio. il por *Newsweek* 113:29 My 8 '89
GIBSON, MEL
about
Mel Gibson [cover story] L. Hirschberg. il pors *Rolling Stone* p38-9+ Ja 12 '89
GIBSON, ROGER
about
Hockey night in Battle Creek. S. Rushin. il por *Sports Illustrated* 70:14 Mr 27 '89

GIBSON, ROGER
about

An expert on risk says you can make money in stocks without losing sleep. C. Willis. il por *Money* 18:205-6 N '89

GIBSON, SHARAN
Classroom dialogues. il *Phi Delta Kappan* 70:553-5 Mr '89

GIBSON, VERNA
about

It's turnaround time for Verna Gibson. S. Phillips. il por *Business Week* p117-18 F 20 '89

GIBSON, WILLIAM, 1948-
Rocket radio. il *Rolling Stone* p84-6+ Je 15 '89
about

Video scans. B. Lindstrom. il *Omni (New York, N.Y.)* 12:166 O '89

GIBSON, WILLIAM E.
about

So you think buying a sick thrift is just a license to print money. K. Kelly. il pors *Business Week* p78-9 Je 19 '89

GIBSON, WILLIAM FRANK
about

NAACP's Gibson urges new tactics to keep set asides. por *Jet* 75:29 Mr 13 '89

GIBSON CAPITAL MANAGEMENT
An expert on risk says you can make money in stocks without losing sleep [views of R. Gibson] C. Willis. il por *Money* 18:205-6 N '89

GIDEON OLIVER [television program] See Television program reviews—Single works

GIDEONSE, HENDRIK
about

NCATE and Texas eyeball to eyeball: who will blink? [interview] D. Watts. il *Phi Delta Kappan* 71:311-18 D '89

GIDRON, DICK
about

Driven by excellence. K. D. Thompson. il pors *Black Enterprise* 19:236-40 Je '89

GIDRON (DICK) CADILLAC & FORD INC. *See* Dick Gidron Cadillac & Ford Inc.

GIEBULTOWICZ, J. M., AND OTHERS
Circadian system controlling release of sperm in the insect testes. bibl f il *Science* 245:1098-100 S 8 '89

GIELGUD, SIR JOHN, 1904-
about

Further thoughts on Olivier. R. Brustein. *The New Republic* 201:25-6 O 9 '89

GIERKE, H. F.
Should a constitutional amendment to prevent flag desecration be approved? [excerpts from testimony, July 20, 1989] *Congressional Digest* 68:218+ Ag/S '89

GIESEKING, HAL
The travel advisor. See issues of Travel Holiday through January 1990

GIFFORD, BARRY, 1946-
about

Grove's 'Wild at heart' gets a running start. *Publishers Weekly* 236:29 D 8 '89

GIFFORD, BERNARD R.
about

A teacher for Apple. A. Edmond, Jr. il pors *Black Enterprise* 19:176-8 F '89

GIFFORD, CHARLIE
about

The Caligari Club. *The New Yorker* 65:39-41 N 27 '89

GIFFORD, FRANK
about

Frank Gifford. H. F. Waters. por *Gentlemen's Quarterly* 59:278-9 N '89

GIFFORD, HENRY
The real thing. il *The New York Review of Books* 36:3-4+ Je 1 '89

GIFT, ROLAND
about

Fine Young Cannibal Roland Gift has it all: great voice, good looks and a juicy Scandal. S. Dougherty. il pors *People Weekly* 31:145-6 My 1 '89
Gift wrapped for a ruckus. J. Cocks. il por *Time* 133:87 My 29 '89
Looking a Gift horse in the mouth [cover story] S. Pond. il pors *Rolling Stone* p44-5+ O 5 '89
Presence. M. Glicksman. por *Film Comment* 25:68-9 Mr/Ap '89
Soul kiss. J. Leland. por *Vogue* 179:256 Ap '89

GIFT *See* Gamete intrafallopian transfer

GIFT FAIRS
The New York International Gift Fair. M. A. Tennenhouse. il *Publishers Weekly* 236:31-2 S 22 '89

GIFT SHOPS
See also
Museum stores

GIFT WRAPPING *See* Wrapping of packages

GIFTED CHILDREN *See* Children, Gifted

GIFTS
See also
Art galleries and museums—Gifts, legacies, etc.
Black colleges and universities—Gifts, legacies, etc.
Books as gifts
Christmas gifts
Colleges and universities—Gifts, legacies, etc.
Diplomatic gifts
Food as gifts
Giving
Money as gifts
Museums—Gifts, legacies, etc.
Phonograph records as gifts
Plants as gifts
Valentine's Day gifts
Video games as gifts
Videotapes as gifts
Wedding gifts
Wine as gifts
Wrapping of packages

Bring me no flowers [hostess gifts] M. Filler. il *House & Garden* 161:68+ F '89
Gandee at large [advice of S. Marcus] C. K. Gandee. il por *House & Garden* 161:178 D '89
Gifts from children. E. Berg. il *Parents* 64:132-3 N '89

Taxation

See also
Gifts to minors
Before the loophole closes. P. Duggan. il *Forbes* 144:239-40 O 2 '89
Your money: should you give your house to your kids? E. Lank. *Modern Maturity* 32:20 Ag/S '89

GIFTS FOR CHILDREN
See also
Christmas gifts for children
Rites of passage III [receiving lamb cake as Confirmation Day present] M. E. Marty. il *The Christian Century* 106:735 Ag 2-9 '89

GIFTS IN BUSINESS
The Black enterprise executive guide to gift giving. J. Torrence-Thompson. il *Black Enterprise* 20:109-13 D '89
Personal computing's executive gift guide. R. Bel Bruno and N. McFeeley. il *Personal Computing* 13:118-25+ D '89

GIFTS TO MINORS
Custodial accounts: saving for college made easy. M. Rowland. *Working Woman* 14:57 O '89
Passing the bucks to your kids. R. R. Roha. il *Changing Times* 43:65-6+ Mr '89
Trimming the tax bite on gifts to grandchildren. T. Segal. il *Business Week* p161 O 23 '89

GIGANTOPITHECUS *See* Primates, Fossil

GIGHA (SCOTLAND)
Aye, laddie, no man is an island, but jack-of-all-trades Seumas McSporran comes close. M. Neill. il pors *People Weekly* 32:84-6 Ag 7 '89

GIGLI, ROMEO
about

Fashion without frontiers. J. Cocks. il pors *Time* 133:94 Mr 20 '89
Romeo, Romeo. C. Petkanas. il por *Harper's Bazaar* 122:148-9+ Ag '89

GIGONDAS (WINE) *See* Wine

GIL-TURNES, M. SOFIA, AND OTHERS
Symbiotic marine bacteria chemically defend crustacean embryos from a pathogenic fungus. bibl f il *Science* 246:116-18 O 6 '89

GILA RIVER TELECOMMUNICATIONS, INC.
Smoke on the line [D. Segress wins cellular licenses for American Indian-owned companies] F. Meeks. il *Forbes* 144:114+ S 4 '89

GILBERT, ARTHUR, 1913-
about

Ah, decadence. C. Brown. il por *Forbes* 143:316+ My 29 '89

GILBERT, BIL
The crow man [interview with L. Kilham] il pors *Life* 12:25-7 Je '89
Enduring earth. il *Life* 12:82-4+ F '89
The incredible odyssey of the president's beasts. il por *Audubon* 91:100-2+ Ja '89
Of time and the river. il *Sports Illustrated* 71:76-80+ Jl 24 '89
One fine crow. il *Reader's Digest* 134:149-52 Ap '89

GILBERT, BRAD
about

It ain't pretty . . . P. Cohen. il por *World Tennis* 37:50-2 D '89

GILBERT, CREIGHTON
(tr) See Michelangelo Buonarroti, 1475-1564. Doubting genius

GILBERT, DEBBIE
Writing on the go. *The Writer* 102:27-8 Mr '89

GILBERT, JAROBIN, JR.
about

After Seoul, Barcelona. T. Paige. il por *Black Enterprise* 19:16 Ja '89

GILBERT, JENNIFER
Omni's *glasnost*. il *Omni (New York, N.Y.)* 11:16 Ag '89

GILBERT, LEWIS
about

Shirley Valentine [film] Reviews
The New Yorker 65:90 S 4 '89. T. Rafferty

GILBERT, LEWIS—about—Shirley Valentine—*cont.*
People Weekly 32:15-16 O 16 '89. R. Novak
GILBERT, PAMELA
(jt. auth) See Waldman, Michael, 1960-, and Gilbert, Pamela
GILBERT, RUTH
Hot line. See issues of New York beginning October 31, 1988
GILBERT, SARA
about
Melissa Gilbert's kid sister Sara has her own hit with Roseanne. S. Dougherty. il pors *People Weekly* 31:111-12 Mr 20 '89
'Roseanne's' terrific TV teens! il pors *'Teen* 33:68 My '89
Talent. T. J. Meyer. il por *Seventeen* 48:75-6+ S '89
GILBERT, SARA D.
Do you know why you eat? il *Glamour* 87:81+ Ap '89
GILBERT, SEAN
about
On deck. il por *Sport (New York, N.Y.)* 80:14 My '89
GILBERT, STEVEN W., AND LYMAN, PETER
Intellectual property in the information age. il *Change* 21:22-8 My/Je '89
GILBERT, SUSAN
Young women, crucial choices. *Glamour* 87:242-3+ N '89
GILBERT, TRIMBLE
about
Shadow over an ancient land. S. K. Reed. il pors *People Weekly* 32:48-53 S 18 '89
GILBERT, ZACK, 1925-
Young lovers [poem] *Essence* 20:112 Je '89
GILBERT (ARTHUR AND ROSALINDE) COLLECTION
See Mosaics—Collectors and collecting
GILBERT AND GEORGE
about
Gilbert & George: the AIDS pictures [cover story] R. Rosenblum. il *Art in America* 77:152-5 N '89
Working stiffs. B. De Lotbiniere. il *Harper's Bazaar* 122:84 S '89
GILBERTIE, SAL
Uncommon scents. il *Organic Gardening* 36:43-6 F '89
GILCHRIST, ALAN, AND HALPER, LOUISE
Jump start. *The Nation* 248:653 My 15 '89
GILCREASE (THOMAS) INSTITUTE OF AMERICAN HISTORY AND ART *See* Thomas Gilcrease Institute of American History and Art
GILDEA, WILLIAM
Father and son. *Reader's Digest* 134:127-30 Ja '89
THE GILDED BAT [ballet] See Ballet reviews—Single works
GILDER, GEORGE F., 1939-
America on the rise: a new breed of innovators. il *Reader's Digest* 135:126-8 Ag '89
Quantum leap. il por *Forbes* 143:138-9 Je 26 '89
Severed heads and wasted resources. il *Forbes* 143:45-6+ Je 26 '89
Where are the microchip billionaires? il *Forbes* 144 Special Issue:378-80+ O 23 '89
The world's next source of wealth [excerpt from Microcosm] il por *Fortune* 120:116-20 Ag 28 '89
about
Mind over matter. T. Bethell. *The American Spectator* 22:11-13 N '89
Who's afraid of the Japanese? P. Elmer-Dewitt. il por *Time* 134:102+ O 23 '89
GILDING
Gilt trip [work of W. Adair] G. Harrell. il por *House & Garden* 161:120+ S '89
GILES, JEFFREY
Talking pictures. *Mother Jones* 14:52 My '89
GILES, JOE W., AND CURTIS, CYNTHIA R.
A state strategy for teacher training: the Tennessee Arts Academy. *Design for Arts in Education* 90:39-42 Jl/Ag '89
GILES, NANCY
about
Showing off her cockeyed humor as a Vietnam deejay, Nancy Giles seizes her own China Beachhead. il por *People Weekly* 31:99 Mr 20 '89
GILETTI, BRUNO J.
(jt. auth) See Fortier, Steven M., and Giletti, Bruno J.
GILGAMESH
Gilgamesh, the king who did not wish to die. J. Bottéro. il *The Unesco Courier* 42:18-21 S '89
GILINSKY, RHODA M.
Bringing up baby. il *Publishers Weekly* 235:20+ Je 9 '89
GILKEY, BERTHA
about
People power transforms a St. Louis housing project. H. C. Boyte. il por *Utne Reader* p46-7 Jl/Ag '89
GILKEY, LANGDON BROWN, 1919-
about
The ultimate and the ordinary: a profile of Langdon Gilkey [cover story] J. L. Price. il por *The Christian Century* 106:380-3 Ap 12 '89
GILL, BRENDAN, 1914-
The faces of Joseph Campbell. il *The New York Review of Books* 36:16+ S 28 '89

Joseph Campbell: an exchange [discussion of September 28, 1989 article, The faces of Joseph Campbell] il *The New York Review of Books* 36:57-61 N 9 '89
Lonely at the top. il pors *House & Garden* 161:32+ Ag '89
The sky line. *The New Yorker* 65:99-104 Mr 6 '89
The sky line. *The New Yorker* 64:73-7 Ja 9 '89
The sky line. *The New Yorker* 65:80-4 Ag 14 '89
What's in a name? il *House & Garden* 161:72+ N '89
about
Bill Moyers angrily defends Joseph Campbell against charges that his wisdom was only a myth. A. Chambers. il pors *People Weekly* 32:64+ N 27 '89
GILL, CARLOS
about
Lotto winner tells why he will share $22 million prize with his family. il pors *Jet* 77:16-17 D 11 '89
GILL, JOCELYN RUTH
about
Affecting eternity. R. D. Hicks. il *Sky and Telescope* 77:236 Mr '89
GILL, JONATHAN
Fox in the coop. *The Nation* 248:40 Ja 9-16 '89
GILL, MARK STUART
The prince of get rich quick. il por *Rolling Stone* p107-8+ F 9 '89
GILL, PAUL G.
A guide to common foot problems. *McCall's* 116:92+ Je '89
GILL, THOMAS J., AND OTHERS
The rat as an experimental animal. bibl f il *Science* 245:269-76 Jl 21 '89
GILLER, ROBERT M., AND MATTHEWS, KATHY, 1949-
25 quick tips to trick off pounds [excerpt from Maximum metabolism] il *Redbook* 172:70-1+ F '89
GILLESPIE, DIANE
Claiming ourselves as teachers. il *Change* 21:56-9 Jl/Ag '89
GILLESPIE, DIZZY, 1917-
about
Bebop's joyful pop. T. Powis. il por *Maclean's* 102:57-8 Mr 20 '89
Dizzy Gillespie's style, its meaning analyzed [reprint] il por *Down Beat* 56:30 S '89
President Bush praises Gillespie and Dunham at White House fete. il pors *Jet* 77:27 D 11 '89
GILLESPIE, JOHN BIRKS *See* Gillespie, Dizzy, 1917-
GILLESPIE, MARCIA ANN
A cry for help. il por *Ms.* 17:32-3 Ja/F '89
Repro woman [interview with F. Wattleton; cover story] por *Ms.* 18:50-3 O '89
GILLESPIE, ROXANI M.
about
A California mission that may be impossible. R. D. Hof. il por *Business Week* p50 Ag 14 '89
GILLESPIE, THOMAS W.
The accidental parson. il *Christianity Today* 33:61+ O 20 '89
GILLESPIE, VICTOR
about
The hunt for western titles: a collector's goals and strategies. S. Sherman. *Publishers Weekly* 235:45 My 5 '89
GILLETT, GEORGE
about
As Vail's trailblazing owner, George Gillett finds there's no business like snow business. F. A. Bernstein. il pors *People Weekly* 31:92-4 F 6 '89
By George! A. H. Greenberg. il pors *Skiing* 41:100+ Ja '89
A vision fulfilled. W. O. Johnson. il pors *Sports Illustrated* 70:70-4+ Ja 30 '89
GILLETT, STACY
Windmill (Nebraska 1982) [poem] *America* 160:537 Je 3 '89
GILLETTE, ARTHUR
The gondola of Venice. il *The Courier (Unesco)* 41:24-9 N '88
GILLETTE, NED, 1945-
Rowing Antarctica's "most mad seas". il map *National Geographic* 175:128-38 Ja '89
GILLETTE CO.
A $200 million close shave [twin blade Gillette Sensor] il *U.S. News & World Report* 107:24 O 16 '89
At Gillette, disposable is a dirty word. K. H. Hammonds. il por *Business Week* p54+ My 29 '89
A better blade [Sensor razor] J. W. Merline. il *Consumers' Research Magazine* 72:38 D '89
Gillette gets sharp. S. Caminiti. il *Fortune* 119:84 My 8 '89
Gillette is looking sharp once again. il *Money* 18:65 O '89
Warren Buffett makes money by making nice [friendly stake in Gillette] L. Jereski. il por *Business Week* p58 Ag 7 '89
GILLIAM, SAM, 1933-
about
Sam Gilliam: working with his seven-league boots on [cover story] C. James. il pors *American Visions* 4:26-30 F '89

GILLIAM, TERRY
about
The adventures of Baron Munchausen [film] Reviews
American Film il 15:70 N '89. P. Rainer
Gentlemen's Quarterly il 59:155+ Mr '89. K. Turan
Maclean's il 102:55 Mr 27 '89. B. D. Johnson
The Nation 248:427-8 Mr 27 '89. S. Klawans
The New Leader 72:21 Mr 6 '89. J. Morrone
The New Republic 200:32-3 Mr 20 '89. S. Kauffmann
New York il 22:73 Mr 20 '89. D. Denby
The New Yorker 65:103-5 Ap 3 '89. P. Kael
Newsweek il 113:69 Mr 13 '89. J. Kroll
People Weekly il 31:15 Mr 13 '89. S. Haller
Theatre Crafts il 23:18 Ap '89. J. Calhoun
Time il 133:82 Mr 13 '89. R. Corliss
Earth to Gilliam. J. Mathews. il por American Film 14:34-9+ Mr '89

GILLIATT, PENELOPE
Profiles [J. Miller] il por The New Yorker 65:52-6+ Ap 17 '89

GILLIGAN, EDMUND
Christmas at Piety Corner [story] il The Saturday Evening Post 261:48-51+ N/D '89

GILLIS, CHRISTOPHER
about
Family dynamics. M. Crabb. pors Maclean's 102:60 My 22 '89

GILLIS, JACK
Recalls: an up-to-date list. See issues of Good Housekeeping beginning May 1987

GILLIS, MARGIE
about
Family dynamics. M. Crabb. pors Maclean's 102:60 My 22 '89

GILLS, ARTIFICIAL
Artificial gill. D. Stover. il Popular Science 234:121-3+ Ap '89

GILMAN, ALFRED G., 1941-
about
Tracing hormone action in the cell. J. L. Marx. il por Science 245:1446-7 S 29 '89

GILMAN, ANDREW
(jt. auth) See Berg, Karen, and Gilman, Andrew

GILMAN, SAUL
about
Saul Gilman: his own salesman. J. Rosen. por Publishers Weekly 235:108+ Ja 20 '89

GILMORE, V. ELAINE
What's new: tools. See issues of Popular Science

GILMOUR, ALLAN D.
about
The Big Three's trio of new leaders for the 1990s. Fortune 120:112 O 23 '89
Ford will need someone to share the driving. J. B. Treece. il por Business Week p28 Ap 24 '89

GILMOUR, DAVID S., AND OTHERS
Drosophila nuclear proteins bind to regions of alternating C and T residues in gene promoters. bibl f il Science 245:1487-90 S 29 '89

GILROY (CALIF.)
Stores
See also
Garlic World (Firm)

GILTENAN, EDWARD
Plastic surgery. il Forbes 143:318 Ja 9 '89

GIMBRONE, MICHAEL A., AND OTHERS
Endothelial interleukin-8: a novel inhibitor of leukocyte-endothelial interactions. bibl f il Science 246:1601-3 D 22 '89

GIMELSON, DEBORAH
Crack pots. il Harper's Bazaar 122:80 O '89
Salon paintings on the rise in New York. il Architectural Digest 46:360+ N '89

GIN
A drink fit for a king. E. Fried. il Black Enterprise 20:144 O '89

GINAVEN, MARLENE
Colorless glass salts. il Antiques & Collecting Hobbies 94:34-6 Je '89

GINDICK, TIA
Tooling around the continent. il Travel Holiday 171:52-9 My '89

GINGER
See also
Cooking—Herbs and spices

GINGERBREAD
Return of the Ginger-Kids . . . and our 1967 Christmas bread [cover story] il Sunset (Central West edition) 183:64-7 D '89

GINGERBREAD HOUSES, ORNAMENTS, ETC. See Cooking, Ornamental

GINGERT, ART
Coming home. il Country Journal 16:39-43 My/Je '89

GINGHER, MARIANNE
Happy after all [story] il Redbook 174:60+ D '89
A passing fancy [story] il Ladies' Home Journal 106:100+ O '89

GINGRICH, NEWT
Toward majority rule. il por Conservative Digest 15:31-4 Ja/F '89
about
Anatomy of a smear. J. M. Barry. il pors Esquire 112:215-20+ O '89
An attack dog, not a lapdog. J. V. Lamar, Jr. il por Time 133:22 Ap 3 '89
Cracking the whip [cover story] T. Bethell. il The American Spectator 22:9-11 Ag '89
Dennis the Menace comes in from the cold. G. Borger. il pors U.S. News & World Report 106:25-6 Mr 27 '89
For the Son of C-SPAN, exposure = power. H. Fineman. il por Newsweek 113:22-3 Ap 3 '89
The GOP's new whip really knows how to lash out. D. Harbrecht. Business Week p47 Ap 3 '89
High noon for Newt [cover story] W. McGurn. il pors National Review 41:21-3 Ag 18 '89
The incumbent party, the party of incumbents. National Review 41:14-15 Je 30 '89
Look who's setting the House on fire. D. Harbrecht. il por Business Week p94+ Ag 14 '89
Master of disaster [cover story] D. Beers. il pors Mother Jones 14:28-9+ O '89
Newtered. F. Barnes. il The New Republic 200:8-10 Ap 24 '89
On the point. National Review 41:12-13 Ap 21 '89
One-man/one-vote Gingrich. W. F. Buckley. National Review 41:62 My 5 '89
The Republicans' pit bull. N. Traver. il Time 133:22 Je 12 '89
Section 89 among House GOP targets. D. C. Bacon. por Nation's Business 77:6 Jl '89

GINN, SAM
about
Pacific Telesis: "noon on a sunny day". N. J. Perry. il por Fortune 120:76 O 9 '89

GINNIE MAE SECURITIES See Mortgage bonds and notes
GINSBERG, ALLEN, 1926-
Graphic winces [poem] Harper's 278:38 Ap '89
Photographs and photography
Indecent exposure? C. Giuliano. il pors Art News 88:31 F '89

GINSBERG, EDWARD, AND GINSBERG, SUSAN
Student loan financing; Student loan default. il Phi Delta Kappan 70:556-8 Mr '89

GINSBERG, SUSAN
When mom goes back to work. il Good Housekeeping 209:114+ S '89

GINSBERG, SUSAN
(jt. auth) See Ginsberg, Edward, and Ginsberg, Susan

GINZBURG, NATALIA
about
Death in Venice, Rome, etc. A. Bernays. il pors Ms. 18:20-1 O '89

GINZBURG, V. L. (VITALIĭ LAZAREVICH), 1916-
High-temperature superconductivity: past, present and future. bibl f il por Physics Today 42:9+ Mr '89
Landau's attitude toward physics and physicists. bibl f il pors Physics Today 42:54-61 My '89

GINZBURG, VITALIĭ LAZAREVICH See Ginzburg, V. L. (Vitaliĭ Lazarevich), 1916-

GIOIA, DANA
All souls' [poem] The New Yorker 65:46 O 9 '89

GIONIS, THOMAS
about
John Wayne's daughter Aissa is brutally beaten, and her ex-husband is soon to stand trial. M. Green. il pors People Weekly 31:106-8 My 29 '89

GIORDANO, UMBERTO, 1867-1948
about
Fedora [opera] Reviews
The New Yorker 65:103-4 F 20 '89. A. Porter

GIORGIANNI, EDWARD J.
(jt. auth) See DeMarsh, LeRoy E., and Giorgianni, Edward J.

GIORGIO CAFE (NEW YORK, N.Y.) See New York (N.Y.)—Restaurants, nightclubs, bars, etc.

GIOTTO COMETARY MISSION See Space flight—Cometary missions

GIOVANELLA, BEPPINO C., AND OTHERS
DNA topoisomerase I-targeted chemotherapy of human colon cancer in xenografts. bibl f il Science 246:1046-8 N 24 '89

GIOVANELLI, RICCARDO
about
A new galaxy vs. old theories. F. Capone. World Press Review 36:67 D '89

GIOVANNINI, JOSEPH
Architectural digest visits: Jaclyn Smith and Tony Richmond [cover story] il pors Architectural Digest 46:180-5+ Ag '89
The geometry of conversation. il House & Garden 161:62+ F '89
Making room for art. il House & Garden 161:132-9 D '89
Manhattan transformation. il Architectural Digest 46:182-7+ Mr '89
Newman's own. il House & Garden 161:22+ Je '89

GIOVANNINI, JOSEPH—*cont.*
Vienna vanguard. il *House & Garden* 161:48 S '89
Village of one's own. il por *House & Garden* 161:116-23
Ap '89
GIPSY KINGS (MUSICAL GROUP)
All heart and no glitter. J. Miller. il *Newsweek* 113:69 Ja 23 '89
Going on the road comes naturally to the latest sensation in ethnic rock and roll, the Gipsy Kings. il *People Weekly* 31:111 Ja 16 '89
GIPSY MOTHS *See* Gypsy moths
GIRAFFE PROJECT
They stick their necks out. R. R. Roha. il *Changing Times* 43:102 My '89
GIRAFFES
Photographs and photography
Serious necking. G. G. Dimijian. il *Natural History* p92-3 S '89
GIRALT-MIRACLE, DANIEL
Gaudí and Dalí, the art of excess. il por *The Courier (Unesco)* 42:32-4 My '89
GIRARD, DOMINIQUE OTHENIN- *See* Othenin-Girard, Dominique
GIRARDEAU, JACQUES, AND OTHERS
Evidence for a heterogeneous upper mantle in the Cabo Ortegal Complex, Spain. bibl f il map *Science* 245:1231-3 S 15 '89
GIRARDET, FREDY, 1936-
about
The best restaurant in the world. D. Shaw. il pors *Gentlemen's Quarterly* 59:196-201 F '89
GIRARDET (CRISSIER, SWITZERLAND: RESTAURANT)
See Crissier (Switzerland)—Restaurants, nightclubs, bars, etc.
GIRDWOOD (ALASKA)
Restaurants, nightclubs, bars, etc.
The last great American roadhouse [Double Musky Inn] P. A. Iseman. il *Esquire* 112:30 Jl '89
GIRL SCOUT COOKIES
Anecdotes, facetiae, satire, etc.
Cookie monsters. W. Geist. il *New York* 22:23 Mr 6 '89
GIRLFRIENDS AND BOYFRIENDS *See* Women and men
GIRLING, SHEILA
about
Caro country: the artist's New York State sculpture studio and fields. K. Wilken. il por *Architectural Digest* 46:192-7+ Ag '89
GIRLS
See also
Sex differences
GIRLS AND VIDEO GAMES *See* Video games and youth
GIRLS CLUB OF NEW YORK
Educating youth about AIDS: a model program. W. Amer-Hirsch. bibl f il *Children Today* 18:16-19 S/O '89
GIRLTALK [television program] *See* Television program reviews—Single works
GIRO D'ITALIA (RACE) *See* Bicycle racing—Italy
GIROLDI, ADELA BONILLA DE *See* Bonilla de Giroldi, Adela
GIROLDI VEGA, MOISÉS
about
The widow of a slain rebel leader looks back in anguish after the failed coup in Panama. B. Hewitt. il pors *People Weekly* 32:101-2 O 30 '89
GIRON, ÁNDRES
about
Mass appeal. M. Cooper. il por *Mother Jones* 14:14 D '89
GIROUARD, MARK, 1931-
Estate of the art. il *House & Garden* 161:58 Mr '89
GIROUX, HENRY A.
Education reform in the age of George Bush. *The Education Digest* 55:3-6 O '89
Rethinking education reform in the age of George Bush. *Phi Delta Kappan* 70:728-30 My '89
GIRZONE, JOSEPH F.
about
Father Joseph Girzone's Joshua parables put a best-selling end to his quiet retirement. L. Smith. il pors *People Weekly* 32:75-6 N 6 '89
PW interviews. W. Griffin. il por *Publishers Weekly* 236:78-9 O 6 '89
GIS *See* Geographic information systems
GISCARD D'ESTAING, VALÉRY, 1926-, AND OTHERS
East-West relations. *Foreign Affairs* 68:1-21 Summ '89
GISELLE [ballet] *See* Ballet reviews—Single works
GISSEN, JAY
Where's Cher? [cover story] il pors *Ladies' Home Journal* 106:36+ Jl '89
GISSEROT, HÉLÈNE
French women today. *America* 160:579-81 Je 17-24 '89
GIT EQUITY TRUST—SPECIAL GROWTH
Buy on weakness. J. Clements. il por *Forbes* 144:150-1 S 4 '89
GITAI, AMOS
about
The films of Amos Gitai. S. Klawans. *The Nation* 248:784-6 Je 5 '89

GITE, LLOYD
Steering safely through setbacks. il pors *Working Woman* 14:39-41+ F '89
GITLER, IRA
'Trane on the track [reprint] il por *Down Beat* 56:48-9 S '89
GITLIN, TODD
Post-modernism: the stenography of surfaces. il *New Perspectives Quarterly* 6:56-9 Spr '89
Postmodernism defined, at last! il *Utne Reader* p52-8+ Jl/Ag '89
GITTELSON, NATALIE
Audrey Hepburn. il pors *McCall's* 116:30-1+ Ag '89
Cissy! Whitney Houston's sweet inspiration. il pors *McCall's* 116:151-2+ My '89
Linda Evans: her second blooming. il pors *McCall's* 116:66-7+ Mr '89
Marie Osmond's all-out holiday celebration. il por *McCall's* 116:23-4+ Ja '89
Meredith Baxter Birney: starting over at 42. il pors *McCall's* 117:109-12 O '89
Shelley Long: her blessings galore. il pors *McCall's* 116:16-18 Ap '89
Tom Selleck settles down . . . il pors *McCall's* 116:83-4+ F '89
GITTINS, SUSAN
Ethical profits. *World Press Review* 36:75 O '89
GIUCA, LINDA
Label ease. il *Organic Gardening* 36:53-6+ N '89
GIUFFRE MEDICAL CENTER (PHILADELPHIA, PA.) *See* Philadelphia (Pa.)—Hospitals
GIULIANI, RUDOLPH W.
about
And the next test will be Giuliani vs. Milken. C. Welles. por *Business Week* p37 Ja 9 '89
Anything goes. A. Logan. *The New Yorker* 65:80-4 Mr 13 '89
The debris in Rudolph Giuliani's wake. C. Welles. pors *Business Week* p36-7 Ja 23 '89
Gandhi vs. Gumby. J. Klein. il pors *New York* 22:42-5 N 6 '89
Gorilla warfare. J. Klein. il pors *New York* 22:24+ Ap 10 '89
Inexakte. A. Logan. *The New Yorker* 65:138-44+ N 6 '89
Jackie Mason tries to talk himself out of trouble [cover story] J. Kasindorf. il pors *New York* 22:36-42 O 16 '89
Jackie Mason's racial remarks about Dinkins, Jews' relations with blacks bring backlash. pors *Jet* 77:5 O 16 '89
The last liberal. J. Klein. il por *New York* 22:14+ Ap 3 '89
London in New York. *National Review* 41:16 Ap 21 '89
Mason bombs in New York. B. Turque. il pors *Newsweek* 114:42 O 9 '89
The mayor's race: Dinkins vs. Giuliani. F. Barnes. *The New Republic* 201:9-10 O 9 '89
Now, the showdown: Dinkins vs. Giuliani in the void left by Koch. J. Klein. il pors *New York* 22:50-3 S 25 '89
Ready for Rudy? [cover story] J. Klein. il pors *New York* 22:30-7 Mr 6 '89
The real thing. J. Klein. il por *New York* 22:16+ N 13 '89
A Rudy awakening. J. Klein. il por *New York* 22:16+ O 16 '89
Rudy's fall from grace: can Ailes put Giuliani's campaign back together again? J. Klein. il pors *New York* 22:40-3 Ag 21 '89
Sorry. A. Logan. *The New Yorker* 65:126-31 O 9 '89
Zinging Rudy. J. Klein. por *New York* 22:14-15 Je 5 '89
GIULIO, ROMANO, 1499?-1546
about
Between the Sistine and Disney. R. Hughes. il *Time* 134:106-7 N 6 '89
GIULIO CESARE [opera] *See* Handel, George Frideric, 1685-1759
GIURGOLA, ROMALDO, 1920-
about
Kimbell times two. J. Kutner. il *Art News* 88:56 O '89
GIUSTINA, NICK
Heaven can wait. il *Travel Holiday* 171:80-2 My '89
GIUSTINO [opera] *See* Handel, George Frideric, 1685-1759
GIVEN NAMES *See* Names, Personal
GIVENS, CHARLES J.
about
The 20% "guarantee". J. Queenan. por *Forbes* 143:260 Je 26 '89
GIVENS, KERRY
about
Making portraits of the microcosm. K. Sferra. il *National Parks* 63:28-31 Mr/Ap '89
On a camera walkabout across the forest floor. P. Skinner. il *Petersen's Photographic Magazine* 17:56-8 Ja '89
GIVENS, ROBIN
about
The champ's biggest fight [cover story] il pors *Ebony* 44:116+ Ja '89
'Free at last,' Tyson says of divorce from actress Robin Givens. il pors *Jet* 76:12-13 Je 19 '89

GIVENS, ROBIN—about—cont.

His Robin flown, the champ pushes on. J. Jerome. il pors *People Weekly* 31:30-5 F 27 '89

Mike Tyson: "the truth about Robin and me". il pors *Jet* 75:59-60 Ja 9 '89

Tyson-Givens split final, $125 million suit ended. il pors *Jet* 75:52 Mr 6 '89

Why Robin Givens has rolled with the punches—and still loves Tyson. M. Murphy. il pors *TV Guide* 37:6-7+ Jl 1-7 '89

GIVENS HALL & ASSOCIATES

The Cayman connection [foreign investments in Coniston Partners may endanger deal for control of UAL] S. Flack. il *Forbes* 144:42-3 D 11 '89

GIVERNY (FRANCE)

Gardens and gardening

Painting with oil sticks [paintings by J. Chesley; cover story] E. Feit. il *American Artist* 53:44-9 Ap '89

GIVING

See also
Charities
Christian giving
Christmas gifts
Corporations—Charitable contributions
Gifts

The best gifts you can give: choose from this lovely assortment of intangibles. J. Stone. il *Glamour* 87:116 D '89

The generosity gap and other scandals. R. J. Neuhaus. *National Review* 41:44 Mr 10 '89

The gift of giving. D. F. Bjorklund and B. Bjorklund. il *Parents* 64:218 D '89

Giving back. See alternate issues of Changing Times beginning January 1989

The philanthropy boom. L. Lenkowsky and P. Frumkin. il *National Review* 41:21-2 D 31 '89

What good are the rich? [exhibiting greater concern for the public good] T. G. Harris and D. Yankelovich. il *Psychology Today* 23:36-9 Ap '89

GIVRAY, CLAUDE DE

(jt. auth) See Truffaut, François, 1932-1984, and Givray, Claude de

GJELSNESS, RUTH

about

The potato queen. D. Blank. il por *Successful Farming* 87:64-5 O '89

GJENVICK, SUSAN

Your health: is hysterectomy necessary? *Modern Maturity* 32:18 F/Mr '89

GLACIAL EPOCHS

After the deluge [Ice Age floods; research by John Shaw] T. Appenzeller. il *Scientific American* 261:22+ D '89

Ancient ice reveals sudden climate shift [Younger Dryas; work of W. Dansgaard] R. Monastersky. *Science News* 135:374 Je 17 '89

Did the roof of the world start an ice age? [research by William Ruddiman] R. A. Kerr. il *Science* 244:1441-2 Je 23 '89

Glacial geology [ancient spruce forest in Wisconsin] J. M. Moran and others. il map *Earth Science* 41:16-18 Wint '88

Glacier bubbles are telling us what was in Ice Age air. J. Weiner. bibl (p164) il *Smithsonian* 20:78-84+ My '89

Great Basin calcite vein and the Pleistocene time scale [discussion of December 2, 1988 article, A 250,000-year climatic record from Great Basin vein calcite: implications for Milankovitch theory] I. J. Winograd and others. *Science* 246:262-3 O 13 '89

Greenland exposed [evidence for melting of ice sheet; research by Roy Koerner] *Discover* 10:14+ N '89

Hills point to catastrophic Ice Age floods [drumlins; work of John Shaw] R. Monastersky. *Science News* 136:213 S 30 '89

Ice cycles [findings in Devil's Hole contradict Milankovitch theory; research by Isaac J. Winograd] R. Kunzig. il *Discover* 10:74-9 My '89

New way to switch earth between hot and cold [ocean dissolved carbon dioxide; research by Edward Boyle] R. A. Kerr. il *Science* 243:480 Ja 27 '89

The next Ice Age. L. Ephron. *The Futurist* 23:38-9 S/O '89

Plankton chronicles rerun [Younger Dryas cooling] *Science News* 135:335 My 27 '89

Rise of Tibet and Rockies set ice-age stage [research by William F. Ruddiman] R. Monastersky. *Science News* 135:309 My 20 '89

Scandinavian, Siberian, and Arctic Ocean glaciation: effect of Holocene atmospheric CO_2 variations. D. R. Lindstrom and D. R. MacAyeal. bibl f il *Science* 245:628-31 Ag 11 '89

What brought on the 'icebox effect' [ice ages caused by winds; research by William Ruddiman and John Kutzbach] *U.S. News & World Report* 106:11 My 22 '89

GLACIER NATIONAL PARK (MONT.)

See also
Waterton-Glacier International Peace Park (Alta. and Mont.)

International hearings on mine near Glacier. il *National Parks* 63:12-13 Ja/F '89

GLACIERS

See also
Aviation—Glacier flying
Glacial epochs

Antarctic meltdown [work of researchers tracking movement of West Antarctica Ice Sheet] M. Parfit. il *Discover* 10:38-40+ S '89

Big ice [Canadian Rockies] D. Thomson. il *Sierra* 74:57 My/Je '89

Holocene-late Pleistocene climatic ice core records from Qinghai-Tibetan Plateau. L. G. Thompson and others. bibl f il maps *Science* 246:474-7 O 27 '89

GLADIEUX, LAWRENCE E.

The student loan quandary. il *Change* 21:35-41 My/Je '89

GLADSTONE, BERNARD

Boatkeeper. See issues of Motor Boating & Sailing
Boatyard. See issues of Motor Boating & Sailing

GLADSTONE, VALERIE

Key West's key lime pie. il *Americana* 16:36-8+ Ja/F '89

Marjory Stoneman Douglas. il pors *Ms.* 17:68-71 Ja/F '89

GLAEG, JAMES

Man in the pink shirt. *America* 161:370-1 N 25 '89

GLAMOUR (PERIODICAL)

Four supermodels tell it like it was [appearing on cover] C. Krupp. il *Glamour* 87:300-3+ Ap '89

Growing up with Glamour. M. A. Kellogg. il *Glamour* 87:356 Ap '89

GLANDS

See also
Adrenal glands
Mammary glands
Pancreas
Pituitary body
Prostate gland
Salivary glands
Thyroid gland

Diseases

See also
Cystic fibrosis

GLANTZ, MICHAEL H.

Datelines. il *World Tennis* 37:72-3 O '89

GLANTZ, RAYMON M.

(jt. auth) See Pfeiffer-Linn, Cindy, and Glantz, Raymon M.

GLANVILLE, JERRY

about

"This is where it starts". J. D. Miller. il por *Sport (New York, N.Y.)* 80:85-8 D '89

Wiseguy. F. Lidz. il pors *Sports Illustrated* 71:58-60+ O 30 '89

GLASER, JAMES K.

In spring [poem] *The Christian Century* 106:301 Mr 22-29 '89

GLASER, MATT

about

Matt Glaser's String Fling: Berklee College/Boston. F. Bouchard. il por *Down Beat* 56:54-5 Ag '89

GLASER, MICHAEL S., 1943-

Apples [poem] *The Christian Century* 106:382 Ap 12 '89

Chance meeting [poem] *America* 161:268 O 21 '89

Pearls [poem] *The Christian Century* 106:197 F 22 '89

Thanksgiving ritual [poem] il *The Christian Century* 106:1079 N 22 '89

GLASER, PAUL MICHAEL

about

Hollywood helps a brave couple raise money for children dying of AIDS. il pors *People Weekly* 32:58-9 N 13 '89

GLASGOW (SCOTLAND)

Arts

Glasgow isn't Paris, but . . . B. Bryson. il *The New York Times Magazine* p34-8+ Jl 9 '89

The lively rebirth of a battered but indomitable Glasgow. S. Meisler. bibl (p229) il *Smithsonian* 20:124-30+ O '89

City planning

Glasgow isn't Paris, but . . . B. Bryson. il *The New York Times Magazine* p34-8+ Jl 9 '89

The lively rebirth of a battered but indomitable Glasgow. S. Meisler. bibl (p229) il *Smithsonian* 20:124-30+ O '89

Historic houses, sites, etc.

Glasgow's Mackintosh revival. A. Hills. il *History Today* 39:6-7 Ap '89

Music

See also
Scottish Opera

GLASHOW, SHELDON L.

Closing the circle. il *Discover* 10:66-70+ O '89

GLASS, ANDREW J.

Bush's budget test. il *The New Leader* 72:3-4 F 20 '89

Bush's politics of evasion. il *The New Leader* 72:3-4 S 18 '89

Good-bye to all that. il *The New Leader* 72:3-4 Ja 23 '89

GLASS, BRETT

Under the hood. See issues of Byte beginning January 1989

GLASS, JIM

Protect what's right. *Outdoor Life* 183:4 Je '89

GLASS, JOANNA M.
about
Yesteryear [drama] Reviews
  Maclean's il 102:47 Ja 23 '89. J. Bemrose
GLASS, JULIE
Animal love. See alternate issues of Glamour beginning July 1987
GLASS, PHILIP
about
Einstein on the beach [opera] Reviews
  Dance Magazine 63:26+ Mr '89. H. Koegler
The fall of the House of Usher [opera] Reviews
  New York il 22:65 Jl 31 '89. P. G. Davis
Anecdotes, facetiae, satire, etc.
Braking Glass. J. Queenan. il *The American Spectator* 22:27 Ap '89
GLASS
See also
  Glassware
  Glazes and glazing (Glass)
  Laminated glass
  Vitrification
  Windows
Bombardment versus quick cooling [relationship between microscopic structure of amorphous material and method used to produce it] I. Peterson. *Science News* 135:207 Ap 1 '89
Fracture
Window on the chemistry of cracking glass [research by Bruce Bunker and Terry Michalske] F. Flam. *Science News* 135:167 Mr 18 '89
GLASS, STAINED *See* Glass painting and staining
GLASS ART SOCIETY
Glass Art Society in Toronto [annual conference] J. Tognini. il *American Craft* 49:72+ Ag/S '89
GLASS BLOCKS AND BRICKS
How to install a glass block window. D. Johnson. il *The Family Handyman* 39:38-9 Mr '89
How to install glass block. P. Barrett. il *Popular Mechanics* 166:95-6 Ag '89
GLASS BLOWING AND WORKING
Double vision [work of J. Kirkpatrick and F. Mace] B. J. Miller. il *American Craft* 49:40-5 O/N '89
GLASS CLEANERS *See* Cleaning compositions
GLASS CONTAINERS
Photographs and photography
The specular and the transparent combined. J. Purcell. il *Petersen's Photographic Magazine* 18:92-3 S '89
GLASS CUTTING
Glass cutting know-how for home projects. P. McCafferty. il *Workbench* 45:48-9 Ja/F '89
Successful glass cutting. K. Collier. il *The Family Handyman* 39:14-15 F '89
GLASS FACTORIES
See also
  Mill (Quechee, Vt.)
GLASS FIBERS *See* Fiberglass
GLASS FIBERS, OPTICAL *See* Fiber optics
GLASS IN HOUSE DECORATION
Restoration glass. B. Vila. il *Popular Mechanics* 166:30-1 Ja '89
GLASS INDUSTRY
See also
  PPG Industries, Inc.
History
See also
  C.F. Monroe Company
  Libbey Glass Company
Ireland
See also
  Waterford Glass Group plc
GLASS PAINTING AND STAINING
See also
  Tiffany glass
Current affairs [work of D. Archer] A. McDonald. il por *Omni (New York, N.Y.)* 11:66-71 S '89
Fill a spice cabinet, memo board and napkin holder with color. M. James. il *Workbench* 45:43-6 Ja/F '89
John La Farge's masterpieces in stained glass. D. D. Thompson. bibl f il *Antiques* 135:708-17 Mr '89
Paul Dufour: line and lucidity. J. McMullan. il por *American Craft* 49:40-5 Je/Jl '89
GLASS SCULPTURE
Double vision [work of J. Kirkpatrick and F. Mace] B. J. Miller. il *American Craft* 49:40-5 O/N '89
Exhibitions
Hank Murta Adams/Dorothy Weiss Gallery. C. White. il *American Craft* 49:80-1 O/N '89
GLASS-STEAGALL ACT *See* Banks and banking—Laws and regulations
GLASSER, WILLIAM, 1925-
Quality is the key to the disciplines. *The Education Digest* 55:24-7 S '89
GLASSES, DRINKING *See* Glassware
GLASSES (SPECTACLES) *See* Eyeglasses
GLASSMAN, BERNIE
about
Livelihood. *The New Yorker* 65:28-9 My 22 '89

GLASSMAN, PETER J., 1945-
Sino-American academic exchanges. il *Change* 21:36-43 Mr/Ap '89
GLASSON, BILL
about
Giving out high marks. J. Diaz. il pors *Sports Illustrated* 70:20-1 Mr 6 '89
GLASSWARE
See also
  Glass Art Society
  Glass sculpture
  Industrial glassware
  Lalique glass
  Opal glass
  Salt and pepper grinders, shakers, etc.
  Snow domes
  Tiffany glass
Collectors and collecting
Brilliant cut glass patterns by Libbey. B. Boggess and L. Boggess. il *Antiques & Collecting Hobbies* 94:26-9 Ap '89
Drink like a Finn. P. Patton. il *Esquire* 112:75 S '89
Nineteenth-century Bohemian glass [cover story] U. Ballay. il *Antiques & Collecting Hobbies* 94:42-5 My '89
Exhibitions
Master of Murano [A. Seguso exhibit at Tiffany & Co.] A. Duncan. il *House & Garden* 161:118 My '89
Nineteenth-century White House glassware. J. S. Spillman. bibl f il *Antiques* 135:950-63 Ap '89
Marketing
China and crystal—not for brides only. M. Rowland. il *Working Woman* 14:102-4+ F '89
Prices
Christie's sale a success [auction of contemporary ceramics and glass] il *American Craft* 49:12 Ap/My '89
GLATFELTER (P. H.) CO. *See* P. H. Glatfelter Co.
GLATTHORN, ALLAN A., 1924-
A "mastery curriculum" for English, grades 5-12. *The Education Digest* 54:40-4 Ja '89
GLATTSTEIN, JUDY
Birds in the winter garden. il *Flower and Garden* 33:20+ N/D '89
Fritillarias. il *Flower and Garden* 33:28-9+ S/O '89
Species tulips. il *Flower and Garden* 33:26-7+ S/O '89
Spire plants. il *Flower and Garden* 33:34-9 My/Je '89
GLAVKOSMOS
Glavcosmos signs Energetics as first U.S. launch customer [Proton rockets] J. R. Asker. il *Aviation Week & Space Technology* 131:40 N 20 '89
Soviets sign space pact, launch military satellites [joint venture between Space Commerce Corp. and Glavcosmos] C. Covault. il *Aviation Week & Space Technology* 130:24-5 Ja 9 '89
GLAXO HOLDINGS PLC
Glaxo's goal: new wonder cures. W. E. Sheeline. il *Fortune* 120:101+ N 6 '89
Prescription for success [E. Mario] J. Zweig. il por *Forbes* 143:178 Je 12 '89
Shakeup at Glaxo [E. Mario becomes CEO] R. A. Melcher. *Business Week* p59 My 22 '89
GLAZER, NATHAN
The enigma. il *The New Republic* 201:13-14 Jl 10 '89
GLAZER, ROBERT I.
about
NIH probes researcher's fundraising. C. Holden. *Science* 243:1000 F 24 '89
GLAZER, STEVEN A.
The pitfalls in protecting your designs from the clutches of others. il *Architectural Record* 177:37+ My '89
GLAZES AND GLAZING
Glazing and marbleizing. B. Vila. il *Popular Mechanics* 166:30-1 S '89
GLAZES AND GLAZING (GLASS)
See also
  Laminated glass
Continuously variable glazing. K. Schachter. il *Popular Science* 235:74-5 N '89
Fabric-saving windows [Southwall Technologies Heat Mirror glazing] V. E. Gilmore. il *Popular Science* 235:38 D '89
Hot and cloudy [Cloud Gel] V. E. Gilmore. il *Popular Science* 235:24 Ag '89
GLEANING
The can people [poor collect aluminum cans in New York City] E. Barnes. il *Life* 12:98-102 Ag '89
GLEASON, HOLLY
Another country. il *Harper's Bazaar* 122:112+ O '89
Dolly Parton: here I come again [cover story] il pors *The Saturday Evening Post* 261:46-9 O '89
GLEASON, JACKIE
about
Jackie Gleason. il pors *People Weekly* 31 Special Issue:24-5 Summ '89
GLEICK, JAMES
After the bomb, a mushroom cloud of metaphors. il *The New York Times Book Review* 94:1+ My 21 '89
GLEMP, JOZEF, CARDINAL
about
Cardinal Glemp's memory lapse. J. M. Wall. *The Christian Century* 106:867 O 4 '89

GLEMP, JOZEF, CARDINAL—about—cont.
The Glemp controversy. *The Christian Century* 106:808 S 13-20 '89
Harsh homily. *Time* 134:77 S 11 '89

GLEN, JOHN
about
Licence to kill [film] Reviews
Motor Boating & Sailing il 163:62-5+ Ap '89. P. Whittell
New York 22:52 Jl 24 '89. D. Denby
Newsweek il 114:52 Jl 17 '89. J. Kroll
People Weekly il 32:11 Jl 17 '89. R. Novak
Time il 134:53 Jl 24 '89. R. Corliss

GLEN, ROBERT
about
In the spirit of the mustangs. il *Southern Living* 24:20 S '89

GLEN CANYON NATIONAL RECREATION AREA (ARIZ. AND UTAH)
Glen Canyon airport expansion under fire. il *National Parks* 63:10-11 Jl/Ag '89

GLEN RIDGE (N.J.)
Crime
Darkness at the heart of town [high school boys arrested for sexually assaulting a retarded girl] P. Wilkinson. il *Rolling Stone* p55-6+ O 5 '89
Gang rape in the suburbs [attack on retarded girl] B. Turque. il *Newsweek* 113:26 Je 5 '89

GLENCOE (ILL.)
Architecture
Good neighbors [Walner House in Glencoe and private residence in Chicago] K. D. Stein. il *Architectural Record* 177:72-81 mid-Ap '89

GLENCONNER, COLIN CHRISTOPHER PAGET TENNANT, 3RD BARON
about
Victorian fantasy. D. J. Ogilvy. il por *House & Garden* 161:176-81 Mr '89

GLENDINNING, NIGEL
Goya and the spirit of enlightenment. il por *USA Today (Periodical)* 117:36-45 Ja '89

GLENDINNING, VICTORIA
about
PW interviews. A. Smith. por *Publishers Weekly* 236:49-50 D 15 '89

GLENDON, MARY ANN, 1938-
A world without Roe. *The New Republic* 200:19-20 F 20 '89

GLENN, CHARLES L.
Just schools for minority children. il *Phi Delta Kappan* 70:777-9 Je '89
Putting school choice in place. il *Phi Delta Kappan* 71:295-300 D '89

GLENN, JEROME C.
Conscious technology: the co-evolution of mind and machine [excerpt from Future mind; cover story] il por *The Futurist* 23:15-20 S/O '89

GLENN, SCOTT
about
Rhymes and reasons. M. Long. il por *Gentlemen's Quarterly* 59:202-3 F '89

GLENN, WILLIAM ELLIS
about
An HDTV with less than meets the eye. A. Fins. il por *Business Week* Special Issue:88 Je 16 '89

GLENNON, LORRAINE
Smart antique hunting. il *New Choices for the Best Years* 29:85-6+ F '89

GLENWOOD SPRINGS (COLO.)
Historic houses, sites, etc.
Colorado cabin fever [1930s log house designed by T. Molesworth] M. Guralnick. il *House & Garden* 161:158-67+ D '89

GLIAL CELLS *See* Nerve cells

GLICK, DANIEL
With an ear to the ground, sea, and sky. il por *Sierra* 74:82-6+ N/D '89

GLICKMAN, JAMES
Homesick [story] il *Ladies' Home Journal* 106:80+ Jl '89

GLICKSMAN, EVE
Daydreams: what they tell us about ourselves. *McCall's* 116:77-8 Jl '89

GLICKSMAN, MARLAINE
Black like who? il *Film Comment* 25:75-6 My/Je '89
Bravo Longo [interview] il por *Film Comment* 25:42-4+ Mr/Ap '89
Presence. por *Film Comment* 25:68-9 Mr/Ap '89
Spike Lee's Bed-Stuy BBQ [interview] il pors *Film Comment* 25:12-16+ Jl/Ag '89
Tempest [interview with E. Palcy] il por *Film Comment* 25:64-6+ S/O '89

GLIDDEN, DAVID
Modern problems, ancient solutions: the philosophy of success. *American Health* 8:114+ Ap '89

GLIDDEN, ROBERT
The K-12 arts agenda: next challenges for higher education. *Design for Arts in Education* 91:11-14 S/O '89

GLIDERS (AVIATION)
See also
Hang gliding
Towing
Towhead. A. Laboda. il *Flying* 116:65 Ag '89

GLIDES (HARDWARE) *See* Casters, glides, etc. (Hardware)

GLIDING AND SOARING *See* Hang gliding

GLIER, MIKE, 1953-
about
Mike Glier at Barbara Gladstone and Wave Hill. H. Cotter. il *Art in America* 77:193 N '89

GLIMMERGLASS OPERA THEATER
Cooperstown, N.Y. W. D. West. *Opera News* 54:61-2 N '89

GLOBAL BLOOD SAFETY INITIATIVE (PROGRAM)
Global Blood Safety Initiative. D. Harris. il *World Health* p28-9 O '89

GLOBAL ENVIRONMENTAL MONITORING SYSTEM *See* United Nations Environment Programme. Global Environmental Monitoring System

GLOBAL MARINE INC.
Now all Global Marine needs is a market. T. Vogel. il *Business Week* p44 Mr 13 '89

GLOBAL NAVIGATION SATELLITE SYSTEM *See* Glonass (Global Navigation Satellite System)

GLOBAL POSITIONING SYSTEM
Collins demonstrates first hand-held Global Positioning System receiver. il *Aviation Week & Space Technology* 130:153 Je 19 '89
Eyes on the Africa-Eurasia vise [research by Kim A. Kastens] R. Monastersky. *Science News* 135:335 My 27 '89
Global Positioning System measurements for crustal deformation: precision and accuracy [California] W. H. Prescott and others. bibl f il *Science* 244:1337-40 Je 16 '89
GPS: the home ranger. F. George. il *Flying* 116:42-3 N '89
Have slide rule, will climb [scientists climb Mount McKinley to measure height via satellite] *U.S. News & World Report* 106:14 Je 12 '89

GLOBAL STUDIES *See* International education

GLOBAL WARMING *See* Greenhouse effect

GLOBALVISION INC.
Covering news where networks fear to tread [South Africa now] C. Reece. il *Channels (New York, N.Y.: 1986)* 9:17 Ja '89
Dark content: getting South Africa news [South Africa now TV show] E. Hedegaard. il *Mother Jones* 14:49 S '89
Globalvision. M. Kelly. il *Utne Reader* p79 Ja/F '89

GLOBE (BOSTON, MASS.) *See* Boston globe

GLOBE AND MAIL (TORONTO, ONT.)
Aftermath of a paper revolution. G. Bain. il *Maclean's* 102:44 F 20 '89
Buying the Times [Globe and mail takes over Financial times of Canada] D. Todd. il *Maclean's* 102:47-8 D 25 '89
End of the Webster era [departure of editor N. Webster] R. Dolphin. *Maclean's* 102:36 Ja 16 '89
A new lineup. B. Came. il *Maclean's* 102:46+ F 13 '89
The Saturday night wars [dispute between editor J. Fraser and writer M. Harris over article on Globe and mail] G. Bain. il *Maclean's* 102:72 N 27 '89
Some sackings are more civil than others. G. Bain. il *Maclean's* 102:46 Ag 28 '89

GLOBE CHALLENGE *See* Yacht racing

GLOBE THEATRE (LONDON, ENGLAND)
Where the Globe was a stage [excavation] il *U.S. News & World Report* 107:19 O 23 '89

GLOBES
See also
George F. Cram Co.
In the trenches [globe of ocean floor relief; work of Pierina R. Nicholson] B. Weber. il *The New York Times Magazine* p110 My 7 '89

O GLOBO (NEWSPAPER)
Brazil's 'Citizen Globo' [R. Marinho] J.-P. Moreau. il por *World Press Review* 36:56 Jl '89

GLOBO TV *See* TV Globo LTDA

GLOBULAR CLUSTERS *See* Stars—Clusters

GLOBULINS
See also
Immunoglobulins
Thymotaxin, a chemotactic protein, is identical to β_2-microglobulin. C. Dargemont and others. bibl f il *Science* 246:803-6 N 10 '89

GLOBUS, RONALD
about
Winky king. *The New Yorker* 65:34-5 My 8 '89

GLOCKNER-FERRARI, DEBORAH A.
about
O rare leviathan. K. Moore. il pors *Sports Illustrated* 70:66-72+ My 29 '89

GLOECKNER, CAROLYN
Life with asthma. il *Current Health 2* 15:10-11 Ap '89
Lung cancer—the smoking gun. il *Current Health 2* 15:14-15 Mr '89

GLONASS (GLOBAL NAVIGATION SATELLITE SYSTEM)
Noisy cosmic neighbors [electromagnetic interference] S. Vogel. il *Discover* 10:28 Ap '89

GLORIFICATION (THEOLOGY) See Glory of God
GLORIOSA DAISIES See Black-eyed Susans
GLORIOUS REVOLUTION, 1688 See Great Britain—History—Revolution of 1688
GLORY [film] See Motion picture reviews—Single works
GLORY! GLORY! [television program] See Television program reviews—Single works
GLORY OF GOD
'So they may see my glory'. K. Koyama. il *The Christian Century* 106:467 My 3 '89
GLOVER, DANNY
about
Why I wear what I wear: Danny Glover, in character [interview] S. Kettmann. il pors *Gentlemen's Quarterly* 59:40+ Jl '89
GLOVER, SAVION
about
The tap dance kid grows up: show-stopping Savion. M. Horosko. il pors *Dance Magazine* 63:38-40 Ag '89
Teenage hoofer Savion Glover helps put tap back on the map. por *People Weekly* 31:81 F 13 '89
GLOVES
See also
Baseball gloves
Space gloves
Don't forget your heat-pipe mittens [research by Amir Faghri] *Science News* 136:62 Jl 22 '89
Hand in glove [sports gloves] T. Imbimbo. il *Health (New York, N.Y.)* 21:31-2 Ja '89
One heart warms many chilly fingers [M. Greenberg distributes gloves to the homeless in New York City] D. Brand. il pors *Time* 133:16+ Ja 2 '89
Spidi Pro One Gloves [for motorcyclists] il *Cycle* 40:60 O '89
GŁOWACKI, JANUSZ
Warsaw scenes: a burned-out light bulb and other tragedies; tr. by Michael Kott. il *The New York Times Magazine* p20-2 Jl 30 '89
GLQ223 (DRUG)
From China, a drug that takes aim at AIDS [work of Michael S. McGrath] J. O. Hamilton. il *Business Week* p29 Ap 24 '89
Genelabs testing promising new AIDS drug. *High Technology Business* 9:33-4 N/D '89
The underground test of Compound Q. D. Wyss. il *Time* 134:18+ O 9 '89
Zeroing in on AIDS. N. Underwood. *Maclean's* 102:58 My 15 '89
GLUCANS
The new bran in town [cholesterol-lowering effects of beta glucans found in rice bran] R. A. Barnett and M. Behen. *American Health* 8:101+ N '89
GLUCK, CHRISTOPH WILLIBALD, RITTER VON, 1714-1787
about
Alceste [opera] Reviews
The *New Yorker* 65:85-6 Ag 14 '89. A. Porter
Iphigénie en Aulide [opera] Reviews
Opera News il 54:43 D 23 '89. J. W. Freeman
Telemaco [opera] Reviews
The *New Yorker* 65:117-18 Ap 17 '89. A. Porter
GLÜCKMAN, GEORG
about
Put another nickel in. D. Galloway. il *Art News* 88:21 D '89
GLUCKSMAN, MARY S.
Across the great divide. il *Omni (New York, N.Y.)* 11:30+ Ap '89
Brain man. il *Omni (New York, N.Y.)* 11:28 My '89
GLUCKSMAN, MARY S., AND SMITH, ELEANOR, 1954-
Fruits de mer. il *Omni (New York, N.Y.)* 11:24+ Ag '89
GLUCOCORTICOID RECEPTORS See Hormone receptors
GLUCOCORTICOIDS See Corticosteroids
GLUCOSE METABOLISM See Carbohydrate metabolism
GLUCOSE TRANSPORT
Localization of the pancreatic beta cell glucose transporter to specific plasma membrane domains. L. Orci and others. bibl f il *Science* 245:295-7 Jl 21 '89
Pretranslational suppression of an insulin-responsive glucose transporter in rats with diabetes mellitus. W. T. Garvey and others. bibl f il *Science* 245:60-3 Jl 7 '89
Sweet success [identification transporter] R. Rusting. *Scientific American* 261:28 Jl '89
GLUE See Adhesives
GLUE GUNS
Glue guns go cordless. P. McCafferty. il *Popular Science* 234:78-9+ F '89
GLUECK, GRACE
And now, a few words from Jenny Holzer. il por *The New York Times Magazine* p42-3+ D 3 '89
GLUTAMATE See Glutamic acid
GLUTAMIC ACID
Tonic activation of NMDA receptors by ambient glutamate enhances excitability of neurons. P. Sah and others. bibl f il *Science* 246:815-18 N 10 '89
GLUTATHIONE
Clues to stimulating AIDS immunity. R. Weiss. *Science News* 136:372 D 9 '89

GLUTTONY
Confessions of a glutton [cover story] M. L. Bringle. *The Christian Century* 106:955-8 O 25 '89
GLYCINE
Effect of serotonergic afferents on quantal release at central inhibitory synapses. I. Mintz and others. bibl f il *Science* 245:190-2 Jl 14 '89
Indole-2-carboxylic acid: a competitive antagonist of potentiation by glycine at the NMDA receptor. J. E. Huettner. bibl f il *Science* 243:1611-13 Mr 24 '89
GLYCOGEN PHOSPHORYLASE See Phosphorylases
GLYCOGENOLYSIS See Carbohydrate metabolism
GLYCOLIPIDS
Signal peptide for protein secretion directing glycophospholipid membrane anchor attachment. I. W. Caras and G. N. Weddell. bibl f il *Science* 243:1196-8 Mr 3 '89
GLYCOLS
See also
Polyethylene glycols
GLYCOPROTEINS
See also
Vascular permeability factor
Autoimmune target in Heymann nephritis is a glycoprotein with homology to the LDL receptor. R. Raychowdhury and others. bibl f il *Science* 244:1163-5 Je 9 '89
Identification of a platelet membrane glycoprotein as a falciparum malaria sequestration receptor. C. F. Ockenhouse and others. bibl f il *Science* 243:1469-71 Mr 17 '89
Identification of the fusion peptide of primate immunodeficiency viruses. M. L. Bosch and others. bibl f il *Science* 244:694-7 My 12 '89
An inducible endothelial cell surface glycoprotein mediates melanoma adhesion. G. E. Rice and M. P. Bevilacqua. bibl f il *Science* 246:1303-6 D 8 '89
Malaria red cell cytoadherence [discussion of March 17, 1989 article, Identification of a platelet membrane glycoprotein as a falciparum malaria sequestration receptor] C. F. Ockenhouse and others. *Science* 246:1051 N 24 '89
The MHC-binding and gp120-binding functions of CD4 are separable. D. Lamarre and others. bibl f il *Science* 245:743-6 Ag 18 '89
Mouse lymph node homing receptor cDNA clone encodes a glycoprotein revealing tandem interaction domains. M. H. Siegelman and others. bibl f il *Science* 243:1165-72 Mr 3 '89
Multidrug resistance in cancer. N. Kartner and V. Ling. bibl il *Scientific American* 260:44-51 Mr '89
A single amino acid interchange yields reciprocal CTL specificities for HIV-1 gp160. H. Takahashi and others. bibl f il *Science* 246:118-21 O 6 '89
Synergism between HIV gp120 and gp120-specific antibody in blocking human T cell activation. R. S. Mittler and M. K. Hoffmann. bibl f il *Science* 245:1380-2 S 22 '89
Tumor resistance: weakening the pulse [research by Thomas P. Miller] R. Weiss. *Science News* 135:348 Je 3 '89
Vaccination with a synthetic zona pellucida peptide produces long-term contraception in female mice. S. E. Millar and others. bibl f il *Science* 246:935-8 N 17 '89
GLYNDEBOURNE FESTIVAL OPERA COMPANY
Glyndebourne. N. Goodwin. il *Opera News* 54:62-3 S '89
Glyndebourne. N. Goodwin. il *Opera News* 54:53 O '89
GLYNN, KEVIN P.
Bethlehem today. il *America* 161:441-2 D 16 '89
GLYNN, PATRICK
The Cuban missiles [discussion of March 1989 article, Nuclear revisionism] *Commentary* 88:9-12 Ag '89
The dangers beyond containment [cover story] *Commentary* 88:15-22 Ag '89
Nuclear revisionism. *Commentary* 87:42-7 Mr '89
Waiting for Wyoming. *The New Republic* 201:14-16 O 2 '89
GM See General Motors Corp.
GM-HUGHES ELECTRONICS CORPORATION
GM/Hughes: vaulting into technology. M. Keller. il *Motor Trend* 41:117 Ja '89
GM, Hughes settle stock fight. B. J. Culliton. *Science* 243:1283 Mr 10 '89
GM's alphabet stocks spelled trouble. J. B. Treece. il *Business Week* p41 Mr 13 '89
GMP See Guanosine monophosphate
GNP See Gross national product
GNRH See Gonadotropin releasing hormone
GO (GAME)
Tournaments
Go [match between K. Kobayashi and M. Takemiya in New York City] *The New Yorker* 64:26-7 F 6 '89
GO-VIDEO INC.
Dual-cassette VCR. W. J. Hawkins. il *Popular Science* 235:90 N '89
A roll of the dice. W. P. Barrett. il *Forbes* 143:81 F 20 '89
GOALIES (HOCKEY PLAYERS) See Hockey players
GOALS (PSYCHOLOGY)
Astound yourself! [setting cycling goals] M. Shermer. il *Bicycling* 30:36-40 S '89
Losing and winning. O. G. Brim. *Current (Washington, D.C.)* 311:12-15 Mr/Ap '89

GOATS
See also
Cashmere
Rocky Mountain goats
GOAT'S MILK
Going for the goat [Jackson-Mitchell dairy] M. Barrier. il
por *Nation's Business* 77:12-13 Ag '89
GOBIE, STEPHEN
about
Another scandal on the Hill. por *Newsweek* 114:24 S 4
'89
Barney Frank's story [cover story; special section; with interview] il pors *Newsweek* 114:14-20 S 25 '89
Letter from Washington. E. Drew. *The New Yorker* 65:106-8+
O 2 '89
A skeleton in Barney's closet. M. B. Carlson. il pors *Time*
134:24 S 25 '89
GOCHMAN, ALICE RUBINSTEIN
Cambridge on the Charles. il *Gourmet* 49:92-7+ S '89
Cooperstown. il *Gourmet* 49:102-7+ O '89
Grand Central Terminal. il *Gourmet* 49:106-11+ N '89
GOD
See also
Atheism
Christianity
Creation
Death of God theology
Faith
Glory of God
Image of God
Jesus Christ
Theism
Trinity
Word of God (Theology)
Badgering God. P. J. Ryan. *America* 161:47 Jl 15-22 '89
Brain and gender: the missing data [discussion of January
4-11, 1989 article, Ways of knowing God: gender and
the brain] J. B. Ashbrook. *The Christian Century* 106:263-4
Mr 8 '89
Can we be good without God? [political meaning of Christianity; cover story] G. Tinder. il *The Atlantic* 264:68-72+
D '89
Cosmic ventures: a meditation on God at war. N. Mailer.
il *Esquire* 112:156-8 D '89
The divine parent. M. E. Marty. *The Christian Century*
106:1215 D 20-27 '89
Does God want to be your macho man? [interview with
A. E. Carr] por *U.S. Catholic* 54:16-22 My '89
God and modern man [views of Rabbi H. Kushner] M.
Starr. il por *Newsweek* 114:74-5 O 23 '89
God is my client. T. J. Reuland. il *Commonweal* 116:527-9
O 6 '89
A God named Abba. T. Stafford. il *Christianity Today* 33:24-5
My 12 '89
The great God blackout [Life magazine removes mention
of God from cover of copies sold in New York City]
M. E. Marty. *The Christian Century* 106:967 O 25 '89
Meeting God in others. K. P. Cecala. il *Commonweal*
116:400-2 Jl 14 '89
Q: Who made me? J. Garvey. *U.S. Catholic* 54:25-7 Jl
'89
They are a stiff-necked people. K. Koyama. il *The Christian
Century* 106:779 Ag 30-S 6 '89
Ways of knowing God: gender and the brain. J. B. Ashbrook.
il *The Christian Century* 106:14-15 Ja 4-11 '89
When bad things happen to good religion [views of H.
Kushner] R. J. Neuhaus. il *National Review* 41:52-4 N
10 '89
Goodness
'May God continue to bless us'. K. Koyama. il *The Christian
Century* 106:442 Ap 26 '89
'Yahweh is generous to all'. K. Koyama. il *The Christian
Century* 106:411 Ap 19 '89
Judgment
Warnings. P. J. Ryan. il *America* 160:159 F 18 '89
Love
See Love (Theology)
Mercy
Lenten meditation:
God's terrifying mercy. R. C. Wood. *The Christian
Century* 106:164-5 F 15 '89
Mercy. P. J. Ryan. *America* 161:150 S 9-16 '89
Proof
Search me and know me [religious reflections on computer
search into existence of finite projective plane of order
10] M. E. Marty. *The Christian Century* 106:247 Mr 1
'89
Suffering
See Suffering of God
Transcendence
See Transcendence of God
Will
Have I done well? [excerpt from Tough questions Christians
ask] D. Neff. il *Christianity Today* 33:22-8 F 17 '89
Visions, voices, and choices. K. S. Kantzer. il *Christianity
Today* 33:8 Ap 21 '89

GOD IN LITERATURE See Religion in literature
GOD IS DEAD THEOLOGY See Death of God theology
GODARD, JEAN LUC, 1930-
about
Hail Mary [film] Reviews
The Christian Century 106:1166-8 D 13 '89. J. K. Larson
GODBER, JOHN
about
Up 'n' under [drama] Reviews
New York il 22:56 Je 26 '89. J. Simon
The New Yorker 65:74 Je 19 '89. E. Oliver
GODDARD, JOHN, 1723-1785
about
The greatest. *The New Yorker* 65:39-40 O 9 '89
GODDARD, NICHOLAS
Royal shows & agricultural progress, 1839-1989. bibl il *History
Today* 39:44-51 Jl '89
GODDARD, ROBERT HUTCHINGS, 1882-1945
about
"The dream of yesterday is the reality of tomorrow". R.
Bruns and B. Kennedy. il pors *American History Illustrated*
24:24-9+ Summ '89
Robert Goddard and his rocket were lonely pioneers of
man's thrust into the limitlessness of space. M. Kernan.
il pors *Smithsonian* 20:46+ N '89
The rocket pioneers. M. R. Chartrand. *Ad Astra* 1:38 Mr
'89
GODDARD, WILLIAM A., III
(jt. auth) See Chen, Guanhua, and Goddard, William A.,
III
GODDESS OF DEMOCRACY
Chinese Goddess of Democracy toppled by troops. J. Gambrell. il *Art in America* 77:29 Jl '89
Notes and comment [Chinese student recounts story of the
Goddess of Democracy] il *The New Yorker* 65:43-4 O
23 '89
GODEAU, ABIGAIL SOLOMON- See Solomon-Godeau,
Abigail
GODFREY, NEALE S.
about
Amassing a small fortune, Neale Godfrey teaches thrift at
the First Children's Bank. R. Arias. il por *People Weekly*
32:127-8 S 18 '89
GODFREY, TONY
An art market for the '90s? il *Art in America* 77:44-5+
O '89
GODIVA CHOCOLATIER
Sweet success in sales automation. J. Pepper. il *Working
Woman* 14:59-60+ Ap '89
GODMILOW, JILL
about
Jill Godmilow [interview] il pors *American Film* 14:20-2+
Je '89
GODOY, JULIO
about
War of words. V. Perera. il por *Mother Jones* 14:19-21
F/Mr '89
GODOY ALCAYAGA, LUCILA See Mistral, Gabriela, 1889-
1957
GODS AND GODDESSES
See also
Izanagi and Izanami (Shinto deities)
The powers of the primeval goddesses. M. R. Lefkowitz.
The American Scholar 58:586-91 Aut '89
THE GODS MUST BE CRAZY II [film] See Motion picture
reviews—Single works
GODWIN, GAIL
My mother, the writer: master of a thousand disguises. il
pors *The New York Times Book Review* 94:7+ Je 11 '89
GODWIN, KATHLEEN See Cole, Kathleen
GODWIN, PHILLIP
Adoption. il pors *Better Homes and Gardens* 67:44+ My
'89
Who will care for mom and dad? il *Better Homes and
Gardens* 67:32+ O '89
GODWIN (TONY) MEMORIAL AWARD See Editors and
editing—Awards
GOELET, ALEXANDRA
about
Wasps' nest [cover story] D. Smith. il pors *New York* 22:30-9
Je 5 '89
GOELL, YOSEF
Israel's Arabs. *The New Republic* 201:16-18 O 23 '89
GOEN, C. C.
about
American ecumenism: separatism, separation and schism
[adaptation of address] M. E. Marty. *The Christian Century*
106:958-61 O 25 '89
GOEPPINGER, SUSAN
about
6,500 'I do's' make for one sturdy marriage for Susan
Goeppinger and fellow actor David Anders. P. Freeman.
il pors *People Weekly* 31:89-90 My 1 '89
GOER, HENCI
The fascinating world of the unborn. *Reader's Digest* 135:150-4
N '89

GOERGENS, CATHY
about
In the depths of a flooded mine, Doug and Cathy Goergens found a Missouri mecca for scuba divers. D. Chu. il pors *People Weekly* 32:81+ N 6 '89

GOERGENS, DOUG
about
In the depths of a flooded mine, Doug and Cathy Goergens found a Missouri mecca for scuba divers. D. Chu. il pors *People Weekly* 32:81+ N 6 '89

GOERTZEN, DONALD
Clamor over Philippine bases. il *The Progressive* 53:15-16 S '89
'No one lives on Rongelap'. *The Progressive* 53:18 N '89

GOES (GEOSTATIONARY OPERATIONAL ENVIRON-MENTAL SATELLITES) *See* Artificial satellites—Meteorological use

GOESSEL (KAN.)
Crime
The startling Shelly Prine case [use of DNA fingerprints to convict O. Smith of murder] P. Michelmore. *Reader's Digest* 135:179-80+ Jl '89

GOETHE, JOHANN WOLFGANG VON, 1749-1832
about
Universality and national identity. A. Finkielkraut. bibl f il pors *The Unesco Courier* 42:30-3 Je '89

GOETTEL, KENNETH A.
about
Goettel is AIP's Congressional Fellow in 1989-90. P. Janowski. *Physics Today* 42:117 O '89

GOETZ, HARRIET
Euthanasia: a bedside view [cover story] *The Christian Century* 106:619-22 Je 21-28 '89

GOFEN, ETHEL
Hey, look me over [cover story] il *Current Health 2* 15:3-8 Ja '89

GOFF, BRUCE, 1904-1982
about
The delirious palace. B. Adams. il *Art in America* 77:136-45 D '89

GOGGLES
Critics fault U.S. Army helicopter training with night vision goggles. *Aviation Week & Space Technology* 130:23 Mr 27 '89
Eyewear [ski equipment] D. White. il *Skiing* 42:234-7 S '89
ITT solves complex problems to produce image intensifiers [night vision goggles] B. D. Nordwall. il *Aviation Week & Space Technology* 130:91+ My 22 '89
New goggles improve night vision but do not match daylight conditions [aviation use] B. D. Nordwall. il *Aviation Week & Space Technology* 130:86-7 Ap 10 '89
Sight savers [sports goggles] T. Imbimbo. il *Health (New York, N.Y.)* 21:32+ Mr '89
Anecdotes, facetiae, satire, etc.
Alpha/theta meditation goggles. M. C. Worley. il *Radio-Electronics* 60:53-7 Ap '89

GOGH, VINCENT VAN, 1853-1890
about
A $60 million van Gogh? R. W. Walker. il *Art News* 88:31 S '89
The anatomy of a deal. R. Hughes. il *Time* 134:66+ N 27 '89
Curse of the muse. B. A. MacAdam. il *Art News* 88:17 Mr '89
Market fever at MOMA. W. Robinson. il *Art in America* 77:33 D '89
Unanswered questions. T. McGhee. il *Art News* 88:56+ O '89
Van Gogh and Gauguin on the couch. B. Collins. bibl f il *Art in America* 77:57+ D '89
Anecdotes, facetiae, satire, etc.
Portraits [van Gogh copies displayed by M. Schacknow] *The New Yorker* 65:36-7 S 18 '89

GOH, JOANNE W., AND PENNEFATHER, PETER S.
A pertussis toxin-sensitive G protein in hippocampal long-term potentiation. bibl f il *Science* 244:980-3 My 26 '89

GOING PUBLIC (SECURITIES) *See* Initial public offerings (Securities)

GOINS, CHARLYNN
about
Charlynn Goins could write the book on job mobility. P. Finch. il por *Business Week* p89 Mr 13 '89

GOIZUETA, ROBERTO C.
Globalization [address, February 9, 1989] *Vital Speeches of the Day* 55:360-2 Ap 1 '89

GOLAN HEIGHTS PEACE FORCE *See* United Nations—Armed Forces—Forces in the Middle East

GOLB, NORMAN
The Dead Sea scrolls: a new perspective. *The American Scholar* 58:177-207 Spr '89
The Dead Sea scrolls—an exchange [discussion of Spring 1989 article] *The American Scholar* 58:626-32 Aut '89

GOLD, ARTHUR RALPH, D. 1988
Paris in the summer of 1988 [poem] *The New Republic* 200:30 Ja 30 '89

GOLD, DON
Max Roach [reprint] il por *Down Beat* 56:42 S '89

GOLD, HEIDI A., AND OTHERS
The RNA processing enzyme RNase MRP is identical to the Th RNP and related to RNase P. bibl f il *Science* 245:1377-80 S 22 '89

GOLD, HERBERT, 1924-
Dear John—look for the lady buying small tins of caviar. il *TV Guide* 37:16-17 Ap 8-14 '89
Father love. il por *American Health* 8:72-3 Ja/F '89
Notes from a 'king' lovingly deposed. il *American Health* 8:68-9 Ja/F '89
On truth and fiction. *The Nation* 249:759-61 D 18 '89

GOLD, PETER
My vasectomy. *Glamour* 87:171+ S '89

GOLD, ROZANNE
about
Rozanne Gold: nearing the top of the food chain. S. Woolley. il por *Business Week* p117 N 6 '89

GOLD, STEPHEN A.
about
Through glasses, darkly. M. Barrier. il pors *Nation's Business* 77:77 Ap '89

GOLD, STEPHEN V.
Charles Dickens got crocked here. il map *The American Spectator* 22:36-7 Ag '89

GOLD, STEVE
Americanization of Vietnamese. il *Society* 27:72-5 N/D '89

GOLD, TODD
Bard of Beverly Hills. il por *Harper's Bazaar* 122:71+ O '89
Earth angels. il *Harper's Bazaar* 122:66-7+ Ja '89
Private eyes: the modern Medicis. il *Harper's Bazaar* 122:98+ My '89
Soul of the plains. il *Harper's Bazaar* 122:20+ Jl '89

GOLD, TRACEY
about
Tracey Gold: prime-time teen talks out! [interview] il pors *'Teen* 33:66 My '89

GOLD
See also
Goldsmithing
Enjoy the gilt! [gold cosmetics packaging] il *Harper's Bazaar* 122:34 Ja '89
Fashioning see-through metal [work of Charles R. Martin and Michael J. Tierney] *Science News* 136:31 Jl 8 '89
Gold: more than glitter. il *National Geographic World* 161:22-5 Ja '89
The liquid state of solid gold particles [research by Laurence D. Marks] I. Peterson. il *Science News* 136:70 Jl 29 '89
Origins and movement of fluids during deformation and metamorphism in the Canadian Cordillera [gold deposits] B. E. Nesbitt and K. Muehlenbachs. bibl f il map *Science* 245:733-6 Ag 18 '89
Orthogonal self-assembled monolayers: alkanethiols on gold and alkane carboxylic acids on alumina. P. E. Laibinis and others. bibl f il *Science* 245:845-7 Ag 25 '89
Prices
A double whammy squashes gold bugs. T. Segal. il *Business Week* p105 F 27 '89
Fool's gold fever? C. Byron. il *New York* 22:16+ D 11 '89
Go for the gold. M. K. Evans. il *Gentlemen's Quarterly* 59:321+ S '89
Gold's new role [views of J. E. Sinclair] R. L. Stern. il por *Forbes* 144:83+ D 25 '89
Gold's up—and therein lies a riddle. T. Segal. il *Business Week* p164 N 27 '89
Good as gold isn't so good these days. T. Segal and G. Weiss. il *Business Week* p116 Je 5 '89
Prospecting for golden opportunities. B. M. Stephens. il *Black Enterprise* 19:83-4 Je '89

GOLD AS AN INVESTMENT
See also
Gold mines and mining—Securities
A double whammy squashes gold bugs. T. Segal. il *Business Week* p105 F 27 '89
Fool's gold fever? C. Byron. il *New York* 22:16+ D 11 '89
The fool's gold rush [dirt-pile mining swindle] B. Mitchell. il *Consumers' Research Magazine* 72:14-15+ Ja '89
Go for the gold. M. K. Evans. il *Gentlemen's Quarterly* 59:321+ S '89
Gold loses its glitter. H. Wheelwright. il *Money* 18:87 D '89
Gold's new role [views of J. E. Sinclair] R. L. Stern. il por *Forbes* 144:83+ D 25 '89
Gold's up—and therein lies a riddle. T. Segal. il *Business Week* p164 N 27 '89
Good as gold isn't so good these days. T. Segal and G. Weiss. il *Business Week* p116 Je 5 '89
Is gold at the end of its rainbow? J. Egan. il *U.S. News & World Report* 107:80 D 18 '89
Is it time to start panning for gold stocks? T. Segal. il *Business Week* p106 Mr 6 '89
Prospecting for golden opportunities. B. M. Stephens. il *Black Enterprise* 19:83-4 Je '89
Waiting for gold to come back to life. E. Schultz. il *Fortune* 120 no10 Special Issue:25 Fall '89

GOLD AS AN INVESTMENT—*cont.*
When you should invest in gold. M. Rowland. il *Working Woman* 14:33-4 F '89
Will gold shine? Yes, but not enough to blind anybody. T. Segal. il *Business Week* p144 D 25 '89-Ja 1 '90

GOLD AS MONEY
Gold [main vault of the Federal Reserve Bank of N. Y.] *The New Yorker* 64:20-1 Ja 2 '89
Golden rule for Russia? [proposal to make the ruble convertible into gold] M. S. Forbes, Jr. il *Forbes* 144:27 O 16 '89

GOLD COINS *See* Coins
GOLD COMPANY *See* Western Michigan University Gold Company
GOLD GLOVE AWARD
Tarnished gold: why don't the best fielders win the Gold Gloves? J. Kaplan. il *Sport (New York, N.Y.)* 80:31-2 O '89

GOLD JEWELRY *See* Jewelry
GOLD METALLURGY
The little bugs that dig for gold [use of Thiobacillus in bioleaching] W. J. Cook. il *U.S. News & World Report* 106:62 Ap 17 '89

GOLD MINES AND MINING
Prospecting for gold in burned sludge? That's right, gold retains its identity through thick and thin. M. Hill. il *Earth Science* 42:36-7 Summ '89

Environmental aspects
Going for the gold. G. Laycock. il *Audubon* 91:70-81 Jl '89

Securities
Is it time to start panning for gold stocks? T. Segal. il *Business Week* p106 Mr 6 '89

Brazil
Warfare over Yanomamö Indians. W. Booth. il *Science* 243:1138-40 Mr 3 '89
Yanomamö survival [discussion of March 3, 1989 article, Warfare over Yanomamö Indians] W. Booth. *Science* 244:11 Ap 7 '89

British Columbia
Gold fever strikes again [Eskay Creek gold find in northern B.C. sends Prime Resources stocks soaring] H. Quinn. il por *Maclean's* 102:33 S 11 '89

California
History
Gold country [in footsteps of Gold Rush ancestor] R. F. Snow. il *American Heritage* 40:30+ My/Je '89
Gold Rush [video game] B. Guerra. il *Compute!* 11:73-4 Ag '89
Opportunities [success of banker D. O. Mills during the California Gold Rush] J. S. Gordon. il *American Heritage* 40:20+ N '89

Canada
See also
Centurion Gold Ltd.
Prime Resources Corporation

Nevada
Invisible gold [mining in the Battle Mountain area] J. Seabrook. *The New Yorker* 65:45-6+ Ap 24 '89
There's holes in them thar hills [open-pit mines in the Carlin Trend] J. M. Nash. il *Time* 134:21-2+ O 23 '89

Ontario
The Pez is golden [Canadian Supreme Court ruling favors Corona Corp. in claim dispute] J. DeMont. il por *Maclean's* 102:39 Ag 21 '89
The tenderfoot and the claim jumper [Corona Corp. wins claim dispute with LAC Minerals] J. Cook. il *Forbes* 144:170+ O 2 '89

South Africa
Apartheid and the Canada connection [Bank of Nova Scotia's involvement in financing Minorco's bid for Consolidated Gold Fields] P. C. Newman. il *Maclean's* 102:29 F 13 '89
Harry Oppenheimer's empire: going for the gold. P. Schmeisser. il por *The New York Times Magazine* p32-3+ Mr 19 '89
Where disinvestment pinches [gold mines] J. Cook. il por *Forbes* 143:62+ Je 26 '89

Soviet Union
The man with the golden headache [M. Gorbachev] P. Fuhrman. il *Forbes* 144:60-3 S 18 '89

Western States
Going for the gold. G. Laycock. il *Audubon* 91:70-81 Jl '89

GOLD RUSH OF 1849 *See* Gold mines and mining—California—History
GOLD STAR SARDINE BAR (CHICAGO, ILL.) *See* Chicago (Ill.)—Restaurants, nightclubs, bars, etc.
GOLD STOCKS *See* Gold mines and mining—Securities
GOLD WORK *See* Goldsmithing
GOLDBARTH, ALBERT
Desert song [poem] *The New Republic* 200:34 Ja 23 '89
Giverny [poem] *The New Republic* 200:34 Ja 23 '89
Poem with 2 lines from a catalogue [poem] *The New Republic* 200:34 Ja 23 '89

GOLDBECK, DAVID
The user-friendly kitchen. il *American Health* 8:87-90+ Jl/Ag '89
(jt. auth) See Goldbeck, Nikki, and Goldbeck, David

GOLDBECK, NIKKI
The blade's the thing. il *American Health* 8:137 Ap '89
GOLDBECK, NIKKI, AND GOLDBECK, DAVID
How to read a food label. il map *The Mother Earth News* 116:72-5 Mr/Ap '89

GOLDBERG, ALAN M., AND FRAZIER, JOHN M.
Alternatives to animals in toxicity testing. bibl il *Scientific American* 261:24-30 Ag '89

GOLDBERG, ARTHUR
about
American stoneware in the collection of Arthur and Esther Goldberg. A. C. Frelinghuysen. bibl f il *Antiques* 136:568-81 S '89

GOLDBERG, BARBARA
(jt. auth) See Wulfhorst, Ellen, and Goldberg, Barbara
GOLDBERG, BERNARD R.
Television insults men, too. il *Reader's Digest* 134:185-6 Je '89

GOLDBERG, GARY DAVID
about
Dad [film] Reviews
Maclean's il 102:82 N 6 '89. B. D. Johnson
The New Yorker 65:119+ N 13 '89. P. Kael
People Weekly il 32:19 N 6 '89. R. Novak
Rolling Stone p38 N 16 '89. P. Travers

GOLDBERG, JAY H.
The technology of Stealth [cover story] il *Technology Review* 92:32-40 My/Je '89

GOLDBERG, JEFF
Bone voyage. il *Omni (New York, N.Y.)* 12:34+ O '89
Desperately seeking Cyborg. il *Omni (New York, N.Y.)* 11:12+ Ag '89
Lunar reflections. il *Omni (New York, N.Y.)* 11:34-6+ Jl '89
Omni's five star travelogue [cover story] il *Omni (New York, N.Y.)* 11:42-4 Mr '89

GOLDBERG, STEVEN
So what if the death penalty deters? *National Review* 41:42+ Je 30 '89

GOLDBERG, VICKI
Margaret Israel's private universe [cover story] il por *American Craft* 49:36-43 Ap/My '89

GOLDBERG, WHOOPI
about
Whoopi Goldberg says her teen daughter is pregnant. il por *Jet* 77:22 N 20 '89

GOLDBERGER, MARVIN L.
about
Institute for Advanced Study: past and future [interview] W. Sweet. por *Physics Today* 42:65-7 Je '89

GOLDBERGER, PAUL
Agrest and Gandelsonas: a sleek Manhattan remodel. il *Architectural Digest* 46:94-7+ Ap '89
Architecture. il *The New York Times Book Review* 94:21+ D 3 '89
Architecture: Franklin D. Israel: Kathryn and Robert Altman's Malibu residence. il pors *Architectural Digest* 46:120-5+ Jl '89
Profiles: Arata Isozaki. il pors *Architectural Digest* 46:174-81+ Mr '89
Works on paper by contemporary architects. il por *Architectural Digest* 46:198+ N '89

GOLDBLATT, HOWARD, 1939-
(tr) See Wang Zengqi. A tail
GOLDBLATT'S DEPARTMENT STORES
Poor customers, rich profits. S. B. Weiner. il *Forbes* 143:145-6 Mr 6 '89

GOLDBLUM, JEFF
about
The couple that stars together . . . R. Gehr. il por *Video* 13:14-15 N '89
Married . . . with chicken [cover story] J. Schneller. il pors *Gentlemen's Quarterly* 59:222-7+ Je '89

GOLDBLUM, ROBERT
Goodbye Thoreau, hello Astaire. il *The New York Times Magazine* p24+ O 29 '89

GOLDEN, JUDITH, 1934-
about
Judith Golden at the MCP. J. Frueh. *Art in America* 77:173 F '89

GOLDEN, MARITA
Raising sons under siege. il *Essence* 20:104 N '89
about
Word star. P. Giddings. por *Essence* 20:32 N '89

GOLDEN, WILLIAM THEODORE, 1909-
How can science best serve the president? *Scientific American* 260:116 F '89

GOLDEN CALF (FIRM)
Tempted by the past [G. Shearing's antique shop] J. M. Laskas. il por *House & Garden* 161:122 My '89

GOLDEN EAGLES *See* Eagles
GOLDEN GATE INTERNATIONAL EXPOSITION (1939-1940)
The other fair. R. Reinhardt. il *American Heritage* 40:42-7+ My/Je '89
Remembering the fairs. il *American History Illustrated* 24:10 Summ '89
Treasure Island looks back 50 years [exhibit at the Treasure Island Museum] il *Sunset (Central West edition)* 182:100 My '89
Vintage images of a fifty-year-old miracle. K. Baker. il *Architectural Digest* 46:186+ My '89
Collectibles
Treasure Island: the forgotten world's fair. D. Stewart. il *Antiques & Collecting Hobbies* 94:29-31 Jl '89
GOLDEN GATE NATIONAL RECREATION AREA (CALIF.)
Golden Gate to get Presidio Army base. il *National Parks* 63:14 Jl/Ag '89
The Presidio: another great park for San Francisco? [cover story] il maps *Sunset (Central West edition)* 183:78-85 N '89
Rockin' in San Francisco [cycling] M. McCloy. il *Bicycling* 30:80-1 O/N '89
GOLDEN GLOBE AWARDS
Win or lose, everyone finds Hollywood's Golden Globes the wackiest ball of all. S. Haller. il *People Weekly* 31:54-6 F 13 '89
GOLDEN HAMSTERS *See* Hamsters
GOLDEN NUGGET, INC.
Tigers, a volcano, dolphins, and Steve Wynn. R. Grover. il por *Business Week* p70-1 N 20 '89
GOLDEN RAIN TREES
Seaside survivors make waves. B. Yinger. il *Flower and Garden* 33:48-9 Jl/Ag '89
GOLDEN RETRIEVERS
Meet Beau, my very own golden boy. N. S. Aronie. il por *Good Housekeeping* 209:124 O '89
GOLDEN STATE MUTUAL LIFE INSURANCE CO.
Reaching for the stars. S. Herbert. il por *Black Enterprise* 19:294-6+ Je '89
GOLDEN VALLEY MICROWAVE FOODS INC.
What's munching away at Golden Valley's success. R. Mitchell. il *Business Week* p30 Jl 10 '89
DER GOLDENE TOPF [opera] *See* Mayer, Eckehard
GOLDENRAIN TREES *See* Golden rain trees
GOLDFARB, DAVID
First word. il *Omni (New York, N.Y.)* 11:8 F '89
GOLDIE, CHRISTINE MATHEWS
I do. il pors *World Tennis* 36:89-90+ Mr '89
The newlywed game. il pors *World Tennis* 36:84-6+ My '89
Summertime blues. il pors *World Tennis* 37:42+ N '89
A tale of two cities. il pors *World Tennis* 37:96+ S '89
A taste of the Orient. il pors *World Tennis* 37:60-1 Ag '89
about
Hearts of Goldie. N. Amdur. il pors *World Tennis* 37:47-8+ D '89
GOLDIE, DAN
On the rebound. il pors *World Tennis* 37:50-1 O '89
One year in the life . . . il por *World Tennis* 36:24+ Ap '89
The pain game. il pors *World Tennis* 37:38-9 Je '89
about
Hard road to the top. N. Amdur. il por *World Tennis* 36:32-4 Ja '89
Hearts of Goldie. N. Amdur. il pors *World Tennis* 37:47-8+ D '89
I do. C. M. Goldie. il pors *World Tennis* 36:89-90+ Mr '89
The newlywed game. C. M. Goldie. il pors *World Tennis* 36:84-6+ My '89
Summertime blues. C. M. Goldie. il pors *World Tennis* 37:42+ N '89
A tale of two cities. C. M. Goldie. il pors *World Tennis* 37:96+ S '89
A taste of the Orient. C. M. Goldie. il pors *World Tennis* 37:60-1 Ag '89
Triumphant returns. J. Schore. il pors *World Tennis* 37:70-1 Jl '89
The turning point. P. Stites. il pors *World Tennis* 36:66-9 F '89
GOLDIN, MARION
about
Women on the verge of a nervy breakthrough [interview] P. Orenstein. il pors *Mother Jones* 14:28-31+ Je '89
GOLDMAN, BARBARA
about
The contemporary general store brings Main Street to Malibu. D. Weil. il por *Working Woman* 14:60-1 Ag '89
GOLDMAN, BARBARA
Help for high blood pressure: less sodium, more potassium. il *Better Homes and Gardens* 67:47 Ap '89
GOLDMAN, BETSY SCHEIN
Karen Horn. il por *American Artist* 53:68-73 Ag '89
Skip Steinworth. il pors *American Artist* 53:46-51+ Je '89
The Torpedo Factory Art Center. il *American Artist* 53:68-73 F '89

GOLDMAN, CALVIN
about
A warning from Ottawa. B. Wallace. il por *Maclean's* 102:38 Ja 30 '89
GOLDMAN, CHARLES REMINGTON, 1930-
Lake Tahoe: preserving a fragile ecosystem [cover story] bibl f il map *Environment* 31:6-11+ S '89
GOLDMAN, JAN
Space commerce, Soviet style. il *Ad Astra* 1:24-30 D '89
GOLDMAN, MARIAN GORDON
(jt. auth) *See* Goldman, Martin, and Goldman, Marian Gordon
GOLDMAN, MARSHALL I.
The future of Soviet economic reform. bibl f *Current History* 88:329-32+ O '89
GOLDMAN, MARTIN, AND GOLDMAN, MARIAN GORDON
Top books: 1988 winners. il *American Health* 8:112+ Ja/F '89
GOLDMAN, MERLE
Vengeance in China. il *The New York Review of Books* 36:5-9 N 9 '89
GOLDMAN, ROBERT K.
(jt. auth) *See* Brown, Cynthia G., 1943-, and Goldman, Robert K.
GOLDMAN, SOL, D. 1987
about
The Midas curse [cover story] D. Smith. il pors *New York* 22:32-40 Ap 3 '89
GOLDMAN, STUART
The blooming of rock 'n' roll [discussion of February 24, 1989 article, That old devil music] il *National Review* 41:44-5 My 5 '89
That old devil music [cover story] il *National Review* 41:28-31+ F 24 '89
about
Face the music. K. Loder. il *Rolling Stone* p57-9+ My 4 '89
GOLDMAN FAMILY
about
The Midas curse [cover story] D. Smith. il pors *New York* 22:32-40 Ap 3 '89
GOLDMAN, SACHS & CO.
Can Goldman stay on top? J. Willoughby. il *Forbes* 144:150+ S 18 '89
The top bear [S. Einhorn] R. Henkoff. il por *Fortune* 119:47+ Ja 2 '89
GOLDREICH, GLORIA
Eight candles of hope [story] il *McCall's* 117:73-7 D '89
GOLDREICH, P., AND OTHERS
Neptune's story. bibl f il *Science* 245:500-4 Ag 4 '89
GOLDRICH, HENRY
about
Manny's happy returns. M. Porter. il *Gentlemen's Quarterly* 59:157-8 Ag '89
GOLDRICH, LAURIE
Dressed to chill. il *Working Woman* 14:88-90 Ag '89
about
Work (and play) in progress. il *Working Woman* 14:162-7 N '89
GOLDSCHMIDT, NICHOLAS
about
A choral cornucopia. P. Young. il *Maclean's* 102:59-60 Je 5 '89
GOLDSMITH, BARBARA
Diary of a duplex: Barbara Goldsmith and Frank Perry on Park. il pors *Architectural Digest* 46:310-15 N '89
GOLDSMITH, E. J., AND OTHERS
Domain separation in the activation of glycogen phosphorylase α. bibl f il *Science* 245:528-32 Ag 4 '89
GOLDSMITH, SIR JAMES, 1933-
Perspective from Europe [address, May 23, 1989] *Vital Speeches of the Day* 55:525-8 Je 15 '89
about
A British war—on Yankee soil. T. Smart and M. Maremont. il *Business Week* p33 S 11 '89
'Goldfinger' is back. L. Reibstein. il por *Newsweek* 114:48-9 Jl 24 '89
Jimmy Goldsmith, leading indicator. C. P. Work. il por *U.S. News & World Report* 107:43-4 Jl 24 '89
Jimmy Goldsmith's gun bearer goes gunning. P. Finch. il por *Business Week* p63+ O 16 '89
A raider returns. J. DeMont. il por *Maclean's* 102:34 Jl 24 '89
Storming a British blue chip. R. A. Melcher. il por *Business Week* p18-19 Jl 24 '89
Take that, Jimmy Goldsmith. R. A. Melcher. il *Business Week* p60-1 O 9 '89
That's a reach, Sir James. J. Castro. il por *Time* 134:36-7 Jl 24 '89
GOLDSMITH, JUDITH
Life's cycles. il por *Organic Gardening* 36:72 My '89
GOLDSMITH, PATRICIA
The heat is on. il *Seventeen* 48:152-3+ O '89
GOLDSMITH, RUSSELL
about
Betting on Republic's bonanza. A. B. Block. il por *Channels (New York, N.Y.: 1986)* 9:48-51 Ja '89

GOLDSMITH, SUZANNE, AND BOO, KATHERINE
The case for the case study. *The Washington Monthly* 21:18-20+ Je '89

GOLDSMITH/JEFFREY (FIRM)
Less is more. B. Kanner. il *New York* 22:16+ O 2 '89

GOLDSMITHING
See also
Gilding
Society of North American Goldsmiths

Exhibitions
African gold comes to America [Metropolitan Museum of Art] il *USA Today (Periodical)* 118:8 D '89
Art à la carte [Gold of Africa] K. Best. il *Travel Holiday* 171:116 Mr '89
Rare artisanry from Africa [Gold of Africa] K. M. Burke. il *Smithsonian* 20:180 Je '89

GOLDSTEIN, ALAN
Galaxy hunting around the Big Dipper. il *Astronomy* 17:78-84 Mr '89
Split a star in two. il *Astronomy* 17:88-91 D '89

GOLDSTEIN, BARRY J.
(jt. auth) See Kahn, C. Ronald, and Goldstein, Barry J.

GOLDSTEIN, CATHERINE, AND GRAY, JEREMY, 1947-
The roots of modern maths. il *The Unesco Courier* 42:42-8 N '89

GOLDSTEIN, LAWRENCE
about
Still in the pinks. T. Jaffe. *Forbes* 143:172-3 F 6 '89

GOLDSTEIN, LEE SCOTT
about
The fan [opera] Reviews
Opera News 54:47-8 O '89. J. Von Rhein

GOLDSTEIN, MARION
Dowsing [poem] *America* 161:220 O 7 '89

GOLDSTEIN, MELVYN C., AND BEALL, CYNTHIA
The remote world of Tibet's nomads. il map *National Geographic* 175:752-81 Je '89

GOLDSTEIN, PATRICK
Return of the money-making slime [cover story] il *Rolling Stone* p52-4+ Je 1 '89

GOLDSTEIN, PAUL, AND BROWNSTEIN, HENRY
The drug-violence nexus. *New Perspectives Quarterly* 6:24 Summ '89

GOLDSTEIN, R. M., AND OTHERS
Remote sensing of ocean currents. bibl f il *Science* 246:1282-5 D 8 '89

GOLDSTEIN, WALTER, 1930-
Economic growth and military power: erosion of the super-powers. *Current (Washington, D.C.)* 309:23-31 Ja '89

GOLDSTROM, DONALD
Notes from a veteran jogger. il *Health (New York, N.Y.)* 21:32-3 O '89

GOLDWATER, BARRY M. (BARRY MORRIS), 1909-
about
Extremists in the mainstream. V. Gold. il *The American Spectator* 22:34-5 Jl '89
Goldwater at 80: in full candor. M. Tulumello. il por *New Choices for the Best Years* 29:8-9 Ja '89
Older, wiser but still prickly as a saguaro, Barry Goldwater remembers when right was wrong. A. Kopkind. il pors *People Weekly* 31:67-70+ F 13 '89
Ready, fire, aim [interview] P. Garrison. il pors *Flying* 116:78-80+ D '89

GOLDWYN, SAMUEL, 1882-1974
about
Goldwynism. J. G. Dunne. il *The New York Review of Books* 36:28-33 My 18 '89
"I made Wuthering Heights. Wyler only directed it". K. Turan. il pors *Gentlemen's Quarterly* 59:105+ My '89
PW interviews [biographer A. S. Berg] L. See. por *Publishers Weekly* 235:49-50 Mr 24 '89
Wuthering Heights. A. S. Berg. il pors *The New York Times Magazine* p46-8+ F 19 '89

GOLEIZOVSKY, KASYAN
about
Before Balanchine: Kasyan Goleizovsky's Russian revolution (I). G. Manor. il pors *Dance Magazine* 63:56-60 Ja '89
Before Balanchine: Kasyan Goleizovsky's Russian revolution (II). G. Manor. il pors *Dance Magazine* 63:60-4 F '89

GOLEM IN ART
Exhibitions
Golem!: Danger, deliverance and art: Jewish Museum. R. Cembalest. il *Art News* 88:150+ F '89

GOLEMAN, DANIEL
Conquering your fears. *McCall's* 117:154+ O '89

GOLENBOCK, PETER, 1946-
about
Foul play by the book. H. F. Waters. por *Newsweek* 114:62 Ag 14 '89

GOLF
See also
Holes in one (Golf)
Miniature golf
Putting (Golf)
For women golfers, life in the rough. A. Engeler. il *The New York Times Magazine* p42+ O 1 '89
Golf guide: the whole in one [cover story] S. Raque. il *Women's Sports & Fitness* 11:44-8+ Jl/Ag '89

The hottest game [cover story; special section; with editorial comment by Kevin Doyle] il *Maclean's* 102:2, 42-4+ Ap 10 '89
On the seventh day he played. C. Gorman. il *Time* 133:66-7 My 8 '89
Tee time for corporate women. D. M. Topolnicki. il *Working Woman* 14:142+ Je '89

Anecdotes, facetiae, satire, etc.
Thanks for the memory. I. Frazier. *The New Yorker* 65:36-7 D 18 '89

Economic aspects
See also
Club Corp. of America
The boom in golf as baby boomers hit the links. W. C. Symonds. il *Business Week* p76-7+ Mr 27 '89

Equipment
See also
Golf balls
Golf clubs (Sticks)

Ethical aspects
Tips for fair play on the fairway. P. Finch. il *Business Week* p164 O 23 '89

Study and teaching
Different strokes for different folks. J. Diaz. il *Money* 18:112-15+ Ap '89
For the love of the game [instructor P. K. Bell] D. Young. il pors *Southern Living* 24:78+ O '89
Fore play [Grand Cypress golf resort in Orlando] J. Queenan. il *Gentlemen's Quarterly* 59:248-57 Je '89

Aids and devices
18 tips from 18 legends of golf; Jack Nicklaus shows you the greatest 18 holes of major championship golf [videos] J. Bessman. il por *Video* 12:90 Ja '89

Tournaments
See also
Ladies Professional Golf Association
PGA Tour Inc.
Another Cup runneth overseas [Great Britain and Ireland team wins Walker Cup] J. Garrity. il *Sports Illustrated* 71:64-5 Ag 28 '89
Augusta overture [Par-3 Contest; reproductions of paintings] R. Wieferich. il *Sports Illustrated* 70:56-65 Ap 10 '89
Beating the devil [J. Inkster wins Nabisco Dinah Shore] D. S. Looney. il por *Sports Illustrated* 70:34+ Ap 10 '89
Bridesmaid revisited [Masters runner-up G. Norman] B. Verdi. il pors *Sports Illustrated* 70:54-7 Ap 24 '89
A British victory in British weather [N. Faldo wins the Masters] H. W. Wind. *The New Yorker* 65:97-103+ My 15 '89
Fit to be tied [Ryder Cup] E. M. Swift. il *Sports Illustrated* 71:30-5 O 2 '89
Getting really mad and good [N. Lopez wins LPGA Championship] G. Sweda. il por *Sports Illustrated* 70:65 My 29 '89
Giving out high marks [B. Glasson wins Doral Ryder Open] J. Diaz. il pors *Sports Illustrated* 70:20-1 Mr 6 '89
Golf's real swingers? Watch the old guys [Senior Tour] M. Durslag. il *TV Guide* 37:22-3 Ag 5-11 '89
High noon at Troon [M. Calcavecchia wins British Open] R. Reilly. il por *Sports Illustrated* 71:20-2+ Jl 31 '89
High, wide and handsome [C. Patton wins U.S. Amateur] J. Garrity. il por *Sports Illustrated* 71:169 S 4 '89
Hoch as in choke [S. Hoch wins Las Vegas tournament after losing Masters on missed putt] R. Reilly. il pors *Sports Illustrated* 70:62-4+ Je 12 '89
Hope for the best [B. Hope star of own tournament] E. M. Swift. il pors *Sports Illustrated* 70:20-2+ Ja 23 '89
It's nifty being 50 [L. Trevino makes Senior Tour debut at Kaanapali Classic] K. Moore. il pors *Sports Illustrated* 71:34-6+ D 18 '89
It's rough to be a duffer at a pro-am. P. Finch. il *Business Week* p94-5 Jl 3 '89
Jolly good show [N. Faldo wins Masters; cover story] E. M. Swift. il pors *Sports Illustrated* 70:18-25 Ap 17 '89
A King is crowned queen [cover story] J. Garrity. il por *Sports Illustrated* 71:71-2 Jl 24 '89
King of the hill [C. Strange wins U.S. Open; cover story] R. Reilly. il pors *Sports Illustrated* 70:20-5 Je 26 '89
Kite finally takes flight [Players Championship] E. M. Swift. il por *Sports Illustrated* 70:26-8+ Mr 27 '89
The Masters blasters [players' complaints about tricky Augusta National course] K. Hannon. il *Sport (New York, N.Y.)* 80:32+ My '89
Michael Jordan launches project to help students in black colleges [celebrity golf tournament to benefit United Negro College Fund] il *Jet* 76:22-5 Ag 14 '89
The Midas touch [T. Kite moves to top of career earnings list with Nabisco Championships victory] J. Garrity. il por *Sports Illustrated* 71:42-3 N 6 '89
No keeping up with Jones [S. Jones wins MONY Tournament of Champions] J. Diaz. il por *Sports Illustrated* 70:34-5 Ja 16 '89
Oh me, oh my, O'Meara! [AT&T Pebble Beach National Pro-Am] R. Reilly. il pors *Sports Illustrated* 70:12-19 F 6 '89
Old Sarge takes charge [O. Moody wins Senior Open] J. Garrity. il *Sports Illustrated* 71:56+ Jl 10 '89

GOLF—Tournaments—*cont.*

Putting on the style [P. Stewart wins PGA Championship] E. M. Swift. il pors *Sports Illustrated* 71:28-9 Ag 21 '89

Sink, blast you! [M. Jordan at St. Jude Pro-Am; cover story] E. M. Swift. il pors *Sports Illustrated* 71:36-9 Ag 14 '89

Strange redux [U.S. Open at Oak Hill] H. W. Wind. *The New Yorker* 65:68-77 Jl 24 '89

The word of mouth on Ted Danson's Hawaiian celeb bash: it was a ball [fund raiser for the American Oceans Campaign] il por *People Weekly* 32:113-15 O 16 '89

Economic aspects

Belles on the ball [LPGA] P. Young. il *Maclean's* 102:68-9 Ap 10 '89

Driving PGA Inc. H. Quinn. il *Maclean's* 102:60-1 Ap 10 '89

Find the golf here? [women's tour] J. Diaz. il *Sports Illustrated* 70:58-60+ F 13 '89

Golf's old greats are really swinging again [Senior Tour] W. C. Symonds. il *Business Week* p122-3 Je 26 '89

History

'80s golf. D. Granger. il *Sport (New York, N.Y.)* 80:84 O '89

Rules

The golf club with a handicap all its own [K. Solheim's Ping irons] P. Finch. il por *Business Week* p126+ My 1 '89

Canada

The hottest game [cover story; special section; with editorial comment by Kevin Doyle] il *Maclean's* 102:2, 42-4+ Ap 10 '89

Japan

Love that golf. R. Reilly. il *Sports Illustrated* 71:70-6+ Ag 21 '89

Western Europe

Will Europe take a divot out of the PGA Tour? W. C. Symonds. il *Business Week* p188-9 S 25 '89

GOLF BALLS

Thar's gold, white gold, in them thar ponds, and golf ball hunter Jim Reid is diving to claim it. A. Abrahams. il *People Weekly* 31:67-8 Je 12 '89

GOLF CLUBS (STICKS)

The golf club with a handicap all its own [K. Solheim's Ping irons] P. Finch. il por *Business Week* p126+ My 1 '89

Put more zing in that swing, with these hot new clubs. P. Finch. il *Business Week* p141 Je 5 '89

GOLF COURSES

See also
Club Corp. of America

America's top 10 golf courses. il *Travel Holiday* 172:59 N '89

Illinois golf course to bear name of Joe Louis. il *Jet* 76:51 S 11 '89

The Masters blasters [players' complaints about tricky Augusta National course] K. Hannon. il *Sport (New York, N.Y.)* 80:32+ My '89

The Pinehurst tradition. J. Y. Bartlett. il *Travel Holiday* 172:50-7 N '89

Roughing it [New York City] J. D'O'Brian. il *New York* 22:42-7 Jl 24 '89

Strange redux [U.S. Open at Oak Hill] H. W. Wind. *The New Yorker* 65:68-77 Jl 24 '89

Design

A golfer's course [Loxahatchee in Jupiter, Fla., designed by J. Nicklaus] il *Maclean's* 102:52 Ap 10 '89

Photographs and photography

Great shots and lovely vistas. il *Maclean's* 102:70-1 Ap 10 '89

Canada

Hunting a game. il *Maclean's* 102:66 Ap 10 '89

Great Britain

A big yen for British courses [Japanese acquisitions] H. J. Steinbreder. il *Sports Illustrated* 71:52-3 Ag 21 '89

GOLF GAMES, ELECTRONIC See Video games

GOLF IN ART

Augusta overture [Par-3 Contest; reproductions of paintings] R. Wieferich. il *Sports Illustrated* 70:56-65 Ap 10 '89

GOLF RESORTS See Resorts

GOLFERS

See also
Ballesteros, Seve
Barr, Dave
Calcavecchia, Mark
Crenshaw, Ben
Faldo, Nick
Gardner, Frank Webb, Jr.
Geiberger, Al
Glasson, Bill
Green, Ken
Hagen, Walter, 1892-1969
Hoch, Scott
Inkster, Juli, 1961?-
Jacklin, Tony
Jones, Rosie
Jones, Steve
King, Betsy
Kite, Tom
Knudson, George

Lopez, Nancy, 1957-
Lyle, Sandy
Martin, Stephanie
Miley, Marion, d. 1941
Moody, Orville
Nicklaus, Jack
Norman, Greg, 1955-
O'Meara, Mark
Patton, Chris
Reid, Mike
Rodriguez, Chi Chi
Stewart, Payne
Strange, Curtis
Trevino, Lee
Woods, Eldrik
Zokol, Richard

The hottest game [cover story; special section; with editorial comment by Kevin Doyle] il *Maclean's* 102:2, 42-4+ Ap 10 '89

Health and hygiene

After beating what seemed bad odds, a top pro is back up to par; ed. by Andrew Abrahams. P. Bradley. il pors *People Weekly* 32:80+ S 18 '89

Salaries, pensions, etc.

Meanwhile, on the links, an Everyman scratches out a living [F. W. Gardner, jr.] G. Waggoner. il pors *Sport (New York, N.Y.)* 80:89+ Je '89

The Midas touch [T. Kite moves to top of career earnings list with Nabisco Championships victory] J. Garrity. il por *Sports Illustrated* 71:42-3 N 6 '89

GOLFO DULCE (COSTA RICA)

The sweet gulf [billfish fishing] B. Stearns. il *Field & Stream* 94:64-6 Ag '89

GOLGI APPARATUS

Clathrin: a role in the intracellular retention of a Golgi membrane protein [yeast] G. S. Payne and R. Schekman. bibl f il *Science* 245:1358-65 S 22 '89

GOLISANO, B. THOMAS

about
Tom Golisano and the red tape factory. F. Meeks. il por *Forbes* 143:80+ My 15 '89

GOLLANCZ (VICTOR) LTD. See Victor Gollancz Ltd.

GOLLEY, FRANK B.

(jt. auth) See Cooley, June H., and Golley, Frank B.

GOLLOB, HERMAN

about
Herman Gollob's bar mitzvah. B. Greene. por *Esquire* 112:33-4 Jl '89

GOLOB, STEVEN

Oases of opportunity. il *Nation's Business* 77:45-6 Jl '89

GOLUB, LEON ALBERT, 1922-

about
Riddled Sphinxes. R. Storr. il *Art in America* 77:126-31 Mr '89

GOLUB, RICHARD

about
The new Roy Cohn [cover story] J. Taylor. il pors *New York* 22:18-25 Ag 7 '89

GOMBROWICZ, WITOLD

On Bruno Schulz; tr. by Lillian Vallee. bibl f il *The New York Review of Books* 36:5-7 Ap 13 '89

GOMEZ, ALAIN

about
Alain Gomez, France's high-tech warrior. T. Peterson. il por *Business Week* p100-2+ My 15 '89

GOMEZ, EDWARD M.

Phototechnology: the future is now. il *Art News* 88:151 Ap '89

GOMPERS, SAMUEL, 1850-1924

about
Samuel Gompers: a half century in labor's front rank. I. Yellowitz. bibl f *Monthly Labor Review* 112:27-33 Jl '89

GONADOTROPIN RECEPTORS See Hormone receptors

GONADOTROPIN RELEASING HORMONE

Hope for endometriosis sufferers. *McCall's* 116:90-1 F '89

GONADS

See also
Testicles

GONDEK, JULIANA

about
Musical events:
Merkin Hall recitals by J. Gondek. A. Porter. *The New Yorker* 65:97-8 O 23 '89

GONDOLAS

The gondola of Venice. A. Gillette. il *The Courier (Unesco)* 41:24-9 N '88

GONE WITH THE WIND [film] See Motion picture reviews—Single works

GONGWER, CALVIN

about
Tri-hull ship [cover story] A. L. Carone and J. Free. il por *Popular Science* 235:60-2 Ag '89

GONICK, JEAN, 1950-

Killing old loves. il *Glamour* 87:256+ N '89

GONIN, JEAN-MARC

(jt. auth) See Legris, Michel, and Gonin, Jean-Marc

GONZAGA, MARYLIS SEVILLA- See Sevilla-Gonzaga, Marylis

GONZÁLES, ELAINE
Say it with chocolate. il *Ladies' Home Journal* 106:156-8 F '89

GONZALES, LAURENCE, 1947-
Toward pure energy. il *Harper's* 279:72-6 Ag '89

GONZÁLEZ, FELIPE
about
Africa no longer starts at the Pyrenees. D. Lawday. il por *U.S. News & World Report* 107:54 O 30 '89
"I used to have little faith in the U.S." [interview] M. Hornblower and J. Walker. il por *Time* 134:54 O 23 '89
Shifting politics in Spain. J. Valls-Russell. il *The New Leader* 72:9-10 N 27 '89
A talk with Felipe González. J. L. Martín Prieto. *World Press Review* 36:25 Mr '89

GONZALEZ, MILDRED
Mirror [poem] *Essence* 19:142 F '89

GONZALEZ-CRUSSI, F.
Hearing pleasures [excerpt from The five senses] il *Health (New York, N.Y.)* 21:64-71 Mr '89

GONZALEZ TORRES, ENRIQUE
about
The great experiment. R. Bautch. *America* 160:316-17 Ap 8 '89

GOOD AND EVIL
See also
Righteousness
Sin
Can we be good without God? [political meaning of Christianity; cover story] G. Tinder. il *The Atlantic* 264:68-72+ D '89
On troubled belief. M. Garvey. *America* 160:164 F 25 '89
A perception of evil [cover story] M. L. West. *America* 161:466-9 D 23-30 '89

GOOD AND EVIL IN MOTION PICTURES
'Crimes' story [work of W. Allen] M. Pally. il por *Film Comment* 25:11-12+ N/D '89

THE GOOD COACH [drama] See Siegler, Ben

GOOD DAY NEW YORK [television program] See Television program reviews—Single works

GOOD FISHING [television program] See Television program reviews—Single works

GOOD FRIDAY
Good Friday. V. S. Owens. il *Christianity Today* 33:21-3 Mr 17 '89

GOOD GUYS INC.
Ron Unkefer: sometimes it pays not to haggle. R. D. Hof. il por *Business Week* p82 Ap 3 '89

GOOD HOUSEKEEPING (PERIODICAL)
Editor's notebook. J. M. Carter. See issues of Good Housekeeping

THE GOOD MOTHER [film] See Motion picture reviews—Single works

GOOD SAMARITANISM See Assistance in emergencies

GOOD SPIRIT (PERIODICAL)
Meet a new magazine for vital living. R. Rodale. il *Prevention (Emmaus, Pa.)* 41:28-31 O '89

GOODALL, JANE
about
Suffer the little chimps. A. Cockburn. *The Nation* 248:222-3 F 20 '89

GOODAVAGE, MARIA
Murky waters. il *Modern Maturity* 32:44-50 Ag/S '89

GOODE, ERICA E.
Secret obsessions. *Vogue* 179:246+ F '89

GOODE, JOE
about
San Francisco's Joe Goode: working hard to be the bad boy of modern dance. J. Ross. il pors *Dance Magazine* 63:46-50 Ja '89

GOODE, RICHARD
about
Richard Goode's late Beethoven. R. Freed. il por *Stereo Review* 54:110 O '89

GOODLAND, ROBERT, 1939-, AND LEDEC, GEORGE
Wildlands: balancing conversion with conservation in World Bank projects [cover story] bibl f il *Environment* 31:6-11+ N '89

GOODLING, WILLIAM F.
Should President Bush's minimum wage proposal be adopted? [excerpts from address, March 23, 1989] *Congressional Digest* 68:140+ My '89

GOODMAN, ALLEGRA
Oral history [story] *Commentary* 87:60-8 F '89

GOODMAN, ANDREW, 1943-1964
about
The '64 civil rights murders: the struggle continues [cover story] J. Kornbluth. il pors *The New York Times Magazine* p16-19+ Jl 23 '89
Back on the bus. P. Dray. il pors *Mother Jones* 14:37-9+ N '89
Honor trio killed by KKK in Mississippi vote drive. il pors *Jet* 76:6-7 Jl 10 '89

GOODMAN, BRENDA J.
Do you disagree with your boss's ethics? il *Glamour* 87:107-8 Ag '89

GOODMAN, CALVIN J.
Benton's enduring American art (I). il pors *American Artist* 53:30-7+ D '89
Supplementing gallery sales. il *American Artist* 53:74-9 Je '89

GOODMAN, ERIC K.
Men and abortion. il *Glamour* 87:178-9+ Jl '89

GOODMAN, FLORENCE JEANNE
What's the good word? il *American Artist* 53:98-101 S '89

GOODMAN, GEORGE J. W. See Smith, Adam, 1930-

GOODMAN, HARRY
about
The lofty dreams of upstart Air Europe. M. Maremont. il por *Business Week* p52+ Ap 17 '89

GOODMAN, HIRSH
Slipping into darkness. *The New Republic* 201:10-12 Jl 3 '89

GOODMAN, JOHN
about
"Getting married is the best thing that's ever happened to me!". V. J. Radovsky. il pors *Redbook* 173:30+ S '89
John Goodman. il por *People Weekly* 32:60-1 D 25 '89-Ja 1 '90
John Goodman, Roseanne Barr's big guy co-star, has a big-time wedding in the Big Easy. il pors *People Weekly* 32:70 N 13 '89
No more wild times with Bruce Willis on the streets of L.A. M. Leahy. il pors *TV Guide* 37:32-3+ F 18-24 '89
Roseanne's main squeeze. E. Sherman. il pors *Ladies' Home Journal* 106:136+ My '89

GOODMAN, JON P.
"Help! My bank just failed". il por *Ladies' Home Journal* 106:22+ Je '89

GOODMAN, MATTHEW
Locker-room tycoons. *Utne Reader* p116-18 N/D '89
Where the boys are. *The Washington Monthly* 21:18-20 Ap '89

GOODMAN, SUSAN
But enough about you . . . why narcissism is on the rise. il *Mademoiselle* 95:143 Mr '89
Jest for the health of it. il *Current Health 2* 15:18-19 Ja '89

GOODMAN, THOMAS
(jt. auth) See Lefrancois, Leo, and Goodman, Thomas

GOODMAN, WALTER
Notes on Italy and England. *The New Leader* 72:7-8 Je 12-26 '89

GOODMAN & HAYLE INFORMATION SYSTEMS, INC.
Back from the brink of bankruptcy [C. Hayle] L. Washer. il pors *Working Woman* 14:61-4 S '89

GOODMARK FOODS INC.
"The chance of a lifetime". P. Duggan. il por *Forbes* 143:140+ Ap 17 '89

GOODNESS GARDENS (FIRM)
A hint of mint. P. Stone. il *The Mother Earth News* 120:53-5 N/D '89

GOODNESS OF GOD See God—Goodness

GOODRICH, CHRIS
Big numbers for innumeracy: Hill & Wang's first bestseller heralds a new direction. il por *Publishers Weekly* 235:46-8 Je 2 '89
Chain reaction. *The Nation* 248:596-8 My 1 '89
Writers and the market—II. *The Nation* 249:24-6+ Jl 3 '89

GOODRICH (B.F.) CO. See B.F. Goodrich Co.

GOODSTEIN, DAVID L., 1939-
Richard P. Feynman, teacher. il *Physics Today* 42:70-5 F '89

GOODWILL IN BUSINESS
Accounting
Britain's goodwill games. D. Wechsler. il *Forbes* 144:65+ O 2 '89
Goodwill is making a lot of people angry. J. M. Laderman. il *Business Week* p73+ Jl 31 '89
Ill will. L. Jereski. il *Forbes* 143:41-2 Ja 23 '89
A peculiar beauty contest [concentration on cash flow vs. earnings in stock valuation as highlighted in Time Inc. merger] D. Wechsler. il *Forbes* 144:43-4+ Jl 10 '89

GOODWILLIE, JOHN MORLEY, 1910-1987
about
Park Avenue Gothic: a family feud turns into a fight to the death. B. Costikyan. il pors *New York* 22:46-50+ Mr 20 '89

GOODWIN, BETTY
The bad Guy finishes first. il pors *TV Guide* 37:28-31 Ja 21-27 '89
The diets that keep stars looking trim. il *TV Guide* 37:26-8 Je 10-16 '89
In high gear. il por *Harper's Bazaar* 122:50-3+ Jl '89
L.A. spreeway. il *Vogue* 179:112+ F '89
Los-Anglophile. il pors *House & Garden* 161:82-9+ Ag '89
The natural. il pors *Vogue* 179:120+ Mr '89
Why Greg Evigan wouldn't come out of the bathroom. il pors *TV Guide* 37:16-18 Ap 15-21 '89

GOODWIN, MARY
about
Classical translation. D. Hall. il por *House & Garden* 161:116-23 Mr '89

GOODWIN, PEGGY

about

Spreading some good words. D. Young. il por *Southern Living* 24:64 Ag '89

GOODWIN, RICHARD N.

about

LBJ's alter ego. G. C. Ward. il *American Heritage* 40:14+ F '89

GOODWIN, ROBERT K.

about

Goodwin leads fed. effort to aid black universities. por *Jet* 76:16 Ag 7 '89

GOODWYN, LAWRENCE

Seize the day. *The Nation* 249:777 D 25 '89

GOODYEAR TIRE & RUBBER COMPANY

Big blue meets the purple eagle eaters [Goodyear and Hoosier vie for NASCAR Winston Cup market] L. Griffin. il *Car and Driver* 34:221-2+ Je '89

The big wheels that may be after Goodyear. G. G. Marcial. il *Business Week* p102 My 29 '89

Can Goodyear pull out of its skid? Z. Schiller. il *Business Week* p41 Mr 20 '89

Great tires, blimp to come [Hoosier Racing Tire vs. Goodyear] J. Harris. il por *Forbes* 143:288+ My 29 '89

The titan of tires [Goodyear dealer M. Brown] M. E. Howard. il pors *Black Enterprise* 20:68-70+ S '89

The Wingfoot Express [early involvement in trucking] W. Jeanes. il map *Car and Driver* 35:121-3 D '89

GOOFY (FICTIONAL CHARACTER)

Collectibles

The Goof. L. Rosenkrantz. il *Antiques & Collecting Hobbies* 94:20+ Mr '89

GOOSE COOKING *See* Cooking—Poultry

GOOSE SHOOTING

Daydreams [Canada geese] G. Hill. il *Field & Stream* 94:10 D '89

Grandpa and the kid [hunting for Christmas goose with Chesapeake Bay retriever] D. Sisson. il *Field & Stream* 94:43+ D '89

H₂Onkers [Canada goose shooting] G. Clancy. il *Outdoor Life* 184:90-1+ N '89

GOP (GRAND OLD PARTY) *See* Republican Party (U.S.)

GOPAL, SARVEPALLI

Makers of modern India. il pors *The Courier (Unesco)* 42:10-11 F '89

GOPNIK, ADAM

The art world. *The New Yorker* 65:88-92 Je 19 '89

The art world. *The New Yorker* 65:132-6+ O 23 '89

The art world. *The New Yorker* 65:107-11 F 20 '89

The art world. *The New Yorker* 65:109-13 Ap 10 '89

GORANSON, LECY

about

'Roseanne's' terrific TV teens! il pors *'Teen* 33:68 My '89

GORBACHEV, MIKHAIL

See also

Bush-Gorbachev summit conference, 1989

Gorbachev speaks to the Council of Europe [excerpts from address, July 6, 1989] *Current History* 88:347 O '89

The international community and change [address, July 6, 1989] *Vital Speeches of the Day* 55:706-11 S 15 '89

Perestroika [address, September 11, 1989] *Vital Speeches of the Day* 56:5-7 O 15 '89

U.S.S.R. arms reduction [address, December 7, 1988] *Vital Speeches of the Day* 55:229-36 F 1 '89

U.S., Soviet Union exchange New Year's messages [remarks, January 1, 1989] *Department of State Bulletin* 89:55 Mr '89

about

The abolitionist. J. Newhouse. *The New Yorker* 64:51-62+ Ja 9 '89

Agreement to disagree. A. Wilson-Smith. il pors *Maclean's* 102:25-6 My 22 '89

American foreign policy: the Bush agenda. R. M. Nixon. *Foreign Affairs* 68 Special Issue:199-219 ['89]

And now for my next trick . . . J. Kohan. il *Time* 133:41-2 My 8 '89

As Kabul teeters, Gorbachev lands on his feet. P. Galuszka and others. il *Business Week* p51 F 20 '89

At the top of Washington's reading list. A. Platt. il *Newsweek* 114:23 O 2 '89

Atari Communists: from hardline to software [cover story; special section; with editorial comment by Nathan Gardels] il *New Perspectives Quarterly* 5:2-60 Wint '88/'89

Back to the future. M. S. Forbes, Jr. il por *Forbes* 143:27 Je 26 '89

The benefits of benign neglect. M. Ruby. il *U.S. News & World Report* 107:68 Jl 31 '89

Can Gorbachev radicalize *perestroika*? S. Bialer. il *U.S. News & World Report* 107:39-40 Ag 7 '89

Can Gorbachev reform the Soviet military? W. E. Odom. il *U.S. News & World Report* 107:43 S 11 '89

Can we trust this nice Mr. Gorbachev? C. W. Weinberger. il *Forbes* 143:37 Ja 9 '89

The China syndrome. F. Coleman. il *Newsweek* 113:36 Je 5 '89

The cold war: a presidential agenda. S. F. Cohen. *Current (Washington, D.C.)* 311:32-8 Mr/Ap '89

Counterpunching Gorbachev. S. V. Roberts. il por *U.S. News & World Report* 106:16-17 My 29 '89

Crises around the clock. H. Anderson. il por *Newsweek* 114:30-1 Ag 7 '89

Dealing warily with a sick Bear. D. Stanglin. il *U.S. News & World Report* 107:32+ S 25 '89

Dear editor: You're fired. Signed, Mikhail Gorbachev. W. R. Doerner. il pors *Time* 134:62-3 O 30 '89

Don't die yet. D. R. Carlin, Jr. *Commonweal* 116:265 My 5 '89

A double standard. A. Nagorski. il *Newsweek* 114:35-6 D 18 '89

The empire breaks up. J. Rupnik. *The New Republic* 200:20-4 F 20 '89

Endgame: pressuring Gorbo. M. Ledeen. il *The American Spectator* 22:29-31 My '89

The enlightened patriot. M. Grondona. *World Press Review* 36:64 Ap '89

Exorcising the 'dead souls'. A. Platt. il por *Newsweek* 113:37 My 8 '89

Face-off on reform. J. Kohan. il pors *Time* 134:20-2 D 25 '89

Farming for dollars: Gorbachev's latest gamble. P. Galuszka. il *Business Week* p44 Ag 28 '89

For Gorbachev, *perestroika II* may mean survival. R. Brady. il *Business Week* p60+ S 25 '89

From now on, the buck stops here. J. Trimble. il *U.S. News & World Report* 107:40 O 2 '89

Giving Gorbachev a boost: Soviet reform is in the U.S. national interest. R. Holbrooke. il *Newsweek* 114:28 S 25 '89

Glasnost in action. A. Wilson-Smith. il por *Maclean's* 102:20+ Je 5 '89

Gorb-aid. *The New Republic* 201:7-8 O 16 '89

Gorba Claus. *The New Republic* 200:5-7 Ja 2 '89

Gorbachev & the U.S. [discussion of August 1989 article, Gorbachev's cultural revolution] C. H. Fairbanks, Jr. *Commentary* 88:2+ N '89

Gorbachev and the '1946 rules'. G. F. Will. il *Newsweek* 114:70 S 25 '89

Gorbachev and the right. W. F. Buckley. *National Review* 41:54-5 Je 16 '89

Gorbachev, freedom fighter. *National Review* 41:9-10 Ag 18 '89

Gorbachev gets out the vote. F. Coleman. il por *Newsweek* 113:36-7 Mr 27 '89

Gorbachev in Armenia. M. Kempton. il *The New York Review of Books* 35:58 Ja 19 '89

The Gorbachev jitters. R. Watson. il *Newsweek* 114:24-6 S 25 '89

Gorbachev lays down the law. R. Watson. il map *Newsweek* 113:52+ Ap 24 '89

The Gorbachev prospect. G. Soros. il *The New York Review of Books* 36:16-18 Je 1 '89

Gorbachev strikes again. H. Anderson. il por *Newsweek* 112:57 My 22 '89

Gorbachev talks but who listens? W. M. Arkin. il por *The Bulletin of the Atomic Scientists* 45:5-6 Mr '89

Gorbachev's challenge to the West [address, April 11, 1989] E. W. Lefever. *Vital Speeches of the Day* 55:588-91 Jl 15 '89

Gorbachev's 'coup'. A. Wilson-Smith. il por *Maclean's* 102:28-30 O 2 '89

Gorbachev's crisis of faith [text of letter] R. Khomeini. *Harper's* 278:21-2 Ap '89

Gorbachev's cultural revolution. C. H. Fairbanks, Jr. *Commentary* 88:23-7 Ag '89

Gorbachev's fate. J. Trimble. il por *U.S. News & World Report* 107:26 D 25 '89-Ja 1 '90

Gorbachev's gamble. A. Wilson-Smith. il por *Maclean's* 102:25-6 Ag 7 '89

Gorbachev's long journey. R. Grenier. il *National Review* 41:27-9 D 31 '89

Gorbachev's nationalities problem. G. W. Lapidus. bibl f *Foreign Affairs* 68:92-108 Fall '89

Gorbachev's new grip on the Kremlin. F. Coleman. il por *Newsweek* 114:22-3 O 2 '89

Gorbachev's new thinking. D. Holloway. bibl f *Foreign Affairs* 68 Special Issue:66-81 ['89]

Gorbachev's not-so-secret weapon: the ballot box. P. Galuszka. il *Business Week* p51 Mr 27 '89

Gorbachev's one-two punch. A. Deming. il *Newsweek* 114:54-5 O 30 '89

Gorbachev's politics. J. F. Hough. bibl f *Foreign Affairs* 68:26-41 Wint '89/'90

Gorbachev's reforms: will they work? [special section] il por *Business Week* p52-7+ Je 5 '89

Gorbachev's strategy, and ours. E. N. Luttwak. *Commentary* 88:29-36 Jl '89

Gorbanomics. R. Parker. *The New Republic* 200:18-20 F 27 '89

Gorbie's choice. S. Anderson. *The New Republic* 200:11-12 Ap 17 '89

Gorby of Mayberry. R. E. Tyrrell. *The American Spectator* 22:10-11 O '89

Gorby the Antichrist [excerpt from Gorbachev! Has the real Antichrist come?] R. W. Faid. *Harper's* 278:24+ Ja '89

GORBACHEV, MIKHAIL—about—cont.

Gorby's farm reform a hard row to hoe. por *U.S. News & World Report* 106:9-10 Mr 27 '89

Gorby's two Achilles' heels. M. S. Forbes, Jr. il *Forbes* 144:27 Jl 24 '89

Hard lessons and unhappy citizens. W. R. Doerner. il por *Time* 133:28-9 Je 19 '89

A hearty da! to democratia. il por *U.S. News & World Report* 106:12 Je 5 '89

His vision thing. B. W. Nelan. il pors *Time* 134:22-3 O 2 '89

How much longer can Gorbachev keep putting out fires? D. Rinehart. il *Business Week* p41 Ag 7 '89

How open shall we be to *glasnost*? C. W. Colson. il *Christianity Today* 33:72 My 12 '89

Is Bush bold enough to answer Gorbachev? W. Greider. il *Rolling Stone* p48+ F 9 '89

Is *glasnost* genuine? [address, November 6, 1988] M. Warder. *Vital Speeches of the Day* 55:341-4 Mr 15 '89

Is Gorbachev's economy doomed to collapse? R. Cornwell. il *World Press Review* 36:20+ S '89

Is Stalin dead? Yes—at last. M. B. Zuckerman. il *U.S. News & World Report* 107:88+ D 4 '89

The Kremlin's talkathon. F. Coleman. il *Newsweek* 113:39 Je 12 '89

A long, mighty struggle. W. Isaacson. il por *Time* 133:48-52+ Ap 10 '89

Madison Avenue, Moscow. G. J. Church. il pors *Time* 133:33-4 My 22 '89

The man with the golden headache. P. Fuhrman. il *Forbes* 144:60-3 S 18 '89

Mikhail Gorbachev. il por *People Weekly* 32:58-9 D 25 '89-Ja 1 '90

Misha and Ron. T. Brewster. il pors *Life* 12:52-4+ Fall '89

Moscow: the struggle for reform. A. Brumberg. bibl f il *The New York Review of Books* 36:37-42 Mr 30 '89

The naysayer and new détente. H. Trewhitt. il pors *U.S. News & World Report* 106:18-19 My 22 '89

New masters of the land. il *Time* 133:53 Mr 27 '89

The new math. R. Wright. *The New Republic* 200:4 Ja 23 '89

The new Russian riddles. *America* 160:387 Ap 29 '89

Nikita Gorbachev? F. Coleman. il pors *Newsweek* 114:39 S 11 '89

Notes and comment. *The New Yorker* 65:25-6 Mr 13 '89

Now, Gorbachev is building a bridge to Japan. A. Borrus. il *Business Week* p70 D 25 '89-Ja 1 '90

On the Atari Communists [discussion of Winter 1988-89 special section, Atari Communists: from hardline to software] *New Perspectives Quarterly* 6:60-1 Spr '89

Party animals. S. F. Starr. *The New Republic* 200:18-21 Je 26 '89

Pavel Palazhchenko: Gorbachev wouldn't leave home without him. W. Plummer. il pors *People Weekly* 32:187-8 D 4 '89

Peace (II). L. Wright. il *Rolling Stone* p54-5+ S 7 '89

Perestroika isn't working. F. Coleman and R. Watson. il por *Newsweek* 113:28-31+ Mr 13 '89

Perestroika shakes Eastern Europe. F. S. Larrabee. il por *The Bulletin of the Atomic Scientists* 45:25-9 Mr '89

Plastics. L. Wieseltier. *The New Republic* 200:4 Ja 2 '89

Reform is risky business. J. Trimble. il por *U.S. News & World Report* 106:27-8 Je 19 '89

Riding a dangerous wave. B. W. Nelan. il por *Time* 134:27 Ag 7 '89

Riding the tiger [cover story] R. Watson. il pors *Newsweek* 114:40-2+ D 4 '89

The rights of Gorbachev [cover story] I. F. Stone. il *The New York Review of Books* 36:3-4+ F 16 '89

Ronald Reagan & Mikhail Gorbachev. B. Darrach. il pors *People Weekly* 32 Special Issue:44-6 Fall '89

Say a prayer for Gorbachev. H. Sidey. il pors *Time* 134:19 Ag 7 '89

Send in the pols. J. Klein. il por *New York* 22:10-11 Ja 9 '89

The shaky fortunes of Gorby Inc. J. Smolowe. il *Time* 133:37 Ja 30 '89

Should the U.S. help Gorbachev? R. M. Nixon. por *Time* 134:94 D 18 '89

The Soviet agony over states' rights. J. Trimble. il map *U.S. News & World Report* 106:34-5 Ap 24 '89

The Soviet challenge to American education. B. T. Trout. *The Education Digest* 54:35-7 Ap '89

Soviet change and Western security. J. Chirac. *Current (Washington, D.C.)* 315:27-32 S '89

The Soviet empire: the military [cover story; special section] il maps *U.S. News & World Report* 106:18-21+ Mr 13 '89

The Soviet empire: the society [cover story; special section; with editorial comment by Mortimer B. Zuckerman] il por maps *U.S. News & World Report* 106:34-9+, 80 Ap 3 '89

Soviet seduction. P. B. Gemma, Jr. il *Conservative Digest* 15:6-7+ Mr/Ap '89

The Soviet Union, 1989 [cover story; special issue] bibl f map (inside back cover) *Current History* 88:321-44+ O '89

The threat to Gorbachev. P. Reddaway. bibl f il *The New York Review of Books* 36:19-24 Ag 17 '89

Twilight of the dinosaurs. *U.S. News & World Report* 106:46 My 8 '89

A usable past. S. F. Starr. *The New Republic* 200:24+ My 15 '89

USSR [cover story] W. R. Doerner. il pors *Time* 133:30-1 Je 5 '89

The view from Moscow. A. Wilson-Smith. il *Maclean's* 102:21-2 N 27 '89

Virtuoso transformations. S. Talbott. il *Time* 133:36 Ja 9 '89

The vote heard round the world. P. Galuszka. il por *Business Week* p26-7 Ap 10 '89

Waiting for Wyoming. P. Glynn. *The New Republic* 201:14-16 O 2 '89

Walking a tight-rope. M. Malkasian. il por *Scholastic Update (Teachers' edition)* 122:20-1 O 20 '89

A warning to Gorbachev. R. Corelli. por *Maclean's* 102:30 S 25 '89

What's behind the 'Sinatra Doctrine'. *U.S. News & World Report* 107:22 N 20 '89

Who's a 'drugstore cowboy'? il *Newsweek* 113:48 My 29 '89

Why Russia is still in the red. R. I. Kirkland, Jr. il *Fortune* 119:173-4+ Ja 30 '89

Will the Soviet Union survive until 1994? [interview with B. Shragin; cover story] D. Evanier. *National Review* 41:24+ Ap 7 '89

The world turned upside down [cover story] M. Kondracke. il *The New Republic* 201:26-9 S 18-25 '89

Yes, he's for real. il por *Time* 134:40-2+ N 6 '89

Anecdotes, facetiae, satire, etc.

The finer points of *perestroika* [imaginary meeting among Gorbachev and his advisers following the Baker mini-summit] R. N. Perle. *U.S. News & World Report* 107:41 O 2 '89

Bibliography

Gorby fever and the publishing body politic. *Publishers Weekly* 236:42 O 27 '89

Salaries, allowances, etc.

A bargain at twice the price. por *U.S. News & World Report* 106:13 F 13 '89

Visit to China, 1989

Diplomacy, Gorbachev-style, looks like a winner in Beijing. D. Lee. il *Business Week* p55 My 15 '89

Marriage of convenience. D. Doder. il pors *U.S. News & World Report* 106:30-2 My 15 '89

Pacific overtures [cover story; special section] il *World Press Review* 36:11-20 My '89

A reunion of comrades [special section] il pors map *Newsweek* 112:46-9+ My 22 '89

Thunder out of China [cover story; special section; with editorial comment by Kevin Doyle] il pors map *Maclean's* 102:2, 28-31+ My 29 '89

Upon my word . . . W. F. Buckley. *National Review* 41:62-3 Je 30 '89

The upstaging of Gorbachev. A. Platt. il por *Newsweek* 113:24 My 29 '89

The view from the guesthouse. J. Kohan. il por *Time* 133:43 My 29 '89

Watching from offshore. C. Ogden. il *Time* 133:45 My 29 '89

Why the Sino-Soviet summit was important. H. Trewhitt. il por *U.S. News & World Report* 106:36 My 29 '89

Visit to Cuba, 1989

The Albania of the Caribbean. R. Grenier. il *National Review* 41:41-3 My 5 '89

Courting a Queen. M. Nemeth. il pors *Maclean's* 102:18-19 Ap 17 '89

Reading between the lines in Havana. pors *U.S. News & World Report* 106:13 Ap 17 '89

Top-level talk in Havana. D. Schorr. *The New Leader* 72:4 Ap 3-17 '89

Whose man in Havana? *The Nation* 248:541 Ap 24 '89

Reporters and reporting

The trouble with anchors away [U.S. television coverage] M. Ruby. il *U.S. News & World Report* 106:80 Ap 17 '89

Visit to France, 1989

'A common home'. H. Jensen. il por *Maclean's* 102:18-19 Jl 17 '89

Muted visit. il por *Time* 134:68 Jl 17 '89

Visit to Germany (East), 1989

The flight to freedom. H. Anderson. il por *Newsweek* 114:40-3+ O 16 '89

'Keep working for socialism'. A. Bilski. *Maclean's* 102:34 O 16 '89

Visit to Germany (West), 1989

Gorbachev lays the cornerstone for his 'common European house'. J. Templeman and G. E. Schares. il por *Business Week* p84 Je 26 '89

The Gorbachev tease [hints at tearing down Berlin Wall] M. Peretz. *The New Republic* 201:14+ Jl 10 '89

"Gorbi! Gorbi! Gorbi!". W. R. Doerner. il por *Time* 133:38 Je 26 '89

Gorbomania in Germany. H. Anderson. il por *Newsweek* 113:31 Je 26 '89

GORBACHEV, MIKHAIL—Visit to Germany (West), 1989 —*cont.*

A hero's welcome. A. Bilski. il por *Maclean's* 102:25 Je 26 '89

Playing the German card. *National Review* 41:16-18 Jl 14 '89

Visit to Great Britain, 1989

And now it's George's turn [seeking dramatic arms proposal to counter M. Gorbachev's initiatives] H. Anderson. il pors *Newsweek* 113:30-2 Ap 17 '89

Courting a Queen. M. Nemeth. il pors *Maclean's* 102:18-19 Ap 17 '89

Visit to the United States, 1988

A day to remember [speech before UN] *Commonweal* 116:4-5 Ja 13 '89

Gorbachev's initiatives. *World Press Review* 36:12 F '89

Gorbachev's triumph. W. F. Buckley. *National Review* 41:70 Ja 27 '89

A new age of world peace . . . breaking the wall of suspicion . . . [R. Reagan and M. Gorbachev address the United Nations] pors *UN Chronicle* 26:31-3 Mr '89

Notes and comment. *The New Yorker* 64:23-4 Ja 16 '89

President Reagan and President Gorbachev meet in New York [remarks, addresses, and news conference, December 3-10, 1988; cover story; special section] R. Reagan. il pors *Department of State Bulletin* 89:1-7 F '89

The suave Gorbachev wears no clothes [cover story] M. Ledeen. il *The American Spectator* 22:16-17 F '89

Visit to the Vatican, 1989

Cross meets Kremlin. R. N. Ostling. il pors *Time* 134:74-6 D 4 '89

Gorby's bow to the Roman legions. il pors *U.S. News & World Report* 107:15 D 11 '89

The higher summit. K. L. Woodward. il pors *Newsweek* 114:36 D 11 '89

The Pope and the pol. K. L. Woodward. il pors *Newsweek* 114:87-90 D 4 '89

Soul of a soulless world. A. Cockburn. *The Nation* 249:778-9 D 25 '89

GORBACHEV, RAISA MAKSIMOVNA

about

Raisa. V. Cadden. il pors *McCall's* 116:110+ F '89

GORCZYNSKI, RENATA

(tr) See Zagajewski, Adam, 1945-. Sails

GORDAY, PETER

Raimundo Panikkar: pluralism without relativism. il por *The Christian Century* 106:1147-50 D 6 '89

GORDIMER, NADINE, 1923-

The gap between the writer and the reader. bibl f il *The New York Review of Books* 36:59-61 S 28 '89

Jump [story] il *Harper's* 279:55-61 O '89

GORDITAS

Pass the gorditas, pilgrim. R. Schrambling. il *Esquire* 112:45 N '89

GORDON, ANNE

about

A harvest of ceramics. C. Petkanas. il pors *House & Garden* 161:28+ Ag '89

GORDON, ANNE J.

The gift. il *American Visions* 4:27-31 D '89

GORDON, BEATE

Recalling art as a way of life: Siberian dancers debut in the U.S.A. il *Dance Magazine* 63:21 Mr '89

GORDON, CHARLES

Another view. See occasional issues of Maclean's

GORDON, DARRYEL

about

Three lives. M. Stone. il pors *New York* 22:35-42 Ja 30 '89

GORDON, DAVID, 1936-

about

United States [dance] Reviews

Dance Magazine 63:94-5 Ap '89. C. Hardy

GORDON, DAVID G.

Hawaii's wet spot: Kauai. il map *Travel Holiday* 171:40-9 Je '89

Tongue Thai'd in Bangkok. il *Travel Holiday* 172:52-7 O '89

A train trilogy. il map *Travel Holiday* 171:60-6 My '89

GORDON, DAWN

Codebusters. il *Video* 12:56+ Mr '89

GORDON, DEXTER

about

Dexter Gordon: making his great leap forward [interview; reprint] C. Berg. il por *Down Beat* 56:82-3 S '89

GORDON, DIANA R.

Can Sessions tame the Bureau? il *The Nation* 249:488-91 O 30 '89

Doing Edgar proud. *The Nation* 249:570-4 N 13 '89

GORDON, ELLEN R.

about

Beyond macho: the power of womanly management [excerpt from Tender power] S. S. Cohen. il pors *Working Woman* 14:77-83 F '89

The practical genius of penny candy. S. Wilkinson. il pors *Working Woman* 14:98-9+ Ap '89

The tight ship lollipop. S. B. Weiner. il por *Forbes* 144:150 D 25 '89

GORDON, FLASH

about

After Live Aid and Farm Aid, hearing aid may be next for unwary victims of rock. N. Geeslin. il pors *People Weekly* 31:95-6 Ja 23 '89

GORDON, GLORIA

Let's communicate. il *World Health* p12-14 Ja/F '89

GORDON, HELEN

Andalusia's age of the Expo. il *World Press Review* 36:76 N '89

GORDON, J. C. (JOHN C.), 1939-

The scientific method [with editorial comment by Paul C. Pritchard] il *National Parks* 63:5, 16-17 My/Je '89

GORDON, JAMES SAMUEL

The cult leader: how absolute power corrupts [excerpt from The golden guru] il por *Utne Reader* p136-7 Mr/Ap '89

GORDON, JOHN C. See Gordon, J. C. (John C.), 1939-

GORDON, JOHN STEELE

The magnitude of J. P. Morgan. bibl il pors *American Heritage* 40:78-9+ Jl/Ag '89

Mephistopheles of Wall Street. il *American Heritage* 40:20+ D '89

Opportunities. il *American Heritage* 40:20+ N '89

The problem of money and time [cover story; with editorial comment by Byron Dobell] il *American Heritage* 40:7, 56-8+ My/Je '89

"The public be damned". il *American Heritage* 40:18+ S/O '89

Rich for a day. il *American Heritage* 40:16+ Ap '89

Technological turkeys. il *American Heritage* 40:18+ My/Je '89

To the swiftest. il *American Heritage* 40:16+ Mr '89

When our ancestors became us. il *American Heritage* 40:106-11+ D '89

Woolworth's cathedral. il *American Heritage* 40:16+ Jl/Ag '89

GORDON, KEITH

about

The chocolate war [film] Reviews

People Weekly il 31:14 Ja 30 '89. P. Travers

GORDON, KENNETH R.

Adaptive nature of skeletal design. bibl f il *BioScience* 39:784-90 D '89

GORDON, LEONID

about

The four *perestroikas* [interview] N. Gardels and W. R. Mead. il *New Perspectives Quarterly* 5:23-6 Wint '88/'89

GORDON, LINDA

32 little diet changes. il *Glamour* 87:74 F '89

Five good reasons to laugh it up when you exercise. il *Glamour* 87:40 Jl '89

Shape-up. See issues of Glamour

GORDON, MAX, 1903-1989

about

Obituary

The New Yorker 65:69-71 Jl 17 '89. W. Balliett

GORDON, MITCHELL

Religion and space technology. il *The Futurist* 23:60 Jl/Ag '89

GORDON, PETER H.

Diamonds are forever: artists & baseball. il *USA Today (Periodical)* 117:76-85 My '89

GORDON, RICHARD H.

about

Richard Gordon plays only one way—hard. R. W. King. il por *Business Week* p50 Ag 28 '89

GORDON (DAVID)/PICK UP COMPANY See David Gordon/Pick Up Company

GORDON RESEARCH CONFERENCES

Gordon Research Conferences. A. M. Cruickshank. il *Science* 246:264-9 O 13 '89

Gordon Research Conferences [cover story] A. M. Cruickshank. *Science* 243:1201-17 Mr 3 '89

GORDON SETTERS

The guru of Gordons [work of N. Sorby] L. Mueller. il por *Outdoor Life* 183:64+ Mr '89

Seize the moment [training techniques of J. Wick and N. Sorby] L. Mueller. il *Outdoor Life* 183:50+ My '89

GORDY, BERRY, JR.

about

Brotherhood Crusade salutes Motown's Berry Gordy. il pors *Jet* 75:32 Ja 30 '89

GORDY, EDWIN

about

Meet Dr. Database. K. J. Novak. il por *Home Office Computing* 7:24-5 Jl '89

GORE, ALBERT, JR.

The ecology of survival. il *The New Republic* 201:26+ N 6 '89

Gore goes for it. il por *American Health* 8:42 Ja/F '89

The new sacred agenda. il *New Perspectives Quarterly* 6:60-1 Summ '89

"What is wrong with us?" [excerpts from address, November 1988] il por *Time* 133:66 Ja 2 '89

about

A plan to help the planet. *Time* 133:57 F 6 '89

GORE, MARY ELIZABETH *See* Gore, Tipper, 1948-
GORE, RICK
　Extinctions [cover story] il supp (folded chart) *National Geographic* 175:662-99 Je '89
GORE, TIPPER, 1948-
　(jt. auth) See Baker, Susan, and Gore, Tipper, 1948-
GORGE-PURGE SYNDROME *See* Bulimia
GORHAM MANUFACTURING COMPANY
　Chantilly [silverware pattern] B. Barol. il *American Heritage* 40:26-7 N '89
GORILLAS
　Gordy and Schroeder growing up [San Diego Wild Animal Park] il *National Geographic World* 165:26-9 My '89
　The gorillas in the mist have a new champion: Diane Doran. B. Johnson. il pors *People Weekly* 32:151-2 D 4 '89
GORILLAS IN THE MIST [film] See Motion picture reviews—Single works
GORKA, JULIE
　The gift of music. il *Parents* 64:88+ Mr '89
GORKY STREET (MOSCOW, SOVIET UNION)
　Gorky Street, fifty years of change. A. Kopp. il *The Unesco Courier* 42:26-9 Ag '89
GORMAN, JAMES, 1949-
　Interview: Jack Horner. il por *Omni (New York, N.Y.)* 11:72-4+ Mr '89
　Nothing to sink your teeth into. il *The New York Times Magazine* p40+ Je 11 '89
　Return of a reptile. il *Sports Illustrated* 70:50-2+ Mr 6 '89
GORMAN, PETER
　Visions of the Matses. il map *Américas* 41 no1:32-7 '89
GORNEY, CYNTHIA
　Escape routes. il por *House & Garden* 161:34+ Ja '89
GORNICK, VIVIAN
　Twice an outsider: on being Jewish and a woman. il *Utne Reader* p95-6 S/O '89
GORNIK, APRIL
　　　　　　　about
　April Gornik's stormy weather [cover story] E. Heartney. il pors *Art News* 88:120-5 My '89
　Portrait of the artists: Eric Fischl and April Gornik on Long Island. S. M. L. Aronson. il pors *Architectural Digest* 46:234-9+ Ap '89
GORR, IVAN W.
　A formula for the future [address, October 19, 1988] *Vital Speeches of the Day* 55:190-2 Ja 1 '89
GORRITI, GUSTAVO A.
　How to fight the drug war. il *The Atlantic* 264:70-2+ Jl '89
　Southern exposure: the view from Peru. il *New Perspectives Quarterly* 6:49-51 Summ '89
GORTARI, CARLOS SALINAS DE *See* Salinas de Gortari, Carlos
GORTNER, MARJOE
　　　　　　　about
　Marjoe. K. Brizzolara. il por *Skiing* 41:36 F '89
GOSCH, DAVID
　Courage on wheels. il por *The Mother Earth News* 119:38-9 S/O '89
GOSPEL FILMS, INC.
　Church, parachurch locked in legal battle [Calvary Chapel vs. Gospel Films over videocassette distribution rights for evangelistic film Fury to freedom] B. Bird. il *Christianity Today* 33:40-3 Ag 18 '89
GOSPEL MUSIC
　　　See also
　Christian contemporary music
　Compact discs—Gospel music
　Spirituals (Songs)
　Whitney Houston is happy to back up BeBe and CeCe Winans, and that's the gospel truth. il pors *People Weekly* 32:44 Jl 3 '89
　　　　　Archives
　　　See also
　Jazz-Blues-Gospel Hall of Fame Archive
　　　　Study and teaching
　New music lesson method can have students playing piano within one month. il por *Jet* 76:14 Ag 28 '89
GOSSAGE, RICH, 1951-
　　　　　　　about
　The Goose again. G. Castle. il pors *Sport (New York, N.Y.)* 80:38-40 Mr '89
GOSSENS, SALVADOR ALLENDE *See* Allende Gossens, Salvador, 1908-1973
GOSSETT, BARRY
　A new look at modular classrooms. *The Education Digest* 54:64-5 Mr '89
GOSSETT, HATTIE, 1942-
　　　　　　　about
　Word star. P. Giddings. por *Essence* 19:40 Ap '89
GOSSETT, LOUIS, JR.
　　　　　　　about
　Minority view: seeing white, being black [interview] R. Hofler. il por *Life* 12:90 Mr '89
GOSSETT, PHILIP
　Up from Beethoven. bibl f il *The New York Review of Books* 36:21-2+ O 26 '89

GOSSIP
　　　See also
　Rumor
　Dear Betty Harragan. B. L. Harragan. il *Working Woman* 14:31-2 Jl '89
　Gossip doesn't pay. E. Kaye. *Mademoiselle* 95:90 Jl '89
　An insider's guide to gossip. *Glamour* 87:86 Ag '89
　Intelligencer. J. Kasindorf. See issues of New York beginning August 19, 1985
　Leak soup [interpreting the grapevine] O. Edwards. il *Gentlemen's Quarterly* 59:224+ Ap '89
　Scandal: taint misbehavin'. Taki. il *Harper's Bazaar* 122:208-9+ Mr '89
　When to listen to the office grapevine. B. Nivens. il *Essence* 19:102 Mr '89
　When you should be an office gossip. M. M. Kennedy. il *Working Woman* 14:34 Ap '89
GOSSIP COLUMNS
　Pretty poison: Anne Crawford skewers Hollywood [columnist for L.A. style] E. J. Carroll. il *Mademoiselle* 95:202-3+ O '89
　　　　　Great Britain
　Low tales of the highborn. M. Pye. il *The New York Times Magazine* p44+ N 12 '89
GOSSIP IN MASS MEDIA
　Loose lips [views of L. Smith] C. Jahr. il por *Ladies' Home Journal* 106:110-12+ Ja '89
　Star reporter [C. Cohen] J. Conant. il pors *Harper's Bazaar* 122:146-7+ N '89
GOSSLER, ACHIM, AND OTHERS
　Mouse embryonic stem cells and reporter constructs to detect developmentally regulated genes. bibl f il *Science* 244:463-5 Ap 28 '89
GOTANDA, PHILIP KAN
　　　　　　　about
　Yankee dawg you die [drama] Reviews
　　The New Yorker 65:97-8 My 29 '89. M. Kramer
GOTCH, TARQUIN
　　　　　　　about
　Tarquin Gotch, soundtrack specialist. S. Roman. il por *Video* 13:18 My '89
GOTH, LOUIS A.
　The parade that's making Milwaukee famous. il *Reader's Digest* 134:154-60 Je '89
GOTHIC CATHEDRALS *See* Cathedrals
GOTHIC REVIVAL ARCHITECTURE *See* Architecture, Gothic revival
GOTHIC REVIVAL HOUSE DECORATION *See* House decoration, Gothic revival
GOTI, JAIME MALAMUD- *See* Malamud-Goti, Jaime
GOTT, JIM
　　　　　　　about
　Life on the lip of a volcano. G. F. Will. il *Newsweek* 113:80 Ap 10 '89
GOTT, RICHARD
　The twilight of the generals. *World Press Review* 36:26+ Jl '89
GOTTFRIED, PAUL
　Nixon visited and revisited. il *National Review* 41:41-2 Jl 14 '89
GOTTI, JOHN
　　　　　　　about
　Cold-blooded King of a Hill under siege [cover story] K. Gross. il pors *People Weekly* 31:70-3+ Mr 27 '89
　In Gotti they trust. P. Hamill. il por *Esquire* 112:63-5 O '89
　John Gotti: running the Mob [cover story] S. Raab. il pors *The New York Times Magazine* p30-3+ Ap 2 '89
　The last Godfather? P. McKillop. il pors *Newsweek* 113:25 F 6 '89
GOTTLIEB, ANNIE
　When it's time for a change. *McCall's* 117:113-14 N '89
　(jt. auth) See Sher, Barbara, and Gottlieb, Annie
GOTTLIEB, DOROTHY WEISS, AND OTHERS
　When the kids call it quits [excerpt from What to do when your son or daughter divorces] il *Modern Maturity* 32:68-70 Je/Jl '89
GOTTLIEB, GIDON
　Israel and the Palestinians. bibl f *Foreign Affairs* 68:109-26 Fall '89
GOTTLIEB, SHERRY GERSHON
　　　　　　　about
　A Change of Hobbit changes its digs once again. M. Jones. il por *Publishers Weekly* 235:34-6 Je 23 '89
GOUDGE, EILEEN
　"From welfare mom to millionaire". il por *Ladies' Home Journal* 106:22+ Ag '89
GOUGH, PAULINE B.
　The editor's page. See issues of Phi Delta Kappan beginning February 1988
GOUGH, PIERS, 1946-
　　　　　　　about
　Prime time. C. K. Gandee. il por *House & Garden* 161:182-7+ Mr '89
GOUGH, TELA
　How to dress a 2-year-old. il *Parents* 64:207-9 Mr '89
GOULD, CAROL
　Hot seats! *World Tennis* 37:40+ Jl '89

GOULD, DALE
about
Weaving their way. G. Harrell. il pors *House & Garden*
161:72 Ap '89
GOULD, GLENN, 1932-1982
about
The enigma variations [excerpts from Glenn Gould: a life
and variations] O. Friedrich. il pors *Maclean's* 102:50-4
My 15 '89
Heart of Gould. E. Rothstein. il *The New Republic* 200:28-32
Je 26 '89
Singing Mahler to the elephants. P. Iyer. il por *Time* 133:115
My 22 '89
GOULD, HERB
Throwing Rice. il por *Sport (New York, N.Y.)* 80:32 S '89
GOULD, IRVING, 1919-
about
Lost opportunity? E. McGlinn. il por *Forbes* 144:288+ N
13 '89
GOULD, JAMES
about
Weaving their way. G. Harrell. il pors *House & Garden*
161:72 Ap '89
GOULD, JAY, 1836-1892
about
Mephistopheles of Wall Street. J. S. Gordon. il *American
Heritage* 40:20+ D '89
GOULD, STEPHEN JAY, 1941-
An asteroid to die for. il *Discover* 10:60-5 O '89
This view of life. See issues of Natural History
about
PW interviews. W. Smith. por *Publishers Weekly* 236:32-3
O 13 '89
We're all lucky to be here. J. Adler. il por *Newsweek* 114:68
N 20 '89
GOULD, WILLIAM L.
Small-scale telescope. il *Sky and Telescope* 77:250-1 Mr '89
GOULD INC.
Gould will use same market strategy under Encore ownership.
E. H. Kolcum. *Aviation Week & Space Technology* 130:53
Ap 17 '89
GOULET, DENIS
The Mexican Church: into the public arena [cover story]
il *America* 160:318-22 Ap 8 '89
GOULSTONE, JOHN, AND SWANTON, MICHAEL JAMES
Carry on cricket: the Duke of Dorset's 1789 tour [cover
story] bibl il *History Today* 39:18-23 Ag '89
GOURGUES REPORT (NEWSLETTER) See Investment news-
letters
GOURLAY, DARLENE
Friends . . . and other creeps [story] il *Teen* 33:39-40+
My '89
GOURMET FOOD DELIVERY SERVICE See Food delivery
service
GOURMETS See Food critics and criticism; Gastronomy
GOURSE, LESLIE
The amazing Andertons. il pors *McCall's* 116:92+ Ja '89
In the limelight: women who play jazz [cover story] il
American Visions 4:32-7 Ap '89
GOVERNMENT, RESISTANCE TO
See also
Coups d'etat
Hunger strikes
Protests, demonstrations, etc.
Revolutions
Tax resistance
Prisoner of conscience [experiences while jailed for antinuclear
activities; cover story] B. Urfer. il *The Progressive* 53:18-21
My '89
Sam Day's example [jailed for trespassing on missile silo
site during protest] E. Knoll. *The Progressive* 53:4 Je '89
GOVERNMENT ACCOUNTING
See also
United States. General Accounting Office
GOVERNMENT ACCOUNTING STANDARDS BOARD
The great GASB. D. Wechsler. il *Forbes* 144:60 D 11 '89
GOVERNMENT ADVERTISING See Government publicity
GOVERNMENT AGENCIES
See also
President's Private Sector Survey on Cost Control (U.S.)
Quasi-government agencies
Regulatory agencies
United States—Executive departments
United States. Cabinet
Federal agencies involved [occupational safety and health]
Congressional Digest 68:99-100 Ap '89
Federal agencies involved [regulation of financial institutions]
Congressional Digest 68:165+ Je/Jl '89
Room at the top [problems in filling top posts in the federal
science bureaucracy] J. Palca. il *Science* 246:566-8 N 3
'89
Turf wars in the federal bureaucracy [various agencies fighting
war on drugs] S. Waldman. il *Newsweek* 113:24-6 Ap
10 '89

Laws and regulations
See also
Sunshine laws

GOVERNMENT AIRPLANES See Airplanes, Government
GOVERNMENT AND AGRICULTURE See Agricultural ad-
ministration
GOVERNMENT AND ART See Art and state
GOVERNMENT AND AVIATION See Aviation and state
GOVERNMENT AND BUSINESS See Industry and state
GOVERNMENT AND CHURCH See Church and state
GOVERNMENT AND DANCE See Dance and state
GOVERNMENT AND LITERATURE See Literature and state
GOVERNMENT AND MEDICINE See Medical policy
GOVERNMENT AND POETRY See Poetry and state
GOVERNMENT AND SCIENCE See Science and state
GOVERNMENT AND SPORTS See Sports and state
GOVERNMENT AND TECHNOLOGY See Technology and
state
GOVERNMENT AND THE ARTS See Arts and state
GOVERNMENT AND THE INDIVIDUAL See Individual
and state
GOVERNMENT AND THE PRESS
See also
Bush, George, 1924——Press relations
Congressmen—Press relations
Journalists in government
Presidents—Press relations
Reagan, Ronald, 1911——Press relations
All the congressmen's men: how Capitol Hill controls the
press. W. Karp. bibl il *Harper's* 279:55-63 Jl '89
As State Department spokesperson, Margaret Tutwiler has
won even the press's respect. M. B. Carlson. il por *Vogue*
179:276+ O '89
Doing it the Army way [charges of censorship at Stars and
stripes] M. Tharp. il *U.S. News & World Report* 107:24
S 25 '89
The ethics police and political leaks. S. J. Hedges. il *U.S.
News & World Report* 106:20 Je 12 '89
Gray matter [leak to press concerning allegations against
Congressman W. H. Gray] T. Eastland. il *The American
Spectator* 22:26-7 S '89
How we got an Official Secrets Act [Supreme Court declines
to review S. L. Morison case] N. Hentoff. il *The Progressive*
53:10-11 Mr '89
Jim Baker, ministering to the media [cover story] T. Bethell.
il *National Review* 41:24-7 My 5 '89
Missing the Tower story [J. Tower nomination and FBI
background investigation] T. Eastland. il *The American
Spectator* 22:34-6 My '89
A mutiny at Stars and stripes [complaints of censorship]
U.S. News & World Report 106:15 Mr 6 '89
Neo-plumbers on the attack [poor journalism due to reliance
on leaks and sensational stories] L. I. Barrett. il *Time*
134:67 S 11 '89
No runs, no drips, no errors [Justice Dept. considers
prosecuting government employees who leak information
obtained from a criminal investigation] T. Eastland. il
The American Spectator 22:30-1 N '89
The quiet coup [case against S. Morison] P. Weiss. il *Harper's*
279:54-65 S '89
Shhhhhh! [Justice Dept.'s anti-leak policy] T. Noah. *The
New Republic* 201:8-10 O 30 '89
Summer spy scoops [F. Bloch and J. V. Hirsch spy cases]
D. Schorr. *The New Leader* 72:3-4 Ag 7-21 '89
Supreme Court press [reporting of affirmative action cases]
T. Eastland. *The American Spectator* 22:32-4 O '89
Welcome to the major leaks. T. Eastland. il *The American
Spectator* 22:23-5 F '89
Where were the media on HUD? M. Riley. il *Time* 134:48
Jl 24 '89
Who decides what is news? (Hint: it's not journalists). W.
Karp. il *Utne Reader* p60-8 N/D '89
Woodward explodes Roe v. Wade [B. Woodward's articles
on the inner workings of the Supreme Court] T. Eastland.
The American Spectator 22:30 Ap '89
History
The news media: fourth branch of government. P. Sudo.
il *Scholastic Update (Teachers' edition)* 122:15-17 S 8 '89
International aspects
New threats in the democracies. *World Press Review* 36:52-7
F '89
Pressing for a free press. S. J. Ungar. *Foreign Policy* 77:132-53
Wint '89/'90
Algeria
Algerian journalists rebel [Movement of Algerian Journalists]
V. Brittain. il *World Press Review* 36:58 Ag '89
Canada
See also
Mulroney, Brian—Press relations
Courtroom chaos [Mountie R. Jordan alleges political inter-
ference at budget leak trial] M. Clark. il por *Maclean's*
102:20 N 20 '89
Damage control [budget leak controversy] T. Tedesco. il
pors *Maclean's* 102:14-16 Je 12 '89
Substance versus fabricated fury [press coverage of refugee
policy] G. Bain. il *Maclean's* 102:37 Ja 23 '89
The subtleties of inside information [leaked budget] G. Bain.
il *Maclean's* 102:48 My 22 '89
The tax squeeze [furor over leaked budget; cover story;
special section; with editorial comment by Kevin Doyle]
il *Maclean's* 102:2, 10-12+ My 8 '89

GOVERNMENT AND THE PRESS—Canada—*cont.*

Wilson's trials [leaks of Finance Minister M. Wilson's budget; with editorial comment by Kevin Doyle] T. Tedesco. il *Maclean's* 102:2, 10-11+ Je 5 '89

Anecdotes, facetiae, satire, etc.

Watergate envy: it's a scandal [furor over budget leaks couched in Watergate terminology] C. Gordon. il *Maclean's* 102:9 Je 26 '89

China

How China manages the press [cover story] M. Hopkins. il *The New Leader* 72:3-4 My 1 '89

Karl Marx, meet Marshall McLuhan. J. Alter. il *Newsweek* 113:28 My 29 '89

Playing the China card [network coverage of student demonstrations] E. Diamond. il *New York* 22:16+ Je 5 '89

Revolution by information. L. Martz. il *Newsweek* 113:28-9 Je 19 '89

Unwilling informants? [candor in news coverage of Tiananmen Square massacre could endanger lives] J. Alter. il *Newsweek* 113:29 Je 26 '89

Cuba

Minority report [Moscow news and Sputnik banned] C. Hitchens. *The Nation* 249:231 S 4-11 '89

Czechoslovakia

Paper back [Lidove noviny] S. J. Ungar. *The New Republic* 201:17-19 D 25 '89

Great Britain

Banned in Britain [issue of Harper's banned for article about British intelligence] E. Knoll. *The Progressive* 53:4 Ja '89

Banned in Britain: a new chapter in the Harrods saga [government outlaws publication of secret report] M. Maremont. pors *Business Week* p36 Ap 17 '89

Britain: under the iron (high) heel? J. O'Sullivan. *Commentary* 88:47-52 S '89

Her majesty's censors [M. Thatcher] M. Friedman. il *The Progressive* 53:30-3 F '89

Thatcher puts a lid on. J. Atlas. il *The New York Times Magazine* p36-8+ Mr 5 '89

Tiny Rowland versus Mohamed Al-Fayed (cont.) [House of Fraser takeover] E. F. Cone. il pors *Forbes* 143:10 My 1 '89

Guatemala

War of words [firebombing of S. Godoy's newspaper La Epoca] V. Perera. il por *Mother Jones* 14:19-21 F/Mr '89

Hungary

Hungary: Red tabloid bares all [Reform] il *Newsweek* 113:36 Ap 17 '89

Israel

Israelis don't hide from the truth [responses to Palestinian intifada] J. B. Miller. *The Christian Century* 106:552-3 My 24-31 '89

Israel's severe censor. E. Pallis. *World Press Review* 36:58 Ap '89

Mexico

To the left of zero [Mexican newspaper editor H. F. Miranda killed in Tijuana] W. Murray. *The New Yorker* 65:57-66 Jl 31 '89

Namibia

As Africa's last colony nears independence [interview with G. Lister] A. Balk. il por *World Press Review* 36:36-8 Jl '89

Nicaragua

Don't call her comrade [publisher V. Chamorro] J. Moody. il por *Time* 133:62-4 Je 12 '89

Northern Ireland

Northern Ireland hit-squad scandal [leak of lists of IRA sympathizers triggers loyalist terrorism] L. Flanders. il *The Nation* 249:491-4 O 30 '89

Paraguay

The dictator and the journalists. W. Steif. il por *The Progressive* 53:16-17 O '89

South Africa

The mystery of Winnie Mandela. G. Bain. il *Maclean's* 102:50 Mr 20 '89

Soviet Union

See also
TASS (Soviet Union)

Dear editor: You're fired. Signed, Mikhail Gorbachev [V. Afanasev and V. Starkov] W. R. Doerner. il pors *Time* 134:62-3 O 30 '89

Gorbachev's one-two punch [scolding the media] A. Deming. il *Newsweek* 114:54-5 O 30 '89

How free is the Soviet press? M. Massing. il *The New York Review of Books* 36:55-8 S 28 '89

International Editor of the Year [V. Korotich, editor of weekly Ogonyok; with interview] il por *World Press Review* 36:22-6 My '89

'Matches in a gas oven'. J. Alter. il *Newsweek* 114:49 D 4 '89

A talk with the editor of 'Ogonyok' [interview with V. Korotich; cover story; with editorial comment] M. Mihajlov. il *The New Leader* 72:2, 10-16 F 20 '89

Typing out the fear. V. Korotich. il *Time* 133:124+ Ap 10 '89

United States

See Government and the press

Yugoslavia

Glasnostradamus. S. Drakulić. *The New Republic* 200:18-20 Ap 24 '89

GOVERNMENT AUCTIONS *See* Auctions

GOVERNMENT BONDS *See* Government securities

GOVERNMENT BUILDINGS *See* Public buildings

GOVERNMENT COMMISSIONS

Autopilot democracy. Z. Citron. *The New Republic* 201:18-20 Jl 10 '89

GOVERNMENT COMMUNICATION *See* Communication in government

GOVERNMENT CONTRACTS *See* Contracts, Government

GOVERNMENT CORPORATIONS

See also
Privatization

Burned by the thrifts, Congress looks at other fire hazards. C. Yang. il *Business Week* p57 O 9 '89

A time bomb for U.S. taxpayers. R. E. Norton. il *Fortune* 120:139+ O 23 '89

Canada

See also
Air Canada
Petro-Canada Inc.
Potash Corporation of Saskatchewan

Great Britain

See also
British Airways plc

Japan

See also
Nippon Telegraph & Telephone Corporation

GOVERNMENT DECENTRALIZATION *See* Decentralization in government

GOVERNMENT DOCUMENTS *See* Government publications

GOVERNMENT EMPLOYEES

See also
Black government employees
Bureaucracy
Civil service
Conflict of interests (Public office)
Congressmen—Staff
Labor unions—Government employees
Postal employees
Presidents—Staff
Public officers
United States. Office of Personnel Management
White House (Washington, D.C.)—Employees

The 'adoption alternative' [adoption recommended to federal workers] B. Kantrowitz. il *Newsweek* 114:84 N 20 '89

Health and hygiene

A boost for drug testing [Supreme Court rulings] A. L. Sanders. il *Time* 133:62 Ap 3 '89

The High Court weighs drug tests [testing of federal employees] il *Newsweek* 113:8 Ap 3 '89

Legal status, laws, etc.

Chilly draft [security clearances and government employment] E. Pell. *The Nation* 248:400 Mr 27 '89

No runs, no drips, no errors [Justice Dept. considers prosecuting government employees who leak information obtained from a criminal investigation] T. Eastland. il *The American Spectator* 22:30-1 N '89

Shhhhhh! [Justice Dept.'s anti-leak policy] T. Noah. *The New Republic* 201:8-10 O 30 '89

Pensions

See Civil service pensions

Recruiting

Too righteous? [ethics rules discourage prospective public servants] J. Cramer. il *Time* 133:32 My 29 '89

Resignation

Beltway brain drain: why civil servants are making tracks. S. B. Garland. il *Business Week* p60-1 Ja 23 '89

Salaries, allowances, etc.

See also
Collective bargaining—Government employees

Beltway brain drain: why civil servants are making tracks. S. B. Garland. il *Business Week* p60-1 Ja 23 '89

Federal pay: only top-to-bottom reform will do. G. S. Becker. il *Business Week* p19 F 13 '89

What Lloyd Cutler could learn from Acme Widget: target pay increases to jobs that are hard to fill. B. Frye. *The Washington Monthly* 21:18-22 Jl/Ag '89

GOVERNMENT EMPLOYEES INSURANCE COMPANY *See* Geico Corp.

GOVERNMENT ENTERTAINING

Oprah Winfrey a hit with White House kitchen staff. il *Jet* 76:61 Jl 17 '89

Welcome to the Bushes'. D. Radcliffe. il pors *The Saturday Evening Post* 261:42+ N/D '89

History

Hello Dolley—on the trail of the Madisons. N. Barry. il por *Gourmet* 49:130+ D '89

Henry Allen explores the history of White House entertaining, concluding that food and fashion are not the point. H. Allen. il *Vogue* 179:450+ N '89

International aspects

The embassy party as geopolitical stethoscope. T. Bethell. *National Review* 41:40 F 10 '89

GOVERNMENT ENTERTAINING—*cont.*

Canada

The protocol of pageantry [royal family visits] T. Tedesco. il *Maclean's* 102:40-1 Jl 24 '89

GOVERNMENT ETHICS *See* Political ethics

GOVERNMENT FINANCE *See* Finance

GOVERNMENT GUARANTY OF LOANS *See* Loans, Bank—Guaranty

GOVERNMENT HOUSING PROJECTS *See* Housing projects

GOVERNMENT INFORMATION

See also

Classified information

Computers—Government use

Executive privilege (Government information)

Freedom of information

Government and the press

Government publications

Official secrets

Tax returns

Telephone—Government use

United States. National Archives and Records Administration

GOVERNMENT INVESTIGATIONS

See also

Exxon Valdez (Ship) oil spill, 1989—Government investigations

Inspectors general (U.S.)

The howl of congressional watchdogs [oversight probes] S. V. Roberts. il *U.S. News & World Report* 107:24-6 S 11 '89

Impeachment by other means [special prosecutor law] T. Eastland. *Commentary* 88:40-4 Ag '89

GOVERNMENT LABORATORIES *See* Laboratories, Government

GOVERNMENT LENDING

See also

Black business enterprises—Federal aid

Export-Import Bank of the United States

Loans, Bank—Guaranty

Savings and loan associations—Federal aid

Small business—Federal aid

United States. Small Business Administration

A different drummer [TV finangelist W. Phillips] C. Poole. il por *Forbes* 143:166 Ap 3 '89

GOVERNMENT LIABILITY

See also

Strategic lawsuits against public participation

Stop the barrister bullies [land use suits brought against local government] P. A. A. Berle. *Audubon* 91:8 Mr '89

GOVERNMENT LOANS *See* Government lending

GOVERNMENT NATIONAL MORTGAGE ASSOCIATION SECURITIES *See* Mortgage bonds and notes

GOVERNMENT OFFICIALS *See* Public officers

GOVERNMENT OPERATIONS COMMITTEE *See* United States. Congress. House. Committee on Government Operations

GOVERNMENT OWNERSHIP

See also

Government corporations

Privatization

Railroads and state

GOVERNMENT PROPERTY

See also

Surplus government property

GOVERNMENT PUBLICATIONS

See also

Classified information

Ask Uncle Sam. il *The Mother Earth News* 115:118+ Ja/F '89

Bibliography

Publications. See issues of Department of State Bulletin

Source material. J. A. Kreslins. See issues of Foreign Affairs beginning Fall 1986

GOVERNMENT PUBLICITY

Brunei

Selling the sultan. J. Levine. il por *Forbes* 144:264-5 Jl 24 '89

Saudi Arabia

Mecca bucks [traveling promotional exhibit] A. Heard. *The New Republic* 201:16-17 S 4 '89

Singapore

Singapore [address, August 1989] J. K. Grace. *Vital Speeches of the Day* 56:76-9 N 15 '89

GOVERNMENT REGULATION OF INDUSTRY *See* Industry and state

GOVERNMENT REGULATORY AGENCIES *See* Regulatory agencies

GOVERNMENT SECRECY *See* Classified information; Official secrets

GOVERNMENT SECURITIES

See also

Municipal bonds

Savings bonds

Treasury bills and notes

How to raise money for the class of 2000 [proposal for government bonds to fund child welfare programs; cover story] F. A. Oski. *The Nation* 248:217+ F 20 '89

Silver lining [thrift bailout bonds from Resolution Funding Corp.] B. Weberman. il *Forbes* 143:179 Ap 3 '89

International aspects

Shouldering arms [M. Markus' idea to securitize U.S. armament loans] M. Schifrin. il por *Forbes* 143:208-9 Ap 17 '89

United States

See Government securities

GOVERNMENT SECURITIES DEALERS

Too many bond traders, too few customers [primary dealers are quitting] F. A. Miller and W. Glasgall. il *Business Week* p71 Ja 30 '89

GOVERNMENT SERVICE *See* Public officers

GOVERNMENT SERVICE CONTRACTS *See* Contracts, Government

GOVERNMENT SPENDING POLICY *See* United States—Appropriations and expenditures

GOVERNMENT STATISTICS

See also

Statistical abstract of the United States

GOVERNMENT TELECOMMUNICATION *See* Telecommunication in government

GOVERNMENT USE OF COMPUTERS *See* Computers—Government use

GOVERNMENTAL ACCOUNTING STANDARDS BOARD *See* Government Accounting Standards Board

GOVERNOR GENERAL'S LITERARY AWARD (CANADA)

A world in one town [won by D. A. Richards' Nights below Station Street] D. Turbide. por *Maclean's* 102:59 Mr 13 '89

GOVERNORS' MANSIONS

Arkansas

Thirty-four years at the governor's mansion [cook E. J. Ashley] R. Brown. il pors *Ebony* 44:52+ Jl '89

Texas

At home with the governor. il *Southern Living* 24:28 My '89

GOW, HAVEN BRADFORD

The true purpose of education. il *Phi Delta Kappan* 70:545-6 Mr '89

GOWDY, CURT

American beauty. il por maps *Popular Mechanics* 166:96-7+ My '89

GOWERS, ANDREW, AND MALLET, VICTOR

The long road to statehood. *World Press Review* 36:14-15 F '89

GOWERS, ANDREW, AND WALKER, TONY

Water war in the Middle East. map *World Press Review* 36:57-8 My '89

GOWNS, WEDDING *See* Wedding clothes

GOYA, FRANCISCO, 1746-1828

about

The art of darkness. A. C. Danto. il *Vogue* 179:186-91 Ja '89

The art world. A. Gopnik. *The New Yorker* 65:88-92 Je 19 '89

Dark knight. K. Larson. il *New York* 22:111-12 My 15 '89

The dark side of Goya. J. Richardson. il *House & Garden* 161:106-11+ F '89

A despairing assault on terminal evil. R. Hughes. il por *Time* 133:70-1 Ja 30 '89

Goya and the spirit of enlightenment. A. C. Danto. *The Nation* 249:66-8 Jl 10 '89

Goya and the spirit of enlightenment. N. Glendinning. il por *USA Today (Periodical)* 117:36-45 Ja '89

Goya and the spirit of revolution. C. Fuentes. il por *Art News* 88:90-5 Ja '89

Goya: visions of the Spanish soul. il *Life* 12:110-14+ F '89

Goya's battle with darkness. J. Kroll. il por *Newsweek* 113:70-2 F 6 '89

The liberal Goya. R. Hughes. il *The New York Review of Books* 36:26-31 Je 29 '89

Minority report. C. Hitchens. *The Nation* 248:838 Je 19 '89

Out of dark dreams and bright hopes, the blazing art of Goya. R. Wernick. bibl (p146) il por *Smithsonian* 19:56-67 Ja '89

Psychological portraits. D. Solomon. il *Harper's Bazaar* 122:28+ Ja '89

The unliberal imagination. J. Brown. il *The New Republic* 200:30-5 My 15 '89

GOYA Y LUCIENTES, FRANCISCO JOSÉ DE *See* Goya, Francisco, 1746-1828

GOZDZIAK, ELZBIETA

New branches . . . distant roots: older refugees in the United States. il *Aging* no359:2-7 '89

GPA GROUP, LTD.

GPA Group poised to order 'well over 200' transports. D. A. Brown. il *Aviation Week & Space Technology* 130:16-17 Ap 17 '89

Large leasing company orders restructure aircraft acquisition [special section] il *Aviation Week & Space Technology* 130:24-7+ Ap 24 '89

A sky-high bet on the plane-leasing business. M. Maremont. il por *Business Week* p120 My 1 '89

GPA JETPROP, LTD.
GPA Jetprop prepares for 1990s with orders for ATRs, Dash 8s. J. M. Lenorovitz. il *Aviation Week & Space Technology* 130:90 Mr 27 '89
GQ (PERIODICAL) *See* Gentlemen's quarterly
GRABER, RICHARD
Take the sting out of criticism. il *Reader's Digest* 134:120-2 Ap '89
GRABLE, RON
Technologue. See issues of Motor Trend
GRACE, PRINCESS OF MONACO, 1929-1982
about
Such good friends. il pors *Harper's Bazaar* 122:110-11+ Je '89
GRACE, J. PETER (JOSEPH PETER)
America needs a "waste czar" [address, September 21, 1989] *Vital Speeches of the Day* 56:37-40 N 1 '89
The deficit time bomb [address, March 13, 1989] *Vital Speeches of the Day* 55:390-4 Ap 15 '89
about
Will Peter Grace call it a day? G. G. Marcial. *Business Week* p146 Mr 20 '89
GRACE, JOHN K.
Singapore [address, August 1989] *Vital Speeches of the Day* 56:76-9 N 15 '89
GRACE, JOSEPH PETER *See* Grace, J. Peter (Joseph Peter)
GRACE, WILLIAM J.
(jt. auth) *See* Hallowell, Edward, and Grace, William J.
GRACE (AESTHETICS)
The case for grace: how to move sleek and sensuous. il *Mademoiselle* 95:232-5 S '89
GRACE (THEOLOGY)
Confessions of a glutton [cover story] M. L. Bringle. *The Christian Century* 106:955-8 O 25 '89
How faith works [Lordship Salvation debate] S. L. Johnson, Jr. il *Christianity Today* 33:21-5 S 22 '89
Old debate finds new life [requirements for salvation] B. Bird. il *Christianity Today* 33:38-40 Mr 17 '89
When mercy hurts. C. Williams. il *Christianity Today* 33:16-19 F 3 '89
GRACE (W.R.) & CO. *See* W.R. Grace & Co.
GRACE COMMISSION *See* President's Private Sector Survey on Cost Control (U.S.)
GRACELAND
Elvis lives. F. Meeks. il por *Forbes* 144:104 Ag 21 '89
GRACIE MANSION (NEW YORK, N.Y.)
Home improvements. *The New Yorker* 65:46-7 O 23 '89
GRADE REPETITION (EDUCATION)
The resistance of conventional wisdom to research evidence: the case of retention in grade. R. P. Doyle. bibl f il *Phi Delta Kappan* 71:215-20 N '89
Testing and retention of young children: moving from controversy to reform. T. Schultz. bibl f il *Phi Delta Kappan* 71:125-9 O '89
GRADING AND MARKING (EDUCATION)
See also
Grade repetition (Education)
School reports and records
Getting great grades: A+ advice [high school students] K. Hinchman. il *Teen* 33:42+ S '89
It's a good score! Just a bad grade. R. L. Canady and P. R. Hotchkiss. il *Phi Delta Kappan* 71:68-71 S '89
Anecdotes, facetiae, satire, etc.
Making the grade: memoirs of a Harvard grader. T. Pappas. *The American Scholar* 58:415-19 Summ '89
GRADING OF MEAT *See* Meat—Grading
GRADISON, HEATHER J.
about
Stormy Heather. J. Cook. il por *Forbes* 143:168+ Je 26 '89
GRADUATE SCHOOLS *See* Colleges and universities—Graduate work
GRADUATE STUDENTS, FOREIGN *See* Foreign students
GRADUATE TEACHING ASSISTANTS
See also
Association of Graduate Student Employees
Collective bargaining—Graduate teaching assistants
GRADUATE WORK *See* Colleges and universities—Graduate work
GRADUATED PAYMENT MORTGAGES *See* Mortgages
GRADUATES, COLLEGE *See* College graduates
GRADUATES, HIGH SCHOOL *See* High school graduates
GRADUATION ADDRESSES *See* Baccalaureate addresses
GRADUATION REQUIREMENTS (HIGH SCHOOL) *See* High schools—Graduation requirements
GRADY, DENISE
My father was an alcoholic. il *Reader's Digest* 135:31-2 S '89
The town that lost two tons. il *Ladies' Home Journal* 106:46+ Je '89
GRADY, PAULINE
Pursuing the rainbow. il *America* 160:146-9 F 18 '89
GRAEDEL, T. E.
Regional and global impacts on the biosphere. bibl f il *Environment* 31:8-13+ Ja/F '89
GRAEDEL, T. E., AND CRUTZEN, PAUL J.
The changing atmosphere. bibl il *Scientific American* 261:58-64+ S '89

GRAF, RUDOLF F.
(jt. auth) *See* Sheets, William, and Graf, Rudolf F.
GRAF, RUDOLF F., AND SHEETS, WILLIAM
Amateur TV transmitter (I). il *Radio-Electronics* 60:45-50 Je '89
One-band shortwave converter. il *Radio-Electronics* 60:49-51 O '89
GRAF, STEFFI
about
Boom Boom [cover story] C. Kirkpatrick. il pors *Sports Illustrated* 71:22-7 S 18 '89
Serving her country. C. Kirkpatrick. il pors *Sports Illustrated* 70:78-82+ Je 26 '89
Shades of greatness. C. Shmerler. por *World Tennis* 37:30-3 Jl '89
Steffi Slam watch: one down, Down Under. il por *Sports Illustrated* 70:10 F 6 '89
The unlucky seven. G. Plimpton. il *Sports Illustrated* 71:28-9 S 18 '89
Unstoppable Steffi [cover story] B. Newman. il pors *Sports Illustrated* 70:32-5 Mr 27 '89
A view from above. C. Evert. il pors *World Tennis* 37:26-8 N '89
Wunderbar! A. Wolff. il pors *Sports Illustrated* 71:14-21 Jl 17 '89
GRAF ZEPPELIN (AIRSHIP)
Out of the blue. J. R. McCormick. il *American Heritage* 40:49-51 D '89
GRÄFENBERG SPOT *See* G spot
GRAFF, DON
A crack in the wall. il map *Travel Holiday* 171:77-81 Mr '89
Scandal Tour. il *Travel Holiday* 172:98 O '89
GRAFF, GERALD, 1937-, AND CAIN, WILLIAM E., 1952-
Peace plan for the canon wars. *The Nation* 248:310-13 Mr 6 '89
GRAFF, HERB
about
Profiles. D. Watt. por *The New Yorker* 65:59-60+ N 20 '89
GRAFF, ILENE
about
'What am I doing wrong?'. E. Warren. por *TV Guide* 37:22-3 Ag 19-25 '89
GRAFF, JONATHAN M., AND OTHERS
Myristoylated and nonmyristoylated forms of a protein are phosphorylated by protein kinase C. bibl f il *Science* 246:503-6 O 27 '89
GRAFF, YVETA SYNEK
Connoisseur's choice. il pors *Opera News* 54:32-3+ S '89
GRAFFITI
Fade to gray in Gotham [retirement of last graffiti-covered subway car] il *U.S. News & World Report* 106:12 My 22 '89
GRAFTING
Grafting apples. J. Vara. il *Country Journal* 16:44-9 Mr/Ap '89
Training "5-n-1" fruit trees [apple trees] I. Merwin. il *Organic Gardening* 36:34-5 Mr '89
GRAFTING OF MOUTH TISSUE *See* Mouth—Transplantation
GRAFTON, SUE
about
Make no bones about it, Sue Grafton's detective heroine is a real pistol. A. Chambers. il por *People Weekly* 32:81-2 Jl 10 '89
GRAFTON (VT.)
Description
Brigadoon, USA. J. Beatty. il *The Atlantic* 264:102-6 S '89
GRAGG, LARRY
The troubled voyage of the Rainbow. bibl il maps *History Today* 39:36-41 Ag '89
GRAGG, ROSA SLADE, D. 1989
about
Obituary
Jet por 75:18 Mr 27 '89
GRAHAM, BILLY, 1918-
about
Billy brings 'em in. A. McCarthy. il *Commonweal* 116:456-7 S 8 '89
Glasnost opens way for Graham. E. E. Plowman. il por *Christianity Today* 33:61 S 8 '89
God and man in Buffalo [cover story] T. C. Muck. il por *Christianity Today* 33:21-6 Ja 13 '89
Soft sell and satellites deliver biggest audience. il por *Christianity Today* 33:48-9 Ag 18 '89
GRAHAM, BRUCE
about
Early one evening at the Rainbow Bar and Grille [drama] Reviews
The New Yorker 65:82 Ap 24 '89. E. Oliver
GRAHAM, CLARE
Dummy boards [cover story] bibl f il *Antiques* 135:1424-31 Je '89
GRAHAM, DALE K.
From the publisher. See issues of Antiques & Collecting Hobbies beginning January 1986

GRAHAM, DENNIS
Giving up guns. il *The New York Times Magazine* p34+ Ag 20 '89
GRAHAM, ELIZABETH, AND OTHERS
On the fringes of conquest: Maya-Spanish contact in colonial Belize. bibl f il map *Science* 246:1254-9 D 8 '89
GRAHAM, FRANK, 1925-
Birdland. See issues of Audubon through January 1989
GRAHAM, HEATHER
about
California cowgirl. K. M. Chanko. il por *New York* 22:30 O 9 '89
GRAHAM, JANIS
Sunscreen roulette. il *Health (New York, N.Y.)* 21:52-7 My '89
GRAHAM, JOHN R.
Those cold calls leave him cold. por *Fortune* 119:326 Ap 24 '89
GRAHAM, JORIE, 1951-
Fission [poem] *The New Yorker* 65:50-1 N 20 '89
The hiding place [poem] *The New Yorker* 65:38-9 My 22 '89
The tree of knowledge [poem] *The New Yorker* 65:38-9 F 27 '89
GRAHAM, KATHARINE
about
Katharine Graham memoirs go to Knopf. *Publishers Weekly* 236:55 N 3 '89
The mastermind of a media empire. M. Rowland. il pors *Working Woman* 14:114-15+ N '89
GRAHAM, LINDACAROL
Do you have a hormone shortage? *Redbook* 172:16 F '89 (ed) See Schulz, Leslie Dunn. "My baby will grow old—but she'll never grow up"
GRAHAM, MARTHA
about
American document [dance] Reviews
New York il 22:156+ O 23 '89. T. Tobias
Frontier of design: Isamu Noguchi 1904-1988. M. U. West. il pors *Dance Magazine* 63:58-60 My '89
Frontier of the mind: Martha Graham at 95 [interview; cover story] M. Horosko. il pors *Dance Magazine* 63:50-7 My '89
Graham assoluta. G. Solomons. il *Dance Magazine* 63:48-51 Mr '89
Graham tomorrow. C. Barnes. *Dance Magazine* 63:130 D '89
Together at a tense moment, two titans of dance turn crisis into creation. M. Small. il pors *People Weekly* 32:42-3 O 16 '89
GRAHAM, MARY
One toke over the line. *The New Republic* 200:20-1 Ap 17 '89
GRAHAM, ROBERT, AND MEAD, GARY
Argentina's return to Peronism. *World Press Review* 36:23-4 Jl '89
GRAHAM, ROBIN LEE
about
When teen sailor Robin Lee Graham came home from his epic voyage, the really rough weather began. S. Toepfer. il pors *People Weekly* 31:82-4 Ja 16 '89
GRAHAM, RONALD L.
(jt. auth) See Bern, Marshall W., and Graham, Ronald L.
GRAHAM, WILLIAM R.
about
Washington ins & outs: Graham departs, Murrin to Commerce, top changes at NASA and Pentagon. I. Goodwin. *Physics Today* 42:47-9 Jl '89
GRAHAM (MARTHA) DANCE COMPANY See Martha Graham Dance Company
GRAHAM-DIXON, ANDREW
Cragg's way. il pors *Art News* 88:132-7 Mr '89
GRAHAM WEBB INTERNATIONAL INC.
A little rest for the weary [R. R. Taylor] C. Siler. il por *Forbes* 144:304 D 11 '89
GRAIN
See also
Bran
Cooking—Grain
Corn
Oats
Psyllium
Rice
Triticale
Wheat
Wholegrains: old and new. B. T. Hunter. il *Consumers' Research Magazine* 72:8-9 O '89
Aeration
Rooftop cooler for flat storage. D. Mowitz. il *Successful Farming* 87:48R N '89
Drying
Dryer differences more than hot air. D. Mowitz. il *Successful Farming* 87:22-3 Ag '89
Handling
See Grain handling
Milling
Homemade cornmeal. W. J. Weber. il *Country Journal* 16:44-7 S/O '89

Storage
The bins are empty! G. Johnston. il *Successful Farming* 87:25 O '89
GRAIN ALCOHOL AS FUEL See Alcohol as fuel
GRAIN HANDLING
Plan to bust handling bottlenecks. D. Mowitz. il *Successful Farming* 87:24-7 Ag '89
Plumb around problems [pneumatic grain conveyors] D. Mowitz. il *Successful Farming* 87:42-3 D '89
Quality grain starts at harvest. il *Successful Farming* 87:49 O '89
GRAIN IN PHOTOGRAPHY See Photography—Grain
GRAIN MILLS See Grain—Milling
GRAIN MIXES
Mixing your own grains . . . to keep on hand for cereal, for salad, for pilaf. il *Sunset (Central West edition)* 182:220+ My '89
GRAIN SUPPLY
The grain drain: the waning of food security [excerpt from State of the world: 1989] L. R. Brown. il por *The Futurist* 23:9-16 Jl/Ag '89
More food for thought. *Science News* 135:111 F 18 '89
The world food crisis. L. R. Brown. il *USA Today (Periodical)* 117:51-3 Mr '89
GRAIN TRADE
See also
Wheat trade
The grain drain: the waning of food security [excerpt from State of the world: 1989] L. R. Brown. il por *The Futurist* 23:9-16 Jl/Ag '89
GRAINGER, DAVID W.
about
DEC has one little word for 30,000 employees: sell. L. Helm. il por *Business Week* p86+ Ag 14 '89
GRAINING
Wood graining. B. Vila. il *Popular Mechanics* 166:32+ F '89
GRAJAL, ALEJANDRO, AND OTHERS
Foregut fermentation in the hoatzin, a neotropical leaf-eating bird [cover story] bibl f il *Science* 245:1236-8 S 15 '89
GRAMERCY CAPITAL MANAGEMENT
This pro's advice: hunt down Wall Street's orphans [views of J. Lappin] C. E. Cohen. il por *Money* 18:205-6 Je '89
GRAMERCY PARK (NEW YORK, N.Y.)
Gramercy Park: Manhattan's private prize. R. Lynes. il *Architectural Digest* 46:128+ N '89
Notes and comment [steam pipe explosion] *The New Yorker* 65:29-30 S 4 '89
The panic in Gramercy Park [asbestos contamination from steam pipe explosion and water main break] il *U.S. News & World Report* 107:14 S 18 '89
Ruptured lives: how the Gramercy Park steam-pipe blast spewed misery with the asbestos. E. Pooley. il *New York* 22:50-4+ O 30 '89
GRAMICIDINS
Righting the antibiotic record [discovery by R. Dubos] R. P. Crease. il pors *Science* 246:883-4 N 17 '89
Transmembrane channels based on tartaric acid-gramicidin A hybrids. C. J. Stankovic and others. bibl f il *Science* 244:813-17 My 19 '89
GRAMINAE See Grasses
GRAMM, PHIL, 1942-
Should a constitutional amendment to prevent flag desecration be approved? [excerpts from testimony, July 18, 1989] *Congressional Digest* 68:210+ Ag/S '89
Should the Congress adopt the "Tender Offer Disclosure and Fairness Act of 1987"? [excerpts from address, June 17, 1988] *Congressional Digest* 68:87+ Mr '89
Should the Senate-passed Immigration Act of 1989 be approved? [excerpts from debate, July 12, 1989] *Congressional Digest* 68:246+ O '89
GRAMM, WILLIAM PHILIP See Gramm, Phil, 1942-
GRAMM-RUDMAN BILL See Budget
GRAMMY AWARDS
. . . and justice for few. D. Handelman. il *Rolling Stone* p15-16 Ap 6 '89
Chapman, McFerrin, Baker are top Grammy nominees. il *Jet* 75:54+ Ja 30 '89
Grammy ratings hit a new low. J. Ressner. *Rolling Stone* p33 My 18 '89
McFerrin, Chapman take top Grammy Award honors. il pors *Jet* 75:54-5 Mr 13 '89
Random notes. S. Rogers. il *Rolling Stone* p9+ Ap 6 '89
Smokey Robinson cited as 'Living Legend' at gala tribute held in Hollywood. il pors *Jet* 77:22 D 18 '89
This year's Grammys: the women have their day. D. Hiltbrand. il pors *TV Guide* 37:6-7+ F 18-24 '89
Anecdotes, facetiae, satire, etc.
These awards were presented earlier. D. Okrent. il *Esquire* 111:52 Mr '89
GRAMONT, SANCHE DE See Morgan, Ted, 1932-
GRAMSCI, ANTONIO, 1891-1937
about
The Gramscists are coming. M. Novak. il por *Forbes* 143:54 Mr 20 '89
GRANADOS, RAMON, AND OTHERS
"Health first" in Bolivia. il *World Health* p14-15 My '89

GRANATA, ROCKY
about
The plush life. R. Miller. il *New York* 22:25 My 29 '89
GRANATO, TONY
about
Oh, you kids, you. A. Murphy. il pors *Sports Illustrated* 70:40-2+ Ja 30 '89
GRAND CANYON (ARIZ.)
See also
Colorado River (Colo.-Mexico)
Curing the interstate blues. P. Berg. il *Car and Driver* 35:158 Ag '89
GRAND CANYON NATIONAL PARK (ARIZ.)
A camper's oasis etched by a prehistoric river. il map *U.S. News & World Report* 106:65-6 My 8 '89
Grand Canyon in winter. il map *Sunset (Central West edition)* 183:26-8+ N '89
Grand Canyon uranium mining assessed. *National Parks* 63:13-14 My/Je '89
Railroad returns to Grand Canyon [Grand Canyon Railway] il *National Parks* 63:9-10 Jl/Ag '89
Return of the rails [Grand Canyon Railway] il *National Parks* 63:48 N/D '89
Study finds source of canyon haze [Navajo Generating Station] il *National Parks* 63:10 Jl/Ag '89
GRAND CANYON RAILWAY
Railroad returns to Grand Canyon. il *National Parks* 63:9-10 Jl/Ag '89
Return of the rails. il *National Parks* 63:48 N/D '89
GRAND CAYMAN (CAYMAN ISLANDS)
See also
Docks, wharves, etc.—Grand Cayman (Cayman Islands)
GRAND CENTRAL TERMINAL (NEW YORK, N.Y.)
Grand Central Terminal. A. R. Gochman. il *Gourmet* 49:106-11+ N '89
GRAND HOTEL (LOS OLIVOS, CALIF.: RESTAURANT)
See Los Olivos (Calif.)—Restaurants, nightclubs, bars, etc.
GRAND HOTEL (MACKINAC ISLAND, MICH.) *See* Hotels, motels, etc.—Mackinac Island (Mich.)
GRAND HOTEL [musical] *See* Musicals, revues, etc.—Reviews—Single works
GRAND HOTEL E LA PACE (MONTECATINI TERME, ITALY) *See* Montecatini Terme (Italy)—Hotels, motels, etc.
GRAND JURY
Frustrated grand jurors say it was no accident Ted Kennedy got off easy [Chappaquiddick incident] J. S. Kunen. il pors *People Weekly* 32:34-6 Jl 24 '89
GRAND METROPOLITAN PLC
Grand Met's recipe for Pillsbury. R. I. Kirkland, Jr. il *Fortune* 119:61+ Mr 13 '89
Trying to get Burger King out of the flames [executive B. J. Gibbons] M. Maremont. il por *Business Week* p29-30 Ja 30 '89
"We've got a serious problem". J. Marcom, Jr. il por *Forbes* 144:48-9+ D 25 '89
GRAND PRIX INTERNATIONAL VIDÉO-DANSE
Grand Prix de Vidéo-Danse. D. Towers. il *Dance Magazine* 63:56-9 Mr '89
GRAND PRIX RACING *See* Automobile racing; Motorcycle racing
GRAND TETON NATIONAL PARK (WYO.)
Last-gasp skiing. J. Schmidt. il *Sierra* 74:58 My/Je '89
Teton, Yellowstone snowmobile issue [proposed trail] il *National Parks* 63:9-10 My/Je '89
Yellowstone: after the fire [bicycle tour] S. Kearin. il map *Bicycling* 30:96-100+ Jl '89
GRAND TRAVERSE BAY REGION (MICH.)
Description and travel
Wandering along Michigan's golden shoreline. K. Rodeghier. il *Travel Holiday* 171:10+ My '89
GRAND UNIFICATION THEORIES *See* Field theory (Physics)
GRAND UNION CO.
The hell with glamour. Give me groceries [G. D. Hirsch] J. H. Dobrzynski. il por *Business Week* p121 My 1 '89
GRANDE GALERIE DE ZOOLOGIE (PARIS, FRANCE)
The once and future museum. C. Gans. il *Natural History* p48-55 Jl '89
GRANDFATHERS *See* Grandparents
GRANDMA MOSES [drama] *See* Pouliot, Stephen
GRANDMOTHERS *See* Grandparents
GRANDMOTHERS FOR PEACE (ORGANIZATION)
Grannies go for peace. D. Pottenger. il *Sierra* 74:27 Mr/Ap '89
GRANDPARENT EDUCATION
Grandparent education [views of Robert Strom] il *The Futurist* 23:55-6 My/Je '89
GRANDPARENTS
A granddaughter's fear. N. Angier. il *The New York Times Magazine* p22+ My 7 '89
Grandma's sewing machine. J. Leonard. il por *Good Housekeeping* 208:56 Ap '89
Grandpa and the kid. D. Sisson. See alternate issues of Field & Stream beginning September 1983
Grandpa Isaak [excerpt from Ours]; tr. by Anne Frydman. S. Dovlatov. *Harper's* 278:24-6 My '89
Grandparents aren't what they used to be. R. D. Turner. il *Ebony* 44:36+ Mr '89

A guide for us grandparents. R. B. Roufberg. il *New Choices for the Best Years* 29:77-9 D '89
How to handle a bossy grandmother. B. Spock. por *Redbook* 172:66 Ja '89
In praise of Mister Rogers [response to child grieving over grandmother's death] B. H. Edgington. il *Parents* 64:120 Mr '89
Love letters from grandma. A. S. Brown. il *New Choices for the Best Years* 29:98+ S '89
'Skip-generation' parents. J. Seligmann. il *Newsweek* 114 Special Issue:46 Wint '89/Spr '90
Trimming the tax bite on gifts to grandchildren. T. Segal. il *Business Week* p161 O 23 '89
The way we are. L. Wyse. il *Good Housekeeping* 208:272 My '89
The way we are [taking grandchildren for a walk] L. Wyse. il *Good Housekeeping* 209:270 D '89
Anecdotes, facetiae, satire, etc.
What my grandmother told me. K. Fury. il *Working Woman* 14:114 Ja '89
GRANDPRÉ, CHANTAL DE
'Slaves of one man'. il *The Unesco Courier* 42:44-7 O '89
LES GRANDS BALLETS CANADIENS
Ann Hutchinson Guest goes back to the source: finding Faune [restaging L'après-midi d'un faune] L. Garafola. il pors *Dance Magazine* 63:32-4 O '89
On its toes again. M. Crabb. il *Maclean's* 102:54 F 27 '89
Reviews:
Performances in Montreal. L. Howe-Beck. *Dance Magazine* 63:84-6 S '89
GRANGE, JACQUES
about
The gilded and the grand. N. Frey. il pors *Harper's Bazaar* 122:110+ Ap '89
Le style Jacques Grange. E. White. il pors *House & Garden* 161:92-105+ Jl '89
GRANGER, DAVID
'80s golf. il *Sport (New York, N.Y.)* 80:84 O '89
Inside the World Series: the laughs that go with the drama. il *TV Guide* 37:2-4 O 14-20 '89
GRANGER, ROBERT C.
The staffing crisis in early childhood education. bibl f il *Phi Delta Kappan* 71:130-4 O '89
GRANITAS *See* Ice cream, ices, etc.
GRANITES, DOLLY NAMPIJINPA
about
Beautiful Dreamings. A. Wallach. il *Ms.* 17:60-4 Mr '89
GRANNY FLATS
Granny flats: another idea for creating affordable housing and strengthening community ties [excerpt from address] A. Duany. *Utne Reader* p72 My/Je '89
GRANT, CARL A.
Urban teachers: their new colleagues and curriculum. bibl f il *Phi Delta Kappan* 70:764-70 Je '89
GRANT, CARY, 1904-1986
about
. . . and Cary. E. Mattlin. por *Film Comment* 25:8-9 N/D '89
A new husband and a new film help Dyan Cannon put her ex, Cary Grant, behind her at last. D. Grogan. il pors *People Weekly* 31:44-5 My 22 '89
GRANT, CURTIS
To make the grade, just go do it. por *Nation's Business* 77:12 D '89
GRANT, DUNCAN JAMES CORROWR, 1885-1978
about
Painting Charleston. J. Johnston. bibl f il pors *Art in America* 77:152-63+ D '89
GRANT, GWENDOLYN GOLDSBY
Just between us. See issues of Essence beginning May 1983
GRANT, JAMES
Michael Milken, meet Sewell Avery. il *Forbes* 144 Special Issue:60-2+ O 23 '89
GRANT, JAMES
Priscilla Presley: never better than now. il pors *McCall's* 116:12-13+ Jl '89
GRANT, JERRY V.
(jt. auth) See Kirk, John T., and Grant, Jerry V.
GRANT, LEE
about
Lee Grant. K. Gross. il pors *People Weekly* 32:105+ O 23 '89
Staying together [film] Reviews
People Weekly il 32:29 N 20 '89. R. Novak
Rolling Stone il por p48 S 21 '89. P. Travers
GRANT, LINDSEY
Foresight: addressing tomorrow's problems today. por *The Futurist* 23:14-17 Ja/F '89
GRANT, R. W., 1929-
Ode to Michael Milken. *Harper's* 279:25-6 Jl '89
GRANT, ROBERTA
Twenty-four going on forty: the new mid-life crisis comes early. il *Mademoiselle* 95:246-7+ S '89
GRANT-KOHRS RANCH NATIONAL HISTORIC SITE (MONT.)
Remembering the frontier. J. Merritt. il map *Americana* 17:34-9 My/Je '89

GRANT STREET NATIONAL BANK
Right with Mike. M. Schifrin. *Forbes* 143:164-5 My 15 '89
GRANTHAM, JEREMY
about
To all yardsticks there is a season. D. Churbuck. il por *Forbes* 144:44+ Ag 21 '89
GRANTHAM, MAYO, VAN OTTERLOO & COMPANY
To all yardsticks there is a season [J. Grantham] D. Churbuck. il por *Forbes* 144:44+ Ag 21 '89
GRANTS, RESEARCH *See* Research grants
GRANTS PASS (OR.)
Clubs
See also
Betty Club
GRANULAR MATERIALS
Dynamic pore-pressure fluctuations in rapidly shearing granular materials. R. M. Iverson and R. G. LaHusen. bibl f il *Science* 246:796-9 N 10 '89
GRANULITE
Origin of granulite terranes and the formation of the lowermost continental crust. S. R. Bohlen and K. Mezger. bibl f il *Science* 244:326-9 Ap 21 '89
GRANULOMATOUS DISEASE, CHRONIC *See* Chronic granulomatous disease
GRANVILLE, GARY N.
Knights of the Far West. il *The Unesco Courier* 42:48-53 S '89
GRANVILLE, JOSEPH ENSIGN, 1923-
about
Joe's back. M. Hulbert. por *Forbes* 144:300 N 27 '89
GRANVILLE MARKET LETTER
Joe's back. M. Hulbert. por *Forbes* 144:300 N 27 '89
GRANZ, NORMAN
about
Lifetime Achievement Award. J. McDonough. il por *Down Beat* 56:21 Ag '89
GRAPE LEAVES
Vintage leaves. C. Fenyvesi. por *Organic Gardening* 36:71 Jl/Ag '89
GRAPEFRUITS
See also
Cooking—Fruit
Peeling
Death to albedo [use of pectinase aids grapefruit peeling] *Discover* 10:14 Ap '89
GRAPES
See also
Viticulture
GRAPH THEORY
A near-optimum parallel planarization algorithm. Y. Takefuji and K.-C. Lee. bibl f il *Science* 245:1221-3 S 15 '89
The shortest-network problem [Steiner problem] M. W. Bern and R. L. Graham. bibl il map *Scientific American* 260:84-9 Ja '89
The sorcerer's apprentice [Graffiti program developed by Siemion Fajtlowicz] B. A. Cipra. il *Science* 244:770 My 19 '89
GRAPHIC ARTS
See also
Book design
Drawing
Etching
Prints
SBG Partners
Graphic design in the age of computers. S. Gamliel. il *Occupational Outlook Quarterly* 32:34-6 Wint '88
Exhibitions
See also
Graphische Sammlung Albertina
MassComm 101: the media vs. modernism [Image world: art and media culture and Graphic design in America] P. Plagens. il *Newsweek* 114:88-9 N 27 '89
A rue with a view [work of P. Bonnard at the Metropolitan Museum of Art] B. Adams. il *Harper's Bazaar* 122:116+ D '89
GRAPHIC METHODS
Hardware hacker. D. Lancaster. il *Radio-Electronics* 60:61-2+ My '89
GRAPHIC NOVELS
Berkley, First and CMG join to revive Classics illustrated. B. Levine. il *Publishers Weekly* 236:48 N 24 '89
GRAPHICAL USER INTERFACES
A guide to GUIs [cover story] F. Hayes and N. Baran. il *Byte* 14:250-7 Jl '89
Mac-like interface brings another look to Unix [Looking Glass] *Byte* 14:17 S '89
OSF/Motif. J. Paul. il *Byte* 14:230-1 My '89
OSF seeking shrink-wrapped Unix software. *Byte* 14:22+ S '89
GRAPHICS, COMPUTER *See* Computer graphics
GRAPHICS TABLETS *See* Digitizing tablets
GRAPHISCHE SAMMLUNG ALBERTINA
Palace evolution [K. Oberhuber] F. Protzman. il por *Art News* 88:117-18 Ap '89
GRAPHITE
Long-range electronic perturbations caused by defects using scanning tunneling microscopy. H. A. Mizes and J. S. Foster. bibl f il *Science* 244:559-62 My 5 '89

Smectic liquid crystal monolayers on graphite observed by scanning tunneling microscopy [cover story] D. P. E. Smith and others. bibl f il *Science* 245:43-5 Jl 7 '89
GRAPHS *See* Graphic methods
GRAPPA
From Romano Levi's grappa . . to exotic comestibles. F. Ferretti. il *Gourmet* 49:70+ S '89
GRASS, GÜNTER, 1927-
about
PW interviews. T. Weyr. il por *Publishers Weekly* 235:54-5 Je 16 '89
GRASS *See* Grasses
GRASS BURNING *See* Burning of land
GRASS SEED *See* Grasses—Seed
GRASSES
See also
Alfalfa
Bamboo
Crabgrass
Fescue
Grazing
Lawns
Sod
Combustible grass winning the West [cheat grass; research by Dwight Billings] J. Raloff. *Science News* 136:127 Ag 19 '89
The South embraces ornamental grasses. L. B. Trigg. il *Southern Living* 24:78-81 N '89
Types of grass. *Flower and Garden* 33:16 S/O '89
Seed
Contamination
Imported weed called threat to sheep and cattle [serrated tussock] S. Christie. *Successful Farming* 87:40A Ag '89
GRASSHOPPER HOLLOW (MO.)
Grasshopper Hollow, Missouri. R. H. Mohlenbrock. il map *Natural History* p60-3 Jl '89
GRASSHOPPERS
Control
An Aussie fungus among us [Entomophaga grylli kills grasshoppers; research by Ray Carruthers] *Science News* 136:46 Jl 15 '89
Return of the locust [African locusts; with editorial comment] J. A. Harriss. il *Reader's Digest* 134:15-16, 122-6 My '89
Embryology
See Embryology—Insects
GRASSLAND FIRES *See* Brush fires
GRASSLANDS
See also
Livestock ranges
Prairies
GRATEFUL DEAD (MUSICAL GROUP)
The Grateful Dead. G. Santoro. *The Nation* 249:695-6 D 4 '89
Jerry Garcia [interview; cover story] F. Goodman. il pors *Rolling Stone* p66-8+ N 30 '89
GRATIFICATION, DELAY OF *See* Delay of gratification
GRATUITIES *See* Tipping
GRAUBARD, STEPHEN RICHARDS
Presidents: the power and the mediocrity. il *The New York Times Book Review* 94:1+ Ja 15 '89
GRAVE LINE TOURS
And now, Hollywood Babble-on. R. Corliss. il *Time* 133:76-7 Ja 16 '89
GRAVES, D. T., AND OTHERS
Identification of monocyte chemotactic activity produced by malignant cells. bibl f il *Science* 245:1490-3 S 29 '89
GRAVES, DALE
about
Are mower repairs worth it? [interview] B. Markovich. il por *Home Mechanix* 86:25-6+ Mr '89
GRAVES, EARL G. (EARL GILBERT), 1935-
Publisher's page. See issues of Black Enterprise
GRAVES, MICHAEL P.
Death wish [poem] *The Christian Century* 106:948 O 25 '89
GRAVES *See* Tombs
GRAVITATION *See* Gravity and gravitation
GRAVITATIONAL LENSES
Einstein's ring and a galaxy's mass [MG 1654 + 1346] il *Sky and Telescope* 77:465-6 My '89
Gravitational lens optics. R. D. Blandford and others. bibl f il *Science* 245:824-30 Ag 25 '89
Starry lens puts a twinkle in quasar's eye [QSO 2237 + 0305; research by M. J. Irwin] I. Peterson. *Science News* 136:375 D 9 '89
GRAVITY AND GRAVITATION
See also
Falling bodies
Fifth force (Physics)
Gravitational lenses
Relativity (Physics)
Weightlessness
Amusement park thrills [role in ride design] il *National Geographic World* 171:20-3 N '89
Gravity under siege [testing Newton's law] T. Waters. il *Discover* 10:18+ Ap '89

GRAVITY AND GRAVITATION—*cont.*
Prediction and theory evaluation: the case of light bending. S. G. Brush. bibl f *Science* 246:1124-9 D 1 '89
Searching for the secrets of gravity. J. Boslough. il *National Geographic* 175:562-83 My '89

Measurement

Einstein's unfinished symphony [laser interferometers in gravity wave detection] M. Bartusiak. il *Discover* 10:62-9 Ag '89

Physiological effects

See also
Geotropism
GRAVITY WAVES *See* Gravity and gravitation
GRAY, ARTHUR, JR., AND LAFFER, ARTHUR B.
Debt and taxes. il *National Review* 41:38-9 S 1 '89
GRAY, BARBARA BRONSON
"We're just ordinary people". il pors *Ladies' Home Journal* 106:88+ Jl '89
(jt. auth) See Farrell, Jane, and Gray, Barbara Bronson
GRAY, BILLY
about
After Father knows best, it was drugs, jail, depression. M. Littwin. il pors *TV Guide* 37:6-8 Je 17-23 '89
GRAY, C. BOYDEN
about
Fraudulence I. R. E. Tyrrell. il *The American Spectator* 22:10 Ap '89
Off on the wrong foot. B. Turque and A. McDaniel. il por *Newsweek* 113:30+ Ap 10 '89
GRAY, C. WILLIAM
The health-care crisis [address, October 27, 1988] *Vital Speeches of the Day* 55:304-7 Mr 1 '89
GRAY, CHARLES L., 1946-, AND ALSON, JEFFREY A., 1956-
The case for methanol. bibl il *Scientific American* 261:108-14 N '89
GRAY, COLIN S.
People, not weapons, make war. *The Bulletin of the Atomic Scientists* 45:34 My '89
GRAY, GORDON C.
about
A golfer's course. il *Maclean's* 102:52 Ap 10 '89
GRAY, HENRY F.
about
Is the radio tube warming up again? W. D. Marbach. il por *Business Week* Special Issue:76 Je 16 '89
GRAY, JACQUELYN
Nigeria. il *Black Enterprise* 20:121-2 D '89
GRAY, JEREMY, 1947-
(jt. auth) See Goldstein, Catherine, and Gray, Jeremy, 1947-
GRAY, JOHN
Can Warsaw and Moscow be friends? *World Press Review* 36:17+ O '89
GRAY, JOHN
The end of history—or of liberalism? *National Review* 41:33-5 O 27 '89
The last socialist? [cover story] il *National Review* 41:27-9+ Je 30 '89
GRAY, JOHN, 1946-
Tangerine dreams. il *Maclean's* 102:50-1 Ag 28 '89
about
Body language. J. Bemrose. il por *Maclean's* 102:58-9 Mr 13 '89
GRAY, LINDA
about
Linda Gray: the butterfly is free. L. Gross. il pors *Ladies' Home Journal* 106:40+ Ag '89
GRAY, PETE, 1915-
about
The Gray matter. J. Howard. il por *Sport (New York, N.Y.)* 80:29 Mr '89
GRAY, PETER F.
Notes from underground. il *The Washington Monthly* 21:19-25 D '89
GRAY, ROBERT H.
Youth, culture, art education, television. bibl f *Design for Arts in Education* 90:23-5 Mr/Ap '89
GRAY, THOMAS A.
about
What you can expect in 1989. il por *Nation's Business* 77:18 Ja '89
GRAY, WILLIAM H., III
about
Former Gray aide denies she's object of FBI probe. por *Jet* 76:6 Je 19 '89
Gray matter. T. Eastland. il *The American Spectator* 22:26-7 S '89
Gray seeks policy shift as Caucus chair. L. Brown. il por *Black Enterprise* 19:29 Mr '89
Gray takes historic step as first black majority whip. S. Booker. il por *Jet* 76:6+ Jl 3 '89
House Speaker Jim Wright resigns; blacks note loss and attack on Bill Gray. il pors *Jet* 76:4-5 Je 19 '89
Putting their House in order. E. Salholz. il pors *Newsweek* 113:18 Je 26 '89
GRAY (HARRY), MEL KLEIN & PARTNERS LP *See* Harry Gray, Mel Klein & Partners LP

GRAY HAIR *See* Hair
GRAY SQUIRRELS *See* Squirrels
GRAY WHALES *See* Whales
GRAYBEAL, SIDNEY N., AND MCFATE, PATRICIA BLISS
Getting out of the STARTing block. il *Scientific American* 261:61-7 D '89
GRAYLING FISHING
The gaudy stranger. P. Barrett. il *Field & Stream* 93:70+ F '89
GRAYSON, DAVID, 1870-1946
The Versailles Treaty and after [reprint from January 1924 issue] *Current History* 88:20-3 Ja '89
GRAYSON, J. PAUL
about
Windows on the world. D. Churbuck. il pors *Forbes* 144:123+ D 25 '89
The wizard of Windows. R. Lockwood. por *Personal Computing* 13:85 Jl '89
GRAYWOLF PRESS
Graywolf: a literary press ponders its problems. J. Ervin, Jr. il *Publishers Weekly* 235:30-1 Ap 14 '89
GRAZING
See also
Forage plants
Holistic resource management
Bovine 'balers' stack big profits [controlled grazing of alfalfa] J. Walter. il *Successful Farming* 87:32-3 mid-Mr '89
Late grazing for low-input cows [stockpiling forage] J. Walter. il *Successful Farming* 87:54+ O '89
Out to pasture, in the money. J. R. Borcherding. il *Successful Farming* 87:29 My '89
Same land, double the herd [intensive grazing management for cattle] J. Walter. il *Successful Farming* 87:30 O '89

Laws and regulations

Going against the graze. D. Zaslowsky. il *Sierra* 74:30+ S/O '89
A land battle in New Mexico [sheep war] J. N. Baker. il *Newsweek* 114:27 S 18 '89
GRAZING LANDS *See* Livestock ranges
GREANVILLE, PATRICE
Animal activists: get green! il *Utne Reader* p52 S/O '89
GREASON, MICHAEL
Here a parcel, there a parcel—fragmented forests. il *The Conservationist* 44:46-9 Jl/Ag '89
GREAT AMERICAN COMMUNICATIONS CORP.
Yabba-dabba-doo. T. Jaffe. *Forbes* 144:172-3 D 25 '89
GREAT AMERICAN MANAGEMENT & INVESTMENT, INC.
Sam Zell, the perpetual dealmaking machine. L. Therrien. il *Business Week* p88-9 Je 26 '89
GREAT ARCH (PARIS, FRANCE) *See* Arche de la Défense (Paris, France)
GREAT ATLANTIC & PACIFIC TEA COMPANY, INC.
A&P is thriving—so why is James Wood still around? A. Rothman. il por *Business Week* p90-1 Ap 10 '89
Has LBO fever struck Europe? [A&P's bid for Gateway] M. Maremont. il *Business Week* p28 Jl 3 '89
GREAT ATTRACTOR (ASTRONOMY)
Looking well beyond the Great Attractor [work of R. Scaramella] I. Peterson. *Science News* 135:230-1 Ap 15 '89
Star attraction [research by Alan Dressler and Sandra Faber] S. Vogel. il *Discover* 10:20+ N '89
GREAT BALLS OF FIRE [film] *See* Motion picture reviews—Single works
GREAT BARRIER REEF (AUSTRALIA)
Crown-of-thorns no Johnny-come-lately [research by A. J. Timothy Jull] S. Hart. *Science News* 136:133 Ag 26 '89
Evidence from sediments of long-term Acanthaster planci predation on corals of the Great Barrier Reef [crown of thorns starfish; cover story] P. D. Walbran and others. bibl f il map *Science* 245:847-50 Ag 25 '89
GREAT BASIN
See also
Geology—Great Basin
GREAT BASIN NATIONAL PARK (NEV.)

Photographs and photography

Great Basin National Park. il *National Geographic* 175:72-5 Ja '89
GREAT BOOKS OF THE WESTERN WORLD
Civilization and its malcontents [politicization of humanities; cover story] S. Hook. il *National Review* 41:30-3 O 13 '89
The great works: who needs them? *Current (Washington, D.C.)* 318:4-11 D '89
Peace plan for the canon wars. G. Graff and W. E. Cain. *The Nation* 248:310-13 Mr 6 '89
The Stanford library [revised Western civilization course] M. Stanford. *The New Republic* 201:18+ O 2 '89
The war of the Great books. B. McArthur. il *American Heritage* 40:57-8+ F '89
What culture should mean. L. S. Robinson. *The Nation* 249:319-21 S 25 '89
Who needs the great works? [Harper's forum; cover story] il *Harper's* 279:43-52 S '89
Whose canon is it, anyway? [place of black literature among classics] H. L. Gates. *The New York Times Book Review* 94:1+ F 26 '89

GREAT BRITAIN

See also

Accounting—Great Britain
Agricultural exhibitions—Great Britain
Agriculture—Great Britain
Airports—Great Britain
Antique dealers—Great Britain
Apprentices—Great Britain
Architecture—Great Britain
Art—Great Britain
Art and state—Great Britain
Art galleries and museums—Great Britain
Astrology—Great Britain
Astronomy—Great Britain
Auctions—Great Britain
Automobile racing—Great Britain
Aviation and state—Great Britain
Balance of payments—Great Britain
Bars and barrooms—Great Britain
Battlefields—Great Britain
Birds—Great Britain
Blacks—Great Britain
Bogs—Great Britain
Booksellers and bookselling—Great Britain
British
Cellular radio—Great Britain
Censorship—Great Britain
Civil rights—Great Britain
Collective settlements—Great Britain
College education and state—Great Britain
Commonwealth of Nations
Costume—Great Britain
Country estates—Great Britain
Cricket (Sport)—Great Britain
Criminal justice, Administration of—Great Britain
Cultural property—Protection—Great Britain
Direct broadcast satellite services—Great Britain
Drug abuse—Great Britain
Drug laws and regulations—Great Britain
Education—Great Britain
Education and state—Great Britain
Educational laws and regulations—Great Britain
Engineering—Study and teaching—Great Britain
Environmental movement—Great Britain
Espionage, Russian—Great Britain
Family—Great Britain
Fertilization in vitro—Laws and regulations—Great Britain
Flower gardens and gardening—Great Britain
Foreign correspondents—Great Britain
Foreign students—Great Britain
Freedom of speech—Great Britain
Gardens and gardening—Great Britain
Genetic research—Great Britain
Germans—Great Britain
Golf courses—Great Britain
Gossip columns—Great Britain
Government and the press—Great Britain
Health education—Great Britain
Historic houses, sites, etc.—Great Britain
Homosexuality—Great Britain
Horse racing—Great Britain
Hunting—Great Britain
Immigration and emigration—Great Britain
Insider trading—Great Britain
Intelligence service—Great Britain
Investments, American—Great Britain
Investments, British
Investments, Egyptian—Great Britain
Investments, Japanese—Great Britain
Investments, Kuwaiti—Great Britain
Investments, South African—Great Britain
Investments, West German—Great Britain
Irish—Great Britain
Irrigation—Great Britain
Jews—Great Britain
Labor—Great Britain
Labor unions—Printers—Great Britain
Law—Great Britain
Leveraged buyouts—Great Britain
Libel and slander—Great Britain
Maritime law—Great Britain
Medical research—Great Britain
Motion picture festivals—Great Britain
Motorcycle racing—Great Britain
Music festivals—Great Britain
Narcotics laws and regulations—Great Britain
Natural history—Great Britain
Nobility—Great Britain
Northern Ireland
Nuclear research—Great Britain
Opera—Great Britain
Organic farming—Great Britain
Preferred stocks—Great Britain
Privatization—Great Britain
Public officers—Great Britain
Queues (Waiting lines)—Great Britain
Radioactive pollution—Great Britain

Research—Great Britain
Roads—Great Britain
Scotland
Shooting preserves—Great Britain
Sikhs—Great Britain
Soccer, Professional—Great Britain
Social classes—Great Britain
Space research—Great Britain
Stone Age—Great Britain
Strikes—Longshore workers—Great Britain
Tabloid newspapers—Great Britain
Telepoint communications—Great Britain
Television broadcasting—Great Britain
Television laws and regulations—Great Britain
Terrorism—Great Britain
Theosophy—Great Britain
Trade waste—Disposal—Great Britain
Upper classes—Great Britain
Wales
Wildlife management—Great Britain
Women—Great Britain
The global zeitgeist checklist: England. M. Kinsley. *The New Republic* 200:29 My 1 '89

Appropriations and expenditures

See also
Budget—Great Britain

Armed Forces

See also
Great Britain. Army
Appropriations and expenditures
U.K. boosts defense spending $1.6 billion to keep weapons programs on schedule. D. A. Brown. *Aviation Week & Space Technology* 130:25 My 8 '89

Civilization

See also
Great Britain—Intellectual life

Colonies

See also
Bermuda
Commonwealth of Nations
Falkland Islands
Hong Kong
United States—History—Colonial period, ca. 1600-1775

Commerce

See also
European Economic Community
Canada
Dangerous cargo [PCB-contaminated wastes from Quebec turned away by British ports] M. Rose. il *Maclean's* 102:10-12 Ag 28 '89
Unwanted garbage: British port blocks ship with Canadian PCBs. A. Phillips. il *Maclean's* 102:43 Ag 21 '89
France
Aerospatiale takes first civilian order for Super Puma Mk. 2 helicopters [Bristow Helicopter Group order] il *Aviation Week & Space Technology* 130:73 Je 26 '89
Jordan
Deficit woes prompt Jordan to postpone Tornado purchase. M. Mecham. *Aviation Week & Space Technology* 130:32-3 Ap 3 '89
Saudi Arabia
Unit set up to finance Saudi military buys from Britain. *Aviation Week & Space Technology* 131:24 D 4 '89
South Africa
Family quarrel [British opposition to sanctions against South Africa at Commonwealth summit in Kuala Lumpur, Malaysia] R. Laver. il *Maclean's* 102:40-1 O 30 '89
A thorny dispute [Britain refuses to endorse call for sanctions against South Africa at Commonwealth conference in Malaysia] R. Laver. il por *Maclean's* 102:36-7 N 6 '89
United States
See United States—Commerce—Great Britain

Cultural relations

Soviet Union
The taste for Bacon [exhibition in Moscow] B. Taylor. il por *Art News* 88:57 Ja '89

Defenses

See also
Airplanes, Military—Great Britain
Great Britain. Army
Great Britain. Royal Navy
Guided missiles, British
Unilateral disarmament—Labor's lost love. N. Moss. il por *The Bulletin of the Atomic Scientists* 45:9-11 O '89

Description and travel

See also
Automobile touring—Great Britain
Armchair excursions [Fodor's Great Britain video] H. B. Livesey. il *Travel Holiday* 172:36-7 N '89
Britain revisited [walking from coast to coast] D. Pollitt. il map *American Health* 8:40 Jl/Ag '89

Diplomatic and consular service

Profiles [former diplomat D. Park] C. Alexander. il por *The New Yorker* 64:57-71 Ja 30 '89
France
Carry on cricket: the Duke of Dorset's 1789 tour [cover story] J. Goulstone and M. J. Swanton. bibl il *History Today* 39:18-23 Ag '89

GREAT BRITAIN—cont.

Economic history

See also

Industrial revolution—Great Britain

Historiography

Words, not numbers: John Harold Clapham. R. Floud. bibl il pors *History Today* 39:42-7 Ap '89

Economic policy

See also

Budget—Great Britain

10 years of Thatcherism. R. Knight. *U.S. News & World Report* 106:56 My 8 '89

Arms and the woman [resignation of Chancellor of the Exchequer N. Lawson] J. O'Sullivan. *National Review* 41:9 N 24 '89

Bad reviews for a one-man show [resignation of Chancellor of the Exchequer N. Lawson triggers anti-Thatcher sentiment] H. Anderson. il pors *Newsweek* 114:46-7 N 6 '89

The beginning of the end of an era [resignation of Chancellor of the Exchequer N. Lawson] R. Knight. por *U.S. News & World Report* 107:50 N 6 '89

Just you move over, 'Enry 'Iggins [changes in the class system attributed to M. Thatcher's economic reforms] R. Knight. il *U.S. News & World Report* 106:40 Ap 24 '89

The moral passion of Mrs. Thatcher. K. R. Minogue. il *National Review* 41:22-5 My 19 '89

Mrs. Thatcher under siege again. C. W. Weinberger. il por *Forbes* 144:31 N 27 '89

A question of judgment [resignation of Chancellor of the Exchequer N. Lawson] A. Phillips. il por *Maclean's* 102:38-9 N 6 '89

Report from Britain. T. Bethell. *The American Spectator* 22:11-13 D '89

Splatcher. M. Elliott. il *The New Republic* 201:14-16 D 11 '89

Thatcher: can an old Tory learn new tricks? R. A. Melcher. por *Business Week* p37 Jl 24 '89

The Thatcher revolution [special section] il pors *Maclean's* 102:30-3+ My 8 '89

What ails Britain. M. Horsman. il *World Press Review* 36:50-1 Ap '89

Economic relations

See also

European Economic Community

Foreign opinion

American

Margaret Thatcher and the revival of the West [cover story] R. Reagan. il *National Review* 41:21-2 My 19 '89

Foreign relations

See also

Espionage, British

A formidable force [Margaret Thatcher] J. Bierman. il *Maclean's* 102:40 My 8 '89

Argentina—History

Whose island story? [Falklands] P. J. Beck. il map *History Today* 39:8-11 F '89

China

Apprehension in Hong Kong [killings in Beijing] A. Phillips. *Maclean's* 102:27 Je 19 '89

Britain's Hong Kong headache has just begun to throb. D. J. Yang. il *Business Week* p83 Jl 17 '89

Britain's shame. M. Elliott. *The New Republic* 201:15-16 Ag 7-14 '89

Broken China [effects of crackdown on students] *The New Republic* 200:5-6 Je 26 '89

Decision time in Hong Kong. F. M. Bordewich. il *Reader's Digest* 134:121-6 Je '89

Fear and anger in Hong Kong [Beijing massacre shakes the colony] W. Stewart. il *Time* 133:22 Je 19 '89

The Hong Kong Church faces 1997 [Catholic Church] M. H. Kelleher. il *America* 161:63-4 Jl 29-Ag 5 '89

Hong Kong gone. W. McGurn. *National Review* 41:22-3 Ap 21 '89

Hong Kong? Just watch China. B. Crozier. *National Review* 41:20 Mr 10 '89

Hong Kong on borrowed time. M. Scott. il *The New York Times Magazine* p30-2+ O 22 '89

The long goodbye [Hong Kong residents who wish to leave and boat people who have arrived] R. Brookhiser. il *National Review* 41:18-19 N 24 '89

Next door and eight years away. J. Greenwald. il *Time* 133:29 Je 5 '89

Preparing for 1997 [Canadian B. Strayer helps draft bill of rights for Hong Kong] J. Keating. *Maclean's* 102:73-4 N 20 '89

The tragedy of Hong Kong. M. Novak. il *Forbes* 144:80-1 Ag 21 '89

What will happen when the Chinese take back their 'fragrant harbor'? [Hong Kong] S. Karnow. bibl (p174) il map *Smithsonian* 20:40-8+ Ap '89

Will the last one to leave please turn out the lights? [reaction to Beijing crackdown in Hong Kong] E. MacFarquhar. il *U.S. News & World Report* 107:36-7 Ag 21 '89

France

See also

Great Britain—Diplomatic and consular service—France

Germany

What can England do about Hitler? [reprint from October 1938 issue] Sir W. Churchill. *Current History* 88:24-5+ Ja '89

Iran

'Shame' [Britain's slow response to threats against S. Rushdie] G. Black. *The Nation* 248:328-9 Mr 13 '89

A shattered deal [release of British hostages in Beirut jeopardized by S. Rushdie affair] il *Newsweek* 113:5 Mr 13 '89

Ireland—History

Strafford in Ireland, 1633-40. H. F. Kearney. il por maps *History Today* 39:20-5 Jl '89

Middle East

Why should Israel trust the PLO? B. Amiel. il *Maclean's* 102:9 Je 5 '89

Middle East—History

The first intifada: rebellion in Palestine, 1936-39. C. Townshend. bibl il *History Today* 39:13-19 Jl '89

Netherlands—History

See also

Anglo-Dutch Wars, 1652-1784

Anglo-Dutch relations, 1940-45 [London conference] il *History Today* 39:61 Jl '89

Poland—History

Were we wrong in 1939? [U.S. refusal to join Anglo-French defense of Poland; with reply by J. P. Roche] D. Carlton. il *National Review* 41:44+ S 29 '89

Soviet Union

See also

Gorbachev, Mikhail—Visit to Great Britain, 1989

Soviet Union—History

Dangerous liaisons [German and British alliances with the Soviet Union during World War II] G. A. Craig. bibl f il *The New York Review of Books* 36:15-19 Mr 30 '89

Spain—History

See also

Spanish Armada, 1588

United States

See United States—Foreign relations—Great Britain

Vietnam

Dashing their dreams [Britain forces repatriation of Vietnamese boat people] W. Stewart. il *Time* 134:26 D 25 '89

Western Europe

A two-speed Europe? T. Garton Ash. il *World Press Review* 36:16+ Ja '89

History

Roman period, 55 B.C.-449 A.D.

Up against the wall [Romans failed to subdue the tribes of northern Britain] W. S. Hanson and L. Macinnes. il maps *Natural History* p80-7 Ap '89

Medieval period, 1066-1485

See also

Hundred Years' War, 1339-1453

Tudors, 1485-1603

See also

Great Britain—History—Elizabethan period, 1558-1603

Younger sons in Tudor and Stuart England. L. A. Pollock. bibl il *History Today* 39:23-9 Je '89

Elizabethan period, 1558-1603

The political magic of John Dee. I. Seymour. bibl il por *History Today* 39:29-35 Ja '89

16th century

See also

Great Britain—History—Tudors, 1485-1603

Stuarts, 1603-1714

Younger sons in Tudor and Stuart England. L. A. Pollock. bibl il *History Today* 39:23-9 Je '89

Civil War, 1642-1649—Campaigns and battles

See also

Naseby (England), Battle of, 1645

Puritan Revolution, 1642-1660

Gerrard Winstanley: England's pioneer Green? I. C. Bradley. bibl il *History Today* 39:12-17 Ag '89

Revolution of 1688

The other, forgotten revolution [Glorious Revolution] M. Barone. il *U.S. News & World Report* 107:49 Jl 17 '89

William and Mary, 1689-1702

The other, forgotten revolution [Glorious Revolution] M. Barone. il *U.S. News & World Report* 107:49 Jl 17 '89

1760-1789

See also

United States—History—Revolution, 1775-1783

1800-1837

See also

United States—History—War of 1812

Victorian period, 1837-1901

See Victorian period

20th century

See also

World War, 1939-1945—Great Britain

1910-1936

Leo Amery, the last imperialist. M. Beloff, Baron. bibl il pors *History Today* 39:13-18 Ja '89

GREAT BRITAIN—History—cont.
Anecdotes, facetiae, satire, etc.
Dead and breakfast. J. Queenan. *The New Republic* 200:12+ Mr 20 '89
Bibliography
Local history. *History Today* 39:53 Ag '89
Exhibitions
Particular places [English local history and the Victoria County history exhibit at the British Library] C. R. Elrington. il *History Today* 39:61-2 Ag '89
Study and teaching
Editorial. *History Today* 39:2 O '89
History tomorrow [teaching of history in Britain's new national curriculum; special section; with editorial comment] il *History Today* 39:6-15 Je '89

Industries
See also
Aerospace industries—Great Britain
Airlines of Britain Holdings plc
Airship Industries, Ltd.
Apple Corps Ltd.
Avdel (Firm)
B A T Industries plc
Baring Brothers & Co. Ltd.
Beecham Group plc
Black business enterprises—Great Britain
Blue Arrow plc
Bodley Head Ltd.
Body Shop International plc
Booksellers and bookselling—Acquisitions and mergers—Great Britain
Bristow Helicopters Ltd.
British Aerospace plc
British Midland Airways Ltd.
British Petroleum Co. plc
British Telecom plc
Brokers—Great Britain
Brooklands Books (Firm)
BTR plc
Cable & Wireless plc
Carlton Communications plc
Century Hutchinson Ltd.
Chatsworth Foods Ltd.
Consolidated Gold Fields plc
Corporations—Acquisitions and mergers—Great Britain
Crown Communications Group plc
David Linley Furniture Ltd.
Distillers Company plc
Doubleday U.K. (Firm)
DRG plc
Electronic industries—Acquisitions and mergers—Great Britain
Faber & Faber Inc.
Ferranti plc
Gateway Foodmarkets Ltd.
General Electric Company plc
Glaxo Holdings plc
Grand Metropolitan plc
Guinness plc
Hamish Hamilton Ltd.
Hanson plc
Hotels, motels, etc.—Acquisitions and mergers—Great Britain
House of Fraser plc
Imperial Tobacco Ltd.
Inchcape & Co. Ltd.
Isosceles plc
J. Floris Ltd.
John Calder Ltd.
Liquor industry—Acquisitions and mergers—Great Britain
Lloyd's of London
Longman Group Ltd.
Macdonald Group
Marconi Co. Ltd.
Marshall of Cambridge (Engineering) Ltd.
Maxwell Communication Corporation plc
Michael Joseph Ltd.
Monarch Airlines
Morgan Grenfell Group plc
Newspaper publishers and publishing—Great Britain
Paper industry—Acquisitions and mergers—Great Britain
Parker Pen plc
Pearson plc
Pentos plc
Plessey Co. plc
Polly Peck International plc
Potteries—Great Britain
Publishers and publishing—Acquisitions and mergers—Great Britain
Publishers and publishing—Great Britain
Rediffusion Simulation Ltd.
Reed International plc
Retail trade—Acquisitions and mergers—Great Britain
Rolls-Royce Ltd.
Saatchi & Saatchi Company plc
Samuel Smith's (Firm)
Shandwick plc

Sheep industry—Great Britain
Sherratt & Hughes
Simon & Schuster Ltd.
Small business—Great Britain
Sock Shop International plc
South Sea Company
Sphere Books Ltd.
Storehouse plc
Tailors—Great Britain
Thorn E M I plc
Trusthouse Forte plc
TVS Entertainment plc
Verso (Firm)
Victor Gollancz Ltd.
Virgin Classics (Firm)
W. H. Smith & Son (Holdings) plc
Waterstone's Booksellers
Wine industry—Great Britain
WPP Group plc
Britain's fallen idols of free enterprise. R. Knight. il *U.S. News & World Report* 107:55+ D 4 '89
Fail Britannia? B. Harrison. il *Technology Review* 92:17 O '89

Intellectual life
See also
Bloomsbury group
The enemies she makes [M. Thatcher] A. Lejeune. *National Review* 41:24 My 19 '89

Kings and rulers
See also
Great Britain—Royal family
Henry VIII, King of England, 1491-1547
Trooping the Color
Victoria, Queen of Great Britain, 1819-1901

Languages
See also
English language in Great Britain

Moral conditions
See also
Prostitution—Great Britain
The moral passion of Mrs. Thatcher. K. R. Minogue. il *National Review* 41:22-5 My 19 '89

Native peoples
Up against the wall [Romans failed to subdue the tribes of northern Britain] W. S. Hanson and L. Macinnes. il maps *Natural History* p80-7 Ap '89

Naval history
See also
Anglo-Dutch Wars, 1652-1784
Bounty Mutiny, 1789
Spanish Armada, 1588
Cromwell's soldier-admirals. M. Baumber. bibl il pors *History Today* 39:42-7 O '89
The rise and fall of the carronade [18th century naval gun] J. E. Talbott. bibl il *History Today* 39:24-30 Ag '89

Politics and government
See also
Conservative Party (Great Britain)
Elections—Great Britain
Great Britain. Cabinet
Great Britain. Parliament
Greater London Council
Green Party (Great Britain)
Labour Party (Great Britain)
Liberalism—Great Britain
Official secrets—Great Britain
Political attitudes—Great Britain
Press and politics—Great Britain
Socialism—Great Britain
After the Thatcher decade. A. Hartley. bibl f *Foreign Affairs* 68:102-18 Wint '89/'90
Has Britain's Iron Lady begun to rust? [M. Thatcher] R. Knight. il por *U.S. News & World Report* 107:82-3 Ag 28-S 4 '89
Is there life after Thatcher? G. Black. *The Nation* 248:620-2 My 8 '89
Is this Denis a menace? [M. Thatcher's husband] W. Mader. il pors *Time* 134:37 Ag 14 '89
Margaret Thatcher and the revival of the West [cover story] R. Reagan. il *National Review* 41:21-2 My 19 '89
Margaret Thatcher holds a finger to the wind—and steps to the left. M. Maremont. il *Business Week* p52 O 30 '89
Portrait of my mother: Margaret Thatcher. C. Thatcher. il pors *Ladies' Home Journal* 106:98+ Je '89
Prime Minister Margaret Thatcher [address, October 19, 1988] J. J. Auer. *Vital Speeches of the Day* 55:276-82 F 15 '89
Remarkable Margaret Thatcher [with interview] P. Johnson. il pors *Reader's Digest* 134:70-81 My '89
The slide at midterm [M. Thatcher] C. S. Manegold. por *Newsweek* 114:32 Jl 3 '89
Thatcher for president. M. Kinsley. il *Time* 133:90 My 15 '89
The Thatcher revolution [special section] il pors *Maclean's* 102:30-3+ My 8 '89

GREAT BRITAIN—Politics and government—*cont.*
Thatcherism isn't working [hope for Labour Party and N. Kinnock] N. Gelb. il *The New Leader* 72:8-9 Jl 10-24 '89

They've come a long way, Maggie. B. Amiel. il *Maclean's* 102:10 Ja 16 '89

Religious institutions and affairs
See also
Arminianism—Great Britain
Church of England
Evangelistic work—Great Britain
Muslims—Great Britain

Roman antiquities
See also
Hadrian's Wall

Royal family
See also
Andrew, Prince, Duke of York, 1960-
Anne, Princess, daughter of Elizabeth II, Queen of Great Britain, 1950-
Beatrice, Princess of York, 1988-
Charles, Prince of Wales, 1948-
Diana, Princess of Wales, 1961-
Elizabeth, Queen, consort of George VI, King of Great Britain, 1900-
Linley, David Albert Charles Armstrong-Jones, Viscount, 1961-
Ogilvy, Marina
Sarah, Duchess of York, 1959-
William, Prince of Great Britain, 1982-
At Ascot, horses finish behind hats and royals. il *People Weekly* 32:54-5 Jl 10 '89
In a season of royal milestones, Di delivers her boys, Fergie her books—and news of a pregnancy. il *People Weekly* 32:101 S 25 '89
Royal family life [excerpt from Royalty revealed; cover story] U. Hall and I. Seward. il *Good Housekeeping* 209:98-9+ Ag '89

Photographs and photography
Days of heir lives. il *Life* 12:75+ Ja '89

Travel
Royal revenge [visits to Canada; cover story; special section; with editorial comment by Kevin Doyle] il pors *Maclean's* 102:4, 36-42+ Jl 24 '89

Social policy
Thatcher's new revolution. R. A. Melcher. il por *Business Week* p42-3 My 1 '89

GREAT BRITAIN. ARMY. BENGAL LANCERS
He remembers when the saber was mightier, but now Bengal Lancer Francis Ingall takes up the pen. K. Gross. il pors *People Weekly* 32:113-15+ S 11 '89

GREAT BRITAIN. CABINET
Top aerospace, defense jobs in British Cabinet change hands. *Aviation Week & Space Technology* 131:25 Jl 31 '89

GREAT BRITAIN. CIVIL AVIATION AUTHORITY
U.S. should establish independent FAA based on Britain's CAA model. A. W. Blackburn. por *Aviation Week & Space Technology* 130:119-20 My 1 '89

GREAT BRITAIN. COURT OF REQUESTS
A social contract? Master against servant in the Court of Requests [case of Bristol notary W. Yeamans and his apprentice T. Alford] P. S. Seaver. il *History Today* 39:50-6 S '89

GREAT BRITAIN. NATIONAL HEALTH SERVICE
Hard cases, strong cure [reforms] G. D. Garcia. il *Time* 133:53 F 13 '89
On the track of a sacred cow. A. Lejeune. *National Review* 41:29 Mr 10 '89
Trouble at the source. A. Phillips. il *Maclean's* 102:38+ F 13 '89
Trouble in Thatcherland. N. Gelb. il *The New Leader* 72:6-7 Mr 20 '89

GREAT BRITAIN. NATIONAL PORTRAIT GALLERY *See* National Portrait Gallery (Great Britain)

GREAT BRITAIN. NAVY *See* Great Britain. Royal Navy

GREAT BRITAIN. OPEN UNIVERSITY *See* Open University

GREAT BRITAIN. PARLIAMENT. HOUSE OF LORDS
Britain's Lords debate embryo research. J. Cherfas. il *Science* 246:1554-5 D 22 '89

GREAT BRITAIN. ROYAL ARMOURIES *See* Royal Armouries (Great Britain)

GREAT BRITAIN. ROYAL NAVY
EH101 antisubmarine version begins flight test program. il *Aviation Week & Space Technology* 131:68 N 13 '89

GREAT BRITAIN. UNIVERSITIES FUNDING COUNCIL *See* Universities Funding Council (Great Britain)

GREAT BRITAIN. UNIVERSITY GRANTS COMMITTEE
See also
Universities Funding Council (Great Britain)

GREAT BRITAIN AND FRANCE
See also
English Channel tunnel

GREAT BRITAIN AND THE UNITED STATES
See also
Great Britain—Foreign opinion—American
United States—Foreign opinion—British

GREAT CENTRAL VALLEY (CALIF.) *See* Central Valley (Calif.)

GREAT CIRCUS PARADE (MILWAUKEE, WIS.) *See* Milwaukee (Wis.)—Parades

GREAT CRANBERRY ISLAND (ME.)
See also
Architecture, Domestic—Great Cranberry Island (Me.)

GREAT DEPRESSION *See* Business depression, 1929-1939

GREAT FALLS PARK (VA.)
Into the breach [kayaking; cover story] T. Kilpatrick. il *National Parks* 63:22-7 Mr/Ap '89

GREAT HORNED OWLS *See* Owls

GREAT LAKES
See also
Cruising—Great Lakes
Lake Erie
Lake Michigan
Water pollution—Great Lakes
The not-so-Great Lakes [effects of global warming on water levels] J. Kaplan. il *Omni (New York, N.Y.)* 11:32 F '89

GREAT LAKES CHEMICAL CORP.
Great Lakes Chemical Corp. J. Slovak. il *Fortune* 119:96 Ja 2 '89

GREAT LAKES REGION
See also
Fish—Great Lakes region
Fishing—Great Lakes region
Hunting—Great Lakes region

Description and travel
See also
Automobile touring—Great Lakes region

Industries
See also
Fisheries—Great Lakes region

GREAT MEN AND WOMEN
See also
Heroes and heroines
Leadership

GREAT MOSQUE HASSAN II (CASABLANCA, MOROCCO)
The King's tall order. B. Weber. il *The New York Times Magazine* p78 Je 18 '89
Megamosque. L. Nickson. il por *Life* 12:47-9+ S '89

GREAT PLAINS
See also
Hunting—Great Plains
Great Plains (I). I. Frazier. *The New Yorker* 65:49-50+ F 20 '89
Great Plains (II). I. Frazier. il *The New Yorker* 65:35-40+ F 27 '89
Great Plains (III). I. Frazier. il *The New Yorker* 65:41-4+ Mr 6 '89
History with a human face [I. Frazier's Great Plains] L. Shapiro. il por *Newsweek* 113:64 Je 12 '89
What's so great about the Great Plains? Ian Frazier took the time to find out. M. Neill. il pors *People Weekly* 32:104-6 Ag 7 '89

GREAT PLAINS IN LITERATURE
Our imaginary plains. M. Horn. il *U.S. News & World Report* 107:51-2+ S 25 '89

GREAT PYRENEES (DOGS)
Outlook for the dog. P. V. Fossel. il *Country Journal* 16:15-16 My/Je '89

GREAT RIVER ROAD
Life by the Mississippi. W. Mueller. il *The Saturday Evening Post* 261:86-8+ Ap '89

GREAT SEAL OF THE UNITED STATES *See* Seals (Numismatics)

GREAT SMOKY MOUNTAINS NATIONAL PARK (N.C. AND TENN.)
See also
Cades Cove (Tenn.)
Great Smoky Mountains. M. Ingebretsen. il *Better Homes and Gardens* 67:172 Ap '89

GREAT SOCIETY *See* United States—Social policy

GREAT TITS (BIRDS) *See* Titmice

GREAT WALL OF CHINA
The Great Wall of China: shattering a myth [visibility from space] il *Sky and Telescope* 78:457 N '89

GREAT WESTERN FINANCIAL CORP.
How to succeed in a lousy business. J. F. Lawrence. il *Fortune* 120:125-6+ Jl 3 '89

GREATER DES MOINES GRAND PRIX *See* Automobile racing

GREATER HOUSTON CONVENTION & VISITORS BUREAU
Houston Convention Bureau affirmative-action plan. L. Gite. il *Black Enterprise* 20:28 N '89

GREATER LONDON COUNCIL
London loses its luster [state of services after the demise of the Greater London Council] N. Gelb. il *The New Leader* 72:12-13 S 18 '89

GREATER NEW YORK SAVINGS BANK
This savings bank has 'em buzzing. G. G. Marcial. *Business Week* p104 D 11 '89

GREATER PITTSBURGH INTERNATIONAL AIRPORT *See* Pittsburgh (Pa.)—Airports

GREATER ROCHESTER CABLEVISION
Norman Lear, meet Adam Smith [owned by Time Warner competes with Act III Broadcasting's independent station in syndicated market] P. Newcomb. il *Forbes* 144:206+ N 27 '89

GREATER YELLOWSTONE *See* Yellowstone National Park region

GREBENSHIKOV, BORIS
about
Glasnost rock. F. Rose. il pors *New York* 22:56-60+ Mr 20 '89
Is Boris good enough? D. Kissinger. il por *Rolling Stone* p16 S 7 '89

GRECKEL, WIL
Bearding the proverbial lion. *Design for Arts in Education* 90:43-7 Mr/Ap '89

GRECO, JOANN
The children's audio challenge: appealing to kids, but selling to parents. il *Publishers Weekly* 235:192-4 F 24 '89

GRECO, PETER
about
Catching the rebound. D. Kortrey. il *Forbes* 144:227 S 18 '89

GRECO-ROMAN CIVILIZATION *See* Civilization, Greco-Roman

GREECE
See also
Athos (Greece)
Corfu (Greece)
Crete
Paleontology—Greece
Terrorism—Greece
Thera (Greece: Island)
Foreign relations
Cyprus
See Cyprus
History
Dinner with Demosthenes [research by A. Dalby] S. J. Evans. il *History Today* 39:3-4 Ja '89
Peloponnesian War, 431-404 B.C.—Bibliography
Athens vs. Sparta. E. N. Luttwak. *Commentary* 87:60-4 Mr '89
Historiography
Herodotus, Alexander, and Rome. G. W. Bowersock. *The American Scholar* 58:407-14 Summ '89
Study and teaching—Aids and devices
Are Plato and the Parthenon copyrighted? [databases about ancient Greece] F. D. Fisher. il *Change* 21:15 My/Je '89
Industries
See also
Wine industry—Greece
Naval history
The trireme sails again. J. F. Coates. bibl il *Scientific American* 260:96-103 Ap '89
Politics and government
See also
Elections—Greece
New Democracy (Greece)
Political campaigns—Greece
Politics, Corruption in—Greece
When a First Lady's husband leaves her for a younger woman [M. Papandreou copes] M. Cohen. il pors *Good Housekeeping* 208:82+ My '89
Religious institutions and affairs
See also
Evangelistic work—Greece
Orthodox Eastern Church—Greece

GREECE, ANCIENT *See* Greece—History
GREED *See* Avarice
GREEK ALPHABET
Who taught Homer his ABC's? [Barry Powell's theory that it was the legendary Palamedes] il *U.S. News & World Report* 106:10 Ja 23 '89

GREEK ART *See* Art, Greek
GREEK ASTRONOMY *See* Astronomy, Greek
GREEK COOKING *See* Cooking, Greek
GREEK LITERATURE
Study and teaching
After smashing the Wedgwood. W. R. Connor. *The American Scholar* 58:533-41 Aut '89
GREEK MATHEMATICS *See* Mathematics, Greek
GREEK MYTHOLOGY *See* Mythology, Greek
GREEK ORTHODOX CHURCH *See* Orthodox Eastern Church
GREEK REVIVAL ARCHITECTURE *See* Architecture, Greek revival
GREEK SCULPTURE *See* Sculpture, Greek
GREEK WINES *See* Wine
GREELEY, ANDREW M., 1928-
Against R.C.I.A. [with reply by R. D. Duggan; cover story] il *America* 161:231-7 O 14 '89
Catholic schools: a golden twilight? *America* 160:106+ F 11 '89
Challenges facing U.S. Catholics. *Commonweal* 116:620 N 17 '89
Don't sell Catholic schools short [with readers' comments] *U.S. Catholic* 54:14-20 Mr '89
Is there an American Catholic elite? *America* 160:426+ My 6 '89

Like a Catholic: Madonna's challenge to her Church. il *America* 160:447-9 My 13 '89
On the margins of the Church: a sociological note. il *America* 160:194-5+ Mr 4 '89
St. Valentine's night [fiction] il por *Good Housekeeping* 209:229-32+ O '89
State of the question [discussion of October 14, 1989 article, Against R.C.I.A.] *America* 161:328-30 N 11 '89

GREELY, JOHN
The spills and spoils of big oil [cover story] il *The Nation* 248:721+ My 29 '89

GREEN, BEVERLY PEURIFOY- *See* Peurifoy-Green, Beverly
GREEN, BILL, 1929-
Should President Bush's minimum wage proposal be adopted? [excerpts from address, March 23, 1989] *Congressional Digest* 68:142+ My '89

GREEN, BUNKY
about
Bunky Green. J. Cunniff. il por *Down Beat* 56:48 My '89
GREEN, DALLAS
about
On the spot [cover story] E. Asinof. il pors *The New York Times Magazine* p28-31+ Mr 26 '89
GREEN, DENNIS
about
Got those smelly gym clothes blues? Try Dennis Green's Sneaker Balls and it's arrivederci, aroma. il por *People Weekly* 32:58 Jl 3 '89
GREEN, HAVIOUS
about
Detroit minister and wife send 8 daughters through college; 2 M.D.s, 3 Ph.D.s. W. Wofford, Jr. il pors *Jet* 75:22-3 F 13 '89
GREEN, JANE
(jt. auth) See Choate, Judith, 1940-, and Green, Jane
GREEN, JESSE
The agony and the exercise. il *Gentlemen's Quarterly* 59:176-9+ Ja '89
More questions than answers: a gay man takes the AIDS test. il *Gentlemen's Quarterly* 59:152+ D '89
GREEN, JULIA
about
Detroit minister and wife send 8 daughters through college; 2 M.D.s, 3 Ph.D.s. W. Wofford, Jr. il pors *Jet* 75:22-3 F 13 '89
GREEN, JUSTIN J., AND WHITMORE, BRIAN
Our pal Pol Pot? *Commonweal* 116:668-9 D 1 '89
GREEN, KEITH S. REID- *See* Reid-Green, Keith S.
GREEN, KEN
about
Just having a fling. M. Bamberger. il pors *Sports Illustrated* 70:54+ Ja 30 '89
GREEN, LARRY
Warning: this job may be hazardous to your health. il *Current Health 2* 15:24-5 My '89
GREEN, LEE
"Hidden fats": key to weight control. il *Reader's Digest* 134:85-7 F '89
GREEN, MALCOLM C.
Should the Senate approve the "Americans with Disabilities Act of 1989"? [excerpts from testimony, May 10, 1909] *Congressional Digest* 68:309 D '89
GREEN, MARK J.
Al's pals. il *The New Republic* 201:16-20 O 30 '89
Filling the deregulatory vacuum [cover story] il *The Nation* 249:441+ O 23 '89
The N.Y.C. scandals of Ed Koch [cover story] *The Nation* 248:397 Mr 27 '89
Progressive values for America [cover story] il *The Nation* 248:109+ Ja 30 '89
GREEN, MICHAEL
Why the Resurrection matters. il *Christianity Today* 33:28-32 Mr 17 '89
GREEN, MICHAEL PHILIP
about
Is this one for real? J. Marcom, Jr. il por *Forbes* 144:252 Jl 24 '89
GREEN, NANCYE
about
Gandee at large. C. K. Gandee. il *House & Garden* 161:218 My '89
Logic plus magic. L. Rosch. il por *Working Woman* 14:142-4 N '89
GREEN, PENELOPE
Greenwich time [cover story] il *House & Garden* 161:120-7 N '89
Sometimes a designer's inspiration comes from a snip of fringe, an old photo, a string of beads. il *Vogue* 179:36-8 Jl '89
GREEN, PETER S.
McConnico unlimited. il por *House & Garden* 161:32+ Jl '89
Tunnel visions. il *House & Garden* 161:164-5 Jl '89
GREEN, PHILIP, 1932-
Abortion: the abusable past. *The Nation* 249:177-9 Ag 7-14 '89
Down the tubes in London. *The Nation* 248:274-7 F 27 '89

GREEN, PIPPA
New wave of defiance in South Africa [cover story] il *The Nation* 249:261+ S 18 '89
GREEN, RICHARD R.
about
Black educators cite late Richard Green, elect new officers at Oregon confab. il por *Jet* 77:28 D 18 '89
Don't ax the mayor [letter to R. Green on New Yorkese spoken by New York City students] E. Koch. *Harper's* 278:21-2 Mr '89
Obituary
Black Enterprise il por 19:14 Jl '89. K. Osborne
Jet il por 76:54-5 My 29 '89
GREEN, ROBERT ALAN
Nineteenth-century jewelers' trade cards. il *Antiques & Collecting Hobbies* 94:64-7 N '89
GREEN, ROCHELLE
Full of beans . . . and better for it. il *Health (New York, N.Y.)* 21:58-61 D '89
GREEN, S. WILLIAM (SEDGWICK WILLIAM) See Green, Bill, 1929-
GREEN, SYLVIA BRIGHT
Toys are ageless. il *Antiques & Collecting Hobbies* 94:62-3 My '89
GREEN, TOM, 1941-
Ted Danson's crusade. il por *Oceans* 22:18-20+ Mr/Ap '89
GREEN, WALON
about
'The wild bunch'. R. Shelton. il por *American Film* 14:18+ Ap '89
GREEN (DENNIS) DESIGN GROUP LTD. See Dennis Green Design Group Ltd.
GREEN BAY (WIS.)
Newspapers
See also
Green Bay news-chronicle
GREEN BAY NEWS-CHRONICLE
Do you sincerely want to publish? R. Koselka. il pors *Forbes* 144:68+ S 18 '89
GREEN BERETS See United States. Army. Special Forces
GREEN FLASH See Sunset phenomena
GREEN MANURING
Fertilizer from the garden. E. Coleman. il *The Mother Earth News* 119:112+ S/O '89
GREEN PARTIES (POLITICS)
Cue the Green god, Ted [cover story] G. Vidal. il *The Nation* 249:153+ Ag 7-14 '89
GREEN PARTY (GERMANY: WEST)
Greens gain in German elections. A. Gyorgy. *Utne Reader* p22 Jl/Ag '89
GREEN PARTY (GREAT BRITAIN)
The year of the Greens. T. Burke. bibl f il *Environment* 31:18-20+ N '89
GREEN PARTY (U.S.)
Can Green politics take root in the U.S.? J. Walljasper. il *Utne Reader* p140-3 S/O '89
Green activists meet to plan national strategy. J. Walljasper. *Utne Reader* p18 My/Je '89
The Greens of Vermont [Burlington mayoral race] J. N. Baker. il *Newsweek* 113:33 F 27 '89
GREEN PARTY (WESTERN EUROPE)
Europe's Green light. D. Johnstone. il *The Progressive* 53:12-13 Jl '89
What the 'Greens' mean for business. S. Tully. il *Fortune* 120:159+ O 23 '89
GREEN TIGER PRESS
Green Tiger bounces back: a cautionary tale. L. See. *Publishers Weekly* 235:191 F 24 '89
GREEN TURTLE CAY (BAHAMAS)
Debut in paradise [maiden voyage of Donzi Z-65] J. Clemans. il *Motor Boating & Sailing* 164:36-41+ S '89
GREENAWAY, PETER
about
Drowning by numbers [film] Reviews
Maclean's 102:86+ N 6 '89. B. D. Johnson
GREENBAUM, STUART
Youth and drug abuse. il *USA Today (Periodical)* 118:45-7 N '89
GREENBERG, ALAN C.
about
'Ace' Greenberg tries to trade up. B. Nussbaum. il por *Business Week* p120-4 Mr 13 '89
GREENBERG, ALFRED H.
Skier-at-large. See issues of Skiing beginning November 1986
GREENBERG, DONALD
Light reflection models for computer graphics. bibl f il *Science* 244:166-73 Ap 14 '89
GREENBERG, JAMES
Our man in Havana. il *American Film* 14:16-18 Mr '89
GREENBERG, JAY
A backhanded compliment. il pors *Sports Illustrated* 71:50-3 O 23 '89
Breaking out. il *Sports Illustrated* 71:32-3 N 6 '89
The face of the future. il pors *Sports Illustrated* 71:86-8 D 11 '89
The honeymooners [cover story] il *Sports Illustrated* 71:44-8+ O 9 '89

NHL preview 1989-90. il *Sports Illustrated* 71:44-8+ O 9 '89
No rattling the Sabres. il pors *Sports Illustrated* 71:40+ D 18 '89
Puzzling Penguins. il por *Sports Illustrated* 71:32-3 N 27 '89
What makes Ron Hextall tick. il pors *Sports Illustrated* 71:62-4+ N 13 '89
GREENBERG, MICHAEL
about
One heart warms many chilly fingers. D. Brand. il pors *Time* 133:16+ Ja 2 '89
GREENBERG, MICHAEL R., AND OTHERS
Media coverage [discussion of March 1989 article, Network television news coverage of environmental risks] il *Environment* 31:2-3 Je '89
Network television news coverage of environmental risks. bibl f *Environment* 31:16-20+ Mr '89
GREENBERG, RICHARD
about
Eastern standard [drama] Reviews
America 160:248 Mr 18 '89. G. G. Seibert
Commonweal 116:210-12 Ap 7 '89. G. C. Weales
New York il 22:79 Ja 16 '89. J. Simon
Vogue 179:266B Mr '89. E. G. Carter
A new, young playwright risks success for his art. K. Hubbard. il pors *People Weekly* 31:125-6 F 13 '89
GREENBERG, ROBERT Y.
about
L.A. Gear is going where the boys are. K. Kerwin. il por *Business Week* p54 Je 19 '89
GREENBERG, STUART
Coping with lead and asbestos. il *The Mother Earth News* 117:26+ My/Je '89
GREENBERGER, LANIE
about
The 'Cotton Club' murder: cocaine and hit men in Hollywood—a 1980s film noir [cover story] J. Kasindorf. il pors *New York* 22:24-33 Jl 24 '89
GREENBRIER (WHITE SULPHUR SPRINGS, W. VA.: RESORT) See Health resorts, watering places, etc.—West Virginia
GREENE, ALAN I.
about
Stocks that pass tough tests [interview] S. Smith. il por *Fortune* 119:36+ Ap 24 '89
GREENE, BERT, 1923-1988
Puttin' on the grits. il *Harper's Bazaar* 122:230+ Mr '89
GREENE, BETTY PATCHIN
The arts and crafts architect's studio in Carmel. il por *Architectural Digest* 46:92+ My '89
GREENE, BOB
American beat. See issues of Esquire through July 1989
The stolen briefcase. il *Reader's Digest* 134:23-4+ Je '89
Your permanent record [condensed from Cheeseburgers] il *Reader's Digest* 134:147-8 Ap '89
GREENE, C. H., AND OTHERS
Predation on ocean krill [discussion of July 15, 1988 article, Acoustical detection of high-density krill demersal layers in the submarine canyons off Georges Bank] *Science* 243:237-8 Ja 13 '89
GREENE, CHARLES SUMNER, 1868-1957
about
The arts and crafts architect's studio in Carmel. B. P. Greene. il por *Architectural Digest* 46:92+ My '89
New house, classic craft. P. Harper. il *Home Mechanix* 85:66-8+ F '89
GREENE, DONALD JOHNSON
A partiality for lords: Evelyn Waugh and snobbery. *The American Scholar* 58:444-5+ Summ '89
GREENE, ELLEN
about
Talk about creating scenes! H. Polskin. il pors *TV Guide* 37:38-40 F 18-24 '89
GREENE, ERICK
Caterpillars and polymorphisms [discussion of February 3, 1989 article, A diet-induced developmental polymorphism in a caterpillar] bibl f *Science* 246:1639-40 D 22 '89
A diet-induced developmental polymorphism in a caterpillar [cover story] bibl f il *Science* 243:643-6 F 3 '89
GREENE, GAEL
Ask Gael: new ideas for places to go in '89. il por *New York* 22:20-8 Ja 2 '89
Eating to the beat: downtown food has attitude, too. il *New York* 22:96-8+ D 25 '89-Ja 1 '90
The insatiable critic. See occasional issues of New York
Inventing a new Colorado vernacular. il por *Architectural Digest* 46:330+ O '89
Sizzling Spain. il *New York* 22:34-41 Jl 24 '89
A thirties revival. il *Architectural Digest* 46:194-201+ Mr '89
GREENE, GRAHAM, 1904-
about
Confrontation and escape: mysteries of Graham Greene [cover story] P. S. Hawkins. il *The Christian Century* 106:934-6 O 18 '89
Of many things [excerpts from interview] G. W. Hunt. *America* 161:226 O 14 '89

GREENHOUSE EFFECT—cont.

Global smog: newest greenhouse projection [research by David Rind] J. Raloff. *Science News* 135:262-3 Ap 29 '89

Global warming [address, February 7, 1989] J. A. Ahladas. *Vital Speeches of the Day* 55:381-4 Ap 1 '89

Global warming: an energy technology R&D challenge. W. Fulkerson and others. bibl f il *Science* 246:868-9 N 17 '89

Global warming becomes hot issue for Bromley. M. Sun. il por *Science* 246:569 N 3 '89

Global warming: blaming the sun [report Scientific perspectives on the greenhouse problem] L. Roberts. il *Science* 246:992-3 N 24 '89

Global warming: inside the greenhouse. A. Fisher. il *Popular Science* 235:63-70 S '89

The global warming is real. R. A. Kerr. il *Science* 243:603 F 3 '89

The global warming panic [cover story] W. T. Brookes. il *Forbes* 144:96-100+ D 25 '89

Global warming: playing dice with earth's climate [with editorial comment by C. P. Gilmore] A. Fisher. il *Popular Science* 235:4, 51-8 Ag '89

Global warming: saving the planet. A. Fisher. il map *Popular Science* 235:51-6+ O '89

Good news for greenhouse worriers [research by James Hansen] *Science News* 136:367 D 2 '89

Goose prelude to global warming [destruction of wetland vegetation due to delayed migration of snow geese; research by Robert Jefferies] J. A. Miller. *BioScience* 39:673 N '89

Governments warm to greenhouse action. J. Raloff. il *Science News* 136:394-5+ D 16 '89

Greenhouse America [EPA study] J. Horgan. map *Scientific American* 260:20-1 Ja '89

The greenhouse effect. C. Pesmen. il *Seventeen* 48:162-3+ Je '89

Greenhouse effect? [viticulture] H. J. De Blij. *Focus (New York, N.Y.: 1950)* 39:37 Spr '89

The greenhouse effect revisited. C. F. Bohren. il *Weatherwise* 42:50-4 F '89

The greenhouse effect: science and policy. S. H. Schneider. bibl f il *Science* 243:771-81 F 10 '89

Greenhouse gas. P. W. Huber. il por *Forbes* 144:226 O 30 '89

Greenhouse gases, climate change, and U.S. forest markets. J. L. Regens and others. bibl f il *Environment* 31:4-5+ My '89

Greenhouse skeptic out in the cold [R. S. Lindzen] R. A. Kerr. por *Science* 246:1118-19 D 1 '89

Hansen and the greenhouse effect [discussion of June 2, 1989 article, Hansen vs. the world on the greenhouse threat] R. A. Kerr. *Science* 245:451-2 Ag 4 '89

Hansen vs. the world on the greenhouse threat. R. A. Kerr. il por *Science* 244:1041-3 Je 2 '89

Has the globe really warmed? il *Technology Review* 92:80 N/D '89

The heat is on: the greenhouse effect and the earth's future. O. S. Owen. il por *The Futurist* 23:34-40 S/O '89

Hi there, Bambi [views of B. McKibben] R. Bailey. il *Forbes* 144:46+ O 16 '89

Higher hints of greenhouse effects [research by David J. Karoly] *Science News* 136:15 Jl 1 '89

A hot issue [OMB censors facts on greenhouse effect] D. Lindorff. *The Nation* 248:724-5 My 29 '89

Hot times on planet earth. M. Jockers. il *Scholastic Update (Teachers' edition)* 121:6-7 Ap 21 '89

How clouds heat and cool the earth [research by V. Ramanathan] *USA Today (Periodical)* 117:3 Je '89

How fast can trees migrate? [climate models predict doom for forests; research by Margaret Davis] L. Roberts. il maps *Science* 243:735-7 F 10 '89

How to fix the clouds in greenhouse models. R. A. Kerr. *Science* 243:28-9 Ja 6 '89

Human activities, greenhouse effect and climate change. il *Physics Today* 42:28-9 My '89

The Intergovernmental Panel on Climate Change. W. A. Nitze. *Environment* 31:44-5 Ja/F '89

Interpretation of cloud-climate feedback as produced by 14 atmospheric general circulation models. R. D. Cess and others. bibl f il *Science* 245:513-16 Ag 4 '89

Interview: Verner Suomi. P. Bagne. por *Omni (New York, N.Y.)* 11:60-2+ Jl '89

Is it all just hot air? S. Begley. il *Newsweek* 114:64-6 N 20 '89

Is it time to build another ark? [concern over sea level changes in the Netherlands] il *U.S. News & World Report* 107:12 N 20 '89

Keeping cool is hot work [use of electrical power contributes to global warming; views of Russell Valentine] il *USA Today (Periodical)* 117:12 Je '89

Looking for Mr. Greenhouse. R. Monastersky. il *Science News* 135:216-17+ Ap 8 '89

Natural gas: for better or for worse? [study by Dean E. Abrahamson] *Science News* 136:127 Ag 19 '89

Not all plants will thrive in 'greenhouse' [research by Chantal D. Reid and Boyd R. Strain] J. Raloff. *Science News* 136:134 Ag 26 '89

The not-so-Great Lakes [effects of global warming on water levels] J. Kaplan. il *Omni (New York, N.Y.)* 11:32 F '89

Not so hot [questioning global warming estimates] T. Beardsley. *Scientific American* 261:17-18 N '89

Panel frets over cash-short climate studies. R. Monastersky. *Science News* 135:150 Mr 11 '89

Paradise lost. D. J. Kevles. bibl f il *The New York Review of Books* 36:32-8 D 21 '89

Peatlands: a global warming threat? [research by Joseph B. Yavitt and R. Kelman Wieder] J. Raloff. *Science News* 136:143 Ag 26 '89

Pinning down clouds [role in climatic change] J. Horgan. il *Scientific American* 260:22+ My '89

Planning for our common future. M. W. Holdgate. bibl f *Environment* 31:14-17+ O '89

Predictions drop for future sea-level rise [views of Mark F. Meier] R. Monastersky. *Science News* 136:397 D 16 '89

Preparing for the greenhouse effect [agriculture] *USA Today (Periodical)* 117:15 Je '89

A question of degree [evidence seen in national parks; cover story] J. Page. il map *National Parks* 63:24-9 Jl/Ag '89

Reactors redux. M. Philips. il *Sierra* 74:56-61 Mr/Ap '89

Recent ocean warming: are satellites right? [research by Alan E. Strong] R. Monastersky. *Science News* 135:247 Ap 22 '89

Report on reports: Greenhouse: planning for climate change. J. Jäger. bibl f *Environment* 31:25-7 Je '89

Researchers irked by changes to testimony [Office of Management and Budget] E. Marshall. *Science* 244:648 My 12 '89

Rising seas may herald global warming [views of W. Richard Peltier] *Science News* 135:367 Je 10 '89

Rough justice in the greenhouse [Northern Hemisphere to suffer more] *Newsweek* 114:65 D 18 '89

Secrets of the sea [advances in climate research; cover story] W. J. Cook. il *U.S. News & World Report* 107:48-52+ Ag 21 '89

Slowing an irreversible experiment. W. Booth. *Science* 243:163 Ja 13 '89

South stays cooler in greenhouse models. R. Monastersky. *Science News* 136:413 D 23-30 '89

To be or not to be? (environmentally speaking) in fall title from Random [work of B. McKibben] C. Goodrich. por *Publishers Weekly* 236:23 Ag 25 '89

Tough carbon budget could slow warming [Energy policy in the greenhouse report] J. Raloff. *Science News* 136:359 D 2 '89

Trees' new role. R. Rodale. il *Organic Gardening* 36:27-8 Ap '89

Trouble in the atmosphere: does your cup of coffee cause forest fires? C. A. Moore. il *International Wildlife* 19:38-45 Mr/Ap '89

Turning down the heat. C. Schneider. il *National Parks* 63:16-17+ Jl/Ag '89

Understanding global change. A. M. Clayson. il *The Unesco Courier* 42:48-9 O '89

Volcanoes can muddle the greenhouse. R. A. Kerr. il *Science* 245:127-8 Jl 14 '89

Warmer clouds could keep earth cooler. R. Monatersky. *Science News* 136:196 S 23 '89

Washington diarist: the end of everything [views of B. McKibben] T. Noah. *The New Republic* 201:54 O 16 '89

We're in hot water [rising ocean temperature and greenhouse effect] *Newsweek* 113:70 My 1 '89

What the greenhouse effect portends. M. E. Murphy. *America* 161:470-2 D 23-30 '89

Whatever the real reasons, the hot, dry weather in Colorado this summer was blamed on the greenhouse effect. R. M. Adams. il *Smithsonian* 20:12 S '89

A White House chill on global warming. *Newsweek* 114:47 N 13 '89

White House global climate plan calls for research by 7 agencies. I. Goodwin. il *Physics Today* 42:52-4 O '89

Will changing your light bulb save the world? C. A. Moore. il *International Wildlife* 19:18-23 My/Je '89

Will earth become another Venus? T. H. Cole. il *Popular Mechanics* 166:18+ Je '89

A world at risk. L. R. Brown and others. il pors *Country Journal* 16:44-8 My/Je '89

World Conference on the Changing Atmosphere: Implications for Global Security [report] P. Usher. *Environment* 31:25-7 Ja/F '89

Worldwide weather threatens millions [views of Philip Johnston] il *USA Today (Periodical)* 117:1-3 Ap '89

Anecdotes, facetiae, satire, etc.

Change the weather. P. Bedard. il *Car and Driver* 35:16 D '89

Economic aspects

Some like it hot. I. M. Stelzer. il *The American Spectator* 22:26-8 Mr '89

When the rivers go dry and the ice caps melt . . . V. Cahan. il *Business Week* p95+ F 13 '89

GREENHOUSES

See also
Cold frames
Conservatories (Greenhouses)

GREENHOUSES—See also—*cont.*
  Garden rooms
  Solar waste water treatment
Choice greenhouses. M. Ferrara. il *Organic Gardening* 36:66-70 N '89
Gardens under glass [vegetable gardening in a solar greenhouse] N. Bubel. il *Country Journal* 16:60-7 S/O '89
Greenhouse gold [organic produce from A. Edey's Solviva Winter Garden] C. Perlmutter. il pors *Organic Gardening* 36:56-60 O '89
Space in the sun [cover story] C. Poole. il *Home Mechanix* 85:24-8+ Ja '89
GREENING, BRUCE
          about
Va. priest fired after announcing plans to join separatist Catholic Church. pors *Jet* 76:26 Ag 21 '89
GREENING, JIM
Pipeline. See issues of Cycle
GREENLAND
          See also
  Eskimos
  Ice—Greenland
              Industries
          See also
  Whaling—Greenland
GREENLEA, SAM
          about
'Spook who sat by door' author Sam Greenlea at work on 4-book odyssey. por *Jet* 75:24 F 27 '89
GREENLEAF (SIMON) SCHOOL OF LAW *See* Simon Greenleaf School of Law
GREENMAIL
What's wrong with a little greenmail? [deals by J. J. Cotter] R. King. il por *Forbes* 143:64+ Mr 6 '89
              Taxation
New trick for greenmailers [Transtech Industries use of personal holding company loophole] J. Zweig. il *Forbes* 144:110 O 30 '89
              Canada
Hoist by their own greenmail [Belzberg takeover of H. H. Robertson] K. Hannon. il *Forbes* 143:156 My 29 '89
GREENMARKETS *See* Farmers' markets
GREENPEACE FOUNDATION
Greenpeace gets boost from R.E.M. K. Terry. *Rolling Stone* p67 Jl 13-27 '89
U.S.S.R. welcomes Greenpeace [debut of benefit album Rainbow warriors] L. Rotcage. il *Rolling Stone* p17 Ap 20 '89
GREENROOMS
The greenroom effect. W. Safire. il *The New York Times Magazine* p16+ Ap 23 '89
GREENS, EDIBLE
          See also
  Cooking—Vegetables
  Herbs
  Kale
  Lettuce
  Pan de zucchero
  Purslane
  Spinach
Weed all about it! Linda Runyon, a wild chef, says we should veg out on crabgrass and clover. D. Chu. il pors *People Weekly* 32:85-6 Jl 24 '89
GREENSBORO (N.C.)
              Education
          See also
  Gateway Education Center (Greensboro, N.C.)
GREENSPAN, ALAN
          about
Caution at the Fed [cover story] L. Uchitelle. il pors *The New York Times Magazine* p18-21+ Ja 15 '89
Collision course: Bush and the Fed. M. McNamee and H. Gleckman. il *Business Week* p34-6 F 27 '89
Greenspan vs. inflation. R. E. Norton. il *U.S. News & World Report* 106:45-6 F 27 '89
Greenspan's moment of truth: can he manage a soft landing without skidding into a recession? [cover story] M. McNamee. il pors *Business Week* p58-62+ Jl 31 '89
GREENSPAN, MARTIN
          about
Obituary. I. Rudnick. por *Physics Today* 42:118-19 S '89
GREENSPAN, STUART
The 11 most uncomfortable chairs. il *House & Garden* 161:30+ Ja '89
The best of the worst: one man's pick of history's most unfortunate furniture styles. il *House & Garden* 161:66+ My '89
Collective spirit. il *House & Garden* 161:156-63 My '89
Driven to collect. il por *House & Garden* 161:32+ Je '89
From soup to sèvres. il *House & Garden* 161:244+ O '89
War at the Armory. il *House & Garden* 161:76+ S '89
GREENSTEIN, GEORGE, 1940-
Through the looking glass. il *Astronomy* 17:20-8 O '89
GREENVILLE (MISS.)
              Historic houses, sites, etc.
Moving a piece of history [pre-Civil War house] J. O'Hagan. il *Southern Living* 24:150-2 S '89

GREENVILLE COUNTY (S.C.)
              Education
Kerns named S.C. school district superintendent. por *Jet* 76:30 My 8 '89
GREENWALD, GERALD
America's stake in the new global economy. il *USA Today (Periodical)* 118:26-8 N '89
The real Masters of the Universe [address, March 2, 1989] *Vital Speeches of the Day* 55:528-30 Je 15 '89
          about
The Big Three's trio of new leaders for the 1990s. *Fortune* 120:112 O 23 '89
GREENWALD, PETER
          about
A man with a mission. D. Bartley. il pors *The Saturday Evening Post* 261:58-61+ N/D '89
GREENWALT, DAVID
          about
Rude awakening [film] Reviews
  Newsweek il 114:68 S 4 '89. D. Ansen
GREENWAY, H. D. S.
The tiger and the crocodile. *The New Yorker* 65:72-83 Jl 17 '89
GREENWICH (CONN.)
              Historic houses, sites, etc.
Greenwich time [restored 1825 farmhouse owned and decorated by S. Brown and R. Jones; cover story] P. Green. il *House & Garden* 161:120-7 N '89
GREENWICH HOUSE POTTERY
Greenwich House Pottery at 80. A. Ross. il *American Craft* 49:44-7 Ap/My '89
GREENWICH VILLAGE (NEW YORK, N.Y.)
          See also
  Stonewall Riot, 1969
East Side story [end of East Village art scene] P. Taylor. il *Vogue* 179:356-61+ My '89
The New York Halloween parade. D. K. Mano. il *National Review* 41:56-8 N 24 '89
Primitive [Halloween parade] *The New Yorker* 65:48-9 N 6 '89
GREENWOOD, HAROLD W., JR.
          about
The downfall of a thrift. J. Hammer. il por *Newsweek* 113:54 F 27 '89
GREENWOOD-ROBINSON, MAGGIE
Carla Dunlap: more than muscle. il por *Women's Sports & Fitness* 11:62 Je '89
Coming on strong: weight training for your sport. il *Women's Sports & Fitness* 11:48-52 My '89
An energizing way to weight train: split routines. il *Women's Sports & Fitness* 11:40-3 Jl/Ag '89
Flex your pecs to shape your chest. il *Women's Sports & Fitness* 11:20 S '89
Shape-onomics: adding muscle where it counts. il *Women's Sports & Fitness* 11:43-7 O '89
Supertoning your hips and thighs. il *Women's Sports & Fitness* 11:18-19 Ja/F '89
There's no place like the home gym. il *Women's Sports & Fitness* 11:62-5 Mr '89
Touching base with the new push-button machines. il *Women's Sports & Fitness* 11:16 My '89
GREER, EBERT
What makes a good dad? il *Good Housekeeping* 208:40 Je '89
GREER, ED
          about
When Ed Greer vanished, a myth was born—and a bitter reality for the family he left behind. G. Stone. il pors *People Weekly* 31:109+ Je 5 '89
GREER, HERB
Letter from Bodrum. *The American Spectator* 22:42-3 D '89
GREETING CARD INDUSTRY
          See also
  Blacks in the greeting card industry
GREETING CARDS
          See also
  Birthday cards
  Christmas cards
  Mother's Day cards
  Valentines
              Collectors and collecting
When you care enough to save the very best. L. Rosenkrantz. il *Antiques & Collecting Hobbies* 94:22+ Ap '89
GREETINGS *See* Salutations
GREGG, COLIN
          about
We think the world of you [film] Reviews
  The Nation 248:24-5 Ja 2 '89. S. Klawans
GREGG, DONALD
          about
Bush's envoy on the grill. R. Parry. il por *Newsweek* 113:40 My 29 '89
Cranston v. Gregg. W. F. Buckley. *National Review* 41:11-12 Je 16 '89
Encore for Iran-contra? L. Howard. il pors *Newsweek* 113:9 Ja 30 '89
Ghost of Iran-contra. *The Progressive* 53:8 Mr '89

GREGG, DONALD—about—*cont.*
Punish the ambassador! D. Bank and P. Leyden. il *Newsweek* 114:40 O 23 '89

GREGG, LINDA
The last night in mithymna [poem] *The Atlantic* 263:78 Ap '89

GREGG, SANDRA R.
Weaving a new spell in Mississippi. il map *American Visions* 4:30-7 Ag '89

GREGOR, HAROLD
about
Harold Gregor at Tibor de Nagy. W. Thompson. *Art in America* 77:213 S '89

GREGOR, KATHERINE
Zen and the art of William T. Wiley. il pors *Art News* 88:184-9 Ap '89

GREGORIAN, VARTAN
about
The man who saved the library: an ode to Vartan Gregorian. C. Trillin. il por *The New York Times Book Review* 94:15 F 5 '89

GREGORY, CYNTHIA
about
Architectural digest visits: Cynthia Gregory. J. Gruen. il pors *Architectural Digest* 46:236-41+ N '89
Reviews:
C. Gregory and F. Bujones at City Center. A. Murphy. *Dance Magazine* 63:82-4 Ja '89

GREGORY, DICK
about
Comedy Awards Show honors Arsenio Hall, salutes Dick Gregory. il por *Jet* 76:53 Je 19 '89
Gregory buys hotel and fattens his diet empire. H. Manly. il por *Black Enterprise* 19:22 Mr '89

GREGORY, GREG
Placebo effect: the power of suggestion. il *Current Health 2* 15:23-5 Ap '89

GREGORY, RICHARD CLAXTON See Gregory, Dick

GREGORY (DICK) HEALTH ENTERPRISES, INC. See Dick Gregory Health Enterprises, Inc.

GREGORY FOREST PRODUCTS INC.
'The spotted owl could wipe us out'. J. B. Levine. il *Business Week* p94+ S 18 '89

GREHAN, RICHARD
Some assembly required. See issues of Byte beginning July 1988

GREIDER, WILLIAM
Gimme shelter: even middle-class Americans now feel the housing crisis. il *Utne Reader* p60-3 My/Je '89
National affairs. See issues of Rolling Stone
about
The deep, dark secret of our government. B. Edmondson. il *Utne Reader* p14-15 Mr/Ap '89

GREIFF, JAMES
When an employee's performance slumps. il *Nation's Business* 77:44-5 Ja '89

GREIL, ARTHUR L.
The religious response to reproductive technology. *The Christian Century* 106:11-14 Ja 4-11 '89

GREIMAN, APRIL, 1948-
about
Color it creative. L. Rosch. il por *Working Woman* 14:109 Ap '89

GREINER, LUDWIG
about
Made in the U.S.A. M. Jailer. il *Antiques & Collecting Hobbies* 94:36-7 Jl '89

GRENADA
See also
Censorship—Grenada
Medical policy—Grenada
Political prisoners—Grenada
Trials—Grenada

Description and travel
Grenada and Carriacou: adventures in the rain forest. A. Dana. *Vogue* 179:314+ N '89
Grenada revisited. A. Reid-Dove. il *Black Enterprise* 19:113-14 My '89
War and remembrance. P. Oliver. il map *Travel Holiday* 172:84-91 Jl '89

Foreign relations
United States
See United States—Foreign relations—Grenada

Politics and government
Club-Med quickie. G. Krist. *The New Republic* 200:10-11 Ap 24 '89

GRENIER, PAUL, AND STUBBS, ERIC
A farewell to arms? The Soviets rethink defense spending. il *USA Today (Periodical)* 118:19-21 N '89

GRENIER, RICHARD, 1926-
The Albania of the Caribbean. il *National Review* 41:41-3 My 5 '89
And in the Ukraine. *National Review* 41:30-1 Ja 27 '89
Gorbachev's long journey. il *National Review* 41:27-9 D 31 '89
Have typewriter, will run. *National Review* 41:33-4 Mr 24 '89

GRENNAN, EAMON
Aloft [poem] *The Nation* 249:468 O 23 '89
Blood, nest, stars [poem] *The Nation* 248:638 My 8 '89
Compass reading [poem] *The New Yorker* 65:56 N 20 '89
Moving [poem] *The New Yorker* 65:34 Jl 31 '89
Reports from the front [poem] *The New Yorker* 65:44 F 20 '89
Room and sun [poem] *The New Yorker* 65:48 O 16 '89
Sign language [poem] *The Nation* 248:497 Ap 10 '89
That ocean [poem] *The New Yorker* 65:38 Ag 28 '89

LA GRENOUILLE (NEW YORK, N.Y.: RESTAURANT) See New York (N.Y.)—Restaurants, nightclubs, bars, etc.

GRESCH, DONALD
Bounce lighting. il *Petersen's Photographic Magazine* 18:24-6+ N '89

GRESHAM, ED
about
Home warranties: peace of mind for a price [interview] il por *Home Mechanix* 85:16+ F '89

GRESHAM, JEWELL HANDY
The politics of family in America. il *The Nation* 249:116-20+ Jl 24-31 '89
(jt. auth) See Wilkerson, Margaret B., and Gresham, Jewell Handy

GRESHAM, JEWELL HANDY, AND WILKERSON, MARGARET B.
The burden of history. *The Nation* 249:115-16 Jl 24-31 '89

GRESS, DAVID
Demystifying the French Revolution. bibl f *Commentary* 88:42-9 Jl '89

GRETTON, TOM
Representing the Revolution. bibl f il *History Today* 39:39-44 My '89

GRETZKY, WAYNE
about
'80s hockey. S. Rosenbloom. il por *Sport (New York, N.Y.)* 80:68-9+ O '89
A backhanded compliment. J. Greenberg. il pors *Sports Illustrated* 71:50-3 O 23 '89
Games men play. H. Quinn. il pors *Maclean's* 102:62 O 23 '89
The Gretzky chase [cover story; special section; with editorial comment by Kevin Doyle] il pors *Maclean's* 102:2, 32-7 F 20 '89
Hockey's only hope. M. Lupica. il *Esquire* 111:55-7 F '89
Masters of the '80s [cover story] R. Reilly. il pors *Sports Illustrated* 71:44-9 D 18 '89
Soviet pretenders to Gretzky's throne. il por *U.S. News & World Report* 107:19 O 30 '89

GREVE, EINAR
about
The shock that zapped Tucson Electric. R. Grover. il por *Business Week* p28-9 Ag 7 '89

GREY, DEBORAH
about
Upset in the West. J. Howse. il por *Maclean's* 102:12-13 Mr 27 '89

GREY, HOWARD M., AND OTHERS
How T cells see antigen. bibl il *Scientific American* 261:56-64 N '89

GREY, RICHARD E.
about
Oopsie-Daisy, guess who's tops in Toyland now? M. Roman. il *Business Week* p102 D 18 '89

GREY ADVERTISING INC.
Mr. Hardball sheds his Grey [H. Siegel's buyout of LBS] J. M. Robins. il pors *Channels (New York, N.Y.: 1986)* 9:62-6 F '89

GREYHOUND CORP.
The other Greyhound isn't winning any races. E. Schine. il *Business Week* p53 Je 19 '89
The "S" factor [surprises tied to stock performance] K. L. Fisher. il *Forbes* 144:116 Ag 21 '89

GREYHOUND LINES, INC.
Greyhound is bringing travelers down to earth again. K. Kelly. il *Business Week* p52-3 Je 19 '89

GREYHOUND RACING
The Bear trap [P. W. Bryant, son of late Alabama coach] W. M. Adler. il por *Esquire* 112:204-6+ S '89
Paws. J. E. Vader. il *Sports Illustrated* 70:46-8+ Je 26 '89
The puppies get plush [greyhound tracks] C. Leerhsen. il *Newsweek* 113:64 Ja 16 '89

GREYSTON BAKERY
Livelihood [Zen Buddhist, B. Glassman, runs Greyston Bakery in Yonkers, N.Y.] *The New Yorker* 65:28-9 My 22 '89

GRICE, AYESHA JIHADA
Sign time. See issues of Essence

GRID SYSTEMS INC.
What's in a name? A lot, says Tandy [selling computers to corporations under the Grid logo] K. Kelly. il *Business Week* p109 F 27 '89

GRIECO, RICHARD
about
Keep an eye on: Richard Grieco. por *'Teen* 33:47 F '89

GRIECO, RICHARD—about—*cont.*
More than One life to live. P. Dell. il pors *'Teen* 33:45-6 D '89
The rebel who makes Hollywood nervous. E. Warren. il pors *TV Guide* 37:18-20 O 28-N 3 '89
Richard Grieco, 21 Jump Street's latest narcissist hunk du jour, is a man with a message: himself. N. Geeslin. il pors *People Weekly* 31:61-2 Je 12 '89
Richard Grieco on the line. B. Stepko. por *Seventeen* 48:60 Jl '89

GRIEF
The cruelest kind of grief [survivors of sudden tragedy] D. Gelman. il *Newsweek* 113:21-3 Ja 2 '89
Farewell to Foxy [family pet] D. D. Zentay. il *The Saturday Evening Post* 261:22 Ja/F '89
Grief's lessons: his and hers. D. Cole. *Psychology Today* 22:60-1 D '88
How sharing grief can ease the pain [interview with H. Seiden] E. E. Goode. il pors *U.S. News & World Report* 106:80 Ja 30 '89
Knocking on death's door [journalists covering tragedies] L. Zuckerman. il *Time* 133:49 F 27 '89
Let go and live. B. Bartocci. *Reader's Digest* 135:103-6 O '89
Message of the pond [rescue of horse trapped in ice helps families cope with grief] P. Michelmore. il *Reader's Digest* 135:106-10 D '89
Still grieving after the death of his young son, Eddie Rabbitt finds solace in country music [Timmy Rabbitt dies from biliary atresia] T. Allis. il pors *People Weekly* 31:83-4 Ap 17 '89
The way we are [letters of sympathy from readers] L. Wyse. il *Good Housekeeping* 209:320 N '89

GRIEF COUNSELING
After Fido dies . . . a support group. *Newsweek* 113:74 Mr 20 '89
Teaching kids how to grieve [program in Watts for children whose lives have been touched by murder] S. Doherty. il *Newsweek* 114:73 N 13 '89

GRIEF IN ART
A grieving mother turns the horror of Pan Am Flight 103 into a monument to her son [S. Lowenstein creates sculptural work entitled Evolution in memory of A. Lowenstein] D. Grogan. il pors *People Weekly* 32:44-6 S 25 '89

GRIER, DAVID
Confronting ethical dilemmas [address, September 19, 1989] *Vital Speeches of the Day* 56:100-4 D 1 '89

GRIESE, ROGER
about
A Catholic taste in clothes. il por *Newsweek* 114:27 S 18 '89

GRIFFEY, KEN, JR.
about
Griffeys Jr. and Sr. make baseball history. il pors *Jet* 76:46 Ap 24 '89
The Griffeys: major-league baseball's first father-and-son pair. il pors *Ebony* 44:78+ S '89
Proving that the son also rises, rookie star Ken Griffey Jr. breaks through the clouds in Seattle. J. Friedman. il pors *People Weekly* 32:77-8 Jl 17 '89

GRIFFEY, KEN, SR.
about
Griffeys Jr. and Sr. make baseball history. il pors *Jet* 76:46 Ap 24 '89
The Griffeys: major-league baseball's first father-and-son pair. il pors *Ebony* 44:78+ S '89

GRIFFIN, ARCHIE, 1954-
about
Didn't you used to be . . . W. Ladson. il por *Sport (New York, N.Y.)* 80:82 Ja '89

GRIFFIN, BEN HILL, JR.
about
The last of the citrus barons. T. Trussell. il pors *Nation's Business* 77:46+ F '89

GRIFFIN, DONALD REDFIELD, 1915-
about
Do bees think? J. Horgan. il por *Scientific American* 260:36-8 My '89

GRIFFIN, GLEN C., AND CASTELLI, WILLIAM P.
All about your cholesterol numbers [excerpt from Good fat, bad fat] il *Prevention (Emmaus, Pa.)* 41:55-9 Mr '89
Fill up on complex carbohydrates [excerpt from Good fat/bad fat] il *The Saturday Evening Post* 261:12-13+ O '89

GRIFFIN, GREGORY *See* Canning, George, 1770-1827

GRIFFIN, JAMES D.
To snare the feet of greatness [address, June 16, 1989] *Vital Speeches of the Day* 55:735-6 S 15 '89

GRIFFIN, JASPER
Greeks, Romans, Jews & others. il *The New York Review of Books* 36:6+ Mr 16 '89

GRIFFIN, JOHN HOWARD, 1920-1980
about
The man who changed his skin. E. Sharpe, Jr. il pors *American Heritage* 40:44-55 F '89

GRIFFIN, LARRY
Sport. See issues of Car and Driver

GRIFFIN, LINDA C., AND DERVAN, PETER B.
Recognition of thymine·adenine base pairs by guanine in a pyrimidine triple helix motif. bibl f il *Science* 245:967-71 S 1 '89

GRIFFIN, MARY D.
The teacher-artist. *The Education Digest* 54:29-31 Ap '89

GRIFFIN, MERV, 1925-
about
The Merv and Don boardwalk game. il por *U.S. News & World Report* 107:17 N 27 '89
Merv Griffin may ground the seaplanes Miami Vice made famous. A. Fins. il *Business Week* p36 D 4 '89
Merv Griffin's last Resort may be bankruptcy. R. Grover. il *Business Week* p34 N 20 '89
The new Merv Griffin show. K. Hannon. il *Forbes* 144:10 Ag 21 '89
The Wheel of Fortune turns badly for Merv Griffin. L. Reibstein. il por *Newsweek* 114:62 N 27 '89
The wheel of misfortune? R. Grover. il *Business Week* p35-6 Ja 16 '89

GRIFFIN, RICHARD *See* Professor Griff

GRIFFIN, ROGER
The radial-velocity revolution. il *Sky and Telescope* 78:263+ S '89

GRIFFIN, WILLIAM
Religious books. See occasional issues of Publishers Weekly beginning July 29, 1983
Religious publishing. See occasional issues of Publishers Weekly beginning July 18, 1986

GRIFFITH, ALINE *See* Aline, Countess of Romanones

GRIFFITH, ANDY, 1926-
about
"I was paralyzed! What was wrong with me?". J. Buck. il pors *Redbook* 173:84+ My '89

GRIFFITH, BRAD, AND OTHERS
Translocation as a species conservation tool: status and strategy. bibl f il *Science* 245:477-80 Ag 4 '89

GRIFFITH, D. W. (DAVID WARK), 1875-1948
about
Intolerance [film] Reviews
Film Comment il 25:28-9 S/O '89. M. Hansen

GRIFFITH, DAVID WARK *See* Griffith, D. W. (David Wark), 1875-1948

GRIFFITH, LEE ELLEN, 1952-
The line-and-berry inlaid furniture of eighteenth-century Chester County, Pennsylvania. bibl f il *Antiques* 135:1202-11 My '89

GRIFFITH, MELANIE
about
America's 10 most beautiful women. J. Stein. il pors *Harper's Bazaar* 122:174+ S '89
A baby for Don and Melanie [cover story] S. Schindehette. il pors *People Weekly* 31:82-4+ F 27 '89
Cozy again [cover story] J. Ellis. il pors *Life* 12:70-4+ Ap '89
Girl talk. J. Feldman. il por *Rolling Stone* p34-5 Ja 26 '89
It's Miami Nice for Don Johnson and Melanie Griffith. pors *TV Guide* 37:8-9 Ja 28-F 3 '89
Melanie Griffith. il pors *'Teen* 33:71 My '89
Melanie Griffith does not take off (all) her clothes. L. Morice. il pors *Mademoiselle* 95:74-5 Ja '89
Melanie Griffith: Working girl makes good. C. McGuigan. il pors *Ladies' Home Journal* 106:106+ Ap '89
A rekindled love proves engaging for Don & Melanie. il pors *People Weekly* 31:46 Ja 9 '89
Working her way to the top. C. McGuigan. il pors *Newsweek* 113:56-7 Ja 2 '89

GRIFFITH, THOMAS
Newswatch. See issues of Time through April 18, 1988
What's so special about news magazines? il *Newsweek* 113:52-3 Je 26 '89

GRIFFITH JOYNER, FLORENCE
about
The 1989 Essence Awards [with editorial comment by Susan L. Taylor] il pors *Essence* 20:57-60+, 69 O '89
Drugs and track. C. Neff. il pors *Sports Illustrated* 71:25-6 O 2 '89
Flo Jo confronts accuser on drug use allegations. il por *Jet* 77:46 O 9 '89
FloJo retires from track to pursue other interests. il por *Jet* 75:12 Mr 13 '89
Florence Griffith Joyner: life in the fast lane [cover story] J. D. Cain. pors *Essence* 19:48-50+ Mr '89
Go with the Flo. S. Mansfield. il por *Vogue* 179:402-5+ Ap '89
No mo FloJo. il por *Runner's World* 24:14 Je '89
The spoils of victory. K. Moore. il pors *Sports Illustrated* 70:50-3+ Ap '89

GRIFFITHS, CHRISTOPHER E. M.
(jt. auth) See Nickoloff, Brian J., and Griffiths, Christopher E. M.

GRIGG, RICHARD W., AND EPP, DAVID
Critical depth for the survival of coral islands: effects on the Hawaiian archipelago. bibl f il map *Science* 243:638-41 F 3 '89

GRIGOROVICH, ÍÙRÏ NIKOLAEVICH, 1927-
about
Don Quixote [ballet] Reviews
  Dance Magazine 63:86 F '89. E. Aschengreen
London critics give Grigorovich the cold shoulder. M. Hunt.
  il *Dance Magazine* 63:23 N '89
GRILIKHES, MICHEL
about
We're off to see the Wizard, live at our local arena, thanks
  to producer Michel Grilikhes. P. Freeman. il *People Weekly*
  31:73-4 My 8 '89
GRILLI, PETER
Ennosuke III and his "Super Kabuki": Kabuki's revolutionary
  traditionalist. il pors *Dance Magazine* 63:30-5 S '89
GRILLING See Barbecue cooking; Broiling
GRILLNER, STEN, 1941-
(jt. auth) See Georgopoulos, Apostolos P., and Grillner, Sten,
  1941-
GRILLS, BARBECUE See Barbecue grills
GRIMES, WILLIAM
The antiquities boom: who pays the price? [cover story]
  il pors *The New York Times Magazine* p16-19+ Jl 16
  '89
Beer from a stone. il *Esquire* 111:30 My '89
The big red one. il *Esquire* 111:58 Mr '89
Oh, Pouilly! il *Esquire* 112:38 Ag '89
Something sublime, with a twist. il *Esquire* 111:40 Je '89
The wine that won the West. il *Esquire* 112:62 S '89
GRIMM, JACOB, 1785-1863
about
Germany's Fairy-tale Road. S. Wilding and A. Del Balso.
  il map *Gourmet* 49:52-5+ Mr '89
Grimm's greatest tale. S. J. Gould. il *Natural History* p20+
  F '89
GRIMM, MARY
Two years [story] *The New Yorker* 65:30-4 Je 19 '89
GRIMM, MICHELE, AND GRIMM, TOM
Travel in focus. See alternate issues of Travel Holiday through
  January 1990
GRIMM, TOM
(jt. auth) See Grimm, Michele, and Grimm, Tom
GRIMM, WILHELM, 1786-1859
about
Germany's Fairy-tale Road. S. Wilding and A. Del Balso.
  il map *Gourmet* 49:52-5+ Mr '89
Grimm's greatest tale. S. J. Gould. il *Natural History* p20+
  F '89
Past present. L. Metzger. *The Nation* 249:801-2 D 25 '89
GRIMSHAW, NICHOLAS THOMAS
about
Heroic transformations. D. Dietsch. il *Architectural Record*
  177:72-83 S '89
GRINDER-MIXERS, FEED See Feed mixers and mixing
GRINDING OF TEETH See Bruxism
GRIPEN AIRPLANES See Airplanes, Military—Sweden
GRIPPO, DAN
Have Catholics found better ways to go to Confession? [cover
  story] il *U.S. Catholic* 54:6-12 Ag '89
GRIS, CHARLES ÉDOUARD JEANNERET- See Le Cor-
  busier, 1887-1965
GRISANTI, MARY LEE
The cesarean epidemic. il *New York* 22:56-61 F 20 '89
GRISCOM, NINA
about
New working class. il pors *Harper's Bazaar* 122:160-75+
  Mr '89
GRISÉ, RICHARD
about
Politics and policing. B. Wallace. il *Maclean's* 102:24 D
  4 '89
GRISEZ, TED
about
Hunting for giants. C. Fergus. il pors *Country Journal* 16:56-61
  Ja '89
GRISOLIA, CYNTHIA
(jt. auth) See Rubin, Hanna, and Grisolia, Cynthia
GRISSIM, JOHN, 1941-
Chairmen of the board [cover story] il *Oceans* 22:22-9+
  Mr/Ap '89
Raise the Rio! il map *Oceans* 22:30-7+ Mr/Ap '89
GRISWOLD, MAC K.
Far afield. il por *House & Garden* 161:108-15 Ap '89
Flower brokers. il *House & Garden* 161:80+ O '89
Green geometry. il por *House & Garden* 161:46+ Jl '89
Princess in the garden. il por *House & Garden* 161:108-13+
  Jl '89
GRITS COOKING See Cooking—Grain
GRIZZLY BEARS See Bears
GROBEL, LAWRENCE
. "My parents never push me". il pors *Redbook* 174:40+ D
  '89
GROBER, MATTHEW S.
Starlight on the reef [cover story] il *Natural History* p72-6+
  O '89
GROBSTEIN, CLIFFORD, 1916-
about
When does life begin? [interview] E. Hall. il pors *Psychology
  Today* 23:42-6 S '89

GROCERY TRADE
See also
American Stores Co.
Circle K Corp.
Computers—Grocery trade use
Fleming Companies, Inc.
Food stores
Great Atlantic & Pacific Tea Company, Inc.
National Convenience Stores Inc.
Optical scanners—Grocery trade use
Rock Store (Calif.)
Safeway Stores, Inc.
Southland Corp.
Supermarkets
Trader Joe's (Firm)
Acquisitions and mergers
Canada
Raising the stakes [bidding war for Steinberg] P. Chisholm.
  il *Maclean's* 102:31 Ag 7 '89
A struggle for Steinberg. P. Chisholm. il *Maclean's* 102:30
  Jl 24 '89
Finance
Food distributors. R. King. il *Forbes* 143:139-40+ Ja 9 '89
Golf balls, motor oil and tomatoes [Wal-Mart's grocery
  business] S. B. Weiner. il *Forbes* 144:130-1+ O 30 '89
Canada
See also
Loblaw Companies Ltd.
Sobeys Stores, Ltd.
Steinberg Inc.
GROCH, JUDITH
Life after work. il *American Health* 8:98+ Mr '89
GROENING, MATT
about
Cartoon from hell. R. Lloyd. il *American Film* 15:112 O
  '89
Is TV the coolest invention ever invented? [cover story]
  S. Elder. il por *Mother Jones* 14:28-31 D '89
Life in hell's Matt Groening goes overboard to make the
  Simpsons the first family of TV 'toons. J. Kaufman. il
  pors *People Weekly* 32:108-10 D 18 '89
GROGAN, BOB
about
The cop who cared too much. G. Dillow. il por *TV Guide*
  37:26-7 Ap 1-7 '89
GROGNET, ALLENE GUSS
Elderly refugees and language learning. il *Aging* no359:8-11
  '89
GROLIER INCORPORATED
Clarke retires amid top shake-up at Grolier. *Publishers Weekly*
  235:14 F 10 '89
GRONDIN, JEAN-LUC
about
Grondin: wings over Canada. J. Watson. il *International
  Wildlife* 19:38-43 Ja/F '89
GRONDONA, MARIANO
The enlightened patriot. *World Press Review* 36:64 Ap '89
GROOMING (PERSONAL CARE) See Beauty, Personal
GROOMS See Weddings
GROOPMAN, JEROME E.
Red scare. il *The New Republic* 200:25-7 Ap 17 '89
Rx for the FDA. *The New Republic* 200:17-18+ F 13 '89
GROOTHUIS, DOUGLAS
Confronting the New Age. il *Christianity Today* 33:36-9 Ja
  13 '89
GROPIUS, WALTER, 1883-1969
about
Architecture: Walter Gropius. K. Frampton. il por
  Architectural Digest 46:82+ F '89
GROSS, ANDREA, 1940-
The good daughter. il *Ladies' Home Journal* 106:216-17+
  N '89
GROSS, DANIEL
The quick fix. *The New Republic* 201:12+ O 16 '89
GROSS, DAVID J.
Can we scale the Planck scale? il por *Physics Today* 42:9+
  Je '89
On the calculation of the fine-structure constant. il por *Physics
  Today* 42:9+ D '89
A week in Beijing. il pors *Physics Today* 42 pt1:9+ Ag
  '89
GROSS, JOHN J.
Shaw and super-Shaw. il *The New York Review of Books*
  36:27-8+ D 21 '89
GROSS, KEN, 1938-
A pathetic bid for sympathy from a long-suffering significant
  other. *Ms.* 17:30 Mr '89
GROSS, LINDEN
Dolly Parton: feeling good again. por *McCall's* 116:87-8+
  S '89
Don't worry, be happy—but how? *Redbook* 174:112-13+ N
  '89
Linda Gray: the butterfly is free. il pors *Ladies' Home
  Journal* 106:40+ Ag '89
Wishing on a star. il *McCall's* 117:64+ N '89
GROSS, MICHAEL
The big deal at Bloomingdale's: Marvin Traub makes a
  run at the top. il pors *New York* 22:56-60+ O 16 '89

GROSS, MICHAEL—*cont.*
The cutting edge. See issues of New York beginning February 22, 1988
The deb of the minute. il pors *New York* 22:42-5 Ag 28 '89
The face [cover story] il pors *New York* 22:32-9 O 30 '89
Favorite son [cover story] il pors *New York* 22:36-44 Mr 20 '89
Patrick Kelly: exuberant style animates the American designer's Paris atelier. il por *Architectural Digest* 46:218-24 S '89
The satanic diaries. il pors *New York* 22:48-56 My 29 '89
Treasure islands. il *New York* 22:120-4+ D 25 '89-Ja 1 '90
The UnHampton. il map *New York* 22:30-2+ Jl 3-10 '89
GROSS, MICHAEL, 1948-
Join the family. il *TV Guide* 37:4-5+ My 13-19 '89
GROSS NATIONAL PRODUCT
After a hot start in the first quarter, growth will cool. M. F. Allyn. il *Fortune* 119:19-20 Mr 27 '89
The consumer shopping spree is still driving growth. J. C. Cooper and K. Madigan. il *Business Week* p23-4 F 13 '89
No apology needed [deficit] E. Rubenstein. il *National Review* 41:16 F 10 '89
Painting without numbers. H. Banks. il *Forbes* 144:10 N 27 '89
Slower growth? The jury still can't reach a verdict. J. C. Cooper and K. Madigan. il *Business Week* p27-8 My 15 '89
What's a woman worth? [unpaid work should be included in figuring; views of M. Waring] Y. Preston. il *Ms.* 18:78 Jl/Ag '89
What's pulling the rug out from under housing. K. Madigan. il *Business Week* p104+ Ja 23 '89
GROSS NATIONAL PRODUCT (COMEDY TROUPE)
Scandal Tour. D. Graff. il *Travel Holiday* 172:98 O '89
GROSSARTH-MATICEK, RONALD
about
The character of controversy. J. Fischman. il *Psychology Today* 22:27 D '88
Health's character. H. J. Eysenck. il pors *Psychology Today* 22:28-32+ D '88
GROSSBERGER, LEWIS
Speaking volumes. il *Vogue* 179:226+ My '89
The unsung unread. il *Vogue* 179:230+ F '89
GROSSBLATT, ROBERT
The drawing board. See issues of Radio-Electronics
GROSSMAN, A. W., AND OTHERS
High-resolution microwave images of Saturn. bibl f il *Science* 245:1211-15 S 15 '89
GROSSMAN, ANN SUE
"My amazing Lisa"; ed. by Susan Lapinski. il por *Redbook* 172:56+ Ap '89
GROSSMAN, DANIEL, AND SHULMAN, SETH
A nuclear dump: the experiment begins. il map *Discover* 10:48-51+ Mr '89
GROSSMAN, DAVID
about
A major Israeli novel. A. L. Mintz. *Commentary* 88:56-60 Jl '89
GROSSMAN, EDITH
(tr) See Paz, Octavio, 1914-. Time's voice
GROSSMAN, FLORENCE
Sledding [poem] *The Nation* 248:464 Ap 3 '89
GROSSMAN, KARL, AND LONG, JUDITH
Nuclear slingshot. *The Nation* 249:336-7 O 2 '89
Plutonium con. *The Nation* 249:589 N 20 '89
GROSSMAN, LARRY
about
The view from Section 117. B. Bethune. il por *Maclean's* 102:47 O 2 '89
GROSSMAN, LENORE
From infertility to adoption. il *Parents* 64:96+ Mr '89
GROSSMAN, LISA
about
"My amazing Lisa"; ed. by Susan Lapinski. A. S. Grossman. il por *Redbook* 172:56+ Ap '89
GROSSMAN, STEPHEN R., AND OTHERS
Turn group input into stellar output [excerpt from Innovation, Inc.] il *Working Woman* 14:36+ D '89
GROSSMAN, YAFFA
Toward a science-based policy on the release of genetically engineered organisms. *BioScience* 39:229 Ap '89
GROSSMANN, JOHN
Big tree for the Big Apple. il pors *National Wildlife* 28:10-13 D '89/Ja '90
GROSSO, SALVADOR See Grosso, Sonny
GROSSO, SONNY
about
Speak loudly and carry a nightstick. D. Friedman. por *Rolling Stone* p37 Ag 10 '89
GROSSO-JACOBSON ENTERTAINMENT
Speak loudly and carry a nightstick [producer and former policeman S. Grosso] D. Friedman. por *Rolling Stone* p37 Ag 10 '89
GROSVENOR, GILBERT M.
Heaven on earth: the race for renewal. il *Harper's Bazaar* 122:59+ Ja '89

Superpowers not so super in geography. il map *National Geographic* 176:816-21 D '89
GRÓSZ, KÁROLY
Visit of Hungarian premier [remarks, July 27, 1988] il por *Department of State Bulletin* 88:36 D '88
Visit to the United States, 1988
Visit of Hungarian premier [remarks, July 27, 1988] R. Reagan; K. Grosz. il por *Department of State Bulletin* 88:36 D '88
GROTH, EDWARD, III
The Alar debate. *Consumers' Research Magazine* 72:28-30 Jl '89
GROUCHO CLUB
The man who put the grouch into Groucho's [J. Bernard] R. Ryan. il por *Gentlemen's Quarterly* 59:31+ Ja '89
GROUND BEEF COOKING *See* Cooking—Meat
GROUND COVER PLANTS
Living mulches. J. A. Van Sweden. il *Organic Gardening* 36:51-4 Mr '89
GROUND CREW (FIRM)
Ruler of the runway [A. Smaltz] S. Rae. il por *Harper's Bazaar* 122:80-1 N '89
GROUND CREWS, AVIATION *See* Airplane mechanics (Persons)
GROUND EFFECT MACHINES *See* Air cushion vehicles
GROUND FAULT CIRCUIT INTERRUPTERS
Ground fault interrupters. M. Henkenius. il *Popular Mechanics* 166:99 Mr '89
Now: an extension cord that can save your life [Guardian] R. Day. il *Popular Science* 234:36 My '89
GROUND FIGURES *See* Geoglyphs
GROUND MEAT COOKING *See* Cooking—Meat
GROUND MEAT MIXES *See* Meat mixes
GROUND PENETRATING RADAR
Radar that sees beneath the ground. N. McAleer. il *Popular Science* 234:113 My '89
GROUND SLOTHS, FOSSIL *See* Sloths, Fossil
GROUND SQUIRRELS
Freeze avoidance in a mammal: body temperatures below 0°C in an Arctic hibernator [cover story] B. M. Barnes. bibl f il *Science* 244:1593-5 Je 30 '89
Rattler battlers. R. G. Coss and D. H. Owings. il *Natural History* p30-5 My '89
Squirrel sleeps at a fluid subzero [research by Brian M. Barnes] *Science News* 136:30 Jl 8 '89
Supercool mammals [body temperature drops below freezing during hibernation; research by Brian Barnes] M. Kemp. il *Discover* 10:24 N '89
GROUND STATIONS (COMMUNICATIONS SATELLITES) *See* Communications satellites—Ground stations
GROUNDHOGS *See* Woodchucks
GROUNDSKEEPING (STADIUMS) *See* Stadiums—Maintenance and repair
GROUNDWATER
See also
Hot springs
Springs
Wells
Great Basin calcite vein and the Pleistocene time scale [discussion of December 2, 1988 article, A 250,000-year climatic record from Great Basin vein calcite: implications for Milankovitch theory] I. J. Winograd and others. *Science* 246:262-3 O 13 '89
GROUNDWATER POLLUTION
Unexpected leakage through landfill liners [diffusion of chemicals through clay] J. Raloff. *Science News* 135:164 Mr 18 '89
Control
Plug-in pollution control. J. Free. il *Popular Science* 234:31 My '89
Protecting your rural well. L. Savage. il *Country Journal* 16:23-7+ S/O '89
California
Source Reduction Research Partnership: a unique joint venture [eliminating groundwater pollution caused by chlorinated solvents] A. Yazdani. bibl f il *Environment* 31:2-4 N '89
Colorado
Land of death . . . and life [wildlife thrive on contaminated grounds of the Rocky Mountain Arsenal] G. Gerhardt. il map *National Wildlife* 28:34-40 D '89/Ja '90
The toxic morass in Denver's backyard [Rocky Mountain Arsenal] S. D. Atchison. il *Business Week* p46 Ja 9 '89
Iowa
Big Spring study: page two tells another story. *Successful Farming* 87:48 N '89
New York (State)
Contaminant Cove: where polluters defile Mohawk land. J. E. Milich. il *The Progressive* 53:23-5 Ja '89
On gushes and seeps—what we do about environmental spills. M. Kadlecek. *The Conservationist* 44:52-3 S/O '89
Utah
See also
Salt Lake City (Utah)—Groundwater pollution
GROUNDWATER PROSPECTING
See also
Dowsing

GROUP COUNSELING
See also
Group psychotherapy
Self help groups

GROUP FOR SWITZERLAND WITHOUT AN ARMY
The Swiss debate their Army's future. A. Schalk. il *Commonweal* 116:331-3 Je 2 '89

GROUP HOMES FOR CHILDREN
See also
Valley Teen Ranch (Madera, Calif.)

GROUP HOMES FOR THE MENTALLY HANDICAPPED
A home of their own [mentally retarded adults living in group homes at former Willowbrook State School] J. L. McCarthy. il *McCall's* 117:66+ D '89
Uncle Sam's NIMBY attack [Justice Dept. suing Chicago Heights] J. P. Shapiro. il *U.S. News & World Report* 107:24 S 18 '89

GROUP LEGAL SERVICES *See* Prepaid legal services
GROUP LIVING ESTABLISHMENTS *See* Collective settlements; Housing, Cooperative
GROUP MATERIAL (GROUP)
Group Material at Dia (Wooster St.). E. Heartney. *Art in America* 77:145 Ja '89
Material world [work of Group Material] W. Olander. il *Art in America* 77:122-9+ Ja '89

GROUP OF SEVEN
Cracks in the G7 front. P. Chisholm. il *Maclean's* 102:30+ Mr 6 '89
The Group of Seven is acting more like the Seven Dwarfs [dollar runup] M. McNamee. il *Business Week* p90 Je 5 '89
The Group of Seven won't be singing harmony [Paris summit] B. Riemer. il *Business Week* p63 Jl 17 '89
Is the Group of Seven on the road to splitsville? M. McNamee. il *Business Week* p29 F 13 '89
Mellow George and the don't worry, be happy summit [Paris economic summit] R. Fly and B. Riemer. por *Business Week* p32 Jl 31 '89
Showdown on the dollar: central banks are attacking the greenback. J. Daly. il *Maclean's* 102:39 O 9 '89

GROUP PSYCHOTHERAPY
See also
Family psychotherapy
Can psychotherapy delay cancer deaths? [research by David Spiegel] M. Barinaga. il *Science* 246:448-9 O 27 '89
Group therapy aids cancer survival [work of David Spiegel] *Science News* 136:302 N 4 '89
Leader of the group [work of S. Scheidlinger] S. Goodman. il por *New York* 22:36 My 15 '89

GROUP RELATIONS TRAINING
See also
Esalen Institute
GROUP UNITED AGAINST RADAR DETECTORS
Detecting trouble. il *Motor Trend* 41:36 Mr '89
We make the insurance hit list. W. Jeanes. il *Car and Driver* 34:7 Ap '89

GROUP W CABLE, INC.
The Baby Bells toddle toward cable [Pacific Telesis' stake in Group W Cable] R. D. Hof. il *Business Week* p40 My 8 '89

GROUP W PRODUCTIONS
A bolder Group W. J. Loftus. il por *Channels (New York, N.Y.: 1986)* 9:24-6 O '89

GROUP WORK IN EDUCATION
Classroom evaluation of cooperative learning. D. Watson and L. Rangel. *The Education Digest* 55:35-7 N '89
Cooperative learning and student achievement. R. E. Slavin. *The Education Digest* 54:15-17 F '89
Cooperative learning and the Native American student. L. Little Soldier. bibl f il *Phi Delta Kappan* 71:161-3 O '89

GROUP WORK IN INDUSTRY *See* Team work in industry
GROUPE BULL
A new CEO is taking Bull by the horns [F. Lorentz] T. Peterson. il por *Business Week* p80 Jl 17 '89
"We still have more to do". C. Siler. il *Forbes* 144:183 D 11 '89
Why Jerry Pearlman gave up his brainchild [selling Zenith's computer unit to Bull] L. Therrien. il por *Business Week* p35 O 16 '89

GROUPE DE LA CITÉ
Cité Group posts strong sales, plans English-language expansion. H. R. Lottman. *Publishers Weekly* 236:12 Jl 21 '89

GROUPERS
Grouper sex in Belize. J. Carter. il *Natural History* p60-9 O '89

GROUPIES
Photographs and photography
True believers. G. Kalogerakis. il *Rolling Stone* p100-2+ S 21 '89

GROUPS (SELF HELP) *See* Self help groups
GROUPS (SOCIOLOGY)
See also
Cliques
Elite (Social sciences)
Peer groups

GROUPS (SPECIAL INTEREST) *See* Special interest groups
GROUPWARE (COMPUTER PROGRAMS)
'Groupware': big breakthrough—or Big Brother? R. Brandt and J. W. Verity. il *Business Week* p130-1 Je 5 '89
Testing
Groping for groupware [Higgins and WordPerfect Office] W. Rash, Jr. il *Byte* 14:135-6+ Ap '89

GROUSE
See also
Ptarmigans
Food and feeding
The tale of the crop. B. W. Dalrymple. il *Field & Stream* 94:44-5+ O '89

GROUSE SHOOTING
The price of things. R. L. Hall. il *Field & Stream* 94:68-9+ N '89
The tale of the crop. B. W. Dalrymple. il *Field & Stream* 94:44-5+ O '89

GROUT, WILLIAM
Inside Skiing. See issues of Skiing beginning September 1986

GROVE, ANDREW S.
How managers should handle staff conflicts [excerpt from One-on-one with Andy Grove] il *Working Woman* 14:146-8 N '89
How to get more done in fewer hours [excerpt from One-on-one with Andy Grove] il *Working Woman* 14:20+ Jl '89
How to give feedback your staff can use [excerpt from One-on-one with Andy Grove] il *Working Woman* 14:54+ S '89

GROVE PARK INN (ASHEVILLE, N.C.) *See* Asheville (N.C.)—Hotels, motels, etc.
GROVE WEIDENFELD (FIRM)
Ann Getty: publish and perish? A. Begley. il pors *The New York Times Magazine* p36-7+ O 22 '89
Green leaves as Grove, Weidenfeld merge. *Publishers Weekly* 235:14 My 19 '89
Grove's 'Wild at heart' gets a running start. *Publishers Weekly* 236:29 D 8 '89

GROVER, LEE, AND GROVER, RAY
From Second sight: the years of two antique dealers [excerpts] pors *Antiques & Collecting Hobbies* 94:36-8+ Ag '89

GROVER, RAY
(jt. auth) See Grover, Lee, and Grover, Ray
GROVER, RICHARD
Kidnapping
Two American missionaries are abducted in Colombia. J. Maust. il pors *Christianity Today* 33:50-1 F 3 '89

GROVER, WAYNE
Dolphins. il *Sea Frontiers* 35:28-30 Ja/F '89

GROVES, DAVID
Step to it. il *Health (New York, N.Y.)* 21:28+ F '89
(jt. auth) See Rippe, James M., and Groves, David

GROVES, LESLIE R., 1896-1970
about
Cool Hand Nuke. R. Scheer. il *Esquire* 112:170-1 O '89

GROWTH
See also
Bone—Growth
Brain—Growth
Growth regulators
Mammary glands—Growth
Maturity
Morphogenesis
Nerve cells—Growth
Regeneration (Biology)
Plants
See also
Geotropism

GROWTH, ECONOMIC *See* Economic development
GROWTH FACTORS *See* Growth regulators
GROWTH HORMONE *See* Pituitary hormones
GROWTH HORMONE, SYNTHETIC *See* Pituitary hormones, Synthetic
GROWTH HORMONE RELEASING FACTOR *See* Pituitary hormone releasing factors
GROWTH INHIBITING SUBSTANCES *See* Growth regulators
GROWTH OF CHILDREN *See* Children—Growth and development
GROWTH OF CITIES AND TOWNS *See* Cities and towns—Growth
GROWTH REGULATORS
See also
Amphiregulin
Ciliary neurotrophic factor
Colony-stimulating factors
Epidermal growth factor
Erythropoietin
Fibroblast growth factor
Interleukin
Keratinocyte growth factor
Mitogens
Nerve growth factor
Pituitary hormones
Platelet-derived growth factor
Transforming growth factor
Vascular endothelial growth factor
Vascular permeability factor

GROWTH REGULATORS—cont.

AIDS-Kaposi's sarcoma-derived cells express cytokines with autocrine and paracrine growth effects. B. Ensoli and others. bibl f il *Science* 243:223-6 Ja 13 '89

Bloodless coup [inhibition of angiogenesis; research by Judah Folkman] T. Beardsley. *Scientific American* 261:18-19 Ag '89

Control of angiogenesis with synthetic heparin substitutes. J. Folkman and others. bibl f il *Science* 243:1490-3 Mr 17 '89

G_1 events and regulations of cell proliferation. A. B. Pardee. bibl f il *Science* 246:603-8 N 3 '89

How we heal. R. Saltus. il *Health (New York, N.Y.)* 21:82-3 F '89

Mouse embryonic stem cells and reporter constructs to detect developmentally regulated genes. A. Gossler and others. bibl f il *Science* 244:463-5 Ap 28 '89

The neuronal growth-associated protein GAP-43 induces filopodia in non-neuronal cells. M. X. Zuber and others. bibl f il *Science* 244:1193-5 Je 9 '89

Production of mammastatin, a tissue-specific growth inhibitor, by normal human mammary cells. P. R. Ervin, Jr. and others. bibl f il *Science* 244:1585-7 Je 30 '89

Substances found to promote bone growth. *High Technology Business* 9:30 My '89

Plants

See also
Auxins
Daminozide
Ethylene

GROWTH STOCK OUTLOOK, INC.

The long and short of it [C. Allmon's performance] M. Hulbert. il *Forbes* 143:217 Mr 20 '89

GROWTH STOCKS *See* Stocks

GRUAU, RENÉ, 1910-

about

Epitome of style. J. McLaughlin. il *Harper's Bazaar* 122:164-7 D '89

GRUBB, KEVIN

Hopeful highlights. il *Dance Magazine* 63:54-5 O '89

Legs Diamond comes to Broadway: give 'em the old razzle-dazzle [cover story] il pors *Dance Magazine* 63:40-4 Ja '89

GRUBB, W. NORTON, AND WILSON, ROBERT HINES

Sources of increasing inequality in wages and salaries, 1960-80. bibl f il *Monthly Labor Review* 112:3-13 Ap '89

GRUBB & ELLIS CO.

But where's the dessert? E. Paris. il por *Forbes* 144:60+ O 2 '89

GRUBBS, ROBERT H., AND TUMAS, WILLIAM

Polymer synthesis and organotransition metal chemistry. bibl f il *Science* 243:907-15 F 17 '89

GRUCHOW, PAUL

The ancient faith of cranes. il *Audubon* 91:40-55 My '89

GRUDEM, WAYNE

Investing in what lasts. il *Christianity Today* 33:31-4 My 12 '89

GRUDER, JAY

Food with thought. il por *Harper's Bazaar* 122:116-17 O '89

Personalities plus. il pors *Harper's Bazaar* 122:173-4 Ag '89

Viva Verdura! il por *Harper's Bazaar* 122:262 S '89

GRUEBY, WILLIAM HENRY

about

Grueby pottery. B. E. Johnson. bibl f il *Antiques & Collecting Hobbies* 94:52-4 O '89

GRUEN, JOHN

Architectural digest visits: Cynthia Gregory. il pors *Architectural Digest* 46:236-41+ N '89

Argentine elan: Amalia Lacroze de Fortabat in Buenos Aires. il por *Architectural Digest* 46:202-7+ Mr '89

The designer's eye for timeless fashion photography. il por *Architectural Digest* 46:78+ S '89

Hamburg's Ivan Liska: starman. il pors *Dance Magazine* 63:36-9 S '89

Jock Soto: portrait of a young artist [cover story] il pors *Dance Magazine* 63:32-7 Ag '89

Killearn Farm: F. William Free's Hudson Valley horse farm. il por *Architectural Digest* 46:182-7+ Je '89

Manhattan revision: an East River penthouse with an old world look. il *Architectural Digest* 46:100-7 F '89

Nelly Arrieta de Blaquier's South American silver. il por *Architectural Digest* 46:102+ O '89

New life for a Water Mill blacksmith shop. il *Architectural Digest* 46:108+ Ag '89

On the Côte d'Azur: Martin and Toni Sosnoff's villa above Nice. il *Architectural Digest* 46:88-93 Ja '89

A woman under the influence. pors *Dance Magazine* 63:52-4 Mr '89

GRUENE (NEW BRAUNFELS, TEX.)

Description

Great old times in Gruene. il *Southern Living* 24:16+ Ag '89

GRUENINGER, WALTER F.

Recorded music in review. See issues of Consumers' Research Magazine

GRUMMAN CORP.

Grumman lab will support variety of systems efforts. S. W. Kandebo. il *Aviation Week & Space Technology* 130:59+ My 1 '89

Grumman prepares for flight tests of advanced capability EA-6B. S. W. Kandebo. il *Aviation Week & Space Technology* 131:41+ S 25 '89

Grumman to roll out new Navy tactical electronic warfare aircraft next month [EA-6B ADVCAP] il *Aviation Week & Space Technology* 131:32 S 11 '89

Grumman using visual simulations to improve electronic warfare capabilities of U.S. Navy. il *Aviation Week & Space Technology* 131:123-4 S 11 '89

Tomcat 21 will include technologies to reduce F-14's radar signature. J. D. Morrocco. il *Aviation Week & Space Technology* 130:30-1 My 22 '89

GRUMPY (FICTIONAL CHARACTER)

Heigh-ho, heigh-ho, it's far, far off we go; or, Grumpynappers give a cement dwarf a joyride [pranksters steal lawn ornament from the home of C. Horne in Mount Marion, N.Y.] il *People Weekly* 31:100-1 Je 26 '89

GRUNDBERG, ANDY

Photography. il *The New York Times Book Review* 94:20+ D 3 '89

GRUNDFEST, JOSEPH A.

Can we prevent another Black Monday? il *USA Today (Periodical)* 117:16-18 My '89

Responsibility and regulation [address, June 26, 1989] *Vital Speeches of the Day* 55:718-22 S 15 '89

GRUNDY, SCOTT M.

Try a healthier way of cooking [excerpt from The American Heart Association low-fat, low-cholesterol cookbook] *Redbook* 173:16 Ag '89

GRUNE, GEORGE V.

Global marketing [address, May 20, 1989] *Vital Speeches of the Day* 55:580-2 Jl 15 '89

GRÜNEN (GERMANY: WEST) *See* Green Party (Germany: West)

GRUNWALD, LISA

Captain Fiction rides again. il por *Esquire* 111:160-2 Mr '89

The passive-aggressive male. il *Esquire* 111:105-8+ Ap '89

Robin Williams has a big premise! [cover story] il *Esquire* 111:108-14+ Je '89

GRUSIN, DAVE

about

Dave Grusin: scoring it big. S. Yanow. il pors *Down Beat* 56:24-6 Jl '89

GRYZINSKI, VILMA

Muddling through in Beirut. il *World Press Review* 36:72 D '89

GSA *See* United States. General Services Administration

GTE CORP.

Blame the phone company: a strategy goes on trial [Home Shopping Network sues GTE] G. DeGeorge. il *Business Week* p30 Je 12 '89

Cincinnati Microwave tries to strengthen its signal [cellular co-marketing deal with GTE] M. Mallory. *Business Week* p29-30 Mr 6 '89

GTE builds muscle with local telephones. il *Money* 18:8 F '89

GTE: computing with connections. il *Personal Computing* 13:81+ S '89

Rocky road. il *Forbes* 143:197 Ja 9 '89

GTE SPRINT COMMUNICATIONS

See also
US Sprint Communications Inc.

GTECH CORPORATION

Automating an ancient business. J. Cook. il *Forbes* 143:52+ Ja 23 '89

GTG ENTERTAINMENT (FIRM)

Pitching USA today. A. Snyder. il *Channels (New York, N.Y.: 1986)* 9:17-18 Mr '89

GTP *See* Guanosine triphosphate

GTPASE *See* Guanosine triphosphatase

GUADALAJARA (MEXICO)

Festivals

Fiestas de Octubre. L. B. Bastian. il *Travel Holiday* 171:50-7 Je '89

GUADELOUPE

See also
Marie-Galante (Guadeloupe)
Terre-de-Haut (Guadeloupe)

GUAM

See also
Birds—Guam
Public health—Guam
Wildlife—Guam

GUANA ISLAND (BRITISH VIRGIN ISLANDS)

Description and travel

Guana Island: a British Virgin Galápagos. R. Alleman. il *Vogue* 179:310 N '89

GUANACASTE NATIONAL PARK (COSTA RICA)

Daniel Janzen's dry idea [dry forest re-creation in Guanacaste National Park] T. A. Lewis. il pors map *International Wildlife* 19:30-6 Ja/F '89

GUANACASTE NATIONAL PARK (COSTA RICA)—*cont.*
Lovely cheetahs, meter-saved [California zoos use old parking meters to raise money] J. Howard. il *Sierra* 74:26 Mr/Ap '89

GUANGDONG PROVINCE (CHINA)
After Tiananmen, what? [Hong Kong investment] il *Forbes* 144:198 Jl 24 '89
Rich China, poor China: the gap keeps growing [contrasting Guangdong with Hunan] D. J. Yang. il *Business Week* p40-1 Je 5 '89

GUANINE
Recognition of thymine · adenine base pairs by guanine in a pyrimidine triple helix motif. L. C. Griffin and P. B. Dervan. bibl f il *Science* 245:967-71 S 1 '89

GUANOSINE
See also
Deoxyguanosine
Prevention of translational frameshifting by the modified nucleoside 1-methylguanosine. G. R. Björk and others. bibl f il *Science* 244:986-9 My 26 '89

GUANOSINE MONOPHOSPHATE
Atrial natriuretic peptide inhibits a cation channel in renal inner medullary collecting duct cells. D. B. Light and others. bibl f il *Science* 243:383-5 Ja 20 '89
New type of receptor found [natriuretic peptide receptor] J. L. Marx. *Science* 244:1140-1 Je 9 '89
The protein kinase domain of the ANP receptor is required for signaling. M. Chinkers and D. L. Garbers. bibl f il *Science* 245:1392-4 S 22 '89

GUANOSINE TRIPHOSPHATASE
The effect of GTPase activating protein upon Ras is inhibited by mitogenically responsive lipids. M.-H. Tsai and others. bibl f il *Science* 243:522-6 Ja 27 '89

GUANOSINE TRIPHOSPHATE
See also
G proteins
Regulatory role for GTP-binding proteins in endocytosis. L. S. Mayorga and others. bibl f il *Science* 244:1475-7 Je 23 '89

GUANYLATE CYCLASE
New type of receptor found [natriuretic peptide receptor] J. L. Marx. *Science* 244:1140-1 Je 9 '89
The protein kinase domain of the ANP receptor is required for signaling. M. Chinkers and D. L. Garbers. bibl f il *Science* 245:1392-4 S 22 '89

GUARANI LANGUAGE
A choice of words [Paraguay] D. Einhorn and S. O. Einhorn. il *Américas* 41 no1:42-7 '89

GUARANTY *See* Warranty
GUARANTY OF LOANS *See* Loans, Bank—Guaranty
GUARANTY OF SECURITIES *See* Securities—Guaranty
GUARD *See* Group United Against Radar Detectors
GUARDIA FONT, ANTONIO DE LA
about
The trial that shook Cuba [cover story] J. Preston. il pors *The New York Review of Books* 36:24-31 D 7 '89

GUARDIAN AND WARD
See also
Capacity and disability
Conservatorships
Custody of children
Parent and child (Law)
The gulag of guardianship [elderly] D. M. Topolnicki. il *Money* 18:140-1+ Mr '89
A will that protects your child [naming a guardian] S. Nielsen. *Good Housekeeping* 208:241 Ap '89

GUARDIAN ANGELS (ORGANIZATION)
Soap star Clayton Prince moonlights on Manhattan's mean streets as a Guardian Angel. J. Kaufman. il pors *People Weekly* 32:195-6 D 4 '89

GUARDIAN GROUP INTERNATIONAL
Protection [use of firearms in self defense; views of S. D'Andrilli] *The New Yorker* 64:22-3 Ja 9 '89

GUARDIAN LIFE INSURANCE CO. OF AMERICA
Bastion of strength. A. Bladen. il *Forbes* 144:136 Jl 10 '89

GUARDS
See also
Bodyguards
Security guards

GUASTAFESTE, AL
about
Sentimental guy. *The New Yorker* 65:28-9 Jl 10 '89

GUATEMALA
See also
Civil rights—Guatemala
Cultural property—Protection—Guatemala
Government and the press—Guatemala
Indians of Central America—Guatemala
Military assistance, American—Guatemala
National parks and reserves—Guatemala
Rain forests—Guatemala
Trifinio (Central America)

Antiquities
See also
Nakbe (Ancient city)
Classic Maya fight to their finish [evidence of warfare at two Guatemala sites] B. Bower. *Science News* 136:365 D 2 '89

Army
Letters [discussion of November 28, 1988 article, Guatemala's new military order] P. Lernoux. *The Nation* 248:254+ F 27 '89
Waging war to prevent war. J. Schirmer. il *The Nation* 248:478-9 Ap 10 '89

Foreign relations
United States
See United States—Foreign relations—Guatemala
History
Revolution, 1954
Quetzal [1954 coup supported by the U.S.] L. H. Lapham. *Harper's* 278:8-10 F '89

Politics and government
Guatemala: What has democracy wrought? S. Kinzer. il *The New York Times Magazine* p32-4+ Mr 26 '89
Letters [discussion of November 28, 1988 article, Guatemala's new military order] P. Lernoux. *The Nation* 248:254+ F 27 '89
Waging war to prevent war. J. Schirmer. il *The Nation* 248:478-9 Ap 10 '89

Religious institutions and affairs
See also
Church and civil rights—Guatemala
Church and social problems—Guatemala
Evangelical churches—Guatemala
Missions—Guatemala

GUATEMALAN COOKING *See* Cooking, Guatemalan
GUBBINS, DAVID
(jt. auth) *See* Bloxham, Jeremy, and Gubbins, David
GUBER, PETER
about
Dynamic duos don't come cheap. C. Gorman. il pors *Time* 134:71 N 6 '89
Making up, Hollywood style. il pors *Time* 134:74 N 27 '89
The producers [cover story] D. K. Shah. il pors *The New York Times Magazine* p26-9+ O 22 '89
Walter Yetnikoff's $300 million mistake. L. Gubernick. il pors *Forbes* 144:108+ D 11 '89

GUBER-PETERS ENTERTAINMENT COMPANY
The producers [cover story] D. K. Shah. il pors *The New York Times Magazine* p26-9+ O 22 '89

GUCCI FAMILY
about
The feuding families of fine goods. C. Dickey. il *Newsweek* 114:42 Ag 7 '89

GUCCI GROUP
The feuding families of fine goods. C. Dickey. il *Newsweek* 114:42 Ag 7 '89

GUCCIONE, BOB, 1930-
about
How Trump plays monopoly. H. Rudnitsky. il *Forbes* 143:128 Ap 17 '89

GUCCIONE, PIERO, 1935-
about
Sicilian perspectives. M. Peppiatt. il por *Architectural Digest* 46:254+ Mr '89

GUENTERT, KENNETH
30 ways to decode liturgy lingo. il *U.S. Catholic* 54:20-4 Jl '89
The Bible is more offensive than you think. *U.S. Catholic* 54:18-20 S '89

GUÉRARD, MICHEL, 1933-
about
Du créateur de la cuisine minceur . . . à la châtelaine d'un restaurant célèbre. F. Ferretti. il *Gourmet* 49:42+ Jl '89

GUERLAIN SA
Soul searching [Samsara fragrance] R. Wiest. il *American Health* 8:20 N '89

GUERRE, DEBRA
Best face forward. il pors *Harper's Bazaar* 122:28+ Ag '89

GUERRERO, EPY
about
Baseball scout Epy Guerrero looks for rough diamonds amid hunger and poverty. W. Plummer. il pors *People Weekly* 31:127-8+ Ap 10 '89

GUERRETTE, LINDA
Sporty skis for women. il *Skiing* 42:180-2+ D '89

GUERRIER-TAKADA, CECILIA, AND OTHERS
Specific interactions in RNA enzyme-substrate complexes. bibl f il *Science* 246:1578-84 D 22 '89

GUERRILLA WARFARE MANEUVERS *See* Military maneuvers

GUERRILLAS
Angola
See also
National Union for the Total Independence of Angola
SWAPO
Burma
Life in the hills. W. Law-Yone. il *The Atlantic* 264:24+ D '89
Cambodia
See also
Khmer Rouge

GUERRILLAS—*cont.*

El Salvador

See also

Farabundo Martí National Liberation Front

Latin America

The world of narcoterrorism. D. Brock. il *The American Spectator* 22:24-8 Je '89

Mozambique

See also

Mozambique National Resistance Movement

Peru

See also

Sendero Luminoso (Guerrilla group)

Philippines

See also

New People's Army (Philippines)

Sudan

See also

Sudan People's Liberation Army

Western Sahara

See also

Polisario Front

GUESS?, INC.

A 'blood war' in the jeans trade [Jordache-Guess battle] C. Welles. il *Business Week* p74-5+ N 13 '89

The great jeans war [Guess? vs. Jordache] C. Byron. il *New York* 22:13-14 Jl 24 '89

The IRS follies [IRS embroiled in jeans war between Nakash family of Jordache and Marciano family of Guess?] C. Byron. il *New York* 22:11-12 Ag 7 '89

GUEST, ANN HUTCHINSON

about

Ann Hutchinson Guest goes back to the source: finding Faune. L. Garafola. il pors *Dance Magazine* 63:32-4 O '89

GUEST, CHRISTOPHER

about

The big picture [film] Reviews

American Film il 14:59 S '89. E. Drucker

Film Comment il 25:6-8 S/O '89. G. Smith

The Nation 249:398-9 O 9 '89. S. Klawans

The New Yorker 65:103-4 S 18 '89. T. Rafferty

People Weekly il 32:12+ O 2 '89. R. Novak

GUEST, JOAN

The biggest divorce. il *Christianity Today* 33:30-2 N 17 '89

GUEST, RAY

Road rallies. *Bicycling* 30:76 Jl '89

GUEST HOUSES

All natural [guest house in Seattle and speculative house in Port Blakely designed by J. Cutler] P. M. Sachner. il *Architectural Record* 177:60-7 mid-Ap '89

Hill Country hideaway [Blanco, Tex. 1860s house] E. Wood. il *Southern Living* 24:124-5 My '89

Living the casual life [pool house/guest suite] L. Hallam. il *Southern Living* 24:56-7 Ag '89

GUEST RANCHES *See* Ranches

GUEST ROOMS

Spare-room make-overs: dual-purpose guest rooms that look great. D. L. Caringer and R. E. Dittmer. il *Better Homes and Gardens* 67:79-86+ Mr '89

GUESTS

See also

Entertaining

Guest work: the good (business) guest's guide to being wined and dined. S. Richardson. il *Working Woman* 14:114+ D '89

Respecting house rules [children] L. G. Katz. il *Parents* 64:200 S '89

Anecdotes, facetiae, satire, etc.

For some overbooked social whirlers, sending a stand-in is the next best thing to being there. W. Norwich. il *Vogue* 179:286 Je '89

Let me entertain you [male house guests] F. Prose. il *Gentlemen's Quarterly* 59:231+ Mr '89

Power sponging. G. Schwartz. il *New York* 22:20 Ag 28 '89

GUETTA, BERNARD

'The need to rethink Leninism' [interview with V. Medvedev] por *World Press Review* 36:23 S '89

GUETZLOE, ELEANOR

School prevention of suicide, violence, and abuse. *The Education Digest* 54:46-9 F '89

GUFFEY, MARY ELLEN

The 25 best cut roses. il *Flower and Garden* 33:26-8+ My/Je '89

GUGGENHEIM (SOLOMON R.) MUSEUM *See* Solomon R. Guggenheim Museum

GUGLIOTTA, GUY F.

Seize the time against cocaine kings. il *U.S. News & World Report* 107:21 S 11 '89

GUICHERD, CATHERINE

Another way to peace. il *Commonweal* 116:704-6 D 15 '89

GUIDANCE, VOCATIONAL *See* Vocational guidance

GUIDANCE COUNSELING, EDUCATIONAL *See* Educational counseling

GUIDANCE COUNSELORS, EDUCATIONAL *See* Educational counselors

GUIDE DOGS

Dash leads the way. A. Potok. il pors *Reader's Digest* 134:44-8 Ja '89

Designer dogs [work of C. Kaman] M. Alpert. il por *Fortune* 119:137 Mr 13 '89

GUIDEBOOKS

See also

Booksellers and bookselling—Guidebooks

Publishers and publishing—Guidebooks

Buying travel books and atlases [Gallup survey] L. A. Wood. il *Publishers Weekly* 235:64 Ja 20 '89

New guides to western camping. *Sunset (Central West edition)* 183:30 O '89

Selling travelers on guidebooks [reader complaints] T. Brosnahan. por *Publishers Weekly* 235:95 Ja 20 '89

Anecdotes, facetiae, satire, etc.

A banana republic Baedeker. W. McGurn. il *The American Spectator* 22:16-18 Mr '89

Bibliography

Exotic shopping & a guide to finding the best book. D. Puccio. il *Travel Holiday* 171:94 My '89

A round-up of 1989 travel books. J. Crichton. il *Publishers Weekly* 235:66-8+ Ja 20 '89

GUIDED MISSILE BASES

Air Force chooses basing sites for rail-mobile MX missile. map *Aviation Week & Space Technology* 131:23 D 4 '89

Army aviation upgrade linked to strategic missile debate [Midgetman vs. MX rail-garrison concept] B. M. Greeley, Jr. il *Aviation Week & Space Technology* 130:67 Ap 24 '89

Breaking the lock on mobile missiles [debate over location of MX missiles] *U.S. News & World Report* 106:13-14 Ap 3 '89

Can mobile missiles give Bush a shot in the arms talks? D. Griffiths and others. il *Business Week* p61 F 27 '89

Cheney endorses MX rail garrison, calls for few cuts in USAF budget. J. D. Morrocco. *Aviation Week & Space Technology* 130:22-3 Ap 24 '89

Defense leaders line up with Scowcroft on Midgetman and carry-hard basing. P. Mann. il *Aviation Week & Space Technology* 130:23-4 F 6 '89

House cuts funding for modernizing USAF's ICBM launch control centers. D. F. Bond. *Aviation Week & Space Technology* 131:69+ Ag 21 '89

Midgetman & Co. D. Housman. *National Review* 41:33-4 My 5 '89

Missile madness [MX and Midgetman] R. E. Powaski. il *America* 161:319-20 N 11 '89

Missiles for strategic deterrence [MX, Midgetman, and Trident] S. V. Cole. il *Conservative Digest* 15:12-15 Mr/Ap '89

Triad, schmiad [ICBM vulnerability] B. M. Blechman. *The New Republic* 200:15-17 F 6 '89

GUIDED MISSILE INDUSTRIES

See also

General Dynamics Corp.

Hercules Aerospace Company

McDonnell Douglas Corp.

Raytheon Co.

Williams International

Export-import trade

Israel's deal with the devil? [collaboration with South Africa on missiles] R. Watson. il *Newsweek* 114:52 N 6 '89

Third world missile proliferation emerges as key arms control issue. il *Aviation Week & Space Technology* 131:31 Jl 3 '89

International aspects

See also

Alliance Defense Corporation

Tight budgets, design conflicts undercut NATO weapon projects. J. D. Morrocco. il *Aviation Week & Space Technology* 131:18-19 S 25 '89

U.S. drops out of modular stand-off weapon program. *Aviation Week & Space Technology* 131:25 S 18 '89

Quality control

Pentagon cites Texas Instruments for quality gains in HARM production. il *Aviation Week & Space Technology* 131:79 S 11 '89

France

See also

Matra SA

GUIDED MISSILE SIMULATORS

See also

Threat simulators

GUIDED MISSILES

A choice of arms [modernizing land-based ICBMs] B. Van Voorst. il *Time* 133:16-17 Ap 3 '89

The decision to modernize U.S. intercontinental ballistic missiles. J. M. Deutch. bibl f *Science* 244:1445-50 Je 23 '89

Defending people by defending rockets. R. N. Perle. il *U.S. News & World Report* 106:39+ Je 26 '89

The general's little missile [Midgetman advocate B. Scowcroft] J. D. Isaacs. il *The Bulletin of the Atomic Scientists* 45:3-4 Mr '89

ICBM modernization [discussion of June 23, 1989 article, The decision to modernize U.S. intercontinental ballistic missiles] J. M. Deutch. *Science* 246:192-4 O 13 '89

GUIDED MISSILES—*cont.*

Land-locked [questioning ICBMs] J. Horgan. il *Scientific American* 261:17+ O '89

Midgetman & Co. D. Housman. *National Review* 41:33-4 My 5 '89

Missile madness [MX and Midgetman] R. E. Powaski. il *America* 161:319-20 N 11 '89

Missiles for strategic deterrence [MX, Midgetman, and Trident] S. V. Cole. il *Conservative Digest* 15:12-15 Mr/Ap '89

One MXed-up debate [MX vs. Midgetman] J. D. Isaacs. il *The Bulletin of the Atomic Scientists* 45:3-4 S '89

U.S. missiles on hair trigger? G. E. Marsh. *The Bulletin of the Atomic Scientists* 45:3 My '89

Accidents and explosions

An absence of spin control [Trident II failure] il *Newsweek* 113:8 Ap 3 '89

Data show guidance system was trying to stabilize SICBM. il *Aviation Week & Space Technology* 130:25 My 22 '89

Navy assesses failure of first Trident 2 underwater launch. E. H. Kolcum. il *Aviation Week & Space Technology* 130:18-19 Mr 27 '89

Pentagon: 0, *glasnost*: 1 [Stealth bomber snafus and Trident II explosion] E. Salholz. il *Newsweek* 114:28-9 Ag 28 '89

Probe blames MX failure on fault in stage 1 joint [collapse of missile in silo in June 1988] *Aviation Week & Space Technology* 130:22 F 20 '89

Second Trident 2 test failure points to missile design flaw. J. D. Morrocco. *Aviation Week & Space Technology* 131:26 Ag 21 '89

Control

See also
Inertial guidance systems

House cuts funding for modernizing USAF's ICBM launch control centers. D. F. Bond. *Aviation Week & Space Technology* 131:69+ Ag 21 '89

Costs

Army aviation upgrade linked to strategic missile debate [Midgetman vs. MX rail-garrison concept] B. M. Greeley, Jr. il *Aviation Week & Space Technology* 130:67 Ap 24 '89

Defense leaders line up with Scowcroft on Midgetman and carry-hard basing. P. Mann. il *Aviation Week & Space Technology* 130:23-4 F 6 '89

House appropriation action signals trouble for ATF, advanced cruise missiles. P. A. Gilmartin. *Aviation Week & Space Technology* 131:27-8 Ag 7 '89

Judge grants motions filed by Northrop [lawsuit involving production of inertial measurement unit for MX missile] *Aviation Week & Space Technology* 130:74 Ja 9 '89

The Pentagon's misguided missile [AMRAAM] P. Cary. il *U.S. News & World Report* 106:33-6 My 1 '89

Trident II misfires in Congress. M. Ross. il *The Bulletin of the Atomic Scientists* 45:11-12 D '89

USAF extends SICBM contracts in face of test, budget hurdles. D. F. Bond. *Aviation Week & Space Technology* 130:23-4 Jl 10 '89

Deactivation

Navy shuns credit for cuts [retirement of three types of missiles from nuclear arsenal] M. Flournoy. il *The Bulletin of the Atomic Scientists* 45:3-4 Jl/Ag '89

Environmental aspects

Arms and the environment. il *Newsweek* 114:30 Ag 28 '89

Defenses

See also
Brilliant Pebbles (Defense system)
North American Aerospace Defense Command
Radar defense networks
Railguns
Strategic Defense Initiative

Army to broaden effort to develop extended-range interceptor. P. A. Gilmartin. il *Aviation Week & Space Technology* 131:30 O 16 '89

Cartwright develops missile attack warning for high-speed tactical aircraft. *Aviation Week & Space Technology* 131:93 S 11 '89

Divided over defense. T. Bethell. *The American Spectator* 22:11-13 O '89

More capable IR-guided weapons prompting improved jammers, decoys. il *Aviation Week & Space Technology* 131:50+ S 11 '89

The muddle on missiles. J. Barry. il *Newsweek* 113:42 F 13 '89

Qaddafi goes ballistic [Accidental Launch Protection System] J. Pike. *The New Republic* 200:14-16 Mr 20 '89

Sanders upgrades IR countermeasures, explores techniques for future systems [coverage against infrared guided missiles] il *Aviation Week & Space Technology* 131:118-19+ S 11 '89

Science and scientists for a nuclear-weapon-free world. Y. P. Velikhov. il *Physics Today* 42:32-3+ N '89

Triad, schmiad [ICBM vulnerability] B. M. Blechman. *The New Republic* 200:15-17 F 6 '89

UV sensors for early-warning systems. *High Technology Business* 9:36 N/D '89

Visit to a laser facility at the Soviet ABM test site. F. Von Hippel. il *Physics Today* 42:34-5 N '89

Design

DARPA presses for continuing role in conventional cruise missile program. *Aviation Week & Space Technology* 130:53 Ja 23 '89

U.S. drops out of modular stand-off weapon program. *Aviation Week & Space Technology* 131:25 S 18 '89

Disarmament

See Disarmament; Strategic Arms Limitation Talks; Strategic Arms Reduction Talks

Electronic equipment

Martin pursues development of autonomous cruise missile. E. H. Kolcum. il *Aviation Week & Space Technology* 130:85-6 My 1 '89

Launchers

See Guided missiles—Propulsion systems

Launching from airplanes

Air Force begins captive-carry tests of advanced cruise missile over Canada. il *Aviation Week & Space Technology* 129:26 Mr 6 '89

Alliance Defense Corp. leads MSOW competition [modular stand-off weapons system] *Aviation Week & Space Technology* 130:33 Je 19 '89

AMRAAM unsuccessful in key test launch; Congress cuts USAF missile programs. J. D. Morrocco. il *Aviation Week & Space Technology* 131:24-5 Ag 14 '89

Britain to get airborne INF. M. Flournoy. *The Bulletin of the Atomic Scientists* 45:4 Jl/Ag '89

Development tests of Tacit Rainbow on Navy A-6 set to begin next week. J. D. Morrocco. il *Aviation Week & Space Technology* 131:21 Jl 3 '89

France approves development of Apache stand-off weapon. il *Aviation Week & Space Technology* 131:20 S 25 '89

Hughes official says Air Force rushed complex AMRAAM test [views of Malcolm R. Currie] *Aviation Week & Space Technology* 131:41 O 9 '89

McDonnell Douglas, Navy prepare SLAM missile for airborne launch [stand-off land attack missile] S. W. Kandebo. il *Aviation Week & Space Technology* 130:31 F 27 '89

New AGM-88C HARM guidance scores five out of five [antiradar missile] il *Aviation Week & Space Technology* 131:69-70 S 11 '89

Ottawa approves USAF request to test advanced cruise missile over Canada. *Aviation Week & Space Technology* 130:24 F 6 '89

The Pentagon's misguided missile [AMRAAM] P. Cary. il *U.S. News & World Report* 106:33-6 My 1 '89

Production-model SLAM scores bull's-eye in first test firing [Stand-off Land Attack Missile] il *Aviation Week & Space Technology* 130:30 Jl 10 '89

Raytheon delivers production AMRAAM; competition expected to reduce costs [advanced medium-range air-to-air missile] *Aviation Week & Space Technology* 130:30 F 27 '89

SLAM missile test conducted successfully at Pacific range [Stand-off Land Attack Missile] *Aviation Week & Space Technology* 131:25 Jl 3 '89

Stealth cruise sneaks into Canada. W. M. Arkin. il *The Bulletin of the Atomic Scientists* 45:6-7 My '89

Tacit Rainbow completes fourth successful test flight. J. D. Morrocco. il *Aviation Week & Space Technology* 131:33-4 S 11 '89

U.S. drops out of modular stand-off weapon program. *Aviation Week & Space Technology* 131:25 S 18 '89

U.S. Navy tests fiber-optic data links for air-launched weapons. il *Aviation Week & Space Technology* 130:275+ Je 12 '89

Why the Stealth bomber should really become invisible [comparison with air launched cruise missiles] D. Griffiths. il *Business Week* p21 Ap 17 '89

Launching from helicopters

Army will equip its LHXs with AH-64 mast-mounted system. B. M. Greeley. il *Aviation Week & Space Technology* 130:25 Ap 17 '89

U.S. Army approves initial design phase of Longbow radar system for AH-64. D. F. Bond. il *Aviation Week & Space Technology* 131:27-8 Jl 31 '89

Launching from ships

See also
Iranian air disaster, 1988

Black Sea experiment only a start [joint Soviet-American nuclear sea-launched cruise missile verification exercise aboard Soviet cruiser] T. B. Cochran. il *The Bulletin of the Atomic Scientists* 45:12-16 N '89

Dispelling myths about verification of sea-launched cruise missiles. G. N. Lewis and others. bibl f il *Science* 246:765-70 N 10 '89

Measurements of radiation from a Soviet warhead [cruise missile] S. Fetter and F. Von Hippel. il *Physics Today* 42:45 N '89

Navy says no PALs for us [permissive action link for nuclear weapons] P. D. Zimmerman. bibl f il *The Bulletin of the Atomic Scientists* 45:36-41 N '89

Navy shuns credit for cuts [retirement of three types of missiles from nuclear arsenal] M. Flournoy. il *The Bulletin of the Atomic Scientists* 45:3-4 Jl/Ag '89

Nuclear weapons at sea, 1989 [table] il *The Bulletin of the Atomic Scientists* 45:48 S '89

GUIDED MISSILES—Launching from ships—*cont.*
Start of Tomahawk flights renews controversy in Maine. D. Hughes. il *Aviation Week & Space Technology* 130:28-9 Ja 23 '89
Weapons scientists retool [verifying limits on sea-launched cruise missiles] V. Kiernan. il *Technology Review* 92:10-11 Ag/S '89
What GLCMs? [Soviets protest announced plan to convert ground-launched cruise missiles to sea-launched ones in violation of INF Treaty] M. Flournoy. il *The Bulletin of the Atomic Scientists* 45:5 My '89
When cruise missiles zoom across Maine. T. DePaul. *The Progressive* 53:12-13 Ja '89

Launching from submarines
An absence of spin control [Trident II failure] il *Newsweek* 113:8 Ap 3 '89
Congress presses treaty objectives on Trident submarine program. D. F. Bond. *Aviation Week & Space Technology* 131:25-6 Ag 21 '89
Navy assesses failure of first Trident 2 underwater launch. E. H. Kolcum. il *Aviation Week & Space Technology* 130:18-19 Mr 27 '89
Navy says Dec. 4 underwater launch of Trident 2 D5 was successful. il *Aviation Week & Space Technology* 131:39 D 11 '89
Navy says no PALs for us [permissive action link for nuclear weapons] P. D. Zimmerman. bibl f il *The Bulletin of the Atomic Scientists* 45:36-41 N '89
Pentagon: 0, *glasnost*: 1 [Stealth bomber snafus and Trident II explosion] E. Salholz. il *Newsweek* 114:28-9 Ag 28 '89
Second Trident 2 test failure points to missile design flaw. J. D. Morrocco. *Aviation Week & Space Technology* 131:26 Ag 21 '89
Trident II misfires in Congress. M. Ross. il *The Bulletin of the Atomic Scientists* 45:11-12 D '89
U.S. Navy conducts successful underwater launch of Lockheed Trident 2 missile off Florida coast. E. H. Kolcum. *Aviation Week & Space Technology* 131:19 Ag 7 '89

Launching sites
See Guided missile bases

Nozzles
Second Trident 2 test failure points to missile design flaw. J. D. Morrocco. *Aviation Week & Space Technology* 131:26 Ag 21 '89

Optical equipment
Infrared detector technology [platinum silicide detectors; special section] il *Aviation Week & Space Technology* 130:51+ Mr 27 '89
U.S. Navy tests fiber-optic data links for air-launched weapons. il *Aviation Week & Space Technology* 130:275+ Je 12 '89

Propulsion systems
Allison will apply GM mass-production experience to expendable engine efforts. S. W. Kandebo. il *Aviation Week & Space Technology* 129:63 Mr 6 '89
Pegasus, MX boosters combined for new Defense launch vehicle [Taurus standard small launch vehicle] C. Covault. il *Aviation Week & Space Technology* 131:47+ S 18 '89

Materials
New source expected to prevent shortage of rayon for NASA, defense rockets [North American Rayon Corp.] *Aviation Week & Space Technology* 131:24 N 27 '89

Radar equipment
Development tests of Tacit Rainbow on Navy A-6 set to begin next week. J. D. Morrocco. il *Aviation Week & Space Technology* 131:21 Jl 3 '89
New AGM-88C HARM guidance scores five out of five [antiradar missile] il *Aviation Week & Space Technology* 131:69-70 S 11 '89
R & D work in low observables shifts emphasis from coatings to structures. il *Aviation Week & Space Technology* 131:109+ S 18 '89
Raytheon team selected to develop ground-launched Tacit Rainbow. J. D. Morrocco. il *Aviation Week & Space Technology* 131:24-5 S 18 '89
Tacit Rainbow completes fourth successful test flight. J. D. Morrocco. il *Aviation Week & Space Technology* 131:33-4 S 11 '89

Specifications
International missiles [tables] il *Aviation Week & Space Technology* 130:165-7 Mr 20 '89
Soviet missiles [tables] il *Aviation Week & Space Technology* 130:171-2 Mr 20 '89
U.S. missiles [tables] il *Aviation Week & Space Technology* 130:168-71 Mr 20 '89

Testing
Air Force begins captive-carry tests of advanced cruise missile over Canada. il *Aviation Week & Space Technology* 129:26 Mr 6 '89
AMRAAM unsuccessful in key test launch; Congress cuts USAF missile programs. J. D. Morrocco. il *Aviation Week & Space Technology* 131:24-5 Ag 14 '89
Hughes official says Air Force rushed complex AMRAAM test [views of Malcolm R. Currie] *Aviation Week & Space Technology* 131:41 O 9 '89
LTV to conduct final TACMS developmental test launch [Tactical Missile System] il *Aviation Week & Space Technology* 131:40 D 11 '89

New AGM-88C HARM guidance scores five out of five [antiradar missile] il *Aviation Week & Space Technology* 131:69-70 S 11 '89
Ottawa approves USAF request to test advanced cruise missile over Canada. *Aviation Week & Space Technology* 130:24 F 6 '89
Pentagon tests new Hellfire platforms as contractors analyze improvements [surface launches] D. F. Bond. il *Aviation Week & Space Technology* 131:32-3 N 6 '89
Production-model SLAM scores bull's-eye in first test firing [Stand-off Land Attack Missile] il *Aviation Week & Space Technology* 130:30 Jl 10 '89
SLAM missile test conducted successfully at Pacific range [Stand-off Land Attack Missile] *Aviation Week & Space Technology* 131:25 Jl 3 '89
Start of Tomahawk flights renews controversy in Maine. D. Hughes. il *Aviation Week & Space Technology* 130:28-9 Ja 23 '89
Stealth cruise sneaks into Canada. W. M. Arkin. il *The Bulletin of the Atomic Scientists* 45:6-7 My '89
U.S. Navy conducts successful underwater launch of Lockheed Trident 2 missile off Florida coast. E. H. Kolcum. *Aviation Week & Space Technology* 131:19 Ag 7 '89
When cruise missiles zoom across Maine. T. DePaul. *The Progressive* 53:12-13 Ja '89

Tracking
SDIO begins measuring booster plumes with Delta Star sensors. E. H. Kolcum. il *Aviation Week & Space Technology* 130:26-7 Ap 3 '89
U.S. developing survivable warning/antimissile satellites [Boost Surveillance Tracking System; cover story] T. M. Foley. il *Aviation Week & Space Technology* 130:34-5+ Ja 23 '89

GUIDED MISSILES, BRITISH
Britain to get airborne INF. M. Flournoy. *The Bulletin of the Atomic Scientists* 45:4 Jl/Ag '89

GUIDED MISSILES, CHINESE
Chinese make strong pitch to sell military hardware, launch services [Dubai '89 Airshow] *Aviation Week & Space Technology* 130:19 F 6 '89

GUIDED MISSILES, DEVELOPING COUNTRIES
Qaddafi goes ballistic [Accidental Launch Protection System] J. Pike. *The New Republic* 200:14-16 Mr 20 '89
Third world missile proliferation emerges as key arms control issue. il *Aviation Week & Space Technology* 131:31 Jl 3 '89

GUIDED MISSILES, EUROPEAN
The battle inside NATO. S. Head. bibl f il *The New York Review of Books* 36:41-6 My 18 '89
The case for the third zero. H. Beach. *The Bulletin of the Atomic Scientists* 45:14-15 D '89

GUIDED MISSILES, FRENCH
France approves development of Apache stand-off weapon. il *Aviation Week & Space Technology* 131:20 S 25 '89
Matra delivers Mistral missiles to French forces. il *Aviation Week & Space Technology* 130:107 F 20 '89

Photographs and photography
A peek at the French missile complex. W. A. Kennedy and M. G. Marshall. il *The Bulletin of the Atomic Scientists* 45:20-3 S '89

GUIDED MISSILES, GERMAN
Can NATO survive détente? R. Mauthner. *World Press Review* 36:22-3 F '89
Europe's short-range missiles nail their first victim [H. D. Genscher] J. Templeman and G. E. Schares. il por *Business Week* p50 Je 12 '89
Germany and the alliance [short range nuclear missiles] il *World Press Review* 36:6 Je '89
Kohl rekindles NATO dispute over upgrading Lance missile. K. F. Mordoff. *Aviation Week & Space Technology* 130:21-2 F 20 '89
Moving on double tracks: deterrence and détente. T. Garton Ash. il *World Press Review* 36:28-9 My '89
U.S. senators threaten troop cutback if West Germany blocks Lance upgrade [with editorial comment] P. A. Gilmartin. *Aviation Week & Space Technology* 130:7, 29 My 8 '89
The war inside NATO [U.S.-German conflict over proposed introduction of new nuclear missiles] D. Johnstone. il *The Progressive* 53:16-18 Ap '89
Will NATO settle for Kohl cuts? T. Risse-Kappen. il *The Bulletin of the Atomic Scientists* 45:9-12 Je '89

GUIDED MISSILES, INDIAN (EAST INDIAN)
India's missiles—with a little help from our friends. G. Milhollin. bibl f il *The Bulletin of the Atomic Scientists* 45:31-5 N '89

GUIDED MISSILES, ISRAELI
Israel's deal with the devil? [collaboration with South Africa on missiles] R. Watson. il *Newsweek* 114:52 N 6 '89

GUIDED MISSILES, ITALIAN
Selenia developing new version of Aspide multirole missile. J. M. Lenorovitz. il *Aviation Week & Space Technology* 131:51 D 4 '89

GUIDED MISSILES, MIDDLE EASTERN
An equality of terror [missiles with chemical warheads] E. Marcuse. il *World Press Review* 36:17-18 Mr '89

GUIDED MISSILES, NORWEGIAN
Norway developing ground-based AMRAAM system for air defense [advanced medium-range air-to-air missile] W. B. Scott. il *Aviation Week & Space Technology* 130:58-9 Ja 23 '89

GUIDED MISSILES, RUSSIAN
Black Sea experiment only a start [joint Soviet-American nuclear sea-launched cruise missile verification exercise aboard Soviet cruiser] T. B. Cochran. il *The Bulletin of the Atomic Scientists* 45:12-16 N '89
Defense Dept. assessment says Soviets deploying improved ICBMs [1989 edition of Soviet military power] D. F. Bond. il *Aviation Week & Space Technology* 131:24-5 O 2 '89
Measurements of radiation from a Soviet warhead [cruise missile] S. Fetter and F. Von Hippel. il *Physics Today* 42:45 N '89
NATO links arms pact to Soviet missile cuts. il *Aviation Week & Space Technology* 130:21 Je 5 '89
Science and scientists for a nuclear-weapon-free world. Y. P. Velikhov. il *Physics Today* 42:32-3+ N '89
Soviet missiles [tables] il *Aviation Week & Space Technology* 130:171-2 Mr 20 '89
Visit to a laser facility at the Soviet ABM test site. F. Von Hippel. il *Physics Today* 42:34-5 N '89

GUIDED MISSILES, SOUTH AFRICAN
Israel's deal with the devil? [collaboration with South Africa on missiles] R. Watson. il *Newsweek* 114:52 N 6 '89

GUIDED PROJECTILES *See* Projectiles
GUIDES
See also
Far North Recreation (Firm)
Table Mountain Outfitters
The care and feeding of fishing guides. E. L. Rogers. il *Outdoor Life* 183:82-3+ Mr '89
Ethical aspects
Outfitters: the good, the bad and the ugly. M. Jones. il *Outdoor Life* 183:78-9+ Ja '89
GUIDES, SAW *See* Saws and sawing—Equipment
GUIDING LIGHT [television program] *See* Television program reviews—Single works
GUIDING OF TELESCOPES *See* Telescopes—Control
GUIDRY, JACQUELINE M.
If I had a hammer. il *Parents* 64:202+ Mr '89
GUILBERT, JAMEE BECKER
about
An American in Paris. J. McCallum. il pors *Sports Illustrated* 70 Special Issue:89-93 F '89
GUILDAMERICA BOOKS
Doubleday introduces new 20-volume Shakespeare series. J. P. Frank. il *Publishers Weekly* 235:54-6 My 5 '89
GUILFOYLE, TOM
(jt. auth) *See* McClure, Bruce A., and Guilfoyle, Tom
GUILLAIN-BARRÉ SYNDROME
"I was paralyzed! What was wrong with me?" [actor A. Griffith] J. Buck. il pors *Redbook* 173:84+ My '89
Woman in bed number 10 [condensation] S. Baier and Z. Schomaker. il *Reader's Digest* 134:199-205+ F '89
GUILLAUME, ROBERT
about
'The Robert Guillaume show' features interracial romance and a nosey dad whose humor adds sparkle to new TV series [cover story] A. Collier. il pors *Jet* 76:58-60 Ap 24 '89
GUILLEM, SYLVIE
about
Dancing:
Grand pas classique with S. Guillem, The spirit of fugue, and Apollo. A. Croce. *The New Yorker* 64:63-4 Ja 16 '89
In step. R. Christiansen. il pors *Vogue* 179:166-71 Jl '89
GUILLÉN LANDRIÁN, NICOLÁS
about
Art, intrigue and human rights. E. Shorris. il *The Nation* 249:14-18 Jl 3 '89
GUILLERMOPRIETO, ALMA, 1949-
Letter from Bogotá. *The New Yorker* 65:112-20+ O 16 '89
GUILLOTINE
Dr. Guillotin's killing machine. il *Maclean's* 102:34 My 15 '89
The heirs of Madame Guillotine [P. Brunet, descendant of executioner C.-H. Sanson] D. Lawday. il por *U.S. News & World Report* 107:46-8 Jl 17 '89
Patrick Brunet, whose ancestor guillotined Louis XVI, swears he's no chip off the old block [executioner C.-H. Sanson] T. Allis. il pors *People Weekly* 31:128+ Je 5 '89
GUILT
Free yourself! [working mother's guilt] A. Van der Meer. *Redbook* 172:93+ Mr '89
If you know he's wrong, are you right to make him feel guilty? C. L. Mithers. *Glamour* 87:170 Ja '89
On leaving [going on assignment and leaving children at home] D. Sobel. il *Ladies' Home Journal* 106:54+ Je '89
Sex-shy: why we're still squeamish after all these years. M. Sandmaier. il *Mademoiselle* 95:155+ Ap '89
Working mother overload. B. J. Berg. *Redbook* 172:92-3+ Mr '89

GUIMOND, RICHARD
about
Change agents. D. Moreau. il por *Changing Times* 43:104 F '89
GUINDON, MYRA
Activists unite! il *Ad Astra* 1:38-40 O '89
GUINEA WORM DISEASE
Towards the end of Guineaworm disease. P. Stroot. il *World Health* p30-1 N '89
GUINNESS, ALEC
about
Man of a thousand faces. J. R. Taylor. il pors *American Film* 14:52-6 Ap '89
GUINNESS PEAT AVIATION
See also
GPA Group, Ltd.
GUINNESS PLC
The crowned heads of Britain in a can [new beer can for Guinness stout works like a keg tap] il *U.S. News & World Report* 107:19 Ag 21 '89
Ernest Saunders markets his innocence [former chairman] M. Maremont. il por *Business Week* p92-3 Ag 14 '89
The House of Guinness. J. Marcom, Jr. il por *Forbes* 143:85+ Je 12 '89
GUINNESS STOUT *See* Stout (Beverage)
GUINZBURG, THOMAS H.
about
The great white hope. M. Webb. il pors *New York* 22:50-3 Ja 16 '89
GUIRLINGER, AUSTIN
about
Cardinal sin. E. Schmuckler. il por *Forbes* 143:14 Ap 17 '89
Cardinal's shaky foundation. S. Phillips. *Business Week* p42+ Mr 20 '89
GUIS *See* Graphical user interfaces
GUITAR MUSIC
See also
Compact discs—Guitar music
Phonograph records—Guitar music
Bill Frisell's solo on "Evidence"—a guitar transcription. J. Dennison. il *Down Beat* 56:56-7 My '89
John Scofield's solo on "Best western"—Phrygian voicings. R. Peckham. il *Down Beat* 56:66-7 D '89
Martinique's 8th World Crossroads of the Guitar. D. Gordon. il *Down Beat* 56:11-12 My '89
Strings and bridges. J. Ephland. il *Down Beat* 56:6 My '89
GUITAR PICKS
Collectors and collecting
Pick men [Chuck Collum's and Rickey Anderson's collections of guitar picks from heavy metal bands] il *The New Yorker* 64:26-7 Ja 30 '89
GUITAR SLIM, JR.
about
Working the Big Easy's hard edge, Guitar Slim Jr. may turn his earthy blues into a Grammy. S. Dougherty. il pors *People Weekly* 31:108-10 F 20 '89
GUITARISTS
See also
Abercrombie, John
Atkins, Chet, 1924-
Baty, Charlie
Beck, Jeff
Beck, Joe
Bertoncini, Gene
Carlton, Larry
Case, Peter
Cray, Robert
Falú, Eduardo
Frisell, Bill
Gale, Eric
Gatton, Danny
Guitar Slim, Jr.
Haque, Fareed
Healey, Jeff
Kaiser, Henry
Lagrene, Bireli
Metheny, Pat
Pizzarelli, Bucky, 1926-
Reid, Vernon
Remler, Emily
Ribot, Marc
Ritenour, Lee
Santana, Carlos, 1947-
Satriani, Joe
Scofield, John
Stuermer, Daryl
Vaughan, Stevie Ray
Walker, Joe Louis
Girls play guitar. A. Romano. il *Seventeen* 48:146-7+ My '89
GUITARISTS, HANDICAPPED
Bluesman Jeff Healey, the blind gonzo guitarist who puts the musical punch in Road house. il por *People Weekly* 31:85 Je 12 '89

GULAGS *See* Concentration camps—Soviet Union
GULF & WESTERN, INC.
Gulf & Western is ready to go off its diet. D. Lieberman. il *Business Week* p31 Ap 24 '89
Paramount's Card Trek [special credit card issued as part of promotional campaign for Star trek] N. Koch. il *Channels (New York, N.Y.: 1986)* 9:52 F '89
GULF & WESTERN INDUSTRIES, INC.
See also
Gulf & Western, Inc.
GULF INTRACOASTAL WATERWAY *See* Intracoastal Waterway
GULF OF AQABA
Duel in the sand [Tri-Country Offshore Powerboat Race] P. Whittell. il *Motor Boating & Sailing* 163:74-7+ Ap '89
GULF OF MAINE
White-water bounty [coccolithophore bloom] C. Mlot. il *BioScience* 39:222-4 Ap '89
GULF OF MEXICO
See also
Petroleum—Gulf of Mexico
Evidence for sediment eruption on deep sea floor, Gulf of Mexico. D. B. Prior and others. bibl f il *Science* 243:517-19 Ja 27 '89
Hole in ocean floor [sediment eruption in the Gulf of Mexico; research by David B. Prior] *Science News* 135:77 F 4 '89

Shellfish fisheries
See Shellfish fisheries
GULF OF SIDRA INCIDENT, 1986 *See* Libyan-American conflict, 1986
GULF POWER CO.
Fatal subtraction [suspicious crash that killed executive J. Horton] J. Carney. il por *Time* 133:87 My 22 '89
GULF STATES UTILITIES CO.
Fast answers make for timely decisions [use of computers by E. L. Draper] C. O'Malley. il por *Personal Computing* 13:83 Ap '89
GULF STREAM
The blue god. W. H. MacLeish. bibl (p170) il map *Smithsonian* 19:44-56+ F '89
Gulf Stream. H. Middleton. il *Southern Living* 24:28+ Jl '89
Painting a portrait of the Stream from miles above—and below. W. H. MacLeish. il *Smithsonian* 19:42-52+ Mr '89
GULFSTREAM AEROSPACE CORP.
Commander lawsuit settled. il *Flying* 116:10 Ag '89
Gulfstream/Soviet SST bizjet. il *Flying* 116:17 S '89
Gulfstream, Soviets expect to select basic supersonic business jet design in November. *Aviation Week & Space Technology* 131:46 O 16 '89
Jaffe Group to replace Gulfstream as partner in SA-30 development. E. H. Phillips. il *Aviation Week & Space Technology* 131:37 S 11 '89
Paulson to build Swearingen jet. il *Flying* 116:14 Ja '89
Soviet/Gulfstream supersonic aircraft hinges on bilateral certification agreement. C. Fotos. *Aviation Week & Space Technology* 131:110-11 D 18-25 '89
The Soviets want to help build a capitalist status symbol [Gulfstream supersonic corporate jet] C. Hawkins and R. Brady. il *Business Week* p42 O 9 '89
Sukhoi, Gulfstream to study supersonic business jet. D. A. Brown. il *Aviation Week & Space Technology* 130:54+ Je 26 '89
U.S.-Soviet team plans to fly supersonic business jet by 1993. E. H. Kolcum. il *Aviation Week & Space Technology* 131:22-4 S 25 '89
GULIY, VITALY
about
Where *perestroika* makes strange bedfellows. J. Trimble. il pors map *U.S. News & World Report* 107:77-8+ Ag 28-S 4 '89
GULLETTE, MARGARET MORGANROTH
Midlife exhilaration. il *The New York Times Magazine* p18+ Ja 29 '89
GULLS
The bad and the beautiful: gulls remind us of us. D. D. Jackson. bibl (p228-9) il *Smithsonian* 20:72-8+ O '89
Gulls: a sea guide. S. J. Kirkpatrick. bibl il *Sea Frontiers* 35:146-51 My/Je '89
New tensions for a rough crowd [nesting space battles for terns and gulls on Rasa Island, Mexico] E. Velarde. il *International Wildlife* 19:20-4 N/D '89
GUM CHEWING *See* Chewing gum
GUMBEL, BRYANT, 1948-
about
A case of morning sickness. J. Adler. il por *Newsweek* 113:61 Mr 13 '89
Gumbel's bumble redux [memo makeover] B. J. Mandel and J. Yellen. il *Working Woman* 14:136-8 S '89
Willard Scott is blowing his top. A. Richman. il pors *People Weekly* 31:44-9 Mr 20 '89
Anecdotes, facetiae, satire, etc.
Life of Bryant. D. Blum. il por *New York* 22:28 Mr 20 '89

GUMPERT, DAVID E., AND DAVIS, DANA
Turning your hobby into a business [cover story; special section] il *New Choices for the Best Years* 29:47-53 O '89
GUMS

Diseases
See also
Dental plaque
Juvenile periodontitis: no laughing matter. L. S. Senz. il *The Saturday Evening Post* 261:76 My/Je '89
Periodontal disease: nothing to smile about. P. A. Feuerstein. il *Current Health 2* 15:28-9 Ja '89
What makes a show-off smile? A. Ranard. il *Health (New York, N.Y.)* 21:50-3+ Ja '89
Causes
Periodontal disease-s-s-s! D. Reese. il *American Health* 8:44 S '89
Where the bad bugs are [role of bacteria in gum disease and tooth decay] C. Sears. il *American Health* 8:50 Ap '89
Diagnosis
Early detection of gum disease [use of filter paper] *Prevention (Emmaus, Pa.)* 41:20-1 Ag '89
Therapy
Better than brushing? [Keyes method] il *Prevention (Emmaus, Pa.)* 41:22 S '89
Boning up on gums. D. Reese and C. Sears. il *American Health* 8:43 S '89
GUMS AND RESINS
See also
Frankincense
Myrrh
Turpentine
GUMS AND RESINS, FOSSIL
See also
Amber
GUN CABINETS *See* Cabinets (Furniture)
GUN CASES
Hard cases for hard travel. D. E. Petzal. il *Field & Stream* 93:50+ Ja '89
GUN CLUBS *See* Firearms—Clubs and societies
GUN CONTROL AND THE PRESS *See* Press and gun control
GUN CONTROL LEGISLATION *See* Firearms—Laws and regulations
GUN DOWN (TERM)
Gun that rumor down. W. Safire. il *The New York Times Magazine* p18+ Ap 9 '89
GUN SIGHTS *See* Firearms—Sights
GUNDAREV, VICTOR
about
K.G.B. defector Gundarev: it's cold coming out [cover story] D. Wise. il *The New York Times Magazine* p36-9+ S 17 '89
GUNMAKERS *See* Firearms industry
GUNN, BILL, D. 1989
about
The forbidden city [drama] Reviews
New York 22:80-1 Ap 17 '89. J. Simon
The New Yorker 65:111-12 Ap 17 '89. M. Kramer
GUNN, E. P.
It's time to put an end to fraternity hazing. *Seventeen* 48:200 Mr '89
GUNNERA
Living on the edge [botanist M. Doyle's studies of gunnera in Alakai Swamp, Kauai] J. Nielsen. il pors *National Wildlife* 27:20-3 O/N '89
GUNNERSON, RONNIE
The second time around. il *Video* 13:68-70 O '89
GUNNISON NATIONAL FOREST (COLO.)
Slumgullion Slide, Colorado. R. H. Mohlenbrock. il map *Natural History* p34-7 Ap '89
GUNRUNNING *See* Smuggling
GUNS, ANTI-AIRCRAFT
Competing GE, FMC armored turrets offer different weapons configurations [Marine Corps Light Armored Vehicle-Air Defense system] D. F. Bond. il *Aviation Week & Space Technology* 131:45+ S 25 '89
GUNS, TOY *See* Toy guns
GUNS (SMALL ARMS) *See* Firearms; Pistols; Revolvers; Rifles; Shotguns
GUNS IN ART

Exhibitions
Cop art [T. Brennan creates sculpture from confiscated guns in Kenmore, Wash.] B. Weber. il *The New York Times Magazine* p94 Ap 30 '89
GUNS N' ROSES (MUSICAL GROUP)
Bringing it all back home. J. Queenan. il *Forbes* 144:152-3 O 2 '89
Guns n' Roses: big noise from L.A. boys! il *Teen* 33:41 Ja '89
The Rolling stone interview: Axl Rose [cover story] D. James. il pors *Rolling Stone* p42-4+ Ag 10 '89
GUNSHOT WOUNDS
How serious are bullet wounds? [views of Steven Barrett] il *USA Today (Periodical)* 117:3-4 Ap '89
GUNSMITHS AND GUNSMITHING
More than a craft. G. Hill. il *Field & Stream* 94:10 N '89

GUNSMOKE [television program] See Television program reviews—Single works
GUNST, KATHY, AND RUDOLPH, JOHN
Record the sounds of childhood. il *Parents* 64:73-6 D '89
GUNST, LAURIE
Johnny-too-bad and the sufferers [cover story] *The Nation* 249:549+ N 13 '89
GUO, PAUL H.
Promoting a healthy environment. il *World Health* p10-11 N '89
GUPTA, VISWA JIT
about
The case of the "misplaced" fossils. R. Lewin. il por *Science* 244:277-9 Ap 21 '89
Cooking the paleontological books? W. F. Allman. il *U.S. News & World Report* 106:61 My 8 '89
GURALNICK, MARGOT
China's polished art. il *House & Garden* 161:78+ My '89
Colorado cabin fever. il *House & Garden* 161:158-67+ D '89
Feast of beasts. il *House & Garden* 161:98+ S '89
Fine lines. il *House & Garden* 161:50+ Je '89
Local color. il *House & Garden* 161:58+ F '89
Paper chase. il *House & Garden* 161:62+ Mr '89
Sleepers awake. il *House & Garden* 161:46-7 Ja '89
Timely obsessions. il pors *House & Garden* 161:94+ S '89
GURAVICH, DAN
about
Winging it. D. Matthews. il *Popular Photography* 96:42-7 Je '89
GUREWITSCH, MATTHEW
How true it Rings. il *Opera News* 53:12-15 Ap 1 '89
A resounding Ring. il *Harper's Bazaar* 122:58 Je '89
The trill of it all. il *Harper's Bazaar* 122:22+ Ja '89
GURGANUS, ALLAN
Reassurance [story] il *Harper's* 279:57-61 N '89
Storied objects. il pors *House & Garden* 161:46+ My '89
Under this very mall [fiction] *Harper's* 278:42-4+ Ap '89
about
He's 42, she's 99—together they make the South rise again. S. K. Reed. il pors *People Weekly* 32:68-70 S 18 '89
Mouth of the South. T. Prince. il por *New York* 22:110-14+ Ag 21 '89
PW interviews. S. Staggs. por *Publishers Weekly* 236:438-9 Ag 11 '89
GURIEVA, DIANA
about
Friend of the family. C. S. Smith. il por *New York* 22:26 Ap 17 '89
GURIN, JOEL, 1953-
Leaner, not lighter. il *Psychology Today* 23:32-4 Je '89
(jt. auth) See Yankelovich, Daniel, and Gurin, Joel, 1953-
GURNETT, D. A., AND OTHERS
First plasma wave observations at Neptune. bibl f il *Science* 246:1494-8 D 15 '89
GURNEY, A. R. (ALBERT RAMSDELL), 1930-
Conversation piece. por *Newsweek* 113:10-11 Je 26 '89
about
The cocktail hour [drama] Reviews
America 160:378 Ap 22 '89. G. G. Seibert
Commonweal 116:280 My 5 '89. G. C. Weales
Laughter, tears and the perfect martini. A. Witchel. il pors *The New York Times Magazine* p42-3+ N 12 '89
Love letters [drama] Reviews
New York il 22:64 S 18 '89. J. Simon
Time il 134:78 S 11 '89. W. A. Henry
Playwright A.R. Gurney Jr.'s Cocktail hour leaves his genteel family shaken, not stirred. P. Freeman. il pors *People Weekly* 31:103-4 Ja 23 '89
GURNEY, ALBERT RAMSDELL See Gurney, A. R. (Albert Ramsdell), 1930-
GURNEY, DAN
about
Birth of an Eagle. L. Griffin. il pors *Car and Driver* 34:175+ My '89
GURU MA See Prophet, Elizabeth Clare
GURUGÉ, ANANDA W. P.
The Mahāvamsa, Sri Lanka's non-stop epic. il *The Unesco Courier* 42:40-3 S '89
GUS AND AL [drama] See Innaurato, Albert
GUSH EMUNIM
The settlers [West Bank] R. I. Friedman. bibl f il *The New York Review of Books* 36:49-56 Je 15 '89
The view from the West Bank. E. Salpeter. il *The New Leader* 72:5-6 Je 12-26 '89
West Bank story [discussion of June 15, 1989 article, The settlers] R. I. Friedman. *The New York Review of Books* 36:59 N 23 '89
GUSLER, WALLACE B.
The tea tables of eastern Virginia. bibl f il *Antiques* 135:1238-57 My '89
GUST, DEVENS, AND MOORE, THOMAS ANDREW
Mimicking photosynthesis. bibl f il *Science* 244:35-41 Ap 7 '89

GUSTAF XVI CARL, KING OF SWEDEN, 1946-
about
A king in Minnesota. G. K. Brushaber. il *Christianity Today* 33:11 Ag 18 '89
GUSTAFSON, ELEANOR H.
Museum accessions. See occasional issues of Antiques
GUSTAITIS, JOSEPH
George Washington's false teeth. il *American History Illustrated* 23:22-3 F '89
The jukebox: America's music machine [cover story] bibl il *American History Illustrated* 24:44-9 N/D '89
A presidential gallery. il *American History Illustrated* 24:20-33 Ap '89
Samuel Slater: father of the American Industrial Revolution. por *American History Illustrated* 24:32-3 My '89
Wernher Von Braun: from Peenemünde to Cape Canaveral. il por *American History Illustrated* 24:30-1 Summ '89
GUSTAITIS, RASA
Infertility hype. il *Glamour* 87:76+ Mr '89
GUSTE, ROY F.
Summer brunch New Orleans style. il *New Choices for the Best Years* 29:64-7 Jl '89
GUSTKE, PATRICIA
Zoo babies. il *Good Housekeeping* 208:60 F '89
GUSTON, PHILIP, 1913-1980
about
An act of salvation. P. Brach. il *Art in America* 77:130-5 Ja '89
GUTFREUND, JOHN
about
Is John Gutfreund dreaming an impossible dream? J. H. Dobrzynski. il por *Business Week* p98-9+ F 27 '89
GUTH, ALAN H.
about
Wormholes in the heavens. M. D. Lemonick. il *Time* 133:55 Ja 16 '89
GUTHRIE, A. B. (ALFRED BERTRAM), 1901-
My West. il por *The Mother Earth News* 118:48-53 Jl/Ag '89
GUTHRIE, ALFRED BERTRAM See Guthrie, A. B. (Alfred Bertram), 1901-
GUTHRIE, ARLO, 1947-
Woodstock remembered: the artists. il pors *Rolling Stone* p88 Ag 24 '89
GUTHRIE, JAMES W.
Why principals should first be teachers. *The Education Digest* 54:13-15 Mr '89
GUTHRIE, JAMES W., AND CLIFFORD, GERALDINE JONÇICH
A brief for professional education. bibl f il *Phi Delta Kappan* 70:380-5 Ja '89
GUTHRIE, MARGARET E.
Dessert warfare. il *The Progressive* 53:50 Ja '89
A Room of One's Own finds a niche of its own. il *Publishers Weekly* 236:66-8 Ag 4 '89
GUTHRIE, WOODY, 1912-1967
about
Library of Congress recordings and Dust Bowl ballads. A. DeCurtis. pors *Rolling Stone* p87-8 My 4 '89
Woody Guthrie. J. Nesin. il por *High Fidelity (New York, N.Y.)* 39:77-8 Ap '89
Woody Guthrie's enduring vision. J. Walljasper. *Utne Reader* p21 Mr/Ap '89
GUTIERREZ, F. JERRY
about
Her eyes see all, her face reveals nothing: Anne Droid is the shoplifter's nemesis. il por *People Weekly* 32:97 O 23 '89
GUTS (GRAND UNIFICATION THEORIES) See Field theory (Physics)
GUTS & GLORY: THE RISE AND FALL OF OLIVER NORTH [television program] See Television program reviews—Single works
GUY, DAVID
A men's group story. il *Utne Reader* p56-7 N/D '89
GUY, JASMINE
about
The bad Guy finishes first. B. Goodwin. il pors *TV Guide* 37:28-31 Ja 21-27 '89
Jasmine Guy is blooming. B. Borns. por *Mademoiselle* 95:73 D '89
Jasmine Guy says making love to Eddie Murphy in 'Harlem nights' is A 'different world' [cover story] R. E. Johnson. il pors *Jet* 77:60-2 D 18 '89
GUY, RAY, 1939-
'A stupefying wrench'. il *Maclean's* 102:22 Ap 3 '89
GUY, RINA, AND OTHERS
Antigen-specific helper function of cell-free T cell products bearing TCR $V_\beta 8$ determinants. bibl f il *Science* 244:1477-80 Je 23 '89
GUY, SHERRY
Palm Beach [special section] il *Horizon (Tuscaloosa, Ala.)* 32:17-30+ Ja/F '89
GUY (MUSICAL GROUP)
Security manager for Guy dead following dispute with New Edition's crew member [murder of A. Bee in Pittsburgh] il *Jet* 76:18 Jl 24 '89

GUY (MUSICAL GROUP)—cont.

Tour rivalry ends in murder: death follows fight between New Edition and Guy. M. Goldberg. *Rolling Stone* p28 Ag 24 '89

GUYANA

See also

Mount Roraima

GUYER, RUTH LEVY, AND KOSHLAND, DANIEL E., JR.

The molecule of the year. il *Science* 246:1543-6 D 22 '89

GUYOT, LAWRENCE

A veteran of Mississippi's 'Freedom Summer' remembers the cause—and the danger; ed. by Jane Sugden. il pors *People Weekly* 32:61-2+ S 18 '89

GUYTON, TYREE

about

Junk magic. S. Yolles. il *Art News* 88:27 O '89

GUZELIMIAN, ARA

Knight of bel canto. il pors *Opera News* 54:10-13 Jl '89

GWICH'IN INDIANS

Beating the drum for caribou [Gwich'in people bordering Arctic National Wildlife Refuge oppose oil development] M. Peale. il *Sierra* 74:32+ My/Je '89

Shadow over an ancient land [T. Gilbert, member of Gwich'in tribe opposing oil development in Alaska] S. K. Reed. il pors *People Weekly* 32:48-53 S 18 '89

GWYN, RICHARD J., 1934-

The spark for a new Mediterranean miracle. il *World Press Review* 36:22-4 Mr '89

GWYNN, CHRIS

about

Gwynn, the Dodger. D. Knobler. il por *Sport (New York, N.Y.)* 80:26 Ag '89

GWYNN, TONY

about

Pssst . . . . heard about Tony Gwynn? [with editorial comment by Kelly Garrett] D. Knobler. il pors *Sport (New York, N.Y.)* 80:3, 22-4+ Ag '89

Way above average. B. Newman. il pors *Sports Illustrated* 71:24-6+ S 25 '89

GYIMAH-BOADI, E.

(jt. auth) See Rothchild, Donald S., and Gyimah-Boadi, E.

GYM CLASSES *See* Physical education and training

GYMNASIUMS

See also

Home gymnasiums

Mind gyms

Now that the health-club singles scene is passé, reports Lia Ilgen, women are beginning to rediscover the benefits of women-only gyms. L. Ilgen. *Vogue* 179:238 O '89

Where the pros train [New York City] M. Bloom. il *New York* 22:48-57 S 18 '89

GYMNASTICS

See also

Rhythmic gymnastics

A dandy Brandy [B. Johnson wins U.S. Gymnastics Championships] J. E. Vader. il pors *Sports Illustrated* 71:24+ Jl 17 '89

Innerview [interview with B. Johnson] por *Women's Sports & Fitness* 11:59 O '89

Leap to the West [Romanian gymnast N. Comaneci] W. O. Johnson and A. Verschoth. il pors *Sports Illustrated* 71:40-1 D 11 '89

Return of the pixies [O. Korbut and M. L. Retton] L. Montville. il pors *Sports Illustrated* 71:34-6+ N 27 '89

GYNECOLOGY

See also

Reproductive organs—Surgery

Top doctors answer your most intimate questions. B. Weinhouse. *Ladies' Home Journal* 106:92+ Je '89

GYORFI, ROBERTA

about

A new year, a new life, a new love. D. Gage. il pors *Good Housekeeping* 208:95+ Ja '89

GYOTAKU (FISH PRINTS) *See* Fish in art

GYPSUM WALLBOARD *See* Wallboard

GYPSY [musical] *See* Musicals, revues, etc.—Reviews—Single works

GYPSY MOTHS

Control

The moth killers [Entomophaga fungus] il *Discover* 10:8 N '89

Sexual behavior

See Sexual behavior—Insects

GYPSY MUSIC

See also

Phonograph records—Gypsy music

GYROPLANES *See* Autogiros

GYROSCOPES

Fiberoptic gyros promise new inertial guidance. il *Popular Mechanics* 166:15 Je '89

Firms research fiber-optic gyros as successors to ring-laser systems. P. J. Klass. il *Aviation Week & Space Technology* 130:79+ F 13 '89

GYROSCOPIC EQUIPMENT

See also

Inertial guidance systems

H

H-2 LOCUS *See* Locus (Genes)

H.B. FULLER COMPANY

Hitting the buzz saw. il *Forbes* 143:104 Ja 9 '89

H-BOMBS *See* Hydrogen bombs

H. H. ROBERTSON CO.

Hoist by their own greenmail [Belzberg takeover] K. Hannon. il *Forbes* 143:156 My 29 '89

H. J. HEINZ CO.

Heinz ain't broke, but it's doing a lot of fixing. G. L. Miles. il por *Business Week* p84-5+ D 11 '89

Heinz might add zest to your portfolio. il *Money* 18:8 Je '89

H-Y ANTIGEN

Can you choose your baby's sex? [research by Kenneth White] il *USA Today (Periodical)* 117:5 Je '89

HA! THE COMEDY NETWORK

Get ready for a mighty battle of wits. H. Polskin. il *TV Guide* 37:14-19 N 11-17 '89

Round-the-clock yucks. R. Zoglin. il *Time* 134:95 N 20 '89

Take my comedy programming, please. D. Lieberman. il *Business Week* p73 D 18 '89

HAACK, ROBERT A., AND MATTSON, WILLIAM J., 1943-

They nibbled while the forests burned. il *Natural History* p56-7 Ja '89

HAAG, ERNEST VAN DEN *See* Van den Haag, Ernest

HAAGS GEMEENTEMUSEUM (NETHERLANDS)

Picassos for sale? [museum director R. H. Fuchs to sell works by Monet and Picasso] J. Turner. il *Art News* 88:84-5+ D '89

HAAS, RICHARD

about

Richard Haas at Brooke Alexander. B. Adams. il *Art in America* 77:210-11 S '89

HAAS, ROBERT B.

about

Splitsville for a hot LBO team. K. Kelly. il pors *Business Week* p34 My 29 '89

HAAS SECURITIES CORPORATION

False securities. J. Crudele. il *New York* 22:25-6 F 6 '89

A penny-stock scam. C. Friday and J. Hammer. il por *Newsweek* 113:51 My 1 '89

HAASS, RICHARD N.

Democracy and tyranny: dealing with friendly tyrants. *Current (Washington, D.C.)* 316:34-40 O '89

HAASSE, HELLA S., 1918-

about

Academy Chicago to publish Dutch bestseller 40 years after original publication in Holland. C. Goodrich. il pors *Publishers Weekly* 235:33-4 Ap 28 '89

HAAVELMO, TRYGVE

about

At long last, laurels. M. J. Mandel. por *Business Week* p66 O 23 '89

Early work rewarded. J. Cherfas. por *Science* 246:328 O 20 '89

Economics. il por *Time* 134:74 O 23 '89

HABASH, GEORGE, 1925-

about

Four decades of blood vengeance; tr. by Richard Flantz. A. Kenan. il *The Nation* 248:154-6 F 6 '89

HABER, EDGAR, AND OTHERS

Innovative approaches to plasminogen activator therapy. bibl f il *Science* 243:51-6 Ja 6 '89

HABER, EDYTHE C.

(tr) See Mishveladze, Revaz. ??? !!!

HABER, JULIAN

Helping learning-disabled children; ed. by Florence Isaacs. il *Good Housekeeping* 209:162+ S '89

HABER, KAREN

Beatrice Berlin. il pors *American Artist* 53:64-7 My '89

HABERFELD, CAROLINE

Varicose veins: the truth behind the thin blue lines. il *Mademoiselle* 95:94+ Je '89

HABERMAN, CLYDE

For Italy's entrepreneurs, the figures are bella. il *The New York Times Magazine* p32-4+ Jl 16 '89

HABERMAN, MARTIN

More minority teachers. bibl f il *Phi Delta Kappan* 70:771-6 Je '89

Thirty-one reasons to stop the school reading machine. bibl f il *Phi Delta Kappan* 71:284-8 D '89

HABITAT FOR HUMANITY INC.

A bootstrap approach to low-cost housing [work of M. Fuller] D. Winbush. il pors *Time* 133:12-13 Ja 16 '89

Raising day [Timber Framers Guild effort in Hanover, Pa.] D. L. Brill. il *Country Journal* 16:57-9 S/O '89

Self-help for the homeless. A. Vuyst. *The Humanist* 49:13+ My/Je '89

HABITS

See also

Nail biting

Bad habits: master these little monsters. M. Conroy. il *Teen* 33:77-8 Je '89

HABITS—*cont.*
A clean break with bad habits. E. Kiester and S. V. Kiester. il *Reader's Digest* 135:165-6+ O '89
Comforting habits [toddlers] J. T. Gibson. il *Parents* 64:208 D '89
Habit forming [survey by Mel Poretz and Barry Sinrod] il *Time* 134:63 N 6 '89
Love stickies. il *Glamour* 87:144 My '89
Nail biting, hair twisting & other nasty habits [bad habits] L. Yarrow. il *Parents* 64:122-5 Je '89
HABITS OF ANIMALS *See* Animals—Habits and behavior
HABITUAL CRIMINALS *See* Recidivists
HABSBURG, HOUSE OF *See* House of Habsburg
HACALA, JOSEPH R.
Two faces in a crowd of graduates. *America* 161:190-1 S 30 '89
HACHETTE SA
Hachette says half its earnings come from outside France. *Publishers Weekly* 236:335 Ag 11 '89
Jean-Luc Lagardere. il *The Nation* 248:818 Je 12 '89
HACINLI, CYNTHIA
All pregnancy tests are not created equal. *Mademoiselle* 95:142 Mr '89
Down East chic. il *Gentlemen's Quarterly* 59:114+ S '89
I'll always be fat . . . and six other overweight myths. il *Mademoiselle* 95:110 D '89
Is your job making you sick? il *Mademoiselle* 95:126 O '89
Life in the fats lane. *Mademoiselle* 95:98 Jl '89
Sick of being tired? News about fatigue. il *Mademoiselle* 95:125-6 F '89
Unmentionables: the six most embarrassing ailments. il *Mademoiselle* 95:152+ S '89
Why you can—or can't—eat another bite. il *Mademoiselle* 95:96+ Jl '89
HACKER, ANDREW
Affirmative action: an exchange [discussion of October 12, 1989 article] *The New York Review of Books* 36:52-3 D 7 '89
Affirmative action: the new look. il *The New York Review of Books* 36:63-8 O 12 '89
HACKER, RANDI, AND KAUFMAN, JACKIE
The sisters Brontë and the sisters Collins: a study in stunning literary parallels. pors *The New York Times Book Review* 94:12-13 Ag 20 '89
HACKER, RICK, 1942-
Success secrets for front loaders. il *Field & Stream* 94:70-1+ N '89
HACKERS (COMPUTER ENTHUSIASTS)
See also
Cyberpunk culture
Free the hacker two. E. Corley. *Harper's* 279:22+ S '89
Goodbye, Mr. Chips. P. Wayner. il *Byte* 14:364 O '89
Hackers: is a cure worse than the disease? M. Lewyn. por *Business Week* p37-8 D 4 '89
Germany (West)
Astronomer Cliff Stoll stars in the espionage game, but for him spying doesn't really compute [responsible for tracking down Hannover, Germany hacker who gained access to U.S. government network] J. S. Kunen. il pors *People Weekly* 32:118+ D 11 '89
German computer spy ring broken. E. Marshall. *Science* 243:1545 Mr 24 '89
Soviet Union
Red hackers, arise! M. Rogers. il *Newsweek* 113:58-9 Mr 20 '89
HACKETT, JAMES T.
Can Brent Scowcroft be converted to SDI? por *Conservative Digest* 15:15 Mr/Ap '89
HACKETT, PAT
(ed) *See* Warhol, Andy, 1928?-1987. Diary of a mad decade
(ed) *See* Warhol, Andy, 1928?-1987. Notes from an endless night
HACKETT, THOMAS
Fire. maps *The New Yorker* 65:50-4+ O 2 '89
HACKMAN, EVETTE
Jump-start your day. il *American Health* 8:118-19+ Ap '89
HACKMAN, GENE, 1931-
about
Hackman: a capper for a craftsman. R. Corliss. por *Time* 133:62 Ja 9 '89
Hollywood's uncommon Everyman [cover story] M. Norman. il pors *The New York Times Magazine* p28-31+ Mr 19 '89
HACKMAN, SANDRA
about
The compleat editor. J. Schlefer. il por *Technology Review* 92:2 Ja '89
HACKMAN, SANDRA, AND HOWARD, ROBERT, 1954-
Health care: confronting the crisis [interview with A. Relman] *Current (Washington, D.C.)* 317:10-15 N '89
HACKWORTH, DAVID H.
about
Self-exiled after Vietnam, Army hero David Hackworth is finally coming home. P. Freeman. il pors *People Weekly* 31:52-4 Je 5 '89

HADAS, RACHEL
Elegy variations I [poem] *The American Scholar* 58:406 Summ '89
HADDAD, ROBERT F.
Blood brothers. *The New Republic* 200:16-18 My 8 '89
HADDEN, JEFFREY
(jt. auth) *See* Barnes, John A., and Hadden, Jeffrey
HADDON, DAYLE
about
Her gaze can daze. R. Wiley. il pors *Sports Illustrated* 70 Special Issue:119-22 F '89
HADID, MOHAMED
about
Puttin' on the Ritz—in New York, Washington, Aspen . . . T. Smart. il por *Business Week* p32+ Ap 24 '89
HADJ *See* Pilgrimages to Mecca
HADLEY, C. J.
Saga of the urban buckarettes. il *The Saturday Evening Post* 261:70-1 Jl/Ag '89
Sanctuary. il *The Saturday Evening Post* 261:82-5 S '89
Slouching through Australia. il *The Saturday Evening Post* 261:82-5+ Mr '89
HADLEY, JENNIFER
about
All God's dangers [drama] Reviews
The New Yorker 65:110 O 30 '89. E. Oliver
HADLEY, LEILA
Offbeat retreat. il *Harper's Bazaar* 122:142-3+ My '89
HADLEY, MALCOLM
Farming the forest. il *The Courier (Unesco)* 42:26-8 Ja '89
HADLEY, MICHAEL
about
All God's dangers [drama] Reviews
The New Yorker 65:110 O 30 '89. E. Oliver
HADRIAN'S WALL
Checkpoint Hadrian. J. J. Wilkes. il maps *Natural History* p64-72 Ap '89
Going to the Wall. R. Burton. il *History Today* 39:5-6 S '89
HAECO *See* Hong Kong Aircraft Engineering Co. Ltd.
HAEDRICH, KEN
Cook's tour. See issues of Country Journal beginning January 1987
HAEFELE, WALTER R.
General George Washington: espionage chief. bibl il pors *American History Illustrated* 24:22-7+ N/D '89
HAERINGER, PHILIPPE
A colourful kaleidoscope. il *The Unesco Courier* 42:22-5 Ag '89
HAFEN, ERNST
(jt. auth) *See* Basler, Konrad, and Hafen, Ernst
HAFEZ, GHADA
A happy ending. il *World Health* p13-15 Jl '89
HAFFIE, TOM
Mendel to Monctezuma: the end-of-term review in genetics. il *BioScience* 39:246-7+ Ap '89
HÁFIZ, 14TH CENT.
about
Hafez: the golden age of Persian literature. C.-H. de Fouchecour. il *The Courier (Unesco)* 42:13-16 My '89
Love sacred and profane. R. Feiz. il *The Courier (Unesco)* 42:12 Mr '89
HAFT, STEVEN
about
Hollywood on the Hudson. B. H. Lynn. il por *New York* 22:24 Je 5 '89
HAGAN, DARIAN
about
A long way from L.A. A. Murphy. il pors *Sports Illustrated* 71:44-6+ D 25 '89-Ja 1 '90
HAGAN, PATTI
Shakespeare in the Park. il *House & Garden* 161:200-3+ O '89
HAGAN, VICTORIA
about
Victoria's secret. L. Snowden. il por *House & Garden* 161:188-91+ My '89
HAGANS, JONATHAN
about
Duped by a mysterious con man, a Florida couple 'find' a missing son only to lose him again. W. Plummer. il pors *People Weekly* 32:59-60 Ag 14 '89
HAGANS, KATHRYN B.
about
How best to heal a shattered child [interview] L. J. Moore. por *U.S. News & World Report* 106:68-9 Ap 10 '89
HAGANS, MARJEAN
about
Duped by a mysterious con man, a Florida couple 'find' a missing son only to lose him again. W. Plummer. il pors *People Weekly* 32:59-60 Ag 14 '89
HAGAR, SAMMY
about
Rock meets dirt. S. Martin. il por *Bicycling* 30:40 O/N '89
Sammy Hagar does the wheel thing. por *Rolling Stone* p39 Jl 13-27 '89

HAGBERG, JAMES
Bicycling's exclusive calorie counter [cover story]; ed. by Nelson Pena. il *Bicycling* 30:100-3 My '89
HAGELSTEIN, PETER
about
In hot water over cold fusion. R. Pool. *Science* 246:1384 D 15 '89
Interview: Peter Hagelstein. B. Moseley. pors *Omni (New York, N.Y.)* 11:74-6+ My '89
HAGEN, CHARLES
The fabulous chameleon. il *Art News* 88:118-23 Summ '89
HAGEN, WALTER, 1892-1969
about
Sir Walter. R. Fimrite. il pors *Sports Illustrated* 70:74-8+ Je 19 '89
HAGGETT, WILLIAM E.
A kinder, gentler Navy? [address, January 18, 1989] *Vital Speeches of the Day* 55:403-5 Ap 15 '89
HAGGIS
Can America stomach it? M. Starr. il *Newsweek* 114:86 O 30 '89
HAGMAN, LARRY
Why America's made him a hero—mean as he is [cover story] il pors *TV Guide* 37:4-6+ F 11-17 '89
about
Larry Hagman. il por *People Weekly* 31 Special Issue:44 Summ '89
HAGNER, JOHN
about
Fame for fall guys. M. Durham. il map *Americana* 17:36-9 N/D '89
HAGUE, MICHAEL, 1948-
about
Drawing for the small screen. O. David. *Publishers Weekly* 235:103 Ja 20 '89
HAHN, JESSICA
about
Look who else is on this month. J. Marion. il por *TV Guide* 37:12 N 4-10 '89
HAHN, JUDITH
Loving a prostitute [cover story] il *The Christian Century* 106:415-16 Ap 19 '89
HAHN, LORNA
China deal. *The New Republic* 201:10-11 O 30 '89
HAID, CHARLES
about
Playing a bad dad. J. Kaye. il por *TV Guide* 37:38 Ap 15-21 '89
HAIDA INDIANS
Haidas on the Seine [work of B. Reid featured at Paris exhibition] N. Jennings. il por *Maclean's* 102:67-8 O 16 '89
HAIGHT, FULTON
Law and medicine [address, September 26, 1988] *Vital Speeches of the Day* 55:180-5 Ja 1 '89
HAIGHT, GRETCHEN
The perilous journey from book to screen. il *Publishers Weekly* 235:137-42 F 24 '89
HAIKU
Poetry in motion at the walking rally [written by participants] M. Bricklin. il *Prevention (Emmaus, Pa.)* 41:144 Jl '89
HAIL MARY [film] See Motion picture reviews—Single works
HAILE SELASSIE I, EMPEROR OF ETHIOPIA, 1891-1975
about
The emperor wore clothes: visiting Haile Selassie in 1943. H. Courlander. *The American Scholar* 58:271-81 Spr '89
HAIM, COREY
about
Celebs speak out on addiction. L. E. Brooks. pors *Teen* 33:30+ S '89
You asked for him: Corey Haim. il pors *Teen* 33:55 Ap '89
HAIMOVITZ, MATT
about
Matt Haimovitz comes of age. R. Freed. il por *Stereo Review* 54:152 O '89
HAINES, JENNIFER
about
Sentence for trespassing. *The Christian Century* 106:256 Mr 8 '89
HAING S. NGOR See Ngor, Haing S.
HAIR
See also
Baldness
Beards
Eyebrows
Hairstyling
Mustaches
Wigs
Does hirsute suit her? L. Kaylin. il *Gentlemen's Quarterly* 59:346-7+ Mr '89
The natural roots of fiber optics [gray hair] I. Amato. il *Science News* 136:414-15 D 23-30 '89
Obsessed by hair. il *Glamour* 87:184-9 F '89
Care
Are you killing your hair? A. P. Lynn. il *Glamour* 87:57 S '89
Can you spot 8 mistakes? il *Redbook* 173:140-1 O '89

Do you want hair with more body? S. Young. il *Glamour* 87:60 Mr '89
A get-fat strategy for thin hair. il *Mademoiselle* 95:52 O '89
Give your summer hair a sporting chance. J. Neal. il *Women's Sports & Fitness* 11:20 My '89
Hair. See issues of Vogue
Hair gets healthy. il *Seventeen* 48:92-5 F '89
Hair on the road. L. F. McCarthy. *Vogue* 179:166 My '89
How to take better care of your hair. L. Heller. il *Redbook* 172:98-9+ Ja '89
Nature girl. il *Seventeen* 48:160 N '89
No-wilt summer hair. il *Glamour* 87:214-17 Ag '89
Silver streak [gray hair] L. Lebowitz. il *Harper's Bazaar* 122:56+ Ag '89
Stressed-out strands. il *Harper's Bazaar* 122:92-5+ Ja '89
Summer hair. il *Seventeen* 48:176-9 My '89
Tress T.L.C. il *'Teen* 33:74-6 Je '89
Tress talk: hair questions answered. il *'Teen* 33:69-76 S '89
Tress tech. il *'Teen* 33:70-1 F '89
Tress trivia. il *'Teen* 33:20 D '89
Winter hair! il *Essence* 20:44 N '89
Winter skin and hair repair. P. Kripke. il *Working Woman* 14:108 Ja '89
Dyeing and bleaching
Color coded: hair's rich and famous hues [highlighting] il *Mademoiselle* 95:166-9 Jl '89
Color: the news in hair—big changes [black women] il *Essence* 19:78-9 Ja '89
Deep, dark secrets [brunette hair] il *'Teen* 33:68+ S '89
A distinctive minority in a world of blonds and brunettes, redheads now have a new range of options in both haircolor and makeup. C. Sullivan. il *Vogue* 179:212+ O '89
From sleek to chic. il *'Teen* 33:60-1 Jl '89
Hair color makeovers. C. Straley. il *Parents* 64:147-9 Ap '89
Hair resistance. C. Sullivan. *Vogue* 179:114 Je '89
Holiday headlines. il *Harper's Bazaar* 122:20+ N '89
Images: hair answers. L. F. McCarthy. *Vogue* 179:66 Jl '89
Keeping color-treated hair healthy, soft, manageable. L. F. McCarty. *Vogue* 179:172 F '89
Pep up your hair with color enhancers. J. Neal. il *Women's Sports & Fitness* 11:70 Mr '89
With an ever-expanding client list and a salon that's already doubled in size, Louis Licari can be called New York's hair man of the moment. il pors *Vogue* 179:182 O '89
Removal
See also
Electrolysis (Hair removal)
Get smooth all over. il *Redbook* 173:8+ Jl '89
Smooth moves. il *Seventeen* 48:150 My '89
Stubble, stubble, toil and trouble. P. Patten. il *Women's Sports & Fitness* 11:60 Jl/Ag '89
Taking it all off. *Essence* 20:54 My '89
Tattletale legs. il *'Teen* 33:66-7 Je '89
The trouble with hairy. A. Tardio. il *Gentlemen's Quarterly* 59:340-5 Mr '89
HAIR CARE PRODUCTS
See also
Baldness remedies
Shampoos
The condition game. *Mademoiselle* 95:28 Jl '89
De-tangling tactics [hair conditioners] C. Duhé. il *Health (New York, N.Y.)* 21:78-80+ S '89
The gel generation [styling gels] il *Mademoiselle* 95:52 My '89
Get a grip on your hair: new ways to shape, style, control. il *Glamour* 87:148-53 Ja '89
Misuse can cancel out many benefits of today's hair tools. Here, proven hair boosters. L. F. McCarthy. *Vogue* 179:160 Ag '89
On one condition . . . il *Essence* 19:52 Ap '89
Some women's hair requires more conditioning than others'. How to choose which conditioners to use. L. F. McCarthy. *Vogue* 179:228 O '89
Winter wrap session. N. Malkin. il *Harper's Bazaar* 122:30+ F '89
You still can't change your hair texture, but now you can change the way it looks and behaves. Here's how. L. F. McCarthy. *Vogue* 179:236 N '89
HAIR CARE PRODUCTS INDUSTRY
See also
Graham Webb International Inc.
J.M. Products Company
Johnson Products Company, Inc.
M&M Products Company
Soft Sheen Products Inc.
Supreme Beauty Products (Firm)
HAIR COLORING *See* Hair—Dyeing and bleaching
HAIR CONDITIONERS *See* Hair care products
HAIR PULLING
Chemistry of compulsive hair pulling [treatment with clomipramine; research by Susan E. Swedo] *Science News* 136:175 S 9 '89
HAIR RESTORERS *See* Baldness remedies
HAIRBRUSHES
Brushing up. il *Seventeen* 48:76 Mr '89

HAIRCUTTING See Hairstyling
HAIRDRESSERS See Hairstylists
HAIRPIECES See Wigs
HAIRSTYLING
See also
Hairstylists
45 tips from the world's top hair stylists. il McCall's 117:21-4 N '89
Alexandre has influenced hairstyles the world over for nearly fifty years. J. Burstall. il pors Vogue 179:285+ S '89
Art of the part. il Vogue 179:160 F '89
Back talk. C. Sullivan. il Vogue 179:212 Mr '89
Be hair awared! il Teen 33:84-7 Ap '89
The big snip: the long-to-short report. il Mademoiselle 95:180-3 Je '89
The bob is back. C. Straley. il Parents 64:92-4+ Ja '89
Class night: women try their luck with the stylists of tomorrow. C. Sullivan. Vogue 179:186 Ap '89
Cropped! Shortcut to summer style. il Glamour 87:138-41 Jl '89
A cut above. L. J. Johnson. il Ladies' Home Journal 106:150-5 Ap '89
Done-up dos. il Teen 33:76-85 N '89
Easy-care hair [short cuts] C. Straley. il Parents 64:159-62 N '89
Easy care summer hair. C. Straley. il Parents 64:115-18 Jl '89
Fabulous hair do-overs. il Redbook 172:100-3 Ja '89
Fast hair fix-its. il Teen 33:62-3 F '89
Five carefree cuts [men] A. Tardio. il Gentlemen's Quarterly 59:306-11 Ap '89
Foolproof holiday eyes and hair. il McCall's 116:18-21 Ja '89
Four great (short!) hairstyles. il Good Housekeeping 209:200-3 S '89
Get the perfect cut. il Redbook 173:106-9 Je '89
Getting the haircut you want. il Glamour 87:95 O '89
Goof-proof kid's haircut. C. Straley. il Parents 64:29 My '89
Guide to great hair. il McCall's 116:23-6 Ap '89
Hair. See issues of Vogue
Hair by design. H. E. Lee. il Vogue 179:147-8 F '89
Hair for the 90's. il Glamour 87:304-7 Ap '89
Hair forecast: a new soft focus. il Harper's Bazaar 122:22+ My '89
Hair necessities. il Teen 33:60-1 Ja '89
Hair now: out of Africa. il Essence 20:36+ Jl '89
Hair say. See issues of Mademoiselle
Hair to the throne [Diana] C. Sullivan. il pors Vogue 179:160 My '89
Hair update: softis sexy. il Glamour 87:238-41 N '89
Hair with flair [black women] il Ebony 44:80-2 Ja '89
Headliners [Paris collections] il Vogue 179:178-9 O '89
Hollywood hair [hair extensions] C. Krupp. il Glamour 87:191 O '89
Hot, hot hair. il Teen 33:96-7 My '89
Hurry-up hair. il Teen 33:82-3 S '89
In the quixotic world of fashion, what's hair today is often gone tomorrow. C. Heimel. il Vogue 179:470 N '89
Je ne sais coif! il Harper's Bazaar 122:82 F '89
The long . . . and short of it. il Seventeen 48:134-7 O '89
Long-hair makeovers. il Teen 33:110-11 Ag '89
Major hair cutbacks now making news. il Mademoiselle 95:160-3 F '89
Men hate short hair, love short skirts. True or false? W. Geist. il Vogue 179:152 Ag '89
A new French twist. il Seventeen 48:22 Jl '89
The new longer short cuts. il Redbook 174:132-5 D '89
The new smooth: the most modern hair has all that shine. il Mademoiselle 95:202-5 S '89
New twists for summer hair; Keeping a cool head [children's styles] N. Brophy and M. Vogel. il Good Housekeeping 208:98-9 Je '89
The new wave. L. F. McCarthy. il Vogue 179:652-5 S '89
On-line looks. il Teen 33:90-3 N '89
One mother's story [reaction to teenage son's Mohawk haircut] J. A. Reimer. il Ladies' Home Journal 106:90+ Ap '89
Parting shots [where to part your hair] il Seventeen 48:124 Je '89
Parts [black hairstyles] il Essence 19:41 Mr '89
Perfect haircut. See occasional issues of Glamour
Permanents solutions. il Teen 33:54-5 D '89
Pin-up girls. il Seventeen 48:90-1 Jl '89
Return of the flip. C. Sullivan. il Vogue 179:198 Mr '89
See the difference! [makeovers for damaged hair] il Redbook 173:138-9 O '89
Short cut to fall. J. J. Buck. il Vogue 179:204-11 Jl '89
Signature haircuts. L. Matthews. il Working Woman 14:173-4+ N '89
Superstar hair. L. J. Johnson. il Ladies' Home Journal 106:126-31 Ag '89
Take a beauty short cut. il Teen 33:28 O '89
Taking it easy [natural look] L. Wells. il The New York Times Magazine p114 My 21 '89
Talking heads [long hair on men] F. Rogers. il The New York Times Magazine p58-9 Jl 23 '89
Tempestt gets a new 'do. il pors Seventeen 48:72 O '89

Ten easy summer hairstyles. il McCall's 116:23-6 Jl '89
Ten steps to a happy haircut. il Seventeen 48:294-7 Ag '89
A trim for him. il Seventeen 48:128 S '89
What a difference! 8 great shape-making haircuts. il Redbook 172:108-11 Mr '89
What they're wearing: short hair. L. Wells. il The New York Times Magazine p56-7 My 28 '89
The wild, wild haircut craze [black men] il Ebony 44:62+ S '89
With help from some wily haircutters, Batman leaves his mark on cropped crusaders. il People Weekly 32:74 Jl 17 '89
World class hairstyles. il Good Housekeeping 208:132-5 Mr '89
HAIRSTYLING SALONS See Beauty shops
HAIRSTYLISTS
See also
Black hairstylists
Dirty rotten scalpers. S. A. Feeney. il Ms. 17:26+ Ap '89
Mane attraction [J. Sahag] il por Harper's Bazaar 122:36+ Mr '89
Anecdotes, facetiae, satire, etc.
Cut down by the hairdresser. P. Rose. il The New York Times Magazine p12+ Ja 15 '89
Training
Class night: women try their luck with the stylists of tomorrow. C. Sullivan. Vogue 179:186 Ap '89
HAISLMAIER, EDMUND F.
The health care quagmire [cover story] il Consumers' Research Magazine 72:10-16 S '89
HAITI
See also
AIDS (Disease)—Haiti
Art—Haiti
Civil rights—Haiti
History
Beyond the mountains (II). M. Danner. maps The New Yorker 65:68+ D 4 '89
Beyond the mountains (III). M. Danner. map The New Yorker 65:100-2+ D 11 '89
Revolution, 1791-1804
In the Antilles, 'liberty for all'. Y. Benot. il The Unesco Courier 42:18-23 Je '89
Politics and government
See also
Elections—Haiti
Beyond the mountains (I). M. Danner. maps The New Yorker 65:55-6+ N 27 '89
Beyond the mountains (III). M. Danner. map The New Yorker 65:100-2+ D 11 '89
Haiti goes back. A. Wilentz. The Nation 249:669-70 D 4 '89
Haiti's prospects under Prosper Avril. S. Rodman. il por The New Leader 72:5-7 S 4 '89
Little priest, big general [J.-B. Aristide and P. Avril] S. Rodman. il National Review 41:24-5 S 29 '89
Revolution on the walls. A. W. Barnett. il Art in America 77:67-9+ Jl '89
Religious institutions and affairs
See also
Catholic Church—Haiti
Christians—Haiti
Church and social problems—Haiti
Missions—Haiti
Voodooism—Haiti
HAITI IN LITERATURE
On truth and fiction [factual basis for book Slave trade involving homosexual boys in Haiti] H. Gold. The Nation 249:759-61 D 18 '89
HAITINK, BERNARD
about
Beethoven's nine, times two. E. Salzman. il pors Stereo Review 54:128 Ja '89
HAJE, KHRYSTYNE
about
Khrystyne Haje. K. Turan. por TV Guide 37:14 S 23-29 '89
HAJJ See Pilgrimages to Mecca
HAKEMACHI, LAURENCE
Macrowave oven. il Radio-Electronics 60:74-5 Ap '89
HAKIM, OMAR
about
Omar Hakim: stickin' it to ya [cover story] J. Levenson. il pors Down Beat 56:16-19 Ap '89
HALABY, LISA See Nur el Hussein, Queen, consort of Hussein, King of Jordan
HALABY, RAOUF
Seeds of diplomacy. il Organic Gardening 36:95 F '89
HALAL, WILLIAM E.
Facing transformation: the great American house move. The Futurist 23:60 S/O '89
HALAT, PETE
about
The murder—and the mayor. J. N. Baker. il por Newsweek 114:32 O 23 '89

HALBERSTAM, DAVID, 1934-
An American romance. il por *Popular Mechanics* 166:48-50+ My '89

The great Joe D. [excerpt from Summer of '49] il pors *New York* 22:42-52 My 8 '89

TV that changed our lives. il *TV Guide* 37:6-8 My 6-12 '89

HALBREICH, KATHY
about
Starting things. C. Giuliano. il por *Art News* 88:32+ Ja '89

HALE, DAVID D.
Must we become Japanese? [cover story] il *National Review* 41:30-2+ O 27 '89

Picking up Reagan's tab. *Foreign Policy* 74:145-67 Spr '89

HALE, ELLEN
The controversial Pap test. il *FDA Consumer* 23:20-3 S '89

Lifting the clouds of cataracts. il *FDA Consumer* 23:26-8+ D '89/Ja '90

HALE, J. R. (JOHN RIGBY), 1923-
1588 and all that. il *The New York Review of Books* 36:30-2 F 16 '89

HALE, JOHN RIGBY *See* Hale, J. R. (John Rigby), 1923-

HALEAKALA NATIONAL PARK (HAWAII)
Downhill all the way [children's bicycling trip] il map *National Geographic World* 170:20-5 O '89

A seabird in the house of the sun [dark-rumped petrels] T. Simons and G. C. Whittow. il *Natural History* p50-3 Mr '89

HALES, DIANNE R., 1950-
Astrology in high places. il *McCall's* 117:83-6 O '89

The baby-baby-baby boom!!! il *Redbook* 172:94-7 Ja '89

Exclusive: Kitty Kelley tells all. il pors *McCall's* 116:67-8+ Ag '89

Quick tips from diet doctors. *Reader's Digest* 135:160-2 D '89

Understanding your personality. il *McCall's* 116:71-4+ Mr '89

Words that can warm up your marriage. il *McCall's* 116:70+ Ap '89

HALES, DIANNE R., 1950-, AND HALES, ROBERT E.
Babes in Stress-land. il *American Health* 8:44-6+ O '89

HALES, ROBERT E.
(jt. auth) *See* Hales, Dianne R., 1950-, and Hales, Robert E.

HALEVY, DAVID
(jt. auth) *See* Livingstone, Neil C., and Halevy, David

HALEVY, DAVID, AND LIVINGSTONE, NEIL C.
An American soldier's death becomes a pawn in a terrorist power struggle. il *U.S. News & World Report* 107:21 O 23 '89

HALEY, ALEX
A different kind of Christmas [story] il pors *Good Housekeeping* 208:147-50+ Ja '89

HALEY, KATHY
Boston faces reality. il *Channels (New York, N.Y.: 1986)* 9:86-7 F '89

Bringing Blair back to life. il por *Channels (New York, N.Y.: 1986)* 9:38-40+ Je '89

Cable learns a new business: PPV. il *Channels (New York, N.Y.: 1986)* 9:68-9 S '89

Righting cable's image wrongs. il *Channels (New York, N.Y.: 1986)* 9:68-9 Jl/Ag '89

Syndicators beware: growth ahead. il *Channels (New York, N.Y.: 1986)* 9:40-1 O '89

HALEY (ALEX) HOUSE MUSEUM *See* Alex Haley House Museum

HALF, ROBERT
about
Finding the right employee (I). B. Stein. il *Home Office Computing* 7:44-5 O '89

Finding the right employee (II). B. Stein. il *Home Office Computing* 7:40+ N '89

HALF DOLLAR COINS *See* Coins

HALF FRAME CAMERAS *See* Cameras

THE HALF OF IT [drama] *See* Krizanc, John

HALFTIME (FOOTBALL GAMES) *See* Football, Professional—Super Bowl—Halftime

HALFTONE PROCESS (PHOTOGRAPHY)
From print shop to stage floor. T. Macie. il *Theatre Crafts* 23:94 Ag/S '89

HALIBUT FISHING
Not just for the halibut [southeast Alaska] B. Stearns. il *Field & Stream* 94:84+ N '89

HALIFAX (N.S.)
Health facilities
A crusader's challenge [H. Morgentaler performs abortions at clinic despite ban] G. Allen. il por *Maclean's* 102:14-15 N 6 '89

Religious institutions and affairs
God and profits [Buddhist firms flourish] il *Maclean's* 102:34-5 Mr 27 '89

HALIFAX COUNTY (N.S.)
Education
School-yard racism [blacks and whites brawl at Cole Harbour District High School] M. Nemeth. il *Maclean's* 102:14 Ja 23 '89

Race relations
School-yard racism [blacks and whites brawl at Cole Harbour District High School] M. Nemeth. il *Maclean's* 102:14 Ja 23 '89

HALITOSIS
Kiss bad breath goodbye. A. Roblin. il *Prevention (Emmaus, Pa.)* 41:58-64 N '89

HALL, ARSENIO
about
All Hall is breaking loose! B. Allen. il pors *Essence* 20:50-2+ Jl '89

Alone at the top. P. Goldstein. il pors *Rolling Stone* p60-2+ N 2 '89

And now, nice-guy talk hosts. R. Zoglin. pors *Time* 133:74 Ja 9 '89

Arsenio Hall. por *People Weekly* 32:50-1 D 25 '89-Ja 1 '90

Arsenio Hall's late arrival. H. F. Waters. il pors *Newsweek* 113:68-9 Ap 10 '89

Arsenio Hall's TV talk show keeps fans awake with fun and famous faces [cover story] A. Collier. il pors *Jet* 76:56-9 Ap 10 '89

Arsenio jokes with 3 champs—Ali, Tyson, Leonard—on show. il pors *Jet* 76:46-7 Ag 21 '89

Comedy Awards Show honors Arsenio Hall, salutes Dick Gregory. il por *Jet* 76:53 Je 19 '89

Getting hotter—but feeling the heat. M. Leahy. il pors *TV Guide* 37:16-19 S 30-O 6 '89

Late-night cool [cover story] M. Norman. il pors *The New York Times Magazine* p28-31+ O 1 '89

"Let's get busy!!" [cover story] R. Zoglin. il pors *Time* 134:92-7 N 13 '89

HALL, BILL
about
From street kids to Royal Knights. J. Coudert. il por *Reader's Digest* 134:141-6 Je '89

HALL, BILL E.
Little girl lost. por *Essence* 20:12 O '89

HALL, BOB
about
The siren song of the open road and the open roof led Bob Hall to the amazing Miata. D. Grogan. il pors *People Weekly* 32:57+ S 4 '89

HALL, CAROL
Deal-makers pull the purse strings. il *Channels (New York, N.Y.: 1986)* 9:82-3 F '89

HALL, DINAH
Classical translation. il por *House & Garden* 161:116-23 Mr '89

HALL, DONALD, 1928-
Death to the death of poetry. il *Harper's* 279:72-6 S '89

Material [poem] *The Atlantic* 264:68 Ag '89

Moon clock [poem] *The New Yorker* 65:98 F 20 '89

Six naps in one day [poem] *The New Yorker* 65:72 N 20 '89

What country doesn't mean. il *Country Journal* 16:70-1 My/Je '89

HALL, ELIZABETH
When does life begin? [interview with C. Grobstein] il pors *Psychology Today* 23:42-6 S '89

HALL, JAMES, III
about
Top secrets for sale? R. Parry. il por *Newsweek* 113:27 Ja 2 '89

HALL, JAMES L.
MTV rocks (and rolls) American youth. il *USA Today (Periodical)* 118:87-8 N '89

HALL, JAMES W. *See* Hall, Jim, 1947-

HALL, JERRY
about
Jerry Hall: spicy as Texas barbecue. C. Krupp. por *Glamour* 87:163 Ag '89

HALL, JIM, 1947-
Women [poem] *The American Scholar* 58:511-12 Aut '89

HALL, JUDITH VIDAL- *See* Vidal-Hall, Judith

HALL, LEON W.
about
Obituary
Jet 77:57 N 27 '89

HALL, OAKLEY M.
Powder River country. il map *American Heritage* 40:43-51 Ap '89

HALL, PHYLLIS A.
Morning walks with Alex. il *Parents* 64:90+ O '89

HALL, ROBERT F., 1906-
The craft of outdoor writing. il *The Conservationist* 44:56 Jl/Ag '89

HALL, STEPHEN S.
A medical messiah? il pors *New Choices for the Best Years* 29:31-6 Ap '89

A molecular code links emotions, mind and health. il *Smithsonian* 20:62-71 Je '89

Standing on those corners, watching all the folks go by. bibl (p171) il por *Smithsonian* 19:119-24+ F '89

HALL, UNITY, AND SEWARD, INGRID
Royal family life [excerpt from Royalty revealed; cover story] il *Good Housekeeping* 209:98-9+ Ag '89

HALL, ZACH W.
(jt. auth) See Ralston, Evelyn, and Hall, Zach W.
HALL CHINA CO.
Keeping things cool in Hall China. L. Rosenkrantz. il *Antiques & Collecting Hobbies* 94:22 My '89
HALL EFFECT
New measurement standards for 1990 [cover story] B. N. Taylor. bibl f il *Physics Today* 42 pt1:23-6 Ag '89
HALL OF SOUTH AMERICAN PEOPLES See American Museum of Natural History. Hall of South American Peoples
HALLEY'S COMET
See also
Space flight—Cometary missions
Active polar region on the nucleus of Comet Halley. H. J. Reitsema and others. bibl f il *Science* 243:198-200 Ja 13 '89
Carbon ratio shows Halley may be alien [research by Susan Wyckoff] F. Flam. *Science News* 135:214 Ap 8 '89
Halley is an alien [carbon ratio; research by Susan Wyckoff] T. Waters. il *Discover* 10:26-7 Ag '89
Halley's birthplace [research by Susan Wyckoff] R. Ruthen. *Scientific American* 260:31 Je '89
The visual recovery of Halley's comet. B. E. Schaefer. *Sky and Telescope* 78:525 N '89
Was Halley's comet interstellar? [research by Susan Wyckoff] *Sky and Telescope* 78:573-4 D '89
HALLIBURTON, KAREN J.
The spirit of Malcolm [poem] *Essence* 20:107 N '89
HALLIBURTON, RICHARD
about
On the royal road to adventures with 'Daring Dick'. D. M. Schwartz. il pors *Smithsonian* 19:159-60+ Mr '89
HALLIDAY, ANTHONY
about
A delicate balance [interview] T. Fennell. por *Maclean's* 102:49 D 18 '89
HALLIDAY, FRED
Moscow's new role in the Middle East [cover story] il *The Nation* 248:361+ Mr 20 '89
Notes on the new political culture. il *The Nation* 249:234-6+ S 4-11 '89
HALLIN, CARLYN K.
(jt. auth) See Bellack, Alison R., and Hallin, Carlyn K.
HALLMARK CARDS, INC.
The Hallmark Photographic Collection: a commitment to fine photography. K. F. Davis. il *USA Today (Periodical)* 117:54-63 Ja '89
HALLOW, RALPH Z.
Man of a thousand lights. *National Review* 41:19-20 My 19 '89
HALLOWEEN
See also
Pumpkin faces
Halloween fright night [arson in Detroit and street crime in New York City] il *Newsweek* 114:49 N 13 '89
The New York Halloween parade. D. K. Mano. il *National Review* 41:56-8 N 24 '89
Primitive [Greenwich Village parade] *The New Yorker* 65:48-9 N 6 '89
Anecdotes, facetiae, satire, etc.
Halloween's here! D. Barry. il *Reader's Digest* 135:89-90 O '89
Bibliography
Frightening books for a frightful holiday. R. Donahue. il *Publishers Weekly* 236:36 S 29 '89
Terminology
Our treat [quiz] il *Seventeen* 48:124 O '89
HALLOWEEN COOKING
Have treats ready. il *Southern Living* 24:164 O '89
Lite eating: terrific Halloween treats. il *McCall's* 117:177 O '89
HALLOWEEN COSTUMES
Fun-to-make Halloween costumes. il *Good Housekeeping* 209:168 S '89
Haunted hats. il *Sunset (Central West edition)* 183:80-1 O '89
Have a happy and safe Halloween. S. Mackenzie. il *Parents* 64:159-62+ O '89
HALLOWEEN MASKS See Masks
HALLOWEEN PARTIES
Boo-tiful Halloween party ideas. il *Redbook* 173:34+ O '89
HALLOWEEN V [film] See Motion picture reviews—Single works
HALLOWELL, EDWARD, AND GRACE, WILLIAM J.
What's your money personality? [excerpt from What are you worth?] il *Good Housekeeping* 208:52+ F '89
HALLS OF FAME
See also
Black Filmmakers Hall of Fame
Business Hall of Fame
Hollywood Stuntmen's Hall of Fame (Moab, Utah)
International Checker Hall of Fame
Jazz-Blues-Gospel Hall of Fame Archive
Labor Hall of Fame
Rock & Roll Hall of Fame
Songwriters' Hall of Fame and Museum
Sports halls of fame

HALLUCINOGENIC DRUGS
See also
LSD
PCP
HALOBACTERIA
The mechanism of DNA transfer in the mating system of an archaebacterium. I. Rosenshine and others. bibl f il *Science* 245:1387-9 S 22 '89
HALOCARBONS
Hydrolysis of carbon tetrachloride [discussion of November 4, 1988 article, Arctic Ocean ventilation studied with a suite of anthropogenic halocarbon tracers] M. Krysell and D. W. R. Wallace. il *Science* 246:1638-9 D 22 '89
HALOGEN BURNERS
Cooking with halogen. V. E. Gilmore. il *Popular Science* 234:143 My '89
HALOPERIDOL
Rat model of tardive dyskinesia gets boost [research by Gaylord Ellison] B. Bower. *Science News* 136:308 N 11 '89
HALOS (ASTRONOMY)
Giant gas ring "weighs" massive halo [elliptical galaxy IC 2006] *Sky and Telescope* 77:587-8 Je '89
Ringing in a new estimate for dark matter [research by Stephen E. Schneider] R. Cowen. il *Science News* 136:84 Ag 5 '89
Spiral arms and dark halos [research by Magnus Thomasson] il *Sky and Telescope* 78:134 Ag '89
HALPER, LOUISE
(jt. auth) See Gilchrist, Alan, and Halper, Louise
HALPERIN, BARRY
about
Child's play. K. Hannon. il *Forbes* 143:101 Ap 3 '89
HALPERIN, MAURICE
about
Child's play. K. Hannon. il *Forbes* 143:101 Ap 3 '89
HALPERIN, MORTON H.
From primer to policy. por *The Bulletin of the Atomic Scientists* 45:31-2 My '89
(jt. auth) See Wales, Jane, and Halperin, Morton H.
about
Has arms control worked? [cover story; special section; with introd. by Michael Krepon] bibl f il *The Bulletin of the Atomic Scientists* 45:26-45 My '89
HALPERN, SUE M.
AIDS: rethinking the risk. il *Ms.* 17:80-2+ My '89
The endangered physical. il *Ms.* 18:18+ N '89
Infertility: a search for solutions. *Reader's Digest* 135:129-30+ Jl '89
Infertility: playing the odds. il *Ms.* 17:146-51+ Ja/F '89
Miracle baby. il pors *Ms.* 18:56-60+ S '89
The rise of the homeless. bibl f il *The New York Review of Books* 36:24-7 F 16 '89
Twilight zones. il *Ms.* 18:26+ S '89
HALPRIN, ANNA, 1920-
about
Halprin takes STEPS for people with AIDS. J. Ross. il pors *Dance Magazine* 63:9 Ap '89
HALS, FRANS, THE ELDER, CA. 1580-1666
about
Clash of the titans. P. Plagens. il pors *Newsweek* 114:84-6 O 9 '89
Frans Hals and American art. D. D. Thompson. bibl f il *Antiques* 136:1170-83 N '89
The painted face. J. Brown. il *Vogue* 179:420-5 O '89
HALSELL (LUCILE) CONSERVATORY See San Antonio Botanical Gardens. Lucile Halsell Conservatory
HALSEY, CHRISTINE
American abroad. il pors *Harper's Bazaar* 122:122-5+ Ag '89
HALSEY, WILLIAM FREDERICK, 1882-1959
about
William F. Halsey, Jr. J. B. Graves. il pors *Conservative Digest* 15:37-41 S/O '89
HALSTED, HANK
Boat handling. See issues of Motor Boating & Sailing
HALSTON
about
The inimitable Halston. N. Darnton. il pors *Newsweek* 114:64-6 Ag 7 '89
HALSTON ENTERPRISES
The inimitable Halston. N. Darnton. il pors *Newsweek* 114:64-6 Ag 7 '89
HALTON, MARK R.
Legislating assimilation: the English-only movement. il *The Christian Century* 106:1119-21 N 29 '89
HALVERSON, THOMAS
(jt. auth) See Mendelsohn, Jack, and Halverson, Thomas
HAM, LEE VAN
Praying with trees. il *The Christian Century* 106:839-40 S 27 '89
HAM
See also
Cooking—Meat
HAM RADIO
Making waves [packet radio] M. Waller. il *Byte* 14:363-4+ D '89

HAM RADIO—*cont.*
No soap radio [operators Charlotte Richardson and Paul Young] J. Stone. il *Discover* 10:82 Ja '89
HAMANN, HILTON
How macho are the Cubans? il *Conservative Digest* 15:54-7 S/O '89
HAMBLEN, KAREN A.
A symposium on skills, knowledge, and creativity in the curriculum. *Design for Arts in Education* 90:25-6 My/Je '89
HAMBLETON, RICHARD
about
Richard Hambleton at Milford. J. Zinsser. il *Art in America* 77:146-7 Ja '89
HAMBLIN, DORA JANE, 1920-
A white marble city that an emperor chose for his own. il *Smithsonian* 19:142-8+ Mr '89
HAMBRECHT, EDWARD C.
The changing retail scene [address, April 25, 1989] *Vital Speeches of the Day* 55:629-32 Ag 1 '89
HAMBRO, ROBIN
about
American abroad. C. Halsey. il pors *Harper's Bazaar* 122:112-5+ Ag '89
HAMBURG, BEATRIX A.
Research on child and adolescent mental disorders. *Science* 246:738 N 10 '89
HAMBURG, JILL
The world and the Kurds. *The Nation* 249:205-6 Ag 21-28 '89
HAMBURG, JOAN
Scam alert! How to avoid a rip-off. il *Ladies' Home Journal* 106:44+ Jl '89
HAMBURG, ROBERT
Assessing the benefits of biogas. bibl f il *Environment* 30:31-2 D '88
HAMBURG (GERMANY)
Galleries and museums
Withered enthusiasms [industrial complex converted to an exhibition hall] D. Galloway. il *Art News* 88:83-4 D '89
HAMBURG BALLET
Hamburg's Ivan Liska: starman. J. Gruen. il pors *Dance Magazine* 63:36-9 S '89
Reviews:
Performance of Peer Gynt at the Hamburg State Opera. H. Koegler. *Dance Magazine* 63:105-7 My '89
HAMBURGER FAST FOOD RESTAURANTS *See* Fast food restaurants
HAMBURGERS
American classics: the hamburger and hot-dog cookbook. il *Ladies' Home Journal* 106:139-40+ Ag '89
Best ever burgers. C. Koury. il *Parents* 64:121-5 Ag '89
Recipe of the week [California cheeseburger skillet] il *Jet* 76:38 S 4 '89
Collectibles
Hamburger heaven: a burger blitz [collection of J. Tennyson] T. Mewborne. il por *Antiques & Collecting Hobbies* 94:22-5 D '89
HAMBY, ALONZO L.
Harry Truman, small-town American. bibl il pors *History Today* 39:17-23 D '89
HAMEL, ALAN
about
A Somers place. P. Viladas. il pors *House & Garden* 161:210-15 S '89
HAMILL, PETE
American journal. See issues of Esquire beginning September 1989
about
New boys on the block. L. Eisenberg. il por *Esquire* 112:51 S '89
HAMILTON, ALEXANDER, 1757-1804
about
The man on the 10-spot turns 200. J. Egan. il *U.S. News & World Report* 107:57 S 18 '89
HAMILTON, ANN
about
Ann Hamilton at Capp Street Project. G. Morris. il *Art in America* 77:221+ O '89
HAMILTON, BRUCE
Unfinished business. il *Sierra* 74:48-51+ S/O '89
HAMILTON, CAROL
Lasting links [poem] *The Christian Century* 106:1109 N 29 '89
HAMILTON, DANIEL
Dateline East Germany: the wall behind the Wall. *Foreign Policy* 76:176-97 Fall '89
HAMILTON, DAVID, 1935-
Their native tongue. il *Opera News* 54:18-20+ Ag '89
HAMILTON, LADY EMMA, 1761?-1815
about
First encounters. E. Sorel and N. C. Sorel. il *The Atlantic* 264:79 S '89
HAMILTON, JANE, 1957-
When I began to understand quantum mechanics [story] il *Harper's* 279:41-9 Ag '89

HAMILTON, JON
Health insurance: weighing the tradeoffs [special section] il *American Health* 8:11-12+ S '89
New treatments for hypertension. il *McCall's* 116:89-90 Je '89
HAMILTON, JOSEPH H.
about
Scuffle in the boardroom. A. A. Lappen. pors *Forbes* 144:112+ O 16 '89
HAMILTON, KIM
The weight-loss perk. il *Health (New York, N.Y.)* 21:32+ Jl '89
HAMILTON, MINARD
Elementary, my dear Watkins. il *The Nation* 248:732-4 My 29 '89
The nuclear waste dilemma. il *USA Today (Periodical)* 117:44-6 Mr '89
HAMILTON, RICHARD
Busted. il pors *Seventeen* 48:122+ O '89
HAMILTON, STEPHANIE RENFROW
Romance away from home. il *Essence* 19:23+ F '89
HAMILTON, WAYNE L.
The sculpturing of Zion [excerpt] il *National Parks* 63:46-7 Jl/Ag '89
HAMILTON, WILLIAM, 1924-
about
The dangerous God: a profile of William Hamilton [cover story] L. H. Steffen. *The Christian Century* 106:844-7 S 27 '89
HAMILTON, WILLIAM, 1939-
Madame Vache. il *Gourmet* 49:68+ Mr '89
HAMILTON-FINLAY, IAN *See* Finlay, Ian Hamilton, 1925-
HAMILTONIAN FUNCTION
Toward protein tertiary structure recognition by means of associative memory Hamiltonians. M. S. Friedrichs and P. G. Wolynes. bibl f il *Science* 246:371-3 O 20 '89
HAMISH HAMILTON LTD.
Heads of Hamish Hamilton and Michael Joseph resign. V. Menkes. *Publishers Weekly* 236:13 Jl 14 '89
HAMIZRACHI, YORAM
Talk with a PLO official [interview with Z. L. al-Terzi] il *World Press Review* 36:17-18 F '89
HAMLIN, GEORGE W.
Boosting operations at underused airports can ease congestion in U.S. por *Aviation Week & Space Technology* 130:173-4+ Je 19 '89
HAMLIN, HARRY
about
Hamlins' hideaway. J. Grant. il pors *Life* 12:119-20 F '89
HAMM, JOHN
Intensive day treatment provides an alternative to residential care. il *Children Today* 18:11-15 S/O '89
HAMM, WILLIAM E.
Honoring the noble sacrifice [address, May 30, 1988] *Vital Speeches of the Day* 55:626-7 Ag 1 '89
HAMMARLUND, MATT
Creating a nostalgic theme assembly. il *Petersen's Photographic Magazine* 17:84-5 Ap '89
HAMMEL, H. B.
Neptune cloud structure at visible wavelengths. bibl f il *Science* 244:1165-7 Je 9 '89
HAMMEL, H. B., AND OTHERS
Neptune's wind speeds obtained by tracking clouds in Voyager images. bibl f il *Science* 245:1367-9 S 22 '89
HAMMEL, LISA
Now voyagers. il *American Craft* 49:34-41 Ag/S '89
HAMMER, ARMAND, 1898-
Armand Hammer, 90, who doesn't have time to retire or die. il por *Forbes* 143:20 Ja 23 '89
about
A philanthropist against cancer. C. SerVaas. il por *The Saturday Evening Post* 261:100-1 Ap '89
The teflon tycoon. S. Weinberg. il pors *Common Cause Magazine* 15:17-21 N/D '89
HAMMER, JOSHUA
Cram scam [cover story] il *The New Republic* 200:15-18 Ap 24 '89
The upstart (slam!) who's reinventing (pow!) the tube (grrr!). il pors *Gentlemen's Quarterly* 59:280-5+ N '89
HAMMER, SIGNE
High tea & totem poles. il *Travel Holiday* 172:82-9 D '89
HAMMERHEAD SHARKS *See* Sharks
HAMMERS
See also
Nail guns
Collectors and collecting
Strapping good hammer. il *Workbench* 45:72 Jl/Ag '89
HAMMERSCHLAG, CARL A.
about
The dance of healing. C. Perlmutter. *Prevention (Emmaus, Pa.)* 41:69-72 S '89
HAMMOND, CAROL
Watermelon. il *Americana* 17:34-6 Jl/Ag '89
HAMMOND, LINDA DARLING- *See* Darling-Hammond, Linda, 1951-
HAMMOND, MARGO
The richest little girl in the world. il pors *McCall's* 117:38-40+ N '89

HAMMOND, MARGO—*cont.*

The Trumps: America's most glamorous two-career couple. il pors *McCall's* 116:22-4+ F '89

HAMMOND, MARY STEWART

Paying respects [poem] *The New Yorker* 65:44 S 18 '89

Saving memory [poem] *The Atlantic* 263:50 F '89

Small talk [poem] *The New Yorker* 65:34 Je 26 '89

HAMMONS, DAVID

about

Chasing the blue train. C. Reid. il *Art in America* 77:196-7 S '89

Hammering the body politic, blacks wreck a portrait of a blond, white Jesse Jackson. il *People Weekly* 32:79 D 18 '89

Jackson cites reality in portrait of him as white. il por *Jet* 77:5 D 18 '89

HAMPL, PATRICIA, 1946-

The lax habits of the free imagination [excerpt from The Houghton Mifflin anthology of short fiction] il *The New York Times Book Review* 94:1+ Mr 5 '89

HAMPSON, THOMAS

about

Rapid transit [cover story] D. G. Winer. il pors *Opera News* 53:8-11+ F 4 '89

HAMPSTEN, ANDY

about

Humility and a pinch of purpose. C. Carpenter-Phinney. il pors *Bicycling* 30:90-2+ Ap '89

HAMPTON, CHRISTOPHER, 1946-

about

Les liaisons dangereuses [drama] Reviews

Theatre Crafts il 23:48-54+ F '89. M. LaRue

HAMPTON, DAN

about

Cool Hand Dan. J. Lieber. il pors *Sports Illustrated* 71:112-18+ O 9 '89

HAMPTON, DUANE

about

Country class. M. Matousek. il pors *Harper's Bazaar* 122:78-83+ Je '89

HAMPTON, LIONEL

about

Lionel Hampton/Chevron Jazz Festival. P. De Barros. il por *Down Beat* 56:50 Je '89

HAMPTON, MARK

Bed and Biedermeier. il *House & Garden* 161:46+ Ag '89

about

As time goes by. C. Vogel. il *The New York Times Magazine* p78-9 O 1 '89

Country class. M. Matousek. il pors *Harper's Bazaar* 122:78-83+ Je '89

Yankee preserve. E. A. Berthold. il *House & Garden* 161:98-103+ Je '89

HAMPTON, MARK, 1923-

about

Minimalism in Miami. J. Taylor. il *Architectural Digest* 46:216-21+ Ap '89

HAMPTON (VA.)

Galleries and museums

See also

Hampton University Museum (Hampton, Va.)

HAMPTON UNIVERSITY MUSEUM (HAMPTON, VA.)

Hampton shares its cultures. il *Southern Living* 24:55 N '89

HAMPTONS (LONG ISLAND, N.Y.) *See* Long Island (N.Y.)

HAMSTERS

Sex lives of the small and furry [frequent sexual encounters weaken immune system of golden hamsters; research by Nancy Ostrowski] il *Discover* 10:10 D '89

Sexual behavior

See Sexual behavior—Rodents

HAN, SANG TAE

Looking ahead. il por *World Health* p3 N '89

HAN XU, 1924-

about

The Chinese ambassador defends his government. W. F. Buckley. *National Review* 41:71 S 29 '89

HANAHAN, DOUGLAS

Transgenic mice as probes into complex systems. bibl f il *Science* 246:1265-75 D 8 '89

HANCE, BILLIE JO

(jt. auth) See Chess, Caron, and Hance, Billie Jo

HANCOCK, JOHN

about

Prancer [film] Reviews

People Weekly 32:17 D 11 '89. R. Novak

HANCOCK CENTER (CHICAGO, ILL.)

Chicago's Hancock Center. A. R. Williams. il *National Geographic* 175:174-85 F '89

HANCOCK FAMILY

about

Blood brothers and bluegrass. W. Nack. il *Sports Illustrated* 71:76-80+ O 30 '89

HAND, DOUGLAS

Breadbasket ecology. il map por *American Health* 8:66-8 S '89

HAND

The gripping story of Paranthropus [evidence of tool use at Swartkrans site; study by Randall L. Susman] P. Shipman. il *Discover* 10:66-71 Ap '89

Care

See also

Manicuring

Deep treats for beautiful hands. il *Glamour* 87:258-61 O '89

A handful of beauty. il *Mademoiselle* 95:32 O '89

Talking hands. H. Burggraf. il *American Health* 8:22-4+ Jl/Ag '89

Wounds and injuries

Helping hands [tennis injuries] P. Stites. il *World Tennis* 36:24+ Mr '89

HAND HELD COMPUTERS *See* Computers

HAND HELD VACUUM CLEANERS *See* Vacuum cleaners

HAND POLLINATION *See* Fertilization of plants

HAND PRINTS *See* Handprints

HAND RAILINGS

Deck under glass. R. Stepler. il *Popular Science* 234:124-6 Ap '89

Grid lets in the light. il *Southern Living* 24:181 N '89

HAND TOOLS *See* Tools

HANDBALL

See also

Racquetball

HANDCLASP INTERNATIONAL

Cinemas on wheels. D. J. Henrich. il *World Health* p10-11 Ja/F '89

HANDEDNESS *See* Left- and right-handedness

HANDEL, GEORGE FRIDERIC, 1685-1759

about

Giulio Cesare [opera] Reviews

The New Yorker 65:117-18 N 20 '89. A. Porter

Giustino [opera] Reviews

Opera News il 54:52 S '89. S. Von Buchau

Hallelujah! P. Yancey. il *Christianity Today* 33:30-3 D 15 '89

Semele [oratorio] Reviews

The New Yorker 65:146-9 D 4 '89. A. Porter

HANDEL FESTIVAL (MD.) *See* Music festivals—Maryland

HANDGUN CONTROL LEGISLATION *See* Firearms—Laws and regulations

HANDGUNS *See* Firearms

HANDICAPPED

See also

Actors and actresses, Handicapped

Amputees

Architecture and the handicapped

Authors, Handicapped

Blind

Cartoonists, Handicapped

Cerebral palsy

Children, Handicapped

Deaf

Drugs and the handicapped

Entertainers, Handicapped

Guitarists, Handicapped

Mentally handicapped

Mentally handicapped children

Mothers, Handicapped

Paralytics

Parents, Handicapped

Parents of the handicapped

Pianists, Handicapped

Scientists, Handicapped

How to lend aid to the disabled. J. Wood. *Modern Maturity* 32:25-6 Ag/S '89

Civil rights

Americans with Disabilities Act. *Congressional Digest* 68:289 D '89

A brave Soviet deputy speaks up for a forgotten minority [I. Zaslavskiy tours U.S.] C. Phillips. il pors *People Weekly* 32:109-10 O 9 '89

Disability bill may go too far for churches [Americans with Disabilities Act of 1989] il *Christianity Today* 33:54-5 Je 16 '89

Disabling America [Americans with Disabilities Act] S. T. Mandel. il *National Review* 41:23-4 S 29 '89

Enabling act [Americans with Disabilities Act] M. Johnson. *The Nation* 249:446 O 23 '89

Liberation day for the disabled [Senate passes Americans with Disabilities Act] J. P. Shapiro. il *U.S. News & World Report* 107:20-2+ S 18 '89

New help for the disabled [Senate passes sweeping legislation that bars discrimination] E. Salholz. il *Newsweek* 114:26 S 18 '89

Notes and comment. *The New Yorker* 65:43-4 N 20 '89

The Peeping Tom Protection Act [Americans with Disabilities Act] D. Seligman. il *Fortune* 120:216 O 23 '89

Education

The impact of policies for handicapped children on future early education policy. J. J. Gallagher. bibl f il *Phi Delta Kappan* 71:121-4 O '89

Employment

See also

United States. Rehabilitation Services Administration

HANDICAPPED—cont.
Equipment
See also
Computers and the handicapped
Volunteers for Medical Engineering
Wheelchairs
Family relationships
See also
Parents of the handicapped
The amazing Andertons [quadraplegic couple] L. Gourse. il pors *McCall's* 116:92+ Ja '89
Psychology
The life my mother chose [coping with paralysis] M. Ragghianti. il *Reader's Digest* 134:7-9+ My '89
The mixed blessings of a movement. P. Glastris. il *U.S. News & World Report* 107:22-3 S 18 '89
Recreation
The playground that Orlando built [All Children's Playground suitable for the handicapped] D. Young. il *Southern Living* 24:159-60 N '89
Sports
See also
Frank Bolling Adaptive Baseball League
Special Olympics
Wheelchair basketball
Wheelchair racing
Able disableds [ski racing] T. Latsis. il *Skiing* 42:286+ S '89
"All I ever wanted was a shot" [one-handed baseball player J. Abbott] J. Howard. il pors *Sport (New York, N.Y.)* 80:26-9 Mr '89
Angel on the ascent [one-handed pitcher J. Abbott makes professional debut] B. Anderson. il por *Sports Illustrated* 70:27 Mr 13 '89
The complete Jim Abbott. C. Leerhsen. il por *Newsweek* 113:60 Je 12 '89
Dreaming the big dreams [one-handed pitcher J. Abbott in California Angels training camp] T. Callahan. il por *Time* 133:78 Mr 20 '89
Grit and a granite will conquer El Capitan [paraplegic M. Wellman makes climb assisted by M. Corbett] M. Brower. il pors *People Weekly* 32:36-9 Ag 14 '89
Heart of an Ironman [arthritis victim G. Yates competes in the triathlon] J. G. Hubbell. il pors *Reader's Digest* 134:13-14+ Mr '89
The man who would not quit [thalidomide victim D. L. Stevens] J. G. Hubbell. il pors *Reader's Digest* 134:115-18 F '89
No more doubts [mid-season report on pitcher J. Abbott] il por *Sports Illustrated* 71:64-5 Jl 24 '89
One for the Angels [J. Abbott] R. Brofman. il pors *Life* 12:118+ Je '89
Travel
Airline groups urge FAA to change proposed rules on handicapped passengers. *Aviation Week & Space Technology* 130:108 Ja 2 '89
Clearing a path for disabled travelers. M. J. Pitzer. il *Business Week* p96 Jl 3 '89
Easy come, easy go? S. Shane. *Travel Holiday* 171:6 Ja '89
FAA seating restrictions clip the wings of handicapped and other flyers. M. Di Landro. il *Travel Holiday* 172:22-3 S '89
Tips for handicapped travelers. H. Gieseking. *Travel Holiday* 171:113-14 Mr '89
Travel books for the disabled. J. Crichton. *Publishers Weekly* 235:60 Ja 20 '89
Unfriendly skies [airlines] M. Ervin. il *The Progressive* 53:28-31 Je '89
Developing countries
Deals on wheels [low cost wheelchairs designed for handicapped in developing countries; work of R. Hotchkiss] B. Weber. il por *The New York Times Magazine* p122 S 17 '89
Soviet Union
A brave Soviet deputy speaks up for a forgotten minority [I. Zaslavskiy tours U.S.] C. Phillips. il pors *People Weekly* 32:109-10 O 9 '89
HANDICAPPED AND ANIMALS
See also
Guide dogs
A boy's best friend [paraplegic T. Berberian's assistance dog] M. Clary. il por *McCall's* 116:75-6 Je '89
HANDICAPPED AS INVENTORS
Tom Houston is a real stand-up guy, thanks to the versatile vertical wheelchair he devised [HiRider] il pors *People Weekly* 32:91-2 Ag 28 '89
HANDICAPPING OF RACE HORSES *See* Horse race betting
HANDICRAFT *See* Arts and crafts
HANDLEMAN CO.
"We are a society of collectors". L. Gubernick. il *Forbes* 144:80 Jl 24 '89
HANDLER, DAVID, 1952-
Is cable now worth the money? il *TV Guide* 37:24-6 Ap 8-14 '89
HANDLER, JOSHUA
(jt. auth) *See* Arkin, William M., and Handler, Joshua

HANDLER, KEN
about
As a tiny plastic star turns 30, the real Barbie and Ken reflect on life in the shadow of the dolls. M. Green. il pors *People Weekly* 31:186-7+ Mr 6 '89
HANDLES
See also
Tool handles
HANDLIN, LILIAN
(jt. auth) *See* Handlin, Oscar, 1915-, and Handlin, Lilian
HANDLIN, OSCAR, 1915-, AND HANDLIN, LILIAN
Who read John Locke? Words and acts in the American Revolution. *The American Scholar* 58:545-56 Aut '89
HANDLING OF FOOD *See* Food handling
HANDLING OF SNAKES (HOLINESS CHURCHES) *See* Snake handling (Holiness churches)
HANDMADE PAPER *See* Paper making
HANDPRINTS
The way the whorls turn [computer reads Down syndrome in parents' handprints] M. R. Meyer. il *Newsweek* 113:73 F 13 '89
HANDRAILS *See* Hand railings
HANDREN, MAURA
about
When Joe Ross rescued little Maura Handren, he didn't know he was really a wife-saver. il pors *People Weekly* 31:94 Ap 17 '89
HANDSAWS *See* Saws and sawing
HANDWRITING RECOGNITION COMPUTERS *See* Pen-based computers
HANDY, BRUCE
A Spy guide to postmodern everything. il *Utne Reader* p55+ Jl/Ag '89
HANDY, JOHN
about
John Handy. A. Lange. il por *Down Beat* 56:14 D '89
HANEY, WALTER, AND MADAUS, GEORGE F.
Searching for alternatives to standardized tests: whys, whats, and whithers. bibl f il *Phi Delta Kappan* 70:683-7 My '89
HANFORD NUCLEAR RESERVATION (WASH.)
Hanford: America's nuclear graveyard. K. D. Steele. bibl f il *The Bulletin of the Atomic Scientists* 45:14-20+ O '89
When a nuclear reactor dies, $98 million is a cheap funeral [Shippingport shutdown] S. Shulman. bibl (p228) il *Smithsonian* 20:56-62+ O '89
HANG GLIDERS *See* Gliders (Aviation)
HANG GLIDING
Ridge runners [ridge soaring in sailplanes over Allegheny Mountains] N. Moll. il *Flying* 116:58-62+ Ag '89
You and the wind [cue from hawk saves life of hang glider] R. Pinkerton. il *Reader's Digest* 135:105-6 Jl '89
HANGERS
No-holes hanger [Sears Hang Fast system] R. Capotosto. il *Popular Mechanics* 166:89 Ag '89
HANGING
Blacks demand probe in death of Missouri youth found hanging from tree [A. Roland] por *Jet* 76:52 Ap 24 '89
HANGING OF PICTURES *See* Pictures—Hanging
HANGING PLANTS
Hanging salads [cover story] il *Sunset (Central West edition)* 182:82-3 F '89
How does Sunset get poinsettias to hang? il *Sunset (Central West edition)* 183:158-9 D '89
HANKE, THOMAS
A dark side of expansion. *World Press Review* 36:18-19 Ja '89
HANKS, CLYDE A.
Before the well runs dry: cutting the cost of retiree health benefits. *USA Today (Periodical)* 117:86-8 My '89
HANKS, TOM
about
Hanks to you [interview] B. Walker. il pors *Film Comment* 25:16-19 Mr/Ap '89
Tom Hanks. N. Anderson. il pors *Good Housekeeping* 208:168+ My '89
HANLEY, DENIS M.
about
Clearly bubbling up from Down Under. S. Hutcheon. il por *Business Week* p115 My 22 '89
HANNA, DANIEL C.
about
Wanna make Dan Hanna wax eloquent? Ask him how he became king of the car wash. il por *People Weekly* 32:84 Ag 21 '89
HANNA ANDERSSON CORPORATION
The new entrepreneurial establishment: 1989 Harriet Alger Award [G. Denhart] il pors *Working Woman* 14:53-6+ N '89
HANNA-BARBERA PRODUCTIONS, INC.
The Hanna-Barbera cartoons: compounding Bible ignorance? [cover story] H. L. Turner and others. il *The Christian Century* 106:231-4 Mr 1 '89
HANNA CAR WASH SYSTEMS (FIRM)
Wanna make Dan Hanna wax eloquent? Ask him how he became king of the car wash. il por *People Weekly* 32:84 Ag 21 '89

HANNA MINING CO.
Hanna the transformed. M. J. Williams. il *Fortune* 120:83 Ag 28 '89

HANNAH, DUNCAN
about
Duncan Hannah: Charles Cowles. A. Corn. il *Art News* 88:162-3 N '89

HANNAM, ANNE
about
Play it again, Anne. K. Williams. il pors *Runner's World* 24:70-5 Ja '89
Woman to watch: road runner Anne Hannam. L. Rothlein. il por *Women's Sports & Fitness* 11:49 Ja/F '89

HANNEMA, DIRK, 1895-1984
Half-truths and treasures. M. K. Talley, Jr. il por *Art News* 88:53-4 F '89

HANNIBAL, JOSEPH T., AND CREASE, FRAY A.
Concrete's a natural. il *Earth Science* 41:19-20 Wint '88

HANNING, JEFFREY
A banking success. il por *The Mother Earth News* 115:46 Ja/F '89

HANNON, KENT
Atlanta. il *Sport (New York, N.Y.)* 80:70-4 Ag '89
The Masters blasters. il *Sport (New York, N.Y.)* 80:32+ My '89
Wheels of fortune. il pors *Sport (New York, N.Y.)* 80:72-4+ Mr '89

HANNUN, YUSUF A., AND BELL, ROBERT MAURICE, 1944-
Functions of sphingolipids and sphingolipid breakdown products in cellular regulation. bibl f il *Science* 243:500-7 Ja 27 '89
Sphingomyelin synthase and PKC activation [discussion of January 27, 1989 article, Functions of sphingolipids and sphingolipid breakdown products in cellular regulation] il *Science* 246:1050 N 24 '89

HANOI (VIETNAM)
Description
Hanoi: the capital today. P. T. White. il maps *National Geographic* 176:558-93 N '89

HANOVER (GERMANY)
Music
See also
Opera—Germany (West)

HANOVER (N.H.)
Galleries and museums
See also
Hood Museum of Art

HANOVER BAND
The "authentic" Beethoven. E. Salzman. il *Stereo Review* 54:126 My '89

HANRAHAN, JOHN, 1938-
Testing ground. il *Common Cause Magazine* 15:13-19+ Ja/F '89
The union-busting Post: labor pains at a liberal paper [cover story] il *The Progressive* 53:18-25 F '89

HANSBERRY, LORRAINE, 1930-1965
about
30th anniversary showing of 'Raisin in the sun' winning rave reviews. il *Jet* 75:38-9 F 20 '89
Look beyond the mad rush to be number one. J. E. Wideman. il *TV Guide* 37:32-4 Ja 28-F 3 '89
A raisin in the sun: the uncut version. D. G. Peerman. *The Christian Century* 106:71-3 Ja 25 '89

HANSEATIC LEAGUE
City freeman? [German enclave in medieval London] D. Keys. il *History Today* 39:4-5 D '89

HANSELL, MICHAEL H. (MICHAEL HENRY), 1940-
Wasp papier-mâché. il *Natural History* p52-61 Ag '89

HANSEN, HOPE
A certain smile. il *Vogue* 179:432-3+ N '89

HANSEN, JACK WINSOR
Werther's way. il *Opera News* 53:18-21+ Mr 18 '89

HANSEN, JAMES E. (JAMES EDWARD), 1941-
about
Doctored data. *Commonweal* 116:325 Je 2 '89
Feeling the heat on the greenhouse. S. Begley. il *Newsweek* 112:79-80 My 22 '89
Hansen and the greenhouse effect [discussion of June 2, 1989 article, Hansen vs. the world on the greenhouse threat] R. A. Kerr. *Science* 245:451-2 Ag 4 '89
Hansen vs. the world on the greenhouse threat. R. A. Kerr. il por *Science* 244:1041-3 Je 2 '89
Researchers irked by changes to testimony. E. Marshall. *Science* 244:648 My 12 '89

HANSEN, JOHN T., AND SLADEK, JOHN R.
Fetal research. bibl f il *Science* 246:775-9 N 10 '89

HANSEN, KENT, AND OTHERS
Making nuclear power work: lessons from around the world [cover story] il *Technology Review* 92:30-8+ F/Mr '89

HANSEN, MICHAEL C.
Ohio natural bridges. il map *Earth Science* 41:10-12 Wint '88

HANSEN, MIRIAM
Griffith's real Intolerance [cover story] il *Film Comment* 25:28-9 S/O '89

HANSEN, PETER M.
Keep your VCR healthy. il *Radio-Electronics* 60:61-4 Mr '89
Keep your VCR healthy. il *Radio-Electronics* 60:55-8 S '89

HANSEN, TOM
In the middle of the journey of our life [poem] *The American Scholar* 58:564-6 Aut '89

HANSEN'S DISEASE *See* Leprosy

HANSMA, PAUL K., 1946-, AND OTHERS
The scanning ion-conductance microscope. bibl f il *Science* 243:641-3 F 3 '89

HANSON, AMY AXT, AND BENNETT, WILLIAM IRA
Trojan eggs. il *The New York Times Magazine* p25-6 Jl 30 '89

HANSON, BETSY, AND NELKIN, DOROTHY
Public responses to genetic engineering. *Society* 27:76-80 N/D '89

HANSON, CHRISTOPHER
Pay dirt. *The New Republic* 201:10-11 D 25 '89

HANSON, DALE
about
Bang for the buck. N. J. Perry. il por *Fortune* 119:37 Ja 2 '89

HANSON, ERIC
Hills alive! il map *Skiing* 41:122-4+ Ja '89

HANSON, HOWARD, 1896-1981
about
Howard Hanson, American romantic. D. Hall. por *Stereo Review* 54:126 S '89

HANSON, WILLIAM S., AND MACINNES, LESLEY
Up against the wall. il maps *Natural History* p80-7 Ap '89

HANSON PLC
A confused agenda for selling the country [Canadian Pacific rumored takeover target] A. Fotheringham. il *Maclean's* 102:56 Ag 14 '89
Did Hanson hide bad news? [Smith Corona spinoff] C. Tucher. *Business Week* p27-8 Ag 28 '89
Hanson, White and Cummins. T. Jaffe. *Forbes* 143:196-7 Je 12 '89
Is Consgold 'just an appetizer' for Hanson? M. Maremont. il *Business Week* p41-2 Jl 10 '89
Why Henry Schacht is watching his rearview mirror [Britain's Hanson's stake in Cummins] J. E. Ellis. il por *Business Week* p43 Ja 9 '89

HANSON TRUST PLC
See also
Hanson plc

HANSSON, LENNART
The lemming phenomenon. il *Natural History* p38-43 D '89

HANUKKAH
See also
Menorah
Chappy Chanukah [English spelling] W. Safire. il *The New York Times Magazine* p26+ D 10 '89
Hanukkah [excerpt from These lights are holy] E. D. Frishman. il *Good Housekeeping* 209:74 D '89
Hanukkah traditions. J. Williams and others. il *Better Homes and Gardens* 67:75-80+ D '89
Interfaith anxiety [Jewish-gentile marriages face Christmas and Hanukkah] il *Psychology Today* 22:6+ D '88
Mixed blessings [Christian-Jewish household] J. Hope. il *Parents* 64:252 D '89

HANUSSEN [film] *See* Motion picture reviews—Single works

HAO, CHARLES
about
Through glasses, darkly. M. Barrier. il pors *Nation's Business* 77:77 Ap '89

HAPGOOD, FRED
Building a better mouse. il *Omni (New York, N.Y.)* 12:22+ N '89
The magic theater. il *Omni (New York, N.Y.)* 12:114-16+ D '89
The quest for oil. il *National Geographic* 176:226-59 Ag '89

HAPGOOD [drama] *See* Stoppard, Tom

HAPPINESS
See also
Fun
Pleasure
Functioning communities. C. A. Murray. *Current (Washington, D.C.)* 311:24-31 Mr/Ap '89
The happiness report. G. Sheehy. il *Glamour* 87:308-13+ Ap '89
Happy parents, happy kids. D. F. Bjorklund and B. Bjorklund. il *Parents* 64:128 Ja '89
How to get lucky in life [excerpt from You'll see it when you believe it] W. W. Dyer. *Redbook* 173:120-1+ Jl '89
The paradox of happiness [cover story] D. Swanbrow. il *Psychology Today* 23:37-9 Jl/Ag '89
Put on a happy face . . . or else. B. Barol. il por *Newsweek* 113:74-5 F 27 '89
Quiz: how happy are you? il *'Teen* 33:22 Ja '89
The secret of true happiness. D. Prager. *Reader's Digest* 134:177-8 Je '89
Tolstoy and the pursuit of happiness. A. Valiunas. *Commentary* 87:33-41 Je '89

HAPPINESS—cont.
What makes a happy person? D. Prager. *Redbook* 172:76-7+ F '89
When she's sad and you're happy . . . shut up! E. Kaye. *Mademoiselle* 95:78 Je '89
HAPSBURG, HOUSE OF *See* House of Habsburg
HAPTOGLOBIN-RELATED PROTEIN
Marker predicts breast cancer recurrence. R. Weiss. *Science News* 136:164 S 9 '89
HAQ, ABDUL
about
Target: Kabul. D. Lorch. il pors map *The New York Times Magazine* p32-5+ F 12 '89
HAQUE, FAREED
about
Fareed Haque. B. Milkowski. por *Down Beat* 56:15 Ag '89
HARARY, KEITH
Womb with a view. il *Omni (New York, N.Y.)* 11:39-40+ Ag '89
HARARY, KEITH, AND WEINTRAUB, PAMELA
Life is but a dream [cover story] il *Omni (New York, N.Y.)* 12:42-4+ N '89
HARASSMENT
See also
Sexual harassment
HARBIN (CHINA)
Festivals
Cold, cold Harbin: China's city of ice [Ice Lantern Festival] il map *National Geographic World* 161:26-31 Ja '89
HARBISON, TAYLOR
about
Captain Hook. D. B. Cowin. il por *House & Garden* 161:110 My '89
HARBOR SEALS *See* Seals (Animals)
HARBOR VILLAGE RESTAURANT (SAN FRANCISCO, CALIF.) *See* San Francisco (Calif.)—Restaurants, nightclubs, bars, etc.
HARBORS
See also
Boston (Mass.)—Harbor
Condominiums (Boat docking)
Docks, wharves, etc.
Houston (Tex.)—Harbor
Marinas
Saint-Tropez (France)—Harbor
Seattle (Wash.)—Harbor
HARCOURT, MICHEL
about
New talents: Michel Harcourt. il por *Harper's Bazaar* 122:85 Mr '89
HARCOURT BRACE JOVANOVICH, INC.
HBJ sells theme parks to Anheuser for $1.1 billion. C. Reid. *Publishers Weekly* 236:11 O 13 '89
If this be victory . . . [onerous debt] S. Flack. il *Forbes* 144:38-9 Ag 7 '89
Mark Helprin's next 10 years (and next six books) with HBJ. il por *Publishers Weekly* 235:33-4 Je 9 '89
Some victory. S. Flack. il *Forbes* 144:10 O 30 '89
What's new at . . . Harcourt Brace Jovanovich [interview with P. Jovanovich] il por *Publishers Weekly* 235:26-7 My 26 '89
HARD DISK MEMORY (COMPUTERS) *See* Computers—Memory systems
HARD OF HEARING *See* Deaf; Deafness
HARDBALL [television program] *See* Television program reviews—Single works
HARDEE FARMS
Successful family farm. B. Freese. il *Successful Farming* 87:36-8 Je '89
HARDEE MEMORIAL HOSPITAL (WAUCHULA, FLA.) *See* Wauchula (Fla.)—Hospitals
HARDEE'S FOOD SYSTEMS, INC.
Burger woes. R. T. Grieves. il por *Forbes* 143:102 Ja 23 '89
HARDENING OF THE ARTERIES *See* Arteriosclerosis
HARDIN, GARRETT JAMES, 1915-
There is no global population problem [cover story] il por *The Humanist* 49:11-13+ Jl/Ag '89
HARDIN, LOUIS *See* Moondog
HARDIN, TED, AND PSIHOYOS, LOUIS
Dream streets. il *New York* 22:58-67 D 25 '89-Ja 1 '90
HARDINESS OF PLANTS *See* Plants—Hardiness
HARDING, RAYMOND B.
about
The last liberal. J. Klein. il por *New York* 22:14+ Ap 3 '89
HARDISON, KADEEM
about
Kadeem Hardison. C. Connors. pors *Seventeen* 48:57+ Jl '89
Kadeem Hardison wants out of A different world. E. Warren. il pors *TV Guide* 37:14-15+ Jl 22-28 '89
HARDMAN, CHRIS
about
Etiquette of the undercaste [drama] Reviews
Mother Jones il por 14:55 Ap '89. M. Berson

HARDNESS
Dreaming up crystals that outdo diamond [work of Marvin L. Cohen and Amy Y. Liu] I. Amato. il *Science News* 136:134 Ag 26 '89
Prediction of new low compressibility solids. A. Y. Liu and M. L. Cohen. bibl f il *Science* 245:841-2 Ag 25 '89
HARDWARE
See also
Casters, glides, etc. (Hardware)
Fasteners
Hinges
Nails
Rivets and riveting
Screws
Washers (Hardware)
HARDWICK, ELIZABETH
Basic Englishing. *The New York Review of Books* 36:67 O 26 '89
HARDWICK, TODD
about
Trapper Todd Hardwick tackles the ultimate varmint, a monster python who won't leave home. M. Neill. il pors *People Weekly* 32:179-80+ D 4 '89
HARDWOOD FLOORING *See* Flooring
HARDWOODS
Taking hardwood cuttings. C. Shirley. il *Organic Gardening* 36:26-7 N '89
HARDY, DOROTHY C.
Salutation [poem] *Essence* 20:149 S '89
HARDY, LELAND
about
A bear in the ring and a bull on Wall Street, Leland Hardy is a broker with a convincing pitch. A. Abrahams. il pors *People Weekly* 32:109-10 S 18 '89
He's bullish on boxing. il por *Sports Illustrated* 71:8 Jl 3 '89
HARDY, PAT
about
An expert offers the ABCs of getting into the B&B biz [interview] J. Wuorio. il por *Money* 18:18 D '89
HARDY, S. J. S.
(jt. auth) See Randall, L. L., and Hardy, S. J. S.
HARDY, THOMAS, 1840-1928
about
Of time and poetry. D. Jacobson. *Commentary* 88:48-53 N '89
HARE, DAVID
The secret rapture [excerpt from drama] il *Harper's* 278:38-9+ F '89
about
Hare apparent. R. Koenig. il por *Vogue* 179:202 F '89
A map of the world [drama] Reviews
Maclean's il 102:56 Mr 6 '89. J. Bemrose
The secret rapture [drama] Reviews
America 161:382 N 25 '89. T. P. O'Malley
Commonweal 116:671+ D 1 '89. G. C. Weales
The Nation 249:766-7 D 18 '89. T. M. Disch
The New Republic 201:29-30 N 20 '89. R. Brustein
New York il 22:132 N 6 '89. J. Simon
The New Yorker 65:106+ N 13 '89. M. Kramer
Newsweek il por 114:89 N 13 '89. J. Kroll
HARES
See also
Rabbits
HARFORD, JOE B.
(jt. auth) See Klausner, Richard D., and Harford, Joe B.
HARGETT, JAMES
Keeping drivers friendly. *Bicycling* 30:58 Ag '89
HARGROVE, BARBARA W.
The future of rural populism. bibl *Society* 26:39-44 Ja/F '89
HARI, RIITTA, AND LOUNASMAA, OLLI V.
Recording and interpretation of cerebral magnetic fields. bibl f il *Science* 244:432-6 Ap 28 '89
HARID CONSERVATORY
Harid still has it. And more. M. Horosko. il *Dance Magazine* 63:90-1 N '89
HARING, BERNARD *See* Häring, Bernhard, 1912-
HÄRING, BERNHARD, 1912-
Building a creative conscience; tr. by Ingrid Knapp. il *Commonweal* 116:433-6 Ag 11 '89
Does God condemn contraception? *Commonweal* 116:69-71 F 10 '89
On Bernard Häring's new book. *America* 161:339-40 N 18 '89
HARING, KEITH, 1958-1990
about
Just say know [interview] D. Sheff. il por *Rolling Stone* p58-9+ Ag 10 '89
HARINGTON, DONALD
about
PW interviews. M. Harris. por *Publishers Weekly* 235:39-40 Mr 31 '89
HARKABI, YEHOSHAFAT, 1921-
about
Israel's fateful hour [interview] R. I. Friedman. *Harper's* 279:28+ Jl '89

HARKABI, YEHOSHAFAT, 1921-—about—cont.
Yehoshafat Harkabi [interview] C. Dreifus. il *The Progressive* 53:36-9 Je '89
HARKIN, TOM, 1939-
about
New hands on the purse strings. W. Booth and others. pors *Science* 243:160 Ja 13 '89
HARKINS, GEORGE
about
George Harkins. M. S. Doherty. il por *American Artist* 53:34-9 My '89
HARKISON, JUDY
I was a flirtatious backwalker for the CIA. il *Smithsonian* 20:128 Jl '89
HARLAN, NEIL EUGENE
about
McKesson dumps another asset: the boss. R. D. Hof. il pors *Business Week* p47 S 25 '89
HARLAND (JOHN H.) CO. *See* John H. Harland Co.
HARLANDS (FRESNO, CALIF.: RESTAURANT) *See* Fresno (Calif.)—Restaurants, nightclubs, bars, etc.
HARLEM (NEW YORK, N.Y.)
See also
Abyssinian Baptist Church (New York, N.Y.)
Birdmen of Harlem [raising pigeons on tenement roofs] J. W. Miller. il *The New York Times Magazine* p48-9+ N 19 '89
From street kids to Royal Knights [B. Hall coaches chess team at J.H.S. 99 in East Harlem] J. Coudert. il por *Reader's Digest* 134:141-6 Je '89
Giving teenagers a new view of their future [work of M. Carrera] M. Ludtke. il por *Time* 133:12+ My 1 '89
Hire education [adopt-a-class program at P.S. 175] K. Emmons. il *Omni (New York, N.Y.)* 11:18+ Je '89
Just another night on crack street [drug dealers in East Harlem] P. Bourgois. il *The New York Times Magazine* p52-3+ N 12 '89
The kids win one in Harlem as, 20 years later, the Little League returns—on drug dealers' turf [organized by I. Raiford] il por *People Weekly* 31:64 Je 19 '89
Profits in a risky business [crack trade] R. Sandza. il *Newsweek* 113:37 My 29 '89
Real choice [junior high school choice program] *National Review* 41:12-13 S 1 '89
"Welcome to new Harlem!". R. Corliss. il map *Time* 133:68-9+ Ap 24 '89
White Harlem minister convicted of sex abuse [case of T. Streitferdt] il por *Jet* 76:32 Je 19 '89
White minister called 'wolf in sheep's clothes' gets 7 years in sex cases [T. Streitferdt] il por *Jet* 76:53 Jl 24 '89
HARLEM (NEW YORK, N.Y.) IN MOTION PICTURES
Eddie Murphy explains why he's making next movie in Hollywood, not Harlem. *Jet* 76:17 Ap 10 '89
HARLEM DANCE THEATRE *See* Dance Theatre of Harlem
HARLEM HOSPITAL CENTER
Princess Di visits infant AIDS victims in Harlem. il pors *Jet* 75:10 F 20 '89
HARLEM INTERNATIONAL TRADE CENTER
Harlem gets trade center. K. Osborne. il *Black Enterprise* 20:22 S '89
HARLEM NIGHTS [film] *See* Motion picture reviews—Single works
HARLEM RENAISSANCE
Harlem's first shining. D. L. Lewis. bibl f il *Modern Maturity* 32:56-61+ F/Mr '89
HARLEQUIN ENTERPRISES LTD.
Harlequin sues Bantam on promotional materials. C. Reid. *Publishers Weekly* 235:14 Ap 14 '89
Writing successful proposals for the romance market. T. Carter. *The Writer* 102:23-5 My '89
HARLEY-DAVIDSON MOTOR CO., INC.
The gentrified hog. M. Marvel. il *Esquire* 112:22+ Jl '89
Hogs. S. Anderson. il *Cycle* 40:7 O '89
Hogs with wheels. S. Smith. *Fortune* 119:38+ Ap 10 '89
How Harley beat back the Japanese [excerpt from Well-made in America] P. C. Reid. il *Fortune* 120:155+ S 25 '89
HARLIN, RENNY
about
A nightmare on Elm Street, part 4: The dream master [film]
Reviews
Video 12:62 F '89. L. Kesten
HARLING, ROBERT, 1951-
Local boy makes good. il por *Life* 12:91+ O '89
about
Star bright. L. Hart. il por *Life* 12:82-4+ O '89
HARLOW, BONNIE
"We're afraid of our son". il pors *Ladies' Home Journal* 106:18+ Mr '89
HARLOW, CHRIS
about
"We're afraid of our son". B. Harlow. il pors *Ladies' Home Journal* 106:18+ Mr '89
HARLOW, HENRY
(jt. auth) *See* Buskirk, Steven, and Harlow, Henry
HARM MISSILES *See* Guided missiles—Launching from airplanes

HARMAN, SUSAN, AND EDELSKY, CAROLE
Literacy acquisition and alienation. *The Education Digest* 55:35-9 D '89
HARMON, DEBBIE
about
She wore serious satin and tulle, but Debbie Harmon made her 'I do's' sheer sitcom. M. Dougherty. il pors *People Weekly* 31:150-1 My 22 '89
HARMON, TONY
The juicy truth about living together. il *Glamour* 87:122+ D '89
HARMONY
See also
Melody
Musical intervals and scales
HARMONY GOLD (FIRM)
Picking on the little guys. A. B. Block. il *Channels (New York, N.Y.: 1986)* 9:76-9 F '89
HARMS, THELMA
The 12 building blocks of discipline. il *Parents* 64:76-8+ Ag '89
HARMS, WARREN
about
An executive turns puzzle maker. D. E. Gumpert and D. Davis. il por *New Choices for the Best Years* 29:50-1 O '89
HARNESS, GERRY
"My gynecologist butchered me!"; ed. by Judith Kelman. il por *Redbook* 173:22+ Jl '89
HARNESS
Efficient horse harnesses [ancient China] R. K. G. Temple. il *The Courier (Unesco)* 41:17-18 O '88
HARNESS RACING
From flight to fancy [aviation pioneer J. Yeager takes up harness racing] B. Harris. il por *Women's Sports & Fitness* 11:64 My '89
HARNISCHFEGER INDUSTRIES, INC.
A company reborn. il *Forbes* 143:156 Ja 9 '89
HAROCHE, SERGE, AND KLEPPNER, DANIEL
Cavity quantum electrodynamics. bibl f il *Physics Today* 42:24-30 Ja '89
HAROUTUNIAN, SAGHATEL
Age [poem]; tr. by Diana Der Hovanessian. il *Good Housekeeping* 209:262 N '89
HARPER, ALFRED E.
about
1989 AIBS Distinguished Service Award to Alfred E. Harper. por *BioScience* 39:499 Jl/Ag '89
HARPER, ANDREW
about
Escape routes. C. Gorney. il por *House & Garden* 161:34+ Ja '89
HARPER, J. J. (JOHN JOSEPH)
about
A death in Winnipeg. P. Kaihla. il por *Maclean's* 102:16 S 11 '89
A final act of despair. B. Bergman. *Maclean's* 102:22 N 13 '89
An unfolding tragedy. P. Kopvillem. il por *Maclean's* 102:23 O 2 '89
HARPER, JACK
about
Jack Harper. B. Tarrant. il por *Field & Stream* 94:156-7 S '89
HARPER, JOHN JOSEPH *See* Harper, J. J. (John Joseph)
HARPER & COLLINS PUBLISHERS LTD.
H&R, Collins and three agents form new Canadian firm. *Publishers Weekly* 235:123 F 24 '89
A shakeup in books. D. Turbide. *Maclean's* 102:53 F 27 '89
HARPER & ROW PUBLISHERS, INC.
Bell to use market research for Harper's new paperback line. M. Reuter. por *Publishers Weekly* 235:15 F 10 '89
H & R to offer free freight, new discount schedule. *Publishers Weekly* 236:9 Ag 25 '89
Harper & Row acquires TDM from McGraw-Hill for Caedmon. P. Sweeting. *Publishers Weekly* 235:16 Je 9 '89
Harper & Row buys Scott, Foresman for $455 million. C. Reid. *Publishers Weekly* 236:8 D 8 '89
Harper & Row, Penguin sign new labor accords. C. Reid. *Publishers Weekly* 235:12 F 3 '89
Murdoch wins Collins, promises autonomy; Craig assesses Harper's new owner. V. Menkes. *Publishers Weekly* 235:16+ Ja 20 '89
On-line on the road: Harper & Row sales reps computerize [using laptops for ordering] J. Mutter. il *Publishers Weekly* 235:50-1 Ja 13 '89
Sparks fly as Colleen McCullough leaves Harper for Hearst. G. Feldman. *Publishers Weekly* 236:40 Jl 21 '89
HARPER BROTHERS (MUSICAL GROUP)
The Harper Brothers: Kimball's/San Francisco, CA. M. Handler. il *Down Beat* 56:54 Jl '89
HARPER PAPERBACKS (FIRM)
Is there room for Harper Paperbacks? G. Feldman. il *Publishers Weekly* 236:24-6 N 17 '89
HARPER'S (PERIODICAL)
Banned in Britain [issue banned for article about British intelligence] E. Knoll. *The Progressive* 53:4 Ja '89

HARPER'S BAZAAR (PERIODICAL)
The Russian revolutionary [A. Brodovitch, former art director]
E. Hartney. il *Harper's Bazaar* 122:324-5+ S '89
HARPISTS
See also
Henson-Conant, Deborah
Vollenweider, Andreas
HARPSICHORD
                    Construction
Stradivari's secret (redux): did baroque artisans "X-ray" wood
with sunlight? J. Horgan. il *Scientific American* 261:21-2
Jl '89
HARR, BARBARA
The meditation of Sarah [poem] *The Christian Century*
106:1036 N 15 '89
HARRAGAN, BETTY LEHAN
Dear Betty Harragan. See issues of Working Woman
HARRELL, GLENN
Back Bay reflections. il por *House & Garden* 161:206-9 S
'89
Custom of the country. il *House & Garden* 161:116-21+
Ag '89
Forever English. il *House & Garden* 161:76 Mr '89
Gilt trip. il por *House & Garden* 161:120+ S '89
Model rooms. il *House & Garden* 161:238-43 O '89
Perfect penmanship. il *House & Garden* 161:68 D '89
HARRELL, MATT
                        about
On deck. il pors *Sport (New York, N.Y.)* 80:16 Ag '89
HARRELL, PHIL
                        about
On deck. il pors *Sport (New York, N.Y.)* 80:16 Ag '89
HARRELSON, WOODY
                        about
Woody Harrelson was out of control. G. Esterly. il pors
TV Guide 37:20-2+ Ag 12-18 '89
Woody Harrelson's horrible secret—"my father's in jail for
murder". M. Morrison. il por *Redbook* 173:42+ S '89
HARRIER AIRPLANES *See* Airplanes, Military
HARRIES, OWEN
Is the cold war really over? il *National Review* 41:40+ N
10 '89
HARRIES, ROBIN
                        about
Designstyle: plenty of hot air. D. L. Umansky. il *Theatre
Crafts* 23:20 D '89
**HARRIET TUBMAN HISTORICAL AND CULTURAL
MUSEUM (MACON, GA.)**
Macon makes a place for black heritage. il *Southern Living*
24:36+ O '89
HARRIGAN, ANTHONY
National character is decisive [address, April 27, 1989] *Vital
Speeches of the Day* 55:507-11 Je 1 '89
HARRIMAN, PAMELA
                        about
A $60 million van Gogh? R. W. Walker. il *Art News* 88:31
S '89
HARRIMAN STATE PARK (N.Y.)
The world of Lily Pond [beaver colony; condensation] H.
Ryden. il *Reader's Digest* 135:189-92+ Ag '89
HARRINGTON, EILEEN
A prayer for July Fourth. il *Reader's Digest* 135:121-2 Jl
'89
HARRINGTON, MICHAEL, 1928-1989
                        about
Obituary
Commonweal il por 116:466-9 S 8 '89
The Nation 249:373-4 O 9 '89. W. Brandt
National Review 41:15-16 S 1 '89
U.S. News & World Report il por 107:16 Ag 14 '89
Utne Reader por p38 N/D '89. H. Meyerson
HARRINGTON, PHIL
The ten best double stars. il *Astronomy* 17:78-83 Jl '89
HARRINGTON, TY
Bring it all back home. il *Video* 13:57-60 Je '89
HARRINGTON-LUEKER, DONNA
Is life too fast for baby boomers' kids? *The Education Digest*
55:29-31 O '89
Protecting schools from outside violence. *The Education Digest*
55:46-9 D '89
HARRIS, ALICE
                        about
"Sweet Alice" Harris. J. Malveaux. il pors *Ms.* 17:72-5 Ja/F
'89
HARRIS, BARBARA C.
                        about
The 1989 Essence Awards [with editorial comment by Susan
L. Taylor] il pors *Essence* 20:57-60+, 69 O '89
A bishop who won't be one of the boys. por *Newsweek*
113:60 F 13 '89
The bold ones. S. Brewer. il pors *New Choices for the Best
Years* 29:37-41 Jl '89
Consecration of bishop stirs Episcopal dissent. R. Walker.
il por *Christianity Today* 33:41+ Mr 17 '89
The first of the 'mitered mamas'. L. Rosellini. por *U.S.
News & World Report* 106:56-7 Je 19 '89
The first woman Episcopal bishop. R. D. Turner. il pors
Ebony 44:40+ My '89

Harris approved. *The Christian Century* 106:104-5 F 1-8
'89
That new time religion. *National Review* 41:16-17 Mr 10
'89
When the Spirit leads. J. Redmont. il por *Commonweal*
116:133-5 Mr 10 '89
HARRIS, BOB
Compassion and principle. il pors *Conservative Digest*
15:13-14+ Ja/F '89
HARRIS, CASSANDRA
                        about
"I have faith my wife will live". V. J. Radovsky. il pors
Redbook 173:36+ My '89
HARRIS, CHRISTOPHER
                        about
The pixie led [drama] Reviews
New York il 22:52+ Jl 31 '89. J. Simon
HARRIS, DALE
Collaborating on the spirit of a new age. il pors *Architectural
Digest* 46:42+ S '89
A legacy of fantasy and grace. il por *Architectural Digest*
46:42+ Ap '89
Mili Weber's world: the artist's fairy-tale house near St.
Moritz. il por *Architectural Digest* 46:174-9 D '89
The Opulent era: Worth, Doucet and Pingat at the Brooklyn
Museum. il *Architectural Digest* 46:66+ S '89
"A Russian musician". il pors *Opera News* 53:30-2 Mr 18
'89
Vieille Russie [cover story] il *Opera News* 54:13-17 S '89
HARRIS, DAMIAN
                        about
The Rachel papers [film] Reviews
Video il 13:88 D '89. I. Robbins
HARRIS, DEREK
Global Blood Safety Initiative. il *World Health* p28-9 O
'89
HARRIS, DORIS
The afterbirth [poem] *Essence* 19:123 Ap '89
HARRIS, ELEANOR
Not just my brother's problem. il *Glamour* 87:218-19+ F
'89
HARRIS, EMMYLOU
                        about
The power of Emmylou Harris. A. Nash. por *Stereo Review*
54:81 Ap '89
HARRIS, FRANK, III
My sister, the cop. por *Essence* 20:6-7 Jl '89
HARRIS, HENRY
When to call the doctor; ed. by Marilyn Mercer. il *Good
Housekeeping* 209:110+ S '89
HARRIS, JAMES, III *See* Jam, Jimmy
HARRIS, JOEL A.
                        about
Fraternity members punished for role in student's death
at Morehouse College. *Jet* 77:13 N 6 '89
HARRIS, JULIE
                        about
Architectural digest visits: Julie Harris. D. Roberts. il por
Architectural Digest 46:140-5+ Je '89
HARRIS, LIS
The Palio. *The New Yorker* 65:83-6+ Je 5 '89
HARRIS, MARK JONATHAN, 1941-
It's so much easier to write about the rich. il *The New
York Times Book Review* 94:46 N 12 '89
HARRIS, MAXINE
                        about
Video publishers reel in profits with avant-garde offerings.
L. Arden. il por *Home Office Computing* 7:45 My '89
HARRIS, MEL
                        about
5 beautiful moms say, "Go for it all!". K. C. Engles. il
por *Redbook* 173:123-7 My '89
HARRIS, MEL, 1942-
                        about
How a rebel rocker became a TV mogul. N. Koch. il por
Channels (New York, N.Y.: 1986) 9:46-7 F '89
HARRIS, MICHAEL
                        about
The Saturday night wars. G. Bain. il *Maclean's* 102:72 N
27 '89
HARRIS, NEIL PATRICK
                        about
Neil Patrick Harris. T. Carlson. il por *TV Guide* 37:11
S 23-29 '89
Would you let this doctor operate on you? [cover story]
B. O'Hallaren. il pors *TV Guide* 37:4-5+ D 16-22 '89
HARRIS, PATRICIA
(jt. auth) See Lyon, David, and Harris, Patricia
HARRIS, PHILIP, 1926-
Toward a space ethos and synergy. *Ad Astra* 1:48 Je '89
HARRIS, RICKY
(jt. auth) See Turner, Sylvia C., and Harris, Ricky
HARRIS, ROBERT
                        about
Thanks to Boat & Breakfast, Bay Area landlubbers can enjoy
the high life on the high seas. J. Boudreau. il pors *People
Weekly* 32:107-8 O 16 '89

HARRIS, ROBERT G.
Telecommunications as a strategic industry [address, December 15, 1988] *Vital Speeches of the Day* 55:377-81 Ap 1 '89
HARRIS, RON
Birth of a video star. il *Video* 12:74-7+ Ja '89
HARRIS, SHARON
Something's fishy. por *Essence* 19:160 F '89
HARRIS, SUSAN
about
A creative collaboration: softening a modern house in Los Angeles. M. Frank. il pors *Architectural Digest* 46:130-7 Ag '89
HARRIS, SUSAN STRAW *See* Straw, Syd
HARRIS, T GEORGE, AND YANKELOVICH, DANIEL
What good are the rich? il *Psychology Today* 23:36-9 Ap '89
HARRIS, TIM
about
Green Bay sacker. P. King. il pors *Sports Illustrated* 71:70-2 O 16 '89
HARRIS, TOM W.
Listen carefully. il *Nation's Business* 77:78 Je '89
HARRIS, WILLIAM HAMILTON, 1944-
about
Wm. H. Harris installed as Texas Southern U. prexy. il pors *Jet* 76:29 Je 5 '89
HARRIS CORP.
Harris plans commercial sales of Night Hawk microcomputer. E. H. Kolcum. il *Aviation Week & Space Technology* 130:59 Mr 13 '89
Harris unit develops advanced GaAs facility to supply MMICs to military [gallium arsenide monolithic microwave integrated circuits] B. W. Henderson. il *Aviation Week & Space Technology* 130:101+ Ap 24 '89
HARRIS CORP.-FEDERAL POLITICAL ACTION COMMITTEE
Is everybody happy? K. Rosenberg. il *Common Cause Magazine* 15:11-12 My/Je '89
HARRIS-TEETER SUPER MARKETS, INC.
Juicy results at an upscale grocer. G. G. Marcial. *Business Week* p104 D 11 '89
HARRISON, ALLEN
about
Allen Harrison: Tortue. P. Hammond. il *Art News* 88:181 Summ '89
HARRISON, BARBARA GRIZZUTI
The importance of being Oprah [cover story] il pors *The New York Times Magazine* p28-30+ Je 11 '89
Jackie: beyond the scandal. il pors *McCall's* 116:31-2+ Jl '89
The private eye. *See* issues of Mademoiselle
HARRISON, BENNETT
[Column] *See* alternate issues of Technology Review beginning July 1988
HARRISON, CHRISTOPHER G.
Crow's nest. il *Sea Frontiers* 35:195 Jl/Ag '89
HARRISON, JEFFREY
Sheet of ice [poem] *Wilderness* 53:55 Wint '89
HARRISON, JIM, 1937-
about
After seven acclaimed novels, Jim Harrison is finding it harder to elude fame. J. Reed. il por *Vogue* 179:502+ S '89
HARRISON, LOU
about
Harrison, Lou: Piano concerto; Suite for violin, piano, and small orchestra. K. R. Schwarz. por *High Fidelity (New York, N.Y.)* 39:56-7 Mr '89
HARRISON, REX
about
British accents. E. MacSweeney. por *Harper's Bazaar* 122:357+ S '89
HARRISON, SHELIA S.
B.E. guide to fellowships and executive training programs. il *Black Enterprise* 19:119-20+ F '89
HARRISON, TONY, 1937-
about
Phaedra Britannica [drama] Reviews
The Nation 248:100-1 Ja 23 '89. T. M. Disch
The New Republic 200:27+ F 13 '89. R. Brustein
HARRISON, V. V., 1942-
about
Those were the days. J. W. Donohue. il *America* 161:258-61 O 21 '89
HARRISON, WALLACE KIRKMAN, 1895-1981
about
Lonely at the top. B. Gill. il pors *House & Garden* 161:32+ Ag '89
HARRISS, JOSEPH A.
A Parisian love affair. il *Reader's Digest* 134:57-8+ Mr '89
Return of the locust [with editorial comment] il *Reader's Digest* 134:15-16, 122-6 My '89
HARRODS, LTD.
Banned in Britain: a new chapter in the Harrods saga [government outlaws publication of secret report] M. Maremont. pors *Business Week* p36 Ap 17 '89

Brawling over Harrods [T. Rowland vs. M. Al-Fayed] S. Lohr. il pors *The New York Times Magazine* p32-3+ O 8 '89
Tit for tat on London's High Street [M. Al-Fayed's takeover] J. Barnes. il pors *U.S. News & World Report* 106:63 Ja 30 '89
HARROIS-MONIN, FRANÇOISE
Sun tantrums. *World Press Review* 36:82-3 O '89
HARRY, JACKEE *See* Jackee
HARRY (DANCE COMPANY)
Wishful thinking [performances at the Joyce Theater] T. Tobias. il *New York* 22:86+ N 27 '89
HARRY GRAY, MEL KLEIN & PARTNERS LP
'A lot of people don't know who Mel Klein is' [bid for American Medical International] T. Vogel. il por *Business Week* p24-5 Jl 24 '89
HARRYMAN, ELIZABETH
(jt. auth) *See* Lasley, Paul, and Harryman, Elizabeth
HARRY'S AT HANOVER SQUARE (NEW YORK, N.Y.: RESTAURANT) *See* New York (N.Y.)—Restaurants, nightclubs, bars, etc.
HARRY'S BAR AND AMERICAN GRILL (LOS ANGELES, CALIF.) *See* Los Angeles (Calif.)—Restaurants, nightclubs, bars, etc.
HARSCO CORP.
The hard facts on Harsco. T. Jaffe. *Forbes* 144:326 D 11 '89
HARSHBARGER, SCOTT
Prosecuting environmental crimes [address, July 17, 1989] *Vital Speeches of the Day* 55:760-3 O 1 '89
HART, ALAN, 1935-
about
Indiana University to publish controversial Arafat biography. il por *Publishers Weekly* 235:43 F 17 '89
HART, BENJAMIN
Rising young stars in the firmament of the right. il *Conservative Digest* 15:18-19+ Ja/F '89
HART, CLYDE E., AND OTHERS
Human chromosome 12 is required for elevated HIV-1 expression in human-hamster hybrid cells. bibl f il *Science* 246:488-91 O 27 '89
HART, EVELYN
about
Slaying the dragons of pain with loyalty and love. D. Jenish. il por *Maclean's* 102:30-1 D 25 '89
HART, JEFFREY PETER, 1930-
The ivory foxhole. See occasional issues of National Review beginning September 26, 1986
While America slept [cover story] *National Review* 41:32-4 S 15 '89
HART, JOHN FRASER
Corn: a photo-essay [cover story] bibl il *Focus (New York, N.Y.: 1950)* 39:4-9 Summ '89
HART, JOHN W., III
Howls [excerpt from The found poetry of Lt. Col. Oliver L. North] *Harper's* 279:30 O '89
HART, KATHLEEN
Is academic freedom bad for business? il por *The Bulletin of the Atomic Scientists* 45:28-31+ Ap '89
HART, LENIE 'T
about
Foster mother to Holland's seals. B. Krist. il por map *International Wildlife* 19:20-4 Jl/Ag '89
HART, LESLIE A.
The horse is dead. bibl f il *Phi Delta Kappan* 71:237-42 N '89
HARTEIS, RICHARD
A race for all seasons [excerpt from Marathon; with editorial comment by George A. Hirsch] il *Runner's World* 24:4, 72-8+ N '89
HARTER, MICHAEL G.
Blessings from and for the poor. il *America* 161:395-8 D 2 '89
HARTFORD, BILL
Imports. *See* issues of Popular Mechanics
HARTFORD (CONN.)
Buildings
Richard Gordon plays only one way—hard. R. W. King. il por *Business Week* p50 Ag 28 '89
Crime
Dealing death [teenage drug dealers in housing projects] il *Scholastic Update (Teachers' edition)* 122:4-6 N 17 '89
Housing
Dealing death [teenage drug dealers in housing projects] il *Scholastic Update (Teachers' edition)* 122:4-6 N 17 '89
Parks and playgrounds
See also
Elizabeth Park (Hartford, Conn.)
HARTFORD STEAM BOILER INSPECTION & INSURANCE CO.
Hartford Steam Boiler Inspection & Insurance Co. R. Abelson. il *Fortune* 120:96 S 25 '89
HARTLEY, ANTHONY
After the Thatcher decade. bibl f *Foreign Affairs* 68:102-18 Wint '89/'90
HARTLEY, KAREN
Elliptical galaxies forged by collision. il *Astronomy* 17:42-5 My '89

HARTLEY, KAREN—*cont.*
A new window on star birth. il *Astronomy* 17:32-6 Mr '89
HARTLEY, MARSDEN, 1877-1943
about
Painter in motion. S. H. Madoff. il por *Art News* 88:81-2
N '89
HARTLIEB, INGRID, 1944-
about
Ingrid Hartlieb at Trabia-Macafee. J. Ash. il *Art in America*
77:172-3 D '89
HARTMAN, ARNIE
about
Arnie and Ginger. J. P. Blank. *Reader's Digest* 134:9-10+
Ja '89
HARTMAN, ARTHUR
about
Perestroika payoff. R. T. Grieves. il por *Forbes* 143:102
Ja 23 '89
HARTMAN, KIMBERLY
about
The Beastie girls. R. Powers. il por *Gentlemen's Quarterly*
59:131+ D '89
HARTMANN, WILLIAM K.
Birth of the moon [cover story] il *Natural History* p68-77
N '89
Piecing together earth's early history. il *Astronomy* 17:24-34
Je '89
What's new on Mars? il *Sky and Telescope* 77:471+ My
'89
HARTNEY, ELEANOR
The Russian revolutionary. il *Harper's Bazaar* 122:324-5+
S '89
HARTOG, JAN DE, 1914-
about
PW interviews. M. Field. por *Publishers Weekly* 236:41-2
Jl 7 '89
HARTOONIAN, MICHAEL
Knowledge and education reform in a democratic republic.
The Education Digest 55:11-14 D '89
HARTT, STANLEY
about
Damage control. T. Tedesco. il pors *Maclean's* 102:14-16
Je 12 '89
HARTUNIAN, PAUL
about
The handwriting's off the wall. J. Queenan. il *Forbes* 144:186+
O 2 '89
HARTWELL, LELAND H., AND WEINERT, TED A.
Checkpoints: controls that ensure the order of cell cycle
events. bibl f il *Science* 246:629-34 N 3 '89
HARTWIG, CLAYTON MICHAEL, D. 1989
about
Foul play on the Iowa? E. Salholz. il pors *Newsweek* 113:22
Je 5 '89
The Iowa inquiry. W. Lowther. *Maclean's* 102:23 Je 5 '89
Mystery aboard the Iowa. F. Trippett. il pors *Time* 133:40
Je 5 '89
The Navy blames a dead man. B. Turque. il *Newsweek*
114:25 S 18 '89
HARTZOG, ANNABETH
about
"Getting married is the best thing that's ever happened
to me!". V. J. Radovsky. il pors *Redbook* 173:30+ S '89
John Goodman, Roseanne Barr's big guy co-star, has a
big-time wedding in the Big Easy. il pors *People Weekly*
32:70 N 13 '89
HARVARD BRIDGE
With a campus legend in peril, members of a fraternity
vow to save the endangered M.I.T. smoot [markings span-
ning the length of the Harvard Bridge created by Lambda
Chi Alpha pledges] N. Geeslin. il pors *People Weekly*
31:93-5 Ap 24 '89
HARVARD BUSINESS SCHOOL *See* Harvard University.
Graduate School of Business Administration
HARVARD MEDICAL SCHOOL
See also
Medical Science Partners
Did the penalty fit the crime? [S. Frazier accused of plagiarism]
M. M. Hunt. il por *The New York Times Magazine* p36-7+
My 14 '89
**HARVARD-SMITHSONIAN CENTER FOR ASTROPHYS-
ICS**
Cosmic correspondence. J. Cornell. il *Sky and Telescope*
77:348 Ap '89
Stellar speedometers: high-tech planet finders. D. W. Latham.
il *Sky and Telescope* 78:264 S '89
HARVARD UNIVERSITY
A beachhead for the beleaguered labor movement [clerical
workers ratify contract] R. Kuttner. il *Business Week* p14
Jl 17 '89
Harvard makeovers. L. Barrett. il *Essence* 20:76-9 Ag '89
Harvard University [theater training opportunities] *Theatre
Crafts* 23:53+ N '89
No patent for Harvard's mouse? [rejection by European Patent
Office] D. Dickson. *Science* 243:1003 F 24 '89
Racist Bigotry 101 at Harvard [week-long program on racism]
R. R. Detlefsen. il *Conservative Digest* 15:40-3 Jl/Ag '89

Seeing Crimson [Harvard graduates as Bush appointees] D.
Wisenberg. il *Common Cause Magazine* 15:7 S/O '89
Shiseido grant: more than skin deep [Japanese funding of
Massachusetts General Hospital-Harvard University's
Cutaneous Biology Research Center] M. Sun. *Science*
245:810-11 Ag 25 '89
Toni Morrison, Kenneth Clark get honorary degrees during
Harvard University graduation. il pors *Jet* 76:13 Je 26
'89
White like me [conference on campus racism] R. R. Detlefsen.
The New Republic 200:18-21 Ap 10 '89
Anecdotes, facetiae, satire, etc.
Making the grade: memoirs of a Harvard grader. T. Pappas.
The American Scholar 58:415-19 Summ '89
**HARVARD UNIVERSITY. AMERICAN REPERTORY
THEATRE** *See* American Repertory Theatre
**HARVARD UNIVERSITY. GRADUATE SCHOOL OF BUSI-
NESS ADMINISTRATION**
Money, power and fame [teaching ethics to MBAs] A. Etzioni.
por *Newsweek* 114:10 S 18 '89
**HARVARD UNIVERSITY. JOHN F. KENNEDY SCHOOL
OF GOVERNMENT** *See* John F. Kennedy School of
Government
HARVARD UNIVERSITY. RUSSIAN RESEARCH CENTER
Bringing Nazi sympathizers to the U.S. [role of T. Parsons;
cover story] J. Wiener. *The Nation* 248:289+ Mr 6 '89
HARVESTING
See also
Cranberries—Harvesting
Vegetables—Harvesting
HARVESTING MACHINERY
See also
Hay handling—Equipment
Deere's new Maximizer combines roll off the line. C. Finck.
il *Successful Farming* 87:26-7 F '89
Equipment
Combine conveniences. D. Mowitz. il *Successful Farming*
87:40-1 O '89
New idea for Uni's [harvesters become chemical sprayers]
D. Mowitz. il *Successful Farming* 87:34AC mid-F '89
HARVEY, BRETT
The great American birth-control crisis. *Mademoiselle*
95:218-21+ Mr '89
The morning after. il *Mother Jones* 14:27-31+ My '89
HARVEY, F. BARTON
A new Enterprise. il por *The Humanist* 49:14-15+ My/Je
'89
HARVEY, HERK
about
Carnival of souls [film] Reviews
The New Yorker 65:88 S 4 '89. T. Rafferty
HARVEY, JOHN J.
about
Cleverness isn't enough. M. Berss. il *Forbes* 144:216 Jl 24
'89
HARVEY, KIT HESKETH- *See* Hesketh-Harvey, Kit
HARVEY, MILES
Jewish publications. il *Utne Reader* p111-13 Mr/Ap '89
HARVEY, PAUL, 1918-
There was a nation . . . il *Reader's Digest* 134:51-3 Ja
'89
HARVEY, PAUL H., 1947-
(jt. auth) See Pagel, Mark D., and Harvey, Paul H., 1947-
HARVEY, PETER R.
about
Cleverness isn't enough. M. Berss. il *Forbes* 144:216 Jl 24
'89
HARVEY, RANDY
They're here. il *Sport (New York, N.Y.)* 80:68-72 D '89
HARVEY, RAYMOND
about
On the upbeat: two young conductors. S. J. Branch. il pors
American Visions 4:22-6 Ag '89
HARVEY, ROBERT D., AND HUME, JOSEPH R.
Autonomic regulation of a chloride current in heart. bibl
f il *Science* 244:983-5 My 26 '89
HARVEY, SHEILA S.
Château d'Amboise [poem] *America* 161:374 N 25 '89
HARVEY MILK SCHOOL (NEW YORK, N.Y.)
A place to be somebody. K. Brady. il *Time* 134:21-2+ N
13 '89
HARVEY NICHOLS (FIRM)
A discerning eye [head buyer A. Verdan] J. McLaughlin.
il por *Harper's Bazaar* 122:54 N '89
HARWELDEN (TULSA, OKLA.: HISTORIC HOUSE) *See*
Tulsa (Okla.)—Historic houses, sites, etc.
HARWIT, MARTIN, 1931-
The universe as afterthought. *Astronomy* 17:8 Ag '89
HASBRO INC.
Hasbro may leave its family home. G. G. Marcial. *Business
Week* p97 Je 26 '89
It's kid brother's turn to keep Hasbro hot [A. Hassenfeld]
L. Jereski. il por *Business Week* p152+ Je 26 '89
Star vehicles [development of Record Breakers toy cars]
B. Kanner. il *New York* 22:20+ D 11 '89
**HASELEY COURT (OXFORDSHIRE, ENGLAND:
HISTORIC HOUSE)** *See* Historic houses, sites, etc.—Great
Britain

HASELKORN, AVIGDOR
Selective terrorism. il *National Review* 41:21-2 S 1 '89
HASELTINE, ROBERT W.
The minimum wage: help or hindrance? *USA Today (Periodical)* 118:31 Jl '89
Tangling with the U.S. economic octopus. il *USA Today (Periodical)* 118:28-30 Jl '89
HASEROT, GERMAINE
about
Systems. R. Day. il *Stereo Review* 54:96-7 Mr '89
HASH
Hashes. K. Haedrich. il *Country Journal* 16:104-9 Mr/Ap '89
HASH HOUSE HARRIERS (ORGANIZATION)
'The Hash': jogging, beer, and song. R. Neff. il *Business Week* p114 Ja 23 '89
HASHISH *See* Marijuana
HASKELL, MOLLY
He drives me crazy. il *The New York Times Magazine* p26+ S 24 '89
HASKINS, RON, AND BROWN, HANK
The day-care reform juggernaut. il *National Review* 41:40-1 Mr 10 '89
HASKINS, TODD
about
America's teen. C. Gammon. il pors *Sports Illustrated* 70:68-9+ Je 12 '89
HASLIP, CLEOPATRA
about
Alabama woman wins $1.2 million in insurance case. *Jet* 77:13 O 23 '89
HASS, NANCY
Playing for real. il pors *New York* 22:60-2+ D 11 '89
HASS, ROBERT
(tr) *See* Miłosz, Czesław. Incarnated
(tr) *See* Miłosz, Czesław. The thistle, the nettle
HASSAN II, KING OF MOROCCO, 1929-
about
The King's tall order. B. Weber. il *The New York Times Magazine* p78 Je 18 '89
Megamosque. L. Nickson. il por *Life* 12:47-9+ S '89
HASSANAL BOLKIAH, SULTAN OF BRUNEI, 1946-
about
Selling the sultan. J. Levine. il por *Forbes* 144:264-5 Jl 24 '89
HASSE, LIZ
Candles in the wind. *The New Republic* 200:24-5 F 20 '89
HASSEBROOK, CHUCK
His farm bill helps family farms and the environment. *Successful Farming* 87:32G S '89
HASSELSTROM, LINDA M.
Journal of a woman rancher. il *Life* 12:88-92+ Jl '89
HASSENFELD, ALAN GEOFFREY, 1948-
about
It's kid brother's turn to keep Hasbro hot. L. Jereski. il por *Business Week* p152+ Je 26 '89
HASSENFELD, STEPHEN DAVID
about
Hasbro may leave its family home. G. G. Marcial. *Business Week* p97 Je 26 '89
HASSRICK, PETER H.
Frederic Remington: masterworks of Western art. il por *USA Today (Periodical)* 117:76-83 Mr '89
HASTEY, STAN
SBC fundamentalists aim to defuse debate. *The Christian Century* 106:548-50 My 24-31 '89
HASTINGS, ALCEE L.
about
Fla. judge Alcee Hastings is removed by U.S. Senate. il por *Jet* 77:12-13 N 6 '89
Hastings impeachment trial slated to begin next month. por *Jet* 75:12 F 27 '89
The leaden wings of Senate justice. il por *U.S. News & World Report* 107:18 O 30 '89
HASTINGS (MINN.)
Festivals
Splash! J. McCallum. il *Sports Illustrated* 71:42-5 Ag 7 '89
HASTORF, CHRISTINE ANN, 1950-
(jt. auth) *See* Johannessen, Sissel, and Hastorf, Christine Ann, 1950-
HAT INDUSTRY
See also
Kirkpatrick Custom Hatters (Firm)
HATAKEYAMA, MASANORI, AND OTHERS
Interleukin-2 receptor β chain gene: generation of three receptor forms by cloned human α and β chain cDNA's. bibl f il *Science* 244:551-6 My 5 '89
HATCH, ORRIN G.
Should the Congress adopt the "High Risk Occupational Disease Notification and Prevention Act of 1987"? [excerpts from statement] *Congressional Digest* 68:107+ Ap '89
HATCH, PETER J., 1949-
about
Greening the South. D. Young. il pors *Southern Living* 24:125-6+ Je '89

HATCHER, EVERETT, D. 1989
about
A federal case. E. Pooley. il por *New York* 22:48-50+ Mr 27 '89
HATCHERIES *See* Fish culture
HATCHING OF EGGS *See* Incubation
HATE
See also
Misogyny
War without hatred. A. Rapoport. il por *The Humanist* 49:14-17+ Jl/Ag '89
HATE CRIMES
The politics of hate [laws dealing with bias-related crime] J. Leo. il *U.S. News & World Report* 107:24 O 9 '89
HATFIELD, KEITH
Camera at Oktoberfest. il *Petersen's Photographic Magazine* 18:48-51 O '89
HATFIELD, MARK O., 1922-
A Congress on the margins [excerpts from address] *Aviation Week & Space Technology* 131:9 S 4 '89
HATHA YOGA *See* Yoga
HATHAWAY, JEANINE
The turning point [poem] *America* 160:329 Ap 8 '89
HATHAWAY, NANCY
Fear of buying: women who save too much. il *Harper's Bazaar* 122:38+ Ja '89
HATLEE, MICHAEL
(jt. auth) *See* Adler, Ruben, and Hatlee, Michael
HATOUM, MONA
about
Mona Hatoum at The Showroom. G. Brett. il *Art in America* 77:205+ N '89
HATRA (IRAQ)
Restoring ancient Hatra. L. Y. Barkho. il *World Press Review* 36:55 Mr '89
HATS
See also
Caps (Hats)
Hat couture: les beaux chapeaux. il *Harper's Bazaar* 122:186 My '89
Haunted hats. il *Sunset (Central West edition)* 183:80-1 O '89
Hints from Eloise [designer M.-R. McDonald] G. Sikes. il por *Harper's Bazaar* 122:66 N '89
The mad modiste [designer A. Moore] J. Craugh. il por *Harper's Bazaar* 122:66 N '89
Not old hat! il *'Teen* 33:12 My '89
What they're wearing: hats. R. La Ferla. il *The New York Times Magazine* p49 Mr 26 '89
Anecdotes, facetiae, satire, etc.
The man in the green hat. J. Epstein. *The American Scholar* 58:167-8+ Spr '89
Photographs and photography
Key in on a theme to help focus your travel shooting [hats of Old Sturbridge Village] L. Dennis. il *Popular Photography* 96:22-3 Mr '89
HATSOPOULOS, G. N. (GEORGE N.)
about
Inventor, teacher, economist—and that's just for starters. K. H. Hammonds. il por *Business Week* p81+ D 18 '89
HATSOPOULOS, GEORGE N. *See* Hatsopoulos, G. N. (George N.)
HATTORI, REIJIRO
about
The last emperor? G. Eisenstodt. il por *Forbes* 144:92+ O 2 '89
HATWOOD, JOSEPHINE
about
Mama and Miss Jordan. M. H. Futrell. il *Reader's Digest* 135:75-80 Jl '89
HAUB, ERIVAN
about
How a German supergrocer gobbled up a winner. A. Rothman. il por *Business Week* p91 Ap 10 '89
HAUCK, GEORGE F. W.
The Roman aqueduct of Nîmes. bibl f map *Scientific American* 260:98-100+ Mr '89
HAUERWAS, STANLEY, 1940-
about
Impolite disengloblments. M. E. Marty. *The Christian Century* 106:487 My 3 '89
HAUERWAS, STANLEY, 1940-, AND WILLIMON, WILLIAM H.
Ministry as more than a helping profession [cover story] il *The Christian Century* 106:282-4 Mr 15 '89
HAUGEN, GREG
about
'Belt the body'. P. Putnam. il pors *Sports Illustrated* 70:44-5 F 27 '89
HAUGHEY, CHARLES
Visit to the United States, 1989
President meets with Irish prime minister [statement, March 17, 1989] G. Bush. *Department of State Bulletin* 89:39 Je '89
HAUKEBO, KIRSTEN
Are you a fashion victim? il *Current Health 2* 15:26-7 Ap '89

HAUNTED HOUSES See Ghosts
HAUPT, JOHN
about
Centerline: John Haupt. M. Sommers. il por *Theatre Crafts* 23:14 Mr '89
HAUPT (ENID A.) GARDEN (WASHINGTON, D.C.) See Enid A. Haupt Garden (Washington, D.C.)
HAUPTMAN, HERBERT AARON, 1917-
The phase problem of X-ray crystallography. bibl f il *Physics Today* 42:24-9 N '89
HAUSER, NAO
To cook a fish. il *American Health* 8:114-17 Je '89
A utensil for all seasonings. il *American Health* 8:134-5 Ap '89
HAUSER, RITA E.
about
Setting Yasser straight. S. Weller. il pors *Ms.* 17:84 Mr '89
HAUSHALTER, ROBERT C., AND OTHERS
Structure of a three-dimensional, microporous molybdenum phosphate with large cavities. bibl f il *Science* 246:1289-91 D 8 '89
HAVANA (CUBA)
Description
Our man in Havana [J. A. Michener] B. Levine. il por *Publishers Weekly* 236:50-1 Jl 14 '89
Historic houses, sites, etc.
The many lives of Old Havana. J. Judge. il map *National Geographic* 176:278-300 Ag '89
Papa's place [E. Hemingway's Finca VigẊia] S. Stapleton. il *Motor Boating & Sailing* 164:45+ S '89
HAVEL, VÁCLAV
A challenge from Citizen Havel. il por *World Press Review* 36:40-1 My '89
A statement to the court. il *The New York Review of Books* 36:41 Ap 27 '89
When you visit Prague. *Harper's* 278:22+ My '89
about
Act of artistic unfreedom. por *Time* 133:45 Mr 6 '89
The conscience of Prague. por *Time* 134:42 D 11 '89
The devil in Eastern Europe. L. Shapiro. il por *Newsweek* 113:77-8 Ap 24 '89
Fueling demands for Czech reform. H. Schwartz. *The Nation* 248:660-3 My 15 '89
Havel: a playwright seizes center stage. M. R. Meyer. il por *Newsweek* 114:34 D 18 '89
A historic encounter. il pors *Time* 133:48 My 29 '89
Temptation [drama] Reviews
New York 22:140-1 Ap 24 '89. J. Simon
The New Yorker 65:111 Ap 17 '89. E. Oliver
Newsweek il 113:77 Ap 24 '89. J. Kroll
Time por 133:71 Ap 17 '89. W. A. Henry
HAVEMAN, ROBERT H.
Targeting the poor: new policy for the new poverty. *Current (Washington, D.C.)* 310:11-19 F '89
HAVEMANN, ERNST
A van for Violet [story] il *The Atlantic* 263:48-51 Ja '89
HAVENS, RICHIE, 1941-
Woodstock remembered: the artists. il pors *Rolling Stone* p77 Ag 24 '89
HAVER, RONALD
He's the man [interview with G. Peck] il pors *American Film* 14:26-30+ Mr '89
HAVERON, BILL
about
Bill Haveron: Art Center Museum. J. Kutner. il *Art News* 88:181 Summ '89
HAVERSTOCK, DONNA
Good food, good health: the puzzling bread picture. il *Better Homes and Gardens* 67:50+ O '89
HAWAII
See also
Architecture, Domestic—Hawaii
Art—Hawaii
Astronomical observatories—Hawaii
Birds—Hawaii
Booksellers and bookselling—Hawaii
Drug abuse—Hawaii
Ecology—Hawaii
Education—Hawaii
Fishing—Hawaii
Haleakala National Park (Hawaii)
Hawaii Volcanoes National Park (Hawaii)
Historic houses, sites, etc.—Hawaii
Homestead law—Hawaii
Honolulu (Hawaii)
Investments, Australian—Hawaii
Kahoolawe (Hawaii)
Kauai (Hawaii)
Kilauea (Hawaii)
Lanai (Hawaii)
Maui (Hawaii)
Molokai (Hawaii)
Motion picture festivals—Hawaii
Paleontology—Hawaii
Rain forests—Hawaii
Resorts—Hawaii

Space centers—Hawaii
Wildlife—Hawaii
Wildlife conservation—Hawaii
Anniversaries, etc.
Hawaii celebrates a Chinese bicentennial. *Sunset (Central West edition)* 182:66 F '89
Defenses
Loose lips in Hawaii [Soviet spying] il *Newsweek* 113:4 Ja 2 '89
Industries
See also
Castle & Cooke, Inc.
Helicopter airlines—Hawaii
Pacific Resources Inc.
Politics and government
Hawaii's dirty secret [native Hawaiians' battle for land tenure; cover story] V. Novak. il *Common Cause Magazine* 15:10-16+ N/D '89
HAWAII INTERNATIONAL FILM FESTIVAL See Motion picture festivals—Hawaii
HAWAII MARITIME CENTER
Kalakaua Boat House . . . a new museum on the tip of Honolulu's Pier 7. il *Sunset (Central West edition)* 182:40 Ja '89
HAWAII VOLCANOES NATIONAL PARK (HAWAII)
Hawaii's lava is still flowing . . . here's where you can watch. il map *Sunset (Central West edition)* 183:54 S '89
HAWAIIAN AIRLINES, INC.
Going, going, gone. K. Hannon. il *Forbes* 144:10 S 18 '89
Hawaiian Airlines board backs $22/share buyout bid. *Aviation Week & Space Technology* 131:71 Ag 28 '89
Investors plan to revamp Hawaiian's operations. *Aviation Week & Space Technology* 131:71 S 4 '89
Peter Ueberroth's Hawaiian adventure. E. Schine. il por *Business Week* p32 S 4 '89
What's Hawaiian for "rotten management"? M. Beauchamp. il por *Forbes* 143:44-5 Je 26 '89
HAWAIIAN COOKING See Cooking, Hawaiian
HAWAIIAN ELECTRIC INDUSTRIES INC.
"Having a mother who loves us". M. Beauchamp. il por *Forbes* 144:117+ O 2 '89
Hawaii six-two. T. Jaffe. *Forbes* 144:349 Jl 24 '89
HAWAIIAN ISLANDS See Hawaii
HAWAIIAN SHIRTS See Shirts
HAWAIIANS
Land tenure
Hawaii's dirty secret [native Hawaiians' battle for land tenure; cover story] V. Novak. il *Common Cause Magazine* 15:10-16+ N/D '89
Mortuary customs
The sacred bones of Maui [plan to build hotel on ancient burial ground stirs strife] W. S. Merwin. il *The New York Times Magazine* p20-1+ Ag 6 '89
HAWARI, COLONEL See Labid, Abdullah Abd al-Hamid
HAWES, JOSIAH JOHNSON, 1808-1901
about
Masters of the daguerreotype. il *American History Illustrated* 24:32-3 S/O '89
HAWK, CARMEN
about
Crazy about Carmen. pors *Seventeen* 48:104-5 D '89
HAWK INN (PLYMOUTH, VT.) See Plymouth (Vt.)—Hotels, motels, etc.
HAWKE, ETHAN
about
Ethan Hawke. C. Connors. por *Seventeen* 48:67 N '89
HAWKE, ROBERT J. L. (ROBERT JAMES LEE), 1929-
Visit of Australian prime minister [remarks, June 27, 1989] il por map *Department of State Bulletin* 89:60-2 O '89
Visit to the United States, 1989
Visit of Australian prime minister [remarks, June 27, 1989] G. Bush; R. J. L. Hawke. il por map *Department of State Bulletin* 89:60-2 O '89
HAWKEN, PAUL
Entrepreneurs: the real cultural revolutionaries [excerpts from address, October 23, 1987] *Utne Reader* p72-3 Ja/F '89
HAWKER DE HAVILLAND AUSTRALIA PTY. LTD.
Hawker de Havilland will use joint programs to spur growth. P. Proctor. il *Aviation Week & Space Technology* 130:43-4 F 6 '89
HAWKING, S. W. (STEPHEN W.)
A brief history of A brief history. il pors *Popular Science* 235:70-2 Ag '89
about
Cosmic quarrel. T. Beardsley. *Scientific American* 261:22+ O '89
Dignifying humanity: the humor of Stephen W. Hawking. T. Organ. por *The Humanist* 49:29-30+ Jl/Ag '89
Stephen Hawking shoots for the stars. il por *Home Office Computing* 7:12 S '89
Wolf Foundation honors Hawking and Penrose for work on relativity. M. Siegel. il por *Physics Today* 42:97-8 Ja '89
HAWKING, STEPHEN W. See Hawking, S. W. (Stephen W.)
HAWKING (STEPHEN) FAN CLUB See Stephen Hawking Fan Club

HAWKINS, AUGUSTUS F.
Should President Bush's minimum wage proposal be adopted? [excerpts from address, March 23, 1989] *Congressional Digest* 68:139+ My '89

HAWKINS, COLEMAN
about
A classic turns 50. K. Whitehead. il por *Down Beat* 56:60-1 N '89

HAWKINS, ERICK
about
Reviews:
Performances at the Joyce Theater, New York City. D. Hering. *Dance Magazine* 63:88-90 Ap '89

HAWKINS, MASON
about
Eyeing companies with lots of cash [interview] A. E. Serwer. il por *Fortune* 119:37-9 F 13 '89

HAWKINS, PETER S.
Annie Dillard: pilgrim at midstream. *The Christian Century* 106:592-5 Je 7-14 '89
Confrontation and escape: mysteries of Graham Greene [cover story] il *The Christian Century* 106:934-6 O 18 '89

HAWKINS, TRIP *See* Hawkins, William M.

HAWKINS, WILLIAM J.
Electronics newsfront. See issues of Popular Science beginning February 1986
What's new in electronics. See issues of Popular Science

HAWKINS, WILLIAM M.
Why multimedia is multiconfusing. por *Personal Computing* 13:220 O '89

HAWKINS, YUSUF
about
Anatomy of a racial murder. J. Derevlany. il pors *Seventeen* 48:108-11+ D '89
Brotherhood week. J. Klein. il por *New York* 22:36+ S 11 '89
The business of us all. *Commonweal* 116:484-5 S 22 '89
Death on a mean street. F. Trippett. il *Time* 134:28 S 11 '89
Fighting the power. A. Logan. il *The New Yorker* 65:108+ S 11 '89
Meditating on Bensonhurst. *America* 161:131 S 9-16 '89
N.Y. gunman surrenders in Hawkins slaying; blacks riot on Brooklyn Bridge. il *Jet* 76:7-8 S 18 '89
New York youth killed in racial attack by whites. il *Jet* 76:52 S 11 '89
A racist ambush in New York. J. N. Baker. il por *Newsweek* 114:25 S 4 '89
The two racisms. M. E. Dyson. *The Nation* 249:300-1 S 25 '89
What really happened in Bensonhurst [cover story] M. Stone. il pors map *New York* 22:46-56 N 6 '89

HAWKINS (ERICK) DANCE COMPANY *See* Erick Hawkins Dance Company

HAWKINSON, TIM
about
Concrete metaphors. H. Drohojowska. il por *Art News* 88:109-10 D '89

HAWKLEY, RENEE
Graduation day. il *Reader's Digest* 134:9-10 Je '89

HAWKS
See also
Caracaras
Falcons
Ospreys
You and the wind [cue from hawk saves life of hang glider] R. Pinkerton. il *Reader's Digest* 135:105-6 Jl '89

HAWLEY, TODD B.
(jt. auth) *See* Diamandis, Peter H., and Hawley, Todd B.

HAWLEY, WILLIS D.
Should we extend teacher preparation? *Society* 26:49-57 My/Je '89
Teacher preparation: should it be changed? *Current (Washington, D.C.)* 318:22-31 D '89

HAWTHORN, INDIAN *See* Indian hawthorn

HAY, JESS THOMAS
about
How much bad luck can one Texan take? T. Mason. il *Business Week* p33 S 18 '89
The last roundup? J. H. Taylor. il por *Forbes* 143:124 Je 12 '89

HAY, ROBERT P.
The day Thomas Jefferson's world fell apart. il *USA Today (Periodical)* 118:90-2 N '89

HAY, VICKY
The multifaceted Donald Locke. il por *American Visions* 4:37-40 O '89

HAY
Harvesting
See Hay handling
Marketing
Bovine 'balers' stack big profits [controlled grazing of alfalfa] J. Walter. il *Successful Farming* 87:32-3 mid-Mr '89
Prices
Hay growers go for quality; then set price! il *Successful Farming* 87:64G Ap '89

HAY FEVER
Fighting hay fever. il *Consumers' Research Magazine* 72:30-3 My '89
It's spring again and allergies are in bloom [cover story] K. Flieger. il *FDA Consumer* 23:16-20 My '89

HAY HANDLING
Equipment
Power feeders: these units shred, slice, chop, unroll and control big bales. B. Eftink. il *Successful Farming* 87:28-30 mid-F '89

HAY HOUSE (FIRM)
Hay House plans Siegel releases. J. Zinsser. *Publishers Weekly* 236:56+ N 3 '89

HAY MAKING *See* Hay handling

HAYAKAWA, S. I.
Bilingualism in America: English should be the only language. il *USA Today (Periodical)* 118:32-4 Jl '89

HAYDAY, ADRIAN
(jt. auth) *See* Richman, Adam, and Hayday, Adrian

HAYDÉE, MARCIA
about
Giselle [ballet] Reviews
Dance Magazine il 63:84-5 D '89. H. Koegler

HAYDEN, DOLORES
Awakening from the American dream: why the suburban, single-family house is outdated [excerpt from Redesigning the American dream] il *Utne Reader* p64-7 My/Je '89

HAYDEN, TOM
about
Jane Fonda enters a new era. A. Sachs. il pors *McCall's* 116:32-4+ S '89
Tom Hayden's original sin. C. Unger. il pors *Esquire* 111:178-80+ Je '89
Will Jane share her wealth? il pors *People Weekly* 32:81 Ag 7 '89

HAYDN, JOSEPH, 1732-1809
about
First encounters. E. Sorel and N. C. Sorel. il *The Atlantic* 264:79 S '89

HAYEK, FRIEDRICH A. VON (FRIEDRICH AUGUST), 1899-
about
The world turns. R. Bailey. il por *Forbes* 143:43-4 My 15 '89

HAYES, BRIAN
Machine dreams. il *Discover* 10:82-7 O '89

HAYES, CHRISTOPHER L.
Financial security: what every woman must know. *McCall's* 117:124+ O '89

HAYES, DAVID
about
Classic David Hayes. J. Chatfield-Taylor. il por *Architectural Digest* 46:210-17 S '89

HAYES, DENNIS
Highest disregard. il *Mother Jones* 14:32-6+ D '89
about
Modems, second act. D. Churbuck. il por *Forbes* 143:119 F 6 '89

HAYES, HAROLD
about
Obituary
Esquire il por 112:17-18+ Ag '89. L. Eisenberg

HAYES, ISAAC
about
Isaac Hayes jailed for failing to pay alimony. il por *Jet* 75:8 Mr 13 '89

HAYES, J. PATRICK
about
Waterford is showing a few cracks. M. Maremont. il *Business Week* p60+ F 20 '89

HAYES, JOHN PHILLIP, 1949-
(ed) *See* Kinch, John E. You can own your own business

HAYES, MARGARET DALY
The U.S. and Latin America: a lost decade? *Foreign Affairs* 68 Special Issue:180-98 ['89]

HAYES MICROCOMPUTER PRODUCTS, INC.
Modems, second act. D. Churbuck. il por *Forbes* 143:119 F 6 '89

HAYFORD, WARREN J.
about
The Marvin and Warren act. R. Reiff. il por *Forbes* 144:52+ S 18 '89

HAYING *See* Hay handling

HAYLE, CLAUDETTE
about
Back from the brink of bankruptcy. L. Washer. il pors *Working Woman* 14:61-4 S '89

HAYNES, AL
about
Capt. Al Haynes. il por *People Weekly* 32:102-3 D 25 '89-Ja 1 '90

HAYNES, CALEB VANCE, 1928-
(jt. auth) *See* Maxwell, Ted A., and Haynes, Caleb Vance, 1928-

HAYNES, NANCY, 1947-
about
Nancy Haynes at John Good. A. F. Collins and B. Collins, Jr. il *Art in America* 77:147 Mr '89

HAYRE, RUTH WRIGHT
about
Underwriting the future: two women will send 146 kids to college. R. Brown. il pors *Ebony* 44:74+ Ap '89
HAYS, CHARLOTTE
The issues game. il *National Review* 41:41-2 F 10 '89
HAYS, CHARLOTTE, AND ROWE, JONATHAN
Reporters are members in good standing of Washington high society. *Utne Reader* p64 N/D '89
HAYSLIP, LE LY
A Vietnam memoir; ed. by Martha K. Babcock. il pors *People Weekly* 32:147-8+ D 18 '89
HAYTON, BEA
Fast friend in the kitchen. bibl il *Current Health 2* 15:14-17 F '89
Nutrition facts & folklore. il *Current Health 2* 15:23-5 Ja '89
Uncooked? Unsafe! il *Current Health 2* 15:13-15 My '89
HAYWARD, GREGORY D.
(jt. auth) See Hayward, Patricia H., and Hayward, Gregory D.
HAYWARD, PATRICIA H., AND HAYWARD, GREGORY D.
Lone ranger of the Rockies. il *Natural History* p78-85 N '89
HAYWORTH, RITA, 1918-1987
about
A candid new biography tells of the shocking childhood that destroyed Rita Hayworth. A. Chambers. il pors *People Weekly* 32:129+ N 13 '89
Goddess of love. W. Thomas. il pors *Harper's Bazaar* 122:156-7 N '89
HAZAN, MARCELLA
about
Battling Spaghetti O taste buds. C. Booth. il por *Time* 133:88-9 My 29 '89
On a visit to Venice, Jeffrey Steingarten learns the mysteries of the deep from an undisputed master of Adriatic seafood, Marcella Hazan. J. Steingarten. il por *Vogue* 179:250+ Ag '89
HAZAN, PIERRE
Hong Kong's lost confidence. il *World Press Review* 36:61 S '89
HAZARDOUS SUBSTANCES
See also
Asbestos
Chemicals
Inflammable materials
Poisons and poisoning
Radioactive substances
Trade waste
Disposal
See also
Love Canal case
Marine Shale Processors Inc.
Radioactive waste disposal
Trade waste—Disposal
Waste disposal in the ocean
Illinois county holds second chemical cleanup. R. Fee. *Successful Farming* 87:26 Ja '89
Land of death . . . and life [wildlife thrive on contaminated grounds of the Rocky Mountain Arsenal] G. Gerhardt. il map *National Wildlife* 28:34-40 D '89/Ja '90
The new midnight dumpers [illegal drug labs creating toxic waste in production of methamphetamine] G. Witkin. il *U.S. News & World Report* 106:57 Ja 9 '89
The toxic morass in Denver's backyard [Rocky Mountain Arsenal] S. D. Atchison. il *Business Week* p46 Ja 9 '89
Toxic responsibility [military and toxic waste disposal] S. Pollack and S. Shulman. il *The Atlantic* 263:26+ Mr '89
Uncle Sam's toxic folly. M. Satchell. il *U.S. News & World Report* 106:20-2 Mr 27 '89
Very [personal pollution [household waste] B. Livermore. il *Health (New York, N.Y.)* 21:42-7+ Mr '89
Laws and regulations
Toxic avengers [New York City's Environmental Police Unit] J. Stone. il *Discover* 10:40-3+ Ag '89
Training
ABC's at the E.P.A. [class in Hazardous Material Incident Response Training] B. Weber. il *The New York Times Magazine* p114 N 12 '89
Fires and fire prevention
Toxic training. T. Kiely. il *Technology Review* 92:10+ My/Je '89
Recycling
Mr. Clean [solar reaction process to destroy toxic chemicals] T. Beardsley. il *Scientific American* 260:83-4 Je '89
HAZE
Haze and hurricanes, tanning and thunderstorms. T. Schlatter. *Weatherwise* 42:218 Ag '89
HAZEL, WILLIAM AUGUSTUS, D. 1929
about
Building on a heritage. L. D. Hutchinson. por *American Visions* 4:11 Ag '89
HAZELDEN FOUNDATION
The last resort. W. W. Prochnau. *Vogue* 179:346-7 F '89

HAZELL, NEWTON
about
N.J. man finds his lotto fortune in cookie jar. il por *Jet* 77:27 N 13 '89
HAZELTINE CORP.
FAA weighs terminating Hazeltine's MLS contract. *Aviation Week & Space Technology* 131:28 Jl 3 '89
FBI charges consultants bribed Navy officials to influence contract awards. J. D. Morrocco. *Aviation Week & Space Technology* 130:22 Ja 9 '89
Hazeltine, FAA work to salvage major MLS production contract. J. T. McKenna. *Aviation Week & Space Technology* 131:70-1 Ag 28 '89
Pentagon suspends Hazeltine, Teledyne following federal charges of fraud. *Aviation Week & Space Technology* 130:23-4 Ja 16 '89
HAZELTON, LYNETTE
First rate conventions you can afford. *Black Enterprise* 19:76-7 Mr '89
HAZELTON, NIKA
Delectations. See occasional issues of National Review
about
Experiencing Nika. P. L. Buckley. *National Review* 41:56-8 Mr 10 '89
HAZELWOOD, JOSEPH J.
about
Captain Hazelwood: what Exxon knew. B. Amero. *Harper's* 279:22-4 Jl '89
He devastated Alaska, but Capt. Jeff Hazelwood, friends say, is an environmentalist. K. Gross. il por *People Weekly* 31:48-50 Ap 24 '89
Joe's bad trip [cover story] R. Behar. il pors map *Time* 134:42-7 Jl 24 '89
HAZELWOOD (MO.)
Education
Student journalists fight for free expression [Supreme Court ruling permits censorship of student press] L. Eskin. il *Scholastic Update (Teachers' edition)* 122:19-21 S 8 '89
HAZER, MELVIN
about
Melvin Hazer: a thinner, happier man. il pors *Ebony* 44:88+ Ja '89
HAZING
Fraternity members punished for role in student's death at Morehouse College. *Jet* 77:13 N 6 '89
It's time to put an end to fraternity hazing. E. P. Gunn. *Seventeen* 48:200 Mr '89
HAZLETON, LESLEY
British soccer: the deadly game. il *The New York Times Magazine* p40-1+ My 7 '89
about
PW interviews. S. Mernit. por *Publishers Weekly* 236:38-9 D 8 '89
HAZLETT, THOMAS W.
Wired. *The New Republic* 200:11-13 My 29 '89
HAZLETTVILLE (DEL.)
Crime
Deaths in the name of life [R. and J. Lynch accused of murder and kidnapping] G. Cerio. il por *Newsweek* 113:29 My 8 '89
HAZZARD, SHIRLEY, 1931-
Breaking faith (I). *The New Yorker* 65:63-4+ S 25 '89
Breaking faith (II). *The New Yorker* 65:74-8+ O 2 '89
HBO See Home Box Office
HDLS (HIGH DENSITY LIPOPROTEINS) See Lipoproteins
HDTV See High definition television
HEACOX, KIM
Fatal attraction? il *International Wildlife* 19:38-43 My/Je '89
Spillwatch. il *Wilderness* 53:15+ Fall '89
HEAD, IVAN L.
South-North dangers. *Foreign Affairs* 68:71-86 Summ '89
HEAD, SIMON
The battle inside NATO. bibl f il *The New York Review of Books* 36:41-6 My 18 '89
HEAD
See also
Face
Wounds and injuries
An alert response to head injury. il *Current Health 2* 16:28-9 D '89
Coming back from head injury [Central Park jogger] D. R. Hales and R. E. Hales. il *American Health* 8:9-10+ N '89
Heads up. P. G. Gill. il *Field & Stream* 94:32+ Jl '89
A near-fatal motorcycle crash changes an actor's life, but not his refusal to wear a helmet; ed. by Jack Kelley. G. Busey. il pors *People Weekly* 31:65-6+ My 15 '89
HEAD IN ART
See also
Portrait painting
Portrait sculpture
HEAD LICE See Lice
HEAD START PROJECT (U.S.) See Project Head Start (U.S.)
HEAD TAX See Poll tax
HEAD-UP DISPLAY SYSTEMS See Air navigation—Aids and devices

HEADACHE

The anatomy of a headache. S. Brownlee. il *U.S. News & World Report* 107:46-8 Jl 31 '89

Making headway against exercise headaches. C. L. Otis. il *Women's Sports & Fitness* 11:10 My '89

Migraines: 6 new ways to fight back. M. C. Stevens. il *Prevention (Emmaus, Pa.)* 41:48-55 Ap '89

New help for headache sufferers. S. Wernick. il *Glamour* 87:82+ S '89

Shooing elephants [migraine and tension headaches] B. H. Dobkin. il *The New York Times Magazine* p54-5 My 14 '89

When aspirin isn't enough [views of Vernon Hofmann] il *USA Today (Periodical)* 118:17 O '89

Where your head aches . . . can tell you why. M. Wolf. il *Redbook* 173:94+ Jl '89

HEADACHE IN ART

Exhibitions

Demons red in tooth and claw [exhibit at Graham Headache Centre in Boston] il *U.S. News & World Report* 107:14 Jl 10 '89

Drawing out the pain [exhibit at Graham Headache Centre in Boston] S. McKee. il *American Health* 8:40 N '89

Images of pain: headache art lends a hand to science [cover story] I. Wickelgren. il *Science News* 136:136-7 Ag 26 '89

HEADGEAR

See also
Hats

HEADHUNTERS

Sabah (Malaysia)

Beware of the headhunters [rumors circulating in Malaysia] M. Liu. il map *Newsweek* 114:62 D 11 '89

HEADHUNTERS, CORPORATE See Executive search consultants

HEADLANDS CENTER FOR THE ARTS (CALIF.)

Brave new world. K. D. Stein. il *Architectural Record* 177:118-25 mid-S '89

HEADLIGHTS, AUTOMOBILE See Automobiles—Lighting

HEADLY, GLENNE

about

Close up. J. E. Fitch. por *American Film* 14:72 Ja/F '89

Funny lady. R. Wetzsteon. il pors *New York* 22:46-8+ F 20 '89

HEADPHONES

Beyerdynamic IRS 690 cordless headphones. J. D. Hirsch. il *Stereo Review* 54:57+ Je '89

Ear shields [pilot headphones that block noise] W. J. Hawkins. il *Popular Science* 235:44 D '89

Headphones that grow on you. W. J. Hawkins. il *Popular Science* 235:30 Jl '89

Hot headphones for cool videos. M. Fleischmann. il *Video* 12:54-7 F '89

Max headset room [David Clark's H10-20 for pilots] J. M. McClellan. il *Flying* 116:33 S '89

Sony's featherweight headset [DR-6010 for pilots] il *Flying* 116:28 Ag '89

Speak softly? Carry headsets and intercom [Concept Industries' Softcomm C-40 headsets and ATC-4 intercom system for pilots and passengers] il *Flying* 116:37 Je '89

Stereo headphones. il *Consumer Reports* 54:109-13 D '89

Stereo headphones: acoustic cocoon. il *Consumer Reports* 54:596-9 S '89

You get quite an earful with these new headphones. S. Woolley. il *Business Week* p106 Je 19 '89

HEADRICK, ROBERT J., JR.

Collecting James Dean memorabilia. il pors *Antiques & Collecting Hobbies* 94:33-6+ Ap '89

HEADS OF STATE

See also
Dictators
Prime ministers

Power to the people. L. Lief. il *U.S. News & World Report* 107:24-5 D 25 '89-Ja 1 '90

The prince and his courtiers: at the White House, the Kremlin, and the Reichschancellery. R. Baker and C. Peters. *The Washington Monthly* 21:38+ F '89

What do you call the boss? D. O. Relin. il *Scholastic Update (Teachers' edition)* 121:23 Ja 13 '89

HEADSETS See Headphones

HEAFITZ, BRUCE

about

Archeology for fun and profit. R. Koselka. il pors *Forbes* 144:146+ D 25 '89

HEALDSBURG (CALIF.)

City planning

Main Street revisited [work of AIA Regional/Urban Design Assistant Team] W. Hoffer. il *Nation's Business* 77:36-8+ Ja '89

Social conditions

Where the living is still easy. J. Foote. il *Newsweek* 114:29 Jl 31 '89

HEALEY, JEFF

about

Bluesman Jeff Healey, the blind gonzo guitarist who puts the musical punch in Road house. il por *People Weekly* 31:85 Je 12 '89

The Jeff Healey Band. E. Miller. il pors *Seventeen* 48:121-2+ Mr '89

HEALEY, NIGEL M.

Danger in a 'dormant' crisis. il *World Press Review* 36:30-2 Ja '89

HEALEY, ROBERT

about

The great experiment. R. Bautch. *America* 160:316-17 Ap 8 '89

HEALEY (JEFF) BAND See Jeff Healey Band

HEALING

See also
Faith cure
Mental healing

55 high-speed healing tips. S. Lally and P. Shimer. il *Prevention (Emmaus, Pa.)* 41:33-57+ D '89

How we heal. R. Saltus. il *Health (New York, N.Y.)* 21:82-3 F '89

Skin deep [wound healing; research by Gregory L. Brown and Lillian B. Nanney] R. Rusting. *Scientific American* 261:38 S '89

Speeding up wound healing the EGF way [research by Gregory L. Brown] R. Cowen. *Science News* 136:39 Jl 15 '89

Vitamin C may hasten healing [tooth extraction; views of Robert A. Halberstein] il *USA Today (Periodical)* 117:4-5 F '89

HEALTH

See also
CD-ROM (Compact disc-Read only memory)—Health use
Computers—Health use
Computers—Medical use
Diet
Environmental health
Exercise
Holistic dentistry
Holistic medicine
Information systems—Health use
Keyboards—Health aspects
Longevity
Medicine
Mental health
Nutrition
Physical fitness
Pilgrimages to Mecca—Health aspects
Public health
Relaxation
Sleep
Therapeutics
Travel—Health aspects
Video display terminals—Health aspects
Video games—Health use
Videotapes—Health use
War—Health aspects
    See also subheads Care and hygiene; Health and hygiene under classes of persons or ethnic groups

The art of healthy living. K. Schmidt. il *World Health* p26 Ja/F '89

Bring back fat. B. G. Harrison. *Mademoiselle* 95:152 Ap '89

Food and your health [special section] A. M. Fletcher. il *McCall's* 117:89+ O '89

Good food, good health: 10 things you can do right now for a healthier you. B. Goldman. il *Better Homes and Gardens* 67:36+ Mr '89

Grandmother was right. G. F. Will. il *Newsweek* 113:68 Ja 16 '89

Health. See issues of Better Homes and Gardens

Health & fitness. See issues of Glamour

Health: the great escape. J. Garvey. il *Commonweal* 116:294-5 My 19 '89

The healthy parent. See issues of Parents beginning October 1987

Just ask us . . . [questions and answers] See issues of Current Health 2

Medical mailbox. C. SerVaas. See issues of The Saturday Evening Post

A question of health. See issues of Consumer Reports

To your health. See issues of The Mother Earth News beginning January/February 1988

Turning points to better health. R. Rodale. il *Prevention (Emmaus, Pa.)* 41:30+ Mr '89

Bibliography

Booklets. See occasional issues of Health (New York, N.Y.)

Health books to give and get. C. Slom. *McCall's* 117:98 D '89

Top books: 1988 winners. M. Goldman and M. G. Goldman. il *American Health* 8:112+ Ja/F '89

Periodicals

See also
Good spirit (Periodical)
Prevention (Periodical)

HEALTH AND HUMAN SERVICES DEPT. (U.S.) See United States. Dept. of Health and Human Services

HEALTH AND RELIGION *See* Medicine and religion
HEALTH AND THE ENVIRONMENT SUBCOMMITTEE
See United States. Congress. House. Committee on Energy
and Commerce. Subcommittee on Health and the Environ-
ment
HEALTH CARE *See* Medical care
HEALTH CARE COSTS *See* Medical care—Costs
HEALTH CARE INDUSTRY *See* Medical care industry
HEALTH CARE POLICY *See* Medical policy
HEALTH CENTERS *See* Health facilities
HEALTH CLINICS *See* Health facilities
HEALTH CLUBS
See also
Clean & Lean (Firm)
The health club with a heart [Brooklyn, N.Y.] B. G. Harrison.
Mademoiselle 95:145 S '89
How to stay fit on the road [hotel health clubs] S. Richmond.
Changing Times 43:122-3 N '89
Is your health club healthy? [bankruptcies] C. Schaeffer.
Changing Times 43:116+ S '89
Pumping iron [Sports Club/LA] K. Roderick. il *Harper's
Bazaar* 122:134-5+ My '89
HEALTH EDUCATION
See also
AIDS (Disease) education
Alzheimer's disease education
Health workers—Training
Nutrition education
Physical education and training
Television broadcasting—Health education programs
Are you teaching your family the facts of health? [quiz]
L. Mendelson and R. Mendelson. il *Good Housekeeping*
209:124+ S '89
Helping students accentuate positive thoughts. C. K. Chandler
and C. A. Kolander. *The Education Digest* 54:52-4 Ja
'89
Needs and concerns for school health education. R. M.
Pigg. *The Education Digest* 54:33-7 My '89
Schoolchildren: health illiterates [study by Ian Newman] *USA
Today (Periodical)* 118:6+ O '89
Awards
WHO award for health education. P. Stroot. il *World Health*
p30 Jl '89
International aspects
"Get them to ask questions" [interview with A. Kern] il
World Health p4-5 Mr '89
Let's talk health [cover story; special issue] il *World Health*
p3-29 Ja/F '89
A sporting partnership [health education through sports] A.
Salahi. il *World Health* p18-19 Jl '89
Canada
Tele-Health. R. Perreault and M.-C. Laurendeau. il *World
Health* p6-7 Mr '89
Great Britain
Save a Life [emergency first aid TV shows] P. Riding. il
World Health p29 Ja/F '89
India
The mini-doctors of Bombay. V. R. Bhalerao. il *World Health*
p20-3 D '88
Middle East
Health education through religion. A. Aly. il *World Health*
p27-8 Jl '89
HEALTH EXAMINATIONS *See* Physical examinations
HEALTH FACILITIES
See also
Abortion clinics
Hospitals
Medical laboratories
Mental health centers
Mobile health facilities
Salick Health Care, Inc.
Trauma care units
Weight loss clinics
The facts of life for infertile couples [survey providing success
rates of IVF clinics; work of Ron Wyden] S. McKee.
il *American Health* 8:11-12 O '89
"Fast-food" medical care [research by David Stewart] il *USA
Today (Periodical)* 118:16 O '89
Help for kids who get sick at night [after-hours pediatric
clinics] L. J. Moore. il *U.S. News & World Report* 107:86
N 13 '89
If a medical problem won't go away, consider a specialty
clinic—carefully. L. Luciano. il *Money* 18:141-2 Jl '89
Trying to fool the infertile [IVF clinics misrepresent success
rates] M. D. Lemonick. il *Time* 133:53 Mr 13 '89
What do infertility clinics really deliver? [misrepresentation
of success rates] S. Findlay. il *U.S. News & World Report*
106:74-5 Ap 3 '89
Architecture
Keeping fit [special section; with introd. by Margaret Gaskie]
il *Architectural Record* 177:78-89 Ap '89
Alabama
See also
West Alabama Health Services, Inc.
California
See also
Community Health Projects Inc.

Canada
Bursting at the seams [pain clinics] B. Came. il *Maclean's*
102:42 F 27 '89
Florida
See also
Pensacola (Fla.)—Health facilities
Maryland
See also
University of Maryland at Baltimore. Health Center
Missouri
See also
Saint Louis (Mo.)—Health facilities
New York (State)
See also
New York (N.Y.)—Health facilities
Nova Scotia
See also
Halifax (N.S.)—Health facilities
HEALTH FOOD *See* Organic food
HEALTH FRAUD *See* Quacks and quackery
HEALTH INSURANCE *See* Insurance, Health
HEALTH LITERATURE
Looking for the good stories. M. Bricklin. il *Prevention
(Emmaus, Pa.)* 41:144+ S '89
HEALTH MAINTENANCE ORGANIZATIONS
See also
Maxicare Health Plans, Inc.
Are companies cutting too close to the bone? [malpractice
claims may arise from new insurance plans designed to
trim costs] M. Galen. il *Business Week* p141+ O 30 '89
Can insurers nurse their HMOs back to health? J. R. Norman.
il *Business Week* p80-1 Ja 16 '89
"Fast-food" medical care [research by David Stewart] il *USA
Today (Periodical)* 118:16 O '89
HEALTH NEWS *See* Medical news
HEALTH NEWSLETTERS *See* Medical newsletters
HEALTH RECORDS *See* Medical records
HEALTH RESEARCH *See* Medical research
HEALTH RESORTS, WATERING PLACES, ETC.
See also
Department stores—Spa services
Mud baths
Pritikin Longevity Centers
Even real men love spas. J. Edgerton. il *Money* 18:100-3+
O '89
Quick-fix revitalizers. S. Bersch. il *Harper's Bazaar* 122:16+
Ja '89
The spa! [weekend spas; cover story] C. Winters and H.
Sweet. il *Health (New York, N.Y.)* 21:45-51+ Ap '89
Spa life [special section] il *The New York Times Magazine*
p75-80+ My 7 '89
Spa update. *Vogue* 179:162+ D '89
Spas [cover story; special section] il *American Health* 8:83+
Ap '89
Spas that fit your fitness program. J. Colbert. il *Women's
Sports & Fitness* 11:54-6+ My '89
Anecdotes, facetiae, satire, etc.
In fitness and in wealth. M. Ivins. il *Ms.* 18:17 N '89
International aspects
Fitness by sea [cruise ship spas] H. Basch and S. Slater.
il *Travel Holiday* 171:79 Ja '89
Spa [special section] il *Harper's Bazaar* 122:132-5+ My '89
Psychological aspects
Head trips [mental fitness programs at spas] L. George.
il *American Health* 8:92+ Ap '89
Alaska
Hot on the trail [hot springs resorts] M. Steere. il map
Travel Holiday 171:55-9 Ja '89
Arizona
Kicking the habit [stop-smoking program at the Canyon
Ranch Spa] H. Sweet. *Vogue* 179:414-15 O '89
Savory splurges [excerpt from The Canyon Ranch health
and fitness program] il *Health (New York, N.Y.)* 21:76-83
Mr '89
Arkansas
See also
Hot Springs (Ark.)
California
See also
Calistoga (Calif.)
Jane Fonda's spa [Laurel Springs Retreat decorated by Barbara
Pohlman] P. Viladas. il por *House & Garden* 161:92-7
Je '89
The smaller the spa, the more personal the attention, as
Rosamond Bernier learned, working out and resting up
at California's Cal-a-Vie. R. Bernier. il *Vogue* 179:150+
D '89
Florida
Gregory buys hotel and fattens his diet empire. H. Manly.
il por *Black Enterprise* 19:22 Mr '89
France
See also
Aix-les-Bains (France)
Germany (West)
See also
Baden-Baden (Germany)

HEALTH RESORTS, WATERING PLACES, ETC.—*cont.*
Italy
See also
Montecatini Terme (Italy)
Jamaica
Miracle waters [Sans Souci] il *Harper's Bazaar* 122:138-41+ My '89
Japan
See also
Ibusuki (Japan)
Mexico
C'mon, work it on out [Rancho La Puerta] D. Wakefield. il *Gentlemen's Quarterly* 59:228-36 F '89
First in fitness [Rancho La Puerta] P. C. Pietschmann. il *Harper's Bazaar* 122:188-9+ Ap '89
New York (State)
The four-hour spa [E. Bruck visits Estée Lauder Spa at Bloomingdale's in Manhattan] L. Washer. il *Working Woman* 14:111-12 F '89
Rocky Mountains region
High-altitude health havens [ski spas] J. Sheehan. il *Travel Holiday* 171:27-31 Ja '89
West Virginia
Goodness gracious, it's the Greenbrier [testing the Range Rover] W. Jeanes. il *Car and Driver* 34:143 F '89
HEALTH, THE MUSICAL [musical] See Musicals, revues, etc.—Reviews—Single works
HEALTH WORKERS
See also
Midwives
Nurses and nursing
A need for information professionals. D. Protti. il *World Health* p26-7 Ag/S '89
Health and hygiene
See also
AIDS (Disease) and health workers
Supply and demand
Allied health professionals. E. McTernan and L. J. Holder. il *World Health* p23-4 My '89
Medicine. il *U.S. News & World Report* 107:62-3 S 25 '89
One physical therapist, 10 job offers. A. Saltzman. il *U.S. News & World Report* 106:67 Je 12 '89
Training
Bolivia's health couriers. C. A. Chelala. il *World Health* p18-19 D '88
Ethiopia's success story [community health workers] G. S. Okubagzhi. il *World Health* p21-2 My '89
Leadership through language training [English as a second language at the WHO Learning Centre] E. N. Francisco. il *World Health* p6 N '89
The RCT proposal and the nursing shortage [registered care technologists; address, January 5, 1989] J. H. Sammons. *Vital Speeches of the Day* 55:373-5 Ap 1 '89
Small patient, big emergency [Pediatric Emergency Medical Services Training Program; work of Jane Ball] B. Portnow. *American Health* 8:120+ Je '89
HEALY, TIMOTHY STAFFORD, 1923-
about
Timothy Healy's sacred secular trust. M. Horn. il por *U.S. News & World Report* 106:52+ Je 5 '89
HEANEY, SEAMUS
Crossings [poem] *The New Yorker* 65:35 Ap 17 '89
HEARD, ALEX
Brat Pack II. il *The American Spectator* 22:27-9 O '89
Danube fever. *The New Republic* 201:16-18 D 4 '89
Gonna party like it's 1999. il *Mother Jones* 14:29-31+ N '89
Hogrolling. *The New Republic* 201:11-12 N 20 '89
Life without LaRouche. *The New Republic* 200:15-17 F 27 '89
Mapplethorpe of my eye. *The New Republic* 201:10-12 Ag 21 '89
Mecca bucks. *The New Republic* 201:16-17 S 4 '89
Oratory in the modern Senate. *The American Spectator* 22:14-15 My '89
Rolfing with Yeltsin. *The New Republic* 201:11-13 O 9 '89
Schlock City. *The New Republic* 200:13-14 F 13 '89
Stop blaming men for everything! (A guy begs for mercy). il *Mademoiselle* 95:182-3+ Ag '89
HEARD, BILL
A lilac primer. il *Flower and Garden* 33:18-20+ Mr/Ap '89
HEARING
See also
Deafness
Ear
Ear, Artificial
Noise—Physiological effects
Psychoacoustics
Sound perception
Speech perception
Hold on to your hearing. D. Benzaia. il *The Saturday Evening Post* 261:40+ Ja/F '89
Infants show keen ear for speech sounds [research by DiAnne Grieser and Patricia K. Kuhl] B. Bower. *Science News* 136:37 Jl 15 '89
Amphibia
In a frog's ear. A. Fisher. *Popular Science* 235:34 N '89

Birds
Owls give a hoot for vision [research by Eric and Phyllis Knudsen] il *Science News* 136:263 O 21 '89
Fish
Good vibrations [sound waves created by fishing boats] P. B. Wright. il *Motor Boating & Sailing* 163:74+ Je '89
Shooing fish with sound [schools of fish] R. Friedman. il *Sea Frontiers* 35:136-41 My/Je '89
Insects
Hearing in honey bees: detection of air-particle oscillations. W. F. Towne and W. H. Kirchner. bibl f il *Science* 244:686-8 My 12 '89
Honey bees listen to the dance [research by William F. Towne] B. Bower. *Science News* 135:318 My 20 '89
HEARING AIDS
Help your hearing. D. Benzaia. il *The Saturday Evening Post* 261:16+ Mr '89
HEARING EDUCATION AND AWARENESS FOR ROCKERS (ORGANIZATION)
After Live Aid and Farm Aid, hearing aid may be next for unwary victims of rock [work of K. Peck and F. Gordon] N. Geeslin. il pors *People Weekly* 31:95-6 Ja 23 '89
HEARING LOSS See Deafness
HEARING PROTECTORS See Ear—Protection
HEARNS, HENRY
about
'Hit Man' Hearns' brother charged in shooting of 'girlfriend' in Michigan. il pors *Jet* 76:51-2 Je 26 '89
HEARNS, THOMAS
about
Another classic [cover story] P. Putnam. il pors *Sports Illustrated* 70:18-21 Je 19 '89
The Hit Man. R. Wiley. il pors *Sports Illustrated* 70:48-50+ Je 5 '89
Leonard-Hearns, again. D. Miller. il pors *Sport (New York, N.Y.)* 80:69-71 Jl '89
Leonard, Hearns rematch finally will take place. pors *Jet* 75:50 F 20 '89
Leonard-Hearns war ends 8-year wait. il pors *Jet* 76:48-50 Je 12 '89
Sugar Ray Leonard and Thomas Hearns battle to a draw in title brawl. il pors *Jet* 76:53-4 Je 26 '89
HEARST TRADE BOOK GROUP
Sparks fly as Colleen McCullough leaves Harper for Hearst. G. Feldman. *Publishers Weekly* 236:40 Jl 21 '89
HEART
See also
Atrial natriuretic factor
Long live the healthy heart! M.-L. Kamberg. bibl il *Current Health 2* 16:4-9 O '89
Abnormalities
See also
Hypoplastic left heart syndrome
Heart defect may lie behind 'bends' [patent foramen ovale; research by Richard E. Moon] *Science News* 135:188 Mr 25 '89
Contraction
See Heart—Muscle—Contraction
Diseases
See also
Arrhythmia
Arteriosclerosis
Cardiacs
Beating heart disease [interviews with A. Watanabe and K. Cooper] C. SerVaas. il pors *The Saturday Evening Post* 261:20-1+ Mr '89
Billows in the heart [mitral valve prolapse] J. Stone. il *The New York Times Magazine* p44-5 Je 18 '89
Compute your heart risk [computer program used by Framingham Heart Study] A. Sprout. il *American Health* 8:14-15 N '89
Finding a silent heart attack can set off some noisy, vital alarms [interview with S. Knoebel; ed. by Giovanna Breu. il por *People Weekly* 32:58 S 18 '89
Have a heart [how to identify a heart attack] P. G. Gill. il *Outdoor Life* 184:59-61 Ag '89
Heart trouble [heart attack fells helicopter pilot] P. Garrison. *Flying* 116:22+ Ja '89
A killer of women, too. J. Silberner. il *U.S. News & World Report* 107:75-6 D 18 '89
Mitral-valve prolapse. J. Kaplan. *Vogue* 179:376+ Mr '89
Was the X factor a factor? [former football player and steroid user S. Courson suffering from cardiomyopathy] por *Sports Illustrated* 70:34 Ap 3 '89
Women and heart disease. J. L. Lippert. il *Ladies' Home Journal* 106:59-60+ O '89
Causes
See also
Arteriosclerosis—Causes
Backfire drugs [Enkaid and Tambocor, used to treat mild arrhythmia, may cause fatalities] J. Ziegler. il *American Health* 8:18 S '89
Bad news bellies [paunchiness linked to diabetes and heart disease in men] D. Grady. il *American Health* 8:20 My '89
Blood pressure: questioning a maxim [research by Michael H. Alderman] S. Hart. *Science News* 136:116 Ag 19 '89

HEART—Diseases—Causes—*cont.*

Cocaine abuse leaves lingering heart risk [research by Koonlawee Nademanee] K. Fackelman. *Science News* 136:358 D 2 '89

Different but deadly [women] E. Rosenthal. il *The New York Times Magazine* p60+ S 17 '89

Diuretic dilemma [Swedish study] *Time* 134:103 O 9 '89

Heart-rhythm drugs found risky for many [encainide and flecainide] R. Weiss. *Science News* 135:260 Ap 29 '89

Hidden heart hazards [high blood insulin levels; cover story] K. Fackelmann. il *Science News* 136:184-6 S 16 '89

Hips hooray! Heartening news for the pear shaped [waist-to-hip ratio; research by C. Wayne Callaway] P. S. Derron. il *Mademoiselle* 95:136 Ag '89

Hot water and your heart [dangers of hot tubs or whirlpool baths] L. Holland. il *Good Housekeeping* 208:241 Ap '89

Hypertension, heart disease and diuretics. R. Weiss. *Science News* 136:254 O 14 '89

The imperfect art of healing [anti-arrhythmia drugs and prostate surgery increase risk of heart attack] *U.S. News & World Report* 106:10-11 My 8 '89

Monoxide heart risk. *Science News* 136:342 N 25 '89

New lifestyles, new diseases [conditions in Bahrain] M. Al-Khateeb. il *World Health* p22-3 Jl '89

Night awakening can trigger heart damage [research by Joan Barry] K. Fackelmann. *Science News* 136:341 N 25 '89

Nighttime danger for blacks [connection between high nocturnal blood pressure and heart damage; research by Michael Murphy and Roberto Lang] il *USA Today (Periodical)* 118:8 O '89

The pace of life [link between high speed cities and heart disease] R. Levine. il *Psychology Today* 23:42-6 O '89

The paunch line [link between waist-to-hip girth ratio and health; research by Richard Terry] J. Poppy. il *Reader's Digest* 135:133-5 Ag '89

The paunch line [link between waist-to-hip girth ratio and health; research by Richard Terry] J. Poppy. il *Esquire* 111:59-60 F '89

Phenomena, comment and notes [heart attack brought on by smoking] J. P. Wiley, Jr. *Smithsonian* 20:32+ Ap '89

The truth about women and heart disease. B. Hersey. il *Working Woman* 14:156+ Ap '89

Weakness for alcohol borne by muscles [research by Emanuel Rubin] I. Wickelgren. *Science News* 135:117 F 25 '89

What causes a coronary? il *USA Today (Periodical)* 117:11 F '89

A woman's heart. J. Ismach. il *American Health* 8:15-16+ Ja/F '89

Women face equal danger [views of Carolyn Corn] *USA Today (Periodical)* 117:4 F '89

Diagnosis

See also
Electrocardiography

Early glimmerings of heart disease [acetylcholine test; work of Joseph A. Vita] K. Fackelmann. *Science News* 136:349 N 25 '89

Healing a broken heart [use of monoclonal antibodies] B. Lawren. il *Omni (New York, N.Y.)* 11:20+ S '89

The heart attack business. C. Messina. il *High Technology Business* 9:22-5 Mr '89

Silent signals. J. Cassidy. il *Current Health 2* 16:14-16 O '89

Tests that can predict heart attacks and strokes. A. C. Mallozzi. il *Good Housekeeping* 209:249-50 O '89

Mortality

See also
Sudden cardiac arrest

Nutritional aspects

See also
Cholesterol

Fill up on complex carbohydrates [excerpt from Good fat/bad fat] G. C. Griffin and W. P. Castelli. il *The Saturday Evening Post* 261:12-13+ O '89

Fish-oil capsules: good for the heart? S. Mahler. *McCall's* 116:108 S '89

A Good Heartkeeping seal of approval [American Heart Association labeling of approved processed foods] C. Jennings-Sauer. il *American Health* 8:16 Je '89

High-carbohydrate diet may pose heart risks [insulin resistance] K. Fackelmann. *Science News* 136:185 S 16 '89

The high price of health approval [HeartGuide seal program] C. Sugarman. il *Consumers' Research Magazine* 72:33-4 N '89

How to be young at heart [role of magnesium in preventing disease] B. SerVaas. il map *The Saturday Evening Post* 261:90+ My/Je '89

How to have a healthier heart. il *McCall's* 116:117+ My '89

A mackerel a day . . . [fish in diet may reduce risk] *Health (New York, N.Y.)* 21:75 My '89

New hope from the fish-oil factor. G. L. Blackburn. il *Prevention (Emmaus, Pa.)* 41:29-30+ Je '89

Revealing the finicky functions of fish oil. I. Wickelgren. *Science News* 135:183 Mr 25 '89

Reversing heart disease [interview with D. Ornish] il *The Saturday Evening Post* 261:42-4 O '89

Tasty foods for a healthy heart. il *Ebony* 44:110+ Jl '89

Prevention

All's well in Wellsburg [public health program in W. Va.] M. Vitez. il *New Choices for the Best Years* 29:10 Je '89

Are you cheating your heart? M. Callahan. il *Parents* 64:220+ Je '89

Aspirin and heart attacks [Physicians' Health Study] il *FDA Consumer* 23:2-3 O '89

Aspirin and heart disease: a final report [research by Julie E. Buring] R. Cowen. *Science News* 136:55 Jl 22 '89

Aspirin on trial [effect on risk of heart attack and stroke] J. Poppy. il *Esquire* 111:89-91 Mr '89

The battle against heart disease begins with children. il *The Saturday Evening Post* 261:12-13+ S '89

A couple of collective tons later, the citizens of Wellsburg, W. Va., are no longer in Fat City [Bayer Wellness Program] M. Brower. il *People Weekly* 31:44-6 F 20 '89

An exercise in longevity [cardiovascular benefits of playing tennis] P. Stites. il *World Tennis* 36:16+ My '89

Facts about kids and cholesterol; ed. by Florence Isaacs. J. H. Moller. il *Good Housekeeping* 209:101+ S '89

The healthy heart [cover story; special issue] il *Current Health 2* 16:4-16+ O '89

The heart part [failure of dentists to treat heart patients with antibiotics to prevent endocarditis] C. Sears. il *American Health* 8:44 Je '89

How fast does your heart beat? [Tecumseh Step Test] C. SerVaas. il *The Saturday Evening Post* 261:96+ My/Je '89

Lifestyle contributes to a healthy heart. K. Fackelmann. *Science News* 136:367 D 2 '89

The town that lost two tons [Bayer Wellness Program] D. Grady. il *Ladies' Home Journal* 106:46+ Je '89

Warm up before shoveling out [reducing heart stress; views of Dan Fintel] *Prevention (Emmaus, Pa.)* 41:12+ D '89

Wellness in Wellsburg [program sponsored by Bayer] P. Stone. il *The Mother Earth News* 115:16+ Ja/F '89

Psychological aspects

The character of controversy [link between disease and personality; work of R. Grossarth-Maticek] J. Fischman. il *Psychology Today* 22:27 D '88

Child's aggression may foretell heart risk [research by Saundra MacD. Hunter] K. Fackelmann. *Science News* 136:15 Jl 1 '89

Danger! A short fuse can kill you [Type A behavior] A. Fischer. il *Redbook* 173:162-3+ S '89

Double jeopardy: cholesterol and Type A [research by Edward Suarez] P. King. il *Psychology Today* 23:26 S '89

Getting to the heart of Type A's [interview with R. B. Williams] S. Findlay. il por *U.S. News & World Report* 106:68 My 15 '89

Happy hearts [depression linked with coronary artery disease; research by Robert M. Carney] *Prevention (Emmaus, Pa.)* 41:10-12 F '89

Health's character [link between personality and disease; research by R. Grossarth-Maticek] H. J. Eysenck. il pors *Psychology Today* 22:28-32+ D '88

The heart of depression [link with coronary artery disease; research by Robert M. Carney] *Science News* 135:13 Ja 7 '89

Hostility boosts risk of heart trouble [research by Redford B. Williams] K. Fackelmann. *Science News* 135:60 Ja 28 '89

Little control=lots of stress [study by Robert Karasek] V. Adler. il *Psychology Today* 23:18-19 Ap '89

Minding your heart [special section] il *Psychology Today* 23:33+ Ja/F '89

Modest treatment yields heartfelt benefits [stress-monitoring program by Nancy Frasure-Smith and Raymond Prince] B. Bower. *Science News* 136:261 O 21 '89

The pretended self [loneliness; research by Dean Ornish] P. Perry. il *Psychology Today* 23:60-1 My '89

A saga of the heart [excerpt from The trusting heart] R. B. Williams. il *Health (New York, N.Y.)* 21:68-9+ Ja '89

Soothing the savage heart [views of R. Williams] J. Poppy. il *Esquire* 112:103-4 O '89

War against the heart [Beirut, Lebanon; study by Abla M. Sibai] *Science News* 136:284 O 28 '89

Your anger can kill you [Type A behavior linked with heart disease; condensed from The trusting heart] R. B. Williams. il *Reader's Digest* 135:183-4+ Ag '89

Statistics

Progress in the fight against heart disease [report by the American Heart Association] K. Fackelmann. *Science News* 135:60 Ja 28 '89

Therapy

See also
Defibrillators
Eminase (Drug)
TPA (Drug)

Balloon trial [questionable value of percutaneous transluminal coronary angioplasty after heart attacks] T. Appenzeller. *Scientific American* 260:32+ My '89

Clot-buster's cost-effectiveness questioned [TPA vs. streptokinase] R. Weiss. *Science News* 135:214 Ap 8 '89

Declogging your own arteries [low fat diet and stress reduction reverse plaque build-up; research by Dean Ornish] D. Grady. il *American Health* 8:18+ Mr '89

HEART—Diseases—Therapy—cont.

Drugs to the rescue of an ailing heart. R. W. Sommi, Jr. il *Current Health 2* 16:22-4 O '89

The heart attack business. C. Messina. il *High Technology Business* 9:22-5 Mr '89

Heart disease in retreat [work of D. Ornish] T. G. Harris. il por *Psychology Today* 23:46+ Ja/F '89

The heart savers. E. Kiester. il *New Choices for the Best Years* 29:51-5 F '89

Heart teamwork [use of aspirin and streptokinase to reduce heart-attack deaths; research by Samuel Z. Goldhaber] il *Prevention (Emmaus, Pa.)* 41:14 Ja '89

Paging Dr. Right [work of D. Ornish] J. Poppy. il *Esquire* 112:49-51 Jl '89

Problems reported with two heart rescues [CPR and sodium bicarbonate injections] S. Hart. *Science News* 136:85 Ag 5 '89

Reversing heart disease [interview with D. Ornish] il *The Saturday Evening Post* 261:42-4 O '89

The two essentials of change [work of Dean Ornish] J. Davidson. il *Psychology Today* 23:32 S '89

When less may be more [drugs as effective as invasive methods] J. Langone. il *Time* 133:61 Mr 20 '89

Zap your plaque. il *Prevention (Emmaus, Pa.)* 41:46-8+ My '89

Metabolism

Rapid β-adrenergic modulation of cardiac calcium channel currents by a fast G protein pathway. A. Yatani and A. M. Brown. bibl f il *Science* 245:71-4 Jl 7 '89

Muscle

Autonomic regulation of a chloride current in heart. R. D. Harvey and J. R. Hume. bibl f il *Science* 244:983-5 My 26 '89

β-adrenergic inhibition of cardiac sodium channels by dual G-protein pathways. B. Schubert and others. bibl f il *Science* 245:516-19 Ag 4 '89

Potassium channels in cardiac cells activated by arachidonic acid and phospholipids. D. Kim and D. E. Clapham. bibl f il *Science* 244:1174-6 Je 9 '89

Two molecular transitions influence cardiac sodium channel gating. D. T. Yue and others. bibl f il *Science* 244:349-52 Ap 21 '89

Contraction

Does voltage affect excitation-contraction coupling in the heart? [discussion of May 19, 1989 article, Regulation of calcium release is gated by calcium current, not gating charge, in cardiac myocytes] M. Näbauer and others. bibl f *Science* 246:1640 D 22 '89

Regulation of calcium release is gated by calcium current, not gating charge, in cardiac myocytes. M. Näbauer and others. bibl f il *Science* 244:800-3 My 19 '89

Surgery

See also

Cardiac catheterization

An affair of the heart [open heart surgery] R. Craft. il *The New York Review of Books* 36:37-8 Ap 13 '89

Carroll O'Connor calls it luck [coronary bypass] G. Esterly. il pors *The Saturday Evening Post* 261:58-9+ O '89

A partnership of the heart [work of surgeon A. Blalock and black assistant V. T. Thomas] K. McCabe. il por *Reader's Digest* 135:91-6 O '89

Scared smokeless [undergoing bypass surgery] J. E. Brown. il *Reader's Digest* 134:117-21 My '89

Should this baby be saved? [performing surgery to correct hypoplastic left heart syndrome] P. Klass. il *Glamour* 87:212-13+ D '89

Will Denton Cooley make medical history again? [cut-rate heart bypasses] M. Ivey. il por *Business Week* p56+ Mr 27 '89

Transplantation

After a heart transplant, a 9-year-old learns the joy of being a normal kid again; ed. by Suzanne Adelson. D. Horn and E. Coleman. il *People Weekly* 32:103+ N 20 '89

The doctor with the heart of gold [excerpt from Transplant] W. H. Frist. il *Redbook* 173:134-6+ Jl '89

Heart transplants: the beat has picked up. J. Rothfeder. il *Business Week* p94-5 Ag 28 '89

A hero of her time [heart-liver transplant recepient S. Jones] S. Christenson. il por *American Health* 8:90 Je '89

I am Joe's new heart. J. Pekkanen. il *Reader's Digest* 134:89-95 Je '89

A new year, a new life, a new love [primary pulmonary hypertension patient R. Gyorfi receives heart-lung transplant] D. Gage. il pors *Good Housekeeping* 208:95+ Ja '89

Transplants in demand. J. Rothfeder. il *The Saturday Evening Post* 261:12-13 N/D '89

The widow of an Israeli soldier gives his heart—and the gift of life—to an Arab, Hanna Khader. il pors *People Weekly* 32:130 D 11 '89

HEART, ARTIFICIAL

The little bionic heart [Hemopump] D. Grady. il *Discover* 10:54-5 Ja '89

HEART ATTACKS *See* Heart—Diseases

HEART BEAT

See also

Arrhythmia

Electrocardiography

Pacemaker, Artificial (Heart)

Pulse

Climbs of the heart [rate increase while exercising] C. L. Otis. il *Women's Sports & Fitness* 11:8 Je '89

A fitter formula [more precise way to figure training heart rate zone] il *Women's Sports & Fitness* 11:14 My '89

How fast does your heart beat? [Tecumseh Step Test] C. SerVaas. il *The Saturday Evening Post* 261:96+ My/Je '89

Is it healthy to be chaotic? R. Pool. bibl il *Science* 243:604-7 F 3 '89

Muscarinic modulation of cardiac rate at low acetylcholine concentrations. D. DiFrancesco and others. bibl f il *Science* 243:669-71 F 3 '89

Racial differences in heart rate [research by Lars G. Ekelund] K. Fackelmann. *Science News* 136:15 Jl 1 '89

Target heart rate [cycling intensity] S. Johnson. il *Bicycling* 30:81 Jl '89

Defibrillators

See Defibrillators

HEART BEAT MONITORS *See* Pulse monitors

HEART CATHETERIZATION *See* Cardiac catheterization

HEART DISEASES *See* Heart—Diseases

HEART IN ART

Heart gallery [Lo del corazón at the Mexican Museum of San Francisco] il *Psychology Today* 23:52+ Ja/F '89

Hearts [excerpt from Mary Emmerling's American country hearts] M. E. Emmerling. il *Good Housekeeping* 208:40+ F '89

HEART-LUNG MACHINES

The luckiest little girl in the world [hypothermia patient M. Funk saved by extracorporeal rewarming] A. Sunshine-Genova. il pors *Ladies' Home Journal* 106:140-1+ Mr '89

HEART MUSCLE *See* Heart—Muscle

HEART OF DIXIE [film] *See* Motion picture reviews—Single works

HEART PATIENTS *See* Cardiacs

HEART PUMPS *See* Heart, Artificial

HEART RATE *See* Heart beat

HEART RESEARCH

See also

American Heart Association

Texas Heart Institute

Ethical aspects

Setting the record straight [retraction of fraudulent papers by R. Slutsky] M. Sun. *Science* 244:911 My 26 '89

HEARTBURN

Help for heartburn. *McCall's* 116:82 Ag '89

HEARTHS *See* Fireplaces

HEARTLAND PARK TOPEKA

A new park in the heartland. T. Swan. il *Popular Mechanics* 166:36 Ap '89

HEARTNEY, ELEANOR

Street scenes. bibl f il *Art in America* 77:230-7+ Ap '89

Visions of Venice. il *Harper's Bazaar* 122:158-9+ N '89

The whole earth show. il *Art in America* 77:90-7 Jl '89

HEARTWATER IN LIVESTOCK *See* Livestock—Diseases and pests

HEAT

See also

Calorimeters and calorimetry

Hot weather

Thermodynamics

Convection

Coming down in sheets [computer model of convection in the earth's mantle; work of Dave Bercovici and others] T. Appenzeller. il *Scientific American* 261:17-18 Ag '89

Giant ocean cataracts. J. A. Whitehead, Jr. bibl il map *Scientific American* 260:50-7 F '89

Three-dimensional spherical models of convection in the earth's mantle. D. Bercovici and others. bibl f il *Science* 244:950-5 My 26 '89

Physiological effects

See also

Cats, Effect of temperature on

Dogs, Effect of temperature on

Fish, Effect of temperature on

Heatstroke

Hyperthermia

The ice is right [running injuries] M. Chasnov. il *Runner's World* 24:24 Jl '89

Radiation and absorption

Heat flow and hydrothermal circulation in the Cascade Range, north-central Oregon. S. E. Ingebritsen and others. bibl f il maps *Science* 243:1458-62 Mr 17 '89

HEAT AND SUNLIGHT [film] *See* Motion picture reviews—Single works

HEAT COLLECTORS, SOLAR *See* Solar collectors

HEAT ENGINES

See also

Stirling engines

HEAT IN ANIMALS *See* Estrus

HEAT PIPES

Don't forget your heat-pipe mittens [research by Amir Faghri] *Science News* 136:62 Jl 22 '89

HEAT PRODUCTION (BIOLOGY) *See* Temperature, Animal and human

HEAT PRODUCTION (BOTANY) *See* Plants—Temperature
HEAT PUMP WATER HEATERS *See* Water heaters
HEAT PUMPS
Advanced heat pump heats water too [Carrier's Hydrotech 2000] E. R. C. Capulong. il *Popular Science* 234:41 F '89
Do-it-all heat pumps [Mac=Pac and HydroTech 2000] M. DiChristina. il *Popular Science* 235:68-70 O '89
Heat pump. T. Klenck. il *Popular Mechanics* 166:97-8 Mr '89
Heat-pump clothes dryer. V. E. Gilmore. il *Popular Science* 235:124+ N '89
The most efficient heating systems. il *Consumers' Research Magazine* 72:25-8 Ja '89
HEAT RADIATION *See* Heat—Radiation and absorption
HEAT REGULATORS *See* Thermostats
HEAT SHOCK PROTEINS
Drosophila nuclear proteins bind to regions of alternating C and T residues in gene promoters. D. S. Gilmour and others. bibl f il *Science* 245:1487-90 S 29 '89
Peptide binding and release by proteins implicated as catalysts of protein assembly. G. C. Flynn and others. bibl f il *Science* 245:385-90 Jl 28 '89
A role for a 70-kilodaton heat shock protein in lysosomal degradation of intracellular proteins. H.-L. Chiang and others. bibl f il *Science* 246:382-5 O 20 '89
T cells against a bacterial heat shock protein recognize stressed macrophages. T. Koga and others. bibl f il *Science* 245:1112-15 S 8 '89
HEAT STROKE *See* Heatstroke
HEATERS
See also
    Solar water heaters
    Water heaters
Add-on heat [electric space heaters] M. LaLiberte. il *The Family Handyman* 39:57-60 Ja '89
Electric heaters: a spot of low-cost warmth. il *Consumer Reports* 54:724-8 N '89
Pulsing room heater [Empulse space heater] E. R. C. Capulong. il *Popular Science* 234:40 F '89
HEATH, ALAN G.
Professional ethics for research biologists. bibl f *BioScience* 39:472-4 Jl/Ag '89
HEATH, ALOISE BUCKLEY
It says here . . . [story] il *National Review* 41:34-6 D 31 '89
HEATH, J. R., AND OTHERS
Diode-laser absorption spectroscopy of supersonic carbon cluster beams: the v_3 spectrum of C_5. bibl f il *Science* 244:564-6 My 5 '89
HEATH, JINGER L.
about
See Dick and Jinger sell. W. P. Barrett. il pors *Forbes* 144:48-9 Ag 7 '89
HEATH, RICHARD W.
about
See Dick and Jinger sell. W. P. Barrett. il pors *Forbes* 144:48-9 Ag 7 '89
HEATHENISM *See* Paganism
HEATHERS [film] *See* Motion picture reviews—Single works
HEATHROW AIRPORT *See* London (England)—Airports
HEATING
See also
    Chimneys
    Fireplaces
    Furnaces
    Insulation (Heat)
    Stoves
    Thermostats
    Wood as fuel
    Wood stoves
Costs
Comparing various heating fuel costs. P. L. Spencer. il *Consumers' Research Magazine* 72:26-8 D '89
HEATING EQUIPMENT
See also
    Furnaces
    Heat pumps
    Stoves
    Wood stoves
House warmers. il *Popular Science* 235:71-3 O '89
HEATING EQUIPMENT INDUSTRY
See also
    Modine Manufacturing Co.
HEATING PADS
Cordless heating pads: one good, one not so hot [Champ Hot Quickwrap and the Spenco Hot Wrap] il *Consumer Reports* 54:287 My '89
HEATSTROKE
Heat success [treating runners] G. Sheehan. il *Runner's World* 24:16 Jl '89
Heatstroke. *Prevention (Emmaus, Pa.)* 41:14 Je '89
HEAVEN
Heaven. K. L. Woodward. il *Newsweek* 113:52-5 Mr 27 '89
Anecdotes, facetiae, satire, etc.
This working woman's heaven. K. Fury. il *Working Woman* 14:170 Ap '89

HEAVEN AND EARTH [film] *See* Motion picture reviews—Single works
HEAVEN IN LITERATURE
An afterlife anthology. D. Gates. *Newsweek* 113:58 Mr 27 '89
HEAVEN ON EARTH [drama] *See* Schenkkan, Robert
HEAVENLY BAMBOO *See* Nandina
HEAVY-ION ACCELERATORS *See* Accelerators (Electrons, etc.)
HEAVY METAL MUSIC
Making it in Metal Mecca [Los Angeles] J. Foote. il *Newsweek* 114:56-8 Ag 7 '89
Vocal coach Elizabeth Sabine, the heavy metal grandma, teaches speech and screech. S. Dougherty. il pors *People Weekly* 31:137-9 My 15 '89
Collectibles
Pick men [Chuck Collum's and Rickey Anderson's collections of guitar picks from heavy metal bands] il *The New Yorker* 64:26-7 Ja 30 '89
Conferences
Head bangers: learning to earn [Foundations Forum] J. Ressner. *Rolling Stone* p33 N 16 '89
HEAVY PETTING [film] *See* Motion picture reviews—Single works
HEAVY WATER *See* Deuterium oxide
HEBEI UNIVERSITY
True power to the people [students join demonstrations] G. Jochnowitz. il *National Review* 41:22-3 Je 30 '89
HEBRIDES (SCOTLAND)
See also
    Gigha (Scotland)
HECHINGER CO.
Trial by fire. J. Drummond. il *Forbes* 144:148+ D 11 '89
HECHT, ANNABEL
Eyes too dry to cry: how Sjögren's syndrome makes the body a 'desert'. il *FDA Consumer* 23:26-30 F '89
HECHT, ANTHONY, 1923-
Naming the animals [poem] *The New York Review of Books* 36:8 Ag 17 '89
HECHT, JULIE
Perfect vision [story] *The New Yorker* 65:34-44+ My 29 '89
HECHT, SUSANNA, AND COCKBURN, ALEXANDER
Defenders of the Amazon [cover story] il *The Nation* 248:695-6+ My 22 '89
Rain forest politics [discussion of May 22, 1989 article, Defenders of the Amazon] *The Nation* 249:262+ S 18 '89
HECHT, TANNIA RUBIANO
about
On top of the world. D. Stathoplos. il pors *Sports Illustrated* 70 Special Issue:109-12 F '89
HECKERLING, AMY
about
Look who's talking [film] Reviews
    People Weekly il 32:67-8 N 13 '89. J. Kaufman
    People Weekly il 32:14 O 30 '89. R. Novak
    Time il 134:98 N 20 '89. R. Corliss
HECKERT, RICHARD EDWIN
Lets apply common sense to chemicals [address, February 21, 1989] *Vital Speeches of the Day* 55:476-8 My 15 '89
HECKSCHER MUSEUM
Unfit for hanging [E. Manet's Bouquet of peonies stolen] R. Cembalest. il *Art News* 88:16 F '89
HECTOR'S TAILORING (FIRM)
Threading the needle. A. A. Knocke. il por *Nation's Business* 77:70 Mr '89
HEDBERG, GUS
Technology that gets you where you live. il *Personal Computing* 13:31-2 O '89
HEDBERG, NANCY ANDERSON
Classing up your concrete: pave the way for stamped-in style underfoot. il *Better Homes and Gardens* 67:117-18 Je '89
HEDDEN, ROB
about
Friday the 13th, part VIII: Jason takes Manhattan [film] Reviews
    People Weekly il 32:17-18 Ag 14 '89. R. Novak
HEDGE SPARROW SEXUAL BEHAVIOR *See* Sexual behavior—Birds
HEDGEHOG CACTUS *See* Cactus
HEDGES, PAT
about
Firestorm! J. L. Moore. il *Reader's Digest* 134:77-82 Mr '89
HEDGES, WILLIAM D.
We must remove elementary teacher training from the state universities. bibl f il *Phi Delta Kappan* 70:623-5 Ap '89
HEDGING (FINANCE)
Got a few million to spare? Head for a hedge fund. G. Weiss. il *Business Week* p126-7 S 11 '89
Hedged bets [views of S. D. Sussman] J. Clements. il por *Forbes* 144 Special Issue:372 O 23 '89
Market advisers get a report card [crop marketing] il *Successful Farming* 87:15 mid-Mr '89

HEDONIC DAMAGES *See* Damages

HEEBNER, KENNETH
about
Companies even better than they look [interview] P. Sellers. il por *Fortune* 120:28-9 Ag 14 '89

HEFFERNAN, MARYCLARE J.
Writing the short story: three basic points. *The Writer* 102:16-18 S '89

HEFLEY, JOEL MAURICE
Should the House-passed wage proposal be enacted? [excerpts from address, March 23, 1989] *Congressional Digest* 68:159 My '89

HEFNER, BILL
Should the Congress adopt the "Textile and Apparel Trade Act of 1987"? [excerpts from address, September 16, 1987] *Congressional Digest* 68:26+ Ja '89

HEFNER, HUGH
about
Hef gains a bride, loses a reputation [cover story] S. Schindehette. il pors *People Weekly* 32:34-9 Jl 17 '89
Mrs. Bunny. J. Ash. il pors *Life* 12:102-6 S '89

HEGG, TOM
A cup of Christmas tea [poem] il *New Choices for the Best Years* 29:26-7 D '89

HEHIR, J. BRYAN
Church/world watch. See occasional issues of Commonweal

HEIDEL, THERESA TROISE
Integrating studio work and outdoor painting. il por *American Artist* 53:44-7+ D '89

THE HEIDI CHRONICLES [drama] *See* Wasserstein, Wendy

HEIFERMAN, MARVIN, 1948-
about
Indelible images. R. Cembalest. il pors *Art News* 88:174-9 Ap '89
Marvin Heiferman's all-encompassing eye has redefined photography. R. B. Woodward. il por *Vogue* 179:284+ N '89

HEIGHT, DOROTHY I.
Self-help—a black tradition. il *The Nation* 249:136-8 Jl 24-31 '89

HEIGHT OF MAN *See* Stature

HEIGHTS, FEAR OF *See* Acrophobia

HEIL, ROBERT A.
Remote A/B switch. il *Radio-Electronics* 60:37+ O '89
Remote control extender. il *Radio-Electronics* 60:41-4 My '89

HEILBRON, J. L., AND KEVLES, DANIEL J.
The "civics" of technology in history textbooks. *The Education Digest* 55:42-4 S '89

HEILBRONER, ROBERT L.
All rich nations need their debt. *The Nation* 248:81-2 Ja 23 '89
The triumph of capitalism. *The New Yorker* 64:98-109 Ja 23 '89
about
No alternative to capitalism [interview] S. K. Sheinbaum and N. Gardels. il *New Perspectives Quarterly* 6:4-10 Fall '89

HEILBRUN, CAROLYN G., 1926-
about
PW interviews. M. Berkley. il por *Publishers Weekly* 235:47-8 Ap 14 '89

HEILBRUNN FAMILY
about
Masters of deception. B. Shaw and D. Van Biema. il *People Weekly* 31:46-51 Je 19 '89

HEILEMANN, JOHN
Congress's watch dog: mostly it still goes for the capillaries. *The Washington Monthly* 21:38-42 N '89
Pop goes the curriculum. *The Washington Monthly* 21:34-5 O '89

HEIM, MICHAEL HENRY
(tr) See Kiš, Danilo. To die for one's country is glorious

HEIMEL, CYNTHIA
On the Marc. il por *Vogue* 179:84-5+ F '89

HEIMLICH MANEUVER
All choked up. P. G. Gill. il *Outdoor Life* 184:60+ S '89

HEIN, CHRISTOPH
East Berlin diary; tr. by Phillip Boehm. il *The New York Times Magazine* p34-7+ D 17 '89

HEINE, ANDREW N.
about
Victor Posner may soon taste his own medicine. G. DeGeorge. il pors *Business Week* p34+ Ap 10 '89

HEINE, HEINRICH, 1797-1856
about
A (Jewish) double helix. C. Raphael. *Commentary* 87:56-8 My '89

HEINEN, KAY, AND PADGETT, MARY ANN
Networking on a shoestring. il *Children Today* 18:30-2 Ja/F '89

HEINLEIN, ROBERT A. (ROBERT ANSON), 1907-1988
This I believe. il por *The Humanist* 49:16 Mr/Ap '89
about
Del Rey digs up Heinlein's 'Grumbles from the grave'. il *Publishers Weekly* 236:55 N 3 '89

HEINO (NETHERLANDS)
Galleries and museums
See also
Kasteel het Nijenhuis (Heino, Netherlands)

HEINRICH, BERND, 1940-
The ravens' feast. il *Natural History* p44-51 F '89

HEINZ (H. J.) CO. *See* H. J. Heinz Co.

HEIRS *See* Inheritance

HEISCHMAN, DANIEL R.
Transmitting a vision: religion in independent schools. *The Christian Century* 106:417-9 Ap 19 '89

HEISE, LORI
The global war against women. il *Utne Reader* p40-5 N/D '89
(jt. auth) See Postel, Sandra, and Heise, Lori

HEISMAN TROPHY
Heisman handicap [top 1989 candidates] M. Francesa. il *Sport (New York, N.Y.)* 80:28 S '89
Houston QB Andre Ware wins '89 Heisman Trophy. il pors *Jet* 77:51 D 18 '89
To h—— with the H——! J. McCallum. por *Sports Illustrated* 71:102 D 4 '89
Who will bag the prize? [cover story] A. Murphy. il *Sports Illustrated* 71:24-6+ N 27 '89

HEISS, GAYLE
Reflecting on priorities in preschool teaching. *The Education Digest* 55:48-51 S '89

HEISS, MICHAEL
Decks that mean business. il *Video* 13:56-8+ My '89

HEJDUK, JOHN, 1929-
about
John Hejduk at Max Protetch. E. Saxon. il *Art in America* 77:164-5 F '89

HELD, AL, 1928-
about
Al Held's Catskill pastoral: the artist's studio and house in Woodstock, New York. D. Solomon. il por *Architectural Digest* 46:170-3+ Je '89
Is bigger necessarily better? P. Plagens. il pors *Newsweek* 113:66-7 Ap 17 '89

HELDMAN, GLADYS M.
The 10 commandments of doubles. il *World Tennis* 37:32+ Ag '89
How to play on hard courts. il *World Tennis* 37:50+ S '89
Power games grip men's tour. il *World Tennis* 36:16-17 F '89
Senior partners. il *World Tennis* 36:66+ Ap '89
A sorority gone sour. il *World Tennis* 37:96 N '89
That was then, this is now. il *World Tennis* 37:34-6 N '89

HELIANTHUS *See* Sunflowers

HELICOPTER AIRLINES
Shuttle service
Helicopters can help unsnarl U.S. city surface gridlock. N. C. Kernstock. il *Aviation Week & Space Technology* 131:89-91 D 18-25 '89
Hawaii
Tourist choppers roil islands. J. Conrow. *The Progressive* 53:16 My '89
Malaysia
See also
Malaysian Helicopter Services

HELICOPTER ASSOCIATION INTERNATIONAL
HAI convention: new helicopter developments [special section] il *Aviation Week & Space Technology* 130:16-19 Ja 23 '89
Helicopter heaven: the HAI show. il *Flying* 116:15-16 Ap '89
Launch of new MDX reflects industry confidence in helicopter market [show] C. A. Shifrin. il *Aviation Week & Space Technology* 130:54-6 F 6 '89

HELICOPTER ENGINES
Defects
Coast Guard weighs replacing troubled Textron Lycoming engines. D. Hughes. il *Aviation Week & Space Technology* 130:19-20 My 15 '89
Design
LHTEC develops commercial version of T800 engine. *Aviation Week & Space Technology* 130:19 Ja 23 '89
Fuel
Soviets testing use of alternate fuels in helicopter powerplants. *Aviation Week & Space Technology* 130:17 Ja 23 '89
Throttle
Twist and shout [questioning need for helicopter pilots to learn piston throttle control] J. M. McClellan. il *Flying* 116:110-11 Je '89

HELICOPTER HIJACKING
With a hijacked copter, she rescued her boyfriend from jail [case of J. Mattox] L. Murray. il por *TV Guide* 37:38 F 11-17 '89

HELICOPTER INDUSTRY
See also
Bell Helicopter Textron Inc.
Boeing Co. Boeing Vertol Company (Div.)
Enstrom Helicopter Corp.
Kaman Corp.
Light Helicopter Turbine Engine Company

HELICOPTER INDUSTRY—See also—*cont.*
McDonnell Douglas Helicopter Company
Orlando Helicopter Airways
Schweizer Aircraft Corp.
Sikorsky Aircraft
Soloy Conversions (Firm)

Export-import trade
Aerospatiale takes first civilian order for Super Puma Mk. 2 helicopters [Bristow Helicopter Group order] il *Aviation Week & Space Technology* 130:73 Je 26 '89
Rising utilization, international demand should spur helicopter sales. C. A. Shifrin. il *Aviation Week & Space Technology* 130:241-4 Mr 20 '89

International aspects
See also
Helicopter Association International
Korean Air negotiates agreement to coproduce Sikorsky UH-60. J. D. Morrocco. il *Aviation Week & Space Technology* 130:225+ Je 12 '89
U.S. Army collaboration 'blueprint' could boost European LHX role. D. F. Bond. il *Aviation Week & Space Technology* 131:25 O 16 '89

Marketing
Launch of new MDX reflects industry confidence in helicopter market [Helicopter Assn. International show] C. A. Shifrin. il *Aviation Week & Space Technology* 130:54-6 F 6 '89

France
See also
Aerospatiale. Helicopter Division

Great Britain
See also
Bristow Helicopters Ltd.

Hungary
Hungary equips ambulance version of Soviet Mi-17. il *Aviation Week & Space Technology* 131:44 Jl 3 '89

Italy
See also
Agusta SpA

Japan
The coming clash over choppers [Heliport Highway 600 project] J. Impoco. il *U.S. News & World Report* 106:47+ F 27 '89

Soviet Union
See also
M. L. Mil Helicopter Design Bureau (Soviet Union)

United States
See Helicopter industry

Western Europe
See also
European Helicopter Industries
European firms told to cut costs of NH-90 by 20% [NATO project] *Aviation Week & Space Technology* 130:31 My 8 '89
U.S. Army collaboration 'blueprint' could boost European LHX role. D. F. Bond. il *Aviation Week & Space Technology* 131:25 O 16 '89

HELICOPTER PILOTS

Health and hygiene
Heart trouble [heart attack] P. Garrison. *Flying* 116:22+ Ja '89

Training
See Aviation—Study and teaching

HELICOPTER SHUTTLE SERVICE *See* Helicopter airlines—Shuttle service
HELICOPTER SIMULATORS *See* Flight simulators
HELICOPTERS
See also
Autogiros

Accidents
Angel of mercy [medical mission helicopter crash] P. Garrison. *Flying* 116:10+ S '89
Critics fault U.S. Army helicopter training with night vision goggles. *Aviation Week & Space Technology* 130:23 Mr 27 '89
Heart trouble [heart attack] P. Garrison. *Flying* 116:22+ Ja '89
Marines ground aircraft to assess safety concerns. B. D. Nordwall. *Aviation Week & Space Technology* 130:72 Je 12 '89
Skid marks [mishap on first solo flight] R. Jackson. il *Flying* 116:100 F '89

Armaments
Navy adds defensive capability to SH-2F, SH-60B helicopters. il *Aviation Week & Space Technology* 130:70-1 My 1 '89

Blades
See Helicopters—Rotors

Cockpits
Simulator, flight tests validate integrated pictorial cockpit display. W. B. Scott. il *Aviation Week & Space Technology* 130:51+ Ja 9 '89

Control
See also
Computers—Aviation use

Costs
Budget cuts put pressure on Army aviators, industry [cover story] D. F. Bond. il *Aviation Week & Space Technology* 131:38-41 Jl 31 '89

European firms told to cut costs of NH-90 by 20% [NATO project] *Aviation Week & Space Technology* 130:31 My 8 '89
GAO criticizes LHX program, claiming R&D work insufficient. M. A. Dornheim. il *Aviation Week & Space Technology* 130:22-4 Ja 30 '89

Design
HAI convention: new helicopter developments [special section] il *Aviation Week & Space Technology* 130:16-19 Ja 23 '89
Heliport 2000 [cover story] F. Mackerodt. il *Popular Mechanics* 166:54-7+ S '89
Launch of new MDX reflects industry confidence in helicopter market [Helicopter Assn. International show] C. A. Shifrin. il *Aviation Week & Space Technology* 130:54-6 F 6 '89
Man-powered helicopter makes first flight [built by Cal Poly students] il *Aviation Week & Space Technology* 131:115 D 18-25 '89
Mil Bureau designing new medium transport helicopter to replace Mi-8 [Russian helicopters] D. Hughes. *Aviation Week & Space Technology* 130:28-9 Je 5 '89
Robinson's millenium [F. Robinson's two-place R-22 piston helicopter] *Flying* 116:30 Je '89

Electronic equipment
See also
Computers—Aviation use
Avionics system lets helicopter crews focus on search, rescue [Bell/Honeywell system] N. C. Kernstock. il *Aviation Week & Space Technology* 130:50-1+ Ap 24 '89
Simulator, flight tests validate integrated pictorial cockpit display. W. B. Scott. il *Aviation Week & Space Technology* 130:51+ Ja 9 '89

Engines
See Helicopter engines

Environmental aspects
Tourist choppers roil islands [Hawaii] J. Conrow. *The Progressive* 53:16 My '89
Whirlybirds not welcome [National Guard helicopters near Black Moshannon State Park, Pa.] S. D. Borowitz. il *Sierra* 74:90-1 N/D '89

Exhibitions
See Aviation—Exhibitions

Hijacking
See Helicopter hijacking

Manufacture
See Helicopter industry

Marketing
See Helicopter industry—Marketing

Military use
See also
Anti-helicopter weapons
Helicopters—Armaments
Helicopters, Training
All aboard Air Oblivion [ineffectiveness and vulnerability of Army helicopters during the Vietnam War] G. Easterbrook. *The Washington Monthly* 21:53+ F '89
Army pursues voice-controlled avionics to improve helicopter pilot performance. B. W. Henderson. il *Aviation Week & Space Technology* 130:43+ My 22 '89
Boeing and Sikorsky near completion of U.S. Army special operations aircraft. S. W. Kandebo. il *Aviation Week & Space Technology* 131:53+ N 27 '89
Boeing rolls out MH-47E Special Operations helicopter. il *Aviation Week & Space Technology* 131:37 D 11 '89
Budget cuts put pressure on Army aviators, industry [cover story] D. F. Bond. il *Aviation Week & Space Technology* 131:38-41 Jl 31 '89
EH101 antisubmarine version begins flight test program. il *Aviation Week & Space Technology* 131:68 N 13 '89
European firms told to cut costs of NH-90 by 20% [NATO project] *Aviation Week & Space Technology* 130:31 My 8 '89
GAO criticizes LHX program, claiming R&D work insufficient. M. A. Dornheim. il *Aviation Week & Space Technology* 130:22-4 Ja 30 '89
Korean Air negotiates agreement to coproduce Sikorsky UH-60. J. D. Morrocco. il *Aviation Week & Space Technology* 130:225+ Je 12 '89
Marines ground aircraft to assess safety concerns. B. D. Nordwall. *Aviation Week & Space Technology* 130:72 Je 12 '89
McDonnell Douglas/Bell team introduces its LHX concept [special section] il *Aviation Week & Space Technology* 129:56-9+ Mr 6 '89
Mil Mi-28 attack helicopter in final tests prior to full-scale production [Soviet helicopter] il *Aviation Week & Space Technology* 130:78-9 Je 5 '89
Navy plans to roll out upgraded SH-2 Seasprite helicopter in October [antisubmarine warfare helicopter] S. W. Kandebo. il *Aviation Week & Space Technology* 130:143+ Je 19 '89
Orlando Helicopter develops simulated Soviet Hind Es [cover story] E. H. Kolcum. il *Aviation Week & Space Technology* 130:34-5+ Ja 9 '89
Revamped, scaled-back LHX may take to the air in the mid-90s. il *Popular Mechanics* 166:13 Mr '89

HELICOPTERS—Military use—*cont.*

Simulators aid LHX design [Army helicopter; cover story; special section] il *Aviation Week & Space Technology* 131:34-5+ N 27 '89

Soviets display export version of Mi-24 at helicopter trade show [Helitech '89 in England] il *Aviation Week & Space Technology* 131:30 S 25 '89

Special report: covert aircraft. il *Popular Mechanics* 166:25 Mr '89

U.S. Army collaboration 'blueprint' could boost European LHX role. D. F. Bond. il *Aviation Week & Space Technology* 131:25 O 16 '89

Western experts impressed by design of Mi-28 prototype [Soviet attack helicopter exhibited at Paris Air Show] D. E. Fink. il *Aviation Week & Space Technology* 130:44-6+ Je 26 '89

Noise

Langley, McDonnell Douglas study methods of reducing rotor noise. E. H. Phillips. il *Aviation Week & Space Technology* 131:75-6 Jl 17 '89

Piloting

Churning up the soup [helicopter IFR flying] J. M. McClellan. il *Flying* 116:30-1 D '89

Helicopter instructors make better hovers. N. Moll. il *Flying* 116:32 Ag '89

Skid marks [mishap on first solo flight] R. Jackson. il *Flying* 116:100 F '89

Radar equipment

Army will equip its LHXs with AH-64 mast-mounted system. B. M. Greeley. il *Aviation Week & Space Technology* 130:25 Ap 17 '89

U.S. Army approves initial design phase of Longbow radar system for AH-64. D. F. Bond. il *Aviation Week & Space Technology* 131:27-8 Jl 31 '89

Rotors

680 rotor system enhances Bell Model 222 performance [cover story] N. C. Kernstock. il *Aviation Week & Space Technology* 130:36-7+ My 15 '89

Langley, McDonnell Douglas study methods of reducing rotor noise. E. H. Phillips. il *Aviation Week & Space Technology* 131:75-6 Jl 17 '89

McDonnell/Bell LHX design will use 680 high-agility rotor. N. C. Kernstock. il *Aviation Week & Space Technology* 129:61 Mr 6 '89

Notar: next year. il *Flying* 116:52 Je '89

Notar reduces pilot workload, improves response in OH-6A [no-tail rotor] N. C. Kernstock. il *Aviation Week & Space Technology* 130:44-5+ F 13 '89

Unconventional helicopter tail rotor offers forward thrust advantage [TailFan; work of M. S. Munski] W. B. Scott. il *Aviation Week & Space Technology* 130:49+ F 13 '89

Specifications

International rotary wing aircraft [tables] il *Aviation Week & Space Technology* 130:157+ Mr 20 '89

U.S. rotary wing aircraft [tables] il *Aviation Week & Space Technology* 130:155-6 Mr 20 '89

Testing

680 rotor system enhances Bell Model 222 performance [cover story] N. C. Kernstock. il *Aviation Week & Space Technology* 130:36-7+ My 15 '89

A+: Agusta A109 MkII Plus [cover story] J. M. McClellan. il *Flying* 116:34-8+ F '89

Day of the Dauphin [Aerospatiale Dauphin 2] J. M. McClellan. il *Flying* 116:76-8+ S '89

EH101 antisubmarine version begins flight test program. il *Aviation Week & Space Technology* 131:68 N 13 '89

The little 'copter that could [Schweizer 300C] J. M. McClellan. il *Flying* 116:58-62+ N '89

MD 500: peak performer. J. M. McClellan. il *Flying* 116:44-8+ Je '89

Mil Mi-28 attack helicopter in final tests prior to full-scale production [Soviet helicopter] il *Aviation Week & Space Technology* 130:78-9 Je 5 '89

Notar reduces pilot workload, improves response in OH-6A [no-tail rotor] N. C. Kernstock. il *Aviation Week & Space Technology* 130:44-5+ F 13 '89

Theft

See also
Helicopter hijacking

HELICOPTERS, MILITARY *See* Helicopters—Military use

HELICOPTERS, REMODELED

Orlando Helicopter develops simulated Soviet Hind Es [cover story] E. H. Kolcum. il *Aviation Week & Space Technology* 130:34-5+ Ja 9 '89

Testing

Turbine powerhouse [Soloy Conversions; cover story] N. Moll. il por *Flying* 116:44-8+ O '89

HELICOPTERS, TRAINING

Design

Army reevaluates plans to procure helicopter total training system. il *Aviation Week & Space Technology* 130:265+ Je 12 '89

New firm to enter modified Bell 206 in growing Army SCAT competition [Imagineering Systems enters competition for Single Contractor Aviation Training program] C. A. Shifrin. il *Aviation Week & Space Technology* 130:47+ Mr 27 '89

SCAT players vie for Army prize [Single Contractor Aviation Training program] *Flying* 116:24 S '89

Schweizer, Enstrom join teams to bid for Army trainer work. il *Aviation Week & Space Technology* 130:18-19 Ja 23 '89

HELICOPTERS IN MEDICAL CARE

Angel of mercy [medical mission helicopter crash] P. Garrison. *Flying* 116:10+ S '89

Hungary equips ambulance version of Soviet Mi-17. il *Aviation Week & Space Technology* 131:44 Jl 3 '89

Litter carrier [Agusta A109] N. Moll. il *Flying* 116:40 F '89

HELICOPTERS IN NARCOTICS REGULATION

Pentagon offers P-3As, utility helicopters for antidrug effort. M. Mecham. il *Aviation Week & Space Technology* 130:27 F 27 '89

HELICOPTERS IN POLICE WORK

Cops above, crime below. T. Jacoby. il *Newsweek* 113:74 Je 5 '89

Eyes in the sky [Supreme Court rules police do not need warrant to spy from helicopter] *Time* 133:60 F 6 '89

HELICOPTERS IN RESCUE WORK

Avionics system lets helicopter crews focus on search, rescue [Bell/Honeywell system] N. C. Kernstock. il *Aviation Week & Space Technology* 130:50-1+ Ap 24 '89

Heroes [Coast Guard rescues shipwrecked sailors from the Lloyd Bermuda container ship] J. A. Fishman. il *Motor Boating & Sailing* 163:52-7+ Mr '89

The hunt for Charles Ridgeway [locating kidney recipient in remote area] J. Shannon. il *Reader's Digest* 135:40-2+ D '89

"Just ten more minutes . . ." [H. Balick, victim of plane crash, rescued] J. McDermott. il *Reader's Digest* 134:89-94 My '89

Life saver [Bell 214ST] J. M. McClellan. il *Flying* 116:52+ Jl '89

HELICOPTERS IN SIGHTSEEING

Tourist choppers roil islands [Hawaii] J. Conrow. *The Progressive* 53:16 My '89

HELICOPTERS IN TELEVISION BROADCASTING

Killer on the loose? [news reporters help capture gunman P. Hutchinson in Denver, Colo.] P. O. D'Aulaire and E. D'Aulaire. il *Reader's Digest* 134:64-70 Ja '89

HÉLION, JEAN, 1904-1987

about

Jean Helion: Rachel Adler. E. Hayt-Atkins. il *Art News* 88:166+ Summ '89

HELIOPAUSE

Listening for hints of the sun's heliopause [research by Ralph L. McNutt] J. Eberhart. *Science News* 136:231 O 7 '89

HELIOSEISMOLOGY

Gazing into the interior of the sun [research by Kenneth G. Libbrecht] M. M. Waldrop. il *Science* 244:31 Ap 7 '89

Looking inside the sun. J. C. LoPresto. il *Astronomy* 17:20-30 Mr '89

Solar revolutions [research by Kenneth G. Libbrecht] A. Fisher. il *Popular Science* 235:12 Jl '89

HELIOSPHERE

Are we living in a "bubble"? [Pioneer 10 data; research by Darrell L. Judge] *USA Today (Periodical)* 117:13 Je '89

The heliosphere as an astrophysical laboratory for particle acceleration. T. Terasawa and M. Scholer. bibl f il *Science* 244:1050-7 Je 2 '89

Probing the heliosphere from India. S. K. Alurkar and R. V. Bhonsle. il map *Sky and Telescope* 78:151 Ag '89

HELIPORTS

Heliport 2000 [cover story] F. Mackerodt. il *Popular Mechanics* 166:54-7+ S '89

The landing zone. P. Scott. il *Flying* 116:38-40+ Mr '89

Japan

The coming clash over choppers [Heliport Highway 600 project] J. Impoco. il *U.S. News & World Report* 106:47+ F 27 '89

HELITECH (AIR SHOW) *See* Aviation—Exhibitions

HELITZER, MELVIN

about

Yukking it up for credit. B. Barol. il *Newsweek* 114:83 D 4 '89

HELIUM

The Crab and kin: the helium Crab [Crab nebula research by Alan Uomoto and Gordon M. MacAlpine] il *Sky and Telescope* 77:9 Ja '89

Isotopes

Moon power [helium-3] M. J. Mackowski. il por *Ad Astra* 1:34-9 Jl/Ag '89

HELIUM, LIQUID *See* Liquid helium

HELLAND, DAVE

Branford Marsalis: the Marsalis tapes [cover story] il pors *Down Beat* 56:16-19 N '89

Greg Osby: open on all sides. il pors *Down Beat* 56:26-8 O '89

Robin Eubanks: a true sense of perspective. il pors *Down Beat* 56:26-8 Ja '89

HELLENISTIC ART *See* Art, Hellenistic
HELLER, KAREN
Your sound and my fury. il *Gentlemen's Quarterly* 59:207+ O '89
HELLER, LINDA
Curves ahead. il *Redbook* 173:81-5 Ag '89
How to take better care of your hair. il *Redbook* 172:98-9+ Ja '89
Keep your bones straight and strong. il *Redbook* 172:22 Mr '89
HELLER, NANCY
about
Bringing it all back home. D. Kern. il por *House & Garden* 161:178-87 My '89
HELLER, ROBERT
AES report. *Theatre Crafts* 23:30-3 F '89
HELLER, ROBERT
about
A rare glimpse inside the Fed [interview] R. E. Norton. il por *Fortune* 120:155-6 S 11 '89
HELLER, SUSANNA
about
Susanna Heller at Tomoko Liguori. R. Berlind. *Art in America* 77:164 F '89
HELLER, YVES
A new kind of leader? *World Press Review* 36:14+ Ag '89
HELLERSTEIN, DAVID
Spying on guys: what men say when women aren't around [special section] il *Mademoiselle* 95:104-9+ Ja '89
HELLINGER (MARK) THEATER (NEW YORK, N.Y.) *See* Mark Hellinger Theater (New York, N.Y.)
HELLMAN, PETER
What's better now [cover story] il *New York* 22:32-9 My 22 '89
HELL'S KITCHEN (NEW YORK, N.Y.)
New York City. K. T. Walsh. il *U.S. News & World Report* 107:48-9 D 18 '89
HELLWIG, MONICA K.
Challenges facing U.S. Catholics. *Commonweal* 116:622 N 17 '89
HELM, BUCK
about
Digging out from under. il pors *People Weekly* 32:46-51 N 6 '89
Out of the ruins, a miracle. il *Newsweek* 114:32 O 30 '89
HELM, CHRISTIANE A., AND OTHERS
Molecular mechanisms and forces involved in the adhesion and fusion of amphiphilic bilayers. bibl f il *Science* 246:919-22 N 17 '89
HELM, MICHAEL
Salvage as salvation: tales from a junk man. il *Utne Reader* p80-1 Jl/Ag '89
HELMBERGER, MARSHALL
Marines hit the beaches in Minnesota. il *The Progressive* 53:17 O '89
HELMET LAWS (MOTORCYCLE) *See* Motorcycles—Laws and regulations
HELMETS
Bike safety: rules for the road. il *Ladies' Home Journal* 106:58 Je '89
Falcon Eye Flir, GEC helmet aid F-16 mission flexibility [cover story] W. B. Scott. il *Aviation Week & Space Technology* 130:34-6+ Ap 17 '89
Helmet buyer's guide. F. Zahradnik. il *Bicycling* 30:160-2+ My '89
Helmet trips [motorcycle helmets] C. Furlong. il *Cycle* 40:20+ Mr '89
How to get your child to wear a helmet. S. Sorensen. il *Bicycling* 30:88+ Je '89
Kaiser improves helmet-mounted display to boost pilot's kill capability. B. W. Henderson. il *Aviation Week & Space Technology* 130:119+ Je 19 '89
NASA, McDonnell Douglas test helmet-mounted landing system. E. H. Phillips. il *Aviation Week & Space Technology* 130:126-7 Je 19 '89
Steady improvements in head-up technology [fighter pilots] il *Popular Mechanics* 166:30 O '89
You are there! [use of remote-control, helmet-mounted camera] R. Doyle. il *Petersen's Photographic Magazine* 18:14-16 Ag '89
HELMINIAK, DANIEL A.
Doing right by women and the Trinity too. il *America* 160:110+ F 11 '89
HELMINTHS
Parasitic protozoa and helminths: biological and immunological challenges. A. A. F. Mahmoud. bibl f il *Science* 246:1015-22 N 24 '89
HELMS, JESSE A.
Should the Senate-passed Immigration Act of 1989 be approved? [excerpts from debate, July 11, 1989] *Congressional Digest* 68:241+ O '89
about
Arts grants under fire. C. McGuigan. il por *Newsweek* 114:23 Ag 7 '89
Compassion and principle. B. Harris. il pors *Conservative Digest* 15:13-14+ Ja/F '89
Jesse Helms on the meaning of art. F. Bruning. il *Maclean's* 102:9 Ag 14 '89

The long, lonely road of rights hero James Meredith ends in a job with Jesse Helms. A. Gonzalez. il pors *People Weekly* 32:40-1 O 16 '89
Meredith readies for post on Sen. Jesse Helms' staff, black leaders bristling. il pors *Jet* 77:12-13 O 16 '89
Our most effective senator [cover story] P. Weyrich. il pors *Conservative Digest* 15:7+ Ja/F '89
Should Congress censor art? M. Horn. il por *U.S. News & World Report* 107:22-4 S 25 '89
HELMS, RICHARD
about
A "light luncheon" with the Führer. H. Sidey. por *Time* 134:50 Ag 28 '89
HELMS-MINDELL, JACALYN
The Black Archives of Mid-America, Inc. il *American Visions* 4:56 Ap '89
HELMSLEY, HARRY B., 1909-
about
A Queen on trial [cover story] H. F. Waters. il pors *Newsweek* 114:46-51 Ag 21 '89
HELMSLEY, LEONA
about
At last, a verdict fit for a Queen. il por *Newsweek* 114:61 S 11 '89
A commoner's royal pain. il por *Newsweek* 114:55 Jl 17 '89
Leona Helmsley: the original Material Girl. B. G. Harrison. *Mademoiselle* 95:104 D '89
The 'Queen' on trial. L. Black. il pors *Maclean's* 102:49+ Ag 14 '89
A Queen on trial [cover story] H. F. Waters. il pors *Newsweek* 114:46-51 Ag 21 '89
Queen, pawns, checkmate [cover story] J. S. Kunen. il pors *People Weekly* 32:94-9 S 11 '89
The Queen stands trial. P. Painton. il por *Time* 134:66 Jl 24 '89
Revenge of the little people. M. B. Carlson. il por *Time* 134:27 S 11 '89
What if Leona leaves the Palace for the pokey? A. Rothman. il por *Business Week* p79+ Jl 24 '89
Who cheats? D. Seligman. il *Fortune* 120:203 O 9 '89
HELMSLEY HOTELS
What if Leona leaves the Palace for the pokey? A. Rothman. il por *Business Week* p79+ Jl 24 '89
HELMUTH, JOHN W.
World hunger amidst plenty. il *USA Today (Periodical)* 117:48-50 Mr '89
HELOISE
Speaker for the house/The Heloise helpline. See issues of Good Housekeeping beginning November 1988
about
The hint maven strikes again. J. Seligmann. il por *Newsweek* 113:70 Ap 10 '89
HELOU, ANISSA
about
Catch of the day. R. Koenig. il por *House & Garden* 161:54-5 Ja '89
HELPER'S NETWORK (FAN CLUB)
The Beastie girls. R. Powers. il por *Gentlemen's Quarterly* 59:131+ D '89
HELPING, ELIZABETH
Ecco Ecomania! il por *Harper's Bazaar* 122:108+ N '89
HELPING BEHAVIOR
See also
Assistance in emergencies
Do religious people help more? Not so you'd notice. A. Kohn. il *Psychology Today* 23:66+ D '89
Evidence for a moral tradition [rescuers of Jews during the Holocaust; study by Samuel Oliner] A. Kohn. il *Psychology Today* 23:72-3 Ja/F '89
How to lend aid to the disabled. J. Wood. *Modern Maturity* 32:25-6 Ag/S '89
I am making myself a doormat [listening to other people's problems] il *Good Housekeeping* 208:20+ Ja '89
When helping hurts. C. R. Berry. *Essence* 19:75-6+ Mr '89
HELPLESSNESS (PSYCHOLOGY)
Are you teaching your staff to be helpless? D. W. Ray. *Working Woman* 14:32 Mr '89
Help for the helpless [learned helplessness] J. E. Loehr. il *World Tennis* 36:14-15 Ja '89
HELPRIN, MARK
about
Mark Helprin's next 10 years (and next six books) with HBJ. il por *Publishers Weekly* 235:33-4 Je 9 '89
HELSINKI HUMAN RIGHTS DAY
Helsinki Human Rights Day, 1989 [proclamation, August 1, 1989] G. Bush. *Department of State Bulletin* 89:42 O '89
HEMANGIOMAS *See* Birthmarks
HEMATOPOIESIS *See* Blood cells—Growth
HEMEROCALLIS *See* Daylilies
HEMINGWAY, ERNEST, 1899-1961
about
Debunking Hemingway's marlin theories. J. Skorupa. il *Popular Mechanics* 166:44 O '89
Hemingway Bar, the Ritz Hotel, Paris. P. Mayle. il *Gentlemen's Quarterly* 59:286-7 N '89

HEMINGWAY, ERNEST, 1899-1961—about—*cont.*
Hemingway: portrait of the artist as an intellectual. P. Johnson. *Commentary* 87:49-59 F '89
Papa, Satchmo, and the Babe. G. C. Ward. il *American Heritage* 40:14+ My/Je '89
Papa's place. S. Stapleton. il *Motor Boating & Sailing* 164:45+ S '89

Anecdotes, facetiae, satire, etc.
Across the river and into Harry's Bar [excerpt from The best of bad Hemingway] G. Plimpton. *The New York Times Book Review* 94:1+ Ap 16 '89

HEMINGWAY, GEORGE R.
Effective transitions. *The Writer* 102:21-3 Ag '89

HEMINGWAY, GERRY
about
Gerry Hemingway. H. Mandel. il por *Down Beat* 56:50-1 Ag '89

HEMINGWAY, MARIEL
about
Mariel's personal best. M. A. Kellogg. il pors *Harper's Bazaar* 122:120-3+ F '89

HEMINWAY, JOHN HYLAN, 1944-
An immigrant artist captured the faces of the New World. il pors *Smithsonian* 20:172-8+ N '89

HEMISPHERIC DOMINANCE *See* Laterality

HEMLEY, R. J.
(jt. auth) *See* Mao, H. K., and Hemley, R. J.

HEMOCHROMATOSIS
Iron man. T. Monmaney. il *Discover* 10:62-5 Jl '89

HEMODIALYSIS
An 'insulin' for anemia sufferers [Epogen replaces erythropoietin in kidney dialysis patients] *U.S. News & World Report* 106:13 Je 12 '89

HEMODIALYSIS EQUIPMENT
Care of filters used in dialysis. *FDA Consumer* 23:4 O '89

HEMOGLOBIN
See also
Blood boosting
Blood from a stone [analysis of hemoglobin residue on tools leads to identification of prehistoric species; work of Thomas Loy] il *Discover* 10:18 N '89
Blood, genes, and malaria. J. M. Diamond. il maps *Natural History* p8+ F '89
Recombinant rodents, human hemoglobin [work of R. R. Behringer] R. Weiss. *Science News* 136:149 S 2 '89
Ritual clues flow from prehistoric blood [analysis of hemoglobin residues from stone slab at Çayönü Tepesi site in Turkey; work of Andrée R. Wood and Thomas H. Loy] B. Brower. *Science News* 136:405 D 23-30 '89
Synthesis of functional human hemoglobin in transgenic mice. R. R. Behringer and others. bibl f il *Science* 245:971-3 S 1 '89

HEMOPHILIA
Therapy
A life in limbo [hemophiliac tests positive for AIDS] P. B. Bayer. il por *The New York Times Magazine* p48+ Ap 2 '89

HEMORRHAGE
See also
Brain—Hemorrhage
Therapy
Raquel Welch: starting over [rollerball technique stems uterine hemorrhage] P. Battelle. il pors *Ladies' Home Journal* 106:46+ My '89

HEMORRHAGIC FEVER
Rat-borne virus may take secret toll [Hantaan virus; research by James W. Le Duc] R. Weiss. *Science News* 135:292 My 13 '89

HEMP
See also
Marijuana

HEMPEL, AMY
Murder [story] il *Mother Jones* 14:34-5 F/Mr '89

HEMPEL, ANOUSKA
about
Anouska Hempel in London. E. Lambert. il por *Architectural Digest* 46:138-45+ S '89
Cozy fan tutte. S. Steward. il por *Harper's Bazaar* 122:101 S '89

HEMPHILL, JULIUS
about
Blindfold test. B. Shoemaker. il por *Down Beat* 56:43 Je '89

HEMPSTEAD, BARBARA L., AND OTHERS
Expression of functional nerve growth factor receptors after gene transfer. bibl f il *Science* 243:373-5 Ja 20 '89

HENDEL, JAYNE
War and remembrance: a new entry from Anne Frank. il por *Seventeen* 48:112-13 Je '89

HENDERSON, CARTER F.
Shedding pounds through surgery. pors *McCall's* 116:100+ Je '89

HENDERSON, GORDON
about
At what price young success? N. Darnton. il por *Newsweek* 114:87 N 20 '89
The flash of Gordon. M. Gross. il por *New York* 22:15 Ag 7 '89

Gordon Henderson. P. H. Starzinger. il por *Vogue* 179:192 S '89

HENDERSON, JOE, 1943-
Joe Henderson's journal. See issues of Runner's World

HENDERSON, KELLY
A prayer of hope: religion as a key to cooperation. por *The Humanist* 49:23-4+ Mr/Ap '89

HENDERSON, LYNNE
about
Image wilting? Help is at hand. R. Conniff. il por *Time* 133:16+ Mr 27 '89

HENDERSON, RICKEY
about
Henderson blames drunks for '88 Yankee downfall. por *Jet* 75:50 Mr 20 '89
Oh, what a show! [cover story] P. Gammons. il pors *Sports Illustrated* 71:30-3+ O 16 '89

HENDERSON, SONYA
3 strikes for you. por *Essence* 19:136 Mr '89

HENDERSON, STEVEN
Patriotic gore: De Palma as sage. *The Christian Century* 106:925-6 O 18 '89

HENDERSON FAMILY
about
Runs in the family. J. Henderson. il *Runner's World* 24:14 Ag '89

HENDERSON-HOLMES, SAFIYA
Harlem/Soweto [poem] *Essence* 19:126 Ap '89

HENDRICK, RICK
about
Rick Hendrick: man on the fast track. J. Ingram. il pors *Motor Trend* 41:116-19+ Ag '89

HENDRICK MANAGEMENT CORPORATION
Rick Hendrick: man on the fast track. J. Ingram. il pors *Motor Trend* 41:116-19+ Ag '89

HENDRICKS, JOHN SAMUEL
about
John Hendricks' big adventure [cover story] P. Pagano. il pors *Channels (New York, N.Y.: 1986)* 9:20-3 O '89

HENDRIX, JIMI
about
The curator of solid gold. S. Fried. il por *Gentlemen's Quarterly* 59:78+ Ja '89

HENDRIX (JIMI) INFORMATION MANAGEMENT INSTITUTE *See* Jimi Hendrix Information Management Institute

HENDRYX, NONA
about
Star quality. M. Johnson. il por *Essence* 20:23 D '89

HENIG, ROBIN MARANTZ
The aging eye. il *The New York Times Magazine* p47-8 Mr 26 '89
Are breast implants too risky? *Vogue* 179:108+ Jl '89
High-tech fortunetelling. il *The New York Times Magazine* p20+ D 24 '89
Is the Pap test valid? il *The New York Times Magazine* p37-8 My 28 '89
Robin Marantz Henig reports on liposuction—cosmetic surgery's most popular body-sculpting procedure—now under federal review. *Vogue* 179:292+ O '89
Stalking the wear-and-tear monster. il *New Choices for the Best Years* 29:59-60+ S '89

HENKE, ELLEN
Bringing orchids down to earth. il *The Saturday Evening Post* 261:46-7 Ap '89
Dutch treats. il *The Saturday Evening Post* 261:64-6 My/Je '89
First Lady of wildflowers. il por *Flower and Garden* 33:61 Mr/Ap '89

HENKIN, JOSH
Individualism unbound: reconsidering modern-day romance. il *Utne Reader* p64-6+ Mr/Ap '89

HENKIN, NANCY Z., AND WEINSTEIN-SHR, GAIL
College students tutor older refugees in English. il *Aging* no359:17-19 '89

HENLEY, BETH
about
Beth's beauties [cover story] K. Jaehne. il pors *Film Comment* 25:9-12+ My/Je '89

HENLEY, DON
about
Building on prime real estate. J. Cocks. il por *Time* 134:64 Jl 31 '89
Don Henley. P. Puterbaugh. por *Stereo Review* 54:132 N '89
Don Henley flies again. A. DeCurtis. il por *Rolling Stone* p61 Jl 13-27 '89

HENLEY, PATRICIA
The secret of cartwheels [story] il *The Atlantic* 263:60-6 Mr '89

HENMUELLER, PAUL
Diamonds of hope [address, June 11, 1989] *Vital Speeches of the Day* 55:680-1 S 1 '89

HENNESSEE, JUDITH ADLER
The love surgeon. il *Mademoiselle* 95:206-7+ Ag '89

HENNESSY, EDMUND
Fresh from the Factory. il *Vogue* 179:323-5+ F '89

HENNESSY, JOHN POPE- See Pope-Hennessy, Sir John
HENNING, DANIEL C.
about
The trouble in China isn't scaring off this trader. D. Greising. il por *Business Week* p108 Je 26 '89
HENNING (TENN.)
Galleries and museums
See also
Alex Haley House Museum
HENNING-KRAJEWSKI TRADING COMPANY
The trouble in China isn't scaring off this trader. D. Greising. il por *Business Week* p108 Je 26 '89
HENRICH, DANIEL J.
Cinemas on wheels. il *World Health* p10-11 Ja/F '89
HENRIOT, PETER
Forgive us our debts . . . *America* 161:420-2+ D 9 '89
HENRY III, KING OF FRANCE, 1551-1589
Assassination
The assassination of Henry III. M. Greengrass. il bibl *History Today* 39:11-17 N '89
HENRY VIII, KING OF ENGLAND, 1491-1547
about
Henry VIII—a malnourished king? S. M. Kybett. bibl il pors *History Today* 39:19-25 S '89
HENRY, AARON
about
Aaron Henry's dangerous journey. S. J. Smith. il *Reader's Digest* 135:116-20 D '89
HENRY, CARL F. H., 1913-
The new coalitions. il *Christianity Today* 33:26-8 N 17 '89
HENRY, ED
How you can save on car insurance. il *Reader's Digest* 134:61-4 My '89
HENRY, JAMES S., AND POMER, MARSHALL
The 1 percent solution. *The New Republic* 200:12-13 F 6 '89
A luxury consumption tax could relieve our budget deficit. *Utne Reader* p88 S/O '89
HENRY, O., 1862-1910
The last leaf [story] il *Reader's Digest* 134:79-82 F '89
HENRY, PATRICK G.
Why Life says we are here. il *The Christian Century* 106:562-3 My 24-31 '89
HENRY, PAUL B.
Morality vs. moralism [address, January 26, 1989] *Vital Speeches of the Day* 55:295-7 Mr 1 '89
Seeking humility in political debate. *The Christian Century* 106:303 Mr 22-29 '89
HENRY, RICHARD C.
Launches into low-earth orbit should be economical, routine. por *Aviation Week & Space Technology* 131:93+ N 27 '89
HENRY, SARA J.
The incredible rhythm of cross-country skiing. il por *Women's Sports & Fitness* 11:54 Ja/F '89
Riding your first century. il *Women's Sports & Fitness* 11:16-17 Ap '89
The sport that lets you laugh at winter. il *Women's Sports & Fitness* 11:54-5 N/D '89
Surviving on two wheels. il *Women's Sports & Fitness* 11:46-9 Je '89
HENRY, WILLIAM
about
Chicago law maker tells grocers to learn English. por *Jet* 77:15 D 25 '89-Ja 1 '90
HENRY, WILLIAM A., 1950-
The meaning of TV. il *Life* 12:66-8+ Mr '89
Private eye. See issues of Channels (New York, N.Y.: 1986)
HENRY FORD MUSEUM AND GREENFIELD VILLAGE
Henry Ford slept here [constructing reproduction wicker bed] K. P. Crombie. il *Workbench* 45:42-6 Mr/Ap '89
HENRY HOLT AND COMPANY
Court splits over fair use language in Hubbard case. M. Reuter. *Publishers Weekly* 236:10 S 22 '89
'Salinger' haunts ruling on Hubbard biography. M. Reuter. *Publishers Weekly* 235:102 My 12 '89
HENRY MOORE SCULPTURE GARDEN
Moore bronzes in urban oasis. il *USA Today (Periodical)* 118:8-9 Ag '89
HENRY R. LUCE CENTER FOR THE STUDY OF AMERI-CAN ART See Metropolitan Museum of Art (New York, N.Y.). Henry R. Luce Center for the Study of American Art
HENRY V [film] See Motion picture reviews—Single works
HENSHALL, NICHOLAS
History tomorrow. *History Today* 39:13-14 Je '89
HENSLER, GUENTER
about
New regime at RCA. T. W. Libbey, Jr. il *High Fidelity (New York, N.Y.)* 39:60 Je '89
HENSON, H. KEITH
The great palladium rush. il *Ad Astra* 1:34-5 N '89
HENSON, JIM
about
Jim Henson [interview] il por *American Film* 15:18-21 N '89

HENSON-CONANT, DEBORAH
about
Deborah Henson-Conant. B. Milkowski. il por *Down Beat* 56:14 Ap '89
HENTOFF, NAT
The Atwater flag sting. il *The Progressive* 53:12-14 N '89
Even in high school. il *The Progressive* 53:13-14 Ag '89
Free speech on the campus. il *The Progressive* 53:12-13 My '89
How we got an Official Secrets Act. il *The Progressive* 53:10-11 Mr '89
Miles [interview with M. Davis; reprint] il por *Down Beat* 56:46-7 S '89
You don't have to believe in God to be prolife. *U.S. Catholic* 54:28-30 Mr '89
HENTZE, MATTHIAS W., AND OTHERS
Oxidation-reduction and the molecular mechanism of a regulatory RNA-protein interaction. bibl f il *Science* 244:357-9 Ap 21 '89
HENWOOD, DOUG
A bankers' world. *The Nation* 249:481 O 30 '89
Business ethics: missing the forest for the trees. *Utne Reader* p58-9 Ja/F '89
Have we really been bingeing? il *The Nation* 248:43-4 Ja 9-16 '89
L.B.O. vapors. *The Nation* 248:257 F 27 '89
HEPARAN SULFATE
Relation of the amyloid β protein precursor to heparan sulfate proteoglycans [discussion of July 8, 1988 article, Amyloid β protein precursor is possibly a heparan sulfate proteoglycan core protein] D. Schubert and others. *Science* 244:826-8 My 19 '89
HEPARIN
. . . and toxic chemicals from the blood [enzyme filters] J. Raloff. *Science News* 135:271 Ap 29 '89
Control of angiogenesis with synthetic heparin substitutes. J. Folkman and others. bibl f il *Science* 243:1490-3 Mr 17 '89
Fat blockers [role of heparin in cholesterol absorption; research by Louis Lange] *Discover* 10:18 N '89
HEPATITIS
Hepatitis C may spread heterosexually. D. E. Loupe. *Science News* 136:151 S 2 '89
Diagnosis
An assay for circulating antibodies to a major etiologic virus of human non-A, non-B hepatitis. G. Kuo and others. bibl f il *Science* 244:362-4 Ap 21 '89
Breaking a fever in the blood [detecting non-A, non-B hepatitis] *U.S. News & World Report* 106:16+ My 1 '89
Coming soon: safer blood [test for non-A, non-B hepatitis virus] J. Langone. il *Time* 133:66 My 1 '89
Hepatitis B mutants hide in blood [research by Girish N. Vyas] I. Wickelgren. *Science News* 135:52 Ja 28 '89
Not necessarily non-A, non-B hepatitis. C. ServAas. *The Saturday Evening Post* 261:100-1 Jl/Ag '89
Path to hepatitis C yields test, clues [research by Michael Houghton] I. Wickelgren. *Science News* 135:246-7 Ap 22 '89
Therapy
Counterattack [interferon used to treat hepatitis C] *Time* 134:96 D 11 '89
Hope for hepatitis C infections [alpha interferon] *Newsweek* 114:92 D 11 '89
Vaccines and vaccination
Chimp test for oral hepatitis B vaccine [research by Michael D. Lubeck and Robert H. Purcell] S. Hart. *Science News* 136:199 S 23 '89
Hepatitis B vaccination [Western Pacific] T. Umenai and H. Suzuki. il *World Health* p24-5 N '89
A vaccine for lovers [hepatitis B] C. Sacra. il *Health (New York, N.Y.)* 21:47 D '89
HEPATITIS VIRUSES
An assay for circulating antibodies to a major etiologic virus of human non-A, non-B hepatitis. G. Kuo and others. bibl f il *Science* 244:362-4 Ap 21 '89
Isolation of a cDNA clone derived from a blood-borne non-A, non-B viral hepatitis genome. Q.-L. Choo and others. bibl f il *Science* 244:359-62 Ap 21 '89
A liver-specific enhancer in the core promoter region of human hepatitis B virus. J.-K. Yee. bibl f il *Science* 246:658-61 N 3 '89
Path to hepatitis C yields test, clues [research by Michael Houghton] I. Wickelgren. *Science News* 135:246-7 Ap 22 '89
Reversible cleavage and ligation of hepatitis delta virus RNA. H.-N. Wu and M. M. C. Lai. bibl f il *Science* 243:652-4 F 3 '89
The ultimate parasite [delta virus] P. Radetsky. il *Discover* 10:20-1 Ag '89
An ultraviolet-sensitive RNA structural element in a viroid-like domain of the hepatitis delta virus. A. D. Branch and others. bibl f il *Science* 243:649-52 F 3 '89
HEPATOCYTES See Cells
HEPBURN, AUDREY, 1929-
about
Audrey Hepburn. N. Gittelson. il pors *McCall's* 116:30-1+ Ag '89

HEPBURN, KATHARINE, 1909-
about
Kate the great. C. P. Andersen. il pors *Ladies' Home Journal* 106:142-4+ S '89
Katharine Hepburn at 80. B. Lovenheim. por *McCall's* 117:125+ N '89
HEPPENHEIMER, T. A., 1947-
The market for transoceanic airliners. il *High Technology Business* 9:22-5 Ja '89
Microbots. il *Discover* 10:78-82+ Mr '89
Taking the crush out of rush hour. il *High Technology Business* 9:26-30 Mr '89
HER ALIBI [film] See Motion picture reviews—Single works
HERALD EXAMINER (LOS ANGELES, CALIF.) See Los Angeles herald examiner
HERB GARDENS See Herbs
HERB WREATHS See Wreaths
HERBAL OILS See Essences and essential oils
HERBER, LEWIS See Bookchin, Murray, 1921-
HERBERS, JOHN
A new heartland. maps *Country Journal* 16:67-9 My/Je '89
HERBERT, BOB
about
Street beat. E. Diamond. il por *New York* 22:16+ Ja 30 '89
HERBERT, ROSEMARY
A chat with Brian W. Aldiss. il por *Publishers Weekly* 236:24 N 10 '89
Science fiction's outer limits? il *Publishers Weekly* 236:18-20+ N 10 '89
HERBERT, SOLOMON
Maximum performance. il *Black Enterprise* 20:86-7 N '89
Reaching for the stars. il por *Black Enterprise* 19:294-6+ Je '89
HERBERT, VICTOR
about
Egyptian love song. F. S. Roffman. il pors *Opera News* 53:32-3+ Ja 7 '89
HERBERT, WRAY
Paranoia: fearful delusions. il *The New York Times Magazine* p62-3 Mr 19 '89
HERBERT-FÖRSTER, THERESE
about
Egyptian love song. F. S. Roffman. il pors *Opera News* 53:32-3+ Ja 7 '89
HERBICIDES
See also
Agent Orange
Chemical weapons for plants. I. S. Abrams. il *Current Health 2* 15:28-9 Ap '89
Why postemerge is looking good. M. Holmberg. il *Successful Farming* 87:20-1 Je '89
Decomposition
New generation of chemicals will disappear quicker. *Successful Farming* 87:33 N '89
Environmental aspects
Coke dusters [U.S. plan to spray Spike on coca plants in Peru] M. Massing. *The New Republic* 200:21-3 Ja 30 '89
Over there [America's drug war abroad] M. J. McConahay and R. Kirk. il *Mother Jones* 14:36-9+ F/Mr '89
Window-box test for carryover [indoor soil bioassay for herbicide residues] B. Freese. il *Successful Farming* 87:48T mid-Mr '89
Handling
Banding! B. Freese. il *Successful Farming* 87:32-4 Ja '89
Biobarrier inhibits root growth [Rootguard] C. M. Fiorillo. *Popular Science* 234:38 F '89
Late hits. M. Holmberg. il *Successful Farming* 87:48F O '89
Injurious effects
Students study ABC's of bean-bar safety. C. Tevis. il *Successful Farming* 87:42 Je '89
Prices
Banding! B. Freese. il *Successful Farming* 87:32-4 Ja '89
HERBIG-HARO OBJECTS
Active young stars in Orion. il *Sky and Telescope* 78:7-8 Jl '89
A young star's active jet. il *Sky and Telescope* 77:9-10 Ja '89
HERBIVORES
Not by grass alone [carnivory by herbivores] R. W. Furness. il *Natural History* p8+ D '89
HERBS
See also
Basil
Cooking—Herbs and spices
Fennel
Goodness Gardens (Firm)
Milk vetch
Nature's Sunshine Products Inc.
Potpourri
Rosemary
Sassafras
Yarrow
Adding a homemade spice to life. G. Abraham and K. Abraham. il *Consumers' Research Magazine* 72:20-3 Je '89

Backyard nursery [D. and M. Keiser's Pennsylvania garden] K. Martin. il pors *Organic Gardening* 36:48-52 D '89
The dooryard garden [cover story] il *Flower and Garden* 33:35-7+ S/O '89
A gallery of garden herbs. N. Bubel. il *Country Journal* 16:25-31 My/Je '89
A passion for herbs [C. Perry's garden in New England] J. A. McKeon. il pors *Better Homes and Gardens* 67:50-4 Ag '89
Thyme for herbs. A. Zabar. il *Seventeen* 48:212-15+ Ap '89
Uncommon scents. S. Gilbertie. il *Organic Gardening* 36:43-6 F '89
Would you like to see my motherworts? [men gardeners] J. H. Kunstler. il *Gentlemen's Quarterly* 59:54+ Ap '89
HERBS, MEDICINAL See Botany, Medical
HERBST, DAN
Three's company. il *Sport (New York, N.Y.)* 80:20-4 D '89
HERCULES (ROMAN MYTHOLOGY)
Art
That dammed Hercules [fresco painted on the face of the Tignes Dam in France for 1992 Olympics] B. Weber. il *The New York Times Magazine* p130 N 5 '89
HERCULES AEROSPACE COMPANY
The winged horse [Pegasus booster] R. G. Nichols. il *Ad Astra* 1:32-6 F '89
HERCULES DEFENSE ELECTRONICS SYSTEMS (FIRM)
Hercules concentrates EW effort on small, low-cost jammers. il *Aviation Week & Space Technology* 131:115+ S 11 '89
HERCULES X-1 (STAR) See Stars, Double
HERD, STAN
about
Cultivating art in the heartland. L. Barash. il *National Wildlife* 27:30-3 Je/Jl '89
The grandest art on earth. G. Sledge. il *Reader's Digest* 134:178-80 My '89
HERDER, JOHANN GOTTFRIED, 1744-1803
Universality and national identity. A. Finkielkraut. bibl f il pors *The Unesco Courier* 42:30-3 Je '89
HEREDITY
See also
Chromosomes
Clones (Biology)
Eugenics
Imprinting (Genetics)
Linkage (Genetics)
Natural selection
Variation (Biology)
HEREDITY AND ENVIRONMENT
The blood-brain barrier [study of adoptees and intelligence by David W. Fulker and John C. DeFries] K. Wright. il *Scientific American* 260:27+ Mr '89
Conservative genes [political attitudes biologically inherited; research by David T. Lykken] D. Seligman. il *Fortune* 120:123 Ag 14 '89
What a child is given. D. Franklin. il *The New York Times Magazine* p36-41+ S 3 '89
HEREDITY AND INTELLIGENCE See Intelligence
HEREDITY OF DISEASE
See also
Alcoholics and alcoholism—Genetic aspects
Alzheimer's disease—Genetic aspects
Angelman syndrome
Autism—Genetic aspects
Cancer—Genetic aspects
Chronic granulomatous disease
Cystic fibrosis
Dental caries—Genetic aspects
Depression, Mental—Genetic aspects
Diabetes—Genetic aspects
Down syndrome
Epilepsy—Genetic aspects
Fanconi anemia
Fragile X syndrome
Gaucher's disease
Gene probes
Gene therapy
Genetic counseling
Genetic screening
Hemophilia
Hypertension—Genetic aspects
Leber's hereditary optic neuropathy
Leukemia—Genetic aspects
Marfan syndrome
Mental illness—Genetic aspects
Multiple sclerosis—Genetic aspects
Muscular dystrophy—Genetic aspects
Neural tube—Diseases
Neurofibromatosis
Prader-Willi syndrome
Schizophrenia—Genetic aspects
Sickle cell anemia
Tay-Sachs disease
The cruel logic of our genes. J. M. Diamond. il *Discover* 10:72-8 N '89
Getting to the heart of genetic disease [special section] J. L. Marx. il *Science* 243:315-16 Ja 20 '89

HEREDITY OF DISEASE—*cont.*

Heritable allele-specific differences in amounts of apoB and low-density lipoproteins in plasma. D. Gavish and others. bibl f il *Science* 244:72-6 Ap 7 '89

Looking for Mr. Good Genes? L. Mosedale. *Glamour* 87:152 O '89

Praying for a miracle [cases of Ryan Clybor, Eric Bottorff and Bruce Rodriquez] J. Lyon. il *Redbook* 173:104-5+ Ag '89

The Quebec phenomenon [high incidence of genetic disorder in Saguenay region] S. Strauss. *World Press Review* 36:68 S '89

HEREK, STEPHEN
about
Bill and Ted's excellent adventure [film] Reviews
People Weekly 31:16 Mr 13 '89. R. Novak

HERENDEEN, DANIEL R., AND OTHERS
Enhancement of bacteriophage T4 late transcription by components of the T4 DNA replication apparatus. bibl f il *Science* 245:952-8 S 1 '89

HERESY
See also
Catholic Church. Congregation for the Doctrine of the Faith
LCMS pastor could face heresy charges [D. Bruch] W. Thorkelson. *Christianity Today* 33:43 Ap 21 '89

HERING, DORIS
Jerome Robbins' Broadway: Jerry's legacy [cover story] il *Dance Magazine* 63:44-51 Ap '89

HERITAGE, PROTECTION OF *See* Cultural property—Protection

HERITAGE EDUCATION
Teaching children to value their architectural heritage. D. L. Weitzman. *The Education Digest* 54:45-7 Ja '89

HERITAGE MINISTRIES
New home for former PTL ministry. *Christianity Today* 33:60 My 12 '89
The remnants of PTL. K. A. Lawton. il por *Christianity Today* 33:36-8 O 6 '89

HERITAGE PLAZA (HOUSTON, TEX.) *See* Houston (Tex.)—Buildings

HERITAGE USA (S.C.)
The remnants of PTL. K. A. Lawton. il por *Christianity Today* 33:36-8 O 6 '89

HERMAN, BURTON
about
Back Bay Victorian. D. Roberts. il *Architectural Digest* 46:152-9 Mr '89

HERMAN, FRANCES
about
Back Bay Victorian. D. Roberts. il *Architectural Digest* 46:152-9 Mr '89

HERMAN, HANK
Flex-time fathers. il *Health (New York, N.Y.)* 21:44-9 Ja '89

HERMAN, LOUIS M.
about
Conversations with the dolphins. S. Chollar. il pors *Psychology Today* 23:52-6 Ap '89
Interview: Louis Herman. J. Kaplan. il pors *Omni (New York, N.Y.)* 11:76-8+ Je '89

HERMAN, MICHELE
A new generation of bicycles offers more comfort and convenience. il *Utne Reader* p92 Mr/Ap '89

HERMAN, STEPHEN P., AND LEVY, ALAN M.
Does peer review have a place in child custody evaluations? il *Children Today* 18:15-18 My/Je '89

HERMAN, WOODY
about
Elegy for the Woodchopper. T. Teachout. *The American Scholar* 58:429-35 Summ '89

HERMAN (STAN) AND ASSOCIATES *See* Stan Herman and Associates

HERMAN MILLER, INC.
Advice to bosses: try a little kindness [views of M. De Pree] J. Greenwald. il por *Time* 134:56 S 11 '89
Hot company, warm culture. K. Labich. il *Fortune* 119:74-6+ F 27 '89
Spatial craft [showroom, Atlanta, Ga.; cover story] K. D. Stein. il *Architectural Record* 177:98-107 Je '89

HERMANN, ALLEN M.
about
A costly lesson in patent law. R. Pool. por *Science* 245:932 S 1 '89
IBM wins a patent for thallium superconductor. R. Pool. *Science* 246:320 O 20 '89
Superconductivity stars move. R. Pool. pors *Science* 244:1141 Je 9 '89

HERMANN, JANE
about
At American Ballet Theatre—Hermann, Smith, and Taras take up the slack. J. H. Mazo. il pors *Dance Magazine* 63:16-17 D '89

HERMES, JOAN GARVEY
Mom, why can't girls be priests? *U.S. Catholic* 54:28-9 Ag '89

HERMÈS (FIRM) *See* House of Hermès (Firm)

HERMÈS (SPACE VEHICLE) *See* Spaceplane, French

HERMÈS MUSEUM
The Hermes Museum. C. Aillaud. il *Architectural Digest* 46:30+ Ja '89

HERMISSENDA LEARNING BEHAVIOR *See* Animal learning

HERMON (ME.)
Crime
A killing in Maine [K. A. Wood killed by hunter D. Rogerson] J. H. Kunstler. il por *The New York Times Magazine* p58-60+ S 10 '89
"My wife shouldn't have died" [K. A. Wood killed by hunter D. Rogerson] J. Hope. il pors *Good Housekeeping* 209:92+ O '89

HERMOSA BEACH (CALIF.)
Architecture
Wedging it in. il *Sunset (Central West edition)* 183:106-7 O '89

HERN, WARREN M.
Abortion as insurrection. por *The Humanist* 49:18-20+ Mr/Ap '89

HERNANDEZ, ANDRES H., AND SCHWEON, CRAIG
Mobile mental health team reaches minorities. il *Aging* no359:12-13 '89

HERNANDEZ, KEITH, 1953-
about
The week that was. B. Newman. il pors *Sports Illustrated* 70:18-20 Mr 13 '89

HERNANDEZ, ROBERTO PERALES
about
Roberto Hernandez battles his arresting similarities to a wanted man with the same name. M. Neill. il pors *People Weekly* 32:95-7 Jl 17 '89

HERNANDEZ GALICIA, JOAQUÍN
about
Bald man on a horse. G. B. Lake. il *National Review* 41:38-9 Mr 10 '89
Robin Hood or robbing hood? G. D. Garcia. il por *Time* 133:39 Ja 23 '89
Salinas declares war on 'the maximum chief' of oil. S. Baker. il *Business Week* p52 Ja 23 '89
Touching the 'untouchable'. S. McGuire. il por *Newsweek* 113:30-1 Ja 23 '89

HEROD ANTIPAS, CA. 21 B.C.-39
about
Alliances. P. J. Ryan. il *America* 160:231 Mr 11 '89

HERODOTUS
about
Herodotus, Alexander, and Rome. G. W. Bowersock. *The American Scholar* 58:407-14 Summ '89

HEROES AND HEROINES
See also
Courage
A different breed of hero. N. V. Peale. il *Good Housekeeping* 209:66 Jl '89
Heroes for today. *Reader's Digest* 135:154-6 S '89
Heroes for today. *Reader's Digest* 134:108-10 Ja '89
Heroes for today. *Reader's Digest* 135:139-40+ Jl '89
Heroes for today. il *Reader's Digest* 134:29+ My '89
Inspirations. il *People Weekly* 32:136-7+ D 25 '89-Ja 1 '90
Look who won our most admired women and men polls. il *Good Housekeeping* 208:48 Ja '89
Mother Jones' third annual Heroes and Heroines. il *Mother Jones* 14:27-35 Ja '89
Splendor on the grass [sports heroes] J. Schulian. il *Gentlemen's Quarterly* 59:142-5+ Ja '89
They did the right thing [special section] S. Kanfer. il *People Weekly* 32 Special Issue:120-1+ Fall '89
Who are your heroes? [use as an interview question] E. Papazian. *Working Woman* 14:72 Mr '89

HEROES AND HEROINES IN TELEVISION
What would Matt Dillon have thought of Sonny Crockett? R. MacKenzie. il *TV Guide* 37:36-9 My 6-12 '89

HEROIN
Lukewarm turkey [drug firms balk at pursuing buprenorphine, a heroin addiction treatment] J. Horgan. *Scientific American* 260:32 Mr '89
The return of a deadly drug called horse. G. Witkin. il map *U.S. News & World Report* 107:31-2 Ag 14 '89
Laws and regulations
See Narcotics laws and regulations
Therapeutic use
A blistering debate [heroin for terminal cancer] R. Dolphin. il *Maclean's* 102:41 F 27 '89

HEROINES *See* Heroes and heroines

HEROISM *See* Courage

HEROLD, GEORG, 1947-
about
Georg Herold: Kunsthalle. E. Beck. il *Art News* 88:224 Ap '89

HERON, KIM
Making country music hot again. il pors *The New York Times Magazine* p28-33+ Je 25 '89
Randy Travis: making country hot again. il por *Reader's Digest* 135:57-8+ N '89
Van Allsburg's express. il por *The New York Times Magazine* p12-15 D 24 '89

HERONS
Game agents foil a gross gros bec feast [night heron massacre in Louisiana] il *Audubon* 91:14 Ja '89

HERPESVIRUSES
See also
Cytomegalovirus
Epstein-Barr virus

Do you know enough about herpes? P. S. Derron. *Mademoiselle* 95:88+ Je '89
Transneuronal transfer of herpes virus from peripheral nerves to cortex and brainstem. G. Ugolini and others. bibl f il *Science* 243:89-91 Ja 6 '89

Immunological aspects
Herpesvirus may boost AIDS expression [study of T cells by Paolo Lusso and Robert C. Gallo] K. Fackelmann. *Science News* 135:55 Ja 28 '89

Therapy
Help for herpes: relax [research by David J. Longo] P. Adelmann. il *Psychology Today* 22:24 D '88

HERPETOLOGISTS
You're a what? Herpetologist. M. Stanton. il *Occupational Outlook Quarterly* 33:37-9 Spr '89

HERR, MICHAEL
King of the Whispers. il *Esquire* 112:191-202 D '89

HERRELL, STEVE
about
I scream, you scream. M. Starr. il por *Newsweek* 113:50 Ja 2 '89

HERRELL'S (FIRM)
I scream, you scream. M. Starr. il por *Newsweek* 113:50 Ja 2 '89

HERRERA, CAROLINA
about
Quality control. il pors *Harper's Bazaar* 122:380-3 S '89

HERRERASAURUS *See* Dinosaurs

HERRHAUSEN, ALFRED
Assassination
The bloody return of the Red Army Faction. il *Newsweek* 114:62 D 11 '89
Taking over the helm of Germany Inc. J. Templeman and G. E. Schares. il por *Business Week* p66-7 D 18 '89
Target for the Red Army Faction. D. Brand. il por *Time* 134:54 D 11 '89

HERRING, JAMES
about
James Herring at SECCA. M. Kangas. il *Art in America* 77:268 Ap '89

HERRINGTON, JOHN S., 1939-
A valentine for Ron [resignation letter, November 9, 1988] *Harper's* 278:20+ F '89

HERRINGTON, ROWDY
about
Jack's back [film] Reviews
Video 12:86 Ja '89. J. Walker
Road house [film] Reviews
New York il 22:64-5 My 29 '89. D. Denby
People Weekly il 31:16+ My 29 '89. S. Haller
Rolling Stone il p34 Je 1 '89. P. Travers

HERRIOT, JAMES
Blossom comes home. il *Good Housekeeping* 208:86 Ja '89
The little dog nobody wanted [excerpt from The market square dog] il *Good Housekeeping* 209:112+ D '89

HERRNSTEIN, RICHARD J.
IQ and falling birth rates. il *The Atlantic* 263:72-6+ My '89
about
A confederacy of dunces. G. Cowley. il por *Newsweek* 112:80+ My 22 '89

HERRON, JERRY, 1949-
Elevate or escalate? *Harper's* 278:27 My '89

HERSCH, FRED
about
Janis Siegel & Fred Hersch. M. Bourne. pors *Down Beat* 56:14 O '89

HERSCH, HANK
Big man on the block. il pors *Sports Illustrated* 70:32-5 My 1 '89
By the skin of his neck. il pors *Sports Illustrated* 70:46-9 Mr 6 '89
Choosing sides. il pors *Sports Illustrated* 71:42-4+ N 27 '89
The comeback chronicles. il pors *Sports Illustrated* 71:38-44+ Jl 24 '89
Fast new pace. il *Sports Illustrated* 71:34-6+ D 25 '89-Ja 1 '90
Gathers 'round the rim. il pors *Sports Illustrated* 70:68-9 F 13 '89
The Gospel and Gaetti. il por *Sports Illustrated* 71:42-4+ Ag 21 '89
Home at last. il *Sports Illustrated* 71:50-3 D 11 '89
A hometown hero. il pors *Sports Illustrated* 70:48-50+ My 15 '89
Look who's on top. il *Sports Illustrated* 70:92-5 Ja 9 '89
Mailman II. il pors *Sports Illustrated* 70:54-6+ Je 26 '89
Not just a tall tale. il pors *Sports Illustrated* 70:42-4+ Mr 20 '89
Rock of a rook. il pors *Sports Illustrated* 70:20-2+ F 6 '89

Scary show at Shea. il *Sports Illustrated* 71:22-5 Ag 14 '89
Sitting Bulls they weren't. il *Sports Illustrated* 70:22-3 My 22 '89
The Sweet 16. il *Sports Illustrated* 71:72-6+ N 20 '89
Time for Big Ben. il pors *Sports Illustrated* 70:54+ My 29 '89

HERSCHMAN, LEO
about
Fans. *The New Yorker* 65:24-5 Jl 24 '89

HERSCU, GEORGE
about
Debacle on 34th Street: how takeover debt helped kill off the venerable B. Altman chain. B. Rudolph. il por *Time* 134:77 D 11 '89
Say g'day to the megamall. S. Phillips. il *Business Week* p29 Mr 6 '89

HERSEY, BROOK
Carey Lowell: the new female Bonding. il por *Glamour* 87:166 Ag '89
How to handle a panic attack. il *Ladies' Home Journal* 106:92 O '89
The surprising eroticism of sound. il *Glamour* 87:190-3 D '89
The truth about women and heart disease. il *Working Woman* 14:156+ Ap '89

HERSEY, JOHN, 1914-
The announcement [story] il *The Atlantic* 264:88-92+ D '89
Could a flawed 46-cent chip cause a nuclear war? il *TV Guide* 37:32-3 Ja 21-27 '89
War: it's hard to get it right. il *The New York Times Book Review* 94:1+ S 10 '89

HERSH, SANDY
Why the dolphins died. il *Sea Frontiers* 35:246-7 Jl/Ag '89

HERSHBERGER, JAMES W.
about
Wake me when it's over. D. Kardong. il por *Runner's World* 24:86-90+ Ap '89

HERSHEY, BARBARA
about
Barbara Hershey—a serious star talks about Beaches, Bette, Temptation, friends . . . and Oscars. D. DeNicolo. il por *Glamour* 87:138 F '89
Hershey kisses the past good-bye. S. Nelson. il por *Mademoiselle* 95:38 Ja '89

HERSHEY FOODS CORP.
The sweet smell of success. A. Kupfer. *Fortune* 119:30+ Ap 24 '89
Why Hershey is smacking its lips. J. Weber, Jr. il por *Business Week* p140 O 30 '89

HERSHISER, OREL
Tommy Lasorda's "Sermon on the mound" [condensed from Out of the blue]; ed. by Jerry B. Jenkins. il por *Reader's Digest* 135:63-5 S '89
about
Calling a game; ed. by Peter Gammons. M. Scioscia. il *Sports Illustrated* 70 Special Issue:34-9 Ap '89
The man with the golden arm. J. Nocera. il pors *Newsweek* 113:42-4+ Ap 10 '89
Orel in Wonderland. S. Ostler. il pors *Sport (New York, N.Y.)* 80:32-4 Mr '89

HERTZ, HEINRICH RUDOLF, 1857-1894
about
Heinrich Hertz and the development of physics. J. F. Mulligan. bibl f il por *Physics Today* 42:50-7 Mr '89

HERTZBERG, ARTHUR, 1921-
What future for American Jews? il *The New York Review of Books* 36:26+ N 23 '89

HERTZBERG, HENDRIK
TRB from Washington. See issues of The New Republic beginning January 30, 1989
Who killed the yuppie? *Utne Reader* p94 Jl/Ag '89

HERVEY, CAROLYN OWENS
about
Looking into a shared past. D. Young. il pors *Southern Living* 24:79+ D '89

HERVIEU, PAUL
about
Books and things. P. Littell. *The New Republic* 201 [Reprint v1]:26 N 6 '89 [N 7 '14]

HERZFELD, THOMAS J.
about
He feasts on ugly duckling funds [interview] E. Schultz. il por *Fortune* 119:44+ Ja 30 '89

HERZOG, CHAIM, 1918-
about
'We can't take chances' [interview] E. Silver. *Maclean's* 102:23 Je 26 '89

HESBURGH, THEODORE MARTIN
about
TV will always expose the phonies. R. Townley. il por *TV Guide* 37:48-50 Ja 7-13 '89

HESIOD, FL. CA. 700 B.C.
about
The powers of the primeval goddesses. M. R. Lefkowitz. *The American Scholar* 58:586-91 Aut '89

HESKETH-HARVEY, KIT
about
Britain's blue-blood bad boys 'Kit and the Widow' make even their royal targets laugh. J. Wadler. il pors *People Weekly* 31:97-9 Ap 24 '89
HESS, DONALD
about
A rich harvest. L. Nilson. il por *Art News* 88:99-100 D '89
HESS COLLECTION WINERY
A rich harvest. L. Nilson. il por *Art News* 88:99-100 D '89
HESSE, EVA, 1936-1970
about
Growing up absurd. A. C. Danto. il por *Art News* 88:118-21 N '89
HESSE, GEORGIA
Pacific and Asian passages. il *Travel Holiday* 171:73-4+ Ap '89
HESSELINK, I. JOHN, 1928-
Emil Brunner: a centennial perspective [cover story] il por *The Christian Century* 106:1171-4 D 13 '89
HESSER, RANDALL G.
Writing the book on employees. il *Nation's Business* 77:50-1 D '89
HESSINGER, DAVID A.
(jt. auth) See Watson, Glen M., and Hessinger, David A.
HESTENES, ROBERTA
about
Roberta Hestenes: taking charge [cover story] T. Stafford. il pors *Christianity Today* 33:16-22 Mr 3 '89
HESTER, RICHARD L.
AAUP censures Southeastern Seminary. *The Christian Century* 106:742-4 Ag 16-23 '89
HESTER, SLEW
No place like home. il *World Tennis* 37:136 S '89
HESTERCOMBE (SOMERSET, ENGLAND: GARDEN) See Somerset (England)—Gardens and gardening
HESTON, CHARLTON
about
Charlton Heston's son has come a long way from the bulrushes: baby Moses is now dad's director. S. Schindehette. il pors *People Weekly* 32:74-6 Jl 3 '89
HESTON, FRASER
about
Charlton Heston's son has come a long way from the bulrushes: baby Moses is now dad's director. S. Schindehette. il pors *People Weekly* 32:74-6 Jl 3 '89
HEWERDINE, BOO
about
Boo Hewerdine & Darden Smith. M. McCormick. pors *Rolling Stone* p30 N 2 '89
HEWES, HAVELOCK
The staff of a lifetime. il *Sport (New York, N.Y.)* 80:44-5+ Je '89
HEWITT, DON, 1922-
about
60 minutes in the garden. C. K. Gandee. il pors *House & Garden* 161:110-17 Je '89
HEWLETT-PACKARD CO.
A buyout guru shares two takeover visions [views of L. Smith] G. G. Marcial. il por *Business Week* p146 Mr 20 '89
Hewlett-Packard's screeching turn toward desktops. J. B. Levine. il por *Business Week* p106-8+ S 11 '89
Hewlett-Packard's whip-cracker [J. Young] il por *Fortune* 119:58 F 13 '89
HP: now no. 1 in workstations [deal for Apollo] J. B. Levine. il *Business Week* p30 Ap 24 '89
Keeping new ideas kicking around. J. B. Levine. il *Business Week* Special Issue:128 Je 16 '89
HEWSON, PAUL See Bono
HEXHAM, IRVING, AND POEWE-HEXHAM, KARLA O.
Charismatic churches and the struggle against apartheid: a dispute [discussion of August 17-24, 1988 article, Charismatics and change in South Africa] *The Christian Century* 106:16+ Ja 4-11 '89
HEXHAM, KARLA O. POEWE- See Poewe-Hexham, Karla O.
HEXTALL, RON
about
What makes Ron Hextall tick. J. Greenberg. il pors *Sports Illustrated* 71:62-4+ N 13 '89
HEY, JEAN
Just two women. il *The New York Times Magazine* p40+ S 10 '89
HEY, WHAT'S ALL THIS TO ME!? [dance] See Dance reviews—Single works
HEYBROCK, CHRISTEL
Digging up Troy. il *World Press Review* 36:57 Ja '89
HEYE MUSEUM (NEW YORK, N.Y.) See Museum of the American Indian—Heye Foundation
HEYERDAHL, THOR
about
Thor Heyerdahl. P. Brock. il pors *People Weekly* 32:181-2+ D 11 '89
HEYMAN, KEN, 1930-
Tinker tailor. il *American Heritage* 40:106-13 N '89

HEYN, DALMA
Bad boys: why we love them sooo . . . il *Seventeen* 48:82-3+ Ja '89
Body hate. il *Ms.* 18:34+ Jl/Ag '89
The intelligent woman's guide to sex. See issues of Mademoiselle beginning December 1986
HEYWOOD, EDDIE, 1915-1989
about
Obituary
Jet il por 75:60 Ja 23 '89
HEYWOOD, PAUL
Why the Republic lost. il *History Today* 39:20-7 Mr '89
HEZLEP, W.
(jt. auth) See Demko, George J., 1933-, and Hezlep, W.
HFCS See Hydrochlorofluorocarbons
HGH (HUMAN GROWTH HORMONE) See Pituitary hormones
HGH (HUMAN GROWTH HORMONE), SYNTHETIC See Pituitary hormones, Synthetic
HHS See United States. Dept. of Health and Human Services
HI-FI SOUND SYSTEMS See Audio systems
HIATT, JOHN
about
Clean & sober. D. Wild. il pors *Rolling Stone* p56-7+ Ja 12 '89
Rocker John Hiatt: as good as his words. P. J. Smith. il por *The New York Times Magazine* p55+ Mr 12 '89
Value for your roots-rock dollar. D. Browne. il pors *Rolling Stone* p28 Mr 23 '89
HIBBS, MARGARET L., AND OTHERS
Mechanisms for regulating expression of membrane isoforms of FcγRIII (CD16). bibl f il *Science* 246:1608-11 D 22 '89
HIBERNATION
Freeze avoidance in a mammal: body temperatures below 0°C in an Arctic hibernator [cover story] B. M. Barnes. bibl f il *Science* 244:1593-5 Je 30 '89
Sleeping beauties [hibernating black bears; study by Ralph Nelson and others] A. C. Revkin. bibl (p84) il *Discover* 10:62-5 Ap '89
Squirrel sleeps at a fluid subzero [research by Brian M. Barnes] *Science News* 136:30 Jl 8 '89
Supercool mammals [body temperature of Arctic ground squirrel drops below freezing during hibernation; research by Brian Barnes] M. Kemp. il *Discover* 10:24 N '89
HIBERNIA CORPORATION
"Our competitors can't touch us". J. H. Taylor. il por *Forbes* 143:86 Mr 20 '89
HIBERNIA OIL FIND See Petroleum—Atlantic Ocean
HIBISCUS
See also
Rose of Sharon
HICCUPS
Hiccups: when to worry! L. Holland. *Good Housekeeping* 209:169 Ag '89
HICKCOX, DAVID H.
Hot spots and cold spots. il *Weatherwise* 42:42-6 F '89
HICKEY, MARY C.
"I love my doctor!". il *Parents* 64:104-7+ Ap '89
HICKEY, WILLIAM
about
Hickey [interview] G. Smith. il pors *Film Comment* 25:52-4 N/D '89
HICKORY
Hickory—the American tree. E. A. Peeples. il *Country Journal* 16:35-8 My/Je '89
HICKS, ALAN
A photographer's guide to Kyoto. il *Petersen's Photographic Magazine* 18:30-5 D '89
Whatever happened to the Allegheny woodrat? il maps *The Conservationist* 43:34-9 Mr/Ap '89
HICKS, DAVID, 1929-
about
Gandee at large. C. K. Gandee. il por *House & Garden* 161:210 Mr '89
A homegrown view. C. Vogel. il *The New York Times Magazine* p68-71 Je 18 '89
HICKS, GLENN R., AND OTHERS
The Diageotropica mutant of tomato lacks high specific activity auxin binding sites. bibl f il *Science* 245:52-4 Jl 7 '89
HICKS, JACK
How her painful divorce helped her on Knots Landing. il pors *TV Guide* 37:18-20 Ag 5-11 '89
TV's battle of the sexes: with Roseanne, it's no holds Barred [cover story] il pors *TV Guide* 37:2-5 Ja 28-F 3 '89
HICKS, JOHN W.
Advance of the red army. il *International Wildlife* 19:4-11 N/D '89
HICKS, ROBERT D.
Affecting eternity. il *Sky and Telescope* 77:236 Mr '89
HICKS, THOMAS O.
about
Splitsville for a hot LBO team. K. Kelly. il pors *Business Week* p34 My 29 '89
HICKS & HAAS
Splitsville for a hot LBO team. K. Kelly. il pors *Business Week* p34 My 29 '89

HIDATSA INDIANS
Minnesota's 'Way to independence' [Memories of a Hidatsa Indian family, 1840-1920] E. Chappell. *The Nation* 249:763-6 D 18 '89

HIDDEN AGENDA (VIDEO GAME)
Compute! choice. K. Sternberg. il *Compute!* 11:84-6 O '89
Hidden Agenda. S. Williams. il *Home Office Computing* 7:70+ Jl '89
Introduction to geopolitics. K. Kane. il *Psychology Today* 23:74-5 O '89

HIDDEN TREASURE *See* Treasure trove
HIDEAWAY REPORT *See* Travel newsletters
HIDES AND SKINS
Export-import trade
Skins to boot [tegu lizards] D. Einhorn. il *Américas* 41 no2:2 '89

HIDING PLACES (SECRET CHAMBERS, ETC.)
Anecdotes, facetiae, satire, etc.
Secret places. P. F. McManus. il *Outdoor Life* 183:120+ Je '89

HIEBERT, MURRAY
(jt. auth) See Tasker, Rodney, and Hiebert, Murray

HIEROGLYPHICS
See also
Rosetta Stone

HIEROGLYPHICS, MAYA *See* Mayas—Writing

HIESEL, RUDOLF, AND OTHERS
RNA editing in plant mitochondria. bibl f il *Science* 246:1632-4 D 22 '89

HIESTAND, EMILY
Holly comes from a cold heaven [poem] *The Nation* 248:66 Ja 9-16 '89
Life [poem] *The Nation* 248:30 Ja 2 '89
Slippery elm [poem] *The Nation* 248:244 F 20 '89
The witch hazel wood [poem] *The Nation* 248:212 F 13 '89

HIGA, MATTHEW
about
Scott and Matthew Higa make their mark as bowling's youngest twin strike force. il pors *People Weekly* 31:98-9 Ja 30 '89

HIGA, SCOTT
about
Scott and Matthew Higa make their mark as bowling's youngest twin strike force. il pors *People Weekly* 31:98-9 Ja 30 '89

HIGBIE, P. R.
(jt. auth) See Hones, Edward W., and Higbie, P. R.

HIGBY, WAYNE, 1943-
Comment. *American Craft* 49:16-17 F/Mr '89

HIGGINS, DAVID
The challenge of dusty dark nebulae. il *Astronomy* 17:86-8 Je '89
The ghostly glow of gaseous nebulae [cover story] il *Astronomy* 17:93-5 O '89

HIGGINS, JOANNA
Notes on carpentry and craft. *The Writer* 102:9-10 Ag '89

HIGGINS, PATRICIA
about
How deregulation spelled opportunity. J. A. Werman. il por *Working Woman* 14:56+ My '89

HIGGINS, PAUL E.
The promised land [poem] *America* 161:380 N 25 '89

HIGGINS, WILLIAM R.
Kidnapping
American hostages in the Middle East [remarks, statement, etc., July 31-August 7, 1989] G. Bush. *Department of State Bulletin* 89:66-9 O '89
An American soldier's death becomes a pawn in a terrorist power struggle [conflicting accounts of W. R. Higgins' death within Hezbollah factions] D. Halevy and N. C. Livingstone. il *U.S. News & World Report* 107:21 O 23 '89
Holding ourselves hostage. H. Fairlie. *The New Republic* 201:12-13 Ag 28 '89
Hostage showdown. R. Watson. il map *Newsweek* 114:14-18 Ag 14 '89
Hostages to terror [cover story; special section; with editorial comment by Kevin Doyle] il pors *Maclean's* 102:2, 20-4+ Ag 14 '89
Inaction is another form of hanging [kidnapping of A. K. Obeid results in murder of W. R. Higgins] R. Rosenblatt. il por *U.S. News & World Report* 107:8-9 Ag 14 '89
"A stupid posting". il por *Time* 134:19 Ag 14 '89

HIGGINS, YVONNE
(jt. auth) See Juskie-Nellis, Joan, and Higgins, Yvonne

HIGGINSEN, VY
about
Show stopper. J. Torrence-Thompson. il por *Black Enterprise* 20:66-8+ Ag '89

HIGGINSEN (VY) INC./REACH ENTERTAINMENT & SPORTS *See* Vy Higginsen Inc./Reach Entertainment & Sports

HIGGISON, PEYTON
about
Sell it yourself. il *American Artist* 53:52 D '89

HIGGS BOSON *See* Particles (Nuclear physics)
HIGH ALTITUDE
E for elevation [research on vitamin E and free radicals in high altitude athletics] il *Women's Sports & Fitness* 11:11 O '89

HIGH ALTITUDE SICKNESS *See* Mountain sickness
HIGH BLOOD PRESSURE *See* Hypertension
HIGH COMMISSIONER FOR REFUGEES *See* United Nations. High Commissioner for Refugees
HIGH DEFINITION TELEVISION
21st century TV. S. A. Booth. il *Popular Mechanics* 166:60-3 D '89
Choosing the TV of the future [cover story; special section] il *Technology Review* 92:30-40 Ap '89
Couching toward HDTV. M. Porter. il *Gentlemen's Quarterly* 59:315+ S '89
Cutting through the high-definition hype. D. Lachenbruch. il *Video* 12:118 Mr '89
Get the picture! G. Kenny. il *Stereo Review* 54:69-73 Ap '89
HDTV inspires a ghostbusting spinoff. D. Lachenbruch. il *Video* 13:138 O '89
HDTV test center gears up. *High Technology Business* 9:35-6 Mr '89
HDTV: the FCC edict. R. Angus. *High Fidelity (New York, N.Y.)* 39:12-13 Ja '89
HDTV: the technology du jour. C. Norman. il *Science* 244:761-4 My 19 '89
HDTV: up for grabs. K. Korman. il *Video* 13:59+ S '89
An HDTV with less than meets the eye [work of W. E. Glenn] A. Fins. il por *Business Week* Special Issue:88 Je 16 '89
HDTV—an alternative viewpoint. D. Lancaster. *Radio-Electronics* 60:78-9 F '89
High definition tele-vision [cover story] L. Feldman. il *Radio-Electronics* 60:35-7+ F '89
High-tech dance film will be screened at World's Fair [HDTV used to produce To dream of roses] C. Lefevre. il *Dance Magazine* 63:14 S '89
I want my HDTV. B. Kanner. il *New York* 22:28+ S 11 '89
IBM-TV? G. F. Gilder. il *Forbes* 143:72-4+ F 20 '89
Low-cost HDTV that beats Japan's? [Summa Medical] G. G. Marcial. *Business Week* p102 My 29 '89
Making a leap in TV technology. W. J. Cook. il *U.S. News & World Report* 106:48-9 Ja 23 '89
Next picture show. S. Levy. il *Rolling Stone* p91-2+ Je 15 '89
Sarnoff Center girds loins for global competition in HDTV. W. Sweet. *Physics Today* 42:63-5 Je '89
Should you wait for picture-perfect TV? *Consumer Reports* 54:118 F '89
Snaring the elusive high-def standard. M. Burgi. il *Channels (New York, N.Y.: 1986)* 9:42 D '89
Some tough choices. T. Wetmore. il *Channels (New York, N.Y.: 1986)* 9:63 Mr '89
Super television [cover story] il *Business Week* p56-9+ Ja 30 '89
Toward a global high-definition TV production standard [statement, March 8, 1989] S. Landau. *Department of State Bulletin* 89:48-51 Je '89
Ultravideo [cover story; special section; with editorial comment by Michael Riggs] il *High Fidelity (New York, N.Y.)* 39:5, 47-8+ Ap '89
Who needs HDTV? L. Winner. por *Technology Review* 92:20 My/Je '89
Why Sony is plugging into Columbia. N. Gross and W. J. Holstein. il *Business Week* p56+ O 16 '89
Federal aid
DARPA poised to award contracts for high-definition display concepts. P. A. Gilmartin. *Aviation Week & Space Technology* 131:32 S 4 '89
DARPA to fund high-density TV. *High Technology Business* 9:33 Ap '89
A focus on advanced television? C. Norman. *Science* 244:137 Ap 14 '89
HDTV: a better buggy whip. *National Review* 41:14-15 Jl 14 '89
High-definition TV: breakthrough, boondoggle—or both? il *Consumer Reports* 54:627-9 O '89
High tech's fickle helping hand [White House wavers on funding] P. Elmer-Dewitt. il *Time* 134:68 D 4 '89
Lawmakers to press for legislation to boost U.S. high-definition TV role. P. A. Gilmartin. *Aviation Week & Space Technology* 130:24 Mr 27 '89
Not a pretty picture [HDTV research funded by DARPA] S. Shulman. il *The Progressive* 53:24-5 S '89
Promoting high-definition TV: the perils for Uncle Sam. P. Magnusson. il *Business Week* p30 My 29 '89
Putting America in the picture. J. Schwartz. il *Newsweek* 113:42-3 My 29 '89
The U.S. electronics industry can be reinvigorated. B. D. Nordwall. il *Aviation Week & Space Technology* 131:40-1 D 18-25 '89
Will the White House torpedo America Inc.? J. Carey. il *Business Week* p80 N 27 '89

HIGH DENSITY LIPOPROTEINS See Lipoproteins
HIGH ENERGY PHYSICS See Nuclear physics
HIGH FIBER DIET See Fiber in diet
HIGH FIDELITY (PERIODICAL)
Reading between the lines [cover story] R. Long. il *High Fidelity (New York, N.Y.)* 39:38-42 F '89
HIGH FIDELITY [film] See Motion picture reviews—Single works
HIGH HEELS (FOOTWEAR) See Footwear
HIGH HOPES [film] See Motion picture reviews—Single works
HIGH INTENSITY DISCHARGE LIGHTING
This bright idea could make GE a billion. M. Mallory. il *Business Week* p120 D 4 '89
HIGH JUMPING
Up where she belongs [Olympic gold medalist L. Ritter] K. Moore. il pors *Sports Illustrated* 70:98-101 Ja 9 '89
HIGH JUMPING RECORDS
The eight-foot feat [J. Sotomayor at Caribbean Zone Track and Field Championship] il por *Newsweek* 114:62 Ag 14 '89
One giant leap [Cuba's J. Sotomayor clears eight feet] M. Noden. il pors *Sports Illustrated* 71:32-3 Ag 7 '89
HIGH PLAINS (U.S.)
   See also
     Wetlands—High Plains (U.S.)
HIGH PRESSURE (SCIENCE)
   See also
     Jet cutting
Hard-pressed [squeezed hydrogen; work of Ho-Kwang Mao and Russell J. Hemley] P. E. Ross and R. Ruthen. *Scientific American* 261:26 N '89
Heavy metal [metallic hydrogen; work of Ho-Kwang Mao and Russell Hemley] *Discover* 10:10+ N '89
Metallic hydrogen. A. Fisher. il *Popular Science* 235:23-5 O '89
Optical studies of hydrogen above 200 gigapascals: evidence for metallization by band overlap [Raman spectra] H. K. Mao and R. J. Hemley. bibl f il *Science* 244:1462-5 Je 23 '89
Putting the squeeze on hydrogen [work of Ho-Kwang Mao and Russell Hemley] R. Pool. *Science* 244:1440 Je 23 '89
Recipe for a bit of deep earth [diamond-anvil cell] R. A. Kerr. il *Science* 246:759 N 10 '89
Silicon coordination and speciation changes in a silicate liquid at high pressures. X. Xue and others. bibl f il *Science* 245:962-4 S 1 '89
Squeezed hydrogen turns semi-metallic [work of Ho-Kwang Mao and Russell J. Hemley] F. Flam. *Science News* 135:327 My 27 '89
X-ray diffraction to 302 gigapascals: high-pressure crystal structure of cesium iodide. H. K. Mao and others. bibl f il *Science* 246:649-51 N 3 '89
HIGH PRESSURE WASHERS See Pressure washers
HIGH SCHOOL AND COLLEGE COOPERATION See Educational cooperation
HIGH SCHOOL ATHLETES See Athletes
HIGH SCHOOL ATHLETES, WOMEN See Women athletes
HIGH SCHOOL ATHLETICS See School athletics
HIGH SCHOOL BUILDINGS See School buildings
HIGH SCHOOL CHOIRS See Choirs
HIGH SCHOOL CREDITS
How to get credit for what you know. il *Occupational Outlook Quarterly* 33:18-19 Summ '89
HIGH SCHOOL DROPOUTS See Dropouts
HIGH SCHOOL EQUIVALENCY TESTS See General educational development tests
HIGH SCHOOL GRADUATES
Where have all the smart girls gone? [study of female valedictorians seven years after high school graduation; work of Terry Denny] M. Conroy. il *Psychology Today* 23:20 Ap '89
HIGH SCHOOL JOURNALISM See College and school journalism
HIGH SCHOOL PRINCIPALS See School superintendents and principals
HIGH SCHOOL PROMS See Proms (Dances)
HIGH SCHOOL REUNIONS
After some rocky times, one class of '59 reunites to roll back the clock thirty years [Birmingham High School, Van Nuys, Calif.] J. Savaiano. il *People Weekly* 32:153-5 S 18 '89
All the girls I've loved. N. Karlen. il *Mademoiselle* 95:191+ N '89
High school . . . the sequel. J. Leigh. il *Health (New York, N.Y.)* 21:52-5 Jl '89
Refugio [class of 1959] J. L. Galloway. il *U.S. News & World Report* 107:51+ D 18 '89
    Anecdotes, facetiae, satire, etc.
Last word. S. N. Farber and J. Killus. il *Omni (New York, N.Y.)* 11:128 Je '89
What we're up to. G. Schwartz. il *New York* 22:14 Jl 17 '89
HIGH SCHOOL STUDENTS
   See also
   High school graduates
   Study
   Teenage pregnancy

High school confidential [Glenbard East High School in Lombard, Ill.] S. Elder. il *American Health* 8:62-3+ O '89
The Seventeen yearbook. T. Imbimbo. il *Seventeen* 48:87-90 My '89
    Admission
   See High schools—Admission
    Attitudes
High school U.S.A.: what's happening at your school? il *Teen* 33:28+ Ag '89
What's your opinion? [beggars and the homeless] D. O. Relin. il *Scholastic Update (Teachers' edition)* 121:3+ F 10 '89
    Civil rights
   See Students—Civil rights
    Dating
   See Dating (Social customs)
    Grading
   See Grading and marking (Education)
    Psychology
I went back to high school . . . and it was hell! [29 year old returns to Langley High School in McLean, Va.] J. Moses. il *Mademoiselle* 95:202-3+ My '89
Learning in style [research by Bernice McCarthy] L. H. Duquin. il *Seventeen* 48:92+ S '89
    Sexual behavior
   See Youth—Sexual behavior
    Volunteer service
   See Volunteer service
HIGH SCHOOL STUDENTS AND DRUGS See Drugs and youth
HIGH SCHOOL YEARBOOKS
Good times [looking through old yearbook] *The New Yorker* 65:30-1 F 20 '89
HIGH SCHOOLS
   See also
   Catholic schools
   Junior high schools
   Secondary education
Inside a New York City high school: snapshots of hope and hopelessness [Seward Park High School] S. G. Freedman. il *The New York Times Magazine* p58-9+ S 17 '89
    Admission
High school choice and students at risk. D. R. Moore and S. Davenport. *The Education Digest* 55:7-10 S '89
    Censorship
   See Censorship
    Curriculum
   See also
   American literature—Study and teaching
   Calculus—Study and teaching
   English language—Study and teaching
   History—Study and teaching
   International education
   Journalism—Study and teaching
   Literature—Study and teaching
   Mathematics—Study and teaching
   Physics—Study and teaching
   Theater—Study and teaching
   Thought and thinking—Study and teaching
How to cut the cost of college [courses taken in high school] R. E. Deck, Jr. il *USA Today (Periodical)* 118:58-9 Jl '89
Let's again talk sense about our schools. J. Georgeoff. bibl f il *Phi Delta Kappan* 71:72-3 S '89
    Enrollment
   See School enrollment
    Entrance requirements
   See High schools—Admission
    Graduation requirements
Why is Pythagoras following me? [mathematics requirements] M. K. Smith. bibl f il *Phi Delta Kappan* 70:446-54 F '89
    Race relations
Building unity across a city street [New York's Martin Luther King Jr. High School and Fiorello H. La Guardia High School of the Arts] L. Eskin. il *Scholastic Update (Teachers' edition)* 121:24-5 Ap 7 '89
School-yard racism [blacks and whites brawl at Cole Harbour District High School in Halifax County, N.S.] M. Nemeth. il *Maclean's* 102:14 Ja 23 '89
Teaching students cultural mediation [Amos Alonso Stagg High School in Stockton, Calif.] B. Huie. *The Education Digest* 55:50-2 O '89
    Standards
   See also
   Coalition of Essential Schools
HIGH SCHOOLS AND BUSINESS See Business and education
HIGH SCHOOLS AND RELIGION See Public schools and religion
HIGH SIERRAS See Sierra Nevada Mountains (Calif. and Nev.)
HIGH SOCIETY See Upper classes
HIGH SPEED ANTIRADIATION MISSILES See Guided missiles—Launching from airplanes

HIGH SPEED PHOTOGRAPHY *See* Photography, High speed
HIGH SPEED TRAINS *See* Railroads—Trains
HIGH SPIRITS [film] *See* Motion picture reviews—Single works
HIGH TECH *See* Technology
HIGH TECH INDUSTRIES *See* Computer industry; Electronic industries
HIGH TEMPERATURES
Intermetallic compounds for high-temperature structural use. A. I. Taub and R. L. Fleischer. bibl f il *Science* 243:616-21 F 3 '89
HIGHCLERE CASTLE
Ancestral style. C. Aslet. il *House & Garden* 161:188-97 Mr '89
HIGHER COMMERCIAL MANAGEMENT SCHOOL (MOSCOW, SOVIET UNION)
Moscow tackles its manager gap. J. Trimble. il *U.S. News & World Report* 107:40+ Jl 31 '89
HIGHER EDUCATION *See* College education; Colleges and universities; Community and junior colleges
HIGHER EDUCATION RESEARCH PROGRAM
On starting a national colloquy. R. Zemsky and S. B. Stine. il *Change* 21:7-9 My/Je '89
HIGHGATE CEMETERY (LONDON, ENGLAND)
Highgate: Victorian extravaganza with a cast of thousands. J. Bainbridge. il *Gourmet* 49:30+ Ag '89
HIGHLIGHTING (HAIR COLORING) *See* Hair—Dyeing and bleaching
HIGHRISE BUILDINGS *See* Skyscrapers
HIGHSMITH, PATRICIA, 1921-
about
Mistress of fright. J. Pearlman. il por *Harper's Bazaar* 122:52+ F '89
HIGHTOWER, HERMA
about
Black woman heads IRS district office in Iowa. por *Jet* 75:6 Mr 6 '89
HIGHTOWER, JIM
Raising issues, hope and hell. il *The Nation* 248:160+ F 6 '89
about
Don't mess around with Jim. R. Woodbury. il por *Time* 133:42 Ap 3 '89
Hightower's view. J. Schutze. il pors *Organic Gardening* 36:32-6 D '89
Jim Hightower: a farmer's friend who goes against the grain. K. Kelly. il por *Business Week* p84 N 6 '89
'A party within a party': Jim Hightower proposes a populist alliance. D. A. Denison. il *The Progressive* 53:22-3 Mr '89
HIGHWAY, TOMSON
about
Dry lips oughta move to Kapuskasing [drama] Reviews *Maclean's* il 102:62 My 8 '89. J. Bemrose
HIGHWAY BEAUTIFICATION *See* Roadside improvement
HIGHWAY TO HEAVEN [television program] *See* Television program reviews—Single works
HIGHWAYS *See* Express highways; Roads
HIGNETT, WILLIAM F.
Designing programs for infant day care. *The Education Digest* 54:62-3 F '89
HIGONNET, ANNE
Where there's a will . . . bibl f il *Art in America* 77:65-7+ My '89
HIJACKING OF BUSES *See* Bus hijacking
HIJACKING OF HELICOPTERS *See* Helicopter hijacking
HIJACKING OF SHIPS *See* Ship hijacking
THE HIJACKING OF THE ACHILLE LAURO [television program] *See* Television program reviews—Single works
HIJAZI, IHSAN A.
Beirut diary. il por *The New York Times Magazine* p30-3+ My 28 '89
HIJUELOS, OSCAR
Lucy and Ricky and the Mambo Kings [fiction] *Harper's* 279:28+ Ag '89
about
PW interviews. M. Coffey. por *Publishers Weekly* 236:42+ Jl 21 '89
HIKING
See also
Backpacks and backpacking
Trails
Adventures of a reluctant Forty-sixer [hiking in the Adirondacks] L. P. Fortin. il *The Conservationist* 44:10-15 N/D '89
A dozen choice trails for day hikers [national forest trails] M. Spilner. il *Prevention (Emmaus, Pa.)* 41:78+ Ap '89
Elko to Eden [hiking in the Ruby Mountains; cover story] T. Kizzia. il map *Sierra* 74:46-54 Mr/Ap '89
Hiking up for Bay views [San Francisco Bay] il *Sunset (Central West edition)* 182:14-16 Ja '89
Many pleasures without names. K. R. Stafford. il *Sierra* 74:68-70 N/D '89
A walk on the wild side [Indian Peaks Wilderness] T. Jenkins. il map *Travel Holiday* 171:46-51 My '89
Equipment
See also
Hiking boots

International aspects
Mini jaunts and major hikes. E. Wetschler. il *Health (New York, N.Y.)* 21:65 S '89
Steppin' out [cover story] C. R. Wolpert. bibl il *Women's Sports & Fitness* 11:20-4 Mr '89
Italy
Footloose [hiking through Tuscany] M. Chabon. il por *Vogue* 179:266+ My '89
Kenya
Walking on the wild side. L. Morrow. il *Time* 134:70 Jl 10 '89
Switzerland
Peak experience [walking tour in the Alps] L. Kleinmann. il *Health (New York, N.Y.)* 21:62-4+ S '89
HIKING BOOTS
No (more) mean feet. G. Williams. il *Sierra* 74:174-5 Ja/F '89
Take a hike. il *Women's Sports & Fitness* 11:45-6+ Mr '89
You don't have to go hiking in clodhoppers. E. Schine. il *Business Week* p182 Jl 17 '89
HILBURN, ANDREW
Help find this mad bomber. il *Reader's Digest* 135:96-100 N '89
HILD, NANCY, AND LIVERMORE, BETH
The pillow chase. il *Health (New York, N.Y.)* 21:70-1+ Jl '89
HILDEBRAND, MILTON, 1918-
The quadrupedal gaits of vertebrates. bibl f il *BioScience* 39:766-75 D '89
Vertebrate locomotion: an introduction. bibl f il *BioScience* 39:764-5 D '89
HILDRETH, JAMES E. K., AND ORENTAS, RIMAS J.
Involvement of a leukocyte adhesion receptor (LFA-1) in HIV-induced syncytium formation. bibl f il *Science* 244:1075-8 Je 2 '89
HILL, EDDIE
about
The big Thrill. D. Wallace. il por *Sport (New York, N.Y.)* 80:66-8 Jl '89
HILL, FIONA
about
In the grasp of romance: my life as Fiona Hill. E. Pall. *The New York Times Book Review* 94:1+ Ap 30 '89
HILL, GENE
Hill country. See issues of Field & Stream
HILL, GEORGE ROY, 1922-
about
Funny farm [film] Reviews
Video il 12:83 Ja '89. J. Walker
HILL, HAL
Scream test. il *Seventeen* 48:117+ O '89
HILL, IAN DARNTON- *See* Darnton-Hill, Ian
HILL, LYNN
about
Cliffhanger [cover story] T. Gabriel. il pors *The New York Times Magazine* p20-5+ D 31 '89
Upward mobility. il pors *Life* 12:104-5 Ag '89
HILL, MARY, 1923-
On earth. See issues of Earth Science
HILL, RICHARD
Equipped for safe solar viewing. il *Astronomy* 17:66-8 F '89
HILL, RICHARD
about
Men working in trees. J. Stuller. il por *Audubon* 91:86-91 Jl '89
HILL, RICHARD, 1941-
Ecology wars. *Omni (New York, N.Y.)* 11:25 Ag '89
HILL, RICK, AND MOHAWK, JOHN
Indian cultures provide ecological wisdom and prophesies. *Utne Reader* p91 N/D '89
HILL, TRACEY
(tr) See Galeano, Eduardo H., 1940-. Sign on the invisible line
HILL, VICTORIA BLYTH
The watchful eye in paper conservation. il *American Artist* 53:22+ Ag '89
HILL, VIRGIL
about
There's no place like home. K. Cook. il pors *Sports Illustrated* 70:90 Je 5 '89
HILL, WALTER, 1942-
about
Johnny Handsome [film] Reviews
American Film il 15:96-7 O '89. R. Seidenberg
The New Yorker 65:110 O 16 '89. P. Kael
People Weekly il 32:14-15 O 16 '89. R. Novak
Red heat [film] Reviews
Video il 12:60 F '89. I. Robbins
HILL & WANG, INC.
Big numbers for innumeracy: Hill & Wang's first bestseller heralds a new direction. C. Goodrich. il por *Publishers Weekly* 235:46-8 Je 2 '89
HILL, HOLLIDAY, CONNORS, COSMOPULOS INC.
Consider the urushi tree—is it not like a luxury car? [campaign for Nissan's Infiniti] L. Armstrong. il *Business Week* p84+ S 4 '89

HILL LODGE (LONDON, ENGLAND) *See* Kensington (London, England)—Historic houses, sites, etc.
HILL STREET BLUES [television program] See Television program reviews—Single works
HILLARD, PAULA ADAMS
As they grow/pregnancy and birth. See issues of Parents
HILLEGASS, CLIFF
about
Shakespeare, Dickens & Hillegass. F. Meeks. il por *Forbes* 144:206+ O 30 '89
HILLENBRAND, CATHERINE
about
Real Comet Press: breaking down categories. J. Barbato. *Publishers Weekly* 236:46 Jl 14 '89
HILLER, ARTHUR
about
See no evil, hear no evil [film] Reviews
The New Republic 200:27 Je 12 '89. S. Kauffmann
New York il 22:71 My 22 '89. D. Denby
People Weekly il 31:15 My 29 '89. R. Novak
HILLER, SUSAN, 1940-
about
Susan Hiller at Pat Hearn. N. Princenthal. *Art in America* 77:154 Ja '89
HILLERMAN, TONY
A canyon, an egret . . . and a mystery. il *Audubon* 91:30-4+ Jl '89
about
In the heart of Navajo country. K. Ames. il por *Newsweek* 113:60-1 Je 19 '89
Navajo cops on the case. A. Ward. il pors *The New York Times Magazine* p38-9+ My 14 '89
HILLIARD, ASA G.
Cultural style in teaching and learning. *The Education Digest* 55:21-3 D '89
HILLIARD, DALTON
Photographs and photography
Outdoor lighting control when the subjects are saints. T. L. Corbell. il pors *Petersen's Photographic Magazine* 18:12-13 My '89
HILLIS, BURTON
Man next door. See issues of Better Homes and Gardens
HILLIS, DANIEL
Richard Feynman and the Connection Machine. il *Physics Today* 42:78-83 F '89
HILLMAN, JAMES
The wonder of wander: walking and the soul of modern society. il *Utne Reader* p93-4 Mr/Ap '89
HILLS, CARLA ANDERSON, 1934-
Status of multilateral trade negotiations [statement, April 11, 1989] *Department of State Bulletin* 89:30-2 Je '89
Trade-related aspects of intellectual property rights [statement, July 25, 1989] *Department of State Bulletin* 89:55-9 N '89
Uruguay Round and U.S. trade policy: a foundation for the future [address, September 14, 1989] *Department of State Bulletin* 89:53-5 N '89
about
Test of wills. M. Nemeth. il pors *Maclean's* 102:63-4 Jl 3 '89
What to do about trade policy. A. R. Dowd. il por *Fortune* 119:106-7+ My 8 '89
HILLS, RUST
Miss Manners lets her hair down. il *Esquire* 111:194-9 Je '89
HILLSIDE ARCHITECTURE
1,200 square feet of efficiency on a rugged site [cabin] il *Sunset (Central West edition)* 183:132 O '89
Home in the mountains [Burnsville, N.C.] il *Southern Living* 24:130-2 Je '89
In the Wright spirit [Hudson River house by Theodore M. Ceraldi] A. Rieselbach. il *Architectural Record* 177:42-9 mid-Ap '89
A lively climb up for a dramatic view [San Francisco] il *Sunset (Central West edition)* 183:115 O '89
Long-legged decks . . . they're steep site solutions. il *Sunset (Central West edition)* 182:100-1 Mr '89
Outpost of civility [Locke House] J. S. Russell. il *Architectural Record* 177:56-9 mid-Ap '89
Three-level answer for a 45° slope [Sherman Oaks, Calif. house] il *Sunset (Central West edition)* 183:84-5 Ag '89
HILLSIDE GARDENS AND GARDENING
Water-stingy but colorful slope garden in Santa Barbara. il *Sunset (Central West edition)* 183:200 O '89
HIMES, CHESTER, 1909-1984
about
Mayhem comes to Harlem. J. Adler. por *Newsweek* 113:72 F 6 '89
HIMMELFARB, GERTRUDE
Victorian values/Jewish values. *Commentary* 87:23-31 F '89
HIMMELFARB, MILTON
American Jews: diehard conservatives. il *Commentary* 87:44-9 Ap '89
The Jewish vote [discussion of April 1989 article, American Jews: diehard conservatives] *Commentary* 88:4-6+ Ag '89
HIMONT INC.
Defying the law of gravity. A. A. Lappen. il por *Forbes* 143:76-7 Ap 3 '89

HINCHMAN, KRISTI
Balancing the family act. il *'Teen* 33:34-5 D '89
Getting great grades: A+ advice. il *'Teen* 33:42+ S '89
Teen mothers: their stories. il *'Teen* 33:32+ N '89
HINDES, GARY E.
about
Yes, Virginia, there is a way to make money in troubled junk. L. Jereski. il pors *Business Week* p87 S 11 '89
HINDUISM
See also
Yoga
HINE, LEWIS WICKES, 1874-1940
about
Time exposures. E. F. Provenzo. il *Society* 26:87-9 S/O '89
HINE, THOMAS, 1947-
Design for eating. il *Gentlemen's Quarterly* 59:78+ N '89
The joy of kitsch. il *Gentlemen's Quarterly* 59:61+ O '89
HINES, ALAN
Artists of different cultures in the New Mexico light. il *American Artist* 53:60-5+ D '89
HINES, GERALD A.
Should the Senate approve the "Americans with Disabilities Act of 1989"? [excerpts from testimony, May 10, 1989] *Congressional Digest* 68:296+ D '89
HINES, GREGORY
about
Sammy Davis, Jr. and Gregory Hines move to the beat in 'Tap' [cover story] il pors *Jet* 75:58-61 F 13 '89
Tap. il pors *Ebony* 44:46+ F '89
HINES, MAURICE
about
Dancescape. A. Barzel. por *Dance Magazine* 63:57 Ap '89
HINES, THOMAS S.
Art: early California watercolors. il *Architectural Digest* 46:296-301+ My '89
HINGES
Installing European hinges. T. H. Jones. il *Home Mechanix* 85:16-17 N '89
Mortising hinges. H. Wicks. il *Home Mechanix* 86:24+ Ap '89
Routing hinge mortises. T. H. Jones. il *Home Mechanix* 85:29-30 O '89
HINGHAM (MASS.)
Historic houses, sites, etc.
History in towns: Hingham, Massachusetts [cover story] M. B. Lehner and M. J. Fannin. bibl f il *Antiques* 136:812-25 O '89
HINNANT, KATHRYN, D. 1989
about
Murder in the safest places. R. Rosenblatt. il *U.S. News & World Report* 106:6-7 Ja 23 '89
The tragedy at Bellevue. E. Salholz. il pors *Newsweek* 113:27 Ja 23 '89
HINRICHSEN, DON
Will the sun ever shine on Budapest? il *International Wildlife* 19:18-23 S/O '89
HINSON, DAVID
about
David Hinson is stretching Midway's wings. J. E. Ellis. il por *Business Week* p84-5 Je 12 '89
HIP CULTURE
The death of hip. J. Kinney. il *Utne Reader* p53-7 S/O '89
Nouveau hip. S. Ruta. il *Utne Reader* p56-7 S/O '89
HIP DYSPLASIA
Dysplasia's end [hunting dogs; work of Dr. W. Belfield] L. Mueller. il pors *Outdoor Life* 183:46+ Ap '89
Hip dysplasia [dogs] R. Kidd. il *The Mother Earth News* 116:42+ Mr/Ap '89
HIP EXERCISES *See* Exercise
HIP-HOP
Hip-hop madness. H. Allen. il *Essence* 19:78-80+ Ap '89
HIP JOINT
A "Fallsafe" against broken hips [tethering system] il *High Technology Business* 9:13-14 N/D '89
HIP JOINT, ARTIFICIAL
New hips for a veteran dancer. M. Beddow. il pors *Dance Magazine* 63:46-50 S '89
HIPPARCOS (ARTIFICIAL SATELLITES)
European space program managers increase expectations for Hipparcos' useful lifetime. *Aviation Week & Space Technology* 131:58 N 13 '89
Hipparcos failure stuns Europeans. S. Mitton. il *Astronomy* 17:14 N '89
Hipparcos: in the low-orbit blues. M. M. Waldrop. *Science* 245:808 Ag 25 '89
Hipparcos remains in transfer orbit, reducing useful astronomy data. J. M. Lenorovitz. il *Aviation Week & Space Technology* 131:28 S 4 '89
Hipparcos satellite's mission success will depend on lifetime in transfer orbit. *Aviation Week & Space Technology* 131:44 O 23 '89
HIPPIES
Canada
Tangerine dreams [1960s] J. Gray. il *Maclean's* 102:50-1 Ag 28 '89

HIPPOCAMPAL NEURONS See Nerve cells
HIPPOCAMPUS (BRAIN) See Brain
HIPPOCRATIC OATH See Physicians' oaths
HIPPOLYTE ET ARICIE [opera] See Rameau, Jean Philippe
HIRABAYASHI, KAORU
about
Kaoru Hirabayashi at Gallery NW House. J. Koplos. il *Art in America* 77:185+ D '89
HIRANO, HISASHI
about
A careful clone of K Mart captivates Japan. T. Holden. il por *Business Week* p115 My 22 '89
HIRANO-NAKANISHI, MARSHA
(jt. auth) See Hsia, Jayjia, and Hirano-Nakanishi, Marsha
HIRATA, NAOHIKO
about
Life after "exam hell". P. Sudo. il por *Scholastic Update (Teachers' edition)* 122:13 D 8 '89
HIRAYAMA, YUJI
Where Japan is second-best. *World Press Review* 36:55 Ja '89
HIRO, DILIP
The Ayatollahs and the Bear. il *The Nation* 249:414-16 O 16 '89
North Yemen: of another age. il *World Press Review* 36:78 S '89
HIROHITO, EMPEROR OF JAPAN, 1901-1989
about
After Hirohito: what remains sacred. I. Buruma. il por *The New York Times Magazine* p28-9+ My 28 '89
A delicate burial. W. R. Doerner. il *Time* 133:34 Ja 23 '89
Hirohito and the fate of the emperor system. Y. Suzuki. *The Christian Century* 106:5-7 Ja 4-11 '89
An imperial farewell. il *Maclean's* 102:24-5 Mr 6 '89
Mourn Hirohito? W. F. Buckley. *National Review* 41:63 Ap 7 '89
Obituary
Maclean's il por 102:20 Ja 16 '89. B. Levin
Maclean's il pors 102:21-2 Ja 16 '89. R. C. Christopher
The Nation il 248:120-2 Ja 30 '89. C. S. Inouye
Newsweek il pors 113:34-6 Ja 16 '89. T. Morganthau
Time il pors 133:30-2 Ja 16 '89. P. Iyer
U.S. News & World Report il por 106:12+ Ja 16 '89
A rite of passage. B. Martin. il por *Newsweek* 113:24-5 F 20 '89
"With grief, we bid you farewell". il *Time* 133:46-7 Mr 6 '89
HIROSHIMA (JAPAN)
Bombardment, 1945
Did Eisenhower oppose A-bomb? [research by Barton J. Bernstein] il por *USA Today (Periodical)* 118:15 Ag '89
Study upgrades radiation risks to humans [National Research Council report] J. Raloff. *Science News* 136:404 D 23-30 '89
The victim and the pilot: a Hiroshima reunion [A. Takahashi meets P. Tibbets] G. Mitchell. il pors *The Progressive* 53:26-8 Ag '89
HIRSCH, BILL
(jt. auth) See Cardozo, Yvette, and Hirsch, Bill
HIRSCH, EDWARD
Memorandums [poem] *The New Yorker* 64:36 F 13 '89
The romance of American communism [poem] *The New Republic* 201:36 N 20 '89
HIRSCH, ERIC DONALD
The primal scene of education. bibl f il *The New York Review of Books* 36:29-35 Mr 2 '89
'The primal scene of education': an exchange [discussion of March 2, 1989 article] il *The New York Review of Books* 36:50 Ap 13 '89
about
Educational misconceptions of a democratic public. W. Feinberg. *The Education Digest* 55:7-10 O '89
In pursuit of cultural literacy. E. H. Schuster. il *Phi Delta Kappan* 70:539-42 Mr '89
Learning by story. N. Postman. il *The Atlantic* 264:119-24 D '89
HIRSCH, GARY D.
about
The hell with glamour. Give me groceries. J. H. Dobrzynski. il por *Business Week* p121 My 1 '89
HIRSCH, GEORGE A.
The inside track. See issues of Runner's World
HIRSCH, JOHN
about
Obituary
Maclean's il por 102:54 Ag 14 '89. D. Turbide
HIRSCH, JOHN VLADIMIR
about
Another spy scandal. *Newsweek* 114:28 Ag 14 '89
Summer spy scoops. D. Schorr. *The New Leader* 72:3-4 Ag 7-21 '89
HIRSCH, JUDD, 1935-
about
'I set out to be the worst person I've ever met'. C. A. Crotta. il por *TV Guide* 37:12-13+ Je 3-9 '89

Judd the obscure. G. Duffy. il por *Rolling Stone* p49+ My 18 '89
HIRSCH, JULIAN D.
Technical talk. See issues of Stereo Review
HIRSCH, JULIAN D., AND STARK, CRAIG
Test reports. See issues of Stereo Review
HIRSCH, KARL F., AND OTHERS
Upper Jurassic dinosaur egg from Utah. bibl f il *Science* 243:1711-13 Mr 31 '89
HIRSCH, LEON C.
about
Now, Lee Hirsch wants to sew up sutures. C. Tucher. il por *Business Week* p74-5 Ag 7 '89
HIRSCH, WENDY AMER- See Amer-Hirsch, Wendy
HIRSCHFIELD, ROBERT
Rabbi Marshall Meyer: a prophet's agenda. *The Christian Century* 106:438-9 Ap 26 '89
HIRSCHL & ADLER FOLK
Frank J. Miele's urban folklore. J. Simpson. il por *Architectural Digest* 46:88+ Je '89
HIRSCHMAN, ALBERT O.
Reactionary rhetoric. il *The Atlantic* 263:63-6+ My '89
HIRSHEY, GERRI
The comedy of hate. il pors *Gentlemen's Quarterly* 59:226-9+ Ag '89
Coupledom uber alles: tyranny of the couples. il *Utne Reader* p48-9+ Mr/Ap '89
The frosted flake [cover story] il pors *Gentlemen's Quarterly* 59:416-21+ S '89
HIRSHHORN MUSEUM AND SCULPTURE GARDEN
Around the Mall and beyond [WORKS site specific series] E. Park. il *Smithsonian* 19:24+ Ja '89
HISPANIC AMERICAN ART See Art, Hispanic American
HISPANIC AMERICAN BUSINESS ENTERPRISES
The importance of Hispanics to our nation [address, February 16, 1989] D. McCormick. *Vital Speeches of the Day* 55:464-7 My 15 '89
HISPANIC AMERICAN MARKET
Barrio makeover [selling Avon products to migrant women] R. Kirk. il *Ms.* 17:73-5 My '89
Dancing to the Latino beat. L. Whitaker. il *Time* 134:114 O 23 '89
Hispanic TV: a great way to make a killing, right? R. Grover. il *Business Week* p61 O 23 '89
The importance of Hispanics to our nation [address, February 16, 1989] D. McCormick. *Vital Speeches of the Day* 55:464-7 My 15 '89
It's a whole nuevo mundo out there. E. Pomice. il *U.S. News & World Report* 106:45-6 My 15 '89
'Se habla español'. il *U.S. News & World Report* 106:15-16 Mr 6 '89
HISPANIC AMERICANS
America in the 21st century [Population Reference Bureau report] *Children Today* 18:2-3 S/O '89
Full-moon wisdom [treatment of the elderly in Hispanic and Indian cultures] R. Coles. il *New Choices for the Best Years* 29:94+ S '89
The Hispanic struggle for success is slowly paying off. B. J. Wattenberg. il *U.S. News & World Report* 107:31 S 25 '89
Lively times in Latino San Francisco [Day of the Dead celebration] il map *Sunset (Central West edition)* 183:32-3+ O '89
A nation within a nation. il *Business Week* p144-5 S 25 '89
Agriculture
See also
Ganados del Valle (Organization)
Education
Can business throw a net under Hispanic dropouts? T. Mason. il *Business Week* p151+ F 20 '89
English classes open up new opportunities for Hispanic New Yorkers. il *Aging* no359:23 '89
Employment
How the Hispanic population boom will hit the work force. G. Koretz. il *Business Week* p21 F 20 '89
Land tenure
A land battle in New Mexico [sheep war] J. N. Baker. il *Newsweek* 114:27 S 18 '89
Nutrition
Learning dietary Spanish [nutrition education programs] J. Steinberg. il *American Health* 8:140-1 Ap '89
Photographs and photography
Inside high villages [N. Warren's work among Hispanic communities in New Mexico] J. Neary. il por *Americana* 17:42-7 Mr/Ap '89
Psychiatric care
Mobile mental health team reaches minorities [Pacific Clinics mental health center in Pasadena, Calif.] A. H. Hernandez and C. Schweon. il *Aging* no359:12-13 '89
Religious life
Realizing the Hispanic dream. J. Miranda. il *Christianity Today* 33:37-40 Mr 3 '89
The success of the sects among Hispanics in the United States. J. J. Diaz Vilar. il *America* 160:174-5+ F 25 '89

HISPANIC AMERICANS—*cont.*
Statistics
Down from the count [Hispanic broadcasters hoping 1990 census will reveal uncounted Hispanic TV viewers] M. Couzens. il *Channels (New York, N.Y.: 1986)* 9:16 My '89

U.S. Hispanics: challenges for the 1990s. il *The Futurist* 23:53 Jl/Ag '89

HISPANIC AMERICANS AND MASS MEDIA
Dancing to the Latino beat. L. Whitaker. il *Time* 134:114 O 23 '89

It's a whole nuevo mundo out there. E. Pomice. il *U.S. News & World Report* 106:45-6 My 15 '89

HISPANIC AMERICANS AND TELEVISION
Down from the count [Hispanic broadcasters hoping 1990 census will reveal uncounted Hispanic viewers] M. Couzens. il *Channels (New York, N.Y.: 1986)* 9:16 My '89

Hispanic viewing close to the mainstream [chart] il *Channels (New York, N.Y.: 1986)* 9:96 Ja '89

HISPANIC HERITAGE WING *See* Museum of International Folk Art (Santa Fe, N.M.). Hispanic Heritage Wing

HISS, TONY
Encountering the countryside (I). il *The New Yorker* 65:40-2+ Ag 21 '89

Encountering the countryside (II). il *The New Yorker* 65:37-40+ Ag 28 '89

Light rail. il *The New Yorker* 65:70-4+ Mr 6 '89

HISTAMINE
    See also
    Scombroid poisoning
Histamine is an intracellular messenger mediating platelet aggregation. S. P. Saxena and others. bibl f il *Science* 243:1596-9 Mr 24 '89

HISTOCOMPATIBILITY *See* Immunological tolerance

HISTOCOMPATIBILITY COMPLEX *See* Major histocompatibility complex

HISTONES
Histone H5 in the control of DNA synthesis and cell proliferation. J.-M. Sun and others. bibl f il *Science* 245:68-71 Jl 7 '89

A protein that binds to a cis-acting element of wheat histone genes has a leucine zipper motif. T. Tabata and others. bibl f il *Science* 245:965-7 S 1 '89

HISTORIANS
    See also
    Children as historians

HISTORIANS, AMERICAN
    See also
    Dawidowicz, Lucy S.
    Fischer, David Hackett
    Russell, Francis, 1910-1989
    Tuchman, Barbara Wertheim

HISTORIANS, ENGLISH
    See also
    Clapham, Sir J. H. (John Harold), 1873-1946
    Fuller, John Frederick Charles, 1878-1966
    Toynbee, Arnold Joseph, 1889-1975

HISTORIANS, FRENCH
    See also
    Renan, Ernest, 1823-1892

HISTORIANS, GERMAN
German historians at war. J. Z. Muller. bibl f *Commentary* 87:33-41 My '89

HISTORIANS, GREEK
    See also
    Herodotus

HISTORIC DEERFIELD, INC.
A walking tour of Historic Deerfield. il *Redbook* 173:106-11 Ag '89

HISTORIC HOUSE MUSEUMS *See* Historic houses, sites, etc.

HISTORIC HOUSES, SITES, ETC.
    See also
    Castles
    Heritage education
    Houses, Restored
    National Register of Historic Places
    Palaces
    Plantations
    Villages, Restored
America's historical cities [Boston, Philadelphia, San Antonio, and San Francisco] il *Better Homes and Gardens* 67:173-4+ O '89

Doing right by Wright. E. M. Gomez. il *Art News* 88:36+ Ja '89

Eyesores into showplaces—even without a tax break [rehabbing] J. Weber, Jr. il *Business Week* p36 Ja 16 '89

Hosts of ghosts [haunted historic houses] G. Turim. il *Americana* 17:21-4 S/O '89

Man in space [preserving relics of the space program] E. Bruske. il *National Parks* 63:32-8 Ja/F '89

New products: windows for historic renovation. il *Architectural Record* 177:114-15+ Ag '89

On the road to glory [historical black sites] W. M. T. Walls. il *Black Enterprise* 19:209-10 F '89

Restoring the rehab tax credit. M. F. Schmertz. *Architectural Record* 177:11 Ag '89

A shrinking market in rehab? Not necessarily. il *Architectural Record* 177:33 O '89

Tacky nostalgia? No, these are landmarks [architecture of the 1950s] J. D. Reed. il *Time* 134:110-11 D 11 '89

Traveling with a sense of history [cover story; special issue] il *American Heritage* 40:34-6+ Ap '89

Conferences
Venturi faults bureaucrats during historic interiors preservation conferences [Interiors Conference and Exposition for Historic Buildings] C. D. W. Koenig. il por *Architectural Record* 177:25 F '89

Alabama
    See also
    Mobile (Ala.)—Historic houses, sites, etc.

Arizona
Restoring a Frank Lloyd Wright jewel [built in 1951 for Raymond Carlson] il *Sunset (Central West edition)* 183:108 O '89

Belgium
    See also
    Knokke-le-Zoute (Belgium)—Historic houses, sites, etc.

Bermuda
Bermuda; "calm clear land". C. Davidson. il *American Heritage* 40:28+ N '89

Brazil
    See also
    Rio de Janeiro (Brazil)—Historic houses, sites, etc.

California
    See also
    Berkeley (Calif.)—Historic houses, sites, etc.
    Beverly Hills (Calif.)—Historic houses, sites, etc.
    Carmel (Calif.)—Historic houses, sites, etc.
    Fresno (Calif.)—Historic houses, sites, etc.
    Hollywood (Calif.)—Historic houses, sites, etc.
    Los Angeles (Calif.)—Historic houses, sites, etc.
    Monterey County (Calif.)—Historic houses, sites, etc.
    Pacific Palisades (Los Angeles, Calif.)—Historic houses, sites, etc.
    Palos Verdes Estates (Calif.)—Historic houses, sites, etc.
    Pasadena (Calif.)—Historic houses, sites, etc.
    Salinas (Calif.)—Historic houses, sites, etc.
    San Francisco (Calif.)—Historic houses, sites, etc.
    San Francisco Bay Area (Calif.)—Historic houses, sites, etc.

Colorado
    See also
    Colorado Springs (Colo.)—Historic houses, sites, etc.
    Glenwood Springs (Colo.)—Historic houses, sites, etc.
    Telluride (Colo.)—Historic houses, sites, etc.

Connecticut
    See also
    Greenwich (Conn.)—Historic houses, sites, etc.
    Lebanon (Conn.)—Historic houses, sites, etc.
    Mystic Seaport Museum
    Washington (Conn.)—Historic houses, sites, etc.
Fast forward [S. and B. Pittman's converted barn] D. Kazanjian. il pors *House & Garden* 161:76-83+ F '89

Rustic frame for a modern collection: the Connecticut house of Katharine and Nicholas Fox Weber [18th century farmhouse and converted barn] R. W. B. Lewis. il *Architectural Digest* 46:200-5+ Je '89

Cuba
    See also
    Havana (Cuba)—Historic houses, sites, etc.

Czechoslovakia
    See also
    Prague (Czechoslovakia)—Historic houses, sites, etc.

Florida
    See also
    Coconut Grove (Miami, Fla.)—Historic houses, sites, etc.
    Miami Beach (Fla.)—Historic houses, sites, etc.
    Palm Beach (Fla.)—Historic houses, sites, etc.
Florida pioneer: a woodland house on the Gulf Coast [home of K. and L. Drummond] B. Dunlop. il *Architectural Digest* 46:174-7+ Je '89

France
    See also
    Albi (France)—Historic houses, sites, etc.
    Autheil (France)—Historic houses, sites, etc.
    Cap d'Antibes (France)—Historic houses, sites, etc.
    Cap Martin (France)—Historic houses, sites, etc.
    Eyrignac (France: Historic house)
    Nice (France)—Historic houses, sites, etc.
    Paris (France)—Historic houses, sites, etc.
    Sologne (France)—Historic houses, sites, etc.
The Désert de Retz, near Paris. P. Deitz. bibl f il *Antiques* 135:718-31 Mr '89

Escape to Normandy [P. Mathieu's and M. Ray's farmhouse; cover story] C. K. Gandee. il pors *House & Garden* 161:96-105+ F '89

The essence of Provence [home of J. and I. Amic] C. Carter. il por *House & Garden* 161:126-31+ Jl '89

The garden of France: history meets geography in the Loire River Valley. B. Warf. il map *Focus (New York, N.Y.: 1950)* 39:26-7+ Fall '89

Norman retreat [N. Worms' 1823 timbered farmhouse] R. Koenig. il *House & Garden* 161:142-7+ Jl '89

HISTORIC HOUSES, SITES, ETC.—France—cont.

A Provençal tale: the house and vineyards of Richeaume [H. Hoesch's estate] D. H. Minassian. il *Architectural Digest* 46:136-41 Ja '89

Georgia

See also
Savannah (Ga.)—Historic houses, sites, etc.

Great Britain

See also
Charleston Manor (Lewes, England)
Chatsworth House (Derbyshire, England)
Chelsea (London, England)—Historic houses, sites, etc.
Chiswick House (Middlesex, England)
Kensington (London, England)—Historic houses, sites, etc.
London (England)—Historic houses, sites, etc.
Penshurst Place (England)

Badminton Court. P. Kinmonth. il por *Vogue* 179:426-35 O '89
Cotswold retreat [S. Falconer's Tughill House] R. B. Shaw. il *House & Garden* 161:124-31+ Mr '89
An education abroad: living and learning in English country houses. E. Lambert. il *Architectural Digest* 46:140-2+ My '89
The functional folly in eighteenth-century Britain. G. Jackson-Stops. bibl f il *Antiques* 135:1412-23 Je '89
The House of Lancaster [Haseley Court; excerpt from Colefax & Fowler] C. Jones. il pors *House & Garden* 161:188-95+ N '89
Hunt country [master of the hunt R. Smith-Ryland's 16th century farmhouse in Warwickshire] G. Nevill. il pors *House & Garden* 161:132-9 Mr '89
Kelmscott Manor [home of W. Morris] J. Marsh. il *History Today* 39:62-3 Ap '89
Monk's House—the author's country retreat in Sussex [V. Woolf] P. Rose. il *Architectural Digest* 46:62+ Jl '89
Red House in Kent [home of W. Morris] E. Lambert. il *Architectural Digest* 46:126+ Ap '89
The scion of Bloomsbury in Sussex [Q. Bell] E. Lambert. il por *Architectural Digest* 46:72+ D '89

Hawaii

A minka revival: Japanese farmhouse traditions reinterpreted in Hawaii. M. Webb. il *Architectural Digest* 46:198-204 Ag '89

Illinois

See also
Chicago (Ill.)—Historic houses, sites, etc.
Lake Forest (Ill.)—Historic houses, sites, etc.
Springfield (Ill.)—Historic houses, sites, etc.

Ireland

See also
Dublin (Ireland)—Historic houses, sites, etc.

Isle of Wight (England)

See also
Osborne House (Isle of Wight, England)

Italy

See also
Milan (Italy)—Historic houses, sites, etc.
Porto Ercole (Italy)—Historic houses, sites, etc.

Jamaica

See also
Sir Noel Coward's Firefly Hill Museum (Jamaica)

A blow to Jamaica's treasure houses [Hurricane Gilbert's effect] A. R. Williams. il *Américas* 41 no1:8-13 '89

Japan

A minka revival: Japanese farmhouse traditions reinterpreted in Hawaii. M. Webb. il *Architectural Digest* 46:198-204 Ag '89

Kentucky

Bluegrass. R. F. Snow. il *American Heritage* 40:26+ Ap '89

Long Island (N.Y.)

A colonial sensibility: restoring a shingled saltbox on eastern Long Island. S. M. Alsop. il *Architectural Digest* 46:132-9 Je '89
Portrait of the artists: Eric Fischl and April Gornik on Long Island [farmhouse renovated by Lee Skolnick] S. M. L. Aronson. il pors *Architectural Digest* 46:234-9+ Ap '89

Maine

See also
Kennebunkport (Me.)—Historic houses, sites, etc.

Maryland

See also
Clara Barton National Historic Site (Md.)

Hugh Newell Jacobsen: refurbishing a colonial house in the Maryland hunt country [Horsehead Farm] il *Architectural Digest* 46:88-90 Ag '89

Massachusetts

See also
Boston (Mass.)—Historic houses, sites, etc.
Chatham (Mass.)—Historic houses, sites, etc.
Fall River (Mass.)—Historic houses, sites, etc.
Hingham (Mass.)—Historic houses, sites, etc.
Historic Deerfield, Inc.
Lincoln (Mass.)—Historic houses, sites, etc.
Monterey (Mass.)—Historic houses, sites, etc.
Salem (Mass.)—Historic houses, sites, etc.

Pure and not so simple [restoration of 18th century house by John Saladino] C. Vogel. il *The New York Times Magazine* p60-5 Ag 20 '89

Michigan

See also
Detroit (Mich.)—Historic houses, sites, etc.

Middle Western States

In the footsteps of the Lincolns. W. T. Anderson. il map *The Saturday Evening Post* 261:64-7+ Jl/Ag '89

Minnesota

See also
Little Falls (Minn.)—Historic houses, sites, etc.

Mississippi

See also
Greenville (Miss.)—Historic houses, sites, etc.
Oxford (Miss.)—Historic houses, sites, etc.
Vicksburg (Miss.)—Historic houses, sites, etc.

Morocco

See also
Essaouira (Morocco)—Historic houses, sites, etc.

Nebraska

See also
Omaha (Neb.)—Historic houses, sites, etc.

New Brunswick

See also
Acadian Historical Village (N.B.)

New England

Leafing through history [black landmarks] B. W. O'Connor. il *Black Enterprise* 20:105-6 S '89
Yankee preserve [interior by M. Hampton] E. A. Berthold. il *House & Garden* 161:98-103+ Je '89

New Jersey

See also
Cape May (N.J.)—Historic houses, sites, etc.
Sayreville (N.J.)—Historic houses, sites, etc.

New York (State)

See also
Bedford (N.Y.)—Historic houses, sites, etc.
Bellport (N.Y.)—Historic houses, sites, etc.
Boscobel Restoration
Columbia County (N.Y.)—Historic houses, sites, etc.
Millbrook (N.Y.)—Historic houses, sites, etc.
Mohonk Mountain House
Muttontown (N.Y.)—Historic houses, sites, etc.
New York (N.Y.)—Historic houses, sites, etc.
Olana State Historic Site (Hudson, N.Y.)
Rose Hill Mansion (Geneva, N.Y.)
Sag Harbor (N.Y.)—Historic houses, sites, etc.
Southampton (N.Y.)—Historic houses, sites, etc.
Water Mill (N.Y.)—Historic houses, sites, etc.

Art of Eastover: Clare and Eugene Thaw in upstate New York. S. M. Alsop. il por *Architectural Digest* 46:118-25+ Je '89
History with a view [Hudson River Valley] H. B. Livesey. il map *Travel Holiday* 172:64-73 D '89
Old light in a new world [1795 Sands House in the Hudson River Valley owned by D. McDermott and P. McGough] C. Black. il pors *House & Garden* 161:176-81+ N '89

Northern Ireland

Mount Stewart vistas: the Northern Ireland estate of Lady Mairi Bury. P. Lauritzen. il *Architectural Digest* 46:222-7+ Ap '89

Oklahoma

See also
Tulsa (Okla.)—Historic houses, sites, etc.

Ontario

See also
Toronto (Ont.)—Historic houses, sites, etc.

Pennsylvania

See also
Philadelphia (Pa.)—Historic houses, sites, etc.

A Philadelphia story: Edgar and Hope Scott at Ardrossan Farms. M. Tree. il por *Architectural Digest* 46:164-9 Je '89

Rhode Island

See also
Newport (R.I.)—Historic houses, sites, etc.

Scotland

See also
Glasgow (Scotland)—Historic houses, sites, etc.
House of Dun (Montrose, Scotland)

South Carolina

See also
Charleston (S.C.)—Historic houses, sites, etc.
Georgetown (S.C.)—Historic houses, sites, etc.

Christmas in the Upcountry [museum houses] C. Engle. il *Southern Living* 24:64-8+ D '89

Southern States

Districts make the difference [zoned historic districts] il *Southern Living* 24:164 N '89
Jefferson Davis called them home. il por *Southern Living* 24:24 Ag '89
Southern exposure [antebellum mansions in use as inns] D. Di Costanzo. il *House & Garden* 161:52+ Ap '89

Soviet Union

See also
Moscow (Soviet Union)—Historic houses, sites, etc.

HISTORIC HOUSES, SITES, ETC.—*cont.*

Spain

See also
Fundación Casa Ducal de Medinaceli
A reign in Spain: the Countess of Romanones in Extremadura and New York [Pascualete] Aline, Countess of Romanones. il pors *Architectural Digest* 46:192-9 Ap '89

Switzerland

See also
Saint Moritz (Switzerland)—Historic houses, sites, etc.

Tennessee

See also
Nashville (Tenn.)—Historic houses, sites, etc.

Texas

See also
Blanco (Tex.)—Historic houses, sites, etc.
Dallas (Tex.)—Historic houses, sites, etc.
Galveston (Tex.)—Historic houses, sites, etc.
San Antonio (Tex.)—Historic houses, sites, etc.
Waco (Tex.)—Historic houses, sites, etc.

United States

See Historic houses, sites, etc.

Vermont

Family ties [S. W. Morgan family's lodge] C. Brown. il *House & Garden* 161:128-35 Je '89
The Vermont farmhouse. il *Esquire* 112:98 O '89

Virginia

See also
Middleburg (Va.)—Historic houses, sites, etc.
Mount Vernon (Va.: Estate)
Richmond (Va.)—Historic houses, sites, etc.
Williamsburg (Va.)
A house worth saving [restoration of Page Meadows, a double-pen log house] L. Hallam. il *Southern Living* 24:168-71 N '89
Interior landscapes [decorated by William Hodgins] P. Carlsen. il *Architectural Digest* 46:172-9 Ag '89

Wales

Journey's end [excerpt from Pleasures of a tangled life] J. Morris. il *House & Garden* 161:128+ S '89

Washington (D.C.)

See Washington (D.C.)—Historic houses, sites, etc.

Washington (State)

See also
Seattle (Wash.)—Historic houses, sites, etc.

West Virginia

Sympathetic, but separate [addition to 200 year old farmhouse] il *Southern Living* 24:120-1 O '89

Yemen Arab Republic

See also
Sanaa (Yemen Arab Republic)—Historic houses, sites, etc.

HISTORIC RUGBY

New life, old dreams on the Cumberland Plateau. D. Young. il *Southern Living* 24:50-5 Ag '89

HISTORIC SITES *See* Historic houses, sites, etc.

HISTORIC TREES

See also
Treaty Oak (Austin, Tex.)

Exhibitions

The object at hand [bullet-riddled tree stump from the Spotsylvania battlefield at the National Museum of American History] M. Kernan. il *Smithsonian* 20:24+ My '89

HISTORICAL FICTION

Authorship

Writing the historical novel for young readers. P. Beatty. *The Writer* 102:17-19 Mr '89

Technique

Writing the historical saga. J. Saunders. *The Writer* 102:22-5 Ja '89

HISTORICAL GEOGRAPHY

See also
Maps, Early

HISTORICAL LITERATURE

See also
Historical fiction
History—Bibliography

HISTORICAL NOVELS *See* Historical fiction

HISTORICAL SOCIETIES

See also
Oregon Historical Society

HISTORIOGRAPHY

See also
Atomic bombs—Historiography
Blacks—History—Historiography
Estonia—History—Historiography
France—History—House of Valois, 1328-1589—Historiography
France—History—Revolution, 1789-1799—Historiography
France—History—February Revolution, 1848—Historiography
Germany—History—1933-1945—Historiography
Great Britain—Economic history—Historiography
Greece—History—Historiography
Holocaust, Jewish (1939-1945)—Historiography
Israel—History—Historiography
Jewish-Arab relations—History—Historiography

Military history—Historiography
Rome—Historiography
Ukraine—History—Historiography
United States—History—Historiography
Women—History—Historiography
World War, 1939-1945—Historiography

HISTORY

See also
Church history
Civilization
Current events
Heroes and heroines
Historical fiction
Local history
Military history
Oral history
Progress
Television and history
See also subhead History under various subjects

Bibliography

Autumn books. il *History Today* 39:56-8 O '89
Book reviews. See issues of History Today
Spring reading for travellers. il *History Today* 39:55-9 Mr '89

Philosophy

The beginning of nonsense [F. Fukuyama's theory of the end of history] S. Talbott. il *Time* 134:39 S 11 '89
The end of history—or of liberalism? [views of F. Fukuyama] J. Gray. *National Review* 41:33-5 O 27 '89
The end of what? [theory of F. Fukuyama] R. E. Tyrrell. *The American Spectator* 22:10 N '89
Endgames [essays by F. Fukuyama and B. McKibben predicting the end of history and the end of nature] L. H. Lapham. *Harper's* 279:10-13 N '89
Entering post-history. F. Fukuyama. il *New Perspectives Quarterly* 6:49-52 Fall '89
Has history come to an end? [views of F. Fukuyama] J. Elson. il por *Time* 134:57 S 4 '89
History's last word? [views of F. Fukuyama] G. F. Will. il *Newsweek* 114:66 Ag 14 '89
The intellectual Hula Hoop [end of history theory by F. Fukuyama] J. Alter. il *Newsweek* 114:39 O 9 '89
Is history over? [views of F. Fukuyama] *National Review* 41:14-15 S 1 '89
Minority report [F. Fukuyama's theory of the end of history] C. Hitchens. *The Nation* 249:302 S 25 '89
Nothing inevitable about democracy. K. Burris. *The Christian Century* 106:807 S 13-20 '89
Stopping time [views of F. Fukuyama] R. Corelli. il *Maclean's* 102:56+ O 2 '89
Washington diarist: the end of everything [views of F. Fukuyama] T. Noah. *The New Republic* 201:54 O 16 '89
What is Fukuyama saying? And to whom is he saying it? [essay on the end of history] J. Atlas. il por *The New York Times Magazine* p38-40+ O 22 '89

Sources

See also
Archives

Study and teaching

See also
United States—History—Study and teaching
Conceptualizing world studies. R. B. Woyack and R. C. Remy. *The Education Digest* 54:32-4 Ap '89
History tomorrow [teaching of history in Britain's new national curriculum; special section; with editorial comment] il *History Today* 39:6-15 Je '89
Teaching history the way it happened [New York plan vs. California plan] J. Leo. il *U.S. News & World Report* 107:73 N 27 '89

Aids and devices

Compute! choice [Where in Time is Carmen Sandiego?] K. Sternberg. il *Compute!* 11:72-4 D '89

Textbooks

See also
United States—History—Textbooks

HISTORY IN MOTION PICTURES

The incredible shrinking epic. A. Barra. il *American Film* 14:40-3+ Mr '89
When Hollywood makes history. il *American Heritage* 40:58-66+ Mr '89

HIT AND RUN ACCIDENTS *See* Traffic accidents

HITACHI, LTD.

Advanced bio class? That's over in Hitachi Hall [Japanese companies setting up labs at U.S. colleges] D. P. Oran. il *Business Week* p73-4 Ag 7 '89
What's behind the Texas Instruments-Hitachi deal. O. Port and T. Mason. il *Business Week* p93+ Ja 16 '89

HITACHI ZOSEN CORP.

The Japanese do it again. A. Tanzer. il *Forbes* 144:40-1 O 16 '89

HITCHCOCK, ALFRED, 1899-1980

about
North by northwest [film] Reviews
Video 12:63-4 Mr '89. M. Fleischmann

HITCHENS, CHRISTOPHER

Contempt for the little colony. il *Harper's* 279:70-6 O '89
Minority report. See issues of The Nation

HITCHENS, CHRISTOPHER—*cont.*
Skeleton at the Inauguration. *National Review* 41:44 F 10 '89

about
On losing one's marbles. J. Gardner. *National Review* 41:53-5 O 27 '89

HITCHES (AUTOMOBILE) *See* Automobile trailers—Towing
HITCHINGS, GEORGE H. (GEORGE HERBERT), 1905-
about
The Nobel pair. K. Bouton. il pors *The New York Times Magazine* p28-9+ Ja 29 '89

HITLER, ADOLF, 1889-1945
about
Angel of light. T. Stafford. il *Christianity Today* 33:16-19 S 8 '89
Correction. N. Birnbaum. *The Nation* 248:617-18 My 8 '89
Double event. H. M. Geduld. il *The Humanist* 49:39-40 Ja/F '89
Dreaming of Hitler. D. Merkin. il *Esquire* 112:75-8+ Ag '89
The Führer's dark legacy. J. Bierman. il pors *Maclean's* 102:32+ My 1 '89
The great Mafia wedding [cover story] J. P. Roche. il *National Review* 41:23-4 S 1 '89
Making way for Hitler. G. A. Craig. bibl f il *The New York Review of Books* 36:11-12+ O 12 '89
The prince and his courtiers: at the White House, the Kremlin, and the Reichschancellery. R. Baker and C. Peters. *The Washington Monthly* 21:38+ F '89
The prince of liars who told the truth. C. C. Aronsfeld. il *History Today* 39:7-9 Ap '89
What can England do about Hitler? [reprint from October 1938 issue] Sir W. Churchill. *Current History* 88:24-5+ Ja '89
World at war [cover story; special section] J. Keegan. il pors maps *U.S. News & World Report* 107:32-6+ Ag 28-S 4 '89
World War II: when darkness fell [cover story; special section] il pors *Time* 134:28-34+ Ag 28 '89

HITOX CORPORATION
"I learn on the job" [R. L. Bowers] W. P. Barrett. il por *Forbes* 144:49-50 Ag 7 '89

HITTLE, ALEX, AND MALAKOFF, DAVID
Perestroika may be both good and bad for Eastern Europe's severe ecological crisis. il *Utne Reader* p86-7 Ja/F '89

HIV VIRUSES
AIDS-Kaposi's sarcoma-derived cells express cytokines with autocrine and paracrine growth effects. B. Ensoli and others. bibl f il *Science* 243:223-6 Ja 13 '89
AIDS paper raises red flag at PNAS [P. H. Duesberg article in the Proceedings of the National Academy of Sciences] W. Booth. *Science* 243:733 F 10 '89
AIDS research focuses on CD4. *High Technology Business* 9:30 Jl/Ag '89
AIDS viral burden far exceeds estimates [patients harbor HIV in CD4-positive T4 cells; research by Miltiades C. Psallidopoulos] R. Weiss. *Science News* 136:54 Jl 22 '89
The arsenal gets larger. M. Patlak. il *Discover* 10:22-3 Ap '89
Blue-green algae kill HIV in culture [research by Michael R. Boyd] *Science News* 136:141 Ag 26 '89
A budding virus [micrographs] P. Gadsby. il *Discover* 10:22-3 My '89
Conserved folding in retroviral proteases: crystal structure of a synthetic HIV-1 protease. A. Wlodawer and others. bibl f il *Science* 245:616-21 Ag 11 '89
Differential effects of *nef* on HIV replication: implications for viral pathogenesis in the host. C. Cheng-Mayer and others. bibl f il *Science* 246:1629-32 D 22 '89
Do sperm spread the AIDS virus? [research by Virginia Scofield] J. L. Marx. il *Science* 245:30 Jl 7 '89
Drug-resistant strains of AIDS virus found [AZT-resistant] J. L. Marx. *Science* 243:1551-2 Mr 24 '89
Factor XIIIa-expressing dermal dendrocytes in AIDS-associated cutaneous Kaposi's sarcomas [with reply by Robert C. Gallo and others] B. J. Nickoloff and C. E. M. Griffiths. bibl f il *Science* 243:1736-7 Mr 31 '89
The Fc and not CD4 receptor mediates antibody enhancement of HIV infection in human cells. J. Homsy and others. bibl f il *Science* 244:1357-60 Je 16 '89
The fickle virus [mutations] M. Patlak. il *Discover* 10:24+ F '89
First 3-D image of AIDS virus protein [work of Manuel A. Navia] R. Weiss. *Science News* 135:100 F 18 '89
Functional analysis of CAR, the target sequence for the Rev protein of HIV-1. E. T. Dayton and others. bibl f il *Science* 246:1625-9 D 22 '89
Fusion factor in AIDS cells identified [role of leukocyte adhesion receptor LFA-1 in syncytium formation; research by James E. K. Hildreth and Rimas J. Orentas] *Science News* 135:366 Je 10 '89
Herpesvirus may boost AIDS expression [study of T cells by Paolo Lusso and Robert C. Gallo] K. Fackelmann. *Science News* 135:55 Ja 28 '89
HIV can linger years with no antibodies [research by David T. Imagawa] R. Weiss. *Science News* 135:340 Je 3 '89

HIV with reduced sensitivity to zidovudine (AZT) isolated during prolonged therapy. B. A. Larder and others. bibl f il *Science* 243:1731-4 Mr 31 '89
Human chromosome 12 is required for elevated HIV-1 expression in human-hamster hybrid cells. C. E. Hart and others. bibl f il *Science* 246:488-91 O 27 '89
The human mouse [infection of SCID-hu mouse by HIV; work of M. McCune; cover story; with editorial comment by Paul Hoffman] G. Montgomery. il por *Discover* 10:4, 48-55 Ag '89
Identification of the fusion peptide of primate immunodeficiency viruses. M. L. Bosch and others. bibl f il *Science* 244:694-7 My 12 '89
Inhibition of antigen-induced lymphocyte proliferation by Tat protein from HIV-1. R. P. Viscidi and others. bibl f il *Science* 246:1606-8 D 22 '89
Interferon-α but not AZT suppresses HIV expression in chronically infected cell lines. G. Poli and others. bibl f il *Science* 244:575-7 My 5 '89
Involvement of a leukocyte adhesion receptor (LFA-1) in HIV-induced syncytium formation. J. E. K. Hildreth and R. J. Orentas. bibl f il *Science* 244:1075-8 Je 2 '89
The MHC-binding and gp120-binding functions of CD4 are separable. D. Lamarre and others. bibl f il *Science* 245:743-6 Ag 18 '89
Molecular modeling of the HIV-1 protease and its substrate binding site. I. T. Weber and others. bibl f il *Science* 243:928-31 F 17 '89
Multiple mutations in HIV-1 reverse transcriptase confer high-level resistance to zidovudine (AZT). B. A. Larder and S. D. Kemp. bibl f il *Science* 246:1155-8 D 1 '89
My life stalking AIDS. R. C. Gallo. il por *Discover* 10:30-3+ O '89
The mystery of 'silent' AIDS infections [deficiencies of standard test] J. Seligmann. il *Newsweek* 113:59 Je 12 '89
NCI team remodels key AIDS virus enzyme. J. L. Marx. il *Science* 245:598 Ag 11 '89
Plasma HIV reflects AIDS progression. K. Fackelmann. *Science News* 136:389 D 16 '89
The reservoir for HIV-1 in human peripheral blood is a T cell that maintains expression of CD4. S. M. Schnittman and others. bibl f il *Science* 245:305-8 Jl 21 '89
Scientists find new HIV-host subtleties. R. Weiss. *Science News* 135:357 Je 10 '89
Shooting the messenger [antisense RNA prevents HIV virus production; research by Jack Cohen] G. Montgomery. il *Discover* 10:32 N '89
Silent AIDS [deficiencies of antibody test] *Time* 133:61 Je 12 '89
A single amino acid interchange yields reciprocal CTL specificities for HIV-1 gp160. H. Takahashi and others. bibl f il *Science* 246:118-21 O 6 '89
Structure of complex of synthetic HIV-1 protease with a substrate-based inhibitor at 2.3 Å resolution. M. Miller and others. bibl f il *Science* 246:1149-52 D 1 '89
Synergism between HIV gp120 and gp120-specific antibody in blocking human T cell activation. R. S. Mittler and M. K. Hoffmann. bibl f il *Science* 245:1380-2 S 22 '89
tat's surprising [HIV protein may derange functioning of cells] R. Rusting. *Scientific American* 260:30+ Mr '89
The virus strikes back [AZT-resistant strains] P. Gadsby. il *Discover* 10:20 Jl '89
Where AIDS takes aim [macrophages; work of Howard Gendelman and Monte Meltzer] P. Gadsby. il *Discover* 10:52-3 Ja '89

HIZZONER! [drama] *See* Shyre, Paul
HJELMELAND, ANDY
Is a rap sheet a legacy? por *Newsweek* 113:10 My 15 '89
HLASEK, JAKOB
about
Jakob climbs the ladder. D. Rosenbaum. il por *World Tennis* 36:8 F '89
HLEBOWITSH, PETER S.
International comparisons and U.S. school reform. *The Education Digest* 55:23-7 N '89
HMONG (ASIAN PEOPLE)
A new collectible art form: the pau dau. R. P. Anjard. il *Antiques & Collecting Hobbies* 94:69 Jl '89
United States
Garden secrets from the Hmong [Montana] C. J. Morris. il *Flower and Garden* 33:36-8 Mr/Ap '89
HMOS *See* Health maintenance organizations
HNATYSHYN, RAMON
about
The Queen's man. M. Clark. il por *Maclean's* 102:16-17 O 16 '89
HO, STANLEY
about
Forging new links. T. Fennell. il pors *Maclean's* 102:26-8 F 20 '89
HO CHI MINH CITY (VIETNAM) *See* Saigon (Vietnam)
HOAGLAND, EDWARD
Buckaroo poets: whoop-ee-ti-yi-yo, git along, little doggerel. il *The New York Times Book Review* 94:3+ Ja 8 '89
Spring. *The Nation* 248:836 Je 19 '89
Too much, too blindly, too fast. il *Harper's* 278:65-8 Je '89
A world worth saving [cover story] il *Life* 12:50-4+ O '89

HOAGLAND, EDWARD—cont.
A writer's journal. *Harper's* 278:30+ F '89
HOAGLAND, K. ELAINE
Global change is key political topic for 1989. *BioScience* 39:151 Mr '89
HOARDING
Hoarding in the Squirrel Society. C. Gordon. il *Maclean's* 102:48 Mr 6 '89
HOATZINS
Alimentary, my dear hoatzin [research by Stuart D. Strahl] R. Cowen. il *Science News* 136:269-70 O 21 '89
Foregut fermentation in the hoatzin, a neotropical leaf-eating bird [cover story] A. Grajal and others. bibl f il *Science* 245:1236-8 S 15 '89
What's a hoatzin? [only bird with foregut fermentation; research by Stuart D. Strahl] J. Horgan. il *Scientific American* 261:30 D '89
HOAXES
See also
    Cardiff giant
Anthropologists debate Tasaday hoax evidence. E. Marshall. il *Science* 246:1113-14 D 1 '89
The Holly Oak shell [discussion of December 2, 1988 article, Mammoth fraud exposed] R. Lewin. *Science* 243:151-2 Ja 13 '89
Pranks a lot! [J. Skaggs] M. Callum. il por *TV Guide* 37:23 Jl 29-Ag 4 '89
The strange case of the Tasaday: were they primitive hunter-gatherers or rain-forest phonies? [cover story] B. Bower. il *Science News* 135:280-1+ My 6 '89
Tasaday controversy grows more curious. B. Bower. *Science News* 136:343 N 25 '89
HOBAN, MICHAEL
about
Leather soul. A. Kahn. il *Vogue* 179:560+ Mr '89
HOBAN, PHOEBE
Design of the dove. il pors *Harper's Bazaar* 122:144-7+ D '89
Getting clean [cover story] il *New York* 22:38-45 F 20 '89
Knit wits. il *New York* 22:46-9 Jl 31 '89
Prodigal son: after the drug bust, Eugene Fodor tries a comeback. il pors *New York* 22:100-2+ D 4 '89
Psycho drama. il pors *New York* 22:40-2+ Je 19 '89
Quick Silver. il pors *New York* 22:72-4+ D 11 '89
Star tech. See occasional issues of New York beginning September 24, 1984
HOBAUGH, MAURICE
about
Hunting for giants. C. Fergus. il pors *Country Journal* 16:56-61 Ja '89
HOBBIE, FRANCES R.
New Jersey's plan for improving education. *The Education Digest* 54:10-12 Ja '89
HOBBIES
See also
    Collectors and collecting
Favorite hobbies of famous faces. il *Ebony* 44:54+ Mr '89
Turning your hobby into a business [cover story; special section] D. E. Gumpert and D. Davis. il *New Choices for the Best Years* 29:47-53 O '89
HOBBIES (PERIODICAL)
A look at an old issue of Hobbies [July 1942] E. Rochette. *Antiques & Collecting Hobbies* 94:64-5 Ap '89
HOBBS, CHARLES R.
How to control the time eaters [excerpt from Time power] *Working Woman* 14:110-11+ My '89
HOBBS, LYNDALL
about
Hobbs's choice. J. Shields. il pors *Vogue* 179:120+ Ap '89
HOBE SOUND NATIONAL WILDLIFE REFUGE (FLA.)
Egging them on [loggerhead turtles] B. Weber. il *The New York Times Magazine* p94 O 1 '89
HOBERMAN, J.
Shelf life [interview with G. Gazdag] il por *Film Comment* 25:50-4+ My/Je '89
HOBHOUSE, JANET, 1948-
Power and flesh [cover story] il por *Art News* 88:112-17 N '89
HOBOES
Catching a westbound freight [traveling with hoboes from Iowa to Washington; cover story] B. Duffy. il map *Harper's* 278:49-55+ Je '89
HOCH, CHARLES, 1948-
When scientists dissent. *Society* 26:8-11 My/Je '89
HOCH, SCOTT
about
Hoch as in choke. R. Reilly. il pors *Sports Illustrated* 70:62-4+ Je 12 '89
HOCHFIELD, SYLVIA
Cast in doubt. il *Art News* 88:108-15 F '89
HOCHMAN, GLORIA
Getting to know my dad . . . again. il *New Choices for the Best Years* 29:82+ Je '89
HOCHMAN, STEVE
(jt. auth) See Petty, Tom, and Hochman, Steve
HOCHSCHILD, ADAM, 1942-
Notes from the former underground. il *Mother Jones* 14:23-6 My '89

HOCHSCHILD, ARLIE RUSSELL, 1940-
The new marriage reality [excerpt from Second shift] il *Glamour* 87:142-5+ Jl '89
about
For working women, having it all may mean doing it all [interview] D. Waggoner. il pors *People Weekly* 32:51+ S 4 '89
The myth of male housework. J. Skow. il *Time* 134:62 Ag 7 '89
Viking to release 'The second shift,' analysis of the two-job marriage. B. Levine. *Publishers Weekly* 235:35-6 Ap 28 '89
Woman's work is never done. J. Miller. il *Newsweek* 114:65 Jl 31 '89
HOCKER, PHILIP, AND UDALL, STEWART L.
What's mined is theirs. il *Sierra* 74:20+ S/O '89
HOCKEY
See also
    Field hockey
    Hockey players
    Table hockey
"I grinned from ear to ear" [playing amateur hockey] N. Santelmann. il *Forbes* 144:278 O 16 '89
The not ready for prime time hockey players [Celebrity All-stars vs. Bruins Legends] S. Harris. il *Sport (New York, N.Y.)* 80:83 Ap '89
Tournaments
Is it nyet or not yet? [V. Fetisov of touring Soviets seeks permission to join NHL] E. M. Swift. il pors *Sports Illustrated* 70:30-3 Ja 16 '89
History
Hello again III [reunion of U.S. 1980 Olympic hockey team] R. Brofman. il *Life* 12:181-3 Fall '89
Soviet Union
The honeymooners [Soviet players in National Hockey League; cover story] J. Greenberg. il *Sports Illustrated* 71:44-8+ O 9 '89
Is it nyet or not yet? [V. Fetisov of touring Soviets seeks permission to join NHL] E. M. Swift. il pors *Sports Illustrated* 70:30-3 Ja 16 '89
A Red-letter day [Soviet Union's S. Priakin makes NHL debut with Calgary] C. Cotton. il por *Sports Illustrated* 70:38-9 Ap 10 '89
Soviet invasion [National Hockey League] J. Howse. il *Maclean's* 102:46-7 O 9 '89
Soviet pretenders to Gretzky's throne [Russian players in National Hockey League] il por *U.S. News & World Report* 107:19 O 30 '89
The winter of discontent. A. Wilson-Smith. il *Maclean's* 102:38-9 F 20 '89
HOCKEY, COLLEGE
The best and the brightest [Harvard] A. Murphy. il *Sports Illustrated* 70:67-8 Ja 30 '89
Tournaments
Minnesota faces were Crimson [Harvard defeats Gophers to win NCAA title] A. Murphy. il *Sports Illustrated* 70:74+ Ap 10 '89
HOCKEY, PROFESSIONAL
See also
    Hockey fans
    Hockey players
    Hockey records
    National Hockey League
Breaking out [New York Rangers] J. Greenberg. il *Sports Illustrated* 71:32-3 N 6 '89
Breaking tradition [Calgary wins Stanley Cup] D. Burke. il *Maclean's* 102:48 Je 5 '89
The Cup heats up [Calgary vs. Montreal] A. Murphy. il *Sports Illustrated* 70:24-6+ My 22 '89
Desperately seeking Stanley [playoff preview] S. Rosenbloom. il *Sport (New York, N.Y.)* 80:62-5 My '89
Dingdong Cup clash [Calgary vs. Montreal] A. Murphy. il *Sports Illustrated* 70:22-3 My 29 '89
The dream series [Montreal and Calgary fight for Cup] J. Howse. il *Maclean's* 102:53 My 29 '89
Dynasty undone [Los Angeles beats Edmonton in playoff series] A. Murphy. il *Sports Illustrated* 70:18-23 Ap 24 '89
Edmonton gets a wake-up call [Oilers vs. Los Angeles Kings in Smythe Division semifinals] A. Murphy. il *Sports Illustrated* 70:26-8+ Ap 17 '89
Fanning the Flames [Calgary] A. Murphy. il *Sports Illustrated* 70:38-40 Mr 13 '89
Montreal goes up in Flames [Calgary wins Stanley Cup] A. Murphy. il *Sports Illustrated* 70:44-7 Je 5 '89
New York, New York . . . New Jersey [Rangers, Islanders, and Devils] J. Rolfe. il *Sport (New York, N.Y.)* 80:34-8 Ja '89
NHL preview 1989-90 [special section] J. Greenberg. il *Sports Illustrated* 71:44-8+ O 9 '89
No rattling the Sabres [Buffalo] J. Greenberg. il pors *Sports Illustrated* 71:40+ D 18 '89
An old habit of the Habs [Montreal vs. Philadelphia in Wales Conference final] A. Murphy. il *Sports Illustrated* 70:34-5 My 15 '89
Puzzling Penguins. J. Greenberg. il por *Sports Illustrated* 71:32-3 N 27 '89

HOCKEY, PROFESSIONAL—*cont.*

The race for first [Calgary Flames] J. Howse. il *Maclean's* 102:56 My 15 '89

The Sport 1989-90 NHL preview. S. Rosenbloom. il *Sport (New York, N.Y.)* 80:24-8+ N '89

Third-degree Burns [Montreal coach P. Burns] A. Murphy. il *Sports Illustrated* 70:50-3 F 27 '89

Toothsome sacrifice [Chicago Blackhawks defeat St. Louis to reach Stanley Cup semifinals] A. Murphy. il *Sports Illustrated* 70:24-6+ My 8 '89

Awards

The 1989 Sport Stanley Cup Finals MVP [A. MacInnis] il por *Sport (New York, N.Y.)* 80:78 Ag '89

Economic aspects

Richard Gordon plays only one way—hard [Whalers' owner] R. W. King. il por *Business Week* p50 Ag 28 '89

Who says Penguins can't fly? [Pittsburgh Penguins] G. L. Miles. il *Business Week* p144-5 Ap 24 '89

Ethical aspects

Fight on [hockey teams turn to boxing trainers for expertise] J. Ryan. il *Sport (New York, N.Y.)* 80:11 My '89

On ice for keeps [NHL bans B. Probert after arrest for importing cocaine] B. Newman. il por *Sports Illustrated* 70:26 Mr 13 '89

Rough the passer, go to jail [implications of the D. Ciccarelli hockey assault decision] S. Rosenbloom. il *Sport (New York, N.Y.)* 80:10 Ja '89

History

'80s hockey. S. Rosenbloom. il por *Sport (New York, N.Y.)* 80:68-9+ O '89

Organization and administration

See also

National Hockey League

Pittsburgh scores [Penguins' revitalization under former general manager E. Johnston] T. Frayne. il por *Maclean's* 102:58-9 My 1 '89

The puck will stop here [what author would do if named commissioner] E. M. Swift. il por *Sports Illustrated* 71:118 O 23 '89

Television broadcasting

See Cable television—Sports; Television broadcasting—Sports

HOCKEY ARENA MODELS *See* Stadium models

HOCKEY CARDS

Making a profitable nostalgia trip. D. Francis. il *Maclean's* 102:9 Ja 23 '89

HOCKEY COACHES

See also

Burns, Pat

Tikhonov, Viktor

Ubriaco, Gene

HOCKEY FANS

The wild blue yonder [New York Ranger fans] G. Plimpton. il *Sports Illustrated* 70:64-6+ Ap 3 '89

HOCKEY PLAYERS

See also

Ciccarelli, Dino

Enga, Richard J.

Fetisov, Viacheslav

Geary, Derek

Granato, Tony

Gretzky, Wayne

Hextall, Ron

Howe, Gordie

Hull, Brett

Lafleur, Guy, 1951-

Leetch, Brian

Lemieux, Mario

Linden, Trevor

Lindros, Eric

MacInnis, Al

Mullen, Brian

Mullen, Joey

Nedved, Petr

Nelson, Chris

Priakin, Sergei

Richer, Stéphane

Shutt, Steve

Stauber, Robb

Turgeon, Pierre

Wregget, Ken

Yzerman, Steve

The NHL's family feud. A. Strachan. il *Sport (New York, N.Y.)* 80:14 Jl '89

Soul on ice: blacks in the National Hockey League. il *Ebony* 44:84+ F '89

Stressed to kill: playoff pressure turns goalies into strange human beings. S. Rosenbloom. il *Sport (New York, N.Y.)* 80:108-11 Je '89

Age

Drafted at the age of nine [link between birth date and hockey ability; research by Roger Barnsley] J. C. Horn. il *Psychology Today* 23:22+ Ja/F '89

HOCKEY RECORDS

A backhanded compliment [W. Gretzky breaks G. Howe's scoring record] J. Greenberg. il pors *Sports Illustrated* 71:50-3 O 23 '89

Games men play [W. Gretzky closes in on G. Howe's scoring record] H. Quinn. il por *Maclean's* 102:62 O 23 '89

Soviet pretenders to Gretzky's throne. il por *U.S. News & World Report* 107:19 O 30 '89

HOCKIN, TOM

about

Breaking barriers. P. Chisholm. il *Maclean's* 102:24-5 F 13 '89

Into the hands of the powerful. D. Francis. il *Maclean's* 102:9 Mr 6 '89

HOCKNEY, DAVID

about

David Hockney's melodic palette. il por *U.S. News & World Report* 107:70-1 N 13 '89

Hockney's Hollywood. D. Thomson. il pors *Film Comment* 25:53-63+ Jl/Ag '89

HODENFIELD, CHRIS

The editing room. See issues of American Film

HODES, RICHARD J., AND OTHERS

Failure of T cell receptor V$_\beta$ negative selection in an athymic environment. bibl f il *Science* 246:1041-4 N 24 '89

HODES, STUART

Transforming dance history: the lost history of rehearsals. bibl f *Design for Arts in Education* 91:10-17 N/D '89

HODGE, FRANCIS P.

Taking the drill out of reading. il *Publishers Weekly* 235:99-100 Ja 20 '89

HODGE, HAMILTON

about

True craftiness. il por *Vogue* 179:112+ My '89

HODGE, MARIE

Teach your kids about money. il *Reader's Digest* 134:54-8 Ja '89

(jt. auth) See Blyskal, Jeff, and Hodge, Marie

HODGE, MARIE, AND BLYSKAL, JEFF

How to help your child choose the right career. il *Reader's Digest* 134:146-8+ F '89

Make the most of your weekends. il *Reader's Digest* 134:9-10+ Ap '89

Who says college campuses are safe? il *Reader's Digest* 135:141-2+ O '89

HODGES, ELAINE R. S.

Scientific illustration: a working relationship between the scientist and artist [cover story] bibl f il *BioScience* 39:104-11 F '89

HODGES, GREGG

An anchorite's lament [poem] *The New Republic* 200:35 F 27 '89

A music [poem] *The New Republic* 201:38 Ag 28 '89

The two cities [poem] *The New Republic* 200:34 My 29 '89

HODGES, HAROLD MELLOR, JR.

On surviving the day after tomorrow. *The Humanist* 49:25-9+ My/Je '89

HODGES, MICHAEL H.

No gays, please, we're British. *The Nation* 248:156-60 F 6 '89

HODGES, PETER

Direct-response selling for the 1990s. il *Publishers Weekly* 235:260+ My 12 '89

HODGES, RALPH

The high end. See issues of Stereo Review beginning June 1984

HODGINS, WILLIAM

about

Back Bay reflections. G. Harrell. il por *House & Garden* 161:206-9 S '89

HODGKIN, HOWARD, 1932-

about

Howard Hodgkin: Knoedler. M. Moorman. il *Art News* 88:129 Ja '89

HODGKIN'S DISEASE

"My husband healed me with love" [case of T. Nelson] J. Wolf. il pors *Redbook* 173:76+ O '89

Therapy

A portrait of healing [use of imagery to combat side effects of chemotherapy] J. Kaplan. il *Omni (New York, N.Y.)* 11:110-12 F '89

HODGSON, BRIAN

about

Clamscam. F. Graham. *Audubon* 91:8+ N '89

HODGSON, JANE

about

Jane Hodgson's odyssey. *U.S. News & World Report* 107:26 D 4 '89

HODIN, RICHARD A., AND OTHERS

Identification of a thyroid hormone receptor that is pituitary-specific. bibl f il *Science* 244:76-9 Ap 7 '89

HODSOLL, FRANK, 1938-

Toward civilization: next responsibilities. *Design for Arts in Education* 90:10-15 Ja/F '89

HOE AVENUE COMMUNITY TENNIS CENTER (BRONX, N.Y.) *See* Tennis centers

HOECHST AG

Court blocks German biotech plant. B. Bachtler. *Science* 246:881 N 17 '89

HOEFT, JACK
about
Hoeft is new president of Bantam Doubleday Dell. D. Maryles. por *Publishers Weekly* 236:9 N 17 '89
HOEHME, GERHARD, 1920-
about
Gerhard Hoehme at Stux. K. Johnson. *Art in America* 77:203-4 S '89
HOEK, ELS
Mondrian in Disneyland. bibl f il *Art in America* 77:136-43+ F '89
HOEKEMA, DAVID A.
The B-2: winning weapon of the last war. *The Christian Century* 106:772-3 Ag 30-S 6 '89
HOEPPNER, GABRIELLE
The pet food dilemma. il *The Saturday Evening Post* 261:26+ O '89
HOERBURGER, ROB
D.J. Jazzy Jeff & the Fresh Prince. il *Seventeen* 48:97-8+ My '89
HOESCH, HENNING
about
A Provençal tale: the house and vineyards of Richeaume. D. H. Minassian. il *Architectural Digest* 46:136-41 Ja '89
HOESCHELE, JOHN P.
A new look at the uncommon common crow. il *The Conservationist* 43:16-19 Mr/Ap '89
HOFFA, HARLAN
Television, cultural history, and arts education. *Design for Arts in Education* 90:15-22 Mr/Ap '89
HOFFENBERG, MARK R.
Falling apartheid. *The New Republic* 201:16-17 Jl 31 '89
HOFFER, MARILYN
(jt. auth) See Hoffer, William, and Hoffer, Marilyn
HOFFER, RICHARD
Lord of the rings. il pors *Sports Illustrated* 71:104-8+ D 11 '89
Still hungry after all these years [cover story] il pors *Sports Illustrated* 71:60-6+ Jl 17 '89
They never gave up. il pors *Sports Illustrated* 71:117-27+ D 25 '89-Ja 1 '90
about
From the publisher. D. J. Barr. il por *Sports Illustrated* 71:4 D 11 '89
HOFFER, WILLIAM
Made in the U.S.A. il por maps *Popular Mechanics* 166:58-60+ My '89
HOFFER, WILLIAM, AND HOFFER, MARILYN
Free fall [condensation] il *Reader's Digest* 134:197-202+ Ap '89
HOFFMAN, ABBIE
Passages [excerpt from Soon to be a major motion picture] il por *Utne Reader* p37 Jl/Ag '89
The young have to be there. il *The Progressive* 53:15 Je '89
about
A message to Abbie Hoffman. P. Krassner. *Utne Reader* p113-15 N/D '89
Obituary
The Nation 248:798+ Je 12 '89
The Nation 248:616 My 8 '89. P. Krassner
National Review 41:14 My 19 '89
The New Yorker 65:26 My 1 '89
Newsweek il pors 113:42 Ap 24 '89. D. Gates
People Weekly il pors 31:100-2+ My 1 '89. J. S. Kunen
Rolling Stone por p49 Je 1 '89. D. Handelman
Time il por 133:23 Ap 24 '89. R. Lacayo
U.S. News & World Report il pors 106:18+ Ap 24 '89
U.S. News & World Report il por 106:61 My 15 '89. J. Leo
HOFFMAN, CARL
(jt. auth) See Page, Jake, and Hoffman, Carl
HOFFMAN, DAVE
about
Broadcast newsman. J. Hester. il por *New York* 22:26 S 4 '89
HOFFMAN, DUSTIN, 1937-
about
Dustin Hoffman is testing his mettle as Shylock on Broadway. J. Heilpern. il *Vogue* 179:198+ O '89
Dustin Hoffman takes a risky shot at Shakespeare. il por *People Weekly* 31:101 Je 19 '89
Who's on first? D. Ansen. il pors *Newsweek* 113:52-6 Ja 16 '89
HOFFMAN, FREDDIE
about
Mileage junkies. S. Martin. il pors *Bicycling* 30:48-50+ Ap '89
HOFFMAN, JAN
TV's new golden girl. il pors *Gentlemen's Quarterly* 59:232-5+ Je '89
HOFFMAN, KENNETH, 1930-, AND STEEN, LYNN ARTHUR, 1941-
Making math education effective. il *Technology Review* 92:22+ N/D '89

HOFFMAN, MICHAEL
about
Some girls [film] Reviews
Newsweek il 113:67 Ap 3 '89. D. Ansen
HOFFMAN, PAUL
From the editor. See issues of Discover beginning September 1987
HOFFMAN, PETER
about
Valentino returns [film] Reviews
People Weekly il 32:11-12 Jl 31 '89. R. Novak
HOFFMAN, STEPHEN L., AND OTHERS
Sporozoite vaccine induces genetically restricted T cell elimination of malaria from hepatocytes. bibl f il *Science* 244:1078-81 Je 2 '89
HOFFMAN-RIEM, CHRISTA
Disclosing adoption. *Society* 26:26-31 My/Je '89
HOFFMANN, MICHAEL K.
(jt. auth) See Mittler, Robert S., and Hoffmann, Michael K.
HOFFMANN, OSWALD C. J.
about
Lutheran power [interview] por *Christianity Today* 33:29 N 3 '89
HOFFMANN, REINHILD
about
Machandel [dance] Reviews
New York 22:109 O 30 '89. T. Tobias
HOFFMANN, STANLEY
Do nuclear weapons matter? bibl f il *The New York Review of Books* 36:28-31 F 2 '89
'Do nuclear weapons matter?': an exchange [discussion of February 2, 1989 article] il *The New York Review of Books* 36:57-8 Ap 27 '89
The European Community and 1992. *Foreign Affairs* 68:27-47 Fall '89
The perfect in-and-outer. bibl f il *The New York Review of Books* 36:13-17 N 23 '89
What should we do in the world? il *The Atlantic* 264:84-8+ O '89
HOFFMANN, STEPHEN A.
Self-care: don't bypass your doctor. por *American Health* 8:83-4 Je '89
UTI's: everything you need to know about urinary tract woes. il *American Health* 8:72-6 Ap '89
HOFFMANN-LA ROCHE INC.
Just what the doctor ordered [plan to recapitalize by splitting stock] J. Greenwald. il *Time* 133:68 My 8 '89
HOFFS, SUSANNA
about
Bangle Susanna Hoffs and actor Donovan Leitch, son of just plain Donovan, mellow together. P. Freeman. il pors *People Weekly* 31:73-4+ Je 12 '89
HOFMANN, ISABELLA
about
Do you know this actress? . . . She thinks you don't. G. Dillow. il pors *TV Guide* 37:25-6+ N 25-D 1 '89
HOFMANN (ALBERT) FOUNDATION See Albert Hofmann Foundation
HOFMANNSTHAL, HUGO VON, 1874-1929
about
The other Frau. S. R. Cerf. il *Opera News* 54:38-9+ D 9 '89
HOFSTADTER, DAN
The far-reaching eye of Venice's Antonio Canaletto. bibl (p245) il *Smithsonian* 20:78-86+ N '89
In one great swoop, country bumpkin to Royal Academy. bibl f (p174) il por *Smithsonian* 20:122-6+ Je '89
Profiles (I) [H. Cartier-Bresson] por *The New Yorker* 65:59-60+ O 23 '89
Profiles (II) [H. Cartier-Bresson] il *The New Yorker* 65:49-52+ O 30 '89
HOFSTADTER, RICHARD, 1916-1970
about
Resurrecting liberalism. B. DeMott. *Current (Washington, D.C.)* 309:14-22 Ja '89
HOG HOUSES See Swine houses
HOGAN, BARBARA, AND ALLEN, BARBARA
Upstairs, downstairs—the ozone dilemma. il *The Conservationist* 44:16-21 N/D '89
HOGAN, CANDACE LYLE
Off & running. il *Runner's World* 24:46-50 My '89
HOGAN, HULK
about
Look out, Hulk—'Macho Man' wants revenge. J. Martel. il pors *TV Guide* 37:20-2 Jl 29-Ag 4 '89
HOGAN, SHERRY HEMMAN
Child's play. il *Reader's Digest* 134:29-30+ Mr '89
HOGE VELUWE NATIONAL PARK (NETHERLANDS)
Country charms [Kroller-Muller Museum's sculpture garden] M. K. Talley, Jr. il *Art News* 88:77-8 Summ '89
HOGS See Swine
HOGS, WILD See Wild boars
HOGUE, WILLIAM P.
My imaginary child. il *Glamour* 87:284 My '89

HOHENDORF, PAUL
about
Before he goes out on a date, Paul Hohendorf has a simple request: 'Just the fax, Ma'am'. il por *People Weekly* 31:107 F 20 '89

HOIG, STAN
The great Oklahoma Land Rush of 1889. il map *American History Illustrated* 24:40-50 Mr '89

HOISTING EQUIPMENT
See also
Winches

HOLBERT, AL
about
Obituary
Car and Driver por 34:141 F '89. L. Griffin
Road & Track il por 40:103 F '89

HOLBROOKE, RICHARD
A dilemma for Washington. il *Newsweek* 113:32 Je 12 '89

HOLDEN, ANN
about
On Audubon Place. N. McKeon. il *House & Garden* 161:94-7+ Ja '89

HOLDEN, ANTHONY, 1947-
Charles and Diana: portrait of a marriage [excerpt from King Charles III] il pors *Ladies' Home Journal* 106:115-17+ F '89

HOLDEN, DONALD, 1931-
about
Donald Holden. M. S. Doherty. il por *American Artist* 53:38-43+ Ap '89

HOLDEN, EDITH, 1871-1920
about
Paradise regained. L. Fleischer. *Publishers Weekly* 235:19 Mr 31 '89

HOLDEN, MARK
Acoustics at Anchorage. il *Architectural Record* 177:106-10 Ap '89

HOLDEN, NATE
about
His object a gentler L.A., a councilman buys up AK-47s. il por *People Weekly* 31:120 F 13 '89

HOLDER, DENNIS
Indie angst in teetering Texas. il *Channels (New York, N.Y.: 1986)* 9:71-3 Ja '89

HOLDER, GEOFFREY
about
Geoffrey Holder. M. S. Doherty. il por *American Artist* 53:38-43 N '89

HOLDER, LEE J.
(jt. auth) See McTernan, Edmund, and Holder, Lee J.

HOLDER, RICHARD G.
The global corporation [address, October 2, 1989] *Vital Speeches of the Day* 56:98-100 D 1 '89

HOLDERS, NAPKIN See Napkin rings, holders, etc.

HOLDGATE, MARTIN W.
Planning for our common future. bibl f *Environment* 31:14-17+ O '89

HOLDING COMPANIES
See also
Bank holding companies
Personal holding companies

HOLDING DEVICES (MACHINE WORK)
See also
Clamps
Jigs (Tools)
Vises

HOLE-IN-THE-WALL GANG CAMP
New frontier [design by Hammond Beeby and Babka] K. D. Stein. il *Architectural Record* 177:86-91 Ja '89
Newman's own [designed by Hammond Beeby and Babka] J. Giovannini. il *House & Garden* 161:22+ Je '89

HOLES IN ONE (GOLF)
Those fabulous four aces [U.S. Open] R. Reilly. il *Sports Illustrated* 70:24-5 Je 26 '89

HOLIDAY, BILLIE, 1915-1959
about
Don't worry 'bout me. J. Berendt. por *Esquire* 112:50 O '89
Sparrow in the sky. H. Mandel. il por *Down Beat* 56:60 Jl '89

HOLIDAY CORP.
For these companies, debt was just what the doctor ordered. M. D. Oneal and others. il *Business Week* p90-1 S 11 '89

HOLIDAY DEPRESSION SYNDROME See Depression, Mental

HOLIDAY ENTERTAINING See Christmas entertaining; Entertaining

HOLIDAY TABLE DECORATION See Table decoration

HOLIDAYS
See also
Christmas
Festivals
Fourth of July
Halloween
Kwanzaa
Martin Luther King Day
Memorial Day
New Year
Thanksgiving Day
Vacations
Valentine's Day
Gobble, gobble [eating sensibly during the holidays] E. Coleman. il *Bicycling* 30:78 D '89
High days and holidays [cover story; special issue] il *The Unesco Courier* 42:8-46 D '89
Holiday ailments: causes and cures. L. Holland. il *Good Housekeeping* 208:167 Ja '89
Holiday guidelines [brochure Religious holidays in the public schools: questions and answers] *Christianity Today* 33:70 N 17 '89
Holiday weather 1988. D. M. Ludlum. *Country Journal* 16:19-20 N/D '89
Holiday weight watching. il *Seventeen* 48:78-9 D '89
Holiday willpower [dancers] J. Scala. il *Dance Magazine* 63:64-5 D '89
How to avoid holiday overindulgence. il *USA Today (Periodical)* 118:10 N '89
Pagan holidays mark earth's yearly cycles. T. Knepher. *Utne Reader* p74-5 N/D '89
Richard Simmons' New Year's revolution [holiday season dieting] P. Perry. il por *The Saturday Evening Post* 261:58-9+ Ja/F '89

HOLINESS
Calling. P. J. Ryan. *America* 160:71 Ja 28 '89

HOLINESS CHURCHES
See also
Church of God
Snake handling (Holiness churches)

HOLINESS FELLOWSHIP OF AMERICA
Trouble brews over charges of "liberalism". D. Disch. por *Christianity Today* 33:42-3 F 17 '89

HOLING, DWIGHT
Outback odyssey. il *New Choices for the Best Years* 29:50-6 S '89
Plain dealing. il map *Sierra* 74:142-7 Ja/F '89

HOLISTIC DENTISTRY
On the cuspid. C. Reuben. il *Ms.* 17:16+ Je '89

HOLISTIC MEDICINE
See also
Wellness Community
Healthy insurance [insurance and alternative medicine] J. F. Wasik. il *Mother Jones* 14:53-4 My '89
The other doctors. J. Bushman. il *Women's Sports & Fitness* 11:10-11 Mr '89

HOLISTIC RESOURCE MANAGEMENT
Reading rangeland. J. Walter. il *Successful Farming* 87:48 F '89

HOLL, STEVEN, 1947-
about
A dreamer who is fussy about the details. K. Andersen. il por *Time* 133:75-6 Mr 20 '89
Holl and Ambasz, in a manner of speaking. R. Kimball. il *Architectural Record* 177:51+ Ap '89
The new faces of modernism on show. il *Architectural Record* 177:47 Mr '89

HOLLAND, BARBARA
'Millard Fillmore was my kind of guy'. il *Smithsonian* 20:238 O '89

HOLLAND, BARRY
Searching for researchers. il *World Press Review* 36:54 Ja '89

HOLLAND, DAVE
about
Dave Holland: creative collaborator. H. Mandel. il pors *Down Beat* 56:20-3 O '89

HOLLAND, E. L.
By dawn's early light. il *Petersen's Photographic Magazine* 18:36-9 D '89

HOLLAND, JOOLS
about
'Sunday night': uncut Jools. B. Flanagan. il por *Rolling Stone* p42+ F 9 '89

HOLLAND, KEATING
Who's first? Good Catholics, good fans. *Commonweal* 116:582-3 N 3 '89

HOLLAND, KIM N.
(jt. auth) See Bushnell, Peter G., and Holland, Kim N.

HOLLAND, LULA
(jt. auth) See Blumenthal, Dale, and Holland, Lula

HOLLAND, MAX, AND NOVAK, VIVECA
Buyouts: the LBO lobby makes its move on Washington [cover story] il *Common Cause Magazine* 15:13-20 S/O '89

HOLLAND, ROBERT G.
The New Dominion. il *National Review* 41:25+ S 29 '89

HOLLAND See Netherlands

HOLLANDER, JOHN
From out of the black [poem] *The Nation* 248:568 Ap 24 '89
Ghazals [poem] *The Nation* 249:68 Jl 10 '89
Into the black [poem] *The Nation* 248:568 Ap 24 '89
An old counting-game [poem] *The New York Review of Books* 36:4 F 2 '89
An old-fashioned song [poem] *The New Republic* 200:30 Mr 27 '89

HOLLANDER, JOHN—cont.
Summer day [poem] *The New Yorker* 65:28 Ag 14 '89
HOLLANDER, PAUL
Social science and social problems in Hungary. *Society* 26:14-21 Ja/F '89
HOLLEIN, HANS, 1934-
Architects' dialogue. il pors *Architectural Digest* 46:72+ Ap '89
HOLLENHORST, LINDA
Growin' bananas. il por *Organic Gardening* 36:54-6+ S '89
HOLLERITH, HERMAN
　　　about
The history of census tabulation. K. S. Reid-Green. bibl il *Scientific American* 260:98-103 F '89
HOLLICK, JULIAN CRANDALL
Pilot error. *The New Republic* 201:13-14 D 4 '89
HOLLIDAY, R. (ROBIN)
A different kind of inheritance. bibl il *Scientific American* 260:60-5+ Je '89
HOLLIDAY, ROBIN *See* Holliday, R. (Robin)
HOLLIFIELD, JOHN
　　　about
Magnesium for farm animals [interview] C. SerVaas. il *The Saturday Evening Post* 261:102 Jl/Ag '89
HOLLINGER, INC.
Media barons are making pilgrimages to Jerusalem [C. M. Black buys Jerusalem post] J. Rossant and N. Sandler. il por *Business Week* p50 My 15 '89
HOLLINGS, ERNEST F., 1922-
Should the Congress adopt the "Financial Institutions Reform, Recovery, and Enforcement Act of 1989"? [excerpts from address, April 19, 1989] *Congressional Digest* 68:171 Je/Jl '89
Should the Congress adopt the "Textile and Apparel Trade Act of 1987"? [excerpts from address, September 15, 1988] *Congressional Digest* 68:12+ Ja '89
　　　about
First and only black to head U.S. Senate committee staff joins 400-lawyer firm. il pors *Jet* 77:37 O 16 '89
HOLLINGSWORTH, JOHN D.
　　　about
American Gothic. V. Contavespi. il pors *Forbes* 144 Special Issue:34-6+ O 23 '89
HOLLINGSWORTH (JOHN D.) ON WHEELS *See* John D. Hollingsworth on Wheels
HOLLIS, ANDREW J., AND MITTON, JACQUELINE
European amateurs study Titan. il *Astronomy* 17:52-4 N '89
HOLLIS, DAVID W.
Fish carvings at Creel Creek. il pors *The Conservationist* 43:36-9 My/Je '89
The snag in Pulaski. il map *Country Journal* 16:68-71+ S/O '89
HOLLIS, PETER B.
　　　about
How Ames is digesting its 'whale'. C. Tucher. il *Business Week* p62 S 11 '89
HOLLITT, RAYE
　　　about
Why she's not saying, 'coffee, tea or milk?'. J. Marion. por *TV Guide* 37:17 O 28-N 3 '89
HOLLOM, CHUCK
　　　about
Fare's fare, but when cabdriver Chuck Hollom goes off the meter, criminals had better look out. W. Plummer. il pors *People Weekly* 32:97-8 S 25 '89
HOLLOWAY, DAVID, 1943-
Gorbachev's new thinking. bibl f *Foreign Affairs* 68 Special Issue:66-81 ['89]
HOLLOWAY, NIGEL
Struggling for financial dominance. *World Press Review* 36:15-17 Ap '89
HOLLOWAY, TREVOR
Eling Tide Mill. bibl il map *Sea Frontiers* 35:114-19 Mr/Ap '89
HOLLY FARMS FOODS, INC.
Don Tyson wins Holly Farms, but his debts aren't chicken feed. K. Kelly. il por *Business Week* p29-30 Jl 10 '89
Flying feathers in the coop [Holly Farms makes lockup deal with ConAgra to prevent takeover by Tyson Foods] il *Time* 133:52 F 6 '89
Shareholders say 'thanks' to these CEOs [R. L. Taylor and A. Born] D. Foust and M. Roman. il pors *Business Week* p48 My 1 '89
HOLLYDAY, CHRIS
　　　about
Christopher Hollyday. J. Levenson. il por *Down Beat* 56:15 S '89
HOLLYWOOD (CALIF.)
　　See also
　　Walk of Fame (Hollywood, Calif.)
　　　Architecture
The Coast [luxury homes] G. Stone. il *Gentlemen's Quarterly* 59:87 Ja '89

　　　Crime
The 'Cotton Club' murder: cocaine and hit men in Hollywood—a 1980s film noir [B. Evans implicated in murder of R. Radin; cover story] J. Kasindorf. il pors *New York* 22:24-33 Jl 24 '89
Letter from Los Angeles [Cotton Club murder case] J. Didion. *The New Yorker* 65:92-9 S 4 '89
　　　Description
Ticket to Hollywood [computer game combines movie trivia and walking tour] T. A. Summers. il *Home Office Computing* 7:84 Mr '89
Ticket to Hollywood [computer game combining movie trivia and walking tour] D. English. il *Compute!* 11:77-8 My '89
　　　Anecdotes, facetiae, satire, etc.
Star trek [Hollywood bike tour] D. Cuerdon. il *Bicycling* 30:66-8 D '89
　　　Education
Michael Jackson gets award from his sixth grade teacher in L.A. il pors *Jet* 77:29 O 30 '89
　　　Gardens and gardening
Hollywood garden tour. L. Fears. il *Ladies' Home Journal* 106:126-30 Jl '89
　　　Historic houses, sites, etc.
A thirties revival [home of H. and R. Wilkinson in the Hollywood Hills] G. Greene. il *Architectural Digest* 46:194-201+ Mr '89
　　　Housing
Hollywood's most outrageous homes. M. Beck. il *TV Guide* 37:10-12+ Ag 12-18 '89
　　　Industries
　　See also
　　Motion picture industry
　　Television industry
The hired and the mighty. E. Stern. il *Gentlemen's Quarterly* 59:242-7+ Je '89
　　　Photographs and photography
Hometown: Hollywood [work of D. Strick] M. Kiwak. il *Petersen's Photographic Magazine* 18:27-9 My '89
　　　Social life and customs
The Coast. G. Stone. See issues of Gentlemen's Quarterly beginning September 1988
How to succeed in Hollywood [networking] I. Chubbuck. il *TV Guide* 37:14-16 O 28-N 3 '89
Pretty poison: Anne Crawford skewers Hollywood [gossip columnist for L.A. style] E. J. Carroll. il *Mademoiselle* 95:202-3+ O '89
　　　Anecdotes, facetiae, satire, etc.
A day. B. Stein. il *The American Spectator* 22:30-1 S '89
HOLLYWOOD BLACKLISTING PERIOD *See* Blacklisting
HOLLYWOOD PARK (INGLEWOOD, CALIF.: RACE TRACK)
Is Hollywood Park on the way to the glue factory? K. Kerwin. il *Business Week* p36 My 29 '89
HOLLYWOOD RECORDS (FIRM)
Add records to Disney's world. *Newsweek* 114:72 D 11 '89
Disney music that isn't Mickey Mouse. *U.S. News & World Report* 107:17-18 D 11 '89
HOLLYWOOD STUNTMEN'S HALL OF FAME (MOAB, UTAH)
Fame for fall guys. M. Durham. il map *Americana* 17:36-9 N/D '89
HOLLYWOOD WOMEN'S POLITICAL COMMITTEE
Choice cuts. A. Ferguson. il *The American Spectator* 22:56 Je '89
HOLM, PETER
　　　about
Living in a land of extremes. E. Pennisi. il por *National Wildlife* 27:14-21 Ap/My '89
HOLMAN, JOHN
Monroe's wedding [story] *The New Yorker* 64:32-7 F 6 '89
HOLMAN, M. CARL
　　　about
Obituary
　　American Visions por 4:10 F '89. B. Barnes
HOLMER, ALAN F., AND BELLO, JUDITH HIPPLER
The 1988 trade bill. *Department of State Bulletin* 89:11-14 Mr '89
HOLMES, DAMON
　　　about
Your friend at the IRS. K. McCormally. il *Changing Times* 43:98 Ja '89
HOLMES, DARRYL
For the same reasons [poem] *Essence* 20:152 S '89
Praise poem [poem] *Essence* 20:134 O '89
Somewhere in the dark [poem] *Essence* 20:146 S '89
HOLMES, H. ALLEN
Biological weapons proliferation [statement, May 17, 1989] *Department of State Bulletin* 89:43-5 Jl '89
Foreign policy implications of biological weapons [statement, July 26, 1989] *Department of State Bulletin* 89:22-4 O '89
FY 1990 security assistance request [statement, March 8, 1989] *Department of State Bulletin* 89:52-4 Je '89

HOLMES, JOHN, D. 1988
about
The devil and John Holmes: drugs, porn and the murders on Wonderland Avenue. M. Sager. il pors *Rolling Stone* p50-2+ Je 15 '89

HOLMES, LARRY
about
Larry Holmes' champion season. C. Meth. il por *Video* 13:18 D '89

HOLMES, MARIAN SMITH
The quest for a black museum. il *American Visions* 4:44-8 D '89

HOLMES, OLIVER WENDELL, 1841-1935
about
Shouting "Fire!". A. M. Dershowitz. il pors *The Atlantic* 263:72-4 Ja '89

HOLMES, SAFIYA HENDERSON- See Henderson-Holmes, Safiya

HOLMES, STEVEN
Retreat on civil rights? il *American Visions* 4:20-4 O '89

HOLMES, SHERLOCK (FICTIONAL CHARACTER) See Sherlock Holmes (Fictional character)

HOLOCAUST, JEWISH (1939-1945)
See also
Auschwitz (Poland: Concentration camp)
Children of Holocaust survivors
Dachau (Germany: Concentration camp)
Kristallnacht, 1938
World War, 1939-1945—War criminals
After the Holocaust [Poland] A. Wilson-Smith. il *Maclean's* 102:51-2 S 4 '89
Catholics and Jews: can we bridge the abyss? [Holocaust martyr E. Stein; adaptation of address, October 16, 1988] S. M. Batzdorff. *America* 160:223-4+ Mr 11 '89
The complete Anne Frank. A. Pons. *World Press Review* 36:73 D '89
Courage to face the truth of the Holocaust [special section] *Society* 26:4-9 Mr/Ap '89
Dreaming of Hitler. D. Merkin. il *Esquire* 112:75-8+ Ag '89
Evidence for a moral tradition [rescuers of Jews during the Holocaust; study by Samuel Oliner] A. Kohn. il *Psychology Today* 23:72-3 Ja/F '89
Healthy talk among Holocaust survivors [study by James W. Pennebaker] *Science News* 136:271 O 21 '89
His brother's keeper [Ukrainian peasant A. Suchinsky honored for hiding Zeiger family] S. Schlegel. *Reader's Digest* 134:112-14 F '89
A lost chance to save the Jews? [failure of German Christianity] C. C. O'Brien. il *The New York Review of Books* 36:27-8+ Ap 27 '89
A lost prisoner of the gulag still holds Moscow hostage [R. Wallenberg case] D. Stanglin. il pors *U.S. News & World Report* 106:34-6 Je 26 '89
Moral heroes of our time: Christian rescuers. E. Fogelman. *America* 161:426-8+ D 9 '89
A pain-filled mystery [Holocaust hero R. Wallenberg] J. Bierman. por *Maclean's* 102:47 O 30 '89
Poland: the ghosts of Jews [excerpt from Mad dreams, saving graces] M. T. Kaufman. il *Commonweal* 116:429-32 Ag 11 '89
The repressed road to trauma recovery [lack of dream recall in Holocaust survivors; research by Peretz Lavie] B. Bower. *Science News* 136:4 Jl 1 '89
War and remembrance: a new entry from Anne Frank [commemoration of her sixtieth birthday] J. Hendel. il por *Seventeen* 48:112-13 Je '89

Caricatures and cartoons
Art Spiegelman [interview] C. Dreifus. il *The Progressive* 53:34-7 N '89

Conferences
Why I won't go to Germany. C. Ozick. *Harper's* 278:16-19 F '89

Exhibitions
See also
U.S. Holocaust Memorial Museum

Historiography
German historians at war. J. Z. Muller. bibl f *Commentary* 87:33-41 My '89
The Holocaust: why the Jews? [book by A. Mayer] T. Jacoby. il por *Newsweek* 113:64-5 My 15 '89
Looking into the mirror of history. R. von Weizsäcker. *Society* 26:6-7 Mr/Ap '89
Perversions of the Holocaust [views of A. Mayer] L. S. Dawidowicz. *Commentary* 88:56-60 O '89
PW interviews [historian L. S. Dawidowicz] W. Gelles. por *Publishers Weekly* 235:264-5 My 12 '89

Memorials
See also
U.S. Holocaust Memorial Museum

Reporters and reporting
In days gone by. M. E. Marty. *The Christian Century* 106:295 Mr 15 '89

HOLOCAUST, JEWISH (1939-1945), IN DRAMA
A conversation with Israeli playwright Joshua Sobol. G. G. Seibert. *America* 160:559-62 Je 10 '89

HOLOCAUST, JEWISH (1939-1945), IN LITERATURE
Haggling presences. D. Donoghue. il *The New York Review of Books* 36:39-43 S 28 '89
The incomprehensible Holocaust [cover story] I. Deak. il *The New York Review of Books* 36:63-72 S 28 '89
The incomprehensible Holocaust: an exchange [discussion of September 28, 1989 article] I. Deak. il *The New York Review of Books* 36:62-5 D 21 '89
A major Israeli novel [D. Grossman's See under: "Love"] A. L. Mintz. *Commentary* 88:56-60 Jl '89
The strange case of Paul de Man. D. Donoghue. il *The New York Review of Books* 36:32-7 Je 29 '89

HOLOCAUST, JEWISH (1939-1945), IN MOTION PICTURES
Lords of the ring [W. Dafoe and R. Loggia in Triumph of the spirit] M. Rochlin. il pors *Harper's Bazaar* 122:103 D '89
Not afraid of the dark [making of Enemies, a love story; cover story] B. Yagoda. il pors *American Film* 15:30-7 N '89

HOLOCAUST, JEWISH (1939-1945), IN TELEVISION
If Hungary's cops don't get you, its telephones will [making Murderers among us: the Simon Wiesenthal story] L. Eisenberg. il *TV Guide* 37:26-9 Ap 22-28 '89

HOLOCENE PERIOD See Paleoclimatology—Holocene

HOLOGRAMS See Holography

HOLOGRAPHIC STORAGE CRYSTALS See Optical storage devices

HOLOGRAPHY
See also
Computer visualization
How to stop worrying about vibration and make holograms viewable in white light. J. Walker. il *Scientific American* 260:134-7 My '89
Innovative imagemakers. K. Geller-Shinn. il *Petersen's Photographic Magazine* 18:75 Jl '89
Japanese researchers push electron holography. S. M. Dambrot. il *Science* 246:31 O 6 '89

Art use
Treasures trapped in light [exhibition of Ukrainian artistic treasures in York, England] A. Morgan. il *History Today* 39:5 Ap '89

HOLSTEIN, ELGIE
The hidden costs of credit cards. il *USA Today (Periodical)* 118:82-3 N '89

HOLT, JOHN CALDWELL, 1923-1985
Learning all the time. il *Parents* 64:112-14+ N '89
about
A note on John Holt. S. Sheffer. il por *Parents* 64:114 N '89

HOLT, RICHARD, 1948-
The medieval mill—a productivity breakthrough? il *History Today* 39:26-31 Jl '89

HOLT, T. HARVEY
A view of the Moonrise. il por *Conservative Digest* 15:36-7+ Ja/F '89

HOLT, TONIE
about
The battle may be o'er, but this couple brings it back for historic site-seers. D. Chu. il pors *People Weekly* 31:129-30 Je 19 '89

HOLT, VALMAI
about
The battle may be o'er, but this couple brings it back for historic site-seers. D. Chu. il pors *People Weekly* 31:129-30 Je 19 '89

HOLT, VICTORIA, 1906-
The captive [fiction] il por *Good Housekeeping* 209:143-6+ Ag '89

HOLT (HENRY) AND COMPANY See Henry Holt and Company

HOLTEL, BOB, AND DARVES, BONNIE
Trail man. il por *Runner's World* 24:66-7 S '89

HOLTZ, LOU
about
All for 1. A. Murphy. il *Sports Illustrated* 71:38-44+ S 4 '89
The fella expects to win. P. A. Witteman. il por *Time* 134:90-2 N 27 '89
Pocket acquires book by Notre Dame football coach Lou Holtz. *Publishers Weekly* 235:61 Ja 13 '89
Shaking down the thunder. G. Kingdom. il pors *The Saturday Evening Post* 261:52-3+ S '89

HOLTZAPFFEL LATHES See Lathes

HOLTZMAN, JOSEPH
about
Mixed company. P. Viladas. il por *House & Garden* 161:66+ N '89

HOLUSHA, ROSEMARY
Impeccable Gregory Peck. il pors *The Saturday Evening Post* 261:66-8+ Ja/F '89

HOLY
See also
Sacred space

HOLY BLOOD AND CRESCENT MOON [opera] See Copeland, Stewart

HOLY COW, INC.
The whole country cowtows as artist Woody Jackson makes his big moove toward udder success. D. Chu. il por *People Weekly* 32:100-1 Ag 28 '89
HOLY DAYS *See* Fasts and feasts
HOLY GHOST *See* Holy Spirit
HOLY LAND
> *See also*
> Bethlehem

Maps
Mapping a Crusade [work of 14th century cartographer M. Sanudo] O. A. W. Dilke and M. Dilke. bibl il maps *History Today* 39:31-5 Ag '89
HOLY PLACES *See* Sacred space
HOLY SATURDAY
Holy Saturday. E. H. Peterson. il *Christianity Today* 33:23-5 Mr 17 '89
HOLY SPIRIT
> *See also*
> Pentecost
> Pentecostalism
> Trinity

Do Catholics let the Spirit move them? J. Deedy. il *U.S. Catholic* 54:21-7 Mr '89
HOLY THURSDAY *See* Maundy Thursday
HOLY WEEK
> *See also*
> Good Friday
> Holy Saturday
> Maundy Thursday
> Palm Sunday

The great reversal [cover story; special section] il *Christianity Today* 33:19-27 Mr 17 '89
HOLYFIELD, EVANDER
> *about*

Beers with . . . Evander Holyfield [interview] P. Fichtenbaum. il pors *Sport (New York, N.Y.)* 80:19-20 Ag '89
Holyfield KO's Dokes, moves toward Tyson bout. il por *Jet* 75:51 Mr 27 '89
Lean and mean. P. Putnam. il pors *Sports Illustrated* 71:24-6+ Jl 24 '89
One angry man. P. Putnam. il pors *Sports Illustrated* 71:38-9 N 13 '89
You're next, Tyson. P. Putnam. il pors *Sports Illustrated* 70:34-5 Mr 20 '89
HOLYOKE (MASS.)
Education
After a year as a fifth-grade Gulliver, author Tracy Kidder speaks up for teachers [writes book about C. Zajac's class] K. Hubbard. il pors *People Weekly* 32:77+ O 9 '89
From 'House' to schoolhouse [T. Kidder's study of C. Zajac, fifth grade teacher] C. Leslie. il por *Newsweek* 114:67 S 11 '89
PW interviews [T. Kidder, author of book about fifth grade class] A. Smith. por *Publishers Weekly* 236:101-2 S 15 '89
HOLZER, ADELA
> *about*

Act two. J. Kasindorf. il pors *New York* 22:46-52+ Ap 10 '89
HOLZER, HAROLD
Baseball Hall of Fame. il *American History Illustrated* 24:12+ N/D '89
Lincoln's new home. il map *Americana* 16:44-9 Ja/F '89
(jt. auth) *See* Neely, Mark E., Jr., and Holzer, Harold
HOLZER, JENNY
> *about*

And now, a few words from Jenny Holzer. G. Glueck. il por *The New York Times Magazine* p42-3+ D 3 '89
In the beginning was the word. K. Larson. il *New York* 22:71 Ap 3 '89
HOLZER, THOMAS L., AND OTHERS
Dynamics of liquefaction during the 1987 Superstition Hills, California, earthquake [cover story] bibl f il map *Science* 244:56-9 Ap 7 '89
HOLZMAN, ADAM
Creative synthesizer technique II—in MIDI Wonderland. il *Down Beat* 56:59-60 F '89
HOMBROICH (NEUSS, GERMANY) *See* Museumsinsel Hombroich (Neuss, Germany)
HOME
> *See also*
> Christmas gifts for the home
> Family

After the hurricane they can't go home again [South Carolina] R. Rosenblatt. il *U.S. News & World Report* 107:6-7 O 9 '89
Finding the way home. J. Jordan. il *The Progressive* 53:15 F '89
Journey's end [excerpt from Pleasures of a tangled life] J. Morris. il *House & Garden* 161:128+ S '89
My house; tr. by Raymond Rosenthal. P. Levi. il *The New York Review of Books* 35:25 Ja 19 '89
The perfect imperfect home [excerpt from No place like home] L. Weltner. il *Utne Reader* p74-5 My/Je '89

HOME ACCIDENTS *See* Accidents
HOME AND THE SCHOOL *See* School and the home
HOME AQUARIUMS *See* Aquariums
HOME AVIARIES *See* Aviaries
HOME BANKING SERVICES
Back to the velvet-roped lines [Chemical Bank cancels system] P. Elmer-Dewitt. il *Time* 133:49 Ja 9 '89
A Banker's Secret [computer program figures amortization schedules] L. Kleinholz. il *Home Office Computing* 7:78-9 F '89
Bits in the bank [CheckFree] P. Scisco. il *Compute!* 11:7 Mr '89
CheckFree [computer program] G. McClure. il *Compute!* 11:72-3 Jl '89
Checkless checkwriting [CheckFree] R. Cullen. il *Home Office Computing* 7:32+ My '89
Electronic banking may have to log off. L. Zinn. il *Business Week* p75 Ap 10 '89
Quicken [checking account management program] S. Anzovin. il *Compute!* 11:72 Ap '89
Quicken vs. Checkwrite Plus. R. Cullen. il *Home Office Computing* 7:28-9 Ag '89
Stocking-stuffer software. K. Davis. *Changing Times* 43:122-3 D '89
HOME BARS *See* Bars for the home
HOME-BASED BUSINESS
101 home business success stories [cover story] P. Edwards. il *Home Office Computing* 7:25-32+ S '89
1989 reader survey. il *Home Office Computing* 7:53-5 S '89
The Barth balance. C. Hurst. il pors *Home Office Computing* 7:51-3 Je '89
Bringing real-estate profits home [cover story] P. G. Miller. il *Home Office Computing* 7:31-6 Jl '89
The buck starts here [making money with a home computer; cover story; special section] il *Compute!* 11:18-22+ Ag '89
Doing business on the home front. M. Scott. il *Black Enterprise* 19:68-70 Ap '89
Editor's note. C. Cohl. *See* issues of Home Office Computing beginning September 1988
Finding the right marketing mix. R. Gunnerson. il *Home Office Computing* 7:37-40 Ag '89
Gambling expert hits a different kind of jackpot [S. Micco] A. Nadler. il pors *Home Office Computing* 7:50-1 Ag '89
The hottest franchises for the home-based [cover story; special section] L. Arden. il *Home Office Computing* 7:41-50 Je '89
How to organize your office [interview with S. Winston] K. Kane. por *Home Office Computing* 7:58 S '89
Life after the corporation: building a business of your own [cover story; with editorial comment by Claudia Cohl] N. Sullivan and W. C. Banks. il *Home Office Computing* 7:6, 43-8 Ja '89
Look who's working at home [cover story] D. C. Bacon. il *Nation's Business* 77:20-3+ O '89
Million-dollar home businesses [cover story; special section] L. Arden. il *Home Office Computing* 7:41-2 My '89
New options for working at home. C. Begole. il *Glamour* 87:324-5+ S '89
Put time on your side. J. Dean. il *Home Office Computing* 7:66-8 D '89
Shoptalk. J. H. Pratt. *See* issues of Home Office Computing beginning September 1988
Stress busters! B. Stein. il *Home Office Computing* 7:49-51 F '89
With a personal computer and some original thinking, you could be rolling in the dough. D. D. Thornburg. il *Compute!* 11:13 Ag '89
Working smarter. P. Edwards and S. Edwards. *See* issues of Home Office Computing beginning September 1988
Worksteading. R. Farmanfarmaian. il *Psychology Today* 23:37-8+ N '89
Workstyles. N. Sullivan. *See* issues of Home Office Computing beginning September 1988
Yes, you can work at home. R. Cohen. il *Parents* 64:64+ Jl '89
Your home office [cover story; special section] il *Compute!* 11:23-6+ N '89
Laws and regulations
Are you harboring an outlawed business? [zoning laws] L. Fleming. il *Home Office Computing* 7:12 Ja '89
A legal checklist for startup businesses. L. Arden. *Home Office Computing* 7:58-9 Mr '89
Public relations
10 ways to give your home business a corporate image. P. Edwards and S. Edwards. il *Home Office Computing* 7:34 Ag '89
Promoting your business on a tight budget. R. Gunnerson. il *Home Office Computing* 7:32 Ag '89
Taxation
Holiday joy! Give less to the IRS. G. Rutman. il *Home Office Computing* 7:62-5 D '89
How to save on taxes: an insider's guide [cover story; special section] S. F. Edwards. il *Home Office Computing* 7:43-8 F '89

HOME BOX OFFICE
The 8000-hour joke [Comedy Channel] T. Minsky. il *Rolling Stone* p66-7+ N 2 '89
No laughing matter. B. Carter. il pors *The New York Times Magazine* p50+ N 5 '89
Smiley's people [Comedy Channel] V. Ziegel. il por *Gentlemen's Quarterly* 59:240-3+ Ag '89
Talk about a running gag [all-comedy channel] H. F. Waters. il *Newsweek* 113:62 My 29 '89
What's so funny about a Comedy Channel? J. Anderson. il *Rolling Stone* p35 Ag 10 '89

HOME BUILDING *See* House construction
HOME BUILDING INDUSTRY *See* Construction industry
HOME-BUILT AIRPLANES *See* Airplanes, Home-built
HOME-BUILT AUTOMOBILES *See* Automobiles, Home-built
HOME BUSINESS *See* Home-based business
HOME BUYING *See* House buying

HOME CARE SERVICES
See also
Cancer patients—Home care
Foster home care
Lifetime Corp.
Progressive Nursing Services
Help with home care. C. Schaeffer. il *Changing Times* 43:75 Ag '89
Home remedies [intravenous therapy] E. Paris. *Forbes* 143:58+ Ja 9 '89

HOME COMPUTERS *See* Computers—Home use
HOME CONSTRUCTION *See* House construction
HOME COOLING *See* Cooling
HOME DECORATION *See* House decoration

HOME DELIVERY SERVICE
Franchising's house calls. M. Whittemore. il *Nation's Business* 77:47-8 D '89

HOME ECONOMICS
See also
Budget, Household
Cooking
Entertaining
Finance, Personal
Food
Homemakers
Household employees
Household records
Households
Houses—Maintenance and repair
Purchasing, Household
Stain removal
Storage in the home
Are dads doing more? K. Levine. il *Parents* 64:73-6 Je '89
For working women, having it all may mean doing it all [interview with A. Hochschild] D. Waggoner. il pors *People Weekly* 32:51+ S 4 '89
The hint maven strikes again [Heloise] J. Seligmann. il por *Newsweek* 113:70 Ap 10 '89
The myth of male housework [views of A. R. Hochschild] J. Skow. il *Time* 134:62 Ag 7 '89
The new marriage reality [sharing the housework; excerpt from Second shift] A. R. Hochschild. il *Glamour* 87:142-5+ Jl '89
Speaker for the house/The Heloise helpline. Heloise. See issues of Good Housekeeping beginning November 1988
Woman's work is never done [views of A. Hochschild] J. Miller. il *Newsweek* 114:65 Jl 31 '89

Anecdotes, facetiae, satire, etc.
Have you seen your wife lately? K. Fury. il *Working Woman* 14:198 N '89

HOME ECONOMICS LITERATURE
See also
Publishers and publishing—Home economics literature

HOME EDUCATION
Home schooling. R. A. Peterson. il *Conservative Digest* 15:54-7 My/Je '89
Home schooling in times of educational reform. V. Roach. *The Education Digest* 54:58-61 F '89
Learning all the time. J. C. Holt. il *Parents* 64:112-14+ N '89
Our dinner table university [father's use of dinner time to teach children; condensed from Papa, my father] L. F. Buscaglia. il *Reader's Digest* 135:78-80 S '89
Why Johnny can't stay home. D. Neff. *Christianity Today* 33:17 N 17 '89

HOME ELECTRICITY *See* Electricity in the home
HOME ELECTRONICS
See also
Audio systems
Audiovisual equipment
Combination disc players
Compact disc interactive
Compact disc players
Compact disc recorders and recording
Compact discs
Media rooms
Phonograph
Radio receivers
Tape recorders and recording
Television receivers
Video equipment
Videodisc players
Videodiscs
Videotape recorders and recording
Videotapes
1990 home tech guide [special section] il *U.S. News & World Report* 107:82-5+ N 20 '89
Consumer electronics 1989 [special section] il *Popular Mechanics* 166:103-6+ O '89
Gadgets under the tree. il *Home Mechanix* 85:74-6+ Ja '89
High-tech gazette. M. Andrews. il *Better Homes and Gardens* 67:144+ D '89
Holiday gift guide. il *Radio-Electronics* 60:51-3+ D '89
New tech. C. Begole. See occasional issues of Glamour
A perfect 10. S. A. Booth. il *Popular Mechanics* 166:60-1 F '89
Technology for the nineties [special section] il *Rolling Stone* p83-6+ Je 15 '89
That's entertainment! [special section] il *Popular Science* 235:85-8+ N '89
The toys of summer. B. Young. il *Rolling Stone* p157+ Jl 13-27 '89

Exhibitions
See also
Consumer Electronics Show

HOME ENERGY CONSERVATION *See* Energy conservation
HOME EQUITY CONVERSION
Cashing in on your big blue chip. W. L. Updegrave. il *Money* 18 Money Guide:83-4+ Fall '89
Consolidate your debts with deductible loans. C. Willis. il *Money* 18:72+ F '89
Finding the way to pay for your dream. T. Thompson. il *U.S. News & World Report* 106:74-5 Ap 17 '89
Home-equity loans: more disclosure coming. W. Giese. il *Changing Times* 43:24 O '89
The home-equity option. M. Hodge. il *New Choices for the Best Years* 29:51-3 N '89
How to find the best home-equity loan. J. Trotsky. il *Changing Times* 43:37-40+ N '89
How to turn your home into cash [reverse mortgages] A. Saltzman. il *U.S. News & World Report* 106:75 Ap 17 '89
Putting your home on the line. *Consumers' Research Magazine* 72:34-6 D '89
Reverse mortgages: a new cash source for older folks. M. Daly. il *Better Homes and Gardens* 67:156-7 Ap '89
Reverse mortgages: an idea whose time is finally coming (again). D. M. Topolnicki. il *Money* 18:169-70 Mr '89
Till death does its part. D. R. Katz. il *Esquire* 111:83-4 Ap '89
Update: home-equity loans. W. Giese. *Changing Times* 43:22 Mr '89
Using your home as an investment. P. Sharif. il *Black Enterprise* 19:57-8+ Ap '89
When your mortgage pays you [reverse mortgages] W. Giese. *Changing Times* 43:24-5 F '89

HOME FIRE PREVENTION *See* Houses—Fires and fire prevention
HOME FIRES BURNING [television program] *See* Television program reviews—Single works
HOME FURNISHINGS *See* Household furnishings
HOME GAMES [drama] *See* Ziegler, Tom
HOME GROUNDS
See also
Landscape gardening
Lawns
Wild ideas [backyard habitats] L. Barash. il *National Wildlife* 27:22-7 Ap/My '89

Safety devices and measures
See Accidents—Prevention

HOME GYMNASIUM EQUIPMENT *See* Exercising equipment
HOME GYMNASIUMS
Private enterprise. il *Harper's Bazaar* 122:136-7+ My '89
There's no place like the home gym [weight training] M. Greenwood-Robinson. il *Women's Sports & Fitness* 11:62-5 Mr '89

HOME IMPROVEMENT CENTERS
See also
Hechinger Co.
K Mart Corp.

Automation
See also
Weyerhaeuser DesignCenters

HOME IMPROVEMENT CONTRACTORS *See* Contractors
HOME IMPROVEMENTS *See* Houses—Maintenance and repair; Houses, Remodeled
HOME INSPECTION *See* Building inspection
HOME INSURANCE *See* Insurance, Homeowners'
HOME LABOR
See also
Home-based business
Telecommuting
Doing home work down on the farm. O. Davidson. il *The Nation* 249:87-8+ Jl 17 '89
Storied objects [writing at home surrounded by personal possessions] A. Gurganus. il pors *House & Garden* 161:46+ My '89

HOME LIBRARIES *See* Libraries, Private

HOME LOAN BANK BOARD *See* United States. Federal Home Loan Bank Board

HOME MECHANIX (PERIODICAL)
'Some doors close, others open'. M. Morris. *Home Mechanix* 86:4 Ap '89

HOME MEDICAL TEST EQUIPMENT *See* Medical equipment

HOME MORTGAGES *See* Mortgages

HOME MOVIES *See* Motion pictures—Amateur films

HOME MOVIES, VIDEO *See* Videotape recorders and recording

HOME OF THE HIRSEL, ALEC DOUGLAS-HOME, BARON, 1903-

about

Postscript to Munich [interview] J. Ranelagh. *National Review* 41:30-1 Je 2 '89

HOME OFFICE COMPUTING (PERIODICAL)
1989 reader survey. il *Home Office Computing* 7:53-5 S '89

HOME OFFICES

See also

Insurance, Home office

Create your space, choose your tools. B. A. McKee. *Nation's Business* 77:23 O '89

Electricity: is your home office safe? il *Home Office Computing* 7:10 S '89

Equipping your home office. S. Esters. il *Black Enterprise* 19:76-7 Ap '89

Equipping your home office. D. Lyon and P. Harris. il *Psychology Today* 23:48-9 N '89

Finishing a family room/office. il *Workbench* 45:48-9 S/O '89

Home-away-from-home office. il *Working Woman* 14:86-7 Jl '89

Home office off the living room . . . it's just closet size. il *Sunset (Central West edition)* 183:136 N '89

Home offices that work. R. Matthews. il *Country Journal* 16:60-4 Jl/Ag '89

Make yourself comfortable. P. Scisco. il *Compute!* 11:28-31 My '89

My office, my castle. N. Sullivan. il *Home Office Computing* 7:104 O '89

Systems [audio system in a home office] R. Day. il *Stereo Review* 54:100-1 O '89

Top 10 home office misconceptions. C. O'Malley. il *Personal Computing* 13:67-8+ N '89

The work-at-home area. il *Good Housekeeping* 208:198-9 Ap '89

Year-end special: great gifts for the home office [cover story] M. Alvich. il *Home Office Computing* 7:56-9 D '89

Your home office [cover story; special section] il *Compute!* 11:23-6+ N '89

Taxation

Deducting your home office: help or hindrance? il *Home Office Computing* 7:64 D '89

Home-office litmus tests. S. F. Edwards. *Home Office Computing* 7:45 F '89

Tax-proofing your home office. R. R. Roha. il *Changing Times* 43:75-6+ Je '89

The tax questions. B. A. McKee. *Nation's Business* 77:30 O '89

Writing off a home office: is it a brilliant deduction or an annual nightmare? G. Hedberg. il *Money* 18:41+ F '89

HOME OWNERSHIP

See also

Apartment houses—Cooperative ownership

Home equity conversion

House buying

Insurance, Mortgage

Mortgages

Viager (Housing finance)

Homeownership is alive and well. S. Nasar. il *U.S. News & World Report* 107:56 D 11 '89

Homeownership: who can afford it? il *Changing Times* 43:34-5 Mr '89

No more home, sweet home? *USA Today (Periodical)* 118:13-14 D '89

HOME RULE, MUNICIPAL *See* Municipal home rule

HOME RUNS (BASEBALL)
When's the last time this guy saw a game? [Chicago's R. Buhrke shags home run balls outside Wrigley Field] G. Castle. il *Sport (New York, N.Y.)* 80:105 F '89

HOME SAFETY DEVICES AND MEASURES *See* Accidents—Prevention

HOME SAVINGS OF AMERICA, A FEDERAL SAVINGS & LOAN ASSN.
How to succeed in a lousy business. J. F. Lawrence. il *Fortune* 120:125-6+ Jl 3 '89

HOME SELLING *See* House selling

HOME SHARING *See* House sharing

HOME SHOPPING, ELECTRONIC *See* Electronic shopping

HOME SHOPPING NETWORK INC.
Blame the phone company: a strategy goes on trial [sues GTE] G. DeGeorge. il *Business Week* p30 Je 12 '89

HOME STORAGE *See* Storage in the home

HOME STUDY COURSES *See* Correspondence schools and courses

HOME SWIMMING POOLS *See* Swimming pools

HOME VIDEOS *See* Videotape recorders and recording

HOME WARRANTY
Home warranties: peace of mind for a price [interview with E. Gresham] il por *Home Mechanix* 85:16+ F '89

HOMEBUILDERS (PROGRAM)
Help without having to leave home. il *Newsweek* 114:69 Jl 31 '89

HOMELESS

See also

Emmaus House, Inc.

Hoboes

Horace McKenna Center

Refugee children

Refugees

Runaways

We Can (Organization)

Address unknown: homelessness in contemporary America. J. D. Wright. bibl *Society* 26:45-53 S/O '89

Autograph [author from Minnesota gives autograph to homeless man in Manhattan] *The New Yorker* 65:30-2 Ag 7 '89

Down and out in suburbia [Westchester County, N.Y.] B. Kessler. il *The Nation* 249:306+ S 25 '89

Gimme shelter: even middle-class Americans now feel the housing crisis. W. Greider. il *Utne Reader* p60-3 My/Je '89

Give the homeless a chance. K. R. Smith. por *Christianity Today* 33:8 Jl 14 '89

Help for the homeless. R. R. Roha. il *Changing Times* 43:100+ Ja '89

Help the homeless [J. Kozol book inspires campaign by American Booksellers Association] L. Fleischer. *Publishers Weekly* 235:446 Ja 27 '89

Home, street home [cover story] B. Spring. il *Christianity Today* 33:15-20 Ap 21 '89

The homeless at Christmas. M. Novak. il *Forbes* 144:70 D 25 '89

Homeless need more than homes. *Society* 26:2 Mr/Ap '89

Homeless need more than shelter. il *USA Today (Periodical)* 117:8 My '89

Homeless rights, community wrongs [efforts to keep New York's homeless out of public parks] J. Leo. il *U.S. News & World Report* 107:56 Jl 24 '89

The homeless take to the water [Austin, Tex.] D. Claitor. il *The Progressive* 53:10-11 F '89

Homelessness [cover story; special section] il map *Scholastic Update (Teachers' edition)* 121:2-23 F 10 '89

Homelessness: a humanist response [cover story; special section] il *The Humanist* 49:7-15+ My/Je '89

How not to help the homeless [McKinney Act mandates turning over surplus buildings to homeless advocates] il *U.S. News & World Report* 107:29 Ag 28-S 4 '89

How to sabotage the homeless. J. Mehrten. il *Conservative Digest* 15:6-7+ My/Je '89

Hushing the homeless. L. T. Sharpe. il *Psychology Today* 23:64-5 D '89

John Wingate's hard fall: a onetime radio star ends up broke and homeless. E. Tivnan. il pors *New York* 22:50-5 Mr 13 '89

Journey to the streets [betrayal of the mentally ill; views of E. F. Torrey] D. Gelman. *Newsweek* 113:58 Ja 23 '89

Kemp OKs use of vacant apartments for homeless [Chicago] il por *Jet* 77:52 N 27 '89

Kris Parker, who came home from life on the streets to become gold record rapper 'KRS-ONE'. S. Dougherty. il pors *People Weekly* 31:101+ F 27 '89

Let's help the homeless [results of poll] I. Groller. il *Parents* 64:31 N '89

Mad Housers help homeless [Atlanta, Ga.] L. S. Bates. il *The Progressive* 53:15 My '89

Middle America: priced out of house and home. K. S. Diegmueller. *Current (Washington, D.C.)* 314:16-21 Jl/Ag '89

"Mommy, are homeless people bad?". J. G. Fitzpatrick. il *Parents* 64:95-8+ F '89

A nightmare on 42nd Street [Port Authority Bus Terminal in New York] G. Hackett and P. McKillop. il *Newsweek* 113:22-4 F 27 '89

One heart warms many chilly fingers [M. Greenberg distributes gloves to the homeless in New York City] D. Brand. il pors *Time* 133:16+ Ja 2 '89

"Rays of hope" for the homeless. *America* 160:3 Ja 7-14 '89

Shattering myths about the homeless. D. Whitman. il *U.S. News & World Report* 106:26+ Mr 20 '89

Shut in but not shut off, actor Dick York gives the time he has left to the homeless. T. Allis. il pors *People Weekly* 31:209-10+ Mr 6 '89

Thoughts on homelessness today. E. Van den Haag. *The American Spectator* 22:36-7 Ap '89

A town with pity [Embry Rucker Shelter in Reston, Va.] M. J. Weiss. il *Ladies' Home Journal* 106:48-9+ D '89

HOMELESS—*cont.*

A tragic harvest [rural areas] R. Matthews. il *Country Journal* 16:10 S/O '89

Washington talk [remarks by J. Kemp] *National Review* 41:16-17 F 24 '89

What it's like to aid the homeless [Washington, D.C.] R. R. Roha. il *Changing Times* 43:80-1 Jl '89

What we can do about the homeless. C. Whitaker. il *Ebony* 44:96+ Je '89

When all the stars are gone [homeless best friend] F. Waitzkin. il *The New York Times Magazine* p20-3+ Jl 16 '89

Anecdotes, facetiae, satire, etc.

Uncivil liberties. C. Trillin. il *The Nation* 248:186 F 13 '89

Fund raising

See also

Comic Relief (Project)

Booksellers rally around the homeless. M. Jones. il *Publishers Weekly* 236:51 N 24 '89

Health and hygiene

See also

AIDS (Disease) and the homeless

Aerobic altruism [classes in Santa Monica, Calif.; work of Lisa de Mondesir] D. Groves. *American Health* 8:37 Je '89

The dynamics of homelessness [study by the Committee on Health Care for Homeless People] *Children Today* 18:2-3 My/Je '89

Homeless in poor mental, physical health. *Science News* 136:302 N 4 '89

Money, medicine and homelessness [Institute of Medicine report; special section] bibl *Society* 26:4-23 My/Je '89

The unhealthy homeless. *The Futurist* 23:56-7 Jl/Ag '89

Political activities

Behind the housing crisis: private-sector forces, not Reagan, killed off affordable rentals [comments on demonstration in Washington] D. Whitman. il *U.S. News & World Report* 107:28+ O 16 '89

A sea of stars [celebrity involvement in Housing Now! march in Washington, D.C.] A. Ferguson. il *National Review* 41:26 N 10 '89

Speaking out for a place to call home [march on Washington, D.C., to protest the plight of the homeless] J. Park. il *People Weekly* 32:40-3 O 23 '89

Anecdotes, facetiae, satire, etc.

Put us in mental institutions, please! [Housing Now! march] P. J. O'Rourke. il *The American Spectator* 22:16-18 D '89

Recreation

Modern dancers reach out to prisoners and to homeless men [New York City] R. Johnson. il *Dance Magazine* 63:15 S '89

Transportation

In Boston, a busing plan that works [nightly busing of the homeless to Braintree] *Newsweek* 113:27 Mr 6 '89

HOMELESS AND AIDS (DISEASE) *See* AIDS (Disease) and the homeless

HOMELESS AS ARTISTS

Brushed-aside artists have their day [exhibit by homeless artists in Chicago] D. Neff. il por *Christianity Today* 33:62 D 15 '89

Chocolate Milk [art gallery in the East Village] *The New Yorker* 65:25-6 Ag 14 '89

HOMELESS AS AUTHORS

Left homeless, Irvin Matus preferred the Bard to a bed [author of scholarly work on W. Shakespeare] K. Gross. il pors *People Weekly* 31:125+ My 22 '89

HOMELESS CHILDREN

See also

Covenant House (New York, N.Y.)

At a California toy store, kids play Santa for the homeless [Where Kids Shop] il por *People Weekly* 32:115 D 18 '89

Before birth control [child abandonment in ancient and medieval Europe; views of John Boswell] L. George. *American Health* 8:114-15 Jl/Ag '89

Lives on hold [children in welfare hotels in New York City] D. O. Relin. il *Scholastic Update (Teachers' edition)* 121:4-7 F 10 '89

Lost youth. R. Coles. il *Vogue* 179:186-9 Jl '89

The unwanted children of times past [child abandonment in ancient and medieval Europe; interview with J. Boswell] A. P. Sanoff. il por *U.S. News & World Report* 106:62 My 1 '89

Education

Can a shelter be a school? C. Leslie. il *Newsweek* 113:51 Ja 23 '89

Educating children of the homeless. E. A. Eddowes and J. R. Hranitz. *The Education Digest* 55:15-17 O '89

First Lady teaches kids at D.C. non-profit center [B. Bush at Martha's Table] il por *Jet* 75:24 F 20 '89

International aspects

On the street of broken dreams. il *UN Chronicle* 26:49-50 S '89

HOMELESS FAMILIES

See also

Better Homes Foundation

Project Family Independence

Homeless couple given $50 tickets to attend a coveted inaugural ball [R. and V. Gaines] il pors *Jet* 75:14 F 13 '89

Lashanda Daniels's outstanding essay on the homeless was no academic exercise—she'd been there [Boston, Mass.] W. Plummer. il pors *People Weekly* 32:39-40 Jl 31 '89

The rise of the homeless [families in N.Y. welfare hotels; view of J. Kozol] S. M. Halpern. bibl f il *The New York Review of Books* 36:24-7 F 16 '89

HOMELESS IN ART

Exhibitions

Martha Rosler at Dia. E. Heartney. *Art in America* 77:186 N '89

HOMELESS WOMEN

Helping the homeless [P. Crowley's work at women's shelter in Chicago] C. Reeve. il por *New Choices for the Best Years* 29:16 F '89

The homeless woman with two homes. G. Talese. il *New York* 22:40-2 O 30 '89

One point of light [New York City homeless woman M. Davis taken in by S. Braun of Honesdale, Pa.] D. Finkel. il pors *Esquire* 112:123-8+ O '89

HOMEMAKERS

See also

Woman's workshop quarterly (Newsletter)

Freaks of nurture [househusbands] H. Straus. il por *American Health* 8:70-1 Ja/F '89

Living with choices. F. Prose. il *Parents* 64:130-3 My '89

Looking to Harriet. D. Seligman. il *Fortune* 120:117 Jl 17 '89

Anecdotes, facetiae, satire, etc.

50 reasons to stay home with your children. M. Fogelman. il *Parents* 64:127-9 Ap '89

Why men make awful wives. D. Burg. il *Harper's Bazaar* 122:118-19+ F '89

HOMEMAKING *See* Home economics

HOMEOBOXES

See also

Engrailed (Gene)

POU! goes the homeobox. J. Benditt. *Scientific American* 260:20+ F '89

Purification of growth hormone-specific transcription factor GHF-1 containing homeobox. J.-L. Castrillo and others. bibl f il *Science* 243:814-17 F 10 '89

The story of life unfolding. W. F. Allman. il *U.S. News & World Report* 106:58-9 My 22 '89

Two cultures find common ground [conference of specialists in mouse and fruit fly development] J. L. Marx. il *Science* 244:652-3 My 12 '89

HOMEOPATHY

Benveniste criticism is diluted [water memory experiment] D. Dickson. *Science* 245:248 Jl 21 '89

Dilutions of grandeur [Nature magazine's investigation of J. Benveniste's water memory experiment] A. C. Revkin. il *Discover* 10:74-5 Ja '89

The natural. M. Donald. il *Gentlemen's Quarterly* 59:151+ My '89

France

Homeopathic chic. M. Carpenter. il *Health (New York, N.Y.)* 21:52-5+ Mr '89

HOMEOWNERS' INSURANCE *See* Insurance, Homeowners'

HOMEOWNERS' WARRANTY *See* Home warranty

HOMER

about

Stargazing with Homer. G. Lovi. il *Sky and Telescope* 77:57-8 Ja '89

Who taught Homer his ABC's? il *U.S. News & World Report* 106:10 Ja 23 '89

Anecdotes, facetiae, satire, etc.

Homer and his publishers. J. Queenan. il *The American Spectator* 22:39 D '89

The quest of lion-browed Andreas [A. Papandreou seeks re-election] D. Lawday. il *U.S. News & World Report* 106:37 Je 19 '89

HOMER, WILLIAM INNES

The Ryder cover-up. il por *Art News* 88:158-61 O '89

HOMEROOM [television program] *See* Television program reviews—Single works

HOMERTON COLLEGE *See* University of Cambridge. Homerton College

HOMES, INSTITUTIONAL

See also

Nursing homes

Orphans and orphanages

St. Vincent's School for Boys (San Rafael, Calif.)

Valley Teen Ranch (Madera, Calif.)

HOMESICKNESS

Sounds of home [sending son in Korea tape recording of thunderstorm] B. V. Moulder. il *Reader's Digest* 135:143-4 Jl '89

HOMESTEAD LAW

Hawaii

Hawaii's dirty secret [native Hawaiians' battle for land tenure; cover story] V. Novak. il *Common Cause Magazine* 15:10-16+ N/D '89

HOMESTEADS

Buttoning up for winter. J. Vivian. il *The Mother Earth News* 119:92-6+ S/O '89

HOMESTEADS—*cont.*

History

See also

Oklahoma—History—Land Rush, 1889

Minnesota

New pioneer spirit as homesteaders look north [Koochiching County] *Successful Farming* 87:26 mid-F '89

Return of the homestead. R. J. Margolis. il *The New Leader* 72:15-16 Ja 23 '89

HOMEWORK

The homework dilemma. J. Stewart. il *Parents* 64:80+ F '89

Homework Writer [computer program] C. S. Holzberg. il *Home Office Computing* 7:75-6 S '89

Homework Writer [computer program] C. S. Holzberg. il *Compute!* 11:70 Ag '89

Homing in on homework [research by Joyce Epstein] G. W. Bracey. *Phi Delta Kappan* 70:732-3 My '89

Kids, parents, and homework. J. Oppenheim. il *Good Housekeeping* 209:148+ S '89

HOMEWORKERS *See* Home labor

HOMICIDE *See* Murder

HOMILIES *See* Sermons

HOMING PIGEONS *See* Pigeons

HOMINIDS *See* Man, Prehistoric

HOMOCHITTO NATIONAL FOREST (MISS.)

Pipes Lake, Mississippi. R. H. Mohlenbrock. il map *Natural History* p74-6 My '89

HOMOLOGY (BIOLOGY)

A G protein gamma subunit shares homology with *ras* proteins. N. Gautam and others. bibl f il *Science* 244:971-4 My 26 '89

Intracellular targeting and structural conservation of a prohormone-processing endoprotease [Sacchasomyces] R. S. Fuller and others. bibl f il *Science* 246:482-6 O 27 '89

Receptor and antibody epitopes in human growth hormone identified by homolog-scanning mutagenesis. B. C. Cunningham and others. bibl f il *Science* 243:1330-6 Mr 10 '89

HOMOPHOBIA

Reducing homophobia among educators and students. R. Schaecher. *The Education Digest* 54:58-61 Ap '89

HOMOSEXUAL LITERATURE

See also

Booksellers and bookselling—Homosexual literature

Publishers and publishing—Homosexual literature

HOMOSEXUALITY

See also

Homophobia

Lesbianism

All in the, er, family [New York ruling on gay couples and rent control] D. Seligman. *Fortune* 120:123-4 Ag 14 '89

Anatomy of a smear [Speaker of the House T. Foley denies rumors of homosexuality] G. Borger. il pors *U.S. News & World Report* 106:40-1 Je 19 '89

Another scandal on the Hill [Congressman B. Frank involved in male homosexual prostitution scandal] por *Newsweek* 114:24 S 4 '89

Arms and the man: a sex scandal rocks Princeton [English professor T. McFarland forced to retire from Princeton] D. Rabinowitz. il pors *New York* 22:30-6 Jl 17 '89

Atwatergate [Republican smear campaign against House Speaker T. Foley] H. Hertzberg. *The New Republic* 201:4 Jl 3 '89

Barney Frank's story [relationship with male prostitute S. Gobie; cover story; special section; with interview] il pors *Newsweek* 114:14-20 S 25 '89

A boy's life [gay black teenager with AIDS] D. L. Kirp. il *Mother Jones* 14:32-8 Jl/Ag '89

Coming out in the age of AIDS. M. Dregni. il *Utne Reader* p19-20 S/O '89

Confirmed but not bachelors? [Andrew Sullivan's case for gay marriage] E. Van den Haag. *National Review* 41:16 S 15 '89

Court OKs re-enlistment of homosexual soldier [case of P. Watkins] il por *Jet* 76:18 My 22 '89

Cousins once removed [English writer and editor J. R. Ackerley] P. Parker. il pors *History Today* 39:7-8 S '89

Dancing gays [gay-lesbian dance at Columbia University] D. K. Mano. *National Review* 41:56-9 F 24 '89

Darrell Yates Rist replies [discussion of February 13, 1989 article, The deadly costs of an obsession] D. Y. Rist. *The Nation* 248:834+ Je 19 '89

The deadly costs of an obsession [concern with AIDS diverts campaign for gay rights; cover story] D. Y. Rist. il *The Nation* 248:181+ F 13 '89

Dirtball politics [homosexual smear perpetrated by Republican National Committee against Speaker of the House T. Foley] T. Morganthau. il pors *Newsweek* 113:32-3 Je 19 '89

Exchange [discussion of February 13, 1989 article, The deadly costs of an obsession] D. Y. Rist. *The Nation* 248:578+ My 1 '89

Forced march in the military [cases challenging regulations banning lesbians and gay men] G. L. Atkins. il *The Nation* 248:16-18 Ja 2 '89

Gay and lesbian couples [parenting] J. Seligmann. il *Newsweek* 114 Special Issue:38-40 Wint '89/Spr '90

Gay kids, mad parents [research by Joyce Hunter] J. Folkenberg. il *American Health* 8:78-9 D '89

Gay politics and AIDS [discussion of February 13, 1989 article, The deadly costs of an obsession] D. Y. Rist. *The Nation* 248:362+ Mr 20 '89

Growing up gay in America [interview with R. Isay] E. E. Goode. il por *U.S. News & World Report* 107:95 N 6 '89

Here comes the groom [case for gay marriage; cover story] A. Sullivan. *The New Republic* 201:20+ Ag 28 '89

Homosexual families and the law. *Newsweek* 114:48 Jl 17 '89

Homosexuality. K. McCoy. *Seventeen* 48:80+ N '89

Homosexuality: who and why? M. Konner. il *The New York Times Magazine* p60-1 Ap 2 '89

House Foleys [rumor of homosexuality of House Speaker T. Foley spread by Republicans and Democrats] T. Eastland. il *The American Spectator* 22:32-3 Ag '89

How to spread a smear [Republican attack on Speaker of the House T. Foley] M. B. Carlson. il pors *Time* 133:33 Je 19 '89

In defense of Barney [Congressman B. Frank involved in male homosexual prostitution scandal] M. Kondracke. *The New Republic* 201:10-11 O 9 '89

Is the gay revolution a flop? [views of H. Madsen and M. Kirk] A. Toufexis. il pors *Time* 134:56 Jl 10 '89

Letter from Washington [Congressman B. Frank's relationship with male prostitute S. Gobie] E. Drew. *The New Yorker* 65:106-8+ O 2 '89

Lovers, liars and other strangers [M. Christian's claim against R. Hudson estate] pors *Newsweek* 113:61 F 27 '89

Mission accomplished [Republican National Committee chairman L. Atwater's involvement in smear campaign against Speaker T. Foley] F. Barnes. il *The New Republic* 201:8-10 Jl 3 '89

The nation's closets [homosexual smear attack against House Speaker T. Foley] *Commonweal* 116:388-9 Jl 14 '89

Non-nuclear proliferation: alternative "family" arrangements grow more common across U.S. D. R. Harris. il *Utne Reader* p22-3 Mr/Ap '89

The Pentagon's fight to keep gays away. P. Cary. il *U.S. News & World Report* 107:57+ N 20 '89

A place to be somebody [Harvey Milk School in New York City] K. Brady. il *Time* 134:21-2+ N 13 '89

Presswatch [Congressman B. Frank's involvement in male prostitution] T. Eastland. *The American Spectator* 22:31-2 N '89

The price of betrayal [M. Christian awarded $21.75 million in lawsuit against estate of R. Hudson] P. Chin. il pors *People Weekly* 31:180-3 Mr 6 '89

Reducing homophobia among educators and students. R. Schaecher. *The Education Digest* 54:58-61 Ap '89

Rethinking homosexuality [David Greenberg's The construction of homosexuality] D. S. Browning. *The Christian Century* 106:911-16 O 11 '89

Rock Hudson. B. Darrach. il pors *People Weekly* 32 Special Issue:65-6 Fall '89

Scenes from the gay life [Lesbian and Gay Pride Weekend in New York City] D. Klinghoffer. *National Review* 41:22-3 Ag 4 '89

Should gays have marriage rights? W. Isaacson. il *Time* 134:101-2 N 20 '89

Should homosexuals be able to serve? [case of P. Watkins] L. Eskin. por *Scholastic Update (Teachers' edition)* 122:22 O 6 '89

A skeleton in Barney's closet [B. Frank's relationship with gay prostitute S. Gobie] M. B. Carlson. il pors *Time* 134:24 S 25 '89

Some gays reverting to risky sex. L. M. Keen. *Utne Reader* p111-12 N/D '89

Stonewall + 20. V. A. Brownworth. *The Nation* 249:5-6 Jl 3 '89

That memo [Republican National Committee attack on House Speaker T. Foley] W. McGurn. por *National Review* 41:22-3 N 10 '89

Trials of Barney [B. Frank involved in male prostitution scandal] *The Nation* 249:371-2 O 9 '89

Where have you gone, Billy boy? M. Milton. il *The New York Times Magazine* p32+ D 10 '89

Why Frank's case is different [congressman involved in male homosexual prostitution scandal] il por *U.S. News & World Report* 107:30 O 2 '89

Winners and sinners: the D'Amato and Frank dossiers. J. Klein. il por *New York* 22:23-4 O 9 '89

History

See also

Stonewall Riot, 1969

Periodicals

See also

New York native (Newspaper)

OUT/LOOK: national lesbian & gay quarterly

Statistics

Prevalence and patterns of same-gender sexual contact among men. R. E. Fay and others. bibl f il *Science* 243:338-48 Ja 20 '89

HOMOSEXUALITY—Statistics—*cont.*
Sex survey provides data on homosexuals. B. Bower. *Science News* 135:54 Ja 28 '89

Canada

Homosexual rights [Maclean's/Decima poll] N. Underwood. il *Maclean's* 102:22+ Ja 2 '89

Great Britain

For queens & country [Gay and Lesbian Film Festival sponsored by the British Film Institute] H. Kennedy. il *Film Comment* 25:15-16 Ja/F '89
No gays, please, we're British. M. H. Hodges. *The Nation* 248:156-60 F 6 '89

HOMOSEXUALITY AND CHRISTIANITY

See also
Church work with homosexuals
Ordination of homosexuals

The battle over gay clergy. R. N. Ostling. il *Time* 134:89-90 N 13 '89
Campolo's views challenged [some people born with homosexual orientation] R. Frame. por *Christianity Today* 33:43 S 8 '89
Ex-gay: can homosexuals really change? [cover story; special section] il *Christianity Today* 33:16-24+ Ag 18 '89
Gay community frowns on disco diva Donna Summer. por *Jet* 76:38 S 18 '89
Let's support civil rights for homosexuals [with readers' comments] G. C. Zahn. *U.S. Catholic* 54:13-18 O '89
Of many things [U.S. Catholic readers' views on homosexuals] G. W. Hunt. *America* 161:310 N 11 '89
Rethinking homosexuality [David Greenberg's The construction of homosexuality] D. S. Browning. *The Christian Century* 106:911-16 O 11 '89
San Francisco set to define 'family' [referendum on affording legal recognition to unmarried heterosexual and homosexual couples] R. Digitale. il *Christianity Today* 33:44-6 O 20 '89
Sort of married. T. K. Jones. il *Christianity Today* 33:14 S 8 '89
Stallings denies charge of a homosexual relationship [black priest] por *Jet* 76:38 S 25 '89

HOMOSEXUALITY IN LITERATURE

See also
Lesbianism in literature

Mainstreaming a cult classic [novels by A. Maupin] T. Clifton. il por *Newsweek* 114:77 O 30 '89
On truth and fiction [factual basis for book Slave trade involving homosexual boys in Haiti] H. Gold. *The Nation* 249:759-61 D 18 '89
Out on the town [novels by A. Maupin] A. Block. il *Mother Jones* 14:54 N '89

HOMOSEXUALITY IN MOTION PICTURES

Dignity in drag [H. Fierstein; cover story] J. Scott. il pors *Film Comment* 25:9-12+ Ja/F '89
Fierstein's Torch song saga. T. Soter. il por *Video* 13:15 Jl '89
For queens & country [Gay and Lesbian Film Festival sponsored by the British Film Institute] H. Kennedy. il *Film Comment* 25:15-16 Ja/F '89

HOMSY, JACQUES, AND OTHERS

The Fc and not CD4 receptor mediates antibody enhancement of HIV infection in human cells. bibl f il *Science* 244:1357-60 Je 16 '89

HONDA (AUTOMOBILE) *See* Automobiles, Foreign; Sports cars

HONDA MOTOR CO., LTD.

1990 preview: Honda [motorcycles; cover story] il *Cycle* 40:28-30 N '89
Arms race on wheels [Grand Prix racing becomes corporate sport] R. Behar. il *Forbes* 143:60+ F 20 '89
Honda seeks response for declining domestic market [motorcycles] N. Voge. il *Cycle* 40:21 N '89
Modern fables [motorcycle business] S. Anderson. il *Cycle* 40:9 N '89
Money fuels the Honda wonder [Grand Prix racing] H. J. Steinbreder. il *Sports Illustrated* 71:58-9 Ag 21 '89

HONDERICH, BELAND H.

about
When a publisher has the last word. G. Bain. il *Maclean's* 102:36 Je 26 '89

HONDURAS

See also
Economic assistance, American—Honduras
Immigration and emigration—Honduras
Peasantry—Honduras
Relief work—Honduras
Trifinio (Central America)
Women—Honduras

Antiquities

See also
Copán (Ancient city)
Tombs—Honduras

Defenses

See also
United States—Armed Forces—Forces in Honduras

Foreign relations

Nicaragua

Cutting the cord in Honduras [contras] W. McGurn. il *National Review* 41:22-3 S 29 '89

Honduras left to push contra pram. J. Eldridge. il *The Nation* 248:734-6+ My 29 '89

HONECKER, ERICH

about
East Germany: clinging to the hard line—and taking a hard fall. G. E. Schares and J. Templeman. il por *Business Week* p28-9 S 4 '89
The flight to freedom. H. Anderson. il por *Newsweek* 114:40-3+ O 16 '89
Honecker and the 'lesson of history'. M. R. Meyer and S. Sullivan. por *Newsweek* 113:45 Je 19 '89
Krenz is cast from Honecker's mold. Now, can he break it? J. Templeman. il por *Business Week* p49 O 30 '89
Krenz takes charge. A. Phillips. il pors *Maclean's* 102:50+ O 30 '89
A model apparatchik. R. Watson. il pors *Newsweek* 114:52-3 O 30 '89
A repressive ruler. J. Bierman. il por *Maclean's* 102:39 O 16 '89
To each according to his greed? R. Knight. il por *U.S. News & World Report* 107:26 D 18 '89
Trading places. J. Smolowe. il por *Time* 134:60-2 O 30 '89

HONES, EDWARD W., AND HIGBIE, P. R.

Distribution and detection of positrons from an orbiting nuclear reactor. bibl f il *Science* 244:448-51 Ap 28 '89

HONESTY

See also
Integrity
Sincerity

Honestly, can we trust you? [pencil-and-paper employment tests] C. Gorman. il *Time* 133:44 Ja 23 '89
In good faith [out-of-work Chicagoan J. Loveras returns contents of missing briefcase to Japanese owner] B. Greene. il pors *Esquire* 111:67-8 Mr '89
Is honesty always the best policy? il *'Teen* 33:20-1+ Ja '89
Job applicants come clean [integrity test; research by Reid Psychological Systems] *USA Today (Periodical)* 118:7-8 Ag '89
Putting honesty in the office—the old-fashioned way [written tests] W. Cole. *Working Woman* 14:14+ Jl '89
The stolen briefcase [J. Loveras returns contents to Japanese owner] B. Greene. il *Reader's Digest* 134:23-4+ Je '89
The truth about lying to a lover. D. Heyn. *Mademoiselle* 95:118 F '89
Watergate figure preaches honesty [J. S. Magruder of Columbus, Ohio] *Christianity Today* 33:47 Ap 21 '89

HONEY

See also
Bees
Cooking—Honey

Honey: nature's sweetener. J. Scala. il *Dance Magazine* 63:64-5 Ag '89

HONEY, I SHRUNK THE KIDS [film] *See* Motion picture reviews—Single works

HONEYBEE LARVAE *See* Larvae

HONEYBEE ROBOTICS (FIRM)

Desperately seeking Cyborg [Flight Telerobotic Servicer for space station assembly] J. Goldberg. il *Omni (New York, N.Y.)* 11:12+ Ag '89

HONEYBEES *See* Bees

HONEYGUIDES (BIRDS)

Honey hunters follow birds to reach bees [research by H. A. Isack and H.-U. Reyer] *Science News* 135:172 Mr 18 '89
Honeyguides and honey gatherers: interspecific communication in a symbiotic relationship. H. A. Isack and H.-U. Reyer. bibl f il *Science* 243:1343-6 Mr 10 '89

HONEYMOON

How to have a second honeymoon (without leaving home). S. F. Enos. il *Redbook* 174:118-19+ N '89
The wonderful husband [F. and E. Roosevelt's European honeymoon in 1905] G. C. Ward. il pors *American Heritage* 40:57-8+ S/O '89

HONEYWELL INC.

Avionics system lets helicopter crews focus on search, rescue. N. C. Kernstock. il *Aviation Week & Space Technology* 130:50-1+ Ap 24 '89
Butt kicking at Honeywell. R. Henkoff. il por *Fortune* 119:141 My 22 '89
Honeywell and GE may be thinking of meshing gears. G. G. Marcial. il *Business Week* p130 Jl 17 '89
Honeywell may still be sweet. G. G. Marcial. *Business Week* p80 Jl 31 '89
Sayonara [New York-Tokyo arbitrage played by Honeywell] S. Flack. il *Forbes* 144:10 Ag 21 '89
"We still have more to do". C. Siler. il *Forbes* 144:183 D 11 '89

HONG KONG

See also
Civil rights—Hong Kong
Hotels, motels, etc.—Hong Kong
Immigration and emigration—Hong Kong
Investments, Foreign—Hong Kong
Investments, Hong Kong
Prostitution—Hong Kong

HONG KONG—cont.

Buildings

Bond Centre, Hong Kong [skyscraper for Bond Corporation] M. F. Schmertz. il *Architectural Record* 177:76-9 Ja '89

Description and travel

Hong Kong. W. McGurn. il *Esquire* 112:229+ S '89

Hong Kong. A. M. Stinchecum. il *Travel Holiday* 172:50-9 S '89

Hong Kong: bound and adrift. B. Wallach. il map *Focus (New York, N.Y.: 1950)* 39:17-25 Fall '89

Economic conditions

A colony living on the edge of chaos. D. Lee. il *Business Week* p34-5 Je 19 '89

Fear and trembling in Hong Kong [violence in Beijing] J. Elliott. *World Press Review* 36:18 Jl '89

Fear in the colony [Hong Kong reacts to Beijing crackdown] T. Fennell. il *Maclean's* 102:32-4 Je 19 '89

Hong Kong? Just watch China. B. Crozier. *National Review* 41:20 Mr 10 '89

Hong Kong revisited. C. W. Weinberger. il *Forbes* 143:31 Je 12 '89

Hong Kong's lost confidence [repression in China] P. Hazan. il *World Press Review* 36:61 S '89

The tragedy of Hong Kong. M. Novak. il *Forbes* 144:80-1 Ag 21 '89

What will happen when the Chinese take back their 'fragrant harbor'? S. Karnow. bibl (p174) il map *Smithsonian* 20:40-8+ Ap '89

Industries

See also

Cathay Pacific Airways Ltd.
Chevalier (OA) Holdings Ltd.
Dickson Concepts Ltd.
Hong Kong Aircraft Engineering Co. Ltd.
Hutchison Whampoa Ltd.
Printing industry—Hong Kong
Semi-Tech Microelectronics (Far East) Ltd.

Photographs and photography

A photographer's guide to Hong Kong. P. Slaughter. il *Petersen's Photographic Magazine* 18:64-7 Je '89

Politics and government

Apprehension in Hong Kong [killings in Beijing] A. Phillips. *Maclean's* 102:27 Je 19 '89

A bad omen for Hong Kong [crackdown on students in mainland China] C. S. Manegold. il *Newsweek* 113:27 Je 19 '89

Britain's Hong Kong headache has just begun to throb. D. J. Yang. il *Business Week* p83 Jl 17 '89

Britain's shame. M. Elliott. *The New Republic* 201:15-16 Ag 7-14 '89

Broken China [effects of crackdown on students] *The New Republic* 200:5-6 Je 26 '89

Decision time in Hong Kong. F. M. Bordewich. il *Reader's Digest* 134:121-6 Je '89

Fear and anger in Hong Kong [Beijing massacre shakes the colony] W. Stewart. il *Time* 133:22 Je 19 '89

Hong Kong [address, October 16, 1989] Sir D. Wilson. *Vital Speeches of the Day* 56:140-3 D 15 '89

Hong Kong gone. W. McGurn. *National Review* 41:22-3 Ap 21 '89

Hong Kong on borrowed time. M. Scott. il *The New York Times Magazine* p30-2+ O 22 '89

Hong Kong's future seems even more in doubt [effects of student protests in China] D. J. Yang and D. Lee. il *Business Week* p41+ Je 12 '89

Next door and eight years away. J. Greenwald. il *Time* 133:29 Je 5 '89

Will the last one to leave please turn out the lights? [reaction to Beijing crackdown] E. MacFarquhar. il *U.S. News & World Report* 107:36-7 Ag 21 '89

Religious institutions and affairs

See also

Catholic Church—Hong Kong
Christians—Hong Kong

Transit systems

Hong Kong. A. M. Stinchecum. il *Travel Holiday* 172:50-9 S '89

Tram's-eye views of Hong Kong street life. il *Sunset (Central West edition)* 182:44 Ju '89

HONG KONG AIRCRAFT ENGINEERING CO. LTD.

Haeco upgrades maintenance facility, employee benefits. P. Proctor. il *Aviation Week & Space Technology* 130:321+ Je 12 '89

HONG KONG AND CHINA *See* China and Hong Kong

HONG KONG AND SHANGHAI BANKING CORPORATION *See* Hongkong and Shanghai Banking Corporation

HONG KONG BANK OF CANADA *See* Hongkong Bank of Canada

HONG KONG CULTURAL CENTRE

Hong Kong opens a new cultural center. D. Ries. il *Dance Magazine* 63:22 N '89

HONG KONG STOCK EXCHANGE

Hong Kong's contrarians [buying stocks] J. Mendes. il *Fortune* 120:30 Jl 17 '89

HONGKONG AND SHANGHAI BANKING CORPORATION

The Bank. A. Tanzer. il por *Forbes* 144:43-4 D 11 '89

Hongkong Bank's quiet invasion. P. C. Newman. il *Maclean's* 102:42 D 18 '89

HONGKONG BANK OF CANADA

Hongkong Bank's quiet invasion. P. C. Newman. il *Maclean's* 102:42 D 18 '89

HONICKER, CLIFFORD T.

The hidden files [cover story] il *The New York Times Magazine* p38-41+ N 19 '89

HONOLULU (HAWAII)

Bookstores

See Booksellers and bookselling—Hawaii

Description

Honolulu lights say "Mele Kalikimaka". il map *Sunset (Central West edition)* 181:50 D '88

Honolulu tours that relive history. *Sunset (Central West edition)* 183:46 Jl '89

Galleries and museums

See also

Contemporary Museum (Honolulu, Hawaii)
Hawaii Maritime Center

Parks and playgrounds

See also

Kapiolani Park (Honolulu, Hawaii)

Waikiki Beach

See Waikiki Beach (Honolulu, Hawaii)

HONOR SYSTEM (EDUCATION)

The onerousness of honor [commission calls for policy changes at U.S. Military Academy] *U.S. News & World Report* 106:17 Je 26 '89

HONORARY DEGREES *See* Degrees, Honorary

HOOD, ANN, 1956-

Bringing the family together [story] il *Redbook* 174:48+ D '89

Fanning an old flame [story] il *Redbook* 172:58+ Mr '89

She's not the daughter we wanted [story] il *Redbook* 172:50+ Ja '89

The Superman affair [story] il *Mademoiselle* 95:106+ Jl '89

HOOD, JOHN

How consumers get taken for a ride. il *Consumers' Research Magazine* 72:31-5 F '89

Must college cost so much? *Reader's Digest* 134:108-10 Ap '89

Private choices for public schools. il *Conservative Digest* 15:70-3 My/Je '89

HOOD, KIT

about

The greening of Degrassi. K. Beck. il pors *Channels (New York, N.Y.: 1986)* 9:62-4 N '89

HOOD MUSEUM OF ART

Orozco's American epic [acquisition of fresco cycle] C. Giuliano. il por *Art News* 88:53+ N '89

HOOD SAILMAKERS, INC.

Sailsmanship [Hood Sailmakers vs. North Sails Group] D. Churbuck. il por *Forbes* 144:50+ Jl 10 '89

HOOGENDORN, CYNTHIA

Jamaica, no problem. il *Black Enterprise* 19:111 My '89

HOOGOVENS ALUMINIUM GMBH

Germany's Hoogovens Aluminum expands with goal of supplying U.S. market. K. F. Mordoff. il *Aviation Week & Space Technology* 130:115-16 My 1 '89

HOOGSTRATEN, LOUISE

about

The passions of Peter Bogdanovich [cover story] J. Wadler. il pors *People Weekly* 31:56-8+ Ja 23 '89

HOOK, SIDNEY, 1902-1989

Civilization and its malcontents [cover story] il *National Review* 41:30-3 O 13 '89

Echoes of the Rosenberg case: an autobiographical postscript. il *The American Spectator* 22:18-20 Ja '89

Hook on democracy. *National Review* 41:4+ Je 2 '89

about

Obituary

Commentary 88:41-7 N '89. J. Epstein
National Review 41:15 Ag 18 '89. P. P. Witonski
National Review 41:55 S 1 '89. W. F. Buckley
The New Leader 72:3-4 Jl 10-24 '89. D. Bell

On being a Jew [interview] N. Podhoretz. *Commentary* 88:28-36 O '89

HOOKED RUGS *See* Rugs and carpets

HOOKER, JOHN LEE

about

Generations of blues. A. DeCurtis. il por *Rolling Stone* p28 N 2 '89

HOOKER CORPORATION LIMITED

Debacle on 34th Street: how takeover debt helped kill off the venerable B. Altman chain. B. Rudolph. il por *Time* 134:77 D 11 '89

Say g'day to the megamall [Forest Fair in Cincinnati] S. Phillips. il *Business Week* p29 Mr 6 '89

HOOKING (CRAFT)

See also

Rugs and carpets

HOOPER, JOSEPH

After the last tango. il *Esquire* 111:140-5 F '89

The hordes' prayer. il *Mother Jones* 14:45-6 F/Mr '89

Not your average family. il pors *The New York Times Magazine* p48-50+ D 10 '89

HOOPER, JUDITH
The hug factor. il *Health (New York, N.Y.)* 21:72-5 O '89
Inputting Sigmund. il *Omni (New York, N.Y.)* 11:20+ Jl '89
Now, where did I put my . . . il *Health (New York, N.Y.)* 21:72-3 N '89
Ode to Cheez Whiz. il *Health (New York, N.Y.)* 21:44+ O '89
Ommm . . . please pass the DHEAS. il *Health (New York, N.Y.)* 21:34 O '89
Sound-and-light wars. il *Omni (New York, N.Y.)* 12:26+ N '89
HOOPER, JUDITH, AND TERESI, DICK
Brain stretches [special section] il *Health (New York, N.Y.)* 21:55-67 Ap '89
HOOPER, SCOTT L., AND MOULINS, MAURICE
Switching of a neuron from one network to another by sensory-induced changes in membrane properties. bibl f il *Science* 244:1587-9 Je 30 '89
HOOPER, WALTER
about
A "hoax" observed. R. Frame. il pors *Christianity Today* 33:64-5 Je 16 '89
Unscrambling the C. S. Lewis 'hoax'. L. W. Dorsett. *The Christian Century* 106:208-9 F 22 '89
HOOSIER (TERM)
Sense and etymology in settlers' English. D. Quayle. *Harper's* 278:19-20 My '89
HOOSIER NATIONAL FOREST (IND.)
Plaster Creek, Indiana [seep springs] R. H. Mohlenbrock. il maps *Natural History* p98-100 N '89
HOOSIER RACING TIRE COMPANY
Big blue meets the purple eagle eaters [Goodyear and Hoosier vie for NASCAR Winston Cup market] L. Griffin. il *Car and Driver* 34:221-2+ Je '89
Blowout. J. Harris. il *Forbes* 143:10 Je 12 '89
Great tires, blimp to come [Hoosier Racing Tire vs. Goodyear] J. Harris. il por *Forbes* 143:288+ My 29 '89
HOOVER, DWIGHT W., 1926-
Magic Middletown [excerpt] il *Society* 26:73-7 Mr/Ap '89
HOOVER, J. EDGAR (JOHN EDGAR), 1895-1972
Bibliography
Doing Edgar proud. D. R. Gordon. *The Nation* 249:570-4 N 13 '89
HOOVER, JOHN EDGAR *See* Hoover, J. Edgar (John Edgar), 1895-1972
HOOVER, MIKE
about
Truth and consequences. il *Time* 134:98 O 9 '89
HOOVER CO.
Can Maytag clean up around the world? [acquisition of Chicago Pacific Corp.] B. Bremner. il *Business Week* p86-7 Ja 30 '89
Maytag's foreign fling isn't much fun after all [Hoover acquisition sours] B. Bremner. *Business Week* p32-3 S 4 '89
HOOVER-DEMPSEY, KATHLEEN V.
(jt. auth) See Plas, Jeanne M., and Hoover-Dempsey, Kathleen V.
HOPE, BARBARA
about
How to manage a grand project. A. M. Russell. il pors *Working Woman* 14:73-7 D '89
HOPE, BOB, 1903-
about
Hope for the best. E. M. Swift. il pors *Sports Illustrated* 70:20-2+ Ja 23 '89
Anecdotes, facetiae, satire, etc.
Thanks for the memory. I. Frazier. *The New Yorker* 65:36-7 D 18 '89
HOPE, CHARLES
The real Leonardo. il *The New York Review of Books* 36:16-18 Ag 17 '89
HOPE, CHRISTOPHER
Seeing is believing. *The New Republic* 201:14-16 D 18 '89
HOPE, GLENDA
Revisioning seminary as ministry-centered [with discussion; cover story] il *The Christian Century* 106:107-11+ F 1-8 '89
Seminary and church: missing ministry [discussion of February 1-8, 1989 article, Revisioning seminary as ministry-centered] *The Christian Century* 106:450-1 Ap 26 '89
HOPE, JACK
Mixed blessings. il *Parents* 64:252 D '89
"My wife shouldn't have died". il pors *Good Housekeeping* 209:92+ O '89
Rebel without a preschool. il *Parents* 64:222+ S '89
HOPE, MARJORIE, AND YOUNG, JAMES, 1916-
Thomas Berry and a new creation story. il por *The Christian Century* 106:750-3 Ag 16-23 '89
HOPE, SAMUEL
National conditions and policy imperatives. bibl f *Design for Arts in Education* 91:15-35 S/O '89
HOPE PLANTATION (WINDSOR, N.C.)
Hope Plantation in North Carolina. J. E. Tyler. bibl f il *Antiques* 135:322-9 Ja '89

HOPKINS, ANN B.
about
Myth America in the workplace. por *U.S. News & World Report* 106:14 My 15 '89
A slap at sex stereotypes. A. Sachs. il por *Time* 133:66 My 15 '89
Smile when you say that, partner. D. L. Jacobs. il por *Ms.* 17:137 Ja/F '89
Wrestling with bias. D. Seligman. il *Fortune* 119:339 Je 5 '89
HOPKINS, CYRIL G.
Cyril Hopkins: a voice for the soil [excerpt from Soil fertility and permanent agriculture] por *Organic Gardening* 36:70 O '89
HOPKINS, ELLEN
Advice and consent. *Harper's Bazaar* 122:201+ Ap '89
The name of the room. il *House & Garden* 161:62+ D '89
Neuroses are a girl's best friend. *Harper's Bazaar* 122:176+ Mr '89
Nowhere to run (I). il *Rolling Stone* p72-4+ Ap 20 '89
Nowhere to run (II). il por *Rolling Stone* p74-6+ My 4 '89
Their fathers' daughters. il pors *Rolling Stone* p76-7+ N 30 '89
HOPKINS, GERARD MANLEY, 1844-1889
Pied beauty [poem] *America* 161:97 Ag 26-S 2 '89
about
The ecstasy of Gerard Manley Hopkins. A. Burgess. il *The New York Times Book Review* 94:15 Ag 27 '89
Gerard Manley Hopkins [cover story] *America* 161:98, 102-9 Ag 26-S 2 '89
HOPKINS, LINDA
about
Linda Hopkins returns to Broadway in new musical 'Black and blue'. il pors *Jet* 76:52-3 Ap 10 '89
HOPKINS, MARK
China's forbidden subject. il *The New Leader* 72:7-9 F 20 '89
How China manages the press [cover story] il *The New Leader* 72:3-4 My 1 '89
Last days of China's old guard [cover story] il *The New Leader* 72:7-8 N 27 '89
The new truth in China [with editorial comment] il *The New Leader* 72:2, 5-7 Jl 10-24 '89
HOPKINS, MARY
Finding bargain air fares [cover story] il *Consumers' Research Magazine* 72:10-12 Jl '89
HOPPE, LESLIE J.
about
What you don't know about the Old Testament could fill a book [interview] il *U.S. Catholic* 54:26-31 S '89
HOPPEN, STEPHANIE
about
Chelsea collector. J. Etra. il *House & Garden* 161:140-5 Mr '89
HOPPER, BILL
about
The energy that drives a national success story. D. Jenish. il por *Maclean's* 102:32-3 D 25 '89
HOPPER, DENNIS
about
Colors [film] Reviews
Video il 12:81-2 Ja '89. I. Robbins
Taking a young, fourth wife, actor Dennis Hopper promises that this time he's playing for keeps. il pors *People Weekly* 32:72-3 Jl 3 '89
HOPPER, EDWARD, 1882-1967
about
Edward Hopper: shades of summer. B. Adams. il pors *Harper's Bazaar* 122:90-3+ Jl '89
HOPPER, GORDON L.
Just for fun. *Bicycling* 30:138-9 My '89
HOPWOOD, DANIEL R.
Whispering giants. il pors *Americana* 17:63-5 My/Je '89
HORACE MCKENNA CENTER
The legacy of Horace McKenna. J. Dear. il *America* 160:170-2 F 25 '89
HORAN, JACK
World nuclear power operators unite. il *The Bulletin of the Atomic Scientists* 45:39-40 Ap '89
HORAN, KEVIN
Big wheel [cover story] il *Modern Maturity* 32:78-82 Je/Jl '89
HORENSTEIN, SIDNEY
Big Apple tusks. il map *Natural History* p96-8+ Mr '89
HORIN, DANIEL BEN- *See* Ben-Horin, Daniel
HORIZON (PERIODICAL)
Arts exchange. See issues of Horizon (Tuscaloosa, Ala.) beginning May 1986
HORIZONTAL OIL WELL DRILLING *See* Oil well drilling
HORKHEIMER, JACK
about
Jack Horkheimer: "Star hustler". S. J. O'Meara. il pors *Sky and Telescope* 77:544-7 My '89
HORMATS, ROBERT D.
Redefining Europe and the Atlantic link. *Foreign Affairs* 68:71-91 Fall '89

HORMEL (GEO. A.) & CO. *See* Geo. A. Hormel & Co.
HORMONE RECEPTORS
See also
Chemoreceptors
1,25-dihydroxyvitamin D-responsive element and glucocorticoid repression in the osteocalcin gene. N. A. Morrison and others. bibl f il *Science* 246:1158-61 D 1 '89
Cloning and sequencing of porcine LH-hCG receptor cDNA: variants lacking transmembrane domain. H. Loosfelt and others. bibl f il *Science* 245:525-8 Ag 4 '89
The EGF receptor kinase substrate p35 in the floor plate of the embryonic rat CNS. J. A. McKanna and S. Cohen. bibl f il *Science* 243:1477-9 Mr 17 '89
High-resolution epitope mapping of hGH-receptor interactions by alanine-scanning mutagenesis. B. C. Cunningham and J. A. Wells. bibl f il *Science* 244:1081-5 Je 2 '89
Human diabetes associated with a deletion of the tyrosine kinase domain of the insulin receptor. M. Taira and others. bibl f il *Science* 245:63-6 Jl 7 '89
Human diabetes associated with a mutation in the tyrosine kinase domain of the insulin receptor. M. Odawara and others. bibl f il *Science* 245:66-8 Jl 7 '89
Identification of a thyroid hormone receptor that is pituitary-specific. R. A. Hodin and others. bibl f il *Science* 244:76-9 Ap 7 '89
In vitro transcription enhancement by purified derivatives of the glucocorticoid receptor. L. P. Freedman and others. bibl f il *Science* 245:298-301 Jl 21 '89
Lutropin-choriogonadotropin receptor: an unusual member of the G protein-coupled receptor family. K. C. McFarland and others. bibl f il *Science* 245:494-9 Ag 4 '89
Molecular cloning of the thyrotropin receptor. M. Parmentier and others. bibl f il *Science* 246:1620-2 D 22 '89
Novel sites of expression of functional angiotensin II receptors in the late gestation fetus. M. A. Millan and others. bibl f il *Science* 244:1340-2 Je 16 '89
Postponement of satiety by blockade of brain cholecystokinin (CCK-B) receptors. C. T. Dourish and others. bibl f il *Science* 245:1509-11 S 29 '89
Pygmy paradox prompts a short answer [shortage of growth hormone receptors] K. Fackelmann. *Science News* 136:22 Jl 8 '89
Pygmy puzzle [defective growth hormone receptor; research by Gerhard Baumann] il *Discover* 10:14 D '89
Recent awakenings in melatonin research [work of Margarita L. Dubocovich] R. Weiss. *Science News* 136:317 N 11 '89
Short-answer question [defective growth hormone receptor in pygmies; research by Gerhard Baumann] J. Benditt. *Scientific American* 261:32-3 S '89
Steroid binding at σ-"opioid" receptors [discussion of April 8, 1988 article, Steroid binding at σ receptors suggests a link between endocrine, nervous, and immune systems] T.-P. Su and others. bibl f il *Science* 246:1635-8 D 22 '89
HORMONES
See also
Angiotensin
Cholecystokinin
Corticosteroids
Epidermal growth factor
Erythropoietin
Insulin
Juvenile hormones
Pheromones
Pituitary hormone releasing factors
Pituitary hormones
Prostaglandins
Steroids
Vasoactive intestinal polypeptide
Identification of a neuropeptide hormone that regulates sex pheromone production in female moths. A. K. Raina and others. bibl f il *Science* 244:796-8 My 19 '89
HORMONES, PLANT
See also
Auxins
HORMONES, SEX
See also
Dehydroepiandrosterone
Estrogen
Progesterone
Progestin
Testosterone
How sex hormones boost—or cut—intellectual ability. D. Kimura. il *Psychology Today* 23:62-6 N '89
The men's club [synthetic male hormones induce feminization in catfish] *Discover* 10:18 Ag '89
Sexual chemistry. R. Ellis. il *Glamour* 87:322-3+ Ap '89
HORMONES, SYNTHETIC
See also
Pituitary hormones, Synthetic
Progestin
HORN, DENISE, AND COLEMAN, ERICA
After a heart transplant, a 9-year-old learns the joy of being a normal kid again; ed. by Suzanne Adelson. il *People Weekly* 32:103+ N 20 '89

HORN, KAREN
about
Karen Horn. B. S. Goldman. il por *American Artist* 53:68-73 Ag '89
HORN, LAURIE
Baryshnikov takes on Swan Lake: something old, something new. il *Dance Magazine* 63:44-9 My '89
Taking care of the roles: Villella victorious, Miami's Prometheus. il *Dance Magazine* 63:44-50 N '89
HORN & HARDART CO.
From takeout to takeover target. il *Money* 18:7 My '89
HORN OF AFRICA *See* East Africa
HORNADAY, ANN
Movies you'll never see. il *Mother Jones* 14:53-4 F/Mr '89
What's a First Lady to do? An open letter to Barbara Bush. *Ms.* 17:98 Ja/F '89
HORNBECK, DAVID W.
Schools: homes away from home. *American Health* 8:50 O '89
HORNBLUM, ALLEN
Condoms in the cells. *The Progressive* 53:12 F '89
HORNE, CAROL
about
Heigh-ho, heigh-ho, it's far, far off we go; or, Grumpynappers give a cement dwarf a joyride. il *People Weekly* 31:100-1 Je 26 '89
HORNE, LENA
about
Lena Horne, 71, reveals she wants to marry again. il pors *Jet* 76:18 My 15 '89
HORNED OWLS *See* Owls
HORNER, JOHN R.
about
Interview: Jack Horner. J. Gorman. il por *Omni (New York, N.Y.)* 11:72-4+ Mr '89
Uncovering the mystery of the dinosaur. E. Ziegler. il *Reader's Digest* 135:163-8 D '89
HORNER, JOHN R., AND WEISHAMPEL, DAVID B.
Dinosaur eggs: the inside story [cover story] il *Natural History* p60-7 D '89
HORNS
Animals
See also
Antlers
Deconstructivist rhinos [thwarting poachers by removing horns in Namibia] il *Discover* 10:12 O '89
Wild things [horn and antler furniture] A. De Moubray. il *House & Garden* 161:28-9 Ja '89
HORNSBY, BRUCE
about
Home on the Range with Bruce Hornsby. P. Puterbaugh. il por *Rolling Stone* p29 Jl 13-27 '89
HOROSCOPES *See* Astrology
HOROSKO, MARIAN
Education. See issues of Dance Magazine
Frontier of the mind: Martha Graham at 95 [interview; cover story] il pors *Dance Magazine* 63:50-7 My '89
The personal you. See issues of Dance Magazine
The tap dance kid grows up: show-stopping Savion. il pors *Dance Magazine* 63:38-40 Ag '89
(jt. auth) See Myers, Martha, and Horosko, Marian
HOROVITZ, ISRAEL
about
The widow's blind date [drama] Reviews
The Nation 249:766 D 18 '89. T. M. Disch
The New Yorker 65:110 N 20 '89. E. Oliver
HOROWITZ, AMITY KAYE
A capital city for kids. il *Publishers Weekly* 235:122-3 My 12 '89
HOROWITZ, DAVID, 1939-
Still taking the Fifth. *Commentary* 88:53-5 Jl '89
(jt. auth) See Collier, Peter, and Horowitz, David, 1939-
about
Radical transformations. S. Churcher. il pors *The New York Times Magazine* p30-1+ Jl 16 '89
HOROWITZ, H. S., AND OTHERS
Submicrometer superconducting $YBa_2Cu_3O_{6+x}$ particles made by a low-temperature synthetic route. bibl f il *Science* 243:66-9 Ja 6 '89
HOROWITZ, IRVING LOUIS
Sociology and subjectivism. *Society* 26:49-54 Jl/Ag '89
HOROWITZ, JONATHAN M., AND OTHERS
Point mutational inactivation of the retinoblastoma antioncogene. bibl f il *Science* 243:937-40 F 17 '89
HOROWITZ, JOY
Hollywood's dirty little secret. il *American Visions* 4:16-21 Ag '89
HOROWITZ, LAWRENCE C.
How to choose a good surgeon [excerpt from Taking charge] por *Prevention (Emmaus, Pa.)* 41:50-3+ Jl '89
HOROWITZ, ROBERT M.
Tighten standards for termination of parental rights. il *Children Today* 18:9-11 My/Je '89
HOROWITZ, VLADIMIR, 1904-1989
about
Obituary
Maclean's il por 102:100 N 20 '89. G. Hayden
National Review 41:55 D 22 '89. W. F. Buckley

HOROWITZ, VLADIMIR, 1904-1989—about—Obituary—cont.
National Review 41:13-14 D 8 '89. S. Chapin
Newsweek il por 114:81 N 20 '89. L. Shapiro
People Weekly il por 32:151 N 20 '89
Time il por 134:120 N 20 '89. M. Walsh
HORROR FILMS *See* Motion pictures—Horror films
HORROR TALES
For goodness sake? [S. King's books banned in public school libraries] H. Wornom. por *Omni (New York, N.Y.)* 12:16+ D '89
Nightmare on game street [horror games] S. Addams. il *Compute!* 11:106-8+ O '89

Authorship
In pursuit of pure horror [horror-story writers develop sequel to E. A. Poe's The tell-tale heart; cover story] il *Harper's* 279:45-53 O '89
HORROR TELEVISION SHOWS *See* Television broadcasting—Horror shows
HORS D'OEUVRES *See* Appetizers
HORSE AUCTIONS
The last of a breed [last son sired by Northern Dancer sold at Keeneland] W. F. Reed. il *Sports Illustrated* 71:10 Jl 31 '89
HORSE BARNS *See* Barns and stables
HORSE BREEDING *See* Horses—Breeding
HORSE CHESTNUT
Of Buckeyes and buckeyes [Ohio buckeye] J. Fleischman. il map *Audubon* 91:112-14+ S '89
HORSE FARMS *See* Horses—Breeding
HORSE FERRIES
Heyday of the horse ferry [teamboat discovered on bottom of Lake Champlain] D. G. Shomette. il map *National Geographic* 176:548-56 O '89
HORSE MANURE
A whiff of things to come [carriage horses to wear canvas bags to catch manure in New York City] il *Newsweek* 113:71 Ap 10 '89
HORSE RACE BETTING
See also
Off-track betting
The daily double [turf writers A. Beyer and S. Crist] G. Norman. il pors *Sports Illustrated* 70:92-6+ Je 5 '89
Easy money [method of W. T. Ziemba; cover story] M. Skinner. il *Omni (New York, N.Y.)* 11:42-4+ My '89
HORSE RACING
See also
Harness racing
Horse race betting
Jockeys
Race horses
Race tracks
Auditions for the Derby. D. Stathoplos. il *Sports Illustrated* 70:78+ Ap 17 '89
Beers with . . . Angel Cordero [interview] I. Cohen. il por *Sport (New York, N.Y.)* 80:41-2 Je '89
The Breeders' Cup runneth low. M. Smith. il *Sport (New York, N.Y.)* 80:14 N '89
The daily double [turf writers A. Beyer and S. Crist] G. Norman. il pors *Sports Illustrated* 70:92-6+ Je 5 '89
Day of reckoning [Kentucky Derby favorite P. Day on Easy Goer] J. E. Vader. il pors *Sports Illustrated* 70:74-6+ My 1 '89
Good hands [jockey's handling · of horse] J. Krone. il por *American Health* 8:64-5 My '89
Loud and clear [Sunday Silence wins Super Derby] D. Stathoplos. il *Sports Illustrated* 71:36-7 O 2 '89
A mystery colt revealed [Houston wins Bay Shore Stakes] D. Stathoplos. il *Sports Illustrated* 70:83-4 Ap 3 '89
Nice and easy [Easy Goer wins Belmont] W. Nack. il *Sports Illustrated* 70:44-5 Je 19 '89
Nose to nose [Sunday Silence outduels Easy Goer at Preakness] D. Stathoplos. il *Sports Illustrated* 70:16-19 My 29 '89
Once again, Easy does it [Easy Goer wins Swale Stakes; Dixieland Brass injured in Florida Derby] D. Stathoplos. il *Sports Illustrated* 70:28+ Mr 13 '89
A perfect horse came up flawed [Houston loses to Sewickley in the Tom Fool Stakes] D. Stathoplos. il *Sports Illustrated* 71:75 Jl 24 '89
She who laughs last . . . [jockey J. Krone; cover story] G. Smith. il pors *Sports Illustrated* 70:84-8+ My 22 '89
Silence roars once more [Sunday Silence wins Breeders' Cup Classic] W. Nack. il *Sports Illustrated* 71:28-30+ N 13 '89
Smelling the roses, pricked by a thorn [trainer D. W. Lukas] P. Axthelm. il pors *Gentlemen's Quarterly* 59:234-9+ My '89
Strike up the band [Dixieland Brass wins Fountain of Youth Stakes] D. Stathoplos. il *Sports Illustrated* 70:48-9 F 27 '89
A Sunday stroll [Sunday Silence beats Easy Goer in Kentucky Derby] W. Nack. il *Sports Illustrated* 70:18-25 My 15 '89
A tale of two horses [Kentucky Derby contenders Houston and Easy Goer] D. Stathoplos. il *Sports Illustrated* 70:78-81+ My 8 '89
The Triple Crown affair. M. Smith. il *Sport (New York, N.Y.)* 80:104-7 Je '89

Turnabout at Belmont [Easy Goer wins] C. Leerhsen. il *Newsweek* 113:67 Je 19 '89

Accidents and injuries
About that picture . . . [N. Hubbard clings to neck of mount to place second in Golden Gate Fields race] il *Sports Illustrated* 70:14 F 20 '89
The longest ride [comeback of jockey R. Davis following accident that killed M. Venezia] W. Nack. il pors *Sports Illustrated* 70:116-20+ Mr 20 '89
The mysterious binoculars [ultrasonic device alleged to be cause of horse throwing jockey in race at Royal Ascot] il *Sports Illustrated* 71:24 N 20 '89

Economic aspects
Gene Klein quits the track—$26 million later. R. Grover. il por *Business Week* p66 Ag 7 '89

Ethical aspects
The mysterious binoculars [ultrasonic device alleged to be cause of horse throwing jockey in race at Royal Ascot] il *Sports Illustrated* 71:24 N 20 '89
Racing's cocaine mystery [race horses test positive] il *Sports Illustrated* 70:14 F 27 '89

History
Breeders' Cup. P. Moran. il *Sports Illustrated* 71:11+ O 23 '89
Forgotten heroes: black winners of the Kentucky Derby. R. A. Frister. il *Ebony* 44:82+ My '89
Kentucky Derby: the Ultimate Derby [fantasy race] W. F. Reed. il *Sports Illustrated* 70:47+ My 1 '89

Uniforms
Horse couture [Aeroform Silks] J. Privman. il *Sport (New York, N.Y.)* 80:14 Ap '89

Great Britain
At Ascot, horses finish behind hats and royals. il *People Weekly* 32:54-5 Jl 10 '89

Italy
See also
Palio di Siena (Italy)
HORSE RACING FANS
Echoes of an equine past [horse-loving teenager at Arlington Park in the 1950s] W. Nack. il *Sports Illustrated* 71:84-8+ S 18 '89
HORSE RACING RECORDS
The Ant gallops toward Joe D [jockey C. Antley's winning streak at Aqueduct reaches 53 days] A. Lennard. il por *Sports Illustrated* 70:16 Ap 24 '89
HORSE SHOE, BATTLE OF THE, 1814
1814. A. Nielson. il por *American Heritage* 40:30 Mr '89
HORSE TRAINERS
See also
Lukas, D. Wayne
McGaughey, Claude R., 1951-
Whittingham, Charlie, 1913-
HORSEBACK RIDING *See* Horsemanship
HORSEBACK TRIPS
See also
Deaf-Blind Trailblazers (Organization)
Big Sky hike [Montana's Bob Marshall Wilderness] J. Zumbo. il *Outdoor Life* 183:88-90+ Mr '89
Fire and glory [Yellowstone National Park] R. Rudner. il *Ms.* 18:34 S '89
Saga of the urban buckarettes [horseback trip from Cottonwood Ranch through the Jarbidge wilderness of Nevada] C. J. Hadley. il *The Saturday Evening Post* 261:70-1 Jl/Ag '89

Accidents and injuries
"Don't let my father die!" [C. Cooke saves father's life after he is seriously injured by horse] P. O. D'Aulaire and E. D'Aulaire. il *Reader's Digest* 134:115-20 Je '89

Anecdotes, facetiae, satire, etc.
Old Ned. G. Hill. il *Field & Stream* 93:19 Mr '89
HORSEFLESH MAHOGANY *See* Sabicu
HORSEMANSHIP
See also
Polo
I'm just wild about horses! L. Cardoso. il por *Women's Sports & Fitness* 11:66 O '89

Study and teaching
Horse sense for aspiring equestrians. G. Weiss. il *Business Week* p110 F 6 '89
Your chaps, sir. V. Klinkenborg. il *Esquire* 111:50+ Je '89
HORSEPOWER (MECHANICS)
Hot-rodders [altering airplane engine's original design to increase horsepower] il *Flying* 116:74 Ag '89
HORSES
See also
Draft horses
Miniature horses
Race horses
Wild horses

Accidents and hazards
Message of the pond [rescue of horse trapped in ice helps families cope with grief] P. Michelmore. il *Reader's Digest* 135:106-10 D '89
The sponger [inadvertently feeding a sponge to a horse] N. Hazelton. *National Review* 41:50+ Ap 21 '89
Anecdotes, facetiae, satire, etc.
Jimmy Kimmery and the saddle horse. B. Tarrant. il por *Field & Stream* 94:102-3 D '89

HORSES—*cont.*

Breeding

Blood brothers and bluegrass [Sunday Silence and Easy Goer products of rival Hancock brothers farms] W. Nack. il *Sports Illustrated* 71:76-80+ O 30 '89

Killearn Farm: F. William Free's Hudson Valley horse farm. J. Gruen. il por *Architectural Digest* 46:182-7+ Je '89

The last of a breed [last son sired by Northern Dancer sold at Keeneland] W. F. Reed. il *Sports Illustrated* 71:10 Jl 31 '89

Raising Arabians can have you rolling in clover. M. Ivey. il *Business Week* p155 Mr 13 '89

Well-groomed or well-bred? [thoroughbred breeding in England] N. Russell. il *History Today* 39:10-12 Ja '89

Equipment

A whiff of things to come [carriage horses to wear canvas bags to catch manure in New York City] il *Newsweek* 113:71 Ap 10 '89

HORSES, DRAFT *See* Draft horses
HORSES, MINIATURE *See* Miniature horses
HORSES, RACE *See* Race horses
HORSES, ROCKING *See* Rocking horses, etc.
HORSES, WILD *See* Wild horses
HORSES AS AN INVESTMENT

It's a long shot. K. Hannon. il *Forbes* 143:262-3 Je 26 '89

An oil heiress looks for pay dirt at the track [fight promoter and race horse breeder J. Abercrombie] T. Vogel. il por *Business Week* p162 My 22 '89

Raising Arabians can have you rolling in clover. M. Ivey. il *Business Week* p155 Mr 13 '89

HORSES IN ART

Equestrian mysteries [interview with D. Butterfield] M. Tucker. il *Art in America* 77:154-7+ Je '89

In the spirit of the mustangs [R. Glen's The mustangs of Las Colinas in Irving, Tex.] il *Southern Living* 24:20 S '89

HORSESHOE BEND, BATTLE OF, 1814 *See* Horse Shoe, Battle of the, 1814
HORSESHOE CRABS

Doing their primal thing [mating on the N.J. shore] M. Riley. il *Time* 134:10-11+ Ag 21 '89

HORSESHOE PITCHING

Tournaments

Pitching a shoe or two [World Horseshoe Tornament] L. Erickson. il *Travel Holiday* 171:130 Mr '89

HORSESHOES

Ten things you never knew about horseshoes. S. Rosenbloom. il *Sport (New York, N.Y.)* 80:125 Je '89

HORSMAN, MATHEW

What ails Britain. il *World Press Review* 36:50-1 Ap '89

HORST, 1906-

about

Horst at Holly Solomon. A. F. Collins. *Art in America* 77:201 N '89

HORSTMAN, JUDITH

The band plays on. il *Country Journal* 16:42-6 Jl/Ag '89

HORSTMAN, NEIL W.

The Mount Vernon Ladies' Association of the Union. il pors *Antiques* 135:454-61 F '89

HORSTMEYER, STEVEN L.

In search of Cincinnati's weather. il *Weatherwise* 42:320-6 D '89

HORSZOWSKI, MIECZYSLAW

about

Horszowski. R. Freed. il por *Stereo Review* 54:126 Mr '89
HORTICULTURAL EXHIBITIONS *See* Garden exhibits
HORTICULTURAL RESEARCH

Looking back . . . and ahead. P. Williams and G. Williams. il *The Mother Earth News* 120:46-7 N/D '89

Federal aid

Support for plant biology. P. H. Abelson. *Science* 246:865 N 17 '89

HORTICULTURE

See also
Forcing (Plants)
Gardens and gardening
Greenhouses
Nurseries (Horticulture)
Vegetable gardens and gardening
HORTICULTURE THERAPY *See* Gardens and gardening—Therapeutic use
HORTON, JACOB F.

about

Fatal subtraction. J. Carney. il por *Time* 133:87 My 22 '89

HORTON, LOWELL

Don't let drug programs send deadly messages. *The Education Digest* 54:38-9 My '89

HORTON, PETER

about

Bachelor #1: Peter Horton. J. Hershel. il por *Mademoiselle* 95:114 S '89

HORTON, TOM

Paradise lost. il *Rolling Stone* p150-1+ D 14-28 '89

HORTON, WILLIE

about

Willie Horton and me. A. Walton. il por *The New York Times Magazine* p52-3+ Ag 20 '89

HORVATH, GAIL

about

Just Desserts Inc.: serving up a model workplace. J. David and K. File. *Working Woman* 14:169+ O '89

HORVATH, HAL

Children and creativity. por *The Humanist* 49:22-3+ Ja/F '89

HORVITZ, WAYNE

about

Wayne Horvitz/The President: Park West/Chicago. E. Guregian. il *Down Beat* 56:54 Ag '89

HORWITZ, SANDIE

How to say the right thing. il *Reader's Digest* 134:161-4 Mr '89

HOSE

See also
Automobile engines—Hoses
Dishwashers—Hoses
Garden hose
HOSENBALL, MARK

The brothers Bush. *The New Republic* 200:19-21 Ap 3 '89

Dear Manny. *The New Republic* 200:9-10 Je 12 '89

The friends of Michael Milken. il por *The New Republic* 201:23-5 Ag 28 '89

Moscow on the HUD [cover story] il *The New Republic* 201:18-21 O 23 '89

HOSENBALL, MARK, AND ISIKOFF, MICHAEL

Pssst. *The New Republic* 200:16+ Ja 2 '89

HOSIERY

See also
Tights (Clothing)
Hosiery. L. Gilliam. il *Essence* 20:36 Ag '89

If you get blisters, check your socks [acrylic fibers more effective than cotton in preventing foot blisters; views of Kirk M. Herring] il *Prevention (Emmaus, Pa.)* 41:12+ Jl '89

Anecdotes, facetiae, satire, etc.

Pantyhoseman! V. S. Sussman. il *Glamour* 87:284+ O '89
HOSIERY INDUSTRY

Advertising

The war of the hoses [pantyhose] B. Kanner. il *New York* 22:12-13 Ja 2 '89

Great Britain

See also
Sock Shop International plc
Switzerland

See also
Fogal AG
HOSIERY STORES

Sock it to me! [sock stores] il *Time* 133:52 Mr 6 '89
HOSKEN, FRAN P., 1919-

Austerity's human toll. il por *The Humanist* 49:17-19+ Ja/F '89

HOSKINS, BOB, 1942-

about

Bob Hoskins' hare raising role. S. Grant. il por *Video* 13:14-15 O '89

HOSKINS, W. LEE

Breaking the inflation-recession cycle [address, September 19, 1989] *Vital Speeches of the Day* 56:158-60 D 15 '89

Financial reform [address, August 29, 1989] *Vital Speeches of the Day* 56:111-14 D 1 '89

HOSLER, KAREN

Sworn to run. il por *Runner's World* 24:30-1+ D '89
HOSMER, RACHEL, D. 1988

Praying with the Klan. *The Christian Century* 106:494-5 My 10 '89

HOSMER, ROBERT E.

Writing with intent [cover story] il pors *Commonweal* 116:233-41 Ap 21 '89

HOSODA, CRAIG

The good parts [excerpt from The bare facts video guide 1989] *Harper's* 279:32+ D '89

HOSPICES

Great Britain

See also
London (England)—Hospices
HOSPITAL BONDS *See* Hospitals—Securities
HOSPITAL CARE

See also
Blacks—Hospital care
Children—Hospital care
Children—Preparation for hospital and medical care
Indians of North America—Hospital care
Infants, Newborn—Hospital care
Intensive care units
Nurses and nursing
Costs

See also
AIDS (Disease)—Costs
Alphabet medicine [effects of Medicare reimbursement cost-cutting] W. F. Allman. il *Health (New York, N.Y.)* 21:34+ Ja '89

HOSPITAL CARE—Costs—cont.

Hospitals: damned if they merge, damned if they don't. S. B. Garland and T. Smart. il *Business Week* p48+ N 6 '89

Looking over the doctor's shoulder [outcome monitoring] S. Findlay. il *U.S. News & World Report* 106:70-1+ Ja 30 '89

Medicare's sickbed [proposed cuts worry hospitals] S. Dentzer. il *U.S. News & World Report* 106:20-1 F 6 '89

On the sick list: rural hospitals. S. B. Garland. il *Business Week* p36 Mr 27 '89

SLC efforts zero in on hospital costs. *Modern Maturity* 32:85 Je/Jl '89

Will Denton Cooley make medical history again? [cut-rate heart bypasses] M. Ivey. il por *Business Week* p56+ Mr 27 '89

HOSPITAL CORP. OF AMERICA

A crazy deal? [sale of psychiatric hospitals to an ESOP] S. Flack. il *Forbes* 144:58 Jl 24 '89

HOSPITAL EMPLOYEES

See also

Nurses and nursing

HOSPITAL EQUIPMENT INDUSTRY

See also

Abbott Laboratories

HOSPITAL FOR SICK CHILDREN (TORONTO, ONT.)

Discoveries of hope at the heart of human life [work of L.-C. Tsui] D. Jenish. il por *Maclean's* 102:22-3 D 25 '89

Nelles's legal gain [Canadian Supreme Court rules in favor of nurse S. Nelles over baby murder mystery] B. Wickens. il por *Maclean's* 102:42 Ag 28 '89

HOSPITAL MANAGEMENT INDUSTRY

See also

American Medical International, Inc.

Hospital Corp. of America

Humana Inc

Health. M. Fritz. il *Forbes* 143:150-1 Ja 9 '89

The prognosis on health care: critical—and getting worse. J. O. Hamilton. il *Business Week* p82 Ja 9 '89

Acquisitions and mergers

A crazy deal? [Hospital Corp. of America to sell its psychiatric hospitals to an ESOP] S. Flack. il *Forbes* 144:58 Jl 24 '89

'A lot of people don't know who Mel Klein is' [bid for American Medical International] T. Vogel. il por *Business Week* p24-5 Jl 24 '89

With all these buyers, AMI must be getting better [American Medical International] P. Cole. *Business Week* p64-5 Je 26 '89

HOSPITAL PATIENTS

Civil rights

Know your rights as a patient! S. Mahler. *McCall's* 116:110+ S '89

Psychology

See also

Munchausen syndrome

Four-legged medicine [pet visits to help patients; work of Jackie McCurdy] B. Portnow. il *American Health* 8:122 Mr '89

HOSPITAL RESIDENTS See Residents (Medicine)

HOSPITAL SHIPS

See also

Americares Foundation

HOSPITAL WASTE DISPOSAL IN THE OCEAN See Medical waste disposal in the ocean

HOSPITALITY

See also

Entertaining

Guests

HOSPITALITY IN THE BIBLE

Entertaining guests. P. J. Ryan. il *America* 161:46 Jl 15-22 '89

If you give a feast, invite the poor. K. Koyama. il *The Christian Century* 106:747 Ag 16-23 '89

HOSPITALS

See also

Children—Hospitals

Hospital care

Nurses and nursing

Nursing homes

Veterinary hospitals

Acquisitions and mergers

Hospitals: damned if they merge, damned if they don't. S. B. Garland and T. Smart. il *Business Week* p48+ N 6 '89

Administration

See also

Hospital management industry

Rx for red ink [nonprofit hospitals set up for profit subsidiaries] E. Paris. il *Forbes* 144:200 O 30 '89

Antitrust cases

Hospitals: damned if they merge, damned if they don't. S. B. Garland and T. Smart. il *Business Week* p48+ N 6 '89

Architecture

Keeping fit [special section; with introd. by Margaret Gaskie] il *Architectural Record* 177:78-89 Ap '89

Emergency services

See also

Trauma care units

Help! This is an emergency! [cutbacks in services] S. Findlay. il *U.S. News & World Report* 107:28+ N 13 '89

Mystery on arrival [difficulties of emergency room diagnosis] E. Rosenthal. il *Discover* 10:78+ D '89

Patients for sale: supply is up, demand down [difficulties moving patients from emergency rooms to psychiatric hospitals] il *U.S. News & World Report* 106:64 Ap 24 '89

Should you go to the emergency room? L. Kramer. il *Glamour* 87:81+ O '89

Photographs and photography

The knife and gun club. E. Richards. il *Life* 12:48-53+ Ap '89

Life and death: scenes from a hospital emergency ward [Bellevue Hospital in New York; cover story] R. Falco. il *USA Today (Periodical)* 118:41-53 Jl '89

Finance

Medicare's sickbed [proposed cuts worry hospitals] S. Dentzer. il *U.S. News & World Report* 106:20-1 F 6 '89

Money for health [Tanzania] S. Ndeki. il *World Health* p11-13 My '89

Intensive care units

See Intensive care units

Lighting

Trouble in the nursery [retinopathy of prematurity] G. Cowley. il *Newsweek* 114:52 Ag 28 '89

Management and regulation

See Hospitals—Administration

Marketing

Curing the empty-bed syndrome. G. B. Bloch. il *Working Woman* 14:57-9 F '89

Maternity care

Austerity's human toll [World Bank and IMF policies concerning African maternity care] F. P. Hosken. il por *The Humanist* 49:17-19+ Ja/F '89

Regulation

See Hospitals—Administration

Securities

Recovery room [hospital bonds] B. Weberman. il *Forbes* 144:157 Ag 7 '89

Subsidiaries

Rx for red ink [nonprofit hospitals set up for profit subsidiaries] E. Paris. il *Forbes* 144:200 O 30 '89

Africa

Austerity's human toll [World Bank and IMF policies concerning maternity care] F. P. Hosken. il por *The Humanist* 49:17-19+ Ja/F '89

Canada

Life-and-death issues [hospitals employing ethics specialists] I. Shapiro. il *Maclean's* 102:56-7 My 1 '89

Sick to death [cover story; special section; with editorial comment by Kevin Doyle] il *Maclean's* 102:2, 32-8+ F 13 '89

Florida

See also

Wauchula (Fla.)—Hospitals

Illinois

See also

Evanston (Ill.)—Hospitals

Iowa

These rural hospitals want to lose their patients. C. Tevis. il *Successful Farming* 87:50AR Ja '89

Middle East

When X-rays are too costly [Basic Radiological System] A. Modjtabai. il *World Health* p29 Jl '89

Mississippi

See also

Jackson (Miss.)—Hospitals

New York (State)

See also

New York (N.Y.)—Hospitals

Queens (New York, N.Y.)—Hospitals

Nicaragua

Going by the book [woman with typhoid fever] T. Dajer. il *Discover* 10:30-3 Ap '89

Pennsylvania

See also

Philadelphia (Pa.)—Hospitals

South Africa

Cutting apartheid to the bone [fight to integrate hospitals] il *U.S. News & World Report* 107:10 Ag 14 '89

Tanzania

Money for health. S. Ndeki. il *World Health* p11-13 My '89

HOSPITALS, CHILDREN'S See Children—Hospitals

HOSPITALS, PSYCHIATRIC

Committed youth. N. Darnton. il *Newsweek* 114:66-9+ Jl 31 '89

A crazy deal? [Hospital Corp. of America to sell its psychiatric hospitals to an ESOP] S. Flack. il *Forbes* 144:58 Jl 24 '89

Patients for sale: supply is up, demand down [difficulties moving patients from emergency rooms to psychiatric hospitals] il *U.S. News & World Report* 106:64 Ap 24 '89

HOSPITALS, PSYCHIATRIC—cont.
Massachusetts
Return of Marie Balter [former patient helps administer Danvers State Hospital] T. Armbrister. il por *Reader's Digest* 135:123-7 Jl '89
Soviet Union
Should world psychiatry readmit the Soviets? P. Reddaway. bibl f il *The New York Review of Books* 36:54-8 O 12 '89
Soviet psychiatry: an exchange [discussion of October 12, 1989 article, Should world psychiatry readmit the Soviets?] P. Reddaway. il *The New York Review of Books* 36:65-6 D 21 '89
HOSPITALS, RURAL
Caring while curing. R. J. Margolis. *The New Leader* 72:11-12 Mr 6 '89
First aid for rural hospitals. C. Tevis. il *Successful Farming* 87:66AE F '89
In America's small-town hospitals, a patient isn't 'just a number'. R. J. Margolis. il *Smithsonian* 20:52-60+ S '89
On the sick list: rural hospitals. S. B. Garland. il *Business Week* p36 Mr 27 '89
These rural hospitals want to lose their patients [Iowa] C. Tevis. il *Successful Farming* 87:50AR Ja '89
HOST-GUEST COMPLEXES (CHEMISTRY)
The man with a new breed of molecule [D. J. Cram] P. Cole. il por *Business Week* Special Issue:74 Je 16 '89
HOST-PARASITE RELATIONSHIPS
Alien influence [wasp larvae manipulation of potato aphid behavior; research by Jacques Brodeur and Jeremy N. McNeil] T. Beardsley. *Scientific American* 261:26 Jl '89
Bacterial blight of soybean: regulation of a pathogen gene determining host cultivar specificity. T. V. Huynh and others. bibl f il *Science* 245:1374-7 S 22 '89
Dying aphids obey wasp's commands [research by Jacques Brodeur and Jeremy N. McNeil] R. Weiss. *Science News* 135:231 Ap 15 '89
Hangers-on [anilocra on heads of fish] L. Bunkley-Williams and E. H. Williams. il *Natural History* p40-1 Ja '89
Plant hybrid zones as sinks for pests [aphids on hybrid cottonwoods] T. G. Whitham. bibl f il *Science* 244:1490-3 Je 23 '89
Seasonal microhabitat selection by an endoparasitoid through adaptive modification of host behavior. J. Brodeur and J. N. McNeil. bibl f il *Science* 244:226-8 Ap 14 '89
HOSTAGES
See also
Beirut airplane hijacking, 1985
Iranian seizure of United States embassy, 1979-1981
Lebanon hostage cases, 1984-
A Kentucky boy's wild cry for help [student D. Pierce holds classmates hostage at Jackson County High School] W. Plummer. il pors *People Weekly* 32:44-7 O 9 '89
HOSTESS GIFTS *See* Gifts
HOSTETLER, KARL
Who says professional ethics is dead? A response to Myron Lieberman. *Phi Delta Kappan* 70:723-5 My '89
HOSTILITY (PSYCHOLOGY)
See also
Anger
Fighting (Psychology)
Danger! A short fuse can kill you [Type A behavior linked with heart disease] A. Fischer. il *Redbook* 173:162-3+ S '89
Getting to the heart of Type A's [interview with R. B. Williams] S. Findlay. il por *U.S. News & World Report* 106:68 My 15 '89
Hostility boosts risk of heart trouble [research by Redford B. Williams] K. Fackelmann. *Science News* 135:60 Ja 28 '89
Soothing the savage heart [views of R. Williams] J. Poppy. il *Esquire* 112:103-4 O '89
The trusting heart [modifying hostile behavior; excerpt] R. B. Williams. il *Psychology Today* 23:36-7+ Ja/F '89
Your anger can kill you [Type A behavior linked with heart disease; condensed from The trusting heart] R. B. Williams. il *Reader's Digest* 135:183-4+ Ag '89
HOSTIN, ROGER N. J.
Lens-scapes: how to put more depth into your scenics. il *Petersen's Photographic Magazine* 17:60-1+ Mr '89
HOT AIR BALLOONS *See* Balloons
HOT DOGS (MEAT) *See* Frankfurters
HOT LINES, INFORMATION *See* Telephone in medical care; Telephone information service
HOT LINES, SPORTS *See* Telephone in sports
HOT LINES, TOLL-FREE *See* Toll-free telephone service
HOT NET (FIRM)
When is a Hot Net not so hot? J. Loftus. il *Channels (New York, N.Y.: 1986)* 9:7 Mr '89
HOT SPOTS (GEOLOGY)
Flood basalts and hot-spot tracks: plume heads and tails. M. A. Richards and others. bibl f il map *Science* 246:103-7 O 6 '89
Heady theory for largest eruptions [work of Mark A. Richards] *Science News* 136:271 O 21 '89
HOT SPRINGS
See also
Megaplumes

Caldron in the sea [Kraternaya Bay] M. V. Propp and V. G. Tarasov. il maps *Natural History* p28-33 Ag '89
Deep-see shrimp [from hydrothermal vents; cover story] R. Monastersky. il *Science News* 135:90-3 F 11 '89
Heat flow and hydrothermal circulation in the Cascade Range, north-central Oregon. S. E. Ingebritsen and others. bibl f il maps *Science* 243:1458-62 Mr 17 '89
Opening the door to the unknown [creatures living near deep sea vents] M. Toner. il *National Wildlife* 27:34-6 Je/Jl '89
The quick recipe for a soup of black gold [research by Bernd R.T. Simoneit] R. Monastersky. *Science News* 136:295 N 4 '89
HOT SPRINGS (ARK.)
Description
Hot Springs, Ark. il *New Choices for the Best Years* 29:13 My '89
HOT SPRINGS RESORTS *See* Health resorts, watering places, etc.
HOT TODDIES *See* Alcoholic beverages
HOT TUBS
A hot tub. P. Butler and M. Butler. il *Outdoor Life* 184:20 Jl '89
Hot tubs, hot times. W. Giese. *Changing Times* 43:20-1 Je '89
Hot water and your heart. L. Holland. il *Good Housekeeping* 208:241 Ap '89
Ponds or spas? il *Sunset (Central West edition)* 183:52-3 Ag '89
Super spa. R. Q. Riley. il *Home Mechanix* 85:74-6 Ag '89
HOT TUNA (MUSICAL GROUP)
Hot Tuna. J. W. Poses. il *Down Beat* 56:46-8 Je '89
HOT WATER HEATERS *See* Water heaters
HOT WATER SUPPLY
See also
Solar water heaters
Water heaters
HOT WEATHER
See also
Droughts
Summer
1988: a summer to remember. A. Fisher. il *Popular Science* 235:55 Ag '89
A season of portents: the long summer of '88: a Wyoming diary. G. Ehrlich. il *Harper's* 279:50-7 Ag '89
Whatever the real reasons, the hot, dry weather in Colorado this summer was blamed on the greenhouse effect. R. M. Adams. il *Smithsonian* 20:12 S '89
Mental and physiological effects
The hazards of overheating. C. Slom. *McCall's* 116:86 Jl '89
Play it cool. C. Straley. il *Parents* 64:26 Jl '89
Summer running [special section] il *Runner's World* 24:66-76+ Jl '89
HOTCHKISS, PHYLLIS R.
(jt. auth) See Canady, Robert Lynn, and Hotchkiss, Phyllis R.
HOTCHKISS, RALF
about
Deals on wheels. B. Weber. il por *The New York Times Magazine* p122 S 17 '89
HOTEL AND RESTAURANT EMPLOYEES AND BARTENDERS INTERNATIONAL UNION *See* Hotel Employees and Restaurant Employees International Union
HOTEL CHARGES *See* Hotels, motels, etc.—Rates
HÔTEL DE CAVOYE (PARIS, FRANCE: HISTORIC HOUSE) *See* Paris (France)—Historic houses, sites, etc.
HOTEL DECORATION
The Grove Park Inn & the arts & crafts movement. B. E. Johnson. il *Antiques & Collecting Hobbies* 94:34-8 O '89
The Hôtel Ritz: Paris' resplendent landmark on the Place Vendôme. C. Aillaud. il *Architectural Digest* 46:120-5+ Ja '89
The Plaza suite [New York hotel] C. Vogel. il por *The New York Times Magazine* p50-2+ Ja 15 '89
Rags to riches [Royalton Hotel decorated by P. Starck] K. D. Stein. il *Architectural Record* 177:94-5 Mr '89
The Royalton treatment [decorated by P. Starck] C. K. Gandee. il por *House & Garden* 161:70-7 Ja '89
HÔTEL DROUOT (PARIS, FRANCE)
Inside the Drouot auctions. J. A. Cuadrado. il *Architectural Digest* 46:180-6+ O '89
HOTEL EMPLOYEES AND RESTAURANT EMPLOYEES INTERNATIONAL UNION
Look for the union label [housing trust fund in contract of Local 26 of Hotel Workers Union in Boston] P. Dreier. il *The Progressive* 53:30 Ap '89
HOTEL MANAGEMENT
See also
Hotels of Distinction (Firm)
An expert offers the ABCs of getting into the B&B biz [interview with P. Hardy] J. Wuorio. il por *Money* 18:18 D '89
So you want to run a country inn. R. R. Roha. il *Changing Times* 43:64-6+ F '89

HOTEL MANAGEMENT—*cont.*

Trouble in paradise [W. Bregman tries resort management in St. Croix] D. Machan. il pors *Forbes* 143:144+ My 15 '89

Study and teaching

To B&B or not to B&B [apprenticeship program at Wildwood Inn, Ware, Mass.] C. McLaughlin. il *New Choices for the Best Years* 29:10-11 Mr '89

HOTEL WORKERS

See also

Collective labor agreements—Hotel workers

Concierges

Hotel Employees and Restaurant Employees International Union

HOTELS, MOTELS, ETC.

See also

Airports—Hotels, motels, etc.

Bed and breakfast accommodations

Interactive video—Hotel use

Resorts

Single room occupancy hotels

Underwater hotels, motels, etc.

Welfare hotels

Great country inns for fall weekends. il *Glamour* 87:191-2+ S '89

Romantic hideaways. il *Glamour* 87:147+ F '89

Room service? Get me milk and cookies [hotel services for children] N. R. Gibbs. il *Time* 134:70-1 Jl 3 '89

So you want to run a country inn. R. R. Roha. il *Changing Times* 43:64-6+ F '89

Splendid splinters. J. Salter. il *Esquire* 112:118-21 Ag '89

Acquisitions and mergers

Puttin' on the Ritz—in New York, Washington, Aspen . . . [M. Hadid's deals] T. Smart. il por *Business Week* p32+ Ap 24 '89

Two guys sitting around with $100 million [E. and T. Slatkin] E. Schine. il pors *Business Week* p76+ O 9 '89

Why Motel 6 is waking up. G. G. Marcial. *Business Week* p206 S 25 '89

International aspects

Hong Kong hoteliers start colonizing the West. D. J. Yang. il *Business Week* p44 Mr 6 '89

Hotelier by default [H. Aoki] H. Katayama. il por *Forbes* 144:240 O 30 '89

Great Britain

Diana slept here [Trusthouse Forte's pursuit of Savoy Hotel plc] J. Marcom, Jr. il *Forbes* 143:116+ My 15 '89

Architecture

The recovery of ornament [Dai-Ichi Tokyo Bay Hotel] R. Kimball. il *Architectural Record* 177:132-7 My '89

Automation

Check yourself out. G. Eichler. il *Esquire* 111:66 F '89

High-tech hotels of the future. *The Futurist* 23:55 Jl/Ag '89

Chain and franchise operations

See also

Days Inns Corp.

Four Seasons Hotels Limited

Helmsley Hotels

Holiday Corp.

Howard Johnson Co.

Hyatt Corp.

Marriott Corporation

Pratt Hotel Corporation

Prime Motor Inns, Inc.

Regent International Hotels

Resorts International Inc.

Ritz-Carlton Hotel Company

Tamar Inns

Wilson Inns

Conservation and restoration

Once and future luxury [Sheraton Palace in San Francisco] B. Weber. il *The New York Times Magazine* p94 O 15 '89

Under the banyan tree [restoring Waikiki's Moana Hotel] C. McGuigan. il *Newsweek* 113:68 Ap 17 '89

A venerable haunt returns [Continental Hotel in Saigon] B. Weber. il *The New York Times Magazine* p70 Ag 13 '89

Decoration

See Hotel decoration

Health clubs

See Health clubs

International aspects

When less is more [small hotels] M. A. Kellogg. il *Travel Holiday* 172:68-73 Ag '89

Management

See Hotel management

Rates

Heartbreak motels. R. Ford. il *Harper's* 279:12-15 Ag '89

Hotels: dial M for muddle. il *Money* 18:17 Ja '89

No cheap room at the inn [yield management used to determine hotel room prices] G. Eichler. il *Esquire* 112:92 O '89

Sleeping cheap [Canada] S. McKay. il *Maclean's* 102:41 Je 5 '89

So little time, so many rooms [budget motels] R. Ford. il pors *Money* 18:102-4+ My '89

Taking "the sting" out of travel. H. Gieseking. il *Travel Holiday* 172:10-11+ D '89

Services

See also

Videotapes—Hotel use

Clubhouse comfort [airline passenger clubs and hotel services for business travelers] R. J. Christmas. il *Black Enterprise* 19:72+ Mr '89

When less is more [small hotels] M. A. Kellogg. il *Travel Holiday* 172:68-73 Ag '89

Suites

Home, suite home. D. Wishik. il *Travel Holiday* 172:92-5+ Jl '89

Telephone service

An end to phone-call gouges [alternative operator services] P. Plawin. *Changing Times* 43:90+ F '89

Atlantic States

Great escapes [country inns] J. Cecil and M. W. Robbins. il *New York* 22:52-6+ Ap 24 '89

California

See also

Los Angeles (Calif.)—Hotels, motels, etc.

San Francisco (Calif.)—Hotels, motels, etc.

West Hollywood (Calif.)—Hotels, motels, etc.

Romance on the rocks [northern coast] P. Viladas. il map *House & Garden* 161:82+ My '89

Canada

See also

Journey's End Motels

Sleeping cheap. S. McKay. il *Maclean's* 102:41 Je 5 '89

Connecticut

See also

North Stonington (Conn.)—Hotels, motels, etc.

Egypt

See also

Alexandria (Egypt)—Hotels, motels, etc.

Florida

See also

Orlando (Fla.)—Hotels, motels, etc.

France

See also

Paris (France)—Hotels, motels, etc.

Gîte d'étape [inexpensive accommodations for cyclists] M. McCloy. *Bicycling* 30:158-9 My '89

The inns of Alsace. J. Lubarsky. il map *Travel Holiday* 171:48-54 Ja '89

Great Britain

See also

London (England)—Hotels, motels, etc.

Savoy Hotel plc

Trusthouse Forte plc

The best of manors [country house hotels] il *House & Garden* 161:84+ Mr '89

Hawaii

See also

Waikiki Beach (Honolulu, Hawaii)—Hotels, motels, etc.

Hong Kong

Hong Kong hoteliers start colonizing the West. D. J. Yang. il *Business Week* p44 Mr 6 '89

India

Emperor of India's hotels [M. S. Oberoi] R. Saksena. il por *World Press Review* 36:73 O '89

Himalayan hideaways. K. Cox. il *Harper's Bazaar* 122:48+ O '89

Italy

See also

Montecatini Terme (Italy)—Hotels, motels, etc.

Japan

See also

Kyoto (Japan)—Hotels, motels, etc.

Nagoya (Japan)—Hotels, motels, etc.

Tokyo (Japan)—Hotels, motels, etc.

Louisiana

See also

New Orleans (La.)—Hotels, motels, etc.

Mackinac Island (Mich.)

Mackinac Island [Grand Hotel] M. Elder. il maps *Gourmet* 49:70-5+ Je '89

Massachusetts

See also

Ware (Mass.)—Hotels, motels, etc.

Williamstown (Mass.)—Hotels, motels, etc.

Maui (Hawaii)

The sacred bones of Maui [plan to build hotel on ancient burial ground stirs strife] W. S. Merwin. il *The New York Times Magazine* p20-1+ Ag 6 '89

New Jersey

See also

Cape May (N.J.)—Hotels, motels, etc.

New York (State)

See also

Bolton Landing (N.Y.)—Hotels, motels, etc.

New York (N.Y.)—Hotels, motels, etc.

North Carolina

See also

Asheville (N.C.)—Hotels, motels, etc.

Pinehurst (N.C.)—Hotels, motels, etc.

HOTELS, MOTELS, ETC.—cont.

Puerto Rico

Rooms to roam in Puerto Rico. L. Thomas. il map *Southern Living* 24:22+ Jl '89

Southern States

Southern exposure [antebellum mansions in use as inns] D. Di Costanzo. il *House & Garden* 161:52+ Ap '89

Sweden

See also

Stockholm (Sweden)—Hotels, motels, etc.

Thailand

See also

Bangkok (Thailand)—Hotels, motels, etc.

United States

See Hotels, motels, etc.

Vermont

See also

Middletown Springs (Vt.)—Hotels, motels, etc.

Plymouth (Vt.)—Hotels, motels, etc.

Land of milk and maple syrup [Rodgers Dairy Farm] C. H. Crowley. il *The Saturday Evening Post* 261:68-9 Jl/Ag '89

Vietnam

See also

Saigon (Vietnam)—Hotels, motels, etc.

Wales

The shooting party [pheasant shooting at Golden Pheasant Inn, Clwyd County] P. Davies. il *Gentlemen's Quarterly* 59:330-4+ O '89

Washington (D.C.)

See Washington (D.C.)—Hotels, motels, etc.

HOTELS OF DISTINCTION (FIRM)

When Alan Tremain checks in, the glitches check out. R. Duffy. il por *Business Week* p89 Mr 13 '89

HOTHOUSE FLOWERS (MUSICAL GROUP)

Hothouse rock. *The New Yorker* 65:33-4 D 25 '89

HOTHOUSES *See* Greenhouses

HOTOL (SPACE VEHICLE) *See* Spaceplane, British

HOTSPOTS (GEOLOGY) *See* Hot spots (Geology)

HOUCK, CATHERINE

How to beat a bad mood. *Reader's Digest* 134:93-5 Ja '89

HOUDAILLE INDUSTRIES, INC.

Junkman in D.C. [Kohlberg Kravis Roberts' buyout of Houdaille points to need to regulate LBOs] M. Holland. *The Nation* 248:365 Mr 20 '89

HOUGH, JERRY F., 1935-

Gorbachev's politics. bibl f *Foreign Affairs* 68:26-41 Wint '89/'90

HOUGHTON, MARY

about

Shorebank Corporation: rebuilding a community. J. David and K. File. *Working Woman* 14:171+ O '89

HOUGHTON, RICHARD A., AND WOODWELL, GEORGE M.

Global climatic change. il maps *Scientific American* 260:36-44 Ap '89

HOUGHTON, ROBERT L.

about

USGS reports a fraud. E. Marshall. *Science* 244:1436 Je 23 '89

HOUGHTON MIFFLIN AUDIO

Houghton Mifflin ships first abridged adult title. P. Sweeting. *Publishers Weekly* 235:49 My 5 '89

HOUGHTON MIFFLIN CO.

An architect of words: Houghton Mifflin's John Sterling. G. Feldman. il por *Publishers Weekly* 235:30-2 Ap 21 '89

HM's Miller to retire, succeeded by Darehshori. il por *Publishers Weekly* 236:16 D 22 '89

Houghton Mifflin to acquire Gollancz. M. Reuter and V. Menkes. *Publishers Weekly* 236:10 O 13 '89

Seymour Lawrence. R. A. Carter. il por *Publishers Weekly* 235:20-2 Mr 17 '89

Targeting the hand-sell [Network puts books in sellers' hands] R. Burroughs. il *Publishers Weekly* 235:52-4 My 19 '89

HOUK, ROSE, 1950-

LBJ Ranch: Heart's home [excerpt] il *National Parks* 63:54-5 N/D '89

HOULIHAN, LOKEY, HOWARD & ZUKIN INVESTMENT MANAGEMENT

Junk buy update [views of M. Budgyk] E. Hardy. il *Forbes* 144:158 D 25 '89

HOULTON, LOYCE

about

Carmina Burana [ballet] Reviews

Dance Magazine 63:100-1 F '89. J. Williams

HOUNDS

A hound's start in life [J. Wick's training suggestions] L. Mueller. il por *Outdoor Life* 183:43-4 F '89

Listening in the dark [coon hounds] B. Tarrant. il *Field & Stream* 93:94+ Ja '89

HOURGLASSES

Meet hourglass maker Frank LaCavera, one retiree who knows how to pass the time. il por *People Weekly* 31:121 Je 5 '89

HOURS OF BUSINESS *See* Business hours

HOURS OF LABOR

See also

Employee vacations

Flextime

Job sharing

Overtime

Body-wise: safe solutions for night work [research by Charles Czeisler] S. Chollar. il *Psychology Today* 23:26 N '89

Safety gets short shrift on long night shift [behavioral effects of circadian rhythms; research by Charles Czeisler] R. Weiss. *Science News* 135:37 Ja 21 '89

Work-time reduction in the U.S. and Western Europe. J. D. Owen. bibl f il *Monthly Labor Review* 111:41-5 D '88

Canada

Running in place. S. McKay. il *Maclean's* 102:66+ N 6 '89

Germany (West)

Is the German featherbed on its way out? G. E. Schares. il *Business Week* p62 Mr 13 '89

Western Europe

Work-time reduction in the U.S. and Western Europe. J. D. Owen. bibl f il *Monthly Labor Review* 111:41-5 D '88

HOUSE, DAVID L.

about

Mr. Chips. C. O'Malley. por *Personal Computing* 13:72 Jl '89

HOUSE, JOHN

Courbet and salon politics. bibl f il *Art in America* 77:160-73+ My '89

HOUSE, KAREN ELLIOTT

Are we underestimating America's future? il *Reader's Digest* 134:185-6+ My '89

HOUSE, MICHAEL

Lebanon's damned inheritance. il *History Today* 39:7-10 Ja '89

HOUSE AUCTIONS *See* Auctions

HOUSE BOATS *See* Houseboats

HOUSE BUILDING *See* House construction

HOUSE BUILDING INDUSTRY *See* Construction industry

HOUSE BUYING

See also

House selling

Housing—Costs

Housing finance

Insurance, Mortgage

Mortgages

Buying real estate out of state. D. LaMaute. il *Black Enterprise* 19:62-4+ Mr '89

Homes across the sea. K. McManus. il *Changing Times* 43:98-103 My '89

How to buy your first house. C. A. Fried. il *Money* 18:137-8+ Ap '89

Inspecting for a safe home. J. Bolger. *Consumers' Research Magazine* 72:29-30 O '89

Now's the time to grab a bargain vacation home. C. A. Fried. il *Money* 18:129-32 O '89

Smart strategies for first-time buyers [special section] S. Sheetz. il *Better Homes and Gardens* 67:41-4+ Ag '89

To buy or to rent is a question for the '90s. A. Saltzman. il *U.S. News & World Report* 106:68-70 Ap 17 '89

HOUSE CALLS (MEDICAL CARE)

Will house calls make a comeback? [views of James Mold] il *USA Today (Periodical)* 118:9 O '89

HOUSE CHURCHES

China

Bishop Ting and China's house churches. R. MacMillan. il *The Christian Century* 106:755-6 Ag 16-23 '89

HOUSE CLEANING

All that glitters is the tub. C. Swartz. il *The New York Times Magazine* p36+ N 5 '89

Cleaning house. K. Childers and D. Prestly. il *The Family Handyman* 39:47-53 F '89

Anecdotes, facetiae, satire, etc.

A neat gift idea [cleaning threshold difference between men and women] P. Chance. il *Psychology Today* 22:58-9 D '88

HOUSE CLEANING SERVICES

The clean machine. H. Rubin. il *Seventeen* 48:122+ My '89

HOUSE CONSTRUCTION

See also

Concrete houses

Houses, Prefabricated

Archome [owner-built barrel vault structure] G. Carlsen. il por *The Mother Earth News* 119:66-71+ S/O '89

Imagining Hill House. P. Theroux. il por *Architectural Digest* 46:32+ D '89

My contractor, my self (I). J. Folds. il *Modern Maturity* 32:62-4+ O/N '89

My contractor, my self (II). J. Folds. il *Modern Maturity* 32:76-8+ D '89/Ja '90

Professional advisor. See issues of Home Mechanix beginning July 1985

Progress report. J. Vara. il *Country Journal* 16:24-5 N/D '89

HOUSE CONSTRUCTION—*cont.*
Costs
Building prices. J. Vara. il *Country Journal* 16:82-3 Jl/Ag
'89

HOUSE CONSTRUCTION INDUSTRY *See* Construction
industry
HOUSE DECORATION
See also
Antiques
Apartments
Art in the home
Bathrooms
Bedrooms
Blinds
Children's rooms
Christmas decorations
Color in house decoration
Curtains and draperies
Dens (Rooms)
Dining alcoves, etc.
Display of antiques, art objects, etc.
Electric lamps
Family rooms
Fireplaces
Fruits, vegetables, etc. in decoration
Furniture
Furniture arrangement
Glass in house decoration
Guest rooms
House painting
Household furnishings
Houses, Remodeled
Interior decorators
Kitchens
Living rooms
Loft apartments
Mantels
Media rooms
Mirrors
Paneling
Pictures—Hanging
Plants in house decoration
Pottery in house decoration
Rooms
Rugs and carpets
Shelves and racks
Table decoration
Textile fabrics
Upholstery
Wall coverings
Wallpaper and wallpapering
Walls
Window shades
Windows
11 character builders to make any place a home. il *Glamour*
87:352-4 Ap '89
Affordable style [home of Becky and Allen Jerdee] D. L.
Caringer and R. E. Dittmer. il *Better Homes and Gardens*
67:81-90 My '89
An agile aesthetic: dancer Barrie Chase's country cottage
in Los Angeles. M. Frank. il por *Architectural Digest*
46:248-55+ O '89
Amazing space. C. Vogel. il *The New York Times Magazine*
p75-83 Je 11 '89
American country houses [cover story; special issue] il
Architectural Digest 46:118-214+ Je '89
Another Nantucket [J. Russo's cottage] G. Harrell. il pors
House & Garden 161:124-31 Ap '89
Architectural digest visits: Charles Bronson and Jill Ireland
[Malibu adobe decorated by King Zimmerman] J. Ireland.
il por *Architectural Digest* 46:98-103+ Jl '89
Architectural digest visits: Jaclyn Smith and Tony Richmond
[cover story] J. Giovannini. il pors *Architectural Digest*
46:180-5+ Ag '89
Architectural digest visits: Joan Rivers [interior by Louis
Malkin] J. Allen. il pors *Architectural Digest* 46:134-9+
F '89
Back Bay reflections [W. Hodgins' 1872 Boston townhouse]
G. Harrell. il por *House & Garden* 161:206-9 S '89
Be a little bold. il *Southern Living* 24:56-7 Jl '89
The big picture [Los Angeles home of J. and M. Nathanson]
P. Viladas. il *House & Garden* 161:160-7 S '89
A blend of new and old. il *Southern Living* 24:120 Jl '89
Bring home the charm [views of designer Mary Meehan]
il *Redbook* 173:92-7 Je '89
Bringing it all back home [N. Heller's Los Angeles house]
D. Kern. il por *House & Garden* 161:178-87 My '89
California design [cover story; special issue] il *Architectural
Digest* 46:36+ My '89
Camping out [Manhattan townhouse of M. O'Donoghue]
Q. Crisp. il por *House & Garden* 161:184-7 O '89
Capital venture [A. Child's Georgetown house] D. Streitfeld.
il por *House & Garden* 161:76-81+ Ag '89
Celebrity homes [M. Forbes' home] M. Fiore. il por *Good
Housekeeping* 208:118-21 Mr '89
Clean sweep [remodeled Southampton farmhouse by Motif
Designs] D. Brenner. il *House & Garden* 161:118-23 Je
'89

Collective spirit [Connecticut home of Paul and Pauline
Briger] S. Greenspan. il *House & Garden* 161:156-63 My
'89
Cottage charm [Tom and Peggy O'Neill's San Francisco
home] S. S. Soria and R. E. Dittmer. il *Better Homes
and Gardens* 67:65-72 Ag '89
Country charm. il *Southern Living* 24:156-7 S '89
Country class [M. and D. Hampton's Long Island cottage]
M. Matousek. il pors *Harper's Bazaar* 122:78-83+ Je '89
Country neoclassic [L. Krieger's Connecticut cottage] W. B.
Logan. il por *House & Garden* 161:216-23+ S '89
Cozy country cottage [blue and white color scheme used
in log cabin] il *McCall's* 116:62-4 Ag '89
A creative collaboration: softening a modern house in Los
Angeles [home of S. Harris and P. J. Witt decorated
by John Saladino] M. Frank. il pors *Architectural Digest*
46:130-7 Ag '89
The cultivated Beene [G. Beene's Long Island country house]
W. Goodman. il por *House & Garden* 161:88-95+ D '89
Decorate under the table, too. il *Southern Living* 24:176
Mr '89
Decorating with dish towels. il *Good Housekeeping*
209:114-15+ Jl '89
Easton meets Midwest [Chicago house decorated by David
Easton] J. Edelstein and L. Wren. il *House & Garden*
161:112-19 F '89
Eccentricities [D. Roos decorates his London house] C. Vogel.
il *The New York Times Magazine* p98-9 Mr 5 '89
For sale: 2 great decorator looks [Laura Ashley and Mario
Buatta furnishings] il *Redbook* 173:164-9 S '89
Formal country [excerpt] P. Ross. il *Redbook* 173:146-51
O '89
From simple to special. C. Engle. il *Southern Living* 24:148-50
Mr '89
Future perfect. il *Ladies' Home Journal* 106:226-31 N '89
Gandee at large [decorator W. Fernandez] C. K. Gandee.
il por *House & Garden* 161:218 N '89
Genial flair on Long Island Sound [decorated by Ruben
de Saavedra] C. McGee. il *Architectural Digest* 46:180-5
D '89
Greenwich time [restored 1825 farmhouse owned and
decorated by S. Brown and R. Jones; cover story] P.
Green. il *House & Garden* 161:120-7 N '89
"Hit the prospect at every emotional level" [fully decorated
model houses] R. Simon. il *Forbes* 143:310-11 Ja 9 '89
Hollywood homestead [home of T. Garr] P. Viladas. il pors
House & Garden 161:98-103 Ag '89
House call [M. A. Tsao's New York townhouse with interiors
by Calvin Tsao and Zack McKown] H. S. MacIsaac. il
pors *House & Garden* 161:232-7 O '89
Instant style-makers. il *Glamour* 87:252-4 Ag '89
Interior landscapes [decorated by William Hodgins] P. Carlsen.
il *Architectural Digest* 46:172-9 Ag '89
International style [L. Meyer's California home decorated
by Anthony Hail] R. Koenig. il *House & Garden* 161:138-43
N '89
Island of calm [R. Chessy's Saint Martin home] B. Howar.
il *House & Garden* 161:140-5 D '89
Lady of the canyon [P. Lipton's house in Bel-Air designed
by John Cottrell] S. M. L. Aronson. il pors *Architectural
Digest* 46:120-7+ F '89
Living with less. il *Glamour* 87:280-2 My '89
Long Island symmetry: reworking a designer's 1920s residence
in Southampton [home of A. E. Smith] P. Warner. il
Architectural Digest 46:138-43 Jl '89
Making an entrance [doors] D. B. Cowin. il *House & Garden*
161:160+ Je '89
Manhattan variations [town house decorated for J. Turken
by J. Montoya] P. Carlsen. il *Architectural Digest* 46:138-43
Ag '89
Middleburg manor [Herman and Monica Greenberg's restored
1740 farmhouse] N. McKeon. il *House & Garden* 161:144-53
Ap '89
My favorite room [actresses] M. Glass and K. Reisler. il
Ladies' Home Journal 106:134-40 F '89
My favorite room [winners of decorating contest] L. Fears.
il *Ladies' Home Journal* 106:158-64+ O '89
Napa renewed [home of W. C. Swanson decorated by Thomas
Britt] J. Simpson. il *Architectural Digest* 46:196-203 O
'89
North of the border [K. Spiegelman's Bel-Air house] D.
Michel. il *House & Garden* 161:92-5 F '89
On Audubon Place [decorator A. Holden's New Orleans
house] N. McKeon. il *House & Garden* 161:94-7+ Ja '89
On the Sound: breezy style for a Long Island estate [interior
by Michael De Santis] P. Carlsen. il *Architectural Digest*
46:128-33 F '89
Our first home [Larry and Kerry Bracken fix up old house]
M. D. Glass. il *Ladies' Home Journal* 106:165-70+ My
'89
The Palm Beach story [Mar-a-Lago estate bought by D.
and I. Trump] C. K. Gandee. il pors *House & Garden*
161:110-19+ D '89
Pared to perfection [work of P. Siskin and P. Valls] M.
Boodro. il *Vogue* 179:282-3+ My '89
Personality design. S. S. Soria. il *Better Homes and
Gardens* 67:62+ O '89

HOUSE DECORATION—cont.
Play of patterns: a designer's vivid realm in Los Angeles [home of M. Smith] H. Hurt. il por *Architectural Digest* 46:192-7 D '89
Private places, private retreats. il *Glamour* 87:282-3 O '89
The quality quandary. M. Cantwell. il *House & Garden* 161:64+ Ap '89
Reader of the Year [C. Andersen] il *McCall's* 117:57-63+ O '89
A Republican heritage in the South: Ambassador and Mrs. Guilford Dudley, Jr., in Nashville and Palm Beach. C. T. Buckley. il pors *Architectural Digest* 46:200-9 Ap '89
Restoration drama [D. Roos' nineteenth century London townhouse] S. Calloway. il por *House & Garden* 161:120-3+ D '89
A Somers place [Palm Springs home of S. Somers and A. Hamel] P. Viladas. il pors *House & Garden* 161:210-15 S '89
Spare sparkle. C. Vogel. il *The New York Times Magazine* p32-3 Ja 1 '89
Special fashion issue [cover story] il *Architectural Digest* 46:29+ S '89
The Sultans of Sag Harbor [home of D. K. Sultan] D. Kazanjian. il por *House & Garden* 161:192-7+ S '89
Summer style [cottage of Doug and Ingrid Leess] il *Glamour* 87:266-9 Je '89
Surface attraction [corner spaces designed by Carolyn Sollis and Anne Foxley] M. Guralnick. il *House & Garden* 161:168-76 Ap '89
Turning a house into a first home [Augusta, Ga. cottage] il *Southern Living* 24:118-19 Jl '89
Tuscan pastoral [G. Giammetti's La Vagnola estate decorated by Renzo Mongiardino; cover story] C. Maclean. il por *House & Garden* 161:146-59+ S '89
The Twin Gables: back to basics [1988 Idea House built in conjunction with the American Wood Council] C. Engle. il *Southern Living* 24:100-2+ Ja '89
Wall-to-wall Waldo means California cool to the likes of Merv and Liz [work of decorator W. Fernandez] H. Shapiro. il pors *People Weekly* 31:131-2 My 1 '89
Work (and play) in progress [Westchester County home of L. Goldrich and B. Wolf] il *Working Woman* 14:162-7 N '89
Yankee preserve [interior of New England house by M. Hampton] E. A. Berthold. il *House & Garden* 161:98-103+ Je '89

Anecdotes, facetiae, satire, etc.
How to redo your house for under $650,000 [condensed from Homes and other black holes] D. Barry. il *Reader's Digest* 134:93-6 Ap '89

Exhibitions
Model rooms [1989 Kips Bay Decorator Show House] G. Harrell. il *House & Garden* 161:238-43 O '89
HOUSE DECORATION, AFRICAN
Grand designs [work of C. Riley, A. Locadia, and T. Miller] D. Sapolin. il pors *Essence* 20:80-1+ Jl '89
HOUSE DECORATION, AMERICAN
See also
Furniture, American
The 200-year-old house that moved [Fall River, Mass. house transported to New York] il *Good Housekeeping* 208:140-3 Je '89
The book of decorating styles [period rooms] il *Good Housekeeping* 209:158-61 N '89
Born in U.S.A. [Riki Gail Zuriff's New York apartment] C. Vogel. il *The New York Times Magazine* p68-9 Ap 16 '89
California brights [southwestern decoration in Glendale, Calif. house] il *Redbook* 172:72-5 F '89
A colonial sensibility: restoring a shingled saltbox on eastern Long Island. S. M. Alsop. il *Architectural Digest* 46:132-9 Je '89
Custom of the country [Long Island house decorated by W. Diamond and A. Baratta] G. Harrell. il *House & Garden* 161:116-21+ Ag '89
Farm-fresh style [home of Liz and Peter Robinson] S. S. Soria and D. A. Jimerson. il *Better Homes and Gardens* 67:75-89 Ap '89
Florida pioneer: a woodland house on the Gulf Coast [home of K. and L. Drummond] B. Dunlop. il *Architectural Digest* 46:174-7+ Je '89
The house and its restoration [Mount Vernon] M. J. Mosca. bibl f il *Antiques* 135:462-73 F '89
Making time for your other life [country home of designer B. Johnson in Columbia County, N.Y.] S. Nelson. il por *Working Woman* 14:102-5 Mr '89
Manhattan country [apartment decorated by W. Diamond] D. Sacks. il por *House & Garden* 161:132-43 Ap '89
Old light in a new world [1795 Sands House in the Hudson River Valley owned by D. McDermott and P. McGough] C. Black. il pors *House & Garden* 161:176-81+ N '89
Pure and not so simple [restoration of 18th century house in Massachusetts by John Saladino] C. Vogel. il *The New York Times Magazine* p60-5 Ag 20 '89
Rethinking the past [early American] S. Calloway. il *House & Garden* 161:42+ Je '89

Southern country [excerpt from Mary Emmerling's American country South] M. E. Emmerling. il *Redbook* 174:97-103 N '89
HOUSE DECORATION, COLONIAL AND EARLY AMERICAN See House decoration, American
HOUSE DECORATION, EDWARDIAN
As time goes by [19th century Manhattan brownstone decorated by M. Hampton] C. Vogel. il *The New York Times Magazine* p78-9 O 1 '89
HOUSE DECORATION, ENGLISH
Caroline Charles: the practical charms of a very English apartment in Knightsbridge. E. Lambert. il por *Architectural Digest* 46:128-31 S '89
Country comfort [English country style in a California Tudor] il *Redbook* 172:128-31 Ap '89
The decorative dandy [eccentrically decorated home of S. Calloway] R. Koenig. il por *House & Garden* 161:42+ Mr '89
English living at its best [special section; with editorial comment by Nancy Novogrod] il *House & Garden* 161:107-98+ Mr '89
The House of Lancaster [Haseley Court; excerpt from Colefax & Fowler] C. Jones. il pors *House & Garden* 161:188-95+ N '89
Inside Fergie's dream house [home of Henry De Kwiatkowski decorated by S. Parish] W. Norwich. il pors *Redbook* 172:92-5 F '89
Los-Anglophile [home of S. Rheinstein] B. Goodwin. il pors *House & Garden* 161:82-9+ Ag '89
The reign of Hardy Amies: the Queen's couturier in London and Gloucestershire. E. Lambert. il por *Architectural Digest* 46:204-9+ S '89
The versatility of English style. il *Southern Living* 24:180 Ap '89
Victor Edelstein: period clarity for the couturier's London flat. E. Lambert. il por *Architectural Digest* 46:184-7+ S '89
HOUSE DECORATION, EUROPEAN
Alpine echoes above Lake Tahoe [Carole and Robert McNeil's adapted alpine chalet designed by Valerian Rybar and Jean-François Daigre] J. Taylor. il *Architectural Digest* 46:84-91 Jl '89
Continental impressions on Nob Hill [San Francisco apartment decorated by Val Arnold for E. Killebrew] H. Junker. il por *Architectural Digest* 46:288-94+ O '89
HOUSE DECORATION, EXTERIOR
See also
Christmas decorations, Outdoor
Dress-up details [special section] K. Collier. il *The Family Handyman* 39:30-7 Ja '89
HOUSE DECORATION, FRENCH
Acts of culture: Jean-Claude Brialy's château in the Marne Valley [interior by Michel van Leempoel] C. Aillaud. il por *Architectural Digest* 46:94-9+ Ja '89
Belle Epoque weekends [1918 carriage house in Bedford, N.Y. designed by Jean-Paul Beaujard] A. Tapert. il *House & Garden* 161:128-37 N '89
Design dialogue: Henri Samuel. C. Aillaud. il por *Architectural Digest* 46:50+ Ja '89
Escape to Normandy [P. Mathieu's and M. Ray's farmhouse; cover story] C. K. Gandee. il pors *House & Garden* 161:96-105+ F '89
The French country look [designed by Pierre Deux] il *Redbook* 172:110-15 Ja '89
Haut Catroux [decorator of Paris apartment] C. Petkanas. il *House & Garden* 161:160-7+ Ap '89
He knows what he likes [M. Galabert's Paris apartment] P. Viladas. il pors *House & Garden* 161:26+ F '89
Hôtel de Cavoye: a Paris house appointed by antiquarian Bernard Steinitz. C. Styles-McLeod. il *Architectural Digest* 46:234-41 O '89
In the light of Provence [D. Dumas' house in Oppède-le-Vieux is former café; cover story] D. Kazanjian. il por *House & Garden* 161:98-107+ Ja '89
Island shelter [K. Keeble's Shelter Island house decorated by Edward Zajac and Richard Callahan] J. Reginato. il por *House & Garden* 161:98-107 Ap '89
Madame Carven: eighteenth-century splendor in her Avenue Foch house. C. Aillaud. il por *Architectural Digest* 46:180-3+ S '89
Master of the house [H. Samuel] M. Filler. il por *House & Garden* 161:42 Jl '89
On the Rue de Rivoli [Paris apartment of M.-P. Pellé] C. K. Gandee. il por *House & Garden* 161:68-77 Jl '89
A page from the past: infusing a Manhattan apartment with period flair [interior by Kevin McNamara] S. Stephens. il *Architectural Digest* 46:174-9 F '89
A Parisian bijou: glittering prizes in a designer's Louis XVI pavilion [designed by Valerian Rybar and J. F. Daigre; cover story] Suzy. il *Architectural Digest* 46:204-11+ O '89
Petit palais [K. Lagerfeld's Paris apartment] A. L. Talley. il por *Vogue* 179:390-1 Ap '89
Royal lineage [J. Garcia's Paris apartment] G. Y. Dryansky. il por *House & Garden* 161:148-55+ Jl '89
Le style Jacques Grange. E. White. il pors *House & Garden* 161:92-105+ Jl '89

HOUSE DECORATION, FRENCH—*cont.*
Undone in Paris [C. Pringle's apartment] E. White. il por *House & Garden* 161:24+ Ja '89
A Victorian Paris: Beatriz Patiño's Plaine Monceau pied-à-terre [interior design by François Catroux] C. Aillaud. il *Architectural Digest* 46:100-7 Ja '89

HOUSE DECORATION, GEORGIAN
A Toronto Georgian [interior by Robert Dirstein and James Robertson] D. Lasker. il *Architectural Digest* 46:114-19 F '89

HOUSE DECORATION, GOTHIC REVIVAL
Anglo-Indian impressions [A. P. Browne's Gothic revival apartment in Georgetown] S. M. Alsop. il por *Architectural Digest* 46:222-6+ Mr '89

HOUSE DECORATION, INDIAN (EAST INDIAN)
Essence of India. il *Seventeen* 48:158-61+ O '89

HOUSE DECORATION, IRISH
Eire apparent [designer S. Connolly] D. Brenner. il por *House & Garden* 161:90+ S '89

HOUSE DECORATION, ITALIAN
The Ruspoli legacy in Italy. C. Aillaud. il pors *Architectural Digest* 46:156-64+ Jl '89

HOUSE DECORATION, MOROCCAN
A Moroccan jewel [residence of B. Willis] C. Aillaud. il *Architectural Digest* 46:126-31+ Jl '89

HOUSE DECORATION, ORIENTAL
Eastern soul [Palos Verdes Peninsula home decorated by Anthony Machado] I. Borger. il *Architectural Digest* 46:308-14+ My '89

HOUSE DECORATION, RUSSIAN
Imperial standard [Manhattan apartment] B. Felner. il *House & Garden* 161:204-13 O '89
Living the history of modern Russia: Nina and Edmund Stevens in Moscow. E. Stevens. il *Architectural Digest* 46:164-7+ F '89

HOUSE DECORATION, SPANISH
Iberian weekends [D. Pinto Coelho's Palacio de los Chaves Mendoza in Trujillo] R. Koenig. il pors *House & Garden* 161:142-53+ F '89

HOUSE DECORATION, SWEDISH
Stockholm on the Hudson [Upper East Side apartment decorated by Peter Marino] S. M. L. Aronson. il *Architectural Digest* 46:296-303 N '89
Swedish fantasies [F. von Celsing's Biby estate] C. Petkanas. il por *House & Garden* 161:126-33+ Ag '89

HOUSE DECORATION, THAI
Exotic themes in Bangkok [residence decorated by Chantaka Puranananda for M. Viravaidya; cover story] W. Warren. il *Architectural Digest* 46:150-5 D '89

HOUSE DECORATION, VICTORIAN
Eminent Victorian [New York City apartment of Christopher Ostafin] M. Bethany. il *New York* 22:48-50 F 6 '89
Mad about Morris [Kurland Zabar] N. F. Weber. il *House & Garden* 161:88 Ap '89
Theatrical menagerie: an English actor's Victorian house in London [T. Jellinek] E. Lambert. il por *Architectural Digest* 46:118-25 D '89
Victorian fantasy [Lord Glenconner's Hill Lodge in Kensington] D. J. Ogilvy. il por *House & Garden* 161:176-81 Mr '89
Victorian revival [Philadelphia 1857 townhouse decorated by R. Denning] B. Adams. il *House & Garden* 161:102-9 D '89

HOUSE DEMOCRATIC CAUCUS (U.S.)
Gray seeks policy shift as Caucus chair. L. Brown. il por *Black Enterprise* 19:29 Mr '89

HOUSE DRAINAGE
See also
Septic tanks

HOUSE EXPANSION *See* Houses, Remodeled
HOUSE GUESTS *See* Guests
HOUSE HEATING *See* Heating
HOUSE HUSBANDS *See* Homemakers
HOUSE INSPECTION *See* Building inspection
HOUSE INSULATION *See* Insulation (Heat)
HOUSE LIGHTING *See* Lighting
HOUSE MODELS
See also
Doll houses
HOUSE MOVING *See* Moving of structures, etc.
HOUSE MUSEUMS *See* Historic houses, sites, etc.
HOUSE MUSIC
House music. D. Gregory and J. Ash. il *Life* 12:96-9 F '89
HOUSE OF COMMONS (CANADA) *See* Canada. Parliament. House of Commons
HOUSE OF DUN (MONTROSE, SCOTLAND)
Dun re-done. T. Aldous. il *History Today* 39:3-4 S '89
HOUSE OF FRASER PLC
Banned in Britain: a new chapter in the Harrods saga [government outlaws publication of secret report] M. Maremont. pors *Business Week* p36 Ap 17 '89
Brawling over Harrods [T. Rowland vs. M. Al-Fayed] S. Lohr. il pors *The New York Times Magazine* p32-3+ O 8 '89
Tiny Rowland versus Mohamed Al-Fayed (cont.). E. F. Cone. il pors *Forbes* 143:10 My 1 '89

HOUSE OF HABSBURG
about
Europe's heads, crowned and otherwise, bury Zita, the last Habsburg Empress. M. Green. il *People Weekly* 31:50-2+ Ap 17 '89
A Hapsburg goes home. N. Darnton. il *Newsweek* 113:41 Ap 10 '89
HOUSE OF HERMÈS (FIRM)
See also
Hermès Museum
Scarves everywhere [show at Hermès Gallery, New York City] *The New Yorker* 64:24-6 Ja 30 '89
A touch of class. Z. Sawaya. il *Forbes* 143:10 My 15 '89
A Waco postman designs Hermès scarves with a western flair [K. Oliver] il pors *People Weekly* 32:162-3 N 13 '89
HOUSE OF LORDS (GREAT BRITAIN) *See* Great Britain. Parliament. House of Lords
HOUSE OF REPRESENTATIVES (U.S.) *See* United States. Congress. House
HOUSE OF STYLE [television program] *See* Television program reviews—Single works
HOUSE OF VALOIS, 1328-1589 *See* France—History—House of Valois, 1328-1589
HOUSE ORGANS
A copy writer's journey into the age of PCs [J. Lane, manager of electronic publishing at MONY] M. Piturro. il por *Personal Computing* 13:146-7 O '89
HOUSE PAINT *See* Paint
HOUSE PAINTING
Energize with paint [spare room/guest room makeover] il *Better Homes and Gardens* 67:84-6+ Mr '89
Exterior period painting. B. Vila. il *Popular Mechanics* 166:38+ Je '89
Painting. il *The Family Handyman* 39:58-66 My '89
Preparing drywall for painting. G. Branson. *Workbench* 45:74 N/D '89
Whole house painting manual [cover story; special section] A. Rooze and D. Prestly. il *The Family Handyman* 39:31-7 Mr '89
HOUSE PLANS *See* Architecture, Domestic—Designs and plans
HOUSE PLANTS
See also
African violets
Artificial light gardening
Bromeliads
Christmas cactus
Garden rooms
Hanging plants
Plants in house decoration
Poinsettias
Schefflera
Soils, Potting
Watering of plants
The 10 most rewarding houseplants [excerpt from Mr. Mother Earth's most rewarding houseplants] J. Rapp. il *Redbook* 172:126-7+ Ap '89
The best new houseplants. T. James. il *Ladies' Home Journal* 106:68+ F '89
Beyond the poinsettia: a dozen other Christmas plants. il *Sunset (Central West edition)* 183:154 D '89
Caring for Christmas plants. *McCall's* 116:67 Ja '89
Christmas legends. J. Rapp. il *Redbook* 174:114-15+ D '89
Doting on houseplants. J. Kaufmann. il por *New Choices for the Best Years* 29:70-3+ O '89
Flowering houseplants: how to keep them blooming. J. A. McKeon. il *Better Homes and Gardens* 67:119+ N '89
Greenery filters out indoor air pollution. J. Raloff. *Science News* 136:212 S 30 '89
House plant make-over: gaunt to chubby [air-layering and repotting] il *Sunset (Central West edition)* 182:130-1 Ja '89
Houseplant questions answered. G. Abraham and K. Abraham. il *Consumers' Research Magazine* 72:29-34 Ja '89
Training
See Plants—Training
HOUSE PRICES *See* Housing—Costs
HOUSE PROTECTION
See also
Alarms
Burglary protection
HOUSE PURCHASING *See* House buying
HOUSE SELLING
Cashing in on your big blue chip. W. L. Updegrave. il *Money* 18 Money Guide:83-4+ Fall '89
Fixed to sell: selective home improvements pay off. S. Sheetz. il *Better Homes and Gardens* 67:58 Ap '89
Home is where the shelter is [taxation rules on house sales] G. W. Padwe. il *Nation's Business* 77:67 Mr '89
IRS traps for the unwary home seller [tax exclusion on profits for those over age 55] L. Wiener. il *U.S. News & World Report* 106:80 My 22 '89
'No thanks, I'll sell it myself' [for sale by owner transactions] A. Miller. il *Newsweek* 114:50 Jl 31 '89
Selling rental real estate: ways to sweeten the deal. il *Changing Times* 43:71-2+ Jl '89

HOUSE SELLING—*cont.*

Uncle Sam's retirement gift [tax exclusion on house sale profits for seniors] M. C. Paulson. *Changing Times* 43:104 Ja '89

Watch out when you sell your home. A. Winter. *Modern Maturity* 32:14 F/Mr '89

HOUSE SHARING

Home sharing as a housing alternative. P. Fornara. *Utne Reader* p71 My/Je '89

Sharing a house of one's own. R. Givens. il *Newsweek* 113:74 Mr 20 '89

HOUSE SWAPPING *See* Real estate exchanges
HOUSE TRADING *See* Real estate exchanges
HOUSE WARRANTY *See* Home warranty
HOUSE WIRING *See* Electric wire and wiring
HOUSE WRECKING *See* Wrecking

HOUSEBOATS

The homeless take to the water [Austin, Tex.] D. Claitor. il *The Progressive* 53:10-11 F '89

The return of the Brandy Bar. R. Trachi. il *The Mother Earth News* 117:82-5 My/Je '89

HOUSECLEANING *See* House cleaning
HOUSEHOLD ACCIDENTS *See* Accidents

HOUSEHOLD APPLIANCES

See also

Clothes dryers
Dishwashers
Household appliances industry
Irons
Kitchen utensils and appliances
Sewing machines
Vacuum cleaners
Washing machines

Are my appliances showing? P. Patton. il *Esquire* 112:19-20 Jl '89

Household help. R. Berendsohn. il *Popular Mechanics* 166:88-9 D '89

Collectors and collecting

Appliance lover Chuck Diehl takes a spin-dry on memory lane. M. Neill. il pors *People Weekly* 31:277-8 Mr 6 '89

Control

Build REACTS: the Radio-Electronics Advanced Control System (XI) [battery-backup power supply] J. Bybee. il *Radio-Electronics* 60:65-8 Ja '89

Maintenance and repair

Appliance clinic. S. Toth. See issues of Popular Mechanics
How to repair. See issues of The Family Handyman beginning January 1988
Why the dealer wins [appliance service contracts] D. Moreau. il *Changing Times* 43:83-4+ Ja '89

Anecdotes, facetiae, satire, etc.

Mourning becomes electric. K. Fury. il *New Choices for the Best Years* 29:88 Je '89

HOUSEHOLD APPLIANCES INDUSTRY

See also

Black & Decker Corp.
Chicago Pacific Corp.
Cuisinarts, Inc.
Maytag Corporation
Rubbermaid Incorporated

Acquisitions and mergers

Can Maytag clean up around the world? [acquisition of Chicago Pacific Corp.] B. Bremner. il *Business Week* p86-7 Ja 30 '89

Maytag's foreign fling isn't much fun after all [Hoover acquisition sours] B. Bremner. *Business Week* p32-3 S 4 '89

International aspects

GE and GEC. F. H. Katayama. il *Fortune* 119:8 F 13 '89

Why GE took a European bride [deal with Britain's General Electric Co. plc] J. R. Norman. il *Business Week* p28-9 Ja 30 '89

Finance

Consumer products. C. Palmeri. il *Forbes* 143:126-7 Ja 9 '89

HOUSEHOLD BANK

Pelf 'R' Us. D. R. Katz. il *Esquire* 111:75-6 Je '89

HOUSEHOLD BUDGET *See* Budget, Household
HOUSEHOLD CHEMICAL DISPOSAL *See* Hazardous substances—Disposal
HOUSEHOLD CHORES, CHILDREN'S *See* Children's chores
HOUSEHOLD CLEANING PRODUCTS *See* Cleaning compositions

HOUSEHOLD EMPLOYEES

See also

House cleaning services
White House (Washington, D.C.)—Employees

Finding live-in help for your child that is loving, loyal and also legal. R. J. Klein. il *Money* 18:155-6 S '89

He works. She works. What about the kids? [au pairs and nannies] J. Zweig. il *Forbes* 143:317-18 Ja 9 '89

My white father [excerpt from Telling memories among southern women] S. Tucker. *Harper's* 279:36+ N '89

Singing the green card blues [hiring a foreigner] N. Henderson. il *Changing Times* 43:71-4 O '89

Take a number and wait [immigration amnesty program] D. Shaw. *The Washington Monthly* 21:28-30+ S '89

Anecdotes, facetiae, satire, etc.

For some overbooked social whirlers, sending a stand-in is the next best thing to being there. W. Norwich. il *Vogue* 179:286 Je '89

Taxation

Household help: avoiding the tax squeeze. N. Henderson. il *Changing Times* 43:56-60+ Ag '89

Your babysitter, the tax liability. H. Wheelwright. il *Money* 18:198+ Je '89

HOUSEHOLD ENERGY CONSERVATION *See* Energy conservation
HOUSEHOLD FINANCE CORPORATION *See* Household International, Inc.

HOUSEHOLD FURNISHINGS

See also

Christmas gifts for the home
Electric lamps
Mirrors

12 best products from the Builders' show. M. Phair. il *Home Mechanix* 85:71-4 Jl '89

100 ideas under $100 [cover story; with editorial comment by David Jordan] J. Williams and J. Severson. il *Better Homes and Gardens* 67:10, 19-24+ Ja '89

Everything's bloomin' tulips! [handcrafted home furnishings] J. Williams and J. Severson. il *Better Homes and Gardens* 67:45-54+ Mr '89

HG guide: New York [stores] D. B. Cowin. il *House & Garden* 161:128+ O '89

Tulipomania. D. B. Cowin. il *House & Garden* 161:166+ Je '89

Design

When old is new. C. Vogel. il *The New York Times Magazine* p66-8 F 12 '89

HOUSEHOLD FURNISHINGS, MOVING OF *See* Moving
HOUSEHOLD FURNISHINGS INDUSTRY

See also

Armstrong World Industries Inc.
Chicago Pacific Corp.

Acquisitions and mergers

Armstrong may get strong-armed. G. G. Marcial. *Business Week* p134 F 20 '89

International aspects

The Belzbergs, again [stake in Armstrong World Industries] T. Jaffe. il *Forbes* 144:316 S 4 '89

Finance

Consumer products. C. Palmeri. il *Forbes* 143:126-7 Ja 9 '89

Marketing

See also

OMO Home (Firm)
Williams-Sonoma, Inc.

HOUSEHOLD INTERNATIONAL, INC.

Spinning gold out of spinoffs [M. Gabelli's interest in Household International spinoffs] G. G. Marcial. *Business Week* p80 Jl 31 '89

HOUSEHOLD LINEN *See* Linen, Household
HOUSEHOLD MANAGEMENT *See* Home economics
HOUSEHOLD MECHANICS *See* Houses—Maintenance and repair

HOUSEHOLD PEST CONTROL

See also

Termites—Control

HOUSEHOLD PESTS

See also

Fleas

HOUSEHOLD PURCHASING *See* Purchasing, Household

HOUSEHOLD RECORDS

Create a homeowner's journal. S. Carmichael. il *Home Mechanix* 85:40-3 Ja '89

The most useful tape you'll ever shoot [home inventory] D. Gordon. il *Video* 13:32-3 O '89

HOUSEHOLDS

See also

House sharing

What's pulling the rug out from under housing. K. Madigan. il *Business Week* p104+ Ja 23 '89

HOUSEHUSBANDS *See* Homemakers
HOUSEKEEPING *See* Home economics

HOUSES

See also

Architecture, Domestic
Brick houses
Bungalows
City houses
Concrete houses
Condominiums
Cottages
Doll houses
Farmhouses
Guest houses
Home ownership
Log cabins, houses, etc.
Plastic houses
Pole houses
Pool houses
Pyramid houses
Ranch houses
Stone houses

HOUSES—See also—cont.
Storage in the home
Suburban homes
Two family houses
Vacation houses

Air pollution
See Indoor air pollution
Automation
See Computers—Home use
Cooling
See Cooling
Electricity
See Electricity in the home
Environmental engineering
See Environmental engineering (Buildings)
Finance
See Housing finance
Fires and fire prevention
Could your family survive a fire? F. Field. il Reader's Digest 135:137-40 N '89
Forest fire strikes home [New York State] E. Jacoby. il The Conservationist 44:40-3 S/O '89
Home fire protection. D. Schoonmaker. il The Mother Earth News 120:64-7 N/D '89
In the aftermath of disaster. D. A. Warren. il Home Mechanix 85:40-3+ S '89
Save your family from a fire. J. H. Sousa. il Parents 64:82+ O '89

Leasing and renting
Bay Area mansions to rent for special occasions. il Sunset (Central West edition) 183:20+ N '89
Selling rental real estate: ways to sweeten the deal. il Changing Times 43:71-2+ Jl '89
To buy or to rent is a question for the '90s. A. Saltzman. il U.S. News & World Report 106:68-70 Ap 17 '89

Maintenance and repair
See also
Insulation (Heat)
Plumbing
Publishers and publishing—Home improvement literature
Slagle & Slagle
Ask Handyman. See issues of The Family Handyman
Buttoning up for winter. J. Vivian. il The Mother Earth News 119:92-6+ S/O '89
Create a homeowner's journal. S. Carmichael. il Home Mechanix 85:40-3 Ja '89
Fixed to sell: selective home improvements pay off. S. Sheetz. il Better Homes and Gardens 67:58 Ap '89
Good housekeeping home improvement guide 1989 [special section] il Good Housekeeping 208:179-82+ Ap '89
Handy hints. See issues of The Family Handyman
Home & shop improvements. See issues of The Family Handyman beginning September 1986
Home improvement helper [special section] A. Arnott. il McCall's 116:93+ Ap '89
Home Q&A. J. Gaynor. See issues of Home Mechanix beginning January 1985
Home tips, ideas, etc. See issues of Southern Living beginning June 1988
Homeowners' clinic. N. Becker. See issues of Popular Mechanics beginning June 1984
The housesmith. J. Vara. See issues of Country Journal beginning October 1986
Old house restoration. B. Vila. See issues of Popular Mechanics beginning May 1986
Tips, tools, and techniques. See occasional issues of Better Homes and Gardens
What's new: home. T. O. Bakke. See issues of Popular Science beginning January 1989
Whole house repair manual [special section] D. Johnson and D. Stoffel. il The Family Handyman 39:44+ S '89
Whole house repair manual [special section] D. Johnson and D. Stoffel. il The Family Handyman 39:69-70+ My '89
Winter prep. H. Spies. il Home Mechanix 85:66-70+ S '89
Workbench solver. See issues of Workbench beginning May/June 1987

Moving
See Moving of structures, etc.
Prices
See Housing—Costs
Radon pollution
See Radon pollution
Warranty
See Home warranty

HOUSES, EARTH SHELTERED
6 summer houses for year-round living. A. W. Lees. il Popular Science 234:128-32+ Ap '89
HOUSES, HISTORIC See Historic houses, sites, etc.
HOUSES, LAKESIDE See Lakeside architecture
HOUSES, MODEL See Model houses
HOUSES, PREFABRICATED
See also
Lindal Cedar Homes, Inc.
Mobile homes
An addition made to order. R. Barnhart. il Home Mechanix 85:38-9+ Ja '89

Build a kit home [home of Paul and Deborah Rogers] il Better Homes and Gardens 67:46+ Ag '89
Elegant—and modular [NEST demonstration house] V. E. Gilmore. il Popular Science 234:26 My '89
Kevin Wilkes: double life of a Princeton prefab. S. Stephens. il por Architectural Digest 46:102-6+ Ap '89

HOUSES, REMODELED
1989 home improvement contest: the winners [special section; cover story] il Better Homes and Gardens 67:77-82+ O '89
Adding on. il Sunset (Central West edition) 182:98-104+ Je '89
Adding up [house in Rosemont area of Alexandria, Va.] il Southern Living 24:158 Ap '89
An addition made to order. R. Barnhart. il Home Mechanix 85:38-9+ Ja '89
Al Held's Catskill pastoral: the artist's studio and house in Woodstock, New York. D. Solomon. il por Architectural Digest 46:170-3+ Je '89
Barn appeal: Ivan and Jane Clark Chermayeff's country house. S. Stephens. il Architectural Digest 46:146-51 Je '89
The barn collectors [S. Spillane's and R. Leech's Connecticut house contructed of reassembled barns] M. Cantwell. il pors House & Garden 161:126-35 F '89
Blasting out the rear wall for light, views. il Sunset (Central West edition) 183:100 D '89
Brave new worlds [downtown, New York City] M. Bethany. il New York 22:114-16+ D 25 '89-Ja 1 '90
Chelsea collector [S. Hoppen's converted carriage house] J. Etra. il House & Garden 161:140-5 Mr '89
Clean sweep [remodeled Southampton farmhouse by Motif Designs] D. Brenner. il House & Garden 161:118-23 Je '89
Coconut Grove Tudor: the Miami residence of Maurice and Mercedes Ferré [remodeled by Bernard Zyscovich] B. Dunlop. il Architectural Digest 46:108-13+ F '89
Creating a family-size home. il Southern Living 24:89 Ag '89
Deciding whether to move or improve. M. Kiernan. il U.S. News & World Report 106:71+ Ap 17 '89
Estimating improvements. W. Giese. Changing Times 43:26-7 D '89
Fast forward [S. and B. Pittman's converted barn in Connecticut] D. Kazanjian. il pors House & Garden 161:76-83+ F '89
Fix a fixer-upper [home of Catherine and Peter Van Allen] il Better Homes and Gardens 67:42-3 Ag '89
Give your house a facelift. il USA Today (Periodical) 118:12-13 Ag '89
Going up [adding a second story] il Sunset (Central West edition) 182:132-8+ My '89
Good housekeeping home improvement guide 1989 [special section] il Good Housekeeping 208:179-82+ Ap '89
Good-neighbor remodels [planned community of Woodbridge in Irvine, Calif.] il Sunset (Central West edition) 183:96-9 N '89
Home remodeling: getting it done right. il Consumers' Research Magazine 72:34-6 S '89
Honor award for a San Francisco remodel. il Sunset (Central West edition) 183:88-9 O '89
How do you remodel an architectural icon? [1914 Berkeley, Calif. house] il Sunset (Central West edition) 183:110 O '89
Kevin Wilkes: double life of a Princeton prefab. S. Stephens. il por Architectural Digest 46:102-6+ Ap '89
A Manhattan sampler [remodeled brownstone owned by M. Malcé and J. Kelter] S. M. L. Aronson. il pors Architectural Digest 46:158-63+ Je '89
The new family room [home of Russell and Alexis Dow] W. L. Nolan and R. E. Dittmer. il Better Homes and Gardens 67:60-8+ S '89
Old house restoration. B. Vila. See issues of Popular Mechanics beginning May 1986
Opening up and "zoning" an 1880s Victorian [San Francisco's Russian Hill] il Sunset (Central West edition) 182:120+ Je '89
"Our dream house made our marriage a nightmare". S. F. Enos. il Ladies' Home Journal 106:14+ Je '89
Our first home [Larry and Kerry Bracken fix up old house] M. D. Glass. il Ladies' Home Journal 106:165-70+ My '89
Portrait of the artists: Eric Fischl and April Gornik on Long Island [farmhouse renovated by Lee Skolnick] S. M. L. Aronson. il pors Architectural Digest 46:234-9+ Ap '89
Private retreat upstairs, space for boys below. il Sunset (Central West edition) 183:104 Jl '89
Professional advisor. See issues of Home Mechanix beginning July 1985
Ranch house remodeled into a "village" [Los Angeles] il Sunset (Central West edition) 183:100 O '89
Remodel strategies: 3 ways to grow. il Sunset (Central West edition) 182:111-18 Ap '89
Remodeling for light, views, outdoor living [San Francisco] il Sunset (Central West edition) 183:98 O '89
Remodeling: hard truths in soft markets. E. Schurenberg. il Money 18:76 Je '89

HOUSES, REMODELED—*cont.*

Reviving a '50s ranch [home of Mike and Nina Snegg] S. Sheetz. il *Better Homes and Gardens* 67:67-77 Ja '89

The southern home [special section] il *Southern Living* 24:95+ O '89

Summer style [cottage of Doug and Ingrid Leess] il *Glamour* 87:266-9 Je '89

They gave up just 6 feet of deck space. il *Sunset (Central West edition)* 182:118 Mr '89

Two wing walls make all the difference. il *Sunset (Central West edition)* 182:94-5 Ja '89

Vintage townhouse for a young family [Alexandria, Va.] il *Southern Living* 24:178-9 N '89

Whole house remodeling. il *The Family Handyman* 39:59-60+ Mr '89

HOUSES, RESTORED

See also
  Historic houses, sites, etc.

Back Bay Victorian [Boston town house decorated by Bruce Gregga for B. and F. Herman] D. Roberts. il *Architectural Digest* 46:152-9 Mr '89

A colonial sensibility: restoring a shingled saltbox on eastern Long Island. S. M. Alsop. il *Architectural Digest* 46:132-9 Je '89

Florida pioneer: a woodland house on the Gulf Coast [home of K. and L. Drummond] B. Dunlop. il *Architectural Digest* 46:174-7+ Je '89

Middleburg manor [Herman and Monica Greenberg's 1740 farmhouse] N. McKeon. il *House & Garden* 161:144-53 Ap '89

The pleasures of Partemi: restoring a ruined castellino on the Tuscan coast [home of D. Burn] I. Borger. il por *Architectural Digest* 46:178-85 Ap '89

Pure and not so simple [restoration of 18th century house in Massachusetts by John Saladino] C. Vogel. il *The New York Times Magazine* p60-5 Ag 20 '89

Restoration respects the original design [Tampa, Fla.] il *Southern Living* 24:142-3 Je '89

Restoring a Frank Lloyd Wright jewel [built in 1951 for Raymond Carlson in Arizona] il *Sunset (Central West edition)* 183:108 O '89

Shingle style revival: new life for a rambling Connecticut residence [home of A. and S. W. Finkelson decorated by Robert Currie] C. D. B. Bryan. il pors *Architectural Digest* 46:152-7+ Je '89

The spirit of '76: saving a pre-Revolutionary house in Sag Harbor [J. and R. K. Lewis] R. Fizdale and A. Gold. il por *Architectural Digest* 46:194-9+ Je '89

A thirties revival [home of H. and R. Wilkinson in the Hollywood Hills] G. Greene. il *Architectural Digest* 46:194-201+ Mr '89

Warm colors, personal style [restored Oxford, Miss. Victorian house] il *Southern Living* 24:172-3 N '89

HOUSES, SEASHORE See Beach architecture

HOUSES, SOLAR See Solar houses

HOUSES, TREE See Tree houses

HOUSES, UNDERGROUND See Houses, Earth sheltered

HOUSES, WOOD See Wood houses

HOUSEWARES See Household appliances

HOUSEWIVES See Homemakers

HOUSEWORK See Home economics

HOUSING

See also
  Aged—Housing
  Black women—Housing
  Blacks—Housing
  Celebrities—Housing
  Children—Housing
  Condominiums
  Congregate housing
  Construction industry
  Discrimination in housing
  Granny flats
  Households
  Housing projects
  Labor—Housing
  Local Initiatives Support Corporation
  National Association of Home Builders (U.S.)
  Poor—Housing
  Single people—Housing
  Unmarried couples—Housing

Local success stories. P. Dreier. il *The Progressive* 53:28 Ap '89

Searching for home [cover story; special section] il *Utne Reader* p58-79 My/Je '89

Tough times for Mr. Levittown [suburban housing pioneer W. Levitt] M. T. Kaufman. il pors *The New York Times Magazine* p42-4+ S 24 '89

Costs

The coming real estate crash. T. McKusick. il *Utne Reader* p9-10 Ja/F '89

Crumbling foundations. A. Bladen. il *Forbes* 143:159 My 15 '89

Down and out in L.A. [California's residential real estate market] H. Rudnitsky. il *Forbes* 144:65+ O 30 '89

Down but not out. C. E. Babin. il por *Forbes* 144:235 S 18 '89

The economies of public housing. W. Tucker. il *The American Spectator* 22:26-9 N '89

Gimme shelter: even middle-class Americans now feel the housing crisis. W. Greider. il *Utne Reader* p60-3 My/Je '89

The great housing bust. A. Miller. il *Newsweek* 114:54-5 D 25 '89

Home affordability, city by city. il *Changing Times* 43:51 My '89

Homeownership is alive and well. S. Nasar. il *U.S. News & World Report* 107:56 D 11 '89

Homeownership: who can afford it? il *Changing Times* 43:34-5 Mr '89

Housing affordability. il *Consumers' Research Magazine* 72:19 Ap '89

Housing policy needs a rehab. L. S. Richman. il *Fortune* 119:84-7+ Mr 27 '89

How to sabotage the homeless. J. Mehrten. il *Conservative Digest* 15:6-7+ My/Je '89

Investors will find that a home is not so sweet. L. Wiener. il *U.S. News & World Report* 107:80+ D 4 '89

It's time to rethink your biggest investment [special section] il *Money* 18:68-74+ Je '89

Middle America: priced out of house and home. K. S. Diegmueller. *Current (Washington, D.C.)* 314:16-21 Jl/Ag '89

Moving in, moving up [cover story; special section] il *U.S. News & World Report* 106:66-71+ Ap 17 '89

No more home, sweet home? *USA Today (Periodical)* 118:13-14 D '89

Outlook: home prices. W. Giese. il maps *Changing Times* 43:48-50+ Ja '89

Renovation and the housing crisis. J. Schlefer. *Technology Review* 92:3+ O '89

A roof, but no shelter. K. R. Sheets. il map *U.S. News & World Report* 106:45-7 Mr 6 '89

Soaring out of reach [Canada] J. DeMont. *Maclean's* 102:29-30 Je 26 '89

This house party is winding down. C. Farrell. il *Business Week* p102-3 Mr 27 '89

Trying to buy a first home? Got a rich uncle? R. Stodghill, II. *Business Week* p106 Ja 23 '89

Unhappy anniversary. A. Bladen. il *Forbes* 144:258 O 2 '89

What do you expect for $2.25 million? [Los Angeles] D. K. Shah. il por *The New York Times Magazine* p54-6+ S 10 '89

When a house is just a home [drop in prices] A. P. Tobias. il *Time* 134:57 D 18 '89

Federal aid

See also
  Federal Home Loan Mortgage Corporation
  Federal National Mortgage Association
  Housing projects
  Housing vouchers
  United States. Dept. of Housing and Urban Development
  United States. Federal Housing Administration

And the latest great housing hope is . . . [public-private partnerships] C. Yang. il *Business Week* p74-5 Jl 10 '89

Behind the housing crisis: private-sector forces, not Reagan, killed off affordable rentals [comments on demonstration in Washington] D. Whitman. il *U.S. News & World Report* 107:28+ O 16 '89

Communities, not carpetbaggers [need for government support of nonprofit housing movement] P. Dreier. il *The Nation* 249:198-200+ Ag 21-28 '89

Fresh ideas on affordable housing. R. Kuttner. il *Utne Reader* p73-5 My/Je '89

House budgeting. R. Coorsh. *Consumers' Research Magazine* 72:4 Ja '89

Housing advocates turn up heat on Congress. M. E. Howard. il *Black Enterprise* 20:39-40 O '89

Housing policy needs a rehab. L. S. Richman. il *Fortune* 119:84-7+ Mr 27 '89

Local success stories [federal government should support nonprofit housing movement] P. Dreier. il *Commonweal* 116:201-2 Ap 7 '89

More housing follies [National Affordable Housing Act] D. Seligman. il *Fortune* 120:124 Ag 14 '89

What Jack Kemp loves about the HUD scandal. R. Stodghill, II and D. Harbrecht. il por *Business Week* p41 Jl 31 '89

Finance

See Housing finance

International aspects

See also
  United Nations. Commission on Human Settlements

California

See also
  Beverly Hills (Calif.)—Housing
  Chico (Calif.)—Housing
  Colton (Calif.)—Housing
  Hollywood (Calif.)—Housing
  Los Angeles (Calif.)—Housing
  Santa Monica (Calif.)—Housing
  Stockton (Calif.)—Housing

HOUSING—California—*cont.*

Blending in with oaks, borrowing from Monterey's history [Palma Grove Homes] il *Sunset (Central West edition)* 183:92-3 O '89

Down and out in L.A. [California's residential real estate market] H. Rudnitsky. il *Forbes* 144:65+ O 30 '89

Canada

Soaring out of reach. J. DeMont. *Maclean's* 102:29-30 Je 26 '89

Connecticut

See also

Hartford (Conn.)—Housing

Denmark

Cohousing: custom-built neighborhoods [cooperative housing; research by Kathryn McCamant and Charles Durrett] il *The Futurist* 23:29-32 S/O '89

Florida

See also

Fort Lauderdale (Fla.)—Housing

Margate (Fla.)—Housing

Georgia

See also

Atlanta (Ga.)—Housing

Germany (West)

See also

Berlin (Germany: West)—Housing

Illinois

See also

Chicago (Ill.)—Housing

Chicago Heights (Ill.)—Housing

Louisiana

See also

New Orleans (La.)—Housing

Maryland

See also

Baltimore (Md.)—Housing

Massachusetts

See also

Boston (Mass.)—Housing

HUDscam revisited [grants during Carter administration] il *National Review* 41:18-19 O 13 '89

Mexico

See also

Mexico City (Mexico)—Housing

Missouri

See also

Saint Louis (Mo.)—Housing

Nebraska

See also

Omaha (Neb.). Housing Authority

New Brunswick

The 'twilight zone'. G. Allen. il *Maclean's* 102:16 Mr 6 '89

New Jersey

See also

Montclair (N.J.)—Housing

New Mexico

See also

Santa Fe (N.M.)—Housing

New York (State)

See also

New York (N.Y.)—Housing

Westchester County (N.Y.)—Housing

South Carolina

After the hurricane they can't go home again. R. Rosenblatt. il *U.S. News & World Report* 107:6-7 O 9 '89

Soviet Union

Moscow on the HUD [involvement of S. R. Pierce in cooperative program with the Soviet Union; cover story] M. Hosenball. il *The New Republic* 201:18-21 O 23 '89

Tennessee

See also

Memphis (Tenn.)—Housing

United States

See Housing

Virginia

See also

Alexandria (Va.)—Housing

Reston (Va.)—Housing

Washington (D.C.)

See Washington (D.C.)—Housing

HOUSING, COOPERATIVE

See also

Apartment houses—Cooperative ownership

House sharing

Cohousing: custom-built neighborhoods [Denmark; research by Kathryn McCamant and Charles Durrett] il *The Futurist* 23:29-32 S/O '89

Good housekeeping: cohousing can reincorporate community into the American dream [excerpt from Cohousing] K. McCamant and C. Durrett. il *Utne Reader* p68-72 My/Je '89

HOUSING AND URBAN DEVELOPMENT DEPT. (U.S.)

See United States. Dept. of Housing and Urban Development

HOUSING BONDS *See Mortgage bonds and notes*

HOUSING CONSTRUCTION INDUSTRY *See Construction industry*

HOUSING FINANCE

See also

Home equity conversion

Housing—Costs

Mortgages

United States. Federal Home Loan Bank Board

Viager (Housing finance)

Gimme shelter [alternative financing] P. Frazer. il *Mother Jones* 14:48+ N '89

Gimme shelter [help for first time buyers] J. Greenwald. il *Time* 133:50-1 F 27 '89

How much home can you afford? [cover story] D. W. Myers. il *Consumers' Research Magazine* 72:11-15 F '89

How to buy your first house. C. A. Fried. il *Money* 18:137-8+ Ap '89

How to pay for your first home. W. Giese. il *Changing Times* 43:48-52+ My '89

Practical tips for first time homebuyers. G. J. Gallagher. il *Black Enterprise* 19:25-6 Jl '89

Smart ways to afford a home of your own. S. Bloch and G. Lichtenstein. il *Reader's Digest* 134:132-6 Je '89

Yes, you can buy a home. il *Glamour* 87:123+ My '89

HOUSING LAWS AND REGULATIONS

See also

Building inspection

Discrimination in housing

Fair Housing Act

Housing vouchers

Rent laws

Renovation and the housing crisis. J. Schlefer. *Technology Review* 92:3+ O '89

HOUSING PROJECTS

See also

Chicago (Ill.)—Housing

Habitat for Humanity Inc.

Hartford (Conn.)—Housing

New York (N.Y.)—Housing

Saint Louis (Mo.)—Housing

Washington (D.C.)—Housing

An enterprising war on poverty [interview with J. Kemp] il *New Perspectives Quarterly* 6:36-9 Summ '89

Evicting the drug dealers [J. Kemp's plan for public housing projects] il *Time* 133:41 My 1 '89

When tenants take charge [J. Kemp's plan] B. Turque. il por *Newsweek* 114:44 N 27 '89

HOUSING VOUCHERS

Abolish HUD. *The New Republic* 201:7-8 Ag 21 '89

The economies of public housing. W. Tucker. il *The American Spectator* 22:26-9 N '89

Housing policy needs a rehab. L. S. Richman. il *Fortune* 119:84-7+ Mr 27 '89

The problem at HUD. S. T. Mandel. il *National Review* 41:21-2 Ag 4 '89

A rental rathole? R. Coorsh. *Consumers' Research Magazine* 72:4 My '89

HOUSMAN, DAMIAN

Midgetman & Co. *National Review* 41:33-4 My 5 '89

HOUSTON, BETH

The news [poem] *Commonweal* 116:46 Ja 27 '89

HOUSTON, CISSY

about

Cissy! Whitney Houston's sweet inspiration. N. Gittelson. il pors *McCall's* 116:151-2+ My '89

Superstars shine as they raise funds to fight against AIDS. C. Waldron. il pors *Jet* 76:56-9 Jl 17 '89

HOUSTON, DICK

The Admiralty's orders were clear: 'sink or destroy the Königsberg'. il map *Smithsonian* 20:130-4+ S '89

HOUSTON, IVAN J., 1925-

about

Reaching for the stars. S. Herbert. il por *Black Enterprise* 19:294-6+ Je '89

HOUSTON, JAMES D.

The dangerous uncle returns. il *Gentlemen's Quarterly* 59:235-8+ D '89

Hawaii's Contemporary Museum. il *Architectural Digest* 46:150+ O '89

HOUSTON, JONAH

Lassoing the cactus bandit. il *Omni (New York, N.Y.)* 11:22 Ag '89

HOUSTON, MARK

about

Kiwi crunch. J. Schlax. il por *Forbes* 143:157 My 1 '89

HOUSTON, STEPHEN D.

(jt. auth) See Stuart, David, and Houston, Stephen D.

HOUSTON, TOM

about

Tom Houston is a real stand-up guy, thanks to the versatile vertical wheelchair he devised. il pors *People Weekly* 32:91-2 Ag 28 '89

HOUSTON, WALTER SCOTT

Deep-sky wonders. See issues of Sky and Telescope

HOUSTON, WHITNEY

about

America's 10 most beautiful women. il pors *Harper's Bazaar* 122:166+ S '89

Cissy! Whitney Houston's sweet inspiration. N. Gittelson. il pors *McCall's* 116:151-2+ My '89

HOUSTON, WHITNEY—about—*cont.*
Superstars shine as they raise funds to fight against AIDS. C. Waldron. il pors *Jet* 76:56-9 Jl 17 '89
Whitney Houston holds a lavish birthday gala. il pors *Jet* 76:60-1 S 11 '89
Whitney Houston is happy to back up BeBe and CeCe Winans, and that's the gospel truth. il pors *People Weekly* 32:44 Jl 3 '89
Whitney's big sound of success. J. Cullen. il pors *Ladies' Home Journal* 106:120+ Mr '89

HOUSTON (TEX.)
Architecture
See also
Houston (Tex.)—Buildings
Auditoriums, convention facilities, etc.
See also
Greater Houston Convention & Visitors Bureau
Buildings
Empty or nearly so in Houston [office buildings] G. W. S. Trow. *The New Yorker* 64:84-91 Ja 30 '89
"You got to look out for yourself" [how A. E. Paulson escaped investment debacle in Heritage Plaza] W. P. Barrett. il *Forbes* 143:43-4+ Ja 23 '89
Economic conditions
Houston's sick economy is taking a little nourishment. M. Ivey. il *Business Week* p102-3 Ja 16 '89
Education
Mentorships and the perceived educational payoffs [program pairing secondary teachers with mathematicians and scientists] L. M. Miller and others. il *Phi Delta Kappan* 70:465-7 F '89
School paper's story on teen mother who's class valedictorian is barred [C. M. Dixon] il por *Jet* 76:31 My 8 '89
Teen mom tells of 'beating odds' to be valedictorian [C. M. Dixon] il pors *Jet* 76:12 Je 26 '89
Teen mother with straight A's tells how education is changing her life [C. M. Dixon] D. M. Cheers. il pors *Jet* 76:28-30 My 22 '89
Valedictorian Carrie Dixon gets top grades in high school—even with a second child on the way. il por *People Weekly* 31:62 My 29 '89
Galleries and museums
See also
Houston Police Museum
Harbor
In port in Houston [Sam Houston tour boat] il *Southern Living* 24:49 S '89
Hospitals
See also
M.D. Anderson Cancer Center
Industries
Indie angst in teetering Texas [independent TV stations] D. Holder. il *Channels (New York, N.Y.: 1986)* 9:71-3 Ja '89
Moral conditions
A smut buster battles sin in the city [D. Hurlbut] R. Woodbury. il pors *Time* 133:22-3+ My 29 '89
Music
See also
Houston Grand Opera Association
Police
"Thank God for people like you" [undercover narcotics officer P. Rosales] M. Siegel. il por *Good Housekeeping* 208:139+ Je '89
Sports
Houston. R. R. Holster, Jr. il *Sport (New York, N.Y.)* 80:112-16 Je '89
Streets
Highways in the city. B. Ouvry-Vial. il *The Unesco Courier* 42:34-7 Ag '89
Tourist trade
See also
Greater Houston Convention & Visitors Bureau

HOUSTON CONVENTION & VISITORS BUREAU *See* Greater Houston Convention & Visitors Bureau

HOUSTON GRAND OPERA ASSOCIATION
Musical events:
M. Tippett's New Year and other productions of the British Opera Festival. A. Porter. *The New Yorker* 65:114-17 N 20 '89
Nixon in China, via Edinburgh. M. S. Eddy. il *Theatre Crafts* 23:42-4+ My '89
Ring in the new [premiere of New Year] P. G. Davis. il *New York* 22:83-5 N 27 '89

HOUSTON-MONTGOMERY, BEAUREGARD
The paparazzi have long been considered the foot soldiers of photography. il *Vogue* 179:274-5 Je '89

HOUSTON POLICE MUSEUM
The law is in order at this museum. il *Southern Living* 24:22+ F '89

HOUSTON ZOOLOGICAL GARDENS
A little piece of paradise in Houston [Tropical Bird House] il *Southern Living* 24:21 D '89

HOUT, MORGAN
about
The last temptation of price. J. D. Miller. il *Sport (New York, N.Y.)* 80:12 Jl '89

HOUTCHENS, C. J.
Washington party power. il *Harper's Bazaar* 122:214+ O '89

HOVENWEEP NATIONAL MONUMENT (COLO. AND UTAH)
NPCA wins appeal on Hovenweep drilling. *National Parks* 63:15 Jl/Ag '89

HOVERCRAFT *See* Air cushion vehicles

HOVERMAN, JAMES J.
about
In the Blue Chips. M. Barrier. il pors *Nation's Business* 77:54 F '89

HOVERSTEN, PAUL
Flying on the edge. il map *Discover* 10:20-1 S '89

HOVIS, GENE
Talking turkey. il *House & Garden* 161:107-10+ N '89
A time for tea. il *The New York Times Magazine* p55-6 Ja 8 '89
The ubiquitous picnic. il *House & Garden* 161:54+ Je '89

HOW-TO ARTICLES *See* Periodical articles

HOW TO GET AHEAD IN ADVERTISING [film] See Motion picture reviews—Single works

HOWAR, BARBARA, 1934-
Island of calm. il *House & Garden* 161:140-5 D '89

HOWARD, CAROLE, 1945-
Integrating public relations into the marketing mix [address, August 7, 1989] *Vital Speeches of the Day* 56:93-6 N 15 '89

HOWARD, DAVID M.
about
Faith at the top [interview] por map *Christianity Today* 33:58-9 Jl 14 '89

HOWARD, DOREEN G.
Everyone can can. il *The Saturday Evening Post* 261:26+ S '89
Growing the "forbidden" fruit. il *The Saturday Evening Post* 261:30+ Ja/F '89

HOWARD, DOROTHY R.
Winter primitive [poem] *McCall's* 116:84 Mr '89

HOWARD, ED
Stacking the deck. il por *Common Cause Magazine* 15:24-6 Ja/F '89

HOWARD, FRANK
about
Paws! C. Kirkpatrick. il pors *Sports Illustrated* 71:98-102+ O 23 '89

HOWARD, GERALD
Mistah Perkins—he dead: publishing today. *The American Scholar* 58:355-69 Summ '89

HOWARD, JEAN
about
Tea & cinema. P. Viladas. il por *House & Garden* 161:60 D '89

HOWARD, JERRY
The lobster man. il por *Modern Maturity* 32:50 Ag/S '89
What's new with zoos? [cover story] il *Modern Maturity* 32:44-9 Ap/My '89

HOWARD, JOHN A. (JOHN ADDISON), 1921-
Higher education and a civilization in trouble [address, November 15, 1988] *Vital Speeches of the Day* 55:314-18 Mr 1 '89

HOWARD, JOHN N.
about
Howard elected 1989 vice president of Optical Society. por *Physics Today* 42:67 Ja '89

HOWARD, JOHNETTE
"All I ever wanted was a shot". il pors *Sport (New York, N.Y.)* 80:26-9 Mr '89

HOWARD, MICHAEL E.
Capital improvements. il *Black Enterprise* 20:53-4+ Ag '89
The titan of tires. il pors *Black Enterprise* 20:68-70+ S '89

HOWARD, RICHARD, 1929-
For Robert Phelps, dead at 66 [poem] *The New Republic* 201:107 N 6 '89

HOWARD, ROBERT, 1954-
(jt. auth) See Hackman, Sandra, and Howard, Robert, 1954-

HOWARD, ROBIN, 1924-1989
about
Obituary
Dance Magazine il por 63:30+ D '89. R. Cohan

HOWARD, RON
about
The nice guy rides again. R. Givens. il pors *Newsweek* 114:56-7 Ag 28 '89
Parenthood [film] Reviews
The American Spectator 22:38 O '89. B. Bawer
Commonweal 116:471-2 S 8 '89. P. D. Baumann
Maclean's il 102:53 Ag 14 '89. P. Young
New York il 22:79-80 Ag 14 '89. D. Denby
The New Yorker 65:75 Ag 7 '89. T. Rafferty
Newsweek il 114:61-2 Ag 7 '89. D. Ansen
People Weekly il 32:17 Ag 14 '89. R. Novak
Rolling Stone p38 Ag 24 '89. P. Travers
Time il 134:54 Ag 7 '89. R. Schickel

HOWARD HUGHES MEDICAL INSTITUTE
GM, Hughes settle stock fight. B. J. Culliton. *Science* 243:1283 Mr 10 '89

HOWARD HUGHES MEDICAL INSTITUTE—*cont.*
GM's alphabet stocks spelled trouble. J. B. Treece. il *Business Week* p41 Mr 13 '89
HOWARD JOHNSON CO.
Reflections on 28 flavors [restaurants fade away] O. Friedrich. il *Time* 133:82 My 1 '89
HOWARD-TILTON MEMORIAL LIBRARY. SOUTHEASTERN ARCHITECTURAL ARCHIVE
Architecture on archive. il *Southern Living* 24:34 S '89
HOWARD UNIVERSITY
Howard students force Atwater's resignation, and push other demands. il *Jet* 75:37 Mr 27 '89
Howard's Cheek to end 20-year career there to take new ambassadorship. il pors *Jet* 76:4-5 Ap 24 '89
Now Willie Horton stalks the GOP [L. Atwater forced to resign from board after student protest] il *U.S. News & World Report* 106:13 Mr 20 '89
Saying no to Lee Atwater [students protest appointment to board of trustees] J. V. Lamar, Jr. il por *Time* 133:27 Mr 20 '89
Student power! R. Powers. por *Essence* 20:122 Ag '89
Students fight naming of Atwater to Howard board. *Jet* 75:11 Mr 20 '89
HOWARD UNIVERSITY. LIBRARIES
See also
Moorland-Spingarn Research Center Library
HOWARD UNIVERSITY. SCHOOL OF COMMUNICATIONS
Howard U. gets Warner Communications grant. il *Jet* 75:47 Mr 13 '89
THE HOWDY DOODY SHOW [television program] *See* Television program reviews—Single works
HOWE, DIANNE S.
At the crossroads: the National Dance Association in the 1990s. *Design for Arts in Education* 90:44-7 My/Je '89
HOWE, GORDIE
about
A backhanded compliment. J. Greenberg. il pors *Sports Illustrated* 71:50-3 O 23 '89
Games men play. H. Quinn. il pors *Maclean's* 102:62 O 23 '89
Three who made history: Cobb, Louis and Howe. J. Lapointe. il pors *Sport (New York, N.Y.)* 80:60 My '89
HOWE, IRVING
The human factor. *The New Republic* 200:30-4 My 8 '89
The treason of the critics. *The New Republic* 200:28-31 Je 12 '89
HOWE, JOHN L.
Home-front vets. por *Essence* 20:12 My '89
HOWE, NANCY LITTERMAN
Feet revenge. il *Runner's World* 24:104 S '89
HOWE, TINA
about
Approaching Zanzibar [drama] Reviews
New York 22:124 My 15 '89. J. Simon
The New Yorker 65:94 My 15 '89. E. Oliver
Time il 133:87 My 15 '89. W. A. Henry
Taking the stage. pors *Harper's Bazaar* 122:150-3+ Ag '89
HOWE, REBECCA (FICTIONAL CHARACTER) *See* Rebecca Howe (Fictional character)
HOWELL, JOHN
Quite contrary [cover story] il pors *Art News* 88:152-7 Mr '89
HOWELL, LLEWELLYN D.
Are Philippine bases essential to U.S. military strategy? il *USA Today (Periodical)* 117:42-5 My '89
HOWELL, MARK D., AND OTHERS
Vaccination against experimental allergic encephalomyelitis with T cell receptor peptides. bibl f il *Science* 246:668-70 N 3 '89
HOWELL, MARTHA C.
about
Economic history, on line. F. Meeks. il por *Forbes* 144:122 Jl 10 '89
HOWELL, ROBERT R.
(jt. auth) *See* Nash, Douglas B., and Howell, Robert R.
HOWELL, RON
Quebec. il *Black Enterprise* 20:123-4 N '89
HOWLAND, NINA D.
The United States and Angola, 1974-88: a chronology. *Department of State Bulletin* 89:16-24 F '89
HOWLAND, REBECCA
about
Rebecca Howland at Willoughby Sharp. E. Myles. il *Art in America* 77:203-4 My '89
HOWLE, MARY JEANETTE
Twinkle, twinkle little star: it's more than just a nursery song. bibl f il *Children Today* 18:18-22 Jl/Ag '89
HOWSE, JOHN
Prairie samurai. il *World Press Review* 36:68-9 N '89
HOY, EDWARD C.
A tray for a Celestron tripod. il *Astronomy* 17:71-2 N '89
HOY, MARK
The most famous farm in America. il por *Audubon* 91:64-7 N '89
Researching the Slough. il map *Audubon* 91:98-105 Mr '89

HOYER, DORE
about
Heart of darkness. T. Tobias. por *New York* 22:124+ N 6 '89
HOYER, STENY H.
Should President Bush's minimum wage proposal be adopted? [excerpts from address, March 23, 1989] *Congressional Digest* 68:145+ My '89
HOYLE, JOHN
Preparing the 21st-century superintendent [adaptation of address, February 1988] bibl f il *Phi Delta Kappan* 70:376-9 Ja '89
HOYOS, BEATRICE, AND OTHERS
Kappa B-specific DNA binding proteins: role in the regulation of human interleukin-2 gene expression. bibl f il *Science* 244:457-60 Ap 28 '89
HOYT, MARY FINCH
"Why I kept my cancer a secret". il pors *Good Housekeeping* 208:154-5+ Je '89
HOYT, THOMAS, JR.
Beyond protocol: the quest for unity. *The Christian Century* 106:926-7 O 18 '89
HPRT (HYPOXANTHINE PHOSPHORIBOSYLTRANSFERASE) *See* Transferases
HPV *See* Human papilloma virus
HRABAL, BOHUMIL, 1914-
The magic flute; tr. by Peter Kussi. *The New York Review of Books* 36:39 My 18 '89
HRANITZ, JOHN R.
(jt. auth) *See* Eddowes, E. Anne, and Hranitz, John R.
HRUSHEVS'KYI, MYKHAiLO, 1866-1934
about
Hrushevsky and the Ukraine's 'lost' history. T. Prymak. bibl il por map *History Today* 39:42-6 Ja '89
HSIA, JAYJIA, AND HIRANO-NAKANISHI, MARSHA
The demographics of diversity. il map *Change* 21:20-7 N/D '89
HTLV VIRUSES
See also
HIV viruses
Amplification and molecular cloning of HTLV-I sequences from DNA of multiple sclerosis patients. E. P. Reddy and others. bibl f il *Science* 243:529-33 Ja 27 '89; Correction. 246:10-11 O 6 '89
High rate of HTLV-II infection in seropositive IV drug abusers in New Orleans. H. Lee and others. bibl f il *Science* 244:471-5 Ap 28 '89
HTLV-I: a new AIDS-like threat? R. Montagna. il por map *The Saturday Evening Post* 261:82-4+ Jl/Ag '89
HTLV-II common among drug abusers [study by Irvin S. Y. Chen] *Science News* 135:284 My 6 '89
Multiple choice [viral fingerprints in blood of MS patients] T. Beardsley. *Scientific American* 260:34-5 Ap '89
PCR analysis of DNA from multiple sclerosis patients for the presence of HTLV-I [discussion of January 27, 1989 article, Amplification and molecular cloning of HTLV-I sequences from DNA of multiple sclerosis patients] E. P. Reddy and others. il *Science* 246:821-4 N 10 '89
HTUN, HAN, AND DAHLBERG, JAMES E.
Topology and formation of triple-stranded H-DNA. bibl f il *Science* 243:1571-6 Mr 24 '89
HU, JIA-LU
about
Reviews:
Retrospective concert presented by Hu Jia-lu in Shanghai. J.-P. Ou. *Dance Magazine* 63:110-11 My '89
HU, YAO-PANG *See* Hu Yaobang, 1915-1989
HU QILI, 1929-
about
Capitalism has no patent on the market [interview] N. Gardels. por *New Perspectives Quarterly* 5:7-11 Wint '88/'89
HU YAOBANG, 1915-1989
about
A look inside the Politburo. il por *Newsweek* 113:35 Je 5 '89
HUAC *See* United States. Congress. House. Committee on Un-American Activities
HUAHINE (FRENCH POLYNESIA)
Description and travel
Gourmet holidays: Society Islands. C. Bates. il map *Gourmet* 49:58-63+ F '89
HUANG, ALLEN
(jt. auth) *See* Wishon, Phillip M., and Huang, Allen
HUANG, MING, AND OTHERS
Immunodeficiency and clonal growth of target cells induced by helper-free defective retrovirus. bibl f il *Science* 246:1614-17 D 22 '89
HUBBARD, H. M.
Photovoltaics today and tomorrow. bibl f il *Science* 244:297-304 Ap 21 '89
HUBBARD, L. RON (LA FAYETTE RON), 1911-1986
about
Court splits over fair use language in Hubbard case. M. Reuter. *Publishers Weekly* 236:10 S 22 '89
L. Ron Hubbard inside the Great Wall. il *Publishers Weekly* 235:36 Ap 28 '89
New Era wins pre-pub review of Hubbard bio. *Publishers Weekly* 236:332 Ag 11 '89

HUBBARD, L. RON (LA FAYETTE RON), 1911-1986—
about—cont.
'Salinger' haunts ruling on Hubbard biography. M. Reuter.
Publishers Weekly 235:102 My 12 '89
HUBBARD, LA FAYETTE RON See Hubbard, L. Ron (La Fayette Ron), 1911-1986
HUBBARD, NATE
                                about
About that picture . . . il Sports Illustrated 70:14 F 20
'89
HUBBARD, WILLIAM B.
(jt. auth) See Brahic, A., and Hubbard, William B.
HUBBELL, JOHN G.
Heart of an Ironman. il pors Reader's Digest 134:13-14+
Mr '89
The man who would not quit. il pors Reader's Digest
134:115-18 F '89
Stickum up, love! Reader's Digest 135:123-5 O '89
Where have all the nurses gone? il Reader's Digest 134:71-6
Je '89
HUBBELL, STEPHEN
Jordan votes the Islamic ticket. il The Nation 249:786+
D 25 '89
HUBBELL, SUE
Be it ever so glitzy, there's no place like the new truck
stop. bibl (p245-6) il Smithsonian 20:94-102+ N '89
Feisty women, family pride. il New Choices for the Best
Years 29:80-1 My '89
The great American pie expedition. The New Yorker 65:75-6+
Mr 27 '89
Its ponds may not always be golden, but the loon still
sings a wild song. il Smithsonian 19:58-67 Mr '89
The Vicksburg ghost. The New Yorker 65:106-17 S 25 '89
HUBBLE, EDWIN POWELL, 1889-1953
                                about
The legacy of Edwin Hubble. B. Jones. il pors Astronomy
17:38-44 D '89
HUBBLE CONSTANT
No go for slow flow [work of R. Brent Tully and J. Richard
Fisher] il Sky and Telescope 77:10-11 Ja '89
HUBBLE SPACE TELESCOPE
Amateur projects selected for Space Telescope. Astronomy
17:16-17 N '89
Ball develops multi-anode microchannel array for Space
Telescope, defense uses. W. B. Scott. il Aviation Week
& Space Technology 130:296-7 Je 12 '89
The big glass [mirror built by Perkin-Elmer Corp.; cover
story] T. Dunkle. il Discover 10:68-81 Jl '89
Building the Hubble Space Telescope. C. R. O'Dell. il Sky
and Telescope 78:31-6 Jl '89
From idea to observation: the Space Telescope at work.
R. Villard. il Astronomy 17:38-44 Je '89
Great telescope, bad service plan. M. M. Waldrop. il Science
246:1551-3 D 22 '89
Heaven's scope. R. Giacconi. il Omni (New York, N.Y.)
11:20 Ag '89
Looking forward to looking back. B. Weber. il The New
York Times Magazine p102 Ap 2 '89
NASA's $60,000 epoxy drops. M. M. Waldrop. Science
243:1281 Mr 10 '89
The new, improved Space Telescope. R. T. Fienberg. il
Sky and Telescope 77:153-5 F '89
Space Telescope delayed (again). M. M. Waldrop. Science
244:912 My 26 '89
Will the Hubble Space Telescope compute? [problems with
operations software] M. M. Waldrop. il Science 243:1437-9
Mr 17 '89
The world's biggest star catalogue [Hubble Space Telescope
Guide star catalog] R. Villard. il Sky and Telescope 78:583-9
D '89
HUBCAP CITY (FIRM)
Hubcap City. The New Yorker 65:26-8 My 1 '89
HUBE, SANDRA BULOW- See Bulow-Hube, Sandra
HUBER, HANK
The environmental kitchen. il Country Journal 16:39 F '89
The versatile sunroom. il Country Journal 16:27-33 Mr/Ap
'89
HUBER, PETER W.
The clinical ecology scam. il por Forbes 144:232 O 2 '89
Electrophobia. por Forbes 144:313 S 4 '89
Greenhouse gas. il por Forbes 144:226 O 30 '89
Litigation thwarts innovation in the U.S. il Scientific American
260:120 Mr '89
The new competitive environment. Society 26:27-31 Jl/Ag
'89
HUBER, ROBERT, 1937-
                                about
Nobel chemists shed light on key structure in photosynthesis.
B. G. Levi. il por Physics Today 42:17-18 F '89
HUBER, VICKI
                                about
The lady in waiting. M. Noden. il pors Sports Illustrated
70:73-4+ Je 5 '89
To be young, gifted & fast [cover story] C. Brennan. il
pors Runner's World 24:42-7 Mr '89
HUBERTS (NEW YORK, N.Y.: RESTAURANT) See New
York (N.Y.)—Restaurants, nightclubs, bars, etc.

HÜBL, MICHAEL
The "Melancholist of virtuosity". il por Art News 88:120-5
F '89
HUCHRA, JOHN
(jt. auth) See Geller, Margaret J., and Huchra, John
HUCK, GABE
Why settle for Communion? Commonweal 116:37-9 Ja 27
'89
HUD See United States. Dept. of Housing and Urban Development
HUD (HEAD-UP DISPLAY) SYSTEMS See Air navigation—
Aids and devices
**HUD-INDEPENDENT   AGENCIES   SUBCOMMITTEE
(HOUSE)** See United States. Congress. House. Committee
on Appropriations. Subcommittee on HUD-Independent
Agencies
HUDAK, JOSEPH
Winterize your yard. il Organic Gardening 36:50-2 S '89
HUDDLES, FOOTBALL See Football huddles
HUDGEL, DONNA
                                about
Trails West rounds up western readers. S. Sherman. il
Publishers Weekly 235:41+ My 5 '89
HUDGINS, ANDREW
An old joke: Christ and the woman take in adultery [poem]
The New Republic 201:38 S 4 '89
Thus [poem] The Atlantic 263:39 Ja '89
HUDSON, BILL
                                about
Cindy Williams and Bill Hudson really do act Just like
family. M. Dougherty. il pors People Weekly 31:61-4 Je
5 '89
HUDSON, CHERYL
Skinny eggs and other dream foods. il Health (New York,
N.Y.) 21:30+ S '89
HUDSON, HENRY E.
                                about
Nobody's laughing at Ill Wind now. P. Dwyer. por Business
Week p34-5 Ja 23 '89
HUDSON, HUGH
                                about
Lost angels [film] Reviews
American Film il 14:61 My '89. E. Drucker
New York 22:72-3 My 22 '89. D. Denby
Video il 13:78 N '89. J. Young
HUDSON, PATRICIA L.
A Vanderbilt Christmas [cover story] il map Americana
17:28-35 N/D '89
HUDSON, ROCK, 1925-1985
                                about
Lovers, liars and other strangers. pors Newsweek 113:61
F 27 '89
The price of betrayal. P. Chin. il pors People Weekly 31:180-3
Mr 6 '89
Rock Hudson. B. Darrach. il pors People Weekly 32 Special
Issue:65-6 Fall '89
HUDSON (N.Y.)
                        Historic houses, sites, etc.
See also
Olana State Historic Site (Hudson, N.Y.)
HUDSON & HUDSON
Finance-a-face-lift. H. Wolinsky. il American Health 8:12
D '89
HUDSON BAY REGION
See also
Birds—Hudson Bay region
HUDSON RIVER (N.Y. AND N.J.) FISHERIES See Fisheries
HUDSON RIVER SCHOOL
The American canvas. L. Bertrand. il por National Parks
63:32-6+ S/O '89
The Hudson River revisited [Olana State Historic Site] R.
I. C. Fisher. il American Artist 53:48-54+ N '89
HUDSON RIVER VALLEY (N.Y. AND N.J.)
                        Description and travel
History with a view. H. B. Livesey. il map Travel Holiday
172:64-73 D '89
HUDSON RIVER VALLEY (N.Y. AND N.J.) IN ART
The Hudson River revisited. R. I. C. Fisher. il American
Artist 53:48-54+ N '89
HUE (VIETNAM)
                        Description
Hue: my city, myself. V. D. Tran. il por map National
Geographic 176:594-603 N '89
HUE-MAN EXPERIENCE BOOKSTORE (DENVER, COLO.)
See Booksellers and bookselling—Colorado
HUEBNER, ALBERT L.
'Real nasty stuff'. il The Progressive 53:26-8 O '89
HUETTNER, JAMES E.
Indole-2-carboxylic acid: a competitive antagonist of potentia-
tion by glycine at the NMDA receptor. bibl f il Science
243:1611-13 Mr 24 '89
HUFBAUER, GARY CLYDE
Beyond GATT. Foreign Policy 77:64-76 Wint '89/'90
                                about
World without borders. E. A. Finn, Jr. il por Forbes 143:118+
Ap 17 '89

HUFF, CAROLINE
about
Caroline Huff. J. Wechsler. il por *American Artist* 53:52-7+ Je '89
HUFFORD, DEBORAH
Fantailed fantasies and other fauna for the pond. il *Flower and Garden* 33:26-30 Jl/Ag '89
Growing an enchanted oasis. il *Flower and Garden* 33:42-6 My/Je '89
On the waterfront. il *Flower and Garden* 33:30-2 N/D '89
Practical reflections on garden pools. il *Flower and Garden* 33:54-8, 60 Mr/Ap '89
Water music. il *Flower and Garden* 33:20-3 S/O '89
HUFFY CORPORATION
Huffy's suitors are pedaling fast. G. G. Marcial. *Business Week* p92 Ap 3 '89
HUFNAGEL, JAMES A.
Foam-core panels. il *Better Homes and Gardens* 67:90+ Mr '89
Install a hardwood floor. il *Better Homes and Gardens* 67:120 My '89
HUFNAGEL, VICKI
about
Maverick doctor: martyr or fraud? K. Moloney. por *Ms.* 18:69-70 N '89
HUFTON, OLWEN
Voilà la citoyenne. bibl il *History Today* 39:26-32 My '89
HUGGING *See* Embracing
HUGGINS, ANDREW WELSH- *See* Welsh-Huggins, Andrew
HUGHES, DAVID
Big, big man. il pors *Sport (New York, N.Y.)* 80:42-3 N '89
HUGHES, DELLA
Running away: a 50-50 chance to survive? il *USA Today (Periodical)* 118:64-6 S '89
HUGHES, FRIEDA
about
Frieda Hughes escapes the shadow of mom Sylvia Plath. F. Hauptfuhrer. il pors *People Weekly* 32:99+ D 4 '89
HUGHES, JOHN
about
Uncle Buck [film] Reviews
The American Spectator 22:39 N '89. B. Bawer
Newsweek il 114:68 S 4 '89. D. Ansen
People Weekly il 32:13-14 S 4 '89. R. Novak
Rolling Stone p32 S 7 '89. P. Travers
HUGHES, KRISTINE FUGAL
about
The Mary Kay of the herb industry. S. D. Atchison. il por *Business Week* p100 My 22 '89
HUGHES, LANGSTON, 1902-1967
about
Suitcase in Harlem. D. Pinckney. bibl f il *The New York Review of Books* 36:38-43 F 16 '89
HUGHES, LARRY, AND SCOTT, SANDY
Canada, carbon dioxide, and the greenhouse effect. bibl f il *Environment* 31:4-5+ N '89
HUGHES, NANCY SCHEPER- *See* Scheper-Hughes, Nancy
HUGHES, ROBERT
Barcelona beauty: the Palau de la Música Catalana. il *Architectural Digest* 46:96-102+ Mr '89
The liberal Goya. il *The New York Review of Books* 36:26-31 Je 29 '89
HUGHES, THOMAS PARKE
U.S. support for Soviet technology: a lesson from history. *Current (Washington, D.C.)* 315:18-26 S '89
about
America's real Founding Fathers [interview] A. P. Sanoff. il por *U.S. News & World Report* 106:64 My 8 '89
HUGHES (HOWARD) MEDICAL INSTITUTE *See* Howard Hughes Medical Institute
HUGHES AIRCRAFT CO.
Ariane 4 vehicle to orbit Hughes payloads in 1990. *Aviation Week & Space Technology* 131:35 Jl 24 '89
General Dynamics will launch first Navy UHF follow-on satellite [Atlas booster] *Aviation Week & Space Technology* 131:22 Ag 21 '89
Hughes/AEL team wins Navy contract for upgraded radar warning receiver. B. W. Henderson. il *Aviation Week & Space Technology* 131:60-1 Ag 28 '89
Hughes developing head-up display for general aviation aircraft. il *Aviation Week & Space Technology* 131:91 Ag 21 '89
Hughes may build lightsat to gather ocean data [SeaWiFS spacecraft] J. R. Asker. *Aviation Week & Space Technology* 131:24 O 16 '89
Hughes moves toward goal of integrating radar, EW [electronic warfare] *Aviation Week & Space Technology* 131:109+ S 11 '89
Hughes official says Air Force rushed complex AMRAAM test [views of Malcolm R. Currie] *Aviation Week & Space Technology* 131:41 O 9 '89
Non-line-of-sight missile will use platinum silicide infrared detectors. il *Aviation Week & Space Technology* 130:67+ Mr 27 '89
HUGHES HELICOPTERS, INC.
See also
McDonnell Douglas Helicopter Company

HUGOZ, JEAN-PIERRE PÉRONCEL- *See* Péroncel-Hugoz, Jean-Pierre, 1940-
HUIE, BARBARA
Teaching students cultural mediation. *The Education Digest* 55:50-2 O '89
HUIZENGA, H. WAYNE
about
Will this video chain stay on fast-forward? P. Engardio and A. Fins. il *Business Week* p72+ Je 12 '89
HUIZHOU (CHINA)
Economic history
The merchants of Huizhou: commerce and Confucianism [cover story] M. Dillon. bibl il map *History Today* 39:24-30 F '89
HUIZINGA, J. H.
When radical chic courted the guillotine. il *The New York Times Book Review* 94:1+ F 5 '89
HULBERT, MARK
Wall Street irregular. See issues of Forbes beginning September 21, 1977
HULCE, TOM
about
Parenthood: raising Tom Hulce. J. E. Fitch. *American Film* 14:57-8 Jl/Ag '89
HULETT, STANLEY W.
Public utilities in transition [address, November 8, 1988] *Vital Speeches of the Day* 55:211-14 Ja 15 '89
HULL, BRETT
about
Another Hull's apoppin'. P. Fichtenbaum. il pors *Sports Illustrated* 71:144+ D 25 '89-Ja 1 '90
HULL, GRETCHEN GAEBELEIN
about
A father's legacy. P. E. Alsdurf. il pors *Christianity Today* 33:58 O 20 '89
HULL, JOHN
about
Bipartisan arm-twisting in Central America [letter from congressmen to O. Arias Sanchez concerning J. Hull] *Harper's* 278:24 Je '89
John Hull, once Oliver North's man in Costa Rica, is now accused of running guns and drugs. R. Arias. il pors *People Weekly* 31:52-4+ My 1 '89
HULL (ENGLAND)
Fortification
Hull's Citadel uncovered. S. Barclay. il *History Today* 39:3-4 Mr '89
HULLETT, SANDRALL
Where a ride to the doctor costs $20. il *Aging* no359:14-16 '89
HULLS (NAVAL ARCHITECTURE)
Don't rock the boat! B. McKeown. il *Popular Science* 234:74-5+ F '89
HUMAN BEHAVIOR *See* Behavior (Psychology)
HUMAN BODY
See also
Lean body mass
Men—Anatomy and physiology
Mind and body
Women—Anatomy and physiology
Lives of the body. S. Tisdale. *Harper's* 279:38+ O '89
Photographs and photography
Bold body graphics. J. Zuckerman. il *Petersen's Photographic Magazine* 18:16-18+ D '89
The sensate body. P. Dixon. il *Esquire* 111:145-50 My '89
HUMAN BODY (THEOLOGY)
Sleeping like spoons. J. G. Milhaven. il *Commonweal* 116:205-7 Ap 7 '89
HUMAN BODY IN MOTION PICTURES
The bloodstream express [special effects in film to be part of Body Wars exhibit at EPCOT] B. Weber. il *The New York Times Magazine* p142 Je 11 '89
HUMAN CAPITAL
See also
Children—Economic value
Women—Economic value
What a life is worth when one is lost [monetary awards in wrongful death cases] *U.S. News & World Report* 106:14+ F 27 '89
HUMAN COLD STORAGE *See* Cryonics
HUMAN DIMENSION CONFERENCES
CSCE Conference on the Human Dimension [statement, May 31, 1989] M. B. Abram. *Department of State Bulletin* 89:88-90 S '89
Helsinki in Paris. W. Korey. il *The New Leader* 72:12-14 Jl 10-24 '89
HUMAN ECOLOGY
See also
Biosphere II
Deep ecology
Environmental refugees
Gaia hypothesis
Holistic resource management
Indians of North America—Influence on nature
Man—Influence of environment
Man—Influence on nature
Man and the Biosphere Programme
Quality of life

HUMAN ECOLOGY—cont.
Beauty and the aesthetics of survival. P. Delattre. il *Utne Reader* p64-7+ Jl/Ag '89
Bringing it all back home. D. Schoonmaker. il *The Mother Earth News* 119:8 S/O '89
Death of a small planet [cover story] M. Bookchin. il *The Progressive* 53:19-23 Ag '89
The ecology of survival. A. Gore, Jr. il *The New Republic* 201:26+ N 6 '89
Ecology wars. R. Hill. *Omni (New York, N.Y.)* 11:25 Ag '89
Facing the habitability crisis [adaptation of address, February 16, 1989] P. R. Ehrlich. *BioScience* 39:480-2 Jl/Ag '89
The futility of global thinking [adaptation of address, June 1989] W. Berry. *Harper's* 279:16-19+ S '89
Man unprepared for challenges [views of Paul R. Ehrlich] *USA Today (Periodical)* 117:7 Ap '89
Neo-modern ecology. A. Touraine. il *New Perspectives Quarterly* 6:33-6 Spr '89
New world, new mind [excerpt] P. R. Ehrlich and R. E. Ornstein. il *New Perspectives Quarterly* 6:26-33 Spr '89
The shadow our future throws [interview] N. Gardels and M. B. Snell. il *New Perspectives Quarterly* 6:20-5 Spr '89
We can't heal the environment without remaking our society. M. Bookchin. il *Utne Reader* p80-2 N/D '89
HUMAN EMBRYO See Fetus
HUMAN ENGINEERING See Ergonomics
HUMAN ERROR
Live and relearn. J. Stone. il *Glamour* 87:134 O '89
Sleep in and smell the coffee [sleep loss linked to human error] M. Adessa. *Psychology Today* 22:18 D '88
When parents make mistakes. P. Colman. *Ladies' Home Journal* 106:106 O '89
Who says it's too late? [rectifying past mistakes] N. V. Peale. *Reader's Digest* 134:23-4 My '89
HUMAN EXPERIMENTATION See Genetic research—Human experimentation; Medical research—Human experimentation; Pharmaceutical research—Human experimentation
HUMAN FIGURE IN ART
See also
Anatomy, Artistic
Nude in art
Portrait drawing
Portrait painting
Portrait sculpture
Women in art
Introspective reflections [C. Carter; cover story] J.-P. Wolf. il por *American Artist* 53:50-5 O '89
HUMAN FRONTIERS SCIENCE PROGRAM
Strasbourg home for Frontiers. D. Dickson. *Science* 245:698 Ag 18 '89
HUMAN GROWTH HORMONE See Pituitary hormones
HUMAN GROWTH HORMONE, SYNTHETIC See Pituitary hormones, Synthetic
HUMAN IMMUNODEFICIENCY VIRUSES See HIV viruses
HUMAN INFORMATION PROCESSING
See also
Artificial intelligence
Neural network computers
Human factors are critical in computer-driven systems. D. Hughes. il *Aviation Week & Space Technology* 131:104-5 D 18-25 '89
Human factors: the gap between humans and machines. E. Weiner and A. Brown. il pors *The Futurist* 23:9-11 My/Je '89
In the blink of an eye [blink rate relates to mental processes] J. A. Stern. il *Reader's Digest* 134:99-101 Ap '89
In the blink of an eye [blink rate relates to mental processes; research by John A. Stern] S. Vogel. il *Discover* 10:62-4 F '89
Organization of the human brain. M. S. Gazzaniga. bibl f il *Science* 245:947-52 S 1 '89
HUMAN LOCOMOTION
See also
Running
Walking
Toe-to-toe with Paranthropus [foot bone gives evidence of bipedality at Swartkrans site; research by Randall Susman] il *Discover* 10:16 Ag '89
HUMAN MECHANICS See Biomechanics
HUMAN MILK See Milk, Human
HUMAN PAPILLOMA VIRUS
The human papilloma virus-16 E7 oncoprotein is able to bind to the retinoblastoma gene product. N. Dyson and others. bibl f il *Science* 243:934-7 F 17 '89
Virus type predicts risky cancer return. K. Fackelmann. *Science News* 136:310 N 11 '89
HUMAN POWERED AIRCRAFT
See also
Daedalus Project
Man-powered helicopter makes first flight [built by Cal Poly students] il *Aviation Week & Space Technology* 131:115 D 18-25 '89
HUMAN POWERED OCEANOGRAPHIC SUBMERSIBLE RACING
Games [first annual International Submarine Races] S. Morris. il *Omni (New York, N.Y.)* 11:120-1 Je '89

HUMAN POWERED OCEANOGRAPHIC SUBMERSIBLES
Muscle subs. P. Britton. il *Popular Science* 234:126-9+ Je '89
HUMAN POWERED VEHICLE RACING
The outer limits [Race Across America] T. Blumenthal. il *Bicycling* 30:36-9 D '89
HUMAN RELATIONS
See also
Affection
Attention seeking
Caring
Child-adult relationship
Communication—Social aspects
Conversation
Courtesy
Criticism, Personal
Dependency (Psychology)
Embracing
Friendship
Helping behavior
Interpersonal attraction
Intimacy
Loneliness
Love
Marriage
Married couples
Monogamy
Neighbors
Parent-child relationship
Personal space
Popularity
Praise
Prejudice
Quarrels
Rejection (Psychology)
Revenge
Romance
Strangers
Sympathy
Toleration
Touch
Women and men
Youth-adult relationship
Alice and the chipmunk. J. M. Laskas. *Reader's Digest* 134:107-8 My '89
Study and teaching
See also
Esalen Institute
HUMAN RIGHTS See Civil rights
HUMAN RIGHTS COMMISSION (UNITED NATIONS) See United Nations. Commission on Human Rights
HUMAN SACRIFICE
See also
Headhunters
Mexico
The believers [M. Kilroy murdered by drug dealers in Matamoros, Mexico] G. D. Garcia. il *Rolling Stone* p46-9+ Je 29 '89
Cult of the red-haired devil [drug dealers practice human sacrifice in Mexico] R. Woodbury. il map *Time* 133:30 Ap 24 '89
The grisly secrets of a lonely ranch [slaying of M. Kilroy and others by drug smugglers in Matamoros, Mexico] A. Richman. il por *People Weekly* 31:44-9 My 1 '89
Magic and murder in Matamoros. J. Burnett. *The Christian Century* 106:815-16 S 13-20 '89
Ritual murder [Matamoros, Mexico] B. Wickens. il *Maclean's* 102:61 Ap 24 '89
Ritual murder in Mexico [practiced by drug dealers] F. Gibney, Jr. il *Newsweek* 113:55 Ap 24 '89
Voodoo in Mexico [practiced by drug dealers] il *U.S. News & World Report* 106:16 Ap 24 '89
Bibliography
Magic! Murder! Mayhem! Drugs! Four new books detail the ritual killings in Matamoros, Mexico. G. Feldman. il *Publishers Weekly* 236:23-4 Ag 18 '89
HUMAN T CELL LEUKEMIA VIRUSES See HTLV viruses
HUMANA FESTIVAL OF NEW AMERICAN PLAYS See Drama festivals—Kentucky
HUMANA INC
All in the family [firms with captive insurance companies win case in continuing battle with IRS] L. Saunders. il *Forbes* 144:214 O 2 '89
Humana regains that healthy glow. S. Phillips. il *Business Week* p127-8 My 22 '89
"We're the low-cost producer". J. Cook. il por *Forbes* 144:65-6 D 25 '89
HUMANISM
See also
Christianity and humanism
Renaissance
For a new humanist militancy. M. Maneli. il por *The Humanist* 49:14-16+ S/O '89
For mutual survival we must bring our world together [address, January 1989; cover story] I. Asimov. il por *The Humanist* 49:5-8+ S/O '89
Geroethics: a humanist issue [treatment of elderly] G. A. Larue. il por *The Humanist* 49:5-10+ Jl/Ag '89

HUMANISM—*cont.*

The greening of Ted Turner [cover story] J. Lanham. il pors *The Humanist* 49:5-7+ N/D '89

Homelessness: a humanist response [cover story; special section] il *The Humanist* 49:7-15+ My/Je '89

Isaac Asimov speaks [interview; cover story] B. Moyers. il pors *The Humanist* 49:5-13+ Ja/F '89

North American Essay Contest [special section] il por *The Humanist* 49:21-9+ Mr/Ap '89

North American Essay Contest [special section] il *The Humanist* 49:20-30+ Ja/F '89

Science fiction writers speak to the future [cover story; special section; with introd. by Bette Chambers] il *The Humanist* 49:5-17+ Mr/Ap '89

The second genesis: future technologies and humanism. A. Bacard. il por *The Humanist* 49:9-11+ S/O '89

Sexual morality for young humanists and their parents. D. Carroll. *The Humanist* 49:41-2+ Jl/Ag '89

What's right about humanism? B. Craig. por *The Humanist* 49:31-2 Jl/Ag '89

HUMANISM FOR KIDS (PROGRAM)

Humanism for Kids. D. Carroll. *The Humanist* 49:37 N/D '89

HUMANISTIC EDUCATION *See* Liberal education

HUMANITIES

See also

Medicine and the humanities

National Endowment for the Humanities

Science and the humanities

Study and teaching

See also

American Association for the Advancement of the Humanities

Blossom time for the humanities. *America* 160:283-4 Ap 1 '89

Civilization and its malcontents [cover story] S. Hook. il *National Review* 41:30-3 O 13 '89

The core of the humanities: can the center hold? T. Todorov. *Current (Washington, D.C.)* 318:12-17 D '89

Crimes against humanities [cover story] T. Todorov. *The New Republic* 201:26-30 Jl 3 '89

Fraudulence II. R. E. Tyrrell. *The American Spectator* 22:10-11 Ap '89

The true purpose of education [cultivation of wisdom and virtue] H. B. Gow. il *Phi Delta Kappan* 70:545-6 Mr '89

HUMBOLDT (SASK.)

Languages

A quiet fury in the west. J. Howse. il *Maclean's* 102:26-7 Mr 20 '89

HUME, BEN

about

Maker. *The New Yorker* 65:28-9 Jl 17 '89

HUME, BRIT

A power trip that's not state of the art. il *Personal Computing* 13:35-6 O '89

about

Meet Brit Hume, ABC's newest rising star. A. Stanley. il por *Vogue* 179:106 Jl '89

HUME, JOSEPH R.

(jt. auth) See Harvey, Robert D., and Hume, Joseph R.

HUMIDIFIERS

Humidifier alert. M. O'Koon. *Good Housekeeping* 208:206 Mr '89

Is your humidifier hazardous to your health? J. O. Hamilton. il *Business Week* p158 Mr 13 '89

Moisturizing the air. L. C. Cook. il *Health (New York, N.Y.)* 21:34-5+ D '89

Safety devices and measures

Humidifier safety. J. W. Merline. *Consumers' Research Magazine* 72:2 D '89

HUMIDITY

See also

Condensation (Meteorology)

Hot weather

It's not the heat, it's the humidity. P. Skalka. il *Reader's Digest* 135:61-4 Jl '89

HUMIDITY METERS *See* Moisture meters

HUMILITY

1989 New Year's resolution: go to heaven. D. E. Koshland, Jr. *Science* 243:9 Ja 6 '89

Lessons in humility. K. Kolenda. *The Humanist* 49:47 Ja/F '89

Lowliness. P. J. Ryan. *America* 161:126-7 Ag 26-S 2 '89

Seeking humility in political debate. P. B. Henry. *The Christian Century* 106:303 Mr 22-29 '89

HUMMEL, RICHARD

about

Here's looking at you, kid. B. Amiel. il *Maclean's* 102:9 Ap 10 '89

HUMMINGBIRD LAUNCH SYSTEMS INC.

Hummingbird Launch Systems update. T. Holmes. il *Ad Astra* 1:7 My '89

HUMMINGBIRDS

Anecdotes, facetiae, satire, etc.

The raccoon and the hummingbird. L. Eisenberg. il *Esquire* 112:43 O '89

HUMOR

See also

Laughter

Limericks

Political humor

Puns and punning

Radio broadcasting—Comedy programs

41 howlers, screamers, and groaners to get you through the holidays [cover story] il *Esquire* 112:163-5+ D '89

Are "JAP" jokes anti-Semitic? [views of Mimi Alperin] *USA Today (Periodical)* 117:5 Ap '89

Clowning around: get serious about your funny factor! il *'Teen* 33:64 Ja '89

JAP jokes are nothing to laugh at [Jewish American Princess jokes] L. Lamb. il *Utne Reader* p30+ My/Je '89

Leopold Fechtner has collected 2¼ million jokes, but his wife says his humor is no laughing matter. il por *People Weekly* 31:123 F 13 '89

Authorship

I could have died laughing [humorous crime fiction] R. Barnard. il *The Writer* 102:15-18 F '89

Ten tips for writing humor. G. M. Down. *The Writer* 102:21-3 Jl '89

Writing short humor. R. Williamson. *The Writer* 102:20-2 My '89

Censorship

The view from Palo Alto [Stanford orders purging of computer humor file that includes ethnic jokes] D. Seligman. il *Fortune* 119:339+ Ap 24 '89

HUMOR, AMERICAN

See also

Algonquin Round Table

53 more cranky opinions from Andy Rooney [excerpt from Not that you asked . . .] A. A. Rooney. il *TV Guide* 37:24-6 Mr 11-17 '89

Madcap airs all [interview with D. Barry] J. Birnbaum. il por *Time* 134:68-9 Jl 3 '89

HUMOR, JAPANESE

Anecdotes, facetiae, satire, etc.

Japun, Inc. J. Queenan. *The New Republic* 201:14-15 O 16 '89

HUMOR, PICTORIAL

See also

Comic books, strips, etc.

Humorous photography

HUMOR, RUSSIAN

Jokes as tiny revolutions. G. F. Will. il *Newsweek* 113:80 Je 5 '89

Let me tell you . . . M. Zhvanetsy. il por *Time* 133:115 Ap 10 '89

Red-faced in Moscow? Would Billy Crystal get his laughs? [taping a TV special] B. Crystal. il por *TV Guide* 37:14-15+ O 21-27 '89

HUMOR IN BUSINESS

Funniest accountant in America [G. Press] il por *Changing Times* 43:29 F '89

The humor prescription. S. Kleinman. il *Health (New York, N.Y.)* 21:40-1 Ag '89

Leave them laughing [humorous speeches] M. B. Marklein. il *Nation's Business* 77:49 O '89

HUMOR IN EDUCATION

The best medicine [research by Avner Ziv] G. W. Bracey. il *Phi Delta Kappan* 70:563-4 Mr '89

HUMOR IN MEDICINE

Humor as antidote. R. Coles. il *New Choices for the Best Years* 29:85-6 Je '89

A jocular doc [B. Conger] S. Brewer. il por *New Choices for the Best Years* 29:8-9 Jl '89

HUMOR IN MOTION PICTURES

See also

Motion pictures—Comedy films

HUMOR IN SCIENCE

Dignifying humanity: the humor of Stephen W. Hawking. T. Organ. por *The Humanist* 49:29-30+ Jl/Ag '89

HUMOR IN TELEVISION

See also

Cable television—Comedy programs

Television broadcasting—Comedy programs

HUMOROUS PHOTOGRAPHY

Building a set with two walls. C. Zsarnay and V. Summerhays. il *Petersen's Photographic Magazine* 17:54-5 Ja '89

Is your photography too serious? Take a break from the "job" and have some fun. J. Shaw. il *Popular Photography* 96:60 Ap '89

Exhibitions

Erwitt gets personal. il *Newsweek* 113:67 Ja 23 '89

HUMOROUS POETRY

Poet to poet. D. Dumars. *The Writer* 102:26-30 Je '89

HUMPBACK WHALES *See* Whales

HUMPHREY, DORIS, 1895-1958

about

The Shakers [ballet] Reviews

Dance Magazine il 63:10-11 Mr '89. G. R. Hubbard

HUMPHREY, PHYLLIS A.

The lease frontier. il *Ms.* 18:38+ O '89

HUMPHREY, WILLIAM
about
PW interviews. J. Yglesias. por *Publishers Weekly* 235:64-5 Je 2 '89
HUN, SEN
about
Better times for a ravaged land. W. Stewart. il *Time* 133:42 My 15 '89
The reluctant prime minister. S. Downe. *World Press Review* 36:36 D '89
Sihanouk on the high wire. A. Platt. il pors *Newsweek* 113:45 My 15 '89
HUNAN PROVINCE (CHINA)
Rich China, poor China: the gap keeps growing [contrasting Guangdong with Hunan] D. J. Yang. il *Business Week* p40-1 Je 5 '89
HUNDRED YEARS' WAR, 1339-1453
Bertrand Du Guesclin—careerist in arms? K. Fowler. bibl il pors *History Today* 39:37-43 Je '89
HUNE, SHIRLEY
Opening the American mind and body: the role of Asian American studies. il *Change* 21:56-63 N/D '89
HUNEYCUTT, LOIS
Medieval queenship. bibl il *History Today* 39:16-22 Je '89
A HUNGARIAN FAIRY TALE [film] See Motion picture reviews—Single works
HUNGARIAN GRAND PRIX *See* Automobile racing—Hungary
HUNGARIAN LUDWIG MUSEUM FOR INTERNATIONAL CONTEMPORARY ART
Ludwig museums go east. J. Gambrell. *Art in America* 77:35+ Je '89
HUNGARIAN PAINTING *See* Painting, Hungarian
HUNGARIAN STATE OPERA AND BALLET
Reviews:
Performances at the Royal Opera House, London. M. E. Willis. *Dance Magazine* 63:54-5 Ag '89
HUNGARIANS
Romania
Romania's reign of terror. il *Reader's Digest* 134:91-5 F '89
United States
Danube fever [Hungarian opposition party leaders study Virginia governor's race] A. Heard. *The New Republic* 201:16-18 D 4 '89
HUNGARY
See also
Automobile racing—Hungary
Budapest (Hungary)
Cemeteries—Hungary
Economic assistance—Hungary
Economic assistance, American—Hungary
Environmental movement—Hungary
Germans—Hungary
Government and the press—Hungary
Hungarians
Investments, American—Hungary
Investments, Canadian—Hungary
Investments, Foreign—Hungary
Jews—Hungary
Motion pictures—Hungary
Pollution—Hungary
Commerce
Looking for markets [magazine Interpress Expo 4/1988] il *The Bulletin of the Atomic Scientists* 45:29 Je '89
United States
See United States—Commerce—Hungary
Commercial policy
Where Adam Smith meets Karl Marx [foreign investment] A. Gabor. il *U.S. News & World Report* 107:36 S 18 '89
Economic conditions
The dark side of democracy. M. Szegedy-Maszak. il *U.S. News & World Report* 107:50-1 N 13 '89
Economic history
Hungary breaks loose. I. T. Berend. il *The Bulletin of the Atomic Scientists* 45:27-31 Je '89
Economic policy
An economy in crisis. M. Nemeth. il *Maclean's* 102:53-4 N 13 '89
From Big Brother to Big Mac [interview with J. Berecz] N. Gardels. il *New Perspectives Quarterly* 5:12-17 Wint '88/'89
Glasnost's twin crucibles. G. E. Schares. il *Business Week* p72-3+ Je 5 '89
The Hungarian miracle. E. von Kuehnelt-Leddihn. *National Review* 41:21-2 My 5 '89
Hungary: dancing in the shackles of the past. I. Völgyes. bibl f *Current History* 88:381-4+ N '89
A Wall Street in Budapest. M. Dini. il *World Press Review* 36:49 Ap '89
Foreign relations
Germany (East)
See Germany (East)—Foreign relations—Hungary
History
Revolution, 1956
Catharsis in Hungary [I. Nagy reburied] il *Time* 133:38 Je 26 '89

Totems and taboos: thoughts in a Budapest graveyard. L. Wieseltier. *The New Republic* 201:21+ Ag 7-14 '89
The tumult of the tomb [proper burial for I. Nagy] M. R. Meyer. il *Newsweek* 113:45 Je 26 '89
Industries
See also
Helicopter industry—Hungary
Malev Hungarian Airlines
Politics and government
See also
Communist Party (Hungary)
Political campaigns—Hungary
Socialist Party (Hungary)
Astonishing reforms [interview with I. Pozsgay] M. Nemeth. por *Maclean's* 102:29+ N 13 '89
Bloc busters [cover story] J. Rupnik. *The New Republic* 200:18+ My 22 '89
The dark side of democracy. M. Szegedy-Maszak. il *U.S. News & World Report* 107:50-1 N 13 '89
A freer, but messier, order. W. Isaacson. il *Time* 134:38-40 Jl 10 '89
The Hungarian miracle. E. von Kuehnelt-Leddihn. *National Review* 41:21-2 My 5 '89
Hungary at a new frontier. R. Knight. il *U.S. News & World Report* 106:43+ Mr 27 '89
Hungary: dancing in the shackles of the past. I. Völgyes. bibl f *Current History* 88:381-4+ N '89
Hungary hearts. T. Aczel. *The New Republic* 201:13-15 D 25 '89
Hungary on the way to democracy. R. L. Tökés. il *The New Leader* 72:9-11 S 18 '89
Hungary's hazy future. R. L. Tökés. il *The New Leader* 72:5-7 O 30 '89
Hungary's heir apparent gambles on radical change [I. Pozsgay] R. Knight. il por map *U.S. News & World Report* 107:32-3 Jl 17 '89
Hungary's quiet revolution. J. Rupnik. *The New Republic* 201:18-20+ N 20 '89
The new Hungarian revolution. P. Keresztes. il *The American Spectator* 22:28-9 Jl '89
Refolution in Hungary and Poland. T. Garton Ash. bibl f il *The New York Review of Books* 36:9-15 Ag 17 '89
Refolution: the springtime of two nations [cover story] T. Garton Ash. bibl f il *The New York Review of Books* 36:3-4+ Je 15 '89
A talk with Hungary's Imre Pozsgay [interview] R. L. Tökés. por *The New Leader* 72:9-12 Je 12-26 '89
Tolerating dissent. A. Phillips. il *Maclean's* 102:20-1+ Mr 27 '89
Totems and taboos: thoughts in a Budapest graveyard. L. Wieseltier. *The New Republic* 201:21+ Ag 7-14 '89
Religious institutions and affairs
See also
Catholic Church—Hungary
Evangelistic work—Hungary
Social conditions
Hungary in April. G. E. Lenski. *Society* 26:11-14 Ja/F '89
Social science and social problems in Hungary. P. Hollander. *Society* 26:14-21 Ja/F '89
HUNGER
See also
Appetite
Famines
Food supply
World Food Day
Frances Moore Lappé's diet for a better world. P. Carroll. il pors *Utne Reader* p42-8 My/Je '89
Hunger in Africa: why it persists, why we must care [cover story; special section] il map *Scholastic Update (Teachers' edition)* 121:2-15 Ja 27 '89
Hunger threat looming over poor countries. il *UN Chronicle* 26:66-7 S '89
World hunger amidst plenty. J. W. Helmuth. il *USA Today (Periodical)* 117:48-50 Mr '89
HUNGER RELIEF *See* Relief work
HUNGER STRIKES
Notes and comment [Korean Americans' hunger strike in front of the United Nations protesting political situation in South Korea] *The New Yorker* 65:33-4 O 30 '89
The triumph of Natan Sharansky [condensed from Fear no evil] N. Sharansky. il por *Reader's Digest* 134:75-80 Ja '89
HUNNICUTT, ELLEN
Developing a specialty in fiction. *The Writer* 102:9-11+ Jl '89
HUNSAKER, JOHANNA, AND HUNSAKER, PHILLIP L.
How to hire the right person for the job [excerpt from Strategies and skills for managerial women] il *Working Woman* 14:28+ Ja '89
HUNSAKER, PHILLIP L.
(jt. auth) See Hunsaker, Johanna, and Hunsaker, Phillip L.
HUNSUCKER, ROBERT D.
about
The list nobody wants to be on. T. Vogel and W. Zellner. il pors *Business Week* p50 My 1 '89

HUNT, BRYAN, 1947-
about
Touched in bronze. S. Westfall. il *Art in America* 77:250-5+
Ap '89
HUNT, CARLOS
about
Choosing sides. H. Hersch. il pors *Sports Illustrated* 71:42-4+
N 27 '89
HUNT, CHERYL YVETTE
When she danced [poem] *Essence* 19:149 F '89
HUNT, GEORGE W., 1937-
American Catholic intellectual life [address, February 1989]
America 160:412-19 My 6 '89
Of many things. See issues of America beginning July 7-14,
1984
HUNT, LAMAR, 1933-
about
The eye of the storm. S. Flink. il por *World Tennis* 36:28+
Mr '89
HUNT, MARILYN
The eleventh Havana International Ballet Festival: la
habanera. il *Dance Magazine* 63:50-2 Je '89
New York City Ballet in Glasgow: dancing on Hope Street.
il *Dance Magazine* 63:40-4 D '89
Seattle strikes gold: Pacific Northwest Ballet's grand pas
de deux. il *Dance Magazine* 63:36-41 Mr '89
Tamas Detrich: an American prince in Europe. il pors *Dance
Magazine* 63:50-3 F '89
Universal Ballet Company: ballet today in Seoul, Korea.
il *Dance Magazine* 63:58-9 Ap '89
HUNT, MORTON M., 1920-
Did the penalty fit the crime? il por *The New York Times
Magazine* p36-7+ My 14 '89
Fighting the good fight. il *New Choices for the Best Years*
29:71-3 Ag '89
Patients' rights. il *The New York Times Magazine* p55-6
Mr 5 '89
HUNT, NELSON BUNKER, 1926-
about
Brothers, are you spared a dime? K. Kelly. il pors *Business
Week* p38 N 20 '89
HUNT, ROBERT J.
about
Posing as an astronaut was just one small step for flimflam
man Robert Hunt. M. Neill. il pors *People Weekly* 31:271-2+
Mr 6 '89
HUNT, WILLIAM HERBERT
about
Brothers, are you spared a dime? K. Kelly. il pors *Business
Week* p38 N 20 '89
HUNT FAMILY
about
Brother, can you spare a dime? K. Hannon. il *Forbes* 144
Special Issue:8 O 23 '89
Brothers, are you spared a dime? K. Kelly. il pors *Business
Week* p38 N 20 '89
HUNTER, BEATRICE TRUM
Food for thought. See issues of Consumers' Research Magazine
HUNTER, D. A., AND GALLAGHER, JOHN SILL, 1947-
Star formation in irregular galaxies. bibl f il *Science*
243:1557-63 Mr 24 '89
HUNTER, DIANNA
Using nature as a model. il *National Parks* 63:40-1 S/O
'89
HUNTER, EVAN, 1926-
Grilling Ed McBain. *The Writer* 102:11-14+ N '89
HUNTER, HOLLY
about
Beth's beauties [cover story] K. Jaehne. il pors *Film Comment*
25:9-12+ My/Je '89
No southern comfort [cover story] J. Mathews. il pors
American Film 15:28-33 D '89
HUNTER, JEFFREY
Camel Fair. il *Petersen's Photographic Magazine* 18:20-3
O '89
A photographer's guide to Iceland. il *Petersen's Photographic
Magazine* 17:66-8 Mr '89
HUNTER, JEFFREY, AND MAKAEA, PAMELA
Southwest! il *Petersen's Photographic Magazine* 18:30-3+ Je
'89
HUNTER, MADELINE C.
about
PET and the pendulum: faddism in education and how
to stop it [cover story] R. E. Slavin. bibl f il *Phi Delta
Kappan* 70:752-8 Je '89
HUNTER, PAUL
about
Paul Hunter at Tibor de Nagy. G. Henry. il *Art in America*
77:179-80 D '89
HUNTER, ROBERT EDWARDS, 1940-
Berlin: forty years on. *Foreign Affairs* 68:41-52 Summ '89
The Reagan administration and the Middle East [reprint
from February 1987 issue] *Current History* 88:41+ Ja '89
HUNTER, ROBERT O.
about
High-energy management stirs up energy research. M. Craw-
ford. il por *Science* 245:1182-3 S 15 '89

HUNTER, SHIREEN T.
Post-Khomeini Iran. *Foreign Affairs* 68:133-49 Wint '89/'90
HUNTER, TIM B.
Finding the best observing site. il *Astronomy* 17:92-3 D
'89
HUNTER [television program] See Television program
reviews—Single works
HUNTER COLLEGE
On changing academic culture from the inside [interview
with D. Shalala] A. Bernstein and S. Mow. il pors *Change*
21:20-9 Ja/F '89
HUNTER MOUNTAIN (N.Y.)
Stalking the real Hunter. K. Brizzolara. il *Skiing* 41:80-4+
F '89
HUNTERS
See also
Farmer-hunter relations
Women hunters
In defense of outdoorsmen. W. G. Tapply. por *Newsweek*
113:10-11 Ap 10 '89
The real environmentalist. R. E. Tyrrell. il *The American
Spectator* 22:10 S '89
Health and hygiene
Shape-up system for hunters. S. Netherby. il *Field & Stream*
94:64-5 Jl '89
Anecdotes, facetiae, satire, etc.
Shaping up. T. Leeson. il *Field & Stream* 94:22 S '89
Psychology
New eyes. G. Hill. il *Field & Stream* 94:12 Jl '89
Patience. T. Leeson. il *Field & Stream* 93:26+ Mr '89
September New Year. B. Woods. il *The Mother Earth News*
115:8 Ja/F '89
HUNTERS AND GATHERERS
A world that never existed [cover story] B. Bower. il *Science
News* 135:264-6 Ap 29 '89
HUNTING
See also
Bear hunting
Buffalo hunting
Computers—Hunting use
Coyote hunting
Decoys (Hunting)
Deer hunting
Duck shooting
Elephant hunting
Elk hunting
Eskimos—Hunting
Farmer-hunter relations
Fox hunting
Game, Dressing of
Game laws
Goose shooting
Grouse shooting
Hunting dogs
Hunting with bow and arrow
Indians of North America—Hunting
Leopard hunting
Market hunting (Game hunting)
Mourning dove shooting
Partridge shooting
Pheasant shooting
Poaching
Pronghorn hunting
Pygmies—Hunting
Quail shooting
Rabbit hunting
Raccoon hunting
Squirrel hunting
Tape recordings—Hunting use
Trapping
Turkey hunting
Walrus hunting
Water bird shooting
Whaling
Wild boar hunting
Woodcock shooting
Doubling back [maneuver to flush tight sitting game] J.
Bashline. il *Field & Stream* 94:69 D '89
Fallen snow. S. Curtis. il *Field & Stream* 94:28 D '89
Grandpa and the kid. D. Sisson. See alternate issues of
Field & Stream beginning September 1983
Hunting & fishing on skis. S. Netherby. il *Field & Stream*
93:30+ F '89
Hunting on the D.O.D. [hunting on military land] G. J.
Sajo. il *Field & Stream* 94:30+ D '89
In stalking feet. W. L. Prothero. il *Outdoor Life* 184:61-3+
D '89
Luck! [reprint from February 1965 issue] T. Trueblood. il
Field & Stream 93:34+ Mr '89
Simple pleasures. R. C. Murray. *Outdoor Life* 183:4 Ja '89
Solunar tables. See issues of Field & Stream
Accidents and injuries
A killing in Maine [K. A. Wood killed by hunter D. Rogerson]
J. H. Kunstler. il por *The New York Times Magazine*
p58-60+ S 10 '89
"My wife shouldn't have died" [K. A. Wood killed by hunter
D. Rogerson in Hermon, Me.] J. Hope. il pors *Good
Housekeeping* 209:92+ O '89

HUNTING—*cont.*

Anecdotes, facetiae, satire, etc.

The marvelous hunt. D. Elliott. il *Field & Stream* 94:29+ N '89

The road hunter. P. F. McManus. il *Outdoor Life* 184:126+ O '89

Bibliography

Books & comments. See occasional issues of Field & Stream beginning April 1985

Equipment

Build a tree stand. D. Carty. il *Field & Stream* 94:32 Je '89

Cold-weather whitetails . . . minus the misery [tree stand hunting] P. Nelson. il *Field & Stream* 94:72-3+ N '89

Field stool. C. Winans. il *Field & Stream* 94:36 D '89

Going light [backpack hunting] S. Netherby. il *Field & Stream* 93:132+ Ap '89

Tom's tree stand. T. Clauss. il *Outdoor Life* 183:58+ My '89

What's new. See issues of Outdoor Life

Ethical aspects

Call me the hunter. T. L. Gibbs; T. Nugent. *Harper's* 278:20 Mr '89

Cutting our losses (I). B. Brister. il *Field & Stream* 94:74+ D '89

Don't shoot a wet doe [myths of shooting lactating mule deer] S. Curtis. il *Field & Stream* 94:88 O '89

Grandpa and the kid. D. Sisson. il *Field & Stream* 93:55+ F '89

Heroes, bears and true baloney. J. Skow. il *Time* 134:122 N 13 '89

Hunting's most wanted. L. Williamson. il *Outdoor Life* 184:40+ Jl '89

Know your limits. G. Hill. il *Field & Stream* 94:12 O '89

A limiting mentality. G. Reiger. il *Field & Stream* 94:14+ D '89

The N.R.A. in a hunter's sights. R. Hughes. il *Time* 133:86 Ap 3 '89

Anecdotes, facetiae, satire, etc.

Lord of the flies. P. F. McManus. il *Outdoor Life* 183:124+ Ja '89

Fees

Fee hunting funds a tree farm [Alabama] O. Miller. il *Successful Farming* 87:51 Ja '89

History

The Jack O'Connor letters (I). il pors *Outdoor Life* 183:66-7+ F '89

The Jack O'Connor letters (II). il pors *Outdoor Life* 183:80-1+ Mr '89

Statistics

Is hunting on its way out? [results of survey] L. Williamson. il *Outdoor Life* 184:46+ S '89

Storm conditions

The mourning after [pursuing a deer by canoe leads to near tragedy during Lake Erie storm] G. Laycock. il *Outdoor Life* 183:68-9+ Je '89

Rainy-day deer. H. Buck. il *Field & Stream* 94:46-7 S '89

Stone cold muleys. B. Journey. il *Outdoor Life* 184:70-1+ O '89

Study and teaching

Drift like smoke [learning to hunt] W. L. Prothero. il *Field & Stream* 93:66-7 Ap '89

Educating New York's hunters. J. E. Ford. il *The Conservationist* 44:34-7 N/D '89

First rifle. W. D. Jorgensen. il *Field & Stream* 94:12 Ag '89

Lessons for a lifetime [raising a daughter to hunt and fish] K. Etling. il *Outdoor Life* 183:76-8+ Je '89

Alabama

Fee hunting funds a tree farm. O. Miller. il *Successful Farming* 87:51 Ja '89

Colorado

Quest for a dream bull [elk] K. Etling. il *Outdoor Life* 183:70-1+ Ja '89

Florida

N.P.S. double cross [no more hunting in Big Cypress] L. Williamson. il *Outdoor Life* 183:34+ F '89

Great Britain

Hunt country [master of the hunt R. Smith-Ryland's 16th century farmhouse in Warwickshire] G. Nevill. il pors *House & Garden* 161:132-9 Mr '89

Great Lakes region

The mourning after [pursuing a deer by canoe leads to near tragedy during Lake Erie storm] G. Laycock. il *Outdoor Life* 183:68-9+ Je '89

Great Plains

George Custer: nomad hunter of the Plains. J. McCafferty. il *Outdoor Life* 184:60-1+ Jl '89

Maine

A killing in Maine [K. A. Wood killed by hunter D. Rogerson] J. H. Kunstler. il por *The New York Times Magazine* p58-60+ S 10 '89

"My wife shouldn't have died" [K. A. Wood killed by hunter D. Rogerson] J. Hope. il pors *Good Housekeeping* 209:92+ O '89

Minnesota

The bear guardian. P. M. Leschak. il *Outdoor Life* 184:54-5+ Jl '89

Mississippi

Hunting the hunters [predators at night with varmint calls] B. Tarrant. il *Field & Stream* 94:95-6 Jl '89

Montana

A firing squad for buffalo [bison hunt] S. Begley. il *Newsweek* 113:51 Mr 6 '89

Following in my footsteps [father and son hunt antelope] D. Small. il *Outdoor Life* 183:62-3+ F '89

Montana hunters, confronting targets big, slow and unwary, take aim at Yellowstone's bison [hunters allowed to shoot bison who wander out of park] D. Grogan. il *People Weekly* 31:110-11 F 27 '89

Solitude. K. McCafferty. il *Field & Stream* 94:48-9+ D '89

Whitetail fingers. S. Curtis. il *Field & Stream* 94:59+ N '89

New Hampshire

Heroes, bears and true baloney. J. Skow. il *Time* 134:122 N 13 '89

New Mexico

Beyond the bugle. J. Byers. il *Outdoor Life* 184:64-5+ Ag '89

New York (State)

1988 Big Buck Club winners. il *The Conservationist* 44:47 S/O '89

Educating New York's hunters. J. E. Ford. il *The Conservationist* 44:34-7 N/D '89

The hated season [deer hunting] S. Lewis. il *The New York Times Magazine* p24+ N 26 '89

Winter rabbit hunting. E. S. Feldmann. il *The Conservationist* 43:14-17 Ja/F '89

Oregon

Grandpa and the kid [grandfather gets lost while deer hunting] D. Sisson. il *Field & Stream* 94:37+ O '89

Southern States

Hard winters and crazy birds [woodcock hunting] H. Middleton. il *Southern Living* 24:36-7 D '89

Soviet Union

Hunting with the Cossacks [wildfowling in the southern Soviet Union] G. Reiger. il *Field & Stream* 93:72-3+ Ap '89

Tanzania

Leopard: a most dangerous game [M. Rowbotham leads safari] J. Carmichel. il *Outdoor Life* 183:58-9+ F '89

Texas

Quail hunting as good as it gets [south Texas] B. Brister. il map *Field & Stream* 93:28-9+ Ja '89

United States

See Hunting

Wales

The shooting party [pheasant shooting at Golden Pheasant Inn, Clwyd County] P. Davies. il *Gentlemen's Quarterly* 59:330-4+ O '89

Western States

Floating for river-bottom bucks [mule deer] W. L. Prothero. il *Field & Stream* 93:52-3+ Mr '89

Whitetails west. J. Barsness. il map *Field & Stream* 93:38-9+ Ja '89

Wild West turkeys. J. Barsness. il *Field & Stream* 93:46-7+ Mr '89

Wyoming

Semi-guided success [Table Mountain Outfitters] S. Netherby. il *Field & Stream* 93:77-8 Mr '89

HUNTING BY ANIMALS *See* Predation (Biology)

HUNTING CLOTHES *See* Clothing and dress—Sports clothes

HUNTING DOGS

See also

Beagles (Dogs)

Hounds

Pointers (Dogs)

Setters (Dogs)

Spaniels

Gun dogs. B. Tarrant. See issues of Field & Stream

Hunting dogs. L. Mueller. See issues of Outdoor Life

Air transport

Teaching bird dogs to fly. L. W. Eckhardt. il *Field & Stream* 93:126 Mr '89

Anecdotes, facetiae, satire, etc.

The longest day [bobwhite shooting] J. M. Vance. il *Field & Stream* 94:21+ D '89

Care

Dysplasia's end [work of Dr. W. Belfield] L. Mueller. il pors *Outdoor Life* 183:46+ Ap '89

Equipment

Chickamauga quail [G. Clements' bird dog training] B. Tarrant. il *Field & Stream* 93:181-2 Ap '89

Great ideas for dogs. L. Mueller. il *Outdoor Life* 184:16+ D '89

More ideas for dogmen. L. Mueller. il *Outdoor Life* 183:66-7 Ja '89

Training

Another bend in the river. B. Tarrant. il *Field & Stream* 93:84+ Mr '89

A bird in hand. B. Tarrant. il *Field & Stream* 94:95-6 Ag '89

The bird launcher. B. Tarrant. il *Field & Stream* 94:132-3 My '89

HUNTING DOGS—Training—*cont.*
Deer chase prevention [breaking hunting dogs from running deer] L. Mueller. il *Outdoor Life* 184:29+ Ag '89
A dog in the hand [bird dog trainer J. Thompson of Rosanky, Tex.] R. Bass. il pors *Esquire* 112:150-4+ O '89
A good retriever conserves wildlife. S. Z. Miller. il *The Conservationist* 43:26-33 Mr/Ap '89
A gun-shy cure that works [using tape recordings on beagles] L. Mueller. il *Outdoor Life* 184:30+ O '89
A hound's start in life [J. Wick's training suggestions] L. Mueller. il por *Outdoor Life* 183:43-4 F '89
Jack Harper. B. Tarrant. il por *Field & Stream* 94:156-7 S '89
Let's not forget [trainer M. Rand] B. Tarrant. il por *Field & Stream* 94:136-8 O '89
Littlebit's first hunt [cottontails] B. Tarrant. il *Field & Stream* 94:110+ N '89
Seize the moment [training techniques of J. Wick and N. Sorby] L. Mueller. il *Outdoor Life* 183:50+ My '89
The sporting springers. L. Mueller. il *Outdoor Life* 184:52+ N '89
HUNTING DOGS, AFRICAN *See* African hunting dogs
HUNTING KNIVES *See* Knives
HUNTING LAWS *See* Game laws
HUNTING LICENSES
Gamble for big game [lottery hunting permits] J. Zumbo. il *Outdoor Life* 183:74-5+ Ja '89
A second chance. J. Spencer. il *Outdoor Life* 183:76-7+ Mr '89
HUNTING RECORDS
A limiting mentality. G. Reiger. il *Field & Stream* 94:14+ D '89
HUNTING RIFLES *See* Rifles
HUNTING SEASON LAWS *See* Game laws
HUNTING STANDS *See* Hunting—Equipment
HUNTING TROPHIES
1988 Big Buck Club winners. il *The Conservationist* 44:47 S/O '89
Blueprinting big bucks [study on hunting trophy whitetails; cover story]; ed. by Kathy Etling. S. Demarais and B. Zaiglin. il *Outdoor Life* 184:61-3+ O '89
A matter of faith [mule deer hunting] J. Barsness. il *Field & Stream* 94:38-9+ O '89
Murphy's pride. P. Johnson. il *Outdoor Life* 183:84-5+ My '89
Quest for a dream bull [elk] K. Etling. il *Outdoor Life* 183:70-1+ Ja '89
Return for a trophy [mule deer] W. L. Prothero. il *Field & Stream* 94:66-7+ N '89
HUNTING WITH BOW AND ARROW
Bowhunting's moment of truth [whitetail deer] T. L. Torget. il *Field & Stream* 94:52-3+ Ag '89
Buck 'n bull bow. R. Hinton. il *Outdoor Life* 184:86-7+ N '89
First rifle. W. D. Jorgensen. il *Field & Stream* 94:12 Ag '89
Practical bow practice. J. Barsness. il *Field & Stream* 94:54-5+ My '89
The voices of wilderness [elk] K. McCafferty. il *Field & Stream* 93:66-7+ F '89
HUNTINGTON (ARCHER M.) ART GALLERY (AUSTIN, TEX.) *See* Archer M. Huntington Art Gallery (Austin, Tex.)
HUNTINGTON (N.Y.)
Galleries and museums
See also
Heckscher Museum
HUNTINGTON (W. VA.)
Crime
See also
Manns, Lindsey Regan—Kidnapping
HUNTINGTON BEACH (CALIF.)
Description
Local motion: life at the Huntington Beach Pier [cover story] R. A. Camp. il map *Focus (New York, N.Y.: 1950)* 39:1-4 Fall '89
HUNTON, DONALD E.
Shuttle glow [cover story] bibl il *Scientific American* 261:92-8 N '89
HUNTOON, BARRY
"I'll always believe she's my daughter"; ed. by Laura Huntoon. il pors *Redbook* 174:79-80+ D '89
HUNTOON, LAURA
(ed) *See* Huntoon, Barry. "I'll always believe she's my daughter"
HUNTSMAN, JON M.
about
"This guy is going to lose everything". P. Berman. il pors *Forbes* 144:169-72+ N 27 '89
HUNTSMAN CHEMICAL CORPORATION
"This guy is going to lose everything" [J. Huntsman] P. Berman. il pors *Forbes* 144:169-72+ N 27 '89
HUNTSVILLE (ALA.)
Airports
First improved terminal radar installed at Huntsville Airport [ASR-9] J. Ott. *Aviation Week & Space Technology* 130:61 Jl 10 '89

HUNTSVILLE INTERNATIONAL AIRPORT *See* Huntsville (Ala.)—Airports
HUPERZINE A
Giving neurotransmitters a second wind [work of Alan P. Kozikowski] *Science News* 135:366 Je 10 '89
HUPPERT, ISABELLE
about
Occupational hazards. W. Fisher. il por *Harper's Bazaar* 122:98 N '89
HURD, GALE ANNE
about
The Hurd instinct [cover story] M. Rosen. il pors *Ms.* 18:66-71 S '89
Teetering over 'The abyss'. B. Walker. il pors *American Film* 14:34-9 Je '89
HURD, MICHAEL D.
The economic status of the elderly. bibl f il *Science* 244:659-64 My 12 '89
HURDLE RACING
Greg Foster marries, returns to competition. il por *Jet* 77:36 D 18 '89
A pair of aces [D. Patrick and S. Farmer-Patrick] M. Noden. il pors *Sports Illustrated* 71:64-6+ O 16 '89
Quest for new conquests [J. Joyner-Kersee wins 400 hurdles at Bruce Jenner's Bud Light Classic] K. Moore. il por *Sports Illustrated* 70:80-1 Je 5 '89
World-class speed, family style [D. Patrick and S. Farmer-Patrick] il pors *Ebony* 45:116+ D '89
HURDLE RACING RECORDS
Roger Kingdom sets world hurdles record. il pors *Jet* 76:46 S 4 '89
Smashing! [world records broken by R. Kingdom in 110-meter hurdles and S. Aouita in 3,000 meters] M. Noden. il pors *Sports Illustrated* 71:16-19 Ag 28 '89
HURLBURT, STEVEN R.
Fleet feet. il *American Health* 8:70+ Je '89
HURLBUT, DAN
about
A smut buster battles sin in the city. R. Woodbury. il pors *Time* 133:22-3+ My 29 '89
HURLEY, BOB
about
Unlikely champs. il pors *Life* 12:68-70+ My '89
HURLEY, DAN
Cycles of craving. il *Psychology Today* 23:54-8 Jl/Ag '89
The end of celebrity. il *Psychology Today* 22:50-3+ D '88
Teaching teens to marry smart. *McCall's* 116:77 My '89
Why are our babies dying? *McCall's* 116:104+ Je '89
HURLEY, DOROTHEA
about
No Don Juan Bon Jovi, Jon marries his high school sweetheart in a Vegas chapel. il pors *People Weekly* 31:46 My 22 '89
HURLEY, ELIZABETH
about
Elizabeth Hurley, British ex-punkster, turns TV heroine with a Christabel that rings true. M. Dougherty. il pors *People Weekly* 31:199-200 Mr 6 '89
HURLEY, JUDITH BENN
Healthy microwaving. *See* issues of Prevention (Emmaus, Pa.) beginning January 1987
New ware for microwaves. *Consumers' Research Magazine* 72:29 D '89
HURLEY, TAMARA R., AND OTHERS
Activators of protein kinase C induce dissociation of CD4, but not CD8, from p56^{lck}. bibl f il *Science* 245:407-9 Jl 28 '89
HURLYBURLY [drama] *See* Rabe, David
HURNE, RALPH
about
The greatest cycling novel ever written. M. E. Mantell. il *Bicycling* 30:82+ Ap '89
HURON-MANISTEE NATIONAL FOREST (MICH.)
Mack Lake, Michigan [Kirtland's warblers] R. H. Mohlenbrock. il map *Natural History* p90-5 O '89
Tuttle Marsh, Michigan. R. H. Mohlenbrock. il maps *Natural History* p72+ Je '89
HURRICANE CAROL, 1954
The siege of New England. H. Cobb. il map *Weatherwise* 42:262-6 O '89
HURRICANE EDNA, 1954
The siege of New England. H. Cobb. il map *Weatherwise* 42:262-6 O '89
HURRICANE FRANCES, 1986
Into the eye of a hurricane [condensed from Jaguars ripped my flesh] T. Cahill. il *Reader's Digest* 135:81-4 S '89
HURRICANE GILBERT, 1988
The aesthetics of storm chasing [cover story] R. Conn. il *Weatherwise* 42:143-7 Je '89
Gilbert's rampage. J. Kluger. il *Discover* 10:39 Ja '89
High school students study Hurricane Gilbert [use of GOES satellite] R. J. Summers. il *Weatherwise* 42:95-6 Ap '89
Economic aspects
A blow to Jamaica's treasure houses. A. R. Williams. il *Américas* 41 no1:8-13 '89
Weathering the storm [effect on Jamaica and Cancun] G. Young. il *Travel Holiday* 171:85-6 My '89

HURRICANE HUGO, 1989
Anarchy in paradise [violence and looting in St. Croix] il *Time* 134:18 O 2 '89
The brutal lesson of Hurricane Hugo [problems of coastal development in South Carolina] il *U.S. News & World Report* 107:13 O 2 '89
'Hugo is a killer. T. Morganthau. il *Newsweek* 114:18-19 O 2 '89
Hurricane Hugo and the Bay Area earthquake: America responds to disaster [cover story; special issue] il maps *Scholastic Update (Teachers' edition)* 122:1-15 D 15 '89
The storm after Hugo [relief efforts] J. N. Baker. il *Newsweek* 114:40 O 9 '89
Surviving Hurricane Hugo [boating] B. Prentiss. il *Motor Boating & Sailing* 164:34+ D '89
The way it should be remembered [impact upon Charleston, S.C.] B. M. Boyd. il *The New York Times Magazine* p44+ N 19 '89
Winds of chaos [Caribbean and the Carolinas] E. Magnuson. il map *Time* 134:16-18 O 2 '89
The winds of fury [Caribbean and Carolinas] M. Nemeth. il *Maclean's* 102:34 O 2 '89
Economic aspects
The Caribbean after Hugo. J. Popkin. il *U.S. News & World Report* 107:110-11 O 16 '89
Charleston, S.C. rebounds from $2-billion destruction by Hugo; Jackson tours state. D. M. Cheers. il *Jet* 77:5-6+ O 9 '89
Hugo may leave a surprising economic wake. K. Pennar. *Business Week* p24 O 16 '89
Hurricane Hugo aftermath: train Caribbean victims in skills needed to rebuild their homes, Jackson says. D. M. Cheers. il pors *Jet* 77:22-3+ O 23 '89
Rebuilding paradise after Hugo. N. R. Gibbs. il map *Time* 134:90-2 D 4 '89
Remembering Hugo. J. J. Kane. il *Time* 134:23 N 6 '89
St. Croix's ravaged tourism. G. DeGeorge. il *Business Week* p47 O 9 '89
Psychological aspects
After the hurricane they can't go home again [South Carolina] R. Rosenblatt. il *U.S. News & World Report* 107:6-7 O 9 '89
A hurricane's haunting legacy. D. Gelman. il *Newsweek* 114:68-9 O 23 '89
Reporters and reporting
Made for television tragedies. P. Sudo. *Scholastic Update (Teachers' edition)* 122:13 D 15 '89
HURRICANE INSURANCE *See* Insurance, Hurricane
HURRICANES
> *See also*
> Aviation—Storm hazards
> Boats and boating—Storm hazards
> Hurricane Carol, 1954
> Hurricane Edna, 1954
> Hurricane Frances, 1986
> Hurricane Gilbert, 1988
> Hurricane Hugo, 1989

Arctic storms resemble tropical hurricanes. il *Earth Science* 42:8-9 Fall '89
House bill supports continued WC-130 use [hurricane hunter aircraft] *Aviation Week & Space Technology* 131:30 S 18 '89
Hurricane hunters. H. Brandli. il *Popular Mechanics* 166:68-70+ S '89
Hurricane prediction: catching the waves [research by Richard L. Pfeffer] D. E. Loupe. *Science News* 136:262 O 21 '89
Nature's one-upmanship [effects of tropical storm on Sanibel Island ecosystem] C. R. Robins. il *Sea Frontiers* 35:192 My/Je '89
Return of the hurricanes [1988] M. B. Lawrence. il map *Weatherwise* 42:22-7 F '89
History
The Antilles cyclonoscope [hurricane observation in the late 1800s]; tr. by Isabella Owen. B. Viñes. il por *Weatherwise* 42:258-61 O '89
The hurricane priest [B. Viñes] D. DeAngelis. il por *Weatherwise* 42:256-7 O '89
HURST, BLAKE
Uncle Sam's farm follies. il *Reader's Digest* 134:124-6 Ja '89
HURST, LYNDA
Waiting for the millennium. il *World Press Review* 36:30+ D '89
HURSTON, ZORA NEALE, 1907-1960
The Ocoee riot. il *Essence* 19:61-2+ F '89
HURT, BOB
about
They never gave up. R. Hoffer. il pors *Sports Illustrated* 71:117-27+ D 25 '89-Ja 1 '90
HURT, EDWARD P., D. 1989
about
Obituary
> *Jet* por 76:50 Ap 17 '89
HURT, HARRY
Architectural digest visits: Steven Spielberg and Amy Irving [cover story] il *Architectural Digest* 46:196-205+ My '89
"I'm at the foot of the ladder . . .". il *Astronomy* 17:22-35 Jl '89

Play of patterns: a designer's vivid realm in Los Angeles. il por *Architectural Digest* 46:192-7 D '89
HURT, HENRY
Portrait of a patriot. il por *Reader's Digest* 135:65-9 Jl '89
HURT, JOHN
about
The outsider [interview] G. Smith. il pors *Film Comment* 25:64-7 Mr/Ap '89
HURT, WILLIAM, 1950-
about
Love, hurt and money [cover story] S. Schindehette. il pors *People Weekly* 32:72-4+ Jl 10 '89
Suing for cash and charging abuse, the mother of his son gives Bill Hurt a Big chill. M. Green. il pors *People Weekly* 31:54-6 Ap 3 '89
HURT, RICHARDSON, GARNER, TODD & CADENHEAD
Atlanta minority law firm shares resources with white firm in unique bar program [Arrington & Hollowell and Hurt, Richardson, Garner, Todd & Cadenhead] il *Jet* 76:24 O 2 '89
HURTER, BILL
One to one. See issues of Petersen's Photographic Magazine
HURTH, ROBERT, AND HURTH, SHEILA
Boudoir photography for fun and profit. il *Petersen's Photographic Magazine* 18:12-15+ N '89
HURTH, SHEILA
(jt. auth) See Hurth, Robert, and Hurth, Sheila
HURWITZ, CHARLES E.
about
California's chain-saw massacre. M. J. Walters. il *Reader's Digest* 135:144-9 N '89
Hurwitz to the max. T. Jaffe. il *Forbes* 144:124-5 Ag 21 '89
Milken, junk bonds and raping redwoods. B. McKibben. *Rolling Stone* p39-40 Ag 10 '89
A raider's ruckus in the redwoods. E. Schultz. il por *Fortune* 119:172-3+ Ap 24 '89
When the safety net is frayed. J. B. Levine. il *Business Week* p158 N 6 '89
HURWITZ, DEENA
The walls are crumbling down. *The Progressive* 53:12 Je '89
HURWITZ, LAURIE S.
Exhibits. See issues of American Artist
HUSARSKA, ANNA
Between issues. *The New Leader* 72:2 Je 12-26 '89
A talk with Adam Michnik [cover story] pors *The New Leader* 72:8-10 Ap 3-17 '89
Up from the underground in Poland. il *The New York Times Book Review* 94:1+ O 8 '89
(tr) See Skalski, Ernest. Ameryka my America
(tr) See Skalski, Ernest. Poland turns to the polls
HUSAYN, ṢADDĀM *See* Hussein, Ṣaddām
HUSBAND AND WIFE *See* Marriage; Married couples
HUSBAND AND WIFE QUARRELS *See* Quarrels
HUSBANDS, JO
(jt. auth) See Stern, Paul C., 1944-, and Husbands, Jo
HUSBANDS
> *See also*
> Adultery
> Divorce
> Marriage
> Married couples
> Runaway husbands
> Widowers
> Wife abuse
> Wives
> Women executives' husbands

Friendly persuasion: how to help your husband help himself. J. Bailey. *Redbook* 172:110-11+ Ap '89
Giving birth—together. A. P. Murphy. il *Parents* 64:8 Ja '89
A husband beyond compare [condensed from Family portraits] M. H. Clark. *Reader's Digest* 135:92-4 D '89
Two of us is one too many [early retirement] H. Bennett. il *The New York Times Magazine* p22+ O 22 '89
Anecdotes, facetiae, satire, etc.
Have you seen your wife lately? K. Fury. il *Working Woman* 14:198 N '89
HUSE, WILLIAM D., AND OTHERS
Generation of a large combinatorial library of the immunoglobulin repertoire in phage lambda. bibl f il *Science* 246:1275-81 D 8 '89
HÜSKER DÜ (MUSICAL GROUP)
New day rising. D. Fricke. por *Rolling Stone* p78-80+ Je 15 '89
HUSLER, DEAN S.
Gotham great grows grim. il *Christianity Today* 33:65 My 12 '89
HUSSEIN, KING OF JORDAN, 1935-
The Middle East [address, April 22, 1989] *Vital Speeches of the Day* 55:486-7 Je 1 '89
Visit of King Hussein I [remarks, April 19, 1989] map *Department of State Bulletin* 89:54-5 Jl '89
about
Bye-bye moderates. por *Time* 134:50 N 20 '89
Contemplating the next step. S. MacLeod. il pors *Time* 133:32-3 Ja 23 '89

HUSSEIN, KING OF JORDAN, 1935- -about-cont.
Getting the royal flush. *Time* 133:45 My 8 '89
Jordan and reverberations of the uprising. R. Satloff. bibl f *Current History* 88:85-8+ F '89
Jordan votes the Islamic ticket. S. Hubbell. il *The Nation* 249:786+ D 25 '89

Visit to Canada, 1989
In search of peace [interview with Queen Noor of Jordan] J. Howse. il por *Maclean's* 102:48 O 30 '89

Visit to the United States, 1989
Visit of King Hussein I [remarks, April 19, 1989] G. Bush; Hussein. il por map *Department of State Bulletin* 89:53-5 Jl '89

HUSSEIN, MAHMOUD
The eagle and the sphinx. il *The Unesco Courier* 42:24-9 Je '89
The poet's tale. il *The Unesco Courier* 42:12-17 S '89

HUSSEIN, MUMTAZ
Afghanistan after the turmoil. il *World Health* p11-12 Jl '89

HUSSEIN, ṢADDĀM
about
Alas, Babylon—can Saddam rebuild it? R. Z. Chesnoff. il por *U.S. News & World Report* 107:37+ S 25 '89
Lose a son, drive a car. P. Fuhrman. il pors *Forbes* 144:256+ D 11 '89

HUSSEINI, FAISAL AL- *See* Al-Husseini, Faisal
HUST, ANNE-MARIE DE CLAVIÈRE D' *See* Clavière d'Hust, Anne-Marie de, comtesse
HUST, BERNARD DE CLAVIÈRE D' *See* Clavière d'Hust, Bernard de, comte
HUSTON, ANJELICA
about
America's 10 most beautiful women. Y. Z. McDonough. il pors *Harper's Bazaar* 122:186+ S '89
Anjelica rising [cover story] J. Kaplan. il pors *The New York Times Magazine* p18-21+ F 12 '89

HUSTON, JOHN, 1906-1987
about
The dead [film] Reviews
Video il 12:82-3 Ja '89. S. L. Siegel
John Huston. R. Seidenberg. il por *American Film* 14:66-7 Je '89

HUTCHENS, JAMES
(jt. auth) *See* Ettinger, Linda F., and Hutchens, James
HUTCHERSON, BOBBY
about
Bobby Hutcherson. R. Tolleson. il por *Down Beat* 56:27 D '89

HUTCHESON, RICHARD G., 1921-
Religion in the Bush White House. *The Christian Century* 106:37-8 Ja 18 '89

HUTCHINS, ROBERT MAYNARD, 1899-1977
about
Requiem for the Hutchins College. F. C. Ward. il por *Change* 21:24-33 Jl/Ag '89
The war of the Great books. B. McArthur. il *American Heritage* 40:57-8+ F '89

HUTCHINSON, ANNE MARBURY, 1591-1643
about
Apologizing to Anne Hutchinson. M. P. Nugent. *The Christian Century* 106:304-5 Mr 22-29 '89

HUTCHINSON, LOUISE DANIEL
Building on a heritage. por *American Visions* 4:11 Ag '89
HUTCHINSON, PHILLIP
Killer on the loose? P. O. D'Aulaire and E. D'Aulaire. il *Reader's Digest* 134:64-70 Ja '89

HUTCHINSON, ROBERT
about
A designer's wanderings in the Yucatán. S. E. Jares. il por *Architectural Digest* 46:270+ Ap '89

HUTCHINSON, SCOTT
A community of remembrance. *The Christian Century* 106:853-6 S 27 '89

HUTCHINSON-GILFORD DISEASE *See* Progeria
HUTCHISON, BRUCE
about
An abiding commitment to the land and the nation. D. Jenish. il por *Maclean's* 102:26-7 D 25 '89

HUTCHISON, FRANK
Coming to grips with an aging church. il *The Christian Century* 106:206-8 F 22 '89

HUTCHISON WHAMPOA LTD.
A $5-billion Canadian solution. P. C. Newman. il *Maclean's* 102:62 D 4 '89

HUTERA, DONALD
Little Dorrit. il *Theatre Crafts* 23:34-7+ Ja '89

HUTH, TOM
A change of peso. il *Gentlemen's Quarterly* 59:438-41+ S '89

HUTSON, DON, 1913-
about
The Bronk and the gazelle. P. Zimmerman. il pors *Sports Illustrated* 71:128-32+ S 11 '89

HUTT, WILLARD ANDRE
about
Historic-trail blazer. il map *National Geographic World* 162:30 F '89

HUTTERIAN BRETHREN
A providential lesson on the need for rules. J. M. Wall. *The Christian Century* 106:611-12 Je 21-28 '89

HUTTERITES *See* Hutterian Brethren
HUTTON, JOHN
about
The man in the perfect chair. P. Patton. il por *Esquire* 111:104-7 Ja '89

HUTTON, LAUREN
about
Collecting vintage dresses with contemporary flair. B. Boehlert. il pors *Architectural Digest* 46:60+ S '89
In her prime. L. George. il por *American Health* 8:70-1 Jl/Ag '89

HUTTON, PAUL ANDREW, 1949-
Davy Crockett—he was hardly king of the wild frontier. il por *TV Guide* 36:24-5 F 4-10 '89

HUTTON, SHIRLEY
about
Sell some, recruit some. L. Washer. il por *Working Woman* 14:95 My '89

HUTTON, WILLIAM R.
The young and the old are not enemies. il *USA Today (Periodical)* 117:63-5 Mr '89

HUWS, URSULA
The cost of flexibility. *World Press Review* 36:48 Je '89

HUXLEY, ALDOUS, 1894-1963
about
Aldous in Wonderland. M. Richler. il *Gentlemen's Quarterly* 59:148+ D '89

HUYGHE, PATRICK
The big yawn. il *Discover* 10:78-81 Je '89
UFO update. il *Omni (New York, N.Y.)* 11:73 F '89
UFO update. il *Omni (New York, N.Y.)* 11:85 S '89
UFO update. il *Omni (New York, N.Y.)* 11:89 Ap '89

HUYNH, THANH V., AND OTHERS
Bacterial blight of soybean: regulation of a pathogen gene determining host cultivar specificity. bibl f il *Science* 245:1374-7 S 22 '89

HUZINEC, MARY
Home base. il pors *Ladies' Home Journal* 106:130+ S '89
HWANG, DAVID HENRY
about
M. Butterfly [drama] Reviews
Time il por 134:62-4 Ag 14 '89. W. A. Henry
When East and West collide. W. A. Henry. il por *Time* 134:62-4 Ag 14 '89

HWANG, TZYH-CHANG, AND OTHERS
Cl⁻ channels in CF: lack of activation by protein kinase C and cAMP-dependent protein kinase. bibl f il *Science* 244:1351-3 Je 16 '89

HWEICHOW (CHINA) *See* Huizhou (China)
HYACINTHS, WATER *See* Water hyacinths
HYALURONATE *See* Hyaluronic acid
HYALURONIC ACID
Preventing postsurgical tissue 'gluing' [use of hyaluronic coatings; work of Eugene P. Goldberg] *Science News* 136:222 S 30 '89

HYAMS, PETER
about
The Presidio [film] Reviews
Video il 12:64 Mr '89. D. Schweiger

HYATT, RALPH
Healthy anger. il *USA Today (Periodical)* 117:75-7 Ja '89
HYATT CORP.
Penny's ante [P. Pritzker runs Hyatt's luxury retirement centers] J. Zweig. il por *Forbes* 144:352 N 13 '89

HYATT REGENCY WAIKOLOA (HAWAII) *See* Resorts—Hawaii
HYBELS, BILL
about
Full house at Willow Creek. B. Dolan. il por *Time* 133:60 Mr 6 '89

HYBRIDIZATION
See also
Apricots—Hybrids
Cell hybridization
Plums—Hybrids

HYBRIDOMAS *See* Cell hybridization
HYDE, CHRISTIE
The "no fair" solution. il *Parents* 64:78+ D '89
HYDE, NINA
The business of chic. il *National Geographic* 176:146-57 Jl '89
HYDE, RICHARD ALLEN
In the name of God, stop the killing. *The Christian Century* 106:1144 D 6 '89

HYDE DE NEUVILLE, ANNE-MARGUERITE-HENRIETTE ROUILLÉ DE MARIGNY, BARONNE, 1749?-1849
about
Banished by Napoleon: the American exile of Baron and Baroness Hyde de Neuville. G.-G. Deák. bibl f il pors *Antiques* 136:1148-57 N '89

HYDE DE NEUVILLE, JEAN-GUILLAUME, BARON, 1776-1857
about
Banished by Napoleon: the American exile of Baron and Baroness Hyde de Neuville. G.-G. Deák. bibl f il pors *Antiques* 136:1148-57 N '89
HYDE IN HOLLYWOOD [drama] See Parnell, Peter
HYDE PARK HOLDINGS INC.
A little cash and a lot of moxie [bid for Universal Foods Corp.] L. J. Nathans. il pors *Business Week* p74 Ja 30 '89
HYDERABAD (INDIA: STATE)
History
Hyderabad: shadow of empire [cover story] A. Bakshian and G. D. Schad. bibl il *History Today* 39:19-28 Ja '89
HYDRAULIC ENGINEERING
Wandering river [bank armor and Iowa vanes prevent meandering] R. Kunzig. il *Discover* 10:68-71 N '89
HYDRAULIC EQUIPMENT
See also
Airplanes—Hydraulic equipment
Airplanes, Jet—Hydraulic equipment
HYDRAZINE
Domesticated mushrooms [hydrazine content linked to cancer] B. T. Hunter. il *Consumers' Research Magazine* 72:8-9 F '89
HYDRO-QUÉBEC
Canadian utility threatens Cree [James Bay II] D. Schulze. il *The Progressive* 53:18 O '89
HYDROCARBONS
And now, the return of the killer trees? *Newsweek* 113:78 Je 5 '89
Leaves of gas [role of hydrocarbons in urban smog in Atlanta, Ga.; research by William Chameides] il *Discover* 10:20 F '89
Tree pollution [role of hydrocarbons in urban smog; research by William Chameides] J. W. Merline. il *Consumers' Research Magazine* 72:38 Ja '89
Spectra and spectroscopy
Spectral reflectance properties of hydrocarbons: remote-sensing implications. E. A. Cloutis. bibl f il *Science* 245:165-8 Jl 14 '89
HYDROCHLOROFLUOROCARBONS
Higher profits from CFC subs. A. A. Layne. *High Technology Business* 9:10 F '89
HYDROCYANIC ACID
Was adenine the first purine? A. W. Schwartz and C. G. Bakker. bibl f il *Science* 245:1102-4 S 8 '89
HYDRODYNAMICS
See also
Drag (Hydrodynamics)
Drops
Viscosity
HYDROELECTRIC DAMS See Dams
HYDROELECTRIC PLANTS
Visions of hydropower. J. Cook. il *Country Journal* 16:27-31 F '89
Canada
See also
James Bay Hydroelectric Project
HYDROELECTRIC POWER
See also
Wave power
Export-import trade
Canadian utility threatens Cree [Hydro-Québec's James Bay II] D. Schulze. il *The Progressive* 53:18 O '89
HYDROFOIL RACING
Winners [H. Brewis] S. Wilson. il por *Motor Boating & Sailing* 163:26+ Mr '89
HYDROGEN
See also
Metallic hydrogen
Chaos in a hydrogen atom. R. Pool. *Science* 243:894 F 17 '89
Isotopes
See also
Tritium
Hydrogen tunneling in enzyme reactions. Y. Cha and others. bibl f il *Science* 243:1325-30 Mr 10 '89
Quantum biology [hydrogen tunneling in enzyme reactions; research by Yuan Cha] J. Kinoshita. *Scientific American* 260:31-2 My '89
HYDROGEN, INTERSTELLAR See Matter, Interstellar
HYDROGEN AS FUEL
Hydrogen: tomorrow's limitless power source. P. C. Cruver. il por *The Futurist* 23:24-6 N/D '89
Light ways of making a future fuel [work of John M. White] *Science News* 135:123 F 25 '89
Researchers explore slush hydrogen as fuel for National Aero-Space Plane. S. W. Kandebo. il *Aviation Week & Space Technology* 130:37-8 Je 26 '89
Road to power [work of John Bockris and others] R. Keating. il *Omni (New York, N.Y.)* 11:66-8+ Je '89
Soaking up the rays to make fuel [liberating hydrogen bound in sea water; work of H. Ti Tien] *Science News* 135:366 Je 10 '89

HYDROGEN BOMBS
Accidents
Classified top secret: H-bomb overboard [rolls off U.S. carrier Ticonderoga headed toward Japanese port] *Newsweek* 113:45 My 15 '89
HYDROGEN CYANIDE See Hydrocyanic acid
HYDROGEN SULFIDE
Hydrogen sulfide on Io: evidence from telescopic and laboratory infrared spectra. D. B. Nash and R. R. Howell. bibl f il *Science* 244:454-7 Ap 28 '89
HYDROGEOLOGY See Groundwater
HYDROLASES
The neuron-specific protein PGP 9.5 is a ubiquitin carboxyl-terminal hydrolase. K. D. Wilkinson and others. bibl f il *Science* 246:670-3 N 3 '89
HYDROLOGIC CYCLE
Water-cycle watch [Penn State experiment part of Earth Observing System] J. A. Yeaple. *Popular Science* 235:93 D '89
HYDROLOGY RESEARCH
Ethical aspects
USGS reports a fraud [case of R. L. Houghton] E. Marshall. *Science* 244:1436 Je 23 '89
HYDROLYSIS
Catalytic antibodies with lipase activity and *R* or *S* substrate selectivity. K. D. Janda and others. bibl f il *Science* 244:437-40 Ap 28 '89
Catalytic hydrolysis of vasoactive intestinal peptide by human autoantibody. S. Paul and others. bibl f il *Science* 244:1158-62 Je 9 '89
HYDROMAGNETIC WAVES See Plasma waves
HYDROPLANE RACING
Final run for a speed legend [death of C. Arfons] J. Skorupa. il por *Popular Mechanics* 166:26 N '89
HYDROPONICS
See also
Goodness Gardens (Firm)
Fresh veggies anywhere. il *The Futurist* 23:51 Mr/Ap '89
Hydroponic gardening. R. K. Collett. il *Flower and Garden* 33:70-2+ Mr/Ap '89
HYDROTHERAPY
See also
Mud baths
HYDROTHERMAL VENTS See Hot springs; Megaplumes
HYDROXYAPATITE
Stone to bone [work of Richard J. Lagow] P. E. Ross. *Scientific American* 261:31+ D '89
HYDROXYCHLOROQUINE
Arthritis relief [rheumatoid arthritis] il *Prevention (Emmaus, Pa.)* 41:8+ O '89
HYDROXYL GROUP
Major enhancement of the affinity of an enzyme for a transition-state analog by a single hydroxyl group. W. M. Kati and R. Wolfenden. bibl f il *Science* 243:1591-3 Mr 24 '89
HYDROXYTRYPTAMINE See Serotonin
HYDROXYUREA
Breaking the sickle cycle [cover story] D. E. Loupe. il *Science News* 136:360-2 D 2 '89
Drug shows promise in sickle cell anemia [research by George J. Dover] I. Wickelgren. *Science News* 135:349 Je 3 '89
HYLAND, CHRISTOPHER
about
Cross references. E. Silberman. il *Vogue* 179:435-7 Mr '89
HYLAND, WILLIAM G., 1929-
Letters [discussion of Winter 1988/1989 article, Setting global priorities] *Foreign Policy* 75:182-9 Summ '89
Setting global priorities. *Current (Washington, D.C.)* 312:26-33 My '89
HYLTON, HILARY
Red-hot peppers. il *New Choices for the Best Years* 29:76-8+ Mr '89
The volunteer angel of San Antonio. il pors *New Choices for the Best Years* 29:76-7+ Ja '89
HYLTON, RICHARD
Social ventures. *Mother Jones* 14:45-6+ Jl/Ag '89
HYMAN, EDWARD S., JR.
about
Why you should own a 'slug' of Treasury bonds [interview] J. Mendes. il por *Fortune* 119:36 F 27 '89
HYMAN, IRWIN A.
The make-believe world of "Lean on me". *The Education Digest* 55:20-2 N '89
HYMANS, SAUL H.
about
No recession—yet. R. Bailey. il por *Forbes* 143:86-7 Ap 17 '89
HYMNALS See Hymns
HYMNS
See also
Gospel music
The hymnal is not enough. C. H. Kraft. por *Christianity Today* 33:8 Ap 7 '89
Mims's hymns: building a community of praise. J. Duin. il por *Christianity Today* 33:60-1 O 6 '89
Singing hymns and hers [revised United Methodist hymnal] R. N. Ostling. il *Time* 133:59 Je 12 '89

HYMNS—cont.
Singing the Lord's songs. A. P. Schantz. il *Christianity Today* 33:53 Ag 18 '89
HYPERACTIVITY
Is your child hyperactive? J. K. Rosemond. il *Better Homes and Gardens* 67:38 Ap '89
The truth about hyperactivity. N. Rubin. il *Parents* 64:110-12+ F '89
Worries about overactive kids. A. Toufexis. il *Time* 133:65 Ja 16 '89

Therapy
Helping children with attention disorder. D. Farley. il *FDA Consumer* 23:10-15 F '89
Hyper, not just active? S. Spedalle. il *Essence* 20:114+ My '89
Is Ritalin necessary? F. Roberts. *Parents* 64:52 My '89
Kids talk about the 'good pill' [psychological side effects of stimulants; research by Peter S. Jensen] B. Bower. *Science News* 135:332 My 27 '89
Ritalin: education's fix-it drug? D. Divoky. bibl f il *Phi Delta Kappan* 70:599-605 Ap '89
Suffer the restless children [use of Ritalin] A. Kohn. il *The Atlantic* 264:90-4+ N '89
HYPERBOLE
Diluting the awe by some. J. Rosenthal. il *The New York Times Magazine* p30+ Ag 20 '89
HYPERCARD (COMPUTER PROGRAM)
See also
Hypermedia
AmandaStories, Vol.1 [children's stories] G. Solomon. il *Home Office Computing* 7:88 F '89
Floppy fiction. C. Zimmer. il *Discover* 10:34+ N '89
Linnaeus: interactive taxonomy using the Macintosh computer and HyperCard. K. W. Estep and others. bibl f il *BioScience* 39:635-8 O '89
Programming never died—it just started talking another language. D. D. Thornburg. il *Compute!* 11:12 My '89
Reports [file management program] H. E. H. Aycock. il *Compute!* 11:94-5 Ja '89
HYPERCHARGE (PHYSICS) See Fifth force (Physics)
HYPERION (SATELLITE) See Saturn (Planet)—Satellites
HYPERKINESIS See Hyperactivity
HYPERMARKETS
Cherchez la store [France's Carrefour opens hypermarket in Philadelphia] D. Fong. il *Forbes* 143:311+ Ja 9 '89
HYPERMEDIA
See also
LinkWay (Computer program)
Hypermedia. D. Stover. il *Popular Science* 234:122-4+ My '89
Hypermedia. T. Waters. il *Discover* 10:72-6 Je '89
Nodes and buttons and links, oh my! H. E. H. Aycock. *Compute!* 11:34-6 My '89
Show and tell. E. Corcoran. il *Scientific American* 261:72+ Jl '89

Educational use
Tutor-Tech. N. Rentschler. il *Compute!* 11:64+ F '89
HYPERPAD (DATABASE)
Desktop manager with hypertext power. A. Reinhardt. il *Byte* 14:90+ Jl '89
HyperCard comes to the PC. C. O'Malley. *Personal Computing* 13:196 S '89
A HyperCard for the PC. B. Stepno. il *Byte* 14:189-90+ S '89
HyperPAD. R. C. Leinecker. il *Compute!* 11:104+ D '89
HYPERSENSITIVITY See Allergy
HYPERSENSITIZED FILM See Photography—Films
HYPERSONICS
Aero-Space Plane leading U.S. hypersonic research [X-30 aircraft] C. Covault. il *Aviation Week & Space Technology* 130:18-19 F 27 '89
Aerojet TechSystems facility to test hypersonic engines designed for NASP [National Aero-Space Plane] il *Aviation Week & Space Technology* 130:263 Je 12 '89
Aeronautical engineering [National Aero-Space Plane; special section] il *Aviation Week & Space Technology* 131:50-1+ O 23 '89
HSCT propulsion studies focus on reducing emissions, noise [cover story] S. W. Kandebo. il *Aviation Week & Space Technology* 130:34-6 Jl 10 '89
HSCT research focuses on environmental issues. J. Ott. il map *Aviation Week & Space Technology* 131:54-6 D 4 '89
Industry, government join in HSCT research. J. Ott. *Aviation Week & Space Technology* 130:53 My 8 '89
International engine manufacturers expect to work on Japan's HSCT propulsion effort [high-speed civil transport] S. W. Kandebo. *Aviation Week & Space Technology* 131:39-40 D 11 '89
Japan to set up R&D programs on advanced engines, heat-resistant materials for supersonic transport. *Aviation Week & Space Technology* 131:138 O 9 '89
Keep the HSCT on track. *Aviation Week & Space Technology* 131:11 S 18 '89
Lack of U.S. interest derails international HSCT consortium. J. Ott. il *Aviation Week & Space Technology* 131:28-9 S 11 '89

Los Alamos expands research focus, explores hypersonic flight issues. il *Aviation Week & Space Technology* 130:20-1 F 27 '89
Nonequilibrium molecular motion in a hypersonic shock wave. G. Pham-Van-Diep and others. bibl f il *Science* 245:624-6 Ag 11 '89
NRC committee supports construction of experimental hypersonic X-30 vehicle. S. W. Kandebo. il *Aviation Week & Space Technology* 130:86 My 8 '89
Preliminary tests bolster Rocketdyne's confidence in NASP propulsion system [National Aero-Space Plane] B. A. Smith. il *Aviation Week & Space Technology* 130:98-9 My 22 '89
Rocketdyne developing facility for hypersonic propulsion tests. W. B. Scott. il *Aviation Week & Space Technology* 130:65 Ja 30 '89
Soviets seek cooperative role in Western hypersonic programs. il *Aviation Week & Space Technology* 130:38 Je 19 '89
HYPERSPACE
A different dimension [fourth dimension's mathematical properties; cover story] I. Peterson. il *Science News* 135:328-30 My 27 '89
HYPERSTUDIO (COMPUTER PROGRAM)
HyperStudio. J. Latimer. il *Compute!* 11:108+ D '89
HYPERTALK (COMPUTER LANGUAGE)
HyperTalk program design. R. D. Lasky. il *Byte* 14 Mac Special Supp:MAC205-MAC211 Ag '89
HYPERTENSION
See also
International Society on Hypertension in Blacks
Blood pressure: questioning a maxim [research by Michael H. Alderman] S. Hart. *Science News* 136:116 Ag 19 '89
Fitness lowers young blacks' blood pressure [study by Gregory A. Harshfield] K. Fackelmann. *Science News* 136:214 S 30 '89
Help for diabetic eyes? [linked with diabetic retinopathy] il *Prevention (Emmaus, Pa.)* 41:18 O '89
Hypertension in pregnancy cuts cancer risk [role of alpha fetoprotein; research by Herbert I. Jacobson] J. Raloff. *Science News* 136:263 O 21 '89
Hypertension predicts diabetic eye-disease risk [retinopathy; work of Ronald Klein] K. Fackelmann. *Science News* 135:383 Je 17 '89
Nighttime danger for blacks [connection between high nocturnal blood pressure and heart damage; research by Michael Murphy and Roberto Lang] il *USA Today (Periodical)* 118:8 O '89

Genetic aspects
A genetic polymorphism in the renin gene of Dahl rats cosegregates with blood pressure. J. P. Rapp and others. bibl f il *Science* 243:542-4 Ja 27 '89
High blood pressure: a loaded inheritance [research by Marvin Zuckerman and Karen Russo] P. King. il *Psychology Today* 23:61 My '89
Treatment with tin prevents the development of hypertension in spontaneously hypertensive rats. D. Sacerdoti and others. bibl f il *Science* 243:388-90 Ja 20 '89

Nutritional aspects
See also
Low sodium cooking
Can fish oil drop B.P.? il *Prevention (Emmaus, Pa.)* 41:8-9 Ag '89
Diet and high blood pressure. J. Schein. il *Consumers' Research Magazine* 72:16-20+ Ja '89
Diet restores youth to aging vessels [research by Ross D. Feldman and Christine Sinkey] K. Fackelmann. *Science News* 136:367 D 2 '89
Fish oil lowers even normal blood pressure [research by Constance Kies] J. Raloff. *Science News* 136:181 S 16 '89
Help for high blood pressure: less sodium, more potassium. B. Goldman. il *Better Homes and Gardens* 67:47 Ap '89
Hypertension triumph: diet may equal drugs. il *Prevention (Emmaus, Pa.)* 41:14 Ag '89
Potassium and high blood pressure [research by Gopal Krishna] il *Prevention (Emmaus, Pa.)* 41:12+ S '89
The salt alarm. W. I. Bennett. il *The New York Times Magazine* p30-1 Ja 22 '89

Therapy
See also
Antihypertensive agents
Diuretics
29 little ways to lower your blood pressure. J. Mullich. il *Prevention (Emmaus, Pa.)* 41:33-40 Je '89
New treatments for hypertension. J. Hamilton. il *McCall's* 116:89-90 Je '89
A new year, a new life, a new love [primary pulmonary hypertension patient R. Gyorfi receives heart-lung transplant] D. Gage. il pors *Good Housekeeping* 208:95+ Ja '89
HYPERTEXT
See also
HyperPad (Database)
AskSam: making order out of chaos [version 4.1] C. Strehlo. il *Personal Computing* 13:200 Ap '89
HYPERTHERMIA
Zapping tumors with microwaves. il *High Technology Business* 9:4 Je '89

HYPERTHYROIDISM
After beating what seemed bad odds, a top pro is back up to par; ed. by Andrew Abrahams. P. Bradley. il pors *People Weekly* 32:80+ S 18 '89
The thyroid mystery (II) [J. M. McMillin traces outbreak of hyperthyroidism to contaminated meat] B. Roueché. il *The Saturday Evening Post* 261:46-9+ Ja/F '89
HYPERVENTILATION
Breathe away your chains of pain. G. McVeigh. il *Prevention (Emmaus, Pa.)* 41:58-64 D '89
HYPNOTICS
Sleeping pills. B. H. Dobkin. il *The New York Times Magazine* p39-40 F 5 '89
HYPNOTISM
See also
Mesmerism
Hypnosis through the years [susceptibility to hypnosis remains consistent] *Science News* 135:141 Mr 4 '89
Educational use
Hypnotize students and improve their ability to learn. L. Casler. il *USA Today (Periodical)* 118:88-90 S '89
HYPOCHONDRIA
Scared sick! Welcome to the age of hypochondria. J. Neimar. il *Mademoiselle* 95:206-7+ N '89
HYPODERMIC SYRINGES *See* Syringes
HYPOGLYCEMIA
Exercise could be dangerous [diabetics; views of Michael MacDonald] *USA Today (Periodical)* 117:5 F '89
The low blood sugar blues: do you have the symptoms? R. N. Podell and A. Fischer. *Redbook* 172:100-1+ Mr '89
HYPOPLASTIC LEFT HEART SYNDROME
Should this baby be saved? [performing surgery to correct hypoplastic left heart syndrome] P. Klass. il *Glamour* 87:212-13+ D '89
HYPOTENSIVE AGENTS *See* Antihypertensive agents
HYPOTHALAMIC HORMONES
See also
Pituitary hormone releasing factors
HYPOTHALAMUS
Clockwork in the brain [transplantation of suprachiasmatic nucleus restores circadian rhythm in hamsters; work of Martin R. Ralph and others] J. A. Miller. il *BioScience* 39:75-8 F '89
HYPOTHERMIA
Hypothermia: cold that kills. il *Current Health 2* 15:16-17 Ja '89
The luckiest little girl in the world [hypothermia patient M. Funk saved by extracorporeal rewarming] A. Sunshine-Genova. il pors *Ladies' Home Journal* 106:140-1+ Mr '89
Medicine man [elderly Navajo man treated for hypothermia] T. Dajer. il *Discover* 10:47-8+ Jl '89
"My son is under the ice—find him!" [rescue and revival of drowning victim]; ed. by Elaine Fein. M. H. Garza. il por *Redbook* 172:44+ Mr '89
HYPOXANTHINE PHOSPHORIBOSYLTRANSFERASE *See* Transferases
HYPRES INC.
Superconducting lives. R. Bailey. *Forbes* 144:259+ Jl 24 '89
HYSLOP, JOHN, 1945-
Portrait of an archeologist. il pors *Natural History* p84+ F '89
HYSTERECTOMY
See also
Posthysterectomy syndrome
15 reasons to say 'no' to hysterectomy. C. Perlmutter. bibl il *Prevention (Emmaus, Pa.)* 41:50-9 Je '89
Subliminal healing [use of positive message tapes during surgery to speed recovery] il *Prevention (Emmaus, Pa.)* 41:12+ Ja '89
Suggestions for recovery [use of positive message tapes during hysterectomy; research by Phil Richardson and Carlton Evans] E. Stark. *Psychology Today* 23:24-5 Mr '89
Three alternatives to hysterectomy. P. G. O'Brien. *Ladies' Home Journal* 106:59 My '89
Your health: is hysterectomy necessary? S. Gjenvick. *Modern Maturity* 32:18 F/Mr '89
HYUNDAI (AUTOMOBILE) *See* Automobiles, Foreign
HYUNDAI GROUP
Ending a battle but not the war: labor unrest at Hyundai. A. Platt. il *Newsweek* 113:37 Ap 10 '89

I

I.C.H. CORP.
This could be the end of a beautiful friendship [ICH stake in First Executive Corp.] K. Kerwin and Z. Schiller. il pors *Business Week* p33-4 S 4 '89
I DO, I DO [musical] *See* Musicals, revues, etc.—Reviews—Single works

I HAVE A DREAM FOUNDATION
The great white hope [T. Guinzburg sponsors Brownsville, Brooklyn class] M. Webb. il pors *New York* 22:50-3 Ja 16 '89
I KNOW MY FIRST NAME IS STEVEN [television program] *See* Television program reviews—Single works
I LOVE LUCY [television program] *See* Television program reviews—Single works
I LOVE YOU PERFECT [television program] *See* Television program reviews—Single works
I SPY [television program] *See* Television program reviews—Single works
IACOCCA, LEE A.
The will to take leadership [address, March 22, 1989] *Vital Speeches of the Day* 55:454-8 My 15 '89
about
The list nobody wants to be on. T. Vogel and W. Zellner. il pors *Business Week* p50 My 1 '89
IACONETTI, JOAN
Bliss on Bequia. il *Travel Holiday* 171:10+ Ap '89
The secret of your success. il *Seventeen* 48:90+ Je '89
IAEA *See* International Atomic Energy Agency
IAM *See* International Association of Machinists and Aerospace Workers
IAN *See* Tyson, Ian, 1933-
IANNI, FRANCIS A. J.
Providing a structure for adolescent development. bibl f il *Phi Delta Kappan* 70:673-82 My '89
IANNINI, ROBERT E.
Programmable phasor property guard [cover story] il *Radio-Electronics* 60:37-41+ D '89
IANNONE, CAROL
The Brodkey question. *Commentary* 87:58-61 Ap '89
Novel events. *National Review* 41:46-7+ S 1 '89
The second coming of J.F. Powers. *Commentary* 87:62-4 Ja '89
A turning of the critical tide? *Commentary* 88:57-9 N '89
IANZELO, TONY
about
The first emperor of China [film] Reviews
Maclean's 102:44 Jl 17 '89. B. D. Johnson
Natural History il p66-9 Jl '89. T. R. Miller
IAPETUS (SATELLITE) *See* Saturn (Planet)—Satellites
IATA *See* International Air Transport Association
IBADITE MUSLIMS *See* Muslims
IBÁRRURI, DOLORES, 1895-1989
about
Obituary
National Review 41:13 D 8 '89
IBBY *See* International Board on Books for Young People
IBD *See* Inflammatory bowel disease
IBEW *See* International Brotherhood of Electrical Workers
IBISES
Rhapsody in red [scarlet ibises in Venezuela] C. S. Luthin. il *International Wildlife* 19:46-51 Jl/Ag '89
IBM *See* International Business Machines Corp.
IBN IYĀS, 1448-CA. 1524
Rivalry in the Red Sea: Portugal's impact on the fortunes of Mamluk Egypt. il *The Courier (Unesco)* 42:30-2 Ap '89
IBRAHIM, ABDULLAH *See* Abdullah Ibrahim
IBS *See* Irritable bowel syndrome
IBSEN, HENRIK, 1828-1906
about
Peer Gynt [drama] Reviews
Maclean's il 102:50 Jl 24 '89. J. Bemrose
The Nation 248:824-5 Je 12 '89. M. Hodgson
The New Republic 200:30+ Je 19 '89. R. Brustein
New York 22:141-2 Ap 24 '89. J. Simon
Rosmersholm [drama] Reviews
The Nation 248:101-2 Ja 23 '89. T. M. Disch
IBUPROFEN
Mixed messages [need for warning labels on over-the-counter ibuprofen] A. E. Young. *Common Cause Magazine* 15:11-12 S/O '89
IBUSUKI (JAPAN)
Sink or swim: Japanese bathing in three easy lessons. M. Di Landro. il *Travel Holiday* 172:74-81 D '89
IC INDUSTRIES, INC.
See also
Whitman Corporation
ICAHN, CARL C.
The case for takeovers. *The New York Times Magazine* p34 Ja 29 '89
about
ALPA prepares for possible sale of all or part of TWA. J. T. McKenna. *Aviation Week & Space Technology* 131:128-9 N 20 '89
Carl Icahn has lots of cash. Will he spend it on TWA? T. Vogel. il por *Business Week* p86-7 Jl 17 '89
Icahn edges closer to taking USX. G. G. Marcial. *Business Week* p180 N 6 '89
Is Icahn taxiing TWA to the auction block? T. Vogel. il *Business Week* p58 D 11 '89
TWA unions attempt to shape strategy for gaining leverage over airline sale. J. T. McKenna. *Aviation Week & Space Technology* 131:32-3 D 4 '89

ICAHN, CARL C.—about—*cont.*
　USX: Icahn's back, and this time he has the cash. G. L.
　　Miles. il por *Business Week* p40 Je 19 '89
　USX: the next apple of Icahn's keen eye? G. G. Marcial.
　　il *Business Week* p134 F 20 '89
　Who's in charge at Texaco now? S. P. Sherman. il pors
　　Fortune 119:68-70+ Ja 16 '89
ICAO *See* International Civil Aviation Organization
ICBM (INTERCONTINENTAL BALLISTIC MISSILES) *See*
　Guided missiles
ICC *See* United States. Interstate Commerce Commission
ICE
　　　See also
　　Color of snow and ice
　　Glaciers
　Ice volcanism on Ariel [discussion of September 9, 1988
　　article, Solid-state ice volcanism on the satellites of Uranus]
　　D. G. Jankowski and S. W. Squyres. *Science* 245:195-6
　　Jl 14 '89

Harvesting
　See Ice harvesting

Photographs and photography
　Five faces of freezing [cover story] C. F. Bohren. il
　　Weatherwise 42:315-19 D '89

Therapeutic use
　The ice is right [running injuries] M. Chasnov. il *Runner's
　　World* 24:24 Jl '89

China
　Holocene-late Pleistocene climatic ice core records from
　　Qinghai-Tibetan Plateau. L. G. Thompson and others.
　　bibl f il maps *Science* 246:474-7 O 27 '89

Greenland
　Ancient ice reveals sudden climate shift [Younger Dryas;
　　work of W. Dansgaard] R. Monastersky. *Science News*
　　135:374 Je 17 '89
　Greenland exposed [evidence for melting of ice sheet; research
　　by Roy Koerner] *Discover* 10:14+ N '89
　Growth of Greenland ice sheet: interpretation. H. J. Zwally.
　　bibl f il map *Science* 246:1589-91 D 22 '89
　Growth of Greenland ice sheet: measurement. H. J. Zwally
　　and others. bibl f il *Science* 246:1587-9 D 22 '89

Polar regions
　Antarctic meltdown [work of researchers tracking movement
　　of West Antarctica Ice Sheet] M. Parfit. il *Discover* 10:38-40+
　　S '89
　Antarctic meteorites reveal ancient ice. il *Sky and Telescope*
　　77:466-7 My '89
　Glacier bubbles are telling us what was in Ice Age air.
　　J. Weiner. bibl (p164) il *Smithsonian* 20:78-84+ My '89
　History of meteorites from the moon collected in Antarctica.
　　O. Eugster. bibl f il *Science* 245:1197-1202 S 15 '89
　Ice sponging off the Antarctic shelf [research by Paul K.
　　Dayton] il *Science News* 136:255 O 14 '89
　Interdecadal variation in an Antarctic sponge and its predators
　　from oceanographic climate shifts. P. K. Dayton. bibl
　　f il *Science* 245:1484-6 S 29 '89
ICE (DRUG)
　The fire of 'ice'. M. A. Lerner. il *Newsweek* 114:37-8+ N
　　27 '89
　The menace of ice. il *Time* 134:28 S 18 '89
　Will new drug 'ice' freeze hope in black communities? A.
　　Carthane. il *Jet* 77:12-15 D 18 '89
ICE ACCIDENTS
　When ice is safe. N. Strung. il *Field & Stream* 93:87 F
　　'89
ICE AGE ART *See* Art, Prehistoric
ICE AGES *See* Glacial epochs
ICE BOATS AND ICE BOATING
　Chilling out. M. Benson. il *Motor Boating & Sailing* 163:78-81
　　F '89
ICE BREAKING VESSELS
　Icebreakers! [cover story] J. Fine. il *Popular Mechanics*
　　166:56-9+ F '89
ICE BREAKING VESSELS, CANADIAN
　Slowdown for the Polar 8. L. Van Dusen. *Maclean's* 102:12
　　My 22 '89
ICE CARVING *See* Ice sculpture
ICE CLIMBING *See* Snow and ice climbing
ICE CREAM, ICES, ETC.
　Dessert in the rough [fruit sherbet] D. Thomas. il *American
　　Health* 8:106+ Jl/Ag '89
　Food [herbal ices and fruit sorbets] J. Steingarten. il *Vogue*
　　179:174+ Je '89
　Frosty, light desserts. H. A. Dorrough. il *Southern Living*
　　24:102+ Ag '89
　'Frosty Paws' ice cream can teach an old dog new licks
　　[developed by W. Tyznik] il *People Weekly* 31:132-3 Je
　　5 '89
　Frozen treats. C. Lyons. il *Ebony* 44:106-8+ Je '89
　Granitas. il *Gourmet* 49:138 Ag '89
　Ice-cream bars. il *Consumer Reports* 54:235-7 D '89
　Ice-cream bars for big kids. il *Consumer Reports* 54:492-6
　　Ag '89
　The ice-cream cookbook. il *Ladies' Home Journal* 106:151-2+
　　Jl '89
　Ice-cream lovers' guide. *Good Housekeeping* 209:132+ Jl '89
　Ice cream treats. il *Good Housekeeping* 208:102 Je '89

Memories are made of this. R. Coyle. il *The New York
　　Times Magazine* p85-6 Mr 5 '89
Pop stars. il *Seventeen* 48:110 Jl '89
Quick! Scoop a dessert. il *Southern Living* 24:210 Mr '89
Sundae afternoons. il *Seventeen* 48:322-3+ Ag '89

Collectibles
Ice cream collectibles. E. M. Plante. il *Antiques & Collecting
　　Hobbies* 94:68-70 Ag '89
ICE CREAM INDUSTRY
　　See also
　　Ben & Jerry's Homemade Inc.
　　Isaly Klondike Company

Marketing
Meltdown [marketing strategy backfires for Klondike ice cream
　　bars] K. Hannon. il por *Forbes* 144:130-1 Ag 7 '89
ICE CREAM MAKERS
　Today's ice-cream makers. il *Better Homes and Gardens*
　　67:156-7 Je '89
ICE CREAM STORES
Chain and franchise operations
　　See also
　　Herrell's (Firm)
ICE CRYSTALS
　　See also
　　Snow crystals
Venus crystals [research by G. P. Können] il *Sky and Telescope*
　　78:13-14 Jl '89
ICE DANCING
Psychological aspects
Synchronicity [ice dancers' views] S. Wynne and J. Druar.
　　il pors *American Health* 8:70-1 Ap '89
ICE FISHING *See* Fishing, Winter
ICE HARVESTING
　Harvesting ice. P. M. Leschak. il *Country Journal* 16:54-8
　　N/D '89

History
Ice harvesting—the way it was [New York State] B. S. Newton.
　　il *The Conservationist* 43:24-5 Ja/F '89
ICE HAZARDS IN AUTOMOBILE DRIVING *See* Automobile
　　driving—Winter driving
ICE HAZARDS IN AVIATION *See* Aviation—Ice hazards
ICE HAZARDS IN BOATING *See* Boats and boating—Ice
　　hazards
ICE HAZARDS IN TRUCK DRIVING *See* Truck driving—
　　Winter driving
ICE HOCKEY *See* Hockey
ICE ON RIVERS, LAKES, ETC.
　Journey to knowledge [Tibetan children travel 100 miles
　　on frozen Zanskar River to go to school] O. Föllmi.
　　il *Life* 12:108-16 D '89
ICE POWER
　Ice power [Bo Nordell uses pressure created by freezing
　　water to power his Icy Rider] D. Scott. il *Popular Science*
　　234:154 Ap '89
ICE SCULPTURE
　Cold, cold Harbin: China's city of ice [Ice Lantern Festival]
　　il map *National Geographic World* 161:26-31 Ja '89
ICE SHOWS
　　See also
　　Next Ice Age (Skating company)
ICE SKATING
　　See also
　　Figure skating
　　Ice dancing
　　Speed skating
ICE SKATING RINKS
Equipment
Hazardous gas strikes hockey rink [excess nitrogen dioxide
　　exposure from malfunctioning ice resurfacer; research by
　　Katrina Hedberg and Kristina L. MacDonald] *Science News*
　　136:396 D 16 '89
ICEBOATS *See* Ice boats and ice boating
ICEBREAKERS *See* Ice breaking vessels
ICELAND
　　See also
　　Americans—Iceland
　　Reykjavik (Iceland)

Photographs and photography
A photographer's guide to Iceland. J. Hunter. il *Petersen's
　　Photographic Magazine* 17:66-8 Mr '89
ICES *See* Ice cream, ices, etc.
ICHIKAWA (KATSU) COMPANY *See* Katsu Ichikawa Com-
　　pany
ICHINOHE, SAEKO
about
Beyond "modern dance with soy sauce": Saeko Ichinohe—an
　　East-West hybrid. K. Matheson. il pors *Dance Magazine*
　　63:46-9 D '89
ICHTHYOSAURS *See* Reptiles, Fossil
ICONS
Exhibitions
The icon cometh [Holy image, holy space: icons and frescoes
　　from Greece] E. Knippers. il *Christianity Today* 33:55
　　Ap 7 '89

ICS *See* Integrated circuits
IDA, MORIHIKO
about
A top analyst sees Tokyo stocks soaring before the big bust. J. Ellis. il por *Money* 18:187-8 Mr '89
IDA, SHIN'YA
Chomin: the Rousseau of the East. il por *The Unesco Courier* 42:40-3 Je '89
IDAHO
See also
Agriculture—Idaho
Birds—Idaho
Frank Church-River of No Return Wilderness (Idaho)
Music festivals—Idaho
Radioactive pollution—Idaho
Wilderness areas—Idaho
IDAHO NATIONAL ENGINEERING LABORATORY
Necessary defense or technological toy? [protest against proposed Special Isotope Separation project] S. Cline. *Sierra* 74:95-6 Mr/Ap '89
IDEAL STATES *See* Utopias
IDEALISM
Consumerism to idealism [young people] N. Ulaby. por *The Humanist* 49:26+ Mr/Ap '89
The lost legacy: idealism in American foreign policy. C. W. Kegley. *USA Today (Periodical)* 117:25-7 Mr '89
Should religion concern itself with political and social questions? [views of J. Macmurray] W. A. Barry. *America* 161:61-2+ Jl 29-Ag 5 '89
IDEAS
See also
Creativity
Brainstorming by computer [IdeaFisher] M. Roberts. il *Psychology Today* 23:51 Jl/Ag '89
The Idea Bank [IdeaFisher] P. McCarthy. il *Omni (New York, N.Y.)* 11:24 S '89
Anecdotes, facetiae, satire, etc.
Are you a midnight genius? H. A. Smith. il *The Saturday Evening Post* 261:54-7+ Mr '89
IDEAS IN BUSINESS
Breaking the cycle that stifles innovation [views of Deborah J. Dougherty] A. Kozlov. il *Psychology Today* 23:18 O '89
How to get good ideas out of quiet employees [corporate meetings] P. Amend. *Working Woman* 14:44+ S '89
Managing your intellectuals [excerpt from Right places, right times] H. Donovan. il pors *Fortune* 120:177-8+ O 23 '89
Nurturing those ideas. R. Mitchell. il *Business Week* Special Issue:106-7+ Je 16 '89
The special art of managing creative people. M. R. Feinberg. *Working Woman* 14:40 Ap '89
Success by surprise. C. A. Jaffe. il *Nation's Business* 77:30+ S '89
Ten ways to fire up your creativity [excerpt from Career tracking] J. Calano and J. Salzman. *Working Woman* 14:94-5 Jl '89
Turn group input into stellar output [brainstorming; excerpt from Innovation, Inc.] S. R. Grossman and others. il *Working Woman* 14:36+ D '89
IDEL, MOSHE, 1947-
about
Jewish mysticism in dispute. R. Alter. *Commentary* 88:53-9 S '89
IDENT-A-KID SERVICES OF AMERICA INC.
Children's products and services. il por *Home Office Computing* 7:45 Je '89
IDENTICAL TWINS *See* Twins
IDENTIFICATION
See also
Bees—Identification
Biometry
Crime and criminals—Identification
DNA fingerprints
Fingerprints
Forensic anthropology
Handprints
Mice—Identification
Pets—Identification
Wine—Identification
IDENTIFICATION CARDS, TAGS, ETC.
See also
Barbara Thomas Enterprises Inc.
Ident-A-Kid Services of America Inc.
IDENTITY (PSYCHOLOGY)
See also
Blacks—Race identity
Developing a sense of self [two-year-olds] B. Weissbourd. il *Parents* 64:211 D '89
Look-alikes: America's new identity crisis. G. F. Kreyche. il *USA Today (Periodical)* 117:98 Ja '89
New-job identity crisis. L. Mosedale. il *Working Woman* 14:97 O '89
Power struggles [teens] D. Elkind. il *Parents* 64:239 O '89
You are what you play [perceived character traits of sports participants; research by Darwyn Linder and others] V. Bozzi. il *Psychology Today* 23:69 O '89

IDENTITY CHURCHES *See* Christian Identity (Movement)
IDEOLOGY
Honey, we shrunk the issues. G. F. Will. il *Newsweek* 114:76 Jl 31 '89
IDIOT SAVANTS *See* Savant syndrome
IDITAROD TRAIL SLED DOG RACE *See* Sled dog racing
IDLE, ERIC
about
Puzzling out his post-Python life leaves Eric Idle with hands full. S. Schindehette. il pors *People Weekly* 31:59+ Ap 24 '89
IDOMENEO [opera] *See* Mozart, Wolfgang Amadeus, 1756-1791
IDONE, CHRISTOPHER
Bites of spring. il *The New York Times Magazine* p53-4 Mr 26 '89
Club comfort. il *The New York Times Magazine* p75-6 Mr 12 '89
Great outdoors. il *The New York Times Magazine* p71-2 My 14 '89
We're all ears. il *The New York Times Magazine* p63-4 Jl 9 '89
IDTV *See* Improved definition television
IEA *See* International Energy Agency
IEC ELECTRONICS CORP.
Winning back the work that got away. I. Breskin. il *Business Week* Special Issue:148 Je 16 '89
IEKEL, JOHN
Civil War weather in Virginia. bibl f il *Weatherwise* 42:268-73 O '89
IFCC *See* International Frequency Coordinating Committee
IFR FLYING *See* Aviation—Instrument flying
IG METALL
A social charter for the E.C.? H. Wainwright. il *The Nation* 249:80-2+ Jl 17 '89
IGBP *See* International Geosphere-Biosphere Program
IGER, ROBERT
about
Stranger in a strange land [interview] N. Koch. il pors *Channels (New York, N.Y.: 1986)* 9:78-9 S '89
IGLITZEN, MARLENE
about
Critical success: Gene Siskel and Marlene Iglitzen's art déco Chicago apartment. C. T. Buckley. il pors *Architectural Digest* 46:256-61+ O '89
IGNATIEFF, MICHAEL
The rise and fall of Vienna's Jews. il *The New York Review of Books* 36:21-5 Je 29 '89
IGNATIUS, OF LOYOLA, SAINT, 1491-1556
about
Thirty days to a stronger soul. R. A. Wild. il *U.S. Catholic* 54:12-13 F '89
IGNATIUS, DAVID, 1950-
Closing up bars and closing up shop on the Monongahela. *The Washington Monthly* 21:62 F '89
IGNITION, GAS AND OIL *See* Gas and oil engines—Ignition
IGNITION, MARINE *See* Marine engines—Ignition
IGNORANCE
Who said ignorance is bliss? A. Furlaud. *The New York Times Magazine* p20+ O 8 '89
IGU *See* International Geographical Union
IGUANAS
Breeding
Iguana conservation and economic development [captive breeding project in Panama; work of D. Werner; cover story] J. P. Cohn. il *BioScience* 39:359-63 Je '89
Iguana mama [work of D. Werner] N. Vietmeyer. il por *International Wildlife* 19:24-7 S/O '89
II MORROW INC.
Lorans of II Morrow. J. M. McClellan. il *Flying* 116:25 Mr '89
I'IDA, YOSHIKUNI, 1923-
about
Yoshikuni Iida at the Meguro Museum and Gatodo Gallery. J. Koplos. il *Art in America* 77:175 F '89
IKANGAA, JUMA
about
Beyond the melting pot. M. Noden. il por *Sports Illustrated* 71:46-8 N 13 '89
IKEA SVENSKA FORSALJNINGS AB
Why competitors shop for ideas at IKEA. J. Bamford. il *Business Week* p88 O 9 '89
IKER, SAM
Struggle for the great wild [cover story] il *National Wildlife* 27:50-9 O/N '89
IKOY PARTNERSHIP
Machine tools [William Davis Computer Research Center at Univ. of Waterloo] M. Gaskie. il *Architectural Record* 177:122-7 O '89
IL PORTO VECCHIO (GENOA, ITALY)
Landfall ho! il *Architectural Record* 177:41 Mr '89
ILÉ AIYÉ: THE HOUSE OF LIFE [television program] *See* Television program reviews—Single works
ÎLE-DE-FRANCE (FRANCE)
Gardens: a philosophy of fragrance: Robert Ricci's floral domain in the Ile-de-France. C. Styles-McLeod. il por *Architectural Digest* 46:142-7 Ja '89

ILEOSTOMY
My second chance [relief for ulcerative colitis] M. Bush. il pors *Ladies' Home Journal* 106:138-9+ Mr '89

ILGEN, LIA
Now that the health-club singles scene is passé, reports Lia Ilgen, women are beginning to rediscover the benefits of women-only gyms. *Vogue* 179:238 O '89

ILIAD
Homer's greatest hits [S. Powelson memorizes the Iliad] J. Stone. il *Discover* 10:78-80+ S '89

ILIZAROV METHOD
A bone-lengthening technique adds inches to a teenager's leg—and answers her prayers [case of M. Yusty] B. Johnson. il pors *People Weekly* 32:49-50+ O 16 '89
Stre-e-e-tch those legs. D. Zevin. il *American Health* 8:25 Mr '89

ILL *See* Sick

ILLEGAL ALIENS *See* Aliens

ILLEGAL LITERATURE *See* Underground literature

ILLEGITIMACY
See also
Paternity
The changing face of out-of-wedlock births. B. J. Wattenberg. il *U.S. News & World Report* 107:29 Jl 3 '89

ILLICH, IVAN, 1926-
about
The shadow our future throws [interview] N. Gardels and M. B. Snell. il *New Perspectives Quarterly* 6:20-5 Spr '89

ILLINOIS
See also
Agriculture—Illinois
Booksellers and bookselling—Illinois
Botany—Illinois
Country estates—Illinois
Crab Orchard National Wildlife Refuge (Ill.)
Criminal justice, Administration of—Illinois
Gardens and gardening—Illinois
Motion picture festivals—Illinois
Music festivals—Illinois
Prairies—Illinois
Women's shelters—Illinois
Climate
Some plants slept [drought] R. H. Mohlenbrock. il *Natural History* p58-60 Ja '89
Description and travel
See also
Cycling—Illinois
Employees
R.N.s get pay fix: nurses lead way for pay equity in state jobs. C. Kleiman. *Ms.* 17:73-4 My '89
Industries
See also
Motion picture industry
Let the lobbying commence [Congressman T. Bruce's industrial constituents express displeasure with new Clean Air Act] A. Plattner. il por *U.S. News & World Report* 106:54 Je 12 '89
Politics and government
Blowing in the wind [J. Thompson] J. R. Coyne, Jr. por *National Review* 41:19-21 N 24 '89

ILLINOIS CENTRAL TRANSPORTATION COMPANY
Ivy League street fighters [Prospect Group's hostile bid] B. Bremner. il *Business Week* p34 F 13 '89
An LBO outfit that goes for the long pull [Prospect Group buys Illinois Central] M. Berss. il por *Forbes* 143:94+ Ap 17 '89

ILLINOIS IN MOTION PICTURES
The state that shoots straight. R. L. Ratny. il *American Film* 15:56-8+ N '89

ILLITERACY *See* Literacy

ILLUMINATION *See* Lighting

ILLUMINATION OF BOOKS AND MANUSCRIPTS
See also
Fraktur
History at the margins: bagpipers in medieval manuscripts. D. Stephens. bibl il *History Today* 39:42-8 Ag '89
Profiles [C. de Hamel, manuscript cataloger at Sotheby's] I. Shenker. il por *The New Yorker* 65:48+ My 29 '89
Exhibitions
Islamic paintings at the Sackler enchant the eye [H. Vever collection] C. Bond. il *Smithsonian* 19:122-7 Ja '89
Old Glory [largest illuminated manuscript in the world made by A. and G. Mungo on view at Fordham University] E. H. Gustafson. il *Antiques* 136:728+ O '89

LES ILLUMINATIONS [ballet] *See* Ballet reviews—Single works

ILLUSIONS, OPTICAL *See* Optical illusions

ILLUSIONS OF NEWS [television program] *See* Television program reviews—Single works

ILLUSTRATED BOOKS
See also
Picture books
Picture books for children
Publishers and publishing—Illustrated books
Bibliography
Gift books for fall. il *Publishers Weekly* 236:35+ S 1 '89

ILLUSTRATION
See also
Forensic illustration
Newspapers—Illustration
Scientific illustration
Chris Van Allsburg, a rare bird among illustrators, brings his art to a fresh Christmas treasure. K. Hubbard. il pors *People Weekly* 32:142-4 D 11 '89
Coming attractions [children's books] il *Publishers Weekly* 236:132-7 Jl 28 '89
Drawing for the small screen [children's illustrator M. Hague's art used on thirtysomething] O. David. *Publishers Weekly* 235:103 Ja 20 '89
Flying starts: new faces of 1989 [children's books] il *Publishers Weekly* 236:26-30+ D 22 '89
Making dimensional illustration. E. Rixford. il *American Artist* 53:70-2+ N '89
PW interviews [children's book illustrator E. Young] D. Brainard. por *Publishers Weekly* 235:208-9 F 24 '89
PW interviews [J. Marshall] L. S. Marcus. il por *Publishers Weekly* 236:202-3 Jl 28 '89
Working with Reader's digest. il *American Artist* 53:42-3+ S '89
Collectors and collecting
Focus on American illustration [cover story; special section; with editorial comment by Frances L. Graham] il *Antiques & Collecting Hobbies* 94:6, 26-30+ N '89
Exhibitions
The bleak history of American illustration. *American Artist* 53:14+ My '89
Three-dimensional illustration comes of age. L. Montana. il *American Artist* 53:34-9 S '89

ILLUSTRATORS
See also
Browne, Anthony
Buckels, Jim
Gruau, René, 1910-
Hague, Michael, 1948-
Knight, Hilary
Marshall, James, 1942-
Potter, Beatrix, 1866-1943
Sendak, Maurice
Smith, Elwood H., 1941-
Staehle, Albert
Tudor, Guy
Wisnewski, Robert
Young, Ed
Tying up the talent: exclusivity deals and brand name publishing [children's book illustrator contracts] K. O. Fakih. *Publishers Weekly* 235:39+ My 19 '89

ILO *See* International Labour Organisation

ILOCOS NORTE (PHILIPPINES)
Description
Habeas corpse [efforts of citizens in Ilocos Norte to have F. Marcos's body returned to the Philippines] A. Berlow. *The New Republic* 201:12+ O 30 '89
The waning (and careful waxing) of a dynasty [Marcos family] T. Friend. il *Harper's* 279:68-71 Ag '89

ILYA OF MUROM (FICTIONAL CHARACTER)
Ilya the invincible. H. Yvert-Jalu. il *The Unesco Courier* 42:32-5 S '89

ILYUSHIN DESIGN BUREAU (SOVIET UNION)
Flight testing of Il-96-300 transport on schedule for certification in 1990. il *Aviation Week & Space Technology* 131:45 Jl 3 '89
Ilyushin Design Bureau plans three new transports for export. il *Aviation Week & Space Technology* 130:65+ Je 5 '89

I'M GONNA GIT YOU SUCKA [film] *See* Motion picture reviews—Single works

IMAGE, BODY *See* Body image

IMAGE (PERIODICAL)
Antidote. G. S. Johnston. il *National Review* 41:49-50 S 1 '89

IMAGE AMPLIFIERS *See* Image intensifiers

IMAGE CONSULTANTS
The art of presentation. D. Kazanjian. il *Vogue* 179:304-5+ S '89
The charisma merchants. D. Machan. il *Forbes* 143:100-1 Ja 23 '89
The image makers. L. Wells. il *The New York Times Magazine* p92 S 17 '89
Image wilting? Help is at hand [work of L. Henderson] R. Conniff. il por *Time* 133:16+ Mr 27 '89
Makeovers for success: is how you dress your company's business? [case of B. Smith] P. R. Satran. il por *Glamour* 87:154-5+ Jl '89
Take stock—then fix what you need to. Now. I. Nelson. *Working Woman* 14:88+ Je '89

IMAGE ENHANCEMENT *See* Image intensifiers

IMAGE INTENSIFIERS
PC Paintbrush IV. D. Atkin. il *Compute!* 11:119+ N '89

IMAGE OF GOD
The face of God. D. Donnelly. *America* 160:212 Mr 11 '89
God & joy unearned. J. Garvey. *Commonweal* 116:108-9 F 24 '89

IMAGE PROCESSING
See also
Computer visualization
Still video cameras
Tomography

Coulomb explosion imaging of small molecules. Z. Vager and others. bibl f il *Science* 244:426-31 Ap 28 '89
Did Billy really die a kid? G. Byrne. il por *Science* 243:610 F 3 '89
Digi-View Gold. S. Anzovin. il *Compute!* 11:80 My '89
Editing in shades of gray [Picture Publisher 1.0] C. O'Malley. il *Personal Computing* 13:194+ My '89
The electronic darkroom [Picture Publisher] J. Fiderio. il *Byte* 14:104-5 Mr '89
Fractals in your future [work of Michael F. Barnsley] T. Waters. il *Discover* 10:26+ Mr '89
Image capture by computer [work of Michael F. Barnsley and Alan D. Sloan] B. A. Cipra. *Science* 243:1288-9 Mr 10 '89
Images through gray glasses. M. Antonoff. il *Personal Computing* 13:61-2+ N '89
Industrial-strength color processing [PhotoMac] T. Thompson. il *Byte* 14:97-8 Ap '89
Low-cost digitizing on the Mac [ComputerEyes] L. H. Loeb and A. F. Lent. il *Byte* 14:98+ Je '89
Oscillating chemical waves process images [research by Lothar Kuhnert and others] *Science News* 135:94 F 11 '89
Phototechnology: the future is now. E. M. Gomez. il *Art News* 88:151 Ap '89
The physics of imaging [cover story; special section] il *Physics Today* 42:22-32+ S '89
Profiting from electronic photography. G. Graff. il *High Technology Business* 9:20-3 My '89
Seeing cracks in three dimensions [work of David Carter] R. Pool. il *Science* 243:1293 Mr 10 '89
Sound and image processing [special section] il *Byte* 14:240-1+ D '89
Splat prints of floppy molecules [Coulomb explosion imaging] *Science News* 136:47 Jl 15 '89
Visual Edge sharpens laser output [printer enhancement] C. O'Malley. il *Personal Computing* 13:192-3 My '89

Astronomical use
Active-optics camera tested [imaging system built for the Canada-France-Hawaii Telescope] il *Sky and Telescope* 78:12-13 Jl '89
Amateurs record Mars with CCD. il *Astronomy* 17:92 F '89
The applications of closure phase to astronomical imaging. T. J. Cornwell. bibl f il *Science* 245:263-9 Jl 21 '89
Computer-age stargazing [eliminating distorting effects of atmosphere; work of Gerry Neugebauer] M. M. Waldrop. il *Science* 245:1191 S 15 '89
Crab close up [CCD images by Sidney van den Bergh and Christopher J. Pritchet] il *Sky and Telescope* 77:586 Je '89
Deep space [observation of extremely faint, bluish galaxies by J. Anthony Tyson] il *Sky and Telescope* 78:455-6 N '89
Imaging to the limit [use of nonredundant masking and fully filled aperture method] il *Sky and Telescope* 78:456-7 N '89
Interpreting CCD images of Mars. S. M. Larson. il *Sky and Telescope* 77:472 My '89
Maximize the entropy, minimize the seeing [views of Nigel Sharp] il *Sky and Telescope* 78:571-2 D '89
Monster CCD's get the big picture [Kitt Peak] il *Sky and Telescope* 78:343-4 O '89
Surveying the scars of ancient Martian floods. M. S. Robinson. il *Astronomy* 17:38-45 O '89

Aviation use
GE simulator image generator offers 3D resolution, fast data base updates [Compu-Scene 5 for use in military mission rehearsal simulation] E. H. Kolcum. il *Aviation Week & Space Technology* 130:286-7+ Je 12 '89
ITT solves complex problems to produce image intensifiers [night vision goggles] B. D. Nordwall. il *Aviation Week & Space Technology* 130:91+ My 22 '89
Navy tests near real-time reconnaissance system using commercial magnetic camera. P. J. Klass. il *Aviation Week & Space Technology* 131:98-9+ O 2 '89

Biological use
Voracious turtle grabs a quick bite [high speed video imaging study by Stephen M. Reilly] A. McKenzie. il *Science News* 136:407 D 23-30 '89

Business use
The paperless office [distributed PC-based document image processing] D. Hough. il *Byte* 14:241-2+ Jl '89
The paperless office comes true [American Automobile Association] P. Carroll. il *Working Woman* 14:73-4+ O '89

Earth sciences use
Remote sensing of the earth: a synoptic view. J. R. Schott. bibl f il *Physics Today* 42:72-9 S '89

Forest fire control use
Airborne surveillance will give Forest Service real-time fire maps. B. D. Nordwall. il *Aviation Week & Space Technology* 130:105+ My 29 '89

Medical use
See also
Radiography, Medical

New test may replace Pap smear [quantitative fluorescent image analysis developed by Jeffrey Smith and George Hemstreet] il *USA Today (Periodical)* 117:7 F '89
Optical fibers in medicine. A. Katzir. bibl il *Scientific American* 260:120-5 My '89
A primer on medical imaging. E. Weck. il *FDA Consumer* 23:12-15 My '89
Zeroing in on cancer [On-line Portal Imaging designed to improve accuracy of radiation therapy] M. Brosnahan. *Maclean's* 102:57 O 16 '89

Oceanographic use
Live broadcasts from the ocean floor. il *Popular Mechanics* 166:13 Ap '89

Space flight use
Ball develops multi-anode microchannel array for Space Telescope, defense uses. W. B. Scott. il *Aviation Week & Space Technology* 130:296-7 Je 12 '89

IMAGE PROCESSING IN CRIMINAL INVESTIGATION
Faces from the future [Scott Barrows and Lewis Sadler use computer system to age photographs of missing children] G. Cowley. il *Newsweek* 113:62 F 13 '89
Hard-driving detectives. L. Kahaner. il *Omni (New York, N.Y.)* 12:24+ D '89
The three faces of John List [fugitive apprehended through use of bust created from computer-aged photograph] il pors *U.S. News & World Report* 106:13 Je 12 '89

IMAGE STABILIZATION
Magnavox VHS camcorder with image stabilization [Magnavox CVJ360AV01] il *Video* 12:37+ Ja '89
No-shake telephoto [image stabilizer built into long lenses] A. Fisher. il *Popular Science* 234:50 Mr '89

IMAGEN (PERIODICAL)
Malaret and Casiano: a voguish women's mag that speaks Spanish. P. Finch. il pors *Business Week* p107 Je 5 '89

IMAGERY (PSYCHOLOGY)
See also
Visualization

Imagery boosts breast milk [research by Stephen D. K. Feher] *Science News* 135:71 F 4 '89
Life is but a dream [alert relaxation techniques for experiencing waking dreams; cover story] K. Harary and P. Weintraub. il *Omni (New York, N.Y.)* 12:42-4+ N '89
Mental rotation of the neuronal population vector [motor cortex of monkeys] A. P. Georgopoulos and others. bibl f il *Science* 243:234-6 Ja 13 '89
Monkey think, monkey do [mental rotation of neuronal population vector in motor cortex; work of Apostolos Georgopoulos] L. Oliwenstein. il *Discover* 10:20 Je '89
Pictures of health [positive imagery techniques; cover story] A. A. Sheikh. il *Omni (New York, N.Y.)* 11:104-10 F '89
A portrait of healing [use of imagery to combat side effects of chemotherapy] J. Kaplan. il *Omni (New York, N.Y.)* 11:110-12 F '89
R.T.'s topsy-turvy world [role of mental rotation in recognition of common objects; research by Martha Farah and Katherine Hammond] J. Rubin. il *Psychology Today* 22:20 D '88
Thinking in circles [mental rotation of neuronal population vector in monkey motor cortex; work of Apostolos Georgopoulos] T. Appenzeller. *Scientific American* 260:26-7 Mr '89

IMAGES, MENTAL *See* Imagery (Psychology)
IMAGINARY ANIMALS *See* Animals, Mythical
IMAGINARY PLAYMATES *See* Imagination in children
IMAGINATION
See also
Creativity
Fantasy
Imagery (Psychology)

The lax habits of the free imagination [excerpt from The Houghton Mifflin anthology of short fiction] P. Hampl. il *The New York Times Book Review* 94:1+ Mr 5 '89

IMAGINATION IN CHILDREN
Flights of fancy: your child's imaginary playmates and monsters. J. K. Rosemond. il *Better Homes and Gardens* 67:22 Ja '89
Memory, imagination, and learning: connected by the story [place of story telling in teaching] K. Egan. bibl f il *Phi Delta Kappan* 70:455-9 F '89
Modern-day monsters [pretend games may allow children to respond appropriately to real-life violence] J. C. Compton. il *Psychology Today* 23:30-1 Mr '89
"We have a problem". J. Marks. il *Parents* 64:64+ My '89

IMAGINEERING SYSTEMS CORPORATION
New firm to enter modified Bell 206 in growing Army SCAT competition [Single Contractor Aviation Training program] C. A. Shifrin. il *Aviation Week & Space Technology* 130:47+ Mr 27 '89

IMAGING SYSTEMS *See* Image processing
IMAN
about
Iman. L. Cunliffe. il pors *Vogue* 179:370-5+ O '89
Where I grew up: Iman [interview] L. Konner. il pors map *Glamour* 87:169 S '89

IMANI TEMPLE AFRICAN-AMERICAN CATHOLIC CONGREGATION

A black Catholic priest's renegade church stirs up an unholy furor [G. A. Stallings] D. Grogan. il pors *People Weekly* 32:28-30 Jl 31 '89

Black Catholics vs. the Church. R. N. Ostling. il por *Time* 134:57 Jl 10 '89

Black priest in schism? [G. A. Stallings] *The Christian Century* 106:649 Jl 5-12 '89

Cardinal bars black D.C. priest from saying Mass [G. A. Stallings] por *Jet* 76:5 Jl 17 '89

D.C. priest splits from Catholic Church; black bishops decry the act [G. Stallings] *Jet* 76:12 Jl 10 '89

Equal rites [G. A. Stallings' rebellion] M. McGough. *The New Republic* 201:11-12 Ag 28 '89

Father Stallings' choices. *America* 161:75 Ag 12-19 '89

Heretic as hero [G. A. Stallings] T. Bethell. il *The American Spectator* 22:11-13 S '89

Is a separate church the answer to blacks' prayers? [G. A. Stallings] D. Pitts. il por *Black Enterprise* 20:28 O '89

Priest seeks to reconcile with Catholic hierarchy; White Chicago priest backs Stallings' stand. il por *Jet* 76:16-17 Jl 24 '89

Stallings denies charge of a homosexual relationship. por *Jet* 76:38 S 25 '89

Va. priest fired after announcing plans to join separatist Catholic Church [B. Greening] pors *Jet* 76:26 Ag 21 '89

What's behind the black rebellion in the Catholic Church? [G. A. Stallings] L. B. Randolph. il pors *Ebony* 45:160-2+ N '89

IMANISHI-KARI, THEREZA
about

The Dingell probe finally goes public. B. J. Culliton. *Science* 244:643-6+ My 12 '89

Whose notes are they? B. J. Culliton. il *Science* 244:765 My 19 '89

IMARI PORCELAIN
Collectors and collecting

Imari: the art of collecting. il *Southern Living* 24:166+ Mr '89

IMATRON INC.

High-speed X-ray CT scanner could meet FAA's explosive detection requirements. B. W. Henderson. il *Aviation Week & Space Technology* 131:78-9 N 13 '89

IMBERT, CLAUDE

The end of French exceptionalism. *Foreign Affairs* 68:48-60 Fall '89

IMBIMBO, TONY

The Seventeen yearbook. il *Seventeen* 48:87-90 My '89

Sight savers. il *Health (New York, N.Y.)* 21:32+ Mr '89

IMF *See* International Monetary Fund

IMHAUSEN-CHEMIE (FIRM)

Bonn finally comes clean [implicated in Libya's chemical weapons plant] M. G. Warner and T. Waldrop. il *Newsweek* 113:32 Ja 23 '89

The new merchants of death [West German link to manufacture of chemical weapons by Libya] il *World Press Review* 36:13-14 Mr '89

On second thought [role in building Libyan gas plant] W. R. Doerner. il *Time* 133:30-1 Ja 23 '89

IMITATION

Baby see, baby do [influence of television; research by Andrew Meltzoff] J. Folkenberg. *American Health* 8:104 My '89

IMITATION ART

The art that tourists bring home may reflect declining standards of craftsmanship, but also innovation. R. M. Adams. il *Smithsonian* 20:12 My '89

IMM *See* International Mobile Machines Corp.

IMMEDIATE FAMILY [film] See Motion picture reviews—Single works

IMMIGRANT LABOR *See* Alien labor

IMMIGRANTS
See also

Aged immigrants
Albanians—United States
Aliens
Asians—United States
British—United States
Cambodians—United States
Canadians—United States
Chinese—United States
Cubans—United States
French—United States
Hmong (Asian people)—United States
Indians (East Indian)—United States
Indochinese—United States
Iranians—United States
Irish—United States
Jamaicans—United States
Japanese—United States
Koreans—United States
Legal assistance to immigrants
Libraries—Services to immigrants
Mexicans—United States
Nicaraguans—United States
Poles—United States
Romanians—United States

Russians—United States
Senegalese—United States
South Africans—United States
Sudanese—United States
Taiwanese—United States
Ugandans—United States
United States. Immigration and Naturalization Service
Vietnamese—United States
West Indians—United States
Yugoslavs—United States

Dark side of the dream. J. J. Treires. il *Newsweek* 113:10-11 Mr 20 '89

The elusive dream of home: the longings of a nation of immigrants. P. Marin. il *Utne Reader* p106-9 Mr/Ap '89

Third world USA [interview with R. Kapuscinski] N. Gardels. *Utne Reader* p105 Mr/Ap '89

Anecdotes, facetiae, satire, etc.

The Emigrants Club. R. Cohen. il *The Atlantic* 264:44+ O '89

Language

The confusion of tongues [cover story] S. Barańczak. il *The New Leader* 72:16-18 F 6 '89

Australia
See also
Asians—Australia

Canada
See also
Americans—Canada
Canada. Office of the Minister of State for Multiculturalism
Chinese—Canada
Japanese—Canada
Poles—Canada
Vietnamese—Canada

An angry racial backlash [cover story; special section; with editorial comment by Kevin Doyle] il *Maclean's* 102:4, 14-21+ Jl 10 '89

Uneasy over newcomers [Maclean's/Decima poll] A. Walmsley. il *Maclean's* 102:28-9 Ja 2 '89

France
See also
Algerians—France
Vietnamese—France

Unsettled immigrants. T. J. Abercrombie. il *National Geographic* 176:120-9 Jl '89

Germany (West)

Old Volk's home [German refugees] K. Breslau. *The New Republic* 200:16+ My 1 '89

Pakistan
See also
Iranians—Pakistan

United States
See Immigrants

IMMIGRANTS AND THE CHURCH *See* Church and social problems

IMMIGRATION AND EMIGRATION
See also
Alien labor
Aliens
Asylum, Right of
Deportation
Legal assistance to immigrants
McCarran-Walter Act
Press and immigration
Refugees
United States. Immigration and Naturalization Service

America helps itself by helping others. J. M. Fallows. il *U.S. News & World Report* 107:47 O 23 '89

As the huddled masses roll across El Norte [U.S. policy] il *U.S. News & World Report* 106:10-11 Ja 30 '89

Borderline cases. M. Kondracke. *The New Republic* 200:8-10 Ap 10 '89

Confronting realities of refugee assistance [address, May 26, 1989] J. Moore. *Department of State Bulletin* 89:85-6 Ag '89

FY 1990 assistance request for refugee programs [statement, March 22, 1989] J. Moore. *Department of State Bulletin* 89:72-3 My '89

Give us your masses—up to a point [increase in Jewish emigrants and low U.S. immigration quotas] il *U.S. News & World Report* 107:12 S 18 '89

Gorbachev opens the door for Jews: the U.S. prepares for an influx. il *World Press Review* 36:16-17 N '89

The Immigration Act of 1989. *Congressional Digest* 68:225-56 O '89

The immigration mess [Central American refugees] J. V. Lamar, Jr. il *Time* 133:14-15 F 27 '89

Knock knock [U.S. policy] *The New Republic* 201:7-8 O 2 '89

Letting their people go [U.S. restricts immigration of Soviet Jews] B. W. Nelan. il *Time* 134:51 O 9 '89

A new Operation Brain Drain [raising U.S. immigration quotas for Europeans and better-educated workers] il *U.S. News & World Report* 107:12 Jl 24 '89

Opening doors for immigrants. J. C. Szabo. il *Nation's Business* 77:48-9 Ag '89

Recent trends in U.S. refugee policy. W. P. Fuller. *America* 161:238-40 O 14 '89

IMMIGRATION AND EMIGRATION—cont.

Roll out America's red carpet for the skilled. M. J. Mandel. il *Business Week* p128 O 30 '89

A troublesome exodus [U.S. policy on Soviet Jews] T. Clifton. il *Newsweek* 114:51-2 S 25 '89

U.S., Vietnam agree on emigration of detainees [joint statement, July 30, 1989] *Department of State Bulletin* 89:63 N '89

Update on immigration and refugee issues [statement, April 6, 1989] J. Moore. *Department of State Bulletin* 89:59-62 Jl '89

A world awash in refugees [U.S. policy] D. Waller. il map *Newsweek* 114:44-5 O 9 '89

History

Evolution of policy. *Congressional Digest* 68:226+ O '89

Trends in immigration. il *Congressional Digest* 68:229-30 O '89

International aspects

The new refugees [cover story; special section] il *U.S. News & World Report* 107:34-7+ O 23 '89

Right of entry fees

Chinese head tax haunts Canada [experience of J. Wing in 1923] C. Bright. il por *The Progressive* 53:13-14 Ap '89

'Give me your rich, your very rich . . .' [Senate immigration bill would grant special preference to millionaires] D. Harbrecht. il *Business Week* p31 S 4 '89

Statistics

Asians dominate recent immigration trends. J. P. Allen and E. Turner. il *Utne Reader* p104 Mr/Ap '89

Austria

Where vacations can last forever [East German refugees reaching Austria via Hungary] map *U.S. News & World Report* 107:16 Ag 14 '89

Canada

See also
Deportation—Canada

Chinese head tax haunts Canada [experience of J. Wing in 1923] C. Bright. il por *The Progressive* 53:13-14 Ap '89

Clearing the logjam [overwhelmed refugee determination system] P. Kaihla. il *Maclean's* 102:16 Ja 9 '89

A cool, steady hand [B. McDougall] M. Clark. il por *Maclean's* 102:20 Jl 10 '89

Cooling the welcome [refugee policy] R. Laver. il *Maclean's* 102:17-18 Jl 10 '89

Doubtful haven in Canada [East Germans] L. Van Dusen. *Maclean's* 102:38 O 16 '89

Escape from danger: Lebanese refugees seek safety in Canada. J. Bierman. il *Maclean's* 102:35 O 2 '89

Substance versus fabricated fury [press coverage of refugee policy] G. Bain. il *Maclean's* 102:37 Ja 23 '89

Germany (West)

Borderline Marxists [East German refugees] *The Nation* 249:333 O 2 '89

The children who come alone [refugees sent by parents from third world countries] M. Fisher. *World Press Review* 36:14+ N '89

East Germans go west. *Commonweal* 116:580-1 N 3 '89

Euphoria & beyond. C. Wilpert. *Commonweal* 116:695-7 D 15 '89

A 'fall to freedom' [East Germans] il *World Press Review* 36:13-14 N '89

Flight to freedom [M. Dürer and family] M. Ryan. il pors *People Weekly* 32:36-9 O 2 '89

The great escape [Hungary grants East Germans passage across Austrian border] J. Smolowe. il map *Time* 134:30-2 S 25 '89

Help definitely wanted [views of Norbert Walter on influx of East Germans] P. Fuhrman. il *Forbes* 144:241 O 30 '89

How to bleed a Red nation white [East German refugees] il *U.S. News & World Report* 107:14 S 25 '89

Is a new economic juggernaut on the way? J. Templeman. il *Business Week* p72+ O 23 '89

Looking for a better life [East Germans] A. Phillips. il *Maclean's* 102:36+ O 16 '89

A mass exodus [East Germans] J. Bierman. il map *Maclean's* 102:28-30 S 25 '89

A mixed blessing for Bonn [East German refugees] H. Anderson. il *Newsweek* 114:33-4 N 27 '89

A mixed welcome for returning Germans [emigration out of East Europe] G. Epp. *The Christian Century* 106:902-3 O 11 '89

One people still divided [ramifications of East Germans' flight into West Germany] H. Anderson. il *Newsweek* 114:27 S 25 '89

A quick leap into a new life [Balzer family flees from East Germany] D. Lawday. il *U.S. News & World Report* 107:37+ O 23 '89

A strange new place called home [List family and S. Schulz, East German refugees] M. Ryan. il pors *Life* 12:34-9 N '89

They came, they saw, they went back to work [East Germans return home after seeing the West] R. Z. Chesnoff and R. Knight. il *U.S. News & World Report* 107:42-3 N 27 '89

Ticket to loneliness [refugee children] N. Darnton. il *Newsweek* 114:43 Ag 28 '89

The welcome can wear thin. P. Clough. *World Press Review* 36:12 N '89

Welcome, East bloc refugees! Well, sort of. J. Templeman. il *Business Week* p50 S 18 '89

Great Britain

The great British brain drain. D. Foote. il *Newsweek* 114:60 Jl 17 '89

Scholar slip [Britain's brain drain] A. Ryan. *The New Republic* 201:14-16 D 4 '89

Honduras

A new life on Block B [Nicaraguan refugee family] A. M. Arrarte. il *U.S. News & World Report* 107:43 O 23 '89

Hong Kong

Boat people, go home. R.-P. Paringaux. *World Press Review* 36:35-6 Je '89

The boat people in peril [Vietnamese] W. Shawcross. il *The New York Review of Books* 36:58-9 N 23 '89

Compassion fatigue: Hong Kong and the boat people [Vietnamese refugees; cover story] D. L. Kirp. il *The American Spectator* 22:16-19 Ap '89

Dashing their dreams [Britain forces repatriation of Vietnamese boat people] W. Stewart. il *Time* 134:26 D 25 '89

Don't keelhaul the boat people [returning Vietnamese boat people from Hong Kong to Vietnam] *National Review* 41:14 D 22 '89

The exodus continues [Vietnamese refugees] B. Came. *Maclean's* 102:24 Jl 10 '89

Exodus creates church leadership shortage. S. Mumper. il *Christianity Today* 33:42+ N 3 '89

Hypocrisy in Hong Kong [forced repatriation of boat people] B. Amiel. il *Maclean's* 102:17 N 20 '89

The limits of mercy [Vietnamese refugees] J. L. Du Sablon. *World Press Review* 36:17-18 N '89

The long goodbye [residents who wish to leave and boat people who have arrived] R. Brookhiser. il *National Review* 41:18-19 N 24 '89

What will the next favorable wind bring? [Vietnamese boat people entering] F. Moan. il *America* 160:86-7 F 4 '89

Israel

A frosty response [U.S. refuses to provide loan guarantees to Israel for housing emigrating Soviet Jews] *Time* 134:45 O 16 '89

Our road to Zion: a memoir [family's move from London to Israel] D. Vital. *Commentary* 87:49-55 My '89

Japan

Japan draws a line. I. Oshima. *World Press Review* 36:18 N '89

Soviet Union

After 58 years in Moscow, prodigal son Abe Stolar comes back to his kind of town [Soviet Jew visits Chicago] W. Plummer. il pors *People Weekly* 32:65-6 Jl 24 '89

For a chance to contribute [Tseytlin family: Jews seeking to leave country] D. Rinehart. il *U.S. News & World Report* 107:40-1 O 23 '89

Free at last [Soviet Jew A. Stolar emigrates to Israel] il por *Newsweek* 113:6 Mr 27 '89

A frosty response [U.S. refuses to provide loan guarantees to Israel for housing emigrating Soviet Jews] *Time* 134:45 O 16 '89

Give us your masses—up to a point [increase in Jewish emigrants and low U.S. immigration quotas] il *U.S. News & World Report* 107:12 S 18 '89

Gorbachev opens the door for Jews: the U.S. prepares for an influx. il *World Press Review* 36:16-17 N '89

How Bush may help open the doors wider for Soviet Jews [Jackson-Vanik waiver] R. Brady and B. Javetski. il *Business Week* p62 My 22 '89

Letting their people go [U.S. restricts immigration of Soviet Jews] B. W. Nelan. il *Time* 134:51 O 9 '89

'Mother Russia' and her exiles. L. Pochivalov. il *World Press Review* 36:30-2 Mr '89

New U.S. policy may stem flow of Soviet Christians. il *Christianity Today* 33:52+ N 3 '89

Soviet exodus strains church resources. K. A. Lawton. il *Christianity Today* 33:50 Je 16 '89

Soviet immigration [Jews] *The Christian Century* 106:1010 N 8 '89

A troublesome exodus [U.S. policy on Soviet Jews] T. Clifton. il *Newsweek* 114:51-2 S 25 '89

U.S. denies refugee status to Soviets. il *Christianity Today* 33:58 Mr 3 '89

Update on immigration and refugee issues [statement, April 6, 1989] J. Moore. *Department of State Bulletin* 89:59-62 Jl '89

The waiting has finally ended [Russian-Jewish mother and daughter reunited in America] N. Zundelevich. il *The New York Times Magazine* p10+ Ja 1 '89

Taiwan

Brain drain in reverse [Taiwan's U.S.-trained returnees] A. Tanzer. il *Forbes* 143:114-15 Ap 17 '89

Thailand

Cambodia's violent border camps. L. Williams. *World Press Review* 36:20 N '89

IMMIGRATION AND EMIGRATION—Thailand—*cont.*
A ghost outside the fence [Khao I Dang Holding Center on the Thai-Kampuchean border] J. Ranney. il *The Progressive* 53:50 Ap '89
Killing time [Cambodian refugee camp] M. Drabble. il *Harper's* 278:69-72 Ap '89
A life of war and waiting [Cambodian refugee family] N. Cumming-Bruce. il *U.S. News & World Report* 107:44-5 O 23 '89
The return of the Khmer Rouge [cover story] S. Erlanger. il map *The New York Times Magazine* p24-7+ Mr 5 '89

United States
See Immigration and emigration

Western Europe
Scorned today, hailed tomorrow? D. Lawday. il *U.S. News & World Report* 106:51-3 Ja 30 '89
IMMIGRATION AND NATURALIZATION SERVICE (U.S.)
See United States. Immigration and Naturalization Service
IMMUNE DEFICIENCY DISEASES *See* Immunologic diseases
IMMUNITY
            See also
    Allergy
    Anaphylaxis
    Antigens and antibodies
    Cancer—Immunological aspects
    Complements (Immunity)
    Depression, Mental—Immunological aspects
    Herpesviruses—Immunological aspects
    Lungs—Diseases—Immunological aspects
    Malaria—Immunological aspects
    Maternally acquired immunity
    Monoclonal antibodies
    Phagocytes and phagocytosis
    Psychoneuroimmunology
    Tuberculosis—Immunological aspects
    Vaccines and vaccination
Are your defenses down? [effect of cycling] N. Pena. il *Bicycling* 30:170-3 Mr '89
As evidence mounts of the strong link between nutrition and immunity, Lori Miller Kase asks: can the use of supplements help in the fight against disease? L. M. Kase. *Vogue* 179:288+ N '89
Breast-milk don'ts [effects of microwaving and mixing; research by John A. Kerner] L. Schroepfer. *American Health* 8:106-7 My '89
Diet and immunity: the new frontier. C. Perlmutter. il *Prevention (Emmaus, Pa.)* 41:46-52+ O '89
The immune system [cover story] J. E. Cohn. bibl il *Current Health 2* 15:4-9 Ap '89
Mechanism of interleukin-2 signaling: mediation of different outcomes by a single receptor and transduction pathway. M. A. Tigges and others. bibl f il *Science* 243:781-6 F 10 '89
A run a day keeps the doctor away? O. Anderson. il *Runner's World* 24:54-7 Ja '89
IMMUNITY (CONGRESSIONAL) *See* United States. Congress—Privileges and immunities
IMMUNITY (PLANTS) *See* Plants—Disease and pest resistance
IMMUNIZATION *See* Vaccines and vaccination
IMMUNOASSAY
An assay for circulating antibodies to a major etiologic virus of human non-A, non-B hepatitis. G. Kuo and others. bibl f il *Science* 244:362-4 Ap 21 '89
Path to hepatitis C yields test, clues [research by Michael Houghton] I. Wickelgren. *Science News* 135:246-7 Ap 22 '89
Testing newborns for cystic fibrosis [measuring immunoreactive trypsinogen; work of Frank J. Accurso] S. Hart and A. McKenzie. *Science News* 136:233 O 7 '89
IMMUNOGENETICS
            See also
    Major histocompatibility complex
Activation of an excluded immunoglobulin allele in a human B lymphoma cell line. N. Berinstein and others. bibl f il *Science* 244:337-9 Ap 21 '89
Key piece found for immunology puzzle? [gene encoding recombinase; work of David Schatz and others] J. L. Marx. il *Science* 246:1561 D 22 '89
IMMUNOGLOBULINS
            See also
    Lectins
    Maternally acquired immunity
Activation of an excluded immunoglobulin allele in a human B lymphoma cell line. N. Berinstein and others. bibl f il *Science* 244:337-9 Ap 21 '89
Allergy-triggering receptor made en masse [work of Jean Pierre Kinet] R. Weiss. *Science News* 135:246 Ap 22 '89
Catalytic hydrolysis of vasoactive intestinal peptide by human autoantibody. S. Paul and others. bibl f il *Science* 244:1158-62 Je 9 '89
Expression of high-affinity binding of human immunoglobulin E by transfected cells. L. Miller and others. bibl f il *Science* 244:334-7 Ap 21 '89
Functionally distinct NF-κB binding sites in the immunoglobulin κ and IL-2 receptor α chain genes. S. L. Cross and others. bibl f il *Science* 244:466-9 Ap 28 '89

Generation of a large combinatorial library of the immunoglobulin repertoire in phage lambda. W. D. Huse and others. bibl f il *Science* 246:1275-81 D 8 '89
Isolation and expression of functional high-affinity Fc receptor complementary DNAs. J. M. Allen and B. Seed. bibl f il *Science* 243:378-81 Ja 20 '89
Mechanisms for regulating expression of membrane isoforms of FcγRIII (CD16). M. L. Hibbs and others. bibl f il *Science* 246:1608-11 D 22 '89
Membrane anchoring of a human IgG Fc receptor (CD16) determined by a single amino acid. L. L. Lanier and others. bibl f il *Science* 246:1611-13 D 22 '89
Repression of the IgH enhancer in teratocarcinoma cells associated with a novel octamer factor. M. J. Lenardo and others. bibl f il *Science* 243:544-6 Ja 27 '89
IMMUNOLOGIC DISEASES
            See also
    AIDS (Disease)
    Allergy
    Lupus erythematosus
    Sjögren's syndrome
The RNA processing enzyme RNase MRP is identical to the Th RNP and related to RNase P [autoimmune disease study] H. A. Gold and others. bibl f il *Science* 245:1377-80 S 22 '89
Therapy
A plea for 'orphan drugs' [severe combined immunodeficiency] A. E. Ashcraft. por *Newsweek* 114:12 O 30 '89
Vaccines and vaccination
Control of experimental autoimmune encephalomyelitis by T cells responding to activated T cells. A. W. Lohse and others. bibl f il *Science* 244:820-2 My 19 '89
Vaccination against experimental allergic encephalomyelitis with T cell receptor peptides. M. D. Howell and others. bibl f il *Science* 246:668-70 N 3 '89
IMMUNOLOGICAL TOLERANCE
Brain and immunity: mapping the link [periaqueductal gray matter of mesencephalon mediates opiate-induced immunosuppression; work of Richard J. Weber and Agu Pert] K. Fackelmann. *Science News* 136:36 Jl 15 '89
Doping the immune system [morphine-induced immunosuppression in rats; research by Richard Weber and Agu Pert] *Discover* 10:14 D '89
Immunologic tolerance: collaboration between antigen and lymphokines. G. J. V. Nossal. bibl f il *Science* 245:147-53 Jl 14 '89
Lifesaver [FK-506 used to prevent organ rejection] *Time* 134:77 O 30 '89
Mechanisms of immunological tolerance. H. R. MacDonald. bibl f *Science* 246:982 N 24 '89
A nondeletional mechanism of thymic self tolerance. F. Ramsdell and others. bibl f il *Science* 246:1038-41 N 24 '89
The periaqueductal gray matter mediates opiate-induced immunosuppression [mesencephalon] R. J. Weber and A. Pert. bibl f il *Science* 245:188-90 Jl 14 '89
Preemptive strike: the body can be made to see foreign cells as "self". T. Beardsley. *Scientific American* 260:26+ Ja '89
Prevention of allogeneic bone marrow graft rejection by H-2 transgene in donor mice. C. Öhlén and others. bibl f il *Science* 246:666-8 N 3 '89
Sex lives of the small and furry [frequent sexual encounters weaken immune system of golden hamsters; research by Nancy Ostrowski] il *Discover* 10:10 D '89
Thymic requirement for clonal deletion during T cell development. A. M. Fry and others. bibl f il *Science* 246:1044-6 N 24 '89
A wonder drug in the transplant ward [FK-506 prevents organ rejection] il *U.S. News & World Report* 107:17 O 30 '89
IMMUNOLOGY *See* Immunity
IMMUNOPATHOLOGY *See* Immunologic diseases
IMMUNOSUPPRESSION *See* Immunological tolerance
IMMUNOSUPPRESSIVE AGENTS
            See also
    Cyclosporine
    FK-506 (Drug)
IMMUNOTHERAPY
            See also
    Cancer—Therapy
IMPACT FEES (REAL ESTATE DEVELOPMENT) *See* Real estate business—Taxation
IMPALAS
Sometimes the graceful flourish [Southern Africa] N. Myers. il *International Wildlife* 19:44-51 Ja/F '89
IMPATIENS
Impatiens: fit for shade. L. B. Trigg. il *Southern Living* 24:54-6 Je '89
IMPEACHMENTS
Fla. judge Alcee Hastings is removed by U.S. Senate. il por *Jet* 77:12-13 N 6 '89
Hastings impeachment trial slated to begin next month. por *Jet* 75:12 F 27 '89
The leaden wings of Senate justice [vote to remove Judge A. L. Hastings] il por *U.S. News & World Report* 107:18 O 30 '89

IMPERIAL OIL LIMITED

Texaco Canada says goodbye [sold to Imperial Oil] J. DeMont. *Maclean's* 102:33 Ja 30 '89

IMPERIAL TOBACCO LTD.

Tobacco green [Norton Formula 1 team backed by Imperial Tobacco] J. Greening. il *Cycle* 40:114 My '89

IMPERIALISM

See also

Colonies

Leo Amery, the last imperialist [British imperialism] M. Beloff, Baron. bibl il pors *History Today* 39:13-18 Ja '89

IMPERSONATION

See also

Elvis impersonators

Kay Kent died the way she lived—as a mirror of Marilyn Monroe. M. Dougherty. il pors *People Weekly* 32:90-1 Jl 3 '89

A kinder, gentler comic. D. Blum. il pors *New York* 22:26 Ja 23 '89

Who says first impressions are lasting? When the U.S. changed presidents, Jim Morris did too. il por *People Weekly* 31:73 My 15 '89

IMPERSONATORS, FEMALE

Ethyl Eichelberger. R. Smith. il pors *Theatre Crafts* 23:28-33+ Ja '89

The man who lived 30 years as a woman [B. Black] il pors *Jet* 75:29 F 20 '89

IMPERSONATORS, MALE

Death discloses Billy Tipton's strange secret: he was a she. P. Chin. il pors *People Weekly* 31:95+ F 20 '89

Death reveals secret of dad, 74: he was a woman [B. Tipton] por *Jet* 75:28 F 20 '89

IMPLANTABLE DEFIBRILLATORS, AUTOMATIC *See* Defibrillators

IMPLANTS, BREAST *See* Surgery, Plastic

IMPLANTS, CONTRACEPTIVE *See* Contraceptives

IMPLANTS, TOOTH *See* Dentures

IMPLEMENTS, UTENSILS, ETC.

See also

Kitchen utensils and appliances

Stone implements and weapons

Tools

IMPORT COMPANIES *See* Trading companies

IMPORT TRADE *See* Export-import trade

IMPOSTORS

See also

Quacks and quackery

Big scam on campus [M. Cortez masquerades as member of Rothschild family] F. Trippett. il por *Time* 134:25 S 25 '89

Duped by a mysterious con man, a Florida couple 'find' a missing son only to lose him again [DNA testing proves that D. Bonnabel is not the son of J. and M. Hagans] W. Plummer. il pors *People Weekly* 32:59-60 Ag 14 '89

Posing as an astronaut was just one small step for flimflam man Robert Hunt. M. Neill. il pors *People Weekly* 31:271-2+ Mr 6 '89

IMPOTENCE

"My husband can't make love". M. D. Rosen. il *Ladies' Home Journal* 106:8+ S '89

"My husband's vasectomy ruined our sex life". H. S. Kaplan. por *Redbook* 173:22 S '89

New cures for impotence. J. Carey. il *U.S. News & World Report* 106:64-6 Ja 16 '89

Not-so-hot seat [cyclists; research by Harin Padma-Nathan] L. Schroepfer. il *American Health* 8:40 O '89

IMPREGNATION, ARTIFICIAL *See* Artificial insemination, Human

IMPRESARIOS

See also

Bagby, Albert Morris

Theatrical agencies and agents

IMPRESSING THE CZAR [ballet] *See* Ballet reviews—Single works

IMPRESSIONISM (ART)

See also

Postimpressionism (Art)

Fleeting impressionism [life in 19th century Paris shown through paintings] J. D. Flam. bibl f il *The New York Review of Books* 36:20-5 S 28 '89

In a different light. J. D. Flam. il *Art News* 88:112-17 Summ '89

Collectors and collecting

Art: Belgian impressionism. D. Solomon. il *Architectural Digest* 46:140-5+ F '89

Exhibitions

The billion-dollar blockbuster [art prices pushing up exhibition expenses] N. Stapen. il *Art News* 88:39-40 S '89

Strength of vision [Masterpieces of impressionism and post-impressionism: the Annenberg Collection at the Philadelphia Museum of Art] H. Drohojowska. il *Harper's Bazaar* 122:204-7+ Ap '89

Will high costs curtail museum exhibitions? D. Grant. il *American Artist* 53:10+ O '89

IMPRINTING (GENETICS)

First impressions: genes from mother don't equal genes from father. T. Beardsley. *Scientific American* 261:33-4 O '89

A genetic gender gap [cover story] R. Weiss. il *Science News* 135:312-15 My 20 '89

Prader lacks fader; Angelman misses mom? [research by Robert D. Nicholls] R. Weiss. *Science News* 136:324 N 18 '89

IMPRISONMENT *See* Prisons

IMPROVED DEFINITION TELEVISION

The best seat in the house [cover story] W. Livingstone. il *Stereo Review* 54:62-8 Ap '89

A few lines about IDTV. D. Ranada. il *High Fidelity (New York, N.Y.)* 39:18 Ja '89

Get the picture! G. Kenny. il *Stereo Review* 54:69-73 Ap '89

Improved definition television. L. Feldman. il *Radio-Electronics* 60:43-5+ Ja '89

Testing

Better picture—at a price [Sony KV27FX120 and Hitachi CT7880K] il *Consumer Reports* 54:629 O '89

Philips improved definition television. il *Video* 13:37+ Je '89

IMPROVISATION (MUSIC)

Exercises for improvisers—Lester Young's solo on Jive at five. J. L. Lieberman. il *Down Beat* 56:56-7 Mr '89

IMPULSE BUYING *See* Compulsive shopping

IMPULSE RADAR *See* Ultra-wideband radar

IMRY, YOSEPH, AND WEBB, RICHARD A.

Quantum interference and the Aharonov-Bohm effect. bibl il *Scientific American* 260:56-62 Ap '89

IMSA *See* International Motor Sports Association

IN A PIG'S VALISE [musical] *See* Musicals, revues, etc.—Reviews—Single works

IN CIRCLES [musical] *See* Musicals, revues, etc.—Reviews—Single works

IN COUNTRY [film] *See* Motion picture reviews—Single works

IN FACT (PERIODICAL)

The FBI and I. G. Seldes. il *The Progressive* 53:50 F '89

IN-LAWS

See also

Mothers-in-law

IN-N-OUT BURGER (FIRM)

Where Bob Hope buys his burgers. E. Paris. il por *Forbes* 144:46+ Jl 24 '89

IN SEARCH OF JUSTICE (ORGANIZATION)

An emerging male backlash. N. Underwood. *Maclean's* 102:47 Ag 14 '89

IN SERVICE EDUCATION (ARTS TEACHERS) *See* Arts teachers—Education in service

IN SERVICE EDUCATION (ENGLISH TEACHERS) *See* English teachers—Education in service

IN SERVICE EDUCATION (MATHEMATICS TEACHERS) *See* Mathematics teachers—Education in service

IN SERVICE EDUCATION (SCIENCE TEACHERS) *See* Science teachers—Education in service

IN SERVICE EDUCATION (TEACHERS) *See* Teachers—Education in service

IN-STORE ADVERTISING

Trolling in the aisles. B. Kanner. il *New York* 22:12+ Ja 16 '89

IN VITRO FERTILIZATION *See* Fertilization in vitro

INAUGURAL PARADES *See* Washington (D.C.)—Parades

INAUGURATIONS

See also

Bush, George, 1924——Inauguration

Presidents—Inaugurations

INBREEDING

Inbreeding costs swamp benefits [research by Katherine Ralls and Jonathan Ballou] R. Lewin. il *Science* 243:482 Ja 27 '89

INCAPACITY (LAW) *See* Capacity and disability

INCARNATION

If there is no God, then Scrooge was right. J. M. Wall. *The Christian Century* 106:1163-4 D 13 '89

Light from light. P. J. Ryan. il *America* 161:459 D 16 '89

INCAS

Antiquities

See also

Machu Picchu (Peru)

INCENSE

See also

Frankincense

INCENSE BURNERS *See* Censers

INCENTIVES IN INDUSTRY

See also

Bonus system

Profit sharing

The hidden cost of golden handshakes [voluntary termination programs] D. Machan. il *Forbes* 143:130+ F 20 '89

INCEST

See also

Foretich, Hilary—Custody case

Avenging years of sexual abuse, twins take their adoptive father to court [case of R. and T. Royce] C. McCall. il pors *People Weekly* 31:54-6+ Je 26 '89

A candid new biography tells of the shocking childhood that destroyed Rita Hayworth [research by B. Leaming] A. Chambers. il pors *People Weekly* 32:129+ N 13 '89

INCEST—cont.

The long road to recovery [victim E. Danica] N. Underwood. il por *Maclean's* 102:64 N 27 '89

Running for their lives [underground railroad for parents fleeing with molested children] J. S. Podesta and D. Van Biema. il *People Weekly* 31:70-8+ Ja 23 '89

"We're afraid of our son" [mentally ill adoptee was abused by natural parents] B. Harlow. il pors *Ladies' Home Journal* 106:18+ Mr '89

INCHCAPE & CO. LTD.

Our vanishing forests . . . it's not just the Amazon [logging in Borneo] il *World Press Review* 36:40-1 O '89

INCHWORMS

Control

What's the diagnosis? [loopers] W. S. Moore. il *Flower and Garden* 33:46 S/O '89

INCINERATION AND INCINERATORS

Garbage burners losing steam. B. Ahlberg. il *Utne Reader* p21-2 S/O '89

Good riddance [address, May 24, 1989] B. M. Thompson. *Vital Speeches of the Day* 55:683-7 S 1 '89

Mass burn is dying. N. Seldman. bibl f *Environment* 31:42-4 S '89

Laws and regulations

Cleaning up after incinerators [EPA proposals] *Science News* 136:381 D 9 '89

Something stinks in Morgan City [case of Marine Shale Processors plant in La.] C. Strickland. il *The Nation* 249:448-51 O 23 '89

Up in smoke. *The Nation* 249:444-5 O 23 '89

INCOME

See also
Gross national product
Minimum wage
Retirement income
Wealth

America's great U-turn [interview with B. Bluestone] il *New Perspectives Quarterly* 6:35-7 Fall '89

America's income gap: the closer you look, the worse it gets. A. Bernstein. il *Business Week* p78-9 Ap 17 '89

Amid prosperity, unequal prospects [baby boom generation; report by Frank Levy and Richard Michel] S. Nazar. il *U.S. News & World Report* 107:73 N 20 '89

As the world turns [global economy and U.S. income inequality] R. B. Reich. *The New Republic* 200:23+ My 1 '89

Creating a chasm. *Commonweal* 116:357-8 Je 16 '89

The debate over how to count the poor [Census Bureau report] B. J. Wattenberg. *U.S. News & World Report* 107:47 O 30 '89

The distribution of income (cont'd.). *National Review* 41:12 Ag 18 '89

Egalityranny. M. Novak. il *Forbes* 143:76 My 15 '89

Income and ideology: the new nexus [liberalism] D. Seligman. il *Fortune* 120:185-6 D 4 '89

Income growth: are we better off? L. S. Richman. il *Current (Washington, D.C.)* 312:4-9 My '89

Interest earnings don't really fatten consumers' wallets. G. Koretz. il *Business Week* p28 F 27 '89

Is the income gap widening? M. Novak. il *Forbes* 144:105 O 2 '89

The rising tide. E. Rubenstein. il *National Review* 41:20 D 8 '89

Social security bridges income gap. *Society* 26:2 My/Je '89

Something seems unbalanced. G. P. Brockway. il *The New Leader* 72:14-15 S 18 '89

Sources of increasing inequality in wages and salaries, 1960-80. W. N. Grubb and R. H. Wilson. bibl f il *Monthly Labor Review* 112:3-13 Ap '89

Spending patterns and income of single and married parents. M. Boyle. bibl f il *Monthly Labor Review* 112:37-41 Mr '89

INCOME MAINTENANCE PROGRAMS

How much poverty is reduced by state income transfers? R. D. Plotnick. bibl f il *Monthly Labor Review* 112:21-6 Jl '89

INCOME OPPORTUNITY REALTY TRUST

From the Mekong to Motown [S. Plum of Charterhouse Inc. bids on Income Opportunity Realty Trust] M. Schifrin. il por *Forbes* 143:324+ My 29 '89

INCOME TAX

See also
Aged—Taxation
Alternative minimum tax
Americans—Foreign countries—Taxation
Artists—Taxation
Blacks—Taxation
Business entertaining—Taxation
Children—Taxation
Computers—Tax return use
Corporations—Taxation
Dividends—Taxation
Employee stock ownership plans—Taxation
Estimated tax
Farmers—Taxation
Fringe benefits—Taxation
Home offices—Taxation
Household employees—Taxation
Independent contractors—Taxation

Interest (Economics)—Taxation
Investments—Taxation
Married couples—Taxation
Middle classes—Taxation
Pensions—Taxation
Poor—Taxation
Reagan, Ronald, 1911——Taxes
Rich—Taxation
Social security—Taxation
Tax evasion
Tax refunds
Tax shelters
United States. Internal Revenue Service
White collar workers—Taxation
Withholding tax

The 12 tax tips of Christmas. A. E. Serwer. il *Fortune* 120:42+ D 18 '89

30 ways to save on your taxes. B. Weinstein. il *McCall's* 116:42+ Mr '89

50 ways to save time & money on your taxes [cover story] K. McCormally. il *Changing Times* 43:26-9+ F '89

The Capitol gains of the well-to-do [Democratic Congress addresses tax cuts] M. Barone. il *U.S. News & World Report* 107:26-7+ O 2 '89

'Congress has done it to us again'. T. Smart. il *Business Week* p38-9 Mr 13 '89

Cut your taxes fast [cover story; special section] il *U.S. News & World Report* 106:75-7+ Mr 27 '89

Dirty little secrets about tax brackets. K. McCormally. il *Changing Times* 43:92+ My '89

Don't hand out prizes for historical ax-grinding [books critical of Reaganomics and tax reform] P. C. Roberts. il *Business Week* p18 My 1 '89

Easing your tax problems. D. LaMaute. *Essence* 19:105+ Ap '89

The fantasy of federal tax policy. J. A. Schnepper. il *USA Today (Periodical)* 117:29 Ja '89

For your tax file. P. N. Strassels. See issues of Nation's Business beginning April 1988

A forgiven debt can mean a tax hike [and other tax tips] L. Wiener. il *U.S. News & World Report* 107:65 Jl 24 '89

Has the Laffer Curve flattened out? [revenues have stalled] H. Banks. *Forbes* 144:33 N 27 '89

Holiday joy! Give less to the IRS. G. Rutman. il *Home Office Computing* 7:62-5 D '89

How fair is the progressive tax? J. A. Schnepper. il *USA Today (Periodical)* 118:17 S '89

Jane Bryant Quinn's tax guide for 1989. J. B. Quinn. il *Newsweek* 113:52-6 Mr 20 '89

Last-minute tax decisions. G. W. Padwe. il *Nation's Business* 77:85 Ap '89

Listen up, tax tinkerers: let's be fair. A. P. Tobias. il *Time* 134:78 O 9 '89

On the Hill, class war over taxes [Democratic plan to raise top rate] E. Clift and R. Thomas. il *Newsweek* 114:24 O 2 '89

Only two weeks till the new (tax) year [year-end maneuvers] L. Wiener. il *U.S. News & World Report* 107:78-9 D 18 '89

The people tax reform left behind. S. Dentzer. il *U.S. News & World Report* 106:24-5 Ap 17 '89

Postcard form promises reform [system devised by Robert E. Hall and Alvin Rabushka] il *USA Today (Periodical)* 118:9-10 D '89

Quick, what is your real tax rate? L. Wiener. il *U.S. News & World Report* 106:60-1 Ja 23 '89

Ready, set . . . go! [cover story; special section] il *Money* 18:54-8+ Ja '89

The short, unhappy life of tax reform. G. Borger. il *U.S. News & World Report* 106:27 F 13 '89

Staying ahead of the IRS. B. M. Stephens and R. E. Barnes. il *Black Enterprise* 20:69-70+ D '89

Tax letter. See issues of Money beginning June 1989

Tax tips for trying times. J. Reese. il *Fortune* 120 no10 Special Issue:201-3 Fall '89

Taxing decisions. G. W. Weinstein. il *Ms.* 17:78+ Mr '89

Timely answers to taxing questions. K. McCormally. il *Changing Times* 43:48-51 Ap '89

Tinkering with tax reform: a bad idea that will just get worse. H. Gleckman. il *Business Week* p104+ N 6 '89

To file is human, to amend divine: changes in the law make it worthwhile to check old returns. L. Wiener. il *U.S. News & World Report* 106:64 Ja 9 '89

Unconditional surrender [steep progressive taxes] D. Seligman. il *Fortune* 119:123 F 13 '89

Year-end tax savers. K. McCormally. il *Changing Times* 43:94-6+ D '89

Your 7 top tax questions. B. G. Quint. *Glamour* 87:134+ Mr '89

Your taxes. See issues of Changing Times beginning January 1989

Your taxes. See issues of Money through March 1989

Auditing

See Tax auditing

Bibliography

Your guide to the 1989 tax guides. G. Hedberg. il *Money* 18:101-2+ Ja '89

INDIA—See also—cont.
    Veterinary hospitals—India
    Volcanoes—India
    Wildlife conservation—India
    Women—India
    Youth—India
    Zanskar River (India)

Army
Forces in Sri Lanka
My half year of living dangerously. W. McGowan. il *Gentlemen's Quarterly* 59:152-7+ Ja '89

Civilization
India: yesterday's heritage, tomorrow's hopes [cover story; special issue] il *The Courier (Unesco)* 42:3-38 F '89

Commerce
Sweden
Gandhi's Watergate? [Bofors arms sale scandal] *Newsweek* 114:42 O 23 '89

Cultural relations
Soviet Union
See Soviet Union—Cultural relations—India

Defenses
See also
Guided missiles, Indian (East Indian)
India, Pakistan's nuclear weapons: all the pieces in place [cover story] D. Albright and T. Zamora. bibl f il map *The Bulletin of the Atomic Scientists* 45:20-6 Je '89

Description and travel
See also
Cycling—India

Foreign relations
Pakistan
Heirs of anger. D. O. Relin. il *Scholastic Update (Teachers' edition)* 121:8-9 Mr 10 '89
India, Pakistan's nuclear weapons: all the pieces in place [cover story] D. Albright and T. Zamora. bibl f il map *The Bulletin of the Atomic Scientists* 45:20-6 Je '89
War at the top of the world [fighting on the Siachen Glacier in the Himalayas] E. W. Desmond. il map *Time* 134:26-7+ Jl 31 '89

History
1500-1765
See also
Mogul Empire
British occupation, 1765-1947
He remembers when the saber was mightier, but now Bengal Lancer Francis Ingall takes up the pen. K. Gross. il pors *People Weekly* 32:113-15+ S 11 '89
Hyderabad: shadow of empire [cover story] A. Bakshian and G. D. Schad. bibl il *History Today* 39:19-28 Ja '89
India's march to freedom. P. E. Rogers. il por *Scholastic Update (Teachers' edition)* 121:18-20 Mr 10 '89

Industries
See also
Motion picture industry—India
Soft drink industry—India

Military policy
The awakening of an Asian power. R. H. Munro. il *Time* 133:32+ Ap 3 '89

Photographs and photography
A photographer's guide to southern India [cover story] P. Slaughter. il *Petersen's Photographic Magazine* 17:38-44 Ap '89

Politics and government
See also
Elections—India
Political campaigns—India
Politics, Corruption in—India
India: state and society diverge. J. Manor. bibl f *Current History* 88:429-32+ D '89
The Indian subcontinent [cover story; special issue] il maps *Scholastic Update (Teachers' edition)* 121:3-26 Mr 10 '89
Caricatures and cartoons
An 'eloquent brush' in India [political cartoonist R. K. Laxman] S. R. Ramanujan. il *World Press Review* 36:58-9 Mr '89

Population
See also
Tibetans—India

Religious institutions and affairs
See also
Church and social problems—India
Jains—India

Social conditions
See also
Caste—India

INDIAN AFFAIRS BUREAU (U.S.) See United States. Bureau of Indian Affairs
INDIAN ART (AMERICAN) See Indians of North America—Art
INDIAN ARTIFACTS (AMERICAN) See Indians of North America—Antiquities
INDIAN ARTISTS (AMERICAN) See Artists, Indian (American)
INDIAN ASTRONOMY (AMERICAN) See Astronomy, Indian (American)

INDIAN BLANKETS, RUGS, ETC. (AMERICAN)
The Navajo blanket. B. Barol. *American Heritage* 40:24 Jl/Ag '89
Space and design: a brief history of the Navajo chief's blanket. J. Baer. bibl f il *Antiques* 136:528-41 S '89
INDIAN CHILD WELFARE ACT OF 1978
Indian Child Welfare: a status report. M. C. Plantz and others. il *Children Today* 18:24-9 Ja/F '89
INDIAN COMMUNICATIONS SATELLITES (EAST INDIAN) See Communications satellites, Indian (East Indian)
INDIAN COOKING (EAST INDIAN) See Cooking, Indian (East Indian)
INDIAN CORN See Corn
INDIAN CREEK (FLA.)
Architecture
No pipe dream, Jim Stewart's house is built of bric-a-brac and mortar [concrete house] il por *People Weekly* 31:101 Ap 24 '89
INDIAN HAWTHORN
Indian hawthorn likes sand, salt, and sun. il *Southern Living* 24:68 Ap '89
INDIAN HOUSE DECORATION (EAST INDIAN) See House decoration, Indian (East Indian)
INDIAN JEWELRY (EAST INDIAN) See Jewelry, Indian (East Indian)
INDIAN LORE (AMERICAN) See Indians of North America—Legends
INDIAN MARKET (SANTA FE, N.M.)
Photographs and photography
Crafts fairs: they're great places to collect pictures. L. Dennis. il *Popular Photography* 96:20+ Je '89
INDIAN MATHEMATICS (EAST INDIAN) See Mathematics, Indian (East Indian)
INDIAN NAMES (AMERICAN) See Names, Indian (American)
INDIAN NATIONAL CONGRESS
A referendum on Rajiv. C. S. Manegold. por *Newsweek* 114:56 N 27 '89
INDIAN OCEAN
See also
Seychelles
United Nations. Ad Hoc Committee on the Indian Ocean
INDIAN PEAKS WILDERNESS (COLO.)
A walk on the wild side. T. Jenkins. il map *Travel Holiday* 171:46-51 My '89
INDIAN PHILOSOPHY (EAST INDIAN) See Philosophy, Indian (East Indian)
INDIAN PUEBLO CULTURAL CENTER (ALBUQUERQUE, N.M.)
A closer look at Pueblos. il *Southern Living* 24:20 Ja '89
INDIAN RELICS (AMERICAN) See Indians of North America—Antiquities
INDIAN RESERVATIONS (AMERICAN) See Indians of North America—Reservations
INDIAN ROCK CARVINGS (AMERICAN) See Petroglyphs
INDIAN RUGS (AMERICAN) See Indian blankets, rugs, etc. (American)
INDIAN TRADING POST (DANBURY, CONN.)
Indian Trading Post [store run by J. Jackson and late husband] *The New Yorker* 65:32-3 Ap 17 '89
INDIANA, ROBERT, 1928-
about
Indiana in Maine. P. Lemos. il pors *Art News* 88:166-9 O '89
INDIANA
See also
Agriculture—Indiana
Booksellers and bookselling—Indiana
Children—Indiana
Hoosier (Term)
Hoosier National Forest (Ind.)
Plaster Creek (Ind.)
INDIANA JONES AND THE LAST CRUSADE [film] See Motion picture reviews—Single works
INDIANA UNIVERSITY, BLOOMINGTON
Sex (research) scandals! [Indiana University asks Kinsey Institute head J. Reinisch to resign] E. E. Goode. il pors *U.S. News & World Report* 106:54-5 Ja 9 '89
INDIANA UNIVERSITY PRESS
Indiana University to publish controversial Arafat biography [work of A. Hart] il por *Publishers Weekly* 235:43 F 17 '89
INDIANAPOLIS (IND.)
Crime
Masters of deception [Heilbrunn family, accused of operating Indianapolis drug ring, now living in Austria] B. Shaw and D. Van Biema. il *People Weekly* 31:46-51 Je 19 '89
Description
Cinderella city. L. Erickson. il *Travel Holiday* 172:83-5 S '89
Galleries and museums
See also
Children's Museum of Indianapolis
Indianapolis Museum of Art
Markets
See also
Indianapolis City Market

INDIANAPOLIS (IND.)—cont.
Sports
Cities get into the game. G. Macnow. il *Nation's Business* 77:48-9+ N '89
INDIANAPOLIS 500 *See* Automobile racing
INDIANAPOLIS CITY MARKET
Traveler's market. D. P. Marshall. il *Travel Holiday* 172:24 D '89
INDIANAPOLIS MUSEUM OF ART
Museum accessions [French pendulum clock] E. H. Gustafson. il *Antiques* 136:1270 D '89
Museum accessions [porcelain French vase acquired] E. H. Gustafson. il *Antiques* 136:76+ Jl '89
INDIANS (AMERICAN)
See also
Indians of Central America
Indians of North America
Indians of South America
Museums and Indians (American)
Paleo-Indians
Antiquities
See also
Paleo-Indians
Health and hygiene
Disease and death in the New World [debate over the size of pre-Columbian populations] L. Roberts. il *Science* 246:1245-7 D 8 '89
INDIANS (AMERICAN) AND MASS MEDIA
The Tonto syndrome. L. Eskin. il *Scholastic Update (Teachers' edition)* 121:21-2 My 26 '89
INDIANS (AMERICAN) AS PRISONERS *See* Indians of North America—Imprisonment
INDIANS (AMERICAN) IN ART
Going back to the past, using collotype art [publication of G. Catlin's North American Indian portfolio] J. P. Frank. il *Publishers Weekly* 236:62-4 Ag 4 '89
Whispering giants [work of carver P. Toth] D. R. Hopwood. il pors *Americana* 17:63-5 My/Je '89
Exhibitions
An immigrant artist captured the faces of the New World [works of R. Winold at the National Portrait Gallery] J. H. Heminway. il pors *Smithsonian* 20:172-8+ N '89
INDIANS (AMERICAN) IN DRAMA
Highway of hope [plays by Tomson Highway] J. Bemrose. il *Maclean's* 102:62 My 8 '89
INDIANS (AMERICAN) IN LITERATURE
A canyon, an egret . . . and a mystery [setting for the novel A thief of time] T. Hillerman. il *Audubon* 91:30-4+ Jl '89
In the heart of Navajo country [books by T. Hillerman] K. Ames. il por *Newsweek* 113:60-1 Je 19 '89
Navajo cops on the case [T. Hillerman] A. Ward. il pors *The New York Times Magazine* p38-9+ My 14 '89
'Slaves of one man' [portrayal of American Indians in 17th and 18th century French literature] C. de Grandpré. il *The Unesco Courier* 42:44-7 O '89
INDIANS (AMERICAN) IN MOTION PICTURES
Highway of dreams [Powwow Highway] B. D. Johnson. il por *Maclean's* 102:62-3 Ap 24 '89
INDIANS (AMERICAN) IN VIDEOTAPES
Space age shamans: the videotape [recording tribal customs of Brazilian Indians] G. Smith. il *Américas* 41 no2:28-31 '89
INDIANS (EAST INDIAN)
See also
Sikhs
United States
In Gandhi's footsteps [A. Gandhi] G. Cowley. il por *Newsweek* 113:48 Mr 6 '89
Inspired by his famous forebear, Mahatma Gandhi's grandson takes a close look at racism in America [A. Gandhi] H. Shapiro. il pors *People Weekly* 31:257-8 Mr 6 '89
INDIANS OF CENTRAL AMERICA
See also
Mayas
Mosquito Indians
Religion and mythology
Blood bond: where Oklahoma and Guatemala meet [Catholic mission] D. Thomson. *America* 161:277-8 O 28 '89
Guatemala
See also
Tzutuhil Indians
Letters [discussion of November 28, 1988 article, Guatemala's new military order] P. Lernoux. *The Nation* 248:254+ F 27 '89
Nicaragua
Nicaragua's English connection [indigenous people on Atlantic coast] A. Hills. il *History Today* 39:3-4 Ag '89
INDIANS OF MEXICO
See also
Aztecs
Antiquities
See Yucatan (Mexico: State)—Antiquities
INDIANS OF NORTH AMERICA
See also
Cherokee Indians
Chippewa Indians
Choctaw Indians
Cree Indians
Dakota Indians
Eskimos
Haida Indians
Hidatsa Indians
Lummi Indians
Mohawk Indians
Navajo Indians
Pueblo Indians
Zuñi Indians
Aged
See also
Sicangu Elderly Concerns, Inc.
Full-moon wisdom [treatment of the elderly in Hispanic and Indian cultures] R. Coles. il *New Choices for the Best Years* 29:94+ S '89
Agriculture
Ancient gardeners conserved water [Pueblo Indian settlements] il *Earth Science* 42:5-6 Fall '89
Origins of agriculture in eastern North America. B. D. Smith. bibl f il map *Science* 246:1566-71 D 22 '89
Antiquities
See also
Colorado—Antiquities
Kentucky—Antiquities
New Mexico—Antiquities
Petroglyphs
Tennessee—Antiquities
'Dead Indians out, live Indians in' [museums return artifacts to Indian tribes] B. E. Johansen. il *The Progressive* 53:15-16 D '89
The Holly Oak shell [discussion of December 2, 1988 article, Mammoth fraud exposed] R. Lewin. *Science* 243:151-2 Ja 13 '89
The plunder of the past. G. Cowley. il *Newsweek* 113:58-60 Je 26 '89
Returning bones of contention [Smithsonian agrees to return Indian remains and burial artifacts] J. Elson. il *Time* 134:61 S 25 '89
Skeletons in our museums' closets: Native Americans want their ancestors' bones back. D. J. Preston. il *Harper's* 278:66-70+ F '89
Skeletons in the attic [Indian remains in museums] C. Spotted Elk. il *Scholastic Update (Teachers' edition)* 121:25 My 26 '89
Smithsonian, Indian leaders call a truce. E. Marshall. il *Science* 245:1184-6 S 15 '89
Walter Echo-Hawk fights for his people's right to rest in peace—not in museums. M. Brower. il pors *People Weekly* 32:42-4 S 4 '89
Art
See also
Eskimos—Art
Indian Market (Santa Fe, N.M.)
Petroglyphs
Thomas Gilcrease Institute of American History and Art
Weave like a Navajo, make jewelry like a Hopi [workshops in Indian arts] il *Sunset (Central West edition)* 182:22-4 Mr '89
Collectors and collecting
Honoring their Cherokee heritage [Kay and Ron Hendricks' log house in north Georgia] C. Engle. il *Southern Living* 24:90-2 O '89
Spirits in the gallery [work of native Canadians] P. Young. il *Maclean's* 102:78+ N 13 '89
Uncovered artifacts. L. Cottingham. il *Harper's Bazaar* 122:14+ Jl '89
Exhibitions
Haidas on the Seine [work of B. Reid featured at Paris exhibition] N. Jennings. il por *Maclean's* 102:67-8 O 16 '89
Indian art in Denver . . . the best work of 300 tribes. il *Sunset (Central West edition)* 182:54+ F '89
Minnesota's 'Way to independence' [Memories of a Hidatsa Indian family, 1840-1920] E. Chappell. *The Nation* 249:763-6 D 18 '89
Tribal rights [handling of Canadian Indian artifacts in museums] S. Jennings. il *Art News* 88:70-1 N '89
Astronomy
See Astronomy, Indian (American)
Baskets, Miniature
By hands so deft [miniature Apache baskets by T. Moonwalker] H. H. Stockel. il por *Americana* 17:64-7 Jl/Ag '89
Children
See also
Indian Child Welfare Act of 1978
Claims
See also
Indians of North America—Land tenure
Dances
See also
American Indian Dance Theatre
Education
Cooperative learning and the Native American student. L. Little Soldier. bibl f il *Phi Delta Kappan* 71:161-3 O '89

INDIANS OF NORTH AMERICA—Education—*cont.*

A Native American CDA: my personal story [Child Development Associate] J. Loretto. il pors *Children Today* 18:26-7 Mr/Ap '89

Storytelling and Native American CDAs [Child Development Associate credential] C. D. Beers. il *Children Today* 18:24-5 Mr/Ap '89

Fishing

Mississippi of the North [protests over Chippewa fishing rights in Wisconsin] D. Parmentier. il por *The Humanist* 49:17-19+ S/O '89

Spearing fish, playing 'chicken' [confrontation over Chippewa Indian fishing rights in Wisconsin] J. Oberly. il *The Nation* 248:844-5+ Je 19 '89

The Wisconsin fishing war [spearfishing by Chippewa Indians] il *Sports Illustrated* 70:16 My 15 '89

Food

A grasshopper in every pot. D. B. Madsen. il *Natural History* p22+ Jl '89

Government relations

See also

Indians of North America—Land tenure

Indians of North America—Reservations

United States. Bureau of Indian Affairs

Bad day at Window Rock [Navajo leader P. MacDonald] S. D. Atchison. il por *Business Week* p32 Mr 6 '89

Casting a long shadow [Navajo leader P. MacDonald under investigation for 1987 land deal] J. N. Baker. por *Newsweek* 113:32 Ja 2 '89

In search of pride [contrasting Indians of Canada and the United States] B. Came. il *Maclean's* 102:40-1 Jl 3 '89

Letting down the tribe [scandal surrounding P. MacDonald, former chairman of the Navajo nation] J. V. Lamar, Jr. il por *Time* 133:30 Mr 6 '89

The new North [native political power in Northwest Territories] J. Howse. il *Maclean's* 102:55 My 1 '89

The new racism is the old power grab [cover story] W. B. Allen. il por *Conservative Digest* 15:16-21 Jl/Ag '89

Showdown at Window Rock [scandal surrounding P. MacDonald; cover story] S. Tolan. il pors *The New York Times Magazine* p28-31+ N 26 '89

Tribal enterprise. D. Cohen. il *The Atlantic* 264:32-4+ O '89

History

A case of misguided good intentions: American Indian policy. K. O'Reilly. il *USA Today (Periodical)* 117:91-3 Ja '89

Tale of tears. D. O. Relin. il *Scholastic Update (Teachers' edition)* 121:17-20 My 26 '89

Tribal rights: who's in charge? S. Manning. il *Scholastic Update (Teachers' edition)* 121:11-12 My 26 '89

History

Pow wow! R. Garon. il *Scholastic Update (Teachers' edition)* 121:4 My 26 '89

Hospital care

Medicine man [elderly Navajo man treated for hypothermia] T. Dajer. il *Discover* 10:47-8+ Jl '89

Hunting

Beating the drum for caribou [Gwich'in people bordering Arctic National Wildlife Refuge oppose oil development] M. Peale. il *Sierra* 74:32+ My/Je '89

Drift like smoke [learning to hunt] W. L. Prothero. il *Field & Stream* 93:66-7 Ap '89

Imprisonment

Choctaw with a mission [activist B. Carnes in Oklahoma] G. S. Phillips. il por *The Progressive* 53:14-15 Jl '89

Industries

See also

Cook Inlet Communications Inc.

Fort Mojave Telecommunications, Inc.

Gila River Telecommunications, Inc.

Indian blankets, rugs, etc. (American)

Bingo! Are Indian tribes hitting the jackpot? S. D. Atchison. il *Business Week* p115 Ap 24 '89

Comeback in Indian country. R. Fitzgerald. *Reader's Digest* 135:29-30+ O '89

Gambling and guns [St. Regis reserve] M. Clark. il *Maclean's* 102:21+ S 18 '89

Tribal enterprise. D. Cohen. il *The Atlantic* 264:32-4+ O '89

Influence on nature

Indian cultures provide ecological wisdom and prophesies. R. Hill and J. Mohawk. *Utne Reader* p91 N/D '89

Land tenure

The 112-year war [Teme-Augama Anishnabai Indians resume blockade of logging road in Ontario's Temagami Wilderness] R. Corelli. il *Maclean's* 102:76-7 O 30 '89

Church leaders support native claim [Lummi Indians vs. development of Madrona Point, Orcas Island, Wash.] J. Magnuson. *The Christian Century* 106:276-7 Mr 15 '89

Disputed land [Black Hills] J. Naughton. il *Scholastic Update (Teachers' edition)* 121:8-10 My 26 '89

Legal status, laws, etc.

See Indians of North America—Government relations

Legends

"But you promised" [legend recounted for youths tempted by drugs] I. E. Cody. il *Reader's Digest* 134:130-1 Je '89

Medicine

The dance of healing [views of C. A. Hammerschlag] C. Perlmutter. *Prevention (Emmaus, Pa.)* 41:69-72 S '89

Mortuary customs

Who owns our past? [pillage of Indian artifacts on Slack Farm excavation site, Ky.] H. Arden. il map *National Geographic* 175:376-93 Mr '89

Museums

See also

Indian Pueblo Cultural Center (Albuquerque, N.M.)

National Museum of the American Indian (U.S.)

Photographs and photography

The vanishing race. il *American History Illustrated* 24:56-7 S/O '89

Religion and mythology

See also

Native American Church of North America

Peyotism

Church leaders support native claim [Lummi Indians vs. development of Madrona Point, Orcas Island, Wash.] J. Magnuson. *The Christian Century* 106:276-7 Mr 15 '89

The lost nations. J. E. Maracle. il *Christianity Today* 33:34-7 Mr 3 '89

Selling Native American soul [cover story] J. Magnuson. il *The Christian Century* 106:1084-7 N 22 '89

Shamans or charlatans? M. Specktor. il *Utne Reader* p15+ Jl/Ag '89

Walking the red road. D. O. Relin. il *Scholastic Update (Teachers' edition)* 121:23-4 My 26 '89

Reservations

See also

Mille Lacs Indian Reservation (Minn.)

Navajo Indian Reservation

Saint Regis Akwesasne Indian Reserve

Wind River Reservation (Wyo.)

Native ground: where America's Indians live. P. M. Jones. il map *Scholastic Update (Teachers' edition)* 121:6-7 My 26 '89

Environmental aspects

The lands the feds forgot. M. Ambler. il *Sierra* 74:44-6+ My/Je '89

Rites and ceremonies

See also

Peyotism

Schools

See Indians of North America—Education

Social conditions

See also

Indians of North America—Reservations

Native Americans: in search of an identity [cover story; special issue] il map *Scholastic Update (Teachers' edition)* 121:2-12+ My 26 '89

Tiospaye Teca: working with young Native American families in the Dakotas [problems associated with teenage pregnancy] A. Floden. il *Children Today* 18:28-32 S/O '89

Suicide

See Suicide

Treatment

Native Americans: in search of an identity [cover story; special issue] il map *Scholastic Update (Teachers' edition)* 121:2-12+ My 26 '89

Women

America's Founding Mothers: our Native American roots [excerpt from The sacred hoop] P. G. Allen. il *Utne Reader* p108-9 Mr/Ap '89

Alaska

See also

Gwich'in Indians

A tale of two villages [natives bordering Arctic National Wildlife Refuge hold opposing viewpoints on oil development] E. Linden. il *Time* 133:62 Ap 17 '89

Canada

See also

Cree Indians

Gwich'in Indians

Teme-Augama Anishnabai Indians

A death in Winnipeg [policeman R. Cross testifies on role in shooting death of native leader J. J. Harper] P. Kaihla. il por *Maclean's* 102:16 S 11 '89

A final act of despair [suicide of K. Dowson, Winnipeg police inspector involved in investigation into shooting death of native J. J. Harper] B. Bergman. *Maclean's* 102:22 N 13 '89

In search of pride [contrasting Indians of Canada and the United States] B. Came. il *Maclean's* 102:40-1 Jl 3 '89

The new North [native political power in Northwest Territories] J. Howse. il *Maclean's* 102:55 My 1 '89

Tribal rights [handling of Canadian Indian artifacts in museums] S. Jennings. il *Art News* 88:70-1 N '89

An unfolding tragedy [suicide of Winnipeg, Man. police inspector K. Dowson disrupts inquiry into shooting death of native leader J. J. Harper] P. Kopvillem. il por *Maclean's* 102:23 O 2 '89

INDIANS OF NORTH AMERICA IN ART *See* Indians (American) in art

INDIANS OF NORTH AMERICA IN MOTION PICTURES
See Indians (American) in motion pictures
INDIANS OF SOUTH AMERICA
   See also
      American Museum of Natural History. Hall of South
         American Peoples
      Yanoama Indians
                    Agriculture
Corn and culture in central Andean prehistory. S. Johannessen
   and C. A. Hastorf. bibl f il *Science* 244:690-2 My 12
   '89
                    Antiquities
   See also
      Chile—Antiquities
      Peru—Antiquities
                    Languages
   See also
      Guarani language
                 Religion and mythology
Dark side of the shaman [Aguaruna Indians of Peru] M.
   F. Brown. *Natural History* p8+ N '89
                    Bolivia
Debt deal stacked against Indians [debt for nature swap]
   M. Collett. *The Progressive* 53:17-18 Ag '89
                    Brazil
   See also
      Cayapo Indians
      Marajoara culture
Space age shamans: the videotape [recording tribal customs
   of Brazilian Indians on videotape] G. Smith. il *Américas*
   41 no2:28-31 '89
                    Chile
   See also
      Chile—Antiquities
Skepticism fades over pre-Clovis man [Tom Dillehay's Monte
   Verde excavations] R. Lewin. *Science* 244:1140 Je 9 '89
                    Peru
   See also
      Aguaruna Indians
      Chavín culture
      Matses Indians
      Moche Indians
      Peru—Antiquities
Long before the Inca. R. L. Burger. il map *Natural History*
   p66-73 F '89
                    Suriname
   See also
      Tirió Indians
INDIANS OF SOUTH AMERICA IN VIDEOTAPES *See*
   Indians (American) in videotapes
INDICATORS, ECONOMIC *See* Economic indicators
INDIGNATION
Indignation on demand [politicians' use of indignation] M.
   Greenfield. il *Newsweek* 114:78 Jl 10 '89
INDIGO (FIRM)
Tracking trends in the city, bringing them to the suburbs.
   D. Weil. il por *Working Woman* 14:62 Ag '89
INDIGO GIRLS (MUSICAL GROUP)
The Indigo Girls' mood isn't blue; they've got a new album
   and their very own tour. il *People Weekly* 32:63 Jl 24
   '89
Indigo Girls: two for the road. M. McCormick. il *Rolling
   Stone* p24 S 21 '89
INDIVIDUAL AND STATE
Individual rights, community claims. J. M. Wall. *The Christian
   Century* 106:707-8 Ag 2-9 '89
INDIVIDUAL DIFFERENCES
   See also
      Sex differences
Appreciating individual differences [nutrition] B. T. Hunter.
   il *Consumers' Research Magazine* 72:8-9 D '89
"Mommy, why is she different?" [answers to sensitive ques-
   tions children ask] L. Derman-Sparks and others. il *Parents*
   64:120-3 D '89
INDIVIDUAL LIBERTY *See* Liberty
INDIVIDUAL RETIREMENT ACCOUNTS
Are IRA's a hazard to your old age? *Newsweek* 114:42 S
   18 '89
Bring back the IRA. B. Kobliner. il *Money* 18:68-9 N '89
The guy who helped invent the IRA tells you how to make
   money in one now [views of R. Murray] J. Edgerton.
   il por *Money* 18:195-6 O '89
How Congress is peddling IRA snake oil. L. Wiener. il
   U.S. News & World Report 107:79 O 9 '89
IRA-II. M. S. Forbes, Jr. il *Forbes* 144:29 S 4 '89
IRAs: calculating your withdrawals. E. M. Abramson. il
   Modern Maturity 32:79-80 Ag/S '89
Moving your IRA, SEP or Keogh into a new home. M.
   Meyer. il *Money* 18:59-60 Ap '89
The nondeductible IRA form. il *Money* 18:96 Ja '89
Nondeductible IRAs can be valuable. G. W. Padwe. il *Nation's
   Business* 77:68 Ag '89
Room at the trough [expansion of program] C. Byron. il
   New York 22:24-5 O 16 '89
Second thoughts about IRAs. H. Banks. *Forbes* 143:33 Ja
   23 '89
Tapping an IRA without penalty. M. A. Leuchter. il *Money*
   18:112+ Jl '89

Tapping retirement savings now [penalty-free withdrawals]
   L. Wiener. il *U.S. News & World Report* 107:80 O 30
   '89
Why George Bush wants to bring IRAs back [cover story]
   H. Banks. il *Forbes* 144:68-71 Ag 21 '89
Your IRA: 9% bank CDs are the deals to beat. il *Money*
   18:36 F '89
INDIVIDUALISM
   See also
      Conformity
      Individual and state
Habits of the hearth [interview with R. Bellah] R. Clapp.
   il pors *Christianity Today* 33:20-4 F 3 '89
INDIVIDUALITY
   See also
      Personality
      Self
The horn of Triton. S. J. Gould. il *Natural History* p18+
   D '89
The risk of being different [address, May 14, 1989] S.
   Schanberg. *Vital Speeches of the Day* 55:700-2 S 1 '89
INDO-EUROPEAN LANGUAGES
The origins of Indo-European languages. C. Renfrew. bibl
   il maps *Scientific American* 261:106-14 O '89
INDOCHINA
   See also
      Cambodia
      Indochinese
      Laos
      Vietnam

                 Foreign relations
                    United States
   See United States—Foreign relations—Indochina
INDOCHINESE
                    United States
                    Psychiatric care
Culture crash. J. Krich. il *Mother Jones* 14:24-7+ O '89
INDOCHINESE REFUGEES *See* Refugees, Indochinese
INDOCTRINATION
   See also
      Brainwashing
INDOLES
To stymie cancer, eat broccoli raw [study by Lloyd D.
   Campbell and Bogdan A. Slominski] *Science News* 136:351
   N 25 '89
INDONESIA
   See also
      Bali (Indonesia)
      Birth control—Indonesia
      East Timor (Indonesia)
      Jakarta (Indonesia)
      Ocean thermal power plants—Indonesia
                 Description and travel
Indonesia. A. Zich. il map *National Geographic* 175:96-127
   Ja '89
                 Native peoples
   See also
      Minangkabau (Indonesian people)
                Photographs and photography
Don't let bad camera karma get in the way of exciting
   pictures. L. Dennis. il *Popular Photography* 96:20+ Jl '89
                 Territorial expansion
Visiting a forgotten war [Pope John Paul II] R. Nordland.
   il map *Newsweek* 114:38 O 23 '89
INDOOR AIR POLLUTION
   See also
      Radon pollution
      Sick building syndrome
Are you home sick? [with editorial comment] D. Schoonmaker.
   bibl il *The Mother Earth News* 116:8, 90+ Mr/Ap '89
The enemy within. A. L. Huebner. il *Women's Sports &
   Fitness* 11:12 Je '89
The fresh air contest [backdraft problems] D. Johnson. il
   The Family Handyman 39:10+ S '89
Greenery filters out indoor air pollution. J. Raloff. *Science
   News* 136:212 S 30 '89
Hazardous gas strikes hockey rink [excess nitrogen dioxide
   exposure from malfunctioning ice resurfacer; research by
   Katrina Hedberg and Kristina L. MacDonald] *Science News*
   136:396 D 16 '89
The hidden menace: indoor pollution. S. Ridley. il *USA
   Today (Periodical)* 118:44-6 S '89
Hog farmers clear the air. C. Tevis. il *Successful Farming*
   87:54-5 D '89
How healthy is your home? Ways to eliminate indoor
   pollution. C. Reuben. il *Utne Reader* p76-9 My/Je '89
Ozone: indoors may offer little protection [research by Charles
   J. Weschler] J. Raloff. il *Science News* 136:198 S 23 '89
Pollution-free housing. J. Bower. bibl il *The Mother Earth
   News* 116:98-100 Mr/Ap '89
Pollution indoors. D. Grossman. il *Technology Review*
   92:13-14 My/Je '89
Toxic gases can penetrate concrete blocks [research by Karina
   Garbesi and Richard G. Sextro] J. Raloff. *Science News*
   136:391 D 16 '89
                 Developing countries
Air pollution. K. R. Smith. bibl f il *Environment* 30:16-20+
   D '88

INDOOR AIR POLLUTION—Developing countries—*cont.*
Air pollution [discussion of December 1988 article] K. R. Smith. il *Environment* 31:2-3 My '89

INDOOR GARDENS AND GARDENING
See also
Artificial light gardening
Greenhouses
House plants
Growing basil indoors. C. Shirley. il *Organic Gardening* 36:26-7 O '89
Indoor gardening. C. Siler. il *Parents* 64:247+ O '89

INDOOR ROCK CLIMBING See Mountaineering
INDOOR WAR GAMES See War games
INDUCTANCE METERS See Electric meters
INDUSTRIAL ACCIDENTS
See also
Bhopal poisonous gas disaster, India, 1984
Insurance, Workers' compensation
Mills—Accidents and explosions
Motion picture production and direction—Accidents
Nuclear facilities—Accidents and explosions
Nuclear power plants—Accidents and explosions
Television production and direction—Accidents
Boom time injuries [research by James Robinson] V. Bozzi. il *Psychology Today* 22:18 D '88
Prevention
See Occupational health and safety

INDUSTRIAL ARTS
See also
Engineering
Mills
Our human heritage as makers and builders [address, April 11, 1989] R. Kanigel. *Vital Speeches of the Day* 55:681-3 S 1 '89

INDUSTRIAL BUILDINGS
See also
Factories

INDUSTRIAL CAPACITY
Capital spending isn't growing where it counts. G. Koretz. il *Business Week* p23 Je 26 '89
Keeping the cow, selling the milk [Air Products' ten year plan contrasted with Federal Reserve anxiety about tight industrial capacity] H. Banks. il por *Forbes* 143:40-1 Mr 20 '89
Lean times loom on the factory floor [capital spending cutbacks] M. W. Karmin. il *U.S. News & World Report* 107:72 N 20 '89

INDUSTRIAL DEMOCRACY See Participative management
INDUSTRIAL DESIGN See Design, Industrial
INDUSTRIAL DISCIPLINE See Labor discipline
INDUSTRIAL DISEASES See Occupational health and safety
INDUSTRIAL DIVERSIFICATION See Diversification in industry
INDUSTRIAL EDUCATION See Vocational-technical education
INDUSTRIAL ENTERTAINING See Business entertaining
INDUSTRIAL EQUIPMENT INDUSTRY
See also
Commercial Intertech Corp.
Emhart Corp.
Harnischfeger Industries, Inc.
Houdaille Industries, Inc.
Lawson Products, Inc.
Machine tool industry
Machinery industry
Petroleum equipment industry
Export-import trade
Are U.S. companies dangerously addicted to foreign equipment? G. Koretz. il *Business Week* p22 Mr 27 '89
Finance
Heavy equipment. J. H. Taylor. il *Forbes* 143:156-7 Ja 9 '89
Securities
Why capital goods stocks look strong for 1989—and beyond. A. E. Serwer. il *Fortune* 119:25-6 Ja 16 '89

INDUSTRIAL EQUIPMENT LEASES
Boxcars and jets are investment vehicles, too. S. Woolley. *Business Week* p108 Ja 16 '89
A limited partnership that's frankly a gamble [options on lease residuals] L. Zinn. *Business Week* p170 O 30 '89

INDUSTRIAL ESPIONAGE See Business intelligence
INDUSTRIAL ETHICS See Business ethics
INDUSTRIAL EXPANSION See Business expansion
INDUSTRIAL FEEDING
See also
Executive dining rooms
INDUSTRIAL FILMS See Motion pictures in industry
INDUSTRIAL FORECASTING See Business forecasting
INDUSTRIAL GLASSWARE
Photographs and photography
Dark-field illumination. K. Collavo. il *Petersen's Photographic Magazine* 18:88-9 My '89
INDUSTRIAL INNOVATIONS See Technological innovations
INDUSTRIAL LAWS AND REGULATIONS
See also
Labor laws and regulations

INDUSTRIAL LIGHT AND MAGIC (STUDIO)
The bloodstream express [special effects in film to be part of Body Wars exhibit at EPCOT] B. Weber. il *The New York Times Magazine* p142 Je 11 '89
Great new Indy Jones special effects. il *Popular Mechanics* 166:18 Jl '89

INDUSTRIAL LOCATION See Location in business and industry
INDUSTRIAL MANAGEMENT See Business management
INDUSTRIAL MICROBIOLOGY
See also
Fermentation
Cell "factories" churn out goods [research by James M. Lee and Bernard J. Van Wie] il *USA Today (Periodical)* 117:11-12 Je '89
Genetic engineering of bacteria from managed and natural habitats. S. E. Lindow and others. bibl f *Science* 244:1300-7 Je 16 '89
In search of the plastic potato [biopolymer engineering] R. Pool. il *Science* 245:1187-9 S 15 '89
The little bugs that dig for gold [use of Thiobacillus in bioleaching] W. J. Cook. il *U.S. News & World Report* 106:62 Ap 17 '89
Microbes to the rescue! S. Begley. il *Newsweek* 113:56-7 Je 19 '89
Patient, heal thyself—with lab-grown cells. N. J. Freundlich. il *Business Week* p148+ Mr 20 '89

INDUSTRIAL MUSEUMS
See also
Youngstown Historical Center of Industry and Labor
INDUSTRIAL PHOTOGRAPHY
See also
Factories—Photographs and photography
Exhibitions
Belief [America worked: the 1950s photographs of Dan Weiner at the Museum of Modern Art] I. Sischy. *The New Yorker* 65:79-82 My 22 '89

INDUSTRIAL POISONS See Poisons and poisoning, Industrial
INDUSTRIAL POLICY See Industry and state
INDUSTRIAL PRODUCTIVITY See Productivity, Industrial
INDUSTRIAL PSYCHOLOGY See Psychology, Industrial
INDUSTRIAL RELATIONS
See also
Church and labor
Collective bargaining
Collective labor agreements
Communication in management
Employee ownership
Featherbedding (Industrial relations)
Labor union busting
Layoffs
Participative management
Productivity, Industrial
Strikes
Team work in industry
United States—Labor policy
Collective bargaining and labor-management relations, 1988. G. Ruben. *Monthly Labor Review* 112:25-39 Ja '89
Developments in industrial relations. G. Ruben. See issues of Monthly Labor Review
Industrial America's suicide pact. P. Keisling. *The Washington Monthly* 21:59-60 F '89
Keeping U.S. business competitive: employers' rights vs. the unions'. T. W. Thee and W. J. Peterson. il *USA Today (Periodical)* 118:38-40 Jl '89
Needed: a replacement for the bargaining table. J. P. Hoerr. il *Business Week* p38-9 Ja 9 '89
The password is 'flexible'. il *Business Week* p152+ S 25 '89
History
Cyrus S. Ching: pioneer in industrial peacemaking. A. H. Raskin. il *Monthly Labor Review* 112:22-35 Ag '89
A look back at "Boulwarism". P. Brimelow. il pors *Forbes* 143:246+ My 29 '89
America
See also
Industrial Relations Congress of the Americas
INDUSTRIAL RELATIONS CONGRESS OF THE AMERICAS
First Industrial Relations Congress of the Americas. H. P. Guzda. *Monthly Labor Review* 112:50-1 My '89
INDUSTRIAL RESEARCH
See also
AT&T Bell Labs
Aviation research
Bell Communications Research, Inc.
David Sarnoff Research Center
Electronics research
Genetic research industry
Inventions
Products, New
Research parks
Technological innovations
Astrophysicist Arno Penzias on making R&D pay off [interview] E. Warner. il por *High Technology Business* 9:24-7 Jl/Ag '89
Inaction on technology programs stirs Congress. C. Norman. *Science* 244:137-8 Ap 14 '89

INDUSTRIAL RESEARCH—*cont.*

Innovation in America [with editorial comment by Stephen B. Shepard] il *Business Week* Special Issue:8-9, 12-18+ Je 16 '89

Technology transfer [research consortiums] E. Corcoran. *Scientific American* 260:98+ My '89

Federal aid

Competitive climate: industry leaders look to the government for a new era. E. Corcoran. il *Scientific American* 260:70+ Mr '89

Washington Inc.? J. Carey. il *Business Week* Special Issue:40-1 Je 16 '89

Finance

Business talks a better R&D game than it plays. G. Koretz. il *Business Week* p20 Ag 21 '89

Do takeovers make managers myopic? [impact on R&D spending] S. Nasar. il *U.S. News & World Report* 107:59 D 4 '89

Financing innovation. C. Farrell. il *Business Week* Special Issue:154-7+ Je 16 '89

Progress isn't drowning in debt—yet [impact of leveraged buyouts and merger mania on R&D] K. Deveny. il *Business Week* Special Issue:110 Je 16 '89

R&D suffers after corporate raids [National Science Foundation survey] M. Crawford. *Science* 243:882 F 17 '89

What LBOs really do to R&D spending. A. Ramirez. il *Fortune* 119:98 Mr 13 '89

Statistics

How R&D spending pays off [R&D scoreboard] il *Business Week* Special Issue:176-81+ Je 16 '89

Management

Wake-up strategies for tired R&D projects. M. Mandell and B. Murphy. il *High Technology Business* 9:22-5 F '89

Where the jobs are. C. A. Gustin. il *High Technology Business* 9:48 S/O '89

Taxation

Fate of R&D tax credit uncertain. M. Crawford. *Science* 243:1659 Mr 31 '89

R&E deductions. M. E. Battersby. il *High Technology Business* 9:14-15 F '89

Canada

See also

Canadian Manufacturing Advanced Technology Exchange

Israel

R&D bounty from Israel. M. Mandell. il *High Technology Business* 9:24-7 Ap '89

Japan

Playing catch-up across the Pacific. M. Tharp. il *U.S. News & World Report* 107:44-5 Jl 10 '89

A wave of ideas, drop by drop. N. Gross. il *Business Week* Special Issue:22+ Je 16 '89

United States

See Industrial research

Western Europe

Adding hustle to Europe's muscle. T. Peterson. il *Business Week* Special Issue:32+ Je 16 '89

INDUSTRIAL REVOLUTION

Great Britain

Business as usual? London and the industrial revolution. T. Barker. bibl il *History Today* 39:45-51 F '89

A tale of two revolutions. O. Scott. il *Conservative Digest* 15:48-51 S/O '89

United States

Samuel Slater: father of the American Industrial Revolution. J. Gustaitis. por *American History Illustrated* 24:32-3 My '89

When our ancestors became us. J. S. Gordon. il *American Heritage* 40:106-11+ D '89

INDUSTRIAL ROBOTS *See* Robots—Industrial use

INDUSTRIAL SAFETY *See* Occupational health and safety

INDUSTRIAL SECRETS *See* Trade secrets

INDUSTRIAL SECURITY MEASURES *See* Industry—Security measures

INDUSTRIAL SUPPLIERS

Contracts [special section] il *Black Enterprise* 19:154-6+ F '89

The front lines of quality [firms scrutinizing vendors] A. Gabor. il *U.S. News & World Report* 107:57-9 N 27 '89

Shaping up your suppliers. J. Dreyfuss. il *Fortune* 119:116+ Ap 10 '89

INDUSTRIAL TOMOGRAPHY *See* Tomography—Industrial use

INDUSTRIAL TOURS

See also

Brewery tours

Batter up for a baseball factory tour [Worth Inc.] il *Southern Living* 24:34 N '89

Factory tours beyond heavy metal. J. Popkin. il *U.S. News & World Report* 107:74-5 S 18 '89

Good to the last drop [Maxwell House factory in Hoboken, N.J.] *The New Yorker* 65:44-5 N 20 '89

INDUSTRIAL WASTE *See* Trade waste

INDUSTRIAL WASTE DISPOSAL *See* Trade waste—Disposal

INDUSTRIEGEWERKSCHAFT METALL *See* IG Metall

INDUSTRY

See also

Big business

Computers—Industrial use

Corporations

Home labor

Location in business and industry

Productivity, Industrial

Science and industry

Small business

Standardization

Ultrasonic waves—Industrial use

See also subhead Industries under names of countries, states, cities, etc.

Elderly services programs

Big business and the granny track. J. P. Shapiro. *U.S. News & World Report* 107:92 Ag 28-S 4 '89

Energy usage

Improving the efficiency of electricity use in manufacturing. M. H. Ross. bibl f il *Science* 244:311-17 Ap 21 '89

History

See also

Industrial revolution

Location

See Location in business and industry

Physical fitness programs

No rush to corporate wellness. il *Fortune* 120:64 S 25 '89

Wellness at work. M. Roberts and T. G. Harris. il *Psychology Today* 23:54-6+ My '89

'Wellness' plans: an ounce of prevention. J. Schwartz. il *Newsweek* 113:51 Ja 30 '89

Wellness works for small firms. H. Rothman. il *Nation's Business* 77:42+ D '89

Prenatal care programs

Spend a dollar, save $3.50—and a baby's life. P. Kruger. *Working Woman* 14:55-6 Je '89

Recreation programs

Take that! B. Rhoden. il *Black Enterprise* 19:330-2 Je '89

Security measures

The new lions who guard the gates [security firms specializing in labor disputes] il *U.S. News & World Report* 107:46 Jl 24 '89

INDUSTRY AND ART *See* Art and industry

INDUSTRY AND CONVICT LABOR *See* Convict labor

INDUSTRY AND DAY CARE *See* Day care and industry

INDUSTRY AND EDUCATION *See* Business and education

INDUSTRY AND STATE

See also

Aerospace industries—Federal aid

Architectural firms—Federal aid

Black business enterprises—Federal aid

Business—Political aspects

Chemicals—Laws and regulations

Contracts, Government

Corporations—Acquisitions and mergers—Laws and regulations

Economic conversion

Electric utilities—Laws and regulations

Factories—Shutdowns—Laws and regulations

Free enterprise

Government corporations

Industrial research—Federal aid

Insurance law

Labor laws and regulations

Lumber industry—Federal aid

Military-industrial complex

Pesticides—Laws and regulations

President's Task Force on Competitiveness

Privatization

Public utilities—Laws and regulations

Railroads and state

Regulatory agencies

Small business—Laws and regulations

Strip mining—Laws and regulations

Transportation—Laws and regulations

U.S. Consumer Product Safety Commission

United States—Labor policy

United States. Federal Trade Commission

United States. Occupational Safety and Health Administration

United States. Small Business Administration

Agenda for change. O. Port. il *Business Week* Special Issue:170-3 Je 16 '89

American free enterprise: shakeups or shakedowns? *America* 161:287-8 N 4 '89

America's economic security [address, May 8, 1989] R. Mosbacher. *Vital Speeches of the Day* 55:554-6 Jl 1 '89

Brady's long-term plans will collide with the deficit [N. Brady's competitiveness policy] H. Gleckman. por *Business Week* p33 Ja 23 '89

Bush goes long. H. Gleckman. il *Business Week* p26-7 F 13 '89

A business guide to Bush country. A. R. Dowd. il *Fortune* 120:93-4+ Jl 17 '89

Congressional alert. See issues of Nation's Business

Corporate safety net. il *The Progressive* 53:8 N '89

Corporatism ousts Reaganomics. I. M. Stelzer. il *The American Spectator* 22:31-4 My '89

Dateline: Washington. See issues of Nation's Business beginning September 1989

INDUSTRY AND STATE—*cont.*

A delicate balance [subsidies under Canada-U.S. free trade agreement; interview with A. Halliday] T. Fennell. por *Maclean's* 102:49 D 18 '89

Deregulation or reregulation? [views of Daniel Spulber] *USA Today (Periodical)* 118:9 Ag '89

Developing healthy state economies: innovation, vision, and strategy. W. S. Edgerly. *USA Today (Periodical)* 118:18-19 S '89

Facing reality in the George Bush era. M. L. Weidenbaum. *Society* 26:25-8 Mr/Ap '89

Filling the deregulatory vacuum [state attorneys general; cover story] M. J. Green. il *The Nation* 249:441+ O 23 '89

Harnessing the American marketplace [special section] bibl *Society* 27:41-71 N/D '89

Holding pep rallies for 1992 [states help U.S. firms with export strategy for Western Europe] J. McCormick. il *Newsweek* 114:60 N 6 '89

In search of exports: the states' new agenda. P. R. Piccigallo. il *USA Today (Periodical)* 118:20-2 S '89

It's time for an American *perestroika*. G. C. Lodge. il *The Atlantic* 263:35-6 Ap '89

Killer regulations. E. Rubenstein. *National Review* 41:20 N 24 '89

Lost horizons [cover story] L. H. Summers. *The New Republic* 200:11-13 Je 26 '89

Manufacturing [address, April 6, 1989] C. H. Chandler. *Vital Speeches of the Day* 55:461-4 My 15 '89

Members only. R. B. Reich. *The New Republic* 200:14+ Je 26 '89

Must we become Japanese? [cover story] D. D. Hale. il *National Review* 41:30-2+ O 27 '89

New name; same bad idea. W. T. Brookes. por *Nation's Business* 77:84 S '89

Politics & policy. See issues of Fortune beginning March 5, 1984

Productivity: key to growth. W. T. Brookes. il *Nation's Business* 77:99 N '89

The quiet crusader [Treasury Secretary N. Brady; cover story] H. Gleckman. il pors *Business Week* p80-3+ S 18 '89

Regulation rises again. T. Smart. il *Business Week* p58-9 Je 26 '89

A right turn, but no free ride for business [Supreme Court] P. Dwyer. il *Business Week* p27 Jl 10 '89

Save us from the reregulators. I. M. Stelzer. il *The American Spectator* 22:25-6 F '89

State funds for start-ups. J. C. Szabo. il *Nation's Business* 77:42+ Je '89

States, technology, and jobs. D. M. Brown. il *Technology Review* 92:16-17 My/Je '89

Tailor-made work forces [customized training targeted to individual companies offered in states' development packages] H. Bacas. il *Nation's Business* 77:33-6 N '89

Trained to order [states providing vocational training as lure to new industry] S. B. Weiner and C. Siler. il *Forbes* 143:73+ Je 26 '89

U.S. credibility and viability in worldwide competition [address, May 25, 1989] N. R. Augustine. *Vital Speeches of the Day* 55:693-7 S 1 '89

What is business? [address, March 17, 1989] E. A. Opitz. *Vital Speeches of the Day* 55:497-500 Je 1 '89

Will business get the bill? [business issues and the 101st Congress] D. Harbrecht. il *Business Week* p28-9 Ja 16 '89

The will to take leadership [increasing America's competitiveness; address, March 22, 1989] L. A. Iacocca. *Vital Speeches of the Day* 55:454-8 My 15 '89

History

Men who made the rules [Thomas K. McCraw's Prophets of regulation] P. Baida. il *American Heritage* 40:18+ F '89

International aspects

Private business and public interest [cover story; special section] *Society* 26:25-58 Mr/Ap '89

Argentina

Can business save Argentina? [Bunge & Born's blueprint] J. Ryser and R. A. Kessler. il pors *Business Week* p46-8 S 18 '89

Canada

A delicate balance [subsidies under Canada-U.S. free trade agreement; interview with A. Halliday] T. Fennell. por *Maclean's* 102:49 D 18 '89

France

The chevalier blanc heading the industry ministry [R. Fauroux] F. J. Comes. il por *Business Week* p64 Mr 13 '89

God is a French Socialist. M. Lilla. il *The American Spectator* 22:27-8 My '89

Japan

See also

Japan. Ministry of International Trade and Industry

Must we become Japanese? [cover story] D. D. Hale. il *National Review* 41:30-2+ O 27 '89

Korea (South)

Asia's next giant. A. H. Amsden. il *Technology Review* 92:46-53 My/Je '89

Korea's powerhouses are under siege. L. Nakarmi and R. Neff. il *Business Week* p52+ N 20 '89

Morocco

"My father-in-law is very demanding" [F. Filali] P. Gupte. il por *Forbes* 143:44-5 My 1 '89

United States

See Industry and state

Western Europe

'Subsidy' becomes a dirty word. J. Kapstein. il *Business Week* p48 Je 19 '89

INDUSTRY AND THE ARTS *See* Arts and industry

INDUSTRY AND THE ENVIRONMENT

See also

Automobile factories—Environmental aspects
Chemical plants—Environmental aspects
Coal industry—Environmental aspects
Electric plants—Environmental aspects
Electronic industries—Environmental aspects
Emission reduction credits
Environmental marketing
Fish culture—Environmental aspects
Forest products industry—Environmental aspects
Gas industry—Environmental aspects
Gold mines and mining—Environmental aspects
Mining industry—Environmental aspects
Nuclear power plants—Environmental aspects
Paper mills—Environmental aspects
Petroleum industry—Environmental aspects
Petroleum refineries—Environmental aspects
Pollution control industries
Resorts—Environmental aspects
Tourist trade—Environmental aspects
Trade waste—Disposal
Uranium industry—Environmental aspects
Valdez Principles

Big dividends from pollution cleanup. *Science News* 136:191 S 16 '89

EPA limits industrial benzene emissions. J. Raloff. *Science News* 136:165 S 9 '89

Getting with the cleanup. G. Carroll. il *Newsweek* 114:35 S 25 '89

Good intentions [socially conscious investments] E. Corcoran. *Scientific American* 261:79 O '89

Grime and punishment. *The New Republic* 200:7-8 F 20 '89

Harnessing market forces to protect the environment [Project 88 report; cover story] R. N. Stavins. bibl f il *Environment* 31:4-7+ Ja/F '89

Keeping tabs on toxics [right to know laws] S. J. Parsons. il *Utne Reader* p11-12 Jl/Ag '89

Let the lobbying commence [Congressman T. Bruce's Illinois industrial constituents express displeasure with new Clean Air Act] A. Plattner. il por *U.S. News & World Report* 106:54 Je 12 '89

Pollution prevention. S. K. Friedlander. bibl f il maps *Environment* 31:10-15+ My '89

Protecting the environment. M. L. Weidenbaum. *Society* 27:49-56 N/D '89

Save the trees—and you may save a bundle. C. McAllister. il *Business Week* p118 S 4 '89

Scrub that smokestack. M. D. Lemonick. il *Time* 134:64 D 18 '89

Silver lining for pollution's cloud? *The Futurist* 23:49 N/D '89

Strategies for manufacturing. R. A. Frosch and N. E. Gallopoulos. bibl il *Scientific American* 261:144-52 S '89

Tanker from hell. J. Edgerton. il *Money* 18:66-7 Je '89

Technology and environment. P. H. Abelson. *Science* 246:429 O 27 '89

Canada

See also

Canada. Centre for Sustainable Economic Development

Environment and economy [address, May 17, 1989] T. D'Aquino. *Vital Speeches of the Day* 55:621-4 Ag 1 '89

Soviet Union

The ecology crisis. M. Sieff. il *National Review* 41:28 Ap 7 '89

United States

See Industry and the environment

Western Europe

The greening of Europe's industries. R. Knight. il *U.S. News & World Report* 106:45+ Je 5 '89

What the 'Greens' mean for business. S. Tully. il *Fortune* 120:159+ O 23 '89

INDUSTRY AND WEATHER

When the rivers go dry and the ice caps melt . . . V. Cahan. il *Business Week* p95+ F 13 '89

INERTIAL CONFINEMENT FUSION *See* Laser fusion

INERTIAL GUIDANCE SYSTEMS

Data show guidance system was trying to stabilize SICBM. il *Aviation Week & Space Technology* 130:25 My 22 '89

Judge grants motions filed by Northrop [lawsuit involving production of inertial measurement unit for MX missile] *Aviation Week & Space Technology* 130:74 Ja 9 '89

INF (INTERMEDIATE NUCLEAR FORCE) REDUCTION
See Disarmament
INFALLIBILITY OF THE POPE *See* Popes—Infallibility
INFANCY OF ANIMALS *See* Animals, Infancy of
INFANT CARRIERS, BICYCLE *See* Bicycles—Equipment
INFANT FORMULA
Laws and regulations
Not like mother made [illegal sale of soy milk as infant formula by Eden Foods] *FDA Consumer* 23:30-1 My '89
INFANT FORMULA INDUSTRY
Advertising
Heating up the bottle battle [controversy over TV ads for Carnation and Gerber infant formulas; cover story] F. A. Oski. *The Nation* 249:665+ D 4 '89
International aspects
See also
Nestle SA—Infant formula boycott case
INFANT LEARNING *See* Infants—Growth and development
INFANT MORTALITY
See also
National Commission to Prevent Infant Mortality (U.S.)
Sudden infant death syndrome
Death without weeping [mother love in shantytowns of Brazil] N. Scheper-Hughes. *Natural History* p8+ O '89
Fighting infant mortality [Momma Mobile] C. SerVaas. il *The Saturday Evening Post* 261:94+ O '89
Preventing infant mortality: an investment in the nation's future [study by the National Commission to Prevent Infant Mortality] P. Rowe. il *Children Today* 18:16-20 Ja/F '89
Saving America's babies. A. Hulbert. *The New Republic* 201:19-21 N 13 '89
Three jailed for selling drug that killed 38 babies [premature infants given solution E-Ferol] C. Carey. il *FDA Consumer* 23:33-4 Jl/Ag '89
Why are our babies dying? D. Hurley. *McCall's* 116:104+ Je '89
INFANT PSYCHOLOGY
See also
Parent-child relationship
Play
Baby faces show the right side of emotion. B. Bower. il *Science News* 135:149 Mr 11 '89
Seeking the source of emotions [amygdala research by Nathan A. Fox] *Science News* 136:175 S 9 '89
Smart from the start. K. Levine. il *Parents* 64:104-8 Je '89
Twinkle, twinkle little star: it's more than just a nursery song. M. J. Howle. bibl f il *Children Today* 18:18-22 Jl/Ag '89
INFANTE, FRANCISCO, 1943-
about
Francisco Infante: International Images. H. Schwalb. il *Art News* 88:186 S '89
INFANTE, LOLA
'If hypocrisy could kill'. il *World Press Review* 36:21 Mr '89
INFANTICIDE *See* Murder
INFANTILE PARALYSIS *See* Poliomyelitis
INFANTS
See also
Drugs and infants
Fetus
Play
Birth defects
See Birth defects
Care and hygiene
See also
Infants—Medical care
Infants—Nutrition
"I'm still doing everything" [sharing child care responsibilities] M. D. Rosen. il *Ladies' Home Journal* 106:20+ N '89
The last 3 months of pregnancy/the first 3 months of parenting. J. Yager. bibl *McCall's* 116:49-50+ Ja '89
Pen pals: our babies' first year. P. Abrams and L. Rosenberg. il pors *Parents* 64:90-4+ N '89
Tender touches [baby massage] A. Finkelstein. il *Parents* 64:102-5 D '89
Crying
Baby, calm thyself [views of William Sammons] W. Gallagher. il *American Health* 8:122 Je '89
The meaning of cries. K. Karlsrud and D. Schultz. il *Parents* 64:224 O '89
What's the best way to get a baby to stop crying? M. Mohler and M. D. Rosen. il *Ladies' Home Journal* 106:58 Jl '89
Day care
See Day care
Equipment
See also
Bellini (Firm)
Cribs (Beds)
A pull-along sled for baby. il *Sunset (Central West edition)* 183:29 D '89

Food and feeding
See Infants—Nutrition
Growth and development
See also
Infant psychology
As they grow/birth to 1 year. K. Karlsrud and D. Schultz. See issues of Parents beginning March 1987
Baby see, baby do [influence of television; research by Andrew Meltzoff] J. Folkenberg. *American Health* 8:104 My '89
The hug factor [effect of close relationships upon health and longevity] J. Hooper. il *Health (New York, N.Y.)* 21:72-5 O '89
Smart from the start. K. Levine. il *Parents* 64:104-8 Je '89
Hearing
See Hearing
Medical care
The first physical. K. Karlsrud and D. Schultz. il *Parents* 64:120 Ja '89
When baby has a fever. P. Klass. il *The New York Times Magazine* p57-8 Ag 20 '89
Memory
See Memory
Nutrition
See also
Gerber Products Co.
Infant formula
Infant formula industry
Milk, Human
Natural Food Products (Firm)
Nestle SA—Infant formula boycott case
Bad apples: in the executive suite [Beech-Nut bogus apple juice case] il *Consumer Reports* 54:294-6 My '89
A choice for the littlest consumers [organic baby food] L. Shapiro. il *Newsweek* 113:26 Mr 27 '89
Starting solids. K. Karlsrud and D. Schultz. il *Parents* 64:187 Mr '89
Psychology
See Infant psychology
Sleep
See Sleep
Vision
See Vision
Testing
See Eye—Examination
INFANTS, NEWBORN
See also
Fetus
As they grow/birth to 1 year. K. Karlsrud and D. Schultz. See issues of Parents beginning March 1987
Birth defects
See Birth defects
Diseases
See also
AIDS (Disease) and children
Retinopathy of prematurity
Diagnosis
Testing newborns for cystic fibrosis [measuring immunoreactive trypsinogen; work of Frank J. Accurso] S. Hart and A. McKenzie. *Science News* 136:233 O 7 '89
Hospital care
See also
Hospitals—Maternity care
Miracle baby [I. Roe, born at 23½ weeks at Cedars-Sinai Medical Center] S. M. Halpern. il pors *Ms.* 18:56-60+ S '89
Three jailed for selling drug that killed 38 babies [premature infants given solution E-Ferol] C. Carey. il *FDA Consumer* 23:33-4 Jl/Ag '89
Trouble in the nursery [hospital lights and retinopathy of prematurity] G. Cowley. il *Newsweek* 114:52 Ag 28 '89
Psychology
See Infant psychology
Sleep
See Sleep
Surgery
Should this baby be saved? [performing surgery to correct hypoplastic left heart syndrome] P. Klass. il *Glamour* 87:212-13+ D '89
Weight
See Birth weight
INFANTS, PREMATURE
See also
Retinopathy of prematurity
Different strokes . . . [tactile stimulation of premature infants; research by Tiffany M. Field and Saul M. Schanberg] T. Beardsley. *Scientific American* 261:34+ S '89
The (liquid) breath of life [perfluorocarbon] M. M. Waldrop. il *Science* 245:1043-5 S 8 '89
Hospital care
See Infants, Newborn—Hospital care
Nutrition
Saving premature babies [work of Laura Hillman] il *USA Today (Periodical)* 118:4 O '89
INFANTS AND PARENTS *See* Parent-child relationship
INFANTS IN VIDEOTAPES
Birth of a video star [making baby videos] R. Harris. il *Video* 12:74-7+ Ja '89

INFECTION
   See also
      Animals as carriers of infection
      Chlamydia infections
      Waterborne infection
Drug abuse: gambling with infection [needle use] K. M. Porterfield. il *Current Health 2* 15:17-19 My '89
Ultrasound can fight infection [work of Larry S. Nichter] il *USA Today (Periodical)* 117:16 F '89
INFECTION, EAR *See* Ear—Diseases
INFECTION, RESISTANCE TO *See* Immunity
INFECTIOUS DISEASES *See* Communicable diseases
INFERTILITY
Baby blues, the sequel [secondary infertility] M. Beck. il *Newsweek* 114:62 Jl 3 '89
The baby chase. K. Barrett and R. Greene. il *Ladies' Home Journal* 106:114+ N '89
Coffee and conception [research by Allen Wilcox and others] P. King. *Psychology Today* 23:25 N '89
Coping with infertility. S. Spedalle. *Essence* 19:98+ Mr '89
A cup of infertility? [linked to use of caffeine; research by Allen Wilcox] J. Rivkin. il *American Health* 8:124 Je '89
From infertility to adoption. L. Grossman. il *Parents* 64:96+ Mr '89
The high cost of fighting infertility. P. Godwin. il *Changing Times* 43:73-4+ Mr '89
Infertility: a search for solutions. S. M. Halpern. *Reader's Digest* 135:129-30+ Jl '89
Infertility hype. R. Gustaitis. il *Glamour* 87:76+ Mr '89
Infertility: playing the odds. S. M. Halpern. il *Ms.* 17:146-51+ Ja/F '89
Latest infertility suspect: caffeine. il *Newsweek* 113:60 Ja 23 '89
Medical technology. G. Legwold. il pors *Better Homes and Gardens* 67:44+ My '89
A reluctant education. P. B. Alden. il *The New York Times Magazine* p44+ D 10 '89
She who laughs gas conceives last [research by Gerard Kugel and Carlos Letelier] F. Flam. *Science News* 135:182 Mr 25 '89
She's not having a baby. A. Ralston. il *Gentlemen's Quarterly* 59:281+ S '89
Upwardly motile. J. Poppy. il *Esquire* 111:67+ Je '89
Will the circle be unbroken? [infertility in Costa Rican banana workers through use of pesticide dibromochloropropane] D. Weir and C. Matthiessen. il *Mother Jones* 14:20-7 Je '89
INFERTILITY CLINICS *See* Health facilities
INFIDELITY, MARITAL *See* Adultery
INFINITI (AUTOMOBILE) *See* Automobiles, Foreign
INFINITI DIVISION *See* Nissan Motor Co. Ltd. Infiniti Division
INFLAMMABLE MATERIALS
        Disposal
Disposing of flammables. il *Better Homes and Gardens* 67:77 My '89
INFLAMMATION
   See also
      Anti-inflammatory agents
Mechanics of stimulated neutrophils: cell stiffening induces retention in capillaries. G. S. Worthen and others. bibl f il *Science* 245:183-6 Jl 14 '89
Stiffened cells lodge in lung capillaries [neutrophils; research by G. Scott Worthen and others] S. Hart. *Science News* 136:39 Jl 15 '89
INFLAMMATORY BOWEL DISEASE
   See also
      Colitis
      Ulcerative colitis
The facts about bowel disease. A. Ferrar. *Ladies' Home Journal* 106:195 Mr '89
Inflammatory bowel disease: incurable and difficult to diagnose. B. Rosenstein. il por *USA Today (Periodical)* 117:91-2 Mr '89
INFLATABLE ART
Designstyle: plenty of hot air [oversized inflatable women designed by R. Harries for Rolling Stones' Steel wheels tour] D. L. Umansky. il *Theatre Crafts* 23:20 D '89
INFLATABLE BOATS *See* Boats and boating
INFLATABLE KAYAKS *See* Kayaks and kayaking
INFLATION (FINANCE)
   See also
      Indexation (Economics)
Aberration inflation. A. C. Brown. il *Forbes* 143:228 Ap 17 '89
Afraid of 'commodities shock'? Well, relax. M. J. Mandel. il *Business Week* p90+ Jl 17 '89
Age vs. wage: how baby boomers may cool inflation. G. Koretz. il *Business Week* p26 F 6 '89
Are we too scared of inflation? C. G. Burck. il *Fortune* 119:105-6+ Je 19 '89
Bankers have the classic COLA. G. P. Brockway. il *The New Leader* 72:14-15 Ja 9 '89
Breaking the inflation-recession cycle [address, September 19, 1989] W. L. Hoskins. *Vital Speeches of the Day* 56:158-60 D 15 '89

Can Congress make inflation illegal? M. J. Mandel. il *Business Week* p123 O 16 '89
Caution at the Fed [A. Greenspan; cover story] L. Uchitelle. il pors *The New York Times Magazine* p18-21+ Ja 15 '89
Collision course: Bush and the Fed. M. McNamee and H. Gleckman. il *Business Week* p34-6 F 27 '89
The CPI should measure inflation. Your mileage may vary. P. Wallich and E. Corcoran. il *Scientific American* 261:76-7 Jl '89
Double trouble ahead from inflation and the budget. V. Brownstein. il *Fortune* 119:21-2 Mr 13 '89
The economy must keep its speed down to swerve away from inflation. J. C. Cooper and K. Madigan. il *Business Week* p31-2 My 8 '89
False confidence. A. Bladen. il *Forbes* 143:118 Ja 23 '89
The Fed seems to be wrestling inflation into submission. J. C. Cooper and K. Madigan. il *Business Week* p31-2 Je 5 '89
The Federal Reserve's dilemma: reduce inflation and keep construction growing. P. E. Kidd. il *Architectural Record* 177:37 O '89
Feeling the heat [Fed's attempt to halt inflation trend] J. Greenwald. il *Time* 133:50-1 Mr 6 '89
A fund investor's guide to fighting inflation. M. Meyer and P. Misra. il *Money* 18:39-40 My '89
A glimmer of hope. A. Bladen. il *Forbes* 143:336 Ja 9 '89
Good news ahead on inflation. S. Nasar. il *U.S. News & World Report* 107:74 N 6 '89
A Greenspan recession? M. S. Forbes, Jr. il *Forbes* 143:27 Ap 3 '89
Greenspan vs. inflation. R. E. Norton. il *U.S. News & World Report* 106:45-6 F 27 '89
Greenspan's moment of truth: can he manage a soft landing without skidding into a recession? [cover story] M. McNamee. il pors *Business Week* p58-62+ Jl 31 '89
A growing shortage of workers is raising inflation risks. V. Brownstein. il *Fortune* 119:33-4 Ap 10 '89
Higher labor costs will keep inflation simmering. V. Brownstein. il *Fortune* 120:17-18 O 9 '89
How clear is that rearview mirror? [faulty indicators] E. A. Finn, Jr. il *Forbes* 143:40-1 Ap 3 '89
Inflation: 'clear for takeoff'. D. Pauly. il *Newsweek* 113:40-1 Mr 6 '89
Inflation II: the sequel [possiblity of a recession] R. E. Norton. il *U.S. News & World Report* 106:18-20+ Ap 3 '89
Inflation is lurking—but Greenspan is on the case. J. C. Cooper and K. Madigan. il *Business Week* p27-8 F 6 '89
Inflation may soon raise the white flag. J. C. Cooper and K. Madigan. il *Business Week* p21-2 Jl 3 '89
Inflation returns to farm country. G. Johnston. *Successful Farming* 87:50A Ja '89
Inflation stages a comeback [special section] il *Business Week* p32-5 Ap 3 '89
Is a distant early warning of inflation flashing? J. C. Cooper and K. Madigan. il *Business Week* p21-2 Ja 30 '89
Is inflation getting better or worse? [conflicting signals of the Producer Price Index vs. the Consumer Price Index] D. Pauly. il *Newsweek* 113:44 Ap 3 '89
Is it inflation? Recession? or just spring fever? J. M. Laderman. il *Business Week* p70-1 Ap 10 '89
Is it inflation yet? D. R. Katz. il *Esquire* 112:121-2 S '89
Just take this medicine. M. Cooper. *The Washington Monthly* 21:28+ My '89
The labor market is a lot looser than it looks. R. Kuttner. il *Business Week* p18 Mr 27 '89
Looking back won't tell you where prices are going. K. Pennar. il *Business Week* p37 Mr 13 '89
A maverick's forecast: high inflation and a boom in Texas stocks [F. Rowe] il por *Money* 18:191-2 My '89
Now the inflation battle is inside the Fed [Washington-based Board of Governors vs regional Fed banks] M. McNamee. il *Business Week* p124+ Mr 13 '89
O.K.—now you can really start to worry about inflation. J. C. Cooper and K. Madigan. il *Business Week* p31-2 F 27 '89
The P-star factor [equation for forecasting inflation rates] P. Chisholm. il *Maclean's* 102:28 Je 26 '89
Reaganism with a human face. il *The Progressive* 53:7-8 Ap '89
Right now, an ounce of prevention is all inflation needs. A. S. Blinder. il *Business Week* p22 Mr 20 '89
Second thoughts on soft landings. M. W. Karmin. *U.S. News & World Report* 107:44 Jl 17 '89
Steeper inflation may be settling in for a long stay. J. C. Cooper and K. Madigan. il *Business Week* p29-30 Ap 3 '89
Stop panicking over inflation. P. C. Roberts. *The Washington Monthly* 21:26-30 My '89
There's nothing fickle about the Fed's war on inflation . . . and if rates rise, capital spending will take the biggest hit. G. Koretz. il *Business Week* p22 S 18 '89
The truth about inflation. G. P. Brockway. il *The New Leader* 72:13-14 F 6 '89

INFLATION (FINANCE)—cont.

We have to conquer inflationary pressures to get building moving again. P. E. Kidd. *Architectural Record* 177:45 Je '89

Welcome to the third world, Uncle Sam. A. Bladen. il *Forbes* 143:167 Mr 6 '89

What happened to Jimmy Carter. G. P. Brockway. il *The New Leader* 72:11-13 N 27 '89

What if inflation returns? J. Aldous. bibl il *Society* 26:76-82 S/O '89

Who's really picking up the tab? [leveraged buyouts and inflation] S. Flack. il *Forbes* 144:38-9 O 30 '89

Why inflation gazers are sending up flares [commodity prices] G. Koretz. il *Business Week* p22 F 13 '89

Why is the Fed still trying to kill the expansion? P. C. Roberts. il *Business Week* p20 Je 26 '89

Why stocks get weaker as inflation gets stronger. M. J. Mandel. il *Business Week* p20 Ap 24 '89

Will corporate debt force the Fed to scrap zero inflation? K. Pennar. il *Business Week* p22 O 23 '89

Winning through inflation. M. W. Karmin. *U.S. News & World Report* 106:47 Je 12 '89

Your best ways to beat inflation [special section] il *Money* 18:58-64+ My '89

Your inflation rate. K. McCormally. il *Changing Times* 43:61-3+ Ja '89

Zero inflation. *National Review* 41:12 D 8 '89

International aspects

As central banks put on the brakes, inflation will skid . . . C. Farrell. *Business Week* p34 S 25 '89

The whole world is adding to inflation pressures. M. F. Allyn. il *Fortune* 119:15-16 My 8 '89

Argentina

Abdication in Argentina [R. Alfonsin resigns] J. Contreras. il por *Newsweek* 113:46-7 Je 26 '89

The fall and fall of Argentina. C. Gorman. il *Time* 133:47 Je 12 '89

Canada

Breaking the inflation-recession cycle [address, September 19, 1989] W. L. Hoskins. *Vital Speeches of the Day* 56:158-60 D 15 '89

China

Inflation and economic reform in China. B. Naughton. bibl f *Current History* 88:269-72+ S '89

Germany (West)

The Bundesbank brakes. P. Fuhrman. il *Forbes* 143:56+ Ja 9 '89

Soviet Union

Gorby's two Achilles' heels. M. S. Forbes, Jr. il *Forbes* 144:27 Jl 24 '89

United States

See Inflation (Finance)

Western Europe

In Europe, inflation is no longer distant thunder. B. Riemer. il *Business Week* p54-5 Mr 20 '89

INFLUENCE (PSYCHOLOGY)

See also

Persuasion (Psychology)

INFLUENCE OF LITERATURE *See* Literature, Influence of

INFLUENZA

America's deadly rendezvous with the 'Spanish Lady' [World War I epidemic] J. Fincher. bibl (p147) il *Smithsonian* 19:130-2+ Ja '89

Cold and flu update. J. Alper. *McCall's* 116:81-2+ Ja '89

A doctor's guide to staying well this winter; ed. by Maxine Abrams. A. Conill. il por *Good Housekeeping* 209:100+ N '89

Help! The stuffy nose, watery eyes, aches and pain, chills and fever, sore throat, colds and flu book; ed. by Seth Rolbein. L. Weinstein. il *Good Housekeeping* 208:56+ Ja '89

Here comes the flu—again [risk of pneumococcal pneumonia] il *USA Today (Periodical)* 118:10-11 O '89

Therapy

Mouse study suggests a cure for influenza [research by Hiroshi Maeda] I. Wickelgren. *Science News* 135:325 My 27 '89

Oxygen radicals in influenza-induced pathogenesis and treatment with pyran polymer-conjugated SOD. T. Oda and others. bibl f il *Science* 244:974-6 My 26 '89

Vaccines and vaccination

Flu shots: do you need one? S. J. Ackerman. il *FDA Consumer* 23:8-11 O '89

INFOCOM (FIRM)

Every picture tells a story. P. Scisco. il *Compute!* 11:82 Mr '89

INFORMANTS *See* Informers

INFORMATION *See* Knowledge

INFORMATION, CLASSIFIED *See* Classified information

INFORMATION, COMMUNICATION OF *See* Communication; Telecommunication

INFORMATION, FREEDOM OF *See* Freedom of information

INFORMATION DISPLAY SYSTEMS

See also

Airplanes, Military—Electronic equipment

Liquid crystal displays

Ovonic Imaging Systems Inc.

Plasma display systems

Private Eye (Display system)

Video display terminals

Virtual reality

A complete circuit [character generator] R. Grossblatt. il *Radio-Electronics* 60:28-9+ Jl '89

A custom-character generator [EPROM character sets for LED displays] R. Grossblatt. il *Radio-Electronics* 60:80-2+ Mr '89

High-contrast flat display [Polyvision] il *High Technology Business* 9:7 Je '89

Let's start programming! [EPROM character sets for LED displays] R. Grossblatt. il *Radio-Electronics* 60:72-3+ My '89

The next picture show. G. McComb. il *Video* 13:56-61+ S '89

INFORMATION FORUMS

CSCE Information Forum [statement, April 21, 1989] L. H. Marks. *Department of State Bulletin* 89:86-7 S '89

INFORMATION MANAGEMENT (COMPUTER SCIENCE)

See Database management

INFORMATION PROCESSING, HUMAN *See* Human information processing

INFORMATION SERVICES

See also

Business—Information services

Medicine—Information services

PC-Link (Database)

Resorts—Information services

Rock music—Information services

Telephone information service

Toll-free telephone service

White House Conference on Library and Information Services

Competition in the information industry [address, October 31, 1988] J. W. Simpson. *Vital Speeches of the Day* 55:284-6 F 15 '89

Fees

A question of information policy [proposed fees for Library of Congress and National Library of Medicine] R. C. Atkinson. *Science* 246:33 N 10 '89

INFORMATION SOCIETY

The computer has triggered a paper explosion. M. S. Forbes. *Forbes* 143:19-21 My 29 '89

Could our current capabilities for information storage and retrieval open a whole new world of ideas? R. M. Adams. il *Smithsonian* 20:12 Ap '89

From Telstar to typefaces, computers bring the information age home. D. D. Thornburg. *Compute!* 11:12 Ap '89

Managing the post-business society [views of P. Drucker] M. Magnet. *Fortune* 120:70-1 Jl 3 '89

The power of ideas and information [address, February 2, 1989] J. Sculley. *Vital Speeches of the Day* 55:565-9 Jl 1 '89

Surfing for information. P. Saffo. il *Personal Computing* 13:213-14 Jl '89

Technology is reshaping both work and workers. J. Sculley. por *Personal Computing* 13:218 O '89

We'll carry the information age with us—in our pockets, purses, and briefcases. P. Scisco. il *Compute!* 11:4 S '89

INFORMATION STORAGE AND RETRIEVAL SYSTEMS

See Information systems

INFORMATION SYSTEMS

See also

Computers

Gateways (Information systems)

Geographic information systems

Hypertext

Knowledge Index (Database)

Libraries—Automation

NewsNet (Information system)

Object-oriented databases

Offices—Automation

Prodigy (Database)

Research libraries—Automation

Text processing (Computer science)

Word processors and processing

Closing up shop, setting up shop [videotex services] M. Couzens. il *Channels (New York, N.Y.: 1986)* 9:80-1 D '89

Computing is the medium for the message. M. Antonoff. il *Personal Computing* 13:163-5 O '89

Electronic bookshelf. R. Scibilia. il *Popular Mechanics* 166:112-13 O '89

Let your keyboard do the walking. D. Churbuck. il *Forbes* 143:316-17 Ja 9 '89

Supercharging your computer with a phone and modem. L. Wiener. bibl il *U.S. News & World Report* 107:90+ N 20 '89

The world through a wire [with editorial comment by Gregg Keizer; cover story] N. Randall. il *Compute!* 11:4, 20-4+ Ap '89

Architectural use

RFP Version 4.0. S. S. Ross. il *Architectural Record* 177:149+ O '89

Art use

Keeping track of sculpture with computers [Inventory of American Sculpture at the National Museum of American Art] il *The Futurist* 23:49 Mr/Ap '89

INFORMATION SYSTEMS—cont.

Astronomical use
Cataloguing one billion stars and more. il *Sky and Telescope* 77:351-2 Ap '89
Deep-sky database [Deepsky 2000] B. Anderson and others. *Astronomy* 17:112 O '89

Aviation use
See also
Direct User Access Terminal System (Database)
Flight Data Center (Database)
Air Force selects Computer Sciences Corp. to develop information processing system [tracking Military Airlift Command aircraft] *Aviation Week & Space Technology* 130:51-2 Ja 23 '89
B-2s built in unique manner. *Aviation Week & Space Technology* 130:19 Ap 3 '89
McDonnell restructures mission planning efforts to gain greater market share. il *Aviation Week & Space Technology* 130:293-4 Je 12 '89
Norden develops system to warn controllers of runway incursions [Runway Incursion Management system] B. D. Nordwall. *Aviation Week & Space Technology* 130:28 My 29 '89
Permanent storage of optical disks finds new uses in aerospace, defense. il *Aviation Week & Space Technology* 130:51+ Jl 10 '89

Banking use
See also
Home banking services
Systematics, Inc.

Biological use
Linnaeus: interactive taxonomy using the Macintosh computer and HyperCard. K. W. Estep and others. bibl f il *BioScience* 39:635-8 O '89
Models, theory, and the matrix of biological knowledge. H. J. Morowitz. bibl f il *BioScience* 39:177-9 Mr '89

Business use
See also
Dow Jones News/Retrieval (Information system)
Executive information systems
Down to business. W. Rash, Jr. See issues of Byte beginning August 1988
Eighty/20. H. F. Beechhold. il *Home Office Computing* 7:76+ Je '89
Get info fast from electronic newsletters. A. Glossbrenner. il *Home Office Computing* 7:32 Ap '89
How you can achieve the information advantage [special section] il *Working Woman* 14:55+ Ap '89
On-line finds [cover story] R. Lockwood. il *Personal Computing* 13:78-81+ D '89
The paperless office comes true [American Automobile Association] P. Carroll. il *Working Woman* 14:73-4+ O '89
Protecting the corporate database. M. Liskin. il *Personal Computing* 13:51-2+ Ag '89
Searching for new business. J. F. Wasik. il *Home Office Computing* 7:38 F '89
Whose data is it anyhow? [file structure for shared databases] M. Liskin. il *Personal Computing* 13:55-6+ Je '89

Dictionaries
290,500 Oxford words to live by [Oxford English dictionary compiled with help of Univ. of Waterloo software] D. Francis. il *Maclean's* 102:9 F 20 '89
Caught in the web of bytes [electronic version of the Oxford English dictionary] C. Murphy. il *The Atlantic* 263:68-70 F '89
Electronic Oxford. E. Giguere. il *Byte* 14:371-2+ D '89
The installation blues [Inductel Reference Series] J. Pournelle. *Byte* 14:121-2+ N '89

Economics use
See also
Medieval & Early Modern Data Bank

Educational use
Are Plato and the Parthenon copyrighted? [databases about ancient Greece] F. D. Fisher. il *Change* 21:15 My/Je '89
Plug into the electronic educational connection. D. Stanton. il *Compute!* 11:80 F '89
The view from Palo Alto [Stanford orders purging of computer humor file that includes ethnic jokes] D. Seligman. il *Fortune* 119:339+ Ap 24 '89

Electrocopying
See Electrocopying

Estate planning use
Database of the dead [For the Record] D. Barker. *Byte* 14:104+ Ja '89

Games
Looking for game opponents? Go on-line. J. Phelan. il *Home Office Computing* 7:65-6+ Jl '89

Genetic research use
Bionet bites the dust. J. L. Marx. *Science* 245:126 Jl 14 '89
Who's minding the store? [loss of Bionet funding] P. Wallich. *Scientific American* 261:20+ O '89

Health use
Informatics and health [cover story; special issue] il *World Health* p2-29 Ag/S '89

Historians' use
See also
Medieval & Early Modern Data Bank

Investment use
See also
Dow Jones News/Retrieval (Information system)
Are you ready for robobroker? [Schwab's TeleBroker system] B. Hager. il *Money* 18:14+ O '89
Discount hunter [closed end fund strategy on a personal computer] D. Churbuck. il *Forbes* 143:252-3 Je 26 '89
Getting investment news and numbers on-line. A. Glossbrenner. il *Home Office Computing* 7:22 Jl '89
Personal newsletter. P. Duggan. il por *Forbes* 143:254 Je 26 '89
Rich prospects, poor technology [ADP taking stock quote market away from Quotron] F. Meeks. il *Forbes* 143:72+ Ap 3 '89
Stock information is just a keystroke away [Telescan Analyzer v2.5 and Telescan Edge v1.0] N. Maffei. il *Home Office Computing* 7:36 Je '89
A tale Dow Jones won't tell [woes of Wall Street journal] A. L. Taylor, III. il *Fortune* 120:100-2+ Jl 3 '89
Watching and buying stocks by computer. B. R. Schlender. il *Fortune* 120:38 D 4 '89
Welcome to Hauppauge, the world's next financial capital [Reuters; cover story] J. Marcom, Jr. il *Forbes* 144:143-9 O 30 '89

Laws and regulations
Corporate Luddism. M. Kinsley. *The New Republic* 201:4 D 25 '89
Telecommunications and the world information revolution [address, July 19, 1989] D. Brenner. *Vital Speeches of the Day* 56:88-91 N 15 '89
Why your service is so primitive [Baby Bells prohibited from creating information services] N. Oliver. il *Consumers' Research Magazine* 72:14-15 Je '89

Legal use
Entrepreneur looks for laws—and finds success [E. Martinez' Search & Research] B. Stein. il por *Home Office Computing* 7:52-3 F '89
Mead tries a new-fangled medium: print [acquisition of Michie Co.] M. Mallory. il *Business Week* p81-2 Ap 10 '89

Management
See Database management

Medical use
Dr. Database [work of the World Research Foundation] A. J. S. Rayl. il *Omni (New York, N.Y.)* 11:100 F '89
Informatics and health [cover story; special issue] il *World Health* p2-29 Ag/S '89
Looking over the doctor's shoulder [outcome monitoring] S. Findlay. il *U.S. News & World Report* 106:70-1+ Ja 30 '89
Meet Dr. Database [use of RapidFile by E. Gordy] K. J. Novak. il por *Home Office Computing* 7:24-5 Jl '89
Supersensitive supersecrecy [databank of professional reprimands against health care practitioners] *Science News* 136:284 O 28 '89

Meteorological use
See also
Direct User Access Terminal System (Database)
Flight Data Center (Database)
NOWrad now [WSI computer briefing services for pilots] A. Laboda. il *Flying* 116:30 S '89
PC flight planning [Aviators Datalog and CompuServe] J. M. McClellan. *Flying* 116:23 Mr '89

Military use
Astronomer Cliff Stoll stars in the espionage game, but for him spying doesn't really compute [responsible for tracking down Hannover, Germany hacker who gained access to U.S. government network] J. S. Kunen. il pors *People Weekly* 32:118+ D 11 '89
German computer spy ring broken. E. Marshall. *Science* 243:1545 Mr 24 '89
Pentagon uses new computer system to help action teams manage crises [crisis management automatic data processing system] B. D. Nordwall. il *Aviation Week & Space Technology* 131:43+ D 4 '89
A search-and-destroy mission—against paper. F. Seghers. il *Business Week* p91+ F 6 '89
Spying and sabotage by computer. J. Peterzell. il *Time* 133:25-6 Mr 20 '89

Pharmaceutical use
Etch-a-drug. I. Chithelen. il *Forbes* 143:154-5 Je 12 '89
Rx for rising costs [computer network coordinating Medicare prescriptions] S. Dentzer. il *U.S. News & World Report* 107:50-1+ S 11 '89

Political use
See also
Public Electronic Network (Santa Monica, Calif.: Database)

Publishing use
The database meets desktop publishing. R. Kendall. il *Home Office Computing* 7:36-7 O '89

Purchasing use
See Electronic shopping

Real estate use
See also
Co-op & Condo Connection (Database)

Reference books
Looking it up. K. Dawson and L. Nixon. il *Publishers Weekly* 236:18+ Jl 14 '89

INFORMATION SYSTEMS—*cont.*
Scientific use
See also
 NSFnet
Electronic networking [sub-Saharan African scientists] B. Gold. il map *Science* 245:538-9 Ag 4 '89
Retrieval of scientific and technical data. P. H. Abelson. *Science* 245:9 Jl 7 '89
Search strategies
See Online searching
Security measures
Protecting the corporate database. M. Liskin. il *Personal Computing* 13:51-2+ Ag '89
Space flight use
Jukeboxes for scientists [coping with upcoming deluge of data] J. Horgan. *Scientific American* 261:24-5 Jl '89
Sports use
See also
 Sports Center (Database)
Telephone directories
PC Yellow Pages. T. A. Summers. il *Home Office Computing* 7:76 Mr '89
Television advertising use
See also
 Hot Net (Firm)
Travel use
Ski info, PC-style. C. Walter. il *Skiing* 42:14 O '89
Africa
Electronic networking [sub-Saharan African scientists] B. Gold. il map *Science* 245:538-9 Ag 4 '89
Brazil
User-friendly videotex [health system in Sao Paulo] I. Fogelman and E. O. C. Chaves. il *World Health* p14-15 Ag/S '89
France
L'informatique videotex [Minitel available in U.S.] P. Scisco. il *Compute!* 11:6 F '89
Minitel: the French connection. M. Antonoff. il *Personal Computing* 13:78 My '89
INFORMED CONSENT (MEDICAL LAW)
Informed consent. J. S. Reed. *Society* 27:25-7 N/D '89
INFORMERS
See also
 Whistle blowing (Public interest)
And why they let anyone be an informant [FBI investigation of Committee in Solidarity with the People of El Salvador] S. Burkholder. *The Washington Monthly* 20:19-20 Ja '89
Outlasting the F.B.I., a determined widow restores her husband's reputation as a loyal Communist [L. Albertson wins lawsuit on behalf of B. Albertson, falsely accused of being an informer] J. S. Kunen. il *People Weekly* 32:171-2 N 20 '89
Snitches on snitching [study of inmates in Swedish prisons] M. Åkerström. bibl *Society* 26:22-6 Ja/F '89
INFRARED ASTRONOMY
Brown dwarf candidates abound. M. M. Waldrop. il *Science* 245:29-30 Jl 7 '89
Brown dwarfs caught in the heat of youth [research by William J. Forrest] I. Peterson. il *Science News* 135:399 Je 24 '89
Brown dwarfs here . . . [research by William J. Forrest] J. Horgan. il *Scientific American* 261:28 S '89
Dwarfs galore [brown dwarfs; research by William Forrest] il *Discover* 10:14 O '89
Hydrogen sulfide on Io: evidence from telescopic and laboratory infrared spectra. D. B. Nash and R. R. Howell. bibl f il *Science* 244:454-7 Ap 28 '89
Infrared observations of the Neptunian system. B. Conrath and others. bibl f il *Science* 246:1454-9 D 15 '89
Inside Orion's stellar nursery. J. Kanipe. il *Astronomy* 17:40-3 Ag '89
The nature of the near-infrared features on the Venus night side. D. Crisp and others. bibl f il *Science* 246:506-9 O 27 '89
New brown dwarf evidence looks promising [research by William Forrest] il *Astronomy* 17:10 S '89
Orion and the Swan: new infrared views [work of Mark McCaughrean and Colin Aspin] il *Sky and Telescope* 77:352-3 Ap '89
Silicate volcanism on Io [research by Torrence V. Johnson] il *Sky and Telescope* 77:355-6 Ap '89
Starbirth's soft glow [image of star forming clouds in Cepheus; research by Adair P. Lane] il *Sky and Telescope* 78:239-40 S '89
INFRARED ASTRONOMY SATELLITE *See* Artificial satellites—Astronomical use
INFRARED COMMUNICATIONS
Remote A/B switch. R. A. Heil. il *Radio-Electronics* 60:37+ O '89
INFRARED DETECTORS *See* Detectors, Infrared
INFRARED FILMS *See* Photography—Films
INFRASONIC WAVES
Elephant talk [cover story] K. Payne. il maps *National Geographic* 176:264-77 Ag '89
INFRASOUND *See* Infrasonic waves
INFRASTRUCTURE *See* Public works
INFRINGEMENT OF COPYRIGHT *See* Copyright infringement

INFRINGEMENT OF PATENTS *See* Patent infringement
ING. C. OLIVETTI & CO., SPA
Can Cassoni get Olivetti off the slippery slope? J. Rossant and T. Peterson. il por *Business Week* p99+ Je 12 '89
INGALL, FRANCIS
about
He remembers when the saber was mightier, but now Bengal Lancer Francis Ingall takes up the pen. K. Gross. il pors *People Weekly* 32:113-15+ S 11 '89
INGBER, RACHEL
Directory assistance. il *World Tennis* 36:48-57 Ja '89
INGEBRETSEN, MARK
America's Caribbean [special section] il map *Better Homes and Gardens* 67:211-12+ N '89
INGEBRITSEN, S. E., AND OTHERS
Heat flow and hydrothermal circulation in the Cascade Range, north-central Oregon. bibl f il maps *Science* 243:1458-62 Mr 17 '89
INGERSOLL, RALPH, II
about
Here comes the Sun, spoiling for a fight in St. Louis. J. E. Ellis. il por *Business Week* p48 S 25 '89
A media baron's suburban strategy. A. Gabor. il por map *U.S. News & World Report* 106:49-50 Ap 24 '89
Sun-rise in St. Louis. W. A. Henry. il por *Time* 134:60 S 25 '89
Why Ingersoll picked St. Louis. J. Heins. il por *Forbes* 144:52+ Jl 24 '89
INGLIS, FRED
Charity begins with gluttony. il *The Nation* 248:446-8 Ap 3 '89
INGRAM BOOK COMPANY
Ingram hosts an open (ware) house. A. Symons. *Publishers Weekly* 235:98-9 Ap 7 '89
INGRAM PUBLISHER SERVICES
Ingram forms publisher fulfillment service [other wholesalers fear conflict of interest] M. Reuter. *Publishers Weekly* 235:17-18 Ap 28 '89
INGREDIENT LABELING OF FOOD *See* Food—Labeling
INGRES, JEAN AUGUSTE DOMINIQUE, 1780-1867
about
Face to face [cover story] S. H. Madoff. il por *Art News* 88:104-7 F '89
Ingres and the modernists. E. Hayt-Atkins. il *Art News* 88:139 F '89
Looking at art [reprint of December 1982 article] H. Brown. bibl f il *American Artist* 53:34+ Ap '89
INHALANT ABUSE
Spray paint sniffers beware [views of Jack Reyes] il *USA Today (Periodical)* 118:7 D '89
INHERITANCE
See also
 Estate planning
 Estates, Decedents'
 Wills
So what are your parents worth? P. Moffitt. il *Esquire* 112:111+ N '89
INHERITANCE OF DISEASES *See* Heredity of disease
INHERITANCE TAX
All in the family [family businesses and estate taxes] J. C. Szabo. il *Nation's Business* 77:73-4 Ap '89
The bad news about estate taxes. L. Saunders. il *Forbes* 143:238-9+ Je 26 '89
Before the loophole closes. P. Duggan. il *Forbes* 144:239-40 O 2 '89
Congress warms to estate freeze. J. C. Szabo. il *Nation's Business* 77:48+ Je '89
Death: the last tax shelter [survivorship or second-to-die life insurance] il *Esquire* 112:88 N '89
How to pay zero estate taxes. D. M. Topolnicki. il *Money* 18 Money Guide:117-18+ Fall '89
Keeping down estate taxes. A. B. Fisher. il *Fortune* 120 no10 Special Issue:189+ Fall '89
Keeping the state out of your estate. R. R. Roha. il *Changing Times* 43:73-8 N '89
This policy takes the sting out of inheritance taxes [survivorship or second-to-die insurance] D. H. Dunn. il *Business Week* p107 Je 12 '89
The trial of Donald and Si Newhouse [cover story] R. Pollak. il *The Nation* 248:325+ Mr 13 '89
What your estate will owe. il *Money* 18 Money Guide:106-7 Fall '89
Your house's hidden problem. R. Wool. il *Money* 18:177-8 N '89
INHIBITED SEXUAL DESIRE *See* Sexual desire
INHIBITION
See also
 Repression (Psychology)
INITIAL PUBLIC OFFERINGS (SECURITIES)
Big bucks at the end of the bridge [bridge financing deals] D. P. Wiener. il *U.S. News & World Report* 107:68 O 2 '89
Born-again stocks [former leveraged buyout companies taken public with new offerings] C. Palmeri. il *Forbes* 143:210-11 Mr 20 '89
But the client is delighted [new stock issue performance] R. L. Stern and C. M. Bartlett, Jr. il *Forbes* 143:130+ Ap 3 '89

INITIAL PUBLIC OFFERINGS (SECURITIES)—*cont.*
Danger: hazardous stocks [environmental companies] R. Simon. il *Forbes* 144:41-2 O 16 '89
First Brands: anatomy of an LBO that worked. T. Vogel. il *Business Week* p104 D 4 '89
How Saint Laurent is skirting sharks [stock goes public] *U.S. News & World Report* 107:11-12 Jl 17 '89
Indianapolis intrigue [B. SerVaas' role in Central Newspapers going public] E. Schmuckler. il por *Forbes* 144:222-3 S 18 '89
IPOs are back—and they're still a treacherous lot. L. Zinn. il *Business Week* p134-5 Ag 14 '89
The Quayle family newspapers: black, white—and green all over. J. F. Siler. il por *Business Week* p29 Ag 28 '89
Reshaping an empire [Bronfmans to sell portion of Edper Enterprises to public] D. Jenish. *Maclean's* 102:43 My 29 '89
The shape of thrifts to come? [People's Bank issues stock] R. W. King. il *Business Week* p102 S 18 '89
Survival of the few [new issues] C. M. Bartlett, Jr. il *Forbes* 143:266-7 Je 26 '89
TLC Beatrice is almost paid for. What's the next course? P. Finch. il por *Business Week* p33-4 N 20 '89
A wake-up call for initial public offerings. L. Helm. *Business Week* p40-1 My 8 '89
INITIALISMS *See* Acronyms
INITIATION RITES
Against R.C.I.A. [Rite of Christian Initiation for Adults; with reply by R. D. Duggan; cover story] A. M. Greeley. il *America* 161:231-7 O 14 '89
Rites of passage II. M. E. Marty. *The Christian Century* 106:703 Jl 19-26 '89
State of the question [discussion of October 14, 1989 article, Against R.C.I.A.] A. M. Greeley. *America* 161:328-30 N 11 '89
INITIATIVE AND REFERENDUM *See* Referendum
INJECTION WELLS FOR WASTE *See* Trade waste—Disposal
INJECTIONS, SCLEROSING *See* Sclerotherapy
INJURIES
See also
Ankle—Wounds and injuries
Arm—Wounds and injuries
Breast—Wounds and injuries
Cats—Wounds and injuries
Exercise—Accidents and injuries
First aid in illness and injury
Foot—Wounds and injuries
Hand—Wounds and injuries
Industrial accidents
Knee—Wounds and injuries
Leg—Wounds and injuries
Neck—Wounds and injuries
Repetitive strain injuries
Sprains
Teeth—Wounds and injuries
Traumatism
INJURIES (LAW) *See* Damages
INJURY HEALING *See* Healing
INK DRAWING *See* Pen drawing
INK-JET PRINTERS
Brighten up your printouts [Hewlett-Packard PaintJet] J. Latimer. il *Home Office Computing* 7:66+ Mr '89
Color printer quells price-tag blues [Tektronix ColorQuick] T. Thompson. il *Byte* 14:187-8 O '89
The DeskJet gets hotter [DeskJet Plus] S. Miastkowski. il *Byte* 14:89 Jl '89
A featherweight printer [Diconix 150 Plus] C. Hlavaty. il *Personal Computing* 13:168 Ag '89
Hewlett-Packard's speedier DeskJet Plus. R. Bel Bruno. il *Personal Computing* 13:164 Ag '89
High-resolution ink-jet printing for the Mac [Hewlett-Packard DeskWriter] D. Hallerman. il *Home Office Computing* 7:80-1 D '89
HP makes a splash with Mac DeskWriter. J. Bell. il *Personal Computing* 13:188 D '89
I usually don't do this, but . . . [DeskJet] A. R. Levitan. il *Compute!* 11:88+ Mr '89
An ink-jet printer for the Mac [DeskWriter] A. F. Lent and L. H. Loeb. il *Byte* 14:82+ O '89
Near-laser quality for less [Hewlett-Packard DeskJet Plus thermal ink jet printer] S. Chen. il *Home Office Computing* 7:61 Ag '89
A portable 24-pin printer [Toshiba ExpressWriter 311] R. Gehorsam. il *Home Office Computing* 7:66+ Je '89
Speed separates two portable printers [Toshiba ExpressWriter 301 and Kodak Diconix 150 Plus] W. Rash, Jr. il *Byte* 14:191-2 O '89
Toshiba puts a handle on 24-pin printing [ExpressWriter 311] R. Bel Bruno. il *Personal Computing* 13:196 Ap '89
Two for the road [Kodak Diconix 150 Plus and Toshiba ExpressWriter 301 portable printers] S. Chen and M. Alvich. il *Home Office Computing* 7:66+ O '89
INK SPOTS (MUSICAL GROUP)
Ink Spots. M. Azerrad. il *Rolling Stone* p87 F 9 '89

INKSTER, JULI, 1961?-
about
Beating the devil. D. S. Looney. il por *Sports Illustrated* 70:34+ Ap 10 '89
INLAND NAVIGATION
See also
Canals
River trips
Inland navigation. S. Stapleton. il *Motor Boating & Sailing* 164:32 D '89
INLAND PASSAGE *See* Inside Passage
INLAY
The line-and-berry inlaid furniture of eighteenth-century Chester County, Pennsylvania. L. E. Griffith. bibl f il *Antiques* 135:1202-11 My '89
INMAC CORP.
Shakeout. F. Meeks. il por *Forbes* 143:120+ Mr 6 '89
INMAN, BOBBY RAY
about
The education of Bobby Inman. K. Kelly. por *Business Week* p50 D 18 '89
INMARSAT *See* International Maritime Satellite Organization
INMARSAT SATELLITES
Carriers, manufacturers assess aerosat communication systems. P. J. Klass. il map *Aviation Week & Space Technology* 130:54-5 Ja 9 '89
GE Astro-Space, Marconi will team to bid for Inmarsat 3 contract. *Aviation Week & Space Technology* 131:79 Ag 21 '89
Management shifts made to resolve Inmarsat 2 development problems. J. M. Lenorovitz. *Aviation Week & Space Technology* 131:44+ O 23 '89
Soviet satellite agency to provide technical aid to Inmarsat. *Aviation Week & Space Technology* 131:81 Ag 21 '89
INNAURATO, ALBERT
What makes great performers? il *Opera News* 54:20+ D 9 '89
about
Gus and Al [drama] Reviews
New York 22:75 Mr 13 '89. J. Simon
The New Yorker 65:74 Mr 13 '89. E. Oliver
INNER CIRCLE (REPUBLICAN PARTY) *See* Republican Senatorial Inner Circle
INNER CIRCLE OF ADVOCATES
Brothers in bucks. L. Spencer. il *Forbes* 144:203 O 16 '89
INNER CITY BROADCASTING CORPORATION
The Dinkins stock crash [D. Dinkins accused of undervaluation of Inner City Broadcasting stock] C. Byron. il *New York* 22:30+ N 6 '89
It's showtime! [cover story] A. Edmond, Jr. il pors *Black Enterprise* 19:46-8+ Ap '89
INNER CITY CHILDREN *See* City children
INNER CITY EDUCATION *See* Urban education
INNER TUBES
Multifactor productivity advances in the tires and inner tubes industry. D. Litz and L. Moore. bibl f il *Monthly Labor Review* 112:19-27 Je '89
Testing
All about inner tubes [bicycles] F. Berto. il *Bicycling* 30:164+ Je '89
INNERVATION OF MUSCLE *See* Muscle—Innervation
INNERVATION OF THE BRAIN *See* Brain—Innervation
INNOCENCE (PSYCHOLOGY)
It's all right to be innocent again [growing trend in children's literature] L. Rosenberg. il *The New York Times Book Review* 94:46 My 21 '89
INNOCENCE MISSION (MUSICAL GROUP)
Innocence Mission. M. Meyer. il *Rolling Stone* p43 N 30 '89
AN INNOCENT MAN [film] *See* Motion picture reviews—Single works
INNOVATIONS, EDUCATIONAL *See* Educational innovations
INNOVATIONS, TECHNOLOGICAL *See* Technological innovations
INNS *See* Hotels, motels, etc.
INNUMERACY *See* Mathematical literacy
INOCULATION *See* Vaccines and vaccination
INOSITOL
See also
Phosphatidylinositol
INOUYE, CHARLES SHIRŌ
Do non-Japanese fear the flame? il *The Nation* 248:120-2 Ja 30 '89
INOUYE, STANLEY K.
The mirror of God. il *Christianity Today* 33:26-8 Mr 3 '89
about
The gift of two cultures. K. H. Sidey. por *Christianity Today* 33:30 Mr 3 '89
INSANITY
Jurisprudence
See Insanity defense
INSANITY AND ART *See* Art and mental illness
INSANITY DEFENSE
See also
Forensic psychiatry

INSANITY DEFENSE—*cont.*
Whose competence? T. S. Szasz. il *National Review* 41:38+ S 15 '89
INSCOM (FIRM)
Brazil, China form space launch venture. E. H. Kolcum. il *Aviation Week & Space Technology* 130:35 My 29 '89
INSCRIPTIONS
See also
Petroglyphs
INSCRIPTIONS, CHINESE
See also
Oracle bones
INSCRIPTIONS, MAYA See Mayas—Writing
INSECT BITES AND STINGS
Bee sting first aid. *Health (New York, N.Y.)* 21:54 Ap '89
INSECT CAMOUFLAGE See Mimicry (Biology)
INSECT COMMUNICATION
Disco-bee [robot bee designed by Wolfgang H. Kirchner and Axel Michelsen] J. Horgan. *Scientific American* 260:31-2 Je '89
Hearing in honey bees: detection of air-particle oscillations. W. F. Towne and W. H. Kirchner. bibl f il *Science* 244:686-8 My 12 '89
Honey bees listen to the dance [research by William F. Towne] B. Bower. *Science News* 135:318 My 20 '89
New dancer in the hive [robot honeybee; cover story] R. Weiss. il *Science News* 136:282-3 O 28 '89
INSECT CONTROL
See also
Aphids—Control
Armyworms—Control
Beetles—Control
Cockroaches—Control
Codling moths—Control
Corn rootworms—Control
Fire ants—Control
Fleas—Control
Grasshoppers—Control
Gypsy moths—Control
Inchworms—Control
Mosquitoes—Control
Pesticides
Tent caterpillars—Control
Termites—Control
Weevils—Control
Controlling pests and pathogens [biocontrol; views of Peter E. Dunn] il *USA Today (Periodical)* 117:14-15 Je '89
Less pesticide, still grows great [Cornell's study on integrated pest management] *Newsweek* 113:53 My 29 '89
Uninvited guests [gardens pests] S. O. Daniels. il *Organic Gardening* 36:38-42 Ap '89
INSECT FEAR FILM FESTIVAL See Motion picture festivals—Illinois
INSECT GENETICS
The apian way [genes linked to honeybee behavior] il *Discover* 10:6 Ja '89
A family of putative potassium channel genes in Drosophila. A. Butler and others. bibl f il *Science* 243:943-7 F 17 '89
Growing old together: fruit flies and you [effects of catalase production on cell aging in Drosophila; research by Glenn Bewley] il *Discover* 10:8 Ap '89
INSECT INTRODUCTION
Hitching a ride with imported insects [viral diseases] R. Weiss. *Science News* 136:202 S 23 '89
INSECT POPULATIONS
See also
Population genetics—Insects
INSECT REPELLENTS
See also
Deet
Debugging your summer. D. Petersen. il *The Mother Earth News* 118:102+ Jl/Ag '89
It takes more than repellent to make flying pests bug off. D. M. Schwartz. il *Smithsonian* 20:76-80+ Jl '89
INSECT SEX ATTRACTANTS
See also
Pheromones—Insects
INSECT SOCIETIES See Insects—Habits and behavior
INSECT SOUNDS
See also
Insect communication
INSECTICIDES See Pesticides
INSECTS
See also
Embryology—Insects
Entomology
Eye—Insects
Forensic entomology
Forest insects
Hearing—Insects
Mutation—Insects
Pheromones—Insects
See also names of insects
Attract these bugs [beneficial in gardens] R. West. il *Organic Gardening* 36:74-5 Mr '89

Anecdotes, facetiae, satire, etc.
Six-legged saboteurs. P. Hoffman. il *Discover* 10:80-3 My '89
Control
See Insect control
Development
See also
Diapause
Caterpillar disguise: you are what you eat [work of Erick Greene with Nemoria arizonaria] I. Wickelgren. il *Science News* 135:70 F 4 '89
Caterpillars and polymorphisms [discussion of February 3, 1989 article, A diet-induced developmental polymorphism in a caterpillar] E. Greene. bibl f *Science* 246:1639-40 D 22 '89
Caterpillars earn their wings. il *National Geographic World* 164:14-19 Ap '89
A diet-induced developmental polymorphism in a caterpillar [Nemoria arizonaria; cover story] E. Greene. bibl f il *Science* 243:643-6 F 3 '89
Identification of an allatotropin from adult Manduca sexta. H. Kataoka and others. bibl f il *Science* 243:1481-3 Mr 17 '89
Is diet destiny? [developmental polymorphism in caterpillars; research by Erick Greene] *Newsweek* 113:62 F 13 '89
Ubiquitous expression of *seventess*: position-dependent specification of cell fate. K. Basler and E. Hafen. bibl f il *Science* 243:931-4 F 17 '89
Eggs
Overwintering insect eggs [tent caterpillar eggs] W. S. Moore. il *Flower and Garden* 33:74 Ja/F '89
Food and feeding
A 48-million-year-old aphid-host plant association and complex life cycle: biogeographic evidence [aphid subtribe Melaphidina and sumac host plant] N. A. Moran. bibl f il map *Science* 245:173-5 Jl 14 '89
A breed apart [sympatric speciation in apple fruit flies; study by Guy L. Bush] K. Wright. il *Scientific American* 260:22+ F '89
Carbon dioxide may spur plant predation. J. Raloff. *Science News* 136:143 Ag 26 '89
The effects of enriched carbon dioxide atmospheres on plant-insect herbivore interactions. E. D. Fajer and others. bibl f il *Science* 243:1198-200 Mr 3 '89
Life in a nutshell [inhabitants of acorns] M. W. Moffett. il *National Geographic* 175:782-96 Je '89
Plant hybrid zones as sinks for pests [aphids on hybrid cottonwoods] T. G. Whitham. bibl f il *Science* 244:1490-3 Je 23 '89
Habits and behavior
See also
Insect communication
Mimicry (Biology)
Parental behavior in insects
Sexual behavior—Insects
Hormonal and genetic control of behavioral integration in honey bee colonies. G. E. Robinson and others. bibl f il *Science* 246:109-12 O 6 '89
Host plants
See Insects—Food and feeding
Molting
See Molting
Photographs and photography
You've got to get up early to catch Mother Nature's crown jewels: dew-covered insects. J. Shaw. il *Popular Photography* 96:18-19 Ag '89
Costa Rica
Trap-jaw ants: set for prey. M. W. Moffett. il *National Geographic* 175:394-400 Mr '89
Japan
Samurai aphids: survival under siege. M. W. Moffett. il *National Geographic* 176:406-22 S '89
Long Island (N.Y.)
Managing New York's mosquito coast. D. Ninivaggi. il por *The Conservationist* 44:26-33 Jl/Ag '89
Vermont
It'll be a scratchy summer [mosquito infestation] il *Newsweek* 114:23 Jl 3 '89
INSECTS, EFFECT OF TEMPERATURE ON
Insect cold-hardiness: to freeze or not to freeze. R. E. Lee, Jr. bibl f il *BioScience* 39:308-13 My '89
INSECTS, STINGING
See also
Insect bites and stings
INSECTS AS CARRIERS OF INFECTION
See also
Mosquitoes as carriers of infection
Ticks as carriers of infection
INSECTS AS FOOD
A grasshopper in every pot. D. B. Madsen. il *Natural History* p22+ Jl '89
Insects, worms, and other tidbits [Mexican cooking] R. Sokolov. il *Natural History* p84+ S '89
INSECTS IN MOTION PICTURES
Education by exaggeration [Insect Fear Film Festival; cover story] R. Weiss. il *Science News* 135:136-7 Mr 4 '89
INSECURITY (PSYCHOLOGY) See Security and insecurity (Psychology)

INSEMINATION, ARTIFICIAL *See* Artificial insemination, Human
INSERVICE EDUCATION (ARTS TEACHERS) *See* Arts teachers—Education in service
INSERVICE EDUCATION (ENGLISH TEACHERS) *See* English teachers—Education in service
INSERVICE EDUCATION (MATHEMATICS TEACHERS) *See* Mathematics teachers—Education in service
INSERVICE EDUCATION (SCIENCE TEACHERS) *See* Science teachers—Education in service
INSERVICE EDUCATION (TEACHERS) *See* Teachers—Education in service
INSIDE BLACK AMERICA [radio program] See Radio program reviews—Single works
INSIDE BOOKS (PERIODICAL)
Freelance writers claim nonpayment by 'Inside books'. C. Reid. *Publishers Weekly* 235:25 Je 30 '89
INSIDE PASSAGE
Alaska—Northwest passages. M. T. O'Keefe. il *The Saturday Evening Post* 261:82-4 My/Je '89
Ferry tales [southeast Alaska] M. Steere. il map *Travel Holiday* 172:58-67 Ag '89
A passage to Alaska. L. Levinger. il map *New Choices for the Best Years* 29:40-5 O '89
INSIDER TRADING
Another Wall Streeter falls [S. Lewis] *Newsweek* 114:46 S 11 '89
Checkmate for the King of Junk Bonds [Drexel Burnham agrees to fire M. Milken] por *U.S. News & World Report* 106:44-5 F 6 '89
Conspiracy of strangers [charges against T. Tabor, R. Wigton and R. Freeman dropped] C. Byron. il pors *New York* 22:16+ S 4 '89
The deal Drexel could not resist [settlement of fraud case] P. Sherrid. il *U.S. News & World Report* 106:46-8 Ja 9 '89
The debris in Rudolph Giuliani's wake. C. Welles. pors *Business Week* p36-7 Ja 23 '89
Drexel is in the doghouse with cities and states. L. J. Nathans. il *Business Week* p81-2 F 13 '89
Drexel pays the piper. D. Pauly. il *Newsweek* 113:40 Ja 16 '89
Drexel's deal with the feds: how much will it hurt? C. Welles. il por *Business Week* p36 F 6 '89
Drexel's profit and potential loss. M. J. Williams. il *Fortune* 119:8+ F 27 '89
The friends of Michael Milken [public relations campaign] M. Hosenball. il por *The New Republic* 201:23-5 Ag 28 '89
From typesetter to insider trader? [J. J. Lynch nabbed for trading on Business week column] C. Welles. *Business Week* p47-8 D 18 '89
G. Robert Blakey versus Michael Milken [author of RICO statute] J. Queenan. il por *Forbes* 143:57+ My 1 '89
Got big deals, big problems, big bucks? Get Arthur Liman [defending M. Milken] M. Galen. il por *Business Week* p112+ My 15 '89
Hitting Milken where it hurts. C. Friday and D. Pauly. il por *Newsweek* 113:49 Ap 10 '89
Inside indication? [Market logic newsletter] M. Hulbert. il *Forbes* 143:120 Ja 23 '89
Insider tips that aren't outside the law. S. Woolley. il *Business Week* p146-7 N 20 '89
The junk bond plague moves north [Drexel Burnham] P. C. Newman. il *Maclean's* 102:32 Ja 16 '89
The Junk King starts anew [M. Milken resigns from Drexel Burnham to start new firm] por *Newsweek* 113:55 Je 26 '89
Just how corrupt is Wall Street? [Drexel Burnham's agreement to plead guilty] C. Welles. il *Business Week* p34-6 Ja 9 '89
Let's make a deal [Drexel pleads guilty to fraud] J. Greenwald. il *Time* 133:84-6 Ja 2 '89
Michael Milken. por *People Weekly* 32:72-3 D 25 '89-Ja 1 '90
Michael Milken. B. Darrach. por *People Weekly* 32 Special Issue:48-9 Fall '89
Nailing the junk kings [Drexel Burnham admits securities fraud] L. Reibstein. il por *Newsweek* 113:44-5+ Ja 2 '89
The phantom of Wall Street: how Ivan Boesky's bitter legacy haunts Mike Milken and his former firm. C. Byron. il pors *New York* 22:52-6 D 4 '89
Predators' fall [M. Milken indicted] *National Review* 41:10-11 My 5 '89
Round up the usual brokers [RICO statute] J. O'Sullivan. *National Review* 41:11 N 10 '89
Taking it all back, plus interest [criminal charges against M. Milken] C. Gorman. il por *Time* 133:42 Ap 10 '89
The transformation of Ivan Boesky [imprisonment in Lompoc] A. Miller. il pors *Newsweek* 114:60 N 27 '89
The U.S. vs. Milken: now the last act begins. C. Welles. il por *Business Week* p29 Ap 10 '89
A verdict that Mike Milken hopes is no warm-up [conviction of five officials of Princeton/Newport Partners and former Drexel Burnham trader] M. Galen. por *Business Week* p46 Ag 14 '89

Welcome to the world of sleaze [conviction of Drexel Burnham Lambert trader and Princeton/Newport Partners executives] il *Time* 134:52 Ag 14 '89
What hath Drexel wrought? [guilty plea] M. J. Williams. il *Fortune* 119:10 Ja 16 '89
What Milken means; Will Mike fight? A. Farnham. il por *Fortune* 119:16-17 Ap 24 '89
Will Michael Milken go to jail? P. Sherrid. il por *U.S. News & World Report* 106:49-50 Ap 10 '89
Will Mike Milken sue? L. Howard. il por *Newsweek* 113:7 F 6 '89

International aspects
The surging markets. J. DeMont. il *Maclean's* 102:26+ F 13 '89

Canada
The Crown's case [former B.C. premier W. Bennett goes on trial in Doman Industries case] H. Quinn. il por *Maclean's* 102:36-7 My 1 '89
A victory for Bennett [former B.C. premier and codefendants acquitted] J. DeMont. il por *Maclean's* 102:28-9 My 22 '89

France
From Balzac to Salvador Dali. D. Singer. il *The Nation* 248:333-4+ Mr 13 '89
Insider-trading shock rocks the Elysee [Triangle affair] B. Riemer. il *Business Week* p54 Ja 23 '89
The Socialists dodge one bullet—but the next? [insider trading Triangle probe] B. Riemer and F. J. Comes. il *Business Week* p46 F 13 '89

Great Britain
Ernest Saunders markets his innocence [former Guinness chairman] M. Maremont. il por *Business Week* p92-3 Ag 14 '89

Japan
The dark side of Japan Inc. [Recruit scandal] J. Hammer. il *Newsweek* 113:41 Ja 9 '89
A fatal money scandal [resignation of N. Takeshita] M. Nemeth. il por *Maclean's* 102:25 My 8 '89
The fine art of kinmyaku [contributions to N. Takeshita from Recruit Company] il por *U.S. News & World Report* 106:18 Ap 24 '89
Insider trading. G. Ellwand. il *Maclean's* 102:22-3 Ja 9 '89
The Japanese scandal [Recruit scandal] il *World Press Review* 36:8 Je '89
Japan's scandal: who's next? S. Solo. il *Fortune* 119:24 Ap 10 '89
'Money politics' makes Tokyo's world go around [Recruit scandal] M. Tharp. il *U.S. News & World Report* 106:48 Ja 9 '89
Now Takeshita really feels the flames of scandal [Recruit scandal] T. Holden. por *Business Week* p55 F 27 '89
A question of ethics [N. Takeshita admits to receiving political donations from Recruit] A. Bilski. *Maclean's* 102:27 Ap 24 '89
The Recruit scandal bubbles to the top. A. Borrus. por *Business Week* p55 Mr 20 '89
Sand in a well-oiled machine [N. Takeshita forced to resign in wake of Recruit scandal] S. MacLeod. por *Time* 133:44 My 8 '89
A scandal that will not die [Recruit scandal] W. R. Doerner. il por *Time* 133:37+ Ap 24 '89
Sinking in a sea of yen [Recruit scandal threatens to topple Prime Minister Takeshita] H. Anderson. il por *Newsweek* 113:49-50 Ap 24 '89
Takeshita talks political reform—but doesn't sound convincing. A. Borrus. il *Business Week* p57 Ja 23 '89
Uniqueness and sleaze [Recruit scandal] W. M. Stern. *National Review* 41:23-4 Je 2 '89
Why time may be running out for Takeshita [Recruit scandal] T. Holden. por *Business Week* p43 Ap 24 '89
Will the Recruit scandal just go away? A. Borrus and N. Gross. il por *Business Week* p40-1 Je 12 '89
You scratch my back . . . [Recruit scandal] J. Greenwald. il *Time* 133:47 Ja 9 '89

Liechtenstein
An insider caper in Liechtenstein [ASEA Brown Boveri helps SEC uncover insider trading during ABB's friendly takeover bid for Combustion Engineering] J. Kapstein. *Business Week* p58-9 D 11 '89

Switzerland
Just smart stock pickers? [Ellis A.G.] R. L. Stern. *Forbes* 144:40-1 S 18 '89

United States
See Insider trading
INSIGNIA
See also
Emblems
Police insignia
U.S.A. space mission patches [shuttle patches] R. V. Simpson. il *Antiques & Collecting Hobbies* 93:50-3 Ja '89
INSOLES
Just how good are those special insoles? [use in running shoes] O. Anderson. il *Women's Sports & Fitness* 11:14 Ja/F '89
INSOMNIA
See also
Hypnotics

INSOMNIA—*cont.*
A bedtime story [cover story] E. Weck. il *FDA Consumer* 23:12-15 O '89
Body's clock keeps insomniacs wide awake [research by Mary Morris] K. Fackelmann. *Science News* 136:13 Jl 1 '89
"It's 3 a.m. . . . where can I get some sleep!". L. David. il *Mademoiselle* 95:130 O '89
Simple steps to a good night's sleep. A. Lake. il *Reader's Digest* 134:33-4+ F '89

INSPECTION
See also
    Airplane engines, Jet—Inspection
    Airplanes, Jet—Inspection
    Airplanes, Light—Inspection
    Building inspection
    Disarmament—Inspection
    Fish inspection
    Food inspection
    Meat inspection

INSPECTOR GENERALS (U.S.) *See* Inspectors general (U.S.)
INSPECTORS GENERAL (U.S.)
The CIA gets a new watchdog. E. Salholz. il *Newsweek* 114:46 D 11 '89
A shorter leash for the Inspectors General? P. Dwyer. il *Business Week* p82+ O 9 '89

INSPIRATION RESOURCES CORP.
Improvised resources? R. Simon. il por *Forbes* 143:88-9 F 20 '89

INSTALMENT PLAN
Renting to own. K. K. Gracey. *Consumers' Research Magazine* 72:2 F '89

INSTANT REPLAY (FIRM)
Codebusters [multistandard VCR's] D. Gordon. il *Video* 12:56+ Mr '89

INSTANT REPLAY (SPORTS)
Best seat in the house. il *People Weekly* 31 Special Issue:140-1 Summ '89
Replay replay [professional football] P. King. il *Sports Illustrated* 71:84 N 27 '89
Scoreboard instant replays can be hazardous to your health. D. Shaw. il *TV Guide* 37:10-12 Mr 18-24 '89

INSTITUT KRASOTY
Reshaping Russia. S. Lord. *Vogue* 179:166+ Ap '89

INSTITUT MERIEUX SA
Connaught's foreign sale. A. Walmsley. il *Maclean's* 102:44-5 D 25 '89
Lament for a cherished asset [proposed sale of Connaught Biosciences to Institut Mérieux] P. C. Newman. il *Maclean's* 102:51 O 16 '89
Science and PR north of the border [sale of Connaught Biosciences to Institut Merieux] D. Powell. *Science* 246:1555-6 D 22 '89
Tempest in a test tube [bidders for Connaught Biosciences] G. W. Taylor. il *Maclean's* 102:42 S 25 '89

INSTITUT PASTEUR (PARIS, FRANCE)
"L'affaire Pasteur" prompts Canadian outcry [decision to publish journals in English] D. Dickson. il *Science* 244:280-1 Ap 21 '89

INSTITUTE FOR 21ST CENTURY STUDIES
21st Century Studies. il *The Futurist* 23:37 N/D '89

INSTITUTE FOR ADVANCED STUDY (PRINCETON, N.J.)
Institute for Advanced Study: past and future [interview with M. L. Goldberger] W. Sweet. por *Physics Today* 42:65-7 Je '89

INSTITUTE FOR PUBLIC POLICY LEADERSHIP
Open for discussion [work of H. Woods] P. Simpson. il por *Ms.* 17:83 Ap '89

INSTITUTE OF MEDICINE (U.S.)
IOM elects new members. *Science* 244:1436 Je 23 '89

INSTITUTE OF THE BROTHERS OF THE CHRISTIAN SCHOOLS *See* Christian Brothers

INSTITUTIONAL INVESTMENTS
See also
    Tactical asset allocation (Investments)
    Workout investments
Another wall comes down [law permitting institutional investors to trade unregistered securities] C. Byron. il *New York* 22:16+ N 27 '89
The best new stocks may never hit the Street [revised SEC rules on private placements] D. Foust. il *Business Week* p47 D 25 '89-Ja 1 '90
The business that brokers would love to ditch [commissions on trades for institutions] J. M. Laderman. il *Business Week* p106 Mr 27 '89
Forbes/TUCS institutional portfolio. S. Kichen. il *Forbes* 144:290 N 27 '89
The Forbes/TUCS institutional portfolio report. S. Kichen. il *Forbes* 144:112-13 Ag 21 '89
The Forbes/TUCS institutional portfolio report. S. Kichen. il *Forbes* 143:142-3 F 20 '89
Moneymen may stop deep-sixing proxies. J. M. Laderman. il *Business Week* p142 Mr 20 '89

INSTITUTIONAL REVOLUTIONARY PARTY (MEXICO)
Democracy wins a round [P. R. I. concedes gubernatorial race in Baja California Norte] G. D. Garcia. il *Time* 134:67 Jl 17 '89
Mexico: true concessions [loses to PAN in Baja] S. McGuire. il *Newsweek* 114:36 Jl 17 '89

No more mañana. R. S. Strother. il *National Review* 41:21-2 N 24 '89

INSTITUTIONS, FINANCIAL *See* Financial institutions
INSTITUTIONS, NONPROFIT *See* Nonprofit institutions

INSTITUTO VALENCIANO DE ARTE MODERNO (SPAIN)
New museum for Valencia. J. Gambrell. il *Art in America* 77:31 Ap '89
Something old, something new. F. Jarque. il *Art News* 88:125-6 O '89

INSTRUCTION *See* Education; Teaching
INSTRUCTION SETS (COMPUTERS)
See also
    Reduced instruction set computers
    Very long instruction word computers
80486, 68040 open new season of CPU power. *Byte* 14:13-14+ Je '89

INSTRUCTIONAL MATERIALS CENTERS *See* Resource centers
INSTRUCTIONAL TECHNOLOGY *See* Educational technology

INSTRUCTORS, COLLEGE *See* College teachers
INSTRUMENT FLYING *See* Aviation—Instrument flying
INSTRUMENTAL ENSEMBLES
See also
    Access (Musical group)
    Canadian Brass (Ensemble)
    Concert Royal
    Jazz groups
    Speculum Musicae (Musical group)
    String quartets
    Trios, Instrumental
Oboe to gamelan . . . want to join a music group? [San Francisco Bay Area] il *Sunset (Central West edition)* 182:50 F '89

INSTRUMENTAL MUSIC
See also
    Guitar music

INSTRUMENTATION AMPLIFIERS *See* Amplifiers
INSTRUMENTATION AND ORCHESTRATION
Cutting the orchestra down to size [various productions of the musical Drood] *Theatre Crafts* 23:54+ Ap '89
Primeval palette [R. Wagner's Ring cycle] R. Markow. il *Opera News* 53:26-9 Ap 1 '89
Realm of sound [Die Frau ohne Schatten] R. Markow. il *Opera News* 54:33+ D 9 '89

INSTRUMENTS
See also
    Musical instruments
    Scientific equipment

INSULATING MATERIALS *See* Insulation (Heat)
INSULATION (HEAT)
See also
    Clothing, Cold weather
    Draft detectors (Air infiltration measurement)
    Space stations—Insulation
    Space vehicles—Insulation
    Weatherproofing
An attic for all seasons. T. O. Bakke. il *Popular Science* 235:80-1 Ag '89
A blanket of restoration [urethane foam insulation for swine buildings] R. Brunoehler. il *Successful Farming* 87:38 My '89
EIF systems: quality lost in the translation? [Exterior Insulation and Finish Systems] J. S. Russell. il *Architectural Record* 177:124-7 Jl '89
Energy efficiency after insulation. D. Johnson. il *The Family Handyman* 39:62-5 S '89
Exteriors and outside insulation. il *Popular Science* 235:65-7 Ag '89
Help in dodging those wintertime drafts. D. H. Dunn. il *Business Week* p204 N 6 '89
High-fiber connectors [Thermomass Foam Sandwich Foundation System] C. M. Fiorillo. il *Popular Science* 235:44+ N '89
Insulation does its stuff. D. Johnson. il map *The Family Handyman* 39:18+ O '89
Product reports 1990. il *Architectural Record* 177:58-60+ D '89
Replace windows and add insulation. il *Workbench* 45:62-5 N/D '89
The sky's the limit [chlorofluorocarbons in foam insulation boards] C. Pearson. il *Architectural Record* 177:134-5 O '89
Sticking with stucco [exterior insulation and finish systems] il *Architectural Record* 177:186-7 D '89
Tiny bubbles [hollow ceramic spheres for insulation] G. Davis. il *Popular Science* 235:42 O '89

INSULATION (SOUND) *See* Soundproofing
INSULIN
See also
    Hypoglycemia
Beta-cell break benefits diabetics [research by Shirish C. Shah] *Science News* 135:156 Mr 11 '89
Diuretic dilemma [Swedish study] *Time* 134:103 O 9 '89
Hidden heart hazards [high blood insulin levels; cover story] K. Fackelmann. il *Science News* 136:184-6 S 16 '89
High-carbohydrate diet may pose heart risks [insulin resistance] K. Fackelmann. *Science News* 136:185 S 16 '89

INSULIN—*cont.*

Hypertension, heart disease and diuretics. R. Weiss. *Science News* 136:254 O 14 '89

Molecular defects in insulin action. C. R. Kahn and B. J. Goldstein. bibl f *Science* 245:13 Jl 7 '89

Pretranslational suppression of an insulin-responsive glucose transporter in rats with diabetes mellitus. W. T. Garvey and others. bibl f il *Science* 245:60-3 Jl 7 '89

INSULIN RECEPTORS *See* Hormone receptors

INSULTS, VERBAL *See* Invective

INSURANCE

Insurance myths you probably believe. P. Plawin. il *Changing Times* 43:31-3 Ag '89

Insurance your kids won't need. N. Henderson. il *Changing Times* 43:111-12+ S '89

Take cover. G. W. Weinstein. il *Ms.* 18:70-2 Jl/Ag '89

Adjustment of claims

See also

Insurance adjusters

A kinder claims court [alternative dispute resolution] il *Esquire* 112:128 S '89

Staking an insurance claim [interview with R. Alford] M. Henkenius. il por *Home Mechanix* 85:40-3 O '89

Claims

See Insurance—Adjustment of claims

Laws and regulations

See Insurance law

Rates and tables

Insurers are arming for another rate war. C. Farrell. il *Business Week* p108-9 Ja 9 '89

'Pennies-a-day' insurance probably isn't worth it. D. H. Dunn. il *Business Week* p98-9 Ja 30 '89

A rate-cut law's distant reach. *Nation's Business* 77:71 Je '89

What will protection cost? M. Rowland. il *Working Woman* 14:64 Ja '89

Reinsurance

Liabilities dangereuses [life insurance accounting] D. Wechsler. il *Forbes* 144:106+ S 18 '89

INSURANCE, ACCIDENT

Compensation for death and dismemberment. C. Thompson. bibl f il *Monthly Labor Review* 112:13-17 S '89

INSURANCE, AGRICULTURAL

See also

Federal Crop Insurance Corporation

INSURANCE, AUTOMOBILE

See also

Insurance, Truck

13 ways to save on car insurance. L. Brenner. *Better Homes and Gardens* 67:166 O '89

Auto insurance reform for consumers [cover story] T. A. Beauchemin and O. S. Kramer. il *Consumers' Research Magazine* 72:11-15 O '89

California insurers won't roll over. R. Grover. il *Business Week* p38 F 27 '89

Car drivers in revolt. J. B. Quinn. il *Newsweek* 113:55 F 13 '89

The collision over collision waivers. A. Fins and C. Power. il *Business Week* p96+ My 1 '89

The compelling case for no-fault insurance. M. C. Paulson. il *Changing Times* 43:49-52 Jl '89

A consumer revolt backfires as auto insurance rates rise [passage of Proposition 103 in California] *Money* 18:17-18 Ja '89

A crash course in when to come clean [reporting accidents] V. S. Sussman. il *U.S. News & World Report* 107:106 N 6 '89

Fill 'er up with no-fault, please [automatic auto insurance via gasoline tax] A. P. Tobias. il *Time* 133:52-3 F 27 '89

The flamboyant force behind California's auto insurance revolt [H. Rosenfield] G. Anrig, Jr. il por *Money* 18:145-6 Jl '89

Free CDW insurance [credit card collision insurance on rentals] K. McCormally. il *Changing Times* 43:120 S '89

Getting what you deserve on a homeowners or auto claim. J. Reid. il *Money* 18:147-8+ Je '89

Hard road ahead for auto insurers. S. Nasar. il *Fortune* 119:99-103 My 8 '89

Hold down your car insurance costs. P. Plawin. *Changing Times* 43:112-13 My '89

Honk if you're for Prop. 103 [car insurance reform in California] H. Hurt. il *Newsweek* 113:34 Mr 27 '89

How safe is your car? [report by Highway Loss Data Institute] il *Consumers' Research Magazine* 72:16-19 N '89

How you can save on car insurance. E. Henry. il *Reader's Digest* 134:61-4 My '89

Leave the coverage to us [credit card collision insurance causes rental rates to rise] B. Rudolph. il *Time* 133:46 Ja 16 '89

May I sue you? [plans allowing individuals to choose between no-fault and at-fault coverage] P. D. Waldstein. il *Esquire* 112:64 Ag '89

"Naaging" guidelines: keeping car-rental ads honest [eliminating collision damage waivers] il *Travel Holiday* 172:14-15 Jl '89

The people vs. the premiums [Proposition 103 in California] il *Esquire* 111:106 Mr '89

The Prop 103 'prairie fire'. S. Waldman. il *Newsweek* 113:50-1 My 15 '89

State Farm's huge harvest in auto insurance. D. Greising. il *Business Week* p78 Ag 21 '89

Tempting proposition [auto insurance industry securities] T. Jaffe. *Forbes* 144:141 Jl 10 '89

The truth about insurance you need (and don't need) in a rented car. E. Henry. il *Changing Times* 43:24 Ap '89

Try to insure that dream car. M. Keller. il *Motor Trend* 41:126 S '89

The war over bent fenders [high priced auto parts] il *Consumer Reports* 54:201 Ap '89

Who needs expensive coverage? [collision damage waiver on rentals] il *Consumer Reports* 54:478-9 Jl '89

Whose no-fault is it, anyway? P. Spiro and D. Mirvish. *The Washington Monthly* 21:24-8 O '89

Will your car coverage vanish? L. Wiener. il *U.S. News & World Report* 106:62 Ja 9 '89

Your money: insurance for rental cars. E. N. Berg. *Modern Maturity* 32:29 Ap/My '89

INSURANCE, AVIATION

Indecent exposure: CFI liability [flight instructors] A. Laboda. il *Flying* 116:36-7 O '89

Risky business. N. Moll. il *Flying* 116:48-50+ My '89

Anecdotes, facetiae, satire, etc.

Crazy claims. P. Boody. il *Flying* 116:70-2+ S '89

INSURANCE, BANK ACCOUNT *See* Bank accounts—Insurance

INSURANCE, BOND *See* Bonds—Insurance

INSURANCE, BUSINESS

See also

Insurance, Home office

More insurance for smaller firms. P. Zinkewicz. il *Nation's Business* 77:67+ Je '89

INSURANCE, DENTAL

Down and out—in the mouth [prohibitive cost of dental care] C. Sears. il *American Health* 8:40 D '89

INSURANCE, DISABILITY

Analyzing short-term disability benefits. J. N. Houff and W. J. Wiatrowski. bibl f il *Monthly Labor Review* 112:3-9 Je '89

Check that you have the coverage you need most. E. Schurenberg. il *Money* 18:77+ F '89

Disability and insurance plans in the public and private sectors. A. Blostin and others. bibl f il *Monthly Labor Review* 111:9-17 D '88

More likely than death. il *Esquire* 111:66 My '89

Plugging the black hole [rising-rate policies] J. B. Quinn. il *Newsweek* 114:47 S 11 '89

INSURANCE, DISASTER

Taxation

Disaster without relief [tax rules on casualty and theft losses] L. Saunders. il *Forbes* 144:124+ N 27 '89

INSURANCE, EARTHQUAKE

Earthquake protection. W. Giese. il *Changing Times* 43:24 D '89

INSURANCE, EMPLOYEE HEALTH *See* Insurance, Health

INSURANCE, HEALTH

See also

AIDS (Disease)—Insurance

Blue Cross & Blue Shield Association

Drug abuse—Insurance

Health maintenance organizations

Insurance, Dental

Insurance, Disability

Insurance, Nursing home care

Medicare

Preferred provider organizations

The $50,000 haircut [recovery from brain aneurysm] F. Swertlow. il pors *Money* 18:84-94+ My '89

Aide denies senator sought mandatory motorcyclist health insurance [Orrin Hatch] *Cycle* 40:26+ O '89

Are companies cutting too close to the bone? [malpractice claims may arise from new insurance plans designed to trim costs] M. Galen. il *Business Week* p141+ O 30 '89

Are you covered? E. Soshensky. il *Travel Holiday* 172:10+ Ag '89

Before the well runs dry: cutting the cost of retiree health benefits. C. A. Hanks. *USA Today (Periodical)* 117:86-8 My '89

Beyond Medicare [cover story; special section] il *Consumer Reports* 54:375-91 Je '89

Bill of health. *The New Republic* 201:5-6 Jl 3 '89

Biting the insurance bullet [national health insurance] S. Waldman. il *Newsweek* 114:46 Ag 28 '89

The calamity of catastrophic coverage. S. Dentzer. *U.S. News & World Report* 106:36 My 8 '89

Can you afford to get sick? [cover story; special section] il *Newsweek* 113:44-52 Ja 30 '89

A Canadian model [clamor for nationalized health insurance in the U.S.] D. Lindorff. il *Maclean's* 102:69 N 27 '89

Can't afford to get sick [health care issue in telephone strike] C. Gorman. il *Time* 134:43 Ag 21 '89

Catastrophic care's impending surgery. *U.S. News & World Report* 107:51 S 11 '89

A checkup on health benefits. R. Thompson. il *Nation's Business* 77:45+ Mr '89

INSURANCE, HEALTH—*cont.*

Confronting the crisis in health care: an interview with Arnold Relman [cover story] S. Hackman and R. Howard. il pors *Technology Review* 92:30-8+ Jl '89

Congress's health-care woes [proposal to scrap catastrophic insurance] M. W. Karmin. *U.S. News & World Report* 107:45 Jl 31 '89

The cost of chaos. R. J. Samuelson. il *Newsweek* 114:52 O 2 '89

The covered city [catastrophic health insurance plan in Montgomery County, Md.] il *Esquire* 111:70 F '89

Covering your longer life. L. Luciano. il *Money* 18 Money Guide:91-2+ Fall '89

Curbing the high cost of health care [cover story] R. Thompson. il *Nation's Business* 77:18-20+ S '89

'Dueling commissions' plot health care into the next century. S. Dentzer. *U.S. News & World Report* 107:31 Ag 21 '89

Easing the cost of catastrophe. A. Quinlan. il *New Choices for the Best Years* 29:45-7 Ap '89

Employees to pay more for benefits. *The Futurist* 23:45 N/D '89

First, you beat the cancer [facing discrimination] J. Silberner. il *U.S. News & World Report* 107:97-8+ N 6 '89

Health care: confronting the crisis [interview with A. Relman] S. Hackman and R. Howard. *Current (Washington, D.C.)* 317:10-15 N '89

Health care cost limitation [address, November 17, 1988] G. L. Musgrave. *Vital Speeches of the Day* 55:273-6 F 15 '89

The health-care crisis [address, October 27, 1988] C. W. Gray. *Vital Speeches of the Day* 55:304-7 Mr 1 '89

A health-care debacle [Medicare Catastrophic Coverage Act] S. Dentzer. il *U.S. News & World Report* 107:16-18 O 9 '89

Health care for a caring America [address, May 23, 1989] H. B. Deets. *Vital Speeches of the Day* 55:636-7 Ag 1 '89

The health care quagmire [cover story] E. F. Haislmaier. il *Consumers' Research Magazine* 72:10-16 S '89

Health costs: what, me worry? il *Esquire* 111:82 Je '89

Health insurance: any way you look at it, business will pay. S. B. Garland. *Business Week* p39 F 13 '89

Health insurance: weighing the tradeoffs [special section] J. Hamilton. il *American Health* 8:11-12+ S '89

Health kick [telephone workers strike over health care insurance] K. Cagney. *The Nation* 249:301 S 25 '89

The health policy crunch. J. B. Quinn. il *Newsweek* 114:62 N 6 '89

Healthy insurance [insurance and alternative medicine] J. F. Wasik. il *Mother Jones* 14:53-4 My '89

Koop de grace. il *The New Republic* 201:7-9 O 23 '89

Living without health insurance. P. Jones. il *Glamour* 87:158+ Ap '89

Mandated benefits' costly trap [impact of Massachusetts law] W. T. Brookes. por *Nation's Business* 77:49 Ap '89

Medical costs hit churches. *The Christian Century* 106:713-14 Ag 2-9 '89

Medicare covers more, but you may still need a medigap policy. D. M. Topolnicki. il *Money* 18:149-50 F '89

Medigap: costs more, covers less. C. Schaeffer. il *Changing Times* 43:57-62 Ap '89

Medigap gets a second opinion—from Congress. S. B. Garland. il *Business Week* p122 My 1 '89

The new bill of health [telephone workers strike over health care] C. Byron. il *New York* 22:16+ Ag 28 '89

No more health care on the house [Fortune poll] A. Farnham. il *Fortune* 119:71-2 F 27 '89

Notes and comment [blood test required as part of application] *The New Yorker* 65:27-8 My 22 '89

The Ohio secession [universal coverage bill] il *Esquire* 112:96 O '89

Older Americans in a changing society [address, March 22, 1989] L. Crooks. *Vital Speeches of the Day* 55:556-8 Jl 1 '89

Ouch! The squeeze on your health benefits [cover story] il *Business Week* p110-13+ N 20 '89

Our goal: quality health care for all. L. Crooks. il *Modern Maturity* 32:10-11 Je/Jl '89

Passing the buck. G. W. Weinstein. il *Ms.* 17:78+ Ap '89

The right medicine. H. Schwartz. il *National Review* 41:26-9 Mr 10 '89

Second opinions: first, talk to your insurer. D. H. Dunn. il *Business Week* p142 Je 5 '89

The short life of catastrophic care [repeal spurs medigap policies] S. Findlay. il *U.S. News & World Report* 107:72-3 D 11 '89

Some of the tough decisions required by a national health plan. L. B. Russell. bibl f il *Science* 246:892-6 N 17 '89

Tackling the health-care crisis. *Modern Maturity* 32:9 Je/Jl '89

To our health [proposed national health care program] R. Ruthen. *Scientific American* 260:18+ Mr '89

To your health. R. Coorsh. *Consumers' Research Magazine* 72:4 Je '89

Too much of a good thing? [medigap insurance] *Modern Maturity* 32:12 O/N '89

Unhealthy, unwealthy, and worse. S. T. Mandel. il *National Review* 41:25-6 O 13 '89

Why insurance fails those who need it most. *McCall's* 116:135 My '89

Accounting

The killer cost stalking business [health benefits] C. J. Loomis. il *Fortune* 119:58-9+ F 27 '89

Retiree benefits: this footnote doesn't have to become a nightmare. J. R. Norman. il *Business Week* p39 F 27 '89

Soothing the sting of an accounting rule [employee health benefits] L. J. Nathans. il *Business Week* p106 S 18 '89

Adjustment of claims

Filling the bills [medical insurance claims manager] B. L. Benderly. il *Health (New York, N.Y.)* 21:32+ My '89

Taxation

Cat scam [repeal of the Medicare Catastrophic Coverage Act] J. Weisberg. *The New Republic* 201:11-12 O 30 '89

Catastrophic follies [Medicare surcharge] P. Longman. *The New Republic* 201:16-18 Ag 21 '89

Catastrophic health benefits translate into catastrophic taxes [Medicare surcharge; cover story] P. J. Ferrara. *Consumers' Research Magazine* 72:11-14 Ap '89

Catastrophic politics [Congress repeals catastrophic health insurance] *National Review* 41:12-13 N 24 '89

Catastrophic tax bite [Medicare surcharge] J. W. Merline. il *Consumers' Research Magazine* 72:38 My '89

Changes ahead for Section 89. D. C. Bacon. il *Nation's Business* 77:6 Je '89

De-taxification [repeal of Catastrophic Health Care Act] D. Corn. *The Nation* 249:480-1 O 30 '89

Doubts multiply on Section 89 [federal benefits law] R. Thompson. il *Nation's Business* 77:17-18+ My '89

The elderly duke it out [Medicare surcharge stirs senior lobby] A. Miller. il *Newsweek* 114:42-3 S 11 '89

Freeing health care. S. M. Butler. il *National Review* 41:34-6 D 22 '89

Giving workers the boss's benefits [Section 89 of tax code] D. L. Boroughs. il *U.S. News & World Report* 106:BC1 Ap 10 '89

"Government gone crazy" [Section 89 of tax code on employee benefits discrimination; cover story] R. Thompson. il *Nation's Business* 77:20-4+ F '89

Health insurance: a tax-reform footnote trips up small business. S. B. Garland. il *Business Week* p45 Ja 30 '89

How the good guys won the battle of Section 89. il *Nation's Business* 77:101 N '89

How to beat the bite of the new Medicare income tax surcharge. *Money* 18:17-18 Mr '89

Invitation to catastrophe [Congress votes to rescind catastrophic health insurance] *Time* 134:33 O 16 '89

Looking beyond Section 89. R. Thompson. il *Nation's Business* 77:27-8 D '89

Medicare tax [municipal bond strategy as way to avoid surtax] B. Weberman. il *Forbes* 143:213 Mr 20 '89

Now you see it . . . [future health benefits for retired employees] J. Novack. il *Forbes* 144:57 Ag 21 '89

A push to repeal Section 89 [strictures on employee benefits] R. Thompson. il *Nation's Business* 77:6 Mr '89

Repeal a bad health bill [Medicare Catastrophic Coverage Act] D. Gergen. il *U.S. News & World Report* 107:76 S 25 '89

Section 89 among House GOP targets. D. C. Bacon. por *Nation's Business* 77:6 Jl '89

Section 89: beyond repair. R. Thompson. il *Nation's Business* 77:65-7 Ap '89

A senior citizen rebellion has Congress retreating in disarray [Medicare tax surcharge] S. B. Garland. il *Business Week* p43 S 11 '89

Taking the teeth out of a new tax bite [Medicare surcharge] L. J. Nathans. *Business Week* p156 Mr 13 '89

There's only one way to clear up this misunderstanding [repeal of Section 89] *Nation's Business* 77:80 Ag '89

The torpedo that slammed into catastrophic health care [National Committee to Preserve Social Security] P. Dwyer. il *Business Week* p70 O 23 '89

A victory for the haves? [Congress votes to trim catastrophic health care due to uproar over income tax surcharge] E. Clift. il *Newsweek* 114:38 O 16 '89

Why shifting investments to beat the Medicare tax can be a bad idea. M. C. Paulson. il *Changing Times* 43:120-2 Ap '89

Canada

A Canadian model. D. Lindorff. il *Maclean's* 102:69 N 27 '89

Health care, Canadian-style. K. Finnegan. *Nation's Business* 77:22 S '89

France

A tale of two eyes [cost of laser eye surgery in France compared to that in U.S.] L. Malkin. *The New Republic* 201:15-16 S 4 '89

Great Britain

See also

Great Britain. National Health Service

INSURANCE, HOME OFFICE

Office insurance: how to guard against wind, rain, fire—and errant skateboards. G. Hedberg. il *Money* 18:155+ Mr '89

INSURANCE, HOMEOWNERS'
See also
Home warranty
Insurance, Home office
Do you have enough property insurance? [guide developed by American Appraisal Associates] il *Consumers' Research Magazine* 72:27-32 Ag '89
Get a homeowners insurance checkup. P. Plawin. *Changing Times* 43:92-3 Je '89
Getting what you deserve on a homeowners or auto claim. J. Reid. il *Money* 18:147-8+ Je '89
Home insurance: what you need to know. H. Porter and S. Richmond. il *Reader's Digest* 134:133-6 Ja '89
Insuring your home. il *Consumer Reports* 54:572-8 S '89
Protecting your prize. C. A. Fried. *Money* 18:142 Ap '89
A simplified guide to homeowners insurance. H. Porter. il *The Family Handyman* 39:44-6+ Mr '89
Staking an insurance claim [interview with R. Alford] M. Henkenius. il por *Home Mechanix* 85:40-3 O '89

INSURANCE, HURRICANE
Where Hugo's winds will keep whipping. T. Vogel. il *Business Week* p46-7 O 9 '89

INSURANCE, INTEREST (ECONOMICS) *See* Interest (Economics)—Insurance

INSURANCE, JEWELRY
Jewelry insurance: make sure it isn't flawed. T. Segal. il *Business Week* p108 F 6 '89

INSURANCE, LEGAL SERVICES *See* Prepaid legal services

INSURANCE, LIABILITY
See also
Insurance, Automobile
Insurance, Aviation
Insurance, Homeowners'
Insurance, Malpractice liability
Insurance, School
Insurance, Space flight
When liability insurance can cover your construction-cost estimate problems [architects] A. Kornblut. por *Architectural Record* 177:31 Ap '89

INSURANCE, LIFE
See also
AIDS (Disease)—Insurance
Annuities
Living benefits (Insurance)
Savings Banks Life Insurance Fund
Do you really need life insurance? B. M. Stephens. il *Black Enterprise* 20:62-4+ N '89
Employer-sponsored life insurance: a new look. A. Z. Bellet. bibl f il *Monthly Labor Review* 112:25-8 O '89
A financial incentive to quit [lower non-smoker insurance rates] il *USA Today (Periodical)* 117:14 Ap '89
Finding lost insurance policies. P. N. Strassels. il *Nation's Business* 77:70 My '89
Good policies are sized right and fit needs that change. T. Thompson. il *U.S. News & World Report* 107:55-6+ Jl 17 '89
Insurance as a financial base. M. Rowland. *Working Woman* 14:82 My '89
Life insurance after 40. J. Kosnett. il *Changing Times* 43:65-6+ My '89
Life insurance: one of your best investments. A. Bladen. il *Forbes* 143:280 Je 26 '89
Life insurance without yawns. M. K. Evans. il *Gentlemen's Quarterly* 59:85+ Jl '89
The money on your life [term insurance] J. B. Quinn. il *Newsweek* 113:46 My 8 '89
The new game in life insurance. T. Paré. il *Fortune* 119:140-4 Mr 27 '89
A primer on new wrinkles in an old standby: life insurance. T. Paré. il *Fortune* 120:25-6 S 25 '89
A shopper's guide to buying the best term policy. R. J. Klein. il *Money* 18:137-8 Ag '89
This expert shares a secret: get your life insurance wholesale and save big bucks [views of G. Daily] L. Luciano. il por *Money* 18:189-90 D '89
You bet your life. M. K. Evans. *Gentlemen's Quarterly* 59:151+ Ag '89
You. bet your life [life insurers' eroding financial base] G. Morgenson. il *Forbes* 144:38-40 Jl 10 '89

Accounting
Big changes in bean counting. *Fortune* 119:144 Mr 27 '89
Liabilities dangereuses. D. Wechsler. il *Forbes* 144:106+ S 18 '89
Surplus loophole [accounting practices of Massachusetts Indemnity & Life Insurance Co.] D. Wechsler. *Forbes* 144:44+ S 4 '89

Policy loans
Tapping your insurance for cash. M. C. Paulson. il *Changing Times* 43:85-6 O '89
When you need a loan, does it pay to tap your life insurance? C. E. Cohen. il *Money* 18:191-2 Ap '89

Taxation
Death: the last tax shelter [survivorship or second-to-die insurance] il *Esquire* 112:88 N '89
Insurance shelters: are they worth the price? T. Segal. il *Business Week* p152-3 Ap 24 '89
Less glamour for single-premium life insurance. *Consumer Reports* 54:7 Ja '89

A price on your head [corporate life insurance for employees] L. Saunders. il *Forbes* 144:80+ S 4 '89
The prospects for single life in the 1990s. il *Esquire* 111:90 Ap '89
This policy takes the sting out of inheritance taxes [survivorship or second-to-die insurance] D. H. Dunn. il *Business Week* p107 Je 12 '89

INSURANCE, MALPRACTICE LIABILITY
Indecent exposure: CFI liability [flight instructors] A. Laboda. il *Flying* 116:36-7 O '89
Law and medicine [address, September 26, 1988] F. Haight. *Vital Speeches of the Day* 55:180-5 Ja 1 '89

INSURANCE, MEDICAL *See* Insurance, Health

INSURANCE, MORTGAGE
Let's make a deal [FHA and Veterans Administration loan guaranty funds] J. Novack. il *Forbes* 143:48 Ja 23 '89

INSURANCE, MOTORCYCLE
Aide denies senator sought mandatory motorcyclist health insurance [Orrin Hatch] *Cycle* 40:26+ O '89
Honda's CBR1000: now you see it, now you don't, and here's why. *Cycle* 40:38+ Ja '89
State Farm and Dairyland abolish superbike blacklists. T. Van Hooydonk. *Cycle* 40:23 My '89

INSURANCE, NURSING HOME CARE
A certain species of helplessness [with editorial comment] R. J. Margolis. il *The New Leader* 72:2, 10-12 Ag 7-21 '89
Collect now, die later [life insurance with long-term health care riders] il *Esquire* 111:54 Ja '89
Financing long-term care. J. B. Quinn. il *Newsweek* 113:52 Ja 30 '89
Getting smart about nursing-home insurance. M. Hodge. il *New Choices for the Best Years* 29:45-7 My '89
Long-term-care insurance: restrictions that can hurt. M. C. Paulson. il *Changing Times* 43:100 F '89
Long-term care takes the spotlight. il *Modern Maturity* 32:96 F/Mr '89
New reports and developments on nursing home insurance. il *Aging* no359:39-41 '89
Nursing home insurance: who needs it? C. Schaeffer. il *Changing Times* 43:59-62 Jl '89
Paying for a nursing home. il *Consumer Reports* 54:664-7 O '89
Paying for long-term care. S. Findlay. il *U.S. News & World Report* 106:56-8 Ja 23 '89
The truth about long-term-care insurance. *Money* 18:166 O '89

INSURANCE, PATENT ENFORCEMENT
Patent enforcement insurance. A. A. Lane. *High Technology Business* 9:8 Ja '89

INSURANCE, PROPERTY AND CASUALTY
See also
Insurance, Automobile
Insurance, Business
Insurance, Disaster
Insurance, Homeowners'
Insurance, Motorcycle

INSURANCE, RACE HORSE *See* Race horses—Insurance

INSURANCE, SCHOOL
Is there a liability insurance crisis? P. A. Zirkel. bibl f il *Phi Delta Kappan* 71:80-1 S '89

INSURANCE, SOCIAL *See* Social security

INSURANCE, SPACE FLIGHT
U.S. sets insurance minimums for commercial space launches. E. H. Kolcum. *Aviation Week & Space Technology* 130:69 Ja 30 '89

INSURANCE, SURETY AND FIDELITY
Guarantees with nothing behind them [Southeastern Insurance Group] A. A. Lappen. il *Forbes* 144:41-2 Jl 24 '89
Worthless guarantees [Southeastern Insurance Group's questionable practices] A. A. Lappen. il *Forbes* 144:10 S 4 '89

INSURANCE, THEATER
Insuring touring. M. Sommers. *Theatre Crafts* 23:78-9 My '89

INSURANCE, TRAVEL
Are you covered? E. Soshensky. il *Travel Holiday* 172:10+ Ag '89
So a quake wrecks your hotel room . . . H. King. il *Business Week* p208 N 27 '89
Travel insurance. B. G. Quint. il *Glamour* 87:66+ Jl '89
Traveler's aid. C. Torcellini. il *Forbes* 143:171-2 Je 12 '89

INSURANCE, TRUCK

Panama
Another Panamanian headache [to duck highway fees, U.S. truckers are registering and insuring their rigs in Panama] D. Fanning. il *Forbes* 144:80 N 13 '89

INSURANCE, UNEMPLOYMENT
Changes in unemployment insurance legislation during 1988. D. Runner. *Monthly Labor Review* 112:59-65 Ja '89
The Supreme Court expands religious freedom [unemployment benefits for individual who refused to work on Sundays] R. F. Drinan. *America* 160:388-9 Ap 29 '89
Unemployment: cutting the costs. R. Thompson. il *Nation's Business* 77:71+ N '89
Unemployment insurance in the United States and Europe, 1973-83. B. G. Reubens. bibl f il *Monthly Labor Review* 112:22-31 Ap '89

INSURANCE LAW—*cont.*
Vermont
Vermont: land of green mountains and self-insurance. L. Jereski. il *Business Week* p77 Ag 21 '89
INSURANCE PREMIUMS *See* Insurance—Rates and tables
INSURANCE RATES *See* Insurance—Rates and tables
INSURANCE STOCKS *See* Insurance companies—Securities
INSURRECTIONS *See* Revolutions
INTEGRATED AMPLIFIERS *See* Amplifiers
INTEGRATED CIRCUITS
See also
Bipolar integrated circuits
Charge coupled devices (Electronics)
Copyright—Integrated circuits
Ferroelectric storage devices
Logic circuits
Microprocessors
Microwave integrated circuits
Random access memory
Read only memory
Reduced instruction set computers
Smart cards
Television circuits
Transistors
Very long instruction word computers
Ciarcia's circuit cellar. S. Ciarcia. See issues of Byte through December 1988
Growing and carving micro-laser forests [chips hosting two million lasers] I. Amato. il *Science News* 136:68 Jl 29 '89
Ignored by the Nobels, engineering and technology are at last being honored by a significant new prize [R. Noyce and J. S. Kilby win Draper Prize] R. M. Adams. il *Smithsonian* 20:12 D '89
Kilby and Noyce win Draper Prize for developing microchips. I. Goodwin. il *Physics Today* 42:52 N '89
Working with counters. R. Marston. il *Radio-Electronics* 60:63-8 Ap '89
Defects
Predicting IC defects. il *Radio-Electronics* 60:6 Je '89
Design
Down-counter cookbook. R. Marston. il *Radio-Electronics* 60:71-7 F '89
New chip may speed genome analysis. L. Roberts. il *Science* 244:655-6 My 12 '89
Maintenance and repair
Broken IC pin. il *Radio-Electronics* 60:8+ D '89
Manufacture
See Electronic industries
Prices
The EC just says no to Japan's cheap chips. T. Peterson. il *Business Week* p46-7 Ja 30 '89
INTEGRATED COMMUNICATION NAVIGATION IDENTIFICATION AVIONICS *See* Airplanes, Military—Electronic equipment
INTEGRATED MICROCOMPUTER SYSTEMS
Listening to an inner voice [J. Yeh of Integrated Microcomputer Systems] A. A. Knocke. il por *Nation's Business* 77:52 F '89
INTEGRATED OFFICE SOFTWARE PLATFORMS
See also
OfficeVision software
INTEGRATED OPTICS
See also
Fiber optics
Optical data processing
Optical wave guides
INTEGRATED PEST MANAGEMENT *See* Insect control
INTEGRATED RESOURCES, INC.
Abandon ship! H. Rudnitsky. il *Forbes* 144:68-9 Jl 10 '89
Charlynn Goins could write the book on job mobility. P. Finch. il por *Business Week* p89 Mr 13 '89
Desperate hours at Integrated Resources. M. D. Oneal. il *Business Week* p44 O 30 '89
Drexel rushes in to save a fallen disciple. L. Light. il *Business Week* p65 Jl 17 '89
Eli Broad's revenge [buying core financial services assets of Integrated Resources] K. Kerwin. il *Business Week* p35 N 20 '89
Integrated Resources: the rise and fall of a debt addict. M. D. Oneal and J. H. Dobrzynski. il *Business Week* p182-4+ N 6 '89
INTEGRATED SERVICES DIGITAL NETWORK
ISDN prototyping telephone (I) [cover story] D. Tousignant. il *Radio-Electronics* 60:35-40 My '89
ISDN prototyping telephone (II). D. Tousignant and K. Sliger. il *Radio-Electronics* 60:61-6 Je '89
INTEGRATED SOFTWARE
See also
AppleWorks (Computer program)
Testing
AlphaWorks. C. Bermant. il *Compute!* 11:74-5 Mr '89
Compute! choice [Better Working Eight-in-One] D. Stanton. il *Compute!* 11:68-70 O '89
The integrated package: how far will it take you? il *Home Office Computing* 7:66-71 S '89
New friends and old [Framework III and Canon Cat] E. Shapiro. il *Byte* 14:139-40+ F '89

T/Master. H. F. Beechhold. il *Home Office Computing* 7:76-7 My '89
Trackball madness [ProPoint trackball and Microsoft Works] E. Shapiro. il *Byte* 14:129-30+ Mr '89
What's new in integrated software. R. Lockwood. il *Personal Computing* 13:107-9+ My '89
WordPerfect Executive. R. Kendall. il *Home Office Computing* 7:76-7 Mr '89
INTEGRATION IN EDUCATION *See* Colleges and universities—Desegregation; Public schools—Desegregation
INTEGRITY
Integrity [address, March 13, 1989] R. W. Roskens. *Vital Speeches of the Day* 55:511-12 Je 1 '89
INTEL CORP.
80486, 68040 open new season of CPU power. *Byte* 14:13-14+ Je '89
The 80486: a hardware perspective. R. Sartore. il *Byte* 14 Special Issue:67-70+ Fall '89
The Intel 80860. N. Margulis. il *Byte* 14:333-4+ D '89
Intel to Motorola: race ya [new 860 chip] O. Port. il *Business Week* p42 Mr 13 '89
Intel's Cray-on-a-chip [80860 RISC microprocessor] F. Hayes. il *Byte* 14:113-14 My '89
Intel's new 80860 CPU aims to be a Cray on a chip. *Byte* 14:11 Ap '89
Intel's plan for staying on top. C. Gottlieb. il *Fortune* 119:98-100 Mr 27 '89
It takes more than a good idea. R. Brandt. il *Business Week* Special Issue:123 Je 16 '89
Mr. Chips [D. House] C. O'Malley. por *Personal Computing* 13:72 Jl '89
The uncertain payoff from Intel's landmark case [microcode copyrights] R. Brandt. il *Business Week* p35 F 20 '89
INTELLECT *See* Mind
INTELLECTUAL DEVELOPMENT OF INFANTS *See* Infants—Growth and development
INTELLECTUAL LIBERTY
See also
Academic freedom
Censorship
Science, Freedom of
INTELLECTUAL PROPERTY
The battle raging over 'intellectual property'. P. Dwyer. il *Business Week* p78-9+ My 22 '89
Cold fusion and property rights. E. Rubenstein. il *National Review* 41:14 Je 16 '89
Crossing 'The thin blue line' [R. D. Adams sues filmmaker E. Morris] M. Lasswell. il por *Rolling Stone* p30 O 19 '89
Exon-Florio an imperfect tool for protecting U.S. technology. V. D. Cohen. por *Aviation Week & Space Technology* 131:68-9 N 6 '89
How can "intellectual property" be "protected?" [academic world; cover story; special section; with editorial comment by Harlan Cleveland] il *Change* 21:10-28 My/Je '89
How to protect your products and ideas. R. Gunnerson. il *Home Office Computing* 7:38+ D '89
Intellectual property. E. Dyson. il *Forbes* 144:202 S 18 '89
Technology licenses: new law closes bankruptcy loophole. M. Shea-Stonum and D. Sloan. il *High Technology Business* 9:15 Mr '89
Three faces of Eve told her story, now Chris Sizemore is battling a major studio over movie rights and wrongs [victim of multiple personality disorder sues Twentieth Century Fox over rights] D. Van Biema. il pors *People Weekly* 31:79-80+ Mr 27 '89
Trade-related aspects of intellectual property rights [statement, July 25, 1989] C. A. Hills. *Department of State Bulletin* 89:55-9 N '89
INTELLECTUALS AND INTELLECTUAL LIFE
See also
Boston (Mass.)—Intellectual life
Catholics—Intellectual life
China—Intellectual life
France—Intellectual life
Great Britain—Intellectual life
Los Angeles (Calif.)—Intellectual life
Paris (France)—Intellectual life
Pseudo-intellectualism
Soviet Union—Intellectual life
United States—Intellectual life
The high priests of knowledge [interview with P. Johnson] R. Knight. il por *U.S. News & World Report* 106:73 Mr 27 '89
Managing your intellectuals [excerpt from Right places, right times] H. Donovan. il pors *Fortune* 120:177-8+ O 23 '89
Minority report [P. Johnson's book, Intellectuals] C. Hitchens. *The Nation* 248:474-5 Ap 10 '89
History
See also
Bloomsbury group
Enlightenment
A must read for students—and parents, too [Paul Johnson's Intellectuals] M. S. Forbes, Jr. il *Forbes* 143:27 Mr 6 '89

INTELLICORP INC.
Cashing in on computer smarts. G. G. Marcial. *Business Week* p122 O 16 '89
INTELLIGENCE
See also
Genius
Intelligence tests
Mind
The blood-brain barrier [study of adoptees and intelligence by David W. Fulker and John C. DeFries] K. Wright. il *Scientific American* 260:27+ Mr '89
Drinking while pregnant risks child's IQ [research by Ann P. Streissguth] B. Bower. *Science News* 135:68 F 4 '89
Reeducating America [interview with R. Ornstein] K. Emmons. il *Omni (New York, N.Y.)* 11:16+ My '89
Athletes
Riding smart: Can intelligence hinder a cyclist? J. Kita. *Bicycling* 30:50 S '89
Blacks
The case of Michael Levin [CCNY professor censored for article on black intelligence] D. Seligman. *National Review* 41:38-40 My 5 '89
Minorities
Race and behavior [controversy over J. P. Rushton's correlation of race to intelligence and behavior] R. Dolphin. il por *Maclean's* 102:44 F 13 '89
Tasting the passing favorite flavors [fuss over racial theories of J. P. Rushton] A. Fotheringham. il *Maclean's* 102:56 F 20 '89
INTELLIGENCE, ANIMAL *See* Animal intelligence
INTELLIGENCE, ARTIFICIAL *See* Artificial intelligence
INTELLIGENCE, BUSINESS *See* Business intelligence
INTELLIGENCE, MILITARY *See* Military intelligence
INTELLIGENCE QUOTIENT *See* Intelligence tests
INTELLIGENCE SERVICE
See also
Association of National Security Alumni
Cryptography
United States. Central Intelligence Agency
United States. Federal Bureau of Investigation
United States. National Security Agency
Can America adjust to the new world of spying? D. L. Wheeler. il *USA Today (Periodical)* 118:16-18 N '89
To catch a terrorist [U.S. captures Arab airplane hijacker F. Yoonis] S. Emerson. il por *Reader's Digest* 135:107-11 O '89
Unintelligence. N. Birnbaum. *The Nation* 248:185-6 F 13 '89
Where spies really matter [efforts to improve U.S. intelligence] P. Cary. il *U.S. News & World Report* 107:24-5 Ag 28-S 4 '89
International aspects
Anti-terrorism networks. S. R. A. Crawshaw. il por *The Futurist* 23:12-13 Mr/Ap '89
Canada
See also
Canada. Communications Security Establishment
Canadian Security Intelligence Service
Royal Canadian Mounted Police
Germany (West)
Unintelligence. N. Birnbaum. *The Nation* 248:185-6 F 13 '89
Great Britain
Banned in Britain [issue of Harper's banned for article about British intelligence] E. Knoll. *The Progressive* 53:4 Ja '89
Mask of treachery [K. Philby; excerpt] J. Costello. il por *Conservative Digest* 15:59+ Ja/F '89
Political spying in 20th-century Britain. B. Porter. il *History Today* 39:7-9 O '89
Bibliography
The upper class and the underworld. N. G. A. Annan, Baron. il *The New York Review of Books* 36:24-9 Ap 13 '89
Soviet Union
See also
KGB
United States
See Intelligence service
INTELLIGENCE TESTS
See also
Aptitude tests
A confederacy of dunces [views of R. J. Herrnstein on IQ and falling birth rates] G. Cowley. il por *Newsweek* 112:80+ My 22 '89
IQ and falling birth rates. R. J. Herrnstein. il *The Atlantic* 263:72-6+ My '89
IQ and intelligence: what's wrong with testing? [excerpt from More like us] J. M. Fallows. *Current (Washington, D.C.)* 315:4-10 S '89
What's wrong with testing? [excerpt from More like us] J. M. Fallows. *The Washington Monthly* 21:12-14+ My '89
INTENSIFIERS, IMAGE *See* Image intensifiers
INTENSIVE CARE UNITS
ICU: the hospital within a hospital. V. Modeland. il *FDA Consumer* 23:31-5 F '89

INTENTION (PSYCHOLOGY)
The perception of intention [study of preschool children] V. Dasser and others. bibl f *Science* 243:365-7 Ja 20 '89
INTER-AGENCY CONSULTATIVE GROUP
Whole earth science. I. Klotz. *Ad Astra* 1:7 Mr '89
INTER-CANADIAN (FIRM)
Fokker initiates North American service with Inter-Canadian. C. Fotos. il *Aviation Week & Space Technology* 130:98 F 13 '89
INTERACTIVE COMPUTER SYSTEMS
Interacting with the tiny and the immense [scientific visualization] C. Mundie. il *Byte* 14:279-80+ Ap '89
INTERACTIVE FICTION *See* Computer novels
INTERACTIVE MARKETING
The coming of audio/video phone-based promotions. I. Mayer. il *Publishers Weekly* 235:73-4 Mr 3 '89
Relationship marketing. G. Slutsker. il *Forbes* 143:145-7 Ap 3 '89
INTERACTIVE NETWORK, INC.
Byte-sized baseball. K. Modesti. il *Sport (New York, N.Y.)* 80:15 D '89
INTERACTIVE PICTURE BOOKS FOR CHILDREN *See* Computer picture books for children
INTERACTIVE VIDEO
Coming for personal computers: full-motion video. J. Free. il *Popular Science* 235:94 N '89
Couch potatoes! Now it's smart TV. B. R. Schlender. il *Fortune* 120:111-12+ N 20 '89
Digital video interactive. B. Glass. il *Byte* 14:283-9 My '89
Finally, a way you and your TV can talk. F. L. Kritz. il *U.S. News & World Report* 106:70 Je 19 '89
IBM-TV? G. F. Gilder. il *Forbes* 143:72-4+ F 20 '89
Inventing the hyperdisc. F. Lovece. il *Video* 13:50-3+ Jl '89
Just call up and watch. M. Burgi. il *Channels (New York, N.Y.: 1986)* 9:92 N '89
PCs: open the video floodgates [digital video interface] il *High Technology Business* 9:6-7 Ja '89
Playing with ITV. M. Mandell. il *High Technology Business* 9:48 Mr '89
Hotel use
Check yourself out. G. Eichler. il *Esquire* 111:66 F '89
INTERCALATION COMPOUNDS
Inclusion systems of organic molecules in restacked single-layer molybdenum disulfide. W. M. R. Divigalpitiya and others. bibl f il *Science* 246:369-71 O 20 '89
INTERCELLULAR JUNCTIONS *See* Junctions (Physiology)
INTERCOLLEGIATE ATHLETICS *See* College athletics
INTERCOM SYSTEMS
See also
Closed circuit television
Speak softly? Carry headsets and intercom [Concept Industries' Softcomm C-40 headsets and ATC-4 intercom system for pilots and passengers] il *Flying* 116:37 Je '89
INTERCOMS *See* Intercom systems
INTERCONNECTED ELECTRIC POWER SYSTEMS
Power goals [merger of Pacificorp and Utah Power & Light] J. Cook. il map *Forbes* 143:116-17 Ap 3 '89
INTERCONSULT (FIRM)
The making of a consultant. il por *Home Office Computing* 7:46 Ja '89
INTERCONTINENTAL BALLISTIC MISSILES *See* Guided missiles
INTERCOURSE, SEXUAL *See* Sexual behavior
INTERCULTURAL COMMUNICATION
Cultures in transition: what the West can learn from developing countries [cover story] W. N. Ellis and M. M. Ellis. il pors *The Futurist* 23:22-5 Mr/Ap '89
People who meet people [meet-the-people programs bring tourists together with residents] B. Wallraff. il *The Atlantic* 263:108+ Ja '89
Shopping makes the world go 'round. N. Janus. *Utne Reader* p83 S/O '89
INTERCULTURAL EDUCATION
The class that deserves cutting [mandatory ethnic studies class at Berkeley] J. Leo. il *U.S. News & World Report* 106:58 My 29 '89
The color of learning [influence of ethnicity upon learning styles of black preschool children; work of Janice Hale-Benson] L. Troiano. il *American Health* 8:76 D '89
Cultural style in teaching and learning. A. G. Hilliard. *The Education Digest* 55:21-3 D '89
Educating language-minority children: challenges and opportunities. B. T. Bowman. il *Phi Delta Kappan* 71:118-20 O '89
The Regents' Round Table [report calling for greater multicultural inclusion in curricula of New York schools] L. Auster. il *National Review* 41:18+ D 8 '89
INTERCULTURAL MARRIAGE *See* Interracial marriage
INTERCULTURAL RESEARCH
The nature and nurture of emotions [relationship between facial expression and the physiology of emotion; research by Paul Ekman and Robert W. Levenson] P. Young. *Science News* 135:59 Ja 28 '89

INTERFAITH ACTION FOR ECONOMIC JUSTICE
How do we solve the global debt crisis? J. W. Skillen.
The Christian Century 106:1004-6 N 8 '89
INTERFAITH COOPERATION *See* Religious cooperation
INTERFAITH MARRIAGE
See also
Children of interfaith parents
How interfaith couples make the most of their differences
[Catholic spouses] R. T. Reilly. il *U.S. Catholic* 54:23-8
My '89
Interfaith anxiety [Jewish-gentile marriages face Christmas
and Hanukkah] il *Psychology Today* 22:6+ D '88
When your child intermarries [Jewish-gentile marriage] G.
Rosenblum. il *New Choices for the Best Years* 29:54-8
Jl '89
INTERFERENCE (ELECTROMAGNETIC) *See* Electromag-
netic waves
INTERFERENCE (LIGHT)
See also
Iridescence
INTERFERENCE (RADAR) *See* Radar interference
INTERFERENCE (RADIO) *See* Radio interference
INTERFERENCE (TELEVISION) *See* Television interference
INTERFEROMETERS AND INTERFEROMETRY
See also
Laser interferometers
The applications of closure phase to astronomical imaging.
T. J. Cornwell. bibl f il *Science* 245:263-9 Jl 21 '89
High-resolution microwave images of Saturn. A. W. Grossman
and others. bibl f il *Science* 245:1211-15 S 15 '89
Imaging to the limit [use of nonredundant masking and
fully filled aperture method] il *Sky and Telescope* 78:456-7
N '89
Mapping deeper within Saturn's clouds [microwave images;
work of A. W. Grossman and others] J. Eberhart. il *Science
News* 136:183 S 16 '89
Special report: optics clear air for astronomers. il *Popular
Mechanics* 166:16 N '89
INTERFERON
Counterattack [used to treat hepatitis C] *Time* 134:96 D
11 '89
Double-stranded ribonuclease coinduced with interferon. J.
M. Meegan and P. I. Marcus. bibl f il *Science* 244:1089-91
Je 2 '89
Drug combo: double whammy with a bonus [AZT and
interferon for AIDS patients with Kaposi's sarcoma; research
by H. Clifford Lane] *Science News* 136:141 Ag 26 '89
Hope for hepatitis C infections. *Newsweek* 114:92 D 11
'89
Hybrid protein may help fight cancer [product of gene for
interferon and gene for tumor necrosis factor] *High
Technology Business* 9:33 Ja '89
Interferon-α but not AZT suppresses HIV expression in
chronically infected cell lines. G. Poli and others. bibl
f il *Science* 244:575-7 My 5 '89
Role of Na$^+$/H$^+$ exchange by interferon-γ in enhanced expres-
sion of JE and I-A$_\beta$ genes. V. Prpic and others. bibl
f il *Science* 244:469-71 Ap 28 '89
INTERFLO MEDICAL INC.
A better gauge for measuring how heart patients are doing.
W. C. Symonds. il *Business Week* p54 Jl 31 '89
INTERGALACTIC CLOUDS *See* Matter, Interstellar
**INTERGOVERNMENTAL COMMITTEE ON SCIENCE
AND TECHNOLOGY FOR DEVELOPMENT** *See* United
Nations. Intergovernmental Committee on Science and
Technology for Development
INTERGOVERNMENTAL FISCAL RELATIONS
See also
Intergovernmental tax relations
INTERGOVERNMENTAL PANEL ON CLIMATE CHANGE
The Intergovernmental Panel on Climate Change. W. A.
Nitze. *Environment* 31:44-5 Ja/F '89
Secretary addresses panel on global climate change [remarks,
January 30, 1989] J. A. Baker, III. *Department of State
Bulletin* 89:13 Ap '89
INTERGOVERNMENTAL TAX RELATIONS
Where does the anti-drug money come from? W. F. Buckley.
National Review 41:62 O 13 '89
INTERIOR AND INSULAR AFFAIRS COMMITTEE *See*
United States. Congress. House. Committee on Interior
and Insular Affairs
INTERIOR DECORATION
See also
Apartments
Apartments, Remodeled
Art in the home
Boat decoration
Hotel decoration
House decoration
Lodge decoration
Nightclub decoration
Office decoration
Restaurant decoration
Store decoration
The best of interior design [1988] il *Business Week* p128
Ja 9 '89

Building an empire [work of architects C. Percier and P.
F. L. Fontaine in early nineteenth century France] O.
Bernier. il *House & Garden* 161:40+ D '89
Design. M. Bethany. See occassional issues of New York
beginning February 20, 1984
A look at the nineties [cover story] M. Bethany. il *New
York* 22:55-81 S 25 '89
Recalling a golden era in Manhattan design [S. Barrows]
P. Carlsen. il por *Architectural Digest* 46:350+ N '89
Awards
Record Interiors 1989 [cover story; special issue; with introd.
by Karen D. Stein] il *Architectural Record* 177:49-125
mid-S '89
Exhibitions
New products: NEOCON 21. il *Architectural Record* 177:154-7
My '89
INTERIOR DECORATORS
See also
American Society of Interior Designers
Arnold, Val
Baratta, Anthony
Biggs, Friederike
Boardman, Pauline
Bonetti, Mattia
Buatta, Mario, 1935-
Burn, Diane
Campbell, Nina
Catroux, François
Childs, Antony
Connolly, Sybil
Daigre, Jean François
Denning, Robert
Diamond, William
Dumas, Dick
D'Urso, Joe, 1943-
Fernandez, Waldo
Garcia, Jacques
Grange, Jacques
Hagan, Victoria
Hampton, Mark
Hicks, David, 1929-
Hodgins, William
Holden, Ann
Holl, Steven, 1947-
Johnson, Jed
Krieger, Lisa
Leen, Jerry
Leff, Naomi
Lewis, Sally Sirkin
Marino, Peter
Mathieu, Paul
Mlinaric, David
Moller, Barbara
Moore, Marnie
Parish, Sister
Pinto Coelho, Duarte
Piva, Paolo
Putman, Andrée
Ray, Michael
Samuel, Henri
Sills, Stephen
Siskin, Paul
Space planners
Spiegelman, Kathleen
Thun, Matteo, 1952-
Valls, Perucho
Wilkinson, Hutton
California designers' favorite shops. J. Chatfield-Taylor. il
Architectural Digest 46:132-9 My '89
New York designers' favorite shops. J. Simpson. il
Architectural Digest 46:146-56+ N '89
Parlors with a pedigree [decorators making furniture] M.
Malone. il *Newsweek* 113:72 Ap 10 '89
Licenses and registration
Agreeing to try to agree. M. F. Schmertz. *Architectural Record*
177:9 F '89
INTERIOR DEPT. (U.S.) *See* United States. Dept. of the
Interior
INTERIOR DESIGNERS *See* Interior decorators
INTERIOR WITH SEVEN FIGURES [dance] *See* Dance
reviews—Single works
INTERIORS IN ART *See* Rooms in art
INTERLEUKIN
Antibody to interleukin-5 inhibits helminth-induced
eosinophilia in mice. R. L. Coffman and others. bibl
f il *Science* 245:308-10 Jl 21 '89
A cancer fighter starts showing its mettle. J. O. Hamilton.
il *Business Week* p96+ Ja 16 '89
COOH-terminal-modified interleukin-3 is retained intracel-
lularly and stimulates autocrine growth. C. E. Dunbar
and others. bibl f il *Science* 245:1493-6 S 29 '89
Endothelial interleukin-8: a novel inhibitor of leukocyte-
endothelial interactions. M. A. Gimbrone and others. bibl
f il *Science* 246:1601-3 D 22 '89
Functionally distinct NF-κB binding sites in the immunoglobulin κ and IL-2 receptor α chain genes. S. L.
Cross and others. bibl f il *Science* 244:466-9 Ap 28 '89

INTERLEUKIN—*cont.*
Interleukin-1 costimulatory activity on the interleukin-2 promoter via AP-1. K. Muegge and others. bibl f il *Science* 246:249-51 O 13 '89
Interleukin-1 mitogenic activity of fibroblasts and smooth muscle cells is due to PDGF-AA. E. W. Raines and others. bibl f il *Science* 243:393-6 Ja 20 '89
Interleukin-2 receptor β chain gene: generation of three receptor forms by cloned human α and β chain cDNA's. M. Hatakeyama and others. bibl f il *Science* 244:551-6 My 5 '89
Kappa B-specific DNA binding proteins: role in the regulation of human interleukin-2 gene expression. B. Hoyos and others. bibl f il *Science* 244:457-60 Ap 28 '89
Mechanism of interleukin-2 signaling: mediation of different outcomes by a single receptor and transduction pathway. M. A. Tigges and others. bibl f il *Science* 243:781-6 F 10 '89
INTERLINE AGREEMENTS, AIRLINE *See* Airlines—Cooperation
INTERMARK, INC.
Intermark keeps pressing its luck—and winning [buying Fuqua] S. Toy. il por *Business Week* p60+ F 6 '89
INTERMARRIAGE, RACIAL *See* Interracial marriage
INTERMARRIAGE, RELIGIOUS *See* Interfaith marriage
INTERMEDIA PARTNERS (FIRM)
New blood for cable. P. Noglows. il *Channels (New York, N.Y.: 1986)* 9:45 O '89
INTERMEDIATE NUCLEAR FORCE REDUCTION *See* Disarmament
INTERMETALLIC COMPOUNDS
Intermetallic compounds for high-temperature structural use. A. I. Taub and R. L. Fleischer. bibl f il *Science* 243:616-21 F 3 '89
INTERMITTENT CLAUDICATION
Don't ignore those achy legs. J. Wood. *Modern Maturity* 32:22 F/Mr '89
INTERNAL MIGRATION *See* Migration, Internal
INTERNAL REVENUE SERVICE (U.S.) *See* United States. Internal Revenue Service
INTERNAL SECURITY
See also
Anti-Communist movements
Industry—Security measures
Loyalty oaths
United States. Congress. House. Committee on Un-American Activities
United States. Federal Bureau of Investigation
United States. National Security Agency
Soviet Union
See also
KGB
INTERNATIONAL AERO ENGINES
IAE plans increased thrust version of V2500 to power A320, MD-90. *Aviation Week & Space Technology* 130:62-3 Ap 17 '89
This engine maker is finally seeing a patch of blue [Engines' Braniff deal] R. W. King. *Business Week* p39-40 Ja 23 '89
INTERNATIONAL AGENCY FOR RESEARCH ON CANCER
World cancer patterns. S. Whelan. il *World Health* p25-7 Je '89
INTERNATIONAL AIR TRANSPORT ASSOCIATION
International airlines in Warsaw [special section] il *Aviation Week & Space Technology* 131:18-21 N 6 '89
INTERNATIONAL AMATEUR ATHLETIC FEDERATION
Starting over [B. Johnson to lose world records in drug use ruling] N. Underwood. il por *Maclean's* 102:66 S 18 '89
INTERNATIONAL ANTIQUE DEALERS SHOW *See* Antiques—Exhibitions
INTERNATIONAL ASSOCIATION OF FIRE FIGHTERS
Fighting the fires of racism. P. Rockwell. il *The Nation* 249:714-16+ D 11 '89
INTERNATIONAL ASSOCIATION OF MACHINISTS AND AEROSPACE WORKERS
Boeing machinists strike hits economy, airline fleet plans. R. G. O'Lone. il *Aviation Week & Space Technology* 131:126-7 N 20 '89
The Boeing strike: both sides are flying. A. Bernstein and others. il *Business Week* p44 N 6 '89
Can Eastern Air Lines survive? D. Pauly. il *Newsweek* 113:42 Mr 13 '89
Collective bargaining at Eastern. *Aviation Week & Space Technology* 130:9 Ja 30 '89
Eastern's labor mess may land in Bush's lap. A. Bernstein. il *Business Week* p26 Mr 6 '89
Going for broke at Eastern [strike] J. Castro. il *Time* 133:42 Mr 13 '89
Grounding a high-flying giant [machinists strike at Boeing] L. Griggs. il *Time* 134:57 O 16 '89
Lorenzo is running out of choices—and time. P. Engardio and G. DeGeorge. il *Business Week* p37-8 Mr 20 '89
No progress reported in second week of strike [Boeing] R. G. O'Lone. il *Aviation Week & Space Technology* 131:18-19 O 16 '89

Pilots will press Eastern to deal or face shutdown. J. T. McKenna and E. H. Kolcum. *Aviation Week & Space Technology* 130:68-9 F 27 '89
The story at Eastern Airlines [strike] W. F. Buckley. *National Review* 41:54 Ap 21 '89
Strike at Boeing cripples production of transports. R. G. O'Lone. *Aviation Week & Space Technology* 131:136-7 O 9 '89
Strike forces Eastern into bankruptcy court [special section; with editorial comment] il *Aviation Week & Space Technology* 130:7, 16-23 Mr 13 '89
Striking machinists return to work at Boeing; restoring full production may take six weeks. R. G. O'Lone. *Aviation Week & Space Technology* 131:85 N 27 '89
U.S. airline industry braces for Eastern machinists' strike. J. Ott. *Aviation Week & Space Technology* 130:92-3 F 13 '89
Why Boeing's hard line didn't pay off [strike ends] A. Bernstein. il *Business Week* p33 D 4 '89
The workingman's man at the takeover table [B. Freeman] C. Tucher. il por *Business Week* p62 S 4 '89
INTERNATIONAL ASTRONAUTICAL FEDERATION
Strengthening IAF's annual congress. *Aviation Week & Space Technology* 131:9 N 6 '89
INTERNATIONAL ATOMIC ENERGY AGENCY
IAEA General Conference deals with nuclear safety, environmental issues. il *UN Chronicle* 26:32 D '89
Safeguards controversy, continued [discussion of December 1988 article, Plutonium for all: leaks in global safeguards] R. Bolt. il *The Bulletin of the Atomic Scientists* 45:38-40 Je '89
INTERNATIONAL BALANCE OF PAYMENTS *See* Balance of payments
INTERNATIONAL BANK FOR RECONSTRUCTION AND DEVELOPMENT *See* World Bank
INTERNATIONAL BANKING *See* Banks and banking, International
INTERNATIONAL BEAUTY SHOW
International Beauty Show. *The New Yorker* 65:32-3 Ap 3 '89
INTERNATIONAL BIENNIAL OF TAPESTRY *See* Tapestry—Exhibitions
INTERNATIONAL BOARD ON BOOKS FOR YOUNG PEOPLE
Children's books in developing countries [workshops] *Publishers Weekly* 235:40-1 Mr 24 '89
INTERNATIONAL BOOK FAIRS *See* Book fairs
INTERNATIONAL BOOKSELLERS FEDERATION
International Booksellers meet. H. Fields. *Publishers Weekly* 235:56 Je 30 '89
INTERNATIONAL BROTHERHOOD OF ELECTRICAL WORKERS
AT&T settlement. *Monthly Labor Review* 112:49-50 Ag '89
Who won what at AT&T? L. A. Winokur. il *The Progressive* 53:29-32 D '89
INTERNATIONAL BROTHERHOOD OF TEAMSTERS, CHAUFFEURS, WAREHOUSEMEN AND HELPERS OF AMERICA
Can reform unhorse Teamsters bosses? [agreement to hold supervised elections to avert federal takeover] il *U.S. News & World Report* 106:12+ Mr 27 '89
Charges against Teamsters resolved. *Monthly Labor Review* 112:58 My '89
The feds drive a wedge into the Teamsters. A. Bernstein. il *Business Week* p90 F 6 '89
Overhauling the Teamsters [racketeering case] A. Bernstein. *Business Week* p35-6 Mr 27 '89
A Soviet election [determining whether Key Airlines employees wish to join Teamsters] D. Seligman. il *Fortune* 120:142+ Jl 3 '89
INTERNATIONAL BUSINESS MACHINES CORP.
Back in the driver's seat in disk drives [3390] J. W. Verity. il *Business Week* p79-80 N 27 '89
Behind the scenes at the fall of Rolm. R. D. Hof. il *Business Week* p82-4 Jl 10 '89
Big Blue bites the bullet. J. Hammer and L. Rosado. il *Newsweek* 114:48 D 18 '89
Big Blue's big overhaul. Z. Schiller. il *Business Week* Special Issue:147 Je 16 '89
A bold move in mainframes [cover story] J. W. Verity. il *Business Week* p72-8 My 29 '89
The chip of tomorrow—in yesterday's machine [IBM to retrofit PS/2 with 1486 microchip] G. Lewis. il *Business Week* p64 Jl 3 '89
Compaq vs. IBM: peace comes to shove. M. Ivey and G. Lewis. il *Business Week* p132 Mr 13 '89
Computer makers are blue—but not IBM. D. A. Depke. il *Business Week* p76 Jl 24 '89
Computers and preschoolers: Head Start/IBM Partnership. L. Tsantis and others. il *Children Today* 18:21-3 Ja/F '89
Defending the realm [J. Cannavino, president of the Entry Systems Division] C. O'Malley. por *Personal Computing* 13:71 Jl '89
A double whammy spooks high-tech investors. J. W. Verity. il *Business Week* p37 Ap 3 '89
The end of application software? [IBM's Systems Application Architecture] F. Langa. *Byte* 14:6 F '89

INTERNATIONAL BUSINESS MACHINES CORP.—*cont.*
An honorable retreat [IBM Palisades Advanced Business Institute, Palisades, N.Y.] C. Pearson. il *Architectural Record* 177:84-91 S '89
How Steve Jobs linked up with IBM [Next computer; cover story] B. R. Schlender. il pors *Fortune* 120:48-51+ O 9 '89
IBM clones a strategy from the clonemakers [mimicking Japanese machines] N. Gross. il *Business Week* p42 Ag 21 '89
IBM: does it have the right connections? C. O'Malley. il *Personal Computing* 13:88-91+ D '89
IBM goes to war. J. Daly. il *Maclean's* 102:46-8 N 27 '89
IBM pioneers a work-at-home program. L. Wu. il *Home Office Computing* 7:14 F '89
IBM special edition [cover story] il *Byte* 14 Special Issue:8+ Fall '89
IBM wins a patent for thallium superconductor [controversial because material first discovered by A. Hermann] R. Pool. *Science* 246:320 O 20 '89
IBM's Micro Channel gets a little respect. S. Gelfond. il *Business Week* p156+ Mr 20 '89
Innovation at Apple and IBM. R. A. Shaffer. il *Personal Computing* 13:45-6 S '89
Reinventing IBM [cover story] J. Dreyfuss. il por *Fortune* 120:30-5+ Ag 14 '89
Rising above the industry chaos [Micro Channel vs. EISA buses] F. Abatemarco. il *Personal Computing* 13:5 F '89
A slimmer IBM may still be overweight. J. W. Verity. il por *Business Week* p107-8 D 18 '89
Suddenly, software houses have a Big Blue buddy. D. A. Depke. il *Business Week* p68-9 Ag 7 '89
Telecomputing lives [IBM's deal with Siemens for Rolm] G. Slutsker and F. Meeks. il *Forbes* 143:51 Ja 9 '89
This Cyclone is out to rain on IBM's parade [Tandem's new mainframe] J. B. Levine. il *Business Week* p114 O 23 '89
What's ailing IBM? More than this year's earnings. J. W. Verity. il por *Business Week* p75+ O 16 '89
Why a change in direction was a step upward [A.-L. Verville] A. M. Russell. il por *Working Woman* 14:64 My '89
Anecdotes, facetiae, satire, etc.
Big Blue nights and dreams of glory. D. Gookin. *Compute!* 11:159 D '89
INTERNATIONAL CAPITAL ACCESS GROUP
The Junk King starts anew [M. Milken resigns from Drexel Burnham to start new firm] por *Newsweek* 113:55 Je 26 '89
INTERNATIONAL CHECKER HALL OF FAME
Squares. *The New Yorker* 65:22-3 Jl 31 '89
INTERNATIONAL CHRISTIAN EMBASSY JERUSALEM (ORGANIZATION)
Ambassadors of Zion. T. Barry and D. Preusch. *The Christian Century* 106:79-81 Ja 25 '89
INTERNATIONAL CIVIL AVIATION ORGANIZATION
British, Czechs push for tighter controls on plastic explosives. D. Hughes. *Aviation Week & Space Technology* 131:26 S 25 '89
ICAO assembly fails to agree on aircraft noise restrictions. D. Hughes. il *Aviation Week & Space Technology* 131:82-3 O 16 '89
ICAO members urged to boost efforts against sabotage. D. Hughes. *Aviation Week & Space Technology* 130:116-17 F 20 '89
ICAO upgrades security unit as part of antiterrorist effort [views of Secretary General S. S. Sidhu] J. Ott. por *Aviation Week & Space Technology* 130:109+ My 1 '89
U.S. airlines ask government to take more active security role. *Aviation Week & Space Technology* 130:62 Ja 9 '89
INTERNATIONAL COFFEE AGREEMENT
Another cartel bites the dust. P. Fuhrman. il *Forbes* 144:41-2 O 30 '89
Negotiations toward a new International Coffee Agreement [address, November 14, 1988] W. A. Wallis. *Department of State Bulletin* 89:15-17 Mr '89
One way to help Colombia [reestablish agreement] *World Press Review* 36:28 N '89
INTERNATIONAL COMMERCIAL POLICY *See* Commercial policy
INTERNATIONAL COMMITTEE FOR THE RESCUE OF SOVIET PRISONERS OF WAR IN AFGHANISTAN
A mission to Moscow. M. G. Harter. *America* 160:28-9 Ja 21 '89
INTERNATIONAL COMPETITION *See* Competition
INTERNATIONAL CONFERENCE ON THE CHANGING ATMOSPHERE: IMPLICATIONS FOR GLOBAL SECURITY
Climate change. N. J. Rosenberg and others. il *Environment* 31:2-3+ Ja/F '89
World Conference on the Changing Atmosphere: Implications for Global Security [report] P. Usher. *Environment* 31:25-7 Ja/F '89
INTERNATIONAL CONFERENCES
See also
Bush-Gorbachev summit conference, 1989
Commonwealth of Nations—Conferences

Conference on Confidence and Security-Building Measures and Disarmament in Europe
Conference on Security and Cooperation in Europe
Economic conferences
European Economic Community—Conferences
Organization of Petroleum Exporting Countries—Conferences
INTERNATIONAL CONVENTION ON THE PREVENTION AND PUNISHMENT OF THE CRIME OF GENOCIDE
The Genocide Convention [ratified by U.S.] *Department of State Bulletin* 88:3 D '88
Genocide Convention Implementation Act of 1987 [remarks and fact sheet, November 4, 1988] R. Reagan. *Department of State Bulletin* 89:38-9 Ja '89
INTERNATIONAL COOKING *See* Cooking, International
INTERNATIONAL COOPERATION
See also
ANZUS Council
ASEAN
Economic assistance
International education
International organization
Internationalism
League of Nations
North Atlantic Treaty Organization
South Asian Association for Regional Cooperation
United Nations
Warsaw Treaty Organization
For mutual survival we must bring our world together [address, January 1989; cover story] I. Asimov. il por *The Humanist* 49:5-8+ S/O '89
INTERNATIONAL CORONA RESOURCES LTD.
See also
Corona Corp.
INTERNATIONAL CORPORATIONS *See* Corporations, International
INTERNATIONAL COURT OF JUSTICE
U.S. refuses to abide by International Court of Justice [reparations owed to Nicaragua] *Utne Reader* p63 S/O '89
INTERNATIONAL COURTS
See also
International Court of Justice
INTERNATIONAL CYCLING UNION
What is the UCI? M. E. Mantell. il *Bicycling* 30:64+ Je '89
INTERNATIONAL DEBTS *See* Debts, External
INTERNATIONAL ECONOMIC POLICY *See* Economic policy
INTERNATIONAL ECONOMIC RELATIONS *See* Economic relations
INTERNATIONAL EDITOR OF THE YEAR AWARD *See* Editors and editing—Awards
INTERNATIONAL EDUCATION
See also
Alaska Sister Schools Network
Internationalism
Language and languages—Study and teaching
Peace studies
Student exchange programs
United Nations—Study and teaching
Conceptualizing world studies. R. B. Woyack and R. C. Remy. *The Education Digest* 54:32-4 Ap '89
Internationalizing college curriculum. R. Smuckler and L. M. Sommers. *The Education Digest* 54:43-7 Mr '89
Internationalizing the community college. M. C. King and S. H. Fersh. *The Education Digest* 54:52-4 My '89
Practicing 'international education'. M. G. Bruce. *Phi Delta Kappan* 70:738-9 My '89
Thinking globally: educating Americans for the 21st century. P. R. Piccigallo. il *USA Today (Periodical)* 118:29-31 N '89
INTERNATIONAL EDUCATIONAL EXCHANGES *See* Educational exchanges
INTERNATIONAL ENERGY AGENCY
International Energy Agency ministers meet in Paris [text of final communique, May 30, 1989] *Department of State Bulletin* 89:83-6 S '89
INTERNATIONAL FINANCE CORPORATION
Ooops, a success. E. F. Cone. il *Forbes* 143:10 Je 26 '89
INTERNATIONAL FLAVORS & FRAGRANCES INC.
Nose job [scent research by B. D. Mookherjee] B. Weber. il pors *The New York Times Magazine* p78 F 5 '89
The search for "living" spices [work of Braja D. Mookherjee] il *USA Today (Periodical)* 117:14 F '89
INTERNATIONAL FOUNDATION FOR THE SURVIVAL AND DEVELOPMENT OF HUMANITY
Foundation for a small planet. S. Shulman. il *Technology Review* 92:15-16 My/Je '89
INTERNATIONAL FREQUENCY COORDINATING COMMITTEE
International Frequency Coordinating Committee. S. Leinwoll. il *Radio-Electronics* 60:72-3+ Ap '89
INTERNATIONAL GEOGRAPHICAL UNION
The 26th Congress of the International Geographical Union [Sydney, Australia] W. Zelinsky. *Focus (New York, N.Y.: 1950)* 39:33-4 Spr '89

INTERNATIONAL GEOLOGICAL CONGRESS
Global change. P. H. Abelson. *Science* 245:449 Ag 4 '89
INTERNATIONAL GEOSPHERE-BIOSPHERE PROGRAM
Mission to Planet Earth revisited [cover story] T. F. Malone and R. Corell. bibl f il *Environment* 31:6-11+ Ap '89
Understanding global change. A. M. Clayson. il *The Unesco Courier* 42:48-9 O '89
INTERNATIONAL HERALD TRIBUNE
Global reach. M. Peretz. *The New Republic* 201:9-11 D 11 '89
INTERNATIONAL IMITATION HEMINGWAY COMPETITION See Fiction—Competitions—Anecdotes, facetiae, satire, etc.
INTERNATIONAL INSTITUTE FOR EDUCATIONAL PLANNING
Educational planners go back to school. map *The Courier (Unesco)* 42:33-4 Mr '89
INTERNATIONAL JEWISH COMMITTEE ON INTERRELIGIOUS CONSULTATIONS
New Jewish secretariat [forum for dialogue with Christian bodies] *The Christian Century* 106:873-4 O 4 '89
INTERNATIONAL JEWISH FEMINIST NETWORK
The Jerusalem agenda [conference] L. C. Pogrebin; A. F. Lewis. il *Ms.* 17:23-7 Mr '89
INTERNATIONAL LABOUR ORGANISATION
Identifying the world's poor. il *UN Chronicle* 26:60-1 S '89
ILO promotes human rights and decent working conditions. il *UN Chronicle* 26:65 Je '89
Rights of indigenous peoples protected by new convention. il *UN Chronicle* 26:54 S '89
INTERNATIONAL LAW
See also
    Airspace (International law)
    Asylum, Right of
    Consuls
    Embargo
    International Court of Justice
    Maritime law
    Passports
    Sanctions (International law)
    Slave trade
    Territorial waters
    United Nations. Legal Committee
    Work visas
The curse of legalism [U.S. policy] C. Krauthammer. il *The New Republic* 201:44+ N 6 '89
The damaged U.S. image [Reagan administration] R. A. Falk. il *The Bulletin of the Atomic Scientists* 45:59-61 Ja/F '89
Nouveau law and foreign policy [U.S. policy] D. J. Scheffer. *Foreign Policy* 76:44-65 Fall '89
INTERNATIONAL LAW COMMISSION (UNITED NATIONS) See United Nations. International Law Commission
INTERNATIONAL LEASE FINANCE CORPORATION
ILFC negotiates pact to buy 16 stretched Airbus A320s. il *Aviation Week & Space Technology* 130:111 Je 5 '89
INTERNATIONAL MANAGEMENT CENTER (BUDAPEST, HUNGARY)
East bloc meets mysterious West. M. Batki. *U.S. News & World Report* 107:42 Jl 31 '89
INTERNATIONAL MARITIME SATELLITE ORGANIZATION
GE Astro-Space, Marconi will team to bid for Inmarsat 3 contract. *Aviation Week & Space Technology* 131:79 Ag 21 '89
Management shifts made to resolve Inmarsat 2 development problems. J. M. Lenorovitz. *Aviation Week & Space Technology* 131:44+ O 23 '89
Soviet satellite agency to provide technical aid to Inmarsat. *Aviation Week & Space Technology* 131:81 Ag 21 '89
INTERNATIONAL MOBILE MACHINES CORP.
A hot phone maker that cooled off fast. J. Weber, Jr. il *Business Week* p104 Je 12 '89
INTERNATIONAL MONETARY FUND
Austerity's human toll [African maternity care] F. P. Hosken. il por *The Humanist* 49:17-19+ Ja/F '89
The best assistance. M. S. Forbes, Jr. il *Forbes* 144:27 O 2 '89
Danger in a 'dormant' crisis. N. M. Healey. il *World Press Review* 36:30-2 Ja '89
Economic restructuring in Sub-Saharan Africa. C. Lancaster. *Current History* 88:213-16+ My '89
Request for U.S. contributions to multilateral development banks [statement, April 17, 1989] N. F. Brady. *Department of State Bulletin* 89:21-30 Je '89
Scenes from the inferno [third world] A. Cockburn. *The Nation* 248:510-11 Ap 17 '89
Surge in IMF resources recommended [views of Michel Camdessus] il *UN Chronicle* 26:63 D '89
Will the U.S. be left holding the bag on third world debt? P. C. Roberts. il *Business Week* p22 O 16 '89
INTERNATIONAL MOTOR SPORTS ASSOCIATION
Bishops, king and queen. L. Griffin. il pors *Car and Driver* 35:161-2+ O '89

INTERNATIONAL MOTORSPORTS HALL OF FAME
The race to history at Talladega. il *Southern Living* 24:22 Ja '89
INTERNATIONAL MUSEUM OF PHOTOGRAPHY AT GEORGE EASTMAN HOUSE
Exposing history. P. Johnston. il *History Today* 39:3-4 D '89
International Museum of Photography opens new center. il *American History Illustrated* 24:8 S/O '89
INTERNATIONAL MUSEUM OF THE RED CROSS
Geneva's museum to the pity of war. A. Hills. il *History Today* 39:4-5 Je '89
INTERNATIONAL NEWS See Foreign news
INTERNATIONAL OCEANOGRAPHIC FOUNDATION
Crow's nest. J. Bradfisch. il *Sea Frontiers* 35:131 My/Je '89
Crow's nest. B. Rosendahl. il *Sea Frontiers* 35:323 N/D '89
Sea winds. See issues of Sea Frontiers beginning January/February 1986
INTERNATIONAL ORGANIZATION
It's a small world after all. *The New Republic* 201:7-8+ S 18-25 '89
One world, max. R. Wright. il *The New Republic* 201:68-72+ N 6 '89
INTERNATIONAL PAPER CO.
A niche papermaker undercuts a giant [P. H. Glatfelter vs. International Paper] il *Business Week* p88 Mr 27 '89
United Paperworkers and 16-month work stoppage. *Monthly Labor Review* 111:47-8 D '88
INTERNATIONAL PEN CLUB See PEN
INTERNATIONAL PHYSICS OLYMPIAD
US high school team garners gold and top score in Physics Olympiad. P. Janowski. il *Physics Today* 42:115-16 O '89
INTERNATIONAL PROGRAM ON CHEMICAL SAFETY
The numbers game. E. Somers. il *World Health* p12-14 D '88
INTERNATIONAL REHABILITATION AND RESEARCH CENTRE FOR TORTURE VICTIMS
Healing the wounds of torture. G. Thomas. *World Press Review* 36:59 My '89
INTERNATIONAL RELATIONS
See also
    Balance of power
    Consuls
    Disarmament
    East and West
    Economic relations
    Geopolitics
    Imperialism
    International cooperation
    International law
    International organization
    International security
    League of Nations
    Nonalignment
    Peace
    United Nations
    War
    World politics
Fear shifts, trouble floats as the cold war ends. J. M. Wall. *The Christian Century* 106:1190-1 D 20-27 '89
A global compact. D. Gergen. il *U.S. News & World Report* 106:87 My 8 '89
International outlook. See issues of Business Week
Is the cold war really over? O. Harries. il *National Review* 41:40+ N 10 '89
Notes on the new political culture. F. Halliday. il *The Nation* 249:234-6+ S 4-11 '89
Security Council permanent members discuss international issues [joint statement, September 29, 1989] *Department of State Bulletin* 89:66 N '89
'We should try to find more common ground': a symposium of leaders and foreign-policy analysts on the post-cold-war era. il *Newsweek* 113:29-30 My 15 '89
Bibliography
Recent books on international relations. L. E. Despard. See issues of Foreign Affairs
Source material. J. A. Kreslins. See issues of Foreign Affairs beginning Fall 1986
Periodicals
See also
    Current history (Periodical)
The third way: publications bridging the East-West gap. M. Specktor. *Utne Reader* p116-19 Ja/F '89
INTERNATIONAL RELATIONS PUBLISHING HOUSE
London's Verso to form joint venture with Soviet house. G. Feldman. *Publishers Weekly* 235:14 Je 16 '89
INTERNATIONAL RICE RESEARCH INSTITUTE
Fading miracle. B. Johnstone. *World Press Review* 36:48 Mr '89
INTERNATIONAL ROCK AWARDS
Rockers finally grow statuesque as their very first annual awards honor Richards, Clapton & Co. il *People Weekly* 31:52-3 Je 19 '89

INTERNATIONAL SATELLITE COMMUNICATION, LTD.
See INSCOM (Firm)
INTERNATIONAL SECURITY
See also
Disarmament
Peace
Peace studies
United Nations. Political and Security Committee
Global security: approaching the year 2000. G. W. Rathjens.
bibl f Current History 88:1-4+ Ja '89
INTERNATIONAL SIGNAL & CONTROL GROUP, PLC
Ferranti defends health of primary business, despite contract irregularities at subsidiary. Aviation Week & Space Technology 131:30 S 25 '89
INTERNATIONAL SOCIETY ON HYPERTENSION IN BLACKS
Doctors to meet in Kenya on high blood pressure. Jet 76:12 Ap 10 '89
INTERNATIONAL SPACE UNIVERSITY
The class of '88. R. Cronise. il Ad Astra 1:19 Mr '89
Educating tomorrow's leaders in space. P. H. Diamandis and T. B. Hawley. il Sky and Telescope 78:4 Jl '89
ISU: teaching cooperation. A. R. Dalby. Ad Astra 1:33 N '89
INTERNATIONAL STANDARD BOOK NUMBERS
See also
Bookland EAN system
INTERNATIONAL STAR REGISTRY
To name a star, for a price. L. A. Shore. il Astronomy 17:114-15+ D '89
INTERNATIONAL STUDIES See International education
INTERNATIONAL SUN-EARTH EXPLORER SATELLITES
See Artificial satellites—Astronomical use
INTERNATIONAL SUN SHADE INC.
Through glasses, darkly. M. Barrier. il pors Nation's Business 77:77 Ap '89
INTERNATIONAL SWIMMING HALL OF FAME
Making waves in Fort Lauderdale. il Southern Living 24:33 Je '89
INTERNATIONAL SWISS INVESTMENTS CORPORATION
Taken to the cleaners in Costa Rica. G. DeGeorge. il por Business Week p78 Ja 23 '89
You can run—but maybe you can't hide in Cuba [penny stock fraud scam by L. Zrnic] G. DeGeorge. il por Business Week p27 Mr 6 '89
INTERNATIONAL TELECHARGE INC.
A bubble ready to burst? F. Meeks. il Forbes 143:57+ Je 12 '89
INTERNATIONAL TELEPHONE AND TELEGRAPH CORPORATION See ITT Corporation
INTERNATIONAL TENNIS CENTER (DELRAY BEACH, FLA.)
Feds: 40 taxpayers: love [FSLIC inherits control] R. L. Stern. il Forbes 144:43-4 S 4 '89
INTERNATIONAL TENNIS FEDERATION
How much is too much? A. Wolff. il Sports Illustrated 71:80-2+ D 11 '89
INTERNATIONAL TRAVEL See Travel
INTERNATIONAL TRUSTEESHIPS
See also
United Nations. Trusteeship Council
INTERNATIONAL UNION OF UNITED AUTOMOBILE, AEROSPACE AND AGRICULTURAL IMPLEMENT WORKERS OF AMERICA See United Automobile, Aerospace and Agricultural Implement Workers of America
INTERNATIONAL WHALING COMMISSION
Letter from San Diego [annual meeting] T. Turner. il The Mother Earth News 120:38-40 N/D '89
INTERNATIONAL YOUTH AND MUSIC FESTIVAL
Song of Eastern High [J. Garrett prepares high school choir in Washington, D.C.] K. McCabe. il Reader's Digest 135:51-6 S '89
INTERNATIONALISM
The end of internationalism? A. Tonelson. The New Republic 200:23-5 F 13 '89
Welcome to the global village. L. Morrow. il Time 133:96 My 29 '89
The world united. K. Kolenda. il The Humanist 49:49-50 N/D '89
INTERNMENT CAMPS See Concentration camps
INTERNMENT OF JAPANESE AMERICANS, 1942-1945
See Japanese Americans—Evacuation and relocation, 1942-1945
INTERNS (BUSINESS)
Giving choices to a new generation [Pepsi-Cola's internship program] C. A. Rhodes. il Black Enterprise 19:184 F '89
Summer industrial intern program in tenth year [physics] il Physics Today 42:110 S '89
Summer jobs that pay off in experience. S. Woolley. il Business Week p160 F 20 '89
INTERNS (EDUCATION) See Student teachers
INTERNS (PHYSICS) See Physics—Study and teaching
INTERNS (SCHOOL MANAGEMENT) See School management and organization—Study and teaching
INTERPERSONAL ATTRACTION
How to increase your sex appeal. il Ebony 45:68+ D '89

Tall, dark first date [effect of height on perceptions of attractiveness; research by Alan Strathman and James Shepperd] V. Bozzi. il Psychology Today 23:67 Jl/Ag '89
Women: if you like heavy metal, don't tell your date [effect of musical preference on perceptions of attractiveness; research by Dolf Zillmann and Azra Bhatia] E. Stark. il Psychology Today 23:14 N '89
INTERPERSONAL COMMUNICATION See Communication—Social aspects
INTERPERSONAL RELATIONS See Human relations
INTERPLACE/TRANSWORLD RECRUIT (FIRM)
'White people, black people' not wanted here? [Japanese employment agencies in U.S. charged with discrimination] M. Galen and L. J. Nathans. il Business Week p31 Jl 10 '89
INTERPLANETARY DUST See Matter, Interstellar
INTERPLANETARY FLIGHT See Space flight
INTERPRESS EXPO 4/1988 (PERIODICAL)
Looking for markets. il The Bulletin of the Atomic Scientists 45:29 Je '89
INTERPRETERS See Translators and translating
INTERPRETIVE PROGRAMS (PARKS) See Parks—Interpretive programs
INTERRACIAL ADOPTION See Adoption and adopted children
INTERRACIAL DATING IN TELEVISION
'The Robert Guillaume show' features interracial romance and a nosey dad whose humor adds sparkle to new TV series [cover story] A. Collier. il pors Jet 76:58-60 Ap 24 '89
INTERRACIAL MARRIAGE
See also
Children of interracial parents
Black women/white men: what's goin' on? L. B. Randolph. il Ebony 44:154+ Mr '89
Cross-culture shock [long-distance editing by Atlantic Monthly Press of J. McIntyre Varawa's book on Fijian marriage] L. Fleischer. Publishers Weekly 235:207 F 24 '89
Joana McIntyre, 58, crosses cultures and generations to marry Fijian Malé Varawa, 28. R. Arias. il pors People Weekly 32:69-70+ Jl 31 '89
INTERREGIONAL GROUP (SOVIET UNION)
Chipping away at an icon [Interregional Group wants to debunk V. Lenin and rewrite the Constitution] B. W. Nelan. il pors Time 134:34-5 Ag 14 '89
INTERREGNUM, PRESIDENTIAL See Presidents—Transition periods
INTERROGATION, POLICE See Police questioning
INTERSTATE COMMERCE COMMISSION (U.S.) See United States. Interstate Commerce Commission
INTERSTATE HIGHWAY SYSTEM See Express highways
INTERSTELLAR COMMUNICATION
See also
Declaration of Principles Concerning Activities Following the Detection of Extraterrestrial Intelligence
Getting ready for SETI. F. White. il Ad Astra 1:3 S '89
Listening for life. L. Frazer. il Ad Astra 1:16-19+ S '89
SETI on video [The Quest for Contact] R. Burnham. Astronomy 17:105 Jl '89
SETI: putting an ear to the universe [cover story] B. D. Gibson. il Ad Astra 1:8-9+ S '89
SETI's guiding light [using supernovas to pick up extraterrestrial signals; theory of William F. Hilton] J. K. Beatty. il Omni (New York, N.Y.) 11:24 Mr '89
UFO update [SETI projects in the Soviet Union] P. McCarthy. il Omni (New York, N.Y.) 12:89 N '89
INTERSTELLAR FLIGHT See Space flight
INTERSTELLAR MATTER See Matter, Interstellar
INTERSTITIAL CYSTITIS See Cystitis
INTERTAN INC.
A Tandy spinoff whose earnings have bloomed. E. Schultz. Fortune 119:26 Mr 13 '89
INTERVAL TRAINING
Interval training [cycling] S. Johnson. Bicycling 30:136-7 My '89
More power to you with interval training [women cyclists] C. Patterson. il por Women's Sports & Fitness 11:18-19 S '89
The new rhythms of fitness. E. Kaufmann. il American Health 8:45-9 D '89
INTERVALS (MUSIC) See Musical intervals and scales
INTERVENING SEQUENCES (GENETICS) See Genetic code
INTERVIEWING
See also
Employment interviewing
The press and power [interviewing the president] D. O. Relin. il Scholastic Update (Teachers' edition) 122:18+ S 8 '89
INTESTINES
See also
Colon (Anatomy)
Physiological constraint on feeding behavior: intestinal membrane disaccharidases of the starling. C. Martinez del Rio and B. R. Stevens. bibl f il Science 243:794-6 F 10 '89
Diseases
See also
Colitis
Diarrhea

INTESTINES—cont.

Surgery

See also
Ileostomy

INTIMACY

See also
Embracing
Kissing

How do you build intimacy in an age of divorce? [cover story] C. Avery. il *Psychology Today* 23:27-31 My '89

How much does he really want to see? il *Glamour* 87:138 Ag '89

Mastering the art of intimacy. S. Nelson. *Working Woman* 14:114-16 Je '89

The new intimacy: rediscovering each other after the kids leave home [cover story] S. Levitt. il *New Choices for the Best Years* 29:38-43 S '89

Staying in love. B. J. Berg. il *Parents* 64:95-9 Je '89

"Why did my husband turn off to me?" [fear of intimacy] H. S. Kaplan. por *Redbook* 174:88 D '89

INTO THE GREAT SOLITUDE [television program] See Television program reviews—Single works

INTOLERANCE *See* Prejudice

INTOLERANCE [film] See Motion picture reviews—Single works

INTOSPACE GMBH

Crystal clear [protein crystallization experiment] W. H. Ganoe. *Ad Astra* 1:47 Ja '89

INTOXICATION *See* Alcoholics and alcoholism

INTRACOASTAL WATERWAY

Barges, boats and big birds [boat traffic eroding whooping crane habitat at Aransas National Wildlife Refuge] T. Turner. il *The Mother Earth News* 118:112 Jl/Ag '89

INTRACRANIAL BLEEDING *See* Brain—Hemorrhage

INTRAPRENEURS

See also
Black intrapreneurs

INTRAUTERINE DEVICES

Is the new IUD for you? S. Young. il *Glamour* 87:60+ Je '89

INTRAVENOUS THERAPY

Costs

Home remedies. E. Paris. *Forbes* 143:58+ Ja 9 '89

Equipment

See also
T² Medical Inc.

INTRODUCTION OF ANIMALS *See* Animal introduction
INTRODUCTION OF BIRDS *See* Bird introduction
INTRODUCTION OF INSECTS *See* Insect introduction
INTRONS *See* Genetic code
INTRUSION ALARM SYSTEMS *See* Alarms
INTUITION

Everyday intuition [cover story] B. L. Benderly. il *Psychology Today* 23:35-8+ S '89

Intuition & strategic planning. W. H. Agor. il por *The Futurist* 23:20-3 N/D '89

INTURRISI, LOUIS

A cool Roman holiday. il *Travel Holiday* 172:98 S '89
Living Chess Game. il *Travel Holiday* 171:92 Ja '89

INUITS *See* Eskimos
INVASION OF PRIVACY *See* Right of privacy
INVASIVE PLANTS

Green invaders. A. Lacy. il por *Organic Gardening* 36:96 Mr '89

INVECTIVE

See also
Racial slurs

When words hurt [parents' use of verbal abuse] B. M. Campbell. il *Essence* 20:88 Jl '89

INVENT AMERICA! (PROGRAM)

Invent America. il *National Geographic World* 166:8-9 Je '89

INVENTIONS

See also
Inventors
Patents
Technological innovations

Far-out inventions. il *National Geographic World* 166:10-13 Je '89

Competitions

See also
Invent America! (Program)

Exhibitions

Reclaiming some talents lost to time [The real McCoy: African-American invention and innovation, 1619-1930 at the Anacostia Museum] K. M. Burke. il *Smithsonian* 20:212 S '89

INVENTORIES

See also
Computer stores—Inventories
Just-in-time system

Are inventories really under control? M. J. Mandel. il *Business Week* p71 Jl 31 '89

Have laser gun, Ballantine reps will travel—faster and smarter [speeding inventory and ordering] J. Mutter. il *Publishers Weekly* 235:53-5 F 17 '89

Taxation

A tax jolt by design [package design costs now must be included in inventory] G. W. Padwe. il *Nation's Business* 77:82 Je '89

INVENTORS

See also
Black inventors
Edison, Thomas A. (Thomas Alva), 1847-1931
Handicapped as inventors
Inventions
Mills, Vic

America's real Founding Fathers [interview with T. P. Hughes] A. P. Sanoff. il por *U.S. News & World Report* 106:64 My 8 '89

INVENTORS' COUNCIL

Helping new inventions meet their makers. J. F. Siler. il *Business Week* p66 Jl 24 '89

INVENTORS' GROUPS

See also
Inventors' Council

Helping new inventions meet their makers. J. F. Siler. il *Business Week* p66 Jl 24 '89

INVENTORY CONTROL *See* Inventories

INVERTEBRATES

See also
Coelenterates
Crustaceans
Eye—Invertebrates
Water bears

Shredders and riparian vegetation [relationship between plant litter and aquatic invertebrate growth] K. W. Cummins and others. bibl f il *BioScience* 39:24-30 Ja '89

Spineless wonders. R. M. Pyle. il *International Wildlife* 19:14-17 S/O '89

INVERTEBRATES, FOSSIL

Oldest animal fossils may not be so old [Ediacaran fossils from Australia; research by Jeffrey F. Mount] *Earth Science* 41:9 Wint '88

INVERTERS, ELECTRIC *See* Electric current inverters
INVESTIGATIONS, GOVERNMENT *See* Government investigations
INVESTIGATORS, PRIVATE *See* Detectives
INVESTMENT ADVISERS

See also
Alliance Capital Management Corp.
Aronson & Fogler
Bailard, Biehl & Kaiser
Berg Partners
Brokers
Burney Company
Capital Group Inc.
Carlyle Group
Cisneros Group
Claremont Economics Institute
Clemente Capital Inc.
Colonial Management Associates, Inc.
Credit Advisors Inc.
Criterion Group Inc.
Cumberland Associates
David J. Greene and Company
Delaware Management Company, Inc.
Edward O. Thorp & Associates
Equitable Capital Management Corporation
Equity Investment Corporation
Fidelity Management & Research Co.
First Capital Partners
GeoCapital Corporation
Gibson Capital Management
Gramercy Capital Management
Grantham, Mayo, Van Otterloo & Company
Growth Stock Outlook, Inc.
Houlihan, Lokey, Howard & Zukin Investment Management
J. & W. Seligman & Co. Inc.
Kellogg Associates
Morgan Stanley Asset Management/Chicago Group
Newell Associates
Pension fund managers
Perrin Long Inc.
Peter B. Cannell & Company
Sandler Capital Management
Sanford C. Bernstein & Co., Inc.
Southeastern Asset Management Inc.
Steinhardt Partners
Tweedy, Browne Inc.
Value Line Inc.
Wells Fargo Investment Advisors
Women investment advisers

The 20% "guarantee" [claims by C. J. Givens] J. Queenan. por *Forbes* 143:260 Je 26 '89

Are these the new Warren Buffetts? B. D. Fromson. il *Fortune* 120 no10 Special Issue:79+ Fall '89

Avoiding fraud and abuse by financial planners. il *Consumers' Research Magazine* 72:25-9 F '89

Betting on the house [fund manager performance] J. Heins. il *Forbes* 144:180-1 S 4 '89

Big-time managers for small-fry investors. E. Schultz. il *Fortune* 120:34+ D 4 '89

INVESTMENT BANKING—Great Britain—*cont.*

Big Bang: big bust, big lessons. R. A. Melcher. il *Business Week* p38-9 Mr 6 '89

Italy

See also
Mediobanca

Japan

See also
Nomura Securities Co. Ltd.
Nomura Wasserstein Perella Company

The hard line coming from Tokyo banks [financing of U.S. leveraged buyouts] T. Holden and W. Glasgall. il *Business Week* p29 O 30 '89

Japan learns the takeover game. G. Hector. il *Fortune* 120:121+ Jl 31 '89

Japanese dealmakers yearn to play QB [Japanese act as silent partners to American investment bankers] J. Friedman. il *Business Week* p82-3 Ja 16 '89

Switzerland

See also
Crédit Suisse

United States
See Investment banking

INVESTMENT BANKING IN LITERATURE

A kiss-and-tell tale from the trading floor [M. Lewis' book Liar's poker about Salomon Inc.] J. Schwartz. il por *Newsweek* 114:62 N 20 '89

One million dollars, no tears [book by M. Lewis] C. Byron. il por *New York* 22:26+ O 9 '89

Playing for keeps when he quit Wall Street, Michael Lewis hits the jackpot with Liar's poker. K. Hubbard. il pors *People Weekly* 32:73-4 D 18 '89

There goes the bonus [M. Lewis' book about Salomon Inc.] J. Queenan. il *Forbes* 144:14 O 30 '89

INVESTMENT CLUBS

See also
AEA Investors, Inc.
Venture capital clubs

Club clout. G. W. Weinstein. il *Ms.* 18:46+ S '89

Clubs where your dues can pay fat dividends. S. Woolley. il *Business Week* p102-3 Ag 21 '89

How to launch an investment club. W. L. Updegrave. il *Money* 18:117-18+ My '89

INVESTMENT COMPANIES *See* Investment trusts

INVESTMENT FRAUD

See also
Ponzi schemes
Real estate investment fraud

Act two [A. Holzer charged with investment fraud] J. Kasindorf. il pors *New York* 22:46-52+ Ap 10 '89

Avoiding fraud and abuse by financial planners. il *Consumers' Research Magazine* 72:25-9 F '89

A backlash against business? [special section] il *Business Week* p30-6 F 6 '89

Beware of penny stocks [excerpt from Investor alert!] il *Consumers' Research Magazine* 72:26-8 Ap '89

Biggest catch [swindler C. D. Noe] A. Farnham. il por *Fortune* 119:59 Ja 2 '89

The fugitive king of penny stocks [J. C. Schidlowski] D. Zigas. il pors *Business Week* p124-5+ N 20 '89

Gentleman scamster [G. Bissell's fraudulent DewKist Plants] R. L. Stern. il por *Forbes* 143:104+ F 20 '89

Have the penny stock police caught a live one? [Power Securities] P. Engardio. il por *Business Week* p132 F 20 '89

Heads you lose, tails you lose [coin investment scams] M. C. Paulson. il *Changing Times* 43:71-6 F '89

"How did I know the guy was calling from jail?" [J. Darder implicated in penny stock fraud over disposable razor] R. L. Stern. il por *Forbes* 143:120+ My 29 '89

Investing in rare coins. il *Consumers' Research Magazine* 72:19-21 My '89

"Like a slaughter-house for hogs" [Mafia manipulation of penny stocks] R. L. Stern and C. Poole. il *Forbes* 144:42-4 D 25 '89

The man who knew too much [involvement of M. Zolp and the Mafia in securities fraud] J. Crudele. il por *New York* 22:16 Mr 6 '89

The many incarnations of Barry Davis. L. J. Nathans and D. Zigas. il por *Business Week* p94 My 29 '89

The most brazen of the penny hustlers? [Power Securities] P. Engardio. il por *Business Week* p130+ N 20 '89

The Moynihan rip-off [municipal bond issues by nonprofit corporations] M. Schifrin. il *Forbes* 144:38-9 D 11 '89

Never, but never, give a sucker an even break [securities fraud charges against A. Kimmes implicate M. Blinder] R. L. Stern and others. il pors *Forbes* 143:46-50 Ja 9 '89

The penny stock scandal [cover story] P. Engardio and G. DeGeorge. il *Business Week* p74-7+ Ja 23 '89

Pyramid scheme [fraud perpetrated by A. Abdul-Fattah in Egypt] W. P. Barrett. il *Forbes* 143:106+ Ap 17 '89

The Ron and John show [R. White and J. Joseph's limited partnerships] R. King. il pors *Forbes* 143:103+ Je 26 '89

The sad saga of a penny-stock company [Sequential Information Systems Inc.] G. Weiss. il por *Business Week* p124-6+ My 15 '89

A taste for art and money [investment fraud by R. Polo] C. Dickey. il por *Newsweek* 113:68 My 29 '89

Telemarketing investment fraud [cover story; special section] *Consumers' Research Magazine* 72:10-12+ Ja '89

Warning: con men want to manage your money. L. Reibstein and C. Friday. il *Reader's Digest* 134:169-70+ My '89

When it sounds too good to be true [prospectus] G. Slutsker. il *Forbes* 143:256-7 Je 26 '89

When the Bubble burst, all of England wound up broke [18th century stock swindle] R. Wernick. bibl (p183) il *Smithsonian* 20:155-6+ D '89

You can run—but maybe you can't hide in Cuba [penny stock fraud scam by L. Zrnic of International Swiss Investments] G. DeGeorge. il por *Business Week* p27 Mr 6 '89

INVESTMENT NEWSLETTERS

See also
BI research (Newsletter)
Chartist (Newsletter)
Granville market letter
Market logic (Newsletter)
McKeever strategy letter (Newsletter)
Prudent speculator (Newsletter)
Stockmarket cycles (Newsletter)
Zweig forecast (Newsletter)

10 stocks that top newsletter editors are recommending now. il *Money* 18:39-43 Ag '89

Beware those high-cost mutual funds [interview with Mutual fund letter publisher G. Perritt] E. Schultz. il por *Fortune* 119:34-5 Mr 13 '89

A Dow theorist sees stocks falling 400 points only to soar again to beyond 3000 [R. L. Evans of Dow theory forecasts] C. E. Cohen. il por *Money* 18:177-8 S '89

Fantasy and reality. D. Machan. il por *Forbes* 144:282+ N 27 '89

Personal newsletter [Personal portfolio manager] P. Duggan. il por *Forbes* 143:254 Je 26 '89

Prophet without honor [H. W. Gourgue's theory that ads in financial planning portend investment disaster] J. Queenan. il por *Forbes* 143:129+ Ap 17 '89

Stock tips and slot machines [Las Vegas meeting for investors sponsored by financial newsletter editors] R. Conniff. il *Time* 133:16-17 My 8 '89

This top-ranked contrarian predicts stocks will hit their pre-crash highs in '89 [Market mania publisher G. Cutler] J. Ellis. il por *Money* 18:163-4 Ja '89

Timing the bull [mutual fund advisory letters] M. Hulbert. il *Forbes* 144:156+ S 4 '89

Wall Street irregular. M. Hulbert. See issues of Forbes beginning September 21, 1977

Prices

How much is astrology worth? M. Hulbert. il *Forbes* 144:259 O 2 '89

INVESTMENT RECORDS *See* Records

INVESTMENT SEMINARS

Stock tips and slot machines [Las Vegas meeting for investors sponsored by financial newsletter editors] R. Conniff. il *Time* 133:16-17 My 8 '89

INVESTMENT TAX CREDIT

Eyesores into showplaces—even without a tax break [rehabbing] J. Weber, Jr. il *Business Week* p36 Ja 16 '89

Help house the poor—and cut your taxes [real estate limited partnerships] T. Segal. *Business Week* p126 D 4 '89

Restoring the rehab tax credit. M. F. Schmertz. *Architectural Record* 177:11 Ag '89

A shrinking market in rehab? Not necessarily. il *Architectural Record* 177:33 O '89

INVESTMENT TRUSTS

See also
44 Wall Street Equity Fund
44 Wall Street Fund
1838 Bond-Debenture Trading Fund
Acorn Fund, Inc.
Americus Shareowner Service Corporation
Baker, Fentress & Co.
Benham Capital Management Group
Brandywine Fund
Capital Preservation Fund
Cash management accounts
Century Shares Trust
College Retirement Equities Fund
Commodity funds
Common Fund
Dodge & Cox Stock Fund
Dreyfus Corp.
Dreyfus Worldwide Dollar Money Market Fund
Fidelity Capital Appreciation Fund
Fidelity Magellan Fund
Fidelity Management & Research Co.
Fidelity Select Leisure & Entertainment Fund
Fidelity Spartan Money Market Fund
First Financial Fund
Foreign exchange cash funds
Freedom Regional Bank Fund
G. T. Europe Growth Fund
Gabelli Growth Fund
Growth Stock Outlook, Inc.
Index funds

INVESTMENT TRUSTS—See also—*cont.*

Legg Mason Value Trust
Loomis Sayles & Co. Inc.
MassMutual Corporate Investors
Natural gas investment trusts
New America High Income Fund, Inc.
Nicholas Fund
Odd-Lot Fund
Oppenheimer Global Fund
Paloma Partners
Petroleum investment trusts
Pilgrim Prime Rate Trust
Pioneer Group, Inc.
Prudential-Bache Utility Fund
Quantum Fund
Quasar Fund
Real estate investment trusts
Scudder Capital Growth Fund
Selected American Shares, Inc.
Sevin Rosen Management Company
Source Capital, Inc.
T. Rowe Price High Yield Fund
T. Rowe Price New Frontier Fund
T. Rowe Price Science & Technology Fund
Templeton Emerging Markets Fund
Tiger Fund
Trend Fund
Twentieth Century Investors, Inc.
United Income Fund
United International Growth Fund
Windsor Fund

The 20% "guarantee" [claims by C. J. Givens] J. Queenan. por *Forbes* 143:260 Je 26 '89

20 superior funds to buy now and hold. C. Willis. il *Money* 18:135-6+ Mr '89

1988: the year the sun came out again—but too few noticed. E. Schurenberg. il *Money* 18:49-51 F '89

Aim for 9% yields with no risk [money market funds] M. Sivy. *Money* 18:85+ D '89

Allocating your assets: you may not need a pro. L. J. Nathans. il *Business Week* p152-3 My 8 '89

The almost-perfect-market thesis [closed-end fund investor S. Bednarski] J. Clements. il por *Forbes* 143:150-1 F 6 '89

Annual fund ratings [cover story; special section] il *Forbes* 144:149-56+ S 4 '89

Are foreign funds set to snap back? J. Egan. il *U.S. News & World Report* 107:60 Jl 10 '89

The best funds for the 1990s [cover story] M. Meyer. il *Money* 18:50-3 Ag '89

The best mutual funds for 1989 [cover story; special section] J. Egan. bibl il *U.S. News & World Report* 106:54-60+ F 6 '89

The best return for the least risk [Mutual fund scoreboard; cover story; special section] J. M. Laderman. il *Business Week* p80-2+ F 20 '89

Big returns in small packages [mutual fund scoreboard] J. M. Laderman. il *Business Week* p74-5 Ap 17 '89

Bond funds that will play the whole fixed-income field for you. J. Mendes. il *Fortune* 119:25-6 Mr 13 '89

Bond funds with an extra kick [closed-end convertible bond funds] L. Zinn. il *Business Week* p98 Ag 28 '89

Bright spots in the year's best quarter [Mutual funds scoreboard] G. Weiss. il *Business Week* p120-1 O 16 '89

The buy-and-hold edge. M. Schiffres. il *Changing Times* 43:20 D '89

Buy munis while the oversupply lasts [no-load funds] T. Paré. il *Fortune* 120:36 O 23 '89

Buying a boatload of munis for less than the price of one [unit trusts and bond mutual funds] il *Money* 18:201-3 N '89

Cash-management checklist. J. F. Wasik. il *Home Office Computing* 7:18 Jl '89

Change agents [B. Bent, inventor of money-market mutual funds] D. Moreau. il por *Changing Times* 43:132 Mr '89

A contrarian case for junk bonds. M. J. Williams. il *Fortune* 120:36 S 11 '89

Convertible bond funds: safety plus the sizzle of stocks. E. Schultz. il *Fortune* 120:29-30 Jl 17 '89

The discount window [closed-end bond funds] B. Weberman. il *Forbes* 144:307 S 4 '89

Don't worry about interest rates [interview with W. E. Donoghue] E. Schultz. il por *Fortune* 119:46+ Je 5 '89

Europe: it's already 1992 [investing in European securities through mutual funds] J. B. Quinn. il *Newsweek* 114:63 N 20 '89

Finding fortunes in funds. P. Sharif. il *Black Enterprise* 20:56 O '89

First aid for a bear bite [all-weather funds; views of Sheldon Jacobs] il *Fortune* 120 no10 Special Issue:76 Fall '89

First-quarter mutual-fund score card. R. J. Morse. il *U.S. News & World Report* 106:72 My 15 '89

Five mutual funds with first-rate managers [no-load funds] J. Mendes. il *Fortune* 120:44 Ag 28 '89

Foreign affairs. R. Addis. il *Forbes* 143:201-2+ Je 26 '89

Fund ratings. il *Forbes* 143:152+ F 6 '89

Fund watch. See issues of Money

The funds. See issues of Forbes

Funds pulled in fat returns in spite of themselves. G. Weiss. il *Business Week* p130-1 D 25 '89-Ja 1 '90

Funds that cut the risk . . . and the reward [asset allocation funds] M. Schiffres. il *Changing Times* 43:43-4+ Jl '89

The "good fund, bad sector" theory [small company funds] J. Clements. il *Forbes* 143:110 Ja 23 '89

Good news [newer mutual funds judged by money manager performance] J. Clements. il *Forbes* 144:228+ O 16 '89

Got a few million to spare? Head for a hedge fund. G. Weiss. il *Business Week* p126-7 S 11 '89

He feasts on ugly duckling funds [closed-end funds; interview with T. J. Herzfeld] E. Schultz. il por *Fortune* 119:44+ Ja 30 '89

Hidden funds [closet investment funds] J. Clements. il *Forbes* 143:264-5 Je 26 '89

How long will junk be king of the bond funds? [Mutual fund scoreboard] J. M. Laderman. il *Business Week* p114-19+ F 27 '89

How mutual funds have battled back. J. M. Laderman. il *Business Week* p100-1 S 18 '89

How savvy fund investors tally the risk [calculating beta] J. Meehan. *Business Week* p118 O 2 '89

How to choose and use money-market funds. il *Consumer Reports* 54:316 My '89

How to evaluate 'ethical' stocks. M. Rowland. il *Working Woman* 14:59-60 Mr '89

How to invest like a millionaire [portfolio of 6 no-load mutual funds] K. Brouwer. il *Forbes* 143:210-13 Je 26 '89

Hunting for treasure in the junkyard. D. Zigas. il *Business Week* p172 O 9 '89

Investing for a better world [socially responsible funds] *Modern Maturity* 32:24+ O/N '89

It's reopening night [equity funds open to new investors] J. Mendes. il *Fortune* 119:42+ Je 5 '89

The latest mutual-fund front-runners. R. J. Morse. il *U.S. News & World Report* 107:65 Jl 31 '89

Market timers and the market march to different drummers. il *Money* 18:17 Je '89

Money-market funds get aggressive. M. Rowland. il *Working Woman* 14:57-8 O '89

Money-market leaders. M. Schiffres. il *Changing Times* 43:16 Je '89

Money market risk. B. Weberman. il *Forbes* 144:317 D 11 '89

The Money rankings. C. Willis. il *Money* 18:92-110+ Ag '89

Most funds are booming, but the biggest bang is in small-caps. D. Zigas. il *Business Week* p98-9 Je 26 '89

Mutual fund update. See issues of Changing Times beginning June 1987

Mutual funds 1989 [cover story; special section] il *Changing Times* 43:27-34+ S '89

Mutual funds demystified (I). il *Consumer Reports* 54:615 O '89

Mutual funds demystified (II). il *Consumer Reports* 54:698 N '89

The new heavyweight money funds [money market mutual funds] T. Thompson. il *U.S. News & World Report* 106:63 Je 12 '89

New souped-up money market mutual funds. B. G. Quint. *Glamour* 87:120 Ag '89

Not quite ready for the junk heap [junk bond funds] J. Egan. il *U.S. News & World Report* 107:69 O 2 '89

Now that interest rates are down, what's up with fixed-income funds? [bond funds] M. Meyer. il *Money* 18:45-8+ S '89

Picks of the mutual fund gurus. D. Lanchner. il *Changing Times* 43:80-3 Mr '89

Pigging out on tax shelters [single state municipal bond funds] K. McCormally. il *Changing Times* 43:45-9+ Je '89

Portfolio monitor. See issues of Changing Times beginning June 1987

Putting your money where your heart is [socially responsible funds] M. Rowland. bibl il *New Choices for the Best Years* 29:57-60 D '89

The risks and rewards of one-country funds. M. Rowland. il *Working Woman* 14:39-40 Ag '89

Save the world! Earn big money! [social mutual funds] J. E. Bahls. *Sierra* 74:18+ Jl/Ag '89

Should you invest in a closed-end fund? M. Rowland. il *Working Woman* 14:75-6 My '89

Small-stock funds with foreign accents. E. Schultz. il *Fortune* 119:34+ My 8 '89

Smart money? [mutual fund managers not buying their own funds] J. Clements. il *Forbes* 143:131 Je 12 '89

The smart way to go global. B. D. Fromson. il *Fortune* 120 no10 Special Issue:103-4+ Fall '89

"Star" funds: three hits, three misses. M. Schiffres. il pors *Changing Times* 43:59-63 My '89

Taking the plunge into a pool of mutual funds. il *Black Enterprise* 19:35-6 Ap '89

These funds move on mood—and the mood is upbeat [closed-end funds] G. Weiss. il *Business Week* p82 F 20 '89

This summer, stock funds were hottest. R. J. Morse. il *U.S. News & World Report* 107:77 O 30 '89

INVESTMENT TRUSTS—*cont.*

Twins but not identical twins [closed-end funds that outperform open-ends] J. Clements. il *Forbes* 143:402-3 My 1 '89

The undiminished allure of investing abroad. J. Egan. il *U.S. News & World Report* 107:76+ D 4 '89

Welcome to the decade of mutual funds. P. Wang. il *Money* 18:91-2+ D '89

What a difference those regular dividends can make [equity income funds] D. P. Wiener. il *U.S. News & World Report* 106:69 My 15 '89

What can go wrong [junk bond unit trusts, higher yield money market mutual funds, and mutual funds with bad records] J. B. Quinn. il *Newsweek* 114:39 Ag 14 '89

Where to keep your cash (I). il *Consumer Reports* 54:153 Mr '89

Who's buying junk? J. Willoughby. il *Forbes* 143:161 Mr 6 '89

Why settle for 6.5% when you can get 9.5%? [money market accounts vs. money market funds] M. Sivy. *Money* 18:76-7 O '89

World funds take a hit. J. B. Quinn. il *Newsweek* 113:55 Je 19 '89

Yielding to total return [closed-end bond funds vs. open-end] J. Clements. il *Forbes* 144:312+ D 11 '89

Young funds with an eye on 1992 [U.S. mutual funds that invest in European stocks] L. J. Nathans. il *Business Week* p116 My 29 '89

Acquisitions and mergers

The Japanese connection [T. Pickens' takeover of Clemente Global Growth Fund thwarted by web of Japanese ties] R. Phalon. il por *Forbes* 143:172+ Ap 3 '89

Musical chairs in mutual funds. L. Jereski. il *Business Week* p126 N 13 '89

What you need to know about mutual fund mergermania. il *Money* 18:46-7 O '89

Advertising

Doesn't honesty sell? [SEC crackdown on bond unit trusts] B. Weberman. il *Forbes* 144:297 O 16 '89

Customer relations

Hand-holding funds. J. Clements. il *Forbes* 143:222-3 Je 26 '89

Directors

The dog that rarely bites. il *Forbes* 144:210 O 2 '89

Dollar cost averaging

A dumb way to buy mutual funds. J. Trotsky and F. W. Frailey. il *Changing Times* 43:58-60+ Mr '89

Laws and regulations

Here's a reform that should fire up fund investors [informing investors of management changes] M. Meyer. il *Money* 18:55-6 D '89

Management fees

Beware those high-cost mutual funds [interview with Mutual fund letter publisher G. Perritt] E. Schultz. il por *Fortune* 119:34-5 Mr 13 '89

Dividend plans that deserve a critical look [fees charged for dividend reinvestment] M. Meyer. *Money* 18:61 Ap '89

Faulty arithmetic [SEC mutual fund management fee calculations] J. Clements. il *Forbes* 143:112 My 15 '89

Funds for tightwads. E. McGlinn. il *Forbes* 143:214 Ap 17 '89

The hazards of small funds. W. Baldwin. il *Forbes* 144:183+ S 4 '89

Hidden costs. G. W. Perritt. il *Forbes* 144:182-3 S 4 '89

How to elude the sharp bite of those submerged fees. A. Rock. il *Money* 18:183-4 Ap '89

Loads vs. no-loads: the winner is . . . M. Schiffres and P. Brandon. il *Changing Times* 43:35-40 F '89

Miracle of the fee-free fund [Dreyfus Corp.] D. P. Wiener. *U.S. News & World Report* 107:80 O 9 '89

Musical chairs in mutual funds. L. Jereski. il *Business Week* p126 N 13 '89

The real cost of buying, keeping and selling a fund. T. Thompson. il *U.S. News & World Report* 106:64 F 6 '89

Taxation

How to keep more profit when you sell a mutual fund. G. Anrig, Jr. il *Money* 18:131-2 Ag '89

However much you think you owe, chances are you're wrong. L. Wiener. *U.S. News & World Report* 106:60 F 6 '89

Making sense of mutual fund taxes. K. McCormally. *Changing Times* 43:118+ Mr '89

Tagging your fund shares. K. McCormally. il *Changing Times* 43:132 N '89

Tax-free unit trusts [municipal bond trusts] B. Weberman. il *Forbes* 143:145 F 20 '89

Tax strategy [funds and capital gains] W. Baldwin. il *Forbes* 144:186+ S 4 '89

'Tis the season of the mutual fund tax boomerang. M. Meyer. il *Money* 18:51 N '89

Austria

See also
Austria Fund

Canada

See also
Cundill Value Fund

Ethical profits [socially responsible funds] S. Gittins. *World Press Review* 36:75 O '89

Voulez-vous visiter Québec? [rules for American investors] J. Clements. il *Forbes* 143:209 Mr 20 '89

Developing countries

See also
Emerging Markets Growth Fund

Exotic returns from exotic lands [closed-end funds bet on emerging markets] J. Meehan. il *Business Week* p124 D 25 '89-Ja 1 '90

Finding the next Korea. M. Berss. il *Forbes* 143:194+ Je 26 '89

Japan

See also
Japan Tilt Fund

Switzerland

See also
Swissbar (Firm)

INVESTMENTS

See also
Annuities
Art as an investment
Bondholders
Bonds
Brokers
Capital investments
Coins as an investment
Colleges and universities—Investments
Computers—Investment use
Contrarian investments
Dividends
Gold as an investment
Government securities
Hedging (Finance)
Horses as an investment
Information systems—Investment use
Institutional investments
Interest (Economics)
Investment clubs
Investment newsletters
Investment trusts
January effect (Investments)
Joint ventures
Mortgage bonds and notes
Palladium as an investment
Postcards as an investment
Precious metals as an investment
Real estate investment
Saving and savings
Securities
Speculation
Stockholders
Stocks
Tactical asset allocation (Investments)
Tankers as an investment
Telephone—Investment use
Television broadcasting—Financial programs
Timber as an investment
Venture capital
Wine as an investment
Workout investments
Wrap accounts

5 super-safe places to save. B. G. Quint. *Glamour* 87:120+ F '89

7 deadly investment sins and how to avoid them. W. Giese. il *Changing Times* 43:54-8 Jl '89

20 ways to cash in on high yields [cover story] M. Schiffres. il *Changing Times* 43:30-9 Ap '89

1990 investment guide [cover story; special section] il *U.S. News & World Report* 107:66-8+ D 4 '89

1990 investor's guide [cover story] il *Fortune* 120 no10 Special Issue:8-9+ Fall '89

Automatic ways to save or invest. il *Consumer Reports* 54:78+ F '89

Beating today's inflation means playing new angles. J. M. Laderman. il *Business Week* p35 Ap 3 '89

Big ideas for a little money. R. J. Maturi. il *Changing Times* 43:67-70 Ag '89

The big shift [investment strategy tied to population trends] J. Crudele. il *New York* 22:21 Mr 27 '89

Black enterprise annual money management issue [special issue] il *Black Enterprise* 20:53-4+ O '89

The buck starts here [special section] il *Harper's Bazaar* 122:38+ Ja '89

Building your fortune. D. P. Wiener. il *U.S. News & World Report* 107:50-2+ Jl 17 '89

Building your own portfolio. M. O'Brien. il *Nation's Business* 77:30+ Ap '89

Capital improvements [results of Black enterprise survey] M. E. Howard. il *Black Enterprise* 20:53-4+ Ag '89

Despite those post-crash highs, be wary of the stock market. J. J. Curran. il *Fortune* 119:25-6+ My 22 '89

Financial bonanzas and bozos of the late, great 1988. il *Money* 18:15-16+ F '89

Five sins to avoid when investing for retirement [experience of Virginia Kinet] E. Schultz. il *Fortune* 119:24+ Mr 27 '89

INVESTMENTS—*cont.*

The Forbes money guide [special section] il *Forbes* 143:176-86+ Je 26 '89

Getting rich $100 at a time [cover story] J. Kosnett. il *Changing Times* 43:20-6 Ag '89

Here's a hot tip with a guaranteed payoff: keep good records. M. T. Smith. *Money* 18:145 Ja '89

How are you doing? [cover story] M. Sivy. il *Money* 18:78-83 O '89

In a slowing economy, good investments are hard to find. il *Fortune* 120:25-7 Ag 14 '89

In God we trust, in dealers we don't [investing in various collectibles] M. K. Evans. il *Gentlemen's Quarterly* 59:217-18+ O '89

Investing during 1989: income now, bonds later. il *Money* 18:34 F '89

Investing in 1989. J. B. Quinn. il *Newsweek* 113:43 Ja 16 '89

Investing in franchising. M. Whittemore. il *Nation's Business* 77:61+ Ag '89

Investment figures of the week. See issues of Business Week beginning January 25, 1988

Investment quandary. A. Armstrong. il *Ms.* 17:76 Mr '89

Investment update. See issues of Changing Times beginning May 1989

Investments: diversification is the key to profits in '89. il *Money* 18:36 Ja '89

Investments you can live without. W. Giese. il *Changing Times* 43:43-4+ N '89

The investor. D. R. Katz. See issues of Esquire through November 1989

Investor's scorecard. See issues of Money through July 1989

Is it inflation yet? D. R. Katz. il *Esquire* 112:121-2 S '89

It may be time to hit the high notes. J. Egan. il *U.S. News & World Report* 106:79 Ap 24 '89

Learning to invest with confidence. M. Rowland. il *Working Woman* 14:61-2+ D '89

Low-stress investments for the decade ahead [portfolio tips from investment advisers; cover story] M. Schiffres. il *Changing Times* 43:29-35 N '89

Markets & investments. See issues of Business Week

Money. M. K. Evans. See issues of Gentlemen's Quarterly

Money angles. A. P. Tobias. See issues of Time beginning June 19, 1989

Money profile. See issues of Money

Money scorecard. See issues of Money beginning August 1989

On coming into money. M. Hodge. il *New Choices for the Best Years* 29:56-9+ Ja '89

Outlook: investing. M. Schiffres. il *Changing Times* 43:40-6 Ja '89

Personal investing. See issues of Fortune

Picking investments that can outrun an economic slowdown. il *Money* 18:7-8 Je '89

Portfolio monitor. See issues of Changing Times beginning June 1987

Put your eggs in several baskets [advice from H. Browne] M. Hulbert. il *Forbes* 143:168 Mr 6 '89

A question of money. M. Rowland. See issues of New Choices for the Best Years beginning January 1989

A recessionist's portfolio. A. G. Shilling. il por *Forbes* 144:234 S 18 '89

Short-run greed, long-run blues. J. Egan. il *U.S. News & World Report* 106:66 Je 19 '89

Stop worrying about the economy and concentrate on finding value. J. J. Curran. il *Fortune* 119:31-2+ F 13 '89

Wall Street. See issues of Money beginning January 1988

What to do with a windfall. M. C. Paulson. il *Changing Times* 43:93-4+ N '89

Where to invest [midyear investment outlook; cover story; special section] il *Business Week* p92-102+ Je 26 '89

Where to invest in 1990 [cover story; special section] il *Business Week* p73-7+ D 25 '89-Ja 1 '90

Where to invest your money now [cover story; special section] il *Money* 18:60-8+ Jl '89

Where to keep your cash (II). il *Consumer Reports* 54:260 Ap '89

Where to put your money in 1990 and beyond [cover story; special section] il *Money* 18:70-6+ D '89

Winning investors know their returns. A. Rock. *Money* 18:149-50 S '89

Worryproof your investments. J. Bodnar. il *Changing Times* 43:75-7 O '89

Your best ways to beat inflation [special section] il *Money* 18:58-64+ My '89

Advertising

Prophet without honor [H. W. Gourgue's theory that ads in Financial planning portend investment disaster] J. Queenan. il por *Forbes* 143:129+ Ap 17 '89

Bibliography

A guide to investing guides. J. Egan. il *U.S. News & World Report* 106:66-8 Ap 3 '89

Seven pillars of wisdom. J. Queenan. il *Forbes* 143:186+ Je 26 '89

Information services

See also
Kellogg Associates
Soft dollar brokers

Psychological aspects

Apples no, whiskey yes [small investors tend to magnify stock market risks] W. Baldwin. il *Forbes* 144:252+ D 11 '89

Lassoing herd instincts for the good of the market. G. S. Becker. il *Business Week* p20 N 20 '89

Social aspects

See also
Community Reinvestment Act of 1977

Clean vs. dirty [J. Dodson of Parnassus Fund vs. K. Roberts of Shearson Fundamental Value] R. O'Connor. il *Mother Jones* 14:56-7 Je '89

Ethical profits [Canadian socially responsible funds] S. Gittins. *World Press Review* 36:75 O '89

Good intentions [socially conscious investments] E. Corcoran. *Scientific American* 261:79 O '89

Green groceries [food industry stocks for ethical investors] S. S. Ross. il *Mother Jones* 14:48-52 F/Mr '89

How to evaluate 'ethical' stocks [mutual funds] M. Rowland. il *Working Woman* 14:59-60 Mr '89

Investing for a better world [socially responsible funds] *Modern Maturity* 32:24+ O/N '89

Putting your money where your heart is [socially responsible funds] M. Rowland. bibl il *New Choices for the Best Years* 29:57-60 D '89

Romantics, radicals and realists [address, April 10, 1989] D. C. Jones. *Vital Speeches of the Day* 55:750-5 O 1 '89

Save the world! Earn big money! [social mutual funds] J. E. Bahls. *Sierra* 74:18+ Jl/Ag '89

Social ventures. R. Hylton. *Mother Jones* 14:45-6+ Jl/Ag '89

When profits meet principles. N. S. Charles. il *Black Enterprise* 19:83-4+ My '89

Anecdotes, facetiae, satire, etc.

I'm irresponsible! J. Rothchild. il *Mother Jones* 14:42-3 S '89

Study and teaching

Aids and devices

Fun with the market [investment games] D. P. Wiener. il *U.S. News & World Report* 106:68 Ap 3 '89

Wealth Insurance [personal investment computer game] G. McClure. il *Compute!* 11:63-4 Ap '89

Wealth Insurance helps you prepare for a roller-coaster economy [personal investment computer game] N. Maffei. il *Home Office Computing* 7:30 Ap '89

Taxation

Money on the move. F. E. Rowe. por *Forbes* 144 Special Issue:400 O 23 '89

Tax tips for trying times. J. Reese. il *Fortune* 120 no10 Special Issue:201-3 Fall '89

INVESTMENTS, AMERICAN

America on the rise: a new breed of innovators. G. F. Gilder. il *Reader's Digest* 135:126-8 Ag '89

Foreign direct investment in a global economy. il *Department of State Bulletin* 89:32-4 Je '89

Risks and opportunities for international business [study by Frost & Sullivan's Political Risk Services] il *USA Today (Periodical)* 118:5 Ag '89

The risks and rewards of one-country funds. M. Rowland. il *Working Woman* 14:39-40 Ag '89

Small-stock funds with foreign accents. E. Schultz. il *Fortune* 119:34+ My 8 '89

The smart way to go global. B. D. Fromson. il *Fortune* 120 no10 Special Issue:103-4+ Fall '89

The undiminished allure of investing abroad. J. Egan. il *U.S. News & World Report* 107:76+ D 4 '89

World funds take a hit. J. B. Quinn. il *Newsweek* 113:55 Je 19 '89

The world is an investor's oyster [views of P. Lynch] M. Magnet. por *Fortune* 120:67-8 Jl 3 '89

Your rivals can be your allies [joint ventures with foreign competitors] L. Kraar. il map *Fortune* 119:66-8+ Mr 27 '89

Asia

The challenge of Asia in the 1990s [cover story] il *Fortune* 120 no13 Special Issue:10-11 Fall '89

Canada

American Airlines, Canadian investors weigh bids for Wardair. C. Fotos. *Aviation Week & Space Technology* 130:108-9 Ap 24 '89

Closing the book on government [publishing industry] D. Francis. il *Maclean's* 102:13 Je 12 '89

Getting the best price [Falconbridge Ltd. favoring AMAX over Noranda in takeover battle; special section] il *Maclean's* 102:34-7 Ag 14 '89

Merger wave rolls on [Consolidated-Bathurst acquired by Stone Container Corp.] D. Jenish. il *Maclean's* 102:28-30 F 6 '89

Voulez-vous visiter Québec? [rules for American investors in Canadian mutual funds] J. Clements. il *Forbes* 143:209 Mr 20 '89

Caribbean region

See also
Caribbean Basin Initiative

INVESTMENTS, AMERICAN—cont.

China

China will always be risky business [interview with G. Browning] C. P. Work. il por *U.S. News & World Report* 107:43 Jl 31 '89

Doing business in China now. F. S. Worthy. il *Fortune* 120 no13 Special Issue:21+ Fall '89

Foreign investors are wary—but they're not running. D. J. Yang and W. Glasgall. il *Business Week* p51 Je 5 '89

How China's chaos affects the West. R. I. Kirkland, Jr. il *Fortune* 119:77-8 Je 19 '89

One company's China debacle [American Motors; excerpt from *Beijing Jeep*] J. Mann. il por *Fortune* 120:145+ N 6 '89

Ready to ride out China's turmoil [Fortune poll] A. Farnham. il *Fortune* 120:117-18 Jl 3 '89

The U.S. in China: letting a new caution bloom. D. Lee. il *Business Week* p47 Ja 30 '89

'We simply can't go rushing back in' [crackdown on pro-democracy movement] B. Powell. il *Newsweek* 114:30 Jl 3 '89

What's next for business in China [crackdown on pro-democracy movement] F. S. Worthy. il *Fortune* 120:110-12 Jl 17 '89

Why there's still promise in China. F. S. Worthy. il *Fortune* 119:95-6+ F 27 '89

Will California's anti-China syndrome spread? [forcing pension funds to divest] M. Shao. il *Business Week* p33 Jl 24 '89

Developing countries

Exotic returns from exotic lands [closed-end funds bet on emerging markets] J. Meehan. il *Business Week* p124 D 25 '89-Ja 1 '90

Finding the next Korea. M. Berss. il *Forbes* 143:194+ Je 26 '89

East Asia

The challenge of Asia in the 1990s [cover story] il *Fortune* 120 no13 Special Issue:10-11 Fall '89

Is the era of cheap Asian labor over? D. J. Yang and L. Nakarmi. il *Business Week* p45-6 My 15 '89

Eastern Europe

Betting money on the East. M. Frankel. il *Newsweek* 114:50 D 18 '89

Go east, young man? R. Ball. il *Time* 134:65 D 4 '89

Pushing capitalism for fun and profit. S. V. Roberts. il *U.S. News & World Report* 107:38-9 D 4 '89

"These countries are up for sale". P. Duggan. il *Forbes* 144:130 D 25 '89

Great Britain

Ford's sporty new number [acquisition of Jaguar] il *Time* 134:83 N 13 '89

Have you driven a Jag, lately? [Ford buys Jaguar] D. Pauly. il *Newsweek* 114:64 N 13 '89

The hole in Ford's doughnut [pursuit of Jaguar and luxury model market] J. Flint. il *Forbes* 144:50+ N 13 '89

A Jaguar buyer may be in for a long, slow drive [GM or Ford] M. Maremont. il *Business Week* p48-9 N 13 '89

The law of the jungle catches up with Jaguar [Ford's bid] R. A. Melcher. il *Business Week* p54 O 2 '89

Operator, can you connect me to the real world? [American investors are bidding up British cellular shares] J. Marcom, Jr. il *Forbes* 144:142 S 18 '89

A sexy new tax shelter from across the Atlantic [British preferred stock] L. Jereski. *Business Week* p108 Je 12 '89

White knight or raider? [H. Kravis' stake in BTR plc] S. Flack. il *Forbes* 144:46 S 18 '89

Why GE took a European bride [deal with Britain's General Electric Co. plc] J. R. Norman. il *Business Week* p28-9 Ja 30 '89

Would you pay $2 billion for a sick cat? [GM and Ford go after Jaguar] M. Maremont. il *Business Week* p58 O 23 '89

Hungary

"These countries are up for sale". P. Duggan. il *Forbes* 144:130 D 25 '89

India

How Pepsi broke into India. S. N. Chakravarty. il *Forbes* 144:43-4 N 27 '89

Iran

See also
Iranian seizure of United States embassy, 1979-1981—Economic aspects

Ireland

Why Irish eyes are smiling [attracting electronics firms] J. Ames. *U.S. News & World Report* 107:47 Jl 10 '89

Italy

Benetton targets a new customer—Wall Street [American depositary receipts] J. Rossant and A. Dunkin. il *Business Week* p32-3 My 29 '89

Why Wall Street is furioso at Raul Gardini [deal to buy out minority holders of Ausimont] J. Rossant and W. Glasgall. il por *Business Week* p48 F 20 '89

Japan

Amway's big, happy family is all smiles—in Japan. T. Holden. il *Business Week* p47+ S 4 '89

A back burner for T. Boone stake [T. B. Pickens denied seat on board of Koito Manufacturing] *U.S. News & World Report* 107:16 Jl 10 '89

Beware the gaijin raider [T. B. Pickens goes after Koito Manufacturing] *Newsweek* 113:48 Ap 17 '89

Boone Pickens, samurai warrior [bid for Koito Manufacturing] M. Ivey. il por *Business Week* p90+ My 8 '89

How d'ya say "liquidator" in Japanese? [I. Jacobs plays Tokyo-New York arbitrage in raids on Shaklee and Avon] S. Flack. il por *Forbes* 143:39-40 Je 12 '89

How to ride Japan Inc.'s raging bull. W. Glasgall and T. Holden. il *Business Week* p108 F 6 '89

IBM clones a strategy from the clonemakers [mimicking Japanese machines] N. Gross. il *Business Week* p42 Ag 21 '89

Kamikaze capitalism [T. B. Pickens buys into Koito Manufacturing] M. Lewis. *The New Republic* 200:19-20 My 1 '89

A new kind of arbitrage [discrepancy between Tokyo and New York P/Es] E. Sturza. il *Forbes* 144:128 Jl 10 '89

Premium pricing [Tokyo/New York arbitrage play in American Family Corp. shares] S. N. Chakravarty. *Forbes* 144:261 O 30 '89

Salomon just can't lose—in Tokyo. T. Holden. il *Business Week* p94 Je 12 '89

Sayonara [New York-Tokyo arbitrage played by Honeywell] S. Flack. il *Forbes* 144:10 Ag 21 '89

T. Boone's declaration of yen-dependence [bid for seat on the board of Koito Manufacturing] M. Tharp. il por *U.S. News & World Report* 106:51 My 1 '89

T. Boone's Tokyo campaign [T. B. Pickens challenges corporate officers at annual meeting of Koito Manufacturing] K. Makihara. il por *Time* 134:45 Jl 10 '89

A Texas raider rocks Club Japan [T. B. Pickens buys into Koito Manufacturing] *U.S. News & World Report* 106:15 Ap 17 '89

Thinking small in Tokyo. R. Phalon. il *Forbes* 143:198+ Je 26 '89

Tokyo's bull has further to run [interview with C. Mitchinson of Salomon Inc.] S. Solo. il por *Fortune* 120:43 Jl 3 '89

U.S. law firms just can't win in Tokyo. T. Holden. il *Business Week* p58+ S 4 '89

Understanding how Japan works. C. Rapoport. il *Fortune* 120 no13 Special Issue:14-15+ Fall '89

Who says you can't break into Japan? [American franchises] T. Holden. il *Business Week* p49 O 16 '89

Libya

U.S. oil companies authorized to resume operations in Libya [White House statement, January 19, 1989] *Department of State Bulletin* 89:71 Mr '89

Mexico

Charlie Crowder sees utopia, and it's a border town [Santa Teresa] S. Baker. il por map *Business Week* p35-6 Jl 31 '89

Philippines

Land-grab in the Philippines [American corporations displace native farmers] B. Miller. il *The Progressive* 53:30-3 N '89

No thrilla in Manila [with interview with C. Aquino] D. J. Yang and K. S. Barnes. il por *Business Week* p64+ N 6 '89

Poland

Lech's American angel [heiress B. Johnson bails out shipyard in Gdańsk, Poland; cover story] D. Margolick. il pors *The New York Times Magazine* p28-31+ O 8 '89

The man who would be magnate [Y. Fromer] M. Schifrin. il por *Forbes* 144:41-4 S 18 '89

One of the great men of our time [visit to U.S. by L. Walesa] M. S. Forbes, Jr. il pors *Forbes* 144:27 D 25 '89

Saudi Arabia

Saudi-U.S. joint ventures formed under AWACS offset program will start operations this year. *Aviation Week & Space Technology* 130:20 F 6 '89

South Africa

Aftermath of the exodus [U.S. disinvestment] J. Jones. il *U.S. News & World Report* 106:49-50 My 1 '89

Dissenting on divestment [Evangelical Lutheran Church in America] *The Christian Century* 106:927 O 18 '89

Divestment update [chart] *Black Enterprise* 19:41 Mr '89

Do South African sanctions make sense? D. Reed. il *Reader's Digest* 134:51-6 F '89

Mobil's big pullout. *Newsweek* 113:42 My 8 '89

Rangel-backed tax law pushes Mobil Oil to sell its S. African holdings. por *Jet* 76:5 My 15 '89

Where disinvestment pinches [gold mines] J. Cook. il por *Forbes* 143:62+ Je 26 '89

Soviet Union

Breakthrough [American Trade Consortium agreement with the Soviet government] *The New Yorker* 65:30-1 Ap 17 '89

Capitalists are bullish on the Bear. il *U.S. News & World Report* 107:15+ D 11 '89

The chill is gone, and U.S. companies are Moscow-bound. P. Galuszka and R. Brady. il *Business Week* p64 Je 5 '89

INVESTMENTS, AMERICAN—Soviet Union—*cont.*

The deal of the decade may get done in Moscow [American Trade Consortium] P. Galuszka and R. Brady. il *Business Week* p54-5 F 27 '89

High risks, distant payoffs [joint ventures] E. Dyson. il *Forbes* 144:114-16+ D 11 '89

Joint misadventures [ventures with U.S. businesses] J. Castro. il *Time* 133:84 Ap 10 '89

Moscow bookstore, with sales of $250,000, starts second year. *Publishers Weekly* 236:9 D 8 '89

Perestroika payoff [U.S.-Soviet joint venture consultant A. Hartman] R. T. Grieves. il por *Forbes* 143:102 Ja 23 '89

Rules of the road to Red Square [code of ethics for investing in the U.S.S.R. developed by Alexander Slepak] E. Pomice. il *U.S. News & World Report* 107:63 N 27 '89

Russia as fourth leg [views of J. B. Fuqua] D. Lataniotis. il por *Forbes* 144 Special Issue:370 O 23 '89

Top U.S. companies move into Russia. L. Kraar. il *Fortune* 120:165-6+ Jl 31 '89

Sweden

Ford is kicking Saab's tires. R. A. Melcher. il *Business Week* p52 S 18 '89

Switzerland

The names of Zurich [views of H. Kaufmann] J. Marcom, Jr. il por *Forbes* 143:206+ Je 26 '89

Venezuela

A crackdown in Caracas sends foreign executives fleeing [currency scheme] G. DeGeorge. il *Business Week* p46 Jl 31 '89

Western Europe

Are U.S. multi-nationals ready for the U.S. of Europe? [pharmaceutical industry; address, May 16, 1989] R. E. Cawthorn. *Vital Speeches of the Day* 55:654-7 Ag 15 '89

Buying a Euro-stake that will thrive on the happenings of 1992. B. Dumaine. il *Fortune* 119:37-8 Ja 30 '89

The coming revival of Europe. M. K. Evans. il *Gentlemen's Quarterly* 59:131-2+ F '89

Detroit's Euro-boom. J. Marcom, Jr. il *Forbes* 143:38-9 Mr 20 '89

Don't tread on us—please [Ford and GM poised to be winners in European car market] J. Flint. il *Forbes* 143:92 Je 12 '89

Europe: it's already 1992 [investing in European securities through mutual funds] J. B. Quinn. il *Newsweek* 114:63 N 20 '89

A European expedition [funds specializing in European stocks] E. Giltenan. il *Forbes* 144:172 S 4 '89

Europe's garbage smells sweet to Waste Management. B. Bremner. il *Business Week* p33 My 29 '89

The future of the European stock exchange system approaching 1992 [address, April 29, 1989] R. V. Rosen. *Vital Speeches of the Day* 56:49-53 N 1 '89

GE and GEC. F. H. Katayama. il *Fortune* 119:8 F 13 '89

How do you say L'eggs in French? [Sara Lee Corp.] S. B. Weiner. il *Forbes* 144:73+ N 27 '89

Investors are grabbing their checkbooks—and heading for Europe. B. Riemer. il *Business Week* p118-19 D 25 '89-Ja 1 '90

It's a bird, it's a plane, it's Euroman [American businessmen] D. Lawday. il *U.S. News & World Report* 107:45 D 25 '89-Ja 1 '90

Jumping into the Euromarket: is it cheaper by the dozen? C. P. Work. il *U.S. News & World Report* 107:44-5+ Jl 3 '89

Two cheers for the new Europe. J. Reid. il *Money* 18:93-4+ Jl '89

UPS buys seven European parcel delivery firms to expand international presence. *Aviation Week & Space Technology* 130:67 Ja 23 '89

Young funds with an eye on 1992 [U.S. mutual funds that invest in European stocks] L. J. Nathans. il *Business Week* p116 My 29 '89

INVESTMENTS, AUSTRALIAN

Hawaii

The price was right [Broken Hill Proprietary acquires Pacific Resources] E. McGlinn. il *Forbes* 143:10 F 20 '89

United States

Debacle on 34th Street: how takeover debt helped kill off the venerable B. Altman chain. B. Rudolph. il por *Time* 134:77 D 11 '89

Leo the Lion is on the loose again [C. Skase's deal to buy MGM/UA falls apart] R. Grover. il por *Business Week* p60 O 23 '89

Say g'day to the megamall [Forest Fair in Cincinnati] S. Phillips. il *Business Week* p29 Mr 6 '89

Stranger in a strange land [C. Skase of Qintex buys MGM/UA Communications] L. Gubernick. il por *Forbes* 144:164+ O 2 '89

INVESTMENTS, BRITISH

Canada

A confused agenda for selling the country [Canadian Pacific rumored takeover target of Hanson Trust] A. Fotheringham. il *Maclean's* 102:56 Ag 14 '89

Killing fields in Old Montreal. P. C. Newman. il *Maclean's* 102:29 F 20 '89

Israel

This year in Jerusalem [media baron R. Maxwell] J. Zweig. il por *Forbes* 144:348+ N 13 '89

North America

Low marks, few sparks [Marks & Spencer] S. B. Weiner. il *Forbes* 144:146-7 S 18 '89

United States

British Telecom is getting less British all the time [buying McDonnell Douglas Corp.'s electronic data communications operations] M. Maremont. il *Business Week* p62 Ag 14 '89

A British war—on Yankee soil [Goldsmith-BAT takeover fight] T. Smart and M. Maremont. il *Business Week* p33 S 11 '89

Brits buy up the ad business [WPP Group and Saatchi & Saatchi; cover story] R. Rothenberg. il por *The New York Times Magazine* p14-19+ Jl 2 '89

Confessions of an advertising man [WPP's M. Sorrell negotiates takeover of Ogilvy] R. I. Kirkland, Jr. il por *Fortune* 119:131-2 Je 5 '89

Craig McCaw goes establishment [selling British Telecom a stake in McCaw Cellular Communications] J. J. Keller. il por *Business Week* p40-1 F 6 '89

An English suitor for Max & Erma's? [Mercury Asset Management] G. G. Marcial. *Business Week* p166 N 27 '89

The 'fax attack' that has Ogilvy fuming [WPP Group plc bids for Ogilvy Group] W. Konrad. il por *Business Week* p36 My 15 '89

Grand Met's recipe for Pillsbury. R. I. Kirkland, Jr. il *Fortune* 119:61+ Mr 13 '89

Hanson, White and Cummins. T. Jaffe. *Forbes* 143:196-7 Je 12 '89

Machiavelli on Madison Avenue [WPP Group's bid for Ogilvy Group] B. Rudolph. il por *Time* 133:58 My 15 '89

The man who would be king of Madison Ave. [M. Sorrell's WPP Group bids for Ogilvy Group] L. Reibstein. il por *Newsweek* 113:52 My 15 '89

Mediums and messages [WPP buys Ogilvy] A. Walmsley. il por *Maclean's* 102:42 My 29 '89

SmithKline thinks Beecham can cure what ails it. J. Weber, Jr. and M. Maremont. il *Business Week* p22 Ap 17 '89

Smoke signals on BAT and American Brands. G. G. Marcial. il *Business Week* p98 S 11 '89

Trying to get Burger King out of the flames [Grand Met executive B. J. Gibbons] M. Maremont. il por *Business Week* p29-30 Ja 30 '89

Victor Posner and the case of the mystery financier [plan to sell Fischbach to an English investor] G. DeGeorge and R. A. Melcher. il por *Business Week* p34 Ag 28 '89

Why Henry Schacht is watching his rearview mirror [Britain's Hanson's stake in Cummins] J. E. Ellis. il por *Business Week* p43 Ja 9 '89

Why MTM isn't the cat's meow [aftermath of TVS takeover] R. A. Melcher and R. Grover. il por *Business Week* p49 S 25 '89

WPP, the new giant of . . . PR? [WPP buys Ogilvy] W. Konrad. *Business Week* p32 My 29 '89

Western Europe

A new British empire. D. Claassen. *World Press Review* 36:50 Jl '89

INVESTMENTS, CANADIAN

China

China's headlong rush to capitalism [Battery Technologies of Canada] P. C. Newman. il *Maclean's* 102:38 Je 12 '89

Hungary

Bay Street comes to the Danube. P. C. Newman. il *Maclean's* 102:44 Ap 17 '89

Israel

Media barons are making pilgrimages to Jerusalem [C. M. Black buys Jerusalem post] J. Rossant and N. Sandler. il por *Business Week* p50 My 15 '89

Northern Ireland

Bombardier of Canada wins competition to buy Short Brothers. *Aviation Week & Space Technology* 130:63 Je 12 '89

Soviet Union

The art of the deal: prying open the Soviet market. M. Gray. il *Maclean's* 102:40 D 4 '89

King Eddy of the dealmakers [E. Cogan puts together group of Canadian entrepreneurs for proposed Leningrad development project] P. C. Newman. il *Maclean's* 102:56 N 13 '89

To Russia with cash [proposed Leningrad development project and other Canadian business ventures; cover story; special section; with editorial comment by Kevin Doyle] il *Maclean's* 102:2, 42-8+ N 13 '89

United States

The acquisitor [Quebecor chairman P. Péladeau acquires control of U.S. printing plants owned by R. Maxwell] J. Daly. il pors *Maclean's* 102:38-9 N 13 '89

The Belzberg brats. S. Flack. il *Forbes* 144:41-2 N 13 '89

The Belzbergs, again [stake in Armstrong World Industries] T. Jaffe. il *Forbes* 144:316 S 4 '89

A burgeoning empire [Irving family in Maine] S. McKay. il *Maclean's* 102:42+ F 6 '89

INVESTMENTS, CANADIAN—United States—*cont.*

Canadian imperialism [R. Cohen and L. Ellen buy into U.S. Trust Co.] J. Willoughby. il por *Forbes* 143:52 Ja 9 '89

A golfer's course [Loxahatchee in Jupiter, Fla., designed by J. Nicklaus] il *Maclean's* 102:52 Ap 10 '89

Hoist by their own greenmail [Belzberg takeover of H. H. Robertson] K. Hannon. il *Forbes* 143:156 My 29 '89

A raider from the north blows into the Windy City [Canada's J. Pattison eyes Whitman Corp.] B. Bremner. il por *Business Week* p34-5 Ja 16 '89

A record year for U.S. buys. H. Jensen. il *Maclean's* 102:38-9 Ag 28 '89

Spreading the net widely [Dominion Textile and Telenet Communications map strategy for U.S.-Canada free trade agreement] J. DeMont. il *Maclean's* 102:76-7 Jl 3 '89

The trade pact is turning into a one-way street—so far. C. Hawkins and W. J. Holstein. il *Business Week* p76-7 Jl 17 '89

A unique monument to urban life [Reichmanns' Yerba Buena Gardens in San Francisco] P. C. Newman. il *Maclean's* 102:33 Mr 13 '89

INVESTMENTS, CHINESE

Canada

A capitalist road. J. DeMont. il *Maclean's* 102:30-1 Ap 24 '89

INVESTMENTS, DUTCH

United States

Front man [A. Checchi fronting for KLM in Northwest takeover] S. Flack. il *Forbes* 144:69 Jl 10 '89

Shopping for bargains [Ahold USA] J. Zweig. il por *Forbes* 144:274 Jl 24 '89

Skinner's limits on NWA buyout fail to dissuade drive for LBO controls. C. Fotos. *Aviation Week & Space Technology* 131:138-9 O 9 '89

U.S. must assess buyout bid's impact on safety at Northwest [KLM's role in Wings Holdings' bid under scrutiny] *Aviation Week & Space Technology* 130:92-3 Je 26 '89

INVESTMENTS, EGYPTIAN

Great Britain

Banned in Britain: a new chapter in the Harrods saga [government outlaws publication of secret report] M. Maremont. pors *Business Week* p36 Ap 17 '89

Brawling over Harrods [T. Rowland vs. M. Al-Fayed] S. Lohr. il pors *The New York Times Magazine* p32-3+ O 8 '89

Tiny Rowland versus Mohamed Al-Fayed (cont.) [House of Fraser takeover] E. F. Cone. il pors *Forbes* 143:10 My 1 '89

Tit for tat on London's High Street [M. Al-Fayed's takeover of Harrods] J. Barnes. il pors *U.S. News & World Report* 106:63 Ja 30 '89

INVESTMENTS, EUROPEAN

United States

Birds of a feather . . . are doing deals together [airlines] C. Power and S. Payne. il *Business Week* p32-3 S 11 '89

Europe's smart money heads back to Wall Street. B. Riemer. il *Business Week* p142 My 22 '89

The new, improved Unilever aims to clean up in the U.S. W. Konrad. il *Business Week* p102+ N 27 '89

Unilever is all made up, with everywhere to go [acquisition of Fabergé and Elizabeth Arden] M. Maremont. il *Business Week* p33-4 Jl 31 '89

INVESTMENTS, FOREIGN

See also
Black business enterprises—International aspects
Business—International aspects
Corporations, International
Debts, External

Algeria

Algeria tries untying the knots of socialism. S. Toy. il por *Business Week* p49 Jl 31 '89

Canada

Takeover fever [special section] il *Maclean's* 102:34-41 Ag 28 '89

A warm welcome from up north. il *U.S. News & World Report* 106:46 My 29 '89

China

Biting the hands that feed them [effects of violence on China's economic ties] il *U.S. News & World Report* 106:26 Je 19 '89

Deng's great leap backward [aftermath of government crackdown on students] H. Anderson. il *Newsweek* 113:26-7 Je 19 '89

Has Beijing burned its bridges with business? W. Glasgall. il *Business Week* p32-3 Je 19 '89

Who's minding the store in China? D. Lee and J. Becker. il *Business Week* p58-9 Ag 14 '89

The year of trouble [following slaughter in Tiananmen Square] J. DeMont. il *Maclean's* 102:28-9 S 11 '89

Developing countries

See also
Emerging Markets Growth Fund

Eastern Europe

Who gains from the new Europe. R. I. Kirkland, Jr. il map *Fortune* 120:83-5+ D 18 '89

Hong Kong

Hong Kong revisited. C. W. Weinberger. il *Forbes* 143:31 Je 12 '89

Hungary

An economy in crisis. M. Nemeth. il *Maclean's* 102:53-4 N 13 '89

Where Adam Smith meets Karl Marx. A. Gabor. il *U.S. News & World Report* 107:36 S 18 '89

Japan

Absorbing Japanese technology. R. DiCicco. il *High Technology Business* 9:9 N/D '89

Big bucks vs. a job for life: why top talent is defecting [Western firms raid Japanese banks and brokerages] T. Holden. il *Business Week* p58 Ja 9 '89

An onslaught from the West: foreign traders and methods are rocking Japan's stock markets. T. Holden. il *Business Week* p140-1 Mr 20 '89

Mexico

Now Mexico looks like a fiesta for investors. S. Baker. il *Business Week* p42-3 Ag 28 '89

Salinas' flashy new step in the Mexican debt dance [relaxing foreign ownership rules] A. Bard. il *Business Week* p28 My 29 '89

Siberia (Soviet Union)

Cold feet in Siberia [joint venture petrochemical projects] P. Galuszka. il *Business Week* p48 Mr 27 '89

South Africa

'Eminent Persons' call for stricter sanctions against South Africa. il *UN Chronicle* 26:61 D '89

Soviet Union

Dialing for rubles. A. Wilson-Smith. il *Maclean's* 102:38-9 Ag 14 '89

The five-percenters, Moscow's pet capitalists [privileged foreign businessmen acting as go-betweens; cover story] P. Berman. il *Forbes* 143:93-7 F 6 '89

Moscow tackles its manager gap [Higher Commercial Management School created in wake of proliferating joint ventures] J. Trimble. il *U.S. News & World Report* 107:40+ Jl 31 '89

United States

See also
United States. Committee on Foreign Investment in the United States

The 100 largest foreign investments in the U.S. il *Forbes* 144:313-16+ Jl 24 '89

America's economic dependence. F. G. Rohatyn. *Foreign Affairs* 68 Special Issue:53-65 ['89]

Beard for hire [airline mergers] S. Flack. il *Forbes* 144:10 O 2 '89

Buy American [views of R. Leuschel of Banque Bruxelles] P. Fuhrman. il por *Forbes* 144:64 Jl 10 '89

Exon-Florio an imperfect tool for protecting U.S. technology. V. D. Cohen. por *Aviation Week & Space Technology* 131:68-9 N 6 '89

Foreign direct investment in a global economy. il *Department of State Bulletin* 89:32-4 Je '89

Foreign intrigue [film industry] S. Emmrich. il *American Film* 14:38-41+ S '89

Foreign-investor worries mean high interest rates a while longer. P. E. Kidd. il *Architectural Record* 177:35 Ja '89

Hogwash [debtor status of U.S.] M. S. Forbes, Jr. il *Forbes* 144 Special Issue:29 O 23 '89

Hollywood or bust. B. Rudolph. il *Time* 134:51-2 S 4 '89

I came, I saw, I blundered [foreign owners of U.S. companies] W. McWhirter. il *Time* 134:72+ O 9 '89

Independence Day blues. I. M. Stelzer. il *The American Spectator* 22:28-9 S '89

Invasion of the studio snatchers. R. Grover. il *Business Week* p52-4 O 16 '89

The myths of foreign investment. R. E. Norton. il *U.S. News & World Report* 106:44-6 My 29 '89

Restrictions on foreign investment [address, September 19, 1989] S. W. Liebeler. *Vital Speeches of the Day* 56:122-4 D 1 '89

The selling of America [cover story] A. K. Selimuddin. il *USA Today (Periodical)* 117:12-14 Mr '89

Selling off America. T. Omestad. *Foreign Policy* 76:119-40 Fall '89

The shoot-out to control Hollywood [foreign investors show interest in motion picture studios] J. Egan. il *U.S. News & World Report* 106:69-72 Mr 20 '89

Sorry, these don't fit [investors overreaching in department store acquisitions] il *Time* 134:77 O 9 '89

Sprechen sie high tech? [foreign buyers love U.S. technology companies] N. Alster. il *Forbes* 143:172-4+ Ap 17 '89

The U.S. role in a changing world economy. P. D. Nigro. il *USA Today (Periodical)* 117:21-2 My '89

What foreigners will buy next. J. J. Curran. il *Fortune* 119:94-8 F 13 '89

Who owns America? E. Rubenstein. il *National Review* 41:14 Ag 18 '89

Why good news isn't bad news. H. Banks. *Forbes* 144:33 Ag 7 '89

Bibliography

America for sale? R. J. Samuelson. *The New Republic* 200:31-5 Je 12 '89

INVESTMENTS, FRENCH

Canada

Connaught's foreign sale [to Institut Mérieux] A. Walmsley. il *Maclean's* 102:44-5 D 25 '89

Lament for a cherished asset [proposed sale of Connaught Biosciences to Institut Mérieux] P. C. Newman. il *Maclean's* 102:51 O 16 '89

Science and PR north of the border [sale of Connaught Biosciences to Institut Merieux] D. Powell. *Science* 246:1555-6 D 22 '89

United States

A case of culture shock along the Wabash [aftermath of GE's sale of consumer electronics division to Thomson SA] L. Therrien. il *Business Week* p102 My 15 '89

Cherchez la store [France's Carrefour opens hypermarket in Philadelphia] D. Fong. il *Forbes* 143:311+ Ja 9 '89

France's beachhead in America. S. Toy. il *Business Week* p48-9 O 16 '89

On the prowl in America [Rhone-Poulenc] J. Zweig. il por *Forbes* 143:154 My 1 '89

Safe harbor [Bénéteau] K. Weisman. il por *Forbes* 144:58+ S 4 '89

That screeching is Michelin doing a U-turn [buying Uniroyal Goodrich] S. Toy and Z. Schiller. il *Business Week* p50 O 9 '89

Why Jerry Pearlman gave up his brainchild [selling Zenith's computer unit to Bull] L. Therrien. il por *Business Week* p35 O 16 '89

INVESTMENTS, HONG KONG

Canada

A $5-billion Canadian solution [Li Ka-shing] P. C. Newman. il *Maclean's* 102:62 D 4 '89

Assault on racism [anti-Asian sentiment in Vancouver] H. Quinn. il *Maclean's* 102:16+ Ap 24 '89

A bubbling urban battle [vacant Expo site in Vancouver] H. Quinn. il por *Maclean's* 102:26-8 Ja 16 '89

Forging new links [Semi-Tech's bid for SSMC] T. Fennell. il pors *Maclean's* 102:26-8 F 20 '89

Hongkong Bank's quiet invasion. P. C. Newman. il *Maclean's* 102:42 D 18 '89

Prosperity and parochialism [influx of Hong Kong Chinese into Vancouver, B.C.] J. L. Graff. il *Time* 133:51 My 22 '89

A watchdog for the Asian connection [D. Lam] P. C. Newman. il *Maclean's* 102:35 Ap 24 '89

China

After Tiananmen, what? il *Forbes* 144:198 Jl 24 '89

United States

Forging new links [Semi-Tech's bid for SSMC] T. Fennell. il pors *Maclean's* 102:26-8 F 20 '89

Hong Kong hoteliers start colonizing the West. D. J. Yang. il *Business Week* p44 Mr 6 '89

Who is James Ting and what will he buy next? [SSMC] C. Hawkins. il por *Business Week* p33 F 13 '89

INVESTMENTS, IRANIAN

United States

See also

Iranian seizure of United States embassy, 1979-1981—Economic aspects

INVESTMENTS, ITALIAN

United States

The man who would be mogul trips up in Tinseltown [G. Parretti] R. Grover and J. Rossant. *Business Week* p31-2 My 1 '89

INVESTMENTS, JAPANESE

Japan's growing global reach. C. Rapoport. il *Fortune* 119:48-50+ My 22 '89

Canada

Hi-tech disagreements [Senator M. Cogger named in Japanese businessman T. Tsuru's lawsuit against entrepreneur G. Montpetit over misspent loans] P. Kaihla. il por *Maclean's* 102:16-17 Je 26 '89

How do you say 'tim-ber' in Japanese? [investment in Alberta-Pacific Forest Industries] T. Mason. il *Business Week* p52 D 4 '89

Investing Japan-style. J. DeMont. il *Maclean's* 102:58-60 N 20 '89

Japan shops the world. P. Chisholm. il *Maclean's* 102:40-1 Ag 28 '89

Great Britain

A big yen for British courses [acquisitions of golf courses] H. J. Steinbreder. il *Sports Illustrated* 71:52-3 Ag 21 '89

The Japanese are coming—and Thatcher is all smiles. R. A. Melcher and M. Maremont. il *Business Week* p46-7 F 20 '89

United States

Advanced bio class? That's over in Hitachi Hall [Japanese companies setting up labs at U.S. colleges] D. P. Oran. il *Business Week* p73-4 Ag 7 '89

After Tokyo, all the world's a bargain [interview with A. Downs] J. Egan. il *U.S. News & World Report* 106:58-9 Ja 30 '89

Ardent's Daddy Warbucks [Kubota Ltd.] J. B. Levine. il *Business Week* p26-7 Je 12 '89

Blytheville's bounty [Japanese-U.S. joint steel mill in Arkansas] il *Time* 133:52 Je 5 '89

Can Bridgestone make the climb? [acquisition of Firestone] Z. Schiller. il *Business Week* p78-9 F 27 '89

Charity begins abroad [Japanese corporations donate to American charities] A. Miller. il *Newsweek* 114:41 Ag 21 '89

Constant improvement? Or speedup? [Mazda's emphasis on kaizen concept fosters union discontent at Michigan plant] J. Flint. il *Forbes* 143:92+ Ap 17 '89

Crazy but harmless [views of J. Fallows] M. Kinsley. *The New Republic* 201:4 D 11 '89

Dai-Ichi's move on CIT: it's bold—and about time. T. Holden. il *Business Week* p202 S 25 '89

Dear Betty Harragan [Japanese management practices in the U.S.] B. L. Harragan. il *Working Woman* 14:50+ S '89

Even for Walter Yetnikoff, this will be a stretch: can Sony's ace juggle both Columbia and CBS Records? D. Lieberman. il por *Business Week* p144-5 O 30 '89

Fast break at Tiffany's [Mitsukoshi's stake] M. Roman. il por *Business Week* p102+ O 9 '89

From Walkman to showman [Sony buys Columbia Pictures] J. Castro. il *Time* 134:70-1 O 9 '89

The hard line coming from Tokyo banks [financing of U.S. leveraged buyouts] T. Holden and W. Glasgall. il *Business Week* p29 O 30 '89

Head 'em up, move 'em out—to Japan [U.S. beef] S. D. Atchison. il *Business Week* p52 Ag 21 '89

Help wanted, room to advance—out the door [American managers quit at Mazda's U.S. plant] W. Zellner. il *Business Week* p42 O 30 '89

Hidden advantages [decision to allow U.S. over-the-counter stocks onto the Tokyo Stock Exchange] R. Phalon. il *Forbes* 144:40-1 N 13 '89

Investing Japan-style. J. DeMont. il *Maclean's* 102:58-60 N 20 '89

Investors' yen for U.S. technology. M. Sun. il *Science* 246:1238-41 D 8 '89

Is Hollywood Japan's field of dreams? P. Sweeting. il *Video* 13:140 N '89

Is the U.S. selling its high-tech soul to Japan? J. B. Levine. il *Business Week* p117-18 Je 26 '89

It's not even flying yet, and already there's a flap [Discovery Airways' financing] J. B. Levine and S. Payne. il *Business Week* p36-7 D 4 '89

Japan: coming on strong [sports and leisure industries] B. Newman. il *Sports Illustrated* 71:48-54+ Ag 21 '89

Japan goes Hollywood [Sony's deal for Columbia Pictures and the competitive challenge to the U.S.; cover story; special section] il *Newsweek* 114:62-9+ O 9 '89

Japan is the biggest U.S. investor—but exactly how big? M. J. Mandel. il *Business Week* p20 My 1 '89

Japan learns the takeover game. G. Hector. il *Fortune* 120:121+ Jl 31 '89

Japan shops the world. P. Chisholm. il *Maclean's* 102:40-1 Ag 28 '89

Japan takes Manhattan [study by Barney Warf] *Focus (New York, N.Y.: 1950)* 38:29 Wint '88

Japanese angels on Broadway. F. H. Katayama. il *Fortune* 119:8 Mr 27 '89

Japanese dealmakers yearn to play QB [Japanese act as silent partners to American investment bankers] J. Friedman. il *Business Week* p82-3 Ja 16 '89

Japan's gung-ho U.S. car plants. L. Kraar. il map *Fortune* 119:98-100+ Ja 30 '89

Japan's search for U.S. colleges [attempts to buy various colleges] S. Tifft. il *Time* 133:57 Ja 23 '89

Japan's secret weapon. J. M. Fallows. il *U.S. News & World Report* 107:46 D 25 '89-Ja 1 '90

The Japs capture Rockefeller Center. W. F. Buckley. il *National Review* 41:53 D 8 '89

The land of the UAW's setting sun [Nissan votes to keep union out] il *U.S. News & World Report* 107:8 Ag 7 '89

"Long Beach is different". E. Paris. il *Forbes* 143:76+ My 29 '89

Losing on both fronts. I. M. Stelzer. il *The American Spectator* 22:37-8 Je '89

Matsushita may tune in to cable [possible bid for General Instrument] G. G. Marcial. *Business Week* p76 Ja 30 '89

Mitsubishi's gamble on a Manhattan jewel [Rockefeller Center] L. Light. il *Business Week* p124 N 13 '89

Next stop, Tinseltown [investments in U.S. films] J. Hammer. il *Newsweek* 114:48-9 Mr 20 '89

Nomura seeks a Yankee skipper [M. Chapman] J. Friedman. il por *Business Week* p96 S 4 '89

'Now they're just rich' [sale of Rockefeller Center to Mitsubishi Estate Co.] C. Friday and J. Hammer. il *Newsweek* 114:62-3 N 13 '89

Our conflicting advice for the Japanese. C. W. Weinberger. il *Forbes* 144:31 Jl 10 '89

Possible Japanese buyout of U.S. chip equipment manufacturer draws fire [Perkin-Elmer Corp. unit; with editorial comment] B. D. Nordwall. il *Aviation Week & Space Technology* 131:9, 26-7 D 4 '89

Revenge of the antisuits [Sony's takeover of CBS Records] S. N. Chakravarty. il *Forbes* 144:49+ D 11 '89

The Rockefeller generation gap [Rockefeller Center sold to Mitsubishi Estate Co.] *U.S. News & World Report* 107:14+ N 13 '89

INVESTMENTS, JAPANESE—United States—cont.

Roundup time for teriyaki beef [Japanese purchase of U.S. beef-producing properties] C. Gorman. il Time 133:47 Mr 13 '89

The Rx for Japan's drug companies: America. A. Borrus. il Business Week p49-50 N 20 '89

Score another for Japan Inc. [Nissan workers vote to keep out union] L. Reibstein. il Newsweek 114:44-5 Ag 7 '89

Shaking up Detroit: how Japanese carmakers are beating the Big Three on their own turf [cover story] J. B. Treece. il Business Week p74-80 Ag 14 '89

Shiseido grant: more than skin deep [Japanese funding of Massachusetts General Hospital-Harvard University's Cutaneous Biology Research Center] M. Sun. Science 245:810-11 Ag 25 '89

Somebody's wrong [Japanese planning to increase production at American plants without reducing imports] J. Flint. il Forbes 144:118 S 18 '89

Sony's big-picture strategy [purchase of Columbia Pictures] J. Egan. il U.S. News & World Report 107:35-6+ O 9 '89

Sure, we'll take Manhattan [sale of Rockefeller Center to Mitsubishi] J. Greenwald. il Time 134:83 N 13 '89

Tokyo brokers beat a retreat from the Street. W. Glasgall. il Business Week p42-3 F 13 '89

The UAW vs. Japan: it's showdown time in Tennessee [Nissan plant election] D. Foust. il Business Week p64-5 Jl 24 '89

An uneasy alliance on the Wabash [Subaru-Isuzu Automotive] J. B. Treece. il Business Week p59 O 23 '89

Unlevel playing field [auto components] N. Alster. il Forbes 143:53+ Je 26 '89

Unwelcome Recruit [Japan's Recruit Co. forces out G. Chichilnisky from management of Financial Telecommunications Inc.] J. Zweig. il por Forbes 143:149 My 15 '89

When Columbia met Sony . . . a love story. R. Grover. il Business Week p44-5 O 9 '89

When U.S. joint ventures with Japan go sour [auto parts] S. Phillips. il Business Week p30-1 Jl 24 '89

'White people, black people' not wanted here? [Japanese employment agencies in U.S. charged with discrimination] M. Galen and L. J. Nathans. il Business Week p31 Jl 10 '89

Why Bridgestone's chairman is making tracks to Akron [T. Eguchi transferred to Firestone] Z. Schiller. il por Business Week p32-3 N 20 '89

Why Sony is plugging into Columbia. N. Gross and W. J. Holstein. il Business Week p56+ O 16 '89

Will Sun get burned by its new partner? [Toshiba] J. B. Levine. Business Week p26-7 Je 12 '89

Yellow-peril journalism: is latent racism coloring business coverage of Japan? E. Cose. il Time 134:79 N 27 '89

A yen for New York: what the Japanese own—what they're after [cover story] D. Burstein. il New York 22:26-36 Ja 16 '89

Anecdotes, facetiae, satire, etc.

Japun, Inc. J. Queenan. The New Republic 201:14-15 O 16 '89

Western Europe

Japanese carmakers flash their cash at the EC. T. Peterson and A. Borrus. il Business Week p43+ F 13 '89

Jumping into the Euromarket: is it cheaper by the dozen? C. P. Work. il U.S. News & World Report 107:44-5+ Jl 3 '89

INVESTMENTS, KOREAN

United States

Here come the Koreans [U.S. real estate market] M. Schifrin. il Forbes 143:40 Mr 6 '89

INVESTMENTS, KUWAITI

Great Britain

BP: making the best of it [buys back half of Kuwait's shares] M. Maremont. Business Week p48 Ja 16 '89

INVESTMENTS, MEXICAN

United States

And now, Tex-Mex banking [Mexicans snap up small Texas banks] M. Ivey and S. Baker. il Business Week p140 O 9 '89

Mexico's giants march north. S. Baker. il Business Week p63+ N 13 '89

INVESTMENTS, SOUTH AFRICAN

Great Britain

Apartheid and the Canada connection [Bank of Nova Scotia's involvement in financing Minorco's bid for Consolidated Gold Fields] P. C. Newman. il Maclean's 102:29 F 13 '89

Harry Oppenheimer's empire: going for the gold. P. Schmeisser. il por The New York Times Magazine p32-3+ Mr 19 '89

United States

A little cash and a lot of moxie [Hyde Park Holdings' bid for Universal Foods Corp.] L. J. Nathans. il pors Business Week p74 Ja 30 '89

INVESTMENTS, SWEDISH

United States

An insider caper in Liechtenstein [ASEA Brown Boveri helps SEC uncover insider trading during ABB's friendly takeover bid for Combustion Engineering] J. Kapstein. Business Week p58-9 D 11 '89

INVESTMENTS, TAIWANESE

United States

A Silicon Valley plum may drop into Taiwan's lap [Wyse Technology] D. J. Yang and M. Shao. il Business Week p38 D 4 '89

Taiwan's U.S. strategy [petrochemicals] R. Simon. il Forbes 143:43-4 My 29 '89

INVESTMENTS, WEST GERMAN

Great Britain

Deutsche Bank nabs a plum—but it didn't come cheap [Morgan Grenfell] J. Templeman. il Business Week p102 D 11 '89

Soviet Union

Soviet adventures in capitalism. World Press Review 36:51 Ja '89

United States

Brain drain [biotech companies being chased out of Germany] R. Bailey. il Forbes 144:261-2 N 27 '89

Springer-Verlag's 25 years in New York. M. Sexton. il Publishers Weekly 236:434+ Ag 11 '89

INVESTOR OWNED HOSPITALS See Hospital management industry

INVESTORS See Bondholders; Investments; Stockholders

INVESTORS CENTER INC.

The final frenzy of a penny stock shop. D. Zigas. il por Business Week p128 Mr 13 '89

Investors Center calling—with a 'really exceptional' deal. D. Zigas. il Business Week p76-7 Ja 23 '89

INVISIBLE FENCE (FIRM)

Behind the Invisible Fence [electronic boundary for dogs] L. Jenson. il Home Mechanix 85:72-3 Ag '89

INVOICES See Billing

IO (SATELLITE) See Jupiter (Planet)—Satellites

IODIDES

See also
Cesium iodide

IODINE

Atomic resolution imaging of adsorbates on metal surfaces in air: iodine adsorption on pt(111) [use of scanning tunneling microscope] B. C. Schardt and others. bibl f il Science 243:1050-3 F 24 '89

IODINE COMPOUNDS

See also
Triiodothyronine

ION BEAM FUSION See Nuclear fusion

ION BEAMS See Ion bombardment

ION BOMBARDMENT

Diamond chips [semiconductor production and doping through carbon in bombardment of silicon; work of Wayne Rabalais] Discover 10:12 Jl '89

Playing three-dimensional pool [use of ion scattering techniques for analyzing surface structure] R. Pool. il Science 246:995-6 N 24 '89

ION CHANNELS

See also
Calcium channels
Chloride channels
Potassium channels
Sodium channels

Atrial natriuretic peptide inhibits a cation channel in renal inner medullary collecting duct cells. D. B. Light and others. bibl f il Science 243:383-5 Ja 20 '89

Block of stretch-activated ion channels in Xenopus oocytes by gadolinium and calcium ions. X.-C. Yang and F. Sachs. bibl f il Science 243:1068-71 F 24 '89

Cell-like biosensor opens ionic floodgates [work of Frances S. Ligler] I. Amato. Science News 135:117 F 25 '89

Quisqualate activates a rapidly inactivating high conductance ionic channel in hippocampal neurons. C.-M. Tang and others. bibl f il Science 243:1474-7 Mr 17 '89

Stretch-inactivated ion channels coexist with stretch-activated ion channels. C. E. Morris and W. J. Sigurdson. bibl f il Science 243:807-9 F 10 '89

Transmembrane channels based on tartaric acid-gramicidin A hybrids. C. J. Stankovic and others. bibl f il Science 244:813-17 My 19 '89

ION EXCHANGE

Plant ion-pump gene cloned, sequenced [work of Michael R. Sussman] I. Wickelgren. Science News 135:135 Mr 4 '89

Role of Na^+/H^+ exchange by interferon-γ in enhanced expression of JE and I-A$_\beta$ genes. V. Prpic and others. bibl f il Science 244:469-71 Ap 28 '89

ION MICROSCOPES

See also
Scanning ion-conductance microscopes

IONIAN ISLANDS (GREECE)

See also
Corfu (Greece)

IONIZATION

See also
Ion exchange
Multiphoton resonance ionization spectroscopy

Electrospray ionization for mass spectrometry of large biomolecules. J. B. Fenn and others. bibl f il Science 246:64-71 O 6 '89

IONIZATION OF GASES
See also
Plasma (Ionized gases)
IONIZING RADIATION See Radiation
IONOPHORES
Self-assembling molecular receptors [research by Alanna Schepartz] *Science News* 136:222 S 30 '89
IONOSPHERE See Atmosphere, Upper
IONS
See also
Metal ions
Micelles
Plasma (Ionized gases)
Basic measurements lead to Physics Nobel [H. Dehmelt and W. Paul for development of ion trap techniques] R. Pool. il pors *Science* 246:327-8 O 20 '89
Building on Nobel research [ion trap used by D. Pritchard] R. Pool. *Science* 246:328 O 20 '89
Cold traps for ion crystals, solid plasmas [research by David J. Wineland] I. Peterson. *Science News* 135:279 My 6 '89
Explosive molecular ionic crystals. W. L. Faust. bibl f il *Science* 245:37-42 Jl 7 '89
Ion sits still for sharp 'picture' of its optical transition. B. G. Levi. il *Physics Today* 42:17-18 S '89
Physics [Nobel Prize awarded to N. Ramsey for separated oscillatory fields technique and to H. Dehmelt and W. Paul for devising ways of trapping ions] il pors *Time* 134:74 O 23 '89
Physics Nobel: traps, clocks, quantum leaps [to H. Dehmelt and W. Paul for development of ion trap techniques] E. Peterson. *Science News* 136:262 O 21 '89
Ramsey, Dehmelt, Paul win Nobel for helping to set high standards [ion trap techniques] B. G. Levi. il pors *Physics Today* 42:17-19 D '89
IORILLO, JEFF
Morning glory. il *Runner's World* 24:104 Jl '89
IOSA GHINI, MASSIMO
about
Dangerous curves. C. K. Gandee. il por *House & Garden* 161:44 My '89
New talents: Massimo Iosa-Ghini. il por *Harper's Bazaar* 122:90 Mr '89
IOWA
See also
Agriculture—Iowa
Booksellers and bookselling—Iowa
Geology—Iowa
Groundwater pollution—Iowa
Hospitals—Iowa
Land—Iowa
Prisons—Iowa
Sports—Iowa
Taxation—Iowa
Wetlands—Iowa
Centennial celebrations, etc.
Collectibles
Who says Iowans are unloved? [centennial commemorative half dollar] E. Rochette. il *Antiques & Collecting Hobbies* 93:50+ F '89
Photographs and photography
The land in between. D. Plowden. il *Americana* 16:39-43 Ja/F '89
IOWA (SHIP) GUN TURRET EXPLOSION, 1989
The dangers of peace. il *U.S. News & World Report* 106:16 My 1 '89
Death on a dreadnought. J. V. Lamar, Jr. il *Time* 133:39 My 1 '89
Foul play on the Iowa? [speculation about suicide or murder] E. Salholz. il pors *Newsweek* 113:22 Je 5 '89
Hell on the Iowa. L. Martz. il *Newsweek* 113:22-4 My 1 '89
The Iowa inquiry [possiblity of murder or suicide raised] W. Lowther. *Maclean's* 102:23 Je 5 '89
Mystery aboard the Iowa [Navy investigation of K. Truitt] F. Trippett. il pors *Time* 133:40 Je 5 '89
The Navy blames a dead man [report cites sabotage by Petty Officer C. Hartwig] B. Turque. il *Newsweek* 114:25 S 18 '89
A tragedy at sea. J. Bierman. il *Maclean's* 102:31 My 1 '89
IOWA CITY (IOWA)
Bookstores
See Booksellers and bookselling—Iowa
Stores
Just saying no to Wal-Mart. T. Padgett. il *Newsweek* 114:65 N 13 '89
IPHIGÉNIE EN AULIDE [opera] See Gluck, Christoph Willibald, Ritter von, 1714-1787
IPOMOEA ALBA See Moonflowers
IPOS See Initial public offerings (Securities)
IQ TESTS See Intelligence tests
IRA See Irish Republican Army
IRAN
See also
Arts and state—Iran
Chemical and biological weapons—Iran
Civil rights—Iran

Kurds—Iran
United Nations—Iran
Commerce
Germany (West)
See Germany (West)—Commerce—Iran
Economic policy
Iran's future held hostage. L. Lief. il *U.S. News & World Report* 106:37-8 F 20 '89
Economic relations
See also
Iranian seizure of United States embassy, 1979-1981—Economic aspects
Foreign relations
Diplomacy in the dark. D. Stanglin. il *U.S. News & World Report* 106:26 Mr 6 '89
Does Teheran want détente? [interview with A. A. Velayati] L. Lief. por *U.S. News & World Report* 107:30 O 9 '89
Iran is trying to shed its outlaw image. J. Rossant and others. il *Business Week* p49 F 13 '89
The West gets tough with Iran—sort of [S. Rushdie affair] R. Watson. il *Newsweek* 113:32-3 Mr 6 '89
When the dust settles, Iran may be facing west. S. Reed. il *Business Week* p50 Je 19 '89
Great Britain
See Great Britain—Foreign relations—Iran
Iraq
See also
Iranian-Iraqi War, 1980-1988
Lebanon
An American soldier's death becomes a pawn in a terrorist power struggle [conflicting accounts of W. R. Higgins' death within Hezbollah factions] D. Halevy and N. C. Livingstone. il *U.S. News & World Report* 107:21 O 23 '89
Soviet Union
See Soviet Union—Foreign relations—Iran
United States
See United States—Foreign relations—Iran
History
The man who would be Shah [Reza Pahlavi] P. Axthelm. il pors *People Weekly* 31:46-51 Ap 3 '89
Revolution, 1979
In the light of history. E. Mortimer. il *World Press Review* 36:64 Mr '89
Industries
See also
Motion picture industry—Iran
Politics and government
See also
Iranian seizure of United States embassy, 1979-1981
Burying the passions Khomeini inflamed. B. Hewitt. il por *Newsweek* 113:44-5 Je 19 '89
Change in Teheran: exit Moses, enter Joshua [R. Khomeini and A. Khamenei] *National Review* 41:15-16 Je 30 '89
The end of the Khomeini era. H. Anderson. il *Newsweek* 113:40 Je 12 '89
A frenzied farewell [funeral of R. Khomeini] J. Smolowe. il *Time* 133:38-9 Je 19 '89
Grief and frenzy [death of Khomeini] R. Corelli. il *Maclean's* 102:20-1 Je 19 '89
The holy terror of Teheran fires his final volley [funeral of R. Khomeini] il *U.S. News & World Report* 106:14-15 Je 19 '89
Iran braces for a power struggle. L. Lief. *U.S. News & World Report* 106:36 Je 19 '89
Iran without Khomeini. M. Ledeen. il *The American Spectator* 22:12-13 Ag '89
Iran's Ayatollah Khomeini: the end of a dream? *World Press Review* 36:31 Jl '89
Islamic wasteland. B. Crozier. il *National Review* 41:17 Mr 24 '89
Khomeini strikes back [murder of A. Al Ahdal in Belgium and downfall of moderate H. Montazeri in Iran] J. Bierman. il pors *Maclean's* 102:25 Ap 10 '89
'Moderate' is no longer a dirty word in Iran. S. Reed and others. il por *Business Week* p54 S 11 '89
A nation in turmoil. F. A. Reed. il *Maclean's* 102:23-5 Ja 16 '89
A new Iran? [cover story; special section] il pors *World Press Review* 36:11-14+ Ag '89
A new 'king' for Iran? [Rafsanjani] A. Platt. il por *Newsweek* 114:31 Jl 3 '89
Now that the millennium has ended [death of R. Khomeini] F. Ajami. il por *U.S. News & World Report* 106:35 Je 19 '89
Post-Khomeini Iran. S. T. Hunter. *Foreign Affairs* 68:133-49 Wint '89/'90
Rafsanjani's no moderate. M. Farhang. il *The Nation* 249:560+ N 13 '89
Rushdie 1, Ayatollah 0 [death of Khomeini] *The New Republic* 200:6-7 Je 26 '89
A standoff in Iran: Rafsanjani is too weak for a deal on the hostages. R. Watson. il por *Newsweek* 114:51-2 N 6 '89
Sword of a relentless revolution [death of Khomeini] il *Time* 133:36+ Je 12 '89
War and revolution in Iran. G. Fuller. bibl f *Current History* 88:81-4+ F '89

IRAN—Politics and government—*cont.*

What Khomeini did. S. Bakhash. il *The New York Review of Books* 36:16-19 Jl 20 '89

When the dust settles, Iran may be facing west. S. Reed. il *Business Week* p50 Je 19 '89

Where God sets prices. F. Ajami. il *U.S. News & World Report* 106:47 F 20 '89

Why the Ayatollah is whipping up a new wave of fanaticism. S. Carter and others. il *Business Week* p47 Mr 6 '89

Will the next Imam please stand up? [R. Khomeini fires heir apparent H. A. Montazeri] il por *U.S. News & World Report* 106:13 Ap 10 '89

Religious institutions and affairs

See also

Christians—Iran

Muslims—Iran

Social conditions

Life after the ayatollah. R. Wilkinson. il *Newsweek* 113:47 Je 26 '89

A nation in turmoil. F. A. Reed. il *Maclean's* 102:23-5 Ja 16 '89

IRAN ARMS-CONTRA AID CASE *See* Iran-contra affair

IRAN-CONTRA AFFAIR

Bush's envoy on the grill [D. Gregg questioned on Iran-contra during confirmation hearings for ambassadorship to South Korea] R. Parry. il por *Newsweek* 113:40 My 29 '89

Christic Institute woes [ordered to pay legal fees to defendants in conspiracy suit] *The Christian Century* 106:224 Mr 1 '89

Contradictions: a decade in documents. P. Kornbluh. il *Mother Jones* 14:26-7 Jl/Ag '89

Cranston v. Gregg [ambassador-designate to South Korea D. Gregg questioned on Iran-contra] W. F. Buckley. *National Review* 41:11-12 Je 16 '89

Deregulating political murder. P. Savoy. il *The Nation* 248:869+ Je 26 '89

Encore for Iran-contra? [possible involvement of D. Gregg and G. Bush] L. Howard. il pors *Newsweek* 113:9 Ja 30 '89

Ghost of Iran-contra [D. Gregg] *The Progressive* 53:8 Mr '89

Iran-contra. F. FitzGerald. *The New Yorker* 65:51-4+ O 16 '89

Media campaigns in the courts [Christic Institute ordered to pay defendants' costs in conspiracy suit] *National Review* 41:13-14 Mr 10 '89

Minority report [link between Iranian hostage case, Reagan's 1980 campaign and contragate] C. Hitchens. *The Nation* 249:78 Jl 17 '89

Minority report [role of G. Bush] C. Hitchens. *The Nation* 248:402 Mr 27 '89

Oliver North. S. Kanfer. il por *People Weekly* 32 Special Issue:55 Fall '89

Ollie's last stand. P. Meyer. il pors *Life* 12:22-6 F '89

Pardon Ollie. *The American Spectator* 22:10-11 Ja '89

Paying the price for political errors. M. Barone. il *U.S. News & World Report* 106:30 My 1 '89

The pitfalls of covert operations. D. Isenberg. il *USA Today (Periodical)* 118:12-14 N '89

Anecdotes, facetiae, satire, etc.

Howls [excerpt from The found poetry of Lt. Col. Oliver L. North] J. W. Hart, III. *Harper's* 279:30 O '89

Bibliography

Rewriting the Iran-contra story. T. Draper. il *The New York Review of Books* 35:38-45 Ja 19 '89

'Rewriting the Iran-contra story': an exchange [discussion of January 19, 1989 article] T. Draper. il *The New York Review of Books* 36:38-9 Mr 2 '89

Canadian participation

Of guns and a guru [dealings of Chandra Swami exposed in S. Martindale's By hook or by crook] M. McDonald. il pors *Maclean's* 102:28-9 Mr 27 '89

Legal aspects

Case closed. W. Dellinger. *The New Republic* 200:14-16 Ja 9-16 '89

Narcotics trade aspects

Bipartisan arm-twisting in Central America [letter from congressmen to O. Arias Sanchez concerning J. Hull] *Harper's* 278:24 Je '89

John Hull, once Oliver North's man in Costa Rica, is now accused of running guns and drugs. R. Arias. il pors *People Weekly* 31:52-4+ My 1 '89

Minority report. C. Hitchens. *The Nation* 248:619 My 8 '89

Public opinion

The verdict on the verdict: a Newsweek poll [O. North trial] il *Newsweek* 113:37 My 15 '89

Special prosecutor

Bud McFarlane: semper fi. B. Brower. il pors *The New York Times Magazine* p26-8 Ja 22 '89

Trials

All-black jury ruled in recent Oliver North trial and prayed for guidance. il por *Jet* 76:7 My 22 '89

The contratration [role of G. Bush] *The Nation* 248:723-4 My 29 '89

A convict of conviction, Oliver North takes the fall. il por *People Weekly* 32:30-1 Jl 24 '89

A courtroom endgame for Ollie North. il *U.S. News & World Report* 106:14 Ap 24 '89

Did he lie? [O. North trial outlines R. Reagan's role] E. Magnuson. il por *Time* 133:42 Mr 27 '89

Fallout from the North verdict. B. Duffy and G. Borger. il por *U.S. News & World Report* 106:20-1 My 15 '89

A folk hero on trial [O. North] M. McDonald. il por *Maclean's* 102:20 F 13 '89

For Denise Anderson, the jury forewoman, passing judgment on Ollie North was a trial by fire. P. Chin. il pors *People Weekly* 31:49-50 My 22 '89

A forgiving sentence [O. North trial] W. Lowther. il por *Maclean's* 102:23 Jl 17 '89

Giving in to "graymail" [L. Walsh drops conspiracy charge against O. North] S. Holmes. il pors *Time* 133:24-5 Ja 16 '89

The guilty parties [evidence of R. Reagan's participation revealed during O. North's trial] il *The Progressive* 53:8-9 Je '89

Hero today, gone tomorrow [O. North] *National Review* 41:10-11 My 19 '89

The hero's clay feet [O. North verdict] L. Martz. il por *Newsweek* 113:32-3+ My 15 '89

Iran-contra: a CIA win [blocking use of classified information in trial of J. Fernandez] *Newsweek* 114:62 D 4 '89

Iran-contra: Reagan's role. il *Newsweek* 113:6 Mr 27 '89

'My bosses made me do it' [claims of O. L. North] *U.S. News & World Report* 106:14 Ap 17 '89

National insecurity [government's refusal to make available documents requested by O. North] *Commonweal* 116:36-7 Ja 27 '89

New North wind? [classified information] *The Nation* 248:327-8 Mr 13 '89

The North case [dismissal of conspiracy and fraud charges] F. FitzGerald. *The Nation* 248:149 F 6 '89

North rains on Bush's parade. *U.S. News & World Report* 106:34-5 Ap 17 '89

Not dumb persons [jurors in trial of O. L. North] M. E. Marty. *The Christian Century* 106:575 My 24-31 '89

Ollie North's big jail break [spared a prison term] il *U.S. News & World Report* 107:10 Jl 17 '89

Ollie North's eleventh-hour stratagem [subpoenas to R. Reagan and G. Bush challenge executive privilege] T. Morganthau. il pors *Newsweek* 113:24 Ja 9 '89

Ollie North's troubles: the sequel. S. J. Hedges and S. Emerson. il por *U.S. News & World Report* 106:24 F 6 '89

Ollie's cash stash. *Time* 133:18 Ap 24 '89

Ollie's short-lived victory [dropping two major counts against O. North] R. Parry. il por *Newsweek* 113:33 Ja 16 '89

Ollie's tarnished image. L. Martz. il por *Newsweek* 113:38 Ap 24 '89

Ollie's trial: the Bush factor. L. Martz. il por *Newsweek* 113:20 Ap 17 '89

Ollie's true colors. E. Alterman. *The New Republic* 200:13-14 Mr 13 '89

On & on it goes [classified documents in O. North case] W. F. Buckley. *National Review* 41:70 F 10 '89

"A partial vindication" [O. North verdict] R. Lacayo. il por *Time* 133:34-5 My 15 '89

Pawn among giants [O. L. North's trial] E. Magnuson. il por *Time* 133:22-3 Ap 17 '89

Reagan's role at Ollie's trial. L. Martz. il pors *Newsweek* 113:29 Ap 10 '89

Revelations of the North trial. T. Draper. bibl f il *The New York Review of Books* 36:54-9 Ag 17 '89

Security blanket [decision to drop conspiracy and fraud charges against O. North] *The Nation* 248:111-12 Ja 30 '89

A silver head and a steady gavel [Judge G. Gesell] il por *U.S. News & World Report* 106:13-14 F 27 '89

A slap on the wrist for Ollie. L. Martz and R. Parry. il por *Newsweek* 114:28-9 Jl 17 '89

Soliciting for the secret war: a chronicle [summary of classified documents submitted as evidence in O. North's trial] *Harper's* 278:17-19+ Je '89

A tale of two governments [testimony of R. Owen at O. North trial] M. Kempton. *The New York Review of Books* 36:43 Mr 30 '89

Top-secret strategy [trial of O. North] G. J. Church. il por *Time* 133:16-17 F 27 '89

Verdict by prayer [O. North found guilty on three counts] M. McDonald. il por *Maclean's* 102:18-19 My 15 '89

What Oliver North's trial means to us. W. Greider. il *Rolling Stone* p45-6 Je 1 '89

What Reagan really knew. E. Salholz. il pors *Newsweek* 113:25 Mr 6 '89

Where, oh where have all the scandals gone? [dropping several charges against O. North] il por *U.S. News & World Report* 106:11-12 Ja 16 '89

Whittling away for Ollie. R. Parry. il pors *Newsweek* 113:20 F 20 '89

Who is Ollie's peer? [selecting jurors for O. North trial] W. F. Buckley. *National Review* 41:62 Mr 10 '89

Winners and losers [O. North verdict] *National Review* 41:12 Je 2 '89

IRAN-CONTRA AFFAIR IN DRAMA

Mastergate—the scandal continues [excerpts from drama] L. Gelbart. il *The Nation* 249:528-30 N 6 '89

IRAN-CONTRA AFFAIR IN TELEVISION
Getting Ollie North right? It was actor vs. director. M. Leahy. il pors *TV Guide* 37:20-3 Ap 29-My 5 '89
IRANIAN AIR DISASTER, 1988
Smarter radar can tell friend or foe. G. Davis. il *Popular Science* 235:78-82 Jl '89
Why was Flight 655 shot down? D. R. Carlson. *Harper's* 279:26-8 N '89

Compensation
Compensation offered for victims of Iran Airbus tragedy [State Dept. statement, July 17, 1989] *Department of State Bulletin* 89:91-2 S '89
U.S. outlines compensation plan for Iran Flight 655. *Aviation Week & Space Technology* 131:36 Jl 24 '89

Retaliation
Bombs across the ocean? [Iranian retaliation suspected in van bombing directed at wife of W. C. Rogers, commander of the Vincennes] E. Magnuson. il *Time* 133:26 Mr 20 '89
Closing in on the Pan Am bombers [Palestinian-Iranian deal in bombing of Pan Am Flight 103; with interview with A. Jibril] B. Duffy and others. il por *U.S. News & World Report* 106:23-4 My 22 '89
The exile of Sharon Rogers [barred from her teaching job in San Diego after bomb attack on her van] J. V. Lamar, Jr. il por *Time* 133:27 Ap 17 '89
An Iranian message to the U.S. Navy? [bombing of Vicennes' commander W. C. Rogers' van in San Diego] *U.S. News & World Report* 106:10+ Mr 20 '89
Pan Am 103: a Teheran connection? il *Newsweek* 112:58 My 22 '89
A terrorist retaliation? [Vincennes' commander W. C. Rogers' van bombed in San Diego] R. Sandza. il por *Newsweek* 113:34 Mr 20 '89
IRANIAN ART See Art, Iranian
IRANIAN CRISIS, 1979-1981 See Iranian seizure of United States embassy, 1979-1981
IRANIAN-IRAQI WAR, 1980-1988
'If hypocrisy could kill' [Iraq's use of chemical weapons] L. Infante. il *World Press Review* 36:21 Mr '89
Peace and mediation
Iran-Iraq peace talks continue in Geneva. map *UN Chronicle* 26:21 S '89
Iran's future held hostage. L. Lief. il *U.S. News & World Report* 106:37-8 F 20 '89
Iraq's changing role in the Persian Gulf. L. Mylroie. bibl f *Current History* 88:89-2+ F '89
Peace plan for Gulf region pursued. il *UN Chronicle* 26:56-7 Mr '89
Renewed efforts asked to implement Resolution 598. *UN Chronicle* 26:23 D '89
Talks aimed at final peace settlement between Iran and Iraq continue; UNIIMOG mandate renewed. il *UN Chronicle* 26:23-5 Je '89
War and revolution in Iran. G. Fuller. bibl f *Current History* 88:81-4+ F '89
IRANIAN NIGHTS [drama] See Ali, Tariq
IRANIAN REFUGEES See Refugees, Iranian
IRANIAN SEIZURE OF UNITED STATES EMBASSY, 1979-1981
Hello again [1989 reunion of the hostages] P. Meyer and J. Mason. il *Life* 12:41-4+ Fall '89
Minority report [link between Iranian hostage case, Reagan's 1980 campaign and contragate] C. Hitchens. *The Nation* 249:78 Jl 17 '89
Economic aspects
Breaking the ice on assets [prospect of settling with Iran at the Claims Tribunal in return for release of the hostages in Lebanon] L. Lief. il *U.S. News & World Report* 107:89-90 Ag 28-S 4 '89
A game of winks and nods [U.S. releases frozen assets to Iran] R. Lacayo. il *Time* 134:65 N 20 '89
Update on U.S.-Iran claims settlement [State Dept. fact sheet, August 9, 1989] *Department of State Bulletin* 89:60 N '89
IRANIAN TERRORISTS See Terrorists, Iranian
IRANIANS
Pakistan
Iranian Christians flee persecution. H. Martyn. *The Christian Century* 106:461-2 My 3 '89
United States
The man who would be Shah [Reza Pahlavi] P. Axthelm. il pors *People Weekly* 31:46-51 Ap 3 '89
IRAQ
See also
Child welfare—Iraq
Civil rights—Iraq
Iranian-Iraqi War, 1980-1988
Kurds—Iraq
United Nations—Iraq
Antiquities
See also
Babylon (Ancient city)
Calah (Ancient city)
Hatra (Iraq)
Mashkan-shapir (Ancient city)

Defenses
See also
Chemical and biological weapons—Iraq
Economic policy
Lose a son, drive a car. P. Fuhrman. il pors *Forbes* 144:256+ D 11 '89
Foreign relations
Persian Gulf region
Iraq's changing role in the Persian Gulf. L. Mylroie. bibl f *Current History* 88:89-2+ F '89
United States
See United States—Foreign relations—Iraq
Politics and government
Alas, Babylon—can Saddam rebuild it? R. Z. Chesnoff. il por *U.S. News & World Report* 107:37+ S 25 '89
Lose a son, drive a car. P. Fuhrman. il pors *Forbes* 144:256+ D 11 '89
The poor man's atomic bomb [use of poison gas against the Kurds] A. C. Revkin. il *Discover* 10:76 Ja '89
Religious institutions and affairs
See also
Muslims—Iraq
IRAS See Individual retirement accounts
IRAS (INFRARED ASTRONOMY SATELLITE) See Artificial satellites—Astronomical use
IRELAND, ANDY
The time has come: bring our troops back from Europe. il *USA Today (Periodical)* 118:16-18 Jl '89
IRELAND, DAVID
about
Brave new world. K. D. Stein. il *Architectural Record* 177:118-25 mid-S '89
David Ireland: Germans Van Eck. L. Holst. il *Art News* 88:160 D '89
David Ireland's accommodations [cover story] B. Berkson. il por *Art in America* 77:178-87+ S '89
David Ireland's art doesn't just hang on a wall—it is the wall. R. Lacayo. il pors *People Weekly* 31:135+ Ap 10 '89
IRELAND, JILL
Architectural digest visits: Charles Bronson and Jill Ireland. il por *Architectural Digest* 46:98-103+ Jl '89
about
Battling the beast within. H. G. Miller. il pors *The Saturday Evening Post* 261:44-5 Jl/Ag '89
Fighting for her own life, Jill Ireland now must mourn the loss of her son Jason. J. Park. il pors *People Weekly* 32:59+ N 27 '89
"I will live . . . ": Jill Ireland fights back. V. Scott. il pors *Good Housekeeping* 208:183+ My '89
Shattered for the second time. B. Kantrowitz. pors *Newsweek* 113:66 My 8 '89
Why me? [interview] il pors *Life* 12:108-9+ Je '89
IRELAND
See also
Abortion—Laws and regulations—Ireland
Astronomy—Ireland
Aviation and state—Ireland
Connemara (Ireland)
Dublin (Ireland)
Galway (Ireland)
Investments, American—Ireland
Irish
Libel and slander—Ireland
Northern Ireland
Publishers and publishing—Laws and regulations—Ireland
Technology and state—Ireland
Antiquities
See also
Tombs—Ireland
Commerce
United States
See United States—Commerce—Ireland
Description and travel
Ireland without the blarney. G. Weiss. il *Business Week* p138-9 O 16 '89
Irish missed. W. Finnegan. il *Mother Jones* 14:41-2 My '89
Foreign relations
Great Britain
See Great Britain—Foreign relations—Ireland
Northern Ireland
See also
Irish unification question
History
1625-1649
Strafford in Ireland, 1633-40. H. F. Kearney. il por maps *History Today* 39:20-5 Jl '89
Industries
See also
Aer Lingus
Electronic industries—Ireland
GPA Group, Ltd.
GPA Jetprop, Ltd.
Ryanair (Firm)
Waterford Glass Group plc

IRELAND—*cont.*

Religious institutions and affairs
See also
Catholic Church—Ireland

Social conditions
Ireland today: life in the big village. K. McQuaid. il map *Focus (New York, N.Y.: 1950)* 39:1-4 Spr '89

Social history
Once I lived in a proper house. M. Keane. il *Gourmet* 49:102+ Ap '89

Union (Proposed)
See Irish unification question

IRELAND, NORTHERN *See* Northern Ireland

IRIDESCENCE
All about iridescence. T. Schlatter. il *Weatherwise* 42:159-60 Je '89

IRIDIUM
Microbes complicate the K-T mystery [research by Betsey D. Dyer] R. Monastersky. *Science News* 136:341 N 25 '89

IRIKI, ATSUSHI, AND OTHERS
Long-term potentiation in the motor cortex. bibl f il *Science* 245:1385-7 S 22 '89

IRION, ROBERT
Inside the rings of Saturn. il *Astronomy* 17:50-1 N '89

IRIS GRAPHICS INC.
Iris: perfect proofs before the presses roll. L. Jereski. il por *Business Week* p61 My 29 '89

IRISES
Iris discovery: Siberian and Japanese. il *Sunset (Central West edition)* 183:184-5 S '89
The Japanese iris. A. McAndrew. il *Flower and Garden* 33:22+ Jl/Ag '89
Love in blooms [work of C. McEwen] E. Tozer. il por *Modern Maturity* 32:56-60 O/N '89

IRISH

Great Britain
British justice, Irish victims [release of Guildford Four who were wrongfully imprisoned in England for terrorist bombings] A. Cockburn. *The Nation* 249:554-5 N 13 '89
Cops above the law [release of Guildford Four who were wrongfully imprisoned in England for being IRA suspects] A. Phillips. il *Maclean's* 102:76+ N 6 '89

United States
See also
Irish Americans
The bloody war in Belfast spills into the U.S. courts [IRA member J. Doherty in U.S. prison] T. Clifton. il por *Newsweek* 114:96+ D 11 '89
The re-greening of America. E. Magnuson. il *Time* 133:30 Mr 20 '89

Religious life
The new Irish immigrant [conference sponsored by National Conference of Catholic Bishops' Committee on Migration] R. Bautch. *America* 160:236-7 Mr 18 '89

IRISH AIRLINES *See* Aer Lingus

IRISH AMERICANS

History
When people cared that Miss Liberty was Irish! [model for Indian-head $10 gold piece] E. Rochette. il *Antiques & Collecting Hobbies* 94:55+ Mr '89

IRISH ELK
Of moose, megaloceros and miracles. D. Petersen. il map *The Mother Earth News* 116:102-7 Mr/Ap '89

IRISH HOUSE DECORATION *See* House decoration, Irish

IRISH NATIONAL BALLET
Reviews:
Performance of Oscar in city of Cork. C. Swift. *Dance Magazine* 63:100+ My '89

IRISH REPUBLICAN ARMY
The bloody war in Belfast spills into the U.S. courts [IRA member J. Doherty in U.S. prison] T. Clifton. il por *Newsweek* 114:96+ D 11 '89
British justice, Irish victims [release of Guildford Four who were wrongfully imprisoned in England for terrorist bombings] A. Cockburn. *The Nation* 249:554-5 N 13 '89
Cops above the law [release of Guildford Four who were wrongfully imprisoned in England for being IRA suspects] A. Phillips. il *Maclean's* 102:76+ N 6 '89
The fighting Irish. P. J. O'Rourke. il *Rolling Stone* p99-100+ F 9 '89
Northern Ireland hit-squad scandal [leak of lists of IRA sympathizers triggers loyalist terrorism] L. Flanders. il *The Nation* 249:491-4 O 30 '89
Vulnerable target, deadly attack [attack on Royal Marines School of Music] *Newsweek* 114:31 O 2 '89
A wave of bloodshed. M. Nemeth. il *Maclean's* 102:34 Ap 3 '89

IRISH UNIFICATION QUESTION
Can Britain ever leave Northern Ireland? C. C. O'Brien. il *World Press Review* 36:56 O '89
Cardinal Ó Fiaich: my vision of a new Ireland [cover story] T. P. O'Mahony. *America* 160:238-40 Mr 18 '89

IRON
See also
Cast iron

Physiological effects
See also
Hemochromatosis

IRON AGE

Bavaria (Germany)
Iron and industry: ancient links [Kelheim excavation; work of Peter S. Wells; cover story] B. Bower. il *Science News* 135:170-1 Mr 18 '89

Denmark
In search of Denmark's bog people [cycling trip] G. Thomson. il map *Bicycling* 30:68-72+ Ag '89

IRON CHLOROSIS (PLANTS) *See* Chlorosis (Plants)

IRON DEFICIENCY ANEMIA *See* Anemia

IRON FENCES *See* Fences

IRON IN THE BODY
See also
Anemia
Ferritin
Charting a sensible course for iron. G. L. Blackburn. il *Prevention (Emmaus, Pa.)* 41:109-10+ O '89
The power of iron. T. Mendoza. il *Current Health 2* 15:14-16 Ap '89
Pumping iron? [cautioning against supplements] L. Applegate. il *Runner's World* 24:22-3 Mr '89
Rust never sleeps [imbalances] J. Scandura. *American Health* 8:151-2 Mr '89
The truth about iron. G. Shockey. il *Women's Sports & Fitness* 11:20-1 Ja/F '89

IRON ORES
See also
Magnetite

THE IRON TRIANGLE [film] *See* Motion picture reviews—Single works

IRONING BOARDS
Fold-away ironing board. A. Rooze. il *The Family Handyman* 39:70-1 N/D '89

IRONS

Collectors and collecting
Flat, pan, sad. C. Walker. il por *Americana* 17:50-3 S/O '89
Grandma had an iron like that! C. Walker and J. Walker. il *Antiques & Collecting Hobbies* 94:23-5+ Mr '89

IRONWORK
See also
Blacksmiths and blacksmithing

IRONY
The irony epidemic: the dark side of Fiestaware and the Flintstones. P. Rudnick and K. Andersen. il *Utne Reader* p34-40 My/Je '89

IRPINIA (ITALY)

Politics and government
Finding gold in the rubble [allegations that officials misused 1980 earthquake relief funds] *Newsweek* 113:35 Ja 9 '89

IRRADIATED FOOD
Food irradiation—scientists' toy or everyman's joy? V. Abramov. il *World Health* p28-9 Ap '89
Radioactive waste and the dangers of food irradiation. *Utne Reader* p61 S/O '89

IRRIGATION
See also
Computers—Irrigation use
Watering of gardens, lawns, etc.

Environmental aspects
Water scarcity threatens food in the '90s [research by Sandra Postel] *Science News* 136:398 D 16 '89

Bali (Indonesia)
The electronic goddess: computerizing Bali's ancient irrigation rites [work of Stephen Lansing and James Kremer] G. Cowley. il *Newsweek* 113:50 Mr 6 '89

Great Britain
History
A watery paradise: Rowland Vaughan and Hereford's 'Golden Vale'. M. Delorme. bibl il *History Today* 39:38-43 Jl '89

IRRIGATION EQUIPMENT
Where's the drip? il *Sunset (Central West edition)* 183:58-9 Ag '89

Control
What can an automatic controller do for your irrigation system? il *Sunset (Central West edition)* 182:228-30 Je '89

Maintenance and repair
Biobarrier inhibits root growth [Rootguard] C. M. Fiorillo. *Popular Science* 234:38 F '89

IRRITABLE BOWEL SYNDROME
Gut emotions. M. Adessa. il *Psychology Today* 23:72+ Mr '89

IRS *See* United States. Internal Revenue Service

IRS RECORDS (FIRM)
If you can't beat 'em . . . [M. Copeland] P. Newcomb. il por *Forbes* 144:152 D 25 '89

IRVIN, GLENN
Pros and cons: a separate piece for general education. il *Change* 21:6-9 Jl/Ag '89

IRVINE, LOUISE
about
The collecting life [interview] il por *Antiques & Collecting Hobbies* 94:50-3+ N '89

ISLAM AND JUDAISM
Time for a new temple? [traditionalist Jews campaign to rebuild temple on Temple Mount] R. N. Ostling. il *Time* 134:64-5 O 16 '89

ISLAM IN LITERATURE
See also
Rushdie, Salman—Satanic verses case

ISLAMIC CONVERTS TO CHRISTIANITY *See* Converts from Islam

ISLAMIC PAINTING *See* Painting, Islamic

ISLAMIC WOMEN *See* Muslim women

ISLAND ECOLOGY
The devil's work in an ark of sand [Sable Island] H. Thurston. il map *Audubon* 91:82-91 Mr '89

Island Pond (Vt.)

Churches (Buildings)
I am the clock winder [tower clock of Christ Episcopal Church] G. Keizer. il *Reader's Digest* 134:113-17 Ap '89

ISLAND RECORDS
"I don't loon off all the time" [C. Blackwell sells Island Records to PolyGram] P. Newcomb. il por *Forbes* 144:344+ N 13 '89
Now it's Chris Blackwell, corporate hipster [Island Records surrenders to PolyGram] R. A. Melcher and D. Lieberman. il por *Business Week* p49 Ag 14 '89

ISLAND SON [television program] *See* Television program reviews—Single works

ISLANDS
See also
Barrier islands
On the waterfront [off-shore island restaurants] M. O'Neill. il *Harper's Bazaar* 122:126+ Jl '89

Australia
Gourmet holidays: islands off the Great Barrier Reef. P. J. Wade and K. Wade. il map *Gourmet* 49:46-51+ Mr '89

Florida
Gourmet holidays: Florida's barrier islands. P. J. Wade and K. Wade. il map *Gourmet* 49:90-5+ O '89

Virginia
See also
Virginia Coast Reserve

ISLANDS, ARTIFICIAL *See* Artificial islands

ISLANDS OF THE PACIFIC
See also
Oceania
Pacific Islands (Trust Territory)

ISLE OF MAN TOURIST TROPHY (RACE) *See* Motorcycle racing—Great Britain

ISLE ROYALE NATIONAL PARK (MICH.)
Wolves of Isle Royale. S. Nash. il *National Parks* 63:20-6+ Ja/F '89

ISLETS OF LANGERHANS *See* Pancreas

ISMAIL, RAGHIB
about
The light and the lightning. R. Wiley. il pors *Sports Illustrated* 71:38-42+ S 25 '89

ISOLATION (SOCIAL) *See* Social isolation

ISOMERASES
DNA topoisomerase I-targeted chemotherapy of human colon cancer in xenografts. B. C. Giovanella and others. bibl f il *Science* 246:1046-8 N 24 '89

ISOMERIZATION
Membranes as the energy source in the endergonic transformation of vitamin A to 11-*cis*-retinol. P. S. Deigner and others. bibl f il *Science* 244:968-71 My 26 '89

ISOSCELES PLC
Europe seems to be losing its appetite for LBOs. R. A. Melcher. il *Business Week* p44 D 18 '89

ISOTEC (FIRM)
If there's a tulip craze, sell trowels [sales of heavy water in wake of cold fusion breakthrough] R. Bailey. il *Forbes* 143:132 My 15 '89

ISOTOPE SEPARATION
See also
Plutonium metallurgy

ISOTOPES
See also
Carbon—Isotopes
Helium—Isotopes
Hydrogen—Isotopes
Nitrogen—Isotopes
Osmium—Isotopes
Rhenium—Isotopes

ISOTRETINOIN
Accutane survival guide [skin tips] *Glamour* 87:52-3 Je '89
Accutane: under attack. J. Kaplan. *Vogue* 179:112-13 Ja '89
A miracle goes sour [Accutane and birth defects] C. Raymond. il *Discover* 10:72 Ja '89

ISOZAKI, ARATA
about
Profiles: Arata Isozaki. P. Goldberger. il pors *Architectural Digest* 46:174-81+ Mr '89

ISPAHANI, MAHNAZ
Middling through. *The New Republic* 201:18+ Jl 3 '89

ISRAEL, BETSY, 1958-
Diaries are a girl's best friend. il *Seventeen* 48:84-5+ Ja '89

ISRAEL, FRANKLIN DAVID, 1945-
about
Architecture: Franklin D. Israel: Kathryn and Robert Altman's Malibu residence. P. Goldberger. il pors *Architectural Digest* 46:120-5+ Jl '89
California modern. P. Viladas. il pors *House & Garden* 161:28+ Je '89
Franklin D. Israel subject of first exhibition in Walker series. G. Rockcastle. il *Architectural Record* 177:69 F '89
With due respect [cover story] D. Dietsch. il *Architectural Record* 177:66-73 Ap '89

ISRAEL, MARGARET, 1930-1987
about
Margaret Israel's private universe [cover story] V. Goldberg. il por *American Craft* 49:36-43 Ap/My '89

ISRAEL
See also
Agriculture—Israel
Americans—Israel
Architecture—Israel
Art—Israel
Banks and banking—Israel
Barta'a (Israel)
Deportation—Israel
Economic assistance, American—Israel
Forests and forestry—Israel
Government and the press—Israel
Immigration and emigration—Israel
Industrial research—Israel
Investments, British—Israel
Investments, Canadian—Israel
Israelis
Jews—Israel
Kibbutzim
Lod (Israel)
Military assistance, American—Israel
Motion pictures—Israel
Negev (Israel)
Paleontology—Israel
Peace movement—Israel
Police—Israel
Political prisoners—Israel
Privatization—Israel
Russians—Israel
Sea of Galilee (Israel)
Sinai (Peninsula)
Stone Age—Israel
Tel Aviv (Israel)
Terrorism—Israel
Theater—Israel
Women—Israel

Antiquities
Boat resurfaces at Sea of Galilee. B. Bower. *Science News* 135:44 Ja 21 '89

Army
Advice for refuseniks [pamphlet distributed to Israeli soldiers by peace group Yesh Gvul] *Harper's* 278:23-4 Ja '89
A crisis of conscience in Israel's Army. R. Watson. il *Newsweek* 113:41 Ja 30 '89
An Israeli soldier lives the 'intifada'. D. Langsam. *World Press Review* 36:38-9 D '89
Israel's troubled Army. R. Watson. il *Newsweek* 113:44+ My 1 '89
A moral dilemma [Israeli Army protests conflicting demands of West Bank duty] J. McGeary. il *Time* 133:32-4 Ja 30 '89
Night of the broken clubs [Israeli actions against Palestinians] Y. Sarid. *Harper's* 279:31-2 S '89
The soldiers: anger and frustration [cover story] J. Brinkley. il *The New York Times Magazine* p30-3+ My 7 '89
The soul-searchers of the West Bank. il *U.S. News & World Report* 106:11 Ja 30 '89
The uprising's hidden toll [comments of Israeli soldiers stationed in the occupied territories]; tr. by Willis Johnson. *Harper's* 279:20-1 Ag '89

Commerce
France
See France—Commerce—Israel
South Africa
Israel's deal with the devil? [collaboration with South Africa on missiles] R. Watson. il *Newsweek* 114:52 N 6 '89

Defenses
See also
Airplanes, Military—Israel
Guided missiles, Israeli
Israel—Army

Economic conditions
The economic underpinnings of the intifada. D. Connell. *Utne Reader* p40-1 S/O '89
Israel has everything it needs—except peace. J. Rossant. il *Business Week* p54+ D 4 '89

Economic policy
Israel. M. S. Forbes, Jr. il *Forbes* 143:29 Ap 17 '89

ISRAEL—cont.
Economic relations
Mexico
Death, intrigue and avocados [Mexico accuses Nucal de Mexico of being part of Israeli scheme to control export market] M. A. Lerner. il *Newsweek* 114:37 Ag 14 '89
Foreign opinion
Israel: a lamentation from the future. N. Podhoretz. *Commentary* 87:15-21 Mr '89
"Lamentation" [discussion of March 1989 article, Israel: a lamentation from the future] N. Podhoretz. *Commentary* 88:4-8+ Jl '89
American
Counterforce [conference of Jewish progressives sponsored by Tikkun] M. L. Sifry. *The Nation* 248:112-13 Ja 30 '89
The diaspora's discontent [American Jews dissatisfied with Israeli handling of occupied territories] L. I. Barrett. il por *Time* 133:18-19 Ap 3 '89
A family quarrel [American Jews and Israel] T. Jacoby. il *Newsweek* 113:58-60 Ap 3 '89
Israel & American Jews [discussion of September 1988 article, Where is Zion?] E. Alexander. *Commentary* 87:8-11 F '89
Israel: some surprising polls [American opinion judged increasingly favorable towards Israel] M. Bard. *Commentary* 88:45-7 Ag '89
No left turn [resurgence of Jewish liberalism in America] R. R. Wisse. *The New Republic* 200:23-7 My 22 '89
Shamir to school kids: drop dead; No pragmatist at heart. A. Cockburn. *The Nation* 248:150-1 F 6 '89
Whither Israel? K. A. Lawton. il *Christianity Today* 33:57+ Ja 13 '89
Foreign relations
See also
 Espionage, Israeli
Israel comes of age. A. Yaniv. bibl f *Current History* 88:69-72+ F '89
Arab countries
See Jewish-Arab relations
Eastern Europe
The Mideast on the back burner. E. Salpeter. il *The New Leader* 72:5-6 N 27 '89
Lebanon
How the Israelis snatched the sheik [kidnapping of A. K. Obeid] H. Goodman. il por map *U.S. News & World Report* 107:24-5 Ag 14 '89
Israel snatches a sheik [A. K. Obeid] por *Newsweek* 114:36 Ag 7 '89
Kidnapping and peace [kidnapping of Sheik A. K. Obeid] *The New Republic* 201:8-9 Ag 21 '89
Salting the tail of the hostage takers [kidnapping of Shiite leader A. K. Obeid] *U.S. News & World Report* 107:9 Ag 7 '89
United States
See United States—Foreign relations—Israel
History
See also
 Zionism
Historiography
Charging Israel with original sin [views of B. Morris and A. Shlaim] S. Teveth. bibl f *Commentary* 88:24-33 S '89
Industries
See also
 El Al Israel Airlines Ltd.
 Electronic industries—Israel
 Israel Aircraft Industries Ltd.
 Newspaper publishers and publishing—Israel
Moral conditions
How Israel has trapped itself. J. M. Wall. *The Christian Century* 106:1003-4 N 8 '89
Israelis don't hide from the truth [responses to Palestinian intifada] J. B. Miller. *The Christian Century* 106:552-3 My 24-31 '89
Politics and government
See also
 Elections—Israel
 Gush Emunim
 Political attitudes—Israel
 Press and politics—Israel
Agonizing reappraisal in Israel [cover story] E. Salpeter. *The New Leader* 72:5-6 Ja 9 '89
Behind "Who is a Jew": a letter from Jerusalem. E. Norden. *Commentary* 87:21-33 Ap '89
Beneath the surface in Israel. E. Salpeter. il *The New Leader* 72:5-6 F 6 '89
Ending the stalemate [Labour and Likud form unity government] B. Levin. *Maclean's* 102:48 Ja 2 '89
Israel comes of age. A. Yaniv. bibl f *Current History* 88:69-72+ F '89
Israel moves right. M. Widlanski. il *National Review* 41:24-5 Je 30 '89
Israel: the rise of the ultra-Orthodox. A. Margalit. il *The New York Review of Books* 36:38-44 N 9 '89
Israel's fateful hour [interview with Y. Harkabi] R. I. Friedman. *Harper's* 279:28+ Jl '89
Masters of double-talk [reports that Y. Shamir has been talking to the PLO] il pors *Time* 134:30-1 Ag 7 '89

The Mideast on the back burner. E. Salpeter. il *The New Leader* 72:5-6 N 27 '89
Never! Never! Never! [interview with A. Sharon] M. J. Gart. por *Time* 133:40-2 Ap 17 '89
Or cut bait. *National Review* 41:15 Ag 4 '89
The politicians: avoiding decisions [cover story] T. L. Friedman. il map *The New York Times Magazine* p34-6+ My 7 '89
Power, not peace [Y. Shamir capitulates to A. Sharon on Palestinian issue] J. Smolowe. il por *Time* 134:66-7 Jl 17 '89
Saying no to Arafat [Y. Shamir forms coalition government and rules out talks with PLO] S. MacLeod. il pors *Time* 133:81-2 Ja 2 '89
Shamir under fire [report concludes that Israel must negotiate with the PLO] J. Bierman. il por *Maclean's* 102:24-5 Ap 3 '89
'Today's word is revenge' [attack on Israeli bus puts latest peace proposals in jeopardy] A. Platt. il *Newsweek* 114:34 Jl 17 '89
"Who is a Jew" [discussion of April 1989 article, Behind "Who is a Jew": a letter from Jerusalem] E. Norden. *Commentary* 88:2-4+ S '89
Why is this man so glum? [Y. Shamir and S. Peres disagree over peace plan] il por *Time* 134:28 Jl 24 '89
The widening gulf [Palestinian attack on Israeli bus throws peace endeavors into chaos] B. Came. il *Maclean's* 102:21 Jl 17 '89
Yehoshafat Harkabi [interview] C. Dreifus. il *The Progressive* 53:36-9 Je '89
Population
See also
 Palestinian Arabs
Religious institutions and affairs
See also
 Christians—Israel
Territorial expansion
See also
 Israel-Arab Wars, 1967- —Territorial questions
ISRAEL AIRCRAFT INDUSTRIES LTD.
IAI develops low-cost, long-range Phalcon airborne early warning system. D. A. Brown. il *Aviation Week & Space Technology* 130:54-5 Je 19 '89
Snecma to deliver Atar 9K50 powerplants for use in prototypes of upgraded Kfir. il *Aviation Week & Space Technology* 131:19 O 30 '89
Star quality [Astra 1125; cover story] F. George. il *Flying* 116:28-32+ Jl '89
ISRAEL AND CENTRAL AMERICA
Ambassadors of Zion [International Christian Embassy Jerusalem] T. Barry and D. Preusch. *The Christian Century* 106:79-81 Ja 25 '89
ISRAEL AND THE UNITED STATES
See also
 Israel—Foreign opinion—American
ISRAEL-ARAB RELATIONS See Jewish-Arab relations
ISRAEL-ARAB WAR, 1948-1949
Personal narratives
Four decades of blood vengeance [death of G. Habash's sister in Lydda during 1948 war; tr. by Richard Flantz] A. Kenan. il *The Nation* 248:154-6 F 6 '89
ISRAEL-ARAB WARS, 1967-
Occupied territories
See Israel-Arab Wars, 1967- —Territorial questions
Peace and mediation
See also
 Israel-Arab Wars, 1967- —Territorial questions
 United Nations—Armed Forces—Forces in the Middle East
Public opinion
Americans neutral on Arab-Israeli conflict [survey by Shibley Telhami and Jon Krosnick] il *USA Today (Periodical)* 118:7 D '89
Reporters and reporting
Film flam [J. Franklin-Trout's controversial PBS documentary Days of rage] S. Emerson. *The New Republic* 201:29-30+ S 18-25 '89
Viewing the intifada stitch by stitch [PBS documentary Days of rage] W. F. Buckley. *National Review* 41:62-3 O 13 '89
Territorial questions
See also
 United Nations—Armed Forces—Forces in the Middle East
Abused and confused [discussion of November 21, 1988 column] A. Cockburn. *The Nation* 248:506+ Ap 17 '89
Advice for refuseniks [pamphlet distributed to Israeli soldiers by peace group Yesh Gvul] *Harper's* 278:23-4 Ja '89
Agonizing reappraisal in Israel [cover story] E. Salpeter. *The New Leader* 72:5-6 Ja 9 '89
Altering the formula for Israel's friends. J. M. Wall. *The Christian Century* 106:4-5 Ja 4-11 '89
Appeals for Tayseer Aruri [letters] *Physics Today* 42:15+ My '89
The Arafat shuffle. il *The New Republic* 200:9-10+ Ja 9-16 '89

ISRAEL-ARAB WARS, 1967—Territorial questions—*cont.*

Arafat to Israel: pardon my French [statement concerning Palestinian National Charter] il por *Newsweek* 113:48 My 15 '89

Arafat's man in New York [E. Said] D. Smith. il pors *New York* 22:40-6 Ja 23 '89

Arafat's types of ambiguity [interpretation of the Palestinian Declaration of Independence] A. Shammas. *Harper's* 278:60-1 Mr '89

Assembly renews call for Middle East peace conference [Geneva debate keynoted by Y. Arafat] il *UN Chronicle* 26:50-4 Mr '89

At the end of his rope [Y. Arafat] A. Platt. il por *Newsweek* 114:35 S 18 '89

Baker: sheepdog diplomacy? M. G. Warner. il *Newsweek* 113:40 Ap 17 '89

Baker takes a risky step to center stage in the Middle East. S. Reed. il *Business Week* p82 O 23 '89

Baker's 'useless' advice [Middle East peace plan] por *Newsweek* 113:42 Je 5 '89

Beat the devil [U.S. agrees to hold talks with the PLO] A. Cockburn. *The Nation* 248:6-7 Ja 2 '89

Beneath the surface in Israel. E. Salpeter. il *The New Leader* 72:5-6 F 6 '89

Beyond reason. J. Klein. il *New York* 22:16+ Ap 17 '89

Blessing both Jew and Palestinian: a religious Zionist view. Y. Landau. *The Christian Century* 106:1196-9 D 20-27 '89

Bunker mentality [delegation of American Jewish leaders meets with PLO] S. K. Sheinbaum. *The Nation* 248:77 Ja 23 '89

The challenge to Bush in the Middle East. il *The Progressive* 53:6-7 Ja '89

A chance to seize the moral high ground. J. M. Wall. *The Christian Century* 106:491-2 My 10 '89

Contemplating the next step [views of Hussein and H. Mubarak] S. MacLeod. il pors *Time* 133:32-3 Ja 23 '89

Counterforce [conference of Jewish progressives sponsored by Tikkun] M. L. Sifry. *The Nation* 248:112-13 Ja 30 '89

A crisis of conscience in Israel's Army. R. Watson. il *Newsweek* 113:41 Ja 30 '89

The critical moment for peace. P. Mattar. *Foreign Policy* 76:141-59 Fall '89

Deadly quarantine [proposed amendment to Prevention of Terrorism Act restricting rights of Palestinians] A. Cockburn. *The Nation* 249:338-9 O 2 '89

Death comes at Ramadan [escalated violence in the West Bank] *Time* 133:36 Ap 24 '89

A defeated compromise [Israel turns down Mubarak plan] J. Bierman. il por *Maclean's* 102:31 O 16 '89

The diaspora's discontent [American Jews dissatisfied with Israeli handling of occupied territories] L. I. Barrett. il por *Time* 133:18-19 Ap 3 '89

Dissenting opinions about Tayseer Aruri [letters] *Physics Today* 42 pt1:13+ Ag '89

Distrust and dissension in the West Bank and Gaza [Y. Shamir's Palestinian election proposal] R. Z. Chesnoff. il *U.S. News & World Report* 107:38-9 Jl 10 '89

Divided together [Soviets press new peace initiative] A. Bilski. il por *Maclean's* 102:26 Mr 6 '89

Divisive diplomacy [Canadian cabinet minister J. Clark seeks stronger ties with PLO] M. Nemeth. por *Maclean's* 102:40 Mr 20 '89

The economic underpinnings of the intifada. D. Connell. *Utne Reader* p40-1 S/O '89

An elusive peace. K. A. Lawton. il *Christianity Today* 33:34-6 Ap 21 '89

Encounter on the West Bank. G. Corea. il *The Progressive* 53:46 S '89

Enemies of peace [America's Mideast plan] M. Kondracke. *The New Republic* 201:14-15 Ag 7-14 '89

Enter the Soviet Union. J. Smolowe. il *Time* 133:40 Mr 6 '89

A false start in the Middle East [J. A. Baker's speech] E. V. Rostow. *Commentary* 88:24-7 O '89

A family quarrel [American Jews and Israel] T. Jacoby. il *Newsweek* 113:58-60 Ap 3 '89

Fear and loathing in Israel [rising tide of violence in West Bank and Gaza] Z. Chafets. il map *U.S. News & World Report* 107:36-8 Jl 10 '89

Fighting fire with fire [Israeli settlers revolt on the West Bank] J. D. Hull. il *Time* 133:39+ Je 26 '89

Film flam [J. Franklin-Trout's controversial PBS documentary Days of rage] S. Emerson. *The New Republic* 201:29-30+ S 18-25 '89

Finding a response to Arafat's yes. J. B. Miller. *The Christian Century* 106:165-6 F 15 '89

Forgive us our press passes [Israeli police masquerading as press in the occupied territories] L. Zuckerman. il *Time* 133:65 My 8 '89

General Assembly asks Security Council to consider ways to protect Palestinian civilians. il *UN Chronicle* 26:16-17 S '89

How Israel has trapped itself. J. M. Wall. *The Christian Century* 106:1003-4 N 8 '89

How the PLO was legitimized [cover story] J. J. Kirkpatrick. *Commentary* 88:21-8 Jl '89

How to move the immovable [forcing Y. Shamir to negotiate with the Palestinians] S. Talbott. il *Time* 133:20 Ap 3 '89

In search of peace [interview with Queen Noor of Jordan] J. Howse. il por *Maclean's* 102:48 O 30 '89

Inch by inch, step by step [Y. Shamir's visit to Washington] S. MacLeod. il por *Time* 133:36+ Ap 17 '89

Inside the intifada [cover story] J. Brinkley. il *The New York Times Magazine* p36-9+ O 29 '89

The internecine war of the West Bank [violence among Palestinians in the occupied territories] R. Z. Chesnoff. il *U.S. News & World Report* 107:38 Ag 21 '89

The intifada's surreal effect. R. Z. Chesnoff. il *U.S. News & World Report* 106:54-5+ Mr 20 '89

Is it safe to travel in Israel? [effect of uprising on Jerusalem] H. R. Lottman. *Publishers Weekly* 235:42 Ja 13 '89

Is the intifadeh losing steam? il *Time* 134:21 S 4 '89

Is the West Bank a vital American interest? [cover story] D. Pipes. *Commentary* 88:19-24 N '89

Israel: a chance for peace? il *Scholastic Update (Teachers' edition)* 122:13 N 3 '89

Israel: a lamentation from the future. N. Podhoretz. *Commentary* 87:15-21 Mr '89

Israel and the Palestinians. *World Press Review* 36:12 Jl '89

Israel and the Palestinians. G. Gottlieb. bibl f *Foreign Affairs* 68:109-26 Fall '89

Israel comes of age. A. Yaniv. bibl f *Current History* 88:69-72+ F '89

Israel has everything it needs—except peace. J. Rossant. il *Business Week* p54+ D 4 '89

Israel: some surprising polls [American opinion judged increasingly favorable towards Israel] M. Bard. *Commentary* 88:45-7 Ag '89

An Israeli draws the line [G. Spiro, co-founder of Yesh Gvul] W. Steif. il por *The Progressive* 53:15 Ap '89

Israeli physicists, and others, comment on case of Palestinian physicist [T. Aruri] W. Sweet. *Physics Today* 42:83-5 S '89

Israeli policies in occupied territories condemned. il *UN Chronicle* 26:55 Mr '89

An Israeli soldier lives the 'intifada'. D. Langsam. *World Press Review* 36:38-9 D '89

An Israeli with a controversial plan for the Palestinians [interview with C. Shur] J. R. Moskin. il por *World Press Review* 36:32-4 Je '89

Israelis don't hide from the truth [responses to Palestinian intifada] J. B. Miller. *The Christian Century* 106:552-3 My 24-31 '89

Israel's Arabs. Y. Goell. *The New Republic* 201:16-18 O 23 '89

Israel's blank check [cover story] S. Zunes. il *The Progressive* 53:20-5 N '89

Israel's dilemma [Palestine question] A. Perlmutter. *Foreign Affairs* 68:119-32 Wint '89/'90

Israel's fateful hour [interview with Y. Harkabi] R. I. Friedman. *Harper's* 279:28+ Jl '89

Israel's prison academies [Palestinians organize while imprisoned by Israelis]; tr. by Ina Friedman. E. Ya'ari. il *The Atlantic* 264:22+ O '89

Israel's troubled Army. R. Watson. il *Newsweek* 113:44+ My 1 '89

It's Arab on Arab two years into the intifada [death squads in the occupied territories] R. Z. Chesnoff. il *U.S. News & World Report* 107:15 D 25 '89-Ja 1 '90

Jerusalem: the future of the past. A. Elon. il *The New York Review of Books* 36:37-9 Ag 17 '89

Jordan/Palestine [discussion of October 1988 article, Is Jordan Palestine?] D. Pipes and A. M. Garfinkle. *Commentary* 87:2+ F '89

Jordan and reverberations of the uprising. R. Satloff. bibl f *Current History* 88:85-8+ F '89

Justice for the Palestinians. M. Singer. il *National Review* 41:40-2 O 13 '89

"Lamentation" [discussion of March 1989 article, Israel: a lamentation from the future] N. Podhoretz. *Commentary* 88:4-8+ Jl '89

Land or life: a biblical dilemma [O. Yosef's views in rabbinical debate over Israeli occupation] R. N. Ostling. il por *Time* 134:67 S 18 '89

Letter from Israel. A. Elon. *The New Yorker* 64:74-80 F 13 '89

A letter to Yasir Arafat. M. Z. Rosensaft. por *Newsweek* 114:14 D 11 '89

Local hero [F. Al-Husseini] *The New Republic* 200:8+ F 20 '89

Massacre in Nahalin [Israeli border police raid on West Bank village] J. Bierman. *Maclean's* 102:26 Ap 24 '89

Masters of double-talk [reports that Y. Shamir has been talking to the PLO] il pors *Time* 134:30-1 Ag 7 '89

The Middle East [address, April 22, 1989] King Hussein. *Vital Speeches of the Day* 55:486-7 Je 1 '89

The Middle East [Palestinian uprising; special section] il *World Press Review* 36:26-9 Ap '89

Middle East [U.S. opens dialogue with PLO; statements and press conferences, November 26-December 18, 1988; special section] *Department of State Bulletin* 89:51-60 F '89

ISRAEL-ARAB WARS, 1967—Territorial questions—*cont.*

Middle East peacemakers. C. T. Oppenheim. *The Progressive* 53:11 Jl '89

The Mideast on the back burner. E. Salpeter. il *The New Leader* 72:5-6 N 27 '89

A moral dilemma [Israeli Army protests conflicting demands of West Bank duty] J. McGeary. il *Time* 133:32-4 Ja 30 '89

Moscow's new role in the Middle East [cover story] F. Halliday. il *The Nation* 248:361+ Mr 20 '89

Mubarak moves to the front lines of the Mideast crisis. B. Slavin and others. il *Business Week* p59 Ja 9 '89

Mubarak's peace plan. il *World Press Review* 36:8 N '89

Much has changed [need to negotiate with PLO] *The Nation* 248:435-6 Ap 3 '89

Nation-building in an occupied land. J. M. Wall. *The Christian Century* 106:459-60 My 3 '89

Never! Never! Never! [interview with A. Sharon] M. J. Gart. por *Time* 133:40-2 Ap 17 '89

The new PLO? [views of B. A. Sharif] S. MacLeod. bibl f il *The New York Review of Books* 36:44-9 Ap 13 '89

Night of the broken clubs [Israeli actions against Palestinians] Y. Sarid. *Harper's* 279:31-2 S '89

No left turn [resurgence of Jewish liberalism in America] R. R. Wisse. *The New Republic* 200:23-7 My 22 '89

No sticks, no aspirins. B. Russett. *Commonweal* 116:336-7 Je 2 '89

No taxation without representation [Palestinian Christians] M. Ward. *America* 161:464-5 D 23-30 '89

No turning back for the Palestinians. J. M. Wall. *The Christian Century* 106:435-6 Ap 26 '89

Notes and comment [U.S. meetings with PLO in Tunis] *The New Yorker* 65:33-4 Ap 10 '89

Null and void [Y. Arafat's statement on the 1964 PLO charter] *Time* 133:45 My 15 '89

Oh, Jerusalem! [election in Jerusalem] E. Norden. *The New Republic* 200:17-18 Mr 27 '89

Or cut bait. *National Review* 41:15 Ag 4 '89

Palestinian Christians join intifada tax protest. L. Cryderman. il por *Christianity Today* 33:42 D 15 '89

Palestinian like me: notes from an undercover Jewish journalist [excerpt from My enemy, my self] Y. Binur. il pors *Utne Reader* p34-45 S/O '89

A Palestinian view of Israel's history. E. W. Said. map *Utne Reader* p38-9 S/O '89

The Palestinians [U.S. refusal of visa to Y. Arafat] il *World Press Review* 36:8+ Ja '89

Palestinians and the intifada: one year later. A. D. Miller. bibl f *Current History* 88:73-6+ F '89

Peace later [J. A. Baker's role in Middle East negotiations] M. Kondracke. *The New Republic* 200:10-12 Mr 27 '89

The peace of Saladin [Yitzhak Shamir's Palestinian election proposal] M. B. Zuckerman. il *U.S. News & World Report* 106:78 My 1 '89

Peace offering [Y. Shamir's plan] *The New Republic* 200:7-8 My 1 '89

The plight of Palestinian schools. S. Tifft. il *Time* 134:56 Jl 31 '89

The PLO [discussion of July 1989 article, How the PLO was legitimized] J. J. Kirkpatrick. *Commentary* 88:7-8 N '89

The politicians: avoiding decisions [cover story] T. L. Friedman. il map *The New York Times Magazine* p34-6+ My 7 '89

The politics of peace in the Mideast [cover story] E. Salpeter. il *The New Leader* 72:5-7 O 2-16 '89

Power, not peace [Y. Shamir capitulates to A. Sharon on Palestinian issue] J. Smolowe. il por *Time* 134:66-7 Jl 17 '89

Prescriptions for the Middle East. M. Morrison. *The American Spectator* 22:16-18 Ja '89

Principles and pragmatism [address, May 22, 1989] J. A. Baker, III. *Vital Speeches of the Day* 55:549-51 Jl 1 '89

Principles and pragmatism: American policy toward the Arab-Israeli conflict [address, May 22, 1989] J. A. Baker, III. *Department of State Bulletin* 89:24-7 Jl '89

"Professor of terror" [discussion of August 1989 article] E. Alexander. *Commentary* 88:2-7+ D '89

Professor of terror [views of E. W. Said] E. Alexander. *Commentary* 88:49-50 Ag '89

A profusion of land mines. M. Cohen. il *Commonweal* 116:275-8 My 5 '89

The rapidly changing world [address, June 14, 1989] M. M. Kampelman. *Vital Speeches of the Day* 55:731-4 S 15 '89

'Realism' and human rights [U.S. report criticizes Israel's practices in the occupied territories] H. Anderson. il *Newsweek* 113:28 F 20 '89

Recent events in the Middle East [statement, September 19, 1989] J. H. Kelly. *Department of State Bulletin* 89:61-3 N '89

Reconquering Palestine [Islamic militants] A. Frachon. *World Press Review* 36:32+ Jl '89

Regrets only [reaction to J. Baker's speech regarding Middle East peace plan] *The New Republic* 200:8 Je 19 '89

The right rights. H. V. Jaffa. *National Review* 41:50 N 10 '89

Ruckus over Days of rage [controversial PBS documentary] R. Zoglin. il *Time* 134:70 S 4 '89

Running out of answers [Israeli tactics fail to stem intifadeh] J. Bierman. il *Maclean's* 102:24 F 6 '89

Sanctum of the strong. E. W. Said. il *The Nation* 249:48-50 Jl 10 '89

Saying no to Arafat [Y. Shamir forms coalition government and rules out talks with PLO] S. MacLeod. il pors *Time* 133:81-2 Ja 2 '89

Secretary Baker's news briefing, Feb. 23, 1989. J. A. Baker, III. il *Department of State Bulletin* 89:1-4 My '89

Secretary meets with Israeli foreign minister [remarks, March 13, 1989] J. A. Baker; M. Arens. *Department of State Bulletin* 89:63 My '89

Secretary's interview on "This week with David Brinkley" [J. A. Baker; transcript of program, April 9, 1989] *Department of State Bulletin* 89:12-14 Je '89

Security Council fails to adopt text on Palestinian rights. il *UN Chronicle* 26:18 S '89

Security Council regrets deportations by Israel of Palestinians. il *UN Chronicle* 26:24 D '89

A seder for peace in the Mideast. A. Waskow. il *The Nation* 248:557+ Ap 24 '89

Send in the pols. J. Klein. il por *New York* 22:10-11 Ja 9 '89

Setting Yasser straight [role of American R. E. Hauser in U.S. recognition of PLO] S. Weller. il pors *Ms.* 17:84 Mr '89

The settlers [West Bank] R. I. Friedman. bibl f il *The New York Review of Books* 36:49-56 Je 15 '89

Shamir gets set for Washington [cover story] E. Salpeter. il *The New Leader* 72:6-8 Mr 6 '89

Shamir molds a peace plan. *Time* 133:53 F 13 '89

Shamir stands his ground [interview with Y. Shamir] R. Rivard and others. il por *Newsweek* 113:42 Ja 2 '89

Shamir to school kids: drop dead; No pragmatist at heart. A. Cockburn. *The Nation* 248:150-1 F 6 '89

Shamir under fire [report concludes that Israel must negotiate with the PLO] J. Bierman. il por *Maclean's* 102:24-5 Ap 3 '89

Shamir's new plan. J. Bierman. il por *Maclean's* 102:20 Ap 17 '89

Should we trust Yasir Arafat? D. Reed. por *Reader's Digest* 135:143-8 S '89

Slipping into darkness. H. Goodman. *The New Republic* 201:10-12 Jl 3 '89

The soldiers: anger and frustration [cover story] J. Brinkley. il *The New York Times Magazine* p30-3+ My 7 '89

The soul-searchers of the West Bank [Israeli Army] il *U.S. News & World Report* 106:11 Ja 30 '89

Sowing dragons' teeth or talking. *America* 161:228 O 14 '89

Spoilers of peace in the Middle East [radical Palestinian groups supported by Syria] R. Z. Chesnoff. il map *U.S. News & World Report* 107:40-1 Jl 10 '89

State of confusion [consequences of an independent Palestinian state; cover story] S. L. Spiegel. *The New Republic* 200:15-18 Ap 10 '89

Still stuck in the Stone Age [Palestinian uprising enters third year] J. D. Hull. il *Time* 134:59-60+ D 11 '89

Straight talk from the U.S. [J. Baker presents plan for peace in Middle East] C. Ogden. il por *Time* 133:32 Je 5 '89

Sustainable development an important element of Palestinian uprising. A. Mitchison. *Utne Reader* p44 S/O '89

Talk to the PLO? More Israelis are thinking about it. N. Sandler and B. Javetski. il *Business Week* p48 Ap 10 '89

A talk with Arafat [cover story] R. O. Freedman. il *The New York Review of Books* 36:8+ Ap 13 '89

Talking to the PLO; A personal triumph [Canada upgrades relations] L. Van Dusen. il por *Maclean's* 102:10-12 Ap 10 '89

Text deploring Israeli policies in occupied territories vetoed. il *UN Chronicle* 26:31 Je '89

A thin green line [Israeli Arabs in Barta'a] D. L. Kirp. il *Mother Jones* 14:16-17+ My '89

Tilling the rocky ground of Mideast peacemaking [Y. Shamir's U.S. visit] L. Lief. il por *U.S. News & World Report* 106:43 Ap 10 '89

Time check. *The Nation* 249:156 Ag 7-14 '89

'Today's word is revenge' [attack on Israeli bus puts latest peace proposals in jeopardy] A. Platt. il *Newsweek* 114:34 Jl 17 '89

True friends and false [J. Baker's speech] *Commonweal* 116:357 Je 16 '89

Turnabout [decision to open talks with PLO] *The Nation* 248:39-40 Ja 9-16 '89

The uprising's hidden toll [comments of Israeli soldiers stationed in the occupied territories]; tr. by Willis Johnson. *Harper's* 279:20-1 Ag '89

The view from the West Bank. E. Salpeter. il *The New Leader* 72:5-6 Je 12-26 '89

Viewing the intifada stitch by stitch [PBS documentary Days of rage] W. F. Buckley. *National Review* 41:62-3 O 13 '89

Vigilantism on the West Bank: Israeli settlers step up their war against Arabs. T. Stanger. il *Newsweek* 113:41 Je 12 '89

ISRAEL-ARAB WARS, 1967—Territorial questions—*cont.*
Virtuoso transformations [Y. Arafat and M. Gorbachev] S. Talbott. il *Time* 133:36 Ja 9 '89
Visit of Egyptian president [remarks, April 3, 1989] G. Bush; H. Mubarak. il por *Department of State Bulletin* 89:40-1 Je '89
Visit of Israeli prime minister [remarks, April 6, 1989] G. Bush; Y. Shamir. il por *Department of State Bulletin* 89:42-3 Je '89
Visit of King Hussein I [remarks, April 19, 1989] G. Bush; Hussein. il por map *Department of State Bulletin* 89:53-5 Jl '89
Waiting for Godot [Israeli opposition to H. Mubarak's peace plan] B. W. Nelan. il por *Time* 134:45 O 16 '89
The walls are crumbling down [peace demonstration in the Negev against Israeli occupation of West Bank] D. Hurwitz. *The Progressive* 53:12 Je '89
'We can't take chances' [interview with C. Herzog] E. Silver. *Maclean's* 102:23 Je 26 '89
West Bank fratricide [violence among the Palestinians] *The New Republic* 201:10-11 S 11 '89
West Bank story [discussion of June 15, 1989 article, The settlers] R. I. Friedman. *The New York Review of Books* 36:59 N 23 '89
What America should say to Arafat. R. N. Perle. il por *U.S. News & World Report* 106:58-9 Mr 20 '89
Whither Israel? K. A. Lawton. il *Christianity Today* 33:57+ Ja 13 '89
Whose Palestine? [cover story; special section] il *World Press Review* 36:13-21 F '89
Why I met with the PLO. M. Z. Rosensaft. por *Newsweek* 113:6 Ja 9 '89
Why is this man so glum? [Y. Shamir and S. Peres disagree over peace plan] il por *Time* 134:28 Jl 24 '89
Why Israel needs a gentle intifadeh victory. M. Kramer. il *Time* 134:68 Jl 24 '89
Why should Israel trust the PLO? B. Amiel. il *Maclean's* 102:9 Je 5 '89
The widening gulf [Palestinian attack on Israeli bus throws peace endeavors into chaos] B. Came. il *Maclean's* 102:21 Jl 17 '89
Willie L. Brown Jr. [advice to George Bush] W. L. Brown, Jr. *National Review* 41:24-5 F 10 '89
Women play key role in opposing the occupation. M. Kaye/Kantrowitz. il *Utne Reader* p42-3 S/O '89
Yehoshafat Harkabi [interview] C. Dreifus. il *The Progressive* 53:36-9 Je '89
Zero-plus game: a strategy for the Middle East. J. B. Hehir. *Commonweal* 116:39-40 Ja 27 '89
ISRAELI ART *See* Art, Israeli
ISRAELI ARTIFICIAL SATELLITES *See* Artificial satellites, Israeli
ISRAELI FICTION
Bibliography
Haggling presences. D. Donoghue. il *The New York Review of Books* 36:39-43 S 28 '89
ISRAELI LITERATURE
Conferences
Jewish guilt and Israeli writers [The writer in the Jewish community: an Israeli-North American dialogue] R. R. Wisse. *Commentary* 87:25-31 Ja '89
ISRAELIS
Colombia
The Israeli connection [mercenaries involved in training Colombian hit squads] E. Magnuson. il *Time* 134:26 S 11 '89
ISRAELOFF, ROBERTA, 1952-
Helping your kids to eat right and have good body images. il *Working Woman* 14:219-22 S '89
Our summer retreat. *Glamour* 87:256 Ag '89
ISSAWI, CHARLES PHILIP
The costs of the French Revolution. *The American Scholar* 58:371-81 Summ '89
Reappraising the French Revolution. il *Current (Washington, D.C.)* 317:4-9 N '89
ISSIGONIS, SIR ALEC, 1906-1988
about
Obituary
Motor Trend por 41:21 Ja '89
ISSUE ADVERTISING *See* Advocacy advertising
ISTANBUL (TURKEY)
Description
Turkish delights. J. Stuart. il *Gentlemen's Quarterly* 59:376+ Mr '89
Music
See also
Opera—Turkey
Protests, demonstrations, etc.
Christians and Muslims unite to oppose The last temptation. B. G. Baker. il *Christianity Today* 33:57 My 12 '89
ISU *See* Independent Steelworkers Union
ISUZU (AUTOMOBILE) *See* Automobiles, Foreign
IT *See* Interval training
ITAL DESIGN (FIRM)
Ital Design Aztec. R. Hutton. il *Car and Driver* 34:87-8 Mr '89

ITALIAN AMERICANS
"Papa was so proud" [excerpt from Papa, my father] L. F. Buscaglia. il pors *Redbook* 173:24+ Je '89
History
"Everybody likes Italian food". J. F. Mariani. il *American Heritage* 40:122-31 D '89
ITALIAN ART *See* Art, Italian
ITALIAN FASHION *See* Fashion
ITALIAN FURNITURE *See* Furniture, Italian
ITALIAN GRAND PRIX *See* Automobile racing—Italy
ITALIAN HOUSE DECORATION *See* House decoration, Italian
ITALIAN JEWELRY *See* Jewelry, Italian
ITALIAN PAINTING *See* Painting, Italian
ITALIAN RESTAURANTS *See* Restaurants
ITALIAN WINES *See* Wine
ITALIANS
United States
See also
Italian Americans
ITALY
See also
Abruzzo National Park (Italy)
Agriculture—Italy
Albaretto della Torre (Italy)
Americans—Italy
Anti-Semitism—Italy
Art—Italy
Automobile racing—Italy
Baseball, Professional—Italy
Basketball, Professional—Italy
Bellagio (Italy)
Bicycle racing—Italy
Country estates—Italy
Courmayeur (Italy)
Cultural property—Protection—Italy
Dance festivals—Italy
Earthquakes—Italy
Emilia-Romagna (Italy)
Florence (Italy)
Game laws—Italy
Investments, American—Italy
Investments, Italian
Irpinia (Italy)
Jazz music—Italy
Lake District (Italy)
Milan (Italy)
Monte Cassino (Monastery: Cassino, Italy)
Montecatini Terme (Italy)
Motion picture festivals—Italy
Motorcycle racing—Italy
Music festivals—Italy
Opera—Italy
Palaces—Italy
Perugia (Italy)
Pietrasanta (Italy)
Porto Ercole (Italy)
Railroads—Italy
Rome (Italy)
Sicily
Siena (Italy)
Tuscany (Italy)
Venice (Italy)
Wildlife conservation—Italy
Women—Italy
The global zeitgeist checklist: Italy. M. Lilla. *The New Republic* 201:20 Jl 10 '89
Antiquities
See also
Pompeii (Ancient city)
Commerce
See also
European Economic Community
North America
Piaggio picks AMR for Avanti [North American sales and support organization] *Flying* 116:14+ Ap '89
Piaggio selects AMR Services to market P. 180 in North America [business aircraft] *Aviation Week & Space Technology* 130:27 Ja 30 '89
Soviet Union
See Soviet Union—Commerce—Italy
Defenses
See also
Airplanes, Military—Italy
Guided missiles, Italian
Description and travel
See also
Automobile touring—Italy
Cycling—Italy
Hiking—Italy
Economic conditions
See also
Underground economy—Italy
Economic policy
See also
Budget—Italy
La dolce deficit. R. Ball. il *Time* 134:58 O 16 '89

ITALY—cont.

Economic relations

See also

European Economic Community

Foreign relations

Eastern Europe

Italy watches an empire stumble. S. F. Senigallia. il *The New Leader* 72:10-11 O 30 '89

North Africa

In Andreotti's tent. B. Crozier. *National Review* 41:20 Ag 18 '89

Soviet Union

See Soviet Union—Foreign relations—Italy

History

1559-1789—Historiography

Power and politics in early modern Italy. R. Oresko. il *History Today* 39:42-9 S '89

Industries

See also

Aeritalia SpA

Aeronautica Macchi

Aerospace industries—Italy

Agusta SpA

Alessi SpA

Arnoldo Mondadori Editore, SpA

Art trade—Italy

Benetton SpA

BPD (Firm)

Corporations—Acquisitions and mergers—Italy

Ferruzzi Group

Fiat SpA

Gucci Group

Ing. C. Olivetti & Co., SpA

Mediobanca

Montedison SpA

Officine Alfieri Maserati SpA

Publishers and publishing—Acquisitions and mergers—Italy

Publishers and publishing—Italy

Rinaldo Piaggio (Firm)

Safilo SpA

Selenia Industrie Elettroniche Associate SpA

Silk industry—Italy

Small business—Italy

Wine industry—Italy

Navy

Italy approves naval use of fixed-wing aircraft [short take-off/vertical landing aircraft] il *Aviation Week & Space Technology* 130:21 F 6 '89

Politics and government

See also

Christian Democratic Party (Italy)

Communist Party (Italy)

Elections—Italy

Fascism—Italy

Religious institutions and affairs

See also

Millennialism—Italy

Social conditions

Italy observed. S. Brint. *Society* 26:71-6 Jl/Ag '89

Italy's re-Renaissance [cover story] J. J. Navone. *America* 161:417-19 D 9 '89

ITAMI, JUZO

about

A taxing woman's return [film] Reviews

The New Republic 201:26-7 Ag 7-14 '89. S. Kauffmann

What's so funny about Japan. V. Canby. il pors *The New York Times Magazine* p26-9+ Je 18 '89

ITCHING

Putting your finger on what makes you itch. N. Brown. il *Nation's Business* 77:75 Ap '89

ITEL CORP.

Sam Zell, the perpetual dealmaking machine. L. Therrien. il *Business Week* p88-9 Je 26 '89

ITŌ, JAKUCHŪ See Jakuchū, 1716-1800

ITO, MASAYOSHI, 1913-

about

Japan's quest for Mr. Clean. B. Martin and H. Takayama. il por *Newsweek* 112:58 My 22 '89

ITO, MIDORI

about

Mite makes right. D. S. Looney. il pors *Sports Illustrated* 70:38-9 Mr 27 '89

IT'S A WONDERFUL LIFE [film] See Motion picture reviews—Single works

ITT CORPORATION

Are raiders ready to take on ITT again? G. G. Marcial. il *Business Week* p130 Ap 24 '89

How I fought off the raiders [excerpts from The ITT wars] R. V. Araskog. il pors *Fortune* 119:110-12+ F 27 '89

ITT Avionics emphasizes development of software, improves electronic system. B. D. Nordwall. il *Aviation Week & Space Technology* 131:83+ Jl 17 '89

ITT solves complex problems to produce image intensifiers [night vision goggles] B. D. Nordwall. il *Aviation Week & Space Technology* 130:91+ My 22 '89

Navy, USAF to award contracts for limited ALQ-165 production [airborne self-protection jamming systems] il *Aviation Week & Space Technology* 131:89+ S 11 '89

Pentagon awards production contracts for ALQ-165 to ITT, Westinghouse [airborne self-protection jammer] P. J. Klass. il *Aviation Week & Space Technology* 131:59+ O 16 '89

ITTER, DIANE, 1946-1989

about

Obituary

American Craft por 49:64 D '89/Ja '90. J. Sauer

IUDS See Intrauterine devices

IVEREM, ESTHER

Diet right. il *Black Enterprise* 19:58-9 Jl '89

IVERMECTIN

Conquering an ancient scourge [river blindness in West Africa; cover story] E. P. Eckholm. il map *The New York Times Magazine* p20-7+ Ja 8 '89

IVERSEN, EDWIN S.

Sushi, sashimi, and sickness: raw fish and parasites. bibl il por *Sea Frontiers* 35:176-83 My/Je '89

IVERSEN, EDWIN S., AND JORY, DARRYL E.

Arms race on the grass flats. il *Sea Frontiers* 35:304-11 S/O '89

IVERSON, BRENT L., AND LERNER, RICHARD A.

Sequence-specific peptide cleavage catalyzed by an antibody. bibl f il *Science* 243:1184-8 Mr 3 '89

IVERSON, RICHARD M., AND LAHUSEN, RICHARD G.

Dynamic pore-pressure fluctuations in rapidly shearing granular materials. bibl f il *Science* 246:796-9 N 10 '89

IVES, EDWARD RILEY

about

Ives: the busy American toymaker. M. Jailer. il *Antiques & Collecting Hobbies* 93:36-8+ Ja '89

IVES, RAY

Getting in gear. *Travel Holiday* 171:42-3 Mr '89

IVES MANUFACTURING CORPORATION

Ives: the busy American toymaker [clockwork-driven toys] M. Jailer. il *Antiques & Collecting Hobbies* 93:36-8+ Ja '89

IVF (IN VITRO FERTILIZATION) See Fertilization in vitro

IVINS, MOLLY

Dumb bankers, mavericks too. il *The Nation* 248:82-4 Ja 23 '89

A few good men. il *Ms.* 17:22 My '89

From CIA to KGB (kinder, gentler Bush) [cover story] il por *Mother Jones* 14:32-7 Ap '89

Good ol debs. il *Ms.* 18:22 Jl/Ag '89

Grin and sell it. il *Ms.* 17:22 Je '89

In fitness and in wealth. il *Ms.* 18:17 N '89

Just say no, fellas. por *Ms.* 18:17 S '89

The Klan: once powerful, now a haven for losers. *TV Guide* 37:25-7 N 4-10 '89

The legislative mangle. il *The New York Times Magazine* p20+ S 17 '89

The memory lingers on. il *Ms.* 17:26-7 Ja/F '89

One Texan, on the rocks. il *Ms.* 17:36 Ap '89

Small favors. See issues of The Progressive beginning March 1986

Stuff it! il *Ms.* 17:46 Mr '89

Too much stuff! Our accumulating crisis. il *Utne Reader* p77-9 Jl/Ag '89

IVORY, JAMES

about

Slaves of New York [film] Reviews

Film Comment il 25:3+ Mr/Ap '89. M. McCreadie

Maclean's il 102:41 Ap 10 '89. B. D. Johnson

The Nation 248:530-1 Ap 17 '89. S. Klawans

The New Republic 200:22-3 Ap 10 '89. S. Kauffmann

New York il 22:69-70 Mr 27 '89. D. Denby

Newsweek il 113:83 Mr 20 '89. D. Ansen

People Weekly il 31:15-16 Ap 24 '89. E. Wurtzel

Time il 133:73 Mr 20 '89. R. Schickel

Video il 13:78+ O '89. I. Robbins

Vogue il 179:192-3 F '89. J. Truman

IVORY, ARTIFICIAL See Tagua

IVORY COAST

See also

Abidjan (Ivory Coast)

IVORY INDUSTRY

Export-import trade

About-face [Japanese ban import of ivory] il *Time* 134:86 O 2 '89

A ban on ivory. M. Nichols. il *Maclean's* 102:86 O 30 '89

Decision time on African ivory trade. J. Cherfas. il *Science* 246:26-7 O 6 '89

Elephants in Alaska [handicrafts made from poached African ivory] F. Graham. *Audubon* 91:27-9 S '89

Elephants look best in ivory [ban on imports] L. Troiano. il *American Health* 8:92 O '89

Global ban sought on ivory trade [to save elephants] R. Lewin. il *Science* 244:1135 Je 9 '89

How to save the African elephant [economic incentives] M. S. Forbes, Jr. *Forbes* 144:29 N 13 '89

International tusk politics. *Science News* 136:94 Ag 5 '89

The ivory dispute [African countries in opposition to trade ban] F. Bridgland. *World Press Review* 36:69 S '89

IVORY INDUSTRY—Export-import trade—*cont.*

Kenya burns $3 mil. in ivory to stop its trade. il *Jet* 76:18 Ag 7 '89

Outlawing ivory [U.S. ban in order to save elephants] il *Time* 133:62 Je 19 '89

Pachyderm policy [elephant herds growing in African countries that permit ivory trading] D. Seligman. il *Fortune* 120:235+ N 20 '89

Reprieve for the giant of beasts [efforts to save the elephant] T. Gup. il *Time* 134:77 O 30 '89

Saving the African elephant. il *The Futurist* 23:49 S/O '89

The shrinking roots of heaven [efforts to stop illegal poaching of elephants by restricting ivory trade] *U.S. News & World Report* 106:11-12 My 22 '89

Symbolic flames [proposed ban on ivory sales] A. Steacy. il *Maclean's* 102:37 Jl 31 '89

Trail of shame [elephants endangered by ivory poachers; cover story] T. Gup. il map *Time* 134:66-9+ O 16 '89

Tusk, tusk [Sotheby's removes elephant tusks from market to alleviate poaching] il *Time* 133:56 My 1 '89

A tussle over tusks [African nations debate ban on ivory trade] J. Bartholet. il *Newsweek* 114:25 Jl 24 '89

History

Arctic treasures: what ruler could resist the allure of white falcons, giant moles, and unicorns? F. Bruemmer. il *Natural History* p38-47 Je '89

In the African interior, the ivory trade and the slave trade helped each other become paying propositions. R. M. Adams. il *Smithsonian* 19:14 Mr '89

IVORY POACHING *See* Poaching

IVRY, BENJAMIN

Captions to certain slide lectures [poem] *The New Republic* 200:42 F 20 '89

Too strong for fantasias. il *Opera News* 53:20-1+ Ja 21 '89

(tr) *See* Zagajewski, Adam, 1945-. Sails

IVY, JOHN

about

Two blacks face murder charges in voodoo scheme. il pors *Jet* 76:52-3 Jl 17 '89

IVY, LEROY

about

Two blacks face murder charges in voodoo scheme. il pors *Jet* 76:52-3 Jl 17 '89

IVY LEAGUE COLLEGES

Is an Ivy degree worth remortgaging the farm? W. Shapiro. *Time* 134:73 S 25 '89

IWO JIMA, BATTLE OF, 1945

Chemical warfare: a forgotten lesson. J. E. van C. Moon. bibl f il *The Bulletin of the Atomic Scientists* 45:40-3 Jl/Ag '89

IYER, PICO

The Tibetan spirit: jolly and rainbowed and welcoming [excerpt from Video night in Kathmandu] il *Utne Reader* p44-6 Mr/Ap '89

IZANAGI AND IZANAMI (SHINTO DEITIES)

The bizarre world of Unishima [American servicemen discover statuettes on island during Korean War] W. J. Buchanan. il *Reader's Digest* 135:71-6 Ag '89

IZYUMOV, ALEXEI

The me generation in Moscow. il *Newsweek* 114:47 D 4 '89

J

J. & W. SELIGMAN & CO. INC.

New broom at Seligman. R. Phalon. il *Forbes* 143:140 F 20 '89

J. C. PENNEY COMPANY, INC.

J.C. Penney takes on a bright new shine. P. Sellers. il *Fortune* 120:26+ S 25 '89

The newly minted Penney: where fashion rules. A. Dunkin. il *Business Week* p88-90 Ap 17 '89

J. CREW (FIRM)

Captain of the Crew [E. Cinader] A. Radakovich. il por *Harper's Bazaar* 122:76+ N '89

The chic is in the mail. B. Rudolph. il *Time* 134:74-5 Jl 17 '89

Storm warnings. G. Morgenson. il *Forbes* 144:140+ D 11 '89

J. E. ROBERT COS.

An odd sort of takeover play [proposed buyout of Federal Asset Disposition Association by J. Robert] J. R. Hayes. il por *Forbes* 143:142 F 6 '89

J. FLORIS LTD.

James Niven: bringing London's toniest scents to the states. il por *Business Week* p107 Je 5 '89

J FREGALETTE JANSEN DANCE

Reviews:

Performances at the Whitney Museum of American Art at Equitable Center, New York City. G. Solomons. *Dance Magazine* 63:86-7 Mr '89

J.G. BOSWELL COMPANY

"Let the growth come by itself". R. King. il pors *Forbes* 143:98+ Ap 17 '89

J. H. WHITNEY & COMPANY

The company they couldn't sell [Prime Computer] G. Slutsker. il *Forbes* 144:227-9 O 2 '89

The Prime buyout is tough to compute [leveraged buyout of Prime Computer Inc.] L. Helm. il *Business Week* p28 Jl 10 '89

J. I. CASE COMPANY

Case study in determination. R. Reiff. il por *Forbes* 144:126-7 O 30 '89

J.M. PRODUCTS COMPANY

Arkansas hair care firm's plant is destroyed by a major fire. il *Jet* 76:27 Ag 21 '89

J. M. SMUCKER CO.

J.M. Smucker Co. J. Slovak. il *Fortune* 119:80 Ja 16 '89

Sorrell Ridge makes Smucker pucker. J. Levine. il *Forbes* 143:166+ Je 12 '89

J. P. MORGAN & CO. INCORPORATED

The magnitude of J. P. Morgan. J. S. Gordon. bibl il pors *American Heritage* 40:78-9+ Jl/Ag '89

J. PAUL GETTY MUSEUM

Nothing to hide [discussion of Summer 1989 article, An outrageous anomaly] A. E. Elsen. il *Art News* 88:190 D '89

An outrageous anomaly [Getty Museum refuses to disclose source of Aphrodite sculpture] A. E. Elsen. il *Art News* 88:196 Summ '89

J.R. EWING (FICTIONAL CHARACTER)

Larry Hagman. il por *People Weekly* 31 Special Issue:44 Summ '89

Why America's made him a hero—mean as he is [cover story] L. Hagman. il pors *TV Guide* 37:4-6+ F 11-17 '89

J. R. SIMPLOT CO.

The magic of 'Mr. Spud' [J. R. Simplot] D. Glick. il por *Newsweek* 114:63 N 27 '89

J. SUNG DYNASTY (NEW YORK, N.Y.: RESTAURANT) *See* New York (N.Y.)—Restaurants, nightclubs, bars, etc.

J. WALTER THOMPSON COMPANY

Madison Avenue's mystery guy [J. Patterson] S. J. Madden. il por *Fortune* 119:192 Ja 30 '89

JABBAR, KAREEM ABDUL- *See* Abdul-Jabbar, Kareem, 1947-

JABS, CAROLYN

Make hard times work for your marriage. *Reader's Digest* 135:145-7 Ag '89

JACK, LAURA

Are liquid diets all wet? il *Mademoiselle* 95:154-5 Ap '89

Is your body bringing you down? il *Mademoiselle* 95:154 S '89

You can talk your way out of a rape. il *Mademoiselle* 95:98 Je '89

JACK DANIEL DISTILLERY, LEM MOTLOW PROP.

Tennessee's legendary sippin' whiskey. J. Rada. il *Southern Living* 24:26+ D '89

JACK-O'-LANTERNS *See* Pumpkin faces

JACKEE

about

Jackée performs exciting dual role in TV movie 'Double your pleasure'. il pors *Jet* 77:16+ O 30 '89

Jackée reveals another side as she debuts in own TV show [cover story] A. Collier. il pors *Jet* 76:58-9 My 22 '89

JACKETS

See also

Blazers (Jackets)

Born to be less wild [motorcycle jacket] il *Gentlemen's Quarterly* 59:249 O '89

Threads with a thousand yarns [brown tweed sports jacket] A. Nelson. il *Gentlemen's Quarterly* 59:71+ S '89

JACKLIN, TONY

about

Captain Marvel. R. Reilly. il pors *Sports Illustrated* 71:60-2+ S 18 '89

JACKNIFE [film] *See* Motion picture reviews—Single works

JACK'S BACK [film] *See* Motion picture reviews—Single works

JACKSON, ANDREW, 1767-1845

about

1814. A. Nielson. il por *American Heritage* 40:30 Mr '89

The ages of Jackson. A. M. Schlesinger. bibl f il *The New York Review of Books* 36:48-51 D 7 '89

Relations with Congress

The president vs. the Senate. B. A. Weisberger. il *American Heritage* 40:22+ S/O '89

JACKSON, ARTHUR RICHARD

about

Vicious crime, double jeopardy. D. Bacon. il pors *People Weekly* 31:44-9 Je 5 '89

JACKSON, BO

about

The big stick [cover story] P. Gammons. il pors *Sports Illustrated* 70:22-7 Je 12 '89

The greatest of them all. T. Callahan. il pors *Newsweek* 114:80-1 D 4 '89

Home run or touchdown—Bo's your man. M. Durslag. il pors *TV Guide* 37:18-19 Ag 12-18 '89

MVP Bo Jackson powers AL to All-star game victory. il pors *Jet* 76:46 Jl 31 '89

JACKSON, CATHY M.
Names can hurt. por *Essence* 19:134 Ap '89
JACKSON, CHRIS
about
Can't hold this Tiger [cover story] C. Kirkpatrick. il pors *Sports Illustrated* 70:48-51 F 20 '89
JACKSON, DERRICK ZANE
An Alaskan cruise. il *Essence* 20:31-2+ My '89
JACKSON, DONALD DALE, 1935-
The bad and the beautiful: gulls remind us of us. bibl (p228-9) il *Smithsonian* 20:72-8+ O '89
Elevating thoughts from Elisha Otis and fellow uplifters. bibl (p247) il por *Smithsonian* 20:210-12+ N '89
'He welted the sphere a prodigious biff'. il *Smithsonian* 20:184 Ap '89
Just another day in paradise. il *Reader's Digest* 134:166-8+ Ap '89
Searching for medicinal wealth in Amazonia. bibl (p171) il pors *Smithsonian* 19:94-103 F '89
Take the oath, put on the badge and do the job. bibl (p174) il *Smithsonian* 20:114-18+ Ap '89
When 20 million tons of water flooded Johnstown. bibl (p163) il *Smithsonian* 20:50-4+ My '89
JACKSON, DOUGLAS W., AND KURZWEIL, PETER R.
A pain in the knee! il *Runner's World* 24:24 D '89
JACKSON, FREDDIE
about
At home with Freddie Jackson. R. D. Turner. il pors *Ebony* 44:124-6+ F '89
JACKSON, GEORGE
Daniel West Dancers. il *Dance Magazine* 63:70-1 S '89
JACKSON, GEORGE T.
about
Presidential Inaugural Parade includes only black builder of float who participated. il por *Jet* 75:57 F 6 '89
JACKSON, JANET
about
Janet Jackson turns serious: 'It's nice to laugh, but don't be the joke' [cover story] R. E. Johnson. il pors *Jet* 77:60-2 N 6 '89
Janet Jackson's 'Nation' under a groove. V. Aletti. il por *Rolling Stone* p81+ O 19 '89
JACKSON, JEREMY B. C., 1942-, AND OTHERS
Ecological effects of a major oil spill on Panamanian coastal marine communities. bibl f il map *Science* 243:37-44 Ja 6 '89
JACKSON, JESSE L., 1941-
History in the making. il por *Harper's Bazaar* 122:138-9+ F '89
about
After visit to African nations, Jesse Jackson urges joint partnership. D. M. Cheers. il pors *Jet* 75:12-14+ Ja 30 '89
American Jews: diehard conservatives. M. Himmelfarb. il *Commentary* 87:44-9 Ap '89
By any other name. K. D. Thompson. il por *Black Enterprise* 19:22 Ap '89
Cambridge diarist. M. Peretz. *The New Republic* 200:43 F 6 '89
Democrats after Dukakis. il *National Review* 41:16-17 F 10 '89
Divided we fell: race and the '88 election. J. Williams. il pors *American Visions* 4:31+ F '89
Drug use is a sin [interview] il *New Perspectives Quarterly* 6:8-11 Summ '89
From 'black' to 'African-American'? *Newsweek* 113:28 Ja 2 '89
The GOP's plan for Jesse. il por *Newsweek* 113:6 F 13 '89
Hit the road, Jack. H. Hertzberg. *The New Republic* 200:4+ Ap 3 '89
Hurricane Hugo aftermath: train Caribbean victims in skills needed to rebuild their homes, Jackson says. D. M. Cheers. il pors *Jet* 77:22-3+ O 23 '89
'It's like I'm the invisible man'. H. Fineman. il por *Newsweek* 114:39 O 16 '89
Jackson action. J. Klein. il por *New York* 22:20+ My 15 '89
Jackson backs Sawyer in Chicago mayoral primary. il pors *Jet* 75:6 F 13 '89
Jackson for D.C. mayor: ready to run? *Newsweek* 113:20 My 8 '89
Jackson makes European-African policy journey. il por *Jet* 76:7-8 Ag 7 '89
Jackson marches against drugs at rally in Boston. il por *Jet* 76:31 Jl 3 '89
Jackson rules. F. Barnes. *The New Republic* 200:14+ My 1 '89
Jackson saluted at his gala 48th birthday bash in D.C. il pors *Jet* 77:6-7 O 23 '89
Jackson strikes out. J. McCormick. il pors *Newsweek* 113:24 Mr 13 '89
Jackson to appear on 'A different world' in new segment on voting. il por *Jet* 76:62 Ap 10 '89
Jackson visits earthquake victims in Soviet Union. D. M. Cheers. il pors *Jet* 75:4-6+ F 20 '89
Jesse: election exposes growth of white voters. por *Jet* 77:18+ N 27 '89

Jesse Jackson. B. Darrach. il por *People Weekly* 32 Special Issue:58-9 Fall '89
Jesse Jackson calls for release of James Brown. pors *Jet* 75:10 Mr 13 '89
Jesse Jackson for mayor? He won't say no [interview] por *Business Week* p43 My 22 '89
Jesse Jackson: newsmaker of the year. G. Wills. *The Christian Century* 106:3-4 Ja 4-11 '89
The Jewish vote [discussion of April 1989 article, American Jews: diehard conservatives] M. Himmelfarb. *Commentary* 88:4-6+ Ag '89
Just say Afro. S. Thernstrom. *The New Republic* 200:10+ Ja 23 '89
Mayor Jesse. R. E. Tyrrell. *The American Spectator* 22:10 Jl '89
'Points of challenge'. *The Nation* 248:433 Ap 3 '89
The racism scam: how liberal black leaders perpetuate dependence. P. B. McGuigan. il por *Conservative Digest* 15:53-5+ Mr/Ap '89
Rainbow future. H. Sklar. *The Nation* 248:113-14 Ja 30 '89
Republicans for Jackson. W. Schneider. il *The Atlantic* 264:48 N '89
'Run Jesse run'—for mayor of Washington. il por *Newsweek* 113:30 Ap 10 '89
Strategies for now—and next time [cover story] A. Kopkind. il *The Nation* 249:297+ S 25 '89
Trying to stop, Jesse, stop. J. N. Baker. il pors *Newsweek* 114:29 Jl 17 '89
What does Jesse Jackson want now? B. Ahlberg. il por *Utne Reader* p22-3 My/Je '89
What must be done. il pors *Ebony* 44:156+ Ag '89
Whither the Rainbow? [discussion of September 25, 1989 article, Strategies for now—and next time] A. Kopkind. *The Nation* 249:738+ D 18 '89
'Why I'm moving to Washington, D.C.' [cover story] il por *Jet* 76:4-6 Ag 7 '89
Statues, portraits, etc.
Hammering the body politic, blacks wreck a portrait of a blond, white Jesse Jackson. il *People Weekly* 32:79 D 18 '89
Jackson cites reality in portrait of him as white. il por *Jet* 77:5 D 18 '89
JACKSON, JOAN
about
Indian Trading Post. *The New Yorker* 65:32-3 Ap 17 '89
JACKSON, JOE, 1887 OR 8-1951
about
Shoeless Joe: his legend survives the man and the scandal. W. Plummer. il pors *People Weekly* 32:99-101 Ag 7 '89
Too good to be left out. N. Dawidoff. por *Sports Illustrated* 70:118 Je 12 '89
JACKSON, KAREN
(ed) See Avery, James. A guide to gemstones
JACKSON, LATOYA
about
Court releases marriage certificate of LaToya. il por *Jet* 77:14 O 30 '89
LaToya at odds with her mother and her church as sex maniac threatens life. il por *Jet* 76:55 Ap 10 '89
LaToya Jackson denies she married her manager; blames possible imposter for rumor. il pors *Jet* 76:57-8 S 25 '89
The LaToya Jackson you didn't know. il pors *Jet* 75:58-61+ F 20 '89
JACKSON, LINDA, 1950-
about
Summer idyll [cover story] P. J. Smith. il pors *Opera News* 53:10-12 Je '89
JACKSON, LISA
Society loves a good victim. por *Newsweek* 114:8 Jl 24 '89
JACKSON, LOGAN
about
"Are you going to cry, Father Jackson?". K. Menehan. il por *Christianity Today* 33:12-13 S 22 '89
JACKSON, MAGA E., AND POLLARD, GAYLE
Mind over money. il *Essence* 20:94+ Jl '89
JACKSON, MAYNARD H.
about
Maynard Jackson enters Atlanta mayor's race against former campaign aide. il por *Jet* 75:4 Mr 6 '89
Maynard Jackson gears for 3rd term as Atlanta mayor. il por *Jet* 77:5 O 23 '89
The unbeatable Jackson. L. Copeland. il por *American Visions* 4:42 O '89
JACKSON, MICHAEL, 1958-
about
All Bad things must come to an end as a tearful Michael Jackson bids bye-bye to the highway. S. Dougherty. por *People Weekly* 31:52-3 F 13 '89
Magical tours. J. Cocks. il por *Time* 133:59 Ja 23 '89
Michael Jackson. R. Lacayo. por *People Weekly* 32 Special Issue:68-9 Fall '89
Michael Jackson and his manager Frank Dileo go their separate ways. il pors *Jet* 75:57 Mr 6 '89
Michael Jackson earns $125 million and remains highest paid entertainer. il por *Jet* 76:26+ O 2 '89

JACKSON, MICHAEL, 1958——about—cont.
Michael Jackson gets award from his sixth grade teacher in L.A. il pors Jet 77:29 O 30 '89
Michael Jackson quits concert stage after world tour sets new records [cover story] R. E. Johnson. il pors Jet 75:54-9 F 27 '89
Michael Jackson says good-bye. M. Hammer. il pors Ladies' Home Journal 106:116+ My '89
Michael Jackson says his 18-month worldwide tour was an 'incredible journey'. il por Jet 75:61 Ja 23 '89
Michael's last tour [cover story] il pors Ebony 44:142-4+ Ap '89
JACKSON, REGINALD
about
Children's products and services. il por Home Office Computing 7:45 Je '89
JACKSON, ROBERT
Skid marks. il Flying 116:100 F '89
JACKSON, ROBERT D.
about
Going for the goat. M. Barrier. il por Nation's Business 77:12-13 Ag '89
JACKSON, RODNEY, AND AHLBORN, GARY
Catching a ghost. il International Wildlife 19:30-3 My/Je '89
JACKSON, STONEWALL, 1824-1863
about
Stonewall Jackson. J. B. Graves. il pors Conservative Digest 15:27-9+ Mr/Ap '89
JACKSON, STU
about
Sports. E. Pooley. il por New York 22:148-9 S 11 '89
JACKSON, THOMAS JONATHAN See Jackson, Stonewall, 1824-1863
JACKSON, TIM
The Tokyo chainsaw massacre. The New Republic 201:20-1 S 11 '89
JACKSON, VICTORIA
about
On a bad night, she gets $500 a word. I. Rudolph. il por TV Guide 37:27 My 27-Je 2 '89
JACKSON, WES
about
Back to Eden [cover story; with editorial comment] E. Eisenberg. il por The Atlantic 264:6, 57-9+ N '89
Breadbasket ecology. D. Hand. il map por American Health 8:66-8 S '89
Prophet of the prairie. J. R. Luoma. il pors map Audubon 91:54-60 N '89
JACKSON, WILLARD
about
Tennis ace Zina Garrison ties Houston love match. il pors Jet 77:52-3 O 23 '89
JACKSON, WILLIAM HENRY, 1843-1942
about
The life and times of William Henry Jackson. R. Findley. il pors map National Geographic 175:216-51 F '89
JACKSON, WOODY
about
The whole country cowtows as artist Woody Jackson makes his big moove toward udder success. D. Chu. il por People Weekly 32:100-1 Ag 28 '89
JACKSON (MISS.)
Architecture
High style—Mississippi style [home of David and Leslie Cox] L. Hallam. il Southern Living 24:94-6 Mr '89
Galleries and museums
See also
Mississippi State Historical Museum
Hospitals
'Dr. Bob' [work of R. Smith] R. D. Turner. il pors Ebony 44:102+ S '89
JACKSON COUNTY (KY.)
Crime
A Kentucky boy's wild cry for help [student D. Pierce holds classmates hostage at Jackson County High School] W. Plummer. il pors People Weekly 32:44-7 O 9 '89
JACKSON FAMILY
about
The Jacksons return to their Gary roots after 18 years away. il Jet 76:24-6 S 25 '89
Jet goes to the Jackson family reunion. il Jet 76:14-17 Ag 21 '89
JACKSON HOLE (WYO.)
Galleries and museums
See also
Wildlife of the American West Art Museum (Jackson, Wyo.)
JACKSON LABORATORY (BAR HARBOR, ME.)
Fire devastates Jackson Lab [research mice destroyed] B. J. Culliton. il Science 244:767-8 My 19 '89
Wanted: $25 million for mouse house [rebuilding after fire] B. J. Culliton. il Science 245:697-8 Ag 18 '89
JACKSON LYNN TRAVERS (FIRM)
A private Mod Squad sets out to prove police harassment—and stirs a fight over its tactics. G. Stone. il People Weekly 32:83-4+ D 11 '89

JACKSON MEMORIAL HOSPITAL (MIAMI, FLA.)
One night in Miami's only trauma unit. A. M. Arrarte. il U.S. News & World Report 107:34 N 13 '89
JACKSON-MITCHELL (FIRM)
Going for the goat. M. Barrier. il por Nation's Business 77:12-13 Ag '89
JACKSON-STOPS, GERVASE
The functional folly in eighteenth-century Britain. bibl f il Antiques 135:1412-23 Je '89
Some sources for the paintings of C. R. Leslie. bibl f il Antiques 135:310-21 Ja '89
JACKSON-VANIK AMENDMENT See United States—Commercial policy
JACKSONS (MUSICAL GROUP)
Jacksons warmly welcomed on European promotion tour. il Jet 76:60 Je 26 '89
JACKSONVILLE (FLA.)
Police
A cop's homage to a slain pal becomes his own tragic farewell [tape made by accident victim R. Shinholser] il por People Weekly 31:43 Ja 30 '89
JACKY, JONATHAN
Throwing stones at "Brilliant Pebbles". il Technology Review 92:20-1+ O '89
JACOB, BONNIE
An eye on ethnicity [cover story] il por American Visions 4:14-19 O '89
JACOB, JOHN E., 1934-
Major issues facing African-Americans [address, August 6, 1989] Vital Speeches of the Day 56:7-12 O 15 '89
JACOB RIIS PARK (NEW YORK, N.Y.)
Gateway theme park plans dropped. J. Weinberg. National Parks 63:13 N/D '89
JACOBBI, MARIANNE, 1951-
Alison's fight for life. il pors Good Housekeeping 209:196-7+ S '89
America's missing women. il Ladies' Home Journal 106:144-6+ Ap '89
Travis comes home. il pors Good Housekeeping 209:103+ Jl '89
What did happen to Kitty Dukakis? il pors Good Housekeeping 208:52+ Je '89
Whose little girl is Kimberly? il pors Good Housekeeping 208:122-3+ Mr '89
JACOBOWITZ (DIANE) DANCE COMPANY See Diane Jacobowitz Dance Company
JACOBS, BRUCE A.
Take a hike! il Black Enterprise 20:79-80+ Ag '89
JACOBS, IRWIN L.
about
Did Irv Jacobs sandbag Outboard Marine? G. DeGeorge. Business Week p38+ F 20 '89
Ding-dong, raider calling. K. Deveny. Business Week p51+ Ag 14 '89
How d'ya say "liquidator" in Japanese? S. Flack. il por Forbes 143:39-40 Je 12 '89
Three raging bulls and two restrained ones. R. King. il pors Forbes 144 Special Issue:362+ O 23 '89
Why Irv Jacobs wants to land Tidewater. R. Mitchell. il Business Week p31-2 Ja 30 '89
JACOBS, JAMES E.
Training the workforce of the future. il Technology Review 92:66-72 Ag/S '89
JACOBS, LAURA A.
On dance. See occasional issues of The New Leader
JACOBS, LUCIA
Cache economy of the gray squirrel. il Natural History p40-7 O '89
JACOBS, MARC, 1963-
about
Life after Perry Ellis. N. Darnton. il por Newsweek 113:67 Ja 2 '89
On the Marc. C. Heimel. il por Vogue 179:84-5+ F '89
Weekend by design. M. Matousek. il pors Harper's Bazaar 122:70-3+ Jl '89
JACOBS, MARK
Stone cowboy on the high plains [story] il The Atlantic 263:66-70+ Je '89
JACOBS, WESLEY A.
about
Two veterinarians guilty in antibiotic case. M. Segal. il FDA Consumer 23:33-4 N '89
JACOB'S PILLOW DANCE FESTIVAL
Reviews:
Gala performance. A. Smith. il Dance Magazine 63:78-9 D '89
Ted Shawn's summer oasis, 1942: Pillow talk [excerpt from American dancesong] S. T. Underwood. il por Dance Magazine 63:28-31 Jl '89
JACOBSEN, CAROL
Two lives: ordinary/extraordinary. bibl f il pors Art in America 77:152-7+ F '89
JACOBSEN, HUGH NEWELL
about
Hugh Newell Jacobsen: refurbishing a colonial house in the Maryland hunt country. il Architectural Digest 46:88-90 Ag '89

JACOBSEN, HUGH NEWELL—about—*cont.*
Village of one's own. J. Giovannini. il por *House & Garden* 161:116-23 Ap '89
JACOBSEN, JOSEPHINE
Next summer [poem] *The New Yorker* 65:65 F 27 '89
Only Alice [poem] *The Atlantic* 263:51 My '89
Reading on the beach [poem] *The New Yorker* 65:36 Ag 14 '89
JACOBSON, DAN
Of time and poetry. *Commentary* 88:48-53 N '89
JACOBSON, ERIK
about
Fury to freedom [film] Reviews
Christianity Today 33:40-3 Ag 18 '89. B. Bird
JACOBSON, HARLAN
Americans abroad. il *Film Comment* 25:67-9 Jl/Ag '89
Born again baseball. il *Film Comment* 25:78-9 My/Je '89
Michael & me [interview with M. Moore; cover story] il pors *Film Comment* 25:16-18+ N/D '89
Truth or consequences [interview with S. Soderbergh] il por *Film Comment* 25:22-4+ Jl/Ag '89
JACOBSON, JODI L.
Recycling our most prolific by-product. *USA Today (Periodical)* 118:88-9 Jl '89
JACOBY, BARBARA
Enhancing the education of college commuters. *The Education Digest* 54:62-4 Ap '89
JACOBY, ED
Forest fire strikes home. il *The Conservationist* 44:40-3 S/O '89
JACOBY, SUSAN
Faith, values & morals. *McCall's* 116:69-71+ My '89
How bigotry affects all our lives. il *Glamour* 87:250-1+ N '89
How to stay cool when the pressure is hot. il *Glamour* 87:218-19+ D '89
Loyalty is admirable. But is it smart? *Glamour* 87:290-1+ S '89
One's single, one's married: can these women still be friends? il *Glamour* 87:162-3+ Ja '89
Soviet women: what does political change mean for them? il *Glamour* 87:268-9+ My '89
When an older woman chooses a younger man. il *New Choices for the Best Years* 29:61-2 Ap '89
JACQUARD COVERLETS *See* Coverlets
JACQUES, MARTIN
New ideas about work. *World Press Review* 36:24 D '89
JACQUET, ILLINOIS
about
Illinois Jacquet. C. Deffaa. il por *Down Beat* 56:14 F '89
Illinois Jacquet's timeless tenor. C. Stern. il por *Rolling Stone* p18 Ap 6 '89
JACQUET, LOU
Does simple living have to be so complicated? il *U.S. Catholic* 54:28-35 Jl '89
Original sin: a new look at the oldest sin in the book [cover story] il *U.S. Catholic* 54:6-12 Je '89
Scripture: now starring in a liturgy near you. il *U.S. Catholic* 54:44-6 S '89
Should parents speak of the devil? il *U.S. Catholic* 54:31-7 Mr '89
JADE PLANTS
Jade and family. il *Sunset (Central West edition)* 183:162-3 D '89
JAEHNE, KAREN
The 18th New Directors/New Films Festival. il *Film Comment* 25:68+ My/Je '89
Beth's beauties [cover story] il pors *Film Comment* 25:9-12+ My/Je '89
Coming attractions. il *Film Comment* 25:46-9 Ja/F '89
Company man. il por *Film Comment* 25:11-15 Mr/Ap '89
The quotable Dolly. il pors *Film Comment* 25:62-3 S/O '89
JAFFA, HARRY V.
The right rights. *National Review* 41:50 N 10 '89
A right to privacy? [with reply by Joseph Sobran] *National Review* 41:51-2 Mr 24 '89
JAFFAR, SAYED
about
War lord. il pors *Life* 12:121-2+ My '89
JAFFE, ANDREW
Firing: there's (almost) always a better way. il *Psychology Today* 23:68-9 Jl/Ag '89
JAFFE, CHARLES A.
Bad debts are worth collecting. il *Nation's Business* 77:53-4+ My '89
The rainbow maker. il por *Nation's Business* 77:41+ N '89
Success by surprise. il *Nation's Business* 77:30+ S '89
JAFFE, DAVE
(jt. auth) *See* Coleman, Mitch, and Jaffe, Dave
JAFFE, DENNIS T., AND SCOTT, CYNTHIA D.
Bridging your workers' "motivation gap". il *Nation's Business* 77:30-2 Mr '89
JAFFE, JOE, AND SYTHE, DAN
Radiation monitor update [with editorial comment by Brian C. Fenton] il *Radio-Electronics* 60:4, 51-5+ Je '89

JAFFE, SHIRLEY, 1923-
about
Shirley Jaffe and Murray Reich at Artists Space. L. Campbell. il *Art in America* 77:199-200 N '89
JAFFE, SUSAN
about
Swan's way. A. L. Ball. il pors *New York* 22:40-4 Je 5 '89
JAFFE AIRCRAFT CORPORATION
Jaffe Group to replace Gulfstream as partner in SA-30 development. E. H. Phillips. il *Aviation Week & Space Technology* 131:37 S 11 '89
Swearingen, Jaffe Group work on schedule for SA-30 business jet development. il *Aviation Week & Space Technology* 131:24 S 25 '89
JAFFREY, MADHUR
Chicken 'n' spice. il *Gourmet* 49:64-5+ Mr '89
JAGDISH BHAGWATI *See* Bhagwati, Jagdish N., 1934-
JÄGER, JILL
Report on reports: Greenhouse: planning for climate change. bibl f *Environment* 31:25-7 Je '89
JAGER, RONALD
Those #!*?@! tool handles. il *Country Journal* 16:66-7 Jl/Ag '89
JÄGER, WOLFGANG
A meeting of motherlands. *World Press Review* 36:24+ Je '89
JAGLOM, HENRY
about
Someone to love [film] Reviews
Psychology Today 23:78 Je '89. W. Herbert
JAGUAR (AUTOMOBILE) *See* Automobiles, Foreign; Sports cars
JAGUAR CARS LTD.
See also
Jaguar plc
JAGUAR PLC
A bid for upward mobility [Ford bids on Jaguar and Saab] A. Gabor. il *U.S. News & World Report* 107:46 O 2 '89
Ford's sporty new number. il *Time* 134:83 N 13 '89
Have you driven a Jag, lately? [Ford buys Jaguar] D. Pauly. il *Newsweek* 114:64 N 13 '89
The hole in Ford's doughnut [pursuit of Jaguar and luxury model market] J. Flint. il *Forbes* 144:50+ N 13 '89
A Jaguar buyer may be in for a long, slow drive [GM or Ford] M. Maremont. il *Business Week* p48-9 N 13 '89
Jaguar—trying to beat the heat. M. Keller. il *Motor Trend* 41:138 O '89
The law of the jungle catches up with Jaguar [Ford's bid] R. A. Melcher. il *Business Week* p54 O 2 '89
Would you pay $2 billion for a sick cat? [GM and Ford go after Jaguar] M. Maremont. il *Business Week* p58 O 23 '89
JAHIEL, ADAM
about
Descent to the Titanic. P. Skinner. il *Petersen's Photographic Magazine* 17:30-3 Mr '89
JAHJOUKA (MOROCCO)
Music
Into the mystic [master musicians] R. Palmer. il *Rolling Stone* p100-3+ Mr 23 '89
JAHN, LAURENCE R.
Maintaining nature's delicate balance. il *USA Today (Periodical)* 118:84-6 N '89
JAHN, ROBERT G.
about
Questions for the cosmos. S. Fishman. il por *The New York Times Magazine* p50+ N 26 '89
JAHR, CLIFF
Amy Irving: mom is her real starring role. il pors *Ladies' Home Journal* 106:114+ Mr '89
Linda Evans: good-bye to Hollywood. il pors *Ladies' Home Journal* 106:44+ Ag '89
Loose lips. il por *Ladies' Home Journal* 106:110-12+ Ja '89
JAILBREAKS *See* Escapes
JAILER, MILDRED
Dolls. See issues of Antiques & Collecting Hobbies beginning March 1985
Toys. See issues of Antiques & Collecting Hobbies beginning November 1985
JAILS *See* Prisons
JAINS
India
Behind the gauze mask. D. R. Ward. il *International Wildlife* 19:14-19 Ja/F '89
JAKARTA (INDONESIA)
Buildings
Dharmala building, Jakarta. M. F. Schmertz. il *Architectural Record* 177:82-5 Ja '89
JAKES, MILOŠ
about
Anatomy of a purge. K. W. Banta. il por *Time* 134:44 D 11 '89
JAKOBSON, CATHRYN
Victim of love. il *Seventeen* 48:204-7+ Ap '89

JAKOBSON, CATHRYN—cont.
Who says you have to have a boyfriend? *Seventeen* 48:108-10+ S '89
JAKUCHŪ, 1716-1800
about
Fantastic voyage. C. McGee. il *New York* 22:98-9 O 30 '89
JALALABAD (AFGHANISTAN)
Fighting for Jalalabad. M. Strmecki. il *The American Spectator* 22:30-2 Je '89
Stalemate at Jalalabad. E. Ahmad. il *The Nation* 249:384-7 O 9 '89
JALAPA (MEXICO)
Galleries and museums
See also
Anthropology Museum of Jalapa (Mexico)
JALU, HÉLÈNE YVERT- *See* Yvert-Jalu, Hélène
JAM, JIMMY
about
Out on the town with Jam and Lewis. il pors *Rolling Stone* p48 Jl 13-27 '89
JAM *See* Jelly, jam, etc.
JAMA *See* Journal of the American Medical Association
JAMAICA
See also
Health resorts, watering places, etc.—Jamaica
Historic houses, sites, etc.—Jamaica
Jamaicans
Kingston (Jamaica)
Narcotics trade—Jamaica
Relief work—Jamaica
Resorts—Jamaica
Economic policy
After the storm [victory of M. Manley] P. Jordan. il *Commonweal* 116:261-3 My 5 '89
Courting capitalism, Manley takes over in Jamaica. M. A. Fortune. il por *Black Enterprise* 19:38 My '89
Industries
See also
Tourist trade—Jamaica
Photographs and photography
Jamaica bound? Head for the hills and harbor towns for some exciting photo opportunities. L. Dennis. il *Popular Photography* 96:20+ My '89
Politics and government
See also
Elections—Jamaica
Political campaigns—Jamaica
JAMAICA HOSPITAL (QUEENS, N.Y.) *See* Queens (New York, N.Y.)—Hospitals
JAMAICANS
United States
Crime
Johnny-too-bad and the sufferers [Jamaican drug posses; cover story] L. Gunst. *The Nation* 249:549+ N 13 '89
JAMES I, KING OF GREAT BRITAIN, 1566-1625
about
A Duke fit for a King. G. Barker. il por *Art News* 88:87+ D '89
JAMES VI, KING OF SCOTLAND *See* James I, King of Great Britain, 1566-1625
JAMES, ANN
Prodigiously lost and found. *The Christian Century* 106:220-1 Mr 1 '89
JAMES, BILL
The watercolor page: Bill James. il por *American Artist* 53:54-7+ Ag '89
JAMES, BILL, 1949-
World Series goats and controversies. il *Sports Illustrated* 71:51+ O 9 '89
JAMES, C. L. R. (CYRIL LIONEL ROBERT), 1901-1989
about
Obituary
The Nation 249:7 Jl 3 '89. C. Hitchens
JAMES, CARYN
Big little magazines: a reader's guide. *The New York Times Book Review* 94:32 Ap 30 '89
JAMES, CURTIA
Sam Gilliam: working with his seven-league boots on [cover story] il pors *American Visions* 4:26-30 F '89
JAMES, CYRIL LIONEL ROBERT *See* James, C. L. R. (Cyril Lionel Robert), 1901-1989
JAMES, DEL
The Rolling stone interview: Axl Rose [cover story] il pors *Rolling Stone* p42-4+ Ag 10 '89
JAMES, ETTA
about
Asking for water. M. Moses. *The New Yorker* 64:83+ F 13 '89
JAMES, GERALDINE
about
The quality of James. R. Koenig. il por *New York* 22:25 D 11 '89
JAMES, HENRY, 1843-1916
The master and Moreau. il *Art News* 88:23 My '89
about
Editorial. W. Garrett. il *Antiques* 136:810-11 O '89

The master at home. J. Bayley. il *The New York Review of Books* 36:21-3 D 7 '89
JAMES, JAMIE
Got a yen for CDs? il *High Fidelity (New York, N.Y.)* 39:46-50 Je '89
Peach of a diva. il por *Opera News* 53:44-5 Ja 7 '89
Stalking the giant ape. il map *Discover* 10:42-6+ F '89
JAMES, P. D.
about
Murder, she writes. K. Flett. il por *Harper's Bazaar* 122:94 S '89
JAMES, RICK
about
Motown sues Rick James. S. Assael. *Rolling Stone* p30 My 18 '89
JAMES, ROGER
Portraits like movie stills. il *Petersen's Photographic Magazine* 18:40-3 N '89
JAMES, THEODORE
The best new houseplants. il *Ladies' Home Journal* 106:68+ F '89
Blooming color. il *New Choices for the Best Years* 29:76-80 S '89
JAMES, WILLIAM, 1929-
about
The final victory. J. Daly. il pors *Maclean's* 102:40-1 O 2 '89
Mr. Perpetual Motion. P. Chisholm. il por *Maclean's* 102:37 Ag 14 '89
JAMES (RAYMOND) & ASSOCIATES, INC. *See* Raymond James & Associates, Inc.
JAMES BAY HYDROELECTRIC PROJECT
Canadian utility threatens Cree. D. Schulze. il *The Progressive* 53:18 O '89
JAMES BOND (FICTIONAL CHARACTER)
Bird, James Bird [character's name taken from real life ornithologist] *Discover* 10:13 Jl '89
James Bond's sizzling new boats [filming Licence to kill] P. Whittell. il *Motor Boating & Sailing* 163:62-5+ Ap '89
JAMESON, ANTONY
Computational aerodynamics for aircraft design [cover story] bibl f il *Science* 245:361-71 Jl 28 '89
JAMESON, RICHARD T.
Life with TNT. il *Film Comment* 25:30-9 Jl/Ag '89
JAMESWAY CORP.
In retail, bigger can be better [Jamesway vs. Wal-Mart] il *Business Week* p90 Mr 27 '89
JAMISON, JUDITH
about
Judith Jamison after Alvin Ailey. F. Washington. por *Newsweek* 114:80 S 18 '89
Reviews:
Performances at the Joyce Theater, New York City. N. V. Dalva. *Dance Magazine* 63:91-3 F '89
JAMISON PROJECT
Judith Jamison after Alvin Ailey. F. Washington. por *Newsweek* 114:80 S 18 '89
Reviews:
Performances at the Joyce Theater, New York City. N. V. Dalva. *Dance Magazine* 63:91-3 F '89
JAMMING OF RADAR *See* Radar interference
JAMMING OF RADIO SIGNALS *See* Radio interference
JAMMU AND KASHMIR (INDIA)
See also
Education—Jammu and Kashmir (India)
JAM'S (SHANGHAI, CHINA: BAR) *See* Shanghai (China)—Restaurants, nightclubs, bars, etc.
JAN BELL MARKETING INC.
Flaws in a jeweler's future? G. G. Marcial. *Business Week* p106 D 4 '89
Jan Bell: on the cutting edge in wholesale jewelry. A. Fins. il *Business Week* p61 My 29 '89
JANÁČEK, LEOŠ, 1854-1928
about
The Makropulos affair [opera] Reviews
Maclean's 102:59 F 6 '89. J. Pearce
JANDA, KIM D., AND OTHERS
Catalytic antibodies with lipase activity and R or S substrate selectivity. bibl f il *Science* 244:437-40 Ap 28 '89
JANEQUIN, CLÉMENT
about
Janequin, Clément. P. Moor. *High Fidelity (New York, N.Y.)* 39:67-8 Ap '89
JANE'S ADDICTION (MUSICAL GROUP)
Hardly a plain Jane. M. Goldberg. il *Rolling Stone* p34 F 9 '89
JANE'S BAR & GRILL (NEW YORK, N.Y.) *See* New York (N.Y.)—Restaurants, nightclubs, bars, etc.
JANE'S DEFENCE WEEKLY
How we got an Official Secrets Act [Supreme Court declines to review S. L. Morison case] N. Hentoff. il *The Progressive* 53:10-11 Mr '89
The quiet coup [case against S. Morison] P. Weiss. il *Harper's* 279:54-65 S '89

JANESH, BARBARA J.
Exercising your flight rights [with editorial comment by Diane P. Marshall] il *Travel Holiday* 171:6, 35-9 Je '89
JANGLISH
Hot-to koh-hee, but hold the creap. M. Shapiro. il *Scholastic Update (Teachers' edition)* 122:22 D 8 '89
JANIS, ERIC M., AND OTHERS
Activation of γδ T cells in the primary immune response to Mycobacterium tuberculosis. bibl f il *Science* 244:713-16 My 12 '89
JANKLOW, MORT
about
Call my agent! T. Gabriel. il pors *The New York Times Magazine* p44-5+ F 19 '89
Morton Janklow sued for $20 million by ex-partner. C. Reid. *Publishers Weekly* 236:8+ N 24 '89
S & S, Janklow, negotiate two-book Reagan deal. *Publishers Weekly* 235:34 F 10 '89
JANKLOW, WILLIAM
about
Court dismisses Janklow suit against Viking and Matthiessen. *Publishers Weekly* 235:14 Je 16 '89
JANKLOW AND NESBIT ASSOCIATES
Call my agent! T. Gabriel. il pors *The New York Times Magazine* p44-5+ F 19 '89
JANKLOW ASSOCIATES
Morton Janklow sued for $20 million by ex-partner. C. Reid. *Publishers Weekly* 236:8+ N 24 '89
JANKO, EDMUND
Knowing is not thinking. il *Phi Delta Kappan* 70:543-4 Mr '89
JANKOWSKI, DAVID G., AND SQUYRES, STEVEN W.
Ice volcanism on Ariel [discussion of September 9, 1988 article, Solid-state ice volcanism on the satellites of Uranus] *Science* 245:195-6 Jl 14 '89
JANOWITZ, TAMA
about
How long can Tama's 15 minutes last? G. Sikes. il por *Mademoiselle* 95:102+ Ap '89
Slaves of New York. il por *Harper's Bazaar* 122:144-5 F '89
JANSEN, JOANN FREGALETTE
about
Reviews:
Performances at the Whitney Museum of American Art at Equitable Center, New York City. G. Solomons. *Dance Magazine* 63:86-7 Mr '89
JANSEN, WALTER
about
Walter and the raffle. P. Kelly. *Reader's Digest* 134:26 Mr '89
JANSEN (J FREGALETTE) DANCE *See* J Fregalette Jansen Dance
JANSSEN, DAVID, 1930-1980
about
David Janssen. il por *People Weekly* 31 Special Issue:67 Summ '89
JANSSEN, PETER A.
At the helm. See issues of Motor Boating & Sailing
JANUARY
The January almanac. il *The Atlantic* 263:14 Ja '89
JANUARY EFFECT (INVESTMENTS)
Bonds' January effect? M. Hulbert. il *Forbes* 144:254 O 30 '89
The fabled January effect may come early this year. J. Willoughby. il *Money* 18:17 D '89
Holiday blues? Play the 'January effect'. S. Woolley. *Business Week* p208 N 27 '89
THE JANUARY MAN [film] See Motion picture reviews—Single works
JANUARY THAW
The January thaw. D. M. Ludlum. il *Country Journal* 16:13-14 Ja '89
JANUS, NOREENE
Shopping makes the world go 'round. *Utne Reader* p83 S/O '89
JANZEN, DANIEL H.
about
Daniel Janzen's dry idea. T. A. Lewis. il pors map *International Wildlife* 19:30-6 Ja/F '89
JAP (TERM) *See* Jewish American Princess (Term)
JAPAN
See also
Aged—Japan
Air traffic control—Japan
Americans—Japan
Anti-nuclear movement—Japan
Anti-Semitism—Japan
Art—Japan
Automobile racing—Japan
Aviation and state—Japan
Aviation research—Japan
Banks and banking—Japan
Bar coding—Japan
Baseball, Professional—Japan
Bathrooms—Japan
Business management—Japan
Capital investments—Japan

Cellular radio—Japan
Chemical research—Japan
Comic books, strips, etc.—Japan
Computer junkyards—Japan
Confession (Law)—Japan
Contracts, Government—Japan
Design, Industrial—Japan
Distribution of goods—Japan
Diversification in industry—Japan
Earthquakes—Japan
Economic assistance, Japanese
Education—Japan
Employment—Japan
Energy policy—Japan
Environmental policy—Japan
Ethnology—Japan
Family—Japan
Franchise system—Japan
Funeral rites and ceremonies—Japan
Gardens and gardening—Japan
Genetic research—Japan
Golf—Japan
Heliports—Japan
Hiroshima (Japan)
Historic houses, sites, etc.—Japan
Ibusuki (Japan)
Immigration and emigration—Japan
Index funds—Japan
Industrial research—Japan
Industry and state—Japan
Insects—Japan
Insider trading—Japan
Investment banking—Japan
Investments, American—Japan
Investments, Foreign—Japan
Investments, Japanese
Japanese
Koyasan (Japan)
Kyoto (Japan)
Labor supply—Japan
Land values—Japan
Law firms—Japan
Market research—Japan
Marketing—Japan
Materials research—Japan
Medical ethics—Japan
Military research—Japan
Money—Japan
Motion pictures—Japan
Motorcycle racing—Japan
Nagasaki (Japan)
Nagoya (Japan)
Nara (Japan)
Nuclear power plants—Japan
Nuclear research—Japan
Organic farming—Japan
Orphans and orphanages—Japan
Osaka (Japan)
Over-the-counter securities markets—Japan
Passports—Japan
Personnel management—Japan
Preventive detention—Japan
Price fixing—Japan
Prices—Japan
Productivity, Industrial—Japan
Program trading (Securities)—Japan
Psychology, Industrial—Japan
Public health—Japan
Public works—Japan
Quality control—Japan
Railroads—Japan
Rapid solidification technology—Japan
Recycling (Waste, etc.)—Japan
Refuse and refuse disposal—Japan
Research—Japan
Retail trade—Laws and regulations—Japan
Rotor aircraft—Japan
Saving and savings—Japan
Science and state—Japan
Securities—Japan
Social classes—Japan
Space research—Japan
Superconductors and superconductivity—Japan
Technology—Japan
Television advertising—Japan
Tokyo (Japan)
Underground structures—Japan
United States—Diplomatic and consular service—Japan
War crime trials—Japan
Young Astronaut Program (Japan)
Youth—Japan
The global zeitgeist checklist: Japan. J. Bailey. *The New Republic* 200:25 Je 26 '89
Japan: what's the secret of its success? [cover story; special issue] il map *Scholastic Update (Teachers' edition)* 122:2-22 D 8 '89

JAPAN—*cont.*

Armed Forces
Appropriations and expenditures
Japan approves 5.9% increase for defense spending in 1989. *Aviation Week & Space Technology* 130:22 F 6 '89
Japan plans to purchase 112 aircraft under $29-billion defense budget. il *Aviation Week & Space Technology* 131:36 S 11 '89
Japan raises defense spending to fund missile, aircraft programs. il *Aviation Week & Space Technology* 130:88+ Mr 20 '89
Spending more on defense. K. Chuma. il *World Press Review* 36:19 Ap '89

Commerce
See also
Balance of trade—Japan
Where Japan will strike next [cover story] G. Bylinsky. il *Fortune* 120:42-6+ S 25 '89
Brazil
See Brazil—Commerce—Japan
Germany (West)
See Germany (West)—Commerce—Japan
Southeast Asia
Wasteful Japan [tropical timber trade] *World Press Review* 36:43+ O '89
Taiwan
Nipponophilia. A. Tanzer. il *Forbes* 143:52 Ap 3 '89
United States
See United States—Commerce—Japan
Western Europe
The EC just says no to Japan's cheap chips. T. Peterson. il *Business Week* p46-7 Ja 30 '89
The Japanese invade Europe. B. Powell. il map *Newsweek* 114:28-9 O 2 '89

Commercial policy
See also
Japan. Ministry of International Trade and Industry
Containing Japan [cover story] J. M. Fallows. il *The Atlantic* 263:40-8+ My '89
Crazy but harmless [views of J. Fallows] M. Kinsley. *The New Republic* 201:4 D 11 '89
Don't expect a caretaker to take care of trade [resignation of N. Takeshita] T. Holden and W. Glasgall. por *Business Week* p37 My 8 '89
Is the door open wide enough? E. M. Reingold. il *Time* 133:54-5 Je 5 '89
Must we become Japanese? [cover story] D. D. Hale. il *National Review* 41:30-2+ O 27 '89
Still only a half-open door. B. Powell. il *Newsweek* 113:48-50 F 13 '89

Cultural relations
United States
See United States—Cultural relations—Japan

Defenses
See also
Airplanes, Military—Japan
Aviation, Military—Japan
United States. Navy—Forces in Japan
Burdensharing and Japan [statement; September 27, 1988] W. Clark, Jr. *Department of State Bulletin* 88:30-1 D '88
Does Japan play fair? [trade and defense issues divide U.S. and Japan] S. Manning. il *Scholastic Update (Teachers' edition)* 122:20-1 D 8 '89
Japan and the U.S.—the security agenda [reprint from November 1983 issue] D. B. H. Denoon. bibl f *Current History* 88:37-8+ Ja '89
Let them defend themselves. J. M. Fallows. il *The Atlantic* 263:17-18+ Ap '89
Tokyo wants its arsenal made in Japan. R. Neff. il *Business Week* p64 S 25 '89
The U.S.-Japan military alliance. A. F. Geyer. *The Christian Century* 106:437-8 Ap 26 '89

Description and travel
Touring from Tokyo. N. Sklarewitz. il *New Choices for the Best Years* 29:28-35 N '89

Economic conditions
See also
Cost and standard of living—Japan
Japan—Industries
Unemployment—Japan
The enigma. N. Glazer. il *The New Republic* 201:13-14 Jl 10 '89
Japan revisited. C. W. Weinberger. il *Forbes* 144:31 N 13 '89
Of cultural gaps and trade talks [effect of Japanese citizens' habits on balance of trade] C. P. Work. *U.S. News & World Report* 107:58 S 18 '89
Robust growth abroad will help keep the U.S. economy on track. R. E. Norton. il *Fortune* 120:15-16 N 6 '89

Economic policy
The enigma of Japanese power [excerpt] K. G. van Wolferen. il por *Fortune* 119:150-3 My 8 '89
How can Japan reduce surplus? [views of Bela Balassa and Marcus Noland] *USA Today (Periodical)* 117:11 Ap '89
"The system" [views of K. G. van Wolferen] A. Tanzer. il por *Forbes* 143:40-1 My 1 '89

Economic relations
Hour of power? [special section] il *Newsweek* 113:14-18+ F 27 '89
Japan and Germany: American concerns. J. E. Garten. il *Foreign Affairs* 68:84-101 Wint '89/'90
Japan's growing global reach. C. Rapoport. il *Fortune* 119:48-50+ My 22 '89
Japan's quiet strength. S. Ōkita. *Foreign Policy* 75:128-45 Summ '89
Japan's shifting role [cover story; special section] il *World Press Review* 36:11-20 Ap '89
East Asia
Asia's 'Tigers' will pounce. K. Kuwabara. *World Press Review* 36:22 D '89
Japan builds a new power base. D. J. Yang and N. Gross. il *Business Week* p42-5 Ap 10 '89
Germany (West)
See Germany (West)—Economic relations—Japan
Soviet Union
See Soviet Union—Economic relations—Japan
United States
See United States—Economic relations—Japan

Foreign opinion
American
Between two cultures. P. Sudo. il *Scholastic Update (Teachers' edition)* 122:2-3 D 8 '89
Charity begins abroad [Japanese corporations donate to American charities] A. Miller. il *Newsweek* 114:41 Ag 21 '89
Is TV news guilty of Japan bashing? E. Diamond and K. O'Neil. il *TV Guide* 37:24-7 My 20-26 '89
Rethinking Japan [cover story] R. Neff and P. Magnusson. il *Business Week* p44-52 Ag 7 '89
Yellow-peril journalism: is latent racism coloring business coverage of Japan? E. Cose. il *Time* 134:79 N 27 '89

Foreign relations
A delicate burial [selection of Hirohito funeral delegations] W. R. Doerner. il *Time* 133:34 Ja 23 '89
Hour of power? [special section] il *Newsweek* 113:14-18+ F 27 '89
Japan's quiet strength. S. Ōkita. *Foreign Policy* 75:128-45 Summ '89
Japan's shifting role [cover story; special section] il *World Press Review* 36:11-20 Ap '89
A rite of passage [Hirohito's funeral] B. Martin. il por *Newsweek* 113:24-5 F 20 '89
Soviet Union
See Soviet Union—Foreign relations—Japan
United States
See United States—Foreign relations—Japan

History
Period of civil wars, 1480-1603
Nobunaga's Ambition [computer simulation of sixteenth-century Japan] N. Randall. il *Compute!* 11:90+ Ja '89
Meiji period, 1868-1912
Chomin: the Rousseau of the East. S. Ida. il por *The Unesco Courier* 42:40-3 Je '89
Allied occupation, 1945-1952
A lesson learned and a lesson forgotten [American businessmen H. Sarasohn and C. Protzman instruct Japanese in management techniques] R. C. Wood. il pors *Forbes* 143:70-2+ F 6 '89

Industries
See also
Aerospace industries—Japan
Airlines—Japan
Airplane industry—Japan
Ajinomoto Co., Inc.
Akai Electric Co., Ltd.
All Nippon Airways Co. Ltd.
Architectural firms—Japan
Automobile equipment industry—Japan
Automobile industry—Japan
Banks and banking—Acquisitions and mergers—Japan
Brewing industry—Japan
Bridgestone Corp.
Brokers—Japan
Canon Inc.
Chemical industries—Japan
Compact disc industry—Japan
Computer industry—Japan
Corporations—Acquisitions and mergers—Japan
Dai-Ichi Kangyo Bank, Ltd.
Daiei, Inc.
Dentsu Inc.
Duskin Co. Ltd.
Engineering construction companies—Japan
Fisheries—Japan
Fuji Photo Film Co., Ltd.
Fujisankei Communications Group
Helicopter industry—Japan
Hitachi, Ltd.
Hitachi Zosen Corp.
Honda Motor Co., Ltd.
Japan Air System (Firm)
Japan Tobacco Inc.
Koito Manufacturing Co. Ltd.
Kubota, Ltd.
Matsushita Electric Industrial Co. Ltd.

JAPAN—Industries—See also—*cont.*
   Mazda Motor Corporation
   Mitsubishi Estate Co. Ltd.
   Mitsubishi Heavy Industries, Ltd.
   Mitsubishi Motors Corp.
   Mitsubishi Rayon Co. Ltd.
   Mitsui Taiyo Kobe Bank
   Mitsukoshi Ltd.
   Mizuno Corporation
   Motion picture industry—Japan
   Mr. Max Corporation
   Munitions—Japan
   Nakamichi Corp.
   Nansay Corporation
   NEC Corp.
   Nikko Securities Co. Ltd.
   Nintendo Co. Ltd.
   Nippon Telegraph & Telephone Corporation
   Nissan Motor Co. Ltd.
   Nomura Securities Co. Ltd.
   Norinchukin Bank
   Panasonic Company
   Petroleum industry—Japan
   PIA Company
   Pioneer Electronic Corp.
   Recruit Company
   Retail trade—Japan
   Seibu Group
   Seibu Railway Co. Ltd.
   Seiko Group
   Shipbuilding—Japan
   Shiseido Company Ltd.
   Sony Corp.
   Telecommunication—Japan
   Television equipment industry—Japan
   Toshiba Corporation
   Tourist trade—Japan
   Toyota Motor Corporation
   Venture capital companies—Japan
   VM Technologies
   Yamaha International Corp.
   Yamaha Motor Co. Ltd.
   Yaohan Department Store Co. Ltd.
Back to basics in Japan. il *World Press Review* 36:54-5 N '89
Japan faces a brain drain [college grads opting out of manufacturing sector] Y. Hoshiai and J. Schwartz. il *Newsweek* 114:47-8 S 4 '89
Japan has a Rust Belt, too. B. Martin. il *Newsweek* 113:48 Ap 17 '89
Japan is like a kid in a candy store—a rich kid. T. Holden. il *Business Week* p50-1 D 4 '89
Japan's big knack for coming back. C. Rapoport. il *Fortune* 120:131+ N 6 '89
What's up—and down—in Japan. il *Fortune* 119:8+ F 27 '89

Kings and rulers
   See also
   Akihito, Emperor of Japan
   Emperor worship, Japanese
   Hirohito, Emperor of Japan, 1901-1989

Maps
Japan in early Portuguese maps. A. P. Marques. il maps *The Courier (Unesco)* 42:14-16 Ap '89

Military policy
   See also
   Japan—Defenses
Japan's new military edge [cover story] J. W. Dower. il *The Nation* 249:1+ Jl 3 '89

Nationalism
After Hirohito: what remains sacred. I. Buruma. il por *The New York Times Magazine* p28-9+ My 28 '89
America-bashing, Japanese style [book The Japan that can say no by A. Morita and S. Ishihara] J. Impoco. pors *U.S. News & World Report* 107:45 O 16 '89
America's self-loathing even has Japan convinced [The Japan that can say no] P. C. Roberts. il *Business Week* p22 D 11 '89
The book that's creating a firestorm [S. Ishihara's The Japan that can say no] A. Borrus. il por *Business Week* p78+ O 23 '89
The country of missing parts. R. Rosenblatt. il *U.S. News & World Report* 106:10-12 Mr 6 '89
Do non-Japanese fear the flame? [death of Hirohito reopens issues of imperialism and nationalism] C. S. Inouye. il *The Nation* 248:120-2 Ja 30 '89
Japan's hardening view of America. R. Neff. il *Business Week* p62-4 D 18 '89
Superiority complex [views of S. Ishihara in The Japan that can say no] H. Jensen. il por *Maclean's* 102:56-7 D 11 '89
Teaching Japan to say no [interview with S. Ishihara] S. Kanise. il por *Time* 134:81-2 N 20 '89
What kind of power to be? *World Press Review* 36:12 Ap '89

Native peoples
   See also
   Ainu (Japanese people)

Politics and government
   See also
   Elections—Japan
   Political campaigns—Japan
   Political candidates—Japan
   Politics, Corruption in—Japan
   Socialist Party (Japan)
An affair to remember [S. Uno's affair with geisha] B. Hillenbrand. il por *Time* 134:33 Jl 10 '89
Cleaning house [new prime minister T. Kaifu] H. Jensen. il por *Maclean's* 102:31 Ag 21 '89
The dirt on 'Mr. Clean' [S. Uno] M. Nemeth. il por *Maclean's* 102:32 Jl 10 '89
The end of the affair? [S. Uno's affair with geisha triggers women's opposition] B. Powell. il por *Newsweek* 114:22-3 Jl 10 '89
The enigma of Japanese power [excerpt] K. G. van Wolferen. il por *Fortune* 119:150-3 My 8 '89
The geisha who knew too much [charges against Prime Minister S. Uno] il *U.S. News & World Report* 106:15-16 Je 19 '89
In Japan, the bosses' man [new prime minister T. Kaifu] D. Benkoil and H. Takayama. il *Newsweek* 114:29 Ag 21 '89
Japan: from 'Inc.' to superpower? B. Crozier. *National Review* 41:20 S 15 '89
Japan's geisha scandal [concerning Prime Minister S. Uno] *World Press Review* 36:6+ Ag '89
Now appearing in the role of Japanese prime minister . . . [T. Kaifu] R. Neff. il por *Business Week* p44 Ag 21 '89
Numero Uno [new prime minister] *Time* 133:35 Je 12 '89
The premier and the geisha [S. Uno] *Newsweek* 113:46 Je 19 '89
"The system" [views of K. G. van Wolferen] A. Tanzer. il por *Forbes* 143:40-1 My 1 '89
Who runs Japan? [bureaucrats] C. Rapoport. il *Fortune* 120:113-14 Ag 28 '89

Race relations
Japanese family fights to remove racially-offensive products in their country [H. Arita] il por *Jet* 76:37 S 4 '89
Trying to mend fences [black Americans and Japanese] G. J. Nagashima. il *Black Enterprise* 20:24 N '89

Religious institutions and affairs
   See also
   Catholics—Japan
   Church and state—Japan
   Protestant churches—Japan

Royal family
   See also
   Akihito, Emperor of Japan
   Fumihito, Prince of Japan, 1965-
   Hirohito, Emperor of Japan, 1901-1989

Social conditions
   See also
   Sexual behavior—Japan
Clash of the old and new. il *Scholastic Update (Teachers' edition)* 122:6-10 D 8 '89
The hard life. J. M. Fallows. il *The Atlantic* 263:16+ Mr '89
Shaking the mold [generation in their late 30s and 40s] A. Platt. il *Newsweek* 113:18 F 27 '89
Understanding how Japan works. C. Rapoport. il *Fortune* 120 no13 Special Issue:14-15+ Fall '89

Social life and customs
   See also
   Geishas

Study and teaching
   See Japanese studies

JAPAN. CONSTITUTION
Chomin: the Rousseau of the East. S. Ida. il por *The Unesco Courier* 42:40-3 Je '89
JAPAN. MINISTRY OF INTERNATIONAL TRADE AND INDUSTRY
Great Japanese mistakes. C. Rapoport. il *Fortune* 119:108-11 F 13 '89
MITI: the sugar daddy to end all sugar daddies. N. Gross. il *Business Week* p112 O 23 '89
World's worst oil policy? A. Tanzer. il *Forbes* 144:245+ Jl 24 '89
JAPAN AIR LINES CO. LTD.
Deregulation, privatization spur JAL to diversify operations. J. Ott. il *Aviation Week & Space Technology* 130:42-3 My 8 '89
Qantas, American, JAL gain shares in Air New Zealand. *Aviation Week & Space Technology* 130:108 Ja 2 '89
JAPAN AIR SYSTEM (FIRM)
Japan Air System begins international flights on competitive route to Korea. J. Ott. il *Aviation Week & Space Technology* 130:46-7 My 8 '89
JAPAN AND THE UNITED STATES
   See also
   Exchanges, Literary and scientific
   Japan—Foreign opinion—American
   United States—Foreign opinion—Japanese
A few pointers. J. M. Fallows. il *The Atlantic* 264:24+ N '89

JAPAN AND THE UNITED STATES—*cont.*
Rediscovering the American spirit. J. M. Fallows. il *U.S. News & World Report* 106:60-1 Ap 10 '89
To our own selves be true [J. M. Fallows' More like us] B. Powell. il *Newsweek* 113:45 Ap 3 '89
JAPAN IN TELEVISION
Is TV news guilty of Japan bashing? E. Diamond and K. O'Neil. il *TV Guide* 37:24-7 My 20-26 '89
JAPAN TILT FUND
Betting on the yen: a way to tilt the odds. S. Woolley. il *Business Week* p234 S 25 '89
JAPAN TOBACCO INC.
A trade threat that worked [Japan opens cigarette market to foreigners] G. Eisenstodt and H. Katayama. il *Forbes* 143:38-9 Ap 3 '89
JAPAN-UNITED STATES AIR AGREEMENTS *See* Aviation and state—International aspects
JAPANESE
Shaking the mold [generation in their late 30s and 40s] A. Platt. il *Newsweek* 113:18 F 27 '89
Canada
Prairie samurai [filming Japanese film Heaven and earth in Alberta] J. Howse. il *World Press Review* 36:68-9 N '89
Prairie samurai: a Japanese epic comes to life in Alberta [Heaven and earth] J. Howse. il *Maclean's* 102:44-5 Ag 21 '89
Sayonara, eh? [filming Japanese samurai epic Heaven and earth in the Canadian Rockies] J. Greenberg. il *American Film* 15:11-12 O '89
Foreign countries
A yen to travel. S. Seibert. il *Newsweek* 114:30-1 Ag 14 '89
United States
See also
Japanese Americans
Comic Tamayo Otsuki is one Japanese import who comes from the Far-out East. por *People Weekly* 32:168 N 20 '89
In good faith [out-of-work Chicagoan J. Loveras returns contents of missing briefcase to Japanese owner] B. Greene. il pors *Esquire* 111:67-8 Mr '89
Japan race project on track [Indianapolis 500] il *The Saturday Evening Post* 261:46-7 N/D '89
The stolen briefcase [J. Loveras returns contents to Japanese owner] B. Greene. il *Reader's Digest* 134:23-4+ Je '89
Teaching a Tokyo whiz kid the art of the deal [H. Kondo from Nikko Securities working for Blackstone Group] J. Friedman. il por *Business Week* p83 Ja 16 '89
A yen for New York: what the Japanese own—what they're after [cover story] D. Burstein. il *New York* 22:26-36 Ja 16 '89
Education
See also
Japanese Weekend School (New York, N.Y.)
The land of rising sons and daughters [first Japanese high school in Sweetwater, Tenn.] il *U.S. News & World Report* 106:12+ My 22 '89
Rising sun over Sweetwater [Tennessee Meiji Gakuin] S. Tifft. il *Time* 133:92 My 22 '89
JAPANESE AMERICAN MARKET
A Japanese mall in—New Jersey? [Yaohan Plaza] L. J. Nathans. il *Business Week* p100 Ja 30 '89
JAPANESE AMERICANS
The new bicoastals: love on Tokyo time [couples who commute between the West Coast and Japan] J. Hammer. il *Newsweek* 113:50 F 13 '89
Tireless Kuniko Terasawa is the force behind a newspaper almost no one can read [Utah nippo] R. Arias. il pors *People Weekly* 32:53-4 S 25 '89
Evacuation and relocation, 1942-1945
On wings of forgiveness [J. Takeshita meets relatives of American civilians killed in explosion of Japanese balloon bomb in Oregon during World War II] J. Fincher. il *Reader's Digest* 134:85-90 Mr '89
'They took away our rights'. P. Sudo. il *Scholastic Update (Teachers' edition)* 122:16-17 D 8 '89
Anecdotes, facetiae, satire, etc.
Uncivil liberties. C. Trillin. *The Nation* 249:374 O 9 '89
Religious life
The gift of two cultures [S. K. Inouye] K. H. Sidey. por *Christianity Today* 33:30 Mr 3 '89
JAPANESE AMERICANS AS CONSUMERS *See* Japanese American market
JAPANESE AND BLACKS
Japanese family fights to remove racially-offensive products in their country [H. Arita] il por *Jet* 76:37 S 4 '89
Trying to mend fences [black Americans and Japanese] G. J. Nagashima. il *Black Enterprise* 20:24 N '89
JAPANESE ART *See* Art, Japanese
JAPANESE AUTOMOBILES *See* Automobiles, Foreign
JAPANESE BATHS
Sink or swim: Japanese bathing in three easy lessons. M. Di Landro. il *Travel Holiday* 172:74-81 D '89
JAPANESE BEETLES *See* Beetles
JAPANESE COMMUNICATIONS SATELLITES *See* Communications satellites, Japanese

JAPANESE COOKING *See* Cooking, Japanese
JAPANESE DANCE *See* Dance, Japanese
JAPANESE DRAMA
See also
Kabuki
JAPANESE GARDENS *See* Gardens and gardening, Japanese
JAPANESE GRAND PRIX *See* Automobile racing—Japan
JAPANESE HUMOR *See* Humor, Japanese
JAPANESE IRISES *See* Irises
JAPANESE LANGUAGE IN JAPAN
Foreign words and phrases
See also
Janglish
JAPANESE LANGUAGE PRESS
See also
Utah nippo (Newspaper)
JAPANESE LITERATURE
See also
Publishers and publishing—Japanese literature
Translations into English
Kodansha brings new Japanese fiction to the U.S. il *Publishers Weekly* 236:57 O 6 '89
JAPANESE PAINTING *See* Painting, Japanese
JAPANESE POETRY
See also
Haiku
JAPANESE RED ARMY
The Japanese Red Army [fact sheet, August 24, 1989] *Department of State Bulletin* 89:64-5 N '89
JAPANESE SPACE VEHICLES *See* Space vehicles, Japanese
JAPANESE SPACEPLANE *See* Spaceplane, Japanese
JAPANESE STUDENTS IN THE UNITED STATES *See* Foreign students—United States
JAPANESE STUDIES
Better ways to watch Japan. M. Mandell. il *High Technology Business* 9:12 Je '89
The Japan-handlers. J. M. Fallows. il *The Atlantic* 264:14+ Ag '89
JAPANESE WEEKEND SCHOOL (NEW YORK, N.Y.)
Tokyo Prep. C. Breslin. il *New York* 22:50-2 Mr 6 '89
JAPANESE WRESTLING *See* Sumo
JAPONICA PARTNERS
Will Japonica bag a railroad—or get derailed? [attack on CNW] G. G. Marcial. il *Business Week* p79 Ap 10 '89
JARDEL, JEAN-PAUL
Knowledge is strength. il *World Health* p3 Je '89
JARDIN DES PLANTES (PARIS, FRANCE)
The once and future museum. C. Gans. il *Natural History* p48-55 Jl '89
JARES, JOE, 1937-
Monday night football. il *Sports Illustrated* 71:5+ S 4 '89
JARES, SUE ELLEN
A designer's wanderings in the Yucatán. il por *Architectural Digest* 46:270+ Ap '89
JARET, PETER
Air quality: unacceptable [cover story] il *Health (New York, N.Y.)* 21:48-51 Mr '89
Risky waters. il *Health (New York, N.Y.)* 21:70-3+ Ag '89
JARMUSCH, JIM
about
Closely watched 'train' [cover story] M. Pally. il *Film Comment* 25:19-21 Jl/Ag '89
Mystery train [film] Reviews
Mademoiselle il 95:78+ D '89. R. Rosenbaum
The Nation 249:726-7 D 11 '89. S. Klawans
The New Republic 201:24 D 11 '89. S. Kauffmann
New York il 22:120+ N 20 '89. D. Denby
Newsweek il 114:78 D 4 '89. D. Ansen
Rolling Stone il p47 N 30 '89. P. Travers
Vogue il por .179:256 N '89. B. Dorminey
JARRAH
Super wood from Down Under. il *Better Homes and Gardens* 67:37 My '89
JARREAU, AL
about
Al Jarreau: a troubadour's new tones. R. Tolleson. il por *Down Beat* 56:24-5 Ap '89
Star quality. M. Southgate. por *Essence* 20:37 My '89
JARRETT, KEITH
about
Keith Jarrett: in search of the perfect E minor chord [cover story; interview] J. Woodard. il pors *Down Beat* 56:16-19 F '89
JARRETT, VERNON
about
Making excellence popular. il pors *Ebony* 44:90+ S '89
JARUZELSKI, WOJCIECH
about
The general's sudden retreat. por *U.S. News & World Report* 107:14 Jl 10 '89
Look who popped up on the firing line. il por *U.S. News & World Report* 107:11 Jl 31 '89
Playing the political odds in Poland. A. Platt. il por *Newsweek* 114:30-1 Ag 7 '89
Thanks a lot, but no thanks. M. Johnson. il por *Time* 134:30 Ag 7 '89
A vote for Jaruzelski. H. Jensen. ·il por *Maclean's* 102:26 Jl 31 '89

JAZZDANCE (DANCE COMPANY)
Zenon and Jazzdance merge. J. Timmis. il *Dance Magazine* 63:17 Je '89
JAZZERCISE, INC.
Dancing to a different drummer [fitness expert J. S. Missett] A. M. Thompson. il por *Women's Sports & Fitness* 11:16 O '89
JAZZIE B.
about
From Soul II gold. S. Bloom. il por *Rolling Stone* p15 S 7 '89
JBL INCORPORATED
The making of an American speaker. I. Masters. il *Stereo Review* 54:75-81 Je '89
JEALOUSY
See also
Envy
JEAN, KAREN
about
A woman's place. J. F. Mariani. il por *Harper's Bazaar* 122:190+ N '89
JEANES, WILLIAM
Eye on the road. See issues of Car and Driver beginning March 1988
Motor sports: racing through 1988. il *Sports Illustrated* 70:37+ F 13 '89
JEANLOZ, RAYMOND
about
A wizard of middle earth under fire. R. A. Kerr. por *Science* 246:758-60 N 10 '89
JEANNERET-GRIS, CHARLES ÉDOUARD See Le Corbusier, 1887-1965
JEANS, MARYLU TERRAL
Love [poem] *Good Housekeeping* 208:228 Je '89
JEANS (CLOTHING)
See also
Gap, Inc.
Levi Strauss & Co.
VF Corp.
America's love affair with denim: it's in our jeans. il *Mademoiselle* 95:184-7 Je '89
Denim delights. A. Holch. il *American Health* 8:34-6 Ap '89
Experimenting with jeans. T. Parker. il *Vogue* 179:126 My '89
Jeans in the genes [S. Toussie and other successful Syrians in the jeans business] P. Patton. il por *New York* 22:40-4+ My 22 '89
Anecdotes, facetiae, satire, etc.
Uncivil liberties. C. Trillin. il *The Nation* 249:6 Jl 3 '89
Prices
Sacrificial brand [VF's Lee brand] G. Morgenson. il *Forbes* 143:41-2 F 6 '89
JEEP AUTOMOBILES
On a Jeep Jamboree: thank heaven for four-wheel drive. J. B. Treece. il *Business Week* p125 D 4 '89
Export-import trade
One company's China debacle [American Motors; excerpt from Beijing Jeep] J. Mann. il por *Fortune* 120:145+ N 6 '89
History
Road warrior [Willys CJ-2A] A. Carey. il *Gentlemen's Quarterly* 59:83+ D '89
Testing
Dustbusters! [Geo Tracker, Isuzu Amigo XS, Jeep Wrangler Islander, and Suzuki Samurai JL in the Mojave Desert] A. Assenza. il *Car and Driver* 35:136-40+ N '89
Mudders [pickup trucks] D. Sherman. il *Popular Science* 235:33-4+ Jl '89
JEEP'S BAR (ALPINE, WYO.) See Alpine (Wyo.)—Restaurants, nightclubs, bars, etc.
JEFF HEALEY BAND
The Jeff Healey Band. E. Miller. il pors *Seventeen* 48:121-2+ Mr '89
JEFFERIES, BOYD L.
about
Five years of hard putting. J. Nocera. il por *Esquire* 112:67-8+ D '89
Life after Boyd? And how. E. Schine. il por *Business Week* p143 Mr 20 '89
Wall Street is glued to the Bilzerian trial. M. Galen. il por *Business Week* p33 My 15 '89
JEFFERIES GROUP INC.
Five years of hard putting [B. L. Jefferies] J. Nocera. il por *Esquire* 112:67-8+ D '89
The house that Boyd built. R. King. il por *Forbes* 144:222 S 18 '89
Life after Boyd? And how. E. Schine. il por *Business Week* p143 Mr 20 '89
Wall Street is glued to the Bilzerian trial. M. Galen. il por *Business Week* p33 My 15 '89
JEFFERSON, KAREN L.
Moorland-Spingarn Research Center. il *American Visions* 4:46-7 Ag '89
JEFFERSON, MARTHA WAYLES SKELTON, 1748-1782
about
The day Thomas Jefferson's world fell apart. R. P. Hay. il *USA Today (Periodical)* 118:90-2 N '89

JEFFERSON, THOMAS, 1743-1826
about
The day Thomas Jefferson's world fell apart [death of M. W. S. Jefferson] R. P. Hay. il *USA Today (Periodical)* 118:90-2 N '89
Going to school with Mr. Jefferson. il *U.S. News & World Report* 107:13 O 9 '89
The incredible odyssey of the president's beasts. B. Gilbert. il por *Audubon* 91:100-2+ Ja '89
The original "Big Cheese". R. Sassaman. il *American History Illustrated* 23:34-5 Ja '89
Reroofing a landmark. D. Rastorfer. il *Architectural Record* 177:124-7 F '89
Religion
Two centuries of Virginia's Act for Religious Freedom. E. Turner. il *USA Today (Periodical)* 117:73-5 Mr '89
JEFFERSON AIRPLANE (MUSICAL GROUP)
Airplane flies again. M. Goldberg. *Rolling Stone* p24 Mr 23 '89
Refueled, retooled and soaring again [New York City concert] D. Fricke. il *Rolling Stone* p32 N 2 '89
Woodstock remembered: the artists. il *Rolling Stone* p75 Ag 24 '89
JEFFERSON CITY (MO.)
Sanitary affairs
Missouri's capital using trash bags made from corn. il *Successful Farming* 87:30 Ja '89
JEFFERSON COUNTY (MISS.)
Water supply
Espy to probe rural Miss. water crisis. *Jet* 76:27 S 11 '89
Taps for Blue Hill. G. Jaynes. il *Life* 12:27 N '89
JEFFERSON PARISH (LA.)
Politics and government
Duke election symptomatic of U.S. racism: Jackson. *Jet* 75:7 Mr 6 '89
An ex-Klansman trades his robes for a cloak of respectability in the Louisiana legislature [D. Duke] D. Grogan. il pors *People Weekly* 31:215-16 Mr 6 '89
The GOP's cross to bear [ex-Klansman D. Duke elected to Louisiana legislature] il pors *U.S. News & World Report* 106:14-15 Mr 6 '89
Hate gets a haircut [state legislature representative D. Duke] L. K. Truscott. il pors map *Esquire* 112:174-6+ N '89
Kluck! Kluck! Kluck! [white supremacist D. Duke wins election to Louisiana legislature] E. Magnuson. il por *Time* 133:29 Mr 6 '89
Louisiana's blow-dried Grand Wizard [D. Duke] il por *Newsweek* 113:27 Ja 23 '89
A seat for the Klansman [D. Duke wins seat in Louisiana legislature] J. Hammer. il por *Newsweek* 113:6 Mr 6 '89
JEFFERSON SMURFIT CORP.
Who needs trees? There's always the Sunday New York times. P. Klebnikov. il *Forbes* 143:108+ Je 26 '89
JEFFERY, DAVID
A renaissance for Michelangelo [cover story] il *National Geographic* 176:688-713 D '89
Yellowstone: the great fires of 1988 [cover story] il supp (folded map) map *National Geographic* 175:252-73 F '89
JEFFREY, TERENCE P.
(jt. auth) See Kirkwood, R. Cort, and Jeffrey, Terence P.
JEFFRIES, WEI-JEN
about
China trade. L. Gubernick. il por *Forbes* 144:287 O 16 '89
JEFF'S PRESERVATION SPECIALTIES, INC.
Freeze-dried memories [J. Weber's service for pet owners] P. Jordan. il por *Time* 133:16-17+ F 13 '89
Frigid pet tricks [J. Weber's service for pet owners] E. Grinnan. il por *Seventeen* 48:31 Jl '89
JEKYLL, GERTRUDE, 1843-1932
about
Best laid plan. M. R. Van Valkenburgh and C. D. Van Valkenburgh. il *House & Garden* 161:150-7 Mr '89
A budding genius. P. Weideger. il por *Ms.* 17:48-9 Mr '89
Miss Jekyll's garden. E. P. Williams. il *House & Garden* 161:166 F '89
JELKS, FREEMAN N.
Searching for value in the stock market [cover story] il *Consumers' Research Magazine* 72:10-13 Mr '89
JELLINEK, TRISTRAM
about
Theatrical menagerie: an English actor's Victorian house in London. E. Lambert. il por *Architectural Digest* 46:118-25 D '89
JELLOUN, TAHAR BEN See Ben Jelloun, Tahar, 1944-
JELLY, JAM, ETC.
See also
J. M. Smucker Co.
Sorrell Ridge (Firm)
Enough jam for a lifetime. M. Kumin. il *Country Journal* 16:56-8 Jl/Ag '89
Preserve fruit the light way. H. A. Dorrough. il *Southern Living* 24:154+ Je '89
Shortcuts to jelly-making [microwaving] il *Southern Living* 24:132 Jl '89
Vintage jellies [made with varietal wines] il *Sunset (Central West edition)* 181:136 D '88

JELLY, JAM, ETC.—*cont.*
Advertising
Sorrell Ridge makes Smucker pucker. J. Levine. il *Forbes* 143:166+ Je 12 '89
JELLYFISH
Jellyfish alert [stings] S. Mahler. *McCall's* 116:88+ Jl '89
Purple-striped jellyfish. il *Sea Frontiers* 35:104-5 Mr/Ap '89
Photographs and photography
Death, where is thy sting? [nudibranch vs. porpita] K. Atkinson. il *Natural History* p80-1 Ag '89
JEMISON, MAE C.
about
Child of the '60s set to become first black woman in space. M. Marshall. il pors *Ebony* 44:50+ Ag '89
First black woman astronaut readies for flight in space. il por *Jet* 77:31 O 30 '89
JEMISON, T. J.
about
$10 million headquarters signals new course for National Baptist Convention, U.S.A. Inc. [cover story] C. L. Sanders. il pors *Ebony* 44:68-70+ O '89
National Baptists build a headquarters. R. Waddle. *The Christian Century* 106:805-7 S 13-20 '89
JENCKS, CHARLES, 1939-
about
Architects' dialogue. H. Hollein. il pors *Architectural Digest* 46:72+ Ap '89
JENCKS, CHRISTOPHER
(jt. auth) See Mayer, Susan E., and Jencks, Christopher
JENCKS, HARLAN W.
The military in China. bibl f *Current History* 88:265-8+ S '89
JENKEL, PAUL
about
A big-gain hunter in small stocks [interview] T. Paré. il por *Fortune* 120:40+ O 23 '89
JENKENS & GILCHRIST
The thrift police [FSLIC files malpractice suit against law firm Jenkens & Gilchrist over its dealings with State Savings & Loan Association of Lubbock] D. Fanning. il *Forbes* 143:74 Ja 9 '89
JENKIN, LEN
about
A country doctor [drama] Reviews
The Nation 248:248 F 20 '89. T. M. Disch
JENKINS, CHARLES J.
about
The vigil [drama] Reviews
The Nation 248:863 Je 19 '89. T. M. Disch
JENKINS, FERGUSON, 1943-
about
Morals and immortals. P. Gammons. il por *Sports Illustrated* 70:78 Ja 23 '89
JENKINS, JEFFREY
about
Jeffrey Jenkins: Stux. D. Rubey. il *Art News* 88:170 N '89
JENKINS, JERRY B.
(ed) See Hershiser, Orel. Tommy Lasorda's "Sermon on the mound"
JENKINS, JOHN A.
Courting disaster. il pors *Gentlemen's Quarterly* 59:214-17+ F '89
JENKINS, JOHN HOLMES, 1940-1989
about
Knowing Johnny Jenkins. C. Trillin. *The New Yorker* 65:79-97 O 30 '89
JENKINS, MARK
An American coup in Paris. il *American Heritage* 40:66-71 Jl/Ag '89
JENKINS, NANCY HARMON
Coastal legacy. il *The New York Times Magazine* p39-40 Ja 22 '89
New England fancy. il *The New York Times Magazine* p65-6 Ap 2 '89
JENKINS, REESE V.
about
Interview: Reese Jenkins. J. Briggs. il por *Omni (New York, N.Y.)* 11:82-4+ Ap '89
JENKINS, SPEIGHT
about
Northern Pacific [interview] S. Von Buchau. il por *Opera News* 53:14-17 Mr 18 '89
JENKINS, TOM
Sell your hidden gold with a query. *The Writer* 102:18-20+ Ag '89
A walk on the wild side. il map *Travel Holiday* 171:46-51 My '89
JENKINS COMPANY
Knowing Johnny Jenkins [controversial rare book dealer who was mysteriously murdered in Bastrop County, Tex.] C. Trillin. *The New Yorker* 65:79-97 O 30 '89
JENNESS, DAVID
(jt. auth) See Jurnovoy, Joyce, and Jenness, David
JENNIFER MULLER/THE WORKS
Reviews:
Performances at the Joyce Theater, New York City. J. Lewis. *Dance Magazine* 63:93-4 S '89

JENNINGER, PHILIPP
about
Jewish victims and German sensitivity [discussion of December 14, 1988 article, Jewish victims and German indifference] J. B. Miller. *The Christian Century* 106:287-8 Mr 15 '89
JENNINGS, PETER, 1938-
Oh, what a year! il por *TV Guide* 37:20-1 D 30 '89-Ja 5 '90
about
The ABCs of Peter Jennings [interview] N. Atkins. por *Rolling Stone* p60-2+ My 4 '89
Peter Jennings ascendant. C. Capuzzi. il por *Channels (New York, N.Y.: 1986)* 9:33 Mr '89
Peter Jennings gets no self-respect. E. Kaye. il pors *Esquire* 112:158-60+ S '89
JENNINGS, REGINA
Assata [poem] *Essence* 20:128 N '89
JENNINGS, SANDRA
about
Love, hurt and money [cover story] S. Schindehette. il pors *People Weekly* 32:72-4+ Jl 10 '89
Suing for cash and charging abuse, the mother of his son gives Bill Hurt a Big chill. M. Green. il pors *People Weekly* 31:54-6 Ap 3 '89
JENSEN, GEORGE
about
The rainbow maker. C. A. Jaffe. il por *Nation's Business* 77:41+ N '89
JENSEN, JIM
A veteran TV anchorman's toughest story was his own—he had to beat drugs and depression; ed. by Jeannie Park. il pors *People Weekly* 32:67-8+ S 4 '89
JENSEN, MICHAEL C.
about
The LBO isn't a superior new species. C. Farrell. il *Business Week* p126 O 23 '89
JENSEN, NANCY
about
Metropolitan reflections: a play of surfaces in a Los Angeles penthouse. M. Webb. il *Architectural Digest* 46:270-5 My '89
JENT, WILLIAM RILEY
about
Presumed guilty. D. Finkel. il pors *Esquire* 111:178-80+ Mr '89
JEOPARDY [television program] See Television program reviews—Single works
JEPPESEN, ELREY BORGE
about
Charting Jeppesen [interview] N. Moll. il pors *Flying* 116:36-41 Ja '89
JEPPESEN (FIRM)
Charting Jeppesen [interview with E. B. Jeppesen]. N. Moll. il pors *Flying* 116:36-41 Ja '89
JEPSON, BARBARA
Who's that man with Marilyn Horne? il *The New York Times Magazine* p32-3+ Ap 16 '89
JEREMY'S PLACE (FIRM)
A birthday presence second to none, Jeremy Sage treats his business like child's play. D. Van Biema. il pors *People Weekly* 31:87-8 My 8 '89
JERKY, MEAT See Meat, Dried
JERMYN, AMANDA
Color blind [story] il *Mademoiselle* 95:128+ Je '89
JERMYN STREET (LONDON, ENGLAND)
Jermyn intelligence. R. Ryan. il *Gentlemen's Quarterly* 59:245-6 D '89
JEROME, FRED
The return of the shuttle syndrome? il *Technology Review* 92:65-6 Ja '89
Science by press conference. il *Technology Review* 92:72-3 Jl '89
JEROME ROBBINS' BROADWAY [musical] See Musicals, revues, etc.—Reviews—Single works
JERRY KRAVAT ENTERTAINMENT SERVICES (FIRM)
The new owner of New Year's Eve [J. Kravat] M. Barrier. il por *Nation's Business* 77:68 Ja '89
JERRY'S (NEW YORK, N.Y.: RESTAURANT) See New York (N.Y.)—Restaurants, nightclubs, bars, etc.
JERSEY (CHANNEL ISLANDS)
See also
Paleontology—Jersey (Channel Islands)
JERSEY CITY (N.J.)
Education
The blackboard jungle revisited. G. Morris. *National Review* 41:18-19 My 5 '89
A case of academic bankruptcy [state-appointed superintendent E. J. Scambio to run school system] *Newsweek* 114:74 O 16 '89
State takeover. *Time* 134:48 O 16 '89
Waterfront
On the waterfront [Port Liberté] S. J. Madden. il por *Fortune* 119:112 F 13 '89
JERUSALEM
See also
Temple Mount (Jerusalem)

JERUSALEM—*cont.*

Antiquities
Beneath the Holy Land. S. Begley. il *Newsweek* 114:44 D 18 '89

Cemeteries
The graveyards of Jerusalem. F. Ajami. *The New Republic* 201:24-5 S 11 '89

City planning
'Bridge' building in Jerusalem [work of M. Safdie in Mamilla district] A. Rabinovich. il por *World Press Review* 36:73 S '89

Description
Is it safe to travel in Israel? [effect of uprising] H. R. Lottman. *Publishers Weekly* 235:42 Ja 13 '89

Newspapers
See also
Jerusalem post

Politics and government
Jerusalem: the future of the past. A. Elon. il *The New York Review of Books* 36:37-9 Ag 17 '89
Oh, Jerusalem! [election] E. Norden. *The New Republic* 200:17-18 Mr 27 '89
JERUSALEM INTERNATIONAL BOOK FAIR *See* Book fairs

JERUSALEM POST
Media barons are making pilgrimages to Jerusalem [C. M. Black buys Jerusalem post] J. Rossant and N. Sandler. il por *Business Week* p50 My 15 '89

JESCHKE, CLAUDIA
about
Ann Hutchinson Guest goes back to the source: finding Faune. L. Garafola. il pors *Dance Magazine* 63:32-4 O '89

JESSI PROJECT
Can Europe survive on chips? D. Dickson. il *Science* 245:246 Jl 21 '89
Europe chips in. G. Lütge. *World Press Review* 36:70-1 O '89
Hands across the chipmaking chasm [U.S. Memories and Sematech to work with JESSI Project] O. Port. *Business Week* p28-9 Jl 3 '89

JESSUP, SHELBY P., AND CARY, ERNESTINE
Geographic information systems: what they are, and how they work. bibl il *Focus (New York, N.Y.: 1950)* 39:10-12 Summ '89

JESUITS
A: The Jeopardy! priest; Q: Who is Tom Smolich? Correct for $39,802! [Jesuit raises money for day care center in East Los Angeles, Calif.] il pors *People Weekly* 32:58 O 9 '89
Barbarity in El Salvador [murder of six priests] *The Christian Century* 106:1112-13 N 29 '89
Confessions of a lay collaborator [cover story] M. R. Carey. *America* 160:500-2 My 27 '89
Death in El Salvador [murder of six Jesuit priests] J. Sobrino. il *Commonweal* 116:693-5 D 15 '89
Grave thoughts [conversation with Jesuit priest I. Ellacuria nine months before his murder in El Salvador] M. Massing. *The New Republic* 201:12-14 D 11 '89
In cold blood [murder of six Jesuit priests in El Salvador] *Time* 134:44 N 27 '89
In solidarity with the slain Jesuits of El Salvador [address, November 22, 1989] J. A. O'Hare. *America* 161:443-6 D 16 '89
In the name of God, stop the killing [priests in El Salvador] R. A. Hyde. *The Christian Century* 106:1144 D 6 '89
'Now you be quiet, Oscar' [death squad killings in El Savador] *America* 161:415 D 9 '89
Of many things [murder of Jesuits in El Salvador] T. H. Stahel. *America* 161:390 D 2 '89

Education
The mission and ministry of Jesuits in higher education [address, June 5, 1989; cover story] F. H. T. Rhodes. *America* 161:54-60 Jl 29-Ag 5 '89
Of many things. G. W. Hunt. *America* 160:570 Je 17-24 '89
The Order of Education. K. L. Woodward. il *Newsweek* 113:59 Je 19 '89

Missions
Re-sounding lost Masses [works by Jesuit composer D. Zípoli] il *Américas* 41 no2:4-5 '89
Tribute to a Latin American martyr [L. Espinal, missionary murdered in Bolivia in 1980] M. O'Sullivan. *America* 160:8-11+ Ja 7-14 '89
JESUS [film] *See* Motion picture reviews—Single works

JESUS CHRIST
See also
Salvation
Second Advent
about
'I am Jesus, whom you persecute'. K. Koyama. *The Christian Century* 106:347 Ap 5 '89

Anecdotes, facetiae, satire, etc.
He's back!!! [cover story] il *Harper's* 278:47-55 Ap '89
Of many things [public relations for Christ's Second Coming] G. W. Hunt. *America* 160:282 Ap 1 '89

Apparitions and miracles
Celebration. P. J. Ryan. *America* 160:22 Ja 7-14 '89

Grateful outcasts. P. J. Ryan. il *America* 161:223 O 7 '89
The prophetic touch. P. J. Ryan. il *America* 160:543 Je 3 '89
This bridge called my back [bent woman in Luke 13] G. E. Ziegenhals. *The Christian Century* 106:343-4 Ap 5 '89
Understanding faith and miracle. P. Perkins. *The Christian Century* 106:555 My 24-31 '89

Art
The emasculation of God. M. S. Podles and L. J. Podles. il *America* 161:372-4 N 25 '89
Taking pains to see. L. Cunningham. il *Commonweal* 116:699+ D 15 '89

Attitudes towards women
Forgiveness [Mary Magdalene] P. J. Ryan. il *America* 160:567 Je 10 '89
Redeemer. P. J. Ryan. il *America* 160:207 Mr 4 '89
This bridge called my back [bent woman in Luke 13] G. E. Ziegenhals. *The Christian Century* 106:343-4 Ap 5 '89

Crucifixion
Dating the Crucifixion. B. E. Schaefer. il *Sky and Telescope* 77:374 Ap '89
Unravelling the mystery of weakness and strength. P. Kreeft. il *Christianity Today* 33:23-5 Ap 21 '89

Art
A Rubens crucifixion on a Chinese export porcelain dish. N. Pearce. bibl f il *Antiques* 136:844-7 O '89

Family
Refugees. P. J. Ryan. *America* 161:491 D 23-30 '89

Humanity
The emasculation of God. M. S. Podles and L. J. Podles. il *America* 161:372-4 N 25 '89
Who's who. H. Fehren. *U.S. Catholic* 54:48-50 S '89

Incarnation
See Incarnation

Messiahship
Christian fulfillment and Jewish-Christian dialogue. I. C. Rottenberg. *The Christian Century* 106:387-91 Ap 12 '89
Divided flock. P. J. Ryan. il *America* 160:355 Ap 8 '89
Identity problems. P. J. Ryan. *America* 160:598 Je 17-24 '89
Shepherd as lamb. P. J. Ryan. il *America* 160:311 Ap 1 '89

Nativity
See also
Epiphany
Incarnation
The divine parent. M. E. Marty. *The Christian Century* 106:1215 D 20-27 '89
Light from light. P. J. Ryan. il *America* 161:459 D 16 '89
The packaging of Jesus. H. Fehren. *U.S. Catholic* 54:38-40 D '89

Parables
He had compassion [Good Samaritan] K. Koyama. il *The Christian Century* 106:651 Jl 5-12 '89
Lenten meditation:
Prodigiously lost and found. A. James. *The Christian Century* 106:220-1 Mr 1 '89
The storyteller visits the vineyard. R. W. Bertram. *The Christian Century* 106:255-6 Mr 8 '89
Mercy. P. J. Ryan. *America* 161:150 S 9-16 '89
Neighbors [Good Samaritan] P. J. Ryan. il *America* 161:23 Jl 1-8 '89
A new beginning [prodigal son] P. J. Ryan. il *America* 160:183 F 25 '89

Passion
Alliances. P. J. Ryan. il *America* 160:231 Mr 11 '89
Something new. P. J. Ryan. il *America* 160:359 Ap 15 '89

Resurrection and Ascension
See also
Easter
Baptized and clothed. P. J. Ryan. il *America* 160:406 Ap 29 '89
Christ's Resurrection and Ascension. G. O'Collins. *America* 160:262-3 Mr 25 '89
Fearlessness. P. J. Ryan. il *America* 160:279 Mr 25 '89
Why the Resurrection matters. M. Green. il *Christianity Today* 33:28-32 Mr 17 '89

Teachings
Christian claims in a pluralistic society. A. M. Watts. *The Christian Century* 106:222-3 Mr 1 '89
Half-baked hearth cakes. H. Fehren. *U.S. Catholic* 54:40-2 Ja '89
Lenten meditation:
When bad things happen. W. H. Willimon. *The Christian Century* 106:198-9 F 22 '89
Promulgation. P. J. Ryan. *America* 160:23 Ja 7-14 '89
Rich wisdom: New Testament teachings on wealth [cover story; special section] il *Christianity Today* 33:27-40 My 12 '89
What is Christ's response? H. Fehren. *U.S. Catholic* 54:38-40 Mr '89

Transfiguration
Patterned on glory. P. J. Ryan. il *America* 160:127 F 11 '89
Radiant victim. P. J. Ryan. il *America* 161:70 Jl 29-Ag 5 '89

JESUS CHRIST IN MOTION PICTURES
An autopsy on 'Temptation'. R. A. Blake. *America* 160:199-201 Mr 4 '89
Christians and Muslims unite to oppose The last temptation [Istanbul] B. G. Baker. il *Christianity Today* 33:57 My 12 '89
Last temptation boycott gets mixed reviews. K. H. Sidey. il *Christianity Today* 33:36-7 Ap 21 '89
Ten-year run for Jesus [film distributed by Campus Crusade for Christ] il *Christianity Today* 33:52 O 20 '89
Unrighteous indignation [The last temptation of Christ] T. C. Muck. il *Christianity Today* 33:14 Ap 7 '89
JESUS CHRIST IN POETRY
Hopkins the mythmaker. J. F. Cotter. *America* 161:106-8 Ag 26-S 2 '89
JESUS CHRIST THE KING, FEAST OF
The Magic Kingdom. P. Perkins. il *The Christian Century* 106:1083 N 22 '89
Royal transfers. P. J. Ryan. il *America* 161:363 N 18 '89
JESUS OF MONTREAL [film] See Motion picture reviews—Single works
JESUS SEMINAR
Do the Gospels put words in Jesus' mouth? B. Doyle. il *U.S. Catholic* 54:32-5 S '89
JET AIRPLANE ENGINES See Airplane engines, Jet
JET AIRPLANES See Airplanes, Jet
JET BOATS
Newport jet set [rally from Narragansett Bay to Nantucket] P. Whittell. il *Motor Boating & Sailing* 164:46-7 S '89
Testing
Megayacht [Octopussy] J. Skorupa. il *Popular Mechanics* 166:132-4 My '89
New U.S. thoroughbred [Trident 105 jetboat Lady Frances] P. Whittell. il *Motor Boating & Sailing* 164:60-3+ N '89
SR-84. L. Rudeen. il *Motor Boating & Sailing* 163:32 Mr '89
State-of-the-art Oceanfast [jet-powered Mercedes 100-foot yacht] P. Whittell. il *Motor Boating & Sailing* 164:50-3+ Ag '89
JET CUTTING
Waterjets. R. Hamilton. il *Technology Review* 92:7+ O '89
JET LAG
Conquering jet lag. E. Barrett-Connor. il *Travel Holiday* 171:18-19 Ap '89
How to beat jet lag drag. P. Lee. il *Black Enterprise* 19:78 Mr '89
Illuminating jet lag [research by Charles Czeisler and Richard Kronauer] R. Pool. il *Science* 244:1256-7 Je 16 '89
Shedding light on jet lag. L. Gilman. il *American Health* 8:46 Je '89
Tennis in good time [effects of circadian rhythms] M. Bloom. il *World Tennis* 36:70-1 F '89
JET PROPULSION
See also
Guided missiles—Propulsion systems
JET PROPULSION LABORATORY (U.S.)
The greatest show off earth [viewing images of the planets] F. Pohl. il *Omni (New York, N.Y.)* 12:14+ N '89
Jet Propulsion Lab looks to life after Voyager. M. M. Waldrop. il *Science* 245:1037 S 8 '89
JPL computer researchers develop hardware for neural networks. B. W. Henderson. il *Aviation Week & Space Technology* 131:129+ O 9 '89
U.S. planetary launch surge [cover story; special section; with editorial comment] il *Aviation Week & Space Technology* 131:19, 44-5+ O 9 '89
JET SKIS
Trouble in their wake. N. R. Gibbs. il *Time* 133:64 Je 19 '89
Laws and regulations
Invasion of the 'water snatchers'. J. Skorupa. il *Popular Mechanics* 166:39+ Ap '89
This land is your land: the battle over PWCs. J. Skorupa. il *Popular Mechanics* 166:24+ Ag '89
JET TRAINERS See Airplanes, Training
JET TRANSPORTS See Airplanes, Jet
JETELOVA, MAGDALENA
about
The powerful and playful forms of Magdalena Jetelova. J. Dornberg. bibl (p164) il pors *Smithsonian* 20:106-12+ My '89
JETHRO TULL (MUSICAL GROUP)
Tull: living in the present. P. Puterbaugh. il *Rolling Stone* p44 N 30 '89
JETT, JOAN
about
The Blackhearts of Broadway. F. Goodman. il por *Rolling Stone* p33 Ap 20 '89
JETT (JOAN) AND THE BLACKHEARTS (MUSICAL GROUP) See Joan Jett and the Blackhearts (Musical group)
JETTEN, ANTON M., AND OTHERS
Persistence of abnormal chloride conductance regulation in transformed cystic fibrosis epithelia. bibl f il *Science* 244:1472-5 Je 23 '89
JETTIES
Hatteras jetty plans set back, not halted. il *National Parks* 63:11 Ja/F '89

JEU DE PAUME MUSÉE (PARIS, FRANCE) See Musée du Jeu de Paume (Paris, France)
JEWEL CAVE NATIONAL MONUMENT (S.D.)
Following the wind [work of J. and H. Conn] M. R. Taylor. il pors *Audubon* 91:90-9 Ja '89
JEWELERS
See also
Lagniappe (Firm)
Ommen, Joke van, 1948-1988
Tiffany & Co.
Town & Country Jewelry Mfg. Co.
Collectibles
Nineteenth-century jewelers' trade cards. R. A. Green. il *Antiques & Collecting Hobbies* 94:64-7 N '89
Ethical aspects
Gems: be on your guard. G. V. Axon. il *Consumers' Research Magazine* 72:24-8 Je '89
France
See also
Cartier (Firm)
JEWELRY
See also
Cuff links
Earrings
Gems
Goldsmithing
Jewelers
Necklaces
Pearls
Pendants (Jewelry)
Buying ethnic jewelry. D. P. Marshall. il *Travel Holiday* 171:72-4 Ja '89
Bygone bijoux [designer T. S. Carr] K. Bruno. il por *Harper's Bazaar* 122:60 N '89
From bear teeth to pearls. C. Clifford. il *Health (New York, N.Y.)* 21:74-9 Ag '89
Gogo Fuller's sassy skeletal jewelry is not for the spineless [bone jewelry created from animal skeletons] M. Dougherty. il pors *People Weekly* 32:101+ O 16 '89
The intimate art. T. L. Wolf. il *Art News* 88:122-9 N '89
Jewelry American style. A. DiNoto. il *American Craft* 49:46-53 Je/Jl '89
Look-good, feel-good jewelry [AllerGuard process] A. Biesada. il *High Technology Business* 9:47 Ja '89
Lumberyard brooches, button pins, high-tech necklaces. il *Sunset (Central West edition)* 181:84-6+ D '88
Walter Bramwell Young's high-stylus jewelry is music to fashionable ears [vinyl jewelry created from melted phonograph records] il por *People Weekly* 32:67 S 18 '89
Collectors and collecting
Costume jewelry: the basics in bangles and beads. E. Baroody. il *Antiques & Collecting Hobbies* 94:26-9 S '89
Exhibitions
An ambiguous art: the jewelry of J. Fred Woell. B. Freudenheim. il *American Craft* 49:32-5 Ap/My '89
The jewelry [Mount Vernon] M. G. Fales. il *Antiques* 135:512-7 F '89
Marketing
See also
Jan Bell Marketing Inc.
Photographs and photography
On becoming a short-order chef of lighting. J. Fruchtman. il por *Petersen's Photographic Magazine* 18:28-9 S '89
Theft
Woman pleads guilty to theft after swallowing $2500 worth of jewelry [L. Riddick of Montclair, N.J.] il por *Jet* 76:18 Jl 10 '89
JEWELRY, AFRICAN
Exhibitions
African gold comes to America [Metropolitan Museum of Art] il *USA Today (Periodical)* 118:8 D '89
Art à la carte [Gold of Africa] K. Best. il *Travel Holiday* 171:116 Mr '89
Rare artisanry from Africa [Gold of Africa] K. M. Burke. il *Smithsonian* 20:180 Je '89
JEWELRY, ASSYRO-BABYLONIAN
The golden treasures of Nimrud. P. Elmer-Dewitt. il *Time* 134:80-1 O 30 '89
JEWELRY, BRITISH
Lost jewels [pieces designed by Pre-Raphaelites] G. C. Munn. bibl f il *Antiques* 136:826-33 O '89
JEWELRY, FRENCH
Exhibitions
Opulent objects by Cartier [Musée du Petit Palais in Paris] A. E. Ledes. il *Antiques* 136:958+ N '89
JEWELRY, INDIAN (EAST INDIAN)
Don't call it a Caine mutiny, but Michael's wife, Shakira, is shaking her baubles, bangles and beads. J. Stark. il pors *People Weekly* 32:105-6 N 27 '89
JEWELRY, ITALIAN
Exhibitions
Viva Verdura! J. Gruder. il por *Harper's Bazaar* 122:262 S '89
JEWELRY BOXES, CASES, ETC.
Elegant jewelry boxes. A. Weaver. il *Workbench* 45:48-51+ N/D '89

JEWELRY INSURANCE *See* Insurance, Jewelry
JEWELRY MAKING *See* Jewelry
JEWELS *See* Gems; Jewelry
JEWELS [ballet] See Ballet reviews—Single works
JEWISH AMERICAN PRINCESS (TERM)
Are "JAP" jokes anti-Semitic? [views of Mimi Alperin] *USA Today (Periodical)* 117:5 Ap '89
JAP jokes are nothing to laugh at. L. Lamb. il *Utne Reader* p30+ My/Je '89
JEWISH-ARAB RELATIONS
See also
Israel-Arab Wars, 1967-
Jerusalem: the future of the past. A. Elon. il *The New York Review of Books* 36:37-9 Ag 17 '89
Palestinian like me: notes from an undercover Jewish journalist [excerpt from My enemy, my self] Y. Binur. il pors *Utne Reader* p34-45 S/O '89
Trying to bridge the gap [moderate Israelis and Arabs] M. Kramer. il *Time* 133:42 Je 26 '89
The widow of an Israeli soldier gives his heart—and the gift of life—to an Arab, Hanna Khader. il pors *People Weekly* 32:130 D 11 '89
History
See also
Israel-Arab War, 1948-1949
Palestine—History—Arab rebellion, 1936-1939
Historiography
Charging Israel with original sin [views of B. Morris and A. Shlaim] S. Teveth. bibl f *Commentary* 88:24-33 S '89
JEWISH-ARAB WAR, 1948-1949 *See* Israel-Arab War, 1948-1949
JEWISH-ARAB WARS, 1967- *See* Israel-Arab Wars, 1967-
JEWISH ART *See* Art, Jewish
JEWISH AUTHORS *See* Authors, Jewish
JEWISH COOKING *See* Cooking, Jewish
JEWISH-GENTILE MARRIAGE *See* Interfaith marriage
JEWISH IDENTITY *See* Jews—Identity
JEWISH LAW
Keep holy the Sabbath: an old ritual worth reconsidering. *Utne Reader* p112 Mr/Ap '89
JEWISH LITERATURE
See also
Israeli literature
Publishers and publishing—Jewish literature
Conferences
Jewish guilt and Israeli writers [The writer in the Jewish community: an Israeli-North American dialogue] R. R. Wisse. *Commentary* 87:25-31 Ja '89
JEWISH NEW YEAR *See* Rosh Hashanah
JEWISH PERIODICALS
See also
Tikkun (Periodical)
Jewish publications. M. Harvey. il *Utne Reader* p111-13 Mr/Ap '89
JEWISH PHILOSOPHY *See* Philosophy, Jewish
JEWISH VOTE *See* Jews—United States—Political activities
JEWISH WOMEN
See also
International Jewish Feminist Network
Jewish American Princess (Term)
National Council of Jewish Women (Canada)
Psychology
Dreaming of Hitler. D. Merkin. il *Esquire* 112:75-8+ Ag '89
Twice an outsider: on being Jewish and a woman. V. Gornick. il *Utne Reader* p95-6 S/O '89
JEWISON, NORMAN
about
In country [film] Reviews
Commonweal 116:591-2 N 3 '89. T. O'Brien
Film Comment il por 25:11-14+ S/O '89. J. Scott
Maclean's il 102:75 S 18 '89. B. D. Johnson
The Nation 249:396-8 O 9 '89. S. Klawans
The New Republic 201:30-1 O 16 '89. S. Kauffmann
New York il 22:129-30 S 25 '89. D. Denby
Newsweek il 114:70 O 2 '89. D. Ansen
People Weekly il 32:16 S 25 '89. R. Novak
Rolling Stone il p27+ O 19 '89. P. Travers
Time il 134:90 O 2 '89
JEWS
See also
Anti-Semitism
Israelis
Converts to Christianity
See Converts from Judaism
Dietary laws
It's kosher [wine] F. J. Prial. il *The New York Times Magazine* p82 Mr 19 '89
Emigration from the Soviet Union
See Immigration and emigration—Soviet Union
Health and hygiene
Mutation revealed for adult Tay-Sachs [work of Ruth Navon and Richard L. Proia] I. Wickelgren. *Science News* 135:167 Mr 18 '89
The mutations in Ashkenazi Jews with adult G_{M2} gangliosidosis, the adult form of Tay-Sachs disease. R. Navon and R. L. Proia. bibl f il *Science* 243:1471-4 Mr 17 '89

History
See also
Holocaust, Jewish (1939-1945)
Identity
Anti-Semitism and Jewish identity. M. A. Meyer. *Commentary* 88:35-40 N '89
Behind "Who is a Jew": a letter from Jerusalem. E. Norden. *Commentary* 87:21-33 Ap '89
Jews of denial. M. Richler. il *Gentlemen's Quarterly* 59:153+ Ap '89
On being a Jew [interview with S. Hook] N. Podhoretz. *Commentary* 88:28-36 O '89
"Who is a Jew" [discussion of April 1989 article, Behind "Who is a Jew": a letter from Jerusalem] E. Norden. *Commentary* 88:2-4+ S '89
Nationalism
See also
Jews—Identity
Zionism
Persecutions
See also
Holocaust, Jewish (1939-1945)
Political activities
See also
Communism and Jews
Israel: a lamentation from the future. N. Podhoretz. *Commentary* 87:15-21 Mr '89
"Lamentation" [discussion of March 1989 article, Israel: a lamentation from the future] N. Podhoretz. *Commentary* 88:4-8+ Jl '89
Psychology
See also
Jews—Identity
Religion
See Judaism
Rites and ceremonies
See also
Bar mitzvah
Bat mitzvah
Hanukkah
Passover
Rosh Hashanah
Seder
Argentina
Rabbi Marshall Meyer: a prophet's agenda. R. Hirschfield. *The Christian Century* 106:438-9 Ap 26 '89
Austria
History
Vienna: complexity, contradictions [handling of return of works of art stolen by Nazis] A. Decker. il *Art News* 88:63 My '89
History—Bibliography
The rise and fall of Vienna's Jews. M. Ignatieff. il *The New York Review of Books* 36:21-5 Je 29 '89
Europe
History
Anti-Semitism [discussion of August 1988 article, Communism, anti-Semitism & the Jews] J. Z. Muller. *Commentary* 87:11-12+ Ja '89
Germany
Danke schön, Herr Doktor: German Jews in Palestine. R. Gay. *The American Scholar* 58:567-77 Aut '89
Germany (West)
Why I won't go to Germany. C. Ozick. *Harper's* 278:16-19 F '89
Great Britain
History
Our road to Zion: a memoir [family's move from London to Israel] D. Vital. *Commentary* 87:49-55 My '89
Victorian values/Jewish values. G. Himmelfarb. *Commentary* 87:23-31 F '89
Hungary
Returning home [S. Schwarcz buried in family cemetery] C. Fenyvesi. por *Organic Gardening* 36:99 Ap '89
Israel
Behind "Who is a Jew": a letter from Jerusalem. E. Norden. *Commentary* 87:21-33 Ap '89
Israel: the rise of the ultra-Orthodox. A. Margalit. il *The New York Review of Books* 36:38-44 N 9 '89
Land or life: a biblical dilemma [O. Yosef's views in rabbinical debate over Israeli occupation] R. N. Ostling. il por *Time* 134:67 S 18 '89
"Who is a Jew" [discussion of April 1989 article, Behind "Who is a Jew": a letter from Jerusalem] E. Norden. *Commentary* 88:2-4+ S '89
Netherlands
History
The complete Anne Frank. A. Pons. *World Press Review* 36:73 D '89
War and remembrance: a new entry from Anne Frank [commemoration of her sixtieth birthday] J. Hendel. il por *Seventeen* 48:112-13 Je '89
Palestine
See also
Zionism
Danke schön, Herr Doktor: German Jews in Palestine. R. Gay. *The American Scholar* 58:567-77 Aut '89

JEWS—Palestine—*cont.*
Minority report [Y. Shamir's involvement with Nazi Germany] C. Hitchens. *The Nation* 249:159 Ag 7-14 '89

Poland
History
After the Holocaust. A. Wilson-Smith. il *Maclean's* 102:51-2 S 4 '89
Poland: the ghosts of Jews [excerpt from Mad dreams, saving graces] M. T. Kaufman. il *Commonweal* 116:429-32 Ag 11 '89

Soviet Union
Emigration
See Immigration and emigration—Soviet Union
History
Why my grandfather Leon Trotsky must be turning in his grave. Y. Akselrod. *Commentary* 87:39-43 Ap '89

Ukraine
History
His brother's keeper [Ukrainian peasant A. Suchinsky honored for hiding Zeiger family during WW2] S. Schlegel. *Reader's Digest* 134:112-14 F '89

United States
See also
American Jewish Committee
What future for American Jews? A. Hertzberg. il *The New York Review of Books* 36:26+ N 23 '89
Political activities
Altering the formula for Israel's friends. J. M. Wall. *The Christian Century* 106:4-5 Ja 4-11 '89
American Jews: diehard conservatives [analysis of 1988 presidential voting] M. Himmelfarb. il *Commentary* 87:44-9 Ap '89
American Jews firmly on the left. *Society* 26:2-3 My/Je '89
Broken vessel [conference of Jewish progressives sponsored by Tikkun] E. Rothstein. *The New Republic* 200:17-20 Mr 6 '89
Bunker mentality [delegation of American Jewish leaders meets with PLO] S. K. Sheinbaum. *The Nation* 248:77 Ja 23 '89
Counterforce [conference of Jewish progressives sponsored by Tikkun] M. L. Sifry. *The Nation* 248:112-13 Ja 30 '89
The diaspora's discontent [American Jews dissatisfied with Israeli handling of occupied territories] L. I. Barrett. il por *Time* 133:18-19 Ap 3 '89
A family quarrel [American Jews and Israel] T. Jacoby. il *Newsweek* 113:58-60 Ap 3 '89
Israel & American Jews [discussion of September 1988 article, Where is Zion?] E. Alexander. *Commentary* 87:8-11 F '89
Israel: some surprising polls [American opinion judged increasingly favorable towards Israel] M. Bard. *Commentary* 88:45-7 Ag '89
The Jewish vote [discussion of April 1989 article, American Jews: diehard conservatives] M. Himmelfarb. *Commentary* 88:4-6+ Ag '89
Liberalism & American Jews [discussion of October 1988 article] I. Kristol. *Commentary* 87:2-3+ Ja '89
No left turn [resurgence of Jewish liberalism in America] R. R. Wisse. *The New Republic* 200:23-7 My 22 '89
Rabbi Marshall Meyer: a prophet's agenda. R. Hirschfield. *The Christian Century* 106:438-9 Ap 26 '89
The rapidly changing world [address, June 14, 1989] M. M. Kampelman. *Vital Speeches of the Day* 55:731-4 S 15 '89
A seder for peace in the Mideast. A. Waskow. il *The Nation* 248:557+ Ap 24 '89
Setting Yasser straight [role of American R. E. Hauser in U.S. recognition of PLO] S. Weller. il pors *Ms.* 17:84 Mr '89
Shamir to school kids: drop dead; No pragmatist at heart. A. Cockburn. *The Nation* 248:150-1 F 6 '89
Why I met with the PLO. M. Z. Rosensaft. por *Newsweek* 113:6 Ja 9 '89

JEWS AND BLACKS
American Jews: diehard conservatives [analysis of 1988 presidential voting] M. Himmelfarb. il *Commentary* 87:44-9 Ap '89
Black Chicago doctor supported Jews with money, time and talent [T. K. Lawless] il por *Jet* 77:5-6 O 16 '89
Blacks and Jews: the uncivil war [Chicago; with editorial comment by Lee Eisenberg] T. Branch. il *Esquire* 111:25, 89-90+ My '89
Different strokes: eleven kids from Brooklyn try life on a kibbutz [project initiated by teacher S. Bialer] J. Taylor. il por *New York* 22:56-8+ Je 12 '89
Jackie Mason tries to talk himself out of trouble [effect of racist remarks on R. Giuliani's New York City mayoral campaign; cover story] J. Kasindorf. il pors *New York* 22:36-42 O 16 '89
Jackie Mason's racial remarks about Dinkins, Jews' relations with blacks bring backlash. pors *Jet* 77:5 O 16 '89
The Jewish vote [discussion of April 1989 article, American Jews: diehard conservatives] M. Himmelfarb. *Commentary* 88:4-6+ Ag '89

Mason bombs in New York [comedian's racial slurs hurt R. Giuliani's mayoral campaign] B. Turque. il pors *Newsweek* 114:42 O 9 '89
Public Enemy number one [S. Lee's reaction to anti-Semitic remarks made by Professor Griff] M. Horowitz. il por *American Film* 14:15 S '89
Conferences
Blacks and Jews [The black-Jewish alliance: reunion and renewal] R. Flick. *National Review* 41:14 Ja 27 '89
JEWS AND CATHOLICS *See* Christianity and other religions
JEWS AND CHRISTIANS *See* Christianity and other religions
JEWS AND EVANGELICALS *See* Christianity and other religions
JEWS AND ISLAM *See* Islam and Judaism
JEWS IN LITERATURE
See also
Holocaust, Jewish (1939-1945), in literature
Goodbye, Newark: Roth remembers his beginnings [preface to 30th anniversary edition of Goodbye, Columbus] P. Roth. por *The New York Times Book Review* 94:14 O 1 '89
JFK ASSASSINATION: AS IT HAPPENED [television program] *See* Television program reviews—Single words
JFK INTERNATIONAL AIRPORT *See* New York (N.Y.)—Airports
JIANG ZEMIN
about
China. *Business Week* p56 O 2 '89
The making of Deng's successor. S. Burton. il por *Time* 134:44 O 9 '89
Old boys' network. J. Mirsky. il por *World Press Review* 36:23 Ag '89
Rise of a perfect apparatchik. W. R. Doerner. il por *Time* 134:32 Jl 10 '89
JIBRIL, AHMED
about
Closing in on the Pan Am bombers [with interview] B. Duffy and others. il por *U.S. News & World Report* 106:23-4 My 22 '89
JIFFY LUBE INTERNATIONAL INC.
The grease guns at Jiffy Lube are squirting red ink. J. Weber, Jr. *Business Week* p42-3 F 27 '89
Water slick [views of stock analyst John Boland] T. Jaffe. il *Forbes* 143:220 Mr 20 '89
JIGS (FISHING) *See* Fishing lures, flies, etc.
JIGS (TOOLS)
Basic hand tool jigs. il *Popular Mechanics* 166:80 N '89
Router jigs to make and buy. il *Workbench* 45:65 Mr/Ap '89
Simple jig helps make cuts for redwood planters. il *Sunset (Central West edition)* 182:118 Je '89
JIGSAW PUZZLES
Aussie jumble [map puzzle of Australia] il *National Geographic World* 172:24 D '89
Jigsaw [video game] H. E. H. Aycock. il *Compute!* 11:74-5 My '89
Piecing together the Milky Way [The Illustrated Milky Way: Sagittarius and Scorpius] R. Bunge. il *Astronomy* 17:108 Je '89
JIJI, JESSICA, AND BERNSTEIN, DENNIS
Filipina activist fights repression. *The Progressive* 53:14 Ap '89
JILLETTE, PENN
See also
Penn & Teller
about
Enter laughing. Teller. il pors *Gentlemen's Quarterly* 59:236-9+ Ag '89
JILLIAN, ANN
"I fear I'm losing my husband". il pors *Redbook* 173:83-4 Jl '89
JIM PATTISON GROUP
A raider from the north blows into the Windy City [J. Pattison eyes Whitman Corp.] B. Bremner. il por *Business Week* p34-5 Ja 16 '89
JIM WALTER CORP.
A lion of the Texas bar snarls at KKR and Drexel [S. Susman builds asbestos case stemming from Jim Walter Corp. LBO] M. Ivey. il por *Business Week* p73+ O 9 '89
JIMÉNEZ, SHERRY LYNN MIMS
Fish oil! Aspirin! Oat bran! il *Health (New York, N.Y.)* 21:36+ N '89
JIMI HENDRIX INFORMATION MANAGEMENT INSTITUTE
Incendiary rocker Jimi Hendrix is gone, but Ken Voss remains the devoted keeper of the flame. J. Hevrdejs. il pors *People Weekly* 32:143-4 D 18 '89
JIMMY THE GREEK
about
The Greek in purgatory. M. Lupica. il *Esquire* 111:43-4+ Ja '89
JIN, SUNGHO
about
The dogged push to overcome resistance. E. T. Smith. il por *Business Week* Special Issue:84 Je 16 '89

JINDO INDUSTRIES LTD.
The rise of Jindo. A. Rawsthorn. *World Press Review* 36:51 Je '89

JM FAMILY ENTERPRISES INC.
Jim Moran, master salesman. G. Button. il pors *Forbes* 144 Special Issue:54-5+ O 23 '89

JMB REALTY TRUST
Bloomie's may be on JMB's Christmas list. D. Greising. il *Business Week* p54 D 25 '89-Ja 1 '90

JOAN JETT AND THE BLACKHEARTS (MUSICAL GROUP)
The Blackhearts of Broadway. F. Goodman. il por *Rolling Stone* p33 Ap 20 '89

THE JOAN RIVERS SHOW [television program] See Television program reviews—Single works

JOANOU, PHIL
about
U2: Rattle and hum [film] Reviews
Rolling Stone p16 Ja 12 '89. J. Ressner
Video il 13:15-16 Ap '89. S. Roman

JOB ACCIDENTS See Industrial accidents
JOB APPLICATIONS
See also
Employment interviewing
Employment references
Finding the right employee (II). B. Stein. il *Home Office Computing* 7:40+ N '89
Getting your name on everyone's lips. D. Cole. il *Working Woman* 14:68-70 Ag '89
How to say no to a job offer and still stay a hot prospect. A. M. Russell. *Working Woman* 14:118 Ap '89
How to write letters that win jobs. M. Swain and R. Swain. il *Working Woman* 14:120-3 Ap '89
Job hunting after 50. *Modern Maturity* 32:36-7 Je/Jl '89
Using contacts to get jobs. P. King. il *Psychology Today* 23:14 Je '89

Ethical aspects
Job applicants come clean [integrity test; research by Reid Psychological Systems] *USA Today (Periodical)* 118:7-8 Ag '89

JOB APTITUDE TESTS See Aptitude tests
JOB ATTENDANCE
See also
Flextime
Hours of labor
JOB CREATING PROGRAMS See Unemployment—Relief measures
JOB DISCRIMINATION See Discrimination in employment
JOB DISEASES See Occupational health and safety
JOB HOPPING See Labor turnover
JOB HUNTING See Job applications
JOB INTERVIEWS See Employment interviewing
JOB MOBILITY See Occupational mobility
JOB PERFORMANCE APPRAISAL See Employees—Rating; Women executives—Rating
JOB PLACEMENT GUIDANCE See Vocational guidance
JOB SATISFACTION
The 50 best places for blacks to work [cover story] il *Black Enterprise* 19:73-8+ F '89
Job satisfaction based on generation, not class. *Society* 27:2 N/D '89
Why you can't get no (job) satisfaction. K. W. Wiley. il *Mademoiselle* 95:122+ Je '89

Anecdotes, facetiae, satire, etc.
Having a nice day. S. Bing. il *Esquire* 111:94 Ap '89

JOB SHARING
Six ways to be "family-friendly". S. Nelton. il *Nation's Business* 77:12-13 Mr '89
Two for one: a working idea. J. E. Bahls. il *Nation's Business* 77:28-30 Je '89

JOB STRESS
Ahhh . . . that feels good [massage in the office] il *Newsweek* 113:53 My 15 '89
Ambition without anxiety [special section] il *Working Woman* 14:123-6+ S '89
A better coffee break [On-Site Massage] V. Brower. il *American Health* 8:34 Jl/Ag '89
The desk stretch: 5 stress stoppers. il *Mademoiselle* 95:30 D '89
Gloom at the top [art museum director burnout] P. Failing. il *Art News* 88:126-31 My '89
How to have an easier homecoming [easing the transition between work and home] J. Bliss. il *Ladies' Home Journal* 106:96 O '89
How to stay cool when the pressure is hot. S. Jacoby. il *Glamour* 87:218-19+ D '89
Is your job driving you crazy? [matching therapy to profession] R. Sandroff. il *Psychology Today* 23:41-5 Jl/Ag '89
Is your job making you sick? C. Hacinli. il *Mademoiselle* 95:126 O '89
A kinder, gentler job: descending the ladder without leaving your company. A. Saltzman. il *U.S. News & World Report* 106:74-6 F 13 '89
Life in the stress lane: diary of a wired day [K. Bunis participates in Gary James' study of key stress points in average day of a working woman] N. Angier. il pors *Mademoiselle* 95:192-5+ F '89

Little control=lots of stress [study by Robert Karasek] V. Adler. il *Psychology Today* 23:18-19 Ap '89
Low control leads to on-the-job stress [study by Robert Karasek] il *USA Today (Periodical)* 117:8-9 Ja '89
Stress busters! [home-based working] B. Stein. il *Home Office Computing* 7:49-51 F '89
Take charge of your job [views of P. Nickerson] R. Thompson. il por *Nation's Business* 77:36-7 Ap '89

JOB SUCCESS See Success
JOB TENURE See Labor turnover; Seniority, Employee
JOB TRAINING See Employees—Training; Unemployment—Relief measures; Vocational-technical education
JOB TRANSFERS See Executives—Transfer; Women executives—Transfer

JOBES, NANCY
about
The extraordinary case of the woman who couldn't die. B. D. Colen. il por *Redbook* 172:126-9+ Mr '89

JOBIM, ANTONIO CARLOS
about
Bye-bye Brazil. E. Pooley. il por *New York* 22:30 Mr 20 '89

JOBS, STEVEN
about
How Steve Jobs linked up with IBM [cover story] B. R. Schlender. il pors *Fortune* 120:48-51+ O 9 '89
A legend's comeback bid. J. Littman. il por *Personal Computing* 13:70 Jl '89
The Next computer: promises to keep. R. A. Shaffer. il *Personal Computing* 13:51-2 Ja '89
Steve Jobs gets the keys to the office PC market. R. Brandt. il por *Business Week* p80-1 Ap 10 '89
Steve Jobs: out for revenge. P. Patton. il por *The New York Times Magazine* p22-3+ Ag 6 '89
Steve Jobs' revolutionary new computer. W. J. Hawkins. il por *Popular Science* 234:68-70+ Ja '89
Steve Jobs's hard sell. *Newsweek* 113:49 Ap 10 '89

JOBS See Employment; Occupations
JOCASSEE WATERSHED (N.C.-S.C.)
Duking it out in the Carolinas [proposed hydroelectric dam to be built by Duke Power] B. Fuller. il *Sierra* 74:96-7 My/Je '89

JOCHNOWITZ, GEORGE
True power to the people. il *National Review* 41:22-3 Je 30 '89
The words of Marx, the methods of Lenin. *National Review* 41:31-2 Ag 4 '89

JOCKEYS
See also
Antley, Chris, 1966?-
Cordero, Angel
Davis, Robbie
Day, Pat, 1954?-
Hubbard, Nate
Krone, Julie
Shoemaker, Bill, 1931-
Turcotte, Ron
Venezia, Mike
Forgotten heroes: black winners of the Kentucky Derby. R. A. Frister. il *Ebony* 44:82+ My '89

Uniforms
See Horse racing—Uniforms

JODHPURS
Riding high: city-smart jodhpurs. il pors *Harper's Bazaar* 122:146-51 F '89

JOE, DALE
Feathering the nest. il *Publishers Weekly* 235:20+ Je 23 '89

JOE L. EVINS APPALACHIAN CENTER FOR CRAFTS
The handmade history of the Upper Cumberland. il *Southern Living* 24:28-9 Ja '89

JOE LOUIS THE CHAMP (RIVERDALE, ILL.: GOLF COURSE) See Golf courses

JOE ROBBIE STADIUM (MIAMI, FLA.)
A Super Sunday victory for Joe Robbie. A. Fins. il por *Business Week* p62 Ja 23 '89

JOE T. GARCIA'S MEXICAN DISHES (FORT WORTH, TEX.: RESTAURANT) See Fort Worth (Tex.)—Restaurants, nightclubs, bars, etc.

JOEL, BILLY, 1949-
about
A $90 million matter of distrust pits Billy Joel against his ex-manager. S. Dougherty. il pors *People Weekly* 32:50-1 O 9 '89
Billy Joel starts a fire. S. Rogers. por *Rolling Stone* p29 N 16 '89

JOËLS, MARIAN, AND KLOET, E. R. DE
Effects of glucocorticoids and norepinephrine on the excitability in the hippocampus. bibl f il *Science* 245:1502-5 S 29 '89

JOELSON, J. R.
From the radical center. See issues of The Humanist beginning May/June 1989

JOE'S STONE CRAB (MIAMI BEACH, FLA.: RESTAURANT) See Miami Beach (Fla.)—Restaurants, nightclubs, bars, etc.

JOFFE, JOSEF
Second thoughts on a unified Germany. il *U.S. News & World Report* 107:46 N 27 '89

JOFFÉ, ROLAND
about
Fat Man and Little Boy [film] Reviews
Commonweal 116:643-4 N 17 '89. T. O'Brien
Esquire il 112:170-1 O '89. R. Scheer
Maclean's il 102:96 O 30 '89. B. D. Johnson
The Nation 249:577-8 N 13 '89. S. Klawans
National Review il 41:63-7 N 10 '89. D. K. Mano
The New Republic 201:28 N 20 '89. S. Kauffmann
New York 22:102+ N 6 '89. D. Denby
The New Yorker 65:121 N 13 '89. P. Kael
Newsweek il 114:75 O 30 '89. D. Ansen
People Weekly il 32:19-20 N 6 '89. R. Novak
Rolling Stone il p37 N 16 '89. P. Travers
Scholastic Update (Teachers' edition) il 122:13 O 6 '89
JOFFREY BALLET
Reviews:
Winter season at City Center. D. Hering. il *Dance
Magazine* 63:22-3+ Mr '89
Something old [opening week of fall season in New York
City] T. Tobias. il *New York* 22:122-3 N 13 '89
The "steady strengthening" of a ballerina [B. Rodriguez;
cover story] S. Anawalt. il pors *Dance Magazine* 63:34-9
N '89
Waltzing to Vienna: the Joffrey Ballet plays the historic
Theater an der Wien [Vienna International Dance Festival]
B. Howard. il *Theatre Crafts* 23:39-41+ My '89
Wishful thinking [winter season at City Center] T. Tobias.
il *New York* 22:86+ N 27 '89
JOGGING *See* Running
JOGGING CLOTHES *See* Clothing and dress—Sports clothes
JOHANNESBURG DANCE FOUNDATION
Dance takes hold in South Africa: rewriting the present.
R. Nelan. il por *Dance Magazine* 63:54-8 F '89
**JOHANNESSEN, SISSEL, AND HASTORF, CHRISTINE
ANN, 1950-**
Corn and culture in central Andean prehistory. bibl f il
Science 244:690-2 My 12 '89
JOHANSEN, BRUCE E. (BRUCE ELLIOTT), 1950-
'Dead Indians out, live Indians in'. il *The Progressive* 53:15-16
D '89
JOHANSON, CONRAD E.
(jt. auth) See Spector, Reynold, and Johanson, Conrad E.
JOHANSSON, INGEMAR
about
Didn't you used to be . . . W. Ladson. pors *Sport (New
York, N.Y.)* 80:78 Jl '89
JOHN, THE BAPTIST
about
More than a prophet. P. J. Ryan. *America* 161:435 D 9
'89
JOHN, ELTON
about
Party hearty Elton John lights 40 candles in the wind for
his manager's birthday. il pors *People Weekly* 32:40-1
S 25 '89
JOHN, OLIVIA NEWTON- *See* Newton-John, Olivia
JOHN A. ROEBLING'S SONS (FIRM)
Landmark [Roebling Eighty-ton Wire Rope Machine] *The
New Yorker* 65:50-1 N 6 '89
JOHN BLAIR & COMPANY
Bringing Blair back to life. K. Haley. il por *Channels (New
York, N.Y.: 1986)* 9:38-40+ Je '89
JOHN BURROUGHS MEDAL
Burroughs Medal [winner L. Kilham] F. Graham. il *Audubon*
91:16+ Jl '89
JOHN CALDER LTD.
John Calder: a sturdy survivor. J. Barbato. *Publishers Weekly*
235:254 My 12 '89
JOHN COLE'S BOOKSHOP (LA JOLLA, CALIF.) *See* Book-
sellers and bookselling—California
**JOHN D. AND CATHERINE T. MACARTHUR FOUNDA-
TION**
MacArthur Foundation confers five physics-related fellow-
ships. M. Siegel. il *Physics Today* 42:123-4+ Mr '89
JOHN D. HOLLINGSWORTH ON WHEELS
American Gothic [J. D. Hollingsworth] V. Contavespi. il
pors *Forbes* 144 Special Issue:34-6+ O 23 '89
JOHN DAY FOSSIL BEDS NATIONAL MONUMENT (OR.)
Fossils of Clarno Basin. C. H. Jones. il *Earth Science* 42:21-3
Spr '89
JOHN F. BLAIR, PUBLISHER
Southern books with an occasional oddity. B. Summer. il
Publishers Weekly 236:19-20 O 20 '89
**JOHN F. KENNEDY CENTER FOR THE PERFORMING
ARTS. OPERA HOUSE**
The Ring: the Deutsche Oper Berlin at Kennedy Center.
B. Howard. il *Theatre Crafts* 23:45+ My '89
JOHN F. KENNEDY INTERNATIONAL AIRPORT *See* New
York (N.Y.)—Airports
JOHN F. KENNEDY SCHOOL OF GOVERNMENT
The case for the case study. S. Goldsmith and K. Boo.
The Washington Monthly 21:18-20+ Je '89
Harvard's Kennedy School: is competence enough? J. A.
Lukas. il *The New York Times Magazine* p36-7+ Mr 12
'89

JOHN F. KENNEDY SPACE CENTER
Consolidation of orbiter logistics speeds repairs, reduces
delays. E. H. Kolcum. il *Aviation Week & Space Technology*
131:45+ Jl 31 '89
Green for go! [National Space Society Shuttle Launch Tour
at Discovery launch] K. McMains. il *Ad Astra* 1:24-7+
Ja '89
Space available. L. Griffin. il *Car and Driver* 34:242 Je
'89
JOHN H. HARLAND CO.
John H. Harland. J. Slovak. il *Fortune* 119:104 Mr 27 '89
JOHN HERRON ART INSTITUTE
See also
Indianapolis Museum of Art
JOHN HUSTON [film] See Motion picture reviews—Single
works
JOHN LABATT LIMITED
A global brew. J. DeMont. il *Maclean's* 102:28-9 Jl 24
'89
JOHN M. COCKERHAM AND ASSOCIATES, INC.
Whistleblowing on U.S. defense contractors is out of control.
J. M. Cockerham. por *Aviation Week & Space Technology*
130:99+ Ap 10 '89
JOHN MORRELL & CO.
Meatpacking company cuts compensation. *Monthly Labor
Review* 112:58-9 My '89
JOHN MUIR TRAIL (CALIF.)
Along the high, wild Sierra. G. A. Rowell. il map *National
Geographic* 175:466-93 Ap '89
JOHN MUIR TRUST
John Muir's Scotland. B. Fuller. il *Sierra* 74:20-1 N/D '89
JOHN PAUL I, POPE, 1912-1978
about
Death in Rome [J. Cornwell's investigation] il por *Time*
133:53 Je 19 '89
Of many things [John Cornwell's A thief in the night: the
mysterious death of John Paul I] G. W. Hunt. *America*
161:286 N 4 '89
JOHN PAUL II, POPE, 1920-
about
All the Pope's men. R. N. Ostling. il por *Time* 133:62
Ja 16 '89
The battle for the Catholic Church. P. Berryman. por *The
Christian Century* 106:523-6 My 17 '89
Beyond protocol: the quest for unity. T. Hoyt, Jr. *The
Christian Century* 106:926-7 O 18 '89
A common quest for understanding. E. McMullin. il *America*
160:100-2+ F 11 '89
Cross meets Kremlin. R. N. Ostling. il pors *Time* 134:74-6
D 4 '89
East-West, North-South. J. B. Hehir. il *Commonweal*
116:614-15 N 17 '89
The El Salvador horror. *The New Republic* 201:7-9 D 11
'89
Gorby's bow to the Roman legions. il pors *U.S. News &
World Report* 107:15 D 11 '89
The higher summit. K. L. Woodward. il pors *Newsweek*
114:36 D 11 '89
John Paul's ecumenical warning. R. N. Ostling. il *Time*
133:96 My 8 '89
The last socialist? [cover story] J. Gray. il *National Review*
41:27-9+ Je 30 '89
My Opus [discussion of April 10, 1989 article, Opus Dei
and the 'perfect society'] P. Lernoux. *The Nation* 249:74+
Jl 17 '89
Opus Dei and the 'perfect society' [cover story] P. Lernoux.
il *The Nation* 248:469+ Ap 10 '89
Peace signals from the papal chimney. il *U.S. News & World
Report* 107:14 O 2 '89
The Pope and the pol. K. L. Woodward. il pors *Newsweek*
114:87-90 D 4 '89
Pope John Paul II and the Jews. K. L. Woodward. il por
Newsweek 114:36 S 11 '89
The Pope of enterprise. M. Novak. il *Forbes* 143:70-1 Je
26 '89
The Pope's critics. J. Duquesne. il por *World Press Review*
36:56 Je '89
A reverence for fundamentalism. P. Lernoux. il *The Nation*
248:513-16 Ap 17 '89
The triumph of John Paul II. S. Kanfer. il pors *Life* 12:34-40+
D '89
Vatican under fire. *Time* 133:57 F 6 '89
Visit to East Timor (Indonesia), 1989
Visiting a forgotten war. R. Nordland. il map *Newsweek*
114:38 O 23 '89
JOHN WILEY & SONS, INC.
'Audubon perspectives' gives Wiley new perspective on trade.
B. Levine. il *Publishers Weekly* 236:31-2 N 10 '89
McGraw-Hill and Wiley quit Iran Fair but decry book
boycotts. C. Reid. *Publishers Weekly* 235:104 My 12 '89
Stubborn patriarch. C. Poole. il por *Forbes* 143:99+ F 6
'89
JOHNNY HANDSOME [film] See Motion picture reviews—
Single works
JOHNNY JOHNSON [musical] See Musicals, revues, etc.—
Reviews—Single works

JOHNNY ROOK (BIRD) *See* Caracaras
JOHNS, JASPER
about
Johns [cover story] W. H. Gass. bibl f il por *The New York Review of Books* 36:22-7 F 2 '89
Pessimist at play. M. Stevens. il *The New Republic* 200:25-6+ Ja 9-16 '89
JOHNS HOPKINS UNIVERSITY
Earth plays to full house at Johns Hopkins University. *Earth Science* 42:7-8 Fall '89
Hopkins hurdle. C. Poole. il *Forbes* 143:10 Mr 20 '89
JOHNSON, ALBERT WESLEY
about
A zestful protector of Canadian values. P. C. Newman. il *Maclean's* 102:34 Ap 10 '89
JOHNSON, ALVIN S.
The cotton crisis. *The New Republic* 201 [Reprint v1]:17-18 N 6 '89 [N 7 '14]
JOHNSON, AMY EDITH
Christmas books: beyond Santa Claus. *The New York Times Book Review* 94:19 D 24 '89
JOHNSON, BARBARA
about
Lech's American angel [cover story] D. Margolick. il pors *The New York Times Magazine* p28-31+ O 8 '89
JOHNSON, BARBARA
about
Hooked. C. Brown. il por *Forbes* 143:158+ Ap 3 '89
JOHNSON, BASIA *See* Johnson, Barbara
JOHNSON, BEN
about
Ben Johnson gets into scuffle with five men. por *Jet* 76:50 My 29 '89
A day of reckoning. il pors *Maclean's* 102:32-3 Je 26 '89
A deepening scandal. B. Wickens. pors *Maclean's* 102:49-50 Je 5 '89
A dirty coach comes clean. M. Noden. il pors *Sports Illustrated* 70:22-3 Mr 13 '89
From dream to nightmare. A. Burfoot and B. Wischnia. il pors *Runner's World* 24:12 Je '89
He has suffered enough. M. Noden. por *Sports Illustrated* 70:98 Je 26 '89
Moses blasts edict to strip Johnson's records. por *Jet* 76:46 O 2 '89
Olympic images. H. Quinn. il *Maclean's* 102:33 Ja 2 '89
A revealing inquiry. M. Noden. il por *Sports Illustrated* 70:19 Je 5 '89
Sabotage at Seoul? R. Dolphin. il por *Maclean's* 102:47 Mr 20 '89
The saga behind the shame. J. Brant. il pors *Runner's World* 24:78-80 Ap '89
Starting over. N. Underwood. il por *Maclean's* 102:66 S 18 '89
The steroid scandal [cover story; special section; with editorial comment by Kevin Doyle] il pors *Maclean's* 102:2, 36-42 Mr 13 '89
Whistle blower. por *Time* 133:50 Mr 13 '89
JOHNSON, BETSEY
about
Making time for your other life. S. Nelson. il por *Working Woman* 14:102-5 Mr '89
JOHNSON, BRANDY
about
A dandy Brandy. J. E. Vader. il pors *Sports Illustrated* 71:24+ Jl 17 '89
Innerview [interview] por *Women's Sports & Fitness* 11:59 O '89
JOHNSON, BRUCE C.
A good race. *America* 160:217-18 Mr 11 '89
JOHNSON, BRUCE E.
The artist and the businessman. il *Antiques & Collecting Hobbies* 94:44-5+ O '89
Dirk van Erp: artistry in metal. bibl f il *Antiques & Collecting Hobbies* 94:32-3+ O '89
The Grove Park Inn & the arts & crafts movement. il *Antiques & Collecting Hobbies* 94:34-8 O '89
Grueby pottery. bibl f il *Antiques & Collecting Hobbies* 94:52-4 O '89
Gustav Stickley and the Craftsman Furniture Workshops. bibl f il *Antiques & Collecting Hobbies* 94:48-9+ O '89
Knock on wood. See issues of Antiques & Collecting Hobbies beginning December 1988
JOHNSON, CATHERINE
about
Getting off the couch for good [interview] E. E. Goode. il por *U.S. News & World Report* 106:62 Ja 23 '89
JOHNSON, CHUCK
about
Soulbeat mines inner-city gold. W. J. Drummond. il por *Channels (New York, N.Y.: 1986)* 9:19 S '89
JOHNSON, CINDY LOU
about
Brilliant traces [drama] Reviews
New York il 22:72 F 20 '89. J. Simon
The New Yorker 65:89-90 F 20 '89. M. Kramer
JOHNSON, CLAUDIA ALTA TAYLOR *See* Johnson, Lady Bird, 1912-

JOHNSON, CLETUS
about
Cletus Johnson at Michael Walls and Leo Castelli. W. Thompson. *Art in America* 77:153-4 Ja '89
JOHNSON, CLIFFORD J.
about
War games. S. Ditlea. il *Omni (New York, N.Y.)* 11:32+ Mr '89
JOHNSON, DANIEL
Supercomputing the universe. il *Astronomy* 17:48-54 D '89
JOHNSON, DENIS, 1949-
The bullet's flight [story] il *Esquire* 111:191-3 Mr '89
JOHNSON, DENNIS
about
Cleaning up. J. Zweig. il por *Forbes* 144:302 D 11 '89
JOHNSON, DIRK
Racial politics—Chicago's raw nerve. il pors *The New York Times Magazine* p34-8+ F 19 '89
JOHNSON, DON
about
A baby for Don and Melanie [cover story] S. Schindehette. il pors *People Weekly* 31:82-4+ F 27 '89
Cozy again [cover story] J. Ellis. il pors *Life* 12:70-4+ Ap '89
Don Johnson: "Relationships are difficult for me". V. J. Radovsky. il pors *Redbook* 172:24+ Ja '89
It's Miami Nice for Don Johnson and Melanie Griffith. pors *TV Guide* 37:8-9 Ja 28-F 3 '89
Meet the new Patti D'Arbanville, star of Wiseguy and Wired, no longer just Don Johnson's ex. M. Dougherty. il pors *People Weekly* 31:58-60 Ap 3 '89
A rekindled love proves engaging for Don & Melanie. il pors *People Weekly* 31:46 Ja 9 '89
Winners. E. Sharp and L. Rudeen. il por *Motor Boating & Sailing* 163:32 Ja '89
JOHNSON, DON, 1934-
The loneliness of the male body. il *American Health* 8:62-3 Ja/F '89
JOHNSON, DOUGLAS W. J.
Winds of change. bibl il *History Today* 39:3-9 My '89
JOHNSON, EARVIN, 1959-
about
Magic vs Bird: 10 years ago they first met in a memorable NCAA title game. W. Ladson and R. Harper. il pors *Sport (New York, N.Y.)* 80:76-7 Ap '89
Magic's fund-raiser nets a cool $1 million for UNCF. il por *Jet* 76:28-9 S 4 '89
Masters of the '80s [cover story] R. Reilly. il pors *Sports Illustrated* 71:44-9 D 18 '89
The Sport Athlete of the Decade: Magic Johnson. il por *Sport (New York, N.Y.)* 80:96-7 O '89
Who's the best—Bird, Magic or Air Jordan? M. Littwin. il pors *TV Guide* 37:20-1+ F 11-17 '89
JOHNSON, EDWARD CROSBY, III
about
Fidelity fights back [cover story] L. Helm. il pors *Business Week* p68-72 Ap 17 '89
JOHNSON, ERIC G.
about
Divorce triggers change in leadership at JPC. S. Chandler. il pors *Black Enterprise* 20:17 D '89
Johnson Products founder names his son president. por *Jet* 75:52 Ja 16 '89
JOHNSON, F. ROSS
about
Biggest bidders, wildest auction. B. Saporito. il pors *Fortune* 119:34-5 Ja 2 '89
How Ross Johnson blew the buyout. B. Saporito. il por *Fortune* 119:296-8+ Ap 24 '89
'They cleaned our clock' [interview] B. Saporito. il por *Fortune* 119:72-4 Ja 2 '89
JOHNSON, FENTON
High in the hollows. il *The New York Times Magazine* p30+ D 17 '89
How I spent my summer vacation. il *The New York Times Magazine* p22+ O 1 '89
JOHNSON, FRANCES
Collecting butter & cheese making tools. il *Antiques & Collecting Hobbies* 94:46-9 Je '89
The joys of collecting wooden tools. il *Antiques & Collecting Hobbies* 94:59-61 S '89
JOHNSON, GEORGE, 1952-
Two sides to every science story. *The New York Times Book Review* 94:1+ Ap 9 '89
JOHNSON, GEORGE E.
about
George E. Johnson resigns as chair, CEO Johnson Products. il *Jet* 77:14 O 16 '89
Johnson Products founder names his son president. por *Jet* 75:52 Ja 16 '89
JOHNSON, GEORGE L.
about
Crunch time. L. Gite. il pors *Black Enterprise* 20:74-6+ S '89

JOHNSON, GREGORY LEE
about
Unimpressed by the freedom to burn Old Glory, Joey Johnson still wants a revolution. D. Grogan. il pors *People Weekly* 32:98-100 Jl 10 '89
JOHNSON, JED
about
Antiquing with Jed Johnson. S. Stephens. il pors *Architectural Digest* 46:80-8+ Mr '89
JOHNSON, JIMMY
about
Big changes in Big D [cover story] P. Zimmerman. il pors *Sports Illustrated* 70:26-8+ Mr 20 '89
'A chapter closed'. W. O. Johnson. il pors *Sports Illustrated* 70:22-4+ Mr 6 '89
Even Cowboys lovers get the blues. L. Rosellini. il pors *U.S. News & World Report* 107:65-6 S 11 '89
Here today, gone today. R. Reilly. por *Sports Illustrated* 70:102 Mr 27 '89
JOHNSON, JOAN B.
about
Divorce triggers change in leadership at JPC. S. Chandler. il pors *Black Enterprise* 20:17 D '89
JOHNSON, JOAN C.
With a little help from her friends. il *Nation's Business* 77:28 Ja '89
Women managers: a certain style. il *Nation's Business* 77:12 Ap '89
JOHNSON, JOEY See Johnson, Gregory Lee
JOHNSON, JOHN H.
How to get your way [condensed from Succeeding against the odds]; ed. by Lerone Bennett. il *Reader's Digest* 135:19-20+ O '89
The untold story of how publisher made millions with a $500 loan [excerpt from Succeeding against the odds]; ed. by Lerone Bennett. il pors *Ebony* 44:48-50+ Je '89
JOHNSON, JOSEPH B.
Is Proposition 42 racist? il por *Ebony* 44:138+ Je '89
JOHNSON, KAREN, 1940-
about
Moving into senior management. J. Ciabattari. il pors *Working Woman* 14:104-6+ My '89
JOHNSON, KEITH
about
Merchant of Memphis. M. Filler. il por *House & Garden* 161:64+ S '89
JOHNSON, KEVIN, 1966-
about
KJ! R. Reilly. il pors *Sports Illustrated* 70:60+ Ap 24 '89
JOHNSON, KIRK
Doomed to equality. il *The New York Times Magazine* p14+ Je 25 '89
JOHNSON, KRISTINA
Making movie magic. il pors *Harper's Bazaar* 122:126-9 Ag '89
JOHNSON, LADY BIRD, 1912-
Bird of paradise. il por *Ms.* 17:32-3 Ap '89
about
Catching up with the Johnson women. L. Carpenter. il pors *Good Housekeeping* 208:88+ Ja '89
First Lady of wildflowers. E. Henke. il por *Flower and Garden* 33:61 Mr/Ap '89
JOHNSON, LAURA
about
Hamlins' hideaway. J. Grant. il pors *Life* 12:119-20 F '89
JOHNSON, LAWRENCE B.
Laser's new populism. il *Video* 13:79-80+ S '89
Power plays [cover story] il *Video* 13:37-40+ Ag '89
JOHNSON, LINDA
Christians and the coalfield conflict. *The Christian Century* 106:868-9 O 4 '89
JOHNSON, LUCI BAINES
about
Catching up with the Johnson women. L. Carpenter. il pors *Good Housekeeping* 208:88+ Ja '89
JOHNSON, LYNDA BIRD See Robb, Lynda Bird Johnson, 1943-
JOHNSON, LYNDON B. (LYNDON BAINES), 1908-1973
about
The Johnson years: a congressman goes to war. R. A. Caro. por *The New Yorker* 65:62-4+ N 6 '89
The Johnson years: buying and selling. R. A. Caro. *The New Yorker* 65:43-8+ D 18 '89
LBJ's alter ego. G. C. Ward. il *American Heritage* 40:14+ F '89
The prince and his courtiers: at the White House, the Kremlin, and the Reichschancellery. R. Baker and C. Peters. *The Washington Monthly* 21:38+ F '89
A Texas-size L.B.J. obsession. R. Z. Sheppard. il pors *Time* 134:98-9 N 13 '89
The unfinished war (II). N. Lemann. il *The Atlantic* 263:52-6+ Ja '89
Homes
LBJ Ranch: Heart's home [excerpt] R. Houk. il *National Parks* 63:54-5 N/D '89

JOHNSON, MAGIC See Johnson, Earvin, 1959-
JOHNSON, MARK A.
Dusk/dark double exposures. il *Petersen's Photographic Magazine* 18:84-5 Ag '89
JOHNSON, MARY
Enabling act. *The Nation* 249:446 O 23 '89
JOHNSON, MICHAEL P., 1941-
Upward in slavery. il *The New York Review of Books* 36:51-5 D 21 '89
JOHNSON, MYRA LANGLEY
When truth isn't stranger than fiction. *The Writer* 102:26-7 F '89
JOHNSON, NICHOLAS L.
The world's "most active spacefaring nation". il *Ad Astra* 1:8-12 My '89
JOHNSON, ORIEN
How to start a religion. por *The Humanist* 49:16-17+ N/D '89
JOHNSON, PAMELA
Do you know the way to Sante Fe? il *Black Enterprise* 19:335-6+ Je '89
They've gotta have it [cover story; with editorial comment by Earl G. Graves] il *Black Enterprise* 19:7, 36-8+ Jl '89
JOHNSON, PAUL, 1928-
Europe and the Reagan years. *Foreign Affairs* 68 Special Issue:28-38 ['89]
Hemingway: portrait of the artist as an intellectual. *Commentary* 87:49-59 F '89
Paul Johnson [advice to George Bush] *National Review* 41:21 F 10 '89
Remarkable Margaret Thatcher [with interview] il pors *Reader's Digest* 134:70-81 My '89
Richard Nixon [discussion of October 1988 article, In praise of Richard Nixon] *Commentary* 87:6-8+ Mr '89
about
The high priests of knowledge [interview] R. Knight. il por *U.S. News & World Report* 106:73 Mr 27 '89
Minority report. C. Hitchens. *The Nation* 248:474-5 Ap 10 '89
JOHNSON, PHILIP CORTELYOU, 1906-
about
House sale. *The New Yorker* 65:29-30 My 29 '89
JOHNSON, PHILLIP
Jewels in the concrete jungle. il *National Wildlife* 27:30-5 Ag/S '89
JOHNSON, R. M., AND OTHERS
Fibroblasts transformed with v-*src* show enhanced formation of an inositol tetrakisphosphate. bibl f il *Science* 246:121-4 O 6 '89
JOHNSON, R. W. (RICHARD WILLIAM)
The Revolution is finally over. il *World Press Review* 36:22-3 Je '89
JOHNSON, RACHEL, 1965-
Falling in line with the British. il *World Press Review* 36:71 D '89
JOHNSON, RALPH P.
about
Obituary
Physics Today il por 42:108+ Je '89. D. B. Langmuir and others
JOHNSON, RANDALL S., AND OTHERS
Targeting of nonexpressed genes in embryonic stem cells via homologous recombination. bibl f il *Science* 245:1234-6 S 15 '89
JOHNSON, RANDY
about
Not just a tall tale. H. Hersch. il pors *Sports Illustrated* 70:42-4+ Mr 20 '89
JOHNSON, RHETA GRIMSLEY, 1953-
about
It's a biography, Charlie Brown!!! J. Crichton. il por *Publishers Weekly* 236:57-8 Ag 4 '89
JOHNSON, RICHARD WILLIAM See Johnson, R. W. (Richard William)
JOHNSON, ROBERT, 1948-
'This man has expired': witness to an execution [cover story] il *Commonweal* 116:9-15 Ja 13 '89
JOHNSON, ROBERT H.
Playing to the home crowd. il *The Bulletin of the Atomic Scientists* 45:24-8 Ja/F '89
JOHNSON, ROBERT LOUIS
about
BET faces music, comes up with talk. K. Beck. por *Channels (New York, N.Y.: 1986)* 9:58-60 Je '89
JOHNSON, ROBERT T., 1948-
about
The new DA in town. K. Osborne. por *Black Enterprise* 19:16 Ja '89
JOHNSON, ROY S.
Hazard to your health. por *Sports Illustrated* 70:77 F 27 '89
about
From the publisher. D. J. Barr. il por *Sports Illustrated* 71:4 N 20 '89
JOHNSON, S. LEWIS, JR.
How faith works. il *Christianity Today* 33:21-5 S 22 '89

JOHNSON, SAM, AND MARCIL, CHRIS
Filofaxed to the max. *Mademoiselle* 95:133+ Jl '89
JOHNSON, SANDRA H.
I wondered if I would pass the test. il *Commonweal* 116:208-10 Ap 7 '89
JOHNSON, SHARON D.
Destruction of a nation [poem] *Essence* 19:128 Ap '89
JOHNSON, STEVE
Bonk. *Bicycling* 30:48 S '89
Cross-training. il *Bicycling* 30:84+ D '89
Interval training. *Bicycling* 30:136-7 My '89
Lactic acid. *Bicycling* 30:60 Ag '89
Road rash. *Bicycling* 30:134 Je '89
Saddle sores. il *Bicycling* 30:74 O/N '89
Target heart rate. il *Bicycling* 30:81 Jl '89
VO₂ max. *Bicycling* 30:130 Ja/F '89
JOHNSON, STEVE
about
Rushdie furor highlights the nature of Islamic faith [interview] il pors *Christianity Today* 33:38-9 Ap 7 '89
JOHNSON, THOMAS
Caviar wishes and vodka dreams [tr. by Betsy Wing] il *Rolling Stone* p47+ Ap 6 '89
JOHNSON, TREVE
Farming sea-ears. bibl il *Sea Frontiers* 35:232-7 Jl/Ag '89
JOHNSON, VANCE
about
Dancescape. H. Ostlere. por *Dance Magazine* 63:9 Ag '89
JOHNSON, WAYNE
Hippies, Indians, buffalo [story] il *The Atlantic* 264:80-2 S '89
JOHNSON, WILLIAM OSCAR
'A chapter closed'. il pors *Sports Illustrated* 70:22-4+ Mr 6 '89
A flight so fancy. il pors *Sports Illustrated* 70:14-21 F 13 '89
In the swim. il *Sports Illustrated* 70 Special Issue:20-4+ F '89
Mountain melodrama. il *Sports Illustrated* 70:32-5 F 20 '89
A vision fulfilled. il pors *Sports Illustrated* 70:70-4+ Ja 30 '89
JOHNSON, WILLIAM OSCAR, AND VERSCHOTH, ANITA
Leap to the West. il pors *Sports Illustrated* 71:40-1 D 11 '89
Out of the shadows. il *Sports Illustrated* 71:16-21 N 27 '89
JOHNSON, WILLIAM WEBER, 1909-
The exhilaration and exaltation of painting the sky [cover story] bibl (p163-4) il *Smithsonian* 20:64-70+ My '89
JOHNSON (BARBARA PIASECKA)-GDAŃSK SHIPYARD COMPANY *See* Barbara Piasecka Johnson-Gdańsk Shipyard Company
JOHNSON (HOWARD) CO. *See* Howard Johnson Co.
JOHNSON (LYNDON B.) NATIONAL HISTORICAL PARK (TEX.) *See* Lyndon B. Johnson National Historical Park (Tex.)
JOHNSON & JOHNSON
Going over the lab wall in search of new ideas. J. Weber, Jr. il *Business Week* Special Issue:132 Je 16 '89
What's behind J&J's odd climb. G. G. Marcial. *Business Week* p84 Je 19 '89
JOHNSON CONTROLS INC.
Bias or safety? [appeals court upholds ban excluding women of childbearing age from hazardous jobs] *Time* 134:61 O 16 '89
Damn the analysts, full speed ahead. A. A. Lappen. il *Forbes* 143:171+ Mr 20 '89
JOHNSON PRODUCTS COMPANY, INC.
Divorce triggers change in leadership at JPC. S. Chandler. il pors *Black Enterprise* 20:17 D '89
George E. Johnson resigns as chair, CEO Johnson Products. il *Jet* 77:14 O 16 '89
Johnson Products founder names his son president. por *Jet* 75:52 Ja 16 '89
JOHNSON PUBLISHING COMPANY, INC.
How to get your way [condensed from Succeeding against the odds]; ed. by Lerone Bennett. J. H. Johnson. il *Reader's Digest* 135:19-20+ O '89
Johnson Publishing wins top honors at CEBA Awards. il *Jet* 77:54-5 D 11 '89
JPC hosts inaugural parade party, guests enjoy food, chit chat. il *Jet* 75:6-7+ F 6 '89
The untold story of how publisher made millions with a $500 loan [excerpt from Succeeding against the odds]; ed. by Lerone Bennett. J. H. Johnson. il pors *Ebony* 44:48-50+ Je '89
JOHNSON SPACE CENTER *See* Lyndon B. Johnson Space Center
JOHNSON WORLDWIDE ASSOCIATES, INC.
The great outdoors. T. Jaffe. *Forbes* 143:188-9 Ap 3 '89
JOHNSTON, DAVID L.
The need to retool vocational education. *The Education Digest* 55:38-9 N '89
JOHNSTON, EDDIE
about
Pittsburgh scores. T. Frayne. il por *Maclean's* 102:58-9 My 1 '89

JOHNSTON, GENE
Gene Johnston. See issues of Successful Farming beginning March 1989
JOHNSTON, JEROME
(jt. auth) See Luker, Richard, and Johnston, Jerome
JOHNSTON, JILL
A Fluxus funeral. il pors *Art in America* 77:42-3+ Mr '89
Painting Charleston. bibl f il pors *Art in America* 77:152-63+ D '89
JOHNSTON, JOE
about
Honey, I shrunk the kids [film] Reviews
People Weekly il 32:13 Jl 10 '89. R. Novak
JOHNSTONE, BOB
Fading miracle. *World Press Review* 36:48 Mr '89
JOHNSTONE, DIANA
Converts to conversion. il *The Progressive* 53:14-15 O '89
Europe's Green light. il *The Progressive* 53:12-13 Jl '89
The war inside NATO. il *The Progressive* 53:16-18 Ap '89
JOHNSTONE, JOHN W., JR.
The war on drugs: saying 'yes' to getting involved [address, December 1, 1988] *Vital Speeches of the Day* 55:325-7 Mr 15 '89
JOHNSTOWN (PA.)
Description
A town rises from the depths. S. Brewer. il *New Choices for the Best Years* 29:11 Ag '89
Flood, 1889
After the flood. D. G. Kinney. il *Life* 12:144-6+ My '89
The day the dam broke. il map *Reader's Digest* 134:193-6+ My '89
Elsie Frum remembers a train's desperate whistle 100 years ago—and the great Johnstown flood. B. Johnson. il pors *People Weekly* 31:85-8 Je 5 '89
A hundred years after the flood. A. Zintl. il *Americana* 17:8 My/Je '89
Johnstown flood. D. M. Ludlum. *Country Journal* 16:18-19 My/Je '89
The Johnstown flood. D. M. Ludlum. il *Weatherwise* 42:88-92 Ap '89
The Johnstown flood. E. Oxford. il *American History Illustrated* 24:12-25 My '89
Johnstown flood centennial. il *American History Illustrated* 24:9 My '89
A town rises from the depths. S. Brewer. il *New Choices for the Best Years* 29:11 Ag '89
When 20 million tons of water flooded Johnstown. D. D. Jackson. bibl (p163) il *Smithsonian* 20:50-4+ My '89
JOINERY *See* Joints (Carpentry)
JOINT BANK ACCOUNTS *See* Bank accounts—Joint accounts
JOINT CENTER FOR POLITICAL STUDIES (U.S.)
Joint Center holds 12th annual dinner, raises record total $550,000. il *Jet* 75:8 Mr 27 '89
JOINT CHIEFS OF STAFF (U.S.) *See* United States. Joint Chiefs of Staff
JOINT CUSTODY OF CHILDREN *See* Custody of children
JOINT EUROPEAN SUBMICRON SILICON PROJECT *See* JESSI Project
JOINT OBSERVATORY FOR COMETARY RESEARCH
An uphill battle for comet research. L. A. Shore. il *Astronomy* 17:46-50 F '89
JOINT OWNERSHIP
See also
Condominiums
Major mergers. G. W. Weinstein. il *Ms.* 17:68+ My '89
JOINT TENANCY *See* Joint ownership
JOINT VENTURES
Aeroflot pursues leases for five A310s, signs CRS and hotel pacts. J. T. McKenna. *Aviation Week & Space Technology* 131:55 O 30 '89
Aeroflot takes off for joint-ventureland. R. Brady and others. il *Business Week* p48-9 O 30 '89
Breakthrough [American Trade Consortium agreement with the Soviet government] *The New Yorker* 65:30-1 Ap 17 '89
Capitalists are bullish on the Bear. il *U.S. News & World Report* 107:15+ D 11 '89
Cold feet in Siberia [joint venture petrochemical projects] P. Galuszka. il *Business Week* p48 Mr 27 '89
The deal of the decade may get done in Moscow [American Trade Consortium] P. Galuszka and R. Brady. il *Business Week* p54-5 F 27 '89
High risks, distant payoffs [ventures with the Soviet Union] E. Dyson. il *Forbes* 144:114-16+ D 11 '89
Joint misadventures [ventures with U.S. businesses] J. Castro. il *Time* 133:84 Ap 10 '89
Joint ventures with the EC. S. Y. Chow. il *High Technology Business* 9:10 Jl/Ag '89
Moscow tackles its manager gap [Higher Commercial Management School created in wake of proliferating joint ventures] J. Trimble. il *U.S. News & World Report* 107:40+ Jl 31 '89
Perestroika payoff [U.S.-Soviet joint venture consultant A. Hartman] R. T. Grieves. il por *Forbes* 143:102 Ja 23 '89
Soviet adventures in capitalism. *World Press Review* 36:51 Ja '89

JOINT VENTURES—cont.
Top U.S. companies move into Russia. L. Kraar. il *Fortune* 120:165-6+ Jl 31 '89
U.S. and Soviets sign 'unique' accord [scientists may initiate joint ventures] *Science News* 135:62 Ja 28 '89
Where Adam Smith meets Karl Marx [foreign investment in Hungary] A. Gabor. il *U.S. News & World Report* 107:36 S 18 '89
Your rivals can be your allies [joint ventures with foreign competitors] L. Kraar. il map *Fortune* 119:66-8+ Mr 27 '89

JOINTERS (WOODWORKING MACHINERY)
Getting straight edges on a jointer. R. J. DeCristoforo. il *Workbench* 45:52-3 Jl/Ag '89
New wave in joining tools [Tru-Match] A. J. Hand. il *Popular Science* 234:140 Je '89
Plate joiner [Sears kit] S. Willson. il *Popular Mechanics* 166:98 S '89
Shopsmith hits the mark [add-on biscuit joiner and strip sander] J. Truini. il *Popular Mechanics* 166:64 Ap '89

JOINTS
      See also
  Hip joint
  Knee
  Wrist
                    Diseases
      See also
  Arthritis
                    Dislocation
      See Dislocations
JOINTS, ARTIFICIAL
      See also
  Hip joint, Artificial
Asbestos again? [cobalt chrome artificial joints may cause bone cancer] L. Scheer. il *Forbes* 143:162+ Je 12 '89
JOINTS (CARPENTRY)
Dovetail joinery. J. Vara. il *Country Journal* 16:92-4 Mr/Ap '89
Dovetails. R. Capotosto. il *Popular Mechanics* 166:87-90+ N '89
How to join wood with dowels. B. Kinghorn. il *The Family Handyman* 39:6+ N/D '89
Joinery and shaping. R. Capotosto. il *Popular Mechanics* 166:81-2+ N '89
Joining landscape timbers. M. Landis and R. N. Hoffman. il *Workbench* 45:49 My/Je '89
Mortising hinges. H. Wicks. il *Home Mechanix* 86:24+ Ap '89
Repairing pegged furniture. M. Varese. il *Workbench* 45:10-11 S/O '89
Routing hinge mortises. T. H. Jones. il *Home Mechanix* 85:29-30 O '89
JOINTS (ENGINEERING)
      See also
  Fasteners
JOKES *See* Humor
JOKES, PRACTICAL *See* Practical jokes
JOLIS, ALAN
City on the verge of a nervous breakdown? il *Vogue* 179:120+ Jl '89
Girls' night out. il *Vogue* 179:406-11 N '89
JOLL, JAMES
No man's land. il *The New York Review of Books* 36:53-6 Ap 27 '89
JOLLEY, ELIZABETH, 1923-
              about
PW interviews. A. Smith. il por *Publishers Weekly* 235:115-16 Ap 7 '89
JOLLEY, VON D.
(jt. auth) *See* Brown, John C., and Jolley, Von D.
JOLLY, WILLIAM L.
Print solarization. il *Petersen's Photographic Magazine* 17:28-33 F '89
JOLO (W. VA.)
          Religious institutions and affairs
Courting death, Appalachia's old-time religionists praise the Lord and pass the snakes [snake handlers] D. Grogan. il pors *People Weekly* 31:79+ My 1 '89
JOMBO, AUGUSTIN B.
              about
Nigerian student can afford family reunion after winning $26 million in N.Y. lotto. *Jet* 75:33 Ja 30 '89
JONAS, GERALD, 1935-
Science fiction. il *The New York Times Book Review* 94:24 Ag 20 '89
Science fiction. il *The New York Times Book Review* 94:32 F 26 '89
Science fiction. il *The New York Times Book Review* 94:40 O 1 '89
Science fiction. il *The New York Times Book Review* 94:4 D 31 '89
Science fiction. *The New York Times Book Review* 94:26 My 21 '89
Science fiction. *The New York Times Book Review* 94:31 Ja 8 '89
Science fiction. il *The New York Times Book Review* 94:38 Ap 9 '89

JONES, ALAN H., AND KOLAR, MARK D.
Readers comment on education. *The Education Digest* 55:40-1 S '89
JONES, ANN
              about
Foreigner affair. W. P. Rayner. il pors *House & Garden* 161:72+ O '89
JONES, BEN
              about
Capitol hillbilly. M. Newman. *The New Republic* 200:13-15 F 6 '89
Mr. Jones goes to D.C. G. Jaynes. il *Life* 12:19 My '89
En route to Congress, actor Ben Jones first beat the bottle, then the incumbent. M. Brower. il pors *People Weekly* 31:38-40 Ja 30 '89
JONES, BILL T.
              about
Bill T. Jones choreographs an anguished tribute to his late partner, a victim of AIDS. M. Small. il pors *People Weekly* 32:44-6 Jl 31 '89
JONES, BRIAN
The legacy of Edwin Hubble. il pors *Astronomy* 17:38-44 D '89
JONES, CARL
Parents and kids: the ESP connection. *McCall's* 116:64+ My '89
JONES, CHARLES, 1932-
Savannah rising [poem] *Wilderness* 53:71 Fall '89
JONES, CHESTER
The House of Lancaster [excerpt from Colefax & Fowler] il pors *House & Garden* 161:188-95+ N '89
JONES, CHRISTINA HAATAINEN
              about
Around the world in 80 days—and 165 masks. L. Stevens. il *Theatre Crafts* 23:56-7+ Ap '89
JONES, CHUCK, 1912-
132 takes/th-th-that's all folks. il por *Film Comment* 25:2-3 Mr/Ap '89
              about
Chuck Jones. P. Brock. il pors *People Weekly* 32:103+ N 13 '89
JONES, CLEVE
              about
And sew it goes. D. Bellm. por *Mother Jones* 14:34-5 Ja '89
JONES, CONNIE HOFFERBER
Fossils of Clarno Basin. il *Earth Science* 42:21-3 Spr '89
JONES, DARRYL
              about
Black elected FOP prexy in Prince Georges County. por *Jet* 77:14 D 25 '89-Ja 1 '90
JONES, DAVID A.
              about
Humana regains that healthy glow. S. Phillips. il *Business Week* p127-8 My 22 '89
"We're the low-cost producer". J. Cook. il por *Forbes* 144:65-6 D 25 '89
JONES, DAVID C.
Romantics, radicals and realists [address, April 10, 1989] *Vital Speeches of the Day* 55:750-5 O 1 '89
JONES, DAVID HUGH, 1934-
              about
Jacknife [film] Reviews
  Maclean's 102:41 Ap 10 '89. B. D. Johnson
  The New Republic 200:24 Mr 6 '89. S. Kauffmann
  People Weekly 31:17 Ap 3 '89. R. Novak
JONES, DAVID PRYCE- *See* Pryce-Jones, David
JONES, DAVID T., AND REED, RANDALL R.
G$_{olf}$: an olfactory neuron specific-G protein involved in odorant signal transduction. bibl f il *Science* 244:790-5 My 19 '89
JONES, DOUGLAS P.
Masi 3V Volumetrica. il por *Bicycling* 30:68-9 Ja/F '89
JONES, E. FAY *See* Jones, Fay, 1921-
JONES, ERNEST, 1879-1958
              about
Free associations. M. Jones. *Society* 27:81-6 N/D '89
JONES, EVAN, 1915-
Christmas in Provence. il *Gourmet* 49:108-9+ D '89
JONES, FAY, 1921-
              about
In the Wright tradition. P. Langdon. il *The Atlantic* 263:83-7 Ap '89
JONES, INIGO, 1573-1652
              about
The brio of a great all-rounder. R. Hughes. il *Time* 133:125 My 22 '89
JONES, IRIS SANDERSON
Yugoslavia's bold coast. il map *Oceans* 22:10-17+ Mr/Ap '89
JONES, JAMES, 1921-1977
A hunger to write [excerpts from To reach eternity] il por *The New York Times Magazine* p28+ Mr 5 '89
              about
A literary friendship. W. Styron. il pors *Esquire* 111:154-8+ Ap '89

JONES, JAMES T., IV
  Betty Carter: look what we've got! il pors *Down Beat* 56:24-6 Ag '89
JONES, JERRAL
  about
  As thousands cheer. M. Ivins. il *The Progressive* 53:35 Ag '89
  'A chapter closed'. W. O. Johnson. il pors *Sports Illustrated* 70:22-4+ Mr 6 '89
  Even Cowboys lovers get the blues. L. Rosellini. il pors *U.S. News & World Report* 107:65-6 S 11 '89
  Hold the tortillas! The Cowboys are in good hands. R. Galloway. il *Sport (New York, N.Y.)* 80:63 Ag '89
  Jerry Jones: the man who fired Tom Landry. K. Kelly. il por *Business Week* p148 Ap 24 '89
JONES, JONATHAN D. G., AND OTHERS
  Visual detection of transposition of the maize element Activator (Ac) in tobacco seedlings. bibl f il *Science* 244:204-7 Ap 14 '89
JONES, JUDY
  Give your lips a lift. il *Redbook* 172:100-3 F '89
  Hayley Mills—a healthy attitude. il pors *Redbook* 172:12+ F '89
  Look who's looking good [special section] il *Redbook* 172:85-91 Ja '89
JONES, KIKI
  about
  On deck. il por *Sport (New York, N.Y.)* 80:38 Je '89
JONES, KIRK BYRON
  The activism of interpretation: black pastors and public life. *The Christian Century* 106:817-18 S 13-20 '89
JONES, LAFAYETTE
  about
  Lafayette Jones forms new company. por *Jet* 75:14 Ja 23 '89
JONES, LANDON Y., 1943-
  Editor's notes. See issues of Money beginning June 1986
JONES, LAWLEY PAISLEY- *See* Paisley-Jones, Lawley
JONES, LUCILE M.
  (jt. auth) See Reasenberg, Paul A., and Jones, Lucile M.
JONES, MARGARET
  Capability's cultivates a gardening clientele. il *Publishers Weekly* 235:42-4 F 10 '89
  A Change of Hobbit changes its digs once again. il por *Publishers Weekly* 235:34-6 Je 23 '89
  The changing style in cookbooks. il *Publishers Weekly* 236:15-16+ S 8 '89
  'Convergence' at the bookstore. il *Publishers Weekly* 236:32-4 N 3 '89
  Getting them out: distribution, how it's done, and how it's doing. il *Publishers Weekly* 235:S22+ My 26 '89
  The light of the Midnight Special. il *Publishers Weekly* 236:50-2 N 24 '89
  New Age on the brink. il *Publishers Weekly* 236:14-16+ N 3 '89
  Scaling the small press hurdle: getting titles onto the shelves. il *Publishers Weekly* 235:37-41 Ap 14 '89
  Shelf-awareness: getting a fix on fixtures. il *Publishers Weekly* 236:18+ Jl 21 '89
  The smart moves of Los Llanos Bookstore. il por *Publishers Weekly* 236:425-6+ Ag 11 '89
  Sorting out the strata. il *Publishers Weekly* 236:20+ N 3 '89
JONES, MERVYN
  Free associations. *Society* 27:81-6 N/D '89
JONES, MICHAEL
  Philippe de Commynes: a courtly middle-man. bibl il *History Today* 39:34-41 Mr '89
JONES, MICHAEL CATON- *See* Caton-Jones, Michael
JONES, MICK, 1944-
  about
  Foreigner affair. W. P. Rayner. il pors *House & Garden* 161:72+ O '89
  A Foreigner takes his solo sojourn. S. Rogers. por *Rolling Stone* p32 S 21 '89
JONES, MICK, 1956-
  about
  Back from the brink of death, former Clash rocker Mick Jones is reborn as the man from B.A.D. S. Dougherty. il pors *People Weekly* 32:99-100 N 20 '89
JONES, MONA
  Being the mother of a black child [poem] *Essence* 19:127 Ja '89
JONES, OWEN T., AND OTHERS
  Localization and mobility of ω-conotoxin-sensitive Ca^{2+} channels in hippocampal CA1 neurons. bibl f il *Science* 244:1189-93 Je 9 '89
JONES, P. M.
  The peasants' revolt? bibl il *History Today* 39:15-19 My '89
JONES, PAM L.
  The backcountry back lot. il *Sierra* 74:115-16 N/D '89
JONES, PAT
  Scoping the solar system. il *Ad Astra* 1:14-18 Mr '89
JONES, PATTI
  Living without health insurance. il *Glamour* 87:158+ Ap '89

JONES, PEARL WILLIAMS- *See* Williams-Jones, Pearl
JONES, PEGGY
  about
  Self-publishers print 100,000 copies (and survive!). J. Barbato. *Publishers Weekly* 236:42 N 10 '89
JONES, RALPH
  about
  Greenwich time [cover story] P. Green. il *House & Garden* 161:120-7 N '89
JONES, RICKIE LEE
  about
  Music and mothering. D. DeNicolo; E. Zimmerman. il pors *Glamour* 87:178 N '89
  Rickie Lee Jones. D. Gates. por *Newsweek* 114:64 O 16 '89
  She's back. J. Cocks. por *Time* 134:110 O 23 '89
JONES, ROBERT, 1934-
  Owl flight [poem] *America* 161:160 S 23 '89
JONES, ROBERT F.
  Man's best friends. il por map *Sports Illustrated* 70:40-2+ Mr 27 '89
JONES, ROBERT TRENT, 1906-
  about
  West meets East. il pors *Esquire* 111:62-5 Ja '89
JONES, RODNEY, 1950-
  In manufacturing [poem] *The Atlantic* 263:64 Mr '89
JONES, ROSIE
  about
  Innerviews. L. Rothlein. il por *Women's Sports & Fitness* 11:51 Ja/F '89
JONES, ROY
  about
  The last Olympian. C. Gammon. il pors *Sports Illustrated* 70:42-4+ My 15 '89
JONES, RUSSELL, 1944-
  Last word [excerpt from The eat a pet cookbook] por *Omni (New York, N.Y.)* 12:128 N '89
JONES, S. GUERNSEY
  A layman's liberal theology [address, November 16, 1988] *Vital Speeches of the Day* 55:253-6 F 1 '89
JONES, SIMON
  Chinese export porcelain. il *Antiques & Collecting Hobbies* 94:26-8+ Jl '89
JONES, STANTON L.
  Homosexuality according to science. il *Christianity Today* 33:26-9 Ag 18 '89
JONES, STEPHEN
  Communism's restless tribes. *World Press Review* 36:12-13 Je '89
JONES, STEPHEN, 1954-
  Lord Leighton's palace of art. il por *Antiques* 135:1466-75 Je '89
JONES, STEVE
  about
  No keeping up with Jones. J. Diaz. il por *Sports Illustrated* 70:34-5 Ja 16 '89
JONES, STEVEN E.
  about
  A cold-fusion pioneer who kept his cool. W. C. Symonds. il por *Business Week* Special Issue:92 Je 16 '89
  Will this tortoise beat the hares? J. Carey and W. C. Symonds. il por *Business Week* p103 My 8 '89
JONES, STORMIE
  about
  A hero of her time. S. Christenson. il por *American Health* 8:90 Je '89
JONES, TERRY, 1942-
  about
  Erik the Viking [film] Reviews
  People Weekly il 32:27+ N 20 '89. R. Novak
JONES, TOD E.
  A humanistic approach toward religionists. *The Humanist* 49:25+ Ja/F '89
JONES, TOMMY LEE
  about
  Star Robert Duvall says: it's going to be like a western Godfather. L. D. Estleman. il pors *TV Guide* 36:14-16+ F 4-10 '89
JONES, WADE HAMPTON
  How to find the perfect doctor . . . bibl il *Modern Maturity* 32:72-4+ Ag/S '89
JONES (BILL T.)/ARNIE ZANE & COMPANY *See* Bill T. Jones/Arnie Zane & Company
JONES TRANSFER CO.
  Wheels of fortune. M. E. Williams. il por *Black Enterprise* 20:100-2+ O '89
JONG, ERICA
  Ziplash: a sexual libertine recants. por *Ms.* 17:49 My '89
  about
  Literary lights. il pors *Harper's Bazaar* 122:58+ Ag '89
JONSON, RAYMOND, 1891-1982
  about
  A modernist surprise. B. B. Stretch. il *Art News* 88:45-6 N '89
JOPLIN, JANIS, 1943-1970
  about
  The uninhibited Janis Joplin [interview; reprint] M. Wolf. il por *Down Beat* 56:65-6 S '89

JORDACHE ENTERPRISES INC.
A 'blood war' in the jeans trade [Jordache-Guess battle] C. Welles. il *Business Week* p74-5+ N 13 '89
The great jeans war [Guess? vs. Jordache] C. Byron. il *New York* 22:13-14 Jl 24 '89
The IRS follies [IRS embroiled in jeans war between Nakash family of Jordache and Marciano family of Guess?] C. Byron. il *New York* 22:11-12 Ag 7 '89

JORDAN, CHUCK
about
Choosing sides. H. Hersch. il pors *Sports Illustrated* 71:42-4+ N 27 '89

JORDAN, DAVID
Editor's letter. See issues of Better Homes and Gardens beginning November 1984

JORDAN, DEANE
Spark up your car collection. il *Popular Mechanics* 166:46 D '89

JORDAN, EILEEN HERBERT
An affair of the hat [story] il *Modern Maturity* 32:46-9+ F/Mr '89

JORDAN, HAMILTON
ATP directive: all systems go. il por *World Tennis* 36:106 My '89

JORDAN, I. KING
about
The bold ones. S. Brewer. il pors *New Choices for the Best Years* 29:37-41 Jl '89
The revolution at Gallaudet. H. Orlans. il pors *Change* 21:8-18 Ja/F '89

JORDAN, JEFFREY
about
Taking charge [cover story] K. D. Thompson and others. il pors *Black Enterprise* 20:42-4+ Ag '89

JORDAN, JOHN PATRICK
President's remarks to the AIBS council. *BioScience* 39:558-9 S '89

JORDAN, JUNE, 1936-
For my brother [poem] *Essence* 20:107 N '89
Just inside the door. See issues of The Progressive beginning February 1989
Solidarity [poem] *The Progressive* 53:18 Je '89
Something like a sonnet for Phillis Miracle Wheatley [poem] *Essence* 20:112 D '89

JORDAN, MARK
about
Designer genes. M. Beauchamp. il por *Forbes* 144:248 O 2 '89

JORDAN, MICHAEL
about
An air of superstardom. C. Leerhsen. il pors *Newsweek* 113:58-60 My 29 '89
Great leapin' lizards! S. B. Donnelly. il por *Time* 133:50-2 Ja 9 '89
The greatest of them all. T. Callahan. il pors *Newsweek* 114:80-1 D 4 '89
Horns of a dilemma. J. McCallum. il pors *Sports Illustrated* 70:34-7 Mr 13 '89
Jordan denies any role in Bulls' coach firing. il pors *Jet* 76:46 Jl 24 '89
Michael Jordan, in his own orbit [cover story] D. Breskin. il pors *Gentlemen's Quarterly* 59:318-23+ Mr '89
Michael Jordan launches project to help students in black colleges. il pors *Jet* 76:22-5 Ag 14 '89
Michael Jordan leaps to success [cover story] L. Ransom. il pors *Jet* 76:52-4 Je 12 '89
Michael Jordan marries mother of his toddler. il pors *Jet* 76:52-3 S 25 '89
Michael Jordan takes a bride: Juanita Vanoy [cover story] il pors *Jet* 77:58-60 O 9 '89
Mission impossible [cover story] J. McCallum. il pors *Sports Illustrated* 71:44-8+ N 6 '89
Sink, blast you! [cover story] E. M. Swift. il pors *Sports Illustrated* 71:36-9 Ag 14 '89
'Un-fath-om-able' [cover story] J. McCallum. il pors *Sports Illustrated* 70:26-8+ My 15 '89
Who's the best—Bird, Magic or Air Jordan? M. Littwin. il pors *TV Guide* 37:20-1+ F 11-17 '89

JORDAN, NEIL, 1951-
about
High spirits [film] Reviews
Video il 13:63 Jl '89. J. Walker
We're no angels [film] Reviews
Newsweek 114:74 D 25 '89. D. Ansen

JORDAN, PAT
Burt Reynolds on the skids . . . will B. L. Stryker be his deliverance? il pors *TV Guide* 37:26-9 Mr 4-10 '89
War of the Roses. il pors *Gentlemen's Quarterly* 59:274-9+ Ap '89

JORDAN, RICHARD
about
Courtroom chaos. M. Clark. il por *Maclean's* 102:20 N 20 '89

JORDAN, ROSA
The end of a war beginning. il *The Progressive* 53:29-31 O '89
Innocent abroad. il *The Progressive* 53:46 Ag '89

JORDAN, SUSAN
'I refused to be a victim to cancer'. il por *New Choices for the Best Years* 29:16+ Ap '89

JORDAN, VERNON
Passages: 1989-2000 [address, January 30, 1989] *Vital Speeches of the Day* 55:406-8 Ap 15 '89

JORDAN, WILLIAM H., JR.
They move, they roar: dinosaurs are here once more. il *Smithsonian* 20:46-52+ Ag '89

JORDAN
Antiquities
See also
Petra (Ancient city)
Commerce
Great Britain
See Great Britain—Commerce—Jordan
Defenses
See also
Airplanes, Military—Jordan
Description and travel
Blazing sandals. T. Young. il *Vogue* 179:250+ F '89
Foreign relations
Middle East
In search of peace [interview with Queen Noor of Jordan] J. Howse. il por *Maclean's* 102:48 O 30 '89
Jordan/Palestine [discussion of October 1988 article, Is Jordan Palestine?] D. Pipes and A. M. Garfinkle. *Commentary* 87:2+ F '89
Jordan and reverberations of the uprising. R. Satloff. bibl f *Current History* 88:85-8+ F '89
The Middle East [address, April 22, 1989] King Hussein. *Vital Speeches of the Day* 55:486-7 Je 1 '89
Israeli occupation, 1967-
See Israel-Arab Wars, 1967- —Territorial questions
Kings and rulers
See also
Hussein, King of Jordan, 1935-
Politics and government
See also
Elections—Jordan
Getting the royal flush [Hussein forces Prime Minister Zaid Rifai to resign in wake of unrest] *Time* 133:45 My 8 '89
Religious institutions and affairs
See also
Muslims—Jordan

JORY, DARRYL E.
(jt. auth) See Iversen, Edwin S., and Jory, Darryl E.

JOSELIT, DAVID
Lessons in public sculpture [cover story] il *Art in America* 77:130-5 D '89
Living on the border. bibl f il *Art in America* 77:120-9 D '89

JOSEPH, FREDERICK H.
about
Can Fred Joseph save Drexel? M. J. Williams. il por *Fortune* 119:89-90+ My 8 '89
'I woke up with my stomach churning'. C. Leinster. il pors *Fortune* 120:120-2 Jl 3 '89

JOSEPH, JOHN B.
about
The Ron and John show. R. King. il pors *Forbes* 143:103+ Je 26 '89

JOSEPH CERNIGLIA WINERY INC.
Trading the Big Apple for an orchard. R. Duffy. il por *Business Week* p91 Je 26 '89

JOSEPH LITTLEJOHN & LEVY
ESOP fable. T. Pouschine. il *Forbes* 143:98+ Je 26 '89

JOSEPHINE, EMPRESS, CONSORT OF NAPOLEON I, EMPEROR OF THE FRENCH, 1763-1814
about
Liberty, equality, absurdity. R. Darnton. il *The New Republic* 200:29-32 Ap 3 '89

JOSEPHS, LARRY
Fighting AIDS all the way. il *The New York Times Magazine* p42+ O 8 '89

JOSEPH'S (FIRM)
Down East chic. C. Hacinli. il *Gentlemen's Quarterly* 59:114+ S '89

JOSEPHSON EFFECT
New measurement standards for 1990 [cover story] B. N. Taylor. bibl f il *Physics Today* 42 pt1:23-6 Ag '89

JOST, JON
End of the indies. il *Film Comment* 25:42-5 Ja/F '89

JOUBERT, CURTIS
about
From offices of excellence. D. Young. il pors *Southern Living* 24:142+ Ap '89

JOUJOUKA (MOROCCO) See Jahjouka (Morocco)

THE JOURNAL [television program] See Television program reviews—Single works

JOURNAL GRAPHICS INC.
If you missed what they said, contact Jim Smith. P. Finch. il por *Business Week* p89 Mr 13 '89

JOURNAL OF THE AMERICAN MEDICAL ASSOCIATION
"It's over, Debbie" [account of mercy killing] L. Oliwenstein. il *Discover* 10:80-1 Ja '89

JOURNALISM
    See also
      Cable television—News
      Celebrities—Press relations
      College and school journalism
      Computers—Journalistic use
      Crime and the press
      Editors and editing
      Environmental news
      Foreign news
      Freedom of the press
      Government and the press
      Interviewing
      Journalistic ethics
      Libel and slander
      Media guide
      News
      Newsletters
      Newspaper and periodical libraries
      Newspapers
      Periodical articles
      Periodicals
      Press
      Race relations and the press
      Radio broadcasting—News
      Reporters and reporting
      Sports journalism
      Television broadcasting—News
      Terrorism and the press
        Awards
    See also
      Alternative Press Awards
      Lawrence R. Klein Award
      Pulitzer prizes
        History
George Seldes, grandfather of the alternative press. J. Wall-jasper. il por *Utne Reader* p142-3 Jl/Ag '89
        Scholarships and fellowships
    See also
      Nieman Fellowships
        Study and teaching
    See also
      Columbia University. Graduate School of Journalism
      Scripps School of Journalism
English and journalism: reaching the same goal [high school instruction] C. Witt. *The Education Digest* 55:51-3 N '89
From here to here [address, September 6, 1988] J. Konner. *Vital Speeches of the Day* 55:238-41 F 1 '89
        Algeria
    See also
      Movement of Algerian Journalists
        Asia
Environmental journalism: guardian of the Asian commons [cover story] S. M. Friedman and K. A. Friedman. bibl f il *Environment* 31:6-9+ Je '89
        Canada
Media watch. G. Bain. See occasional issues of Maclean's
        United States
    See Journalism
JOURNALISM, AMATEUR
        History
Desk-top publishing [after Civil War] P. E. Petrik. bibl il *History Today* 39:12-26 O '89
JOURNALISM, AUTOMOTIVE
      Anecdotes, facetiae, satire, etc.
The auto journalist acid test. J. R. Nerad. il *Motor Trend* 41:14-15 Mr '89
JOURNALISM, COMMERCIAL
America's no. 1 tipster [stock market journalist D. Dorfman] J. Egan. il por *U.S. News & World Report* 107:59-60 Ag 21 '89
The little guy's little guy [financial columnist D. Dorfman] J. Nocera. il *Esquire* 112:109+ S '89
JOURNALISM, LABOR *See* Labor unions and the press
JOURNALISM, MEDICAL
Fish oil! Aspirin! Oat bran! [pitfalls of relying upon medical news] S. L. M. Jiménez. il *Health (New York, N.Y.)* 21:36+ N '89
JOURNALISM, MILITARY
    See also
      Stars and stripes (Newspaper)
      World War, 1939-1945—Reporters and reporting
TV vs. the military: it's an unfair fight. J. F. Lehman. il *TV Guide* 37:32-4 N 4-10 '89
JOURNALISM, RELIGIOUS
    See also
      Church and the press
JOURNALISM, SCIENTIFIC
Don't believe everything you read . . . [inaccurate newspaper accounts of sex hormone research by Doreen Kimura and Elizabeth Hampson] B. L. Benderly. il *Psychology Today* 23:67-9 N '89
The process of publication [Science magazine's attempts to avert fraud] D. E. Koshland, Jr. *Science* 245:573 Ag 11 '89
What's wrong with this prose? N. D. Mermin. por *Physics Today* 42:9+ My '89

Writing about science. D. Bane. *The Writer* 102:25-7 N '89
JOURNALISTIC ETHICS
    See also
      Confidential communications—Press
      Photography, Journalistic—Ethical aspects
All the fiction fit to print—or broadcast. L. Ackland. *The Bulletin of the Atomic Scientists* 45:2 N '89
Are journalists basically liars? [J. Malcolm's criticism of J. McGinniss in the New Yorker] F. Bruning. il *Maclean's* 102:11 Ap 24 '89
The art of the deals. J. Alter. il *Newsweek* 113:58-9 Ja 9 '89
Buckrakers Anonymous. M. Kondracke. *The New Republic* 200:42 Ja 9-16 '89
Dog-bites-dog journalism [decline in fact checking] L. I. Barrett. il *Time* 134:87 O 30 '89
Editor, heal thyself [code for British tabloids] D. Brand. il *Time* 134:89 D 11 '89
The era of the big blur [blurring lines between advertising and editorial content] J. Alter. il *Newsweek* 112:73+ My 22 '89
Free advice [Massachusetts psychologists investigated for speculating about K. Dukakis in the press] por *Time* 134:71 D 4 '89
From here to here [address, September 6, 1988] J. Konner. *Vital Speeches of the Day* 55:238-41 F 1 '89
Holier than thou [J. Malcolm's attack on J. McGinniss in the New Yorker] J. Taylor. il pors *New York* 22:32-7 Mr 27 '89
Is it right to publish rumors? W. Shapiro. il *Time* 134:53 Jl 10 '89
The journalist and the murderer (I) [convicted murderer J. MacDonald's suit against author J. McGinniss] J. Malcolm. *The New Yorker* 65:38-42+ Mr 13 '89
The journalist and the murderer (II) [convicted murderer J. MacDonald's suit against author J. McGinniss] J. Malcolm. *The New Yorker* 65:49-50+ Mr 20 '89
Knocking on death's door [covering tragedies] L. Zuckerman. il *Time* 133:49 F 27 '89
McGinniss: a travesty of libel [J. MacDonald's breach of contract suit against J. McGinniss] M. Garbus. *Publishers Weekly* 235:69 Ap 21 '89
Neo-plumbers on the attack [poor journalism due to reliance on leaks and sensational stories] L. I. Barrett. il *Time* 134:67 S 11 '89
Pain behind the camera [covering crash of Pan Am 103 on local TV] K. Frankola. por *Newsweek* 113:9 F 6 '89
Prefab news [video news releases] S. E. Davis. il *Technology Review* 92:6-7 O '89
A reporter isn't a friend [J. Malcolm's piece on J. McGinniss' ethics in the New Yorker] J. Alter and G. Cowley. il por *Newsweek* 113:62 Mr 27 '89
Reporters as stunt men [French journalists test airport security] J. Alter. il *Newsweek* 113:47+ Ja 16 '89
The talk of the town [J. Malcolm's piece on J. McGinniss' ethics in the New Yorker] *The Nation* 248:469 Ap 10 '89
Truth and consequences [CBS's alleged use of faked footage of Afghan war] il *Time* 134:98 O 9 '89
What role do advertisers play in deciding the news? [excerpt from Inventing reality] M. Parenti. *Utne Reader* p66 N/D '89
When a publisher has the last word [views of retired Toronto star publisher B. H. Honderich] G. Bain. il *Maclean's* 102:36 Je 26 '89
JOURNALISTIC PHOTOGRAPHY *See* Photography, Journalistic
JOURNALISTS
    See also
      Black journalists
      Drugs and journalists
      Foreign correspondents
      Women journalists
        See also names of journalists
        Attitudes
Media's liberal slant on the news. B. Baker. il *USA Today (Periodical)* 118:64-6 Jl '89
Notes and comment [views of Chinese journalists in the U.S. on student protests in China] *The New Yorker* 65:35-7 Je 12 '89
JOURNALISTS AS BANKERS
Hello sweetheart, get me mergers and acquisitions [S. Rattner] P. Weiss. *The Washington Monthly* 21:67-8 F '89
JOURNALISTS IN GOVERNMENT
Androgyny and Dr. Broder. T. Eastland. il *The American Spectator* 22:28-9 Mr '89
Buckrakers Anonymous. M. Kondracke. *The New Republic* 200:42 Ja 9-16 '89
JOURNALS *See* Periodicals
JOURNALS, PERSONAL *See* Diaries
THE JOURNEY OF CARLOS FUENTES: CROSSING BORDERS [television program] See Television program reviews—Single works
JOURNEY'S END MOTELS
Sleeping cheap. S. McKay. il *Maclean's* 102:41 Je 5 '89
JOVANOVIC, PETAR
Satellite medicine. il *World Health* p18-19 Ja/F '89

JOVANOVICH, PETER
about
What's new at . . . Harcourt Brace Jovanovich [interview] il por *Publishers Weekly* 235:26-7 My 26 '89
JOY
God & joy unearned. J. Garvey. *Commonweal* 116:108-9 F 24 '89
Joy in our times [address, May 7, 1989] G. A. Geyer. *Vital Speeches of the Day* 55:666-8 Ag 15 '89
JOYCE, ED, 1932-
Is network news getting better—or worse? il *TV Guide* 37:10-12 My 13-19 '89
JOYCE, JAMES, 1882-1941
about
Miami J'yce: love walks right out of a 'Ulysses' symposium. B. Maddox. il *The New York Times Book Review* 94:7 F 26 '89
The new 'Ulysses': grave matters [discussion of December 8, 1988 article, The new 'Ulysses': the hidden controversy] C. Rossman. il *The New York Review of Books* 36:43-5 Mr 30 '89
The new 'Ulysses': unanswered questions [discussion of December 8, 1988 article, The new 'Ulysses': the hidden controversy] C. Rossman. *The New York Review of Books* 35:58-9 Ja 19 '89
'The scandal of Ulysses': yet another exchange [discussion of June 30, 1988 article] J. Kidd. il *The New York Review of Books* 36:40-1 Je 1 '89
JOYCE, PEGGY HOPKINS, 1893-1957
about
Peggy Hopkins Joyce, Inc. D. Grafton. il pors *Forbes* 144 Special Issue:68+ O 23 '89
JOYCE TRISLER DANSCOMPANY
Reviews:
Performances at the Joyce Theater, New York City. D. Hering. *Dance Magazine* 63:88-9 Ja '89
JOYNER, FLORENCE GRIFFITH *See* Griffith Joyner, Florence
JOYNER-KERSEE, JACKIE
about
Can world's greatest woman athlete cash in on Olympic gold? il pors *Ebony* 44:96+ Ap '89
Jackie Joyner-Kersee brings a gold-medal glow back to hard-pressed East St. Louis. D. Chu. il pors *People Weekly* 31:44-5 Ja 30 '89
The Jackie nobody knows [cover story] J. D. Cain. pors *Essence* 20:62-4+ Ag '89
Quest for new conquests. K. Moore. il por *Sports Illustrated* 70:80-1 Je 5 '89
JOYSTICKS
Answers to my Mac mess [preventing hard disk crashes and MouseStick] E. Shapiro. il *Byte* 14:129-30+ Ap '89
JPL *See* Jet Propulsion Laboratory (U.S.)
JUAREZ, FRANCISCO ALVARADO- *See* Alvarado-Juarez, Francisco
JUAREZ, ROBERTO, 1952?-
about
Roberto Juarez at Robert Miller. K. Johnson. il *Art in America* 77:209 S '89
JUBA (SUDAN)
Juba: a city under siege. R. Wilkinson. il map *Newsweek* 113:47 Mr 20 '89
JUDAISM
See also
Bar mitzvah
Bat mitzvah
Catholic Church—Relations—Judaism
Converts from Judaism
Hanukkah
Jews
Menorah
Passover
Rosh Hashanah
Seder
Talmud
Zionism
Liturgy and ritual
Hanukkah [excerpt from These lights are holy] E. D. Frishman. il *Good Housekeeping* 209:74 D '89
JUDAISM AND CHRISTIANITY *See* Christianity and other religions
JUDAISM AND ECONOMICS
Victorian values/Jewish values. G. Himmelfarb. *Commentary* 87:23-31 F '89
JUDAISM AND ISLAM *See* Islam and Judaism
JUDD, DONALD, 1928-
about
Boxed metaphors. E. Heartney. il *Art News* 88:143 F '89
Red desert & Arctic dreams. D. B. Kuspit. il *Art in America* 77:120-5 Mr '89
JUDGE, HARRY GEORGE
Is there a crisis in British secondary schools? bibl f *Phi Delta Kappan* 70:813-16 Je '89
JUDGE, JOSEPH
The many lives of Old Havana. il map *National Geographic* 176:278-300 Ag '89

JUDGES
See also
Bork, Robert H., 1927-
Gardner, Thomas, III
Gesell, Gerhard
Judicial ethics
Judicial power
Kaufman, Irving R.
Kennedy, Anthony M.
Marshall, Thurgood
Moore, Andrew G. T., II
Rothwax, Harold
United States. Supreme Court
Wapner, Frederick
Wapner, Joseph A.
Women judges
Impeachment
See Impeachments
Rating
Rating the judiciary [list of Canada's best and worst judges in Canadian lawyer] N. Underwood. il *Maclean's* 102:56 My 22 '89
Salaries, allowances, etc.
Hard times. *The Nation* 248:112 Ja 30 '89
One for the Gypper. F. Barnes. *The New Republic* 200:14-15 F 27 '89
The quiet crisis in America's courts [Miami federal judges are fed up with salaries] S. J. Hedges. il *U.S. News & World Report* 106:30+ Ap 3 '89
Thurgood Marshall still Court's poorest justice. il por *Jet* 76:13 Je 5 '89
JUDGES AS AUTHORS
Edwin Torres. L. Carcaterra. il pors *People Weekly* 32:155-6+ D 4 '89
JUDGING OF PHOTOGRAPHS *See* Photography—Criticism, interpretation, etc.
JUDGMENT (ETHICS)
Son of man [sic], will you judge? [judging by current standards] M. E. Marty. *The Christian Century* 106:1103 N 22 '89
JUDGMENT DAY
Weariness in well-doing. P. Perkins. il *The Christian Century* 106:1011 N 8 '89
JUDGMENT OF GOD *See* God—Judgment
JUDGMENTS
See also
Stare decisis
JUDICIAL ERROR *See* Miscarriage of justice
JUDICIAL ETHICS
Disorder in the court [Canadian provincial court judges under fire] N. Underwood. il *Maclean's* 102:55-6 Ap 24 '89
Fla. judge Alcee Hastings is removed by U.S. Senate. il por *Jet* 77:12-13 N 6 '89
Hastings impeachment trial slated to begin next month. por *Jet* 75:12 F 27 '89
Justice for sale [Texas] E. H. Methvin. *Reader's Digest* 134:131-6 My '89
The leaden wings of Senate justice [vote to remove Judge A. L. Hastings] il por *U.S. News & World Report* 107:18 O 30 '89
JUDICIAL POWER
The case against political judging [cover story] R. H. Bork. il por *National Review* 41:23-8 D 8 '89
Constitutional law [discussion of December 1988 article, Rewriting the Constitution] S. C. Brubaker. *Commentary* 87:2-4+ My '89
'The tempting of America' [views of R. Bork] G. F. Will. il *Newsweek* 114:96 D 4 '89
Why courts are always making law [employment-at-will issue] G. E. Frug. il por *Fortune* 120:245+ S 25 '89
JUDICIARY *See* Courts; Judges; Judicial power
JUDICIARY AND THE PRESS *See* Government and the press
JUDICIARY COMMITTEE (SENATE) *See* United States. Congress. Senate. Committee on the Judiciary
JUDIS, JOHN B.
Can we sort out the mail mess? il *Reader's Digest* 134:189-90+ Ap '89
Herbert Croly's promise. por *The New Republic* 201:84-7 N 6 '89
An officer and a gentleman. *The New Republic* 200:19-22 Ja 23 '89
Rev. Moon's rising political influence. il *U.S. News & World Report* 106:27-9+ Mr 27 '89
JUDITH KRANTZ'S TILL WE MEET AGAIN [television program] *See* Television program reviews—Single works
JUDITH'S ROOM (NEW YORK, N.Y.: BOOKSTORE) *See* Booksellers and bookselling—New York (State)
JUFFER, JANE
Roundup on the Rio Grande. il *The Progressive* 53:32-3 Ap '89
JUG WINES *See* Wine
JUGENDSTIL *See* Art nouveau
JUGGLERS AND JUGGLING
Cruise control [interview with A. Lucas] S. McKee. il por *American Health* 8:66-7 D '89

JUICE, APPLE *See* Apple juice
JUICE, ORANGE *See* Orange juice
JUIN RACHELE COSMETICS INC.
Battle of the vanities [cover story] A. Edmond, Jr. il por *Black Enterprise* 19:42-3+ Mr '89
JUKEBOX SATURDAY NIGHT II [television program] See Television program reviews—Single works
JUKEBOXES
Collectors and collecting
The Wurlitzer 1015. B. Barol. il *American Heritage* 40:28-9 S/O '89
History
The jukebox: America's music machine [cover story] J. Gustaitis. bibl il *American History Illustrated* 24:44-9 N/D '89
JULES FISHER & PAUL MARANTZ, INC.
Living on borrowed light. J. S. Russell. il *Architectural Record* 177:150-3 My '89
JULES' UNDERSEA LODGE (FLA.) *See* Underwater hotels, motels, etc.
JULIA, RAUL
about
Of many things. G. W. Hunt. *America* 160:162 F 25 '89
JULIAN, AUDREY
about
Folk art, friends and good food [excerpt from Mary Emmerling's American country cooking] M. E. Emmerling. il *Working Woman* 14:100-2 Ja '89
JULIAN (CALIF.)
Architecture
Avant-garde in the desert [home of Phil and Wendy Gay] J. S. Eakin. il *New Choices for the Best Years* 29:36-8 Je '89
JULIE AND CAROL: TOGETHER AGAIN [television program] See Television program reviews—Single works
JULIUS, DAVID, AND OTHERS
Ectopic expression of the serotonin 1c receptor and the triggering of malignant transformation. bibl f il *Science* 244:1057-62 Je 2 '89
JULIUS CAESAR [drama] See Shakespeare, William, 1564-1616
JULY
The July almanac. il *The Atlantic* 264:12 Jl '89
JULYAN, BOB
The gray ghost. il *Runner's World* 24:96 Ag '89.
JUMEAU DOLLS *See* Dolls
JUMP ROPE *See* Rope jumping
JUMP STARTING, AUTOMOBILE *See* Automobiles—Starting
JUMPER CABLES *See* Storage batteries—Booster cables
JUMPING
See also
Bungee jumping
High jumping
Hurdle racing
Ski jumping
JUMPING GENES *See* Transposons
JUMPING ROPE *See* Rope jumping
JUMPING SPIDERS *See* Spiders
JUNCTIONS (PHYSIOLOGY)
See also
Plasmodesmata
Cloning and expression of a Xenopus embryonic gap junction protein. L. Ebihara and others. bibl f il *Science* 243:1194-5 Mr 3 '89
JUNE
The June almanac. il *The Atlantic* 263:14 Je '89
JUNEAU, PIERRE
about
'I am very pessimistic' [interview] P. Young. il por *Maclean's* 102:39 Ag 7 '89
JUNEK, ELISABETH
about
Flying lady. B. Visnic. il pors *Car and Driver* 35:141-4+ Jl '89
JUNG, ANEES
India's lifeline. il *The Courier (Unesco)* 42:22-4 F '89
JUNGLE *See* Rain forests
JUNGSTEDT, SANDRA
about
Prosaic to professional. G. Lee. il pors *Harper's Bazaar* 122:22+ Je '89
JUNI-HITOE *See* Kimonos
JUNIOR ACHIEVEMENT, INC.
Senior achievement. R. Bailey. il *Forbes* 143:174+ Je 12 '89
JUNIOR COLLEGE TEACHERS *See* College teachers
JUNIOR COLLEGE TEACHING *See* College teaching
JUNIOR COLLEGES *See* Community and junior colleges
JUNIOR HIGH SCHOOL JOURNALISM *See* College and school journalism
JUNIOR HIGH SCHOOLS
See also
Middle schools
Middle school versus junior high. F. Roberts. *Parents* 64:47-8+ N '89
JUNIOR TENNIS PLAYERS *See* Tennis players
JUNIOR TENNIS TOURNAMENTS *See* Tennis—Tournaments

JUNK
Anecdotes, facetiae, satire, etc.
Just say no to junk. R. E. Kotzsch. *Utne Reader* p79 Jl/Ag '89
JUNK ART
A heavy metal message [nuclear sculptor T. Price] J. Neary. il por *Life* 12:146-8 Mr '89
Junk magic [work of artist T. Guyton in Detroit] S. Yolles. il *Art News* 88:27 O '89
Things [motorcycle parts] C. Furlong. il *Cycle* 40:27-30 Ja '89
JUNK BONDS
And the next test will be Giuliani vs. Milken. C. Welles. por *Business Week* p37 Ja 9 '89
The balloon bursts for Wall Street arbs. J. Egan. il *U.S. News & World Report* 107:71 N 6 '89
Big yields from little deals [MassMutual Corporate Investors] S. Manolatos. il por *Forbes* 144:234 O 16 '89
The bills are coming due [leverage binge winds down; cover story] C. Farrell. il *Business Week* p84-7+ S 11 '89
Bondholders are mad as hell—and they're not going to take it anymore. C. Farrell. il *Business Week* p82-3 F 6 '89
The bondholders' cold new world. G. Hector. il *Fortune* 119:83-4+ F 27 '89
Can Fred Joseph save Drexel? M. J. Williams. il por *Fortune* 119:89-90+ My 8 '89
The Canadian who sparked the crash [decline in value of R. Campeau's junk bonds before Friday the 13th plunge] P. C. Newman. il *Maclean's* 102:75 O 30 '89
Coelho under fire [congressman given easy deal on hard-to-get junk bonds] *Newsweek* 112:41 My 22 '89
A contrarian case for buying certain junk bond funds now. M. Meyer. il *Money* 18:51-2+ N '89
A contrarian case for junk bonds. M. J. Williams. il *Fortune* 120:36 S 11 '89
Corporate America wants out from under its junk pile. L. Light. il *Business Week* p80-1 Ag 21 '89
Does junk have lasting value? Probably. J. M. Laderman. il *Business Week* p118-19 My 1 '89
Don't put away the smelling salts yet. D. Zigas and L. Light. il *Business Week* p92-3 O 2 '89
Drexel rushes in to save a fallen disciple [bailout of Integrated Resources] L. Light. il *Business Week* p65 Jl 17 '89
Drexel's deal with the feds: how much will it hurt? C. Welles. il por *Business Week* p36 F 6 '89
First Boston: trying to shake off the junk-bond jitters. J. Friedman. il *Business Week* p90 O 2 '89
He who lives by the junk bond . . . [T. Spiegel's fall at Columbia Savings & Loan] K. Kerwin. il por *Business Week* p46-7 D 25 '89-Ja 1 '90
High-grade junk. B. Weberman. il *Forbes* 144:115 Ag 21 '89
History is bunk, the future is junk [interview with M. R. Milken] S. K. Sheinbaum and others. il *New Perspectives Quarterly* 6:12-20 Fall '89
How long will junk be king of the bond funds? [Mutual fund scoreboard] J. M. Laderman. il *Business Week* p114-19+ F 27 '89
Hunting for treasure in the junkyard. D. Zigas. il *Business Week* p172 O 9 '89
The infighting that kept Salomon behind in junk bonds. J. H. Dobrzynski. *Business Week* p102-3 F 27 '89
Is Wasserstein's star tarnished? L. J. Nathans. il por *Business Week* p88-90 O 2 '89
It's not all junk. J. Heins. il *Forbes* 143:244-5 Je 26 '89
Jewels in the junk. C. Byron. il *New York* 22:23-4 O 30 '89
John Kissick. E. Schine. il por *Business Week* Special Issue:95 Ap 14 '89
Junk after Milken. G. Hector. il por *Fortune* 120:121+ N 6 '89
The junk bond plague moves north [Drexel Burnham] P. C. Newman. il *Maclean's* 102:32 Ja 16 '89
Junk bonds are climbing out of the grave. L. J. Nathans. il *Business Week* p134 D 25 '89-Ja 1 '90
Junk bonds face the big unknown. J. P. Newport, Jr. il *Fortune* 119:129-30 My 22 '89
Junk buy update [views of M. Budgyk] E. Hardy. il *Forbes* 144:158 D 25 '89
Junk danger. *The American Spectator* 22:11+ Ja '89
The junk funk. M. Schiffres. il *Changing Times* 43:12+ Je '89
The junk market's black hole. L. J. Nathans. il *Business Week* p156-7 N 27 '89
A junk pile for junk bonds? C. Friday and D. Pauly. il *Newsweek* 113:42 My 8 '89
Junk: the weak and the strong. S. E. Kuhn. il *Fortune* 120:17 O 23 '89
The loud clank of junk. L. Reibstein. il *Newsweek* 114:32-3 S 25 '89
Meeting with Milken. W. F. Buckley. *National Review* 41:71 N 10 '89
Michael Milken, meet Sewell Avery. J. Grant. il *Forbes* 144 Special Issue:60-2+ O 23 '89
Milken's shadow hovers over Fred Carr [First Executive Corp.] K. Kerwin. il por *Business Week* p24 Ap 17 '89
Not quite ready for the junk heap [bond funds] J. Egan. il *U.S. News & World Report* 107:69 O 2 '89

JUNK BONDS—*cont.*

Not so junky junk [Minstar Inc.] T. Jaffe. il *Forbes* 144:267 O 2 '89

Panic in the junk pile. il *Time* 134:54 S 25 '89

Quid pro junk? [federal probe of junk bond fund managers' personal portfolios] R. L. Stern and P. Berman. il *Forbes* 144:39-40 Ag 7 '89

The rape of the bondholder. A. Sloan. il *Forbes* 143:67-9 Ja 23 '89

Riklis' fancy footwork may be tripping him up. A. Rothman. il por *Business Week* p86-8 Je 19 '89

Trouble in the market. L. Black. il *Maclean's* 102:42 O 2 '89

True junk [New America High Income Fund] G. Morgenson. il por *Forbes* 144:202 O 2 '89

Turning America into junk. J. Mysak. il *The American Spectator* 22:28-9 Ap '89

Wall Street's junk-bond jitters. P. Sherrid. il *U.S. News & World Report* 106:53 My 8 '89

What can go wrong [junk bond unit trusts, higher yield money market mutual funds, and mutual funds with bad records] J. B. Quinn. il *Newsweek* 114:39 Ag 14 '89

What hath Drexel wrought? [guilty plea] M. J. Williams. il *Fortune* 119:10 Ja 16 '89

When the smoke clears [RJR Nabisco] B. Weberman. il *Forbes* 144:131 Jl 10 '89

When vultures get food poisoning [investing in distressed companies] H. Rudnitsky. il *Forbes* 144:53+ O 16 '89

Who's buying junk? [funds] J. Willoughby. il *Forbes* 143:161 Mr 6 '89

Without Milken, can Drexel still be Drexel? E. Schine. il pors *Business Week* p34 Mr 27 '89

Your junk bond surprise. W. L. Updegrave and C. A. Fried. il *Money* 18:52-3 Ja '89

Taxation

Takeovers: Congress comes out swinging a wet noodle. H. Gleckman. *Business Week* p29 Jl 24 '89

JUNK CERTIFICATES OF DEPOSIT

Bad deals in high yields. M. Feinberg. il *Changing Times* 43:63-7 Je '89

JUNK IN SPACE *See* Space debris

JUNK MAIL *See* Advertising, Direct mail

JUNKER, HOWARD

Continental impressions on Nob Hill. il por *Architectural Digest* 46:288-94+ O '89

Nob Hill epigram: an antiquarian's San Francisco apartment. il por *Architectural Digest* 46:250-5 My '89

San Francisco protocol: Charlotte Mailliard Swig in Pacific Heights. il por *Architectural Digest* 46:238-43+ My '89

JUNKYARDS

See also
Automobile junkyards
Computer junkyards

Salvage as salvation: tales from a junk man. M. Helm. il *Utne Reader* p80-1 Jl/Ag '89

JUNOR, PENNY

Diana comes of age. il pors *McCall's* 117:38-41 O '89

The furor over Fergie. il por *McCall's* 116:48-50+ F '89

JUPITER (PLANET)

See also
Space flight to Jupiter

A green flash of Jupiter. G. L. Verschuur. *Sky and Telescope* 77:259 Mr '89

Jupiter on your shortwave. D. A. Rosenthal. il *Sky and Telescope* 78:628 D '89

Jupiter's changing rhythms. R. Shaffer. il *Astronomy* 17:65 O '89

The longitude of Jupiter's central meridian [computer program] R. W. Sinnott. il *Sky and Telescope* 78:640-1 D '89

Atmosphere

Focus on Jupiter's atmosphere. R. Shaffer. il *Astronomy* 17:63-4 D '89

Galileo to perform first dedicated study of Jupiter's atmosphere and satellites. M. A. Dornheim. il *Aviation Week & Space Technology* 131:69-70+ O 9 '89

Jupiter's darkening red spot. A. MacRobert. il *Sky and Telescope* 78:508-9 N '89

Jupiter's major belt nearly fades away. J. Olivarez and P. W. Budine. il *Sky and Telescope* 78:396 O '89

Photographs and photography

Photographing details on Jupiter. il *Astronomy* 17:99-102 N '89

Satellites

Jupiter and its mobile moons [Basic program] O. S. Correa. il *Sky and Telescope* 77:650-1 Je '89

Jupiter's moon dance. A. MacRobert. il *Sky and Telescope* 78:626-7 D '89

Geology

Silicate volcanism on Io [research by Torrence V. Johnson] il *Sky and Telescope* 77:355-6 Ap '89

Surface

Hydrogen sulfide on Io: evidence from telescopic and laboratory infrared spectra. D. B. Nash and R. R. Howell. bibl f il *Science* 244:454-7 Ap 28 '89

The shocking surface of Io. *Science News* 136:143 Ag 26 '89

JURASSIC PERIOD *See* Paleontology—Jurassic

JURICH, JAMES P.

(tr) *See* Samway, Patrick H. The French Church in crisis

JURIED ART COMPETITIONS *See* Art—Competitions

JURISPRUDENCE

See also
Medical jurisprudence

JURNOVOY, JOYCE, AND JENNESS, DAVID

Jars for smart cookies. bibl il *New Choices for the Best Years* 29:101-3 S '89

JURY

See also
Grand jury

All-black jury ruled in recent Oliver North trial and prayed for guidance. il por *Jet* 76:7 My 22 '89

Experimental research on jury decision-making. R. J. MacCoun. bibl f *Science* 244:1046-50 Je 2 '89

For Denise Anderson, the jury forewoman, passing judgment on Ollie North was a trial by fire. P. Chin. il pors *People Weekly* 31:49-50 My 22 '89

From the publisher. D. K. Graham. *Antiques & Collecting Hobbies* 94:80 N '89

Not dumb persons [jurors in trial of O. L. North] M. E. Marty. *The Christian Century* 106:575 My 24-31 '89

A not-too severe mercy. T. C. Muck. il *Christianity Today* 33:14 Jl 14 '89

Waking up the jury box. T. Jacoby. il *Newsweek* 114:51 Ag 7 '89

Who is Ollie's peer? [selecting jurors for O. North trial] W. F. Buckley. *National Review* 41:62 Mr 10 '89

JURY DUTY *See* Jury

JUSKIE-NELLIS, JOAN, AND HIGGINS, YVONNE

The portable poetry workshop. *The Writer* 102:21-2 O '89

JUST, WARD S.

about

Compromising positions. D. Baldwin. il por *Common Cause Magazine* 15:34-8 Mr/Ap '89

Inside-the-Beltway intrigue [interview] A. P. Sanoff. por *U.S. News & World Report* 106:60 F 20 '89

JUST DESSERTS INC.

Just Desserts Inc.: serving up a model workplace. J. David and K. File. *Working Woman* 14:169+ O '89

JUST-IN-TIME SYSTEM

Are inventories really under control? M. J. Mandel. il *Business Week* p71 Jl 31 '89

Software's dirty little secret [On Demand Systems tries to bring just-in-time distribution to computer software] D. Churbuck. il *Forbes* 143:128 My 15 '89

JUST-US-BOOKS

Black toymakers brace for increased competition. D. Whittingham-Barnes. il *Black Enterprise* 20:24 D '89

JUST WAR DOCTRINE

What are the rules for revolution? A. L. Sherman. il *Christianity Today* 33:54-5 Ja 13 '89

JUSTICE, BLAIR

The ties that heal: how family and friends keep you healthy. il *Better Homes and Gardens* 67:48+ N '89

JUSTICE

See also
Religion and justice

Recoiling from reason [views of A. MacIntyre] M. C. Nussbaum. bibl f il *The New York Review of Books* 36:36-41 D 7 '89

JUSTICE, ADMINISTRATION OF

See also
Actions and defenses
Arbitration and award
Courts
Criminal justice, Administration of
Judges
Jury
Juvenile justice, Administration of
Legal procedure
Miscarriage of justice
Political prisoners
Public prosecutors
Searches and seizures
United States. Dept. of Justice

JUSTICE, MISCARRIAGE OF *See* Miscarriage of justice

JUSTICE DENIED [television program] *See* Television program reviews—Single works

JUSTICE DEPT. (U.S.) *See* United States. Dept. of Justice

JUSTICES *See* Judges

JUSTICES, SUPREME COURT *See* United States. Supreme Court

JUSTIFICATION

For the sake of ten. K. Koyama. *The Christian Century* 106:683 Jl 19-26 '89

JUSTLIFE (ORGANIZATION)

"Prolife": what does it really mean? [cover story; special section] il *Christianity Today* 33:27-38 Jl 14 '89

JUVENILE DELINQUENTS AND DELINQUENCY

See also
Gangs
Juvenile justice, Administration of
School violence
Wilding (Group violence)

JUVENILE DELINQUENTS AND DELINQUENCY—*cont.*
Adding up violent vulnerabilities [research by Dorothy Otnow Lewis] B. Bower. *Science News* 135:318 My 20 '89
Darkness at the heart of town [high school boys arrested for sexually assaulting a retarded girl in Glen Ridge, N.J.] P. Wilkinson. il *Rolling Stone* p55-6+ O 5 '89
Gang rape in the suburbs [attack on retarded girl in Glen Ridge, N.J.] B. Turque. il *Newsweek* 113:26 Je 5 '89
Is a rap sheet a legacy? A. Hjelmeland. por *Newsweek* 113:10 My 15 '89
A Kentucky boy's wild cry for help [student D. Pierce holds classmates hostage at Jackson County High School] W. Plummer. il pors *People Weekly* 32:44-7 O 9 '89
Kids who kill. R. Wright. il *Good Housekeeping* 209:54+ Ag '89
Meltdown in our cities [crimes by black youths] M. B. Zuckerman. il *U.S. News & World Report* 106:74 My 29 '89
Our violent kids. A. Toufexis. il *Time* 133:52-5+ Je 12 '89
Teenagers and crime. A. C. Mallozzi. *Good Housekeeping* 209:270 N '89
Teenagers and sex crimes. A. Toufexis. il *Time* 133:60 Je 5 '89

Imprisonment
The abuse of America's incarcerated children. *Utne Reader* p63 S/O '89
A dose of discipline for first offenders [use of paramilitary treatment] J. J. Kane. il *Time* 134:17-18 O 16 '89
Experiments in boot camp [military-style camps for young offenders] B. Turque. il *Newsweek* 112:42+ My 22 '89
JUVENILE HORMONES
Hormonal and genetic control of behavioral integration in honey bee colonies. G. E. Robinson and others. bibl f il *Science* 246:109-12 O 6 '89
Hormone triggers moth mating [research by Michel Cusson and Jeremy N. McNeil] *Science News* 135:46 Ja 21 '89
Identification of an allatotropin from adult Manduca sexta. H. Kataoka and others. bibl f il *Science* 243:1481-3 Mr 17 '89
Involvement of juvenile hormone in the regulation of pheromone release activities in a moth. M. Cusson and J. N. McNeil. bibl f il *Science* 243:210-12 Ja 13 '89
JUVENILE JUSTICE, ADMINISTRATION OF
See also
Juvenile delinquents and delinquency—Imprisonment
Bad news for death row [Supreme Court okays execution of juvenile and retarded criminals] A. L. Sanders. il *Time* 134:48-9 Jl 10 '89
High Court ruling upholds states' rights to execute young killers, retarded. *Jet* 76:4 Jl 10 '89
Is it fair to punish parents for crimes of their children? il *Jet* 76:12-14 My 29 '89
Now, parents on trial. B. Kantrowitz. il *Newsweek* 114:54-5 O 2 '89
When parents pay for their kids' sins [parental liability laws] J. P. Shapiro. il *U.S. News & World Report* 107:26 Jl 24 '89

Canada
Children of crime. R. Dolphin. il *Maclean's* 102:43-4 Ja 30 '89

Missouri
Too young to die? [case of H. Wilkins; cover story] R. Rosenbaum. il pors *The New York Times Magazine* p32-5+ Mr 12 '89

Pennsylvania
See also
Kunkletown (Pa.)—Juvenile justice, Administration of
JUVENILE LITERATURE *See* Children's literature
JUVENILE-TYPE DIABETES *See* Diabetes
JV DIALOGUE (FIRM)
High risks, distant payoffs. E. Dyson. il *Forbes* 144:114-16+ D 11 '89
JVC JAZZ FESTIVAL *See* Music festivals—New York (State)

K

K-9 [film] *See* Motion picture reviews—Single works
K-DRON
From here to infinity [invention of J. Kapusta] C. S. Smith. il por *New York* 22:24 Mr 6 '89
K MART CORP.
Attention, K Mart shoppers [chairman J. Antonini] P. Sellers. il por *Fortune* 119:41 Ja 2 '89
Attention K Mart shoppers [stock price] G. G. Marcial. il *Business Week* p80 Jl 10 '89
Why K Mart has stalled. F. Rice. il *Fortune* 120:79 O 9 '89
K.O.S. (GROUP) *See* Tim Rollins + K.O.S. (Group)
K. T.'S KITCHENS INC.
Kathy Taggares: her fast foods are really cooking. D. Castellon. il por *Business Week* p69 D 4 '89

KABBALAH *See* Cabala
KABUKI
Ennosuke III and his "Super Kabuki": Kabuki's revolutionary traditionalist. P. Grilli. il pors *Dance Magazine* 63:30-5 S '89
Exquisitely oriented [I. Ennosuke] L. A. Jacobs. *The New Leader* 72:23 S 18 '89
Witchcraft [Ennosuke's Kabuki in New York City] T. Tobias. il *New York* 22:121-2 S 25 '89
KABUL (AFGHANISTAN)
Afghan sitzkrieg. R. Sikorski. il *National Review* 41:37-8 Ap 21 '89
A city under siege. M. Nemeth. il *Maclean's* 102:22 F 6 '89
A city under siege. B. Levin. il *Maclean's* 102:28 F 27 '89
Inside a frightened city. M. Liu. il *Newsweek* 113:36+ Mr 13 '89
Still-life by shellfire. R. Sikorski. il *National Review* 41:22-3 Ap 7 '89
Target: Kabul. D. Lorch. il pors map *The New York Times Magazine* p32-5+ F 12 '89
KACHOYEANOS, MARY
(jt. auth) *See* Kraegel, Janet M., and Kachoyeanos, Mary
KACKEL, DOUGLAS
What can we learn from Amish education? *The Education Digest* 55:61-3 N '89
KADDAFI, MUAMMAR *See* Qaddafi, Muammar al-, 1942-
KADLECEK, MARY
On gushes and seeps—what we do about environmental spills. *The Conservationist* 44:52-3 S/O '89
Some saving thoughts in a time of plenty. il *The Conservationist* 44:52-3 N/D '89
KADOHATA, CYNTHIA
Devils [story] *The New Yorker* 65:38-41 S 18 '89
KADOKAWA, HARUKI
about
Heaven and earth [film] Reviews
American Film il 15:11-12 O '89. J. Greenberg
Prairie samurai. J. Howse. il *World Press Review* 36:68-9 N '89
Prairie samurai: a Japanese epic comes to life in Alberta. J. Howse. il *Maclean's* 102:44-5 Ag 21 '89
KADREY, RICHARD, 1957-
Becoming Cindy [fiction] il *Omni (New York, N.Y.)* 11:74-6+ S '89
KAEL, PAULINE
The current cinema. *See* issues of The New Yorker
about
She lost it at the movies. J. Podhoretz. *The American Scholar* 58:117-22 Wint '89
KAFKA, BARBARA
An opinionated palate. *See* issues of Gourmet beginning August 1989
Pleasing the palette. il *Art News* 88:162-5 O '89
KAGAN, DONA M.
The cost of avoiding research. bibl f il *Phi Delta Kappan* 71:220-4 N '89
KAGAN, DONALD
about
Yale strikes gold. J. P. Hart. *National Review* 41:24 Je 2 '89
KAGAN, ROBERT
Ballot blocks. *The New Republic* 200:21-2 Je 12 '89
KAGAN, SHARON LYNN
Early care and education: beyond the schoolhouse doors. bibl f il *Phi Delta Kappan* 71:107-12 O '89
Early care and education: tackling the tough issues. *The Education Digest* 54:17-20 My '89
Early care and education: tackling the tough issues [cover story] bibl f il *Phi Delta Kappan* 70:432-9 F '89
KAHANE, MELANIE, 1910-1988
about
Evolution of a classic: a Fifth Avenue signature by the late Melanie Kahane. S. Stephens. il *Architectural Digest* 46:242-9+ N '89
KAHANER, LARRY
Hard-driving detectives. il *Omni (New York, N.Y.)* 12:24+ D '89
Something in the air. il *Wilderness* 52:18-27 Wint '88
KAHIN, BRIAN
Software patents: franchising the information infrastructure. *Change* 21:24-5 My/Je '89
KAHLE, RON
about
You can come home again. B. Freese. il pors *Successful Farming* 87:15 D '89
KAHLE, STEVE
about
You can come home again. B. Freese. il pors *Successful Farming* 87:15 D '89
KAHLER, GERALD
about
Washington memorabilia from the Kahler Collection. J. C. Weaver. il pors *Antiques & Collecting Hobbies* 93:28-30 F '89

KAHN, ALICE, 1943-
Desperately seeking . . . anyone [excerpt from My life as a gal] il *Utne Reader* p67 Mr/Ap '89
Leather soul. il *Vogue* 179:560+ Mr '89
KAHN, C. RONALD, AND GOLDSTEIN, BARRY J.
Molecular defects in insulin action. bibl f *Science* 245:13 Jl 7 '89
KAHN, E. J., 1947-
(ed) See McDonald, Steven, and McDonald, Patti Ann. To serve and protect
KAHN, NED
about
Spouting off. B. Weber. il por *The New York Times Magazine* p110 Mr 19 '89
KAHN, PHILIPPE
Designing software to span the globe. por *Personal Computing* 13:224 O '89
KAHN, RICHARD
Europe: the new destination. il *Travel Holiday* 171:45-6+ Mr '89
KAHN, ROGER
about
Waiting for the final chapter. C. Leerhsen. il pors *Newsweek* 113:71 Ap 10 '89
KAHOOLAWE (HAWAII)
Island under fire. D. Kloepfer. *Wilderness* 53:29 Wint '89
KAI, NUBIA
Drums [poem] *Essence* 19:130 Mr '89
Golden lotus (for Sheik Hassan Cissi) [poem] *Essence* 19:130 Mr '89
KAIFU, TOSHIKI
Visit of Japanese prime minister [remarks, September 1, 1989] il por *Department of State Bulletin* 89:51-3 N '89
about
Cleaning house. H. Jensen. il por *Maclean's* 102:31 Ag 21 '89
In Japan, the bosses' man. D. Benkoil and H. Takayama. il *Newsweek* 114:29 Ag 21 '89
Japanese voters may settle for the LDP—warts and all. R. Neff. il por *Business Week* p70 N 13 '89
Now appearing in the role of Japanese prime minister . . . R. Neff. il por *Business Week* p44 Ag 21 '89
Same old story. por *Time* 134:36 Ag 14 '89
Visit to the United States, 1989
Visit of Japanese prime minister [remarks, September 1, 1989] G. Bush; T. Kaifu. il por *Department of State Bulletin* 89:51-3 N '89
KAIHARA, SHIGEKOTO
Information explosion. il *World Health* p6-8 Ag/S '89
KAISER, EMIL THOMAS, 1938-1988, AND OTHERS
Peptide and protein synthesis by segment synthesis-condensation. bibl f il *Science* 243:187-92 Ja 13 '89
KAISER, HENRY
about
Henry Kaiser. R. Tolleson. il por *Down Beat* 56:48+ My '89
KAISER, STEVE
Blazing the lonesome trail. il *Ad Astra* 1:32-4+ O '89
KAISER AEROSPACE & ELECTRONICS CORP.
Kaiser improves helmet-mounted display to boost pilot's kill capability. B. W. Henderson. il *Aviation Week & Space Technology* 130:119+ Je 19 '89
KAISER PERMANENTE MEDICAL CENTER (LOS ANGELES, CALIF.)
Every mother's nightmare comes true when a hospital nursery mix-up sends two babies home with the wrong parents [N. Kirks and W. Mailett] M. Brower. il pors *People Weekly* 31:123-4 Ap 3 '89
KAKADU NATIONAL PARK (AUSTRALIA)
Crocodile attack! [V. Plumwood attacked; condensation] H. Edwards. il *Reader's Digest* 135:70-5 O '89
KAKANIAS, KONSTANTIN
about
Konstantin Kakanias takes inspiration for his witty prints from mummies in Egypt, the guillotine in France. J. Shields. il por *Vogue* 179:132 S '89
KALACHE, ALEXANDRE
Youth and the elderly. il *World Health* p8-9 Mr '89
KALAHARI DESERT
How meat-eaters rule each other [cover story] D. Owens and M. Owens. il *International Wildlife* 19:4-11 Jl/Ag '89
KALAMAZOO (MICH.)
Monuments, statues, etc.
Statue of King erected in Kalamazoo, Mich. il por *Jet* 77:38 O 23 '89
KALAMAZOO RIVER (MICH.)
Of time and the river. B. Gilbert. il *Sports Illustrated* 71:76-80+ Jl 24 '89
KALAMBAY, SUMBU
about
This time Nunn chose not to run. P. Putnam. il pors *Sports Illustrated* 70:80 Ap 3 '89
KALAMU YA SALAAM, 1947-
Drug frenzy is nothing new in the U.S. *Utne Reader* p78 Mr/Ap '89
The hidden war in Mozambique. il *Utne Reader* p27 N/D '89

KALE
Vegetables that think they're flowers [ornamentals; cover story] L. B. Trigg. il *Southern Living* 24:50-1 O '89
KALER, ERIC W., AND OTHERS
Spontaneous vesicle formation in aqueous mixtures of single-tailed surfactants. bibl f il *Science* 245:1371-4 S 22 '89
KALER, KEITH
The Blue Lake rhinoceros. il map *Earth Science* 42:22-4 Fall '89
KALIBA, LAYDING LUMUMBA
Blues children (for Bessie Smith) [poem] *Essence* 20:149 S '89
Tribute [poem] *Essence* 19:142 F '89
KALIKOW, PETER
about
The newest new Post. E. Diamond. il por *New York* 22:28-9 Je 12 '89
Sunday, bloody Sunday. E. Diamond. il por *New York* 22:26+ Ap 24 '89
KALIL, RONALD E.
Synapse formation in the developing brain. bibl il *Scientific American* 261:76-9+ D '89
KALIN, NED H., AND SHELTON, STEVEN E.
Defensive behaviors in infant rhesus monkeys: environmental cues and neurochemical regulation. bibl f il *Science* 243:1718-21 Mr 31 '89
KALISH, GILBERT
about
A century, and more, of American song. K. R. Schwarz. *High Fidelity (New York, N.Y.)* 39:52 Mr '89
KALLIR, OTTO
about
Keeping the flame. A. Decker. il *Art News* 88:28+ O '89
KALOMIRAKIS, THEODORE
about
Basement bijou. M. Fleischmann. il *Video* 13:46-8+ Je '89
KALPAKIAN, LAURA
The overnight letter [story] il *McCall's* 116:136 My '89
KALTOFEN, MARCO
about
The toxic avenger strikes at corporate polluters. M. Satchell. il por *U.S. News & World Report* 106:28 Je 26 '89
KALVEN, JAMIE
At war with the First Amendment. *The Bulletin of the Atomic Scientists* 45:56-9 Ja/F '89
KAMALI, NORMA
about
No place like Home. M. Boodro. il por *Vogue* 179:267 F '89
Norma Kamali plays house. il *Seventeen* 48:36 Je '89
KAMAN, CHARLES H.
about
Designer dogs. M. Alpert. il por *Fortune* 119:137 Mr 13 '89
KAMAN CORP.
Designer dogs [work of C. Kaman] M. Alpert. il por *Fortune* 119:137 Mr 13 '89
Navy plans to roll out upgraded SH-2 Seasprite helicopter in October [antisubmarine warfare helicopter] S. W. Kandebo. il *Aviation Week & Space Technology* 130:143+ Je 19 '89
KAMBER, VICTOR
How to write labor's obit. por *Newsweek* 114:10-11 S 11 '89
KAMBERG, MARY-LANE
Long live the healthy heart! bibl il *Current Health 2* 16:4-9 O '89
The pet prescription. il *Current Health 2* 15:10-12 My '89
Respiratory system [cover story] bibl il *Current Health 2* 16:4-9 N '89
A sad state of mind. il *Current Health 2* 16:17-19 D '89
Selling your car: how to make the best deal. *Better Homes and Gardens* 67:121 Ag '89
The sound-, light-, and sleep-show in your room. il *Current Health 2* 15:26-7 Ja '89
Stroke: the brain disrupted [cover story] il *Current Health 2* 15:3-9 F '89
Why you're shy. il *Current Health 2* 16:27-9 N '89
KAMEL-REID, SUZANNE, AND OTHERS
A model of human acute lymphoblastic leukemia in immune-deficient SCID mice. bibl f il *Science* 246:1597-600 D 22 '89
KAMEN, AL
(jt. auth) See Williams, Marjorie C., and Kamen, Al
KAMEN, JEFF
(jt. auth) See Kupperman, Robert H., 1935-, and Kamen, Jeff
KAMERMAN, SHEILA B.
An international overview of preschool programs. bibl f il *Phi Delta Kappan* 71:135-41 O '89
KAMIN (VICTOR) INC. See Booksellers and bookselling—Maryland
KAMMERER, MIKE
about
Mike Kammerer's unwired world. C. Reece. por *Channels (New York, N.Y.: 1986)* 9:30 Ap '89

KAMPELMAN, MAX M., 1920-
Arms control and Soviet relations [address, March 1, 1989] *Vital Speeches of the Day* 55:386-90 Ap 15 '89
Comment and correspondence. *Foreign Affairs* 68:160-2 Summ '89
Diplomacy in an election year and beyond [address, October 7, 1988] *Department of State Bulletin* 88:38-40 D '88
The rapidly changing world [address, June 14, 1989] *Vital Speeches of the Day* 55:731-4 S 15 '89
KAMPMANN & COMPANY
Bankrupt Kampmann & Co. faces counter suits. C. Reid. *Publishers Weekly* 235:15 Ap 21 '89
Judge releases books in Connecticut warehouse. C. Reid. *Publishers Weekly* 236:10 Ag 4 '89
Kampmann bankruptcy order threatens 65 firms. C. Reid. *Publishers Weekly* 236:10-11 Jl 21 '89
Tentative pact joins Kampmann & Co. with National Book Network. C. Reid. *Publishers Weekly* 235:16 My 26 '89
KAMPUCHEA *See* Cambodia
KAMPUCHEANS *See* Cambodians
KAN, YUE-SAI
about
China star. *The New Yorker* 64:20-2 Ja 9 '89
KANAI-PAK, MASAKO
(jt. auth) See Anders, Robert L., and Kanai-Pak, Masako
KANAN, SEAN
about
Critically injured in filming, Karate Kid bad boy Sean Kanan rallies to fight to the finish. M. Dougherty. il pors *People Weekly* 32:51-2 Jl 17 '89
KANASCO, LTD.
A shaggy drug tale. il *FDA Consumer* 23:39-40 Ap '89
KANBAN SYSTEM *See* Just-in-time system
KANDEL, ERIC R.
about
Molecules of memory [cover story] G. Montgomery. il por *Discover* 10:46-50+ D '89
KANDINSKY, WASSILY, 1866-1944
about
Kandinsky's Moscow. M. Werenskiold. bibl f il *Art in America* 77:96-111 Mr '89
KANE, BILL, 1951-
about
Bill Kane at Foster Goldstrom. C. Little. il *Art in America* 77:177-8 D '89
KANE, BOB
My son, the Batman: a proud memoir by the artist who sired Gotham's defender; ed. by Michael Alexander. il pors *People Weekly* 32:33-4+ Jl 31 '89
KANE, BRIAN A., AND BERNARD, RUEL
Puerto Rico: nation or state? il *The Progressive* 53:32-5 S '89
KANE, EDWARD J.
The unending deposit insurance mess. bibl f il *Science* 246:451-6 O 27 '89
KANE, JOE
about
Joe Kane ran the mighty Amazon and lived to tell the tale. K. McMurran. il pors *People Weekly* 32:83+ Jl 17 '89
KANE, KAREN
The best learning software. il *Psychology Today* 23:66+ S '89
KANE, THERESA
Challenges facing U.S. Catholics. *Commonweal* 116:623 N 17 '89
KANE, TIM D.
A new world order? il *USA Today (Periodical)* 117:23 My '89
KANE/MILLER BOOK PUBLISHERS
Australian books in the U.S.: two small companies find success. il *Publishers Weekly* 235:38-40 Mr 24 '89
KANEDA, YASUFUMI, AND OTHERS
Increased expression of DNA cointroduced with nuclear protein in adult rat liver. bibl f il *Science* 243:375-8 Ja 20 '89
KANEKO, JUN, 1942-
about
Jun Kaneko/Brendan Walter Gallery. M. McCloud. il *American Craft* 49:80-1 Ag/S '89
KANELLOS, NICOLÁS
about
Arte Publico: keeping Hispanic literature alive. J. Barbato. *Publishers Weekly* 235:42 Je 9 '89
KANEW, JEFF
about
Troop Beverly Hills [film] Reviews
People Weekly il 31:17 Ap 10 '89. T. Cunneff
KANEZASHI, MASAO
Japan's new political activism. *World Press Review* 36:52-3 S '89
KANFER, STEFAN
The triumph of John Paul II. il pors *Life* 12:34-40+ D '89
K'ANG-HSI, EMPEROR OF CHINA, 1654-1722
about
An education emperor: teachings from the life of K'ang-hsi. B. DeMott. *Change* 21:62 Mr/Ap '89

KANGAROO RATS
A most exclusive neighborhood [preserve in Riverside County, Calif. financed through impact fees] il *U.S. News & World Report* 106:16 Mr 6 '89
KANGAS, MATTHEW
Clay at a crossroads. il *American Craft* 49:18-23 Je/Jl '89
KANIGEL, ROBERT
Our human heritage as makers and builders [address, April 11, 1989] *Vital Speeches of the Day* 55:681-3 S 1 '89
KANIN, GARSON, 1912-
about
Born yesterday [drama] Reviews
America 160:176 F 25 '89. G. G. Seibert
The Nation 248:354-5 Mr 13 '89. T. M. Disch
New York il 22:76-7 F 13 '89. J. Simon
The New Yorker 64:81-2 F 13 '89. M. Kramer
Time il 133:80 F 6 '89. W. A. Henry
KANIUK, YORAM
about
PW interviews. P. Kaganoff. por *Publishers Weekly* 235:56+ Ap 28 '89
KANNAPELL, ANDREA
Outrage over omnipresent violence: where to aim it? il *Utne Reader* p46-9 N/D '89
KANNER, BERNICE
Mind games [cover story] il *New York* 22:34-40 My 8 '89
On Madison Avenue. See issues of New York
Salute to military moms. il *Parents* 64:130-4+ D '89
KANOKVIJITJALEARN, PORNTIP
My mother. il *World Health* p29 Mr '89
KANSAI INTERNATIONAL AIRPORT *See* Osaka (Japan)—Airports
KANSAS
See also
Flint Hills (Kan. and Okla.)
National parks and reserves—Kansas
Prairies—Kansas
Ranches—Kansas
Social life and customs
Harold and Louie [excerpt from Bird, Kansas] T. Parker. *Harper's* 278:35-6+ My '89
KANSAS CITY (MO.)
Airports
Kansas City rebuilding after Braniff bankruptcy. C. Fotos. *Aviation Week & Space Technology* 131:56-7 D 4 '89
Crime
A string of sixty murders. B. Turque. il *Newsweek* 114:64 D 4 '89
Description
K.C.'s Christmas is in the cards. W. Mueller. il *The Saturday Evening Post* 261:82-5 N/D '89
Education
Affirmative reaction [dissatisfaction with desegregation plan] R. Nadler and T. Donelson. il *National Review* 41:28-9 S 15 '89
The billionaire and the students [students helped to stay drug free by E. M. Kauffman] D. Narine. il pors *Ebony* 44:146+ Ag '89
When desegregation backfires [black parents sue the state to pay for private schools because magnet plan is not working] P. King. il *Newsweek* 114:56 Jl 31 '89
Galleries and museums
See also
Black Archives of Mid-America
Gardens and gardening
The city Eden of Sarah and Virginia Weatherly. R. Haskell. il *Flower and Garden* 33:44-8 Ja/F '89
Flower & garden's own garden. R. Snyder. il *Flower and Garden* 33:84-8 Ja/F '89
KANSAS CITY INTERNATIONAL AIRPORT *See* Kansas City (Mo.)—Airports
KANSAS CITY SOUTHERN INDUSTRIES, INC.
Is there a 'buyout' sign on this railroad's route? G. G. Marcial. il *Business Week* p206 S 25 '89
KANSBOD, LENA
about
The best of both worlds. J. McCallum. il pors *Sports Illustrated* 70 Special Issue:149-51 F '89
KANTER, ROSABETH MOSS
The changing basis for pay. bibl *Society* 26:54-65 S/O '89
How the kinder, more cooperative corporation wins [excerpt from When giants learn to dance] *Working Woman* 14:118-20 My '89
Why cowboy management is bad for American business [excerpt from When giants learn to dance] il por *Working Woman* 14:134-6+ Ap '89
KANTROWITZ, BARBARA
Upgrading the schools: a primer for parents. il *Ladies' Home Journal* 106:70+ S '89
KANTROWITZ, MELANIE KAYE/ *See* Kaye/Kantrowitz, Melanie
KAPIOLANI PARK (HONOLULU, HAWAII)
They'll be strumming and humming at Kapiolani Park. il *Sunset (Central West edition)* 182:64 Je '89
KAPITAN, JUNE, AND SZABO, BILL
Reaching the trade: advice from two publishers turned booksellers. il pors *Publishers Weekly* 235:26+ Je 16 '89

KAPLAN, BERNARD
about
A Florida composition. C. McGee. il *Architectural Digest* 46:144-9 Jl '89
KAPLAN, BETH
Anemic and considered dangerous. il *Current Health 2* 16:10-11 N '89
KAPLAN, DAVID A.
The players' main man. il por *The New York Times Magazine* p46+ O 29 '89
KAPLAN, DAVID MICHAEL
Stand [story] il *The Atlantic* 264:62-9 Jl '89
Unfinished business [story] il *Redbook* 173:48+ S '89
KAPLAN, HELEN SINGER, 1929-
Help! My husband's always working. por *Redbook* 172:42 F '89
Keep your marriage sexy: 10 mistakes to avoid. *Redbook* 172:114-15+ Ap '89
"My husband's vasectomy ruined our sex life". por *Redbook* 173:22 S '89
"Why did my husband turn off to me?". por *Redbook* 174:88 D '89
KAPLAN, JAMES
Anjelica rising [cover story] il pors *The New York Times Magazine* p18-21+ F 12 '89
Block Island light. il pors *House & Garden* 161:84-91 Je '89
Inside the Club. il *The New York Times Magazine* p62+ Je 11 '89
Profiles [P. Shaffer] il *The New Yorker* 64:36-40+ Ja 16 '89
Sneak attacks. il *Vogue* 179:178+ My '89
KAPLAN, JIM
Tarnished gold: why don't the best fielders win the Gold Gloves? il *Sport (New York, N.Y.)* 80:31-2 O '89
KAPLAN, JONATHAN
about
The accused [film] Reviews
  The American Spectator il 22:35-6 Ja '89. B. Bawer
  Video il 13:62+ Jl '89. J. Young
Immediate family [film] Reviews
  Commonweal 116:670 D 1 '89. T. O'Brien
  Maclean's il 102:98 O 30 '89. B. D. Johnson
  New York il 22:102+ N 6 '89. D. Denby
  People Weekly il 32:17 N 13 '89. R. Novak
  Time il 134:84 N 6 '89. R. Corliss
KAPLAN, JUSTIN
A Connecticut Yankee in hell. il *American Heritage* 40:97-102+ N '89
about
For editor Justin Kaplan, updating Bartlett's is as easy as shopping for a new quote. M. Neill. il por *People Weekly* 31:141-2 Ap 10 '89
KAPLAN, JUSTINE
The day of the dolphins. il *Omni (New York, N.Y.)* 11:42-4+ Je '89
Interview: Louis Herman. il pors *Omni (New York, N.Y.)* 11:76-8+ Je '89
The not-so-Great Lakes. il *Omni (New York, N.Y.)* 11:32 F '89
A portrait of healing. il *Omni (New York, N.Y.)* 11:110-12 F '89
KAPLAN, MICHAEL
Brief encounter. il *Gentlemen's Quarterly* 59:204+ Mr '89
The drill is gone. il *Gentlemen's Quarterly* 59:170+ N '89
KAPLAN, MICHELE
about
A Florida composition. C. McGee. il *Architectural Digest* 46:144-9 Jl '89
KAPLAN, ROBERT D.
Europe's third world. il *The Atlantic* 264:16-18+ Jl '89
Postmortem. il *The Atlantic* 263:26+ Ap '89
KAPLAN, ROBERT S.
Management accounting for advanced technological environments. bibl f il *Science* 245:819-23 Ag 25 '89
KAPLAN, ROGER
U.S. out of NATO? A French scenario. il *The American Spectator* 22:32-3 F '89
KAPLAN, SHEILA, AND TINSLEY, ADRIAN
Women in administration of higher education. *The Education Digest* 55:24-7 D '89
KAPLAN, STEVE
The drugstore that ate South Dakota. il *Travel Holiday* 171:90 Je '89
E.T. come home. il *Travel Holiday* 171:104 My '89
Orlando without Mickey. il *Travel Holiday* 172:86-90 S '89
Roadside fantasies. il *Travel Holiday* 172:98 N '89
KAPLAN, STEVEN B.
(jt. auth) See Sienkiewicz-Mercer, Ruth, and Kaplan, Steven B.
KAPOOR, SHASHI
about
Shashi Kapoor branches out. P. Saxena. il por *World Press Review* 36:75 S '89
KAPOSI'S SARCOMA
AIDS-Kaposi's sarcoma-derived cells express cytokines with autocrine and paracrine growth effects. B. Ensoli and others. bibl f il *Science* 243:223-6 Ja 13 '89

Drug combo: double whammy with a bonus [AZT and interferon for AIDS patients with Kaposi's sarcoma; research by H. Clifford Lane] *Science News* 136:141 Ag 26 '89
Factor XIIIa-expressing dermal dendrocytes in AIDS-associated cutaneous Kaposi's sarcomas [with reply by Robert C. Gallo and others] B. J. Nickoloff and C. E. M. Griffiths. bibl f il *Science* 243:1736-7 Mr 31 '89
KAPPEL-SMITH, DIANA
Locking time: life at the edge of winter. il *Country Journal* 16:73-6 N/D '89
KAPPEN, THOMAS RISSE- *See* Risse-Kappen, Thomas
KAPPLER, JOHN, AND OTHERS
Vβ-specific stimulation of human T cells by staphyloccocal toxins. bibl f il *Science* 244:811-13 My 19 '89
KAPUŚCIŃSKI, RYSZARD
Uganda: after the terror. il por map *The New York Times Magazine* p38-41+ Mr 12 '89
The writer as combatant. *New Perspectives Quarterly* 6:54-5 Spr '89
about
Third world USA [interview] N. Gardels. *Utne Reader* p105 Mr/Ap '89
KAPUSTA, JANUSZ, 1951-
about
From here to infinity. C. S. Smith. il por *New York* 22:24 Mr 6 '89
KAPUSTIN, ANATOLY
about
Where *perestroika* makes strange bedfellows. J. Trimble. il pors map *U.S. News & World Report* 107:77-8+ Ag 28-S 4 '89
KAR-BEN COPIES INC.
Kar-Ben Copies. W. Wollheim and R. S. Frank. il *Publishers Weekly* 235:36-8 Mr 3 '89
KARA JURO (THEATER COMPANY)
Traveling show [Tadao Ando's Karaza Theater building] K. D. Stein. il *Architectural Record* 177:90-3 Mr '89
KARABAKH AUTONOMOUS OBLAST (SOVIET UNION)
See Nagorno-Karabakh Autonomous Oblast (Soviet Union)
KARAJAN, HERBERT VON
about
Musical events:
  H. von Karajan conducting at Carnegie Hall. A. Porter. *The New Yorker* 65:90-1 Mr 20 '89
Now, a grab for new chairs. M. Walsh. il pors *Time* 133:90-1 My 8 '89
Obituary
  Maclean's il por 102:44 Jl 31 '89. D. Turbide
  National Review 41:13-14 Ag 18 '89. S. Chapin
  Opera News il pors 54:30-3 N '89. N. Lebrecht
  Opera News por 54:44 S '89. P. J. Smith
Olympian games. P. G. Davis. il por *New York* 22:113-14 D 11 '89
One of a kind. T. W. Libbey, Jr. il *High Fidelity (New York, N.Y.)* 39:57 My '89
KARAN, DONNA
about
Donna Karan. il por *People Weekly* 32:104-5 D 25 '89-Ja 1 '90
High style for the 9-to-5 set. B. Rudolph. il por *Time* 134:70 O 23 '89
New working class. il pors *Harper's Bazaar* 122:160-75+ Mr '89
Prima Donna. S. Mansfield. il pors *Vogue* 179:290-7+ Ag '89
Turning rags into riches. N. Darnton. il por *Newsweek* 113:84 Ap 24 '89
KARAN (DONNA) COMPANY *See* Donna Karan Company
KARAOKES
The yen for karaoke. E. Grinnan. il *Seventeen* 48:44 O '89
KARAOSMANOGLU, ATTILA
Environment, poverty and growth [address, February 9, 1989] *Vital Speeches of the Day* 55:396-400 Ap 15 '89
THE KARATE KID, PART III [film] See Motion picture reviews—Single works
KARDISH, LAURENCE
CineSanJuan. il *Film Comment* 25:4+ Ja/F '89
KARDON, JANET
about
Janet Kardon named director of American Craft Museum. por *American Craft* 49:10 Ag/S '89
KARDONG, DON
Picture this. il pors *Runner's World* 24:66-71 Ag '89
KARELIS, CHARLES
No to separate checks [discussion of March/April 1989 article, Price as a lever for reform] *Change* 21:5 Jl/Ag '89
Price as a lever for reform. il *Change* 21:20-8 Mr/Ap '89
THE KAREN CARPENTER STORY [television program] See Television program reviews—Single works
KARENS
Burma
Life in the hills. W. Law-Yone. il *The Atlantic* 264:24+ D '89
KARESH, LANCE
about
Past as prologue. R. La Ferla. il pors *The New York Times Magazine* p56-7 F 19 '89

KARI, THEREZA IMANISH- See Imanishi-Kari, Thereza
KARIBA WEEDS
Waterweed invasions. S. C. H. Barrett. bibl il map *Scientific American* 261:90-7 O '89
KARKOWSKY, NANCY
Exercise with care—fitness is not risk-free. il *FDA Consumer* 23:24-7 My '89
KARL, INGRID
about
Cool Noir. A. Lange. il por *Down Beat* 56:60 Mr '89
KARLE, JEROME, 1918-
Macromolecular structure from anomalous dispersion [cover story] bibl f il *Physics Today* 42:22-9 Je '89
KARLEN, NEAL
All the girls I've loved. il *Mademoiselle* 95:191+ N '89
For $2,400, Gordon Lish will tell you how to reach God. il *Gentlemen's Quarterly* 59:240-3+ My '89
Wild Bill. il por *Gentlemen's Quarterly* 59:306-11+ D '89
KARLSRUD, KATHERINE, AND SCHULTZ, DODI
As they grow/birth to 1 year. See issues of Parents beginning March 1987
KARNOW, STANLEY
Setting Marcos adrift. il pors *The New York Times Magazine* p50+ Mr 19 '89
What will happen when the Chinese take back their 'fragrant harbor'? bibl (p174) il map *Smithsonian* 20:40-8+ Ap '89
KAROFF, BARBARA
Chilies. il *Gourmet* 49:114-17+ O '89
KARP, IVAN C., 1926-
A curious relationship. il *Art in America* 77:51+ Mr '89
KARP, JANE
Walter Karp, 1934-1989 [interview] il por *American Heritage* 40:166-7 N '89
KARP, VICKIE
Stars [poem] *The New Yorker* 65:40 Mr 13 '89
KARP, WALTER
All the congressmen's men: how Capitol Hill controls the press. bibl il *Harper's* 279:55-63 Jl '89
The quiz-show scandal. il pors *American Heritage* 40:76-84+ My/Je '89
Who decides what is news? (Hint: it's not journalists). il *Utne Reader* p60-8 N/D '89
about
Obituary
Harper's il 279:8+ O '89. L. H. Lapham
Walter Karp, 1934-1989 [interview] J. Karp. il por *American Heritage* 40:166-7 N '89
KARPA, STEVE
about
Why did Steve Karpa build this humongous pool table? Chalk it up to whimsy. il por *People Weekly* 31:74 Ap 3 '89
KARPATI, RON
A scientist: 'I am the enemy'. por *Newsweek* 114:12-13 D 18 '89
KARPATKIN, RHODA H.
Memo to members. See issues of Consumer Reports
KARR, RICK G.
Not so Simple. il *Stereo Review* 54:103-5 N '89
KARRAS, GREG
Pollution prevention: the Chevron story. bibl f *Environment* 31:4-5+ O '89
KARRAS, JOHN
How to live to be 100. *Better Homes and Gardens* 67:36-7+ S '89
KARRIEM, JALLELAH
A poem [poem] *Essence* 19:120 Ja '89
A quarter for your thoughts [poem] *Essence* 19:124 Ap '89
KARSH, YOUSUF, 1908-
about
'Karsh of Ottawa'. R. Dolphin. il por *Maclean's* 102:50 Ap 24 '89
Portraits of power through the eyes of a master. D. Jenish. il por *Maclean's* 102:16-17 D 25 '89
KARSTEN MANUFACTURING CORPORATION
The golf club with a handicap all its own [K. Solheim's Ping irons] P. Finch. il por *Business Week* p126+ My 1 '89
KARTNER, NORBERT, AND LING, VICTOR
Multidrug resistance in cancer. bibl il *Scientific American* 260:44-51 Mr '89
KARWOSKI, CHESTER J., AND OTHERS
Spatial buffering of light-evoked potassium increases by retinal Müller (Glial) cells. bibl f il *Science* 244:578-80 My 5 '89
KASARDA, JOHN D.
Opportunity foreclosure zones. il *New Perspectives Quarterly* 6:16-21 Summ '89
KASDAN, LAWRENCE
about
The accidental tourist [film] Reviews
America 160:113+ F 11 '89. R. A. Blake
The American Spectator il 22:30+ Mr '89. B. Bawer
Commonweal 116:81 F 10 '89. T. O'Brien
The Nation 248:65-6 Ja 9-16 '89. S. Klawans
National Review 41:56 Mr 10 '89. J. Simon
The New Yorker 64:90-1 Ja 23 '89. P. Kael

He knew what he wanted. B. Cronenworth. il pors *American Film* 14:46-52 Ja/F '89
KASEM, CASEY, 1932-
about
Casey Kasem's flip side. B. Ohanian. il pors *Mother Jones* 14:21-3+ O '89
The top 40 times two. B. Barol. il por *Newsweek* 113:56 F 6 '89
KASER, JOYCE S.
(jt. auth) See Raizen, Senta A., and Kaser, Joyce S.
KASHIWA, HANK
Free skiing to better technique. il *Skiing* 41:74 F '89
Get the racer's edge. il *Skiing* 41:72 Ja '89
Racing for the whole family. il *Skiing* 41:27 Mr '89
KASID, U., AND OTHERS
Effect of antisense c-*raf*-1 on tumorigenicity and radiation sensitivity of a human squamous carcinoma. bibl f il *Science* 243:1354-6 Mr 10 '89
KASINDORF, JEANIE
Abortion in New York [cover story] il *New York* 22:32-8+ S 18 '89
Act two. il pors *New York* 22:46-52+ Ap 10 '89
The 'Cotton Club' murder: cocaine and hit men in Hollywood—a 1980s film noir [cover story] il pors *New York* 22:24-33 Jl 24 '89
How Bess got out of the mess. il pors *New York* 22:38-48 Ja 16 '89
Intelligencer. See issues of New York beginning August 19, 1985
Jackie Mason tries to talk himself out of trouble [cover story] il pors *New York* 22:36-42 O 16 '89
Mommy oldest: having babies at 45 and beyond [cover story] il *New York* 22:22-9 Jl 17 '89
Stepping out. il pors *New York* 22:36-44 D 18 '89
KASPAROV, GARY
about
Computer chess: a masterful lesson. I. Peterson. *Science News* 136:276 O 28 '89
Humanity 2, computers 0. M. M. Waldrop. il por *Science* 246:572-3 N 3 '89
It's mind over matter, 2-0. F. Lidz. il por *Sports Illustrated* 71:97 O 30 '89
The winning edge. R. Chelminski. il por *Reader's Digest* 135:175-6+ D '89
KASPER, OTTO
Noodle doodles [photographs] il *Life* 12:122-4 F '89
KASPER, RAPHAEL G.
about
Washington ins & outs: moves from House Science Panel; new positions at NSF and SSC. I. Goodwin. *Physics Today* 42:50-1 My '89
KASPER, STEPHEN
Cool comfort in the hot sun. il *Sierra* 74:102-3 Mr/Ap '89
KASS, LEON
Genesis 1 [discussion of November 1988 article, Evolution and the Bible] *Commentary* 87:2+ Ap '89
What's wrong with Babel? *The American Scholar* 58:41-60 Wint '89
KASSALOW, EVERETT MALCOLM
Employee representation on U.S., German boards. bibl f *Monthly Labor Review* 112:39-42 S '89
KASSEBAUM, JOHN PHILIP
about
John Philip Kassebaum's unparalleled ceramics in Charleston. J. S. Wamsley. il pors *Architectural Digest* 46:86+ D '89
KASSEBAUM, LLEWELLYN
about
John Philip Kassebaum's unparalleled ceramics in Charleston. J. S. Wamsley. il pors *Architectural Digest* 46:86+ D '89
KASTEEL HET NIJENHUIS (HEINO, NETHERLANDS)
Half-truths and treasures. M. K. Talley, Jr. il por *Art News* 88:53-4 F '89
KASTEN, ROBERT W.
Should the Congress adopt the "High Risk Occupational Disease Notification and Prevention Act of 1987"? [excerpts from address, March 29, 1988] *Congressional Digest* 68:121+ Ap '89
KASTNER, JOSEPH
When spelling—Pow!—wurdz can get you down. il *Smithsonian* 20:140 Ag '89
KATAHN, MARTIN
Diet the T-factor way [condensed from The T-factor diet] *Reader's Digest* 135:119-22 O '89
KATALYSIS FOUNDATION
Growing third world pride. J. E. Eppinger. il *New Choices for the Best Years* 29:12-13 Je '89
KATAOKA, HIROSHI, AND OTHERS
Identification of an allatotropin from adult Manduca sexta. bibl f il *Science* 243:1481-3 Mr 17 '89
KATAOKA, TETSUYA
Stop bashing Japan for U.S. deficits. il *USA Today (Periodical)* 117:26-8 Ja '89
KATARINCIC, JOSEPH A.
Real victim of the takeover fever [address, April 7, 1989] *Vital Speeches of the Day* 55:540-4 Je 15 '89

KATCHEN, CAROLE, 1944-
Bring out the artist in your child. il *Parents* 64:80+ Je '89

KATES, DON B., 1941-
about
Should you own a gun for protection? [interview] il *U.S. News & World Report* 106:28 My 8 '89

KATE'S DIARY [drama] See Tolan, Kathleen

KATHAKALI
Reviews:
Olé! Shabash! at the American Theatre of Actors, New York City. C. Hardy. *Dance Magazine* 63:115-16 My '89

KÄTHE WOHLFAHRT'S CHRISTKINDLMARKT
The gift that blessed the giver. S. Wilding. il *Good Housekeeping* 209:234+ D '89

KATI, WARREN M., AND WOLFENDEN, RICHARD
Major enhancement of the affinity of an enzyme for a transition-state analog by a single hydroxyl group. bibl f il *Science* 243:1591-3 Mr 24 '89

KATSU ICHIKAWA COMPANY
Hardware hill. B. Weber. il *The New York Times Magazine* p74 Je 25 '89

KATYDIDS
Life as a leaf [katydid mimicry] J. L. Castner. il *International Wildlife* 19:18-21 Mr/Ap '89

KATYN FOREST MASSACRE, 1940
Between issues. *The New Leader* 72:2 Mr 6 '89
To tell the truth. E. K. Valkenier. *The New Republic* 200:20-1 My 22 '89

KATZ, DONALD R.
The investor. See issues of Esquire through November 1989

KATZ, JAMES EVERETT
Pivotal issues. bibl *Society* 26:5-10 Jl/Ag '89

KATZ, JONATHAN
about
Lights! Camera! Hammer and nails! M. Barrier. il por *Nation's Business* 77:12+ Je '89

KATZ, LILIAN G.
As they grow/3 and 4. See issues of Parents

KATZ, LILLIAN VERNON
about
Growing a business [interview] B. Stein. il por *Home Office Computing* 7:56 S '89

KATZ, NATASHA
about
Impressions vs. effects. S. Flatow. il pors *Theatre Crafts* 23:56-60+ N '89

KATZ, RUTH J.
Skin care. il *New York* 22:118+ My 15 '89
Tip sheet. il *New York* 22:54-6+ D 18 '89

KATZ, SUSAN
The collector. il *Ladies' Home Journal* 106:122+ My '89

KATZEN, MOLLIE, 1950-
about
Warmth and whimsy. S. Margolis. il por *Health (New York, N.Y.)* 21:64-7+ Ja '89

KATZIR, ABRAHAM
Optical fibers in medicine. bibl il *Scientific American* 260:120-5 My '89

KATZMAN, JOHN
about
Cram scam [cover story] J. Hammer. il *The New Republic* 200:15-18 Ap 24 '89

KATZMAN, LISA
Festivals. il *Film Comment* 25:68-70 N/D '89
'Opening night': moment by moment. il *Film Comment* 25:34-9 My/Je '89

KAUAI (HAWAII)
See also
Alakai Swamp (Kauai, Hawaii)
Botany—Kauai (Hawaii)
Children—Kauai (Hawaii)
Description and travel
Hawaii's wet spot: Kauai. D. G. Gordon. il map *Travel Holiday* 171:40-9 Je '89
High on Kauai. D. Freeman. il *Vogue* 179:396+ Mr '89
Kauai: next link on the chain. M. Ashley. il *The Saturday Evening Post* 261:92-5 Ja/F '89

KAUCHAK, THERESE
Roxanne Black's Long Distance Love. il por *Seventeen* 48:68 Je '89

KAUFFMAN, EWING M., 1916-
about
The billionaire and the students. D. Narine. il pors *Ebony* 44:146+ Ag '89

KAUFFMAN, JANET, 1945-
How sunlight figures in [story] *The New Yorker* 65:31-4 F 27 '89

KAUFFMANN, JEAN-PAUL
Kidnapping
'I feel as if I'm a thief' [interview] B. de Koster and C. Dickey. il por *Newsweek* 113:42 Je 5 '89

KAUFFMANN, STANLEY, 1916-
Stanley Kauffmann on films. See issues of The New Republic

KAUFFMANN, SYLVIE
'The transition to normalcy' [interview with T. Mazowiecki] *World Press Review* 36:15-17 O '89

KAUFMAN, BEL
Tales from "the author of" an education best-seller [excerpt from preface to the 25th anniversary edition of Up the down staircase] *The Education Digest* 54:41-4 Ap '89

KAUFMAN, HENRY
about
Henry Kaufman: corporate debt erodes competition [interview] J. H. Dobrzynski. por *Business Week* p40 Mr 20 '89

KAUFMAN, HUGH
about
Nebraska's new favorite son. B. Turque. il por *Newsweek* 114:21 Jl 10 '89

KAUFMAN, IRVING R.
about
Echoes of the Rosenberg case: an autobiographical postscript. S. Hook. il *The American Spectator* 22:18-20 Ja '89

KAUFMAN, JACKIE
(jt. auth) See Hacker, Randi, and Kaufman, Jackie

KAUFMAN, JOANNE
The face on the back of the book. il *The New York Times Book Review* 94:1+ Je 25 '89
Last look. il *Ladies' Home Journal* 106:47-8+ N '89
My mother died too soon. il por *Glamour* 87:144+ N '89
Raised on Monkee business, Micky Dolenz's daughter Ami takes her swing at film acting. il pors *People Weekly* 31:59-60 My 1 '89
Stardom, she wrote. il pors *Ladies' Home Journal* 106:56+ D '89

KAUFMAN, MARGO
Cancer: facts vs. feelings. por *Newsweek* 113:10 Ap 24 '89
For better, for worst: why are men such babies when they get sick? *Reader's Digest* 134:49-50 F '89

KAUFMAN, MICHAEL, 1951-
Manley returns. *The Nation* 248:293 Mr 6 '89

KAUFMAN, MICHAEL T.
Poland: the ghosts of Jews [excerpt from Mad dreams, saving graces] il *Commonweal* 116:429-32 Ag 11 '89
Tough times for Mr. Levittown. il pors *The New York Times Magazine* p42-4+ S 24 '89

KAUFMAN, PHILIP
about
The unbearable lightness of being [film] Reviews
Video il 12:63 Mr '89. S. L. Siegel

KAUFMAN, PHILIP S.
Autocracy isn't the Catholic style. il *Commonweal* 116:110-14 F 24 '89

KAUFMAN, SHIRLEY
The status quo [poem] *The New Republic* 201:32 Jl 3 '89

KAUFMAN & BROAD, INC.
See also
Broad, Inc.

KAUFMAN & BROAD HOME CORP.
A hot homebuilder. D. Sylvester. il *Fortune* 119:89 Ap 10 '89

KAUFMANN, ELIZABETH
The new rhythms of fitness. il *American Health* 8:45-9 D '89
Shoe biz. il *Health (New York, N.Y.)* 21:60-1 S '89

KAUFMANN, HANS
about
The names of Zurich. J. Marcom, Jr. il por *Forbes* 143:206+ Je 26 '89

KAUFMANN, JERRY
Doting on houseplants. il por *New Choices for the Best Years* 29:70-3+ O '89

KAUFMANN, JOHN H.
The wood turtle stomp. il *Natural History* p8+ Ag '89

KAUFMANN, P., AND OTHERS
Effects of the large June 1975 meteoroid storm on earth's ionosphere. bibl f il map *Science* 246:787-90 N 10 '89

KAUS, MICKEY
Abolish the Fifth Amendment. *The Washington Monthly* 21:69-70 F '89
Watch what you call welfare. *The Washington Monthly* 21:45-6 Mr '89

KAUS, ROBERT M. See Kaus, Mickey

KAWAKUBO, REI
about
Tailor made. K. D. Stein. il *Architectural Record* 177:92-3 Ja '89

KAWASHIMA, KIKO
about
The Emperor's second son falls in love with a commoner—and so does the rest of Japan. il pors *People Weekly* 32:54-5 S 18 '89

KAY, ALAN
about
Interview: Alan Kay. D. Sobel. il por *Omni (New York, N.Y.)* 12:80-2+ N '89
PCs for the year 2000. M. Rogers. il por *Newsweek* 114:36 O 2 '89

KAY, JANE HOLTZ
Testing toxins at $100 a day. il *The Nation* 248:300-2 Mr 6 '89

KAYAK RACING
See also
Running rapids—Competitions

KAYAKS AND KAYAKING
See also
Running rapids
Boat-in-a-box? It's an inflatable kayak. il *Sunset (Central West edition)* 183:70-1 D '89
Kayaking the wilderness waterways of southern Alaska. il map *Sunset (Central West edition)* 182:70+ Je '89
KAYAPO INDIANS *See* Cayapo Indians
KAYE, CATHRYN BERGER
Essentials for successful community service programs. *The Education Digest* 55:57-60 N '89
KAYE, ELIZABETH
"He's late. He's been in an accident. He's dead in a ditch. And I'll never, ever meet another man . . . ". il *Mademoiselle* 95:176+ Ap '89
Peter Jennings gets no self-respect. il pors *Esquire* 112:158-60+ S '89
Sly's progress [cover story] il pors *Esquire* 111:96-102+ F '89
about
Stallone with our thoughts. L. Eisenberg. por *Esquire* 111:25 F '89
KAYE, JEFF
(ed) See Falk, Peter. Columbo returns! What you can expect from him now
KAYE, KATHLEEN
First love [poem] il *Good Housekeeping* 208:226 Ap '89
KAYE, SUSAN, 1945-
A movable feast in Mexico. il *World Press Review* 36:62 Ja '89
KAYE/KANTROWITZ, MELANIE
Women play key role in opposing the occupation. il *Utne Reader* p42-3 S/O '89
KAYSER-THREDE GMBH
Soviets book new commercial payloads, grant greater access to space facilities [microgravity missions] J. M. Lenorovitz. *Aviation Week & Space Technology* 131:121+ O 9 '89
KAZA, JURIS
Fighting for 'socialist pluralism' in Latvia. il map *The New Leader* 72:12-14 Ja 23 '89
KAZANJIAN, DODIE
The Bushes of Kennebunkport [interview with B. Bush] il pors *House & Garden* 161:140-5 Je '89
Fast forward. il pors *House & Garden* 161:76-83+ F '89
He's the tops. il pors *House & Garden* 161:120-5+ F '89
In the light of Provence [cover story] il por *House & Garden* 161:98-107+ Ja '89
Inside Newport. il *House & Garden* 161:54-67+ Ag '89
Sanctuary for art [interview with M. Morley] il por *House & Garden* 161:150-5+ My '89
The Sultans of Sag Harbor. il por *House & Garden* 161:192-7+ S '89
KAZAS, TOM
Looks like wood. il pors *Americana* 17:54-8 S/O '89
KAZHDAN, A. P. (ALEKSANDR PETROVICH), 1922-
Byzantium: the emperor's new clothes? [cover story] bibl il map *History Today* 39:26-34 S '89
KAZHDAN, ALEKSANDR PETROVICH *See* Kazhdan, A. P. (Aleksandr Petrovich), 1922-
KAZIN, ALFRED, 1915-
American Gothic. il *The New York Review of Books* 36:45-6 N 23 '89
The New republic: a personal view. il *The New Republic* 201:78-80+ N 6 '89
KAZIN, MICHAEL, 1948-
The new historians recapture the flag. il *The New York Times Book Review* 94:1+ Jl 2 '89
KAZIS, RICHARD, 1952-
Rags to riches? il *Technology Review* 92:42-53 Ag/S '89
KAZOO
Electronic kazoo [Vocalizer 1000 synthesizer] D. Stover. il *Popular Science* 234:33 Je '89
KAZUO, KURIMOTO
Under new management. il *The Unesco Courier* 42:28-33 Jl '89
KBTN (NEOSHO, MO.: RADIO STATION) *See* Radio stations
KC-10 AIRPLANES *See* Tank airplanes
KEALING SPACE CENTER
The cosmic classroom. J. K. Strickland, Jr. il *Ad Astra* 1:20-3 Mr '89
KEAN, THOMAS H.
Timidity [address, April 6, 1989] *Vital Speeches of the Day* 55:488-90 Je 1 '89
about
New Jersey's battle for better schools. T. Armbrister. *Reader's Digest* 135:159-64 N '89
KEANE, GEORGE
about
Big money manager on campus. G. G. Marcial. il por *Business Week* p88 Ag 21 '89
KEANE, GLEN, 1954-
about
Mermaid artist Glen Keane grew up in a Family circus. C. Sanz. il pors *People Weekly* 32:127-8 D 11 '89

KEANE, MICHAEL
about
Masterpieces. A. Shreve. il por *Motor Boating & Sailing* 163:58-61+ Ja '89
KEANE, MOLLY
Once I lived in a proper house. il *Gourmet* 49:102+ Ap '89
KEARIN, SCOTT
Yellowstone: after the fire. il map *Bicycling* 30:96-100+ Jl '89
KEARNEY, CAROL MORSE
Joel's room [poem] *McCall's* 117:102 N '89
KEARNEY, HUGH F.
Strafford in Ireland, 1633-40. il por maps *History Today* 39:20-5 Jl '89
KEARNEY, JOHN
about
With an instinct for the extinct, John Kearney brings back the dinosaurs—bumper-to-bumper. il por *People Weekly* 32:94 O 16 '89
KEARNS, JERRY
about
Jerry Kearns at Kent. K. Johnson. il *Art in America* 77:142 Jl '89
KEATES, JONATHAN
From gods to citizens. il *Opera News* 54:27-9 Jl '89
Viewpoint. *Opera News* 53:4 Ja 7 '89
KEATING, CHARLES H., JR.
about
$1 billion worth of influence. M. B. Carlson. il por *Time* 134:27-8 N 6 '89
Bob Bennett: on the trail of the 'Keating Five'. T. Smart. il por *Business Week* p60 D 11 '89
CC calls for ethics inquiry of five senators. J. Denny. *Common Cause Magazine* 15:28 N/D '89
Charlie Keating in the Show Me state. G. Morgenson. il por *Forbes* 143:12 My 29 '89
Financier Charles Keating is the $2 billion man of the savings and loan crisis. B. Hewitt. il pors *People Weekly* 32:78-80 D 4 '89
For Charlie Keating, the best defense is a lawsuit. K. Kerwin. il por *Business Week* p32+ My 1 '89
Good timing, Charlie. H. Rudnitsky. il por *Forbes* 144:140-2+ N 27 '89
Is Danny Wall on the way out? C. Yang and P. Dwyer. *Business Week* p59 N 13 '89
Keating takes the Fifth. M. B. Carlson. il por *Time* 134:46 D 4 '89
"A legal bank robbery". M. B. Carlson. il pors *Time* 134:29 N 27 '89
The man who tried to buy Washington. G. Borger and S. J. Hedges. il pors *U.S. News & World Report* 107:18-21+ N 27 '89
Now it's broke. J. R. Adams. *The New Republic* 201:16-18 N 13 '89
The S&L scandal's biggest blowout. T. Morganthau. il por *Newsweek* 114:35-6 N 6 '89
The seduction of Senator Alan Cranston. P. Dwyer. il pors *Business Week* p82-4 D 4 '89
KEATING, ROBERT
Road to power. il *Omni (New York, N.Y.)* 11:66-8+ Je '89
KEATING, THOMAS
about
Contemplative prayer: taking time to hang out with God [interview; cover story] il por *U.S. Catholic* 54:6-13 Mr '89
KEATING-EDH, BARBARA
Supreme Court delivers blow to consumers. *Consumers' Research Magazine* 72:20-1 S '89
KEATON, DIANE
about
Unnatural actresses. R. Rosenbaum. il pors *Mademoiselle* 95:46+ Ja '89
KEATON, MICHAEL
about
Batman [cover story] B. Zehme. il pors *Rolling Stone* p38-42+ Je 29 '89
Movies. E. G. Carter. il pors *Vogue* 179:128-30 Je '89
KECK, PAMELA J., AND OTHERS
Vascular permeability factor, an endothelial cell mitogen related to PDGF. bibl f il *Science* 246:1309-12 D 8 '89
KECK OBSERVATORY (HAWAII) *See* Astronomical observatories—Hawaii
KEDDIE, B. ANDREW, AND OTHERS
The pathway of infection of Autographa californica nuclear polyhedrosis virus in an insect host. bibl f il *Science* 243:1728-30 Mr 31 '89
KEDOURIE, ELIE
The limitations of liberalism. *The American Scholar* 58:265-70 Spr '89
The lives of Lawrence. *The New Republic* 201:37 Ag 21 '89
KEEBLE, KEZIA
about
Island shelter. J. Reginato. il por *House & Garden* 161:98-107 Ap '89

KEEL, WILLIAM C.
Crashing galaxies, cosmic fireworks [cover story] il *Sky and Telescope* 77:18-21+ Ja '89
KEELER, CHRISTINE, 1941?-
about
The faded flower of a great British scandal, Christine Keeler heeds a last call to the limelight. M. Green. il pors *People Weekly* 31:76-7+ Ap 24 '89
Party-girl Scandal. B. D. Johnson. il pors *Maclean's* 102:58-9 My 22 '89
Undercovers. G. Fuller. il por *Film Comment* 25:56-8+ Mr/Ap '89
KEELS
Repairing fiberglass keels. L. W. Taylor. il *Motor Boating & Sailing* 163:87 Je '89
KEEN, LISA M.
Some gays reverting to risky sex. *Utne Reader* p111-12 N/D '89
KEEN, MARY, LADY
about
The vicar's walk [excerpt from Private landscape] C. Seebohm. il *House & Garden* 161:174-8 S '89
KEEN, SAM
The Inc.ed man. il *American Health* 8:70-1 Ja/F '89
Original blessing, not original sin [interview with M. Fox] il pors *Psychology Today* 23:54-8 Je '89
The stories we live by [cover story] il *Psychology Today* 22:42-7 D '88
KEEN, SAM, AND ZUR, OFER
Who is the new ideal man? il *Psychology Today* 23:54+ N '89
KEENAN, TED
Fuji's fastest black-and-white. il *Popular Photography* 96:60-3 Ja '89
KEENELAND YEARLING SALES *See* Horse auctions
KEEPNEWS, PETER
Rouse & Nica. il *Down Beat* 56:59-60 Ap '89
KEEPSAKES *See* Souvenirs (Keepsakes)
KEESEY, LORI
Need money? Good luck! il *Ad Astra* 1:17-21 D '89
KEESHAN, BOB
Banning corporal punishment in the classroom. *The Education Digest* 54:19-22 Ap '89
KEFIR
Liquid gold [Lifeway Foods] M. Barrier. il por *Nation's Business* 77:14 Jl '89
KEGLEY, CHARLES W.
The lost legacy: idealism in American foreign policy. *USA Today (Periodical)* 117:25-7 Mr '89
KEH, DAVID
about
Leaner-than-ever Chinese cuisine. T. Ney. il por *Prevention (Emmaus, Pa.)* 41:75-8+ F '89
KEILLOR, GARRISON
A Christmas story [story] *The New Yorker* 65:40-2 D 25 '89
The Chuck show. *The New Yorker* 65:26-9 Jl 24 '89
How the savings and loans were saved. *The New Yorker* 65:42 O 16 '89
When you kick a liberal. il *Harper's* 278:72-5 Ja '89
Where there's smoke there's ire . . . il por *American Health* 8:50-3 D '89
about
Wild seed in the Big Apple. J. Skow. il por *Time* 134:109 D 11 '89
KEIM FAMILY BAKERY
Cooking up a future. M. E. Johnson and S. Brewer. il *New Choices for the Best Years* 29:6 D '89
KEIRSTEAD, S. A., AND OTHERS
Electrophysiologic responses in hamster superior colliculus evoked by regenerating retinal axons. bibl f il *Science* 246:255-7 O 13 '89
KEISER, DENNIS
about
Backyard nursery. K. Martin. il pors *Organic Gardening* 36:48-52 D '89
KEISLING, PHILLIP
Industrial America's suicide pact. *The Washington Monthly* 21:59-60 F '89
The ozone's shot, the oceans stink—so what has the Monthly had to say? *The Washington Monthly* 21:36-7 Mr '89
KEISLING, PHILLIP, AND ALTER, JONATHAN
35 ways to cut the defense budget. *The Washington Monthly* 21:50+ F '89
KEITA, SALIF
about
Salif Keita. R. Givens. por *Stereo Review* 54:150 N '89
KEITH, DAVID
about
David Keith gets back in uniform as Ollie North, the officer and gentleman of Guts & glory. M. Dougherty. il pors *People Weekly* 31:113+ My 1 '89
Getting Ollie North right? It was actor vs. director. M. Leahy. il pors *TV Guide* 37:20-3 Ap 29-My 5 '89
KEITH-RYAN, HEATHER
about
An Anglo rebellion. M. Rose. il *Maclean's* 102:13 Ag 28 '89

KEIZER, GARRET
I am the clock winder. il *Reader's Digest* 134:113-17 Ap '89
KEIZER, GREGG
Editorial license. See issues of Compute! beginning May 1988 through June 1989
The gulag on the Rue des Grandes Augustins [fiction] il *Omni (New York, N.Y.)* 11:96-103 Ja '89
KELHEIM (GERMANY)
Antiquities
Iron and industry: ancient links [work of Peter S. Wells; cover story] B. Bower. il *Science News* 135:170-1 Mr 18 '89
KELLEHER, HERBERT DAVID
about
Southwest Airlines: flying high with 'Uncle Herb'. K. Kelly. il por *Business Week* p53+ Jl 3 '89
KELLEHER, MATTHEW H.
The Hong Kong Church faces 1997. il *America* 161:63-4 Jl 29-Ag 5 '89
KELLER, BILL
Comrade Engver goes to Moscow [cover story] il pors *The New York Times Magazine* p24-7+ Ag 27 '89
Moscow's other mastermind [cover story] il pors *The New York Times Magazine* p30-3+ F 19 '89
KELLER, GEORGE, 1928-
Learning to love bibliospeak. *Change* 21:19 Ja/F '89
Pavlov lives: who's to blame for educational failures? il *Change* 21:54 My/Je '89
Slouching toward solvency. *Change* 21:7 S/O '89
KELLER, HOLLY
Maxine in the middle [story] il *Parents* 64:141-2+ D '89
KELLER, JÖRG
(jt. auth) See Krafft, Maurice, and Keller, Jörg
KELLER, KATHRYN
Could you have a hidden allergy? il *Redbook* 173:142-3+ O '89
KELLER, MARYANN
Streetwise. See issues of Motor Trend beginning September 1986
KELLERMAN, LAWRENCE R.
An open letter to educators. *Ad Astra* 1:14 Ap '89
KELLEY, DEAN M.
Statism, not separationism, is the problem. *The Christian Century* 106:48-51 Ja 18 '89
KELLEY, KATHLEEN
about
Lobbyist in the winter/farmer in the summer. il por *Successful Farming* 87:39 Ja '89
KELLEY, KEVIN J.
Condos where cows once grazed. il *The Progressive* 53:28 N '89
KELLEY, KITTY
about
Exclusive: Kitty Kelley tells all. D. R. Hales. il pors *McCall's* 116:67-8+ Ag '89
KELLEY, TERRY
about
The hometown boys. J. H. Taylor. il por *Forbes* 144:253-4 O 16 '89
KELLING, GEORGE L.
(jt. auth) See Wilson, James Q., and Kelling, George L.
KELLMAN, BARNET
about
Family man. C. S. Smith. il por *New York* 22:32 Je 12 '89
KELLMAN, JOSEPH
about
"We decided to show how things can work". S. B. Weiner. il por *Forbes* 144:180-1+ S 18 '89
KELLOGG, MARY ALICE
Growing up with Glamour. il *Glamour* 87:356 Ap '89
Mariel's personal best. il pors *Harper's Bazaar* 122:120-3+ F '89
When less is more. il *Travel Holiday* 172:68-73 Ag '89
KELLOGG, WILL KEITH
about
The U.S. Business Hall of Fame. W. Guzzardi. il por *Fortune* 119:135 Mr 13 '89
KELLOGG ASSOCIATES
"Eventually, it all topples". D. Wechsler. il *Forbes* 143:48 My 29 '89
Spotting stocks in trouble before they drop. K. Kerwin. il *Business Week* p41 My 22 '89
KELLOGG CO.
Big G is growing fat on oat cuisine [General Mills' cereals gain on Kellogg's] R. Mitchell. il *Business Week* p29 S 18 '89
Kellogg rides the health craze. W. Zellner. il *Business Week* Special Issue:28-31 Ap 14 '89
This one spells o-o-p-s [presidents puzzle wrongly includ-- name of J. Davis] il *Newsweek* 113:50 My 1
KELLOW, BRIAN
Alter ego. il por *Opera News* 54:22-3 D 23 '89
Stages. il por *Opera News* 54:18-22 S '89

KELLY, COLLEEN
about
Careers by design. il pors *Harper's Bazaar* 122:188-91+ Mr '89
KELLY, DELIA ROCHE- *See* Roche-Kelly, Delia
KELLY, FRANKLIN
Frederic Church and the enterprise of landscape painting [with editorial comment by Wendell Garrett] bibl f il *Antiques* 136:1108-23 N '89
KELLY, GENE, 1912-
about
Singin' in the rain [film] Reviews
Video il 12:63-4 Mr '89. M. Fleischmann
KELLY, GRACE *See* Grace, Princess of Monaco, 1929-1982
KELLY, HENRY, AND WYCKOFF, ANDREW
Distorted image: how government statistics misrepresent the economy. il *Technology Review* 92:52-60 F/Mr '89
Statistics and policy: distorting economic activity. *Current (Washington, D.C.)* 314:22-7 Jl/Ag '89
KELLY, JAMES R.
Catholic abortion rates and the abortion controversy. *America* 160:82-5 F 4 '89
Data and mystery: a decade of studies on Catholic leadership. *America* 161:345-6+ N 18 '89
Winning Webster v. Reproductive Health Services: the crisis of the pro-life movement. *America* 161:79-83 Ag 12-19 '89
KELLY, JOHN H.
Recent events in the Middle East [statement, September 19, 1989] *Department of State Bulletin* 89:61-3 N '89
U.S. diplomacy in the Middle East [statement, July 12, 1989] *Department of State Bulletin* 89:44-5 O '89
KELLY, KATHY
A note from prison. *America* 161:230 O 14 '89
KELLY, KEN, 1955-
about
Ken Kelly at Cliff Michel. M. Kangas. il *Art in America* 77:183+ D '89
KELLY, KRISTIN
Is it time to raise the gasoline tax? *Utne Reader* p88 Mr/Ap '89
KELLY, MARJORIE
The Body Shop. por *Utne Reader* p76 Ja/F '89
Revolution in the marketplace. il *Utne Reader* p54-62 Ja/F '89
KELLY, MICHAEL
"Ten steps, then we shoot," says Ron Brown. "I've got my AK-47," replies Lee Atwater. "What've you got?". il pors *Gentlemen's Quarterly* 59:142-7+ Jl '89
KELLY, PATRICK
about
An original American in Paris. M. Hornblower. il por *Time* 133:66-8 Ap 3 '89
Paris has exploded in buttons, bows, fruits, and festivities since America's irrepressible Patrick Kelly came to town. J. Reed. il por *Vogue* 179:778+ S '89
Patrick Kelly: exuberant style animates the American designer's Paris atelier. M. Gross. il por *Architectural Digest* 46:218-24 S '89
Patrick Kelly: prince of Paris [cover story] P. Johnson. il pors *Essence* 20:90-3+ My '89
KELLY, PATRICK, AND STUART, OTIS
Neoromanticism, men, and the eighties: dancing the difference. il *Dance Magazine* 63:34-8 Ja '89
KELLY, PHILLIP
Walter and the raffle. *Reader's Digest* 134:26 Mr '89
KELLY, ROBERT N.
Realigning federal student aid policy. *The Education Digest* 55:61-3 O '89
KELLY, SHELDON
Attack from the ocean deep. il *Reader's Digest* 134:67-72 F '89
Midnight race for freedom. il pors *Reader's Digest* 135:198-202+ S '89
"That car is going to explode!". il pors *Reader's Digest* 134:96-100 Ja '89
KELM, JACK
about
Pushing his luck—and his blood pressure—an aged bank robber is caught red-handed. il por *People Weekly* 31:108 Ap 17 '89
KELMAN, JUDITH
Book sightings: a new source of author income? por *Publishers Weekly* 235:65 Mr 17 '89
Families who believe their houses are haunted—do you? il *Redbook* 173:40+ O '89
Getting crafty! il *Ladies' Home Journal* 106:120+ O '89
Motherhood 1989: the state of the art. il *Ladies' Home Journal* 106:63-4+ My '89
(ed) See Bird, Val. "I saved my baby from crib death"
(ed) See Harness, Gerry. "My gynecologist butchered me!"
KELMSCOTT MANOR (OXFORDSHIRE, ENGLAND) *See* Historic houses, sites, etc.—Great Britain
KELP
Magnification of secondary production by kelp detritus in coastal marine ecosystems. D. O. Duggins and others. bibl f il *Science* 245:170-3 Jl 14 '89

Photographs and photography
Fish faces in the kelp forest. N. Wu. il *Sea Frontiers* 35:366-9 N/D '89
KELSO, LOUIS O.
about
Louis Kelso's baby is making daddy proud. J. B. Levine. il por *Business Week* p130 My 8 '89
KELSO AND COMPANY
Louis Kelso's baby is making daddy proud [ESOPs] J. B. Levine. il por *Business Week* p130 My 8 '89
KELTER, JOLIE
about
A Manhattan sampler. S. M. L. Aronson. il pors *Architectural Digest* 46:158-63+ Je '89
KELTON, NANCY
Dating at forty. il *Parents* 64:126-8 S '89
Resolutions for 1989. il *Parents* 64:77-9 Ja '89
Turning 40. il *Parents* 64:132-3 Mr '89
KELVIN, ALICE
Cheek to cheek is doubly chic, the second time around [cover story] il *Smithsonian* 19:84-90+ Mr '89
KEMP, GEOFFREY
Middle East opportunities. *Foreign Affairs* 68 Special Issue:139-58 ['89]
KEMP, JACK
about
Can Jack Kemp clean up the HUD mess? S. V. Roberts. il por *U.S. News & World Report* 107:26-7 Jl 3 '89
Cleaning house at HUD—and then some. H. Gleckman and others. il por *Business Week* p72-4 Jl 10 '89
A conservative war on poverty. J. P. Shapiro. il por *U.S. News & World Report* 106:20-3 F 27 '89
An enterprising war on poverty [interview] il *New Perspectives Quarterly* 6:36-9 Summ '89
Evicting the drug dealers. il por *Time* 133:41 My 1 '89
Has Bush assigned Kemp a mission impossible? R. Stodghill, II. por *Business Week* p51 Ja 9 '89
Housing Dept.'s Kemp takes Atlanta fact-finding tour. il por *Jet* 75:46 Mr 6 '89
HUD Sec. Kemp visits as Chicago gives control of housing unit to tenants. il por *Jet* 76:26 My 29 '89
HUD without politics? S. Waldman and C. Bingham. il *Newsweek* 114:38 O 9 '89
Jack be nimble, Jack be quick. E. Magnuson. il por *Time* 134:20 Jl 24 '89
Jack Kemp faces reality. J. Traub. il pors *The New York Times Magazine* p38-9+ My 7 '89
The Kemp cure-all. D. Osborne. *The New Republic* 200:21+ Ap 3 '89
Kemp OKs use of vacant apartments for homeless. il por *Jet* 77:52 N 27 '89
The Kemp plan for rebuilding the city. C. Oglesbee. *The Christian Century* 106:340-1 Ap 5 '89
Kemp's brave new world. A. McDaniel. il por *Newsweek* 113:26 Ja 2 '89
Looking beyond the HUD scandal. B. Cohn. il por *Newsweek* 114:19 Ag 21 '89
Perseverance pays, HUD Secretary Jack Kemp tells Central State U. students. il pors *Jet* 76:16+ Je 19 '89
The poverty thing. F. Barnes. *The New Republic* 200:13-15 Ja 30 '89
The 'Reverend Jack' believes—now he has to deliver. R. Stodghill, II. il por *Business Week* p86+ Je 12 '89
Washington talk. *National Review* 41:16-17 F 24 '89
What Jack Kemp loves about the HUD scandal. R. Stodghill, II and D. Harbrecht. il por *Business Week* p41 Jl 31 '89
What will be the impact on new construction under Jack Kemp's tutelage at HUD? P. Hoffmann. por *Architectural Record* 177:23 F '89
When tenants take charge. B. Turque. il por *Newsweek* 114:44 N 27 '89
KEMP, JAMES C.
about
Obituary
Physics Today il por 42:94-5 D '89. R. J. Donnelly
KEMP, JAN
about
Jan Kemp. S. Kanfer. il por *People Weekly* 32 Special Issue:124 Fall '89
KEMP, JOHN R., 1945-
Beginning a career as a watercolorist. il por *American Artist* 53:72-5+ Jl '89
KEMP, SHARON D.
(jt. auth) See Larder, Brendan A., and Kemp, Sharon D.
KEMP, SHAWN
about
Sonic boon. J. McCallum. il pors *Sports Illustrated* 71:78+ N 27 '89
KEMPAINEN, ROBERT
about
Captain Crunch. B. Miller. il por *Runner's World* 24:93 D '89
KEMPER, VICKI
Members only. *Common Cause Magazine* 15:6-7 N/D '89
KEMPINGER, HERWIG
about
Body doubles. M. Haus. il por *Art News* 88:107-8 S '89

KEMPTON, BEVERLY GARY

Bowing out: a tough choice. por *New Choices for the Best Years* 29:20+ O '89

Great transformations. il *Working Woman* 14:88-92 Ja '89

Just call me Mary Rose. il pors *New Choices for the Best Years* 29:52-5 D '89

KEMPTON, MURRAY

Another dirty secret. *The New York Review of Books* 36:52 D 7 '89

The GOP blues. il *The New York Review of Books* 36:4 Mr 16 '89

Gorbachev in Armenia. il *The New York Review of Books* 35:58 Ja 19 '89

Mad about guns. *The New York Review of Books* 36:62 D 21 '89

A tale of two governments. *The New York Review of Books* 36:43 Mr 30 '89

Why Noriega wins. il *The New York Review of Books* 36:10 Je 15 '89

KEMPTON-SMITH, DEBBI

Horoscope. See issues of Seventeen beginning March 1985 through February 1990

KENAN, AMOS

Four decades of blood vengeance; tr. by Richard Flantz. il *The Nation* 248:154-6 F 6 '89

KENAN, RANDALL

about

Gone to Carolina. C. McGee. il por *New York* 22:24 Ag 14 '89

KENDALL, DAVE

Acupuncture wins the West. il *The Mother Earth News* 117:42+ My/Je '89

KENDALL, ELIZABETH, 1947-

Company as community: DTH at 20 [cover story] il por *Dance Magazine* 63:40-2 Je '89

KENDALL, MARIE

about

A town that looked just so. G. Robinson. il *American Heritage* 40:92-9 Jl/Ag '89

KENEALLY, THOMAS

about

Never a question of easy grace. P. D. Baumann. il por *Commonweal* 116:395-400 Jl 14 '89

KENMORE (WASH.)

Monuments, statues, etc.

Cop art [T. Brennan creates sculpture from confiscated guns] B. Weber. il *The New York Times Magazine* p94 Ap 30 '89

KENNAN, GEORGE FROST, 1904-

After the cold war. il *The New York Times Magazine* p32-3+ F 5 '89

The history of Arnold Toynbee [address, November 13, 1988] il *The New York Review of Books* 36:19-22 Je 1 '89

The last wise man [excerpts from Sketches from a life; cover story] il pors *The Atlantic* 263:39-47+ Ap '89

about

The Eliotic Kennan. B. Gewen. *The New Leader* 72:3-4 My 15-29 '89

Guest of the age. R. Steel. il *The New York Review of Books* 36:3-5 Ag 17 '89

An icon of the cold war. E. Thomas. il por *Newsweek* 113:34 Ap 17 '89

Kennan's lament: American mass culture uncontained. A. Stephanson. il *New Perspectives Quarterly* 6:54-7 Fall '89

Bibliography

Mr. X. S. Hoffmann. il *The New Republic* 201:35-8 O 2 '89

KENNEALLY, JOYCE A.

Microwave cooking tips. See issues of Good Housekeeping beginning October 1985

KENNEBEC RIVER (ME.)

Fish and power in a riverine rivalry [call for the removal of Edwards Dam in Augusta, Me. in order to restore Kennebec River fisheries] B. Carpenter. il map *U.S. News & World Report* 107:90+ O 16 '89

KENNEBUNKPORT (ME.)

Description

A small town goes prime-time [effect of G. Bush's election] S. Allis. il *Time* 133:14+ Ja 9 '89

Historic houses, sites, etc.

The Bushes of Kennebunkport [interview with B. Bush] D. Kazanjian. il pors *House & Garden* 161:140-5 Je '89

KENNEDY, ANTHONY M.

about

Are you smiling, Robert Bork? il por *U.S. News & World Report* 106:10 Je 26 '89

The Court spins right. A. McDaniel. il por *Newsweek* 113:16-18 Je 26 '89

KENNEDY, BRUCE R.

about

"We're vulnerable". M. Beauchamp. il por *Forbes* 143:80+ Mr 6 '89

KENNEDY, BRYAN

(jt. auth) See Bruns, Roger, and Kennedy, Bryan

KENNEDY, CAROLINE

about

The family's first year. L. David. il pors *McCall's* 116:12-14 Ag '89

Jackie: a mother's journey. C. Avery. il *Ladies' Home Journal* 106:142-4+ Mr '89

KENNEDY, CORA WRIGHT

Tools & techniques. See issues of Popular Photography through August 1989

KENNEDY, DAN

The great sleep-out. il *Parents* 64:170 Ag '89

KENNEDY, DIANA

about

Beyond combination plates. L. Shapiro. il por *Newsweek* 114:105 N 13 '89

Quinta Diana. S. O. Daniels. il pors map *Organic Gardening* 36:40-6 Jl/Ag '89

KENNEDY, DIANE

Selective weeding. il *Organic Gardening* 36:79-80 F '89

KENNEDY, EDWARD MOORE, 1932-

Grabbing the creative initiative: a new Democratic opportunity. por *USA Today (Periodical)* 118:35-7 Jl '89

Should the Congress adopt the "High Risk Occupational Disease Notification and Prevention Act of 1987"? [excerpts from address, March 22, 1988] *Congressional Digest* 68:106+ Ap '89

Should the Senate approve the "Americans with Disabilities Act of 1989"? [excerpts from testimony, May 9, 1989] *Congressional Digest* 68:294+ D '89

Should the Senate-passed Immigration Act of 1989 be approved? [excerpts from debate, July 11, 1989] *Congressional Digest* 68:236+ O '89

about

Ted and I agree. R. E. Tyrrell. il *The American Spectator* 22:10-11+ My '89

Chappaquiddick incident, July 1969

All washed up. P. Terzian. il *The American Spectator* 22:49 Jl '89

Chappaquiddick. T. Mathews. il *Newsweek* 114:52-3 Jl 3 '89

Frustrated grand jurors say it was no accident Ted Kennedy got off easy. J. S. Kunen. il pors *People Weekly* 32:34-6 Jl 24 '89

Memories of Mary Jo. J. Farrell. il pors *Ladies' Home Journal* 106:108-10+ Jl '89

KENNEDY, HARLAN

For queens & country. il *Film Comment* 25:15-16 Ja/F '89

Gondola wind. *Film Comment* 25:72+ N/D '89

The new wizards of Oz. il *Film Comment* 25:73-4+ S/O '89

KENNEDY, HOWARD E.

about

A nose for success. K. Osborne and C. C. Williams. por *Black Enterprise* 19:32 F '89

KENNEDY, JOHN F. (JOHN FITZGERALD), 1917-1963

about

"I'm staying right here". H. Sidey. il por *Time* 133:40 F 13 '89

JFK Jr. to narrate 'Profiles in courage' for Harper Audio. il pors *Publishers Weekly* 236:28 D 1 '89

JFK remembered [videotape] R. S. Rothenberg. il por *USA Today (Periodical)* 117:97 Ja '89

Letters [discussion of December 5, 1988 article, J.F.K.'s legacy] A. Kopkind. *The Nation* 248:218 F 20 '89

Addresses, messages, etc.

Present at the construction [genesis of speech at the Berlin Wall] H. Sidey. il por *Time* 134:33 N 20 '89

Assassination

The cross fire over Jack Ruby's gun. il por *U.S. News & World Report* 107:10 D 25 '89-Ja 1 '90

Guardians of Infinity: To Save Kennedy [interactive text game] E. Ferrell. il *Compute!* 11:65 Jl '89

Guardians of Infinity: To Save Kennedy [video game] S. Williams. il por *Home Office Computing* 7:90 My '89

Jack Ruby's family and lawyer battle for possession of the gun that killed Lee Harvey Oswald. W. Plummer. il por *People Weekly* 31:42-3 My 22 '89

Lights and shadows: destiny in Dallas. E. Oxford. bibl f il por *American History Illustrated* 23:12-17+ Ja '89

Man in the pink shirt. J. Glaeg. *America* 161:370-1 N 25 '89

World of mirrors. E. Oxford. bibl il *American History Illustrated* 23:34-45 F '89

Exhibitions

Reflections on a tragedy [Texas School Book Depository] D. Bedwell. il *Travel Holiday* 172:96+ Ag '89

"The sixth floor". il *American History Illustrated* 23:42-3 F '89

A tragic dilemma [discussion of August 1989 article, Reflections on a tragedy] D. Bedwell. il *Travel Holiday* 172:8 N '89

Reporters and reporting

The best TV documentary of 1988 [JFK assassination: as it happened] T. Teachout. il *The American Spectator* 22:27-8 F '89

Media-watch. H. David. il *History Today* 39:5-7 Mr '89

KENNEDY, JOHN F., 1960-

about

Favorite son [cover story] M. Gross. il pors *New York* 22:36-44 Mr 20 '89

KENNEDY, JOHN F., 1960—about—*cont.*
Jackie: a mother's journey. C. Avery. il *Ladies' Home Journal* 106:142-4+ Mr '89
JFK Jr. to narrate 'Profiles in courage' for Harper Audio. il pors *Publishers Weekly* 236:28 D 1 '89

KENNEDY, JOSEPH PATRICK, II
about
Facing divorce Joe Kennedy says no to higher office—for now. P. Chin. il pors *People Weekly* 31:45-6 Mr 27 '89
New Kennedy, old solutions. S. T. Mandel. *National Review* 41:22-3 Jl 14 '89
Sticking it to the taxpayers. D. Corn. il *The Nation* 249:238-40 S 4-11 '89

KENNEDY, KATHLEEN *See* Townsend, Kathleen
KENNEDY, LINDA
(jt. auth) *See* Stinespring, John A., and Kennedy, Linda
KENNEDY, MARILYN MOATS, 1943-
Job strategies. *See* issues of Glamour
Manager's tipsheet: keeping minimum-wage workers motivated. *Working Woman* 14:32 O '89

KENNEDY, PATRICK J.
about
New talents: Patrick J. Kennedy. il por *Harper's Bazaar* 122:118 Mr '89

KENNEDY, PAUL M., 1945-
Can the US remain number one? [cover story] il *The New York Review of Books* 36:36-42 Mr 16 '89
The challenges to America—long-term, short-term, or both? *New Perspectives Quarterly* 5:62-3 Wint '88/'89
Economic and military security [address, February 22, 1989] *Vital Speeches of the Day* 55:594-7 Jl 15 '89
about
New century, new players [interview] il *Life* 12:76 F '89

KENNEDY, RANDALL
Brown plus 35. *The Nation* 248:725 My 29 '89
KENNEDY, ROBERT T., AND OTHERS
Microcolumn separations and the analysis of single cells. bibl f il *Science* 246:57-63 O 6 '89

KENNEDY, ROGER G.
A young nation builds its temples to the future. bibl (p230) il *Smithsonian* 20:170-5 O '89
about
The stuff of history. B. Barol. il por *Newsweek* 113:80-1 Ap 24 '89

KENNEDY, SEAN
Last word. por *Omni (New York, N.Y.)* 12:168 O '89
KENNEDY, TED *See* Kennedy, Edward Moore, 1932-
KENNEDY, WALLACE
Managing the influence of television through the discipline of video. bibl f *Design for Arts in Education* 90:26-8 Mr/Ap '89

KENNEDY, WILLIAM, 1928-
about
Fathers & their sons. D. M. Murtaugh. il por *Commonweal* 116:298-302 My 19 '89

KENNEDY, WILLIAM A., AND MARSHALL, MARK G.
A peek at the French missile complex. il *The Bulletin of the Atomic Scientists* 45:20-3 S '89

KENNEDY (JOHN F.) SCHOOL OF GOVERNMENT *See* John F. Kennedy School of Government

KENNEDY FAMILY
about
The young Kennedys carry on. E. Mehren. il *McCall's* 116:40-2+ Je '89

KENNEDY INTERNATIONAL AIRPORT *See* New York (N.Y.)—Airports
KENNEDY SPACE CENTER *See* John F. Kennedy Space Center

KENNELLY, BARBARA B.
Should the House-passed wage proposal be enacted? [excerpts from address, March 23, 1989] *Congressional Digest* 68:156+ My '89

KENNELS
The dog house [made from plastic barrels] B. Tarrant. il *Field & Stream* 94:94+ Je '89
One dandy doghouse packed with style, storage, and fun [combined with storage shed] J. Franck. il *Better Homes and Gardens* 67:124 Jl '89
The ultimate kennel. L. Mueller. il *Outdoor Life* 183:38+ Je '89
Exhibitions
Mondo cane [Going to the dogs show in Kentucky] il *American Craft* 49:52-3 O/N '89

KENNER, HUGH
Ear culture. *Harper's* 278:26-7+ Mr '89
Out my computer window. il *Harper's* 279:76-80 N '89
Print queue. *See* issues of Byte beginning July 1989

KENNETH
about
He's the tops. D. Kazanjian. il pors *House & Garden* 161:120-5+ F '89

KENNEY, JAMES J.
(jt. auth) *See* Pritikin, Robert, and Kenney, James J.
KENNEY, JOHN
Grave waters. il map *National Parks* 63:18-23+ Jl/Ag '89
KENNICOTT, PHILIP
Christmas dream work. il *Dance Magazine* 63:67 D '89

KENNY, GLENN
Get the picture! il *Stereo Review* 54:69-73 Ap '89
KENSINGTON (LONDON, ENGLAND)
Historic houses, sites, etc.
Victorian fantasy [Lord Glenconner's Hill Lodge in Kensington] D. J. Ogilvy. il por *House & Garden* 161:176-81 Mr '89
KENSIT, PATSY
about
Patsy Kensit. S. Mills. il pors *Seventeen* 48:60 D '89
Patsy Kensit's sultry beauty lights the fuse in Lethal weapon 2. il por *People Weekly* 32:50-1 Jl 31 '89

KENT, DEBRA
Baby boom. il *Seventeen* 48:117-18+ Je '89
The daddy trap. il *Mademoiselle* 95:182-3+ D '89
How to have a boyfriend without losing your friends. il *Seventeen* 48:155-6+ My '89
Thin thighs, heavy heart. il *Mademoiselle* 95:166+ S '89

KENT, KAY
about
Kay Kent died the way she lived—as a mirror of Marilyn Monroe. M. Dougherty. il pors *People Weekly* 32:90-1 Jl 3 '89

KENT, LINDA
about
The fat firmers. P. Nicoll. pors *Harper's Bazaar* 122:34+ Ag '89
A mover moves on. S. Reiter. il por *Dance Magazine* 63:38 Ap '89

KENTUCKY
See also
Big South Fork National River and Recreation Area (Tenn. and Ky.)
Country estates—Kentucky
Drama festivals—Kentucky
Educational laws and regulations—Kentucky
Historic houses, sites, etc.—Kentucky
Jackson County (Ky.)
Marion County (Ky.)
Medical care—Kentucky
Wetlands, Artificial—Kentucky
Antiquities
Who owns our past? [pillage of Indian artifacts on Slack Farm excavation site] H. Arden. il map *National Geographic* 175:376-93 Mr '89
Description and travel
See also
Automobile touring—Kentucky
Celebrate a Kentucky Christmas. J. T. Black. il map *Southern Living* 24:40+ D '89
Industries
See also
Strip mining—Kentucky
Politics and government
Congressional miracle: Natcher runs, but he won't take the money. J. S. Kunen. il pors *People Weekly* 31:45+ Je 26 '89

KENTUCKY CENTRAL LIFE INS. CO.
This insurer may be up for grabs. G. G. Marcial. *Business Week* p104 Ag 14 '89
KENTUCKY COOKING *See* Cooking, American
KENTUCKY DERBY *See* Horse racing
KENYA
See also
Amboseli National Park (Kenya)
Birds—Kenya
Crime and criminals—Kenya
Game preserves—Kenya
Hiking—Kenya
Masai Mara Game Reserve (Kenya)
Medical care—Kenya
Nomads—Kenya
Paleontology—Kenya
Railroads—Kenya
Relief work—Kenya
Sex education—Kenya
Tsavo National Park (Kenya)
Wildlife—Kenya
Wildlife conservation—Kenya
Women—Kenya
Industries
See also
Evikar International
Native peoples
See also
Boran (African people)
Kipsigis (African people)
Masai (African people)
Rendile (African people)
Photographs and photography
Above Kenya. Y. Arthus-Bertrand. il *Life* 12:90-5 Ag '89
KENYON, JANE
At the dime store [poem] *The Atlantic* 264:76 O '89
At the Public Market Museum: Charleston, South Carolina [poem] *The New Yorker* 65:73 Ag 14 '89
Geranium [poem] *The Nation* 248:388 Mr 20 '89

KENYON, JEAN
Northern Hemisphere albatrosses. bibl il *Sea Frontiers* 35:342-7 N/D '89
KENYON, MICHAEL
Following the Tour de France. il *Gourmet* 49:72+ Jl '89
A Texas Thanksgiving. il *Gourmet* 49:138+ N '89
Worcestershire sauce. il *Gourmet* 49:122+ O '89
KENYON COLLEGE
Homophobiaphobia [feminist linguistic course taught by lesbian] T. Short. *National Review* 41:19-20 Ag 18 '89
KEOGH PLANS
Moving your IRA, SEP or Keogh into a new home. M. Meyer. il *Money* 18:59-60 Ap '89
KEOHANE, MICHAEL
about
Kid Keohane. M. Will-Weber. il por *Runner's World* 24:101 Jl '89
KEOUGH, BILL
Bean bounty [cover story] il *Organic Gardening* 36:30-2+ F '89
KEOUGH, DANIELLE RILEY
about
The Presleys' newest star [cover story] M. Green. il pors *People Weekly* 31:108-10+ Je 19 '89
KEOWN, IAN
Gourmet holidays: Amsterdam. il *Gourmet* 49:74-9+ Ap '89
KEPPLER, HERBERT
SLR world. See issues of Popular Photography beginning September 1987
KERATINOCYTE GROWTH FACTOR
Human KGF is FGF-related with properties of a paracrine effector of epithelial cell growth. P. W. Finch and others. bibl f il *Science* 245:752-5 Ag 18 '89
KERATINOCYTES
Detection of cell-affecting agents with a silicon biosensor [silicon microphysiometer] J. W. Parce and others. bibl f il *Science* 246:243-7 O 13 '89
Listening to the breaths of 1,000 cells [silicon microphysiometer] *Science News* 136:286 O 28 '89
KERATOCONJUNCTIVITIS SICCA *See* Eye—Diseases and defects
KERCHIEFS *See* Scarves
KERCKERINCK, JOSEF, BARON
about
Bambi and the baron. D. Machan. il por *Forbes* 144:298+ D 11 '89
KÉRÉKOU, MATHIEU
about
Pass the ammunition. P. R. Michaud. *The New Republic* 200:14 Mr 13 '89
KEREM, BAT-SHEVA, AND OTHERS
Identification of the cystic fibrosis gene: genetic analysis. bibl f il *Science* 245:1073-80 S 8 '89
KEREN, DAVID F.
(jt. auth) See Silbart, Lawrence K., and Keren, David F.
KERESZTES, PETER
The new Hungarian revolution. il *The American Spectator* 22:28-9 Jl '89
KERMAN, JOSEPH, 1924-
Mozart à la mode. bibl f il *The New York Review of Books* 36:50-2 My 18 '89
KERMIT (MUPPET)
Kermit the Frog. il *People Weekly* 31 Special Issue:58 Summ '89
KERN, ANN
about
"Get them to ask questions" [interview] il *World Health* p4-5 Mr '89
KERN, BLAINE
about
Larger than life. B. Weber. il *The New York Times Magazine* p70 Ja 22 '89
KERN, DALE
Bringing it all back home. il por *House & Garden* 161:178-87 My '89
KERN, PASCAL
about
Pascal Kern: Galerie Zabriskie. G. Danto. il *Art News* 88:164 F '89
KERN, PORTIA
about
Pit players. D. Sherman. il pors *Ms.* 18:62-4+ N '89
KERN (NORMAN) & COMPANY *See* Norman Kern & Company
KERNAN, MICHAEL
The chicks that stayed home in the range. il *Smithsonian* 20:214 S '89
Fit only for the fire: the Adirondack chair. il *Smithsonian* 20:192 D '89
In 1789 a farmer went to New York to become president. bibl f (p174) il *Smithsonian* 20:94-6+ Je '89
Robert Goddard and his rocket were lonely pioneers of man's thrust into the limitlessness of space. il pors *Smithsonian* 20:46+ N '89
William and Henry Walters, and their fever for the fine arts. bibl (p135) il pors *Smithsonian* 20:102-8+ Ag '89

KERNS, JOANNA
about
Alan Thicke loves Joanna Kerns—and does he have plans for her! H. Newton. il por *TV Guide* 37:6-7+ Jl 22-28 '89
KERNS, THOMAS E.
about
Kerns named S.C. school district superintendent. por *Jet* 76:30 My 8 '89
KERNSTOCK, NICHOLAS C.
Market focus. See issues of Aviation Week & Space Technology beginning October 3, 1988
KEROUAC, JACK, 1922-1969
about
On the road to nowhere. S. Birkerts. il *Harper's* 279:74-6 Jl '89
KERR, BLAKE, AND ACKERLY, JOHN
Witness to repression. il *Utne Reader* p42-3 Mr/Ap '89
KERR, CHRISTOPHER
Medical publishers enlist expert advice on the future. il *Publishers Weekly* 235:43-4 Ap 14 '89
KERR, D. STEVEN, AND OTHERS
Corticosteroid modulation of hippocampal potentials: increased effect with aging. bibl f il *Science* 245:1505-9 S 29 '89
KERR, DAVID A.
The satanic verses and beyond. *The Christian Century* 106:354-8 Ap 5 '89
KERR, GEORGE T.
Synthetic zeolites [cover story] bibl il *Scientific American* 261:100-5 Jl '89
KERR, STEPHEN T.
Reform in Soviet and American education: parallels and contrasts. bibl f il *Phi Delta Kappan* 71:19-28 S '89
KERR, STEVE
about
Steve Kerr: comeback kid. L. Elliott. il por *Reader's Digest* 134:37-8+ Ap '89
KERR-MCGEE CORP.
Does Pennzoil see a gusher in Kerr-McGee? G. G. Marcial. il *Business Week* p134 My 8 '89
Playing with the majors. T. Mack. il por *Forbes* 144:92+ N 13 '89
KERREY, ROBERT
Should a constitutional amendment to prevent flag desecration be approved? [excerpts from address, July 18, 1989] *Congressional Digest* 68:205+ Ag/S '89
Should the Congress adopt the "Financial Institutions Reform, Recovery, and Enforcement Act of 1989"? [excerpts from address, April 19, 1989] *Congressional Digest* 68:191 Je/Jl '89
about
Senator perfect [cover story] J. Weisberg. por *The New Republic* 201:16-20 D 18 '89
KERRIDGE, JOHN F., 1937-
What has caused the secular increase in solar nitrogen-15? bibl f il *Science* 245:480-6 Ag 4 '89
KERSEE, JACKIE JOYNER- *See* Joyner-Kersee, Jackie
KERTES, TOM
'80s basketball. il *Sport (New York, N.Y.)* 80:62-4+ O '89
Fearless Final Fourcast. il *Sport (New York, N.Y.)* 80:66-70 Ap '89
Guru of the glass. il por *Sport (New York, N.Y.)* 80:68-71 Mr '89
Life at the top. il *Sport (New York, N.Y.)* 80:31-7 Jl '89
The NBA's entrance exam. il *Sport (New York, N.Y.)* 80:40-1+ Ja '89
The Sport 1989-90 college hoops preview [cover story] il *Sport (New York, N.Y.)* 80:36-40+ D '89
KESEY, KEN
Remember this: write what you don't know. *The New York Times Book Review* 94:1+ D 31 '89
about
Ken Kesey's eclectic writing acid test. D. Weddle. il por *Rolling Stone* p119-20+ O 5 '89
KESLER, CHARLES R.
about
Paleo right and natural right. P. J. Stanlis. *National Review* 41:44 O 27 '89
KESSLER, BRAD
Down and out in suburbia. il *The Nation* 249:306+ S 25 '89
KESSLER, BRUCE
12,000 mile dream cruise (I). il maps *Motor Boating & Sailing* 163:70-3+ Mr '89
12,000 mile dream cruise (II). map *Motor Boating & Sailing* 163:78-9+ Ap '89
12,000 mile dream cruise (III). il *Motor Boating & Sailing* 163:68-9+ My '89
KESSLER, DAVID
about
David Kessler: home nursing for AIDS patients. D. Castellon. il por *Business Week* p117 N 6 '89
KESSLER, KAYE W.
20 years ago the Ohio State Buckeyes won the Big Ten's last national championship. il *Sport (New York, N.Y.)* 80:74-5 Ja '89

KESSLER, KEVIN J.
Humankind's global steps in humanist directions. por *The Humanist* 49:21+ Mr/Ap '89

KESSLER, RICHARD A.
Peronists seek "nuclear greatness". il por *The Bulletin of the Atomic Scientists* 45:13-15 My '89

KESSLER, RONALD
Moscow station: how the KGB penetrated the American embassy [excerpts; cover story] il *Time* 133:50-2+ F 20 '89

KESTEN, LOU
New products. See issues of Video through October 1989

KESTENBAUM, STUART J.
(jt. auth) See Bither, Eve M., and Kestenbaum, Stuart J.

KESTNER, JOSEPH
Beyond reason [cover story] il *Opera News* 53:8-11+ F 18 '89
Born of obsession. il *Opera News* 53:24-6+ Mr 4 '89

KESWICK, WILLIAM
about
Sir William Keswick's sculptural landscape in Scotland. J. McEwen. il por *Architectural Digest* 46:324+ O '89

KETCHAM, DIANA
Time pieces. il pors *Art News* 88:152-7 O '89
Who's afraid of James Stirling? il por *Art News* 88:98-103 F '89

KETCHUM, RICHARD M., 1922-
For sale: rural America. il *Country Journal* 16:80-3 My/Je '89
Yesterday, December 7, 1941 [with editorial comment by Byron Dobell] il *American Heritage* 40:5, 52-6+ N '89

KETELSEN, JAMES L.
about
Case study in determination. R. Reiff. il por *Forbes* 144:126-7 O 30 '89

KETEMA, INC.
Ametek backwards. T. Jaffe. *Forbes* 143:124-5 Ja 23 '89

KETEYIAN, ARMEN
Follow that girl. il pors *New York* 22:38-43 Mr 6 '89

KETOCONAZOLE
Lung power [use of ketoconazole to prevent respiratory failure from fluid in the lungs] *Prevention (Emmaus, Pa.)* 41:16+ Ag '89

KETTLE'S YARD GALLERY
Ede's corner. C. Rose. il por *Art News* 88:103-4 N '89

KETTMANN, STEVE
The San Francisco treat [interview with J. Rice] il pors *Gentlemen's Quarterly* 59:121+ O '89
Why I wear what I wear: Danny Glover, in character [interview] il pors *Gentlemen's Quarterly* 59:40+ Jl '89

KEVLAR
Step aside, Superman [Kevlar vs. Spectra Shield] A. A. Lappen. il *Forbes* 143:124+ F 6 '89

KEVLES, BARBARA
Walking tall. il *Women's Sports & Fitness* 11:26 Ap '89
When you haven't got time for the pain. il *Women's Sports & Fitness* 11:12 Jl/Ag '89

KEVLES, DANIEL J.
Paradise lost. bibl f il *The New York Review of Books* 36:32-8 D 21 '89
(jt. auth) See Heilbron, J. L., and Kevles, Daniel J.

KEVORKIAN, JACK
about
Death-row murderers could be lifesavers. *Newsweek* 113:49 Ja 9 '89

KEW GARDENS (GREAT BRITAIN) See Royal Botanic Gardens (Kew, England)

KEWEENAW PENINSULA (MICH.)
Climate
The land of lavish snow. K. Walters. il map *Country Journal* 16:56-9 F '89

KEWPIE DOLLS
Collectors and collecting
Kewpies: love at first sight [R. O'Neill's dolls] M. Jailer. il *Antiques & Collecting Hobbies* 94:33-4+ My '89

KEY, DOUGLAS
(jt. auth) See Matzke, Gordon, and Key, Douglas

KEY, FRANCIS SCOTT, 1779-1843
about
Key on display. J. Nassar. il por *Americana* 17:10 N/D '89

KEY AIRLINES
A Soviet election [determining whether employees wish to join Teamsters] D. Seligman. il *Fortune* 120:142+ Jl 3 '89

KEY BOOK SERVICES
Judge releases books in Connecticut warehouse. C. Reid. *Publishers Weekly* 236:10 Ag 4 '89

KEY LIME PIE See Pie

KEY WEST (FLA.)
City planning
Pritam Singh's strange career [developing the Truman Annex] R. Conniff. il por *Time* 134:21-2+ D 11 '89
Description
Romancing the Keys. M. Chabon. il *Vogue* 179:234-5+ D '89

Restaurants, nightclubs, bars, etc.
Key West's key lime pie. V. Gladstone. il *Americana* 16:36-8+ Ja/F '89

KEYBOARD INSTRUMENTS
See also
Piano
Keys to the kingdom [electronic keyboards] J. Cocks. il *Time* 133:64 Mr 6 '89

KEYBOARDS
Cures for mushy keyboard syndrome [OmniKey/102; Zeos/RS] C. O'Malley. il *Personal Computing* 13:202 Ap '89
Search for a perfect keyboard, continued. S. R. Reed. il *Personal Computing* 13:229 N '89
Stalking the 8-bit spectrum. T. Thompson. il *Byte* 14:333-4+ S '89
A useful alternative to macro software [AutoKey macro keyboard] R. Bel Bruno. il *Personal Computing* 13:202 D '89
Writing your way [customizing keyboard commands] C. Bermant. il *Home Office Computing* 7:24+ My '89
Health aspects
Computeritis [carpal tunnel syndrome] R. Trubo. il *Glamour* 87:56+ D '89

KEYES, ALAN
Alan Keyes [advice to George Bush] il *National Review* 41:27-8 F 10 '89

KEYES, RALPH
Classics. il *Gentlemen's Quarterly* 59:146-51 Ja '89
Help! My wife may throw me away! il *Good Housekeeping* 208:109-10 Mr '89

KEYES, WILLIAM A.
Blacks and Republicans. il *Conservative Digest* 15:47-9 Jl/Ag '89

KEYFITZ, NATHAN, 1913-
The growing human population. il map *Scientific American* 261:118-26 S '89

KEYISHIAN, ELIZABETH
Pillow talk. il *Glamour* 87:168 Ja '89

KEYNES, JOHN MAYNARD, 1883-1946
about
Keynes the able. R. Kuttner. por *The New Republic* 201:62+ N 6 '89

KEYNESIAN ECONOMICS See Economics

KEYS, MICHAEL
about
Steroids built Mike Keys up; then they tore him down. M. Brower. il pors *People Weekly* 31:107-8 Mr 20 '89

KEYS See Locks and keys

KEYSER, BARBARA
The risk of breaking rules. il *American Artist* 53:20+ O '89
Support systems for paintings (I). il *American Artist* 53:20+ D '89

KEYWORTH, GEORGE A., AND ABELL, BRUCE
The third generation of the space age. *Science* 245:16 Jl 7 '89

KFIR AIRPLANES See Airplanes, Military—Israel

KGB
Inside the KGB. il *Time* 133:54-5 F 13 '89
K.G.B. defector Gundarev: it's cold coming out [cover story] D. Wise. il *The New York Times Magazine* p36-9+ S 17 '89
Mask of treachery [K. Philby; excerpt] J. Costello. il por *Conservative Digest* 15:59+ Ja/F '89
The Moscow bug hunt [no evidence that Marines C. Lonetree and A. Bracy allowed Soviets into the U.S. embassy] J. Peterzell. il pors *Time* 134:26-8 Jl 10 '89
Moscow station: how the KGB penetrated the American embassy [Marine guard spy case; excerpts; cover story] R. Kessler. il *Time* 133:50-2+ F 20 '89

KGO (SAN FRANCISCO, CALIF.: TELEVISION STATION) See Television stations

KHADAFY, MOAMMAR See Qaddafi, Muammar al-, 1942-

KHADER, HANNA
about
The widow of an Israeli soldier gives his heart—and the gift of life—to an Arab, Hanna Khader. il pors *People Weekly* 32:130 D 11 '89

KHALATNIKOV, I. M.
Reminiscences of Landau. il pors *Physics Today* 42:34-41 My '89

KHALID, S. M.
Namibia: independent at last—we hope. map *American Visions* 4:51-2 Je '89

KHALIL, AMER
about
Notes and comment. il *The New Yorker* 65:23-4 Ag 28 '89

KHALILZAD, ZALMAY
The United States in South Asia. map *Current History* 88:417-20+ D '89

KHAMENEI, HOJATOLESLAM ALI, 1940-
about
Change in Teheran: exit Moses, enter Joshua. *National Review* 41:15-16 Je 30 '89

KHAN, KAUSAR S., AND ISLAM, KAMAL
A health care paradox. il *World Health* p5-7 My '89

KHANGA, YELENA
    Black Russian. il pors *Essence* 20:59-60+ Ag '89
KHASHOGGI, ADNAN
        about
    From jet set to jail cell. C. Dickey. il por *Newsweek* 113:10
        My 1 '89
    Of guns and a guru. M. McDonald. il pors *Maclean's* 102:28-9
        Mr 27 '89
    Scandal, sex and the stir. S. Slewka and N. Le Quesne.
        il pors *Life* 12:28-31 Je '89
    Stepping out. J. Kasindorf. il pors *New York* 22:36-44 D
        18 '89
KHATEEB, MUHAMMAD AL- *See* Al-Khateeb, Muhammad
KHMER ROUGE
    Back to the killing fields. A. Deming. il *Newsweek* 114:40
        S 11 '89
    Cambodia's test of wills—and arms. R. Tasker and M. Hiebert.
        il *World Press Review* 36:34+ D '89
    Civil war in Cambodia? N. Chanda. *Foreign Policy* 76:26-43
        Fall '89
    A firm no to the Tiger [Paris conference] S. Talbott. il
        Time 134:36 Ag 14 '89
    Healing Cambodia's wounds [Paris conference] S. H. Green-
        berg. il *Newsweek* 114:29 Ag 14 '89
    Journey to freedom [condensed from A Cambodian odyssey];
        ed. by Roger Warner. H. S. Ngor. il *Reader's Digest*
        134:209-13+ Mr '89
    Killing fields II. E. Becker. *The New Republic* 200:10+ Ja
        2 '89
    The killing fields revisited. S. Talbott. il *Time* 133:47 My
        1 '89
    Never again? A. Berlow. il *Harper's* 279:62-8 O '89
    Old war, China card & Sihanouk. S. Blaustein. il *The Nation*
        249:485-6+ O 30 '89
    The return of the Khmer Rouge [cover story] S. Erlanger.
        il map *The New York Times Magazine* p24-7+ Mr 5
        '89
    Return to the killing fields [cover story] P. Dith. il pors
        The New York Times Magazine p30-3+ S 24 '89
    Sihanouk on the high wire. A. Platt. il pors *Newsweek* 113:45
        My 15 '89
    The specter of the Khmer Rouge. M. K. Magistad. *The
        Nation* 248:228+ F 20 '89
    Stop Pol Pot. il *The New Republic* 200:7-9 Ap 3 '89
    The tiger and the crocodile. H. D. S. Greenway. *The New
        Yorker* 65:72-83 Jl 17 '89
    The unmaking of a quagmire. N. Cooper. il map *Newsweek*
        113:38-40 Ja 30 '89
    Who's the puppet? [Norodom Sihanouk's ties with the Khmer
        Rouge] A. Berlow. *The New Republic* 201:16-18 O 2 '89
    Zbig deal in Cambodia [U.S. responsibility for continued
        strength of Khmer Rouge] *The Nation* 248:109 Ja 30
        '89
KHOKHA, RAMA, AND OTHERS
    Antisense RNA-induced reduction in murine TIMP levels
        confers oncogenicity on Swiss 3T3 cells. bibl f il *Science*
        243:947-50 F 17 '89
KHOMEINI, AHMAD
        about
    Battle of the heirs: son of Ayatollah vs. son of Shah. E.
        Flores. il pors *World Press Review* 36:16 Ag '89
KHOMEINI, RUHOLLAH
    Gorbachev's crisis of faith [text of letter] *Harper's* 278:21-2
        Ap '89
        about
    The Ayatollah, the novelist, and the West [cover story]
        D. Pipes. *Commentary* 87:9-17 Je '89
    Book world reacts to Khomeini's threats [special section;
        with editorial comment by John F. Baker] *Publishers Weekly*
        235:22, 26-8+ Mr 3 '89
    Burying the passions Khomeini inflamed. B. Hewitt. il por
        Newsweek 113:44-5 Je 19 '89
    Deadly defiance. A. Phillips. il por *Maclean's* 102:18-19
        Mr 6 '89
    Diplomacy in the dark. D. Stanglin. il *U.S. News & World
        Report* 106:26 Mr 6 '89
    Embroiled Salman. M. Peretz. *The New Republic* 200:50
        Mr 20 '89
    A frenzied farewell. J. Smolowe. il *Time* 133:38-9 Je 19
        '89
    The holy terror of Teheran fires his final volley. il *U.S.
        News & World Report* 106:14-15 Je 19 '89
    Hunted by an angry faith. W. E. Smith. il pors *Time* 133:28-33
        F 27 '89
    In the light of history. E. Mortimer. il *World Press Review*
        36:64 Mr '89
    Iran braces for a power struggle. L. Lief. *U.S. News &
        World Report* 106:36 Je 19 '89
    Iran's threats against author [statement, March 8, 1989] A.
        P. Adams, Jr. *Department of State Bulletin* 89:78-80 My
        '89
    Islamic wasteland. B. Crozier. il *National Review* 41:17 Mr
        24 '89
    Khomeini strikes back. J. Bierman. il pors *Maclean's* 102:25
        Ap 10 '89
    A love poem. W. Chittick and P. Clawson. *The New Republic*
        201:35 S 4 '89

Minority report. C. Hitchens. *The Nation* 248:332 Mr 13
    '89
The new Satans. W. E. Smith. il por *Time* 133:36-8 Mr
    6 '89
Now that the millennium has ended. F. Ajami. il por *U.S.
    News & World Report* 106:35 Je 19 '89
Obituary
    Maclean's il por 102:20-1 Je 19 '89. R. Corelli
    The Nation 248:869 Je 26 '89
    National Review 41:15-16 Je 30 '89
    The New Republic 200:6-7 Je 26 '89
    The New York Review of Books il 36:16-19 Jl 20 '89.
        S. Bakhash
    Newsweek por 113:40 Je 12 '89. H. Anderson
    Time il pors 133:36+ Je 12 '89
    World Press Review 36:20 Ag '89. G. H. Jansen
    World Press Review 36:31 Jl '89
On blasphemy: advice for the Ayatollah. R. Goetz. *The
    Christian Century* 106:253-5 Mr 8 '89
Prosaic justice all around. P. Iyer. il *Time* 133:84 Mr 6
    '89
The Rushdie affair [discussion of June 1989 article, The
    Ayatollah, the novelist, and the West] D. Pipes.
    Commentary 88:11-12+ O '89
Salman Rushdie: a collage of comment [special section; with
    introd. by Nathan Gardels] il *New Perspectives Quarterly*
    6:48-55 Spr '89
The 'Satanic' furor [cover story; special section; with editorial
    comment by Kevin Doyle] il pors *Maclean's* 102:2, 16-22+
    F 27 '89
A 'Satanic' fury [cover story] R. Watson. il pors *Newsweek*
    113:34-6+ F 27 '89
Secular sermon. H. Hertzberg. *The New Republic* 200:4+
    Mr 20 '89
'Shame'. G. Black. *The Nation* 248:328-9 Mr 13 '89
Two cheers for blasphemy. *The New Republic* 200:7-9 Mr
    13 '89
War and revolution in Iran. G. Fuller. bibl f *Current History*
    88:81-4+ F '89
War of the words. *Commonweal* 116:131-2 Mr 10 '89
The West gets tough with Iran—sort of. R. Watson. il
    Newsweek 113:32-3 Mr 6 '89
Why the Ayatollah is whipping up a new wave of fanaticism.
    S. Carter and others. il *Business Week* p47 Mr 6 '89
Will the next Imam please stand up? il por *U.S. News
    & World Report* 106:13 Ap 10 '89
Zealots with fear in their eyes. R. Rosenblatt. il por *U.S.
    News & World Report* 106:8-11 F 27 '89
KHOROSHILOV, PAVEL
        about
    Can a socialist win in a free market? Pavel Khoroshilov
        as Leo Castelli? M. Esterow. il pors *Art News* 88:51-2+
        S '89
KHRUSCHEV, NIKITA *See* Khrushchev, Nikita Sergeevich,
        1894-1971
KHRUSHCHEV, NIKITA SERGEEVICH, 1894-1971
        about
    Commentary: the Cuban missile crisis. R. S. Cline. bibl
        f *Foreign Affairs* 68:190-6 Fall '89
    Nikita Gorbachev? F. Coleman. il pors *Newsweek* 114:39
        S 11 '89
    Remember Khrushchev. M. Tatu. *World Press Review* 36:24
        F '89
KHUN SA
        about
    Burma's 'Money Tree'. M. Liu. il por map *Newsweek* 113:42-3
        My 15 '89
KI-ZERBO, JOSEPH
        about
    An African view of the debt [interview] H. Ziady. il por
        World Press Review 36:50 Ag '89
KIBBUTZIM
    Different strokes: eleven kids from Brooklyn try life on
        a kibbutz [project initiated by teacher S. Bialer] J. Taylor.
        il por *New York* 22:56-8+ Je 12 '89
KID ANTRIM *See* Billy, the Kid
KIDD, BILLY
    Kids page. See issues of Skiing beginning September 1984
    'Race Country USA'. il *Skiing* 41:94-5+ Ja '89
KIDD, JOHN
    'The scandal of Ulysses': yet another exchange [discussion
        of June 30, 1988 article] il *The New York Review of
        Books* 36:40-1 Je 1 '89
        about
    Miami J'yce: love walks right out of a 'Ulysses' symposium.
        B. Maddox. il *The New York Times Book Review* 94:7
        F 26 '89
KIDD, JULIA
        about
    Julia Kidd at Anne Plumb. K. Johnson. *Art in America*
        77:153 Mr '89
KIDD, RANDY
    The aging pet. *The Mother Earth News* 118:34-6 Jl/Ag '89
    Feline leukemia. il *The Mother Earth News* 119:34+ S/O
        '89
    Hip dysplasia. il *The Mother Earth News* 116:42+ Mr/Ap
        '89

KIDD, RANDY—*cont.*
Pets and the holidays. il *The Mother Earth News* 120:33-4 N/D '89
KIDDER, TRACY
about
After a year as a fifth-grade Gulliver, author Tracy Kidder speaks up for teachers. K. Hubbard. il pors *People Weekly* 32:77+ O 9 '89
From 'House' to schoolhouse. C. Leslie. il por *Newsweek* 114:67 S 11 '89
PW interviews. A. Smith. por *Publishers Weekly* 236:101-2 S 15 '89
KIDDER, PEABODY & CO., INCORPORATED
The body count keeps growing at Kidder Peabody. J. R. Norman and J. Friedman. il *Business Week* p128-9 F 20 '89
Michael Carpenter. J. Friedman. il por *Business Week* Special Issue:154 Ap 14 '89
KIDDIEPORN LAWS *See* Obscenity (Law)
KIDNAPPING
See also
Anderson, Terry—Kidnapping
Camarena Salazar, Enrique—Murder case
Cicippio, Joseph—Kidnapping
Custody kidnapping
Della Casa, Nicholas—Kidnapping
Gibson, Matthew—Kidnapping
Grover, Richard—Kidnapping
Higgins, William R.—Kidnapping
Kauffmann, Jean-Paul—Kidnapping
Libby, Roy—Kidnapping
Manns, Lindsey Regan—Kidnapping
Obeid, Abdul Karim—Kidnapping
Olson, Bruce—Kidnapping
Stayner, Steven—Kidnapping
Weflen, Julie—Kidnapping
Wetterling, Jacob—Kidnapping
"We had to kidnap our son from the hospital" [D. Pagán jailed after husband takes leukemia-stricken son from Memorial Sloan-Kettering Cancer Center] J. L. Block. il pors *Good Housekeeping* 209:144-5+ O '89
KIDNEY DIALYSIS *See* Hemodialysis
KIDNEY STONES
Are you stone prone? L. Holland. *Good Housekeeping* 209:275 S '89
Therapy
The good news on stones. A. J. Sheinman. il *New Choices for the Best Years* 29:55-7 Ag '89
Say goodbye to kidney stones. K. Pechter. il *Prevention (Emmaus, Pa.)* 41:58-61 S '89
KIDNEYS
See also
Adrenal glands
Urine
Atrial natriuretic peptide inhibits a cation channel in renal inner medullary collecting duct cells. D. B. Light and others. bibl f il *Science* 243:383-5 Ja 20 '89
Cancer
Genetic aspects
One Wilms' tumor gene is cloned; are there more? M. Hoffman. *Science* 246:1387 D 15 '89
Diseases
See also
Nephritis
Causes
Analgesics can harm kidney [research by Dale P. Sandler] *Science News* 135:294 My 13 '89
Transplantation
Count Dracula makes an offer [letter sent to bankrupt persons offering to buy one of their kidneys in West Germany]; tr. by Elliott Rabin. R. R. Adelmann von Adelmannsfelden. *Harper's* 278:23-4 Mr '89
An enigma named Gloria [woman with cytomegalovirus pneumonia] T. Dajer. il *Discover* 10:86-9 N '89
Expert doubts success rate of transplants in blacks [views of Clive Callender] il *Jet* 76:51 Je 19 '89
The hunt for Charles Ridgeway [locating kidney recipient in remote area] J. Shannon. il *Reader's Digest* 135:40-2+ D '89
KIDNEYS, ARTIFICIAL
See also
Hemodialysis
KIDS AS CAPITAL *See* Children—Economic value
KIDS IN THE HALL (COMEDY TROUPE)
Oh, those darn Kids. B. Barol. il *Newsweek* 114:67 O 2 '89
Their first gig? The Loose Moose Theater! H. M. Rosenthal. il *TV Guide* 37:23 N 18-24 '89
KIDS OF SURVIVAL (GROUP) *See* Tim Rollins + K.O.S. (Group)
KIECHEL, CONRAD
Something happened. *National Review* 41:23-4 Jl 14 '89
KIECHEL, WALTER
Office hours. See alternate issues of Fortune
KIEFER, ANSELM, 1945-
about
Anselm Kiefer at MOMA. J. Gardner. *National Review* 41:52-3+ Mr 10 '89

Art. A. C. Danto. *The Nation* 248:26-8 Ja 2 '89
KIEFER, MICHAEL
'80s Olympics. il *Sport (New York, N.Y.)* 80:82-3 O '89
Chicago. il *Sport (New York, N.Y.)* 80:62-6 Mr '89
Down to size. il *The New York Times Magazine* p18+ Ja 8 '89
Fall of the Garden of Eden. il *International Wildlife* 19:38-43 Jl/Ag '89
KIEHNE, ERNEST
about
Will the real Ben Graham please stand up? J. Clements. il pors *Forbes* 144:310+ D 11 '89
KIEKHAEFER, CARL
about
Fifty years in the fast lane. J. Skorupa. il *Popular Mechanics* 166:22-3 Ja '89
KIENHOLZ, EDWARD, 1927-
about
Social work. K. Larson. il *New York* 22:113-14 N 6 '89
KIENHOLZ, NANCY REDDIN
about
Social work. K. Larson. il *New York* 22:113-14 N 6 '89
KIERKEGAARD, SØREN, 1813-1855
about
A faith that trembles and dances. V. S. Owens. il *Christianity Today* 33:19-22 Jl 14 '89
A playing field for the boys of eternity. J. M. Wall. *The Christian Century* 106:515-16 My 17 '89
KIERNAN, VINCENT
How far to the galaxies? [cover story] il *Astronomy* 17:48-54 Je '89
KIERSH, EDWARD
Why Robert Culp's not happy with Bill Cosby. pors *TV Guide* 37:13-15 O 7-13 '89
KIESELSTEIN-CORD, BARRY
about
Creative collaborators. il pors *Harper's Bazaar* 122:116-21 Je '89
KIESELSTEIN-CORD, CECE
about
Creative collaborators. il pors *Harper's Bazaar* 122:116-21 Je '89
KIESER, ELLWOOD, 1929-
about
Celluloid evangelism. S. Ulstein. il por *Christianity Today* 33:77-8 N 3 '89
KIESLING, STEPHEN
Hell's angels. il pors *Sports Illustrated* 70:82-7+ Mr 27 '89
KIESTER, EDWIN
He's praying for a Quantum leap—right into the movies. por *TV Guide* 37:14-15 D 23-29 '89
KIESTER, EDWIN, AND KIESTER, SALLY VALENTE
Bring fun back to your marriage. il *Reader's Digest* 134:81-4 Ja '89
A clean break with bad habits. il *Reader's Digest* 135:165-6+ O '89
Everyday math for grownups. *Reader's Digest* 135:43-4+ O '89
How to improve your child's test scores. il *Reader's Digest* 134:84-8 My '89
KIESTER, SALLY VALENTE
(jt. auth) See Kiester, Edwin, and Kiester, Sally Valente
KIEV (UKRAINE)
See also
Soviet Union—History—Kievan period, 862-1237
KIHL, YOUNG W., 1932-
South Korea's rise to prominence. bibl f *Current History* 88:165-8+ Ap '89
KILA, GETI
(jt. auth) See Mills, John, and Kila, Geti
KILAUEA (HAWAII)
Volcano exhibit to travel U.S. il *Earth Science* 42:5-6 Summ '89
KILBY, JACK ST. CLAIR
about
Ignored by the Nobels, engineering and technology are at last being honored by a significant new prize. R. M. Adams. il *Smithsonian* 20:12 D '89
Kilby and Noyce win Draper Prize for developing microchips. I. Goodwin. il *Physics Today* 42:52 N '89
KILDAY, GREGG
The eighties: the industry. il *Film Comment* 25:60+ N/D '89
Green light. See issues of American Film beginning April 1989
Movie villains were once the equal of their enemies; now they're copycat clichés. il *Vogue* 179:196-8 Ag '89
KILDERY, PAUL
about
Think small, play big. J. E. Loehr. il por *World Tennis* 36:12-13 F '89
KILHAM, LAWRENCE, 1910-
about
Burroughs Medal. F. Graham. il *Audubon* 91:16+ Jl '89
The crow man [interview] B. Gilbert. il pors *Life* 12:25-7 Je '89
KILIMANJARO, MOUNT (TANZANIA) *See* Mount Kilimanjaro (Tanzania)

KILLEA, LUCY
about
Barred from Communion. *The Christian Century* 106:1193-4 D 20-27 '89
A mistake in San Diego. *America* 161:416 D 9 '89
KILLEBREW, ELEANOR
about
Continental impressions on Nob Hill. H. Junker. il por *Architectural Digest* 46:288-94+ O '89
KILLEN, MARY
Fit for a queen. il *Vogue* 179:406 My '89
KILLER BEES *See* Bees
KILLER CELLS
Prevention of allogeneic bone marrow graft rejection by H-2 transgene in donor mice. C. Öhlén and others. bibl f il *Science* 246:666-8 N 3 '89
Setting the stage for infection [lowered response rate of natural killer cells; research by Sandra M. Levy] B. Bower. *Science News* 136:141 Ag 26 '89
KILLER WHALES
Dropping in on orcas at their summer home. il map *Sunset (Central West edition)* 182:90-1 My '89
Killer encounters [boats attacked] M. Benson. il *Motor Boating & Sailing* 164:50-1+ N '89
Staying alive [B. Butler and his wife survive 66 days on a raft after their boat was sunk by killer whales] S. Stapleton. il pors *Motor Boating & Sailing* 164:48-51+ N '89
KILLGORE, JOHN, AND OTHERS
Nutritional importance of pyrroloquinoline quinone. bibl f il *Science* 245:850-2 Ag 25 '89
KILLIAN, ANITA M.
Playing dice with the solar system. il *Sky and Telescope* 78:136-8+ Ag '89
KILLIFISH
See also
Rivulus
Tolerance and stress in a polluted environment [killifish in New Jersey waters] J. S. Weis and P. Weis. bibl f il *BioScience* 39:89-95 F '89
KILLINGTON (VT.: RESORT) *See* Resorts—Vermont
KILLUS, JAMES
(jt. auth) *See* Farber, Sharon N., and Killus, James
KILMAN, LARRY
France dance: le nouveau stuff. il *Dance Magazine* 63:46-8 F '89
KILPATRICK, DAVID
about
A Highland collector and his collection. A. Bahar. il *Antiques & Collecting Hobbies* 94:47-50 Ap '89
KILPATRICK, TERRY
Into the breach [cover story] il *National Parks* 63:22-7 Mr/Ap '89
KILRAIN, JAKE
about
1889. A. Nielson. il por *American Heritage* 40:30+ Jl/Ag '89
KILROY, MARK
about
The believers. G. D. Garcia. il *Rolling Stone* p46-9+ Je 29 '89
The grisly secrets of a lonely ranch. A. Richman. il por *People Weekly* 31:44-9 My 1 '89
KILWORTH, GARRY
Filming the making of the film of the making of 'Fitzcarraldo' [story] il *Omni (New York, N.Y.)* 11:52-4+ Mr '89
KIM, ALBERT
Are their days numbered? il *Sports Illustrated* 70:46-8+ My 22 '89
KIM, CHONG IL *See* Kim, Jong Il
KIM, DONGHEE, AND CLAPHAM, DAVID E.
Potassium channels in cardiac cells activated by arachidonic acid and phospholipids. bibl f il *Science* 244:1174-6 Je 9 '89
KIM, ELAINE
about
Muse of Melrose. L. Berger. il por *Harper's Bazaar* 122:72 N '89
KIM, HYUN HEE
about
The 'virgin terrorist'. S. Begley. il por *Newsweek* 113:8 Mr 20 '89
KIM, IL SUNG, 1912-
about
Great Leader to Dear Leader. N. D. Kristof. il por *The New York Times Magazine* p44-7+ Ag 20 '89
Kim Il Sung's 'socialist paradise'. B. Martin. il pors *Newsweek* 114:38-9 Ag 7 '89
People's democratic revue. A. Daniels. *National Review* 41:19-20 S 1 '89
KIM, JONG IL
about
Great Leader to Dear Leader. N. D. Kristof. il por *The New York Times Magazine* p44-7+ Ag 20 '89
KIM, SUK-WON
about
His father's son. A. Tanzer. il por *Forbes* 143:148+ My 29 '89

KIM, WILLA
about
Willa Kim. B. Howard. il *Theatre Crafts* 23:28-33+ Mr '89
KIM, WOO-CHOONG
Challenges and issues for Asia and the Pacific [address, June 7, 1989] *Vital Speeches of the Day* 55:642-4 Ag 15 '89
KIMBALL, CHARLES A.
Bishops' principles for Middle East peace. *The Christian Century* 106:972-3 N 1 '89
KIMBALL, ROGER
Holl and Ambasz, in a manner of speaking. il *Architectural Record* 177:51+ Ap '89
The riddle of the pyramid. il *Architectural Record* 177:58-61 Ja '89
KIMBALL, WILLIAM R.
(ed) *See* Block, Mickey. Me and the Preacher Man
KIMBELL, LARRY
about
"Panic in Wall Street, good times coming". R. Bailey. il por *Forbes* 144:68+ N 27 '89
KIMBELL ART MUSEUM
Kimbell times two [addition designed by R. Giurgola] J. Kutner. il *Art News* 88:56 O '89
Portrait: Ted Pillsbury. B. Gill. il por *Architectural Digest* 46:72+ O '89
KIMBER, ROBERT
Made for the country. *See* issues of Country Journal beginning October 1986
KIMBERLY-CLARK CORP.
Huggable shares. T. Jaffe. *Forbes* 143:346 My 29 '89
KIMBROUGH, ANN
Feeling the heat. il *Black Enterprise* 19:265-6+ Je '89
KIMELBERG, HAROLD K., AND NORENBERG, MICHAEL D.
Astrocytes. bibl il *Scientific American* 260:66-72+ Ap '89
KIMMAGE, PAUL
Never say die [cover story; with editorial comment by James C. McCullagh] il pors *Bicycling* 30:10, 30-4+ O/N '89
KIMMEL, MICHAEL S.
The sixties without metaphor. *Society* 26:78-84 Mr/Ap '89
KIMMELMAN, MICHAEL
Unnerving art [cover story] il por *The New York Times Magazine* p40-3+ Ag 20 '89
KIMMES, ARNOLD
about
Never, but never, give a sucker an even break. R. L. Stern and others. il pors *Forbes* 143:46-50 Ja 9 '89
KIMONOS
Best dress [juni-hitoe] *The New Yorker* 65:32-3 D 18 '89
KIMURA, DOREEN
How sex hormones boost—or cut—intellectual ability. il *Psychology Today* 23:62-6 N '89
KIMURA, MOTOO, 1924-
about
Through a lens, darkly. S. J. Gould. il *Natural History* p16+ S '89
KIN SELECTION
Limits to DNA fingerprinting [use in animal population biology] R. Lewin. il *Science* 243:1549-51 Mr 24 '89
KINABALU NATIONAL PARK (BORNEO)
It's a jungle in there [tourist walkway] E. McGowan. il *Travel Holiday* 172:26-7 Ag '89
KINAMORE, ANGELA
African American woman [poem] *Essence* 19:142 F '89
'Home' girls [poem] *Essence* 19:112 Ja '89
The warrior spirit [poem] *Essence* 19:152 F '89
KINASES
See also
Protein kinase
Streptokinase
The cell cycle coming under control. J. L. Marx. il *Science* 245:252-5 Jl 21 '89
The EGF receptor kinase substrate p35 in the floor plate of the embryonic rat CNS. J. A. McKanna and S. Cohen. bibl f il *Science* 243:1477-9 Mr 17 '89
Human diabetes associated with a deletion of the tyrosine kinase domain of the insulin receptor. M. Taira and others. bibl f il *Science* 245:63-6 Jl 7 '89
Human diabetes associated with a mutation in the tyrosine kinase domain of the insulin receptor. M. Odawara and others. bibl f il *Science* 245:66-8 Jl 7 '89
KINCAID, JAMAICA
Mariah [story] *The New Yorker* 65:32-8 Je 26 '89
Poor visitor [story] *The New Yorker* 65:28-30 F 27 '89
The tongue [story] *The New Yorker* 65:44-54 O 9 '89
KINCH, JOHN E.
You can own your own business [condensed from Franchising; ed. by John Phillip Hayes. il *Reader's Digest* 134:187-90+ F '89
KINCHELOE, JOE L.
Building strong academic backgrounds for teachers. *The Education Digest* 55:20-3 S '89

KINDER, GARY
about
Atlantic Monthly uncovers buried riches. *Publishers Weekly* 236:48-9 N 24 '89
KINDER, MELVYN, AND COWAN, CONNELL
Surprising key to the happiest couples [condensed from Husbands and wives] il *Reader's Digest* 135:149-52 Jl '89
KINDER-CARE LEARNING CENTERS INC.
Has this problem child learned its lesson? D. Foust. il *Business Week* p28 Je 12 '89
Lost and found? M. Schifrin. il *Forbes* 144:10 Ag 7 '89
Ring around the rosie at Kinder-Care. C. Hawkins. il *Business Week* p45-6 D 18 '89
Small tots, big biz. T. Lewin. il *The New York Times Magazine* p30-1+ Ja 29 '89
KINDERGARTEN
Delaying kindergarten. F. Roberts. *Parents* 64:66+ Mr '89
The first test of childhood [kindergarten screenings] P. Wilkes. por *Newsweek* 114:8 Ag 14 '89
From half day to full day. C. Leslie and P. Wingert. il *Newsweek* 113:62 Je 26 '89
High-stakes testing in kindergarten. S. J. Meisels. *The Education Digest* 55:25-8 O '89
"Is my daughter learning too fast?". F. Roberts. il *Parents* 64:52 O '89
The kindergarten wars [holding children back to ensure academic success] B. Brophy. il *U.S. News & World Report* 106:53-4 Ap 10 '89
Off to kindergarten! J. Oppenheim. il *Good Housekeeping* 209:134+ S '89
The redshirt solution [delaying kindergarten] J. Elson. il *Time* 134:102 N 13 '89
KINDRED, DAVE
The Final 4. il *Sports Illustrated* 70:49+ Mr 20 '89
Pass the gravy, please. il por *Sports Illustrated* 70:96 My 15 '89
KINESIOLOGY *See* Biomechanics
KINETIC ART
Collectors and collecting
"If it doesn't work, it isn't art" [D. Bermant's collection] C. Brown. il por *Forbes* 143:142 My 15 '89
KINETIC KILL VEHICLES
See also
Brilliant Pebbles (Defense system)
Army HEDI launch complex ready for summer test [High Endoatmospheric Defense Interceptor] *Aviation Week & Space Technology* 130:49-50 Ap 3 '89
Defense Dept. to launch competition for exoatmospheric interceptor design. P. A. Gilmartin. *Aviation Week & Space Technology* 131:27+ N 6 '89
Delay of first HEDI test launch caused by flight destruct system replacement [High Endoatmospheric Defense Interceptor] P. A. Gilmartin. *Aviation Week & Space Technology* 131:21 O 30 '89
Do we really need a space-based defense? *National Review* 41:12-13 F 10 '89
Lockheed integrating components of SDI exoatmospheric interceptor. B. W. Henderson. il *Aviation Week & Space Technology* 130:50 Ja 2 '89
Space interceptor model hovers during laboratory tests at Edwards. T. M. Foley. il *Aviation Week & Space Technology* 130:49 Ja 2 '89
KING, ANDREA
TV's best new sitcom: The famous Teddy Z. il por *Glamour* 87:194 O '89
KING, B. B.
about
Mississippi homecoming. F. Schruers. il pors *Rolling Stone* p87-92+ N 30 '89
KING, BERNICE
about
Bernice King. P. Cleage. por *Essence* 19:69-70+ Ja '89
KING, BETSY
about
A King is crowned queen. J. Garrity. il por *Sports Illustrated* 71:71-2 Jl 24 '89
KING, BILLIE JEAN
The best shots in tennis; ed. by Herma M. Rosenthal. il *TV Guide* 37:6-7+ Je 24-30 '89
Service winner: pros who teach. por *World Tennis* 36:72+ Ja '89
KING, BOB
about
Lost brother. K. King. il pors *Life* 12:94-8+ N '89
KING, CHARLES C.
about
A suntan can be a fun tan with this new way to change your oil. il *People Weekly* 31:116-17 My 29 '89
KING, CHARLES E.
Homelessness in America. il *The Humanist* 49:8+ My/Je '89
KING, DEXTER
about
Dexter King installed as King Center prexy on 21st anniversary of dad's death. il pors *Jet* 76:6 Ap 24 '89
Dexter King steps forth. N. McCall. il por *Black Enterprise* 19:20 Ap '89

Rev. King's son, Dexter, resigns from position as president of the King Center. il por *Jet* 76:8 Ag 28 '89
Son Dexter to take reins of the King Center in Atlanta. il por *Jet* 75:36-7 F 6 '89
KING, DON, 1929-
about
Tyson no 'slave,' King testifies against Cayton. por *Jet* 75:47 Mr 6 '89
KING, DOUGLAS B.
Doctor visits made easy. il *Parents* 64:237-8 D '89
KING, ERIKA
about
Corporate art. D. C. Bacon. il por *Nation's Business* 77:20 N '89
KING, FLORENCE
Benched: life after sex. il por *Ms.* 17:43-5 My '89
KING, FRANK
about
Toward a kinder, gentler Lotus. E. S. Ely. por *Personal Computing* 13:73 Jl '89
KING, GWENDOLYN S.
about
Gwendolyn King is first black social security chief. il por *Jet* 76:4 Ag 21 '89
KING, JAMES OLIVER, JR.
about
Death of black in small Texas town questioned. il *Jet* 77:5 D 11 '89
KING, KIT
Lost brother. il pors *Life* 12:94-8+ N '89
KING, LARRY, 1933-
about
All alone by his telephone, big talker Larry King reaches out and marries someone. W. Plummer. il pors *People Weekly* 32:115+ O 23 '89
We talk to Larry King. A. Ebert. il por *Good Housekeeping* 209:131+ O '89
KING, LARRY L.
about
The night Hank Williams died [drama] Reviews
Commonweal 116:210-12 Ap 7 '89. G. C. Weales
The Nation 248:355-6 Mr 13 '89. T. M. Disch
New York 22:92-3 F 6 '89. J. Simon
The New Yorker 65:89 F 20 '89. E. Oliver
KING, MARTIN LUTHER, 1929-1968
See also
Martin Luther King Day
about
Abernathy cuts book tour because of controversy. il pors *Jet* 77:14 N 13 '89
Abernathy takes a cheap shot. J. M. Wall. por *The Christian Century* 106:971-2 N 1 '89
A bitter battle erupts over the last hours of Martin Luther King. J. S. Kunen. il pors *People Weekly* 32:40-2 O 30 '89
Eyewitness statements on King's death dispute Abernathy's accounts. il pors *Jet* 77:57-9 N 6 '89
Fall of the Berlin Wall fits Rev. King's dream. il por *Jet* 77:53-4 N 27 '89
A fight among Dr. King's faithful. il por *Newsweek* 114:31 O 23 '89
The greening of a martyr [interview with T. Branch] A. P. Sanoff. il por *U.S. News & World Report* 106:22 Ja 23 '89
Hot writers. A. DeCurtis. il pors *Rolling Stone* p117-18+ My 18 '89
In the churches, in the streets: Taylor Branch on 'the King years'. R. Westbrook. *The Christian Century* 106:351-4 Ap 5 '89
King's dream becomes a reality in Selma. il *Jet* 75:10-11 F 13 '89
'Martin'. D. Moore. il *American Visions* 4:34-9 D '89
Martin Luther King: the preacher as virtuoso [cover story] M. E. Marty. *The Christian Century* 106:348-50 Ap 5 '89
On the humanity of saints. P. Marin. il *The Nation* 249:784-6 D 25 '89
Ralph Abernathy's book denounced for 'painful distortions' about King. il pors *Jet* 77:8-10 O 30 '89
Remembering Dr. King [special section] il pors *Ebony* 44:37+ Ja '89
Sexual charges and Martin Luther King. F. Bruning. il *Maclean's* 102:13 N 6 '89
Tattletale memoir. por *Time* 134:42 O 23 '89
Their fathers' daughters. E. Hopkins. il pors *Rolling Stone* p76-7+ N 30 '89
Homes
Birthplace of a national hero. R. D. Turner. il *Ebony* 44:40-2 Ja '89
Statues, portraits, etc.
Statue of King erected in Kalamazoo, Mich. il por *Jet* 77:38 O 23 '89
Vandals desecrate King's statue in Birmingham park. il *Jet* 76:32 My 29 '89
KING, MAXWELL C., AND FERSH, SEYMOUR H.
Internationalizing the community college. *The Education Digest* 54:52-4 My '89

KING, MICHAEL GORDON
about
Big bucks, tough tactics. T. Dunkel. il pors *The New York Times Magazine* p56-7+ S 17 '89
KING, MICHAEL P., AND ATTARDI, GIUSEPPE
Human cells lacking mtDNA: repopulation with exogenous mitochondria by complementation. bibl f il *Science* 246:500-3 O 27 '89
KING, NANCY
The simplest and hardest of education reforms. *Design for Arts in Education* 91:2-9 N/D '89
KING, P. E. (PATRICK E.)
When accidents happen to kids. *McCall's* 116:51 Jl '89
KING, PAM
The night the Lakers got psyched out of a victory. il *TV Guide* 37:8-9 Je 3-9 '89
KING, PATRICK E. *See* King, P. E. (Patrick E.)
KING, PETER, 1957-
Back to basics [cover story] il pors *Sports Illustrated* 71:14-18+ Ag 7 '89
Fight to the finish. il *Sports Illustrated* 71:26-31 D 25 '89-Ja 1 '90
Green Bay sacker. il pors *Sports Illustrated* 71:70-2 O 16 '89
A happy homecoming. por *Sports Illustrated* 71:76 Jl 31 '89
Inside the NFL. See issues of Sports Illustrated published during the football season beginning September 11, 1989
Jilted Jim's big McLove-in. il pors *Sports Illustrated* 71:20-1 Ag 28 '89
Now it gets grisly. il *Sports Illustrated* 71:40+ D 4 '89
Onward, Christian. il pors *Sports Illustrated* 71:74-6+ D 11 '89
Sudden impact [cover story] il pors *Sports Illustrated* 71:42-4+ O 23 '89
That man again [cover story] il por *Sports Illustrated* 71:52-4 O 2 '89
about
From the publisher. D. J. Barr. il por *Sports Illustrated* 71:4 S 11 '89
KING, RICK
about
Forced march [film] Reviews
People Weekly il 32:20+ N 27 '89. R. Novak
KING, ROBERT D.
Treason and traitors. bibl *Society* 26:39-48 Jl/Ag '89
KING, ROGER MONROE
about
Big bucks, tough tactics. T. Dunkel. il pors *The New York Times Magazine* p56-7+ S 17 '89
KING, STEPHEN, 1947-
about
For goodness sake? H. Wornom. por *Omni (New York, N.Y.)* 12:16+ D '89
Genre. *The New Yorker* 65:27 F 27 '89
Horror's heaviest hitter. F. Lovece. il por *Video* 13:46-9+ Ag '89
Stephen King. G. Schwartz. il por *People Weekly* 32 Special Issue:90 Fall '89
Stephen King: limited edition for a bestselling author. C. Reid. il *Publishers Weekly* 235:37-8 Mr 31 '89
KING, STEVEN S.
It's show time for business. il *Nation's Business* 77:54-6 Ap '89
KING, SUSAN
Emmys '89. il *American Film* 14:46-7 Jl/Ag '89
KING, WAYNE
Bad times on the bayou. il *The New York Times Magazine* p56-9+ Je 11 '89
Carter redux [cover story] il pors *The New York Times Magazine* p38-41+ D 10 '89
KING, YOLANDA
about
Their fathers' daughters. E. Hopkins. il pors *Rolling Stone* p76-7+ N 30 '89
KING (MARTIN LUTHER JR.) CENTER FOR NONVIOLENT SOCIAL CHANGE *See* Martin Luther King, Jr. Center for Nonviolent Social Change
KING ARTHUR [opera] *See* Purcell, Henry, 1659-1695
KING WORLD PRODUCTIONS, INC.
Big bucks, tough tactics [R. and M. King] T. Dunkel. il pors *The New York Times Magazine* p56-7+ S 17 '89
KINGDOM, GERRY
Shaking down the thunder. il pors *The Saturday Evening Post* 261:52-3+ S '89
KINGDOM, ROGER
about
Roger Kingdom sets world hurdles record. il pors *Jet* 76:46 S 4 '89
Smashing! M. Noden. il pors *Sports Illustrated* 71:16-19 Ag 28 '89
KINGDOM OF GOD
Christian fulfillment and Jewish-Christian dialogue. I. C. Rottenberg. *The Christian Century* 106:387-91 Ap 12 '89
Equal opportunity. P. J. Ryan. *America* 161:95 Ag 12-19 '89
Fit for the reign of God. P. Perkins. il *The Christian Century* 106:618 Je 21-28 '89

A king in Minnesota. G. K. Brushaber. il *Christianity Today* 33:11 Ag 18 '89
The Kingdom of God: what role do we play? W. A. Barry. *America* 161:165-6 S 23 '89
The Magic Kingdom. P. Perkins. il *The Christian Century* 106:1083 N 22 '89
Royal transfers. P. J. Ryan. il *America* 161:363 N 18 '89
KINGS AND RULERS
See also
France—Kings and rulers
Queens
KINGS POINT (N.Y.)
Architecture
On the Sound: breezy style for a Long Island estate [interior by Michael De Santis] P. Carlsen. il *Architectural Digest* 46:128-33 F '89
KING'S X (MUSICAL GROUP)
King's X. K. Neely. il *Rolling Stone* p43 N 30 '89
KINGSLEY, BEN
about
Ben Kingsley. B. Golightly. il pors *Horizon (Tuscaloosa, Ala.)* 32:52-6 Mr/Ap '89
KINGSOLVER, BARBARA
The lost language of love [fiction] il *Mademoiselle* 95:150+ My '89
Precious little time [story] il *Redbook* 173:28+ Jl '89
KINGSTON, MAXINE HONG
The novel's next step. il *Mother Jones* 14:37-41 D '89
about
'The Tao is up'. M. Loke. il pors *The New York Times Magazine* p28-9+ Ap 30 '89
KINGSTON (JAMAICA)
Poor
Blessings from and for the poor [work of Food for the Poor] M. G. Harter. il *America* 161:395-8 D 2 '89
KINGSTON (N.Y.)
Stores
See also
Nekos Pharmacy
KINISON, SAM
about
The comedy of hate. G. Hirshey. il pors *Gentlemen's Quarterly* 59:226-9+ Ag '89
The devil and Sam Kinison [cover story] D. Handelman. il pors *Rolling Stone* p24-6+ F 23 '89
Sam Kinison, tastefully. A. Meisler. il pors *Gentlemen's Quarterly* 59:89+ Je '89
KINJITE [film] *See* Motion picture reviews—Single works
KINKO'S GRAPHICS CORPORATION
Eight publishers sue photocopying chain. C. Reid. *Publishers Weekly* 235:100 My 12 '89
KINMONTH, PATRICK
Badminton Court. il por *Vogue* 179:426-35 O '89
Classic lines. il *Vogue* 179:344-6 Ap '89
Fine & dandy. il *Vogue* 179:334-9 Ag '89
The New Curiosity Shop. il por *House & Garden* 161:78+ Mr '89
KINNANE-ROELOFSMA, DERK
The more things change . . . il *National Review* 41:17-19 My 19 '89
KINNEAR, JAMES W., 1928-
about
Jim Kinnear is pumping new life into Texaco. M. Ivey. il por *Business Week* p50+ Ap 17 '89
Who's in charge at Texaco now? S. P. Sherman. il pors *Fortune* 119:68-70+ Ja 16 '89
KINNELL, GALWAY, 1927-
When one has lived a long time alone [poem] il *The Atlantic* 264:82-3 O '89
KINNEY, JAY
The death of hip. il *Utne Reader* p53-7 S/O '89
Déjà vu: the hidden history of the New Age [excerpt from The fringes of reason] il *Utne Reader* p109 S/O '89
KINNOCK, NEIL
about
Thatcherism isn't working. N. Gelb. il *The New Leader* 72:8-9 Jl 10-24 '89
Unilateral disarmament—Labor's lost love. N. Moss. il por *The Bulletin of the Atomic Scientists* 45:9-11 O '89
KINO, GORDON S., AND CORLE, TIMOTHY R.
Confocal scanning optical microscopy. bibl f il *Physics Today* 42:55-62 S '89
KINOSHITA, JUNE
Neptune. il *Scientific American* 261:82-91 N '89
KINSELLA, W. P.
about
Baseball like it oughta be [interview] A. Knight. il *American Film* 14:76 My '89
KINSEY INSTITUTE FOR RESEARCH IN SEX, GENDER AND REPRODUCTION
Sex (research) scandals! [Indiana University asks Kinsey Institute head J. Reinisch to resign] E. E. Goode. il pors *U.S. News & World Report* 106:54-5 Ja 9 '89
KINSEY REPORT (MUSICAL GROUP)
The Kinsey Report. L. Birnbaum. il *Down Beat* 56:46-7 F '89

KINSLEY, MICHAEL
Now you're thinking like a lawyer. *The Washington Monthly* 21:44+ F '89
The rich don't serve—so what? il *The Washington Monthly* 21:26-7 Mr '89
about
Kinsley does it again. R. E. Tyrrell. *The American Spectator* 22:10-11 D '89
KINSMAN, JOHN
about
Rural exchange program makes links. J. Miller. il por *The Progressive* 53:12-13 Ap '89
KINZER, STEPHEN
Guatemala: What has democracy wrought? il *The New York Times Magazine* p32-4+ Mr 26 '89
KINZIE, MARY
Lunar frost [poem] *The New Yorker* 64:34-5 F 6 '89
The shed [poem] *The New Republic* 200:32 Je 5 '89
Small birthday poem [poem] *The American Scholar* 58:270 Spr '89
KIPLING, RUDYARD, 1865-1936
about
Kipling's Simla. *Gourmet* 49:232 N '89
KIPLINGER, AUSTIN HUNTINGTON, 1918-, AND KIPLINGER, KNIGHT
America's bright global future [excerpt from America in the global '90s] il *Changing Times* 43:111-12+ O '89
KIPLINGER, KNIGHT
(jt. auth) See Kiplinger, Austin Huntington, 1918-, and Kiplinger, Knight
KIPSIGIS (AFRICAN PEOPLE)
A Kipsigis parable. R. E. Daniels. il *Natural History* p66+ Je '89
KIRALY, KARCH, 1961?-
about
Their final shots. B. Anderson. il pors *Sports Illustrated* 71:24-5 Jl 10 '89
KIRBY, BRUNO
about
Some character. K. M. Chanko. il por *New York* 22:16 Jl 17 '89
KIRBY, DAVID K.
The poet within you. *The Writer* 102:19-21 F '89
KIRBY, LOWRY DALE
about
The Lowry Dale Kirby Collection of old Sheffield plate. J. D. Davis. il *Antiques* 136:848-59 O '89
KIRBY, MARY E.
Picnics past. il *Gourmet* 49:94+ Je '89
KIRCH, LEO
about
Four titans carve up European TV [cover story] W. Fisher and M. Schapiro. il *The Nation* 248:37+ Ja 9-16 '89
KIRCHHOFF, SUSAN
(jt. auth) See Denner, Barbara W., and Kirchhoff, Susan
KIRCHNER, WOLFGANG H.
(jt. auth) See Towne, William F., and Kirchner, Wolfgang H.
KIRCHWEY, FREDA
about
Battle hymns, ancient and modern. A. Cockburn. *The Nation* 249:266-7 S 18 '89
KIRCHWEY, KARL
German nudists, Kalamaki, Crete [poem] *The New Yorker* 65:38 S 4 '89
In passing [poem] *The Nation* 248:103 Ja 23 '89
KIRK, JAMES
about
Down in the dumps. R. Simon. il por *Forbes* 143:104+ My 1 '89
KIRK, JOHN T., AND GRANT, JERRY V.
Forty untouched masterpieces of Shaker design. il *Antiques* 135:1226-37 My '89
KIRK, MARSHALL
about
Is the gay revolution a flop? A. Toufexis. il pors *Time* 134:56 Jl 10 '89
KIRK, ROBIN
(jt. auth) See McConahay, Mary Jo, and Kirk, Robin
KIRKLAND, WILLIAM, 1768-1836
about
Ayr Mount on the Eno River, near Hillsborough, North Carolina. J. L. Sanders. bibl f il por *Antiques* 135:1190-201 My '89
KIRKPATRICK, CURRY
Becker the Yankee wrecker. il *Sports Illustrated* 71:56-7 Jl 31 '89
The bluegrass isn't so blue. il pors *Sports Illustrated* 71:54-6+ D 11 '89
Boom Boom [cover story] il pors *Sports Illustrated* 71:22-7 S 18 '89
Born to serve. il pors *Sports Illustrated* 70:64-8+ Mr 13 '89
Bustin' loose. il *Sports Illustrated* 71:46-52 N 20 '89
Can't hold this Tiger [cover story] il pors *Sports Illustrated* 70:48-51 F 20 '89
Crass and class. il pors *Sports Illustrated* 71:56-9+ N 20 '89

Dodging a bullet [cover story] il *Sports Illustrated* 70:24-6+ My 29 '89
Face-off! il *Sports Illustrated* 71:18-23 D 18 '89
Giant killers. il pors *Sports Illustrated* 70:34-6+ Je 19 '89
Illini on the rise. il *Sports Illustrated* 70:12-15 Ja 23 '89
Mister Clutch [cover story] il *Sports Illustrated* 70:16-23 Ap 10 '89
Much ado about a 'do. il pors *Sports Illustrated* 70:52-4+ Ja 16 '89
The NCAAs from A to Z. il por *Sports Illustrated* 70:136 Mr 20 '89
Older and better. il pors *Sports Illustrated* 70 Special Issue:95+ F '89
Paws! il pors *Sports Illustrated* 71:98-102+ O 23 '89
Serving her country. il pors *Sports Illustrated* 70:78-82+ Je 26 '89
Sitting pretty in Rome. il pors *Sports Illustrated* 71:26-8+ O 9 '89
Special D from this Courier. il pors *Sports Illustrated* 70:84+ Je 12 '89
Team Turmoil triumphs. il *Sports Illustrated* 70:22-5 Mr 20 '89
'They don't pay nobody to be humble' [cover story] il pors *Sports Illustrated* 71:52-6+ N 13 '89
(ed) See Evert, Chris. 'Tennis was my showcase'
KIRKPATRICK, JEANE J., 1926-
How the PLO was legitimized [cover story] *Commentary* 88:21-8 Jl '89
Jeane J. Kirkpatrick [advice to George Bush] *National Review* 41:28 F 10 '89
The PLO [discussion of July 1989 article, How the PLO was legitimized] *Commentary* 88:7-8 N '89
The withering away of the state? il *New Perspectives Quarterly* 5:34-7 Wint '88/'89
KIRKPATRICK, JOEY
about
Double vision. B. J. Miller. il *American Craft* 49:40-5 O/N '89
KIRKPATRICK, SEAN J.
Gulls: a sea guide. bibl il *Sea Frontiers* 35:146-51 My/Je '89
KIRKPATRICK, SHEILA
about
Montanans say hot hatter Sheila Kirkpatrick makes the best brims under the Big Sky. M. L. Gavenas. il pors *People Weekly* 31:85-6 My 15 '89
KIRKPATRICK CUSTOM HATTERS (FIRM)
Montanans say hot hatter Sheila Kirkpatrick makes the best brims under the Big Sky. M. L. Gavenas. il pors *People Weekly* 31:85-6 My 15 '89
KIRKS, NICHOLAS BRIAN
about
Every mother's nightmare comes true when a hospital nursery mix-up sends two babies home with the wrong parents. M. Brower. il pors *People Weekly* 31:123-4 Ap 3 '89
KIRKWOOD, R. CORT, AND JEFFREY, TERENCE P.
Quis custodiet? il *National Review* 41:35-6 Ap 21 '89
KIRN, WALTER
Yellow stars of Utah [story] *Esquire* 112:117-19 Jl '89
KIROV BALLET
The ballerinas and the bodybuilders: body and soul [encounter between Soviet dancers and bodybuilders in Philadelphia] T. Tobias. il *Dance Magazine* 63:46 Jl '89
Dancing:
   Performances at the Metropolitan Opera House. A. Croce. *The New Yorker* 65:89-92 Ag 7 '89
   Performances at the Metropolitan Opera House. A. Croce. *The New Yorker* 65:72-3 Jl 31 '89
Freed by *glasnost*, the Kirov Ballet arrives in America this month with new prima ballerina Altynai Asylmuratova. D. Daniel. por *Vogue* 179:84-5 Jl '89
From Leningrad with love. M. Duffy. il *Time* 134:90-1 Jl 17 '89
Kiroviana: the *glasnost* difference [cover story] M. E. Willis. il *Dance Magazine* 63:36-41 Jl '89
The Kirov's timeless virtues. L. A. Jacobs. *The New Leader* 72:22-3 Ag 7-21 '89
Leningrad miracle. L. Shapiro. il *Newsweek* 114:58 Jl 24 '89
Makarova returns to the Kirov: going home. N. Alovert. il pors *Dance Magazine* 63:36-7 My '89
The new improved Kirov: an interview with Oleg Vinogradov. N. Alovert. il por *Dance Magazine* 63:42-4 Jl '89
The red shoes dance modern [will perform works of G. Balanchine] il por *U.S. News & World Report* 106:16 F 27 '89
Reviews:
   Performance of Potemkin in Leningrad; tr. by Susan Cook Summer. A. Degen. il *Dance Magazine* 63:52-3 Jl '89
   Performances at the Metropolitan Opera House, New York City. D. Hering. il *Dance Magazine* 63:74+ N '89
Shipwrecked [performance of Le corsaire] T. Tobias. il *New York* 22:56-7 Jl 24 '89
Touchstones [New York City performances] T. Tobias. il *New York* 22:61-2 Jl 31 '89

KIROV BALLET—*cont.*
Two decades of Kirov danseurs: generation in shadow. N. Alovert. il *Dance Magazine* 63:52-5 Ap '89
Worlds apart. T. Tobias. il *New York* 22:50-1 Ag 7 '89

KIRP, DAVID L.
A boy's life. il *Mother Jones* 14:32-8 Jl/Ag '89
Compassion fatigue: Hong Kong and the boat people [cover story] il *The American Spectator* 22:16-19 Ap '89
Education: the movie [cover story] il pors *Mother Jones* 14:36-45 Ja '89
A thin green line. il *Mother Jones* 14:16-17+ My '89
(jt. auth) See Timar, Thomas, and Kirp, David L.

KIRP, DAVID L., AND EPSTEIN, STEVEN
AIDS in America's schoolhouses: learning the hard lessons [cover story; with editorial comment by Pauline B. Gough] il *Phi Delta Kappan* 70:578, 584-93 Ap '89

KIRSCH, JACK F.
(jt. auth) See Toney, Michael D., and Kirsch, Jack F.

KIRSCHENBAUM, JILL
Women at work: Lois Greenfield. il pors *Ms.* 18:42-4 S '89

KIRSCHNER, MARC W.
(jt. auth) See Murray, Andrew W., and Kirschner, Marc W.

KIRSEBOM, VENDELA
about
The face of the '90s may belong to Vendela, Swedish supermodel and Grace Kelly look-alike. il pors *People Weekly* 31:103-5 Mr 27 '89

KIRSHENBAUM, JERRY
An American disgrace. il *Sports Illustrated* 70:16-19 F 27 '89
(jt. auth) See Demak, Richard, and Kirshenbaum, Jerry

KIRSHENBAUM, RICHARD
about
The ad brats. J. Taylor. il pors *New York* 22:50-6 N 13 '89

KIRSHENBAUM & BOND
The ad brats. J. Taylor. il pors *New York* 22:50-6 N 13 '89

KIRSTEIN, LINCOLN, 1907-
Walker Evans: American photographs. il *USA Today (Periodical)* 117:54-9 Mr '89

KIRSTEIN, PETER N.
The atomic museum. bibl f il *Art in America* 77:44-5+ Je '89

KIRTLAND, ROBERT
The last time I was in Mexico. il *America* 161:7-9 Jl 1-8 '89

KIRTLAND'S WARBLERS
Mack Lake, Michigan. R. H. Mohlenbrock. il map *Natural History* p90-5 O '89

KIRWAN, JACK D.
Buggy whips on starships. *Ad Astra* 1:46 Ap '89

KIS, DANILO
To die for one's country is glorious [story]; tr. by Michael Henry Heim. *Harper's* 278:32+ F '89

KISATCHIE NATIONAL FOREST (LA.)
Kisatchie Hills, Louisiana. R. H. Mohlenbrock. il map *Natural History* p30-2 F '89

KISER, ROSEMARIE
Woodpecker [story] il *New Choices for the Best Years* 29:58-63 Ag '89

KISHIMOTO, TAKASHI KEI, AND OTHERS
Neutrophil Mac-1 and MEL-14 adhesion proteins inversely regulated by chemotactic factors. bibl f il *Science* 245:1238-41 S 15 '89

KISIEL, CAROLINE M.
(tr) See Zárate Macías, Rosa Marta. Cantico de mujer

KISMARIC, CAROLE, 1942-
Forced out: the tragic plight of the world's refugees [excerpts] il *People Weekly* 31:98-102+ Ap 17 '89
about
Four houses join forces to publicize the plight of the world's refugees. il *Publishers Weekly* 235:42-3 Mr 24 '89

KISS, ZOLTAN J.
about
Burnt bulb? J. Cook and R. Addis. il por *Forbes* 144:10 Ag 7 '89

KISSELL, GEORGE
about
The College of Cardinals. J. Garrity. il pors *Sports Illustrated* 71:64-8+ Ag 14 '89

KISSICK, JOHN H.
about
John Kissick. E. Schine. il por *Business Week* Special Issue:95 Ap 14 '89
Without Milken, can Drexel still be Drexel? E. Schine. il pors *Business Week* p34 Mr 27 '89

KISSIN, EVGENY
about
Evgeny Kissin's debut. R. Freed. por *Stereo Review* 54:84 Ap '89

KISSING
Kissing in the boardroom. *Harper's* 279:27+ S '89

KISSINGER, HENRY, 1923-
How Kissinger sees it. il *Newsweek* 114:45 O 16 '89
Living with the inevitable. il *Newsweek* 114:51-2+ D 4 '89

Seeking a new balance in Asia. il *Newsweek* 112:51-2+ My 22 '89
about
The Kissinger clique. M. G. Warner and others. il por *Newsweek* 113:30+ Mr 27 '89
Kissinger vs. Nixon. pors *Time* 134:32 D 25 '89
Minority report. C. Hitchens. *The Nation* 248:764 Je 5 '89
The out-of-office reign of Henry I. il por *U.S. News & World Report* 106:10 Mr 27 '89
What's wrong with Yalta II. S. Talbott. il *Time* 133:36 Ap 24 '89

KISSINGER ASSOCIATES INC.
The Kissinger clique. M. G. Warner and others. il por *Newsweek* 113:30+ Mr 27 '89
The out-of-office reign of Henry I. il por *U.S. News & World Report* 106:10 Mr 27 '89

KISTIAKOWSKY, VERA
Keep Pentagon out of civilian economy. *The Bulletin of the Atomic Scientists* 45:5 Ap '89

KISZCZAK, CZESLAW, 1925-
about
Crisis in Poland. M. Nemeth. il por *Maclean's* 102:16-17 Ag 14 '89
The general's sudden retreat. por *U.S. News & World Report* 107:14 Jl 10 '89
To the brink—and back again. J. Smolowe. il por *Time* 134:38-9 Ag 14 '89

KIT AIRPLANES *See* Airplanes, Home-built
KIT AND THE WIDOW (MUSICAL GROUP)
Britain's blue-blood bad boys 'Kit and the Widow' make even their royal targets laugh. J. Wadler. il pors *People Weekly* 31:97-9 Ap 24 '89
KIT CARS *See* Automobiles, Home-built
KIT HOUSES *See* Houses, Prefabricated
KITCHELL, JENNIFER A., AND MACLEOD, NORMAN S.
Asymmetries of clade shape and the direction of evolutionary time [discussion of May 27, 1988 article, Macroevolutionary interpretations of symmetry and synchroneity in the fossil record] *Science* 243:1613-15 Mr 24 '89
KITCHEN BOARDS *See* Cutting boards
KITCHEN CABINETS
Buying cabinets. K. Childers. il *The Family Handyman* 39:38-42 S '89
The cabinet choice. il *Sunset (Central West edition)* 182:68-73 Ja '89
KITCHEN FURNITURE
See also
Kitchen cabinets
6 great products for kitchens and baths. A. Arnott. il *Home Mechanix* 85:66-7 O '89
Slabs of color [composite kitchen counters] C. M. Fiorillo. il *Popular Science* 234:138-41+ Je '89
Surface materials. J. Vara. il *Country Journal* 16:47-9 F '89
Tech tops [FormStone, ARP and Craftwood laminates] T. O. Bakke. il *Popular Science* 235:88+ D '89
KITCHEN KNIVES *See* Knives
KITCHEN RANGES *See* Stoves
KITCHEN TOWELS *See* Towels
KITCHEN UTENSILS AND APPLIANCES
See also
Blenders (Appliances)
Bread makers (Appliances)
Convection ovens
Cutting boards
Dishwashers
Drink mixers (Appliances)
Food processors (Appliances)
Ice cream makers
Microwave cookware
Microwave ovens
Mixers (Appliances)
Popcorn poppers
Pressure cookers
Stoves
Thermometers, Cooking
Best kitchen gear and gadgets. il *McCall's* 116:52 Ap '89
Cook away your cholesterol. J. B. Hurley. il *Prevention (Emmaus, Pa.)* 41:83-4+ S '89
Easy meals from your slow cooker [spiced beef brisket] il *Better Homes and Gardens* 67:136 Mr '89
Going cordless. D. Moreau. il *Changing Times* 43:81-2 Je '89
If there's a nutrition-minded cook in your kitchen. il *Sunset (Central West edition)* 183:124 D '89
Kitchen-counter intelligence. C. Christman. il *New Choices for the Best Years* 29:75+ My '89
Kitchen tech [special section] A. Arnott. il *Home Mechanix* 86:56+ Ap '89
Kitchen VIP's* *(very important pieces of equipment). A. Mandel. il *Working Woman* 14:140-2 Ap '89
Machine dreams. B. Shacochis. il *Gentlemen's Quarterly* 59:358+ O '89
Stocking-stuffers for cooks of all ages. il *Sunset (Central West edition)* 181:120 D '88

KITCHEN UTENSILS AND APPLIANCES—*cont.*
Anecdotes, facetiae, satire, etc.
Mice in the kitchen [Apple Computer] D. Gookin. *Compute!* 11:143 N '89
Collectors and collecting
Collecting butter & cheese making tools. F. Johnson. il *Antiques & Collecting Hobbies* 94:46-9 Je '89
Materials
A cook's tour of cookware materials. *Consumers' Research Magazine* 72:32-6 Ap '89
KITCHEN UTENSILS AND APPLIANCES INDUSTRY See Household appliances industry
KITCHENS
See also
Dining alcoves, etc.
3 eat-in kitchens. W. L. Nolan. il *Better Homes and Gardens* 67:58-62 Ag '89
12 square feet was all they had to add. il *Sunset (Central West edition)* 182:84 Ja '89
The after 5:00 kitchen. T. Jackson. il *Better Homes and Gardens* 68:77-82 F '89
Bow-bay for sink, counter. il *Sunset (Central West edition)* 182:136 Ap '89
Boxy kitchen and dining room became one bright space. il *Sunset (Central West edition)* 182:164+ My '89
Chef's special [L. Panish's kitchen designed by Anderson/ Schwartz Architects] H. S. MacIsaac. il por *House & Garden* 161:90-3 Ja '89
Come into the kitchen. il *McCall's* 116:98 Ap '89
Counter revolutionary. B. Shacochis. il *Gentlemen's Quarterly* 59:482+ S '89
Do-it-yourself kitchen guide [cover story] A. Rooze. il *The Family Handyman* 39:31-7 S '89
Family kitchens. N. Wing. il *Parents* 64:202-5 O '89
How big is this kitchen? Mirrors keep you guessing. il *Sunset (Central West edition)* 183:99 D '89
Jann's dream kitchen [Jann Miller-Chavez, winner of kitchen makeover contest] il *Good Housekeeping* 209:140-1 O '89
Kitchen cuts cost, not design. il *Southern Living* 24:166 Ap '89
A kitchen for the family. L. Hallam. il *Southern Living* 24:104-5 My '89
A kitchen for two cultures and three little boys. il *Sunset (Central West edition)* 182:142-3 Mr '89
Kitchens full of handy ideas. il *Good Housekeeping* 209:92-7+ Ag '89
Lightening up [update of old farmhouse kitchen] N. Cooper. il *Home Mechanix* 85:30-2+ Ag '89
Little room, big kitchen. H. Wicks. il *Home Mechanix* 85:28-35+ F '89
Lofty kitchen replaces the old patio. il *Sunset (Central West edition)* 182:88 Ja '89
Made to measure [Gina and Paul Hiatt's remodeled kitchen] il *Better Homes and Gardens* 67:94-5 O '89
Mini-kitchen remodel. D. Stover. il *Popular Science* 234:144-5 My '89
Multi-cook kitchen: duplicate workstations keep cooking duo happy. S. Sheetz. il *Better Homes and Gardens* 67:74+ S '89
New kitchen, antique character. il *Southern Living* 24:190 N '89
New porch and additions help unbury small, dark kitchen. il *Sunset (Central West edition)* 182:138-9 Mr '89
No longer an "afterthought" kitchen. il *Sunset (Central West edition)* 182:106-8 Mr '89
The practical country kitchen [cover story; special section] il *Country Journal* 16:33-49 F '89
Prefab storefront unit opens kitchen to view. il *Sunset (Central West edition)* 182:146 My '89
Recipes for kitchens. il *Good Housekeeping* 208:180-2+ Ap '89
Same space, new kitchen. C. Engle. il *Southern Living* 24:66-71 S '89
Streamlined kitchen makes the most of the view. il *Sunset (Central West edition)* 182:116 Je '89
They wanted more privacy and more storage. il *Sunset (Central West edition)* 182:146 My '89
Three rooms in one. il *Southern Living* 24:100 F '89
Three zones in one spacious, well-organized kitchen. il *Sunset (Central West edition)* 182:174 My '89
Tile a kitchen floor and backsplash. A. Rooze. il *The Family Handyman* 39:40-3 O '89
The ultimate kitchen remodel. A. W. Lees. il *Popular Science* 234:138-41 My '89
The user-friendly kitchen. D. Goldbeck. il *American Health* 8:87-90+ Jl/Ag '89
A white, bright kitchen. il *Southern Living* 24:172 Mr '89
Wide-open kitchen redo. S. Sheetz. il *Better Homes and Gardens* 67:66+ N '89
Years of idea-collecting paid off in this small but efficient kitchen. il *Sunset (Central West edition)* 182:128+ Ap '89
Anecdotes, facetiae, satire, etc.
Ghosts of kitchens past. B. H. Pierce. il *Gourmet* 49:144+ N '89
History
The kitchen at Montgeoffroy. L. Langseth-Christensen. il *Gourmet* 49:50-1+ Jl '89

Scotland's Brodick Castle kitchen. L. Langseth-Christensen. il *Gourmet* 49:82-3+ My '89
KITCHENWARE See Kitchen utensils and appliances
KITE, TOM
about
Kite finally takes flight. E. M. Swift. il por *Sports Illustrated* 70:26-8+ Mr 27 '89
The Midas touch. J. Garrity. il por *Sports Illustrated* 71:42-3 N 6 '89
KITELEY, DAVID
about
Side by side. K. H. Sidey. il pors *Christianity Today* 33:33 Mr 3 '89
KITES
The exhilaration and exaltation of painting the sky [cover story] W. W. Johnson. bibl (p163-4) il *Smithsonian* 20:64-70+ My '89
Kites are flying to a high-tech high. J. Frouman. il *Business Week* p105 Ag 21 '89
Photographs and photography
Kite festivals. A. Baget and L. Baget. il *Petersen's Photographic Magazine* 17:30-3 Ap '89
KITS, MEDICAL See Medical equipment
KITS, PREGNANCY See Pregnancy—Signs and diagnosis
KITSCH
Elitist kitsch. K. Dieckmann. *Utne Reader* p36 My/Je '89
Fontana's base materialism. Y.-A. Bois. bibl f il *Art in America* 77:238-49+ Ap '89
Kitsch in synch. J. Perl. il *Vogue* 179:326-7+ F '89
Anecdotes, facetiae, satire, etc.
The art of inventing the unnecessary. V. S. Sussman. il *U.S. News & World Report* 106:70 Je 26 '89
KITT, MICHAEL T.
Eight lunar wonders [cover story] il *Astronomy* 17:66-71 Mr '89
Observe the Apollo landing sites. il *Astronomy* 17:66-72 Jl '89
KITT PEAK NATIONAL OBSERVATORY
Monster CCD's get the big picture. il *Sky and Telescope* 78:343-4 O '89
KITTLE, HUB
about
The College of Cardinals. J. Garrity. il pors *Sports Illustrated* 71:64-8+ Ag 14 '89
KITTREDGE, WILLIAM
Showdown at Yucca Mountain: the high stakes of a nuclear waste dump. il *Utne Reader* p44-9 Ja/F '89
KITZHABER, JOHN
about
Drawing the line. I. Mothner. il por *American Health* 8:72-4+ Jl/Ag '89
KIWI FRUIT
A fuzz-less kiwi? [hardy kiwi] il *Sunset (Central West edition)* 182:160-1 F '89
KIWI FRUIT INDUSTRY
See also
California Kiwifruit Commission
KIZZIA, TOM
Elko to Eden [cover story] il map *Sierra* 74:46-54 Mr/Ap '89
KKK See Ku Klux Klan
KKRZ (PORTLAND, OR.: RADIO STATION) See Radio stations
KLADY, LEONARD
Practice made perfect. *Film Comment* 25:39 N/D '89
The scarlet letter. il pors *American Film* 15:15-16 D '89
KLAMATH BASIN NATIONAL WILDLIFE REFUGES (CALIF. AND OR.) See Wildlife sanctuaries—Pacific Northwest
KLAMATH RIVER (OR. AND CALIF.)
Most reliable rafter's river? Perhaps the Klamath. il map *Sunset (Central West edition)* 182:38-40 My '89
KLAMON, LAWRENCE P.
about
Under new management. A. A. Lappen. il por *Forbes* 144:164 S 18 '89
KLARE, MICHAEL T., 1942-
Stopping the war against the third world [adaptation of address, September 1988] il *The Progressive* 53:14-16 Ja '89
KLASS, PERRI, 1958-
AIDS: the youngest victims. il *The New York Times Magazine* p34-5+ Je 18 '89
Child abuse: the interrogation. il *The New York Times Magazine* p53-4 F 26 '89
Nutrition and medical newsletters offer information-hungry readers new food for thought. *Vogue* 179:554+ S '89
The perfect baby? il *The New York Times Magazine* p45-6 Ja 29 '89
Should this baby be saved? il *Glamour* 87:212-13+ D '89
Vital signs. See alternate issues of Discover beginning April 1985
Watching for red flags. il *The New York Times Magazine* p56-7 Ap 23 '89
When baby has a fever. il *The New York Times Magazine* p57-8 Ag 20 '89
When child's play isn't fun. il *The New York Times Magazine* p31-2 Ag 6 '89

KLAUSNER, RICHARD D., AND HARFORD, JOE B.
Cis-trans models for post-transcriptional gene regulation. bibl f il *Science* 246:870-2 N 17 '89

KLAVAN, ELLEN
Mother to mother. il *Parents* 64:74+ F '89
Pick the best after-school care. il *Parents* 64:72+ S '89

KLAYMAN, DANIEL L.
Weeding out malaria. il *Natural History* p18+ O '89

KLEBER, HERBERT D.
about
Kleber offers expert and blunt opinions on addiction. C. Holden. por *Science* 246:1381 D 15 '89

KLEENE, STEVE
The diving seal [adaptations of harbor seals] bibl il *Sea Frontiers* 35:370-4 N/D '89

KLEHR, HARVEY
(jt. auth) See Evanier, David, and Klehr, Harvey

KLEIBER, CARLOS
about
Music. P. G. Davis. il *New York* 22:78-9 S 11 '89

KLEIMAN, CAROL
How to get 'em on track. il *Ms.* 18:64 Jl/Ag '89
R.N.s get pay fix: nurses lead way for pay equity in state jobs. *Ms.* 17:73-4 My '89

KLEIMAN, DEVRA G.
Reintroduction of captive mammals for conservation [cover story] bibl f il *BioScience* 39:152-61 Mr '89

KLEIN, ARTHUR C.
(jt. auth) See Sobel, Dava, and Klein, Arthur C.

KLEIN, DEBORAH PISETZNER
(jt. auth) See Norwood, Janet L., and Klein, Deborah Pisetzner

KLEIN, EDWARD, 1936-
Jackie: her friends finally talk! il pors *Good Housekeeping* 209:60+ N '89
Winning Diane: how ABC's Roone Arledge snatched her away from CBS [cover story] il pors *New York* 22:36-43 Mr 13 '89

KLEIN, ELIZABETH
Bonus baby. il *The New York Times Magazine* p22+ Ag 27 '89

KLEIN, GENE
about
Gene Klein quits the track—$26 million later. R. Grover. il por *Business Week* p66 Ag 7 '89

KLEIN, HELEN
about
Woman of the century. P. L. Potts. il pors *Runner's World* 24:34-6 Je '89

KLEIN, JEANNE
K-12 drama/theatre research for the 1990s: an agenda for dramatic action. bibl f *Design for Arts in Education* 91:27-34 N/D '89

KLEIN, JILL
about
Batters know that where there's smoke, there's Jill Klein. il pors *People Weekly* 31:60 My 22 '89

KLEIN, JOE, 1946-
Been down so long it looks like up to me. il por *New York* 22:34-7 F 20 '89
Can Dinkins do it? [cover story] il pors *New York* 22:30-7 Jl 31 '89
Gandhi vs. Gumby. il pors *New York* 22:42-5 N 6 '89
The lion in summer: Koch on the comeback trail. il pors *New York* 22:38-42 S 4 '89
The new mayor and the crisis of New York [cover story] il pors *New York* 22:36-40 N 20 '89
Now, the showdown: Dinkins vs. Giuliani in the void left by Koch. il pors *New York* 22:50-3 S 25 '89
Race: the issue [cover story] il *New York* 22:32-8 My 29 '89
Ready for Rudy? [cover story] il pors *New York* 22:30-7 Mr 6 '89
Rudy's fall from grace: can Ailes put Giuliani's campaign back together again? il pors *New York* 22:40-3 Ag 21 '89
The sorrow and the city [cover story] il *The New Republic* 201:24-8 N 13 '89
Spike Lee replies: "Say it ain't so, Joe" [discussion of June 26, 1989 article, Spiked?] il por *New York* 22:6 Jl 17 '89

KLEIN, LARRY
Audio update. See issues of Radio-Electronics beginning January 1987
Crosstalk. See issues of High Fidelity (New York, N.Y.) beginning March 1987 through July 1989

KLEIN, MELVYN N.
about
'A lot of people don't know who Mel Klein is'. T. Vogel. il por *Business Week* p24-5 Jl 24 '89

KLEIN, RALPH
about
Alberta's 'loose cannon'. J. Howse. il por *Maclean's* 102:12 Ja 23 '89

KLEIN, SIEGFRIED
about
The impossible achieved? R. Hodges. il *Stereo Review* 54:136 Je '89

KLEIN, YVES, 1928-1962
about
Yves Klein's market: flying high. R. W. Walker. il por *Art News* 88:37 My '89

KLEIN (LAWRENCE R.) AWARD *See* Lawrence R. Klein Award

KLEINER, ART
What do you want from fashion right now! il *Glamour* 87:207+ Mr '89

KLEINER, KURT
Union victory in a copper refinery. il *The Progressive* 53:13 S '89

KLEINER, PERKINS, CAUFIELD & BYERS
Making money the new-fashioned way [J. Doerr] E. S. Ely. por *Personal Computing* 13:74 Jl '89

KLEINFIELD, N. R.
Children's books: inside the Baby-sitters Club. *The New York Times Book Review* 94:42 Ap 30 '89

KLEINMAN, SUSAN, 1964-
The humor prescription. il *Health (New York, N.Y.)* 21:40-1 Ag '89

KLEINMANN, LEANNE
Condom alert: the rubber you're using may not be as safe as you think. il *Glamour* 87:250-1 Ag '89

KLEINSCHMIDT, EDWARD
Orchestrion [poem] *The New Yorker* 65:54 N 6 '89

KLEINZAHLER, AUGUST
Sunday in November [poem] *The New Yorker* 65:74 My 1 '89

KLEISER, RANDAL
about
Big top Pee-wee [film] Reviews
   Video il 12:61 F '89. B. Walters
Getting it right [film] Reviews
   Commonweal 116:338 Je 2 '89. T. O'Brien

KLENICKI, LEON, AND MALLON, ELIAS D.
Close enough to step on toes: tensions between Jews & Catholics. il *Commonweal* 116:521-6 O 6 '89

KLENSCH, ELSA
about
Leading a stylish revolution in the fashion media. P. Warner. il por *Architectural Digest* 46:29+ S '89

KLEPPNER, DANIEL
A passion for precision. il por *Physics Today* 42:9+ N '89
(jt. auth) See Haroche, Serge, and Kleppner, Daniel

KLIGMAN, ALBERT MONTGOMERY
about
Top hat and tall tales. L. N. Vreeland. il por *Money* 18:76 Ap '89

KLIMT, GUSTAV, 1862-1918
about
Gustav Klimt: Galerie St. Etienne. il *Art News* 88:200 O '89

KLINE, DAVID
An Amish drought journal. il *The Mother Earth News* 118:60-1 Jl/Ag '89

KLINE, EDWARD
(tr) See Sakharov, Andreï Dmitrievich, 1921-1989. A speech to the People's Congress

KLINE, ELIZABETH
Pittsburgh Ballet Theatre forges ahead: the future is now [cover story] il *Dance Magazine* 63:37-42 O '89

KLINE, S. ALLAN
about
The hidden files [cover story] C. T. Honicker. il *The New York Times Magazine* p38-41+ N 19 '89

KLINE-CHESSON, KATHLEEN
The living word: dance as a language of faith. il *The Christian Century* 106:314-16 Mr 22-29 '89

KLINGER, JUDSON
In pursuit of crazy language [interview with T. McGuane] il por *American Film* 14:42-5+ Ap '89

KLINGHOFFER, DAVID
Random notes. *National Review* 41:44 Jl 14 '89
Scenes from the gay life. *National Review* 41:22-3 Ag 4 '89

KLINGLER, JENNIFER
(jt. auth) See Klingler, Tim, and Klingler, Jennifer

KLINGLER, TIM, AND KLINGLER, JENNIFER
The rain maps. maps *Bicycling* 30:134 Ap '89

KLINKENBORG, VERLYN
Meeting her family. il *Glamour* 87:232 F '89
Thomas Hart Benton came from Missouri—and he showed 'em [cover story] bibl (p174) il pors *Smithsonian* 20:82-101 Ap '89
Your chaps, sir. il *Esquire* 111:50+ Je '89

KLINT, HILMA AF, 1862-1944
about
Back from the beyond. M. Moorman. il por *Art News* 88:85-6 Summ '89
Contemplating the rose hip. B. Adams. il *Art in America* 77:164-7 D '89

KLINTWORTH, GARY
What Vietnam achieved in Cambodia. *World Press Review* 36:35 D '89

KLM ROYAL DUTCH AIRLINES
Belgium will sell British Airways, KLM 20% stakes in new Sabena. *Aviation Week & Space Technology* 130:95 Je 26 '89
Dutch treat. T. Jaffe. il *Forbes* 144:238 S 18 '89
Front man [A. Checchi fronting for KLM in Northwest takeover] S. Flack. il *Forbes* 144:69 Jl 10 '89
Skinner's limits on NWA buyout fail to dissuade drive for LBO controls. C. Fotos. *Aviation Week & Space Technology* 131:138-9 O 9 '89
U.S. must assess buyout bid's impact on safety at Northwest [KLM's role in Wings Holdings' bid under scrutiny] *Aviation Week & Space Technology* 130:92-3 Je 26 '89

KLOCKENBRINK, MYRA
Cleansing waters. il map *American Health* 8:72 S '89

KLOEPFER, DEANNE
Island under fire. *Wilderness* 53:29 Wint '89

KLOET, E. R. DE
(jt. auth) See Joëls, Marian, and Kloet, E. R. de

KLOPPENBURG, ALOKA
about
Aloka: now and then. il pors *Seventeen* 48:152-5 S '89

KLOSE, MONIKA, AND BENTLEY, DAVID R.
Transient pioneer neurons are essential for formation of an embryonic peripheral nerve [cover story] bibl f il *Science* 245:982-4 S 1 '89

KLOTZ, IRENE
Commercial launches: getting the business? il *Ad Astra* 1:16-19 Ap '89
Spaceport 2000. il map *Ad Astra* 1:39-42 F '89

KLOVES, STEVE
about
The fabulous Baker Boys [film] Reviews
Commonweal 116:644 N 17 '89. T. O'Brien
Maclean's il 102:66 O 23 '89. B. D. Johnson
The New Republic 201:28-9 N 20 '89. S. Kauffmann
New York il 22:73-5 O 16 '89. D. Denby
The New Yorker 65:107-9 O 16 '89. P. Kael
Newsweek il 114:84-5 O 23 '89. D. Ansen
People Weekly il 32:19 O 23 '89. R. Novak
Rolling Stone il p36 N 2 '89. P. Travers
Time il 134:85 O 23 '89. R. Schickel

KLRT (LITTLE ROCK, ARK.: TELEVISION STATION) See Television stations

KLUGE, JOHN WERNER
about
Pikers need not apply. J. Zweig. il por *Forbes* 143:142 F 6 '89
Pop goes the wallet. J. Zweig. por *Forbes* 144:138 Ag 7 '89

KLUGE SUBOTNICK PERKOWSKI & COMPANY
Pikers need not apply. J. Zweig. il por *Forbes* 143:142 F 6 '89

KNABUSCH, CHARLES T.
about
Rocking the recliners. M. Schifrin. il por *Forbes* 144:194+ O 16 '89

KNAPP, ED
The era of the fabulous Hollywood fan magazine. il *Antiques & Collecting Hobbies* 94:34-8 Mr '89

KNAPP, EDWARD A.
about
Knapp resigns from URA leadership; Truly to pilot NASA, Fields at DARPA. I. Goodwin. *Physics Today* 42:42-4 Je '89

KNAPP, INGRID
(tr) See Häring, Bernhard, 1912-. Building a creative conscience

KNAPPERTSBUSCH, GERDA
about
Greener fields. C. Joritz. il por *Women's Sports & Fitness* 11:58-9 N/D '89

KNEE
Surgery
New knee options [reconstructing dancers' anterior cruciate ligaments] M. Horosko. il *Dance Magazine* 63:96-7 Je '89
Transplantation
"Please save my leg!" [transplant replaces knee destroyed by tumor] ed. by Elaine Fein. S. Lazarchick. il por *Redbook* 172:68+ Ja '89
Wounds and injuries
A pain in the knee! [iliotibial band syndrome] D. W. Jackson and P. R. Kurzweil. il *Runner's World* 24:24 D '89
Ski trips. il *Prevention (Emmaus, Pa.)* 41:10+ Ja '89
Take care of your knees [views of Dennis Phelps] *USA Today (Periodical)* 117:7-8 F '89
What can be done about knee injuries? [skiers' anterior cruciate ligament sprains] C. Ettlinger. il *Skiing* 41:85-7+ Mr '89

KNEPHER, TOM
Pagan holidays mark earth's yearly cycles. *Utne Reader* p74-5 N/D '89

KNEPPER, MIKE, 1943-
Affordable four-doors: perfect cars for young families. il *Better Homes and Gardens* 67:187-8+ N '89
New-car lingo: a buyer's guide to today's technological wonders. il *Better Homes and Gardens* 67:176 My '89

KNEUPPER, WILLIE MAE
First lines. *The Writer* 102:27+ O '89

KNEVETT, CHARLES
The prince and the architects. il *Architectural Record* 177:57+ O '89

KNICKERBOCKER, SUZY See Suzy

KNICKERS
Knickers. J. Berendt. il *Esquire* 111:46 Ap '89

KNIEVEL, EVEL
about
Daredevil Robbie Knievel heads for Vegas to show his famous dad he's more than a little Evel. P. Axthelm. il pors *People Weekly* 31:62-3 Ap 10 '89
Returning good for Evel. F. Lidz. il pors *Sports Illustrated* 70:26-7 Ap 24 '89

KNIEVEL, ROBBIE
about
Daredevil Robbie Knievel heads for Vegas to show his famous dad he's more than a little Evel. P. Axthelm. il pors *People Weekly* 31:62-3 Ap 10 '89
Returning good for Evel. F. Lidz. il pors *Sports Illustrated* 70:26-7 Ap 24 '89

KNIFE SHARPENING See Sharpeners and sharpening

KNIFEFISH
See also
Spinal cord

KNIGHT, ANN
Baseball like it oughta be [interview] il *American Film* 14:76 My '89

KNIGHT, BOBBY
about
The Knight I knew [excerpt from Playing for Knight]; ed. by John Garrity. S. Alford. il pors *The Saturday Evening Post* 261:66-8+ N/D '89

KNIGHT, C. A., AND DEVRIES, ARTHUR L.
Melting inhibition and superheating of ice by an antifreeze glycopeptide. bibl f il *Science* 245:505-7 Ag 4 '89

KNIGHT, CHUCK
about
Shades of Geneen at Emerson Electric. il por *Fortune* 119:39 My 22 '89

KNIGHT, DENNIS H., AND WALLACE, LINDA L.
The Yellowstone fires: issues in landscape ecology. bibl f il *BioScience* 39:700-6 N '89

KNIGHT, ERIC
Lassie come home [story] il *The Saturday Evening Post* 261:34-6+ Mr '89

KNIGHT, FRANK
The Shawangunk Mountains. il *The Conservationist* 44:26-33 S/O '89

KNIGHT, GLADYS
about
Gladys Knight goes solo and tells why [cover story] R. E. Johnson. il pors *Jet* 76:56-9 My 8 '89

KNIGHT, HILARY
about
Hilary of the Plaza. E. Newhall. il por *New York* 22:22 Ja 16 '89

KNIGHT, STEFAN, AND OTHERS
Reexamination of the three-dimensional structure of the small subunit of RuBisCo from higher plants. bibl f il *Science* 244:702-5 My 12 '89

KNIGHT, VIRGINIA CURTIN
Namibia's transition to independence. bibl f *Current History* 88:225-8+ My '89

KNIGHTSBRIDGE MEDICAL PUBLISHING (FIRM)
Getting information to the masses. J. Bethune. il *Publishers Weekly* 235:38 Ap 21 '89

KNIPPERS, EDWARD
Hellfire of the banalities. il *Christianity Today* 33:26-7 S 22 '89
The icon cometh. il *Christianity Today* 33:55 Ap 7 '89

KNITTING
Everything's coming up roses [cover story] il *Good Housekeeping* 208:198-9+ My '89
The knitting image [summer top] il *Seventeen* 48:45+ Jl '89

KNITTING FACTORY (NEW YORK, N.Y.: NIGHTCLUB) See New York (N.Y.)—Restaurants, nightclubs, bars, etc.

KNITTING FACTORY JAZZ FESTIVAL (NEW YORK, N.Y.) See Music festivals—New York (State)

KNIVES
See also
Swiss Army knives
The blade's the thing [kitchen knives] N. Goldbeck. il *American Health* 8:137 Ap '89
Kitchen knives. il *Consumer Reports* 54:294-8 D '89
A lockback lineup [hunting knives] D. E. Petzal. il *Field & Stream* 93:68-9+ Ap '89
The new edges for outdoors. il *Outdoor Life* 184:76-7 N '89
A utensil for all seasonings [kitchen knives] N. Hauser. il *American Health* 8:134-5 Ap '89
Collectors and collecting
Art of the knife. B. Winter. il *Popular Mechanics* 166:86-8 Mr '89

KNIVES—cont.
Photographs and photography
Object on a complementary background [hunting knife against black reflective background] D. Palmer. il *Petersen's Photographic Magazine* 18:48-9 Jl '89

KNOBLER, DANNY
'80s baseball. il *Sport (New York, N.Y.)* 80:54-6+ O '89
Best of the best. il *Sport (New York, N.Y.)* 80:23-6 My '89
The boys of spring. il *Sport (New York, N.Y.)* 80:24-5 Mr '89
The college baseball boom. il *Sport (New York, N.Y.)* 80:48+ Ap '89
Oh-and-two: when the count goes to two strikes, the pitcher-hitter battle really gets interesting. il *Sport (New York, N.Y.)* 80:98-100+ Je '89
The power rabbits [cover story] il pors *Sport (New York, N.Y.)* 80:22-4+ Jl '89
Pssst . . . . heard about Tony Gwynn? [with editorial comment by Kelly Garrett] il pors *Sport (New York, N.Y.)* 80:3, 22-4+ Ag '89
To rise again. il *Sport (New York, N.Y.)* 80:47-8+ S '89
Top secret. il *Sport (New York, N.Y.)* 80:72-4 N '89

KNOCK, ENGINE See Automobile engines—Detonation
KNOEBEL, SUZANNE B., 1926-
about
Finding a silent heart attack can set off some noisy, vital alarms [interview]; ed. by Giovanna Breu. il por *People Weekly* 32:58 S 18 '89

KNOKKE-LE-ZOUTE (BELGIUM)
Historic houses, sites, etc.
Surreal note in Belgium: artist Roger Nellens' collection at Knokke. E. White. il *Architectural Digest* 46:142-9+ D '89

KNOLL, ERWIN
Memo. See issues of The Progressive
KNOT THEORY See Topology
KNOTS LANDING [television program] See Television program reviews—Single works
KNOTT, M. LEON
Sharpen images with a cardboard mask. il *Astronomy* 17:84-5 F '89

KNOWLEDGE
See also
Facts
Freedom of information
Ignorance
Intuition
Science
Skepticism
Could our current capabilities for information storage and retrieval open a whole new world of ideas? R. M. Adams. il *Smithsonian* 20:12 Ap '89
Knowing is not thinking. E. Janko. il *Phi Delta Kappan* 70:543-4 Mr '89
Overcome "information anxiety" [condensed from Information anxiety] R. S. Wurman. il *Reader's Digest* 134:127-30 My '89

KNOWLEDGE, THEORY OF
See also
Cognition
Perception
Subjectivity
Truth
A nation still at risk [cover story] C. E. Finn. *Commentary* 87:17-23 My '89
What to do about the schools [discussion of May 1989 article, A nation still at risk] C. E. Finn. *Commentary* 88:4-6+ O '89

KNOWLEDGE INDEX (DATABASE)
The Knowledge Index: a low-cost, easy-to-use, on-line database. A. Glossbrenner. il *Home Office Computing* 7:44 N '89

KNOX, CHARLES E.
Remotely incensed: the search for profits [cover story] il *Ad Astra* 1:22-4+ Ap '89
KNOX, MARGARET L.
Horns of a dilemma. il *Sierra* 74:58-67 N/D '89
No nation an island. il *Sierra* 74:78-84 My/Je '89
KNOXVILLE (MD.)
Gardens and gardening
Bearing fruit [W. Ehrhardt's fruit garden] K. Martin. il pors *Organic Gardening* 36:68-72 Mr '89
KNUCKLES, JEFFREY
Angela [poem] *Essence* 20:106 Jl '89
KNUDSON, GEORGE
about
He had a dream. L. Rubenstein. il por *Maclean's* 102:74 Ap 10 '89
Obituary
Maclean's il por 102:51 F 6 '89. T. Frayne
KNUDSON, TOM
Rancho Seco decked again. il *The Bulletin of the Atomic Scientists* 45:7-8 D '89
KNUDSON-BENSON ASSOCIATES
Centerline: Robert L. Benson. M. Sommers. il por *Theatre Crafts* 23:28-9 My '89

KNUTSON-LYCHOLAT, CINDY
about
Basement finishing options [interview] il por *Home Mechanix* 85:18+ D '89
KO SAMUI (THAILAND) See Samui (Thailand)
KOBAYASHI, KOICHI
about
Go. *The New Yorker* 64:26-7 F 6 '89
KOBILINSKY, LAWRENCE
(jt. auth) See Levine, Louis, 1921-, and Kobilinsky, Lawrence
KOBILKA, BRIAN K., AND OTHERS
Analysis of ligand binding specificity of receptor chimeras [discussion of June 3, 1988 article, Chimeric α_2-,β_2-adrenergic receptors: delineation of domains involved in effector coupling and ligand binding specificity] *Science* 243:236-7 Ja 13 '89
KØBKE, CHRISTEN SCHJELLERUP, 1810-1848
about
Storm beneath the calm. Sir M. Levey. il por *Art News* 88:79-80 F '89
KOBLER, JOHN
Bernhardt in America. il pors *American Heritage* 40:52-4+ Jl/Ag '89
Beverly Sills hits all the high notes. il pors *New Choices for the Best Years* 29:36-40 Mr '89
KOBRAK, FRED
The international PSP market: an update. *Publishers Weekly* 236:44-5 N 10 '89
This year in Moscow. il *Publishers Weekly* 236:23-4 O 13 '89
KOCH, BILL
The double pole. il *Skiing* 41:30 Ja '89
My favorite touring centers. il *Skiing* 42:28+ D '89
Technique terrorists. il *Skiing* 42:40+ N '89
KOCH, ED, 1924-
Don't ax the mayor [letter to R. Green on New Yorkese spoken by New York City students] *Harper's* 278:21-2 Mr '89
Edward I. Koch [advice to George Bush] *National Review* 41:22 F 10 '89
How'd I do? il pors *The New York Times Magazine* p26-7+ D 31 '89
Mayor Koch and Cardinal O'Connor: a conversation [excerpts from His Eminence and Hizzoner] il por *Good Housekeeping* 208:148+ My '89
about
Around City Hall (Koch administration). A. Logan. See occasional issues of The New Yorker through December 25, 1989
Been down so long it looks like up to me. J. Klein. il por *New York* 22:34-7 F 20 '89
Big Ben: has Police Commissioner Ward become a liability to Koch? P. Blauner. il pors *New York* 22:48-50+ Ap 3 '89
A call for racial harmony. E. Salholz. il pors *Newsweek* 114:21-2 S 25 '89
Dinkins readies for N.Y.C. mayoral race after major primary election victory. il pors *Jet* 76:4+ O 2 '89
Enough already? J. Klein. il *New York* 22:14+ Je 12 '89
Gotham rainbow. *The Nation* 249:335-6 O 2 '89
It's a dirty job—but a lot of people want to do it. H. Collingwood. il por *Business Week* p26 Ap 17 '89
Koch against Koch. S. Roberts. il pors *The New York Times Magazine* p32-4+ Je 11 '89
Koch lives. J. Klein. il por *New York* 22:9-10 Ag 7 '89
The lion in summer: Koch on the comeback trail. J. Klein. il pors *New York* 22:38-42 S 4 '89
Mayor culpa. J. B. Rose. *The New Republic* 200:18-20+ My 8 '89
Mayor Koch's wrinkled brow. W. F. Buckley. *National Review* 41:62-3 Mr 10 '89
The N.Y.C. scandals of Ed Koch [cover story] M. J. Green. *The Nation* 248:397 Mr 27 '89
New York's first and last hurrahs. D. Baer. il pors *U.S. News & World Report* 107:26-7 S 25 '89
Now, the showdown: Dinkins vs. Giuliani in the void left by Koch. J. Klein. il pors *New York* 22:50-3 S 25 '89
The prophet motive. J. Klein. il pors *New York* 22:12+ Mr 20 '89
The race for New York: Edward Koch loses a bid for a new term. H. Mackenzie. il pors *Maclean's* 102:32-3 S 25 '89
So long, Ed. W. F. Buckley. *National Review* 41:63 O 27 '89
Zinging Rudy. J. Klein. por *New York* 22:14-15 Je 5 '89
KOCH, EDWIN B., 1937-
about
The subjective object. H. M. Sayre. il por *American Artist* 53:70-5+ D '89
KOCH, STEPHEN
Journey's beginning: a talk with Diana Trilling. il por *The New York Times Book Review* 94:1+ F 19 '89
KOCHER, CAMERON
about
A murder rap at age 10. *Newsweek* 114:24 Ag 14 '89

KOCINSKI, JOHN
about
Heir apparent. H. R. Abrams. il pors *Cycle* 40:52-4+ N '89
Schwantz, Kocinski win at Japanese GP. T. Van Hooydonk. il *Cycle* 40:24 Je '89
KOCKELMAN, JOHN
about
The wonderful world of bungee jumping. E. Grinnan. il por *Seventeen* 48:132 Ag '89
KOCOL, CLEO
Feminist update. See issues of The Humanist beginning September/October 1986
KODAK CAMERAS *See* Cameras
KODAK COMPANY *See* Eastman Kodak Co.
KODANSHA INTERNATIONAL USA LTD.
Kodansha brings new Japanese fiction to the U.S. il *Publishers Weekly* 236:57 O 6 '89
KOELREUTERIA *See* Golden rain trees
KOENIG, BRUCE
Audience chime system. il *Theatre Crafts* 23:76-7 O '89
KOENIG, RHODA
Carving out a niche. il por *House & Garden* 161:218-23 O '89
Catch of the day. il por *House & Garden* 161:54-5 Ja '89
The decorative dandy. il por *House & Garden* 161:42+ Mr '89
The down patrol: the book on downtown fiction. il *New York* 22:147-8+ D 25 '89-Ja 1 '90
Gardens of delight. il *House & Garden* 161:46+ F '89
Hare apparent. il por *Vogue* 179:202 F '89
Iberian weekends. il pors *House & Garden* 161:142-53+ F '89
International style. il *House & Garden* 161:138-43 N '89
Murder on the moon—the crimebuster's wearing a strapless sheath. il pors *TV Guide* 37:24-6+ Ap 29-My 5 '89
Norman retreat. il *House & Garden* 161:142-7+ Jl '89
Reads: paperbacks by the sack for when the pressure's off. il *New York* 22:138+ Jl 3-10 '89
KOENIGSWARTER, PANNONICA DE, BARONESS, 1913-1988
about
Obituary
Down Beat il 56:59-60 Ap '89. P. Keepnews
KOENKER, DIANE, 1947-
Strike's back. *The New Republic* 201:14-16 O 23 '89
KOEPPEL, BARBARA
A company town decays. il *The Progressive* 53:12-13 F '89
Victor Reuther [interview] il *The Progressive* 53:25-8 D '89
KOERNER, CHRISTINE
Report from Tweeriviere. il *UN Chronicle* 26:11 D '89
KOERNER, ROBERT M., 1933-
Ice core evidence for extensive melting of the Greenland ice sheet in the last interglacial. bibl f il map *Science* 244:964-8 My 26 '89
KOESTENBAUM, WAYNE
Fantasia on my father's gift [poem] *The Nation* 248:706-7 My 22 '89
KOESTLER, ARTHUR, 1905-1983
about
Darkness at noon; tr. by Barry J. Rubin. V. Chubinsky. il *The New Republic* 200:28-30 F 20 '89
KOGA, TETSUYA, AND OTHERS
T cells against a bacterial heat shock protein recognize stressed macrophages. bibl f il *Science* 245:1112-15 S 8 '89
KOGER, IRA M.
about
Chacun à son pocketbook. C. Brown. il pors *Forbes* 144:144-5 D 25 '89
KOHL, HELMUT, 1930-
Chancellor Kohl on "heirless" art. il por *Art News* 88:17 Summ '89
Chancellor Kohl's visit [remarks, November 15, 1988] il por *Department of State Bulletin* 89:56-7 Mr '89
Federal Republic of Germany [address, April 27, 1989] *Vital Speeches of the Day* 55:482-6 Je 1 '89
Painful questions. *Society* 26:7-9 Mr/Ap '89
Remarks and question-and-answer session, Bonn, May 30, 1989. *Department of State Bulletin* 89:33-4 Ag '89
about
The assertive chancellor. D. C. Marsh. *World Press Review* 36:30-1 My '89
Fighting off the beer-hall boys. N. Birnbaum. il *The Nation* 248:588-9+ My 1 '89
Kohl isn't quite out, but he sure is down. J. Templeman. il por *Business Week* p52 S 11 '89
Kohl rekindles NATO dispute over upgrading Lance missile. K. F. Mordoff. *Aviation Week & Space Technology* 130:21-2 F 20 '89
Kohl takes on topic A. D. Benjamin. il *Time* 134:45 D 11 '89
The Kohl war. *The New Republic* 200:7-8 My 22 '89
One people, one country: a scenario. K. Breslau. il por *Newsweek* 114:34 D 11 '89
The perilous trek of Helmut Kohl. R. Knight. il *U.S. News & World Report* 106:28-9 Je 5 '89
Western Europe's man in the middle. D. Lawday. il por *U.S. News & World Report* 107:45 D 11 '89

Why Kohl is right. S. Talbott. il por *Time* 133:26 My 15 '89
Visits to the United States, 1988
Chancellor Kohl's visit [remarks, November 15, 1988] R. Reagan; H. Kohl. il por *Department of State Bulletin* 89:56-7 Mr '89
KOHL, LARRY
Above China. il maps *National Geographic* 175:278-311 Mr '89
KOHL (WALTER A.) SALES (FIRM) *See* Walter A. Kohl Sales (Firm)
KOHLBERG, JEROME
about
Churning in the shark tank. B. Rudolph. il por *Time* 134:58 S 11 '89
Clash of the titans. C. Byron. il por *New York* 22:33-4 S 25 '89
KOHLBERG KRAVIS ROBERTS & CO.
Biggest bidders, wildest auction [RJR Nabisco takeover] B. Saporito. il pors *Fortune* 119:34-5 Ja 2 '89
Bonds that bind [Swiss court intervention in Kohlberg Kravis Roberts' bid for RJR Nabisco] D. Fanning. il *Forbes* 143:48 My 1 '89
Churning in the shark tank [suit by J. Kohlberg] B. Rudolph. il por *Time* 134:58 S 11 '89
Clash of the titans [suit by J. Kohlberg] C. Byron. il por *New York* 22:33-4 S 25 '89
'Greed really turns me off' [RJR Nabisco buyout; interview with H. Kravis] C. Leinster. il por *Fortune* 119:69-71 Ja 2 '89
Has the Beatrice LBO gone pffft? C. J. Loomis. il *Fortune* 120:113+ Jl 31 '89
How KKR stubbed its toe [SCI TV deal] L. J. Nathans. il *Business Week* p56 Ag 7 '89
How Ross Johnson blew the buyout [RJR Nabisco] B. Saporito. il por *Fortune* 119:296-8+ Ap 24 '89
Junkman in D.C. [Kohlberg Kravis Roberts' buyout of Houdaille points to need to regulate LBOs] M. Holland. *The Nation* 248:365 Mr 20 '89
KKR tiptoes into Texas [pumps capital into MCorp] T. Mason. il *Business Week* p33 Ja 16 '89
KKR to buy Macmillan Book Clubs and Intertec for $310 million. *Publishers Weekly* 235:16 Je 16 '89
A lion of the Texas bar snarls at KKR and Drexel [S. Susman builds asbestos case stemming from Jim Walter Corp. LBO] M. Ivey. il por *Business Week* p73+ O 9 '89
See you in bankruptcy court [leveraged buyout of Seaman Furniture turns into headache for Kohlberg Kravis Roberts] S. Flack. il *Forbes* 144:77+ O 16 '89
'They cleaned our clock' [RJR Nabisco buyout; interview with F. R. Johnson] B. Saporito. il por *Fortune* 119:72-4 Ja 2 '89
White knight or raider? [H. Kravis' stake in BTR plc] S. Flack. il *Forbes* 144:46 S 18 '89
Anecdotes, facetiae, satire, etc.
How to save communism: a modest prospectus [leveraged buyout of Soviet Union] M. D. Coleman. *National Review* 41:36-7 Mr 24 '89
KOHLER CO.
Kohler Co. R. Koselka and others. il *Forbes* 144:216+ D 11 '89
KOHLMEYER, IDA, 1912-
about
Catch a curator's eye. il *American Artist* 53:48 D '89
KOHLS, ANN
(jt. auth) See Conforti, Michael, and Kohls, Ann
KOHN, ALFIE
After happily ever after. il *Psychology Today* 23:66-70 Ja/F '89
Do religious people help more? Not so you'd notice. il *Psychology Today* 23:66+ D '89
Doing good. *Current (Washington, D.C.)* 309:4-6 Ja '89
The new discipline. il *Ladies' Home Journal* 106:190 N '89
Raising kids who care. il *Ladies' Home Journal* 106:112 D '89
Suffer the restless children. il *The Atlantic* 264:90-4+ N '89
KOHN, HOWARD
Company town. il *Rolling Stone* p67-8+ Ap 6 '89
Fields of dreams: old farming is new again. il *Rolling Stone* p41-2 O 5 '89
The last farmer [condensation] il *Reader's Digest* 134:115-20 Mr '89
about
Picking up the PC's. M. Porter. il por *Gentlemen's Quarterly* 59:203+ Ap '89
KOITO MANUFACTURING CO. LTD.
A back burner for T. Boone stake [T. B. Pickens denied seat on board of Koito Manufacturing] *U.S. News & World Report* 107:16 Jl 10 '89
Beware the gaijin raider [T. B. Pickens] *Newsweek* 113:48 Ap 17 '89
Boone Pickens, samurai warrior [bid for Koito Manufacturing] M. Ivey. il por *Business Week* p90+ My 8 '89
Kamikaze capitalism [T. B. Pickens buys into Koito Manufacturing] M. Lewis. *The New Republic* 200:19-20 My 1 '89

KOITO MANUFACTURING CO. LTD.—*cont.*
T. Boone's declaration of yen-dependence [bid for seat on the board of Koito Manufacturing] M. Tharp. il por *U.S. News & World Report* 106:51 My 1 '89
T. Boone's Tokyo campaign [T. B. Pickens challenges corporate officers at annual meeting] K. Makihara. il por *Time* 134:45 Jl 10 '89
A Texas raider rocks Club Japan [T. B. Pickens buys into Koito Manufacturing] *U.S. News & World Report* 106:15 Ap 17 '89

KOKERNAK, ROBERT
On the trail of a shot. il por *Country Journal* 16:37-41 Ja '89

KOKERNOT, HERBERT, JR.
about
The best little ballpark in Texas (or anywhere else). N. Dawidoff. il *Sports Illustrated* 71:58-64+ Jl 31 '89

KOKERNOT FIELD (ALPINE, TEX.)
The best little ballpark in Texas (or anywhere else). N. Dawidoff. il *Sports Illustrated* 71:58-64+ Jl 31 '89

KOKH, PETER
The moon is . . . *Ad Astra* 1:64 Jl/Ag '89

KOLANDER, CHERYL A.
(jt. auth) See Chandler, Cynthia K., and Kolander, Cheryl A.

KOLAR, MARK D.
(jt. auth) See Jones, Alan H., and Kolar, Mark D.

KOLATA, GINA
The lost voice. il *The New York Times Magazine* p33-4 Ja 15 '89
Operating on the unborn. il *The New York Times Magazine* p34-5+ My 14 '89
Vital opinions. il *The New York Times Magazine* p46-7 Ap 16 '89
When they say it's cancer. *Reader's Digest* 135:151-3 S '89
Who should stop using the pill? *Glamour* 87:250-1+ My '89
Women and AIDS: what you must know now. il *Ladies' Home Journal* 106:98+ N '89

KOLB, ELENE
When women finally got the word. il *The New York Times Book Review* 94:1+ Jl 9 '89

KOLBERT, KATHRYN
(jt. auth) See Copelon, Rhonda, and Kolbert, Kathryn

KOLBOWSKI, SILVIA
about
Silvia Kolbowski at Postmasters. J. Zinsser. il *Art in America* 77:265-6 Ap '89

KOLESNIKOVS, GEORGS
about
Winners. L. Rudeen. il por *Motor Boating & Sailing* 164:20 Ag '89

KOLLEK, AMOS
about
Forever, Lulu [film] Reviews
Video il 12:85 Ja '89. D. Wheeler

KOLLEK, TEDDY
about
Oh, Jerusalem! E. Norden. *The New Republic* 200:17-18 Mr 27 '89

KOLLEKTIEF (WILLEM BREUKER) (MUSICAL GROUP)
See Willem Breuker Kollektief (Musical group)

KOLLMORGEN CORP.
Kollmorgen could get ambushed. G. G. Marcial. *Business Week* p136 N 20 '89

KOLMOGOROV, ANDREI N., 1903-1987
about
Obituary
Physics Today por 42:148+ O '89. V. I. Arnol'd

KOLONIA, PETER
In the dark. See issues of Popular Photography beginning April 1989

KOLOVAKOS, GREGORY
AIDS words. *The Nation* 248:598-602 My 1 '89

KOLTNOW, EMILY
about
Emily Koltnow: the fired woman's best friend. il por *Business Week* p68 S 18 '89

KOMA
about
Thirst [dance] Reviews
The New Leader 72:22 Ja 9 '89. L. A. Jacobs
Tree [dance] Reviews
The New Leader 72:22 Ja 9 '89. L. A. Jacobs

KOMA, DEBRA MARTIN
How to choose a good travel agent. il *Travel Holiday* 172:58-61 O '89
Smooth operators? il *Travel Holiday* 171:67-70 My '89
Spur-of-the-moment travel. il *Travel Holiday* 171:32-8 Mr '89

KOMAR, CHRIS
about
Chris Komar expands his work as a Cunningham dancer. il pors *Dance Magazine* 63:12 Mr '89

KOMAR, VITALI, 1943-
about
Bayonne. *The New Yorker* 65:32-3 Ap 24 '89

Komar & Melamid at Ronald Feldman Fine Arts. N. Princenthal. *Art in America* 77:206 S '89

KOMISARUK, SUSAN
about
Who will yell fire when the house is ablaze? R. E. Burns. *U.S. Catholic* 54:2 F '89

KOMORNY, ANNIE
Dear sweepstakes computer [poem] il *Good Housekeeping* 209:273 O '89

KOMSOMOLTZ (SUBMARINE)
Disaster strikes a Soviet sub. D. Benjamin. il map *Time* 133:38 Ap 17 '89
An undersea prize for the taking. L. Martz. il map *Newsweek* 113:33 Ap 17 '89

KONA VILLAGE (HAWAII: RESORT) *See* Resorts—Hawaii

KONCAK, JON
about
Millions from heaven. R. Telander. il pors *Sports Illustrated* 71:56-8+ N 6 '89

KONCHALOVSKY, ANDREI
about
Shy people [film] Reviews
Video il 12:84 Ja '89. T. Soter

KONDO, HIROYUKI
about
Teaching a Tokyo whiz kid the art of the deal. J. Friedman. il por *Business Week* p83 Ja 16 '89

KONDRACKE, MORTON
Secretary's interview for "American interests" [J. A. Baker; transcript of program, April 22, 1989] *Department of State Bulletin* 89:14-19 Je '89

KÖNIGSBERG (CRUISER)
The Admiralty's orders were clear: 'sink or destroy the Königsberg' [British-German encounter off the East African coast] D. Houston. il map *Smithsonian* 20:130-4+ S '89

KONISHI, MASAKAZU, AND OTHERS
Contributions of bird studies to biology. bibl f il *Science* 246:465-72 O 27 '89

KONISHIKI, YASOKICHI
about
An American wins big. S. Smith. il por *Sports Illustrated* 71:30 D 11 '89
Charge of the unlight brigade. il por *U.S. News & World Report* 107:14-15 D 11 '89
They've got Rockefeller Center, but we've got Konishiki, the world's best sumo wrestler. il por *People Weekly* 32:133 D 11 '89

KONNER, JOAN
From here to here [address, September 6, 1988] *Vital Speeches of the Day* 55:238-41 F 1 '89

KONNER, LINDA
Where I grew up: Blair Brown [interview] il pors *Glamour* 87:172 Mr '89
Where I grew up: Iman [interview] il pors map *Glamour* 87:169 S '89
Where I grew up: Shelley Long [interview] il pors map *Glamour* 87:155 My '89

KONNER, MELVIN
Homosexuality: who and why? il *The New York Times Magazine* p60-1 Ap 2 '89
The long haul. il *The New York Times Magazine* p55-6 Jl 9 '89
The loss of self. il *The New York Times Magazine* p42-3 Je 25 '89
Where should baby sleep? il *The New York Times Magazine* p39-40 Ja 8 '89

KONRÁD, GYÖRGY
Notes on your Central Europe—and mine; tr. by James A. Tucker. *Harper's* 278:22-4 F '89

KOONCE, MICHAEL P.
(jt. auth) See McIntosh, J. Richard, and Koonce, Michael P.

KOONS, JEFF, 1955-
about
The art world. A. Gopnik. *The New Yorker* 65:107-11 F 20 '89
Artist Jeff Koons makes, and earns, giant figures. R. Lacayo. il pors *People Weekly* 31:127-8+ My 8 '89

KOONTZ, KATY
Just me. il pors *Health (New York, N.Y.)* 21:38-9 F '89

KOOP, C. EVERETT
The health care mess. por *Newsweek* 114:10 Ag 28 '89
about
C. Everett Koop. S. Kanfer. il por *People Weekly* 32 Special Issue:127 Fall '89
Chicken Koop. R. E. Tyrrell. il *The American Spectator* 22:34-5 Je '89
Citizen Koop. *Commonweal* 116:420-1 Ag 11 '89
Cooing over Koop. *National Review* 41:17-18 F 10 '89
A doctor prescribes hard truth. M. B. Carlson. por *Time* 133:82-4 Ap 24 '89
The embattled career of Dr. Koop [cover story] P. Yancey. il por *Christianity Today* 33:16-21 O 20 '89
Koop de grace. il *The New Republic* 201:7-9 O 23 '89
Koop finds abortion evidence "inconclusive". C. Holden. *Science* 243:730-1 F 10 '89
Notes and comment. *The New Yorker* 65:29-30 Ag 7 '89

KOOP, C. EVERETT—about—*cont.*
An officer and a gentleman. J. B. Judis. *The New Republic* 200:19-22 Ja 23 '89
Surgeon General Koop is good medicine. B. G. Harrison. *Mademoiselle* 95:126 My '89
A Surgeon General's warnings: C. Everett Koop is not about to abandon his public platform [interview] P. Yancey. il pors *Christianity Today* 33:30-3 N 3 '89

KOOPMAN, GEORGE A., D. 1989
about
Obituary
Ad Astra por 1:43-4 S '89. M. Jordan

KOPECHNE, GWEN
about
Memories of Mary Jo. J. Farrell. il pors *Ladies' Home Journal* 106:108-10+ Jl '89

KOPECHNE, JOSEPH
about
Memories of Mary Jo. J. Farrell. il pors *Ladies' Home Journal* 106:108-10+ Jl '89

KOPECHNE, MARY JO, 1941-1969
about
Frustrated grand jurors say it was no accident Ted Kennedy got off easy. J. S. Kunen. il pors *People Weekly* 32:34-6 Jl 24 '89
Memories of Mary Jo. J. Farrell. il pors *Ladies' Home Journal* 106:108-10+ Jl '89

KOPECKY, GINI
The gifts heaven sent: five true stories to touch your heart. il *Redbook* 174:108-9+ D '89

KOPECKY, ROBERT J.
(jt. auth) See Rinella, Sal D., and Kopecky, Robert J.

KOPFF COMETARY MISSION See Space flight—Cometary missions

KOPKIND, ANDREW
Older, wiser but still prickly as a saguaro, Barry Goldwater remembers when right was wrong. il pors *People Weekly* 31:67-70+ F 13 '89
Whither the Rainbow? [discussion of September 25, 1989 article, Strategies for now—and next time] *The Nation* 249:738+ D 18 '89

KOPLIN, RICHARD S.
The save-your-sight eye book; ed. by Florence Isaacs. il *Good Housekeeping* 208:69-72 F '89

KOPLOS, JANET
Through the looking glass. il *Art in America* 77:98-107+ Jl '89

KOPLOVITZ, KAY
about
Never look down. D. Machan. il por *Forbes* 144:270+ Jl 24 '89
When Murder & Vice are no longer enough [interview] il pors *Channels (New York, N.Y.: 1986)* 9:70-1 Ap '89

KOPP, ANATOLE
Gorky Street, fifty years of change. il *The Unesco Courier* 42:26-9 Ag '89

KOPPEL, TED
The video revolution no one expected. il por *Video* 13:154 D '89
about
The case against Ted Koppel [cover story] M. Miller. il *The Washington Monthly* 21:34-6+ My '89
Mock crisis, real players. B. Van Voorst. il por *Time* 134:88 D 11 '89

KOPPEL, TOM
Cocos Island. il *Travel Holiday* 172:88-90+ N '89

THE KOPPEL REPORT: THE BLUE X CONSPIRACY [television program] See Television program reviews—Single works

KORBUT, OLGA
about
Return of the pixies. L. Montville. il pors *Sports Illustrated* 71:34-6+ N 27 '89

KORČULA (YUGOSLAVIA: ISLAND)
Description and travel
An Adriatic idyll. C. Maclean. il *House & Garden* 161:68+ S '89

KORDA, MICHAEL, 1933-
about
"Power" revisited. O. Edwards. il *Gentlemen's Quarterly* 59:164+ Je '89

KOREA
See also
Korean Demilitarized Zone (Korea)

KOREA (NORTH)
See also
Americans—Korea (North)
Civil rights—Korea (North)
United Nations—Korea (North)

Commerce
Korea (South)
See Korea (South)—Commerce—Korea (North)
Foreign relations
Korea (South)
See Korea (South)—Foreign relations—Korea (North)
United States
See United States—Foreign relations—Korea (North)
Politics and government
Great Leader to Dear Leader. N. D. Kristof. il por *The New York Times Magazine* p44-7+ Ag 20 '89
Kim Il Sung's 'socialist paradise'. B. Martin. il pors *Newsweek* 114:38-9 Ag 7 '89
People's democratic revue. A. Daniels. *National Review* 41:19-20 S 1 '89
Religious institutions and affairs
See also
Christians—Korea (North)

KOREA (PEOPLE'S REPUBLIC) See Korea (North)
KOREA (REPUBLIC) See Korea (South)
KOREA (SOUTH)
See also
Bombing and gunnery ranges—Korea (South)
Botany—Korea (South)
Copyright infringement—Korea (South)
Industry and state—Korea (South)
Investments, Korean
Labor unions—Korea (South)
Protests, demonstrations, etc.—Korea (South)
Strikes—Korea (South)
Student protests, demonstrations, etc.—Korea (South)
United Nations—Korea (South)
United States—Diplomatic and consular service—Korea (South)
Wages and salaries—Korea (South)
Air Force
FX fighter program to set stage for Air Force modernization plan. J. D. Morrocco. il *Aviation Week & Space Technology* 130:191+ Je 12 '89
Armed Forces
Air, naval and ground forces participate in Team Spirit '89 [U.S./Korean exercises; special section] il *Aviation Week & Space Technology* 130:68-9+ Ap 24 '89
Commerce
See also
Balance of trade—Korea (South)
Asia's next giant. A. H. Amsden. il *Technology Review* 92:46-53 My/Je '89
Korea (North)
The Pyongyang puzzle: trick or trade? L. Nakarmi. il *Business Week* p47-8 F 20 '89
United States
See United States—Commerce—Korea (South)
Defenses
See also
Airplanes, Military—Korea (South)
Aviation, Military—Korea (South)
United States. Air Force—Forces in Korea (South)
Leaving Korea. D. Bandow. *Foreign Policy* 77:77-93 Wint '89/'90
Economic policy
Can South Korea bat in the big leagues? M. Tharp. il *U.S. News & World Report* 106:35-8 F 27 '89
Has the Korean miracle run out of magic? R. Neff and L. Nakarmi. il *Business Week* p38-9 Jl 3 '89
Is the Korean miracle running on empty? P. Maass. il *U.S. News & World Report* 107:55-6 S 18 '89
Economic relations
Eastern Europe
Is the 'wall' between the two Koreas starting to wobble? L. Nakarmi. il *Business Week* p75 N 27 '89
Soviet Union
See Soviet Union—Economic relations—Korea (South)
Foreign relations
Korea (North)
See also
Korean reunification question
Is the 'wall' between the two Koreas starting to wobble? L. Nakarmi. il *Business Week* p75 N 27 '89
The 'virgin terrorist' [Kim Hyun Hee stands trial for bombing KAL Flight 858 in 1987] S. Begley. il por *Newsweek* 113:8 Mr 20 '89
United States
See United States—Foreign relations—Korea (South)
Industries
See also
Aerospace industries—Korea (South)
Asiana Airlines
Daewoo Corporation
Electronic industries—Korea (South)
Hyundai Group
Jindo Industries Ltd.
Korean Air Lines Co. Ltd.
Samsung Aerospace Industries Ltd.
SSangyong Group
Asia's next giant. A. H. Amsden. il *Technology Review* 92:46-53 My/Je '89

KOREA (SOUTH)—Industries—*cont.*
Korea's powerhouses are under siege. L. Nakarmi and R. Neff. il *Business Week* p52+ N 20 '89
The tigers behind Korea's prowess [chaebol] L. Kraar. il *Fortune* 120 no13 Special Issue:36-7+ Fall '89
Labor policy
It's time for the main bout: Roh vs. labor. L. Nakarmi. il *Business Week* p45-6 Ap 10 '89
Politics and government
Has Bush helped paint Roh into a corner? L. Nakarmi. il pors *Business Week* p61-2 Mr 13 '89
Korea—land in transition. C. W. Weinberger. il *Forbes* 143:31 Je 26 '89
Notes and comment [Korean Americans' hunger strike in front of the United Nations protesting political situation] *The New Yorker* 65:33-4 O 30 '89
The Republic of Korea [address, March 9, 1989] R. H. Myers. *Vital Speeches of the Day* 55:418-20 My 1 '89
Roh on Korea's referendum: no go. *Newsweek* 113:33 Ap 3 '89
South Korea. *Business Week* p60 Ap 3 '89
South Korea. L. Nakarmi. *Business Week* p55 My 15 '89
South Korea's rise to prominence. Y. W. Kihl. bibl f *Current History* 88:165-8+ Ap '89
Religious institutions and affairs
See also
Church and state—Korea (South)
KOREAN AIR LINES CO. LTD.
Korean Air adds international routes, but faces first domestic competition. J. Ott. *Aviation Week & Space Technology* 130:54-5 My 8 '89
Korean Air, Asiana order U.S. transports valued at $1.35 billion. J. Ott. *Aviation Week & Space Technology* 130:17 Ap 17 '89
Korean Air negotiates agreement to coproduce Sikorsky UH-60. J. D. Morrocco. il *Aviation Week & Space Technology* 130:225+ Je 12 '89
KOREAN AIR LINES FLIGHT 007 DISASTER, 1983
KAL 007: the cover-up continues. R. W. Lee. il *Conservative Digest* 15:28-31 S/O '89
KOREAN AMERICAN BUSINESS ENTERPRISES
Minding the family store [greengrocers in New York City] C. Koehl. il *Newsweek* 114 Special Issue:4 Wint '89/Spr '90
KOREAN AMERICANS
Political activities
Notes and comment [hunger strike in front of the United Nations protesting political situation in South Korea] *The New Yorker* 65:33-4 O 30 '89
Religious life
For Koreans in America, growth and growing pains. D. Moul. il *Christianity Today* 33:56+ Mr 3 '89
Pastors given rare glimpse of North Korea [Korean-American Southern Baptist pastors attend Easter service] D. Burton. *Christianity Today* 33:63 Je 16 '89
KOREAN DEMILITARIZED ZONE (KOREA)
Description and travel
Pilgrimage to the perimeter. C. N. Barnard. il map *Modern Maturity* 32:62-8+ F/Mr '89
A return to no man's land. B. E. Trainor. il *The New York Times Magazine* p22+ Mr 19 '89
KOREAN HELICOPTERS *See* Helicopters
KOREAN LITERATURE
See also
Publishers and publishing—Korean literature
KOREAN REUNIFICATION QUESTION
Koreans yearn for reunification [trip to North by Moon Ik Hwan] D. G. Peerman. map *The Christian Century* 106:580-2 Je 7-14 '89
North and South Korea in General Assembly present proposals on reunification. il *UN Chronicle* 26:66-7 Mr '89
KOREAN WAR, 1950-1953
Aerial operations
Hitler: eternal springtime [aerial bombing by American forces] A. Cockburn. *The Nation* 248:654-5 My 15 '89
American participation
The bizarre wind of Unishima [American servicemen discover statuettes of Shinto deities Izanagi and Izanami on island] W. J. Buchanan. il *Reader's Digest* 135:71-6 Ag '89
Sentimental guy [A. Guastafeste, piano accompanist to actress M. Monroe when she entertained troops] *The New Yorker* 65:28-9 Jl 10 '89
Personal narratives
A return to no man's land. B. E. Trainor. il *The New York Times Magazine* p22+ Mr 19 '89
KOREANS
United States
See also
Korean Americans
Problems [B. Seitz teaches Koreans attending the New York School of Drycleaning] *The New Yorker* 65:40-1 O 9 '89
KOREY, WILLIAM
Advancing the Helsinki process. il *The New Leader* 72:7-9 F 6 '89
Helsinki in Paris. il *The New Leader* 72:12-14 Jl 10-24 '89

KORFMANN, MANFRED
about
Digging up Troy. C. Heybrock. il *World Press Review* 36:57 Ja '89
KORIETH, KARYN
Restoring the restored. il por map *Americana* 17:44-9 S/O '89
KORN, LESTER B.
How the next CEO will be different. il *Fortune* 119:157-8+ My 22 '89
KORN, PETER
Big men, big problems. il pors *Sport (New York, N.Y.)* 80:71-3+ Ap '89
Old catchers never die . . . il pors *Sport (New York, N.Y.)* 80:44-9 Jl '89
KORN, WENDY
Skin symptoms you must not ignore. il *Ladies' Home Journal* 106:66+ S '89
KORNBLUH, PETER
Contradictions: a decade in documents. il *Mother Jones* 14:26-7 Jl/Ag '89
The edge of might. *Omni (New York, N.Y.)* 11:46 Ja '89
Will Bush keep his word with the death squads? *Mother Jones* 14:26-7 Ap '89
KORNBLUT, ARTHUR
Watch out for this new "model" owner/design-professional agreement. il por *Architectural Record* 177:29+ F '89
When liability insurance can cover your construction-cost estimate problems. por *Architectural Record* 177:31 Ap '89
KORNBLUTH, JESSE
The '64 civil rights murders: the struggle continues [cover story] il pors *The New York Times Magazine* p16-19+ Jl 23 '89
KOROTICH, VITALY
Typing out the fear. il *Time* 133:124+ Ap 10 '89
about
International Editor of the Year [with interview] il por *World Press Review* 36:22-6 My '89
A talk with the editor of 'Ogonyok' [interview; cover story; with editorial comment] M. Mihajlov. il *The New Leader* 72:2, 10-16 F 20 '89
KORPIVAARA, ARI
Hands across the ages [cover story] il *New Choices for the Best Years* 29:41-3+ Ag '89
KORS, MICHAEL
about
View. D. Kazanjian. il por *Vogue* 179:60-2 Je '89
KORT, MICHELE
All bases covered. il pors *Women's Sports & Fitness* 11:48-51 O '89
KORY, ROBERT B.
(ed) See Bloomfield, Harold H., 1944-, and Vettese, Sirah. Healthy love
(ed) See Bloomfield, Harold H., 1944-, and Vettese, Sirah. How to have an affair with your husband
KOSCHNICK, WOLFGANG J., 1942-
"I can think of more important things than being loved by everybody" [interview with R. Murdoch] il pors *Forbes* 144:98+ N 27 '89
KOSHELNYK, WILLIAM J.
Pride and prejudice: an examination of the economics of black America. il *Conservative Digest* 15:23-6 Jl/Ag '89
KOSHER FOOD *See* Jews—Dietary laws
KOSHER RESTAURANTS
Untapped market [restaurant at J. Schlang's Palm Beach Plaza Hotel] *The New Yorker* 64:24-5 Ja 16 '89
KOSHLAND, DANIEL E., JR.
(jt. auth) See Guyer, Ruth Levy, and Koshland, Daniel E., Jr.
KOSICKA, JADWIGA
(tr) See Kott, Jan. Caesar at the Bastille
KOSKAN FAMILY
about
Successful family farm. J. Walter. il *Successful Farming* 87:46-8 D '89
KOSKOTAS, GEORGE
about
The looting of Greece. R. Ajemian. il pors *Time* 133:32-5 Mr 13 '89
"No mud touches me". W. R. Doerner. il por *Time* 133:37 Mr 20 '89
Out of office, into the dock? por *Time* 134:38 S 25 '89
KOSLOW, JULES
My son the tour guide. il *New Choices for the Best Years* 29:77+ Jl '89
KOSOVO (YUGOSLAVIA)
Riots
Nationalist rage. A. Bilski. il *Maclean's* 102:24 Ap 10 '89
KOSS CLASSICS (FIRM)
Recording American. W. Livingstone. il *Stereo Review* 54:32 S '89
KOSTER, OTILIA DE
about
Rights of spring. E. Pall. il por *Mother Jones* 14:16 Ap '89

KOSTKA, GLORIA
Tipping the scales for vibrant health; ed. by Deborah Grandinetti. il pors *Prevention (Emmaus, Pa.)* 41:102-4 Ag '89
KOSTMAN, CHRIS
The double century. *Bicycling* 30:160-1 Ap '89
KOSTMAYER, PETER H.
about
Stacking the deck. E. Howard. il por *Common Cause Magazine* 15:24-6 Ja/F '89
KOSZUTA, LAURIE EINSTEIN
An aerobic walkout. il *Current Health 2* 15:20-1 My '89
Elements of fitness for those of strong heart and muscle. il *Current Health 2* 16:12-13 S '89
Exercise the right way. il *Current Health 2* 15:12-13 Ap '89
Fitness: getting to the heart of the matter. il *Current Health 2* 16:10-11 O '89
Homestyle fitness. il *Current Health 2* 15:28-9 F '89
Low-impact, high-value exercise. il *Current Health 2* 15:26-7 Mr '89
Putting fat in its place. il *Current Health 2* 16:14-16 N '89
KOTCHEFF, TED, 1931-
about
Weekend at Bernie's [film] Reviews
People Weekly il 32:12-13 Jl 24 '89. R. Novak
Winter people [film] Reviews
People Weekly il 31:11 My 1 '89. R. Novak
KOTROSITS, LYNN
A no-tears trip to the hospital. il *Parents* 64:85-6+ Je '89
KOTSILIBAS-DAVIS, JAMES
Autumn [cover story] il *Travel Holiday* 172:38-43 O '89
KOTT, JAN
Caesar at the Bastille; tr. by Jadwiga Kosicka. il *The New York Review of Books* 36:40-2 O 12 '89
KOTT, MICHAEL
(tr) See Głowacki, Janusz. Warsaw scenes: a burned-out light bulb and other tragedies
KOTTLER, HOWARD, 1930-1989
about
Obituary
American Craft il por 49:69 Ap/My '89. J. S. Schwartz
KOTZSCH, RONALD E.
Just say no to junk. *Utne Reader* p79 Jl/Ag '89
KOTZWINKLE, WILLIAM
about
PW interviews. W. Gelles. por *Publishers Weekly* 236:46-7 N 10 '89
KOUF, JIM
about
Disorganized crime [film] Reviews
People Weekly il 31:11-12 My 1 '89. R. Novak
KOVACS, ERNIE, 1919-1962
about
Ernie Kovacs. il pors *People Weekly* 31 Special Issue:64-5 Summ '89
KOVALENKO, Y., AND POLIANOVSKY, E.
Joseph Brodsky's Nobel Prize; tr. by Barry J. Rubin. il *The New Republic* 200:38-40 F 20 '89
KOWAL, JOAN
about
A change for the better. K. Burke. pors *McCall's* 116:92-3 Jl '89
KOWALSKI, ROBERT E.
Cholesterol and your family. il por *Parents* 64:169+ O '89
Helping kids with high cholesterol [excerpt from Cholesterol and children] il *Psychology Today* 23:30 S '89
KOYAMA, KŌSUKE, 1929-
For the sake of ten. *The Christian Century* 106:683 Jl 19-26 '89
He had compassion. il *The Christian Century* 106:651 Jl 5-12 '89
'I am Jesus, whom you persecute'. *The Christian Century* 106:347 Ap 5 '89
If you give a feast, invite the poor. il *The Christian Century* 106:747 Ag 16-23 '89
'May God continue to bless us'. il *The Christian Century* 106:442 Ap 26 '89
'So they may see my glory'. il *The Christian Century* 106:467 My 3 '89
Speak my word faithfully. *The Christian Century* 106:716 Ag 2-9 '89
They are a stiff-necked people. il *The Christian Century* 106:779 Ag 30-S 6 '89
'Yahweh is generous to all'. il *The Christian Century* 106:411 Ap 19 '89
'You prepare a table for me'. il *The Christian Century* 106:379 Ap 12 '89
KOYASAN (JAPAN)
Description
Koyasan . . . an island of quiet not far from Osaka. il map *Sunset (Central West edition)* 182:44+ F '89
KOZAK, MICHAEL G.
Cuba: a threat to peace and security in our hemisphere [statement, August 2, 1989] *Department of State Bulletin* 89:75-9 N '89

FY 1990 assistance request for Latin America and the Caribbean [statement, March 2, 1989] il *Department of State Bulletin* 89:59-66 Je '89
KOZARICH, JOHN W., AND OTHERS
Sequence-specific isotope effects on the cleavage of DNA by bleomycin. bibl f il *Science* 245:1396-9 S 22 '89
KOZDEN, SHARON
Childhood revisited. il *Antiques & Collecting Hobbies* 94:27+ D '89
KOZLOV, ALEX
The automation generation. il *Omni (New York, N.Y.)* 11:18+ Mr '89
Brave new mouse. il *Discover* 10:78 Ja '89
KOZOL, JONATHAN
The new untouchables. il *Newsweek* 114 Special Issue:48-9+ Wint '89/Spr '90
A report card on schools after 20 years. *The Education Digest* 54:7-9 Ja '89
about
Help the homeless. L. Fleischer. *Publishers Weekly* 235:446 Ja 27 '89
The rise of the homeless. S. M. Halpern. bibl f il *The New York Review of Books* 36:24-7 F 16 '89
KRACHT FAMILY
about
Solomon's choice. D. Zegart. il *Ms.* 17:78-83 Je '89
KRAEGEL, JANET M., AND KACHOYEANOS, MARY
The nurses [excerpt from Just a nurse] il *Ladies' Home Journal* 106:62+ Je '89
KRAFCIK, JOHN F.
A new diet for U.S. manufacturing. il *Technology Review* 92:28-34+ Ja '89
KRAFFT, MAURICE, AND KELLER, JÖRG
Temperature measurements in carbonatite lava lakes and flows from Oldoinyo Lengai, Tanzania. bibl f il *Science* 245:168-70 Jl 14 '89
KRAFT, CHARLES E.
I read it in the paper. il *Antiques & Collecting Hobbies* 94:74-7 Mr '89
KRAFT, CHARLES H.
The hymnal is not enough. por *Christianity Today* 33:8 Ap 7 '89
KRAFT, DAVID
Forced field. il *Flying* 116:134 Ag '89
KRAFT, EUGENE
As I step down from the train [poem] *The Christian Century* 106:932 O 18 '89
KRAFT GENERAL FOODS GROUP
A cup of Jell-O, Velveeta to taste . . . L. Therrien. il *Business Week* p74+ My 8 '89
How Philip Morris diversified right. S. P. Sherman. il por *Fortune* 120:120-2+ O 23 '89
Is bigger better for Philip Morris? [interview with H. Maxwell] C. Leinster. il por *Fortune* 119:66-71 My 8 '89
Michael Miles. L. Therrien. il por *Business Week* Special Issue:126 Ap 14 '89
Philip Morris's big bite [cover story] L. J. Davis. il por *The New York Times Magazine* p30-3+ Ap 9 '89
KRAFT INC.
Why Celestial Seasonings wasn't Kraft's cup of tea. S. D. Atchison. il por *Business Week* p76 My 8 '89
KRAINES, ARLENE
about
Art déco revisited: a Beverly Hills residence marked by period flair. il *Architectural Digest* 46:154-9 Ag '89
KRAIZER, SHERRYLL, AND OTHERS
Child sexual abuse prevention programs: what makes them effective in protecting children? bibl f *Children Today* 18:23-7 S/O '89
KRAJICK, KEVIN
Don't touch! What makes a guy lose his lust. il *Mademoiselle* 95:189-90+ N '89
Lust he must: the nature of a man's desire. por *Mademoiselle* 95:108-9+ Ja '89
KRAKAUER, JON
Daredevil pilots take glacier flying to new heights [cover story] bibl (p147) il *Smithsonian* 19:96-100+ Ja '89
Gidget has grown up, but surfing is still a 'totally happening' sport. bibl f (p174) il *Smithsonian* 20:106-10+ Je '89
In the San Juan Islands: driftwood and sod shape a Seattle architect's residence [cover story] il *Architectural Digest* 46:188-93 Je '89
KRAKER, JOSEPH H.
On our knees. *America* 160:141-5 F 18 '89
KRAM, MARK
Brando. il pors *Esquire* 112:156-62+ N '89
Great men die twice. il pors *Esquire* 111:210-14+ Je '89
The next Brando. il pors *Esquire* 111:78-85 Ja '89
KRAMER, ARTHUR
Pro view. See issues of Popular Photography beginning March 1989
KRAMER, BILL
about
Sidney Kramer Books: the big turnaround. H. Fields. il *Publishers Weekly* 235:128-9 My 12 '89
KRAMER, CAROL
Candice. il pors *McCall's* 117:20-2+ O '89

KRAMER, IRWIN
about
Nassau via New York. Suzy. il *Architectural Digest* 46:142-51 Mr '89
KRAMER, JACK, 1921-
about
Mr. Kramer and Mr. Becker. H. W. Wind. il *The New Yorker* 65:85-96+ O 16 '89
KRAMER, JANE
Climbing Mt. Manhattan. il *House & Garden* 161:188-9+ O '89
Floral decorum. il *House & Garden* 161:112+ S '89
Letter from Europe. *The New Yorker* 64:72-4+ Ja 30 '89
Letter from Europe. *The New Yorker* 65:81-94 My 1 '89
Prisoners of taste. il *House & Garden* 161:106-7 Jl '89
KRAMER, LOUISE
Should you go to the emergency room? il *Glamour* 87:81+ O '89
KRAMER, MARK, 1944-
Can Gorbachev feed Russia? il *The New York Times Magazine* p42-3+ Ap 9 '89
KRAMER, MARK, 1959-
Soviet military policy. bibl f *Current History* 88:337-40+ O '89
KRAMER, MARTIN A.
Caught in the web: the agenda of enrollments, costs, and student aid. il *Change* 21:8 Mr/Ap '89
Empty chairs: what happens to students who don't go to college. *Change* 21:6-7 Ja/F '89
Four contributions to a checklist. il *Change* 21:16 S/O '89
The sirens' song: trying to do all things for all students. *Change* 21:42 My/Je '89
A tale of two candidates. *Change* 20:9+ N/D '88
KRAMER, MIMI, 1957-
The theatre. See issues of The New Yorker beginning June 8, 1987
KRAMER, ORIN S.
(jt. auth) See Beauchemin, Timothy A., and Kramer, Orin S.
KRAMER, RITA
(jt. auth) See Kramer, Yale, and Kramer, Rita
KRAMER, TERRY ALLEN
about
Nassau via New York. Suzy. il *Architectural Digest* 46:142-51 Mr '89
KRÄMER, TONI
about
Son of the forest. H. E. Phillips. il por *Opera News* 53:51-2 Ap 1 '89
KRAMER, YALE, AND KRAMER, RITA
Eastside story. il *The American Spectator* 22:21-4 Ag '89
KRAMERS, HENDRIK ANTHONY, 1894-1952
about
The long chain from Kramers's polymer work [discussion of September 1988 article, Kramers's contributions to statistical mechanics] M. Dresden. bibl *Physics Today* 42:13+ O '89
KRANE, JONATHAN D.
about
Look who's got a box-office smash. R. Grover. il por *Business Week* p142 D 11 '89
KRANTZ, JUDITH
about
Author Judith Krantz tells: why TV strips the sex out of my novels [cover story] B. Davidson. il por *TV Guide* 37:2-4 N 18-24 '89
KRANZ, RACHEL
Toward a new definition of singleness: building a life with close friends. il *Utne Reader* p56-7+ Mr/Ap '89
KRAPU, GARY L.
The last watering holes on the prairie. il *Natural History* p66-9 Ja '89
KRASNOV, VLADISLAV
The Soviet Union and the Asian-Pacific region in the 1990s [address, November 11, 1988] *Vital Speeches of the Day* 55:164-6 Ja 1 '89
KRASNOW, ERWIN G., AND CONRAD, ROBIN S.
Managing your lawyer. il *Nation's Business* 77:70-2 Ap '89
KRASOTY INSTITUT See Institut Krasoty
KRASS, DEBORAH B.
Behind closed doors. il por *World Tennis* 37:96 D '89
KRASSNER, PAUL
A message to Abbie Hoffman. *Utne Reader* p113-15 N/D '89
Talkin' 'bout a revolution. il *Vogue* 179:84+ Ja '89
KRATERNAYA BAY (SOVIET UNION)
Caldron in the sea. M. V. Propp and V. G. Tarasov. il maps *Natural History* p28-33 Ag '89
KRAUS, CAROLYN
Water witching. *The New Yorker* 65:97+ O 9 '89
KRAUS, JON
Economic adjustment and regime creation in Nigeria. *Current History* 88:233-7+ My '89
KRAUSE, BERNIE
about
Laying down animal tracks. D. Glick. il por *Newsweek* 114:62 Jl 31 '89

Pet shop boy. E. Smith. il *Omni (New York, N.Y.)* 12:20+ D '89
With an ear to the ground, sea, and sky. D. Glick. il por *Sierra* 74:82-6+ N/D '89
KRAUSHAR, JON
(ed) See Ailes, Roger, 1940-. How to make a good impression
KRAUTHAMMER, CHARLES, 1950-
Don't blame "society". *Reader's Digest* 135:54-5 Ag '89
KRAUZE, JAN
The U.S. mainstream now flows to the right. *World Press Review* 36:26-7 Ja '89
KRAVAT, JERRY
about
The new owner of New Year's Eve. M. Barrier. il por *Nation's Business* 77:68 Ja '89
KRAVAT (JERRY) ENTERTAINMENT SERVICES (FIRM)
See Jerry Kravat Entertainment Services (Firm)
KRAVIS, HENRY R.
about
Biggest bidders, wildest auction. B. Saporito. il pors *Fortune* 119:34-5 Ja 2 '89
Carolyne Roehm: an opulent aesthetic for the designer's Manhattan residence. Suzy. il por *Architectural Digest* 46:112-19 S '89
'Greed really turns me off [interview] C. Leinster. il por *Fortune* 119:69-71 Ja 2 '89
White knight or raider? S. Flack. il *Forbes* 144:46 S 18 '89
KRAVITZ, LENNY
about
New kids chip off the old block. A. DeCurtis. il *Rolling Stone* p75-6 S 7 '89
No more Mr. Lisa Bonet, rocker Lenny Kravitz makes a name for himself with a hot debut album. S. Dougherty. il pors *People Weekly* 32:142-3 N 6 '89
KRAWCZYK, FRANK
about
Calling all shipmates. S. Brewer. il por *New Choices for the Best Years* 29:12-13 My '89
KREBS, ROBERT D., 1942-
about
Almost everybody wants to break up Santa Fe. B. Bremner and C. Hawkins. il por *Business Week* p67 Mr 6 '89
KREEFT, PETER
Unravelling the mystery of weakness and strength. il *Christianity Today* 33:23-5 Ap 21 '89
KREIN, DARREN
about
Here today, gone today. R. Reilly. por *Sports Illustrated* 70:102 Mr 27 '89
KREISBERG, PAUL H.
Containment's last gasp. *Foreign Policy* 75:146-63 Summ '89
KREITMAN, STANLEY
about
From munis to money. J. Zweig. il por *Forbes* 143:134 F 20 '89
KREMENTZ, JILL
Fighting for their lives. il *American Health* 8:62+ N '89
KREMLINOLOGY See Soviet studies
KRENS, THOMAS
about
A megamuseum in a mill town. D. Weisgall. il por *The New York Times Magazine* p32-5+ Mr 5 '89
New talents: Thomas Krens. C. Ratcliff. il por *Harper's Bazaar* 122:108 Mr '89
KRENZ, EGON
about
The choice for East Germany. D. R. Shanor. il por *The New Leader* 72:3-4 O 30 '89
'Egon, here we come'. M. R. Meyer. il *Newsweek* 114:52 N 13 '89
He stopped the shooting [interview] J. O. Jackson and F. Ungeheuer. por *Time* 134:46-7 D 11 '89
In East Germany, 'order' crumbles and danger grows. P. R. Range. il *U.S. News & World Report* 107:24-5 D 18 '89
Krenz is cast from Honecker's mold. Now, can he break it? J. Templeman. il por *Business Week* p49 O 30 '89
Krenz takes charge. A. Phillips. il pors *Maclean's* 102:50+ O 30 '89
A model apparatchik. R. Watson. il pors *Newsweek* 114:52-3 O 30 '89
No longer if but when. J. Borrell. il por *Time* 134:42-4 N 13 '89
Trading places. J. Smolowe. il por *Time* 134:60-2 O 30 '89
Up against the Wall in East Berlin. G. E. Schares. il *Business Week* p48-9 N 20 '89
KREPON, MICHAEL, 1946-
Peacemakers or rent-a-spies? il *The Bulletin of the Atomic Scientists* 45:12-15 S '89
Spying from space. *Foreign Policy* 75:92-108 Summ '89
KRESA, KENT
about
The good soldier Kresa steps up at Northrop. E. Schine. il por *Business Week* p39 My 8 '89

KRESLINS, JANICE A.
Source material. See issues of Foreign Affairs beginning Fall 1986
KRESS, G. MAYER- *See* Mayer-Kress, G. (Gottfried), 1954-
KRETZMANN, JOHN
(jt. auth) See Fish, John H., and Kretzmann, John
KREUTER, RODNEY A.
Active antenna. il *Radio-Electronics* 60:51-2+ F '89
KREUTTNER, JOHN
John Kreuttner's world. il *National Review* 41:20-1 Ap 7 '89
KREYCHE, GERALD F.
"Bon mots". il *USA Today (Periodical)* 118:98 Jl '89
Day care: the new surrogacy. il *USA Today (Periodical)* 118:91-3 S '89
Food for thought. il *USA Today (Periodical)* 117:98 Mr '89
Living in an ambiguous world. il *USA Today (Periodical)* 118:98 N '89
Look-alikes: America's new identity crisis. il *USA Today (Periodical)* 117:98 Ja '89
The mustache—man's last bastion of individuality. il *USA Today (Periodical)* 118:98 S '89
A nation afraid. il *USA Today (Periodical)* 117:98 My '89
Yellowstone: crown jewel of the national park system [cover story] il *USA Today (Periodical)* 118:34-43 S '89
KRICH, JOHN, 1951-
Culture crash. il *Mother Jones* 14:24-7+ O '89
Postmodern tours. il por *Mother Jones* 14:42-4 Jl/Ag '89
Travel books. il *The New York Times Book Review* 94:12+ Je 11 '89
KRICKSTEIN, AARON
about
Aaron: on the mend. E. Strauss. il por *World Tennis* 36:12-13 Ja '89
KRIDER, E. PHILIP
(jt. auth) See Campins, Humberto, and Krider, E. Philip
(jt. auth) See Faidley, Warren E., and Krider, E. Philip
(jt. auth) See Uman, Martin A., and Krider, E. Philip
KRIECKHAUS, STEVE
about
Points in space. T. Tobias. il *New York* 22:84-5 Mr 20 '89
KRIEGER, LISA
about
Country neoclassic. W. B. Logan. il por *House & Garden* 161:216-23+ S '89
KRIEGER, SHOSHANA
Tuned out. il *Seventeen* 48:84-5+ Je '89
KRIEGSTEIN, ROMAN
about
Down to the sea in ship models. C. Brown. il *Forbes* 144:336+ N 13 '89
KRILL
Predation on ocean krill [discussion of July 15, 1988 article, Acoustical detection of high-density krill demersal layers in the submarine canyons off Georges Bank] C. H. Greene and others. *Science* 243:237-8 Ja 13 '89
KRIM, MATHILDE, 1926-
about
The bold ones. S. Brewer. il pors *New Choices for the Best Years* 29:37-41 Jl '89
KRIMIGIS, STAMATIOS M., AND OTHERS
Hot plasma and energetic particles in Neptune's magnetosphere. bibl f il *Science* 246:1483-9 D 15 '89
KRIMSKY, SHELDON, AND OTHERS
Controlling risk in biotech. il *Technology Review* 92:62-8+ Jl '89
KRIPKE, PAM
Winter skin and hair repair. il *Working Woman* 14:108 Ja '89
KRIST, BOB
Foster mother to Holland's seals. il por map *International Wildlife* 19:20-4 Jl/Ag '89
KRIST, GARY
Club-Med quickie. *The New Republic* 200:10-11 Ap 24 '89
KRISTALLNACHT, 1938
Father Coughlin and the Jews: a broadcast remembered [justifying Kristallnacht] R. Modras. *America* 160:219-22 Mr 11 '89
Jewish victims and German sensitivity [discussion of December 14, 1988 article, Jewish victims and German indifference] J. B. Miller. *The Christian Century* 106:287-8 Mr 15 '89
Kristallnacht reflections. L. H. Gann. il *The American Spectator* 22:25-6 Ja '89
Painful questions. H. Kohl. *Society* 26:7-9 Mr/Ap '89
KRISTAN, WILLIAM B., JR.
(jt. auth) See Loer, Curtis M., and Kristan, William B., Jr.
KRISTIANSEN, INGRID
about
Chasing legends. A. Burfoot. il pors *Runner's World* 24:34-41 Jl '89
KRISTIN, JACK
The many faces of Eve: the changing image of the sex goddess. il *American Film* 14:38-41+ Ap '89

KRISTOF, NICHOLAS D., 1959-
China erupts . . . the reasons why [cover story] il *The New York Times Magazine* p26-9+ Je 4 '89
Great Leader to Dear Leader. il por *The New York Times Magazine* p44-7+ Ag 20 '89
How the hardliners won [cover story] il *The New York Times Magazine* p38-41+ N 12 '89
KRISTOL, ELIZABETH
Just the facts, ma'am. il *The American Spectator* 22:39-41 Jl '89
KRISTOL, IRVING
Liberalism & American Jews [discussion of October 1988 article] *Commentary* 87:2-3+ Ja '89
KRITSICK, STEPHEN
about
He talks to the animals . . . M. Siegel. il por *Good Housekeeping* 209:56+ Jl '89
KRIZANC, JOHN
about
The half of it [drama] Reviews
Maclean's il 102:76 D 4 '89. J. Bemrose
KROC, JOAN
about
All my Padres. S. Wulf. il *Sports Illustrated* 70 Special Issue:42-6+ Ap '89
KROGSTAD, E. J., AND OTHERS
Plate tectonics 2.5 billion years ago: evidence at Kolar, South India. bibl f il map *Science* 243:1337-40 Mr 10 '89
KROK SISTERS
about
Bye-bye razors, so long wax—if you want a clean shave, the Krok Sisters are at the EPIcenter. K. S. Schneider. il *People Weekly* 32:89-90 D 11 '89
KRÖLLER-MÜLLER NATIONAL MUSEUM (OTTERLO, NETHERLANDS)
Country charms [sculpture garden in Hoge Veluwe National Park] M. K. Talley, Jr. il *Art News* 88:77-8 Summ '89
KRONAN (SHIP)
Kronan: remnants of a warship's past. A. Franzén. il map *National Geographic* 175:438-65 Ap '89
KRONDL, MICHAEL
Come on over for take-out [special section] il *McCall's* 116:81-2+ S '89
KRONE, JULIE
Good hands. il por *American Health* 8:64-5 My '89
about
She who laughs last . . . [cover story] G. Smith. il pors *Sports Illustrated* 70:84-8+ My 22 '89
KRONOS QUARTET
Classical flash. S. Fried. il *Gentlemen's Quarterly* 59:240+ S '89
Fanatic champions of the new. J. Elson. il *Time* 133:86 Je 26 '89
KROODSMA, DONALD E.
What, when, where, and why warblers warble [cover story] il *Natural History* p50-9 My '89
KROOS, LEE, AND OTHERS
Switch protein alters specificity of RNA polymerase containing a compartment-specific sigma factor. bibl f il *Science* 243:526-9 Ja 27 '89
KRS-ONE
about
Kris Parker, who came home from life on the streets to become gold record rapper 'KRS-ONE'. S. Dougherty. il pors *People Weekly* 31:101+ F 27 '89
KRUEGER, FREDERICK W., 1943-
about
Environmental crisis: put Christian virtues at your disposal [interview] por *U.S. Catholic* 54:25-30 O '89
KRUEGER, FREDDY (FICTIONAL CHARACTER) *See* Freddy Krueger (Fictional character)
KRUGER, BARBARA
about
Barbara Kruger at Mary Boone. K. Johnson. il *Art in America* 77:260-1 Ap '89
Barbara Kruger: Mary Boone. N. Grimes. il *Art News* 88:200 Ap '89
Genre. *The New Yorker* 65:27 F 27 '89
Stephen King: limited edition for a bestselling author. C. Reid. il *Publishers Weekly* 235:37-8 Mr 31 '89
Talking pictures. J. Giles. *Mother Jones* 14:52 My '89
KRUGER, PAMELA
An executive's guide to volunteering. *Working Woman* 14:86-8 D '89
What attracts the best workers. *Working Woman* 14:76+ Mr '89
KRUMHANSL, JAMES A.
about
Krumhansl protests China situation, urges support for scholars in USA. *Physics Today* 42 pt1:79 Ag '89
KRUMHOLZ, PHILLIP
The barber pole: symbol with a past and a future. il *Antiques & Collecting Hobbies* 94:69-72 Mr '89
KRUMM, DANIEL JOHN, 1926-
about
Damned if you do . . . K. Hannon. il por *Forbes* 143:201 Mr 20 '89

KRUMME, RICHARD
Across the editor's desk. See issues of Successful Farming
KRUMRIE, TIM
about
Broken but unbowed. J. Lieber. il pors *Sports Illustrated* 70:104-7 Mr 20 '89
KRUPINSKI, JOHN, AND OTHERS
Adenylyl cyclase amino acid sequence: possible channel- or transporter-like structure. bibl f il *Science* 244:1558-64 Je 30 '89
KRUPP, CHARLA
People. See issues of Glamour
KRUPP CASH PLUS L.P.
Please read fine print. M. Schifrin. il *Forbes* 143:62+ Mr 6 '89
KRUSHCHEV, NIKITA *See* Khrushchev, Nikita Sergeevich, 1894-1971
KRUYS, VÉRONIQUE, AND OTHERS
Translational blockade imposed by cytokine-derived UA-rich sequences. bibl f il *Science* 245:852-5 Ag 25 '89
KRYSELL, M., AND WALLACE, D. W. R.
Hydrolysis of carbon tetrachloride [discussion of November 4, 1988 article, Arctic Ocean ventilation studied with a suite of anthropogenic halocarbon tracers] il *Science* 246:1638-9 D 22 '89
KRYSTAL, ARTHUR
On writing: let there be less. il *The New York Times Book Review* 94:1+ Mr 26 '89
KRZEMINSKI, ADAM
(jt. auth) See Baczynski, Jerzy, and Krzeminski, Adam
KTBC (AUSTIN, TEX.: RADIO STATION) *See* Radio stations
KU KLUX KLAN
Ala. Klan must take course on civil rights: settlement. il *Jet* 76:7 Ag 14 '89
Duke election symptomatic of U.S. racism: Jackson. *Jet* 75:7 Mr 6 '89
Duke shows his true colors [D. Duke to run for the Senate from Louisiana] B. Turque. il por *Newsweek* 114:53 D 25 '89
An ex-Klansman trades his robes for a cloak of respectability in the Louisiana legislature [D. Duke] D. Grogan. il pors *People Weekly* 31:215-16 Mr 6 '89
The GOP's cross to bear [ex-Klansman D. Duke elected to Louisiana legislature] il pors *U.S. News & World Report* 106:14-15 Mr 6 '89
Hate gets a haircut [Louisiana state legislature representative D. Duke] L. K. Truscott. il pors map *Esquire* 112:174-6+ N '89
The Klan: once powerful, now a haven for losers. M. Ivins. *TV Guide* 37:25-7 N 4-10 '89
Kluck! Kluck! Kluck! [white supremacist D. Duke wins election to Louisiana legislature] E. Magnuson. il por *Time* 133:29 Mr 6 '89
Let's tear off their hoods. B. Bayh. por *Newsweek* 113:8 Ap 17 '89
Louisiana's blow-dried Grand Wizard [D. Duke] il por *Newsweek* 113:27 Ja 23 '89
Praying with the Klan [evening of dialogue sponsored by Tennessee seminary students in 1981] R. Hosmer. *The Christian Century* 106:494-5 My 10 '89
Republican racist [D. Duke of Louisiana] L. Cohler. *The New Republic* 201:11-14 S 18-25 '89
A seat for the Klansman [D. Duke wins seat in Louisiana legislature] J. Hammer. il por *Newsweek* 113:6 Mr 6 '89
Skinheads + Klan = trouble. D. J. Dent. il *Black Enterprise* 19:22 Ap '89
Woman awarded $7 million against KKK dies without will; daughters administer [B. M. Donald] pors *Jet* 76:12 Ap 24 '89
KUBOTA, LTD.
Ardent's Daddy Warbucks. J. B. Levine. il *Business Week* p26-7 Je 12 '89
KUBRICK, STANLEY
about
2001: a space odyssey [film] Reviews
Video 12:63-4 Mr '89. M. Fleischmann
'Lolita'. P. Schrader. il *American Film* 15:18-20+ O '89
KUCHNIR, DEBORAH
about
Kuchnir and Simon are co-winners of undergraduate Apker Award. pors *Physics Today* 42:85 D '89
KUDZU (COMIC STRIP)
Discrimination isn't comic [Chicago tribune replaces Kudzu with Pogo] M. E. Marty. *The Christian Century* 106:215 F 22 '89
KUEHNELT-LEDDIHN, ERIK VON
From the Continent. See occasional issues of National Review
KUENZI, DAVID
The mantis' prayer [poem] *The Nation* 248:138 Ja 30 '89
KUGHN, DICK
about
Dick Kughn had so much fun with his Lionel trains that he bought the whole railroad. D. Chu. il por *People Weekly* 32:119-20 D 18 '89

KUGLER, D. D.
about
Newhouse [drama] Reviews
Maclean's il 102:63 My 1 '89. J. Bemrose
KUHARSKI, MARY ANN
Dry times at Slick's Bar. il pors *Christianity Today* 33:14-15 Mr 17 '89
A love of family affairs. por *Newsweek* 114:8 Ag 21 '89
KUHLMAN CORPORATION
Kuhlman Corp. S. L. Kirsch. il *Fortune* 120:128 D 18 '89
KUHN, DWIGHT
Secrets of a small pond [photographs] il *Country Journal* 16:53-5 My/Je '89
KUHN, HANS PETER
about
Creating an audio environment: Hans Peter Kuhn's Forest sounds. J. Calhoun. il por *Theatre Crafts* 23:46-8+ Ja '89
KUHN, THOMAS R.
Striving for balanced growth [address, May 16, 1989] *Vital Speeches of the Day* 55:637-40 Ag 1 '89
KUHN, LOEB & COMPANY
Jacob Schiff and the Northern Pacific corner [1901 battle with J. P. Morgan for control of company] J. S. Gordon. il por *American Heritage* 40:86-7 Jl/Ag '89
KUIPER AIRBORNE OBSERVATORY *See* Airplanes in astronomy
KUIPERS, DEAN
The silencing of 'Radio Sarah'. il *The Nation* 248:559+ Ap 24 '89
KUIPERS, OSCAR P., AND OTHERS
Enhanced activity and altered specificity of phospholipase A_2 by deletion of a surface loop. bibl f il *Science* 244:82-5 Ap 7 '89
KUITER, RUDIE
Father does best [photograph] il *International Wildlife* 19:12-13 Ja/F '89
KUKICH, DIANE
The unwritten rules of the pool. il *Women's Sports & Fitness* 11:80-1 Ap '89
KULCINSKI, GERALD
about
Moon power. M. J. Mackowski. il por *Ad Astra* 1:34-9 Jl/Ag '89
KULSKI, JULIAN
Stalling for time. il *Flying* 116:110 My '89
KUMIN, MAXINE, 1925-
Enough jam for a lifetime. il *Country Journal* 16:56-8 Jl/Ag '89
Long road home to an upland farm. il *Country Journal* 16:75-9 My/Je '89
Looking for luck in Bangkok [poem] *The New Yorker* 65:42 Je 12 '89
KUMMER, CORBY
A better omelet. il *The Atlantic* 264:99-101 O '89
Holiday-spanning bread. il *The Atlantic* 263:84+ Mr '89
Over the coals. il *The Atlantic* 263:83-6 Je '89
KUMON (MATHEMATICS INSTRUCTION)
Samurai math gets a tryout [Sumiton, Ala.] A. Murr. il *Newsweek* 113:60 Ap 10 '89
KUMP, THERESA
Miniatures: a world at your fingertips. il *New Choices for the Best Years* 29:74+ Ag '89
KUMQUATS
Kumquats. *Good Housekeeping* 209:230 D '89
KUNC, MILAN
about
Milan Kunc at Robert Miller. J. Zinsser. *Art in America* 77:160 F '89
KUNES, ELLEN
American myopia. *Omni (New York, N.Y.)* 11:33 Mr '89
Suckers for science. *Omni (New York, N.Y.)* 11:25 Jl '89
Troubled water. *Omni (New York, N.Y.)* 11:46+ S '89
KÜNG, HANS, 1928-
about
The Church in China [interview] P. H. Samway. *America* 160:374-6+ Ap 22 '89
KUNG FU MASTER [film] See Motion picture reviews—Single works
KUNIN, ARTHUR
about
Two first gentlemen. C. Reeve. il pors *New Choices for the Best Years* 29:14-15 F '89
KUNIN, MADELEINE
Madeleine Kunin [excerpt from address] il por *Ladies' Home Journal* 106:62 N '89
KUNK, M. J., AND OTHERS
^{40}Ar-^{39}Ar dating of the Manson impact structure: a Cretaceous-Tertiary boundary crater candidate. bibl f il *Science* 244:1565-8 Je 30 '89
KUNKEL, KENNETH E.
A drought's unyielding cycle. il *Natural History* p48-9 Ja '89
KUNKLETOWN (PA.)
Juvenile justice, Administration of
A murder rap at age 10 [C. Kocher] *Newsweek* 114:24 Ag 14 '89

KUNSTHISTORISCHES MUSEUM (VIENNA, AUSTRIA)
Double departure [resignation of directors] F. Protzman. *Art News* 88:77 O '89

KUNSTLER, JAMES HOWARD
For sale [cover story] il *The New York Times Magazine* p22-5+ Je 18 '89
A killing in Maine. il por *The New York Times Magazine* p58-60+ S 10 '89
Would you like to see my motherworts? il *Gentlemen's Quarterly* 59:54+ Ap '89

KUO, GEORGE, AND OTHERS
An assay for circulating antibodies to a major etiologic virus of human non-A, non-B hepatitis. bibl f il *Science* 244:362-4 Ap 21 '89

KUO, LAWRENCE C., AND OTHERS
Triggering of allostery in an enzyme by a point mutation: ornithine transcarbamoylase. bibl f il *Science* 245:522-4 Ag 4 '89

KUPFER, FERN
Between mother and daughter [story] il *Redbook* 172:60+ Ap '89
No regrets [story] il por *Redbook* 173:50+ Ag '89

KUPFERBERG, HERBERT
Anne-Sophie Mutter. il pors *Stereo Review* 54:63-5 Jl '89
Jeffrey Tate. il pors *Stereo Review* 54:86-8 My '89

KUPPERMAN, ROBERT H., 1935-, AND KAMEN, JEFF
When terrorists strike . . . the lessons TV must learn. il *TV Guide* 37:18-22 S 23-29 '89

KURAOKA, NOBUYOSHI
about
Fugu, taxis, and Tender Buttons. H. Bridges. il *Gourmet* 49:48+ S '89

KURDS
Iran
A precarious refuge in Iran [Iraqi Kurds] F. A. Reed. il *Maclean's* 102:25 Ja 16 '89
Iraq
Flanders Fields revisited [Iraqi use of poison gas against Kurds] I. O'Keeffe. il *World Press Review* 36:12-13 Mr '89
The poor man's atomic bomb [use of poison gas against the Kurds] A. C. Revkin. il *Discover* 10:76 Ja '89
A precarious refuge in Iran [Iraqi Kurds] F. A. Reed. il *Maclean's* 102:25 Ja 16 '89
The world and the Kurds. J. Hamburg. *The Nation* 249:205-6 Ag 21-28 '89

KUREISHI, HANIF
Esther [story] il *The Atlantic* 263:56-62 My '89

KURLAND ZABAR (FIRM)
Mad about Morris. N. F. Weber. il *House & Garden* 161:88 Ap '89

KURLANSKY, MARK
In the land of the blind caudillo. il pors *The New York Times Magazine* p24-6+ Ag 6 '89

KUROSAWA, AKIRA, 1910-
about
Akira Kurosawa. G. Peary. il pors *American Film* 14:80-2 Ap '89
A funny thing happened on the way to the Film Forum. D. Denby. il *New York* 22:66+ F 6 '89
Japan's emperor of film. I. Buruma. il pors *The New York Times Magazine* p42-5+ O 29 '89

KURYOKHIN, SERGEY
about
Sergey Kuryokhin: the Russian Martian arrives. H. Mandel. il pors *Down Beat* 56:26-8 Ap '89

KURZWEIL, PETER R.
(jt. auth) See Jackson, Douglas W., and Kurzweil, Peter R.

KURZWEIL, RAYMOND
Beyond pattern recognition. il *Byte* 14:277+ D '89

KUSAMA, YAYOI, 1929-
about
Social work. K. Larson. il *New York* 22:113-14 N 6 '89

KUSCSIK, NINA
How to improve your 5K and 10K times. il *Women's Sports & Fitness* 11:30-5 My '89
That first marathon. il *Women's Sports & Fitness* 11:20-5 O '89

KUSHNER, HAROLD S., 1935-
about
God and modern man. M. Starr. il por *Newsweek* 114:74-5 O 23 '89
Two from the heart [interview] M. Lodge. il pors *Ladies' Home Journal* 106:78+ D '89
When bad things happen to good religion. R. J. Neuhaus. il *National Review* 41:52-4 N 10 '89

KUSNET, DAVID
A dirty business. *Commonweal* 116:107-8 F 24 '89

KUSPIT, DONALD B. (DONALD BURTON), 1935-
Red desert & Arctic dreams. il *Art in America* 77:120-5 Mr '89

KUSSI, PETER
(tr) See Hrabal, Bohumil, 1914-. The magic flute

KUTCHIN INDIANS *See* Gwich'in Indians

KUTS, VLADIMIR
about
Red Army vet Vladimir Kuts joins up with his GI pals 44 years after battling the Nazis together. W. Plummer. il por *People Weekly* 32:86-8 Ag 21 '89

KUTTNER, ROBERT
Economic viewpoint. See issues of Business Week
Fresh ideas on affordable housing. il *Utne Reader* p73-5 My/Je '89
Keeping the market in its place. *Utne Reader* p67 Ja/F '89
Ron Brown's party line. il pors *The New York Times Magazine* p44+ D 3 '89

KUWABARA, KONOSUKE
Asia's 'Tigers' will pounce. *World Press Review* 36:22 D '89

KUWAIT
See also
Investments, Kuwaiti

KUZNIK, FRANK
Divide & conquer. il *Common Cause Magazine* 15:13-16 My/Je '89

KVANT (PERIODICAL)
Soviet magazine for high schoolers to appear in English. P. Janowski. *Physics Today* 42:116-17 O '89

KWANGTUNG PROVINCE (CHINA) *See* Guangdong Province (China)

KWANZAA
Kwanzaa: celebrate in holiday style! il *Essence* 20:50-8 D '89
Rejoice! S. L. Taylor. il *Essence* 20:49 D '89

KWAPIS, KEN
about
Vibes [film] Reviews
Video il 12:62 F '89. D. Schweiger

KWIK, PHILL
Pittston power. *The Nation* 249:409 O 16 '89

KWONG, PETER, AND MIŠČEVIČ, DUŠANKA
China gropes toward a way out [cover story] il *The Nation* 249:73+ Jl 17 '89

KYBETT, SUSAN MACLEAN
Henry VIII—a malnourished king? bibl il pors *History Today* 39:19-25 S '89

KYLIÁN, JIŘÍ
about
Reviews:
Performance of works by J. Kylián in Stuttgart. H. Koegler. *Dance Magazine* 63:73-4 Ap '89

KYNAR *See* Polyvinylidene fluoride

KYOTO (JAPAN)
Hotels, motels, etc.
Kyoto comforts. M. Filler. il *House & Garden* 161:74+ D '89

Photographs and photography
A photographer's guide to Kyoto. A. Hicks. il *Petersen's Photographic Magazine* 18:30-5 D '89

L

L-5 SOCIETY
See also
National Space Society (U.S.)

L.A. GEAR INC.
L.A. Gear is going where the boys are. K. Kerwin. il por *Business Week* p54 Je 19 '89
Will this runner finally stumble? [stock outlook] J. Egan. il *U.S. News & World Report* 106:72 Mr 13 '89

L.A. LAW [television program] *See* Television program reviews—Single works

L.A. STYLE (PERIODICAL)
Pretty poison: Anne Crawford skewers Hollywood [gossip columnist] E. J. Carroll. il *Mademoiselle* 95:202-3+ O '89

L.F. ROTHSCHILD HOLDINGS INC.
Ernest Fleischer finally tastes humble pie [filing for bankruptcy] D. Zigas. il por *Business Week* p67 Jl 17 '89

L.M. ERICSSON TELEPHONE CO.
Ericsson's true calling. J. Kapstein. *Business Week* p42+ Mr 6 '89

L-TRYPTOPHAN *See* Tryptophan

LA CHAPELLE, DAVID, 1963-
about
David LaChapelle at Trabia-MacAfee. J. Ash. *Art in America* 77:173 Je '89

LA CORTE, JOHN N.
about
Telephone. *The New Yorker* 65:34-5 O 30 '89

LA FALAISE, LUCIE DE
about
Young talent. N. Frey. il pors *Harper's Bazaar* 122:110-13 Jl '89

LA FARGE, JOHN, 1835-1910
about
John La Farge's masterpieces in stained glass. D. D. Thompson. bibl f il *Antiques* 135:708-17 Mr '89
LA FRESSANGE, INÈS DE
about
In a clash of symbols, Chanel's top model falls from the runway. M. H. J. Farrell. il pors *People Weekly* 32:51+ Ag 14 '89
LA GUARDIA, FIORELLO HENRY, 1882-1947
about
Novik and LaGuardia. *The New Yorker* 65:24-6 Ag 28 '89
The sorrow and the city [cover story] J. Klein. il *The New Republic* 201:24-8 N 13 '89
LA GUARDIA AIRPORT *See* New York (N.Y.)—Airports
LA JOLLA (SAN DIEGO, CALIF.)
Bookstores
See Booksellers and bookselling—California
LA LA LA HUMAN STEPS (DANCE COMPANY)
Bodies in collision. P. Young. il *Maclean's* 102:90-1 N 6 '89
LA NASA, KATHERINE
about
Taking a young, fourth wife, actor Dennis Hopper promises that this time he's playing for keeps. il pors *People Weekly* 32:72-3 Jl 3 '89
LA NIÑA (OCEAN CURRENT)
Far-off clues to nearby weather [drought research by Kevin Trenberth] B. Carpenter. il map *U.S. News & World Report* 106:56 Ja 16 '89
The wayward winds. K. E. Trenberth. maps *Natural History* p44-5 Ja '89
LA NOUE, TERENCE, 1941-
about
Terence La Noue: Dorothy Goldeen. P. Hammond. il *Art News* 88:190 S '89
LA PASIONARIA *See* Ibárruri, Dolores, 1895-1989
LA PLATA COUNTY (COLO.)
Description and travel
La Plata County, Colorado [cover story] D. Petersen. il map *The Mother Earth News* 119:56-63 S/O '89
LA QUINA *See* Hernandez Galicia, Joaquín
LA RIVIÈRE, J. W. M.
Threats to the world's water. bibl il map *Scientific American* 261:80-4+ S '89
LA RUTA MAYA
La Ruta Maya [cover story] W. E. Garrett. il supp (folded map) maps *National Geographic* 176:424-78 O '89
Treasures of the Guatemala rain forest. A. Wade. il *The New Leader* 72:11-13 Ap 3-17 '89
LA SCALA OPERA *See* Opera—Italy
LA-Z-BOY CHAIR CO.
Rocking the recliners [proxy fight] M. Schifrin. il por *Forbes* 144:194+ O 16 '89
LABATT (JOHN) LIMITED *See* John Labatt Limited
LABCOM *See* U.S. Army Laboratory Command
LABELLE, PATTI
about
Patti LaBelle says 'forget my hair and costumes because my voice is the real me' [cover story] R. L. Haywood. il pors *Jet* 76:24-7 Je 26 '89
LABER, JERI
Cruel and usual punishment. il *The New York Review of Books* 36:34-5 Jl 20 '89
Fighting back in Prague. il *The New York Review of Books* 36:39-41 Ap 27 '89
LABERGE, SUZAN
about
Daughter of Manson victims finds forgiveness. J. Shaver. il pors *Christianity Today* 33:50-1 S 22 '89
LABIANCA, DOMINICK A.
How reliable is breath-alcohol testing? il *USA Today (Periodical)* 118:71-2 S '89
LABID, ABDULLAH ABD AL-HAMID
about
French court convicts Palestinian terrorist [statement and fact sheet, October 31, 1988] *Department of State Bulletin* 89:64-5 F '89
LABOR
See also
Church and labor
Employment
Home labor
Hours of labor
Job satisfaction
Socialism
Strikes
Unemployment
Work
Labor month in review. See issues of Monthly Labor Review
Year of the blue-collar guy. S. Olson. por *Newsweek* 114:16 N 6 '89
Education
See also
Apprentices
Workers' Educational Association (Great Britain)

American workers lack training [report by the American Society for Training and Development] *USA Today (Periodical)* 118:6-7 D '89
Coping with the coming labor shortage [address, May 11, 1989] G. M. Smith. *Vital Speeches of the Day* 55:669-71 Ag 15 '89
Do more-educated workers fare better following job displacement? P. Swaim and M. Podgursky. bibl f il *Monthly Labor Review* 112:43-6 Ag '89
Education and employment. il *Black Enterprise* 20:53 D '89
Education reform and economic competition [address, August 15, 1989] W. Wilkinson. *Vital Speeches of the Day* 56:40-3 N 1 '89
The forgotten half [undereducated work force; cover story] D. Whitman. il *U.S. News & World Report* 106:44-9+ Je 26 '89
Intellectual decapitalization. *America* 161:252 O 21 '89
Performance of U.S. educational system threatens defense base, economic position. S. W. Kandebo. *Aviation Week & Space Technology* 131:34-5 D 18-25 '89
A prescription for solving the crisis in the work force [Investing in people: strategy to address America's workforce crisis] H. Brand. *Monthly Labor Review* 112:82-6 N '89
Training the workforce of the future. J. E. Jacobs. il *Technology Review* 92:66-72 Ag/S '89
What the boardroom has to offer the schoolroom. E. Flax. *Working Woman* 14:26+ D '89
When you know your ABCs. W. F. Buckley. *National Review* 41:62 O 27 '89
Health and hygiene
See Occupational health and safety
History
See also
Labor Hall of Fame
Photographs and photography
Tinker tailor [19th century tintypes] K. Heyman. il *American Heritage* 40:106-13 N '89
Housing
Look for the union label [housing trust fund in contract of Local 26 of Hotel Workers Union in Boston] P. Dreier. il *The Progressive* 53:30 Ap '89
Periodicals
See also
Monthly labor review
Psychology
See Psychology, Industrial
Statistics
See also
United States. Bureau of Labor Statistics
Conference papers [papers at the Sesquicentennial Program of the American Statistical Association] *Monthly Labor Review* 112:29-33 O '89
Current labor statistics. See issues of Monthly Labor Review
Developing statistics to meet society's needs. J. L. Norwood and D. P. Klein. bibl f *Monthly Labor Review* 112:14-19 O '89
Statistics and public policy [excerpts from address, August 8, 1989] J. L. Norwood. *Monthly Labor Review* 112:2 S '89
Great Britain
See also
Bristol (England)—Labor
New ideas about work. M. Jacques. *World Press Review* 36:24 D '89
History
See also
Workers' Educational Association (Great Britain)
Enterprise past and present [working class entrepreneurs in late 19th and early 20th century] J. Benson. il *History Today* 39:5-7 Ag '89
Massachusetts
See also
Boston (Mass.)—Labor
West Virginia
See also
Ward (W. Va.)—Labor
LABOR (NEWSPAPER)
Deaths in the family. E. Knoll. *The Progressive* 53:4 Mr '89
LABOR (OBSTETRICS) *See* Childbirth
LABOR AGREEMENTS *See* Collective labor agreements
LABOR CAMPS *See* Concentration camps
LABOR CONTRACTS
See also
Collective labor agreements
First it was poison pills—now it's 'people pills' [resignation pact for top managers] C. Farrell. *Business Week* p33-4 Ja 16 '89
LABOR COSTS
See also
Collective labor agreements
Measuring the precision of the Employment Cost Index. K. O'Conor and W. Wong. il *Monthly Labor Review* 112:29-36 Mr '89

LABOR COSTS—*cont.*
International aspects
How to keep the home forges burning—and profitable [manufacturers shifting overseas operations back to U.S.] P. Sherrid. il *U.S. News & World Report* 107:48-9 Jl 3 '89

International comparisons of hourly compensation costs. P. Capdevielle. il *Monthly Labor Review* 112:10-12 Je '89

International comparisons of productivity and unit labor cost trends in manufacturing. A. Neef and J. Thomas. bibl f il *Monthly Labor Review* 111:27-33 D '88
East Asia
Is the era of cheap Asian labor over? D. J. Yang and L. Nakarmi. il *Business Week* p45-6 My 15 '89

LABOR DEPT. (U.S.) *See* United States. Dept. of Labor

LABOR DISCIPLINE
The lost art of kicking ass. O. Edwards. il *Gentlemen's Quarterly* 59:239-42 O '89

LABOR DISPUTES
See also
   Collective bargaining
   Labor union busting
   Strikes

LABOR FORCE *See* Labor supply

LABOR HALL OF FAME
New Labor Hall of Fame. *Monthly Labor Review* 112:45 My '89

New Labor Hall of Fame. *Monthly Labor Review* 112:29 Je '89

LABOR IN ART
Ideal union [work of R. Fasanella] N. Gill. il por *Mother Jones* 14:16 N '89

LABOR IN MASS MEDIA
Working-class heroes no more. B. Ehrenreich. *Harper's* 279:22+ D '89

LABOR IN POLITICS *See* Labor unions—Political activities

LABOR INCENTIVES *See* Incentives in industry

LABOR LAWS AND REGULATIONS
See also
   Boycott
   Factories—Shutdowns—Laws and regulations
   Hours of labor
   Insurance, Workers' compensation
   Minimum wage
   Occupational health and safety—Laws and regulations
   United States. Dept. of Labor

Above the law? [Congress] J. Novack. il *Forbes* 143:250 My 29 '89

The courts shouldn't become pink-slip police. G. S. Becker. il *Business Week* p14 Ag 28 '89

Legal rulings. *Monthly Labor Review* 112:43 Ap '89

Needed: a replacement for the bargaining table. J. P. Hoerr. il *Business Week* p38-9 Ja 9 '89

New bill to define rights of workers in union dealings. il *Nation's Business* 77:8 Je '89

See you in court [cover story] D. C. Bacon. il *Nation's Business* 77:16-18+ Jl '89

State labor legislation enacted in 1988. R. R. Nelson. *Monthly Labor Review* 112:40-58 Ja '89

Supreme Court ruling lets airlines assure jobs to strike breakers [case of TWA vs. Independent Federation of Flight Attendants] M. Mecham. *Aviation Week & Space Technology* 129:67 Mr 6 '89
International aspects
Economic patriotism in a global economy [address, December 8, 1988] W. W. Winpisinger. *Vital Speeches of the Day* 55:220-2 Ja 15 '89
Soviet Union
In the school of democracy [dealing with strikes] A. Blackman. il *Time* 134:44 O 16 '89

Is the Soviet economy too sick for *perestroika*? R. Brady and M. McNamee. *Business Week* p33 O 16 '89

Strike's back. D. Koenker. *The New Republic* 201:14-16 O 23 '89
Texas
Farm workers don't have to be poor. T. Rosenberg. *The Washington Monthly* 21:22-4+ Ap '89
Western Europe
The cost of flexibility. U. Huws. *World Press Review* 36:48 Je '89

A dark side of expansion. T. Hanke. *World Press Review* 36:18-19 Ja '89

A social charter for the E.C.? H. Wainwright. il *The Nation* 249:80-2+ Jl 17 '89

LABOR LEADERS *See* Labor unions—Officials

LABOR-MANAGEMENT COOPERATION *See* Participative management

LABOR-MANAGEMENT RELATIONS *See* Industrial relations

LABOR MARKET *See* Labor supply

LABOR MOBILITY
See also
   Black executives—Relocation
   Executives—Relocation
   Labor turnover
   Occupational mobility
Easing the moving blues. K. Springen and A. Miller. il *Newsweek* 114:40-1 Jl 3 '89

LABOR MOVEMENT *See* Labor unions—History

LABOR PARTY (GREAT BRITAIN) *See* Labour Party (Great Britain)

LABOR PRODUCTIVITY *See* Productivity, Industrial

LABOR RELATIONS *See* Industrial relations

LABOR SHORTAGE *See* Labor supply

LABOR STATISTICS *See* Employment—Statistics; Labor—Statistics; Unemployment—Statistics

LABOR STATISTICS BUREAU (U.S.) *See* United States. Bureau of Labor Statistics

LABOR STUDIES
Blue-collar scholar: a former steelworker hits the books. L. Evans. il *The Progressive* 53:22-5 Ap '89

LABOR SUPPLY
See also
   Aged—Employment
   Alien labor
   Blacks—Employment
   Cancer patients—Employment
   Cardiacs—Employment
   Children—Employment
   College graduates—Employment
   Contingent workers
   Convict labor
   Farm labor
   Farm women—Employment
   Forced labor
   Hispanic Americans—Employment
   Labor mobility
   Married women—Employment
   Migrant labor
   Minorities—Employment
   Part time employment
   Poor—Employment
   Skilled labor
   Slavery
   Temporary employment
   White collar workers
   Women—Employment
   Women college graduates—Employment
   Youth—Employment

The changing work force [excerpts from address, February 23, 1989] J. L. Norwood. *Monthly Labor Review* 112:2 Mr '89

Characteristics of occupational entrants. M. L. Carey. il *Occupational Outlook Quarterly* 33:8-17 Summ '89

Coping with the coming labor shortage [address, May 11, 1989] G. M. Smith. *Vital Speeches of the Day* 55:669-71 Ag 15 '89

Flexible future for workforce [study by the National Association of Temporary Services] *USA Today (Periodical)* 118:6 D '89

Future shock [population trends point to labor shortage and increase in minority birth rate; cover story] D. E. Bloom and N. G. Bennett. *The New Republic* 200:18-20+ Je 19 '89

A growing shortage of workers is raising inflation risks. V. Brownstein. il *Fortune* 119:33-4 Ap 10 '89

The hiring crisis of the '90s. R. Sandroff. il *Working Woman* 14:92-4 F '89

Labor force projections. il *Monthly Labor Review* 112:2 Ja '89

Labor market changes and adjustments: how do the U.S. and Japan compare? R. W. Bednarzik and C. R. Shiells. bibl f il *Monthly Labor Review* 112:31-42 F '89

Labor market completes sixth year of expansion in 1988. W. J. Howe and W. Parks, II. il *Monthly Labor Review* 112:3-14 F '89

Labor shortages: menace or mirage? J. Sargent. il *Occupational Outlook Quarterly* 32:27-33 Wint '88

New challenges in the workplace [Workforce 2000] L. Crooks. il *Modern Maturity* 32:10-11 F/Mr '89

Outlook 2000 [cover story; special issue] bibl f il *Monthly Labor Review* 112:2-74 N '89

Plenty of workers are waiting in the wings. M. J. Mandel. il *Business Week* p90+ Mr 13 '89

A prescription for solving the crisis in the work force [Investing in people: strategy to address America's workforce crisis] H. Brand. *Monthly Labor Review* 112:82-6 N '89
Germany (West)
Euphoria & beyond. C. Wilpert. *Commonweal* 116:695-7 D 15 '89

Help definitely wanted [views of Norbert Walter on influx of East Germans] P. Fuhrman. il *Forbes* 144:241 O 30 '89

Is a new economic juggernaut on the way? [wave of émigrés] J. Templeman. il *Business Week* p72+ O 23 '89
Japan
Japan Inc. hangs out a help-wanted sign. A. Borrus. il *Business Week* p32 Jl 24 '89

Labor market changes and adjustments: how do the U.S. and Japan compare? R. W. Bednarzik and C. R. Shiells. bibl f il *Monthly Labor Review* 112:31-42 F '89
United States
See Labor supply

LABOR TURNOVER
See also
   Executives—Resignation

LABOR TURNOVER—*cont.*

Tuition payments cut job turnover [Burger King in downtown Detroit] S. D. Rinella and R. J. Kopecky. il por *Nation's Business* 77:25-6 Ag '89

LABOR UNION BUSTING

A dirty business [anti-union consulting] D. Kusnet. *Commonweal* 116:107-8 F 24 '89

The union-busting Post: labor pains at a liberal paper [cover story] J. Hanrahan. il *The Progressive* 53:18-25 F '89

LABOR UNIONS

See also
AFL-CIO
Boycott
Collective bargaining
Collective labor agreements
Communications Workers of America
Industrial relations
International Brotherhood of Teamsters, Chauffeurs, Warehousemen and Helpers of America
Laborers' International Union of North America
Strikes
United Automobile, Aerospace and Agricultural Implement Workers of America
United Food and Commercial Workers International Union

How to write labor's obit. V. Kamber. por *Newsweek* 114:10-11 S 11 '89

Is labor ready to break the siege? [cover story] J. Slaughter. il *The Progressive* 53:20-1+ D '89

Labor month in review. See issues of Monthly Labor Review

Labor's bark is back, but not its bite. R. A. Taylor. il *U.S. News & World Report* 106:54 My 22 '89

Labor's 'deal' is undone [increased militancy] S. Aronowitz. il *The Progressive* 53:18-19 D '89

The Vegas connection [decline of labor movement] D. Seligman. *Fortune* 120:223 S 11 '89

Why organized labor is unlikely to make a comeback. R. A. Taylor. *U.S. News & World Report* 107:31 S 11 '89

Air pilots

See also
Air Line Pilots Association

Air traffic controllers (Persons)

See also
National Air Traffic Controllers Association

Airline employees

See also
Independent Federation of Flight Attendants
International Association of Machinists and Aerospace Workers

Board decisions muddle rules on union role after mergers [National Mediation Board rulings] J. Ott. *Aviation Week & Space Technology* 131:68 Ag 28 '89

Crashing Eastern [unions urging re-regulation of airlines] il *National Review* 41:12 Ap 7 '89

TWA unions attempt to shape strategy for gaining leverage over airline sale. J. T. McKenna. *Aviation Week & Space Technology* 131:32-3 D 4 '89

Ueberroth woos unions in bid to take over Eastern, resume flight operations. J. T. McKenna and E. H. Kolcum. *Aviation Week & Space Technology* 130:89 Ap 10 '89

Union plan for Eastern takeover released at congressional hearing. il *Aviation Week & Space Technology* 130:22 Mr 13 '89

Unions face struggle to reverse 1980s' setbacks. J. T. McKenna. *Aviation Week & Space Technology* 131:77+ D 18-25 '89

Unions fly high. I. M. Stelzer. il *The American Spectator* 22:30-1 Jl '89

Artists

Soviet Union

See also
Artists Union (Soviet Union)

Authors

See also
National Writers Union

Automobile industry workers

See also
United Automobile, Aerospace and Agricultural Implement Workers of America

Blacks

The growing clout of black labor leaders. D. C. Lyons. il *Ebony* 44:40+ Je '89

Coal miners

The good war [coal miners in Ward, W. Va. during the 1930s] E. Wilson. *The New Republic* 200:21 My 29 '89

Copper miners

Mexico

Salinas strikes before the miners can. S. Baker. il map *Business Week* p50 S 4 '89

Corporate campaigns

The battle ahead: labor's new playbook. S. Waldman. il *Newsweek* 113:24 Mr 20 '89

Dancers

See also
American Guild of Musical Artists

Dues, fees, etc.

Jobs with justice? [right of workers not to fund union political activities] S. T. Mandel. *National Review* 41:17 Ag 18 '89

Elections

Can reform unhorse Teamsters bosses? [agreement to hold supervised elections to avert federal takeover] il *U.S. News & World Report* 106:12+ Mr 27 '89

The land of the UAW's setting sun [Nissan votes to keep union out] il *U.S. News & World Report* 107:8 Ag 7 '89

Score another for Japan Inc. [Nissan workers vote to keep out union] L. Reibstein. il *Newsweek* 114:44-5 Ag 7 '89

So where does the UAW go from here? [loss at Nissan plant in Smyrna, Tenn.] W. Zellner. il *Business Week* p77 Ag 14 '89

A Soviet election [determining whether Key Airlines employees wish to join Teamsters] D. Seligman. il *Fortune* 120:142+ Jl 3 '89

Struggle for the soul of the union [New Directions movement of the United Auto Workers] J. Schwartz. il *The Nation* 249:8-10 Jl 3 '89

The UAW vs. Japan: it's showdown time in Tennessee [Nissan plant election] D. Foust. il *Business Week* p64-5 Jl 24 '89

Electric workers

See also
United Electrical, Radio and Machine Workers of America

Electronics workers

Malaysia

Dreaming of the forty-hour week. D. MacShane. *The Nation* 248:658-60 My 15 '89

Firefighters

See also
International Association of Fire Fighters

Government employees

Can employee associations negotiate new growth? S. A. Levitan and F. Gallo. bibl f il *Monthly Labor Review* 112:5-14 Jl '89

Canada

See also
Canadian Union of Public Employees

Graduate teaching assistants

See also
Association of Graduate Student Employees

History

Glory days [cover story] T. Geoghegan. *The New Republic* 200:18-23 My 29 '89

The tolerated unions. *The New Republic* 201 [Reprint v1]:11-12 N 6 '89 [N 7 '14]

Hotel workers

See also
Hotel Employees and Restaurant Employees International Union

International aspects

See also
International Labour Organisation

Membership

See also
Labor unions—Blacks

Unions must woo young and women [views of James B. Dworkin] il *USA Today (Periodical)* 118:10 Ag '89

See also
Labor union busting
Labor unions—Corporate campaigns

The good war [coal miners in Ward, W. Va. during the 1930s] E. Wilson. *The New Republic* 200:21 My 29 '89

New believers [union organizers in Boston] B. McKibben. il *Mother Jones* 14:38-41+ Ap '89

Miners

See also
United Mine Workers of America

Musicians

See also
American Guild of Musical Artists

Newspaper employees

See also
Newspaper Guild

Officials

The growing clout of black labor leaders. D. C. Lyons. il *Ebony* 44:40+ Je '89

Organizing activities

See Labor unions—Membership drives

Petroleum workers

Mexico

Bald man on a horse [C. Salinas de Gortari takes action against head of union] G. B. Lake. il *National Review* 41:38-9 Mr 10 '89

Robin Hood or robbing hood? [arrest of union official J. Hernández Galicia] G. D. Garcia. il por *Time* 133:39 Ja 23 '89

Salinas declares war on 'the maximum chief' of oil [union strongman J. Hernández Galicia] S. Baker. il *Business Week* p52 Ja 23 '89

Touching the 'untouchable' [C. Salinas de Gortari arrests head of oil 'workers' union] S. McGuire. il por *Newsweek* 113:30-1 Ja 23 '89

Membership drives

LABOR UNIONS—cont.
Police
The .44-caliber mouthpiece [San Antonio, Tex. police union head H. Flammia] W. P. Barrett. il *Forbes* 144:166 S 18 '89
Political activities
Jobs with justice? [right of workers not to fund union political activities] S. T. Mandel. *National Review* 41:17 Ag 18 '89
Parting shot: a labor leader blasts the Democrats. W. W. Winpisinger. il *The Progressive* 53:28-30 Jl '89
Postal employees
See also
National Post Office Mail Handlers Union
Printers
Great Britain
The bloke buckled [Britain's union bashing publisher E. Shah] E. McGlinn. il por *Forbes* 143:10 F 6 '89
Railroad workers
See also
United Transportation Union
Reporters and reporting
See Labor unions and the press
Restaurant employees
See also
Hotel Employees and Restaurant Employees International Union
Rubber industry workers
Brazil
Chronicle of a death foretold [murder of environmentalist C. Mendes Filho] M. Beck. il por *Newsweek* 113:62 Ja 9 '89
Defenders of the Amazon [cover story] S. Hecht and A. Cockburn. il *The Nation* 248:695-6+ My 22 '89
Extractive reserves in Brazilian Amazonia [rubber workers' proposal to fight deforestation] P. M. Fearnside. bibl f il map *BioScience* 39:387-93 Je '89
In memory of Chico Mendes [union leader and ecologist slain] J. D. Hair. il *International Wildlife* 19:30 Mr/Ap '89
Murder in the Amazon [union leader and ecologist C. Mendes Filho slain] J. Bierman. il por *Maclean's* 102:21 Ja 9 '89
Notes and comment [murder of environmentalist C. Mendes Filho] il *The New Yorker* 65:27-8 F 20 '89
Rain forest politics [discussion of May 22, 1989 article, Defenders of the Amazon] S. Hecht and A. Cockburn. *The Nation* 249:262+ S 18 '89
Whose hands will shape the future of the Amazon's green mansions? [plight of the rubber tappers; cover story] M. Parfit. bibl (p245) il maps *Smithsonian* 20:58-68+ N '89
Service industries
New believers [union organizers in Boston] B. McKibben. il *Mother Jones* 14:38-41+ Ap '89
Steel workers
See also
Independent Steelworkers Union
United Steelworkers of America
Teachers
See also
National Education Association of the United States
Who says professional ethics is dead? A response to Myron Lieberman [discussion of October 1988 article, Professional ethics in public education: an autopsy] M. Lieberman. *Phi Delta Kappan* 70:723-7 My '89
Telephone workers
Mexico
Salinas goes after another monster: the phone system. S. Baker. il *Business Week* p42 Mr 6 '89
Television workers
See also
National Association of Broadcast Employees and Technicians
Unions learn to go with the flow [automation] D. Bollier. il *Channels (New York, N.Y.: 1986)* 9:44-5 My '89
Tin miners
Bolivia
Tin miners' radio on the ropes. J. Slaughter. il *The Progressive* 53:11 F '89
Asia
Dreaming of the forty-hour week. D. MacShane. *The Nation* 248:658-60 My 15 '89
Brazil
Rural workers face murder. W. Steif. il *The Progressive* 53:26 Je '89
Korea (South)
Labor stirrings in Korea. J. West. il *The Progressive* 53:12 Mr '89
Latin America
See also
American Institute for Free Labor Development
Philippines
The AFL-CIO meddles in the Philippines. K. Scipes. il *The Progressive* 53:33 N '89
Poland
See also
Solidarity (Labor union)

United States
See Labor unions
LABOR UNIONS AND FOREIGN RELATIONS
See also
Asian American Free Labor Institute
LABOR UNIONS AND THE CHURCH *See* Church and labor
LABOR UNIONS AND THE PRESS
Beat the devil [coverage of the strike against Eastern and of the struggle in El Salvador] A. Cockburn. *The Nation* 248:438-9 Ap 3 '89
Their miners and ours (II) [poll indicating more people know about the Soviet coal miners strike than the Pittston strike] A. Cockburn. *The Nation* 249:410-11 O 16 '89
LABORATORIES
See also
AT&T Bell Labs
Bell Communications Research, Inc.
Connaught Biosciences Inc.
David Sarnoff Research Center
Environmental research laboratories
Jackson Laboratory (Bar Harbor, Me.)
Medical laboratories
National Technical Systems (Firm)
Nuclear research laboratories
Photographic laboratories
Stanford University. Near West Science Campus
Independent labs play key role in aerospace testing, verification. W. B. Scott. il *Aviation Week & Space Technology* 130:110-11 My 22 '89
Environmental aspects
The new midnight dumpers [illegal drug labs creating toxic waste in production of methamphetamine] G. Witkin. il *U.S. News & World Report* 106:57 Ja 9 '89
Fires and fire prevention
Fire devastates Jackson Lab [research mice destroyed] B. J. Culliton. il *Science* 244:767-8 My 19 '89
Wanted: $25 million for mouse house [rebuilding Jackson Lab after fire] B. J. Culliton. il *Science* 245:697-8 Ag 18 '89
LABORATORIES, GOVERNMENT
See also
Air Force Wright Aeronautical Laboratories
Argonne National Laboratory
Fermi National Accelerator Laboratory
Idaho National Engineering Laboratory
Lawrence Livermore National Laboratory
Los Alamos National Laboratory
Oak Ridge National Laboratory
Sandia National Laboratories
U.S. Army Laboratory Command
Profitable technology from Uncle Sam. R. Schneiderman. il map *High Technology Business* 9:26-30 F '89
LABORATORY ANIMALS
See also
Animal experimentation
Chimpanzees
Diseases—Animal models
Fish
Mammals
Mice
Monkeys
Rats
LABORATORY COMMAND (U.S.) *See* U.S. Army Laboratory Command
LABORATORY FOR EXPERIMENTAL MEDICINE AND SURGERY IN PRIMATES
Suffer the little chimps [J. Goodall bitten] A. Cockburn. *The Nation* 248:222-3 F 20 '89
LABORERS' INTERNATIONAL UNION OF NORTH AMERICA
Struggling for union democracy. D. Corn. il *The Nation* 248:48-50+ Ja 9-16 '89
LABOUR PARTY (GREAT BRITAIN)
Albert Mansbridge and a fresh coat of paint. D. Thompson. il pors *History Today* 39:7-9 Ag '89
Billy Bragg: of Labour and love. D. Fricke. por *Rolling Stone* p18 Ja 12 '89
The dockers who won [1889] J. Crossland. il *History Today* 39:9-10 O '89
Thatcherism isn't working [hope for N. Kinnook] N. Gelb. il *The New Leader* 72:8-9 Jl 10-24 '89
Unilateral disarmament—Labor's lost love. N. Moss. il por *The Bulletin of the Atomic Scientists* 45:9-11 O '89
LABRADOR (NFLD.)
See also
Fishing—Labrador (Nfld.)
LABRADOR RETRIEVERS
Another bend in the river. B. Tarrant. il *Field & Stream* 93:84+ Mr '89
LABRECQUE, THOMAS G., 1938-
Strengthening U.S. export performance [address, March 23, 1989] *Vital Speeches of the Day* 55:500-2 Je 1 '89
LABYRINTHS
Building a better mouse [robots that negotiate mazes; work of D. Otten] F. Hapgood. il *Omni (New York, N.Y.)* 12:22+ N '89

LABYRINTHS—cont.

Down and out in a daze and Links: working on the name chain. S. Morris. il *Omni (New York, N.Y.)* 11:96-7 My '89

Escaping the maze. D. Cater. il *Health (New York, N.Y.)* 21:64-9 Je '89

LAC MINERALS LTD.

The Pez is golden [Canadian Supreme Court ruling favors Corona Corp. in claim dispute] J. DeMont. il por *Maclean's* 102:39 Ag 21 '89

The tenderfoot and the claim jumper [Corona Corp. wins claim dispute with LAC Minerals] J. Cook. il *Forbes* 144:170+ O 2 '89

LACADRE, INC.

Lacadre to certify Avtec 400A aircraft. E. H. Phillips. *Aviation Week & Space Technology* 131:138 N 20 '89

LACAVERA, FRANK J.

about

Meet hourglass maker Frank LaCavera, one retiree who knows how to pass the time. il por *People Weekly* 31:121 Je 5 '89

LACE

You just cut out and stuff lace. il *Sunset (Central West edition)* 181:108 D '88

LACE (ARTIFICIAL SATELLITE)

SDI experiments set for launch in January. P. A. Gilmartin. il *Aviation Week & Space Technology* 131:35 S 11 '89

LACEFIELD, PATRICK

The generals don't repent. *Commonweal* 116:583-4 N 3 '89

The war continues. il *Commonweal* 116:197-9 Ap 7 '89

LACEY, STEPHEN

Scents and sensibility. il *House & Garden* 161:80+ Ap '89

LACHENBRUCH, DAVID

Cutting through the high-definition hype. il *Video* 12:118 Mr '89

A dumb idea whose time has come? il *Video* 13:106 Ap '89

Four video fancies that never took flight. il *Video* 13:116 Jl '89

HDTV inspires a ghostbusting spinoff. il *Video* 13:138 O '89

Screening the new TVs. il *New Choices for the Best Years* 29:86+ S '89

Video news. See issues of Radio-Electronics

Your stereophonic, digitized media center is waiting. il *TV Guide* 37:18-19 My 6-12 '89

LACHMAN, ANDREW

Where the sidewalk ends. il map *National Parks* 63:30-6 N/D '89

LACK, RICHARD

Classical realism: the other 20th century. il *Utne Reader* p59 Jl/Ag '89

LACKI, MELANIE

Watercolor page: winning color combinations. il por *American Artist* 53:44-7+ N '89

LACMA See Los Angeles County Museum of Art

LACOUTURE, JEAN

about

Champollion, a hero of the Enlightenment [interview] il por *The Unesco Courier* 42:4-9 O '89

LACQUER AND LACQUERING

Lacquer [ancient China] R. K. G. Temple. il *The Courier (Unesco)* 41:30-1 O '88

LACROIX, CHRISTIAN

about

Couture's future. C. Donovan. il pors *The New York Times Magazine* p48 Ag 27 '89

LACROIX, SUSAN

Jailing mothers for drug abuse. il *The Nation* 248:585-6+ My 1 '89

LACROSSE, PROFESSIONAL

See also

Major Indoor Lacrosse League

LACTAMASES

Inhibition of a class C β-lactamase by a specific phosphonate monoester. R. F. Pratt. bibl f il *Science* 246:917-19 N 17 '89

LACTATION

Don't shoot a wet doe [myths of shooting lactating mule deer] S. Curtis. il *Field & Stream* 94:88 O '89

Imagery boosts breast milk [research by Stephen D. K. Feher] *Science News* 135:71 F 4 '89

LACTIC ACID

Lactic acid [responsible for burning sensation during cycling] S. Johnson. *Bicycling* 30:60 Ag '89

LACTOBACILLUS ACIDOPHILUS MILK *See* Milk, Acidophilus

LACTOSE

Sweet solution to tainted poultry [use of lactose in drinking water; research by John R. DeLoach] *Science News* 135:349 Je 3 '89

LACTOSE INTOLERANCE

Controlling dairy food intolerance. *USA Today (Periodical)* 117:6 F '89

Milk for people who can't drink milk [Lactaid] il *Consumer Reports* 54:133 Mr '89

LACY, ALLEN, 1935-

Asters again. il *Organic Gardening* 36:60-4 N '89

Gardening books. il *The New York Times Book Review* 94:30 Je 11 '89

Green invaders. il por *Organic Gardening* 36:96 Mr '89

Our real roots. il *Organic Gardening* 36:73-6+ F '89

LACY, STEVE

about

An American in Paris. F. Davis. il por *The Atlantic* 264:120+ N '89

Lacy & Co. [discography] A. Lange. il por *Down Beat* 56:32 O '89

LADA (AUTOMOBILE) *See* Automobiles, Foreign

LADD FURNITURE INC.

Sitting pretty at Ladd. G. G. Marcial. *Business Week* p96 Je 12 '89

LADDERS

Easy attic access. R. Barnhart. il *Home Mechanix* 85:58+ F '89

The ladder of success [safety tips] il *Home Mechanix* 85:17 My '89

LADENIS, NICO

about

The River Cafe, Very Simply Nico, Chez Nico. J. Bainbridge. il por *Gourmet* 49:52+ N '89

LADIES' HOME JOURNAL

Editor's journal. M. Blyth. See issues of Ladies' Home Journal

LADIES PROFESSIONAL GOLF ASSOCIATION

Belles on the ball. P. Young. il *Maclean's* 102:68-9 Ap 10 '89

Find the golf here? J. Diaz. il *Sports Illustrated* 70:58-60+ F 13 '89

For women golfers, life in the rough. A. Engeler. il *The New York Times Magazine* p42+ O 1 '89

THE LADY IN QUESTION [drama] *See* Busch, Charles

LADY MACBETH OF MTSENSK [opera] *See* Shostakovich, Dmitrii Dmitrievich, 1906-1975

LADY OF THE CAMELLIAS [ballet] *See* Ballet reviews—Single works

LADYBIRDS

A bug you can take home to mother. il *U.S. News & World Report* 107:11 Ag 7 '89

The lady wears red. H. Middleton. il *Southern Living* 24:46+ My '89

LADYBUGS *See* Ladybirds

LAFALCE, JOHN J.

Should the Congress adopt the "Textile and Apparel Trade Act of 1987"? [excerpts from address, September 16, 1987] *Congressional Digest* 68:27+ Ja '89

LAFAYETTE, MARIE JOSEPH PAUL YVES ROCH GILBERT DU MOTIER, MARQUIS DE, 1757-1834

about

Lafayette: man and monument. A. E. Ledes. il *Antiques* 136:58+ Jl '89

Collectibles

Lafayette, you are here! S. Sifton. il pors *American Heritage* 40:46-51 Jl/Ag '89

LAFF, EUGENE

about

A penny-stock scam. C. Friday and J. Hammer. il por *Newsweek* 113:51 My 1 '89

LAFFER, ARTHUR B.

(jt. auth) See Gray, Arthur, Jr., and Laffer, Arthur B.

LAFFOLEY, PAUL

about

Paul Laffoley: Kent Fine Art. E. Heartney. il *Art News* 88:166-7 D '89

LAFLECHE, HEIDI J.

Lunch box [cover story] il por *Antiques & Collecting Hobbies* 94:24-5+ Jl '89

LAFLEUR, GUY, 1951-

about

Guy Lafleur, hockey's faded flower, blooms anew in New York. A. Richman. il pors *People Weekly* 31:57+ F 6 '89

LAFONTAINE, MARIE-JO

about

Marie Jo Lafontaine at Jack Shainman. B. Adams. *Art in America* 77:209-10 O '89

LAFONTANT, JEWEL S.

about

Atty. Jewel Lafontant weds international businessman in D.C. church ceremony. il pors *Jet* 77:43 D 25 '89-Ja 1 '90

Lafontant oversees refugee affairs in new State post. il por *Jet* 76:9 Ag 7 '89

LAFRANCE, CLAUDE

about

Transport Canada official resigns as Gander controversy intensifies. D. Hughes. *Aviation Week & Space Technology* 130:33 Mr 27 '89

LAGARDÈRE, JEAN-LUC

about

Jean-Luc Lagardere. il *The Nation* 248:818 Je 12 '89

LAGERFELD, KARL

about

Couture's future. C. Donovan. il pors *The New York Times Magazine* p48 Ag 27 '89

Facing up to the 90's. L. Wells. il por *The New York Times Magazine* p66-7 S 24 '89

LAGERFELD, KARL—about—*cont.*

In a clash of symbols, Chanel's top model falls from the runway. M. H. J. Farrell. il pors *People Weekly* 32:51+ Ag 14 '89

Petit palais. A. L. Talley. il por *Vogue* 179:390-1 Ap '89

Royalist leanings. G. Howell. il *Vogue* 179:380-9+ Ap '89

LAGNIAPPE (FIRM)

Saga of a business start-up (I). L. Washer. il pors *Working Woman* 14:45-6+ D '89

LAGRENE, BIRELI

about

Bireli Lagrene. B. Milkowski. il por *Down Beat* 56:14 My '89

LAGROUW, CORNEL

about

Notes and comment. *The New Yorker* 65:29-31 Ap 3 '89

LAGUNA VERDE NUCLEAR POWER PLANT (MEXICO)

See Nuclear power plants—Mexico

LAHTI, CHRISTINE

about

After a feminist journey Heidi would envy, Christine Lahti soars as a working mom. M. H. J. Farrell. il pors *People Weekly* 32:85-6+ D 4 '89

LAHUE, R. S., AND OTHERS

DNA mismatch correction in a defined system. bibl f il *Science* 245:160-4 Jl 14 '89

LAHUSEN, RICHARD G.

(jt. auth) *See* Iverson, Richard M., and LaHusen, Richard G.

LAI, MICHAEL M. C.

(jt. auth) *See* Wu, Huey-Nan, and Lai, Michael M. C.

LAIBINIS, PAUL E., AND OTHERS

Orthogonal self-assembled monolayers: alkanethiols on gold and alkane carboxylic acids on alumina. bibl f il *Science* 245:845-7 Ag 25 '89

LAIDLAW, MARC

His powder'd wig, his crown of thornes [fiction] il *Omni (New York, N.Y.)* 11:50-2+ S '89

LAIDLAW (R. A.) CENTER/BETTY OLIPHANT THEATRE (TORONTO, ONT.) *See* R. A. Laidlaw Center/Betty Oliphant Theatre (Toronto, Ont.)

LAIMANEE, SUWAN *See* Suwan Laimanee

LAINE, CLEO

about

Two new sides where Sondheim shines. R. Hoffman. il por *Business Week* p120 Mr 27 '89

LAIRD, JEAN E., 1930-

Over-the-counter addictions. *Better Homes and Gardens* 67:40+ S '89

LAISE, C. STEVENS

A. J. Davis and American classicism [cover story] bibl f il por *Antiques* 136:1320-33 D '89

LAISSEZ FAIRE *See* Free enterprise

LAITY

Catholic Church

Beautiful feet [lay apostolate] H. Fehren. *U.S. Catholic* 54:39-41 Ap '89

Catholics won't settle for half a Mass [priestless liturgies; with readers' comments] T. Unsworth. *U.S. Catholic* 54:13-19 Je '89

A Church without priests [San Patricio's, Throckmorton, Tex.] A. G. Mojtabai. il *The New York Times Magazine* p16-17+ D 24 '89

Confessions of a lay collaborator [lay-Jesuit collaboration; cover story] M. R. Carey. *America* 160:500-2 My 27 '89

Confessions of a modern Catholic layman [cover story] M. Finley. *America* 160:366-8 Ap 22 '89

God is my client. T. J. Reuland. il *Commonweal* 116:527-9 O 6 '89

Guidelines for preaching by the laity: another step backward? J. A. Wallace. *America* 161:139-41 S 9-16 '89

I wondered if I would pass the test. S. H. Johnson. il *Commonweal* 116:208-10 Ap 7 '89

Lay Catholics: are the silent partners finding their voice? M. J. Cook. il *U.S. Catholic* 54:34-9 Ja '89

Lay leadership in the 1990's [cover story] E. C. Sellner. *America* 161:133-8 S 9-16 '89

Lecturing (sigh!) the laity [report from 1987 synod] il *Commonweal* 116:132-3 Mr 10 '89

Meeting God in others. K. P. Cecala. il *Commonweal* 116:400-2 Jl 14 '89

Our task is to create worlds. E. Antonucci. il *Commonweal* 116:334-5 Je 2 '89

Priestless rites: Catholic bishops okay services led by nuns and lay people. il *Time* 134:98 N 20 '89

Standing in the way of worship. P. E. Dinter. il *Commonweal* 116:367-70 Je 16 '89

Standing in the way of worship [discussion of June 16, 1989 article] P. E. Dinter. *Commonweal* 116:495+ S 22 '89

When laity lead. J. Figueroa. *Commonweal* 116:470-1 S 8 '89

Why settle for Communion? [in the absence of priests] G. Huck. *Commonweal* 116:37-9 Ja 27 '89

You and your parish deserve more from each other [interview with C. Thero] por *U.S. Catholic* 54:20-7 Ag '89

Preaching

See Preaching

LAKE, ALICE, 1916-

Simple steps to a good night's sleep. il *Reader's Digest* 134:33-4+ F '89

LAKE, GEORGE BYRAM

Bald man on a horse. il *National Review* 41:38-9 Mr 10 '89

LAKE CHAMPLAIN

Heyday of the horse ferry [teamboat discovered] D. G. Shomette. il map *National Geographic* 176:548-56 O '89

LAKE CONSTANCE

Gourmet holidays: Lake Constance. L. Langseth-Christensen. il map *Gourmet* 49:60-5+ Je '89

LAKE DISTRICT (ITALY)

Description and travel

Italian Lake District. D. Simanaitis. il map *Road & Track* 40:80+ My '89

LAKE ECOLOGY

Lake Tahoe: preserving a fragile ecosystem [cover story] C. R. Goldman. bibl f il map *Environment* 31:6-11+ S '89

Playa lakes: prairie wetlands of the Southern High Plains. E. G. Bolen and others. bibl f il map *BioScience* 39:615-23 O '89

Protecting water clarity in Lake George [role of Nitella] R. Stross and B. Rottier. il *The Conservationist* 44:44-6 S/O '89

X-ray microanalysis of leaf-litter decomposition in lakes [scanning microscope] J. A. Perry and others. bibl f il *BioScience* 39:260-3 Ap '89

LAKE ERIE

An alien invasion [zebra mussels] A. Steacy. *Maclean's* 102:97 N 6 '89

Showdown at mussel beach [zebra mussel invasion] G. Cowley. il *Newsweek* 114:66 N 20 '89

Hunting

See Hunting—Great Lakes region

LAKE FISHING *See* Fishing

LAKE FOREST (ILL.)

Historic houses, sites, etc.

Prairie in flower [Ragdale estate designed by H. Shaw] D. G. Lowe. il *House & Garden* 161:68-75+ Ag '89

LAKE GEORGE (N.Y.)

Protecting water clarity in Lake George [role of Nitella] R. Stross and B. Rottier. il *The Conservationist* 44:44-6 S/O '89

LAKE GEORGE OPERA FESTIVAL *See* Music festivals—New York (State)

LAKE HOUSES *See* Lakeside architecture

LAKE LANIER (GA.)

Summer splash. M. Benson. il *Motor Boating & Sailing* 164:54-7 Ag '89

LAKE LOUISE (ALTA.)

Of moose and men. J. Maxwell. il *Esquire* 112:50+ N '89

Royal Canadian. N. Howe. il *Skiing* 42:122-6+ D '89

LAKE MICHIGAN

High spirits [Cruisers 36 Esprit] D. Fales. il *Motor Boating & Sailing* 164:56-9+ D '89

Fisheries

See Fisheries—Great Lakes region

Water pollution

See Water pollution—Great Lakes

LAKE NYOS (CAMEROON)

Nyos, the killer lake, may be coming back. R. A. Kerr. il *Science* 244:1541-2 Je 30 '89

LAKE OF THE WOODS

Lake of the Woods. E. L. Rogers. il *Outdoor Life* 183:94-6+ Ap '89

LAKE PLACID OLYMPICS, 1980 *See* Olympic Games—1980—Winter Olympics

LAKE POLLUTION *See* Water pollution

LAKE POWELL (UTAH AND ARIZ.)

See also

Rainbow Bridge (Utah and Ariz.)

LAKE SAINT CLAIR (MICH. AND ONT.)

An alien invasion [zebra mussels] A. Steacy. *Maclean's* 102:97 N 6 '89

LAKE SENECA (N.Y.) *See* Seneca Lake (N.Y.)

LAKE SUPERIOR

See also

Silver Bay State Park (Minn.)

LAKE TAHOE (CALIF. AND NEV.)

Lake Tahoe: preserving a fragile ecosystem [cover story] C. R. Goldman. bibl f il map *Environment* 31:6-11+ S '89

LAKE TAHOE REGION (CALIF. AND NEV.)

See also

Architecture, Domestic—Lake Tahoe region (Calif. and Nev.)

Environmental policy—Lake Tahoe region (Calif. and Nev.)

Resorts—Lake Tahoe region (Calif. and Nev.)

Skiing—Lake Tahoe region (Calif. and Nev.)

Description and travel

The four faces of Tahoe. C. Canter. il map *Travel Holiday* 171:88-95 Mr '89

LAKE TROUT FISHING *See* Trout fishing
LAKE WORTH (FLA.)
Galleries and museums
See also
Lannan Museum (Lake Worth, Fla.)
Palm Beach Community College. Lannon Gallery
LAKES
See also
Great Lakes
Playas
Water pollution
Acid rain: lowdown on health of lakes [research by David W. Schindler] J. Raloff. *Science News* 135:311 My 20 '89
The variety of lakes in the world is vast, but they all have certain characteristics in common. M. Hill. il *Earth Science* 42:37 Fall '89
Temperature
Temperature measurements in carbonatite lava lakes and flows from Oldoinyo Lengai, Tanzania. M. Krafft and J. Keller. bibl f il *Science* 245:168-70 Jl 14 '89
Water temperature cycle. B. Volkart. il *Field & Stream* 94:34+ D '89
Arizona
See also
Peck's Lake (Ariz.)
California
See also
Mono Lake (Calif.)
East Africa
See also
Project PROBE
Snippets from Nyanja chronicles. B. Rosendahl. il por map *Sea Frontiers* 35:292-302 S/O '89
Michigan
See also
Mack Lake (Mich.)
Bridges. J. Dennis. il *Audubon* 91:46-7 Jl '89
Minnesota
See also
Mille Lacs Lake (Minn.)
Mississippi
See also
Pipes Lake (Miss.)
New York (State)
See also
Seneca Lake (N.Y.)
Acid highs and lows in Adirondack lakes. J. Raloff. *Science News* 135:165 Mr 18 '89
Ice harvesting—the way it was. B. S. Newton. il *The Conservationist* 43:24-5 Ja/F '89
Pennsylvania
Damaged lakes can be rescued [use of limestone; research by Patricia Bradt] il *USA Today (Periodical)* 117:2 Je '89
LAKES IN ART
Storm beneath the calm [View on a lake in Copenhagen by C. Købke] Sir M. Levey. il por *Art News* 88:79-80 F '89
LAKESIDE ARCHITECTURE
Amelia's island [weekend lakeside retreat owned by A. Fatt] S. Nelson. il pors *Working Woman* 14:198-202 S '89
Contemporary traditions on Lake Tahoe [lodge remodeled by Robert V. Arrigoni and decorated by Charles Pfister] J. Chatfield-Taylor. il *Architectural Digest* 46:270-5+ O '89
Lively cottage for the weekend [Lake Pontchartrain; cover story] L. Hallam. il *Southern Living* 24:106-7 Jl '89
LAL, RATNESHWAR, AND FRIEDLANDER, MICHAEL J.
Gating of retinal transmission by afferent eye position and movement signals. bibl f il *Science* 243:93-6 Ja 6 '89
LALANNE, CLAUDE
about
Claude and François-Xavier Lalanne at Marisa del Re. L. Campbell. il *Art in America* 77:166-7 F '89
LALANNE, FRANÇOIS-XAVIER, 1924-
about
Claude and François-Xavier Lalanne at Marisa del Re. L. Campbell. il *Art in America* 77:166-7 F '89
LALIBERTE, RICHARD
Unguarded moments [cover story] il *Health (New York, N.Y.)* 21:52-7 Ag '89
LALIQUE GLASS
Dancescape [Lalique "Suzanne" statuette inspired by dance] L. Garafola. il *Dance Magazine* 63:8 Ag '89
LALLINGER, MANUELA VON CHIELANSKI- *See* Chielanski-Lallinger, Manuela von
LAM, DAVID
about
A watchdog for the Asian connection. P. C. Newman. il *Maclean's* 102:35 Ap 24 '89
LAMA (TONY) COMPANY *See* Tony Lama Company
LAMANNA, DEAN
(jt. auth) *See* Sirkin, Elliott, and Lamanna, Dean

LAMAR, BERT
about
Jake and the Rad Man. D. White. il pors *Skiing* 42:238-40+ D '89
LAMAR UNIVERSITY. COLLEGE OF EDUCATION
Attracting bright adolescents to teaching careers [program developed by Lamar University and Beaumont School District, Tex.] M. J. Cooper and others. il *Phi Delta Kappan* 70:566-7 Mr '89
LAMARRE, DANIEL, AND OTHERS
The MHC-binding and gp120-binding functions of CD4 are separable. bibl f il *Science* 245:743-6 Ag 18 '89
LAMAS
See also
Dalai Lama XIV, 1935-
LAMAUTE, DENISE
Easing your tax problems. *Essence* 19:105+ Ap '89
LAMB, DAVID
about
Did Refco help take Uncle Sam to the cleaners? D. Greising. il *Business Week* p33-4 O 2 '89
LAMB, DENIS
EC project 1992: the dynamics of change [address, September 9, 1988] *Department of State Bulletin* 89:31-5 F '89
LAMB, JOHN M.
(jt. auth) *See* Rauf, Tariq, and Lamb, John M.
LAMB, KEVIN
Ditka's Bad News Bears: what's next? [cover story] il *Sport (New York, N.Y.)* 80:66-73 Ja '89
LAMB, RAEL
about
Martin [ballet] Reviews
American Visions il pors 4:34-9 D '89. D. Moore
LAMB, YANICK RICE
Lighting the way for youth. il *Black Enterprise* 19:205-7 F '89
Rack 'em up. il *Black Enterprise* 20:115-16+ D '89
Romancing the isle. il *Black Enterprise* 19:116 My '89
Sentimental returns. il *Black Enterprise* 20:79-80+ D '89
LAMB (MEAT)
See also
Cooking—Meat
LAMB STEW *See* Stew
LAMBERG, LYNNE
Voyeurs in the kingdom of sleep. il *Health (New York, N.Y.)* 21:66-9 Jl '89
LAMBERT, DAVID D., AND OTHERS
Rhenium-osmium and samarium-neodymium isotopic systematics of the Stillwater Complex. bibl f il *Science* 244:1169-74 Je 9 '89
LAMBERT, MARY
about
Pet sematary [film] Reviews
People Weekly il 31:13 My 15 '89. R. Novak
LAMBERT, PHYLLIS, 1927-
about
A capital of design. P. Young. il por *Maclean's* 102:54-5 My 22 '89
The fire behind a fight for livable cities. D. Jenish. il por *Maclean's* 102:18-19 D 25 '89
Hard-hatted woman. D. Brenner. il pors *House & Garden* 161:38+ My '89
LAMBERTSON, DAVID F.
Burma: political situation and human rights [statement, March 2, 1989] map *Department of State Bulletin* 89:40-3 My '89
Future prospects for the Philippines [statement, March 7, 1989] *Department of State Bulletin* 89:43-9 My '89
Update on Cambodia [statement, March 1, 1989] map *Department of State Bulletin* 89:37-40 My '89
LAMBORGHINI (AUTOMOBILE) *See* Sports cars
LAMBRECHT, DORA
(jt. auth) *See* Lambrecht, Frank L., and Lambrecht, Dora
LAMBRECHT, FRANK L., AND LAMBRECHT, DORA
The Seychelles (Treasure) Islands. il map *Focus (New York, N.Y.: 1950)* 39:35-6+ Spr '89
LAMBS
Peddero. A. Friedman. il *Country Journal* 16:50-5 F '89
LAMINAR FLOW
Langley uses Learjet to study wave disturbances in laminar flow. il *Aviation Week & Space Technology* 130:270-1 Je 12 '89
LAMINATED CONSTRUCTION
See also
Delamination
LAMINATED GLASS
New products: laminated glass. il *Architectural Record* 177:116-17 Ap '89
LAMINATED METALS
Metal laminate. il *Popular Mechanics* 166:121-2 Ap '89
LAMINATED PLASTICS
Tech tops [FormStone, ARP and Craftwood laminates] T. O. Bakke. il *Popular Science* 235:88+ D '89
LAMINATED WOOD
Tech tops [FormStone, ARP and Craftwood laminates] T. O. Bakke. il *Popular Science* 235:88+ D '89

LAMING, JAMES
about
The mysterious binoculars. il *Sports Illustrated* 71:24 N 20 '89
LAMM, HARVEY H.
about
Counterattack. S. N. Chakravarty. il *Forbes* 144:56+ N 13 '89
LAMM, RICHARD D.
Confronting minority failure [address, January 26, 1989] *Vital Speeches of the Day* 55:433-5 My 1 '89
Lawyers and lawyering [address, October 1, 1988] *Vital Speeches of the Day* 55:206-9 Ja 15 '89
LAMME, LINDA LEONARD
Whole-language instruction: teaching authorship. *The Education Digest* 55:46-50 N '89
LAMONT, BARBARA
about
Broadcast news. L. Gite. il pors *Black Enterprise* 20:100-3+ D '89
LAMOTTE, BERNARD
about
The man upstairs. W. Goodman. il pors *New York* 22:54-9 Je 19 '89
LAMPERT, MURRAY A., 1921-1988
about
Obituary
Physics Today por 42 pt1:84 Ag '89. A. Rose and others
LAMPREDI, AURELIO, 1917-1989
about
Obituary
Road & Track por 41:45 D '89. J. Thompson
LAMPRON, VELNA
Bluebirds are funny. il *Southern Living* 24:118 Ap '89
LAMPS
See also
Electric lamps
Tiffany lamps
Burning the midnight oil. R. Kimber. il *Country Journal* 16:110-13 Mr/Ap '89
Collectors and collecting
Brass student lamps and night lamps. A. G. McDonald. bibl il *Antiques & Collecting Hobbies* 93:20-3 Ja '89
LAMPS (LIGHT AIRBORNE MULTI-PURPOSE SYSTEM) HELICOPTERS *See* Helicopters—Military use
LAMPSHADES
Cover a shade with fabric. il *Southern Living* 24:170 Mr '89
LAMPSON, BERT C., AND OTHERS
Reverse transcriptase in a clinical strain of Escherichia coli: production of branched RNA-linked msDNA. bibl f il *Science* 243:1033-8 F 24 '89
LAMY, MICHELE
about
Los Angeles à la mode. M. Rochlin. il por *Harper's Bazaar* 122:50 N '89
LANAI (HAWAII)
Description and travel
Hawaii's adventure islands: Lanai and Molokai. il maps *Sunset (Central West edition)* 182:68-73 F '89
Planning a trip to Lanai or Molokai? il map *Sunset (Central West edition)* 182:52-3 F '89
LANCASHIRE (ENGLAND)
History
Threads of Lancashire history [Young Historians Scheme's History Day] D. Gregory. il *History Today* 39:4-5 O '89
LANCASTER, CAROL
Economic restructuring in Sub-Saharan Africa. *Current History* 88:213-16+ My '89
LANCASTER, DON
Hardware hacker. See issues of Radio-Electronics beginning January 1988
LANCASTER, LYNNE C.
(jt. auth) See Rapoza, Rita S., and Lancaster, Lynne C.
LANCASTER, NANCY
about
The House of Lancaster [excerpt from Colefax & Fowler] C. Jones. il pors *House & Garden* 161:188-95+ N '89
LANCASTER COUNTY (PA.)
Description and travel
In country [Amish country] il map *Seventeen* 48:182-8 S '89
Lancaster County [cover story] S. Wilding. il *Gourmet* 49:112-17+ N '89
LANCIA (AUTOMOBILE) *See* Automobiles, Foreign
LAND, LESLIE
And so to bed. il *The New York Times Magazine* p59-60 Ap 23 '89
Down East blues. il *Life* 12:41-2 S '89
Loafing around. il *The New York Times Magazine* p73-4 S 24 '89
LAND, THOMAS
The drowning delta. *World Press Review* 36:64-5 N '89
LAND
See also
Burning of land
Public lands
Real estate business

Real property
Reclamation of land
Wetlands
Land. See occasional issues of Successful Farming
Prices
See Land values
Purchasing
See Real estate investment
Taxation
See Real property—Taxation
Iowa
Iowa farmland up 20% in a year. R. Fee. *Successful Farming* 87:6 mid-F '89
Middle Western States
Midwest land up 3% for quarter, 11% for year [farmland] R. Fee. *Successful Farming* 87:10 Ap '89
Price explosion continues [farmland] R. Fee. *Successful Farming* 87:14 mid-Mr '89
LAND, POSTING OF *See* Trespass
LAND AND WATER CONSERVATION FUND GRANT ASSISTANCE PROGRAM (U.S.)
Finding funding for parks. E. Seaborg. il *Sierra* 74:30-2 My/Je '89
LAND-ATMOSPHERE INTERACTION *See* Soil-atmosphere interaction
THE LAND BEFORE TIME [film] See Motion picture reviews—Single works
LAND BUYING *See* Real estate investment
LAND DEVELOPMENT BUSINESS *See* Real estate business
LAND INSTITUTE (KAN.)
Back to Eden [work of W. Jackson; cover story; with editorial comment] E. Eisenberg. il por *The Atlantic* 264:6, 57-9+ N '89
Breadbasket ecology [work of W. Jackson] D. Hand. il map por *American Health* 8:66-8 S '89
Prophet of the prairie [work of W. Jackson] J. R. Luoma. il pors map *Audubon* 91:54-60 N '89
LAND MANAGEMENT BUREAU (U.S.) *See* United States. Bureau of Land Management
LAND PLANNING *See* Land utilization
LAND RECLAMATION *See* Reclamation of land
LAND REFORM
Farm futures [adaptation of 1987 address] D. Terry. il *Mother Jones* 14:6-8 O '89
Brazil
Assassination in Brazil [land reform activist J. F. Alevino] B. Tyson. *The Christian Century* 106:384-7 Ap 12 '89
El Salvador
The colony of El Salvador. T. Bethell. il *The American Spectator* 22:11-13 My '89
Mexico
History
The land question at Aguascalientes. *The New Republic* 201 [Reprint v1]:10-11 N 6 '89 [N 7 '14]
Soviet Union
Comrade Gorbachev's leap in the dark. *National Review* 41:13-14 Ap 21 '89
Gorby's farm reform a hard row to hoe. por *U.S. News & World Report* 106:9-10 Mr 27 '89
New masters of the land. il *Time* 133:53 Mr 27 '89
LAND RUSH, 1889 *See* Oklahoma—History—Land Rush, 1889
LAND SALES BUSINESS *See* Real estate business
LAND SLIDES *See* Landslides
LAND SPECULATION *See* Real estate investment
LAND SPEED RECORDS
Call me Speedo [W. Stakes' Sonic Wind] B. Weber. il por *The New York Times Magazine* p94 Ap 9 '89
Freud's greatest adventure: full moon over Bonneville [G. Freudenberger sets 750 class land speed record for motorcycles] K. Vreeke. il pors *Cycle* 40:65-7+ F '89
The glory and the dream [driver F. Lockhart dies attempting to set land speed record in 1928] J. A. Wren. il por *Road & Track* 40:106-7 My '89
High-speed hauler [record set at Bonneville in a GMC S-15 Club Coupe] L. Frank. il *Popular Mechanics* 166:52-3 D '89
King of the salt [D. Vesco] P. Lyons. il pors *Cycle* 40:48-51+ D '89
LAND TAX *See* Real property—Taxation
LAND TENURE
See also
Hawaiians—Land tenure
Hispanic Americans—Land tenure
Homestead law
Indians of North America—Land tenure
Land reform
Peasantry
Real property
Trespass
International aspects
See also
Native peoples—Land tenure
Barbuda (Antigua and Barbuda)
Ancient rights [controversy over land rights and development] R. Coram. *The New Yorker* 64:76-86+ F 6 '89
LAND TITLES
See also
Adverse possession

LAND TITLES—See also—*cont.*
  Deeds
  This land is my land . . . or is it? D. Fanning. il *Forbes* 143:62 Ja 23 '89
LAND TRUSTS
  See also
    Texas Pacific Land Trust
  Preserving land through local land trusts. C. Elfring. il *BioScience* 39:71-4 F '89
  Protect your view and get a tax break, too [conservation easements] G. Morgenson. il *Forbes* 144:276-7 O 16 '89
    Scotland
    See also
      John Muir Trust
LAND USE *See* Land utilization
LAND UTILIZATION
  See also
    Land trusts
    Shore protection
    Soil conservation
  Death and taxes. G. Reiger. il *Field & Stream* 93:18+ Ap '89
    Laws and regulations
    See also
      Zoning
  Stop the barrister bullies [land use suits brought against local government] P. A. A. Berle. il *Audubon* 91:8 Mr '89
  This land is whose land? [public land mismanagement] E. T. Smith. il *Business Week* p48-51 Ap 24 '89
    Florida
  Florida's great red tape swamp. J. Drummond. il *Forbes* 144:193+ O 30 '89
    New York (State)
  For sale [Adirondack Park; cover story] J. H. Kunstler. il *The New York Times Magazine* p22-5+ Je 18 '89
  A wild island of hope [Adirondack Park] J. G. Mitchell. il *Wilderness* 53:42-51 Fall '89
LAND VALUES
  See also
    Real property—Valuation
  Bill Helming. B. Helming. il *Successful Farming* 87:17 mid-Mr '89
  Buyers and sellers cautious. R. Fee. *Successful Farming* 87:18 D '89
  Iowa farmland up 20% in a year. R. Fee. *Successful Farming* 87:6 mid-F '89
  Midwest land up 3% for quarter, 11% for year [farmland] R. Fee. *Successful Farming* 87:10 Ap '89
  National survey shows land up. R. Fee. *Successful Farming* 87:10 Ag '89
  Price explosion continues [farmland] R. Fee. *Successful Farming* 87:14 mid-Mr '89
    Japan
  After Tokyo, all the world's a bargain [interview with A. Downs] J. Egan. il *U.S. News & World Report* 106:58-9 Ja 30 '89
LANDAU, LEV DAVIDOVICH, 1908-1968
    about
  Landau's attitude toward physics and physicists. V. L. Ginzburg. bibl f il pors *Physics Today* 42:54-61 My '89
  Reminiscences of Landau. I. M. Khalatnikov. il pors *Physics Today* 42:34-41 My '89
LANDAU, MARTIN
    about
  From heavy to Everyman. C. McGuigan. il por *Newsweek* 114:67 O 16 '89
LANDAU, SAUL
  After Castro [cover story] il por *Mother Jones* 14:20-6+ Jl/Ag '89
LANDAU, SONIA
  Toward a global high-definition TV production standard [statement, March 8, 1989] *Department of State Bulletin* 89:48-51 Je '89
LANDAU, TERRY
  No fooling [excerpt from About faces; cover story] il *Health (New York, N.Y.)* 21:49-51+ My '89
LANDAU, YEHEZKEL
  Blessing both Jew and Palestinian: a religious Zionist view. *The Christian Century* 106:1196-9 D 20-27 '89
LANDAUER, ROLF
  Can we switch by control of quantum mechanical transmission? bibl f *Physics Today* 42:119+ O '89
LANDER, DONALD
    about
  The man for the job. G. W. Taylor. il por *Maclean's* 102:36 O 9 '89
LANDERS, ANN
    about
  Living by the letter [interview] E. Taylor. il pors *Time* 134:62-3 Ag 21 '89
  Mr. Lonelyhearts. J. Zaslow. il *The New York Times Magazine* p59-60+ O 29 '89
LANDES, DAVID S.
  Rich country, poor country [cover story] il *The New Republic* 201:23-7 N 20 '89

LANDFILLS, SANITARY *See* Sanitary landfills
LANDI, ANN
  When having everything isn't enough [cover story] il *Psychology Today* 23:27-30 Ap '89
LANDING FEES, AIRPORT *See* Airports—Fees
LANDING GEAR, AIRPLANE *See* Airplanes, Jet—Landing gear; Airplanes, Military—Landing gear
LANDING OF AIRPLANES *See* Airplanes—Landing; Airplanes, Freight—Landing; Airplanes, Jet—Landing
LANDING SYSTEMS, MICROWAVE *See* Microwave landing systems
LANDIS, JAMES MCCAULEY, 1899-1964
    about
  Men who made the rules. P. Baida. il *American Heritage* 40:18+ F '89
LANDIS, JOHN
    about
  Coming to America [film] Reviews
    Video il 13:16-17 Je '89. J. Bernard
    Video il 13:73 My '89. R. Gehr
LANDLORD AND TENANT
  See also
    Eviction
    Farm tenancy
  HUD Sec. Kemp visits as Chicago gives control of housing unit to tenants. il por *Jet* 76:26 My 29 '89
  Pity the New York landlord [rent control] W. Tucker. il *The American Spectator* 22:19-22 F '89
  "The tenants could do a better job of managing" [Chicago housing project] M. M. McDowell. il *Black Enterprise* 19:16 Jl '89
  Tenants' rights movement presses for quality affordable housing. J. Atlas and P. Dreier. il *Utne Reader* p66-7 My/Je '89
  When tenants take charge [J. Kemp's plan] B. Turque. il por *Newsweek* 114:44 N 27 '89
LANDLORD BLUES [film] *See* Motion picture reviews—Single works
LANDMARKS, HISTORIC *See* Historic houses, sites, etc.
LANDOLT, ARLO W.
    about
  The first winter. il por *Sky and Telescope* 77:600 Je '89
LANDRIÁN, NICOLÁS GUILLÉN *See* Guillén Landrián, Nicolás
LANDRY, DONALD W., AND OTHERS
  Purification and reconstitution of chloride channels from kidney and trachea. bibl f il *Science* 244:1469-72 Je 23 '89
LANDRY, TOM
    about
  'A chapter closed'. W. O. Johnson. il pors *Sports Illustrated* 70:22-4+ Mr 6 '89
  Fired after 29 years as coach of the Cowboys, Tom Landry drops his bland, stoic mask. P. Axthelm. por *People Weekly* 31:44-5 Mr 13 '89
  Once more, with feeling. il por *Sports Illustrated* 70:14 My 1 '89
LANDS' END, INC.
  Big picture strategy. R. Addis. il *Forbes* 143:70+ Ja 9 '89
  The chic is in the mail. B. Rudolph. il *Time* 134:74-5 Jl 17 '89
  A mail-order romance: Lands' End courts unseen customers. S. Caminiti. il *Fortune* 119:44-5 Mr 13 '89
LANDSAT SATELLITES *See* Artificial satellites—Earth sciences use
LANDSCAPE ARCHITECTURE
    See also
      Farm Beautiful! (Project)
      Follies (Architecture)
      Miniature landscapes
      Sand in landscape architecture
      Water in landscape architecture
  D-I-Y Landscaping Contest: the winners. D. Colby. il *Home Mechanix* 86:47-58+ Mr '89
  Entry is now more spacious, attractive. il *Southern Living* 24:95 D '89
  Face-lift for a fifties house. il *Southern Living* 24:62 N '89
  Garden architecture [special section] il *Flower and Garden* 33:39-44+ Jl/Ag '89
  Landscaping blooms in Raleigh. il *Southern Living* 24:122 My '89
  Living outdoors and loving it [home of Carol and Steve Higgins] J. A. McKeon. il *Better Homes and Gardens* 67:65-70 Je '89
  Nothing timid about it [Irvine, Calif.] il *Sunset (Central West edition)* 182:178-9 My '89
  Now this garden's on the level. il *Southern Living* 24:80-1 Ap '89
  Privacy, parking, and a side-yard patio. il *Sunset (Central West edition)* 183:86-7 Ag '89
  Putt, swim, play paddle tennis, relax . . . here's a garden that was planned for action. il *Sunset (Central West edition)* 182:218-19 Ap '89
  They started with just a lawn, a wall, and a steep bank. il *Sunset (Central West edition)* 183:88-9 S '89

LANDSCAPE ECOLOGY
Phenomena, comment and notes [A. Leopold] J. P. Wiley, Jr. il por *Smithsonian* 20:38+ N '89
LANDSCAPE GARDENING
See also
Decks, patios, terraces, etc.
Garden borders
Garden steps
Ground cover plants
Hillside gardens and gardening
Lawns
Miniature landscapes
Shrubs
Xeriscaping
Artificial nature: the synthetic landscape of the future [cover story] R. Vick. il por *The Futurist* 23:29-32 Jl/Ag '89
Charleston charm, minimal maintenance. il *Southern Living* 24:50 Jl '89
Designing your own landscape. bibl il *Sunset (Central West edition)* 182:214+ Ap '89
Eight months of weekends. il *Sunset (Central West edition)* 182:100-3 Ap '89
Expanding their Denver garden gave them more space for outdoor living. il *Sunset (Central West edition)* 182:220-1 Je '89
Foundation plantings. K. Childers. il *The Family Handyman* 39:60-2 Jl/Ag '89
Gardens that say welcome [entry garden] R. W. Strickland. il *Southern Living* 24:94-7 My '89
Green geometry [gardens at the Bastille Opera designed by P. Cribier] M. K. Griswold. il por *House & Garden* 161:46+ Jl '89
If you live in wildfire country [California] il *Sunset (Central West edition)* 183:96+ S '89
Living tapestry in Santa Fe. il *Sunset (Central West edition)* 182:90-1 Je '89
No longer in a fishbowl. il *Southern Living* 24:60 O '89
One garden, many moods [New Orleans] R. W. Strickland. il *Southern Living* 24:88-90 Je '89
Side yards: useful places, not wasted spaces. R. W. Strickland. il *Southern Living* 24:78-80 S '89
Spring landscaping [special section] il *Organic Gardening* 36:60-70+ Ap '89
Tori Thomas: agricultural abstractions in a Virginia landscape. il por *Architectural Digest* 46:100-1 Ap '89
Exhibitions
San Francisco's big landscape show. il *Sunset (Central West edition)* 182:234 Ap '89
LANDSCAPE IN ART
See also
Landscape painting
LANDSCAPE PAINTING
See also
Hudson River School
Topographic painting
April Gornik's stormy weather [cover story] E. Heartney. il pors *Art News* 88:120-5 My '89
Art: primitive landscapes [American folk artists] J. R. Mellow. il *Architectural Digest* 46:186-91 D '89
Art: Victorian landscapes. P. Fuller. il *Architectural Digest* 46:160-5+ Ag '89
Boundless landscapes [work of B. Berns] L. Anderson. il *American Artist* 53:86-91+ S '89
Energizing landscape paintings [B. Sullivan] L. S. Zelenko. il *American Artist* 53:66-71 O '89
George Harkins. M. S. Doherty. il por *American Artist* 53:34-9 My '89
Linden Frederick. E. Feit. il por *American Artist* 53:48-53+ Jl '89
Michael Scott. L. S. Hurwitz. il por *American Artist* 53:46-7 Ag '89
Nature as teacher: the art of Jim McVicker. E. Feit. il *American Artist* 53:38-43+ D '89
An unusual approach to acrylics [mixed with gel and extruded through syringes] H. J. Drexler. il por *American Artist* 53:44-9 F '89
Exhibitions
Chris Pfister at Bess Cutler. J. Ash. *Art in America* 77:195 N '89
Frederic Church and the enterprise of landscape painting [with editorial comment by Wendell Garrett] F. Kelly. bibl f il *Antiques* 136:1108-23 N '89
In the halcyon days when pictures of the land came first [works by F. Church] J. Sherman. bibl (p229) il por *Smithsonian* 20:88-96+ O '89
LANDSCAPE PHOTOGRAPHY See Photography—Landscapes
LANDSCAPE PROTECTION
See also
Environmental movement
Roadside improvement
Shore protection
Stream conservation
Wilderness areas
A bend in the road. C. Fletcher. *Wilderness* 52:12+ Wint '88
The landscape connection. G. F. White. *Environment* 31:inside cover Ap '89

LANDSCHULZ, WILLIAM H., AND OTHERS
The DNA binding domain of the rat liver nuclear protein C/EBP is bipartite. bibl f il *Science* 243:1681-8 Mr 31 '89
LANDSLIDES
Dynamic pore-pressure fluctuations in rapidly shearing granular materials. R. M. Iverson and R. G. LaHusen. bibl f il *Science* 246:796-9 N 10 '89
Slumgullion Slide, Colorado. R. H. Mohlenbrock. il map *Natural History* p34-7 Ap '89
LANDSTEINER, KARL, 1868-1943
about
What's your type? il *Current Health 2* 16:12-13 O '89
LANDY, EUGENE
about
Brian Wilson's Svengali has his wings clipped as he gives up his license to shrink. il pors *People Weekly* 31:97 Ap 17 '89
Landy loses license. M. Goldberg. pors *Rolling Stone* p27 My 18 '89
LANDY, JOANNE
(jt. auth) See Morton, Brian, and Landy, Joanne
LANE, ARTHUR L., AND OTHERS
Photometry from Voyager 2: initial results from the Neptunian atmosphere, satellites, and rings. bibl f il *Science* 246:1450-4 D 15 '89
LANE, BELDEN C., 1943-
Blending salt and spice, joining wisdom and prophecy [cover story] il *The Christian Century* 106:499-502 My 10 '89
Fierce landscapes and the indifference of God [cover story] *The Christian Century* 106:907-10 O 11 '89
The power of myth: lessons from Joseph Campbell. il *The Christian Century* 106:652-4 Jl 5-12 '89
LANE, BILL
Back from Australia, looking ahead at Sunset and the West. il pors *Sunset (Central West edition)* 183:164 Jl '89
LANE, BRENDA
You can go home again. il *American Visions* 4:24-7 Ap '89
LANE, CHARLES
Death's democracy. il *The Atlantic* 263:18+ Ja '89
The war that will not end [cover story] *The New Republic* 201:23-7 O 16 '89
LANE, CHARLES
about
Dim lights, sad city. P. Hoban. il por *New York* 22:36 N 6 '89
LANE, DIANE
about
Diane Lane, with a new husband and no fear of flying, takes wing again in Lonesome dove. M. Dougherty. il pors *People Weekly* 31:77+ F 13 '89
LANE, HELEN R.
(tr) See Vargas Llosa, Mario, 1936-. The writer reflects
LANE, JOE
about
A copy writer's journey into the age of PCs. M. Piturro. il por *Personal Computing* 13:146-7 O '89
LANE, JOHN J. (JOHN JOSEPH), 1935-, AND WALBERG, HERBERT J., 1937-
Site-managed schools: the Chicago plan [excerpt from Organizing for learning] *The Education Digest* 55:28-31 N '89
LANE, LAURENCE W., JR. See Lane, Bill
LANE, NANCY
about
The human factor flourishes in the new biz. A. L. Ball. il pors *Working Woman* 14:135-6 O '89
LANE, SANDY
about
For a yellow color. A. Arndt. il por *Americana* 17:34-7 S/O '89
LANE, VINCENT
about
Can business save public housing? R. Henkoff. il por *Fortune* 120:121+ N 20 '89
Can Chicago beat the odds? J. McCormick. il por *Newsweek* 113:24-6 Ja 2 '89
High noon at the housing project. il pors *Ebony* 44:130+ Ag '89
The man who's giving Chicago's projects some r-e-s-p-e-c-t. B. Bremner. por *Business Week* p88 Je 12 '89
LANE COMMUNITY COLLEGE
An accident of birth delivers a most unusual scholarship [J. Lester, born on campus, receives scholarship] il por *People Weekly* 32:81 O 23 '89
LANEY, JAMES T.
Lawyers and leveraged buyouts [address, November 16, 1988] *Vital Speeches of the Day* 55:318-20 Mr 1 '89
LANEY, SHAREEN
My dad's on death row. il *Seventeen* 48:68+ My '89
LANFORD, SHEILA WILENSKY- See Wilensky-Lanford, Sheila
LANG, DARREL, AND LANG, LADELL
Dressing for exercise. il *Current Health 2* 16:14-15 D '89
LANG, K. D.
about
K.D. Lang. A. Nash. il por *Stereo Review* 54:75 Ag '89

LANG, LADELL
(jt. auth) See Lang, Darrel, and Lang, LaDell
LANG, STEPHEN
about
Kindled spirit. D. Ryll. *Omni (New York, N.Y.)* 11:70 Ag '89
Martial artist. J. Weinberg. il por *New York* 22:45 D 4 '89
LANGACKER, P., AND MANN, ALFRED K.
The unification of electromagnetism with the weak force. bibl f il *Physics Today* 42:22-31 D '89
LANGAN, MARIANNE
Food tips to clip. See issues of McCall's beginning May 1986
LANGAN, PETER, D. 1988
about
A fine madness. P. Wilkinson. il por *Gentlemen's Quarterly* 59:430-5+ S '89
LANGAN'S BRASSERIE (CENTURY CITY, CALIF.) *See* Century City (Los Angeles, Calif.)—Restaurants, nightclubs, bars, etc.
LANGDON, JOHN
A quiet revolution—the horse in agriculture, 1100-1500. bibl il map *History Today* 39:32-7 Jl '89
LANGDON, PHILIP
Glorified bathrooms. il *The Atlantic* 264:102+ O '89
In the Wright tradition. il *The Atlantic* 263:83-7 Ap '89
LANGE, ART
Sting speaks [interview; reprint from December 1985 issue] il por *Down Beat* 56:93-4 S '89
LANGE, DAVID
about
New Zealand takes on the U.S. [interview] M. Gawenda. il por *Time* 133:45 My 8 '89
LANGELLIER, JEAN-PIERRE
The challenge of reclaiming Islam from extremists. *World Press Review* 36:30-1 Jl '89
LANGENFASS, ROLF
about
Sewing down a dream. G. Schmidgall. il pors *Opera News* 53:30-2 Ap 1 '89
LANGER, CASSANDRA
The art of healing. il *Ms.* 17:132-3 Ja/F '89
LANGER, ELLEN J., 1947-
The mindset of health [excerpt from Mindfulness] il *Psychology Today* 23:48-51 Ap '89
One-track thinking [excerpt from Mindfulness] il *Health (New York, N.Y.)* 21:72-5+ Mr '89
LANGER, J. S.
Dendrites, viscous fingers, and the theory of pattern formation. bibl f il *Science* 243:1150-6 Mr 3 '89
LANGERHANS, ISLETS OF *See* Pancreas
LANGLEY RESEARCH CENTER (U.S.)
Langley, McDonnell Douglas study methods of reducing rotor noise. E. H. Phillips. il *Aviation Week & Space Technology* 131:75-6 Jl 17 '89
Langley uses Learjet to study wave disturbances in laminar flow. il *Aviation Week & Space Technology* 130:270-1 Je 12 '89
Modified LEBU devices could cut skin-friction drag. E. H. Phillips. il *Aviation Week & Space Technology* 131:71+ Ag 21 '89
NASA Langley expands flight envelope of F-106B equipped with vortex flaps. E. H. Phillips. il *Aviation Week & Space Technology* 130:22-3 Je 5 '89
NASA prepares to reopen transonic wind tunnel after major fan repairs. E. H. Phillips. il *Aviation Week & Space Technology* 131:61 Ag 7 '89
NASA tests indicate heavy rainfall can reduce lift at high angles of attack [transport aircraft wings] E. H. Phillips. il *Aviation Week & Space Technology* 131:64-5 Ag 28 '89
NASA will study heavy rain effects on wing aerodynamics [cover story] E. H. Phillips. il *Aviation Week & Space Technology* 130:38-9+ F 13 '89
Pratt & Whitney scramjet design for NASP tested in NASA-Langley facility at Mach 8 [National Aero-Space Plane] il *Aviation Week & Space Technology* 131:26 O 16 '89
LANGLOIS, JUAN CARLOS, 1926-
. . . a fragile heritage. il *The Courier (Unesco)* 42:5 My '89
LANGLOIS, STEVE
about
Steve Langlois is out to prove that haute cuisine and oat cuisine are not the same in the Midwest. D. Chu. il pors *People Weekly* 32:143-4 N 27 '89
LANGMUIR, IRVING
Pathological science [address, December 18, 1953] bibl f il por *Physics Today* 42:36-48 O '89
LANGSAM, DAVID
An Israeli soldier lives the 'intifada'. *World Press Review* 36:38-9 D '89
LANGSETH-CHRISTENSEN, LILLIAN
Fudge fudgery. il *Gourmet* 49:110-11+ D '89
Gourmet holidays: Lake Constance. il map *Gourmet* 49:60-5+ Je '89
The kitchen at Montgeoffroy. il *Gourmet* 49:50-1+ Jl '89
New Year's in Munich. il *Gourmet* 49:42-3+ Ja '89

Scotland's Brodick Castle kitchen. il *Gourmet* 49:82-3+ My '89
Shopping in Scottsdale. il *Gourmet* 49:70-5+ F '89
LANGSTON, J. WILLIAM
(jt. auth) See Tetrud, James W., and Langston, J. William
LANGSTON, MARK
about
Richest of the rich. F. Lidz. il pors *Sports Illustrated* 71:64-6+ D 11 '89
A wanted man. R. Fimrite. il pors *Sports Illustrated* 70:34-6 Ap 24 '89
LANGUAGE AND EDUCATION
See also
Bilingual education
Educating language-minority children: challenges and opportunities. B. T. Bowman. il *Phi Delta Kappan* 71:118-20 O '89
LANGUAGE AND LANGUAGES
See also
Alphabet
Artists—Language
Bilingualism
Canada—Languages
Children—Language
Communication
Conversation
Czech language
Deaf children—Language
Diplomats—Language
English language
French language
Humboldt (Sask.)—Languages
Immigrants—Language
Indo-European languages
Legislators—Language
Linguistics
Metaphor
Montreal (Québec)—Languages
Multilingualism
Native language
New Brunswick—Languages
Ontario—Languages
Paraguay—Languages
Rhetoric
Russian language
Sex discrimination in language
Sign language
Spanish language
Spanish language in the United States
Speech
Translators and translating
Origin
Grimm's greatest tale. S. J. Gould. il *Natural History* p20+ F '89
On the origins of speech [address, February 1, 1989] G. P. Rice. *Vital Speeches of the Day* 55:400-3 Ap 15 '89
The origins of Indo-European languages. C. Renfrew. bibl il maps *Scientific American* 261:106-14 O '89
Talk of ages [Neanderthal hyoid bone from Kebara cave site, Israel; cover story] B. Bower. il *Science News* 136:24-6 Jl 8 '89
Political aspects
See also
Moldavia (Soviet Union)—Languages
Québec (Province)—Languages
Study and teaching
Diving right into a new language. S. Woolley. il *Business Week* p100 Jl 10 '89
Foreign language studies making slight rebound [degree programs] il *Change* 20:27-31 N/D '88
How adults could learn languages as well as children [study by Elissa L. Newport and Ted Supalla] J. Rubin. il *Psychology Today* 23:21 Ap '89
Aids and devices
See also
Tape recordings—Language study use
Speaking in tongues [foreign language software] T. Netsel. *Compute!* 11:108-10+ N '89
LANGUAGE ARTS
Study and teaching
Learning to read and write [four year study of children from low income families by Connie Juel] G. W. Bracey. il *Phi Delta Kappan* 70:559-60 Mr '89
Literacy acquisition and alienation [whole language learning] S. Harman and C. Edelsky. *The Education Digest* 55:35-9 D '89
Taking the drill out of reading [whole language instruction] F. P. Hodge. il *Publishers Weekly* 235:99-100 Ja 20 '89
Whole-language instruction: teaching authorship [elementary students] L. L. Lamme. *The Education Digest* 55:46-50 N '89
LANGUAGE DEVELOPMENT *See* Children—Language
LANGUAGE OF ANIMALS *See* Animal communication
LANGUAGE POETRY
Publishing language poets. J. Barbato. *Publishers Weekly* 235:60 Ja 13 '89

LANGWAY, LYNN
The she decade. il *Ladies' Home Journal* 106:211-14 N '89

LANHAM, JULIE
The greening of Ted Turner [cover story] il pors *The Humanist* 49:5-7+ N/D '89

LANIER, LEWIS L., AND OTHERS
Membrane anchoring of a human IgG Fc receptor (CD16) determined by a single amino acid. bibl f il *Science* 246:1611-13 D 22 '89

LANIER, LAKE (GA.) *See* Lake Lanier (Ga.)

LANK, EDITH
Your money: should you give your house to your kids? *Modern Maturity* 32:20 Ag/S '89

LANKER, BRIAN
I dream a world [excerpts; with introd. by M. Angelou] il *National Geographic* 176:206-25 Ag '89
about
'Ordinary women of grace'. M. McLoughlin. il *U.S. News & World Report* 106:50-5+ F 13 '89

LANMON, LORRAINE WELLING, 1932-, AND ROENKE, H. MERRILL, JR.
Rose Hill near Geneva, New York. il *Antiques* 136:144-53 Jl '89

LANNAN MUSEUM (LAKE WORTH, FLA.)
Walls without a museum. E. Turner. il *Art News* 88:31-2 Ja '89

LANNON GALLERY *See* Palm Beach Community College. Lannon Gallery

LANOIL, GEORGIA WITKIN- *See* Witkin-Lanoil, Georgia

LANOIS, DANIEL
about
Chairman of the boards. M. Goldberg. il por *Rolling Stone* p39 N 30 '89

LANOUETTE, WILLIAM J.
Bumbling toward the bomb. bibl f il por *The Bulletin of the Atomic Scientists* 45:7-11 S '89
Plutonium—no supply, no demand? il *The Bulletin of the Atomic Scientists* 45:42-5 D '89

LANS *See* Local area networks

LANSBURY, ANGELA
about
Angela Lansbury: "It's always just beginning!". S. Price. il pors *McCall's* 116:76-7+ Ap '89
Stardom, she wrote. J. Kaufman. il pors *Ladies' Home Journal* 106:56+ D '89

LANSDOWNE (PA.)
Race relations
What would our children think of us? [segregation at Lansdowne Swim Club] J. T. Ryan. il *Commonweal* 116:115-17 F 24 '89

LANSING, DON
about
For Field of dreams fans who trek to Don Lansing's Iowa farm, the diamond is forever. M. Donovan. il pors *People Weekly* 32:120-1 O 23 '89

LANSING, SHERRY
about
Making movie magic. K. Johnson. il pors *Harper's Bazaar* 122:126-9 Ag '89
Producer. M. Beller. il pors *Life* 12:79-80 Spr '89

LANSKY, VICKI
Shower your kids with love [excerpt from 101 ways to tell your child "I love you"] il *Redbook* 172:28+ F '89

LANTERNS
Coleman's diamond in the rough [gasoline lanterns] R. Kimber. il *Country Journal* 16:22 My/Je '89

LANTING, FRANS
Down and out: feathered victims in living color [photographs] il *Omni (New York, N.Y.)* 11:58-63 Ag '89
Eggs to see [photographs] il *Omni (New York, N.Y.)* 11:58-63 My '89
If heaven were wild [cover story] il *International Wildlife* 19:4-13 S/O '89
On the trail of lemurs [cover story] il *International Wildlife* 19:4-13 My/Je '89

LANTIRN NIGHT SENSOR SYSTEM *See* Detectors, Infrared

LANVIN, BERNARD
about
Tailored perfection. N. Frey. il por *Harper's Bazaar* 122:70 Ap '89

LANZEROTTI, LOUIS J., AND UBEROI, CHANCHAL
The planets' magnetic environments. il *Sky and Telescope* 77:149-52 F '89

LAOS
See also
Temples—Laos
Economic policy
Lao Communists do an about-face. N. Cumming-Bruce. il *U.S. News & World Report* 107:35-6 Jl 3 '89
Native peoples
See also
Hmong (Asian people)
Politics and government
Lao Communists do an about-face. N. Cumming-Bruce. il *U.S. News & World Report* 107:35-6 Jl 3 '89

LAP DESKS *See* Desks

LAPHAM, LEWIS H.
Notebook. See issues of Harper's
A political opiate [cover story] bibl f il *Harper's* 279:43-8 D '89

LAPIDUS, ALAN H.
about
The temples of Lapidus. J. Adler. il por *Newsweek* 113:64-5 Je 26 '89

LAPIDUS, GAIL WARSHOFSKY
Gorbachev's nationalities problem. bibl f *Foreign Affairs* 68:92-108 Fall '89

LAPIDUS, GAIL WARSHOFSKY, AND DALLIN, ALEXANDER
The pacification of Ronald Reagan. il *The Bulletin of the Atomic Scientists* 45:14-17 Ja/F '89

LAPIERRE, WAYNE
about
Should more limits be placed on guns? [interview] il *U.S. News & World Report* 106:32 Ap 10 '89

LAPINSKI, SUSAN
(ed) See Grossman, Ann Sue. "My amazing Lisa"

LAPLACA, ALISON
about
Alison LaPlaca. K. Turan. por *TV Guide* 37:4 S 23-29 '89

LAPLINK (COMPUTER PROGRAM)
File transfer with LapLink III. il *Radio-Electronics* 60 ComputerDigest:77-9 S '89
Have LapLink, will travel. C. Lee. *Personal Computing* 13:204 N '89

LAPOINTE, BRIAN E.
Caribbean coral reefs: are they becoming algal reefs? il *Sea Frontiers* 35:82-91 Mr/Ap '89

LAPOINTE, JOE
Detroit. il *Sport (New York, N.Y.)* 80:56-61 My '89

LAPPÉ, FRANCES MOORE
Lappé to world: start talking [excerpt from Rediscovering America's values] *Utne Reader* p48 My/Je '89
Saving the family farm can benefit all of us. il *Utne Reader* p86 Jl/Ag '89
about
Frances Moore Lappé's diet for a better world. P. Carroll. il pors *Utne Reader* p42-8 My/Je '89
A small planet revisited [interview] S. McInerney. il por *Country Journal* 16:7-8 S/O '89

LAPPIN, JOAN
about
This pro's advice: hunt down Wall Street's orphans. C. E. Cohen. il por *Money* 18:205-6 Je '89

LAPTOP COMPUTERS *See* Computers

LAQUEUR, WALTER, 1921-
Confessions of a self-made Sovietologist. *Society* 26:5-9 S/O '89

L'AQUITAINE (FIRM)
SoHo grandee [owner C. F. Llamas] M. Guralnick. il por *House & Garden* 161:96 O '89

LARA, JOE
about
Model Joe Lara answers the call of the jungle as TV's new Tarzan. M. Dougherty. il pors *People Weekly* 31:65-6 Ap 17 '89

LARA CASTRO, CARMEN DE
about
Hope for Paraguay. W. Steif. *The Progressive* 53:16-17 Jl '89

LARCENY *See* Stealing

LARDER, BRENDAN A., AND KEMP, SHARON D.
Multiple mutations in HIV-1 reverse transcriptase confer high-level resistance to zidovudine (AZT). bibl f il *Science* 246:1155-8 D 1 '89

LARDER, BRENDAN A., AND OTHERS
HIV with reduced sensitivity to zidovudine (AZT) isolated during prolonged therapy. bibl f il *Science* 243:1731-4 Mr 31 '89

LARGE EDDY BREAKUP DEVICES
Modified LEBU devices could cut skin-friction drag. E. H. Phillips. il *Aviation Week & Space Technology* 131:71+ Ag 21 '89

LARGE PRINT BOOKS
See also
Publishers and publishing—Large print books

LARGELY NEW YORK [drama] *See* Irwin, Bill

LARGEMOUTH BASS FISHING *See* Bass fishing

LARGENT, LINNY
about
Carving a new Thanksgiving tradition. J. Rogers. il por *Prevention (Emmaus, Pa.)* 41:67-71+ N '89

LARKIN, PETER
about
Peter Larkin. G. M. Loney. il por *Theatre Crafts* 23:38-45+ Ja '89

LARKIN, PHILIP
about
The master of the ordinary. D. Walcott. il *The New York Review of Books* 36:37-40 Je 1 '89

LARKO, VALERI, 1959-
about
Valeri Larko. R. I. C. Fisher. il por *American Artist* 53:40-1 Ag '89
LARKSPURS *See* Delphiniums
LARMER, PAUL
A clearcutting ban for the birds. il *Sierra* 74:28-30 Mr/Ap '89
LAROUCHE, LYNDON H.
about
Debtor's prison. por *Time* 133:33 F 6 '89
Anecdotes, facetiae, satire, etc.
Life without LaRouche. A. Heard. *The New Republic* 200:15-17 F 27 '89
LARRABEE, F. STEPHEN
Perestroika shakes Eastern Europe. il por *The Bulletin of the Atomic Scientists* 45:25-9 Mr '89
LARROQUETTE, JOHN
about
John Larroquette: "I was born an alcoholic". B. Weinhouse. il pors *Redbook* 172:30+ Ap '89
LARSEN, BOB
about
The natural. B. Wischnia. il pors *Runner's World* 24:30-1+ Jl '89
LARSEN, CHRISTIAN GRØNHØJ, AND OTHERS
The neutrophil-activating protein (NAP-1) is also chemotactic for T lymphocytes. bibl f il *Science* 243:1464-6 Mr 17 '89
LARSON, BOB
about
Questions raised about Bob Larson campaign. L. Cryderman. il *Christianity Today* 33:47-8 Mr 3 '89
LARSON, BRUCE L.
An American childhood in Little Falls. il por *Architectural Digest* 46:36+ Je '89
LARSON, D. W.
(jt. auth) *See* Duchesne, Luc C., and Larson, D. W.
LARSON, ELWIN S., 1926-
about
"We had to get more sophisticated". J. Cook. il por *Forbes* 143:57+ Mr 20 '89
LARSON, ERIK
I scream, you scream . . . il *Utne Reader* p64-6+ Ja/F '89
Remembrance of Cheerios past. il *Parents* 64:268+ N '89
What sort of car-rt-sort am I? il *Harper's* 279:64-9 Jl '89
LARSON, GARY
about
The Far side of science. T. R. Miller. il *Natural History* p78 My '89
LARSON, KAY
Art. *See* issues of New York
The art of the newest. il *New York* 22:76-8 D 25 '89-Ja 1 '90
LARSON, RICHARD C.
The new crime stoppers. il *Technology Review* 92:26-31 N/D '89
LARSON (BOB) MINISTRIES *See* Bob Larson Ministries
LARSSON, OLLE
Learn from watching the best. il *Skiing* 41:69-73 F '89
LARUE, GERALD A.
Geroethics: a humanist issue. il por *The Humanist* 49:5-10+ Jl/Ag '89
LARVAE
See also
Caterpillars
Attraction of the parasitic mite Varroa to the drone larvae of honey bees by simple aliphatic esters. Y. Le Conte and others. bibl f il *Science* 245:638-9 Ag 11 '89
Baby bee odor lures cradle-robbing mites [research by Guy Ourisson] S. Hart. *Science News* 136:103 Ag 12 '89
A little thirst can aid plant defenses [soybeans and Mexican bean beetle larvae; research by Edward F. Connor and Grant McQuate] J. Raloff. *Science News* 136:37 Jl 15 '89
Meanderings of larval fish. il *Sea Frontiers* 35:199 Jl/Ag '89
LARVAE AS FOOD
Insects, worms, and other tidbits [Mexican cooking] R. Sokolov. il *Natural History* p84+ S '89
LARYNGITIS
The lost voice. G. Kolata. il *The New York Times Magazine* p33-4 Ja 15 '89
Sharpening the silence. C. Anderson. *Commonweal* 116:230 Ap 21 '89
LARYNX
Talk of ages [Neanderthal hyoid bone from Kebara cave site, Israel; cover story] B. Bower. il *Science News* 136:24-6 Jl 8 '89
Cancer
Genetic aspects
Effect of antisense c-*raf*-1 on tumorigenicity and radiation sensitivity of a human squamous carcinoma. U. Kasid and others. bibl f il *Science* 243:1354-6 Mr 10 '89
Diseases
See also
Spastic dysphonia

LAS VEGAS (NEV.)
Las Vegas hits the jackpot [Money magazine ranking] M. T. Smith. il *Money* 18:132 S '89
Hotels, motels, etc.
See also
Mirage (Las Vegas, Nev.: Casino)
Centerline: Ed Peterson [show room designer] M. Sommers. il por *Theatre Crafts* 23:18 D '89
Religious institutions and affairs
The cross and the casino [Southern Baptists] il *Christianity Today* 33:50 Jl 14 '89
LASAGA, ANTONIO C.
(jt. auth) *See* Berner, Robert A., 1935-, and Lasaga, Antonio C.
LASAGNE COOKING *See* Cooking—Pasta
LASCAUX (SAN FRANCISCO, CALIF.: RESTAURANT) *See* San Francisco (Calif.)—Restaurants, nightclubs, bars, etc.
LASDUN, JAMES
Powder compact [poem] *The New Yorker* 65:40 Mr 20 '89
LASER ARMS (FIRM)
The man who knew too much [involvement of M. Zolp and the Mafia in securities fraud] J. Crudele. il por *New York* 22:16 Mr 6 '89
LASER DATA PROCESSING *See* Optical data processing
LASER DISC PLAYERS *See* Compact disc players
LASER DISC RECORDERS *See* Compact disc recorders and recording
LASER DISCS *See* Compact discs
LASER DISCS, VIDEO *See* Videodiscs
LASER FAX MACHINES *See* Fax machines
LASER FUSION
Flash point [security restrictions on inertial confinement fusion] J. Horgan. il *Scientific American* 260:18+ Ap '89
Fusion plan ignites controversy at DOE [shifting funds from magnetic fusion to laser program] M. Crawford. il *Science* 244:1434-5 Je 23 '89
Laser-controlled fusion. il *Popular Mechanics* 166:16 Mr '89
LASER HOLOGRAPHY *See* Holography
LASER INTERFEROMETERS
Einstein's unfinished symphony [gravity wave detection] M. Bartusiak. il *Discover* 10:62-9 Ag '89
LASER OPTICAL DISC RECORDING *See* Optical storage devices
LASER PRINTERS
400-dpi printer shines in graphics [Genicom 6142 laser printer] T. Thompson. il *Byte* 14:288+ N '89
Buyer's guide. il *Personal Computing* 13:123-7+ S '89
Canon's swift laser printer [Canon LBP-811 T laser beam printer] S. Chen. il *Home Office Computing* 7:56 Jl '89
The language of lasers. K. Quirk. il *Byte* 14 Special Issue:203-6+ Fall '89
Laser printing for the masses [Hewlett-Packard Laserjet IIP] M. Antonoff. il *Personal Computing* 13:192 D '89
Nonstandard language unleashes this laser's power [Office Automation Systems LaserPro Express Series II] H. F. Beechhold. il *Home Office Computing* 7:65-6 Ja '89
Panasonic's speedy Laser Partner. C. O'Malley. il *Personal Computing* 13:192+ F '89
Plug and play PostScript [PacificPage PostScript emulation cartridge] M. Antonoff. il *Personal Computing* 13:206 D '89
Postscript power with a Canon engine [QMS PS-820] J. Pepper. il *Personal Computing* 13:190-1 Jl '89
Refilling SX cartridges [toner cartridges for copiers and laser printers] D. Lancaster. il *Radio-Electronics* 60:27+ Ap '89
Toner refilling tools. D. Lancaster. *Radio-Electronics* 60:71-2 Jl '89
A variety of laser printers for every need. H. F. Beechhold. il *Home Office Computing* 7:58+ Ap '89
Visual Edge sharpens laser output [printer enhancement] C. O'Malley. il *Personal Computing* 13:192-3 My '89
The wait for color laser printers. P. Honan. il *Personal Computing* 13:113 Ap '89
The well-equipped laser. M. Antonoff. il *Personal Computing* 13:93-5+ Jl '89
LASER RANGING, LUNAR *See* Lasers—Astronomical use
LASER SHOWS
Twilite glow [injurious effects of laser show at Twilite Club in Los Angeles] il *FDA Consumer* 23:34 N '89
LASER SPECTROSCOPY *See* Spectrum analysis
LASER WELDING
Zap! G. Slutsker. il *Forbes* 143:193-4 Ap 17 '89
LASERS
See also
Free electron lasers
Stereolithography
Electrons may shed light for X-ray lasers [research by David B. Chang and James C. McDaniel] R. Cowen. *Science News* 136:183 S 16 '89
Growing and carving micro-laser forests [chips hosting two million lasers] I. Amato. il *Science News* 136:68 Jl 29 '89
How quantum theory works in lasers and transistors. il *Fortune* 119:114 Ja 30 '89
Laser resources. D. Lancaster. *Radio-Electronics* 60:68-70 O '89

LASERS—*cont.*

Lift-off laser: GaAs on glass. R. Pool. il *Science* 243:1009-10 F 24 '89

Little lenses for little lasers. *Science News* 136:62 Jl 22 '89

Reflected light. G. T. Forrest. il *Byte* 14:249-54+ O '89

Semiconductor devices transfer like decals [epitaxial liftoff] I. Amato. *Science News* 135:101 F 18 '89

"Utah effect" strikes again? [purported X ray laser] R. Pool. *Science* 244:420 Ap 28 '89

Astronomical use

An unsung legacy of the first lunar landing [lunar laser ranging] D. C. Morrison. il *Science* 246:447-8 O 27 '89

Chemical use

Chemical cartography: finding the keys to the kinetic labyrinth. G. W. Flynn. bibl f il *Science* 246:1009-15 N 24 '89

Volatilization of high molecular weight DNA by pulsed laser ablation of frozen aqueous solutions [mass spectrometry] R. W. Nelson and others. bibl f il *Science* 246:1585-7 D 22 '89

Communication use

Laser-based communication system eyed. *High Technology Business* 9:35 F '89

Conferences

CLEO-QELS to be held in Baltimore [Conference on Lasers and Electro-Optics and Quantum Electronics and Lasers Science Conference] il *Physics Today* 42:50-2 Ap '89

Dental use

Casting light on gums. H. Wolinsky. il *American Health* 8:38 O '89

Tooth tech: the new dentistry. A. Biesada. il *High Technology Business* 9:28-31 Ap '89

Energy usage

Superfast switch speeds development [work of Martin A. Gundersen] *USA Today (Periodical)* 117:10 Je '89

Universal laser power supply [cover story] G. McComb. il *Radio-Electronics* 60:33-7 Mr '89

Injurious effects

Twilite glow [laser show at Twilite Club in Los Angeles] il *FDA Consumer* 23:34 N '89

Measurement use

See also
Lasers—Time measurement use

Medical use

Dye laser clears children's birthmarks [research by Oon Tian Tan] K. Fackelmann. *Science News* 135:118 F 25 '89

Erasing port-wine stains. S. Begley. il *Newsweek* 113:65 F 27 '89

Excimer laser surgery. A. Biesada. il *High Technology Business* 9:9 F '89

Is there a laser in the house? P. Elmer-Dewitt. il *Time* 134:97 S 18 '89

Lasers take lead in angioplasty treatment. *High Technology Business* 9:37-8 Ap '89

Lasers used to weld tissue. *High Technology Business* 9:31 Je '89

Lasers vs. skin cancer [removal of precancerous patches; work of William Dobes] *USA Today (Periodical)* 118:13-14 O '89

Latest ways to remove scars and birthmarks. L. Holland. il *Good Housekeeping* 209:179 Jl '89

Optical fibers in medicine. A. Katzir. bibl il *Scientific American* 260:120-5 My '89

Solid-state research promises tunable lasers. *High Technology Business* 9:36-7 My '89

A tale of two eyes [cost of laser eye surgery in France compared to that in U.S.] L. Malkin. *The New Republic* 201:15-16 S 4 '89

Military use

See also
Relay Mirror Experiment (Artificial satellite)

Alpha missile defense laser is fired for first time [Zenith Star project] il *Aviation Week & Space Technology* 130:23-4 Ap 17 '89

Energy Dept. plans to cut spending on nuclear directed-energy weapons. T. M. Foley. *Aviation Week & Space Technology* 130:132-3 F 20 '89

Interview: Peter Hagelstein [resignation from Lawrence Livermore's SDI X ray laser work] B. Moseley. pors *Omni (New York, N.Y.)* 11:74-6+ My '89

Laser-based communication system eyed. *High Technology Business* 9:35 F '89

U.S., Soviet scientists propose system to monitor laser ASATs. T. M. Foley. *Aviation Week & Space Technology* 130:31 My 15 '89

USAF demonstrates technique for brighter laser beam [Chemical Oxygen Iodine Laser] il *Aviation Week & Space Technology* 130:58+ My 15 '89

USAF stresses development of semiconductor laser. il *Aviation Week & Space Technology* 130:57-8 Ja 30 '89

Visit to a laser facility at the Soviet ABM test site. F. Von Hippel. il *Physics Today* 42:34-5 N '89

Mirrors

See also
Relay Mirror Experiment (Artificial satellite)

Photographic use

See also
Holography

Physics use

See also
Multiphoton resonance ionization spectroscopy

Atomic fountain springs from a light touch [work of Steven Chu] I. Peterson. il *Science News* 136:117 Ag 19 '89

Chilling an atom in solitary confinement. I. Amato. *Science News* 136:103 Ag 12 '89

Ion sits still for sharp 'picture' of its optical transition. B. G. Levi. il *Physics Today* 42:17-18 S '89

Laser optics of neutral atomic beams. V. I. Balykin and V. S. Letokhov. bibl f il *Physics Today* 42:23-8 Ap '89

'Optical matter' emerges under laser [work of Michael M. Burns and Jean Marc Fournier] I. Amato. *Science News* 136:212 S 30 '89

Surgical use

See Lasers—Medical use

Time measurement use

Atomic timekeeping. R. Henson. il *Technology Review* 92:12-13 Ag/S '89

Traffic control use

Laser thwarts auto radar detectors. il *Popular Mechanics* 166:11 S '89

LASERS IN CRIMINAL INVESTIGATION, ESPIONAGE, ETC.

Lifting 'latents' is now very much a high-tech matter. J. Fincher. bibl (p230) il *Smithsonian* 20:201-2+ O '89

LASHANSKY, MICHAEL

Digital capacitance meter. il *Radio-Electronics* 60:38-43 Jl '89

R-C decade box. il *Radio-Electronics* 60:39-42+ N '89

LASISI, JOE

about

There's no place like home. K. Cook. il pors *Sports Illustrated* 70:90 Je 5 '89

LASKAS, JEANNE MARIE

Alice and the chipmunk. *Reader's Digest* 134:107-8 My '89

A tale of two brothers. il pors *Life* 12:84-5+ D '89

Tempted by the past. il por *House & Garden* 161:122 My '89

LASKER, DAVID

A Toronto Georgian. il *Architectural Digest* 46:114-19 F '89

LASKER MEDICAL RESEARCH AWARDS

Lasker Award goes to four signal scientists. J. L. Marx. il *Science* 245:1447 S 29 '89

LASKEY, R. A., AND OTHERS

S phase of the cell cycle. bibl f il *Science* 246:609-14 N 3 '89

LASKI, HAROLD JOSEPH, 1893-1950

about

The inventor of 'pluralism'. L. S. Feuer. por *The New Leader* 72:12-13 S 4 '89

Presidents: the power and the mediocrity. S. R. Graubard. il *The New York Times Book Review* 94:1+ Ja 15 '89

LASKO, WARREN

about

Cyclical calm. R. T. Grieves. il por *Forbes* 143:322 Ja 9 '89

LASLEY, PAUL, AND HARRYMAN, ELIZABETH

Palm Springs: a celebration of film. il *American Film* 15:59-60+ D '89

LASLEY, THOMAS J.

A teacher development model for classroom management. bibl f il *Phi Delta Kappan* 71:36-8 S '89

LASORDA, TOM

about

Business secrets of Tommy Lasorda [interview] B. Dumaine. il pors *Fortune* 120:130-2+ Jl 3 '89

Tommy Lasorda's "Sermon on the mound" [condensed from Out of the blue; ed. by Jerry B. Jenkins. O. Hershiser. il por *Reader's Digest* 135:63-5 S '89

With less linguine, he's not managing so well. M. Durslag. il pors *TV Guide* 37:20-1 Ag 26-S 1 '89

LASSALLE, GILBERT DUCLOS- *See* Duclos-Lassalle, Gilbert

LASSELL, WILLIAM, 1799-1880

about

Neptune's forgotten ring. R. Baum and R. W. Smith. il por *Sky and Telescope* 77:610-11 Je '89

LASSEN VOLCANIC NATIONAL PARK (CALIF.)

All's quiet at Lassen. il maps *Sunset (Central West edition)* 183:16-17+ Ag '89

Lassen Volcanic [excerpt] E. Richard. il *National Parks* 63:46-7 Mr/Ap '89

LASSER, STUART

about

The right way to buy a car [interview] K. Zino. il por *Home Mechanix* 85:28+ S '89

LAST, JOHN M., 1926-

Ethics and epidemiology. il *World Health* p22-4 Je '89

LAST JUDGMENT *See* Judgment Day

LAST POST (CONN.)

Room with a mew. il *Life* 12:122-3 Je '89

Three hundred pampered felines retire in style to the best little cat house in Connecticut [old age home for cats] M. Neill. il *People Weekly* 31:165-7 My 15 '89

THE LAST TEMPTATION OF CHRIST [film] *See* Motion picture reviews—Single works

LASTFOGEL, ABE, 1898-1984
about
Roots: the man who discovered Chaplin, and the world's fastest golfer. L. Gubernick. il por *Forbes* 143:52 Je 12 '89
LATCHES
Jammed door latch fix [automobiles] P. Brand. il *The Family Handyman* 39:73-4 N/D '89
LATCHKEY CHILDREN *See* Children of working parents
LATE NIGHT WITH DAVID LETTERMAN [television program] *See* Television program reviews—Single works
LATEEF, YUSEF
about
Yusef Lateef. D. Helland. il por *Down Beat* 56:54-5 D '89
LATERAL SCLEROSIS *See* Amyotrophic lateral sclerosis
LATERALITY
See also
Left- and right-handedness
Split brain
Baby faces show the right side of emotion. B. Bower. il *Science News* 135:149 Mr 11 '89
The gender gap [differences in men's and women's mental skills] C. Tavris. *Vogue* 179:302+ Ap '89
A 'handy' guide to primate evolution. B. Bower. il *Science News* 135:10-12 Ja 7 '89
Ocular dominance column development: analysis and simulation [visual cortex] K. D. Miller and others. bibl f il *Science* 245:605-15 Ag 11 '89
Ways of knowing God: gender and the brain. J. B. Ashbrook. il *The Christian Century* 106:14-15 Ja 4-11 '89
LATHAM, CAROLINE
"Where's Mommy?". il *Forbes* 144 Special Issue:86-8+ O 23 '89
LATHAM, JOHN A., AND CECH, THOMAS R.
Defining the inside and outside of a catalytic RNA molecule. bibl f il *Science* 245:276-82 Jl 21 '89
LATHES
See also
Turning (Machine work)
The ultimate lathe [Holtzapffel lathe] P. D. Ungerer. il *Popular Science* 234:116-20 Ap '89
LATIN AMERICA
See also
Airlines—Routes—Latin America
Baseball, Professional—Latin America
Books and reading—Latin America
Capital movements—Latin America
Direct broadcast satellite services—Latin America
Drug abuse—Latin America
Freedom of information—Latin America
Guerrillas—Latin America
Loans, Bank—Latin America
Military assistance, Cuban—Latin America
Motion pictures—Latin America
Narcotics laws and regulations—Latin America
Narcotics trade—Latin America
Poor—Latin America
Rain forests—Latin America
Rich—Latin America
Terrorism—Latin America
United Nations—Latin America
Regional report: Latin America. L. Rogers. See issues of *World Press Review* beginning September 1986 through March 1989
Armed Forces
The twilight of the generals. R. Gott. *World Press Review* 36:26+ Jl '89
Bibliography
Book reviews. *Current History* 88:142-3+ Mr '89
Books. See issues of *Américas*
Commerce
United States
See United States—Commerce—Latin America
Defenses
See also
United States—Armed Forces—Forces in Latin America
Economic conditions
See also
Underground economy—Latin America
A chasm of misery [gap between rich and poor] F. Ungeheuer. il *Time* 134:64-6 N 6 '89
Economic history
Why Latin America is poor. M. Novak. il *Forbes* 143:76-7 Ap 17 '89
Economic policy
Down and out in Latin America. S. Baker. il *Business Week* p44-5 Jl 10 '89
Latin populism at a dead end. *World Press Review* 36:80 N '89
Perestroika goes south. A. Miller. il *Newsweek* 114:53 N 6 '89
Self-made crisis [debt crisis] M. S. Forbes, Jr. il *Forbes* 143:27 F 20 '89
Why Asian countries blossomed while Latin America wilted [income inequality] G. Koretz. il *Business Week* p16 Ag 28 '89
Will democracy in Latin America simply mean plunder? P. C. Roberts. il *Business Week* p18 S 18 '89

Foreign relations
Canada
See Canada—Foreign relations—Latin America
United States
See United States—Foreign relations—Latin America
Industries
See also
Airlines—Latin America
Languages
See also
Spanish language in Latin America
Politics and government
See also
Politics, Corruption in—Latin America
Populism—Latin America
Commitment to democracy and economic progress in Latin America [address, May 2, 1989] G. Bush. il por *Department of State Bulletin* 89:1-2 Je '89
Hemispheric bigthink. H. Hertzberg. *The New Republic* 200:4+ Mr 13 '89
The open society and its friends [address, October 11, 1988] G. P. Shultz. *Department of State Bulletin* 88:13-16 D '88
South America, 1989 [cover story; special issue] bibl f map (inside back cover) *Current History* 88:113-54 Mr '89
Spitting distance. G. Black. *The Nation* 248:5 Ja 2 '89
The trials of democracy Latin style. C. A. Robbins. il *U.S. News & World Report* 106:36-7 Ap 17 '89
The U.S. and Latin America: a lost decade? M. D. Hayes. *Foreign Affairs* 68 Special Issue:180-98 ['89]
Uncle Sam, stay home [adaptation of address, May 1988] C. Fuentes. *Harper's* 278:14-17 Ja '89
A year of decision—and democracy [special section] il *World Press Review* 36:22-4+ Jl '89
Religious institutions and affairs
See also
Catholic Church—Latin America
Church and social problems—Latin America
Evangelical churches—Latin America
Latin American Council of Churches
LATIN AMERICAN ART *See* Art, Latin American
LATIN AMERICAN BOOK FAIR (NEW YORK, N.Y.) *See* Book fairs
LATIN AMERICAN COUNCIL OF CHURCHES
A new Pentecost: hope in solidarity [assembly in Indaiatuba, Brazil] J. H. Sinclair. il *The Christian Century* 106:83-4 Ja 25 '89
LATIN AMERICAN DANCE *See* Dance, Latin American
LATIN AMERICAN LITERATURE
Literary detection and Latin American writing. F. Ainsa. il *The Courier (Unesco)* 42:21-3 My '89
Bibliography
Best sellers in the Americas. M. del C. Prodoscimi. il *Américas* 41 no2:54-6 '89
Best sellers in the Americas. M. del C. Prodoscimi. *Américas* 41 no1:50-1 '89
LATIN AMERICAN MANUSCRIPTS *See* Manuscripts, Latin American
LATIN AMERICAN MUSIC *See* Music, Latin American
LATIN AMERICAN PAINTING *See* Painting, Latin American
LATIN AMERICANS
United States
See also
Hispanic Americans
LATINOS (U.S.) *See* Hispanic Americans
LATITUDE
Biologists disagree over bold signature of nature [species-richness gradient; views of George Stevens] R. Lewin. il *Science* 244:527-8 My 5 '89
LATKES
Hanukkah latkes. il *Redbook* 174:50 D '89
Hanukkah latkes. il *Gourmet* 49:126-7+ D '89
LATTER-DAY SAINTS *See* Mormons and Mormonism
LATTICE FENCES *See* Fences
LATTICE THEORY
See also
Crystals—Lattices
Sphere packing
LATTICEWORK
Arbors and lattice. il *Sunset (Central West edition)* 182:166-7 F '89
At last, durable lattice. il *Southern Living* 24:76 Ap '89
LATTIMORE, OWEN, 1900-1989
about
Obituary
The Nation 248:873 Je 26 '89
Owen Lattimore and the 'cold war'; Lattimore & Wicker. W. F. Buckley. *National Review* 41:54-5 Ag 18 '89
Owen Lattimore, RIP [excerpt from column, September 1979] W. F. Buckley. *National Review* 41:18-20 Je 30 '89
Why are the liberals whitewashing? W. F. Buckley. *National Review* 41:60 Jl 14 '89
LATTIN, JOHN D.
(jt. auth) *See* Stanton, Nancy L., and Lattin, John D.
LATVIA
Nationalism
Breaking away. J. Kaza. il *The American Spectator* 22:34-5 N '89

LATVIA—Nationalism—*cont.*
Fighting for 'socialist pluralism' in Latvia. J. Kaza. il map *The New Leader* 72:12-14 Ja 23 '89
LAU, BARBARA
Big job on little rooms. il *Americana* 17:30-3 My/Je '89
LAUCALA (FIJI)
Description and travel
Malcolm Forbes in Fiji: the publisher's private island in the South Seas. J. Taylor. il por *Architectural Digest* 46:180-8+ F '89
LAUDER, ESTÉE
about
How Leonard Lauder is making his mom proud. K. Deveny. il pors *Business Week* p68-9+ S 4 '89
LAUDER, EVELYN
about
The beauty elite. il pors *Harper's Bazaar* 122:40+ Ag '89
LAUDER, SIR HARRY, 1870-1950
about
The Scottish minstrel: Harry Lauder (II). B. Ault. il por *Antiques & Collecting Hobbies* 93:32-5 Ja '89
The Scottish minstrel: Harry Lauder (III). B. Ault. por *Antiques & Collecting Hobbies* 93:66-9 F '89
LAUDER, LEONARD
about
Acceptably sexy. S. N. Chakravarty. il por *Forbes* 144:122+ N 13 '89
How Leonard Lauder is making his mom proud. K. Deveny. il pors *Business Week* p68-9+ S 4 '89
LAUDER, RONALD S., 1944-
about
Anything goes. A. Logan. *The New Yorker* 65:80-4 Mr 13 '89
The big spender who would be mayor. A. Rothman. il por *Business Week* p72-3 S 4 '89
Great-man theory. J. Klein. pors *New York* 22:16+ F 13 '89
Zinging Rudy. J. Klein. por *New York* 22:14-15 Je 5 '89
LAUGHING GAS *See* Nitrous oxide
LAUGHLIN, DON
about
A desert fox. G. Buchalter. il pors map *Forbes* 144:244+ O 16 '89
LAUGHLIN, MEG
Is he in career arrest—or is there life after Miami Vice? il pors *TV Guide* 37:18-21 O 21-27 '89
LAUGHLIN (NEV.)
Economic conditions
A desert fox [D. Laughlin] G. Buchalter. il pors map *Forbes* 144:244+ O 16 '89
Hotels, motels, etc.
See also
Riverside Resort Hotel & Casino
LAUGHTER
See also
Humor
Smiles
Psychological aspects
Five good reasons to laugh it up when you exercise. L. Gordon. il *Glamour* 87:40 Jl '89
Jest for the health of it. S. Goodman. il *Current Health* 2 15:18-19 Ja '89
Lighten up: laugh your way to good health. N. Gallo. *Better Homes and Gardens* 67:31-2 Ag '89
Norman Cousins helps other patients as he once helped himself—by laughing [excerpt from Head first] N. Cousins. il por *Good Housekeeping* 209:92 N '89
Proving the power of laughter. N. Cousins. il *Psychology Today* 23:22-5 O '89
Why we need to laugh. J. Brothers. il *TV Guide* 37:18-19 N 11-17 '89
Anecdotes, facetiae, satire, etc.
One laugh = 3 tbsp. oat bran. J. Leo. il *U.S. News & World Report* 106:55 Ja 23 '89
LAUMANN, EDWARD O., AND OTHERS
Monitoring the AIDS epidemic in the United States: a network approach. bibl f il *Science* 244:1186-9 Je 9 '89
Monitoring the U.S. AIDS epidemic [discussion of June 9, 1989 article, Monitoring the AIDS epidemic in the United States: a network approach] *Science* 245:908-10 S 1 '89
LAUNCHERS FOR GUIDED MISSILES *See* Guided missiles—Propulsion systems
LAUNCHERS FOR SPACE VEHICLES *See* Space vehicles—Propulsion systems
LAUNCHING OF BOATS *See* Boats and boating—Launching
LAUNCHING OF SPACE VEHICLES *See* Space vehicles—Launching
LAUNCHING PADS, SITES, ETC. FOR SPACE VEHICLES *See* Space vehicles—Launching pads, sites, etc.
LAUNDERING OF MONEY
See also
Iran-contra affair
Battling crime through the banks. D. Francis. il *Maclean's* 102:13 My 29 '89
The Bulgarian connection [drugs and money laundering] P. Fuhrman. il map *Forbes* 143:40-4 Ap 17 '89

A bungled deal with Panama [DEA money laundering crackdown utilizes M. Noriega's forces] il por *Newsweek* 113:25 Ap 10 '89
City of Angels, indeed [Los Angeles banks involved in laundering drug money] il *U.S. News & World Report* 106:14 Ap 10 '89
Crackdown on the Swiss laundry. C. Gorman. il *Time* 133:53 Ap 24 '89
A drug crackdown in the Alps [Switzerland] C. Dickey. il *Newsweek* 113:40 Ap 10 '89
The drug-money hunt. P. R. Range. il map *U.S. News & World Report* 107:22-5 Ag 21 '89
The drug war—European style. B. Riemer. *Business Week* p31-2 O 2 '89
Getting banks to just say 'no'. P. Dwyer and P. Engardio. il *Business Week* p16-17 Ap 17 '89
'He started at the top and worked his way down' [R. Silberman] K. Kerwin. il por *Business Week* p139 My 1 '89
Hiding the drug money [Canada; cover story; special section; with editorial comment by Kevin Doyle] H. Jensen. il *Maclean's* 102:2, 42-4+ O 23 '89
A torrent of dirty dollars [cover story] J. Beaty and R. Hornik. il *Time* 134:50-3+ D 18 '89
LAUNDROMATS
See also
Clean & Lean (Firm)
Oasis Laundries Inc.
Beautiful laundrettes. A. Miller. il *Newsweek* 113:42 Ja 9 '89
LAUNDRY
See also
Stain removal
LAUNDRY CHUTES
Tile hides laundry chute. il *Sunset (Central West edition)* 182:168 My '89
LAUNDRY DETERGENTS *See* Detergents
LAUNDRY EQUIPMENT
See also
Clothes dryers
Ironing boards
Washing machines
LAUNDRY PRODUCTS
See also
Detergents
LAUPER, CYNDI
about
Lauper shakes her bad vibes. F. Goodman. por *Rolling Stone* p28 Je 1 '89
LAURA, ROLAND LEGIARDI- *See* Legiardi-Laura, Roland
LAURA CASPARI LTD./SHE, INC.
Taking charge [M. Williams] D. Machan. il pors *Forbes* 143:154-6 Mr 6 '89
LAUREL, DOY *See* Laurel, Salvador
LAUREL, SALVADOR
about
Why is this man smirking? por *Time* 134:29 D 18 '89
LAUREL SPRINGS RETREAT (SANTA BARBARA, CALIF.: SPA) *See* Health resorts, watering places, etc.—California
LAUREN, RALPH
about
Ralph Lauren. C. Dowling. il pors *Life* 12:136-40+ My '89
What's it all about, Ralphie? Ralph Lauren and the New Traditionalism. B. Edmondson. il por *Utne Reader* p21-2 Jl/Ag '89
LAURENCE, DUNCAN, AND WYNNE, BRIAN, 1947-
Transporting waste in the European Community: a free market? bibl f il *Environment* 31:12-17+ Jl/Ag '89
LAURENCE, LESLIE
Forget the mall—it's in the mail. il *New Choices for the Best Years* 29:72-3+ F '89
LAURENCE, TIMOTHY
about
A crisis rocks a royal marriage [cover story] J. Kaufman. il pors *People Weekly* 31:66-8+ Ap 24 '89
LAURENDEAU, MARIE-CLAIRE
(jt. auth) *See* Perreault, Robert, and Laurendeau, Marie-Claire
LAURENZO, NINFA MARIA
about
Steering safely through setbacks. L. Gite. il pors *Working Woman* 14:39-41+ F '89
LAURIN, GINETTE
about
Chagall [dance] Reviews
Dance Magazine 63:104-5 My '89. L. Howe-Beck
LAURISTIN, MARJU
about
Pushing forward. J. Kohan. il por *Time* 133:66+ Ap 10 '89
LAUSANNE COMMITTEE FOR WORLD EVANGELIZATION
Global camp meeting [Lausanne II in Manila] L. Cryderman. il *Christianity Today* 33:39-41 Ag 18 '89
High hopes for Lausanne II [Manila] W. Conard. il *Christianity Today* 33:44 F 17 '89
Lausanne II: reshaping world evangelicalism. R. V. Pierard. *The Christian Century* 106:740-2 Ag 16-23 '89
Lausanne lives on. *Christianity Today* 33:15 S 8 '89

LAUSANNE COMMITTEE FOR WORLD EVANGELIZATION—*cont.*

Manila Manifesto to undergo further study. L. Cryderman. il *Christianity Today* 33:62-3 S 8 '89

The Prayboy Club [attending Lausanne II in Manila] J. I. Packer. il *Christianity Today* 33:11 O 20 '89

LAUSANNE CONSULTATION ON JEWISH EVANGELISM

Lausanne group addresses anti-Semitism. il *Christianity Today* 33:56 Je 16 '89

LAUTNER, JOHN

about

Playing the angles. D. Dietsch. il *Architectural Record* 177:76-9 mid-S '89

LAUTREC, HENRI DE TOULOUSE- *See* Toulouse-Lautrec, Henri de, 1864-1901

LAV (LIGHT ARMORED VEHICLES) *See* Motor vehicles, Military

LAV VIRUSES *See* HIV viruses

LAVA

See also

Basalt

The Blue Lake rhinoceros [lava mold found in Washington State] K. Kaler. il map *Earth Science* 42:22-4 Fall '89

Hawaii's lava is still flowing . . . here's where you can watch. il map *Sunset (Central West edition)* 183:54 S '89

Temperature measurements in carbonatite lava lakes and flows from Oldoinyo Lengai, Tanzania. M. Krafft and J. Keller. bibl f il *Science* 245:168-70 Jl 14 '89

LAVA SCULPTURE

Kindled spirit [work of S. Lang] D. Ryll. *Omni (New York, N.Y.)* 11:70 Ag '89

LAVALLIERE, MIKE

about

The throwback. P. Korn. il por *Sport (New York, N.Y.)* 80:49 Jl '89

LAVE, JUDITH R.

Band-aid solutions. *Society* 26:11-12 My/Je '89

LAVEGA, AGUSTIN SANCHEZ- *See* Sanchez-Lavega, Agustin

LAVELLE, MICHAEL J.

Religion in Czechoslovakia, 1989. *America* 161:375-7 N 25 '89

LAVENDER, DAVID SIEVERT, 1910-

The Mudgetts equation. il map *Wilderness* 52:28-39 Wint '88

LAVENTHOL, DAVID A.

about

Los Angeles's changing times. M. Beck. il por *Newsweek* 114:65 S 11 '89

LAVER, ROD

about

What a blast! S. Flink. il por *World Tennis* 37:22+ S '89

LAVERDIERE, EUGENE

Eucharist and tradition in the Middle Kingdom. *America* 161:162-4 S 23 '89

There's no such thing as a Catholic fundamentalist. il *U.S. Catholic* 54:36-8 S '89

LAVERNE, ANDY

Chick Corea's "Folk song"—an exercise in arranging. il *Down Beat* 56:56-7 Ag '89

about

Andy Laverne. M. Bourne. il por *Down Beat* 56:13 Jl '89

LAVIN, LEONARD H., 1919-

about

Washing the gray out at Alberto-Culver. J. F. Siler. il pors *Business Week* p138 Je 26 '89

LAVOISIER, ANTOINE LAURENT, 1743-1794

about

The passion of Antoine Lavoisier. S. J. Gould. *Natural History* p16+ Je '89

LAW, BRETT

about

A high school football record gets smashed in the name of Law. J. Friedman. il pors *People Weekly* 32:61-2 O 23 '89

LAW, GEORGE

about

To the swiftest. J. S. Gordon. il *American Heritage* 40:16+ Mr '89

LAW

See also

Arbitration and award

Civil rights

Compensation (Law)

Confession (Law)

Contracts

Copyright

Corporation law

Courts

Criminal law

Divorce

Feminist law

Homestead law

Information systems—Legal use

Inheritance

International law

Jury

Justice

Lawyers

Legal ethics

Legal procedure

Liability (Law)

Libel and slander

Maritime law

Mining law

Narcotics laws and regulations

Natural law

Power of attorney

Publicity (Law)

Rescission (Law)

Sunshine laws

Television broadcasting—Trials

United States. Supreme Court

Wills

See also subheads Law; Laws and regulations; Legal status, laws, etc. under various subjects

Blank check laws [deliberately vague wording] D. E. Koshland, Jr. *Science* 243:585 F 3 '89

Periodicals

See also

Canadian lawyer (Periodical)

'Academic poverty-pimping' [discussion of September 4-11, 1989 article, Law profs fight the power] J. Wiener. *The Nation* 249:442+ O 23 '89

Law profs fight the power [works by minority scholars] J. Wiener. *The Nation* 249:246-8 S 4-11 '89

Philosophy

The godfather of the American Constitution [Montesquieu] R. Wernick. il *Smithsonian* 20:183-4+ S '89

Religious aspects

See Religion and law

Study and teaching

See also

Law clerks

Law schools

Aids and devices

Law school lite [using course outlines and summaries] D. Pink. *The Washington Monthly* 21:20-3 N '89

China

See also

Criminal law—China

Connecticut

The country lawyer remembered [Windham County, Conn. in 1930s] W. Domnarski. *The American Scholar* 58:283-8 Spr '89

Florida

The defenders of abortion win one [Florida Supreme Court decision] il *U.S. News & World Report* 107:24+ O 16 '89

Tiny fingers on the trigger [Florida proposal authorizing prison terms for parents whose children misuse guns] il *U.S. News & World Report* 107:11-12 Jl 3 '89

With a new law, Florida heeds a child's plaintive cry to 911: 'I shot her—I didn't mean to'. M. Green. il *People Weekly* 32:56-8+ Jl 10 '89

France

See also

Paris (France)—Ordinances

Great Britain

Hard cases, strong cure [deregulation of legal profession] G. D. Garcia. il *Time* 133:53 F 13 '89

History

Evolution, not revolution [roles of solicitors and barristers] N. Dalton. il *History Today* 39:10-11 Ag '89

Indiana

See also

Gary (Ind.)—Ordinances

Louisiana

Louisiana: back to the 'dark ages'? [abortion laws] il *Newsweek* 114:34-5 O 9 '89

Maryland

The meaning of Maryland [gun control] D. E. Petzal. il *Field & Stream* 93:24-5 Mr '89

Massachusetts

See also

Cambridge (Mass.)—Ordinances

Michigan

A boost for abortion's foes. *Newsweek* 113:26 Ap 3 '89

Missouri

If fetuses are people . . . W. Saletan. *The New Republic* 201:18-20 S 18-25 '89

New York (State)

See also

New York (N.Y.)—Ordinances

No pleasure for lawyers [rules against hedonic damages] *Newsweek* 113:48 Mr 6 '89

Pennsylvania

In search of a compromise on abortion. S. V. Roberts. il *U.S. News & World Report* 107:31 N 6 '89

United States

See Law

Western Europe

See also

Antitrust law—Western Europe

LAW (THEOLOGY)
   See also
   Jewish law
Not through the law. P. Perkins. *The Christian Century* 106:587 Je 7-14 '89
'The power of sin is the law'. P. Perkins. il *The Christian Century* 106:1044 N 15 '89
LAW AND CHRISTIANITY *See* Religion and law
LAW AND RELIGION *See* Religion and law
LAW CLERKS
   See also
   Black law clerks
While justice sleeps [Supreme Court justices' reliance on clerks; cover story] T. Eastland. il *National Review* 41:24-6 Ap 21 '89
LAW ENFORCEMENT
   See also
   Computers—Police use
   Police
   United States. Federal Bureau of Investigation
   United States. Marshals Service
LAW ENFORCEMENT INTELLIGENCE UNIT
America's secret police network, part II. *Utne Reader* p62 S/O '89
LAW ENFORCEMENT TELEVISION NETWORK
Cops on camera. A. L. Sanders. il *Time* 134:77 N 13 '89
LAW FIRMS
   See also
   Baker & McKenzie
   Black law firms
   Christensen, White, Miller, Fink & Jacobs
   Hurt, Richardson, Garner, Todd & Cadenhead
   Jenkens & Gilchrist
   Touby & Smith P.A.
     Acquisitions and mergers
       Canada
A matter of size. B. Wickens. il *Maclean's* 102:72-3 N 6 '89
       Japan
U.S. law firms just can't win in Tokyo. T. Holden. il *Business Week* p58+ S 4 '89
LAW IN CABLE TELEVISION
Lawyers on screen [Law line cable TV show] D. Fanning. il *Forbes* 143:136 Je 26 '89
LAW IN TELEVISION
The verdict on Judge Wapner. A. J. Mikva. il pors *TV Guide* 37:12-14 Ap 22-28 '89
LAW LINE [television program] *See* Television program reviews—Single works
LAW OF NATURE *See* Natural law
LAW REVIEWS *See* Law—Periodicals
LAW SCHOOL ADMISSIONS TEST
Mastering the LSAT [computer program] C. S. Holzberg. *Compute!* 11:132+ N '89
LAW SCHOOLS
   See also
   Simon Greenleaf School of Law
   University of Chicago. Law School
Law school lite [using course outlines and summaries] D. Pink. *The Washington Monthly* 21:20-3 N '89
     Admission
   See also
   Law School Admissions Test
LAW SOCIETIES
   See also
   American Bar Association
LAW TEACHERS
   See also
   Minority law teachers
LAW-YONE, WENDY
Life in the hills. il *The Atlantic* 264:24+ D '89
LAWANSON, RUTH
     about
Woman to watch: volleyball pro Ruth Lawanson. F. D'Addesa. il por *Women's Sports & Fitness* 11:66 Mr '89
LAWHEAD, STEPHEN R. *See* Lawhead, Steve, 1950-
LAWHEAD, STEVE, 1950-
     about
Crossway's crossover novelist. B. Summer. il por *Publishers Weekly* 236:28+ O 6 '89
LAWLER, ANDREW
Desperately seeking station. il *Ad Astra* 1:8-11 Je '89
LAWLER, LOUISE
     about
Louise Lawler at Metro Pictures. K. Johnson. *Art in America* 77:191 N '89
LAWLESS, THEODORE K., D. 1971
     about
Black Chicago doctor supported Jews with money, time and talent. il por *Jet* 77:5-6 O 16 '89
LAWN CARE INDUSTRY
Lawn services. K. K. Gracey. il *Consumers' Research Magazine* 72:2 Ap '89
LAWN EQUIPMENT
   See also
   Blowers (Machinery)
   Leaf balers
   Toro Company

9 best new yard and garden tools. B. Markovich. il *Home Mechanix* 85:48+ Je '89
The best of lawn and garden equipment in 1989. H. E. Gibson. il *Flower and Garden* 33:51-2 N/D '89
Bladeless revolution [string trimmers] B. Gloege. il *Home Mechanix* 85:54-9+ Je '89
Garden gear. il *Popular Mechanics* 166:92-3 Jl '89
Muss busters. B. Markovich. il *Home Mechanix* 85:60-2+ S '89
New yard tools. D. Mowitz. il *Successful Farming* 87:32D-32E Ag '89
Power blowers [leaf blowers] il *Consumer Reports* 54:371-5 D '89
Power players. il *Popular Mechanics* 166:144-5 My '89
Spring '89 yard power. T. O. Bakke. il *Popular Science* 234:40+ Mr '89
String trimmers. il *Consumer Reports* 54:366-71 D '89
String trimmers. M. Ferrara. il *Organic Gardening* 36:55-8 F '89
     Maintenance and repair
Cold storage. B. Markovich. il *Home Mechanix* 85:114-18+ N '89
Organizing Neighborhood Cooperative Machine Maintenance Day. D. Sprockett. *Flower and Garden* 33:50-1 Jl/Ag '89
     Safety devices and measures
Be careful outdoors. *USA Today (Periodical)* 118:13 Ag '89
LAWN MOWERS
   See also
   Tractors
Robo-mower [Lawn Ranger] il *The Futurist* 23:39 Ja/F '89
     Accidents
What every mother fears [riding mower severs the foot of 17 month old daughter] B. Phelps. il por *Ladies' Home Journal* 106:20+ Jl '89
     Maintenance and repair
Are mower repairs worth it? [interview with D. Graves] B. Markovich. il por *Home Mechanix* 86:25-6+ Mr '89
How to be a good service customer. D. Sprockett. *Flower and Garden* 33:98-100+ Mr/Ap '89
How to sharpen a lawnmower blade. R. Capotosto. il *Popular Mechanics* 166:106 Mr '89
New motors for old mowers. M. Hood. il *Successful Farming* 87:64X Ap '89
Preparing mowers for winter storage. D. Smittle. il *Flower and Garden* 33:17 S/O '89
Sure summer start-ups. B. Markovich. il *Home Mechanix* 85:78 Ag '89
"Won't start!". P. Stone. il *The Mother Earth News* 117:96+ My/Je '89
     Safety devices and measures
Lawn mower safety. P. A. Seefeldt. *Good Housekeeping* 209:169 Ag '89
     Starting
Replace a starter rope. M. J. Schultz. il *The Family Handyman* 39:81 Jl/Ag '89
     Testing
The cutting edge: eight state-of-the-art midpriced mowers. B. Gloege. il *Home Mechanix* 85:52-7+ Jl '89
Easy riders. B. Markovich. il *Home Mechanix* 86:80-3+ Ap '89
Self-propelled lawn mowers. il *Consumer Reports* 54:361-6 D '89
Sicklebar mowers [Troy-Bilt Trail Blazer] il *Organic Gardening* 36:59 F '89
Walk-behind mowers. M. Ferrara. il *Organic Gardening* 36:79-84+ Ap '89
What's new in lawn mowers. S. Nesbitt. il *Flower and Garden* 33:93-7 Mr/Ap '89
LAWN MOWING *See* Lawns
LAWN ORNAMENTS *See* Garden ornaments
LAWN SEED *See* Grasses—Seed
LAWN TRACTORS *See* Tractors
LAWNS
   See also
   Lawn care industry
   Robots—Lawn care use
5 steps to a better lawn. K. Childers. il *The Family Handyman* 39:56+ O '89
Crabgrass wars: my father's surrender. W. French. il *Commonweal* 116:421-2 Ag 11 '89
Don't forget to rake [leaf raking] il *Southern Living* 24:61 O '89
A flowering lawn [wildflowers] G. Logsdon. il *Organic Gardening* 36:44-8 My '89
How to restore your lawn. D. Prestly. il *The Family Handyman* 39:62-6+ Ap '89
In praise of lawns. *Harper's* 278:31-2 My '89
Putting the lawn to bed for a long winter's night. D. Smittle. il *Flower and Garden* 33:15-16 S/O '89
Restore your lawn [drought damage] B. Pleasant. il *Organic Gardening* 36:74-8 Ap '89
The southern gardener [special section] il *Southern Living* 24:99+ Mr '89
TFH lawn care guide. D. Prestly. il map *The Family Handyman* 39:78+ My '89
Walk-on meadow . . . it's blooming yarrow. il *Sunset (Central West edition)* 183:212 N '89

LAWNS—*cont.*
Why mow? The case against lawns [cover story] M. Pollan. il *The New York Times Magazine* p22-7+ My 28 '89
LAWREN, BILL
Apocalypse now? il *Psychology Today* 23:38-9+ My '89
The creative computer. il *Omni (New York, N.Y.)* 11:28+ Je '89
Healing a broken heart. il *Omni (New York, N.Y.)* 11:20+ S '89
The high cost of neglecting wildlife. il *National Wildlife* 27:4-9 Ap/My '89
Seating for success. il *Psychology Today* 23:16+ S '89
LAWRENCE, ARNIE
about
Arnie Lawrence. M. Bourne. il por *Down Beat* 56:46-7 O '89
LAWRENCE, JIM
about
Earning his stripes [cover story] J. Reginato. il pors *House & Garden* 161:224-7+ O '89
LAWRENCE, KATHLEEN ROCKWELL
Flimsy excuses. il *The New York Times Magazine* p14+ F 12 '89
LAWRENCE, LINDA
(ed) See Baird, Forrest E. My dream house and my boy
LAWRENCE, MILES B.
Return of the hurricanes. il map *Weatherwise* 42:22-7 F '89
LAWRENCE, MURRAY
about
High stakes. K. Hannon. il por *Forbes* 143:326+ My 29 '89
LAWRENCE, PAMELA MOFFAT
about
Earning his stripes [cover story] J. Reginato. il pors *House & Garden* 161:224-7+ O '89
LAWRENCE, SEYMOUR, 1926-
about
Seymour Lawrence. R. A. Carter. il por *Publishers Weekly* 235:20-2 Mr 17 '89
LAWRENCE, T. E. (THOMAS EDWARD), 1888-1935
about
The fallen hero. W. Pfaff. *The New Yorker* 65:105-15 My 8 '89
The lives of Lawrence. E. Kedourie. *The New Republic* 201:37 Ag 21 '89
LAWRENCE, THOMAS EDWARD *See* Lawrence, T. E. (Thomas Edward), 1888-1935
LAWRENCE (CYRUS J.) INCORPORATED *See* Cyrus J. Lawrence Incorporated
LAWRENCE (MASS.)
Criminal justice, Administration of
Putting the heat on dealers [drug dealing] *Newsweek* 114:32 Jl 31 '89
Education
In-school breakfasts improve test scores. J. Raloff. *Science News* 136:247 O 14 '89
LAWRENCE LIVERMORE NATIONAL LABORATORY
Advances in induction-type FEL add to its antimissile potential [free electron laser] B. W. Henderson. il *Aviation Week & Space Technology* 130:81+ My 8 '89
Interview: Peter Hagelstein [resignation from SDI X ray laser work] B. Moseley. pors *Omni (New York, N.Y.)* 11:74-6+ My '89
Weapons scientists retool [verifying limits on sea-launched cruise missiles] V. Kiernan. il *Technology Review* 92:10-11 Ag/S '89
LAWRENCE OF ARABIA [film] *See* Motion picture reviews—Single works
LAWRENCE R. KLEIN AWARD
Klein Award. il *Monthly Labor Review* 112:2 Ap '89
LAWS *See* Law
LAWSON, EDDIE
about
The art of losing. K. Vreeke. il por *Cycle* 40:16 Ja '89
Eddie keeps the crown. M. Oxley. il por *Cycle* 40:19-20 D '89
Lawson closes on Rainey in 500 GPs. M. Oxley. il por *Cycle* 40:24+ O '89
Lawson, Kanemoto: adding up victory. K. Cameron. il por *Cycle* 40:20 D '89
Lawson on Roberts. *Cycle* 40:48 Ja '89
Lawson takes GP point lead as Rainey crashes. M. Oxley. il pors *Cycle* 40:24 N '89
Lawson wins Spanish GP; riders boycott in Italy. M. Oxley. il *Cycle* 40:22 Ag '89
The secret life of Eddie Lawson. K. Vreeke. il por *Cycle* 40:58-61+ Ag '89
LAWSON, ELLEN NICKENZIE
Children of the Amistad. il *American Visions* 4:38-41 F '89
LAWSON, JENNIFER
about
Civil rights movement led Lawson to her PBS career. *Jet* 77:38 D 18 '89
LAWSON, KAROL ANN
A vision of our nation. il *USA Today (Periodical)* 117:52-61 My '89

LAWSON, NIGEL
about
Arms and the woman. J. O'Sullivan. *National Review* 41:9 N 24 '89
Bad reviews for a one-man show. H. Anderson. il pors *Newsweek* 114:46-7 N 6 '89
The beginning of the end of an era. R. Knight. por *U.S. News & World Report* 107:50 N 6 '89
A question of judgment. A. Phillips. il por *Maclean's* 102:38-9 N 6 '89
LAWSON PRODUCTS, INC.
A fresh start after 40 [S. Port] R. Thompson. il pors *Nation's Business* 77:62+ Ap '89
LAWSUITS *See* Actions and defenses
LAWTON, JOHN H.
(jt. auth) *See* Churcher, Peter B., and Lawton, John H.
LAWYERS
See also
Alderson, Sandy
American Bar Association
Attorneys general
Bennett, Robert S.
Black lawyers
Coale, John P.
Diamond, Bobby
Divorce lawyers
Echo-Hawk, Walter
Felder, Raoul
Golub, Richard
Gray, C. Boyden
Janklow, Mort
Law clerks
Law firms
Legal aid
Legal ethics
Liman, Arthur L.
Marks, Leonard
Mayer, Jules F.
Morgan, Robert M.
Pitts, Lewis
Public prosecutors
Right to counsel
Slotnick, Barry Ivan
Sullivan, Brendan V.
Thomson, Joe
Tribe, Laurence H.
Women lawyers
The country lawyer remembered [Windham County, Conn. in 1930s] W. Domnarski. *The American Scholar* 58:283-8 Spr '89
The drug lawyers. S. Waldman and M. Miller. il *Newsweek* 114:41+ N 13 '89
Evolution, not revolution [roles of solicitors and barristers in Great Britain] N. Dalton. il *History Today* 39:10-11 Ag '89
Expensive habits: lawyers. P. Mayle. il *Gentlemen's Quarterly* 59:65+ F '89
Hard cases, strong cure [deregulation of legal profession in Great Britain] G. D. Garcia. il *Time* 133:53 F 13 '89
Have law degree, will travel. A. Sachs. il *Time* 134:106 D 11 '89
Now you're thinking like a lawyer. M. Kinsley. *The Washington Monthly* 21:44+ F '89
Revenge of the nerds: patent lawyers grab the spotlight. P. Dwyer. il *Business Week* p82 My 22 '89
Advertising
Lawyers on screen [Law line cable TV show] D. Fanning. il *Forbes* 143:136 Je 26 '89
Malpractice
See Malpractice
Religious life
God is my client. T. J. Reuland. il *Commonweal* 116:527-9 O 6 '89
Salaries, fees, etc.
See also
Prepaid legal services
Christic Institute woes [ordered to pay legal fees to defendants in conspiracy suit] *The Christian Century* 106:224 Mr 1 '89
Court orders: dealing with porn and drugs [Supreme Court rules on drug lawyers' fees] *Newsweek* 114:20 Jl 3 '89
Media campaigns in the courts [Christic Institute ordered to pay defendants' costs in conspiracy suit] *National Review* 41:13-14 Mr 10 '89
The plaintiff attorneys' great honey rush [with list of best paid lawyers in America; cover story] il *Forbes* 144:197-200+ O 16 '89
Supply and demand
Law. il *U.S. News & World Report* 107:69-70 S 25 '89
LAWYERS AND CLIENTS
See also
Confidential communications—Lawyers
Managing your lawyer. E. G. Krasnow and R. S. Conrad. il *Nation's Business* 77:70-2 Ap '89
LAWYERS' OFFICES
Trial and elegance [attorney K. A. Touby] L. Rosch. il por *Working Woman* 14:90-1 F '89

LAWYERS' PERIODICALS See Law—Periodicals
LAWYERS' WIVES
Anecdotes, facetiae, satire, etc.
Lawyers in love. K. Lowry. il *Gentlemen's Quarterly* 59:90+ Ja '89
LAXATIVES
Advertising
The breakfast drug [FDA reviews use of psyllium in cereal to determine if it is a food or drug] J. Newman. *American Health* 8:82+ D '89
Does this cereal belong in the medicine cabinet? [P&G claims that General Mills' cholesterol-reducing Benefit is a drug; Metamucil also contains psyllium] R. Mitchell and others. il *Business Week* p22-3 Jl 24 '89
LAXMAN, R. K.
about
An 'eloquent brush' in India. S. R. Ramanujan. il *World Press Review* 36:58-9 Mr '89
LAY, KENNETH LEE, 1942-
about
The hour before the dawn. J. Cook. il por *Forbes* 143:52+ My 15 '89
THE LAY OF CORNET CHRISTOPH RILKE'S LOVE AND DEATH [opera] See Matthus, Siegfried, 1934-
LAY PREACHING See Preaching
LAYCOCK, DOUGLAS
Peyote, wine and the First Amendment. *The Christian Century* 106:876-80 O 4 '89
LAYCOCK, GEORGE
The baptism of Prince William Sound. il map *Audubon* 91:74-9+ S '89
LAYER COMPOUNDS See Intercalation compounds
LAYMEN See Laity
LAYNE, ABNER A.
The market for American architectural services in Japan comes of age. il *Architectural Record* 177:33+ Mr '89
Pay phones pay off. il *High Technology Business* 9:24-7 N/D '89
LAYNE, CHRISTOPHER
Superpower disengagement. *Foreign Policy* 77:17-40 Wint '89/'90
(jt. auth) See Tonelson, Alan, and Layne, Christopher
LAYNG, ANTHONY
What keeps women "in their place"? il *USA Today (Periodical)* 117:89-91 My '89
LAYOFFS
How layoffs affect survivors. M. Chinnici. *Psychology Today* 23:20 O '89
Managing survivors in the wake of cutbacks [views of Lynn Isabella] J. A. Werman. *Working Woman* 14:22+ D '89
PWA Corp. to lay off 1,900 airline personnel [combining Canadian Airlines International and Wardair into one airline] *Aviation Week & Space Technology* 131:45 D 11 '89
A sad time for brokers. P. Chisholm. il *Maclean's* 102:40-1 D 18 '89
LAYTONVILLE (CALIF.)
Education
A boy sides with Dr. Seuss's Lorax, and puts a town at loggerheads [parents of S. Bailey call for removal of title from reading list] R. Arias. il pors *People Weekly* 32:67-8 O 23 '89
LAZAR, ELYSA
about
It's a jungle out there, so savvy buyers let Elysa Lazar guide them on their shopping safaris. S. Carswell. il por *People Weekly* 32:105-6 O 30 '89
LAZAR, JERRY
Tracey Ullman makes a face. il pors *The New York Times Magazine* p28-9+ O 15 '89
LAZARCHICK, SUSAN
"Please save my leg!"; ed. by Elaine Fein. il por *Redbook* 172:68+ Ja '89
LAZARD FRÈRES ET CIE
Tough guys with a genteel manner. P. Berman. il por *Forbes* 144:75-80 Jl 10 '89
LAZARD, DAVID
In defense of confidentiality. *Physics Today* 42:57-9 O '89
LAZARUS, ELEANOR
Equality and excellence education in arts. bibl f *Design for Arts in Education* 90:30-2 Jl/Ag '89
LAZARUS, FRED
Arts education in the 1990s: are we ready to move forward? *Design for Arts in Education* 90:33-8 Jl/Ag '89
LAZELL, JAMES
Pushy wildlife: animals that thrive on human habitat. il *National Parks* 63:18-25 S/O '89
LAZINESS
See also
Procrastination
What happens when the acceleration syndrome backfires? Welcome to the dawning age of sloth. M. Dezell. *Utne Reader* p42-3 Ja/F '89
LBS COMMUNICATIONS (FIRM)
Mr. Hardball sheds his Grey [H. Siegel's buyout of LBS from Grey Advertising] J. M. Robins. il pors *Channels (New York, N.Y.: 1986)* 9:62-6 F '89

LC See Library of Congress
LCDS See Liquid crystal displays
LCMV See Lymphocytic choriomeningitis virus
LDCS (LESS DEVELOPED COUNTRIES) See Developing countries
LDDC See London Docklands Development Corporation
LDLS (LOW DENSITY LIPOPROTEINS) See Lipoproteins
LE BOEUF, BURNEY J.
Incredible diving machines [cover story] il *Natural History* p34-41 F '89
LE BOURHIS, KATELL
about
The emperor's old clothes. D. Lida. il por *Harper's Bazaar* 122:71 N '89
LE BROCK, KELLY
about
America's 10 most beautiful women. B. Foley. il pors *Harper's Bazaar* 122:170+ S '89
LE CARRÉ, JOHN, 1931-
'Personal for Mr. Bartholomew Scott Blair, urgent' [fiction] il *The New York Times Book Review* 94:1+ Ap 23 '89
about
In from the cold [cover story] T. Mathews. il pors *Newsweek* 113:52-7 Je 5 '89
Romance in Russia. D. Kucherawy. il por *Maclean's* 102:55 Je 19 '89
Spies who come in from the cold war [interview] V. Orlik. il por *World Press Review* 36:28+ O '89
The thawing of the old spymaster [interview] A. P. Sanoff. il por *U.S. News & World Report* 106:59-61 Je 19 '89
LE CLEZIO, SYLVIE
about
Miracle baby. S. M. Halpern. il pors *Ms.* 18:56-60+ S '89
LE CONTE, YVES, AND OTHERS
Attraction of the parasitic mite Varroa to the drone larvae of honey bees by simple aliphatic esters. bibl f il *Science* 245:638-9 Ag 11 '89
LE CORBUSIER, 1887-1965
about
My Le Corbusier home. H. McNulty. il *Gourmet* 49:140+ N '89
LE GUIN, URSULA K., 1929-
The hand that rocks the cradle writes the book. il *The New York Times Book Review* 94:1+ Ja 22 '89
In and out [story] *The New Yorker* 64:30-5 Ja 16 '89
Read my lips: on the joys—and the necessity—of reading aloud [excerpt from *Dancing at the edge of the world*] il *Utne Reader* p126-7 Jl/Ag '89
So much for Prince Charming [excerpt from *Dancing at the edge of the world*] il *Ms.* 17:101-2+ Ja/F '89
LE MANS ENDURANCE RACE (AUTOMOBILE RACE) See Automobile racing—France
LE SIEG, THEO See Seuss, Dr.
LEACH, RICK
about
The dream team. S. Stevenson. il pors *World Tennis* 37:53-4+ Jl '89
LEACH, ROBIN
about
Tracking the rich and famous. H. G. Miller. por *The Saturday Evening Post* 261:30-1 My/Je '89
LEACHING
Cistern water: soft—and corrosive. *Science News* 135:191 Mr 25 '89
The little bugs that dig for gold [use of Thiobacillus in bioleaching] W. J. Cook. il *U.S. News & World Report* 106:62 Ap 17 '89
LEACHMAN, CLORIS
about
Playing Grandma Moses, Cloris Leachman paints a new picture of old age. K. Hubbard. il pors *People Weekly* 31:112-13 My 22 '89
LEAD
See also
Gasoline—Lead content
LEAD BASED PAINT
Lead in paint: the asbestos issue of the '90s? P. Hoffmann. il *Architectural Record* 177:35 My '89
Possible ban of some artists' materials. il *American Artist* 53:22+ N '89
LEAD IN THE BODY
See also
Lead poisoning
LEAD MINES AND MINING
Missouri
See also
Bonne Terre Mine (Firm)
LEAD PAINT See Lead based paint
LEAD PENCILS See Pencils
LEAD POISONING
Blood-lead climbs as old bones decline [aged women at risk] J. Raloff. *Science News* 135:181 Mr 25 '89
Cistern water: soft—and corrosive. *Science News* 135:191 Mr 25 '89
Clues to how lead impairs growth, vision [children] J. Raloff. *Science News* 136:87 Ag 5 '89

LEAD POISONING—*cont.*

A cure that's worse than the ailment [folk remedies containing lead; research by Robert T. Trotter] *Science News* 135:60 Ja 28 '89

Get the lead out. M. Morse. il *Utne Reader* p8-9 S/O '89

Getting the lead out [comparison of modern and ancient lead levels; research by Jonathon E. Ericson] B. Bower. *Science News* 135:44 Ja 21 '89

Gun buffs risk loading lungs with lead [handgun hobbyists using indoor firing ranges] *Science News* 136:126 Ag 19 '89

Lead effects show in child's balance [research by Amit Bhattacharya] J. Raloff. il *Science News* 135:54 Ja 28 '89

Lead toxicity: bones tell the real story [children] *Science News* 135:111 F 18 '89

Lead upsets menstrual cycle in monkeys [research by Nellie K. Laughlin] A. McKenzie. *Science News* 136:373 D 9 '89

Minnesotans struggle to save their poisoned swans [P. Redig's efforts to treat trumpeters at the University of Minnesota's Raptor Center] M. Nelson. il *People Weekly* 31:103-5 Mr 13 '89

The pottery problem: some dishes cause lead poisoning. il *Better Homes and Gardens* 67:156 O '89

Prevention

Coping with lead and asbestos. S. Greenberg. il *The Mother Earth News* 117:26+ My/Je '89

Lead in ceramic dishes. A. W. Simpson. il *Consumers' Research Magazine* 72:2 O '89

Lead in paint: the asbestos issue of the '90s? P. Hoffmann. il *Architectural Record* 177:35 My '89

Solving the lead dilemma. S. Pollack. il *Technology Review* 92:22-31 O '89

An unwanted souvenir: lead in ceramic ware. D. Blumenthal. il *FDA Consumer* 23:18-21 D '89/Ja '90

LEADED GASOLINE *See* Gasoline—Lead content

LEADER, CHARLES

Japan unlikely to parlay FSX work into civilian aircraft leadership role. por *Aviation Week & Space Technology* 130:97+ Mr 27 '89

Making total quality management work: lessons from industry. por *Aviation Week & Space Technology* 131:65+ O 30 '89

LEADERS, FISHING *See* Fishing tackle

LEADERSHIP

See also

> Black leadership
> Christian leadership
> Elite (Social sciences)
> Executives
> Followership
> Heads of state
> Presidents
> Women executives

Bring in the leaders. J. A. Skidmore, Jr. il *USA Today (Periodical)* 118:79-80 N '89

The courage of Sam Bird [example set by U.S. Army captain in Vietnam] B. T. Collins. il *Reader's Digest* 134:49-54 My '89

Creativity in turbulent times. B. I. Page and R. Theobald. il pors *The Futurist* 23:25-8 S/O '89

The Esquire register 1989 [special section] il *Esquire* 112:93+ D '89

How to be a leader. S. S. Cohen. il *Reader's Digest* 135:98-100 Ag '89

John Gardner: the serious optimist. D. Baldwin. por *Common Cause Magazine* 15:34-8 S/O '89

The leaders we deserve [political leaders] F. Ajami. il *U.S. News & World Report* 107:22-3 D 25 '89-Ja 1 '90

Restructuring leadership [West German model] A. Shanker. *The Education Digest* 54:3-5 F '89

Twenty guidelines for leadership. P. M. Smith. il *Nation's Business* 77:60-1 S '89

LEADERSHIP NETWORK (FIRM)

The hottest product is Brand X. il *Fortune* 120:128 S 25 '89

LEAF BALERS

Leaf baler. M. Ferrara. il *Organic Gardening* 36:68-9 S '89

LEAF BLOWERS *See* Blowers (Machinery)

LEAF RAKING *See* Lawns

LEAFLETS *See* Pamphlets

LEAFY SPURGE

Control

Weed from outer space. J. Walter. il *Successful Farming* 87:71 N '89

LEAGUE OF ARAB STATES *See* Arab League

LEAGUE OF NATIONS

The Versailles Treaty and after [reprint from January 1924 issue] D. Grayson. *Current History* 88:20-3 Ja '89

LEAKAGE

See also

> Automobiles—Leakage

LEAKEY, RICHARD E., 1944-

about

Elephant man. W. F. Allman. il por *U.S. News & World Report* 107:58+ O 2 '89

Leakey leaves Kenya museums. R. Lewin. il por *Science* 243:473 Ja 27 '89

LEAKS, GOVERNMENT *See* Government and the press

LEAMER, LAURENCE

Johnny Carson [excerpt from King of the night] il pors *Good Housekeeping* 209:104-5+ Jl '89

LEAMING, BARBARA

about

A candid new biography tells of the shocking childhood that destroyed Rita Hayworth. A. Chambers. il pors *People Weekly* 32:129+ N 13 '89

LEAN, DAVID

about

Abrams buys authorized bio of filmmaker David Lean. B. Levine. il por *Publishers Weekly* 235:43 Mr 24 '89

David Lean is back [interview] T. Sotinel. il por *World Press Review* 36:59 Ag '89

Lawrence of Arabia [film] Reviews

> *America* 160:226 Mr 11 '89. R. A. Blake
> *American Film* por 14:44 Mr '89. A. Barra
> *The New Republic* 200:26-8 F 20 '89. S. Kauffmann
> *The New Republic* 201:37 Ag 21 '89. E. Kedourie
> *New York* il 22:78 F 13 '89. D. Denby
> *Newsweek* il por 113:75 F 6 '89. D. Ansen
> *People Weekly* 31:11-12 F 27 '89. S. Haller
> *People Weekly* il 31:36-7 F 27 '89
> *Time* il por 133:62-3 F 6 '89. R. Corliss

LEAN, J.

Contribution of ultraviolet irradiance variations to changes in the sun's total irradiance. bibl f il *Science* 244:197-200 Ap 14 '89

LEAN BODY MASS

Can you preserve a lean body? [loss is part of the aging process; study by Margaret Flynn] il *USA Today (Periodical)* 118:6 O '89

LEAN ON ME [film] *See* Motion picture reviews—Single works

LEANDER, GEORG A., 1948-1988

about

Obituary

> *Physics Today* 42:100-1 My '89. J. Dudek and J. B. McGrory

LEANING TOWER OF PISA

Secrets of Pisa's Tower. P. Brogi. *World Press Review* 36:75 D '89

LEAR, FRANCES

about

A maturing woman unleashed. M. Smilgis. il por *Time* 133:70-2 My 15 '89

A new magazine's mercurial midwife. P. Sellers. il por *Fortune* 119:42-3 Ja 2 '89

LEAR, JOHN OLSON

about

UFO update. P. Huyghe. il *Omni (New York, N.Y.)* 11:85 S '89

LEAR, WILLIAM POWELL, 1902-1978

about

Mister Bill. P. Garrison. il por *Flying* 116:66 S '89

LEARJETS *See* Airplanes, Business

LEARN-TO-FLY MONTH

An invitation to fly. W. Garvey. il *Flying* 116:56-8 Je '89

LEARNED HELPLESSNESS *See* Helplessness (Psychology)

LEARNING, PSYCHOLOGY OF

See also

> Animal learning
> Conditioned responses
> Group work in education
> Learning disabilities
> Memory
> Psychology, Educational
> Students—Psychology

The best medicine [humor and learning; research by Avner Ziv] G. W. Bracey. il *Phi Delta Kappan* 70:563-4 Mr '89

Cultural style in teaching and learning. A. G. Hilliard. *The Education Digest* 55:21-3 D '89

The horse is dead [brain-compatible approach to restructuring schools] L. A. Hart. bibl f il *Phi Delta Kappan* 71:237-42 N '89

How adults could learn languages as well as children [study by Elissa L. Newport and Ted Supalla] J. Rubin. il *Psychology Today* 23:21 Ap '89

How kids learn [cover story; special section] B. Kantrowitz and P. Wingert. il *Newsweek* 113:50-7 Ap 17 '89

It's like, you know . . . [young children's abilities to use analogies to acquire information; research by Stella Vosniadou and Marlene Schommer] G. W. Bracey. il *Phi Delta Kappan* 70:560-1 Mr '89

Learning all the time. J. C. Holt. il *Parents* 64:112-14+ N '89

Learning in style [research by Bernice McCarthy] L. H. Duquin. il *Seventeen* 48:92+ S '89

Marijuana and learning: grass gets an F. K. M. Porterfield. il *Current Health 2* 15:20-2 Ja '89

Memory, imagination, and learning: connected by the story [place of story telling in teaching] K. Egan. bibl f il *Phi Delta Kappan* 70:455-9 F '89

LEARNING, PSYCHOLOGY OF—*cont.*

Now, which kind of preschool? E. R. Shell. il *Psychology Today* 23:52-3+ D '89

Preschool? [fetal learning; cover story] P. Weintraub. il *Omni (New York, N.Y.)* 11:34-8+ Ag '89

Reading, revising, and remembering [research by Bruce Britton and others] G. W. Bracey. *Phi Delta Kappan* 71:246-7 N '89

Some thoughts on treasure-keeping. T. C. O'Brien. bibl f il *Phi Delta Kappan* 70:360-4 Ja '89

Toward a unified theory of literacy learning and instructional practices [cover story] D. Taylor. bibl f il *Phi Delta Kappan* 71:184-93 N '89

Which tests teach most? [research by Ronald P. Fisher and Paul W. Foos] C. Potera. *Psychology Today* 23:28 Mr '89

LEARNING ALLIANCE

Environmental Trojan horse [Learning Alliance courses] D. K. Mano. *National Review* 41:50-1 Ag 4 '89

LEARNING AND SCHOLARSHIP

See also
Education
Humanism
Intellectuals and intellectual life
Knowledge
Scholarly publishing
Student achievements
Study
Wisdom

LEARNING CENTERS See Resource centers

LEARNING DISABILITIES

See also
Attention deficit disorder
Dyslexia
Reading disability

Educating students with learning problems. M. Will. *The Education Digest* 54:54-7 Ap '89

Helping learning-disabled children; ed. by Florence Isaacs. J. Haber. il *Good Housekeeping* 209:162+ S '89

Helping your learning-disabled child. J. Friedman. il *Parents* 64:106-8+ D '89

Is your child learning-disabled? L. O. Townsend. il *Essence* 20:118 O '89

Labeling away problem kids. J. Rachlin. il *U.S. News & World Report* 106:59-61 Mr 13 '89

Learning-disabled students: the masks they wear. S. L. Smith. *The Education Digest* 55:50-3 D '89

Look what I did! [software for learning disabled children] M. Furst. il *Home Office Computing* 7:82+ F '89

"My son needed to feel needed" [learning disabled teenage volunteer] M. B. White. il *Parents* 64:84+ Ap '89

LEARNING IN INFANTS See Infants—Growth and development

LEARNING TECHNOLOGY See Educational technology

LEARNING THEORY See Learning, Psychology of

LEAR'S (PERIODICAL)

A maturing woman unleashed [publisher F. Lear] M. Smilgis. il por *Time* 133:70-2 My 15 '89

A new magazine's mercurial midwife [F. Lear] P. Sellers. il por *Fortune* 119:42-3 Ja 2 '89

LEARY, MARY ELLEN

Liberalism's future may depend on social movements. *Utne Reader* p74 Mr/Ap '89

LEARY, TIMOTHY FRANCIS, 1920-

Czar Bennett and his holy war on drugs. *New Perspectives Quarterly* 6:62 Fall '89

LEASE AND RENTAL SERVICES

See also
Airplanes—Leasing and renting
Airplanes, Jet—Leasing and renting
Automobiles—Leasing and renting
Automobiles in business—Leasing and renting
Boats and boating—Leasing and renting
Clothing and dress—Leasing and renting
Computers—Leasing and renting
Dance studios—Leasing and renting
Employee leasing
Fishing boats—Leasing and renting
Houses—Leasing and renting
Itel Corp.
Motor boats—Leasing and renting
Offices—Leasing and renting
Railroads—Cars—Leasing and renting
Ryder System, Inc.
Space stations—Leasing and renting
Trucks in business—Leasing and renting
Vacation houses—Leasing and renting
Video cameras—Leasing and renting
Yachts and yachting—Leasing and renting

Firms now lease everything but time. K. R. Sheets. il *U.S. News & World Report* 107:45-6 Ag 14 '89

LEASE OR BUY DECISIONS

Renting to own. K. K. Gracey. *Consumers' Research Magazine* 72:2 F '89

LEASES

See also
Coal leases
Eviction

Industrial equipment leases
Municipal leases
Oil and gas leases
Triple net partnership

LEASEWAY TRANSPORTATION CORP.

Leaseway may set a standard for ailing LBOs. Z. Schiller. il *Business Week* p81 N 27 '89

LEATHER, ELA MILOSZEWSKI RIGBY- See Rigby-Leather, Ela Miloszewski

LEATHER, GEOFFREY RIGBY- See Rigby-Leather, Geoffrey

LEATHER

See also
Hides and skins

LEATHER, ARTIFICIAL

Faking it! il *Glamour* 87:220 O '89

LEATHER GARMENTS

Best defense [leather riding suits for motorcyclists] J. P. Burns. il *Cycle* 40:60-6 S '89

Designs on leather. il *Essence* 20:40 N '89

Leather soul [work of M. Hoban] A. Kahn. il *Vogue* 179:560+ Mr '89

Rawhide [leather motorcycle riding suits after suffering accidents] K. Vreeke. il *Cycle* 40:67 S '89

LEATHER GOODS

See also
Coach Leatherware (Firm)

LEATHERS, ROBERT

about

Wherever he goes, architect Robert Leathers leaves another new playground behind. N. Geeslin. il pors *People Weekly* 32:63+ S 25 '89

LEAVE IT TO BEAVER [television program] See Television program reviews—Single works

LEAVES

See also
Color of leaves
Grape leaves
Phyllotaxis

Recycling

The trouble with leaves. N. Shute. il *National Wildlife* 27:18-19 O/N '89

LEAVES IN ART

Bark with a bite [R. Carroll's egg tempera paintings] E. Agar. il *American Artist* 53:92-7 S '89

LEAVES OF ABSENCE

See also
Clergy—Leaves of absence
Maternity leaves
Parental leaves
Paternity leaves

The corporate sabbatical: a win-win approach. M. Olivero. *Working Woman* 14:22+ Je '89

John Sculley on sabbatical. B. O'Reilly. il por *Fortune* 119:79-80 Mr 27 '89

Psychological aspects

Separation (from work) anxiety. S. Person. il *Working Woman* 14:61+ Jl '89

LEAVITT, DAVID, 1961-

The way I live now. il *The New York Times Magazine* p28-32+ Jl 9 '89

LEAVITT, GREG A.

about

Heady metal. L. Stains. il por *Home Mechanix* 85:14-16+ Je '89

LEAVITT, PETER

about

Weather or not? J. Zweig. il por *Forbes* 144:120 Jl 10 '89

LEAVITT, ROBERT

Bush's chintzy offer at Vienna. *The Bulletin of the Atomic Scientists* 45:13 O '89

LEBANESE REFUGEES See Refugees, Lebanese

LEBANON

See also
Beirut (Lebanon)
British—Lebanon
Crime and criminals—Lebanon
Espionage, American—Lebanon
Terrorism—Lebanon
United Nations—Lebanon
United States—Diplomatic and consular service—Lebanon

Republic of Lebanon. map *Department of State Bulletin* 88:48-53 D '88

Defenses

See also
Syria—Armed Forces—Forces in Lebanon
United Nations—Armed Forces—Forces in Lebanon

Foreign relations

Iran

See Iran—Foreign relations—Lebanon

Israel

See Israel—Foreign relations—Lebanon

Saudi Arabia

Charade in Taif. *The New Republic* 201:8 N 20 '89

Syria

The nation that has made hell routine. L. Lief. il por *U.S. News & World Report* 106:46-7 My 1 '89

LEBANON—Foreign relations—Syria—*cont.*
Syria and Lebanon in 1988. I. Rabinovich. bibl f *Current History* 88:77-80+ F '89
United States
See United States—Foreign relations—Lebanon
History
Lebanon's damned inheritance. M. House. il *History Today* 39:7-10 Ja '89
Industries
See also
Almashrek Bank
Banque du Liban
Politics and government
See also
Elections—Lebanon
Agony in Beirut [bomb kills President R. Moawad] L. Marlowe. il *Maclean's* 102:26-7 D 4 '89
The agony of Beirut. J. Bierman. il *Maclean's* 102:20-2 Ag 28 '89
The assassination of hope [killing of president R. Moawad] R. Wilkinson. il *Newsweek* 114:68 D 4 '89
Beirut days: life and death. S. Issa. il map *Newsweek* 114:58+ N 13 '89
Beirut diary. I. A. Hijazi. il por *The New York Times Magazine* p30-3+ My 28 '89
Beleaguered Beirut [Arab League calls another ceasefire] L. Marlowe. il *Maclean's* 102:26-7 My 8 '89
Blood brothers. R. F. Haddad. *The New Republic* 200:16-18 My 8 '89
Bloody chaos in Beirut. H. Anderson. il *Newsweek* 113:43 My 1 '89
A bomb aimed at peace. [assassination of R. Moawad] J. F. O. McAllister. il por *Time* 134:52 D 4 '89
Charade in Taif. *The New Republic* 201:8 N 20 '89
Continued fighting in Lebanon [State Dept. statements, March 16 and 29, 1989] *Department of State Bulletin* 89:65 My '89
Death throes of a capital. J. Bartholet and S. Issa. il *Newsweek* 114:24-6 Ag 21 '89
An inside view of Lebanon. J. J. Donohue. *America* 161:378-81 N 25 '89
Lebanon: at the crossroads [address, October 29, 1988] R. W. Murphy. *Department of State Bulletin* 88:45-7 D '88
Lebanon: from change and turmoil to cantonization? G. Rowley. il maps *Focus (New York, N.Y.: 1950)* 39:9-16 Fall '89
Lebanon's last battle? K. H. Sidey. *Christianity Today* 33:46-8 Je 16 '89
Muddling through in Beirut. V. Gryzinski. il *World Press Review* 36:72 D '89
A nation of hostages where memory is a curse. S. V. Roberts. il *U.S. News & World Report* 107:10-11 Ag 21 '89
The nation that has made hell routine. L. Lief. il por *U.S. News & World Report* 106:46-7 My 1 '89
Nearing the point of no return. il *Time* 133:36 Ap 17 '89
A preview of the apocalypse [continued fighting in Beirut] J. Smolowe. il map *Time* 134:23-4 Ag 28 '89
Recent events in the Middle East [statement, September 19, 1989] J. H. Kelly. *Department of State Bulletin* 89:61-3 N '89
Security Council members call for cease-fire in Lebanon. *UN Chronicle* 26:20 S '89
Situation in Lebanon [State Dept. and White House statements, April 3-20, 1989] *Department of State Bulletin* 89:43-4 Je '89
Syria and Lebanon in 1988. I. Rabinovich. bibl f *Current History* 88:77-80+ F '89
Who killed Lebanon? A list of culprits. R. Slusser. *The Christian Century* 106:900-1 O 11 '89
Why the carnage does not stop. R. Backmann and P. Blanchet. *World Press Review* 36:24-5 O '89
Population
Lebanon: from change and turmoil to cantonization? G. Rowley. il maps *Focus (New York, N.Y.: 1950)* 39:9-16 Fall '89
Religious institutions and affairs
See also
Christians—Lebanon
Muslims—Lebanon
LEBANON (CONN.)
Historic houses, sites, etc.
Revolutionary village. C. Weeks. il map *American Heritage* 40:80-91 Ap '89
LEBANON (N.H.)
Airports
First federal MLS is commissioned [microwave landing system] il map *Flying* 116:20 Jl '89
LEBANON HOSTAGE CASES, 1984-
See also
Anderson, Terry—Kidnapping
Cicippio, Joseph—Kidnapping
Higgins, William R.—Kidnapping
Iran-contra affair
Kauffmann, Jean-Paul—Kidnapping
American hostages in the Middle East [remarks, statement, etc., July 31-August 7, 1989] G. Bush. *Department of State Bulletin* 89:66-9 O '89

The bazaar is open [negotiations] J. McDowell. il *Time* 134:23 Ag 21 '89
Beware bad deals at the bazaar [improved relations with Iran] D. Gergen. il *U.S. News & World Report* 107:27 Ag 21 '89
Breaking the ice on assets [prospect of settling with Iran at the Claims Tribunal in return for release of the hostages] L. Lief. il *U.S. News & World Report* 107:89-90 Ag 28-S 4 '89
Concern for the hostages rises. *Christianity Today* 33:48 Je 16 '89
Frenetic caution [G. Bush's handling of the hostage crisis] F. Barnes. *The New Republic* 201:10-11 Ag 28 '89
A game of winks and nods [U.S. releases frozen assets to Iran] R. Lacayo. il *Time* 134:65 N 20 '89
Hanging hostage questions. D. Schorr. il *The New Leader* 72:4 Ag 7-21 '89
Holding ourselves hostage. H. Fairlie. *The New Republic* 201:12-13 Ag 28 '89
Hostage showdown. R. Watson. il map *Newsweek* 114:14-18 Ag 14 '89
Hostages to terror [cover story; special section; with editorial comment by Kevin Doyle] il pors *Maclean's* 102:2, 20-4+ Ag 14 '89
'I feel as if I'm a thief' [interview with J.-P. Kauffmann] B. de Koster and C. Dickey. il por *Newsweek* 113:42 Je 5 '89
Inaction is another form of hanging [kidnapping of A. K. Obeid results in murder of W. R. Higgins] R. Rosenblatt. il por *U.S. News & World Report* 107:8-9 Ag 14 '89
Israel snatches a sheik [A. K. Obeid] por *Newsweek* 114:36 Ag 7 '89
Kidnapping and peace [kidnapping of Sheik A. K. Obeid] *The New Republic* 201:8-9 Ag 21 '89
The man who holds the hostages [I. Mughniyah] il *Time* 133:42 Mr 20 '89
Mixed signals. J. Bierman. il *Maclean's* 102:28-9 Ag 21 '89
New hostage hope? il *Newsweek* 113:7 Ja 16 '89
News conference of August 15 (excerpts). G. Bush. *Department of State Bulletin* 89:13-15 O '89
Not again [dealing with death threats against U.S. hostages; cover story] R. Lacayo. il *Time* 134:14-20+ Ag 14 '89
On the other hand . . . *National Review* 41:14-15 S 15 '89
The president held hostage. *National Review* 41:9-10 S 1 '89
Salting the tail of the hostage takers [kidnapping of Shiite leader A. K. Obeid] *U.S. News & World Report* 107:9 Ag 7 '89
Security Council condemns hostage-taking and abduction; UNIFIL mandate renewed. il *UN Chronicle* 26:25-6 D '89
A shattered deal [release of British hostages in Beirut jeopardized by S. Rushdie affair] il *Newsweek* 113:5 Mr 13 '89
Some reflections on terrorists and hostages. C. W. Weinberger. il *Forbes* 144:31 S 4 '89
A standoff in Iran: Rafsanjani is too weak for a deal on the hostages. R. Watson. il por *Newsweek* 114:51-2 N 6 '89
Talk firmly and send the ships [special section; with editorial comment by Mortimer B. Zuckerman] B. Duffy. il *U.S. News & World Report* 107:22-6+, 72 Ag 14 '89
To deal or not to deal? H. Anderson. il *Newsweek* 114:26 Ag 21 '89
A voice of the Hizballah [interview with M. H. Fadlallah] W. Dowell. por *Time* 134:58-9 O 9 '89
What's a life worth? il *The Progressive* 53:9-10 S '89
Public opinion
Comment as cautious as the president himself. J. Cassidy. il *World Press Review* 36:11-12 S '89
Reporters and reporting
The hostages. *World Press Review* 36:6 S '89
LEBARON, DEAN
Fund managers play 'me too' and fail. por *Fortune* 120:148 Jl 3 '89
LEBER'S HEREDITARY OPTIC NEUROPATHY
Mom's legacy [linked to faulty mitochondrial genes; research by Douglas Wallace] J. Spencer. il *American Health* 8:22+ Mr '89
LEBLANC, RENA DICTOR
Avalanche! il *Reader's Digest* 135:129-33 D '89
LEBLOND, BILLY
about
"We're just ordinary people". B. B. Gray. il pors *Ladies' Home Journal* 106:88+ Jl '89
LEBLOND, DOROTHY BUSH
about
"Dear Doro . . . Devotedly, Dad". G. Bush. il pors *Good Housekeeping* 208:120-1+ Ap '89
"We're just ordinary people". B. B. Gray. il pors *Ladies' Home Journal* 106:88+ Jl '89
LEBOW, EDWARD
ASU Art Museum. il por *American Craft* 49:64-9 Ag/S '89
LEBOW, FRED
about
Piece of cake. il por *Runner's World* 24:48-9 N '89

LEBOWITZ, FRAN
about
Great nappers [interview] il por *House & Garden* 161:164-7
My '89
LEBOWITZ, LISA
Silver streak. il *Harper's Bazaar* 122:56+ Ag '89
LEBRECHT, NORMAN, 1948-
Abbado takes Berlin. il por *Opera News* 54:16-17 D 23
'89
Serious music, serious money. *World Press Review* 36:51
Ag '89
Silver rush. il *Opera News* 54:8-10 Ag '89
Tippett's New Year. il pors *Opera News* 54:22+ O '89
LEBUS *See* Large eddy breakup devices
LECH (AUSTRIA)
The once and future Lech. J. Skow. il *Skiing* 42:182-7 O
'89
LECHNER, FRANK J.
Fundamentalism revisited. bibl *Society* 26:51-9 Ja/F '89
LECHNER, SHERYL
Amazing Glades. il *Sierra* 74:134-40 Ja/F '89
LECITHIN
Potassium channels in cardiac cells activated by arachidonic
acid and phospholipids. D. Kim and D. E. Clapham.
bibl f il *Science* 244:1174-6 Je 9 '89
LECLERC DU SABLON, JEAN
(jt. auth) See L'Ecotais, Yann de, and Leclerc du Sablon,
Jean
LECOMTE, DOUGLAS
The rains return to the tropics. il *Weatherwise* 42:8-12 F
'89
A sun-baked summer in the U.S. il *Weatherwise* 42:13-16
F '89
LECONTE, HENRI
about
Frenchman on the fringe. M. August. il por *World Tennis*
37:59-62 Je '89
**L'ECOTAIS, YANN DE, AND LECLERC DU SABLON,
JEAN**
Who is going to govern Europe? [interview with J. Delors]
il por *World Press Review* 36:28+ S '89
LECTINS
A chitin-binding lectin from stinging nettle rhizomes with
antifungal properties. W. F. Broekaert and others. bibl
f il *Science* 245:1100-2 S 8 '89
Lectins as cell recognition molecules. N. Sharon and H.
Lis. bibl f il *Science* 246:227-34 O 13 '89
LA LECTRICE [film] See Motion picture reviews—Single works
LECTURERS AND LECTURING (PUBLIC SPEAKING) *See*
Public speaking
LED (LIGHT-EMITTING DIODES) *See* Diodes
LEDBETTER, JAMES
New members, new problems. il *The Nation* 248:442-4 Ap
3 '89
LEDDIHN, ERIK VON KUEHNELT- *See* Kuehnelt-Leddihn,
Erik von
LEDEC, GEORGE
(jt. auth) See Goodland, Robert, 1939-, and Ledec, George
LEDEEN, MICHAEL, 1941-
The curious case of chemical warfare. *Commentary* 88:37-41
Jl '89
LEDERER, ESTHER PAULINE See Landers, Ann
LEDERER, RICHARD, 1938-
Down-to-earth language. il *Country Journal* 16:48-9 Ja '89
Haunted words. il *The New York Times Magazine* p14+
S 3 '89
about
Lederer's "linguistic ludicrousness" lands at Pocket Books.
G. Corcoran. il *Publishers Weekly* 235:34 Je 9 '89
LEDERMAN, LEON M.
Observations in particle physics from two neutrinos to the
standard model. bibl f il *Science* 244:664-72 My 12 '89
about
Interview: Leon Lederman. D. Teresi. pors *Omni (New York,
N.Y.)* 12:98-100+ O '89
Nobel Prize in Physics. P. F. Schewe. bibl f *Physics Today*
42:S67 Ja '89
Physics Nobel Prize to Lederman, Schwartz and Steinberger.
B. M. Schwarzschild. bibl f il *Physics Today* 42:17-20
Ja '89
LEDES, ALLISON ECKARDT
Books about antiques. See issues of Antiques
Current and coming. See issues Antiques beginning April
1988
The Mexican War in print and photograph. il *Antiques*
136:1242 D '89
LEDESMA, RODOLFO G.
How to check your credit rating. il *Consumers' Research
Magazine* 72:30-3 S '89
LEDGER, CHARLES, 1818-1905
about
He gave quinine to the world. J. Bland. il *World Health*
p28-9 D '88
LEDOGAR, STEPHEN J.
CFE talks end round two [statement, July 13, 1989]
Department of State Bulletin 89:75 S '89

European security negotiations open in Vienna [conventional
armed forces; statements and text of Western position
paper, March 9, 1989] *Department of State Bulletin* 89:33-4
My '89
LEDUC, GILBERT
Mlle. Liberty at 200. il *World Press Review* 36:26 Je '89
LEE, BARBARA
10 questions to ask your broker. *Harper's Bazaar* 122:54+
Ja '89
LEE, BENJAMIN, AND LEE, LEO OU-FAN
The Goddess of Democracy deconstructed. il *New Perspectives
Quarterly* 6:58-61 Fall '89
LEE, BERTRAM M.
about
Blacks buy NBA Nuggets; 1st black-owned pro team. il
pors *Jet* 76:51+ Jl 24 '89
Blacks conclude deal to buy NBA Denver Nuggets. *Jet* 77:51
N 6 '89
Crossing the last sports color line. il *Newsweek* 114:52 Jl
24 '89
The NBA scores a first in the front office. K. H. Hammonds
and W. C. Symonds. il pors *Business Week* p26 Jl 24
'89
Nuggets buy makes history. Will it crumble barrier? P.
Raybon. il pors *Black Enterprise* 20:17-18 S '89
Sale of Denver Nuggets to two blacks is delayed. pors *Jet*
77:37 O 30 '89
Welcome to the owners' club. M. Jaffe. il por *Sports Illustrated*
71:12 Jl 24 '89
LEE, BRENDAN, AND OTHERS
Identification of the molecular defect in a family with
spondyloepiphyseal dysplasia. bibl f il *Science* 244:978-80
My 26 '89
LEE, CATHLEEN COLLINS
Mothering my way. il *Parents* 64:85-6+ S '89
LEE, DAVID
Left-wing miracles. *National Review* 41:34 S 29 '89
LEE, DON
El Niño [story] il *Gentlemen's Quarterly* 59:224+ O
'89
LEE, DOUGLAS
Tragedy in Alaska waters. il map *National Geographic*
176:260-3 Ag '89
LEE, G.
All Souls' Day [poem] *America* 161:278 O 28 '89
LEE, GIL, AND OTHERS
Scanning tunneling microscopy of nucleic acids. bibl f il
Science 244:475-7 Ap 28 '89
LEE, GLENDA
A Gallic gala comes to America. il *Harper's Bazaar* 122:26+
Ap '89
Prosaic to professional. il pors *Harper's Bazaar* 122:22+
Je '89
LEE, HELEN, AND OTHERS
High rate of HTLV-II infection in seropositive IV drug
abusers in New Orleans. bibl f il *Science* 244:471-5 Ap
28 '89
LEE, KAI N.
The Columbia River basin [cover story] bibl f il map
Environment 31:6-11+ Jl/Ag '89
LEE, KUAN YEW
about
Singapore—an ally we need. C. W. Weinberger. il por *Forbes*
143:31 My 29 '89
LEE, KUO-CHUN
(jt. auth) See Takefuji, Yoshiyasu, and Lee, Kuo-Chun
LEE, KYUNG-SIK
Nurses and the community. il *World Health* p4 N '89
LEE, LEO OU-FAN
(jt. auth) See Lee, Benjamin, and Lee, Leo Ou-fan
LEE, MICHELE
about
The bittersweet truth about love triangles. J. Lazar. il por
TV Guide 37:9 O 21-27 '89
How her painful divorce helped her on Knots Landing.
J. Hicks. il pors *TV Guide* 37:18-20 Ag 5-11 '89
LEE, MIN S., AND OTHERS
Three-dimensional solution structure of a single zinc finger
DNA-binding domain [cover story] bibl f il *Science*
245:635-7 Ag 11 '89
LEE, P. C.
(jt. auth) See Foley, R. A., and Lee, P. C.
LEE, PAULINE L., AND OTHERS
Purification and complementary DNA cloning of a receptor
for basic fibroblast growth factor. bibl f il *Science* 245:57-60
Jl 7 '89
LEE, PETER, AND OTHERS
Anomalous scattering study of the Bi distribution in the
2212 superconductor: implications for Cu valency. bibl
f il *Science* 244:62-3 Ap 7 '89
LEE, PHYLLIS
Basic training. il *Black Enterprise* 19:52-3 Jl '89
How to beat jet lag drag. il *Black Enterprise* 19:78 Mr
'89
LEE, RENSSELAER W.
South American cocaine: why the U.S. can't stop it. *Current
(Washington, D.C.)* 313:22-31 Je '89

LEE, RICHARD E., JR.
Insect cold-hardiness: to freeze or not to freeze. bibl f il *BioScience* 39:308-13 My '89
LEE, RICKY
Perils of privilege. il *Harper's Bazaar* 122:72 O '89
LEE, RUSSELL
about
In the footsteps of Russell Lee. E. Margolis. il *Society* 26:77-83 Ja/F '89
LEE, SPIKE
Spike to Spike: the filmmaker interviews himself. il pors *Essence* 20:55-6 Jl '89
about
Do the right thing [film] Reviews
America 161:86-7 Ag 12-19 '89. R. A. Blake
Commonweal 116:562-3 O 20 '89. B. B. Morton
Commonweal 116:402-3 Jl 14 '89. T. O'Brien
Essence il pors 20:55-6 Jl '89
Mademoiselle il por 95:94+ Ag '89. R. Rosenbaum
Mother Jones il por 14:35+ S '89. A. White
The Nation 249:98-100 Jl 17 '89. S. Klawans
National Review il 41:45-6+ Ag 4 '89. J. Simon
The New Leader 72:21-2 S 18 '89. J. Morrone
The New Republic 201:24-6 Jl 3 '89. S. Kauffmann
New York il por 22:53-4 Je 26 '89. D. Denby
The New York Review of Books il 36:37-8 S 28 '89. M. Kempton
The New Yorker 65:78-81 Jl 24 '89. T. Rafferty
People Weekly il por 32:13-14 Jl 3 '89. R. Novak
Rolling Stone il p27+ Je 29 '89. P. Travers
Time il por 134:62 Jl 3 '89. R. Corliss
Vogue il pors 179:76-7+ Jl '89. D. McLane
Do the right thing: a jarring look at racism. J. M. Wall. *The Christian Century* 106:739-40 Ag 16-23 '89
Doing the controversial thing. A. P. Sanoff. por *U.S. News & World Report* 107:51 Jl 10 '89
He's got to have it his way. J. McDowell. il por *Time* 134:92-4 Jl 17 '89
How hot is too hot? [special section] il *Newsweek* 114:64-6 Jl 3 '89
Insight to riot. D. Handelman. il por *Rolling Stone* p104-5+ Jl 13-27 '89
Knocking on Hollywood's door [cover story] B. Sharkey. il pors *American Film* 14:22-7+ Jl/Ag '89
Local hero. T. Davis. il pors *American Film* 14:26-7 Jl/Ag '89
Public Enemy number one. M. Horowitz. il por *American Film* 14:15 S '89
Spike Lee. il por *People Weekly* 32:78-9 D 25 '89-Ja 1 '90
Spike Lee explores racial conflict in 'Do the right thing' [cover story] T. S. Moore. il pors *Jet* 76:36-9 Jl 10 '89
Spike Lee inflames the critics with a film he swears is The right thing. J. S. Kunen. il pors *People Weekly* 32:67-8 Jl 10 '89
Spike Lee replies: "Say it ain't so, Joe" [discussion of June 26, 1989 article, Spiked?] J. Klein. il por *New York* 22:6 Jl 17 '89
Spike Lee: the man behind the movies and the controversy. L. Norment. il pors *Ebony* 44:140+ O '89
Spike Lee's Bed-Stuy BBQ [interview] M. Glicksman. il pors *Film Comment* 25:12-16+ Jl/Ag '89
Spiked? J. Klein. il pors *New York* 22:14-15 Je 26 '89
Spike's riot [cover story] P. Orenstein. il pors *Mother Jones* 14:32-5+ S '89
Uplifting his race. D. O. Relin and T. Beller. il por *Scholastic Update (Teachers' edition)* 121:27 Ap 7 '89
The 'vision' thing. D. Ansen. il por *Newsweek* 114:37 O 2 '89
The world according to Spike Lee [cover story] M. Morrison. por *National Review* 41:24-5 Ag 4 '89
LEE, STAN
about
Stan Lee comic-book hero. A. Roth. il *American Film* 15:12 O '89
LEE, WILL, AND OTHERS
Secretion of activin by interstitial cells in the testis. bibl f il *Science* 243:396-8 Ja 20 '89
LEE, WILL
about
The World's Most Dangerous sidemen. il pors *Down Beat* 56:18 O '89
LEECH, ROBIN
about
The barn collectors. M. Cantwell. il pors *House & Garden* 161:126-35 F '89
LEECH, THOMAS
Suminagashi: black ink floating. *Focus (New York, N.Y.: 1950)* 39:3 Summ '89
LEECHES
Nervous system
See Nervous system—Annelids
LEEDS, DOROTHY
How to be sure your speech is a success [excerpt from Powerspeak] *Working Woman* 14:98-9 Mr '89
LEEDS, JEFFREY T.
Impeccable judgments or tainted policies? il *The New York Times Magazine* p72+ S 10 '89

LEEDS (ENGLAND)
Music
See also
Opera North
LEEN, JERRY
about
Nob Hill epigram: an antiquarian's San Francisco apartment. H. Junker. il por *Architectural Digest* 46:250-5 My '89
LEES-MILINE, JAMES
Portraits of houses: contemporary masters of a venerable genre. il *Architectural Digest* 46:118+ Mr '89
LEESTAMPER, ROBERT E.
Run Richmond graduates, run [address, May 11, 1989] *Vital Speeches of the Day* 56:156-7 D 15 '89
LEETCH, BRIAN
about
Oh, you kids, you. A. Murphy. il pors *Sports Illustrated* 70:40-2+ Ja 30 '89
LEEWARD ISLANDS (WEST INDIES)
See also
Nevis (Saint Kitts-Nevis)
Saint Barthélemy (Guadeloupe)
LEFALLE-COLLINS, LIZZETTA
Sandra Rowe: practitioner of a healing art [cover story] il pors *American Visions* 4:27-9 Ag '89
LEFEBVRE, MARCEL
about
The Lefebvrite-feminist coalition? M. McGough. il *The American Spectator* 22:28-9 Ag '89
LEFEVER, ERNEST W.
Gorbachev's challenge to the West [address, April 11, 1989] *Vital Speeches of the Day* 55:588-91 Jl 15 '89
LEFF, LEONARD J., AND SIMMONS, JEROLD, 1941-
No trollops, no tomcats [excerpt from The dame in the kimono] il por *American Film* 15:40-3+ D '89
LEFF, NAOMI
about
Minding the store. C. Vogel. il por *The New York Times Magazine* p34-7 Jl 30 '89
LEFFINGWELL, EDWARD
São Paulo diary. il *Art in America* 77:55-7+ Ja '89
LEFKOWITZ, ALAN
about
Comedy shrink. P. Mehlman. il *Gentlemen's Quarterly* 59:218 Ag '89
LEFKOWITZ, MARY R., 1935-
The powers of the primeval goddesses. *The American Scholar* 58:586-91 Aut '89
LEFRANCOIS, LEO, AND GOODMAN, THOMAS
In vivo modulation of cytolytic activity and thy-1 expression in TCR-γδ⁺ intraepithelial lymphocytes. bibl f il *Science* 243:1716-18 Mr 31 '89
LEFT (POLITICAL SCIENCE) *See* Communism; Liberalism; Radicalism; Socialism
LEFT AND RIGHT (POLITICAL SCIENCE) *See* Right and left (Political science)
LEFT- AND RIGHT-HANDEDNESS
Bat those eyes! [crossed eye-hand dominance in baseball players; research by Jose Portal and Paul Romano] S. McKee. il *American Health* 8:16 O '89
A 'handy' guide to primate evolution. B. Bower. il *Science News* 135:10-12 Ja 7 '89
Lefties and longevity: look again [disagreement between Stanley Coren and Max Anderson] R. Weiss. *Science News* 136:180 S 16 '89
Now, on the other hand [left-handed people more accident prone] il *U.S. News & World Report* 107:18 Ag 21 '89
On the other hand. J. T. Gibson. il *Parents* 64:171 F '89
Psychologist Stanley Coren's bad news comes out of left field—lefties lead riskier, shorter lives [interview] D. K. Bacon. il por *People Weekly* 32:115-16+ N 6 '89
Sinister stats [shorter life expectancy for lefties; study by Diane F. Halpern and Stanley Coren] T. Waters. il *Discover* 10:26 Ap '89
Anecdotes, facetiae, satire, etc.
Do we want a leftist in the White House? D. Seligman. il *Fortune* 119:135-6 Ja 16 '89
LEFTOVERS *See* Cooking—Leftovers
LEG
See also
Knee
Fall signals: legs. S. Orlean. il *Vogue* 179:164-5 Jl '89
Care
The smoothest legs ever. S. Young. il *Glamour* 87:56 My '89
Wounds and injuries
After the fall [skier P. Fletcher recovers from fracture] S. Nelson. il por *Health (New York, N.Y.)* 21:28-9 Mr '89
Broken but unbowed [Cincinnati's T. Krumrie recuperates from leg fracture suffered in Super Bowl] J. Lieber. il pors *Sports Illustrated* 70:104-7 Mr 20 '89
Last legs [running] M. Tymn. il *Runner's World* 24:24 Mr '89
LEG, ARTIFICIAL
Helping amputees walk again [work of David Thompson] il *USA Today (Periodical)* 117:12 F '89

LEG EXERCISES See Exercise
LEGACIES
See also
Wills
LEGAL AID
See also
Legal Defense and Educational Fund
Legal Services Corporation
Defending the poor: a harder task [cover story] G. M. Anderson. il *America* 160:4-7 Ja 7-14 '89
The pro bono hustle. L. Mundy. *The Washington Monthly* 21:10-14+ S '89

South Africa
See also
Legal Resources Center (South Africa)
LEGAL ASSISTANCE TO IMMIGRANTS
An inquisitor becomes an ally [Canada] P. Kaihla. *Maclean's* 102:18 Jl 10 '89
LEGAL COMMITTEE (UNITED NATIONS) See United Nations. Legal Committee
LEGAL DEFENSE AND EDUCATIONAL FUND
Guarding the civil rights dream. C. Whitaker. il *Ebony* 45:31-2+ N '89
NAACP/LDEF sues Shoney's. L. Brown. *Black Enterprise* 20:20 Ag '89
LEGAL EDUCATION See Law—Study and teaching; Law schools
LEGAL ETHICS
See also
Confidential communications—Lawyers
Judicial ethics
The drug lawyers. S. Waldman and M. Miller. il *Newsweek* 114:41+ N 13 '89
The flowering of legal ethics in America [cover story] R. F. Drinan. il *America* 161:76-8 Ag 12-19 '89
Lawyers and leveraged buyouts [address, November 16, 1988] J. T. Laney. *Vital Speeches of the Day* 55:318-20 Mr 1 '89
The pro bono hustle. L. Mundy. *The Washington Monthly* 21:10-14+ S '89
Stop the barrister bullies [land use suits brought against local government] P. A. A. Berle. *Audubon* 91:8 Mr '89
LEGAL FEES See Cost (Law); Lawyers—Salaries, fees, etc.
LEGAL MALPRACTICE See Malpractice
LEGAL MEDICINE See Medical jurisprudence
LEGAL NEWSLETTERS
See also
Bowker's legal publishing preview (Newsletter)
LEGAL PERIODICALS See Law—Periodicals
LEGAL PHILOSOPHY See Law—Philosophy
LEGAL PROCEDURE
See also
Actions and defenses
Arbitration and award
Bail
Confession (Law)
Executions and executioners
Extradition
Grand jury
Jury
Public prosecutors
Searches and seizures
Trials
Do-it-yourself law. K. L. Bundy. *Essence* 19:103 Ja '89
LEGAL PROFESSION See Lawyers
LEGAL RESOURCES CENTER (SOUTH AFRICA)
Taking apartheid to court. B. W. Nelan. il *Time* 134:44 Ag 14 '89
LEGAL SERVICES CORPORATION
Fox in the coop [chairman M. Wallace] J. Gill. *The Nation* 248:40 Ja 9-16 '89
Off the record. Cato. *National Review* 41:56 D 22 '89
Right cross [conservatives fight nomination of M. C. Butler] F. Barnes. *The New Republic* 201:10-12 O 16 '89
LEGAL TECHNICIANS
Perry Mason they're not. M. Shao. il *Business Week* p83+ N 20 '89
LEGALIZATION OF NARCOTICS
Accepting the presence of drugs. A. S. Trebach. il *New Perspectives Quarterly* 6:40-4 Summ '89
Can government outlaw drugs? [debate between Victorians H. Spencer and J. F. Stephen] M. Cranston. pors *National Review* 41:43-5 O 13 '89
Drug decriminalization [discussion of September 1, 1989 article, Drug prohibition in the United States: costs, consequences, and alternatives] E. A. Nadelmann. *Science* 246:1102-5 D 1 '89
Drug prohibition in the United States: costs, consequences, and alternatives. E. A. Nadelmann. bibl f *Science* 245:939-47 S 1 '89
Drug talk across the way. W. F. Buckley. *National Review* 41:63 My 5 '89
The enemy within. M. B. Zuckerman. il *U.S. News & World Report* 107:91 S 11 '89
First word. K. Schmoke. il *Omni (New York, N.Y.)* 11:8 Ap '89
Is legalization the answer? il *World Press Review* 36:27-8 N '89

Should drugs be legalized?:
No. R. Coles. *Utne Reader* p80 Mr/Ap '89
Yes. E. Scigliano. *Utne Reader* p80 Mr/Ap '89
Taking on the legalizers. T. Morganthau. il *Newsweek* 114:46-8 D 25 '89
A war for the Surgeon General, not the Attorney General. K. Schmoke. il *New Perspectives Quarterly* 6:12-15 Summ '89

Anecdotes, facetiae, satire, etc.
When the feds turned drug dealer. J. Leo. il *U.S. News & World Report* 107:75 N 13 '89
The year they legalized drugs. V. Gold. il *The American Spectator* 22:33 N '89
Public opinion
This is what you thought: 89% say drugs should not be legalized! [results of survey] il *Glamour* 87:49 Ja '89
Netherlands
The Dutch model. E. Engelsman. *New Perspectives Quarterly* 6:44-5 Summ '89
Western Europe
A Common Market of crack? C. Dickey. il *Newsweek* 114:37 S 18 '89
LEGAT, JOHN
about
A European expedition. E. Giltenan. il *Forbes* 144:172 S 4 '89
LEGEND (WORD PROCESSOR PROGRAM) See Word processors and processing—Programming
LEGENDS
See also
Indians of North America—Legends
Mythology
Romeo and Juliet (Legend)
LEGERE, ALLAN
about
Blood on the cross. G. W. Taylor. il por *Maclean's* 102:71 N 27 '89
The end of a manhunt. P. Kopvillem. por *Maclean's* 102:25 D 4 '89
LEGETTE, CYNTHIA
Branch office big shot. il *Black Enterprise* 19:129-30+ F '89
How to improve your negotiation skills. il *Black Enterprise* 20:106-8+ O '89
LEGG MASON VALUE TRUST
Will the real Ben Graham please stand up? [stock pickers E. Kiehne and W. H. Miller] J. Clements. il pors *Forbes* 144:310+ D 11 '89
LEGGE, KATE
Abortion debate. *World Press Review* 36:46 F '89
LEGGE, MICHAEL
Sharing the U.S. burden: a British view. il *Current (Washington, D.C.)* 313:15-21 Je '89
LEGIARDI-LAURA, ROLAND
about
Azul [film] Reviews
The Nation 248:786-7 Je 5 '89. S. Klawans
LEGISLATION
See also
Law
Referendum
United States. Congress
Veto
When is a ladybug a matter of state? [designation of state symbols by state legislatures] W. Ecenbarger. il *Reader's Digest* 135:134-6 D '89
Canada
See also
Canada. Parliament
LEGISLATIVE BODIES
See also
State legislatures
United States. Congress
LEGISLATORS
See also
Congressmen
Congresswomen
Senators
Conflict of interests
See Conflict of interests (Public office)
Language
Anecdotes, facetiae, satire, etc.
The legislative mangle. M. Ivins. il *The New York Times Magazine* p20+ S 17 '89
LEGISLATURES, STATE See State legislatures
LEGOLAND PARK (BILLUND, DENMARK)
Spring cleanup at Legoland Park [cover story] il *National Geographic World* 171:4-9 N '89
LEGRAND, CATHERINE
The little girl without a smile. il *Reader's Digest* 135:107-12 Ag '89
LEGRAND, TERESA M.
about
GE whiz. M. Alpert. il por *Fortune* 119:151 Mr 27 '89
LEGRIS, MICHEL, AND GONIN, JEAN-MARC
Paradox for Switzerland. *World Press Review* 36:63 D '89

LEGS *See* Leg
LEGS DIAMOND [musical] See Musicals, revues, etc.—
Reviews—Single works
LEGUIN, URSULA *See* Le Guin, Ursula K., 1929-
LEGUMES
See also
Alfalfa
Beans
Cooking—Vegetables
Peas
Soybeans
LEGVOLD, ROBERT
The revolution in Soviet foreign policy. bibl f *Foreign Affairs*
68 Special Issue:82-98 ['89]
LEGVOLD, GARY
Fitness matters. See issues of Better Homes and Gardens
beginning October 1987
Medical technology. il pors *Better Homes and Gardens* 67:44+
My '89
LEHMAN, DAVID, 1948-
Literal lives [poem] *The New Republic* 201:32 D 18
'89
One size fits all: a critical essay [poem] *The New York
Review of Books* 36:19 Jl 20 '89
With tenure [poem] *The New York Review of Books*
36:23 F 16 '89
LEHMAN, JOHN F.
TV vs. the military: it's an unfair fight. il *TV Guide* 37:32-4
N 4-10 '89
about
Man the pumps! C. W. Weinberger. il *Forbes* 143:31 My
1 '89
LEHMAN, MICHAEL
about
The case of the tick and the tic. A. Roblin. il *Prevention
(Emmaus, Pa.)* 41:104-5+ Jl '89
LEHMAN, PAUL R.
"Toward civilization" in music education. *The Education
Digest* 54:46-9 My '89
LEHMAN, WENDY
about
Carving out a niche. R. Koenig. il por *House & Garden*
161:218-23 O '89
New working class. il pors *Harper's Bazaar* 122:160-75+
Mr '89
LEHMANN, DANIEL J.
Financial worries darken ELCA assembly. *The Christian
Century* 106:804-5 S 13-20 '89
Whatever happened to Sunday school? il *The Christian
Century* 106:404-5 Ap 19 '89
LEHMANN, MICHAEL
about
Heathers [film] Reviews
American Film il 14:10 Ja/F '89. L. Ochoa
The American Spectator il 22:42-3 Je '89. B. Bawer
Gentlemen's Quarterly il 59:123+ Ap '89. K. Turan
The Nation 248:530 Ap 17 '89. S. Klawans
New York il 22:68+ Ap 3 '89. D. Denby
The New Yorker 65:115-16 Ap 17 '89. P. Kael
Newsweek 113:67 Ap 3 '89. D. Ansen
Rolling Stone il p38 Ap 20 '89. S. Pond
Time il 133:83 Ap 17 '89. R. Corliss
Video il 13:88+ S '89. I. Robbins
LEHMANN, RICHARD J.
about
Thumb in the dike. J. H. Taylor. il por *Forbes* 144:76
Ag 21 '89
LEHN, JOSEPH
about
Just for pretty: Joseph Lehn's boxes. il *Americana* 17:36
S/O '89
LEHNER, MONIQUE B., AND FANNIN, MINXIE J.
History in towns: Hingham, Massachusetts [cover story] bibl
f il *Antiques* 136:812-25 O '89
LEHNHOFF, NIKOLAUS
about
Five minutes to midnight. P. O'Connor. il pors *Opera News*
53:14-16+ Mr 4 '89
LEHRER, JOHN
Be the master of your machine. il *Women's Sports & Fitness*
11:16+ Jl/Ag '89
Take a ride in the great indoors. il *Women's Sports &
Fitness* 11:14 O '89
Ten tips toward a better ride. il *Women's Sports & Fitness*
11:16 Mr '89
LEHRER, LINDA
More than she bargained for. il *Ms.* 17:111-14 Ja/F '89
LEHRER, MERRILL C.
California caravan: the Parlor Car way. il *USA Today
(Periodical)* 117:36-41 My '89
Compact discs. See issues of USA Today (Periodical) beginning
January 1988
Has the Orient totally conquered U.S. electronics? Seven
companies say no [cover story] il *USA Today (Periodical)*
117:16-22 Ja '89
MGM Grand: affluence in the air. il *USA Today (Periodical)*
117:34-7 Mr '89

LEHRER, SHERWIN S., AND OTHERS
Assembly of the native heterodimer of Rana esculenta
tropomyosin by chain exchange. bibl f il *Science* 246:926-8
N 17 '89
LEHTINEN, DEXTER
about
Last gasp for the Everglades. J. Carney. il por map *Time*
134:26-7 S 25 '89
LEHTINEN, ILEANA ROS- *See* Ros-Lehtinen, Ileana
LEIBNER, RICHARD
about
When Leibner calls, the networks listen. B. Yagoda. il pors
The New York Times Magazine p36-8+ Je 18 '89
LEIBOVIT, MARK
about
Is this a blow-off? M. Hulbert. il *Forbes* 143:191 Je 12
'89
LEIFERMANN, HENRY
Head for the hills. il *New Choices for the Best Years* 29:58-64
Mr '89
The other Georgia [cover story] il map *New Choices for
the Best Years* 29:46-52 Jl '89
LEIGH, CHRISTIAN
about
A big influence. H. Muschamp. il por *Vogue* 179:98+ Ja
'89
LEIGH, JULIA
High school . . . the sequel. il *Health (New York, N.Y.)*
21:52-5 Jl '89
LEIGH, MIKE, 1943-
about
High hopes [film] Reviews
Commonweal 116:212 Ap 7 '89. T. O'Brien
The Nation 248:352-3 Mr 13 '89. S. Klawans
The New Leader 72:22-3 F 20 '89. J. Morrone
The New Republic 200:26-7 Mr 13 '89. S. Kauffmann
New York il 22:142-3 F 27 '89. D. Denby
The New Yorker 65:96-8 F 20 '89. P. Kael
Newsweek il 113:69 F 27 '89. D. Ansen
Time il 133:72-3 Mr 20 '89. R. Schickel
LEIGH, PAMELA
Not-so-tough talk from Clint Eastwood. il pors *Ladies' Home
Journal* 106:38+ Je '89
Tom Selleck: one man and a baby. il por *Ladies' Home
Journal* 106:38+ Mr '89
LEIGH STOWELL & COMPANY
Knocking newspapers [WVEC's campaign for advertising
dollar in Norfolk, Va.] A. Snyder. il *Channels (New York,
N.Y.: 1986)* 9:32-3 F '89
LEIGHT, WARREN D.
His. See issues of Mademoiselle beginning December 1987
LEIGHTON, JAN
about
Man of a thousand faces. B. Kanner. il pors *New York*
22:20-1 My 29 '89
LEIGHTON, MARK
about
Interdependence. F. Graham. il *Audubon* 91:14+ My '89
LEIGHTON HOUSE ART GALLERY AND MUSEUM (LON-
DON, ENGLAND)
Lord Leighton's palace of art. S. Jones. il por *Antiques*
135:1466-75 Je '89
LEIGHTON OF STRETTON, FREDERIC LEIGHTON,
BARON, 1830-1896
about
Lord Leighton's palace of art. S. Jones. il por *Antiques*
135:1466-75 Je '89
LEIKEN, ROBERT S., 1939-
The Soviet Union and Nicaragua [reprint from October 1984
issue] *Current History* 88:39-40+ Ja '89
LEIMBACH, MARTI
about
Marti Leimbach's first novel clocks up $500,000 in advances.
J. Crichton. por *Publishers Weekly* 235:46-7 Je 16 '89
LEINBAUGH, HAROLD P.
about
The secret of the soldiers who didn't shoot. F. P. Smoler.
il pors *American Heritage* 40:5, 36-45 Mr '89
LEINWOLL, STANLEY
Shortwave radio. See issues of Radio-Electronics beginning
April 1988
LEIPZIG (GERMANY)
Protests, demonstrations, etc.
Church in East Germany helps create die Wende. J. P.
Burgess. *The Christian Century* 106:1140-2 D 6 '89
Leipzig: hotbed of protest. K. W. Banta. il *Time* 134:41
N 27 '89
LEISHMAN, KATIE
The outsider. il por *Rolling Stone* p75-6+ Mr 23 '89
LEISHMANIASIS
Therapy
Receptor-mediated drug delivery to macrophages in
chemotherapy of leishmaniasis. A. Mukhopadhyay and
others. bibl f il *Science* 244:705-7 My 12 '89
LEISURE, MARY JO, AND WENTZ, MARGY
Santa is everything that is Christmas [excerpt from Homes
for the holiday with painted treasures] il *Good Housekeeping*
209:166-7 D '89

LEISURE
    See also
    Fidelity Select Leisure & Entertainment Fund
    Hobbies
    Recreation
    Vacations
13 ways to a perfect summer weekend. il *Glamour* 87:85 Ag '89
Helping students use leisure time effectively [social studies] W. W. Crowder. *The Education Digest* 55:54-6 N '89
How to spend time, not save it. L. Mosedale. il *Glamour* 87:236-9 Ag '89
Leisure and recreation. D. Fanning. il *Forbes* 143:168-9 Ja 9 '89
Lovers' weekend: a stay-at-home guide to romance. il *Glamour* 87:190-3+ F 19 '89
Make the most of your weekends [families] M. Hodge and J. Blyskal. il *Reader's Digest* 134:9-10+ Ap '89
Making time for your other life [special section] il *Working Woman* 14:101-8+ Mr '89
Present tense. J. Reed. il *Vogue* 179:426-9 N '89
Rediscovering the rat race. R. J. Samuelson. il *Newsweek* 113:57 My 15 '89
Time out to recharge [weekend activities; special section] il *Working Woman* 14:107-116+ Je '89
Unguarded moments [cover story] R. Laliberte. il *Health (New York, N.Y.)* 21:52-7 Ag '89
LEISURE HOMES *See* Vacation houses
LEITCH, DONOVAN, 1967-
    about
Bangle Susanna Hoffs and actor Donovan Leitch, son of just plain Donovan, mellow together. P. Freeman. il pors *People Weekly* 31:73-4+ Je 12 '89
LEITHAUSER, BRAD
Rain & snow [poem] *The New Yorker* 65:146 N 13 '89
Your natural history [poem] *The Atlantic* 264:78 N '89
LEITZKE, MARCIE
Red Wing stoneware soars. il *Antiques & Collecting Hobbies* 93:26-7+ F '89
LEIU *See* Law Enforcement Intelligence Unit
LEIVENBERG, RICHARD
Holiday gift guide: what to buy the sports nut who's seen and played everything. il *Sport (New York, N.Y.)* 80:76-7 Ja '89
Tru confessions. il pors *Harper's Bazaar* 122:362-3+ S '89
LEJEUNE, ANTHONY, 1928-
It's not all Brideshead revisited. il *National Review* 41:27-9 O 13 '89
No quick drug fix. *National Review* 41:21-3 Mr 24 '89
On the track of a sacred cow. *National Review* 41:29 Mr 10 '89
The rise and fall of the western [cover story] il *National Review* 41:23-6 D 31 '89
LEKACHMAN, ROBERT
F.D.R. changed, and so can you. il por *The Nation* 248:117-18 Ja 30 '89
    about
Obituary
    The Nation 248:148-9 F 6 '89
    The New Leader 72:2 Ja 23 '89
LELAND, JOHN, 1754-1841
    about
The original "Big Cheese". R. Sassaman. il *American History Illustrated* 23:34-5 Ja '89
LELAND, MICKEY
What African-Americans can do about starvation in Africa. il *Ebony* 44:80-2+ O '89
    about
Before death, Leland wrote in Ebony about starvation in Africa. il pors *Jet* 76:16-18+ Ag 28 '89
Fatal flight in Ethiopia. C. S. Manegold. il por map *Newsweek* 114:37 Ag 21 '89
Obituary
    Black Enterprise il 20:11 O '89. E. G. Graves
    Black Enterprise il por 20:21 O '89. S. Jones
    Jet il pors 76:10-13+ Ag 28 '89
    Jet il 76:54-5 S 11 '89
    Jet il pors 76:6-13+ S 4 '89
    The New Yorker 65:31-2 S 11 '89
    People Weekly il pors 32:83 Ag 28 '89
    The Progressive il 53:37 O '89. M. Ivins
    Time por 134:12 Ag 28 '89
LEMAÎTRE, PHILIPPE
First aid. il *World Press Review* 36:16 O '89
LEMANN, NANCY
Creole comforts. il por *House & Garden* 161:180-5+ S '89
LEMANN, NICHOLAS
Act II, winning an election. *The Washington Monthly* 21:30+ Mr '89
"Gung ho on O'B". il *The Atlantic* 263:26+ Je '89
Lessons from the poverty front. *The Washington Monthly* 21:33-5 D '89
Me and my fish fetish. il *Esquire* 112:70+ S '89
Stressed out in suburbia. il *The Atlantic* 264:34+ N '89
The unfinished war (II). il *The Atlantic* 263:52-6+ Ja '89

Whistling in the Pentagon. bibl f il *The New York Review of Books* 36:3-4+ O 26 '89
LEMIEUX, MARIO
    about
The Gretzky chase [cover story; special section; with editorial comment by Kevin Doyle] il pors *Maclean's* 102:2, 32-7 F 20 '89
Make room for Lemieux [cover story] A. Murphy. il pors *Sports Illustrated* 70:28-30+ F 6 '89
LEMIRE, SARAH
    about
Inside Cosby's closet [interview] J. Marion. il *TV Guide* 37:9 Ap 1-7 '89
LEMMON, JACK
This Lemmon gets sweeter with age [ed. by Patricia Nolan] il pors *New Choices for the Best Years* 29:16+ Mr '89
LEMNA *See* Duckweeds
LEMON GROVE (CALIF.)
    Education
Still hungry for knowledge at 105, Gertrude Palmer is one for the books [named Senior Adult Student of the Year] il pors *People Weekly* 31:116-17 Mr 20 '89
LEMONADE
Naturally pink lemonade. il *Sunset (Central West edition)* 183:176 O '89
LEMOND, GREG, 1961?-
    about
Beating the clock—and all the odds—cyclist Greg LeMond triumphs in the Tour de France. C. Nolan and others. il pors *People Weekly* 32:51-3 Ag 7 '89
CoreStates. T. Blumenthal. il *Bicycling* 30:14 S '89
Le Grand LeMond [cover story] E. M. Swift. il pors map *Sports Illustrated* 71:54-8+ D 25 '89-Ja 1 '90
LeMond's ultimate challenge. G. Drake. il pors *Bicycling* 30:60-2+ My '89
Never say die [cover story; with editorial comment by James C. McCullagh] P. Kimmage. il pors *Bicycling* 30:10, 30-4+ O/N '89
Vive LeMond! [cover story] F. Lidz. il pors *Sports Illustrated* 71:12-17 Jl 31 '89
World beater. G. Drake. il por *Bicycling* 30:28-32+ D '89
LEMONICK, MICHAEL D.
Back to the future. il *Discover* 10:42-3+ Ja '89
The two faces of Nereid. il *Discover* 10:18-19 Ja '89
LEMONS (AUTOMOBILES) *See* Automobiles—Defects
LEMOS, PETER
Indiana in Maine. il pors *Art News* 88:166-9 O '89
LEMOYNE, JAMES
El Salvador's forgotten war. *Foreign Affairs* 68:105-25 Summ '89
The guns of Salvador [cover story] il *The New York Times Magazine* p18-21+ F 5 '89
LEMPER, UTE
    about
German chanteuse Ute Lemper proves you don't have to be 50 to take a walk on the Weill side. T. Kahn. il pors *People Weekly* 31:113-14 Mr 13 '89
LEMURS
    Photographs and photography
On the trail of lemurs [Madagascar; cover story] F. Lanting. il *International Wildlife* 19:4-13 My/Je '89
LENA FIORE INC.
Women are gobbling up the Massullo sisters' turkey-feather coats. il *People Weekly* 32:154-5 N 27 '89
LENARDO, MICHAEL J., AND OTHERS
Repression of the IgH enhancer in teratocarcinoma cells associated with a novel octamer factor. bibl f il *Science* 243:544-6 Ja 27 '89
LEND ME A TENOR [drama] *See* Ludwig, Ken
LENDING OF SECURITIES *See* Securities—Lending
LENDING RIGHTS (OF AUTHORS) *See* Public lending rights (of authors)
LENDL, IVAN
    about
Ivan: this one's for you. S. Flink. il *World Tennis* 37:20+ Jl '89
Obsession [cover story] T. Schwartz. il pors *New York* 22:30-41 Je 26 '89
LENFESTEY, JAMES P.
Catch of a lifetime. il *Reader's Digest* 134:111-12 F '89
LENGTH, STANDARDS OF *See* Standards of length
LENGTH OF DAY *See* Day
LENGTH OF LIFE *See* Longevity
LENGTH OF SCHOOL DAY *See* School day
LENGTH OF SERVICE (EMPLOYMENT) *See* Labor turnover; Seniority, Employee
LENIN, VLADIMIR IL'ICH, 1870-1924
    about
Chipping away at an icon. B. W. Nelan. il pors *Time* 134:34-5 Ag 14 '89
The power of an idea. S. Manning. il por *Scholastic Update (Teachers' edition)* 121:22 My 5 '89
LENINGRAD (SOVIET UNION)
    Restaurants, nightclubs, bars, etc.
Freedom and skepticism: snapshots of the *glasnost* era [restaurant owner Y. Bu014chevsky] N. Marcus. il por *Scholastic Update (Teachers' edition)* 121:18-20 My 5 '89

LENINGRAD (SOVIET UNION)—*cont.*
Theater
See also
DEREVO (Theater company)
Waterfront
King Eddy of the dealmakers [E. Cogan puts together group of Canadian entrepreneurs for proposed Leningrad development project] P. C. Newman. il *Maclean's* 102:56 N 13 '89
To Russia with cash [proposed Leningrad development project and other Canadian business ventures in Soviet Union; cover story; special section; with editorial comment by Kevin Doyle] il *Maclean's* 102:2, 42-8+ N 13 '89
LENINGRAD THEATER OF CONTEMPORARY BALLET
Reviews:
   Winter season in Moscow; tr. by Susan Cook Summer. V. Vanslov. *Dance Magazine* 63:53+ Jl '89
LENKIEWICZ, R. O.
                    about
When Robert Lenkiewicz paints the town in Plymouth, England, some people see only red. R. Wolmuth. il pors *People Weekly* 31:108-11 Ja 23 '89
LENKOWSKY, LESLIE, 1946-, AND FRUMKIN, PETER
The philanthropy boom. il *National Review* 41:21-2 D 31 '89
LENNARD, DAVID
"Why did I hit my daughter?". il *Redbook* 173:50+ Je '89
LENNON, JOHN, 1940-1980
                    about
John Lennon: good guy—or as bad as his critics say? C. Flippo. il pors *TV Guide* 37:16-19 Mr 4-10 '89
LENNON, JULIAN
                    about
Julian Lennon: the next generation. N. Malkin. por *Mademoiselle* 95:88+ O '89
LENO, JAY
                    about
Jawing with Jay Leno. M. Billard. il pors *Gentlemen's Quarterly* 59:220-5+ Ag '89
The joker. E. G. Carter. il pors *Rolling Stone* p46-8+ N 2 '89
Meet the multimillionaire comic who can't order room service. J. Kalter. il pors *TV Guide* 37:20-2+ Je 10-16 '89
Not just another funny face. P. Tauber. il pors *The New York Times Magazine* p26-7+ F 26 '89
LENOIRE, ROSETTA
                    about
In the sun. *The New Yorker* 65:24-5 F 27 '89
LENORE MARSHALL/NATION POETRY PRIZE
The Lenore Marshall/Nation Poetry Prize—1989 [awarded to T. McGrath for his book Selected poems: 1938-1988] A. Clampitt. *The Nation* 249:534-5 N 6 '89
LENSER, JOHN
                    about
Music to their ears. M. Barrier. il pors *Nation's Business* 77:69-70 Mr '89
LENSER, MARCIA
                    about
Music to their ears. M. Barrier. il pors *Nation's Business* 77:69-70 Mr '89
LENSES
         See also
         Contact lenses
         Eyeglasses
         Gravitational lenses
         Magnifiers
Giving the etch to superior optics [work of Wilfrid B. Veldkamp] I. Peterson. *Science News* 135:287 My 6 '89
Little lenses for little lasers. *Science News* 136:62 Jl 22 '89
LENSES, PHOTOGRAPHIC
28-210mm zoom too short? How about a 35-300mm? H. Keppler. il *Popular Photography* 96:36 My '89
Lens lineup shows more autofocus from independents [Photokina] il *Popular Photography* 96:96+ Ja '89
No-shake telephoto [image stabilizer built into long lenses] A. Fisher. il *Popular Science* 234:50 Mr '89
So you thought zoom lenses always stay in focus as you zoom, eh? Well, they don't! H. Keppler. il *Popular Photography* 96:38-9+ Jl '89
The standard lens. R. Bishop. il por *Petersen's Photographic Magazine* 17:16-18+ Ja '89
There are no good ways to change lenses, but some are better than others. Here's my own compromise with gravity. H. Keppler. il *Popular Photography* 96:28-9 F '89
Wide-angle. J. Schneider and others. il *Popular Photography* 96:44-55 Ag '89
You just bought a view camera for not too many bucks. Now you find that the lens alone in twice the price! A. Kramer. il *Popular Photography* 96:84+ Je '89
Testing
4 new Tamron lenses. B. Hurter. il *Petersen's Photographic Magazine* 17:62-3+ Ap '89
Canon, EF L-series lenses. il *Petersen's Photographic Magazine* 18:58-9 N '89
Canon EOS-1. D. Brooks. il *Petersen's Photographic Magazine* 18:78-81 D '89

Intelligent teleconverters [Cambron MC4 and MC7 for Maxxum lenses] il *Popular Photography* 96:118 Jl '89
Nikon El-Nikkor enlarging lenses. il *Petersen's Photographic Magazine* 18:70-1 N '89
'Normal' SLR lenses. il *Consumer Reports* 54:229-30 D '89
Schneider Apo-Symmar lenses. il *Petersen's Photographic Magazine* 18:75 N '89
Schneider lenses APO-Componon HM. B. Hurter. il *Petersen's Photographic Magazine* 18:61 My '89
SP 17mm f/3.5 & 24mm f/2.5 lenses. il *Petersen's Photographic Magazine* 18:66 N '89
Tamron SP series lenses. il *Petersen's Photographic Magazine* 18:52-3 My '89
Zoom lenses. il *Consumer Reports* 54:225-8 D '89
LENSKI, GERHARD EMMANUEL, 1924-
Hungary in April. *Society* 26:11-14 Ja/F '89
LENT, PETER C.
Return of the mighty muskox. il *Natural History* p50-9 N '89
LENT
         See also
         Ash Wednesday
         Easter
         Good Friday
         Holy Saturday
         Holy Week
         Maundy Thursday
         Palm Sunday
Lenten meditation:
         God's terrifying mercy. R. C. Wood. *The Christian Century* 106:164-5 F 15 '89
         Prodigiously lost and found [parable of the prodigal son] A. James. *The Christian Century* 106:220-1 Mr 1 '89
         The storyteller visits the vineyard. R. W. Bertram. *The Christian Century* 106:255-6 Mr 8 '89
         When bad things happen. W. H. Willimon. *The Christian Century* 106:198-9 F 22 '89
A new beginning [prodigal son] P. J. Ryan. il *America* 160:183 F 25 '89
Patterned on glory. P. J. Ryan. il *America* 160:127 F 11 '89
Professing faith. P. J. Ryan. *America* 160:95 F 4 '89
Warnings. P. J. Ryan. il *America* 160:159 F 18 '89
LENTS, JAMES
                    about
"Moderately radical". M. Beauchamp. il por *Forbes* 143:148 My 15 '89
LENYA, LOTTE, 1898-1981
                    about
Threepenny romance. P. Moor. il pors *High Fidelity (New York, N.Y.)* 39:50-3 My '89
The woman behind the songs. J. Simon. *The New Leader* 72:12-15 My 15-29 '89
LENZ, KAY
                    about
After riding a lifetime of ups and downs, Kay Lenz hits her stride with a role in Midnight caller. J. Park. il pors *People Weekly* 32:83-4 N 20 '89
LENZ, RANDOLPH W.
                    about
Parlaying the winnings. R. Reiff. il por *Forbes* 144:45-6 Jl 24 '89
LEÓN, JUANA PONCE DE *See* Ponce de León, Juana
LEONARD, BILL
Fragmentation grows for Southern Baptists. *The Christian Century* 106:644-6 Jl 5-12 '89
LEONARD, ELMORE, 1925-
                    about
Delacorte's Dutch treat. M. Simson. il *Publishers Weekly* 236:24 O 20 '89
LEONARD, FRANCES
Pensions: off balance. il *Modern Maturity* 32:78+ O/N '89
LEONARD, GEORGE BURR, 1923-
Sex and other pleasures [cover story; special section] il *Esquire* 111:129-32+ My '89
LEONARD, JOAN
Grandma's sewing machine. il por *Good Housekeeping* 208:56 Ap '89
How we survived our first night out. il *Parents* 64:97-8+ N '89
Post-baby beach days. il *Parents* 64:90-2 Jl '89
LEONARD, JOHN
Bad-boy books. il *Ms.* 17:124+ Ja/F '89
Television. See issues of New York beginning November 28, 1983
LEONARD, RAY CHARLES *See* Leonard, Sugar Ray
LEONARD, SUGAR RAY
                    about
Another classic [cover story] P. Putnam. il pors *Sports Illustrated* 70:18-21 Je 19 '89
The Hit Man. R. Wiley. il pors *Sports Illustrated* 70:48-50+ Je 5 '89
Leonard bashing. D. Miller. il pors *Sport (New York, N.Y.)* 80:73-5 D '89
Leonard dances to win as Duran has 'no mas'. il pors *Jet* 77:51-2 D 25 '89-Ja 1 '90

LEONARD, SUGAR RAY—about—*cont.*

Leonard-Hearns, again. D. Miller. il pors *Sport (New York, N.Y.)* 80:69-71 Jl '89

Leonard, Hearns rematch finally will take place. pors *Jet* 75:50 F 20 '89

Leonard-Hearns war ends 8-year wait. il pors *Jet* 76:48-50 Je 12 '89

One for the ages. P. Putnam. il pors *Sports Illustrated* 71:24-5 D 18 '89

One more time! J. Torres. pors *TV Guide* 37:34-6 D 2-8 '89

Sugar and wife separated, set no plans for divorce. il por *Jet* 76:46+ My 22 '89

Sugar Ray Leonard and Thomas Hearns battle to a draw in title brawl. il pors *Jet* 76:53-4 Je 26 '89

The world according to Ray. G. Smith. il pors *Sports Illustrated* 71:80-6+ D 4 '89

LEONARD, THOM

Hand pollinating corn. il *Organic Gardening* 36:28-9 My '89

LEONARDO, DA VINCI, 1452-1519

Leonardo's lessons [excerpt from Leonardo on painting] il *Art News* 88:24 D '89

about

Leonardo's manor house in France. il *Sunset (Central West edition)* 181:24 D '88

Picking up the pieces. B. Taylor. il *Art News* 88:43+ F '89

The real Leonardo. C. Hope. il *The New York Review of Books* 36:16-18 Ag 17 '89

What becomes a legend most [cover story] G. Danto. il *Art News* 88:148-51 Summ '89

LEONARDO DA VINCI AIRPORT (ROME, ITALY) See Rome (Italy)—Airports

LEONE, SERGIO, 1921-1989

about

Leonesque. D. Thomson. il por *American Film* 14:26-31+ S '89

Obituary

Film Comment il pors 25:77-8 Jl/Ag '89. B. Bertolucci

LEONG, RUSSELL C.

Discovering a rich resource: literature by and about Asian Americans. *Change* 21:64-8 N/D '89

LEOPARD HUNTING

Leopard: a most dangerous game [M. Rowbotham leads safari in Tanzania] J. Carmichel. il *Outdoor Life* 183:58-9+ F '89

LEOPARDS

Catching a ghost [monitoring snow leopards in Nepal] R. Jackson and G. Ahlborn. il *International Wildlife* 19:30-3 My/Je '89

Care

Around the Mall and beyond [capture and tracking of a clouded leopard in Royal Chitwan National Park, Nepal] E. Dinerstein. il *Smithsonian* 20:24+ Ap '89

LEOPOLD, ALDO, 1886-1948

Thinking like a mountain. il *The Mother Earth News* 117:10 My/Je '89

about

Phenomena, comment and notes. J. P. Wiley, Jr. il por *Smithsonian* 20:38+ N '89

LEP (LARGE ELECTRON-POSITRON) COLLIDING-BEAM ACCELERATOR See Accelerators (Electrons, etc.)

LEPAGE, ROBERT

about

Echo [drama] Reviews

Maclean's il 102:95+ N 20 '89. J. Bemrose

LEPERS See Leprosy

LEPIDOPTERA

See also

Butterflies

Moths

LÉPINE, MARC

about

The man who hated women. W. R. Doerner. il por *Time* 134:30 D 18 '89

Massacre in Montreal. B. Turque. il por *Newsweek* 114:39 D 18 '89

Montreal massacre [cover story; special section] il *Maclean's* 102:14-19+ D 18 '89

LEPROSY

Leprosy: out of the Dark Ages. J. P. Cohn. il *FDA Consumer* 23:24-7 S '89

LEPROSY IN THE BIBLE

Grateful outcasts. P. J. Ryan. il *America* 161:223 O 7 '89

LEPTOMONAS

Expression of a bacterial gene in a trypanosomatid protozoan. V. Bellofatto and G. A. M. Cross. bibl f il *Science* 244:1167-9 Je 9 '89

LERITZ, LEN

What mothers know and managers must learn. il *Working Woman* 14:32+ My '89

LERMAN, LEO

The cookbook shelf. il *Gourmet* 49:80+ N '89

The cookbook shelf. il *Gourmet* 49:82+ F '89

A grand surprise. il *House & Garden* 161:156-61 N '89

LERNER, JONATHAN

Fresh air antiques. il *House & Garden* 161:72+ Je '89

LERNER, MAX, 1902-

It is later than you think: 1989. *Society* 26:83-6 S/O '89

LERNER, MICHAEL

about

Daring to care. V. Brower. il por *American Health* 8:62-4 Ap '89

LERNER, PRESTON

A fast comeback. il pors *The New York Times Magazine* p42+ O 15 '89

LERNER, RALPH E., 1943-, AND BRESLER, JUDITH

Obscenity: what the Supreme Court says [excerpt from Art law] il *Art News* 88:144-5 O '89

LERNER, RICHARD A.

(jt. auth) See Iverson, Brent L., and Lerner, Richard A.

LERNER, ROBERT

(jt. auth) See Rothman, Stanley, 1927-, and Lerner, Robert

LERNER, ROBERT M.

Woody and Ed. il *Organic Gardening* 36:104 Ja '89

LERNOUX, PENNY, 1940-1989

Letters [discussion of November 28, 1988 article, Guatemala's new military order] *The Nation* 248:254+ F 27 '89

My Opus [discussion of April 10, 1989 article, Opus Dei and the 'perfect society'] *The Nation* 249:74+ Jl 17 '89

Opus Dei and the 'perfect society' [cover story] il *The Nation* 248:469+ Ap 10 '89

Playing golf while drugs flow. il *The Nation* 248:188-90+ F 13 '89

A reverence for fundamentalism. il *The Nation* 248:513-16 Ap 17 '89

about

The battle for the Catholic church. P. Berryman. por *The Christian Century* 106:523-6 My 17 '89

Obituary

The Nation 249:480 O 30 '89

LESBIAN AND GAY BIG APPLE CORPS MARCHING BAND

Details [participates in bicentennial celebration of George Washington's inauguration] *The New Yorker* 65:28-9 Jl 3 '89

LESBIANISM

Court backs two-mom family [lesbians recognized as legal parents in Washington State] K. Monagle. il *Ms.* 18:69 O '89

Double lives: what it's like to be lesbian today [excerpt from Invisible lives] M. B. Barrett. il *Glamour* 87:316-17+ S '89

Forced march in the military [cases challenging regulations banning lesbians and gay men] G. L. Atkins. il *The Nation* 248:16-18 Ja 2 '89

Gay and lesbian couples [parenting] J. Seligmann. il *Newsweek* 114 Special Issue:38-40 Wint '89/Spr '90

Homophobiaphobia [feminist linguistic course taught by lesbian at Kenyon College] T. Short. *National Review* 41:19-20 Ag 18 '89

Just friends [black woman's friendship with lesbian] R. Weems. il *Essence* 20:60-2+ My '89

The Pentagon's fight to keep gays away. P. Cary. il *U.S. News & World Report* 107:57+ N 20 '89

This is what you thought: 50% say doctors should turn down lesbians for artificial insemination [survey results] il *Glamour* 87:141 Ag '89

When a church supports a lesbian seminarian [United Church of Christ in Carbondale, Ill.] T. A. Braun. *The Christian Century* 106:516-17 My 17 '89

Witch hunt at Parris Island: the Marine Corps targets lesbians. J. Lynch. il *The Progressive* 53:24-7 Mr '89

LESBIANISM AND CHRISTIANITY See Homosexuality and Christianity

LESBIANISM IN ADVERTISING

Breaking the last taboo [M. Roux's erotic ad for La Grande Passion liqueur] I. Bosch. il *Mother Jones* 14:49 My '89

LESBIANISM IN LITERATURE

Lesbian writer fights feminist censors [J. Nestle] H. Metz. il por *The Progressive* 53:16-17 Ag '89

LESCHAK, PETER M.

Hellroaring: fighting last summer's fires. il *Harper's* 279:70-3 Jl '89

LESE (AFRICAN PEOPLE)

The Efe: archers of the African rain forest. R. C. Bailey. il maps *National Geographic* 176:664-86 N '89

LESHER, RICHARD L.

about

Free-market economics: antidote for war and poverty. il *Nation's Business* 77:71 D '89

LESHINSKIE, KATHLEEN

about

A chilling effect on evaluation? P. A. Zirkel. il *Phi Delta Kappan* 71:164-5 O '89

LESIONS, BRAIN See Brain damage

LESLIE, ALFRED, 1927-

Watercolors that transport [excerpt from 100 views along the road] il *American Artist* 53:66-9+ Ap '89

LESLIE, CHARLES ROBERT, 1794-1859

about

Some sources for the paintings of C. R. Leslie. G. Jackson-Stops. bibl f il *Antiques* 135:310-21 Ja '89

LESLIE, KIMBERLY K.

(jt. auth) See Queenan, John T., and Leslie, Kimberly K.

LESLIE, MARY
(jt. auth) See Barnes, Barbara, and Leslie, Mary
L'ESPERANCE QUINTUPLETS See Quintuplets
LESS DEVELOPED COUNTRIES See Developing countries
LESSARD, SUZANNAH
Busting our mental blocks on drugs and crime. *The Washington Monthly* 21:70 F '89
Profiles [V. Rieti] il por *The New Yorker* 64:32-6+ Ja 9 '89
Taste, class, and Mary Tyler Moore. *The Washington Monthly* 21:33-4 F '89
LESSAY, JEAN
Thomas Paine: the antimonarchist who tried to save a king [excerpt from L'Américain de la Convention] por *The Unesco Courier* 42:18 Je '89
LESSEM, DON
Secrets of the Gobi Desert. il map *Discover* 10:40-6 Je '89
LESSING, DORIS MAY, 1919-
Among the roses [story] il por *Ladies' Home Journal* 106:96+ Ap '89
LESTER, DEEGEE
The mystery of the mall [story] il *'Teen* 33:38+ D '89
The mystery of the mall [story] il *'Teen* 33:36+ N '89
LESTER, JOHN
about
An accident of birth delivers a most unusual scholarship. il por *People Weekly* 32:81 O 23 '89
LESTON, KIMBERLEY
Neneh Cherry, Britain's rising new rapper, is a self-styled Buffalo girl. il pors *Vogue* 179:154+ O '89
LET NATIONAL CORPORATION
Czech regional transport designed for rugged operations. J. M. Lenorovitz. il *Aviation Week & Space Technology* 130:96 F 13 '89
Czechs seek wider market for L410, L610 transports [cover story] J. M. Lenorovitz. il *Aviation Week & Space Technology* 130:36-8+ Ap 3 '89
LETHAL WEAPON 2 [film] See Motion picture reviews—Single works
LETOKHOV, V. S.
(jt. auth) See Balykin, Victor I., and Letokhov, V. S.
LET'S GET LOST [film] See Motion picture reviews—Single works
LETTER PAPER See Stationery
LETTER WRITING See Letters
LETTERING
See also
Calligraphy
LETTERMAN, DAVID
about
David Letterman. il pors *People Weekly* 31 Special Issue:74-5 Summ '89
He's no Johnny Carson [interview] R. Zoglin. il por *Time* 133:66-8 F 6 '89
LETTERS
See also
Authors—Correspondence, reminiscences, etc.
Business writing
Chain letters
Christmas letters
Fan mail
Love letters
Pen pals
Thank-you notes
After 58 years, a round-robin letter keeps on delivering [women graduates of the College of Wooster maintain contact] W. Plummer. il *People Weekly* 31:99-100 Ja 16 '89
The lost art of letter writing. R. Epstein. il *Utne Reader* p92 My/Je '89
Love letters from grandma. A. S. Brown. il *New Choices for the Best Years* 29:98+ S '89
Pen ultimate [letter writing] H. Fairlie. il *Vogue* 179:268+ Ap '89
LETTERS OF CREDIT
On the front lines in the trade war. S. A. Rondel. il *Nation's Business* 77:10 Je '89
LETTERS OF RECOMMENDATION
See also
Employment references
LETTERS TO LEGISLATORS See Lobbyists and lobbying
LETTERS TO THE EDITOR See Newspapers—Letters to the editor; Periodicals—Letters to the editor
LETTRE INTERNATIONALE (PERIODICAL)
The smallest giant [A. Liehm] B. Müller-Ullrich. il por *World Press Review* 36:67 N '89
LETTUCE
About lettuce. S. Pacher. il *The Mother Earth News* 115:26-7+ Ja/F '89
Hanging salads [cover story] il *Sunset (Central West edition)* 182:82-3 F '89
Lettuce vogue [cover story] S. Ogden. il pors *Organic Gardening* 36:30-5 My '89

LEUCINE
Cognate DNA binding specificity retained after leucine zipper exchange between GCN4 and C/EBP. P. Agre and others. bibl f il *Science* 246:922-6 N 17 '89
The DNA binding domain of the rat liver nuclear protein C/EBP is bipartite [support for leucine zipper hypothesis] W. H. Landschulz and others. bibl f il *Science* 243:1681-8 Mr 31 '89
Evidence that the leucine zipper is a coiled coil. E. K. O'Shea and others. bibl f il *Science* 243:538-42 Ja 27 '89
Leucine repeats and an adjacent DNA binding domain mediate the formation of functional cFos-cJun heterodimers [proposed function of the leucine zipper] R. Turner and R. Tjian. bibl f il *Science* 243:1689-94 Mr 31 '89
Parallel association of Fos and Jun leucine zippers juxtaposes DNA binding domains. R. Gentz and others. bibl f il *Science* 243:1695-9 Mr 31 '89
Preferential heterodimer formation by isolated leucine zippers from Fos and Jun. E. K. O'Shea and others. bibl f il *Science* 245:646-8 Ag 11 '89
A protein that binds to a cis-acting element of wheat histone genes has a leucine zipper motif. T. Tabata and others. bibl f il *Science* 245:965-7 S 1 '89
Scissors-grip model for DNA recognition by a family of leucine zipper proteins. C. R. Vinson and others. bibl f il *Science* 246:911-16 N 17 '89
LEUKEMIA
'A little bit of wonder' [opera singer J. Carreras] K. Ames. il por *Newsweek* 113:74 My 1 '89
Cancer claimed the heart of this family. C. Tevis. il *Successful Farming* 87:62 S '89
A life cut short [Syracuse running back E. Davis] W. Nack. il pors *Sports Illustrated* 71:136-46 S 4 '89
Genetic aspects
elk, tissue-specific *ets*-related genes on chromosomes X and 14 near translocation breakpoints. V. N. Rao and others. bibl f il *Science* 244:66-70 Ap 7 '89
The gene for enhancer binding proteins E12/E47 lies at the t(1;19) breakpoint in acute leukemias. J. D. Mellentin and others. bibl f il *Science* 246:379-82 O 20 '89
Lineage-specific requirement of c-*abl* function in normal hematopoiesis [chronic myelogenous leukemia] D. Caracciolo and others. bibl f il *Science* 245:1107-10 S 8 '89
A model of human acute lymphoblastic leukemia in immune-deficient SCID mice. S. Kamel-Reid and others. bibl f il *Science* 246:1597-600 D 22 '89
The myeloperoxidase gene in acute promyelocytic leukemia [discussion of May 6, 1988 article, Translocation and rearrangement of myeloperoxidase gene in acute promyelocytic leukemia] S. C. Weil and others. il *Science* 244:823-6 My 19 '89
Therapy
Hopes heighten for new leukemia drug [use of fludarabine in chronic lymphocytic leukemia; research by Michael J. Keating] R. Weiss. *Science News* 135:348 Je 3 '89
Increasing survival rates [marrow transplant program at the University of Michigan Medical Center] *USA Today (Periodical)* 118:9-10 O '89
Marrow donors: reaching beyond family [chronic myelogenous leukemia] R. Weiss. *Science News* 135:348 Je 3 '89
"We had to kidnap our son from the hospital" [D. Pagán jailed after husband takes leukemia-stricken son from Memorial Sloan-Kettering Cancer Center] J. L. Block. il pors *Good Housekeeping* 209:144-5+ O '89
LEUKEMIA CELLS See Cancer cells
LEUKEMIA IN CATS See Cats—Diseases and pests
LEUKEMIA VIRUSES
See also
HIV viruses
HTLV viruses
Bovine leukemia's hidden toll [research by Harris A. Lewin] *Science News* 135:123 F 25 '89
LEUKOCYTES
See also
Phagocytes and phagocytosis
Antibody to interleukin-5 inhibits helminth-induced eosinophilia in mice. R. L. Coffman and others. bibl f il *Science* 245:308-10 Jl 21 '89
Endothelial cell gene expression of a neutrophil chemotactic factor by TNF-α, LPS, and IL-1β. R. M. Strieter and others. bibl f il *Science* 243:1467-9 Mr 17 '89
Endothelial interleukin-8: a novel inhibitor of leukocyte-endothelial interactions. M. A. Gimbrone and others. bibl f il *Science* 246:1601-3 D 22 '89
Endothelial leukocyte adhesion molecule 1: an inducible receptor for neutrophils related to complement regulatory proteins and lectins. M. P. Bevilacqua and others. bibl f il *Science* 243:1160-5 Mr 3 '89
Fusion factor in AIDS cells identified [role of leukocyte adhesion receptor LFA-1 in syncytium formation; research by James E. K. Hildreth and Rimas J. Orentas] *Science News* 135:366 Je 10 '89
Identification of monocyte chemotactic activity produced by malignant cells. D. T. Graves and others. bibl f il *Science* 245:1490-3 S 29 '89

LEUKOCYTES—cont.

Involvement of a leukocyte adhesion receptor (LFA-1) in HIV-induced syncytium formation. J. E. K. Hildreth and R. J. Orentas. bibl f il *Science* 244:1075-8 Je 2 '89

Mechanics of stimulated neutrophils: cell stiffening induces retention in capillaries. G. S. Worthen and others. bibl f il *Science* 245:183-6 Jl 14 '89

The neutrophil-activating protein (NAP-1) is also chemotactic for T lymphocytes. C. G. Larsen and others. bibl f il *Science* 243:1464-6 Mr 17 '89

Neutrophil Mac-1 and MEL-14 adhesion proteins inversely regulated by chemotactic factors. T. K. Kishimoto and others. bibl f il *Science* 245:1238-41 S 15 '89

New family of adhesion proteins discovered. J. L. Marx. *Science* 243:1144 Mr 3 '89

Recombinant 47-kilodalton cytosol factor restores NADPH oxidase in chronic granulomatous disease [neutrophil cytosol factor] K. J. Lomax and others. bibl f il *Science* 245:409-12 Jl 28 '89; Correction. 246:987 N 24 '89

Stiffened cells lodge in lung capillaries [neutrophils; research by G. Scott Worthen and others] S. Hart. *Science News* 136:39 Jl 15 '89

LEUKOPLAKIA, ORAL

Carrot 'chemo'? Beta-carotene may shrink oral precancers. il *Prevention (Emmaus, Pa.)* 41:8 N '89

Got a light? This carrot keeps going out [research by Harinder Garewal] R. Weiss. *Science News* 135:348 Je 3 '89

LEUNG, DAVID W., AND OTHERS

Vascular endothelial growth factor is a secreted angiogenic mitogen. bibl f il *Science* 246:1306-9 D 8 '89

LEUSCHEL, ROLAND

about

Buy American. P. Fuhrman. il por *Forbes* 144:64 Jl 10 '89

LEVA, MICHAEL

about

Michael Leva. P. H. Starzinger. il por *Vogue* 179:206 S '89

LEVAMISOLE

Death-defying drug therapy [use of 5-fluorouracil and levamisole to treat colon cancer] il *Time* 134:76+ O 16 '89

Drug availability is an issue for cancer patients, too [levamisole-5-fluorouracil therapy for colon cancer] J. L. Marx. il *Science* 245:346-7 Jl 28 '89

Drug duo takes on deadly colon cancer [levamisole and 5-fluorouracil; research by Charles G. Moertel] K. Fackelmann. *Science News* 136:228-9 O 7 '89

LEVELLERS (POLITICAL MOVEMENT)

Gerrard Winstanley: England's pioneer Green? I. C. Bradley. bibl il *History Today* 39:12-17 Ag '89

LEVELS (TOOLS)

Electronics on the level [Anglesensor and SmartLevel] R. J. DeCristoforo. il *Popular Science* 234:74+ My '89

LEVENE, STEPHEN D., AND ZIMM, BRUNO H.

Understanding the anomalous electrophoresis of bent DNA molecules: a reptation model. bibl f il *Science* 245:396-9 Jl 28 '89

LEVENSON, JEFF

Jack DeJohnette: multidirectional musician [interview; cover story] il pors *Down Beat* 56:16-19 D '89

Omar Hakim: stickin' it to ya [cover story] il pors *Down Beat* 56:16-19 Ap '89

Ray Anderson: slidin' into first. il pors *Down Beat* 56:27-9 Ag '89

What'd I say—a conversation with Ray Charles [cover story] il pors *Down Beat* 56:16-19 Ja '89

LEVENTER, MARTINE

The 'Amerippon' alliance. *World Press Review* 36:48-9 Ag '89

LEVENTHAL, ALICE WALKER *See* Walker, Alice, 1944-

LEVEQUE, JAMES

Cook Islands [cover story] il *Travel Holiday* 172:40-9 S '89

LEVER BROTHERS COMPANY

The new, improved Unilever aims to clean up in the U.S. W. Konrad. il *Business Week* p102+ N 27 '89

LEVERAGE (FINANCE)

See also

Parking (Securities)

Be wise, equitize [deleveraging of U.S. business] P. Berman. il *Forbes* 144:38-40 N 27 '89

The bills are coming due [leverage binge winds down; cover story] C. Farrell. il *Business Week* p84-7+ S 11 '89

The debt addiction. F. G. Rohatyn. il *The New York Review of Books* 36:39-42 Ap 13 '89

Is now the time for leverage? M. Gianturco. por *Forbes* 144:120 Ag 21 '89

Michael Milken, meet Sewell Avery. J. Grant. il *Forbes* 144 Special Issue:60-2+ O 23 '89

LEVERAGED BUYOUTS

See also

Hicks & Haas

The acquisition boom has lost a lot of its thunder . . . but takeover candidates still thrill Wall Street. G. Koretz. il *Business Week* p18 Je 12 '89

After euphoria, reality. F. E. Rowe. il *Forbes* 144:372 N 13 '89

Airline takeovers: who's in play, what's at stake? [special section; with editorial comment] il *Aviation Week & Space Technology* 131:9, 18-22 Ag 14 '89

America pays the price. R. B. Reich. il *The New York Times Magazine* p32-3+ Ja 29 '89

American free enterprise: shakeups or shakedowns? *America* 161:287-8 N 4 '89

The benefits of leverage [R. H. Macy] S. N. Chakravarty. il por *Forbes* 143:42 My 1 '89

Biggest bidders, wildest auction [RJR Nabisco takeover] B. Saporito. il pors *Fortune* 119:34-5 Ja 2 '89

The biggest buy-out in history means hard decisions for a chemist and his wife [RJR Nabisco stockholders Don and Nancy Roberts] H. Wheelwright. il *Money* 18:129-30 F '89

Billion-dollar mind [W. Farley's acquisition of West Point-Pepperell] C. Bruck. *The New Yorker* 65:76-88 Ag 7 '89

The bills are coming due [leverage binge winds down; cover story] C. Farrell. il *Business Week* p84-7+ S 11 '89

Bob Bass may have to settle for a quick profit on this one [disappointing results of Bell & Howell leveraged buyout] J. F. Siler. il por *Business Week* p48+ O 9 '89

Bondholders are mad as hell—and they're not going to take it anymore. C. Farrell. il *Business Week* p82-3 F 6 '89

The bondholders' cold new world. G. Hector. il *Fortune* 119:83-4+ F 27 '89

Bonds that bind [Swiss court intervention in Kohlberg Kravis Roberts' bid for RJR Nabisco] D. Fanning. il *Forbes* 143:48 My 1 '89

Born-again stocks [former leveraged buyout companies taken public with new offerings] C. Palmeri. il *Forbes* 143:210-11 Mr 20 '89

Brady, buyouts, and Purolator [Nicholas Brady's role in thwarted buyout bid] il *Fortune* 119:66 My 22 '89

Buying out the boss [ESOPs in leveraged buyouts] M. Berss. il *Forbes* 143:41-2 Ap 3 '89

Can bankers sell groceries [Merrill Lynch leveraged buyout of Supermarkets General] G. Morgenson. il *Forbes* 144:54+ O 30 '89

The case for takeovers. C. C. Icahn. *The New York Times Magazine* p34 Ja 29 '89

Cleverness isn't enough [buyouts engineered by Artra Group] M. Berss. il *Forbes* 144:216 Jl 24 '89

Concerns about leverage cool market for airline takeovers. N. C. Kernstock. il *Aviation Week & Space Technology* 131:71-4 N 20 '89

Corporate takeovers [address, February 7, 1989] J. G. Smale. *Vital Speeches of the Day* 55:330-2 Mr 15 '89

Cruel October [Friday the 13th stock plunge] *The Nation* 249:515-16 N 6 '89

Dangerous shapes [inverted yield curve pushes up short term rates] J. Willoughby. il *Forbes* 143:39-40 Ja 23 '89

Deals, yes. Maniac deals, no [aftermath of Friday the 13, 1989 stock plunge] J. H. Dobrzynski. il *Business Week* p30-1 O 30 '89

The debt addiction. F. G. Rohatyn. il *The New York Review of Books* 36:39-42 Ap 13 '89

Debt on trial [special section] il *U.S. News & World Report* 106:60-3+ F 13 '89

A dogfight for dominance of the skies [airline takeover battles] K. R. Sheets and P. Dworkin. il *U.S. News & World Report* 107:54-5 S 11 '89

Don't blame me [L. Funston's failed leveraged buyout of O'Day Corp.] A. A. Lappen. il por *Forbes* 144:102-3+ S 4 '89

The education of Bobby Inman [Tracor LBO] K. Kelly. por *Business Week* p50 D 18 '89

An employee LBO could be a buy [Modine Mfg.] G. G. Marcial. *Business Week* p134 F 20 '89

Engineering your own LBO. T. Thompson. il *U.S. News & World Report* 106:74-6 Ja 30 '89

First Brands: anatomy of an LBO that worked. T. Vogel. il *Business Week* p104 D 4 '89

'Greed really turns me off' [RJR Nabisco buyout; interview with H. Kravis] C. Leinster. il por *Fortune* 119:69-71 Ja 2 '89

The hard line coming from Tokyo banks [financing of U.S. leveraged buyouts] T. Holden and W. Glasgall. il *Business Week* p29 O 30 '89

Has the Beatrice LBO gone pfft? C. J. Loomis. il *Fortune* 120:113+ Jl 31 '89

The hell with glamour. Give me groceries [G. D. Hirsch] J. H. Dobrzynski. il por *Business Week* p121 My 1 '89

Henry Kaufman: corporate debt erodes competition [interview] J. H. Dobrzynski. por *Business Week* p40 Mr 20 '89

How KKR stubbed its toe [SCI TV deal] L. J. Nathans. il *Business Week* p56 Ag 7 '89

How Ross Johnson blew the buyout [RJR Nabisco] B. Saporito. il por *Fortune* 119:296-8+ Ap 24 '89

"If something could go wrong, it did" [D. Beldock's BASIX] E. Giltenan. il por *Forbes* 143:70+ My 29 '89

Ill will [goodwill accounting] L. Jereski. il *Forbes* 143:41-2 Ja 23 '89

Is privacy the goal of Mapco's maneuvers? G. G. Marcial. il *Business Week* p62 Jl 24 '89

Junk danger. *The American Spectator* 22:11+ Ja '89

KKR to buy Macmillan Book Clubs and Intertec for $310 million. *Publishers Weekly* 235:16 Je 16 '89

LEVERAGED BUYOUTS—*cont.*

The last fundamentalist? [A. Galef] R. King. il por *Forbes* 144:132+ N 27 '89

The LBO isn't a superior new species [views of M. Jensen] C. Farrell. il *Business Week* p126 O 23 '89

An LBO outfit that goes for the long pull [Prospect Group] M. Berss. il por *Forbes* 143:94+ Ap 17 '89

The LBO sails down Madison Avenue. T. Mason and others. il *Business Week* p69+ S 18 '89

LBOs: greed, good business—or both? J. P. Newport, Jr. il *Fortune* 119:66-8 Ja 2 '89

LBOs: let's bail out. J. Greenwald. il *Time* 134:50-1 Ag 14 '89

Leaseway may set a standard for ailing LBOs. Z. Schiller. il *Business Week* p81 N 27 '89

Life after debt: how LBOs do it. B. D. Fromson. il *Fortune* 119:91-2+ Mr 13 '89

Living out every manager's dream [buying and then selling off former CBS magazine group] P. G. Diamandis. il por *Fortune* 120:109+ O 9 '89

The loud clank of junk. L. Reibstein. il *Newsweek* 114:32-3 S 25 '89

Louis Kelso's baby is making daddy proud [ESOPs] J. B. Levine. il por *Business Week* p130 My 8 '89

Man oh Manischewitz [A. E. Levine puts LBO deal together] K. Kerwin. il por *Business Week* p25 Jl 24 '89

Mr. Hardball sheds his Grey [H. Siegel's buyout of LBS from Grey Advertising] J. M. Robins. il pors *Channels* (New York, N.Y.: 1986) 9:62-6 F '89

Off we go into the hazy blue yonder. C. Power. il *Business Week* p26-7 S 18 '89

One man's poison . . . [competitors take advantage of leveraged rivals] N. Alster. il *Forbes* 144:38-9 O 16 '89

Pikers need not apply [Kluge Subotnick Perkowski & Co.] J. Zweig. il por *Forbes* 143:142 F 6 '89

The Prime buyout is tough to compute [J. H. Whitney's leveraged buyout of Prime Computer Inc.] L. Helm. il *Business Week* p28 Jl 10 '89

Progress isn't drowning in debt—yet [impact of leveraged buyouts and merger mania on R&D] K. Deveny. il *Business Week* Special Issue:110 Je 16 '89

Railroaded [clearcutting by Plum Creek Timber Company spurred on by LBO fever] A. Porterfield. il *Common Cause Magazine* 15:21-3 S/O '89

Running the biggest LBO [L. Gerstner of RJR Nabisco; cover story] J. H. Dobrzynski. il pors *Business Week* p72-5+ O 2 '89

See you in bankruptcy court [leveraged buyout of Seaman Furniture turns into headache for Kohlberg Kravis Roberts] S. Flack. il *Forbes* 144:77+ O 16 '89

Sifting ashes on Wall Street: turnaround artists prosper rescuing failed LBOs. D. Pauly. il *Newsweek* 114:42-3 S 4 '89

Sitting pretty at Ladd. G. G. Marcial. *Business Week* p96 Je 12 '89

Take the money and run [stock that becomes target] M. J. Williams. il *Fortune* 119:26 Ja 2 '89

Takeovers [address, February 23, 1989] J. R. Munro. *Vital Speeches of the Day* 55:470-3 My 15 '89

The Texas chain store massacre [Southland's] J. H. Taylor. il *Forbes* 143:54+ F 6 '89

'They cleaned our clock' [RJR Nabisco buyout; interview with F. R. Johnson] B. Saporito. il por *Fortune* 119:72-4 Ja 2 '89

This year, LBO means 'let's back off'. L. J. Nathans. il *Business Week* p123+ My 8 '89

Turning America into junk. J. Mysak. il *The American Spectator* 22:28-9 Ap '89

Wanted: ailing companies. Call: Leonard Shaykin. P. Finch. il por *Business Week* p75+ F 27 '89

When the smoke clears [RJR Nabisco junk bonds] B. Weberman. il *Forbes* 144:131 Jl 10 '89

Where all the money comes from. V. Brownstein. il *Fortune* 119:75-6+ Ja 2 '89

Who's really picking up the tab? [leveraged buyouts and inflation] S. Flack. il *Forbes* 144:38-9 O 30 '89

Why Celestial Seasonings wasn't Kraft's cup of tea. S. D. Atchison. il por *Business Week* p76 My 8 '89

Will the Big Three buy Chrysler? [Chrysler executives leveraging a buyout] il *Motor Trend* 41:29 O '89

The wolves of Wall Street. D. R. Katz. il *Esquire* 111:99-100 Mr '89

Yesterday's bad deals are today's new business. L. Light. il *Business Week* p96-7 D 11 '89

Accounting

A colossal case of apples and oranges [banks disclosing information about their lending to highly leveraged transactions] P. Wang. il *Forbes* 143:48+ Mr 20 '89

Hassling the dealmakers. D. Wechsler. il *Forbes* 143:40-1 My 15 '89

Anecdotes, facetiae, satire, etc.

How to save communism: a modest prospectus [leveraged buyout of Soviet Union] M. D. Coleman. *National Review* 41:36-7 Mr 24 '89

Laws and regulations

Buyouts: the LBO lobby makes its move on Washington [cover story] M. Holland and V. Novak. il *Common Cause Magazine* 15:13-20 S/O '89

The debt presidency. I. M. Stelzer. il *The American Spectator* 22:26-7 Ja '89

The heat is on airline deals. S. Payne. il por *Business Week* p32 O 2 '89

House tax panel probes airline bailout threat. M. Mecham. il *Aviation Week & Space Technology* 131:52-3 O 30 '89

Junkman in D.C. [Kohlberg Kravis Roberts' buyout of Houdaille points to need to regulate LBOs] M. Holland. *The Nation* 248:365 Mr 20 '89

L.B.O. vapors. D. Henwood. *The Nation* 248:257 F 27 '89

Lawmakers fear LBOs threaten fitness of U.S. airline industry. M. Mecham. *Aviation Week & Space Technology* 131:104-5+ Jl 31 '89

Lawyers and leveraged buyouts [address, November 16, 1988] J. T. Laney. *Vital Speeches of the Day* 55:318-20 Mr 1 '89

A lion of the Texas bar snarls at KKR and Drexel [S. Susman builds asbestos case stemming from Jim Walter Corp. LBO] M. Ivey. il por *Business Week* p73+ O 9 '89

The old boy and the new boys. C. Bruck. *The New Yorker* 65:81-90+ My 8 '89

Skinner's limits on NWA buyout fail to dissuade drive for LBO controls. C. Fotos. *Aviation Week & Space Technology* 131:138-9 O 9 '89

Transportation Dept. considers standards for regulating LBOs [airline industry] *Aviation Week & Space Technology* 131:128 S 11 '89

Uncle Sam won't defend against raiders. H. Banks. *Forbes* 143:33 Mr 6 '89

Washington's war against LBO debt. A. R. Dowd. il *Fortune* 119:91-2 F 13 '89

White House, Hill clash over airline takeovers [with editorial comment] M. Mecham. *Aviation Week & Space Technology* 131:7, 16-17 O 23 '89

Why Reagan's regulators are taking aim at takeovers. T. Smart. il *Business Week* p43 Ja 16 '89

Why Washington may not lay a glove on LBOs. H. Gleckman. il *Business Week* p86 F 6 '89

Taxation

Takeovers: Congress comes out swinging a wet noodle. H. Gleckman. *Business Week* p29 Jl 24 '89

Tax adagio. R. Phalon. *Forbes* 143:42-3 F 20 '89

Germany (West)

Sprechen sie LBO? P. Fuhrman. il por *Forbes* 144:43-4 O 16 '89

Great Britain

Europe seems to be losing its appetite for LBOs. R. A. Melcher. il *Business Week* p44 D 18 '89

Has LBO fever struck Europe? [A&P's bid for Gateway] M. Maremont. il *Business Week* p28 Jl 3 '89

Is Consgold 'just an appetizer' for Hanson? M. Maremont. il *Business Week* p41-2 Jl 10 '89

Western Europe

Europe seems to be losing its appetite for LBOs. R. A. Melcher. il *Business Week* p44 D 18 '89

'Nothing is sacred, and no one is too big'. R. A. Melcher. il *Business Week* p44-5 Jl 31 '89

LEVEY, JAY

about

UHF [film] Reviews

People Weekly il 32:11-12 Ag 7 '89. R. Novak

LEVI, PRIMO, 1919-1987

Beetlemania [excerpt from Other people's trades]; tr. by Raymond Rosenthal. *Harper's* 278:27-8 F '89

The mark of the chemist [excerpt from Other people's trades]; tr. by Raymond Rosenthal. il *Discover* 10:70-5 F '89

My house; tr. by Raymond Rosenthal. il *The New York Review of Books* 35:25 Ja 19 '89

LEVI, ROMANO

about

From Romano Levi's grappa . . to exotic comestibles. F. Ferretti. il *Gourmet* 49:70+ S '89

LEVI STRAUSS & CO.

For these companies, debt was just what the doctor ordered. M. D. Oneal and others. il *Business Week* p90-1 S 11 '89

LEVIATHAN [film] See Motion picture reviews—Single works

LEVICOFF, STEVE

Upholding students' religious freedom. *The Christian Century* 106:1108-9 N 29 '89

LEVIN, ARTHUR

. . . and be the perfect patient. *Modern Maturity* 32:73-4 Ag/S '89

LEVIN, DIANE E.

(jt. auth) See Carlsson-Paige, Nancy, and Levin, Diane E.

LEVIN, DORON P.

Breaking up is hard to do. il pors *The New York Times Magazine* p36-7+ Mr 26 '89

LEVIN, IRA

about

Cantorial [drama] Reviews

The Nation 248:462-3 Ap 3 '89. T. M. Disch

LEVIN, JENNIFER DAWN, D. 1986

Murder case

Art imitates death in The preppie murder. J. S. Kunen. il pors *People Weekly* 32:36-9 S 25 '89

LEVIN, JENNIFER DAWN, D. 1986—Murder case—cont.
'There was no sex diary': Jennifer Levin wasn't asking for trouble [TV movie The preppie murder] P. H. Brown. il pors *TV Guide* 37:24-7 S 23-29 '89
Wasted lives: the shocking case of "the preppie murder" [excerpt from Wasted] L. Wolfe. il pors *Redbook* 173:170-2+ S '89

LEVIN, MICHAEL E.
about
The case of Michael Levin. D. Seligman. *National Review* 41:38-40 My 5 '89

LEVIN, MYRON
Fighting fire with P.R. il *The Nation* 249:52-5 Jl 10 '89

LEVIN, SUSANNA
The new anticancer agenda. il *Mademoiselle* 95:143-4 Mr '89
Think zinc, cure a cold. il *Mademoiselle* 95:64-6 Ja '89

LEVINE, AL
Troubles they've seen: African-American Catholics. il *Commonweal* 116:550-1 O 20 '89

LEVINE, ART
Blitzed. *The New Republic* 200:16-17 Ja 9-16 '89
Have you got what it takes to write for the Washington monthly? *The Washington Monthly* 21:54 F '89
What Charlie Peters can learn from Jerry Brown. *The Washington Monthly* 21:34-5 Mr '89
(jt. auth) See Crawford, Alan Pell, and Levine, Art

LEVINE, ARTHUR E.
about
Man oh Manischewitz. K. Kerwin. il por *Business Week* p25 Jl 24 '89

LEVINE, BETH
How to improve your . . . oh, yeah, memory. il *Seventeen* 48:38+ Ja '89

LEVINE, CAROL
God's will vs. doctor's orders. il *Parents* 64:220+ Mr '89

LEVINE, ERIK
about
Curves ahead. por *Vogue* 179:63 Ja '89

LEVINE, I. S.
The case of the vanishing pinup. il pors *Rolling Stone* p167+ N 16 '89

LEVINE, JAMES A.
How schools help families. il *Good Housekeeping* 209:141-2 S '89

LEVINE, KAREN
Negotiating the best parental leave. il *Parents* 64:74+ My '89

LEVINE, KEN
Are you up on your facts about fat? il *Reader's Digest* 134:87-90 F '89

LEVINE, LAWRENCE W.
about
How high the brow? D. Gates. il *Newsweek* 113:51 F 20 '89

LEVINE, LOUIS, 1921-, AND KOBILINSKY, LAWRENCE
DNA typing and parentage. *BioScience* 39:588-9 O '89

LEVINE, MARK, 1958-
(jt. auth) See Pollan, Stephen M., and Levine, Mark, 1958-

LEVINE, MICHAEL
about
Deal maker for Canada's stars. B. D. Johnson. il por *Maclean's* 102:43 Ja 16 '89

LEVINE, NORMAN D.
Evolution and extinction. *BioScience* 39:38-40 Ja '89

LEVINE, PHILIP, 1928-
Fire [poem] *The New Yorker* 65:32 Jl 17 '89
M. Degas teaches art & science at Durfee Intermediate School [poem] *The New Yorker* 65:42 Ap 17 '89
Overtime [poem] *The New Yorker* 65:46 Mr 20 '89
Perennials [poem] *The New Yorker* 64:38 Ja 16 '89
Snails [poem] *The New Yorker* 65:54 D 4 '89

LEVINE, ROBERT
The pace of life. il *Psychology Today* 23:42-6 O '89

LEVINE, ROBERT
Spain. il map *New Choices for the Best Years* 29:50-3 Ap '89

LEVINE, ROBERT A.
Informal moves work, too. *The Bulletin of the Atomic Scientists* 45:42-3 My '89

LEVINE, ROBERT J.
Fetal research: the underlying issue. *Scientific American* 261:112 Ag '89

LEVINE, SARAH L., 1946-, AND OSBOURNE, SALLY
Living and learning with dyslexia. bibl il *Phi Delta Kappan* 70:594-8 Ap '89

LEVINE, SHERRIE, 1947-
about
Sherrie Levine at Mary Boone. H. Cotter. *Art in America* 77:187 N '89

LEVINE, SOL, 1922-
about
The changes at Revlon are more than just cosmetic. M. Roman. il por *Business Week* p74+ N 20 '89

LEVINE, STEVEN I.
The uncertain future of Chinese foreign policy. bibl f *Current History* 88:261-4+ S '89

LEVINE, TESSLER, LEICHTMAN & COMPANY
Man oh Manischewitz [A. E. Levine puts LBO deal together] K. Kerwin. il por *Business Week* p25 Jl 24 '89

LEVINGER, LARRY
A passage to Alaska. il map *New Choices for the Best Years* 29:40-5 O '89
Taking a lesson from dad. il *New Choices for the Best Years* 29:79-80 Ja '89

LEVINSON, BARRY
about
A Hollywood record: six movies, no car chases. A. P. Sanoff. il por *U.S. News & World Report* 106:58 Ja 9 '89
The making of 'Rain Man' [interview] D. Rensin. il por *Rolling Stone* p30 Ja 12 '89
Rain Man [film] Reviews
    Commonweal 116:49 Ja 27 '89. T. O'Brien
    The Humanist il 49:39-40 Mr/Ap '89. H. M. Geduld
    The Nation 248:66-7 Ja 9-16 '89. S. Klawans
    National Review 41:52+ F 24 '89. J. Simon
    The New Republic 200:24-5 Ja 9-16 '89. S. Kauffmann
    New York 22:46-7 Ja 2 '89. D. Denby
    The New Yorker 64:95-6 F 6 '89. P. Kael
    Newsweek il 113:52-6 Ja 16 '89. D. Ansen
    People Weekly il 31:36-41 Ja 23 '89. D. Chu

LEVIO, ROSE
Elegant effervescence. il *Harper's Bazaar* 122:48 Ap '89

LEVIS, ART
Channel one. See issues of Video beginning July 1989

LEVITAN, ARLAN R.
Levitations. See issues of Compute! beginning May 1988 through July 1989

LEVITAN, IRWIN B.
The basic defect in cystic fibrosis. bibl f *Science* 244:1423 Je 23 '89

LEVITAN, SAR A., AND GALLO, FRANK
Can employee associations negotiate new growth? bibl f il *Monthly Labor Review* 112:5-14 Jl '89
Collective bargaining and private sector professionals. bibl f il *Monthly Labor Review* 112:24-33 S '89

LEVITATION
Levitation in physics [cover story] E. H. Brandt. bibl f il *Science* 243:349-55 Ja 20 '89

LEVITATION, MAGNETIC *See* Magnetic suspension

LEVITIN, SONIA, 1934-
Who are these people? Knowing your fiction characters. *The Writer* 102:15-17 N '89

LEVITSKY, MELVYN
Cuba and narcotics trafficking [statement, July 26, 1989] *Department of State Bulletin* 89:46-8 O '89

LEVITT, ARTHUR, JR.
about
The play's the thing. J. Zweig. il por *Forbes* 144:246 O 2 '89

LEVITT, SHELLEY
The new intimacy: rediscovering each other after the kids leave home [cover story] il *New Choices for the Best Years* 29:38-43 S '89

LEVITT, WILLIAM
about
Tough times for Mr. Levittown. M. T. Kaufman. il pors *The New York Times Magazine* p42-4+ S 24 '89

LEVONORGESTREL *See* Progestin

LEVOY, GREGG
Accelerated medicine. il *Omni (New York, N.Y.)* 11:26+ Mr '89
Born rivals. il *Psychology Today* 23:67-8 Je '89
Born rivals. *Utne Reader* p101-2 S/O '89
A place to belong. il *Health (New York, N.Y.)* 21:54-7 F '89

LEVY, ALAN M.
(jt. auth) See Herman, Stephen P., and Levy, Alan M.

LEVY, BERNARD HENRI
about
20th-century rebels. L. Nesselson. il pors *Harper's Bazaar* 122:106 Ap '89

LEVY, DAVID A.
Is our eye on the wrong ball? il por *Forbes* 143:232 Ap 17 '89

LEVY, DAVID H., 1948-
StarTrails. See issues of Sky and Telescope beginning January 1988
Who gets the credit? *Astronomy* 17:8 O '89

LEVY, ELLEN
Saving the land. *The Nation* 249:418 O 16 '89

LEVY, FAYE
Fruits de mer. il *Gourmet* 49:60-1+ Jl '89

LEVY, GUSTAVE
about
Gus and Mike. J. Willoughby. il por *Forbes* 144:158 S 18 '89

LEVY, LAURENCE
about
A little cash and a lot of moxie. L. J. Nathans. il pors *Business Week* p74 Ja 30 '89

LEVY, MARJORIE, AND CHRISTIE-BLICK, NICHOLAS
Pre-Mesozoic palinspastic reconstruction of the eastern Great Basin (western United States) [cover story] bibl f il maps *Science* 245:1454-62 S 29 '89

LEVY, PAUL, 1941-
Channel crossings. il *House & Garden* 161:96+ Mr '89
LÉVY, RAYMOND
about
Is Renault's new engine built for the long haul? S. Toy. il por *Business Week* p38-9 Ag 21 '89
LEVY, SCOTT
about
He shoots baseball cards: a dentist with a passion for spring training. S. Martin. il por map *Petersen's Photographic Magazine* 18:32-5 My '89
LEVY, STEVEN
Next picture show. il *Rolling Stone* p91-2+ Je 15 '89
LEWEX, INC.
Limited prospects [L. Wexner's oil forays] J. Zweig. il por *Forbes* 144:142 S 4 '89
LEWIN, DAN'L
Higher education: beyond personal computers. por *Personal Computing* 13:242 O '89
LEWIN, TAMAR
Small tots, big biz. il *The New York Times Magazine* p30-1+ Ja 29 '89
LEWINGTON, JENNIFER
Time to define his presidency at home. il *World Press Review* 36:19 S '89
LEWIS, ANN F., 1938-
Alaskan housekeeping. il *Ms.* 17:76 Je '89
If women ran the drug war. *Ms.* 18:73 N '89
The Jerusalem agenda [conference] il *Ms.* 17:23+ Mr '89
New club rules. il *Ms.* 17:78-9 My '89
New congresswomen squeak into office. il *Ms.* 17:140-1 Ja/F '89
Optimist at last. *Ms.* 18:71 O '89
Thanks, guys. il *Ms.* 18:86 S '89
LEWIS, ANNE C.
The not so extracurricular. il *Phi Delta Kappan* 70:K1-K8 My '89
Washington commentary. See issues of Phi Delta Kappan
Washington news. See issues of The Education Digest beginning September 1986
LEWIS, ANTHONY, 1927-
The intimidated press. il *The New York Review of Books* 35:26-8 Ja 19 '89
about
Anthony agonistes. H. Catto. il *National Review* 41:34-7+ S 1 '89
LEWIS, BARBARA A.
The children's cleanup crusade. il *Sierra* 74:62-6 Mr/Ap '89
LEWIS, BARRY
about
Station-dealing blues. P. Noglows. il *Channels (New York, N.Y.: 1986)* 9:89 F '89
LEWIS, BARRY
Lewis, Clark & the old fartleks. il *Runner's World* 24:64-5 S '89
LEWIS, BERNARD
The map of the Middle East. *The American Scholar* 58:19-38 Wint '89
LEWIS, C. S. (CLIVE STAPLES), 1898-1963
about
C. S. Lewis, sins and all [excerpt from C. S. Lewis] A. N. Wilson. il por *The New York Times Book Review* 94:1+ D 24 '89
A "hoax" observed. R. Frame. il pors *Christianity Today* 33:64-5 Je 16 '89
Unscrambling the C. S. Lewis 'hoax'. L. W. Dorsett. *The Christian Century* 106:208-9 F 22 '89
LEWIS, CARL
about
Drugs and track. C. Neff. il pors *Sports Illustrated* 71:25-6 O 2 '89
Missed opportunity. M. Bloom. il por *Runner's World* 24:60-2+ Ja '89
LEWIS, CARLTON
about
Getting in on the biotech revolution. F. Brown, Jr. *American Visions* 4:12+ Je '89
LEWIS, CHRISTOPHER
Mondo Longo. il *Art in America* 77:35+ Mr '89
LEWIS, CLIVE STAPLES *See* Lewis, C. S. (Clive Staples), 1898-1963
LEWIS, DANIEL DAY- *See* Day-Lewis, Daniel
LEWIS, DAVID L. (DAVID LEVERING)
Harlem's first shining. bibl f il *Modern Maturity* 32:56-61+ F/Mr '89
LEWIS, DOUGLAS B.
After an oil spill: saving the birds. il *Sea Frontiers* 35:200-5 Jl/Ag '89
LEWIS, EDNA
about
Food with thought. J. Gruder. il por *Harper's Bazaar* 122:116-17 O '89
Making Brooklyn cook again. S. Wyndham. il por *New York* 22:24 Jl 31 '89
LEWIS, GEORGE N., AND OTHERS
Dispelling myths about verification of sea-launched cruise missiles. bibl f il *Science* 246:765-70 N 10 '89

LEWIS, JERRY
Space: more than a program. *Ad Astra* 1:16 D '89
LEWIS, JERRY, 1926-
about
Jerry Lewis telethon raises $78.4 million; Sammy Davis performs. il por *Jet* 76:28 S 25 '89
LEWIS, JERRY LEE
about
Dennis Quaid stokes rock's Fire. I. Robbins. il pors *Video* 13:16-17 D '89
Goodness gracious! [cover story] J. E. Bradley. il pors *Esquire* 111:136-42+ Mr '89
Playing the Killer. N. Tosches. il pors *Vogue* 179:182-5 Jl '89
Simmer down, son [cover story] R. Palmer. il pors *American Film* 14:26-33+ Je '89
Surviving marriage to the Killer. V. Balfour. il pors *People Weekly* 32:48-53 Jl 10 '89
Too hot to handle. B. D. Johnson. il por *Maclean's* 102:46-7 Jl 10 '89
LEWIS, JO ANN
Long-lasting impressions. il *Harper's Bazaar* 122:48+ Je '89
LEWIS, JOY
about
The spirit of '76: saving a pre-Revolutionary house in Sag Harbor. R. Fizdale and A. Gold. il por *Architectural Digest* 46:194-9+ Je '89
LEWIS, MERIWETHER, 1774-1809
about
Meriwether Lewis. J. B. Graves. il por *Conservative Digest* 15:29-33 Jl/Ag '89
LEWIS, MICHAEL
Dallas Down Under. *The New Republic* 200:14+ My 22 '89
Kamikaze capitalism. *The New Republic* 200:19-20 My 1 '89
Leave home without it [cover story] il *The New Republic* 201:19-20+ S 4 '89
St. Buddy. il *The New Republic* 200:16+ Mr 20 '89
about
A kiss-and-tell tale from the trading floor. J. Schwartz. il por *Newsweek* 114:62 N 20 '89
One million dollars, no tears. C. Byron. il por *New York* 22:26+ O 9 '89
Playing for keeps when he quit Wall Street, Michael Lewis hits the jackpot with Liar's poker. K. Hubbard. il pors *People Weekly* 32:73-4 D 18 '89
There goes the bonus. J. Queenan. il *Forbes* 144:14 O 30 '89
LEWIS, NORMAN, 1909-1979
about
Norman Lewis: pathfinder. C. James. il por *American Visions* 4:19-23 Je '89
LEWIS, PETER
Simplifying French. il *World Press Review* 36:56 Mr '89
LEWIS, R. W. B. (RICHARD WARRINGTON BALDWIN)
Rustic frame for a modern collection: the Connecticut house of Katharine and Nicholas Fox Weber. il *Architectural Digest* 46:200-5+ Je '89
LEWIS, REGINALD F.
about
TLC Beatrice is almost paid for. What's the next course? P. Finch. il por *Business Week* p33-4 N 20 '89
LEWIS, RICHARD WARRINGTON BALDWIN *See* Lewis, R. W. B. (Richard Warrington Baldwin)
LEWIS, RICKI
Baculovirus for biocontrol and biotech. il *BioScience* 39:431-4 Jl/Ag '89
Biological recognition repackaged. il *BioScience* 39:288-91 My '89
Genetics meets forensics. il *BioScience* 39:6-9 Ja '89
Making sense out of antisense. il *BioScience* 39:590-3 O '89
LEWIS, ROBERT K.
about
The spirit of '76: saving a pre-Revolutionary house in Sag Harbor. R. Fizdale and A. Gold. il por *Architectural Digest* 46:194-9+ Je '89
LEWIS, SALLY SIRKIN
about
Contemporary Southwest. R. Morris. il *Architectural Digest* 46:148-55 Ap '89
LEWIS, SANDY
about
Another Wall Streeter falls. *Newsweek* 114:46 S 11 '89
LEWIS, SARA E.
In training to be famous [story] il *Mademoiselle* 95:196+ Ap '89
LEWIS, STEVEN
The hated season. il *The New York Times Magazine* p24+ N 26 '89
LEWIS, SUSAN
Double-exposing two media. il *Petersen's Photographic Magazine* 17:76-7 Mr '89
LEWIS, TERRY
about
Out on the town with Jam and Lewis. il pors *Rolling Stone* p48 Jl 13-27 '89

LEWIS, THOMAS A., 1942-
Daniel Janzen's dry idea. il pors map *International Wildlife* 19:30-6 Ja/F '89
Fighting for the past. il map *Audubon* 91:56-72 S '89
Slow creature caught in a fast world. il *National Wildlife* 28:42-9 D '89/Ja '90
Tragedy in Alaska. il map *National Wildlife* 27:4-9 Je/Jl '89

LEWIS, TONY
Make your own etching tank. il *Radio-Electronics* 60:45-50 D '89

LEWIS AND CLARK EXPEDITION (1804-1806)
The incredible odyssey of the president's beasts [transporting live specimens to T. Jefferson] B. Gilbert. il por *Audubon* 91:100-2+ Ja '89
Lewis, Clark & the old fartleks [Trail Run ultramarathon across Washington] B. Lewis. il *Runner's World* 24:64-5 S '89
Meriwether Lewis. J. B. Graves. il por *Conservative Digest* 15:29-33 Jl/Ag '89

LEWIS-BRENT, LANA JANE
about
The champion of the modern corner store. P. O'Toole. il pors *Working Woman* 14:114-15+ S '89

LEWISOHN, MARK
about
Tracking the Beatles. J. Ressner. il *Rolling Stone* p15-17 F 9 '89

LEWITCH, JOSEPH *See* Lewis, Jerry, 1926-

LEWITZKY, BELLA, 1916-
about
Reviews:
    Performances in Los Angeles. D. Perlmutter. *Dance Magazine* 63:26 Ja '89

LEWITZKY DANCE COMPANY
Reviews:
    Performances in Los Angeles. D. Perlmutter. *Dance Magazine* 63:26 Ja '89

LEWONTIN, RICHARD C., 1929-
The science of metamorphoses. bibl f il *The New York Review of Books* 36:18-22 Ap 27 '89

LEXINGTON (AIRCRAFT CARRIER)
Five die on Lexington as student pilot crashes. *Aviation Week & Space Technology* 131:31 N 6 '89

LEXINGTON (KY.)
Crime
A golf great cut down in her prime [M. Miley murdered in 1941] B. K. Bell. il por *Women's Sports & Fitness* 11:60 O '89

LEXINGTON GARDENS (FIRM)
Cultivated pleasures. W. B. Logan. il *House & Garden* 161:65-6 Je '89

LEXIS SYSTEM *See* Information systems—Legal use

LEXITEL CORPORATION
See also
ALC Communications Corporation

LEXUS (AUTOMOBILE) *See* Automobiles, Foreign

LEXUS DIVISION *See* Toyota Motor Corporation. Lexus Division

LEYNER, MARK
The size of love [story] *Esquire* 112:122-3 Jl '89

LEYS, SIMON
After the massacres. bibl f il *The New York Review of Books* 36:17-19 O 12 '89
The curse of the man who could see the little fish at the bottom of the ocean. il *The New York Review of Books* 36:29 Jl 20 '89
The wrong march. *The New Republic* 200:11-12+ Je 19 '89

LEZOTTE, LAWRENCE W.
Features of effective school improvement plans. *The Education Digest* 55:15-17 D '89

LHON *See* Leber's hereditary optic neuropathy

LHTEC *See* Light Helicopter Turbine Engine Company

LI, KA-SHING
about
A $5-billion Canadian solution. P. C. Newman. il *Maclean's* 102:62 D 4 '89
A bubbling urban battle. H. Quinn. il por *Maclean's* 102:26-8 Ja 16 '89

LI, MING, AND OTHERS
Regulation of chloride channels by protein kinase C in normal and cystic fibrosis airway epithelia. bibl f il *Science* 244:1353-6 Je 16 '89

LI, P'ENG *See* Li Peng, 1928-

LI, VICTOR
about
A bubbling urban battle. H. Quinn. il por *Maclean's* 102:26-8 Ja 16 '89

LI CHANG, AND LI DAO-HE
Theatre architecture now and then. il *Theatre Crafts* 23:88+ Ap '89

LI DAO-HE
(jt. auth) *See* Li Chang, and Li Dao-He

LI PENG, 1928-
about
China's economy is careening out of control. D. J. Yang. il *Business Week* p54+ Ap 3 '89

LIABILITY (LAW)
See also
Airlines—Suits and claims
Airplane industry—Suits and claims
Asbestos industry—Suits and claims
Banks and banking—Suits and claims
Bhopal poisonous gas disaster, India, 1984—Suits and claims
Blood banks—Suits and claims
Computer industry—Suits and claims
Computer service industries—Suits and claims
Damages
Drug industry—Suits and claims
Exxon Valdez (Ship) oil spill, 1989—Suits and claims
Federal Employers' Liability Act
Government liability
Insurance, Liability
Malpractice
Motion picture industry—Suits and claims
Pollution liability
Prize contests—Suits and claims
Railroads—Suits and claims
Telephone companies—Suits and claims
Theatrical agencies and agents—Suits and claims
Torts
How to control liability costs. G. L. Priest. il por *Fortune* 119:323-4 Ap 24 '89
Innovation on trial: punitive damages versus new products. R. J. Mahoney and S. E. Littlejohn. bibl f *Science* 246:1395-9 D 15 '89
Limiting the damage from liability suits. T. Gest. *U.S. News & World Report* 106:50 My 15 '89
Litigation thwarts innovation in the U.S. P. W. Huber. il *Scientific American* 260:120 Mr '89
The plaintiff attorneys' great honey rush [with list of best paid lawyers in America; cover story] il *Forbes* 144:197-200+ O 16 '89
Products liability reform. J. L. Coleman. *Society* 27:57-66 N/D '89
Reform the product-liability system to prevent further economic harm. il *Nation's Business* 77:86 S '89
A seat on the board is getting hotter. M. Galen. il *Business Week* p72-3 Jl 3 '89
See you in court [cover story] D. C. Bacon. il *Nation's Business* 77:16-18+ Jl '89
This safety ruling could be hazardous to employers' health [OSHA decision opens business to more criminal charges] S. B. Garland. il *Business Week* p34 F 20 '89
Whose responsibility is it, anyway? [child welfare worker liability] J. P. Shapiro. il *U.S. News & World Report* 106:29-30 Ja 9 '89
You little tort [views of R. Neely on product liability] D. A. Farber. *The Washington Monthly* 20:49-50+ Ja '89

LIABILITY INSURANCE *See* Insurance, Liability

LES LIAISONS DANGEREUSES [drama] *See* Hampton, Christopher, 1946-

LIBARIDIAN, GERARD J.
Armenian earthquakes and Soviet tremors. *Society* 26:59-63 Mr/Ap '89

LIBBEY GLASS COMPANY
Brilliant cut glass patterns by Libbey. B. Boggess and L. Boggess. il *Antiques & Collecting Hobbies* 94:26-9 Ap '89

LIBBY, H. MORTON
about
A neat little package. B. Stack. il por *Nation's Business* 77:16 Je '89

LIBBY, ROY
Kidnapping
Two American missionaries are abducted in Colombia. J. Maust. il pors *Christianity Today* 33:50-1 F 3 '89

LIBBY PERSZYK KATHMAN (FIRM)
A neat little package. B. Stack. il por *Nation's Business* 77:16 Je '89

LIBBY PRISON (RICHMOND, VA.)
1864 [Union prisoners escape] A. Nielsen. il *American Heritage* 40:36-7 F '89

LIBEL AND SLANDER
See also
Blasphemy
Appeal Court reverses libel ruling against Doubleday's 'Nutcracker'. C. Reid. *Publishers Weekly* 235:22 Ja 6 '89
Court dismisses Janklow suit against Viking and Matthiessen. *Publishers Weekly* 235:14 Je 16 '89
The F.B.I. man who cried libel [suit brought by D. Price] M. Garbus. il *The Nation* 249:564+ N 13 '89
Limiting our rights [recent Supreme Court decisions] M. Garbus. *Publishers Weekly* 236:21 Ag 18 '89
McGinniss: a travesty of libel [J. MacDonald's breach of contract suit against J. McGinniss] M. Garbus. *Publishers Weekly* 235:69 Ap 21 '89
Media won record 40% of libel cases in past two years. H. Fields. *Publishers Weekly* 236:10 S 8 '89
The right to fake quotes [J. Masson's suit against J. Malcolm dismissed] W. A. Henry. por *Time* 134:49 Ag 21 '89
Supreme Court upholds public figure libel charge; High Court refuses to place limits on jury awards in civil suits. H. Fields. *Publishers Weekly* 236:12 Jl 14 '89

LIBEL AND SLANDER—*cont.*

Viking, Matthiessen win in Price libel suit. *Publishers Weekly* 236:8 S 1 '89

Why does libel law need reform? R. A. Smolla. *Society* 26:67-70 Jl/Ag '89

Great Britain

A reprieve for the Eye [court of appeal reduces libel award] B. Wickens. *Maclean's* 102:86 O 30 '89

The troubled Eye [libel costs threaten Private eye] A. Phillips. il *Maclean's* 102:44 Je 19 '89

Ireland

Irish publishers attempt to reform libel laws. *Publishers Weekly* 236:336 Ag 11 '89

LIBER (BOOK FAIR) *See* Book fairs

LIBERAL ARTS EDUCATION *See* Liberal education

LIBERAL-DEMOCRATIC PARTY (JAPAN)

Cleaning house [new prime minister T. Kaifu] H. Jensen. il por *Maclean's* 102:31 Ag 21 '89

In Japan, the bosses' man [new prime minister T. Kaifu] D. Benkoil and H. Takayama. il *Newsweek* 114:29 Ag 21 '89

Japanese voters may settle for the LDP—warts and all. R. Neff. il por *Business Week* p70 N 13 '89

Japan's quest for Mr. Clean [M. Ito declines to run for prime minister] B. Martin and H. Takayama. il por *Newsweek* 112:58 My 22 '89

A mountain moves [results of vote for the upper house of parliament] J. Smolowe. il *Time* 134:24-6 Ag 7 '89

Now appearing in the role of Japanese prime minister . . . [T. Kaifu] R. Neff. il por *Business Week* p44 Ag 21 '89

Real reform in Japan? Don't hold your breath. T. Holden. il *Business Week* p51 My 29 '89

The road warriors of Japan's politics [candidate S. Sato] M. Tharp. il pors map *U.S. News & World Report* 107:28-30 Jl 24 '89

Same old story [T. Kaifu nominated for prime minister] por *Time* 134:36 Ag 14 '89

Sex, lies, and Japanese politics. M. Sayle. *The New Republic* 201:18-22 S 11 '89

Sex, taxes and 'the Madonna factor' [T. Doi's Socialist Party wins parliamentary elections] J. Impoco. il por *U.S. News & World Report* 107:36 Ag 7 '89

The Socialists' stunning win. B. Powell and others. il *Newsweek* 114:33 Ag 7 '89

Upset in Japan [vote for upper house of parliament] H. Jensen. il pors *Maclean's* 102:22-3 Ag 7 '89

Will the Recruit scandal just go away? A. Borrus and N. Gross. il por *Business Week* p40-1 Je 12 '89

With the LDP on the rocks, Japan may be rudderless. R. Neff. il *Business Week* p47 Jl 10 '89

Would a socialist Japan be the same old Japan? R. Neff. il *Business Week* p67 Ag 14 '89

LIBERAL EDUCATION

See also

Consortium for Excellence in Teacher Education

Apocalypse now in U.S. higher education [cover story] F. Oakley. *America* 160:286-7+ Ap 1 '89

General education [cover story; special section; with editorial comment by Arthur Levine] il *Change* 21:4, 10-33 Jl/Ag '89

Go, oh thoughts, on wings of gold [address, October 7, 1988] M. Ross. *Vital Speeches of the Day* 55:282-4 F 15 '89

Marks of distinction [liberal arts colleges] il *U.S. News & World Report* 107:76-9 O 16 '89

Of many things [views of A. B. Giamatti] G. W. Hunt. *America* 160:338 Ag 15 '89

Preserving quality: teacher training from a liberal arts perspective [program at Willamette University] J. B. Engel. il *Phi Delta Kappan* 70:475-7 F '89

Pros and cons: a separate piece for general education [separate faculty] G. Irvin. il *Change* 21:6-9 Jl/Ag '89

Remember the Ph.D. glut? Colleges will go begging [shortage of liberal arts professors] D. L. Boroughs. il *U.S. News & World Report* 107:55 S 25 '89

Small and superb [liberal arts colleges] il *U.S. News & World Report* 107:69-71 O 16 '89

LIBERAL PARTY (CANADA)

Chrétien tests the pool. P. Kaihla. il por *Maclean's* 102:22 O 9 '89

Combat in Ontario [Peterson government] T. Tedesco. il por *Maclean's* 102:14-15 Ja 30 '89

In search of unity [B. Tobin] R. Laver. il por *Maclean's* 102:12 Mr 6 '89

Jean Chrétien's race for the fastest track. P. C. Newman. il *Maclean's* 102:28 Je 5 '89

John Turner: a man out of time. A. Fotheringham. il *Maclean's* 102:64 My 15 '89

The leaders in waiting. R. Laver. il pors *Maclean's* 102:10-12 Mr 6 '89

Leaders of Canada's Liberal Party may seek hearings on Gander crash [1985 crash] D. Hughes. *Aviation Week & Space Technology* 130:24-5 F 27 '89

The leadership issue. B. Wallace. il por *Maclean's* 102:18+ My 1 '89

Liberal controversies [three high-profile resignations in Ontario] P. Kaihla. il por *Maclean's* 102:17 Je 19 '89

A Liberal landslide [Prince Edward Island] G. Allen. il por *Maclean's* 102:17 Je 12 '89

Old powers, new strengths [Senate] B. Wallace. il *Maclean's* 102:27-8 O 30 '89

Ready to run [J. Chrétien] R. Laver. il por *Maclean's* 102:10-12 Je 26 '89

The rest of the pack [D. Peterson considering race for Liberal Party leadership] T. Tedesco. il por *Maclean's* 102:14-15 Je 26 '89

Return of the red tide [Liberals return to power in Newfoundland] G. Allen. il por *Maclean's* 102:12-13+ My 1 '89

Stepping down [J. Turner; special section; with editorial comment by Kevin Doyle] il por *Maclean's* 102:2, 10-12+ My 15 '89

Testing the waters [Liberal hopefuls] B. Wallace. il *Maclean's* 102:12-13 Ag 14 '89

A time for riding off in all directions. P. C. Newman. il *Maclean's* 102:34 F 27 '89

The tragedy of John Napier Turner. P. C. Newman. il *Maclean's* 102:48 My 15 '89

Waiting for a leader [constitutional accord debate] B. Wallace. *Maclean's* 102:24 N 6 '89

Anecdotes, facetiae, satire, etc.

All the comedy that's fit to print [J. Chrétien's delay in announcing leadership bid] A. Fotheringham. il *Maclean's* 102:112 N 20 '89

LIBERAL PARTY OF NEW YORK STATE

The last liberal [possibility that Liberal Party leader R. Harding will support R. Giuliani for mayor] J. Klein. il por *New York* 22:14+ Ap 3 '89

LIBERALISM

See also

Conservatism

American Jews firmly on the left. *Society* 26:2-3 My/Je '89

Anticommunism redefined. M. Greenfield. il *Newsweek* 113:72 Je 12 '89

Beyond the legal right: why liberals and feminists don't like to talk about the morality of abortion [cover story] J. DeParle. *The Washington Monthly* 21:28-9+ Ap '89

The brief life of liberal anti-communism. P. Coleman. il *National Review* 41:34-6 S 15 '89

Broken vessel [conference of Jewish progressives sponsored by Tikkun] E. Rothstein. *The New Republic* 200:17-20 Mr 6 '89

The Democrats [discussion of February 1989 article, Why the Democrats lost again] J. Muravchik. *Commentary* 87:2-5 Je '89

The Duke did his best. R. E. Tyrrell. *The American Spectator* 22:10 Ja '89

The end of history—or of liberalism? [views of F. Fukuyama] J. Gray. *National Review* 41:33-5 O 27 '89

Filling in the gaps of liberal culture [Robert Booth Fowler's Unconventional partners: religion and liberal culture in the United States] M. E. Marty. *The Christian Century* 106:1019-20+ N 8 '89

The gospel reconsidered [neoliberal philosophy of the Washington monthly; cover story; special section] *The Washington Monthly* 21:26-30+ Mr '89

Henry Luce, call your medium [Time's new liberal agenda] L. B. Bozell, III and B. Baker. *National Review* 41:37 S 15 '89

How big business bankrolls the left. W. T. Poole. il *National Review* 41:34-7 Mr 10 '89

Income and ideology: the new nexus. D. Seligman. il *Fortune* 120:185-6 D 4 '89

The intellectuals & the cold war. G. Szamuely. *Commentary* 88:54-6 D '89

Is liberalism still possible? R. H. Bates. *National Review* 41:17 D 31 '89

Israel's blank check [cover story] S. Zunes. il *The Progressive* 53:20-5 N '89

JFK's children: the class of '74 [neoliberal Democrats; cover story] W. Schneider. il por *The Atlantic* 263:35-40+ Mr '89

Lenny explains [L. Bernstein] W. F. Buckley. *National Review* 41:71 Ja 27 '89

Liberal establishment on Tory Row [neighborhood opposition forces departure of predominantly black Commonwealth Day School from Cambridge, Mass.] E. W. Wagner. il *National Review* 41:19-21 D 31 '89

Liberalism & American Jews [discussion of October 1988 article] I. Kristol. *Commentary* 87:2-3+ Ja '89

Liberalism's future may depend on social movements. M. E. Leary. *Utne Reader* p74 Mr/Ap '89

Liberals and Catholics: political economy in our time. M. Novak. *Current (Washington, D.C.)* 311:20-3 Mr/Ap '89

The limitations of liberalism. E. Kedourie. *The American Scholar* 58:265-70 Spr '89

Looking for Mr. Liberal [Franklin and Eleanor Roosevelt Institute conference] D. Seligman. *Fortune* 120:235 N 20 '89

Looking leftward [most liberal congressmen] D. Seligman. il *Fortune* 120:228+ S 11 '89

Media's liberal slant on the news. B. Baker. il *USA Today (Periodical)* 118:64-6 Jl '89

Mr. Superliberal [C. Pell] D. Seligman. il *Fortune* 119:195-6 Je 19 '89

LIBERALISM—cont.

No left turn [resurgence of Jewish liberalism in America] R. R. Wisse. *The New Republic* 200:23-7 My 22 '89

O'Sullivan's first law [Amnesty International's opposition to death penalty shows abandonment of political neutrality] J. O'Sullivan. *National Review* 41:14 O 27 '89

Portrait of a liberal [senators with highest liberal rankings] D. Seligman. il *Fortune* 119:341 Je 5 '89

The professor and the L-word. M. Decter. *Commentary* 87:39-48 F '89

Progressive values for America [cover story] M. J. Green. il *The Nation* 248:109+ Ja 30 '89

Razing the liberal plantation [cover story; special section] *National Review* 41:27-32 N 10 '89

Reagan, Bush, and the liberal revolution [address, December 8, 1988] E. H. Crane. *Vital Speeches of the Day* 55:265-8 F 15 '89

A rebirth of virtue: religion and liberal renewal. K. Townsend. *The Washington Monthly* 21:36-7 F '89

Resurrecting liberalism [1950's analysis by R. Merton, P. Hofstadter and L. Trilling distorted by neoconservatives] B. DeMott. *Current (Washington, D.C.)* 309:14-22 Ja '89

Ted and I agree. R. E. Tyrrell. il *The American Spectator* 22:10-11+ My '89

That memo [Republican National Committee attack on House Speaker T. Foley] W. McGurn. por *National Review* 41:22-3 N 10 '89

What ever happened to neoliberalism? D. D'Souza. *National Review* 41:34-6 Je 2 '89

What liberals haven't learned & why [presidential election] F. F. Siegel. il *Commonweal* 116:16-20 Ja 13 '89

Why are the liberals whitewashing? [case of O. Lattimore] W. F. Buckley. *National Review* 41:60 Jl 14 '89

Why do the liberals rage? [opposition to author's nomination to Supreme Court] R. H. Bork. *National Review* 41:26-7 D 8 '89

Why 'liberal' has become a dirty word. D. Moberg. il *Utne Reader* p70-1+ Mr/Ap '89

Why the Democrats lost again [presidential election] J. Muravchik. *Commentary* 87:13-22 F '89

Wright's real wrongs [J. Wright's move to left] D. Seligman. il *Fortune* 119:167 My 22 '89

Anecdotes, facetiae, satire, etc.

When you kick a liberal. G. Keillor. il *Harper's* 278:72-5 Ja '89

Canada

Double standards on Canada's left. B. Amiel. il *Maclean's* 102:9 S 25 '89

In defense of the 'L' word [address, March 15, 1989] D. R. Peterson. *Vital Speeches of the Day* 55:420-3 My 1 '89

Great Britain
Bibliography

Paperback history. B. Schwarz. *History Today* 39:54 Jl '89

Soviet Union

Back to the future. M. S. Forbes, Jr. il por *Forbes* 143:27 Je 26 '89

A usable past [M. Gorbachev's reforms evoke Russia's past liberalism] S. F. Starr. *The New Republic* 200:24+ My 15 '89

LIBERALISM (RELIGION)

In search of the hero: masculine spirituality and liberal Christianity [cover story] P. M. Arnold. il *America* 161:206-10 O 7 '89

A layman's liberal theology [address, November 16, 1988] S. G. Jones. *Vital Speeches of the Day* 55:253-6 F 1 '89

State of the question [discussion of October 7, 1989 article, In search of the hero: masculine spirituality and liberal Christianity] P. M. Arnold. *America* 161:304-6 N 4 '89

Where is the 'mainline' headed? [cover story; special section] il *The Christian Century* 106:1012-20+ N 8 '89

LIBERATION MOVEMENTS, NATIONAL *See* National liberation movements

LIBERATION THEOLOGY
See also
Mujerista theology

From 'liberation' to 'exile': a new image for church mission. E. Radner. *The Christian Century* 106:931-4 O 18 '89

Left-wing miracles [views of C. Boff] D. Lee. *National Review* 41:34 S 29 '89

Liberation theology adapts & endures [excerpt from Liberation theology and its critics] A. F. McGovern. il *Commonweal* 116:587-90 N 3 '89

Liberation theology and the Peruvian Church [cover story] J. A. McCoy. *America* 160:526-30 Je 3 '89

Of many things [Harvey Cox's The silencing of Leonardo Boff] G. W. Hunt. *America* 160:98 F 11 '89

The Peruvian Church and liberation theology [discussion of June 3, 1989 article, Liberation theology and the Peruvian Church] J. A. McCoy. *America* 161:84-5+ Ag 12-19 '89

What every North American should know about liberation theology [interview with R. M. Brown] por *U.S. Catholic* 54:21-8 Ap '89

LIBERIA
See also
Economic assistance, American—Liberia

Economic policy

Treasure for pleasure [American money managers leave Liberia] B. Martin. il *Newsweek* 113:39 F 13 '89

LIBERMAN, ALVIN M., AND MATTINGLY, IGNATIUS G.

A specialization for speech perception. bibl f il *Science* 243:489-94 Ja 27 '89

A specialization for speech perception? [discussion of January 27, 1989 article, A specialization for speech perception] *Science* 244:1530-1 Je 30 '89

LIBERT, FRÉDÉRICK, AND OTHERS

Selective amplification and cloning of four new members of the G protein-coupled receptor family. bibl f il *Science* 244:569-72 My 5 '89

LIBERTARIANISM
See also
Cato Institute
Christian Reconstruction movement

LIBERTY
See also
Civil rights
Democracy
Freedom of information
Freedom of speech
Freedom of the press
Religious liberty

1789: an idea that changed the world [cover story; special issue] il *The Unesco Courier* 42:4-58 Je '89

Capitalism and freedom. R. J. Samuelson. il *Newsweek* 113:46 Je 12 '89

Freedom gusts on. P. Yancey. il *Christianity Today* 33:80 O 20 '89

Individual rights, community claims. J. M. Wall. *The Christian Century* 106:707-8 Ag 2-9 '89

Old Glory. L. H. Lapham. *Harper's* 279:11-13 S '89

Outlines of a new world of freedom [address, September 25, 1989] G. Bush. il pors *Department of State Bulletin* 89:27-31 N '89

A prayer for July Fourth [mother's hope for son] E. Harrington. il *Reader's Digest* 135:121-2 Jl '89

Reflections on the revolution in China. C. Krauthammer. il *Time* 133:90 Je 5 '89

Structures of interest, structures of love: a response to Michael Novak [discussion of January 28, 1989 article, Structures of virtue, structures of sin: a theology of natural liberty] M. Novak. *America* 160:369-71 Ap 22 '89

Structures of virtue, structures of sin: a theology of natural liberty [address, May 5, 1988; cover story] M. Novak. *America* 160:54-60 Ja 28 '89

Word of the year: freedom. W. Safire. il *The New York Times Magazine* p10+ D 31 '89

LIBERTY BAPTIST COLLEGE
See also
Liberty University

LIBERTY UNIVERSITY

The last temptation of price [J. Falwell fires Liberty University football coach M. Hout] J. D. Miller. il *Sport (New York, N.Y.)* 80:12 Jl '89

Thou shalt not lose. L. Montville. il *Sports Illustrated* 71:82-6+ N 13 '89

LIBIOULLE, ANDRE

Rediscovering 'the Islands of the Moon'. il *The Courier (Unesco)* 42:31-2 Mr '89

LIBRARIANS

Dear Betty Harragan. B. L. Harragan. il *Working Woman* 14:49-50 Ap '89

LIBRARIES
See also
College libraries
Librarians
National libraries
Newspaper and periodical libraries
Presidential libraries
Research libraries

Architecture
See Library architecture

Automation

Library research. D. Lancaster. *Radio-Electronics* 60:25-6 Mr '89

Censorship
See Censorship

Circulation, loans, etc.
See also
Overdue library books
Public lending rights (of authors)

Manuscript collections

Libraries to the rescue [preserving contemporary manuscripts] G. Cartier. il *The Courier (Unesco)* 42:6-8 My '89

Periodical collections

The serials pricing controversy. G. Feldman. il *Publishers Weekly* 235:68-70 Ja 13 '89

Services to immigrants

Spreading some good words [librarian P. Goodwin's program for foreign users of Walnut Creek Branch Library in Garland, Tex.] D. Young. il por *Southern Living* 24:64 Ag '89

LIBRARIES—cont.
Technical processes
See also
Books—Conservation and restoration
Microwaves—Library use
Alabama
See also
Birmingham (Ala.)—Libraries
Egypt
See also
Alexandria (Egypt)—Libraries
France
See also
Bibliothèque de France
Georgia
See also
Norcross (Ga.)—Libraries
New York (State)
See also
New York (N.Y.)—Libraries
New York Public Library
Oregon
See also
West Salem (Or.)—Libraries
Texas
See also
Garland (Tex.)—Libraries
LIBRARIES, PRIVATE
Build a home library [cover story] K. Collier. il *The Family Handyman* 39:32-9 Jl/Ag '89
The library doctor [K. Thometz] L. Kaylin. il por *Gentlemen's Quarterly* 59:89+ D '89
LIBRARIES, SPECIAL
See also
Data Center (Oakland, Calif.)
LIBRARIES AND AUTHORS
See also
Public lending rights (of authors)
LIBRARIES AND BLACKS
See also
Moorland-Spingarn Research Center Library
LIBRARIES AND PUBLISHERS
Dispelling more myths about marketing to libraries. M. Sexton. *Publishers Weekly* 236:38 D 22 '89
Replacing the myths about marketing to libraries. M. Sexton. *Publishers Weekly* 235:56-7 Mr 10 '89
LIBRARY ARCHITECTURE
An architect for Mitterrand's new library [D. Perrault] N. Marmer. il *Art in America* 77:31 O '89
LIBRARY BUILDINGS *See* Library architecture
LIBRARY CONFERENCES
See also
White House Conference on Library and Information Services
LIBRARY OF AMERICA (FIRM)
Library of America considers publication of biographies. J. P. Frank. *Publishers Weekly* 235:15 My 19 '89
LIBRARY OF CONGRESS
America's amazing treasure chest. R. Fitzgerald. il *Reader's Digest* 134:47-8+ Je '89
A question of information policy [proposed fees] R. C. Atkinson. *Science* 246:33 N 10 '89
Scholarly Librarian of Congress to knock on publishers' doors [J. Billington] H. Fields. il por *Publishers Weekly* 235:26 Ja 13 '89
The secret in the stacks: how the Library of Congress hid Pentagon spending. il *Time* 134:29 O 9 '89
LIBRETTISTS
See also
Hofmannsthal, Hugo von, 1874-1929
LIBRETTOS
Words and music [collaboration with G. Stein] V. Thomson. il *The New York Review of Books* 36:43 Ap 13 '89
LIBROS REVOLUCIÓN (LOS ANGELES, CALIF.: BOOKSTORE) *See* Booksellers and bookselling—California
LIBYA
See also
Investments, American—Libya
Commerce
See also
Libyan-American conflict, 1986—Economic aspects
Germany (West)
See Germany (West)—Commerce—Libya
Soviet Union
See Soviet Union—Commerce—Libya
Defenses
See also
Airplanes, Military—Libya
Chemical and biological weapons—Libya
Foreign relations
United States
See United States—Foreign relations—Libya
Industries
See also
Petroleum industry—Libya
Politics and government
Libya's 'green *perestroika*'. C. Wallace. *World Press Review* 36:30 F '89

Social conditions
Qaddafi's revolution. P. G. Coy. *Commonweal* 116:552-3 O 20 '89
LIBYAN-AMERICAN CONFLICT, 1986
Economic aspects
U.S. oil companies authorized to resume operations in Libya [White House statement, January 19, 1989] *Department of State Bulletin* 89:71 Mr '89
LICARI, LOUIS, 1951-
about
With an ever-expanding client list and a salon that's already doubled in size, Louis Licari can be called New York's hair man of the moment. il pors *Vogue* 179:182 O '89
LICE
Hairy hassle [coping with head lice] L. Brown. il *American Health* 8:88 O '89
Of lice and children: going to the head of the class [head lice] T. A. Young and J. Willis. il *FDA Consumer* 23:28-31 N '89
LICENCE TO KILL [film] *See* Motion picture reviews—Single works
LICENSES
See also
Air pilots—Licenses
Architects—Licenses and registration
Automobile drivers—Licenses
Cellular radio—Licenses
Contractors—Licenses
Fishing boats—Licenses
Fishing licenses
Hunting licenses
Interior decorators—Licenses and registration
Marriage licenses
Psychotherapists—Licenses
LICENSING AGREEMENTS
See also
Computer industry—Licensing agreements
Drug industry—Licensing agreements
LICHINE, ALEXIS, 1913-1989
about
The battle of 1855. F. J. Prial. il *The New York Times Magazine* p78 Ag 20 '89
LICHT, STUART, AND OTHERS
Time and spatial dependence of the concentration of less than 10^5 microelectrode-generated molecules. bibl f il *Science* 243:1176-8 Mr 3 '89
LICHTBLAU, JOHN H.
about
A microchip in hand beats oil in the ground [interview] T. Mack. il por *Forbes* 144:150 O 30 '89
LICHTENSTEIN, GRACE
Bicycle days. il *Harper's Bazaar* 122:36+ S '89
Days of glory. il *Vogue* 179:202-3+ Ap '89
Getting zee drift. il *Ms.* 17:122 Ja/F '89
Glide through a 'snow forest'. il *New Choices for the Best Years* 29:54-5 Ja '89
A wheel good time [cover story] il *New Choices for the Best Years* 29:39-42 Ap '89
(jt. auth) *See* Bloch, Sonny, and Lichtenstein, Grace
LICHTENSTEIN, ROY, 1923-
about
The work of Roy Lichtenstein in the age of Walter Benjamin's and Jean Baudrillard's popularity [cover story] C. Ratcliff. il *Art in America* 77:110-23+ F '89
LICKONA, THOMAS
Educating the moral child. *The Education Digest* 55:45-7 S '89
LIDA, DAVID
A misunderstood misanthrope. il por *Harper's Bazaar* 122:76+ My '89
Well-read women. il pors *House & Garden* 161:228-31 O '89
LIDDY, G. GORDON
Rules of the game. il *Omni (New York, N.Y.)* 11:42-4+ Ja '89
LIDGARD, SCOTT
(jt. auth) *See* Crane, Peter R., and Lidgard, Scott
LIDOVE NOVINY (CZECHOSLOVAKIA: NEWSPAPER)
Paper back. S. J. Ungar. *The New Republic* 201:17-19 D 25 '89
LIDZ, FRANZ
Birdland. il pors *Sports Illustrated* 71:22-5 S 11 '89
The boys on the bus. il *Sports Illustrated* 71:58-62+ Jl 3 '89
Call it the Loving Cup. il pors *Sports Illustrated* 70:76 Ap 17 '89
Granny and the Giant. il pors *Sports Illustrated* 70:36-8+ Je 26 '89
It's mind over matter, 2-0. il por *Sports Illustrated* 71:97 O 30 '89
The pixie pioneer. il pors *Sports Illustrated* 70 Special Issue:59-61 F '89
Richest of the rich. il pors *Sports Illustrated* 71:64-6+ D 11 '89
Suddenly, a door-Mats. il pors *Sports Illustrated* 70:38-40 My 15 '89
Vive LeMond! [cover story] il pors *Sports Illustrated* 71:12-17 Jl 31 '89

LIDZ, FRANZ—cont.
What is 'Jeopardy!'? il *Sports Illustrated* 70:94-8+ My 1 '89
Wiseguy. il pors *Sports Illustrated* 71:58-60+ O 30 '89
Yearning for Howard. por *Sports Illustrated* 70:86 My 29 '89

LIE, TRYGVE, 1896-1968
about
Breaking faith (I). S. Hazzard. *The New Yorker* 65:63-4+ S 25 '89

LIE DETECTORS AND DETECTION
How to comply with the polygraph law. il *Nation's Business* 77:36-7 D '89

LIEBELER, SUSAN W.
Restrictions on foreign investment [address, September 19, 1989] *Vital Speeches of the Day* 56:122-4 D 1 '89

LIEBENTHAL, JEAN
Blessed to receive [story] il *Redbook* 174:54+ D '89

LIEBER, CHARLES M.
(jt. auth) See Wu, Xian Liang, and Lieber, Charles M.

LIEBER, IRWIN
about
Ballast. R. Phalon. il por *Forbes* 144:138 N 13 '89

LIEBER, JAMES
The case of the frozen embryos. il *The Saturday Evening Post* 261:50-3 O '89
A piece of yourself in the world. il *The Atlantic* 263:76-80 Je '89

LIEBER, JILL
Broken but unbowed. il pors *Sports Illustrated* 70:104-7 Mr 20 '89
Cool Hand Dan. il pors *Sports Illustrated* 71:112-18+ O 9 '89
Dreams do come true. il pors *Sports Illustrated* 71:74-8 O 23 '89
Hitter with heart. il pors *Sports Illustrated* 70:44-8 Ja 23 '89
Maximum exposure. il pors *Sports Illustrated* 70:38-40+ My 1 '89
No bones about it. il pors *Sports Illustrated* 71:54-8+ Ag 28 '89
Rocky flight into first. il por *Sports Illustrated* 71:36-8+ N 20 '89
Taking care of business. il *Sports Illustrated* 70:49-50 Ja 9 '89
The woman warrior. il pors *Sports Illustrated* 70 Special Issue:131-4 F '89
(jt. auth) See Neff, Craig, and Lieber, Jill

LIEBER, JILL, AND NEFF, CRAIG
The case against Pete Rose [cover story] il pors *Sports Illustrated* 71:10-20+ Jl 3 '89
An idol banned. il pors *Sports Illustrated* 71:29-30 S 4 '89

LIEBERMAN, ANNETTE R.
(jt. auth) See Lindner, Vicki, 1944-, and Lieberman, Annette R.

LIEBERMAN, JULIE LYONN
Exercises for improvisers—Lester Young's solo on Jive at five. il *Down Beat* 56:56-7 Mr '89

LIEBERMAN, MYRON, 1919-
Who says professional ethics is dead? A response to Myron Lieberman [discussion of October 1988 article, Professional ethics in public education: an autopsy] *Phi Delta Kappan* 70:723-7 My '89

LIEBERMAN, SUSAN
Downtown redevelopment. il *Theatre Crafts* 23:40-3+ D '89
Six characters in Madrid: American Repertory Theatre tours to Europe. il *Theatre Crafts* 23:34-5+ My '89

LIEBERSON, JONATHAN
TV: a day in the life. bibl f il *The New York Review of Books* 36:15-16+ Ap 13 '89

LIEBERSON, STANLEY, 1933-
When right results are wrong. *Society* 26:60-6 Jl/Ag '89

LIEBMAN, DAVE
about
The Liebman connection. J. Roberts. il por *Down Beat* 56:37 Ag '89

LIEBMANN-SMITH, JOAN
Two friends with one dream: "She gave me my baby". *Redbook* 172:122-3+ Mr '89

LIECHTENSTEIN
See also
Insider trading—Liechtenstein

LIEDTKE, J. HUGH
about
What does Liedtke want? M. Ivey and M. Shao. il por *Business Week* p42-3 D 25 '89-Ja 1 '90

LIEHM, ANTONÍN J., 1924-
about
The smallest giant. B. Müller-Ullrich. il por *World Press Review* 36:67 N '89

LIEPA, ANDRIS
about
Andris Liepa leaps to the U.S., but with *glasnost* the Bolshoi star can go home again. R. Arias. il pors *People Weekly* 31:50-2 My 29 '89
Dance steppes. D. Daniel. por *Vogue* 179:254 Ap '89

LIEPA, MARIS, 1936-1989
about
Obituary
Dance Magazine il por 63:28 Je '89

LIES See Lying

LIFE
See also
Conduct of life
Death
Quality of life
Don't act your age! [life stages] C. Tavris. il *American Health* 8:50-2+ Jl/Ag '89
Why Life says we are here [symposium in Life magazine] P. G. Henry. il *The Christian Century* 106:562-3 My 24-31 '89

Economic value
See Human capital

LIFE (BIOLOGY)
See also
Biosphere
Longevity
Is an embryo a person? C. A. Gardner. il *The Nation* 249:557-9 N 13 '89
Opening the door to the unknown. M. Toner. il *National Wildlife* 27:34-6 Je/Jl '89
When does life begin? [interview with C. Grobstein] E. Hall. il pors *Psychology Today* 23:42-6 S '89

Origin
See also
Creation
Comets and meteorites: harbingers of life on earth . . . and destructors of Mars. il *Sky and Telescope* 78:242 S '89
Comets may have supplied earth with chemicals of life. *Earth Science* 42:6-7 Summ '89
Did life really start out in an RNA world? M. M. Waldrop. il *Science* 246:1248-9 D 8 '89
How do you read from the palimpsest of life? M. M. Waldrop. il *Science* 246:578-9 N 3 '89
How old is the genetic code? Statistical geometry of tRNA provides an answer. M. Eigen and others. bibl f il *Science* 244:673-9 My 12 '89
The impact giveth . . . [amino acids found in Cretaceous-Tertiary boundary clay; research by Meixun Zhao and Jeffrey L. Bada] J. Horgan. *Scientific American* 261:24+ S '89
In the beginning [work of Jack W. Szostak and Jennifer Doudna] J. P. Rennie. *Scientific American* 261:28+ S '89
RNA offers clue to life's start [self-replicating RNA from ribozymes; work of Jack W. Szostak and Jennifer A. Doudna] I. Amato. *Science News* 135:372 Je 17 '89
Tracing living signs of ancient life forms [research by Andrew D. Ellington] I. Amato. *Science News* 136:229 O 7 '89
Was adenine the first purine? A. W. Schwartz and C. G. Bakker. bibl f il *Science* 245:1102-4 S 8 '89

LIFE (PERIODICAL)
The great God blackout [removes mention of God from cover of copies sold in New York City] M. E. Marty. *The Christian Century* 106:967 O 25 '89
Why Life says we are here [symposium] P. G. Henry. il *The Christian Century* 106:562-3 My 24-31 '89

LIFE CARE COMMUNITIES
Marketing
Penny's ante [P. Pritzker runs Hyatt's luxury retirement centers] J. Zweig. il por *Forbes* 144:352 N 13 '89
Tea, sympathy and direct mail [Marriott's marketing] J. Novack. il *Forbes* 144:210-11 S 18 '89

LIFE DETECTORS
Life detector. G. Davis. il *Popular Science* 235:59 Ag '89

LIFE EXPECTANCY See Longevity
LIFE EXPERIENCE COLLEGE CREDITS See College credits
LIFE GOES ON [television program] See Television program reviews—Single works
LIFE IN HELL (COMIC STRIP)
Is TV the coolest invention ever invented? S. Elder. il por *Mother Jones* 14:28-31 D '89
LIFE INSURANCE See Insurance, Life
LIFE JACKETS See Life preservers
LIFE ON MARS
Bringing Mars to life. *The Futurist* 23:42 Ja/F '89
Mars: remembrance of life past. M. Tennesen. il *Discover* 10:82-8 Jl '89
Solving a mystery in the sands of Mars [research by Robert C. Plumb] J. Eberhart. *Science News* 135:266 Ap 29 '89
LIFE ON OTHER PLANETS
See also
Interstellar communication
Life on Mars
UFOs
If we are alone, what on earth are we doing? G. L. Verschuur. il *Sky and Telescope* 78:452 N '89
Is anyone out there? il *Life* 12:48-53+ Jl '89
A new age of enlightenment? L. Frazer. il *Ad Astra* 1:20-1 S '89

Anecdotes, facetiae, satire, etc.
Alien rations. G. Schwartz. il *New York* 22:34 N 6 '89
Last word. B. Butterworth. por *Omni (New York, N.Y.)* 12:156 D '89

LIFE PRESERVERS
Vested interest. L. Green. il *Home Mechanix* 85:70-1+ Ag '89
LIFE PROGRAM
Families on welfare foster children with special needs. M. G. Myers. il *Children Today* 18:6-9+ Jl/Ag '89
LIFE SAVING *See* Rescue work
LIFE SAVING EQUIPMENT
See also
  Airplanes, Military—Escape devices
  Life detectors
  Life preservers
LIFE SCIENCES
See also
  Biology
LIFE SPAN *See* Longevity
LIFE SUPPORT SYSTEMS (SPACE ENVIRONMENT)
See also
  Biosphere II
Ins and outs of astronauts. M. R. Chartrand. *Ad Astra* 1:37 O '89
LIFESTYLES
Acceleration syndrome: does everyone live in the fast lane nowadays? T. Schwartz. il *Utne Reader* p36-43 Ja/F '89
Adding faces to ratings [VALS 2 psychographic profiles of selected markets] il *Channels (New York, N.Y.: 1986)* 9:80 S '89
Adding it up: the life style factor. H. Wheelwright. il *Money* 18 Money Guide:14-18+ Fall '89
Franchising's pathfinders [capitalizing on lifestyle trends] N. C. Baker and M. Whittemore. il *Nation's Business* 77:61-3+ F '89
How America has run out of time [living at an accelerated pace; cover story] N. R. Gibbs. il *Time* 133:58-61+ Ap 24 '89
Lifestyle contributes to a healthy heart. K. Fackelmann. *Science News* 136:367 D 2 '89
The pace of life [link between high speed cities and heart disease] R. Levine. il *Psychology Today* 23:42-6 O '89
Psycho-selling [VALS 2 typology of American consumers] C. Reece. il *Channels (New York, N.Y.: 1986)* 9:14 Jl/Ag '89
Rediscovering the rat race. R. J. Samuelson. il *Newsweek* 113:57 My 15 '89
Waste a lot, want a lot: our all-consuming quest for style. S. Ewen. il *Utne Reader* p81-4 S/O '89
Periodicals
Writing for life style magazines (II). il *The Writer* 102:28-30 Ja '89
LIFESTYLES OF THE RICH AND FAMOUS [television program] *See* Television program reviews—Single works
LIFETIME (FIRM)
If at first you don't succeed . . . M. Burgi. il *Channels (New York, N.Y.: 1986)* 9:66-7 S '89
LIFETIME CORP.
Michael Sinclair: health care's whirling dervish. R. A. Melcher. il por *Business Week* p69 D 4 '89
LIFEWAY FOODS INC.
Liquid gold. M. Barrier. il por *Nation's Business* 77:14 Jl '89
LIFSON, BEN
Perfect exposure. il por *House & Garden* 161:40+ F '89
LIFTING AND CARRYING
See also
  Weight lifting
LIGACHEV, YEGOR K.
about
Back-alley politics in the Kremlin. D. Brand. il por *Time* 133:48 My 29 '89
LIGAMENTS
Wounds and injuries
See also
  Sprains
LIGANDS
Analysis of ligand binding specificity of receptor chimeras [discussion of June 3, 1988 article, Chimeric α_2-,β_2-adrenergic receptors: delineation of domains involved in effector coupling and ligand binding specificity] B. K. Kobilka and others. *Science* 243:236-7 Ja 13 '89
Molecular recognition and metal ion template synthesis. T. J. McMurry and others. bibl f il *Science* 244:938-43 My 26 '89
LIGETI, GEORGE B.
about
Building a brewery is no small beer. il pors *Business Week* p40-1 Jl 24 '89
LIGHT, DOUGLAS B., AND OTHERS
Atrial natriuretic peptide inhibits a cation channel in renal inner medullary collecting duct cells. bibl f il *Science* 243:383-5 Ja 20 '89
LIGHT, JUDITH
Q. Why did Judith Light smash a window in anger? A. Her emotions spilled over playing the mother of a son with AIDS; ed. by Jeff Kaye. il por *TV Guide* 37:14-15 Ja 7-13 '89
about
Tony Danza, my husband, and me. V. Scott. il pors *Good Housekeeping* 208:86+ Ap '89

LIGHT
See also
  Airglow
  Color
  Doppler effect
  Fiber optics
  Lasers
  Luminescence
  Photochemistry
  Photography—Light and lighting
  Photons
  Polarization (Light)
  Reflection (Optics)
  Refraction
  Refraction, Double
  Sunlight
Photographs and photography
See also
  Reflections (Photography)
Funlights [time exposure] N. Ballenger and J. Tulley. il *Petersen's Photographic Magazine* 17:58-60 Ap '89
Pure light [photo of studio lights] J. Frunchtman. il *Petersen's Photographic Magazine* 17:58-9 Mr '89
Physiological effects
See also
  Photoperiodism
  Photoreceptors
  Phototherapy
  Plants, Effect of light on
  Seasonal affective disorder
  Ultraviolet rays—Physiological effects
Bright light induction of strong (type O) resetting of the human circadian pacemaker. C. A. Czeisler and others. bibl f il *Science* 244:1328-33 Je 16 '89
Illuminating jet lag [research by Charles Czeisler and Richard Kronauer] R. Pool. il *Science* 244:1256-7 Je 16 '89
A light touch changes the biological clock [research by Charles A. Czeisler] K. Fackelmann. *Science News* 135:374 Je 17 '89
Modulation of rod-cone coupling by light. X.-L. Yang and S. M. Wu. bibl f il *Science* 244:352-4 Ap 21 '89
Scattering
See also
  Rayleigh scattering
The nude in the shower phenomenon. C. F. Bohren. il *Weatherwise* 42:278-80 O '89
Strange footprints in snow. C. F. Bohren. il *Weatherwise* 42:168-70 Je '89
LIGHT, ZODIACAL *See* Zodiacal light
LIGHT AIRPLANES *See* Airplanes, Light
LIGHT ARMORED VEHICLES *See* Motor vehicles, Military
LIGHT BOXES
Boxes shed light up, down and out. A. R. Gould. il *Workbench* 45:38-41 Ja/F '89
LIGHT BULBS IN ART *See* Light in art
LIGHT COMMUNICATION SYSTEMS
See also
  Fiber optics
  Infrared communications
  Lasers—Communication use
Light beam communicator (I) [cover story] R. Sonntag. il *Radio-Electronics* 60:31-4 Jl '89
Light beam communicator (II). R. Sonntag. il *Radio-Electronics* 60:52-5+ Ag '89
LIGHT DETECTORS
Ball develops multi-anode microchannel array for Space Telescope, defense uses. W. B. Scott. il *Aviation Week & Space Technology* 130:296-7 Je 12 '89
LIGHT-EMITTING DIODES *See* Diodes
LIGHT FILTERS
10 best filters. il *Petersen's Photographic Magazine* 18:56-61 Ag '89
Color gels. C. Place. il *Petersen's Photographic Magazine* 17:64-7 Ap '89
Color in light; Beyond plastic filters: a look ahead. M. S. Eddy. il *Theatre Crafts* 23:40+ Ap '89
Equipped for safe solar viewing. R. Hill. il *Astronomy* 17:66-8 F '89
Filters for viewing [Chroma-Scan pocket filters] R. Burnham. il *Astronomy* 17:96 Ap '89
Quick-change artist for filters [Pro 4 filter system] il *Popular Photography* 96:118-19 Jl '89
Schneider B+W filters. il *Petersen's Photographic Magazine* 18:79 N '89
Secrets of city astrophotography. K. R. Brasch. il *Astronomy* 17:90-5 Ja '89
Subject got a contrast range that's as wide as all outdoors? It may be time to graduate. J. Shaw. il *Popular Photography* 96:38-9 N '89
Viewing sunspots with just a filter. A. MacRobert. il *Sky and Telescope* 78:289+ S '89
LIGHT GARDENING, ARTIFICIAL *See* Artificial light gardening
LIGHT HELICOPTER TURBINE ENGINE COMPANY
LHTEC develops commercial version of T800 engine. *Aviation Week & Space Technology* 130:19 Ja 23 '89

LIGHT IN ART
See also
Chiaroscuro
Camera, lights, action! [work of E. Staller] il por *National Geographic World* 165:30-5 My '89
Games [B. Bell's LED sculptures] S. Morris. il *Omni (New York, N.Y.)* 11:128 F '89
Twinkle, twinkle, little car [E. Staller's Lightmobile and Roly-Poly] B. Weber. il por *The New York Times Magazine* p82 Mr 26 '89

Exhibitions
See also
Museum of Neon Art (Los Angeles, Calif.)
Keith Sonnier: Barbara Gladstone; Leo Castelli. H. Cotter. il *Art News* 88:197-8 Ap '89
When neon signs were art [L. Davidson's restorations in Philadelphia] J. O'Dwyer. il pors *Americana* 17:50-5 My/Je '89

LIGHT INTENSIFICATION See Image intensifiers
LIGHT METERS See Exposure meters
LIGHT PENS
FTG improves on-screen penmanship [FT-1000 light pen and PXL-480 micro channel light pen board] B. Krasnoff. il *Personal Computing* 13:189 Je '89
LIGHT POLLUTION, OUTDOOR See Lighting, Outdoor
LIGHT PRODUCTION IN ANIMALS AND PLANTS See Bioluminescence
LIGHT RAIL SYSTEMS
Light rail [proposals for New York City] T. Hiss. il *The New Yorker* 65:70-4+ Mr 6 '89
LIGHT SHOWS
See also
Laser shows
Around the Mall and beyond [WORKS site specific series at the Hirshhorn] E. Park. il *Smithsonian* 19:24+ Ja '89
LIGHT THERAPY See Phototherapy
LIGHT VERSE See Humorous poetry
LIGHT-YEARS See Astronomical measurements
LIGHTFEATHER, MELODY
about
Fancy footwork. J. O'Dwyer. il por *Americana* 16:6 Ja/F '89
LIGHTFOOT, DALE
(jt. auth) See Lightfoot, Victoria, and Lightfoot, Dale
LIGHTFOOT, GORDON, 1938-
about
Gordon Lightfoot. B. Altman. il por *High Fidelity (New York, N.Y.)* 39:73-4 Jl '89
LIGHTFOOT, VICTORIA, AND LIGHTFOOT, DALE
Revealing the ancient world through high technology. il *Technology Review* 92:54-61 My/Je '89
LIGHTHOUSE POINT (FLA.)
Crime
Hit-and-run: a family's nightmare [A. Story struck and killed by car of C. Breeding] D. M. Mazie. il *Reader's Digest* 135:152-7 D '89
LIGHTHOUSE TENDERS
Twilight time for lightkeepers. S. McInerney. il *Country Journal* 16:15 Jl/Ag '89
LIGHTHOUSES
See also
National Lighthouse Day
A bright 200th anniversary. il *Southern Living* 24:37 Ag '89
Photographs and photography
Two centuries of light [cover story] il *Americana* 17:43-9 Jl/Ag '89
LIGHTING
See also
Agricultural equipment—Lighting
Art galleries and museums—Lighting
Automobiles—Lighting
Bathrooms—Lighting
Bicycles—Lighting
Candles and candleholders
Daylight
Electric lamps
High intensity discharge lighting
Hospitals—Lighting
Light boxes
Lighting fixtures
Opera—Stage lighting
Photography—Light and lighting
Skylights
Theater—Stage lighting
Videotape recorders and recording—Light and lighting
High-tech lighting for your home [special section] il *Popular Science* 235:79-90+ S '89
Light touches. N. Cooper. il *Home Mechanix* 85:46-8+ F '89
Lighting defines spaces. il *Southern Living* 24:104+ O '89
Living on borrowed light [architectural use of daylight] J. S. Russell. il *Architectural Record* 177:150-3 My '89
Control
See also
Electric switches
AC lighting controls. D. Lancaster. il *Radio-Electronics* 60:26-8+ Mr '89

Programmed mood lighting. T. O. Bakke. il *Popular Science* 235:86-7 S '89
LIGHTING, OUTDOOR
See also
Christmas decorations, Outdoor
Centerline: John Haupt [lighting designer for Disney World's live shows] M. Sommers. il por *Theatre Crafts* 23:14 Mr '89
Low-voltage outdoor lighting. D. Prestly. il *The Family Handyman* 39:34-8 Je '89
Michigan light victory [light pollution and John Rogers Observatory] il *Astronomy* 17:16 Ap '89
Night magic [cover story] R. Cornwell. il *Home Mechanix* 85:36-40+ Ag '89
Outdoor lighting . . . art and technology [home yards; cover story] il *Sunset (Central West edition)* 183:72-8+ Jl '89
The shot heard round the universe [shooting out light to watch occultation] W. Allen. *Astronomy* 17:110-11 Ja '89
Sodium lights repel turtles [allowing Florida loggerheads to find ocean] il *Sea Frontiers* 35:69 Mr/Ap '89
Space pollution obscures night sky. il *Earth Science* 42:9 Spr '89
Who will miss the night sky? [light pollution] D. L. Crawford. *Astronomy* 17:8 Mr '89
Laws and regulations
Court rules against light polluter [yard light interferes with astronomical observatory] il *Astronomy* 17:16 Jl '89
Lights out in Flagstaff. *Astronomy* 17:12+ Jl '89
LIGHTING DESIGNERS
See also
Devin, Richard
Haupt, John
Katz, Natasha
Musser, Tharon
Skelton, Tom
Sullivan, Joan
A guide for assistant lighting designers. C. Miller. il *Theatre Crafts* 23:22-7 Ja '89
You're a what? Lighting designer. M. Stanton. il *Occupational Outlook Quarterly* 32:37-9 Wint '88
LIGHTING FIXTURES
See also
Lanterns
Crafty lighting: one-of-a-kind fixtures—make 'em yourself and save! il *Better Homes and Gardens* 67:71 S '89
High-tech lighting for your home [special section] il *Popular Science* 235:79-90+ S '89
Medicine cabinets and recessed lights. il *Popular Mechanics* 166:118-20 Ap '89
Collectors and collecting
Benson's burners [art nouveau fixtures by W. A. S. Benson] M. Filler. il *House & Garden* 161:52 Ja '89
LIGHTMAN, ALAN P., 1948-
Magic on the mind: physicists' use of metaphor. *The American Scholar* 58:97-101 Wint '89
LIGHTNING
See also
Cycling—Lightning hazards
Thunderstorms
Bolts from the blue: researchers seek forecasting clues from lightning patterns. il *U.S. News & World Report* 107:54-5 Jl 24 '89
Letters [discussion of November 1988 article, The electrification of thunderstorms] E. R. Williams. *Scientific American* 261:8 Jl '89
Lightning in your life. T. Schlatter. il *Weatherwise* 42:332-4 D '89
Natural and artificially initiated lightning [cover story] M. A. Uman and E. P. Krider. bibl f il *Science* 246:457-64 O 27 '89
Stalking the wild thunderbolt. S. J. Nadis. il *Technology Review* 92:15-16 F/Mr '89
Photographs and photography
A lucky strike. W. E. Faidley and E. P. Krider. bibl f il *Weatherwise* 42:136-9 Je '89
LIGHTNING OVER BRADDOCK: A RUSTBOWL FANTASY [film] See Motion picture reviews—Single works
LIGHTNING PROTECTION
Lightning. S. Curtis. il *Field & Stream* 94:20 Ag '89
Shock therapy. il map *The Mother Earth News* 118:66-9 Jl/Ag '89
When lightning strikes . . . . C. Slom. *McCall's* 116:90 Jl '89
LIGHTPENS See Light pens
LIGHTS, FISHING See Fishing lights
LIGNIN
Land plants' algal roots [research by Charles F. Delwiche] *Science News* 136:70 Jl 29 '89
Lignin-like compounds and sporopollenin in Coleochaete, an algal model for land plant ancestry. C. F. Delwiche and others. bibl f il *Science* 245:399-401 Jl 28 '89
LIGURIAN COOKING See Cooking, Italian
LIH, LARS T.
The transition era in Soviet politics. bibl f *Current History* 88:333-6+ O '89
LIKHACHEV, DMITRII SERGEEVICH
Doctor Zhivago; tr. by Barry J. Rubin. il *The New Republic* 200:30+ F 20 '89

LIKUD PARTY (ISRAEL)
Israel moves right. M. Widlanski. il *National Review* 41:24-5 Je 30 '89

LILA ACHESON WALLACE WING *See* Metropolitan Museum of Art (New York, N.Y.). Lila Acheson Wallace Wing

LILAC TIME (MUSICAL GROUP)
Folklure. J. Leland. por *Vogue* 179:280 Mr '89

LILACS
A lilac primer. B. Heard. il *Flower and Garden* 33:18-20+ Mr/Ap '89
Sweet lilacs. G. Morris. il *Americana* 17:44-9 My/Je '89

LILBURNE, GEOFFREY R.
Neighbor [poem] *The Christian Century* 106:230 Mr 1 '89

LILIEN, COPIE
about
Copie Lilien: hefty sales in hefty kids' togs. R. Duffy. il por *Business Week* p98 My 8 '89

LILIES
See also
Daylilies
Fritillarias

LILIES, VOODOO *See* Voodoo lilies

LILLA, MARK
The global zeitgeist checklist: France. *The New Republic* 200:21 Ap 10 '89
The global zeitgeist checklist: Italy. *The New Republic* 201:20 Jl 10 '89
God is a French Socialist. il *The American Spectator* 22:27-8 My '89
Vive la télé. *The New Republic* 200:24 Ja 23 '89

LILLE (FRANCE)
Economic conditions
Lille gets ready for '92. J. Ardagh. il map *The New York Times Magazine* p58-60+ D 3 '89

LILLEHAMMER OLYMPICS, 1994 *See* Olympic Games— 1994—Winter Olympics

LILLIAN VERNON CORPORATION
Growing a business [interview with L. V. Katz] B. Stein. il por *Home Office Computing* 7:56 S '89

LILLIENSTEIN, MAXWELL J.
Pitfalls and penalties lurk in Child Obscenity Act. *Publishers Weekly* 235:21+ Ja 20 '89

LILLY, JOHN CUNNINGHAM, 1915-
about
The man who talked to dolphins. S. Chollar. il por *Psychology Today* 23:56 Ap '89

LILLY ENDOWMENT, INC.
The high priest of scholarship [R. W. Lynn] K. L. Woodward. il por *Newsweek* 114:52 Ag 7 '89

LILLYWHITE, HARVEY B., AND DONALD, JOHN A.
Pulmonary blood flow regulation in an aquatic snake. bibl f il *Science* 245:293-5 Jl 21 '89

LIMA (PERU)
Buildings
Bankers' trust [Banco de Credito designed by Arquitectonica; cover story] K. D. Stein. il *Architectural Record* 177:90-9 F '89
Poor
Squalor in the "City of God" [work of D. Wroughton] P. Yancey. il *Christianity Today* 33:12-13 F 17 '89

LIMAN, ARTHUR L.
about
Got big deals, big problems, big bucks? Get Arthur Liman. M. Galen. il por *Business Week* p112+ My 15 '89
The verdict on Arthur Liman. T. Friend. il por *Esquire* 111:66-75 Ja '89

LIMBIC SYSTEM (BRAIN) *See* Brain

LIMBS (ANATOMY)
See also
Arm
Surgery
See also
Ilizarov method

LIMERICKS
Competitions
Time out for nonsense [winners of International wildlife's animal limerick contest] il *International Wildlife* 19:42-4 S/O '89

LIMESTONE
Damaged lakes can be rescued [use of limestone; research by Patricia Bradt] il *USA Today (Periodical)* 117:2 Je '89

LIMING ENGINE MANUFACTURING CORPORATION
Liming Engine plant seeks foreign parts contracts, nonaerospace work. il *Aviation Week & Space Technology* 131:87-8 D 11 '89

LIMITATION OF ARMS *See* Disarmament

LIMITED, INC.
Is there no limit to The Limited's growth? S. Phillips. il *Business Week* p192+ N 6 '89
It's turnaround time for Verna Gibson. S. Phillips. il por *Business Week* p117-18 F 20 '89

LIMITED EDITION PUBLISHING *See* Publishers and publishing—Limited editions

LIMITED PARTNERSHIP
See also
Airlie Group
Boston Celtics Limited Partnership
Centennial Group, Inc.
Corporate Partners LP
Harry Gray, Mel Klein & Partners LP
InterMedia Partners (Firm)
Krupp Cash Plus L.P.
Master limited partnership
Medical Science Partners
Mesa Limited Partnership
OKC Limited Partnership
Perkins Family Restaurants LP
Triple net partnership
Boxcars and jets are investment vehicles, too. S. Woolley. *Business Week* p108 Ja 16 '89
Co-op quake [shaky limited partnership deals used to finance co-op conversion in New York City] C. Byron. il *New York* 22:22+ N 20 '89
Funds that profit from jump-starting the startups. L. Light. *Business Week* p128 S 18 '89
Know-nothing investments. J. B. Quinn. il *Newsweek* 113:50 Je 5 '89
The limited future of limited partnerships. M. Schiffres. il *Changing Times* 43:27-30 Ag '89
A limited partnership that's frankly a gamble [options on lease residuals] L. Zinn. *Business Week* p170 O 30 '89
Real estate partnerships are sinking, with no lifeboats in sight. L. Jereski and L. Light. il *Business Week* p74-5 Jl 3 '89
RELPs: is it better to bail out—or mutiny? L. Jereski. *Business Week* p80 Ag 7 '89
Taxation
Help house the poor—and cut your taxes [real estate limited partnerships] T. Segal. *Business Week* p126 D 4 '89
Landlord, beware [real estate partnerships in low income housing] H. Rudnitsky. il *Forbes* 144:44-5 Jl 24 '89

LIMOUSINES
Mary Wilson to have her Beatles' limo auctioned. il por *Jet* 76:14 Ap 10 '89

LIMULUS *See* Horseshoe crabs

LIN, LEU-FEN H., AND OTHERS
Purification, cloning, and expression of ciliary neurotrophic factor (CNTF). bibl f il *Science* 246:1023-5 N 24 '89

LIN, MAYA YING
about
First she looks inward. J. Coleman. il pors *Time* 134:90-2+ N 6 '89
Maya Lin lets healing waters flow over her Civil Rights Memorial. D. Grogan. il por *People Weekly* 32:78-80 N 20 '89

LIN BROADCASTING CORP.
The cellular bidding war will get even hotter [McCaw's offer for LIN] R. D. Hof. il *Business Week* p39-40 Je 19 '89
For Craig McCaw, it's do-or-die time. C. Hawkins and R. D. Hof. il *Business Week* p34 D 4 '89
This cellular hookup could jam the competition [LIN and BellSouth's merger] J. J. Keller. il *Business Week* p45 S 25 '89
Will McCaw be ensnared by the net of his dreams? R. D. Hof. map *Business Week* p43-4 D 18 '89
Winning is only the first step [McCaw Cellular gains control] F. Meeks. il pors map *Forbes* 144:80-3 D 25 '89

LINCOLN, ABRAHAM, 1809-1865
Addresses, messages, etc.
A. Lincoln, writer. G. C. Ward. il *American Heritage* 40:14+ S/O '89
Lincoln's tragic heroism. T. Fleming. por *National Review* 41:38-40 D 8 '89
To the Gettysburg station. A. Delbanco. il *The New Republic* 201:31-6+ N 20 '89
Bibliography
Abe, honestly and otherwise [juvenile biographies] H. Mayer. *The New York Times Book Review* 94:24 F 12 '89
Collectibles
Lincolniana in 1988. F. J. Williams. il pors *Antiques & Collecting Hobbies* 93:35-7 F '89
Correspondence
A. Lincoln, writer. G. C. Ward. il *American Heritage* 40:14+ S/O '89
Lincoln's tragic heroism. T. Fleming. por *National Review* 41:38-40 D 8 '89
To the Gettysburg station. A. Delbanco. il *The New Republic* 201:31-6+ N 20 '89
Gettysburg address
Anecdotes, facetiae, satire, etc.
Aside from that, Sam, how did you like the speech? V. Gold. *The American Spectator* 22:20 Ja '89
Homes
The house at Eighth and Jackson. G. C. Ward. bibl il por *American Heritage* 40:68-72+ Ap '89
In the footsteps of the Lincolns. W. T. Anderson. il map *The Saturday Evening Post* 261:64-7+ Jl/Ag '89
Lincoln's new home [Lincoln Home National Historic Site, Springfield, Ill.] H. Holzer. il map *Americana* 16:44-9 Ja/F '89

LINCOLN, ABRAHAM, 1809-1865—Homes—*cont.*
Mr. Lincoln's Springfield. W. T. Anderson. il *American History Illustrated* 24:26-31 Mr '89
Press relations
Anecdotes, facetiae, satire, etc.
Aside from that, Sam, how did you like the speech? V. Gold. *The American Spectator* 22:20 Ja '89
Statues, portraits, etc.
Lincoln walks in Charleston. il por *Southern Living* 24:32 Je '89

LINCOLN, NAN
The summer of Cecily. il *Reader's Digest* 134:84-8 Je '89

LINCOLN (ENGLAND)
Antiquities
The new York? D. Byrne. il *History Today* 39:7-8 Jl '89

LINCOLN (MASS.)
Historic houses, sites, etc.
Architecture: Walter Gropius [Gropius House] K. Frampton. il por *Architectural Digest* 46:82+ F '89

LINCOLN (VT.)
Social conditions
A neighborly sort of way. C. A. Bohjalian. il *Reader's Digest* 134:71-2 Ja '89

LINCOLN CENTER FOR THE PERFORMING ARTS. METROPOLITAN OPERA HOUSE *See* Metropolitan Opera House (New York, N.Y.)

LINCOLN HIGH SCHOOL BAND (EAST SAINT LOUIS, ILL.)
Award-winning director faces layoff [band director R. Carter] D. Helland. il *Down Beat* 56:12 Ag '89

LINCOLN HOME NATIONAL HISTORIC SITE (ILL.)
The house at Eighth and Jackson. G. C. Ward. bibl il por *American Heritage* 40:68-72+ Ap '89
Lincoln's new home. H. Holzer. il map *Americana* 16:44-9 Ja/F '89
Mr. Lincoln's Springfield. W. T. Anderson. il *American History Illustrated* 24:26-31 Mr '89

LINCOLN-MERCURY DIVISION *See* Ford Motor Co. Lincoln-Mercury Division

LINCOLN PARK ZOO
At Chicago's Lincoln Park Zoo, artistic elephants and chimps are living the easel life. il *People Weekly* 32:108-9 Ag 28 '89

LINCOLN PROPERTY COMPANY
"The dinosaurs are dying". J. H. Taylor. il *Forbes* 143:92+ My 1 '89
Nothing to Crow about. K. Hannon. il *Forbes* 144:10 S 18 '89

LINCOLN SAVINGS & LOAN ASSOCIATION
$1 billion worth of influence [C. Keating's dealings with five senators] M. B. Carlson. il por *Time* 134:27-8 N 6 '89
Asleep at the S&L switch [M. D. Wall] R. Thomas and E. Clift. il por *Newsweek* 114:71 D 11 '89
Bob Bennett: on the trail of the 'Keating Five' [Senate Ethics inquiry into scandal] T. Smart. il por *Business Week* p60 D 11 '89
CC calls for ethics inquiry into five senators [dealings with C. Keating in the Lincoln Savings & Loan affair] J. Denny. *Common Cause Magazine* 15:28 N/D '89
Financier Charles Keating is the $2 billion man of the savings and loan crisis. B. Hewitt. il pors *People Weekly* 32:78-80 D 4 '89
For Charlie Keating, the best defense is a lawsuit [declares American Continental bankrupt as feds close in on Lincoln Savings & Loan] K. Kerwin. il por *Business Week* p32+ My 1 '89
Good timing, Charlie [C. Keating] H. Rudnitsky. il por *Forbes* 144:140-2+ N 27 '89
Is Danny Wall on the way out? [tainted by scandal] C. Yang and P. Dwyer. *Business Week* p59 N 13 '89
Keating takes the Fifth. M. B. Carlson. il por *Time* 134:46 D 4 '89
"A legal bank robbery". M. B. Carlson. il pors *Time* 134:29 N 27 '89
The man who tried to buy Washington [C. Keating's dealings with five senators] G. Borger and S. J. Hedges. il pors *U.S. News & World Report* 107:18-21+ N 27 '89
Now it's broke [D. Regan's role in S&L scandal] J. R. Adams. *The New Republic* 201:16-18 N 13 '89
The S&L scandal's biggest blowout. T. Morganthau. il por *Newsweek* 114:35-6 N 6 '89
The seduction of Senator Alan Cranston. P. Dwyer. il pors *Business Week* p82-4 D 4 '89
The tumbling of Danny Wall. S. J. Hedges. *U.S. News & World Report* 107:55 D 11 '89

LINCOLN UNIVERSITY (PA.)
Clifton Davis of 'Amen' gets honorary degree at Lincoln U. commencement. il pors *Jet* 76:16 My 29 '89
Frederick Douglass statue unveiled at Lincoln Univ. il *Jet* 77:36-7 N 20 '89
Niara Sudarkasa: educator for the 1990's. E. B. Washington. il pors *Essence* 20:106-8+ My '89

LIND, ROBERT H.
(jt. auth) See Armstrong, Lawrence E., and Lind, Robert H.

LINDAL CEDAR HOMES, INC.
An American builds in Japan. A. R. Gould. il *Workbench* 45:12 S/O '89

LINDBERG, TOD
The world according to Moyers [cover story] il *National Review* 41:22-5 Mr 10 '89

LINDBERGH, CHARLES, 1902-1974
about
An American childhood in Little Falls. B. L. Larson. il por *Architectural Digest* 46:36+ Je '89
Collectibles
It's the heroes who give us specialized fields of collecting [medals commemorating flight] E. Rochette. il *Antiques & Collecting Hobbies* 93:66-7 Ja '89

LINDBERGH FLIGHT *See* Aviation—Transatlantic flights—History

LINDBLAD, GUNILLA
about
Best face forward. D. Guerre. il pors *Harper's Bazaar* 122:28+ Ag '89

LINDEMAN, BARD
The family gathering. il *New Choices for the Best Years* 29:78-9 Ag '89

LINDEN, RON
about
Ron Linden at Ovsey. F. Colpitt. il *Art in America* 77:204-5 My '89

LINDEN, TREVOR
about
Medicine man for Vancouver. A. Murphy. il pors *Sports Illustrated* 70:91-2 Ap 3 '89

LINDEN
Around the Mall and beyond [death of hundred year old tree in the Enid A. Haupt Garden] E. Park. il *Smithsonian* 20:26+ Je '89

LINDMAYER, JOSEPH
about
Quantum leap. G. F. Gilder. il por *Forbes* 143:138-9 Je 26 '89

LINDNER, LAWRENCE
Type A diet traps. il *Health (New York, N.Y.)* 21:36-7 Ag '89

LINDNER, LAWRENCE, AND ZYLA, GAIL
Attention dieters . . . il *Redbook* 173:14 S '89

LINDNER, VICKI, 1944-, AND LIEBERMAN, ANNETTE R.
What's your money personality? *Redbook* 172:124-5+ Ap '89

LINDORFF, DAVID
A hot issue. *The Nation* 248:724-5 My 29 '89

LINDOW, STEVEN E., AND OTHERS
Genetic engineering of bacteria from managed and natural habitats. bibl f *Science* 244:1300-7 Je 16 '89

LINDROS, ERIC
about
The face of the future. J. Greenberg. il pors *Sports Illustrated* 71:86-8 D 11 '89

LINDSAY, KAREN
about
Karen Lindsay was overdue at the library; so they threw the book at her. il pors *People Weekly* 32:113 N 27 '89

LINDSAY, S. M., AND OTHERS
Images of the DNA double helix in water [cover story] bibl f il *Science* 244:1063-4 Je 2 '89

LINDSAY OLIVE GROWERS
The thoroughly modern olive. R. Sokolov. il *Natural History* p102-4 Ap '89

LINDSAY-POLAND, JOHN
Unwelcome in El Salvador. il *The Progressive* 53:32-5 My '89

LINDSEY, BILL
about
Working for our cities. D. Young. il pors *Southern Living* 24:141-2+ S '89

LINDSEY, LUCI
about
Cultivating the gray. D. Machan. il pors *Forbes* 144:126+ S 4 '89

LINDSEY, RICHARD ARLEN
about
Private mercy [excerpt from Public justice, private mercy]; ed. by Dick Adler. E. G. Brown. il *Common Cause Magazine* 15:28-33 Jl/Ag '89

LINDSEY, WILLIAM H. *See* Lindsey, Bill

LINDSKOOG, KATHRYN ANN
about
A "hoax" observed. R. Frame. il pors *Christianity Today* 33:64-5 Je 16 '89
Unscrambling the C. S. Lewis 'hoax'. L. W. Dorsett. *The Christian Century* 106:208-9 F 22 '89

LINDSMITH, BETH
Shed a tear for shoulder pads. il *Glamour* 87:148 N '89

LINDSTEN, TULLIA, AND OTHERS
Regulation of lymphokine messenger RNA stability by a surface-mediated T cell activation pathway. bibl f il *Science* 244:339-43 Ap 21 '89

LINDSTROM, ALETHA
A diary for living. il *Reader's Digest* 134:158-60 F '89
LINDSTROM, BOB
Video scans. See issues of Omni (New York, N.Y.) beginning February 1989 through December 1989
LINDSTROM, D. R., AND MACAYEAL, D. R.
Scandinavian, Siberian, and Arctic Ocean glaciation: effect of Holocene atmospheric CO_2 variations. bibl f il *Science* 245:628-31 Ag 11 '89
LINDZEN, RICHARD S.
about
Greenhouse skeptic out in the cold. R. A. Kerr. por *Science* 246:1118-19 D 1 '89
LINE, LES
Etcetera. See issues of Audubon
LINE ITEM VETO *See* Veto
LINEBACKERS (FOOTBALL PLAYERS) *See* Football players
LINEBERGER, KATHRYN
Colonial collectibles. il *Harper's Bazaar* 122:92 O '89
LINEN, HOUSEHOLD
See also
Bedding
Pillow cases
Towels
West Point-Pepperell, Inc.
New life for old linens. J. Williams and J. Severson. il *Better Homes and Gardens* 67:113-15 Je '89
Care
Resurrect old linens. D. Dunne. il *Americana* 17:14-16 Mr/Ap '89
LINEN CLOSETS *See* Closets
LINER, ELAINE
Weighing the workouts. il *Video* 13:54-6 Ag '89
LINERS *See* Ocean liners
LINES, FISHING *See* Fishing tackle
LINES, WAITING *See* Queues (Waiting lines)
LING, ALISTER
Rewarding star clusters. il *Astronomy* 17:86-9 Ag '89
Standout winter star clusters. il *Astronomy* 17:98-103 Ja '89
LING, JACK
The media's role. il *World Health* p24-5 Ja/F '89
LING, PETER
Sex and the automobile in the Jazz Age. bibl il *History Today* 39:18-24 N '89
LING, VICTOR
(jt. auth) See Kartner, Norbert, and Ling, Victor
LINGUISTICS
A linguistic "nay" to channeling [work of Sarah Thomason] M. Roberts. il *Psychology Today* 23:64-5 O '89
LINK, PERRY
The Chinese intellectuals and the revolt. il *The New York Review of Books* 36:38-41 Je 29 '89
(tr) See Fang Lizhi. China's despair and China's hope
LINKAGE (GENETICS)
See also
Genetic mapping
Restriction fragment length polymorphisms
Troubles encountered in gene linkage land [difficulty in replicating mental disorder studies] D. M. Barnes. *Science* 243:313-14 Ja 20 '89
LINKE, FRANCESCA
about
In Time flies when you're alive, actor Paul Linke turns the last years of his wife's life into art. J. Kaufman. il pors *People Weekly* 32:59-60 Ag 21 '89
LINKE, PAUL
about
In Time flies when you're alive, actor Paul Linke turns the last years of his wife's life into art. J. Kaufman. il pors *People Weekly* 32:59-60 Ag 21 '89
LINKE, SUSANNE
about
Heart of darkness. T. Tobias. por *New York* 22:124+ N 6 '89
LINKLATER, ANDRO
The rhino's last stand. il *Reader's Digest* 134:106-10 F '89
LINKWAY (COMPUTER PROGRAM)
LinkWay. D. Stanton. *Compute!* 11:62 S '89
LINLEY, DAVID ALBERT CHARLES ARMSTRONG-JONES, VISCOUNT, 1961-
about
The crafty Viscount. L. Distelheim. il pors *Life* 12:165-6 Mr '89
The Viscount Linley: at home with a royal entrepreneur. E. Lambert. il por *Architectural Digest* 46:50+ F '89
LINLEY (DAVID) FURNITURE LTD. *See* David Linley Furniture Ltd.
LINNAEUS, CARL *See* Linné, Carl von, 1707-1778
LINNÉ, CARL VON, 1707-1778
about
Where the wild things grow. J. Bosveld. il *Omni (New York, N.Y.)* 11:56-61 Ap '89
LINNELL, JOHN
about
Giant steps. P. Tyre. il pors *New York* 22:52-5 F 6 '89

LINOLEIC ACID
Cheese source of dietary anticancer agent [research by Michael W. Pariza] J. Raloff. *Science News* 135:87 F 11 '89
LINOLENIC ACID
It's not fish oil, but . . . [conversion of vegetable-derived linolenic acid in the body; research by Edward A. Emken] *Science News* 135:237 Ap 15 '89
LINSON, SUSAN
The new softball bats: great at the plate. il *Women's Sports & Fitness* 11:86 Ap '89
LINTAS: WORLDWIDE (FIRM)
The quiet combination rocking Madison Avenue. W. Konrad. il *Business Week* p54+ Ja 16 '89
LINTON, MICHAEL MANLEY
about
Nowhere to run (I). E. Hopkins. il *Rolling Stone* p72-4+ Ap 20 '89
Nowhere to run (II). E. Hopkins. il por *Rolling Stone* p74-6+ My 4 '89
LINTON, RENEE
about
Nowhere to run (I). E. Hopkins. il *Rolling Stone* p72-4+ Ap 20 '89
Nowhere to run (II). E. Hopkins. il por *Rolling Stone* p74-6+ My 4 '89
LINXE, ROBERT
about
La Maison du Chocolat. A. W. Salmon. il *Gourmet* 49:80-5+ S '89
LINZEY, ANDREW
about
An uncaged vision of nonhuman creation. J. M. Wall. *The Christian Century* 106:947-8 O 25 '89
LIONEL TRAINS INC.
Dick Kughn had so much fun with his Lionel trains that he bought the whole railroad. D. Chu. il por *People Weekly* 32:119-20 D 18 '89
LIONS
Death in the African bush [murder of lion enthusiast G. Adamson in Kenya] C. S. Manegold. il *Newsweek* 114:32 S 4 '89
The murder of innocence in Africa [death of lion enthusiast G. Adamson] M. Vollers. il *People Weekly* 32:46-51 S 11 '89
LIONS, MOUNTAIN *See* Pumas
LIOTTA, LOUIE
Candid cameraman; ed. by Joyce Wadler. il pors *People Weekly* 32:171+ D 11 '89
LIOUNIS, AUDREY
Summer smoothers. il *Health (New York, N.Y.)* 21:58-61 Jl '89
LIP MAKEUP *See* Makeup
LIPASES
Catalytic antibodies with lipase activity and R or S substrate selectivity. K. D. Janda and others. bibl f il *Science* 244:437-40 Ap 28 '89
Enhanced activity and altered specificity of phospholipase A_2 by deletion of a surface loop. O. P. Kuipers and others. bibl f il *Science* 244:82-5 Ap 7 '89
Studies of inositol phospholipid-specific phospholipase C. S. G. Rhee and others. bibl f *Science* 244:546-50 My 5 '89
LIPECTOMY *See* Liposuction
LIPIDS
See also
Cholesterol
Glycolipids
Lipoproteins
Phosphatides
Sphingolipids
Steroids
Lipid analysis in microbial ecology. J. R. Vestal and D. C. White. bibl f il *BioScience* 39:535-41 S '89
LIPKIN, RICHARD
Stalking the super storms. il *Reader's Digest* 134:76-80 Ap '89
LIPKING, LAWRENCE
Competitive reading. *The New Republic* 201:28-30+ O 2 '89
LIPKIS, ANDY
about
Planting trees of life. il por *Time* 133:23 Ja 9 '89
LIPMAN, JEAN, 1909-
Folk, or art? bibl f *Antiques* 135:280 Ja '89
LIPMAN, SAMUEL
Does the piano have a future? *Commentary* 88:48-53 D '89
The NEA: looking back, and looking ahead. *Design for Arts in Education* 90:2-9 Ja/F '89
A new look at Prokofiev. *Commentary* 87:53-8 Ap '89
LIPOPROTEIN RECEPTORS *See* Protein receptors
LIPOPROTEINS
Do you know your HDL? J. Raloff. il *Science News* 136:171-3 S 9 '89
HDL at your finger tips [cholesterol screening] J. Ziegler. il *American Health* 8:14 D '89

LIPOPROTEINS—*cont.*
Heritable allele-specific differences in amounts of apoB and low-density lipoproteins in plasma. D. Gavish and others. bibl f il *Science* 244:72-6 Ap 7 '89
The mysteries of lipoprotein(a). G. Utermann. bibl f il *Science* 246:904-10 N 17 '89
Too little cholesterol? [HDL levels] *Prevention (Emmaus, Pa.)* 41:16 My '89
What's your HDL level? [cholesterol guidelines] L. Husten. il *American Health* 8:20 Ap '89
Working women take one benefit to heart [higher HDL cholesterol than non-working women in West Germany; study by Ursula Haertel] K. Fackelmann. *Science News* 135:389 Je 24 '89

LIPOSUCTION
Liposuction makeovers. G. Maleskey. il *Prevention (Emmaus, Pa.)* 41:52-7 N '89
Robin Marantz Henig reports on liposuction—cosmetic surgery's most popular body-sculpting procedure—now under federal review. R. M. Henig. *Vogue* 179:292+ O '89
Sculpting the body. N. Underwood. il *Maclean's* 102:58 O 9 '89
Unloading those saddlebags for good. il *U.S. News & World Report* 106:70-1 My 1 '89

LIPPER, KENNETH
What needs to be done? il *The New York Times Magazine* p28+ D 31 '89

LIPPERT, BARBARA
Auto erotica. il *Vogue* 179:430 Mr '89

LIPPERT, JOAN L.
Women and heart disease. il *Ladies' Home Journal* 106:59-60+ O '89

LIPPMAN, BERNARD A.
about
Obituary
Physics Today por 42:110 Je '89. J. B. Keller

LIPREADING
My toughest campaign: hearing loss. C. H. Percy. il por *Modern Maturity* 32:88-91 Ap/My '89

LIPS
Give your lips a lift. J. Jones. il *Redbook* 172:100-3 F '89
Kiss me now. il *Seventeen* 48:96-7 F '89
Kissable lips. il *Glamour* 87:218-19 Ag '89
The provocative pout: hot lips. J. Logan. il *Harper's Bazaar* 122:178-9+ Ap '89
Winter tips for luscious lips. P. Boyer. il *Prevention (Emmaus, Pa.)* 41:92-3+ D '89
The word on lips. il *'Teen* 33:30 O '89

LIPSCOMB, BELINDA
about
Tuning up & trimming down. il pors *Ebony* 44:68+ Ap '89

LIPSET, SEYMOUR MARTIN
Critics and crusaders on neoconservatism [discussion of July/August 1988 article, Neoconservatism: myth and reality] *Society* 26:5-9 Ja/F '89
about
The continental divide [interview] P. Kaihla. *Maclean's* 102:39 O 30 '89

LIPSKE, MIKE
Living legacies. il por *National Wildlife* 27:14-16 Je/Jl '89

LIPSKY, DAVID
Answers [story] il *Seventeen* 48:160-1+ Je '89

LIPSKY, LARRY
Scuba photography. il *Petersen's Photographic Magazine* 17:36-8+ Mr '89

LIPSON, EDEN ROSS
Reading along with Barbara Bush: the endings are mostly happy. il por *The New York Times Book Review* 94:36+ My 21 '89

LIPSTADT, HÉLÈNE
Revolutionary Fêtes '89. il *Art in America* 77:198-203+ O '89

LIPSTICK
Lips that last. il *Mademoiselle* 95:52 Ap '89
Spring zing. il *'Teen* 33:82-3 Ap '89
Anecdotes, facetiae, satire, etc.
Red my lips. C. Morgan. il *Seventeen* 48:161 Ag '89

LIPSTICK APPLICATION *See* Makeup

LIPTON, PEGGY
about
Lady of the canyon. S. M. L. Aronson. il pors *Architectural Digest* 46:120-7+ F '89

LIQUEURS
See also
Absinthe
Aquavit
Luscious liqueurs, the perfect finish. E. Fried. il *Black Enterprise* 19:85 Mr '89

LIQUID CARBON
Supercomputing the liquid state of carbon [work of Richard M. Martin] I. Peterson. *Science News* 136:166 S 9 '89

LIQUID CRYSTAL DISPLAYS
Breaking away [Ovonic Imaging Systems] R. Reiff. il por *Forbes* 144:132+ D 25 '89
Color's here—could be better [NEC's ProSpeed CSX] P. Honan. il *Personal Computing* 13:79 N '89

Navy chooses LCD technology for new A-12 color displays. B. D. Nordwall. il *Aviation Week & Space Technology* 131:56-7 S 4 '89

LIQUID CRYSTAL SHUTTER PRINTERS
A giant leap for small footprints [Fortis DP600P page printer] R. Nelson. il *Personal Computing* 13:190 D '89

LIQUID CRYSTALS
An appetite for liquid-crystal spaghetti [work of Peter Palffy-Muhoray] I. Peterson. il *Science News* 135:181 Mr 25 '89
Liquids, crystals and liquid crystals [cover story] J. D. Brock and others. bibl f il *Physics Today* 42:52-9 Jl '89
Smectic liquid crystal monolayers on graphite observed by scanning tunneling microscopy [cover story] D. P. E. Smith and others. bibl f il *Science* 245:43-5 Jl 7 '89
The world's strongest plastics [thermotropic liquid crystalline polymers] R. P. Heggs. il *High Technology Business* 9:20-3 Je '89

LIQUID DIETS
Are liquid diets all wet? L. Jack. il *Mademoiselle* 95:154-5 Ap '89
Are liquid diets for you? L. Villarosa. il *Essence* 20:11-12 Je '89
Diet in a glass. C. Lowe. il *Health (New York, N.Y.)* 21:48+ O '89
Do the new liquid diets really work? C. Rohlfing. il *Reader's Digest* 134:15-18 Je '89
Fast food [Optifast program] M. Rosen. il *Ms.* 17:36+ Ja/F '89
The liquid-diet craze: why doctors say "Watch out". L. Holland. il *Good Housekeeping* 208:205-6 Mr '89
Liquid diets. S. Young. il *Glamour* 87:94+ Ap '89
A new look at liquid diets. G. L. Blackburn. il *Prevention (Emmaus, Pa.)* 41:100-2 Ap '89
Should you go on a very-low-calorie diet? P. M. Barrier. il *Nation's Business* 77:61 Jl '89
What have you got to lose? [views of Theodore Van Itallie] C. Jennings-Sauer. *American Health* 8:155-6+ Mr '89
Wind beneath my wings [cover story] O. Winfrey. il pors *Essence* 20:44-6+ Je '89
With less linguine, he's not managing so well [T. Lasorda] M. Durslag. il pors *TV Guide* 37:20-1 Ag 26-S 1 '89

LIQUID DROPS *See* Drops
LIQUID FERTILIZERS AND MANURES *See* Fertilizers and manures

LIQUID HELIUM
Superfluid transition in porous media shows puzzling features. A. Khurana. bibl f il *Physics Today* 42:21-5 Jl '89

LIQUID HYDROGEN
See also
Hydrogen as fuel

LIQUID PROTEIN DIETS *See* Liquid diets
LIQUIDATION
Brothers, are you spared a dime? [Hunts] K. Kelly. il pors *Business Week* p38 N 20 '89

LIQUIDITY (ECONOMICS)
How you can put your rainy-day cash to work and still have it for emergencies. R. J. Klein. il *Money* 18:175-6 My '89
Where all the money comes from [cash for deals] V. Brownstein. il *Fortune* 119:75-6+ Ja 2 '89

LIQUIDS
See also
Viscosity
Putting the squeeze on liquid films [research by Steve Granick and John Van Alsten] I. Peterson. *Science News* 135:207 Ap 1 '89

LIQUOR INDUSTRY
See also
Brown-Forman Corp.
Jack Daniel Distillery, Lem Motlow Prop.
Acquisitions and mergers
Great Britain
The House of Guinness [acquisition of Distillers Co.] J. Marcom, Jr. il por *Forbes* 143:85+ Je 12 '89
Advertising
Breaking the last taboo [M. Roux's erotic ad for La Grande Passion liqueur] I. Bosch. il *Mother Jones* 14:49 My '89
Export-import trade
See also
Carillon Importers Ltd.
Marketing
Absolut marketing [vodka] E. McGlinn. il por *Forbes* 144:282+ D 11 '89
Kansas hooch in Scandinavian bottles [Brown-Forman's marketing strategy for Icy vodka] J. Levine. il *Forbes* 144:131 Ag 7 '89
A thirst for slicker liquor [superpremium brands] M. Mabry. il *Newsweek* 114:60 O 16 '89
What stirs the spirit makers: vodka, vodka, vodka. A. Dunkin. il *Business Week* p54-5 Je 12 '89
Canada
See also
Seagram Company Ltd.
France
See also
Rémy Martin et Compagnie SA

LIQUOR INDUSTRY—*cont.*
Great Britain
See also
Distillers Company plc
Grand Metropolitan plc
Scotland
Single malt scotch whisky. G. Asher. il *Gourmet* 49:94-9+
D '89
LIQUOR LAWS AND REGULATIONS
See also
Prohibition
LIQUOR PROBLEM
See also
Alcohol—Physiological effects
Alcohol and artists
Alcohol and automobile drivers
Alcohol and celebrities
Alcohol and employment
Alcohol and motorcyclists
Alcohol and politicians
Alcohol and religion
Alcohol and seamen
Alcohol and sports
Alcohol and the aged
Alcohol and women
Alcohol and youth
Alcoholics and alcoholism
LIQUOR TRAFFIC
See also
Prohibition
LIQUORS
See also
Brandy
Cocktails
Cooking—Liquors
Gin
Liqueurs
Rum
Scotch whiskey
Tequila
Vodka
Whiskey
Holiday spirits guide. il *Essence* 20:88 N '89
Prices
A thirst for slicker liquor [superpremium brands] M. Mabry.
il *Newsweek* 114:60 O 16 '89
LIS, HALINA
(jt. auth) See Sharon, Nathan, and Lis, Halina
LISA LISA
about
Lisa Lisa's West Side story. il por *Rolling Stone* p31 Jl
13-27 '89
LISBON (N.D.)
Description
Lisbon. W. J. Cook. il *U.S. News & World Report* 107:63-4
D 18 '89
THE LISBON TRAVIATA [drama] See McNally, Terrence,
1939-
LISC See Local Initiatives Support Corporation
LISH, GORDON
about
Captain Fiction rides again. L. Grunwald. il por *Esquire*
111:160-2 Mr '89
For $2,400, Gordon Lish will tell you how to reach God.
N. Karlen. il *Gentlemen's Quarterly* 59:240-3+ My '89
LISKA, A. JAMES
Wynton & Branford Marsalis: a common understanding
[interview; reprint from December 1982 issue] il pors *Down
Beat* 56:94-5+ S '89
LISKA, IVAN, 1950-
about
Hamburg's Ivan Liska: starman. J. Gruen. il pors *Dance
Magazine* 63:36-9 S '89
LISKIN, MIRIAM
Data base management. See issues of Personal Computing
beginning June 1987
LISP (COMPUTER LANGUAGE)
Lisp's future linked to other languages. *Byte* 14:18+ Ag '89
microExplorer in action! A. Lane. il *Byte* 14:247-8+ N '89
LIST, JOHN
about
In hiding for 18 years, a wanted man is caught by the
FBI and a TV posse. K. Gross. il pors *People Weekly*
31:69-70+ Je 19 '89
Murder, they broadcast. T. Jacoby. pors *Newsweek* 113:58
Je 12 '89
The three faces of John List. il pors *U.S. News & World
Report* 106:13 Je 12 '89
LIST FAMILY
about
A strange new place called home. M. Ryan. il pors *Life*
12:34-9 N '89
LISTENING
Hearing what we ought to hear [address, May 8, 1989]
W. F. Eadie. *Vital Speeches of the Day* 55:587-8 Jl 15
'89
Listen carefully. T. W. Harris. il *Nation's Business* 77:78
Je '89

LISTENING DEVICES, ELECTRONIC See Electronics in
criminal investigation, espionage, etc.
LISTENING DEVICES, LASER See Lasers in criminal investi-
gation, espionage, etc.
LISTER, GEORGE
Good news: our human rights policy [address, October 3,
1988] *Department of State Bulletin* 89:36-8 Ja '89
LISTER, GWEN
about
As Africa's last colony nears independence [interview] A.
Balk. il por *World Press Review* 36:36-8 Jl '89
LISTER, GWEN, AND VERBAAN, MARK
Peace at last in Namibia? il *The Nation* 248:18+ Ja 2 '89
LISTER, PAMELA
Beauty's new horizon. il *American Health* 8:78-80+ Ap '89
Dream creams. il *American Health* 8:82-3 Ja/F '89
Putting the wrap on wrinkles. il *New Choices for the Best
Years* 29:41-6 D '89
LISTER, SAMUEL CUNLIFFE See Masham, Samuel Cunliffe
Lister, 1st Baron, 1815-1906
LISTERIA INFECTIONS See Listeriosis
LISTERIOSIS
Lethal Listeria surfaces on fresh vegetables. I. Wickelgren.
Science News 136:119 Ag 19 '89
Minute shrimp [boiling time required to reduce risk] D.
Blumenthal. il *FDA Consumer* 23:29-30 My '89
LISTS
See also
Wine lists
List Manager techniques. J. Eugenides. il *Byte* 14 Mac Special
Supp:MAC199-MAC203 Ag '89
Anecdotes, facetiae, satire, etc.
To-do or not to-do? J. W. Boeldt. il *New Choices for the
Best Years* 29:88 Ag '89
LISZT, FRANZ, 1811-1886
about
A Chicago grad student strikes a career high note, finding
a long-lost Liszt. il por *People Weekly* 31:113 Ap 10
'89
LITE (TERM)
Charge of the Lite Brigade. il *People Weekly* 32 Special
Issue:95 Fall '89
LITE COOKING See Low calorie cooking
LITE FOOD See Food
LITERACY
See also
Biblical literacy
Cultural literacy
Mathematical literacy
Reading
Scientific literacy
Arthur: a tale of disempowerment. L. V. Rosow. bibl f
il *Phi Delta Kappan* 71:194-9 N '89
Baltimore, the city that reads. B. Prete. *Publishers Weekly*
236:71-2 Ag 4 '89
The illiteracy epidemic. M. B. Zuckerman. il *U.S. News
& World Report* 106:72 Je 12 '89
Toward a unified theory of literacy learning and instructional
practices [cover story] D. Taylor. bibl f il *Phi Delta Kappan*
71:184-93 N '89
LITERACY EDUCATION
See also
Barbara Bush Foundation for Family Literacy
Business Council for Effective Literacy
Literacy Volunteers of New York City
America's need to read [work of B. Bush] L. Smith. il
por *Harper's Bazaar* 122:70-1 Ja '89
Baltimore mayor Schmoke cites city's Read-A-Thon. il por
Jet 76:23-4 Ag 28 '89
Help America banish illiteracy. L. Crooks. il *Modern Maturity*
32:10-11 Ag/S '89
How did I get through school when I couldn't read? [D.
Manley] L. B. Randolph. il pors *Ebony* 44:102+ O '89
I read and write. F. A. Bragg. por *Essence* 20:148 My '89
Letter to the First Lady. K. Fury. *Working Woman* 14:136
F '89
Literacy acquisition and alienation [whole language learning]
S. Harman and C. Edelsky. *The Education Digest* 55:35-9
D '89
Overselling literacy [adaptation of address, May 1988; cover
story; with editorial comment by Pauline B. Gough] F.
Smith. bibl f il *Phi Delta Kappan* 70:346, 352-9 Ja '89
Terrorizing Dexter Manley tearfully testifies that he learned
to read at age 28. il pors *Jet* 76:50 Je 5 '89
Until he tackled his illiteracy, the Redskins' gridiron terror
lived in fear of the ABC's; ed. by Marilyn Balamaci.
D. Manley. il pors *People Weekly* 32:49-50+ S 25 '89
The way we are. L. Wyse. il *Good Housekeeping* 209:308
S '89
When you know your ABCs. W. F. Buckley. *National Review*
41:62 O 27 '89
Federal aid
Adult education: more than moonlighting? [Southport Institute
report] A. C. Lewis. il *Phi Delta Kappan* 70:500-1 Mr
'89
Defensive end Manley in poignant plea for federal literacy
aid. H. Fields. *Publishers Weekly* 235:10 Je 9 '89

LITERACY EDUCATION—Federal aid—*cont.*
The federal role in adult literacy. F. Chisman. *The Education Digest* 55:11-14 O '89
Publishers testify at Senate and House literacy hearings. H. Fields. *Publishers Weekly* 236:10 N 17 '89
LITERACY TESTING *See* Reading—Testing
LITERACY VOLUNTEERS OF NEW YORK CITY
With Barbara Bush present, literacy event raises $215,000. il por *Publishers Weekly* 235:10 Je 9 '89
LITERARY AGENCIES AND AGENTS
     See also
     Acton and Dystel Inc.
     Book packagers
     Janklow and Nesbit Associates
     Janklow Associates
     Writers House (Firm)
Call my agent! T. Gabriel. il pors *The New York Times Magazine* p44-5+ F 19 '89
A good agent is not hard to find—if you know how, when, and where to look. T. Schaffner. *The Writer* 102:14-16 Ja '89
How a one-woman show becomes a big-bucks business [J. Naggar] E. Prescott. il pors *Working Woman* 14:51-3+ Mr '89
The naughty schoolboy [A. Wylie] P. Painton. il por *Time* 133:46 Je 12 '89
Quality lit [V. Barber] K. Pryor. il por *New York* 22:26 Mr 27 '89
Washington's Rafe Sagalyn. G. Feldman. il por *Publishers Weekly* 235:246+ My 12 '89
LITERARY BEGINNINGS *See* Beginnings, Literary
LITERARY CHARACTERS *See* Characters in literature
LITERARY COLLABORATION *See* Authorship—Collaboration
LITERARY CONTESTS *See* Literature—Competitions
LITERARY CRITICS AND CRITICISM
     See also
     Benjamin, Walter, 1892-1940
     Book reviews and reviewing
     Deconstruction
     Feminist literary criticism
     Literature—Appreciation and interpretation
     Textual criticism
     Woolf, Virginia, 1882-1941
The duty of harsh criticism [English literature] Dame R. West. *The New Republic* 201 [Reprint v1]:18-20 N 6 '89 [N 7 '14]
Fighting words. J. P. Tompkins. *Harper's* 278:33-5 Mr '89
The treason of the critics. I. Howe. *The New Republic* 200:28-31 Je 12 '89
LITERARY ENDINGS *See* Endings, Literary
LITERARY ERRORS
Who's minding the store? [errors found in S. Winters' autobiography] L. Fleischer. *Publishers Weekly* 236:49 S 8 '89
LITERARY ETHICS
Autobiography and the craft of embellishment. A. P. Sanoff. il *U.S. News & World Report* 107:64 O 23 '89
LITERARY FANTASIES *See* Fantasies, Literary
LITERARY PERIODICALS
     See also
     Lettre internationale (Periodical)
Big little magazines: a reader's guide. C. James. *The New York Times Book Review* 94:32 Ap 30 '89
Literary cross-pollination [using literary magazines to identify potential book authors] W. Nixon. il *Publishers Weekly* 235:30+ Mr 31 '89
LITERARY PRIZES
     See also
     Booker Prize
     Carey-Thomas Awards
     Governor General's Literary Award (Canada)
     National Book Awards
     National Book Critics Circle Awards
     Nobel prizes
     Pulitzer prizes
Literary prizes and awards. *Publishers Weekly* 235:40-1 Mr 10 '89
Los Angeles-based AIDS project gives first literary awards [Words Project for AIDS] L. See. il *Publishers Weekly* 235:38 Ap 7 '89
The Washington monthly annual Political Book Award. il *The Washington Monthly* 21:23 Mr '89
The year's top prizes. *Publishers Weekly* 235:54 Ja 6 '89
     Anecdotes, facetiae, satire, etc.
Worst books of the year [J. Gordon Coogler Award] R. E. Tyrrell. il *The American Spectator* 22:10 My '89
LITERARY RECREATIONS
     See also
     Riddles
LITERARY STYLE *See* Style, Literary
LITERATURE
     See also
     American literature
     Anthropological literature
     Arabic literature
     Art and literature
     Arts and crafts literature
     Asian American literature

     Authorship
     Autobiography
     Best sellers
     Bible—Literary character
     Books and reading
     Censorship
     Characters in literature
     Children's literature
     Chinese literature
     Classical literature
     Computers—Literary use
     Economics literature
     Educational literature
     Fiction
     Food literature
     French literature
     Health literature
     Horror tales
     Japanese literature
     Jewish literature
     Literary critics and criticism
     Mass media and literature
     Mathematics and literature
     Medical literature
     Military literature
     New Age literature
     Parody (Literature)
     Physics literature
     Plagiarism
     Poetry
     Postmodernism (Literature)
     Realism in literature
     Russian literature
     Scientific literature
     Self help literature
     Spy stories
     Television and literature
     Travel literature
     Ukrainian literature
     Underground literature
     Young adults' literature
     Appreciation and interpretation
Competitive reading. L. Lipking. *The New Republic* 201:28-30+ O 2 '89
     Awards
     See Literary prizes
     Competitions
Prize offers. See issues of The Writer
     Moral and religious aspects
     See also
     Religion in literature
Answering Faulkner. L. Phillips. il *America* 160:452-3 My 13 '89
Robin Hood, Huck Finn and me. R. Coles. il *New Choices for the Best Years* 29:90+ N '89
     Periodicals
     See Literary periodicals
     Study and teaching
     See also
     Cliff's Notes Inc.
George P. Elliott and the common reader. L. C. Tisdale. *The American Scholar* 58:421-8 Summ '89
Letting great books speak to students. J. Agresto. *The Education Digest* 54:33-4 F '89
     Technique
     See also
     Fiction—Technique
Three surefire ways to write and sell nonfiction. S. S. Baker. *The Writer* 102:11-13 Mr '89
     Themes
     See also
     Accounting in literature
     AIDS (Disease) literature
     Animals in literature
     Apartheid in literature
     Baby sitters in literature
     Baseball in literature
     Bicycle racing in literature
     Biology in literature
     Blacks in literature
     Boxing in literature
     Business in literature
     Childbirth in literature
     Children's literature—Themes
     Current events in literature
     Deforestation in literature
     Economics in literature
     Education in literature
     Emotions in literature
     Great Plains in literature
     Haiti in literature
     Heaven in literature
     Homosexuality in literature
     Indians (American) in literature
     Investment banking in literature
     Lesbianism in literature
     Mississippi in literature
     Moon in literature

LITERATURE—Themes—*See also—cont.*
  Music in literature
  New York (N.Y.) in literature
  Newspapers in literature
  Nuclear warfare in literature
  Okies in literature
  Opera in literature
  Organized crime in literature
  Parent-child relationship in literature
  Parents in literature
  Politics in literature
  Poor in literature
  Priests in literature
  Property in literature
  Religion in literature
  Rome in literature
  Simla (India) in literature
  South Africa in literature
  Soviet Union in literature
  United States in literature
  Vampires in literature
  War in literature
  Washington (D.C.) in literature
  Weather in literature
  Wilderness areas in literature
  Women in literature
LITERATURE, INFLUENCE OF
  Educated by novels. J. Epstein. *Commentary* 88:33-9 Ag
    '89
  Novels [discussion of August 1989 article, Educated by novels]
    J. Epstein. *Commentary* 88:8-9 N '89
LITERATURE, MEDIEVAL
    See also
    Arthurian romances
  When women finally got the word [women of medieval
    Japan and Europe, writing in the vernacular, prefigured
    modern literature] E. Kolb. il *The New York Times Book
    Review* 94:1+ Jl 9 '89
LITERATURE AND SCIENCE
    See also
    Science fiction
LITERATURE AND STATE
            Central Europe
  The telltale scar. C. Miłosz. *The New Republic* 201:27-9
    Ag 7-14 '89
                China
  In praise of Wang Meng. W. Barnstone. *The Nation* 249:502-3
    O 30 '89
  In praise of Wang Meng. H. Calisher. *The Nation* 249:500-2
    O 30 '89
            Czechoslovakia
  Czech writers: politicians in spite of themselves. J. Škvorecký.
    The New York Times Book Review 94:1+ D 10 '89
  Notes and comment [views of Z. Urbánek] *The New Yorker*
    65:31-2 D 18 '89
              Soviet Union
  The *glasnost* papers [cover story; special section] il *The
    New Republic* 200:28-30+ F 20 '89
  Glasnost writing: so where's the golden age? C. R. Whitney.
    il *The New York Times Book Review* 94:1+ Mr 19 '89
  The two *perestroikas.* D. Fanger. *The New Republic* 201:26-30
    O 23 '89
  A very partial reclamation project [G. Orwell's Animal farm
    and 1984] J. Rodden. il *Commonweal* 116:78-80 F 10
    '89
                Taiwan
  Creative progress in Taiwan. S. Pasquier. *World Press Review*
    36:86 O '89
LITHIUM
    See also
    Lithium Corporation of America
  Pride and prejudice [cosmic lithium abundance and open
    vs. closed universe; research by Lawrence M. Krauss]
    T. Rothman. *Scientific American* 261:16-17 Ag '89
          Therapeutic use
  Lithium dissolves as alcoholism treatment [research by Walter
    Dorus] B. Bower. *Science News* 135:309 My 20 '89
LITHIUM CORPORATION OF AMERICA
  A fusion flier. M. Gianturco. il por *Forbes* 143:161 My
    15 '89
LITHOGRAPHS
              Exhibitions
  George Bellows, great printmaker. il *USA Today (Periodical)*
    117:8-9 Ap '89
  The use and abuse of realism [G. Bellows] B. W. Bloch.
    The New Leader 72:22-3 O 2-16 '89
LITHOGRAPHY
    See also
    Collotypes
    Nanolithography
    Stereolithography
    X ray lithography
LITHOSPHERE *See* Earth—Crust
LITHOTRIPSY
  Gallstone quick-fix [percutaneous lithotripsy] *Prevention
    (Emmaus, Pa.)* 41:18 N '89

LITIGATION *See* Actions and defenses
LITITZ (PA.)
            Galleries and museums
    See also
    Candy Americana Museum (Lititz, Pa.)
LITTELL, MARY ANN
  Mother & child. See issues of Good Housekeeping beginning
    March 1987
LITTLE, MALCOLM *See* Malcolm X, 1925-1965
LITTLE BIG HORN, BATTLE OF THE, 1876
    See also
    Custer Battlefield National Monument (Mont.)
LITTLE CHARLIE AND THE NIGHTCATS (MUSICAL
    GROUP)
  Little Charlie and the Nightcats. D. Whiteis. il por *Down
    Beat* 56:15 D '89
LITTLE DORRIT [film] See Motion picture reviews—Single
    works
LITTLE FALLS (MINN.)
          Historic houses, sites, etc.
  An American childhood in Little Falls [C. Lindbergh] B.
    L. Larson. il por *Architectural Digest* 46:36+ Je '89
LITTLE LEAGUE BASEBALL
  Fields of dreams. K. E. Franklin. il *Sport (New York, N.Y.)*
    80:64-6 S '89
  The kids win one in Harlem as, 20 years later, the Little
    League returns—on drug dealers' turf [organized by I.
    Raiford] il por *People Weekly* 31:64 Je 19 '89
  Out in left field [Little League dad] A. Gelb. il *Parents*
    64:218 Ap '89
  Parents keep out! J. Feldman. por *Newsweek* 112:8 My 22
    '89
          Anecdotes, facetiae, satire, etc.
  Little League blues. D. Barry. il *Reader's Digest* 135:56-8
    Ag '89
                World Series
  Boy, oh boy, what a year! [C. Drury, member of Trumbull,
    Conn. championship team] D. S. Looney. il pors *Sports
    Illustrated* 71:76-80+ D 25 '89-Ja 1 '90
  Way to go, gang [Trumbull, Conn., beats Taiwan] E. M.
    Swift. il *Sports Illustrated* 71:32-5 S 4 '89
                Taiwan
  World Series dynasty: why Taiwan reigns. T. Mulgannon.
    il *Sport (New York, N.Y.)* 80:67 S '89
THE LITTLE MERMAID [film] See Motion picture reviews—
    Single works
LITTLE MONSTERS [film] See Motion picture reviews—Single
    works
LITTLE PROFESSOR BOOK CENTERS
  Little Professor Book Centers: happy at last. M. J. O'Brien.
    il *Publishers Weekly* 235:50-3 Je 2 '89
LITTLE RICKY ROCKO *See* Rogoway, Sam
LITTLE ROCK (ARK.)
                Architecture
  Touched by new traditions [house of Becky and William
    Ketcher] il *Southern Living* 24:152-4 Ap '89
                Blacks
  Former Arkansas gov. Orval Faubus honors Daisy Bates.
    pors *Jet* 76:30 Ag 21 '89
  Thirty-four years at the governor's mansion [cook E. J.
    Ashley] R. Brown. il pors *Ebony* 44:52+ Jl '89
                Education
  Ark. to pay $118 mil. in school bias settlement. *Jet* 75:10
    Mr 20 '89
                Industries
  Mutual aid society [joint promotion of Storer Cable and
    KLRT] A. Snyder. il *Channels (New York, N.Y.: 1986)*
    9:22-3 Ja '89
                Riots
  Flag-burning attempt in Little Rock incites a race riot at
    the capitol. il *Jet* 76:6-7 Jl 24 '89
                Stores
  The magic is back in Little Rock [MainStreet] il *Southern
    Living* 24:33 Mr '89
LITTLE SAINT SIMONS ISLAND (GA.)
          Description and travel
  The other Georgia [cover story] H. Leifermann. il map *New
    Choices for the Best Years* 29:46-52 Jl '89
LITTLE SOLDIER, LEE
  Cooperative learning and the Native American student. bibl
    f il *Phi Delta Kappan* 71:161-3 O '89
LITTLE TENNESSEE RIVER VALLEY
  Strawberry fields, almost forever [prehistoric Native Ameri-
    cans] J. Chapman and others. il maps *Natural History*
    p50-8 S '89
THE LITTLE THIEF [film] See Motion picture reviews—Single
    works
LITTLE TIKES COMPANY
  Why Little Tikes' managers picked up their toys and left.
    M. Mallory. il *Business Week* p83 N 27 '89
LITTLE VERA [film] See Motion picture reviews—Single works
LITTLEFIELD, EVERETT
  Uses for rigid-swivel based casters. il *Theatre Crafts* 23:97
    Ap '89
LITTLEJOHN, STEPHEN E.
  (jt. auth) See Mahoney, Richard John, and Littlejohn, Stephen
    E.

LITTLETON, MARK R., 1950-
The fine art of encouragement. *Reader's Digest* 135:141-3 N '89

LITTMAN, MARK S.
Poverty in the 1980's: are the poor getting poorer? bibl f il *Monthly Labor Review* 112:13-18 Je '89
Reasons for not working: poor and nonpoor householders. bibl f il *Monthly Labor Review* 112:16-21 Ag '89

LITTMANN, MARK, 1939-
Where is Planet X? il *Sky and Telescope* 78:596-9 D '89

LITTON INDUSTRIES, INC.
GAO advises Air Force to cancel Loral's advanced radar warning receiver contract [allegations of illegally receiving information about competing Litton system] *Aviation Week & Space Technology* 130:23 My 22 '89
Litton gets share of ALR-56M program in Ill Wind plea agreement by Loral. D. F. Bond. *Aviation Week & Space Technology* 131:115 D 18-25 '89
Litton protest raises questions about new Loral operation [USAF award for F-16 radar warning receivers] P. J. Klass. *Aviation Week & Space Technology* 130:57 F 6 '89
Makers of EW components adopt fresh strategies as programs dwindle. *Aviation Week & Space Technology* 131:115+ S 18 '89
USAF urges GAO to reconsider criticism of Loral contract award [Litton protest of contract] B. W. Henderson. *Aviation Week & Space Technology* 130:31 Je 5 '89

LITTWIN, MIKE
After Father knows best, it was drugs, jail, depression. il pors *TV Guide* 37:6-8 Je 17-23 '89
No longer the center of things. il *TV Guide* 37:8-9 Ap 29-My 5 '89
Who's the best—Bird, Magic or Air Jordan? il pors *TV Guide* 37:20-1+ F 11-17 '89

LITURGICAL OBJECTS
See also
Menorah
Votive candles

LITWINSKI, MIECZYSLAW
about
Air. *The New Yorker* 65:29-30 Je 5 '89

LIU, AMY Y., AND COHEN, MARVIN L.
Prediction of new low compressibility solids. bibl f il *Science* 245:841-2 Ag 25 '89

LIU, PIN-YEN *See* Liu Binyan, 1925-

LIU, PU, AND OTHERS
Isolation of human transcribed sequences from human-rodent somatic cell hybrids. bibl f il *Science* 246:813-15 N 10 '89

LIU BINYAN, 1925-
Deng's pyrrhic victory [cover story] *The New Republic* 201:21-4 O 2 '89
about
The Great Wall endures [interview] O. Schell and N. Gardels. il *New Perspectives Quarterly* 5:42-6 Wint '88/'89
Pantheon to publish autobiography of Chinese dissident next spring. por *Publishers Weekly* 235:29-30 My 26 '89
The price China has paid: an interview with Liu Binyan [with introduction by Merle Goldman] N. Gardels. il *The New York Review of Books* 35:31+ Ja 19 '89
Two dissidents challenge 'feudal communism' [interview] J. L. Du Sablon. il pors *World Press Review* 36:26-7 F '89

LIU HAO XUE
about
The first emperor of China [film] Reviews
Maclean's 102:44 Jl 17 '89. B. D. Johnson
Natural History il p66-9 Jl '89. T. R. Miller

LIULICHANG STREET (BEIJING, CHINA) *See* Beijing (China)—Streets

LIVE BAIT *See* Bait

LIVE TELEVISION PROGRAMS
Umberto Eco: a memo to Roone [excerpt from The open work]; tr. by Anna Cancogni. U. Eco. *Harper's* 278:31-3 Je '89

LIVER
The DNA binding domain of the rat liver nuclear protein C/EBP is bipartite [support for leucine zipper hypothesis] W. H. Landschulz and others. bibl f il *Science* 243:1681-8 Mr 31 '89
Increased expression of DNA cointroduced with nuclear protein in adult rat liver. Y. Kaneda and others. bibl f il *Science* 243:375-8 Ja 20 '89

Cancer
Causes
Clues to a new class of liver carcinogens [peroxisome-proliferating chemicals; research by Janardan Reddy] J. Raloff. *Science News* 135:119 F 25 '89
Surgery
"Swiss cheese" cancer surgery [work of John Minton] *USA Today (Periodical)* 118:17 O '89

Diseases
See also
Biliary atresia
Hepatitis
Nutritional aspects
Weight loss builds a healthy liver [research by Melissa Palmer] K. Fackelmann. *Science News* 135:332 My 27 '89

Transplantation
A family account at the organ bank [A. Smith receives piece of mother's liver] il por *U.S. News & World Report* 107:17 D 11 '89
A hero of her time [heart-liver transplant recepient S. Jones] S. Christenson. il por *American Health* 8:90 Je '89
Lifesaving surgery [A. Smith receives segment of mother's liver] H. Jensen. il por *Maclean's* 102:54 D 11 '89
Liver-transplant surgeons use living donor [A. Smith receives segment of mother's liver] K. Fackelmann. *Science News* 136:358 D 2 '89
A mother's gift of life [A. Smith gets transplant from her mother] B. Dolan. il por *Time* 134:96 D 11 '89
A mother's gift of love and life [A. Smith receives liver] M. Beck. il pors *Newsweek* 114:91-2 D 11 '89
New way of keeping donor livers healthy [Belzer's solution] K. Fackelmann. *Science News* 135:69 F 4 '89
The power of plastics [use in transplantation of liver cells; work of Joseph Vacanti] L. Oliwenstein. il *Discover* 10:18 D '89
Transplant emergency! [victims of amanita poisoning receive liver transplants; work of C. W. Pinson] J. Fincher. il *Reader's Digest* 135:43-8 Jl '89

LIVER AS FOOD
Among the liver eaters [channel catfish] J. M. Vance. il *Field & Stream* 94:16-17 Je '89

LIVER CELLS *See* Cells

LIVERMORE, BETH
(jt. auth) *See* Hild, Nancy, and Livermore, Beth

LIVERMORE (LAWRENCE) NATIONAL LABORATORY
See Lawrence Livermore National Laboratory

LIVERMORE VALLEY (CALIF.)
Description and travel
Sampling Livermore Valley by bike. il map *Sunset (Central West edition)* 183:18 O '89

LIVERSIDGE, ANTHONY
Interview: Neil Sloane. il pors *Omni (New York, N.Y.)* 11:78-80+ S '89

LIVESEY, HERBERT BAILEY
History with a view. il map *Travel Holiday* 172:64-73 D '89
Separating good from bad. il *Travel Holiday* 171:108-12 Mr '89

LIVESTOCK
See also
Cattle
Cows
Donkeys
Ducks
Horses
Mules
Poultry
Sheep
Swine
The climatic advantages of pigging out [study by Florentin Krause] *Science News* 136:381 D 9 '89
How livestock make my organic methods possible. J. Bender. il *Successful Farming* 87:17 Ap '89

Breeding
The barnyard restoration. L. Drew. il *Newsweek* 113:50-1 My 29 '89
Biotech on the farm: geneticists in the pasture. G. E. Seidel. *Current (Washington, D.C.)* 316:21-6 O '89
The farm animals of tomorrow. il *The Futurist* 23:47-8 N/D '89
Genetic engineering of livestock. V. G. Pursel and others. bibl f il *Science* 244:1281-8 Je 16 '89
Geneticists in the pasture. G. E. Seidel. il *Technology Review* 92:42-50+ Ap '89
Sperm sorter ensures sex-linked litters. *Science News* 136:175 S 9 '89

Diseases and pests
Pheromone-mediation of host-selection in bont ticks (Amblyomma hebraeum Koch) [carriers of heartwater disease] R. A. I. Norval and others. bibl f il *Science* 243:364-5 Ja 20 '89
Ticks follow fellows to tastiest cows [carriers of heartwater disease; research by Conrad E. Yunker and others] *Science News* 135:123 F 25 '89

Marketing
Marketing. *See* issues of Successful Farming

Treatment
See Animals—Treatment

LIVESTOCK FENCES, ELECTRIC *See* Fences, Electric

LIVESTOCK IN TELEVISION
The big round-up [Lonesome dove] M. Loeffler. il *Theatre Crafts* 23:47+ F '89

LIVESTOCK OF THE VALLEY (ORGANIZATION) *See* Ganados del Valle (Organization)

LIVESTOCK RANGES
See also
Holistic resource management
Today's embattled cowboys. H. L. Lund. *National Review* 41:26 D 31 '89

LIVING *See* Conduct of life; Life

LIVING, COST AND STANDARD OF *See* Cost and standard of living

LIVING BENEFITS (INSURANCE)
Collect now, die later [life insurance with long-term health care riders] il *Esquire* 111:54 Ja '89
A gift for the dying—or sheer ghoulishness? S. D. Atchison. il *Business Week* p79 Je 19 '89
Life insurance that pays off while you're still around. D. H. Dunn. il *Business Week* p100-1 Jl 31 '89
You can't take it with you. J. Schwartz. il *Newsweek* 113:45 My 8 '89
LIVING BENEFITS INC.
A gift for the dying—or sheer ghoulishness? S. D. Atchison. il *Business Week* p79 Je 19 '89
You can't take it with you. J. Schwartz. il *Newsweek* 113:45 My 8 '89
LIVING BRIDGES INTERNATIONAL
The great experiment [debt exchange with Catholic priest E. Gonzalez Torres in Mexico] R. Bautch. *America* 160:316-17 Ap 8 '89
LIVING CHESS GAME (MAROSTICA, ITALY)
Living Chess Game. L. Inturrisi. il *Travel Holiday* 171:92 Ja '89
LIVING COLOUR (MUSICAL GROUP)
Basic black. F. Brown. il *Mother Jones* 14:14 Je '89
Living Colour turns to gold. M. Goldberg. il *Rolling Stone* p24 Ap 6 '89
One of rock's liveliest new bands comes to you in Living Colour. D. Grogan. il por *People Weekly* 32:84-5 Ag 21 '89
LIVING DOLLS [television program] See Television program reviews—Single works
LIVING FOSSILS
'Living fossils' [Australia] il *The Courier (Unesco)* 41:30-1 D '88
LIVING HISTORY FARMS (DES MOINES, IOWA)
Iowa pioneer days. M. K. Shanley. il *Travel Holiday* 171:96-99 Mr '89
LIVING IN FAMILY ENVIRONMENTS PROGRAM See LIFE Program
LIVING ROOMS
Gabled addition pushes living room into the garden. il *Sunset (Central West edition)* 183:114 N '89
Layered by design [parlor] C. Engle. il *Southern Living* 24:96-7 F '89
Lovely living rooms [Laura Ashley designs] il *Good Housekeeping* 208:188-91 My '89
A modest wall makes the room special. il *Southern Living* 24:82-3 N '89
They added a tall-ceilinged living room. il *Sunset (Central West edition)* 182:136 Mr '89
LIVING TRUSTS
A trust to live without? K. Davis. *Changing Times* 43:125-6 N '89
LIVING WILLS
The extraordinary case of the woman who couldn't die [coma patient N. Jobes kept alive because she had no living will] B. D. Colen. il por *Redbook* 172:126-9+ Mr '89
The faulty promise of 'living wills'. J. Carey. il *U.S. News & World Report* 107:63-4 Jl 24 '89
Why everyone should write a living will. R. J. Klein. il *Money* 18:165-6 Je '89
LIVINGSTONE, NEIL C.
(jt. auth) See Halevy, David, and Livingstone, Neil C.
LIVINGSTONE, NEIL C., AND HALEVY, DAVID
The search for Lauren. il pors *Reader's Digest* 135:77-84 Ag '89
LIZ CLAIBORNE, INC.
Can Ms. Fashion bounce back? [cover story] K. Deveny. il pors *Business Week* p64-7+ Ja 16 '89
LIZARDS
See also
Iguanas
Tuataras
Cost accounting for lizards [size differences among lizards of the Galapagos Islands; research by Howard L. Snell] J. A. Miller. il *BioScience* 39:674-5 N '89
Get a grip, gecko! [tokay gecko] il *National Geographic World* 170:26-9 O '89
A lizard foretold [search for Gymnophthalmus species by chromosome comparison] C. J. Cole and others. map *Natural History* p12+ My '89
Skins to boot [tegu lizards] D. Einhorn. il *Américas* 41 no2:2 '89
LLADRO, SA
Lladro: the art of Spanish porcelain. il *USA Today (Periodical)* 117:78-83 Ja '89
LLAMAS, CARLOS FERNANDEZ
about
SoHo grandee. M. Guralnick. il por *House & Garden* 161:96 O '89
LOS LLANOS BOOKSTORE (SANTA FE, N.M.) See Booksellers and bookselling—New Mexico
LLC CORP.
See also
Valhi Inc.
LLEWELLYN, J. BRUCE
about
Llewellyn plugs into $420 million NYT cable deal. K. D. Thompson. por *Black Enterprise* 19:17 Mr '89

LLOSA, MARIO VARGAS See Vargas Llosa, Mario, 1936-
LLOYD, EMILY
about
Emily Lloyd's star is rising in America, but is America ready for a star like Emily Lloyd? N. Karlen. pors *Rolling Stone* p94-7 O 5 '89
LLOYD, JOHN, 1946-
From the rubble. il *National Review* 41:31-2 Ja 27 '89
Here come the '*glasnost* generals'. *World Press Review* 36:38-9 Mr '89
LLOYD, ROBERT
Pals. il pors *American Film* 14:28-33+ Jl/Ag '89
LLOYD, ROBERT A.
Artists or teachers? Arts education in independent schools. *Design for Arts in Education* 90:42-5 Ja/F '89
LLOYD, RUTH L.
Exploring west of the Rockies on souvenir spoons. il *Antiques & Collecting Hobbies* 94:30-4 S '89
LLOYD'S OF LONDON
High stakes [insures race horses] K. Hannon. il por *Forbes* 143:326+ My 29 '89
Of piracy and payoffs [ships diverted into Lebanese ports] J. Penycate. *World Press Review* 36:53 My '89
LO, CECILIA W.
(jt. auth) See Richa, Jean, and Lo, Cecilia W.
LO, EILEEN YIN-FEI
China trade. il *The New York Times Magazine* p117-18 Je 11 '89
LO, SHYH-CHING
about
AIDS researchers upset by refusal to share probes on mysterious microbe. W. Booth. *Science* 244:416 Ap 28 '89
LOA See Library of America (Firm)
LOAFERS (SHOES) See Footwear
LOAN ASSOCIATIONS See Savings and loan associations
LOAN COMPANIES See Finance companies
LOANS
See also
Credit
Government lending
Insurance, Life—Policy loans
Interest (Economics)
Mortgages
LOANS, AMERICAN
Mexico
A vote of confidence. L. Meyer. il *World Press Review* 36:64 Ja '89
LOANS, ART See Art loans
LOANS, AUTOMOBILE See Automobile loans
LOANS, BANK
See also
Agricultural credit
Asset-backed financing
Bridge loans
Banking on television. H. D. Shapiro. il *Channels (New York, N.Y.: 1986)* 9:40-3 Ap '89
Banking on women owners [lending to women entrepreneurs] il *Nation's Business* 77:28 My '89
Taking the banker to court [lender liability] C. Friday and L. Reibstein. il *Newsweek* 113:44 My 8 '89
Three ways banks can help your business. M. Stevens. il *Working Woman* 14:34 Ag '89
Guaranty
The $5 trillion shock. S. Waldman. il *Newsweek* 114:26-8 D 18 '89
Let's make a deal [FHA and Veterans Administration loan guaranty funds] J. Novack. il *Forbes* 143:48 Ja 23 '89
International aspects
The onset of big-debt blues [Paris summit] J. Egan. il maps *U.S. News & World Report* 107:20-2 Jl 24 '89
Africa
An African view of the debt [interview with J. Ki-Zerbo] H. Ziady. il por *World Press Review* 36:50 Ag '89
Banking on African conservation [debt-for-nature swaps] *Science News* 135:62 Ja 28 '89
Economic restructuring in Sub-Saharan Africa. C. Lancaster. *Current History* 88:213-16+ My '89
Asia
Environment, poverty and growth [address, February 9, 1989] A. Karaosmanoglu. *Vital Speeches of the Day* 55:396-400 Ap 15 '89
Bolivia
Debt deal stacked against Indians [debt for nature swap] M. Collett. *The Progressive* 53:17-18 Ag '89
Brazil
Using red ink to keep tropical forests green [debt-for-nature swaps] C. P. Work and G. Smith. il map *U.S. News & World Report* 106:48-9 Mr 6 '89
The world puts the heat on Brazil [forgiving part of debt in exchange for help in protecting nature] *World Press Review* 36:38 My '89
China
How bad will China's debt crunch get? D. Lee. il *Business Week* p62 S 25 '89
Costa Rica
Capital conservation [debt for nature swaps] J. Zweig. por *Forbes* 143:208 Ap 17 '89

LOANS, BANK—*cont.*

Developing countries

See also

Foundation for International Community Assistance

The alarming truth about the World Bank. J. Bovard. *Reader's Digest* 134:108-12 Je '89

And now, back to the issues: budget, trade, banking and debtors [address, November 10, 1988] W. C. Butcher. *Vital Speeches of the Day* 55:241-3 F 1 '89

At debt's door [effect of loan repayment on women] J. Steinberg. il *Ms.* 18:74-9 N '89

Attack on problem of external debt urged by Assembly. il *UN Chronicle* 26:75 Mr '89

Banks are getting those third world jitters again [push for higher reserves] J. Meehan and W. Glasgall. il *Business Week* p200+ S 25 '89

Big bank stocks rise on hopes of a third world deal. J. Mendes. il *Fortune* 120:39+ Jl 31 '89

Children are paying the third world debt with their lives. *Utne Reader* p62 S/O '89

Danger in a 'dormant' crisis. N. M. Healey. il *World Press Review* 36:30-2 Ja '89

Dealing with the international debt crisis [remarks, March 10, 1989] N. F. Brady. *Department of State Bulletin* 89:53-6 My '89

Debt and forgiveness [Brady plan] S. Talbott. *Time* 134:25 Jl 31 '89

Debt: killer of third world children. il *UN Chronicle* 26:48 S '89

The debt presidency. I. M. Stelzer. il *The American Spectator* 22:26-7 Ja '89

The dilemma of third world debt. C. W. Weinberger. il *Forbes* 143:31 My 15 '89

Easing third world debt [exit bonds] J. Williamson. il *USA Today (Periodical)* 117:28-9 Mr '89

Favor debt cancellation [U.S. Catholic bishops' statement] *The Christian Century* 106:976-7 N 1 '89

The Fed lifts the Brady plan out of its sickbed [relaxing reserve accounting rules] M. McNamee and W. Glasgall. il *Business Week* p43 O 9 '89

Forgive us our debts . . . P. Henriot. *America* 161:420-2+ D 9 '89

A global Chapter 11. B. J. Cohen. *Foreign Policy* 75:109-27 Summ '89

How do we solve the global debt crisis? [statement by Interfaith Action for Economic Justice] J. W. Skillen. *The Christian Century* 106:1004-6 N 8 '89

International Bank for Ruination and Destruction [World Bank] M. S. Tammen. il *Conservative Digest* 15:45+ Mr/Ap '89

IOU's and third world blues. S. Dentzer. il *U.S. News & World Report* 107:51 O 2 '89

It's not all that complicated [Relieving third world debt; a statement released by the U.S. bishops] *America* 161:263-4 O 28 '89

Making the Brady plan work. J. D. Sachs. bibl f il *Foreign Affairs* 68:87-104 Summ '89

Nature reaps a cash bonanza [debt-for-nature swaps] T. A. Lewis. il *International Wildlife* 19:37 Ja/F '89

An offer they can't refuse [IRS ruling limits tax advantages banks get for writing off foreign loan losses] L. Saunders. il *Forbes* 143:144 My 29 '89

Saving forests—with debt [less money for environmentally destructive projects] P. Adams. il *World Press Review* 36:47 O '89

Scenes from the inferno. A. Cockburn. *The Nation* 248:510-11 Ap 17 '89

Triple play [U.S. Catholic bishops' statement on third world debt] *Commonweal* 116:581-2 N 3 '89

What are they waiting for? [reserve boosts by banks with third world loans] P. Duggan. il *Forbes* 144:45-6 O 2 '89

Who swallows the debt? L. Stoléru. *World Press Review* 36:80 S '89

Will the U.S. be left holding the bag on third world debt? P. C. Roberts. il *Business Week* p22 O 16 '89

Latin America

The banker plan [disclosure of J. Baker's Chemical Bank holdings clouds his policy on Latin American debt relief] *The New Republic* 200:7-8 Mr 6 '89

Brady bailout II. *National Review* 41:10 My 5 '89

Can this flight be grounded? [exodus of capital from Latin debtor nations] M. McNamee. il *Business Week* p74 Ap 10 '89

Debt and the Brady plan. il *World Press Review* 36:9 My '89

The debt plan Brady floated is still, well, floating. M. McNamee. por *Business Week* p51 My 8 '89

The dirty little debt secret [capital flight] D. Pauly. il *Newsweek* 113:46 Ap 17 '89

Enter the Brady plan. B. Rudolph. il por *Time* 133:54 Mr 20 '89

Half a loaf for third world debtors. M. W. Karmin. *U.S. News & World Report* 107:48 Ag 7 '89

The Harvard debt doctor's controversial cure [views of J. Sachs] J. Greenwald. il por *Time* 134:66 N 6 '89

Jim Baker's conflict-of-interest problems. W. Greider. il *Rolling Stone* p43-5 Ap 20 '89

A Latin debt plan that might work [Brady plan] J. Main. il *Fortune* 119:205+ Ap 24 '89

Loan sharks [Brady plan to ease Latin debt] B. D. Nossiter. *The Nation* 248:652-3 My 15 '89

Making the Brady plan work. J. D. Sachs. bibl f il *Foreign Affairs* 68:87-104 Summ '89

A new plan for debt [Canadian banks wary of Brady plan] J. DeMont. il *Maclean's* 102:32-3 Mr 27 '89

The new spelling of relief [Brady plan to ease Latin debt] D. Pauly. il por *Newsweek* 113:32 Mr 20 '89

The next liberator? [C. A. Perez's approach to debt crisis] M. Collett. il *The Atlantic* 263:29+ F '89

No relief on Latin debt—without World Bank reform. P. C. Roberts. il *Business Week* p15 My 6 '89

On drugs, debt and poverty [interview with C. A. Perez] J. Moody and S. Talbott. il por *Time* 134:12-14 N 27 '89

Robbin' hoods [big banks and debt relief; cover story] J. D. Sachs. il *The New Republic* 200:19-20+ Mr 13 '89

Self-made crisis [debt crisis] M. S. Forbes, Jr. il *Forbes* 143:27 F 20 '89

Sounding the alarm. G. D. Garcia. il *Time* 133:32-3 Ja 9 '89

Third world deadbeats. I. M. Stelzer. il *The American Spectator* 22:34-5 Ap '89

Third world hydraulics. T. Bethell. il *The American Spectator* 22:9-11 Je '89

Washington's new, softer line on Latin debt [Brady plan] M. McNamee. il por *Business Week* p58 Mr 20 '89

What Bush owes. M. Nadle. *The Nation* 248:400-1 Mr 27 '89

Mexico

Giving a little to save a lot [debt problems] E. A. Finn, Jr. il *Forbes* 143:38-9 Mr 6 '89

The great experiment [Living Bridges International arranges debt exchange with Catholic priest E. Gonzalez Torres] R. Bautch. *America* 160:316-17 Ap 8 '89

A little easing. R. Koselka. il *Forbes* 144:10 Ag 21 '89

The Mexican kleptocracy. T. Bethell. il *The American Spectator* 22:11-13 Jl '89

Rhodes to Latin America [Citibank loan negotiator] J. Zweig. il por *Forbes* 144:142+ S 4 '89

Salinas' flashy new step in the Mexican debt dance [relaxing foreign ownership rules] A. Bard. il *Business Week* p28 My 29 '89

A small sigh of relief. W. Glasgall. il *Business Week* p33 Jl 24 '89

So what took them so long? [agreement reached with creditor banks] C. Gorman. il *Time* 134:38 Ag 7 '89

South Africa

The Thatcher factor [banks reschedule debt] R. Laver. il *Maclean's* 102:42 O 30 '89

Soviet Union

The coming Soviet crash [excerpt] J. Shelton. il *Conservative Digest* 15:63+ Mr/Ap '89

The common defense [disproportionate burden shouldered by U.S. compounded by Western loans to Soviet Union] E. Rubenstein. il *National Review* 41:19 Je 30 '89

Comrade, can you spare a dime? E. Van den Haag. *National Review* 41:35-7 Mr 24 '89

Endgame: pressuring Gorbo. M. Ledeen. il *The American Spectator* 22:29-31 My '89

Financing Gorbachev's economic program: a bad investment for the West? S. Symms. il *USA Today (Periodical)* 118:25-7 Jl '89

Vladimir Bukovsky [advice to George Bush] V. Bukovsky. il *National Review* 41:22-3 F 10 '89

The West should not bankroll *perestroika*. B. Bradley. *USA Today (Periodical)* 118:22-4 Jl '89

Venezuela

Debt and politics in Venezuela. J. Ewell. bibl f *Current History* 88:121-4+ Mr '89

The next liberator? [C. A. Perez's approach to debt crisis] M. Collett. il *The Atlantic* 263:29+ F '89

LOANS, EAST EUROPEAN

Developing countries

Moscow's debt crisis. P. Fuhrman. il *Forbes* 143:40-1 My 29 '89

LOANS, FOREIGN

See also

Export-Import Bank of the United States

International Monetary Fund

World Bank

LOANS, GOVERNMENT *See* Government lending

LOANS, PERSONAL

See also

Automobile loans

Boat loans

Insurance, Life—Policy loans

A banker tells the secrets of the vault [interview with E. Mrkvicka] E. M. MacDonald. il pors *Money* 18:95-6+ Je '89

Borrowing money: smart moves in today's money market. N. Dunnan. *Better Homes and Gardens* 67:90+ Je '89

Bridging the gap. P. N. Strassels. il *Nation's Business* 77:90 N '89

Finance-a-face-lift [loans for plastic surgery from Hudson & Hudson] H. Wolinsky. il *American Health* 8:12 D '89

LOANS, PERSONAL—*cont.*
How to cope with lending rate gloom. G. Anrig, Jr. il *Money* 18:70-2+ My '89
LOANS, RUSSIAN
Developing countries
Moscow's debt crisis. P. Fuhrman. il *Forbes* 143:40-1 My 29 '89
LOBACK, JUDITH
Sunday is no day for shopping. il *Christianity Today* 33:8 Mr 3 '89
LOBBYING *See* Lobbyists and lobbying
LOBBYISTS AND LOBBYING
See also
American Association of Retired Persons
American Oceans Campaign
Anti-nuclear movement
Chamber of Commerce of the United States of America
Children's Defense Fund (U.S.)
Citizens for Rational Traffic Laws
Common Cause (U.S.)
Environmental movement
Federation of American Scientists
Moral Majority
National Audubon Society
National Committee to Preserve Social Security and Medicare
National Rifle Association of America
Political action committees
Sierra Club
Spacecause
Tobacco Institute
Universities Research Association
Wildlife Legislative Fund of America
Women lobbyists and lobbying
Abolish the lobbyist maintenance tax! J. Rowe. *The Washington Monthly* 21:14+ Jl/Ag '89
A business guide to Bush country. A. R. Dowd. il *Fortune* 120:93-4+ Jl 17 '89
Buyouts: the LBO lobby makes its move on Washington [cover story] M. Holland and V. Novak. il *Common Cause Magazine* 15:13-20 S/O '89
The elderly duke it out [Medicare surcharge stirs senior lobby] A. Miller. il *Newsweek* 114:42-3 S 11 '89
For the civil-rights lobby, a time to regroup. S. V. Roberts. *U.S. News & World Report* 107:30 Jl 10 '89
The gloves are off in lobbying for defense programs. P. A. Gilmartin. *Aviation Week & Space Technology* 131:29 D 18-25 '89
Hogrolling [helmet law opposition] A. Heard. *The New Republic* 201:11-12 N 20 '89
Politics & policy. See issues of Fortune beginning March 5, 1984
Reformers 3, S&L lobby 1 [House vote] D. Pauly. il *Newsweek* 113:55 Je 26 '89
The S&Ls' last stand against Congress. C. Yang. il *Business Week* p30-1 Jl 3 '89
A senior citizen rebellion has Congress retreating in disarray [Medicare tax surcharge] S. B. Garland. il *Business Week* p43 S 11 '89
Want action in Washington? Write a letter. D. Harbrecht. il *Business Week* p172 O 9 '89
Writing a letter that gets noticed [letters to congressmen] *U.S. News & World Report* 107:56 Ag 7 '89
Laws and regulations
None dare call it lobbying! R. Cowan. il *Common Cause Magazine* 15:13-16 Mr/Ap '89
Canada
See also
National Action Committee on the Status of Women (Canada)
LOBLAW COMPANIES LTD.
The chill wind from Canada [store brands] J. Levine. il *Forbes* 143:308+ My 29 '89
A divisive alliance [Pollution Probe and Friends of the Earth endorse Loblaw's environmentally friendly line of products] *Maclean's* 102:40 Jl 17 '89
LOBLOLLY PINE *See* Pine
LOBSENZ, NORMAN M., 1919-
Tips for closer family ties. *Reader's Digest* 134:139-42 F '89
LOBSTERS
See also
Cooking—Shellfish
Nervous system
See Nervous system—Crustaceans
LOCADIA, ALEX
about
Grand designs. D. Sapolin. il pors *Essence* 20:80-1+ Jl '89
LOCAL AREA NETWORKS
See also
AppleTalk (Local area network)
NetBIOS (Local area network)
Anatomy of a LAN operating system. M. L. Van Name and B. Catchings. il *Byte* 14:157-8+ Je '89
Battle of the network stars [LAN operating systems] S. Apiki and others. il *Byte* 14:154-6+ Jl '89

Breaking down the barriers [linking PCs and Macs on a LAN] M. L. Van Name and B. Catchings. il *Byte* 14:155-6 O '89
Current events [CarrierNET, carrier current system] R. L. Mitchell. il *Byte* 14:97 Mr '89
Discovering the promised LAN. S. Esters. il *Black Enterprise* 20:122-4+ O '89
E-mail for LANs: redefining corporate networking. E. Kay. il *Personal Computing* 13:127-31 N '89
Everyone into the pool [asynchronous gateways] B. Nance. il *Byte* 14:167-8+ N '89
Getting into bigger LANs. W. Rash, Jr. il *Byte* 14:145-7 F '89
Growing pains [choosing a LAN operating system] J. Y. Bryce. il *Byte* 14:135-6+ Ag '89
The LAN road to OSI. M. L. Van Name and B. Catchings. il *Byte* 14:148-50+ Jl '89
LAN supplement [special section] il *Byte* 14:211-14+ S '89
The LAN terminal alternative [Wyse WY-212 and TeleVideo TS2 TeleStation diskless PCs] B. Catchings and M. L. Van Name. il *Byte* 14:211-14 N '89
The Mac makes connections. B. N. Meeks. il *Byte* 14:171-2+ My '89
The mailman cometh. M. L. Van Name and B. Catchings. il *Byte* 14:143-4+ S '89
Networking with Unix [workstations] G. Comeau. il *Byte* 14:265-7+ F '89
The opposite tack. M. L. Smith and G. White. il *Byte* 14:216-17 Jl '89
PC communications [special section] il *Byte* 14:249+ Ja '89
The promised LAN. C. Strehlo. il *Personal Computing* 13:92-6+ Ja '89
So, maybe you do need a LAN. W. Rash, Jr. il *Byte* 14:135-6+ Ja '89
The spotlight turns to database servers. M. Liskin. il *Personal Computing* 13:53-6 N '89
UNIX workstation connect. D. Fiedler. il *Byte* 14:123-6 D '89
What a LAN consultant will tell you. C. Strehlo. il *Personal Computing* 13:97-9+ Ap '89
When one drive is enough [diskless PCs] M. L. Van Name and B. Catchings. il *Byte* 14:141-2+ D '89
Which LAN? R. Watson. il *Byte* 14 Special Issue:195-8+ Fall '89
Failure
Is there a doctor in the house? [software to diagnose failures in local area networks from Network General] J. Pitta. il *Forbes* 144:254+ N 27 '89
Security measures
The data bandits. W. M. Adney and D. E. Kavanagh. il *Byte* 14:267-70 Ja '89
Standards
How to lose a lead [3Com Corp. let Novell gain lead in LANs] J. Pitta. il *Forbes* 144:126 Ag 7 '89
LAN standards: do you need them? J. Schmidt. il *Byte* 14:212-14+ S '89
The light at the end of the LAN [Fiber Distributed Data Interface standard] B. Glass. il *Byte* 14:269-72+ Jl '89
The Token Ring. B. Glass. bibl il *Byte* 14:363-8+ Ja '89
Terminology
How to talk LANspeak. C. Strehlo. il *Personal Computing* 13:102-5+ F '89
LOCAL CONTROL OF SCHOOLS *See* School management and organization
LOCAL FINANCE
See also
Municipal finance
The state and local budget squeeze. H. Banks. *Forbes* 143:35 My 1 '89
LOCAL GOVERNMENT
See also
Decentralization in government
A free market in government. D. J. Devine. *National Review* 41:40-1 O 27 '89
Life at the local level: a Soviet journalist examines our 'grass-roots' politics. V. Nikolayev. *World Press Review* 36:34-6 N '89
United States
See Local government
LOCAL HISTORY
Bibliography
Local history [Britain] *History Today* 39:53 Ag '89
Exhibitions
Particular places [English local history and the Victoria County history exhibit at the British Library] C. R. Elrington. il *History Today* 39:61-2 Ag '89
LOCAL INITIATIVES SUPPORT CORPORATION
An unlikely source. K. D. Thompson. *Black Enterprise* 19:15 Ja '89
LOCAL POLITICS *See* Municipal government
LOCAL SERVICE AIRLINES *See* Airlines—Local service
LOCAL TAXATION
See also
New York (N.Y.)—Taxation
LOCAL TRANSIT
See also
Chicago (Ill.)—Transit systems
Hong Kong—Transit systems

LOCAL TRANSIT—See also—*cont.*
  Light rail systems
  New Orleans (La.)—Transit systems
  New York (N.Y.)—Subways
  New York (N.Y.)—Transit systems
  Rome (Italy)—Transit systems
  Trolleys
Mass transit and the poor. G. M. Anderson. il *America* 161:399-402 D 2 '89
Transportation tomorrow. M. Renner. il por *The Futurist* 23:14-16+ Mr/Ap '89
Federal aid
How consumers get taken for a ride. J. Hood. il *Consumers' Research Magazine* 72:31-5 F '89
U.S. transit subsidy policy: in need of reform. M. Wachs. bibl f il *Science* 244:1545-9 Je 30 '89
Developing countries
The transportation crisis in the third world. M. Renner. il *The Futurist* 23:17 Mr/Ap '89
LOCALIZATION OF BRAIN FUNCTIONS *See* Brain—Localization of functions
LOCATION IN BUSINESS AND INDUSTRY
  See also
  Automobile factories—Location
  Business districts
  Offshore offices
America's boom towns [cover story] M. W. Karmin. il maps *U.S. News & World Report* 107:54-6+ N 13 '89
The best cities for business [cover story; special section] il *Fortune* 120:56-8+ O 23 '89
Big fish in small ponds. K. L. Fisher. il *Forbes* 143:278 Je 26 '89
Doing business in the 'burbs [women entrepreneurs; special section] D. Weil. il *Working Woman* 14:58-62+ Ag '89
Escape from high costs [businesses and individuals leaving Toronto] P. Chisholm. il *Maclean's* 102:62+ N 20 '89
Favorite cities for tomorrow's workers. il *The Futurist* 23:52 Jl/Ag '89
Great stock buys [cover story] J. Kosnett and R. J. Maturi. il *Changing Times* 43:28-38 O '89
Holdup in the Windy City [tax incentives spur Sears' move to suburbs] P. Glastris. il *U.S. News & World Report* 107:40-1 Jl 17 '89
Houston's sick economy is taking a little nourishment. M. Ivey. il *Business Week* p102-3 Ja 16 '89
How to keep the home forges burning—and profitable [manufacturers shifting overseas operations back to U.S.] P. Sherrid. il *U.S. News & World Report* 107:48-9 Jl 3 '89
In search of exports: the states' new agenda. P. R. Piccigallo. il *USA Today (Periodical)* 118:20-2 S '89
Migratory habits of the 500 [Fortune 500] A. Farnham. il map *Fortune* 119:400-1 Ap 24 '89
Not mad about Manhattan [Exxon moves headquarters to Texas] il *Time* 134:69 N 6 '89
States, technology, and jobs. D. M. Brown. il *Technology Review* 92:16-17 My/Je '89
Surviving the slowdown: diversity is key. K. Madigan. il *Business Week* p57-8 Jl 3 '89
Tailor-made work forces [customized training targeted to individual companies offered in states' development packages] H. Bacas. il *Nation's Business* 77:33-6 N '89
Trained to order [states providing vocational training as lure to new industry] S. B. Weiner and C. Siler. il *Forbes* 143:73+ Je 26 '89
What's the best city? [Columbus, Ohio] W. E. Sheeline. il *Fortune* 119:11 Ja 2 '89
Where will the jobs go? [software jobs] K. K. Wiegner. il *Forbes* 144:270-2 D 11 '89
Will Wall Street fade? J. Cook. il *Forbes* 144:138-9 O 16 '89
LOCATION TRANSPARENCY (DATABASE MANAGEMENT)
"Location transparency" next hurdle for database technology. *Byte* 14:12+ Ap '89
LOCK UP [film] See Motion picture reviews—Single works
LOCKE, DONALD
  about
The multifaceted Donald Locke. V. Hay. il por *American Visions* 4:37-40 O '89
LOCKE, JOHN, 1632-1704
  about
Who read John Locke? Words and acts in the American Revolution. O. Handlin and L. Handlin. *The American Scholar* 58:545-56 Aut '89
LOCKE, LAWRENCE F.
General education: in search of facts. il *Change* 21:20-3 Jl/Ag '89
LOCKE, SONDRA
  about
Suing Clint Eastwood, Sondra Locke strikes with Magnum force. J. Kaufman. il pors *People Weekly* 31:58-60 My 15 '89
When Harry left Sondra. il pors *People Weekly* 32:68-9 Ag 7 '89
LOCKERBIE, D. BRUCE
The trouble with being open-minded [address, July 18, 1989] *Vital Speeches of the Day* 55:723-7 S 15 '89

LOCKERBIE (SCOTLAND) AIR DISASTER, 1988 *See* Pan American Flight 103 disaster, 1988
LOCKHART, FRANK
  about
The glory and the dream. J. A. Wren. il por *Road & Track* 40:106-7 My '89
LOCKHEED AIR TERMINAL, INC.
Buyers are starting to circle the airports [new era in privatization] S. Payne and E. Schine. il *Business Week* p38 O 2 '89
LOCKHEED CORP.
Additional P-7A design work may cost Lockheed $300 million. il *Aviation Week & Space Technology* 131:22-3 N 27 '89
Aeronautics/propulsion [development of Stealth technology; aerospace laureate] il *Aviation Week & Space Technology* 130:15 Ja 2 '89
A beleaguered Boeing may be on Lockheed's tail. G. G. Marcial. il *Business Week* p130 Mr 13 '89
Boeing borrows skilled workers from Lockheed for 747-400 program. R. G. O'Lone. *Aviation Week & Space Technology* 130:66 Mr 13 '89
Daewoo wins contract to assemble wing panels for Lockheed P-7A. M. A. Dornheim. *Aviation Week & Space Technology* 131:29 S 4 '89
Lockheed develops threat warning system for U.S. military satellites [Satellite On-board Attack Warning System] B. W. Henderson. il *Aviation Week & Space Technology* 131:61+ Jl 3 '89
Lockheed dons new armor to keep the raiders at bay. E. Schine. il *Business Week* p20-1 Ap 17 '89
Lockheed establishes military avionics unit in Sanders affiliate. D. Hughes. il *Aviation Week & Space Technology* 130:92-3+ Ap 24 '89
Lockheed implements restructuring to focus on primary businesses. B. A. Smith. *Aviation Week & Space Technology* 130:31 Ap 10 '89
Lockheed integrating components of SDI exoatmospheric interceptor. B. W. Henderson. il *Aviation Week & Space Technology* 130:50 Ja 2 '89
Lockheed nears completion of work on new Palmdale composite facility. il *Aviation Week & Space Technology* 130:26 My 1 '89
Lockheed renovates clean room for work on large satellites. il *Aviation Week & Space Technology* 130:303 Je 12 '89
Lockheed weighs investment risks of developing new C-130 version. E. H. Kolcum. il *Aviation Week & Space Technology* 131:45+ N 27 '89
NASA selects Lockheed/Aerojet to build shuttle's advanced solid rocket motor. T. M. Foley. il *Aviation Week & Space Technology* 130:31-2 My 1 '89
New tape laying machine eases preparation of thermoplastic material. il *Aviation Week & Space Technology* 131:83 S 18 '89
OSHA threatens to fine Lockheed $1.5 million. *Aviation Week & Space Technology* 130:20 Ap 3 '89
Tests to verify airworthiness of new ES-3A configuration. B. D. Nordwall. il *Aviation Week & Space Technology* 131:36-7+ S 25 '89
U.S., West Germany may delay P-7 agreement until September [antisubmarine warfare aircraft] J. D. Morrocco. il *Aviation Week & Space Technology* 130:62 Je 19 '89
LOCKLEAR, HEATHER
  about
Then & now: Heather Locklear. il pors *'Teen* 33:52 Je '89
LOCKMAN, HEATHER
Asia in a day. il *Travel Holiday* 172:90-5 Ag '89
LOCKRIDGE, PATRICIA A.
Volcanoes and tsunamis [cover story] il *Earth Science* 42:24-5 Spr '89
LOCKS AND KEYS
Games [trick for opening a locked change purse invented by M. Weber] S. Morris. il *Omni (New York, N.Y.)* 12:118 N '89
Locks without keys [electronic door locks] H. B. Cohen. il *Home Mechanix* 85:32+ D '89
Open-and-shut case [trick for opening a locked change purse invented by M. Weber] S. Morris. il *Omni (New York, N.Y.)* 12:164-5+ O '89
LOCKWOOD, VICTORIA
  about
'Champagne Charlie,' Di's dashing brother, takes a bride decked in . . . gold. M. H. J. Farrell. il pors *People Weekly* 32:42-5 O 2 '89
Lord Althorp, Di's impetuous brother, proposes to a model he met only two months ago. T. Allis. il pors *People Weekly* 32:32-3 Jl 24 '89
LOCOMOTION
  See also
  Animal locomotion
  Human locomotion
LOCOMOTIVES
Born again [steam trains; cover story] W. Hoffer. il *Popular Mechanics* 166:117-19+ My '89
LOCONTI, KATHLENE M.
(jt. auth) See Decker, Daniel J., and Loconti, Kathlene M.
LOCTITE CORP.
Loctite Corp. R. Abelson. il *Fortune* 119:148 Je 19 '89

LOCUS (GENES)
See also
Restriction fragment length polymorphisms
Altering the genome by homologous recombination [gene targeting] M. R. Capecchi. bibl f il *Science* 244:1288-92 Je 16 '89
Cloning of breakpoints of a chromosome translocation identifies the AN2 locus [aniridia] M. Gessler and others. bibl f il *Science* 244:1575-8 Je 30 '89
Cystic fibrosis: cloning and genetics [cover story; special section; with editorial comment by Daniel E. Koshland] *Science* 245:1029, 1059-80 S 8 '89
Cystic fibrosis gene and protein identified [work of Francis S. Collins and Lap-Chee Tsui] K. Fackelmann. *Science News* 136:149 S 2 '89
The cystic fibrosis gene is found [work of Lap-Chee Tsui and Francis Collins] J. L. Marx. il *Science* 245:923-5 S 1 '89
Cystic fibrosis: hunting down a killer gene. J. Seligmann. il *Newsweek* 114:60-1 S 4 '89
elk, tissue-specific *ets*-related genes on chromosomes X and 14 near translocation breakpoints. V. N. Rao and others. bibl f il *Science* 244:66-70 Ap 7 '89
Fighting heredity: doctors identify the cystic fibrosis gene. R. Corelli. il *Maclean's* 102:63 S 4 '89
The gene for enhancer binding proteins E12/E47 lies at the t(1;19) breakpoint in acute leukemias. J. D. Mellentin and others. bibl f il *Science* 246:379-82 O 20 '89
A genetic link to epilepsy [juvenile myoclonic epilepsy; research by Antonio Delgado] *USA Today (Periodical)* 118:12-13 O '89
A medical breakthrough gives new hope to David Reitz—and all kids with cystic fibrosis [research by Francis Collins and Lap-Chee Tsui] R. Arias. il *People Weekly* 32:83-4+ S 11 '89
A new DNA marker tightly linked to the fragile X locus (FRAXA). G. K. Suthers and others. bibl f il *Science* 246:1298-1300 D 8 '89
p53: a frequent target for genetic abnormalities in lung cancer. T. Takahashi and others. bibl f il *Science* 246:491-4 O 27 '89
Physical mapping of a translocation breakpoint in neurofibromatosis. J. W. Fountain and others. bibl f il *Science* 244:1085-7 Je 2 '89
Prevention of allogeneic bone marrow graft rejection by H-2 transgene in donor mice. C. Öhlén and others. bibl f il *Science* 246:666-8 N 3 '89
A Salmonella locus that controls resistance to microbicidal proteins from phagocytic cells. P. I. Fields and others. bibl f il *Science* 243:1059-62 F 24 '89
Scientists home in on tooth enamel gene [amelogenin; research by Eduardo C. Lau] *Science News* 135:269 Ap 29 '89
Selection for precise chromosomal targeting of a dominant marker by homologous recombination. J. R. Dorin and others. bibl f il *Science* 243:1357-60 Mr 10 '89
Winning candidate [identification of cystic fibrosis gene by Lap-Chee Tsui and John R. Riordan] T. Beardsley. *Scientific American* 261:28+ N '89

LOCUST TREES
Flowering locusts. E. A. Peeples. il *Country Journal* 16:13-14 N/D '89

LOCUSTS *See* Grasshoppers

LOD (ISRAEL)
Four decades of blood vengeance [death of G. Habash's sister in Lydda during 1948 war]; tr. by Richard Flantz. A. Kenan. il *The Nation* 248:154-6 F 6 '89

LODER, GILES
about
Gardens: High Beeches: preserving a woodland heritage in Sussex. E. Lambert. il *Architectural Digest* 46:150-3+ Ag '89

LODESTAR GROUP
Ring around the rosie at Kinder-Care. C. Hawkins. il *Business Week* p45-6 D 18 '89

LODGE, DAVID, 1935-
about
PW interviews. A. Smith. por *Publishers Weekly* 236:41-2 Ag 18 '89

LODGE, GEORGE C.
It's time for an American *perestroika*. il *The Atlantic* 263:35-6 Ap '89

LODGE, MICHELLE
How to heal yourself [interview with B. S. Siegel] por *Ladies' Home Journal* 106:108+ Je '89
Learning the business. il *Publishers Weekly* 235:19-23 Mr 24 '89
Two from the heart [interviews with E. Bombeck and H. Kushner] il pors *Ladies' Home Journal* 106:78+ D '89
When you eat too much. il *Ladies' Home Journal* 106:42+ D '89

LODGE DECORATION
Jane Fonda's spa [Laurel Springs Retreat decorated by Barbara Pohlman] P. Viladas. il por *House & Garden* 161:92-7 Je '89

LODGES
Call of the wild [luxury lodges in the wilderness; survey by T. Zagat] N. M. Better. il *House & Garden* 161:46+ Je '89

Contemporary traditions on Lake Tahoe [lodge remodeled by Robert V. Arrigoni and decorated by Charles Pfister] J. Chatfield-Taylor. il *Architectural Digest* 46:270-5+ O '89
Family ties [S. W. Morgan family's Vermont lodge] C. Brown. il *House & Garden* 161:128-35 Je '89
Lodges on the run [floating lodges for salmon fishing in British Columbia] J. Gibbs. il *Outdoor Life* 183:86-7+ My '89

LODOLETTA [opera] *See* Mascagni, Pietro, 1863-1945

LODZ GHETTO [film] *See* Motion picture reviews—Single works

LOEB, GERALD E.
Neural control of locomotion. bibl f il *BioScience* 39:800-4 D '89

LOEB, JACQUES, 1859-1924
about
The science of metamorphoses. R. C. Lewontin. bibl f il *The New York Review of Books* 36:18-22 Ap 27 '89

LOEB, MARSHALL
Editor's desk. See issues of Fortune beginning June 9, 1986

LOEHR, JAMES E.
The mental game. See issues of World Tennis

LOER, CURTIS M., AND KRISTAN, WILLIAM B., JR.
Central synaptic inputs to identified leech neurons determined by peripheral targets. bibl f il *Science* 244:64-6 Ap 7 '89

LOESCHHORN, JOHN
Sand dudes. il *Runner's World* 24:58-9 S '89

LOEWS CORPORATION
The Loews-some dove stock play. il *Money* 18:8 Ap '89

LOEWY, RAYMOND FERNAND, 1893-1986
about
Raymond Loewy's four-door Avanti. S. Kichen. il por *Forbes* 144:180 O 2 '89

LOFGREN, GARY E.
(jt. auth) See Beard, James S., and Lofgren, Gary E.

LOFT APARTMENTS
Another country [Peter and Olga Gee's loft and roof garden in New York's SoHo] M. Bethany. il *New York* 22:84-8+ Jl 3-10 '89
An architectural presence in the Manhattan art world [L. H. Skolnick] K. Andersen. il por *Architectural Digest* 46:170+ N '89
A downtown aesthetic: the residence and studio of artist Jennifer Bartlett. D. Solomon. il por *Architectural Digest* 46:316-21+ N '89
An educated palette [Manhattan loft of R. Rosenblum and J. Kaplowitz] J. Russell. il pors *House & Garden* 161:136-9+ Je '89
Lofty ambitions [R. Bleckner's Manhattan loft] L. Kaylin. il pors *Gentlemen's Quarterly* 59:208-11+ F '89
Playing for keeps [M. Schwartz's collection of eighties art in Manhattan loft] J. Saltz. il pors *House & Garden* 161:162-9 O '89
SoHo salon [Manhattan loft of P. Arnell and S. Nolan] M. Filler. il pors *House & Garden* 161:170-3 O '89
Vass horizons [Manhattan loft] J. Etra. il por *House & Garden* 161:60-9+ Ja '89

LOG CABINS, HOUSES, ETC.
See also
House decoration
Alan Flusser upstate: an offbeat cabin designed with humor in New York. S. M. L. Aronson. il pors *Architectural Digest* 46:192-7+ S '89
Colorado cabin fever [1930s log house in Glenwood Springs designed by T. Molesworth] M. Guralnick. il *House & Garden* 161:158-67+ D '89
For the love of art [addition to 1840 log house in Nashville, Tenn.] il *Southern Living* 24:130 O '89
Honoring their Cherokee heritage [Kay and Ron Hendricks' log house in north Georgia] C. Engle. il *Southern Living* 24:90-2 O '89
A house worth saving [restoration of Page Meadows, a double-pen log house in Virginia] L. Hallam. il *Southern Living* 24:168-71 N '89
West by southwest: a Telluride log house with mining camp roots [designed by Theodore Brown] J. Naisbitt and P. Aburdene. il pors *Architectural Digest* 46:206-14 Je '89

LOGAN, ANDY
Around City Hall (Koch administration). See occasional issues of The New Yorker through December 25, 1989

LOGAN, JULIE
Making the most of it. il *American Health* 8:88+ Ap '89
The provocative pout: hot lips. il *Harper's Bazaar* 122:178-9+ Ap '89

LOGAN, LIZ
Rooms at the top. il *House & Garden* 161:118+ O '89

LOGAN, ONNIE LEE
What I know about deliverin' babies come from motherwit, common sense. God gave it to me [excerpt from Motherwit: an Alabama midwife's story]; ed. by Katherine Clark. il pors *Life* 12:19-21 Je '89

LOGAN, WILLIAM, 1950-
New Year's at the methodists [poem] *The Nation* 248:826 Je 12 '89
The shadow-line [poem] *The New Yorker* 64:30 F 6 '89

LOGAN, WILLIAM BRYANT
Beyond the box step. il *House & Garden* 161:82+ N '89
Country neoclassic. il por *House & Garden* 161:216-23+ S '89
Cultivated pleasures. il *House & Garden* 161:65-6 Je '89
Peach heaven [cover story] il *Organic Gardening* 36:40-5 Mr '89
LOGAN INTERNATIONAL AIRPORT See Boston (Mass.)—Airports
LOGBOOKS
StarTrails [keeping an observing log] D. H. Levy. *Sky and Telescope* 77:659 Je '89
LOGÉ, DAN
about
Dan Logé—an artist in touch with the river. H. W. Trimm. il *The Conservationist* 44:10-15 S/O '89
LOGGERHEAD TURTLES See Turtles
LOGGIA, ROBERT
Don't wait until you're 40. por *World Tennis* 36:96 F '89
about
Lords of the ring. M. Rochlin. il pors *Harper's Bazaar* 122:103 D '89
LOGGING See Lumbering
LOGGING ON (COMPUTERS)
Logging on from Lagos to Lima. S. Baker. il *Business Week* p158 My 15 '89
LOGIC, SYMBOLIC AND MATHEMATICAL
See also
Fuzzy systems (Computer science)
Proof theory
LOGIC ANALYZERS
Precision Motion 20-MHz logic analyzer. il *Radio-Electronics* 60:22+ D '89
LOGIC CIRCUITS
See also
Programmable logic devices
How smart is your disk drive? K. K. Wiegner. il *Forbes* 144:219+ O 30 '89
Speed demons. K. K. Wiegner. il *Forbes* 143:302-3 Ja 9 '89
Design
Elenco XK-220 Digital Trainer. il *Radio-Electronics* 60:22 S '89
LOGO (COMPUTER LANGUAGE)
Learning with LogoWriter, Home Edition. C. S. Holzberg. il *Home Office Computing* 7:86-7 My '89
Logo and geography teaching. M. Eichen. bibl *Focus (New York, N.Y.: 1950)* 39:25-6 Summ '89
LOGOS See Trade marks and trade names
LOGOTHETIS, NIKOS K., AND SCHALL, JEFFREY D.
Neuronal correlates of subjective visual perception. bibl f il *Science* 245:761-3 Ag 18 '89
LOGSDON, GENE
Finding Christmas. il *Country Journal* 16:82-7 N/D '89
A flowering lawn. il *Organic Gardening* 36:44-8 My '89
Sporting pleasures. il *Country Journal* 16:36-41 Jl/Ag '89
Who says the family farm is dead? Welcome to future farming's best bet. il *Utne Reader* p82-8 Jl/Ag '89
LOGSDON, JOHN M.
Do we really need a Space Council? il *Ad Astra* 1:3 F '89
LOGSDON, JOHN M., AND WILLIAMSON, RAY A., 1938-
U.S. access to space. bibl il *Scientific American* 260:34-40 Mr '89
LOH, ELWYN Y., AND OTHERS
Polymerase chain reaction with single-sided specificity: analysis of T cell receptor δ chain. bibl f il *Science* 243:217-20 Ja 13 '89
LOHMANN, JEANNE
Skeletal [poem] *America* 160:445 My 13 '89
LOHR, KATHY
Raise the Arabia! il *The Saturday Evening Post* 261:48-9+ Jl/Ag '89
LOHR, PETER
Should you be in business for yourself? il *Reader's Digest* 135:49-52 Jl '89
LOHR, STEVE
Brawling over Harrods. il pors *The New York Times Magazine* p32-3+ O 8 '89
LOHSE, ANSGAR W., AND OTHERS
Control of experimental autoimmune encephalomyelitis by T cells responding to activated T cells. bibl f il *Science* 244:820-2 My 19 '89
LOIRE RIVER VALLEY (FRANCE)
The garden of France: history meets geography in the Loire River Valley. B. Warf. il map *Focus (New York, N.Y.: 1950)* 39:26-7+ Fall '89
LOJACK CORPORATION
To catch a thief [LoJack tracking equipment] C. Torcellini. il *Forbes* 143:202 Ap 17 '89
LOKE, MARGARETT
'The Tao is up'. il pors *The New York Times Magazine* p28-9+ Ap 30 '89
LOMA PRIETA (CALIF.) EARTHQUAKE, 1989 See San Francisco Bay Area (Calif.)—Earthquake, 1989

LOMAS FINANCIAL CORP.
How much bad luck can one Texan take? [J. Hay's plan to remake Lomas Financial] T. Mason. il *Business Week* p33 S 18 '89
The last roundup? J. H. Taylor. il por *Forbes* 143:124 Je 12 '89
"Not another Texas bank". il *Forbes* 143:136 Ja 9 '89
LOMAX, KAREN J., AND OTHERS
Recombinant 47-kilodalton cytosol factor restores NADPH oxidase in chronic granulomatous disease. bibl f il *Science* 245:409-12 Jl 28 '89; Correction. 246:987 N 24 '89
LOMBARD, CAROLE, 1908-1942
about
Carole Lombard. A. Sarris. il pors *American Film* 14:62-4 Mr '89
LOMBARD (ILL.)
Education
High school confidential [Glenbard East High School] S. Elder. il *American Health* 8:62-3+ O '89
LOMBARDI, JOHN
Frank Rizzo without prejudice. il por *Esquire* 112:114-17 Ag '89
LOMBREGLIA, RALPH
Jungle video [story] *The New Yorker* 65:30-9 Ag 21 '89
LOMON, KEVIN
about
Felled by the fall. J. Rodewald. il por *Sports Illustrated* 71:16 O 9 '89
LOMPOC PENITENTIARY (CALIF.) See Prisons—California
LONDON, GABRIELLE
about
Blueprint for growth: (not always) an easy alliance. A. L. Ball. il pors *Working Woman* 14:138+ O '89
LONDON, HERBERT IRA
about
London in New York. *National Review* 41:16 Ap 21 '89
LONDON, JACK, 1876-1916
The original big one. il *U.S. News & World Report* 107:34 O 30 '89
LONDON, RACHEL
about
With flowers as her trademark, fashion designer Rachel London's career goes into full bloom. H. Shapiro. il pors *People Weekly* 31:77-8 My 8 '89
LONDON (ENGLAND)
See also
Chelsea (London, England)
Kensington (London, England)
Marylebone (London, England)
Seven Dials (London, England)
Airports
Biggin Hill. N. Moll. il *Flying* 116:76-80+ Ja '89
Change of transport ministers leaves new rules for British airports in doubt. D. A. Brown. *Aviation Week & Space Technology* 131:82-3 Ag 7 '89
Security levels increased at Frankfurt, Heathrow [following Pan Am Flight 103 bombing] K. F. Mordoff. il *Aviation Week & Space Technology* 130:28-9 Ja 9 '89
Antiquities
City freeman? [Hanseatic League's German enclave in medieval London] D. Keys. il *History Today* 39:4-5 D '89
To build or not to build. A. Toufexis. il *Time* 133:64-5 My 29 '89
Where the Globe was a stage [excavation of Globe Theater] il *U.S. News & World Report* 107:19 O 23 '89
Architecture
See also
London (England)—Buildings
Prime time [J. Street-Porter's house designed by P. Gough] C. K. Gandee. il por *House & Garden* 161:182-7+ Mr '89
Whose Britain is it? [criticisms by Prince Charles] J. Adler. il por *Newsweek* 114:84-6 N 13 '89
Banks
Big Bang: big bust, big lessons. R. A. Melcher. il *Business Week* p38-9 Mr 6 '89
Bookstores
See Booksellers and bookselling—Great Britain
Buildings
Heroic transformations [designs by R. Rogers, N. Foster and N. Grimshaw] D. Dietsch. il *Architectural Record* 177:72-83 S '89
Cemeteries
See also
Highgate Cemetery (London, England)
Churches (Buildings)
St Martin's, Gospel Oak. P. Conrad. il *History Today* 39:59-60 Jl '89
City planning
See also
London Docklands Development Corporation
Clubs
See also
Groucho Club
Description
London. C. Carlisle. il *Esquire* 112:185+ D '89

LONDON (ENGLAND)—Description—*cont.*
London journal. J. Bainbridge. See occasional issues of *Gourmet*
Paris/London: the chic beat. J. M. Adams. il *Seventeen* 48:172+ Ap '89
A young person's guide to London. M. Elder. il *Gourmet* 49:108-13+ O '89

Docks, wharves, etc.
See also
London Docklands Development Corporation

Economic history
Business as usual? London and the industrial revolution. T. Barker. bibl il *History Today* 39:45-51 F '89

Galleries and museums
See also
Bank of England Museum
British Museum
Design Museum (London, England)
Leighton House Art Gallery and Museum (London, England)
Museum of the Moving Image (London, England)
National Gallery (Great Britain)
National Portrait Gallery (Great Britain)
Tate Gallery
Victoria and Albert Museum

Historic houses, sites, etc.
See also
Number 10 Downing Street (London, England)
Restoration drama [D. Roos' nineteenth century townhouse] S. Calloway. il por *House & Garden* 161:120-3+ D '89
Theatrical menagerie: an English actor's Victorian house in London [T. Jellinek] E. Lambert. il por *Architectural Digest* 46:118-25 D '89

Hospices
Lead me safely through death [St. Joseph's Hospice; cover story] W. F. Carr. *America* 160:264-7 Mr 25 '89

Hotels, motels, etc.
See also
Savoy Hotel plc
Cozy fan tutte [Blakes Hotel run by A. Hempel] S. Steward. il por *Harper's Bazaar* 122:101 S '89
London's Sunday antiques fairs. J. Robinson. il *Gourmet* 49:66-9+ Je '89
A room of her own [Reeves hotel for businesswomen] N. R. Gibbs. il por *Time* 134:58-9 Ag 21 '89
Steeped in tradition [tea at Brown's Hotel] S. Steward. il *Harper's Bazaar* 122:96 S '89
Suite perfection [Connaught Hotel] P. Mayle. il *Gentlemen's Quarterly* 59:284-91 D '89

Intellectual life
See also
Bloomsbury group

Maps
See also
London Topographical Society

Monuments, statues, etc.
Sunrise at Seven Dials [replica of 17th-century column erected] T. Aldous. il *History Today* 39:6 Jl '89

Municipal services
London loses its luster [state of services after the demise of the Greater London Council] N. Gelb. il *The New Leader* 72:12-13 S 18 '89

Music
See also
English National Opera
Opera—Great Britain
Royal Opera House (London, England)

Newspapers
See also
Daily telegraph (London, England)

Photographs and photography
A photographer's guide to London. P. Slaughter. il *Petersen's Photographic Magazine* 18:38-42 Ag '89

Politics and government
See also
Greater London Council

Popular culture
Inside London [special section] il *Harper's Bazaar* 122:45-8+ S '89
Sights & sounds. C. Worthington. il *Harper's Bazaar* 122:48+ Mr '89

Restaurants, nightclubs, bars, etc.
The Bank of England Museum and Sweetings. J. Bainbridge. il *Gourmet* 49:36+ My '89
Channel crossings [Mosimann's and Bibendum] P. Levy. il *House & Garden* 161:96+ Mr '89
A fine madness [restaurateur P. Langan] P. Wilkinson. il pors *Gentlemen's Quarterly* 59:430-5+ S '89
The River Cafe, Very Simply Nico, Chez Nico. J. Bainbridge. il por *Gourmet* 49:52+ N '89

Social history
Retrieved riches: Charles Booth's Life and labour of the people in London. R. O'Day. bibl il por map *History Today* 39:29-35 Ap '89

Social life and customs
The man who put the grouch into Groucho's [J. Bernard at the Groucho Club] R. Ryan. il por *Gentlemen's Quarterly* 59:31+ Ja '89

Stores
See also
Harrods, Ltd.
Marks & Spencer plc
Rigby & Peller (Firm)
SCP Ltd.
Buying British [antique furniture] B. Singer. il *House & Garden* 161:198+ Mr '89
A cut above the best [clothiers] J. McLaughlin. il *Harper's Bazaar* 122:118 S '89
The empire's new clothes. S. James. il *Harper's Bazaar* 122:150 S '89
The merchant of style [clothing stores of J. Ettedgui] C. K. Gandee. il por *House & Garden* 161:46 Ap '89

Streets
See also
Jermyn Street (London, England)

Theater
See also
Globe Theatre (London, England)
National Theatre (Great Britain)
Old Vic Theatre (London, England)
Rose Theatre (London, England)
The Bard stripped bare. V. Radin. il *Vogue* 179:248-51 Ap '89
Dustin Hoffman takes a risky shot at Shakespeare. il por *People Weekly* 31:101 Je 19 '89
'Iranian nights': but will it play in Teheran? [play based on S. Rushdie affair] il *Newsweek* 113:43 My 1 '89
The ladies of London. J. Kroll. il *Newsweek* 113:52-3 Ja 9 '89
London sets the stage for theater. C. Griffith-Roberts. il *Southern Living* 24:30 O '89
The play's the (available) thing. J. Marcom, Jr. il *Forbes* 143:312-14 My 29 '89
The theater of "received pronunciation". R. Brustein. *The New Republic* 200:26-8 Mr 6 '89
Theater preservation update: London 1989. A. Robins. il *Architectural Record* 177:79 N '89
Theater under the London sun. G. G. Seibert. *America* 161:145 S 9-16 '89
A trio of triumphs in London. W. A. Henry. il *Time* 134:73 Jl 3 '89
Upstaging Broadway. R. T. Marin. il *The American Spectator* 22:48 My '89

LONDON (ENGLAND). GREATER LONDON COUNCIL
See Greater London Council

LONDON (ENGLAND) FASHION SHOWS *See* Fashion shows

LONDON & ATLANTIC METAL BROKERS
Did Refco help take Uncle Sam to the cleaners? [dodging taxes through phony London trading] D. Greising. il *Business Week* p33-4 O 2 '89

LONDON BOOK FAIR *See* Book fairs

LONDON CLASSICAL PLAYERS
Beethoven lite. P. G. Davis. il por *New York* 22:60-1 Ag 28 '89
A man for all seasons [director R. Norrington] S. Cantrell. il pors *High Fidelity (New York, N.Y.)* 39:46-8 Mr '89
Roger Norrington's Beethoven. P. Mattick, Jr. *The Nation* 249:326-8 S 25 '89

LONDON DOCKLANDS DEVELOPMENT CORPORATION
The worst of Thames. D. Sudjic. il *House & Garden* 161:56 Mr '89

LONDON FESTIVAL BALLET
See also
English National Ballet
Reviews:
Performances in London. J. Percival. *Dance Magazine* 63:25-7 F '89

LONDON STOCK EXCHANGE
Big Bang: big bust, big lessons. R. A. Melcher. il *Business Week* p38-9 Mr 6 '89

LONDON TOPOGRAPHICAL SOCIETY
London Topographical Society. R. Cavendish. il *History Today* 39:60-1 S '89

LONDONDERRY (NORTHERN IRELAND)
Social conditions
Daughters of Derry [Catholic women] N. McCafferty. il *Ms.* 18:72-7 S '89

LONE STAR INDUSTRIES, INC.
Home, sweet cement [J. E. Stewart] M. Alpert. il por *Fortune* 119:121 F 27 '89
Which of Lone Star's suitors will get the dance? G. G. Marcial. il *Business Week* p80 Jl 31 '89

LONE STAR OBSERVATORY (TEX.)
Backyard observatory, Texas style. *Astronomy* 17:18 Ag '89

LONE STAR TECHNOLOGIES INC.
Bad news for Beasley. R. Reiff. il por *Forbes* 143:180 Je 12 '89

LONELINESS
The pretended self [loneliness and heart disease; research by Dean Ornish] P. Perry. il *Psychology Today* 23:60-1 My '89

LONESOME DOVE [television program] *See* Television program reviews—Single works

LONETREE, CLAYTON
about
The Moscow bug hunt. J. Peterzell. il pors *Time* 134:26-8 Jl 10 '89
LONEY, GLENN MEREDITH, 1928-
The sleeping Prince. il *Opera News* 53:14+ My '89
LONG, EARL K.
about
The cockeyed world of Ron Shelton. J. Silverman. il pors *American Film* 15:34-9+ D '89
Stripper Blaze Starr recalls her affair with the governor; ed. by Margie Bonnett Sellinger. B. Starr. il pors *People Weekly* 32:157+ D 18 '89
LONG, J. V.
Walking the tightrope of mystery. il por *Commonweal* 116:555-8 O 20 '89
LONG, JUDITH
(jt. auth) See Grossman, Karl, and Long, Judith
LONG, LYNETTE
How educators can help latchkey children. *The Education Digest* 54:53-7 Mr '89
LONG, MARION
Rhymes and reasons. il por *Gentlemen's Quarterly* 59:202-3 F '89
LONG, MICHAEL E.
High tech: the future is now. il maps *National Geographic* 176:92-101 Jl '89
LONG, PERRIN
about
Perrin Long: the loner everybody listens to. J. Friedman. il por *Business Week* p58 Jl 24 '89
LONG, RICHARD, 1945-
about
Richard Long: Sperone Westwater. L. Holst. il *Art News* 88:162-3 Summ '89
LONG, ROBERT
Rotel RTC-850 tuner/preamplifier. il *High Fidelity (New York, N.Y.)* 39:26-7+ Jl '89
Tape tracks. See issues of High Fidelity (New York, N.Y.) beginning May 1986 through July 1989
LONG, SHELLEY
about
Shelley Long: her blessings galore. N. Gittelson. il pors *McCall's* 116:16-18 Ap '89
Where I grew up: Shelley Long [interview] L. Konner. il pors map *Glamour* 87:155 My '89
LONG (PERRIN) INC. See Perrin Long Inc.
LONG AGO & FAR AWAY [television program] See Television program reviews—Single works
LONG BEACH (CALIF.)
Economic conditions
"Long Beach is different" [Japanese investment] E. Paris. il *Forbes* 143:76+ My 29 '89
LONG BEACH CITY COLLEGE
Faculty development from the inside [holistic assessment and placement project for composition classes] K. Burne and others. pors *Change* 21:43-9 My/Je '89
LONG BEACH GRAND PRIX See Automobile racing
LONG BEACH MARATHON See Marathon running
LONG DISTANCE LOVE (ORGANIZATION)
Roxanne Black's Long Distance Love. T. Kauchak. il por *Seventeen* 48:68 Je '89
LONG DISTANCE TELEPHONE SERVICE See Telephone—Long distance service
LONG-DURATION EXPOSURE FACILITY (ARTIFICIAL SATELLITE)
The decline and fall of LDEF. P. Jones. il *Ad Astra* 1:36-7 N '89
LDEF decay sparks move for early retrieval mission. E. H. Kolcum. il *Aviation Week & Space Technology* 131:20-1 Ag 21 '89
Left in space [cover story] I. Amato. il *Science News* 136:314-15 N 11 '89
NASA racing the sun to save a satellite. R. A. Kerr. il *Science* 244:1443 Je 23 '89
SDI urges NASA to accelerate satellite retrieval with shuttle. C. Covault. il *Aviation Week & Space Technology* 130:80-1 My 8 '89
Shuttle Columbia poised to retrieve LDEF satellite, deploy Navy Syncom. C. Covault. il *Aviation Week & Space Technology* 131:35-6 D 11 '89
LONG ISLAND (N.Y.)
See also
Agriculture—Long Island (N.Y.)
Architecture, Domestic—Long Island (N.Y.)
Beaches—Long Island (N.Y.)
Country estates—Long Island (N.Y.)
Flower gardens and gardening—Long Island (N.Y.)
Gardens and gardening—Long Island (N.Y.)
Gardiners Island (N.Y.)
Historic houses, sites, etc.—Long Island (N.Y.)
Insects—Long Island (N.Y.)
Wetlands—Long Island (N.Y.)
Climate
Haze and hurricanes, tanning and thunderstorms. T. Schlatter. *Weatherwise* 42:218 Ag '89

Description and travel
Island hopping with Debbie Gibson. il por *Rolling Stone* p17 Jl 13-27 '89
Industries
See also
Wine industry
Social life and customs
Budd Schulberg in Great Gatsby land [Hamptons] A. Fotheringham. il *Maclean's* 102:56 Ag 28 '89
Anecdotes, facetiae, satire, etc.
Next summer, I'll be married [house sharing in the Hamptons] P. Mehlman. il *The New York Times Magazine* p44+ My 21 '89
A summer place [taking a summer share in the Hamptons] M. McCully. il *Gentlemen's Quarterly* 59:143-4+ Je '89
LONG ISLAND CITY FINANCIAL
Hidden values for 1989. B. D. Fromson. il *Fortune* 119:28 Ja 2 '89
LONG MARCH, 1934-1935
The Long March to revolution. L. Eskin. il por *Scholastic Update (Teachers' edition)* 121:21 My 5 '89
LONG-NOSED BATS See Bats
LONG RANGE NAVIGATION See Loran
LONG TERM CARE INSURANCE See Insurance, Nursing home care
LONG-TERM POTENTIATION See Electrophysiology
LONGEVITY
See also
Aging
Centenarians
Pritikin Longevity Centers
Catchers die young, infielders live longest [research by John Waterbor] S. McKee. il *American Health* 8:18 Ap '89
Health secrets of the long-lived Japanese. R. Rodale. il *Prevention (Emmaus, Pa.)* 41:30+ N '89
Heaven can wait, but for how long? *U.S. News & World Report* 107:9-10 Ag 7 '89
How to live to be 100. J. Karras. *Better Homes and Gardens* 67:36-7+ S '89
Lefties and longevity: look again [disagreement between Stanley Coren and Max Anderson] R. Weiss. *Science News* 136:180 S 16 '89
The life expectancy gap widens for blacks, whites. il *Jet* 76:37 Ap 10 '89
Longevity blooms with younger grooms [research by Laurel Klinger-Vartabedian] J. Davidson. *Psychology Today* 23:72 D '89
The longevity gap [men and women] E. Berlow. il *New Choices for the Best Years* 29:10 N '89
Ommm . . . please pass the DHEAS [effects of transcendental meditation upon levels of dehydroepiandrosterone] J. Hooper. il *Health (New York, N.Y.)* 21:34 O '89
Psychologist Stanley Coren's bad news comes out of left field—lefties lead riskier, shorter lives [interview] D. K. Bacon. il por *People Weekly* 32:115-16+ N 6 '89
Sinister stats [shorter life expectancy for lefties; study by Diane F. Halpern and Stanley Coren] T. Waters. il *Discover* 10:26 Ap '89
Survivors' exercise guide (revised ed.) [study by the Institute for Aerobics Research] il *U.S. News & World Report* 107:18+ N 13 '89
Take a walk—and live [mild exercise can postpone death; research by the Institute for Aerobics Research] M. D. Lemonick. il *Time* 134:90 N 13 '89
To live longer, take a walk [benefits of moderate exercise; study by the Institute of Aerobics Research] C. Leerhsen. il *Newsweek* 114:77 N 13 '89
When death does us part: the difference between widows and widowers [study by Ken R. Smith] M. M. Breecher. *Psychology Today* 23:14 N '89
Who lives longer? P. Skalka. *McCall's* 116:91+ Ag '89
LONGFELLOW, HENRY WADSWORTH, 1807-1882
about
Longfellow's lovers. W. Schemmel. *Travel Holiday* 171:45 F '89
LONGITUDE
The longitude of Jupiter's central meridian [computer program] R. W. Sinnott. il *Sky and Telescope* 78:640-1 D '89
LONGMAN, PHILLIP
Catastrophic follies. *The New Republic* 201:16-18 Ag 21 '89
LONGMAN GROUP LTD.
Rix to retire as Longman plans further global expansion. V. Menkes. *Publishers Weekly* 236:336 Ag 11 '89
LONGO, ROBERT
about
Bravo Longo [interview] M. Glicksman. il por *Film Comment* 25:42-4+ Mr/Ap '89
Mondo Longo. C. Lewis. il *Art in America* 77:35+ Mr '89
Pop provocateur. H. Drohojowska. il *Harper's Bazaar* 122:222 S '89
Riding the apocalypse. J. Kroll. *Newsweek* 114:80 O 23 '89
Robert Longo: Metro Pictures. J. Sturman. il *Art News* 88:132 Ja '89
What makes Longo run? P. Plagens. il *Newsweek* 114:80 O 23 '89

LONGO, TONY
about
Tony Longo: Madonna's new boy toy. L. Morice. il por *Mademoiselle* 95:40 Ja '89
LONGO TOYOTA (FIRM)
"I never learned anything from another car dealer except what to do wrong". M. Beauchamp. il *Forbes* 143:148+ Je 26 '89
LONGSHORE WORKERS
See also
Strikes—Longshore workers
Health and hygiene
Disabling injuries in longshore operations. A. Lettman. il *Monthly Labor Review* 112:37-8 O '89
LONGSHOREMEN *See* Longshore workers
LONGUEVILLE, BERTRAND DU GUESCLIN, COMTE DE *See* Du Guesclin, Bertrand, comte de Longueville, ca. 1320-1380
LOOK WHO'S TALKING [film] *See* Motion picture reviews—Single works
LOOM (VIDEO GAME)
New game interfaces feel more real. O. S. Card. il *Compute!* 11:104 O '89
LOOMIS, KRISTIN
AIDS: the numbers game. il map *New York* 22:44-9 Mr 6 '89
LOOMIS, SUSAN HERRMANN
Basque in it. il *The New York Times Magazine* p83-4 N 26 '89
Beyond the burrito. il *The New York Times Magazine* p47-8 S 3 '89
Golden gates. il *The New York Times Magazine* p49-50 F 12 '89
Pacific Provençal: a food pro at home. il pors *Working Woman* 14:112-16 Mr '89
Prize catch [excerpts from The great American seafood cookbook] il *Ladies' Home Journal* 106:166-8+ Ap '89
Winter warmth. il *The New York Times Magazine* p35-6 Ja 15 '89
LOOMIS SAYLES & CO. INC.
Companies even better than they look [interview with K. Heebner] P. Sellers. il por *Fortune* 120:28-9 Ag 14 '89
LOON MOUNTAIN (N.H.: RESORT) *See* Resorts—New Hampshire
LOONEY, DOUGLAS S.
The ax falls at Toledo. il por *Sports Illustrated* 71:32-3 D 25 '89-Ja 1 '90
Beating the devil. il por *Sports Illustrated* 70:34+ Ap 10 '89
The best just became better. il por *Sports Illustrated* 71:53 Jl 3 '89
Boy, oh boy, what a year! il pors *Sports Illustrated* 71:76-80+ D 25 '89-Ja 1 '90
Bring back Bonnie. il pors *Sports Illustrated* 70:32-3 Mr 6 '89
A Cardinal virtue. il pors *Sports Illustrated* 71:94-6 N 20 '89
Futility U. il *Sports Illustrated* 71:82-5+ S 4 '89
Ho hum, it's Harvard. il *Sports Illustrated* 70:64 Je 26 '89
Life in the slow lane. il por *Sports Illustrated* 70:92 My 1 '89
The luck of the Irish. il *Sports Illustrated* 71:36-9 O 30 '89
Mite makes right. il pors *Sports Illustrated* 70:38-9 Mr 27 '89
A most unusual man. il pors *Sports Illustrated* 71:118-24+ S 4 '89
On the road again. il pors *Sports Illustrated* 70:52-6+ F 20 '89
On top of the world. il pors *Sports Illustrated* 71:54-6+ O 16 '89
Paddling the straight and narrow. il pors *Sports Illustrated* 70:56+ Je 19 '89
The pearls of Paulina. il pors *Sports Illustrated* 70 Special Issue:191+ F '89
A run for the Roses. il *Sports Illustrated* 71:34-5 N 20 '89
Shake-up in Title Town. il *Sports Illustrated* 71:34-7 Ag 28 '89
These Reds look Rosy. il *Sports Illustrated* 70:42-3 Je 5 '89
Whole lot of Carays going on. il *Sports Illustrated* 71:87 Ag 14 '89
LOONIES (COINS) *See* Coins
LOONS
The common loon cries for help [cover story] J. McIntyre. il map *National Geographic* 175:510-24 Ap '89
Its ponds may not always be golden, but the loon still sings a wild song. S. Hubbell. il *Smithsonian* 19:58-67 Mr '89
LOOPERS *See* Inchworms
LOOPERS, CABBAGE *See* Cabbage loopers
LOOPHOLES, TAX *See* Taxation, Exemption from
LOOS, MARY ANITA
A celebration of Mexican tastes. il *Gourmet* 49:124-5+ N '89

LOOS, RYLAND
A view from Marcy. il *The Conservationist* 43:20-3 My/Je '89
LOOSFELT, HUGUES, AND OTHERS
Cloning and sequencing of porcine LH-hCG receptor cDNA: variants lacking transmembrane domain. bibl f il *Science* 245:525-8 Ag 4 '89
LOOTING *See* Pillage
LOPAPA, ALBERTO F.
about
At this medical lab, only the bills were real. P. Dwyer. *Business Week* p38 O 16 '89
LOPES, JOSE LUIS FERNANDES *See* Fernandes Lopes, Jose Luis
LOPES, ROSALY
Is an astronomy degree useful? il *Sky and Telescope* 78:236 S '89
LOPEZ, BARRY HOLSTUN, 1945-
Mapping the real geography. *Harper's* 279:19-21+ N '89
Our frail planet in cold, clear view [cover story] il *Harper's* 278:43-9 My '89
about
Barry Lopez finds a new home at Knopf. por *Publishers Weekly* 235:30-1 Je 23 '89
LOPEZ, JANE FORD
Poinsettia and the men in her life. il *Flower and Garden* 33:41-2 N/D '89
LOPEZ, NANCY, 1957-
about
Getting really mad and good. G. Sweda. il por *Sports Illustrated* 70:65 My 29 '89
LOPOKOV, FYODOR VASILIEVICH *See* Lopukhov, Fyodor Vasilievich, 1887?-1973
LOPRESTO, JAMES CHARLES
Looking inside the sun. il *Astronomy* 17:20-30 Mr '89
LOPUKHOV, FYODOR VASILIEVICH, 1887?-1973
about
From St. Petersburg to Leningrad: Lopukhov's legacy. N. Alovert. il pors *Dance Magazine* 63:42-6 Mr '89
LOQUASTO, SANTO, 1944-
about
Paul Taylor, Santo Loquasto and Speaking in tongues: the right mix. N. V. Dalva. il *Dance Magazine* 63:36-8 Ap '89
LORAL CORP.
GAO advises Air Force to cancel Loral's advanced radar warning receiver contract [allegations of illegally receiving information about competing Litton system] *Aviation Week & Space Technology* 130:23 My 22 '89
Litton gets share of ALR-56M program in Ill Wind plea agreement by Loral. D. F. Bond. *Aviation Week & Space Technology* 131:115 D 18-25 '89
Litton protest raises questions about new Loral operation [USAF award for F-16 radar warning receivers] P. J. Klass. *Aviation Week & Space Technology* 130:57 F 6 '89
Loral to produce advanced radar warning systems for USAF. *Aviation Week & Space Technology* 130:34 Ja 2 '89
More capable IR-guided weapons prompting improved jammers, decoys. il *Aviation Week & Space Technology* 131:50+ S 11 '89
Operation Ill Wind whips through Loral. M. D. Oneal. il *Business Week* p68 Je 12 '89
USAF urges GAO to reconsider criticism of Loral contract award [Litton protest of contract] B. W. Henderson. *Aviation Week & Space Technology* 130:31 Je 5 '89
LORAN
Gap sealer [mid-continent gap in Loran C signal coverage to be closed by 1990] *Flying* 116:18 My '89
KLN 88: every inch a King. F. George. il *Flying* 116:30 O '89
Loran to go [Azure Locator] J. M. McClellan. il *Flying* 116:38-9 Je '89
Lorans of II Morrow. J. M. McClellan. il *Flying* 116:25 Mr '89
Motion pictures [Argus 5000 moving map] N. Moll. il *Flying* 116:66-7 Ja '89
Multichain Loran C on the horizon. F. George. *Flying* 116:100 S '89
Riding radio waves to your fish. J. Gibbs. il *Outdoor Life* 184:66-7+ Ag '89
Sophisticated navigators [Arnav Lorans] J. M. McClellan. il *Flying* 116:28 Ap '89
STS 120MC Loran. J. M. McClellan. il *Flying* 116:22+ F '89
Super Bandit: it's a steal [II Morrow Apollo 618] J. M. McClellan. il *Flying* 116:96+ S '89
LORANCE, PATRICIA
about
One step forward, two steps back. P. Simpson. il por *Ms.* 18:96 S '89
LORCH, DONATELLA
Target: Kabul. il pors map *The New York Times Magazine* p32-5+ F 12 '89
LORD, BETTE BAO
These people have no fear. il *Newsweek* 113:29 My 29 '89
'Warn Americans not to be fooled'. il *Newsweek* 113:28 Je 12 '89

LORD, ELIZABETH M.
(jt. auth) See Sanders, L. C., and Lord, Elizabeth M.
LORD, RICHARD
about
Fulton Fish Market and Urban Archaeology Ltd. H. Bridges. il *Gourmet* 49:36+ Mr '89
LORD, WINSTON
China and America: beyond the big chill. *Foreign Affairs* 68:1-26 Fall '89
The view from the Forbidden City. il por *Newsweek* 114:36 D 18 '89
LORD AUCH See Bataille, Georges, 1897-1962
LORDS, TRACI
about
Lord's prayer. R. J. Smith. il por *Film Comment* 25:2+ Jl/Ag '89
LORD'S DAY See Sunday
LORD'S SUPPER
'You prepare a table for me'. K. Koyama. il *The Christian Century* 106:379 Ap 12 '89
L'OREAL SA
Beauty at a fair price [B. Dautresme] il pors *Harper's Bazaar* 122:192-3+ Mr '89
LOREN, ALLAN Z.
about
Allan Loren. M. Shao. il por *Business Week* Special Issue:158 Ap 14 '89
LOREN, SOPHIA, 1934-
about
Sophia Loren: the private woman. M. F. Shyer. il pors *McCall's* 116:36-7+ My '89
LORENTZ, FRANCIS
about
A new CEO is taking Bull by the horns. T. Peterson. il por *Business Week* p80 Jl 17 '89
LORENZ, EDWARD
about
Franklin Institute honors Lorenz, Oatley and Madey. M. Siegel. pors *Physics Today* 42:113 S '89
LORENZ, KONRAD
about
Obituary
U.S. News & World Report il por 106:13 Mr 13 '89
LORENZO, FRANCISCO A.
about
Advantage, Lorenzo. G. DeGeorge and S. Payne. il por *Business Week* p24-6 Jl 10 '89
Air sickness. H. Fairlie. *The New Republic* 200:14-16+ Je 5 '89
Back to you, Frank. A. Bernstein and C. Power. il pors *Business Week* p24-6 Ap 24 '89
A boss they love to hate. J. Schwartz. il por *Newsweek* 113:20-4 Mr 20 '89
Creditors pose key threat to Eastern revival effort. J. T. McKenna. *Aviation Week & Space Technology* 130:106-7 Ap 24 '89
Eastern: does anybody win? W. Woods. il por *Fortune* 119:14 Ap 10 '89
Eastern goes bust. J. Castro. il por *Time* 133:52-3 Mr 20 '89
Eastern unions losing bid to unseat Lorenzo. J. T. McKenna. il *Aviation Week & Space Technology* 130:108-9 My 29 '89
GAO will review Ritchie, Lorenzo plans for Eastern. J. T. McKenna. *Aviation Week & Space Technology* 131:100-1 Jl 31 '89
Judge threatens to auction Eastern after buyout fails. J. T. McKenna and E. H. Kolcum. *Aviation Week & Space Technology* 130:60-1 Ap 17 '89
Lorenzo is running out of choices—and time. P. Engardio and G. DeGeorge. il *Business Week* p37-8 Mr 20 '89
Lorenzo weighs selling stake in Continental. *Aviation Week & Space Technology* 131:69-70 S 4 '89
Suicide pact at Eastern Air Lines [with interview] T. Moore and C. P. Work. il por *U.S. News & World Report* 106:18-21 Mr 20 '89
Texas Air: empire in jeopardy [special section] il por *Business Week* p28-31 Mr 27 '89
LORENZO, FRANK See Lorenzo, Francisco A.
LORETTO, JUDITH
A Native American CDA: my personal story. il pors *Children Today* 18:26-7 Mr/Ap '89
LORGE, BARRY
Grand Slam: only the strong survive. il *Sports Illustrated* 70:55-6+ Je 5 '89
LORING, DAGMAR
Reverend father. *The Humanist* 49:21-3+ Jl/Ag '89
LOROS, JENNIFER J., AND OTHERS
Molecular cloning of genes under control of the circadian clock in Neurospora. bibl f il *Science* 243:385-8 Ja 20 '89
LOS ALAMOS [opera] See Neikrug, Marc
LOS ALAMOS NATIONAL LABORATORY
The hidden files [1946 accident; cover story] C. T. Honicker. il *The New York Times Magazine* p38-41+ N 19 '89
Los Alamos expands research focus, explores hypersonic flight issues. il *Aviation Week & Space Technology* 130:20-1 F 27 '89

Los Alamos free electron laser altered for higher-power tests. T. M. Foley. il *Aviation Week & Space Technology* 130:88-9 F 13 '89
LOS ALAMOS SCIENTIFIC LABORATORY
See also
Los Alamos National Laboratory
LOS ANGELES (CALIF.)
Air pollution
Blueprint for clear skies. M. Cone. il *Sierra* 74:16+ Jl/Ag '89
Clean air? Don't hold your breath. E. Marshall. il *Science* 244:517-20 My 5 '89
A drastic plan to banish smog. P. Elmer-Dewitt. il *Time* 133:65 Mr 27 '89
Getting a clearer view of smog [supercomputer pollution model developed by G. J. McRae] M. Schroeder. il por *Business Week* Special Issue:73 Je 16 '89
L.A. fights for breath [cover story] A. Weisman. il *The New York Times Magazine* p14-17+ Jl 30 '89
"Moderately radical". M. Beauchamp. il por *Forbes* 143:148 My 15 '89
To live and breathe in L.A. J. E. Basu. il maps *American Health* 8:52-4+ S '89
Why no one's safe [effects of smog on residents] J. E. Basu. maps *American Health* 8:64 S '89
Airports
A sense of place [Terminal 5, Delta Air Lines] M. Gaskie. il *Architectural Record* 177:134-7 Je '89
Anecdotes, facetiae, satire, etc.
Smart money. D. Blum. il *New York* 22:42 D 4 '89
Architecture
40 years old, it's a "classic modern" [Case Study program exhibition at the Museum of Contemporary Art, Los Angeles] il *Sunset (Central West edition)* 183:224 O '89
California modern [work of F. D. Israel] P. Viladas. il pors *House & Garden* 161:28+ Je '89
Ranch house remodeled into a "village". il *Sunset (Central West edition)* 183:100 O '89
With due respect [work of F. D. Israel; cover story] D. Dietsch. il *Architectural Record* 177:66-73 Ap '89
Art
L.A.: outward bound. P. Clothier. il *Art News* 88:126-31 D '89
Smoggy euphoria. P. Clothier. il *Art News* 88:50+ My '89
Banks
See also
Far East National Bank
GBC Bancorp
City of Angels, indeed [laundering drug money] il *U.S. News & World Report* 106:14 Ap 10 '89
Blacks
See also
Watts (Los Angeles, Calif.)
Go west, young entrepreneur. S. L. Hilliard and J. Shiver. il *Black Enterprise* 19:112+ Je '89
Bookstores
See Booksellers and bookselling—California
Buildings
Mythic proportions [Los Angeles offices of Propaganda Films designed by Franklin Israel] il *Architectural Record* 177:68-71 Ap '89
Churches (Buildings)
See also
FaithDome (Los Angeles, Calif.)
City planning
Booming L.A.: brave new urbanism? A. Betsky. il *Architectural Record* 177:71+ F '89
Courts
While his father rules TV's People's court, judge Fred Wapner delivers real crooks to jail time. L. Armstrong. il pors *People Weekly* 32:139-40 D 18 '89
Crime
Bail is set at $2 mil. for Bridges; faces more charges [T. Bridges] por *Jet* 75:12 Mr 20 '89
Bridges held on attempted murder charge in L.A. por *Jet* 75:54 F 20 '89
Bridges' mother blames son's problems on drugs [T. Bridges] il por *Jet* 75:52 F 27 '89
Death among the innocent [gang related murders] A. Gregor. il *Maclean's* 102:38 My 22 '89
The devil and John Holmes: drugs, porn and the murders on Wonderland Avenue. M. Sager. il pors *Rolling Stone* p50-2+ Je 15 '89
A fatal obsession with the stars [murder of actress R. Schaeffer and other incidents] A. Toufexis. il por *Time* 134:43-4 Jl 31 '89
His object a gentler L.A., a councilman buys up AK-47s [N. Holden's cash-for-guns scheme to combat crime] il por *People Weekly* 31:120 F 13 '89
An innocent life, a heartbreaking death [actress R. Schaeffer killed by obsessive fan] P. Axthelm. il por *People Weekly* 32:60-2+ Jl 31 '89
To deal and die in L.A. [drugs] A. Collier. il *Ebony* 44:106+ Ag '89
Todd Bridges tells how Hollywood destroyed his life and how God is rebuilding it. il pors *Jet* 76:28-30 Ap 10 '89

LOS ANGELES (CALIF.)—Crime—cont.
When you're a Crip (or a Blood) [discussion with L.A. gang members] *Harper's* 278:51-9 Mr '89

Dance
Pacific HIGHWAYS [alternative performance space for Los Angeles area dancers and artists] E. Zimmer. il *Dance Magazine* 63:52-3 S '89
Reviews:
> HIGHWAYS opening benefit, Santa Monica, Calif. *Dance Magazine* 63:86-7 N '89

Description
L.A. il *Esquire* 112:105+ Ag '89
Tone-Lōc: hanging with the homeboys. il por *Rolling Stone* p20 Jl 13-27 '89

Education
Jana Taylor gives new focus to the lives of inner-city kids [teaching photography] S. Schindehette. il pors *People Weekly* 31:126-7+ Ap 3 '89
L.A. law helps latchkey pupils; extends hours for after-school play. il *Jet* 75:38 Ja 16 '89
Miracle worker at Garfield High [calculus teacher J. Escalante; condensed from Escalante] J. Mathews. il pors *Reader's Digest* 134:165-70+ Ja '89
The new apple of teachers' eyes [teachers pushing for school-based management] il *U.S. News & World Report* 106:11 My 29 '89
Teaching kids how to grieve [program in Watts for children whose lives have been touched by murder] S. Doherty. il *Newsweek* 114:73 N 13 '89
Vote to continue programs for latchkey kids in L.A. il *Jet* 77:52 O 9 '89

Galleries and museums
See also
Gene Autry Western Heritage Museum
Los Angeles County Museum of Art
Museum of Neon Art (Los Angeles, Calif.)

Historic houses, sites, etc.
An agile aesthetic: dancer Barrie Chase's country cottage in Los Angeles. M. Frank. il por *Architectural Digest* 46:248-55+ O '89
Architectural digest visits: Jaclyn Smith and Tony Richmond [cover story] J. Giovannini. il pors *Architectural Digest* 46:180-5+ Ag '89
Architecture and music in Los Angeles [Chamber Music in Historic Sites program] M. Webb. il *Architectural Digest* 46:116+ My '89
Million-dollar "birthday cakes" [homes demolished in wealthy neighborhoods] N. R. Gibbs. il *Time* 133:79 My 1 '89
North of the border [K. Spiegelman's Bel-Air house] D. Michel. il *House & Garden* 161:92-5 F '89

Hospitals
See also
Cedars-Sinai Medical Center (Los Angeles, Calif.)
Kaiser Permanente Medical Center (Los Angeles, Calif.)

Hotels, motels, etc.
See also
Ambassador Hotel (Los Angeles, Calif.)
L.A. luxe. E. Paris. il *Forbes* 143:140-2 My 15 '89

Housing
"Can I get a bulldozer down the driveway?" [teardowns of houses] E. Paris. il *Forbes* 144 Special Issue:48-9+ O 23 '89
What do you expect for $2.25 million? D. K. Shah. il por *The New York Times Magazine* p54-6+ S 10 '89

Industries
Go west, young entrepreneur. S. L. Hilliard and J. Shiver. il *Black Enterprise* 19:112+ Je '89
L.A. goes Hispanic [TV stations] K. Beck. il *Channels (New York, N.Y.: 1986)* 9:22+ Je '89

Intellectual life
Anecdotes, facetiae, satire, etc.
Makeovers of the mind: L.A.'s new intellectuals [celebrities] D. Denicolo. il *Glamour* 87:164 Ag '89

Monuments, statues, etc.
A dying sculptor fights vandals over Myrna Loy [W. Van Orden restores statue outside Venice High School] il por *People Weekly* 31:111 My 29 '89

Motion picture theaters
Black theater gets new run [Baldwin Entertainment Complex] S. Herbert. *Black Enterprise* 20:18 Ag '89

Music
See also
Los Angeles Music Center Opera
Los Angeles Philharmonic Orchestra
Walt Disney Concert Hall (Los Angeles, Calif.)
Architecture and music in Los Angeles [Chamber Music in Historic Sites program] M. Webb. il *Architectural Digest* 46:116+ My '89
Making it in Metal Mecca [heavy metal rockers] J. Foote. il *Newsweek* 114:56-8 Ag 7 '89
Remo bash for cash [Drums in Concert fundraiser at UCLA] L. J. Scheuerell. *Down Beat* 56:11 D '89

Newspapers
See also
Los Angeles herald examiner
Los Angeles times

Police
The cop who cared too much [detective B. Grogan's work on Hillside Strangler case] G. Dillow. il por *TV Guide* 37:26-7 Ap 1-7 '89
"I like to get the bad guys" [detective C. Polak] W. Urbanska. il pors *McCall's* 116:134+ F '89
The priest who loves gangsters [mission for gang members run by G. J. Boyle; cover story] E. Shorris. il *The Nation* 249:737+ D 18 '89

Politics and government
Bradley: down and nearly out? E. Schine. *Business Week* p29 Ag 7 '89
Hard times for Teflon Tom. E. M. Reingold. por *Time* 133:35 My 22 '89
How to make boring beautiful. M. B. Carlson. il *Time* 133:20 Ap 24 '89
L.A.'s teflon mayor [T. Bradley] M. Reese. il por *Newsweek* 113:33 Ap 10 '89
Letter from Los Angeles [T. Bradley's re-election] J. Didion. *The New Yorker* 65:88+ Ap 24 '89
Tom Bradley wins an unprecedented fifth term as mayor of L.A. il por *Jet* 76:4 My 1 '89
Where Angelenos fear to tread [proposed ethics code for city officials] S. Tifft. *Time* 134:70-1 D 4 '89

Popular culture
L.A. international. B. Bull. il *Vogue* 179:332-5 F '89

Population
Undertow: LA copes with the flood of Soviet émigrés. E. Schrader. *The New Republic* 201:11-12 D 4 '89

Public welfare
Undertow: LA copes with the flood of Soviet émigrés. E. Schrader. *The New Republic* 201:11-12 D 4 '89

Religious institutions and affairs
See also
Crenshaw Christian Center
A: The Jeopardy! priest; Q: Who is Tom Smolich? Correct for $39,802! [Jesuit raises money for day care center in East Los Angeles, Calif.] il pors *People Weekly* 32:58 O 9 '89
The priest who loves gangsters [mission for gang members run by G. J. Boyle; cover story] E. Shorris. il *The Nation* 249:737+ D 18 '89

Anecdotes, facetiae, satire, etc.
The ultimate church [cover story] T. Raabe. *The Christian Century* 106:717-21 Ag 2-9 '89

Restaurants, nightclubs, bars, etc.
Across the river and into Harry's Bar [International Imitation Hemingway Competition; excerpt from The best of bad Hemingway] G. Plimpton. *The New York Times Book Review* 94:1+ Ap 16 '89
Bright chefs, big City [recipes of M. Milliken and S. Feniger, owners of City] S. Carlton. il pors *Health (New York, N.Y.)* 21:78-81 F '89
California steamin' [Campanile and Patina] D. Shaw. il *Gentlemen's Quarterly* 59:190+ D '89
Out with the stars. L. Gubernick. il *Forbes* 143:141 My 15 '89
Spécialités de la maison:
> Gardens, Rangoon Racquet Club, Yanks. C. Bates. il *Gourmet* 49:48+ Ap '89
> Tulipe, Al Amir. C. Bates. il *Gourmet* 49:40+ N '89
To live and dine in L.A. [Rex, Pazzia and Fennel] D. Shaw. il por *Gentlemen's Quarterly* 59:161+ Ap '89
Twilite glow [injurious effects of laser show at Twilite Club] il *FDA Consumer* 23:34 N '89

Savings and loan associations
See also
Family Savings & Loan Association (Los Angeles, Calif.)
Founders Savings & Loan Association

Schools
See Los Angeles (Calif.)—Education

Social conditions
The Basin runneth over. G. F. Will. il *Newsweek* 113:80 Ja 30 '89
Falling out of love with L.A. P. Farrelly. por *Newsweek* 114:8 S 25 '89

Social life and customs
A long way from the Rue de la Paix [culture shock experienced by journalist transferred to Los Angeles from Paris] J. Bonfante. il *Time* 133:70 Je 19 '89
Moving from the East to the West, as Claire Scovell found out, doesn't just mean a change of climate. C. Scovell. il *Vogue* 179:162-4 Ag '89
On the West Coast, fitness has moved beyond the pursuit of the perfect body. H. Hansen. il *Vogue* 179:166+ Ag '89

Anecdotes, facetiae, satire, etc.
The Los Angeles man. C. Scovell. il *Gentlemen's Quarterly* 59:139-40 Ag '89

Social work
See also
Parents of Watts (Organization)

Sports
Los Angeles [special section] il *Sport (New York, N.Y.)* 80:22-6+ Ja '89

Stores
See also
Ecru (Firm)

LOS ANGELES (CALIF.)—Stores—cont.
L.A. spreeway. B. Goodwin. il *Vogue* 179:112+ F '89
Street traffic
See also
Los Angeles (Calif.)—Traffic regulations
You can't tell the players without a program. J. Miller.
il *Motor Trend* 41:135 F '89
Traffic regulations
Some L.A. law-breakers claim Steve Verret's stand-up comedy
traffic class is just the ticket [World Famous Improvisation
Traffic School] T. Allis. il pors *People Weekly* 31:117-18
Je 19 '89
Water supply
A deal that might save a Sierra gem [Mono Lake] R. Conniff.
il *Time* 133:8+ Ap 3 '89
Youth
L.A. international. B. Bull. il *Vogue* 179:332-5 F '89
Arleta
See Arleta (Los Angeles, Calif.)
Brentwood
See Brentwood (Los Angeles, Calif.)
Century City
See Century City (Los Angeles, Calif.)
Pacific Palisades
See Pacific Palisades (Los Angeles, Calif.)
Watts
See Watts (Los Angeles, Calif.)
LOS ANGELES COMPUTER AIDED DESIGN RESEARCH,
INC. *See* Lacadre, Inc.
LOS ANGELES COUNTY (CALIF.)
Police
A private Mod Squad sets out to prove police harassment—
and stirs a fight over its tactics [Jackson Lynn Travers
detective agency] G. Stone. il *People Weekly* 32:83-4+
D 11 '89
LOS ANGELES COUNTY MUSEUM OF ART
LACMA revisited. H. Drohojowska. il por *Architectural Digest*
46:172+ My '89
LOS ANGELES COUNTY MUSEUM OF ART. PAVILION
FOR JAPANESE ART
The delirious palace [designed by B. Goff] B. Adams. il
Art in America 77:136-45 D '89
LOS ANGELES HERALD EXAMINER
Final edition. il *Time* 134:77 N 13 '89
Los Angeles herald examiner, R.I.P. il *Newsweek* 114:74
N 13 '89
LOS ANGELES INTERNATIONAL AIRPORT *See* Los
Angeles (Calif.)—Airports
LOS ANGELES MARATHON *See* Marathon running
LOS ANGELES MUSIC CENTER OPERA
Ferocious parable [The rise and fall of the city of Mahagonny]
O. Friedrich. il *Time* 134:76 S 25 '89
Los Angeles. D. Perlmutter. il *Opera News* 54:62 D 9 '89
LOS ANGELES PHILHARMONIC ORCHESTRA
Now, a grab for new chairs [choosing successor to A. Previn]
M. Walsh. il pors *Time* 133:90-1 My 8 '89
LOS ANGELES TIMES
Los Angeles's changing times [publisher D. A. Laventhol]
M. Beck. il por *Newsweek* 114:65 S 11 '89
LOS ANGELES ZOO
Assignment: poster [fund raising poster] B. Hurter. il *Petersen's
Photographic Magazine* 17:24-7 Mr '89
LOS OLIVOS (CALIF.)
Restaurants, nightclubs, bars, etc.
Carving a new Thanksgiving tradition [work of L. Largent,
chef at the Grand Hotel] J. Rogers. il por *Prevention
(Emmaus, Pa.)* 41:67-71+ N '89
LOSH, J. MICHAEL
about
Teaching an Oldsmobile new tricks. J. B. Treece. il por
Business Week p52 S 25 '89
LOSING *See* Failure (Psychology)
LOSS DEDUCTIONS *See* Income tax—Loss deductions
LOSS OF CONSCIOUSNESS
See also
Coma
LOST AND FOUND ART *See* Art—Missing and found works
LOST ANGELS [film] *See* Motion picture reviews—Single
works
LOST ARROW INC.
The man is the message [Y. Chouinard] F. Meeks. il por
Forbes 143:148+ Ap 17 '89
LOST CHILDREN *See* Missing children
LOST JEWELRY
See also
Jewelry—Theft
LOST MONEY
See also
Found money
LOST PERSONS *See* Missing persons
LOST PETS
When pets stray. M. Behen. il *American Health* 8:102 My
'89
LOST WAX PROCESS
See also
Bronze founding

LOT (FRANCE)
Description and travel
The Lot. F. Sagan. il por *Architectural Digest* 46:22+ Ja
'89
LOTAN, ILANA, AND OTHERS
Specific block of calcium channel expression by a fragment
of dihydropyridine receptor cDNA. bibl f il *Science*
243:666-9 F 3 '89
LOTH, RENEE
Celebrating my change of life. il por *New Choices for the
Best Years* 29:16+ My '89
A conscientious objector. il por *New Choices for the Best
Years* 29:16+ S '89
LOTT, BRET
Another bad dream [story] il *Redbook* 173:60+ S '89
LOTT, GEORGE
The best ever [cover story] il pors *World Tennis* 36:25-8
F '89
LOTT, RONNIE, 1959-
about
Hitter with heart. J. Lieber. il pors *Sports Illustrated* 70:44-8
Ja 23 '89
LOTTERIES
Gamble for big game [lottery hunting permits] J. Zumbo.
il *Outdoor Life* 183:74-5+ Ja '89
The great cellular giveaway [rural cellular licenses] H. Rudnit-
sky. il *Forbes* 144:40-1 D 25 '89
How worthy are these causes? [charity sweepstakes] *Modern
Maturity* 32:12 F/Mr '89
In the grip of gambling [state lotteries] G. F. Will. il *Newsweek*
113:78 My 8 '89
The lottery plague. G. K. Brushaber. *Christianity Today*
33:15 S 8 '89
Lottomania. J. Cook. il *Forbes* 143:92-6 Mr 6 '89
A national lottery is not such a long shot. P. Magnusson.
il *Business Week* p57 Ap 10 '89
The phone flushaway [FCC lottery for distribution of cellular
telephone licenses] D. Ellen. *The New Republic* 201:13-15
O 9 '89
Playing the lottery is idolatry. T. Watson. por *Christianity
Today* 33:8 N 3 '89
The states like the odds. il *Time* 134:19 Jl 10 '89
This is what you thought: 87% approve of state-sponsored
lotteries [results of survey] *Glamour* 87:137 D '89
To keep the tax promise, try a lottery. A. Rabushka and
M. S. Bernstam. pors *Fortune* 119:126 F 27 '89
A touchdown for sports gambling [Oregon lottery to offer
pro football betting] *U.S. News & World Report* 107:11+
Jl 31 '89
Walter and the raffle [migrant workers send boss W. Jansen
to Puerto Rico] P. Kelly. *Reader's Digest* 134:26 Mr '89
Automation
Automating an ancient business [Gtech] J. Cook. il *Forbes*
143:52+ Ja 23 '89
Taxation
Higher 'sin' taxes: a low blow to the poor. G. S. Becker.
il *Business Week* p23 Je 5 '89
LOTTERY WINNERS
Black family wins $22 million in Illinois lottery [L. Pierce]
il pors *Jet* 76:24-6 Jl 31 '89
Black mechanic is among 14 Ohioans splitting 8.25 mil.
winning share in Pa. lottery [B. Shavers] il por *Jet* 76:6
My 15 '89
Calif. lottery moves to get back $3.4 mil. win by Los Angeles
woman [D. Barnett] por *Jet* 76:25 My 22 '89
Chicago couple wins $6 mil. in Illinois state lottery [R.
Anderson] il por *Jet* 76:10 S 25 '89
Los Angeles nurse finally named $3M lottery winner [D.
Barnett] il pors *Jet* 76:24 Ap 24 '89
Lotto winner tells why he will share $22 million prize with
his family [C. Gill] il pors *Jet* 77:16-17 D 11 '89
N.J. man finds his lotto fortune in cookie jar [N. Hazell]
il por *Jet* 77:27 N 13 '89
New ruling favors Barnett in Calif. lottery battle. por *Jet*
76:36 Je 26 '89
Nigerian student can afford family reunion after winning
$26 million in N.Y. lotto [A. B. Jombo] *Jet* 75:33 Ja
30 '89
Nursing assistant, 25, wins $37.4 million in Fla. lotto [G.
Mitchem] il por *Jet* 75:27 Mr 27 '89
LOTTMAN, HERBERT R.
International front. See occasional issues of Publishers Weekly
beginning May 27, 1983
LOTUS
The lotus. il *Flower and Garden* 33:46 My/Je '89
LOTUS (AUTOMOBILE) *See* Sports cars
LOTUS 1-2-3 (COMPUTER PROGRAM) *See* Spreadsheets
(Computer programs)
LOTUS DEVELOPMENT CORPORATION
Jim Manzi. K. H. Hammonds. il por *Business Week* Special
Issue:147 Ap 14 '89
Lotus at war [cover story; with editorial comment by Fred
Abatemarco] J. Schwartz. il *Personal Computing* 13:5, 70-5+
Je '89
The spreadsheet that nearly wore Lotus out [Release 3]
K. H. Hammonds. il por *Business Week* p62-4 Jl 3 '89
Toward a kinder, gentler Lotus. E. S. Ely. por *Personal
Computing* 13:73 Jl '89

LOTUS DEVELOPMENT CORPORATION—*cont.*
What not doing Windows costs Lotus. K. H. Hammonds. il *Business Week* p152 O 30 '89
LOU, RAY
Model minority? Getting behind the veil. il *Change* 21:16-17 N/D '89
LOUD, LANCE
An extra's tale. il por *American Film* 14:92 Ap '89
Famous and Andy. il *American Film* 15:80 D '89
LOUDSPEAKERS
How to buy speakers. I. Masters. il *Stereo Review* 54:100-4 S '89
The quest for speakers [cover story] D. Ranada. il *High Fidelity (New York, N.Y.)* 39:32-7+ Je '89
The speaker gap. K. C. Pohlmann. *Stereo Review* 54:24 O '89
Speakers. il *Stereo Review* 54:114-16+ F '89
Video sound solution: powered speakers. I. Berger. il *Video* 12:28-9 My '89
What's new in outdoor speakers? il *Sunset (Central West edition)* 183:76+ Ag '89

Design
Big sound, small boxes. C. P. Gilmore. il *Popular Science* 235:76-8 S '89
The black hole of bass [Phantom Acoustics Shadow] R. Hodges. il *Stereo Review* 54:136 My '89
Getting good sound the wireless way. I. Berger. il *Video* 13:24+ Jl '89
The impossible achieved? [tweeter designed by S. Klein] R. Hodges. il *Stereo Review* 54:136 Je '89
The making of an American speaker [JBL] I. Masters. il *Stereo Review* 54:75-81 Je '89
The Ohm/Walsh driver. R. Hodges. il *Stereo Review* 54:112 Ap '89
Speaker design. J. D. Hirsch. il *Stereo Review* 54:115-18+ N '89

History
The history and theory of the dynamic loudspeaker. L. Klein. il *Radio-Electronics* 60:70+ My '89

Maintenance and repair
Loudspeakers and things [antique radios] R. D. Fitch. il *Radio-Electronics* 60:91-2 F '89

Specifications
Reading speaker specs. D. Ranada. *High Fidelity (New York, N.Y.)* 39:37 Je '89

Testing
Advent Baby II loudspeaker. R. Long. il *High Fidelity (New York, N.Y.)* 39:33-5 Mr '89
Advent Prodigy Tower speaker system. J. D. Hirsch. il *Stereo Review* 54:47-8 My '89
Allison AL 120 speaker system. J. D. Hirsch. il *Stereo Review* 54:47-8 S '89
Altec Lansing Model 511 speaker system. J. D. Hirsch. il *Stereo Review* 54:84+ N '89
Audio Concepts G-2 loudspeaker. R. Long. il *High Fidelity (New York, N.Y.)* 39:39-40 Ap '89
B&W Matrix 3 Series 2 loudspeaker. R. Long. il *High Fidelity (New York, N.Y.)* 39:21+ Je '89
Bose 10.2 Series II speaker system. J. D. Hirsch. il *Stereo Review* 54:46+ F '89
Bose 401 loudspeaker. R. Long. il *High Fidelity (New York, N.Y.)* 39:30-1 Je '89
Celestion 3 speaker system. J. D. Hirsch. il *Stereo Review* 54:42+ Je '89
Celestion DL-8 Series Two loudspeaker. M. Riggs. il *High Fidelity (New York, N.Y.)* 39:50+ Ja '89
Design Acoustics PS-3 Micro-Monitor speaker system. J. D. Hirsch. il *Stereo Review* 54:69-70+ D '89
Epicure Model 1 speaker system. J. D. Hirsch. il *Stereo Review* 54:78+ O '89
Four more ears [Cambridge SoundWorks Ensemble speaker system] P. Schneider. il *Esquire* 111:54+ Mr '89
Goodmans Maxim 2 loudspeaker. M. Riggs. il *High Fidelity (New York, N.Y.)* 39:35-6 F '89
Jamo Concert II speaker. J. D. Hirsch. il *Stereo Review* 54:28-9 Jl '89
Loudspeakers: the make-or-break component. il *Consumer Reports* 54:166 Mr '89
Meridian D600 digital active speaker. J. D. Hirsch. il *Stereo Review* 54:108-12 S '89
Mission Cyrus 781 speaker system. J. D. Hirsch. il *Stereo Review* 54:53+ O '89
Mordaunt-Short MS-10 Series 2 loudspeaker. R. Long. il *High Fidelity (New York, N.Y.)* 39:44-5 Ja '89
Mordaunt-Short MS35Ti speaker system. J. D. Hirsch. il *Stereo Review* 54:62+ My '89
Ohm CAM-16 loudspeaker. R. Long. il *High Fidelity (New York, N.Y.)* 39:26+ Je '89
Ohm CAM 16 speaker. J. D. Hirsch. il *Stereo Review* 54:39-40 Ap '89
Paradigm Export Monitor speaker system. J. D. Hirsch. il *Stereo Review* 54:38+ Jl '89
Pioneer TZ-9 loudspeaker. D. Ranada. il *High Fidelity (New York, N.Y.)* 39:28-9 My '89
Polk's SDA Mobile Monitors [car speakers] B. C. Fishkind. il *High Fidelity (New York, N.Y.)* 39:16 Ap '89
Precise Monitor 3 loudspeaker. R. Long. il *High Fidelity (New York, N.Y.)* 39:24-6 Je '89

Precise Monitor 5 speaker system. J. D. Hirsch. il *Stereo Review* 54:39-40 Ag '89
Sight and sound: maverick speakers. H. Fantel. il *Opera News* 54:36-7 D 23 '89
Six-inch overachiever [Yamaha's AST-S1] R. Hodges. il *Stereo Review* 54:104 Jl '89
Small loudspeakers. il *Consumer Reports* 54:113-17 D '89
Speaker of the house [in-wall speakers] W. Berger. il *Stereo Review* 54:91-5 Mr '89
Subjective evaluations. J. D. Hirsch. il *Stereo Review* 54:42 Ja '89
Thiel CS1.2 speaker system. J. D. Hirsch. il *Stereo Review* 54:53-4 Ja '89
Wharfedale Diamond III speaker system. J. D. Hirsch. il *Stereo Review* 54:43-4 Mr '89
Yamaha NS-1 speaker. J. D. Hirsch. il *Stereo Review* 54:39-40 F '89

LOUGHEED, PETER, 1928-
about
The most influential corporate director. P. C. Newman. il *Maclean's* 102:53 S 18 '89
LOUIE, ELAINE
Bloom service deluxe. il por *Harper's Bazaar* 122:134+ Je '89
LOUIS XVI, KING OF FRANCE, 1754-1793
about
Patrick Brunet, whose ancestor guillotined Louis XVI, swears he's no chip off the old block. T. Allis. il pors *People Weekly* 31:128+ Je 5 '89
Thomas Paine: the antimonarchist who tried to save a king [excerpt from L'Américain de la Convention] J. Lessay. por *The Unesco Courier* 42:18 Je '89
LOUIS, FATHER *See* Merton, Thomas, 1915-1968
LOUIS, ERROL T.
Jazz makes a new sound with soul, pop and computers. bibl (p230) il *Smithsonian* 20:176-8+ O '89
LOUIS, JOE, 1914-1981
about
Illinois golf course to bear name of Joe Louis. il *Jet* 76:51 S 11 '89
Three who made history: Cobb, Louis and Howe. J. Lapointe. il pors *Sport (New York, N.Y.)* 80:60 My '89
LOUIS, MURRAY
On then & now. See issues of Dance Magazine beginning October 1989
about
Nikolais and Louis discuss their future together. R. Johnson. pors *Dance Magazine* 63:17 O '89
LOUIS-DREYFUS, ROBERT
about
Saatchi says this change is for real. R. A. Melcher. il por *Business Week* p50 O 30 '89
Sibling setbacks. J. Castro. il *Time* 134:66-7 D 25 '89
LOUIS VUITTON (FIRM)
See also
LVMH Moët Hennessy Louis Vuitton
LOUISE, TINA, 1934-
about
Tina Louise. il pors *Redbook* 172:87 Ja '89
LOUISIANA
See also
Architecture, Domestic—Louisiana
Avery Island (La.)
Colleges and universities—Louisiana
Criminal justice, Administration of—Louisiana
Festivals—Louisiana
Game laws—Louisiana
Geology—Louisiana
Jefferson Parish (La.)
Kisatchie National Forest (La.)
Law—Louisiana
Music festivals—Louisiana
Plantations—Louisiana
Taxation—Louisiana
Wetlands—Louisiana

History
Stripper Blaze Starr recalls her affair with the governor [E. Long]; ed. by Margie Bonnett Sellinger. B. Starr. il pors *People Weekly* 32:157+ D 18 '89
See also
Shellfish culture

Industries
See also
Shellfish culture

Legislature
Hate gets a haircut [Representative D. Duke] L. K. Truscott. il pors map *Esquire* 112:174-6+ N '89
Republican racist [D. Duke] L. Cohler. *The New Republic* 201:11-14 S 18-25 '89

Politics and government
See also
Louisiana—Legislature
Bad times on the bayou. W. King. il *The New York Times Magazine* p56-9+ Je 11 '89
Duke shows his true colors [D. Duke to run for the Senate] B. Turque. il por *Newsweek* 114:53 D 25 '89
St. Buddy [B. Roemer] M. Lewis. il *The New Republic* 200:16+ Mr 20 '89

LOUISIANA—cont.
Social conditions
Bad times on the bayou. W. King. il *The New York Times Magazine* p56-9+ Je 11 '89
LOUISIANA NATURE AND SCIENCE CENTER
Getting back to nature. il *Southern Living* 24:27 My '89
LOUISIANA-PACIFIC CORP.
Louisiana-Pacific's acres of assets. G. G. Marcial. *Business Week* p79 Ap 10 '89
LOUISIANA STATE UNIVERSITY, BATON ROUGE. RURAL LIFE MUSEUM AND BURDEN RESEARCH PLANTATION See LSU Rural Life Museum and Burden Research Plantation
LOUISVILLE (COLO.)
Bookstores
See Booksellers and bookselling—Colorado
LOUISVILLE (KY.)
Crime
'I told them I'd be back' [J. T. Wesbecker's murder spree] J. N. Baker. il *Newsweek* 114:22 S 25 '89
The shots heard 'round the Congress [J. T. Wesbecker's murder spree with AK-47] il *U.S. News & World Report* 107:15 S 25 '89
Theater
See also
Actors Theater of Louisville
LOUISVILLE BALLET
Louisville puts Shakers into an apt setting. G. R. Hubbard. il *Dance Magazine* 63:10-11 Mr '89
Reviews:
Performances at Kentucky Center for the Arts. G. R. Hubbard. *Dance Magazine* 63:90-2 Mr '89
LOUNASMAA, OLLI V.
Nuclear magnetic ordering at nanokelvin temperatures. bibl f il *Physics Today* 42:26-33 O '89
(jt. auth) See Hari, Riitta, and Lounasmaa, Olli V.
LOURDEAUX, LEE
American Dance Festival. il *Dance Magazine* 63:74-6 D '89
LOURENÇO, EDUARDO
The Lusiads: from national epic to universal myth. il *The Courier (Unesco)* 42:26-7 Ap '89
LOURIE, RICHARD, 1940-
Gulag capitalism. *The New Republic* 201:18-19 O 16 '89
LOURIE, RICHARD, 1940-, AND MIKHALEV, ALEKSEI
Why you'll never have fun in Russian. *The New York Times Book Review* 94:1+ Je 18 '89
LOUVERS
New products [automated louvers] il *Architectural Record* 177:112 S '89
LOUVRE MUSEUM See Musée du Louvre
LOVE, BEN F., 1924-
about
It's back to square 2 for Texas Commerce. M. Ivey. il por *Business Week* p125-6 Jl 17 '89
LOVE, BOB
Inside stuttering basketball star Bob Love was an intelligent man struggling to be understood; ed. by Priscilla Turner. il pors *People Weekly* 31:111 Ap 3 '89
about
The second time around. R. Fimrite. il pors *Sports Illustrated* 70:110-14+ Ja 9 '89
LOVE, HOWARD M.
about
Last chance for Love? G. L. Miles. *Business Week* p31-2 Ap 24 '89
National Intergroup: how Pete Love went wrong. G. L. Miles. il pors *Business Week* p56-7+ Mr 6 '89
LOVE
See also
Affection
Crushes (Emotions)
Erotomania
Romance
10 ways to keep love alive. il *Ebony* 44:116+ Mr '89
The dialectic of marriage [love-centered marriage] I. Sarnoff and S. Sarnoff. il *Psychology Today* 23:54-7 O '89
A fine romance [special section] il *Harper's Bazaar* 122:200-1+ Ap '89
Good love. S. L. Taylor. il *Essence* 19:51 F '89
Healthy love [excerpt from Lifemates; ed. by Robert B. Kory. H. H. Bloomfield and S. Vettese. il *Health (New York, N.Y.)* 21:24+ F '89
It's a love story. K. J. Gergen and M. M. Gergen. *Psychology Today* 22:48-9 D '88
Love gone loco: when breakups go too far! E. Karlsberg. il *Teen* 33:36-7+ F '89
Love moments. il *Glamour* 87:202-5 F '89
Love proverbs are universal, says an expert—and like love itself, they can bite [compiler W. Meider] il por *People Weekly* 31:112-13 F 20 '89
Lovestruck: reigniting an old romance. G. D. Moore. il por *Ms.* 17:45-9 My '89
A midsummer night's dream: the sequel. P. Iyer. il *Time* 134:66 Ag 7 '89
'My first love' [black celebrities] L. B. Randolph. il *Ebony* 44:144+ F '89

New Age loving [cover story] P. Johnson. il *Essence* 19:65-6+ F '89
Shower your kids with love [excerpt from 101 ways to tell your child "I love you"] V. Lansky. il *Redbook* 172:28+ F '89
That crazy little thing called love. G. Schwartz. il *Seventeen* 48:48 F '89
What love really means. B. Plain. *Reader's Digest* 134:62-4 F '89
What men really mean when they say "I love you". il *Glamour* 87:182-3+ F '89
Anecdotes, facetiae, satire, etc.
Can this be love? B.-J. Raphael. See issues of Glamour through January 1989
Exclusive! Bill Cosby's newest, funniest book [excerpt from Love and marriage] B. Cosby. il pors *Good Housekeeping* 208:126+ Je '89
"Help! My wife drives me crazy!" [excerpt from Love and marriage] B. Cosby. il por *Redbook* 173:114-15+ Jl '89
A man who can't love (dedicated to women who love too much). G. W. S. Trow. *The New Yorker* 64:29 Ja 16 '89
What is love? B. Adler. il *McCall's* 116:106 F '89
LOVE, MATERNAL
Death without weeping [mother love in shantytowns of Brazil] N. Scheper-Hughes. *Natural History* p8+ O '89
LOVE (THEOLOGY)
The cantata of love [Song of songs; book by Blaise Arminjon] P. V. Ahern. *America* 160:53 Ja 28 '89
Did Jesus really mean it when he said "Love your enemies"? J. H. Forest. il *U.S. Catholic* 54:35-8 Je '89
Love takes you a long way [activist lawyer L. Pitts] W. H. Willimon. *The Christian Century* 106:460-1 My 3 '89
More than know. J. Garvey. *Commonweal* 116:615-16 N 17 '89
Scared? H. Fehren. *U.S. Catholic* 54:38-40 Ag '89
Something new. P. J. Ryan. il *America* 160:359 Ap 15 '89
They are a stiff-necked people. K. Koyama. il *The Christian Century* 106:779 Ag 30-S 6 '89
Unravelling the mystery of weakness and strength. P. Kreeft. il *Christianity Today* 33:23-5 Ap 21 '89
LOVE AND ANGER [drama] See Walker, George F.
LOVE AND HATE: THE STORY OF COLIN AND JOANN THATCHER [television program] See Television program reviews—Single works
LOVE AND ROCKETS (MUSICAL GROUP)
From bauhaus to our house. J. Ressner. il *Rolling Stone* p23 S 21 '89
Gloom-rockers Love and Rockets splash down in the mainstream. il *People Weekly* 32:69 S 25 '89
LOVE CANAL CASE
A toxic ghost town. M. H. Brown. il *The Atlantic* 264:23-4+ Jl '89
LOVE IN MOTION PICTURES
Coming attractions. K. Jaehne. il *Film Comment* 25:46-9 Ja/F '89
What's love got to do with it? J. Cameron. il *American Film* 14:30-3+ Ap '89
Why Hollywood ignores black love and intimacy. A. Collier. il *Ebony* 44:41-4 Ap '89
LOVE IN TELEVISION
The hottest love stories on daytime soaps [cover story] C. Passalacqua. il *TV Guide* 37:2-5 Je 24-30 '89
LOVE LETTERS
How to write the ultimate valentine. H. O'Neill. il *Gentlemen's Quarterly* 59:45+ F '89
Never put anything in writing. D. Heyn. il *Mademoiselle* 95:126 Ag '89
LOVE LETTERS [drama] See Gurney, A. R. (Albert Ramsdell), 1930-
LOVE POETRY
A love poem [written by R. Khomeini] W. Chittick and P. Clawson. *The New Republic* 201:35 S 4 '89
Love sacred and profane [works of Hafiz] R. Feiz. il *The Courier (Unesco)* 42:12 Mr '89
LOVE SONG WALTZES [ballet] See Ballet reviews—Single works
LOVECE, FRANK
Learning to play in sweet harmony. il *Channels (New York, N.Y.: 1986)* 9:68-70 Ja '89
LOVEJOY, ANN
Consider the daylilies. il *House & Garden* 161:68+ Je '89
Rooms with a view. il *Organic Gardening* 36:66-70 Ap '89
LOVEJOY, THOMAS E.
about
Tom Lovejoy and the last crusade. R. Migler. il pors *Gentlemen's Quarterly* 59:286-9+ O '89
LOVELOCK, JAMES
Planetary medicine. il por *American Health* 8:86-8 Mr '89
about
Gaia. il por *People Weekly* 32:63-4 D 25 '89-Ja 1 '90
Gaia. T. Beardsley. il *Scientific American* 261:35-6 D '89
How the earth maintains life. E. Linden. il *Time* 134:114 N 13 '89
James Lovelock: toward a new planetary perspective [interview] S. Pacher. il por *The Mother Earth News* 119:44-6+ S/O '89

LOVELOCK, JAMES—about—*cont.*
What Gaia hath wrought: the story of a scientific controversy. F. Lyman. il *Technology Review* 92:54-61 Jl '89
LOVENHEIM, BARBARA
Katharine Hepburn at 80. por *McCall's* 117:125+ N '89
LOVERAS, JOSEPH J.
about
In good faith. B. Greene. il pors *Esquire* 111:67-8 Mr '89
The stolen briefcase. B. Greene. il *Reader's Digest* 134:23-4+ Je '89
LOVERBOY [film] See Motion picture reviews—Single works
LOVERRO, THOM
Baltimore & Washington. il *Sport (New York, N.Y.)* 80:74-8 S '89
Mountains of men. il pors *Sport (New York, N.Y.)* 80:58-62 F '89
LOVERS' QUARRELS See Quarrels
LOVE'S LABOR'S LOST [drama] See Shakespeare, William, 1564-1616
LOVETT, JON
Tracing the roots of the world's favorite houseplant. il *International Wildlife* 19:34-7 Mr/Ap '89
LOVETT, LYLE
about
Lyle Lovett's large band. A. Nash. il por *Stereo Review* 54:104+ My '89
LOVETTE, BONNIE
about
The triumph of Bonnie Lovette. L. Marsa. il pors *Good Housekeeping* 209:72+ Ag '89
LOVI, GEORGE
Rambling through the skies. See issues of Sky and Telescope
LOVINGER, DAVID M., AND OTHERS
Ethanol inhibits NMDA-activated ion current in hippocampal neurons. bibl f il *Science* 243:1721-4 Mr 31 '89
LOVOOS, JANICE
Paradise revisited. il por *American Artist* 53:64-7+ Ag '89
LOW ALTITUDE FLYING See Aviation—Altitude flying
LOW CALORIE COOKING
See also
Project LEAN
As good as fried. il *Redbook* 172:93-5+ Ap '89
Carving a new Thanksgiving tradition [work of L. Largent, chef at the Grand Hotel in Los Olivos, Calif.] J. Rogers. il por *Prevention (Emmaus, Pa.)* 41:67-71+ N '89
Chicken, shrimp, rice-beans: low-fat main dishes. il *Sunset (Central West edition)* 183:110 S '89
Chinese lessons. N. Simonds. il *American Health* 8:114-16+ S '89
Culinary crossroads [recipes of M. Chiarello from Tra Vigne in Saint Helena, Calif.] D. Welch. il por *Health (New York, N.Y.)* 21:74-9+ Ap '89
Diet dinners [tropical fruit] J. B. Hurley. il *Prevention (Emmaus, Pa.)* 41:76-8+ Ja '89
Diet—with pleasure! J. B. Hurley. il *Prevention (Emmaus, Pa.)* 41:74-6+ My '89
Down home at the diner. R. A. Barnett. il *American Health* 8:104-6+ Ja/F '89
Eat healthy, eat thin [carbohydrates] il *Glamour* 87:286-7 O '89
Eat light! [recipes from famous chefs] il *Redbook* 173:125-8+ Je '89
Eat thin! [excerpts from Weight Watchers quick success program cookbook] il *Redbook* 172:63-9+ F '89
The egg-lover's guide to low-cholesterol breakfasts. J. B. Hurley. il *Prevention (Emmaus, Pa.)* 41:83-6+ Ap '89
Fat-finding mission [altering recipes] M. Shakespeare. il *Health (New York, N.Y.)* 21:30-1 Mr '89
Finger-food feasts. il *Health (New York, N.Y.)* 21:76-83 D '89
Food for life. C. Lyons. il *Ebony* 44:82-4+ Ag '89
Food to keep fit on. il *Good Housekeeping* 208:134+ My '89
Good food, good health: low-fat strategies. B. Goldman. il *Better Homes and Gardens* 67:33+ Ja '89
Healthful high-fiber, low-fat recipes. il *The Saturday Evening Post* 261:32 N/D '89
Healthy eating. J. Nash. *Essence* 20:84+ Je '89
Healthy hearts across America [American Heart Association Food Festival] M. Roberts. *Psychology Today* 23:33 S '89
High comfort low calorie. R. Sax. il *Working Woman* 14:106-8 F '89
Holiday classics with a big fat difference. J. B. Hurley. il *Prevention (Emmaus, Pa.)* 41:66-70+ D '89
Leaner-than-ever Chinese cuisine [recipes of D. Keh, owner of David K's] T. Ney. il por *Prevention (Emmaus, Pa.)* 41:75-8+ F '89
Light & lean. C. Lyons. il *Ebony* 44:72-4+ Ja '89
Light and easy. See issues of Good Housekeeping beginning March 1989
Light food [views of M. R. Shulman] L. Troiano. il *American Health* 8:147-8 Ap '89
Lite eating. See issues of McCall's beginning August 1986
Low-cal cooking: treats that trim. C. Thomas and S. Young. il *Teen* 33:30+ Ap '89
Master your microwave: cut the fat. A. Johnson. il *Parents* 64:175-7 Ap '89

Meal makeovers: from greasy to good-for-you. il *Ladies' Home Journal* 106:184-6+ S '89
Microwaves: the machines that fire your diet. E. Kunes. il *Mademoiselle* 95:226 N '89
A month of slimming dinners. J. Nash. il *Essence* 19:83-6+ Mr '89
The new American picnic [Fourth of July barbecue] J. B. Hurley. il *Prevention (Emmaus, Pa.)* 41:72-6+ Jl '89
The new BBQ. M. Burros. il *American Health* 8:102+ Jl/Ag '89
The "new" food [recipes from William Moulin at Pritikin Longevity Center] il *Health (New York, N.Y.)* 21:69-71+ O '89
On the light side [special section] il *Southern Living* 24:73+ F '89
The parties of winter [appetizers] R. A. Barnett. il *American Health* 8:68-70+ D '89
Redbook's fastest, easiest diet dishes. il *Redbook* 173:99-101+ My '89
Savory splurges [excerpt from The Canyon Ranch health and fitness program] il *Health (New York, N.Y.)* 21:76-83 Mr '89
Slimming summer suppers [work of chef K. Mills at the Clift Hotel in San Francisco] T. Ney. il por *Prevention (Emmaus, Pa.)* 41:66-8+ Ag '89
Split the difference. R. Schrambling. il *The New York Times Magazine* p85-6 My 7 '89
Sweet cheats. il *Ladies' Home Journal* 106:128-9 Ja '89
Tête à tête dining. B. Gibbons. il *Modern Maturity* 32:72-4+ Ap/My '89
Trimming Christmas [desserts] N. Hauser. il *American Health* 8:92 D '89
Try a healthier way of cooking [excerpt from The American Heart Association low-fat, low-cholesterol cookbook] S. M. Grundy. *Redbook* 173:16 Ag '89
Vermont French light [recipes from the New England Culinary Institute] R. Barral. il *American Health* 8:140+ Mr '89
What's cooking, good looking? [recipes from Canyon Ranch spa] K. Cobb. il *American Health* 8:100-1 Ap '89
Whipping up a new self [chef A. Sturges] R. A. Barnett. il por *American Health* 8:135 S '89
LOW CALORIE DIET See Diet
LOW DENSITY LIPOPROTEINS See Lipoproteins
LOW FAT COOKING See Low calorie cooking
LOW IMPACT AEROBICS See Aerobics
LOW INCOME HOUSING See Housing
LOW-POWER ATMOSPHERIC COMPENSATION EXPERIMENT SATELLITE See LACE (Artificial satellite)
LOW POWER TELEVISION
A low-wire act. R. Katz. il *Channels (New York, N.Y.: 1986)* 9:92 D '89
LOW SODIUM COOKING
Pour salt-free freshness on salads. J. P. Day. il *The Saturday Evening Post* 261:18-21 O '89
LOW TAR CIGARETTES See Cigarettes
LOW TEMPERATURES
See also
Cold
Magnetic refrigeration
Refrigerators
Supercooling
Superfluidity
Nuclear magnetic ordering at nanokelvin temperatures. O. V. Lounasmaa. bibl f il *Physics Today* 42:26-33 O '89
LOWE, CARL
Diet in a glass. il *Health (New York, N.Y.)* 21:48+ O '89
LOWE, DAVID GARRARD
Prairie in flower. il *House & Garden* 161:68-75+ Ag '89
LOWE, DONALD R., AND OTHERS
Geological and geochemical record of 3400-million-year-old terrestrial meteorite impacts. bibl f il *Science* 245:959-62 S 1 '89
LOWE, MARCIA D.
Pushing pedalers: bicycles may be the key to unlocking our traffic woes. il *Utne Reader* p90-2 Mr/Ap '89
LOWE, ROB
about
Rob Lowe's girl trouble. M. Sager. il por *Rolling Stone* p92-3+ Ag 24 '89
A video romp in the buff gives heartbreaker Rob Lowe a little too much southern exposure. S. Dougherty. il pors *People Weekly* 31:79-80 Je 5 '89
LOWE, WENDY
Summoning the sandman. il *Better Homes and Gardens* 67:39-40 Je '89
LOWE TUCKER METCALF (FIRM)
British intelligence. B. Kanner. il *New York* 22:22+ N 13 '89
LOWELL, CAREY
about
Carey Lowell: the new female Bonding. B. Hersey. il por *Glamour* 87:166 Ag '89
Suitable girl. P. H. Starzinger. il *Vogue* 179:484-7 Mr '89
LOWELL, JOHN
Mr. Eliot's guide to quantum theory. il *Physics Today* 42:46-7 Ap '89

LOWELL, ROBERT, 1917-1977
The immortals [poem] *The New York Review of Books* 36:4 N 23 '89
LOWELL (MASS.)
Education
The future school: is Lowell pointing us toward a revolution in education? [City Magnet School] G. Richmond. il *Phi Delta Kappan* 71:232-6 N '89
LOWENKRON, LOU
about
Root beer gloat. E. Giltenan. il por *Forbes* 144:156+ D 11 '89
LOWENSTEIN, ALEXANDER
about
A grieving mother turns the horror of Pan Am Flight 103 into a monument to her son. D. Grogan. il pors *People Weekly* 32:44-6 S 25 '89
LOWENSTEIN, JEROLD
Landfall. See issues of Oceans through March/April 1989
LOWENSTEIN, LOUIS
Regulate the Wall Street casino. il por *Fortune* 119:125-6 F 27 '89
LOWENSTEIN, SUSE
about
A grieving mother turns the horror of Pan Am Flight 103 into a monument to her son. D. Grogan. il pors *People Weekly* 32:44-6 S 25 '89
LOWENSTEIN, TIM K., AND OTHERS
Origin of ancient potash evaporites: clues from the modern nonmarine Qaidam basin of western China. bibl f il map *Science* 245:1090-2 S 8 '89
LOWER CALIFORNIA See Baja California (Mexico: Peninsula)
LOWER MISSISSIPPI DELTA ECONOMIC COMMISSION
For poverty-ridden Delta, Commission is sign of hope. G. Simmons. il *Black Enterprise* 20:20 D '89
LOWRY, CORINNA
about
Dance takes hold in South Africa: rewriting the present. R. Nelan. il por *Dance Magazine* 63:54-8 F '89
LOWRY, DONALD S.
about
Victims of the Church of Love were only the lonely. J. Friedman. il por *People Weekly* 31:77-8+ Ja 30 '89
LOWRY, KATHARINE
Lawyers in love. il *Gentlemen's Quarterly* 59:90+ Ja '89
LOWRY, LOIS
Calling it quits. *The Writer* 102:13-14+ Ap '89
LOXAHATCHEE (JUPITER, FLA.: GOLF COURSE) See Golf courses
LOY, MYRNA
about
A dying sculptor fights vandals over Myrna Loy. il por *People Weekly* 31:111 My 29 '89
LOYALISTS, AMERICAN See American loyalists
LOYALTY
See also
Corporate loyalty
Loyalty is admirable. But is it smart? S. Jacoby. *Glamour* 87:290-1+ S '89
LOYALTY OATHS
See also
Pledge of Allegiance
Catholic Church
Catholic oaths and academic freedom. M. B. Lukens. *The Christian Century* 106:982-4 N 1 '89
Inflating the oath [document issued by the Congregation for the Doctrine of the Faith] J. A. Coriden. il *Commonweal* 116:455-6 S 8 '89
New loyalty oath. *The Christian Century* 106:377 Ap 12 '89
Profession of faith and the 'oath of fidelity'. L. M. Orsy. *America* 160:345-7+ Ap 15 '89
A university perspective on the 'oath of fidelity'. Q. L. Quade. *America* 160:348-9 Ap 15 '89
Anecdotes, facetiae, satire, etc.
Forged teaching [revised loyalty oath] M. E. Marty. *The Christian Century* 106:455 Ap 26 '89
LOZANO, WILLIAM
about
Miami cop who killed two blacks and incited riot guilty of manslaughter. il por *Jet* 77:4-5 D 25 '89-Ja 1 '90
Miami: 'We got justice'. G. Hackett. il por *Newsweek* 114:30 D 18 '89
LOZANSKY, EDWARD D. (EDWARD DMITRIEVICH), 1941-
about
From Russia with love. il pors *U.S. News & World Report* 107:16 O 2 '89
LPGA See Ladies Professional Golf Association
LSAT See Law School Admissions Test
LSD
Encyclopedia psychedelia [Albert Hofmann Foundation established by LSD researchers] A. J. S. Rayl. il *Omni (New York, N.Y.)* 11:30+ Je '89
LSU RURAL LIFE MUSEUM AND BURDEN RESEARCH PLANTATION
Real life on a plantation. il *Southern Living* 24:39 Mr '89

LTU LUFTTRANSPORT UNT GMBH & CO. KG
West Germany's LTU expands fleet with Boeing 767-300ERs. B. A. Smith. il *Aviation Week & Space Technology* 130:92-3 Mr 27 '89
LTV AEROSPACE & DEFENSE CO.
Army to broaden effort to develop extended-range interceptor. P. A. Gilmartin. il *Aviation Week & Space Technology* 131:30 O 16 '89
LTV begins flight tests of reengined A-7F for Air Guard mission. D. A. Brown. il *Aviation Week & Space Technology* 131:19-21 D 4 '89
LTV, BPD consider building increased-lift Scout 2 launcher. J. M. Lenorovitz. *Aviation Week & Space Technology* 130:25 Ap 10 '89
LTV to conduct final TACMS developmental test launch [Tactical Missile System] il *Aviation Week & Space Technology* 131:40 D 11 '89
USAF, LTV probe wing cracks that grounded Air Guard A-7s. E. H. Phillips. il *Aviation Week & Space Technology* 130:29-30 My 29 '89
LTV STEEL CO.
Why a big steelmaker is mimicking the minimills [Birmingham vs. LTV] il *Business Week* p92 Mr 27 '89
LUBARSKY, JARED
The inns of Alsace. il map *Travel Holiday* 171:48-54 Ja '89
Thailand's secluded paradise. il *Travel Holiday* 171:8-13 Je '89
LUBBOCK (TEX.)
Savings and loan associations
See also
State Savings & Loan Association of Lubbock
LUBECK, JACKIE
about
Notes and comment. il *The New Yorker* 65:23-4 Ag 28 '89
The story of Kufur Shamma [drama] Reviews *New York* 22:45 Ag 7 '89. J. Simon
LUBECK, SALLY
Issues on four-year-olds and public schooling. *The Education Digest* 55:21-4 O '89
LUBIN, DIANE
(jt. auth) See Lubin, Jim, and Lubin, Diane
about
'A once-in-a-lifetime challenge'. il pors *UN Chronicle* 26:16 Je '89
LUBIN, JIM
about
'A once-in-a-lifetime challenge'. il pors *UN Chronicle* 26:16 Je '89
LUBIN, JIM, AND LUBIN, DIANE
Letters from Okakarara. map *UN Chronicle* 26:11 S '89
LUBIN, PETER
How to dismantle communism [interview with I. Birman] il *National Review* 41:29-33 D 8 '89
A word edgewise. See issues of National Review beginning October 13, 1989
LUBOWSKI, ANTON, D. 1989
about
Namibia holds its breath. S. Reiss. il *Newsweek* 114:31 S 25 '89
LUBRANO, ALFRED
Bricklayer's boy. il *Gentlemen's Quarterly* 59:171-2+ Je '89
LUBRICATION AND LUBRICANTS
See also
Airplanes—Lubrication and lubricants
Automobiles—Lubrication and lubricants
Bicycles—Lubrication and lubricants
Boats and boating—Lubrication and lubricants
Motorcycles—Lubrication and lubricants
Quaker State Corporation
LUBRIZOL CORP.
Tough and slippery. C. Siler. il *Forbes* 143:42-3 My 29 '89
LUCAS, ALBERT
about
Cruise control [interview] S. McKee. il por *American Health* 8:66-7 D '89
LUCAS, STEVE
Legendary faint galaxies. il *Astronomy* 17:80-2 F '89
LUCAS, STEVE
Spectacular swimwear [cover story] il *Petersen's Photographic Magazine* 18:24-9+ Jl '89
LUCAS, WILLIAM
about
Cool Hand Lucas. W. McGurn. *National Review* 41:21-2 Je 2 '89
Fractured gospel. *The New Republic* 201:4 S 4 '89
Guess who's (not) coming to dinner. W. McGurn. il *National Review* 41:18-19 S 1 '89
A low-profile civil-rights march. por *U.S. News & World Report* 107:11 Ag 14 '89
Lucas gets liaison post within U.S. Justice Dept. por *Jet* 76:22 S 4 '89
Lucas's battle for confirmation. S. J. Hedges. il por *U.S. News & World Report* 106:33 My 8 '89
Missed opportunity. *National Review* 41:14 S 15 '89

LUCAS, WILLIAM—about—cont.
Mixed signals on civil rights. M. Miller. por Newsweek 113:20 My 8 '89
Politics and double standards. N. Traver. il por Time 134:29 Ag 14 '89
Token enforcer. F. Barnes. The New Republic 200:10-11 Je 19 '89
William Lucas choice to head Civil Rights Division. por Jet 75:6 Mr 13 '89
LUCAS (KAN.)
Historic houses, sites, etc.
See also
Concrete Garden of Eden (Lucas, Kan.)
LUCASFILM LTD.
Real hi-fi at the movies? [Lucasfilm THX sound system] J. D. Hirsch. il Stereo Review 54:48+ N '89
LUCASFILM LTD. INDUSTRIAL LIGHT AND MAGIC (STUDIO) See Industrial Light and Magic (Studio)
LUCCHESE, ALPHONSE M.
about
Iris: perfect proofs before the presses roll. L. Jereski. il por Business Week p61 My 29 '89
LUCCI, SUSAN
about
Susan Lucci: raising Kane for two decades. M. Logan. il pors TV Guide 37:16-19 D 30 '89-Ja 5 '90
Photographs and photography
Beauty session basics. G. Bernstein. il por Petersen's Photographic Magazine 18:30-1 Ag '89
LUCE, PEGGY
about
What it takes to reach the summit. J. Skow. il pors Time 133:14-15+ Mr 6 '89
LUCE (CLARE BOOTHE) FUND See Clare Boothe Luce Fund
LUCE (HENRY R.) CENTER FOR THE STUDY OF AMERICAN ART See Metropolitan Museum of Art (New York, N.Y.). Henry R. Luce Center for the Study of American Art
LUCIA DI LAMMERMOOR [opera] See Donizetti, Gaetano, 1797-1848
LUCIANI, ALBINO See John Paul I, Pope, 1912-1978
LUCID DREAMS See Dreams
LUCIENTES, FRANCISCO JOSÉ DE GOYA Y See Goya, Francisco, 1746-1828
LUCIFERASE
Beetlejuice genes now in biotechnicolor [click beetles; research by Keith V. Wood and William D. McElroy] R. Weiss. il Science News 135:308 My 20 '89
Complementary DNA coding click beetle luciferases can elicit bioluminescence of different colors. K. V. Wood and others. bibl f il Science 244:700-2 My 12 '89
Kittyboo colors [gene tagging with luciferase from click beetles; research by Keith Wood and others] il Discover 10:12 N '89
LUCILE HALSELL CONSERVATORY See San Antonio Botanical Gardens. Lucile Halsell Conservatory
LUCINDA CHILDS DANCE COMPANY
Folk movements. L. A. Jacobs. The New Leader 72:22-3 O 30 '89
The new Lucinda Childs. I. M. Fanger. il pors Dance Magazine 63:48-53 O '89
LUCK
Luck! [reprint from February 1965 issue] T. Trueblood. il Field & Stream 93:34+ Mr '89
LUCKY STAR RANCH
Bambi and the baron [J. Kerckerinck's efforts to persuade Americans to eat venison] D. Machan. il por Forbes 144:298+ D 11 '89
LUCKY STORES INC.
American: can it mine Lucky Stores' magic? R. Grover. il Business Week p141+ Ap 24 '89
LUCONA (SHIP)
Social climber's guide to Vienna [Socialist Party officials linked to U. Proksch and deliberate sinking of the Lucona] E. von Kuehnelt-Leddihn. National Review 41:42 Mr 10 '89
LUCY MARSDEN (FICTIONAL CHARACTER)
He's 42, she's 99—together they make the South rise again [creation of A. Gurganis] S. K. Reed. il pors People Weekly 32:68-70 S 18 '89
LUDLUM, DAVID M., 1910-
Alaskan weather. See issues of Weatherwise
Almanac. See issues of Country Journal beginning October 1986
Weatherwatch. See issues of Weatherwise
(jt. auth) See Robinson, David A., and Ludlum, David M., 1910-
LUDMANN, JEAN-DANIEL
about
Curators in court. B. Grauman. il Art News 88:72-4 Ap '89
Scandals rock French museums. W. Robinson. il por Art in America 77:21+ F '89
LUDVIGSON, SUSAN
Au premier coup [poem] The Nation 248:676 My 15 '89
Laura [poem] America 161:82 Ag 12-19 '89

There are reasons [poem] The Nation 248:353 Mr 13 '89
LUDWIG, KEN
about
Lend me a tenor [drama] Reviews
The Nation 248:534-5 Ap 17 '89. M. Hodgson
New York 22:74-5 Mr 13 '89. J. Simon
The New Yorker 65:74 Mr 13 '89. E. Oliver
LUDWIG, PETER, 1925-
about
Ludwig museums go east. J. Gambrell. Art in America 77:35+ Je '89
LUDWIG RUDOLPH, OF HANOVER
about
Obituary
People Weekly il pors 31:51-2 Ja 9 '89. M. Brower
LUDWIGSBURG FESTIVAL See Music festivals—Germany (West)
LUE, NEAL F., AND OTHERS
Initiation by yeast RNA polymerase II at the adenoviral major late promoter in vitro. bibl f il Science 246:661-4 N 3 '89
LUECKE, RICHARD
Saul Alinsky: homo ludens for urban democracy. il por The Christian Century 106:1050-3 N 15 '89
LUEKER, DONNA HARRINGTON- See Harrington-Lueker, Donna
LUFT, KLAUS
about
This German company's days of freedom may be numbered. G. E. Schares. il por Business Week p51-2 D 4 '89
LUFTHANSA
Air France, Lufthansa sign pact for broad cooperative policies. J. M. Lenorovitz. il Aviation Week & Space Technology 131:108 S 25 '89
The boys from Bremen [pilot training program] W. Garvey. il Flying 116:72-7 Je '89
Lufthansa boosts firm order total for Airbus A321-100 transports. C. A. Shifrin. Aviation Week & Space Technology 131:58-9 Ag 14 '89
Lufthansa prepares for expansion into new European, world markets. il Aviation Week & Space Technology 131:95+ N 20 '89
LUGBILL, JON
about
The best just became better. D. S. Looney. il por Sports Illustrated 71:53 Jl 3 '89
Paddling the straight and narrow. D. S. Looney. il pors Sports Illustrated 70:56+ Je 19 '89
LUGER, KAROLIN, AND OTHERS
Correct folding of circularly permuted variants of a βα barrel enzyme in vivo. bibl f il Science 243:206-10 Ja 13 '89
LUGGAGE
See also
Packing of luggage
Best bags to take on board [carry-on luggage] D. Moreau. il Changing Times 43:111-12+ Ap '89
The elegant man [garment bags] H. Sterne. il Gentlemen's Quarterly 59:244-5 O '89
LUGGAGE, MOTORCYCLE See Motorcycles—Equipment
LUGGAGE HANDLING, AIRLINE See Airlines—Luggage handling
LUGINBILL, MICHAEL, AND SPIEGLER, ALLAN
Specialized foster family care: a community-based program for children with special needs. il Children Today 18:5-9 Ja/F '89
LUHRS, WARREN
about
Thursday's child triumphs. L. Rudeen. il por map Motor Boating & Sailing 163:66-71+ Ap '89
LUIGI PECCI CENTER FOR CONTEMPORARY ART (PRATO, ITALY) See Centro per l'Arte Contemporaneo Luigi Pecci (Prato, Italy)
LUIGS, CHARLES RUSSELL
about
Now all Global Marine needs is a market. T. Vogel. il Business Week p44 Mr 13 '89
LUITJENS, JACOB
about
A race against time. N. Underwood. pors Maclean's 102:44 Ja 23 '89
LUJAN, MANUEL, JR.
about
Half Watt. B. Reed. il The New Republic 201:20-2 O 16 '89
Lujan to lead Interior Department. il por National Parks 63:9-10 Mr/Ap '89
Thoughts. F. Graham. il Audubon 91:13-14 Jl '89
LUKACS, ATTILA RICHARD
about
Attila Richard Lukacs at 49th Parallel. K. Johnson. Art in America 77:204 S '89
LUKACS, JOHN, 1924-
America's true power. il American Heritage 40:74-9 Mr '89
The coming of the Second World War. Foreign Affairs 68:165-74 Fall '89

LUKAS, D. WAYNE
about
Smelling the roses, pricked by a thorn. P. Axthelm. il pors *Gentlemen's Quarterly* 59:234-9+ My '89

LUKAS, J. ANTHONY, 1933-
Harvard's Kennedy School: is competence enough? il *The New York Times Magazine* p36-7+ Mr 12 '89

LUKE, JOY TURNER
New federal legislation on art material labeling. *American Artist* 53:24+ Je '89
Toxicity of artists' materials. *American Artist* 53:22+ Jl '89

LUKE, GOSPEL OF *See* Bible. N.T. Luke

LUKENS, DONALD E.
about
U.S. rep. convicted for having sex with a minor. il pors *Jet* 76:8 Je 12 '89
U.S. Rep. Lukens gets 30-day jail term, fine in sex with minor case. il pors *Jet* 76:33 Jl 24 '89

LUKENS, MICHAEL B.
Catholic oaths and academic freedom. *The Christian Century* 106:982-4 N 1 '89

LUKENS, PEGGY
Probing the "myths" about Japanese education. *The Education Digest* 54:13-16 My '89

LUKER, RICHARD, AND JOHNSTON, JEROME
Television in adolescent social development. *The Education Digest* 54:50-1 F '89

LULA *See* Silva, Luis Inácio da

LULLABIES
Twinkle, twinkle little star: it's more than just a nursery song. M. J. Howle. bibl f il *Children Today* 18:18-22 Jl/Ag '89

LULLY, JEAN BAPTISTE, 1632-1687
about
Atys [opera] Reviews
New York il 22:60+ Je 5 '89. P. G. Davis
The New Yorker 65:90-2 Je 12 '89. A. Porter
Opera News il 53:20+ My '89. M. Swed

LUMA (NEW YORK, N.Y.: RESTAURANT) *See* New York (N.Y.)—Restaurants, nightclubs, bars, etc.

LUMBER
See also
Sawmills
Innovative lumber. il *Popular Science* 235:68-9 Ag '89
Transportation
Convoys set for Yellowstone. il *National Parks* 63:8-9 N/D '89

LUMBER INDUSTRY
See also
Collective bargaining—Lumber industry
Gregory Forest Products Inc.
Louisiana-Pacific Corp.
Pacific Lumber Co.
Plum Creek Timber Company, Inc.
Potlatch Corp.
Timber
Weyerhaeuser Company
A boy sides with Dr. Seuss's Lorax, and puts a town at loggerheads [parents of S. Bailey call for removal of title from school reading list in Laytonville, Calif.] R. Arias. il pors *People Weekly* 32:67-8 O 23 '89
Oregon's not-so-Sweet Home [decline in logging and mill jobs] S. Doherty. il *Newsweek* 114:55 D 11 '89
Acquisitions and mergers
California's chain-saw massacre [clearcutting of redwood by Pacific Lumber] M. J. Walters. il *Reader's Digest* 135:144-9 N '89
Milken, junk bonds and raping redwoods [C. Hurwitz accelerates logging following takeover] B. McKibben. *Rolling Stone* p39-40 Ag 10 '89
A raider's ruckus in the redwoods [accelerated logging following Maxxam's takeover of Pacific Lumber] E. Schultz. il por *Fortune* 119:172-3+ Ap 24 '89
When the safety net is frayed [takeover of Pacific Lumber by Charles E. Hurwitz causes pension plan termination] J. B. Levine. il *Business Week* p158 N 6 '89
Employees
See Lumber workers
Export-import trade
Wasteful Japan [tropical timber trade] *World Press Review* 36:43+ O '89
Federal aid
Deforestation hits home: U.S. Forest Service levels our landscape. K. E. Franklin. il *Utne Reader* p52 My/Je '89
Forest Service: admissions and additions [losing money on timber sales] *Wilderness* 52:v-vi Spr '89
Timber! K. E. Franklin. *The New Republic* 200:12-14 Ja 2 '89
Finance
Sawmills are starting to drop like trees. J. B. Levine. il *Business Week* p42 F 6 '89

LUMBER WORKERS
Oregon's not-so-Sweet Home [decline in logging and mill jobs] S. Doherty. il *Newsweek* 114:55 D 11 '89

Salaries, pensions, etc.
When the safety net is frayed [takeover of Pacific Lumber by Charles E. Hurwitz causes pension plan termination] J. B. Levine. il *Business Week* p158 N 6 '89

LUMBERING
See also
Clearcutting
Park-quality sequoias logged [Sequoia National Forest] il *National Parks* 63:8-9 My/Je '89
Please don't eat the trees [damage caused by black bears in the commercial forests of the Northwest] B. J. Bashin. il *Sierra* 74:22-4 Jl/Ag '89
Competitions
The world's best woodcutters [Lumberjack World Championships] H. Nuwer. il *Country Journal* 16:21-6 F '89

LUMBERJACKS
Competitions
See Lumbering—Competitions

LUMINESCENCE
See also
Airglow
Bioluminescence
Does the moon spark like a Life Saver? [theory of Richard R. Zito] J. Eberhart. *Science News* 136:375 D 9 '89
Shuttle glow [cover story] D. E. Hunton. bibl il *Scientific American* 261:92-8 N '89

LUMINOUS CLOUDS *See* Noctilucent clouds

LUMMI INDIANS
Church leaders support native claim [Lummi Indians vs. development of Madrona Point, Orcas Island, Wash.] J. Magnuson. *The Christian Century* 106:276-7 Mr 15 '89

LUMPECTOMY *See* Breast—Cancer—Surgery

LUMPKIN, SUSAN
(ed) *See* Seidensticker, John. Playing possum is serious business for our only marsupial

LUN, K. C.
Hand-held computers. il *World Health* p9-11 Ag/S '89

LUNAR AND PLANETARY INSTITUTE
The planetologists' home. B. Nolley. il *Ad Astra* 1:29-30 Mr '89

LUNAR BASES
Apollo 11 [cover story; special issue; with editorial comment by Charles Walker] il *Ad Astra* 1:2, 8-12+ Jl/Ag '89
The art of the possible. G. R. Woodcock. il *Ad Astra* 1:8-13 O '89
Bush: 'the inescapable challenge' [excerpts from address, July 20, 1989] G. Bush. *Aviation Week & Space Technology* 131:13 Jl 31 '89
Chalk talk [Bush space plan] L. David. il *Ad Astra* 1:37 S '89
Extending the limits of our frontiers [address, July 20, 1989; with editorial comment by Charles D. Walker] G. Bush. il pors *Ad Astra* 1:2, 38-40 S '89
Fletcher supports moon outpost by 2004. il *Ad Astra* 1:46 Ja '89
From footprints to foothold. R. G. Nichols. il *Astronomy* 17:48-53 Jl '89
If they turned me loose on the moon . . . I. Asimov. il por *TV Guide* 37:6-7+ Jl 15-21 '89
Is the man in the White House moonstruck? il *U.S. News & World Report* 107:10 Jl 24 '89
Japan's moonhouses. A. Brown. il *Omni (New York, N.Y.)* 11:17 Jl '89
'A journey into tomorrow' [G. Bush speech on space program] J. Schwartz and M. Hager. il por *Newsweek* 114:31 Jl 31 '89
Manned lunar base, Mars initiative raised in secret White House review [with editorial comment] C. Covault. il *Aviation Week & Space Technology* 131:7, 24-6 Jl 17 '89
Moon base made easy. il *Popular Mechanics* 166:14 Ja '89
NASA accelerates lunar base planning as station changes draw European fire. C. Covault. il *Aviation Week & Space Technology* 131:26-7 S 18 '89
NASA declares a bold agenda for 21st century. il *Popular Mechanics* 166:11 My '89
NASA offers five alternatives for landing humans on Mars by 2018. J. R. Asker. il *Aviation Week & Space Technology* 131:30-1 N 27 '89
The people's space program. T. Morgan. *Ad Astra* 1:48 Ja '89
President's message. C. D. Walker. il *Ad Astra* 1:2 N '89
Soviet moon base? P. Jackson and L. David. il *Ad Astra* 1:6-7 Jl/Ag '89
Space station changes for lunar base would cost NASA more than $1 billion. C. Covault. il *Aviation Week & Space Technology* 131:34-5 O 9 '89
Taking the next 'giant leap'. *Astronomy* 17:14+ Ap '89
To the moon or Mars. il *Popular Science* 235:72-4 Jl '89
Astronomical use
A robot-built lunar observatory. B. D. Gibson. il *Astronomy* 17:14 Jl '89

LUNAR ECLIPSES *See* Eclipses, Lunar

LUNAR GEOLOGY
See also
Moon—Surface

LUNAR GEOLOGY—cont.
Cordierite-spinel troctolite, a new magnesium-rich lithology from the lunar highlands. U. B. Marvin and others. bibl f il map *Science* 243:925-8 F 17 '89
Does the moon spark like a Life Saver? [theory of Richard R. Zito] J. Eberhart. *Science News* 136:375 D 9 '89
Earth's largest lunar meteorite announced [MAC88105] *Science News* 136:62 Jl 22 '89
History of meteorites from the moon collected in Antarctica. O. Eugster. bibl f il *Science* 245:1197-1202 S 15 '89
How Apollo changed the moon. R. Burnham. il *Astronomy* 17:40-2 Jl '89
Lunar prospecting [cover story] W. R. Farrand. il *Ad Astra* 1:8-12 F '89
Moonrock tells of little-known lunar layer [cordierite] *Science News* 135:126 F 25 '89
Moonrocks [specimens brought back from Apollo missions] L. Hart and others. il *Life* 12:58-9+ Jl '89
Moonstruck. T. Waters. il *Discover* 10:90-5 Jl '89
A piece of the rock [Lunar Sample Loan Program] il *Ad Astra* 1:54 Jl/Ag '89
Rock of ages [lunar rocks curator John W. Dietrich] B. Nolley. il *Ad Astra* 1:7+ Jl/Ag '89
Treasuring the moon for 20 years [moon rocks collected by Apollo astronauts] R. A. Kerr. il *Science* 243:1552 Mr 24 '89
LUNAR LASER RANGING *See* Lasers—Astronomical use
LUNAR POWER RESOURCES
Extraterrestrial energy [NASA Lunar Energy Enterprise Case Study Task Force] il *Ad Astra* 1:6-7 N '89
Moon power [helium-3] M. J. Mackowski. il por *Ad Astra* 1:34-9 Jl/Ag '89
What has caused the secular increase in solar nitrogen-15? J. F. Kerridge. bibl f il *Science* 245:480-6 Ag 4 '89
LUNAR RESEARCH *See* Moon
LUNCH, MILT
about
Who will design buildings for human habitation? (I) [interview] C. M. Sapers. pors *Architectural Record* 177:41+ Je '89
Who will design buildings for human habitation? (II) [interview] C. M. Sapers. il por *Architectural Record* 177:41-2 Jl '89
LUNCH BOXES
Collectors and collecting
Lunch box [cover story] H. J. LaFleche. il por *Antiques & Collecting Hobbies* 94:24-5+ Jl '89
Timely obsessions [P. Reginato's and F. De Chabris' collection of lunchboxes] M. Guralnick. il pors *House & Garden* 161:94+ S '89
LUNCHBOXES *See* Lunch boxes
LUNCHEONS
See also
Brunches
Easter luncheon. il *Gourmet* 49:96-102+ Mr '89
Gather the ladies for lunch. S. Payne. il *Southern Living* 24:118-20 Ja '89
A lovely luncheon for 12. il *Southern Living* 24:108-9 Ag '89
Luncheon among the rhododendrons. il *Gourmet* 49:108-15 Je '89
A poolside Spanish luncheon. il *Gourmet* 49:78-84 Ag '89
A spring luncheon. il *Gourmet* 49:128-36 Ap '89
LUNCHEONS, BUSINESS *See* Business entertaining
LUNCHEONS IN ART
The luncheon [C. Monet painting] Sir M. Levey. il por *Art News* 88:91-2 O '89
LUNCHES
See also
Brunches
School lunches
Club comfort [private clubs] C. Idone. il *The New York Times Magazine* p75-6 Mr 12 '89
Tempting lunchbox treats. H. A. Dorrough. il *Southern Living* 24:168+ S '89
LUNCHES, BUSINESS *See* Business entertaining
LUND, HERTHA L.
Today's embattled cowboys. *National Review* 41:26 D 31 '89
LUND, PETER
about
The art and advantage of conversation [interview] il pors *Channels (New York, N.Y.: 1986)* 9:54-5 My '89
LUNDE, ANDERS S.
Oil well pump whirligig. il *Workbench* 45:22-4 Jl/Ag '89
LUNDEN, JOAN
about
Watch out for her surprise offensive. D. Hill. il pors *TV Guide* 37:12-14 S 2-8 '89
LUNGS
See also
Respiration
Full of hot air [Darwin's theory that lungs evolved from swim bladders] S. J. Gould. il *Natural History* p28+ O '89
Cancer
Sweet sorrow [mother's battle with lung cancer] A. Rosen. il *Ms.* 18:24-5 N '89

Causes
Cancer prevention strategy at the NCI [interview with S. Broder] C. SerVaas. il por *The Saturday Evening Post* 261:50-1+ My/Je '89
Lung cancer—the smoking gun. C. Gloeckner. il *Current Health 2* 15:14-15 Mr '89
Diagnosis
Fighting cancer [use of monoclonal antibodies to detect lung cancer cells in sputum] il *Prevention (Emmaus, Pa.)* 41:16+ Mr '89
Genetic aspects
p53: a frequent target for genetic abnormalities in lung cancer. T. Takahashi and others. bibl f il *Science* 246:491-4 O 27 '89
Nutritional aspects
More veggies join fight against lung cancer [research by Loïc Le Marchand] I. Wickelgren. *Science News* 136:102 Ag 12 '89
Therapy
The horror is worth it. V. Williams. por *Newsweek* 114:14 O 9 '89
Diseases
See also
Cystic fibrosis
Emphysema
Pneumonia
Tuberculosis
Cooking up chest illness [use of wood stoves and respiratory problems in children; research by J. Osborne Scott and Richard E. Honicky] il *Prevention (Emmaus, Pa.)* 41:10+ D '89
Hog farmers clear the air. C. Tevis. il *Successful Farming* 87:54-5 D '89
Lung power [use of ketoconazole to prevent respiratory failure from fluid in the lungs] *Prevention (Emmaus, Pa.)* 41:16+ Ag '89
Why no one's safe [effects of smog on residents in Los Angeles basin] J. E. Basu. maps *American Health* 8:64 S '89
Immunological aspects
Smoking inhibits lung's immune cells [research by Mohan L. Sopori and George M. Shopp] *Science News* 135:255 Ap 22 '89
Nutritional aspects
Vitamin C for healthy lungs? [research by Joel Schwartz] il *Prevention (Emmaus, Pa.)* 41:10+ O '89
Therapy
The (liquid) breath of life [perfluorocarbon] M. M. Waldrop. il *Science* 245:1043-5 S 8 '89
Dust diseases
Asbestos fiber shape may trigger radicals [study by Andrij Holian] D. E. Loupe. *Science News* 136:167 S 9 '89
Respiratory hazards in the shop. M. Lane. il *Workbench* 45:66-9 Ja/F '89
Transplantation
Double-lung transplant. C. SerVaas. il *The Saturday Evening Post* 261:98-100 Mr '89
A new year, a new life, a new love [primary pulmonary hypertension patient R. Gyorfi receives heart-lung transplant] D. Gage. il pors *Good Housekeeping* 208:95+ Ja '89
LUNINE, JONATHAN I.
Origin and evolution of outer solar system atmospheres. bibl f il *Science* 245:141-7 Jl 14 '89
about
Lunine receives Urey Prize for planetary science. *Physics Today* 42:128 Mr '89
LUOMA, JON R.
Doomed canaries of Tadoussac. il por map *Audubon* 91:92-7 Mr '89
Prophet of the prairie. il pors map *Audubon* 91:54-60 N '89
Storming Montana's wilderness. il *The New York Times Magazine* p34-6+ Ap 16 '89
Terror and triage at the laundry. il *Audubon* 91:92-101 S '89
LUONGO, PINO
about
Mothers of invention. R. D. Story. il por *New York* 22:46-51 Je 5 '89
LUPER, JERRY
about
Aging gracefully. F. J. Prial. il por *The New York Times Magazine* p68 Ap 2 '89
LUPICA, MIKE
The sporting life. See issues of Esquire beginning October 1987
LUPUS ERYTHEMATOSUS
Living with lupus. D. Stehlin. il *FDA Consumer* 23:8-12 D '89/Ja '90
Lupus: master of disguise. J. Cassidy. il *Current Health 2* 16:26-7 D '89
The wolf at the door [lupus-induced catatonia] E. Rosenthal. il *Discover* 10:34+ F '89
LURES, FISHING *See* Fishing lures, flies, etc.
LURIE, ALISON
A dictionary for deconstructors. il *The New York Review of Books* 36:49-50 N 23 '89

LURIE, ALISON—cont.
Fat people [story] *Vogue* 179:438-9+ O '89
LUSHING, GLORIA
about
A California collection: sleek spaces for art in Beverly Hills.
B. D. Colen. il *Architectural Digest* 46:126-33 D '89
LUSHING, JERRY
about
A California collection: sleek spaces for art in Beverly Hills.
B. D. Colen. il *Architectural Digest* 46:126-33 D '89
LUSSIER, ROGER
about
Framer's art. S. Barron. il por *House & Garden* 161:150-7+
D '89
LUSTER, JORY
about
Jory Luster is elected new AHBAI chairman. por *Jet* 76:31
S 25 '89
LUSTIG, WILLIAM
about
Relentless [film] Reviews
People Weekly il 32:13-14 S 18 '89. R. Novak
LUTEN, C. J.
Verdi redivivus. il *Opera News* 54:46-9 S '89
LÜTGE, GUNHILD
Europe chips in. *World Press Review* 36:70-1 O '89
LUTHERAN CHURCH
Sweden
Reforms enliven the Church of Sweden. K.-E. Williams.
The Christian Century 106:52-5 Ja 18 '89
United States
America's Lutherans [cover story; special section; with
editorial comment by Kenneth S. Kantzer] il *Christianity
Today* 33:14, 18-29 N 3 '89
Church exchange strengthens urban/rural ties [Brooklyn's Zion
Lutheran Church and Elstad-Highland Prairie Churches,
Minn.] B. Heidtke. *Successful Farming* 87:F4 D '89
LCMS pastor could face heresy charges [D. Bruch] W.
Thorkelson. *Christianity Today* 33:43 Ap 21 '89
Meeting the quota for church conservatives [Evangelical
Lutheran Church in America] R. E. Saltzman. *The Christian
Century* 106:975 N 1 '89
Missouri Synod doctrine [views of Alvin J. Schmidt and
Daniel Bruch on women in ministry] *The Christian Century*
106:681 Jl 19-26 '89
Missouri Synod Lutherans seek harmony. R. Frame. il
Christianity Today 33:45 Ag 18 '89
Finance
Dissenting on divestment [Evangelical Lutheran Church in
America] *The Christian Century* 106:927 O 18 '89
Financial worries darken ELCA assembly. D. J. Lehmann.
The Christian Century 106:804-5 S 13-20 '89
LUTHIN, CHARLES S.
Rhapsody in red. il *International Wildlife* 19:46-51 Jl/Ag
'89
LUTHY, RICHARD G.
Personnel and research shortages: policy recommendations
for the environmental professions. bibl f *Environment*
31:4-5+ Ap '89
LUTIN, MICHAEL
Horoscope. See issues of Vogue beginning January 1989
through November 1989
LUTOSLAWSKI, WITOLD, 1913-
about
Musical events:
Messiaen's Et exspecto, Lutoslawski's Piano concerto,
and Rorem's Violin concerto. A. Porter. *The New
Yorker* 64:65-6 Ja 16 '89
LUTTER, JOSEPH
about
Joseph Lutter carves carousel horses by giving rein to his
gifts. H. Shapiro. il pors *People Weekly* 32:167-8 D 11
'89
LUTTMANN, GAIL
How to write a how-to that sells. *The Writer* 102:19-20+
Jl '89
Starting with geese. il *Country Journal* 16:77-81 N/D '89
LUTTWAK, EDWARD N.
'A' is for autonomy. *The New Republic* 200:15-16 Ap 17
'89
Athens vs. Sparta. *Commentary* 87:60-4 Mr '89
Books you may have missed. il *The American Spectator*
22:46-7 Mr '89
Gorbachev's strategy, and ours. *Commentary* 88:29-36 Jl
'89
LUTYENS, SIR EDWIN LANDSEER, 1869-1944
about
Best laid plan. M. R. Van Valkenburgh and C. D. Van
Valkenburgh. il *House & Garden* 161:150-7 Mr '89
LUTZ, ROBERT A.
about
From the top. il pors *Car and Driver* 35:93-6+ O '89
How a top boss manages his day. A. L. Taylor, III. il
pors *Fortune* 119:95-7+ Je 19 '89
Interview: Robert A. Lutz. J. Miller. il pors *Motor Trend*
41:61-5 Ja '89

LUTZOMYIA *See* Moth flies
LUXEMBURG, ROSA, 1871-1919
Photographs and photography
Two lives: ordinary/extraordinary. C. Jacobsen. bibl f il pors
Art in America 77:152-7+ F '89
LUXURIES
Little luxuries: why live without them? A. Stoddard. il
McCall's 117:184 O '89
LUXURY TAX *See* Consumption tax
LUZ INTERNATIONAL LTD.
Warming trend. J. Cook. il *Forbes* 143:68+ F 20 '89
LVMH MOËT HENNESSY LOUIS VUITTON
Avant le deluge at Moet Hennessy Louis Vuitton. S. Toy.
il *Business Week* p44 Ap 24 '89
King of chic—and artful deals [B. Arnault] S. Tully. il por
Fortune 119:40 Ja 2 '89
A luxury fight to the finish. S. Greenhouse. il pors *The
New York Times Magazine* p38-9+ D 17 '89
The new king of luxury [B. Arnault] C. Dickey. il por
Newsweek 114:40-2 Ag 7 '89
Tough guys with a genteel manner [Lazard Frères & Cie]
P. Berman. il por *Forbes* 144:75-80 Jl 10 '89
LYCAON PICTUS *See* African hunting dogs
LYCHOLAT, CINDY KNUTSON- *See* Knutson-Lycholat,
Cindy
LYDDA (ISRAEL) *See* Lod (Israel)
LYING
See also
Lie detectors and detection
Munchausen syndrome
Dating, dishonesty and AIDS [study by Susan Cochran] M.
Roberts. il *Psychology Today* 22:60 D '88
Is she/he telling you the truth? How to tell. il *Glamour*
87:83 F '89
The lies men tell. D. Seeley. il *Mademoiselle* 95:172-3+ Je
'89
The Pinocchio syndrome. K. S. Kantzer. il *Christianity Today*
33:13 O 6 '89
Sexual lies: his and yours. L. Dormen. il *Glamour* 87:262-3+
O '89
The truth about liars [views of Gordon Deckert] il *USA
Today (Periodical)* 117:9 My '89
The truth about lying. M. Jaworski. il *Ladies' Home Journal*
106:58+ F '89
The untruthful interviewee. *Working Woman* 14:162 Mr
'89
Who's lying now? [politics] D. Baldwin. il *Common Cause
Magazine* 15:32-7 My/Je '89
LYING IN CHILDREN
Creative lying [lying as a child helpful to adult fiction writers]
J. VanOosting. *The Writer* 102:7-8 O '89
The figments of childhood [views of P. Ekman] *U.S. News
& World Report* 107:62-3 O 23 '89
The lighter side of lying. W. Sayres. il *Parents* 64:131-4
Je '89
Understanding kids' lies [views of P. Ekman] N. Darnton.
il *Newsweek* 114:62-3 O 2 '89
What do you do when your child tells a lie? B. Spock.
por *Redbook* 172:36 Mr '89
Would a child lie? P. Ekman. il *Psychology Today* 23:62-5
Jl/Ag '89
LYLE, SANDY
about
Britannia rules again. S. Ballard. il pors *Sports Illustrated*
71:60-4+ Jl 10 '89
LYLES, BARBARA
What to call people of color. por *Newsweek* 113:8-9 F 27
'89
LYMAN, FRANCESCA
What Gaia hath wrought: the story of a scientific controversy.
il *Technology Review* 92:54-61 Jl '89
LYMAN, PETER
(jt. auth) See Gilbert, Steven W., and Lyman, Peter
LYME DISEASE
At the drop of a tick [cover story] I. Wickelgren. il *Science
News* 135:184-7 Mr 25 '89
Bad news from a tiny tick. il *Southern Living* 24:28 Ag
'89
Beware the new tick invasion! M. Rhodes. il *Redbook* 173:14
Jl '89
Dairyman adjusts to life after Lyme disease. C. Tevis. il
Successful Farming 87 no4:52 Mr '89
En garde against Tick Garde. il *Consumer Reports* 54:489
Ag '89
How to keep those ticks at bay. S. Woolley. il *Business
Week* p97 Jl 3 '89
How you can prevent Lyme disease. *Prevention (Emmaus,
Pa.)* 41:110 Jl '89
The latest on Lyme disease. il *The Mother Earth News*
118:21-2 Jl/Ag '89
The Lyme disease invasion. T. J. Daniels and R. C. Falco.
il *Natural History* p4+ Jl '89
Lyme disease: not just deer ticks: mosquitoes, pets, even
rabbits, can transmit the germ. J. Hamilton. il *American
Health* 8:13-14 Je '89
Lyme on the lam [antibodies unable to recognize Borrelia
bacteria; research by Tom Schwan] il *Discover* 10:10 S
'89

LYME DISEASE—*cont.*

The mounting toll of Lyme disease. J. Pekkanen. il *Reader's Digest* 134:88-92 Ap '89

Rising star Neneh Cherry discovers that the lowly deer tick is a showstopper, too. S. Dougherty. il por *People Weekly* 32:124-5 O 9 '89

A tick buster's guide to bug repellents. J. Silberner. il *U.S. News & World Report* 107:57 Ag 7 '89

Tick tactics. N. Tannenhaus. il *Travel Holiday* 171:88 Je '89

Tick, tick, tick. M. E. Makover. il *New York* 22:77-8 My 22 '89

Tiny tick, big worry [cover story] J. Seligmann. il map *Newsweek* 112:66-70+ My 22 '89

Diagnosis

The case of the tick and the tic [case of M. Lehman] A. Roblin. il *Prevention (Emmaus, Pa.)* 41:104-5+ Jl '89

Is it Lyme disease? [excerpt from Protect yourself from Lyme disease] D. Benzaia. il *Health (New York, N.Y.)* 21:72-5 Je '89

Looking for Lyme in the nervous system [research by John J. Halperin] I. Wickelgren. *Science News* 135:390 Je 24 '89

New test homes in on evasive Lyme disease [research by Patricia A. Rosa and Tom G. Schwan] K. Fackelmann. *Science News* 136:374 D 9 '89

Vaccines and vaccination

Tick-tock: still no shot. R. Weiss. *Science News* 135:186 Mr 25 '89

LYMPHADENOPATHY-ASSOCIATED VIRUSES *See* HIV viruses

LYMPHATIC SYSTEM

T cell receptor gene trans-rearrangements: chimeric γ-δ genes in normal lymphoid tissues. B. Tycko and others. bibl f il *Science* 245:1242-6 Mr 10 '89

Cancer

See also

Hodgkin's disease

Genetic aspects

Four steps to lymphoma [research by Charles L. Sidman] P. Young. *Science News* 136:92 Ag 5 '89

Normal expression of a rearranged and mutated c-*myc* oncogene after transfection into fibroblasts [Burkitt's lymphoma] A. Richman and A. Hayday. bibl f il *Science* 246:494-7 O 27 '89

Therapy

Tumor resistance: weakening the pulse [research by Thomas P. Miller] R. Weiss. *Science News* 135:348 Je 3 '89

LYMPHOCYTES

See also

B cells

CD4 proteins

Killer cells

T cells

Blood cells yield cystic fibrosis clues [cyclic adenosine monophosphate-regulated chloride channel in lymphocytes; research by Jennifer H. Chen and others] *Science News* 135:110 F 18 '89

A cAMP-regulated chloride channel in lymphocytes that is affected in cystic fibrosis. J. H. Chen and others. bibl f il *Science* 243:657-60 F 3 '89

Designing cells to deliver drugs. B. J. Culliton. *Science* 246:746 N 10 '89

Fighting cancer with designer cells [immunotherapy using tumor-infiltrating lymphocytes; work of S. A. Rosenberg] B. J. Culliton. il por *Science* 244:1430-3 Je 23 '89

Gene transfer test: so far, so good [treatment of advanced melanoma with tumor-infiltrating lymphocytes; work of Steven A. Rosenberg] B. J. Culliton. *Science* 245:1325 S 22 '89

Immunology's designer genes [tumor-infiltrating lymphocytes; work of S. A. Rosenberg] S. Brownlee. il por *U.S. News & World Report* 107:65-6 O 30 '89

Inhibition of antigen-induced lymphocyte proliferation by Tat protein from HIV-1. R. P. Viscidi and others. bibl f il *Science* 246:1606-8 D 22 '89

Is regulation of a chloride channel in lymphocytes affected in cystic fibrosis? [discussion of February 3, 1989 article, A cAMP-regulated chloride channel in lymphocytes that is affected in cystic fibrosis] J. H. Chen and others. *Science* 246:1049-50 N 24 '89

Smoking inhibits lung's immune cells [research by Mohan L. Sopori and George M. Shopp] *Science News* 135:255 Ap 22 '89

LYMPHOCYTIC CHORIOMENINGITIS VIRUS

Viral alteration of cell function. M. B. A. Oldstone. bibl il *Scientific American* 261:42-8 Ag '89

LYMPHOCYTIC LEUKEMIA *See* Leukemia

LYMPHOID TISSUE *See* Lymphatic system

LYMPHOKINES

See also

Interleukin

Immunologic tolerance: collaboration between antigen and lymphokines. G. J. V. Nossal. bibl f il *Science* 245:147-53 Jl 14 '89

Regulation of lymphokine messenger RNA stability by a surface-mediated T cell activation pathway. T. Lindsten and others. bibl f il *Science* 244:339-43 Ap 21 '89

LYMPHOMA CELLS *See* Cancer cells

LYMPHOMAS *See* Lymphatic system—Cancer

LYNCH, DAVID

about

The angriest painter in the world. R. Gehr. il *American Film* 14:12 Ap '89

LYNCH, JERRY, 1942-

Relax to the max. il *Runner's World* 24:38-40 Mr '89

LYNCH, JIM

Witch hunt at Parris Island: the Marine Corps targets lesbians. il *The Progressive* 53:24-7 Mr '89

LYNCH, JOHN JOSEPH

about

From typesetter to insider trader? C. Welles. *Business Week* p47-8 D 18 '89

LYNCH, JOYCE

about

Deaths in the name of life. G. Cerio. il por *Newsweek* 113:29 My 8 '89

LYNCH, KELLY

about

Isn't it romantic? T. Hamilton. il pors *Rolling Stone* p181-6 N 16 '89

Kelly Lynch, ex-model, plays Drugstore's spunky junkie. I. Lacher. il pors *People Weekly* 32:137+ N 6 '89

Unique star quality. Y. Z. McDonough. il pors *Harper's Bazaar* 122:208-15+ Ap '89

LYNCH, KEVIN

Henry Threadgill: composer, bandleader, and alchemist. il pors *Down Beat* 56:20-2 F '89

LYNCH, MICHAEL J.

about

Michael J. Lynch [cover story] M. S. Doherty. il por *American Artist* 53:36-41 F '89

LYNCH, PETER

One up on Wall Street [excerpt]; ed. by J. Rothchild. il pors *Money* 18:128-9+ Ja '89

The power of common knowledge [condensed from One up on Wall Street]; ed. by John Rothchild. *Reader's Digest* 135:85-9 Ag '89

about

Can Lynch live up to his reputation? J. Clements. il por *Forbes* 143:174+ Ap 3 '89

Inside traitor. M. K. Evans. il *Gentlemen's Quarterly* 59:153-4 Je '89

Investing: how to beat the pros [interview; cover story] il pors *Changing Times* 43:32-4+ My '89

Johnson and Lynch: an odd couple with a hit formula. J. Friedman. il por *Business Week* p73 Ap 17 '89

Lynch's law? M. Hulbert. il *Forbes* 143:230 Ap 17 '89

Peter Lynch's seven rules for making money. il por *Money* 18:74-5 D '89

Think like an amateur, profit like a pro [interview] pors *U.S. News & World Report* 106:86+ Mr 20 '89

What Magellan's man at the top is buying. G. G. Marcial. por *Business Week* p142 O 9 '89

The world is an investor's oyster. M. Magnet. por *Fortune* 120:67-8 Jl 3 '89

LYNCH, RICHARD

about

Deaths in the name of life. G. Cerio. il por *Newsweek* 113:29 My 8 '89

LYNCH, TIMOTHY B.

(jt. auth) *See* Friedman, Louis, and Lynch, Timothy B.

LYNCH CORP.

Berkshire Hathaway II? [M. Gabelli] J. Clements. il por *Forbes* 144:40-1 Jl 24 '89

LYNCHBURG (TENN.)

Description

Tennessee's legendary sippin' whiskey. J. Rada. il *Southern Living* 24:26+ D '89

LYNCHBURG (VA.)

Galleries and museums

See also

Maier Museum of Art (Lynchburg, Va.)

LYNCHING

The business of us all [racial murders of Y. Hawkins and E. Till] *Commonweal* 116:484-5 S 22 '89

Ida B. Wells-Barnett: an Afro-American prophet. E. M. Townes. *The Christian Century* 106:285-6 Mr 15 '89

Woman awarded $7 million against KKK dies without will; daughters administer [B. M. Donald] pors *Jet* 76:12 Ap 24 '89

LYND, HELEN MERRELL, 1896-

about

Magic Middletown [excerpt] D. W. Hoover. il *Society* 26:73-7 Mr/Ap '89

LYND, ROBERT STAUGHTON, 1892-

about

Magic Middletown [excerpt] D. W. Hoover. il *Society* 26:73-7 Mr/Ap '89

LYNDON B. JOHNSON NATIONAL HISTORICAL PARK (TEX.)

LBJ Ranch: Heart's home [excerpt] R. Houk. il *National Parks* 63:54-5 N/D '89

LYNDON B. JOHNSON SPACE CENTER

NASA flight controllers become AI pioneers. M. M. Waldrop. il *Science* 244:1044-5 Je 2 '89

LYNES, JOSEPH RUSSELL See Lynes, Russell, 1910-
LYNES, RUSSELL, 1910-
Gramercy Park: Manhattan's private prize. il *Architectural Digest* 46:128+ N '89
LYNN, LORETTA
about
So close . . . and yet so far apart. N. Hickey. il pors *TV Guide* 37:10-12 Ag 19-25 '89
LYNN, MICHAEL E., III
about
Look who's paying big bucks to football players. T. Kennedy. il por *Business Week* p54 O 30 '89
Rocky flight into first. J. Lieber. il por *Sports Illustrated* 71:36-8+ N 20 '89
LYNN, ROBERT WOOD
about
The high priest of scholarship. K. L. Woodward. il por *Newsweek* 114:52 Ag 7 '89
LYNN, VANESSA S.
Forced dialogue: Do craft symposia serve the field? *American Craft* 49:14 Je/Jl '89
LYNX (CONSTELLATION) See Constellations
LYNXES
See also
Bobcats
LYO, IN-WHAN, AND AVOURIS, PHAEDON
Negative differential resistance on the atomic scale: implications for atomic scale devices. bibl f il *Science* 245:1369-71 S 22 '89
LYON, DAVID, AND HARRIS, PATRICIA
Equipping your home office. il *Psychology Today* 23:48-9 N '89
LYON, JEFF
Praying for a miracle. il *Redbook* 173:104-5+ Ag '89
LYON, RICK
Almost autumn [poem] *The Nation* 248:708 My 22 '89
The Island [poem] *The Nation* 248:708 My 22 '89
LYON (FRANCE)
Industries
See also
Silk industry—France
LYONS, CHARLOTTE
Date with a dish. See issues of Ebony
LYONS, EMILIO
The Sax Doctor rides again; ed. by Fred Bouchard. il por *Down Beat* 56:61 F '89
LYONS, PAUL
The hidden dangers of yuppie bashing. il *Utne Reader* p92-8 Jl/Ag '89
LYONS (ILL.)
Politics and government
The unlikely tamer of Lyons [Mayor J. Petrucci] P. Alson. il por *Life* 12:29-30 N '89
LYONS DANCE FESTIVAL See Dance festivals—France
LYPHOMED INC.
Lyphomed's vital signs are stabilizing. J. F. Siler. il *Business Week* p46 Jl 3 '89
LYRIC OPERA CENTER FOR AMERICAN ARTISTS
Chicago. J. Von Rhein. *Opera News* 54:47-8 O '89
LYRIC OPERA OF CHICAGO
Chicago. J. Von Rhein. il *Opera News* 53:37-8 Mr 4 '89
Chicago. J. Von Rhein. il *Opera News* 54:38 Ag '89
Chicago at its prime. T. Willis. il *Opera News* 54:12-14+ O '89
Chicago on the air (I). il *Opera News* 53:41-4 My '89
Chicago on the air (II). il *Opera News* 53:37-40 Je '89
Chicago plans for the millennium. P. J. Smith. *Opera News* 54:12 D 9 '89
From Chicago with love. A. Kuflik. il *Newsweek* 114:73-4 D 18 '89
Ring in the new. P. G. Davis. il *New York* 22:83-5 N 27 '89
LYRICISTS
See also
Gershwin, Ira, 1896-1983
Razaf, Andy, 1895-1973
LYRICS (ROCK MUSIC) See Rock music
LYSERGIC ACID DIETHYLAMIDE See LSD
LYSILOMA LATISILIQUA See Sabicu
LYSINE
See also
Feeds—Lysine content
A multiubiquitin chain is confined to specific lysine in a targeted short-lived protein. V. Chau and others. bibl f il *Science* 243:1576-83 Mr 24 '89
LYSIS
Second cytotoxic pathway of diphtheria toxin suggested by nuclease activity. M. P. Chang and others. bibl f il *Science* 246:1165-8 D 1 '89
LYSIS CORPORATION
Computers, customers and hand-holding. E. Dyson. il *Forbes* 144:128 Ag 7 '89
LYSOSOMES
A role for a 70-kilodaton heat shock protein in lysosomal degradation of intracellular proteins. H.-L. Chiang and others. bibl f il *Science* 246:382-5 O 20 '89

LYSOZYMES
Control of enzyme activity by an engineered disulfide bond. M. Matsumura and B. W. Matthews. bibl f il *Science* 243:792-4 F 10 '89
Splicing on-off switches into proteins [disulfide bond; research by Brian W. Matthews and Masazumi Matsumura] *Science News* 135:123 F 25 '89
LYSTAD, MARY H.
20 years on Sesame Street. bibl f il *Children Today* 18:20-2 S/O '89
Taming the Wild Things. bibl f il *Children Today* 18:16-19 Mr/Ap '89

M

M/A-COM INC.
M/A-COM uses gallium-arsenide facility to become EW subsystem supplier. *Aviation Week & Space Technology* 131:103 S 18 '89
M-BASE (MUSICAL GROUP)
Jazz makes a new sound with soul, pop and computers. E. T. Louis. bibl (p230) il *Smithsonian* 20:176-8+ O '89
M-Base [performance at Brooklyn Academy of Music] B. Milkowski. il *Down Beat* 56:50-1 Mr '89
M. BUTTERFLY [drama] See Hwang, David Henry
M.D. ANDERSON CANCER CENTER
Medical Center lifeline [computer use] C. Strehlo. il *Personal Computing* 13:97 Ja '89
M. H. DE YOUNG MEMORIAL MUSEUM
A master showman imbues clothes with life [S. de Pietri, curator of costume exhibits] C. R. Milbank. il por *Architectural Digest* 46:88+ S '89
M. L. MIL HELICOPTER DESIGN BUREAU (SOVIET UNION)
Mil Bureau designing new medium transport helicopter to replace Mi-8. D. Hughes. *Aviation Week & Space Technology* 130:28-9 Je 5 '89
Mil Mi-28 attack helicopter in final tests prior to full-scale production [Soviet helicopter] il *Aviation Week & Space Technology* 130:78-9 Je 5 '89
Western experts impressed by design of Mi-28 prototype [attack helicopter exhibited at Paris Air Show] D. E. Fink. il *Aviation Week & Space Technology* 130:44-6+ Je 26 '89
M&M PRODUCTS COMPANY
M&M Products purchased by Boston minority firm [BML Associates] il *Jet* 76:16-17 Jl 17 '89
Negotiations end between M&M Products and BML. il *Jet* 76:36 Ag 14 '89
With M&M buy, B.M.L. moves into hair-care business. N. McCall. il *Black Enterprise* 20:17 Ag '89
MA, GURU See Prophet, Elizabeth Clare
MA, YO-YO, 1955-
about
Cellist for today. P. G. Davis. il por *New York* 22:68 My 29 '89
Profiles. D. Blum. il *The New Yorker* 65:41-2+ My 1 '89
MAASS, PEGGY
about
The daily record. G. Knuth and L. Rothlein. il por *Women's Sports & Fitness* 11:62+ My '89
MABA See Mid-Atlantic Booksellers Association
MABUS, RAY
about
Miss. Rep. Espy, Gov. Mabus blaze new political trail to push progress in state. S. Booker. il pors *Jet* 75:26-7 Ja 16 '89
MAC SYSTEM 7.0 OPERATING SYSTEM See System 7.0 operating system
MACADAMS, LEWIS
Populism offers a progressive alternative to liberalism. il *Utne Reader* p72 Mr/Ap '89
MACANDREWS & FORBES GROUP, INCORPORATED
Ron Perelman's $640 million unsure thing [acquisition and resale of Technicolor, Inc.] R. King. il por *Forbes* 144:42-4+ O 30 '89
MACAO
See also
Airports—Macao
MACAQUES
Ms. Monkey [female macaque's social climbing; study in La Forêt des Singes, France] M. F. Small. il *Natural History* p10+ Ja '89
Training
On Malay Peninsula picking coconuts is monkey business. R. S. Peffer. bibl (p147) il *Smithsonian* 19:110-12+ Ja '89
MACARENA, SERRANÍA DE LA (COLOMBIA) See Serranía de la Macarena (Colombia)

MACARONI PRODUCTS *See* Pasta
MACARTHUR (JOHN D. AND CATHERINE T.) FOUNDA-
TION *See* John D. and Catherine T. MacArthur Foundation
MACAULEY, ROBERT CONOVER
about
With an entrepreneur's energy, Americares' Bob Macauley
brings help to the world's needy. K. Hubbard. il pors
People Weekly 31:71+ My 29 '89
MACAYEAL, D. R.
(jt. auth) *See* Lindstrom, D. R., and MacAyeal, D. R.
MACCALLUM, LEE
Your pregnancy. *See* issues of Glamour
MACCOUN, ROBERT J.
Experimental research on jury decision-making. bibl f *Science*
244:1046-50 Je 2 '89
MACCULLOCH, DIARMAID
Arminius and the Arminians. il por *History Today* 39:27-34
O '89
MACDONALD, H. ROBSON
Mechanisms of immunological tolerance. bibl f *Science*
246:982 N 24 '89
MACDONALD, JEFFREY R.
about
Are journalists basically liars? F. Bruning. il *Maclean's* 102:11
Ap 24 '89
The journalist and the murderer (I). J. Malcolm. *The New
Yorker* 65:38-42+ Mr 13 '89
The journalist and the murderer (II). J. Malcolm. *The New
Yorker* 65:49-50+ Mr 20 '89
McGinniss: a travesty of libel. M. Garbus. *Publishers Weekly*
235:69 Ap 21 '89
A reporter isn't a friend. J. Alter and G. Cowley. il por
Newsweek 113:62 Mr 27 '89
MACDONALD, JERRY P.
about
Tracking the early Permian. L. S. Bowlds. il pors *Earth
Science* 42:16-19 Summ '89
MACDONALD, PETER
about
Bad day at Window Rock. S. D. Atchison. il por *Business
Week* p32 Mr 6 '89
Casting a long shadow. J. N. Baker. por *Newsweek* 113:32
Ja 2 '89
Letting down the tribe. J. V. Lamar, Jr. il por *Time* 133:30
Mr 6 '89
Showdown at Window Rock [cover story] S. Tolan. il pors
The New York Times Magazine p28-31+ N 26 '89
MACDONALD, RICHARD J.
The meaning of achievement. por *Channels (New York, N.Y.:
1986)* 9:37 Jl/Ag '89
MACDONALD GROUP
Penguin Group sells Sphere to Maxwell's Macdonald Publish-
ing. V. Menkes. *Publishers Weekly* 235:40 Ap 7 '89
MACDOUGALL, A. KENT
about
Confessions of a closet leftist. L. Zuckerman. il por *Time*
133:58 F 6 '89
MACDOWELL, ANDIE
about
Dandy Andie. S. Orlean. pors *Rolling Stone* p36-9+ O 19
'89
Sex, lies, and Andie MacDowell. E. Pooley. il pors *New
York* 22:38-42 Jl 17 '89
Why is Andie MacDowell talking dirty? A. Elliot. por
Mademoiselle 95:90 Ag '89
MACE, FLORA CARRIE
about
Double vision. B. J. Miller. il *American Craft* 49:40-5 O/N
'89
MACE, RON
Should the Senate approve the "Americans with Disabilities
Act of 1989"? [excerpts from testimony, May 10, 1989]
Congressional Digest 68:300+ D '89
MACEACHEN, ALLAN JOSEPH
about
A Red-Chamber power broker. L. Van Dusen. *Maclean's*
102:28 O 30 '89
MACFADDEN, GARY D.
Are we there yet? map *Bicycling* 30:152 Je '89
MACFADDEN HOLDINGS, INC.
Alien beancounters invade the Enquirer. A. Fins. il *Business
Week* p35 S 11 '89
Peter Callahan: an acquiring mind [buyout of National en-
quirer] A. Rothman. il por *Business Week* p139-40 My
15 '89
MACFARQUHAR, NEIL
Go down, Moses. il *Esquire* 112:56 D '89
MACFARQUHAR, RODERICK
The end of the Chinese revolution [cover story] il *The
New York Review of Books* 36:8-10 Jl 20 '89
MACH, PETER
about
In the mood. B. Schwalberg. il *Popular Photography* 96:47-8
Mr '89
MACH OPERATING SYSTEM
Mach: the model for future Unix. A. Tevanian, Jr. and
B. Smith. *Byte* 14:411-12+ N '89

MACHADO, ANTONIO, 1875-1939
about
Spanish dreams from a French cemetery. J. Valls-Russell.
il *The New Leader* 72:10-11 Mr 20 '89
MACHAN, TIBOR R.
Are human rights real? por *The Humanist* 49:28-9+ N/D
'89
MACHANDEL [dance] *See* Dance reviews—Single works
MACHINE GUNS
Guns 'R' Us. M. Maranz. *The New Republic* 200:12+ Ja
23 '89
MACHINE THEORY
See also
Artificial intelligence
Cellular automata
Computational complexity
Turing machines
MACHINE TOOL INDUSTRY
See also
Bendix Corp.
Houdaille Industries, Inc.
Export-import trade
The allies: fools or tools? [U.S. raises objection to machine
tool exports to the Soviets] *Newsweek* 114:54 O 30 '89
MACHINE TRANSLATING
The accidental tourist [S. A. Rondel's Voice computer] M.
Barrier. il por *Nation's Business* 77:78 Ap '89
Instant spoken translation [S. A. Rondel's Voice computer]
W. J. Hawkins. il por *Popular Science* 234:78+ My '89
Trying to decipher babel [Japanese systems] B. Hillenbrand.
il *Time* 134:62 Jl 24 '89
Why can't computers talk? D. Fong. il *Forbes* 143:130 My
1 '89
MACHINE VISION
Machine vision focuses on profits [cover story] G. T. Pope.
il *High Technology Business* 9:14-17 Ja '89
MACHINERY
See also
Agricultural equipment
Conveying equipment
Harvesting machinery
Stands, tables, etc.
Benchtop router table. L. Okrend. il *Workbench* 45:68-9
Mr/Ap '89
Hands-off router. R. J. DeCristoforo. il *Popular Science*
234:114-16 Mr '89
How to build a router table. R. Capotosto. il *Popular
Mechanics* 166:75-7 S '89
Mobile miter box. R. J. DeCristoforo. il *Popular Science*
234:86-8 F '89
MACHINERY INDUSTRY
See also
Agricultural equipment industry
Emhart Corp.
Harnischfeger Industries, Inc.
Machine tool industry
Finance
Machine makers enjoy the ride—while it lasts. Z. Schiller.
il *Business Week* p71 Ja 9 '89
MACHINES *See* Machinery
MACHINISTS
See also
International Association of Machinists and Aerospace
Workers
MACHLOWITZ, DAVID S.
Take the best home videos. il *Parents* 64:64+ Ag '89
MACHOVER, TOD, 1953-
about
VALIS [opera] Reviews
The New Yorker 65:67-8 Jl 31 '89. A. Porter
Opera News il 54:20-2 Jl '89. P. J. Smith
MACHU PICCHU (PERU)
At last: city in the sky. C. N. Barnard. il map *Modern
Maturity* 32:48-55+ Je/Jl '89
On the trail to Machu Picchu. C. N. Barnard. il map *Modern
Maturity* 32:80-4+ Ap/My '89
MACHUA, WILFRED
A Kenyan tycoon. il por *World Press Review* 36:52 Jl '89
MACIE, TOM
From print shop to stage floor. il *Theatre Crafts* 23:94
Ag/S '89
MACINNES, LESLEY
(jt. auth) *See* Hanson, William S., and Macinnes, Lesley
MACINNES, PATRICIA
The tunnel [story] il *Seventeen* 48:164-7+ S '89
MACINNIS, AL
about
The 1989 Sport Stanley Cup Finals MVP. il por *Sport (New
York, N.Y.)* 80:78 Ag '89
MACINNIS, JEFF
Braving the Northwest Passage. il map *National Geographic*
175:584-601 My '89
MACINNIS, ROBERTA
To the rescue. il pors *Runner's World* 24:36-8 Ag '89
MACINTOSH (COMPUTER) *See* Computers
MACINTOSH OPERATING SYSTEMS
See also
MultiFinder operating system

MACINTOSH OPERATING SYSTEMS—See also—*cont.*
System 7.0 operating system
Answers to my Mac mess [preventing hard disk crashes and MouseStick] E. Shapiro. il *Byte* 14:129-30+ Ap '89
The Mac interface: showing its age. D. E. Crabb. *Byte* 14 Mac Special Ed:MAC235-MAC237 Je '89
Macintosh vs. MS-DOS: which system is better for page layout? S. Morgenstern. il *Home Office Computing* 7:32+ F '89
An MS-DOS user eyes the Mac. N. Sullivan. il *Home Office Computing* 7:80 Jl '89
A tale of two operating systems. D. E. Crabb. il *Byte* 14:137-9 D '89
Virtual memory, "hot links" coming to the Mac OS. *Byte* 14:17-18+ Jl '89
A virtual toolkit for Windows and the Mac [XVT 1.1] R. Valdés. il *Byte* 14:209-10+ Mr '89

MACINTYRE, ALASDAIR C.
about
Recoiling from reason. M. C. Nussbaum. bibl f il *The New York Review of Books* 36:36-41 D 7 '89

MACIOCHA, EDWARD
Baubiologie: Germany's natural home movement. il *Utne Reader* p78-9 My/Je '89

MACISAAC, HEATHER SMITH
Chef's special. il por *House & Garden* 161:90-3 Ja '89
Coming home. il *House & Garden* 161:36+ D '89
Curtain call. il por *House & Garden* 161:60+ N '89
Getting plastered. il *House & Garden* 161:56 Ja '89
House call. il pors *House & Garden* 161:232-7 O '89

MACK, JOHN
Ways of the ancestors. il *Natural History* p24+ Ap '89

MACK, JOHN PAUL
about
All the Wright moves. J. H. Fund. il *National Review* 41:19-20 Je 16 '89
Capitol offense. por *Time* 133:38 My 15 '89
One of the boys. M. B. Carlson. *The New Republic* 200:11-13 Je 5 '89
The protégé and the victim. E. Clift. il pors *Newsweek* 113:38 My 15 '89
A victim's story. K. Ringle. pors *Reader's Digest* 135:49-54 Ag '89
A Washington morality tale. il por *U.S. News & World Report* 106:22 My 22 '89
Wright's aide: too little, too late. E. Clift. il pors *Newsweek* 112:41 My 22 '89

MACK, KEVIN
about
Brown's Mack a free man, returns to football team. il por *Jet* 77:48 N 27 '89

MACK, MICHAEL
Vigil lights: there's something special about an old flame. *U.S. Catholic* 54:29-30 Ap '89

MACK, STAN
Heard at the Super Bowl. il por *Sports Illustrated* 70:86 Ja 30 '89

MACK LAKE (MICH.)
Mack Lake, Michigan [Kirtland's warblers] R. H. Mohlenbrock. il map *Natural History* p90-5 O '89

MACKAY, HARVEY
about
How to swim with the sharks [interview] P. Edwards and S. Edwards. il por *Home Office Computing* 7:46-8 Ap '89

MACKE, KENNETH
about
From punching bag to retailing black belt. R. Mitchell. il por *Business Week* p62+ N 20 '89

MACKENDRICK, ALEXANDER, 1912-
about
Sweet smell of success [film] Reviews
Video 13:64 Jl '89. M. Fleischmann

MACKENZIE, JAMES J., 1939-, AND EL-ASHRY, MOHAMED T.
Ill winds: air pollution's toll on trees and crops. il map *Technology Review* 92:64-71 Ap '89

MACKENZIE, ROBERT
A busy person's guide to TV [cover story] il *TV Guide* 37:2-5 Ap 8-14 '89
What would Matt Dillon have thought of Sonny Crockett? il *TV Guide* 37:36-9 My 6-12 '89

MACKENZIE, ROBERT
Rescue in Mozambique [with editorial comment by James R. Whelan] il pors map *Conservative Digest* 15:39+, 70 Mr/Ap '89

MACKENZIE, SALLY
Have a happy and safe Halloween. il *Parents* 64:159-62+ O '89

MACKENZIE, WARREN, 1924-
about
Down-to-earth idealist. R. Silberman. bibl f il por *American Craft* 49:32-9 Je/Jl '89

MACKENZIE, WILL
about
Worth winning [film] Reviews
People Weekly il 32:18-19 N 13 '89. R. Novak

MACKERODT, FRED
Aviation. See issues of Popular Mechanics beginning April 1987

MACKERRAS, SIR CHARLES, 1925-
about
Mackerras's Schubert ninth. R. Freed. il por *Stereo Review* 54:144 F '89

MACKEY, BETTY BARR
Spring crocus. il *Flower and Garden* 33:30 S/O '89

MACKIE, BOB
about
Bob Mackie: casual comfort in Beverly Hills. J. Allen. il por *Architectural Digest* 46:146-51+ S '89

MACKINAC ISLAND (MICH.)
See also
Hotels, motels, etc.—Mackinac Island (Mich.)
Description and travel
Mackinac Island. M. Elder. il maps *Gourmet* 49:70-5+ Je '89

MACKINNON, DOUGLAS, AND BALDANZA, JOSEPH
Footprints on the moon [cover story] il *American History Illustrated* 24:18-23 Summ '89

MACKINNON, RODERICK, AND MILLER, CHRISTOPHER, 1946-
Mutant potassium channels with altered binding of charybdotoxin, a pore-blocking peptide inhibitor. bibl f il *Science* 245:1382-5 S 22 '89

MACKINTOSH, CAMERON
about
A box office superstar. P. Young. il por *Maclean's* 102:44 Mr 27 '89
The 'middlebrow' maestro of megahits. E. Behr. il por *Newsweek* 114:68-9 O 2 '89

MACKINTOSH, CHARLES RENNIE, 1868-1928
about
Glasgow's Mackintosh revival. A. Hills. il *History Today* 39:6-7 Ap '89

MACKLIN, ELIZABETH
I imagine back [poem] *The New Yorker* 65:70 S 4 '89
Instructions: early epiphanies [poem] *The New Yorker* 65:48 Je 12 '89
Looking to console the maker [poem] *The New Yorker* 65:101 Mr 13 '89
Our fall [poem] *The New Yorker* 65:66 O 23 '89
Reassurance in a hot summer [poem] *The New Yorker* 65:34 Jl 24 '89
Surface tension [poem] *The New Yorker* 64:36 Ja 30 '89
Two poems [poem] *The New Yorker* 65:52 D 11 '89

MACKLOWE, HARRY
about
Notes and comment. *The New Yorker* 65:26 Je 26 '89

MACKOFF, BARBARA
Career workshop. See occasional issues of Ladies' Home Journal beginning February 1988 through February 1989

MACKOWN, DIANA
about
The art of the feud: sculptor Louise Nevelson's tangled legal legacy. D. Rabinowitz. il pors *New York* 22:82-8+ S 25 '89
A battle over a legacy pits sculptor Louise Nevelson's son against her loyal aide. P. Freeman. il pors *People Weekly* 32:42-4 Jl 17 '89

MACKOWSKI, MAURA J.
Home on the Esrange. il *Ad Astra* 1:39-40+ My '89
Moon power. il por *Ad Astra* 1:34-9 Jl/Ag '89

MACKRELL, JUDITH
Trinidad Sevillano's special promise: straight from the heart. il pors *Dance Magazine* 63:24-7 Jl '89

MACLAINE, SHIRLEY
about
Shirley MacLaine. B. Darrach. il por *People Weekly* 32 Special Issue:86-7 Fall '89
Shirley MacLaine: the prime of her lives. J. Rovin. il pors *Ladies' Home Journal* 106:74+ Ap '89
Steel magnolias. J. E. Fitch. il por *American Film* 15:62 N '89

MACLEAN, AMY
about
Tour de Tundra: cyclist Amy McClean caps the grueling Iditabike. Y. Samer. il *Women's Sports & Fitness* 11:56-7 Je '89

MACLEAN, CHARLES, 1946-
An Adriatic idyll. il *House & Garden* 161:68+ S '89
Forging ahead. il por *House & Garden* 161:150-5+ N '89
Tropical Scotland. il *House & Garden* 161:136-41+ F '89
Tuscan pastoral [cover story] il por *House & Garden* 161:146-59+ S '89

MACLEAN, JOHN N.
CNN takes on the big boys. il *Reader's Digest* 135:148-52 Ag '89

MACLEAN HUNTER LTD.
Assuring the regulators [purchase of Selkirk Communications] J. DeMont. il *Maclean's* 102:36 Je 12 '89

MACLEAN'S (PERIODICAL)
From the editor's desk. K. Doyle. See issues of Maclean's beginning March 14, 1983

MACLEAN'S PHOTO CONTEST *See* Photography—Competitions

MACLEISH, WILLIAM H., 1928-
The blue god. bibl (p170) il map *Smithsonian* 19:44-56+ F '89
Painting a portrait of the Stream from miles above—and below. il *Smithsonian* 19:42-52+ Mr '89
about
Around the Mall and beyond. E. Park. il por *Smithsonian* 19:24+ Mr '89

MACLEOD, NORMAN S.
(jt. auth) *See* Kitchell, Jennifer A., and MacLeod, Norman S.

MACLEOD, SCOTT
The new PLO? bibl f il *The New York Review of Books* 36:44-9 Ap 13 '89

MACLEOD, STEWART
A community of small communities. por *Maclean's* 102:64 Je 5 '89
The favor of Erik Nielsen's silence. por *Maclean's* 102:64 S 11 '89
Helping taxpayers by using fewer 'jerks'. por *Maclean's* 102:64 Mr 13 '89
The PM's black, travelling cloud. por *Maclean's* 102:68 S 4 '89
Subsidizing the hyphenated Canadian. por *Maclean's* 102:48 Ja 9 '89
'Well-educated, dynamic man seeks . . .'. por *Maclean's* 102:64 My 29 '89

MACMANUS, DECLAN PATRICK ALOYSIUS *See* Costello, Elvis

MACMILLAN, RON
Bishop Ting and China's house churches. il *The Christian Century* 106:755-6 Ag 16-23 '89

MACMILLAN, INC.
KKR to buy Macmillan Book Clubs and Intertec for $310 million. *Publishers Weekly* 235:16 Je 16 '89
Macmillan/Shultz deal, take two. por *Publishers Weekly* 236:53 N 3 '89

MACMILLAN BLOEDEL LIMITED
A towering fight [proposed logging of Sitka spruce on Vancouver Island] H. Quinn. il *Maclean's* 102:46 Je 5 '89

MACMILLAN/MCGRAW-HILL SCHOOL PUBLISHING COMPANY
Macmillan, McGraw-Hill combine elhi businesses. M. Reuter. il *Publishers Weekly* 235:24+ Je 2 '89

MACMURRAY, JOHN, 1891-1976?
about
Should religion concern itself with political and social questions? W. A. Barry. *America* 161:61-2+ Jl 29-Ag 5 '89

MACNAB, ROY
For honour alone. il *History Today* 39:5-7 Ja '89

MACNEALE, PEGGY
Notes for new gardeners. *See* issues of Flower and Garden

MACNEIL, KAREN
Whiskey codes. il *Ms.* 18:35 N '89

MACNEIL, ROBERT, 1931-
Spell of a storyteller [condensed from Wordstruck] bibl *Reader's Digest* 135:181-2+ O '89

MACNEILL, JIM
Strategies for sustainable economic development. bibl il *Scientific American* 261:154-9+ S '89

MACNICOL, PETER
about
Striking out with Sigourney, social slimer Peter MacNicol still scores in Ghostbusters II. J. Kaufman. il pors *People Weekly* 32:91-2 Jl 17 '89

MACNOW, GLEN
Buffalo's Rich baseball legacy. il por *Nation's Business* 77:42-5 F '89
Cities get into the game. il *Nation's Business* 77:48-9+ N '89
From calamity to conglomerate. il por *Nation's Business* 77:48-50+ My '89
Sports tie-ins help firms score. il *Nation's Business* 77:36-8 S '89

MACON (GA.)
Galleries and museums
See also
Harriet Tubman Historical and Cultural Museum (Macon, Ga.)

MACPHERSON, ELLE
about
What's the big deal? E. M. Swift. il pors *Sports Illustrated* 70 Special Issue:207+ F '89

MACPHERSON STRUT SHOCK ABSORBERS *See* Automobiles—Shock absorbers

MACQUEEN, GLENDA, AND OTHERS
Pavlovian conditioning of rat mucosal mast cells to secrete rat mast cell protease II. bibl f il *Science* 243:83-5 Ja 6 '89

MACRAE, MEREDITH
about
Meredith MacRae. il pors *Redbook* 172:90-1 Ja '89

MACROBERT, ALAN
Backyard astronomy. *See* occasional issues of Sky and Telescope beginning August 1983

Celestial calendar. *See* issues of Sky and Telescope beginning October 1984
The sun, moon, and planets this month. *See* issues of Sky and Telescope beginning April 1988

MACROMIND INC.
Multimedia for the MAC may make them multimillions. M. Shao. il *Business Week* p155 O 9 '89

MACROMOLECULES
Macromolecular crystals. A. McPherson. bibl il *Scientific American* 260:62-9 Mr '89
Macromolecular structure from anomalous dispersion [cover story] J. Karle. bibl f il *Physics Today* 42:22-9 Je '89

MACROPHAGES
Bringing home the bacon [nitric oxide secreted by macrophages; research by Michael Marletta and Dennis Stuehr] S. Vogel. il *Discover* 10:42 Jl '89
Identification of monocyte chemotactic activity produced by malignant cells. D. T. Graves and others. bibl f il *Science* 245:1490-3 S 29 '89
Receptor-mediated drug delivery to macrophages in chemotherapy of leishmaniasis. A. Mukhopadhyay and others. bibl f il *Science* 244:705-7 My 12 '89
T cells against a bacterial heat shock protein recognize stressed macrophages. T. Koga and others. bibl f il *Science* 245:1112-15 S 8 '89
Where AIDS takes aim [work of Howard Gendelman and Monte Meltzer] P. Gadsby. il *Discover* 10:52-3 Ja '89

MACROPHOTOGRAPHY
A world of coral harmonies. S. Rudavsky. il *Omni (New York, N.Y.)* 11:58-63 Je '89

MACROPROCESSORS
Make word processing easier with macros and menus. R. Kendall. il *Home Office Computing* 7:20-1 Ag '89
PRD+. S. Morgenstern. il *Home Office Computing* 7:80 Je '89
Slashing time with macros. R. Blodgett. il *Personal Computing* 13:53-4+ Jl '89
A useful alternative to macro software [AutoKey macro keyboard] R. Bel Bruno. il *Personal Computing* 13:202 D '89

MACSHANE, DENIS
Dreaming of the forty-hour week. *The Nation* 248:658-60 My 15 '89

MACSWEENEY, EVE
Affairs of the art. il *Harper's Bazaar* 122:168-73 D '89
Angst of the spirit. il *Harper's Bazaar* 122:174-5+ O '89

MACULAR DEGENERATION
Diet and light may affect sight [research by Lynette Feeney-Burns] *USA Today (Periodical)* 118:5-6 O '89

MACUNAIMA [film] *See* Motion picture reviews—Single works

MACWATTERS, VIRGINIA
about
Forever Adele. M. Dismore. il por *Opera News* 53:34-5 Ja 7 '89

MACY (R. H.) & CO., INC. *See* R. H. Macy & Co., Inc.

MACY'S THANKSGIVING DAY PARADE
Miracle on 34th Street. P. Oliver. il *Travel Holiday* 172:82-7 N '89

MAD (PERIODICAL)
Acquisition of the year: Mad magazine [impact of Time-Warner deal] il *Newsweek* 113:50 Mr 20 '89

MAD HOUSERS (ORGANIZATION)
Mad Housers help homeless [Atlanta, Ga.] L. S. Bates. il *The Progressive* 53:15 My '89

MAD LIBS (GAME)
Homework [Mad Libs program] H. E. H. Aycock. il *Compute!* 11:98 O '89

MADAGASCAN ART *See* Art, Madagascan

MADAGASCAR
See also
Environment—Madagascar
Funeral rites and ceremonies—Madagascar
Wildlife—Madagascar
Social life and customs
Exhibitions
Art à la carte [Madagascar: island of the ancestors at the American Museum of Natural History] C. Mac Connie. il *Travel Holiday* 171:92 My '89
Ways of the ancestors. J. Mack. il *Natural History* p24+ Ap '89

MADAGASCAR PERIWINKLE *See* Periwinkle

MADAME C. J. WALKER COMPANY
Madam C. J. Walker: first black woman millionaire. K. Doyle. por *American History Illustrated* 24:24-5 Mr '89

MADAME SOUSATZKA [film] *See* Motion picture reviews—Single works

MADAUS, GEORGE F.
(jt. auth) *See* Haney, Walter, and Madaus, George F.
about
New ways of thinking about testing [interview] M. C. McClellan. por *Phi Delta Kappan* 70:642-5 Ap '89

MADCAAP (ORGANIZATION)
A new kind of moving day [houses relocated for the poor in Canton, Miss.] D. S. Levy. il *Time* 134:25-7 O 30 '89

MADDOX, BRENDA
Miami J'yce: love walks right out of a 'Ulysses' symposium. il *The New York Times Book Review* 94:7 F 26 '89

MADDOX, BRENDA—*cont.*
Out of Amazonia. il por *Ms.* 18:54-7 O '89
MADDOX, TOM
Baby strange [fiction] il *Omni (New York, N.Y.)* 11:70-2+ Ap '89
MADDREY, ERWIN E.
about
Iconoclasts. R. Addis. il pors *Forbes* 143:49+ Ap 17 '89
MADE IN USA [film] *See* Motion picture reviews—Single works
MADEIRA (MADEIRA ISLANDS)
Description and travel
An island for individualists. D. Wachholz. il *World Press Review* 36:62 Ap '89
MADEJA, STANLEY S.
The corporation and arts education: a new merger? *Design for Arts in Education* 90:20-4 N/D '88
MADELEINE GALLAY (FIRM)
New talents: Madeleine Gallay. N. Malkin. il por *Harper's Bazaar* 122:134 Mr '89
MADELEY, JOHN
Choking off the supply. il *World Health* p28-9 Je '89
MADELIN, HENRI
The Church in France since the second Vatican Council. il *America* 160:582-4+ Je 17-24 '89
MADENSKI, MELISSA
The watercolor page: Michael Schlicting. il pors *American Artist* 53:42-5+ Je '89
MADEWOOD PLANTATION (NAPOLEONVILLE, LA.) IN ART
Ten artists respond to a southern plantation [cover story] M. S. Doherty. il *American Artist* 53:32-43 Ja '89
MADEY, J. M. J.
about
Franklin Institute honors Lorenz, Oatley and Madey. M. Siegel. pors *Physics Today* 42:113 S '89
MADISON, DEBORAH
Hot, hearty stews. il *Organic Gardening* 36:38-42 F '89
MADISON, DOLLEY, 1768-1849
about
Hello Dolley—on the trail of the Madisons. N. Barry. il por *Gourmet* 49:130+ D '89
MADISON, JAMES, 1751-1836
about
Hello Dolley—on the trail of the Madisons. N. Barry. il por *Gourmet* 49:130+ D '89
The spirit of '89. W. L. Miller. *The New Republic* 200:21-4 Je 26 '89
Religion
Two centuries of Virginia's Act for Religious Freedom. E. Turner. il *USA Today (Periodical)* 117:73-5 Mr '89
MADISON (WIS.)
Bookstores
See Booksellers and bookselling—Wisconsin
MADISON AVENUE (NEW YORK, N.Y.)
At home on Madison. A. Foxley. il *House & Garden* 161:206+ My '89
MADISON COUNTIANS ALLIED AGAINST POVERTY (ORGANIZATION) *See* MadCAAP (Organization)
MADISON SQUARE GARDEN NETWORK
The Yankee dollar [Cablevision and MSG battle over cable rights to Yankee baseball] C. Byron. il *New York* 22:20+ Je 5 '89
MADOFF, BERNARD L.
about
Living off the spread. R. L. Stern. il *Forbes* 144:66-7 Jl 10 '89
MADOFF, STEVEN HENRY
Face to face [cover story] il por *Art News* 88:104-7 F '89
MADOFF (BERNARD L.) INVESTMENT SECURITIES *See* Bernard L. Madoff Investment Securities
MADONNA
about
Gal pals Sandra Bernhard and Madonna monkey around to save the jungle. il pors *People Weekly* 31:54-6 Je 12 '89
Like a Catholic: Madonna's challenge to her Church. A. M. Greeley. il *America* 160:447-9 My 13 '89
'Like a prayer': Madonna's true confessions. J. D. Considine. il *Rolling Stone* p79-80 Ap 6 '89
Madonna. por *People Weekly* 32:83 D 25 '89-Ja 1 '90
Madonna. R. Lacayo. pors *People Weekly* 32 Special Issue:50-1 Fall '89
Madonna [interview; cover story] B. Zehme. il pors *Rolling Stone* p50-3+ Mr 23 '89
Madonna holds court. V. Woods. il pors *Vogue* 179:342-51 My '89
Madonna: the message behind the makeovers. C. Krupp. il pors *Glamour* 87:200-1 My '89
Madonna's "Like a prayer". P. Puterbaugh. il por *Stereo Review* 54:67 Jl '89
Surprise! It's splits, fits and quits again for Sean and Madonna. J. S. Kunen. il pors *People Weekly* 31:44-6 Ja 23 '89
What no one will admit about race in America. R. Rosenbaum. il *Mademoiselle* 95:94+ Ag '89
MADRAS SHIRTS *See* Shirts
MADRAZO, MARIANO FORTUNY Y *See* Fortuny y Madrazo, Mariano

LE MADRI (NEW YORK, N.Y.: RESTAURANT) *See* New York (N.Y.)—Restaurants, nightclubs, bars, etc.
MADRID (SPAIN)
Galleries and museums
See also
Museo del Prado (Madrid, Spain)
Industries
See also
Publishers and publishing—Spain
Restaurants, nightclubs, bars, etc.
City on the verge of a nervous breakdown? A. Jolis. il *Vogue* 179:120+ Jl '89
Theater
Six characters in Madrid: American Repertory Theatre tours to Europe. S. Lieberman. il *Theatre Crafts* 23:34-5+ My '89
MADRID (SPAIN) FASHION SHOWS *See* Fashion shows
MADSEN, DAVID B.
A grasshopper in every pot. il *Natural History* p22+ Jl '89
MADSEN, HUNTER
about
Is the gay revolution a flop? A. Toufexis. il pors *Time* 134:56 Jl 10 '89
MADSEN, VIRGINIA
about
First, she threw the script in the garbage. L. Farr. il pors *TV Guide* 37:6-7+ My 27-Je 2 '89
Virginia real. J. Schulian. il pors *Gentlemen's Quarterly* 59:204-7 F '89
MADSON, JOHN
Point of view. il *National Wildlife* 27:42-4 O/N '89
MAEDER, THOMAS
Wounded healers [cover story] il *The Atlantic* 263:37-47 Ja '89
MAEROFF, GENE I.
The principles of teacher empowerment. *The Education Digest* 54:6-9 F '89
MAFIA
Bring back the Mafia. R. Moran. por *Newsweek* 114:8 Ag 7 '89
A change of command for the Chicago Mob [death of J. Ferriola] *Newsweek* 113:34 Mr 27 '89
Charges against Teamsters resolved. *Monthly Labor Review* 112:58 My '89
Cold-blooded King of a Hill under siege [J. Gotti; cover story] K. Gross. il pors *People Weekly* 31:70-3+ Mr 27 '89
The feds drive a wedge into the Teamsters. A. Bernstein. il *Business Week* p90 F 6 '89
In Gotti they trust. P. Hamill. il por *Esquire* 112:63-5 O '89
Italian justice on the run [Sicilian Mafia] S. F. Senigallia. il *The New Leader* 72:10-11 S 4 '89
John Gotti: running the Mob [cover story] S. Raab. il pors *The New York Times Magazine* p30-3+ Ap 2 '89
The last Godfather? [arrest of J. Gotti] P. McKillop. il pors *Newsweek* 113:25 F 6 '89
"Like a slaughter-house for hogs" [manipulation of penny stocks] R. L. Stern and C. Poole. il *Forbes* 144:42-4 D 25 '89
The man who knew too much [involvement of M. Zolp and the Mafia in securities fraud] J. Crudele. il por *New York* 22:16 Mr 6 '89
MCA suspends video head for allegedly funneling funds to Mafia [E. F. Giaquinto] P. Sweeting. *Publishers Weekly* 235:27 Ja 13 '89
Overhauling the Teamsters [racketeering case] A. Bernstein. *Business Week* p35-6 Mr 27 '89
Tour shakedowns alleged [N. Walters accused by M. Franzese] J. Capeci. il por *Rolling Stone* p20 My 4 '89
The wild and crazy gangster: Michael Markowitz's twisted American dream. P. Blauner. il pors *New York* 22:52-6+ O 9 '89
MAGAININ SCIENCES INC.
Magainin: the penicillin of the 1990s? J. Weber, Jr. il por *Business Week* Special Issue:167 Je 16 '89
MAGAININS
Magainin: the penicillin of the 1990s? J. Weber, Jr. il por *Business Week* Special Issue:167 Je 16 '89
MAGAZINE, ALAN H.
Competing by cooperating [address, May 9, 1989] *Vital Speeches of the Day* 55:604-8 Jl 15 '89
Human resources [address, January 19, 1989] *Vital Speeches of the Day* 55:502-7 Je 1 '89
MAGAZINE, MOUNT (ARK.) *See* Mount Magazine (Ark.)
MAGAZINE ADVERTISING *See* Advertising, Magazine
MAGAZINE ARTICLES *See* Periodical articles
MAGAZINE COVERS *See* Periodical covers
MAGAZINE DESIGN *See* Periodical design
MAGAZINE ILLUSTRATION *See* Illustration
MAGAZINE PUBLISHING *See* Publishers and publishing—Periodicals
MAGAZINE VENDORS *See* Periodical vendors
MAGAZINES *See* Periodicals
MAGDOFF, HARRY
about
Beat the devil [interview] A. Cockburn. il *The Nation* 248:726-7 My 29 '89

MAGELLAN FLIGHTS *See* Space flight to Venus
MAGGIO, MICHAEL
about
Chicago style. A. Witchel. il por *New York* 22:14 Ag 7 '89
MAGHERINI, GRAZIELLA
about
The Stendhal syndrome causes museum-goers to make an exhibition of themselves. il *People Weekly* 32:109 Jl 17 '89
That swooning feeling. J. Turner. il por *Art News* 88:150-3 D '89
MAGI
See also
Epiphany
Physics and Christmas. *National Review* 41:15 D 31 '89
MAGIC
See also
Conjuring
THE MAGIC CHRISTIAN [film] *See* Motion picture reviews—Single works
MAGIC MARKER INDUSTRIES INC.
Brand-new start [Magic Markers to be marketed by Binney & Smith] E. F. Cone. il *Forbes* 143:10 Mr 6 '89
MAGIC SQUARES AND CUBES
See also
K-dron
MAGICIANS
See also
Penn & Teller
Weber, Michael
MAGICIENS DE LA TERRE (EXHIBITION)
Magicians of the earth: Centre Georges Pompidou Grande Halle at La Villette. G. Danto. *Art News* 88:222 O '89
The whole earth show. E. Heartney. il *Art in America* 77:90-7 Jl '89
The whole earth show [interview with J.-H. Martin] H. D. Buchloh. il *Art in America* 77:150-9+ My '89
MAGILL, DAN
about
For the love of the game. D. Young. il pors *Southern Living* 24:78+ O '89
MAGISTAD, MARY KAY
The specter of the Khmer Rouge. *The Nation* 248:228+ F 20 '89
MAGISTRETTI, ADRIANO
about
Roman revival. J. Turner. il por *House & Garden* 161:114-19+ Ja '89
MAGLEV TRAINS
310-mph flying trains—in the '90s—in the U.S. D. Scott and J. Free. il *Popular Science* 234:132-5+ My '89
Federal aid
How to lose: the story of maglev. D. P. Moynihan. *Scientific American* 261:130 N '89
MAGLIOZZI, RAY
about
Motor mouths. E. Yoffe. il pors *Rolling Stone* p163-4+ N 16 '89
Ray and Tom Magliozzi get stalled auto owners in gear with nuts-and-bolts Car talk. A. Schulman. il pors *People Weekly* 32:93-4+ Ag 7 '89
MAGLIOZZI, TOM
about
Motor mouths. E. Yoffe. il pors *Rolling Stone* p163-4+ N 16 '89
Ray and Tom Magliozzi get stalled auto owners in gear with nuts-and-bolts Car talk. A. Schulman. il pors *People Weekly* 32:93-4+ Ag 7 '89
MAGMA
Drilling begins in search of molten energy [Long Valley Caldera] R. Monastersky. il *Science News* 136:101 Ag 12 '89
The furnace beneath us [drilling to the magma in California] G. Carroll. il *Newsweek* 114:55 Ag 28 '89
Magma reservoir seen under ocean ridge [study by Mark S. Burnett and others] R. Monastersky. il *Science News* 135:326 My 27 '89
Rhenium-osmium and samarium-neodymium isotopic systematics of the Stillwater Complex. D. D. Lambert and others. bibl f il *Science* 244:1169-74 Je 9 '89
Underplating and partial melting: implications for melt generation and extraction. G. W. Bergantz. bibl f il *Science* 245:1093-5 S 8 '89
MAGNA INTERNATIONAL INC.
Magna steps on the brake. J. Daly. il por *Maclean's* 102:44-6 O 16 '89
MAGNELLI, ALBERTO, 1888-1971
about
Alberto Magnelli: Palazzo Vecchio. J. Turner. il *Art News* 88:163 F '89
MAGNESIUM
See also
Feeds—Magnesium content
MAGNESIUM IN THE BODY
The case of the missing mineral [S. Driscoll combats deficiency] A. Roblin. il *Prevention (Emmaus, Pa.)* 41:120+ F '89

How to be young at heart [role in preventing cardiovascular disease] B. SerVaas. il map *The Saturday Evening Post* 261:90+ My/Je '89
Magnesium for farm animals [interview with J. Hollifield] C. SerVaas. il *The Saturday Evening Post* 261:102 Jl/Ag '89
Magnesium for moms-to-be. il *Prevention (Emmaus, Pa.)* 41:8+ Ja '89
New clues to the power of magnesium. A. Roblin. il map *Prevention (Emmaus, Pa.)* 41:33-9 Ap '89
MAGNESIUM SILICATES
Deep water: "phase B" is decoded. R. Pool. *Science* 246:887 N 17 '89
Elasticity of $MgSiO_3$ in the perovskite structure. A. Yeganeh-Haeri and others. bibl f il *Science* 243:787-9 F 10 '89
MAGNESYS CORPORATION
Bubble memory's ruggedness revives interest for military use. il *Aviation Week & Space Technology* 130:52-3+ Ja 16 '89
MAGNET SCHOOLS
Affirmative reaction [dissatisfaction with desegregation plan in Kansas City, Mo.] R. Nadler and T. Donelson. il *National Review* 41:28-9 S 15 '89
After busing: education and choice. D. J. Armor. *Current (Washington, D.C.)* 316:14-20 O '89
Developing magnet programs. *The Education Digest* 54:22-4 F '89
The future school: is Lowell pointing us toward a revolution in education? [City Magnet School] G. Richmond. il *Phi Delta Kappan* 71:232-6 N '89
Just schools for minority children. C. L. Glenn. il *Phi Delta Kappan* 70:777-9 Je '89
Magnet schools. F. Roberts. il *Parents* 64:48+ S '89
When desegregation backfires [black parents sue the state to pay for private schools because magnet plan is not working; Kansas City, Mo.] P. King. il *Newsweek* 114:56 Jl 31 '89
MAGNETIC BEARINGS *See* Magnetic suspension
MAGNETIC FIELDS
See also
Superconductors and superconductivity—Magnetic properties
Measurement
See also
Magnetoencephalography
SQUIDs (Superconducting quantum interference devices)
Physiological effects
Biomagnetism attracts diverse crowd. R. P. Crease. il *Science* 245:1041-3 S 8 '89
Show me the way you go home [homing pigeons] C. Walcott. *Natural History* p40+ N '89
MAGNETIC FIELDS (ASTROPHYSICS)
See also
Magnetosphere
Mars (Planet)—Magnetic properties
Neptune (Planet)—Magnetic properties
Planets—Magnetic properties
Sun—Magnetic properties
Uranus (Planet)—Magnetic properties
Dr. Zodiac [theories of S. Percy] D. Sobel. il pors *Omni (New York, N.Y.)* 12:60-2+ D '89
MAGNETIC FUSION
Fusion chief reassigned as program is refocused [removal of J. F. Clarke] M. Crawford. por *Science* 243:303 Ja 20 '89
Fusion plan ignites controversy at DOE [shifting funds from magnetic fusion to laser program] M. Crawford. il *Science* 244:1434-5 Je 23 '89
MAGNETIC GLASSES *See* Spin glasses
MAGNETIC LEVITATION *See* Magnetic suspension
MAGNETIC LEVITATION VEHICLES *See* Maglev trains
MAGNETIC MEASUREMENTS
See also
Magnetometers
MAGNETIC MOMENTS
Nuclear magnetic ordering at nanokelvin temperatures. O. V. Lounasmaa. bibl f il *Physics Today* 42:26-33 O '89
MAGNETIC RECORDERS AND RECORDING *See* Tape recorders and recording
MAGNETIC REFRIGERATION
Magna fridge. J. L. Schefter. il *Popular Science* 234:93+ Mr '89
MAGNETIC RESONANCE IMAGING
Crystal versus solution structures of enzymes: NMR spectroscopy of a crystalline serine protease. S. O. Smith and others. bibl f il *Science* 244:961-4 My 26 '89
'Magic angle' reveals zeolite reactions [work of Jacek Klinowski and Michael Anderson] F. Flam. *Science News* 135:310 My 20 '89
Magic angle spin. A. Fisher. il *Popular Science* 234:8+ Mr '89
Magnetic resonance finds new applications. *High Technology Business* 9:34-5 Mr '89
Nuclear magnetic ordering at nanokelvin temperatures. O. V. Lounasmaa. bibl f il *Physics Today* 42:26-33 O '89
Some developments in nuclear magnetic resonance of solids [cover story] B. F. Chmelka and A. Pines. bibl f il *Science* 246:71-7 O 6 '89

MAGNETIC RESONANCE IMAGING—*cont.*
Three-dimensional solution structure of a single zinc finger DNA-binding domain [cover story] M. S. Lee and others. bibl f il *Science* 245:635-7 Ag 11 '89

Chemical use
A connoisseur's SNIF: magnetic resonance aids in identification of wines [work of Gerard Martin] E. Corcoran. *Scientific American* 261:76 Jl '89
Protein structure determination in solution by nuclear magnetic resonance spectroscopy. K. Wüthrich. bibl f il *Science* 243:45-50 Ja 6 '89

Geological use
Nuclear magnetic resonance spectroscopy in the earth sciences: structure and dynamics. J. F. Stebbins and I. Farnan. bibl f il *Science* 245:257-63 Jl 21 '89

Medical use
The anatomy of memory loss [abnormality in the hippocampal formation of amnesia patients; research by Gary A. Press] *Science News* 136:204 S 23 '89
Fixing a child's heart [used to view aortic coarctation] J. Stone. il *The New York Times Magazine* p37-8 Ag 13 '89
Magnetic resonance images take place of X-rays. il *Radio-Electronics* 60:4 D '89
Magnetic resonance opens new frontiers. il *Radio-Electronics* 60:6 Ja '89

MAGNETIC SOUND RECORDING AND REPRODUCING
See Sound—Recording and reproducing

MAGNETIC SUSPENSION
See also
    Maglev trains
Levitation in physics [cover story] E. H. Brandt. bibl f il *Science* 243:349-55 Ja 20 '89
Levitation without superconductors. *High Technology Business* 9:8 My '89
Look, Ma, no bearings. K. K. Wiegner. il *Forbes* 143:136+ My 1 '89
Short-pulse thrusters for SDI require new instrumentation [magnetic suspension test stand for Lightweight Exoatmospheric Projectile] M. A. Dornheim. il *Aviation Week & Space Technology* 131:53+ Ag 28 '89
Super (conductor) man [inventor F. Reick] A. Fisher. il por *Popular Science* 235:76-7 D '89
Suspending disbelief over superconductivity. B. Schechter. il *Discover* 10:59-60 Ja '89

MAGNETIC TAPE *See* Tape, Magnetic

MAGNETISM
See also
    Electromagnetism
    Superconductors and superconductivity—Magnetic properties
Chemico-viscous remanent magnetization in the Fe_3O_4-γFe_2O_3 system. Ö. Özdemir and D. J. Dunlop. bibl f il *Science* 243:1043-7 F 24 '89

Physiological effects
See Magnetic fields—Physiological effects

MAGNETISM, TERRESTRIAL
See also
    Auroras
    Magnetosphere
    Paleomagnetism
    Polar wander
Digi-compass. T. E. Black. il *Radio-Electronics* 60:43-5+ N '89
Earth as egg: hard-boiled or raw? [research by Richard Muller and Donald Morris] R. Monastersky. *Science News* 135:319 My 20 '89
The evolution of the earth's magnetic field. J. Bloxham and D. Gubbins. bibl il maps *Scientific American* 261:68-75 D '89
Geomagnetic origin for transient particle events from nuclear reactor-powered satellites [experiment on Solar Maximum Mission satellite] G. H. Share and others. bibl f il *Science* 244:444-8 Ap 28 '89
Hidden chemistry [core-mantle boundary; research by Raymond Jeanloz] T. Appenzeller. *Scientific American* 260:17-18 F '89
Is our view of the core obscured by "clouds"? [core-mantle boundary] R. A. Kerr. *Science* 243:739 F 10 '89
Magnetic signal preceded October quake. R. Monastersky. *Science News* 136:390 D 16 '89
A wizard of middle earth under fire [R. Jeanloz] R. A. Kerr. por *Science* 246:758-60 N 10 '89

MAGNETITE
Chemico-viscous remanent magnetization in the Fe_3O_4-γFe_2O_3 system. Ö. Özdemir and D. J. Dunlop. bibl f il *Science* 243:1043-7 F 24 '89

MAGNETOENCEPHALOGRAPHY
Electric brain waves: acid test [use in combating epilepsy] J. Partridge. il *Omni (New York, N.Y.)* 12:34+ D '89
Recording and interpretation of cerebral magnetic fields. R. Hari and O. V. Lounasmaa. bibl f il *Science* 244:432-6 Ap 28 '89

MAGNETOHYDRODYNAMICS
See also
    Plasma waves

MAGNETOMETERS
A jam-jar magnetometer as "aurora detector". R. J. Livesey. il *Sky and Telescope* 78:426-32 O '89

MAGNETORESISTANCE
See also
    Aharonov-Bohm effect
    Aharonov-Casher effect

MAGNETOSPHERE
Distribution and detection of positrons from an orbiting nuclear reactor [observations by Solar Maximum Mission satellite] E. W. Hones and P. R. Higbie. bibl f il *Science* 244:448-51 Ap 28 '89
The dynamic aurora [cover story] S.-I. Akasofu. bibl il *Scientific American* 260:90-7 My '89
Seeing is believing! [Echo 7 sounding rocket experiment photographs electrons spiraling around earth's magnetic field lines] il *Sky and Telescope* 77:130-1 F '89

MAGNETS
See also
    Refrigerator magnets

THE MAGNIFICENT AMBERSONS [film] See Motion picture reviews—Single works

MAGNIFIERS
Let's take a closer look. N. Schreiber. il *New Choices for the Best Years* 29:79-81 Ap '89

MAGNIFYING GLASSES See Magnifiers

MAGNITUDES OF PLANETS See Planets—Magnitudes

MAGNITUDES OF STARS See Stars—Magnitudes

MAGNUM MOTOR COACH (FIRM)
A Bronco with a stretch. T. Opre. il *Outdoor Life* 183:28+ F '89

MAGNUSON, ANN
Footnotes from history: Ann Magnuson. il *Vogue* 179:122+ O '89

MAGNUSON, JON
Church leaders support native claim. *The Christian Century* 106:276-7 Mr 15 '89
Selling Native American soul [cover story] il *The Christian Century* 106:1084-7 N 22 '89

MAGOON, JOHN H., JR.
about
What's Hawaiian for "rotten management"? M. Beauchamp. il por *Forbes* 143:44-5 Je 26 '89

MAGOWAN, PETER A.
about
Safeway: it's confounding critics. R. D. Hof. il por *Business Week* p141 Ap 24 '89

MAGPIES
The incredible odyssey of the president's beasts [transporting live specimens from the Lewis and Clark Expedition to T. Jefferson] B. Gilbert. il por *Audubon* 91:100-2+ Ja '89

MAGRANE, JOE
about
Beers with . . . Joe Magrane [interview] B. Chastain. il pors *Sport (New York, N.Y.)* 80:19-21 S '89
Joe Magrane strikes back. G. Collins. il pors *Gentlemen's Quarterly* 59:260-3 Ap '89

MAGRIEL, PAUL DAVID, 1906-
about
Raider of the lost art. M. Filler. il por *House & Garden* 161:36+ Ap '89

MAGRUDER, JEB STUART, 1934-
about
Watergate figure preaches honesty. *Christianity Today* 33:47 Ap 21 '89

MAGUIRE, JACK
about
The stuff of dreams. C. B. Fleming. il *Health (New York, N.Y.)* 21:28+ D '89

MAGUIRE, THOMAS P.
Big lakers on Seneca. il *The Conservationist* 43:10-13 My/Je '89

MAGUIRE THOMAS PARTNERS
Nice profits from better city life. J. F. Lawrence. il *Fortune* 120:117-19+ O 9 '89

MAGUS VIDEO PRODUCTIONS
The Barth balance. C. Hurst. il pors *Home Office Computing* 7:51-3 Je '89

MAH, SY, D. 1988
about
Obituary
Runner's World il por 24:12 Ap '89. J. Henderson

MAHĀBHĀRATA
Jean-Claude Carrière: the Mahabharata, the great history of mankind [interview] il pors *The Unesco Courier* 42:4-9+ S '89

THE MAHABHARATA [drama] See Brook, Peter, 1925-

MAHADEVAN, RAJAN
about
Rajan Mahadevan is a memorable master of presto digittation. il por *People Weekly* 32:121 N 6 '89

MAHAN, MARVIN
about
New trick for greenmailers. J. Zweig. il *Forbes* 144:110 O 30 '89
Untouchable. J. Zweig. il *Forbes* 144:10 Jl 24 '89

MAHARAJ, CHANDRA *See* Chandra Maharaj, Swami
MAHARIDGE, DALE, AND WILLIAMSON, MICHAEL
The long journey home [excerpt from And their children after them] il *Rolling Stone* p87-96 Mr 23 '89
MAHARISHI INTERNATIONAL UNIVERSITY
Levitation U. D. Starr. il *Omni (New York, N.Y.)* 11:66-8+ My '89
MAHĀVAMSA
The Mahāvamsa, Sri Lanka's non-stop epic. A. W. P. Gurugé. il *The Unesco Courier* 42:40-3 S '89
MAHDI, SADIQ EL *See* El Mahdi, Sadiq, 1936-
MAHER, DANIEL
about
"That car is going to explode!". S. Kelly. il pors *Reader's Digest* 134:96-100 Ja '89
MAHER, JOHN
about
Delancey Street's road to success. C. Males and J. Raskin. il por *Reader's Digest* 134:108-12 Mr '89
MAHER, LEO
about
Barred from Communion. *The Christian Century* 106:1193-4 D 20-27 '89
A mistake in San Diego. *America* 161:416 D 9 '89
MAHER, LOUIS J., III, AND OTHERS
Inhibition of DNA binding proteins by oligonucleotide-directed triple helix formation. bibl f il *Science* 245:725-30 Ag 18 '89
MAHFOUZ, NAGUIB *See* Mahfūz, Najīb, 1912-
MAHFŪZ, NAJĪB, 1912-
about
Interview with Najib Mahfouz. V. Massuh. il por *The Unesco Courier* 42:4-6 D '89
Naguib Mahfouz [interview] W. Steif. il *The Progressive* 53:38-9 F '89
A Nobelist's inspiration [interview] H. Abu Ahmed. il por *World Press Review* 36:61 Ja '89
The shroud of Mahfouz. A. Shammas. il *The New York Review of Books* 36:19-21 F 2 '89
MAHKEE, WELLS
My search for identity. il *Scholastic Update (Teachers' edition)* 121:3 My 26 '89
MAHLER, GUSTAV, 1860-1911
about
Mahler from a master. D. Hurwitz. il por *High Fidelity (New York, N.Y.)* 39:62-3 Ja '89
MAHLER, RICHARD
New Mexico shoot-out. il *Channels (New York, N.Y.: 1986)* 9:84-5 Ja '89
MAHMOUD, ADEL A. F.
Parasitic protozoa and helminths: biological and immunological challenges. bibl f il *Science* 246:1015-22 N 24 '89
MAHOGANY
Wood you believe? E. H. Gustafson. bibl f il *Antiques* 135:1102+ My '89
MAHON, GIGI
S.I. Newhouse and Conde Nast: taking off the white gloves [cover story] il pors *The New York Times Magazine* p46-51+ S 10 '89
MAHON, MAXINE
about
California Ballet at twenty: staking a claim. W. E. Fark. il por *Dance Magazine* 63:52-5 Ja '89
MAHONE, CATHY
about
The search for Lauren. N. C. Livingstone and D. Halevy. il pors *Reader's Digest* 135:77-84 Ag '89
MAHONEY, PETER P.
The wounds of two wars. il *The New York Times Magazine* p60-1+ Je 11 '89
MAHONEY, RICHARD JOHN
about
Blood, sweat and profits. R. Reiff. il por *Forbes* 143:110+ Mr 6 '89
Why Monsanto is plunking down its chips on R&D. J. E. Ellis. il por *Business Week* p66-7 Ag 21 '89
MAHONEY, RICHARD JOHN, AND LITTLEJOHN, STEPHEN E.
Innovation on trial: punitive damages versus new products. bibl f *Science* 246:1395-9 D 15 '89
MAHONY, PHILLIP, 1955-
about
Beat poet. A. Rosenstein. il por *New York* 22:24 Ag 28 '89
MAHORN, RICK
about
A master of intimidation. R. Wiley. il pors *Sports Illustrated* 70:66-8 Ap 10 '89
MAHRAN, MAHER
Islam and family planning. il *World Health* p22-3 Ap '89
MAHRE, PHIL
about
The boys are back! P. Oliver. il pors *Skiing* 41:38-40 Mr '89
Year of the rookie. P. Oliver. il por *Skiing* 42:137+ O '89

MAHRE, STEVE
about
The boys are back! P. Oliver. il pors *Skiing* 41:38-40 Mr '89
MAHURIN, MATT, 1959?-
about
In the dark. J. Farber. por *Rolling Stone* p75 Ap 6 '89
MAI BASIC FOUR, INC.
Caveat raider [MAI Basic Four's battle for Prime Computer sours customer relations] K. K. Wiegner. il *Forbes* 143:160 Je 12 '89
MAIER, CHARLES S.
Nineteen thirty-nine. *The New Republic* 201:16-17 S 11 '89
MAIER, H. JOHN
A touch of magic. il pors *Sports Illustrated* 70 Special Issue:153-6 F '89
MAIER MUSEUM OF ART (LYNCHBURG, VA.)
American art in the Maier Museum of Art, Randolph-Macon Woman's College, Lynchburg, Virginia. D. M. Sokol. il *Antiques* 136:1138-47 N '89
MAIL ADVERTISING *See* Advertising, Direct mail
MAIL AUCTIONS *See* Auctions
MAIL BOXES *See* Mailboxes
MAIL FRAUD
Behind those fast-buck ads. D. P. Wiener. il *U.S. News & World Report* 106:70-1 Ap 24 '89
Is shopping by mail safe? [photographic equipment] J. Augustine. il *Petersen's Photographic Magazine* 18:6 N '89
Sure you can get bargains when you order by mail, but you've got to know how to do it [photographic equipment] H. Keppler. il *Popular Photography* 96:75-7 Mr '89
There are good dealers like good car salesmen, but the rotters can spoil it for everyone [photographic equipment] H. Keppler. il *Popular Photography* 96:42+ Jl '89
The trouble with angels [mail order fraud perpetrated against single men by Church of Love] il *New Choices for the Best Years* 29:13+ Ap '89
Unordered merchandise. J. W. Merline. il *Consumers' Research Magazine* 72:38 N '89
Victims of the Church of Love were only the lonely [mail order scam perpetrated by D. S. Lowry] J. Friedman. il por *People Weekly* 31:77-8+ Ja 30 '89
Watch out! Latest mail & phone frauds. S. Nielsen. *Good Housekeeping* 209:163-4 Ag '89
"You have definitely won a fabulous prize!". M. C. Paulson. il *Changing Times* 43:34-6+ Ag '89
MAIL HANDLING
See also
Mailrooms
United States Postal Service—Automation
Can we sort out the mail mess? [Postal Service] J. B. Judis. il *Reader's Digest* 134:189-90+ Ap '89
Mail and the moving man. R. Phalon. il *Forbes* 143:133-4 F 6 '89
MAIL ORDER BUSINESS
See also
Capability's Books (Firm)
CML Group, Inc.
Computer Express, Inc.
Day-Timers (Firm)
Eddie Bauer Inc.
Faith Mountain Company
Hanna Andersson Corporation
Holy Cow, Inc.
Inmac Corp.
J. Crew (Firm)
Lands' End, Inc.
Lillian Vernon Corporation
Quill Corporation
Sears, Roebuck and Co.
Spiegel, Inc.
Tweeds (Firm)
Award-winning mail order strategies [computers; cover story; special section] R. Lockwood. il *Personal Computing* 13:78-81+ F '89
Creating mail-order art. D. Grant. il *American Artist* 53:10+ N '89
Death by mail [firearms and accessories] J. Sugarmann. *The Nation* 248:450 Ap 3 '89
Direct-mail dining, gourmet style. il *USA Today (Periodical)* 118:95 S '89
From the Sugarplum Fairy: wonderful things to eat. il *Glamour* 87:232-3 D '89
Gifts of food by phone. il *Gourmet* 49:112-14 D '89
Hold the phone! D. W. Englander. il *Money* 18:85-6+ Jl '89
Low-cost 386-based computers [buying by mail] H. F. Beechhold. il *Home Office Computing* 7:61-5 O '89
Mail-order meals beyond the ordinary. J. Thornton. il *U.S. News & World Report* 107:66-7+ D 11 '89
Mail-order success only looks easy . . . [R. Fortune] D. E. Gumpert. il pors *Working Woman* 14:37-8+ Jl '89
Minimum-order hassles [electronics parts] D. Lancaster. *Radio-Electronics* 60:26-7 Ap '89
Salmon to salsa . . . mail-order treasures of the Northwest and the Southwest. il *Sunset (Central West edition)* 183:162+ N '89

MAIL ORDER BUSINESS—*cont.*
These dealers pay cash for your clutter. il *Good Housekeeping* 208:247 My '89

Taxation
Catalog firms bite the hand that squeezes [move to impose state sales tax] E. Pomice. il *U.S. News & World Report* 107:44 Jl 31 '89
If you catalog-shop [state sales tax] R. Coorsh. il *Consumers' Research Magazine* 72:4 Jl '89
Tax by mail. D. Fanning. il *Forbes* 143:126+ Ap 3 '89

Netherlands
The Johnny Appleseed of pot [marijuana seed salesman N. Schoenmakers] R. Z. Chesnoff. il *U.S. News & World Report* 107:30 N 6 '89

MAIL ORDER BUSINESS FRAUD See Mail fraud
MAIL ORDER CATALOGS See Catalogs, Commercial
MAIL SERVICE See Postal service; United States Postal Service
MAILBOXES
Cedar-shingle mailbox. T. Wolfe. il *Flower and Garden* 33:96 Ja/F '89
Raising the red flag. A. Meyer. il *The Mother Earth News* 118:46 Jl/Ag '89

Photographs and photography
Checking up on what the mail must go through. B. Py-Lieberman. il *Smithsonian* 20:186-9 N '89

MAILER, NORMAN
Cosmic ventures: a meditation on God at war. il *Esquire* 112:156-8 D '89

about
Moonraker [interview] T. Piazza. por *Omni (New York, N.Y.)* 11:18+ Jl '89

MAILING FRANK See Franking privilege
MAILING LISTS
See also
Computers—Mailing list use
Use the mail to build your business [special section] L. Arden. il *Home Office Computing* 7:49-55 Mr '89

MAILLET, WASIM
about
Every mother's nightmare comes true when a hospital nursery mix-up sends two babies home with the wrong parents. M. Brower. il pors *People Weekly* 31:123-4 Ap 3 '89

MAILROOMS
What goes on in your mailroom? A. Farnham. il *Fortune* 119:105-6+ F 27 '89

MAIN, JEREMY
Third world economies: a new proposal. *Current (Washington, D.C.)* 314:38-40 Jl/Ag '89

MAIN, TOM
about
Where disinvestment pinches. J. Cook. il por *Forbes* 143:62+ Je 26 '89

MAINE
See also
Acadia National Park (Me.)
Aviation, Military—Maine
Criminal justice, Administration of—Maine
Education—Maine
Environmental movement—Maine
Game laws—Maine
Hunting—Maine
Income tax—Maine
Kennebec River (Me.)
Moosehorn National Wildlife Refuge (Me.)
Mount Desert Island (Me.)
Public welfare—Maine
Wilderness areas—Maine

Fisheries
See Fisheries

Industries
See also
Blueberry industry
A burgeoning empire [Canada's Irving family] S. McKay. il *Maclean's* 102:42+ F 6 '89

Legislature
Mr. Smith goes to Augusta. J. N. Diamond. *The Washington Monthly* 21:36-8 Jl/Ag '89

Politics and government
See also
Maine—Legislature
Tenants Harbor diarist. N. Von Hoffman. *The New Republic* 200:50 My 15 '89

MAINE, GULF OF See Gulf of Maine
MAINE STATE MUSEUM
Museum accessions [J. D. Poor murals acquired] E. H. Gustafson. il *Antiques* 136:402+ S '89

MAINFRAME COMPUTER INDUSTRY See Computer industry
MAINIERI, MIKE
about
Mike Mainieri & Steps Ahead: hitting it heavy. M. Bourne. il pors *Down Beat* 56:20-2 Jl '89

MAINLINE (TERM)
If it's not 'mainline,' what is it? M. E. Marty. *The Christian Century* 106:1031 N 8 '89
Mainline or mainstream? M. E. Marty. *The Christian Century* 106:1183 D 13 '89

Tracing the mainline. M. E. Marty. *The Christian Century* 106:1159 D 6 '89

MAINSTREAMING (EDUCATION) See Children, Handicapped—Education
MAIOLICA See Majolica
MAIRE, PASCAL, AND OTHERS
The role of cis-acting promoter elements in tissue-specific albumin gene expression. bibl f il *Science* 244:343-6 Ap 21 '89

MAISEL, JAY, 1931-
about
Jay Maisel directs the compacts. il *Petersen's Photographic Magazine* 17:56-7 Mr '89

MAISLEN, ALAN D.
In search of historic Elvis. il *Rolling Stone* p196-201 D 14-28 '89

LA MAISON DU CHOCOLAT (FIRM)
La Maison du Chocolat [chocolate maker R. Linxe] A. W. Salmon. il *Gourmet* 49:80-5+ S '89

MAIZE See Corn
MAJKOWSKI, DON
about
The Majik show. P. Zimmerman. il por *Sports Illustrated* 71:34-9 D 11 '89

MAJOLICA
Collectors and collecting
A grand surprise [Victorian majolica] L. Lerman. il *House & Garden* 161:156-61 N '89

MAJOR, KEVIN, 1949-
about
Boyhood on the Rock. D. Turbide. il por *Maclean's* 102:61 Ap 17 '89

MAJOR & MRS. HOLT'S BATTLEFIELD TOURS (FIRM)
The battle may be o'er, but this couple brings it back for historic site-seers [work of V. and T. Holt] D. Chu. il pors *People Weekly* 31:129-30 Je 19 '89

MAJOR DAD [television program] See Television program reviews—Single works

MAJOR HISTOCOMPATIBILITY COMPLEX
Class II MHC molecules are specific receptors for staphylococcus enterotoxin A. J. A. Mollick and others. bibl f il *Science* 244:817-20 My 19 '89
How T cells see antigen. H. M. Grey and others. bibl il *Scientific American* 261:56-64 N '89
Influence of the major histocompatibility complex on positive thymic selection of $V_\beta 17a^+$ T cells. M. A. Blackman and others. bibl f il *Science* 244:214-17 Ap 14 '89
The MHC-binding and gp120-binding functions of CD4 are separable. D. Lamarre and others. bibl f il *Science* 245:743-6 Ag 18 '89
Murine MHC polymorphism and T cell specificities. S. Roy and others. bibl f il *Science* 244:572-5 My 5 '89
A new cluster of genes within the human major histocompatibility complex. T. Spies and others. bibl f il *Science* 243:214-17 Ja 13 '89
Prevention of allogeneic bone marrow graft rejection by H-2 transgene in donor mice. C. Öhlén and others. bibl f il *Science* 246:666-8 N 3 '89
Role of Na^+/H^+ exchange by interferon-γ in enhanced expression of JE and $I\text{-}A_\beta$ genes. V. Prpic and others. bibl f il *Science* 244:469-71 Ap 28 '89
Structure and specificity of a class II MHC alloreactive γδ T cell receptor heterodimer. L. A. Matis and others. bibl f il *Science* 245:746-9 Ag 18 '89
Transgenic mice with I-A on islet cells are normoglycemic but immunologically intolerant. J. Böhme and others. bibl f il *Science* 244:1179-83 Je 9 '89

MAJOR INDOOR LACROSSE LEAGUE
What's as gory as hockey and as upscale as squash? R. Duffy. il *Business Week* p42 Ap 17 '89

MAJOR LEAGUE [film] See Motion picture reviews—Single works

MAJOR LEAGUE BASEBALL PLAYERS ASSOCIATION
The players' main man [D. Fehr, executive director] D. A. Kaplan. il por *The New York Times Magazine* p46+ O 29 '89
The union rep who changed baseball [M. Miller] J. Nocera. il por *Newsweek* 113:46 Ap 10 '89

MAJOR LEAGUE BASEBALL PRODUCTIONS
Baseball moments are missing; no film at 11. G. Castle. il *Sport (New York, N.Y.)* 80:35 Je '89

MAJORS, LEE, JR.
Photographs and photography
Like father, like son. G. Bernstein. il por *Petersen's Photographic Magazine* 17:12-13 F '89

MAKAEA, PAMELA
(jt. auth) See Hunter, Jeffrey, and Makaea, Pamela

MAKAROVA, NATALIA, 1940-
about
La bayadère [ballet] Reviews
Dance Magazine il 63:76-7 O '89. L. Svedin
Makarova returns to the Kirov: going home. N. Alovert. il pors *Dance Magazine* 63:36-7 My '89

MAKELA, MARIA
Munich's design for living. bibl f il *Art in America* 77:144-51 F '89

MÄKELÄ, MARIKA
about
Marika Mäkelä: Kunsthalle. E. Beck. il *Art News* 88:163-4 F '89
MAKEOVERS, BEAUTY *See* Beauty, Personal
MAKEUP
See also
Computers—Makeup use
Paramedical camouflage
10 perfect makeups. il *Harper's Bazaar* 122:180-1+ Ap '89
Act now to age-proof your eyes. il *Glamour* 87:270-3 O '89
Au naturel [makeup colors] L. Wells. il *The New York Times Magazine* p70 Mr 26 '89
Bare but there! il *'Teen* 33:100-2 My '89
Beautiful imperfections. il *Harper's Bazaar* 122:82-5 Ja '89
Beauty break. il *Redbook* 173:12 S '89
Bejeweled. il *'Teen* 33:8 D '89
Best face forward. D. Guerre. il pors *Harper's Bazaar* 122:28+ Ag '89
Bright thinking [fall makeup] L. Cunliffe. il *Vogue* 179:688-91 S '89
The bronze rage [blushers to enhance or create tans] il *Seventeen* 48:130 Je '89
Brush up on blusher. C. Straley. il *Parents* 64:129-32 F '89
Cheek to cheek [blusher application] il *Mademoiselle* 95:22 Jl '89
Cheek to chic [blusher application] il *'Teen* 33:92-3 O '89
Class colors: makeup news 'n hues. il *'Teen* 33:84-7 S '89
Color! Shades of you. A. G. Britton. il *American Health* 8:26-8+ Ja/F '89
Daily de-aging: how to take years off your looks every morning. il *Ladies' Home Journal* 106:116-19+ Ja '89
The deep: fall makeup colors are absolutely profound. il *Mademoiselle* 95:176-9 O '89
Easy! Makeup hints from Hollywood [views of makeup artist Joe Blasco] il *Redbook* 174:14+ D '89
The face of the nineties [natural shades] L. George. il *American Health* 8:102-3 S '89
Fire! Winter makeup hits a warming trend. il *Mademoiselle* 95:200-3 F '89
Foolproof holiday eyes and hair. il *McCall's* 116:18-21 Ja '89
Freckle face. il *Seventeen* 48:90-1 Ja '89
The fresh faces of spring. il *Glamour* 87:272-5 Mr '89
Gilt trips/hi, ho silver. il *'Teen* 33:72-5 N '89
Glitz takes a powder [matte makeup] L. Wells. il *The New York Times Magazine* p96 N 19 '89
Going public. L. Wells. il *The New York Times Magazine* p52 O 22 '89
Grooming goes public. A. Russell. il *Working Woman* 14:109 S '89
Holiday beauty tips. C. Straley. il *Parents* 64:166-7 D '89
Hot desert colors. N. Malkin. il *Harper's Bazaar* 122:16+ Jl '89
In the nude: shy makeup colors come on strong. il *Mademoiselle* 95:202-5 Mr '89
Join the party! One girl/three looks. il *Mademoiselle* 95:198-201 N '89
Kiss kiss [lip makeup] il *Mademoiselle* 95:248-51 S '89
Lashing out. il *'Teen* 33:68-9 F '89
Lip service. C. Sullivan. il *Vogue* 179:164-5 Ap '89
Makeup makeovers. il *'Teen* 33:88-91 O '89
Makeup secrets of famous faces [TV stars] il *Ladies' Home Journal* 106:32 F '89
Makeup—the undercover story. il *Mademoiselle* 95:48 N '89
Matte & shine. J. Shields. il *Vogue* 179:400-5 N '89
Moonlighting. il *Seventeen* 48:250-3 Mr '89
The new eye. C. Sullivan. il *Vogue* 179:148-50 F '89
New looks for your eyes. il *Redbook* 172:100-3 Ap '89
The new unmakeup. il *Glamour* 87:276-81 S '89
Nude study. C. Warren. il *Vogue* 179:372-83 N '89
One little eye buy gets you three big looks. il *Mademoiselle* 95:122-3 Ja '89
Passport to beauty. il *Seventeen* 48:260-5 Mr '89
Prime-time pretties. il *'Teen* 33:70-1 Mr '89
Read my lips! il *Seventeen* 48:182 O '89
Saturday faces. il *Glamour* 87:224-7 N '89
Shades of summer. L. J. Johnson. il *Ladies' Home Journal* 106:130-5 Je '89
So simple, so super. il *'Teen* 33:52-3 Ja '89
Spices are hot! il *Redbook* 173:10+ O '89
Spring colors. N. Malkin. il *Harper's Bazaar* 122:104-7+ Ja '89
Sugar 'n spice. il *'Teen* 33:112-13 Ag '89
Taking it easy [natural look] L. Wells. il *The New York Times Magazine* p114 My 21 '89
Tender dreams [Victorian face] il *Seventeen* 48:170-1 Je '89
True blues [eye makeup] il *'Teen* 33:62-3 Jl '89
What boys really think about makeup. D. Seeley. il *Seventeen* 48:52-3+ Jl '89
What's your eye-cue? il *Seventeen* 48:356 Ag '89
When should your daughter start wearing makeup? [views of experts] il *Good Housekeeping* 209:139+ S '89

MAKEUP, THEATRICAL
Dick Smith: on aging a woman 40 years in five minutes for live '50s TV. D. Smith. il por *People Weekly* 31 Special Issue:106 Summ '89
Ellen Barkin and the man behind her new look [A. Di Biase] C. Krupp. pors *Glamour* 87:192 O '89
Not another pretty face [creating makeup for R. England's Freddy Krueger character] B. Weber. il pors *The New York Times Magazine* p66 Jl 16 '89
What's in a gnome? [F. Mazura's makeup for Das Rheingold] G. Downer. il pors *Opera News* 53:34-5 Ap 1 '89
MAKEUP ARTISTS
See also
Aucoin, Kevyn
MAKEUP AS ART MATERIAL
Artistry in makeup [works by N. Rielle, N. Marshall and M. Geiger] M. Gazzaniga. il pors *Harper's Bazaar* 122:26+ D '89
MAKHIJANI, ARJUN
(jt. auth) *See* Alvarez, Robert, and Makhijani, Arjun
MAKI, FUMIHIKO, 1928-
about
Tokyo collage. L. Breslin. il *Architectural Record* 177:84-93 O '89
MAKIN, JOHN H.
Conservative Keynesian. *National Review* 41:48-9 Ja 27 '89
Let's keep our cool on U.S.-Japan trade. il por *Fortune* 120:147-8 Jl 3 '89
MAKOS, JEFF, AND MORSE, LIBBY
Cookbook sales beyond the bookstore. il *Publishers Weekly* 236:30+ S 8 '89
MAKOUL, RUDY
The living end. il *The Writer* 102:7-8 F '89
MAKOVER, MICHAEL E.
Tick, tick, tick. il *New York* 22:77-8 My 22 '89
THE MAKROPULOS AFFAIR [opera] *See* Janáček, Leoš, 1854-1928
MALABAR FARM STATE PARK (LUCAS, OHIO)
The most famous farm in America. M. Hoy. il por *Audubon* 91:64-7 N '89
MALACINSKI, GEORGE M., AND OTHERS
Developmental biology in outer space. bibl f il *BioScience* 39:314-20 My '89
MALAKHOV, VLADIMIR
about
Vladimir Malakhov challenges Soviet male stereotypes. N. Chernova. por *Dance Magazine* 63:24 D '89
MALAKOFF, DAVID
(jt. auth) *See* Hittle, Alex, and Malakoff, David
MALAMUD-GOTI, JAIME
Cry, Argentina. *The Nation* 249:517-18 N 6 '89
MALARET, MARISOL
about
Malaret and Casiano: a voguish women's mag that speaks Spanish. P. Finch. il pors *Business Week* p107 Je 5 '89
MALARIA
Body's protein does malaria's dirty work [research by Kathleen L. Miller] F. Flam. *Science News* 135:293 My 13 '89
Identification of a platelet membrane glycoprotein as a falciparum malaria sequestration receptor. C. F. Ockenhouse and others. bibl f il *Science* 243:1469-71 Mr 17 '89
Malaria red cell cytoadherence [discussion of March 17, 1989 article, Identification of a platelet membrane glycoprotein as a falciparum malaria sequestration receptor] C. F. Ockenhouse and others. *Science* 246:1051 N 24 '89
Immunological aspects
Blood, genes, and malaria. J. M. Diamond. il maps *Natural History* p8+ F '89
Prevention and control
See also
Antimalarials
Quinine
Bednets that kill mosquitos. L. S. Self. il *World Health* p20-2 N '89
Malaria researcher indicted [W. Siddiqui charged with embezzling research funds at the University of Hawaii] E. Marshall. *Science* 245:1326 S 22 '89
Therapy
Fish oil: new hope in fighting malaria [research by Orville A. Levander and Arba L. Ager] *Science News* 135:237 Ap 15 '89
Vaccines and vaccination
Circumsporozoite protein heterogeneity in the human malaria parasite Plasmodium vivax. R. Rosenberg and others. bibl f il *Science* 245:973-6 S 1 '89
Conserved repetitive epitope recognized by CD4$^+$ clones from a malaria-immunized volunteer. E. H. Nardin and others. bibl f il *Science* 246:1603-6 D 22 '89
Sporozoite vaccine induces genetically restricted T cell elimination of malaria from hepatocytes. S. L. Hoffman and others. bibl f il *Science* 244:1078-81 Je 2 '89
Studies begun for malaria vaccine. *High Technology Business* 9:34 Mr '89
MALARIAL PARASITES *See* Plasmodium (Parasite)
MALATESTA, EDWARD J.
China friendships after June 4. *America* 161:132 S 9-16 '89

MALAWI
See also
Paleontology—Malawi
Description and travel
Malawi: faces of a quiet land. P. Theroux. il map *National Geographic* 176:370-89 S '89
MALAYSIA
See also
Airports—Malaysia
Labor unions—Electronics workers—Malaysia
Wildlife—Malaysia
Description and travel
Beyond Singapore. il map *Sunset (Central West edition)* 182:82+ Ap '89
Economic conditions
Asia's reluctant growth champs. F. S. Worthy. il *Fortune* 119:283-4+ Ap 24 '89
Industries
See also
Airod Sendirian Berhad
Malaysia Airlines
Malaysian Helicopter Services
MALAYSIA AIRLINES
Annual Moslem pilgrimage to Mecca spurs surge in Malaysia Airline traffic. il *Aviation Week & Space Technology* 131:63 O 30 '89
Malaysia Airlines receives first aircraft ordered under fleet upgrade plan. P. Proctor. il *Aviation Week & Space Technology* 131:58-9+ O 30 '89
MALAYSIAN HELICOPTER SERVICES
Malaysian Helicopter Services prepares for surge in demand. il *Aviation Week & Space Technology* 131:66 N 6 '89
MALCÉ, MICHAEL
about
A Manhattan sampler. S. M. L. Aronson. il pors *Architectural Digest* 46:158-63+ Je '89
MALCOLM, ANDREW H., 1943-
The ultimate decision [cover story] il pors *The New York Times Magazine* p38-41+ D 3 '89
MALCOLM, BEATRICE BOWLES
about
The ultimate decision [cover story] A. H. Malcolm. il pors *The New York Times Magazine* p38-41+ D 3 '89
MALCOLM, JANET
The journalist and the murderer (I). *The New Yorker* 65:38-42+ Mr 13 '89
The journalist and the murderer (II). *The New Yorker* 65:49-50+ Mr 20 '89
about
Are journalists basically liars? F. Bruning. il *Maclean's* 102:11 Ap 24 '89
Holier than thou. J. Taylor. il pors *New York* 22:32-7 Mr 27 '89
A reporter isn't a friend. J. Alter and G. Cowley. il por *Newsweek* 113:62 Mr 27 '89
The right to fake quotes. W. A. Henry. por *Time* 134:49 Ag 21 '89
The talk of the town. *The Nation* 248:469 Ap 10 '89
MALCOLM BALDRIGE NATIONAL QUALITY AWARD
How the Baldrige winners did it. D. C. Bacon. il *Nation's Business* 77:32+ Ja '89
MALCOLM X, 1925-1965
Just say no [excerpts from The autobiography of Malcolm X] il *New Perspectives Quarterly* 6:26-32 Summ '89
The legacy of Malcolm X [excerpts from lectures and speeches] il pors *Ebony* 44:156+ My '89
about
Their fathers' daughters. E. Hopkins. il pors *Rolling Stone* p76-7+ N 30 '89
MALCOMSON, SCOTT L.
Stranger than paradise. il map *Mother Jones* 14:19-21+ Ja '89
MALE GARDENERS See Gardeners
MALE IMPERSONATORS See Impersonators, Male
MALE PROSTITUTION
Another scandal on the Hill [Congressman B. Frank involved in male homosexual prostitution scandal] por *Newsweek* 114:24 S 4 '89
Art of the voyeur [Washington party giver C. Spence involved in male prostitution scandal] T. Noah. por *The New Republic* 201:16+ Ag 7-14 '89
Barney Frank's story [relationship with male prostitute S. Gobie; cover story; special section; with interview] il pors *Newsweek* 114:14-20 S 25 '89
The death of a man who disappeared [C. Spence] por *Newsweek* 114:55 N 20 '89
In defense of Barney [Congressman B. Frank involved in male homosexual prostitution scandal] M. Kondracke. *The New Republic* 201:10-11 O 9 '89
Letter from Washington [Congressman B. Frank's relationship with male prostitute S. Gobie] E. Drew. *The New Yorker* 65:106-8+ O 2 '89
Presswatch [Congressman B. Frank's involvement] T. Eastland. *The American Spectator* 22:31-2 N '89
A season of scandal takes its final toll on mysterious lobbyist Craig Spence. il por *People Weekly* 32:103 N 27 '89

A skeleton in Barney's closet [B. Frank's relationship with gay prostitute S. Gobie] M. B. Carlson. il pors *Time* 134:24 S 25 '89
Trials of Barney [B. Frank involved in male prostitution scandal] *The Nation* 249:371-2 O 9 '89
Washington's man from nowhere [party giver C. Spence's use of male prostitution service] M. B. Carlson. il por *Time* 134:24 Jl 24 '89
Why Frank's case is different [congressman involved in male homosexual prostitution scandal] il por *U.S. News & World Report* 107:30 O 2 '89
Winners and sinners: the D'Amato and Frank dossiers. J. Klein. il por *New York* 22:23-4 O 9 '89
MALE PSYCHOLOGY See Masculinity (Psychology); Men—Psychology
MALEC, WILLIAM FRANK, 1940-
about
Sheer challenge. J. Zweig. il por *Forbes* 143:166-7 Ap 3 '89
MALEDICTION See Swearing
MALES, CAROLYN
Italian provincial. il map *Travel Holiday* 172:60-71 N '89
A sporting good time in Bermuda. il *Travel Holiday* 171:9-10+ F '89
MALES, CAROLYN, AND RASKIN, JULIE
Delancey Street's road to success. il por *Reader's Digest* 134:108-12 Mr '89
MALEV HUNGARIAN AIRLINES
Malev takes delivery of Western transports, reviews fleet needs. D. A. Brown. *Aviation Week & Space Technology* 130:111+ Ja 2 '89
MALEVICH, KAZIMIR SEVERINOVICH, 1878-1935
about
Behind the suprematist mirror. C. Douglas. bibl f il *Art in America* 77:164-77 S '89
MALI
See also
Sikasso (Mali)
MALIBU (CALIF.)
Architecture
Architectural digest visits: Charles Bronson and Jill Ireland [Malibu adobe decorated by King Zimmerman] J. Ireland. il por *Architectural Digest* 46:98-103+ Jl '89
Architecture: Franklin D. Israel: Kathryn and Robert Altman's Malibu residence. P. Goldberger. il pors *Architectural Digest* 46:120-5+ Jl '89
Galleries and museums
See also
J. Paul Getty Museum
Sanitary affairs
The sewers of Malibu. M. Beauchamp. il *Forbes* 144:120-1 Ag 7 '89
Social life and customs
Anecdotes, facetiae, satire, etc.
Malibu diary. B. Stein. il *The American Spectator* 22:33-5 Ja '89
Point Doom. B. Stein. il *The American Spectator* 22:34-6 D '89
Stores
See also
Malibu Art & Design (Firm)
MALIBU ART & DESIGN (FIRM)
The contemporary general store brings Main Street to Malibu. D. Weil. il por *Working Woman* 14:60-1 Ag '89
MALIK, ALEXANDER JOHN
about
Evangelical view [interview] por *Christianity Today* 33:46 Jl 14 '89
MALIN, P. E., AND OTHERS
Microearthquake imaging of the Parkfield asperity. bibl f il *Science* 244:557-9 My 5 '89
MALINA, ROGER F.
Art in the computer age. il *Technology Review* 92:71-2+ O '89
MALINOW, ROBERTO, AND OTHERS
Inhibition of postsynaptic PKC or CaMKII blocks induction but not expression of LTP. bibl f il *Science* 245:862-6 Ag 25 '89
MALKIEL, BURTON GORDON, 1932-
The case for bonds. il *Forbes* 143:180-5 Je 26 '89
The efficient market hypothesis [discussion of March 10, 1989 article, Is the stock market efficient?] *Science* 244:1424-5 Je 23 '89
Is the stock market efficient? bibl f il *Science* 243:1313-18 Mr 10 '89
MALKIN, LAWRENCE
A tale of two eyes. *The New Republic* 201:15-16 S 4 '89
MALKIN, MORT
about
Shoe scoop [interview] V. Brower. il *American Health* 8:34 N '89
MALKIN, NINA
Dressing thin: the real black magic. il *Harper's Bazaar* 122:90-1 Ja '89
Fashion fidelity. il *Vogue* 179:104-5+ My '89
Winter wrap session. il *Harper's Bazaar* 122:30+ F '89
You're on: diary of a 14-hour day. il *Working Woman* 14:156+ O '89

MALL OF AMERICA (BLOOMINGTON, MINN.)
The Minnesota mallers. il *U.S. News & World Report* 106:12 Je 26 '89
MALLARMÉ, STÉPHANE, 1842-1898
about
Prince of poets. J. Barnes. il *The New York Review of Books* 36:10+ N 9 '89
MALLE, LOUIS, 1932-
about
20th-century rebels. L. Nesselson. il pors *Harper's Bazaar* 122:106 Ap '89
Au revoir les enfants [film] Reviews
Video il 13:60 Ap '89. R. Gehr
Louis Malle [interview] il por *American Film* 14:22-4+ Ap '89
MALLET, VICTOR
(jt. auth) See Gowers, Andrew, and Mallet, Victor
MALLEY, JAMES B.
Old friends and new problems. *America* 161:275-6 O 28 '89
MALLEY, STEPHEN
Diet daze. il *Runner's World* 24:86-8 O '89
MALLICK, GEORGE A.
about
Speaker Jim Wright's old pal George Mallick is rarin' for a fight with Congress. M. Green. il pors *People Weekly* 31:101-2 My 15 '89
MALLIHOUANA (ANGUILLA: RESORT) *See* Resorts—Anguilla
MALLON, ELIAS D.
Offense and counter-offense. il *America* 160:327-9 Ap 8 '89
(jt. auth) See Klenicki, Leon, and Mallon, Elias D.
MALLON, MARY *See* Typhoid Mary, d. 1938
MALLON, THOMAS, 1951-
All's well that's Boswell. il *Gentlemen's Quarterly* 59:75+ D '89
One small shelf for literature. il *The New York Times Book Review* 94:1+ Jl 16 '89
The people next door. il *The American Spectator* 22:22-6 D '89
MALLOVE, EUGENE F., AND MATLOFF, GREGORY L.
We can outlive our star. *Astronomy* 17:8 D '89
MALLOY, EDWARD ALOYSIUS
From Rome with hope. *America* 160:548-9+ Je 10 '89
MALLS, SHOPPING *See* Shopping centers
MALNUTRITION
Bread of dreams [effects of malnutrition and adulterated bread on the poor of medieval Europe; cover story] P. Camporesi. il *History Today* 39:14-21 Ap '89
Give them their daily bread [improvements in health result in economic growth; views of Robert Fogel] S. Nasar. *U.S. News & World Report* 107:64 O 30 '89
MALODY, KAREN
about
Pacific Provençal: a food pro at home. S. H. Loomis. il pors *Working Woman* 14:112-16 Mr '89
MALONE, JOHN
about
Malone alone [cover story] P. Ainslie. il por *Channels (New York, N.Y.: 1986)* 9:30-2+ Je '89
Want this stock? It's up 91,000%. C. Knowlton. il por *Fortune* 120:97+ Jl 31 '89
MALONE, KARL
about
Mailman II. H. Hersch. il pors *Sports Illustrated* 70:54-6+ Je 26 '89
Utah's Mailman delivers in 39th NBA All-star game. il por *Jet* 75:51 F 27 '89
MALONE, MICHAEL J.
about
Mike Malone and the slumbering giant. M. Beauchamp. il por *Forbes* 143:90+ F 20 '89
MALONE, THOMAS F., AND CORELL, ROBERT
Mission to Planet Earth revisited [cover story] bibl f il *Environment* 31:6-11+ Ap '89
MALONE, TOM
Self-fulfillment through service to others. *The Humanist* 49:24+ Ja/F '89
MALONE (TEX.)
Crime
Death of black in small Texas town questioned [J. O. King] il *Jet* 77:5 D 11 '89
MALONEY, E. S.
Notices to boatmen. See issues of Motor Boating & Sailing
MALONEY, SUSAN
Curran loses—so does Catholic education. *The Christian Century* 106:278-9 Mr 15 '89
MALPRACTICE
See also
Clergy malpractice
Insurance, Malpractice liability
Are companies cutting too close to the bone? [malpractice claims may arise from new insurance plans designed to trim costs] M. Galen. il *Business Week* p141+ O 30 '89
Brian Wilson's Svengali has his wings clipped as he gives up his license to shrink [E. Landy] il pors *People Weekly* 31:97 Ap 17 '89

James Burt's 'love surgery' was supposed to boost pleasure, but some patients say it brought pain [faces suits for experimental gynecological surgery] M. Brower. il por *People Weekly* 31:97-6+ Mr 27 '89
Landy loses license [E. Landy] M. Goldberg. pors *Rolling Stone* p27 My 18 '89
Law and medicine [address, September 26, 1988] F. Haight. *Vital Speeches of the Day* 55:180-5 Ja 1 '89
The love surgeon [experimental gynecological surgery performed by J. Burt] J. A. Hennessee. il *Mademoiselle* 95:206-7+ Ag '89
Maverick doctor: martyr or fraud? [V. Hufnagel loses medical license] K. Moloney. por *Ms.* 18:69-70 N '89
"My gynecologist butchered me!" [J. Burt performs experimental reconstructive surgery]; ed. by Judith Kelman. G. Harness. il por *Redbook* 173:22+ Jl '89
See you in court! [suits against doctors; excerpt] F. J. Edwards. il por *Health (New York, N.Y.)* 21:52+ N '89
Supersensitive supersecrecy [databank of professional reprimands against health care practitioners] *Science News* 136:284 O 28 '89
The thrift police [FSLIC files malpractice suit against law firm Jenkens & Gilchrist over its dealings with State Savings & Loan Association of Lubbock] D. Fanning. il *Forbes* 143:74 Ja 9 '89
The unhappiest part of medicine, says author John Pekkanen, may be the physicians who practice it. M. Brower. il pors *People Weekly* 31:85+ Ja 9 '89
Worrying about medical costs [views of Herbert Berger] W. F. Buckley. *National Review* 41:63 Mr 10 '89
MALPRACTICE LIABILITY INSURANCE *See* Insurance, Malpractice liability
MALTA
Description and travel
Malta. W. S. Ellis. il maps *National Geographic* 175:700-17 Je '89
MALTA SUMMIT, 1989 *See* Bush-Gorbachev summit conference, 1989
MALTER, JAMES S.
Identification of an AUUUA-specific messenger RNA binding protein. bibl f il *Science* 246:664-6 N 3 '89
MALTHUS, T. R. (THOMAS ROBERT), 1766-1834
about
Malthus and his ghost. R. Percival. *National Review* 41:30-3 Ag 18 '89
MALTHUS, THOMAS ROBERT *See* Malthus, T. R. (Thomas Robert), 1766-1834
MALVASIA (NEW YORK, N.Y.: RESTAURANT) *See* New York (N.Y.)—Restaurants, nightclubs, bars, etc.
MALVEAUX, JULIANNE
Economics and you. See issues of Essence beginning August 1987
One jazzy lady. il pors *New Choices for the Best Years* 29:54-8 N '89
"Sweet Alice" Harris. il pors *Ms.* 17:72-5 Ja/F '89
MAMA I WANT TO SING [musical] *See* Musicals, revues, etc.—Reviews—Single works
MAMA MONTEGO (FICTIONAL CHARACTER)
M.M. [Mama Montego radio broadcast on WRKS in New York City] *The New Yorker* 65:36-7 O 30 '89
MAMELUKES
Rivalry in the Red Sea: Portugal's impact on the fortunes of Mamluk Egypt. Ibn Iyās. il *The Courier (Unesco)* 42:30-2 Ap '89
MAMET, DAVID
Dodge [excerpt from drama] il *Harper's* 278:43-4 F '89
about
Bobby Gould in hell [drama] Reviews
New York il 22:105 D 18 '89. J. Simon
The New Yorker 65:77-8+ D 25 '89. M. Kramer
Time il 134:78 D 18 '89. W. A. Henry
Things change [film] Reviews
The Humanist il 49:39 Mr/Ap '89. H. M. Geduld
Video 13:63 Je '89. M. Pierson
MAMLUKS *See* Mamelukes
MAMMALS
See also
Bats
Carnivores
Marine mammals
Pinnipedia
Primates
Rodents
Whales
Beyond the lab rat [unusual mammals] J. P. Cohn. il *BioScience* 39:518-22 S '89
Mammalian terrestrial locomotion and size. A. A. Biewener. bibl f il *BioScience* 39:776-83 D '89
Scaling body support in mammals: limb posture and muscle mechanics. A. A. Biewener. bibl f il *Science* 245:45-8 Jl 7 '89
MAMMARY GLANDS
See also
Breast
Growth
Production of mammastatin, a tissue-specific growth inhibitor, by normal human mammary cells. P. R. Ervin, Jr. and others. bibl f il *Science* 244:1585-7 Je 30 '89

MAMMI, ALESSANDRA
Italy's crumbling heritage [interview with G. Urbani] il *World Press Review* 36:74 D '89
MAMMOGRAPHY
Mammograms save lives. *McCall's* 116:107 S '89
Mammography: who needs it? M. Weber. *Vogue* 179:114 Ja '89
MAN

Economic value
See Human capital

Evolution
See Evolution

Influence of environment
See also
Environmental health
Why I went to the woods. K. Ziembinska. por *The Humanist* 49:22+ Mr/Ap '89

Influence on nature
See also
Desertification
Environmental policy
Indians of North America—Influence on nature
Man and the Biosphere Programme
Pollution
Amid nature's glory, a writer urgently warns of its passing [interview with B. McKibben] S. K. Reed. il pors *People Weekly* 32:55-6+ O 16 '89
A bend in the road. C. Fletcher. *Wilderness* 52:12+ Wint '88
Cave man started it [environmental destruction] H. de Saint-Blanquat. *World Press Review* 36:41 O '89
The earth . . . strikes back. il *Life* 12:8-15+ Ja '89
The ecology of survival. A. Gore, Jr. il *The New Republic* 201:26+ N 6 '89
The end of nature. B. McKibben. *The New Yorker* 65:47-8+ S 11 '89
Endgames [essays by F. Fukuyama and B. McKibben predicting the end of history and the end of nature] L. H. Lapham. *Harper's* 279:10-13 N '89
Enduring earth. B. Gilbert. il *Life* 12:82-4+ F '89
The etiquette of freedom. G. Snyder. il *Sierra* 74:74-7+ S/O '89
Evolution and extinction [species preservers trying to stop the clock; with reply by N. Meyers] N. D. Levine. *BioScience* 39:38-40 Ja '89
Fall of the Garden of Eden [prehistoric man and the environment] M. Kiefer. il *International Wildlife* 19:38-43 Jl/Ag '89
Fear in a handful of numbers. D. Overbye. il *Time* 134:119-20 O 9 '89
Hi there, Bambi [views of B. McKibben] R. Bailey. il *Forbes* 144:46+ O 16 '89
Human activities, greenhouse effect and climate change. il *Physics Today* 42:28-9 My '89
Looking for Mr. Greenhouse. R. Monastersky. il *Science News* 135:216-17+ Ap 8 '89
Managing planet earth [cover story; special section] il *Scientific American* 261:46-54+ S '89
Our fragile earth. J. Schell. il *Discover* 10:44-7+ O '89
Save the whales, screw the shrimp. J. Williams. il *Esquire* 111:89-95 F '89
To be or not to be? (environmentally speaking) in fall title from Random [work of B. McKibben] C. Goodrich. por *Publishers Weekly* 236:23 Ag 25 '89
Trouble in the atmosphere: does your cup of coffee cause forest fires? C. A. Moore. il *International Wildlife* 19:38-45 Mr/Ap '89

Anecdotes, facetiae, satire, etc.
Last word. T. Runté. por *Omni (New York, N.Y.)* 11:116 S '89

Migrations
The bones from Brazil [evidence of earlier New World migration date; work of Maria Beltrão and Niède Guidon] H. Pringle. il *Omni (New York, N.Y.)* 11:26+ Ap '89
Migration evolves Down Under [views of Milford H. Wolpoff] B. Bower. *Science News* 136:365 D 2 '89
Teeth and prehistory in Asia [reconstructing the great migrations] C. G. Turner, II. bibl il map *Scientific American* 260:88-91+ F '89

Origin and antiquity
See Man, Prehistoric
MAN, PREHISTORIC
See also
Archeology
Art, Prehistoric
Bog people
Cardiff giant
Cave drawings and paintings
Paleo-Indians
Stone implements and weapons
Asian human-origin theory gets new teeth [research by Christy G. Turner] B. Bower. *Science News* 136:100 Ag 12 '89
Bamboo and human evolution. G. G. Pope. il map *Natural History* p48-57 O '89
Cave man started it [environmental destruction] H. de Saint-Blanquat. *World Press Review* 36:41 O '89
Cold water on the fire [doubtful research by Steven R. James] J. Benditt. *Scientific American* 260:21-2 My '89

An essay on a pig roast [role of F. Osborn's erroneous Nebraska Man theory in the creationism debate] S. J. Gould. il *Natural History* p14+ Ja '89
European prehistory gets even older. S. Ackerman. il *Science* 246:28-30 O 6 '89
Fall of the Garden of Eden [prehistoric man and the environment] M. Kiefer. il *International Wildlife* 19:38-43 Jl/Ag '89
Finite social space, evolutionary pathways, and reconstructing hominid behavior. R. A. Foley and P. C. Lee. bibl f il *Science* 243:901-6 F 17 '89
The first humans [Homo habilis fossils of Olduvai Gorge; cover story] W. F. Allman. il *U.S. News & World Report* 106:52-9 F 27 '89
The great leap forward [human evolution; cover story; with editorial comment by Paul Hoffman] J. M. Diamond. il map *Discover* 10:4, 50-60 My '89
Greek contact for humans, Neanderthals? [research by Curtis Runnels] B. Bower. *Science News* 135:39 Ja 21 '89
The gripping story of Paranthropus [evidence of tool use at Swartkrans site; study by Randall L. Susman] P. Shipman. il *Discover* 10:66-71 Ap '89
Human origins. E. L. Simons. bibl f il *Science* 245:1343-50 S 22 '89
Human origins recede in southern Asia [research by Kenneth A. R. Kennedy] B. Bower. *Science News* 135:388 Je 24 '89
The hunt for Proconsul. A. Walker and M. Teaford. il map *Scientific American* 260:76-82 Ja '89
Migration evolves Down Under [views of Milford H. Wolpoff] B. Bower. *Science News* 136:365 D 2 '89
Modern humans take a spin back in time [electron spin resonance dating of Skhul site; research by Christopher B. Stringer] B. Bower. *Science News* 135:263 Ap 29 '89
My granddad, Neanderthal? S. Begley. il map *Newsweek* 114:70-1 O 16 '89
Neanderthals get an evolutionary face-lift [evidence for early stage in the Near East] B. Bower. *Science News* 135:229 Ap 15 '89
Paranthropus yields mosaic arm bone [work of Randall L. Susman and Frederick E. Grine] B. Bower. *Science News* 135:251 Ap 22 '89
Prehistoric barbecue [evidence of fire use at Swartkrans; research by C. K. Brain and Andrew Sillen] *Discover* 10:14-15 Mr '89
Species questions in modern human origins. R. Lewin. il *Science* 243:1666-7 Mr 31 '89
Stone tips on ancient hunting [work of John J. Shea] *Science News* 136:13 Jl 1 '89
Talk of ages [Neanderthal hyoid bone from Kebara cave site, Israel; cover story] B. Bower. il *Science News* 136:24-6 Jl 8 '89
Tasmania's earliest settlers [research by Richard Cosgrove] *Science News* 135:223 Ap 8 '89
Teeth and prehistory in Asia [reconstructing the great migrations] C. G. Turner, II. bibl il map *Scientific American* 260:88-91+ F '89
Thirty thousand years of human colonization in Tasmania: new Pleistocene dates. R. Cosgrove. bibl f il map *Science* 243:1706-8 Mr 31 '89
Toe-to-toe with Paranthropus [foot bone gives evidence of bipedality at Swartkrans site; research by Randall Susman] il *Discover* 10:16 Ag '89
A walk back through evolution [study of gaits and footprints of modern people who walk barefooted indicates Laetoli prints are not Australopithecus afarensis; work of Russell H. Tuttle] B. Bower. *Science News* 135:251 Ap 22 '89

Diseases
See Paleopathology

Mortuary customs
Grave doubts [Neanderthal burials; research by Robert H. Gargett] J. Benditt. il *Scientific American* 260:32-3 Je '89
MAN (THEOLOGY)
See also
Fall of man
MAN AND NATURE *See* Man—Influence of environment; Man—Influence on nature
MAN AND SUPERMAN [drama] *See* Shaw, Bernard, 1856-1950
MAN AND THE BIOSPHERE PROGRAMME
Biosphere reserves: what, where and why? il map *Focus (New York, N.Y.: 1950)* 39:17-19 Spr '89
A MAN CALLED HAWK [television program] *See* Television program reviews—Single works
MAN RAY *See* Ray, Man, 1890-1976
MAN WITH THE PICTURES (TERM)
The Man with the pictures. W. Safire. il *The New York Times Magazine* p14+ Je 18 '89
MANAGEMENT
See also
Arts—Management
Business management
Communication in management
Farm management
Organization
School management and organization
Time management
Wildlife management

MANAGEMENT—See also—*cont.*
Yield management
How to manage a grand project [work of J. Pepper, B. Hope and M. Patrick] A. M. Russell. il pors *Working Woman* 14:73-7 D '89

MANAGEMENT ACCOUNTING
Management accounting for advanced technological environments. R. S. Kaplan. bibl f il *Science* 245:819-23 Ag 25 '89

MANAGEMENT AND BUDGET OFFICE (U.S.) See United States. Office of Management and Budget

MANAGEMENT COMPANY ENTERTAINMENT GROUP INC.
Look who's got a box-office smash. R. Grover. il por *Business Week* p142 D 11 '89

MANAGEMENT CONSULTANTS See Business consultants

MANAGEMENT DEVELOPMENT PROGRAMS See Executives—Training

MANAGEMENT OF CHILDREN See Children—Management and training

MANAGERS See Black executives; Executives; Women executives

MANAGERS, BASEBALL See Baseball managers

MANAGEWARE INC.
Consultant in a bind [business modeling program Compete!] D. Churbuck. il por *Forbes* 144:285-6 N 13 '89

MANAS, BLANKA
Police uniform buttons. il *Antiques & Collecting Hobbies* 94:52-3 My '89

MANAS (NEWSPAPER)
Deaths in the family. E. Knoll. *The Progressive* 53:4 Mr '89
A man and his "paper". R. Grossman. il *Utne Reader* p32 My/Je '89

MANASSAS NATIONAL BATTLEFIELD PARK (VA.)
Manassas: where our nation marched to war. D. Young. il *Southern Living* 24:36+ My '89
The third battle of Manassas [defeat of proposed mall] A. Hills. il *History Today* 39:4-5 Mr '89

MANATEES
Slow creature caught in a fast world [Florida] T. A. Lewis. il *National Wildlife* 28:42-9 D '89/Ja '90

LA MANCHA PRIVATE CLUB & VILLAS (PALM SPRINGS, CALIF.: RESORT) See Resorts—California

MANCHESTER, WILLIAM
The last lion: alone [excerpt] il pors *Conservative Digest* 15:63+ Jl/Ag '89

MANCHIN, A. JAMES, 1927-
about
A mountainous loss in West Virginia. G. L. Miles. il *Business Week* p42 Ap 3 '89

MANCHURIA (CHINA)
See also
Forests and forestry—Manchuria (China)
Description and travel
Postmodern tours. J. Krich. il por *Mother Jones* 14:42-4 Jl/Ag '89

MANCINI, BOOM BOOM
about
Fat City for rusty pugs. W. Nack. il pors *Sports Illustrated* 70:36-7 Mr 20 '89
A Ray of hope. J. E. Loehr. il pors *World Tennis* 37:36-8+ Ag '89

MANCINI, MARC
Professor Gore. il *Film Comment* 25:8 S/O '89

MANCINI, PATTI F.
The politics of power [address, April 1, 1989] *Vital Speeches of the Day* 55:657-62 Ag 15 '89

MANCUSO, FBI [television program] See Television program reviews—Single works

MANDARICH, TONY
about
The big enchilada [cover story] R. Telander. il pors *Sports Illustrated* 70:40-2+ Ap 24 '89
If you think Tony Mandarich gets paid too much, you'll have a short stay in Green Bay. R. Arias. il pors *People Weekly* 32:139+ D 11 '89
Tackling the NFL. D. Burke. il por *Maclean's* 102:49+ My 8 '89
Tale of the tape. il pors *Sports Illustrated* 70:14 My 29 '89

MANDARIN ORANGES
Diseases and pests
Biological pest control [Chinese use of carnivorous ants to protect mandarin oranges] R. K. G. Temple. il *The Courier (Unesco)* 41:24 O '88

MANDARIN PAPERBACKS (FIRM)
Mandarin, U.K.'s first mass market line in 15 years, poised for launch. V. Menkes. il *Publishers Weekly* 235:18 F 10 '89

MANDATED BENEFITS LEGISLATION See Fringe benefits—Laws and regulations

MANDEL, ABBY
Kitchen VIP's* *(very important pieces of equipment). il *Working Woman* 14:140-2 Ap '89

MANDEL, BARRETT J., AND YELLEN, JUDITH
Mastering the memo. il *Working Woman* 14:134-7 S '89

MANDEL, HOWARD
Dave Holland: creative collaborator. il pors *Down Beat* 56:20-3 O '89
Gil Evans: the lone arranger [reprint from April 1984 issue] por *Down Beat* 56:92 S '89
John Scofield: restless guitar player [cover story] il pors *Down Beat* 56:16-19 Mr '89
Sergey Kuryokhin: the Russian Martian arrives. il pors *Down Beat* 56:26-8 Ap '89

MANDEL, SALLY
A time to sing [fiction] il pors *Good Housekeeping* 208:213-16+ Je '89

MANDEL, SUSAN T.
Avoiding the Burtonmander. *National Review* 41:17 D 22 '89
Disabling America. il *National Review* 41:23-4 S 29 '89
Jobs with justice? *National Review* 41:17 Ag 18 '89
New Kennedy, old solutions. *National Review* 41:22-3 Jl 14 '89
The problem at HUD. il *National Review* 41:21-2 Ag 4 '89
Suffer the little children. il *National Review* 41:20-1 S 1 '89
Unhealthy, unwealthy, and worse. il *National Review* 41:25-6 O 13 '89

MANDEL, SUSAN T., AND MCGURN, WILLIAM
How the Democrats hold on to Congress. *National Review* 41:37-40 N 24 '89

MANDELA, NELSON
about
A glimmer of peace. C. Erasmus. il por *Maclean's* 102:26 Jl 24 '89
Meeting of different minds. S. MacLeod. il pors *Time* 134:28 D 25 '89
Teatime in Pretoria. C. S. Manegold. il *Newsweek* 114:24 Jl 24 '89
Then there was one. S. MacLeod. il *Time* 134:49-50 O 23 '89
An unlikely tea for two. B. W. Nelan. il pors *Time* 134:29 Jl 24 '89
Word from South Africa [interview with Z. M. Dlamini] S. L. Taylor and E. B. Washington. il por *Essence* 20:42-4+ Jl '89

MANDELA, WINNIE
about
A call for unity. S. L. Taylor. il *Essence* 20:59 My '89
Decline and fall of a heroine. B. W. Nelan. il por *Time* 133:36 F 27 '89
Free Winnie! E. Brown. por *Essence* 20:128 Je '89
Mrs. Mandela's disgrace. S. Reiss. il por *Newsweek* 113:44 F 27 '89
The mystery of Winnie Mandela. G. Bain. il *Maclean's* 102:50 Mr 20 '89
Pedestal politics. *The Nation* 248:325 Mr 13 '89
Scandal in Soweto: black rights leaders disown Winnie Mandela. J. Bierman. il por *Maclean's* 102:26-7 F 27 '89
Soweto's 'Winnie problem'. S. Reiss. il por *Newsweek* 113:35 F 13 '89
The sudden unmaking of Winnie Mandela. il por *U.S. News & World Report* 106:13 F 27 '89
Winnie the shrew. S. Mufson. *The New Republic* 200:14-16 Mr 13 '89
Word from South Africa [interview with Z. M. Dlamini] S. L. Taylor and E. B. Washington. il por *Essence* 20:42-4+ Jl '89

MANDELA HOUSE (OAKLAND, CALIF.)
A hand and a home for pregnant addicts [work of M. Thomas] D. Wyss. il pors *Time* 133:10+ F 27 '89

MANDELA UNITED FOOTBALL CLUB
Decline and fall of a heroine [W. Mandela] B. W. Nelan. il por *Time* 133:36 F 27 '89
Fighting back [W. Mandela battles accusers] J. Bierman. il por *Maclean's* 102:20 Mr 6 '89
Mandela's mess [W. Mandela] il por *World Press Review* 36:42 Ap '89
Mrs. Mandela's disgrace. S. Reiss. il por *Newsweek* 113:44 F 27 '89
The mystery of Winnie Mandela. G. Bain. il *Maclean's* 102:50 Mr 20 '89
Pedestal politics [controversy over W. Mandela] *The Nation* 248:325 Mr 13 '89
Scandal in Soweto: black rights leaders disown Winnie Mandela. J. Bierman. il por *Maclean's* 102:26-7 F 27 '89
Soweto's 'Winnie problem'. S. Reiss. il por *Newsweek* 113:35 F 13 '89
The sudden unmaking of Winnie Mandela. il por *U.S. News & World Report* 106:13 F 27 '89
Winnie the shrew. S. Mufson. *The New Republic* 200:14-16 Mr 13 '89

MANDELBAUM, MICHAEL
Ending the cold war. bibl f *Foreign Affairs* 68:16-36 Spr '89
Facts, not pacts. *The Bulletin of the Atomic Scientists* 45:44-5 My '89

MANDELBAUM, PAUL
A question of trust. il *The New York Times Magazine* p14+ Ag 6 '89

MANDELBROT, BENOIT B.
Temperature fluctuation: a well-defined and unavoidable notion. il *Physics Today* 42:71+ Ja '89
MANDELBROT SET *See* Fractals
MANDELKOW, ECKHARD, AND OTHERS
Spatial patterns from oscillating microtubules. bibl f il *Science* 246:1291-3 D 8 '89
MANDELL, MEL
Take charge of your phones. il *Nation's Business* 77:25-6 Ja '89
MANDELL, PATRICIA
Details, details, details. il map *Americana* 17:48-54 N/D '89
Extra Ordinary. il pors map *Americana* 17:26-31+ Mr/Ap '89
A hands-on guide to camcorders. *Working Woman* 14:168+ N '89
MANDEL'STAM, NADEZHDA, 1899-1980
about
Memoirs; tr. by Barry J. Rubin. M. Polivanov. il *The New Republic* 200:34-7 F 20 '89
MANDESE, JOE
Cable advertising goes past the wire. il *Channels (New York, N.Y.: 1986)* 9:62 Ap '89
Finding gold in your hometown. il *Channels (New York, N.Y.: 1986)* 9:79-81 Ja '89
MANDIL, SALAH
Health informatics. il *World Health* p2-5 Ag/S '89
MANELI, MIECZYSŁAW
For a new humanist militancy. il por *The Humanist* 49:14-16+ S/O '89
MANET, ÉDOUARD, 1832-1883
about
Unfit for hanging. R. Cembalest. il *Art News* 88:16 F '89
MANEUVERS, MILITARY *See* Military maneuvers
MANGAN, MARGARET
The poor [poem] *Commonweal* 116:461 S 8 '89
MANGANESE
The manganese site of the photosynthetic water-splitting enzyme. G. N. George and others. bibl f il *Science* 243:789-91 F 10 '89
MANGER GROUPS *See* Christmas cribs
MANGINO, BOB
Last word. il *Omni (New York, N.Y.)* 11:132 Ap '89
MANGOES
See also
Cooking—Fruit
MANGRUM, TOMONTRA
about
Girl who sued prom date gets $81.28 in settlement. il por *Jet* 76:29 Jl 10 '89
Giving courtship a new meaning, a Florida teen sues the date who stood her up for the school prom. il por *People Weekly* 31:101 My 29 '89
MANHATTAN BEACH (CALIF.)
Crime
Making history—of a dubious sort [McMartin Preschool trial] *U.S. News & World Report* 106:20 My 1 '89
Restaurants, nightclubs, bars, etc.
Spécialités de la maison:
Saint Estèphe. C. Bates. il *Gourmet* 49:38+ F '89
MANHATTAN CABLE TV SERVICES
Manhattan takes Bravo. C. Capuzzi. *Channels (New York, N.Y.: 1986)* 9:45 Ap '89
MANHATTAN PROJECT *See* Atomic bombs—History
MANHATTAN SAVINGS BANK
Dividends [D. Scardino plays piano] *The New Yorker* 65:38-9 O 2 '89
MANHATTAN SCHOOL OF MUSIC
Musical events:
Performances of operas Arlecchino and The nightingale. A. Porter. *The New Yorker* 64:68+ Ja 16 '89
MANHEIM EXOTIC AUCTION
Rinard at Manheim. J. A. McPhee. *The New Yorker* 65:150-2 D 4 '89
MANHUNT . . . LIVE! [television program] See Television program reviews—Single works
MANHUNT: SEARCH FOR THE NIGHT STALKER [television program] See Television program reviews—Single works
MANIC DEPRESSION *See* Depression, Mental
MANICURING
See also
Nail care industry
Getting and maintaining a good manicure. L. F. McCarty. *Vogue* 179:176 F '89
Give yourself a perfect 10. il *Ladies' Home Journal* 106:28+ Je '89
Healthy nails for a polished look. P. Patten. il *Women's Sports & Fitness* 11:22 Je '89
The nail file [special section] L. Daigneault. il *Health (New York, N.Y.)* 21:64-9 Ag '89
Nail know-how & news. il *Redbook* 172:118-21 Mr '89
Nails: hands-down winning treatments. il *Glamour* 87:248-51 Mr '89
Nails: turn yours into a perfect 10! il *Good Housekeeping* 208:126+ My '89
Three weeks to great nails. il *McCall's* 117:81 O '89

Today's products go the distance toward preventing chipping and staining. S. Lord. il *Vogue* 179:344 S '89
MANICURING SALONS *See* Beauty shops
MANIFOLDS
See also
Automobile engines—Manifolds
MANIFOLDS (MATHEMATICS)
A different dimension [fourth dimension's mathematical properties; cover story] I. Peterson. il *Science News* 135:328-30 My 27 '89
MANILA (PHILIPPINES)
Airports
Manila will expand airport to serve as major Pacific hub. il *Aviation Week & Space Technology* 131:106 Ag 21 '89
MANILA INTERNATIONAL AIRPORT *See* Manila (Philippines)—Airports
MANIOC *See* Cassavas
MANIPULATION (PSYCHOLOGY)
Outmaneuver manipulators. B. A. Baldwin. il *Reader's Digest* 134:118-20 Ap '89
MANIPULATORS (MECHANISM)
Robotic arms aid handicapped kids [increases learning ability; work of Richard Howell] il *USA Today (Periodical)* 117:6-7 F '89
MANISCHEWITZ (B.) CO. *See* B. Manischewitz Co.
MANITOBA
See also
Churchill (Man.)
Fishing—Manitoba
Trials—Manitoba
Wildlife—Manitoba
Winnipeg (Man.)
Indians
See Indians of North America—Canada
Politics and government
Feuding Tories [Winnipeg-Ottawa relations] P. Kopvillem. il por *Maclean's* 102:20 My 29 '89
A parallel accord [Manitoba politicians near agreement on Meech Lake constitutional accord] G. W. Taylor. il *Maclean's* 102:15+ Jl 24 '89
Stormy weather [Premier G. Filmon withdraws support for Meech Lake constitutional accord] B. Wallace. il por *Maclean's* 102:12-14 Ja 16 '89
Test in the West [public hearings on Meech Lake constitutional accord] R. Laver. il por *Maclean's* 102:12-14 Ap 24 '89
Under the gun [Meech Lake constitutional accord; with interview with F. McKenna] il por *Maclean's* 102:10-13 F 27 '89
MANKARIOUS, NAGUIB SOBY
about
Atty. Jewel Lafontant weds international businessman in D.C. church ceremony. il pors *Jet* 77:43 D 25 '89-Ja 1 '90
MANLEY, DEXTER
about
Defensive end Manley in poignant plea for federal literacy aid. H. Fields. *Publishers Weekly* 235:10 Je 9 '89
How did I get through school when I couldn't read? L. B. Randolph. il pors *Ebony* 44:102+ O '89
Redskins' Manley aims for NFL reinstatement. por *Jet* 77:48 D 11 '89
Terrorizing Dexter Manley tearfully testifies that he learned to read at age 28. il pors *Jet* 76:50 Je 5 '89
MANLEY, ELIZABETH
about
Innerviews [interview] por *Women's Sports & Fitness* 11:58 Je '89
MANLEY, MICHAEL, 1924-
about
After the storm. P. Jordan. il *Commonweal* 116:261-3 My 5 '89
A comeback in Jamaica [with interview] E. Calonius. il por *Newsweek* 113:29 F 20 '89
Courting capitalism, Manley takes over in Jamaica. M. A. Fortune. il por *Black Enterprise* 19:38 My '89
Manley returns. M. Kaufman. *The Nation* 248:293 Mr 6 '89
Manley wins national election in Jamaica. il por *Jet* 75:14 F 27 '89
Once more, with moderation. G. D. Garcia. il por *Time* 133:48 F 20 '89
Polling in paradise. J. Bierman. il pors *Maclean's* 102:20 F 6 '89
A sweet victory. A. Bilski. il por *Maclean's* 102:22 F 20 '89
MANN, ALFRED K.
(jt. auth) See Langacker, P., and Mann, Alfred K.
MANN, CAROL
Past echoes, future challenges [adaptation of address, January 1989] il *Women's Sports & Fitness* 11:88 Ap '89
MANN, CHARLES C.
Armies of physicists struggle to discover proof of a Scot's brainchild. bibl (p191) il *Smithsonian* 19:106-10+ Mr '89
MANN, JIM, 1946-
One company's China debacle [excerpt from Beijing Jeep] il por *Fortune* 120:145+ N 6 '89

MANN, JONATHAN M.
AIDS and discrimination. il *World Health* p14-15 Ap '89
Global AIDS into the 1990s. il *World Health* p6-7 O '89

MANN, LEE
One lens, one film, one frosty morning. il *Petersen's Photographic Magazine* 18:30-3 N '89

MANN, MARY BETH
Victims of abuse: paying the price for the sins of others. *U.S. Catholic* 54:36-8 Jl '89

MANN, MAURICE
Internationalization of the Pacific Stock Exchange [address, November 2, 1988] *Vital Speeches of the Day* 55:214-17 Ja 15 '89

MANN, MICHAEL
about
Guadalajara vice. M. Christensen. il por *Rolling Stone* p53 N 30 '89

MANN, MURRAY GELL- *See* Gell-Mann, Murray, 1929-

MANN, PEGGY
Dogged crusader against drugs. il por *Reader's Digest* 134:102-6 My '89
The truth about calcium. il *Reader's Digest* 134:70-4 Mr '89

MANN, RON, 1958-
about
Comic book confidential [film] Reviews
   The New Republic 201:24-5 Jl 17-24 '89. S. Kauffmann

MANNED MANEUVERING UNIT *See* Space flight—Extravehicular activity

MANNED SPACE FLIGHTS *See* Space flight

MANNEQUINS (FIGURES)
See also
Adel Rootstein Inc.

MANNEQUINS (FIGURES) IN CRIME PREVENTION
For the woman who has everything [dummy called Gregory] il *Newsweek* 112:64 My 22 '89
Her eyes see all, her face reveals nothing: Anne Droid is the shoplifter's nemesis [mannequin with built-in surveillance system; developed by F. J. Gutferrez] il por *People Weekly* 32:97 O 23 '89

MANNERS AND CUSTOMS
See also
Clothing and dress
Courtesy
Dating (Social customs)
Drinking customs
Etiquette
Funeral rites and ceremonies
Holidays
Rites and ceremonies
Salutations
Tipping

MANNES COLLEGE OF MUSIC
Musical events:
Performances of Donizetti's Rita and Rossini's L'occasione fa il ladro. A. Porter. *The New Yorker* 65:118-19 Ap 17 '89

MANNEY, HENRY N., 1922-1988
about
Miscellaneous ramblings. T. L. Bryant. il pors *Road & Track* 40:35-6 Jl '89

MANNHART, J., AND OTHERS
Spatially resolved observation of supercurrents across grain boundaries in YBaCuO films. bibl f il *Science* 245:839-41 Ag 25 '89

MANNHEIMER, STEVE
Litigators of the lost art. il *The Saturday Evening Post* 261:62-8 O '89

MANNING-MIMS, MADELINE
about
The second time around. R. Fimrite. il pors *Sports Illustrated* 70:110-14+ Ja 9 '89

MANNINGHAM MILLS (BRADFORD, ENGLAND)
Manningham Mills, Bradford. A. Briggs. il por *History Today* 39:62-3 O '89

MANNS, LINDSEY REGAN
Kidnapping
Babies were Linda German's obsession—was she crazy or just madly in love? [victim of pseudocyesis charged with baby snatching in Huntington, W. Va.] G. Stone. il pors *People Weekly* 31:84-8 Mr 20 '89

MANNY'S MUSICAL INSTRUMENTS & ACCESSORIES INC.
Manny's happy returns. M. Porter. il *Gentlemen's Quarterly* 59:157-8 Ag '89

MANO, D. KEITH
The gimlet eye. See occasional issues of National Review

MANOFF, DINAH
about
It's Dinah vs. the dog—and she's growling. B. O'Hallaren. il pors *TV Guide* 37:12-14 Je 24-30 '89

MANOOGIAN, RICHARD
about
American paintings in the Manoogian Collection. N. Cikovsky. il *Antiques* 136:132-43 Jl '89

MANOR, GIORA
Before Balanchine: Kasyan Goleizovsky's Russian revolution (I). il pors *Dance Magazine* 63:56-60 Ja '89

Before Balanchine: Kasyan Goleizovsky's Russian revolution (II). il pors *Dance Magazine* 63:60-4 F '89

MANOR, JAMES
India: state and society diverge. bibl f *Current History* 88:429-32+ D '89

MANOR, JASON *See* Hall, Oakley M.

MANOR CARE, INC.
Thank you, Medicare. il *Forbes* 143:150 Ja 9 '89

MANPOWER
See also
Labor supply

MANPOWER, INC.
Betting on the man who built Manpower. G. G. Marcial. il *Business Week* p106 D 4 '89
For Mitchell Fromstein, how sweet it is. R. A. Melcher and J. E. Ellis. il por *Business Week* p32 Ja 30 '89

MANPOWER AND EDUCATION *See* Labor—Education

MANPOWERED AIRCRAFT *See* Human powered aircraft

MANRY, DAVID E.
Mainland China's perfect metropolis. il *Travel Holiday* 171:12+ Ja '89

MANSBRIDGE, ALBERT
about
Albert Mansbridge and a fresh coat of paint. D. Thompson. il pors *History Today* 39:7-9 Ag '89

MANSE (MONTEREY, MASS.) *See* Monterey (Mass.)—Historic houses, sites, etc.

MANSEL, PHILIP, 1961-
On the Bosphorus. il *Opera News* 53:36-7 My '89

MANSELL, NIGEL
about
Mansell the magician. I. Ireland. il *Road & Track* 41:124-5+ D '89
Red hot! I. Ireland. il *Road & Track* 40:102-4+ Jl '89

MANSFIELD, MIKE
The U.S. and Japan: sharing our destinies. *Current (Washington, D.C.)* 316:27-33 O '89
The U.S. and Japan: sharing our destinies. *Foreign Affairs* 68:3-15 Spr '89

MANSFIELD, STEPHANIE
Go with the Flo. il por *Vogue* 179:402-5+ Ap '89
Nobody beats the Miz. il por *Vogue* 179:294-9+ F '89
Why I wear what I wear: Eric the dark [interview] il pors *Gentlemen's Quarterly* 59:94+ D '89

MANSHIP, PAUL, 1885-1966
about
Reintroducing Manship's art. K. M. Burke. il *Smithsonian* 20:168 My '89

MANSIONS, GOVERNORS' *See* Governors' mansions

MANSO, LEO, 1914-
about
Leo Manso at Armstrong. L. Campbell. il *Art in America* 77:156-7 Ja '89

MANSON, CHARLES, 1934-
about
Daughter of Manson victims finds forgiveness. J. Shaver. il pors *Christianity Today* 33:50-1 S 22 '89
Manson. J. Adler. por *Newsweek* 114:54-5 Jl 3 '89

MANSOURI, LOTFI
about
Detail man. S. Von Buchau. il pors *Opera News* 54:24-7 S '89

MANSTEIN, DIETMAR J., AND OTHERS
Expression and characterization of a functional myosin head fragment in Dictyostelium discoideum. bibl f il *Science* 246:656-8 N 3 '89

MANTEGNA, JOE, 1948?-
about
Bleacher bums [drama] Reviews
   Sports Illustrated il 70:16 Je 26 '89. R. Berler

MANTELL, MATTHEW E.
The greatest cycling novel ever written. il *Bicycling* 30:82+ Ap '89
Waiting for the black Merckx. il *Bicycling* 30:90-1+ My '89
What is the UCI? il *Bicycling* 30:64+ Je '89

MANTELS
How to build a fireplace mantle. P. Barrett. il *Popular Mechanics* 166:75-8 F '89
Mantel masterpiece. D. Vandervort. il *Home Mechanix* 85:109-11 N '89
Playing with fire [fabric wall coverings and coordinated mantel decoration] il *House & Garden* 161:132-7 Ja '89

MANTI-LASAL NATIONAL FOREST (UTAH AND COLO.)
Brumley Ridge, Utah. R. H. Mohlenbrock. il map *Natural History* p68-71 S '89

MANTIS SHRIMP EYE *See* Eye—Crustaceans

MANTLE, MARGARET
It takes one to know one: a mom's-eye view of the Blessed Mother. *U.S. Catholic* 54:29-31 My '89

MANTLE, MICKEY, 1931-
about
Mickey Mantle's field of dreams. C. Meth. il pors *Video* 13:12 Ag '89

MANTLE OF THE EARTH *See* Earth—Internal structure
MANUAL TYPEWRITERS *See* Typewriters
MANUFACTURED HOUSES *See* Houses, Prefabricated
MANUFACTURING IN SPACE *See* Space processing
MANUFACTURING INDUSTRIES
    See also
    Canadian Manufacturing Advanced Technology Exchange
    Design for manufacturability and assembly
    Industrial capacity
    Mills
Competing by cooperating [address, May 9, 1989] A. H. Magazine. *Vital Speeches of the Day* 55:604-8 Jl 15 '89
The economy's landing gear may have a defect: manufacturing. J. C. Cooper and K. Madigan. il *Business Week* p23-4 S 4 '89
Factories throttle down fast—and that could backfire on the economy. J. C. Cooper and K. Madigan. il *Business Week* p57-8 Jl 17 '89
The funk at the factory gums up the big picture. J. C. Cooper and K. Madigan. il *Business Week* p27-8 O 16 '89
How to keep the home forges burning—and profitable [shifting overseas operations back to U.S.] P. Sherrid. il *U.S. News & World Report* 107:48-9 Jl 3 '89
How to regain the productive edge [excerpts from MIT report Made in America] il *Fortune* 119:92-4+ My 22 '89
Idle smokestacks probably won't drag the economy down. J. C. Cooper and K. Madigan. il *Business Week* p37-8+ D 18 '89
If manufacturing slows much more, watch out for recession. J. C. Cooper and K. Madigan. il *Business Week* p37-8 N 6 '89
Improving the efficiency of electricity use in manufacturing. M. H. Ross. bibl f il *Science* 244:311-17 Ap 21 '89
International comparisons of productivity and unit labor cost trends in manufacturing. A. Neef and J. Thomas. bibl f il *Monthly Labor Review* 111:27-33 D '88
Japan faces a brain drain [college grads opting out of manufacturing sector] Y. Hoshiai and J. Schwartz. il *Newsweek* 114:47-8 S 4 '89
M.B.A.s with blue collars [manufacturers should recruit best and brightest young managers] A. G. Shilling. il por *Forbes* 144:300 O 16 '89
Manufacturing [address, April 6, 1989] C. H. Chandler. *Vital Speeches of the Day* 55:461-4 My 15 '89
MIT study confirms productivity slipping in key U.S. industries [Made in America report] *Aviation Week & Space Technology* 131:69-70 D 4 '89
Productivity [cover story; special section; with editorial comment by Jonathan Schlefer] il *Technology Review* 92:2, 27-40+ Ag/S '89
Regaining the productive edge (I). C. W. Weinberger. il *Forbes* 144:31 O 2 '89
Regaining the productive edge (II). C. W. Weinberger. il *Forbes* 144:31 O 16 '89
Revitalizing our economy: manufacturing is the key. J. J. Jasinowski. il *USA Today (Periodical)* 117:23-4 Ja '89
U.S. companies lack trade aggressiveness. W. T. Brookes. por *Nation's Business* 77:13 F '89
The U.S. gets back in fighting shape. A. L. Taylor, III. il *Fortune* 119:42-5+ Ap 24 '89
Why smokestack America doesn't quake at the word 'recession'. M. Schroeder. il *Business Week* p100-1+ S 11 '89
MANURE *See* Horse manure
MANURE HANDLING *See* Fertilizers and manures—Handling
MANURES AS FERTILIZERS *See* Fertilizers and manures
MANUSCRIPTS
    See also
    Illumination of books and manuscripts
    Cataloging
Profiles [C. de Hamel, manuscript cataloger at Sotheby's] I. Shenker. il por *The New Yorker* 65:48+ My 29 '89
    Collectors and collecting
    See also
    Libraries—Manuscript collections
    Conservation and restoration
Modern manuscripts: a fragile heritage [cover story; special issue] il *The Courier (Unesco)* 42:3-25 My '89
MANUSCRIPTS, AMERICAN
    Forgeries
Lone Star fakes [T. Taylor tracks down forgeries of Texas historical documents] L. Belkin. il pors *The New York Times Magazine* p66+ D 10 '89
MANUSCRIPTS, HEBREW
    See also
    Dead Sea scrolls
MANUSCRIPTS, LATIN AMERICAN
Literary detection and Latin American writing. F. Ainsa. il *The Courier (Unesco)* 42:21-3 My '89
MANVILLE CORPORATION
Free at last for a second try [W. T. Stephens] C. Leinster. il por *Fortune* 119:36 Ja 2 '89
He won't travel far without his laptop [W. T. Stephens] C. O'Malley. il por *Personal Computing* 13:75 Ap '89
Just when Manville thought it was safe . . . [furious pace of settling claims] S. D. Atchison. *Business Week* p36 N 20 '89

MANZI, JIM P.
Software must work the way people do. por *Personal Computing* 13:211 O '89
    about
Jim Manzi. K. H. Hammonds. il por *Business Week* Special Issue:147 Ap 14 '89
The spreadsheet that nearly wore Lotus out. K. H. Hammonds. il por *Business Week* p62-4 Jl 3 '89
MAO, H. K., AND HEMLEY, R. J.
Optical studies of hydrogen above 200 gigapascals: evidence for metallization by band overlap. bibl f il *Science* 244:1462-5 Je 23 '89
MAO, H. K., AND OTHERS
X-ray diffraction to 302 gigapascals: high-pressure crystal structure of cesium iodide. bibl f il *Science* 246:649-51 N 3 '89
MAO, TSE-TUNG *See* Mao Zedong, 1893-1976
MAO ZEDONG, 1893-1976
    about
The battle over the Chairman. R. Wilkinson. il *Newsweek* 114:31 Ag 14 '89
The incredible shrinking man. J. Mirsky. il *The New York Review of Books* 36:18-20 Je 29 '89
The Long March to revolution. L. Eskin. il por *Scholastic Update (Teachers' edition)* 121:21 My 5 '89
Mao lives. W. F. Buckley. *National Review* 41:62 Je 30 '89
MAORIS
    Health and hygiene
The well-being of the Maori. H. R. Broughton. il *World Health* p20-1 Je '89
MAP CONTOURS *See* Contours (Cartography)
MAP MAKING *See* Cartography
A MAP OF THE WORLD [drama] *See* Hare, David
MAP PROJECTIONS *See* Cartography
MAP PUZZLES *See* Puzzles
MAPCO INC.
Is privacy the goal of Mapco's maneuvers? G. G. Marcial. il *Business Week* p62 Jl 24 '89
MAPES, ALAN
The World Series of Birding. il *The Conservationist* 43:20-5 Mr/Ap '89
MAPLE
Maple: the biogeography of popular species. S. D. Garber. *Focus (New York, N.Y.: 1950)* 38:32-3+ Wint '88
    Diseases and pests
Plight of the maples [cover story] R. Matthews. il *Country Journal* 16:50-4+ Mr/Ap '89
MAPLE SUGAR
Sweet sugar maple memories. N. Eggleston. il *The Conservationist* 43:2-5 Mr/Ap '89
MAPLE SUGAR INDUSTRY
Plight of the maples [cover story] R. Matthews. il *Country Journal* 16:50-4+ Mr/Ap '89
Where has all the syrup gone? J. Seligmann. *Newsweek* 113:67 My 8 '89
MAPLE SYRUP
Tapping the source [sugaring season in western Mass.] D. Grant. il *New York* 22:70+ Mr 20 '89
MAPP, ERICA
The garden of St. Paul's Hospital in Arles [poem] *Commonweal* 116:564 O 20 '89
Mountains at St. Remy [poem] *Commonweal* 116:564 O 20 '89
Tarascon diligence [poem] *Commonweal* 116:564 O 20 '89
MAPPLETHORPE, ROBERT
    about
Art and taxpayers. A. C. Danto. *The Nation* 249:192-3 Ag 21-28 '89
Corcoran showdown. C. McGuigan. il pors *Newsweek* 114:111+ O 9 '89
Exhibitionism. *The New Republic* 201:6 Jl 17-24 '89
Mad about Mapplethorpe. A. Ferguson. *National Review* 41:20-1 Ag 4 '89
Mapplethorpe of my eye. A. Heard. *The New Republic* 201:10-12 Ag 21 '89
The pleasure of the chase. C. McGuigan. il pors *Newsweek* 113:62-3 Ja 30 '89
Robert Mapplethorpe. il por *People Weekly* 32:100-1 D 25 '89-Ja 1 '90
Robert Mapplethorpe at Robert Miller. B. Berkson. il *Art in America* 77:258 Ap '89
Robert Mapplethorpe: Washington Project for the Arts. A. D. Coleman. il *Art News* 88:213 O '89
A "sacrificial lamb"? S. Hochfield. il por *Art News* 88:62 N '89
Some women [cover story] J. Didion. il por *Esquire* 112:214-23 S '89
White and black. I. Sischy. *The New Yorker* 65:124+ N 13 '89
Whose art is it, anyway? M. B. Carlson. il *Time* 134:21 Jl 3 '89
MAPS
    See also
    Atlases
    Australia—Maps
    Aviation charts

MAPS—See also—*cont.*
Cartography
Computer maps
Egypt—Maps
Forest fires—Maps
Geology—Maps
Globes
Holy Land—Maps
Japan—Maps
Mars (Planet)—Maps
Moon—Maps
Moscow (Soviet Union)—Maps
New York (N.Y.)—Maps
Ocean bottom—Maps
Orienteering (Sport)
Road maps, guides, etc.
Soviet Union—Maps
Topographic maps
Weather maps
Western States—Maps
World maps
Bringing maps home. M. Eichen. il *Parents* 64:143-6 S '89
What's new in maps & atlases. J. Crichton. il *Publishers Weekly* 235:91-4 Ja 20 '89

MAPS, ASTRONOMICAL *See* Astronomy—Charts, diagrams, etc.

MAPS, EARLY
Japan in early Portuguese maps. A. P. Marques. il maps *The Courier (Unesco)* 42:14-16 Ap '89
Mapping the world. L. Eskin. il *Scholastic Update (Teachers' edition)* 122:8-9 S 22 '89
Collectors and collecting
Caught mapping [S. Schwartz' collection] C. Brown. il por *Forbes* 144:134 S 4 '89

MAR-A-LAGO (PALM BEACH, FLA.: HISTORIC HOUSE)
See Palm Beach (Fla.)—Historic houses, sites, etc.

MARACAIBO (VENEZUELA)
Theater
Curtains up! [restoration of Baralt Theater] il *Américas* 41 no2:3-4 '89

MARACLE, JOHN E.
The lost nations. il *Christianity Today* 33:34-7 Mr 3 '89
about
Looking for a chance. K. H. Sidey. por *Christianity Today* 33:35 Mr 3 '89

MARAJÓ ISLAND (BRAZIL)
Antiquities
Lost civilizations of the lower Amazon. A. C. Roosevelt. il map *Natural History* p74-83 F '89

MARAJOARA CULTURE
Lost civilizations of the lower Amazon. A. C. Roosevelt. il map *Natural History* p74-83 F '89

MARAN, STEPHEN P.
Little missions, big returns. il *Astronomy* 17:34-40 Ja '89
Sky reporter. See occasional issues of Natural History through May 1989

MARANO, ROCCO J.
U.S. technical leadership is threatened by investment pressure [address, May 8, 1989] *Vital Speeches of the Day* 55:601-3 Jl 15 '89

MARANZ, MATTHEW
Guns 'R' Us. *The New Republic* 200:12+ Ja 23 '89

MARAT, JEAN PAUL, 1743-1793
about
First encounters. E. Sorel and N. C. Sorel. il *The Atlantic* 264:77 Jl '89

MARATHON DES SABLES *See* Desert running

MARATHON RUNNING
See also
Ultramarathon running
Alive & kicking [J. Welzel's recovery from auto accident] J. Brant. il pors *Runner's World* 24:52-5 F '89
Better late than never [J. Campbell] R. Robinson. il pors *Runner's World* 24:62-5 Ag '89
Beyond a shadow of a doubt [Twin Cities Marathon] H. Higdon. il *Runner's World* 24:40-1+ Ja '89
Beyond the melting pot [J. Ikangaa wins New York City Marathon] M. Noden. il por *Sports Illustrated* 71:46-8 N 13 '89
California steamin' [Los Angeles Marathon] B. Wischnia. il *Runner's World* 24:38-40+ Je '89
Chasing legends [A. Mekonnen and I. Kristiansen win Boston Marathon; special section] A. Burfoot. il pors *Runner's World* 24:34-41 Jl '89
Dog-eared days [journey from obesity and smoking to running the marathon] P. A. Schreivogel. il por *Runner's World* 24:86 F '89
Flying at the finish [A. Mekonnen wins Boston Marathon] M. Noden. il por *Sports Illustrated* 70:28 Ap 24 '89
The gentle man of Verona [G. Bordin] M. Bloom. il pors *Runner's World* 24:60-5 N '89
Great races to run in 1989. il *Women's Sports & Fitness* 11:40-3 Ja/F '89
Hill, yes! [training for the St. George Marathon] J. Ullyot. il por *Runner's World* 24:24-5 Ap '89
In the culture of fitness [Los Angeles Marathon director B. Burke] por *Runner's World* 24:52 Ja '89

Is this your first time? B. Glover. il *Runner's World* 24:22 O '89
"Just give it a go". P. Welch. il pors *Runner's World* 24:54-7 Ag '89
Life in the Filutze lane [B. Filutze] M. Bloom. il pors *Runner's World* 24:68-72 Je '89
Made for each other [Los Angeles Marathon] il *Runner's World* 24:46-7 Ja '89
Man with a mission [E. Eyestone] C. Negron. il por *Runner's World* 24:101 N '89
A marathon of marathons [1989 calendar] il *Runner's World* 24:76-9 Ja '89
Nobody does it faster [Rotterdam Marathon] B. Wischnia. il *Runner's World* 24:62-5 Jl '89
On top of the world [Los Angeles Marathon] N. Ditz. il por *Runner's World* 24:50 Ja '89
Package deal [volunteers stuff goody bags for the New York City Marathon] G. Averbuch. il *Runner's World* 24:50+ N '89
Piece of cake [New York City marathon director F. Lebow] il por *Runner's World* 24:48-9 N '89
A pilgrim's progress [black South African marathoner M. Plaatjes] J. Brant. il pors *Runner's World* 24:66-71 D '89
A race for all seasons [running the New York Marathon; excerpt from Marathon; with editorial comment by George A. Hirsch] R. Harteis. il *Runner's World* 24:4, 72-8+ N '89
Remembering Sy [S. Mah] J. Henderson. il *Runner's World* 24:12 Ap '89
Revival of the fittest [New York City Marathon] M. Bloom. il *Runner's World* 24:30-5 Ja '89
The road to recovery [post-race guidelines] H. Higdon. il *Runner's World* 24:44-6+ N '89
Runaround Sue [S. Marchiano] M. Post. il por *Runner's World* 24:101 S '89
Same old style [Chicago Marathon] D. Kardong. il *Runner's World* 24:36-9 Ja '89
Speedy septuagenarians. M. Tymn. il *Runner's World* 24:26 N '89
Starting over [running in the Long Beach Marathon for pleasure] J. Henderson. il por *Runner's World* 24:12 O '89
Swift Swiss [G. Andersen] M. Will-Weber. il por *Runner's World* 24:93 Ja '89
That first marathon [training advice for women] N. Kuscsik. il *Women's Sports & Fitness* 11:20-5 O '89
Time travelers [Athens International Marathon] M. Will-Weber. il *Runner's World* 24:56-7 S '89
To Sur with love [Big Sur Marathon] il *Runner's World* 24:68-71 S '89
When the saints go running in [comparison between a marathon and a 10K race] G. Sheehan. il *Runner's World* 24:14 O '89
Woman to watch: runner Sue Marchiano. K. Williams. il por *Women's Sports & Fitness* 11:62 S '89
Anecdotes, facetiae, satire, etc.
Bubble vision. M. Campagne. il *Runner's World* 24:96 Mr '89
A view to a thrill [watching the Boston Marathon] F. Reese. il *Runner's World* 24:120 Ap '89
Economic aspects
Take the money and run [payment of guarantees to stars] P. Gambaccini. il *Sport (New York, N.Y.)* 80:14 Mr '89
Ethical aspects
Did Ria or didn't she? [disqualification of woman marathon runner R. van Landeghem for failing Olympic drug test] *Runner's World* 24:42-3 Ja '89
History
Burning bright [G. Muhrcke, first winner of the New York City Marathon] P. Gambaccini. il por *Runner's World* 24:56-7 N '89

MARATHON RUNNING RECORDS
It's another day, another marathon, as Richard Bird ends a record year on the run [breaks world record for most marathons in a year] J. Friedman. il pors *People Weekly* 31:103+ Ap 24 '89

MARATHON SWIMMING
The other New York marathon [swimmer S. Taylor-Smith] J. Ridge. il *Women's Sports & Fitness* 11:56-7 N/D '89
Rough, ready, and wet [women swimmers] T. Slear. *Ms.* 18:54 Jl/Ag '89
History
"Queen of Hell Gate" [A. Trapp, endurance swimming's female pioneer] A. Garrard. il pors *Ms.* 18:52-5 Jl/Ag '89

MARBERRY, CRAIG
Don't say no! por *Essence* 19:12 Ap '89

MARBLE
Authenticating ancient marble sculpture. S. V. Margolis. bibl il map *Scientific American* 260:104-10 Je '89

MARBLES (GAME)
The big shot. S. Clark. il *Southern Living* 24:146 S '89

MARBLING
See also
Suminagashi
Glazing and marbleizing. B. Vila. il *Popular Mechanics* 166:30-1 S '89

MARBLING—cont.
Mimicking marble [kit from Plaid Enterprises] N. J. Freundlich. il *Popular Science* 235:88-9 Jl '89
MARC, ALESSANDRA
about
Alessandra the great. D. Daniel. il por *Vogue* 179:211 F '89
MARC V. *See* V., Marc
MARCADE GROUP INC.
Can't get no respect. T. Jaffe. *Forbes* 144:316-17 S 4 '89
MARCEAU, SOPHIE
about
Offbeat sex appeal. M. Matousek. pors *Harper's Bazaar* 122:54+ Ap '89
MARCH, BABETTE
about
The pixie pioneer. F. Lidz. il pors *Sports Illustrated* 70 Special Issue:59-61 F '89
MARCH
The March almanac. il *The Atlantic* 263:12 Mr '89
MARCH FOR PARKS
March for Parks. P. C. Pritchard. il *National Parks* 63:5 N/D '89
MARCHANT, FREDERICK J.
Mayan figures in stone (Coba, Yucatan) [poem] *America* 160:216 Mr 11 '89
MARCHE INTERNATIONAL DES FILMS ET DES PROGRAMMES POUR LA TV, LA VIDEO, LE CABLE ET LE SATELLITE
At MIPCOM: a buyer's life. P. Ainslie. il pors *Channels (New York, N.Y.: 1986)* 9:36-40 Mr '89
MARCHESE, RICHARD T.
about
Have the penny stock police caught a live one? P. Engardio. il por *Business Week* p132 F 20 '89
The most brazen of the penny hustlers? P. Engardio. il por *Business Week* p130+ N 20 '89
MARCHETTE, ANN
about
A single mom bets it all on herself. S. Seixas. il pors *Money* 18:127-32 Ap '89
MARCHIANO, SUE
about
Runaround Sue. M. Post. il por *Runner's World* 24:101 S '89
Woman to watch: runner Sue Marchiano. K. Williams. il por *Women's Sports & Fitness* 11:62 S '89
MARCHING BANDS *See* Bands (Music)
MARCIAL, GENE G.
Inside Wall Street. See issues of Business Week
MARCIANO FAMILY
about
A 'blood war' in the jeans trade. C. Welles. il *Business Week* p74-5+ N 13 '89
The great jeans war. C. Byron. il *New York* 22:13-14 Jl 24 '89
The IRS follies. C. Byron. il *New York* 22:11-12 Ag 7 '89
MARCIE-RIVIÈRE, JEAN-PIERRE
about
Buenos Aires alchemy: Jean-Pierre and Rosemarie Marcie-Rivière's city apartment. Suzy. il pors *Architectural Digest* 46:220-7 O '89
MARCIE-RIVIÈRE, ROSEMARIE
about
Buenos Aires alchemy: Jean-Pierre and Rosemarie Marcie-Rivière's city apartment. Suzy. il pors *Architectural Digest* 46:220-7 O '89
MARCIL, CHRIS
(jt. auth) See Johnson, Sam, and Marcil, Chris
MARCIULIONIS, SARUNAS
about
A Soviet hoopster in the Promised Land. P. De Jonge. il pors *The New York Times Magazine* p64+ N 5 '89
MARCONI CO. LTD.
GE Astro-Space, Marconi will team to bid for Inmarsat 3 contract. *Aviation Week & Space Technology* 131:79 Ag 21 '89
MARCOS, FERDINAND E., 1917-1989
about
From jet set to jail cell. C. Dickey. il por *Newsweek* 113:10 My 1 '89
Habeas corpse. A. Berlow. *The New Republic* 201:12+ O 30 '89
Obituary
National Review 41:22 O 27 '89
Newsweek il por 114:59 O 9 '89. R. Watson
Time il por 134:52 O 9 '89. H. G. Chua-Eoan
U.S. News & World Report por 107:12 O 9 '89
Setting Marcos adrift. S. Karnow. il pors *The New York Times Magazine* p50+ Mr 19 '89
Stepping out. J. Kasindorf. il pors *New York* 22:36-44 D 18 '89
The waning (and careful waxing) of a dynasty. T. Friend. il *Harper's* 279:68-71 Ag '89
MARCOS, IMELDA
about
Imelda's 'hell in paradise'. T. Clifton. il por *Newsweek* 113:38 My 8 '89

Stepping out. J. Kasindorf. il pors *New York* 22:36-44 D 18 '89
MARCOS, JOSEFA EDRALIN
about
The waning (and careful waxing) of a dynasty. T. Friend. il *Harper's* 279:68-71 Ag '89
MARCOS FAMILY
about
The waning (and careful waxing) of a dynasty. T. Friend. il *Harper's* 279:68-71 Ag '89
MARCUM, JOHN A.
Africa: a continent adrift. bibl f *Foreign Affairs* 68 Special Issue:159-79 ['89]
MARCUS, BEN
North Shore deliverance. il *Sport (New York, N.Y.)* 80:96-8 F '89
MARCUS, EGERTON
about
Top middleweight Marcus learned ropes from mom. pors *Jet* 76:50 Ag 21 '89
MARCUS, GREIL
The eighties: the art. il *Film Comment* 25:61-4 N/D '89
MARCUS, JEFF
about
Off the beach, back into cable. J. Stilson. por *Channels (New York, N.Y.: 1986)* 9:20 N '89
MARCUS, LEONARD S., 1950-
PW interviews [J. Marshall] il por *Publishers Weekly* 236:202-3 Jl 28 '89
MARCUS, PHILIP I.
(jt. auth) See Meegan, James M., and Marcus, Philip I.
MARCUS, STANLEY, 1905-
about
Gandee at large. C. K. Gandee. il por *House & Garden* 161:178 D '89
MARCUSE, ELIE
An equality of terror. il *World Press Review* 36:17-18 Mr '89
MARCY, MOUNT (N.Y.) *See* Mount Marcy (N.Y.)
MARDEN, BRICE, 1938-
about
Making his mark. J. Yau. il pors *Vogue* 179:190-5 Jl '89
MARDER, AMY R.
Your healthy pet. See issues of Prevention (Emmaus, Pa.) beginning July 1987
MARDER, BRUCE
about
Smooth take-off. P. Viladas. il por *House & Garden* 161:42 Ap '89
MARDER, SETH R., AND OTHERS
Synthesis of organic salts with large second-order optical nonlinearities. bibl f il *Science* 245:626-8 Ag 11 '89
MARDI GRAS *See* Carnival (Pre-Lenten festival)
MARDON, GRAEME, AND OTHERS
Duplication, deletion, and polymorphism in the sex-determining region of the mouse Y chromosome. bibl f il *Science* 243:78-80 Ja 6 '89
MAREK, ELIZABETH
The lives of teenage mothers. il *Harper's* 278:56-8+ Ap '89
MARESCA, JOHN J., 1937-
European security negotiations open in Vienna [conventional armed forces; statements and text of Western position paper, March 9, 1989] *Department of State Bulletin* 89:35-6 My '89
MARFAN SYNDROME
Marfan syndrome: the silent killer. C. Williams. il *USA Today (Periodical)* 118:64-5 N '89
MARGALIT, AVISHAI
Israel: the rise of the ultra-Orthodox. il *The New York Review of Books* 36:38-44 N 9 '89
MARGARINE
Butter & margarine. il *Consumer Reports* 54:249-53 D '89
Butter vs. margarine. il *Consumer Reports* 54:551-6 S '89
MARGARITONDO, GIORGIO, 1946-, AND OTHERS
Photoemission spectroscopy of the high-temperature superconductivity gap. bibl f il *Science* 246:770-5 N 10 '89
MARGATE (FLA.)
Housing
Home rule [condominium refuses to permit daughter J. Swartz to live with father] I. Nelson. il por *New Choices for the Best Years* 29:12-13 Ap '89
MARGERIE, EMMANUEL DE
Bicentennial events worth commemorating; tr. by Patrick H. Samway. *America* 160:572-3 Je 17-24 '89
MARGIN BUYING *See* Stocks—Margin buying
MARGOLICK, DAVID
Lech's American angel [cover story] il pors *The New York Times Magazine* p28-31+ O 8 '89
MARGOLIS, ERIC
In the footsteps of Russell Lee. il *Society* 26:77-83 Ja/F '89
MARGOLIS, HOWARD, AND MCCABE, PATRICK P.
Easing the adjustment to mainstreaming programs. *The Education Digest* 55:58-61 S '89
MARGOLIS, RICHARD J.
Caring while curing. *The New Leader* 72:11-12 Mr 6 '89
A certain species of helplessness [with editorial comment] il *The New Leader* 72:2, 10-12 Ag 7-21 '89

MARGOLIS, RICHARD J.—cont.
How the West was lost. *The New Leader* 72:13-14 N 27 '89
In America's small-town hospitals, a patient isn't 'just a number'. il *Smithsonian* 20:52-60+ S '89
Return of the homestead. il *The New Leader* 72:15-16 Ja 23 '89
This is Mexico? *The New Leader* 72:11-12 My 1 '89

MARGOLIS, STANLEY V.
Authenticating ancient marble sculpture. bibl il map *Scientific American* 260:104-10 Je '89

MARGOSHES, PAMELA
It's not all absinthe and croissants. *The Writer* 102:5-6 Jl '89

MARGRY, JACQUES G.
about
Penmanship with a flourish. J. Marcom, Jr. il por *Forbes* 143:152+ Ap 3 '89

MARGULES, MATTHEW
about
Matt's biggest race. S. L. Englebardt. il pors *Reader's Digest* 135:53-8 Jl '89

MARGULIS, LYNN, 1938-
about
A biologist whose heresy redraws earth's tree of life. J. McDermott. bibl (p135) il pors *Smithsonian* 20:72-6+ Ag '89
Rethinking evolution. G. Cowley. il por *Newsweek* 114:38 O 2 '89

MARIA STUARDA [opera] See Donizetti, Gaetano, 1797-1848
MARIAN DEVOTION See Mary, Blessed Virgin, Saint—Devotions

MARIANI, JOHN F.
Cheers! The best new restaurants of 1989. il *Esquire* 112:187-8+ N '89
"Everybody likes Italian food". il *American Heritage* 40:122-31 D '89
Spirits locker. See alternate issues of Motor Boating & Sailing
A woman's place. il por *Harper's Bazaar* 122:190+ N '89

MARIANNE (FRENCH NATIONAL SYMBOL) IN ART
In a clash of symbols, Chanel's top model falls from the runway [I. de la Fressange selected to be model for bust] M. H. J. Farrell. il pors *People Weekly* 32:51+ Ag 14 '89

MARICH, ROBERT
Shifting windows: an indie dilemma. il *Channels (New York, N.Y.: 1986)* 9:76-8 Ja '89

MARICULTURE See Aquaculture
MARIE-GALANTE (GUADELOUPE)
Description and travel
Les Saintes and Marie-Galante: the Saint Barts of the nineties? R. Urquhart. il map *Vogue* 179:304-5+ N '89

MARIHUANA See Marijuana
MARIJUANA
The chemistry of reefer madness [THC receptor; research by Allyn Howlett] L. Wallach. il *Omni (New York, N.Y.)* 11:18+ Ag '89
Dogged crusader against drugs [G. G. Nahas] P. Mann. il por *Reader's Digest* 134:102-6 My '89
The downside of smoking tobacco and marijuana. W. Steele. il *Current Health 2* 16:24-6 N '89
Marijuana and learning: grass gets an F. K. M. Porterfield. il *Current Health 2* 15:20-2 Ja '89
Marijuana mangles memory [research by Richard H. Schwartz] *Science News* 136:332 N 18 '89
Pot peril [smokers risk mercury poisoning; work of Barbara and Sanford Siegel] P. McCarthy. il *American Health* 8:16 D '89

Laws and regulations
Apollonia arrested for marijuana; claims buy was research for movie. il por *Jet* 77:31 O 23 '89
The greening of America, '80s style [crusade against domestic growers] il *U.S. News & World Report* 106:12 My 29 '89
High in the hollows [growing marijuana in Marion County, Ky.] F. Johnson. il *The New York Times Magazine* p30+ D 17 '89
Inside the high-flying pot industry [rise in domestic growers] G. Witkin. il *U.S. News & World Report* 107:27-8+ N 6 '89
Masters of deception [Heilbrunn family, accused of operating Indianapolis drug ring, now living in Austria] B. Shaw and D. Van Biema. il *People Weekly* 31:46-51 Je 19 '89

MARIJUANA RECEPTORS See Drug receptors
MARIJUANA TRADE See Narcotics trade
MARILLION (MUSICAL GROUP)
Marillion. A. Nash. il *High Fidelity (New York, N.Y.)* 39:73 Jl '89

MARIMOLIN (MUSICAL GROUP)
Marimolin. D. Helland. il *Down Beat* 56:14 Ag '89

MARIN, MAGUY
about
Hey, what's all this to me!? [dance] Reviews *New York* il 22:114+ N 20 '89. T. Tobias

MARIN, PETER
The elusive dream of home: the longings of a nation of immigrants. il *Utne Reader* p106-9 Mr/Ap '89

On the humanity of saints. il *The Nation* 249:784-6 D 25 '89

MARIN, RICHARD T.
The big donut. il *The American Spectator* 22:49 N '89
Upstaging Broadway. il *The American Spectator* 22:48 My '89

MARIN COUNTY (CALIF.)
Description and travel
Marin's lake country: hiking, fishing, biking. il map *Sunset (Central West edition)* 182:14+ Ap '89

MARIN COUNTY COMMUNITY COLLEGE
Bookstores
See College bookstores

MARINACCIO, JIM
about
East meets West Side: James and Marilyn Marinaccio's Japanese ethos. A. Berman. il pors *Architectural Digest* 46:304-9+ N '89

MARINACCIO, MARILYN
about
East meets West Side: James and Marilyn Marinaccio's Japanese ethos. A. Berman. il pors *Architectural Digest* 46:304-9+ N '89

MARINADES
Marinated cheeses. il *Sunset (Central West edition)* 182:66-7 Ja '89
Sauced. B. Shacochis. il *Gentlemen's Quarterly* 59:95+ Jl '89

MARINAS
See also
Condominiums (Boat docking)
Docking in a new marina. S. Stapleton. il *Motor Boating & Sailing* 164:30-1 Ag '89
Million-dollar marinas [East Coast] L. Rudeen. il *Motor Boating & Sailing* 164:50-3+ O '89

MARINATOS, SPYRIDON
about
The Thera theory. A. Chen. il maps *Discover* 10:76-80+ F '89

MARINE ACCIDENTS
See also
Boats and boating—Accidents
Nuclear submarines—Accidents and explosions
Ocean liners—Accidents
Shipwrecks
Yacht racing—Accidents and injuries

MARINE ARCHEOLOGY See Archeology, Submarine
MARINE BACTERIA See Bacteria, Marine
MARINE BATTERIES See Storage batteries
MARINE BIOLOGY
See also
Marine ecology
Marine fauna
Marine pharmacology
Marine sediments
Plankton
Spawning

Bibliography
Reviews. See issues of Oceans through March/April 1989
MARINE CHARTS See Nautical charts
MARINE CORPS (U.S.) See United States. Marine Corps
MARINE DEPOSITS See Marine sediments
MARINE ECOLOGY
See also
Brown tide
Food chains (Ecology)
Red tide
Seashore ecology
Ecological effects of a major oil spill on Panamanian coastal marine communities. J. B. C. Jackson and others. bibl f il map *Science* 243:37-44 Ja 6 '89
Managing the oceans. T. M. Hawley. il *Technology Review* 92:18 F/Mr '89
Monitoring ocean nutrients [Benthic Lander developed by Douglas E. Hammond] il *USA Today (Periodical)* 117:6-7 Je '89
The touch of the sea [cover story; special issue] il *Audubon* 91:10-12+ Mr '89

MARINE ECOSYSTEMS See Marine ecology
MARINE EDUCATION See Oceanographic education
MARINE ELECTRICITY See Boats and boating—Electric equipment
MARINE ELECTRONICS See Boats and boating—Electronic equipment
MARINE ENGINES
See also
Diesel engines, Marine
Motor boat engines
Engine room. T. P. Banse. See issues of Motor Boating & Sailing

Fuel
Leaded fuel update '89. T. P. Banse. il *Motor Boating & Sailing* 164:97 Ag '89

Ignition
Marine ignition update. T. P. Banse. il *Motor Boating & Sailing* 164:91 O '89

MARINE ENGINES—*cont.*
Lubrication and lubricants
See Boats and boating—Lubrication and lubricants
Maintenance and repair
Engine checks underway. S. Stapleton. il *Motor Boating & Sailing* 163:42 Je '89
MARINE FARMING *See* Aquaculture
MARINE FAUNA
See also
Coelenterates
Coral reef fauna
Fish
Horseshoe crabs
Marine mammals
Octopuses
Sea anemones
Shrimp
Sponges
Starfish
An alarming catch [critics condemn use of drift nets] M. Nichols. il *Maclean's* 102:49 Je 12 '89
Almost human? Marine animal models. M. Root. il *BioScience* 39:520-1 S '89
Caldron in the sea [Kraternaya Bay] M. V. Propp and V. G. Tarasov. il maps *Natural History* p28-33 Ag '89
Don't leave the dock [exotic marine life off Cayman Kai dock] F. J. Viola. il *Sea Frontiers* 35:336-41 N/D '89
An expert warns of the dangers of driftnets, lethal curtains that reap fish—and controversy—by the ton [interview with J. Coe] J. H. Blackman. il pors *People Weekly* 31:145-6+ My 15 '89
Fish mining on the open seas [U.S. attempt to curb Japanese use of drift nets that ensnare various types of marine life] il *Time* 133:70 Je 5 '89
Ocean creatures resent man's noise [research by Arthur A. Myrberg, Jr.] il *USA Today (Periodical)* 117:7 Je '89
Opening the door to the unknown [creatures living near deep sea vents] M. Toner. il *National Wildlife* 27:34-6 Je/Jl '89
Sea of trouble [plastics pollution] K. Brower. il *Omni (New York, N.Y.)* 11:20+ Ap '89
Food and feeding
See also
Food chains (Ecology)
Photographs and photography
New Zealand's magic waters. D. Doubilet. il map *National Geographic* 176:506-29 O '89
MARINE FAUNA, FOSSIL
See also
Burgess Shale fossils
Asymmetries of clade shape and the direction of evolutionary time [discussion of May 27, 1988 article, Macroevolutionary interpretations of symmetry and synchroneity in the fossil record] J. A. Kitchell and N. S. MacLeod. *Science* 243:1613-15 Mr 24 '89
"Diary in stone" traces extinction [extinction evidence found in Changxing quarry in China; research by David J. Bottjer] *USA Today (Periodical)* 118:10 Ag '89
MARINE FLORA
See also
Algae
Seaweed
MARINE GEOLOGY *See* Submarine geology
MARINE MAMMAL PROGRAM (U.S.) *See* United States. Navy. Marine Mammal Program
MARINE MAMMALS
See also
Cetacea
Dolphins
Manatees
Pinnipedia
Sea otters
Seals (Animals)
Walruses
Whales
Laws and regulations
Save our sea mammals. K. Brower. il *Omni (New York, N.Y.)* 11:26+ Je '89
MARINE MICROBIOLOGY
See also
Bacteria, Marine
MARINE MINERAL RESOURCES
See also
Exclusive Economic Zone
Petroleum in submerged lands
MARINE NAVIGATION *See* Navigation
MARINE PAINT, ANTIFOULING *See* Paint, Protective
MARINE PAINTING
See also
Ships in art
Exhibitions
The canvas sea [Sounding the depths: 150 years of American seascape] il *Modern Maturity* 32:66-9 D '89/Ja '90
MARINE PHARMACOLOGY
Fruits de mer. M. S. Glucksman and E. Smith. il *Omni (New York, N.Y.)* 11:24+ Ag '89
Medicines from the sea. J. Lowenstein. il *Oceans* 22:72 Mr/Ap '89

MARINE PHOTOGRAPHY
See also
Underwater photography
MARINE POLLUTION
See also
Medical waste disposal in the ocean
Oil pollution
Radioactive waste disposal in the ocean
Waste disposal in the ocean
At the beaches this summer, the dirty word is plastics. M. Satchell. *U.S. News & World Report* 107:30 Jl 17 '89
Deep trouble under the sea. L. Eskin. il *Scholastic Update (Teachers' edition)* 121:8 Ap 21 '89
Murky waters. M. Goodavage. il *Modern Maturity* 32:44-50 Ag/S '89
'The sea has its limits'. C. Denis. il *World Press Review* 36:55 Je '89
Sea of trouble [plastics pollution] K. Brower. il *Omni (New York, N.Y.)* 11:20+ Ap '89
Seagate [failure of Sea World to inform public about ocean pollution] D. Adcroft. *Omni (New York, N.Y.)* 11:33 Je '89
Stopping coastline pollution at the sewer and the farm. S. Brownlee. il *U.S. News & World Report* 107:52 Ag 21 '89
Control
See also
American Oceans Campaign
Laws and regulations
Coastal waters in jeopardy. *Oceans* 22:69 Mr/Ap '89
MARINE PROPELLERS *See* Boats and boating—Propellers
MARINE RADIOTELEPHONE *See* Radiotelephone on ships, boats, etc.
MARINE RESEARCH *See* Oceanography
MARINE RESOURCES
See also
Fisheries
Petroleum in submerged lands
MARINE SCIENCE *See* Oceanography
MARINE SCIENCE EDUCATION *See* Oceanographic education
MARINE SEDIMENTS
See also
Ocean Drilling Program
Caught in an abyssal storm [sediment upheaval due to benthic current encountered on Alvin mission] R. Gannon. il map *Earth Science* 42:18-20 Spr '89
Crown-of-thorns no Johnny-come-lately [Great Barrier Reef; research by A. J. Timothy Jull] S. Hart. *Science News* 136:133 Ag 26 '89
Evidence for sediment eruption on deep sea floor, Gulf of Mexico. D. B. Prior and others. bibl f il *Science* 243:517-19 Ja 27 '89
Evidence from sediments of long-term Acanthaster planci predation on corals of the Great Barrier Reef [crown of thorns starfish; cover story] P. D. Walbran and others. bibl f il map *Science* 245:847-50 Ag 25 '89
Hole in ocean floor [sediment eruption in the Gulf of Mexico; research by David B. Prior] *Science News* 135:77 F 4 '89
Inner space. C. T. Feazel. il *Sea Frontiers* 35:49-52 Ja/F '89
MARINE SHALE PROCESSORS INC.
Something stinks in Morgan City. C. Strickland. il *The Nation* 249:448-51 O 23 '89
MARINE SPARK PLUGS *See* Spark plugs
MARINE TURTLES *See* Turtles
MARINER MARK II MISSIONS *See* Space flight—Mariner Mark II missions
MARINER'S MUSEUM (NEWPORT NEWS, VA.). CHESAPEAKE BAY GALLERY
Of menhaden and watermen. E. Crews. il map *Americana* 17:40-3 S/O '89
MARINES (U.S.) *See* United States. Marine Corps
MARINHO, ROBERTO
about
Brazil's 'Citizen Globo'. J.-P. Moreau. il por *World Press Review* 36:56 Jl '89
MARINO, PETER
about
Peter the Great. C. K. Gandee. il pors *House & Garden* 161:174-83+ O '89
MARINO (P. MICHAEL) ASSOCIATES *See* P. Michael Marino Associates
MARINOV, VSEVOLOD
What the comrades say. il *Time* 133:62-3 Ap 10 '89
MARIO, ERNEST, 1938-
about
Prescription for success. J. Zweig. il por *Forbes* 143:178 Je 12 '89
Shakeup at Glaxo. R. A. Melcher. *Business Week* p59 My 22 '89
MARION, JANE
(ed) *See* Stayner, Kay. My son was kidnapped for seven years

MARION (ILL.)

Prisons and reformatories

Toxins on tap? [contaminated water supply at Marion Federal Penitentiary] L. Rocawich. il *The Progressive* 53:24-7 My '89

Water pollution

Toxins on tap? [contaminated water supply at Marion Federal Penitentiary] L. Rocawich. il *The Progressive* 53:24-7 My '89

MARION COUNTY (KY.)

Crime

High in the hollows [growing marijuana] F. Johnson. il *The New York Times Magazine* p30+ D 17 '89

MARION FEDERAL PENITENTIARY *See* Marion (Ill.)— Prisons and reformatories

MARION LABORATORIES, INC.

Marion Laboratories Inc. J. Slovak. il *Fortune* 119:144 My 22 '89

MARIONI, TOM, 1937-

about

Tom Marioni at Margarete Roeder. K. Johnson. il *Art in America* 77:167-8 F '89

MARIS, ROGER, 1934-1985

about

Baseball lives [excerpt] M. Bryan. il por *Sports Illustrated* 70:85+ Ap 24 '89

MARISOL, 1930-

about

Who is Marisol? P. Gardner. il por *Art News* 88:146-51 My '89

MARITAL INFIDELITY *See* Adultery

MARITAL QUARRELS *See* Quarrels

MARITIME CENTER (NORWALK, CONN.)

Under the Long Island Sound. R. W. Cox. il *Travel Holiday* 171:103-7 Mr '89

MARITIME LAW

See also

Boats and boating—Laws and regulations
Convention on the Law of the Sea (1982)
Exclusive Economic Zone
Rule of the road at sea
Slave trade
Territorial waters
United Nations. Preparatory Commission for the International Sea-Bed Authority and the International Tribunal for the Law of the Sea

Great Britain

Drawing the line at safety [S. Plimsoll's reform campaign in 19th century Britain] A. Thomas. il por map *History Today* 39:5-7 F '89

United States

See Maritime law

MARITIME PROVINCES

Economic conditions

Atlantic chill. G. Allen. il *Maclean's* 102:14-16 My 29 '89

MARK, MARY ELLEN, 1940-

Victories of the spirit [photographs] il *The New York Times Magazine* p28-31 Ag 27 '89

about

Mary Ellen Mark. M. Moorman. il por *Art News* 88:152-3 Ap '89

MARK, NORMAN

about

Norman Mark gets the last nyah-hah-hah-hah-hah. R. Powers. il por *Gentlemen's Quarterly* 59:125-6+ My '89

MARK HELLINGER THEATER (NEW YORK, N.Y.)

His prayers answered, evangelist David Wilkerson has a divine hit running on the Great White Way [Times Square Church] R. Arias. il pors *People Weekly* 32:63-4 S 4 '89

MARK MORRIS DANCE GROUP

See also

Monnaie Dance Group/Mark Morris

MARK ROTHKO FOUNDATION

Rothko's legacy. A. Decker. il por *Art News* 88:41+ S '89

MARK TWAIN NATIONAL FOREST (MO.)

Grasshopper Hollow, Missouri. R. H. Mohlenbrock. il map *Natural History* p60-3 Jl '89

MARKERS

See also

Plant labels

MARKET GARDENING *See* Truck farming

MARKET GUNNING *See* Market hunting (Game hunting)

MARKET HUNTING (GAME HUNTING)

Hunting's most wanted. L. Williamson. il *Outdoor Life* 184:40+ Jl '89

MARKET LOGIC (NEWSLETTER)

Inside indication? M. Hulbert. il *Forbes* 143:120 Ja 23 '89

Murphy's law. M. Hulbert. il *Forbes* 144:232 S 18 '89

MARKET MANIA (NEWSLETTER) *See* Investment newsletters

MARKET RESEARCH

See also

Arbitron Ratings Company
Gartner Group Inc.
Leigh Stowell & Company
Nielsen Media Research
People meters (TV audience research)

Q ratings
Single-source research (TV audience research)
Strategic Information Inc.

Adding faces to ratings [VALS 2 psychographic profiles of selected markets] il *Channels (New York, N.Y.: 1986)* 9:80 S '89

Do marketers control what we see? D. M. Topolnicki. il *Psychology Today* 23:73-5 Je '89

Feasibility studies [need for theater building] M. LaRue. *Theatre Crafts* 23:78-83 D '89

Psycho-selling [VALS 2 typology of American consumers] C. Reece. il *Channels (New York, N.Y.: 1986)* 9:14 Jl/Ag '89

Japan

Will next year's hot gift be an insect orchestra? [test marketing new products] N. Gross. il *Business Week* p67-8 D 25 '89-Ja 1 '90

MARKET SHARE

Companies that compete best [cover story] B. Saporito. il *Fortune* 119:36-8+ My 22 '89

One man's poison . . . [competitors take advantage of leveraged rivals] N. Alster. il *Forbes* 144:38-9 O 16 '89

Stealing the right shoppers [expanding market share] J. Levine. *Forbes* 144:104-5 Jl 10 '89

MARKETEL INTERNATIONAL INC.

Computers may turn the world into one big commodities pit. R. Kuttner. il *Business Week* p17 S 11 '89

MARKETING

See also

Advertising
Aged market
Auctions
Direct selling
Distribution of goods
Electronic marketing
Environmental marketing
Franchise system
Hispanic American market
Interactive marketing
Japanese American market
Mail order business
Merchandising
Micro marketing
Middle age market
National Association of Market Developers
Price policies
Products, New
Rebates
Roadside marketing
Sales promotion
Samples (Merchandising)
Society for Marketing Professional Services
Trade loading
Wholesale trade
Youth market
See also subhead Marketing under various subjects

But in the office, no [brand names] J. Levine. il *Forbes* 144:272-3 O 16 '89

Finding the right marketing mix. R. Gunnerson. il *Home Office Computing* 7:37-40 Ag '89

Growing pains—and gains [established brand names used on new products] B. Kanner. il *New York* 22:22+ Mr 13 '89

Selling on a shoestring. N. C. Baker. il *Nation's Business* 77:78-80 N '89

International aspects

Global marketing [address, May 20, 1989] G. V. Grune. *Vital Speeches of the Day* 55:580-2 Jl 15 '89

Globalization [address, February 9, 1989] R. C. Goizueta. *Vital Speeches of the Day* 55:360-2 Ap 1 '89

Social aspects

I gave at the supermarket [cause related marketing] J. Levine. il *Forbes* 144:138+ D 25 '89

Japan

P&G goes global by acting like a local. Z. Schiller and T. Holden. il *Business Week* p58 Ag 28 '89

Ready, set, sell—Japan is buying. C. Rapoport. il *Fortune* 120:159-60+ S 11 '89

To sell in Japan, meet the Japanese. R. C. Dorney. il *Nation's Business* 77:10 F '89

Western Europe

How do you say L'eggs in French? [Sara Lee Corp.] S. B. Weiner. il *Forbes* 144:73+ N 27 '89

MARKETING AS A PROFESSION

To market, to market: job opportunities in marketing. M. C. White. il *Occupational Outlook Quarterly* 33:2-11 Spr '89

MARKETING CHANNELS

New ways to reach your customers [teaming up with distributors] P. D. Moore. por *Fortune* 120:210 N 6 '89

MARKETING CONSULTANTS

See also

Agricultural consultants
Bronner Slosberg Associates
Donovan & Green

Perestroika payoff [U.S.-Soviet joint venture consultant A. Hartman] R. T. Grieves. il por *Forbes* 143:102 Ja 23 '89

MARKETING CONSULTANTS—cont.
Acquisitions and mergers
International aspects
Saatchi beats a retreat back to Mad Ave. [wants out of consulting] W. Konrad and R. A. Melcher. il *Business Week* p70-1 Jl 10 '89
MARKETING INNOVATIONS INTERNATIONAL
"Merchandise that motivates". M. Barrier. il pors *Nation's Business* 77:64 My '89
MARKETING MANAGERS
See also
Women marketing managers
MARKETING ORDERS AND AGREEMENTS *See* Agricultural administration
MARKETING RESEARCH *See* Market research
MARKETS
See also
Farmers' markets
Flea markets
Germany (West)
See also
Berlin (Germany: West)—Markets
Indiana
See also
Indianapolis City Market
Louisiana
See also
French Market (New Orleans, La.)
Maine
See also
Damariscotta (Me.)—Markets
New York (State)
See also
New York (N.Y.)—Markets
MARKETS, BLACK *See* Black markets
MARKETS, ROADSIDE *See* Roadside marketing
MARKETS FOR AUTHORS *See* Authors and publishers
MARKETS FOR PHOTOGRAPHERS *See* Photographs—Marketing
MARKING (EDUCATION) *See* Grading and marking (Education)
MARKLEIN, MARY BETH
Leave them laughing. il *Nation's Business* 77:49 O '89
A sickness in the air. *The Progressive* 53:17 D '89
MARKOVICH, BOB
Preventive maintenance. See issues of Home Mechanix beginning September 1988
MARKOW, ROBERT
Primeval palette. il *Opera News* 53:26-9 Ap 1 '89
Realm of sound. il *Opera News* 54:33+ D 9 '89
MARKOWITZ, MICHAEL
about
The wild and crazy gangster: Michael Markowitz's twisted American dream. P. Blauner. il pors *New York* 22:52-6+ O 9 '89
MARKS, CYNTHIA
The absolutely, positively last word on the pill (for now). il *Mademoiselle* 95:170+ D '89
Brand-name or generic: what your body does—and doesn't—know. il *Mademoiselle* 95:128+ O '89
Eye workouts that don't work. il *Mademoiselle* 95:142 N '89
Is your medicine an Rx for disaster? il *Mademoiselle* 95:130+ My '89
The new breast-implant scare. *Mademoiselle* 95:124+ F '89
MARKS, JANE
"We have a problem". See issues of Parents beginning February 1987
MARKS, LEONARD
about
All my children. P. Newcomb. il por *Forbes* 144:287 N 27 '89
MARKS, LEONARD H.
CSCE Information Forum [statement, April 21, 1989] *Department of State Bulletin* 89:86-7 S '89
MARKS & SPENCER PLC
Low marks, few sparks. S. B. Weiner. il *Forbes* 144:146-7 S 18 '89
MARKUS, JULIA, 1939-
Two years after his death, the curtain rises on Andy Warhol. bibl (p170) il pors *Smithsonian* 19:62-8+ F '89
MARKUS, MARVIN
about
Shouldering arms. M. Schifrin. il por *Forbes* 143:208-9 Ap 17 '89
MARKUSEN, ANN R.
Cold war economics. bibl f il *The Bulletin of the Atomic Scientists* 45:41-4 Ja/F '89
MARLER, PETER
(jt. auth) See Nelson, Douglas A., and Marler, Peter
MARLEY, BOB
about
Marley's estate sparks bitter court battle. il por *Jet* 75:16 Mr 6 '89
MARLIN, KATE ANDERS
The underground ecumenist. See issues of The Christian Century beginning October 25, 1989

MARLIN, STEVE
Art for whose sake? *National Review* 41:21-2 Ap 21 '89
MARLIN FISHING
Before Cabo. R. R. Holster, Jr. il *Sport (New York, N.Y.)* 80:62-5 Ja '89
Debunking Hemingway's marlin theories. J. Skorupa. il *Popular Mechanics* 166:44 O '89
Fishing Cuba's forbidden waters. S. Stapleton. il *Motor Boating & Sailing* 164:42-4+ S '89
Numero Uno [marlin fishing off Cabo San Lucas in a Barattucci 82-foot sportsfisher] N. Rabinowitz. il *Motor Boating & Sailing* 163:52-7+ Ap '89
Oh Magnifica! [giant marlin hooked off the Azores] E. M. Swift. il *Sports Illustrated* 71:154-8+ S 4 '89
Pacifica shootout [West Coast Marlin Shootout] B. Duke. il *Motor Boating & Sailing* 163:134+ Mr '89
A reel revolutionary [fisherwoman M. Bierman] P. Hoover. il por *Women's Sports & Fitness* 11:78 Ap '89
MARMER, NANCY
Boltanski: the uses of contradiction [cover story] bibl f il *Art in America* 77:168-81+ O '89
MAROE, JIM
(jt. auth) See Diamond, Edwin, and Maroe, Jim
MARONCELLI, MARK, AND OTHERS
Polar solvent dynamics and electron-transfer reactions. bibl f il *Science* 243:1674-81 Mr 31 '89
MAROSTICA (ITALY)
Festivals
See also
Living Chess Game (Marostica, Italy)
MARPLES, DAVID R.
No soap, say striking Soviet miners. bibl f il *The Bulletin of the Atomic Scientists* 45:38-40 D '89
Ukraine fallout debate. bibl f il *The Bulletin of the Atomic Scientists* 45:9-11 D '89
MARQUES, ALFREDO PINHEIRO
Japan in early Portuguese maps. il maps *The Courier (Unesco)* 42:14-16 Ap '89
MÁRQUEZ, GÁBRIEL GARCÍA *See* García Márquez, Gabriel, 1928-
MARQUIS, KEN
about
Cages that soar. T. Sweeney. il por *Home Mechanix* 85:26-7 F '89
MARRIAGE
See also
Adultery
Common law marriage
Divorce
Family
Farm marriage
Honeymoon
Husbands
Interfaith marriage
Interracial marriage
Marriage of priests
Married couples
Married women
Monogamy
Remarriage
Weddings
Wife abuse
Wives
6 questions that can warm up a cool marriage. J. Viorst. *Redbook* 172:40+ Mr '89
Bring fun back to your marriage. E. Kiester and S. V. Kiester. il *Reader's Digest* 134:81-4 Ja '89
Can this marriage be saved? See issues of Ladies' Home Journal
Confirmed but not bachelors? [Andrew Sullivan's case for gay marriage] E. Van den Haag. *National Review* 41:16 S 15 '89
The dialectic of marriage [love-centered marriage] I. Sarnoff and S. Sarnoff. il *Psychology Today* 23:54-7 O '89
Dr. Ruth asks, "Are you having fun together?" [with quiz] R. Westheimer. il por *Redbook* 172:116-18 Ja '89
First-time brides after 40. R. D. Turner. il *Ebony* 45:84+ N '89
Here comes the groom [case for gay marriage; cover story] A. Sullivan. *The New Republic* 201:20+ Ag 28 '89
How to keep your man monogamous [excerpt] A. Penney. il por *Ladies' Home Journal* 106:70+ Jl '89
How to make a marriage work. il *Ebony* 44:29-30+ O '89
How to share bed and bath (and stay happily married!). A. Stoddard. il *McCall's* 116:182 My '89
Is married better? [sisters exchange places] S. Nelson and L. Nelson. il pors *Glamour* 87:274-5+ O '89
It takes two to tangle. P. Weideger. il *Ms.* 17:106-7+ Ja/F '89
Just married (the inside story). J. Marshall. il *Mademoiselle* 95:164-5+ Ag '89
Love and marriage [questions and answers] C. Deutsch. See issues of Parents
Make hard times work for your marriage. C. Jabs. *Reader's Digest* 135:145-7 Ag '89
Marital myths: what we "know" hurts [quiz] P. Adelmann. il *Psychology Today* 23:68-9 My '89

MARRIAGE—*cont.*

Marriage's unfulfilled promise [importance of women's friendships with other women; research by Stacey Oliker] P. King. il *Psychology Today* 23:71-2 D '89

Men: what do they expect from marriage today? N. Dawidoff. il *Glamour* 87:236-9+ My '89

New dilemma for black professionals: 'living together' or marriage? R. Brown. il *Ebony* 45:96+ D '89

The new intimacy: rediscovering each other after the kids leave home [cover story] S. Levitt. il *New Choices for the Best Years* 29:38-43 S '89

Oh men, oh women! [symposium] il *Ladies' Home Journal* 106:90+ S '89

One's single, one's married: can these women still be friends? S. Jacoby. il *Glamour* 87:162-3+ Ja '89

Planning it all: the new calendar girls [trying to fit marriage into timetable] E. Weiner. il *Mademoiselle* 95:130-3+ Jl '89

Reaching the other shore: marriages that last [research by Sylvia Weishaus and Dorothy Field] P. King. il *Psychology Today* 23:64 Mr '89

Relationships tote emotional baggage [views of Jacque Cook] *USA Today (Periodical)* 118:10 S '89

Staying in love. B. J. Berg. il *Parents* 64:95-9 Je '89

Surprising key to the happiest couples [condensed from Husbands and wives] M. Kinder and C. Cowan. il *Reader's Digest* 135:149-52 Jl '89

What took me so long. D. McDonough. il *Glamour* 87:282-3+ S '89

Women with cold feet. L. Mosedale. il *Glamour* 87:200-1+ D '89

Words that can warm up your marriage [paying compliments] D. R. Hales. il *McCall's* 116:70+ Ap '89

Anecdotes, facetiae, satire, etc.

"Dear Katie, so you want to get married . . .". J. Viorst. il *Redbook* 172:38+ Ap '89

Exclusive! Bill Cosby's newest, funniest book [excerpt from Love and marriage] B. Cosby. il pors *Good Housekeeping* 208:126+ Je '89

"Help! My wife drives me crazy!" [excerpt from Love and marriage] B. Cosby. il por *Redbook* 173:114-15+ Jl '89

How to have a happy marriage [advice from fourth graders] il *Good Housekeeping* 208:64 Je '89

A kinder, gentler marriage. M. G. Stoddard. il *The Saturday Evening Post* 261:56-7+ S '89

Marred bliss. M. O'Donnell. il *The Atlantic* 263:30-1 Ap '89

Catholic Church

Do Catholic couples view having kids as a given? D. Morris. il *U.S. Catholic* 54:32-7 My '89

How to find time for faith in a two-career marriage. D. Curran. il *U.S. Catholic* 54:19-24 O '89

The scary fidelity of Jesus. M. Garvey. il *Commonweal* 116:173-4 Mr 24 '89

Statistics

The postmarital society: Americans now spend more of their lives single. M. F. Riche. il *Utne Reader* p50-1 Mr/Ap '89

United States

See Marriage

Western Europe

The Eurowife: foreign aid. A. Morgan. *Harper's Bazaar* 122:119+ F '89

MARRIAGE CONTRACTS

Divvying up before you split [postnuptial agreements] N. Santelmann. il *Forbes* 144:276+ N 27 '89

Prenuptial agreements. B. G. Quint. il *Glamour* 87:132+ N '89

Those pre-marriage contracts: a guide for the bride. S. Berkman. il *Good Housekeeping* 208:243 Je '89

MARRIAGE COUNSELING

Can this marriage be saved? See issues of Ladies' Home Journal

Churches unite, take a stand to prevent divorce [Modesto, Calif.] J. Williams. il *Christianity Today* 33:65-6 S 8 '89

Healthy love [excerpt from Lifemates]; ed. by Robert B. Kory. H. H. Bloomfield and S. Vettese. il *Health (New York, N.Y.)* 21:24+ F '89

Saving my marriage. M. Beaubien. por *Essence* 19:6 Mr '89

The thoughts that wound [cognitive therapy] D. Gelman. il *Newsweek* 113:46-8 Ja 9 '89

MARRIAGE CUSTOMS AND RITES

See also

Weddings

MARRIAGE EDUCATION *See* Family education

MARRIAGE IN MOTION PICTURES

Media mates: role model marriages. L. Phillips. *Harper's Bazaar* 122:119+ F '89

MARRIAGE IN TELEVISION

Media mates: role model marriages. L. Phillips. *Harper's Bazaar* 122:119+ F '89

Relationships now: what TV couples are telling us. C. Krupp. il *Glamour* 87:183 Mr '89

MARRIAGE LAW

See also

Marriage contracts

Caribbean region

Romancing the isle [arranging weddings in the Caribbean] Y. R. Lamb. il *Black Enterprise* 19:116 My '89

Wisconsin

1914: January 20 [law requiring premarital testing for veneral disease declared unconstitutional] A. Nielson. il *American Heritage* 40:40-1 F '89

MARRIAGE LICENSES

High 'I do' blood-test dues [mandatory AIDS testing for marriage license applicants in Illinois] *Science News* 135:357 Je 10 '89

MARRIAGE OF PRIESTS

Of many things [M. Dally's account of acceptance of married Episcopal priest into Catholic priesthood] J. W. Donohue. *America* 160:362 Ap 22 '89

MARRIED COUPLES

See also

Dinks

Wedding anniversaries

10 most exciting couples [black celebrities] L. Norment. il *Ebony* 44:164-6+ F '89

Are you out of sync with each other? [differing circadian rhythms; research by Jeffry Larson] K. Locitzer. il *Psychology Today* 23:66 Jl/Ag '89

Coupledom uber alles: tyranny of the couples. G. Hirshey. il *Utne Reader* p48-9+ Mr/Ap '89

'How we met' [black celebrity couples] il *Ebony* 44:158-61 F '89

Invasion of the couple people: what's a happily single girl to do? M. McNamara. il *Mademoiselle* 95:206-7+ S '89

It hyphened one night [hyphenated surnames] H. G. Chua-Eoan. il *Time* 133:78 Ap 17 '89

Longevity blooms with younger grooms [research by Laurel Klinger-Vartabedian] J. Davidson. *Psychology Today* 23:72 D '89

Two of us is one too many [husband takes early retirement] H. Bennett. il *The New York Times Magazine* p22+ O 22 '89

Anecdotes, facetiae, satire, etc.

Help! My wife may throw me away! R. Keyes. il *Good Housekeeping* 208:109-10 Mr '89

Love lessons learned from famous couples. il *Glamour* 87:111 F '89

Employment

See also

Children of working parents

Commuter marriage: does it work? E. C. Ray. il *Essence* 19:103+ F '89

Doing the double juggle. G. Averbuch. il *Ms.* 17:115-16 Ja/F '89

Entrepreneurial couples [views of Frank and Sharan Barnett] il *The Futurist* 23:50 My/Je '89

For working women, having it all may mean doing it all [interview with A. Hochschild] D. Waggoner. il pors *People Weekly* 32:51+ S 4 '89

How entrepreneurial couples work together. F. Barnett and S. Barnett. il pors *Working Woman* 14:77-80 Ap '89

How to find time for faith in a two-career marriage. D. Curran. il *U.S. Catholic* 54:19-24 O '89

Marrying into a family business. S. Nelton. il *Nation's Business* 77:42-3+ Ap '89

Mastering the art of intimacy. S. Nelson. *Working Woman* 14:114-16 Je '89

Moscow yuppies? Nyet quite! [I. Zvereva and S. Burak] E. B. Fein. il *Mademoiselle* 95:222-3+ O '89

The myth of male housework [views of A. R. Hochschild] J. Skow. il *Time* 134:62 Ag 7 '89

The new bicoastals: love on Tokyo time [couples who commute between the West Coast and Japan] J. Hammer. il *Newsweek* 113:50 F 13 '89

The new marriage reality [sharing the housework; excerpt from Second shift] A. R. Hochschild. il *Glamour* 87:142-5+ Jl '89

New rules for today's black couples. D. Narine. il *Ebony* 44:46+ S '89

Partners in entrepreneurship [research by Frank and Sharan Barnett] S. Nelton. il *Nation's Business* 77:38-9 Mr '89

Running in place [Canada] S. McKay. il *Maclean's* 102:66+ N 6 '89

She's the boss [husbands working for wives] D. Michals. il *Ms.* 18:58-61 N '89

Six ways to be "family-friendly". S. Nelton. il *Nation's Business* 77:12-13 Mr '89

Spending patterns and income of single and married parents. M. Boyle. bibl f il *Monthly Labor Review* 112:37-41 Mr '89

A spouse's income costs as well as pays. P. N. Strassels. il *Nation's Business* 77:66 Mr '89

Viking to release 'The second shift,' analysis of the two-job marriage [work of A. R. Hochschild] B. Levine. *Publishers Weekly* 235:35-6 Ap 28 '89

Wedded to their work [entreprenurial couples; views of Frank and Sharan Barnett] S. Brewer. il *New Choices for the Best Years* 29:13 Jl '89

Woman's work is never done [views of A. Hochschild] J. Miller. il *Newsweek* 114:65 Jl 31 '89

Working parents [cover story] T. B. Brazelton. il por *Newsweek* 113:66-70 F 13 '89

MARRIED COUPLES—Employment—*cont.*
Working parents: how to get the most from 2 incomes [cover story] K. McManus. il *Changing Times* 43:22-8 Jl '89
A working wife. D. A. Williams. por *Essence* 20:12-13 Ag '89

Health and hygiene
In sickness and in health [study by Dee Edington and Louis Yen] V. Bozzi. *Psychology Today* 23:22 Ap '89

Quarrels
See Quarrels

Sexual behavior
Attention busy women . . . are you neglecting your sex life? R. Westheimer. *Redbook* 173:142-3+ S '89
Don't let these sex myths ruin your marriage. J. G. Patrick. *Reader's Digest* 135:211-12 N '89
A fine romance. L. C. Pogrebin. il *Ms.* 17:21 My '89
Help! My husband's always working. H. S. Kaplan. por *Redbook* 172:42 F '89
How to have an affair with your husband [excerpt from Lifemates]; ed. by Robert B. Kory. H. H. Bloomfield and S. Vettese. il *Ladies' Home Journal* 106:52+ Ap '89
The joys of (quickie) sex. R. Westheimer. por *Redbook* 173:112-13+ Jl '89
Keep your marriage sexy: 10 mistakes to avoid. H. S. Kaplan. *Redbook* 172:114-15+ Ap '89
The most-asked sex questions; ed. by Nelly Edmondson Gupta. D. O'Connor. *Ladies' Home Journal* 106:72+ F '89
"My husband's vasectomy ruined our sex life". H. S. Kaplan. por *Redbook* 173:22 S '89
"No sex, please, we're married". D. G. Weiss. il *Ladies' Home Journal* 106:176+ N '89
Not tonight, honey . . . [lovelife after childbirth] S. F. Enos. il *Ladies' Home Journal* 106:42 Ja '89
Sex during pregnancy. K. B. Fader. il *Glamour* 87:64+ F '89
Take 6 steps to better sex. D. O'Connor. *Redbook* 172:90-1+ F '89
What happy couples say about sex. B. Zilbergeld. *Reader's Digest* 134:13-14+ F '89
Who has time for sex? K. Levine. il *Parents* 64:61-2+ N '89
"Why did my husband turn off to me?" [fear of intimacy] H. S. Kaplan. por *Redbook* 174:88 D '89

Taxation
Facing the new facts of life [older married couples] S. Weinman. il *Money* 18:178+ D '89

MARRIED TO THE MOB [film] See Motion picture reviews—Single works
MARRIED . . . WITH CHILDREN [television program] See Television program reviews—Single works

MARRIED WOMEN
See also
Mothers
First-time brides after 40. R. D. Turner. il *Ebony* 45:84+ N '89
A husband of one's own. W. Diagana. il *World Health* p10 Mr '89
A married woman's crush. D. Porretto. *Glamour* 87:114 F '89
Single women, married women: can we be friends? B. M. Campbell. il *Essence* 20:47-8+ Jl '89
The state of the union [special section] il *Harper's Bazaar* 122:118-19+ F '89

Employment
See also
Farm women—Employment
Mothers—Employment
My wife, the sportswriter. M. Winerip. il *Glamour* 87:188 Jl '89
Wage hikes and family troubles for women [views of James P. Smith and Michael Ward] il *The Futurist* 23:52-3 S/O '89
A working wife. D. A. Williams. por *Essence* 20:12-13 Ag '89

MARRINER, NEVILLE, 1924-
about
Keeping score. E. MacSweeney. il por *Harper's Bazaar* 122:48 S '89

MARRIOTT, CARY
The domes of Paris. il map *Gourmet* 49:52-9+ Jl '89

MARRIOTT, J. WILLARD, 1932-
about
How master lodger Bill Marriott prophesied profit and prospered. il por *Fortune* 119:56-7 Je 5 '89
Rooms at the inn. E. C. Baig. il por *Fortune* 119:62 Ja 2 '89

MARRIOTT, MICHEL
Can men be faithful? il *Essence* 20:61-2+ N '89

MARRIOTT CORPORATION
Aeroflot, Marriott cooperate on in-flight catering service. J. Ott. *Aviation Week & Space Technology* 130:64-5 Ja 23 '89
A buyback backfires. T. Smart. il *Business Week* p29 My 1 '89
How master lodger Bill Marriott prophesied profit and prospered. il por *Fortune* 119:56-7 Je 5 '89

Rooms at the inn [J. W. Marriott] E. C. Baig. il por *Fortune* 119:62 Ja 2 '89
Tea, sympathy and direct mail [marketing of lifecare facilities] J. Novack. il *Forbes* 144:210-11 S 18 '89

MARROW
Marrow rebuilt with umbilical-cord blood [work of Arleen D. Auerbach] A. McKenzie. *Science News* 136:293 N 4 '89
Thymotaxin, a chemotactic protein, is identical to β_2-microglobulin. C. Dargemont and others. bibl f il *Science* 246:803-6 N 10 '89

Transplantation
Bone marrow transplants approved [radiation victims] J. L. Marx. il *Science* 244:768 My 19 '89
Bone voyage. J. Goldberg. il *Omni (New York, N.Y.)* 12:34+ O '89
Increasing survival rates [leukemia; program at the University of Michigan Medical Center] *USA Today (Periodical)* 118:9-10 O '89
Marrow donors: reaching beyond family [chronic myelogenous leukemia] R. Weiss. *Science News* 135:348 Je 3 '89
Prevention of allogeneic bone marrow graft rejection by H-2 transgene in donor mice. C. Öhlén and others. bibl f il *Science* 246:666-8 N 3 '89

MARRYSHOW, TERRY
about
A doctor's dilemma. W. Steif. il por *The Progressive* 53:10 Ja '89

MARS (NEW YORK, N.Y.: NIGHTCLUB) *See* New York (N.Y.)—Restaurants, nightclubs, bars, etc.

MARS (PLANET)
See also
Life on Mars
Mars vehicles
Space flight to Mars
Clear view of Mars delights observers. D. J. Eicher. il *Astronomy* 17:108-9 Ja '89
Have earth rocks gone to Mars? [research by S. A. Phinney] J. Eberhart. *Science News* 135:191 Mr 25 '89
Life on Mars: cultivating a planet—and ourselves [cover story] F. Turner. il *Harper's* 279:33-40 Ag '89
Mars' grand finale. D. C. Parker and others. il *Sky and Telescope* 77:369-72 Ap '89
Mars: remembrance of life past. M. Tennesen. il *Discover* 10:82-8 Jl '89
Memories of Mars [cover story] D. J. Eicher and D. M. Troiani. il *Astronomy* 17:74-9 Ap '89
The red planet shows off. J. D. Beish and others. il *Sky and Telescope* 77:30-5 Ja '89

Atmosphere
The Martian atmosphere: old versus new. J. Eberhart. il *Science News* 135:21 Ja 14 '89
Signs of old Mars: written in the dust [evidence for warmer period, complete with water; research by Ted L. Roush] J. Eberhart. *Science News* 135:173 Mr 18 '89

Geology
Calcium carbonate found in 'Mars' meteorites [research by James L. Gooding] *Astronomy* 17:14 Je '89
Meteorite may carry organic Martian cargo [EETA 79001; research by Ian P. Wright] I. Amato. *Science News* 136:53 Jl 22 '89
Surveying the scars of ancient Martian floods. M. S. Robinson. il *Astronomy* 17:38-45 O '89

Magnetic properties
Phobos 2 asks, "Is Mars magnetic?". il *Sky and Telescope* 77:464 My '89

Maps
Drawing Mars from video. R. N. Clark. il *Sky and Telescope* 77:476 My '89

Photographs and photography
Amateurs record Mars with CCD. il *Astronomy* 17:92 F '89
The best telescopic pictures of Mars. G. H. de Vaucouleurs. il *Sky and Telescope* 77:15-17 Ja '89
Images [Candor Chasma] il *Sky and Telescope* 77:144-5 F '89
Mars from Tennessee. L. Koehn. il *Sky and Telescope* 77:676-7 Je '89
What's new on Mars? W. K. Hartmann. il *Sky and Telescope* 77:471+ My '89

Satellites
Fear of Phobos [moving closer to planet's face] il *Discover* 10:13 Jl '89
New views of Mars and Phobos [Phobos mission] R. Burnham. il *Astronomy* 17:28-32 S '89
Radar detection of Phobos. S. J. Ostro and others. bibl f il *Science* 243:1584-6 Mr 24 '89
Sizing up Phobos. P. Stooke. il *Sky and Telescope* 77:477-9 My '89
Soviet findings from Phobos and Mars. il *Science News* 136:286 O 28 '89
Soviet Mars probe collects data in preparation for Phobos flyby. il *Aviation Week & Space Technology* 130:26 Mr 27 '89
Soviet probe enters Mars orbit; landers to descend on Phobos. C. Covault. il *Aviation Week & Space Technology* 130:24-5 F 13 '89
Target: Phobos. K. Croswell. il *Ad Astra* 1:16-21 Ja '89

MARS (PLANET)—Satellites—*cont.*
Watching Mars' elusive moons. D. Di Cicco. il *Sky and Telescope* 77:446-7 Ap '89
Surface
Envisioning the waters of Phobos [research by Fraser P. Fanale and James R. Salvail] *Science News* 135:287 My 6 '89
Martian impacts and Phobos' grooves [study by Peter H. Schultz and David A. Crawford] J. Eberhart. *Science News* 136:334 N 18 '89
Phobos: moonlet of the pits. J. Eberhart. il *Science News* 136:301 N 4 '89
Surface
A balloonful of earth to help study Mars. *Science News* 135:223 Ap 8 '89
A different view of Mars [radar map by Duane O. Muhleman] J. Eberhart. il *Science News* 135:75 F 4 '89
Drawing Mars in 1988. D. C. Parker and others. il *Sky and Telescope* 77:429-30 Ap '89
For how long did the Martian waters run? [research by Michael H. Carr] *Science News* 135:351 Je 3 '89
Mapping Mars. il *Sky and Telescope* 77:431 Ap '89
Mars Observer begins new era using proven spacecraft design. M. Mecham. il *Aviation Week & Space Technology* 131:79+ O 9 '89
Muddy evidence [study of volcanic debris flow strengthens case for water; work of Eric H. Christiansen] B. D. Schwartz. *Scientific American* 260:28+ Je '89
Muddying the waters [channels of volcanic debris as evidence for water on Mars; research by Eric Christiansen] il *Discover* 10:10 N '89
NASA ponders the Mars Rover. il *Astronomy* 17:16 Mr '89
NASA scientists hope Mars Rover will be precursor to manned flight. B. W. Henderson. il *Aviation Week & Space Technology* 131:85-6+ O 9 '89
Searching for the waters of Mars [cover story] S. W. Squyres. il *Astronomy* 17:20-8 Ag '89
Signs of old Mars: written in the dust [evidence for warmer period, complete with water; research by Ted L. Roush] J. Eberhart. *Science News* 135:173 Mr 18 '89
Solving a mystery in the sands of Mars [research by Robert C. Plumb] J. Eberhart. *Science News* 135:266 Ap 29 '89
Viking missions are principal source of scientists' knowledge about Mars. il *Aviation Week & Space Technology* 131:95 O 9 '89

MARS (PLANET) IN ART
Capturing Mars on paper. il *Astronomy* 17:90-1 Mr '89
Drawing Mars in 1988. D. C. Parker and others. il *Sky and Telescope* 77:429-30 Ap '89

MARS (PLANET) IN MOTION PICTURES
New views of Mars [Mars the movie and Samara probe] T. H. Cole. il *Popular Mechanics* 166:36 S '89

MARS VEHICLES
Design
NASA ponders the Mars Rover. il *Astronomy* 17:16 Mr '89
NASA scientists hope Mars Rover will be precursor to manned flight. B. W. Henderson. il *Aviation Week & Space Technology* 131:85-6+ O 9 '89

MARSA, LINDA
Addiction and IQ. il *Omni (New York, N.Y.)* 12:24+ O '89
Live and let die. *Omni (New York, N.Y.)* 11:40-2 S '89
Phoenix rising [cover story] il *Omni (New York, N.Y.)* 12:50-4+ D '89
The triumph of Bonnie Lovette. il pors *Good Housekeeping* 209:72+ Ag '89

MARSALIS, BRANFORD
about
Branford Marsalis: blowing his own horn. C. Waldron. il pors *Ebony* 44:66+ F '89
Branford Marsalis: the Marsalis tapes [cover story] D. Helland. il pors *Down Beat* 56:16-19 N '89
Wynton & Branford Marsalis: a common understanding [interview; reprint from December 1982 issue] A. J. Liska. il pors *Down Beat* 56:94-5+ S '89

MARSALIS, WYNTON
Christmas meant football and turkey—and a swig o' cranberry bog; ed. by Herma M. Rosenthal. il pors *TV Guide* 37:12-14 D 16-22 '89
about
Music to our ears (I). J. Ephland. il por *Down Beat* 56:6 Jl '89
A star too soon. T. Outhwaite. *National Review* 41:49-50 D 31 '89
Wynton & Branford Marsalis: a common understanding [interview; reprint from December 1982 issue] A. J. Liska. il pors *Down Beat* 56:94-5+ S '89
Wynton Marsalis journeys to the heart of New Orleans. B. Cullman. il por *Vogue* 179:206 Ag '89

MARSCHALEK, ROLF, AND OTHERS
Transfer RNA genes: landmarks for integration of mobile genetic elements in Dictyostelium discoideum. bibl f il *Science* 244:1493-6 Je 23 '89

MARSCHALL, LAURENCE A.
Supernova aftermath [cover story] il *Astronomy* 17:40-2 F '89

MARSDEN, MICHAEL T.
Headlights. See issues of Motor Trend beginning January 1987 through February 1989
MARSDEN, LUCY (FICTIONAL CHARACTER) See Lucy Marsden (Fictional character)
MARSEILLES (FRANCE)
Population
Unsettled immigrants. T. J. Abercrombie. il *National Geographic* 176:120-9 Jl '89
MARSH, DAVID C. (DAVID CHARLES)
The assertive chancellor. *World Press Review* 36:30-1 My '89
The Procession of Holy Blood. il map *Travel Holiday* 171:64-71 Mr '89
MARSH, FREDDIE
When in Tokyo . . . *World Press Review* 36:55 My '89
MARSH, GERALD E.
U.S. missiles on hair trigger? *The Bulletin of the Atomic Scientists* 45:3 My '89
MARSH, HUGH
about
Hugh Marsh. D. Ouellette. por *Down Beat* 56:14 Jl '89
MARSH, JAN
Kelmscott Manor. il *History Today* 39:62-3 Ap '89
MARSH, PETER
(jt. auth) See White, David, and Marsh, Peter
MARSH, WILLIAM
(jt. auth) See Chen, Milton, and Marsh, William
MARSH PLANTS
See also
Cattails
MARSHALL, COLIN M.
about
From 'Bloody Awful' to bloody awesome. C. Power. il por *Business Week* p97+ O 9 '89
MARSHALL, EDWARD, 1942-
See also
Marshall, James, 1942-
MARSHALL, GAIL
Evaluating research on school computer use. *The Education Digest* 54:30-3 Ja '89
MARSHALL, GARRY, 1934-
Garry Marshall: on the Happy days all-stars and discovering Robin Williams. il por *People Weekly* 31 Special Issue:139 Summ '89
about
Beaches [film] Reviews
Glamour il 87:186 Mr '89. J. G. Boyum
New York il 22:58+ Ja 16 '89. D. Denby
The New Yorker 64:91-2 Ja 23 '89. P. Kael
People Weekly il 31:12 Ja 9 '89. P. Travers
Video il 13:80+ O '89. R. Gehr
MARSHALL, JAMES, 1942-
about
PW interviews. L. S. Marcus. il por *Publishers Weekly* 236:202-3 Jl 28 '89
MARSHALL, JENNIFER
Just married (the inside story). il *Mademoiselle* 95:164-5+ Ag '89
MARSHALL, MARGARET A.
(jt. auth) See Timberlake, William E., and Marshall, Margaret A.
MARSHALL, MARIA
about
Blind faith [excerpt] J. McGinniss. il pors *Ladies' Home Journal* 106:62+ Ap '89
MARSHALL, MARK G.
(jt. auth) See Kennedy, William A., and Marshall, Mark G.
MARSHALL, NEIL
about
Artistry in makeup. M. Gazzaniga. il pors *Harper's Bazaar* 122:26+ D '89
MARSHALL, NOREEN
The land of 'Lion Mountain'. il *World Press Review* 36:62 Je '89
MARSHALL, PENNY
about
Big [film] Reviews
Video il 13:57 Ap '89. J. Young
MARSHALL, ROB
about
Blind faith [excerpt] J. McGinniss. il pors *Ladies' Home Journal* 106:62+ Ap '89
MARSHALL, S. L. A. (SAMUEL LYMAN ATWOOD), 1900-1977
about
The secret of the soldiers who didn't shoot. F. P. Smoler. il pors *American Heritage* 40:5, 36-45 Mr '89
MARSHALL, SAMUEL LYMAN ATWOOD See Marshall, S. L. A. (Samuel Lyman Atwood), 1900-1977
MARSHALL, SUSAN
about
Interior with seven figures [dance] Reviews
Dance Magazine 63:81-2 Mr '89. C. Hardy

MARSHALL, THURGOOD
about

Thurgood Marshall hires two black Ivy League law clerks. il pors *Jet* 77:4+ N 13 '89

Thurgood Marshall still Court's poorest justice. il por *Jet* 76:13 Je 5 '89

Thurgood's way. D. Seligman. il *Fortune* 119:165+ My 8 '89

MARSHALL (BOB) WILDERNESS (MONT.) *See* Bob Marshall Wilderness (Mont.)
MARSHALL (LENORE) POETRY PRIZE *See* Lenore Marshall/Nation Poetry Prize
MARSHALL (SUSAN) AND COMPANY *See* Susan Marshall and Company
MARSHALL OF CAMBRIDGE (ENGINEERING) LTD.
British cargo conversion of TriStar offered to airline operators. D. A. Brown. il *Aviation Week & Space Technology* 131:63+ Ag 21 '89

MARSHALL PLAN
The Marshall Plan [reprint from September 1947 issue] S. B. Fay. *Current History* 88:30-1+ Ja '89

MARSHALS SERVICE (U.S.) *See* United States. Marshals Service
MARSHES
See also

Arcata Marsh and Wildlife Sanctuary (Calif.)
Bogs
Dyke Marsh (Va.)
Everglades (Fla.)
Tuttle Marsh (Mich.)

MARSI, RICK
January—the Dog, the stars, the president [excerpt from Wheel of seasons] il *The Conservationist* 43:56 Ja/F '89

MARSTON, RAY
Basic op-amps. il *Radio-Electronics* 60:69-72+ Mr '89
Bilateral switches. il *Radio-Electronics* 60:54-8 N '89
CMOS PLL's. il *Radio-Electronics* 60:55-8 D '89
Compound op-amps. il *Radio-Electronics* 60:69-72+ Ja '89
Down-counter cookbook. il *Radio-Electronics* 60:71-7 F '89
Op-amp oscillators. il *Radio-Electronics* 60:51-5 Jl '89
Op-amps in instrumentation. il *Radio-Electronics* 60:59-63 S '89
Working with counters. il *Radio-Electronics* 60:63-8 Ap '89
Working with op-amps. il *Radio-Electronics* 60:54-8 My '89

MARSUPIALS
See also

Opossums
Sugar gliders (Animals)
Wombats

MARSYAS (GREEK DEITY) IN ART
Hubris before the gods [Titian painting] M. K. Talley, Jr. il por *Art News* 88:75-6 My '89

MARTEL, JAY
Look out, Hulk—'Macho Man' wants revenge. il pors *TV Guide* 37:20-2 Jl 29-Ag 4 '89

MARTENS
Hunting for an elusive hunter [field studies in Wyoming] S. Buskirk and H. Harlow. il *National Wildlife* 28:20-3 D '89/Ja '90

MARTHA GRAHAM DANCE COMPANY
Flags flying [revival of American document] T. Tobias. il *New York* 22:156+ O 23 '89

Folk movements. L. A. Jacobs. *The New Leader* 72:22-3 O 30 '89

Frontier of the mind: Martha Graham at 95 [interview; cover story] M. Horosko. il pors *Dance Magazine* 63:50-7 My '89

Graham assoluta [fall season at City Center] G. Solomons. il *Dance Magazine* 63:48-51 Mr '89

Graham tomorrow. C. Barnes. *Dance Magazine* 63:130 D '89

Together at a tense moment, two titans of dance turn crisis into creation [M. Baryshnikov and M. Graham] M. Small. il pors *People Weekly* 32:42-3 O 16 '89

A woman under the influence [dancer T. Capucilli] J. Gruen. pors *Dance Magazine* 63:52-4 Mr '89

MARTHA'S VINEYARD (MASS.)
See also

Architecture, Domestic—Martha's Vineyard (Mass.)
Felix Neck Wildlife Sanctuary (Mass.)

Blacks

Creating a racquet [Martha's Vineyard Racquet & Fitness Club] B. W. O'Connor. il *Black Enterprise* 19:54-5 Jl '89

Martha's Vineyard. il *Ebony* 44:36-40 Jl '89

Description and travel

East to Eden. J. Sedgwick. il *Gentlemen's Quarterly* 59:370-4+ Mr '89

Martha's Vineyard [popularity among blacks] il *Ebony* 44:36-40 Jl '89

MARTHA'S VINEYARD RACQUET & FITNESS CLUB *See* Sports clubs
MARTIAL ARTS
See also

Capoeira (Dance)

MARTIGNETTE, CHARLES
American advertising art. il *Antiques & Collecting Hobbies* 94:32-4 N '89

American illustration: the real art of America. il *Antiques & Collecting Hobbies* 94:26-9+ N '89

American pin-up, calendar and glamour art. il por *Antiques & Collecting Hobbies* 94:44-5+ N '89

Arthur Sarnoff: American artist and illustrator. il por *Antiques & Collecting Hobbies* 94:40-1+ N '89

about

An introduction to Charles Martignette: art historian, author, dealer and collector. il por *Antiques & Collecting Hobbies* 94:30 N '89

MARTIKA
about

Martika: more talent than you know! il por *'Teen* 33:56 N '89

One name, one album, one goal: cool hand Martika believes she is destined to be a princess of pop. S. Dougherty. il pors *People Weekly* 32:75+ O 30 '89

MARTIN, AGNES, 1912-
about

Agnes Martin at Pace. H. Cotter. il *Art in America* 77:257 Ap '89

MARTIN, ANN M., 1955-
about

Ann Martin stirs up a tiny tempest in Preteen Land with her best-selling Baby-sitters Club. K. McMurran. il pors *People Weekly* 32:55-6 Ag 21 '89

Children's books: inside the Baby-sitters Club. N. R. Kleinfield. *The New York Times Book Review* 94:42 Ap 30 '89

MARTIN, BJORN, AND OTHERS
Restriction fragment length polymorphisms associated with water use efficiency in tomato. bibl f il *Science* 243:1725-8 Mr 31 '89

MARTIN, DAVID, 1929-
Speaking in Latin tongues [cover story] il *National Review* 41:30-5 S 29 '89

MARTIN, FRANK
about

John Huston [film] Reviews

American Film il 14:66-7 Je '89. R. Seidenberg

MARTIN, FRANKLIN D.
Let Freedom ring! il *Sky and Telescope* 77:460-1 My '89

The U.S. space station: a commitment to technological advancement [cover story] il *USA Today (Periodical)* 117:30-4 My '89

MARTIN, GUY
Back in the USSA. *Utne Reader* p97-8 S/O '89

MARTIN, I. MAXIMILIAN
about

Stand & deliver. K. Dumas. il por *Black Enterprise* 19:276-8+ Je '89

MARTIN, JEAN-HUBERT
about

The whole earth show [interview] H. D. Buchloh. il *Art in America* 77:150-9+ My '89

MARTIN, JERRY
about

He fixed it. J. Schwarz. il pors map *Americana* 16:57-60 Ja/F '89

MARTIN, JOHN
about

Penniless poet to laureate of lowlife. il por *U.S. News & World Report* 106:52 Ja 9 '89

MARTIN, JOHN
Action at local level. il *World Health* p3-4 My '89

MARTIN, JUDITH, 1938-
about

Miss Manners lets her hair down. R. Hills. il *Esquire* 111:194-9 Je '89

Miss Manners on office etiquette [interview] B. Dumaine. il por *Fortune* 120:155+ N 6 '89

MARTIN, MAHLON
about

Mahlon A. Martin heads Winthrop Rockefeller Foundation. il pors *Ebony* 44:56+ Ag '89

Martin named head of Rockefeller Foundation. por *Jet* 76:24 My 22 '89

MARTIN, MARCEL
'*Glasnost*' on film. il *World Press Review* 36:60 Jl '89

MARTIN, MARY, 1913-
about

Back from legal Never-never Land, Mary Martin's magical Peter Pan soars on the airwaves again. T. Allis. il pors *People Weekly* 31:55-6+ Mr 27 '89

MARTIN, NICHOLAS
Revenge of the nerds. il *The Washington Monthly* 20:21-2+ Ja '89

MARTIN, PATRICIA
Money moves. See issues of Essence beginning March 1988

MARTIN, PAUL, 1938-
about

The leaders in waiting. R. Laver. il pors *Maclean's* 102:10-12 Mr 6 '89

MARTIN, PHYLLIS M. (PHYLLIS MARY)
Peace in Angola? bibl f *Current History* 88:229-32+ My '89

MARTIN, PHYLLIS RODGERS
The artful interview: how to find out everything you want to know in an hour or two. *Working Woman* 14:71-4+ Mr '89

MARTIN, RICHARD
Why the hammer head? il *Sea Frontiers* 35:142-5 My/Je '89

MARTIN, STAN
He shoots baseball cards: a dentist with a passion for spring training. il por map *Petersen's Photographic Magazine* 18:32-5 My '89

MARTIN, STEPHANIE
about
On deck. il por *Sport (New York, N.Y.)* 80:16 O '89

MARTIN, STEVE, 1945?-
about
Steve Martin: wild and serious guy [cover story] C. Millner. il pors *The Saturday Evening Post* 261:52-5 N/D '89

MARTIN, TOVAH
Window box beauties. il *Country Journal* 16:32-5 Jl/Ag '89

MARTIN [ballet] See Ballet reviews—Single works

MARTIN LUTHER KING DAY
Arizona finally gets a M. L. King state holiday. il *Jet* 77:18 O 9 '89
M.L.K. Jr. bill reaches another snag in Arizona. *Jet* 76:38 Jl 24 '89
Nation celebrates 4th holiday honoring King. il *Jet* 75:6+ Ja 16 '89
Notes and comment [programs at the Cathedral of St. John the Divine] *The New Yorker* 64:23-4 Ja 30 '89
President Reagan declares Martin Luther King, Jr. Day. R. Reagan. il por *Jet* 75:6+ Ja 23 '89
Son Dexter to take reins of the King Center in Atlanta. il por *Jet* 75:36-7 F 6 '89

MARTIN LUTHER KING, JR. CENTER FOR NONVIOLENT SOCIAL CHANGE
Dexter King installed as King Center prexy on 21st anniversary of dad's death. il pors *Jet* 76:6 Ap 24 '89
Dexter King steps forth. N. McCall. il por *Black Enterprise* 19:20 Ap '89
Rev. King's son, Dexter, resigns from position as president of the King Center. il por *Jet* 76:8 Ag 28 '89
Son Dexter to take reins of the King Center in Atlanta. il por *Jet* 75:36-7 F 6 '89

MARTIN LUTHER KING, JR. NATIONAL HISTORIC SITE AND PRESERVATION DISTRICT
Birthplace of a national hero. R. D. Turner. il *Ebony* 44:40-2 Ja '89

MARTIN MARIETTA CORP.
ALS cost, efficiency to depend heavily on process improvements [Advanced Launch System program] W. B. Scott. il *Aviation Week & Space Technology* 131:41+ O 23 '89
Blast off. T. Jaffe. *Forbes* 143:236-7 Ap 17 '89
First commercial Titan prepared for September launch. il *Aviation Week & Space Technology* 130:97 My 1 '89
Martin Marietta robotic device will aid in space station assembly [Flight Telerobotic Servicer] B. D. Nordwall. il *Aviation Week & Space Technology* 130:53 My 15 '89
Martin pursues development of autonomous cruise missile. E. H. Kolcum. il *Aviation Week & Space Technology* 130:85-6 My 1 '89

MARTIN PRIETO, JOSÉ LUIS
A talk with Felipe González. *World Press Review* 36:25 Mr '89

MARTINDALE, STEVEN
about
Of guns and a guru. M. McDonald. il pors *Maclean's* 102:28-9 Mr 27 '89

MARTINE, JEAN KINKEAD
The happily married woman [story] il *Good Housekeeping* 209:146-7 O '89

MARTINEZ, A
about
'I wake up and wonder what it was that woke me'. E. Warren. il pors *TV Guide* 37:24-6 N 11-17 '89

MARTíNEZ, BOB, 1934-
about
With friends like Bob Martinez, the GOP doesn't need . . . G. DeGeorge and R. Fly. il por *Business Week* p47 O 30 '89

MARTINEZ, CECILIA
(jt. auth) See Byrne, John, 1949-, and Martinez, Cecilia

MARTINEZ, EDIE
about
Entrepreneur looks for laws—and finds success. B. Stein. il por *Home Office Computing* 7:52-3 F '89

MARTINEZ, ELIANA
about
AIDS: students in glass houses? P. A. Zirkel. bibl f il *Phi Delta Kappan* 70:646-8 Ap '89

MARTINEZ, MATTHEW G.
Should President Bush's minimum wage proposal be adopted? [excerpts from address, March 23, 1989] *Congressional Digest* 68:149 My '89

MARTINEZ DEL RIO, CARLOS, AND STEVENS, BRUCE R.
Physiological constraint on feeding behavior: intestinal membrane disaccharidases of the starling. bibl f il *Science* 243:794-6 F 10 '89

MARTíNEZ ROMERO, EDUARDO
about
Passing the extradition test. M. S. Serrill. il por *Time* 134:48 S 18 '89

MARTINI, FEDERICO
about
Federico Martini. por *Cycle* 40:37 Ag '89

MARTINIQUE
See also
Music festivals—Martinique

MARTINO, ANTONIO
What is the 'right' amount of saving? *National Review* 41:31 Je 16 '89

MARTINO, DONALD, 1931-
about
Musical events:
D. Martino's Concerto for alto saxophone. A. Porter. *The New Yorker* 65:92-3 Mr 6 '89

MARTINS, PETER
about
Dancing:
P. Martins' Beethoven romance, Mozart serenade, and The waltz project. A. Croce. *The New Yorker* 65:101-2 F 20 '89
Echo [ballet] Reviews
New York il 22:53-4 Jl 17 '89. T. Tobias
A fool for you [ballet] Reviews
Dance Magazine il 63:59 O '89. J. Gruen

MARTINSBURG (W. VA.)
Crime
Crack invades the countryside. M. McConnell. il *Reader's Digest* 134:73-8 F '89

MARTINU, BOHUSLAV, 1890-1959
about
Firkušný plays Martinů. R. Freed. por *Stereo Review* 54:126 D '89

MARTON, ANDREW
Ad makers zap back. il *Channels (New York, N.Y.: 1986)* 9:30-1 S '89

MARTY, MARTIN E., 1928-
American ecumenism: separatism, separation and schism [adaptation of address] *The Christian Century* 106:958-61 O 25 '89
The establishment that was. *The Christian Century* 106:1045-7 N 15 '89
Filling in the gaps of liberal culture. *The Christian Century* 106:1019-20+ N 8 '89
M.E.M.O. See issues of The Christian Century
Mainline or mainstream? *The Christian Century* 106:1183 D 13 '89
Martin Luther King: the preacher as virtuoso [cover story] *The Christian Century* 106:348-50 Ap 5 '89
Rites of passage. por *Christianity Today* 33:20 N 3 '89
Sophisticated primitives then, primitive sophisticates now [adaptation of address; cover story] il *The Christian Century* 106:588-91 Je 7-14 '89
The years of the evangelicals [cover story] il *The Christian Century* 106:171-4 F 15 '89

MARTYN, HOWARD
Iranian Christians flee persecution. *The Christian Century* 106:461-2 My 3 '89

MARTZ, JOHN D.
Colombia's search for peace. bibl f *Current History* 88:125-8+ Mr '89

MARTZ, KARL
about
People & places. il por *American Craft* 49:13 Ap/My '89

MARTZLOFF, JEAN-CLAUDE
π in the sky. il *The Unesco Courier* 42:22-8 N '89

MARVEL, MARK
The gentrified hog. il *Esquire* 112:22+ Jl '89

MARVIN, URSULA B., AND OTHERS
Cordierite-spinel troctolite, a new magnesium-rich lithology from the lunar highlands. bibl f il map *Science* 243:925-8 F 17 '89

MARVULLO, JOE
Civil War photo diary: re-creating Gettysburg: summer of 1863. il *Petersen's Photographic Magazine* 18:24-6+ Ag '89
Colorvision: seeing the true character of color. il *Petersen's Photographic Magazine* 18:40-3 O '89
A photographer's guide to Bermuda. il map *Petersen's Photographic Magazine* 18:50-3+ Jl '89

MARX, GROUCHO, 1891-1977
about
My dinner with Groucho. F. Oursler. il por *Esquire* 111:130-2+ Je '89

MARX, JULIUS H. See Marx, Groucho, 1891-1977

MARX, LOUIS, JR.
about
An LBO outfit that goes for the long pull. M. Berss. il por *Forbes* 143:94+ Ap 17 '89

MARX, RICHARD
about
Richard Marx, music's mane man. A. Elliot. por *Mademoiselle* 95:56 Je '89
MARX, ROBERT
Directions. il *Opera News* 54:28-30+ O '89
Grand finale. il *Opera News* 54:14-16+ Jl '89
MARX BROTHERS
See also
Marx, Groucho, 1891-1977
MARXISM *See* Communism; Socialism
MARXISM AND EDUCATION *See* Socialism and education
MARY, BLESSED VIRGIN, SAINT
about
It takes one to know one: a mom's-eye view of the Blessed Mother. M. Mantle. *U.S. Catholic* 54:29-31 My '89
More than a prophetess. P. J. Ryan. il *America* 161:435 D 9 '89
Annunciation
Living with mystery. P. J. Ryan. il *America* 161:491 D 23-30 '89
Wrestling with Advent [film Hail Mary] J. K. Larson. *The Christian Century* 106:1166-8 D 13 '89
Devotions
It's time to push over Our Lady of the Pedestal. R. E. Burns. *U.S. Catholic* 54:2 My '89
MARY BOONE GALLERY
Dealer's choice. J. J. Buck. il por *Vogue* 179:336-45+ F '89
MARY KAY COSMETICS, INC.
Sell some, recruit some [S. Hutton] L. Washer. il por *Working Woman* 14:95 My '89
MARY MAGDALENE, SAINT
about
Forgiveness. P. J. Ryan. il *America* 160:567 Je 10 '89
MARY POPPINS (FICTIONAL CHARACTER)
Mary Poppins, force of nature. H. Carpenter. *The New York Times Book Review* 94:29 Ag 27 '89
MARY RICHARDS (FICTIONAL CHARACTER)
From Mary to Murphy: codependent no more. V. Rebeck. *The Christian Century* 106:948+ O 25 '89
THE MARY TYLER MOORE SHOW [television program] *See* Television program reviews—Single works
MARYLAND
See also
Antietam National Battlefield (Md.)
Booksellers and bookselling—Maryland
Charles County (Md.)
Fairs—Maryland
Historic houses, sites, etc.—Maryland
Insurance law—Maryland
Law—Maryland
Montgomery County (Md.)
Music festivals—Maryland
Prince Georges County (Md.)
Talbot County (Md.)
MARYLAND HANDEL FESTIVAL *See* Music festivals—Maryland
MARYLEBONE (LONDON, ENGLAND)
Description
Notes and comment. *The New Yorker* 65:47-8 S 25 '89
MARY'S DANISH (MUSICAL GROUP)
Mary's Danish. J. Ressner. il *Rolling Stone* p18 S 7 '89
MARYSTOWN (NFLD.)
Economic conditions
Facing the future. G. Allen. il *Maclean's* 102:19 Ap 3 '89
MARZOLLO, JEAN
After the baby: easing your return to work. il *Parents* 64:106-10 O '89
Help your husband be a great dad. il *Parents* 64:98-102 S '89
How 3-year-olds learn best. il *Parents* 64:124-6+ Mr '89
MARZORATI, GERALD
Can a novelist save Peru? [cover story] il pors *The New York Times Magazine* p44-7+ N 5 '89
Fiction's embattled infidel [cover story] il pors *The New York Times Magazine* p24-7+ Ja 29 '89
True confessions of an exiled Afrikaner. il pors *The New York Times Magazine* p32-3+ Ag 27 '89
MASAI (AFRICAN PEOPLE)
The Masai. J. Horgan. il map *Scientific American* 261:38+ S '89
MASAI MARA GAME RESERVE (KENYA)
Junk food monkeys [olive baboons feeding on humans' garbage] R. M. Sapolsky. il *Discover* 10:48-51 S '89
MASA'S (SAN FRANCISCO, CALIF.: RESTAURANT) *See* San Francisco (Calif.)—Restaurants, nightclubs, bars, etc.
MASCAGNI, PIETRO, 1863-1945
about
Lodoletta [opera] Reviews
The New Yorker 65:80 My 8 '89. A. Porter
Le maschere [opera] Reviews
The New Yorker 65:132-3 D 11 '89. A. Porter
Music. P. G. Davis. il *New York* 22:58-9 S 4 '89
MASCARAS
The fashionable lash. il *Mademoiselle* 95:172-5 D '89
Lash flash: the latest mascaras. il *Harper's Bazaar* 122:58 My '89

Magic wands. il *Seventeen* 48:130 S '89
MASCELLI, ANNE
Unwind! Relax and enjoy life. il *Essence* 19:59-62 Ja '89
LE MASCHERE [opera] *See* Mascagni, Pietro, 1863-1945
MASCOTS
Fight! Fauna fight! [college sports mascots named for animals] R. Telander. il *National Wildlife* 27:14-16 F/Mr '89
MASCULINITY (PSYCHOLOGY)
In search of the hero: masculine spirituality and liberal Christianity [cover story] P. M. Arnold. il *America* 161:206-10 O 7 '89
Macho drinks. J. F. Mariani. il *Motor Boating & Sailing* 163:48 My '89
Redefining roles [New Men] N. Underwood. il *Maclean's* 102:46-7 Ag 14 '89
State of the question [discussion of October 7, 1989 article, In search of the hero: masculine spirituality and liberal Christianity] P. M. Arnold. *America* 161:304-6 N 4 '89
Strong, silent and suffering. S. R. Morris. por *Newsweek* 113:10-11 Ap 3 '89
Who is the new ideal man? [survey results] S. Keen and O. Zur. il *Psychology Today* 23:54+ N '89
The wimp factor [cover story] B. Curtis. il *American Heritage* 40:40-4+ N '89
Anecdotes, facetiae, satire, etc.
Is that rouge, Son? S. Bing. il *Esquire* 112:45-6 Jl '89
The new improved New Man ['90s Man] W. D. Leight. *Mademoiselle* 95:128 Mr '89
MASER (ITALY)
Historic houses, sites, etc.
See also
Villa Barbaro (Maser, Italy)
MASERATI (AUTOMOBILE) *See* Automobiles, Foreign
MASERATI SPA *See* Officine Alfieri Maserati SpA
MASERS, CELESTIAL
When a red giant swallows its planets [theory of Curtis Struck-Marcell] il *Sky and Telescope* 77:7 Ja '89
M*A*S*H [television program] *See* Television program reviews—Single works
MASHAM, SAMUEL CUNLIFFE LISTER, 1ST BARON, 1815-1906
about
Manningham Mills, Bradford. A. Briggs. il por *History Today* 39:62-3 O '89
MASHBURN, RICK
A modern armor maker dresses men in knights' clothing. bibl (p183) il pors *Smithsonian* 20:116-20+ D '89
Plantation home. il pors map *Americana* 16:50-4 Ja/F '89
MASHED POTATOES *See* Cooking—Potatoes
MASHKAN-SHAPIR (ANCIENT CITY)
Iraqi dig uncovers Mesopotamian city [work of Elizabeth C. Stone and Paul E. Zimansky] B. Bower. il *Science News* 135:198 Ap 1 '89
MASHPEE (MASS.)
City planning
Back to the future [Mashpee Commons designed by Andres Duany and Elizabeth Plater-Zyberk] V. E. Gilmore. il *Popular Science* 235:22 S '89
Common sense [Mashpee Commons] P. M. Sachner. il *Architectural Record* 177:84-9 Mr '89
MASI, THOMAS A., AND DORDEVIC, DEAN M.
Age 60: a widower, no dependents. il pors *Fortune* 120 no10 Special Issue:140 Fall '89
MASINI, ALFRED M.
about
Caviar dreams for couch potatoes. J. B. Newman. il pors *Channels (New York, N.Y.: 1986)* 9:32-6 Ja 16 '89
MASKING (PHOTOGRAPHY) *See* Photography—Masking
MASKS
See also
Dust masks
Gas masks
Telescopes—Masks
Around the world in 80 days—and 165 masks [work of C. H. Jones] L. Stevens. il *Theatre Crafts* 23:56-7+ Ap '89
A Halloween recall [Spencer Gifts withdraws mask of sheik after Arab American protests] il *Newsweek* 114:61 N 6 '89
Anecdotes, facetiae, satire, etc.
All about tigers. E. Zern. il *Field & Stream* 94:140 N '89
MASOCHISM
See also
Sadomasochism
MASON, BELINDA
about
AIDS commissioner Belinda Mason speaks with ringing authority about the disease: she has it. L. Kramer. il pors *People Weekly* 32:147+ D 11 '89
MASON, BOBBIE ANN
Piano fingers [fiction] il por *Ladies' Home Journal* 106:78+ N '89
MASON, CHRISTOPHER
about
A society songster who (gently) bites the hands that feed. N. Geeslin. il pors *People Weekly* 31:249-50 Mr 6 '89

MASON, JACKIE

about

Jackie Mason tries to talk himself out of trouble [cover story] J. Kasindorf. il pors *New York* 22:36-42 O 16 '89

Jackie Mason's racial remarks about Dinkins, Jews' relations with blacks bring backlash. pors *Jet* 77:5 O 16 '89

A jesting Jackie in the box. H. F. Waters. il por *Newsweek* 114:70 S 18 '89

Mason bombs in New York. B. Turque. il pors *Newsweek* 114:42 O 9 '89

Television. J. Leonard. il por *New York* 22:60-1 S 11 '89

The Yiddish Will Rogers. J. McCollister. il por *The Saturday Evening Post* 261:44-5 Mr '89

MASON, JOHN M., AND CASEY, JOHN G.

Monsters of the deep—delights for the palate [cover story] il *The Conservationist* 44:2-9+ S/O '89

MASON, JUDI ANN

A Hollywood success story [story] il *Essence* 19:79-80+ Mr '89

MASON, LISA

Tomorrow's child [fiction] il *Omni (New York, N.Y.)* 12:94-6+ D '89

MASON, ROBERT T., AND OTHERS

Sex pheromones in snakes. bibl f il *Science* 245:290-3 Jl 21 '89

MASON, PERRY (FICTIONAL CHARACTER) See Perry Mason (Fictional character)

MASONRY

See also

Brick construction

Stone construction

Maintenance and repair

Mortar scraper and shaper [Jointmaster] D. Scott. il *Popular Science* 234:160 Ap '89

MASS

See also

Sign of peace (Catholic liturgy)

Don't miss it! H. Fehren. *U.S. Catholic* 54:38-40 My '89

Equal rites. M. McGough. *The New Republic* 201:11-12 Ag 28 '89

Let's cancel the Creed at Sunday Mass [with readers' comments] T. Unsworth. *U.S. Catholic* 54:13-17 Ja '89

MASS (MUSIC)

See also

Requiems

Mass appeal [Bach's B. Minor Mass by New York Philharmonic] P. G. Davis. il *New York* 22:152 O 23 '89

Musical events:

Performance of Mass by J. Obrecht. A. Porter. *The New Yorker* 65:69-70 F 27 '89

Re-sounding lost Masses [works by Jesuit composer D. Zípoli] il *Américas* 41 no2:4-5 '89

MASS (PHYSICS)

See also

Dark matter (Astronomy)

The concept of mass. L. B. Okun'. bibl f il *Physics Today* 42:31-6 Je '89

Einstein's ring and a galaxy's mass [MG 1654 + 1346] il *Sky and Telescope* 77:465-6 My '89

Zeroing in on the Z° mass. *Science News* 136:69 Jl 29 '89

Zs for two: a critical mass [Fermilab vs. SLAC] M. M. Waldrop. *Science* 245:350 Jl 28 '89

MASS. BAY BREWING COMPANY

Building a brewery is no small beer. il pors *Business Week* p40-1 Jl 24 '89

MASS DEMOCRATIC MOVEMENT (SOUTH AFRICA)

A cry from the masses. D. Jenish. il *Maclean's* 102:38-9 S 18 '89

New wave of defiance in South Africa [cover story] P. Green. il *The Nation* 249:261+ S 18 '89

MASS EXTINCTION OF SPECIES

^{40}Ar-^{39}Ar dating of the Manson impact structure: a Cretaceous-Tertiary boundary crater candidate [north-central Iowa] M. J. Kunk and others. bibl f il *Science* 244:1565-8 Je 30 '89

An asteroid to die for. S. J. Gould. il *Discover* 10:60-5 O '89

A combination of impact and volcano is dismissed. *Science* 243:479 Ja 27 '89

The cycle of fate. J. S. Trefil. bibl il por *Modern Maturity* 32:60-4 D '89/Ja '90

"Diary in stone" traces extinction [marine fauna extinction evidence found in Changxing quarry in China; research by David J. Bottjer] *USA Today (Periodical)* 118:10 Ag '89

Evolution and extinction [species preservers trying to stop the clock; with reply by N. Meyers] N. D. Levine. *BioScience* 39:38-40 Ja '89

Extinctions [cover story] R. Gore. il supp (folded chart) *National Geographic* 175:662-99 Je '89

Giant meteor impacts and great eruptions: dinosaur killers? G. S. Paul. bibl f il *BioScience* 39:162-72 Mr '89

The impact giveth . . . [amino acids found in Cretaceous-Tertiary boundary clay; research by Meixun Zhao and Jeffrey L. Bada] J. Horgan. *Scientific American* 261:24+ S '89

Manson, Iowa: where the 'big one' struck? [crater; research by M. J. Kunk] *Astronomy* 17:10-11 O '89

Microbes complicate the K-T mystery [research by Betsey D. Dyer] R. Monastersky. *Science News* 136:341 N 25 '89

New impact evidence: amino acids from space [Cretaceous-Tertiary boundary clay; research by Meixun Zhao and Jeffrey L. Bada] *Astronomy* 17:11+ O '89

The next doomsday impact. C. R. Chapman and D. Morrison. *Astronomy* 17:8 N '89

Planetary scientists focus on impact geology [Lunar and Planetary Science Conference] *Astronomy* 17:14+ Ag '89

Rare amino acids support impact theory [Cretaceous-Tertiary boundary clays; research by Jeffrey L. Bada] R. Monastersky. *Science News* 135:356 Je 10 '89

Signs of an ancient worldwide wallop [stishovite discovery in New Mexico; research by John McHone] R. Monastersky. *Science News* 135:132 Mr 4 '89

Stishovite at the Cretaceous-Tertiary boundary, Raton, New Mexico. J. F. McHone and others. bibl f il *Science* 243:1182-4 Mr 3 '89

Tires to sandals. S. J. Gould. *Natural History* p8+ Ap '89

The wheel of fortune and the wedge of progress. S. J. Gould. *Natural History* p14+ Mr '89

A world in crisis. P. H. Raven. il *USA Today (Periodical)* 117:48-50 My '89

MASS MEDIA

See also

AIDS (Disease) in mass media

Business and mass media

Gossip in mass media

Hispanic Americans and mass media

Hypermedia

Indians (American) and mass media

Journalistic ethics

Labor in mass media

Massachusetts Institute of Technology. Media Laboratory

Motion pictures

Multimedia

Newspapers

Periodicals

Press

Radio broadcasting

Television broadcasting

Vampires in mass media

Women and mass media

1990 field guide to the electronic environment. il *Channels (New York, N.Y.: 1986)* 9:8+ D '89

Marshall McLuhan: 'televisionary' or crackpot? N. Hickey. il por *TV Guide* 37:30-2 Je 10-16 '89

Media: winners and sinners of 1989. E. Diamond. il *New York* 22:20+ D 25 '89-Ja 1 '90

History

Mass media: marketing marketing [1980s] B. Duffy. il *U.S. News & World Report* 107:116 D 25 '89-Ja 1 '90

International aspects

The lords of the global village [cover story; with editorial comment] B. Bagdikian. *The Nation* 248:799-800, 805-8+ Je 12 '89

Moral and religious aspects

See also

Mass media in religion

Sex in mass media

Violence in mass media

Periodicals

Media watchdogs. J. Reid. il *Utne Reader* p110-12 My/Je '89

Political aspects

See also

Press and politics

Radio and politics

Television and politics

Missing from the news. B. Bagdikian. il *The Progressive* 53:32-4 Ag '89

The top 10 censored stories of 1988 [underreported or overlooked by the media; views of Project Censored] il *Utne Reader* p59-63 S/O '89

Social aspects

Style vs. substance. J. Saltzman. il *USA Today (Periodical)* 117:87 Ja '89

Study and teaching

See also

Annenberg School of Communications

Media literacy mandated in Ontario English curriculum. T. McConaghy. *Phi Delta Kappan* 71:332-3 D '89

Canada

Media watch. G. Bain. See occasional issues of *Maclean's*

United States

See Mass media

MASS MEDIA AND ART

Exhibitions

The '80s: stop making sense [Los Angeles Museum of Contemporary Art's exhibition A forest of signs; cover story] H. Drohojowska. il *Art News* 88:146-51 O '89

Image maker [Image world: art and media culture at the Whitney Museum curated by L. Phillips] B. Smith. il por *Harper's Bazaar* 122:88+ D '89

MASS MEDIA AND ART—Exhibitions—*cont.*

MassComm 101: the media vs. modernism [Image world: art and media culture and Graphic design in America] P. Plagens. il *Newsweek* 114:88-9 N 27 '89

Mucking with media [Image world: art and media culture at the Whitney Museum] R. Hughes. il *Time* 134:93 D 25 '89

Notes from an unseen exhibition [Image world: art and media culture at the Whitney Museum] R. Gehr. il *American Film* 15:15 N '89

MASS MEDIA AND LITERATURE

Are books holding their own? [Gallup survey of entertainment activities] L. A. Wood. il *Publishers Weekly* 235:445 Ja 27 '89

MASS MEDIA AND PUBLIC HEALTH

"Get them to ask questions" [interview with A. Kern] il *World Health* p4-5 Mr '89

The media's role. J. Ling. il *World Health* p24-5 Ja/F '89

MASS MEDIA AND YOUTH

Understanding the news: how the media shapes your world [cover story; special issue] il *Scholastic Update (Teachers' edition)* 122:3-25 S 8 '89

MASS MEDIA BROKERS

See also

Communications Equity Associates

Canada

Deal maker for Canada's stars [M. Levine] B. D. Johnson. il por *Maclean's* 102:43 Ja 16 '89

MASS MEDIA IN RELIGION

See also

Direct broadcast satellite services—Religious programs

Radio broadcasting—Religious programs

Television broadcasting—Religious programs

World Association for Christian Communication

The Church's response to the media: twenty-five years after Inter mirifica [Vatican II decree] R. P. Waznak. *America* 160:36-40 Ja 21 '89

MASS MEDIA INDUSTRY

See also

Blacks in the mass media industry

Capital Cities/ABC Inc.

Fox Inc.

Gulf & Western, Inc.

John Blair & Company

Macfadden Holdings, Inc.

MCA Inc.

MGM/UA Communications Co.

Minorities in the mass media industry

Multimedia, Inc.

Newhouse Broadcasting Corporation

Paramount Communications Inc.

Price Communications Corp.

Publishers and publishing

Quantum Media, Inc.

Radio industry

Television industry

Time Inc.

Time Warner Inc.

Warner Communications Inc.

Washington Post Co.

1990 field guide to the electronic environment. il *Channels (New York, N.Y.: 1986)* 9:8+ D '89

The Channels achievers [cover story; special section] il *Channels (New York, N.Y.: 1986)* 9:21+ Jl/Ag '89

Communications media. L. Gubernick. il *Forbes* 143:111-12 Ja 9 '89

Do marketers control what we see? D. M. Topolnicki. il *Psychology Today* 23:73-5 Je '89

Acquisitions and mergers

All hitched up and ready to go [Delaware court OKs Time Warner] J. Greenwald. *Time* 134:39 Ag 7 '89

Banking on Time [role of Toronto Dominion and Bank of Nova Scotia in Paramount Communications' hostile bid for Time Inc.] P. Chisholm and J. DeMont. il *Maclean's* 102:34-5 Jl 10 '89

Cashing in on the news. L. Kramer. il *Scholastic Update (Teachers' edition)* 122:22 S 8 '89

Clash of the titans [Paramount challenges merger of Time and Warner Communications] J. Greenwald. il *Time* 133:42-5 Je 19 '89

The counterattack [Time Inc. moves to buy Warner in countermove against Paramount; cover story] J. Schwartz. il *Newsweek* 113:48-53 Je 26 '89

A deal heard round the world [merger of Time and Warner] C. P. Alexander. il *Time* 133:55-6 Mr 20 '89

Deals that were, or almost were. M. Brown. il *Channels (New York, N.Y.: 1986)* 9:36 D '89

Even behind the scenes, the Time-Warner drama has its stars [money managers F. Sarofim and O. Aboodi] M. Ivey; J. Friedman. il pors *Business Week* p55-6 Jl 31 '89

Feeding frenzy [Paramount's hostile bid to stop Time-Warner merger] C. Byron. il *New York* 22:24-8 Je 26 '89

First salvos in the fight for Time [bid by Paramount Communications] B. Saporito. il *Fortune* 120:12 Jl 3 '89

Gentlemen's agreement [merger of Time and Warner] E. Diamond. il *New York* 22:16+ Mr 20 '89

Gulf & Western is ready to go off its diet. D. Lieberman. il *Business Week* p31 Ap 24 '89

Heading for D-Day in Delaware [court to decide whether Time Inc. up for sale] J. Castro. il *Time* 134:44 Jl 10 '89

Heading for 'War Time'? [Time Inc. mega deal with Warner Communications] L. Reibstein. il *Newsweek* 113:50 Mr 20 '89

How the rich get richer [tax breaks in affirmative action media buys] H. Rudnitsky. il *Forbes* 143:38-9 My 15 '89

How Time Warner will look when the fog clears; Pondering Time's fate over chicken gumbo. il *Business Week* p24-5 Ag 7 '89

How to drive off a raider [battle over Time Inc.] J. Schwartz. il *Newsweek* 114:43 Ag 7 '89

In or out of the game? [Narragansett Capital] P. Noglows. il *Channels (New York, N.Y.: 1986)* 9:67 Mr '89

In the nick of Time? [rumor of Cap Cities/ABC bid for Time Inc.] S. N. Chakravarty. il *Forbes* 144:14 Jl 10 '89

The inside story of Time Warner. B. Saporito. il *Fortune* 120:164-6+ N 20 '89

A legal battle that could kill off friendly mergers [court to decide if Time-Warner stock swap will put Time in play] M. Galen. il *Business Week* p27 Jl 3 '89

A legal victory for the long term [Delaware court allows Time Inc. to buy Warner and repel Paramount's hostile bid] B. Saporito. il *Fortune* 120:56-9 Ag 14 '89

Missing from the news. B. Bagdikian. il *The Progressive* 53:32-4 Ag '89

The moguls of Media, Inc. [merger of Time Inc. and Warner Communications] E. Pomice. il *U.S. News & World Report* 106:66-7 Mr 20 '89

A new march on Time [Paramount bid] P. Chisholm. il *Maclean's* 102:37 Je 19 '89

A new media powerhouse [Time Inc. and Warner] J. DeMont. il por *Maclean's* 102:42-4 Mr 20 '89

A nice, simple Time-Warner deal was too good to last [bid by Paramount Communications] D. Lieberman. il *Business Week* p38-9 Je 19 '89

One for the books [Delaware court rejects Paramount's challenge to Time-Warner deal] J. Greenwald. il *Time* 134:34-6 Jl 24 '89

Paramount bid for Time launches all-out battle. *Publishers Weekly* 235:8 Je 23 '89

Paramount raises its ante [increases hostile bid for Time] J. Greenwald. il *Time* 134:42 Jl 3 '89

A peculiar beauty contest [concentration on cash flow vs. earnings in stock valuation as highlighted in Time Inc. merger] D. Wechsler. il *Forbes* 144:43-4+ Jl 10 '89

The Rattner years [departure of S. Rattner] P. Noglows. il por *Channels (New York, N.Y.: 1986)* 9:73 Jl/Ag '89

Return to sender [Paramount's hostile bid for Time] J. Greenwald. il *Time* 133:54-5 Je 26 '89

Steve Ross' big sweet deal [merger of Warner Communications and Time] G. Morgenson. il por *Forbes* 143:14 Ap 3 '89

Temple of gloom [A. Temple quits as Time Inc. director because he opposes proposed merger with Warner Communications] J. Zweig. il por *Forbes* 143:168 Je 26 '89

Time + Dallas = ? [New York times coverage of Time Inc. acquisition of Warner Communications] R. Pollak. *The Nation* 248:401 Mr 27 '89

Time Inc. gets a green light [Delaware judge OKs Warner bid] J. Schwartz and C. Friday. il *Newsweek* 114:50 Jl 24 '89

Time Inc. goes Hollywood [buyout of Warner Communications] L. Reibstein. il *Newsweek* 113:41-2 Mr 13 '89

Time Inc. will have to pull a Houdini [Paramount's hostile bid] D. Lieberman. il *Business Week* p62 Je 26 '89

Time out [merger of Time Inc. and Warner Communications] J. Bennet. *The New Republic* 200:20+ Ap 24 '89

Time rejects Paramount's sweetened $12 billion bid. *Publishers Weekly* 236:8 Jl 7 '89

Time vs. its shareholders [Paramount's hostile bid to stop merger with Warner] J. Egan. il *U.S. News & World Report* 107:38-40 Jl 3 '89

The Time Warner challenge. M. Brown. il *Channels (New York, N.Y.: 1986)* 9:20 My '89

Time-Warner heads receive cordial hearing by House Judiciary unit. H. Fields. *Publishers Weekly* 235:14 Mr 31 '89

Time-Warner: this close to victory [Delaware court decision; special section] il *Business Week* p26-9 Jl 31 '89

Time-Warner: three's a crowd: Bob Bass may stop the merger. K. Kelly and D. Lieberman. il por *Business Week* p38 Ap 3 '89

Time's bad fortune with money people [Paramount's bid for Time Inc.] *U.S. News & World Report* 106:14 Je 19 '89

Time's counterattack is drawing acid reviews [Warner bid] D. Lieberman. il *Business Week* p26 Jl 3 '89

Time's next battleground [Delaware Chancery Court] R. Sandza. *Newsweek* 114:31 Jl 10 '89

Upping the ante for Time [Paramount's new bid] J. Schwartz. il *Newsweek* 114:42 Jl 3 '89

MASS MEDIA INDUSTRY— Acquisitions and mergers— *cont.*

The war over Time Inc. [Paramount's hostile bid threatens Warner merger] J. Schwartz. il *Newsweek* 113:48-9+ Je 19 '89

Why doesn't Time Inc. just put itself on the block? J. H. Dobrzynski. il *Business Week* p63 Je 26 '89

Will it happen? And will it work? [Time-Warner deal; special section] il *Business Week* p32-6 Mr 20 '89

The wizards of 'Wasserella' [role in Time Inc. takeover] J. Schwartz and C. Friday. il pors *Newsweek* 114:30-1 Jl 10 '89

Anecdotes, facetiae, satire, etc.

Let's do a deal [Nation bids for Time, Inc.] V. S. Navasky. *The Nation* 249:3-4 Jl 3 '89

Sharp elbows and the media barons [bidders for Time Inc.] A. Fotheringham. il *Maclean's* 102:56 Je 26 '89

Time is money [discussion of July 3, 1989 article, Let's do a deal] V. S. Navasky. *The Nation* 249:75-6 Jl 17 '89

International aspects

Even Rupert Murdoch has his limits [financial strains] C. Welles. il por *Business Week* p34-5 O 2 '89

"I can think of more important things than being loved by everybody" [interview with R. Murdoch] W. J. Koschnick. il pors *Forbes* 144:98+ N 27 '89

Keeping up with the Murdochs. D. Lieberman. il *Business Week* p32-4 Mr 20 '89

The lords of the global village [cover story; with editorial comment] B. Bagdikian. *The Nation* 248:799-800, 805-8+ Je 12 '89

Media wars [cover story; special section; with editorial comment by Kevin Doyle] il *Maclean's* 102:2, 26-32+ Jl 17 '89

The myth of global synergy. J. Hammer. il *Newsweek* 113:54 Je 26 '89

Uncle Sam is pop culture to the world. il *U.S. News & World Report* 107:9 Ag 7 '89

Canada

Assuring the regulators [Maclean Hunter Ltd.'s purchase of Selkirk Communications] J. DeMont. il *Maclean's* 102:36 Je 12 '89

Securities

Achieving on the exchange [tables] il *Channels (New York, N.Y.: 1986)* 9:76 Jl/Ag '89

Deals that were, or almost were. M. Brown. il *Channels (New York, N.Y.: 1986)* 9:36 D '89

Inside the market. F. M. Seegal. il por *Channels (New York, N.Y.: 1986)* 9:89 Ja '89

Making millions on media [top money managers] il *Channels (New York, N.Y.: 1986)* 9:53-4 Jl/Ag '89

The meaning of achievement. R. J. MacDonald. por *Channels (New York, N.Y.: 1986)* 9:37 Jl/Ag '89

The usual suspects. T. Jaffe. *Forbes* 143:188 Ap 3 '89

Taxation

How the rich get richer [tax breaks in affirmative action media buys] H. Rudnitsky. il *Forbes* 143:38-9 My 15 '89

Canada

See also

Selkirk Communications Limited

Media wars [cover story; special section; with editorial comment by Kevin Doyle] il *Maclean's* 102:2, 26-32+ Jl 17 '89

Germany (West)

See also

Bertelsmann AG

Great Britain

See also

Carlton Communications plc

Maxwell Communication Corporation plc

Japan

See also

Fujisankei Communications Group

MASS MOCA *See* Massachusetts Museum of Contemporary Art and Architecture

MASS MURDER *See* Murder

MASS SPECTROMETERS *See* Spectrometers

MASS SPECTROMETRY *See* Spectrum analysis

MASS SPECTROMETRY, ACCELERATOR *See* Accelerator mass spectrometry

MASS TRANSIT *See* Local transit

MASSACHUSETTS

See also

Arts and crafts—Massachusetts

Berkshire Hills (Mass.)

Booksellers and bookselling—Massachusetts

Cape Cod National Seashore (Mass.)

Concord River (Mass.)

Education—Massachusetts

Environmental movement—Massachusetts

Express highways—Massachusetts

Finance—Massachusetts

Historic houses, sites, etc.—Massachusetts

Hospitals, Psychiatric—Massachusetts

Housing—Massachusetts

Insurance law—Massachusetts

Martha's Vineyard (Mass.)

Merrimack River (N.H. and Mass.)

Music festivals—Massachusetts

Prisons—Massachusetts

Shore protection—Massachusetts

Walden Pond (Mass.)

History

The troubled voyage of the Rainbow [Massachusetts colony confronts issue of slave trade] L. Gragg. bibl il maps *History Today* 39:36-41 Ag '89

Politics and government

The losses keep mounting [personal and political difficulties faced by K. and M. Dukakis] R. Ajemian. il pors *Time* 134:66 N 20 '89

Playing single-issue politics: abortion and the Massachusetts governor's race. M. Starr. il *Newsweek* 114:22 Ag 14 '89

Population

A tale of two states [views of Carl Haub] *The Futurist* 23:51-2 My/Je '89

MASSACHUSETTS COUNCIL ON THE ARTS AND HUMANITIES

Bad news for arts budgets in Massachusetts. *Art in America* 77:224 N '89

MASSACHUSETTS EYE AND EAR INFIRMARY

Hospital faulted for dry eye study [Harvard-affiliated] W. Booth. *Science* 243:1000 F 24 '89

MASSACHUSETTS FURNITURE *See* Furniture, American

MASSACHUSETTS INDEMNITY & LIFE INS. CO.

Surplus loophole [accounting practices] D. Wechsler. *Forbes* 144:44+ S 4 '89

MASSACHUSETTS INSTITUTE OF TECHNOLOGY

Intellectual exports [Industrial Liaison Program] T. Beardsley. *Scientific American* 261:17+ S '89

Is academic freedom bad for business? [denial of tenure to professor D. Noble] K. Hart. il por *The Bulletin of the Atomic Scientists* 45:28-31+ Ap '89

March 4, 1969 [conference on political awareness] J. Schlefer. *Technology Review* 92:2 Ap '89

MIT-industry links draw congressional attention. M. Crawford. il *Science* 244:1136 Je 9 '89

Reporter: a digest of news from M.I.T. See occasional issues of Technology Review

With a campus legend in peril, members of a fraternity vow to save the endangered M.I.T. smoot [markings spanning the length of the Harvard Bridge created by Lambda Chi Alpha pledges] N. Geeslin. il pors *People Weekly* 31:93-5 Ap 24 '89

MASSACHUSETTS INSTITUTE OF TECHNOLOGY. MEDIA LABORATORY

The wizards of the Media Lab. J. J. Barron. il *Byte* 14:353-6+ D '89

MASSACHUSETTS MUSEUM OF CONTEMPORARY ART AND ARCHITECTURE

A megamuseum in a mill town. D. Weisgall. il por *The New York Times Magazine* p32-5+ Mr 5 '89

MASSACHUSETTS MUTUAL LIFE INSURANCE CO.

Why technical skill alone isn't enough [P. Wallington] J. Pepper. il por *Working Woman* 14:64+ My '89

MASSACHUSETTS PORT AUTHORITY

Court grounds Logan fees. il *Flying* 116:12 N '89

Massport drops PACE to avoid loss of U.S. aid [landing fee schedule at Logan International Airport] *Aviation Week & Space Technology* 130:109 Ja 2 '89

Massport suspends Logan's higher fees. *Flying* 116:12-13 Mr '89

MASSACRES

China

See also

Tiananmen Square (China) student occupation, 1989

Vietnam

See also

My Lai Massacre, 1968

Zaire

25 years later, life still springs from death [slain medical missionary P. Carlson] il por *Christianity Today* 33:56+ N 17 '89

MASSAGE

See also

Chiropractic

Ahhh . . . that feels good [massage in the office] il *Newsweek* 113:53 My 15 '89

The beauty magic of touch. il *Glamour* 87:240-3 Ag '89

A better coffee break [On-Site Massage] V. Brower. il *American Health* 8:34 Jl/Ag '89

Facial massage. D. Carter. il *American Health* 8:22 O '89

A hands-on career. il *New Choices for the Best Years* 29:13 O '89

Hands-on healing hints [excerpts from Hands-on healing] il *Prevention (Emmaus, Pa.)* 41:105-8+ Ag '89

The magic of massage. il *Essence* 20:52 O '89

Tender touches [baby massage] A. Finkelstein. il *Parents* 64:102-5 D '89

A touch of calm in a mad world. il *Mademoiselle* 95:40 Mr '89

MASSE, MARCEL

about

Culture in crisis. P. Young. il por *Maclean's* 102:58-60 My 8 '89

MASSELINK, BEN
Chased out of the sea. il *Sea Frontiers* 35:256 Jl/Ag '89
MASSENET, JULES, 1842-1912
about
Werther [opera] Reviews
Opera News il 53:18-21+ Mr 18 '89. J. W. Hansen
Opera News il 53:22-5 Mr 18 '89
MASSEY, RUTH
Wat Phou: saving a treasure of Khmer civilization. il *The Courier (Unesco)* 41:20-3 N '88
MASSEY, WALTER E.
Science education in the United States: what the scientific community can do [with editorial comment by Richard S. Nicholson] bibl f il *Science* 245:905, 915-21 S 1 '89
about
Dr. Walter E. Massey. D. C. Lyons. il pors *Ebony* 44:62-3+ Ag '89
MASSINE, LEONIDE, 1896-1979
about
Diaghilev sits out WWI in Spain: Iberian idyll. J. R. Acocella. il pors *Dance Magazine* 63:45-8 Je '89
MASSING, MICHAEL
Coke dusters. *The New Republic* 200:21-3 Ja 30 '89
Crack's destructive sprint across America. il *The New York Times Magazine* p38-41+ O 1 '89
Desperate over drugs [cover story] il *The New York Review of Books* 36:22-6 Mr 30 '89
Grave thoughts. *The New Republic* 201:12-14 D 11 '89
How free is the Soviet press? il *The New York Review of Books* 36:55-8 S 28 '89
Sad new El Salvador. il *The New York Review of Books* 36:53-60 My 18 '89
'The war on cocaine': an exchange [discussion of December 22, 1988 article] il *The New York Review of Books* 36:40 Mr 2 '89
MASSIVELY PARALLEL SUPERCOMPUTERS
Richard Feynman and the Connection Machine. D. Hillis. il *Physics Today* 42:78-83 F '89
These gee-whiz machines are finding an audience. L. Jereski. il *Business Week* p154+ My 22 '89
MASSMUTUAL CORPORATE INVESTORS
Big yields from little deals. S. Manolatos. il por *Forbes* 144:234 O 16 '89
MASSON, J. MOUSSAIEFF (JEFFREY MOUSSAIEFF), 1941-
about
The anti-shrinks. M. DiLeo. pors *Mother Jones* 14:13 Jl/Ag '89
Holier than thou. J. Taylor. il pors *New York* 22:32-7 Mr 27 '89
The right to fake quotes. W. A. Henry. por *Time* 134:49 Ag 21 '89
MASSON, JEFFREY MOUSSAIEFF See Masson, J. Moussaieff (Jeffrey Moussaieff), 1941-
MASSON EDITEUR
French trade publisher Belfond joins Masson medical group. H. R. Lottman. *Publishers Weekly* 236:11 N 17 '89
MASSUH, VICTOR
Interview with Najib Mahfouz. il por *The Unesco Courier* 42:4-6 D '89
MASSULLO SISTERS
about
Women are gobbling up the Massullo sisters' turkey-feather coats. il *People Weekly* 32:154-5 N 27 '89
MAST CELLS
Pavlovian conditioning of rat mucosal mast cells to secrete rat mast cell protease II. G. MacQueen and others. bibl f il *Science* 243:83-5 Ja 6 '89
MASTECTOMY
Breast cancer: playing the odds [additional therapy for mastectomy patients] il *Newsweek* 113:46-7 Mr 6 '89
How I fought the no. 1 cancer killer of black women. A. Gale. il pors *Ebony* 44:58+ Je '89
"I will live . . . ": Jill Ireland fights back. V. Scott. il pors *Good Housekeeping* 208:183+ My '89
New treatment may reduce breast surgeries [chemotherapy followed by lumpectomy and radiation; work of Gianni Bonadonna] R. Weiss. *Science News* 135:325-6 My 27 '89
Tempering the trauma [research shows lumpectomy and mastectomy are equally effective] *U.S. News & World Report* 106:17 Ap 10 '89
MASTECTOMY IN ART
The art of healing [work of H. Wilke and N. Fried] C. Langer. il *Ms.* 17:132-3 Ja/F '89
THE MASTER AND MARGARITA [ballet] See Ballet reviews—Single works
MASTER CLASSES (SINGING INSTRUCTION) See Singing—Study and teaching
MASTER DUPLICATORS (FIRM)
Audiotape business reels in profits. R. Gunnerson. il pors *Home Office Computing* 7:63-4 N '89
MASTER LIMITED PARTNERSHIP
See also
ServiceMaster Limited Partnership
Partnerships with a plus. M. Schiffres. il *Changing Times* 43:47-8+ O '89
MASTERGATE [drama] See Gelbart, Larry

MASTERMEDIA LTD.
How to choose a distributor. S. S. Stautberg. por *Publishers Weekly* 236:429 Ag 11 '89
MASTERS, DEBORAH
about
Loft Tenants. *The New Yorker* 64:25-6 Ja 16 '89
MASTERS, DEXTER, 1908-1989
about
Obituary
Consumer Reports il por 54:134 Mr '89
MASTERS, IAN
Audio Q&A. See issues of Stereo Review beginning October 1986
MASTERS, KIM
Syndication's Magic Kingdom. il *Channels (New York, N.Y.: 1986)* 9:39-42 Ja 16 '89
MASTERS RUNNING See Running
MASTERSON, MARY STUART
about
Finding dignity in a pregnant teen, Mary Stuart Masterson waits to be discovered—again. C. Sanz. il pors *People Weekly* 32:151+ N 13 '89
Will Mary Stuart Masterson be as big as her name? L. Morice. il por *Mademoiselle* 95:73-4 D '89
MASTERSON, PETER
about
Night game [film] Reviews
People Weekly il 32:11-12 O 2 '89. R. Novak
MASTODONS
Big Apple tusks [mastodon fossils in New York City] S. Horenstein. il map *Natural History* p96-8+ Mr '89
MASTRANTONIO, MARY ELIZABETH
about
Can 'The abyss' make Mary Elizabeth Mastrantonio an even bigger name? D. Wild. il pors *Rolling Stone* p83-6 Ag 10 '89
MASTURBATION
Anecdotes, facetiae, satire, etc.
Pro-life pro. P. Roth. il *The New York Review of Books* 36:5 Ag 17 '89
MASURSKY, HAROLD, 1922-, AND STROBELL, MARY
Memorials on the moon. il *Sky and Telescope* 77:265 Mr '89
MASZAK, MARIANNE SZEGEDY- See Szegedy-Maszak, Marianne
MATA HARI [film] See Motion picture reviews—Single works
MATADOR [film] See Motion picture reviews—Single works
MATAMOROS (TAMAULIPAS, MEXICO)
Crime
The believers [M. Kilroy murdered by drug dealers] G. D. Garcia. il *Rolling Stone* p46-9+ Je 29 '89
Cult of the red-haired devil [drug dealers practice human sacrifice] R. Woodbury. il map *Time* 133:30 Ap 24 '89
The grisly secrets of a lonely ranch [human sacrifice slaying of M. Kilroy and others by drug smugglers] A. Richman. il por *People Weekly* 31:44-9 My 1 '89
Magic and murder in Matamoros. J. Burnett. *The Christian Century* 106:815-16 S 13-20 '89
Ritual murder. B. Wickens. il *Maclean's* 102:61 Ap 24 '89
Ritual murder in Mexico [human sacrifice practiced by drug dealers] F. Gibney, Jr. il *Newsweek* 113:55 Ap 24 '89
Voodoo in Mexico [human sacrifice practiced by drug dealers] il *U.S. News & World Report* 106:16 Ap 24 '89
Bibliography
Magic! Murder! Mayhem! Drugs! Four new books detail the ritual killings in Matamoros, Mexico. G. Feldman. il *Publishers Weekly* 236:23-4 Ag 18 '89
MATERIALISM
The faces of Joseph Campbell. B. Gill. il *The New York Review of Books* 36:16+ S 28 '89
Good-bye to materialism? M. Novak. il *Forbes* 144:108-9 N 27 '89
Having it all: '60s idealism, $100 haircuts, and a confused conscience. M. Orth. il *Utne Reader* p70 S/O '89
Hellfire of the banalities [work of A. Warhol] E. Knippers. il *Christianity Today* 33:26-7 S 22 '89
Joseph Campbell: an exchange [discussion of September 28, 1989 article, The faces of Joseph Campbell] B. Gill. il *The New York Review of Books* 36:57-61 N 9 '89
MATERIALS
See also
Airplanes, Jet—Materials
Artists' materials
Building materials
Ceramics
Composite materials
Raw materials
Failure
Making concrete smarter than it looks [work of Robert E. Shannon and William G. Clark Jr.] I. Amato. *Science News* 135:284 My 6 '89
A relation to describe rate-dependent material failure. B. Voight. bibl f il *Science* 243:200-3 Ja 13 '89
MATERIALS, FLAMMABLE See Inflammable materials
MATERIALS PROCESSING IN SPACE See Space processing
MATERIALS RESEARCH
See also
Beijing Institute of Aeronautical Materials

MATERIALS RESEARCH—See also—*cont.*
    Intospace GmbH
    Making new materials molecule by molecule. I. Amato. *Science News* 135:166 Mr 18 '89
    Making new materials with nature's help. R. Pool. *Science* 246:1389 D 15 '89
    Making the right stuff. I. Amato. il *Science News* 136:108-10 Ag 12 '89
    Materials research for the 1990s [National Research Council report] R. Pool. *Science* 245:1449 S 29 '89
    New materials by design [work of Rustum Roy] *USA Today (Periodical)* 117:8-9 Je '89
    New probes reveal atomic structures [position sensing atom probe] il *Popular Mechanics* 166:14 My '89
    Reshaping our lives: advanced materials. T. Y. Canby. il *National Geographic* 176:746-81 D '89
    Smart materials. S. R. Tessler. il *Technology Review* 92:8-9 Ap '89

Japan
    Progress in advanced materials. M. Mandell. il *High Technology Business* 9:12 Jl/Ag '89
MATERIALS RESEARCH SOCIETY
    MRS meets in Boston. il *Physics Today* 42:55-7 N '89
MATERKA, PAT ROESSIE
    Managing your time [excerpt from Time in, time out, time enough] il *Essence* 20:120+ My '89
MATERNAL BEHAVIOR See Mothers
MATERNAL BEHAVIOR IN ANIMALS See Parental behavior in animals
MATERNAL DEPRIVATION
    Understanding kids. L. Balter. il *Ladies' Home Journal* 106:92 Ap '89
MATERNAL-FETAL EXCHANGE
    See also
    Maternally acquired immunity
MATERNAL LOVE See Love, Maternal
MATERNAL MORTALITY See Mothers—Mortality
MATERNALLY ACQUIRED IMMUNITY
    Maternal immunity via molecular ferry [research on FcRn by Neil E. Simister and Keith E. Mostov] R. Weiss. *Science News* 135:20 Ja 14 '89
MATERNITY See Mothers
MATERNITY CARE, HOSPITAL See Hospitals—Maternity care
MATERNITY CLOTHES See Clothing and dress—Maternity clothes
MATERNITY LEAVES
    After the baby: easing your return to work. J. Marzollo. il *Parents* 64:106-10 O '89
    Helping your company become family-friendly. R. Sandroff. il *Working Woman* 14:136-7+ N '89
    Job rights for mothers-to-be. P. A. Seefeldt. il *Good Housekeeping* 209:272 N '89
    Negotiating the best parental leave. K. Levine. il *Parents* 64:74+ My '89
    When the boss becomes pregnant. B. Hamer. il *Psychology Today* 23:14+ Ja/F '89
MATHABANE, MARK
    Color picture out of focus. il *World Tennis* 37:27+ Je '89
MATHEMATICAL ANALYSIS
    See also
    Mathematical optimization
MATHEMATICAL ILLITERACY See Mathematical literacy
MATHEMATICAL LITERACY
    Are you an innumerate? [views of John Paulos] K. Bartlett. il *por The Saturday Evening Post* 261:36 S '89
    Big numbers for innumeracy: Hill & Wang's first bestseller heralds a new direction. C. Goodrich. il *por Publishers Weekly* 235:46-8 Je 2 '89
    An eminent math professor says "innumeracy" rivals illiteracy as a cause for concern in America [interview with J. Paulos] D. Chu. il *pors People Weekly* 31:95-6+ My 29 '89
    The odds are you're innumerate. J. A. Paulos. il *The New York Times Book Review* 94:1+ Ja 1 '89
    To conquer fear of counting [views of J. A. Paulos] S. Kanfer. il *Time* 133:66 Ja 30 '89
MATHEMATICAL MODELS
    See also
    Brain—Mathematical models
    Ecological models
    Game theory
    Monte Carlo method
    Securities—Mathematical models
    Systems analysis
MATHEMATICAL OPTIMIZATION
    The optimizers are coming [investment programs] M. Gianturco. il *Forbes* 144:270 O 16 '89
MATHEMATICAL PHYSICS
    See also
    Ergodic theory
    Fractals
    Statistical mechanics
    What's wrong with these equations? N. D. Mermin. il *por Physics Today* 42:9+ O '89
MATHEMATICAL PROOF See Proof theory
MATHEMATICAL RECREATIONS
    Games. S. Morris. See issues of Omni (New York, N.Y.)

NumberMaze [computer game] G. Solomon. il *Home Office Computing* 7:87 Mr '89
MATHEMATICIANS
    See also
    Penrose, Roger
    Ramanujan Aiyangar, Srinivasa, 1887-1920
MATHEMATICS
    See also
    Algebra
    Algorithms
    Arithmetic
    Biomathematics
    Calculus
    Combinatorial analysis
    Computers—Mathematical use
    Fractions
    Game theory
    Geometry
    Graphic methods
    Mathematical recreations
    Probabilities
    Series (Mathematics)
    Topology

History
    A mathematical mystery tour [cover story; special issue] il *The Unesco Courier* 42:10-48 N '89
Study and teaching
    See also
    Arithmetic—Study and teaching
    Calculus—Study and teaching
    Geometry—Study and teaching
    Kumon (Mathematics instruction)
    Mathematics teachers
    Big changes urged for precollege math [standards formulated by the National Council of Teachers of Mathematics] C. Holden. il *Science* 243:1655 Mr 31 '89
    Bring back the old math [curriculum and evaluation standards for school mathematics by National Council of Teachers of Mathematics] C. Nelson. il *The American Spectator* 22:36-7 N '89
    Educating John Q. Public. M. Estren. *High Technology Business* 9:3 Je '89
    Essential mathematics for the twenty-first century. I. M. Carl. *The Education Digest* 55:40-2 D '89
    Everyday math for grownups. E. Kiester and S. V. Kiester. *Reader's Digest* 135:43-4+ O '89
    The huge problem in American schools [address, December 6, 1988] L. F. Cavazos. *Vital Speeches of the Day* 55:236-8 F 1 '89
    In her majesty's service [National Research Council report] B. M. Smith. *Phi Delta Kappan* 70:426 F '89
    Making math education effective. K. Hoffman and L. A. Steen. il *Technology Review* 92:22+ N/D '89
    Math education reform [report of the National Research Council] *The Education Digest* 54:29-32 My '89
    More math means more money [positive correlation between number of mathematics courses a person takes and earnings] B. A. Cipra. *Science* 243:314 Ja 20 '89
    Overhaul urged for math teaching [National Research Council report] G. Byrne. il *Science* 243:597 F 3 '89
    Reforming math education [National Research Council report] *Science News* 135:70 F 4 '89
    Scientific competency through fun. D. E. Koshland, Jr. *Science* 243:989 F 24 '89
    Spearheading mathematics reform [report of the National Research Council] il *Children Today* 18:4-5 My/Je '89
    Three reports on mathematics emphasize reasoning over rote. C. S. Powell. *Physics Today* 42:45 Ap '89
    U.S. students flunk math, science [study by the Educational Testing Service] G. Byrne. *Science* 243:729 F 10 '89
    When "everybody counts," perhaps no one will [National Research Council report] E. G. Effros. *The Education Digest* 55:18-20 O '89
    Why is Pythagoras following me? [mathematics requirements in high schools] M. K. Smith. bibl f il *Phi Delta Kappan* 70:446-54 F '89
    Writing off our future? M. Estren. *High Technology Business* 9:5 F '89

Aids and devices
    Math Blaster Mystery. J. Zornberg. il *Home Office Computing* 7:98 N '89
MATHEMATICS, ARABIC
    Where geometry and algebra intersect [interview with R. Rashed] il *The Unesco Courier* 42:36-41 N '89
MATHEMATICS, ASSYRO-BABYLONIAN
    Prime numbers. J. Ritter. il *The Unesco Courier* 42:12-17 N '89
MATHEMATICS, CHINESE
    π in the sky. J.-C. Martzloff. il *The Unesco Courier* 42:22-8 N '89
MATHEMATICS, EGYPTIAN
    Prime numbers. J. Ritter. il *The Unesco Courier* 42:12-17 N '89
MATHEMATICS, GREEK
    The odyssey of reason. B. Vitrac. il *The Unesco Courier* 42:28-35 N '89

MATHEMATICS, INDIAN (EAST INDIAN)
Lilavati, gracious lady of arithmetic. F. Zimmermann. il *The Unesco Courier* 42:18-21 N '89
MATHEMATICS AND LITERATURE
The odds are you're innumerate. J. A. Paulos. il *The New York Times Book Review* 94:1+ Ja 1 '89
MATHEMATICS TEACHERS
Education in service
Mentorships and the perceived educational payoffs [Houston program pairing secondary teachers with mathematicians and scientists] L. M. Miller and others. il *Phi Delta Kappan* 70:465-7 F '89
MATHESON, KATY
Beyond "modern dance with soy sauce": Saeko Ichinohe—an East-West hybrid. il pors *Dance Magazine* 63:46-9 D '89
MATHESON, RICHARD, 1926-
Eyes [story] *Omni (New York, N.Y.)* 11:52-3 Ap '89
MATHEWS, DAVID
Teaching politics as public work [excerpt from Public leadership education] *The Education Digest* 55:32-4 D '89
MATHEWS, EVERETTE
about
In praise of amateur status. S. Griswold. il por *Petersen's Photographic Magazine* 17:50-3 F '89
MATHEWS, JACK
Earth to Gilliam. il por *American Film* 14:34-9+ Mr '89
No southern comfort [cover story] il pors *American Film* 15:28-33 D '89
MATHEWS, JAY, 1945-
Miracle worker at Garfield High [condensed from Escalante] il pors *Reader's Digest* 134:165-70+ Ja '89
MATHEWS, JESSICA TUCHMAN
Redefining security. *Foreign Affairs* 68:162-77 Spr '89
MATHEWS, LAURA
Books. See issues of Glamour
MATHEWS, MAX V.
about
Different drum uses computer, radio waves. *Byte* 14:14+ Mr '89
MATHEWS, NANCY MOWLL
Mary Cassatt in the 1890's: the color prints in context. bibl f il *Antiques* 136:860-71 O '89
MATHEWS-BERENSON, MARGARET
The Pollock-Krasner Foundation: special assistance for needy artists. il *American Artist* 53:80-3 Je '89
MATHIEU, PAUL
about
Escape to Normandy [cover story] C. K. Gandee. il pors *House & Garden* 161:96-105+ F '89
The gilded and the grand. N. Frey. il pors *Harper's Bazaar* 122:110+ Ap '89
MATHIS, WELDON L.
about
The feds drive a wedge into the Teamsters. A. Bernstein. il *Business Week* p90 F 6 '89
MATICEK, RONALD GROSSARTH- *See* Grossarth-Maticek, Ronald
MATING BEHAVIOR *See* Sexual behavior
MATINYI, MOBHARE
Grandad learns about smoking. il *World Health* p25-6 Mr '89
MATIS, LOUIS A., AND OTHERS
Structure and specificity of a class II MHC alloreactive γδ T cell receptor heterodimer. bibl f il *Science* 245:746-9 Ag 18 '89
MATLACK, FRED
Six useful projects for the woodworking shop. il por *Country Journal* 16:65-71 N/D '89
MATLIN, MARLEE
about
Actress Marlee Matlin builds A bridge to silence to star in her first speaking role. P. Freeman. il pors *People Weekly* 31:158-60 Ap 10 '89
Marlee Matlin: breaking the silence. L. A. Walker. il pors *Ladies' Home Journal* 106:42+ Ap '89
Marlee Matlin comes on . . . loud and clear. M. Leahy. il pors *TV Guide* 37:18-20+ Ap 8-14 '89
MATLOFF, GREGORY L.
(jt. auth) See Mallove, Eugene F., and Matloff, Gregory L.
MATOUSEK, MARK
Offbeat sex appeal. pors *Harper's Bazaar* 122:54+ Ap '89
Rio with love. il por *Harper's Bazaar* 122:390+ S '89
Spirit! Ring in the season. il pors *Harper's Bazaar* 122:154-7+ D '89
MATRA SA
ESA council endorses French Matra design for polar platform [Columbus space station] *Aviation Week & Space Technology* 131:24 O 30 '89
ESA director general selects Matra polar platform design. il *Aviation Week & Space Technology* 130:26 F 27 '89
France approves development of Apache stand-off weapon. il *Aviation Week & Space Technology* 131:20 S 25 '89
France's Matra will cooperate with Spain to develop Hispasat satellite network. J. M. Lenorovitz. maps *Aviation Week & Space Technology* 131:93 Jl 17 '89

French approval of Spot 4 ensures earth imaging services through 1990s. J. M. Lenorovitz. il *Aviation Week & Space Technology* 131:43 Ag 14 '89
Matra delivers Mistral missiles to French forces. il *Aviation Week & Space Technology* 130:107 F 20 '89
MATRIMONY *See* Marriage
MATS FOR PICTURES *See* Pictures—Trimming, mounting, etc.
MATSES INDIANS
Visions of the Matses. P. Gorman. il map *Américas* 41 no1:32-7 '89
MATSON, HOWARD
The case of the misplaced faith [story] por *The Humanist* 49:10-11+ N/D '89
MATSON, MANDY
Working mothers: these make the best of both worlds. il *Good Housekeeping* 208:46+ Mr '89
MATSUI, TOSHIMITSU, AND OTHERS
Isolation of a novel receptor cDNA establishes the existence of two PDGF receptor genes. bibl f il *Science* 243:800-4 F 10 '89
MATSUMURA, MASAZUMI, AND MATTHEWS, BRIAN W.
Control of enzyme activity by an engineered disulfide bond. bibl f il *Science* 243:792-4 F 10 '89
MATSUSHITA ELECTRIC INDUSTRIAL CO. LTD.
Matsushita may tune in to cable [possible bid for General Instrument] G. G. Marcial. *Business Week* p76 Ja 30 '89
MATT, TONI, D. 1989
about
Obituary
Skiing il por 42:36+ S '89. N. Howe
MATTA, 1911-
about
Noble riddles and surrealist fruits. I. Stavans. il *Art News* 88:29 N '89
MATTAR, PHILIP, 1944-
The critical moment for peace. *Foreign Policy* 76:141-59 Fall '89
MATTEL INC.
Mattel is putting its dollhouse in order. P. Cole. il por *Business Week* p66-7 Ag 28 '89
Toyland turnaround. il *Forbes* 143:168 Ja 9 '89
MATTER, DARRYL E., AND MATTER, ROXANA MARIE
Mementos of a champ: Max Schmeling, world's heavyweight boxing champion, 1930-1932. il pors *Antiques & Collecting Hobbies* 94:59-60 Jl '89
The science-fiction fantasy world of A. Merritt. il *Antiques & Collecting Hobbies* 93:47-9 F '89
MATTER, ROXANA MARIE
(jt. auth) See Matter, Darryl E., and Matter, Roxana Marie
MATTER
See also
Antimatter
Compression
Mass (Physics)
Particles (Nuclear physics)
Surfaces
Condensed matter physics. bibl f *Physics Today* 42:S22-S32 Ja '89
A matter fabricator provides matter for thought [Banach-Tarski paradox] A. K. Dewdney. il *Scientific American* 260:116-19 Ap '89
'Optical matter' emerges under laser [work of Michael M. Burns and Jean Marc Fournier] I. Amato. *Science News* 136:212 S 30 '89
Richard Feynman and condensed matter physics. D. Pines. bibl f il *Physics Today* 42:61-6 F '89
Searching for strange matter [study of quarks] I. Peterson. il *Science News* 135:138-9 Mr 4 '89
Strange matter [quarks; cover story] S. Vogel. il *Discover* 10:62-7 N '89
MATTER, INTERSTELLAR
See also
Dark matter (Astronomy)
Masers, Celestial
Nebulae
Oort clouds
Astronomers find evidence of galaxies still forming [interstellar hydrogen cloud found by Riccardo Giovanelli and Martha Haynes] *Earth Science* 42:9-10 Fall '89
Carrying fuel into the galactic center [Paul T. P. Ho identifies stream of gas] I. Peterson. *Science News* 135:21 Ja 14 '89
Cloud links quasars to Seyfert galaxies [hydrogen cloud; work of Kimiaki Kawara] A. McKenzie. *Science News* 136:215 S 30 '89
Comets and meteorites: harbingers of life on earth . . . and destructors of Mars. il *Sky and Telescope* 78:242 S '89
Comets may have supplied earth with chemicals of life. *Earth Science* 42:6-7 Summ '89
Diamonds from heaven and earth. *Sky and Telescope* 77:244-5 Mr '89
Feeding the hole [stream of gas near Milky Way; research by Paul Ho] il *Discover* 10:14 Je '89

MATTER, INTERSTELLAR—*cont.*
Feeding the monster in the middle [Milky Way's black hole; research by Paul Ho] M. M. Waldrop. il *Science* 243:478 Ja 27 '89
Fractal-shaped dust [work of Edward L. Wright] il *Sky and Telescope* 78:240 S '89
Galactic birth? [intergalactic hydrogen cloud discovered by Riccardo Giovanelli and Martha Haynes] *Time* 134:66 S 11 '89
Galactic cannonballs [research by Jane C. Charlton and Edwin E. Salpeter] *Sky and Telescope* 78:246 S '89
The hidden lives of massive stars [role of molecular clouds; research by Edward B. Churchwell and Douglas O. S. Wood] *Science News* 135:88 F 11 '89
How a star is born [Submillimeter Wave Astronomy Satellite project by Gary Melnick] K. Hartley. il *Astronomy* 17:14 D '89
In the beginning was a cloud [intergalactic hydrogen cloud discovered by Riccardo Giovanelli and Martha Haynes] S. Begley. *Newsweek* 114:66 S 11 '89
Island gas cloud may be protogalaxy [intergalactic hydrogen cloud discovered by Martha P. Haynes and Riccardo Giovanelli] il *Astronomy* 17:10 D '89
The Lazarus star [cloud of gas emitted from white dwarf star; research by Howard Bond] il *Discover* 10:10 My '89
Leo's intergalactic ring [research by Stephen E. Schneider] il *Sky and Telescope* 78:8-9 Jl '89
Looking down on the Milky Way [map of molecular clouds by Philip M. Solomon and A. R. Rivolo] il *Sky and Telescope* 78:127 Ag '89
The making of interstellar grit [silicon carbide; research by Michael Frenklach] *Science News* 135:351 Je 3 '89
New echoes of Supernova 1987A [light echoes from dust clouds; work of Arlin P. S. Crotts and William E. Kunkel] I. Peterson. *Science News* 136:12 Jl 1 '89
A new window on star birth [submillimeter astronomy] K. Hartley. il *Astronomy* 17:32-6 Mr '89
Pumping gas to fuel a galaxy's active core [computer simulation by Lars Hernquist] I. Peterson. *Science News* 136:150 S 2 '89
Star formation in irregular galaxies. D. A. Hunter and J. S. Gallagher. bibl f il *Science* 243:1557-63 Mr 24 '89
Starbirth's soft glow [image of star forming clouds in Cepheus; research by Adair P. Lane] il *Sky and Telescope* 78:239-40 S '89
Starlight shadows protogalaxy finding [intergalactic hydrogen cloud discovered by Martha P. Haynes and Riccardo Giovanelli] R. Cowen. il *Science News* 136:164 S 9 '89
Stillborn [interstellar hydrogen cloud found by Riccardo Giovanelli and Martha P. Haynes] J. Horgan. *Scientific American* 261:28 N '89
Supernova burps rid galaxies of hot gas [work of Jane C. Charlton and Edwin E. Salpeter] I. Peterson. *Science News* 136:310 N 11 '89
A surprise near Virgo [intergalactic hydrogen cloud discovered by Riccardo Giovanelli and Martha Haynes] J. Palca. *Science* 245:933 S 1 '89
Unveiling the hidden Milky Way [molecular cloud mapping] E. S. Palmer. il *Astronomy* 17:32-40 N '89
MATTERA, JOANNE
Clothes strategies. See issues of Glamour beginning October 1986
MATTERA, RAFAEL, AND OTHERS
Splice variants of the α subunit of the G protein G$_s$ activate both adenylyl cyclase and calcium channels. bibl f il *Science* 243:804-7 F 10 '89
MATTERN, EVELYN
Legacy [poem] *America* 161:64 Jl 29-Ag 5 '89
MATTHEW BENDER & CO.
A new Federal tax service from Matthew Bender. J. Wisdom. il *Publishers Weekly* 236:50 S 8 '89
MATTHEWS, BRIAN W.
(jt. auth) See Matsumura, Masazumi, and Matthews, Brian W.
MATTHEWS, DAVID, 1943-
Composers tune out. *World Press Review* 36:71 N '89
MATTHEWS, DENISE See Vanity
MATTHEWS, DOWNS
Winging it. il *Popular Photography* 96:42-7 Je '89
MATTHEWS, GEOFFREY
'Good sons' who kill. il *World Press Review* 36:26-7 N '89
MATTHEWS, KATHY, 1949-
(jt. auth) See Giller, Robert M., and Matthews, Kathy, 1949-
MATTHEWS, RANDY
about
Wilderness reclamation [interview] D. Coran. il por *Christianity Today* 33:63 D 15 '89
MATTHEWS, RICHARD
Articles for the rural and country market. *The Writer* 102:28-9 N '89
A good vane. il *Country Journal* 16:50-5 Ja '89
Home offices that work. il *Country Journal* 16:60-4 Jl/Ag '89
Plight of the maples [cover story] il *Country Journal* 16:50-4+ Mr/Ap '89
A tragic harvest. il *Country Journal* 16:10 S/O '89

MATTHEWS, WESTINA
about
Women who go for it! B. M. Campbell. il pors *Essence* 20:48-50+ Ag '89
MATTHEWS, WILLIAM, 1942-
The blues [poem] *The Atlantic* 264:60 S '89
Mood indigo [poem] *The New Yorker* 65:40 Jl 10 '89
MATTHEWS, WILLIAM HENRY, 1919-
Superstition to science. il *Earth Science* 42:12-16 Fall '89
MATTHIESSEN, CONSTANCE
(jt. auth) See Weir, David, 1947-, and Matthiessen, Constance
MATTHIESSEN, PETER
Old hometown. il pors *Architectural Digest* 46:52+ N '89
about
Court dismisses Janklow suit against Viking and Matthiessen. *Publishers Weekly* 235:14 Je 16 '89
The F.B.I. man who cried libel. M. Garbus. il *The Nation* 249:564+ N 13 '89
In the workshop of Peter Matthiessen. il por *Esquire* 111:118-19 My '89
Viking, Matthiessen win in Price libel suit. *Publishers Weekly* 236:8 S 1 '89
MATTHUS, SIEGFRIED, 1934-
about
The lay of Cornet Christoph Rilke's love and death [opera] Reviews
The New Yorker 65:128-9 N 6 '89. A. Porter
MATTICK, PAUL, JR.
Roger Norrington's Beethoven. *The Nation* 249:326-8 S 25 '89
MATTINGLY, DON
about
The hit man hits back. P. Gammons. il pors *Sports Illustrated* 70:54-8+ F 6 '89
MATTINGLY, IGNATIUS G.
(jt. auth) See Liberman, Alvin M., and Mattingly, Ignatius G.
MATTISON, ALICE
A winding stair [story] *The New Yorker* 65:35-40 Je 19 '89
MATTLIN, EVERETT
. . . and Cary. por *Film Comment* 25:8-9 N/D '89
MATTOX, JOYCE
about
With a hijacked copter, she rescued her boyfriend from jail. L. Murray. il por *TV Guide* 37:38 F 11-17 '89
MATTRESS PADS
Electric blankets & mattress pads. il *Consumer Reports* 54:711-14 N '89
MATTSON, WILLIAM J., 1943-
(jt. auth) See Haack, Robert A., and Mattson, William J., 1943-
MATULKA, JAN, 1890-1972
about
Jan Matulka at Schoelkopf. L. Campbell. il *Art in America* 77:148-9 Mr '89
MATURI, RICHARD J.
Maintain the right. il *American History Illustrated* 24:32-9 Mr '89
MATURITY
Are you grown up? J. Stone. il *Glamour* 87:190 Ap '89
The generation blur. B. D. Colen. il *Health (New York, N.Y.)* 21:30-1 O '89
How do you know when you're grown up? J. Groch. il *American Health* 8:117-18 Jl/Ag '89
Why boys have more fun. J. Schaefers. il *Seventeen* 48:68-9 Jl '89
Young beyond their years [postponing move into adulthood] K. L. Woodward. il *Newsweek* 114 Special Issue:54-5+ Wint '89/Spr '90
MATURITY, SEXUAL See Puberty
MATURITY NEWS SERVICE
'Rookie' reporter plies MNS beat [J. Volz] il por *Modern Maturity* 32:88 Je/Jl '89
MATUS, IRVIN
about
Left homeless, Irvin Matus preferred the Bard to a bed. K. Gross. il pors *People Weekly* 31:125+ My 22 '89
MATUSADONA NATIONAL PARK (ZIMBABWE)
African safari adventure [students from Eiffel Flats Primary School explore Matusadona National Park; cover story] il map *National Geographic World* 168:3-8 Ag '89
MATZ, ANNE L., AND MATZ, MILTON
Turning arguments into agreements. *Nation's Business* 77:74 Je '89
MATZ, MILTON
(jt. auth) See Matz, Anne L., and Matz, Milton
MATZEN, THOMAS
about
Sprechen sie LBO? P. Fuhrman. il por *Forbes* 144:43-4 O 16 '89
MATZKE, GORDON, AND KEY, DOUGLAS
Wildfire in the West's woods: fire policy in the wake of the fires of 1988. il *Focus (New York, N.Y.: 1950)* 39:1-2+ Summ '89

MAU, TURIA *See* Payot, Turia Mau
MAUCHER, HELMUT
about
Nestlé shows how to gobble markets. S. Tully. il por map *Fortune* 119:74-6+ Ja 16 '89
MAUDLIN, MICHAEL G.
America's Lutherans: where they are going. il *Christianity Today* 33:26-9 N 3 '89
MAUGHAM, SOMERSET *See* Maugham, W. Somerset (William Somerset), 1874-1965
MAUGHAM, W. SOMERSET (WILLIAM SOMERSET), 1874-1965
about
The circle [drama] Reviews
New York il 22:166-7 D 4 '89. J. Simon
The New Yorker 65:142 D 4 '89. E. Oliver
MAUGHAM, WILLIAM SOMERSET *See* Maugham, W. Somerset (William Somerset), 1874-1965
MAUI (HAWAII)
See also
Architecture, Domestic—Maui (Hawaii)
Arts and crafts—Maui (Hawaii)
Birds—Maui (Hawaii)
Hotels, motels, etc.—Maui (Hawaii)
Antiquities
The sacred bones of Maui [plan to build hotel on ancient burial ground stirs strife] W. S. Merwin. il *The New York Times Magazine* p20-1+ Ag 6 '89
Description and travel
See also
Automobile touring—Maui (Hawaii)
Cycling—Maui (Hawaii)
MAUNA KEA OBSERVATORY *See* Astronomical observatories—Hawaii
MAUNDY THURSDAY
Maundy Thursday. W. Wangerin. il *Christianity Today* 33:19-21 Mr 17 '89
MAUNEY, KAREN
Brother, can you spare a grand? *Opera News* 53:12 Ap 15 '89
MAUPIN, ARMISTEAD
about
Mainstreaming a cult classic. T. Clifton. il por *Newsweek* 114:77 O 30 '89
Out on the town. A. Block. il *Mother Jones* 14:54 N '89
MAUPIN, DARRELL
about
Personalities plus. J. Gruder. il pors *Harper's Bazaar* 122:173-4 Ag '89
MAURER, ALLAN
Deep-sea cinema. il *Omni (New York, N.Y.)* 11:14+ Ag '89
MAURER, BRIAN A.
(jt. auth) See Brown, James H., and Maurer, Brian A.
MAURER, MARC
Language and the future of the blind [address, July 8, 1989] *Vital Speeches of the Day* 56:16-22 O 15 '89
about
"Blindness isn't a handicap—it's a nuisance". D. Scoblionkov. il pors *McCall's* 117:49-52 O '89
MAURER, PATRICIA
about
"Blindness isn't a handicap—it's a nuisance". D. Scoblionkov. il pors *McCall's* 117:49-52 O '89
MAURICE (NEW YORK, N.Y.: RESTAURANT) *See* New York (N.Y.)—Restaurants, nightclubs, bars, etc.
MAURITIUS
See also
Public health—Mauritius
Description and travel
Gourmet holidays: Mauritius. N. Barry. il maps *Gourmet* 49:96-101+ N '89
MAUS, WARREN
Living with your neighbors' fowl habits. *Flower and Garden* 33:64+ Mr/Ap '89
MAUTHNER, ROBERT
Can NATO survive détente? *World Press Review* 36:22-3 F '89
MAX, LEON
about
Heavy metal. A. Betsky. il *Architectural Record* 177:86-93 mid-S '89
MAX & ERMA'S RESTAURANTS
An English suitor for Max & Erma's? [Mercury Asset Management] G. G. Marcial. *Business Week* p166 N 27 '89
MAXICARE HEALTH PLANS, INC.
Even heroic measures may not save Maxicare. P. Cole. il por *Business Week* p96+ Mr 27 '89
MAXILLA & MANDIBLE (FIRM)
All that's left [proprietor H. Galiano] *The New Yorker* 65:35-6 O 30 '89
MAXIMS
Can you trust a rule of thumb? Only with a grain of salt [financial maxims] B. Kobliner. il *Money* 18:187-8 Ap '89
MAXIMUM STEADY-STATE PACE TRAINING *See* Tempo training
MAXSON, GLORIA A.
Credo [poem] *The Christian Century* 106:983 N 1 '89

MAXWELL, BRUCE
Not so fast. il *Common Cause Magazine* 15:24-5 S/O '89
MAXWELL, DAPHNE *See* Reid, Daphne Maxwell
MAXWELL, DAVID OGDEN
about
Fannie Mae helps put a roof over the nation's poor. C. Yang. il por *Business Week* p113 Je 5 '89
MAXWELL, HAMISH
about
From soup to nuts. A. Farnham. il por *Fortune* 119:43 Ja 2 '89
Is bigger better for Philip Morris? [interview] C. Leinster. il por *Fortune* 119:66-71 My 8 '89
Philip Morris's big bite [cover story] L. J. Davis. il por *The New York Times Magazine* p30-3+ Ap 9 '89
MAXWELL, JESSICA
Of moose and men. il *Esquire* 112:50+ N '89
MAXWELL, ROBERT
about
The acquisitor. J. Daly. il pors *Maclean's* 102:38-9 N 13 '89
Four titans carve up European TV [cover story] W. Fisher and M. Schapiro. il *The Nation* 248:37+ Ja 9-16 '89
Getting ready for takeoff. A. Farnham. il por *Fortune* 119:52-3 Ja 2 '89
Macmillan/Shultz deal, take two. por *Publishers Weekly* 236:53 N 3 '89
Robert Maxwell. il *The Nation* 248:814 Je 12 '89
This year in Jerusalem. J. Zweig. il por *Forbes* 144:348+ N 13 '89
MAXWELL, TED A., AND HAYNES, CALEB VANCE, 1928-
Large-scale, low-amplitude bedforms (chevrons) in the Selima sand sheet, Egypt. bibl f il map *Science* 243:1179-82 Mr 3 '89
MAXWELL, WILLIAM, 1908-
Billie Dyer [story] *The New Yorker* 65:40-52+ My 15 '89
MAXWELL COMMUNICATION CORPORATION PLC
Getting ready for takeoff [R. Maxwell] A. Farnham. il por *Fortune* 119:52-3 Ja 2 '89
Robert Maxwell. il *The Nation* 248:814 Je 12 '89
MAXWELL HOUSE COFFEE COMPANY
Drip, drip, drip . . . drip [ad campaign] J. Levine. il *Forbes* 143:196+ Ap 17 '89
Good to the last drop [touring factory in Hoboken, N.J.] *The New Yorker* 65:44-5 N 20 '89
Just say no: boycotts at the barricades [prochoice boycott of Domino's Pizza and prolife boycott of Maxwell House coffee] *Newsweek* 114:21 Ag 14 '89
MAXWELL LABORATORIES, INC.
'Pulse power' fuels a bid [Jaycor's bid for Maxwell Labs] E. Schine. il *Business Week* p64 Je 26 '89
MAXXAM GROUP INC.
Hurwitz to the max. T. Jaffe. il *Forbes* 144:124-5 Ag 21 '89
Milken, junk bonds and raping redwoods [C. Hurwitz accelerates logging following takeover] B. McKibben. *Rolling Stone* p39-40 Ag 10 '89
A raider's ruckus in the redwoods [accelerated logging following takeover of Pacific Lumber] E. Schultz. il por *Fortune* 119:172-3+ Ap 24 '89
When the safety net is frayed [takeover of Pacific Lumber by Charles E. Hurwitz causes pension plan termination] J. B. Levine. il *Business Week* p158 N 6 '89
MAXYMUIK, J.
Bubbles can be beautiful. il *Popular Photography* 96:60-1 Je '89
MAY, A. W.
Big science, big thinking [address, June 27, 1989] *Vital Speeches of the Day* 56:114-17 D 1 '89
MAY, CLIFFORD, 1908-
about
View from Wappo Hill: Robert and Margrit Mondavi's Napa Valley vineyard. B. D. Colen. il pors *Architectural Digest* 46:276-83 My '89
MAY, LELAND C.
Bomba the Jungle Boy: the series. il *Antiques & Collecting Hobbies* 94:40+ Jl '89
MAY, MARIAN
Waikiki hotel gardens. il *Flower and Garden* 33:16-17 Mr/Ap '89
MAY, PETER
about
Nelson Peltz: shopping to chase the blues. K. Deveny. il pors *Business Week* p143 Je 26 '89
MAY, ROBERT LEWIS
about
The story behind Rudolph the Red-Nosed Reindeer. S. A. Frankel. il *Good Housekeeping* 209:126+ D '89
MAY, STEFAN
Budapest reborn. il *World Press Review* 36:62 Jl '89
MAY
The May almanac. il *The Atlantic* 263:16 My '89
MAY DEPARTMENT STORES CO.
Milking the cow, hard. C. Siler. il *Forbes* 143:49-50 F 6 '89

MAYA COOKING *See* Cooking, Maya
MAYAS
Antiquities
See also
Caracol site (Belize)
Chichén Itzá (Mexico)
Copán (Ancient city)
La Ruta Maya
Nakbe (Ancient city)
Classic Maya fight to their finish [evidence of warfare at two Guatemala sites] B. Bower. *Science News* 136:365 D 2 '89
How Maya culture withstood colonial force [Tipu and Lamanai sites; research by Elizabeth Graham] B. Bower. *Science News* 136:373 D 9 '89
Late Maya culture gets an island lift [Marco Gonzalez site excavations by Elizabeth Graham and David M. Pendergast] B. Bower. *Science News* 136:20 Jl 8 '89
On the fringes of conquest: Maya-Spanish contact in colonial Belize [Tipu and Lamanai sites] E. Graham and others. bibl f il map *Science* 246:1254-9 D 8 '89
Walking on ancestral gods [Mayan ruins damaged by modern Mayas in Yucatan] T. Padgett. il *Newsweek* 114:83 O 9 '89
Tombs
Copán: a royal Maya tomb discovered. R. A. Fasquelle and W. L. Fash. il map *National Geographic* 176:480-7 O '89
Writing
Maya writing. D. Stuart and S. D. Houston. bibl il *Scientific American* 261:82-9 Ag '89
MAYBANK, VANESSA TURNER- *See* Turner-Maybank, Vanessa
MAYBECK, BERNARD RALPH, 1862-1957
about
The 1909 Leon K. Roos house in San Francisco. S. B. Woodbridge. il *Architectural Digest* 46:162+ My '89
MAYER, ARIE, AND OTHERS
Degradation of proteins with acetylated amino termini by the ubiquitin system. bibl f il *Science* 244:1480-3 Je 23 '89
MAYER, ARNO J.
about
The Holocaust: why the Jews? T. Jacoby. il por *Newsweek* 113:64-5 My 15 '89
Perversions of the Holocaust. L. S. Dawidowicz. *Commentary* 88:56-60 O '89
MAYER, ECKEHARD
about
Der goldene Topf [opera] Reviews
Opera News il 54:59 S '89. J. H. Sutcliffe
MAYER, HENRY, 1941-
Abe, honestly and otherwise. *The New York Times Book Review* 94:24 F 12 '89
MAYER, IRA
The coming of audio/video phone-based promotions. il *Publishers Weekly* 235:73-4 Mr 3 '89
MAYER, JEFFREY
about
For the tidy sum of $250 an hour, Jeffrey Mayer does top-drawer desk cleaning. il por *People Weekly* 32:49 Jl 31 '89
MAYER, JULES F.
about
The cross fire over Jack Ruby's gun. il por *U.S. News & World Report* 107:10 D 25 '89-Ja 1 '90
Jack Ruby's family and lawyer battle for possession of the gun that killed Lee Harvey Oswald. W. Plummer. il por *People Weekly* 31:42-3 My 22 '89
MAYER, MARTIN, 1928-
Art and taxes. il *Opera News* 53:14-17 Ap 15 '89
A capital enterprise. il pors *Opera News* 54:24-9+ N '89
Credit unions: a primer. il *Modern Maturity* 32:84-6+ D '89/Ja '90
MAYER, RALEIGH
Defensive moves. il *Health (New York, N.Y.)* 21:90-1 S '89
MAYER, RALPH, 1895-1979
Technical page. *American Artist* 53:26+ F '89
Technical page. *American Artist* 53:22+ Mr '89
MAYER, ROBERT E.
New Heico chemicals. il *Petersen's Photographic Magazine* 17:46-7 Ja '89
MAYER, SUSAN E., AND JENCKS, CHRISTOPHER
Growing up in poor neighborhoods: how much does it matter? bibl f *Science* 243:1441-5 Mr 17 '89
MAYER-KRESS, G. (GOTTFRIED), 1954-
about
Nonlinear thinking. J. Horgan. *Scientific American* 260:26+ Je '89
MAYER-KRESS, GOTTFRIED *See* Mayer-Kress, G. (Gottfried), 1954-
MAYHALL, JANE
My uncle's canary [poem] *The American Scholar* 58:18 Wint '89
MAYHEW, DAVID R., AND RUSSETT, BRUCE
How the Democrats can win in '92. *The New Leader* 72:13 Ja 9 '89

MAYLE, PETER
Expensive habits. See alternate issues of Gentlemen's Quarterly
MAYNARD, CHRIS
about
Under the hood. *The New Yorker* 65:26-7 Ag 14 '89
MAYNARD, FREDELLE BRUSER
The age of independence [with editorial comment by Ann Pleshette Murphy] il *Parents* 64:6, 122-5+ Ap '89
Can you praise a child too much? il *Parents* 64:93-6 S '89
MAYNARD, JOYCE, 1953-
Books. See issues of Mademoiselle beginning January 1985
MAYNARD-REID, PEDRITO U.
Called to share. il *Christianity Today* 33:37-9 My 12 '89
MAYNES, CHARLES WILLIAM
Coping with the '90s. bibl f *Foreign Policy* 74:42-62 Spr '89
MAYO, BARRY
about
Broadcast news. L. Gite. il pors *Black Enterprise* 20:100-3+ D '89
MAYONNAISE
Quick mayonnaises. il *Gourmet* 49:234 My '89
MAYOR, FEDERICO
The World Decade for Cultural Development. il *The Courier (Unesco)* 41:4-7 N '88
about
Federico Mayor [interview] il pors *The Unesco Courier* 42:4-9 N '89
The more things change . . . D. Kinnane-Roelofsma. il *National Review* 41:17-19 My 19 '89
MAYOR ZARAGOZA, FEDERICO *See* Mayor, Federico
MAYORGA, LUIS S., AND OTHERS
Regulatory role for GTP-binding proteins in endocytosis. bibl f il *Science* 244:1475-7 Je 23 '89
MAYORS
See also
Black mayors
Women mayors
What can a mayor do to save a city? D. Baer. il *U.S. News & World Report* 106:22-3 My 15 '89
MAYRON, MELANIE
about
Around thirtysomething: Melanie Mayron's got muscle—just ask Peter Horton. L. Farr. il pors *TV Guide* 37:12-14 Jl 15-21 '89
Melanie Mayron: success and the single girl. C. Jakobson. por *Mademoiselle* 95:78 My '89
MAYS, CHRIS
about
Dinosaurs in 3-D. J. Schwartz. il por *Newsweek* 114:51 O 2 '89
MAYS, KIMBERLY
about
Every parent's nightmare: a hospital nursery swap throws two Florida families into disarray. M. Green. il pors *People Weekly* 32:77-8+ D 11 '89
Whose little girl is Kimberly? M. Jacobbi. il pors *Good Housekeeping* 208:122-3+ Mr '89
MAYS, ROBERT W.
about
Every parent's nightmare: a hospital nursery swap throws two Florida families into disarray. M. Green. il pors *People Weekly* 32:77-8+ D 11 '89
Whose little girl is Kimberly? M. Jacobbi. il pors *Good Housekeeping* 208:122-3+ Mr '89
MAYS, WILLIE, 1931-
about
Willie Mays called shots as Giants centerfielder. *Jet* 76:47 Ap 10 '89
MAYTAG CORPORATION
Can Maytag clean up around the world? [acquisition of Chicago Pacific Corp.] B. Bremner. il *Business Week* p86-7 Ja 30 '89
Damned if you do . . . K. Hannon. il por *Forbes* 143:201 Mr 20 '89
Maytag may be back in the takeover cycle. G. G. Marcial. il *Business Week* p78 Ag 28 '89
Maytag's foreign fling isn't much fun after all [Hoover acquisition sours] B. Bremner. *Business Week* p32-3 S 4 '89
Wake up, Maytag man! J. Harris. il *Forbes* 144:308+ N 13 '89
MAYWEATHER, ROGER
about
Stop meeting like this. P. Putnam. il pors *Sports Illustrated* 70:75 My 22 '89
MAZDA (AUTOMOBILE) *See* Automobiles, Foreign; Sports cars
MAZDA MOTOR CORPORATION
Constant improvement? Or speedup? [emphasis on kaizen concept fosters union discontent at Michigan plant] J. Flint. il *Forbes* 143:92+ Ap 17 '89
Designer genes [Miata designer M. Jordan] M. Beauchamp. il por *Forbes* 144:248 O 2 '89
Help wanted, room to advance—out the door [American managers quit at Mazda's U.S. plant] W. Zellner. il *Business Week* p42 O 30 '89

MAZDA MOTOR CORPORATION—*cont.*
Mazda rolls out a poor man's Maserati [Miata] L. Armstrong. il *Business Week* p66 Je 26 '89
Romancing the roadster [Mazda Miata] S. C. Gwynne. il *Time* 134:39 Jl 24 '89

MAZES *See* Labyrinths

MAZIE, DAVID M.
Hit-and-run: a family's nightmare. il *Reader's Digest* 135:152-7 D '89

MAZIQUE (EDWARD C.) PARENT-CHILD CENTER (WASHINGTON, D.C.) *See* Edward C. Mazique Parent-Child Center (Washington, D.C.)

MAZLISH, ELAINE
(jt. auth) *See* Faber, Adele, and Mazlish, Elaine

MAZOWIECKI, TADEUSZ
about
Dawn in Poland. D. Singer. il *The Nation* 249:265 S 18 '89
An epochal shift. M. Johnson. il por *Time* 134:16-18 Ag 28 '89
Freedom's turn [cover story; special section] il pors *Newsweek* 114:16-23+ Ag 28 '89
'The government must have credibility' [interview] S. Smith and M. R. Meyer. *Newsweek* 114:46 O 9 '89
An offer you can't refuse. *America* 161:99 Ag 26-S 2 '89
"People are impatient" [interview] por *Time* 134:35 S 11 '89
Solidarity in power. J. Bugajski. *The New Republic* 201:12-14 S 11 '89
Solidarity makes a choice [cover story] D. Warszawski. il *The New Leader* 72:3-4 S 4 '89
Solidarity's glorious game. *National Review* 41:12-13 S 15 '89
Solidarity—the road to power. D. Singer. il *The Nation* 249:376-80 O 9 '89
'The transition to normalcy' [interview] S. Kauffmann. *World Press Review* 36:15-17 O '89
Walesa's revolution [cover story; special section; with editorial comment by Kevin Doyle] il pors *Maclean's* 102:2, 24-30 Ag 28 '89

MAZUR, MICHAEL, 1935-
about
Michael Mazur at Macalester College Galleries. C. Waddington. il *Art in America* 77:170-1 F '89

MAZURA, FRANZ
about
What's in a gnome? G. Downer. il pors *Opera News* 53:34-5 Ap 1 '89

MAZURSKY, PAUL
about
Enemies, a love story [film] Reviews
American Film il 15:30-7 N '89. B. Yagoda
New York 22:103-4 D 18 '89. D. Denby
The New Yorker 65:73-4 D 25 '89. P. Kael
Newsweek il 114:69 D 18 '89. D. Ansen
Moon over Parador [film] Reviews
Video il 13:59 Ap '89. J. Walker

MAZZAPICA, DOUG
Hometown photo essay. il *Petersen's Photographic Magazine* 18:34-7 S '89
October brides. il *Petersen's Photographic Magazine* 18:46-7 O '89
So, you want to be a news photographer? il *Petersen's Photographic Magazine* 17:60-2+ F '89
Super strobo basketball: bringing light to the pros who shoot the NBA. il *Petersen's Photographic Magazine* 18:20-3+ Je '89

MAZZIOTTI, RICHARD
Fog bound. il *Flying* 116:100 Ja '89

MAZZOCCO, ROBERT
1815 [poem] *The New Yorker* 65:28 Jl 24 '89
Aubade [poem] *The New Yorker* 65:44 Ap 3 '89
Loneliness in the city [poem] *The New Yorker* 65:56 My 15 '89
Rimbaud [poem] *The New Yorker* 65:46 O 2 '89

MBAS (MASTERS OF BUSINESS ADMINISTRATION) *See* Business schools—Graduates

MBB *See* Messerschmitt-Bölkow-Blohm GmbH

MCA INC.
Are MCA and Disney ready to co-star? G. G. Marcial. il *Business Week* p97 Je 26 '89
Co-starring soon: MCA and Cineplex? G. G. Marcial. *Business Week* p87 Ja 16 '89
Every trick in the books [Cineplex Odeon's accounting techniques] D. Wechsler. il por *Forbes* 143:46+ My 29 '89
MCA suspends video head for allegedly funneling funds to Mafia [E. F. Giaquinto] P. Sweeting. *Publishers Weekly* 235:27 Ja 13 '89
Showdown at Cineplex [G. Drabinsky battles to regain control] J. DeMont. il por *Maclean's* 102:46-7 My 8 '89

MCAFEE, JOHN
about
If your computer catches a virus on Friday the 13th, who you gonna call? John McAfee. il por *People Weekly* 32:77 O 16 '89

MCAFEE, LARRY
about
Death wish. *Time* 134:67 S 18 '89

Last rights. M. G. Maudlin. *Christianity Today* 33:15 N 3 '89

MCAFEE, ROBERT E.
To be a physician [address, March 4, 1989] *Vital Speeches of the Day* 55:697-700 S 1 '89

MCALEER, NEIL, 1942-
Getting creative: birth of a notion. il *Omni (New York, N.Y.)* 11:112-19 Ap '89
On creativity [cover story] il *Omni (New York, N.Y.)* 11:42-4+ Ap '89

MCALLASTER, ELVA, 1922-
Listening, under protest [poem] *Wilderness* 52:72 Spr '89

MCALLISTER, BRUCE, 1946-
Little boy blue [story] il *Omni (New York, N.Y.)* 11:100-8 Je '89

MCALLISTER, EUGENE J.
Aviation's role in shaping today's world [address, June 20, 1989] *Department of State Bulletin* 89:33-5 O '89

MCALPINE, KEN
The jitter bug. il *Runner's World* 24:24 S '89

MCALPINE (ALISTAIR) (FIRM) *See* Alistair McAlpine (Firm)

MCALPINE OF WEST GREEN, ROBERT ALISTAIR MCALPINE, BARON, 1942-
about
The New Curiosity Shop. P. Kinmonth. il por *House & Garden* 161:78+ Mr '89

MCANALLY, GENE
I was homeless. il *The Humanist* 49:12 My/Je '89

MCANDREW, ANNETTE
The Japanese iris. il *Flower and Garden* 33:22+ Jl/Ag '89

MCARTHUR, BENJAMIN
The war of the Great books. il *American Heritage* 40:57-8+ F '89

MCARTHUR, CHERYL
about
Cheryl McArthur: discount outlets for mall mavens. P. Y. Hong. il por *Business Week* p117 N 6 '89

MCARTHUR/GLEN GROUP
Cheryl McArthur: discount outlets for mall mavens. P. Y. Hong. il por *Business Week* p117 N 6 '89

MCAT *See* Medical College Admissions Test

MCAULIFFE, JACK
about
The collecting life [interview] il pors *Antiques & Collecting Hobbies* 94:54-6+ Ag '89

MCAULIFFE, KATHLEEN
Moral propaganda. *Omni (New York, N.Y.)* 12:41 O '89

MCAULIFFE, RUTHIE
about
The collecting life [interview] il pors *Antiques & Collecting Hobbies* 94:54-6+ Ag '89

MCAVINNEY, PAUL
about
Computers you control with a wave of your hand. M. Schroeder. il por *Business Week* p142+ F 20 '89

MCBEE, GARY
about
Pushing his luck—and his blood pressure—an aged bank robber is caught red-handed. il por *People Weekly* 31:108 Ap 17 '89

MCBIRNEY, EDWIN, III
about
The bust of '89 [cover story] T. Moore. il por *U.S. News & World Report* 106:36-43 Ja 23 '89

MCBRIDE, BOB, AND MCBRIDE, BUNNY
Greetings from Cleveland Ohio. il *Travel Holiday* 172:52-6 Ag '89

MCBRIDE, BRENT A.
Educators can promote involvement of fathers. *The Education Digest* 55:43-5 N '89

MCBRIDE, BUNNY
Acadia National Park puts its best seasons forward. il map *Travel Holiday* 171:48-55 F '89
(jt. auth) *See* McBride, Bob, and McBride, Bunny

MCBRIDE, CHRISTIAN
about
All-Philadelphia Jazz. R. Woessner. il por *Down Beat* 56:24-5 O '89

MCBRIDE, DAVID
about
Missionaries to Nepal, Colombia find freedom. K. H. Sidey. il pors *Christianity Today* 33:47+ Ap 7 '89

MCBRIDE, GAIL
Liz Taylor's aching back and yours! il por *Ladies' Home Journal* 106:80+ Je '89

MCBRIDE, JIM
about
Great balls of fire [film] Reviews
American Film il 14:26-33+ Je '89. R. Palmer
Maclean's il 102:46-7 Jl 10 '89. B. D. Johnson
The New Leader 72:21 Ag 7-21 '89. J. Morrone
Newsweek il 114:72 Jl 10 '89. D. Ansen
People Weekly 32:12+ Jl 17 '89. R. Novak
Rolling Stone il p118-21+ Jl 13-27 '89. S. Pond
Rolling Stone p33 Ag 10 '89
Time il 134:67 Jl 10 '89. R. Schickel
Video il 13:16-17 D '89. I. Robbins

MCBRIDE, JIM—about—Great balls of fire—*cont.*
Vogue il 179:182-5 Jl '89. N. Tosches
MCBRIDE, PATRICIA
about
Heroines. T. Tobias. il *New York* 22:59-60 Je 26 '89
MCBRIDE, STEWART
Paris by night. il *Travel Holiday* 172:60-9 Jl '89
The ultimate fast lane. il *Travel Holiday* 171:72-6 Mr '89
MCCABE, JOE
The evil men do—and why they do it. il *Mademoiselle* 95:186-7+ N '89
MCCABE, KATIE
A partnership of the heart. il por *Reader's Digest* 135:91-6 O '89
Song of Eastern High. il *Reader's Digest* 135:51-6 S '89
MCCABE, PATRICK P.
(jt. auth) See Margolis, Howard, and McCabe, Patrick P.
MCCAFFERTY, NELL
Daughters of Derry. il *Ms.* 18:72-7 S '89
MCCAFFERTY, TAYLOR
Mama was right [story] il *Redbook* 173:48+ O '89
MCCAIG, DONALD
Rural firemen. il *Country Journal* 16:79-83 Mr/Ap '89
MCCAIN, WARREN E.
about
Food for thought. M. Beauchamp. il por *Forbes* 143:73 Ap 17 '89
MCCALL, BRUCE
Wings ahoy! il *The New Yorker* 65:30-3 My 1 '89
MCCALLA, GARY E.
Life at Southern living. See issues of Southern Living
MCCALL'S (PERIODICAL)
From our editor. E. Sloan-Bubrick. See issues of McCall's beginning March 1986 through December 1989
Reader of the Year [C. Andersen] il *McCall's* 117:57-63+ O '89
MCCALLUM, JACK, 1949-
An American in Paris. il pors *Sports Illustrated* 70 Special Issue:89-93 F '89
And the winner is . . . il pors *Sports Illustrated* 70:34-6 Mr 6 '89
Ask me again, next year. por *Sports Illustrated* 70:130 Ja 9 '89
The Bad Boys get better. il *Sports Illustrated* 70:29-31 Je 5 '89
The best of both worlds. il pors *Sports Illustrated* 70 Special Issue:149-51 F '89
Failure most foul. il *Sports Illustrated* 70:96-8+ Mr 20 '89
The final agenda. il *Sports Illustrated* 70:30-2+ Je 12 '89
He's the Spur of the moment. il por *Sports Illustrated* 71:72-3 N 13 '89
Horns of a dilemma. il pors *Sports Illustrated* 70:34-7 Mr 13 '89
Hub of emotion [cover story] il pors *Sports Illustrated* 71:42-4+ D 11 '89
Is anybody happy here? il por *Sports Illustrated* 70:22-4+ Ja 16 '89
Joy ride. il *Sports Illustrated* 71:53-4+ Jl 17 '89
Life on a small but fast track. il pors *Sports Illustrated* 71:58+ Ag 14 '89
Many happy returns. il *Sports Illustrated* 71:110-16+ N 6 '89
Mission impossible [cover story] il pors *Sports Illustrated* 71:44-8+ N 6 '89
A new face, but the same old Magic. il *Sports Illustrated* 70:16-21 My 22 '89
A perfect fit. il pors *Sports Illustrated* 71:52-4+ D 18 '89
The power of the press [cover story] il por *Sports Illustrated* 70:22-6 F 13 '89
A raft of fun. il pors *Sports Illustrated* 71:4, 34-7 Jl 10 '89
A real Bulls market. il *Sports Illustrated* 70:20-1 My 29 '89
School of hard knocks. il *Sports Illustrated* 71:85 Ag 28 '89
Sonic boon. il pors *Sports Illustrated* 71:78+ N 27 '89
Splash! il *Sports Illustrated* 71:42-5 Ag 7 '89
Take us out to the ball game. il *Sports Illustrated* 71:32-4+ Jl 24 '89
They had one whale of a time. il *Sports Illustrated* 71:94+ Ag 21 '89
To h—— with the H——! por *Sports Illustrated* 71:102 D 4 '89
'Un-fath-om-able' [cover story] il pors *Sports Illustrated* 70:26-8+ My 15 '89
An unhappy ending [cover story] il pors *Sports Illustrated* 70:30-4 Ja 23 '89
A vacation from a vacation. il *Sports Illustrated* 71:32-4+ Jl 31 '89
Who's Most Valuable? il *Sports Illustrated* 70:42-4+ Ap 17 '89
about
From the publisher. D. J. Barr. il por *Sports Illustrated* 71:4 Jl 10 '89

MCCALLUM, JASON
about
Fighting for her own life, Jill Ireland now must mourn the loss of her son Jason. J. Park. il pors *People Weekly* 32:59+ N 27 '89
Shattered for the second time. B. Kantrowitz. pors *Newsweek* 113:66 My 8 '89
MCCALLUM, NAPOLEON
about
The comeback chronicles. H. Hersch. il pors *Sports Illustrated* 71:38-44+ Jl 24 '89
MCCAMANT, KATHRYN, 1959-, AND DURRETT, CHARLES, 1955-
Good housekeeping: cohousing can reincorporate community into the American dream [excerpt from Cohousing] il *Utne Reader* p68-72 My/Je '89
MCCANDLESS, ALFRED A.
Should the "balanced budget constitutional amendment" be adopted? [excerpts from statement, November 17, 1987] *Congressional Digest* 68:270+ N '89
MCCANDLESS, HOLLOWAY
How sexual ghosts can haunt your—and his—love life. il *Glamour* 87:138-9+ Ja '89
MCCARRAN-WALTER ACT
McMurtry and others decry continuing use of McCarran Act. H. Fields. *Publishers Weekly* 235:15 My 26 '89
Non-alien speech [decision striking down alien deportation provisions] D. Cole. *The Nation* 248:220-1 F 20 '89
MCCARRY, CHARLES
Two revolutions. il *National Geographic* 176:50-5 Jl '89
MCCARTHER TWINS See Siamese twins
MCCARTHY, ABIGAIL
Challenges facing U.S. Catholics. *Commonweal* 116:618-19 N 17 '89
Of several minds. See alternate issues of Commonweal
MCCARTHY, GLENN HERBERT, 1907-1988
about
Self-made and self-unmade. S. G. Sheehy. il pors *Forbes* 144 Special Issue:72-3 O 23 '89
MCCARTHY, JOSEPH L.
A home of their own. il *McCall's* 117:66+ D '89
MCCARTHY, LAURA FLYNN
The mind-body connection. il *Working Woman* 14:145-8 Ap '89
Rules of attraction: why you're hot—or not. il *Mademoiselle* 95:125-6 F '89
Swimsuit anxiety. il *Health (New York, N.Y.)* 21:43+ My '89
MCCARTHY, MARY, 1912-1989
A memory of James Baldwin. il *The New York Review of Books* 36:48-9 Ap 27 '89
about
Obituary
National Review 41:14-15 N 24 '89
Newsweek il por 114:91 N 6 '89. C. McGuigan
People Weekly il pors 32:75-6 N 13 '89. J. Wadler
Time il por 134:87 N 6 '89. M. Duffy
U.S. News & World Report il por 107:16 N 6 '89
MCCARTHY, PAUL
The Idea Bank. il *Omni (New York, N.Y.)* 11:24 S '89
UFO update. il *Omni (New York, N.Y.)* 11:89 Je '89
UFO update. il *Omni (New York, N.Y.)* 12:89 N '89
MCCARTHY, STEPHEN
about
Oregon original. F. J. Prial. il *The New York Times Magazine* p56 F 5 '89
MCCARTHY, STEVE
about
British boxer's mom takes bout into her own hands. il por *Jet* 77:52-3 O 16 '89
MCCARTHY, TODD
Speed of light. il *Film Comment* 25:32-4+ S/O '89
MCCARTHY, WILLIAM J.
about
The feds drive a wedge into the Teamsters. A. Bernstein. il *Business Week* p90 F 6 '89
MCCARTHYISM See Anti-Communist movements—History
MCCARTNEY, BOB
about
Greening the South. D. Young. il pors *Southern Living* 24:125-6+ Je '89
MCCARTNEY, PAUL
about
Can Paul McCartney get back? [cover story] J. Henke. il pors *Rolling Stone* p40-4+ Je 15 '89
Getting back on track. B. Barol. il por *Newsweek* 113:67 Mr 13 '89
Paul gets back. N. Jennings. il pors *Maclean's* 102:68-70 O 2 '89
Yesterday and today. A. Sweeting. il por *Rolling Stone* p22 N 16 '89
MCCARTY, HENRY See Billy, the Kid
MCCARVER, TIM
Presenting . . . Tim McCarver's all-star screwball team. il *TV Guide* 37:21-2 Jl 8-14 '89

MCCAW, CRAIG

about

The cellular bidding war will get even hotter. R. D. Hof. il *Business Week* p39-40 Je 19 '89

Craig McCaw goes establishment. J. J. Keller. il por *Business Week* p40-1 F 6 '89

For Craig McCaw, it's do-or-die time. C. Hawkins and R. D. Hof. il *Business Week* p34 D 4 '89

Will McCaw be ensnared by the net of his dreams? R. D. Hof. map *Business Week* p43-4 D 18 '89

Winning is only the first step. F. Meeks. il pors map *Forbes* 144:80-3 D 25 '89

MCCAW CELLULAR COMMUNICATIONS INC.

The cellular bidding war will get even hotter [McCaw's offer for LIN] R. D. Hof. il *Business Week* p39-40 Je 19 '89

Craig McCaw goes establishment [selling British Telecom a stake] J. J. Keller. il por *Business Week* p40-1 F 6 '89

For Craig McCaw, it's do-or-die time [battle for LIN Broadcasting] C. Hawkins and R. D. Hof. il *Business Week* p34 D 4 '89

This cellular hookup could jam the competition [LIN and BellSouth's merger] J. J. Keller. il *Business Week* p45 S 25 '89

Will McCaw be ensnared by the net of his dreams? [LIN acquisition] R. D. Hof. map *Business Week* p43-4 D 18 '89

Winning is only the first step [control of LIN Broadcasting] F. Meeks. il pors map *Forbes* 144:80-3 D 25 '89

MCCGWIRE, MICHAEL K., 1924-

About face: how the Soviets stopped planning for world war. il *Technology Review* 92:32-6+ N/D '89

MCCLANE, A. J. (ALBERT JULES), 1922-

Pass the buck. il *Esquire* 112:50+ D '89

Run, rabbit. il *Esquire* 111:40 F '89

Sea pig on rye, please. il *Esquire* 111:39-40 Je '89

A sworded affair. il *Esquire* 111:50+ Ap '89

MCCLANE, ALBERT JULES See McClane, A. J. (Albert Jules), 1922-

MCCLATCHY, J. D., 1945-

Heads [poem] *The New Yorker* 64:30 Ja 30 '89

Indispensable. il por *Opera News* 53:16-18 F 18 '89

Medea in Tokyo [poem] *The New Republic* 200:40 Ja 9-16 '89

Night piece [poem] *The New Yorker* 65:56 N 13 '89

Spenser's tower [poem] *The Nation* 248:601 My 1 '89

Weeds [poem] *The New Republic* 201:34 O 2 '89

MCCLAURIN, IRMA

Caribbean interlude (Joseph House, St. Croix) [poem] *Essence* 19:114 Ap '89

Harriet Tubman [poem] *Essence* 19:117 Mr '89

Love poem #6 [poem] *Essence* 19:130 Mr '89

MCCLEARY, KATHLEEN

Performance plus? il *Health (New York, N.Y.)* 21:88-9 Mr '89

MCCLELLAN, GARY

New radios, new problems, new solutions (I). il *Radio-Electronics* 60:57-60 Jl '89

New radios, new problems, new solutions (II). il *Radio-Electronics* 60:60-3 Ag '89

MCCLELLAN, LAWRENCE, JR.

Curtis Fuller's solo on "Blues after all"—a trombone transcription. il *Down Beat* 56:56 Jl '89

MCCLELLAN, MARY C.

New ways of thinking about testing [interview with G. Madaus] por *Phi Delta Kappan* 70:642-5 Ap '89

MCCLINTOCK, MIKE

A useful family space. il pors *Country Journal* 16:40-6 F '89

MCCLINTON, KATHARINE MORRISON

American Eastlake furniture. il *Antiques & Collecting Hobbies* 94:28-30+ My '89

MCCLOSKEY, LIZ LEIBOLD

Hearing and healing Hedda Nussbaum. *The Christian Century* 106:178-9 F 15 '89

MCCLOSKEY, MICHAEL J.

A green Blueprint for Bush. il *Sierra* 74:36-8 Ja/F '89

MCCLOUD, MAC

Jun Kaneko/Brendan Walter Gallery. il *American Craft* 49:80-1 Ag/S '89

MCCLOY, JOHN JAY, 1895-1989

about

Obituary

Foreign Affairs 68:1-2 Spr '89. W. G. Hyland

The Nation 248:437 Ap 3 '89. M. Holland

MCCLOY, KRISTIN

The wrong man. il *Gentlemen's Quarterly* 59:171-2+ My '89

about

In contemplation of sex, death and bikers, Kristin McCloy writes a racy first novel, Velocity. S. Dougherty. il pors *People Weekly* 31:107+ F 13 '89

MCCLOY, MARJORIE

Gîte d'étape. *Bicycling* 30:158-9 My '89

Rockin' in San Francisco. il *Bicycling* 30:80-1 O/N '89

Taming Seattle's Tiger. il *Bicycling* 30:84 O/N '89

MCCLURE, BRUCE A., AND GUILFOYLE, TOM

Rapid redistribution of auxin-regulated RNAs during gravitropism. bibl f il *Science* 243:91-3 Ja 6 '89

MCCLURE, JESSICA

about

To the rescue. R. MacInnis. il pors *Runner's World* 24:36-8 Ag '89

MCCLURG, EDIE

about

A $13,000 job—or $75 a week as an actress? E. Warren. il por *TV Guide* 37:9 Ag 19-25 '89

MCCOLL, BILL

about

The second time around. R. Fimrite. il pors *Sports Illustrated* 70:110-14+ Ja 9 '89

MCCOLL, HUGH L., JR.

about

Getting big fast. J. Huey. il por *Fortune* 119:63 Ja 2 '89

Hugh McColl. D. Foust. il por *Business Week* Special Issue:148 Ap 14 '89

Why Hugh McColl is courting an Atlanta belle. D. Foust and S. Ticer. il por *Business Week* p19-20 Ap 17 '89

MCCOLLAM, JAMES G.

Antique or junque. See issues of Antiques & Collecting Hobbies beginning October 1988

MCCOLLISTER, BETTY

The eggs. por *The Humanist* 49:39 N/D '89

MCCOLLISTER, JOHN

Doc Severinsen's musical medicine. il por *The Saturday Evening Post* 261:64-5+ N/D '89

Phyllis Diller's about-face. il pors *The Saturday Evening Post* 261:30-2 Ap '89

Spring training for writers. *The Writer* 102:7-8 Ap '89

What's cooking in Hollywood? il *The Saturday Evening Post* 261:18+ My/Je '89

The Yiddish Will Rogers. il por *The Saturday Evening Post* 261:44-5 Mr '89

MCCOLLUM, SHAUNE

about

Teenager in trouble: 'I lied. I stole. I cheated'. il pors *Ebony* 44:120+ Ag '89

MCCOMB, GORDON

Universal laser power supply [cover story] il *Radio-Electronics* 60:33-7 Mr '89

MCCONAGHY, TOM

Media literacy mandated in Ontario English curriculum. *Phi Delta Kappan* 71:332-3 D '89

A provincial vision of Canadian education. il *Phi Delta Kappan* 70:648-9 Ap '89

The quiet revolution: school-based budgeting. il *Phi Delta Kappan* 70:486-7 F '89

Teacher education in Ontario: a case for tuning the whole instrument. bibl f il *Phi Delta Kappan* 70:830-1 Je '89

MCCONAHAY, MARY JO, AND KIRK, ROBIN

Over there. il *Mother Jones* 14:36-9+ F/Mr '89

MCCONNELL, ALICIA

about

The short good-bye. C. Shmerler. *Women's Sports & Fitness* 11:56 Jl/Ag '89

MCCONNELL, BOB

(jt. auth) See Nichol, Liz, and McConnell, Bob

MCCONNELL, JEAN

A week in the country [story] il *Good Housekeeping* 208:107-11 Je '89

MCCONNELL, MALCOLM

Crack invades the countryside. il *Reader's Digest* 134:73-8 F '89

(jt. auth) See Aldrin, Buzz, and McConnell, Malcolm

MCCONNELL, MICHAEL

Why 'separation' is not the key to church-state relations [cover story; with reply by D. M. Kelley] il *The Christian Century* 106:43-52 Ja 18 '89

MCCONNELL, MITCH

Should the Congress adopt the "High Risk Occupational Disease Notification and Prevention Act of 1987"? [excerpts from address, March 29, 1988] *Congressional Digest* 68:125+ Ap '89

MCCONNELL, SUSAN K., AND OTHERS

Subplate neurons pioneer the first axon pathway from the cerebral cortex. bibl f il *Science* 245:978-82 S 1 '89

MCCONNICO, HILTON

about

McConnico unlimited. P. S. Green. il por *House & Garden* 161:32+ Jl '89

MCCOO, MARY H., D. 1989

about

Obituary

Jet il por 77:16 O 23 '89

MCCORD, RICHARD

Rachel remembers. *Reader's Digest* 135:170-2 D '89

MCCORD, ROBERT

about

Helping Congress look ahead [interview] T. Willard and D. M. Fields. il pors *The Futurist* 23:23-7 My/Je '89

MCCORD, SUSAN
about
Susan McCord's quilts: a farmwife's legacy at Henry Ford Museum. il *Antiques & Collecting Hobbies* 94:37-8 Ap '89
Through her quilts, one women's life unfolds. il *Americana* 17:26 N/D '89
MCCORKINDALE, DAN
Our own garden. See issues of Flower and Garden beginning January/February 1989
MCCORMACK, RICHARD T.
Competitiveness in the global marketplace [address, May 11, 1989] *Department of State Bulletin* 89:49-53 Jl '89
MCCORMICK, DICK
The importance of Hispanics to our nation [address, February 16, 1989] *Vital Speeches of the Day* 55:464-7 My 15 '89
MCCORMICK, JOHN R.
Out of the blue. il *American Heritage* 40:49-51 D '89
MCCORVEY, NORMA
about
Attacking the real 'Jane Roe'. S. Waldman. il por *Newsweek* 113:22 Ap 17 '89
Save my law. G. H. Colt. il pors *Life* 12:111-12+ My '89
The woman behind Roe v. Wade. M. Green. il pors *People Weekly* 31:36-41 My 22 '89
MCCOSH, DAN
Automotive newsfront. See issues of Popular Science beginning January 1986
MCCOURTIE, CHERYL
Where I enter. por *Essence* 19:83-4+ Ap '89
MCCOY, ANN, 1946-
about
Ann McCoy at ACA Contemporary. B. Adams. il *Art in America* 77:144-5 Ja '89
MCCOY, DORIS LEE
Golf's Good Samaritan. il por *The Saturday Evening Post* 261:52-3 Mr '89
MCCOY, FRANK
Ready for the world. il *Black Enterprise* 19:162-4+ Je '89
Toward a more perfect union. il *Black Enterprise* 20:86-8+ O '89
MCCOY, JOHN A.
Liberation theology and the Peruvian Church [cover story] *America* 160:526-30 Je 3 '89
The Peruvian Church and liberation theology [discussion of June 3, 1989 article, Liberation theology and the Peruvian Church] *America* 161:84-5+ Ag 12-19 '89
MCCOY, JOHN BONNET
about
How Banc One moved to the front of the line. S. Phillips. il por *Business Week* p76 Jl 3 '89
MCCOY, KATHLEEN, 1945-
Is your child flirting with sex? il *Reader's Digest* 135:111-14 S '89
Sex and your body. See issues of Seventeen beginning June 1983 through January 1990
MCCOY, KATHY *See* McCoy, Kathleen, 1945-
MCCOY, MICHAEL
Out of the ashes. il *Bicycling* 30:100+ Jl '89
MCCRADY, DONNER T.
about
Outdoor medicine. H. Middleton. il *Southern Living* 24:26+ Ag '89
MCCRADY, KENNETH A.
about
Limited options. K. Wandycz. il por *Forbes* 144:166 N 27 '89
MCCRAW, DAVID
A funny thing happened on the way to the legislature. I lost. *The Washington Monthly* 21:30-2+ Jl/Ag '89
MCCREADIE, MARSHA, 1943-
Big bad Apple. il *Film Comment* 25:3+ Mr/Ap '89
MCCREDIE, SCOTT
They're still slimy, but naked snails are finding new friends. bibl (p171) il *Smithsonian* 19:134-41 F '89
MCCRUM, LINDSAY
about
Different strokes: a touch of splash. S. Nelson. il pors *Harper's Bazaar* 122:124-7+ F '89
MCCULLAGH, JAMES C., 1941-
Inside. See issues of Bicycling
A mother's crusade [cover story] il pors *Organic Gardening* 36:32-7 Ap '89
MCCULLERS, CARSON, 1917-1967
about
The member of the wedding [drama] Reviews
The Nation 248:825 Je 12 '89. M. Hodgson
New York il 22:100 Ap 10 '89. J. Simon
The New Yorker 65:114 Ap 10 '89. E. Oliver
MCCULLOCH, ALBERT DONALD, JR.
about
Living off the fat of the land. M. Schifrin. il por *Forbes* 144:186-7+ N 13 '89
MCCULLOCH, DANIEL
about
Dolphins: your most willing and joyous subjects ever! F. Cameron. il por *Petersen's Photographic Magazine* 18:32-4 O '89

MCCULLOUGH, COLLEEN, 1937-
about
Sparks fly as Colleen McCullough leaves Harper for Hearst. G. Feldman. *Publishers Weekly* 236:40 Jl 21 '89
MCCULLOUGH, JULIE
about
Growing pains's Julie McCullough tries to bury her bare-all past. J. Kaufman. il pors *People Weekly* 32:57+ O 30 '89
MCCULLY, MARTHA
A summer place. il *Gentlemen's Quarterly* 59:143-4+ Je '89
MCCUNE, J. M. *See* McCune, Mike
MCCUNE, KATE
The Odyssey Book Shop: a long voyage home. il *Publishers Weekly* 235:63-5 Mr 3 '89
MCCUNE, MIKE
about
The human mouse. G. Montgomery. il por *Discover* 10:4, 48-55 Ag '89
MCCURDY, HAROLD
An ancient glass medallion [poem] *America* 160:33 Ja 21 '89
The fountain [poem] *The Christian Century* 106:414 Ap 19 '89
Gethsemane [poem] *The Christian Century* 106:317 Mr 22-29 '89
MCCURDY, HOWARD E.
Piece by piece. il *Ad Astra* 1:24-8 F '89
MCCUTCHEN, NORMA
Oklahoma Land Rush. il *Americana* 17:32-5 Mr/Ap '89
MCCUTCHEON, ROBERT A.
Stalin's purge of Soviet astronomers. il *Sky and Telescope* 78:352-7 O '89
MCDANIEL, NEIL G.
Arms and the man. il *Oceans* 22:38-45 Mr/Ap '89
MCDANIEL, THOMAS R.
Demilitarizing public education: school reform in the era of George Bush. bibl f il *Phi Delta Kappan* 71:15-18 S '89
MCDERMOTT, DAVID
about
Old light in a new world. C. Black. il pors *House & Garden* 161:176-81+ N '89
MCDERMOTT, JAMES
"Just ten more minutes . . .". il *Reader's Digest* 134:89-94 My '89
MCDERMOTT, JEANNE
A biologist whose heresy redraws earth's tree of life. bibl (p135) il pors *Smithsonian* 20:72-6+ Ag '89
MCDERMOTT, JOHN V.
A grammarian's dilemma [poem] *America* 160:349 Ap 15 '89
MCDERMOTT, ROBERT F., 1920-
about
You're in the office of the future now. B. Brophy. il por *U.S. News & World Report* 106:50-2 Ap 17 '89
MCDERMOTT (EUGENE) CONCERT HALL (DALLAS, TEX.) *See* Eugene McDermott Concert Hall (Dallas, Tex.)
MCDONALD, AMY
Current affairs. il por *Omni (New York, N.Y.)* 11:66-71 S '89
MCDONALD, ANN GILBERT
Brass student lamps and night lamps. bibl il *Antiques & Collecting Hobbies* 93:20-3 Ja '89
MCDONALD, BEN
about
Time for Big Ben. H. Hersch. il pors *Sports Illustrated* 70:54+ My 29 '89
MCDONALD, BOB
about
Comedian Bob McDonald gets jail term for scam. il pors *Jet* 77:25 D 25 '89-Ja 1 '90
MCDONALD, JOE, 1941-
Woodstock remembered: the artists. il pors *Rolling Stone* p87 Ag 24 '89
MCDONALD, JOSEPH P.
When outsiders try to change schools from the inside. bibl f il *Phi Delta Kappan* 71:206-12 N '89
MCDONALD, KENT L.
(jt. auth) See McIntosh, J. Richard, and McDonald, Kent L.
MCDONALD, MARY-REA
about
Hints from Eloise. G. Sikes. il por *Harper's Bazaar* 122:66 N '89
MCDONALD, PATTI ANN
(jt. auth) See McDonald, Steven, and McDonald, Patti Ann
MCDONALD, RANDAL B.
about
Randal McDonald. il por *Business Week* Special Issue:160 Ap 14 '89
MCDONALD, STEVEN, AND MCDONALD, PATTI ANN
To serve and protect [condensed from The Steven McDonald story]; ed. by E. J. Kahn. il pors *Reader's Digest* 135:201-4+ O '89
MCDONALD, TOM
Who speaks for the child? *Children Today* 18:11+ My/Je '89

MCDONALD, WALTER
Digging in a footlocker [poem] *The New York Review of Books* 36:19 O 12 '89
Feeding the winter cattle [poem] *America* 161:454 D 16 '89
Hawks in a bitter blizzard [poem] *The Atlantic* 264:82 S '89

MCDONALD OBSERVATORY
Director of McDonald Observatory honored [H. J. Smith] il por *Astronomy* 17:12 Ja '89

MCDONALD'S CORP.
The burger wars were just a warmup for McDonald's. B. Bremner. il *Business Week* p67+ My 8 '89
Crunch time [vendor Quality Croutons] L. Gite. il pors *Black Enterprise* 20:74-6+ S '89
Inside the Golden Arches. M. Mabry. il *Newsweek* 114:46-7 D 18 '89
A Mac attack on plastic wrapping [restaurants to recycle food containers] il *U.S. News & World Report* 107:15 N 6 '89
McDonald's stoops to conquer [discounts and new menus] B. Bremner. il *Business Week* p120+ O 30 '89
Two Big Macs, large fries—and a pepperoni pizza, please. B. Bremner. il *Business Week* p33 Ag 7 '89
You deserve a pizza today? J. Schwartz. il *Newsweek* 114:46 S 11 '89

MCDONALD'S RESTAURANTS OF CANADA LTD.
Unpopular packaging [Canadians protest chlorofluorocarbons] M. Nichols. *Maclean's* 102:51 D 25 '89

MCDONNELL, ANNA
Wild pitches. il *American Film* 15:44-5+ D '89

MCDONNELL, CLAUDIA
How working mothers fit God in their schedule. il *U.S. Catholic* 54:28-33 N '89

MCDONNELL, KILIAN
Eucharistic exposition: an obsolete relic? [cover story] il *America* 160:166-9 F 25 '89

MCDONNELL DOUGLAS CORP.
Airframe makers exploit boom by adding production capacity. il *Aviation Week & Space Technology* 130:95+ My 29 '89
Bumpy flight at McDonnell Douglas. R. Henkoff. il *Fortune* 120:79-80 Ag 28 '89
Commercial airframe makers take conservative approach. R. G. O'Lone. il *Aviation Week & Space Technology* 130:197-9 Mr 20 '89
Douglas asks NTSB to reopen probe of Northwest MD-82 crash [charging that pilots disconnected warning system that could have prevented August 1987 crash in Detroit] C. Fotos. *Aviation Week & Space Technology* 130:106 My 1 '89
Douglas grapples with delays in three transport programs. B. A. Smith. il *Aviation Week & Space Technology* 130:88-9 Ap 10 '89
Douglas launches MD90 transport with Delta order. B. A. Smith. il *Aviation Week & Space Technology* 131:34-5 N 20 '89
Douglas management revamped to focus on transport programs. B. A. Smith. *Aviation Week & Space Technology* 130:29 F 20 '89
Douglas may offer three MD-90 versions with V2500 powerplants. C. A. Shifrin. il *Aviation Week & Space Technology* 131:56-7 Jl 3 '89
Douglas prepares initial MD-11 for first flight. il *Aviation Week & Space Technology* 131:19 O 23 '89
Douglas prepares to flight test PW-Allison propfan powerplant. il *Aviation Week & Space Technology* 130:35 Ja 2 '89
Douglas receiving strong customer interest in MD90-30 version of proposed new twinjet. B. A. Smith. il *Aviation Week & Space Technology* 131:85 O 16 '89
Douglas transport losses ease; reorganization issues persist. B. A. Smith. il *Aviation Week & Space Technology* 131:16-19 O 30 '89
McDonnell Douglas: an order boom, but an operating loss. J. E. Ellis. il *Business Week* p34-5 My 8 '89
McDonnell Douglas, Navy prepare SLAM missile for airborne launch [stand-off land attack missile] S. W. Kandebo. il *Aviation Week & Space Technology* 130:31 F 27 '89
McDonnell restructures mission planning efforts to gain greater market share. il *Aviation Week & Space Technology* 130:293-4 Je 12 '89
MD-82 transport assembly accelerates at Shanghai. il *Aviation Week & Space Technology* 131:68-9 D 11 '89
MD90, 737 transport orders set stage for Delta's increased share of U.S. market. il *Aviation Week & Space Technology* 131:35+ N 20 '89
Midway triples MD-80 order; Douglas predicts more delays. *Aviation Week & Space Technology* 130:34 Ap 3 '89
Multibillion-dollar MD-11 order [American Airlines; special section] il *Aviation Week & Space Technology* 130:16-21 F 13 '89
NASA, McDonnell Douglas test helmet-mounted landing system. E. H. Phillips. il *Aviation Week & Space Technology* 130:126-7 Je 19 '89
Navy, McDonnell Douglas agree on modifications to T-45A trainer. *Aviation Week & Space Technology* 131:21 S 25 '89
Officials fear reorganization could threaten Douglas' sales [with editorial comment] B. A. Smith. il *Aviation Week & Space Technology* 130:7, 16-18 My 15 '89
Shanghai will deliver No. 13 MD-82 ahead of schedule. il *Aviation Week & Space Technology* 131:61-2 D 11 '89
Shutoff valve to isolate DC-10 tail hydraulics. *Aviation Week & Space Technology* 131:32 S 25 '89
Team correcting deficiencies in Navy's T-45A trainer aircraft. E. H. Phillips. il *Aviation Week & Space Technology* 131:46-8 O 30 '89
U.S. reenters commercial launch arena with private Delta mission [launch of British television relay spacecraft Marcopolo] E. H. Kolcum. il *Aviation Week & Space Technology* 131:24-5 S 4 '89
USAF controllers, F-15 pilots train for combat using multiship simulation. S. W. Kandebo. il *Aviation Week & Space Technology* 130:71+ Mr 27 '89
USAF, McDonnell Douglas prepare to deploy F-15E for winter testing. W. B. Scott. il *Aviation Week & Space Technology* 130:79+ Ja 2 '89

MCDONNELL DOUGLAS CORP. MCDONNELL DOUGLAS INFORMATION SYSTEMS CO.
British Telecom is getting less British all the time [buying electronic data communications operations] M. Maremont. il *Business Week* p62 Ag 14 '89

MCDONNELL DOUGLAS HELICOPTER COMPANY
Langley, McDonnell Douglas study methods of reducing rotor noise. E. H. Phillips. il *Aviation Week & Space Technology* 131:75-6 Jl 17 '89
McDonnell Douglas/Bell team introduces its LHX concept [special section] il *Aviation Week & Space Technology* 129:56-9+ Mr 6 '89
McDonnell Douglas launches MDX helicopter production. C. A. Shifrin. il *Aviation Week & Space Technology* 130:16-18 Ja 23 '89
Notar reduces pilot workload, improves response in OH-6A [no-tail rotor] N. C. Kernstock. il *Aviation Week & Space Technology* 130:44-5+ F 13 '89

MCDONOUGH, DAVID
What took me so long. il *Glamour* 87:282-3+ S '89

MCDONOUGH, YONA ZELDIS
Christina's world. il pors *Harper's Bazaar* 122:160-1+ N '89

MCDOUGALL, BARBARA
about
A cool, steady hand. M. Clark. il por *Maclean's* 102:20 Jl 10 '89

MCDOWALL, RODDY, 1928-
Double exposure [excerpts] il *Good Housekeeping* 209:162-7 N '89
about
Liz toasts Roddy McDowall's photo book, and the old pals make quite a picture. il pors *People Weekly* 32:91-2+ N 6 '89

MCDOWELL, BART
Cartagena nights. il maps *National Geographic* 175:494-509 Ap '89

MCDOWELL, DAVID
The achievements of New Zealand's new Department of Conservation. il *Environment* 31:42-3 Ap '89

MCDOWELL, MELODY M.
Banking on new territory. il por *Black Enterprise* 19:256-8+ Je '89
Cutting deals at conventions. il *Black Enterprise* 20:114-16+ O '89

MCELROY, MICHAEL, 1939-, AND SALAWITCH, ROSS J.
Changing composition of the global stratosphere. bibl f il *Science* 243:763-70 F 10 '89

MCENROE, JOHN
about
As he sees fit [cover story] N. Amdur. il pors *World Tennis* 37:34-6 Jl '89
Call it the Loving Cup. F. Lidz. il pors *Sports Illustrated* 70:76 Ap 17 '89
Mac's last stand. J. Feinstein. il pors *World Tennis* 37:58-60+ S '89
McEnroe: coming around again. S. Flink. il por *World Tennis* 36:20+ My '89
A new Mac attack. C. Kirkpatrick. il pors *Sports Illustrated* 70:20-1 Mr 13 '89

MCENTIRE, REBA
about
Reba McEntire to fans: 'Relax, I'm not popping out of country'. T. Allis. il pors *People Weekly* 32:135-6 S 18 '89

MCEWEN, BROOKS
about
Two inventive mothers hit the tot charts with Baby songs. L. Lague. il pors *People Weekly* 31:95-6 Ja 16 '89

MCEWEN, CURRIER
about
Love in blooms. E. Tozer. il por *Modern Maturity* 32:56-60 O/N '89

MCEWEN, JOHN, 1942-
Sir William Keswick's sculptural landscape in Scotland. il por *Architectural Digest* 46:324+ O '89

MCEWEN, MARK
about
This morning's weatherman: dependably breezy. J. Marion. il por *TV Guide* 37:36 S 30-O 6 '89

MCFADDEN, MARY
about
She's 51, her fourth husband is 22—but designer Mary McFadden simply couldn't care less. D. Hutchings. il pors *People Weekly* 32:53-4+ O 23 '89

MCFALL, GARDNER
Moves [poem] *The Nation* 248:707 My 22 '89

MCFARLAND, DENNIS
The music room [story] *The New Yorker* 65:26-38+ Jl 31 '89
Nothing to ask for [story] *The New Yorker* 65:55-62 S 25 '89

MCFARLAND, K. C., AND OTHERS
Lutropin-choriogonadotropin receptor: an unusual member of the G protein-coupled receptor family. bibl f il *Science* 245:494-9 Ag 4 '89

MCFARLAND, STUART
about
Epic task. J. Novack. il por *Forbes* 143:142+ F 6 '89

MCFARLAND, THOMAS, 1926-
about
Arms and the man: a sex scandal rocks Princeton. D. Rabinowitz. il pors *New York* 22:30-6 Jl 17 '89

MCFARLANE, ROBERT C.
about
Bud McFarlane: semper fi. B. Brower. il pors *The New York Times Magazine* p26-8 Ja 22 '89

MCFATE, PATRICIA BLISS
(jt. auth) See Graybeal, Sidney N., and McFate, Patricia Bliss

MCFERRIN, BOBBY
about
McFerrin, Chapman take top Grammy Award honors. il pors *Jet* 75:54-5 Mr 13 '89
Put on a happy face . . . or else. B. Barol. il por *Newsweek* 113:74-5 F 27 '89

MCGARVEY, ROBERT
Easy does it. il *Travel Holiday* 172:28-31 O '89
Head coaches. il *Sport (New York, N.Y.)* 80:92-4 F '89
Sports gambling '90s style. il *Sport (New York, N.Y.)* 80:57-9 Ap '89

MCGAUGHEY, CLAUDE R., 1951-
about
Tops at the track. W. Nack. il pors *Sports Illustrated* 70:38-41+ F 6 '89

MCGAVRAN, DONALD ANDERSON, 1897-
Beyond the maintenance mentality. il *Christianity Today* 33:28-9 F 3 '89

MCGEE, CELIA
Cosmopolitan mise-en-scéne. il *Architectural Digest* 46:186-91 Ap '89
A Florida composition. il *Architectural Digest* 46:144-9 Jl '89
Genial flair on Long Island Sound. il *Architectural Digest* 46:180-5 D '89
Maestro at the Met. il por *House & Garden* 161:50+ S '89

MCGHEE, JULIA ANNE
about
Academics and athletics: 'What price victory?'. P. A. Zirkel. il *Phi Delta Kappan* 70:564-5 Mr '89

MCGILLIGAN, PATRICK
Corey-ography [interview with J. Corey] il pors *Film Comment* 25:38-9+ N/D '89

MCGINNIS, SID
about
The World's Most Dangerous sidemen. il pors *Down Beat* 56:18 O '89

MCGINNISS, JOE
Blind faith [excerpt] il pors *Ladies' Home Journal* 106:62+ Ap '89
about
Are journalists basically liars? F. Bruning. il *Maclean's* 102:11 Ap 24 '89
Holier than thou. J. Taylor. il pors *New York* 22:32-7 Mr 27 '89
The journalist and the murderer (I). J. Malcolm. *The New Yorker* 65:38-42+ Mr 13 '89
The journalist and the murderer (II). J. Malcolm. *The New Yorker* 65:49-50+ Mr 20 '89
McGinniss: a travesty of libel. M. Garbus. *Publishers Weekly* 235:69 Ap 21 '89
A reporter isn't a friend. J. Alter and G. Cowley. il por *Newsweek* 113:62 Mr 27 '89
The talk of the town. *The Nation* 248:469 Ap 10 '89

MCGINTY, BRIAN
Steinbeck country. il *American History Illustrated* 24:18+ S/O '89

MCGOFF, ROBIN
Time in the curriculum: the dilemma for arts education, K-6. *Design for Arts in Education* 90:44-6 N/D '88

MCGOUGH, MICHAEL
Equal rites. *The New Republic* 201:11-12 Ag 28 '89

The Lefebvrite-feminist coalition? il *The American Spectator* 22:28-9 Ag '89

MCGOUGH, PETER
about
Old light in a new world. C. Black. il pors *House & Garden* 161:176-81+ N '89

MCGOURTY, BRIAN M.
Shaping a new industrial Canada [address, September 11, 1989] *Vital Speeches of the Day* 56:104-8 D 1 '89

MCGOURTY, FREDERICK
Chi-chi plants. il *Flower and Garden* 33:80 My/Je '89
Easing into spring. il *Flower and Garden* 33:120 Mr/Ap '89
Gardener-at-large. il *Flower and Garden* 33:64 S/O '89
Keys to a classic perennial garden [excerpt from The perennial gardener] il *Country Journal* 16:32-8 S/O '89
Oh, the buzzing of the words. il *Flower and Garden* 33:64 N/D '89
Swoe is me! il *Flower and Garden* 33:64 Jl/Ag '89
Thoughts for the new year. il *Flower and Garden* 33:112 Ja/F '89

MCGOVERN, ARTHUR F.
Liberation theology adapts & endures [excerpt from Liberation theology and its critics] il *Commonweal* 116:587-90 N 3 '89

MCGOVERN, DENNIS
Trusting herself. il pors *Opera News* 53:16+ Ja 7 '89

MCGOVERN, JOE
about
When theater meets big business. S. P. Herman. il pors *Home Office Computing* 7:56-7 Mr '89

MCGOVERN, MARGARET
about
When theater meets big business. S. P. Herman. il pors *Home Office Computing* 7:56-7 Mr '89

MCGOWAN, JO
In India, they abort females. por *Newsweek* 113:12 Ja 30 '89

MCGOWAN, WILLIAM
My half year of living dangerously. il *Gentlemen's Quarterly* 59:152-7+ Ja '89

MCGRATH, DEANN
about
Art of the spiel. J. McLaughlin. il por *Harper's Bazaar* 122:54 N '89

MCGRATH, DOUGLAS
Exhaust-op and the p.-rind flap. il por *The Nation* 249:456-8 O 23 '89

MCGRATH, ELLIE
When it's time to change careers. il *New Choices for the Best Years* 29:45-9 S '89

MCGRATH, JOSEPH
about
The magic Christian [film] Reviews *Video* il 13:74 My '89. I. Robbins

MCGRATH, THOMAS, 1916-
Afternoon of a McGrath [poem] *The Nation* 249:535-6 N 6 '89
Mediterranean [poem] *The Nation* 249:536 N 6 '89
Up the dark valley [poem] *The Nation* 249:535 N 6 '89
about
The Lenore Marshall/Nation Poetry Prize—1989. A. Clampitt. *The Nation* 249:534-5 N 6 '89

MCGRATH, TOM
Forty hours. il *U.S. Catholic* 54:20-7 N '89

MCGRAW, ALICE
The 'Catwoman' case. B. Wickens. il *Maclean's* 102:39 Jl 31 '89
The 'Catwoman' of Atlanta. por *Newsweek* 113:29 My 8 '89

MCGRAW-HILL, INC.
Harper & Row acquires TDM from McGraw-Hill for Caedmon. P. Sweeting. *Publishers Weekly* 235:16 Je 9 '89
McGraw-Hill and Wiley quit Iran Fair but decry book boycotts. C. Reid. *Publishers Weekly* 235:104 My 12 '89
McGraw-Hill shuts down general books unit. *Publishers Weekly* 236:15 D 22 '89
A revolutionary new system customizes textbooks. J. P. Frank. il *Publishers Weekly* 236:63-4 N 3 '89

MCGREW, HERB
Provence: a walk in the sun. il map *Gourmet* 49:96-8+ My '89

MCGRIFF, FRED
about
Hit it a mile. R. Wiley. il pors *Sports Illustrated* 70:34-6+ My 8 '89

MCGROTHA, ROSEMARY
about
American in Paris. N. Frey. il pors *Harper's Bazaar* 122:106-9 Jl '89

MCGUANE, THOMAS, 1939-
about
He's left no stone unturned. G. D. Garcia. il por *Time* 134:70-2 D 25 '89

MCGUANE, THOMAS, 1939— *about—cont.*
His carousing days behind him, author Tom McGuane is at home—and at peace—on the range. J. Diamond. il pors *People Weekly* 32:57-8+ S 25 '89
In plains English. K. Black. il por *Harper's Bazaar* 122:88+ O '89
In pursuit of crazy language [interview] J. Klinger. il por *American Film* 14:42-5+ Ap '89
PW interviews. M. Harris. por *Publishers Weekly* 236:50+ S 29 '89

MCGUIGAN, CATHLEEN
Melanie Griffith: Working girl makes good. il pors *Ladies' Home Journal* 106:106+ Ap '89

MCGUIRE, ELINOR
about
On Stinson Beach: Pacific spaces for John and Elinor McGuire. J. Chatfield-Taylor. il pors *Architectural Digest* 46:206-13 My '89

MCGUIRE, JOHN
about
On Stinson Beach: Pacific spaces for John and Elinor McGuire. J. Chatfield-Taylor. il pors *Architectural Digest* 46:206-13 My '89

MCGUIRE, MEREDITH B.
Healing rituals hit the suburbs [cover story] il *Psychology Today* 23:57-64 Ja/F '89

MCGUIRE, RICHARD
Agriculture and animal rights [address, July 27, 1989] *Vital Speeches of the Day* 55:766-8 O 1 '89
Biotechnology and agriculture [address, November 3, 1989] *Vital Speeches of the Day* 56:147-50 D 15 '89

MCGUIRE, RICK
A classy joint. il *Women's Sports & Fitness* 11:52-5 O '89
Mixing it up—the cross-training alternative. il *Women's Sports & Fitness* 11:26-8+ Jl/Ag '89

MCGURN, WILLIAM
Advance Australia fair. *National Review* 41:45 S 15 '89
A banana republic Baedeker. il *The American Spectator* 22:16-18 Mr '89
The brave new world of Suzie Wong. il *Esquire* 111:45 Je '89
Cool Hand Lucas. *National Review* 41:21-2 Je 2 '89
Cutting the cord in Honduras. il *National Review* 41:22-3 S 29 '89
The Dodd Doctrine. il *National Review* 41:27-8 S 15 '89
Drug czar in search of a throne [cover story] il por *National Review* 41:22-4 Je 16 '89
Exit stage Wright. *National Review* 41:23 Je 30 '89
Guess who's (not) coming to dinner. il *National Review* 41:18-19 S 1 '89
High noon for Newt [cover story] il pors *National Review* 41:21-3 Ag 18 '89
Hong Kong. il *Esquire* 112:229+ S '89
Hong Kong gone. *National Review* 41:22-3 Ap 21 '89
Losing well is the best revenge. *National Review* 41:16 D 8 '89
Mr. Wright's wrongs. *National Review* 41:16 My 19 '89
No room at the inn. *National Review* 41:26 Je 30 '89
That memo. por *National Review* 41:22-3 N 10 '89
Washington shows Solidarity. *National Review* 41:24-5 O 27 '89
What the people really say. il *National Review* 41:26-9 D 22 '89
(jt. auth) See Mandel, Susan T., and McGurn, William

MCHENRY, STEPHEN P.
The 'education president' meets with Catholic educators. *America* 161:52-3 Jl 29-Ag 5 '89

MCHENRY, SUSAN, AND SMALL, LINDA LEE
Does part-time pay off? il *Ms.* 17:88-94 Mr '89

MCHONE, JOHN F., AND OTHERS
Stishovite at the Cretaceous-Tertiary boundary, Raton, New Mexico. bibl f il *Science* 243:1182-4 Mr 3 '89

MCHUGH, MARY
Festive days, festive nights! [cover story] il map *Travel Holiday* 172:36-47 D '89

MCHUGH-ROLLINS ASSOCIATES, INC.
Masters of realism. M. Sommers. il *Theatre Crafts* 23:16+ F '89

MCI COMMUNICATIONS CORP.
MCI's new problem: 'how to spend all this cash'. T. Smart. il *Business Week* p94 Ag 21 '89
Smooth operator. C. Gorman. il *Time* 134:60-1 S 18 '89

MCILHENNY CO.
Salt and pepper flavor this island [Avery Island, home of Tabasco sauce maker] il map *Southern Living* 24:34-5 Mr '89

MCILVAINE, BILL
Things to come: the 1939 New York World's Fair. il *American History Illustrated* 24:32-47 Summ '89

MCINERNEY, JAY
Raymond Carver: a still, small voice. il por *The New York Times Book Review* 94:1+ Ag 6 '89
The writers of wrong: a novelist carves the critics [cover story] il por *Esquire* 112:104-8+ Jl '89
about
Bright light in the big city. C. K. Gandee. il pors *House & Garden* 161:190-5 O '89

Anecdotes, facetiae, satire, etc.
The Calphalon candidate. D. Blum. por *New York* 22:31 Ap 24 '89

MCINERNEY, JOSEPH D.
University scientists as precollege science curriculum developers [discussion of September 1988 article, The role of universities in developing precollege science curricula] bibl f *BioScience* 39:102-3 F '89

MCINTIRE, SAMUEL, 1757-1811
about
Restoring the restored. K. Korieth. il por map *Americana* 17:44-9 S/O '89

MCINTOSH, J. RICHARD, AND KOONCE, MICHAEL P.
Mitosis. bibl f il *Science* 246:622-8 N 3 '89

MCINTOSH, J. RICHARD, AND MCDONALD, KENT L.
The mitotic spindle. bibl il *Scientific American* 261:48-56 O '89

MCINTOSH, NASH
Incident at Ossabaw. il *Reader's Digest* 135:112-14 N '89

MCINTYRE, JUDITH
The common loon cries for help [cover story] il map *National Geographic* 175:510-24 Ap '89

MCINTYRE, ROBERT S.
Tax Americana. *The New Republic* 200:18-20 Mr 27 '89
Tax deform. *The New Republic* 201:18-21 Ag 21 '89

MCKANNA, JAMES A., AND COHEN, STANLEY, 1922-
The EGF receptor kinase substrate p35 in the floor plate of the embryonic rat CNS. bibl f il *Science* 243:1477-9 Mr 17 '89

MCKEAN, MICHAEL
about
The big picture. E. Drucker. il por *American Film* 14:59 S '89

MCKEEVER, JAMES
about
Risk rewarded? M. Hulbert. il por *Forbes* 143:149 F 20 '89
An ungraceful retreat. M. Hulbert. il *Forbes* 144:320 D 11 '89

MCKEEVER STRATEGY LETTER (NEWSLETTER)
Risk rewarded? M. Hulbert. il por *Forbes* 143:149 F 20 '89
An ungraceful retreat. M. Hulbert. il *Forbes* 144:320 D 11 '89

MCKENNA, FRANK
about
Under the gun [with interview] il por *Maclean's* 102:10-13 F 27 '89

MCKENNA, GEORGE
about
Education: the movie [cover story] D. L. Kirp. il pors *Mother Jones* 14:36-45 Ja '89

MCKENNA, HORACE
about
The legacy of Horace McKenna. J. Dear. il *America* 160:170-2 F 25 '89

MCKENNA, KRISTINE
Tough, passionate, persuasive. il por *American Film* 14:32-7 S '89

MCKENNA (HORACE) CENTER *See* Horace McKenna Center

MCKENZIE, ALECIA
Cooking up profits in Europe. por *Black Enterprise* 20:79-80 N '89

MCKENZIE, DAN P.
(jt. auth) See White, Robert S., and McKenzie, Dan P.

MCKENZIE, MARY BETH
Resolving a painting [excerpt from A painterly approach] il *American Artist* 53:64-9 Ja '89

MCKENZIE, RICHARD B.
The decline of America: myth or fate? *Society* 27:41-8 N/D '89
How big is the displaced worker problem? *Society* 26:43-8 Mr/Ap '89
Kickbacks in university textbook adoptions. *BioScience* 39:326-7 My '89

MCKEON, JACK
about
Beers with . . . Jack McKeon [interview] S. Delsohn. il pors *Sport (New York, N.Y.)* 80:19+ Jl '89

MCKEON, NANCY, 1967-
about
I'm doing this movie to keep Buck Thurman from getting out of jail. S. Littwin. por *TV Guide* 37:24-6 S 30-O 6 '89

MCKEON, NANCY
Capital ideas. il *House & Garden* 161:180+ Ap '89
Middleburg manor. il *House & Garden* 161:144-53 Ap '89
On Audubon Place. il *House & Garden* 161:94-7+ Ja '89

MCKEOWN, BILL
Boating. See issues of Outdoor Life beginning May 1983

MCKEOWN, PAM
Esophageal pain: another price of success. il *Nation's Business* 77:89 N '89

MCKERROW, AMANDA
about
Amanda McKerrow takes stage: the real thing. O. Stuart. il pors *Dance Magazine* 63:40-3 Ap '89

MCKESSON CORP.
McKesson dumps another asset: the boss [T. W. Field] R. D. Hof. il pors *Business Week* p47 S 25 '89

MCKIBBEN, BILL
The end of nature. *The New Yorker* 65:47-8+ S 11 '89
Hero of the wilderness. il por *The New York Review of Books* 36:20+ N 9 '89
New believers. il *Mother Jones* 14:38-41+ Ap '89
about
Amid nature's glory, a writer urgently warns of its passing [interview] S. K. Reed. il pors *People Weekly* 32:55-6+ O 16 '89
Endgames. L. H. Lapham. *Harper's* 279:10-13 N '89
Hi there, Bambi. R. Bailey. il *Forbes* 144:46+ O 16 '89
To be or not to be? (environmentally speaking) in fall title from Random. C. Goodrich. por *Publishers Weekly* 236:23 Ag 25 '89
Washington diarist: the end of everything. T. Noah. *The New Republic* 201:54 O 16 '89

MCKINLEY, MOUNT (ALASKA) *See* Mount McKinley (Alaska)

MCKINNA, J. S.
Working underwater. il *Sea Frontiers* 35:348-55 N/D '89

MCKINNEY, CARYN
about
Innerviews [interview] il por *Women's Sports & Fitness* 11:57 N/D '89

MCKINNEY, KEVIN
Desert son. il *Omni (New York, N.Y.)* 12:16+ N '89

MCKINNEY, TAMARA
about
A flight so fancy. W. O. Johnson. il pors *Sports Illustrated* 70:14-21 F 13 '89

MCKINNEY, WILLIAM, 1946-
Revisioning the future of oldline Protestantism. *The Christian Century* 106:1014-16 N 8 '89

MCKINNEY AVENUE (DALLAS, TEX.)
McKinney Avenue: great street in the heart of Dallas. L. Thomas. il map *Southern Living* 24:62-7 O '89

MCKINNISS, RICK
Our flag is not sacred. por *Christianity Today* 33:8 S 8 '89

MCKNIGHT, ROBERT B.
about
Hey, dude, check out these boardshorts. L. Armstrong. il por *Business Week* p96 My 22 '89

MCKOWN, DELOS BANNING
Demythologizing natural human rights. por *The Humanist* 49:21-4+ My/Je '89

MCLAIN, DENNY, 1944-
about
The road may not be ready, but Denny McLain and Leon Spinks are getting their acts together. M. Green. il pors *People Weekly* 31:130-1 F 13 '89

MCLAREN, MALCOLM
about
Radical cheek. M. Boodro. il por *Art News* 88:114-17 Ja '89

MCLAUGHLIN, AUDREY
about
Challenge seeker. E. K. Fulton. il por *Maclean's* 102:18+ D 4 '89
The new face of the NDP. il pors *Maclean's* 102:2, 20-4+ D 11 '89
A race without stars. C. Wood. il por *Maclean's* 102:16-17 Je 5 '89

MCLAUGHLIN, JOHN
From Washington straight. See issues of National Review

MCLAUGHLIN, JOHN
Feats with pleats. il *Harper's Bazaar* 122:128+ O '89

MCLAUGHLIN, JUDITH, AND RIESMAN, DAVID, 1909-
The shady side of sunshine. il *Change* 21:44-57 Ja/F '89

MCLAUGHLIN, WILLIAM I.
Voyager's decade of wonder. il *Sky and Telescope* 78:16-20 Jl '89

MCLEAN, ODILE
Will we have a space age? il *Ad Astra* 1:48 O '89

MCLEAN (VA.)
Education
I went back to high school . . . and it was hell! [29 year old returns to Langley High School] J. Moses. il *Mademoiselle* 95:202-3+ My '89
Social history
Where I grew up: Blair Brown [interview] L. Konner. il pors *Glamour* 87:172 Mr '89

MCLEAN INDUSTRIES INC.
ESOP fable. T. Pouschine. il *Forbes* 143:98+ Je 26 '89

MCLEMORE, LAMONTE
about
A singer and his camera. il por *Ebony* 45:92-4+ N '89

MCLEOD, CATHERINE STYLES- *See* Styles-McLeod, Catherine

MCLIN, CLARENCE JOSEF, 1921-1989
about
Obituary
Jet por 75:17-18 Ja 23 '89

MCLOUGHLIN, MERRILL
Sandra Day O'Connor: woman in the middle. por *Ladies' Home Journal* 106:218-19+ N '89

MCLUHAN, MARSHALL, 1911-1980
about
Marshall McLuhan: 'televisionary' or crackpot? N. Hickey. il por *TV Guide* 37:30-2 Je 10-16 '89

MCMAHON, ED
about
Ed McMahon, late-night TV's favorite foil, decides it's time to wrap up his 13-year marriage. J. Kaufman. il pors *People Weekly* 32:87-8 Ag 14 '89

MCMAHON, EDWARD T., 1947-
Open roads: keeping America's scenic roads free of billboard blight. il *National Parks* 63:14-15 N/D '89

MCMAHON, JIM
about
Jilted Jim's big McLove-in. P. King. il pors *Sports Illustrated* 71:20-1 Ag 28 '89
A lot of McMoney at stake. G. Castle. il *Sport (New York, N.Y.)* 80:13 Ag '89
Photographs and photography
Jim McMahon and the art of the celebrity poster. T. L. Corbell. il por *Petersen's Photographic Magazine* 17:64-5 Mr '89

MCMAHON, VICTORIA
about
Ed McMahon, late-night TV's favorite foil, decides it's time to wrap up his 13-year marriage. J. Kaufman. il pors *People Weekly* 32:87-8 Ag 14 '89

MCMAHON, VINCE, JR.
about
The upstart (slam!) who's reinventing (pow!) the tube (grrr!). J. Hammer. il pors *Gentlemen's Quarterly* 59:280-5+ N '89

MCMANUS, FREDERICK R.
Academic freedom and the Catholic University of America. *America* 160:506-9 My 27 '89

MCMANUS, PATRICK F.
The last laugh. See issues of Outdoor Life
Wet behind the ears. il *Outdoor Life* 183:128+ F '89
about
Inside Pat McManus. M. Finley. il pors *Outdoor Life* 184:74-6+ O '89
PW interviews. W. Brisick. por *Publishers Weekly* 235:42-3 Je 23 '89

MCMANUS, ROBERT J.
Bishops, politicians and abortion [cover story] *America* 161:294-6+ N 4 '89

MCMARTIN FAMILY
about
Making history—of a dubious sort. *U.S. News & World Report* 106:20 My 1 '89

MCMICHAEL, RICHARD B.
How to get the best from your consulting engineers. por *Architectural Record* 177:35 N '89

MCMILLAN, HERMAN
about
N.Y. couple charged with abusing their 9 children. il por *Jet* 76:38 S 11 '89

MCMILLAN, TERRY
Zora and Franklin [fiction] il *Essence* 20:67-8+ Ag '89

MCMILLIN, J. MICHAEL, 1940-
about
The thyroid mystery (II). B. Roueché. il *The Saturday Evening Post* 261:46-9+ Ja/F '89

MCMULLAN, JEAN
Paul Dufour: line and lucidity. il por *American Craft* 49:40-5 Je/Jl '89

MCMULLIN, ERNAN, 1924-
A common quest for understanding. il *America* 160:100-2+ F 11 '89

MCMURRY, THOMAS J., AND OTHERS
Molecular recognition and metal ion template synthesis. bibl f il *Science* 244:938-43 My 26 '89

MCMURTRY, LARRY
about
Court enjoins Dove's distribution of 'Lonesome dove' audio. J. Tangorra. *Publishers Weekly* 236:12 S 22 '89
Dueling 'Doves': acrimony clouds copyright issue. P. Sweeting. il *Publishers Weekly* 235:54-6 Je 2 '89

MCNABB, JANET, AND ROSETH, GENE
Phonlink II (I). il *Radio-Electronics* 60:44-9 F '89
Phonlink II (II). il *Radio-Electronics* 60:46-9 Mr '89

MCNALLY, BRIAN
about
Hotter than hot: why they kill to get into 150 Wooster. G. Greene. il por *New York* 22:44-9 O 30 '89

MCNALLY, PAUL JOSEPH
about
Genetic fingerprints. R. Laver. il *Maclean's* 102:54 Ap 17 '89

MCNALLY, TERRENCE, 1939-
about
The Lisbon Traviata [drama] Reviews
The Nation 249:766 D 18 '89. T. M. Disch
New York il 22:71 Je 19 '89. J. Simon

MCNALLY, TERRENCE, 1939- — about — The Lisbon Traviata—*cont.*
New York 22:130-1 N 13 '89. J. Simon
The New Yorker 65:74-6 Je 19 '89. M. Kramer
Time il 134:120 N 13 '89. W. A. Henry

MCNAMAR, R. T.
New issues for the economic summit [address, May 18-19, 1989] *Vital Speeches of the Day* 56:60-4 N 1 '89

MCNAMARA, JOSEPH D.
A nation of certified killers. il *Harper's* 278:58-9 My '89

MCNAMARA, MARY
Invasion of the couple people: what's a happily single girl to do? il *Mademoiselle* 95:206-7+ S '89

MCNAMARA, ROBERT S., 1916-
The lessons of October. il por *Newsweek* 113:47 F 13 '89

MCNAMARA, WILLIAM
about
William McNamara. G. Sikes. il por *Seventeen* 48:108-9 My '89

MCNAMEE, GREGORY
On reading that William Butler Yeats lies forgotten in a pauper's grave [poem] *America* 161:242 O 14 '89

MCNAMEE, JOHN
Clay vessels [poem] *America* 161:454 D 16 '89

MCNAMEE, LOUISE R.
about
The image of creative control. L. Rosch. il por *Working Woman* 14:132-3 S '89

MCNAMEE, ROGER
about
Technology time? C. Torcellini. il por *Forbes* 144:362+ N 13 '89

MCNAY, DON
about
Chasing the ambulance chasers. L. Spencer. il por *Forbes* 144:352+ N 13 '89

MCNAY FINANCIAL SERVICES
Chasing the ambulance chasers. L. Spencer. il por *Forbes* 144:352+ N 13 '89

MCNEAL, JOSEPH
Audition for tragedy. *Commonweal* 116:228-31 Ap 21 '89

MCNEAL, TOM
The knowing wife [story] il *Redbook* 173:46+ My '89

MCNEALY, SCOTT
about
High noon for Sun [cover story] J. B. Levine. il pors *Business Week* p70-5 Jl 24 '89
Scott McNealy. J. B. Levine. il por *Business Week* Special Issue:100 Ap 14 '89

MCNEELY, JEFFREY A.
Report on reports: World resources 1988-89. bibl f *Environment* 31:25-8 Ap '89

MCNEIL, DEAN
about
Strangers on the line. A. Prud'homme. il por *Art News* 88:26 Summ '89

MCNEIL, DONALD R.
Technology in college: where is its impact? *The Education Digest* 55:58-9 D '89

MCNEIL, FREEMAN
about
Remorse? Not in the NFL. B. Newman. il por *Sports Illustrated* 71:112 O 16 '89

MCNEIL, JEREMY N.
(jt. auth) See Brodeur, Jacques, and McNeil, Jeremy N.
(jt. auth) See Cusson, Michel, and McNeil, Jeremy N.

MCNEIL, R. EDWARD
Blowing in the wind. *Omni (New York, N.Y.)* 11:25 S '89

MCNEIL RIVER STATE GAME SANCTUARY (ALASKA)
It's a good thing McNeil's big bears get plenty to eat [work of L. Aumiller with brown bears] B. Norton. il pors *Smithsonian* 20:56-60+ Ap '89

MCNICHOL, KRISTY
about
'I was crying all the time' [cover story] S. Haller. il pors *People Weekly* 31:88-90+ Ap 3 '89

MCNULTY, FAITH
Children's books for Christmas. il *The New Yorker* 65:134-44 N 27 '89

MCNULTY, HENRY
My Le Corbusier home. il *Gourmet* 49:140+ N '89

MCORP
It's back to square 2 for Texas Commerce [failed bid for MCorp banks] M. Ivey. il por *Business Week* p125-6 Jl 17 '89
KKR tiptoes into Texas [Kohlberg Kravis Roberts pumps capital into MCorp] T. Mason. il *Business Week* p33 Ja 16 '89
Why Robert Abboud wants MCorp in his corral. T. Vogel. il por *Business Week* p31 Ap 10 '89

MCPHEE, JOHN A.
Rinard at Manheim. *The New Yorker* 65:150-2 D 4 '89

MCPHERSON, ALEXANDER
Macromolecular crystals. bibl il *Scientific American* 260:62-9 Mr '89

MCPHERSON, FRANK A., 1933-
about
Playing with the majors. T. Mack. il por *Forbes* 144:92+ N 13 '89

MCQUAID, E. PATRICK
The rising tide of mediocre education coverage. *The Education Digest* 54:7-10 Ap '89
A story at risk: the rising tide of mediocre education coverage. il *Phi Delta Kappan* 70:K1-K8 Ja '89

MCQUAID, KIM
Ireland today: life in the big village. il map *Focus (New York, N.Y.: 1950)* 39:1-4 Spr '89

MCRAE, GREGORY J.
about
Getting a clearer view of smog. M. Schroeder. il por *Business Week* Special Issue:73 Je 16 '89

MCRAE, MIKE
Presenting crazy Alan Root. il pors *International Wildlife* 19:30-5 N/D '89

MCRANEY, GERALD
about
Delta Burke and Gerald McRaney: their first screen kiss turned into real-life love. S. Littwin. il pors *TV Guide* 37:32-5 Ja 14-20 '89
Delta Burke: "The man who taught me to love again" [cover story] V. Scott. pors *Good Housekeeping* 208:76+ F '89
Of hearts, flowers and wedding bliss [cover story] S. Schindehette. il pors *People Weekly* 31:86-7+ Je 12 '89
The ultimate prime-time love story [cover story] G. Esterly. il pors *TV Guide* 37:4-5+ O 7-13 '89

MCSHANE, JOSEPH MICHAEL, 1949-
The Catholic experience at taming pluralism [cover story] il *The Christian Century* 106:443-6 Ap 26 '89
The centennial of Andrew Carnegie's "Gospel of wealth". *America* 161:211-13 O 7 '89

MCSHANN, JAY
about
Alvin Ailey's Opus McShann: City Center Theatre/New York. B. S. Comer. il *Down Beat* 56:47-9 Ap '89

MCSHERRY, MARY
You can't go home again. il *National Review* 41:37-8+ D 22 '89

MCSPORRAN, SEUMAS
about
Aye, laddie, no man is an island, but jack-of-all-trades Seumas McSporran comes close. M. Neill. il pors *People Weekly* 32:84-6 Ag 7 '89

MCSWIGGEN, JAMES A., AND CECH, THOMAS R.
Stereochemistry of RNA cleavage by the Tetrahymena ribozyme and evidence that the chemical step is not rate-limiting. bibl f il *Science* 244:679-83 My 12 '89

MCTERNAN, EDMUND, AND HOLDER, LEE J.
Allied health professionals. il *World Health* p23-4 My '89

MCTIERNAN, JOHN
about
Die hard [film] Reviews
Video il 12:61 Mr '89. L. Kesten

MCTIGUE, GERARD
Bicycling the back roads of China [cover story] il map *Travel Holiday* 171:40-5 My '89

MCVICKER, JIM
about
Nature as teacher: the art of Jim McVicker. E. Feit. il *American Artist* 53:38-43+ D '89

MCVITTIE, GEORGE C., 1904-1988
about
Obituary
Physics Today por 42:128-30+ Mr '89. G. W. Swenson

MCWEY, MICHAEL
Tall, dark & clingy [story] il *'Teen* 33:40-3 Ap '89

MCWHORTER, DIANE
Since Mississippi burned. il *People Weekly* 31:36-43 Ja 9 '89

MCWILLIAMS, WILSON CAREY
A republic of couch potatoes [cover story] il *Commonweal* 116:138-40 Mr 10 '89

MD-11 AIRPLANES *See* Airplanes, Jet

MDMA (DRUG)
The agony of Ecstasy. S. Rae. il *Mademoiselle* 95:158-61+ Je '89
Dangerous new drugs [speed and Ecstasy] M. O'Koon. il *Good Housekeeping* 208:235-6 Ap '89

MEAD, CARVER
about
Mead's Silicon Retina points toward brain-like processing. *Byte* 14:11 F '89

MEAD, CHRIS
(jt. auth) See Emmerling, Mary Ellisor, and Mead, Chris

MEAD, GARY
(jt. auth) See Graham, Robert, and Mead, Gary

MEAD, MARK N., AND OTHERS
The fate of the earth depends on the fate of the trees. il *Utne Reader* p49-57 My/Je '89

MEAD, REBECCA
(jt. auth) See Diamond, Edwin, and Mead, Rebecca

MEAD, WALTER RUSSELL
Environmental Keynesianism. *New Perspectives Quarterly* 6:62-3 Summ '89

MEAD CORPORATION. MEAD IMAGING DIVISION
Bubble film [Cycolor film] J. Free. il *Popular Science* 234:78-9 Ja '89

MEAD DATA CENTRAL, INC.
Mead tries a new-fangled medium: print [acquisition of Michie Co.] M. Mallory. il *Business Week* p81-2 Ap 10 '89

MEADOWOOD (CALIF.: RESORT) *See* Resorts—California

MEADOWS, ANNE
Watch the birdie! il por *Américas* 41 no2:61-3 '89
(jt. auth) *See* Buck, Daniel, and Meadows, Anne

MEADOWS, CHRISTINE
The furniture. bibl f il *Antiques* 135:480-9 F '89

MEALS
See also
Breakfasts
Brunches
Buffet meals
Cooking
Diet
Dinners and dining
Entertaining
Luncheons
Lunches
Menus
Outdoor meals
Snacks
Suppers
Table setting
30-minute menu. *See* issues of Good Housekeeping
50 fast meals. J. T. Hazard. il *Ladies' Home Journal* 106:250-2+ N '89
A cross-country skiing weekend. il *Gourmet* 49:90-6+ F '89
Don't skip family meals [with readers' comments] J. Breig. *U.S. Catholic* 54:13-19 Jl '89
Easy as 1-2-3. *See* issues of Ladies' Home Journal
Easy weekend eating. R. Sax. il *Working Woman* 14:191-4 S '89
Express-lane cook [excerpts from Twenty minute menus] M. Burros. il *Working Woman* 14:146-8 O '89
Fun family food. D. Barton. il *American Health* 8:98+ My '89
Gourmet classics in 20 minutes. M. Burros. il *Ladies' Home Journal* 106:170-2+ S '89
Heat busters. J. Voltz. il *Modern Maturity* 32:62-4+ Je/Jl '89
Hurry-up one-dish dinners. il *McCall's* 116:74-6+ Ja '89
Making mealtime family time. J. Taylor. il *Better Homes and Gardens* 67:178 N '89
Meal makeovers: from greasy to good-for-you. il *Ladies' Home Journal* 106:184-6+ S '89
One-dish dinners for two. il *Southern Living* 24:180 O '89
Perfect meals. J. T. Hazard. il *Ladies' Home Journal* 106:206-8+ My '89
Quick! One-dish meals. il *Southern Living* 24:128-9 Jl '89
Rescuing the family meal. E. Satter. il *American Health* 8:93-8 My '89
Spring ephemerals. R. Haskell. il *Flower and Garden* 33:86-9 Mr/Ap '89
Togetherness that counts [family meals] J. K. Rosemond. il *Better Homes and Gardens* 67:23 O '89
Tray meals. il *Gourmet* 49:70-2+ Mr '89

MEALWORMS
Homegrown bait. B. Volkart. il *Field & Stream* 94:134 My '89

MEANING (PHILOSOPHY)
The fear of insignificance. D. Taylor. il *Christianity Today* 33:25-6 F 3 '89

MEARS, HENRIETTA C. (HENRIETTA CORNELIA), 1890-
about
In the footsteps of a grand vision. por *Christianity Today* 33:20 Mr 3 '89

MEARS, RICK
All-American highways. il por maps *Popular Mechanics* 166:66-8+ My '89
about
Rocket Rick burns up the track. S. Moses. il por *Sports Illustrated* 70:69-70 My 22 '89

MEASLES
. . . and measles, too. il *FDA Consumer* 23:15 Jl/Ag '89
Mumps and measles make a comeback. J. Willis. il *Consumers' Research Magazine* 72:23-6 S '89
Vaccines and vaccination
Measles busters: Chicago's vaccine plan. J. N. Baker. il *Newsweek* 114:22 Ag 21 '89

MEASLES, GERMAN *See* Rubella

MEASURE FOR MEASURE [drama] *See* Shakespeare, William, 1564-1616

MEASUREMENT
See also
Astronomical measurements
Distances—Measurement
Particles (Nuclear physics)—Measurement
Time measurement

MEASURING EQUIPMENT
See also
Gages
Digital peak detector. R. D. Secura. il *Radio-Electronics* 60:59-62 Ap '89

MEASURING WORMS *See* Inchworms

MEAT
See also
Beef
Carving (Meat, etc.)
Cooking—Meat
Pork
Rabbit meat
Grading
Big profits, big losses for lean, clean beef. *Successful Farming* 87:36 S '89
Inspection
See Meat inspection

MEAT, DRIED
Gnaw this [beef jerky made by Leroy and Geneva Rabke] G. Waggoner. *Esquire* 111:28+ Ja '89

MEAT CONTAMINATION
See also
Poultry contamination
The ironies behind beef imports. P. Smith. *Successful Farming* 87:32C Ag '89
The thyroid mystery (II) [J. M. McMillin traces outbreak of hyperthyroidism to contaminated meat] B. Roueché. il *The Saturday Evening Post* 261:46-9+ Ja/F '89

MEAT CUTTING
See also
Game, Dressing of

MEAT EATING ANIMALS *See* Carnivores

MEAT INDUSTRY
See also
Cattle industry
Collective labor agreements—Meat industry
Farmstead Foods (Firm)
Geo. A. Hormel & Co.
John Morrell & Co.
Acquisitions and mergers
Pac-Man packers gobble up the competition. B. Eftink. il *Successful Farming* 87 no4:6-7 Mr '89
International aspects
Head 'em up, move 'em out—to Japan [U.S. beef] S. D. Atchison. il *Business Week* p52 Ag 21 '89
Roundup time for teriyaki beef [Japanese purchase of U.S. beef-producing properties] C. Gorman. il *Time* 133:47 Mr 13 '89
Export-import trade
Beef, pork, and history [German ban on American pork in 1880s over trichinosis concerns] B. A. Weisberger. il *American Heritage* 40:20+ Jl/Ag '89
Bill Eftink [EEC hormone ban on U.S. beef imports] B. Eftink. il *Successful Farming* 87:19 mid-Mr '89
Europe bans boeuf's à l'estradiol. E. Marshall. *Science* 243:161-2 Ja 13 '89
A food fight as big as the Atlantic [EEC threatens ban on U.S. meat] *Newsweek* 113:41 Ja 9 '89
Head 'em up, move 'em out—to Japan [U.S. beef] S. D. Atchison. il *Business Week* p52 Ag 21 '89
The ironies behind beef imports. P. Smith. *Successful Farming* 87:32C Ag '89
Is the beef flap a taste of trade wars to come? [U.S. vs. European Community] F. J. Comes and P. Magnusson. il *Business Week* p47 Ja 16 '89
The politics of pork [dispute over U.S. import duty on Canadian pork] R. Laver. il *Maclean's* 102:17 S 11 '89
What's the beef? [European Community's ban on imports of beef injected with growth hormones] W. E. Sheeline. il *Fortune* 119:8 Ja 30 '89
Why the beef over hormones? [European Community bans import of U.S. meat from animals treated with hormones] J. Castro. il *Time* 133:44 Ja 16 '89
Laws and regulations
See also
Meat inspection
Marketing
Big profits, big losses for lean, clean beef. *Successful Farming* 87:36 S '89
Contented pigs? [Tyson Food's drive to popularize pork] M. Fritz. il *Forbes* 144:118-19 Ag 7 '89
Canada
See also
Gainers Inc.

MEAT INDUSTRY WORKERS
See also
Strikes—Meat industry workers
United Food and Commercial Workers International Union
Health and hygiene
Profiles in safety and health: occupational hazards of meat-packing. M. E. Personick and K. Taylor-Shirley. bibl f il *Monthly Labor Review* 112:3-9 Ja '89
Salaries, pensions, etc.
Meatpacking company cuts compensation [John Morrell & Co.] *Monthly Labor Review* 112:58-9 My '89

MEAT INSPECTION
History
Beef, pork, and history [German ban on American pork in 1880s over trichinosis concerns] B. A. Weisberger. il *American Heritage* 40:20+ Jl/Ag '89

MEAT MIXES
Make-ahead meat mix [ground meat mix] il *Southern Living* 24:162 Je '89
MEAT PACKING INDUSTRY WORKERS *See* Meat industry workers
MEAT SAUCES *See* Sauces
MEAT THERMOMETERS *See* Thermometers, Cooking
MEATLESS MEALS *See* Vegetarianism
MECCA (SAUDI ARABIA)
See also
Pilgrimages to Mecca
MECH, L. DAVID
Stubborn hunter in a harsh land. il map *National Wildlife* 27:20-4 Ag/S '89
about
White wolf: living with an Arctic legend [condensation] J. Brandenburg. il *Reader's Digest* 134:126-32 Mr '89
MECHAI, VIRAVAIDYA
about
The good news: Thailand controls a baby boom. il por *Time* 133:50 Ja 2 '89
MÉCHAIN, PIERRE-FRANÇOIS-ANDRÉ, 1744-1804
about
Deep-sky wonders. W. S. Houston. il *Sky and Telescope* 77:570-2 My '89
MECHAM, EVAN
about
A 'Christian nation' in the Far West. *U.S. News & World Report* 106:14 Mr 27 '89
How hot is it? J. Toobin. *The New Republic* 201:12-14 Ag 7-14 '89
The resurrection of Evan Mecham. K. V. Smith. il por *National Review* 41:42-3 My 19 '89
MECHANICAL BANKS *See* Banks, Coin
MECHANICAL TOYS *See* Toys
MECHANICS
See also
Fracture mechanics
Horsepower (Mechanics)
Micromechanics
Statistical mechanics
Strains and stresses
MECHANICS, CELESTIAL
See also
Solar system—Motion in space
MECHANICS, HOUSEHOLD *See* Houses—Maintenance and repair
MECHANICS (PERSONS)
See also
Airplane mechanics (Persons)
Motorcycle mechanics (Persons)
MECHANORECEPTORS *See* Sensory receptors
MECHCATIE, ELIZABETH
Surgery's darlings. il *Health (New York, N.Y.)* 21:74-7+ N '89
MECUM, SHADE M.
about
Once burned, twice the CEO? S. Ticer. il por *Business Week* Special Issue:169 Je 16 '89
MEDAL OF ARTS, NATIONAL *See* National Medal of Arts
MEDAL OF SCIENCE, NATIONAL *See* National Medal of Science
MEDAL OF TECHNOLOGY, NATIONAL *See* National Medal of Technology
MEDALLA, DAVID
about
Impromptus: David Medalla. G. Brett. bibl f il pors *Art in America* 77:156-63+ N '89
MEDALS
Collectors and collecting
It's the heroes who give us specialized fields of collecting [commemorating C. Lindbergh's flight] E. Rochette. il *Antiques & Collecting Hobbies* 93:66-7 Ja '89
MEDALS OF HONOR
21 years after losing the Pueblo, Lloyd Bucher wins honors for its crew. M. Brower. il pors *People Weekly* 32:26-7 Jl 31 '89
MEDAVOY, PATRICIA DUFF
about
West Coast wonder woman. M. A. Kellogg. il por *Harper's Bazaar* 122:168-71+ Ap '89
MEDELLIN (COLOMBIA)
Crime
Company town [cocaine trade] H. Kohn. il *Rolling Stone* p67-8+ Ap 6 '89
'Good sons' who kill. G. Matthews. il *World Press Review* 36:26-7 N '89
Religious institutions and affairs
Violence in Colombia unites evangelicals. J. Maust. *Christianity Today* 33:49 S 22 '89
MEDIA *See* Mass media
MEDIA BROKERS *See* Mass media brokers
MEDIA GUIDE
Pigging out. E. Diamond. il por *New York* 22:22+ Ap 17 '89

MEDIA INDUSTRY *See* Mass media industry
MEDIA ROOMS
Basement bijou [home theater of T. Kalomirakis] M. Fleischmann. il *Video* 13:46-8+ Je '89
The best seat in the house [cover story] W. Livingstone. il *Stereo Review* 54:62-8 Ap '89
Creating your own home theater [cover story; with editorial comment by Stan Pinkwas] F. Lovece. il *Video* 13:6, 42-5+ Je '89
Electronics: today's hearth. il *Southern Living* 24:136+ O '89
Systems [Wayne Mackey's garage becomes media room] R. Day. il *Stereo Review* 54:82-3 Je '89
MEDIA STUDIES *See* Mass media—Study and teaching
MEDIA WATCH (ORGANIZATION)
The woman warrior [A. Simonton] J. Lieber. il pors *Sports Illustrated* 70 Special Issue:131-4 F '89
MEDIATION *See* Arbitration and award
MEDIATION, COMMERCIAL *See* Arbitration, Commercial
MEDIATION, SPORTS *See* Arbitration, Sports
MEDICAID
Do only the suckers pay? [fraud perpetrated by elderly seeking shelter from nursing home costs] J. B. Quinn. il *Newsweek* 114:52 D 18 '89
Drawing the line [Oregon] I. Mothner. il por *American Health* 8:72-4+ Jl/Ag '89
Health care for all or an excuse for cutbacks? [Oregon cuts] S. B. Garland. il *Business Week* p68 Je 26 '89
Rainy-day plan [New York State program] D. Wise. il *New York* 22:121-2+ D 4 '89
MEDICAL BOTANY *See* Botany, Medical
MEDICAL CARE
See also
Aged—Medical care
Airplanes in medical care
Blacks—Medical care
Children—Medical care
Chiropractic
Diagnosis
First aid in illness and injury
Health facilities
Helicopters in medical care
Home care services
Hospitals
House calls (Medical care)
Infants—Medical care
Medical ethics
Minorities—Medical care
Missions, Medical
Nurses and nursing
Palestinian Arabs—Medical care
Physicians
Physicians and patients
Poor—Medical care
Quacks and quackery
Rich—Medical care
Single men—Medical care
Taxicabs in medical care
Telephone in medical care
Trauma care units
Veterans—Medical care
Women prisoners—Medical care
Youth—Medical care
The body snatchers [proposed Health Care Rights Amendment] R. E. Borgman. *Omni (New York, N.Y.)* 12:41 D '89
Health care in the United States: rights and reality. R. J. Barnet. *America* 160:268-71 Mr 25 '89
New doctor roles for 21st century [views of Richard A. Wright] il *USA Today (Periodical)* 118:11 Ag '89
Phoenix rising [influence of AIDS on changes in health care; cover story] L. Marsa. il *Omni (New York, N.Y.)* 12:50-4+ D '89
Self-care: don't bypass your doctor. S. A. Hoffmann. por *American Health* 8:83-4 Je '89
Anecdotes, facetiae, satire, etc.
Sick of the sick. B. Ehrenreich. il *Mother Jones* 14:7+ N '89
Costs
See also
AIDS (Disease)—Costs
Dental fees
Hospital care—Costs
Nursing homes—Costs
Physicians—Salaries, fees, etc.
The $50,000 haircut [recovery from brain aneurysm] F. Swertlow. il pors *Money* 18:84-94+ My '89
Are companies cutting too close to the bone? [malpractice claims may arise from new insurance plans designed to trim costs] M. Galen. il *Business Week* p141+ O 30 '89
Before the well runs dry: cutting the cost of retiree health benefits. C. A. Hanks. *USA Today (Periodical)* 117:86-8 My '89
Bill of health. *The New Republic* 201:5-6 Jl 3 '89
Can insurers nurse their HMOs back to health? J. R. Norman. il *Business Week* p80-1 Ja 16 '89
Can you afford to get sick? [cover story; special section] il *Newsweek* 113:44-52 Ja 30 '89

MEDICAL CARE—Costs—*cont.*

Challenges, choices and concerns [address, May 8, 1989] R. A. Schoellhorn. *Vital Speeches of the Day* 56:56-9 N 1 '89

Confronting the crisis in health care: an interview with Arnold Relman [cover story] S. Hackman and R. Howard. il pors *Technology Review* 92:30-8+ Jl '89

The cost of chaos. R. J. Samuelson. il *Newsweek* 114:52 O 2 '89

Costs and cures. S. Findlay and J. Silberner. il *U.S. News & World Report* 107:68-9 D 25 '89-Ja 1 '90

Curbing the high cost of health care [cover story] R. Thompson. il *Nation's Business* 77:18-20+ S '89

Employees to pay more for benefits. *The Futurist* 23:45 N/D '89

Freeing health care. S. M. Butler. il *National Review* 41:34-6 D 22 '89

Got a moment? How about some knee surgery? [rising need for evaluating outpatient care] E. Paris. il *Forbes* 144:58 Jl 10 '89

Health care: confronting the crisis [interview with A. Relman] S. Hackman and R. Howard. *Current (Washington, D.C.)* 317:10-15 N '89

Health care cost limitation [address, November 17, 1988] G. L. Musgrave. *Vital Speeches of the Day* 55:273-6 F 15 '89

The health-care crisis [address, October 27, 1988] C. W. Gray. *Vital Speeches of the Day* 55:304-7 Mr 1 '89

The health care quagmire [cover story] E. F. Haislmaier. il *Consumers' Research Magazine* 72:10-16 S '89

Health costs: what, me worry? il *Esquire* 111:82 Je '89

The health of nations. E. Rubenstein. *National Review* 41:11 S 1 '89

The high cost of fighting infertility. P. Godwin. il *Changing Times* 43:73-4+ Mr '89

High-tech health care: who will pay? J. O. Hamilton and others. il *Business Week* p74-6+ F 6 '89

How to control U.S. health costs. A. Robbins. *Scientific American* 261:158 D '89

The killer cost stalking business [health benefits] C. J. Loomis. il *Fortune* 119:58-9+ F 27 '89

Koop de grace. il *The New Republic* 201:7-9 O 23 '89

Living without health insurance. P. Jones. il *Glamour* 87:158+ Ap '89

Medical costs hit churches. *The Christian Century* 106:713-14 Ag 2-9 '89

No more health care on the house [Fortune poll] A. Farnham. il *Fortune* 119:71-2 F 27 '89

Ouch! The squeeze on your health benefits [cover story] il *Business Week* p110-13+ N 20 '89

Rationing medical care. J. Elson. il *Time* 133:84+ My 15 '89

Retiree benefits: this footnote doesn't have to become a nightmare. J. R. Norman. il *Business Week* p39 F 27 '89

The right medicine. H. Schwartz. il *National Review* 41:26-9 Mr 10 '89

Sick to death [cover story; special section; with editorial comment by Kevin Doyle] il *Maclean's* 102:2, 32-8+ F 13 '89

Soothing the sting of an accounting rule [employee health benefits] L. J. Nathans. il *Business Week* p106 S 18 '89

A tale of two eyes [cost of laser eye surgery in France compared to that in U.S.] L. Malkin. *The New Republic* 201:15-16 S 4 '89

Unhealthy, unwealthy, and worse. S. T. Mandel. il *National Review* 41:25-6 O 13 '89

Worrying about medical costs [views of Herbert Berger] W. F. Buckley. *National Review* 41:63 Mr 10 '89

Evaluation

Challenges, choices and concerns [address, May 8, 1989] R. A. Schoellhorn. *Vital Speeches of the Day* 56:56-9 N 1 '89

Got a moment? How about some knee surgery? [rising need for evaluating outpatient care] E. Paris. il *Forbes* 144:58 Jl 10 '89

Looking over the doctor's shoulder [outcome monitoring] S. Findlay. il *U.S. News & World Report* 106:70-1+ Ja 30 '89

Physician, inform thyself [patient-outcomes research] M. Ludtke. il *Time* 133:71 Je 26 '89

International aspects

The health of nations. E. Rubenstein. *National Review* 41:11 S 1 '89

Live and let die. L. Marsa. *Omni (New York, N.Y.)* 11:40-2 S '89

Reach out for health [primary health care; cover story; special issue] il *World Health* p3-24 My '89

Alabama

What I know about deliverin' babies come from motherwit, common sense. God gave it to me [excerpt from Motherwit: an Alabama midwife's story]; ed. by Katherine Clark. O. L. Logan. il pors *Life* 12:19-21 Je '89

Bolivia

"Health first" in Bolivia. R. Granados and others. il *World Health* p14-15 My '89

Canada

The pain barrier [special section] il *Maclean's* 102:36-42 F 27 '89

Sick to death [cover story; special section; with editorial comment by Kevin Doyle] il *Maclean's* 102:2, 32-8+ F 13 '89

Developing countries

Reach out for health [primary health care; cover story; special issue] il *World Health* p3-24 My '89

Ethiopia

Ethiopia's success story [training community health workers] G. S. Okubagzhi. il *World Health* p21-2 My '89

Great Britain

See also

Great Britain. National Health Service

Kentucky

Coal miner's doctor [country doctor A. A. Bates] J. Ralston. il pors *McCall's* 116:70+ S '89

Kenya

District approach to primary health care [Reach out for health video] il *World Health* p20 My '89

Out of Africa. E. Rosenthal. il *Discover* 10:37-9 Ag '89

Mississippi

'Dr. Bob' [work of R. Smith] R. D. Turner. il pors *Ebony* 44:102+ S '89

Norway

Light at the end of the tunnel. G. Bolstad. il *World Health* p8-10 My '89

Pakistan

A health care paradox. K. S. Khan and K. Islam. il *World Health* p5-7 My '89

United States

See Medical care

Washington (D.C.)

See Washington (D.C.)—Medical care

MEDICAL CARE, RURAL

See also

Hospitals, Rural

Coal miner's doctor [country doctor A. A. Bates in Kentucky] J. Ralston. il pors *McCall's* 116:70+ S '89

Help wanted: boon docs. F. Maier. il *Newsweek* 113:58-9 F 27 '89

Rural health. C. Tevis. See issues of Successful Farming beginning March 1989

MEDICAL CARE, STATE

See also

Great Britain. National Health Service

Medicaid

Medicare

MEDICAL CARE INDUSTRY

See also

Hospital management industry

Lifetime Corp.

Salick Health Care, Inc.

Summit Health Ltd.

T^2 Medical Inc.

Health. M. Fritz. il *Forbes* 143:150-1 Ja 9 '89

The prognosis on health care: critical—and getting worse. J. O. Hamilton. il *Business Week* p82 Ja 9 '89

Soviet Union

How to get rich off *perestroika* [eye surgeon and entrepreneur S. Fyodorov] P. Péan. il pors *Fortune* 119:145-6 My 8 '89

MEDICAL CARE PROXIES

New York looks at health-care proxies. *Modern Maturity* 32:93 Ap/My '89

MEDICAL CENTERS *See* Health facilities; Hospitals

MEDICAL COLLEGE ADMISSIONS TEST

MCAT to stress thinking, writing. C. Holden. *Science* 243:1431 Mr 17 '89

MEDICAL COLLEGE OF OHIO

Ombudsmen train young doctors [nursing home ombudsmen and Medical College of Ohio program] il *Aging* no359:24-5 '89

MEDICAL COLLEGES

See also

Harvard Medical School

Medical College of Ohio

Meharry Medical College

University of Pittsburgh. School of Medicine

Entrance examinations

See also

Medical College Admissions Test

MEDICAL EDUCATION

See also

Residents (Medicine)

MEDICAL ELECTRONICS

See also

Biosensors

Biotelemetry

Computers—Medical use

Defibrillators

Magnetic resonance imaging—Medical use

Radiography, Medical

Volunteers for Medical Engineering

Special report: orthopedic engineering. il *Popular Mechanics* 166:17 S '89

MEDICAL ELECTRONICS INDUSTRY
See also
　Therapeutic Technologies Inc.
MEDICAL EQUIPMENT
See also
　Heart-lung machines
　Hemodialysis equipment
　Image processing—Medical use
　Medical electronics
　Polymers in medicine
　Surgical equipment
　Syringes
A guide to home medical tests. C. Slom. il *McCall's* 117:103 N '89
Home medical tests. S. Squires. *Ladies' Home Journal* 106:56 F '89
Home medical tests: what they can tell you. L. Holland. il *Good Housekeeping* 208:245 Je '89
House calls—or bad calls? [do-it-yourself medical kits] K. Doheny. il *Modern Maturity* 32:92-4 D '89/Ja '90
Outdoor medicine [D. T. McCrady supplies medical kit after author slips on rock] H. Middleton. il *Southern Living* 24:26+ Ag '89
The ready and fit kit. P. G. Gill, Jr. il *Outdoor Life* 184:58-9 D '89
The well-stocked first aid kit. B. Tilton. il *Field & Stream* 94:106-7 N '89
MEDICAL EQUIPMENT INDUSTRY
See also
　Cordis Corporation
　Imatron Inc.
　InterFlo Medical Inc.
　Stryker Corp.
MEDICAL ETHICS
See also
　Cancer research—Ethical aspects
　Epidemiology—Ethical aspects
　Euthanasia
　Fertilization in vitro—Ethical aspects
　Fetal tissue—Transplantation—Ethical aspects
　Gamete intrafallopian transfer—Ethical aspects
　Gene therapy—Ethical aspects
　Genetic research—Ethical aspects
　Genetic research—Human experimentation
　Heart research—Ethical aspects
　Informed consent (Medical law)
　Medical laboratories—Ethical aspects
　Medical referral—Ethical aspects
　Medical research—Ethical aspects
　Medical research—Human experimentation
　Pharmaceutical research—Ethical aspects
　Pharmaceutical research—Human experimentation
　Psychiatric research—Ethical aspects
　Right to die
　Transplantation of organs, tissues, etc.—Ethical aspects
　Vision research—Ethical aspects
A doctor and his critics [F. Tennant of Community Health Projects Inc.] R. Demak and J. Kirshenbaum. il *Sports Illustrated* 71:46-7 Jl 10 '89
Doctor fear [interview with R. Cook] M. Segell. il *American Health* 8:82-4+ S '89
Miracle baby [I. Roe, born at 23½ weeks at Cedars-Sinai Medical Center] S. M. Halpern. il pors *Ms.* 18:56-60+ S '89
Pitching doctors [drug companies] M. S. Wilkes and M. Shuchman. il *The New York Times Magazine* p88+ N 5 '89
The prolongation of life [address, December 3, 1988] E. M. Skinner. *Vital Speeches of the Day* 55:271-3 F 15 '89
Tough cases, hard choices [bioethicists J. Arras and N. N. Dubler at Montefiore Medical Center, Bronx, N.Y.] A. Rosenfeld. il pors *New York* 22:32-7 Ja 9 '89
The unhappiest part of medicine, says author John Pekkanen, may be the physicians who practice it. M. Brower. il pors *People Weekly* 31:85+ Ja 9 '89
When doctors say no [patients who have been denied care] R. Trubo. il *Good Housekeeping* 209:82+ Ag '89
International aspects
Ethics and health [special issue] il *World Health* p2-25 Ap '89
Canada
Life-and-death issues [hospitals employing ethics specialists] I. Shapiro. il *Maclean's* 102:56-7 My 1 '89
Sex, law and ethics [commission formed to examine questions raised by new reproductive technologies] L. Van Dusen. il *Maclean's* 102:16 N 13 '89
Japan
Whose life is it, anyway? [patients' rights] N. Darnton. il *Newsweek* 113:61 Ja 23 '89
MEDICAL EXAMINATIONS *See* Physical examinations
MEDICAL EXAMINERS (LAW)
Coroners who miss all the clues [lack of skills in forensic pathology] A. Toufexis. il *Time* 134:61 Ag 14 '89

MEDICAL FACILITIES *See* Health facilities
MEDICAL FAKERS *See* Quacks and quackery
MEDICAL FILMS *See* Motion pictures—Medical films
MEDICAL GENETICS *See* Heredity of disease
MEDICAL GEOGRAPHY
Reducing the incidence of disease: clues from the environment [esophageal cancer] H. D. Foster. bibl f il maps *Environment* 31:12-17+ Ap '89
Sizing up SADness according to latitude [research by Norman E. Rosenthal] B. Bower. *Science News* 136:198 S 23 '89
MEDICAL HISTORIES *See* Medical records
MEDICAL INSURANCE *See* Insurance, Health
MEDICAL JARGON *See* Medicine—Terminology
MEDICAL JOURNALISM *See* Journalism, Medical
MEDICAL JURISPRUDENCE
See also
　Forensic dentistry
　Forensic psychiatry
　Medical examiners (Law)
Caution urged on DNA fingerprinting [ruling in J. Castro case] C. Norman. *Science* 245:699 Ag 18 '89
DNA analysis in forensic science. M. D. Moody. bibl f il *BioScience* 39:31-6 Ja '89
DNA on trial. il *Time* 134:63 Ag 28 '89
DNA takes the stand. R. Weiss. il *Science News* 136:74-6 Jl 29 '89
DNA typing is called flawed [J. Castro case] R. Lewin. il *Science* 245:355 Jl 28 '89
DNA typing on the witness stand [challenging reliability of forensic DNA fingerprinting; case of J. Castro] R. Lewin. il *Science* 244:1033-5 Je 2 '89
Genetic fingerprints [used in convicting Ottawa rapist P. J. McNally] R. Laver. il *Maclean's* 102:54 Ap 17 '89
Genetics meets forensics [DNA fingerprints] R. Lewis. il *BioScience* 39:6-9 Ja '89
Maine case deals blow to DNA fingerprinting. C. Norman. il *Science* 246:1556-8 D 22 '89
Misprint [reliability of genetic fingerprinting] M. Thompson. *The New Republic* 200:14-15 Ap 3 '89
Misprints [problems with forensic DNA typing; case of J. Castro] J. Kinoshita. *Scientific American* 261:12+ Ag '89
Science in court. C. Holden. *Science* 243:1658-9 Mr 31 '89
The startling Shelly Prine case [use of DNA fingerprints to convict O. Smith of murder in Goessel, Kan.] P. Michelmore. *Reader's Digest* 135:179-80+ Jl '89
A trial of high-tech detectives [challenge to reliability of DNA analysis; case of J. Castro] D. Thompson. il por *Time* 133:63 Je 5 '89
MEDICAL KITS *See* Medical equipment
MEDICAL LABORATORIES
See also
　Metpath Inc.
　National Health Laboratories, Inc.
Ethical aspects
At this medical lab, only the bills were real [fake tests cheat insurers; fraud scheme of A. F. Lopapa] P. Dwyer. *Business Week* p38 O 16 '89
Laws and regulations
Making medical labs measure up. T. Kiely. il *Technology Review* 92:14-15 Jl '89
MEDICAL LAWS AND REGULATIONS *See* Medical policy
MEDICAL LIBRARIES
See also
　National Library of Medicine (U.S.)
　World Research Foundation
MEDICAL LITERATURE
See also
　Publishers and publishing—Medical literature
Collectors and collecting
Can onions prevent baldness? [rare medical book collection of C. C. Tandy] C. Brown. il por *Forbes* 144:135 Ag 7 '89
MEDICAL MISSIONS *See* Missions, Medical
MEDICAL NEWS
See also
　Journalism, Medical
Big help for little ailments. D. Pine. il *Ladies' Home Journal* 106:112+ Ap '89
Biggest medical breakthroughs of the decade. D. Webb. il *Ladies' Home Journal* 106:90+ N '89
Family doctor. A. E. Nourse. See issues of Good Housekeeping
Health front. See issues of Prevention (Emmaus, Pa.)
Medical mailbox. C. SerVaas. See issues of The Saturday Evening Post
Medical report. See issues of Glamour
Medinews. See issues of Ladies' Home Journal
News. M. Sandmaier. See issues of Mademoiselle
News from the world of medicine. See issues of Reader's Digest
A question of health. See issues of Consumer Reports
Quick studies: from chores to chili. il *New Choices for the Best Years* 29:11 Ap '89
Stethoscope. See issues of Current Health 2
Surgery's darlings. E. Mechcatie. il *Health (New York, N.Y.)* 21:74-7+ N '89
Top medical news of 1989. C. Slom. *McCall's* 117:97 D '89
Vital signs. See issues of McCall's beginning October 1983

MEDICAL NEWS—*cont.*
Well wishers. il *Harper's Bazaar* 122:34 Je '89
What's new in the world of medicine. il *U.S. News & World Report* 106:80 F 20 '89

MEDICAL NEWSLETTERS
Nutrition and medical newsletters offer information-hungry readers new food for thought. P. Klass. *Vogue* 179:554+ S '89
Paper medicine [physicians' personalized newsletters] E. Paris. il *Forbes* 143:92 Ja 23 '89
Take two of these and call us in the morning to cure the scare of the week. R. Sandroff. il *Money* 18:53-4 My '89

MEDICAL PHYSICS
Medical physics. bibl f *Physics Today* 42:S49-S52 Ja '89

MEDICAL POLICY
See also
Hospital care—Costs
Informed consent (Medical law)
Medical laboratories—Laws and regulations
Quarantine
United States. Dept. of Health and Human Services
United States. Surgeon-General's Office
At risk. P. C. Montgomery. il *Common Cause Magazine* 15:28-33 Mr/Ap '89
The body snatchers [proposed Health Care Rights Amendment] R. E. Borgman. *Omni (New York, N.Y.)* 12:41 D '89
Confronting the crisis in health care: an interview with Arnold Relman [cover story] S. Hackman and R. Howard. il pors *Technology Review* 92:30-8+ Jl '89
The debate at home [medical care crisis] D. Schorr. *The New Leader* 72:4 O 2-16 '89
Health care: confronting the crisis [interview with A. Relman] S. Hackman and R. Howard. *Current (Washington, D.C.)* 317:10-15 N '89
Health care for a caring America [address, May 23, 1989] H. B. Deets. *Vital Speeches of the Day* 55:636-7 Ag 1 '89
The health care mess. C. E. Koop. por *Newsweek* 114:10 Ag 28 '89
The health care quagmire [cover story] E. F. Haislmaier. il *Consumers' Research Magazine* 72:10-16 S '89
Health policy for the elderly. S. P. Wallace and C. L. Estes. bibl f *Society* 26:66-75 S/O '89
How to control U.S. health costs. A. Robbins. *Scientific American* 261:158 D '89
Koop de grace. il *The New Republic* 201:7-9 O 23 '89
Phoenix rising [influence of AIDS on changes in health care; cover story] L. Marsa. il *Omni (New York, N.Y.)* 12:50-4+ D '89
Rationing medical care. J. Elson. il *Time* 133:84+ My 15 '89
The right medicine. H. Schwartz. il *National Review* 41:26-9 Mr 10 '89
Some of the tough decisions required by a national health plan. L. B. Russell. bibl f il *Science* 246:892-6 N 17 '89
Tackling the health-care crisis. *Modern Maturity* 32:9 Je/Jl '89
To our health [proposed national health care program] R. Ruthen. *Scientific American* 260:18+ Mr '89
Washington health watch. C. Slom. *McCall's* 117:98 D '89
France
France introduces bioethics law. D. Dickson. *Science* 243:1284 Mr 10 '89
Grenada
A doctor's dilemma [Cuban-trained doctor T. Marryshow not permitted to practice] W. Steif. il por *The Progressive* 53:10 Ja '89
New York (State)
New York looks at health-care proxies. *Modern Maturity* 32:93 Ap/My '89
Rainy-day plan [Medicaid program] D. Wise. il *New York* 22:121-2+ D 4 '89
Oregon
Drawing the line [Medicaid] I. Mothner. il por *American Health* 8:72-4+ Jl/Ag '89
Health care for all or an excuse for cutbacks? S. B. Garland. il *Business Week* p68 Je 26 '89

MEDICAL RADIOGRAPHY *See* Radiography, Medical
MEDICAL RECORDS
Unwilling players in the name game [sale of credit and medical information to direct marketing companies] A. Mundy. il *U.S. News & World Report* 106:52+ My 1 '89

MEDICAL REFERRAL
Ethical aspects
Check out eye doctor referrals. J. Wood. *Modern Maturity* 32:24 F/Mr '89
MEDICAL RESEARCH
See also
Animal experimentation
Cancer research
Heart research
Howard Hughes Medical Institute
National Institute of Allergy and Infectious Diseases (U.S.)

National Institutes of Health (U.S.)
Pharmaceutical research
Psychiatric research
Vision research
Bypassing the ban [neuroscientists seek alternatives to research on human fetal cells] R. Weiss. il *Science News* 136:378-9 D 9 '89
Fostering more orphan-disease research [report of National Commission on Orphan Diseases] *Science News* 135:255 Ap 22 '89
Ethical aspects
The epilepsy "cure": bold claims, weak data [controversy over peer-reviewed article by Phodios A. Anninos and N. Tsagas in International journal of neuroscience] R. P. Crease. il *Science* 245:1444-5 S 29 '89
Fraud and the "glare of the TV camera" [views of L. W. Sullivan] G. Byrne. por *Science* 244:1038 Je 2 '89
Misconduct cases probed. *Science News* 136:20 Jl 8 '89
NIH grapples with conflict of interest. J. Palca. il *Science* 245:23 Jl 7 '89
Peer review comes under peer review [biomedical publishing] M. Sun. il *Science* 244:910-12 My 26 '89
Publication bias: looking for missing data [survey by Colin B. Begg] I. Peterson. *Science News* 135:5 Ja 7 '89
Experimentation on man
See Medical research—Human experimentation
Federal aid
See also
National Institutes of Health (U.S.)—Appropriations and expenditures
Human experimentation
Artificial organs: living with risk. P. M. Galletti. *Current (Washington, D.C.)* 311:16-19 Mr/Ap '89
France
See also
Institut Pasteur (Paris, France)
Germany (West)
Germany to ban embryo use. D. Kirk. *Science* 245:464 Ag 4 '89
Great Britain
Britain's Lords debate embryo research. J. Cherfas. il *Science* 246:1554-5 D 22 '89
Fetal tissue transplants win U.K. approval. D. Dickson. il *Science* 245:464-5 Ag 4 '89

MEDICAL RESEARCH COUNCIL (GREAT BRITAIN)
Britain launches genome program. D. Dickson. *Science* 243:1657 Mr 31 '89
MEDICAL SCIENCE *See* Medicine
MEDICAL SCIENCE PARTNERS
Harvard chases biotech bucks. J. Wiener. il *The Nation* 248:12-16 Ja 2 '89
MEDICAL SELF CARE *See* Medical care
MEDICAL SERVICE *See* Medical care
MEDICAL SOCIETIES
See also
American Medical Association
Institute of Medicine (U.S.)
Society for the Social History of Medicine
MEDICAL STUDENTS
See also
Women medical students
MEDICAL TECHNOLOGY
Challenges, choices and concerns [address, May 8, 1989] R. A. Schoellhorn. *Vital Speeches of the Day* 56:56-9 N 1 '89
Genies in the medicine bottle. D. R. Katz. il *Esquire* 112:73-4 D '89
High-tech health care: who will pay? J. O. Hamilton and others. il *Business Week* p74-6+ F 6 '89
MEDICAL TELEVISION PROGRAMS *See* Television broadcasting—Medical programs
MEDICAL TERMINOLOGY *See* Medicine—Terminology
MEDICAL ULTRASONICS *See* Ultrasonic waves—Medical use
MEDICAL WASTE DISPOSAL IN THE OCEAN
Hype tide [medical waste and beaches] A. Burdick. *The New Republic* 200:15-18 Je 12 '89
Medical waste just one threat to beaches. il *National Parks* 63:9-10 Ja/F '89
Tracking seaside medical wastes. *Science News* 136:191 S 16 '89
MEDICAL WORKERS *See* Health workers
MEDICARE
See also
Medicaid
National Committee to Preserve Social Security and Medicare
Alphabet medicine [effects of reimbursement cost-cutting] W. F. Allman. il *Health (New York, N.Y.)* 21:34+ Ja '89
Applying a scalpel to doctors' wallets [Congress lowers reimbursements] il *U.S. News & World Report* 107:11 D 4 '89
Beyond Medicare [cover story; special section] il *Consumer Reports* 54:375-91 Je '89
The calamity of catastrophic coverage. S. Dentzer. *U.S. News & World Report* 106:36 My 8 '89
Cat scam [repeal of the Medicare Catastrophic Coverage Act] J. Weisberg. *The New Republic* 201:11-12 O 30 '89

MEDICARE—*cont.*

Catastrophic care's impending surgery. *U.S. News & World Report* 107:51 S 11 '89

Catastrophic follies [Medicare surcharge] P. Longman. *The New Republic* 201:16-18 Ag 21 '89

Catastrophic health benefits translate into catastrophic taxes [Medicare surcharge; cover story] P. J. Ferrara. *Consumers' Research Magazine* 72:11-14 Ap '89

Catastrophic politics [Congress repeals catastrophic health insurance] *National Review* 41:12-13 N 24 '89

Catastrophic tax bite [Medicare surcharge] J. W. Merline. il *Consumers' Research Magazine* 72:38 My '89

Congress's health-care woes [proposal to scrap catastrophic insurance] M. W. Karmin. *U.S. News & World Report* 107:45 Jl 31 '89

De-taxification [repeal of Catastrophic Health Care Act] D. Corn. *The Nation* 249:480-1 O 30 '89

Dig deeper for Medicare. M. C. Paulson. il *Changing Times* 43:103 Ja '89

'Dueling commissions' plot health care into the next century. S. Dentzer. *U.S. News & World Report* 107:31 Ag 21 '89

Easing the cost of catastrophe. A. Quinlan. il *New Choices for the Best Years* 29:45-7 Ap '89

The elderly duke it out [Medicare surcharge stirs senior lobby] A. Miller. il *Newsweek* 114:42-3 S 11 '89

A health-care debacle [Medicare Catastrophic Coverage Act] S. Dentzer. il *U.S. News & World Report* 107:16-18 O 9 '89

Help with Medicare forms. C. Schaeffer. *Changing Times* 43:76-7 Jl '89

How to beat the bite of the new Medicare income tax surcharge. *Money* 18:17-18 Mr '89

Invitation to catastrophe [Congress votes to rescind catastrophic health insurance] *Time* 134:33 O 16 '89

Is this operation necessary? *Society* 26:3 My/Je '89

Medicare covers more, but you may still need a medigap policy. D. M. Topolnicki. il *Money* 18:149-50 F '89

Medicare tax [municipal bond strategy as way to avoid surtax] B. Weberman. il *Forbes* 143:213 Mr 20 '89

Medicare's catastrophe? *U.S. News & World Report* 106:58 Ja 23 '89

Medicare's sickbed [proposed cuts worry hospitals] S. Dentzer. il *U.S. News & World Report* 106:20-1 F 6 '89

Medigap: costs more, covers less. C. Schaeffer. il *Changing Times* 43:57-62 Ap '89

Medigap gets a second opinion—from Congress. S. B. Garland. il *Business Week* p122 My 1 '89

On the sick list: rural hospitals. S. B. Garland. il *Business Week* p36 Mr 27 '89

Repeal a bad health bill [Medicare Catastrophic Coverage Act] D. Gergen. il *U.S. News & World Report* 107:76 S 25 '89

Rx for rising costs [computer network coordinating prescriptions] S. Dentzer. il *U.S. News & World Report* 107:50-1+ S 11 '89

A senior citizen rebellion has Congress retreating in disarray [tax surcharge] S. B. Garland. il *Business Week* p43 S 11 '89

The short life of catastrophic care [repeal spurs medigap policies] S. Findlay. il *U.S. News & World Report* 107:72-3 D 11 '89

Some groups are raising funds by raising fears about social security and Medicare. M. C. Paulson. il *Changing Times* 43:124-6 D '89

Taking the teeth out of a new tax bite [surcharge] L. J. Nathans. *Business Week* p156 Mr 13 '89

A tale of two eyes [cost of laser eye surgery in France compared to that in U.S.] L. Malkin. *The New Republic* 201:15-16 S 4 '89

Thank you, Medicare [Manor Care, Inc.] il *Forbes* 143:150 Ja 9 '89

Too much of a good thing? [medigap insurance] *Modern Maturity* 32:12 O/N '89

The torpedo that slammed into catastrophic health care [National Committee to Preserve Social Security] P. Dwyer. il *Business Week* p70 O 23 '89

A victory for the haves? [Congress votes to trim catastrophic health care due to uproar over income tax surcharge] E. Clift. il *Newsweek* 114:38 O 16 '89

What you need to know about Medicare. F. C. Marshman. il *Money* 18 Money Guide:99-100 Fall '89

What'll it cost, doc? [fairer price scale for payments; study by William Hsiao] J. Hamilton. il *American Health* 8:15-16 Ap '89

Why shifting investments to beat the Medicare tax can be a bad idea. M. C. Paulson. il *Changing Times* 43:120-2 Ap '89

Canada
See Insurance, Health—Canada

MEDICINAL PLANTS *See* Botany, Medical

MEDICINE
See also
Accelerators (Electrons, etc.)—Medical use
Acupuncture
Anesthesia and anesthetics
Balloons—Medical use
Computers—Medical use

Dentistry
Diseases
Folk medicine
Holistic medicine
Homeopathy
Humor in medicine
Image processing—Medical use
Indians of North America—Medicine
Information systems—Medical use
Lasers—Medical use
Medical research
Microwaves—Medical use
Nuclear medicine
Paleopathology
Polymers in medicine
Quacks and quackery
Robots—Medical use
Space medicine
Surgery
Telecommunication in medicine
Tropical medicine
Ultrasonic waves—Medical use
Veterinary medicine

Awards
See also
Lasker Medical Research Awards

Equipment
See Medical equipment

Information services
The advice network. C. Caruana. il *Parents* 64:208+ Ap '89

Laws and regulations
See Medical policy

Periodicals
See also
Journal of the American Medical Association
Peer review comes under peer review [biomedical publishing] M. Sun. il *Science* 244:910-12 My 26 '89

Practice
See Physicians

Quotations
Forsooth, did Shakespeare know best? *USA Today (Periodical)* 117:13 F '89

Terminology
Medical terms—what do those words mean? A. Brown. il *Current Health 2* 15:28-9 My '89

Textbooks
Pirated textbooks come to U.S. shores [unauthorized medical texts at the L.A. Chiropractic College] *Publishers Weekly* 236:50-1 S 8 '89

Burkina Faso
The old and the new. A. J. Ouédraogo. il *World Health* p23-4 Mr '89

Great Britain
History
See also
Society for the Social History of Medicine

Pacific region
Priority areas in traditional medicine. K. Tsutani. il *World Health* p26-8 N '89

Tanzania
Notes on Tanzania. C. Michael. il *World Health* p19-20 Mr '89

United States
See Medicine

MEDICINE, CHINESE
Immuni-tea [effects of astragalus on T cell activity; research by Giora Mavligit and Da-Tong Chu] J. Barone. il *American Health* 8:100 O '89

Immunology [ancient China] R. K. G. Temple. il *The Courier (Unesco)* 41:34 O '88

MEDICINE, MILITARY
See also
Afghanistan—Russian invasion, 1979-1989—Medical and sanitary affairs
United States. Army—Medical and sanitary affairs
United States. Army Nurse Corps
World War, 1914-1918—Medical and sanitary affairs
World War, 1939-1945—Medical and sanitary affairs

MEDICINE, PREVENTIVE
See also
Vaccines and vaccination
The healthy elite . . . are you a member, too? [Prevention Index] M. Bricklin. il *Prevention (Emmaus, Pa.)* 41:144+ Ag '89

More talking, less testing [U.S. Preventive Services Task Force report] J. Carey. il *U.S. News & World Report* 106:62-3+ My 15 '89

'Report card' on health habits [Prevention Index] il *FDA Consumer* 23:4 N '89

MEDICINE, PSYCHOSOMATIC
See also
Faith cure
Hospital patients—Psychology
Hypochondria
Mental healing
Munchausen syndrome
Psychoneuroimmunology

MEDICINE, PSYCHOSOMATIC—*cont.*

Bare your soul and beat disease [excerpt from *Healthy pleasures*] R. E. Ornstein and D. S. Sobel. il *Prevention (Emmaus, Pa.)* 41:100+ Jl '89

Doctor love [B. Siegel; cover story] T. Schwartz. il pors *New York* 22:40-9 Je 12 '89

Doctors and patients must talk [condensed from Head first] N. Cousins. *Reader's Digest* 135:133-4+ O '89

The health personality test. *Psychology Today* 22:34 D '88

Healthy pleasures [excerpt; with editorial comment by Joel Gurin] R. E. Ornstein and D. S. Sobel. il *American Health* 8:53-8+, 116 My '89

How to heal yourself! [excerpt from Peace, love and healing] B. S. Siegel. *Redbook* 173:110-11+ Je '89

How to heal yourself [interview with B. S. Siegel] M. Lodge. por *Ladies' Home Journal* 106:108+ Je '89

The hug factor [effect of close relationships upon health and longevity] J. Hooper. il *Health (New York, N.Y.)* 21:72-5 O '89

Is your job making you sick? C. Hacinli. il *Mademoiselle* 95:126 O '89

Jest for the health of it. S. Goodman. il *Current Health 2* 15:18-19 Ja '89

The Lazarus file [spontaneous remission] H. Straus. il *American Health* 8:67-8+ My '89

Lighten up: laugh your way to good health. N. Gallo. *Better Homes and Gardens* 67:31-2 Ag '89

Mind over matter. E. Rosenthal. il *Discover* 10:36-8 Je '89

The mindset of health [excerpt from Mindfulness] E. J. Langer. il *Psychology Today* 23:48-51 Ap '89

Norman Cousins helps other patients as he once helped himself—by laughing [excerpt from Head first] N. Cousins. il por *Good Housekeeping* 209:92 N '89

The pleasure principle [views of Robert Ornstein and David Sobel] S. Thompson. il *Health (New York, N.Y.)* 21:28-9 Ag '89

Proving the power of laughter. N. Cousins. il *Psychology Today* 23:22-5 O '89

The ties that heal: how family and friends keep you healthy. B. Justice. il *Better Homes and Gardens* 67:48+ N '89

When truth doesn't hurt [research by Michael S. Shutty] P. Chance. *Psychology Today* 22:11 D '88

Why lovers live longer [effect of close relationships upon health] L. Moll. il *Mademoiselle* 95:132+ My '89

Wish me well [battling cancer] R. Shereff. il *Ms.* 18:26+ O '89

Anecdotes, facetiae, satire, etc.

One laugh = 3 tbsp. oat bran. J. Leo. il *U.S. News & World Report* 106:55 Ja 23 '89

MEDICINE AND ART

See also
Anatomy, Artistic

MEDICINE AND RELIGION

The church's challenge in health care [Carter Center conference] J. P. Wind. *The Christian Century* 106:1201-4 D 20-27 '89

Doctors agree: prayer works. T. C. Muck. *Christianity Today* 33:17 Mr 17 '89

Finitude, contingency, transience. M. E. Marty. *The Christian Century* 106:639 Je 21-28 '89

Health education through religion [Middle East] A. Aly. il *World Health* p27-8 Jl '89

MEDICINE AND STATE See Medical policy

MEDICINE AND THE HUMANITIES

Humanism and the art of medicine [address, June 21, 1989] A. R. Nelson. *Vital Speeches of the Day* 56:91-3 N 15 '89

MEDICINE BOTTLES

Adultproof cap [medication event monitoring system uses computer chips in medicine bottle caps] *Time* 133:70 Je 5 '89

MEDICINE CABINETS

Medicine cabinets and recessed lights. il *Popular Mechanics* 166:118-20 Ap '89

MEDICINE MEN

See also
Shamans and shamanism

Just another day in paradise [M. Plotkin's work with the Tirió Indians of Suriname] D. D. Jackson. il *Reader's Digest* 134:166-8+ Ap '89

Medicine man [elderly Navajo man treated for hypothermia] T. Dajer. il *Discover* 10:47-8+ Jl '89

Searching for medicinal wealth in Amazonia [M. Plotkin's work with Tirió Indians of Suriname] D. D. Jackson. bibl (p171) il pors *Smithsonian* 19:94-103 F '89

MEDICINES See Drugs

MEDICINES, NONPRESCRIPTION

See also
Cold (Disease) remedies
Mouthwashes

Can P&G commandeer more shelves in the medicine chest? [prescription drug marketing] Z. Schiller. il *Business Week* p64+ Ap 10 '89

Doing more good than harm with children's medications. S. J. Ackerman. il *FDA Consumer* 23:28-31 Mr '89

Our get-well guide to the best medicine you can buy [special section] il *Redbook* 174:91-4+ D '89

Over-the-counter addictions. J. E. Laird. *Better Homes and Gardens* 67:40+ S '89

MEDIEVAL & EARLY MODERN DATA BANK

Economic history, on line. F. Meeks. il por *Forbes* 144:122 Jl 10 '89

MEDIEVAL LITERATURE See Literature, Medieval

MEDIEVAL PHILOSOPHY See Philosophy, Medieval

MEDIGAP INSURANCE See Insurance, Health

MEDINA, LESLIE DAWSON- See Dawson-Medina, Leslie

MEDINA, NOE J.

(jt. auth) See Neill, D. Monty, and Medina, Noe J.

MEDINA SANCHEZ, JOSE GUILLERMO

about

A curious retirement. *Time* 133:44 F 20 '89

MEDINACELI DUCAL HOUSE FOUNDATION See Fundación Casa Ducal de Medinaceli

MEDIOBANCA

"The good drawing room". K. Weisman. *Forbes* 144:136 Jl 24 '89

MEDITATION

See also
Transcendental meditation

Contemplative prayer: taking time to hang out with God [interview with T. Keating; cover story] il por *U.S. Catholic* 54:6-13 Mr '89

Bibliography

Book reviews [Challenge program] P. Pilgram. *America* 160:44-5 Ja 21 '89

MEDITERRANEAN COOKING See Cooking, Mediterranean

MEDITERRANEAN REGION

See also
Malta
Public health—Mediterranean region

Defenses

See also
United States. Navy—Forces in the Mediterranean region

MEDIUM WELL DONE (FIRM)

When bigger doesn't mean better. K. J. Novak. il por *Home Office Computing* 7:60-1 D '89

MÉDOC WINES See Wine

MEDROXYPROGESTERONE

When the spirit takes wing [Provera victim D. Able born without arms or legs] M. Grant. il pors *People Weekly* 31:50-5 My 15 '89

MEDVED, DIANE

The trouble with divorce [condensed from The case against divorce] *Reader's Digest* 134:96-9 My '89

MEDVEDEV, ROY ALEKSANDROVICH, 1925-

about

A million here, a million there. A. Cockburn. *The Nation* 248:294-5 Mr 6 '89

Stalin's victims [discussion of March 6, 1989 article, A million here, a million there] A. Cockburn. *The Nation* 249:154+ Ag 7-14 '89

MEDVEDEV, VADIM

Turning Marx on his head [adaptation of address, October 4, 1988] il *New Perspectives Quarterly* 5:4-6 Wint '88/'89

about

'The need to rethink Leninism' [interview] B. Guetta. por *World Press Review* 36:23 S '89

MEE, MARGARET, 1909-1988

about

Out of Amazonia. B. Maddox. il por *Ms.* 18:54-7 O '89

MEEGAN, JAMES M., AND MARCUS, PHILIP I.

Double-stranded ribonuclease coinduced with interferon. bibl f il *Science* 244:1089-91 Je 2 '89

MEEHAN, JAMES

about

What goes up must come down. J. Zweig. pors *Forbes* 143:200 Mr 20 '89

MEEHAN, MARY

about

Antiquing in Scotland. J. Allen. il pors maps *Architectural Digest* 46:166-73+ O '89

New York story: romantic traditions fill a designer's East Side residence. S. M. L. Aronson. il por *Architectural Digest* 46:112-19+ Jl '89

MEEK, BOB

about

Mussel man Bob Meek runs a seafood farm built on mutual shellfishness. N. Geeslin. il pors *People Weekly* 31:135-6 My 1 '89

MEEKER, AMY

Do awards sell books? il *Publishers Weekly* 236:32+ Ag 25 '89

MEEKS, BROCK N.

COM1. See issues of Byte beginning August 1988 through May 1989

MEESE, EDWIN, III

about

Holt to publish Meese's memoirs of his years with Reagan. il por *Publishers Weekly* 235:25 Mr 17 '89

One for the Gypper. F. Barnes. *The New Republic* 200:14-15 F 27 '89

MEET ME IN ST. LOUIS [musical] See Musicals, revues, etc.—Reviews—Single works

MEETINGS
See also
Conventions
Corporations—Meetings
Stockholders' meetings
MEFLOQUINE
New drug for malaria. il *FDA Consumer* 23:4-5 S '89
MEGALITHIC MONUMENTS
France
Tantalizing to scholars and tourists, Carnac's megaliths remain an enigma. D. Roberts. il *Smithsonian* 20:146-54+ S '89
MEGALOCEROS GIGANTEUS *See* Irish elk
MEGAPLUMES
Second megaplume found in Pacific [work of Edward T. Baker] *Science News* 136:239 O 7 '89
MEGARRY, A. ROY
about
A new lineup. B. Came. il *Maclean's* 102:46+ F 13 '89
MEGAYACHTS *See* Yachts and yachting
MEHARRY MEDICAL COLLEGE
Bill and Camille Cosby give $1.5 million to Meharry and Bethune-Cookman colleges. il pors *Jet* 75:5-6 Ja 9 '89
MEHERANI, CANDYCE
Make the grade. il *Seventeen* 48:154-5+ Ap '89
MEHL, B. MAX
about
A look at an old issue of Hobbies. E. Rochette. *Antiques & Collecting Hobbies* 94:64-5 Ap '89
MEHLE, AILEEN *See* Suzy
MEHLINGER, HOWARD D.
American textbook reform: what can we learn from the Soviet experience? bibl f il *Phi Delta Kappan* 71:29-35 S '89
MEHLMAN, PETER
The endless winter. il pors *Gentlemen's Quarterly* 59:336-9+ Mr '89
My game is mud. il *Gentlemen's Quarterly* 59:302-7 O '89
Next summer, I'll be married. il *The New York Times Magazine* p44+ My 21 '89
MEHR, CHRISTIAN
Are the Swiss forests in peril? il map *National Geographic* 175:636-51 My '89
MEHREN, ELIZABETH
I was an unwed stepmother. por *Newsweek* 114:12-13 O 23 '89
The young Kennedys carry on. il *McCall's* 116:40-2+ Je '89
MEHRTEN, JOSEPH
How to sabotage the homeless. il *Conservative Digest* 15:6-7+ My/Je '89
MEHTA, GITA
about
Literary lights. il pors *Harper's Bazaar* 122:58+ Ag '89
MEHTA, HARKISHAN
EPI: a dream come true. il *World Health* p12-13 N '89
MEHTA, KETAN
about
Spices [film] Reviews
The Nation 249:399 O 9 '89. S. Klawans
MEHTA, ZUBIN
about
Passing the baton. P. G. Davis. il *New York* 22:82-6+ My 15 '89
Strictures at an institution. E. Rothstein. *The New Republic* 200:27-31 Mr 13 '89
MEIER, DEBORAH
about
Education: the movie [cover story] D. L. Kirp. il pors *Mother Jones* 14:36-45 Ja '89
MEIER, RICHARD, 1934-
about
New directions. D. Dietsch. il *Architectural Record* 177:70-7 Ag '89
MEIGS, JAMES B.
Home video. See alternate issues of Popular Mechanics beginning January 1986
MEINDERSMA, CHRISTA
Massacre in the Forbidden Kingdom. il *Reader's Digest* 135:126-30 O '89
MEINKE, PETER
Soldiers with green leggings [poem] *America* 160:446 My 13 '89
MEIOSIS (BIOLOGY) *See* Cell division (Biology)
MEIROSE, CARL E.
The faces of fear. il *America* 160:372-3 Ap 22 '89
MEISELS, SAMUEL J.
High-stakes testing in kindergarten. *The Education Digest* 55:25-8 O '89
MEISLER, ANDY
Baby boom! [cover story] il pors *TV Guide* 37:4-7+ D 30 '89-Ja 5 '90
It's a good nudes, bad nudes game. il *TV Guide* 37:16-18 Ag 26-S 1 '89
Sam Kinison, tastefully. il pors *Gentlemen's Quarterly* 59:89+ Je '89
What to expect from your favorite show [cover story] il *TV Guide* 37:2-6+ S 16-22 '89

The women of L.A. law: are they doing justice to their roles? [cover story] il *TV Guide* 37:4-5+ Ap 1-7 '89
MEISLER, STANLEY
Casting a *glasnost* glow on once-obscured artists. bibl (p183) il *Smithsonian* 20:130-6+ D '89
The lively rebirth of a battered but indomitable Glasgow. bibl (p229) il *Smithsonian* 20:124-30+ O '89
DIE MEISTERSINGER VON NURNBERG [opera] *See* Wagner, Richard, 1813-1883
MEKONNEN, ABEBE
about
Chasing legends. A. Burfoot. il pors *Runner's World* 24:34-41 Jl '89
Flying at the finish. M. Noden. il por *Sports Illustrated* 70:28 Ap 24 '89
MELAMED, LEO
about
A bid to salvage a go-go legacy. W. McWhirter. il por *Time* 133:52 F 6 '89
Leo Melamed. K. A. Behof. il por *Business Week* Special Issue:123 Ap 14 '89
MELAMID, ALEKSANDR, 1945-
about
Bayonne. *The New Yorker* 65:32-3 Ap 24 '89
Komar & Melamid at Ronald Feldman Fine Arts. N. Princenthal. *Art in America* 77:206 S '89
MELANCHOLIA *See* Depression, Mental
MELANCHOLY IN ART
Exhibitions
Saturn in Europe: Ancienne Douane; Oeuvre Nôtre Dame; Palais Rohan. M. Hübl. il *Art News* 88:159 Ja '89
MELANESIA
See also
Fiji
MELANIE, 1947-
Woodstock remembered: the artists. il pors *Rolling Stone* p79 Ag 24 '89
MELANOMA *See* Skin—Cancer
MELANOMA CELLS *See* Cancer cells
MELATONIN RECEPTORS *See* Hormone receptors
MELBA, NELLIE
about
Peach of a diva. J. James. il por *Opera News* 53:44-5 Ja 7 '89
MELBA [television program] *See* Television program reviews—Single works
MELBOURNE (AUSTRALIA)
Music
See also
Opera—Australia
MELCHIOR, LAURITZ, 1890-1973
about
He knew his Wagner. W. H. Youngren. il *The Atlantic* 264:83-5 Jl '89
MELENDEZ, BILL
about
He's a howling success at bringing comics to life. M. Barrier. il por *Nation's Business* 77:16+ O '89
MELENDEZ, TONY
Faith of a family: the Tony Melendez story [condensed from A gift of hope]; ed. by Mel White. il *Reader's Digest* 134:209-12+ Je '89
MELENDEZ (BILL) PRODUCTIONS *See* Bill Melendez Productions
MELITTA-WERKE BENTZ & SOHN
Helmut Radtke: no grind at selling coffee. il por *Business Week* p68 S 18 '89
MELLENCAMP, JOHN COUGAR
about
The further maturation of 'Big Daddy'. S. Pond. il por *Rolling Stone* p85-7 Je 1 '89
John Mellencamp's void in the Heartland. A. DeCurtis. il pors *Rolling Stone* p32-5+ Je 29 '89
MELLENTIN, JULIA D., AND OTHERS
The gene for enhancer binding proteins E12/E47 lies at the t(1;19) breakpoint in acute leukemias. bibl f il *Science* 246:379-82 O 20 '89
MELLO, FERNANDO COLLOR DE *See* Collor de Mello, Fernando
MELLO, NANCY K., AND OTHERS
Buprenorphine suppresses cocaine self-administration by rhesus monkeys. bibl f il *Science* 245:859-62 Ag 25 '89
MELLON, PAUL
about
The fine art of giving [interview] S. Allis. il por *Time* 134:86-7 S 18 '89
MELLON (ANDREW W.) FOUNDATION *See* Andrew W. Mellon Foundation
MELLON BANK NA
Selling your problems to others. il por *Forbes* 143:97 Ja 9 '89
MELLOW, JAMES R.
Art: primitive landscapes. il *Architectural Digest* 46:186-91 D '89
MELMAN, LARRY BUD
about
Larry "Bud" Melman bakes a video potato. J. Bernard. il por *Video* 12:14 Mr '89

MELODY

Composers tune out [serious contemporary music] D. Matthews. *World Press Review* 36:71 N '89

MELONS

See also

Cooking—Fruit

Watermelons

Mad about melons! R. Haskell. il *Flower and Garden* 33:48-50+ My/Je '89

Ripening

Melon meter [research by Gerald Dull] J. A. Yeaple. *Popular Science* 235:130 N '89

MELTING

Effect of water on the composition of partial melts of greenstone and amphibolite. J. S. Beard and G. E. Lofgren. bibl f il *Science* 244:195-7 Ap 14 '89

Explaining and exploiting a winter worry [work of J. G. Dash on frost heave] A. McKenzie. *Science News* 136:407 D 23-30 '89

A grazing view of melting [research by Sean Brennan] I. Peterson. *Science News* 135:77 F 4 '89

Liquids, crystals and liquid crystals [cover story] J. D. Brock and others. bibl f il *Physics Today* 42:52-9 Jl '89

Thermomolecular pressure in surface melting: motivation for frost heave. J. G. Dash. bibl f il *Science* 246:1591-3 D 22 '89

Underplating and partial melting: implications for melt generation and extraction. G. W. Bergantz. bibl f il *Science* 245:1093-5 S 8 '89

MELTON, D. A.

(jt. auth) See Whitman, Malcolm, and Melton, D. A.

MELTON, FRANK

about

Broadcast news. L. Gite. il pors *Black Enterprise* 20:100-3+ D '89

MELTZER, ALLAN H.

Monetarist. *National Review* 41:47-8 Ja 27 '89

MELVILLE, HERMAN, 1819-1891

Anecdotes, facetiae, satire, etc.

Moby Dick 2.1. K. Sheldon. *Byte* 14:344 Jl '89

MELVILLE CORPORATION

Melville has a whale of a good story. J. Mendes. il *Fortune* 119:26 Ja 16 '89

MELVIN, JAMES E.

(jt. auth) See Foskett, J. Kevin, and Melvin, James E.

MELVIN SIMON & ASSOCIATES, INC.

No more plastic plants. S. B. Weiner. il por *Forbes* 143:107-8 Mr 20 '89

MELZACK, RONALD

about

Making a breakthrough. C. Wood. il por *Maclean's* 102:40-1 F 27 '89

THE MEMBER OF THE WEDDING [drama] See McCullers, Carson, 1917-1967

MEMBRANE TRANSPORT SYSTEMS See Biological transport

MEMBRANES (BIOLOGY)

See also

Blood-brain barrier

Calcium channels

Chloride channels

Epithelium

Ion channels

Mitochondrial membranes

Mucous membranes

Potassium channels

Protein transport

Sodium channels

Cellulose and the evolution of plant life [plant cell walls] L. C. Duchesne and D. W. Larson. bibl f il *BioScience* 39:238-41 Ap '89

DNA's extended domain [cover story] I. Wickelgren. il *Science News* 136:234-7 O 7 '89

Fluid membranes repel one another; solid membranes may not crumple. A. Khurana. bibl f il *Physics Today* 42 pt1:17-21 Ag '89

Hydrophobic organization of membrane proteins [Rhodobacter] D. C. Rees and others. bibl f il *Science* 245:510-13 Ag 4 '89

Land plants' algal roots [research by Charles F. Delwiche] *Science News* 136:70 Jl 29 '89

Lignin-like compounds and sporopollenin in Coleochaete, an algal model for land plant ancestry [study of cell walls] C. F. Delwiche and others. bibl f il *Science* 245:399-401 Jl 28 '89

Localization of the pancreatic beta cell glucose transporter to specific plasma membrane domains. L. Orci and others. bibl f il *Science* 245:295-7 Jl 21 '89

Mechanism of membrane anchoring affects polarized expression of two proteins in MDCK cells. D. A. Brown and others. bibl f il *Science* 245:1499-501 S 29 '89

Physiological constraint on feeding behavior: intestinal membrane disaccharidases of the starling. C. Martinez del Rio and B. R. Stevens. bibl f il *Science* 243:794-6 F 10 '89

Proton motive force involved in protein transport across the outer membrane of Aeromonas salmonicida. K. R. Wong and J. T. Buckley. bibl f il *Science* 246:654-6 N 3 '89

Purification and reconstitution of chloride channels from kidney and trachea [plasma membranes] D. W. Landry and others. bibl f il *Science* 244:1469-72 Je 23 '89

Signal peptide for protein secretion directing glycophospholipid membrane anchor attachment. I. W. Caras and G. N. Weddell. bibl f il *Science* 243:1196-8 Mr 3 '89

MEMBRANES (TECHNOLOGY)

See also

Memtec Ltd.

Molecular mechanisms and forces involved in the adhesion and fusion of amphiphilic bilayers. C. A. Helm and others. bibl f il *Science* 246:919-22 N 17 '89

Spontaneous vesicle formation in aqueous mixtures of single-tailed surfactants. E. W. Kaler and others. bibl f il *Science* 245:1371-4 S 22 '89

Synthetic membranes. P. H. Abelson. *Science* 244:1421 Je 23 '89

MEMENTOS See Souvenirs (Keepsakes)

MEMO PADS

Stickum up, love! [family communication via Post-It Notes] J. G. Hubbell. *Reader's Digest* 135:123-5 O '89

MEMOIRS See Autobiography

MEMORABILIA See Souvenirs (Keepsakes)

MEMORANDUMS

Mastering the memo. B. J. Mandel and J. Yellen. il *Working Woman* 14:134-7 S '89

Memo makeover: from fog to clarity [business memorandums] J. Pharriss. *Working Woman* 14:130-1 D '89

Memo of the month. See issues of The Washington Monthly

MEMORIAL DAY

Honoring the noble sacrifice [address, May 30, 1988] W. E. Hamm. *Vital Speeches of the Day* 55:626-7 Ag 1 '89

Collectibles

America's Memorial Day coin! [half-dollar commemorating 75th anniversary of the Battle of Gettysburg] E. Rochette. il *Antiques & Collecting Hobbies* 94:68-9 My '89

MEMORIAL SLOAN-KETTERING CANCER CENTER

Breast-cancer care: a state-of-the-art treatment site. *Vogue* 179:228 D '89

"We had to kidnap our son from the hospital" [D. Pagán jailed after husband takes leukemia-stricken son] J. L. Block. il pors *Good Housekeeping* 209:144-5+ O '89

MEMORIALS

See also

Crazy Horse, Sioux Chief, ca. 1842-1877—Memorials

Mount Rushmore National Memorial (S.D.)

War memorials

MEMORY

See also

Amnesia

Attention

Mnemonics

Past

Recognition (Psychology)

Boosting memory in the blink of an eye [use of nimodipine with aging rabbits; work of Richard A. Deyo] B. Bower. *Science News* 135:86 F 11 '89

Disorders of memory. C. Krauthammer. il *Time* 134:74 Jl 3 '89

Fading remembrances of television past [use of programs cancelled after one year to study long-term memory; work of Larry R. Squire] B. Bower. *Science News* 135:167 Mr 18 '89

Homer's greatest hits [S. Powelson memorizes the Iliad] J. Stone. il *Discover* 10:78-80+ S '89

Investigating eyewitness memory mishaps. B. Bower. *Science News* 135:134 Mr 4 '89

Marijuana mangles memory [research by Richard H. Schwartz] *Science News* 136:332 N 18 '89

Memories are made of this. S. Blakeslee. il *New Choices for the Best Years* 29:41-2+ N '89

Memories are made of this [cover story] K. Flieger. il *FDA Consumer* 23:14-19 S '89

Memory, imagination, and learning: connected by the story [place of story telling in teaching] K. Egan. bibl f il *Phi Delta Kappan* 70:455-9 F '89

Memory storage and neural systems. D. L. Alkon. il *Scientific American* 261:42-50 Jl '89

Molecules of memory [neurobiologist E. R. Kandel's work with Aplysia; cover story] G. Montgomery. il por *Discover* 10:46-50+ D '89

Nimodipine facilitates associative learning in aging rabbits [could counteract memory loss in the aged] R. A. Deyo and others. bibl f il *Science* 243:809-11 F 10 '89

Now, where did I put my . . . [effects of aging on memory] J. Hooper. il *Health (New York, N.Y.)* 21:72-3 N '89

Rabbit punch [use of nimodipine to boost memory in aging rabbits] il *Discover* 10:12 Je '89

Rajan Mahadevan is a memorable master of presto digit-tation [ability to memorize numbers] il por *People Weekly* 32:121 N 6 '89

The stuff memories are made of [role of neural synapses; research by William Greenough] il *U.S. News & World Report* 107:16+ N 13 '89

Womb with a view [techniques for remembering your own birth] K. Harary. il *Omni (New York, N.Y.)* 11:39-40+ Ag '89

MEMORY—*cont.*

You must remember this. B. Bryson. il *Gentlemen's Quarterly* 59:169+ Ap '89

Anecdotes, facetiae, satire, etc.

Selective memory. M. E. Marty. *The Christian Century* 106:863 S 27 '89

MEMORY CARDS *See* Smart cards

MEMORY DEVICES (COMPUTERS) *See* Computers—Memory systems

MEMOS *See* Memorandums

MEMPHIS (FIRM)

Merchant of Memphis [American distributor K. Johnson] M. Filler. il por *House & Garden* 161:64+ S '89

MEMPHIS (TENN.)

Architecture

On May Woods Lane. il *Southern Living* 24:132 My '89

Galleries and museums

See also

National Civil Rights Center (Memphis, Tenn.)

Historic houses, sites, etc.

See also

Graceland

Housing

Why Memphis sings the overbuilt blues. E. Schurenberg. il *Money* 18:73 Je '89

MEMTEC LTD.

Clearly bubbling up from Down Under. S. Hutcheon. il por *Business Week* p115 My 22 '89

MEN

See also

Beauty, Personal—Men

Christmas gifts for men

Cooking by men

Fathers

Heroes and heroines

Husbands

Mustaches

Sex differences

Single men

Widowers

Young men

About men. See issues of The New York Times Magazine

The American male: altered egos [comparison of 1929, 1959, and 1989] il *Vogue* 179:238-9 Je '89

Look who won our most admired women and men polls. il *Good Housekeeping* 208:48 Ja '89

Our men in crisis [black men; cover story; with editorial comment by Susan L. Taylor] il *Essence* 20:47, 49-52+ N '89

Anatomy and physiology

Bad news bellies [paunchiness linked to diabetes and heart disease] D. Grady. il *American Health* 8:20 My '89

The paunch line [link between waist-to-hip girth ratio and health; research by Richard Terry] J. Poppy. il *Esquire* 111:59-60 F '89

The paunch line [link between waist-to-hip girth ratio and health; research by Richard Terry] J. Poppy. il *Reader's Digest* 135:133-5 Ag '89

Anecdotes, facetiae, satire, etc.

The Bing report. S. Bing. See issues of Esquire beginning July 1989

Attitudes

The American man in transition [survey] il *American Health* 8:59-61 Ja/F '89

The happiness report. G. Sheehy. il *Glamour* 87:308-13+ Ap '89

His. W. D. Leight. See issues of Mademoiselle beginning December 1987

Jake: a man's opinion. See issues of Glamour

Men at work: is sex on their minds—or what? [survey results] il *Glamour* 87:124-9 Ja '89

Men hate short hair, love short skirts. True or false? W. Geist. il *Vogue* 179:152 Ag '89

Men: what do they expect from marriage today? N. Dawidoff. il *Glamour* 87:236-9+ My '89

Obsessed by hair. il *Glamour* 87:184-9 F '89

Oh men, oh women! [views on marriage; symposium] il *Ladies' Home Journal* 106:90+ S '89

Say, brother. See issues of Essence beginning May 1983

Spying on guys: what men say when women aren't around [special section] D. Hellerstein. il *Mademoiselle* 95:104-9+ Ja '89

What men love about the women of summer. J. P. Davis. il *Glamour* 87:170-1+ Jl '89

What men want (I). S. Cook. il *Gentlemen's Quarterly* 59:294-301+ O '89

What men want (II). S. Cook. il *Gentlemen's Quarterly* 59:272-7+ N '89

Who is the new ideal man? [survey results] S. Keen and O. Zur. il *Psychology Today* 23:54+ N '89

Women we love [cover story; special section] il *Esquire* 112:86-101 Ag '89

Clothing and dress

See Clothing and dress—Men

Hairstyling

See Hairstyling

Health and hygiene

See also

Beauty, Personal—Men

Active health. J. Poppy. See issues of Esquire beginning June 1988

Body and soul: health. C. Sherman. See issues of Gentlemen's Quarterly

Photographs and photography

Rites of man. P. Brown. il *Mother Jones* 14:25-31 S '89

Psychology

See also

Beauty, Personal—Psychological aspects

Masculinity (Psychology)

50 ways to scare your lover. W. D. Leight. *Mademoiselle* 95:84 Je '89

The American man in transition [cover story; special section] il *American Health* 8:59-73 Ja/F '89

. . . and the woman who loves him [relationship with a Casanova] E. Royte. il *Mademoiselle* 95:190+ My '89

Fighting violence against women is a man's job too. J. Stoltenberg. *Utne Reader* p44 N/D '89

The hit & run lover. D. Heyn. *Mademoiselle* 95:130 Mr '89

How men's hearts break. W. D. Leight. *Mademoiselle* 95:49 Ap '89

How to criticize a man. J. Stone. il *Glamour* 87:146 Je '89

The lies men tell. D. Seeley. il *Mademoiselle* 95:172-3+ Je '89

Male pride: a pain in the ego. W. D. Leight. *Mademoiselle* 95:60 Ja '89

The man who couldn't be faithful [confessions of a Casanova] P. Trachtenberg. il *Mademoiselle* 95:188-9+ My '89

The man who loves misery—yours. D. Heyn. *Mademoiselle* 95:120 N '89

The man who would be bossy. W. D. Leight. *Mademoiselle* 95:97 D '89

Men and abortion. E. K. Goodman. il *Glamour* 87:178-9+ Jl '89

Men have feelings too [special section] il *Mademoiselle* 95:186-7+ N '89

Midlife crises in men: are women to blame? S. Amsterdam. il *TV Guide* 37:18-20 Jl 22-28 '89

My imaginary child [coping with wife's miscarriage] W. P. Hogue. il *Glamour* 87:284 My '89

The no-regrets ultimatum. C. Bushnell. il *Mademoiselle* 95:186+ Ap '89

The passive-aggressive male. L. Grunwald. il *Esquire* 111:105-8+ Ap '89

Splendor on the grass [sports heroes] J. Schulian. il *Gentlemen's Quarterly* 59:142-5+ Ja '89

Spying on guys: what men say when women aren't around [special section] D. Hellerstein. il *Mademoiselle* 95:104-9+ Ja '89

Support for partners [male response to rape] D. Burden. *Psychology Today* 23:72-3 S '89

Unsportsmanlike conduct. L. L. Riskin. il *The New York Times Magazine* p14+ Ja 22 '89

What is it with guys and baseball? R. Rosenbaum. il *Mademoiselle* 95:66+ Jl '89

What men really mean when they say "I love you". il *Glamour* 87:182-3+ F '89

What men really want in bed. J. P. Davis. il *Glamour* 87:256-7+ Je '89

What men want in bed [excerpt from How to keep your man monogamous] A. Penney. il *Ladies' Home Journal* 106:80+ Ag '89

What took me so long [getting married] D. McDonough. il *Glamour* 87:282-3+ S '89

Who, him? Worry about his body? D. Seeley. il *Mademoiselle* 95:258-9+ Ap '89

Who, me—angry? How guys hide their ire. D. Heyn. *Mademoiselle* 95:76 Je '89

Why home plate is where his heart is. W. D. Leight. *Mademoiselle* 95:111 O '89

Anecdotes, facetiae, satire, etc.

For better, for worst: why are men such babies when they get sick? M. Kaufman. *Reader's Digest* 134:49-50 F '89

If it's broke, I can't fix it [men who aren't mechanically inclined] W. D. Leight. *Mademoiselle* 95:82 Jl '89

Mid-life sax [middle-aged men taking up saxophone] J. Nocera. il *Esquire* 111:52 Ap '89

Reading

Action! Adventure! Sales! [men's adventure series] D. E. Showalter. il *Publishers Weekly* 235:20-2+ My 5 '89

Religious life

In search of the hero: masculine spirituality and liberal Christianity [cover story] P. M. Arnold. il *America* 161:206-10 O 7 '89

State of the question [discussion of October 7, 1989 article, In search of the hero: masculine spirituality and liberal Christianity] P. M. Arnold. *America* 161:304-6 N 4 '89

MEN—*cont.*

Sexual behavior

See Sexual behavior

Statistics

Where the boys are: proportion of the 18-to-44 age group that is male, by county. B. Edmondson and B. Cutler. map *The Atlantic* 263:67 F '89

MEN [television program] See Television program reviews—Single works

MEN AND WOMEN *See* Women and men

MEN GARDENERS *See* Gardeners

MEN IN ADVERTISING

Television insults men, too. B. R. Goldberg. il *Reader's Digest* 134:185-6 Je '89

MEN IN LITERATURE *See* Characters in literature

MEN IN TELEVISION

A fun-house mirror on American men [thirtysomething's male characters; cover story] S. Fried. il *Gentlemen's Quarterly* 59:264-9+ Ap '89

The male eunuch [shows about abandoned men] R. Powers. il *Gentlemen's Quarterly* 59:108+ F '89

Stop bashing men! J. Cohen. il *TV Guide* 37:27-9 Ag 12-18 '89

TV's ideal men? H. Stein. il *TV Guide* 37:8-11 Mr 25-31 '89

MEN, WOMEN AND GOD: CHRISTIANS FOR BIBLICAL EQUALITY (ORGANIZATION)

New statement affirms equality of men, women. M. G. Maudlin. *Christianity Today* 33:38 Ag 18 '89

MENACKER, JULIUS, AND OTHERS

School order and safety as community issues. bibl f il *Phi Delta Kappan* 71:39-40+ S '89

MENCKEN, H. L. (HENRY LOUIS), 1880-1956

Mencken's diaries: sustained by scorn and beer [excerpts from The diary of H. L. Mencken]; ed. by Charles A. Fecher. il por *The New York Times Book Review* 94:1+ D 17 '89

about

First encounters. E. Sorel and N. C. Sorel. il *The Atlantic* 264:101 N '89

The lost Mencken. G. C. Ward. il *American Heritage* 40:14+ D '89

A member of the 'booboisie'. J. Alter. il por *Newsweek* 114:66 D 18 '89

MENCKEN, HENRY LOUIS See Mencken, H. L. (Henry Louis), 1880-1956

MEND (ORGANIZATION)

Can you say "apple pie" in Russian? [Soviet women visit America] E. Sloan-Bubrick. il *McCall's* 116:10 Jl '89

Mothers on a diplomatic mission. V. Cadden. il *McCall's* 116:86+ Ap '89

MENDEL, RICHARD A.

(jt. auth) See Stubbing, Richard A., and Mendel, Richard A.

MENDELSOHN, ERICH, 1887-1953

about

Pioneering the modern movement in Palestine. J. Rykwert. il por *Architectural Digest* 46:82+ O '89

MENDELSOHN, JACK

START deals cut at Jackson Hole. il pors *The Bulletin of the Atomic Scientists* 45:25-7 D '89

MENDELSOHN, JACK, AND HALVERSON, THOMAS

The conventional balance: a TKO for NATO? [cover story] bibl f il *The Bulletin of the Atomic Scientists* 45:30-4+ Mr '89

MENDELSOHN, JOHN, 1949-

about

John Mendelsohn at Michael Walls. K. Johnson. *Art in America* 77:155 Ja '89

MENDELSON, LOTTIE, AND MENDELSON, ROBERT

Are you teaching your family the facts of health? [quiz] il *Good Housekeeping* 209:124+ S '89

MENDELSON, ROBERT

(jt. auth) See Mendelson, Lottie, and Mendelson, Robert

MENDES, JONATHAN DE SOLA

about

Park Avenue Gothic: a family feud turns into a fight to the death. B. Costikyan. il pors *New York* 22:46-50+ Mr 20 '89

MENDES FILHO, CHICO

about

Chronicle of a death foretold. M. Beck. il por *Newsweek* 113:62 Ja 9 '89

Defenders of the Amazon [cover story] S. Hecht and A. Cockburn. il *The Nation* 248:695-6+ My 22 '89

In memory of Chico Mendes. J. D. Hair. il *International Wildlife* 19:30 Mr/Ap '89

Murder in the Amazon. J. Bierman. il por *Maclean's* 102:21 Ja 9 '89

Notes and comment. il *The New Yorker* 65:27-8 F 20 '89

Rain forest politics [discussion of May 22, 1989 article, Defenders of the Amazon] S. Hecht and A. Cockburn. *The Nation* 249:262+ S 18 '89

Anecdotes, facetiae, satire, etc.

Gold diggers of '89. J. Queenan. il *The American Spectator* 22:34 O '89

Bibliography

Five books to explore the life and work of Chico Mendes. C. Goodrich. il *Publishers Weekly* 236:22-3 Ag 18 '89

MENDEZ, RAYMOND A.

Hanging tough [photograph] il *Natural History* p116-17 N '89

MENDLOWITZ, BENJAMIN

Classic wooden boats [excerpt from Wood, water and light] il *Oceans* 22:46-53 Mr/Ap '89

MENDOCINO (CALIF.)

Restaurants, nightclubs, bars, etc.

The taste of Mendocino [Cafe Beaujolais] M. Barrier. il por *Nation's Business* 77:11-12 Je '89

Wine industry

See Wine industry

MENDOCINO COUNTY (CALIF.)

Description and travel

Mendocino vacation rentals. *Sunset (Central West edition)* 182:31 Ap '89

MENDOZA, TERRI

Diet, cancer, and common sense. il *Current Health 2* 16:18-21 N '89

Fats and sodium in your diet. il *Current Health 2* 16:18-21 O '89

Good morning sugar, salt, and fat. il *Current Health 2* 15:22-5 Mr '89

Mighty minerals in mini-doses. il *Current Health 2* 16:22-5 D '89

The power of iron. il *Current Health 2* 15:14-16 Ap '89

Sizing up food servings. il *Current Health 2* 16:20-2 S '89

MENDOZA (ARGENTINA)

Municipal improvement

Turning a new leaf. D. Einhorn. il *Américas* 41 no1:2-3 '89

MENEM, CARLOS SAÚL

about

Abdication in Argentina. J. Contreras. il por *Newsweek* 113:46-7 Je 26 '89

Argentina drifts toward disaster [cover story] A. Evans-Pritchard. il *The American Spectator* 22:19-21+ S '89

Argentina gets ready for 'surgery without anesthetic' [with interview] J. Ryser and R. A. Kessler. il por *Business Week* p46+ O 2 '89

Can business save Argentina? J. Ryser and R. A. Kessler. il pors *Business Week* p46-8 S 18 '89

Carlos Menem: a Peronist who may rule like a pragmatist. J. Ryser and R. A. Kessler. il por *Business Week* p41 Jl 3 '89

Carlos Menem in the driver's seat. A. M. Shapiro. il *The New Leader* 72:10-11 Jl 10-24 '89

Cry, Argentina. J. Malamud-Goti. *The Nation* 249:517-18 N 6 '89

The generals don't repent. P. Lacefield. *Commonweal* 116:583-4 N 3 '89

"Get up and walk!". G. D. Garcia. il por *Time* 134:39 Jl 24 '89

Menem's dangerous maneuvers. A. M. Shapiro. il *The New Leader* 72:12-13 N 13 '89

A Peronist triumph. M. Nemeth. il por *Maclean's* 102:24 My 29 '89

Peronists seek "nuclear greatness". R. A. Kessler. il por *The Bulletin of the Atomic Scientists* 45:13-15 My '89

Peron's latest hurrah. E. Ehrmann. *National Review* 41:20-1 Je 16 '89

Return of the Peronists? J. Contreras. il por *Newsweek* 113:48 My 15 '89

Should anyone cry for Argentina? C. A. Robbins and J. Staubus. il por *U.S. News & World Report* 107:51+ O 30 '89

A test for Latin democracy. G. D. Garcia. il por *Time* 133:46 My 15 '89

The voice of Argentine voters will echo through Latin America. R. A. Kessler and J. Ryser. il por *Business Week* p60 Mr 20 '89

We cry for you, Argentina. C. A. Robbins. il *U.S. News & World Report* 107:22 Jl 24 '89

MENENDEZ, RAMON

about

Stand and deliver [film] Reviews

Video il 12:82 Ja '89. J. Young

MENGES, CHRIS

about

A world apart [film] Reviews

American Film il 15:102 O '89. P. Rainer

MENGIN, CHRISTIANE

The Friedrichstrasse, a link in the chain of history. il map *The Unesco Courier* 42:10-14 Ag '89

MENGISTU HAILE-MARIAM

about

Fizzled coup. *Time* 133:61 My 29 '89

MENINGITIS

In the grip of a plague [meningitis strikes Africa] S. Seibert. il map *Newsweek* 113:38 Ap 10 '89

Diagnosis

Watching for red flags [signs in small children] P. Klass. il *The New York Times Magazine* p56-7 Ap 23 '89

MENNEN COMPANY
Sweating it out [Real deodorant] C. Poole. il *Forbes* 144:274 O 16 '89
MENNONITES
See also
Amish
MENOPAUSE
The anti-aging patch for women [transdermal patch releases estrogen] S. Fields and L. Holland. il *Good Housekeeping* 208:163-4 F '89
Celebrating my change of life [D. L. Siegal] R. Loth. il por *New Choices for the Best Years* 29:16+ My '89
Estrogen effects assessed [risk of breast cancer in postmenopausal women] *Science News* 136:86 Ag 5 '89
Estrogen use linked to breast cancer. J. L. Marx. *Science* 245:593 Ag 11 '89
Hard looks at hormones [estrogen and progestin may increase risk of breast cancer] J. Langone. il *Time* 134:56 Ag 14 '89
Hormone replacement therapy: is it for you? S. Mahler. *McCall's* 117:149 O '89
The (meno)pause that refreshes [depression aspect; research by Sonja and John McKinlay] P. King. il *Psychology Today* 22:11 D '88
The miracles and misfires of medicine [progestin and estrogen increase risk of breast cancer in postmenopausal women] *U.S. News & World Report* 107:16+ Ag 14 '89
Should you take estrogen? [hormone replacement therapy] C. Perlmutter. il *Prevention (Emmaus, Pa.)* 41:42-51 N '89
An update on estrogen-replacement therapy. N. Simon. il *Working Woman* 14:148+ My '89
MENORAH
Christmas in July [crèche and menorah decision issued by the Supreme Court] *America* 161:27 Jl 15-22 '89
Court and crèche [Supreme Court ruling on religious symbols on public property] *The Christian Century* 106:713 Ag 2-9 '89
Ignore a menorah [Supreme Court rules on public religious displays] S. Bates. *The New Republic* 201:14-16 Jl 31 '89
Is the Court hostile to religion? [Christmas crèche-menorah display decision] R. N. Ostling. il *Time* 134:80 Jl 17 '89
MEN'S CLOTHES *See* Clothing and dress—Men
MEN'S EARRINGS *See* Earrings
MEN'S FRIENDSHIPS *See* Friendship
MEN'S HAIRSTYLING *See* Hairstyling
MEN'S LIBERATION MOVEMENT
See also
In Search of Justice (Organization)
Connecting with the wild man inside all males [interview with R. Bly] K. Thompson. *Utne Reader* p58 N/D '89
Mano a mano [attending gatherings hosted by R. Bly] M. Ventura. il *American Health* 8:64-5 Ja/F '89
A men's group story. D. Guy. il *Utne Reader* p56-7 N/D '89
Methinks I see my father. A. Meyer. il *American Health* 8:66-7 Ja/F '89
Of hawks and men: a weekend in the male wilderness [men's retreat run by S. Bliss] J. Tevlin. il *Utne Reader* p50-7+ N/D '89
The wild man [interview with R. Bly] A. Meyer. *American Health* 8:67-8 Ja/F '89
Canada
Redefining roles. N. Underwood. il *Maclean's* 102:46-7 Ag 14 '89
MEN'S SHIRTS *See* Shirts
MEN'S TENNIS COUNCIL
Power games grip men's tour. G. M. Heldman. il *World Tennis* 36:16-17 F '89
MENSAH, ANASTASIA
about
Black female student from Russia to attend U. of D.C. il por *Jet* 76:24 Ag 21 '89
MENSAH, BARBARA
about
DNA test says Ali isn't father of Houston girl. il pors *Jet* 75:52 F 20 '89
MENSTRUAL CYCLE *See* Menstruation
MENSTRUATION
See also
Menopause
The fertility cycle. L. Villarosa. il *Essence* 19:18+ F '89
Anecdotes, facetiae, satire, etc.
Pro-life pro. P. Roth. il *The New York Review of Books* 36:5 Ag 17 '89
Disorders
See also
Premenstrual syndrome
Lead upsets menstrual cycle in monkeys [research by Nellie K. Laughlin] A. McKenzie. *Science News* 136:373 D 9 '89
No periods and not pregnant. P. A. Hillard. il *Parents* 64:162+ F '89
Therapy
See also
Ibuprofen

How to make your period less of a pain. S. Young. il *Glamour* 87:70 Ja '89
MENTAL DEPRESSION *See* Depression, Mental
MENTAL DEVELOPMENT OF INFANTS *See* Infants—Growth and development
MENTAL HEALING
See also
Faith cure
Healing hands [noncontact therapeutic touch] M. Schecter. il *Psychology Today* 23:28+ Jl/Ag '89
Healing rituals hit the suburbs [excerpt from Ritual healing in suburban America; cover story] M. B. McGuire. il *Psychology Today* 23:57-64 Ja/F '89
The healing touch. M. Brown. il *Utne Reader* p20 My/Je '89
MENTAL HEALTH
See also
Maturity
Mental illness
Mind and body
National Institute of Mental Health (U.S.)
Psychiatry
Psychotherapy
Relaxation
Mind health. C. Tavris. See issues of Vogue
Research
See Psychiatric research
Middle East
Mental health adds quality to life. N. N. Wig. il *World Health* p24-6 Jl '89
MENTAL HEALTH CENTERS
Mobile mental health team reaches minorities [Pacific Clinics mental health center in Pasadena, Calif.] A. H. Hernandez and C. Schweon. il *Aging* no359:12-13 '89
MENTAL HEALTH LAWS
See also
Mentally handicapped—Civil rights
MENTAL HOSPITALS *See* Hospitals, Psychiatric
MENTAL ILLNESS
See also
Art and mental illness
Autism
Depression, Mental
Mentally ill
Nervous breakdown
Paranoia
Schizophrenia
Sociopaths, suicide and serotonin. R. Cowen. *Science News* 136:250 O 14 '89
Spare the rod, spare the child [adult emotional problems can result from harsh discipline as a child; research by Sandra Holmes and Lee Robins] N. Jordan. il *Psychology Today* 23:16 Je '89
Diagnosis
The diagnostic dilemma [revision of the Diagnostic and statistical manual of mental disorders] B. Bower. il *Science News* 135:120-2 F 25 '89
Marcus Welby, J.D. [mental illness diagnosis and legal defense; cover story] W. Saletan and N. Watzman. *The New Republic* 200:19-22+ Ap 17 '89
Genetic aspects
Mysteries of the mind. il *Good Housekeeping* 208:46+ Ja '89
Troubles encountered in gene linkage land [difficulty in replicating mental disorder studies] D. M. Barnes. *Science* 243:313-14 Ja 20 '89
Research
See Psychiatric research
Therapy
See also
Psychopharmacology
Psychotherapy
Order on the couch [treatments of psychiatric disorders] J. Alper. il *The Atlantic* 263:24-7+ My '89
MENTAL IMAGES *See* Imagery (Psychology)
MENTAL PRAYER *See* Meditation
MENTALLY HANDICAPPED
See also
Angelman syndrome
Fragile X syndrome
Group homes for the mentally handicapped
Prader-Willi syndrome
Savant syndrome
Civil rights
Bad news for death row [Supreme Court okays execution of juvenile and retarded criminals] A. L. Sanders. il *Time* 134:48-9 Jl 10 '89
Execute an 8-year-old? The Johnny Penry case [mentally retarded adult awaiting execution in Texas] R. F. Drinan. *The Christian Century* 106:199-200 F 22 '89
High Court ruling upholds states' rights to execute young killers, retarded. *Jet* 76:4 Jl 10 '89
Uncle Sam's NIMBY attack [Justice Dept. suing Chicago Heights] J. P. Shapiro. il *U.S. News & World Report* 107:24 S 18 '89

MENTALLY HANDICAPPED—*cont.*

Crimes against

Darkness at the heart of town [high school boys arrested for sexually assaulting a retarded girl in Glen Ridge, N.J.] P. Wilkinson. il *Rolling Stone* p55-6+ O 5 '89

Gang rape in the suburbs [attack on retarded girl in Glen Ridge, N.J.] B. Turque. il *Newsweek* 113:26 Je 5 '89

Family relationships

Severing the cord [son with fetal alcohol syndrome; excerpt from The broken cord] M. Dorris. il *Mother Jones* 14:47-8 S '89

Institutional care

See also

Staten Island Developmental Center

Driven by an unquenchable spirit, a Massachusetts woman writes an impossible book [confinement of cerebral palsy patient R. Sienkiewicz-Mercer to Belchertown State School] L. Smith. il pors *People Weekly* 32:107+ S 11 '89

I raise my eyes to say yes [confinement of cerebral palsy patient to Belchertown State School in Massachusetts; excerpts] R. Sienkiewicz-Mercer and S. B. Kaplan. il *Glamour* 87:280-1+ O '89

Rehabilitation

Back in the land of the living [65 year old retarded man named Paul adjusts to the world after living in a Maryland attic for decades] M. S. Holmes. il *People Weekly* 31:42-7 My 29 '89

MENTALLY HANDICAPPED CHILDREN

See also

Autism

Down syndrome

Parents of the mentally handicapped

Brain risk seen in sickle cell kids [study by Andrea V. Swift] R. Weiss. *Science News* 136:404 D 23-30 '89

Care and treatment

See also

LIFE Program

Education

AIDS: students in glass houses? [case of E. Martinez in Tampa, Fla.] P. A. Zirkel. bibl f il *Phi Delta Kappan* 70:646-8 Ap '89

MENTALLY ILL

See also

Drugs and the mentally ill

Care and treatment

See also

Hospitals, Psychiatric

Journey to the streets [betrayal of the mentally ill; views of E. F. Torrey] D. Gelman. *Newsweek* 113:58 Ja 23 '89

When mental illness hits home [with case study of schizophrenic J. Alexander; cover story; special section] E. E. Goode. il pors *U.S. News & World Report* 106:54-7+ Ap 24 '89

Family relationships

Lost brother [coping with schizophrenic] K. King. il pors *Life* 12:94-8+ N '89

Memories of Frank [manic-depressive brother who committed suicide] M. K. Blakely. il *Psychology Today* 23:48-50+ O '89

Out of the ashes, a family restored [P. Daniluk reunited with mother who is a patient in mental institution after separation of 64 years] M. Dougherty. il pors *People Weekly* 31:46-51 F 13 '89

Rehabilitation

Return of Marie Balter [former patient helps administer Danvers State Hospital] T. Armbrister. il por *Reader's Digest* 135:123-7 Jl '89

MENTALLY ILL CHILDREN

See also

Autism

Care and treatment

Childhood mental disorders. *The Futurist* 23:46 N/D '89

MENTALLY RETARDED *See* Mentally handicapped

MENTALLY RETARDED CHILDREN *See* Mentally handicapped children

MENTORS

See also

Business mentors

When it's time for a change. A. Gottlieb. *McCall's* 117:113-14 N '89

MENTORS IN EDUCATION *See* Educational counseling

MENUS

See also

Breakfasts

Brunches

Buffet meals

Dinners and dining

Lunches

Meals

Gourmet's menus. See issues of Gourmet

[Month] menus. See issues of Sunset (Central West edition)

MENUS (COMPUTER PROGRAMMING)

Make word processing easier with macros and menus. R. Kendall. il *Home Office Computing* 7:20-1 Ag '89

MENZEL, PAT

about

Toughest job. G. H. Colt. il pors *Life* 12:100-4+ My '89

MEOLA, TONY

about

A glue-fingered U.S. goalie keeps opponents' net profits to zero. R. Arias. il pors *People Weekly* 32:105-6 D 18 '89

MERCALDO, STEVE

Taking care of your car. See issues of Popular Science through April 1989

MERCANTILE TEXAS CORP.

See also

MCorp

MERCAPTANS *See* Mercapto compounds

MERCAPTO COMPOUNDS

Orthogonal self-assembled monolayers: alkanethiols on gold and alkane carboxylic acids on alumina. P. E. Laibinis and others. bibl f il *Science* 245:845-7 Ag 25 '89

MERCE CUNNINGHAM DANCE COMPANY

Chris Komar expands his work as a Cunningham dancer. il pors *Dance Magazine* 63:12 Mr '89

Dancing:

Performances of Five stone wind, Cargo X, and Field and figures. A. Croce. *The New Yorker* 65:106-8 Ap 3 '89

Mature talents. L. A. Jacobs. il *The New Leader* 72:23 Ap 3-17 '89

Points in space [performance of Five stone wind] T. Tobias. il *New York* 22:84-5 Mr 20 '89

Reviews:

Performances at City Center, New York City. N. V. Dalva. il por *Dance Magazine* 63:66+ Je '89

MERCEDES-BENZ (AUTOMOBILE) *See* Automobiles, Foreign; Convertibles (Automobiles)

MERCENARIES (SOLDIERS) *See* Mercenary troops

MERCENARY TROOPS

See also

United Nations. Ad Hoc Committee on the Drafting of an International Convention against the Recruitment, Use, Financing and Training of Mercenaries

The Israeli connection [mercenaries involved in training Colombian hit squads] E. Magnuson. il *Time* 134:26 S 11 '89

MERĆEP, MLADEN, AND OTHERS

Activation-driven programmed cell death and T cell receptor $\zeta\eta$ expression. bibl f il *Science* 246:1162-5 D 1 '89

MERCER, MARILYN

Infidelity. il *New Choices for the Best Years* 29:58-62 Je '89

(ed) See Harris, Henry. When to call the doctor

MERCER, RUTH SIENKIEWICZ- *See* Sienkiewicz-Mercer, Ruth

MERCHANDISE *See* Commercial products

MERCHANDISE, QUALITY OF *See* Quality of products

MERCHANDISE, SECONDHAND *See* Secondhand trade

MERCHANDISING

See also

Marketing Innovations International

Rebates

Samples (Merchandising)

Anger on the Island [dispute over Anne of Green Gables merchandising] R. Corelli. il *Maclean's* 102:40 Jl 10 '89

Who makes it? G. Williams. il *Home Mechanix* 85:72-3+ F '89

MERCHANT, CAROLYN

Ecofeminists draw the connections between sexism and environmental degradation. il *Utne Reader* p76 N/D '89

MERCHANT, NATALIE

about

10,000 Maniacs break loose. A. DeCurtis. il pors *Rolling Stone* p64-6+ Je 15 '89

Like 10,000 Maniacs, the band she leads, Natalie Merchant demands to be heard. J. Leland. por *Vogue* 179:82 Jl '89

MERCHANT BANKING *See* Investment banking

THE MERCHANT OF VENICE [drama] *See* Shakespeare, William, 1564-1616

MERCHANT SEAMEN

Water transportation occupations. D. E. Hecker. il *Occupational Outlook Quarterly* 33:20-3 Spr '89

MERCK & CO., INC.

A culture that just keeps dishing up success. J. Weber, Jr. il *Business Week* Special Issue:120 Je 16 '89

Merck wants to be alone—but with lots of friends. J. Weber, Jr. il *Business Week* p62 O 23 '89

Suspect vaccine [K. Fox files suit after developing rubella vaccine side effects] H. S. Miller. il por *Ms.* 17:81-2 Ap '89

MERCURY

See also

Plants—Mercury content

MERCURY (PLANET)

Atmosphere

Mercury's atmosphere: an inside source? J. Eberhart. *Science News* 136:311 N 11 '89

Internal structure

Iron planet [theory that Mercury was formed due to impacts with other planets] R. Kunzig. il *Discover* 10:66-9 F '89

MERCURY ASSET MANAGEMENT (FIRM)

An English suitor for Max & Erma's? G. G. Marcial. *Business Week* p166 N 27 '89

MERCURY DIVISION See Ford Motor Co. Lincoln-Mercury Division
MERCURY IN THE BODY
See also
Mercury poisoning
Dentist's device [Amalgameter to measure mercury vapor emitted from fillings] il *FDA Consumer* 23:35-6 O '89
Scared of the dentist's chair? [hazards of filling cavities with silver-mercury amalgams] C. Fahey. il *Utne Reader* p16+ N/D '89
MERCURY MARINE (FIRM)
Fifty years in the fast lane [C. Kiekhaefer] J. Skorupa. il *Popular Mechanics* 166:22-3 Ja '89
MERCURY POISONING
Hold the tuna [risk from cat food] V. Adler. *American Health* 8:110 Jl/Ag '89
Pot peril [smokers of marijuana; work of Barbara and Sanford Siegel] P. McCarthy. il *American Health* 8:16 D '89
A tuna a day makes the cat slow to play [research by Katherine A. Houpt] *Science News* 135:111 F 18 '89
MERCY
A not-too severe mercy. T. C. Muck. il *Christianity Today* 33:14 Jl 14 '89
When mercy hurts. C. Williams. il *Christianity Today* 33:16-19 F 3 '89
MERCY KILLING See Euthanasia
MERCY KILLING OF ANIMALS See Euthanasia—Animals
MERCY OF GOD See God—Mercy
MEREDITH, JAMES
about
The long, lonely road of rights hero James Meredith ends in a job with Jesse Helms. A. Gonzalez. il pors *People Weekly* 32:40-1 O 16 '89
Meredith readies for post on Sen. Jesse Helms' staff, black leaders bristling. il pors *Jet* 77:12-13 O 16 '89
MEREDITH, NIKKI
Into the Battlezone: the making of a woman warrior. *Health (New York, N.Y.)* 21:70-1 Je '89
MERINGUE
Christmas meringues. il *The Mother Earth News* 120:42-4 N/D '89
MERIT CERTIFICATES See Certificates of merit
MERIT PAY
The changing basis for pay. R. M. Kanter. bibl *Society* 26:54-65 S/O '89
Does greater merit mean better money? J. Scandura. il *Working Woman* 14:76 Ja '89
Group therapy: the answer to merit pay. S. Waldman. *The Washington Monthly* 21:38+ Mr '89
What's new in employee paychecks? W. Cole. *Working Woman* 14:25-7 My '89
MERKIN, DAPHNE
Dreaming of Hitler. il *Esquire* 112:75-8+ Ag '89
Ready, willing and wary. il *The New York Times Magazine* p12+ Jl 16 '89
MERKIN, RICHARD, 1938-
Merkin on style. See issues of Gentlemen's Quarterly beginning March 1988
MERKLING, FRANK
Details! Details! il *Opera News* 54:18-20+ N '89
The furtive tear. il *Opera News* 53:28-9 Ap 15 '89
MERLINE, JOHN W.
Calling all consumers. See issues of Consumers' Research Magazine
MERMIN, N. DAVID
Prizes and their problems [discussion of January 1989 article, What's wrong with these prizes?] *Physics Today* 42:97-102 D '89
What's wrong with these equations? il por *Physics Today* 42:9+ O '89
What's wrong with these prizes? il por *Physics Today* 42:9+ Ja '89
What's wrong with this pillow? il *Physics Today* 42:9+ Ap '89
What's wrong with this prose? por *Physics Today* 42:9+ My '89
about
Can you help the Mets by watching on TV? R. Pool. il por *Science* 244:773-4 My 19 '89
Physics' unseen hand. W. F. Allman. il *U.S. News & World Report* 107:65 O 23 '89
Quantum baseball [cover story] I. Peterson. il por *Science News* 136:88-9 Ag 5 '89
MERMIN, ROB
about
Feel like clowning around? Step right up to Rob Mermin's big top camp, Circus Smirkus. A. Chambers. il pors *People Weekly* 32:99-101 Ag 14 '89
MERNIT, SUSAN
The day-care deadline. *Harper's Bazaar* 122:65+ Jl '89
MERRIFIELD, LEWIS B., III
about
"We satisfy egos". R. King. il por *Forbes* 144:101 Jl 24 '89
MERRILL, GEORGE
about
Boy Meets Girl: a star-quality couple! D. McCue. il pors *Teen* 33:45 Jl '89

Boy Meets Girl! Boy loses girl! But now they're back together, and singing in an altared state. il pors *People Weekly* 31:69 Ja 16 '89
MERRILL, JAMES INGRAM
Overdue pilgrimage to Nova Scotia [poem] *The New Yorker* 65:50 O 23 '89
Quatrains for Pegasus [poem] *The Nation* 248:601 My 1 '89
MERRILL LYNCH & CO., INC.
The $1.2 billion-dollar man [D. J. Peterson] E. S. Ely. por *Personal Computing* 13:72 Jl '89
The broker who wouldn't grow up [A. G. Edwards vs. Merrill Lynch] il *Business Week* p94 Mr 27 '89
The market is high but cash is a trap [interview with C. Clough] J. Mendes. il por *Fortune* 120:37 O 9 '89
The remaking of Merrill Lynch. J. Friedman. il por *Business Week* p122-5 Jl 17 '89
MERRILL LYNCH CANADA INC.
Revolution at Merrill Lynch. P. C. Newman. il *Maclean's* 102:66 N 20 '89
MERRILL LYNCH CAPITAL MARKETS
Can bankers sell groceries [Merrill Lynch leveraged buyout of Supermarkets General] G. Morgenson. il *Forbes* 144:54+ O 30 '89
MERRIMACK RIVER (N.H. AND MASS.)
Another week on the Concord and Merrimack [H. D. Thoreau's trip] R. Crum. *Wilderness* 53:11-12+ Fall '89
MERRIN, EDWARD H.
about
The antiquities boom: who pays the price? [cover story] W. Grimes. il pors *The New York Times Magazine* p16-19+ Jl 16 '89
MERRITT, ABRAHAM, 1882-1943
about
The science-fiction fantasy world of A. Merritt. D. E. Matter and R. M. Matter. il *Antiques & Collecting Hobbies* 93:47-9 F '89
MERRITT, CHRIS
about
Knight of bel canto. A. Guzelimian. il pors *Opera News* 54:10-13 Jl '89
MERRITT, JIM
Design of life. bibl il *Modern Maturity* 32:42-7 Je/Jl '89
Here Custer died. il por map *Americana* 16:30-5 Ja/F '89
Remembering the frontier. il map *Americana* 17:34-9 My/Je '89
MERRITT, JOHN I. See Merritt, Jim
MERRITT ISLAND (FLA.)
See also
Architecture, Domestic—Merritt Island (Fla.)
MERRY-GO-ROUND ENTERPRISES, INC.
Hot streak. E. F. Cone. il por *Forbes* 143:10 Je 26 '89
MERRY-GO-ROUNDS See Carousels
MERSER, CHERYL
Alone at last [excerpt from Grownups] il *Utne Reader* p62-3 Mr/Ap '89
MERTON, LOUIS THOMAS See Merton, Thomas, 1915-1968
MERTON, ROBERT KING, 1910-
about
Resurrecting liberalism. B. DeMott. *Current (Washington, D.C.)* 309:14-22 Ja '89
MERTON, THOMAS, 1915-1968
about
Thomas Merton's three gifts: a review essay. W. H. Shannon. *America* 161:267-73+ O 21 '89
MERWIN, IAN
Training "5-n-1" fruit trees. il *Organic Gardening* 36:34-5 Mr '89
MERWIN, W. S. (WILLIAM STANLEY), 1927-
The morning train [poem] *The New Yorker* 65:32 Ag 21 '89
Mushrooms [poem] il *The Atlantic* 264:61 Jl '89
One story [poem] *The Nation* 248:859 Je 19 '89
The sacred bones of Maui. il *The New York Times Magazine* p20-1+ Ag 6 '89
MERWIN, WILLIAM STANLEY See Merwin, W. S. (William Stanley), 1927-
MERZ, MARIO, 1925-
about
Coming round again. K. Larson. il *New York* 22:149 O 23 '89
Italian artist Mario Merz turns a museum into a dream. M. Small. il por *People Weekly* 32:176-7 N 20 '89
Mario Merz. A. C. Danto. *The Nation* 249:613-16 N 20 '89
MESA (ARIZ.)
Police
The electronic cop [Custom Electronics Model DXT Mobile Data Terminal] D. C. Ross. il *Motor Trend* 41:70 Je '89
MESA AIRLINES, INC.
Is Mesa Airlines facing a dogfight? [stake by StatesWest Airlines] G. G. Marcial. *Business Week* p130 Jl 17 '89
MESA LIMITED PARTNERSHIP
T. Boone for governor? T. Vogel. il por *Business Week* p43 F 27 '89

MESENCEPHALON *See* Brain
MESMER, FRANZ ANTON, 1734-1815
about
The chain of reason vs. the chain of thumbs. S. J. Gould. il *Natural History* p12+ Jl '89
MESMERISM
France
The chain of reason vs. the chain of thumbs. S. J. Gould. il *Natural History* p12+ Jl '89
MESOPOTAMIA
See also
Babylon (Ancient city)
Mashkan-shapir (Ancient city)
MESOSCOPIC PHYSICS
Can we switch by control of quantum mechanical transmission? R. Landauer. bibl f *Physics Today* 42:119+ O '89
MESSENGER RNA
Access to a messenger RNA sequence or its protein product is not limited by tissue or species specificity. G. Sarkar and S. S. Sommer. bibl f il *Science* 244:331-4 Ap 21 '89
Are tissues a patch quilt of ectopic gene expression? [discussion of April 21, 1989 article, Access to a messenger RNA sequence or its protein product is not limited by tissue or species specificity] G. Sarkar and S. S. Sommer. *Science* 246:261 O 13 '89
G_1/S transition in normal human T-lymphocytes requires the nuclear protein encoded by c-*myb*. A. M. Gewirtz and others. bibl f il *Science* 245:180-3 Jl 14 '89
Identification of an AUUUA-specific messenger RNA binding protein. J. S. Malter. bibl f il *Science* 246:664-6 N 3 '89
Limbic seizures increase neuronal production of messenger RNA for nerve growth factor. C. M. Gall and P. J. Isackson. bibl f il *Science* 245:758-61 Ag 18 '89
Making sense out of antisense [using a gene's complementary sequence to turn off gene expression] R. Lewis. il *BioScience* 39:590-3 O '89
A novel mRNA of the A4 amyloid precursor gene coding for a possibly secreted protein. F. De Sauvage and J.-N. Octave. bibl f il *Science* 245:651-3 Ag 11 '89
Oxidation-reduction and the molecular mechanism of a regulatory RNA-protein interaction. M. W. Hentze and others. bibl f il *Science* 244:357-9 Ap 21 '89
Regulation of lymphokine messenger RNA stability by a surface-mediated T cell activation pathway. T. Lindsten and others. bibl f il *Science* 244:339-43 Ap 21 '89
Shooting the messenger [antisense RNA prevents HIV virus production; research by Jack Cohen] G. Montgomery. il *Discover* 10:32 N '89
Translational blockade imposed by cytokine-derived UA-rich sequences [Xenopus oocytes] V. Kruys and others. bibl f il *Science* 245:852-5 Ag 25 '89
The turnover of messenger RNA. J. Ross. bibl il *Scientific American* 260:48-55 Ap '89
Unusual pattern of accumulation of mRNA encoding EGF-related protein in sea urchin embryos. Q. Yang and others. bibl f il *Science* 246:806-8 N 10 '89
MESSENGERS
See also
Couriers
MESSERSCHMITT-BÖLKOW-BLOHM GMBH
Aerospatiale and MBB disagree on A320/A321 assembly location. J. M. Lenorovitz. il *Aviation Week & Space Technology* 131:70 O 23 '89
Daimler accepts German constraints on its buyout of MBB. *Aviation Week & Space Technology* 131:31 S 18 '89
The even-bigger shadow Daimler could cast [MBB takeover] J. Templeman. il por *Business Week* p54-5 My 22 '89
German Cartel Office raises antitrust issues in MBB takeover [acquisition by Daimler-Benz] *Aviation Week & Space Technology* 130:271 Mr 20 '89
U.S. criticizes E.C. plan to shield MBB from fluctuations in exchange rate. M. Mecham. *Aviation Week & Space Technology* 130:91 Mr 27 '89
MESSIAEN, OLIVIER
about
Musical events:
Messiaen's Et exspecto, Lutoslawski's Piano concerto, and Rorem's Violin concerto. A. Porter. *The New Yorker* 64:65-6 Ja 16 '89
MESSIAH
See also
Jesus Christ—Messiahship
MESSIAH (ORATORIO) *See* Oratorio
MESSINA, CHRIS
The heart attack business. il *High Technology Business* 9:22-5 Mr '89
MESSINA, JIM
about
Jim Messina. P. Puterbaugh. il por *Rolling Stone* p54 Ag 10 '89
MESSINA, TONY
Building a MIDI studio. il *Down Beat* 56:56-7 Je '89
MESSINESS
The truth about desk mess. K. A. Samon. il *Working Woman* 14:107 Ap '89

Anecdotes, facetiae, satire, etc.
I confess: I'm a mess. S. Nelson. il *Seventeen* 48:168-9 S '89
MESSNER VETERE BERGER CAREY SCHMETTER (FIRM)
Alphabet troupe. B. Kanner. il *New York* 22:34+ O 23 '89
METABOLISM
See also
Arachnids—Metabolism
Bioenergetics
Carbohydrate metabolism
Cells—Metabolism
Heart—Metabolism
Lean body mass
Plants—Metabolism
Proteins—Metabolism
25 quick tips to trick off pounds [excerpt from Maximum metabolism] R. M. Giller and K. Matthews. il *Redbook* 172:70-1+ F '89
Bicycling's exclusive calorie counter [cover story]; ed. by Nelson Pena. J. Hagberg. il *Bicycling* 30:100-3 My '89
Burn, baby, burn [effect of running on weight loss] D. Kardong. il *Runner's World* 24:32-7 F '89
Can running lower metabolism? [views of Kelly Brownell] A. M. Fletcher. *American Health* 8:152-3 Mr '89
Exercise: some routines burn fat better than others. il *Psychology Today* 23:34 Je '89
Flab-to-muscle pill? [use of dehydroepiandrosterone to burn body fat] A. Dane. *American Health* 8:18 Jl/Ag '89
The gastrointestinal tract in growth and reproduction. K. Uvnäs-Moberg. bibl il *Scientific American* 261:78-83 Jl '89
The new Hilton Head diet [excerpt from The Hilton Head over 35 diet] P. M. Miller. il *Ladies' Home Journal* 106:88+ F '89
Nicotine boosts a busy body's metabolism [research by Kenneth A. Perkins] R. Weiss. *Science News* 135:214 Ap 8 '89
Striking a balance [effect of running] L. Applegate. il *Runner's World* 24:22-3 D '89
The weight-loss perk [effect of caffeine] K. Hamilton. il *Health (New York, N.Y.)* 21:32+ Jl '89
Why diets are weighted against you. M. Rosen. *Ms.* 17:41 Ja/F '89

Disorders
See also
Adenosine deaminase deficiency disorder
Anorexia nervosa
Chronic granulomatous disease
Cystic fibrosis
Diabetes
Gangliosidosis
Gaucher's disease
Lactose intolerance
Prader-Willi syndrome
METAL BONDING
See also
Rapid solidification technology
METAL CUTTING TOOLS *See* Cutting tools
METAL FOILS
See also
Aluminum foil
METAL INDUSTRY
See also
Aluminum industry
AMAX Inc.
Steel industry
Wyman-Gordon Co.
METAL IONS
Molecular recognition and metal ion template synthesis. T. J. McMurry and others. bibl f il *Science* 244:938-43 My 26 '89
METAL MINING INDUSTRY *See* Mining industry
METAL OXIDE SEMICONDUCTORS
Bilateral switches [CMOS switches] R. Marston. il *Radio-Electronics* 60:54-8 N '89
CMOS PLL's [phase-locked loop] R. Marston. il *Radio-Electronics* 60:55-8 D '89
Flashing LED's [CMOS 4017 device] il *Radio-Electronics* 60:12+ My '89
METAL POISONING
See also
Lead poisoning
METAL POWDERS
Preparation of organometallic compounds from highly reactive metal powders. R. D. Rieke. bibl f il *Science* 246:1260-4 D 8 '89
METAL ROOFS *See* Roofs and roofing
METAL SCULPTURE
See also
Bronzes
Reginato's improvisations [colored steel sculpture] C. Ratcliff. bibl f il *Art in America* 77:146-51 D '89
METAL WORK
See also
Art metal work
Welding

METAL WORKER'S UNION (GERMANY: WEST) *See* IG
Metall
METALLIC HYDROGEN
Hard-pressed [squeezed hydrogen; work of Ho-Kwang Mao
and Russell J. Hemley] P. E. Ross and R. Ruthen. *Scientific
American* 261:26 N '89
Heavy metal [work of Ho-Kwang Mao and Russell Hemley]
Discover 10:10+ N '89
Metallic hydrogen. A. Fisher. il *Popular Science* 235:23-5
O '89
Optical studies of hydrogen above 200 gigapascals: evidence
for metallization by band overlap [Raman spectra] H.
K. Mao and R. J. Hemley. bibl f il *Science* 244:1462-5
Je 23 '89
Putting the squeeze on hydrogen [work of Ho-Kwang Mao
and Russell Hemley] R. Pool. *Science* 244:1440 Je 23
'89
Squeezed hydrogen turns semi-metallic [work of Ho-Kwang
Mao and Russell J. Hemley] F. Flam. *Science News* 135:327
My 27 '89
METALLICA (MUSICAL GROUP)
Heavy metal justice. D. Fricke. il *Rolling Stone* p44-6+ Ja
12 '89
METALLOORGANIC COMPOUNDS *See* Organometallic
compounds
METALLOPROTEINASES
See also
Tissue inhibitor of metalloproteinases
METALLURGY
See also
Electrodeposition of metals
Electrometallurgy
Plutonium metallurgy
Steel metallurgy
Uranium metallurgy
METALS
See also
Electrodeposition of metals
Intermetallic compounds
Laminated metals
Mines and mineral resources
Platinum metals
See also names of metals
Corrosion
See Corrosion and anticorrosives
Fatigue
Old, tired, and rusty [structural failures] il *Discover* 10:68-70
Ja '89
METALS IN THE BODY
See also
Iron in the body
Zinc in the body
METAMORPHISM (GEOLOGY)
Origins and movement of fluids during deformation and
metamorphism in the Canadian Cordillera [gold deposits]
B. E. Nesbitt and K. Muehlenbachs. bibl f il map *Science*
245:733-6 Ag 18 '89
Rates of tectonometamorphic processes from rubidium and
strontium isotopes in garnet [southeast Vermont] J. N.
Christensen and others. bibl f il *Science* 244:1465-9 Je
23 '89
METAMORPHOSIS
See also
Insects—Development
METAMORPHOSIS [drama] *See* Berkoff, Steven
METAPHOR
Magic on the mind: physicists' use of metaphor. A. P.
Lightman. *The American Scholar* 58:97-101 Wint '89
Metaphors of the world, unite! [attempt to define the age
in which we live] L. Morrow. il *Time* 134:96 O 16 '89
Now, metaphor as illness [S. Sontag's AIDS and its metaphors]
D. Gates. il por *Newsweek* 113:79 Ja 30 '89
METAPHYSICS
See also
Absolute
METASTASIS
Enzyme suggests breast cancer spread [cathepsin-D; research
by Henri Rochefort] J. Raloff. *Science News* 136:325 N
18 '89
How cancer cells spread in the body. J. L. Marx. il *Science*
244:147-8 Ap 14 '89
An inducible endothelial cell surface glycoprotein mediates
melanoma adhesion. G. E. Rice and M. P. Bevilacqua.
bibl f il *Science* 246:1303-6 D 8 '89
Marker predicts breast cancer recurrence [haptoglobin-related
protein] R. Weiss. *Science News* 136:164 S 9 '89
Metastatic hibernomas in transgenic mice expressing an
α-amylase-SV40 T antigen hybrid gene. N. Fox and others.
bibl f il *Science* 244:460-3 Ap 28 '89
Nontoxic drugs halt cancer spread in mice [anti-metastatic
compounds; research by George Martin] J. Raloff. il *Science
News* 135:228 Ap 15 '89
METAVIEW (FIRM)
The ad killers. D. Churbuck. *Forbes* 143:76 F 20 '89
METCALF, JOEL HASTINGS, 1866-1925
about
A remarkable New England amateur. J. E. Bortle. il por
Sky and Telescope 78:435-6 O '89

METCALF, LAURIE, 1955?-
about
Her idea of fun? Getting muddy with Roseanne. J. Marion.
il por *TV Guide* 37:17 Jl 22-28 '89
METEOR BURST COMMUNICATION
The meteor is the message. il *Sky and Telescope* 78:245-6
S '89
Tracking trucks without satellites. il *High Technology Business*
9:27 My '89
METEOR CRATER (ARIZ.)
Dating craters [beryllium-aluminum dating of rocks; work
of James Arnold] J. A. Yeaple. *Popular Science* 235:128
N '89
METEORITES
Antarctic meteorites reveal ancient ice. il *Sky and Telescope*
77:466-7 My '89
Calcium carbonate found in 'Mars' meteorites [research by
James L. Gooding] *Astronomy* 17:14 Je '89
Carbonaceous meteorites and asteroids. J. Eberhart. *Science
News* 136:334 N 18 '89
Comets and meteorites: harbingers of life on earth . . .
and destructors of Mars. il *Sky and Telescope* 78:242
S '89
Diamonds from heaven and earth. *Sky and Telescope* 77:244-5
Mr '89
Earth as egg: hard-boiled or raw? [research by Richard Muller
and Donald Morris] R. Monastersky. *Science News* 135:319
My 20 '89
Earth's largest lunar meteorite announced [MAC88105] *Science
News* 136:62 Jl 22 '89
Effects of the large June 1975 meteoroid storm on earth's
ionosphere [very low frequency radio wave propagation
anomalies] P. Kaufmann and others. bibl f il map *Science*
246:787-90 N 10 '89
Geological and geochemical record of 3400-million-year-old
terrestrial meteorite impacts [South Africa] D. R. Lowe
and others. bibl f il *Science* 245:959-62 S 1 '89
Giant meteor impacts and great eruptions: dinosaur killers?
G. S. Paul. bibl f il *BioScience* 39:162-72 Mr '89
Have earth rocks gone to Mars? [research by S. A. Phinney]
J. Eberhart. *Science News* 135:191 Mr 25 '89
History of meteorites from the moon collected in Antarctica.
O. Eugster. bibl f il *Science* 245:1197-1202 S 15 '89
The impact giveth . . . [amino acids found in Cretaceous-
Tertiary boundary clay; research by Meixun Zhao and
Jeffrey L. Bada] J. Horgan. *Scientific American* 261:24+
S '89
Meteorite may carry organic Martian cargo [EETA 79001;
research by Ian P. Wright] I. Amato. *Science News* 136:53
Jl 22 '89
The new age of the sun [research by David B. Guenther]
Science News 135:269 Ap 29 '89
New impact evidence: amino acids from space [Cretaceous-
Tertiary boundary clay; research by Meixun Zhao and
Jeffrey L. Bada] *Astronomy* 17:11+ O '89
On the trail of a meteorite. C. E. Spratt. il *Astronomy*
17:70-6 Ag '89
Phyllosilicate absorption features in main-belt and outer-belt
asteroid reflectance spectra. F. Vilas and M. J. Gaffey.
bibl f il *Science* 246:790-2 N 10 '89
Rare amino acids support impact theory [Cretaceous-Tertiary
boundary clays; research by Jeffrey L. Bada] R. Monaster-
sky. *Science News* 135:356 Je 10 '89
Rhenium-osmium isotope systematics of carbonaceous chon-
drites [resonance ionization mass spectrometry] R. J. Walker
and J. W. Morgan. bibl f il *Science* 243:519-22 Ja 27
'89
Signs of an ancient worldwide wallop [stishovite discovery
in New Mexico; research by John McHone] R. Monastersky.
Science News 135:132 Mr 4 '89
Spatially resolved organic analysis of the Allende meteorite.
R. Zenobi and others. bibl f il *Science* 246:1026-9 N
24 '89
Stishovite at the Cretaceous-Tertiary boundary, Raton, New
Mexico. J. F. McHone and others. bibl f il *Science*
243:1182-4 Mr 3 '89
Age
Do meteorite ages tell of comet storms? [H-chondrites; re-
search by Saul Perlmutter and Richard A. Muller]
Astronomy 17:12+ Ja '89
METEOROIDS *See* Meteors
METEOROLOGICAL EQUIPMENT
See also
Anemometers
Cyclonoscopes
METEOROLOGICAL MODELS
An astrophysical guide to the weather on earth [Piecewise
Parabolic Method developed by Paul Woodward] B. A.
Cipra. il *Science* 246:212-13 O 13 '89
Carbon dioxide: where does it all go? [research by Pieter
P. Tans] R. Monastersky. *Science News* 136:132 Ag 26
'89
Climate and the earth's radiation budget [cover story] V.
Ramanathan and others. bibl f il *Physics Today* 42:22-7+
My '89
Cloud-radiative forcing and climate: results from the Earth
Radiation Budget Experiment. V. Ramanathan and others.
bibl f il maps *Science* 243:57-63 Ja 6 '89

METEOROLOGICAL MODELS—*cont.*

Clouds clearing from climate predictions [Earth Radiation Budget Experiment; research by V. Ramanathan] R. Monastersky. *Science News* 135:6 Ja 7 '89

Clouds in the greenhouse [data from Earth Radiation Budget Satellite] A. C. Revkin. map *Discover* 10:24 Je '89

Global smog: newest greenhouse projection [research by David Rind] J. Raloff. *Science News* 135:262-3 Ap 29 '89

Great Basin calcite vein and the Pleistocene time scale [discussion of December 2, 1988 article, A 250,000-year climatic record from Great Basin vein calcite: implications for Milankovitch theory] I. J. Winograd and others. *Science* 246:262-3 O 13 '89

Greenhouse models vs. reality. R. A. Kerr. *Science* 244:1042 Je 2 '89

Greenhouse skeptic out in the cold [R. S. Lindzen] R. A. Kerr. por *Science* 246:1118-19 D 1 '89

Hot spot [Pangaea; research by Thomas J. Crowley] J. Horgan. il *Scientific American* 261:20+ S '89

How to fix the clouds in greenhouse models. R. A. Kerr. *Science* 243:28-9 Ja 6 '89

Hurricane prediction: catching the waves [research by Richard L. Pfeffer] D. E. Loupe. *Science News* 136:262 O 21 '89

Ice cycles [findings in Devil's Hole contradict Milankovitch theory; research by Isaac J. Winograd] R. Kunzig. il *Discover* 10:74-9 My '89

Interpretation of cloud-climate feedback as produced by 14 atmospheric general circulation models. R. D. Cess and others. bibl f il *Science* 245:513-16 Ag 4 '89

Is it all just hot air? [greenhouse effect] S. Begley. il *Newsweek* 114:64-6 N 20 '89

Is something strange about the weather? [researchers using tools from the study of chaos] R. Pool. bibl il *Science* 243:1290-3 Mr 10 '89

Not so hot [questioning global warming estimates] T. Beardsley. *Scientific American* 261:17-18 N '89

Pinning down clouds [role in climatic change] J. Horgan. il *Scientific American* 260:22+ My '89

Predictions drop for future sea-level rise [views of Mark F. Meier] R. Monastersky. *Science News* 136:397 D 16 '89

Scandinavian, Siberian, and Arctic Ocean glaciation: effect of Holocene atmospheric CO_2 variations. D. R. Lindstrom and D. R. MacAyeal. bibl f il *Science* 245:628-31 Ag 11 '89

Up in smoke [nuclear winter modeling based on shape of soot particles; work of Jenny Nelson] S. Vogel. il *Discover* 10:26 N '89

Warmer clouds could keep earth cooler. R. Monatersky. *Science News* 136:196 S 23 '89

METEOROLOGICAL OPTICS

See also
   Airglow
   Haze
   Mirages
   Noctilucent clouds

A field guide to atmospheric optics [cover story] F. Schaaf. bibl il *Sky and Telescope* 77:254-9 Mr '89

Refraction by earth's atmosphere [computer program] B. E. Schaefer. il *Sky and Telescope* 77:311-13 Mr '89

METEOROLOGICAL PHOTOGRAPHY

1989 Photo Contest winners [Weatherwise Contest; cover story] il *Weatherwise* 42:197-204 Ag '89

METEOROLOGICAL RESEARCH *See* Meteorology

METEOROLOGISTS

See also
   Bluestein, Howard
   Suomi, Verner
   Viñes, Benito

METEOROLOGISTS, AMATEUR

See also
   Association of American Weather Observers

METEOROLOGY

See also
   Airplanes in meteorology
   Artificial satellites—Meteorological use
   Atmosphere
   Auroras
   Boundary layer (Meteorology)
   Climate
   Clouds
   Computers—Meteorological use
   Condensation (Meteorology)
   Dew
   Floods
   Fog
   Forensic meteorology
   Humidity
   Hurricanes
   Information systems—Meteorological use
   Lightning
   Motion pictures—Meteorological films
   Radar meteorology
   Rain and rainfall
   Snow
   Soil-atmosphere interaction
   Storms
   Sun and meteorology

   Thunderstorms
   Tornadoes
   Videotapes—Meteorological use
   Weather
   Weather forecasting
   Weather maps
   Winds

Low-tech earth observation. E. Marshall. il *Science* 244:1249 Je 16 '89

Federal aid

Panel frets over cash-short climate studies. R. Monastersky. *Science News* 135:150 Mr 11 '89

Study and teaching

Aids and devices

Audio visuals about the weather. E. Brotak. *Weatherwise* 42:55 F '89

High school students study Hurricane Gilbert [use of GOES satellite] R. J. Summers. il *Weatherwise* 42:95-6 Ap '89

Weather prediction in the classroom [Accu-Weather Forecaster] M. Eichen. *Focus (New York, N.Y.: 1950)* 39:27+ Spr '89

Cuba

History

The hurricane priest [B. Viñes] D. DeAngelis. il por *Weatherwise* 42:256-7 O '89

METEOROLOGY, AGRICULTURAL *See* Plants, Effect of climate on

METEOROLOGY, AVIATION

See also
   Computers—Meteorological use
   Information systems—Meteorological use
   Radar meteorology
   Wind shear

Grave expectations [flying an approach into low IFR weather] J. M. McClellan. il *Flying* 116:39-40 O '89

The road warrior [low altitude VFR scud running] P. Garrison. *Flying* 116:84-5 My '89

VFR in IMC: taking it to the limit [flying VFR in instrument meteorological conditions; NTSB accident statistics] J. M. McClellan. *Flying* 116:38 S '89

METEOROLOGY, MARITIME

See also
   Ocean-atmosphere interaction

METEOROLOGY, MILITARY

History

See also
   France—History—Revolution, 1789-1799—Meteorological aspects
   United States—History—Civil War, 1861-1865—Meteorological aspects

METEORS

1989's first meteor shower [Quadrantids] il *Astronomy* 17:66 Ja '89

Catch these falling stars! [Perseids] T. Dunkle. il *Reader's Digest* 135:41-2+ Ag '89

Catching the Perseids. il *Sky and Telescope* 78:180-1 Ag '89

Geminids provide year-end sky show. D. J. Eicher. il *Astronomy* 17:84-5+ Ap '89

Geologic events. See issues of Earth Science

Meteors from asteroids. il *Sky and Telescope* 77:245-6 Mr '89

Perseids provide sky show. D. J. Eicher. il *Astronomy* 17:109+ D '89

Spinning meteors [theory of Martin Beech] il *Sky and Telescope* 77:11-12 Ja '89

Watching meteors by radar [work of Graham Poole and David Roux] il *Sky and Telescope* 78:244-5 S '89

METEORS IN POETRY

William Blake and August's fiery meteors. D. W. Olson and M. S. Olson. il *Sky and Telescope* 78:192-4 Ag '89

METEOSAT WEATHER SATELLITES *See* Artificial satellites—Meteorological use

METER (STANDARD OF LENGTH) *See* Metric system

METER READING

What's a dog to do? [remote meter reading] V. E. Gilmore. il *Popular Science* 235:42+ N '89

METERS

See also
   Data meters
   Electric meters
   Exposure meters
   Gas meters
   Moisture meters

METHADONE CLINICS

California

See also
   Community Health Projects Inc.

New York (State)

See also
   Addiction Research and Treatment Corporation

METHAMPHETAMINE

Dangerous new drugs [speed and Ecstasy] M. O'Koon. il *Good Housekeeping* 208:235-6 Ap '89

The new midnight dumpers [illegal drug labs creating toxic waste] G. Witkin. il *U.S. News & World Report* 106:57 Ja 9 '89

METHAMPHETAMINE—*cont.*
Role for excitatory amino acids in methamphetamine-induced nigrostriatal dopaminergic toxicity. P. K. Sonsalla and others. bibl f il *Science* 243:398-40 Ja 20 '89
METHANE
See also
Bacteria, Methanogenic
Coalbed methane
Bovine madness [cattle burps as source of atmospheric methane] J. Stone. il *Discover* 10:38+ F '89
Carbon-14 in methane sources and in atmospheric methane: the contribution from fossil carbon. M. Wahlen and others. bibl f il *Science* 245:286-90 Jl 21 '89
Carbon copies [Cretaceous cold-seep communities in the Canadian Arctic; research by Renoit Beauchamp] *Discover* 10:15 Ag '89
Cloudy memories of Krakatau [research by Gary E. Thomas] il *Discover* 10:14 Ag '89
Cretaceous cold-seep communities and methane-derived carbonates in the Canadian Arctic. B. Beauchamp and others. bibl f il map *Science* 244:53-6 Ap 7 '89
Methane clouding up the twilight [research by Gary E. Thomas] *Science News* 135:255 Ap 22 '89
Methane key to Arctic mystery mounds [research by Benoit Beauchamp] R. Monastersky. *Science News* 135:215 Ap 8 '89
Methane rain on Titan? il *Sky and Telescope* 77:246 Mr '89
Plankton to petroleum [origin of oil and gas] W. W. Dickinson. il *Earth Science* 41:21-3 Wint '88
Soil nitrogen leaves methane up in the air [research by Paul A. Steudler] D. E. Loupe. *Science News* 136:213 S 30 '89
Triton: do we see to the surface? D. P. Cruikshank and others. bibl f il *Science* 245:283-6 Jl 21 '89
Utah researchers probe coalbed methane. *High Technology Business* 9:36-7 Ap '89
METHANOGENIC BACTERIA *See* Bacteria, Methanogenic
METHANOL
The any-fuel engine. D. McCosh. il *Popular Science* 234:73+ F '89
The bumpy road to 'clean fuels'. il *U.S. News & World Report* 106:10-11 Je 26 '89
The case for methanol. C. L. Gray and J. A. Alson. bibl il *Scientific American* 261:108-14 N '89
Coalaholics [methanol-powered cars from Chevrolet, Ford and Chrysler] M. Allen. il *Popular Mechanics* 166:60-2 N '89
Fill'er up with methyl. G. Cowley. il *Newsweek* 113:67 My 1 '89
Fuel fantasies [alternative fuels for cars] J. Flint. il *Forbes* 143:66-7 My 29 '89
Fuel for thought. T. Beardsley. *Scientific American* 261:20 D '89
Fuels in your future. M. Knepper. il *Popular Mechanics* 166:55-7 N '89
Gasoline: the unclean fuel? E. Marshall. il *Science* 246:199-201 O 13 '89
The methanol car in your future. A. Kupfer. il *Fortune* 120:71+ S 25 '89
Methanol may be clean, but it's a dirty word to big oil. M. Ivey. il *Business Week* p106 S 4 '89
Report gives methanol thumbs down. *High Technology Business* 9:37 Ap '89
METHENY, PAT
about
Pat Metheny: the interview from home [cover story; interview] J. Roberts. il pors *Down Beat* 56:16-19 Ag '89
METHENY (PAT) GROUP *See* Pat Metheny Group
METHODIST CHURCH
Fiji
Sabbath laws split Methodists in Fiji. D. C. White. *The Christian Century* 106:406-7 Ap 19 '89
United States
See also
United Methodist Church
METHOXATIN
Nutritional importance of pyrroloquinoline quinone. J. Killgore and others. bibl f il *Science* 245:850-2 Ag 25 '89
METHUEN (FIRM)
See also
Routledge, Chapman & Hall
METHVIN, EUGENE H.
Beauty and the beast. il pors *Reader's Digest* 134:132-8 F '89
Crusader for Peru's have-nots. il *Reader's Digest* 134:137-40 Ja '89
Justice for sale. *Reader's Digest* 134:131-6 My '89
The unquiet ghosts of Stalin's victims. *National Review* 41:24-5+ S 1 '89
METHYL ALCOHOL *See* Methanol
METHYL ISOCYANATE
See also
Bhopal poisonous gas disaster, India, 1984
METHYL-PHENYL-TETRAHYDROPYRIDINE *See* MPTP (Drug)

METHYLATION
A different kind of inheritance [DNA methylation as an epigenetic mechanism] R. Holliday. bibl il *Scientific American* 260:60-5+ Je '89
Genomic sequencing and methylation analysis by ligation mediated PCR. G. P. Pfeifer and others. bibl f il *Science* 246:810-13 N 10 '89
METHYLCHLOROFORM
Just when the ozone war looked winnable . . . V. Cahan. il *Business Week* p56 Je 12 '89
METHYLENE-DIOXY-METHAMPHETAMINE *See* MDMA (Drug)
METHYLGUANOSINE *See* Guanosine
METHYLPHENIDATE
Is Ritalin necessary? F. Roberts. *Parents* 64:52 My '89
The Ritalin controversy. N. Rubin. *Parents* 64:112 F '89
Ritalin: education's fix-it drug? D. Divoky. bibl f il *Phi Delta Kappan* 70:599-605 Ap '89
Suffer the restless children [use of Ritalin] A. Kohn. il *The Atlantic* 264:90-4+ N '89
METOYER, MARIA THERESA COINCOIN *See* Coincoin, Maria Theresa
METPATH INC.
Clinical case. I. Chithelen. il *Forbes* 143:178+ Mr 20 '89
METRIC SYSTEM
Accelerate U.S. metrification. *Aviation Week & Space Technology* 131:7 N 27 '89
Do you speak metric? [measuring race distances] J. Henderson. il *Runner's World* 24:12 Ja '89
It pays to go the extra meter. L. Williams. il *Nation's Business* 77:42-3 S '89
Make mine metric. D. Fong. il *Forbes* 143:106-7 Je 26 '89
METRO (NEW YORK, N.Y.: RESTAURANT) *See* New York (N.Y.)—Restaurants, nightclubs, bars, etc.
METRO AIRLINES, INC.
Phoenix Airlines may get its wings clipped. D. Foust. il por *Business Week* p114 Mr 13 '89
METROMEDIA, INC.
Pop goes the wallet [J. Kluge] J. Zweig. por *Forbes* 144:138 Ag 7 '89
METROPOLITAN AREAS
See also
City planning
Exurbs
Suburbs
The best places to live in America. R. Eisenberg and M. T. Smith. il *Money* 18:124-6+ S '89
METROPOLITAN MUSEUM OF ART (NEW YORK, N.Y.)
American pastels [American pastels in the Metropolitan Museum of Art: 1880-1930] A. E. Ledes. il *Antiques* 136:650+ O '89
Art chic. J. Levine. il *Forbes* 144:94+ Ag 21 '89
Party palace: the high life at the gilded Metropolitan Museum [cover story] J. Taylor. il *New York* 22:20-30 Ja 9 '89
"Please have your tickets ready for 'Degas'". M. Esterow. il *Art News* 88:198 Mr '89
Raider of the lost art [tours by P. D. Magriel] M. Filler. il por *House & Garden* 161:36+ Ap '89
METROPOLITAN MUSEUM OF ART (NEW YORK, N.Y.). AMERICAN WING
Silvia Kolbowski at Postmasters [show based on Metropolitan Museum's American Wing] J. Zinsser. il *Art in America* 77:265-6 Ap '89
METROPOLITAN MUSEUM OF ART (NEW YORK, N.Y.). COSTUME INSTITUTE
The emperor's old clothes [Age of Napoléon exhibit] D. Lida. il por *Harper's Bazaar* 122:71 N '89
Franco Moschino [designer visits exhibition of Victorian costumes] *The New Yorker* 64:19-20 Ja 9 '89
METROPOLITAN MUSEUM OF ART (NEW YORK, N.Y.). DEPT. OF EUROPEAN PAINTINGS
Maestro at the Met [New York apartment of Metropolitan Museum of Art curator E. Fahy] C. McGee. il por *House & Garden* 161:50+ S '89
METROPOLITAN MUSEUM OF ART (NEW YORK, N.Y.). HENRY R. LUCE CENTER FOR THE STUDY OF AMERICAN ART
Embarrassment of riches unveiled. B. Wallis. il *Art in America* 77:23+ F '89
A new resource for scholars and collectors. A. E. Ledes. il *Antiques* 135:62+ Ja '89
METROPOLITAN MUSEUM OF ART (NEW YORK, N.Y.). LILA ACHESON WALLACE WING
Miller high style [shows by design curator R. C. Miller] M. Filler. il por *House & Garden* 161:48 Ja '89
METROPOLITAN OPERA (NEW YORK, N.Y.)
Almost lost [Metropolitan Opera premiere of Don Carlos in 1920] il *Opera News* 53:22-3 F 4 '89
Details! Details! [G. Fitzgerald's Annals of the Metropolitan Opera] A. Porter; F. Merkling. il pors *Opera News* 54:18-20+ N '89
How's this for openers? P. G. Davis. il *New York* 22:88+ O 9 '89
A human comedy [performance of Don Carlos] P. G. Davis. il *New York* 22:66-7 F 20 '89
Indispensable [chorus master D. Stivender] J. D. McClatchy. il por *Opera News* 53:16-18 F 18 '89

METROPOLITAN OPERA (NEW YORK, N.Y.)—*cont.*
Interior decoration [performance of Bluebeard's castle and Erwartung] P. G. Davis. il *New York* 22:54 Ja 30 '89
Lost in Crete [performance of Idomeneo] P. G. Davis. il *New York* 22:144+ F 27 '89
Making it at the Met [work of designers and craftspeople] M. Sommers. il *Theatre Crafts* 23:50-5+ O '89
The Met's new "Walküre" [recording] D. P. Stearns. il *Stereo Review* 54:134 Ja '89
Music [Bluebeard's castle and Erwartung] E. W. Said. *The Nation* 248:314-17 Mr 6 '89
Musical events:
   Aida. A. Porter. *The New Yorker* 64:66-8 Ja 16 '89
   Bluebeard's castle and Erwartung. A. Porter. *The New Yorker* 64:98+ F 6 '89
   Die Frau ohne Schatten. A. Porter. *The New Yorker* 65:134 D 11 '89
   Salome. A. Porter. *The New Yorker* 65:90 Mr 20 '89
   Wagner's Ring. A. Porter. *The New Yorker* 65:89-90 My 22 '89
New man in charge [interview with H. Southern] P. J. Smith. il por *Opera News* 54:16-17 N '89
New York City. J. W. Freeman. il *Opera News* 53:46-7 Je '89
New York City. J. W. Freeman. il *Opera News* 53:36-7 Mr 4 '89
New York City. G. Schmidgall. il *Opera News* 53:36-7 F 4 '89
New York City. G. Schmidgall. il *Opera News* 54:37 Jl '89
New York City. G. Schmidgall. il *Opera News* 53:53 Ap 1 '89
New York City. J. W. Freeman; B. Kellow. il *Opera News* 54:39 D 23 '89
No offense [Rigoletto] P. G. Davis. il *New York* 22:118 N 20 '89
Party girl [Salome] P. G. Davis. il *New York* 22:101-2 Mr 6 '89
A plodding 'Porgy'. P. G. Davis. il *New York* 22:105-6 O 16 '89
Pyramid club [Aida] P. G. Davis. il *New York* 22:43 Ja 2 '89
Der Ring des Nibelungen [cover story; special issue; with editorial comment by Gerald Fitzgerald] il *Opera News* 53:6, 12-16+ Ap 1 '89
A Ring for the '80s [German Romantic roots of new production] B. Adams. il *Art in America* 77:222-9 Ap '89
Ring resounding. P. G. Davis. il *New York* 22:85-6 My 8 '89
Star power [fiftieth anniversary of Texaco sponsorship of broadcasts; cover story] bibl il *Opera News* 54:10-12+ N '89
Strictures at an institution. E. Rothstein. *The New Republic* 200:27-31 Mr 13 '89
Texaco-Metropolitan Opera radio network: 1989-90 season. il *Opera News* 54:50 D 9 '89
Trimming 'Traviata'. P. G. Davis. il *New York* 22:107 O 30 '89
Viewpoint [radio broadcasts] P. J. Smith. *Opera News* 54:6 D 9 '89
Viewpoint [rationale for new productions] P. J. Smith. *Opera News* 54:4 D 23 '89
Vitalized with fresh talent, the Met's new season heralds the return of opera mania. D. Daniel. il *Vogue* 179:470+ S '89
Wagnerian celebration [new Ring] K. Ames. il *Newsweek* 113:68-9 My 8 '89
Welcome to the 20th century [B. Bartok's Bluebeard's castle and A. Schoenberg's Erwartung] K. Ames. il *Newsweek* 113:70 Ja 30 '89
   Photographs and photography
Metropolitan Express [Kodak's Duratrans photo in Grand Central Station] J. L. Poole. il *Opera News* 53:30-1 Je '89
METROPOLITAN OPERA HOUSE (NEW YORK, N.Y.)
Big sky [new cyclorama installed] *The New Yorker* 65:30-1 S 4 '89
METROPOLITAN OPERA NATIONAL COUNCIL AUDITIONS *See* Singing—Competitions
METROPOLITAN PERFORMING ARTS CENTER (SPOKANE, WASH.)
Spokane shows how to create space for the performing arts. S. English. *Dance Magazine* 63:14 Ja '89
METROPOLITAN TRANSPORTATION AUTHORITY
Heavy metal [Auction and Tag Sale] *The New Yorker* 65:46-7 D 11 '89
METTKE, JÖRG
Thaw on the Bering Strait. il *World Press Review* 36:58 Ja '89
METZ, DALE
   about
Going to bat for special children. D. Young. il pors *Southern Living* 24:100+ Jl '89
METZ, HOLLY
Lesbian writer fights feminist censors. il por *The Progressive* 53:16-17 Ag '89

METZ, SHIRLEY
   about
South Pole or bust. B. Sims. il por *Skiing* 42:18 O '89
METZENBAUM, HOWARD M.
Should a constitutional amendment to prevent flag desecration be approved? [excerpts from testimony, July 13, 1989] *Congressional Digest* 68:203+ Ag/S '89
Should the Congress adopt the "Financial Institutions Reform, Recovery, and Enforcement Act of 1989"? [excerpts from address, April 18, 1989] *Congressional Digest* 68:171+ Je/Jl '89
Should the Congress adopt the "High Risk Occupational Disease Notification and Prevention Act of 1987"? [excerpts from address, March 22, 1988] *Congressional Digest* 68:114+ Ap '89
METZGER, LOIS
Past present. *The Nation* 249:801-2 D 25 '89
METZGER, ROBERT O.
The ominous exporting of U.S. clerical jobs. il *USA Today (Periodical)* 117:30-1 Mr '89
METZLER, JOANN
Succession. il *Sierra* 74:71-2+ N/D '89
METZNER, SHEILA
   about
Sheila Metzner. P. Haldeman. il por *Art News* 88:166-7 Ap '89
MEUCCI, ANTONIO, 1808-1889
   about
Telephone. *The New Yorker* 65:34-5 O 30 '89
MEWBORNE, TYLER
Hamburger heaven: a burger blitz. il por *Antiques & Collecting Hobbies* 94:22-5 D '89
MEWSHAW, MICHAEL, 1943-
Noble Roman. il por *House & Garden* 161:128-39+ My '89
MEXICAN AMERICAN ART *See* Art, Mexican American
MEXICAN AMERICAN AUTHORS *See* Authors, Mexican American
MEXICAN AMERICANS
To the border. R. Rodriguez. il *Harper's* 278:31-2+ Ap '89
   Education
Miracle worker at Garfield High [calculus teacher J. Escalante; condensed from Escalante] J. Mathews. il pors *Reader's Digest* 134:165-70+ Ja '89
MEXICAN BEAN BEETLE LARVAE *See* Larvae
MEXICAN COOKING *See* Cooking, Mexican
MEXICAN FREETAIL BATS *See* Bats
MEXICAN GRAND PRIX *See* Automobile racing—Mexico
MEXICAN RESTAURANTS *See* Restaurants
MEXICAN REVOLUTION, 1910-1920 *See* Mexico—History—Revolution, 1910-1920
MEXICAN WAR, 1845-1848 *See* United States—History—War with Mexico, 1845-1848
MEXICANOS *See* Mexican Americans
MEXICANS
   United States
   See also
   Mexican Americans
Actor's son Cheyney Ryan brings migrant workers a theater that could save their lives. A. Chambers. il pors *People Weekly* 32:175-6 O 4 '89
Border crossing. W. P. Norton. il *The Progressive* 53:46 O '89
The last time I was in Mexico. R. Kirtland. il *America* 161:7-9 Jl 1-8 '89
Mexico's flower children [flower sellers in New York City] R. Miller. il *New York* 22:31 O 16 '89
Raids, racism and the I.N.S. [on trial for harassing Mexican immigrants in California] E. Shorris. il *The Nation* 248:628-30 My 8 '89
   Crime
Every agent's a drug agent [U.S. Border Patrol] F. Gibney, Jr. il *Newsweek* 113:27 My 1 '89
MEXICO
   See also
   Aliens—Mexico
   Automobile racing—Mexico
   Automobile rallies—Mexico
   Baja California (Mexico: Peninsula)
   Baja California Norte (Mexico)
   Banks and banking—Mexico
   Cancún (Mexico)
   Christmas—Mexico
   Ciudad Juarez (Mexico)
   Collective bargaining—Telephone workers—Mexico
   Cozumel Island (Mexico)
   Criminal justice, Administration of—Mexico
   Cuernavaca (Mexico)
   Festivals—Mexico
   Government and the press—Mexico
   Guadalajara (Mexico)
   Health resorts, watering places, etc.—Mexico
   Human sacrifice—Mexico
   Investments, American—Mexico
   Investments, Foreign—Mexico
   Investments, Mexican
   Labor unions—Copper miners—Mexico
   Labor unions—Petroleum workers—Mexico

MEXICO—See also—*cont.*
    Labor unions—Telephone workers—Mexico
    Land reform—Mexico
    Loans, American—Mexico
    Loans, Bank—Mexico
    Matamoros (Tamaulipas, Mexico)
    Mexicans
    Mexico City (Mexico)
    Narcotics laws and regulations—Mexico
    Narcotics trade—Mexico
    Nuclear power plants—Mexico
    Oaxaca (Mexico)
    Oaxaca (Mexico: State)
    Organic gardens and gardening—Mexico
    Pinacate Mountains region (Mexico)
    Prisons—Mexico
    Privatization—Mexico
    Public health—Mexico
    Puerto Vallarta (Mexico)
    Railroads—Mexico
    Rain forests—Mexico
    Rasa Island (Mexico)
    Sex education—Mexico
    Sian Ka'an Biosphere Reserve (Mexico)
    Sonoran Desert
    Strikes—Teachers—Mexico
    Taxco (Mexico)
    Tijuana (Mexico)
    United States—Diplomatic and consular service—Mexico
    Yelapa (Mexico)
    Yucatan (Mexico: State)

Boundaries
The last time I was in Mexico. R. Kirtland. il *America* 161:7-9 Jl 1-8 '89

Commerce
United States
See United States—Commerce—Mexico

Commercial policy
A free-for-all for carmakers south of the border [easing of Mexico's local content restrictions] S. Baker. il *Business Week* p32 O 16 '89

Description and travel
¡Hola! ¡Gracias! ¡Destapador! [Pacific coast] R. Reilly. il *Sports Illustrated* 70 Special Issue:258-62+ F '89
One of the world's best train rides [Chihuahua al Pacifico] L. Sutherland. il map *New Choices for the Best Years* 29:34-9 O '89

Economic policy
Bienvenidos to a fire sale. C. P. Work and J. Bussey. il por *U.S. News & World Report* 107:96+ O 16 '89
Giving a little to save a lot [debt problems] E. A. Finn, Jr. il *Forbes* 143:38-9 Mr 6 '89
A Gorbo for Mexico [C. Salinas de Gortari] M. Kondracke. *The New Republic* 200:11-12+ F 20 '89
Here is a pebble of a project [Polyconomics to study Mexico] M. S. Forbes, Jr. il *Forbes* 144:27 Jl 10 '89
If Washington can learn, Mexico can teach. *America* 160:411 My 6 '89
The Mexican kleptocracy. T. Bethell. il *The American Spectator* 22:11-13 Jl '89
No more mañana. R. S. Strother. il *National Review* 41:21-2 N 24 '89
One tough hombre [C. Salinas de Gortari] S. Baker and E. Weiner. il pors *Business Week* p50-3 Ap 3 '89
Wimp no more [President C. Salinas de Gortari] G. D. Garcia. il por *Time* 133:28-9 Ap 24 '89

Economic relations
Israel
See Israel—Economic relations—Mexico

Foreign relations
United States
See United States—Foreign relations—Mexico

History
Conquest, 1519-1540
Before the Conquest. R. Sokolov. il *Natural History* p76-9 Ag '89
Revolution, 1910-1920
The land question at Aguascalientes. *The New Republic* 201 [Reprint v1]:10-11 N 6 '89 [N 7 '14]
Revolution, 1910-1920—Photographs and photography
Pancho Villa and friends on film in Mexico City [exhibit at the Museo Nacional de la Revolución] il *Sunset (Central West edition)* 182:96 My '89

Industries
See also
    Automobile industry—Mexico
    Compañía Minera de Cananea SA
    Nucal de Mexico (Firm)
    Petroleos Mexicanos
    Teléfonos de México, SA
    Tourist trade—Mexico
    Xabre SA

Politics and government
See also
    Institutional Revolutionary Party (Mexico)
    Partido Acción Nacional (Mexico)
    Politics, Corruption in—Mexico

A Gorbo for Mexico [C. Salinas de Gortari] M. Kondracke. *The New Republic* 200:11-12+ F 20 '89
The power politics of Carlos Salinas. C. A. Robbins. il por *U.S. News & World Report* 106:61-2+ Mr 20 '89
Three scenarios for Mexico's future. S. Galico. il por *The Futurist* 23:17-19 Jl/Ag '89

Religious institutions and affairs
See also
    Catholic Church—Mexico
    Christianity and economics—Mexico
    Church and social problems—Mexico
    Missions—Mexico

MEXICO, GULF OF *See* Gulf of Mexico

MEXICO CITY (MEXICO)
Air pollution
Asphyxiation by progress [excerpts from Christopher unborn; with introd. by Nathan Gardels and Marilyn Berlin Snell] C. Fuentes. il *New Perspectives Quarterly* 6:43-7 Spr '89
The death of a masterpiece. H. Aridjis. il *New Perspectives Quarterly* 6:40-3 Spr '89
Mexican cleanup. S. J. Nadis. il *Technology Review* 92:10-11 N/D '89

Housing
Not to be confused with bird or plane, Mexico's caped crusader packs a political paunch [Super Barrio] A. Gonzalez. il *People Weekly* 31:114-15 Ap 10 '89

Municipal improvement
Reviving Mexico City neighborhood by neighborhood. J. H. Fish and J. Kretzmann. il *The Christian Century* 106:1116-18 N 29 '89

Religious institutions and affairs
Reviving Mexico City neighborhood by neighborhood. J. H. Fish and J. Kretzmann. il *The Christian Century* 106:1116-18 N 29 '89-

MEYER, ALFRED, 1935-
Methinks I see my father. il *American Health* 8:66-7 Ja/F '89
Open road. See issues of The Mother Earth News beginning September/October 1988

MEYER, EDWARD C.
(jt. auth) See Owen, Henry, and Meyer, Edward C.

MEYER, LORENZO
A vote of confidence. il *World Press Review* 36:64 Ja '89

MEYER, LUCERO
about
International style. R. Koenig. il *House & Garden* 161:138-43 N '89

MEYER, MARIANNE
Kidvid. See issues of Video
Reel great gifts. il *Redbook* 174:37 D '89

MEYER, MARSHALL THEODORE, 1930-
about
Rabbi Marshall Meyer: a prophet's agenda. R. Hirschfield. *The Christian Century* 106:438-9 Ap 26 '89

MEYER, MICHAEL A.
Anti-Semitism and Jewish identity. *Commentary* 88:35-40 N '89

MEYER, TARO
about
Shining star daughters and their amazing moms. il pors *'Teen* 33:46-7 D '89

MEYER, THOMAS J.
Fred Savage. il pors *Seventeen* 48:105-6+ Je '89

MEYERBEER, GIACOMO, 1791-1864
about
L'Africaine [opera] Reviews
    Opera News il 54:52 D 9 '89

MEYERS, ARI
about
Shining star daughters and their amazing moms. il pors *'Teen* 33:46-7 D '89

MEYERS, LAURA
about
Laura Meyers creates software that talks friendly to help disabled kids find their voices. S. Adelson. il por *People Weekly* 32:165-6 D 4 '89

MEYERS, PERLA
Skillet skills. il *The New York Times Magazine* p31-2 Jl 30 '89

MEYERS, ROBERT L.
Greening of the farm bill. *BioScience* 39:599 O '89

MEYERSON, MORTON H.
about
Mort Meyerson is raring to slip the leash. K. Kelly. il por *Business Week* p58 S 11 '89
The power behind Pan Am's bid for Northwest. C. Power and K. Kelly. il por *Business Week* p29 Je 12 '89

MEYERSON (MORTON H.) SYMPHONY CENTER (DALLAS, TEX.) *See* Morton H. Meyerson Symphony Center (Dallas, Tex.)

MEYO, RAYMOND D., 1943-
about
The little company that had trouble growing up. M. Fritz. il por *Forbes* 144:118+ D 25 '89

MEYROWITZ, ROBERT
about
Dig in, Robert. P. Newcomb. il por *Forbes* 143:328 My 29 '89

MEZGER, K.
(jt. auth) See Bohlen, S. R., and Mezger, K.
MEZZACAPPA, LIZ
about
Hampton classic. K. Whiteside. il *House & Garden* 161:82-9 Ja '89
MG (AUTOMOBILE) *See* Sports cars
MGM GRAND AIR INC.
MGM Grand: affluence in the air. M. C. Lehrer. il *USA Today (Periodical)* 117:34-7 Mr '89
MGM/UA COMMUNICATIONS CO.
Leo the Lion is on the loose again [C. Skase's deal to buy MGM/UA falls apart] R. Grover. il por *Business Week* p60 O 23 '89
Stranger in a strange land [C. Skase of Qintex buys MGM/UA Communications] L. Gubernick. il por *Forbes* 144:164+ O 2 '89
MGS ARCHITECTS
On the go [America restaurant in Washington, D.C.] C. Pearson. il *Architectural Record* 177:80-5 mid-S '89
MHC *See* Major histocompatibility complex
MI CASA RESOURCE CENTER FOR WOMEN (DENVER, COLO.)
Where there's a skill, there's a way. A. Bonavoglia. il *Ms.* 18:67-8 O '89
MIAMI (FLA.)
Airports
Pan Am will use Jetstreams to bolster Miami operations. J. T. McKenna. *Aviation Week & Space Technology* 131:82-3 N 27 '89
Architecture
Minimalism in Miami [house by architect M. Hampton] J. Taylor. il *Architectural Digest* 46:216-21+ Ap '89
Courts
The quiet crisis in America's courts [federal judges are fed up with salaries] S. J. Hedges. il *U.S. News & World Report* 106:30+ Ap 3 '89
Crime
The day death came into Carrie Edmondson's yard [children caught in shootout] S. J. Hedges. il *U.S. News & World Report* 106:22-3 Ap 10 '89
The littlest victim [interview with five year old murder witness J. Royal] V. Gladstone. il pors *Life* 12:16+ O '89
The littlest witness may testify about her friend's killing [four year old J. Royal to testify against M. Ward in murder trial] M. Brower. il pors *People Weekly* 31:108-10 Ap 24 '89
Description
Miami. J. Achenbach and M. Stapp. il *Esquire* 112:209+ O '89
Health facilities
See also
University of Miami. Comprehensive Pain and Rehabilitation Center
Hospitals
See also
Jackson Memorial Hospital (Miami, Fla.)
Industries
Inside an 'enterprise zone'. M. Miller. il *Newsweek* 113:43 Mr 6 '89
Municipal improvement
See also
TACOLCY Economic Development Corporation, Inc.
Police
'All of us are in trouble' [riots] G. Hackett. il *Newsweek* 113:36-7 Ja 30 '89
A brightly colored tinderbox [riots following police shooting of motorcyclist in Overtown] J. V. Lamar, Jr. il *Time* 133:28-9 Ja 30 '89
A city waiting for an explosion [police shooting trial could spark riots] A. M. Arrarte. il *U.S. News & World Report* 107:37 N 27 '89
Commission seeks answers to the violence in Miami. *Jet* 75:16 F 13 '89
Miami cop who killed two blacks and incited riot guilty of manslaughter [W. Lozano] il por *Jet* 77:4-5 D 25 '89-Ja 1 '90
Miami: 'We got justice' [policeman W. Lozano found guilty for shootings that resulted in race violence] G. Hackett. il por *Newsweek* 114:30 D 18 '89
Miami's racial fires [police shooting sparks riots] A. Bilski. il *Maclean's* 102:23-5 Ja 30 '89
Too close for comfort [TV news show Eye on crime shows police in action] J. M. Robins. il *Channels (New York, N.Y.: 1986)* 9:24+ Mr '89
Politics and government
Caught up in Miami's Cuban politics [deportation case of O. Bosch] B. Turque. il por *Newsweek* 114:24 S 4 '89
Miami advice [campaign of victorious congressional candidate I. Ros-Lehtinen] W. McGurn. *National Review* 41:39 N 24 '89
Off-key notes in an ethnic symphony [I. Ros-Lehtinen wins House seat] il por *U.S. News & World Report* 107:10 S 11 '89
Population
Washington isn't mellowing on Cuba—but Miami is. A. Fins. il *Business Week* p41 Ap 17 '89

Will the contras' next home be Miami? il *Newsweek* 114:29 Ag 21 '89
Race relations
A city waiting for an explosion [police shooting trial could spark riots] A. M. Arrarte. il *U.S. News & World Report* 107:37 N 27 '89
Miami cop who killed two blacks and incited riot guilty of manslaughter [W. Lozano] il por *Jet* 77:4-5 D 25 '89-Ja 1 '90
Miami: 'We got justice' [policeman W. Lozano found guilty for shootings that resulted in race violence] G. Hackett. il por *Newsweek* 114:30 D 18 '89
Restaurants, nightclubs, bars, etc.
Miami's restaurant scene. R. Sax. il *Gourmet* 49:84+ O '89
Riots
'All of us are in trouble'. G. Hackett. il *Newsweek* 113:36-7 Ja 30 '89
A brightly colored tinderbox [riots following police shooting of motorcyclist in Overtown] J. V. Lamar, Jr. il *Time* 133:28-9 Ja 30 '89
Commission seeks answers to the violence in Miami. *Jet* 75:16 F 13 '89
Miami's racial fires [police shooting sparks riots] A. Bilski. il *Maclean's* 102:23-5 Ja 30 '89
Tension in Miami. J. Maust. il *Christianity Today* 33:40-1 F 17 '89
Savings and loan associations
See also
CenTrust Savings Bank
MIAMI BEACH (FLA.)
Description
Gloria Estefan is a very nautical girl. il por *Rolling Stone* p36 Jl 13-27 '89
Historic houses, sites, etc.
Photographs and photography
Think architecture is boring? Take a shot at Miami Beach's art deco district. L. Dennis. il *Popular Photography* 96:32-3 O '89
Religious institutions and affairs
Tension in Miami. J. Maust. il *Christianity Today* 33:40-1 F 17 '89
Restaurants, nightclubs, bars, etc.
Also on the menu—tradition [Joe's Stone Crab] D. Young. il *Southern Living* 24:110-12+ My '89
Social life and customs
John Cristi, who sees 300 plays and concerts a year, may be the greatest show man on earth. S. Dougherty. il pors *People Weekly* 32:81+ O 2 '89
MIAMI CITY BALLET
Reviews:
Season in Miami. J. Eldridge. *Dance Magazine* 63:79-80 Ap '89
Taking care of the roles: Villella victorious, Miami's Prometheus. L. Horn. il *Dance Magazine* 63:44-50 N '89
MIAMI-DADE COMMUNITY COLLEGE
Finding the call to teach [Miami-Dade Community College teacher spends year at Evergreen State] B. Hilbert. il *Change* 21:6+ Mr/Ap '89
MIAMI INTERNATIONAL AIRPORT *See* Miami (Fla.)—Airports
MIAMI INTERNATIONAL BOAT SHOW *See* Boats and boating—Exhibitions
MIAMI SOUND MACHINE (MUSICAL GROUP)
Gloria Estefan. G. Flowers and J. Nash. il por *Seventeen* 48:70+ D '89
MIAS (AFGHANISTAN INVASION) *See* Afghanistan—Russian invasion, 1979-1989—Missing in action
MICCO, SAM
about
Gambling expert hits a different kind of jackpot. A. Nadler. il pors *Home Office Computing* 7:50-1 Ag '89
MICE
Fire devastates Jackson Lab [research mice destroyed] B. J. Culliton. il *Science* 244:767-8 My 19 '89
Gene-transfer method fails test [trying to replicate; work of Corrado Spadafora] M. Barinaga. *Science* 246:446 O 27 '89
The human mouse [infection of SCID-hu mouse by HIV; work of M. McCune; cover story; with editorial comment by Paul Hoffman] G. Montgomery. il por *Discover* 10:4, 48-55 Ag '89
Making transgenic mice: is it really that easy? [trying to replicate work of Corrado Spadafora] M. Barinaga. il *Science* 245:590-1 Ag 11 '89
The molecular basis of muscular dystrophy in the *mdx* mouse: a point mutation. P. Sicinski and others. bibl f il *Science* 244:1578-80 Je 30 '89
Transgenic mice as probes into complex systems. D. Hanahan. bibl f il *Science* 246:1265-75 D 8 '89
Two cultures find common ground [conference of specialists in mouse and fruit fly development] J. L. Marx. il *Science* 244:652-3 My 12 '89
Wanted: $25 million for mouse house [rebuilding Jackson Lab after fire] B. J. Culliton. il *Science* 245:697-8 Ag 18 '89
Breeding
Brave new mouse [first animal patent for cancer-prone mouse] A. Kozlov. il *Discover* 10:78 Ja '89

MICE—Breeding—*cont.*
No patent for Harvard's mouse? [rejection by European Patent Office] D. Dickson. *Science* 243:1003 F 24 '89
A tiny mouse came forth [patented oncomouse] E. Corcoran. *Scientific American* 260:73 F '89
Control
See also
Mousetraps
Embryology
See Embryology—Rodents
Identification
Probing secrets of small critters: fuchsia mice and bar-coded bees. L. Ware. il *Audubon* 91:12 Ja '89
Reproduction
See Rodents—Reproduction
MICE, ROBOTIC *See* Micromice
MICELLES
Molecular dynamics simulation of a phospholipid micelle. J. J. Wendoloski and others. bibl f il *Science* 243:636-8 F 3 '89
MICHAEL, PRINCE OF GREECE, 1939-
A Spanish heritage: the Duke of Segorbe's crusade to preserve the family estates. il por *Architectural Digest* 46:198-207+ D '89
MICHAEL, CHARLES
Notes on Tanzania. il *World Health* p19-20 Mr '89
MICHAEL, GEORGE, 1919-
Antiques & Americana. See issues of Antiques & Collecting Hobbies beginning October 1988
MICHAEL FOODS INC.
Michael Foods. J. Slovak. il *Fortune* 119:188 Ap 24 '89
MICHAEL JOSEPH LTD.
Heads of Hamish Hamilton and Michael Joseph resign. V. Menkes. *Publishers Weekly* 236:13 Jl 14 '89
MICHAEL ZOCHE (FIRM)
West German firm developing diesel engines for general aviation aircraft. *Aviation Week & Space Technology* 131:57+ Ag 28 '89
MICHAELIS, GEORGE H.
about
Compound interest machines. J. Clements. il por *Forbes* 144:43-4 Ag 21 '89
MICHAELS, AL
about
"We're having an . . .". S. Smith. il por *Sports Illustrated* 71:35 O 30 '89
MICHAELS, JOHN PATRICK, JR.
about
CEA's entertaining mix. M. Brown. il por *Channels (New York, N.Y.: 1986)* 9:73 S '89
MICHAELS, LEONARD, 1933-
Diary of an ex. *Harper's* 279:31-2 D '89
MICHAELS, LORNE
about
Up all night. C. Reece. il pors *Channels (New York, N.Y.: 1986)* 9:39-41 N '89
MICHAELSEN, MARK G.
My life as a congressional candidate. *The American Spectator* 22:24-5 N '89
MICHAELSON, LORI
"My baby really didn't have a chance . . . it has to be a miracle"; ed. by Beth Weinhouse. il *Redbook* 174:130-2+ N '89
MICHALS, DEBRA
Great escapes. il *Harper's Bazaar* 122:106+ D '89
The new rack pack. il *Harper's Bazaar* 122:82+ O '89
She's the boss. il *Ms.* 18:58-61 N '89
Voice of choice. il pors *Harper's Bazaar* 122:110-13+ Ag '89
MICHALS, DUANE, 1932-
about
Duane Michals. R. B. Woodward. il por *Art News* 88:156-7 Ap '89
MICHALSKY, WALT
The Vatican heresy. il *The Humanist* 49:27+ N/D '89
MICHAUD, MICHAEL A. G.
Cooperation in space: the real world. il *Sky and Telescope* 77:4 Ja '89
Planetary partners [cover story] il *Ad Astra* 1:24-8 Mr '89
MICHAUD, PAUL R.
Pass the ammunition. *The New Republic* 200:14 Mr 13 '89
MICHEL, ANDRÉE
Marina, Sarah, Michel and Jean. il *The Unesco Courier* 42:34-7 Jl '89
MICHEL, DEBORAH
North of the border. il *House & Garden* 161:92-5 F '89
MICHEL, HARRIET RICHARDSON
about
Beyond macho: the power of womanly management [excerpt from Tender power] S. S. Cohen. il pors *Working Woman* 14:77-83 F '89
MICHEL, HARTMUT, 1948-
(jt. auth) See Deisenhofer, Johann, 1943-, and Michel, Hartmut, 1948-
about
Nobel chemists shed light on key structure in photosynthesis. B. G. Levi. il por *Physics Today* 42:17-18 F '89

MICHEL, ROBERT H., 1923-
Should a constitutional amendment to prevent flag desecration be approved? [excerpts from testimony, July 13, 1989] *Congressional Digest* 68:202+ Ag/S '89
Should President Bush's minimum wage proposal be adopted? [excerpts from address, March 23, 1989] *Congressional Digest* 68:138+ My '89
about
Little big man. Z. Citron. *The New Republic* 200:12-14 F 27 '89
MICHELANGELI, ARTURO BENEDETTI
about
Michelangeli plays Debussy. R. Freed. il por *Stereo Review* 54:70 Jl '89
MICHELANGELO BUONARROTI, 1475-1564
Doubting genius [poem]; tr. by Creighton Gilbert. il *Art News* 88:13 Ja '89
about
The real Leonardo. C. Hope. il *The New York Review of Books* 36:16-18 Ag 17 '89
A renaissance for Michelangelo [cover story] D. Jeffery. il *National Geographic* 176:688-713 D '89
MICHELE, MICHAEL
about
Comic Eddie Murphy hit with $75 million suit charging sex harassment. pors *Jet* 76:60 My 29 '89
Pink-slipped by Eddie Murphy, Michael Michele vows their only date will be in court. S. Schindehette. il pors *People Weekly* 31:48-9 My 29 '89
MICHELIN ET CIE
Inside mission to Michelin [radial motorcycle tire development] K. Cameron. il *Cycle* 40:55-7+ F '89
Michelin subsidiary developing tires for hypervelocity aircraft program. il *Aviation Week & Space Technology* 130:269 Je 12 '89
That screeching is Michelin doing a U-turn [buying Uniroyal Goodrich] S. Toy and Z. Schiller. il *Business Week* p50 O 9 '89
MICHELMORE, PETER
Beware the health hucksters. *Reader's Digest* 134:114-18 Ja '89
Kids crusade to save our streams. il *Reader's Digest* 134:98-102 Je '89
The long nightmare of Ruth Finley. il por *Reader's Digest* 134:97-104 Mr '89
Message of the pond. il *Reader's Digest* 135:106-10 D '89
"Pull me out". il *Reader's Digest* 135:120-5 Ag '89
The startling Shelly Prine case. *Reader's Digest* 135:179-80+ Jl '89
MICHELS, ALLEN H.
about
"I love the tumult". J. Pitta. il pors *Forbes* 144:296-8 N 13 '89
MICHELS, BRUCE
about
Managing your company's money. N. Sullivan. por *Home Office Computing* 7:60 S '89
MICHELS, DOUG
about
Bringing Unix to PCs. C. O'Malley. por *Personal Computing* 13:83 Jl '89
MICHENER, CHARLES
She's not Meryl Streep, but she's Close. il pors *Esquire* 112:136-8+ N '89
MICHENER, JAMES A. (JAMES ALBERT), 1907-
about
Our man in Havana. B. Levine. il por *Publishers Weekly* 236:50-1 Jl 14 '89
MICHIE COMPANY
Mead tries a new-fangled medium: print [acquisition of Michie Co.] M. Mallory. il *Business Week* p81-2 Ap 10 '89
MICHIGAN
See also
Agriculture—Michigan
Birds—Michigan
Finance—Michigan
Grand Traverse Bay region (Mich.)
Huron-Manistee National Forest (Mich.)
Isle Royale National Park (Mich.)
Kalamazoo River (Mich.)
Keweenaw Peninsula (Mich.)
Lake Saint Clair (Mich. and Ont.)
Lakes—Michigan
Law—Michigan
Mack Lake (Mich.)
Mackinac Island (Mich.)
Tuttle Marsh (Mich.)
Water pollution—Michigan
Wildlife management—Michigan
MICHIGAN, LAKE *See* Lake Michigan
MICHIGAN EDUCATION TRUST
New deal. J. A. Barnes and J. Hadden. *The New Republic* 200:20+ My 1 '89
MICHNIK, ADAM
about
A talk with Adam Michnik [cover story] A. Husarska. pors *The New Leader* 72:8-10 Ap 3-17 '89

MICKEY MOUSE (FICTIONAL CHARACTER)
Collectibles
Mickey Mouse cameras. E. S. Lothrop. il *Popular Photography* 96:52-3 Jl '89

MICKLUS, SAM
about
Mind Odyssey [interview] N. Guccione. il *Omni (New York, N.Y.)* 11:16 Ap '89

MICRO CHANNEL (COMPUTER BUS)
ALR revs up MCA [MicroFlex 7000] B. Catchings and M. L. Van Name. il *Byte* 14:165-9 S '89
The case for Micro Channel architecture. J. Blackford. il *Personal Computing* 13:209-10 Jl '89
EISA sets the stage for open standards. J. Blackford. il *Personal Computing* 13:301-2 Ja '89
IBM's Micro Channel gets a little respect. S. Gelfond. il *Business Week* p156+ Mr 20 '89
The light at the end of the Channel. R. Nelson. *Personal Computing* 13:26 D '89
MCA meets SX [IBM PS/2 Model 55 SX and the American Mitac MPS2386] M. L. Van Name and B. Catchings. il *Byte* 14:181-4 O '89
A PS/2 in Channel only [Tandy 5000 MC] M. L. Van Name. il *Byte* 14:197-200+ F '89
Rising above the industry chaos [Micro Channel vs. EISA buses] F. Abatemarco. il *Personal Computing* 13:5 F '89

MICRO MARKETING
Stalking the new consumer [cover story] Z. Schiller. il *Business Week* p54-8+ Ag 28 '89

MICROBIAL DEGRADATION *See* Biodegradation

MICROBIAL ECOLOGY
Lipid analysis in microbial ecology. J. R. Vestal and D. C. White. bibl f il *BioScience* 39:535-41 S '89
Microbial life in deep terrestrial subsurfaces [sediments from Savannah River Plant] C. B. Fliermans and D. L. Balkwill. bibl f il *BioScience* 39:370-7 Je '89
X-ray microanalysis of leaf-litter decomposition in lakes [scanning microscope] J. A. Perry and others. bibl f il *BioScience* 39:260-3 Ap '89

MICROBIAL GENETICS
See also
Gene transfection
Gene transfer
Chromosomal location and evolutionary rate variation in enterobacterial genes. P. M. Sharp and others. bibl f il *Science* 246:808-10 N 10 '89
Chromosomal rearrangement generating a composite gene for a developmental transcription factor [Bacillus subtilis] P. Stragier and others. bibl f il *Science* 243:507-12 Ja 27 '89
Construction of large DNA segments in Escherichia coli. M. O'Connor and others. bibl f il *Science* 244:1307-12 Je 16 '89
Coordinate regulation and sensory transduction in the control of bacterial virulence. J. F. Miller and others. bibl f il *Science* 243:916-22 F 17 '89
Evolution set fast-forward [viral genetics] *BioScience* 39:512-13 S '89
Expression of a bacterial gene in a trypanosomatid protozoan [Leptomonas] V. Bellofatto and G. A. M. Cross. bibl f il *Science* 244:1167-9 Je 9 '89
Genetic engineering of bacteria from managed and natural habitats. S. E. Lindow and others. bibl f *Science* 244:1300-7 Je 16 '89
Hungry to evolve? [controversy over John Cairns' work with Escherichia coli mutations] J. P. Rennie. *Scientific American* 261:20+ N '89
A liver-specific enhancer in the core promoter region of human hepatitis B virus. J.-K. Yee. bibl f il *Science* 246:658-61 N 3 '89
Microbes to aid plants from within [corn field trials of genetically altered Clavibacter xyli] J. A. Miller. *BioScience* 39:227-8 Ap '89
Microbial census hints at biotech hurdles [study of pseudomonas by Michael H. Smith] R. Weiss. *Science News* 135:4 Ja 7 '89
Reverse transcriptase in a clinical strain of Escherichia coli: production of branched RNA-linked msDNA. B. C. Lampson and others. bibl f il *Science* 243:1033-8 F 24 '89
Spiders of industry [genetically engineered bacteria produce silk; work of Nick Ashley] il *Discover* 10:8 F '89
Switch protein alters specificity of RNA polymerase containing a compartment-specific sigma factor [Bacillus subtilis] L. Kroos and others. bibl f il *Science* 243:526-9 Ja 27 '89

MICROBIAL PESTICIDES *See* Pesticides

MICROBIOLOGY
See also
Biodegradation
Fermentation
Industrial microbiology
Mouth—Microbiology
Soil microbiology
Water—Microbiology

Ecology
See Microbial ecology

MICROCIRCUITS *See* Integrated circuits

MICROCOMPUTER INDUSTRY *See* Computer industry

MICROCONTROLLERS
68705 microcontroller (I). T. Henry. il *Radio-Electronics* 60 ComputerDigest:82-6 S '89
68705 microcontroller (II). T. Henry. il *Radio-Electronics* 60:83+ O '89

MICRODOSES
Benveniste criticism is diluted [water memory experiment] D. Dickson. *Science* 245:248 Jl 21 '89
Dilutions of grandeur [Nature magazine's investigation of J. Benveniste's water memory experiment] A. C. Revkin. il *Discover* 10:74-5 Ja '89

MICROELECTRODES
Time and spatial dependence of the concentration of less than 10^5 microelectrode-generated molecules. S. Licht and others. bibl f il *Science* 243:1176-8 Mr 3 '89

MICROELECTRONICS
See also
Integrated circuits
Molecular electronics
Vacuum microelectronics
The incredible shrinking machine. P. Elmer-Dewitt. il *Time* 134:108+ N 20 '89
Mind over matter [G. Gilder's Microcosm] T. Bethell. *The American Spectator* 22:11-13 N '89
Negative differential resistance on the atomic scale: implications for atomic scale devices. I.-W. Lyo and P. Avouris. bibl f il *Science* 245:1369-71 S 22 '89
A small, small, very small diode [tunnel diode] R. Pool. il *Science* 246:1251 D 8 '89
The world's next source of wealth [excerpt from Microcosm] G. F. Gilder. il por *Fortune* 120:116-20 Ag 28 '89

MICROELECTRONICS AND COMPUTER TECHNOLOGY CORPORATION
Advancing U.S. technology [address, December 6, 1988] G. A. Dove. *Vital Speeches of the Day* 55:268-70 F 15 '89
A high-tech think tank thinks big bucks. K. Kelly. il *Business Week* p222+ S 25 '89

MICROELECTRONICS INDUSTRY *See* Electronic industries

MICROFILMS
Theft
Microfilm thieves hit university libraries [Patent Depository Library] J. Palca. *Science* 245:248 Jl 21 '89

MICROFORMS
See also
Microfilms

MICROGRAFX, INC.
Windows on the world [Microsoft's Presentation Manager strategy in conflict with Micrografx' Windows business] D. Churbuck. il pors *Forbes* 144:123+ D 25 '89
The wizard of Windows [J. P. Grayson] R. Lockwood. por *Personal Computing* 13:85 Jl '89

MICROMARKETING *See* Micro marketing

MICROMECHANICS
The incredible shrinking machine. P. Elmer-Dewitt. il *Time* 134:108+ N 20 '89
Micro-machines. S. Strauss. il *Technology Review* 92:10-11 Ja '89
Micromachine magic [cover story] R. Gannon. il *Popular Science* 234:88-92+ Mr '89
Motors 100 times smaller than any known today. il *Radio-Electronics* 60:4 Mr '89
Small things considered [cover story] I. Amato. il *Science News* 136:8-10 Jl 1 '89

MICROMICE
Building a better mouse [robots that negotiate mazes; work of D. Otten] F. Hapgood. il *Omni (New York, N.Y.)* 12:22+ N '89

MICRONESIA
See also
Pacific Islands (Trust Territory)

MICROORGANISMS
See also
Amebas
Bacteria
Microbial ecology
Staphylococci
Viruses

MICROORGANISMS, FOSSIL *See* Micropaleontology

MICROORGANISMS, PATHOGENIC
See also
Mycoplasmas
Protozoa, Pathogenic

MICROPALEONTOLOGY
See also
Conodonts
Microbes complicate the K-T mystery [research by Betsey D. Dyer] R. Monastersky. *Science News* 136:341 N 25 '89

MICROPHONES
Wireless FM microphone. M. Spiwak. il *Radio-Electronics* 60:43-5 Mr '89

MICROPHOTOGRAPHY
See also
Photomicrography

MICROPROCESSORS

See also
Microcontrollers

32 bits and above [special section; with editorial comment by Jane Morrill Tazelaar] il *Byte* 14:296-7+ N '89

The 486 systems are coming. J. Blackford. il *Personal Computing* 13:231-2 D '89

80486, 68040 open new season of CPU power. *Byte* 14:13-14+ Je '89

Build an 80386SX motherboard (I). B. A. McIlhany. il *Radio-Electronics* 60 ComputerDigest:79+ Je '89

Build an 80386SX motherboard (II). B. A. McIlhany. il *Radio-Electronics* 60 ComputerDigest:81 Jl '89

Build an 80386SX motherboard (III). B. A. McIlhany. il *Radio-Electronics* 60 ComputerDigest:75+ Ag '89

Checking out the new 80486 and 68040. F. Langa. il *Byte* 14:8 Je '89

The chip of tomorrow—in yesterday's machine [IBM to retrofit PS/2 with I486 microchip] G. Lewis. il *Business Week* p64 Jl 3 '89

Configuring parallel programs (I) [Occam Transpiler] D. Pountain. il *Byte* 14:349-52 D '89

Does everyone need an 80386-based computer? *High Technology Business* 9:31-2 Ja '89

Hip-deep and rising [making upgrade decisions] F. Langa. il *Byte* 14:8 O '89

Hold onto your hat (and your wallet) [Apricot 80486-based machine] F. Langa. il *Byte* 14:8 Ag '89

Inside Intel's 80386 (I). N. Margulis. il *Radio-Electronics* 60 ComputerDigest:90-5+ Ja '89

Inside Intel's 80386 (II). N. Margulis. il *Radio-Electronics* 60 ComputerDigest:103-8 F '89

Inside Intel's 80386 (III). J. Kardach and N. Margulis. il *Radio-Electronics* 60 ComputerDigest:98-101 Mr '89

The latest 386-based computers. E. Rutsch. il *Home Office Computing* 7:54-8 Je '89

The long view on chip technology [SX chip] J. Blackford. il *Personal Computing* 13:249 My '89

Making sense of the SX. R. Lockwood. il *Personal Computing* 13:82-6 Je '89

Microprocessor challenge. R. C. Wood. il *High Technology Business* 9:12+ My '89

More bang for your bucks [80486-based systems from Cheetah and ALR] F. Langa. il *Byte* 14 Special Issue:8 Fall '89

A PC run circles around a Cray? [coprocessors and transputers] T. J. Byers. il *Radio-Electronics* 60 ComputerDigest:77+ Ap '89

Protected mode. B. Glass. bibl il *Byte* 14:377-84 D '89

Revenge of the CISCs. M. Slater and J. H. Wharton. il *Byte* 14:323-4+ N '89

The wages of sin. P. Wilson. il *Byte* 14 Special Issue:276 Fall '89

What drew Canon to Motorola? Passion, of course [microprocessor for EOS camera] N. Gross. il *Business Week* p118 N 13 '89

Testing

The 486s are here! [Apricot VX FT Server; cover story] P. Lavin and M. E. Nadeau. il *Byte* 14:95-8 S '89

80386SX performance trials. R. Lockwood. il *Personal Computing* 13:87-9+ Ag '89

The 80486: a hardware perspective. R. Sartore. il *Byte* 14 Special Issue:67-70+ Fall '89

Battle of the chips [Intel 80286, 80386, and 80386SX; cover story] F. Hayes. il *Byte* 14:274-7+ Mr '89

Building an OmniView application. M. Toutonghi. il *Radio-Electronics* 60 ComputerDigest:80-4 Ag '89

Desktop power to go [80386 portables] S. Diehl and S. J. Wszola. il *Byte* 14:142-6+ Ag '89

EISA arrives [Vectra 486; cover story] N. Baran. il *Byte* 14:93-6+ N '89

The fastest 80386s ever? [cover story] R. Malloy. il *Byte* 14:109-12 Je '89

The fastest PCs in the world [ALR FlexCache 33/386, AST Premium 386/33, Compaq Deskpro 386/33, Everex Step 386/33, Zenith Z-386/33, Zeos 386/33] P. Honan. il *Personal Computing* 13:95-7+ S '89

The last word on the SX? F. Langa. il *Byte* 14:8 D '89

MCA meets SX [IBM PS/2 Model 55 SX and the American Mitac MPS2386] M. L. Van Name and B. Catchings. il *Byte* 14:181-4 O '89

Megahertz madness [15 of the world's fastest PCs] il *Byte* 14 Special Issue:13-18+ Fall '89

OmniView and a 386 [DOS multitasking operating environment] M. Toutonghi. il *Radio-Electronics* 60 ComputerDigest:73 Jl '89

Speed-up board gives decent return for your money [Orchid TwinTurbo 12] H. F. Beechhold. il *Home Office Computing* 7:62 Ja '89

What's new in accelerator boards. R. Bel Bruno. il *Personal Computing* 13:103-5+ Ag '89

MICROROBOTS

Microbots. T. A. Heppenheimer. il *Discover* 10:78-82+ Mr '89

MICROSCOPES

See also
Acoustic microscopes
Atomic force microscopes
Confocal microscopes
Electron microscopes
Photomicrography
Scanning electron microscopes
Scanning ion-conductance microscopes
Scanning tunneling microscopes
X ray microscopes

Micro magic. S. Shulman. il *Technology Review* 92:11-12 N/D '89

Scanned-probe microscopes. H. K. Wickramasinghe. il *Scientific American* 261:98-105 O '89

Space flight use

Robotic microscope could allow R&D in space. *High Technology Business* 9:36-7 F '89

MICROSOFT CORPORATION

Meanwhile, back among the fir trees at Microsoft . . . il *Fortune* 120:61 O 9 '89

'Microsoft is like an elephant rolling around, squashing ants'. R. Brandt. il *Business Week* p148-9+ O 30 '89

The once and future evangelist [W. H. Gates] S. R. Reed. por *Personal Computing* 13:75 Jl '89

Windows on the world [Microsoft's Presentation Manager strategy in conflict with Micrografx' Windows business] D. Churbuck. il pors *Forbes* 144:123+ D 25 '89

MICROSOFT WORD (WORD PROCESSOR PROGRAM)

See Word processors and processing—Programming

MICROSPHERES

Mapping neuronal inputs to REM sleep induction sites with carbachol-fluorescent microspheres. J. J. Quattrochi and others. bibl f il *Science* 245:984-6 S 1 '89

MICROTUBULES

Direct measurements of sliding between outer doublet microtubules in swimming sperm flagella [sea urchins] C. J. Brokaw. bibl f il *Science* 243:1593-6 Mr 24 '89

The mitotic spindle. J. R. McIntosh and K. L. McDonald. bibl il *Scientific American* 261:48-56 O '89

Spatial patterns from oscillating microtubules. E. Mandelkow and others. bibl f il *Science* 246:1291-3 D 8 '89

MICROWAVE COMMUNICATION SYSTEMS

See also
Multichannel multipoint distribution service

MICROWAVE COOKING

See also
Golden Valley Microwave Foods Inc.

30-minute main dish [couscous- and shrimp-stuffed zucchini; low wattage microwaving] il *Better Homes and Gardens* 67:101 Ja '89

30 terrific ways to use your microwave. il *Ladies' Home Journal* 106:137-8+ Ja '89

Breakfast sandwiches. il *Southern Living* 24:130-1 Ja '89

Breast-milk don'ts [effects on immune protection; research by John A. Kerner] L. Schroepfer. *American Health* 8:106-7 My '89

Doughnut detonator [R. Schiffmann tests microwaveable foods] J. Zweig. il por *Forbes* 143:154+ My 1 '89

Easy entrées for two. il *Southern Living* 24:132 F '89

Fast friend in the kitchen. B. Hayton. bibl il *Current Health 2* 15:14-17 F '89

Fast snacks. il *Southern Living* 24:168 My '89

Few ingredients, lots of flavor. il *Southern Living* 24:94 Ag '89

Fish in the microwave. S. Bashline. il *Field & Stream* 94:68 Ag '89

Fun foods for moms and kids to make. *Good Housekeeping* 209:224 N '89

Ginger bass, salsa trout . . . in the microwave. il *Sunset (Central West edition)* 183:90 Ag '89

Healthy microwaving. J. B. Hurley. See issues of Prevention (Emmaus, Pa.) beginning January 1987

High-tech game cookery. S. Bashline. il *Field & Stream* 94:30 O '89

Hurry-up vegetables. *Good Housekeeping* 209:238 N '89

Mad about muffins. *Good Housekeeping* 209:212+ N '89

Master your microwave. See issues of Parents beginning February 1989

Meals in a micro-wave [on board a boat] J. F. Mariani. il *Motor Boating & Sailing* 163:50-1 F '89

A meditation on the microwave. M. Visser. il *Psychology Today* 23:38+ D '89

Micro-cooking meat: five steps for success. *Better Homes and Gardens* 67:151 Ap '89

Micro-way cooking. See issues of McCall's beginning March 1986

The microwave at Thanksgiving. il *Gourmet* 49:126-7+ N '89

The microwave cookbook. See issues of Good Housekeeping beginning November 1985

Microwave cookbook for summer-fresh vegetables. B. Goldman. il *Better Homes and Gardens* 67:95-100+ Ag '89

Microwave cookery [special section] il *Southern Living* 24:109+ Je '89

Microwave cooking tips. J. A. Kenneally. See issues of Good Housekeeping beginning October 1985

Microwave entertaining [excerpt] M. Cone and T. Snyder. il *Ladies' Home Journal* 106:273+ N '89

Microwave harvests [winter squash and fruit] N. Hauser. il *American Health* 8:104 O '89

Microwave magic. C. Lyons. il *Ebony* 44:104-6+ Ap '89

MICROWAVE COOKING—cont.

Microwave poultry. il *Better Homes and Gardens* 67:153-4 Je '89

Microwave side dishes. il *Better Homes and Gardens* 67:141-2 Mr '89

Microwave snacks. il *Better Homes and Gardens* 67:159-60 S '89

Microwave snacks for kids. M. Cone and T. Snyder. il *Working Woman* 14:224 S '89

Microwave the main dish. il *Southern Living* 24:166 O '89

Microwave top ten [popular things to make] il *Seventeen* 48:173 Je '89

Microwaves: the machines that fire your diet. E. Kunes. il *Mademoiselle* 95:226 N '89

Savvy ways with meat. il *Southern Living* 24:206+ Mr '89

Shortcuts to jelly-making. il *Southern Living* 24:132 Jl '89

Speedy microwave pizza starts with a flour tortilla. il *Sunset (Central West edition)* 182:194 Ap '89

Spring-fresh microwave meals. L. Holderness. il *Better Homes and Gardens* 67:153-4 Ap '89

Tex-Mex microwave [excerpt from Kids cook microwave] il *National Geographic World* 169:10-11 S '89

Timesaving barbecue. il *Southern Living* 24:192 Ap '89

Treat yourself to apples and pears. il *Southern Living* 24:184 S '89

Turkey breast, fast and flavorful. il *Southern Living* 24:200-1 N '89

Anecdotes, facetiae, satire, etc.

The 60-second gourmet. D. Blum. il *New York* 22:27 F 20 '89

MICROWAVE COOKWARE

A fast way to cook mediocre stew [Nordic Ware's Tender Cooker] il *Consumer Reports* 54:677 N '89

New ware for microwaves. J. B. Hurley. *Consumers' Research Magazine* 72:29 D '89

Utensils for the microwave oven. *Consumers' Research Magazine* 72:36 Ap '89

MICROWAVE DETECTORS

Advanced weather sensor enhances next-generation defense satellite [Aerojet ElectroSystems' Special Sensor Microwave Imager Sounder] B. W. Henderson. il *Aviation Week & Space Technology* 131:47+ Ag 14 '89

MICROWAVE INTEGRATED CIRCUITS

Electronic warfare (II) [cover story; special section] il *Aviation Week & Space Technology* 131:84-5+ S 18 '89

Harris unit develops advanced GaAs facility to supply MMICs to military [gallium arsenide monolithic microwave integrated circuits] B. W. Henderson. il *Aviation Week & Space Technology* 130:101+ Ap 24 '89

Sanders develops MMIC for phased array systems [monolithic microwave integrated circuit device] *Aviation Week & Space Technology* 130:291 Je 12 '89

MICROWAVE INTERFEROMETERS *See* Interferometers and interferometry

MICROWAVE LANDING SYSTEMS

American offers to use its pilots, simulators to evaluate MLS curved approach capabilities. il *Aviation Week & Space Technology* 129:69 Mr 6 '89

ATA will establish task force to critique MLS programs. J. T. McKenna. il *Aviation Week & Space Technology* 129:68-9 Mr 6 '89

Canada, airlines develop plan to test MLS capabilities. J. T. McKenna. *Aviation Week & Space Technology* 131:70-1 S 4 '89

FAA refines MLS plan. *Flying* 116:21 My '89

FAA weighs terminating Hazeltine's MLS contract. *Aviation Week & Space Technology* 131:28 Jl 3 '89

First federal MLS is commissioned [Lebanon Municipal Airport, N.H.] il *Flying* 116:20 Jl '89

Hazeltine, FAA work to salvage major MLS production contract. J. T. McKenna. *Aviation Week & Space Technology* 131:70-1 Ag 28 '89

Nice, but necessary? J. M. McClellan. il *Flying* 116:104 Mr '89

MICROWAVE OVENS

Aluminum in microwaves. K. K. Gracey. *Consumers' Research Magazine* 72:2 Ja '89

Concern shifts to the food. *Consumer Reports* 54:693 N '89

A home for your microwave. il *Southern Living* 24:146-7 Je '89

How it works: microwave oven. T. Klenck. il *Popular Mechanics* 166:78-9 S '89

The little waves that could. M. B. Roman. il *Discover* 10:54-8+ N '89

Microwave/convection ovens. il *Consumer Reports* 54:580-6 S '89

Microwave/convection ovens. il *Consumer Reports* 54:287-94 D '89

Microwave ovens. il *Consumer Reports* 54:145-51 Mr '89

Mid-sized microwave ovens. il *Consumer Reports* 54:282-7 D '89

Small microwave ovens. il *Consumer Reports* 54:692-7 N '89

What's all the fuss about wattage? il *Southern Living* 24:115 D '89

Anecdotes, facetiae, satire, etc.

Macrowave oven. L. Hakemachi. il *Radio-Electronics* 60:74-5 Ap '89

MICROWAVE RECEIVERS

Digital receiver offers many benefits for EW. *Aviation Week & Space Technology* 131:91 S 18 '89

Need to detect signals instantly spurs call for digital components. il *Aviation Week & Space Technology* 131:104-5 S 18 '89

MICROWAVE SEWAGE DISPOSAL

Waste zapper. J. A. Yeaple. *Popular Science* 235:49 Jl '89

MICROWAVE SPECTROSCOPY

New range opens for spectroscopy. il *Radio-Electronics* 60:4 Jl '89

MICROWAVES

Library use

Microwaves that save manuscripts [deacidification] D. Sergent. il *The Courier (Unesco)* 42:9 My '89

Medical use

The little waves that could. M. B. Roman. il *Discover* 10:54-8+ N '89

Zapping tumors with microwaves. il *High Technology Business* 9:4 Je '89

Physiological effects

The hazards of electromagnetic fields (II) [Pave Paws radar] P. Brodeur. *The New Yorker* 65:47-9+ Je 19 '89

MID-ATLANTIC BOOKSELLERS ASSOCIATION

Stormy weather in Atlantic City [NYRBA-MABA joint meeting] M. J. O'Brien. il *Publishers Weekly* 236:26-7 O 20 '89

MID-ATLANTIC RIDGE *See* Ocean bottom

MIDDLE AGE

F-F-F-Fortysomething? [black men] E. V. Tait. il *Essence* 20:16+ N '89

Fifty, fabulous and flaunting it [black celebrities] R. D. Turner. il *Ebony* 44:34+ O '89

First-time brides after 40. R. D. Turner. il *Ebony* 45:84+ N '89

Fortysomething is a wonderful age! J. Viorst. *Redbook* 173:42+ Je '89

Look who's looking good [stars from '60s sitcoms; special section] J. Jones. il *Redbook* 172:85-91 Ja '89

Over-40 special [cover story; special issue] il *Harper's Bazaar* 122:28+ Ag '89

Anecdotes, facetiae, satire, etc.

Mid-life sax [middle-aged men taking up saxophone] J. Nocera. il *Esquire* 111:52 Ap '89

Psychology

The mid-life fitness peak [study by Charles A. Garfield] M. Rozak. il *Psychology Today* 23:32-3 Jl/Ag '89

Midlife crises in men: are women to blame? S. Amsterdam. il *TV Guide* 37:18-20 Jl 22-28 '89

Midlife exhilaration [women] M. M. Gullette. il *The New York Times Magazine* p18+ Ja 29 '89

Old and in the way. G. Jaynes. il *Life* 12:14 Ag '89

Reflections on middle age. R. Coles. il *New Choices for the Best Years* 29:90+ O '89

Sixteen—the third time around. I. Davis. il *The New York Times Magazine* p22+ D 17 '89

Turning 40. N. Kelton. il *Parents* 64:132-3 Mr '89

Anecdotes, facetiae, satire, etc.

Dating at forty. N. Kelton. il *Parents* 64:126-8 S '89

Religious aspects

Faith lift: how to navigate midlife's mysteries. B. Dodds. il *U.S. Catholic* 54:31-5 O '89

Have I done well? [excerpt from Tough questions Christians ask] D. Neff. il *Christianity Today* 33:22-8 F 17 '89

MIDDLE AGE MARKET

The age wave—and how to ride it. C. Farrell. il *Business Week* p112+ O 16 '89

As time goes by [cosmetics ads] L. Wells. il *The New York Times Magazine* p86 Mr 19 '89

MIDDLE AGE PREGNANCY *See* Pregnancy

MIDDLE AGES

See also
Crusades

Bread of dreams [effects of malnutrition and adulterated bread on the poor of medieval Europe; cover story] P. Camporesi. il *History Today* 39:14-21 Ap '89

The medieval mill—a productivity breakthrough? R. Holt. il *History Today* 39:26-31 Jl '89

Medieval queenship. L. Huneycutt. bibl il *History Today* 39:16-22 Je '89

MIDDLE CLASSES

See also
Black middle class

The case against Joe Nocera [exodus of white middle class from public schools] J. Nocera. *The Washington Monthly* 21:22-4+ F '89

Is the middle class getting squeezed? il *Changing Times* 43:30-1 Mr '89

A plague without boundaries [upper middle class crack users] P. Elmer-Dewitt. il *Time* 134:95+ N 6 '89

Taxation

Fighting a taxing burden [Canada] P. Chisholm. il *Maclean's* 102:64-5 N 6 '89

MIDDLE CLASSES—Taxation—*cont.*
Taxing the already overburdened [Canada's proposed Goods and Services Tax] P. C. Newman. il *Maclean's* 102:69 N 6 '89

Canada
Destroying the middle class [special section; with editorial comment by Kevin Doyle] il *Maclean's* 102:2, 56-8+ N 6 '89
Taxing the already overburdened [proposed Goods and Services Tax] P. C. Newman. il *Maclean's* 102:69 N 6 '89

India
Puppies and consumer boomers. E. W. Desmond. il *Time* 134:53+ N 13 '89

MIDDLE EAST
See also
Economic assistance, American—Middle East
Espionage, American—Middle East
Health education—Middle East
Holy Land
Hospitals—Middle East
Iran
Iraq
Israel
Jerusalem
Jordan
Lebanon
Mental health—Middle East
Midwives—Middle East
Munitions—Middle East
Oman
Paleontology—Middle East
Public health—Middle East
Syria
Television and politics—Middle East
Terrorism—Middle East
Turkey
United Nations—Middle East
United Nations Relief and Works Agency for Palestine Refugees in the Near East
Water supply—Middle East
Regional report: the Middle East. S. Pope. See issues of World Press Review beginning June 1986

Civilization
The map of the Middle East. B. Lewis. *The American Scholar* 58:19-38 Wint '89

Commerce
Cuba
See Cuba—Commerce—Middle East
Germany (West)
See Germany (West)—Commerce—Middle East

Defenses
See also
Chemical and biological weapons—Middle East
Guided missiles, Middle Eastern
United Nations—Armed Forces—Forces in the Middle East
United States. Army—Forces in the Middle East

Foreign relations
Canada
See Canada—Foreign relations—Middle East
Egypt
See Egypt—Foreign relations—Middle East
Great Britain
See Great Britain—Foreign relations—Middle East
Jordan
See Jordan—Foreign relations—Middle East
Soviet Union
See Soviet Union—Foreign relations—Middle East
Syria
See Syria—Foreign relations—Middle East
United States
See United States—Foreign relations—Middle East

History
See also
Israel-Arab War, 1948-1949
The map of the Middle East. B. Lewis. *The American Scholar* 58:19-38 Wint '89

Politics and government
See also
Israel-Arab Wars, 1967-
Jewish-Arab relations
Bishops' principles for Middle East peace [draft of U.S. Catholic bishops' pastoral letter] C. A. Kimball. *The Christian Century* 106:972-3 N 1 '89
Contemplating the next step [views of Hussein and H. Mubarak] S. MacLeod. il pors *Time* 133:32-4 Ja 23 '89
Hands off by the superpowers. R. Fisk. il *World Press Review* 36:26-7 O '89
The Middle East, 1989 [cover story; special issue] bibl f map (inside back cover) *Current History* 88:65-107 F '89
Middle East opportunities. G. Kemp. *Foreign Affairs* 68 Special Issue:139-58 ['89]
PW interviews [T. L. Friedman] S. Staggs. por *Publishers Weekly* 236:54-5 Jl 14 '89
Triple play [U.S. Catholic bishops' statement] *Commonweal* 116:581-2 N 3 '89
Whodunit? [conspiracy theory belief] D. Pipes. il *The Atlantic* 263:18+ My '89

Religious institutions and affairs
See also
Middle East Council of Churches
Muslims—Middle East
MIDDLE EAST COUNCIL OF CHURCHES
A partisan 'holy cow' in the Middle East. J. M. Wall. *The Christian Century* 106:923-4 O 18 '89
MIDDLE EAST IN OPERA
The God who cries: an opera on the Mideast [S. Copeland's Holy blood and crescent moon] H. W. Eberts. *The Christian Century* 106:1174-8 D 13 '89
MIDDLE EUROPE *See* Central Europe
MIDDLE MANAGERS *See* Executives
MIDDLE SCHOOLS
Building an atmosphere of success in a middle school [Roosevelt Middle School in Eugene, Or.] R. E. Rubinstein. *Phi Delta Kappan* 71:328-9 D '89
Help for at-risk kids [Carnegie proposals] S. Tifft. il *Time* 133:51 Je 26 '89
Middle school versus junior high. F. Roberts. *Parents* 64:47-8+ N '89
Schools: homes away from home [report of the Carnegie Task Force on Education of Young Adolescents] D. W. Hornbeck. *American Health* 8:50 O '89
Upgrading education in local public schools [Nathaniel Rochester Community School in Rochester, N.Y.] B. Delatiner. *The Education Digest* 55:28-30 S '89
Which way the middle school? P. S. George. *The Education Digest* 54:13-16 Ja '89

Curriculum
See also
Special education
MIDDLE WESTERN STATES
See also
Agriculture—Middle Western States
Fishing—Middle Western States
Great Plains
Historic houses, sites, etc.—Middle Western States
Land—Middle Western States
Resorts—Middle Western States
Restaurants—Middle Western States
Skiing—Middle Western States
Heartland vs. Sunbelt [quality of life; study by Dowell Myers] il *USA Today (Periodical)* 118:4-5 D '89

Climate
A drought's unyielding cycle. K. E. Kunkel. il *Natural History* p48-9 Ja '89

Description and travel
Anecdotes, facetiae, satire, etc.
Plains? Great! P. Nelson. il *Mother Jones* 14:53-4 Je '89

Industries
See also
Paper industry
MIDDLEBURG (VA.)

Historic houses, sites, etc.
Middleburg manor [Herman and Monica Greenberg's restored 1740 farmhouse] N. McKeon. il *House & Garden* 161:144-53 Ap '89
MIDDLETON, DREW, 1913-1990
The world has never been quite the same. il *The New York Times Magazine* p28-30+ S 3 '89
MIDDLETOWN SPRINGS (VT.)

Hotels, motels, etc.
Curl up in a country inn [Middletown Springs Inn] J. O'Reilly. il *New Choices for the Best Years* 29:51-4 Ja '89
MIDDLETOWN SPRINGS INN (VT.) *See* Middletown Springs (Vt.)—Hotels, motels, etc.
MIDGET AUTOMOBILE RACING
The secret life of Eddie Lawson. K. Vreeke. il por *Cycle* 40:58-61+ Ag '89
Tiny terrors [D. Schilling] L. Griffin. il *Car and Driver* 35:158-9+ D '89
MIDGETMAN (MISSILE) *See* Guided missiles
MIDGETMAN (MISSILE) BASING SYSTEM *See* Guided missile bases
MIDGETS *See* Dwarfs and dwarfism
MIDI (MUSICAL INSTRUMENT DIGITAL INTERFACE)
Building a MIDI studio [schools] T. Messina. il *Down Beat* 56:56-7 Je '89
Creative synthesizer technique II—in MIDI Wonderland [West L.A. Music's Keyboard and MIDI Show] A. Holzman. il *Down Beat* 56:59-60 F '89
MIDI equipment. M. M. Rosenthal. il *Radio-Electronics* 60:34-41 Ag '89
Musical Instrument Digital Interface [cover story] J. Simonton. il *Radio-Electronics* 60:33-41 Ag '89

Programming
MIDI and the theatre: a guide to music software applications. J. Roper. *Theatre Crafts* 23:70+ O '89
MIDKIFF, DALE

about
He lives just down the road from fame. S. Littwin. il por *TV Guide* 37:32 S 2-8 '89
MIDLAND DOHERTY FINANCIAL CORP.
An audacious gambler bucks the trends [P. Campbell] P. C. Newman. il *Maclean's* 102:41 Ja 30 '89

MIDLER, BETTE
about
Bankable Bette [cover story] M. Rosen. il pors *Ms.* 17:52-7 Mr '89
Bette Midler gets serious. E. Sherman. il pors *Ladies' Home Journal* 106:58+ Ja '89
Bette Midler is Big business. S. Grant. il por *Video* 13:14 Ap '89
The private Bette Midler—a big surprise! D. Ephron. il pors *Redbook* 172:28+ Mr '89
Trouble for copycats. P. Young. il por *Maclean's* 102:92 N 20 '89
A U.S. patent on famous voices. il por *U.S. News & World Report* 107:19 N 13 '89
MIDNIGHT BASKETBALL LEAGUE
Midnight rescue [founded in Md. to combat youth drug abuse] B. A. McKee. il por *Nation's Business* 77:86 N '89
MIDNIGHT CALLER [television program] See Television program reviews—Single works
MIDNIGHT RUN [film] See Motion picture reviews—Single works
MIDNIGHT SPECIAL (LOS ANGELES, CALIF.: BOOKSTORE) See Booksellers and bookselling—California
MIDWAY AIRLINES, INC.
David Hinson is stretching Midway's wings. J. E. Ellis. il por *Business Week* p84-5 Je 12 '89
Is a nutsy-boltsy company out to nail Midway Airlines? [Ampco-Pittsburgh] M. Schroeder. il *Business Week* p26 Ag 21 '89
Midway triples MD-80 order; Douglas predicts more delays. *Aviation Week & Space Technology* 130:34 Ap 3 '89
MIDWAY ISLANDS
See also
Birds—Midway Islands
MIDWEST See Middle Western States
MIDWEST EXPRESS
Air Kleenex. C. Poole. il *Forbes* 143:10 Mr 20 '89
MIDWEST FEDERAL SAVINGS & LOAN ASSOCIATION OF MINNEAPOLIS
The downfall of a thrift. J. Hammer. il por *Newsweek* 113:54 F 27 '89
MIDWESTERN COOKING See Cooking, American
MIDWIVES
Midwives: tapping every woman's strength. P. Armstrong and S. Feldman. il *American Health* 8:74-6+ Ja/F '89
What I know about deliverin' babies come from motherwit, common sense. God gave it to me [excerpt from Motherwit: an Alabama midwife's story]; ed. by Katherine Clark. O. L. Logan. il pors *Life* 12:19-21 Je '89
Algeria
Midwives in Algeria. O. Zémor. il *World Health* p15-16 D '88
Middle East
A happy ending [assisting at difficult birth leads to training of birth attendants] G. Hafez. il *World Health* p13-15 Jl '89
MIEDER, WOLFGANG
about
Love proverbs are universal, says an expert—and like love itself, they can bite. il por *People Weekly* 31:112-13 F 20 '89
MIELE, FRANK
about
Frank J. Miele's urban folklore. J. Simpson. il por *Architectural Digest* 46:88+ Je '89
MIFEPRISTONE See RU 486 (Drug)
MIG AIRPLANES See Airplanes, Military
MIGHTY MOUSE (FICTIONAL CHARACTER)
The last angry mouse. R. Powers. il por *Gentlemen's Quarterly* 59:106+ Ag '89
THE MIGHTY QUINN [film] See Motion picture reviews—Single works
MIGLER, RACHAEL
Tom Lovejoy and the last crusade. il pors *Gentlemen's Quarterly* 59:286-9+ O '89
MIGLIN-BEITLER DEVELOPMENT INC.
Able to leap the Sears Tower in a single bound? [125 story skyscraper to be built in Chicago] D. Greising. il *Business Week* p94 Je 5 '89
MIGRAINE See Headache
MIGRANT LABOR
See also
Okies
Actor's son Cheyney Ryan brings migrant workers a theater that could save their lives. A. Chambers. il pors *People Weekly* 32:175-6 D 4 '89
Barrio makeover [selling Avon products to Hispanic women] R. Kirk. il *Ms.* 17:73-5 My '89
Big sugar (I) [cutting sugar cane in Florida] A. Wilkinson. il *The New Yorker* 65:41-2+ Jl 17 '89
Big sugar (II) [cutting sugar cane in Florida] A. Wilkinson. il *The New Yorker* 65:42-3+ Jl 24 '89
Farm workers don't have to be poor [Texas] T. Rosenberg. *The Washington Monthly* 21:22-4+ Ap '89
Walter and the raffle [migrant workers send boss W. Jansen to Puerto Rico] P. Kelly. *Reader's Digest* 134:26 Mr '89

Why I am homeless. C. C. Bruno. il por *The Humanist* 49:10-11+ My/Je '89
MIGRATION
See also
Birds—Migration
Butterflies—Migration
Cranes (Birds)—Migration
Deer—Migration
Dinosaurs—Migration
Ducks, Wild—Migration
Geese, Wild—Migration
Man—Migrations
Polar bears—Migration
Rodents—Migration
Shore birds—Migration
Swans—Migration
Turtles—Migration
Water birds—Migration
MIGRATION, INTERNAL
See also
Blacks—Migration
Cities and towns—Growth
Labor mobility
Student mobility
A new heartland. J. Herbers. maps *Country Journal* 16:67-9 My/Je '89
Canada
Escape from high costs [businesses and individuals leaving Toronto] P. Chisholm. il *Maclean's* 102:62+ N 20 '89
Escaping the money squeeze [leaving large urban centers] *Maclean's* 102:58 N 6 '89
Anecdotes, facetiae, satire, etc.
A world-class exit from the fast lane [people leaving Toronto] C. Gordon. il *Maclean's* 102:15 S 18 '89
MIGRATION FROM CITIES See Migration, Internal
MIGRATORY WORKERS See Migrant labor
MIHAJLOV, MIHAJLO
A talk with the editor of 'Ogonyok' [interview with V. Korotich; cover story; with editorial comment] il *The New Leader* 72:2, 10-16 F 20 '89
about
Between issues. *The New Leader* 72:2 Mr 20 '89
MIHARA, KOICHIRO, AND OTHERS
Cell cycle-dependent regulation of phosphorylation of the human retinoblastoma gene product. bibl f il *Science* 246:1300-3 D 8 '89
MIKAN, GEORGE
about
Big George. R. Fimrite. il pors *Sports Illustrated* 71:128-34+ N 6 '89
MIKHALEV, ALEKSEI
(jt. auth) See Lourie, Richard, 1940-, and Mikhalev, Aleksei
MIKOYAN DESIGN BUREAU (SOVIET UNION)
Mikoyan Design Group upgrading MiG-29 with fly-by-wire controls, new cockpit. il *Aviation Week & Space Technology* 130:81 Je 5 '89
MIKULSKI, BARBARA A.
Should the Congress adopt the "Financial Institutions Reform, Recovery, and Enforcement Act of 1989"? [excerpts from address, April 19, 1989] *Congressional Digest* 68:188+ Je/Jl '89
Should the Senate-passed Immigration Act of 1989 be approved? [excerpts from debate, July 13, 1989] *Congressional Digest* 68:255 O '89
about
New hands on the purse strings. W. Booth and others. pors *Science* 243:160 Ja 13 '89
MIKVA, ABNER J.
The verdict on Judge Wapner. il pors *TV Guide* 37:12-14 Ap 22-28 '89
MIL (M. L.) HELICOPTER DESIGN BUREAU (SOVIET UNION) See M. L. Mil Helicopter Design Bureau (Soviet Union)
MILAN (ITALY)
Historic houses, sites, etc.
Wally Toscanini: Milan's first lady of opera [Casa Toscanini] C. Aillaud. il pors *Architectural Digest* 46:58+ Mr '89
Industries
See also
Memphis (Firm)
Publishers and publishing—Italy
Music
See also
Opera—Italy
Restaurants, nightclubs, bars, etc.
A fashionable love affair with food [favorite restaurants of fashion designers] C. Petkanas. il *Harper's Bazaar* 122:81+ Ja '89
MILAN (ITALY) FASHION DESIGNERS See Fashion designers
MILAN (ITALY) FASHION SHOWS See Fashion shows
MILAN FURNITURE FAIR See Furniture, Italian—Exhibitions
MILANKOVITCH CYCLES See Meteorological models
MILANO, ALYSSA
about
The worries are what to do about love, sex, religion—and where to have pizza Friday night. M. Murphy. il por *TV Guide* 37:12-13 F 11-17 '89

MILANO, CAROL
Small-budget start-ups. il *Essence* 20:124+ O '89
MILANOV, ZINKA, 1906-1989
about
Obituary
Opera News 54:36 Ag '89
Opera News il pors 54:45 Jl '89. P. J. Smith
MILBANK, CAROLINE RENNOLDS
American independents. il *Vogue* 179:106-7+ D '89
George Stavropoulos: a master of classical line in Manhattan.
il pors *Architectural Digest* 46:158-61+ S '89
A master showman imbues clothes with life. il por
Architectural Digest 46:88+ S '89
Metropolitan flair: telling details for Jackie Rogers in Manhattan. il por *Architectural Digest* 46:286-9 N '89
MILE RUNNING *See* Track and field athletics
MILER, MARTIN C.
about
"Our competitors can't touch us". J. H. Taylor. il por *Forbes*
143:86 Mr 20 '89
MILES, ARLENE B.
Cultivate a budding gardener. il *Parents* 64:78-9+ Ap '89
MILES, CHARLENE
about
Black hairdresser turns six-chair salon into a multimillion
$ business. il pors *Jet* 76:28-30+ Je 12 '89
MILES, IAN CHICHESTER- *See* Chichester-Miles, Ian
MILES, JACK
The novelist and the liar. *New Perspectives Quarterly* 6:53-4
Spr '89
MILES, MICHAEL A.
about
A cup of Jell-O, Velveeta to taste . . . L. Therrien. il
Business Week p74+ My 8 '89
How Philip Morris diversified right. S. P. Sherman. il por
Fortune 120:120-2+ O 23 '89
Michael Miles. L. Therrien. il por *Business Week* Special
Issue:126 Ap 14 '89
MILES, SARA, AND OSTERTAG, BOB
'Absolute, diabolical terror'. il *Mother Jones* 14:22-7+ Ap
'89
MILEY, MARION, D. 1941
about
A golf great cut down in her prime. B. K. Bell. il por
Women's Sports & Fitness 11:60 O '89
MILHAVEN, JOHN GILES
Sleeping like spoons. il *Commonweal* 116:205-7 Ap 7 '89
MILHOLLIN, GARY
India's missiles—with a little help from our friends. bibl
f il *The Bulletin of the Atomic Scientists* 45:31-5 N '89
MILICH, JOHN E.
Contaminant Cove: where polluters defile Mohawk land.
il *The Progressive* 53:23-5 Ja '89
Environmental sleuth battles bureaucrats. il por *The
Progressive* 53:15-16 N '89
MILICI, MARILYN L.
Of false tongues and Sunday bread. il *Américas* 41 no1:58-9
'89
MILITARY ACCIDENTS *See* United States—Armed Forces—
Accidents and injuries; United States. Marine Corps—Accidents and injuries; United States. Navy—Accidents and
injuries
MILITARY ADMINISTRATION
See also
United States—Armed Forces—Management
MILITARY AIR TRAFFIC CONTROL *See* Air traffic control,
Military
MILITARY AIRLIFT COMMAND (U.S.) *See* United States.
Air Force. Military Airlift Command
MILITARY AIRPLANES *See* Airplanes, Military
MILITARY AND TELEVISION *See* Television and the military
MILITARY AND THE ENVIRONMENT
See also
Guided missiles—Deactivation—Environmental aspects
Death of a small country [U.S. military presence and the
environment in Costa Rica] M. I. Niman. il *The Progressive*
53:24-5 Ag '89
Environment and security. N. Myers. *Foreign Policy* 74:23-41
Spr '89
Land of death . . . and life [wildlife thrive on contaminated
grounds of the Rocky Mountain Arsenal] G. Gerhardt.
il map *National Wildlife* 28:34-40 D '89/Ja '90
The toxic morass in Denver's backyard [Rocky Mountain
Arsenal] S. D. Atchison. il *Business Week* p46 Ja 9 '89
Toxic responsibility [military and toxic waste disposal] S.
Pollack and S. Shulman. il *The Atlantic* 263:26+ Mr '89
Uncle Sam's toxic folly. M. Satchell. il *U.S. News & World
Report* 106:20-2 Mr 27 '89
MILITARY ART AND SCIENCE
See also
Camouflage
Computers—Military use
Electronics—Military use
Superconductors and superconductivity—Military use
Television and the military
United States. Air Force Weapons Laboratory
War

War games
MILITARY ASSISTANCE, AMERICAN
Budget, trade deficits could spur restrictive trade legislation
[U.S. military exports and aid] il *Aviation Week & Space
Technology* 130:73+ Mr 20 '89
Building a better coup [CIA wants clarification on political
assassinations] C. S. Manegold. il *Newsweek* 114:55 O
30 '89
Christic Institute woes [ordered to pay legal fees to defendants
in conspiracy suit] *The Christian Century* 106:224 Mr
1 '89
The cop and the benefactor [U.S. and Japan] R. Watson.
il *Newsweek* 113:36+ F 6 '89
Damned if you coup . . . [history of covert action] E.
Salholz. il *Newsweek* 114:34 O 16 '89
FY 1990 security assistance request [statement, March 8,
1989] H. A. Holmes. *Department of State Bulletin* 89:52-4
Je '89
Media campaigns in the courts [Christic Institute ordered
to pay defendants' costs in conspiracy suit] *National Review*
41:13-14 Mr 10 '89
Mr. Webster has it exactly wrong [CIA policy on assassinations] W. F. Buckley. *National Review* 41:62-3 N 24
'89
Over there [America's drug war abroad] M. J. McConahay
and R. Kirk. il *Mother Jones* 14:36-9+ F/Mr '89
The pitfalls of covert operations. D. Isenberg. il *USA Today
(Periodical)* 118:12-14 N '89
Reopening a deadly debate: the CIA wants to have a freer
hand during coups. J. Peterzell. il *Time* 134:54 O 30
'89
Shouldering arms [M. Markus' idea to securitize U.S. armament loans] M. Schifrin. il por *Forbes* 143:208-9 Ap 17
'89
Wright turn [J. Wright postpones House action on covert
operations legislation] *The Nation* 248:255-6 F 27 '89
Afghanistan
Misplaced optimism [mujahedin gaining little ground] J. Elson.
il *Time* 133:40-1 My 15 '89
A U.S. victory begins to unravel [failure of mujahedin to
oust Communist regime] L. Lief. il *U.S. News & World
Report* 107:38 Jl 24 '89
Why are we in Afghanistan? R. Wright. *The New Republic*
201:23-5 S 4 '89
Angola
The end of the affair [J. Savimbi and U.S. support for
UNITA] B. Turque. il por *Newsweek* 114:54 O 16 '89
Minority report [J. Savimbi] C. Hitchens. *The Nation* 248:690
My 22 '89
Cambodia
As China agonizes, the U.S. wavers and Cambodia waits.
L. Lief. il *U.S. News & World Report* 107:34 Jl 3 '89
Holiday in Cambodia. J. R. Thomson. il *National Review*
41:26-7 O 13 '89
Stop Pol Pot. il *The New Republic* 200:7-9 Ap 3 '89
U.S. policy in Asia [address, June 22, 1989] D. Quayle.
Vital Speeches of the Day 55:610-13 Ag 1 '89
Central America
Central America: Bush may be reduced to a supporting
player. B. Javetski and A. Arana. il *Business Week* p60
Ap 3 '89
The deal in Central America. E. Abrams. *Commentary*
87:29-32 My '89
El Salvador [discussion of May 1989 article, The deal in
Central America] E. Abrams. *Commentary* 88:8-9 S '89
Notes and comment. *The New Yorker* 65:41-3 D 4 '89
China
The warlords [weapons supplied by U.S. used against students]
The Nation 248:871-2 Je 26 '89
Colombia
Bennett: 'It's their fight right now' [interview with W. J.
Bennett] M. Miller. il *Newsweek* 114:32 S 11 '89
Can the drug lords be dethroned? P. Dwyer. il *Business
Week* p28-30 S 11 '89
The cocaine war: Washington and Bogotá battle the drug
lords. M. Nemeth. il *Maclean's* 102:18-19 S 4 '89
Emergency package for Colombia's drug flight [statement,
August 25, 1989] G. Bush. *Department of State Bulletin*
89:47 O '89
Going too far [U.S. and Colombia step up war on drug
lords] G. J. Church. il *Time* 134:12-15 S 4 '89
Hitting the drug lords. T. Morganthau. il map *Newsweek*
114:18-23 S 4 '89
Now, for the real drug war. B. Duffy. il map *U.S. News
& World Report* 107:18-20 S 11 '89
Costa Rica
Death of a small country [U.S. military presence and the
environment] M. I. Niman. il *The Progressive* 53:24-5
Ag '89
Developing countries
Dealing arms. J. Cobb and J. M. Zindar. il *Common Cause
Magazine* 15:23-7 Mr/Ap '89
Playing to the home crowd [Reagan Doctrine] R. H. Johnson.
il *The Bulletin of the Atomic Scientists* 45:24-8 Ja/F '89
Stopping the war against the third world [low intensity conflict;
adaptation of address, September 1988] M. T. Klare. il
The Progressive 53:14-16 Ja '89

MILITARY ASSISTANCE, AMERICAN—*cont.*

El Salvador

Adolf's heirs [electoral victory by Arena] A. Cockburn. *The Nation* 248:655 My 15 '89

Back burner, front burner. il *The Progressive* 53:8-9 My '89

Bush's Central American albatross [A. Cristiani rejects rebel cease-fire offer] L. Lief. *U.S. News & World Report* 107:33 D 4 '89

Demonizing D'Aubuisson [role in assassination of Archbishop O. Romero] J. Morley. il *The Nation* 248:624-6 My 8 '89

Eichmann with a smile [G. Bush's comments] *The Nation* 249:701 D 11 '89

El Salvador's Army: a force unto itself. J. Millman. il *The New York Times Magazine* p46-7+ D 10 '89

El Salvador's forgotten war. J. LeMoyne. *Foreign Affairs* 68:105-25 Summ '89

Hanging in the balance: El Salvador's future & the limits of U.S. power. L. S. Robinson. il *Commonweal* 116:242-5 Ap 21 '89

In freedom's name. A. Cockburn. *The Nation* 249:706-7 D 11 '89

In Salvador time waits for no one [cover story] R. Zamora. *The Nation* 248:253+ F 27 '89

In the name of God, stop the killing. R. A. Hyde. *The Christian Century* 106:1144 D 6 '89

Losing gamble [U.S. military aid continues despite human rights abuses] *The Nation* 249:704 D 11 '89

Negotiations or total war [possible FMLN compromise settlement] F. Smyth. il *The Nation* 249:164-6 Ag 7-14 '89

'Now you be quiet, Oscar' [death squad killings] *America* 161:415 D 9 '89

The return of the right. C. Lane. il por *Newsweek* 113:38+ Mr 20 '89

Save El Salvador. *Commonweal* 116:660-1 D 1 '89

Secretary's news conference [November 14, 1988] G. P. Shultz. *Department of State Bulletin* 89:13 Ja '89

The Sheraton siege. D. Brand. il *Time* 134:50-1 D 4 '89

Tet in Salvador. *The Nation* 249:667-8 D 4 '89

The war continues. P. Lacefield. il *Commonweal* 116:197-9 Ap 7 '89

The war that will not end [cover story] C. Lane. *The New Republic* 201:23-7 O 16 '89

'What has our money got for 10 years?'. H. Anderson. il *Newsweek* 114:55 N 27 '89

Will Bush keep his word with the death squads? P. Kornbluh. *Mother Jones* 14:26-7 Ap '89

France

A bad rap for the force de frappe? [views of Richard H. Ullman] C. Dickey. il *Newsweek* 113:35 Je 12 '89

The covert French connection [nuclear] R. H. Ullman. *Foreign Policy* 75:3-33 Summ '89

Guatemala

Friendly death squads. *The Progressive* 53:9 N '89

Israel

The sinews of Israel: why Israeli strength is vital to the U.S. Y. Atlas. il map *Conservative Digest* 15:58-60 S/O '89

Nicaragua

See also

Iran-contra affair

Are the contras finished? E. Abrams. *National Review* 41:30-1 Mr 10 '89

Blown opportunities in Central America [failure of George Bush to enact policies] C. A. Robbins. il *U.S. News & World Report* 106:28 F 27 '89

Catching the administration napping [Nicaragua's pledge of reforms prompts Central American neighbors to remove U.S.-backed contras] *Newsweek* 113:43 F 27 '89

Central America. *World Press Review* 36:9-10 Ap '89

Confronting the Sandinistas. R. J. Bresler. il *USA Today (Periodical)* 118:5 N '89

Contradictions: a decade in documents. P. Kornbluh. il *Mother Jones* 14:26-7 Jl/Ag '89

Cutting the cord in Honduras [contras] W. McGurn. il *National Review* 41:22-3 S 29 '89

Disarming the rebels [accord signed by Central American presidents] M. Nemeth. il *Maclean's* 102:33+ Ag 21 '89

The "disposal problem" [Tela plan to disband contras] J. Smolowe. il *Time* 134:32 Ag 21 '89

The Dodd Doctrine [bipartisan accord on aid to contras] W. McGurn. il *National Review* 41:27-8 S 15 '89

Enlarging the cloth [Tela agreement disbanding and resettling the contras] *Commonweal* 116:451-2 S 8 '89

Honduras left to push contra pram. J. Eldridge. il *The Nation* 248:734-6+ My 29 '89

Lethal aid. J. Wypijewski. *The Nation* 248:580 My 1 '89

Look out, gringo [Bush administration policies] M. Kondracke. *The New Republic* 201:12-13 S 4 '89

Look—we've come through. G. Black. il *The Nation* 249:166-8+ Ag 7-14 '89

Minority report. C. Hitchens. *The Nation* 249:671 D 4 '89

Mr. Yankee goes home. A. Cruz, Jr. *Commentary* 88:47-8 Ag '89

Nicaragua [cease fire suspension] il *World Press Review* 36:6 D '89

Now the Sandinistas can't blame it on the contras. B. Javetski and S. Baker. il *Business Week* p47 Ag 21 '89

The old gringos [D. Ortega's announcement ending the cease-fire] A. Kopkind. *The Nation* 249:625 N 27 '89

Ortega's ploy [ends cease fire] *The New Republic* 201:9 N 20 '89

Planning for peace [summit of Central American presidents] A. Bilski. il *Maclean's* 102:29 F 27 '89

A Reagan Doctrine? *National Review* 41:12-13 Ja 27 '89

A slim hope for freedom in Nicaragua [agreement to disband contras] C. W. Weinberger. il *Forbes* 144:31 S 18 '89

Termination time [move to disband contras] *The Nation* 249:227-8 S 4-11 '89

U.S. refuses to abide by International Court of Justice. *Utne Reader* p63 S/O '89

Undoing the 'Reagan Doctrine' [Bush administration] D. Schorr. *The New Leader* 72:3-4 Ap 3-17 '89

'We will not fight another war' [peace activist J. Barnette] R. Chepesiuk. il por *The Progressive* 53:17 N '89

Will the contras' next home be Miami? il *Newsweek* 114:29 Ag 21 '89

Pakistan

Debating the Pakistan dilemma. N. Cooper. il *Newsweek* 113:34 F 13 '89

The new phase in U.S.-Pakistani relations. T. P. Thornton. *Foreign Affairs* 68:142-59 Summ '89

Panama

Panama contras? T. Avirgan. *The Nation* 249:263-5 S 18 '89

Philippines

Civilians caught in Philippine 'total war'. D. Cunningham. *The Christian Century* 106:1036-7 N 15 '89

MILITARY ASSISTANCE, CUBAN

Angola

The Angola/Namibia accords. C. W. Freeman. *Foreign Affairs* 68:126-41 Summ '89

Angola/Namibia accords [special section] il maps *Department of State Bulletin* 89:10-23 F '89

How macho are the Cubans? H. Hamann. il *Conservative Digest* 15:54-7 S/O '89

Namibia: the making of a new nation [tripartite agreement among Angola, Cuba, and South Africa; cover story; special section] il map *UN Chronicle* 26:34-48 Mr '89

Namibian independence and troop withdrawal from Angola [statement, March 31, 1989] J. A. Baker, III. *Department of State Bulletin* 89:29 My '89

Peace at last in Namibia? G. Lister and M. Verbaan. il *The Nation* 248:18+ Ja 2 '89

Peace in Angola? P. M. Martin. bibl f *Current History* 88:229-32+ My '89

Latin America

Off the record [Cuban-Palestinian arms smuggling network] *National Review* 41:18 F 24 '89

MILITARY ASSISTANCE, NICARAGUAN

El Salvador

The evidence in the bean field: Nicaragua's fingerprints in El Salvador's war. C. S. Manegold. il *Newsweek* 114:67-8 D 4 '89

A Soviet missile mystery [plane crash in El Salvador reveals arms flow through Nicaragua] D. Waller. il *Newsweek* 114:35 D 11 '89

MILITARY ASSISTANCE, RUSSIAN

Central America

Soviet policy in Central America [White House statement, April 5, 1989] *Department of State Bulletin* 89:67 Je '89

Developing countries

"New thinking" and Soviet third world policy. C. R. Saivetz. bibl f *Current History* 88:325-8+ O '89

El Salvador

A Soviet missile mystery [plane crash in El Salvador reveals arms flow through Nicaragua] D. Waller. il *Newsweek* 114:35 D 11 '89

Nicaragua

The Soviet Union and Nicaragua [reprint from October 1984 issue] R. S. Leiken. *Current History* 88:39-40+ Ja '89

Who's a 'drugstore cowboy'? [M. Fitzwater's comments concerning M. Gorbachev's announcement that Russian arms shipments to Nicaragua have stopped] il *Newsweek* 113:48 My 29 '89

MILITARY ASTRONAUTICS *See* Space flight—Military use

MILITARY AVIATION *See* Aviation, Military

MILITARY BASES

See also

Air bases

Guided missile bases

Navy yards and naval stations

Are Philippine bases essential to U.S. military strategy? L. D. Howell. il *USA Today (Periodical)* 117:42-5 My '89

Clamor over Philippine bases. D. Goertzen. il *The Progressive* 53:15-16 S '89

The Presidio: another great park for San Francisco? [cover story] il maps *Sunset (Central West edition)* 183:78-85 N '89

A sense of foreboding in the Philippines [assassination of U.S. Army colonel N. Rowe] B. Duffy. il *U.S. News & World Report* 106:35-6 My 15 '89

MILITARY BASES—*cont.*

Singapore offers U.S. military greater access to its facilities. map *Aviation Week & Space Technology* 131:69 Ag 21 '89

U.S.-Philippines military bases agreement review, 1988 [texts of agreement, remarks, and letter, October 17, 1988] *Department of State Bulletin* 88:24-7 D '88

Why Filipinos oppose U.S. military bases. R. M. Brown. *The Christian Century* 106:100-1 F 1-8 '89

Shutdowns

After fat years come the lean. map *U.S. News & World Report* 106:10-11 Ja 9 '89

Closing a base opens doors [Mineral Wells, Tex.] D. C. Bacon. il map *Nation's Business* 77:9+ My '89

Five Air Force bases are among 86 slated for closure. *Aviation Week & Space Technology* 130:40 Ja 2 '89

Golden Gate to get Presidio Army base. il *National Parks* 63:14 Jl/Ag '89

House endorses military base closing plan. *Aviation Week & Space Technology* 130:34 Ap 24 '89

Taps for old bases. J. V. Lamar, Jr. il *Time* 133:28 Ja 9 '89

This congressman beat the system [R. Armey pushes through amendment to close obsolete bases] R. Fitzgerald. il por *Reader's Digest* 134:125-8 Ap '89

MILITARY BASES, CANADIAN

Shutdowns

A call to arms. T. Tedesco. il *Maclean's* 102:16 My 22 '89

Military manoeuvres. M. Clark. il *Maclean's* 102:19 My 8 '89

MILITARY BUDGET *See* United States. Dept. of Defense—Appropriations and expenditures

MILITARY BUDGETS, INTERNATIONAL *See* Armed Forces—Appropriations and expenditures

MILITARY CADETS, WOMEN *See* Women cadets

MILITARY CHAPLAINS *See* Chaplains, Military

MILITARY COMMUNICATIONS *See* Communications, Military

MILITARY COMMUNICATIONS SATELLITES *See* Communications satellites—Military use

MILITARY DRAFT *See* Draft

MILITARY EDUCATION

See also

Military training

Military training camps

United States Military Academy

France

See also

École de Cavalerie

Soviet Union

Building a military machine. J. Trimble. il *U.S. News & World Report* 106:31-2+ Mr 13 '89

MILITARY ELECTRONICS *See* Electronics—Military use; Superconductors and superconductivity—Military use

MILITARY EXPENDITURES *See* United States. Dept. of Defense—Appropriations and expenditures

MILITARY EXPENDITURES, INTERNATIONAL *See* Armed Forces—Appropriations and expenditures

MILITARY EXPORTS *See* Munitions—Export-import trade

MILITARY HISTORY

See also

United States—Military history

Historiography

Theory from practice—Major General J.F.C. Fuller. B. H. Reid. bibl il pors *History Today* 39:44-9 Je '89

MILITARY-INDUSTRIAL COMPLEX

See also

Pentagon procurement scandal

Administration officials say defense cuts will not endanger industrial base. P. A. Gilmartin. *Aviation Week & Space Technology* 130:139+ Je 19 '89

Cold war economics [militarization of economy under Reagan administration] A. R. Markusen. bibl f il *The Bulletin of the Atomic Scientists* 45:41-4 Ja/F '89

Converts to conversion. D. Johnstone. il *The Progressive* 53:14-15 O '89

Defense contractors must change to survive competition in 1990s. W. V. Dee. por *Aviation Week & Space Technology* 131:99+ Jl 17 '89

Dollars and defense. J. McCartney. il map *Scholastic Update (Teachers' edition)* 122:9-10 O 6 '89

De facto industrial policymaking. H. Banks. *Forbes* 143:33 F 20 '89

Heard on the Street [Wall Street defense watchers] L. Feinstein. il *Common Cause Magazine* 15:12-15 Jl/Ag '89

Keep Pentagon out of civilian economy. V. Kistiakowsky. *The Bulletin of the Atomic Scientists* 45:5 Ap '89

Keeping semiconductors safe for democracy. D. Charles. il *The Bulletin of the Atomic Scientists* 45:8-10 N '89

New name; same bad idea. W. T. Brookes. por *Nation's Business* 77:84 S '89

The peace outbreak sparks a war on defense spending. S. Dentzer. il *U.S. News & World Report* 107:51-2 D 4 '89

Preparing for a different world [views of F. Rohatyn] P. Mann. il *Aviation Week & Space Technology* 130:17 Mr 20 '89

Rethinking the military's role in the economy: an interview with Harvey Brooks and Lewis Branscomb. S. Hackman and R. Howard. il pors *Technology Review* 92:54-60+ Ag/S '89

Star Wars won't die. T. Engelhardt. il *The Progressive* 53:22-3 S '89

Top brass [congressional defense complex] J. Cobb. il *Common Cause Magazine* 15:23-7 My/Je '89

Total quality management [address, November 29, 1988] B. P. Randolph. *Vital Speeches of the Day* 55:322-4 Mr 15 '89

U.S. defense industry faces difficult times. B. L. Schwartz. por *Aviation Week & Space Technology* 131:71+ D 4 '89

The watershed decade [address, June 20, 1989] J. D. Cosgrove. *Vital Speeches of the Day* 55:744-7 O 1 '89

MILITARY INTELLIGENCE

Crowe calls for review of military intelligence. *Aviation Week & Space Technology* 131:31 N 20 '89

MILITARY JOURNALISM *See* Journalism, Military

MILITARY LIFESTYLE (PERIODICAL)

Targeting the military market. L. Williams. il pors *Nation's Business* 77:66+ My '89

MILITARY LITERATURE

Paperback fighter [T. Clancy's unrealistic depiction of the military in his novels] S. Shuger. il *The Washington Monthly* 21:10-14+ N '89

MILITARY MANEUVERS

Air, naval and ground forces participate in Team Spirit '89 [U.S./Korean exercises; special section] il *Aviation Week & Space Technology* 130:68-9+ Ap 24 '89

Dame at sea [four day Navy tour] J. M. Stapleton. *The New Republic* 200:42 My 22 '89

Pentagon streamlines Reforger exercise [Return of Forces to Germany] *Aviation Week & Space Technology* 130:31 F 13 '89

Protests threaten to cripple USAF training operations [Koon-Ni gunnery range in South Korea] J. D. Morrocco. il *Aviation Week & Space Technology* 130:239+ Je 12 '89

War and peace in the White Mountains [Army's Firestorm '88 guerrilla exercises in N.H.] A. Alpert. il *The Progressive* 53:13-14 Mr '89

MILITARY MEN *See* Servicemen

MILITARY MINIATURES

Floor wars [toy warriors] C. Schine. il *The New York Times Magazine* p28-31+ Ag 13 '89

MILITARY MOTOR VEHICLES *See* Motor vehicles, Military

MILITARY MUSEUMS

The atomic museum. P. N. Kirstein. bibl f il *Art in America* 77:44-5+ Je '89

Where Patton prepared for North Africa in southern California [site of Camp Young, headquarters for Desert Training Center] il *Sunset (Central West edition)* 182:63 F '89

MILITARY PENSIONS *See* Pensions, Military

MILITARY PILOTS *See* Air pilots

MILITARY POLICY

See also

China—Military policy

India—Military policy

Japan—Military policy

Soviet Union—Military policy

United States—Military policy

MILITARY RADAR *See* Radar—Military use

MILITARY RECONNAISSANCE

See also

Aerial reconnaissance

MILITARY RESEARCH

See also

Fiber Optic Technology Center (U.S.)

National Technical Systems (Firm)

Rome Air Development Center

U.S. Army Laboratory Command

United States. Defense Advanced Research Projects Agency

Eat hot lead, R2D2. J. Adam. il *The New Republic* 201:14+ Jl 17-24 '89

De facto industrial policymaking. H. Banks. *Forbes* 143:33 F 20 '89

Keep Pentagon out of civilian economy. V. Kistiakowsky. *The Bulletin of the Atomic Scientists* 45:5 Ap '89

Keeping semiconductors safe for democracy. D. Charles. il *The Bulletin of the Atomic Scientists* 45:8-10 N '89

More for the military [Reagan administration] J. Reppy. bibl f il *The Bulletin of the Atomic Scientists* 45:46-8 Ja/F '89

Rethinking the military's role in the economy: an interview with Harvey Brooks and Lewis Branscomb. S. Hackman and R. Howard. il pors *Technology Review* 92:54-60+ Ag/S '89

U.S. defense budget cuts could imperil nation's research and development effort. B. W. Henderson. il *Aviation Week & Space Technology* 131:35+ D 18-25 '89

U.S. leaders cite need for national technology plan. S. W. Kandebo. il *Aviation Week & Space Technology* 131:27-8 O 2 '89

International aspects

U.S. pressed by allies on critical technology research, Pentagon says. M. Mecham. *Aviation Week & Space Technology* 130:52-3+ Ap 3 '89

MILITARY RESEARCH—*cont.*

Japan

Japan's new military edge [cover story] J. W. Dower. il *The Nation* 249:1+ Jl 3 '89

Let's make a deal: the U.S.-Japan co-technology sphere. S. K. Vogel. *The New Republic* 200:14+ Je 19 '89

Soviet Union

Red tech rising [cover story] T. H. Cole. il *Popular Mechanics* 166:28, 84-92+ Ap '89

MILITARY RESERVATIONS

Hunting on the D.O.D. [hunting on military land] G. J. Sajo. il *Field & Stream* 94:30+ D '89

MILITARY SATELLITES *See* Artificial satellites—Military use

MILITARY SECRETS, CLASSIFIED *See* Classified information

MILITARY SERVICE, COMPULSORY *See* Draft

MILITARY SURPLUSES *See* Surplus military property

MILITARY TELESCOPES *See* Telescopes, Military

MILITARY TRAINING

See also
Military maneuvers
Naval Strike Warfare Center (U.S.)

Marine training prepares crews for combined operations. il *Aviation Week & Space Technology* 130:48-9 F 27 '89

Training for 'high-intensity peace' [Marines] P. Cary. il *U.S. News & World Report* 107:29 D 11 '89

MILITARY TRAINING CAMPS

A dose of discipline for first offenders [use of paramilitary treatment for juvenile offenders] J. J. Kane. il *Time* 134:17-18 O 16 '89

Experiments in boot camp [military-style camps for young offenders] B. Turque. il *Newsweek* 112:42+ My 22 '89

Welcome to the U.S. Army [basic training at Fort Knox] D. Johnson. il *Scholastic Update (Teachers' edition)* 122:18-19 O 6 '89

Where Patton prepared for North Africa in southern California [site of Camp Young, headquarters for Desert Training Center] il *Sunset (Central West edition)* 182:63 F '89

MILITARY TRANSPORTATION *See* Transportation, Military

MILK

See also
Goat's milk
Skim milk
Soybean milk

Milk for people who can't drink milk [Lactaid] il *Consumer Reports* 54:133 Mr '89

Composition

See also
Lactose

Contamination

See Milk contamination

Fat content

Bovine leukemia's hidden toll [research by Harris A. Lewin] *Science News* 135:123 F 25 '89

Microbiology

See also
Milk, Acidophilus
Milk as carrier of infection

Prices

Dairymen say 'Happy New Year,' to prices in 1989. J. R. Borcherding. *Successful Farming* 87:62 F '89

Milk prices up, trucks roll south to fill shortage. *Successful Farming* 87:35 N '89

Production

A furious battle over milk [furor over use of bovine somatotropin to increase milk production] D. Wyss. il *Time* 133:77 My 29 '89

Just say moo [backlash against use of bovine growth hormone] W. P. Norton. il *The Progressive* 53:26-9 N '89

Market sours on milk hormone [bovine somatotropin] M. Sun. il *Science* 246:876-7 N 17 '89

Milking Bossy for all she's worth [bovine somatotropin] il *FDA Consumer* 23:23 Ap '89

Rations for all cow seasons. J. R. Borcherding. il *Successful Farming* 87:46-7 S '89

MILK, ACIDOPHILUS

See also
Yogurt

The 'life force' food factor [probiotics] G. McVeigh. *Prevention (Emmaus, Pa.)* 41:47-51 Ag '89

MILK, FERMENTED

See also
Kefir

MILK, HUMAN

See also
Milk as carrier of infection

Breast-milk don'ts [effects of microwaving and mixing on immune protection; research by John A. Kerner] L. Schroepfer. *American Health* 8:106-7 My '89

MILK (HARVEY) SCHOOL (NEW YORK, N.Y.) *See* Harvey Milk School (New York, N.Y.)

MILK AND HONEY [film] See Motion picture reviews—Single works

MILK AS CARRIER OF INFECTION

Keeping breast milk safe [AIDS testing at milk banks] H. Wolinsky. il *American Health* 8:20+ Ja/F '89

MILK CONTAINERS

FDA finds dioxin in milk. *Science News* 136:165 S 9 '89

MILK CONTAMINATION

FDA finds dioxin in milk. *Science News* 136:165 S 9 '89

Keeping drug residues out of milk [sulfamethazine] F. E. Young. il *FDA Consumer* 23:7 Mr '89

Sulfamethazine residues in food. B. T. Hunter. il *Consumers' Research Magazine* 72:36-8 F '89

MILK INDUSTRY

Ethical aspects

Where Elsie needs a lawyer [allegations concerning Borden, Inc.] N. Alster. *Forbes* 144:108 D 25 '89

MILK PRODUCTION *See* Milk—Production

MILK PRODUCTS *See* Dairy products

MILK VETCH

Immuni-tea [effects of astragalus on T cell activity; research by Giora Mavligit and Da-Tong Chu] J. Barone. il *American Health* 8:100 O '89

MILKEN, MICHAEL R.

about

And the next test will be Giuliani vs. Milken. C. Welles. por *Business Week* p37 Ja 9 '89

Checkmate for the King of Junk Bonds. por *U.S. News & World Report* 106:44-5 F 6 '89

Disowning a billion-dollar baby. B. Rudolph. il por *Time* 133:86 Ja 2 '89

Drexel's deal with the feds: how much will it hurt? C. Welles. il por *Business Week* p36 F 6 '89

The friends of Michael Milken. M. Hosenball. il por *The New Republic* 201:23-5 Ag 28 '89

G. Robert Blakey versus Michael Milken. J. Queenan. il por *Forbes* 143:57+ My 1 '89

Got big deals, big problems, big bucks? Get Arthur Liman. M. Galen. il por *Business Week* p112+ My 15 '89

Hard times. *The Nation* 248:544 Ap 24 '89

History is bunk, the future is junk [interview] S. K. Sheinbaum and others. il *New Perspectives Quarterly* 6:12-20 Fall '89

Hitting Milken where it hurts. C. Friday and D. Pauly. il por *Newsweek* 113:49 Ap 10 '89

Junk after Milken. G. Hector. il por *Fortune* 120:121+ N 6 '89

The Junk King starts anew. por *Newsweek* 113:55 Je 26 '89

Meeting with Milken. W. F. Buckley. *National Review* 41:71 N 10 '89

Michael Milken. por *People Weekly* 32:72-3 D 25 '89-Ja 1 '90

Michael Milken. B. Darrach. por *People Weekly* 32 Special Issue:48-9 Fall '89

Milken's shadow hovers over Fred Carr. K. Kerwin. il por *Business Week* p24 Ap 17 '89

Nailing the junk kings. L. Reibstein. il por *Newsweek* 113:44-5+ Ja 2 '89

No bad debt—only bad managers [interview] por *U.S. News & World Report* 106:61 F 13 '89

The phantom of Wall Street: how Ivan Boesky's bitter legacy haunts Mike Milken and his former firm. C. Byron. il pors *New York* 22:52-6 D 4 '89

Predators' fall. *National Review* 41:10-11 My 5 '89

Taking it all back, plus interest. C. Gorman. il por *Time* 133:42 Ap 10 '89

The U.S. vs. Milken: now the last act begins. C. Welles. il por *Business Week* p29 Ap 10 '89

Vanity press. D. Ellen. *The New Republic* 201:25 Ag 28 '89

A verdict that Mike Milken hopes is no warm-up. M. Galen. por *Business Week* p46 Ag 14 '89

What Milken means; Will Mike fight? A. Farnham. il por *Fortune* 119:16-17 Ap 24 '89

Why blacks like Mike Milken. J. Lieblich. il por *Fortune* 119:10 My 22 '89

Why Mike Milken was so eager to help Peter Ueberroth. A. Bernstein. *Business Week* p30 My 1 '89

Will Michael Milken go to jail? P. Sherrid. il por *U.S. News & World Report* 106:49-50 Ap 10 '89

Will Mike Milken sue? L. Howard. il por *Newsweek* 113:7 F 6 '89

Without Milken, can Drexel still be Drexel? E. Schine. il pors *Business Week* p34 Mr 27 '89

Anecdotes, facetiae, satire, etc.

Ode to Michael Milken. R. W. Grant. *Harper's* 279:25-6 Jl '89

MILKING PARLORS

Spick-and-span for 629 cows. J. R. Borcherding. il *Successful Farming* 87 no4:37 Mr '89

MILKOWSKI, BILL

Gary Burton: vibes alive! [interview] il pors *Down Beat* 56:20-3 Ap '89

Steve Miller: the Joker gets jazzy. il pors *Down Beat* 56:24-6 F '89

Terri Lyne Carrington: real-life heartbeats. il pors *Down Beat* 56:20-2 Je '89

MILKWEED

Gene Johnston. G. Johnston. il *Successful Farming* 87:17 Je '89

MILKY WAY

Carrying fuel into the galactic center [Paul T. P. Ho identifies stream of gas] I. Peterson. *Science News* 135:21 Ja 14 '89

Far-out star. il *Sky and Telescope* 78:573 D '89

Feeding the hole [stream of gas near Milky Way; research by Paul Ho] il *Discover* 10:14 Je '89

Feeding the monster in the middle [black hole; research by Paul Ho] M. M. Waldrop. il *Science* 243:478 Ja 27 '89

Gamma-ray confusion at the galactic center. il *Sky and Telescope* 77:584-5 Je '89

Great globs of fire [age of globular clusters challenges fast collapse theory of Milky Way's birth; research by Michael Bolte and Peter Stetson] T. Waters. il *Discover* 10:26 S '89

The hidden lives of massive stars [role of molecular clouds; research by Edward B. Churchwell and Douglas O. S. Wood] *Science News* 135:88 F 11 '89

High-energy summer for astrophysics [gamma ray source at center flickers out] M. M. Waldrop. *Science* 245:129 Jl 14 '89

Looking down on the Milky Way [map of molecular clouds by Philip M. Solomon and A. R. Rivolo] il *Sky and Telescope* 78:127 Ag '89

The Milky Way's jet. il *Sky and Telescope* 78:127-8 Ag '89

The Milky Way's third population [thick-disc stars; research by Bruce W. Carney] *Science News* 135:155 Mr 11 '89

Milky Way's youngest supernova? [G25.5 + 0.2 discovered by John J. Cowan] il *Sky and Telescope* 78:348-9 O '89

Missing by more than a mile [gamma ray source; research by Thomas A. Prince] I. Peterson. *Science News* 135:44 Ja 21 '89

Out of the center: gamma-ray redux [research by Marvin Leventhal and Jeffrey E. McClintock] I. Peterson. *Science News* 135:303 My 13 '89

Standout winter star clusters. A. Ling. il *Astronomy* 17:98-103 Ja '89

A star-hop from Capella. A. MacRobert. il *Sky and Telescope* 77:140-2 F '89

Starburst Milky Way [research by Don C. Barry] il *Sky and Telescope* 77:589-90 Je '89

Swirls and threads at the Milky Way's core. il *Science News* 136:279 O 28 '89

Treasures of the winter Milky Way. D. J. Eicher. il *Astronomy* 17:76-83 N '89

Unveiling the hidden Milky Way [molecular cloud mapping] E. S. Palmer. il *Astronomy* 17:32-40 N '89

A young Milky Way? [theory of Harvey Butcher] *Sky and Telescope* 78:349-50 O '89

MILL (QUECHEE, VT.)

Pleasures of the table: Simon Pearce. Z. E. Zakroff. il por *Gourmet* 49:56-61+ Ag '89

MILL WORK (WOODWORK) *See* Millwork (Woodwork)

MILLAN, MONICA A., AND OTHERS

Novel sites of expression of functional angiotensin II receptors in the late gestation fetus. bibl f il *Science* 244:1340-2 Je 16 '89

MILLAR, M. STUART

about

Piper may still be carrying excess baggage. G. DeGeorge. il por *Business Week* p76 Je 12 '89

MILLAR, SARAH E., AND OTHERS

Vaccination with a synthetic zona pellucida peptide produces long-term contraception in female mice. bibl f il *Science* 246:935-8 N 17 '89

MILLBROOK (N.Y.)

Historic houses, sites, etc.

Killearn Farm: F. William Free's Hudson Valley horse farm. J. Gruen. il por *Architectural Digest* 46:182-7+ Je '89

MILLE LACS INDIAN RESERVATION (MINN.)

State of the Band, January 14, 1989 [address] A. Gashbow. *Vital Speeches of the Day* 55:409-13 Ap 15 '89

MILLE LACS LAKE (MINN.)

Home is where the fish are [ice fishing for walleyes] T. Dickson. il *National Wildlife* 27:24-8 F/Mr '89

MILLE MIGLIA (RACE) *See* Automobile racing—Italy

MILLEMANN, BETH

Wretched refuse off our shores. il *Sierra* 74:26-8 Ja/F '89

MILLENARIANISM *See* Millennialism

MILLENNIALISM

Italy

Savonarola—preacher and patriot? D. Weinstein. bibl il por *History Today* 39:30-6 N '89

MILLENNIUM

See also

Millennialism

One thousand (Year)

100 years of attitude [end-of-century effect in creative endeavors; excerpt from American renaissance] M. J. Cetron and O. Davies. il *Omni (New York, N.Y.)* 12:18+ O '89

Apocalypse now? B. Lawren. il *Psychology Today* 23:38-9+ My '89

MILLENNIUM [film] *See* Motion picture reviews—Single works

MILLER, AARON DAVID

Palestinians and the intifada: one year later. bibl f *Current History* 88:73-6+ F '89

MILLER, AK

about

Ak Miller and his "Caballo de hierro". D. Prieto. il pors *Motor Trend* 41:108-9 Ja '89

MILLER, ALAN S.

Report on reports: three reports on Japan and the global environment. bibl f *Environment* 31:25-9 Jl/Ag '89

MILLER, ALLAN

about

High fidelity [film] Reviews
The New Republic 201:34+ S 18-25 '89. S. Kauffmann
New York 22:75 O 2 '89. D. Denby

MILLER, ARTHUR, 1915-

about

My moments with Marilyn. M. A. Miller. il por *Esquire* 111:161-4+ Je '89

MILLER, BEBE

about

Bebe Miller comes home. E. Zimmer. il pors *Dance Magazine* 63:34-8 D '89

MILLER, BILL

about

Paging Dr. Funny Bone: comedy doc leaves 'em in stitches. S. Carrell. il *American Health* 8:22 My '89

MILLER, BONNIE J.

Double vision. il *American Craft* 49:40-5 O/N '89

MILLER, BRAD

Land-grab in the Philippines. il *The Progressive* 53:30-3 N '89

MILLER, CARL

about

Big tree for the Big Apple. J. Grossmann. il pors *National Wildlife* 28:10-13 D '89/Ja '90

MILLER, CHARLES

Headline: commercial space dies . . . *Ad Astra* 1:13 F '89

MILLER, CHARLES P.

Holy cow! It's Harry Caray. il pors *The Saturday Evening Post* 261:54-5+ O '89

MILLER, CHRISTOPHER, 1946-

(jt. auth) See MacKinnon, Roderick, and Miller, Christopher, 1946-

MILLER, CLAUDE

about

The little thief [film] Reviews
American Film il 15:97 O '89. D. Yakir
Film Comment il 25:6 Jl/Ag '89. M. Pally
The New Yorker 65:89 S 4 '89. T. Rafferty
Newsweek 114:55 S 11 '89. D. Ansen
People Weekly 32:14 S 18 '89. R. Novak

MILLER, CRAIG

A guide for assistant lighting designers. il *Theatre Crafts* 23:22-7 Ja '89

MILLER, DALE A.

The American paradox [address, October 31, 1989] *Vital Speeches of the Day* 56:150-3 D 15 '89

The biological future of pest control [address, November 15, 1988] *Vital Speeches of the Day* 55:337-40 Mr 15 '89

MILLER, DAVIS

Leonard bashing. il pors *Sport (New York, N.Y.)* 80:73-5 D '89

Leonard-Hearns, again. il pors *Sport (New York, N.Y.)* 80:69-71 Jl '89

My dinner with Ali. il pors *Sport (New York, N.Y.)* 80:70-2+ My '89

MILLER, DENNIS

about

Why I wear what I wear: Miller time. G. Collins. il pors *Gentlemen's Quarterly* 59:65+ Ag '89

MILLER, DEREK

about

An outbreak of teen alcoholism [interview] G. Breu. il por *People Weekly* 31:81 Ja 16 '89

MILLER, EARNEST LEE

about

Presumed guilty. D. Finkel. il pors *Esquire* 111:178-80+ Mr '89

MILLER, EDWIN

Spotlight. See issues of Seventeen through March 1989

MILLER, FERDINAND, JR.

Your own piece of the solar system [with editorial comment by Richard Berry] il *Astronomy* 17:6, 73-7 Mr '89

MILLER, GLENN

about

Glenn Miller: an American icon (I). S. M. Stroff. il pors *Antiques & Collecting Hobbies* 94:44-7+ S '89

Glenn Miller: an American icon (II). S. M. Stroff. il pors *Antiques & Collecting Hobbies* 94:60-3 N '89

MILLER, HAROLD TAYLOR, 1923-

about

HM's Miller to retire, succeeded by Darehshori. il por *Publishers Weekly* 236:16 D 22 '89

MILLER, HARRIET SUGAR

Suspect vaccine. il por *Ms.* 17:81-2 Ap '89

MILLER, J. B.
about
The magic mating-call letters for Desperate and dateless singles are WKRC in Cincinnati. il por *People Weekly* 32:59 Jl 24 '89
MILLER, J. DAVID (JOSEPH DAVID), 1964-
'80s football. il *Sport (New York, N.Y.)* 80:48-50+ O '89
The dirty dozen. il *Sport (New York, N.Y.)* 80:45-50 N '89
Filling the Bills. il *Sport (New York, N.Y.)* 80:38-43 My '89
"Let's play football!". il pors *Sport (New York, N.Y.)* 80:22-3+ O '89
Run 'n' Shoot. il por *Sport (New York, N.Y.)* 80:38-40+ Jl '89
The Sport 1989 pro football preview [cover story; special section] il *Sport (New York, N.Y.)* 80:30-2+ Ag '89
Super Bowl game plan. il *Sport (New York, N.Y.)* 80:25-6+ F '89
Then there was Nunn. il pors *Sport (New York, N.Y.)* 80:54-7 S '89
"This is where it starts". il por *Sport (New York, N.Y.)* 80:85-8 D '89
MILLER, JACK
Rural exchange program makes links. il por *The Progressive* 53:12-13 Ap '89
MILLER, JAMES EDWARD
A short history of NATO. il *Department of State Bulletin* 89:1-5 Ag '89
MILLER, JEFF F., AND OTHERS
Coordinate regulation and sensory transduction in the control of bacterial virulence. bibl f il *Science* 243:916-22 F 17 '89
MILLER, JOHN W.
Birdmen of Harlem. il *The New York Times Magazine* p48-9+ N 19 '89
MILLER, JON
Reinventing the brake. *Commonweal* 116:105-7 F 24 '89
MILLER, JONATHAN, 1934-
about
Profiles. P. Gilliatt. il por *The New Yorker* 65:52-6+ Ap 17 '89
MILLER, JONI
Adopt-a-Stream. il *Harper's Bazaar* 122:64-5 Ja '89
Dial-a-dinner party. il *Harper's Bazaar* 122:221+ Mr '89
The vision thing. il *Ms.* 17:30+ Je '89
MILLER, JOSEPH DAVID *See* Miller, J. David (Joseph David), 1964-
MILLER, JUDEA B.
Finding a response to Arafat's yes. *The Christian Century* 106:165-6 F 15 '89
Israelis don't hide from the truth. *The Christian Century* 106:552-3 My 24-31 '89
Jewish victims and German sensitivity [discussion of December 14, 1988 article, Jewish victims and German indifference] *The Christian Century* 106:287-8 Mr 15 '89
MILLER, JUDITH, AND MILLER, MARK
Supertrain: a solution to U.S. transportation woes. il *USA Today (Periodical)* 118:27-9 S '89
MILLER, KEN
New waves. il *Seventeen* 48:114+ My '89
MILLER, KENNETH D., AND OTHERS
Ocular dominance column development: analysis and simulation. bibl f il *Science* 245:605-15 Ag 11 '89
MILLER, KEVIN
We ask for poor sermons. por *Christianity Today* 33:10 D 15 '89
MILLER, LARRY, AND OTHERS
Expression of high-affinity binding of human immunoglobulin E by transfected cells. bibl f il *Science* 244:334-7 Ap 21 '89
MILLER, LAURENCE
To beat stress, don't relax: get tough. il *Psychology Today* 23:62-3 D '89
What biofeedback does (and doesn't) do. il *Psychology Today* 23:22-4 N '89
MILLER, LEE, 1907-1977
about
Surreal to real. C. Squiers. il por *Vogue* 179:214+ F '89
MILLER, LESLIE M., AND OTHERS
Mentorships and the perceived educational payoffs. il *Phi Delta Kappan* 70:465-7 F '89
MILLER, LOIS K.
(jt. auth) *See* O'Reilly, David R., and Miller, Lois K.
MILLER, MARIA, AND OTHERS
Structure of complex of synthetic HIV-1 protease with a substrate-based inhibitor at 2.3 Å resolution. bibl f il *Science* 246:1149-52 D 1 '89
MILLER, MARK
(jt. auth) *See* Miller, Judith, and Miller, Mark
MILLER, MARK CRISPIN
Barbara Walters's theater of revenge. *Harper's* 279:40-1+ N '89
MILLER, MARVIN
about
The union rep who changed baseball. J. Nocera. il por *Newsweek* 113:46 Ap 10 '89

MILLER, MARY SUSAN
1989 Teacher of the Year. il por *Good Housekeeping* 208:152+ My '89
MILLER, MATTHEW
The case against Ted Koppel [cover story] il *The Washington Monthly* 21:34-6+ My '89
"Ma'am, what you need is a new improved Hoover". il por *The Washington Monthly* 20:10-14+ Ja '89
MILLER, MORTON A., 1914-
My moments with Marilyn. il por *Esquire* 111:161-4+ Je '89
MILLER, PENELOPE ANN
about
Penelope Miller hopes a hot scene with Don Johnson means she won't be stood up by stardom again. S. Dougherty. il pors *People Weekly* 31:79-80 Ap 17 '89
The pleasures of being Penelope. S. Pocharski. por *Mademoiselle* 95:84 F '89
MILLER, PETER, 1934-
A castle under the Louvre. il *National Geographic* 176:102-7 Jl '89
MILLER, PETER M.
Pan Am winter games: for the sport of it [cover story] il map *Américas* 41 no2:42-5 '89
MILLER, PETER MICHAEL, 1942-
The new Hilton Head diet [excerpt from The Hilton Head over 35 diet] il *Ladies' Home Journal* 106:88+ F '89
MILLER, R. CRAIG
about
Miller high style. M. Filler. il por *House & Garden* 161:48 Ja '89
MILLER, RICHARD W.
about
Wang's turnaround specialist prepares for surgery. G. McWilliams. il por *Business Week* p108-9 D 11 '89
MILLER, ROBERT C.
about
Management by parking your car. J. Pitta. il por *Forbes* 144:92 Ag 21 '89
MIPS' strategy in the RISC race: pressing the flesh. R. D. Hof. il por *Business Week* p196 N 27 '89
Why MIPS is the one to beat. R. D. Hof. il por *Business Week* p40-1 F 27 '89
MILLER, ROBERT F.
Getting your money's worth. *Travel Holiday* 172:82 S '89
MILLER, ROBERT L.
A letter from the publisher. *See* issues of Time beginning February 9, 1987
MILLER, ROBERT L.
The woman-managed firm: how big a deal? il pors *Architectural Record* 177:47+ Je '89
MILLER, ROBIN
"Gentlemen, start your engines . . .". il *Sport (New York, N.Y.)* 80:60-2+ Je '89
MILLER, RUSSELL
about
'Salinger' haunts ruling on Hubbard biography. M. Reuter. *Publishers Weekly* 235:102 My 12 '89
MILLER, SANDY ZEH
A good retriever conserves wildlife. il *The Conservationist* 43:26-33 Mr/Ap '89
MILLER, STEPHEN
PC buyer's guide. il *Essence* 20:107-8+ D '89
MILLER, STEPHEN, 1941-
Totalitarianism, dead and alive. *Commentary* 88:28-32 Ag '89
MILLER, STEVE, 1943-
about
Steve Miller: the Joker gets jazzy. B. Milkowski. il pors *Down Beat* 56:24-6 F '89
MILLER, SUSAN
about
For dear life [drama] Reviews
  New York 22:56 Ja 23 '89. J. Simon
MILLER, TOM
"It's a wonderful lie". il *Consumers' Research Magazine* 72:24-5 D '89
MILLER, TOM, 1945-
about
Grand designs. D. Sapolin. il pors *Essence* 20:80-1+ Jl '89
MILLER, VIRGIL
about
Videotaping services. il por *Home Office Computing* 7:43 Je '89
MILLER, WALTER ERNEST
about
Of guns and a guru. M. McDonald. il pors *Maclean's* 102:28-9 Mr 27 '89
MILLER, WILLIAM H.
about
Will the real Ben Graham please stand up? J. Clements. il pors *Forbes* 144:310+ D 11 '89
MILLER, WILLIAM LEE
The spirit of '89. *The New Republic* 200:21-4 Je 26 '89
MILLER (BEBE) AND COMPANY *See* Bebe Miller and Company

MILLER (HERMAN) INC. See Herman Miller, Inc.
MILLER BREWING COMPANY
How Miller got dunked in Matilda Bay [wine cooler] J.
  F. Siler. il *Business Week* p54 S 25 '89
Miller guy life [spring break beer ads] T. Riordan. *The
  New Republic* 200:16-17 Mr 27 '89
MILLER BROTHERS
              about
Brother act. M. Barrier. il *Nation's Business* 77:41-2 Ja '89
MILLER TABAK HIRSCH & COMPANY
The hell with glamour. Give me groceries [G. D. Hirsch]
  J. H. Dobrzynski. il por *Business Week* p121 My 1 '89
MILLET
        See also
        Cooking—Grain
MILLHAUSER, STEVEN
The illusionist [story] il *Esquire* 112:214-20+ D '89
MILLI VANILLI (MUSICAL GROUP)
Pop's hair apparent. J. Giles. il *Rolling Stone* p25-6 N 30
  '89
MILLIGAN, TOM
              about
Successful family farm. M. Holmberg. il pors *Successful
  Farming* 87:60-2 O '89
MILLIKEN, MARY SUE
              about
Bright chefs, big City. S. Carlton. il pors *Health (New York,
  N.Y.)* 21:78-81 F '89
MILLIKEN, ROGER
              about
Can Roger Milliken emulate William Randolph Hearst? A.
  A. Lappen. il por *Forbes* 143:52+ My 29 '89
MILLIKEN & COMPANY
Can Roger Milliken emulate William Randolph Hearst? A.
  A. Lappen. il por *Forbes* 143:52+ My 29 '89
Chink in the armor [Stroud family sells small stake in Milliken
  & Co. to Delta Woodside Industries] A. A. Lappen. il
  Forbes 144:84+ N 13 '89
MILLINERY See Hats
MILLIONAIRES
'Give me your rich, your very rich . . .' [Senate immigration
  bill would grant special preference to millionaires] D.
  Harbrecht. il *Business Week* p31 S 4 '89
How to make a million dollars. C. Whitaker. il *Ebony* 44:134+
  S '89
Millionaire bachelors: the 20 most wanted. S. Bidel. il *Harper's
  Bazaar* 122:46+ Ja '89
When $2 million isn't enough. P. Moffitt. il *Esquire* 111:79+
  My '89
Wrap session [retirement income strategy] B. Weberman.
  il *Forbes* 144 Special Issue:395 O 23 '89
MILLISECOND PULSARS See Pulsars
MILLMAN, JOEL
El Salvador's Army: a force unto itself. il *The New York
  Times Magazine* p46-7+ D 10 '89
MILLMAN, ROBERT B.
Drugs: no exit. il *American Health* 8:68 O '89
MILLNER, CORK, 1931-
Not-so-plain Jane Seymour [cover story] il pors *The Saturday
  Evening Post* 261:42-3+ My/Je '89
Steve Martin: wild and serious guy [cover story] il pors
  The Saturday Evening Post 261:52-5 N/D '89
MILLNER, GUY W.
              about
Temporary assignment. M. Barrier. il pors *Nation's Business*
  77:34+ O '89
MILLS, DARIUS OGDEN, 1825-1910
              about
Opportunities. J. S. Gordon. il *American Heritage* 40:20+
  N '89
MILLS, DONNA
Inside Knots Landing: my life as a troublemaker [cover
  story] pors *TV Guide* 37:2-4 Je 17-23 '89
MILLS, ENOS, 1870-1922
              about
Hero of the wilderness. B. McKibben. il por *The New York
  Review of Books* 36:20+ N 9 '89
MILLS, HAYLEY, 1946-
              about
Hayley Mills—a healthy attitude. J. Jones. il pors *Redbook*
  172:12+ F '89
MILLS, HERBERT, 1912-1989
              about
Obituary
  Jet il pors 76:54 My 1 '89
MILLS, JESSICA
              about
Beauty on ice. il pors *'Teen* 33:86-7 N '89
MILLS, JOHN, AND KILA, GETI
Village development: working together. il *World Health* p5
  N '89
MILLS, JUDY
End of the line for French bears? il *International Wildlife*
  19:4-11 Ja/F '89
Great explorations. bibl il *Ms.* 17:58-62 Je '89

MILLS, KELLY
              about
Slimming summer suppers. T. Ney. il por *Prevention
  (Emmaus, Pa.)* 41:66-8+ Ag '89
MILLS, NICOLAUS
Doing the right thing(s). *Commonweal* 116:488-9 S 22 '89
MILLS, SARAH
Abortion under siege. il *Ms.* 18:48-51 Jl/Ag '89
MILLS, SIMON
Patsy Kensit. il pors *Seventeen* 48:60 D '89
MILLS, VIC
              about
Change agents. D. Moreau. il por *Changing Times* 43:108
  My '89
MILLS
        See also
        Millwork (Woodwork)
        Paper mills
        Steel works
        Water mills
              Accidents and explosions
Job hazards underscored in woodworking study. M. E. Per-
  sonick and E. A. Biddle. bibl f il *Monthly Labor Review*
  112:18-23 S '89
MILLWORK (WOODWORK)
Job hazards underscored in woodworking study. M. E. Per-
  sonick and E. A. Biddle. bibl f il *Monthly Labor Review*
  112:18-23 S '89
MILNE, ROBERT D.
Age 40: married with kids 2 and 4. il por *Fortune* 120
  no10 Special Issue:132 Fall '89
MILNER, RON, 1938-
              about
Checkmates [drama] Reviews
  Commonweal 116:21-2 Ja 13 '89. G. C. Weales
MILO
        See also
        Feeds—Milo
MILOŠEVIĆ, SLOBODAN
              about
Yugoslavia's new political truth. S. Drakulić. il *The Nation*
  248:297-8+ Mr 6 '89
MIŁOSZ, CZESŁAW
A few words on Bruno Schulz. il *The New Republic* 200:30-1
  Ja 2 '89
Incarnated [poem]; tr. by the author and Robert Hass.
  The New Yorker 65:40 D 18 '89
The telltale scar. *The New Republic* 201:27-9 Ag 7-14 '89
The thistle, the nettle [poem]; tr. by the author and Robert
  Hass. *The New Yorker* 65:46 N 27 '89
              about
Minority report. C. Hitchens. *The Nation* 248:259 F 27
  '89
MILSTAR SATELLITES See Communications satellites—Mili-
  tary use
MILSTEIN, MICHAEL
The quiet kill. il *National Parks* 63:18-25 My/Je '89
MILTON, MICHAEL
Where have you gone, Billy boy? il *The New York Times
  Magazine* p32+ D 10 '89
MILWARD, JOHN
The Lovesexy lord of flick and funk. il por *TV Guide*
  37:24-5 D 16-22 '89
MILWAUKEE (WIS.)
              Arts
Milwaukee [special section] il *Horizon (Tuscaloosa, Ala.)*
  32:17-32 Mr/Ap '89
              Description
The BoDeans' blue-collar cool-out. C. Mundy. il *Rolling
  Stone* p52 Jl 13-27 '89
Milwaukee [special section] il *Horizon (Tuscaloosa, Ala.)*
  32:17-32 Mr/Ap '89
              Education
Jazz Experience [Milwaukee Jazz Experience] J. Lehman.
  il *Down Beat* 56:11+ F '89
              Festivals
Fabulous festivals. M. Wade. il *Horizon (Tuscaloosa, Ala.)*
  32:24 Mr/Ap '89
              Galleries and museums
        See also
        Milwaukee Public Museum
              Music
        See also
        Florentine Opera Company
        Skylight Comic Opera Ltd.
Jazz Experience [Milwaukee Jazz Experience] J. Lehman.
  il *Down Beat* 56:11+ F '89
              Parades
The Circus Parade. B. Golightly. il *Horizon (Tuscaloosa,
  Ala.)* 32:23 Mr/Ap '89
The parade that's making Milwaukee famous [Great Circus
  Parade] L. A. Goth. il *Reader's Digest* 134:154-60 Je '89
              Theater
        See also
        Milwaukee Repertory Theater
MILWAUKEE BALLET
        See also
        Pennsylvania and Milwaukee Ballet

MILWAUKEE BALLET—*cont.*
Repertoire of growth. il *Horizon (Tuscaloosa, Ala.)* 32:20 Mr/Ap '89

MILWAUKEE PUBLIC MUSEUM
Jungle cries in Milwaukee [Rain forest: exploring life on earth] D. Einhorn. il *Américas* 41 no1:3 '89

MILWAUKEE REPERTORY THEATER
Master builders. M. Wade. il *Horizon (Tuscaloosa, Ala.)* 32:21-2 Mr/Ap '89

MILWAUKEE SYMPHONY ORCHESTRA
The stunning success of Milwaukee's Symphony Orchestra reflects the city's own achievement. B. Golightly. il *Horizon (Tuscaloosa, Ala.)* 32:17-18 Mr/Ap '89

MIMICRY (BIOLOGY)
Banded octopus: uncommon mimic. il *Sea Frontiers* 35:375 N/D '89
The frogfish: disappearing angler. il *Sea Frontiers* 35:231 Jl/Ag '89
Life as a leaf [katydid mimicry] J. L. Castner. il *International Wildlife* 19:18-21 Mr/Ap '89
The owl that traded a hoot for a hiss [burrowing owl] M. Rowe. il *Natural History* p32-3 My '89

MIMS, GEORGE
about
Mims's hymns: building a community of praise. J. Duin. il por *Christianity Today* 33:60-1 O 6 '89

MIMS, MADELINE MANNING- *See* Manning-Mims, Madeline

MINANGKABAU (INDONESIAN PEOPLE)
The nature and nurture of emotions [cross cultural study of relationship between facial expression and the physiology of emotion; research by Paul Ekman and Robert W. Levenson] P. Young. *Science News* 135:59 Ja 28 '89
Underneath, we're all the same [cross cultural study of relationship between facial expression and the physiology of emotion; research by Paul Ekman] C. Raymond. il *Psychology Today* 23:17 Je '89

MINASI, MARK
OS/2 notebook. See issues of Byte beginning August 1988

MINASSIAN, DANIEL H.
The collectors: neoclassical aesthetic: fashion designer Gaston Choron in Wiesbaden. il por *Architectural Digest* 46:240-6+ Ap '89
Gardens: wonders of Scherrer Park. il *Architectural Digest* 46:228-33 O '89
Legends of Villa Cypris. il *Architectural Digest* 46:126-31 Ja '89
Portrait of Picasso's tailor. il pors *Architectural Digest* 46:62+ F '89
A Provençal tale: the house and vineyards of Richeaume. il *Architectural Digest* 46:136-41 Ja '89

MINCEMEAT
Homemade mincemeat. B. Johnson. il *Better Homes and Gardens* 67:177 N '89

MIND
See also
Brain
Genius
Intelligence
Memory
Wisdom
Life after work [stretching the mind] J. Groch. il *American Health* 8:98+ Mr '89
Anecdotes, facetiae, satire, etc.
The other 90% [increasing brain power] P. Chance. il *Psychology Today* 23:20-1 N '89

MIND AND BODY
See also
Biofeedback training
Bodywork (Biomechanics)
Consciousness
Holistic medicine
Hypnotism
Hypochondria
Medicine, Psychosomatic
Mental healing
Mind gyms
Parapsychology
Psychology, Physiological
Psychoneuroimmunology
Sleep
The mind-body connection. L. F. McCarthy. il *Working Woman* 14:145-8 Ap '89
The skin and mind connection. S. Lord. *Vogue* 179:205 Ja '89
Anecdotes, facetiae, satire, etc.
No sense lending my body an ear. R. Blount. il *The Atlantic* 263:34-5 Ja '89

MIND CONTROL *See* Brainwashing

MIND GYMS
Exercise your mind. R. Flippin. il *Working Woman* 14:122+ F '89
Pumping intellect: can mind machines build up our brains? C. H. Otis. il *Utne Reader* p32-3 Ja/F '89
Sound-and-light wars [Synchro-Energizer] J. Hooper. il *Omni (New York, N.Y.)* 12:26+ N '89

Synchro Energize me! [visit to C. Zerrer's brain salon in Manhattan] D. Teresi. il *Health (New York, N.Y.)* 21:59 Ap '89

MINDELL, JACALYN HELMS- *See* Helms-Mindell, Jacalyn

MINDFULNESS
One-track thinking [excerpt from Mindfulness] E. J. Langer. il *Health (New York, N.Y.)* 21:72-5+ Mr '89

MIND'S EYE (FIRM)
Mind's Eye lands BBC catalogue [radio dramas] P. Sweeting. il *Publishers Weekly* 235:61 Ja 6 '89

MINDWRITE (WORD PROCESSOR PROGRAM) *See* Word processors and processing—Programming

MINER, ELLIS D.
Voyager's last encounter. il *Sky and Telescope* 78:26-9 Jl '89
(jt. auth) See Stone, E. C., and Miner, Ellis D.

MINERAL RESOURCES *See* Mines and mineral resources

MINERAL WATER
See also
Bottled water

MINERAL WELLS (TEX.)
Industries
Closing a base opens doors. D. C. Bacon. il map *Nation's Business* 77:9+ My '89

MINERALS
See also
Color of minerals
Meteorites
Mines and mineral resources
Water—Mineral content

MINERALS, EFFECT OF RADIATION ON
Giant radiation-induced color halos in quartz: solution to a riddle. A. L. Odom and W. J. Rink. bibl f il *Science* 246:107-9 O 6 '89

MINERALS & RESOURCES CORPORATION
See also
Minorco (Firm)

MINERALS IN THE BODY
See also
Boron in the body
Calcium in the body
Iron in the body
Magnesium in the body
Vitamins
America's big on vitamins, minerals. il *FDA Consumer* 23:3-4 D '89/Ja '90
Body mechanics: how well does your engine run? il *'Teen* 33:75 Ja '89
Mighty minerals in mini-doses. T. Mendoza. il *Current Health 2* 16:22-5 D '89
Mineral deposits [enhancing running ability] L. Applegate. il *Runner's World* 24:18-19+ O '89
Sequence-specific peptide cleavage catalyzed by an antibody. B. L. Iverson and R. A. Lerner. bibl f il *Science* 243:1184-8 Mr 3 '89
Squaring off over vitamins [debate over nutritional requirements and supplements] S. Findlay. il *U.S. News & World Report* 106:62-4 Ap 10 '89
You are what you eat. P. Cobe. il *Ladies' Home Journal* 106:164-6+ Mr '89

MINERS
See also
Coal miners
United Mine Workers of America
Health and hygiene
'Worse than Robben Island' [Zinc and Lead Company (Namibia) Ltd.] J. Apter. *The Progressive* 53:15-16 Jl '89

MINES, MILITARY
See also
Mines, Submarine

MINES, SUBMARINE
See also
Minesweepers
Submersible acrobat [Scorpio Scout mine hunting vehicle] P. Britton. il *Popular Science* 234:96 Ap '89

MINES AND MINERAL RESOURCES
See also
Coal mines and mining
Gold mines and mining
Mining industry
Ore deposits
Platinum mines and mining
Space mineral resources
Space mining
Strip mining
Tin mines and mining
Uranium mines and mining
Antarctic regions
Mine! Mine! Mine! *The Progressive* 53:10 D '89
'Why tempt the devil?'. C. Dickey and F. Gleizes. il *Newsweek* 114:39 O 23 '89

MINES AND MINERAL RESOURCES—cont.
United States
See Mines and mineral resources
MINES AND MINING
Laws and regulations
See Mining law
MINESWEEPERS
New brooms against deadly weapons [Manta minehunter developed by Sea Industries] P. C. Newman. il *Maclean's* 102:28 Ja 9 '89
MINETA, NORMAN Y.
Will there be life in our space program? *Ad Astra* 1:20 N '89
MING DYNASTY, 1368-1644 *See* China—History—Ming dynasty, 1368-1644
MINGO, FRANK
about
Obituary
Jet il por 77:32 N 20 '89
MINGUS, CHARLES, 1922-1979
An open letter to Miles Davis [reprint] il por *Down Beat* 56:48 S '89
about
Jazz. W. Balliett. *The New Yorker* 65:87-9 Ag 21 '89
MINGUS DYNASTY (MUSICAL GROUP)
Jazz. W. Balliett. *The New Yorker* 65:91-2 F 20 '89
MINH-HA, TRINH T. *See* Trinh, T. Minh-Ha, 1952-
MINI (AUTOMOBILE) *See* Automobiles, Foreign
MINIATURE ANIMALS *See* Animals, Miniature
MINIATURE GOLF
Welcome to putter's paradise. S. Monroe. il *Time* 134:73 S 11 '89
MINIATURE GOLF, ELECTRONIC *See* Video games
MINIATURE HORSES
The little-horse ranch in Texas: miniature thoroughbreds mean big bucks for the nuns of St. Clare. H. Phillips. il *Travel Holiday* 172:106 Jl '89
MINIATURE LANDSCAPES
His garden is a railway. il *Sunset (Central West edition)* 183:142 Jl '89
MINIATURE OBJECTS
See also
Architectural models
Automobile models
Books—Microscopic and miniature editions
Cameras, Miniature
Military miniatures
Models of cities, towns, etc.
Room models
Ship and boat models
Miniatures. A. Bahar. See issues of Antiques & Collecting Hobbies beginning March 1985
Collectors and collecting
Connoisseur Orville Elton is definitely small-minded: he has amassed 40,000 tiny treasures. D. Chu. il por *People Weekly* 32:197-8 D 4 '89
A Highland collector and his collection [D. Kilpatrick] A. Bahar. il *Antiques & Collecting Hobbies* 94:47-50 Ap '89
Miniatures: a world at your fingertips. T. Kump. il *New Choices for the Best Years* 29:74+ Ag '89
MINIATURE PAINTING
Exhibitions
Islamic paintings at the Sackler enchant the eye [H. Vever collection] C. Bond. il *Smithsonian* 19:122-7 Ja '89
Portraits in miniature [permanent gallery at the Worcester Art Museum] A. E. Ledes. il *Antiques* 136:1242+ D '89
MINIATURE ROSES *See* Roses
MINIMAL ARCHITECTURE
Minimalism in Miami [house by architect M. Hampton] J. Taylor. il *Architectural Digest* 46:216-21+ Ap '89
MINIMAL ART
Exhibitions
New shows of minimalism and conceptualism prove the power of ideas. il *Vogue* 179:534 S '89
MINIMALISM (ART) *See* Minimal art
MINIMILLS, STEEL *See* Steel minimills
MINIMUM COMPETENCY TESTS FOR TEACHERS *See* Teachers—Examinations
MINIMUM WAGE
The 30¢ gap [minimum wage bill vetoed] por *Time* 133:58 Je 26 '89
"Antibusiness bills" reappear. D. C. Bacon. il *Nation's Business* 77:6 Ap '89
Congress' minimum-wage bill: what the outcome will say about who's in charge. il *Nation's Business* 77:87 My '89
A deal on minimum wage. il *Newsweek* 113:5 Mr 6 '89
The fight for a new minimum wage. M. E. Howard. il *Black Enterprise* 20:27 Ag '89
A flip of fate on the subminimum wage [training wage] il *U.S. News & World Report* 107:14 N 13 '89
It's sacred—but is it smart? E. Clift and R. Thomas. il *Newsweek* 113:24 Ap 17 '89
Manager's tipsheet: keeping minimum-wage workers motivated. M. M. Kennedy. *Working Woman* 14:32 O '89
The minimum wage: help or hindrance? R. W. Haseltine. *USA Today (Periodical)* 118:31 Jl '89

Minimum wage legislation. il *Congressional Digest* 68:131-60 My '89
Minimum wage vs. maximum confusion. G. P. Brockway. il *The New Leader* 72:14-15 Ap 3-17 '89
The next battle in the war on poverty [proposed increase] D. Whitman. il *U.S. News & World Report* 106:18 My 29 '89
A pay hike for the poor. R. Lacayo. il *Time* 134:36 N 13 '89
Why the nickel-and-diming over the minimum wage? S. B. Garland. il *Business Week* p35 Mr 27 '89
Winners in the minimum-wage fight. M. W. Karmin. *U.S. News & World Report* 106:53 Ap 24 '89
MINING *See* Mines and mineral resources
MINING, PETROLEUM *See* Petroleum engineering
MINING INDUSTRY
See also
AMAX Inc.
Hanna Mining Co.
Inspiration Resources Corp.
Stillwater Mining Company
Acquisitions and mergers
International aspects
Getting the best price [Falconbridge Ltd. favoring AMAX over Noranda in takeover battle; special section] il *Maclean's* 102:34-7 Ag 14 '89
Canada
The final victory [Noranda's takeover of Falconbridge] J. Daly. il pors *Maclean's* 102:40-1 O 2 '89
Environmental aspects
The pastures of Class-L heaven [climbing Clark Mountain in the East Mojave Scenic Area] D. Darlington. il *Sierra* 74:70-3+ S/O '89
What's mined is theirs [General Mining Act] P. Hocker and S. L. Udall. il *Sierra* 74:20+ S/O '89
Finance
Metals [nonferrous mining industry] R. Reiff. il *Forbes* 143:172-3 Ja 9 '89
The mining industry climbs out of the pits. S. D. Atchison. il *Business Week* p61-3 Je 19 '89
International aspects
See also
Minorco (Firm)
Canada
See also
Corona Corp.
Falconbridge Limited
LAC Minerals Ltd.
Noranda Inc.
MINING LAW
What's mined is theirs [General Mining Act] P. Hocker and S. L. Udall. il *Sierra* 74:20+ S/O '89
MINING LEASES
See also
Coal leases
Oil and gas leases
MINING TOWNS
See also
Battle Mountain (Nev.)
MINISERIES (TELEVISION) *See* Television broadcasting—Miniseries
MINISKIRTS *See* Skirts (Clothing)
MINISTERS (CLERGY) *See* Black clergy; Clergy
MINISTRY *See* Church work
MINISTRY OF INTERNATIONAL TRADE AND INDUSTRY (JAPAN) *See* Japan. Ministry of International Trade and Industry
MINIT-LUBE (FIRM)
Quaker State switches into a quick-change artist. M. Schroeder. il por *Business Week* p126-7 O 16 '89
MINITEL (VIDEOTEX SYSTEM) *See* Information systems—France
MINITEL USA
L'informatique videotex. P. Scisco. il *Compute!* 11:6 F '89
MINIVANS *See* Vans
MINK
about
Mink. *The New Yorker* 65:38-9 Je 12 '89
MINK COATS, WRAPS, ETC. *See* Fur coats, wraps, etc.
MINKOW, BARRY
about
How Barry Minkow fooled the auditors. D. Akst. il pors *Forbes* 144:126-7+ O 2 '89
MINKOWITZ, NORMA, 1937-
about
Norma Minkowitz: shadow boxes. M. Shermeta. il *American Craft* 49:38-41 D '89/Ja '90
MINNEAPOLIS (MINN.)
Banks
See also
First Bank System Inc.
Buildings
Photographs and photography
Minneapolis, D.C. [Foshay Building] il *American Heritage* 40:106-7 Jl/Ag '89

MINNEAPOLIS (MINN.)—*cont.*
Criminal justice, Administration of
Minneapolis judge lets victim set punishment [W. Posten lets rape victim decide sentence] por *Jet* 75:24 Ja 30 '89
Putting the heat on dealers [drug dealing] *Newsweek* 114:32 Jl 31 '89
Description
Out on the town with Jam and Lewis. il pors *Rolling Stone* p48 Jl 13-27 '89
Festivals
Reviews:
Out There, festival in Minneapolis. J. Timmis. *Dance Magazine* 63:118-19 My '89
Galleries and museums
See also
Walker Art Center
Restaurants, nightclubs, bars, etc.
Dry times at Slick's Bar. M. A. Kuharski. il pors *Christianity Today* 33:14-15 Mr 17 '89
Savings and loan associations
See also
Midwest Federal Savings & Loan Association of Minneapolis
Sports
The Twin Cities. D. Barreiro. il *Sport (New York, N.Y.)* 80:76-9 D '89
Water supply
When the Land of Lakes went dry. L. P. Gerlach and E. D. Whitaker. il *Natural History* p62-4 Ja '89
MINNELLI, LIZA
about
Shedding her past, Liza Minnelli reinvents herself as a postdisco dance queen. D. Toop. il por *Vogue* 179:260 O '89
MINNERUP, GÜNTER
Opening up a new Europe? il *The Nation* 249:672-4 D 4 '89
MINNESOTA
See also
Boundary Waters Canoe Area (Minn.)
Criminal justice, Administration of—Minnesota
Educational laws and regulations—Minnesota
Fishing—Minnesota
Homesteads—Minnesota
Hunting—Minnesota
Lake of the Woods (Minn.)
Mille Lacs Lake (Minn.)
Voyageurs National Park (Minn.)
Water supply—Minnesota
Climate
The forest is for burning [influence of climate on forest fires] J. S. Clark. il *Natural History* p50-3 Ja '89
Description and travel
See also
Cycling—Minnesota
Forest fires
See Forest fires
Parks and reserves
See also
Silver Bay State Park (Minn.)
MINNESOTA. DEPT. OF HUMAN SERVICES
Old pines in the land of ten thousand lakes [social service program for Vietnamese in Minnesota] il *Aging* no359:22 '89
MINNESOTA MINING & MFG. CO.
Masters of innovation: how 3M keeps its new products coming [cover story] R. Mitchell. il *Business Week* p58-63 Ap 10 '89
Mining the work force for ideas. R. Mitchell. il *Business Week* Special Issue:121 Je 16 '89
MINNESOTA MULTIPHASIC PERSONALITY INVENTORY
This is your life [psychological evaluation test administered by Target Stores] *Harper's* 279:19-20+ D '89
MINNESOTA OPERA
Transformations. P. Gainsley. il *Opera News* 53:24-7 F 4 '89
MINNESOTA POWER
Deft management. J. Cook. il por *Forbes* 144:96+ D 11 '89
MINNETONKA INC.
Bob Taylor wants to walk away from his Obsession. M. J. Pitzer. il por *Business Week* p44 Mr 20 '89
MINOAN ANTIQUITIES *See* Crete—Antiquities
MINOANS
The Thera theory [evidence against S. Marinatos' hypothesis that the disappearance of the Minoans was linked to volanic eruption on Thera] A. Chen. il maps *Discover* 10:76-80+ F '89
MINOGUE, KENNETH R., 1930-
The moral passion of Mrs. Thatcher. il *National Review* 41:22-5 My 19 '89
MINOGUE, KYLIE
about
Kylie Minogue. B. Stepko. por *Seventeen* 48:132 Mr '89
Rockers on a roll. K. Turman. il por *'Teen* 33:43 Ja '89

MINOR LEAGUE BASEBALL *See* Baseball, Professional—Minor leagues
MINOR PLANETS *See* Asteroids
MINORCO (FIRM)
Apartheid and the Canada connection [Bank of Nova Scotia's involvement in financing bid for Consolidated Gold Fields] P. C. Newman. il *Maclean's* 102:29 F 13 '89
Harry Oppenheimer's empire: going for the gold. P. Schmeisser. il por *The New York Times Magazine* p32-3+ Mr 19 '89
MINORITIES
See also
Discrimination
Intelligence—Minorities
Confronting minority failure [address, January 26, 1989] R. D. Lamm. *Vital Speeches of the Day* 55:433-5 My 1 '89
Loaded terms. E. K. Braxton. *Commonweal* 116:328-9 Je 2 '89
Civil rights
See also
United Nations. Sub-commission on Prevention of Discrimination and Protection of Minorities
'Academic poverty-pimping' [discussion of September 4-11, 1989 article, Law profs fight the power] J. Wiener. *The Nation* 249:442+ O 23 '89
Civil rights: a presidential agenda. T. Eastland. *Current (Washington, D.C.)* 310:36-8 F '89
Law profs fight the power. J. Wiener. *The Nation* 249:246-8 S 4-11 '89
Education
See also
Bilingual education
National Scholars Program
Public schools—Desegregation
Cultural style in teaching and learning. A. G. Hilliard. *The Education Digest* 55:21-3 D '89
Educating language-minority children: challenges and opportunities. B. T. Bowman. il *Phi Delta Kappan* 71:118-20 O '89
Education: the movie [principals J. Clark, G. McKenna, D. Meier; cover story] D. L. Kirp. il pors *Mother Jones* 14:36-45 Ja '89
Ethnic groups' SAT scores rising. *USA Today (Periodical)* 118:15 Ag '89
The great white hope [T. Guinzburg sponsors Brownsville, Brooklyn class] M. Webb. il pors *New York* 22:50-3 Ja 16 '89
Hire education [adopt-a-class program at P.S. 175 in Harlem] K. Emmons. il *Omni (New York, N.Y.)* 11:18+ Je '89
Just schools for minority children. C. L. Glenn. il *Phi Delta Kappan* 70:777-9 Je '89
Minority and disadvantaged students [address, February 2, 1989] M. Coughlin. *Vital Speeches of the Day* 55:569-72 Jl 1 '89
The Regents' Round Table [report calling for greater multicultural inclusion in curricula of New York schools] L. Auster. il *National Review* 41:18+ D 8 '89
The search for minorities [colleges] S. Tifft. il *Time* 134:64-5 Ag 21 '89
Bibliography
Affirmative action: an exchange [discussion of October 12, 1989 article] A. Hacker. *The New York Review of Books* 36:52-3 D 7 '89
Affirmative action: the new look. A. Hacker. il *The New York Review of Books* 36:63-8 O 12 '89
Opportunities for minorities: new focus on concern for higher education. G. Orfield. il *Change* 21:50-3 My/Je '89
Employment
See also
United States. Equal Employment Opportunity Commission
Are the courts retreating on civil rights? T. Gest. *U.S. News & World Report* 106:47 Je 19 '89
Can your kid become president? M. Magnet. il *Fortune* 119:271+ Je 5 '89
FBI moving to improve its minority employment. *Jet* 75:8 Mr 20 '89
The FBI's new most wanted list [efforts to boost minority hiring] G. Witkin. il *U.S. News & World Report* 106:23-4 My 29 '89
Holding firm on affirmative action [Fortune poll] A. Farnham. il *Fortune* 119:87-8 Mr 13 '89
A question of statistics [Supreme Court decision on racial discrimination at Alaskan fish canneries] T. Jacoby. il *Newsweek* 113:58 Je 19 '89
Health and hygiene
See also
AIDS (Disease) and minorities
Medical care
Minority health: an enigma to solve. J. Wood. *Modern Maturity* 32:22+ F/Mr '89
Political activities
Ambitious visions for a GOP majority. G. Borger. il por *U.S. News & World Report* 106:18-19 Ja 23 '89
End of the rainbow [voting patterns of poor and minorities] R. A. Teixeira. il *The New Republic* 200:11-12+ Ap 3 '89

MINORITIES—*cont.*

Reading

ANPA publisher says minorities key to future survival of newspapers [views of David Lawrence Jr.] *Jet* 76:21 My 15 '89

Religious life

Listening to America's ethnic churches [special section] il *Christianity Today* 33:25-42 Mr 3 '89

Statistics

Finding out who counts [undercounting minorities and aliens in the census] S. Rabinove. il *Commonweal* 116:360-1 Je 16 '89

Future shock [population trends point to labor shortage and increase in minority birth rate; cover story] D. E. Bloom and N. G. Bennett. *The New Republic* 200:18-20+ Je 19 '89

The politics of minority statistics. H. Orlans. *Society* 26:24-5 My/Je '89

Who should count in the 1990 census? C. Norman. il *Science* 243:601-2 F 3 '89

Will 1990 census undercount minorities? il *USA Today (Periodical)* 118:8-9 N '89

Vocational-technical education

See also

Mi Casa Resource Center for Women (Denver, Colo.)

Canada

See also

Canada. Office of the Minister of State for Multiculturalism

Uneasy over newcomers [Maclean's/Decima poll] A. Walmsley. il *Maclean's* 102:28-9 Ja 2 '89

Poland

A letter to the Polish electorate. L. Wałęsa. *The New York Review of Books* 36:72 S 28 '89

Soviet Union

Dateline USSR: ethnic tremors. P. Cockburn. *Foreign Policy* 74:168-84 Spr '89

The empire breaks up. J. Rupnik. *The New Republic* 200:20-4 F 20 '89

Gorbachev lays down the law. R. Watson. il map *Newsweek* 113:52+ Ap 24 '89

Gorbachev's crisis of faith; tr. by Michael Davies. R. Debray. *Harper's* 278:22+ Ap '89

Gorbachev's nationalities problem. G. W. Lapidus. bibl f *Foreign Affairs* 68:92-108 Fall '89

Identity crisis in the Soviet west. A. J. Motyl. map *The Bulletin of the Atomic Scientists* 45:21-4 Mr '89

The nationalities crisis. M. Sieff. *National Review* 41:27 Ap 7 '89

Russia's shuddering empire. R. Pipes. il *The New Republic* 201:52+ N 6 '89

The Soviet agony over states' rights. J. Trimble. il map *U.S. News & World Report* 106:34-5 Ap 24 '89

The Soviet republics. *World Press Review* 36:10 Ja '89

The Soviet Union's nationalities question. S. L. Burg. bibl f map *Current History* 88:341-4+ O '89

USSR and its ethnics: the desire for autonomy. P. Cockburn. *Current (Washington, D.C.)* 315:33-9 S '89

When God fails, Russia remains. R. Debray. il *New Perspectives Quarterly* 5:30-3 Wint '88/'89

United States

See Minorities

MINORITIES IN ADVERTISING

It's a small world after all [advertisers use ethnic models] S. Scott. il *Time* 134:56 S 25 '89

MINORITIES IN THE MASS MEDIA INDUSTRY

FCC distress-sale policy overturned. S. M. Williams. *Black Enterprise* 19:54 Je '89

How the rich get richer [tax breaks in affirmative action media buys] H. Rudnitsky. il *Forbes* 143:38-9 My 15 '89

MINORITY ATHLETES, WOMEN *See* Women athletes

MINORITY BUSINESS DEVELOPMENT AGENCY (U.S.) *See* United States. Minority Business Development Agency

MINORITY BUSINESS ENTERPRISES

See also

Black business enterprises

Hispanic American business enterprises

Korean American business enterprises

Palestinian Arab business enterprises

Chicago law maker tells grocers to learn English [W. Henry] por *Jet* 77:15 D 25 '89-Ja 1 '90

Franchising draws minorities. M. Whittemore. il *Nation's Business* 77:68 Ap '89

Federal aid

See also

United States. Minority Business Development Agency

MINORITY ENGINEERS

See also

National Action Council for Minorities in Engineering

MINORITY LAW TEACHERS

'Academic poverty-pimping' [discussion of September 4-11, 1989 article, Law profs fight the power] J. Wiener. *The Nation* 249:442+ O 23 '89

Law profs fight the power. J. Wiener. *The Nation* 249:246-8 S 4-11 '89

MINORITY PHYSICISTS

Roster of minority members in physics and newsletter are available. *Physics Today* 42:121 Mr '89

MINORITY TEACHERS

Recruiting

More minority teachers. M. Haberman. bibl f il *Phi Delta Kappan* 70:771-6 Je '89

Recruiting minority teachers [Pittsburgh, Pa.] L. B. Nicklos and W. S. Brown. *The Education Digest* 55:28-31 D '89

MINORS, EMPLOYMENT OF *See* Children—Employment

MINORS (LAW) *See* Parent and child (Law)

MINOT, SUSAN

The feather in the toque [story] *Harper's* 278:30-1 Je '89

How love goes [story] il *Mademoiselle* 95:146+ F '89

about

The story of her life. K. Pryor. il pors *New York* 22:52-5 Je 12 '89

Why Susan Minot isn't Tama Janowitz. J. Maynard. il por *Mademoiselle* 95:56+ Jl '89

MINOXIDIL

Hair today [low-key ads for Rogaine] B. Kanner. il *New York* 22:20+ O 30 '89

Minoxidil—better known under its brand name Rogaine—has been found to have about a 60 percent success rate for women with thinning hair. R. M. Henig. *Vogue* 179:560+ S '89

Thin, thinning, gone [treating baldness in women] E. Baum. *Health (New York, N.Y.)* 21:74-6 Ja '89

MINSHALL, G. WAYNE, AND OTHERS

Wildfires and Yellowstone's stream ecosystems. bibl f il maps *BioScience* 39:707-15 N '89

MINSKY, LEONARD, AND NOBLE, DAVID F.

Corporate takeover on campus [cover story] il *The Nation* 249:477+ O 30 '89

MINSKY, MARVIN LEE, 1927-

The intelligence transplant. il por *Discover* 10:52-6+ O '89

MINSTAR INC.

Not so junky junk. T. Jaffe. il *Forbes* 144:267 O 2 '89

MINT JULEPS (MUSICAL GROUP)

Mint Juleps mix it up. J. Giles. il *Rolling Stone* p33 N 16 '89

MINTER, MARILYN

about

Marilyn Minter at White Columns. S. Westfall. il *Art in America* 77:170 Je '89

MINTS

See also

United States. Mint

MINTZ, ALAN L.

A major Israeli novel. *Commentary* 88:56-60 Jl '89

MINTZ, ANN EMMONS

The Futures Center: tomorrow's science and technology. il por *The Futurist* 23:19-24 Ja/F '89

MINTZ, ISABELLE, AND OTHERS

Effect of serotonergic afferents on quantal release at central inhibitory synapses. bibl f il *Science* 245:190-2 Jl 14 '89

MIOU MIOU

about

Offbeat sex appeal. M. Matousek. pors *Harper's Bazaar* 122:54+ Ap '89

MIPCOM *See* Marche International des Films et des Programmes pour la TV, la Video, le Cable et le Satellite

MIPS COMPUTER SYSTEMS INC.

Management by parking your car. J. Pitta. il por *Forbes* 144:92 Ag 21 '89

MIPS' strategy in the RISC race: pressing the flesh. R. D. Hof. il por *Business Week* p196 N 27 '89

Why MIPS is the one to beat. R. D. Hof. il por *Business Week* p40-1 F 27 '89

MIR (SPACE STATION) *See* Space stations, Russian

MIRA (STAR) *See* Stars, Variable

MIRABELLA, GRACE

about

What's in a name? N. Darnton. il pors *Newsweek* 113:62-3 Je 5 '89

MIRABELLA (PERIODICAL)

What's in a name? N. Darnton. il pors *Newsweek* 113:62-3 Je 5 '89

MIRACLE, DANIEL GIRALT- *See* Giralt-Miracle, Daniel

MIRACLE MILE [film] *See* Motion picture reviews—Single works

MIRACLES

See also

Faith cure

Jesus Christ—Apparitions and miracles

Signs and wonders movement

The gifts heaven sent: five true stories to touch your heart. G. Kopecky. il *Redbook* 174:108-9+ D '89

The other half of the gospel? C. Brown. il *Christianity Today* 33:26-9 Ap 21 '89

Small miracles [condensed from All I really need to know I learned in kindergarten] R. Fulghum. il *Reader's Digest* 134:67-9 My '89

MIRAGE (LAS VEGAS, NEV.: CASINO)

Tigers, a volcano, dolphins, and Steve Wynn. R. Grover. il por *Business Week* p70-1 N 20 '89

MIRAGE AIRPLANES *See* Airplanes, Military
MIRAGES
Highway mirages. C. F. Bohren. il *Weatherwise* 42:224-7 Ag '89
MIRAMAX FILMS (FIRM)
"We don't want to be Walt Disney". L. Gubernick. il pors *Forbes* 144:109-10 O 16 '89
Will success spoil the Weinstein brothers? A. Thompson. il pors *Film Comment* 25:72+ Jl/Ag '89
MIRAMICHI RIVER REGION (N.B.)
Crime
Blood on the cross [series of killings] G. W. Taylor. il por *Maclean's* 102:71 N 27 '89
The end of a manhunt [capture of A. Legere, suspect in string of murders] P. Kopvillem. por *Maclean's* 102:25 D 4 '89
MIRAMONTES, OCTAVIO
Wooing Mexico to nuclear power. bibl f il *The Bulletin of the Atomic Scientists* 45:36-8 Jl/Ag '89
MIRANDA, HECTOR FELIX
about
To the left of zero. W. Murray. *The New Yorker* 65:57-66 Jl 31 '89
MIRANDA, JESSE
Realizing the Hispanic dream. il *Christianity Today* 33:37-40 Mr 3 '89
MIRMAN, SOPHIE
about
Queen of pantyhose. D. Fong. il por *Forbes* 143:72+ Mr 20 '89
MIRO, CARLOS I.
about
Did this insurance whiz undercut and run? T. Smart. il por *Business Week* p120+ O 23 '89
MIRO & ASSOCIATES RISK MANAGEMENT INC.
Did this insurance whiz undercut and run? [C. Miro] T. Smart. il por *Business Week* p120+ O 23 '89
MIROJNICK, ELLEN
about
'Can you imagine them making love?'. C. Troy. il por *American Film* 14:46-51+ Je '89
MIRONENKO, VLADIMIR
about
"In a neutral zone". S. Hochfield. il pors *Art News* 88:47-8 D '89
MIRROR FRAMES AND FRAMING
Simple frame, fancy finish. il *Southern Living* 24:106+ F '89
MIRRORS
See also
Mirror frames and framing
Telescopes—Mirrors
How big is this kitchen? Mirrors keep you guessing. il *Sunset (Central West edition)* 183:99 D '89
'Magic mirrors' [ancient Chinese mirrors] R. K. G. Temple. il *The Courier (Unesco)* 41:16-17 O '88
True reflections [wall mirror] L. M. Dalsgaard. il *Home Mechanix* 85:72-3 D '89
MIRSKY, JONATHAN
The incredible shrinking man. il *The New York Review of Books* 36:18-20 Je 29 '89
Old boys' network. il por *World Press Review* 36:23 Ag '89
Stories from the Ice Age. bibl f il *The New York Review of Books* 36:27-8+ O 26 '89
Zhao fights for his political life. *World Press Review* 36:15-16 My '89
MIRVISH, DANIEL
(jt. auth) *See* Spiro, Peter, and Mirvish, Daniel
MIRVISH, DAVID
about
Transatlantic impresarios. P. Young. il pors *Maclean's* 102:45-6 Mr 27 '89
MIRVISH, EDWIN
about
The lights, sound and action of a community man. D. Jenish. il por *Maclean's* 102:28-9 D 25 '89
Transatlantic impresarios. P. Young. il pors *Maclean's* 102:45-6 Mr 27 '89
MISCARRIAGE
Anita Baker suffers a miscarriage in Detroit. il por *Jet* 75:17 F 27 '89
Selecting survivors: mother knows best? [selective abortion hypothesis; research by Stephen C. Stearns and Jan Koslowski] D. E. Loupe. *Science News* 136:331 N 18 '89
VDT radiation [risk of miscarriage] M. A. Pinsky. *The Nation* 248:41 Ja 9-16 '89
Psychological aspects
A delicate balance [strain on women's friendship] K. W. Wiley. il *Health (New York, N.Y.)* 21:30+ My '89
My imaginary child. W. P. Hogue. il *Glamour* 87:284 My '89
MISCARRIAGE OF JUSTICE
'Because I was a nobody' [wrongful jailing of R. D. Adams as depicted in The thin blue line] D. Hill. il pors *TV Guide* 37:20-2 My 20-26 '89

British justice, Irish victims [release of Guildford Four who were wrongfully imprisoned in England for terrorist bombings] A. Cockburn. *The Nation* 249:554-5 N 13 '89
Convicted of murdering one of his children, James Richardson hopes the truth will set him free [Florida man imprisoned for 1967 poisonings] P. Chin. il pors *People Weekly* 31:191-2+ Mr 6 '89
Cops above the law [release of Guildford Four who were wrongfully imprisoned in England for being IRA suspects] A. Phillips. il *Maclean's* 102:76+ N 6 '89
Crossing a line that is not thin at all, Randall Dale Adams wins release from a Texas prison. M. Brower. il pors *People Weekly* 31:155-6 Ap 10 '89
Crossing 'The thin blue line' [R. D. Adams sues filmmaker E. Morris] M. Lasswell. il por *Rolling Stone* p30 O 19 '89
Department of amplification [R. D. Adams, wrongly convicted for murder, released from Texas jail] M. Singer. *The New Yorker* 65:119-20 Ap 10 '89
From tragedy to travesty [questioning the guilt of J. Richardson who served 21 years in Florida for poisoning his children] J. N. Baker. il por *Newsweek* 113:68 Ap 24 '89
Jailed for a rape that never happened, Gary Dotson has his name cleared at last. M. Brower. il pors *People Weekly* 32:80-1 Ag 28 '89
A movie for the defense [R. D. Adams murder case and film The thin blue line] J. N. Baker. il por *Newsweek* 113:27 Mr 13 '89
No happy ending [R. Adams denied parole in Texas] J. E. Gallagher. il por *Time* 133:56 Mr 6 '89
Presumed guilty [half brothers E. L. Miller and W. R. Jent released from Florida's death row after new evidence uncovered concerning 1979 murder case] D. Finkel. il pors *Esquire* 111:178-80+ Mr '89
Recrossing The thin blue line [R. Adams released from jail] M. B. Carlson. il por *Time* 133:23 Ap 3 '89
Roberto Hernandez battles his arresting similarities to a wanted man with the same name. M. Neill. il pors *People Weekly* 32:95-7 Jl 17 '89
That's outrageous! *Reader's Digest* 135:19-20+ S '89
That's outrageous! *Reader's Digest* 134:41-2+ F '89
Why did Randall Adams almost die? F. Bruning. il *Maclean's* 102:9 Mr 27 '89
MISCEGENATION *See* Interracial marriage
MIŠČEVIĆ, DUŠANKA
(jt. auth) *See* Kwong, Peter, and Miščević, Dušanka
MISCHEL, WALTER, AND OTHERS
Delay of gratification in children. bibl f il *Science* 244:933-8 My 26 '89
MISCONDUCT IN OFFICE
See also
Politics, Corruption in
LES MISÉRABLES [musical] *See* Musicals, revues, etc.—Reviews—Single works
MISHVELADZE, REVAZ
??? !!! [story]; tr. by Edythe C. Haber. *Harper's* 279:34+ D '89
MISKELLY, GORDON M., AND OTHERS
Analysis of the published calorimetric evidence for electrochemical fusion of deuterium in palladium. bibl f il *Science* 246:793-6 N 10 '89
MISKITO INDIANS *See* Mosquito Indians
MISOGYNY
The roots of misogyny. C. Kocol. il *The Humanist* 49:35-6 My/Je '89
MISREPRESENTATION *See* Fraud
MISS, MARY, 1944-
about
Space exploration. A. Berman. il pors *Art News* 88:130-5 N '89
MISS AMERICA PAGEANT
Debbye Turner: new Miss America says, 'Beauty is content of character' [cover story] R. E. Johnson. il pors *Jet* 77:54-7 O 23 '89
Miss America: black, beautiful, brainy and born-again [D. Turner; cover story] L. Norment. il pors *Ebony* 45:132-4+ D '89
Miss America—was last year's voting suspect? L. DePaulo. il pors *TV Guide* 37:4-7 S 2-8 '89
Missouri veterinary coed in Miss America contest [D. Turner] il por *Jet* 76:27 Jl 31 '89
New Miss America is black Missouri coed, born-again Christian [D. Turner] il pors *Jet* 76:12-14 O 2 '89
On the road with Miss America [G. E. Carlson] A. Cook. il pors *Ladies' Home Journal* 106:38+ S '89
Sew red [clothes designer J. Duroché] B. Weber. il por *The New York Times Magazine* p66 Ag 27 '89
MISS FIRECRACKER [film] *See* Motion picture reviews—Single works
MISS LIBERTY (SYMBOL) IN ART
When people cared that Miss Liberty was Irish! [model for Indian-head $10 gold piece] E. Rochette. il *Antiques & Collecting Hobbies* 94:55+ Mr '89
MISS SAIGON [musical] *See* Musicals, revues, etc.—Reviews—Single works
MISS TEENAGE AMERICA PAGEANT
Get-ups to go! [C. Bliss] il pors *'Teen* 33:78-81 S '89

MISS TEENAGE AMERICA PAGEANT—*cont.*

Miss Teenage America 1989: taking it to the top [winner C. Bliss] il pors *'Teen* 33:60-1 F '89

Nautical & nice. il *'Teen* 33:52-9 F '89

Teen to teen. C. Bliss. See issues of *'Teen* beginning February 1989 through December 1989

MISS UNIVERSE PAGEANT

One beauty married a terrorist, another was sentenced to jail. J. K. Tree. il *TV Guide* 37:27 My 20-26 '89

MISSETT, JUDI SHEPPARD

about

Dancing to a different drummer. A. M. Thompson. il por *Women's Sports & Fitness* 11:16 O '89

MISSILE BASES *See* Guided missile bases

MISSILES, GUIDED *See* Guided missiles

MISSING AIRPLANES

See also

Bermuda Triangle

MISSING AND FOUND ART *See* Art—Missing and found works

MISSING CHILDREN

See also

Runaways

Duped by a mysterious con man, a Florida couple 'find' a missing son only to lose him again [DNA testing proves that D. Bonnabel is not the son of J. and M. Hagans] W. Plummer. il pors *People Weekly* 32:59-60 Ag 14 '89

Keeping hope alive. B. Kantrowitz. il *Newsweek* 114:95-6 N 27 '89

Photographs and photography

Faces from the future [Scott Barrows and Lewis Sadler use computer system to age photographs of missing children] G. Cowley. il *Newsweek* 113:62 F 13 '89

Ethiopia

African tribe rears white siblings found after 20 yrs. [H. and T. Gadessa] pors *Jet* 76:25 Ag 21 '89

MISSING IN ACTION

See also

Afghanistan—Russian invasion, 1979-1989—Missing in action

MISSING PERSONS

See also

Fugitives from justice

Runaway husbands

America's missing women. M. Jacobbi. il *Ladies' Home Journal* 106:144-6+ Ap '89

A disquieting mystery: St. John's rallies behind an abandoned girl [known as Christina] G. Allen. il por *Maclean's* 102:18-19 Ag 7 '89

Resolving a riddle [identity of girl known as Christina is discovered in St. John's, Nfld.] B. Came and H. Quinn. il por *Maclean's* 102:40-2 Ag 21 '89

MISSING PETS *See* Lost pets

MISSING SHIPS

See also

Bermuda Triangle

MISSION FURNITURE

Collectors and collecting

Gustav Stickley and the Craftsman Furniture Workshops. B. E. Johnson. bibl f il *Antiques & Collecting Hobbies* 94:48-9+ O '89

Mission accomplished [New York City loft of Theo Westenberger] M. Bethany. il *New York* 22:64-9 O 30 '89

Mission oak: a solid investment. J. H. Pluenneke. il *Business Week* p101 Jl 31 '89

Square roots [Hudson Valley home of Mark McDonald and Ralph Cutler] C. Vogel. il *The New York Times Magazine* p64-5 F 19 '89

MISSION: IMPOSSIBLE [television program] See Television program reviews—Single works

MISSION OF THE CHURCH

AD 2000: eleven years to reach the world [Global Consultation on World Evangelization by AD 2000 and beyond] A. Toalston. il *Christianity Today* 33:48+ F 3 '89

Beyond the maintenance mentality. D. A. McGavran. il *Christianity Today* 33:28-9 F 3 '89

From 'liberation' to 'exile': a new image for church mission. E. Radner. *The Christian Century* 106:931-4 O 18 '89

Kairos international: call to conversion. R. M. Brown. il *The Christian Century* 106:1091-3 N 22 '89

Willimon's project: does it make sense? W. L. Sachs. *The Christian Century* 106:412-14 Ap 19 '89

MISSION SOCIETY FOR UNITED METHODISTS

Mission Society complains. *The Christian Century* 106:681-2 Jl 19-26 '89

MISSION TO PLANET EARTH (PROJECT)

Mission to Planet Earth. il *Popular Science* 235:69-70 Jl '89

Mission to Planet Earth [cover story; special section; with editorial comment] il *Aviation Week & Space Technology* 130:7, 34-7+ Mr 13 '89

The next giant leap for mankind may be saving planet earth. J. Carey. il *Business Week* p90-2 Jl 31 '89

Taking the earth's vital signs. il *Time* 133:72-4 Je 5 '89

MISSIONARIES

See also

Black missionaries

Children of missionaries

Missions

The cost of loving Jesus [interview with H. Roseveare] por *Christianity Today* 33:45 My 12 '89

Protection

Some high-risk outposts for missions work. *Christianity Today* 33:48 My 12 '89

Supply and demand

Debts pose problems for missions candidates. K. H. Sidey. il *Christianity Today* 33:36-8 S 22 '89

MISSIONS

See also

Atlanta (Ga.)—Missions

Black missionaries

Jesuits—Missions

Mission Society for United Methodists

Missionaries

World Vision (Organization)

Evangelical voice heard at World Council meeting [conference on Mission and Evangelism] R. Frame. il *Christianity Today* 33:45-6 Jl 14 '89

Good news from missionaries: God was already there [interview with J. Donders] por *U.S. Catholic* 54:26-33 Ja '89

Missions and the translatable Gospel [L. Sanneh's Translating the message; cover story] J. B. Carman. *The Christian Century* 106:786+ Ag 30-S 6 '89

'Solidarity' meets 'evangelism' in WCC [World Conference on Mission and Evangelism at Trinity University] J. C. Lyles. *The Christian Century* 106:613-15 Je 21-28 '89

Study and teaching

Debts pose problems for missions candidates. K. H. Sidey. il *Christianity Today* 33:36-8 S 22 '89

Afghanistan

Room for missions in Afghan War? il *Christianity Today* 33:50 Mr 3 '89

Bolivia

Tribute to a Latin American martyr [L. Espinal, Jesuit missionary murdered in 1980] M. O'Sullivan. *America* 160:8-11+ Ja 7-14 '89

Colombia

Freed missionary tells story of survival [B. Olson] K. H. Sidey. il por *Christianity Today* 33:47 S 22 '89

Missionaries assess risks in Colombia [drug-related violence] J. Maust. *Christianity Today* 33:52 O 6 '89

Two American missionaries are abducted in Colombia [R. Grover and R. Libby] J. Maust. il pors *Christianity Today* 33:50-1 F 3 '89

El Salvador

Fear in the midst of war [army detains church workers] M. Nemeth. il *Maclean's* 102:48 D 4 '89

Guatemala

Blood bond: where Oklahoma and Guatemala meet [Catholic mission] D. Thomson. *America* 161:277-8 O 28 '89

Haiti

Voodoo sect members attack missionaries. il *Christianity Today* 33:43+ Ap 21 '89

Mexico

Paying the price [Westmont College students killed in auto accident while doing missions work] K. H. Sidey. il *Christianity Today* 33:44-6 My 12 '89

Molokai (Hawaii)

History

Father Damien, citizen of the world [care for lepers on Molokai] por *The Unesco Courier* 42:47 D '89

Nepal

Missionaries to Nepal, Colombia find freedom [D. McBride and M. Budd] K. H. Sidey. il pors *Christianity Today* 33:47+ Ap 7 '89

New Mexico

See New Mexico—Missions

MISSIONS, MEDICAL

Developing countries

Operating in danger zones. M. Johnson. il *Time* 133:56-8 Ja 16 '89

Tanzania

The farming doctor [I. Williams] A. L. Berry. il por *American Visions* 4:44-5 Ag '89

Zaire

25 years later, life still springs from death [slain medical missionary P. Carlson] il por *Christianity Today* 33:56+ N 17 '89

MISSISSIPPI

See also

Architecture, Domestic—Mississippi

Blacks—Mississippi

Crime and criminals—Mississippi

Homochitto National Forest (Miss.)

Hunting—Mississippi

Jefferson County (Miss.)

Medical care—Mississippi

Pipes Lake (Miss.)

Wetlands—Mississippi

Yazoo River (Miss.)

Description and travel

Mississippi: where to go, what to see. S. R. Gregg. map *American Visions* 4:34-7 Ag '89

MISSISSIPPI—cont.

History
Photographs and photography
Southern exposure [E. Welty's photographs] G. Jaynes. il por *Life* 12:58-60+ N '89

Politics and government
Miss. Rep. Espy, Gov. Mabus blaze new political trail to push progress in state. S. Booker. il pors *Jet* 75:26-7 Ja 16 '89

Race relations
The business of us all [racial murders of Y. Hawkins and E. Till] *Commonweal* 116:484-5 S 22 '89
The new Mississippi: is it really better than 'up north'? C. Whitaker. il *Ebony* 44:30+ Ag '89
A veteran of Mississippi's 'Freedom Summer' remembers the cause—and the danger [drive for black voter registration conducted by SNCC in 1964]; ed. by Jane Sugden. L. Guyot. il pors *People Weekly* 32:61-2+ S 18 '89

MISSISSIPPI BURNING [film] See Motion picture reviews—Single works
MISSISSIPPI DELTA ECONOMIC COMMISSION See Lower Mississippi Delta Economic Commission
MISSISSIPPI IN LITERATURE
Faulkner's Mississippi [cover story] W. Morris. il por *National Geographic* 175:312-39 Mr '89
MISSISSIPPI IN MOTION PICTURES
Fire this time [Mississippi burning; cover story] R. Corliss. il *Time* 133:56-62 Ja 9 '89
Hollywood and civil rights [shortcomings of Mississippi burning] D. Bogle. il *Essence* 19:32 Mr '89
Hollywood: the dustbin of history [Mississippi burning] P. Arthur. il *USA Today (Periodical)* 117:35 My '89
Mississippi theater won't show controversial movie [Philadelphia, Miss. theater won't show Mississippi burning] il *Jet* 75:51 Ja 23 '89
MISSISSIPPI RIVER
See also
Great River Road
Tooling down the Mississippi [M. S. Forbes' motorcycling tour] B. Sipchen. il pors map *Forbes* 144:22-3 O 30 '89

Delta
See also
Lower Mississippi Delta Economic Commission
MISSISSIPPI STATE HISTORICAL MUSEUM
A walk through time in Jackson. il *Southern Living* 24:33 Ja '89
MISSOURI
See also
Abortion clinics—Missouri
Criminal justice, Administration of—Missouri
Education—Missouri
Fishing—Missouri
Grasshopper Hollow (Mo.)
Juvenile justice, Administration of—Missouri
Law—Missouri

Description and travel
Small-town America: an endangered species. G. Smith. il map *National Geographic* 175:186-215 F '89

History
Photographs and photography
Small-town America: an endangered species. G. Smith. il map *National Geographic* 175:186-215 F '89
MISSOURI SYNOD OF THE LUTHERAN CHURCH See Lutheran Church—United States
MISTER ROGERS' NEIGHBORHOOD [television program] See Television program reviews—Single works
MISTRAL, GABRIELA, 1889-1957
about
Gabriela Mistral: poet and humanist. G. von dem Bussche. pors *The Unesco Courier* 42:49 N '89
MIT See Massachusetts Institute of Technology
MITCHAM, MARYLEE
Opus in a drawer: on having written an unpublished novel. il *Commonweal* 116:296-7 My 19 '89
MITCHELL, ANNE W.
Old baggage, new visions: shaping policy for early childhood programs [cover story; with editorial comment by Pauline B. Gough] bibl f il *Phi Delta Kappan* 70:658, 664-72 My '89
MITCHELL, ARTHUR, 1934-
about
Company as community: DTH at 20 [cover story] E. Kendall. il por *Dance Magazine* 63:40-2 Je '89
Stepping out with Arthur Mitchell. H. Sterne. il por *Gentlemen's Quarterly* 59:428-9 S '89
MITCHELL, BOB
The fool's gold rush. il *Consumers' Research Magazine* 72:14-15+ Ja '89
MITCHELL, CLARENCE, JR.
about
Mitchell family home in Baltimore up for auction due to default on loan. *Jet* 76:9 Jl 3 '89
MITCHELL, DANIEL J.
Gramm-Rudman: a potent weapon for spending restraint. il *USA Today (Periodical)* 118:22-4 N '89
MITCHELL, DEAN, 1957-
The watercolor page. il por *American Artist* 53:50-5+ F '89

MITCHELL, GREG, 1947-
The victim and the pilot: a Hiroshima reunion. il pors *The Progressive* 53:26-8 Ag '89
MITCHELL, JOHN G.
War in the woods: Swan song. il map *Audubon* 91:92-102+ N '89
A wild island of hope. il *Wilderness* 53:42-51 Fall '89
MITCHELL, KEVIN
about
Granny and the Giant. F. Lidz. il pors *Sports Illustrated* 70:36-8+ Je 26 '89
Putting the mean streets behind him, slugger Kevin Mitchell now does his hitting on the field. S. K. Reed. il pors *People Weekly* 31:93+ Je 19 '89
MITCHELL, MARGARET, 1900-1949
about
Back with the wind. il por *Time* 134:51 O 9 '89
MITCHELL, MARGARET M.
Social teaching and social history: learning from the early church. *The Christian Century* 106:724-5 Ag 2-9 '89
MITCHELL, NORMAN See Lobsenz, Norman M., 1919-
MITCHELL, PAMELA J., AND TJIAN, ROBERT
Transcriptional regulation in mammalian cells by sequence-specific DNA binding proteins. bibl f il *Science* 245:371-8 Jl 28 '89
MITCHELL, SASHA
about
Sasha Mitchell. S. Littwin. por *TV Guide* 37:15 S 23-29 '89
Sasha Mitchell. B. Stepko. il por *Seventeen* 48:104-5 F '89
MITCHELL, SCOTT
about
Big, big man. D. Hughes. il pors *Sport (New York, N.Y.)* 80:42-3 N '89
MITCHELL, SEAN
Don't worry, be unhappy. il pors *American Film* 14:44-9 My '89
MITCHELL, SHANE
Images: beauty to go. il *Vogue* 179:62 Jl '89
MITCHELL, SHANNON
about
Hand-scribed missals: calligraphed masterpieces in miniature. A. Bahar. il por *Antiques & Collecting Hobbies* 94:60-3 D '89
MITCHELL, STEPHEN
Spinoza [poem] *The New Yorker* 65:36 Ag 7 '89
Tao-chi [poem] *The Nation* 249:608 N 20 '89
(tr) See Pagis, Dan. Ein Leben
(tr) See Pagis, Dan. A moment at the Louvre
MITCHELL, WILLIAM L., 1912-1988
about
Obituary
Road & Track il por 40:150 Ja '89. S. MacMinn
MITCHELSON, MARVIN M., 1928-
about
A struggle for splitsville's bucks. J. D. Reed. il pors *Time* 133:53 Ja 9 '89
MITCHEM, GLORIA
about
Nursing assistant, 25, wins $37.4 million in Fla. lotto. il por *Jet* 75:27 Mr 27 '89
MITCHINSON, CHRISTOPHER
about
Tokyo's bull has further to run [interview] S. Solo. il por *Fortune* 120:43 Jl 3 '89
MITCHISON, AMANDA
Sustainable development an important element of Palestinian uprising. *Utne Reader* p44 S/O '89
MITER BOXES, GAGES, ETC.
Miter gauge stop rod. R. J. DeCristoforo. il *Workbench* 45:66 My/Je '89
Stands, tables, etc.
See Machinery—Stands, tables, etc.
MITES
Attraction of the parasitic mite Varroa to the drone larvae of honey bees by simple aliphatic esters. Y. Le Conte and others. bibl f il *Science* 245:638-9 Ag 11 '89
Baby bee odor lures cradle-robbing mites [research by Guy Ourisson] S. Hart. *Science News* 136:103 Ag 12 '89
Photographs and photography
Mite riders. R. Noonan. il *Natural History* p80-1 My '89
MITGANG, HERBERT
about
Ballantine releases updated edition of 'Dangerous dossiers'. B. Levine. il *Publishers Weekly* 235:27 Mr 17 '89
MITHERS, CAROL LYNN
Love me tender. il *Ladies' Home Journal* 106:90+ Mr '89
Sexual ethics. See issues of Glamour beginning April 1987
Turning point. il *Ladies' Home Journal* 106:94 O '89
The war against women. il *Ladies' Home Journal* 106:137-9+ O '89
What male friends can & can't teach you about love. il *Glamour* 87:338-9+ Ap '89
MITHRAISM
The Mithraic mysteries. D. Ulansey. bibl il map *Scientific American* 261:130-5 D '89

MITI *See* Japan. Ministry of International Trade and Industry
MITNICK, KEVIN
about
Drop the phone. por *Time* 133:49 Ja 9 '89
MITOCHONDRIA
RNA editing in plant mitochondria [Oenothera] R. Hiesel and others. bibl f il *Science* 246:1632-4 D 22 '89
MITOCHONDRIAL DNA
See also
Polymerase chain reaction
Cellular aging [evidence that mitochondrial DNA damage leads to decrease in cellular respiration; research by Anthony Linnane and others] *Discover* 10:13-14 S '89
Cutting away DNA the mitochondrial way [work of Douglas C. Wallace] P. Young. *Science News* 136:85 Ag 5 '89
A direct repeat is a hotspot for large-scale deletion of human mitochondrial DNA [neuromuscular disorders characterized by ocular myopathy and ophthalmoplegia] E. A. Schon and others. bibl f il *Science* 244:346-9 Ap 21 '89
Dusky legacy [extinct dusky seaside sparrow; research by John Avise] L. Oliwenstein. il *Discover* 10:38 Jl '89
Fungal duo teaches evolutionary lesson [research by Jeffrey D. Palmer] B. Bower. *Science News* 135:318 My 20 '89
Human cells lacking mtDNA: repopulation with exogenous mitochondria by complementation. M. P. King and G. Attardi. bibl f il *Science* 246:500-3 O 27 '89
Molecular genetic relationships of the extinct dusky seaside sparrow. J. C. Avise and W. S. Nelson. bibl f il map *Science* 243:646-8 F 3 '89
Mom's legacy [Leber's hereditary optic neuropathy linked to faulty mitochondrial genes; research by Douglas Wallace] J. Spencer. il *American Health* 8:22+ Mr '89
Nature's family archives. J. C. Avise. *Natural History* p24+ Mr '89
A sparrow's fall [dusky seaside sparrow; research by John C. Avise and William S. Nelson] T. Appenzeller. *Scientific American* 260:32+ Ap '89
MITOCHONDRIAL MEMBRANES
Vitamin E fights radicals—again and again [research by Lester Packer] J. Raloff. *Science News* 135:327 My 27 '89
MITOGENS
The effect of GTPase activating protein upon Ras is inhibited by mitogenically responsive tissues. M.-H. Tsai and others. bibl f il *Science* 243:522-6 Ja 27 '89
Vascular endothelial growth factor is a secreted angiogenic mitogen. D. W. Leung and others. bibl f il *Science* 246:1306-9 D 8 '89
MITOSIS (BIOLOGY) *See* Cell division (Biology)
MITRAL VALVE PROLAPSE *See* Heart—Diseases
MITRANI, ANNE
about
Is this kid for real? Artist Anne Mitrani's dolls can fool you even in the, er, flesh. G. Oliver. il por *People Weekly* 32:157-9 N 27 '89
MITRE CORP.
Digital network could improve aircraft links to operations, ATC. P. J. Klass. il *Aviation Week & Space Technology* 131:121+ N 20 '89
MITSUBISHI (AUTOMOBILE) *See* Automobiles, Foreign
MITSUBISHI ESTATE CO. LTD.
Mitsubishi's gamble on a Manhattan jewel [Rockefeller Center] L. Light. il *Business Week* p124 N 13 '89
'Now they're just rich' [sale of Rockefeller Center to Mitsubishi Estate Co.] C. Friday and J. Hammer. il *Newsweek* 114:62-3 N 13 '89
The Rockefeller generation gap [Rockefeller Center sold to Japan's Mitsubishi Estate Co.] *U.S. News & World Report* 107:14+ N 13 '89
Sure, we'll take Manhattan [sale of Rockefeller Center to Mitsubishi] J. Greenwald. il *Time* 134:83 N 13 '89
MITSUBISHI HEAVY INDUSTRIES, LTD.
Japan explores liquid air cycle engine for future rocket propulsion needs. *Aviation Week & Space Technology* 130:58 Ap 3 '89
A 'little old agreement' on the F-16 [FSX deal with General Dynamics] *Newsweek* 113:34 Ja 30 '89
Mitsubishi plans to test experimental liquefied air cycle engine based on LE-5. il *Aviation Week & Space Technology* 131:33 Jl 31 '89
Technology concerns delay approval of FS-X agreement [sharing F-16 technology with Japan] M. Mecham. il *Aviation Week & Space Technology* 130:16-17 F 20 '89
MITSUBISHI MOTORS CORP.
Mitsubishi is souping up its image. L. Armstrong. il *Business Week* p56 F 27 '89
MITSUBISHI RAYON CO. LTD.
Severed heads and wasted resources [Fibermedia charged with stealing trade secrets from Advance Display Technologies Inc.] G. F. Gilder. il *Forbes* 143:45-6+ Je 26 '89
MITSUI TAIYO KOBE BANK
The birth of a behemoth. T. Holden. il *Business Week* p52 S 11 '89
MITSUKOSHI LTD.
Fast break at Tiffany's [Mitsukoshi's stake] M. Roman. il por *Business Week* p102+ O 9 '89

MITTELEUROPA *See* Central Europe
MITTERRAND, FRANÇOIS, 1916-
President meets with French president [news conference, May 21, 1989] il por *Department of State Bulletin* 89:79-83 Ag '89
about
L'édifice, c'est moi. A. J. Blinken. *The New Republic* 200:16+ My 15 '89
An exclusive interview with the president of the French Republic: François Mitterrand. pors *The Unesco Courier* 42:4-9 Je '89
France's Mitterrand: a study in ambition. R. Chelminski. il pors *Reader's Digest* 134:141-6 Ap '89
God is a French Socialist. M. Lilla. il *The American Spectator* 22:27-8 My '89
Paris à la Mitterrand. R. Hughes. il *Time* 134:88-90+ S 18 '89
What price glory. M. Filler. il *House & Garden* 161:118-25+ Jl '89
Visit to Czechoslovakia, 1988
When you visit Prague. V. Havel. *Harper's* 278:22+ My '89
Visit to the United States, 1989
President meets with French president [news conference, May 21, 1989] F. Mitterrand; G. Bush. il *Department of State Bulletin* 89:79-83 Ag '89
MITTLER, ROBERT S., AND HOFFMANN, MICHAEL K.
Synergism between HIV gp120 and gp120-specific antibody in blocking human T cell activation. bibl f il *Science* 245:1380-2 S 22 '89
MITTON, JACQUELINE
(jt. auth) *See* Hollis, Andrew J., and Mitton, Jacqueline
MITTON, JOHN N.
Make a telescope for $500: model 3. il por *Sky and Telescope* 77:488-91 My '89
MIXED DRINKS *See* Cocktails
MIXED MARRIAGE *See* Interfaith marriage
MIXERS, VIDEO *See* Video mixers
MIXERS (APPLIANCES)
See also
Drink mixers (Appliances)
Maintenance and repair
Replacing a mixer switch. C. Maxwell. il *The Family Handyman* 39:76 Mr '89
MIXES, FOOD *See* Food mixes
MIYATANI, SEIJI, AND OTHERS
Neural cadherin: role in selective cell-cell adhesion. bibl f il *Science* 245:631-5 Ag 11 '89
MIYAZAKI, TSUTOMU
about
The Tokyo chainsaw massacre. T. Jackson. *The New Republic* 201:20-1 S 11 '89
MIZES, H. A., AND FOSTER, J. S.
Long-range electronic perturbations caused by defects using scanning tunneling microscopy. bibl f il *Science* 244:559-62 My 5 '89
MIZRAHI, ISAAC
about
In Isaac Mizrahi's perfect packable wardrobe, every piece has nine lives. L. J. Nonkin. il *Vogue* 179:126+ N '89
Nobody beats the Miz. S. Mansfield. il por *Vogue* 179:294-9+ F '89
Shaped & draped. il pors *Harper's Bazaar* 122:140-3+ F '89
What makes Isaac run. M. Gross. il por *New York* 22:38+ S 25 '89
MIZUNO, MASATO
about
Grandpa would be pleased. S. Smith. il por *Sports Illustrated* 71:62-3 Ag 21 '89
MIZUNO CORPORATION
Grandpa would be pleased. S. Smith. il por *Sports Illustrated* 71:62-3 Ag 21 '89
MLINARIC, DAVID
about
Mlinaric: now and then. M. Ruthven. il pors *House & Garden* 161:164-73 Mr '89
MLOT, CHRISTINE
Blueprint for conserving plant diversity. il *BioScience* 39:364-8 Je '89
MMDS *See* Multichannel multipoint distribution service
MMPI *See* Minnesota Multiphasic Personality Inventory
MMU (MANNED MANEUVERING UNIT) *See* Space flight—Extravehicular activity
MNATSAKANYAN, RUBEN ARTYOMOVICH
(jt. auth) *See* Altshuler, Igor Izodorovich, and Mnatsakanyan, Ruben Artyomovich
MNEMONICS
A balk down memory lane [mnemonics in aviation] P. Garrison. *Flying* 116:38-9 O '89
How to improve your . . . oh, yeah, memory. B. Levine. il *Seventeen* 48:38+ Ja '89
Remember names better than a computer. A. Roblin. il *Prevention (Emmaus, Pa.)* 41:105-6+ D '89
MOAN, FRANK
What will the next favorable wind bring? il *America* 160:86-7 F 4 '89

MOANA HOTEL (WAIKIKI BEACH, HAWAII) See Waikiki Beach (Honolulu, Hawaii)—Hotels, motels, etc.
MOATS, ALICE-LEONE
about
Obituary
National Review 41:14-15 Je 16 '89
MOAWAD, RENÉ
about
Celebrations and bombs. A. Bilski. il por Maclean's 102:42-3 N 20 '89
Assassination
Agony in Beirut. L. Marlowe. il Maclean's 102:26-7 D 4 '89
The assassination of hope. R. Wilkinson. il Newsweek 114:68 D 4 '89
A bomb aimed at peace. J. F. O. McAllister. il por Time 134:52 D 4 '89
MOB (CRIMINALS) See Mafia
THE MOB [drama] See Galsworthy, John, 1867-1933
MOBERG, DAVID
Why 'liberal' has become a dirty word. il Utne Reader p70-1+ Mr/Ap '89
MOBERG, KERSTIN UVNÄS- See Uvnäs-Moberg, Kerstin
MOBIL CORPORATION
Double jeopardy [proposed oil exploration in Zambezi Valley, Zimbabwe] M. L. Knox. il Sierra 74:66-7 N/D '89
Mobil is waging a Hefty war on 'wimpy' wastebaskets. M. Mallory. Business Week p70 My 29 '89
Mobil's big pullout [South Africa] Newsweek 113:42 My 8 '89
Rangel-backed tax law pushes Mobil Oil to sell its S. African holdings. por Jet 76:5 My 15 '89
MOBILE (ALA.)
Arts
Mobile [special section] il Horizon (Tuscaloosa, Ala.) 32:73-88 Mr/Ap '89
Child welfare
Alabama police investigate "gift babies" [Unification Church members give infants to Mobile, Ala. families] Christianity Today 33:43-4 Mr 17 '89
Description
Mobile [special section] il Horizon (Tuscaloosa, Ala.) 32:73-88 Mr/Ap '89
Historic houses, sites, etc.
Beauty by design. D. Kerr. il Horizon (Tuscaloosa, Ala.) 32:75-6 Mr/Ap '89
Music
See also
Mobile Opera
Race relations
Woman awarded $7 million against KKK dies without will; daughters administer [B. M. Donald] pors Jet 76:12 Ap 24 '89
MOBILE BALLET
Making the leap. J. McAdams. il Horizon (Tuscaloosa, Ala.) 32:77 Mr/Ap '89
MOBILE HEALTH FACILITIES
Fighting infant mortality [Momma Mobile] C. SerVaas. il The Saturday Evening Post 261:94+ O '89
MOBILE HOME INDUSTRY
See also
Skyline Corp.
MOBILE HOME INDUSTRY WORKERS
Health and hygiene
Profiles in safety and health: work hazards of mobile homes. M. E. Personick and J. R. Daley. bibl f il Monthly Labor Review 112:15-20 Jl '89
MOBILE HOMES
View from a trailer. J. R. Sullivan. il Country Journal 16:84-5 Mr/Ap '89
MOBILE MOTION PICTURE THEATERS
Cinemas on wheels [health communication] D. J. Henrich. il World Health p10-11 Ja/F '89
MOBILE OFFICES
Office gear on the go. S. Advokat. il Nation's Business 77:56+ N '89
MOBILE OPERA
A grand tradition. J. Schonbak. il Horizon (Tuscaloosa, Ala.) 32:80 Mr/Ap '89
MOBILE SATELLITE SYSTEM See Communications satellites—Radiotelephone use
MOBILE TELECOMMUNICATIONS TECHNOLOGIES (FIRM)
Why new beepers vibrate. F. Meeks. il por Forbes 144:72-3 Ag 21 '89
MOBILE TELEPHONES See Cellular radio; Radiotelephone
MOBILIER NATIONAL (PARIS, FRANCE)
A nation's storehouse. P. Corbett. il House & Garden 161:52+ Jl '89
MOBILITY, RESIDENTIAL See Migration, Internal
MOBILITY, SOCIAL See Social mobility
MOBILITY OF ELECTRONS See Electron mobility
MOBILNET INC.
Cincinnati Microwave tries to strengthen its signal [cellular co-marketing deal with GTE] M. Mallory. Business Week p29-30 Mr 6 '89
MOBLEY, JANE
Paradise for sale. il Travel Holiday 171:118 Ap '89

MOBRIDGE (S.D.)
Weed all about it! Tumbleweeds invade South Dakota town! Houses buried! Folks mighty upset! il People Weekly 32:153 N 27 '89
MOBUTU SESE SEKO, 1930-
Visit of Zaire's president [remarks, June 29, 1989] il por map Department of State Bulletin 89:15-17 O '89
about
'Peacemaker' Mobutu is under fire. S. Askin and B. Javetski. il por Business Week p42 Jl 10 '89
Visit to the United States, 1989
Visit of Zaire's president [remarks, June 29, 1989] G. Bush; Mobutu Sese Seko. il por map Department of State Bulletin 89:15-17 O '89
Zaire's president Mobutu confers with Bush in D.C. il por Jet 76:4 Jl 17 '89
MOBY DICK (FICTIONAL CHARACTER)
Anecdotes, facetiae, satire, etc.
Moby Dick 2.1. K. Sheldon. Byte 14:344 Jl '89
MOCHE INDIANS
Thor Heyerdahl [tombs in El Purgatorio, Peru] P. Brock. il pors People Weekly 32:181-2+ D 11 '89
MOCK, RICHARD BASIL
about
Richard Mock at Souyun Yi. N. Princenthal. Art in America 77:210 O '89
MOCKINGBIRDS
Who listens to the mockingbird? R. Breitwisch. il Natural History p6+ Je '89
Sexual behavior
See Sexual behavior—Birds
MODEL CARS See Automobile models
MODEL HOUSES
Elegant—and modular [NEST demonstration house] V. E. Gilmore. il Popular Science 234:26 My '89
"Hit the prospect at every emotional level" [fully decorated model houses] R. Simon. il Forbes 143:310-11 Ja 9 '89
The Twin Gables: back to basics [1988 Idea House built in conjunction with the American Wood Council] C. Engle. il Southern Living 24:100-2+ Ja '89
MODEL MUGGING (PROGRAM)
Girls fight back. T. Imbimbo. il Seventeen 48:134 Ag '89
Women to their own defense. P. King. il Psychology Today 23:71-2 S '89
MODELING AGENCIES
See also
Click Agency
Ford Model Agency
MODELS
See also
Airplane models
Astronomical models
Automobile models
Ecological models
Geological models
Meteorological models
Miniature objects
Molecular models
Paleontological models and exhibits
Railroad models
Remotely piloted vehicle models
Rocket models
Room models
Ship and boat models
Space station models
Space vehicle models
Stadium models
Telescope models
MODELS, ARTISTS'
Affairs of the art [artists' models who were also mistresses] E. MacSweeney. il Harper's Bazaar 122:168-73 D '89
MODELS (PERSONS)
See also
Alexis, Kim
Alt, Carol
Bay, Willow
Bippus, Sunny
Black models (Persons)
Brinkley, Christie
Bunte, Donna
Campbell, Naomi
Carey, Jacqueline
Chyna
Crawford, Cindy
Gastineau, Erin
Guilbert, Jamee Becker
Haddon, Dayle
Hawk, Carmen
Hecht, Tannia Rubiano
Kansbod, Lena
Kirsebom, Vendela
Kloppenburg, Aloka
La Fressange, Inès de
Lockwood, Victoria
Lynch, Kelly
MacDowell, Andie
Macpherson, Elle
March, Babette

MODELS (PERSONS)—See also—*cont.*
McGrotha, Rosemary
Models, Artists'
Noble, Jennifer
O'Reilly, Toni
Otis, Carré
Payot, Turia Mau
Percival, Marilyn Tindall
Peterson, Sue
Porizkova, Paulina
Reece, Gabrielle
Roscoe, Sheila
Simonton, Ann
Smith, Mandy
Snowball, Emma
Soto, Talisa
Sousa, Maria João Leal de
Sylvander, Yvette
Sylvander, Yvonne
Tiegs, Cheryl
Turlington, Christy
Wilander, Sonya
Williams, Rachel
Young, Kara
Everybody's all-American. S. Lord. il *Vogue* 179:312-19 F '89
Facing up to the 90's [views of K. Lagerfeld] L. Wells. il por *The New York Times Magazine* p66-7 S 24 '89
Family valentines. il *Good Housekeeping* 208:112-15 F '89
Four supermodels tell it like it was [appearing on cover of *Glamour* magazine] C. Krupp. il *Glamour* 87:300-3+ Ap '89
It's a small world after all [advertisers use ethnic models] S. Scott. il *Time* 134:56 S 25 '89
Modeling: behind the glitter & glitz. J. Romberger. il *'Teen* 33:38-9+ F '89
The new top models. il *Glamour* 87:252-7 My '89
New year, new you. il *Seventeen* 48:64-5 Ja '89
Putting their best face forward [cosmetics firms hunting for images that will appeal to age and ethnic groups] E. Pomice. il *U.S. News & World Report* 106:45-6 Je 12 '89
Tall isn't all. il *'Teen* 33:50+ My '89
Those lips, those eyebrows. M. Gross. il *New York* 22:24-5 F 13 '89
West Coasting. il map *Seventeen* 48:40-5 F '89
What makes a model? il *Seventeen* 48:142 My '89
Competitions
Cover models hit New York [finalists in Seventeen's 1989 Cover Model Contest] il *Seventeen* 48:80+ S '89
The Dove/LHJ classic model discovery winners! il *Ladies' Home Journal* 106:29-30 Mr '89
The Great Model Search 1989 [special section] il pors *'Teen* 33:76-85 O '89
She's a winner [S. C. Swainson wins Gentle-Treatment Model Search] C. Morris. por *Essence* 19:42+ Mr '89
MODELS OF CITIES, TOWNS, ETC.
E. Nesbit's Magic Cities. A. Bahar. il por *Antiques & Collecting Hobbies* 94:64-8 Jl '89
Exhibitions
See also
Tiny Town (Colo.)
MODEMS
See also
Hayes Microcomputer Products, Inc.
The ABCs of X-, Y-, and ZMODEM [file transfer protocols] B. N. Meeks. il *Byte* 14:163-6 F '89
Boxes that let computers talk. il *U.S. News & World Report* 107:85 N 20 '89
Brother bundles fax, modem, and software [Brother IntelliFax board] C. Lee. il *Personal Computing* 13:186 Je '89
Fax and a whole lot more [Connection coprocessor] C. O'Malley. il *Personal Computing* 13:194-5 Jl '89
Fax it by modem. A. Glossbrenner. il *Home Office Computing* 7:38 O '89
A great communicator [Connection CoProcessor PC facsimile board] N. Baran. il *Byte* 14:195-6+ Ja '89
Mac goes fax [InterFax, AppleFax, FaxSTF modems] D. E. Crabb. il *Byte* 14:208C-208D+ My '89
Modern modem methods. B. Glass. il *Byte* 14:321-4+ Je '89
The protocol pack [XMODEM and its file transfer heirs] B. N. Meeks. il *Byte* 14:155-6+ Mr '89
Reasonably priced modem software [Mirror III] T. A. Summers. il *Home Office Computing* 7:83-4 N '89
Thoroughly modern modems. T. J. Byers. il *Radio-Electronics* 60:83+ N '89
Whither the modem? J. H. Humphrey and G. S. Smock. il *Byte* 14:281-3 Ja '89
X.25 pads performance [V-series Smartmodem] S. Satchell. il *Byte* 14:233-5 N '89
Speed
2400-baud external modems help data move faster. H. F. Beechhold. il *Home Office Computing* 7:64-5 Je '89
2400-bps external modem [Racal-Vadic 2400LC] H. F. Beechhold. il *Home Office Computing* 7:71 O '89
4800 bits, no errors [2400-bps modems] S. Apiki and S. Diehl. il *Byte* 14:162-70+ Je '89

A real deal: 2400-bps modem for $95 [CCC Model 2400] D. Allen. il *Byte* 14:102+ Mr '89
Why I traded up to a 2400-bps modem. A. Glossbrenner. il *Home Office Computing* 7:30 Ag '89
MODERN ARCHITECTURE *See* Architecture, Modern
MODERN ART *See* Art, Modern
MODERN CIVILIZATION *See* Civilization
MODERN DANCE *See* Dance
MODERN MUSIC *See* Music, Modern
MODERN SUPPLY COMPANY
Fans [owner L. Herschman] *The New Yorker* 65:24-5 Jl 24 '89
MODERNISM (AESTHETICS)
The good side of bad taste. H. Muschamp. il *House & Garden* 161:50 Ja '89
Modernism outmoded [fashion] H. Brubach. *The New Yorker* 65:102-9 N 20 '89
MODERNISM (ART) *See* Art, Modern
MODERNIZATION *See* Social change
MODES, MUSICAL *See* Musical intervals and scales
MODESTO (CALIF.)
Religious institutions and affairs
Churches unite, take a stand to prevent divorce. J. Williams. il *Christianity Today* 33:65-6 S 8 '89
MODIFIED AIRPLANES *See* Airplanes, Remodeled
MODINE MANUFACTURING CO.
An employee LBO could be a buy. G. G. Marcial. *Business Week* p134 F 20 '89
MODJTABAI, ATAROD
When X-rays are too costly. il *World Health* p29 Jl '89
MODRAS, RONALD
Father Coughlin and the Jews: a broadcast remembered. *America* 160:219-22 Mr 11 '89
MODULA-2 (COMPUTER LANGUAGE)
Modula-2 and OS/2 join forces. A. Schulman. il *Byte* 14:171-4 Ag '89
TopSpeed Modula-2. B. Nance. il *Byte* 14:211-14 My '89
MODULAR CONSTRUCTION
See also
Cardinal Industries Inc.
Houses, Prefabricated
School buildings, Prefabricated
Elegant—and modular [NEST demonstration house] V. E. Gilmore. il *Popular Science* 234:26 My '89
MODULAR ENERGY COMPANY
From sawdust to sawbucks. R. W. Simpson. il *Nation's Business* 77:14 D '89
MODULAR FURNITURE *See* Furniture
MODULATION (ELECTRONICS)
See also
Pulse code modulation
Radio frequency modulation
MODULATORS
See also
Modems
MOE, DOUG
about
Beers with . . . Doug Moe [interview] B. Diddlebock. il pors *Sport (New York, N.Y.)* 80:21-2 Jl '89
MOE, MICHAEL K., AND ROSEN, SIMON PETER
Double-beta decay. bibl il *Scientific American* 261:48-52+ N '89
MOEGERLE, GIL ALEXANDER- *See* Alexander-Moegerle, Gil
MOELLER, DADE W.
How to control radon gas. il *Consumers' Research Magazine* 72:19-23 F '89
Radon zapper. il map *Popular Science* 235:78-80 O '89
MOELLER, JAMES
Will it be clear tonight? il *Astronomy* 17:74-7 D '89
MOELLER, ROBERT C.
about
Living with a laptop. M. Antonoff. il pors *Personal Computing* 13:94-5+ F '89
MOELLER, SUSAN D.
about
How photography shapes the face of battle [interview] A. P. Sanoff. il *U.S. News & World Report* 106:62-3 Ap 3 '89
MOËT HENNESSY
See also
LVMH Moët Hennessy Louis Vuitton
MOFFETT, JAMES R.
about
"When preparation meets opportunity". K. Hannon. il por *Forbes* 143:266+ My 29 '89
MOFFETT, LUISA
The Brussels chapter begins: Mark Morris comes to town (Brussels). il *Dance Magazine* 63:32-3 F '89
MOFFETT, MARK W.
Life in a nutshell. il *National Geographic* 175:782-96 Je '89
Samurai aphids: survival under siege. il *National Geographic* 176:406-22 S '89
Trap-jaw ants: set for prey. il *National Geographic* 175:394-400 Mr '89

MOFFITT, PHILLIP
So what are your parents worth? il *Esquire* 112:111+ N '89
When $2 million isn't enough. il *Esquire* 111:79+ My '89

MOGADISHU (SOMALIA)
Social history
Where I grew up: Iman [interview] L. Konner. il pors map *Glamour* 87:169 S '89

MOGADOR (MOROCCO) *See* Essaouira (Morocco)

MOGUL EMPIRE
Hyderabad: shadow of empire [cover story] A. Bakshian and G. D. Schad. bibl il *History Today* 39:19-28 Ja '89

MOHAMED, KHALID
Close-up on Indian cinema. il *The Courier (Unesco)* 42:12-15 F '89

MOHAMMED REZA PAHLAVI, SHAH OF IRAN, 1919-1980
about
The man who would be Shah. P. Axthelm. il pors *People Weekly* 31:46-51 Ap 3 '89

MOHAMMEDANISM *See* Islam

MOHAVE DESERT (CALIF.) *See* Mojave Desert (Calif.)

MOHAWK, JOHN
(jt. auth) *See* Hill, Rick, and Mohawk, John

MOHAWK INDIANS
Contaminant Cove: where polluters defile Mohawk land [New York State] J. E. Milich. il *The Progressive* 53:23-5 Ja '89
Gambling and guns [St. Regis reserve] M. Clark. il *Maclean's* 102:21+ S 18 '89

MOHLENBROCK, ROBERT H., 1931-
Brumley Ridge, Utah. il map *Natural History* p68-71 S '89
Grasshopper Hollow, Missouri. il map *Natural History* p60-3 Jl '89
Kisatchie Hills, Louisiana. il map *Natural History* p30-2 F '89
Mack Lake, Michigan. il map *Natural History* p90-5 O '89
Paint Rock, North Carolina. il maps *Natural History* p64-7 Ag '89
Pipes Lake, Mississippi. il map *Natural History* p74-6 My '89
Plaster Creek, Indiana. il maps *Natural History* p98-100 N '89
Slumgullion Slide, Colorado. il map *Natural History* p34-7 Ap '89
Some plants slept. il *Natural History* p58-60 Ja '89
Tom Miner Basin, Montana. il maps *Natural History* p14-16 D '89
Tuttle Marsh, Michigan. il maps *Natural History* p72+ Je '89
Workman Creek Falls, Arizona. il map *Natural History* p86-9 Mr '89

MOHLER, MARY, AND ROSEN, MARGERY D.
Parents' journal. *See* issues of Ladies' Home Journal beginning September 1987

MOHN, REINHARD, 1921-
about
Reinhard Mohn. il *The Nation* 248:810 Je 12 '89

MOHNEN, VOLKER A.
Letters [discussion of August 1988 article, The challenge of acid rain] *Scientific American* 260:7 Ja '89

MOHONK MOUNTAIN HOUSE
The Mohonk Mountain House. R. Brookhiser. il *The American Spectator* 22:39 Je '89
Mohonk Mountain House—the last best summer place. B. Gill. il *Architectural Digest* 46:70+ Je '89

MOHR, JANE
Love multiplied by three; ed. by Elaine Fein. il pors *Redbook* 173:100-1+ Ag '89

MOHR, NANCY L.
Treasures on an island. il *American Visions* 4:29-31 O '89

MOHR TRIPLETS *See* Triplets

MOIR, ROB, AND PARKER, JACKSON
Massachusetts waterfowl decoys [cover story] bibl f il *Antiques* 136:516-27 S '89

MOIS, JYRI
A Soviet cure for the S&L mess. il por *Fortune* 120:207+ N 6 '89

MOISEYEV DANCE COMPANY
From the USSR to the NYCB. L. A. Jacobs. il *The New Leader* 72:22-3 F 6 '89
Ground work [New York City performances] T. Tobias. il *New York* 22:90 F 6 '89

MOISTURE
See also
Humidity
Wood—Moisture
Too much moisture. il *The Family Handyman* 39:6 Ap '89

MOISTURE METERS
About wood moisture meters. il *Workbench* 45:70 S/O '89
Humidity sensors. D. Lancaster. il *Radio-Electronics* 60:65-9+ S '89

MOISTURIZERS *See* Cosmetics

MOITOSO DE VARGAS, LINA, AND OTHERS
DNA looping generated by DNA bending protein IHF and the two domains of lambda integrase. bibl f il *Science* 244:1457-61 Je 23 '89

MOJAVE DESERT (CALIF.)
See also
Clark Mountain (Calif.)
Dustbusters! [Geo Tracker, Isuzu Amigo XS, Jeep Wrangler Islander, and Suzuki Samurai JL] A. Assenza. il *Car and Driver* 35:136-40+ N '89

MOJER, LINDA
Racquetball: grace, grit, and greatness. il por *Women's Sports & Fitness* 11:72 Mr '89

MOJTABAI, A. G., 1937-
A Church without priests. il *The New York Times Magazine* p16-17+ D 24 '89

MOLDAVIA (SOVIET UNION)
Languages
The language of unrest. W. R. Doerner. il *Time* 134:40 S 11 '89
War of the words [controversy over Russian as official language] R. Knight. *U.S. News & World Report* 107:32 Jl 31 '89
Nationalism
'Happy' Moldavia. A. Wilson-Smith. il *Maclean's* 102:32+ N 13 '89

MOLDED SALADS *See* Salads

MOLDINGS (ARCHITECTURE)
Coping with molding. il *Better Homes and Gardens* 67:79 My '89
Moldings enrich a stark room. T. H. Jones. il *Workbench* 45:16+ Mr/Ap '89
Moldings: what's in a name? T. H. Jones. il *Workbench* 45:14+ Jl/Ag '89
Trim molding. il *The Family Handyman* 39:40-2+ My '89

MOLDS (BOTANY)
See also
Slime molds

MOLDS (BUTTER) *See* Butter molds

MOLECULAR BIOLOGY
See also
Water memory theory
The science of metamorphoses [J. Loeb] R. C. Lewontin. bibl f il *The New York Review of Books* 36:18-22 Ap 27 '89

MOLECULAR CLONING *See* Clones (Biology)
MOLECULAR CLOUDS *See* Matter, Interstellar
MOLECULAR DYNAMICS
Hidden thermodynamics of mutant proteins: a molecular dynamics analysis. J. Gao and others. bibl f il *Science* 244:1069-72 Je 2 '89
Molecular dynamics simulation of a phospholipid micelle. J. J. Wendoloski and others. bibl f il *Science* 243:636-8 F 3 '89
Nonequilibrium molecular motion in a hypersonic shock wave. G. Pham-Van-Diep and others. bibl f il *Science* 245:624-6 Ag 11 '89
Shear forces in molecularly thin films. M. Schoen and others. bibl f il *Science* 245:1223-5 S 15 '89

MOLECULAR ELECTRONICS
Meet MIT's Mr. Biochips [M. S. Wrighton's work on molecular computers] R. Duffy. il por *Business Week* Special Issue:80 Je 16 '89
Mimicking photosynthesis. D. Gust and T. A. Moore. bibl f il *Science* 244:35-41 Ap 7 '89
The quest for the molecular computer. M. A. Clarkson. il *Byte* 14:268-73 My '89

MOLECULAR GENETICS
See also
DNA fingerprints
Restriction fragment length polymorphisms
Conquering the gene. D. Baltimore. il *Discover* 10:74-6+ O '89
Dusky legacy [mitochondrial DNA of extinct dusky seaside sparrow; research by John Avise] L. Oliwenstein. il *Discover* 10:38 Jl '89
Grimm's greatest tale. S. J. Gould. il *Natural History* p20+ F '89
How do you read from the palimpsest of life? M. M. Waldrop. il *Science* 246:578-9 N 3 '89
Molecular genetic relationships of the extinct dusky seaside sparrow. J. C. Avise and W. S. Nelson. bibl f il map *Science* 243:646-8 F 3 '89
Molecular genetics of human blue cone monochromacy. J. Nathans and others. bibl f il *Science* 245:831-8 Ag 25 '89
Nature's family archives [mitochondrial DNA analysis] J. C. Avise. *Natural History* p24+ Mr '89
Phylogeny and molecular data [discussion of February 12, 1988 article, Molecular phylogeny of the animal kingdom] K. G. Field and others. *Science* 243:548-51 Ja 27 '89
A sparrow's fall [DNA of the dusky seaside sparrow; research by John C. Avise and William S. Nelson] T. Appenzeller. *Scientific American* 260:32+ Ap '89
Through a lens, darkly. S. J. Gould. il *Natural History* p16+ S '89
Time bomb [DNA clock; work of Charles G. Sibley and Jon E. Ahlquist] J. Horgan. *Scientific American* 260:24+ Mr '89
Tracing living signs of ancient life forms [research by Andrew D. Ellington] I. Amato. *Science News* 136:229 O 7 '89

MOLECULAR MODELS

Molecular modeling of the HIV-1 protease and its substrate binding site. I. T. Weber and others. bibl f il *Science* 243:928-31 F 17 '89

Systems analysis at the molecular scale. H. Rabitz. bibl f il *Science* 246:221-6 O 13 '89

MOLECULAR RECOGNITION

Calicheamicin γ_1^1 and DNA: molecular recognition process responsible for site-specificity. N. Zein and others. bibl f il *Science* 244:697-9 My 12 '89

Molecular recognition and metal ion template synthesis. T. J. McMurry and others. bibl f il *Science* 244:938-43 My 26 '89

MOLECULAR ROTATION

A rotationally resolved fluorescence excitation spectrum of all-trans-1,4-diphenyl-1,3-butadiene. J. F. Pfanstiel and others. bibl f il *Science* 245:736-8 Ag 18 '89

MOLECULES

See also
Macromolecules
Polymers

. . . and self-assembling chemical parts [trinacrene formed by structure-directed synthesis] *Science News* 136:349 N 25 '89

Coulomb explosion imaging of small molecules. Z. Vager and others. bibl f il *Science* 244:426-31 Ap 28 '89

Electrospray ionization for mass spectrometry of large biomolecules. J. B. Fenn and others. bibl f il *Science* 246:64-71 O 6 '89

Making new materials molecule by molecule. I. Amato. *Science News* 135:166 Mr 18 '89

Splat prints of floppy molecules [Coulomb explosion imaging] *Science News* 136:47 Jl 15 '89

Sweet and sour [sweetness determined by shape of molecule; work of Murray Goodman] T. Beardsley. *Scientific American* 261:22+ N '89

Models
See Molecular models

MOLECULES, INTERSTELLAR See Matter, Interstellar

MOLECULON RESEARCH CORPORATION

Grantsmanship [career of A. Obermayer] I. Cithelen. il por *Forbes* 144:310+ N 13 '89

MOLES (DERMATOLOGY)

Leg moles? Get out the sunblocker [susceptibility to melanoma; research by Martin A. Weinstock] *Science News* 136:30 Jl 8 '89

Those little brown 'moles'. J. Clayton. il *Essence* 20:22 My '89

MOLESTING, CHILD See Child molesting

MOLESWORTH, THOMAS, 1890-1977
about

Colorado cabin fever. M. Guralnick. il *House & Garden* 161:158-67+ D '89

MOLITAR, NANCY K.

Cross-country skiing: the anywhere winter sport. il *Current Health 2* 15:13-15 Ja '89

MOLL, LUCY

Rev up. il *Health (New York, N.Y.)* 21:45-6 Je '89

Why lovers live longer. il *Mademoiselle* 95:132+ My '89

Writing for Vegetarian times. il *The Writer* 102:25-6 Ap '89

MOLLER, BARBARA
about

New life for a Water Mill blacksmith shop. J. Gruen. il *Architectural Digest* 46:108+ Ag '89

MOLLER, JAMES H. (JAMES HERMAN)

Facts about kids and cholesterol; ed. by Florence Isaacs. il *Good Housekeeping* 209:101+ S '89

MOLLER, PAUL
about

Flier Paul Moller is a former alien with a real flying saucer. W. Plummer. il pors *People Weekly* 31:149-50 Je 19 '89

MOLLICK, JOSEPH A., AND OTHERS

Class II MHC molecules are specific receptors for staphylococcus enterotoxin A. bibl f il *Science* 244:817-20 My 19 '89

MOLLINO, CARLO, 1905-1973
about

Fifties flyer. J. Turner. il por *Art News* 88:117-18 O '89

MOLLUSKS

See also
Nautilus
Nervous system—Mollusks
Octopuses
Shells (Conchology)
Slugs
Snails
Squid

Arms race on the grass flats [mollusks and their predators] E. S. Iversen and D. E. Jory. il *Sea Frontiers* 35:304-11 S/O '89

MOLLY MAID INC.

Housekeeping services. il pors *Home Office Computing* 7:42 Je '89

MOLNAR, JEEP
about

Chrysler would prefer a bar by any other name, but Jeep Molnar would rather fight than switch. il por *People Weekly* 31:63 Ap 3 '89

MOLNAR, THOMAS STEVEN

Recentralizing Europe. *National Review* 41:34+ N 24 '89

MOLOKAI (HAWAII)

See also
Missions—Molokai (Hawaii)

Description and travel

Hawaii's adventure islands: Lanai and Molokai. il maps *Sunset (Central West edition)* 182:68-73 F '89

Planning a trip to Lanai or Molokai? il map *Sunset (Central West edition)* 182:52-3 F '89

Parks and reserves

See also
Molokai Ranch Wildlife Park (Hawaii)

MOLOKAI RANCH WILDLIFE PARK (HAWAII)

Reflections of Africa in the Aloha State. K. Best. il map *Travel Holiday* 171:68-72 Ap '89

MOLONEY, KATHLEEN

Do you know light from lite? [excerpt from The Canyon Ranch health and fitness program] il *Health (New York, N.Y.)* 21:32+ F '89

Making sense of food labels [condensed from The Canyon Ranch health and fitness program] *Reader's Digest* 135:117-20 Jl '89

Maverick doctor: martyr or fraud? por *Ms.* 18:69-70 N '89

MOLSON BREWERIES

A global brew. J. DeMont. il *Maclean's* 102:28-9 Jl 24 '89

MOLSON COMPANIES LIMITED

See also
Molson Breweries

In search of a bigger gulp [merger of Molson and Carling] B. Came. il *Maclean's* 102:36 Ja 30 '89

MOLTEN METALS

See also
Rapid solidification technology

MOLTING

A baculovirus blocks insect molting by producing ecdysteroid UDP-glucosyl transferase. D. R. O'Reilly and L. K. Miller. bibl f il *Science* 245:1110-12 S 8 '89

What's the diagnosis? [insect cast skins] W. S. Moore. il *Flower and Garden* 33:8 Mr/Ap '89

MOLTON, WARREN LANE

First calling [poem] *The Christian Century* 106:551 My 24-31 '89

MOLYBDENUM PHOSPHATE

Structure of a three-dimensional, microporous molybdenum phosphate with large cavities. R. C. Haushalter and others. bibl f il *Science* 246:1289-91 D 8 '89

MOLYBDENUM SULFIDES

Inclusion systems of organic molecules in restacked single-layer molybdenum disulfide. W. M. R. Divigalpitiya and others. bibl f il *Science* 246:369-71 O 20 '89

MOMA See Museum of Modern Art (New York, N.Y.)

MOMENTS OF INERTIA

See also
Angular momentum

MOMENTUM, ANGULAR See Angular momentum

MOMMSEN, THOMAS P., AND WALSH, PATRICK J.

Evolution of urea synthesis in vertebrates: the piscine connection. bibl f il *Science* 243:72-5 Ja 6 '89

MOMMY DOLLS

The Mommy doll cues kids on the new reality: mother's place is wherever she wants to be! [developed by C. Stern and S. Ogden] il *People Weekly* 32:112-13 Ag 7 '89

MOMMY TRACK

Advocating a 'mommy track' [views of F. Schwartz] B. Kantrowitz. il por *Newsweek* 113:45 Mr 13 '89

Blowing the whistle on the "mommy track" [views of F. Schwartz] B. Ehrenreich and D. English. il *Ms.* 18:56-8 Jl/Ag '89

The daddy track. R. J. Samuelson. il *Newsweek* 113:47 Ap 3 '89

Forget the mommy track: make room for daddy. il *Glamour* 87:156 Je '89

Is the mommy track a blessing—or a betrayal? [discussion of March 20, 1989 article, The mommy track] il *Business Week* p98-9 My 15 '89

The mommy track [cover story] E. Ehrlich. il *Business Week* p126-9+ Mr 20 '89

Mommy tracks that lead somewhere good [women lawyers] L. Dusky. il *Working Woman* 14:132-4 N '89

Mothers in careers: business makes adjustments. F. N. Schwartz. *Current (Washington, D.C.)* 314:4-11 Jl/Ag '89

Reality check for harassed parents [views of F. N. Schwartz] J. Leo. il *U.S. News & World Report* 106:64 Ap 3 '89

Rolling along the mommy track. J. Castro. il *Time* 133:72 Mr 27 '89

What makes a good leader? A. M. Smith. *Working Woman* 14:2 My '89

Anecdotes, facetiae, satire, etc.

How to get 'em on track. C. Kleiman. il *Ms.* 18:64 Jl/Ag '89

MOMMY TRACK—Anecdotes, facetiae, satire, etc.—*cont.*
The mommy test. B. Ehrenreich. il *Mother Jones* 14:8-9 Jl/Ag '89
MON CHER TONTON (NEW YORK, N.Y.: RESTAURANT)
See New York (N.Y.)—Restaurants, nightclubs, bars, etc.
MONACELLA, SUZANA
about
Rio with love. M. Matousek. il por *Harper's Bazaar* 122:390+ S '89
MONACO, JAMES
Into the '90s. il *American Film* 14:24-7 Ja/F '89
MONACO
See also
Automobile racing—Monaco
Monte Carlo (Monaco)
Royal family
See also
Grace, Princess of Monaco, 1929-1982
Rainier III, Prince of Monaco, 1923-
Monaco's royal family: who will inherit the throne? S. Piersanti. il *McCall's* 116:14-16+ Mr '89
MONACO GRAND PRIX *See* Automobile racing—Monaco
MONAGHAN, THOMAS
about
Pie in the sky. K. Shyne. il pors *Runner's World* 24:34-6 N '89
Tom Monaghan. P. Alson and J. Greenwalt. il pors *People Weekly* 32:102-3+ S 25 '89
Tom Monaghan kneads the dough. E. Stern. il pors *Gentlemen's Quarterly* 59:136-41+ Jl '89
Why the pizza king may abdicate the throne. W. Zellner. il por *Business Week* p46 S 25 '89
MONAGLE, KATIE
Nice girls do or want to. il *Ms.* 17:50+ My '89
MONARCH AIRLINES
Monarch Airlines will expand EROPS 757 service to Far East [extended range overwater operations] D. A. Brown. *Aviation Week & Space Technology* 130:71 Ja 9 '89
MONARCH BUTTERFLIES *See* Butterflies
MONARCHY
See also
Queens
Religious aspects
A king in Minnesota. G. K. Brushaber. il *Christianity Today* 33:11 Ag 18 '89
Sunday monarchists and Monday citizens? W. J. Everett. *The Christian Century* 106:503-5 My 10 '89
MONASTERIES
Greece
See also
Athos (Greece)
Italy
See also
Monte Cassino (Monastery: Cassino, Italy)
MONASTICISM
See also
Benedictines
History
All I want is a cave somewhere [Desert Fathers] J. Garvey. il *U.S. Catholic* 54:8-10 F '89
MONDADORI (ARNOLDO) EDITORE, SPA *See* Arnoldo Mondadori Editore, SpA
MONDAVI, MARGRIT BIEVER- *See* Biever-Mondavi, Margrit
MONDAVI, ROBERT
about
View from Wappo Hill: Robert and Margrit Mondavi's Napa Valley vineyard. B. D. Colen. il pors *Architectural Digest* 46:276-83 My '89
MONDRIAN, PIET, 1872-1944
about
Mondrian in Disneyland. E. Hoek. bibl f il *Art in America* 77:136-43+ F '89
MONDRIAN (NEW YORK, N.Y.: RESTAURANT) *See* New York (N.Y.)—Restaurants, nightclubs, bars, etc.
MONDRIAN (WEST HOLLYWOOD, CALIF.: HOTEL) *See* West Hollywood (Calif.)—Hotels, motels, etc.
MONET, CLAUDE, 1840-1926
about
The luncheon. Sir M. Levey. il por *Art News* 88:91-2 O '89
MONETARY POLICY (U.S.) *See* Federal Reserve System (U.S.)
MONEY, EDDIE
about
Eddie Money. C. Eddy. por *High Fidelity (New York, N.Y.)* 39:70-1 Jl '89
MONEY
See also
Checks
Coins
Credit
Deflation (Finance)
Finance
Found money
Gold as money
Inflation (Finance)
Interest (Economics)
Laundering of money

Liquidity (Economics)
Paper money
Time value of money
Tokens
United States. Dept. of the Treasury
Wealth
Anti-dollarism. D. Seligman. il *Fortune* 120:215 N 6 '89
As central banks put on the brakes, inflation will skid . . . C. Farrell. *Business Week* p34 S 25 '89
Currency strategies that will pay off big if the dollar drops. S. Nasar. il *Fortune* 120:29+ Jl 3 '89
Does the buck stop here? [strong dollar] J. Edgerton. il *Money* 18:48-9 Ag '89
The dollar bubble will float back down to earth. V. Brownstein. il *Fortune* 119:19-20 Je 19 '89
The dollar comes roaring back. M. McNamee and W. Glasgall. il *Business Week* p26-7 My 29 '89
The dollar's value can affect your job, your mortgage rate and your investments. M. Schiffres. il *Changing Times* 43:20 F '89
Ease, please. T. Jaffe. *Forbes* 143:196 Je 12 '89
An end to monetary instability? [privatizing money] P. Brimelow. il *Forbes* 143:120+ Ap 3 '89
A fair exchange [handling money abroad] D. Wishik. il *Travel Holiday* 172:58-63 D '89
Following the money trail [U.S. policy] J. Egan. *U.S. News & World Report* 107:56 S 11 '89
A forecast for '89: exporters will profit as the dollar declines. J. Edgerton and M. T. Smith. il *Money* 18:7 Ja '89
The great dollar mystery. L. Reibstein. il *Newsweek* 113:44 My 29 '89
The Group of Seven is acting more like the Seven Dwarfs [dollar runup] M. McNamee. il *Business Week* p90 Je 5 '89
Interest rates could take the dollar on a ride downhill. G. Koretz. il *Business Week* p18 Jl 10 '89
Money & banking. See issues of Business Week
Save the dollar [devaluation] M. S. Forbes, Jr. il *Forbes* 144:29 O 30 '89
The shadow bankers [currency brokers control dollar's fate] B. Powell. il *Newsweek* 114:47-8 O 23 '89
Showdown on the dollar: central banks are attacking the greenback. J. Daly. il *Maclean's* 102:39 O 9 '89
Soaring dollar, easier money. M. W. Karmin and P. Sherrid. *U.S. News & World Report* 106:51 My 29 '89
The soaring U.S. dollar. T. Fennell. il *Maclean's* 102:26-7 Je 5 '89
The trade deficit is still heading the right way. V. Brownstein. il *Fortune* 119:27-8 F 13 '89
Try to stop me, if you can [strong dollar] il *Time* 133:69 My 29 '89
Vertigo and the soaring dollar. M. W. Karmin. *U.S. News & World Report* 106:54 Je 26 '89
What your bucks will buy abroad this summer. K. McManus and B. Stauffer. il *Changing Times* 43:72-4+ My '89
International aspects
See also
Capital movements
Foreign exchange
Gold as money
International Monetary Fund
Not much danger from the dollar. S. Nasar. *U.S. News & World Report* 107:41 O 9 '89
Psychological aspects
See also
Rich—Psychology
Fear of buying: women who save too much. N. Hathaway. il *Harper's Bazaar* 122:38+ Ja '89
Living grandly on less. M. Phillips and others. il *Utne Reader* p85-6 S/O '89
Mind over money. M. E. Jackson and G. Pollard. il *Essence* 20:94+ Jl '89
More than she bargained for [how differences in salaries may affect relationships] L. Lehrer. il *Ms.* 17:111-14 Ja/F '89
What's your money personality? V. Lindner and A. R. Lieberman. *Redbook* 172:124-5+ Ap '89
What's your money personality? [quiz; excerpt from What are you worth?] E. Hallowell and W. J. Grace. il *Good Housekeeping* 208:52+ F '89
When having everything isn't enough [cover story] A. Landi. il *Psychology Today* 23:27-30 Ap '89
Quotations
Money talks. il *People Weekly* 32 Special Issue:99-100 Fall '89
Social aspects
From Balzac to Salvador Dali. D. Singer. il *The Nation* 248:333-4+ Mr 13 '89
A penny for your values. M. G. Maudlin. *Christianity Today* 33:17 Je 16 '89
Eastern Europe
The West German mark may soon rule the East. B. Riemer and J. Kapstein. il *Business Week* p65 N 27 '89
Germany (West)
The West German mark may soon rule the East. B. Riemer and J. Kapstein. il *Business Week* p65 N 27 '89

MONEY—cont.

Japan

Struggling for financial dominance [yen vs. dollar] N. Holloway. *World Press Review* 36:15-17 Ap '89

Soviet Union

See also

Foreign exchange—Laws and regulations—Soviet Union

Golden rule for Russia? [proposal to make the ruble convertible into gold] M. S. Forbes, Jr. il *Forbes* 144:27 O 16 '89

'I'll take it. What is it?' The shopping spree in Russia. P. Galuszka. il *Business Week* My 1 '89

Now it's more like real money. R. Hornik. il *Time* 134:52 N 6 '89

Soviet T-bonds? They're only the beginning. R. Brady. il *Business Week* p46 N 13 '89

Soviet Union. *Business Week* p70 N 6 '89

United States

See Money

Venezuela

See also

Foreign exchange—Laws and regulations—Venezuela

Western Europe

See also

European Currency Unit

European Monetary System

MONEY (PERIODICAL)

Anecdotes, facetiae, satire, etc.

How one family handles its finances [J. Wright] J. Queenan. *Forbes* 143:42-3 Je 12 '89

MONEY AS GIFTS

Gracious gifts of money [Christmas gifts] G. Worth. il *Working Woman* 14:78-9+ D '89

MONEY CARDS *See* Debit cards

MONEY IN THE BIBLE

Rich wisdom: New Testament teachings on wealth [cover story; special section] il *Christianity Today* 33:27-40 My 12 '89

Sharp dealing. P. J. Ryan. *America* 161:151 S 9-16 '89

MONEY LENDING *See* Loans, Personal

MONEY MANAGEMENT *See* Budget, Household; Finance, Personal; Financial services; Investment advisers

MONEY MANAGEMENT ACCOUNTS *See* Cash management accounts

MONEY MARKET ACCOUNTS (BANKING) *See* Bank accounts—Interest (Economics)

MONEY MARKET FUNDS *See* Investment trusts

MONEY MARKETS

See also

Foreign exchange

MONEY, POWER, MURDER [television program] *See* Television program reviews—Single works

MONEY RAISING CAMPAIGNS *See* Fund raising

MONEY RATES *See* Interest (Economics)

MONEY SUPPLY

See also

Federal Reserve System (U.S.)

Economists find a new straw floating in the wind [world dollar base] K. Pennar. il *Business Week* p30 O 9 '89

MONEY TRADERS *See* Foreign exchange brokers

MONFORT, CHARLES A.

ASATs: Star Wars on the cheap. bibl f il *The Bulletin of the Atomic Scientists* 45:10-13 Ap '89

MONG TAI REVOLUTIONARY ARMY

Burma's 'Money Tree' [drug lord Khun Sa] M. Liu. il por map *Newsweek* 113:42-3 My 15 '89

MONGOLIA

See also

Paleontology—Mongolia

MONGOLIAN POETRY

See also

Epic poetry, Mongolian

MONGOLISM *See* Down syndrome

MONIN, FRANÇOISE HARROIS- *See* Harrois-Monin, Françoise

MONITORING

See also

Brokers—Monitoring

Employees—Monitoring

MONITORS, VIDEO *See* Video monitors

MONK, DENNIS C.

The mind's ear. bibl f *Design for Arts in Education* 90:17-29 Jl/Ag '89

MONK, THELONIOUS, 1917-1982

about

Rouse & Nica. P. Keepnews. il *Down Beat* 56:59-60 Ap '89

Thelonious Monk: Philharmonic Hall, Lincoln Center, New York City [reprint] I. Gitler. il por *Down Beat* 56:64 S '89

MONK (THELONIOUS) INSTITUTE OF JAZZ *See* Thelonious Monk Institute of Jazz

MONKEYS

See also

Baboons

Macaques

Defensive behaviors in infant rhesus monkeys: environmental cues and neurochemical regulation. N. H. Kalin and S. E. Shelton. bibl f il *Science* 243:1718-21 Mr 31 '89

Treatment

Monkey euthanasia stalled by activists [work of People for the Ethical Treatment of Animals] C. Holden. *Science* 244:1437 Je 23 '89

MONKS, BUDDHIST *See* Buddhist monks

MONK'S HOUSE (SUSSEX, ENGLAND) *See* Historic houses, sites, etc.—Great Britain

MONMANEY, TERENCE

Iron man. il *Discover* 10:62-5 Jl '89

MONNAIE DANCE GROUP/MARK MORRIS

An American in Brussels [M. Morris] J. Dupont. il pors *The New York Times Magazine* p22-3+ Ja 22 '89

The Brussels chapter begins: Mark Morris comes to town (Brussels). L. Moffett. il *Dance Magazine* 63:32-3 F '89

Dancing:

Brussels debut. A. Croce. *The New Yorker* 64:61-3 Ja 16 '89

Heroines [performance of Dido and Aeneas] T. Tobias. il *New York* 22:59-60 Je 26 '89

Kiss kiss, bang bang [fall program in Brussels] T. Tobias. il *New York* 22:106+ D 11 '89

Like Bejart before him, Morris scandalizes Brussels. L. Moffett. il por *Dance Magazine* 63:12 Jl '89

Reviews:

Performance of Dido and Aeneas in Brussels. L. Moffett. il *Dance Magazine* 63:62 Je '89

MONO-HA (GROUP)

Mono-ha: University of Rome, "La Sapienza". E. M. Gomez. *Art News* 88:191 Mr '89

MONO LAKE (CALIF.)

A deal that might save a Sierra gem. R. Conniff. il *Time* 133:8+ Ap 3 '89

MONOCLONAL ANTIBODIES

See also

Catalytic antibodies

Antibody to interleukin-5 inhibits helminth-induced eosinophilia in mice. R. L. Coffman and others. bibl f il *Science* 245:308-10 Jl 21 '89

Compelling cancer cells to self-destruct [use of anti-APO-1] S. Hart. *Science News* 136:69 Jl 29 '89

Fighting cancer [used to detect lung cancer cells in sputum] il *Prevention (Emmaus, Pa.)* 41:16+ Mr '89

Generation of a large combinatorial library of the immunoglobulin repertoire in phage lambda. W. D. Huse and others. bibl f il *Science* 246:1275-81 D 8 '89

Healing a broken heart. B. Lawren. il *Omni (New York, N.Y.)* 11:20+ S '89

Learning how to bottle the immune system [work of Richard Lerner] J. L. Marx. il *Science* 246:1250-1 D 8 '89

Monoclonal antibody-mediated tumor regression by induction of apoptosis [leukemia cells] B. C. Trauth and others. bibl f il *Science* 245:301-5 Jl 21 '89

Receptor and antibody epitopes in human growth hormone identified by homolog-scanning mutagenesis. B. C. Cunningham and others. bibl f il *Science* 243:1330-6 Mr 10 '89

Sequence-specific peptide cleavage catalyzed by an antibody. B. L. Iverson and R. A. Lerner. bibl f il *Science* 243:1184-8 Mr 3 '89

Taming the wily rhinovirus [work of Michael Rossmann and Richard Colonno] P. Radetsky. il *Discover* 10:38-43 Ap '89

MONOCYTES *See* Leukocytes

MONOGAMY

How to keep your man monogamous [excerpt] A. Penney. il por *Ladies' Home Journal* 106:70+ Jl '89

Will he cheat? Men tell why they do—or don't [excerpt from How to keep your man monogamous] A. Penney. il *Glamour* 87:220-3+ Ag '89

MONONGAHELA RIVER VALLEY

Closing up bars and closing up shop on the Monongahela. D. Ignatius. *The Washington Monthly* 21:62 F '89

When workers become entrepreneurs [steel mills] B. Harrison. il *Technology Review* 92:19+ Jl '89

MONOPOD CAMERA SUPPORTS *See* Camera supports

MONORAIL CAMERAS *See* Cameras

MONOTONES [ballet] *See* Ballet reviews—Single works

MONROE, MARILYN, 1926-1962

about

Kay Kent died the way she lived—as a mirror of Marilyn Monroe. M. Dougherty. il pors *People Weekly* 32:90-1 Jl 3 '89

My moments with Marilyn. M. A. Miller. il por *Esquire* 111:161-4+ Je '89

Sentimental guy. *The New Yorker* 65:28-9 Jl 10 '89

MONROE, RONALD

about

Execute Ronald Monroe? W. F. Buckley. *National Review* 41:63 S 15 '89

Only two weeks to live. G. Carroll and A. Press. il por *Newsweek* 114:62-4 Ag 21 '89

Ronald Monroe fights a Louisiana verdict of murder for a crime many think he did not commit. J. S. Kunen. il por *People Weekly* 32:95-6+ Ag 28 '89

MONROE (C.F.) COMPANY *See* C.F. Monroe Company
MONROY DE VELASCO, ANAMELI
Talking to teenagers about sex. il *World Health* p15 Ja/F '89
MONSANTO COMPANY
Blood, sweat and profits. R. Reiff. il por *Forbes* 143:110+ Mr 6 '89
Why Monsanto is plunking down its chips on R&D. J. E. Ellis. il por *Business Week* p66-7 Ag 21 '89
MONSOONS
India
India's lifeline. A. Jung. il *The Courier (Unesco)* 42:22-4 F '89
MONSTER FACTORY
To get a hold on a pro career, wrestlers pin their hopes on Larry Sharpe's Monster Factory. M. Neill. il pors *People Weekly* 31:131+ My 15 '89
MONSTERS
Monster mania. il *National Geographic World* 168:22-5 Ag '89
MONTAGE
See also
Photomontage
MONTAGNA, RICHARD
HTLV-I: a new AIDS-like threat? il por map *The Saturday Evening Post* 261:82-4+ Jl/Ag '89
MONTAGNE, BILL
about
Propeller-driven machbuster. M. Lamm. il por *Popular Mechanics* 166:48+ Ag '89
MONTAGNIER, LUC
(jt. auth) See Gallo, Robert C., and Montagnier, Luc
MONTAGU, EDWARD JOHN BARRINGTON DOUGLAS-SCOTT-MONTAGU *See* Montagu of Beaulieu, Edward John Barrington Douglas-Scott-Montagu, Baron, 1926-
MONTAGU OF BEAULIEU, EDWARD JOHN BARRING-TON DOUGLAS-SCOTT-MONTAGU, BARON, 1926-
History tomorrow. il *History Today* 39:7-8 Je '89
MONTALVO, JUAN, 1832-1889
about
The mighty pen. M. A. Vasco. por *Américas* 41 no2:57 '89
MONTANA, CLAUDE
about
Chez Claude. C. Petkanas. il pors *Harper's Bazaar* 122:104-9+ Je '89
Claude Montana: an avant-garde elegance on the Left Bank. C. Aillaud. il por *Architectural Digest* 46:120-7 S '89
The great state of Montana. M. Gross. il por *New York* 22:22-3 Jl 31 '89
Selling Montana. H. Brubach. *The New Yorker* 64:110+ Ja 23 '89
MONTANA, JENNIFER
Photographs and photography
Strobe-assist—the order of the day [fashion ad featuring J. and J. Montana] G. Bernstein. il pors *Petersen's Photographic Magazine* 18:12 S '89
MONTANA, JOE
about
Joe Montana: state of the art [cover story] I. Muchnick. il pors *The New York Times Magazine* p26-9+ D 17 '89
Masters of the '80s [cover story] R. Reilly. il pors *Sports Illustrated* 71:44-9 D 18 '89
Montana's passing fancy. C. Leerhsen. il pors *Newsweek* 113:54-5 Ja 23 '89
Tell a friend: Joe Montana may be the best ever. G. Dickey. il por *Sport (New York, N.Y.)* 80:55 Ag '89
That man again [cover story] P. King. il por *Sports Illustrated* 71:52-4 O 2 '89
Photographs and photography
Strobe-assist—the order of the day [fashion ad featuring J. and J. Montana] G. Bernstein. il pors *Petersen's Photographic Magazine* 18:12 S '89
MONTANA, LOUIS
Three-dimensional illustration comes of age. il *American Artist* 53:34-9 S '89
MONTANA
See also
Bighorn River (Wyo. and Mont.)
Birds—Montana
Bob Marshall Wilderness (Mont.)
Cannon Mountain (Mont.)
Cross country skiing—Montana
Custer Battlefield National Monument (Mont.)
Finance—Montana
Fishing—Montana
Gallatin National Forest (Mont. and Wyo.)
Geology—Montana
Glacier National Park (Mont.)
Grant-Kohrs Ranch National Historic Site (Mont.)
Hunting—Montana
National Bison Range (Mont.)
Paleobotany—Montana
Paleontology—Montana
Powder River Valley (Wyo. and Mont.)
Resorts—Montana
Vegetable gardens and gardening—Montana

Waterton-Glacier International Peace Park (Alta. and Mont.)
Wilderness areas—Montana
Antiquities
Park dig yields Custer artifacts [excavations at Custer Battlefield National Monument] il *National Parks* 63:12-13 N/D '89
Climate
Bluebirds liked it hot. H. Power. maps *Natural History* p61 Ja '89
Weather report [cold front] *The New Yorker* 65:28-9 F 20 '89
Description and travel
Montana: not a movie. S. Chapple. il *Mother Jones* 14:40-1 S '89
Forest fires
See Forest fires
Industries
See also
Platinum mines and mining—Montana
MONTAND, YVES
about
Architectural digest visits: Yves Montand. C. Aillaud. il pors *Architectural Digest* 46:82-7+ Ja '89
MONTANO, LINDA
The performance artist's training manual. *Harper's* 279:36-7 Jl '89
MONTARA (CALIF.)
Architecture
Spend on the design, save on the extras [small one-of-a-kind house] il *Sunset (Central West edition)* 182:148-50 Ap '89
MONTAZERI, HUSSEIN ALI
about
Khomeini strikes back. J. Bierman. il pors *Maclean's* 102:25 Ap 10 '89
Will the next Imam please stand up? il por *U.S. News & World Report* 106:13 Ap 10 '89
MONTCLAIR (N.J.)
Crime
Woman pleads guilty to theft after swallowing $2500 worth of jewelry [L. Riddick] il por *Jet* 76:18 Jl 10 '89
Housing
The family suburban. il *Esquire* 112:89 N '89
MONTE CARLO (MONACO)
Description
Girls' night out. A. Jolis. il *Vogue* 179:406-11 N '89
MONTE CARLO METHOD
Nonequilibrium molecular motion in a hypersonic shock wave. G. Pham-Van-Diep and others. bibl f il *Science* 245:624-6 Ag 11 '89
Shear forces in molecularly thin films. M. Schoen and others. bibl f il *Science* 245:1223-5 S 15 '89
MONTE CASSINO (MONASTERY: CASSINO, ITALY)
Letter from Cassino. W. Murray. *The New Yorker* 65:112-20 My 15 '89
MONTE VISTA NATIONAL WILDLIFE REFUGE (COLO.)
The numbers game puts birds at risk [avian disease] F. Graham. il map *Audubon* 91:18+ Ja '89
MONTECATINI EDISON *See* Montedison SpA
MONTECATINI TERME (ITALY)
Hotels, motels, etc.
From the waters of Montecatini [Grand Hotel e La Pace] F. Ferretti. il *Gourmet* 49:78+ D '89
Restaurants, nightclubs, bars, etc.
From the waters of Montecatini [PierAngelo] F. Ferretti. il *Gourmet* 49:78+ D '89
MONTECINO, MARCELO
Sixteen years under Pinochet. il por *The Progressive* 53:34-7 D '89
MONTECITO (CALIF.)
Gardens and gardening
Call it a California impressionist garden. il *Sunset (Central West edition)* 183:94-5 N '89
Restaurants, nightclubs, bars, etc.
Spécialités de la maison:
Stonehouse Restaurant, Pane e Vino. C. Bates. il *Gourmet* 49:38+ S '89
MONTEDISON SPA
Why Wall Street is furioso at Raul Gardini [deal to buy out minority holders of Ausimont] J. Rossant and W. Glasgall. il por *Business Week* p48 F 20 '89
MONTEFIORE HOSPITAL AND MEDICAL CENTER (NEW YORK, N.Y.)
Tough cases, hard choices [bioethicists J. Arras and N. N. Dubler] A. Rosenfeld. il pors *New York* 22:32-7 Ja 9 '89
MONTEGO, MAMA (FICTIONAL CHARACTER) *See* Mama Montego (Fictional character)
MONTELLO, JOSUE
Camões and Brazil. il *The Courier (Unesco)* 42:28-9 Ap '89
MONTEREY (MASS.)
Historic houses, sites, etc.
The Manse in Monterey, Berkshire County, Massachusetts. W. Garrett. il *Antiques* 136:282-91 Ag '89

MONTEREY (TENN.)
Monuments, statues, etc.
Monterey's mysterious stone [Standing Stone Monument] il *Southern Living* 24:31 F '89
MONTEREY COUNTY (CALIF.)
Historic houses, sites, etc.
Steinbeck country. B. McGinty. il *American History Illustrated* 24:18+ S/O '89
Wine industry
See Wine industry
MONTEREY HISTORIC AUTOMOBILE RACES *See* Automobile racing
MONTEREY JAZZ FESTIVAL *See* Music festivals—California
MONTEREY PENINSULA (CALIF.)
Description and travel
The marvelous Monterey Peninsula. S. Birnbaum. il *Good Housekeeping* 209:16+ O '89
MONTERO, ROSA
A novelist copes with the critics [interview with M. Puig] por *World Press Review* 36:60 Mr '89
MONTESQUIEU, CHARLES DE SECONDAT, BARON DE, 1689-1755
about
The godfather of the American Constitution. R. Wernick. il *Smithsonian* 20:183-4+ S '89
MONTEVECCHI, LILIANE
about
Tutu much. M. Matousek. il por *Harper's Bazaar* 122:180+ O '89
MONTEVERDI, CLAUDIO, 1567-1643
about
Musical events:
  Monteverdi's Orfeo, L'incoronatione di Poppea, and Il ritorno d'Ulisse [Skylight Comic Opera] A. Porter. *The New Yorker* 65:78-9 My 8 '89
  Il ritorno d'Ulisse in patria [opera] Reviews *The New Yorker* 65:133-4 D 11 '89. A. Porter
MONTGOMERY, BEAUREGARD HOUSTON- *See* Houston-Montgomery, Beauregard
MONTGOMERY, GEOFFREY
The human mouse [cover story; with editorial comment by Paul Hoffman] il por *Discover* 10:4, 48-55 Ag '89
The infant brain. il *Discover* 10:30+ Ag '89
The mind in motion [cover story] il *Discover* 10:58-61+ Mr '89
Molecules of memory [cover story] il por *Discover* 10:46-50+ D '89
Shooting the messenger. il *Discover* 10:32 N '89
Turning cancer off. il *Discover* 10:66-7 Ja '89
MONTGOMERY, JOHN WARWICK
about
Problems derail law school founder. R. Frame. *Christianity Today* 33:48 Mr 17 '89
MONTGOMERY, JOSEPH
about
Ten-speed to grow on. R. Koselka. il por *Forbes* 144:224+ N 27 '89
MONTGOMERY, L. M. (LUCY MAUD), 1874-1942
about
Anger on the Island. R. Corelli. il *Maclean's* 102:40 Jl 10 '89
MONTGOMERY, LUCY MAUD *See* Montgomery, L. M. (Lucy Maud), 1874-1942
MONTGOMERY, M. R.
Impalpable dust. il *The New Yorker* 65:94-111 Mr 27 '89
MONTGOMERY, MAURICE R.
about
Impalpable dust. M. R. Montgomery. il *The New Yorker* 65:94-111 Mr 27 '89
MONTGOMERY, SY
Digging is their game. il *International Wildlife* 19:46-50 Mr/Ap '89
MONTGOMERY (ALA.)
Monuments, statues, etc.
See also
Civil Rights Memorial (Montgomery, Ala.)
MONTGOMERY COUNTY (MD.)
The covered city [catastrophic health insurance plan] il *Esquire* 111:70 F '89
MONTGOMERY COUNTY (PA.)
Education
A chilling effect on evaluation? [case of teacher K. Leshinskie] P. A. Zirkel. il *Phi Delta Kappan* 71:164-5 O '89
MONTGOMERY-FATE, TOM
The hidden reality in Guatemala. il *The Christian Century* 106:820-2 S 13-20 '89
MONTHLY LABOR REVIEW
Klein Award. il *Monthly Labor Review* 112:2 Ap '89
Labor month in review. *Monthly Labor Review* 112:2 Ag '89
MLR: 1915-1990. H. Lowenstern. il *Monthly Labor Review* 112:2-4 Jl '89
MONTHLY REVIEW
Tilters. *The Nation* 248:328 Mr 13 '89
MONTHS
See also
April
August

December
February
January
July
March
May
November
October
September
MONTICELLO (VA.: ESTATE)
Gardens
Greening the South. D. Young. il pors *Southern Living* 24:125-6+ Je '89
MONTOYA, JUAN
about
Manhattan variations. P. Carlsen. il *Architectural Digest* 46:138-43 Ag '89
MONTPETIT, GUY
about
Hi-tech disagreements. P. Kaihla. il por *Maclean's* 102:16-17 Je 26 '89
MONTRACHET (NEW YORK, N.Y.: RESTAURANT) *See* New York (N.Y.)—Restaurants, nightclubs, bars, etc.
MONTREAL (QUÉBEC)
Architecture
See also
Canadian Centre for Architecture (Montreal, Québec)
Banks
A tale of three cities. A. Walmsley. il *Maclean's* 102:40-1 Ja 23 '89
Crime
The man who hated women [M. Lépine murders women at the University of Montreal] W. R. Doerner. il por *Time* 134:30 D 18 '89
Massacre in Montreal [M. Lépine's murder spree] B. Turque. il por *Newsweek* 114:39 D 18 '89
Meaner streets. D. Burke. il *Maclean's* 102:56 Ap 17 '89
Montreal massacre [M. Lépine guns down women at Univ. of Montreal; cover story; special section] il *Maclean's* 102:14-19+ D 18 '89
Quebec fire storm [language disputes and arson] L. Van Dusen. il por *Maclean's* 102:12-13 F 6 '89
Description
Gourmet holidays: Montreal. G. Asher. il *Gourmet* 49:64-9+ My '89
Montreal. il *Better Homes and Gardens* 67:156 Mr '89
Education
A study in fear [school violence] D. Burke. il *Maclean's* 102:42 My 22 '89
Galleries and museums
See also
Canadian Centre for Architecture (Montreal, Québec)
Industries
Killing fields in Old Montreal. P. C. Newman. il *Maclean's* 102:29 F 20 '89
Languages
Killing fields in Old Montreal. P. C. Newman. il *Maclean's* 102:29 F 20 '89
'To remind them that we're here' [English-speaking community] S. Page. *World Press Review* 36:42 F '89
Music festivals
See Music festivals—Québec (Province)
Race relations
A study in fear [school violence] D. Burke. il *Maclean's* 102:42 My 22 '89
Theater
See also
Théâtre 1774 (Theater company)
MONTREAL FILM FESTIVAL *See* Motion picture festivals—Québec (Province)
MONTREAL FORUM
Hockey night in Battle Creek [R. Gibson builds facsimile] S. Rushin. il por *Sports Illustrated* 70:14 Mr 27 '89
MONTREUX JAZZ FESTIVAL *See* Music festivals—Switzerland
MONTVILLE, LEIGH
The face of genius. il pors *Sports Illustrated* 71:58-62+ S 25 '89
Hey, Tyson, I'm The Man! il *Sports Illustrated* 71:116 O 2 '89
Holy cow, what digs! il pors *Sports Illustrated* 71:122-7 N 6 '89
In the nick of time. il *Sports Illustrated* 71:104-6+ N 6 '89
It's Back to the Bambino. il por *Sports Illustrated* 71:100 D 18 '89
Letters and more letters. il *Sports Illustrated* 70 Special Issue:276+ F '89
No legs to stand on. il pors *Sports Illustrated* 71:44-6+ D 4 '89
Return of the pixies. il pors *Sports Illustrated* 71:34-6+ N 27 '89
See Larry run. il pors *Sports Illustrated* 71:26-9 Jl 3 '89
Special delivery. il pors *Sports Illustrated* 71:64-9 N 20 '89
Thou shalt not lose. il *Sports Illustrated* 71:82-6+ N 13 '89

MONTVILLE, LEIGH—*cont.*

about

From the publisher. D. J. Barr. il por *Sports Illustrated* 71:1 S 25 '89

MONTY PYTHON'S FLYING CIRCUS [television program] See Television program reviews—Single works

MONUMENTS

See also

San Antonio (Tex.)—Monuments, statues, etc.

War memorials

Sacred places. J. Updike. il por maps *Popular Mechanics* 166:26-30 My '89

Nebraska

See also

Alliance (Neb.)—Monuments, statues, etc.

United States

See Monuments

MONUMENTS, MEGALITHIC *See* Megalithic monuments

MONVILLE, FRANCOIS-NICOLAS-HENRI RACINE, BARON DE, 1737-1794

about

The Désert de Retz, near Paris. P. Deitz. bibl f il *Antiques* 135:718-31 Mr '89

MONY *See* Mutual Life Insurance Co. of New York

MOOD DISORDERS *See* Depression, Mental

MOODS

How to beat a bad mood. C. Houck. *Reader's Digest* 134:93-5 Ja '89

MOODY, JIM

Should the "balanced budget constitutional amendment" be adopted? [excerpts from statement, November 17, 1987] *Congressional Digest* 68:269+ N '89

MOODY, MARK D.

DNA analysis in forensic science. bibl f il *BioScience* 39:31-6 Ja '89

MOODY, ORVILLE

about

Old Sarge takes charge. J. Garrity. il *Sports Illustrated* 71:56+ Jl 10 '89

MOODY GARDENS (GALVESTON, TEX.)

A garden of hope and recovery. D. Dietsch. il *Architectural Record* 177:94-9 N '89

MOODY'S INVESTORS SERVICE, INC.

Soothing the sting of an accounting rule [employee health benefits] L. J. Nathans. il *Business Week* p106 S 18 '89

MOOKHERJEE, BRAJA D.

about

Nose job. B. Weber. il pors *The New York Times Magazine* p78 F 5 '89

MOON, IK HWAN

about

Koreans yearn for reunification. D. G. Peerman. map *The Christian Century* 106:580-2 Je 7-14 '89

MOON, JOHN ELLIS VAN COURTLAND

Chemical warfare: a forgotten lesson. bibl f il *The Bulletin of the Atomic Scientists* 45:40-3 Jl/Ag '89

MOON, SUN MYUNG

about

Rev. Moon's rising political influence. J. B. Judis. il *U.S. News & World Report* 106:27-9+ Mr 27 '89

A view of the Moonrise. T. H. Holt. il por *Conservative Digest* 15:36-7+ Ja/F '89

MOON

See also

Eclipses, Lunar

Lunar geology

Space flight to the moon

Tides

An afternoon occultation for the south [Regulus] il *Sky and Telescope* 77:407+ Ap '89

A bright-moon Regulus occultation. il maps *Sky and Telescope* 77:73 Ja '89

Crescent moon nicks the Pleiades. D. W. Dunham. il *Sky and Telescope* 77:405-6 Ap '89

Follow the moon. T. D. Nicholson. *Natural History* p108+ O '89

Lunar occultation highlights for 1989. D. W. Dunham. il map *Sky and Telescope* 77:68-9+ Ja '89

The moon in time and space. M. R. Chartrand. *Ad Astra* 1:60-1 Jl/Ag '89

A plethora of lunar occultations. R. Shaffer. il *Astronomy* 17:57-9 Ap '89

Regulus occulted. *Astronomy* 17:98-9 My '89

The sun, moon, and planets this month. A. MacRobert. See issues of Sky and Telescope beginning April 1988

Ups and downs of the moon [computer program] R. W. Sinnott. il *Sky and Telescope* 78:78-80 Jl '89

Waning crescent moon in the Pleiades. D. W. Dunham. il *Sky and Telescope* 78:64-5 Jl '89

Atmosphere

The moon's atmosphere [work of Andrew E. Potter and Thomas H. Morgan] *Sky and Telescope* 77:589 Je '89

Evolution

Birth of the moon [cover story] W. K. Hartmann. il *Natural History* p68-77 N '89

Making the moon, remaking earth [giant impact theory] R. A. Kerr. il *Science* 243:1433-5 Mr 17 '89

Exploration

See also

Lunar bases

Influence on man

Don't blame the moon. M. A. Frasca. il *Sky and Telescope* 78:340 O '89

Pull of the moon. P. Steinhart. il *Audubon* 91:32-4 S '89

Maps

Lunar prospecting [cover story] W. R. Farrand. il *Ad Astra* 1:8-12 F '89

Origin

See Moon—Evolution

Phases

Breaking the new-moon record. D. Di Cicco. il *Sky and Telescope* 78:322-3 S '89

Results of the July Moonwatch. L. E. Doggett and B. E. Schaefer. il map *Sky and Telescope* 77:373+ Ap '89

Photographs and photography

A busy spring for the moon. il *Astronomy* 17:92-3 Ag '89

Lunar flash mystery: solved or deepened? [satellite hypothesis] il *Sky and Telescope* 78:461 N '89

Moon slides. R. Burnham. *Astronomy* 17:96-7 Ap '89

Mysterious flash photographed on moon [work of G. Kolovos] il *Sky and Telescope* 77:468-9 My '89

Surface

Eight lunar wonders [cover story] M. T. Kitt. il *Astronomy* 17:66-71 Mr '89

Memorials on the moon [craters named for astronauts] H. Masursky and M. Strobell. il *Sky and Telescope* 77:265 Mr '89

Moon river [search for water] G. K. O'Neill. il *Omni (New York, N.Y.)* 11:20+ My '89

Observe the Apollo landing sites. M. T. Kitt. il *Astronomy* 17:66-72 Jl '89

Return to Tranquillity Base. S. J. O'Meara. il *Sky and Telescope* 78:84 Jl '89

Three lunar challenges [craters] il *Sky and Telescope* 77:520-1 My '89

MOON BASES *See* Lunar bases

MOON IN LITERATURE

Chaucer and the moon's speed. D. W. Olson and L. E. Jasinski. il *Sky and Telescope* 77:376-7 Ap '89

One small shelf for literature. T. Mallon. il *The New York Times Book Review* 94:1+ Jl 16 '89

MOON IN RELIGION, FOLKLORE, ETC.

Moon myths. il *National Geographic World* 167:25 Jl '89

MOON OVER PARADOR [film] See Motion picture reviews—Single works

MOON ROCKS *See* Lunar geology

MOON VINE *See* Moonflowers

MOONDOG

about

New York has something to howl about again—legendary street musician Moondog. M. Small. il pors *People Weekly* 32:109-10 N 27 '89

MOONEY, PATRICIA

Mountain biking just gets better and better. il por *Women's Sports & Fitness* 11:74 My '89

MOONEY AIRCRAFT CORPORATION

Socata, Mooney proceed with TBM 700 production. J. M. Lenorovitz. il *Aviation Week & Space Technology* 130:53-4 Je 26 '89

MOONEYHAM, ERIC

about

World Vision. B. Brander. il *Petersen's Photographic Magazine* 18:24-6+ Je '89

MOONFLOWERS

Moonflower brightens the night. L. A. Weathers. il *Southern Living* 24:68 Mr '89

MOONLIGHT

Elk in the full moon [night feeding myths] H. Buck. il *Field & Stream* 94:40 D '89

Winter's moon. H. Borland. il *Audubon* 91:37 Ja '89

MOONLIGHTING *See* Supplementary employment

MOONLIGHTING [television program] See Television program reviews—Single works

MOONS *See* Satellites

MOONWALKER, TU

about

By hands so deft. H. H. Stockel. il por *Americana* 17:64-7 Jl/Ag '89

MOORE, ANDREW G. T., II

about

The betting is that Judge Moore won't stop Time. M. Galen. por *Business Week* p27 Jl 31 '89

MOORE, ANNE

about

The mad modiste. J. Craugh. il por *Harper's Bazaar* 122:66 N '89

MOORE, ARCHIE, 1913-

about

The ageless warrior. F. Deford. il pors *Sports Illustrated* 70:102-6+ My 8 '89

MOORE, BLANCHE KISER TAYLOR

about

Arsenic and old lace. E. Salholz. il por *Newsweek* 114:24 Ag 14 '89

MOORE, BRIAN, 1921-
about
Walking the tightrope of mystery. J. V. Long. il por *Commonweal* 116:555-8 O 20 '89
MOORE, CARLOS
about
Word star. P. Giddings. por *Essence* 20:24 D '89
MOORE, CLEMENT CLARKE, 1779-1863
Anecdotes, facetiae, satire, etc.
St. Nicholas: a textual scandal [cover story] R. R. Lingeman and T. M. Disch. *The Nation* 248:1+ Ja 2 '89
MOORE, CURTIS A.
Trouble in the atmosphere: does your cup of coffee cause forest fires? il *International Wildlife* 19:38-45 Mr/Ap '89
Will changing your light bulb save the world? il *International Wildlife* 19:18-23 My/Je '89
MOORE, DAVID E.
Creating a global constituency for free trade [address, September 13-15, 1989] *Vital Speeches of the Day* 56:108-10 D 1 '89
MOORE, DAVID M.
about
Crunch time. L. Gite. il pors *Black Enterprise* 20:74-6+ S '89
MOORE, DEBORAH KAYE
about
Court papers say Bond denies fathering baby. por *Jet* 77:55 N 27 '89
MOORE, DEEDEE
'Martin'. il *American Visions* 4:34-9 D '89
Shooting straight: the many worlds of Gordon Parks. bibl (p174) il pors *Smithsonian* 20:66-72+ Ap '89
MOORE, DIANNE-JO
The big scoop on sugar. il *New Choices for the Best Years* 29:71-3 Je '89
MOORE, DONALD R., AND DAVENPORT, SUZANNE
High school choice and students at risk. *The Education Digest* 55:7-10 S '89
MOORE, DONNIE, 1954-1989
about
Ex-Angels reliever Moore shoots wife, kills self. il por *Jet* 76:48 Ag 7 '89
MOORE, FRAZIER
More sound for less. il *Channels (New York, N.Y.: 1986)* 9:72 Jl/Ag '89
Speeding up the cutting. il *Channels (New York, N.Y.: 1986)* 9:72 S '89
MOORE, GILBERT DEERING
Lovestruck: reigniting an old romance. il por *Ms.* 17:45-9 My '89
MOORE, HENRY, 1898-1986
about
Henry Moore: more means less. R. W. Walker. *Art News* 88:41 Ap '89
Henry Moore: Royal Academy of Arts. P. Failing. il *Art News* 88:222 Ap '89
MOORE, JOHN
about
Whose spleen is it? D. Andrews. il por *Technology Review* 92:14 N/D '89
MOORE, JOHN A.
NRDC report flawed. *Consumers' Research Magazine* 72:15 My '89
MOORE, JOHN L.
Firestorm! il *Reader's Digest* 134:77-82 Mr '89
MOORE, JOHN L.
about
John L. Moore at Tomoko Liguori. R. Berlind. *Art in America* 77:212 O '89
MOORE, JONATHAN
Confronting realities of refugee assistance [address, May 26, 1989] *Department of State Bulletin* 89:85-6 Ag '89
Developing solutions for Central American refugee problems [address, May 30, 1989] *Department of State Bulletin* 89:87-8 Ag '89
FY 1990 assistance request for refugee programs [statement, March 22, 1989] *Department of State Bulletin* 89:72-3 My '89
Update on immigration and refugee issues [statement, April 6, 1989] *Department of State Bulletin* 89:59-62 Jl '89
MOORE, JUDITH, 1940-
Save your life: notes on the value of keeping a diary. il *Utne Reader* p90-3 My/Je '89
MOORE, KENNETH, 1930-
Solidarity's many faces. il *Commonweal* 116:391-2 Jl 14 '89
MOORE, KENNY, 1943-
Back on the track. il *Sports Illustrated* 70:26-7 Je 26 '89
Big splash in Hawaii. il pors *Sports Illustrated* 71:62-4+ O 23 '89
Bionic man. il pors *Sports Illustrated* 71:80-2+ O 23 '89
Eight is not enough. il pors *Sports Illustrated* 70:40-2+ Je 12 '89
Good neighbor Sam. il pors *Sports Illustrated* 71:92-6+ S 11 '89
Hell on wheels. il pors *Sports Illustrated* 71:44-6+ Jl 17 '89

It's nifty being 50. il pors *Sports Illustrated* 71:34-6+ D 18 '89
Life without a problem. il pors *Sports Illustrated* 70 Special Issue:83-5 F '89
O rare leviathan. il pors *Sports Illustrated* 70:66-72+ My 29 '89
Quest for new conquests. il por *Sports Illustrated* 70:80-1 Je 5 '89
The spoils of victory. il pors *Sports Illustrated* 70:50-3+ Ap 10 '89
The times of their lives. il *Sports Illustrated* 71:44-7 Ag 14 '89
Up where she belongs. il pors *Sports Illustrated* 70:98-101 Ja 9 '89
Uplifted, gently, by sport. il por *Sports Illustrated* 71 Special Issue:234 N 15 '89
MOORE, KENNY, 1943-, AND VADER, J. E.
Living a dream. il pors *Sports Illustrated* 71:70+ N 27 '89
MOORE, LORRIE
The Jewish hunter [story] *The New Yorker* 65:48-58 N 13 '89
Two boys [story] il *Gentlemen's Quarterly* 59:211+ Ap '89
You're ugly, too [story] *The New Yorker* 65:30-40 Jl 3 '89
MOORE, MARNIE
about
Keeping it in the family. D. Guerre. il pors *Harper's Bazaar* 122:174-7+ Ap '89
MOORE, MARY ROSALIE
Tapestries in Spain [poem] *America* 160:513 My 27 '89
MOORE, MARY TYLER
about
Mary Tyler Moore. il pors *People Weekly* 31 Special Issue:34-5 Summ '89
MOORE, MICHAEL
about
Goodbye, Michael. W. Balliett. *The New Yorker* 65:133-7 N 6 '89
MOORE, MICHAEL
about
Michael & me [interview; cover story] H. Jacobson. il pors *Film Comment* 25:16-18+ N/D '89
Roger & me [film] Reviews
American Film il por 15:14 N '89. A. Insdorf
The Nation 249:505-6 O 30 '89. S. Klawans
New York 22:102-3 D 18 '89. D. Denby
Newsweek il por 114:113 O 9 '89. C. Leerhsen
MOORE, PETER D.
New ways to reach your customers. por *Fortune* 120:210 N 6 '89
MOORE, RAY
A race against time. il *World Tennis* 37:96 O '89
MOORE, SHELLEY
Riding the wind. il *Black Enterprise* 19:119 My '89
MOORE, SYLVIA
Health across barriers. il *World Health* p18-19 My '89
MOORE, THOMAS ANDREW
(jt. auth) See Gust, Devens, and Moore, Thomas Andrew
MOORE, THOMAS J., 1944-
The cholesterol myth [excerpt from Heart failure; cover story] il *The Atlantic* 264:37-40+ S '89
about
Cholesterol confusion. G. Cowley. il *Newsweek* 114:68-9 S 18 '89
Don't go back to butter. A. Purvis. il *Time* 134:108+ O 9 '89
Taking aim at doctors' dire warnings, Thomas Moore triggers a cholesterol debate. M. H. J. Farrell. il pors *People Weekly* 32:125-6 N 13 '89
MOORE, WAYNE S.
What's the diagnosis? See issues of Flower and Garden beginning February/March 1984
MOORE (HENRY) SCULPTURE GARDEN See Henry Moore Sculpture Garden
MOOREA (FRENCH POLYNESIA)
Description and travel
Gourmet holidays: Society Islands. C. Bates. il map *Gourmet* 49:36-41+ Ja '89
MOORING OF BOATS See Anchorage
MOORLAND-SPINGARN RESEARCH CENTER LIBRARY
Moorland-Spingarn Research Center. K. L. Jefferson. il *American Visions* 4:46-7 Ag '89
MOORMAN, MARGARET
States of grace. il por *Art News* 88:118-22 Ja '89
MOOSE
Contamination
Swedish moose a la cesium 137 [high concentration of radiation in muscle tissue following Chernobyl accident] il *Environment* 31:22-3 My '89
MOOSEHORN NATIONAL WILDLIFE REFUGE (ME.)
Unnatural habitat [woodcock preservation] K. Morrison. il *Country Journal* 16:39-43 S/O '89
MOOSHEI, BRUNO
about
The martini master. S. Kettmann. il por *Gentlemen's Quarterly* 59:72+ My '89

MORA, PHILIPPE, 1949-
about
Communion [film] Reviews
  People Weekly il 32:19 N 27 '89. R. Novak
MORAIN, MARY
Population update. See issues of The Humanist beginning
  July/August 1986
MORAL CODES *See* Ethics
MORAL DEVELOPMENT
Beginners' ethics. L. G. Katz. il *Parents* 64:213 D '89
MORAL EDUCATION
Catch of a lifetime [son learns about ethics from fishing
  with father] J. P. Lenfestey. il *Reader's Digest* 134:111-12
  F '89
Communicating your values. B. Weissbourd. il *Parents* 64:207
  My '89
Educating the moral child [elementary students] T. Lickona.
  The Education Digest 55:45-7 S '89
Ethics education for the gifted. A. Roeper. *The Education
  Digest* 54:37-9 F '89
Explaining today to yesterday [cover story] W. J. O'Malley.
  il *America* 161:254-7 O 21 '89
Higher education and a civilization in trouble [address,
  November 15, 1988] J. A. Howard. *Vital Speeches of
  the Day* 55:314-18 Mr 1 '89
The journey to justice [cover story] W. J. O'Malley. *America*
  161:28-31 Jl 15-22 '89
The new moral classroom. E. Smith. il *Psychology Today*
  23:32-6 My '89
Parents: sixties hippies, eighties babies. Ram Dass. il *American
  Health* 8:54 O '89
Taking a lesson from dad. L. Levinger. il *New Choices
  for the Best Years* 29:79-80 N '89
Teaching character development [Child Development Project
  in Danville, Calif.] W. Streshly and E. Schaps. *The
  Education Digest* 54:25-8 Mr '89
Teaching your kids values. J. P. Comer. il *Parents* 64:220
  N '89
The third wave of school reform [excerpt from The blackboard
  fumble; cover story] E. L. Boyer. il *Christianity Today*
  33:16-19 S 22 '89
The trouble with being open-minded [address, July 18, 1989]
  D. B. Lockerbie. *Vital Speeches of the Day* 55:723-7 S
  15 '89
The true purpose of education [cultivation of wisdom and
  virtue] H. B. Gow. il *Phi Delta Kappan* 70:545-6 Mr
  '89
MORAL JUDGMENT *See* Judgment (Ethics)
MORAL MAJORITY
Exit right. L. Cryderman. *Christianity Today* 33:15 Ag 18
  '89
Falwell claims victory, dissolves Moral Majority. R. Walker.
  por *Christianity Today* 33:58-9 Jl 14 '89
Scrapping the Moral Majority. *Time* 133:26 Je 26 '89
MORAL PHILOSOPHY *See* Ethics
MORAL THEOLOGY *See* Christian ethics
MORALE
  See also
  Employee morale
  Optimism
The dance of revolution. J. Jordan. il *The Progressive* 53:11-12
  Ag '89
MORALE, NATIONAL
The American adventure. G. Bush. il por *Popular Mechanics*
  166:22-3 My '89
Fear of living [cover story] H. Fairlie. *The New Republic*
  200:14+ Ja 23 '89
How Reagan changed America [cover story] G. F. Will.
  il pors *Newsweek* 113:12-17 Ja 9 '89
National character is decisive [address, April 27, 1989] A.
  Harrigan. *Vital Speeches of the Day* 55:507-11 Je 1 '89
Timidity [address, April 6, 1989] T. H. Kean. *Vital Speeches
  of the Day* 55:488-90 Je 1 '89
Where have all the risk takers gone? [address, March 29,
  1989] C. J. Silas. *Vital Speeches of the Day* 55:530-3
  Je 15 '89
The wonder year. *The Nation* 249:551-2 N 13 '89
Argentina
Have a nice day! F. Rellim. il *World Press Review* 36:56
  Ag '89
Australia
My bicentenary message [address, December 2, 1988] A.
  H. Pollard. *Vital Speeches of the Day* 55:346-9 Mr 15
  '89
Canada
Canadians cope, Americans conquer. A. Fotheringham. *World
  Press Review* 36:36 Ap '89
Signing away Canada's soul [free trade agreement with the
  U.S.; adaptation of address, May 1988] R. Davies. il
  Harper's 278:43-7 Ja '89
A spotlight on Canadians [Maclean's/Decima poll; cover
  story; special section; with introd. by Allan R. Gregg
  and editorial comment by Kevin Doyle] il *Maclean's* 102:2,
  8-20+ Ja 2 '89
  Anecdotes, facetiae, satire, etc.
Oy, Canada [J. Queenan's views] M. Richler. il *Gentlemen's
  Quarterly* 59:181+ Mr '89

Germany (West)
The hazards of an unusable past. J. M. Wall. *The Christian
  Century* 106:195-6 F 22 '89
Soviet Union
Punk *perestroika* [pessimistic mood in Moscow; cover story]
  M. Walker. il *The New Republic* 201:22+ D 4 '89
What *glasnost* has destroyed. L. Aron. *Commentary* 88:30-4
  N '89
United States
  See Morale, National
MORALES, FERNANDO SOLANA *See* Solana Morales, Fer-
  nando
MORALITY *See* Ethics
MORALITY AND RELIGION *See* Christian ethics
MORALS *See* Ethics
MORALS AND LITERATURE *See* Literature—Moral and
  religious aspects
MORALS AND POLITICS *See* Political ethics
MORALS AND WAR *See* War and morals
MORAN, JIM
  about
Jim Moran, master salesman. G. Button. il pors *Forbes*
  144 Special Issue:54-5+ O 23 '89
MORAN, JOSEPH M., AND OTHERS
Glacial geology. il map *Earth Science* 41:16-18 Wint '88
MORAN, NANCY A.
A 48-million-year-old aphid-host plant association and com-
  plex life cycle: biogeographic evidence. bibl f il map *Science*
  245:173-5 Jl 14 '89
MORAN, PAUL
Breeders' Cup. il *Sports Illustrated* 71:11+ O 23 '89
MORAN, RICHARD
Bring back the Mafia. por *Newsweek* 114:8 Ag 7 '89
MORAVEC, HANS P.
  about
Interview: Hans Moravec. E. Regis. por *Omni (New York,
  N.Y.)* 11:74-6+ Ag '89
MORAVIAN CHURCH
  Nicaragua
Faith and endurance in eastern Nicaragua. M. D. Wilde.
  The Christian Century 106:973-4 N 1 '89
MORAVIAN POTTERY *See* Pottery, Moravian
MORDDEN, ETHAN, 1947-
"Show boat" crosses over. *The New Yorker* 65:79-94 Jl 3
  '89
MOREAU, GUSTAVE, 1826-1878
  about
The master and Moreau. H. James. il *Art News* 88:23 My
  '89
MOREAU, JEAN-PIERRE
Brazil's 'Citizen Globo'. il por *World Press Review* 36:56
  Jl '89
MORECAMBE (ENGLAND)
  Theater
  See also
  Winter Gardens (Morecambe, England)
MOREHOUSE COLLEGE
Fraternity members punished for role in student's death
  at Morehouse College. *Jet* 77:13 N 6 '89
Oprah Winfrey gives gift of $1 million to Morehouse to
  help educate black men. il por *Jet* 76:4 Je 5 '89
MOREHOUSE SCHOOL OF MEDICINE
Dr. Sullivan to get $215,000 in severance pay; Senators
  see no conflict in HHS post. il por *Jet* 76:38 Ap 17
  '89
MOREII (WORD PROCESSOR PROGRAM) *See* Word proc-
  essors and processing—Programming
MOREIRA, RAFAEL DE FARIA D.
Portuguese art in the maritime era. il *The Courier (Unesco)*
  42:35-6 Ap '89
MORELLA, JOE, AND EPSTEIN, EDWARD Z.
Paul and Joanne—their real life story [excerpt] pors *Good
  Housekeeping* 208:72+ Ja '89
MORELLO, JOE
  about
Joe Morello. D. Helland. il por *Down Beat* 56:14 D '89
MOREM, SALLY
Taking full measure. *Ad Astra* 1:48 F '89
MORETTI, LAURA
(jt. auth) See Toussaint, Danielle, and Moretti, Laura
MORGAN, AMANDA
Happy stepfamilies: what are they doing right? il *Redbook*
  173:128-9+ My '89
MORGAN, CARRIE
Red my lips. il *Seventeen* 48:161 Ag '89
MORGAN, DAVID
The Protestant struggle with the image. il *The Christian
  Century* 106:308-11 Mr 22-29 '89
Stalking the spiritual in the visual arts [cover story] il *The
  Christian Century* 106:1152-5 D 6 '89
MORGAN, DEBBI
  about
Debbi Morgan: feeling good. J. D. Cain. il pors *Essence*
  20:105-6+ S '89
MORGAN, DIANA VIVIAN
Finding the exerciser in you. il *Health (New York, N.Y.)*
  21:38-9 Mr '89

MORGAN, DIANE
The cave [poem] *Wilderness* 52:xiii Spr '89
MORGAN, DONNA
about
Fashion statement. S. Stephens. il *Architectural Digest* 46:92-7
Jl '89
MORGAN, ELIZABETH, 1947-
about
A courageous mother's first taste of freedom [cover story]
J. S. Podesta and P. Chin. il pors *People Weekly* 32:78-80+
O 16 '89
Elizabeth Morgan. il pors *People Weekly* 32:97-8 D 25 '89-Ja
1 '90
Elizabeth Morgan's brother risks jail as he joins her in
defying a Washington judge. D. Grogan. il pors *People
Weekly* 32:38-40 Jl 3 '89
A hard case of contempt. J. Elson. il por *Time* 134:66
S 18 '89
Morganatic marriage. *The New Republic* 201:4+ Jl 31 '89
A mother's 759 days of defiance. il por *U.S. News & World
Report* 107:12-13 O 9 '89
Stalemate for high stakes. P. Chin and J. S. Podesta. il
pors *People Weekly* 31:84-5 Ja 23 '89
Update on Elizabeth Morgan. il por *Glamour* 87:116 S '89
Vowing to protect her child from rape, Elizabeth Morgan
faces her 23rd month in jail. P. Chin. il pors *People
Weekly* 31:113-15+ Je 12 '89
Who's to judge? M. Szegedy-Maszak. il pors *The New York
Times Magazine* p28-9+ My 21 '89
MORGAN, ELIZABETH L.
Parent-teacher communication techniques. *The Education
Digest* 55:32-5 O '89
MORGAN, FRANK
about
Thirty years of hard practice. D. Okrent. il por *Esquire*
112:28 Jl '89
MORGAN, J. W.
(jt. auth) See Walker, R. J., and Morgan, J. W.
MORGAN, JAMES
Loafer with the fringe on top. il *Gentlemen's Quarterly* 59:39
Je '89
MORGAN, JOAN
Sexism comes in all colors. *Utne Reader* p48-9 N/D '89
MORGAN, JOHN PIERPONT, 1837-1913
about
The magnitude of J. P. Morgan. J. S. Gordon. bibl il pors
American Heritage 40:78-9+ Jl/Ag '89
MORGAN, LEN
Vectors. See issues of Flying
MORGAN, LESLIE
Desperate odds. *Seventeen* 48:257+ Mr '89
Why are girls obsessed with their weight? il *Seventeen*
48:118-19+ N '89
MORGAN, MARY, 1943-
about
Baby guru Dr. Spock grows up in memoir from Pantheon.
J. Crichton. pors *Publishers Weekly* 236:25 O 13 '89
MORGAN, MICHAEL
about
On the upbeat: two young conductors. S. J. Branch. il pors
American Visions 4:22-6 Ag '89
MORGAN, MIKE
about
Pitching like a new man. B. Anderson. il por *Sports Illustrated*
70:73 Je 26 '89
MORGAN, MONROE T.
A world fit to live in. il *World Health* p25-7 My '89
MORGAN, NEIL BOWEN, 1924-
Where two Californias meet: San Diego. il map *National
Geographic* 176:176-205 Ag '89
MORGAN, ROBERT M.
about
Elizabeth Morgan's brother risks jail as he joins her in
defying a Washington judge. D. Grogan. il pors *People
Weekly* 32:38-40 Jl 3 '89
MORGAN, ROBIN
The demon lover [excerpt] il *Ms.* 17:68-72 Mr '89
MORGAN, SHERLEY WARNER
about
Family ties. C. Brown. il *House & Garden* 161:128-35 Je
'89
MORGAN, TED, 1932-
L'affaire Touvier: opening old wounds. il pors *The New
York Times Magazine* p32-3+ O 1 '89
MORGAN, THOMAS BRUCE, 1926-
John Vachon: a certain look [cover story] il por *American
Heritage* 40:94-109 F '89
MORGAN, TIMOTHY
The people's space program. *Ad Astra* 1:48 Ja '89
MORGAN (J. P.) & CO. INCORPORATED See J. P. Morgan
& Co. Incorporated
MORGAN (PIERPONT) LIBRARY See Pierpont Morgan
Library
MORGAN CITY (LA.)
Pollution
Something stinks in Morgan City [case of Marine Shale
Processors plant] C. Strickland. il *The Nation* 249:448-51
O 23 '89

MORGAN CREEK PRODUCTIONS
From cars to stars. P. Newcomb. il pors *Forbes* 143:60-1
Ja 23 '89
MORGAN GRENFELL GROUP PLC
Deutsche Bank nabs a plum—but it didn't come cheap.
J. Templeman. il *Business Week* p102 D 11 '89
MORGAN STANLEY AND COMPANY
Count your blessings? [involved in dispute with investors
over Silgan Corp. buyout] R. L. Stern. il *Forbes* 144:14
N 13 '89
Hello sweetheart, get me mergers and acquisitions [S. Rattner]
P. Weiss. *The Washington Monthly* 21:67-8 F '89
A last hurrah for stocks? [interview with B. Biggs] J. Mendes.
il por *Fortune* 120:46-8 Ag 28 '89
The Rattner years [departure of S. Rattner] P. Noglows.
il por *Channels (New York, N.Y.: 1986)* 9:73 Jl/Ag '89
**MORGAN STANLEY ASSET MANAGEMENT/CHICAGO
GROUP**
Telltale signs of bargain stocks [interview with T. S. White]
il por *Fortune* 119:30+ Ja 16 '89
MORGENROTH, LYNDA
High-risk pain pills. il *The Atlantic* 264:36+ D '89
MORGENSTEIN, GARY
Are these huddles? Or muddles? il *TV Guide* 37:37-8 N
18-24 '89
MORGENSTERN, JOE
The banker who robbed banks. il pors *The New York Times
Magazine* p54-6+ N 12 '89
The recording angel. il *The New York Times Magazine*
p20+ O 15 '89
Tim Burton, Batman and the Joker. il por *The New York
Times Magazine* p44-6+ Ap 9 '89
TV's big turnoff [cover story] il por *The New York Times
Magazine* p12-15+ Ja 1 '89
MORGENTALER, HENRY
about
A crusader's challenge. G. Allen. il por *Maclean's* 102:14-15
N 6 '89
A network of clinics. P. Kopvillem. il por *Maclean's* 102:19
Jl 31 '89
MORGENTHAU, HANS JOACHIM, 1904-
U.S. misadventure in Vietnam [reprint from January 1968
issue] *Current History* 88:32-4+ Ja '89
MORI, HANAE
about
Hanae Mori: East meets West in the designer's Paris residence.
C. Aillaud. il por *Architectural Digest* 46:152-7 S '89
MORIMURA, YASUMASA
about
Yasumasa Morimura at NW House. J. Koplos. il por *Art
in America* 77:189 Je '89
MORISON, SAMUEL LORING
about
How we got an Official Secrets Act. N. Hentoff. il *The
Progressive* 53:10-11 Mr '89
The quiet coup. P. Weiss. il *Harper's* 279:54-65 S '89
MORITA, AKIO
about
America-bashing, Japanese style. J. Impoco. pors *U.S. News
& World Report* 107:45 O 16 '89
A Japanese view: why America has fallen behind. por *Fortune*
120:52 S 25 '89
Morita: 'We need American leadership' [interview] J. Schwartz.
il por *Newsweek* 114:66 O 9 '89
Sony's Morita bashes back. por *Business Week* p58 O 16
'89
MORLEY, JEFFERSON
Aftermath of a crack article. il *The Nation* 249:592+ N
20 '89
Contradictions of cocaine capitalism [cover story] il *The
Nation* 249:341-7 O 2 '89
Demonizing D'Aubuisson. il *The Nation* 248:624-6 My 8
'89
What crack is like. *The New Republic* 201:12-13 O 2 '89
about
Attitude problem. *The New Republic* 201:4+ O 9 '89
Kinsley does it again. R. E. Tyrrell. *The American Spectator*
22:10-11 D '89
MORLEY, MALCOLM
about
Malcolm Morley at Pace. K. Johnson. il *Art in America*
77:159-60 F '89
Sanctuary for art [interview] D. Kazanjian. il por *House
& Garden* 161:150-5+ My '89
MORMONS AND MORMONISM
See also
Brigham Young University
Converts from Mormonism
Why Mormonism is the fastest growing religion in the West.
W. J. Whalen. il *U.S. Catholic* 54:28-34 Je '89
MORNING GLORIES
See also
Moonflowers
MOROCCAN HOUSE DECORATION See House decoration,
Moroccan

MOROCCAN MUSIC *See* Music, Moroccan
MOROCCO
   See also
     Essaouira (Morocco)
     Geology—Morocco
     Industry and state—Morocco
     Jahjouka (Morocco)
     Palaces—Morocco
     Skiing—Morocco
     Tangier (Morocco)
     United Nations—Morocco
      Description and travel
Casablanca going south. P. Schneider. il *Esquire* 111:22+ Ja '89
      Industries
   See also
     Omnium Nord-Africain (Firm)
     Photographs and photography
A photographer's guide to Morocco. P. Slaughter. il *Petersen's Photographic Magazine* 17:76-7 F '89
      Territorial expansion
   See also
     Western Sahara conflict, 1975-
MOROWITZ, HAROLD J.
Models, theory, and the matrix of biological knowledge. bibl f il *BioScience* 39:177-9 Mr '89
MORPHOGENESIS
   See also
     Differentiation (Biology)
Morphogenesis of the polarized epithelial cell phenotype. E. Rodriguez-Boulan and W. J. Nelson. bibl f il *Science* 245:718-25 Ag 18 '89
MORPHOLOGY
   See also
     Body size
     Cyclomorphosis
     Homology (Biology)
     Morphogenesis
     Phyllotaxis
Spiral effect [shapes occuring in nature] J. Carey. il *National Wildlife* 27:52-9 Ap/My '89
MORPHONIOS, ELLEN
Crime & punishment: a view from a broad; ed. by Linda Marx. il pors *People Weekly* 32:79-80+ Jl 3 '89
MORPHOSIS (FIRM)
Heavy metal [L. Max showroom in Los Angeles] A. Betsky. il *Architectural Record* 177:86-93 mid-S '89
Morphosis at the Walker Arts Center [Three houses exhibit] D. R. Suisman. il *Architectural Record* 177:65 Jl '89
MORRELL (JOHN) & CO. *See* John Morrell & Co.
MORRIS, BENNY, 1948-
     about
Charging Israel with original sin. S. Teveth. bibl f *Commentary* 88:24-33 S '89
MORRIS, BERNADINE
Adolfo in New York. il por *Architectural Digest* 46:132-7 S '89
MORRIS, BOB
35mm motions. il *Film Comment* 25:47-9 Mr/Ap '89
MORRIS, CARL A., 1911-
     about
Carl Morris at Foster/White. M. Kangas. il *Art in America* 77:271 Ap '89
MORRIS, CAROL J.
Garden secrets from the Hmong. il *Flower and Garden* 33:36-8 Mr/Ap '89
MORRIS, CATHERINE E., AND SIGURDSON, WADE J.
Stretch-inactivated ion channels coexist with stretch-activated ion channels. bibl f il *Science* 243:807-9 F 10 '89
MORRIS, CHARLES R.
The coming global boom [cover story; with editorial comment] il *The Atlantic* 264:6, 51-8+ O '89
Deficit figuring doesn't add up. il *The New York Times Magazine* p36+ F 12 '89
MORRIS, DANIEL
Do Catholic couples view having kids as a given? il *U.S. Catholic* 54:32-7 My '89
Families in trouble: how to know when to get help. il *U.S. Catholic* 54:30-6 Ag '89
Mom liked you best: how Christians outgrow sibling rivalry [cover story] il *U.S. Catholic* 54:6-12 Ja '89
MORRIS, DAVID J.
The materials we need to create a sustainable society lie close to home. il *Utne Reader* p84-5+ N/D '89
MORRIS, EDMUND
Mr. Woodcutter, spare that tree! il *The New York Times Magazine* p20+ Mr 5 '89
MORRIS, ERROL
     about
'Because I was a nobody'. D. Hill. il pors *TV Guide* 37:20-2 My 20-26 '89
Crossing 'The thin blue line'. M. Lasswell. il por *Rolling Stone* p30 O 19 '89
Department of amplification. M. Singer. *The New Yorker* 65:119-20 Ap 10 '89
A movie for the defense. J. N. Baker. il por *Newsweek* 113:27 Mr 13 '89

Profiles. M. Singer. por *The New Yorker* 64:38-40+ F 6 '89
The thin blue line [film] Reviews
   America 160:94-5 F 4 '89. R. A. Blake
MORRIS, FRED B.
What can Central America expect from the Bush administration? il *The Christian Century* 106:472-5 My 3 '89
MORRIS, GEOFFREY, 1932-
The blackboard jungle revisited. *National Review* 41:18-19 My 5 '89
The mark of Kean. *National Review* 41:17-18 Je 16 '89
MORRIS, GITTA
Sweet lilacs. il *Americana* 17:44-9 My/Je '89
MORRIS, JAMES, 1926-
   See also
     Morris, Jan, 1926-
MORRIS, JAN, 1926-
Journey's end [excerpt from Pleasures of a tangled life] il *House & Garden* 161:128+ S '89
MORRIS, JIM
     about
A kinder, gentler comic. D. Blum. il pors *New York* 22:26 Ja 23 '89
Who says first impressions are lasting? When the U.S. changed presidents, Jim Morris did too. il por *People Weekly* 31:73 My 15 '89
MORRIS, JOE
     about
Joe says it's so: New York Giants star Joe Morris reconditions for the long road back. A. Tardio. il pors *Gentlemen's Quarterly* 59:314-18+ N '89
MORRIS, LOIS B.
Putting pessimism in its place. il *Health (New York, N.Y.)* 21:62-3 Ag '89
Social anxiety. il *Health (New York, N.Y.)* 21:50-1+ S '89
Spotting Mr. Wrong . . . early. il *Health (New York, N.Y.)* 21:34-5 N '89
MORRIS, MARK
     about
L'allegro, il penseroso ed il moderato [dance] Reviews
   The New Yorker 64:61-3 Ja 16 '89. A. Croce
An American in Brussels. J. Dupont. il pors *The New York Times Magazine* p22-3+ Ja 22 '89
The Brussels chapter begins: Mark Morris comes to town (Brussels). L. Moffett. il *Dance Magazine* 63:32-3 F '89
Dancing:
   Comparison of W. Forsythe and M. Morris. A. Croce. *The New Yorker* 65:70-2 Jl 31 '89
Dido and Aeneas [dance] Reviews
   Dance Magazine il por 63:62 Je '89. L. Moffett
   New York il por 22:59 Je 26 '89. T. Tobias
Kiss kiss, bang bang. T. Tobias. il *New York* 22:106+ D 11 '89
Like Bejart before him, Morris scandalizes Brussels. L. Moffett. il por *Dance Magazine* 63:12 Jl '89
MORRIS, MICHAEL
Editor's notes. See issues of Home Mechanix beginning February 1989
MORRIS, PHIL
     about
Mission: possible. il pors *Ebony* 44:70+ Je '89
MORRIS, ROBERT, 1734-1806
     about
What your country can do for you. J. Willoughby. il por *Forbes* 144 Special Issue:104+ O 23 '89
MORRIS, ROBERT, 1931-
Three folds in the fabric and four autobiographical asides as allegories (or interruptions). il *Art in America* 77:142-51 N '89
MORRIS, ROBERT T., JR.
     about
Hackers: is a cure worse than the disease? M. Lewyn. por *Business Week* p37-8 D 4 '89
Revenge of the nerds. N. Martin. il *The Washington Monthly* 20:21-2+ Ja '89
MORRIS, ROGER
Contemporary Southwest. il *Architectural Digest* 46:148-55 Ap '89
MORRIS, S. CONWAY *See* Conway Morris, S.
MORRIS, SAMUEL SOLOMON, D. 1989
     about
Obituary
   Jet por 76:51 Ap 17 '89
MORRIS, SCOT
Games. See issues of Omni (New York, N.Y.)
MORRIS, STEPHEN R.
Strong, silent and suffering. por *Newsweek* 113:10-11 Ap 3 '89
MORRIS, STEVELAND *See* Wonder, Stevie
MORRIS, WILLIAM, 1834-1896
     about
Kelmscott Manor. J. Marsh. il *History Today* 39:62-3 Ap '89
Red House in Kent. E. Lambert. il *Architectural Digest* 46:126+ Ap '89
MORRIS, WILLIE
Faulkner's Mississippi [cover story] il por *National Geographic* 175:312-39 Mr '89

MORRIS, WRIGHT, 1910-
Uno más [story] *The New Yorker* 64:28-31 F 6 '89
MORRIS (WILLIAM) AGENCY *See* William Morris Agency
MORRIS CHAIRS *See* Chairs
MORRISON, BRUCE A.
about
Sticking it to the taxpayers. D. Corn. il *The Nation* 249:238-40 S 4-11 '89
MORRISON, DAVID
about
Bar Harbor, RFD. R. Sassaman. il por *Country Journal* 16:76-80 S/O '89
MORRISON, DAVID, 1940-
(jt. auth) See Chapman, Clark R., and Morrison, David, 1940-
MORRISON, DAVID C.
The build-down. il *The Atlantic* 263:60-4 Je '89
MORRISON, FREDERIC, D. 1989
about
Obituary
Jet il pors 76:9 Ag 14 '89
MORRISON, JAMES
about
James Morrison. B. Milkowski. il por *Down Beat* 56:14 N '89
MORRISON, JIM, 1943-1971
about
The night the Lizard King came to dinner [excerpt from Wonderland Avenue] D. Sugerman. il *Rolling Stone* p31-3+ F 23 '89
MORRISON, KEN, 1918-
Unnatural habitat. il *Country Journal* 16:39-43 S/O '89
MORRISON, MAGGIE
How much is too much sun? il *Redbook* 173:12 Ag '89
Natural herbal remedies. il *Redbook* 174:18 D '89
MORRISON, MARK
"It's hard being the child of movie stars" [cover story] il pors *Redbook* 173:98+ O '89
Woody Harrelson's horrible secret—"my father's in jail for murder". il por *Redbook* 173:42+ S '89
MORRISON, MICAH
The world according to Spike Lee [cover story] por *National Review* 41:24-5 Ag 4 '89
MORRISON, NIGEL A., AND OTHERS
1,25-dihydroxyvitamin D-responsive element and glucocorticoid repression in the osteocalcin gene. bibl f il *Science* 246:1158-61 D 1 '89
MORRISON, PHILIP
Books. See issues of Scientific American
MORRISON, STEVEN A., 1951-, AND WINSTON, CLIFFORD, 1952-
Airline deregulation and public policy. bibl f *Science* 245:707-11 Ag 18 '89
MORRISON, TONI, 1931-
about
The pain of being black [interview] B. Angelo. il por *Time* 133:120-2 My 22 '89
The Toni award. *The New Republic* 200:9-10 Je 19 '89
Toni Morrison, Kenneth Clark get honorary degrees during Harvard University graduation. il pors *Jet* 76:13 Je 26 '89
MORRISON-KNUDSEN CO., INC.
Bill Agee gets a second chance. C. Knowlton. il por *Fortune* 119:94-6 Mr 27 '89
This time for sure. il *Forbes* 143:124 Ja 9 '89
MORRISSEY, KEVIN
about
Season to Taste Books: a comfy (and kitschy) culinary store. M. McQuade. il pors *Publishers Weekly* 236:45-6 S 8 '89
MORRISSEY, PAUL
about
Spike of Bensonhurst [film] Reviews
Video 13:59 Ap '89. J. Walker
MORRO BAY (CALIF.)
Kayaking, biking, or hiking around Morro Bay. il map *Sunset* (*Central West edition*) 183:14+ O '89
MORROW, JAMES
The best children's shows on cable. il *TV Guide* 37:16-17+ F 25-Mr 3 '89
The best children's shows on TV [cover story] il *TV Guide* 37:12-14+ F 18-24 '89
MORROW, RICHARD H.
New weapons. il *World Health* p9-11 Je '89
MORROW, RICHARD MARTIN
about
First-rate company. J. Cook. il por *Forbes* 143:84+ My 1 '89
MORROW, TRACY L.
about
Atlanta suit to examine black-on-black bias. *Jet* 76:7 Je 12 '89
MORROW (WILLIAM) & CO., INC. *See* William Morrow & Co., Inc.
MORSE, LIBBY
(jt. auth) See Makos, Jeff, and Morse, Libby

MORSE, SUZANNE W.
Developing the citizen leader [address, August 18, 1989] *Vital Speeches of the Day* 56:79-81 N 15 '89
MORSVIAZSPUTNIK
Soviet satellite agency to provide technical aid to Inmarsat. *Aviation Week & Space Technology* 131:81 Ag 21 '89
MORTALITY
See also
Asthma—Mortality
Blacks—Mortality
Cancer—Mortality
Celebrities—Mortality
Death
Dolphins—Mortality
Esophagus—Cancer—Mortality
Executives—Mortality
Infant mortality
Mothers—Mortality
Scientists—Mortality
Veterans—Mortality
Acid rain—one of America's worst killers. il *Utne Reader* p61-2 S/O '89
Chernobyl fallout. S. Shulman. il *Technology Review* 92:12-13 F/Mr '89
The deadly cost of 65 mph [study of rural interstate highway fatalities in New Mexico] J. Raloff. *Science News* 136:294 N 4 '89
U.S. health: the good and the bad. *Science News* 135:188 Mr 25 '89
Developing countries
Maternal death: a preventable tragedy. il *UN Chronicle* 26:46-7 S '89
MORTAR
Repoint mortar joints. il *The Family Handyman* 39:48-9 S '89
MORTGAGE BANKERS ASSOCIATION OF AMERICA
Cyclical calm [views of W. Lasko] R. T. Grieves. il por *Forbes* 143:322 Ja 9 '89
MORTGAGE BANKS
See also
Mortgage Bankers Association of America
MORTGAGE BONDS AND NOTES
See also
Real estate mortgage investment conduits
At 20% yields, these CMO REITS make junk bonds look safe. il *Money* 18:16+ Ap '89
Back to basics [Ginnie Maes] B. Weberman. il *Forbes* 143:405 My 1 '89
Carving up mortgages [collateralized mortgage obligation residuals] B. Weberman. il *Forbes* 143:165 Mr 6 '89
For serious buyers only [tax-frees; views of Michael C. Brilley] B. Weberman. il *Forbes* 144:163 D 25 '89
Freddie and Fannie clean up after the S&L mess. C. Yang. il *Business Week* p112-13 Je 5 '89
Ginnie's and Freddie's more predictable cousins [collateralized mortgage obligations] D. H. Dunn. *Business Week* p104 F 13 '89
Going-out-of-business sale [Ginnie Mae outlook brightens as CD rates go down] B. Weberman. il *Forbes* 144:229 S 18 '89
A good time to meet Fannie, Freddie, or Ginnie. D. Zigas. *Business Week* p128 S 11 '89
Hidden options. B. Weberman. il *Forbes* 144:255 O 2 '89
How a real estate highflier flamed out [Residential Resources Mortgage Investments Corp.] D. Zigas. il *Business Week* p90 Mr 6 '89
Time for another date with Ginnie Mae? [collateralized mortgage obligations] T. Thompson. il *U.S. News & World Report* 107:77 O 9 '89
Zombie bonds [thrifts] M. Schifrin. il *Forbes* 143:70 Ap 3 '89
MORTGAGE BROKERS
See also
Equity Programs Investment Corporation
Puller Mortgage Associates, Inc.
The mortgage maze. G. W. Weinstein. il *Ms.* 17:36+ Je '89
Federal aid
Another financial mess [defaults in HUD's program that deputizes firms to issue and underwrite mortgages] M. Schifrin. il *Forbes* 144:10 Jl 10 '89
Come and get it [federal government deputizes mortgage brokers to approve and coinsure FHA mortgages] M. Schifrin. il *Forbes* 143:41-2 My 15 '89
The plot thickens [defaults in HUD's program that deputizes brokers to underwrite mortgages] M. Schifrin. il *Forbes* 144:10 O 30 '89
MORTGAGE INSURANCE *See* Insurance, Mortgage
MORTGAGES
See also
Discrimination in mortgages
Equity sharing mortgages
Federal Agricultural Mortgage Corporation
Federal Home Loan Mortgage Corporation
Federal National Mortgage Association
Foreclosure
Home equity conversion
Insurance, Mortgage

MORTGAGES—See also—*cont.*

United States. Federal Home Loan Bank Board

A break on big mortgages. W. Giese. il *Changing Times* 43:22 Mr '89

Crumbling foundations. A. Bladen. il *Forbes* 143:159 My 15 '89

Digging their own graves? [adjustable rate mortgages' impact on thrifts] H. Rudnitsky. il *Forbes* 143:44-5 My 29 '89

Do you know where your mortgage is? Or whether your property taxes and insurance premiums have been paid? il *Consumer Reports* 54:441 Jl '89

Financing options for today's home buyers. G. James-Gallagher and R. E. Barnes. il *Black Enterprise* 20:41-2 N '89

Finding the way to pay for your dream [price level adjusted and adjustable rate mortgages] T. Thompson. il *U.S. News & World Report* 106:74-5 Ap 17 '89

Happy returns in home loans. A. P. Tobias. il *Time* 134:44 Jl 3 '89

How to cope with lending rate gloom. G. Anrig, Jr. il *Money* 18:70-2+ My '89

Making homes affordable [price level adjusted mortgages] J. A. Schnepper. il *USA Today (Periodical)* 118:25 N '89

Mortgages to warm your home and wallet [energy efficient mortgages] I. Hellman. il *Money* 18:24+ N '89

My banker wouldn't back my building [futile attempt to obtain mortgage for office space] J. DeParle. il *The Washington Monthly* 20:30-1 Ja '89

New pluses in adjustable-rate mortgages. M. Rowland. *Working Woman* 14:59 Mr '89

The next big housing scandal [excessively high mortgage loans made by DRG Funding] il *U.S. News & World Report* 107:27 Jl 3 '89

On the home front [lifetime mortgages] D. P. Wiener. il *U.S. News & World Report* 107:80 D 25 '89-Ja 1 '90

PLAM! [price level-adjusted mortgages] R. Bailey. il *Forbes* 143:38-9 Ja 23 '89

Rising rates may finally curb the urge to splurge. G. Koretz. *Business Week* p20 Mr 20 '89

A scary mortgage idea [price level adjusted mortgages] P. Godwin. il *Changing Times* 43:20 Jl '89

Short-doc woes [bad mortgage loans made by the Dime Savings Bank] C. Byron. *New York* 22:23 Je 5 '89

Shortening your mortgage in a tough market. G. J. Gallagher. il *Black Enterprise* 19:51-2 My '89

When home buyers should consider graduated mortgages. S. Weiss. il *Money* 18:18+ Jl '89

Zap mortgages; ARMs: difficult adjustments. W. Giese. il *Changing Times* 43:20 Je '89

Advertising

New standard for loan ads. W. Giese. *Changing Times* 43:18 Ag '89

Default

Another financial mess [defaults in HUD's program that deputizes firms to issue and underwrite mortgages] M. Schifrin. il *Forbes* 144:10 Jl 10 '89

Come and get it [federal government deputizes mortgage brokers to approve and coinsure FHA mortgages] M. Schifrin. il *Forbes* 143:41-2 My 15 '89

The plot thickens [defaults in HUD's program that deputizes brokers to underwrite mortgages] M. Schifrin. il *Forbes* 144:10 O 30 '89

Who checks the checkers? [HUD's reliance on incomplete credit reports] M. Schifrin. il *Forbes* 144:64 Ag 7 '89

Prepayment

The right and wrong ways to cut your mortgage costs. E. M. MacDonald. il *Money* 18:24+ D '89

Refinancing

The mad rush to refinance. W. Giese. il *Changing Times* 43:41-5 O '89

Paying off your home the old-time way [fixed rate mortgages] T. Thompson. il *U.S. News & World Report* 107:60 Ag 7 '89

Teasing the teasers [adjustable rate mortgage refinancing's impact on shaky thrifts] J. Willoughby. il *Forbes* 143:68 Ap 3 '89

When to refinance—and when to stay put. J. Meehan. *Business Week* p96 Ag 28 '89

Taxation

House-hunting? Read this first [interest deduction; cover story] L. Saunders. il *Forbes* 143:119-21 Mr 20 '89

Mortgage mine field. L. Saunders. il *Forbes* 144:256+ O 16 '89

MORTIMER, EDWARD

Bring down the Wall. *World Press Review* 36:31 My '89

Closing the door. il *World Press Review* 36:22 N '89

In the light of history. il *World Press Review* 36:64 Mr '89

MORTIMER, ROBERT A.

Maghreb matters. *Foreign Policy* 76:160-75 Fall '89

MORTIMER, SENGA

Bermuda in bloom. il *House & Garden* 161:144-9+ N '89

MORTIMER'S (NEW YORK, N.Y.: RESTAURANT) *See* New York (N.Y.)—Restaurants, nightclubs, bars, etc.

MORTISE AND TENON JOINTS *See* Joints (Carpentry)

MORTMAN, DORIS

Rightfully mine [fiction] il por *Good Housekeeping* 209:153-6+ Jl '89

MORTON, BRIAN, AND LANDY, JOANNE

Independent activists challenge the status quo across Eastern Europe. il *Utne Reader* p81-3+ Ja/F '89

MORTON, BRIDGET BALTHROP

Daniel: beloved by God & by me. *Commonweal* 116:562-3 O 20 '89

MORTON, JASON

Standing on shaky ground. il *World Tennis* 37:98 Je '89

THE MORTON DOWNEY JR. SHOW [television program]

See Television program reviews—Single works

MORTON H. MEYERSON SYMPHONY CENTER (DALLAS, TEX.)

The perfectionist [architect I. M. Pei] C. McGuigan. il por *Newsweek* 114:60-1+ S 25 '89

MOS *See* Metal oxide semiconductors

MOSAICS

Court orders return of looted art [Cypriot mosaics] *Art in America* 77:256 O '89

In Indiana, a battle over stolen mosaics [Cypriot mosaics] D. Tsiantar. il *Newsweek* 113:66-7 My 29 '89

Litigators of the lost art [Cypriot mosaics] S. Mannheimer. il *The Saturday Evening Post* 261:62-8 O '89

Raiders of the lost art, the nonmovie [Cypriot mosaics] il *U.S. News & World Report* 106:13 Je 12 '89

Rightful owners [court decisions involving Cypriot mosaics and Peruvian pre-Columbian art] R. W. Walker and L. Nilson. il *Art News* 88:51+ O '89

Collectors and collecting

Ah, decadence [Arthur and Rosalinde Gilbert Collection] C. Brown. il por *Forbes* 143:316+ My 29 '89

MOSAICS (BIOLOGY)

Activation of bacterial porin gene expression by a chimeric signal transducer in response to aspartate. R. Utsumi and others. bibl f il *Science* 245:1246-9 S 15 '89

Analysis of ligand binding specificity of receptor chimeras [discussion of June 3, 1988 article, Chimeric α_2-,β_2-adrenergic receptors: delineation of domains involved in effector coupling and ligand binding specificity] B. K. Kobilka and others. *Science* 243:236-7 Ja 13 '89

Germ-line transmission of a *c-abl* mutation produced by targeted gene disruption in ES cells [cover story] P. L. Schwartzberg and others. bibl f il *Science* 246:799-803 N 10 '89

Introduction of human DNA into mouse eggs by injection of dissected chromosome fragments. J. Richa and C. W. Lo. bibl f il *Science* 245:175-7 Jl 14 '89

Of birds and brains [quail-chick chimeras produce modified songs; research by Evan Balaban and others] il *Discover* 10:14 F '89

T cell receptor gene trans-rearrangements: chimeric γ-δ genes in normal lymphoid tissues. B. Tycko and others. bibl f il *Science* 245:1242-6 S 15 '89

MOSASAURS *See* Reptiles, Fossil

MOSBACHER, GEORGETTE

about

Independent spirits. C. Cozzone. il pors *Harper's Bazaar* 122:44-9 Jl '89

Neoclassical overtones: Georgette Mosbacher's Sutton Place pied-á-terre. Suzy. il por *Architectural Digest* 46:258-63 N '89

MOSBACHER, ROBERT

America's economic security [address, May 8, 1989] *Vital Speeches of the Day* 55:554-6 Jl 1 '89

MOSCA, MATTHEW JOHN

The house and its restoration. bibl f il *Antiques* 135:462-73 F '89

MOSCHINO, FRANCO

about

Cheek chic. L. Chua. il por *Rolling Stone* Fashion Collection:63+ S 7 '89

Fashion's antifascist. C. Heimel. il por *Vogue* 179:144-5+ Mr '89

Franco Moschino. *The New Yorker* 64:19-20 Ja 9 '89

MOSCO, VINCENT

Déjà vu all over again? bibl *Society* 26:31-8 Jl/Ag '89

MOSCOW (SOVIET UNION)

Art

Rauschenberg goes to Moscow. A. Wallach. il por *Art in America* 77:21+ Mr '89

The ROCI road show [R. Rauschenberg show] M. L. Kotz. il por *Art News* 88:48+ Summ '89

The taste for Bacon [exhibition in Moscow] B. Taylor. il por *Art News* 88:57 Ja '89

Bookstores

See Booksellers and bookselling—Soviet Union

Description

Destination: Moscow. P. Galuszka. il *Business Week* p78-9 Ag 7 '89

Life in two capitals. L. Doder. il *Maclean's* 102:37 My 29 '89

Then and now. S. W. Cloud. il *Time* 133:60-1 Ap 10 '89

Economic conditions

A family of three in 323 square feet [Taldikin family] il *U.S. News & World Report* 107:29 N 20 '89

Perestroika up close. R. Rand. il *Reader's Digest* 135:115-19 Ag '89

MOSCOW (SOVIET UNION)—*cont.*
Galleries and museums
See also
    Pushkin Museum of Fine Arts (Moscow, Soviet Union)
Ludwig museums go east. J. Gambrell. *Art in America* 77:35+ Je '89
Health facilities
See also
    Institut Krasoty
Historic houses, sites, etc.
Living the history of modern Russia: Nina and Edmund Stevens in Moscow. E. Stevens. il *Architectural Digest* 46:164-7+ F '89
Rodchenko in Moscow: miraculous survival of the constructivist's historic studio. M. Ruthven. il pors *Architectural Digest* 46:53+ O '89
Maps
Lost and found [government issues revised map] *Time* 134:49 Jl 24 '89
Restaurants, nightclubs, bars, etc.
Dining in Moscow [contrasting dinners at the Ukraine hotel and U Persomany] R. D. Novak. *National Review* 41:30-1 D 8 '89
A raised *glasnost* [Kropotkinskaya 36] E. B. Fein. il *Gentlemen's Quarterly* 59:106+ O '89
Social conditions
Moscow yuppies? Nyet quite! [I. Zvereva and S. Burak] E. B. Fein. il *Mademoiselle* 95:222-3+ O '89
Punk *perestroika* [pessimistic mood; cover story] M. Walker. il *The New Republic* 201:22+ D 4 '89
Streets
See also
    Gorky Street (Moscow, Soviet Union)
Theater
Soviet theater. N. Rzhevsky. *The Nation* 249:180-1 Ag 7-14 '89
Voices from the inner depths. W. A. Henry. il *Time* 133:112+ Ap 10 '89
MOSCOW (SOVIET UNION) IN ART
Kandinsky's Moscow. M. Werenskiold. bibl f il *Art in America* 77:96-111 Mr '89
MOSCOW BOOK FAIR *See* Book fairs
MOSCOW CIRCUS
For a journalist in the Moscow Circus, gathering the bear facts is a clowning achievement. C. A. Azizian. il *People Weekly* 31:66-8 Ja 16 '89
MOSCOW CLASSICAL BALLET
Reviews:
    Performances of Swan Lake in Boston. C. Hardy. *Dance Magazine* 63:94-5 Mr '89
MOSCOW COSMETOLOGICAL CLINIC *See* Institut Krasoty
MOSCOZO, FLORE CÉLESTINE THÉRÈSE HENRIETTE TRISTAN Y *See* Tristan, Flora, 1803-1844
MOSEDALE, LAURA
All-in-the-family birth. il *Health (New York, N.Y.)* 21:85-6+ S '89
He spies/she spies: why we snoop in the name of love. il *Glamour* 87:162-3+ Jl '89
Women right now. See issues of Glamour
Women with cold feet. il *Glamour* 87:200-1+ D '89
MOSELEY, BILL
Interview: Peter Hagelstein. pors *Omni (New York, N.Y.)* 11:74-6+ My '89
MOSEN, PETER
about
Who you gonna call if you want your kid's party to gel? Try faux Ghostbuster Peter Mosen. il por *People Weekly* 32:115 Jl 17 '89
MOSER, CHARLOTTE, 1947-
Burning bridges. il *Art in America* 77:64-5+ N '89
MOSER, DON, 1932-
A salesman for the heavens wants to rope you in. bibl (p174) il pors *Smithsonian* 20:102-6+ Ap '89
MOSER, MARVIN, 1924-
Outsmarting the 'silent killer' [excerpt from Lower your blood pressure and live longer] *Prevention (Emmaus, Pa.)* 41:53-9 O '89
MOSER, PENNY WARD
Are cats smart? il *Reader's Digest* 135:112-16 O '89
A climate for death. il *Sports Illustrated* 70:48-50+ Mr 13 '89
Good scouts indeed. il pors *Sports Illustrated* 70:46-9 F 6 '89
MOSES, BILLY
about
"My husband healed me with love". J. Wolf. il pors *Redbook* 173:76+ O '89
MOSES, BOB
about
Blindfold test. F. Bouchard. por *Down Beat* 56:48 Jl '89
MOSES, EDWIN
about
Moses blasts edict to strip Johnson's records. por *Jet* 76:46 O 2 '89
MOSES, FRED
about
Boyhood dreams, adult realities. K. D. Thompson and J. Coleman. il por *Black Enterprise* 19:73 Je '89

MOSES, JENNIFER
I went back to high school . . . and it was hell! il *Mademoiselle* 95:202-3+ My '89
MOSES, KNOLLY
Giving computers an ethnic edge. il *American Visions* 4:12 D '89
MOSES, MARK
Popular music. See occasional issues of The New Yorker beginning February 1, 1988 through April 24, 1989
about
Obituary
    The New Yorker 65:124 S 11 '89
MOSES, REBECCA
about
In the world of fashion, a designer's name can be her most important asset. S. Mansfield. il por *Vogue* 179:88+ D '89
MOSES, ROBERT, 1888-1981
about
Reconsidering Robert Moses: power vs. paralysis. J. S. Russell. il por *Architectural Record* 177:49+ Ap '89
Robert Moses: the master builder. J. H. Kay. *The Nation* 248:569-71 Ap 24 '89
MOSES, SAM
About time, fella. il por *Sports Illustrated* 70:46-7 F 27 '89
All sorts of horse power. il pors *Sports Illustrated* 70:40-2+ My 29 '89
A bumper-car Indy. il *Sports Illustrated* 70:32-4+ Je 5 '89
Close call for a millionaire. il por *Sports Illustrated* 71:90-1 N 27 '89
Daytona's park-in. il *Sports Illustrated* 70:30-1 F 13 '89
Fast lane for Phoenix. il *Sports Illustrated* 70:28-9 Je 12 '89
One family's mountain. il por *Sports Illustrated* 71:22-3 Jl 17 '89
Ready to trade some paint. il pors *Sports Illustrated* 71:43-4+ Jl 3 '89
Rocket Rick burns up the track. il por *Sports Illustrated* 70:69-70 My 22 '89
MOSHER, LAWRENCE
Amazing boon. il *Américas* 41 no2:32-40 '89
What happened to cheap water? il *National Wildlife* 27:18-23 Je/Jl '89
MOSHOESHOE II, KING OF LESOTHO, 1938-
Visit to the United States, 1989
Lesotho King Moshoeshoe II lauded at Lincoln Univ.; hosted in D.C. by Quayle. il por *Jet* 77:26 N 6 '89
MOSIER, JOHN
Film. See issues of Américas
MOSIMANN'S (LONDON, ENGLAND: RESTAURANT) *See* London (England)—Restaurants, nightclubs, bars, etc.
MOSKIN, J. ROBERT
Aspen Forum: looking toward 2000. *Publishers Weekly* 235:28-9 Ap 21 '89
MOSKOS, CHARLES C.
about
National policies to encourage service [interview; cover story; with editorial comment by Susan Stroud] F. Newman. il *Change* 21:4, 8-17 S/O '89
MOSKOWITZ, ROBERT S., 1935-
about
Out of the abstract murk. P. Plagens. il *Newsweek* 114:63 Jl 31 '89
Robert Moskowitz: Hirshhorn Museum and Sculpture Garden. V. H. Winner. il *Art News* 88:213+ O '89
Second that emotion. K. Larson. il *New York* 22:46-7 Ag 7 '89
MOSLEM BROTHERHOOD (EGYPT) *See* Muslim Brotherhood (Egypt)
MOSLEMS *See* Muslims
MOSQUITO INDIANS
Faith and endurance in eastern Nicaragua. M. D. Wilde. *The Christian Century* 106:973-4 N 1 '89
A Hobson's choice for Miskito refugees. M. D. Wilde. il *The Christian Century* 106:726-8 Ag 2-9 '89
MOSQUITOES
It'll be a scratchy summer [infestation in Vermont] il *Newsweek* 114:23 Jl 3 '89
Control
See also
    Malaria—Prevention and control
Managing New York's mosquito coast. D. Ninivaggi. il por *The Conservationist* 44:26-33 Jl/Ag '89
MOSQUITOES AS CARRIERS OF INFECTION
See also
    Malaria
Hitching a ride with imported insects [viral diseases] R. Weiss. *Science News* 136:202 S 23 '89
MOSS, JULIE
about
The first unforgettable Ironman performance. K. McAlpine. *Women's Sports & Fitness* 11:27 Je '89
MOSS, LYDIA
Traveling with Lydia. See issues of McCall's beginning May 1989

MOSS, NORMAN
Unilateral disarmament—Labor's lost love. il por *The Bulletin of the Atomic Scientists* 45:9-11 O '89

MOSS, RICHARD
about
Time on his hands. C. Brown. il por *Forbes* 144:110+ Jl 10 '89

MOSS LANDING (CALIF.)
Stores
Whaling village becomes an antiques center . . . Moss Landing. il map *Sunset (Central West edition)* 182:12 Mr '89

MOSTLY MOZART FESTIVAL *See* Music festivals—New York (State)

MOTA, ROSA
about
Rosa Mota. B. Wischnia. il por *Runner's World* 24:49 F '89

MOTAVALLI, JIM
Coal wars again. il *The Progressive* 53:24-7 Jl '89

MOTEL 6, INC.
Why Motel 6 is waking up. G. G. Marcial. *Business Week* p206 S 25 '89

MOTELS *See* Hotels, motels, etc.

MOTH-EYE TECHNOLOGY
Moth-eye magic. J. L. Schefter. il *Popular Science* 234:136-7+ My '89

MOTH FLIES
A novel vasodilatory peptide from the salivary glands of the sand fly Lutzomyia longipalpis. J. M. C. Ribeiro and others. bibl f il *Science* 243:212-14 Ja 13 '89

MOTHER FUSSIN' RAPPERS (MUSICAL GROUP)
Rap as a second language. G. Collins. il *Ms.* 17:56-8 Ja/F '89

MOTHER JONES (PERIODICAL)
Mother Jones' third annual Heroes and Heroines. il *Mother Jones* 14:27-35 Ja '89
Writing for Mother Jones. J. A. Cabello. il *The Writer* 102:28 O '89

MOTHER LOVE *See* Love, Maternal
MOTHER TONGUE *See* Native language
MOTHER YORK
about
The church picnic goes to jail. R. Clapp. il por *Christianity Today* 33:14-15 Je 16 '89

MOTHERHOOD *See* Mothers
MOTHERS
See also
Childbirth
Homemakers
Love, Maternal
Maternal deprivation
Overprotective parents
Parent education
Pregnancy
Single mothers
Stepparents and stepchildren
Surrogate mothers
Baby chic: what's behind the new diaper rush? N. Angier. il *Mademoiselle* 95:194-5+ Je '89
Gay and lesbian couples. J. Seligmann. il *Newsweek* 114 Special Issue:38-40 Wint '89/Spr '90
Giving up the God role. E. Berg. il *Parents* 64:138-40 Mr '89
Growing up with a famous mother. il *Ebony* 44:122+ My '89
The hand that rocks the cradle writes the book. U. K. Le Guin. il *The New York Times Book Review* 94:1+ Ja 22 '89
It takes one to know one: a mom's-eye view of the Blessed Mother. M. Mantle. *U.S. Catholic* 54:29-31 My '89
Life with mother [motherhood from the 1920s through the 1980s] il *Good Housekeeping* 208:186-7 My '89
The loneliness of motherhood [giving up job to raise son] L. George. il *American Health* 8:114+ Mr '89
Mommy oldest: having babies at 45 and beyond [cover story] J. Kasindorf. il *New York* 22:22-9 Jl 17 '89
Mother to mother. E. Klavan. il *Parents* 64:74+ F '89
Motherhood 1989: the state of the art. J. Kelman. il *Ladies' Home Journal* 106:63-4+ My '89
Mothering. See issues of Essence
Mothering my way. C. C. Lee. il *Parents* 64:85-6+ S '89
The mothers' page. See issues of McCall's beginning January 1984
Pen pals: our babies' first year. P. Abrams and L. Rosenberg. il pors *Parents* 64:90-4+ N '89
This is what you thought: 50% say doctors should turn down lesbians for artificial insemination [survey results] il *Glamour* 87:141 Ag '89
Tough guys talk about mom. il *New Choices for the Best Years* 29:48-50+ My '89
When mom's feeling ill. J. T. Gibson. il *Parents* 64:197 S '89
A young mother's story. See issues of Redbook
Anecdotes, facetiae, satire, etc.
Are you a '90s mom? M. Mohler and M. D. Rosen. il *Ladies' Home Journal* 106:188 N '89

Attitudes
Are schools flunking out? [LHJ Roper poll] il *Ladies' Home Journal* 106:72+ S '89
Stay-at-home moms speak out [excerpts from letters] il *Ladies' Home Journal* 106:194 N '89
Employment
See also
Children of working parents
Maternity leaves
Mommy track
Woman's workshop quarterly (Newsletter)
5 beautiful moms say, "Go for it all!". K. C. Engles. il por *Redbook* 173:123-7 My '89
After the baby: easing your return to work. J. Marzollo. il *Parents* 64:106-10 O '89
The Barth balance. C. Hurst. il pors *Home Office Computing* 7:51-3 Je '89
Corporate nannies for a new decade [businesses coping with family issues] B. Brophy. il *U.S. News & World Report* 107:70+ D 25 '89-Ja 1 '90
The corporation vs. the family: can the conflict be resolved? [special section] il *Working Woman* 14:125-7+ N '89
Dear Betty Harragan. B. L. Harragan. il *Working Woman* 14:31+ D '89
Families of working wives spending more on services and nondurables [Consumer Expenditure Survey] E. Jacobs and others. bibl f il *Monthly Labor Review* 112:15-23 F '89
Free yourself! [working mother's guilt] A. Van der Meer. *Redbook* 172:93+ Mr '89
Good-bye, June Cleaver [working mother's anxiety over fixing breakfast for her children] L. Flaherty. il *Ladies' Home Journal* 106:62+ Jl '89
How working mothers fit God in their schedule. C. McDonnell. il *U.S. Catholic* 54:28-33 N '89
Living with choices. F. Prose. il *Parents* 64:130-3 My '89
Managing your career and family. B. Nivens. il *Essence* 19:104 Ja '89
Morning madness [suggestions by Ronni Eisenberg and Kate Kelly] K. Levine. il *Parents* 64:68+ F '89
A mother's dilemma. K. Triedman. il *Ms.* 18:59-63 Jl/Ag '89
Music and mothering [N. Cherry and R. Jones] D. DeNicolo; E. Zimmerman. il pors *Glamour* 87:178 N '89
My mother, the doctor [pediatricians who are also mothers] M. Siegel. il *Good Housekeeping* 209:90+ S '89
Not your typical family-business wife [M. Forthman] S. Nelton. il por *Nation's Business* 77:40 Ag '89
On leaving [going on assignment and leaving children at home] D. Sobel. il *Ladies' Home Journal* 106:54+ Je '89
The role of "mom". J. L. Ward and L. Sorenson. il *Nation's Business* 77:40-1 Ag '89
The search for quality time [panel discussion] il *Ladies' Home Journal* 106:192 N '89
Stop ironing the diapers. B. Ehrenreich. il *Ms.* 17:30-1 Ap '89
Success and the second child. K. Levine. il *Parents* 64:57-8+ Jl '89
Toughest job [daily schedule of working mother P. Menzel] G. H. Colt. il pors *Life* 12:100-4+ My '89
The trials and triumphs of working mothers. L. Norment. il *Ebony* 44:38+ S '89
Viking to release 'The second shift,' analysis of the two-job marriage [work of A. R. Hochschild] B. Levine. *Publishers Weekly* 235:35-6 Ap 28 '89
When mom goes back to work. S. Ginsberg. il *Good Housekeeping* 209:114+ S '89
"Why my mom works". K. Levine. il *Parents* 64:77-80 O '89
Wife, mother, entrepreneur. S. Nelton. il *Nation's Business* 77:10 Ap '89
Will you be penalized for having a baby? il *Glamour* 87:106+ F '89
Working moms gripe [advice from panel of experts] A. Fischer. *Redbook* 173:126-7+ O '89
The working mom's handbook [special section] il *Ladies' Home Journal* 106:55-6+ Ag '89
The working mom's obstacle course. K. Levine. il *Parents* 64:67-8+ D '89
Working mother overload. B. J. Berg. *Redbook* 172:92-3+ Mr '89
Working mothers: these make the best of both worlds. M. Matson. il *Good Housekeeping* 208:46+ Mr '89
Bibliography
"Diary of a mad supermom". S. Faludi. il *Mother Jones* 14:39-41 Je '89
Language
Anecdotes, facetiae, satire, etc.
The mother tongue. P. Volk. il *The New York Times Magazine* p20+ My 14 '89
Mortality
Maternal death: a preventable tragedy. il *UN Chronicle* 26:46-7 S '89
Recreation
See also
Mother's Camp (Calif.)
Religious life
How working mothers fit God in their schedule. C. McDonnell. il *U.S. Catholic* 54:28-33 N '89

MOTHERS, HANDICAPPED
"I have to save my baby!" [paraplegic C. Dunlop rescues daughter from swimming pool] J. Stuller. il *Reader's Digest* 134:65-70 Ap '89
MOTHERS, UNMARRIED *See* Single mothers
MOTHERS AGAINST GANGS (ORGANIZATION)
Frances Sandoval. S. Kanfer. il por *People Weekly* 32 Special Issue:126 Fall '89
MOTHERS AND CHILDREN *See* Parent-child relationship
MOTHER'S CAMP (CALIF.)
At a California camp where no husbands are allowed, moms get a weekend on chore leave [founded by C. Smith-Carter] M. Neill. il por *People Weekly* 32:85-6 Jl 3 '89
No Pampers, pampering. J. Gordon. il por *Newsweek* 114:76 Jl 10 '89
A MOTHER'S COURAGE: THE MARY THOMAS STORY [television program] *See* Television program reviews—Single works
MOTHER'S DAY CARDS
Here are the top-winning cards in the 1989 Mother's Day contest! il *Good Housekeeping* 208:56+ My '89
MOTHER'S DAY DINNERS *See* Dinners and dining
MOTHERS EMBRACING NUCLEAR DISARMAMENT (ORGANIZATION) *See* MEND (Organization)
MOTHER'S HELPERS *See* Household employees
MOTHERS-IN-LAW
My mother-in-law is for the birds. S. H. Shetterly. il *New Choices for the Best Years* 29:89-92 Mr '89
MOTHERS IN TELEVISION
Anecdotes, facetiae, satire, etc.
Three popular shows offer motherhood role models. C. Schine. il *Vogue* 179:262+ N '89
MOTHERS' MILK *See* Milk, Human
MOTHERWELL, ROBERT
about
Novel ideas. R. B. Woodward. il *Art News* 88:127 Ap '89
Robert Motherwell: forty-five years of printmaking: Associated American Artists. C. Lyon. il *Art News* 88:173-4 Mr '89
MOTHS
See also
Bagworms
Caterpillars
Codling moths
Gypsy moths
Identification of a neuropeptide hormone that regulates sex pheromone production in female moths. A. K. Raina and others. bibl f il *Science* 244:796-8 My 19 '89
Development
See Insects—Development
Sexual behavior
See Sexual behavior—Insects
MOTION
See also
Precession
Rotation
Solar system—Motion in space
Stars—Motion
MOTION, HUMAN *See* Biomechanics
MOTION DETECTORS
Ball Aerospace stresses simplicity in space-based motion sensor design [Remote Attitude Measurement Sensor] W. B. Scott. il *Aviation Week & Space Technology* 130:100-2 Je 5 '89
MOTION PERCEPTION
Neural integration of information specifying structure from stereopsis and motion. M. Nawrot and R. Blake. bibl f il *Science* 244:716-18 My 12 '89
Neuronal correlates of subjective visual perception. N. K. Logothetis and J. D. Schall. bibl f il *Science* 245:761-3 Ag 18 '89
Ocular responses to linear motion are inversely proportional to viewing distance. U. Schwarz and others. bibl f il *Science* 245:1394-6 S 22 '89
Tracking down the neurons of perception [research by Jeffrey D. Schall and Nikos K. Logothetis] I. Amato. il *Science News* 136:118 Ag 19 '89
MOTION PICTURE ACTORS AND ACTRESSES
See also
Academy Awards
Motion Picture and Television Country House and Hospital (Woodland Hills, Calif.)
New York Film Critics' Circle Awards
Youth as actors and actresses
See also names of motion picture actors and actresses
Actors face the truth. G. Smith. il *Film Comment* 25:32-5 Ja/F '89
And now, Hollywood Babble-on [Grave Line Tours] R. Corliss. il *Time* 133:76-7 Ja 16 '89
Cast of characters [character actors; special section] il *Film Comment* 25:31-6+ N/D '89
An extra's tale [Scenes from the class struggle in Beverly Hills] L. Loud. il por *American Film* 14:92 Ap '89
Goddesses. J. Salter. il *Gentlemen's Quarterly* 59:282-5+ O '89
Hollywood's rising stars. J. Calio and J. Rachlin. il *Ladies' Home Journal* 106:138+ N '89
Invasion of the TV people [TV actors in movies] R. Rosen-baum. il *Mademoiselle* 95:100+ My '89

Like mother . . . like daughter [cover story] J. Ardmore. il *Good Housekeeping* 209:110-11+ Jl '89
The many faces of Eve: the changing image of the sex goddess. J. Kristin. il *American Film* 14:38-41+ Ap '89
New faces of '88. L. O'Toole. il *Film Comment* 25:54-5 Ja/F '89
Summer breakout [TV stars in movies; cover story] K. Turan. il *TV Guide* 37:2-5 Jl 1-7 '89
Photographs and photography
Hollywood 1939-1989 [cover story; special issue] il *Life* 12:8-14+ Spr '89
Political activities
See also
Hollywood Women's Political Committee
Sarandon, seriously [cover story] A. L. Ball. pors *Mother Jones* 14:30-3+ F/Mr '89
Susan Sarandon [interview] C. Dreifus. il *The Progressive* 53:33-6 O '89
Religious life
Of many things [Catholics R. Julia and B. Shields] G. W. Hunt. *America* 160:162 F 25 '89
Salaries, pensions, etc.
The Club [actors who command $5 million per picture] C. Fleming. *American Film* 14:13 Ap '89
Fat times for studios, fatter times for stars. R. Grover. il *Business Week* p48 Jl 24 '89
The price club. R. Natale. il *American Film* 14:42-4+ Je '89
MOTION PICTURE ADAPTATIONS
See also
Comic books, strips, etc. and motion pictures
Dickens on stage and screen [cover story] R. Samuel. il por *History Today* 39:44-51 D '89
Dolled up in Dixie [filming of Steel magnolias] B. D. Johnson. il *Maclean's* 102:84+ N 20 '89
The hottest dead man in Hollywood [J. Fante] F. Spotnitz. il pors *American Film* 14:40-4+ Jl/Ag '89
Mirror, mirror . . . [In country] J. Scott. il *Film Comment* 25:11-14 S/O '89
Not afraid of the dark [making of Enemies, a love story; cover story] B. Yagoda. il pors *American Film* 15:30-7 N '89
Rights. P. S. Nathan. See issues of Publishers Weekly
Slaves of New York [production of T. Janowitz's novel] il por *Harper's Bazaar* 122:144-5 F '89
Star bright [filming of R. Harling's play Steel magnolias; special section] L. Hart. il por *Life* 12:82-4+ O '89
MOTION PICTURE AND TELEVISION COUNTRY HOUSE AND HOSPITAL (WOODLAND HILLS, CALIF.)
A fete honoring Clint, Julio and Bette Davis turns into a blast from the past. il *People Weekly* 31:106-7 Ja 23 '89
MOTION PICTURE ASSOCIATION OF AMERICA
Fighting for Hollywood's fair share [interview with J. Valenti] il pors *Channels (New York, N.Y.: 1986)* 9:98-9 N '89
MOTION PICTURE AUDIENCES
Notes and comment [watching C. Chaplin's City lights] *The New Yorker* 64:19 Ja 9 '89
MOTION PICTURE AUTHORSHIP
Darkness at the edge of Towne. M. Sragow. il por *American Film* 14:40-5+ Ja/F '89
The hottest dead man in Hollywood [J. Fante] F. Spotnitz. il pors *American Film* 14:40-4+ Jl/Ag '89
In pursuit of crazy language [interview with T. McGuane] J. Klinger. il por *American Film* 14:42-5+ Ap '89
Jeffrey Boam's two scripts make him a Lethal box office weapon after a long Crusade for success. M. H. J. Farrell. il pors *People Weekly* 32:47-8 S 4 '89
John Patrick Shanley [interview] il pors *American Film* 14:20-4 S '89
Paul Schrader [interview] il pors *American Film* 14:16-21 Jl/Ag '89
The screenplay's the thing. B. Bawer. il *The American Spectator* 22:33-4 F '89
Secrets from the cutting room [screenwriters' laments] R. Rosenbaum. il pors *Mademoiselle* 95:64+ Je '89
Strictly movie [account of getting started as a screenwriter in Hollywood] D. Fuchs. *Commentary* 88:38-46 S '89
Visually speaking [interview with H. Pinter] M. Ciment. il por *Film Comment* 25:20-2 My/Je '89
With Sea of love, novelist Richard Price drops anchor among Hollywood's writer elite. T. Allis. il pors *People Weekly* 32:68+ N 27 '89
MOTION PICTURE CAMERAS
See also
Film-to-video transfer system
MOTION PICTURE CARTOONS *See* Motion pictures—Animated films
MOTION PICTURE COLLECTIONS
See also
Archive Film Productions Inc.
Cinephiles (Organization)
National Film Registry
Tyler, Texas Black Film Collection
Wesleyan College. Cinema Archive
Gems [R. Prelinger's collection of educational, safety, and promotional films] *The New Yorker* 65:32-3 S 11 '89

MOTION PICTURE COLLECTIONS—*cont.*
Profiles [H. Graff] D. Watt. por *The New Yorker* 65:59-60+ N 20 '89
MOTION PICTURE CRITICS AND CRITICISM
See also
Kael, Pauline
Motion picture reviews
Television broadcasting—Motion picture criticism programs
Two thumbs down. A. White. il *Film Comment* 25:37-9 Ja/F '89
MOTION PICTURE DIRECTORS
See also
Allen, Woody
Almodóvar, Pedro
Annaud, Jean-Jacques
Bogdanovich, Peter, 1939-
Brittain, Donald
Brooks, James L., 1940-
Cassavetes, John
Cocteau, Jean, 1889-1963
Costa-Gavras
Craven, Wes
De Palma, Brian
De Vito, Danny
Demme, Jonathan
Dreyer, Carl Theodor, 1889-1968
Duncan, Patrick
Edwards, Blake, 1922-
Egoyan, Atom
Fellini, Federico
Forman, Miloš
Frankenheimer, John
Friedman, Ken
Gazdag, Gyula
Gilliam, Terry
Gitai, Amos
Heston, Fraser
Howard, Ron
Itami, Juzo
Jarmusch, Jim
Kadokawa, Haruki
Kapoor, Shashi
Kasdan, Lawrence
Kurosawa, Akira, 1910-
Lean, David
Leone, Sergio, 1921-1989
Levinson, Barry
Lynch, David
Malle, Louis, 1932-
Morris, Errol
Paradjanov, Sergei
Preminger, Otto, 1906-1986
Reiner, Rob
Ritt, Martin
Roche, Luis Armando
Schatzberg, Jerry, 1927-
Schrader, Paul
Scorsese, Martin
Soderbergh, Steven
Sokurov, Alexander
Spielberg, Steven, 1947-
Towne, Robert, 1936-
Truffaut, François, 1932-1984
Weir, Peter, 1944-
Wellman, William Augustus, 1896-1975
Wilder, Billy, 1906-
Women motion picture directors
The disappearing director. B. Walker. il *Film Comment* 25:28-31 Ja/F '89
First-time directors. L. Ochoa. il *American Film* 14:46-51+ Ap '89
Rebel filmmakers. il *Rolling Stone* p113 D 14-28 '89
When directors get personal [autobiographical films] M. Sragow. il *American Film* 14:64-6 My '89
MOTION PICTURE EDITING See Motion pictures—Editing
MOTION PICTURE FESTIVALS
'Glasnost' documentaries [Glasnost Film Festival in the U.S.] J. E. Fitch. *American Film* 14:12 Jl/Ag '89
California
Palm Springs: a celebration of film. P. Lasley and E. Harryman. il *American Film* 15:59-60+ D '89
Cuba
Our man in Havana [Festival of New Latin American Cinema] J. Greenberg. il *American Film* 14:16-18 Mr '89
France
See also
Cannes Film Festival
Low-life serenade [Deauville Film Festival] K. Turan. il *Gentlemen's Quarterly* 59:59-60 Jl '89
Germany (West)
A film journey to the Lodz ghetto [Berlin Film Festival] J. M. Wall. *The Christian Century* 106:251-2 Mr 8 '89
Great Britain
For queens & country [Gay and Lesbian Film Festival sponsored by the British Film Institute] H. Kennedy. il *Film Comment* 25:15-16 Ja/F '89

Hawaii
Speak your peace [Vietnam Film Project at the Hawaii International Film Festival] K. Jaehne. il *Film Comment* 25:14 Mr/Ap '89
Illinois
Education by exaggeration [Insect Fear Film Festival; cover story] R. Weiss. il *Science News* 135:136-7 Mr 4 '89
Italy
Gondola wind [Venice Film Festival] H. Kennedy. *Film Comment* 25:72+ N/D '89
New York (State)
The 18th New Directors/New Films Festival. K. Jaehne; A. White. il *Film Comment* 25:68-70+ My/Je '89
Festivals [New York Film Festival] L. Katzman. il *Film Comment* 25:68-70 N/D '89
Ontario
Big-screen frontiers [Toronto's Festival of Festivals] B. D. Johnson. il *Maclean's* 102:72-4 S 18 '89
Cinema of rage [Toronto's Festival of Festivals] B. D. Johnson. il *Maclean's* 102:58+ S 25 '89
Toronto wigs out [Festival of Festivals] D. Chute. *Film Comment* 25:70+ N/D '89
Puerto Rico
CineSanJuan. L. Kardish. il *Film Comment* 25:4+ Ja/F '89
Québec (Province)
Ecumenical jury winners at Montreal [Montreal World Film Festival] J. W. Arnold. *America* 161:252-3 O 21 '89
Jesus and others at Montreal festival [Montreal World Film Festival] J. M. Wall. *The Christian Century* 106:835-6 S 27 '89
Montreal: just 35 millimeters from Latin America [Montreal World Film Festival] J. Mosier. il *Américas* 41 no2:8-9 '89
Utah
Utah's mecca for mavericks [U.S. Film Festival] M. Pierson. *Video* 13:18 My '89
MOTION PICTURE FILMS
Conservation and restoration
See Motion pictures—Conservation and restoration
MOTION PICTURE INDUSTRY
See also
Amblin Entertainment
Blacks in the motion picture industry
Cannon Group Inc.
Columbia Pictures Entertainment Inc.
Fox Inc.
Gospel Films, Inc.
Guber-Peters Entertainment Company
Lucasfilm Ltd.
MCA Inc.
MGM/UA Communications Co.
Miramax Films (Firm)
Morgan Creek Productions
Motion Picture Association of America
Motion picture production and direction
Motion picture theaters
Motown Productions
New Line Cinema Corp.
New World Entertainment Ltd.
Pathe Communications Corp.
Republic Pictures Corporation
Showscan Film Corporation
Steinhardt Baer Pictures Company
Tribeca Film Center
Twentieth Century-Fox Film Corp.
Universal Pictures
Walt Disney Company
Warner Bros. Inc.
Weintraub Entertainment Group Inc.
Women in the motion picture industry
The '90s: future tense [special section] il *Film Comment* 25:27-39+ Ja/F '89
Industry. See issues of Film Comment
Into the '90s [special section] il *American Film* 14:24-39+ Ja/F '89
A man who hates Rambo [interview with D. Puttnam] E. Linden. il por *Time* 133:62-3 My 1 '89
The state that shoots straight [Illinois] R. L. Ratny. il *American Film* 15:56-8+ N '89
Acquisitions and mergers
International aspects
Even for Walter Yetnikoff, this will be a stretch: can Sony's ace juggle both Columbia and CBS Records? D. Lieberman. il por *Business Week* p144-5 O 30 '89
Foreign intrigue. S. Emmrich. il *American Film* 14:38-41+ S '89
From Walkman to showman [Sony buys Columbia Pictures] J. Castro. il *Time* 134:70-1 O 9 '89
Hollywood or bust [foreign investment] B. Rudolph. il *Time* 134:51-2 S 4 '89
Invasion of the studio snatchers. R. Grover. il *Business Week* p52-4 O 16 '89
Is Hollywood Japan's field of dreams? P. Sweeting. il *Video* 13:140 N '89
Japan goes Hollywood [Sony's deal for Columbia Pictures and the competitive challenge to the U.S.; cover story; special section] il *Newsweek* 114:62-9+ O 9 '89

MOTION PICTURE INDUSTRY — Acquisitions and mergers—International aspects—*cont.*

Leo the Lion is on the loose again [C. Skase's deal to buy MGM/UA falls apart] R. Grover. il por *Business Week* p60 O 23 '89

The man who would be mogul trips up in Tinseltown [G. Parretti] R. Grover and J. Rossant. *Business Week* p31-2 My 1 '89

Puzzle in Movieland: the case of the mystery moguls [G. Parretti and F. Fiorini] J. Rossant. il pors *Business Week* p80-1+ Mr 13 '89

The shoot-out to control Hollywood [foreign investors show interest] J. Egan. il *U.S. News & World Report* 106:69-72 Mr 20 '89

Sony's big-picture strategy [purchase of Columbia Pictures] J. Egan. il *U.S. News & World Report* 107:35-6+ O 9 '89

Stranger in a strange land [C. Skase of Qintex buys MGM/UA Communications] L. Gubernick. il por *Forbes* 144:164+ O 2 '89

When Columbia met Sony . . . a love story. R. Grover. il *Business Week* p44-5 O 9 '89

Why Sony is plugging into Columbia. N. Gross and W. J. Holstein. il *Business Week* p56+ O 16 '89

Advertising

Tyson pockets $150,000 for 'Lean on me' plug. por *Jet* 75:48 Mr 20 '89

Communist activities

Postscript on Lucy [L. Ball's testimony before House Committee on Un-American Activities] *The Nation* 248:685 My 22 '89

The real blacklist. J. Farah. *National Review* 41:42-3 O 27 '89

Ethical aspects

The 'Cotton Club' murder: cocaine and hit men in Hollywood—a 1980s film noir [B. Evans implicated in murder of R. Radin; cover story] J. Kasindorf. il pors *New York* 22:24-33 Jl 24 '89

Letter from Los Angeles [Cotton Club murder case] J. Didion. *The New Yorker* 65:92-9 S 4 '89

Export-import trade

As the world turns. D. Denby. il *New York* 22:116 D 11 '89

Hollywood reaps a windfall from television's richest endeavor [British direct broadcast satellite services] K. Pearce. il *Channels (New York, N.Y.: 1986)* 9:9 Mr '89

No flying buns for a bully boy [J. Valenti campaigns against Canadian efforts to reduce U.S. domination of movie distribution business] A. Fotheringham. il *Maclean's* 102:116 O 30 '89

Finance

The 14th annual grosses gloss. A. Thompson. il *Film Comment* 25:70-4 Mr/Ap '89

Batprofits smooth big takeover [Batman earns big profits for Warner] E. Pomice. il *U.S. News & World Report* 107:44 Jl 24 '89

Boffo Bat B.O. buoys biz. B. Miner. *National Review* 41:56 S 15 '89

Boffo box office big boost to biz. D. Ansen. il *Newsweek* 114:60-2 Jl 31 '89

Bono less than boffo at box office [U2: Rattle and hum] J. Ressner. *Rolling Stone* p16 Ja 12 '89

. . . but the rest of the holiday flicks look mostly ho-ho-hum. R. Grover. il *Business Week* p51 N 13 '89

End of the indies. J. Jost. il *Film Comment* 25:42-5 Ja/F '89

Fat times for studios, fatter times for stars. R. Grover. il *Business Week* p48 Jl 24 '89

In the race for viewers, the networks fall further behind. R. Grover and D. Lieberman. il *Business Week* p80-1 Ja 9 '89

Next stop, Tinseltown [Japanese investments in U.S. films] J. Hammer. il *Newsweek* 113:48-9 Mr 20 '89

One eye on art, one on profits [independent filmmakers] D. Ansen. il *Newsweek* 113:66 Ap 3 '89

Retread IV: return of the son of sequel [upcoming summer movies] R. Grover. il *Business Week* p38 My 15 '89

The shoot-out to control Hollywood [foreign investors show interest] J. Egan. il *U.S. News & World Report* 106:69-72 Mr 20 '89

The year in movies [1989] P. Travers. il *Rolling Stone* p21+ D 14-28 '89

History

14-karat oomph [1930s at Warner Bros] R. Corliss. il *Film Comment* 25:40-6 Jl/Ag '89

100 years of filmmaking in New York [special section] il *American Film* 15:57-68+ O '89

The eighties: the industry. G. Kilday. il *Film Comment* 25:60+ N/D '89

"I made Withering Heights. Wyler only directed it" [S. Goldwyn] K. Turan. il pors *Gentlemen's Quarterly* 59:105+ My '89

Strictly movie [account of getting started as a screenwriter in Hollywood] D. Fuchs. *Commentary* 88:38-46 S '89

Ticket to Hollywood [computer game combines movie trivia and walking tour] T. A. Summers. il *Home Office Computing* 7:84 Mr '89

Ticket to Hollywood [computer game combining movie trivia and walking tour] D. English. il *Compute!* 11:77-8 My '89

Bibliography

Goldwynism. J. G. Dunne. il por *The New York Review of Books* 36:28-33 My 18 '89

International aspects

Shashi Kapoor branches out [Indo-Soviet production Ajooba] P. Saxena. il por *World Press Review* 36:75 S '89

Laws and regulations

See Motion picture laws and regulations

Suits and claims

Hollywood's hottest hired gun [T. N. Christensen] R. Grover. il por *Business Week* p132 N 13 '89

Africa

Richard Attenborough [interview] C. Vieler-Porter. il pors *The Unesco Courier* 42:4-7 Ag '89

Australia

The Australian cinema. K. Williams. il *The Courier (Unesco)* 41:34-7 D '88

Canada

The Maple Leaf Mafia [Canadians in Hollywood] B. D. Johnson. il *Maclean's* 102:78-80+ Jl 3 '89

No flying buns for a bully boy [J. Valenti campaigns against Canadian efforts to reduce U.S. domination of movie distribution business] A. Fotheringham. il *Maclean's* 102:116 O 30 '89

Prairie samurai [filming Japanese film Heaven and earth in Alberta] J. Howse. il *World Press Review* 36:68-9 N '89

Prairie samurai: a Japanese epic comes to life in Alberta [Heaven and earth] J. Howse. il *Maclean's* 102:44-5 Ag 21 '89

Sayonara, eh? [filming Japanese samurai epic Heaven and earth in the Canadian Rockies] J. Greenberg. il *American Film* 15:11-12 O '89

China

See also
Xi'an Film Studio

India

Close-up on Indian cinema. K. Mohamed. il *The Courier (Unesco)* 42:12-15 F '89

Iran

Nonviolent shooting in Iran. G. Peary. il *American Film* 15:14-15 N '89

Japan

Next stop, Tinseltown [Japanese investments in U.S. films] J. Hammer. il *Newsweek* 113:48-9 Mr 20 '89

Soviet Union

In Moscow with 'Fayfer' and 'Oh-Oh-Seven' [shooting The Russia house] C. Bogert. il *Newsweek* 114:66-7 N 6 '89

Rubles of the game. A. Williamson. il *Film Comment* 25:23-4+ Ja/F '89

United States

See Motion picture industry

MOTION PICTURE INDUSTRY IN VIDEOTAPES

Cinema of the unknown [documentaries about filmmaking] F. Thompson. il *American Film* 15:64-6+ N '89

MOTION PICTURE LAWS AND REGULATIONS

The networks are hungry for homegrown hits. D. Lieberman. il *Business Week* p88+ N 13 '89

Canada

No flying buns for a bully boy [J. Valenti campaigns against Canadian efforts to reduce U.S. domination of movie distribution business] A. Fotheringham. il *Maclean's* 102:116 O 30 '89

MOTION PICTURE LITERATURE

See also
Publishers and publishing—Motion picture literature

MOTION PICTURE MAKEUP *See* Makeup, Theatrical

MOTION PICTURE MUSEUMS

See also
American Museum of the Moving Image (New York, N.Y.)
Museum of the Moving Image (London, England)

MOTION PICTURE MUSIC *See* Motion pictures—Music

MOTION PICTURE PHOTOGRAPHY

See also
Cinematographers
Motion pictures—Amateur films
Motion pictures—Special effects
Photography, Time-lapse
Showscan process
Underwater cinematography

History

Time and motion. il pors *American History Illustrated* 24:62-3 S/O '89

MOTION PICTURE POSTERS *See* Posters

MOTION PICTURE PREMIERES

1939 [Gone with the wind] A. Nielsen. il *American Heritage* 40:43-5 D '89

The belles blossom at the premiere of Steel magnolias. il *People Weekly* 32:66-7 N 20 '89

Great balls of fire! opens with a whole lot of shakin' on both coasts. il *People Weekly* 32:40-1 Jl 17 '89

Harry and Sally meet a big squeeze in Beverly Hills. il *People Weekly* 32:24-5 Jl 31 '89

MOTION PICTURE PREMIERES—*cont.*

Hollywood helps a brave couple raise money for children dying of AIDS [P. and E. Glaser host premiere of Immediate family] il pors *People Weekly* 32:58-9 N 13 '89

Nights for bats, ghosts and stars [Batman premiere in Hollywood] il *People Weekly* 32:34-5 Jl 3 '89

Violence darkens the bright opening of Eddie Murphy's plush, flush Harlem nights [eruption of violence in cities around U.S.] il *People Weekly* 32:76-7 D 4 '89

With giggles, ghouls and glamour, celebs break loose for Ghostbusters II [Hollywood premiere] il *People Weekly* 32:36-7 Jl 3 '89

MOTION PICTURE PRODUCERS

See also
Daly, John, 1937-
Evans, Bob, 1930-
Goldwyn, Samuel, 1882-1974
Guber, Peter
Haft, Steven
Management Company Entertainment Group Inc.
Peters, Jon
Pressman, Edward
Selznick, David O., 1902-1965
Shamberg, Michael
Winkler, Irwin

Anecdotes, facetiae, satire, etc.

Wild pitches [story ideas pitched to producers] A. McDonnell. il *American Film* 15:44-5+ D '89

MOTION PICTURE PRODUCT PLACEMENT

Dangerous liaisons. L. P. Sheinfeld. il *Film Comment* 25:70-2 S/O '89

Plugging away in Hollywood [commercial products featured in movies] J. D. Reed. il *Time* 133:103 Ja 2 '89

Talk about 'placements' . . . [Ramses condoms in Lethal weapon 2] il *Newsweek* 114:50 Jl 31 '89

When screens become billboards. J. Silberg. il *American Film* 14:12 My '89

MOTION PICTURE PRODUCTION AND DIRECTION

See also
Motion picture directors
Motion pictures—Setting and scenery

The abyss. J. Calhoun. il *Theatre Crafts* 23:44-6+ Ag/S '89

The cockeyed world of Ron Shelton [making of Blaze] J. Silverman. il pors *American Film* 15:34-9+ D '89

Dance of the independent [D. Weisman's Naked tango] G. Kilday. il *American Film* 14:16+ S '89

Deep-sea cinema [making of The abyss] A. Maurer. il *Omni (New York, N.Y.)* 11:14+ Ag '89

Dialogue on film. See issues of American Film

Earth to Gilliam [making of The adventures of Baron Munchausen] J. Mathews. il por *American Film* 14:34-9+ Mr '89

The Hurd instinct [cover story] M. Rosen. il pors *Ms.* 18:66-71 S '89

Little Dorrit. D. Hutera. il *Theatre Crafts* 23:34-7+ Ja '89

The making of 'Rain Man' [interview with B. Levinson] D. Rensin. il por *Rolling Stone* p30 Ja 12 '89

Michael Shamberg [interview] il por *American Film* 14:16-18+ Ja/F '89

Production: The adventures of Baron Munchausen. J. Calhoun. il *Theatre Crafts* 23:18 Ap '89

Return of the money-making slime [Ghostbusters II; cover story] P. Goldstein. il *Rolling Stone* p52-4+ Je 1 '89

Ron's rules of order [R. Shelton's Blaze] P. Jordan. il pors *Gentlemen's Quarterly* 59:300-5+ D '89

She devil [interview with S. Seidelman] D. DeNicolo. il por *Glamour* 87:158+ D '89

The Steel magnolias scrapbook. J. Rachlin and J. Rovin. il *Ladies' Home Journal* 106:126+ N '89

Teetering over 'The abyss' [producer G. A. Hurd] B. Walker. il pors *American Film* 14:34-9 Je '89

Unforgettable Gone with the wind. J. Culhane. il *Reader's Digest* 135:146-51 D '89

Wave of the future [making of The abyss] J. Calhoun. il *Theatre Crafts* 23:46-7+ Ag/S '89

What hath John Waters wrought? A musical with a cast you wouldn't believe [Cry baby] M. Dougherty. il *People Weekly* 32:54-6 S 11 '89

Who's on first? [making Rain Man] D. Ansen. il pors *Newsweek* 113:52-6 Ja 16 '89

Accidents

Critically injured in filming, Karate Kid bad boy Sean Kanan rallies to fight to the finish. M. Dougherty. il pors *People Weekly* 32:51-2 Jl 17 '89

MOTION PICTURE REMAKES

Imported inspiration [She-devil and other American remakes of foreign films] G. Kilday. il *American Film* 14:14 My '89

The remake hall of fame [videos] M. G. Stevenson. il *Video* 12:22 Ja '89

MOTION PICTURE REVIEWS

The big screen scene. il *Teen* 33:42 F '89

Christmas at the movies. D. DeNicolo. il *Glamour* 87:156 D '89

Cue: a complete entertainment guide for the week. See issues of New York

The current cinema. P. Kael. See issues of The New Yorker

Film. J. Simon. See occasional issues of National Review

Film review. H. M. Geduld. See issues of The Humanist

Films. See issues of Maclean's

Goings on about town. See issues of The New Yorker

The gold rush [summer preview] P. Travers. il *Rolling Stone* p73-4+ Je 15 '89

Illuminations. See issues of American Film

Imitation of life. J. Greenberg. il *American Film* 14:13-14 S '89

Independents' day [summer releases] G. Peary. il *American Film* 14:45 Je '89

Intimate stories. B. D. Johnson. il *Maclean's* 102:44-5 Ja 9 '89

Kid stuff: our panel of young experts rate the summer movies. L. Barry. il *American Film* 14:72 S '89

Macho under fire. P. Travers. il *Rolling Stone* p27+ O 19 '89

Movie muses [summer preview] M. Flamm. il *Harper's Bazaar* 122:86-91+ Je '89

Movies. il *Vogue* 179:247+ O '89

Movies. J. G. Boyum. See issues of Glamour

Movies. D. Denby. See issues of New York

Movies [fall preview] N. Dolin. il *New York* 22:56-9 S 11 '89

Movies. R. Rosenbaum. See issues of Mademoiselle

Movies. K. Turan. See issues of Gentlemen's Quarterly

Movies to see. See issues of Jet beginning February 10, 1986

People picks & pans. See issues of People Weekly

Post-Vietnam survival tactics. J. M. Wall. *The Christian Century* 106:961-3 O 25 '89

Screen. il *People Weekly* 32:74-7 S 4 '89

Screen. T. O'Brien. See occasional issues of Commonweal beginning February 10, 1984

Screenings. See issues of American Film

Sneak preview. il *Teen* 33:48 D '89

Spotlight. E. Miller. See issues of Seventeen through March 1989

Stanley Kauffmann on films. S. Kauffmann. See issues of The New Republic

Summer film guide. il *Teen* 33:48-9 Je '89

Summer of superheroes. B. D. Johnson. il *Maclean's* 102:50-3 Je 26 '89

The talkies. B. Bawer. See issues of The American Spectator

The year in movies [1989] P. Travers. il *Rolling Stone* p21+ D 14-28 '89

Single works

36 fillette
  The Nation 248:174 F 6 '89. S. Klawans
  The New Republic 200:24 F 6 '89. S. Kauffmann
  New York 22:83 F 6 '89. D. Denby
  People Weekly 31:19-20 Ja 16 '89. P. Travers

84 Charlie MoPic
  Commonweal 116:278 My 5 '89. T. O'Brien
  Film Comment il 25:11-15 Mr/Ap '89. K. Jaehne
  The New Republic 200:24-5 Ap 24 '89. S. Kauffmann
  Newsweek 113:67+ Ap 3 '89. D. Ansen
  People Weekly il 31:12 My 1 '89. R. Novak
  Rolling Stone il p32 My 4 '89. J. Marchese
  Time il 133:83 Ap 17 '89. R. Schickel

2001: a space odyssey
  Video 12:63-4 Mr '89. M. Fleischmann

The abandoned field
  The New Yorker 65:25-6 Jl 17 '89

Above the law
  Video 12:83-4 Ja '89. D. Schweiger

The abyss
  American Film il 14:34-9 Je '89. B. Walker
  Ms. il 18:66-71 S '89. M. Rosen
  New York il 22:126+ Ag 21 '89. D. Denby
  The New Yorker 65:89-90 S 4 '89. T. Rafferty
  Newsweek il 114:56 Ag 14 '89. D. Ansen
  Omni (New York, N.Y.) il 11:14+ Ag '89. A. Maurer
  People Weekly il 32:17-18 Ag 28 '89. R. Novak
  Rolling Stone il p37 Ag 24 '89. P. Travers
  Theatre Crafts il 23:44-7+ Ag/S '89. J. Calhoun
  Time il 134:79 Ag 14 '89. R. Schickel

The accidental tourist
  America 160:113+ F 11 '89. R. A. Blake
  The American Spectator il 22:30+ Mr '89. B. Bawer
  Commonweal 116:81 F 10 '89. T. O'Brien
  The Nation 248:65-6 Ja 9-16 '89. S. Klawans
  National Review 41:56 Mr 10 '89. J. Simon
  The New Yorker 64:90-1 Ja 23 '89. P. Kael

The accused
  The American Spectator il 22:35-6 Ja '89. B. Bawer
  Video il 13:62+ Jl '89. J. Young
  Video il 13:14 My '89. S. Roman

The adventures of Baron Munchausen
  American Film il 14:34-9+ Mr '89. J. Mathews
  American Film il 15:70 N '89. P. Rainer
  Gentlemen's Quarterly il 59:155+ Mr '89. K. Turan
  Maclean's il 102:55 Mr 27 '89. B. D. Johnson
  The Nation 248:427-8 Mr 27 '89. S. Klawans
  The New Leader 72:21 Mr 6 '89. J. Morrone
  The New Republic 200:32-3 Mr 20 '89. S. Kauffmann
  New York 22:73 Mr 20 '89. D. Denby
  The New Yorker 65:103-5 Ap 3 '89. P. Kael
  Newsweek il 113:69 Mr 13 '89. J. Kroll

MOTION PICTURE REVIEWS — Single works — The adventures of Baron Munchausen—*cont.*
    People Weekly il 31:15 Mr 13 '89. S. Haller
    Theatre Crafts il 23:18 Ap '89. J. Calhoun
    Time il 133:82 Mr 13 '89. R. Corliss
Ajooba
    World Press Review il 36:75 S '89. P. Saxena
Alien nation
    Video il 13:60 Ag '89. J. Walker
All dogs go to heaven
    American Film il 15:17 D '89. R. Lloyd
    Newsweek il 114:72-3 N 20 '89. B. Barol
    People Weekly il 32:21 D 4 '89. R. Novak
    Time il 134:91 N 20 '89. R. Corliss
Animal behavior
    Newsweek 114:92 N 13 '89. J. Kroll
    People Weekly 32:19 N 13 '89. R. Novak
Another woman
    Video 13:62+ Je '89. I. Robbins
Arena brains
    Art in America il 77:35+ Mr '89. C. Lewis
Au revoir les enfants
    Video il 13:60 Ap '89. R. Gehr
Azul
    The Nation 248:786-7 Je 5 '89. S. Klawans
Babar: the movie
    Maclean's il 102:48 Ag 7 '89. G. Hayden
    People Weekly il 32:18-19 S 11 '89. R. Novak
Babette's feast
    Video il 13:60 Ap '89. R. Gehr
Baby, it's you
    Video il 13:78+ N '89. J. Young
Back to the future, part II
    Maclean's il 102:70+ D 4 '89. B. D. Johnson
    The New Republic 201:26 D 25 '89. S. Kauffmann
    The New Yorker 65:139-40 D 11 '89. P. Kael
    Newsweek il 114:78 D 4 '89. D. Ansen
    People Weekly 32:17 D 11 '89. R. Novak
    Time il 134:101 D 4 '89. R. Schickel
Bagdad Cafe
    Video il 12:61-2 F '89. M. Coyle
Batman
    Commonweal il 116:503 S 22 '89. P. D. Baumann
    Film Comment il 25:76+ N/D '89. A. White
    Life il 12:84-6 Spr '89. L. Nickson
    Motor Trend il 41:56-9+ Jl '89. P. Bingham
    The Nation 249:100-1 Jl 17 '89. S. Klawans
    National Review 41:46+ Ag 18 '89. J. Simon
    National Review 41:55-7 S 15 '89. M. Sieff
    The New Republic 201:24 Jl 31 '89. S. Kauffmann
    New York il 22:45-6 Jl 17 '89. D. Denby
    The New York Times Magazine il p44-6+ Ap 9 '89. J. Morgenstern
    The New Yorker 65:83-5 Jl 10 '89. P. Kael
    Newsweek il 113:68-9 Ja 23 '89. J. Kroll
    Newsweek il 113:70-4 Je 26 '89. B. Barol
    People Weekly il 32:13 Jl 3 '89. R. Novak
    Popular Mechanics il 166:13 O '89
    Rolling Stone il p38-42+ Je 29 '89. B. Zehme
    Theatre Crafts il 23:21 Ag/S '89. A. Pirani
    Time il 133:60-2 Je 19 '89. R. Corliss
    Video il 13:80-1+ D '89. B. Eder
    Vogue il 179:128-30 Je '89. E. G. Carter
Batteries not included
    Video il 12:89 Ja '89. M. Coyle
Beaches
    Glamour il 87:186 Mr '89. J. G. Boyum
    New York il 22:58+ Ja 16 '89. D. Denby
    The New Yorker 64:91-2 Ja 23 '89. P. Kael
    People Weekly il 31:12 Ja 9 '89. P. Travers
    Video il 13:80+ O '89. R. Gehr
The bear
    Commonweal il 116:706-7 D 15 '89. T. O'Brien
    Film Comment il 25:2+ S/O '89. A. Thompson
    Gentlemen's Quarterly il 59:129-30+ N '89. K. Turan
    Life il 12:89-91 Spr '89. T. Skari
    Maclean's il por 102:94+ O 30 '89. B. D. Johnson
    New York il 22:70 O 30 '89. D. Denby
    The New Yorker 65:121-3 N 13 '89. P. Kael
    Newsweek il 114:92 N 13 '89. D. Ansen
    People Weekly il 32:87-8 N 6 '89. I. Lacher
    Time il 134:97 O 30 '89. R. Schickel
Bert Rigby, you're a fool
    Time il 133:82 F 27 '89. R. Schickel
Betrayed
    Video il 13:60 Ap '89. R. Gehr
Big
    Video il 13:57 Ap '89. J. Young
The big picture
    American Film il 14:59 S '89. E. Drucker
    Film Comment il 25:6-8 S/O '89. G. Smith
    The Nation 249:398-9 O 9 '89. S. Klawans
    The New Yorker 65:103-4 S 18 '89. T. Rafferty
    People Weekly il 32:12+ O 2 '89. R. Novak
Big top Pee-wee
    Video il 12:61 F '89. B. Walters
Bill and Ted's excellent adventure
    People Weekly 31:16 Mr 13 '89. R. Novak

Bird
    Down Beat il 56:6 F '89. K. Whitehead
    The New Republic il 200:25-31 F 27 '89. S. Crouch
Black rain
    Commonweal 116:565-6 O 20 '89. P. D. Baumann
    Life il 12:79-80 Spr '89. M. Beller
    Maclean's 102:65+ O 2 '89. B. D. Johnson
    The New Republic 201:31-2 O 16 '89. S. Kauffmann
    New York il 22:66+ O 2 '89. D. Denby
    Newsweek il 114:70-1 O 2 '89. D. Ansen
    People Weekly il 32:17 O 9 '89. R. Novak
    Time 134:90 O 2 '89. R. Corliss
Blade runner
    American Film il 15:72 D '89. D. Rochester
Blaze
    American Film il 15:35-9+ D '89. J. Silverman
    Gentlemen's Quarterly il 59:300-5+ D '89. P. Jordan
    Maclean's il 102:53-4 D 25 '89. B. D. Johnson
    The New Yorker 65:136+ D 11 '89. P. Kael
    Newsweek il 114:69+ D 18 '89. D. Ansen
    Time il 134:93 D 18 '89. R. Corliss
The blob
    Video il 12:86+ Ja '89. M. Pierson
Blue steel
    American Film 14:59 S '89. N. Mills
    Gentlemen's Quarterly il 59:162+ O '89. K. Turan
    Rolling Stone il p47-8 S 21 '89. P. Travers
Born on the Fourth of July
    New York il 22:101-2 D 18 '89. D. Denby
    Newsweek il 114:74 D 25 '89. D. Ansen
    Time il por 134:75-9 D 25 '89. R. Corliss
Breaking in
    The New Republic 201:24-5 O 23 '89. S. Kauffmann
    The New Yorker 65:109-10 O 16 '89. P. Kael
    People Weekly 32:14 O 16 '89. R. Novak
Bull Durham
    Video il 12:16 F '89. L. Kesten
    Video il 12:61-2 Mr '89. D. Schweiger
The 'burbs
    Newsweek il 113:58 Mr 6 '89. D. Ansen
    People Weekly il 31:17 Mr 6 '89. R. Novak
    Time il 133:81-2 F 27 '89. R. Corliss
    Video il 13:91+ S '89. J. Young
Burning secret
    People Weekly il 31:19 Ja 16 '89. P. Travers
Buy & cell
    People Weekly 31:16+ F 13 '89. S. Haller
Camille Claudel
    Vogue il 179:498-503+ Mr '89. A.-E. Moutet
    World Press Review il 36:61 Mr '89. M. Braudeau
Carnival of souls
    The New Yorker 65:88 S 4 '89. T. Rafferty
Casualties of war
    The Christian Century 106:925-6 O 18 '89. S. Henderson
    Commonweal 116:502-3 S 22 '89. P. D. Baumann
    Film Comment il 25:49-52 Jl/Ag '89. G. Smith
    Gentlemen's Quarterly il 59:201+ S '89. K. Turan
    Maclean's il 102:46 Ag 21 '89. P. Hluchy
    The Nation 249:252 S 4-11 '89. S. Klawans
    National Review il 41:63-4 S 29 '89. J. Simon
    The New Republic 201:26-8 O 2 '89. S. Kauffmann
    New York il 22:53+ Ag 28 '89. D. Denby
    The New York Times Magazine il p24-7+ My 21 '89. B. Weber
    The New Yorker 65:76-9 Ag 21 '89. P. Kael
    Newsweek il 114:58 Ag 21 '89. D. Ansen
    People Weekly il 32:47+ Ag 28 '89. M. H. J. Farrell
    People Weekly il 32:17 Ag 28 '89. R. Novak
    Rolling Stone il p31 S 7 '89. P. Travers
    Time il 134:54 Ag 21 '89. R. Schickel
Champions forever
    Sport (New York, N.Y.) il 80:11 D '89. D. Miller
Chances are
    Maclean's il 102:59 Mr 20 '89. B. D. Johnson
    Newsweek 113:83 Mr 20 '89. D. Ansen
    People Weekly il 31:11 Mr 27 '89. R. Novak
Cheetah
    People Weekly il 32:13 S 4 '89. R. Novak
Chocolat
    America 161:124-5 Ag 26-S 2 '89. R. A. Blake
    The New Republic 200:28-9 Ap 17 '89. S. Kauffmann
    Newsweek il 113:68 Mr 27 '89. J. Kroll
    Vogue il 179:268 Mr '89. K. Bishop
The chocolate war
    People Weekly il 31:14 Ja 30 '89. P. Travers
A chorus of disapproval
    The New Republic 201:26-7 S 11 '89. S. Kauffmann
City lights
    The New Yorker 64:19 Ja 9 '89
Clean and sober
    Video il 13:76 My '89. J. Young
Cocktail
    Video il 13:61 Je '89. J. Young
Cocoon: the return
    Video 13:60+ Ag '89. J. Walker
Cold feet
    People Weekly il 31:13 Je 19 '89. R. Novak

MOTION PICTURE REVIEWS—Single works—*cont.*

Colors
  Video il 12:81-2 Ja '89. I. Robbins
Comic book confidential
  The New Republic 201:24-5 Jl 17-24 '89. S. Kauffmann
Coming to America
  Video il 13:73 My '89. R. Gehr
  Video il 13:16-17 Je '89. J. Bernard
Communion
  People Weekly il 32:19 N 27 '89. R. Novak
Cookie
  The New Yorker 65:90 S 4 '89. T. Rafferty
  Newsweek 114:68 S 4 '89. D. Ansen
  People Weekly il 32:17 S 11 '89. R. Novak
  Rolling Stone il por p48 S 21 '89. P. Travers
  Time il 134:64 Ag 28 '89. R. Corliss
The Cotton Club
  New York il 22:24-33 Jl 24 '89. J. Kasindorf
Cousins
  Commonweal 116:177-8 Mr 24 '89. T. O'Brien
  Glamour il 87:226 Ap '89. D. Denicolo
  The New Yorker 65:97-8 Mr 6 '89. P. Kael
  Newsweek il 113:65 F 20 '89. D. Ansen
  People Weekly 31:17-18 F 20 '89. S. Haller
  Video il 13:77+ N '89. J. Walker
  Vogue il 179:268 Mr '89. J. Sherman
Crimes and misdemeanors
  America 161:429-30 D 9 '89. R. A. Blake
  The Christian Century il por 106:991 N 1 '89. J. M. Wall
  Commonweal 116:706 D 15 '89. T. O'Brien
  Film Comment il 25:11-12+ N/D '89. M. Pally
  Maclean's il por 102:68 O 23 '89. B. D. Johnson
  The Nation 249;575-6 N 13 '89. S. Klawans
  National Review il 41:46-8 D 8 '89. J. Simon
  The New Republic 201:22-3 N 13 '89. S. Kauffmann
  The New Republic 201:43 N 27 '89. L. Wieseltier
  New York il 22:124+ O 23 '89. D. Denby
  The New Yorker 65:76-8 O 30 '89. P. Kael
  Newsweek il 114:67 O 16 '89. J. Kroll
  People Weekly il por 32:13 O 16 '89. R. Novak
  Rolling Stone il p35 N 2 '89. P. Travers
  Time il por 134:82 O 16 '89. R. Schickel
Criminal law
  The Humanist il 49:47-8 Jl/Ag '89. H. M. Geduld
  People Weekly il 31:13+ Je 5 '89. R. Novak
Crossing Delancey
  Video il 13:75 My '89. J. Bernard
Crusoe
  The New Yorker 65:114-15 Ap 17 '89. P. Kael
  People Weekly 31:13 My 15 '89. S. Haller
Cry-baby
  Film Comment il por 25:2+ Jl/Ag '89. R. J. Smith
  People Weekly il 32:54-6 S 11 '89. M. Dougherty
Cry freedom
  The Unesco Courier il 42:4-7 Ag '89. C. Vieler-Porter
A cry in the dark
  American Film il 14:72 Je '89. P. Rainer
  Glamour il 87:103-4 Ja '89. J. G. Boyum
  Mademoiselle il 95:46+ Ja '89. R. Rosenbaum
  Video il 13:62 Jl '89. J. Young
Dad
  Maclean's il 102:82 N 6 '89. B. D. Johnson
  The New Yorker 65:119+ N 13 '89. P. Kael
  People Weekly il 32:19 N 6 '89. R. Novak
  Rolling Stone p38 N 16 '89. P. Travers
Dangerous liaisons
  America 160:88 F 4 '89. R. A. Blake
  American Film il 14:64 Jl/Ag '89. P. Rainer
  The American Spectator 22:38 My '89. B. Bawer
  Commonweal 116:147 Mr 10 '89. T. O'Brien
  Glamour il 87:186+ Mr '89. J. G. Boyum
  The Humanist il 49:45-6 My/Je '89. H. M. Geduld
  Mademoiselle 95:92 F '89. R. Rosenbaum
  The Nation 248:173-4 F 6 '89. S. Klawans
  National Review 41:54-5 F 24 '89. J. Simon
  The New Republic 200:24-5 Ja 2 '89. S. Kauffmann
  New York il 22:52+ Ja 9 '89. D. Denby
  The New York Times Magazine il p72 F 19 '89. La Ferla Ruth
  The New Yorker 64:78-80 Ja 9 '89. P. Kael
  Time il 133:64 Ja 16 '89. R. Corliss
  Video il 13:59 Ag '89. J. Bernard
The dead
  Video il 12:82-3 Ja '89. S. L. Siegel
Dead-bang
  People Weekly il 31:17-18 Ap 10 '89. R. Novak
Dead calm
  Newsweek 113:72 Ap 17 '89. D. Ansen
  People Weekly il 31:17+ Ap 17 '89. S. Haller
  Video il 13:79 N '89. J. Silberg
Dead Poets Society
  America 161:40 Jl 15-22 '89. R. A. Blake
  American Film il 14:57 Jl/Ag '89. R. Seidenberg
  The American Spectator il 22:39-40 Ag '89. B. Bawer
  Commonweal 116:372 Je 16 '89. T. O'Brien
  The Humanist il 49:41-2 S/O '89. H. M. Geduld
  Life il 12:64-8 Spr '89

  Maclean's il 102:52 Je 12 '89. B. D. Johnson
  National Review 41:54-5 S 15 '89. J. Simon
  The New Republic 200:26-7 Je 26 '89. S. Kauffmann
  New York il 22:77-8 Je 12 '89. D. Denby
  The New Yorker 65:70-1 Je 26 '89. P. Kael
  Newsweek il 113:67 Je 12 '89. D. Ansen
  Newsweek il 114:74 Jl 3 '89. G. F. Will
  People Weekly il 31:17 Je 12 '89. R. Novak
  Rolling Stone il p29 Je 29 '89. P. Travers
  Time il 133:78 Je 5 '89. R. Schickel
Dead ringers
  Video il 13:62+ Je '89. I. Robbins
  Video il 13:17-18 Je '89. D. Schweiger
Dealers
  People Weekly il 32:19-20 N 27 '89. R. Novak
Deepstar six
  People Weekly 31:16 Ja 30 '89. P. Travers
Depeche Mode 101
  Rolling Stone il p36 My 18 '89. J. Farber
Die hard
  Video il 12:61 Mr '89. L. Kesten
Dirty rotten scoundrels
  The New Republic 200:28-9 Ja 30 '89. S. Kauffmann
  New York 22:60 Ja 16 '89. D. Denby
  The New Yorker 64:92-3 Ja 23 '89. P. Kael
  Rolling Stone il p44 F 9 '89. A. White
  Video il 13:63 Jl '89. J. Walker
Disorganized crime
  People Weekly il 31:11-12 My 1 '89. R. Novak
Distant voices, still lives
  The Nation 249:252-3 S 4-11 '89. S. Klawans
  The New Yorker il 65:88-9 S 4 '89. T. Rafferty
  Time il 134:78-9 Ag 14 '89. R. Corliss
Do the right thing
  America 161:86-7 Ag 12-19 '89. R. A. Blake
  The Christian Century 106:739-40 Ag 16-23 '89. J. M. Wall
  Commonweal 116:562-3 O 20 '89. B. B. Morton
  Commonweal 116:402-3 Jl 14 '89. T. O'Brien
  Essence il pors 20:55-6 Jl '89
  Film Comment il 25:12-16+ Jl/Ag '89. M. Glicksman
  Jet il 76:36-9 Jl 10 '89. T. S. Moore
  Mademoiselle il por 95:94+ Ag '89. R. Rosenbaum
  Mother Jones il 14:32-5+ S '89. P. Orenstein
  Mother Jones il por 14:35+ S '89. A. White
  The Nation 249:98-100 Jl 17 '89. S. Klawans
  National Review il 41:45-6+ Ag 4 '89. J. Simon
  National Review 41:24-5 Ag 4 '89. M. Morrison
  The New Leader 72:21-2 S 18 '89. J. Morrone
  The New Republic 201:24-6 Jl 3 '89. S. Kauffmann
  New York 22:6 Jl 17 '89. S. Lee
  New York il 22:14-15 Je 26 '89. J. Klein
  New York il 22:53-4 Je 26 '89. D. Denby
  The New York Review of Books il 36:37-8 S 28 '89. M. Kempton
  The New Yorker 65:78-81 Jl 24 '89. T. Rafferty
  Newsweek il 114:64-6 Jl 3 '89
  People Weekly il 32:67-8 Jl 10 '89. J. S. Kunen
  People Weekly il por 32:13-14 Jl 3 '89. R. Novak
  Rolling Stone il p104-5+ Jl 13-27 '89. D. Handelman
  Rolling Stone il p27+ Je 29 '89. P. Travers
  Time il por 134:62 Jl 3 '89. R. Corliss
  U.S. News & World Report il 107:51 Jl 10 '89
  Vogue il pors 179:76-7+ Jl '89. D. McLane
The dream team
  American Film il 14:77-8 Ap '89. F. Spotnitz
  The New Yorker 65:113-14 Ap 17 '89. P. Kael
  People Weekly il 31:18 Ap 10 '89. S. Haller
  Video il 13:77 N '89. J. Walker
The dressmaker
  New York 22:56-7 Mr 6 '89. D. Denby
  Newsweek 113:54 Ja 9 '89. D. Ansen
  People Weekly 31:20 Ja 16 '89. P. Travers
Driving Miss Daisy
  Jet il 77:51 D 4 '89. S. P. Flanagan
  Maclean's 102:52 D 25 '89. B. D. Johnson
  The New Yorker 65:74-6 D 25 '89. P. Kael
  Newsweek il 114:68-9 D 18 '89. D. Ansen
  People Weekly il 32:15-16 D 18 '89. R. Novak
  Time il 134:91 D 18 '89. R. Schickel
Drowning by numbers
  Maclean's 102:86+ N 6 '89. B. D. Johnson
Drugstore cowboy
  Gentlemen's Quarterly il por 59:59-60 Jl '89. K. Turan
  Maclean's 102:84 N 6 '89. B. D. Johnson
  New York il 22:82-3 O 9 '89. D. Denby
  The New Yorker 65:74+ O 30 '89. P. Kael
  Newsweek il 114:84 O 23 '89. D. Ansen
  Rolling Stone il p50 N 30 '89. C. Arrington
A dry white season
  America 161:353 N 18 '89. R. A. Blake
  American Film il 14:32-7 S '89. K. McKenna
  Essence il 20:31-2 O '89. M. Southgate
  Film Comment il 25:64-6+ S/O '89. M. Glicksman
  Jet il 77:63 O 23 '89
  Ms. il 18:18+ O '89. M. Rosen
  The Nation 249:507-8 O 30 '89. S. Klawans
  National Review il 41:56-8 O 27 '89. J. Simon

MOTION PICTURE REVIEWS — Single works — A dry
white season—*cont.*
  The New Republic 201:24-5 O 9 '89. S. Kauffmann
  New York 22:75 O 2 '89. D. Denby
  The New Yorker 65:101 O 2 '89. P. Kael
  People Weekly il 32:16-17 S 25 '89. R. Novak
  People Weekly il 32:71-2 O 16 '89. I. Lacher
  Rolling Stone il p36 O 5 '89
  Time il 134:78 S 25 '89. R. Schickel
E.T. the extra-terrestrial
  People Weekly il 32 Special Issue:91 Fall '89. B. Darrach
  Rolling Stone il p127 F 9 '89. J. B. Meigs
Earth girls are easy
  New York il 22:101 My 15 '89. D. Denby
  People Weekly 31:15-16 My 29 '89. R. Novak
  Time il 133:74-5 My 15 '89. R. Corliss
  Video il 13:14-15 N '89. R. Gehr
  Vogue il 179:212 My '89. J. Lazar
Eat a bowl of tea
  The New Leader 72:20-1 Ag 7-21 '89. J. Morrone
Eat the rich
  Video 12:85 Ja '89. I. Robbins
Enemies, a love story
  American Film il 15:30-7 N '89. B. Yagoda
  New York 22:103-4 D 18 '89. D. Denby
  The New Yorker 65:73-4 D 25 '89. P. Kael
  Newsweek il 114:69 D 18 '89. D. Ansen
Erik the Viking
  People Weekly il 32:27+ N 20 '89. R. Novak
The exorcist 1990
  People Weekly 32:44-6 Ag 14 '89. M. Dougherty
The fabulous Baker Boys
  Commonweal 116:644 N 17 '89. T. O'Brien
  Maclean's il 102:66 O 23 '89. B. D. Johnson
  The New Republic 201:28-9 N 20 '89. S. Kauffmann
  New York il 22:73-5 O 16 '89. D. Denby
  The New Yorker 65:107-9 O 16 '89. P. Kael
  Newsweek il 114:84-5 O 23 '89. D. Ansen
  People Weekly il 32:19 O 23 '89. R. Novak
  Rolling Stone il p36 N 2 '89. P. Travers
  Time il 134:85 O 23 '89. R. Schickel
Far north
  Glamour il 87:104 Ja '89. J. G. Boyum
Fat Man and Little Boy
  Commonweal 116:643-4 N 17 '89. T. O'Brien
  Esquire il 112:170-1 O '89. R. Scheer
  Maclean's il 102:96 O 30 '89. B. D. Johnson
  The Nation 249:577-8 N 13 '89. S. Klawans
  National Review il 41:63-7 N 10 '89. D. K. Mano
  The New Republic 201:28 N 20 '89. S. Kauffmann
  New York 22:102+ N 6 '89. D. Denby
  The New Yorker 65:121 N 13 '89. P. Kael
  Newsweek il 114:75 O 30 '89. D. Ansen
  People Weekly il 32:19-20 N 6 '89. R. Novak
  Rolling Stone il p37 N 16 '89. P. Travers
  Scholastic Update (Teachers' edition) il 122:13 O 6 '89
Field of dreams
  American Film 14:62 My '89. J. E. Fitch
  The Christian Century 106:515-16 My 17 '89. J. M. Wall
  Commonweal 116:303 My 19 '89. T. O'Brien
  Film Comment il 25:78-9 My/Je '89. H. Jacobson
  Maclean's il 102:66 My 1 '89. B. D. Johnson
  Mademoiselle il 95:66+ Jl '89. R. Rosenbaum
  The Nation 248:678 My 15 '89. S. Klawans
  The New Republic 200:26+ My 8 '89. S. Kauffmann
  New York il 22:96+ Ap 24 '89. D. Denby
  The New Yorker 65:76-7 My 1 '89. P. Kael
  Newsweek il 113:72-3 Ap 24 '89. D. Ansen
  Newsweek il 113:68 Je 12 '89. D. Ansen
  People Weekly il 32:120-1 O 23 '89. M. Donovan
  People Weekly il 31:13-14 My 15 '89. R. Novak
  Sports Illustrated il 70:81 My 1 '89. S. Wulf
  Time 133:78 Ap 24 '89. R. Corliss
  Vogue il 179:204 My '89
The final season
  Maclean's il 102:85-6 N 13 '89. B. D. Johnson
The first emperor of China
  Forbes il 144:20 Ag 7 '89. M. S. Forbes
  Maclean's 102:44 Jl 17 '89. B. D. Johnson
  Natural History il p66-9 Jl '89. T. R. Miller
A fish called Wanda
  American Film il 14:16-18+ Ja/F '89
  Video 13:59 Ap '89. J. Walker
Five easy pieces
  Video il 12:84-5 Ja '89. F. Lovece
Fletch lives
  Newsweek il 113:83 Mr 20 '89. D. Ansen
  People Weekly il 31:11-12 Mr 27 '89. R. Novak
The fly II
  People Weekly 31:11 F 27 '89. R. Novak
  Video il 13:81 O '89. D. Schweiger
For queen and country
  The New Leader 72:21 My 1 '89. J. Morrone
Forced march
  People Weekly il 32:20+ N 27 '89. R. Novak
Forever, Lulu
  Video il 12:85 Ja '89. D. Wheeler

A forgotten tune for the flute
  Commonweal 116:119 F 24 '89. T. O'Brien
Four adventures of Reinette and Mirabelle
  The New Republic 201:26-7 Ag 28 '89. S. Kauffmann
  People Weekly 32:18 Ag 14 '89. R. Novak
The French Revolution
  American Film il 15:12-13 O '89. N. Mills
Friday the 13th, part VIII: Jason takes Manhattan
  People Weekly il 32:17-18 Ag 14 '89. R. Novak
Friendship's death
  People Weekly 31:18+ Ja 23 '89. P. Travers
Funny
  The New Republic 201:25 Jl 17-24 '89. S. Kauffmann
  Theatre Crafts il 23:12-13 Ja '89. J. Calhoun
Funny farm
  Video il 12:83 Ja '89. J. Walker
Fury to freedom
  Christianity Today 33:40-3 Ag 18 '89. B. Bird
Getting it right
  Commonweal 116:338 Je 2 '89. T. O'Brien
Ghostbusters II
  New York il 22:46 Jl 17 '89. D. Denby
  The New Yorker 65:85 Jl 10 '89. P. Kael
  Newsweek il 113:68 Je 26 '89. D. Ansen
  People Weekly il 32:14-15 Jl 3 '89. R. Novak
  Rolling Stone il por p52-4+ Je 1 '89. P. Goldstein
  Time il 133:89 Je 26 '89. R. Schickel
  Video il 13:87 D '89. J. Young
Glory
  American Visions il 4:24 D '89. R. Faulcon
  Essence il 20:30 D '89. M. Southgate
  Newsweek 114:73 D 18 '89. D. Ansen
  Time il 134:91 D 18 '89. R. Schickel
The gods must be crazy II
  American Film il 15:97+ O '89. E. Drucker
Gone with the wind
  American Heritage il 40:43-5 D '89. A. Nielsen
  The New Yorker 64:27 F 13 '89
  Reader's Digest il 135:146-51 D '89. J. Culhane
The good mother
  The American Spectator 22:36 Ja '89. B. Bawer
  Glamour il 87:103 Ja '89. J. G. Boyum
  Mademoiselle il 95:46+ Ja '89. R. Rosenbaum
Gorillas in the mist
  Video il 13:64 Je '89. S. L. Siegel
Great balls of fire
  American Film il 14:26-33+ Je '89. R. Palmer
  Maclean's il 102:46-7 Jl 10 '89. B. D. Johnson
  The New Leader 72:21 Ag 7-21 '89. J. Morrone
  Newsweek il 114:72 Jl 10 '89. D. Ansen
  People Weekly 32:12+ Jl 17 '89. R. Novak
  Rolling Stone il p118-21+ Jl 13-27 '89. S. Pond
  Rolling Stone p33 Ag 10 '89
  Time il 134:67 Jl 10 '89. R. Schickel
  Video il 13:16-17 D '89. I. Robbins
  Vogue il 179:182-5 Jl '89. N. Tosches
Hail Mary
  The Christian Century 106:1166-8 D 13 '89. J. K. Larson
Halloween V
  People Weekly 32:14-15 O 30 '89. R. Novak
Hanussen
  The New Republic 200:22 Ap 10 '89. S. Kauffmann
Harlem nights
  American Film il 15:63 N '89. C. Fleming
  Jet il pors 77:60-2 D 18 '89. R. E. Johnson
  Jet il 77:56-60 N 20 '89
  Jet il 77:56-8 D 11 '89
  Maclean's il por 102:74 N 27 '89. B. D. Johnson
  The New Republic 201:24-5 D 18 '89. S. Kauffmann
  Newsweek il por 114:92 N 27 '89. D. Ansen
  People Weekly 32:16+ D 18 '89. R. Novak
  People Weekly il 32:76-7 D 4 '89
  Time il por 134:88 N 27 '89. R. Schickel
Heart of Dixie
  American Film il 14:58 S '89. J. E. Fitch
Heat and sunlight
  The New Republic 200:31 My 1 '89. S. Kauffmann
Heathers
  American Film il 14:10 Ja/F '89. L. Ochoa
  The American Spectator 22:42-3 Je '89. B. Bawer
  Gentlemen's Quarterly il 59:123+ Ap '89. K. Turan
  The Nation 248:530 Ap 17 '89. S. Klawans
  New York il 22:68+ Ap 3 '89. D. Denby
  The New Yorker 65:115-16 Ap 17 '89. P. Kael
  Newsweek 113:67 Ap 3 '89. D. Ansen
  Rolling Stone il p38 Ap 20 '89. S. Pond
  Time il 133:83 Ap 17 '89. R. Corliss
  Video il 13:88+ S '89. I. Robbins
Heaven and earth
  American Film il 15:11-12 O '89. J. Greenberg
  Maclean's il 102:44-5 Ag 21 '89. J. Howse
  World Press Review il 36:68-9 N '89. J. Howse
Heavy petting
  Mother Jones il 14:50 S '89. J. Farber
  Psychology Today il 23:67-8 O '89. M. Nelson
Henry V
  American Film il por 15:62-3 N '89. R. Seidenberg
  Film Comment il 25:2+ N/D '89. G. Fuller

MOTION PICTURE REVIEWS—Single works—Henry V— cont.

   Maclean's il por 102:89-90 N 20 '89. B. D. Johnson
   The Nation 249:724-6 D 11 '89. S. Klawans
   The New Republic 201:28-30 D 4 '89. S. Kauffmann
   New York il por 22:74+ N 27 '89. D. Denby
   The New Yorker 65:104-5 N 27 '89. P. Kael
   Rolling Stone il p49 N 30 '89. P. Travers
   Time il 134:119-20 N 13 '89. R. Corliss
Her alibi
   The New Republic 200:24 Mr 6 '89. S. Kauffmann
   People Weekly il 31:15 F 6 '89. P. Travers
   Video il 13:79 O '89. M. Pierson
High fidelity
   The New Republic 201:34+ S 18-25 '89. S. Kauffmann
   New York 22:75 O 2 '89. D. Denby
High hopes
   Commonweal 116:212 Ap 7 '89. T. O'Brien
   The Nation 248:352-3 Mr 13 '89. S. Klawans
   The New Leader 72:22-3 F 20 '89. J. Morrone
   The New Republic 200:26-7 Mr 13 '89. S. Kauffmann
   New York il 22:142-3 F 27 '89. D. Denby
   The New Yorker 65:96-8 F 20 '89. P. Kael
   Newsweek il 113:69 F 27 '89. D. Ansen
   Time il 133:72-3 Mr 20 '89. R. Schickel
High spirits
   Video il 13:63 Jl '89. J. Walker
Honey, I shrunk the kids
   People Weekly il 32:13 Jl 10 '89. R. Novak
How to get ahead in advertising
   The Nation 248:676-7 My 15 '89. S. Klawans
   The New Leader 72:21 My 1 '89. J. Morrone
   The New Republic 200:28-9 Je 5 '89. S. Kauffmann
   New York il 22:71-2 My 22 '89. D. Denby
   People Weekly il 31:16+ Je 26 '89. R. Novak
   Time il 133:110 My 22 '89. R. Schickel
   Vogue il 179:204 My '89
A Hungarian fairy tale
   The Nation 248:175 F 6 '89. S. Klawans
I'm gonna git you sucka
   Jet il 75:28-30 Ja 16 '89
   The Nation 248:208 F 13 '89. S. Klawans
   People Weekly il 31:16+ Ja 23 '89. P. Travers
Immediate family
   Commonweal 116:670 D 1 '89. T. O'Brien
   Maclean's il 102:98 O 30 '89. B. D. Johnson
   New York il 22:102+ N 6 '89. D. Denby
   People Weekly il 32:17 N 13 '89. R. Novak
   Time il 134:84 N 6 '89. R. Corliss
In country
   Commonweal 116:591-2 N 3 '89. T. O'Brien
   Film Comment il por 25:11-14+ S/O '89. J. Scott
   Maclean's il 102:75 S 18 '89. B. D. Johnson
   The Nation 249:396-8 O 9 '89. S. Klawans
   The New Republic 201:30-1 O 16 '89. S. Kauffmann
   New York il 22:129-30 S 25 '89. D. Denby
   Newsweek il 114:70 O 2 '89. D. Ansen
   People Weekly il 32:16 S 25 '89. R. Novak
   Rolling Stone il p27+ O 19 '89. P. Travers
   Time il 134:90 O 2 '89
Indiana Jones and the last crusade
   America 160:591 Je 17-24 '89. R. A. Blake
   Commonweal 116:403-4 Jl 14 '89. T. O'Brien
   Film Comment il por 25:9-11 Jl/Ag '89. A. White
   Maclean's il 102:56 Je 5 '89. B. D. Johnson
   The Nation 248:862 Je 19 '89. S. Klawans
   The New Republic 200:28-9 Je 19 '89. S. Kauffmann
   New York il 22:58-9 Je 5 '89. D. Denby
   The New Yorker il 65:103-5 Je 12 '89. P. Kael
   Newsweek il 113:69 My 29 '89. D. Ansen
   People Weekly il 31:13 Je 5 '89. R. Novak
   Popular Mechanics il 166:18 Jl '89
   Rolling Stone il p31 Je 15 '89. P. Travers
   Time il 133:82-4 My 29 '89. R. Corliss
An innocent man
   People Weekly il 32:17 O 23 '89. R. Novak
Intolerance
   Film Comment il 25:28-9 S/O '89. M. Hansen
The iron triangle
   People Weekly il 31:17 Mr 6 '89. R. Novak
It's a wonderful life
   Common Cause Magazine il 15:26-30 S/O '89. J. Cobb
   Modern Maturity il 32:38-43 D '89/Ja '90. N. Dillon
Jacknife
   Maclean's 102:41 Ap 10 '89. B. D. Johnson
   The New Republic 200:24 Mr 6 '89. S. Kauffmann
   People Weekly 31:17 Ap 3 '89. R. Novak
Jack's back
   Video 12:86 Ja '89. J. Walker
The January man
   Maclean's il 102:45 Ja 23 '89. B. D. Johnson
   The New Leader 72:23 Ja 23 '89. J. Morrone
   The New Republic 200:24-5 F 6 '89. S. Kauffmann
   Newsweek 113:70 Ja 30 '89. D. Ansen
   People Weekly il 31:16 Ja 23 '89. P. Travers
   Time il 133:59 Ja 23 '89. R. Schickel
Jesus
   Christianity Today il 33:52 O 20 '89

Jesus of Montreal
   Maclean's il por 102:54-5 My 29 '89. B. D. Johnson
   Maclean's il 102:74 S 18 '89. B. D. Johnson
John Huston
   American Film il 14:66-7 Je '89. R. Seidenberg
Johnny Handsome
   American Film il 15:96-7 O '89. R. Seidenberg
   The New Yorker 65:110 O 16 '89. P. Kael
   People Weekly il 32:14-15 O 16 '89. R. Novak
K-9
   People Weekly il 31:13 My 22 '89. R. Novak
The Karate Kid, part III
   People Weekly il 32:13-14 Jl 10 '89. R. Novak
Kinjite
   People Weekly 31:15-16 F 6 '89. P. Travers
Kung Fu Master
   American Film il por 14:67 Je '89. J. E. Fitch
   The New Republic 200:27 Je 26 '89. S. Kauffmann
The land before time
   Video il 13:80 N '89. M. Meyer
Landlord blues
   The Nation 248:862 Je 19 '89. S. Klawans
The last temptation of Christ
   America 160:199-201 Mr 4 '89. R. A. Blake
   American Film il 14:12 Jl/Ag '89. C. Koseluk
   Christianity Today 33:36-7 Ap 21 '89. K. H. Sidey
   Christianity Today il 33:14 Ap 7 '89. T. C. Muck
   Christianity Today il por 33:57 My 12 '89. B. G. Baker
   Video il 13:78 O '89. I. Robbins
Lawrence of Arabia
   America 160:226 Mr 11 '89. R. A. Blake
   American Film por il 14:44 Mr '89. A. Barra
   The New Republic 200:26-8 F 20 '89. S. Kauffmann
   The New Republic 201:37 Ag 21 '89. E. Kedourie
   New York il 22:78 F 13 '89. D. Denby
   Newsweek il por 113:75 F 6 '89. D. Ansen
   People Weekly il 31:36-7 F 27 '89
   People Weekly 31:11-12 F 27 '89. S. Haller
   Time il por 133:62-3 F 6 '89. R. Corliss
Lean on me
   Commonweal 116:245 Ap 21 '89. T. O'Brien
   The Education Digest 55:20-2 N '89. I. A. Hyman
   Jet il 75:24-6 Mr 6 '89. T. S. Moore
   Jet il 75:48 Mr 20 '89
   New York 22:73-5 Mr 20 '89. D. Denby
   People Weekly 31:19-20 Mr 20 '89. T. Cunneff
   Time il 133:82 Mr 13 '89. R. Schickel
   Video il 13:78+ N '89. J. Young
La lectrice
   Commonweal 116:278-9 My 5 '89. T. O'Brien
   The New Leader 72:21 Ap 3-17 '89. J. Morrone
Lethal weapon 2
   Commonweal 116:530 O 6 '89. P. D. Baumann
   Newsweek il 114:53 Jl 17 '89. D. Ansen
   Newsweek il 114:50 Jl 31 '89
   People Weekly il 32:12 Jl 24 '89. R. Novak
   Time il 134:53 Jl 24 '89. R. Corliss
Let's get lost
   American Film il 14:50-4 My '89. R. Seidenberg
   Maclean's il 102:85-6 N 13 '89. B. D. Johnson
   The New Yorker 65:75-6 My 1 '89. P. Kael
   Newsweek 113:69 My 29 '89. D. Ansen
   Rolling Stone il p19 My 4 '89. C. Stern
Leviathan
   People Weekly il 31:18 Ap 3 '89. N. Geeslin
Licence to kill
   Motor Boating & Sailing il 163:62-5+ Ap '89. P. Whittell
   New York 22:52 Jl 24 '89. D. Denby
   Newsweek il 114:52 Jl 17 '89. J. Kroll
   People Weekly il 32:11 Jl 17 '89. R. Novak
   Time il 134:53 Jl 24 '89. R. Corliss
Lightning over Braddock: a Rustbowl fantasy
   American Film il por 14:11-12 Je '89. P. Aufderheide
Little Dorrit
   Maclean's il 102:47 Ja 16 '89. J. Bemrose
   The New York Review of Books il 36:16-18 F 2 '89. G. Wills
   Theatre Crafts il 23:34-7+ Ja '89. D. Hutera
The little mermaid
   American Film 15:17 D '89. R. Lloyd
   The New Republic 201:26-7 D 25 '89. S. Kauffmann
   New York il 22:143 D 4 '89. D. Denby
   The New Yorker 65:140 D 11 '89. P. Kael
   Newsweek il 114:72-3 N 20 '89. B. Barol
   People Weekly il 32:123-5 D 11 '89. C. Sanz
   People Weekly il 32:27 N 20 '89. R. Novak
   Time il 134:91 N 20 '89. R. Corliss
Little monsters
   Teen il 33:50 O '89
The little thief
   American Film il 15:97 O '89. D. Yakir
   Film Comment il 25:6 Jl/Ag '89. M. Pally
   The New Yorker 65:89 S 4 '89. T. Rafferty
   Newsweek 114:55 S 11 '89. D. Ansen
   People Weekly 32:14 S 18 '89. R. Novak
Little Vera
   America 161:116+ Ag 26-S 2 '89. R. A. Blake
   The American Spectator 22:43 Je '89. B. Bawer

MOTION PICTURE REVIEWS—Single works—Little Vera
—*cont.*
   Film Comment il 25:23-4+ Ja/F '89. A. Williamson
   Maclean's 102:54 Je 12 '89. B. D. Johnson
   The Nation 248:675-6 My 15 '89. S. Klawans
   The New Republic 200:30-1 My 1 '89. S. Kauffmann
   New York il 22:61-2 Ap 17 '89. D. Denby
   Newsweek il 113:71 Ap 17 '89. J. Kroll
Lock up
   People Weekly il 32:13 Ag 21 '89. R. Novak
Lodz ghetto
   The Christian Century 106:251-2 Mr 8 '89. J. M. Wall
Look who's talking
   Business Week il p142 D 11 '89. R. Grover
   People Weekly il 32:14 O 30 '89. R. Novak
   People Weekly il 32:67-8 N 13 '89. J. Kaufman
   Time il 134:98 N 20 '89. R. Corliss
Lost angels
   American Film il 14:61 My '89. E. Drucker
   New York 22:72-3 My 22 '89. D. Denby
   Video il 13:78 N '89. J. Young
Loverboy
   People Weekly il 31:12 My 22 '89. R. Novak
Macunaima
   The Unesco Courier il 42:14-17 O '89. A. Rodrigues
Madame Sousatzka
   Video 13:59 Ag '89. J. Bernard
Made in USA
   Mother Jones il 14:53-4 F/Mr '89. A. Hornaday
The magic Christian
   Video il 13:74 My '89. I. Robbins
The magnificent Ambersons
   American Film il 15:72 D '89. D. Rochester
Major league
   The New Republic 200:26 My 8 '89. S. Kauffmann
   People Weekly il 31:15 Ap 24 '89. R. Novak
   Sports Illustrated il 70:84 Ap 17 '89. S. Wulf
   Time il 133:78 Ap 24 '89. R. Corliss
   Video il 13:77 N '89. J. Walker
Married to the Mob
   Video il 12:62 Mr '89. S. L. Siegel
   Video il 12:12 Mr '89. M. Fleischmann
Mata Hari
   American Film il por 14:80 Je '89. R. Tierney
Matador
   American Film il por 15:70 N '89. P. Rainer
Midnight run
   Video il 13:74+ My '89. I. Robbins
The Mighty Quinn
   Jet il 75:46-8 F 20 '89
   New York il 22:56 Mr 6 '89. D. Denby
   People Weekly 31:11 Mr 27 '89. S. Haller
Milk and honey
   People Weekly il 32:11-12 Jl 17 '89. R. Novak
Millennium
   People Weekly il 32:13 S 18 '89. R. Novak
Miracle mile
   People Weekly 31:15-16 Je 5 '89. R. Novak
Miss Firecracker
   American Film il 14:60-1 My '89. C. Hodenfield
   Commonweal 116:338 Je 2 '89. T. O'Brien
   Film Comment il 25:9-12+ My/Je '89. K. Jaehne
   The Nation 248:677-8 My 15 '89. S. Klawans
   The New Republic 200:26-7 Je 12 '89. S. Kauffmann
   New York il 22:101-2 My 15 '89. D. Denby
   The New Yorker 65:103-4 My 29 '89. P. Kael
   Newsweek il 113:75 My 1 '89. J. Kroll
   People Weekly 31:15 My 29 '89. S. Haller
   Time 133:68 My 1 '89. R. Corliss
Mississippi burning
   Christianity Today il 33:56 Ap 7 '89. S. Ulstein
   Commonweal 116:20 Ja 13 '89. T. O'Brien
   Essence il 19:32 Mr '89. D. Bogle
   Glamour il 87:140+ F '89. J. G. Boyum
   Jet il 75:51 Ja 23 '89
   Mademoiselle 95:92 F '89. R. Rosenbaum
   Mother Jones il 14:37-9+ N '89. P. Dray
   The Nation 248:26 Ja 2 '89. S. Klawans
   National Review 41:55-6 Mr 10 '89. J. Simon
   The New Republic 200:24 Ja 9-16 '89. S. Kauffmann
   People Weekly il 31:36-43 Ja 9 '89. D. McWhorter
   Time il 133:56-62 Ja 9 '89. R. Corliss
   USA Today (Periodical) 117:35 My '89. P. Arthur
   Video il 13:57 Ag '89. S. L. Siegel
Moon over Parador
   Video il 13:59 Ap '89. J. Walker
The music teacher
   The New Republic 201:24-5 Jl 31 '89. S. Kauffmann
My left foot
   American Film il 15:64-5 D '89. A. Insdorf
   Harper's Bazaar il 122:84+ N '89
   Maclean's il 102:87 N 13 '89. B. D. Johnson
   The New Republic 201:25-6 N 27 '89. S. Kauffmann
   New York il 22:109-10 N 13 '89. D. Denby
   The New Yorker 65:98-100 O 2 '89. P. Kael
   Newsweek 114:90 N 27 '89. D. Ansen
   Rolling Stone il p38 N 16 '89. P. Travers
   Time il 134:84 N 6 '89. R. Corliss

My stepmother is an alien
   Video 13:63 Jl '89. J. Walker
Mystery train
   Film Comment il 25:19-21 Jl/Ag '89. M. Pally
   Mademoiselle il 95:78+ D '89. R. Rosenbaum
   The Nation 249:726-7 D 11 '89. S. Klawans
   The New Republic 201:24 D 11 '89. S. Kauffmann
   New York il 22:120+ N 20 '89. D. Denby
   Newsweek il 114:78 D 4 '89. D. Ansen
   Rolling Stone il p47 N 30 '89. P. Travers
   Vogue il por 179:256 N '89. B. Dorminey
The naked gun
   Video 13:91 S '89. J. Young
Naked tango
   American Film il 14:16+ S '89. G. Kilday
National Lampoon's Christmas vacation
   People Weekly il 32:17-18 D 11 '89. R. Novak
The navigator
   American Film il 14:61-2 My '89. A. Klein
   Christianity Today 33:66 My 12 '89. S. Ulstein
   Commonweal 116:437-8 Ag 11 '89. T. O'Brien
   Gentlemen's Quarterly 59:119-20 Je '89. K. Turan
   Newsweek il 113:72 Ap 17 '89. D. Ansen
New York stories
   America 160:353 Ap 15 '89. R. A. Blake
   The American Spectator il 22:37-8 My '89. B. Bawer
   Commonweal 116:212-13 Ap 7 '89. T. O'Brien
   Maclean's il pors 102:62 Mr 13 '89. B. D. Johnson
   The Nation 248:426-7 Mr 27 '89. S. Klawans
   National Review 41:45+ Je 16 '89. J. Simon
   The New Leader il 72:20-1 Mr 6 '89. J. Morrone
   The New Republic 200:24-6 Mr 27 '89. S. Kauffmann
   New York il 22:63-4 Mr 13 '89. D. Denby
   The New Yorker 65:93-6 Mr 20 '89. P. Kael
   Newsweek il 113:58 Mr 6 '89. D. Ansen
   People Weekly il 31:15-16 Mr 13 '89. S. Haller
   Time il 133:68 Mr 6 '89. R. Schickel
Night game
   People Weekly il 32:11-12 O 2 '89. R. Novak
A nightmare on Elm Street, part 4: The dream master
   Video 12:62 F '89. L. Kesten
A nightmare on Elm Street, part 5: The dream child
   Teen il 33:50 O '89
No holds barred
   People Weekly il 31:13+ Je 19 '89. R. Novak
   Sports Illustrated il 70:91 Je 19 '89. F. Lidz
North by northwest
   Video 12:63-4 Mr '89. M. Fleischmann
Not of this earth
   Video il 12:85-6 Ja '89. R. Swan
La nouba des femmes du mont Chenoua
   The Unesco Courier il 42:34-7 O '89. A. Djebar
Off limits
   Video 12:83 Ja '89. D. Schweiger
Old gringo
   Maclean's il 102:60-1 O 16 '89. B. D. Johnson
   People Weekly il 32:17 O 23 '89. R. Novak
   Theatre Crafts il 23:56-7 O '89. J. Calhoun
Only a buck
   People Weekly il 31:107 Ap 10 '89
Out cold
   The New Yorker 65:95 Mr 6 '89. P. Kael
   People Weekly il 31:19 Mr 20 '89. R. Novak
The package
   Newsweek 114:68 S 4 '89. D. Ansen
   People Weekly il 32:13 S 4 '89. R. Novak
Paperhouse
   Newsweek 113:65 F 20 '89. D. Ansen
Parenthood
   The American Spectator 22:38 O '89. B. Bawer
   Commonweal 116:471-2 S 8 '89. P. D. Baumann
   Maclean's il 102:53 Ag 14 '89. P. Young
   New York il 22:79-80 Ag 14 '89. D. Denby
   The New Yorker 65:75 Ag 7 '89. T. Rafferty
   Newsweek il 114:61-2 Ag 7 '89. D. Ansen
   Newsweek il 114:56-7 Ag 28 '89. R. Givens
   People Weekly il 32:17 Ag 14 '89. R. Novak
   Rolling Stone p38 Ag 24 '89. P. Travers
   Time il 134:54 Ag 7 '89. R. Schickel
Parents
   Maclean's il 102:55 F 13 '89. B. D. Johnson
   The Nation 248:206-7 F 13 '89. S. Klawans
   The New Yorker 65:95-7 Mr 6 '89. P. Kael
   Newsweek il 113:79 F 13 '89. D. Ansen
   People Weekly il 31:14+ Ja 30 '89. P. Travers
   Video il 13:62 Je '89. I. Robbins
The Peking Opera blues
   New York il 22:66 F 6 '89. D. Denby
Pelle the conqueror
   America 160:88+ F 4 '89. R. A. Blake
   National Review 41:54-6+ My 5 '89. J. Simon
   The New Republic 200:26-7 Ja 23 '89. S. Kauffmann
   New York 22:54-5 Ja 9 '89. D. Denby
   Newsweek il 113:54 Ja 9 '89. D. Ansen
   People Weekly il 31:19 Ja 16 '89. P. Travers
   Time il 133:94 Ja 2 '89. R. Schickel
   Video 13:59+ Ag '89. J. Bernard

MOTION PICTURE REVIEWS—Single works—*cont.*
Penn & Teller get killed
  The New Republic 201:25 O 30 '89. S. Kauffmann
  The New Yorker 65:100-1 O 2 '89. P. Kael
  People Weekly il 32:17+ O 9 '89. R. Novak
  Rolling Stone il por p38 N 2 '89. N. Scovell
Pet sematary
  People Weekly il 31:13 My 15 '89. R. Novak
Peter Pan
  People Weekly il 32:11 Jl 31 '89. R. Novak
Physical evidence
  People Weekly il 31:20 F 13 '89. R. Novak
Pin
  Maclean's il 102:55 F 13 '89. B. D. Johnson
Pink Cadillac
  Newsweek il 113:67 Je 12 '89. D. Ansen
  People Weekly il 31:18-19 Je 12 '89. R. Novak
  Time il 133:78 Je 5 '89. J. Skow
The plot against Harry
  American Film il 15:16-17 D '89. R. Seidenberg
  New York 22:82 O 9 '89. D. Denby
Powwow Highway
  Maclean's il 102:62-3 Ap 24 '89. B. D. Johnson
  The New Republic 200:24 Ap 24 '89. S. Kauffmann
  Newsweek 113:70 Ap 3 '89. D. Ansen
Prancer
  People Weekly 32:17 D 11 '89. R. Novak
The Presidio
  Video il 12:64 Mr '89. D. Schweiger
The prince of Pennsylvania
  Video il 13:58+ Ag '89. I. Robbins
Punchline
  Video 12:62-3 Mr '89. R. Granger
Queen of hearts
  Commonweal 116:591 N 3 '89. T. O'Brien
  Maclean's 102:86 N 6 '89. B. D. Johnson
  The New Leader 72:21 O 2-16 '89. J. Morrone
  Time 134:90 O 2 '89. R. Corliss
The Rachel papers
  Video il 13:88 D '89. I. Robbins
The radicals
  Christianity Today il 33:60 O 6 '89. D. Beard
Rain Man
  Commonweal 116:49 Ja 27 '89. T. O'Brien
  The Humanist il 49:39-40 Mr/Ap '89. H. M. Geduld
  The Nation 248:66-7 Ja 9-16 '89. S. Klawans
  National Review 41:52+ F 24 '89. J. Simon
  The New Republic 200:24-5 Ja 9-16 '89. S. Kauffmann
  New York 22:46-7 Ja 2 '89. D. Denby
  The New Yorker 64:95-6 F 6 '89. P. Kael
  Newsweek il 113:52-6 Ja 16 '89. D. Ansen
  People Weekly il 31:36-41 Ja 23 '89. D. Chu
  Rolling Stone il p30 Ja 12 '89. D. Rensin
  Video il 13:87 S '89. S. Isler
The rainbow
  America 161:40+ Jl 15-22 '89. R. A. Blake
  American Film il 14:11-12 My '89. J. Greenberg
  Commonweal 116:337-8 Je 2 '89. T. O'Brien
  Film Comment 25:2+ My/Je '89. G. Fuller
  Gentlemen's Quarterly il 59:117-19 Je '89. K. Turan
  The New Republic 200:28 My 15 '89. S. Kauffmann
  New York 22:65 My 29 '89. D. Denby
  The New Yorker 65:102-3 My 29 '89. P. Kael
  Newsweek il 113:70 My 8 '89. J. Kroll
  People Weekly il 31:15-16 Je 26 '89. R. Novak
  Rolling Stone il p36 Je 1 '89
  Time il 133:75 My 15 '89. R. Schickel
Red heat
  Video il 12:60 F '89. I. Robbins
Relentless
  People Weekly il 32:13-14 S 18 '89. R. Novak
Renegades
  People Weekly il 31:15 Je 19 '89. R. Novak
  Rolling Stone p29 Je 29 '89. P. Travers
The rescuers
  People Weekly il 31:17-18 Ap 3 '89. R. Novak
Return of the killer tomatoes: the sequel
  Video 12:86+ Ja '89. M. Pierson
Reunion
  Film Comment il 25:16-22 My/Je '89. M. Ciment
Road house
  New York il 22:64-5 My 29 '89. D. Denby
  People Weekly il 31:16+ My 29 '89. S. Haller
  Rolling Stone il p34 Je 1 '89. P. Travers
Roger & me
  American Film il por 15:14 N '89. A. Insdorf
  Film Comment il 25:16-18+ N/D '89. H. Jacobson
  The Nation 249:505-6 O 30 '89. S. Klawans
  New York 22:102-3 D 18 '89. D. Denby
  Newsweek il por 114:113 O 9 '89. C. Leerhsen
Romero
  America 161:167+ S 23 '89. R. A. Blake
  The Christian Century il 106:870-2 O 4 '89. D. G. Peerman
  Christianity Today il 33:77-8 N 3 '89. S. Ulstein
  Commonweal 116:471 S 8 '89. T. O'Brien
  The New Republic 201:26 S 11 '89. S. Kauffmann

Rude awakening
  Newsweek il 114:68 S 4 '89. D. Ansen
The Russia house
  Newsweek il por 114:66-7 N 6 '89. C. Bogert
A rustling of leaves: inside the Philippine revolution
  Maclean's il 102:63 Ap 24 '89. B. D. Johnson
Salaam Bombay!
  American Film il 14:64 S '89. P. Rainer
  Christianity Today il 33:64 F 3 '89. S. Ulstein
  Video il 13:80 O '89. R. Gehr
Say anything
  The New Yorker 65:122-3 My 15 '89. P. Kael
  Newsweek 113:72 Ap 17 '89. D. Ansen
  People Weekly il 31:16 Ap 24 '89. S. Haller
  Scholastic Update (Teachers' edition) il 121:12 Ap 21 '89
  Scholastic Update (Teachers' edition) il 121:TE4 Ap 21 '89
  Video il 13:88 D '89. I. Robbins
Scandal
  American Film il 14:10-11 Mr '89. A. Barra
  The American Spectator il 22:37-8 Jl '89. B. Bawer
  Commonweal 116:371-2 Je 16 '89. T. O'Brien
  Film Comment il 25:56-8+ Mr/Ap '89. G. Fuller
  Gentlemen's Quarterly il 59:328-31 Mr '89
  Glamour il 87:226+ Ap '89. D. Denicolo
  Maclean's il 102:58-9 My 22 '89. B. D. Johnson
  The Nation 248:787-8 Je 5 '89. S. Klawans
  National Review 41:53-4+ Je 30 '89. J. Simon
  The New Leader 72:20-1 My 1 '89. J. Morrone
  The New Republic 200:24-5 My 29 '89. S. Kauffmann
  New York il 22:78+ My 8 '89. D. Denby
  The New Yorker 65:121-2 My 15 '89. P. Kael
  Newsweek il 113:76 My 1 '89. J. Kroll
  People Weekly 31:12 My 22 '89. S. Haller
  Rolling Stone p40 Ap 20 '89. J. Kaplan
  Rolling Stone il p39 My 18 '89. P. Travers
  Time il 133:68 My 1 '89. R. Corliss
  Video il 13:76 N '89. I. Robbins
  Vogue il 179:506-9 Mr '89. A. Waugh
Scenes from the class struggle in Beverly Hills
  America 161:116 Ag 26-S 2 '89. R. A. Blake
  American Film il 14:92 Ap '89. L. Loud
  The Nation 248:860-1 Je 19 '89. S. Klawans
  The New Republic 201:26+ Jl 10 '89. S. Kauffmann
  Newsweek il 113:68 Je 12 '89. D. Ansen
  Time il 133:73 Je 12 '89. R. Corliss
  Video il 13:76+ N '89. I. Robbins
  Vogue il 179:204 My '89
Scrooged
  Video il 13:14 N '89. L. Kesten
  Video il 13:89 D '89. R. Gehr
Sea of love
  Commonweal 116:565 O 20 '89. P. D. Baumann
  National Review il 41:61-2 N 10 '89. J. Simon
  New York il 22:70-1 S 18 '89. D. Denby
  The New Yorker il 65:100+ S 18 '89. T. Rafferty
  Newsweek il 114:81 S 18 '89. D. Ansen
  People Weekly il 32:14 S 18 '89. R. Novak
  Rolling Stone il p35 O 5 '89. P. Travers
Second sight
  People Weekly 32:29-30 N 20 '89. R. Novak
The secret
  Américas il 41 no1:63 '89. J. Mosier
See no evil, hear no evil
  Jet il 76:36-8 Je 5 '89
  The New Republic 200:27 Je 12 '89. S. Kauffmann
  New York il 22:71 My 22 '89. D. Denby
  People Weekly il 31:15 My 29 '89. R. Novak
See you in the morning
  Commonweal 116:302-3 My 19 '89. T. O'Brien
  Glamour 87:186 Mr '89. J. G. Boyum
  The New Republic 200:28-9 My 15 '89. S. Kauffmann
  People Weekly il 31:19-20 My 8 '89. R. Novak
sex, lies, and videotape
  American Film il 14:76-7 Ap '89. R. Seidenberg
  The American Spectator il 22:38-9 N '89. B. Bawer
  Commonweal 116:529-30 O 6 '89. P. D. Baumann
  Film Comment il 25:22-4+ Jl/Ag '89. H. Jacobson
  Maclean's il 102:61 S 25 '89. B. D. Johnson
  The Nation 249:250+ S 4-11 '89. S. Klawans
  National Review 41:62-3 N 10 '89. J. Simon
  The New Leader 72:20-1 O 2-16 '89. J. Morrone
  The New Republic 201:26-7 S 4 '89. S. Kauffmann
  New York il 22:40+ Ag 7 '89. D. Denby
  The New Yorker 65:73-4 Ag 7 '89. T. Rafferty
  Newsweek il 114:61 Ag 7 '89. D. Ansen
  People Weekly il 32:14-15 S 4 '89. R. Novak
  Rolling Stone il p81+ My 18 '89. T. Minsky
  Rolling Stone il p38 Ag 24 '89. P. Travers
  Time il 134:65+ Jl 31 '89. R. Corliss
  Vogue il 179:454-5 S '89. P. Rainer
Shag: the movie
  People Weekly 32:12 Ag 7 '89. R. Novak
She-devil
  American Film il 14:14 My '89. G. Kilday
  American Film il 15:64 D '89. J. Ressner
  Glamour il 87:158+ D '89. D. DeNicolo

MOTION PICTURE REVIEWS—Single works—She-devil—
cont.

> *Maclean's* il 102:59 D 18 '89. B. D. Johnson
> *Newsweek* 114:88 D 11 '89. D. Ansen
> *People Weekly* il 32:18 D 18 '89. R. Novak
> *Time* il 134:93 D 11 '89. R. Corliss

She's out of control
> *People Weekly* il 31:19 My 8 '89. T. Cunneff

Shirley Valentine
> *The New Yorker* 65:90 S 4 '89. T. Rafferty
> *People Weekly* 32:15-16 O 16 '89. R. Novak

Shocker
> *People Weekly* il 32:17-18 N 13 '89. R. Novak

Shy people
> *Video* il 12:84 Ja '89. T. Soter

Sidewalk stories
> *New York* il 22:36 N 6 '89. P. Hoban

Sing
> *People Weekly* il 31:17 Ap 17 '89. R. Novak
> *Time* 133:83 Ap 17 '89. R. Corliss

Singin' in the rain
> *Video* il 12:63-4 Mr '89. M. Fleischmann

Skin deep
> *Maclean's* 102:59 Mr 20 '89. B. D. Johnson
> *Newsweek* 113:69 Mr 13 '89. J. Kroll
> *People Weekly* il 31:20-1 Mr 20 '89. S. Haller
> *Video* il 13:76+ N '89. I. Robbins

Slaves of New York
> *Film Comment* il 25:3+ Mr/Ap '89. M. McCreadie
> *Harper's Bazaar* il 122:144-5 F '89
> *Maclean's* il 102:41 Ap 10 '89. B. D. Johnson
> *The Nation* 248:530-1 Ap 17 '89. S. Klawans
> *The New Republic* 200:22-3 Ap 10 '89. S. Kauffmann
> *New York* il 22:69-70 Mr 27 '89. D. Denby
> *Newsweek* il 113:83 Mr 20 '89. D. Ansen
> *People Weekly* il 31:15-16 Ap 24 '89. E. Wurtzel
> *Time* il 133:73 Mr 20 '89. R. Schickel
> *Video* il 13:78+ O '89. I. Robbins
> *Vogue* il 179:192-3 F '89. J. Truman

Some girls
> *Newsweek* il 113:67 Ap 3 '89. D. Ansen

Someone to love
> *Psychology Today* 23:78 Je '89. W. Herbert

Spices
> *The Nation* 249:399 O 9 '89. S. Klawans

Spike of Bensonhurst
> *Video* 13:59 Ap '89. J. Walker

Stand and deliver
> *Video* il 12:82 Ja '89. J. Young

Star trek V: the final frontier
> *New York* il por 22:68 Je 19 '89. D. Denby
> *Newsweek* il 113:63+ Je 19 '89. D. Ansen
> *People Weekly* il por 31:15 Je 26 '89. R. Novak
> *Rolling Stone* il p75 Jl 13-27 '89. P. Travers
> *Time* il 133:89 Je 26 '89. R. Schickel

Staying together
> *People Weekly* il 32:29 N 20 '89. R. Novak
> *Rolling Stone* il por p48 S 21 '89. P. Travers

Steel magnolias
> *American Film* il 15:62 N '89. J. E. Fitch
> *Ladies' Home Journal* il 106:126+ N '89. J. Rachlin
> *Life* il 12:82-4+ O '89
> *Maclean's* il 102:84+ N 20 '89. B. D. Johnson
> *New York* 22:78 N 27 '89. D. Denby
> *Newsweek* il 114:90 N 27 '89. D. Ansen
> *People Weekly* il 32:21-2 D 4 '89. R. Novak
> *Time* il 134:92 N 20 '89. R. Schickel

Stepfather II
> *'Teen* il 33:50 O '89

Story of women
> *Film Comment* il 25:16-18+ S/O '89. M. Pally
> *Harper's Bazaar* il por 122:98 N '89. W. Fisher
> *Mademoiselle* il 95:104+ N '89. R. Rosenbaum
> *The Nation* 249:576-7 N 13 '89. S. Klawans
> *The New Republic* 201:24-5 O 30 '89. S. Kauffmann
> *New York* il 22:70+ O 30 '89. D. Denby
> *Rolling Stone* p36 N 2 '89. P. Travers

Sullivan's travels
> *Video* 13:64 Jl '89. M. Fleischmann

Sunnyside
> *The New Republic* 200:28 My 22 '89. S. Kauffmann

Superstar
> *American Film* il 15:80 D '89. L. Loud

Surname Viet given name Nam
> *The Nation* 248:529-30 Ap 17 '89. S. Klawans

Sweet smell of success
> *Video* 13:64 Jl '89. M. Fleischmann

Talk radio
> *The American Spectator* 22:32 Mr '89. B. Bawer
> *Commonweal* 116:20-1 Ja 13 '89. T. O'Brien
> *Film Comment* il 25:64-70 Ja/F '89. R. Corliss
> *The Nation* 248:67 Ja 9-16 '89. S. Klawans
> *National Review* 41:46-9 Mr 24 '89. J. Simon
> *The New Republic* 200:26 F 13 '89. S. Kauffmann
> *Newsweek* il 113:54 Ja 9 '89. D. Ansen
> *People Weekly* 31:15 Ja 9 '89. P. Travers
> *Video* il 13:59+ Ag '89. J. Bernard

Tap
> *Ebony* il 44:46+ F '89
> *Jet* il 75:58-61 F 13 '89
> *The New Republic* 200:32 Mr 20 '89. S. Kauffmann
> *The New Yorker* 64:74-5 F 6 '89. A. Croce
> *Newsweek* 113:79 F 13 '89. D. Ansen
> *People Weekly* il 31:16 F 13 '89. R. Novak

A taxing woman's return
> *The New Republic* 201:26-7 Ag 7-14 '89. S. Kauffmann

Tequila sunrise
> *American Film* il 14:40-5+ Ja/F '89. M. Sragow
> *Mademoiselle* il 95:91-2 F '89. R. Rosenbaum
> *The Nation* 248:25-6 Ja 2 '89. S. Klawans
> *National Review* 41:54 F 24 '89. J. Simon
> *Video* il 13:94 S '89. R. Gehr

Thelonious Monk: straight, no chaser
> *Down Beat* il 56:6 N '89. A. Lange
> *The Nation* 249:506-7 O 30 '89. S. Klawans
> *People Weekly* il 32:15-16 O 30 '89. R. Novak
> *Rolling Stone* il p19 My 4 '89. C. Stern

The thin blue line
> *America* 160:94-5 F 4 '89. A. Blake
> *Newsweek* il 113:27 Mr 13 '89. J. N. Baker
> *Rolling Stone* il p30 O 19 '89. M. Lasswell
> *TV Guide* il 37:20-2 My 20-26 '89. D. Hill

Things change
> *The Humanist* il 49:39 Mr/Ap '89. H. M. Geduld
> *Video* 13:63 Je '89. M. Pierson

Three fugitives
> *The New Republic* 200:24-5 Mr 6 '89. S. Kauffmann
> *The New Yorker* 65:98 F 20 '89. P. Kael
> *Newsweek* il 113:79 F 13 '89. D. Ansen
> *People Weekly* 31:16 F 6 '89. P. Travers

Three men and a baby
> *Video* 12:59-60 F '89. J. Young

To dream of roses
> *Dance Magazine* il 63:14 S '89. C. Lefevre

Tom Jones
> *Gentlemen's Quarterly* il 59:93+ Ag '89. K. Turan
> *People Weekly* il 32:11 O 2 '89. R. Novak

Torch song trilogy
> *Film Comment* il 25:9-12+ Ja/F '89. J. Scott
> *Glamour* il 87:140 F '89. J. G. Boyum
> *Maclean's* il 102:53 F 20 '89. B. D. Johnson
> *National Review* 41:46-8 Mr 24 '89. J. Simon
> *Newsweek* il 113:58 Ja 2 '89. D. Ansen
> *People Weekly* il 31:12+ Ja 9 '89. P. Travers

Triumph of the spirit
> *Harper's Bazaar* il 122:103 D '89. M. Rochlin
> *The New Republic* 201:26 D 25 '89. S. Kauffmann
> *Newsweek* il 114:90 D 11 '89. J. Kroll

Troop Beverly Hills
> *People Weekly* il 31:17 Ap 10 '89. T. Cunneff

True believer
> *Harper's Bazaar* il 122:50+ F '89. B. Borns
> *Maclean's* il 102:55 F 27 '89. B. D. Johnson
> *The New Republic* 200:26-7 F 13 '89. S. Kauffmann
> *New York* il 22:70-1 F 20 '89. D. Denby
> *The New Yorker* 65:95-6 F 20 '89. P. Kael
> *People Weekly* il 31:11 F 27 '89. S. Haller
> *Time* il 133:94 F 20 '89. R. Schickel
> *Video* il 13:58 Ag '89. I. Robbins
> *Vogue* il 179:76-7 Ja '89. H. Edwards

True love
> *Rolling Stone* il por p48 S 21 '89. P. Travers

Tucker: the man and his dream
> *Video* il 13:76 My '89. J. Young

Turner & Hooch
> *Newsweek* il 114:56 Ag 14 '89. D. Ansen
> *People Weekly* il 32:11 Ag 7 '89. R. Novak
> *Time* il 134:54 Ag 7 '89. R. Schickel

Twins
> *The Humanist* il 49:39 Mr/Ap '89. H. M. Geduld
> *Video* il 13:61 Jl '89. J. Bernard

The two Jakes
> *New York* il por 22:54-5 S 11 '89. D. Denby

U2: Rattle and hum
> *Rolling Stone* p16 Ja 12 '89. J. Ressner
> *Video* il 13:15-16 Ap '89. S. Roman

UHF
> *People Weekly* il 32:11-12 Ag 7 '89. R. Novak

The unbearable lightness of being
> *Video* il 12:63 Mr '89. S. L. Siegel

Uncle Buck
> *The American Spectator* 22:39 N '89. B. Bawer
> *Newsweek* il 114:68 S 4 '89. D. Ansen
> *People Weekly* il 32:13-14 S 4 '89. R. Novak
> *Rolling Stone* p32 S 7 '89. P. Travers

Under the sun of Satan
> *The New Republic* 200:26-8 Ap 3 '89. S. Kauffmann

Valentino returns
> *People Weekly* il 32:11-12 Jl 31 '89. R. Novak

Valmont
> *Commonweal* 116:670-1 D 1 '89. T. O'Brien
> *Life* il 12:70-5 Spr '89. T. Skari
> *Maclean's* il 102:82-3 N 20 '89. B. D. Johnson
> *The Nation* 249:727-8 D 11 '89. S. Klawans
> *The New Republic* 201:24-5+ D 11 '89. S. Kauffmann

MOTION PICTURE REVIEWS—Single works—Valmont—
cont.

New York 22:122 N 20 '89. D. Denby
The New Yorker 65:105-7 N 27 '89. P. Kael
Newsweek il 114:77 N 20 '89. J. Kroll
Rolling Stone il p48 N 30 '89. P. Travers
Time il 134:92 N 20 '89. R. Schickel
Vogue il 179:252-3 N '89. J. Morgenstern

Vampire's kiss
American Film il 14:67-8 Je '89. J. E. Fitch
New York 22:68-9 Je 19 '89. D. Denby
The New Yorker 65:105-6 Je 12 '89. P. Kael
People Weekly il 31:17-18 Je 12 '89. R. Novak

Vibes
Video il 12:62 F '89. D. Schweiger

Voices of Sarafina!
The Nation 248:174-5 F 6 '89. S. Klawans

The War of the Roses
Maclean's il por 102:62-4 D 11 '89. B. D. Johnson
Newsweek il 114:88 D 11 '89. D. Ansen
People Weekly il 32:15 D 18 '89. R. Novak
Rolling Stone il p40 N 16 '89. J. Ressner
Time il 134:93 D 11 '89. R. Schickel

We the living
National Review 41:52-3 Ja 27 '89. J. Sobran

We think the world of you
The Nation 248:24-5 Ja 2 '89. S. Klawans

Weapons of the spirit
Newsweek il 114:81 S 18 '89. D. Ansen

Weekend at Bernie's
People Weekly il 32:12-13 Jl 24 '89. R. Novak

Welcome home
People Weekly il 32:22-3 N 27 '89. R. Novak

We're no angels
Newsweek 114:74 D 25 '89. D. Ansen

When Harry met Sally . . .
American Film il 14:28-33+ Jl/Ag '89. R. Lloyd
The American Spectator 22:38-40 O '89. B. Bawer
Commonweal 116:472 S 8 '89. P. D. Baumann
Maclean's il 102:51 Jl 24 '89. B. D. Johnson
The New Republic 201:26-8 Ag 21 '89. S. Kauffmann
New York il 22:50+ Jl 24 '89. D. Denby
The New Yorker 65:74-5 Ag 7 '89. T. Rafferty
Newsweek il 114:52 Jl 17 '89. D. Ansen
People Weekly il 32:13-14 Jl 24 '89. R. Novak
Rolling Stone il p32 Ag 10 '89
Time il 134:65 Jl 31 '89. R. Corliss

Who framed Roger Rabbit
Video il 13:77 O '89. S. L. Siegel
Video il 13:14-15 O '89. S. Grant

Who killed Vincent Chin?
Mother Jones 14:54 Jl/Ag '89. D. Sachs

Who's Harry Crumb?
The American Spectator 22:38-9 Ap '89. B. Bawer
People Weekly il 31:17 F 20 '89. R. Novak

The wild bunch
American Film il 14:18+ Ap '89. R. Shelton

Winter people
People Weekly il 31:11 My 1 '89. R. Novak

Wired
American Film il 14:72 Jl/Ag '89. M. Rochlin
The Humanist il 49:45-6 N/D '89. H. M. Geduld
Maclean's il 102:52-3 Ag 28 '89. P. Young
Newsweek 114:68 S 4 '89. D. Ansen
People Weekly il 32:17-18 S 11 '89. R. Novak
Rolling Stone il p32 S 7 '89. P. Travers
Time il 134:64 Ag 28 '89. R. Corliss
Time il 133:90 Ap 24 '89. R. Zoglin

Withnail and I
Video 12:86 Ja '89. I. Robbins

Without a clue
Video il 13:63 Je '89. M. Pierson

The Wizard of Oz
People Weekly il 31:38-40 Je 26 '89. M. Neill
Video il 12:63-4 Mr '89. M. Fleischmann

A woman of Paris
The New Republic 200:28-9 My 22 '89. S. Kauffmann

Women on the verge of a nervous breakdown
America 160:41+ Ja 21 '89. R. A. Blake
American Film il 15:70 D '89. P. Rainer
Maclean's il 102:50 Ja 30 '89. B. D. Johnson

Working girl
The American Spectator 22:38 Ap '89. B. Bawer
Commonweal 116:48-9 Ja 27 '89. T. O'Brien
Fortune il 119:124 F 13 '89. D. Seligman
Glamour il 87:140 F '89. J. G. Boyum
The New Republic 200:28 Ja 30 '89. S. Kauffmann
New York il 22:45-6 Ja 2 '89. D. Denby
The New Yorker 64:80-1 Ja 9 '89. P. Kael
Newsweek il 113:57 Ja 2 '89. D. Ansen
Video il 13:75 N '89. J. Bernard

A world apart
American Film il 15:102 O '89. P. Rainer

Worth winning
People Weekly il 32:18-19 N 13 '89. R. Novak

Wuthering Heights
American Film il 14:77 Ap '89. J. E. Fitch

The New York Times Magazine il por p46-8+ F 19
'89. A. S. Berg

Young Einstein
Gentlemen's Quarterly il 59:93+ Ag '89. K. Turan
Mademoiselle il 95:106 S '89. L. Morice
People Weekly il 32:13-14 Ag 21 '89. R. Novak

Young guns
Video il 12:60-1 F '89. D. Wheeler

MOTION PICTURE SCRIPTS
The Coast [C. Proser's Interface] G. Stone. il Gentlemen's
Quarterly 59:118 F '89
Fellini's magical '8½'. F. Pierson. il por American Film 14:16-17
Je '89
'The little thief': scenes from the last Truffaut. F. Truffaut
and C. de Givray. il Film Comment 25:17-22 Ja/F '89
'Lolita'. P. Schrader. il American Film 15:18-20+ O '89
'The wild bunch' [analysis of W. Green's screen play] R.
Shelton. il por American Film 14:18+ Ap '89

Anecdotes, facetiae, satire, etc.
Wild pitches [story ideas pitched to producers] A. McDonnell.
il American Film 15:44-5+ D '89

MOTION PICTURE SEQUELS
Going home to the '70s. D. Rochester. il American Film
14:13 S '89
Hollywood's summer of the sequel. M. Silver. il U.S. News
& World Report 106:67 Je 26 '89
Oh, no, not again. P. Travers. il Rolling Stone p31 Ag
10 '89
Retread IV: return of the son of sequel. R. Grover. il Business
Week p38 My 15 '89
The return of the return of the summer sequel. B. Sharkey.
il American Film 14:40-1 Je '89

MOTION PICTURE SETS See Motion pictures—Setting and
scenery

MOTION PICTURE SOCIETIES
See also
American Film Institute

MOTION PICTURE SOUND RECORDING
One hand clapping [digital audio] K. Wright. Scientific
American 260:35-7 Je '89
Real hi-fi at the movies? [Lucasfilm THX sound system]
J. D. Hirsch. il Stereo Review 54:48+ N '89
Save that Studer, continued [Dolby SR] R. Hodges. il Stereo
Review 54:176 F '89

MOTION PICTURE STUDIO TOURS
See also
Disney-MGM Studios Theme Park (Fla.)
Behind the scenes in Hollywood [visiting active studios]
il Sunset (Central West edition) 183:70+ N '89
Movie studio tours—the new, fun vacation! S. Birnbaum.
il Good Housekeeping 208:36+ Je '89

MOTION PICTURE STUNTS See Stunts

MOTION PICTURE THEATERS
See also
Cineplex Odeon Corporation
Drive-in theaters
Los Angeles (Calif.)—Motion picture theaters
Mobile motion picture theaters
Pacific Theatres Corporation
Philadelphia (Miss.)—Motion picture theaters

Accounting
Every trick in the books [Cineplex Odeon's accounting tech-
niques] D. Wechsler. il por Forbes 143:46+ My 29 '89

Electronic sound control
Real hi-fi at the movies? [Lucasfilm THX sound system]
J. D. Hirsch. il Stereo Review 54:48+ N '89

Sound systems
See Motion picture theaters—Electronic sound control

Canada
See also
Famous Players Ltd.

MOTION PICTURES
See also
Advertising mediums—Motion pictures
Cable television—Motion pictures
Characters in motion pictures
Copyright—Motion pictures
Direct broadcast satellite services—Motion pictures
Film-to-video transfer system
Television broadcasting—Motion pictures
Videodiscs—Motion pictures
Videotapes—Motion pictures
Violence in motion pictures
The '90s: future tense [special section] il Film Comment
25:27-39+ Ja/F '89
Into the '90s [special section] il American Film 14:24-39+
Ja/F '89

Advertising
See Motion picture industry—Advertising

Aesthetics
Borrowed images [special section] il Film Comment 25:27-30+
Mr/Ap '89

Amateur films
The recording angel. J. Morgenstern. il The New York Times
Magazine p20+ O 15 '89

Animated films
See also
Computer animation

MOTION PICTURES—Animated films—See also—*cont.*
    Goofy (Fictional character)
    Mickey Mouse (Fictional character)
    Walt Disney Company
Carrot and shtick [Warner Bros. cartoons] T. Teachout. il *The American Spectator* 22:30-1 O '89
Chuck Jones. P. Brock. il pors *People Weekly* 32:103+ N 13 '89
Comic relief. J. Etra. il *Harper's Bazaar* 122:31-2 Jl '89
Mermaid artist Glen Keane grew up in a Family circus. C. Sanz. il pors *People Weekly* 32:127-8 D 11 '89
Those faces! Those voices! behind The little mermaid's box office splash are some surprising folks. C. Sanz. il *People Weekly* 32:123-5 D 11 '89
'Toons: good, bad and ugly. B. Barol. il *Newsweek* 114:72-3 N 20 '89
When toons really knew how to talk. *U.S. News & World Report* 107:12 Jl 17 '89

        Collectibles
Mickey mania. C. Brown. il *Forbes* 144:230-2 O 30 '89
        Audiences
    See Motion picture audiences
        Awards
    See also
    Academy Awards
    Black Oscar Nominees (Awards)
    Golden Globe Awards
    New York Film Critics' Circle Awards
        Anecdotes, facetiae, satire, etc.
1988 & all that. S. Harvey and R. Corliss. il *Film Comment* 25:52-3 Ja/F '89
        Best films
American film critics poll: the '80s. P. McGilligan and M. Rowland. il *American Film* 15:23-9 N '89
Best films of 1988—critic's pick. *Film Comment* 25:52-3 Ja/F '89
Best of '88. il *Time* 133:94 Ja 2 '89
The eighties: the art. G. Marcus. il *Film Comment* 25:61-4 N/D '89
Movies of the eighties. P. Travers. il *Rolling Stone* p23 D 14-28 '89
Out on a limb [1988] T. O'Brien. *Commonweal* 116:80-1 F 10 '89
The pick of 1988. il *Maclean's* 102:60-1+ Ja 2 '89
Ten best movies [1980s] J. Connors. il *Seventeen* 48:72+ D '89
Ten films to see from the '88 releases. J. M. Wall. *The Christian Century* 106:35-7 Ja 18 '89
You must remember these. M. Zolotow. il *Reader's Digest* 134:129-35 Ap '89
        Bibliography
Books. See issues of Film Comment
        Censorship
G-men at the movies [FBI memo on A. Warhol's Lonesome cowboys] *Harper's* 278:26 Je '89
No trollops, no tomcats [J. Breen and the Production Code; excerpt from The dame in the kimono] L. J. Leff and J. Simmons. il por *American Film* 15:40-3+ D '89
Student-crushing China cows Natural History Museum [film The first emperor of China not shown by American Museum of Natural History] M. S. Forbes. il *Forbes* 144:20 Ag 7 '89
        Children's films
Saturday-matinee menagerie. R. Corliss. il *Time* 134:93-4 S 18 '89
        Classification
    See Motion pictures—Ratings
        Collectibles
The collectibles of Oz. R. Reed. il *Antiques & Collecting Hobbies* 94:32-4 Jl '89
        Coloring
    See also
    American Film Technologies Inc.
Oman urges extension of authors' moral rights [Copyright Office's views on colorization] H. Fields. *Publishers Weekly* 235:35 Ap 7 '89
Up the barbarians. D. Seligman. il *Fortune* 119:342 Ap 24 '89
        Comedy films
All that ZAZ [D. Zucker, J. Abrahams and J. Zucker] I. Slifkin. il pors *Video* 13:14 S '89
Movies [comedy films] K. Turan. il *Gentlemen's Quarterly* 59:93+ Ag '89
        Conservation and restoration
    See also
    National Film Registry
At long last, the real Lawrence. A. Barra. il *American Film* 14:44 Mr '89
Breaking the silents. B. Paris. il *American Film* 14:11-12 Ap '89
Griffith's real Intolerance [cover story] M. Hansen. il *Film Comment* 25:28-9 S/O '89
Hollywood's sheikh elite shows up to toast the restored Lawrence of Arabia. il *People Weekly* 31:36-7 F 27 '89
A masterpiece restored to the screen [Lawrence of Arabia] R. Corliss. il *Time* 133:62-3 F 6 '89
Saved from the sands of time [Lawrence of Arabia] D. Ansen. il *Newsweek* 113:75 F 6 '89

Survival of the fittest. P. Arthur. il *USA Today (Periodical)* 117:67 Ja '89
        Anecdotes, facetiae, satire, etc.
The new face of film restoration. M. Feintisch-Ng. *Film Comment* 25:4 My/Je '89
        Costs
    See Motion picture industry—Finance
        Costume
    See Costume, Theatrical
        Crime films
        Anecdotes, facetiae, satire, etc.
"Are you tryin' t' give me the business?" [phrases culled from American gangster films of the 1930s and 40s] R. Merkin. il *Gentlemen's Quarterly* 59:104+ D '89
        Dance films
Dancefilms. See occasional issues of Dance Magazine
Sammy Davis, Jr. and Gregory Hines move to the beat in 'Tap' [cover story] il pors *Jet* 75:58-61 F 13 '89
Tap [G. Hines film] il pors *Ebony* 44:46+ F '89
        Documentary films
Cinema of the unknown [documentaries about filmmaking on video] F. Thompson. il *American Film* 15:64-6+ N '89
In the eye of the beholder: poetic documentaries about technology [work of H. Bitomsky and H. Farocki] K. Rosenberg. il *Technology Review* 92:62-8 F/Mr '89
Profiles [director E. Morris] M. Singer. por *The New Yorker* 64:38-40+ F 6 '89
        Editing
    See also
    Motion pictures—Sound editing
Brando says studio sold him out on 'Dry white season'. il por *Jet* 77:63 O 23 '89
Movies you'll never see [dispute between K. Friedman and J. Daly over editing of Made in USA] A. Hornaday. il *Mother Jones* 14:53-4 F/Mr '89
        Educational films
    See Motion pictures in education
        Experimental films
The invisible films of Guy Debord. C. Phillips. il por *Art in America* 77:190 O '89
Voices from the underground. P. Arthur. il *USA Today (Periodical)* 118:33 S '89
        Foreign language films
Films [Cutting edge II series] S. Klawans. *The Nation* 248:206-9 F 13 '89
The five nominees and how they grew [Oscar nominations] H. A. Rodman. *Film Comment* 25:8+ Mr/Ap '89
Imported inspiration [She-devil and other American remakes of foreign films] G. Kilday. il *American Film* 14:14 My '89
        History
1939: twelve months of magic. G. Clarke. il *Time* 133:72-4 Mr 13 '89
Concurrent lives. S. Kauffmann. *The New Republic* 201:88-90 N 6 '89
Dressed for excess [films of the 1980s] D. Edelstein. il *Vogue* 179:186-7+ D '89
Hollywood 1939-1989 [cover story; special issue] il *Life* 12:8-14+ Spr '89
No trollops, no tomcats [J. Breen and the Production Code; excerpt from The dame in the kimono] L. J. Leff and J. Simmons. il por *American Film* 15:40-3+ D '89
Old gold [special section] il *Film Comment* 25:29-48 Jl/Ag '89
Profiles [actress L. Basquette] B. Paris. il por *The New Yorker* 64:54-73 F 13 '89
Wuthering Heights. A. S. Berg. il pors *The New York Times Magazine* p46-8+ F 19 '89
        Horror films
After A nightmare on Elm Street, director Wes Craven dreams up Shocker's maniacal killer. M. H. J. Farrell. il pors *People Weekly* 32:159+ N 13 '89
Horror's heaviest hitter [S. King on video] F. Lovece. il por *Video* 13:46-9+ Ag '89
"It's great for a date" [films from New Line Cinema] L. Gubernick. il por *Forbes* 143:110+ F 6 '89
Not another pretty face [creating makeup for R. England's Freddy Krueger character] B. Weber. il pors *The New York Times Magazine* p66 Jl 16 '89
Professor Gore [W. Craven] M. Mancini. il *Film Comment* 25:8 S/O '89
        Anecdotes, facetiae, satire, etc.
Scream test [quiz] H. Hill. il *Seventeen* 48:117+ O '89
        Laws and regulations
    See Motion picture laws and regulations
        Medical films
Cinemas on wheels [health communication] D. J. Henrich. il *World Health* p10-11 Ja/F '89
        Meteorological films
Audio visuals. E. Brotak. *Weatherwise* 42:335 D '89
        Moral and religious aspects
    See also
    Good and evil in motion pictures
    Jesus Christ in motion pictures
    Motion pictures—Censorship
    Sex in motion pictures
    Violence in motion pictures

MOTION PICTURES—Moral and religious aspects—*cont.*

Ecumenical jury winners at Montreal [Montreal World Film Festival] J. W. Arnold. *America* 161:252-3 O 21 '89

Jesus and others at Montreal festival [Montreal World Film Festival] J. M. Wall. *The Christian Century* 106:835-6 S 27 '89

The magical kingdom's box office [summer movies] R. M. Anker. il *Christianity Today* 33:70 S 8 '89

A playing field for the boys of eternity [Field of dreams] J. M. Wall. *The Christian Century* 106:515-16 My 17 '89

Wrestling with Advent [film Hail Mary] J. K. Larson. *The Christian Century* 106:1166-8 D 13 '89

Music

See also

Compact discs—Motion picture music
Phonograph records—Motion picture music
Tape recordings—Motion picture music

At long last, jazz [B. Weber's Let's get lost] R. Seidenberg. il pors *American Film* 14:50-4 My '89

Celluloid songs. A. White. il *Film Comment* 25:36-9 Mr/Ap '89

Dave Grusin: scoring it big. S. Yanow. il pors *Down Beat* 56:24-6 Jl '89

Messy life, perfect art [C. Parker film biography Bird] K. Whitehead. il por *Down Beat* 56:6 F '89

Prince of the City [Batman music videos by Prince] A. White. il pors *Film Comment* 25:76+ N/D '89

Tarquin Gotch, soundtrack specialist. S. Roman. il por *Video* 13:18 My '89

Test your movie music memory! il *'Teen* 33:70 My '89

Periodicals

Collectors and collecting

The era of the fabulous Hollywood fan magazine. E. Knapp. il *Antiques & Collecting Hobbies* 94:34-8 Mr '89

Philosophy

See also

Motion pictures—Aesthetics

Plots, themes, etc.

See also

Abortion in motion pictures
Animals in motion pictures
Apartheid in motion pictures
Arabs in motion pictures
Architecture in motion pictures
Art in motion pictures
Automobiles in motion pictures
Baseball fields in motion pictures
Baseball in motion pictures
Bears in motion pictures
Beauty contests in motion pictures
Bedford-Stuyvesant (New York, N.Y.) in motion pictures
Bicycle racing in motion pictures
Blacks in motion pictures
Boats in motion pictures
Business in motion pictures
Cats in motion pictures
China in motion pictures
Christmas in motion pictures
Comic books, strips, etc. and motion pictures
Cycling in motion pictures
Dance in motion pictures
Diving equipment in motion pictures
Dogs in motion pictures
Drug abuse in motion pictures
Dwarfs and dwarfism in motion pictures
El Salvador in motion pictures
Family in motion pictures
Germans in motion pictures
Good and evil in motion pictures
Harlem (New York, N.Y.) in motion pictures
History in motion pictures
Holocaust, Jewish (1939-1945), in motion pictures
Homosexuality in motion pictures
Human body in motion pictures
Illinois in motion pictures
Indians (American) in motion pictures
Insects in motion pictures
Jesus Christ in motion pictures
Love in motion pictures
Marriage in motion pictures
Mars (Planet) in motion pictures
Mississippi in motion pictures
Natchitoches (La.) in motion pictures
National socialism in motion pictures
New York (N.Y.) in motion pictures
Nineteen hundred and sixties in motion pictures
Nuclear warfare in motion pictures
Nudity in motion pictures
Parent-child relationship in motion pictures
Pizza restaurants in motion pictures
Race relations in motion pictures
Rape in motion pictures
SoHo (New York, N.Y.) in motion pictures
Southerners in motion pictures
Soviet Union in motion pictures
Strangers in motion pictures
Twins in motion pictures

United States in motion pictures
Villains in motion pictures
Violence in motion pictures
Women and men in motion pictures
Women in motion pictures

Bringing up baby [adult films] D. Edelstein and A. Thompson. il *Vogue* 179:246-7 O '89

Why movies come in bunches. G. Kilday. *American Film* 14:14+ Ap '89

Political films

See Politics in motion pictures

Promotion

See Motion picture industry—Advertising

Ratings

Movies. See issues of Consumer Reports

What the critics say about movies. See issues of Consumers' Research Magazine

Religious films

See also

Gospel Films, Inc.

Remakes

See Motion picture remakes

Science fiction films

See also

Star trek

Creatures from inner space. C. Aziza. il *The Unesco Courier* 42:12-13 O '89

Earthling: take me to your teacher [teaching science through science fiction films] G. Byrne. il *Science* 244:919 My 26 '89

Anecdotes, facetiae, satire, etc.

Last word. B. Butterworth. por *Omni (New York, N.Y.)* 12:156 D '89

Setting and scenery

Designer [B. Ringwood's and A. Furst's work on Batman] L. Nickson and N. Le Quesne. il pors *Life* 12:84-6 Spr '89

Heightening realities [work of production designer K. Zea] J. Calhoun. il por *Theatre Crafts* 23:58-67 Ap '89

Old gringo. J. Calhoun. il *Theatre Crafts* 23:56-7 O '89

The place is the thing. P. Arthur. il *USA Today (Periodical)* 118:93 N '89

Prairie samurai [filming Japanese film Heaven and earth in Alberta] J. Howse. il *World Press Review* 36:68-9 N '89

Prairie samurai: a Japanese epic comes to life in Alberta [Heaven and earth] J. Howse. il *Maclean's* 102:44-5 Ag 21 '89

Production: Batman. A. Pirani. il *Theatre Crafts* 23:21 Ag/S '89

Richard Sylbert [interview] il pors *American Film* 15:22-6 D '89

Sayonara, eh? [filming Japanese samurai epic Heaven and earth in the Canadian Rockies] J. Greenberg. il *American Film* 15:11-12 O '89

The state that shoots straight [Illinois] R. L. Ratny. il *American Film* 15:56-8+ N '89

Silent films

Breaking the silents. B. Paris. il *American Film* 14:11-12 Ap '89

Social aspects

See also

Motion pictures and youth

Strangers on the screen [cover story; special issue] il *The Unesco Courier* 42:10-43 O '89

Songs

See Motion pictures—Music

Sound editing

See also

Dubbing of motion pictures

Stick it in your ear. F. Spotnitz. il *American Film* 15:40-5 O '89

Sound recording

See Motion picture sound recording

Spanish language films

The rub in the dubbing [films and serials meant for TV screening to be dubbed in Argentina] I. Pardal. *Américas* 41 no2:64 '89

Special effects

See also

Showscan process

The bloodstream express [special effects in film to be part of Body Wars exhibit at EPCOT] B. Weber. il *The New York Times Magazine* p142 Je 11 '89

Chemist Gary Zeller wins an Academy Award for playing (safely) with fire. K. Hubbard. il pors *People Weekly* 31:98-100 Ap 3 '89

Filmmakers press limits of special-effects tech. il *Popular Mechanics* 166:12 My '89

Great new Indy Jones special effects [created by Industrial Light and Magic] il *Popular Mechanics* 166:18 Jl '89

How does Hollywood zap a planet? With high-definition help. P. Cole and R. Brandt. il *Business Week* p62 Ja 30 '89

Seeing double on the set of Dead ringers [optical supervisor Lee Wilson] D. Schweiger. il *Video* 13:17-18 Je '89

MOTION PICTURES—cont.
Study and teaching
See also
Sundance Institute
Film school confidential [college programs] J. Diamond. il *American Film* 14:34-9+ Jl/Ag '89
Stunts
See Stunts
Titling
A new look for subtitles. J. Bernard. il *Video* 13:15+ O '89
War films
See also
France—History—Revolution, 1789-1799—Motion pictures
United States—History—Civil War, 1861-1865—Motion pictures
Vietnamese War, 1957-1975, in motion pictures
World War, 1914-1918, in motion pictures
Westerns
Knights of the Far West [cowboys] G. N. Granville. il *The Unesco Courier* 42:48-53 S '89
The rise and fall of the western [cover story] A. Lejeune. il *National Review* 41:23-6 D 31 '89
Wide screen films
The letterbox advantage [scanned and letterboxed versions of wide screen films] M. Fleischmann. il *Video* 13:21-3 Jl '89
Wildlife films
Presenting crazy Alan Root. M. McRae. il pors *International Wildlife* 19:30-5 N/D '89
Algeria
Behind the veil [portrayal of Algerian women] A. Djebar. il *The Unesco Courier* 42:34-7 O '89
Australia
The new wizards of Oz. H. Kennedy. il *Film Comment* 25:73-4+ S/O '89
Canada
See also
National Film Board of Canada
Big-screen frontiers [Toronto's Festival of Festivals] B. D. Johnson. il *Maclean's* 102:72-4 S 18 '89
Turning homespun ideas into truth on the screen [A. Wheeler] D. Jenish. il por *Maclean's* 102:24-5 D 25 '89
Denmark
Dreyer [Museum of Modern Art retrospective] A. White. il por *Film Comment* 25:24-6 My/Je '89
Films [Museum of Modern Art retrospective of C. Dreyer's films] S. Klawans. *The Nation* 248:353 Mr 13 '89
France
Germans screened through French eyes. R. Prédal. il *The Unesco Courier* 42:18-23 O '89
The invisible films of Guy Debord. C. Phillips. il por *Art in America* 77:190 O '89
Louis Malle [interview] il por *American Film* 14:22-4+ Ap '89
Très blasé: why aren't French films any fun anymore? R. Rosenbaum. il *Mademoiselle* 95:78+ D '89
Germany (West)
In the eye of the beholder: poetic documentaries about technology [work of H. Bitomsky and H. Farocki] K. Rosenberg. il *Technology Review* 92:62-8 F/Mr '89
Nazi film machine [current films] G. Peary. il *American Film* 14:11-12 Jl/Ag '89
Hungary
Shelf life [interview with G. Gazdag] J. Hoberman. il por *Film Comment* 25:50-4+ My/Je '89
India
India's dream makers. R. Bharadwat. il *Scholastic Update (Teachers' edition)* 121:24-5 Mr 10 '89
Israel
The films of Amos Gitai [International Film Circuit retrospective at New York City Public Theater] S. Klawans. *The Nation* 248:784-6 Je 5 '89
Japan
Akira Kurosawa. G. Peary. il pors *American Film* 14:80-2 Ap '89
A funny thing happened on the way to the Film Forum [A. Kurosawa movies] D. Denby. il *New York* 22:66+ F 6 '89
Japan's emperor of film [A. Kurosawa] I. Buruma. il pors *The New York Times Magazine* p42-5+ O 29 '89
What's so funny about Japan. V. Canby. il pors *The New York Times Magazine* p26-9+ Je 18 '89
Latin America
Film. J. Mosier. See issues of *Américas*
Montreal: just 35 millimeters from Latin America [Montreal World Film Festival] J. Mosier. il *Américas* 41 no2:8-9 '89
Our man in Havana [Festival of New Latin American Cinema] J. Greenberg. il *American Film* 14:16-18 Mr '89
Nicaragua
Cine Sandino. G. Fuller. il *Film Comment* 25:2+ Ja/F '89
Soviet Union
Censors' day off. R. Corliss. il *Time* 133:127+ Ap 10 '89
'Glasnost' documentaries [Glasnost Film Festival in the U.S.] J. E. Fitch. *American Film* 14:12 Jl/Ag '89

'Glasnost' on film. M. Martin. il *World Press Review* 36:60 Jl '89
How Soviet cinema went Hollywood. K. Rosenberg. il *Technology Review* 92:76-7 Ap '89
Natalya Negoda knocks Soviet cinema reeling. M. Green. il pors *People Weekly* 31:40-2 Mr 27 '89
Prisoner [work of S. Paradjanov] A. Williamson. il pors *Film Comment* 25:57-60+ My/Je '89
Sokurov's 'Lonely voice'. A. Vogel. il por *Film Comment* 25:64+ My/Je '89
Tristan and Pavlova through the looking glass [how Soviet movies depict the United States] M. Fellous. il *The Unesco Courier* 42:30-3 O '89
Spain
Pedro on the verge of a nervy breakthrough [P. Almodóvar] R. Corliss. il por *Time* 133:68-9 Ja 30 '89
A winner from Spain [P. Almodóvar] M. Bayón. il por *World Press Review* 36:60 Ap '89
Vietnam
Speak your peace [Vietnam Film Project at the Hawaii International Film Festival] K. Jaehne. il *Film Comment* 25:14 Mr/Ap '89
The Vietnam Film Project. J. Burton. *The Nation* 248:825-7 Je 12 '89
MOTION PICTURES AND CHILDREN
See also
Motion pictures—Children's films
MOTION PICTURES AND LITERATURE
See also
Motion picture adaptations
MOTION PICTURES AND PHOTOGRAPHY
Film stills. R. Woodward. il *Film Comment* 25:51-2+ Mr/Ap '89
MOTION PICTURES AND TAPE RECORDINGS
Movie tie-ins proliferate for spoken audio publishers. P. Sweeting. il *Publishers Weekly* 235:103-4 Ap 7 '89
MOTION PICTURES AND TELEVISION
See also
Cable television—Motion pictures
Television broadcasting—Motion picture criticism programs
Fighting for Hollywood's fair share [interview with J. Valenti] il pors *Channels (New York, N.Y.: 1986)* 9:98-9 N '89
Invasion of the TV people [TV actors in movies] R. Rosenbaum. il *Mademoiselle* 95:100+ My '89
The networks are hungry for homegrown hits. D. Lieberman. il *Business Week* p88+ N 13 '89
Summer breakout [TV stars in movies; cover story] K. Turan. il *TV Guide* 37:2-5 Jl 1-7 '89
MOTION PICTURES AND THEATER
See also
Motion picture adaptations
MOTION PICTURES AND YOUTH
G.W.T.W. [young woman's devotion to Gone with the wind] *The New Yorker* 64:27 F 13 '89
Kid stuff: our panel of young experts rate the summer movies. L. Barry. il *American Film* 14:72 S '89
Yikes! Nightmares from Hollywood [cover story] R. M. Anker. il *Christianity Today* 33:18-23 Je 16 '89
MOTION PICTURES IN EDUCATION
Video technology: its effects on teaching English and film. B. Gallagher. *The Education Digest* 54:29-32 Mr '89
MOTION PICTURES IN INDUSTRY
Enterprise and meaning: sponsored film, 1939-1949. W. L. Bird. bibl il *History Today* 39:24-30 D '89
Now for something completely . . . [business training films; interview with J. Cleese] A. P. Sanoff. por *U.S. News & World Report* 107:105 O 16 '89
MOTION SICKNESS
Misery in motion [seasickness] P. G. Gill. il *Outdoor Life* 183:52+ Ap '89
MOTIVATION (EDUCATION)
Quality is the key to the disciplines. W. Glasser. *The Education Digest* 55:24-7 S '89
MOTIVATION (PSYCHOLOGY)
See also
Goals (Psychology)
Risk taking (Psychology)
12 ways to better team building. E. J. Belzer. il *Working Woman* 14:12+ Ag '89
13 ways to re-energize your staff. A. J. Bernstein and S. C. Rozen. il *Working Woman* 14:45-6 Ap '89
Bridging your workers' "motivation gap". D. T. Jaffe and C. D. Scott. il *Nation's Business* 77:30-2 Mr '89
Business secrets of Tommy Lasorda [interview] B. Dumaine. il pors *Fortune* 120:130-2+ Jl 3 '89
A good start for new hires. G. Geromel. il *Nation's Business* 77:21+ Ja '89
Manager's tipsheet: keeping minimum-wage workers motivated. M. M. Kennedy. *Working Woman* 14:32 O '89
MOTOCROSS RACING See Motorcycle racing
MOTOR ABILITY
Neural control of locomotion. G. E. Loeb. bibl f il *BioScience* 39:800-4 D '89
Visuomotor coordination in reaching and locomotion. A. P. Georgopoulos and S. Grillner. bibl f *Science* 245:1209-10 S 15 '89

MOTOR BOAT ENGINES
See also
Mercury Marine (Firm)
Outboard Marine Corp.
The silent approach [electric trolling motors] B. Stearns. il *Field & Stream* 94:70+ Je '89
Stern drive roundup '89. T. P. Banse. il *Motor Boating & Sailing* 163:99-100 Mr '89
Year of the sterndrive. J. Wooldridge. il *Popular Mechanics* 166:98-100+ F '89

Fuel
Gone fishing [oilless gasoline causes engine failure during Canadian fishing trip] D. Sprockett. *Flower and Garden* 33:104-7 Ja/F '89

History
Fifty years in the fast lane [C. Kiekhaefer] J. Skorupa. il *Popular Mechanics* 166:22-3 Ja '89

Maintenance and repair
Rx for outboards. T. P. Banse. il *Motor Boating & Sailing* 163:88-90 Je '89

Superchargers
California muscle boats [racing boat engines] J. Skorupa. il *Popular Mechanics* 166:58-61 S '89

Testing
Big block stern drives. T. P. Banse. il *Motor Boating & Sailing* 163:74-6+ My '89
Outboards '89. T. P. Banse. il *Motor Boating & Sailing* 163:122-4 F '89
Outboards—new for '90. B. McKeown. il *Outdoor Life* 184:34+ O '89
Stern-drive update. B. Stearns. il *Field & Stream* 94:62-3 Jl '89
Sterndrive muscle. B. McKeown. il *Outdoor Life* 184:22+ Ag '89

MOTOR BOAT RACING
See also
Hydrofoil racing
Hydroplane racing
Duel in the sand [Tri-Country Offshore Powerboat Race in the Gulf of Aqaba] P. Whittell. il *Motor Boating & Sailing* 163:74-7+ Ap '89
Rough water roulette [S. Casiraghi wins World Offshore Championship in Atlantic City] P. Whittell. il por *Motor Boating & Sailing* 164:46-9+ D '89
Winners. See issues of Motor Boating & Sailing beginning January 1989

Ethical aspects
Wanted: winners. P. A. Janssen. il *Motor Boating & Sailing* 163:21 Ja '89

MOTOR BOATING AND SAILING (PERIODICAL)
At the helm. P. A. Janssen. See issues of Motor Boating & Sailing

MOTOR BOATS
See also
Cruisers (Pleasure boats)
Fishing boats
Big dreams in small packages. J. Skorupa. il *Popular Mechanics* 166:86-7 F '89
Finest of the fleet. B. McKeown. il *Outdoor Life* 183:28+ Ja '89
Sportboats. M. Benson. il *Motor Boating & Sailing* 164:60-2 S '89
Trends '90 [special section] il *Motor Boating & Sailing* 164:54-65 S '89

Design
Porsche's new speedboat. M. Benson. il *Motor Boating & Sailing* 163:70-1 Ja '89

Equipment
Transom treatments. B. Stearns. il *Field & Stream* 93:76+ F '89

Handling
Driving tips from the pros. J. A. Fishman. il *Motor Boating & Sailing* 164:62-3+ Jl '89

Leasing and renting
Directories
Motor boating & sailing worldwide charter directory [special section] il *Motor Boating & Sailing* 164:59-66+ Ag '89

Materials
Bright work [Chris-Craft reissues 1930's mahogany runabout] M. Benson. il *Motor Boating & Sailing* 164:40-3+ D '89

Specifications
High performance buyer's guide specs. il *Motor Boating & Sailing* 164:82+ Jl '89

Stability and stabilizers
Transom treatments [trim tabs] B. Stearns. il *Field & Stream* 93:76+ F '89

Testing
90 MPH-guaranteed [Cigarette; cover story] P. A. Janssen. il *Motor Boating & Sailing* 164:48-9 Jl '89
Arriva 2450. L. Rudeen. il *Motor Boating & Sailing* 163:36 F '89
Baja 420. T. P. Banse. il *Motor Boating & Sailing* 163:32 Ap '89
Blue water marauder [Chaparral Villain IV] T. P. Banse. il *Motor Boating & Sailing* 163:70-3+ Je '89
Bright work [Chris-Craft reissues 1930's mahogany runabout] M. Benson. il *Motor Boating & Sailing* 164:40-3+ D '89

California muscle boats. J. Skorupa. il *Popular Mechanics* 166:58-61 S '89
Cobalt 252. D. Fales. il *Motor Boating & Sailing* 164:26 O '89
Cross-country cruise [Miami to Los Angeles in Tempest powerboats] J. Catlett. il map *Motor Boating & Sailing* 163:72-5+ F '89
Donzi Black Widow. P. A. Janssen. il *Motor Boating & Sailing* 163:28 Mr '89
Firebreathers [tunnel boats] J. Skorupa. il *Popular Mechanics* 166:62-5+ Ja '89
Four Winns 220. L. Rudeen. il *Motor Boating & Sailing* 164:24 N '89
Maelstrom 23. D. Fales. il *Motor Boating & Sailing* 163:32 My '89
Package deals. J. Skorupa. il *Popular Mechanics* 166:68-71 Mr '89
Picking up performance. B. McKeown. il *Outdoor Life* 183:54+ My '89
Power lunch [Baja Sport 280] M. Benson. il *Motor Boating & Sailing* 163:48-51+ Mr '89
Power plays [Aronow 37, Birger 38, Cigarette 35 Cafe Racer, Euromarine 42, Formula 357 SR-1, Fountain 36 Fever and Wellcraft Scarab 38 Excel] L. Rudeen. il *Motor Boating & Sailing* 164:38-47+ Jl '89
Ski odyssey [skiing behind the Ski Challenger 2081 off Corfu] L. Rudeen. il *Motor Boating & Sailing* 164:58-61+ Jl '89
Slickcraft 268 SL. M. Benson. il *Motor Boating & Sailing* 164:27 N '89
Space-age speedster [Glastron Carlson 33; cover story] P. A. Janssen. il *Motor Boating & Sailing* 164:38-41 N '89
Weekend fast lane [Stingray 235] T. P. Banse. il *Motor Boating & Sailing* 164:58-9+ O '89

MOTOR CAMPING *See* Camping
MOTOR CLUBS *See* Automobile clubs
MOTOR CORTEX *See* Brain
MOTOR FUELS
See also
Automobile engines—Fuel
Diesel fuels
Gasoline
MOTOR HOMES *See* Campers, Truck
MOTOR OILS, AIRPLANE *See* Airplanes—Lubrication and lubricants
MOTOR OILS, AUTOMOTIVE *See* Automobiles—Lubrication and lubricants
MOTOR OILS, MARINE *See* Boats and boating—Lubrication and lubricants
MOTOR SCOOTER TOURING
Europe
Anecdotes, facetiae, satire, etc.
A rendezvous in Warsaw. A. Fotheringham. il *Maclean's* 102:88 N 27 '89
MOTOR SCOOTERS
"Go for it, lady!". J. Coudert. il *Reader's Digest* 134:121-3 Ja '89

Testing
Honda Elite 250. il *Cycle* 40:61-2+ D '89
MOTOR TREND (PERIODICAL)
Change, the only constant. J. R. Nerad. il *Motor Trend* 41:8 Ag '89
Motor trend's 40th anniversary [cover story; special section] il *Motor Trend* 41:68-72+ My '89
MOTOR TREND AWARDS
40 years of winners. il *Motor Trend* 41:120-1+ My '89
1989 Car of the Year [Ford Thunderbird SC; cover story] il *Motor Trend* 41:48-56+ F '89
1989 Car of the Year preview. D. C. Ross. il *Motor Trend* 41:82-5 Ja '89
1989 Import Car of the Year [Mitsubishi Galant GS] il *Motor Trend* 41:86-91+ Mr '89
Motor trend's 1989 Truck of the Year [Toyota Xtracab SR5 V-6] il *Motor Trend* 41:108-12+ Ap '89
Preview: 1989 Import Car of the Year. B. J. Hoffman. il *Motor Trend* 41:120-1 F '89
Recollections of an ICOY princess [Import Car of the Year tests] J. Manfredi. *Motor Trend* 41:142 Mr '89
Anecdotes, facetiae, satire, etc.
Moto rooter: giant Auto of the Year issue! il *Car and Driver* 34:101+ Ap '89
MOTOR VEHICLE DRIVING
Dirty driving [off-road motoring] L. Frank and R. Millen. il *Popular Mechanics* 166:130 Mr '89
Fighting instinct. S. L. White. il *Field & Stream* 94:78+ My '89
MOTOR VEHICLE ENGINES
Puzzles and principles. K. Cameron. il *Cycle* 40:11 My '89
Energy usage
The road to fuel efficiency in the passenger vehicle fleet. S. E. Plotkin. bibl f il *Environment* 31:18-20+ Jl/Ag '89
MOTOR VEHICLE INDUSTRIES *See* Automobile industry; Truck industry
MOTOR VEHICLE RACING
See also
Automobile racing
Drag racing
Motor vehicle rallies
Motorcycle racing

MOTOR VEHICLE RACING—*cont.*
Intruders in the dirt [Binion's Nissan Mint 400] P. Berg. il *Car and Driver* 35:145+ Ag '89

Baja California (Mexico: Peninsula)
Beat the Baja [1988 1,000 mile race] T. Carlson. il map *Sport (New York, N.Y.)* 80:66-9 My '89

MOTOR VEHICLE RALLIES
On a Jeep Jamboree: thank heaven for four-wheel drive. J. B. Treece. il *Business Week* p125 D 4 '89

MOTOR VEHICLES
See also
  All terrain vehicles
  Automobiles
  Four wheel drive vehicles
  Jeep automobiles
  Motor scooters
  Motorcycles
  Recreational vehicles
  Snowmobiles and snowmobiling
  Station wagons
  Trucks
  Vans

Maintenance and repair
Pre-trip checklist. S. L. White. il *Field & Stream* 94:66-7 Jl '89

MOTOR VEHICLES, MILITARY
Competing GE, FMC armored turrets offer different weapons configurations [Marine Corps Light Armored Vehicle-Air Defense system] D. F. Bond. il *Aviation Week & Space Technology* 131:45+ S 25 '89

Export-import trade
A lemon? Don't tell the Saudis [Bradley Fighting Vehicle] B. Bremner. il *Business Week* p40 Ja 23 '89

MOTOR YACHTS *See* Yachts and yachting
MOTORBIKES *See* Motorcycles
MOTORBOATS *See* Motor boats
MOTORCYCLE ACCIDENTS *See* Motorcycling—Accidents and injuries
MOTORCYCLE BRAKES *See* Brakes, Motorcycle
MOTORCYCLE DEALERS
See also
  Walter A. Kohl Sales (Firm)
MOTORCYCLE ENGINEERING
Hardware, software [adjusting to advanced technology] K. Cameron. il *Cycle* 40:10+ N '89
MOTORCYCLE ENGINES
See also
  Carburetors
The great raft adventure [motorcycle-powered raft trip up the Yukon River] K. Schubert. il map *Cycle* 40:38-41+ Jl '89

Camshafts
Cam timing: how to do it. K. Cameron. il *Cycle* 40:50-2 S '89
Secrets of the ancient cam timers. K. Cameron. il *Cycle* 40:45-9+ S '89

Crankshafts
Broken shafts. K. Cameron. il *Cycle* 40:10 D '89

Design
Inside the ZX-7 [Kawasaki] il *Cycle* 40:35-7 Ap '89
Laughing stock and beyond [success of Norton-Wankel in World TT Formula One] J. Greening. il *Cycle* 40:12 F '89
V-twins [Ducati 851 engine] S. Anderson. il *Cycle* 40:7 S '89

Fuel feeding
Fuel-injected ZX-10 [Kawasaki with experimental engine; cover story] K. Cameron. il *Cycle* 40:30-5+ D '89
Fuel injection tech. *Cycle* 40:36+ D '89
Moto Guzzi finishing R&D on fuel injection. B. De Prato. il *Cycle* 40:19 Jl '89

Lubrication
See Motorcycles—Lubrication and lubricants
MOTORCYCLE HELMET LAWS *See* Motorcycles—Laws and regulations
MOTORCYCLE HELMETS *See* Helmets
MOTORCYCLE INDUSTRY
See also
  Buell Motor Company
  Harley-Davidson Motor Co., Inc.
Advertising
Business cycles. K. Cameron. il *Cycle* 40:19 F '89
Marketing
600s top 1989 bestseller lists. il *Cycle* 40:23 D '89
Market diversity. K. Cameron. il *Cycle* 40:8 O '89
Japan
See also
  Honda Motor Co., Ltd.
  Yamaha Motor Co. Ltd.
MOTORCYCLE INSURANCE *See* Insurance, Motorcycle
MOTORCYCLE JACKETS *See* Jackets
MOTORCYCLE MECHANICS (PERSONS)
A team mechanic's life. J. Smith. il *Cycle* 40:21 O '89
MOTORCYCLE OWNERSHIP
Money [Bimota owner S. Bernstein] S. Anderson. il *Cycle* 40:7 Ag '89

MOTORCYCLE PARTS
See also
  Walter A. Kohl Sales (Firm)
Things [motorcycle parts for junk art] C. Furlong. il *Cycle* 40:27-30 Ja '89
MOTORCYCLE RACE TRACKS *See* Speedways
MOTORCYCLE RACERS (PERSONS) *See* Motorcyclists
MOTORCYCLE RACING
See also
  Speedways
Air Time [motocross racer G. Cooper] T. Carlson. il pors *Sport (New York, N.Y.)* 80:53-6 Ja '89
Daytona '89. il *Cycle* 40:40-5 Je '89
Heir apparent [J. Kocinski] H. R. Abrams. il pors *Cycle* 40:52-4+ N '89
Kocinski hurt, Russell rebounds at Road Atlanta. K. Cameron. il *Cycle* 40:22+ Ag '89
Pipeline. J. Greening. See issues of Cycle
Project DTX: the sequel [racing a dirt track bike built from a motocrosser] K. Vreeke. il *Cycle* 40:61+ O '89
Rumors in flight [500 cc Grand Prix racing] K. Vreeke. il *Cycle* 40:100 Mr '89
Sport for sale [American road racing] K. Cameron. il *Cycle* 40:54-8+ Mr '89
A team mechanic's life. J. Smith. il *Cycle* 40:21 O '89
USGP: the second coming. K. Cameron. il *Cycle* 40:51-60+ Jl '89
Video review: the road to Laguna Seca. il *Cycle* 40:79 Mr '89
When push comes to shove [sliding the front tire while cornering in 500GP racing] K. Cameron. il *Cycle* 40:60-3+ My '89

Accidents and injuries
Fall from grace [B. Shobert injured during cool-off lap at Laguna Seca] K. Cameron. il *Cycle* 40:8 Ag '89
Rawhide [leather motorcycle riding suits after suffering accidents] K. Vreeke. il *Cycle* 40:67 S '89

Economic aspects
Superbike shuffle [difficulty in finding sponsors for the World Superbike Series] J. Greening. il *Cycle* 40:82 Jl '89
Tobacco green [Norton Formula 1 team backed by Imperial Tobacco] J. Greening. il *Cycle* 40:114 My '89

History
A racer of the purest kind [J. Surtees] M. Nicks. il pors *Road & Track* 40:74-6+ Je '89

International aspects
1989 race calendar. il *Cycle* 40:26 Ap '89
Border patrols. K. Cameron. il *Cycle* 40:8 S '89
Eddie keeps the crown [500cc World Championship road racing title won by E. Lawson] M. Oxley. il por *Cycle* 40:19-20 D '89
Grand Prix evolution. J. Greening. il *Cycle* 40:82 N '89
Sidecars. K. Cameron. il *Cycle* 40:37-9+ S '89
Star search [Grand Prix circuit after retirement of F. Spencer] J. Greening. il *Cycle* 40:82 D '89
Superbike season recap. K. Vreeke. il *Cycle* 40:108 Ap '89

Study and teaching
Hickman Haul-Ass Club (II) [K. Robert's private training camp for team riders] K. Vreeke. il pors *Cycle* 40:45-8+ Ja '89

Australia
Gardner tops Rainey at Australian GP. il *Cycle* 40:24 Jl '89

Europe
Schwantz and Rainey top Euro Grands Prix. M. Oxley. il *Cycle* 40:24 S '89

Great Britain
Class structure. J. Greening. il *Cycle* 40:100 Je '89
Classic action. J. Greening. il *Cycle* 40:104 Ap '89
Lawson takes GP point lead as Rainey crashes [E. Lawson wins Swedish GP; K. Schwantz wins British GP] M. Oxley. il pors *Cycle* 40:24 N '89
Norton at the Isle of Man. C. Fox. il *Cycle* 40:36-41 O '89
Power plays [Donington awarded British Grand Prix over Brands Hatch] J. Greening. il *Cycle* 40:82 Ag '89
Renfrow nips Quarterley at Loudon National. K. Cameron. il *Cycle* 40:26 S '89
Tobacco green [Norton Formula 1 team backed by Imperial Tobacco] J. Greening. il *Cycle* 40:114 My '89

Italy
Lawson wins Spanish GP; riders boycott in Italy. M. Oxley. il *Cycle* 40:22 Ag '89

Japan
Schwantz, Kocinski win at Japanese GP. T. Van Hooydonk. il *Cycle* 40:24 Je '89

Spain
Lawson wins Spanish GP; riders boycott in Italy. M. Oxley. il *Cycle* 40:22 Ag '89

Sweden
Lawson takes GP point lead as Rainey crashes [E. Lawson wins Swedish GP; K. Schwantz wins British GP] M. Oxley. il pors *Cycle* 40:24 N '89

Western Europe
Laughing stock and beyond [success of Norton-Wankel in World TT Formula One] J. Greening. il *Cycle* 40:12 F '89

MOTORCYCLE RACING—Western Europe—*cont.*
Lawson closes on Rainey in 500 GPs. M. Oxley. il por
Cycle 40:24+ O '89
MOTORCYCLE RIDING *See* Motorcycling
MOTORCYCLE SPEED RECORDS
Freud's greatest adventure: full moon over Bonneville [G.
Freudenberger sets 750 class land speed record] K. Vreeke.
il pors *Cycle* 40:65-7+ F '89
MOTORCYCLE TIRES *See* Tires, Motorcycle
MOTORCYCLE TOURING *See* Motorcycling
MOTORCYCLES
See also
Motor scooters
Motorcycling
Advertising
See Motorcycle industry—Advertising
Brakes
See Brakes, Motorcycle
Carburetors
See Carburetors
Design
1990 preview: Honda. il *Cycle* 40:28-30 N '89
1990 preview: Honda. il *Cycle* 40:38-40+ D '89
1990 preview: Yamaha. il *Cycle* 40:31-2 N '89
Federico Martini [designer of the Bimota YB6] por *Cycle*
40:37 Ag '89
Honda seeks response for declining domestic market. N.
Voge. il *Cycle* 40:21 N '89
Kawasaki, Suzuki create new standards [ZR400 Zephyr and
Bandit] T. Van Hooydonk. il *Cycle* 40:19+ S '89
The missing center [need for better general-purpose bike]
S. Anderson. il *Cycle* 40:11 May '89
Post-industrial motorcycle design [Honda Pacific Coast] B.
Finlayson. il *Cycle* 40:38-9 Je '89
Yamaha, Honda bring GP wars to the street [TZR250 and
NSR250R] T. Van Hooydonk. il *Cycle* 40:19-20 Ag '89
Yamaha unveils a Genesis twin [XTZ750 Super Ténéré]
T. Van Hooydonk. il *Cycle* 40:23 Mr '89
Equipment
Aerostich Courier Bag. il *Cycle* 40:40 S '89
The bottom line: cures for saddle sores. T. Van Hooydonk.
il *Cycle* 40:57-9 D '89
Galindo designs tank bag. il *Cycle* 40:80 Ja '89
Lockhart Buckle Buster and Fanny Tank Pack. il *Cycle*
40:68-9 O '89
Tail bags. il *Cycle* 40:78-80 My '89
Frames
Frames: state of the art. T. Tsuji. il *Cycle* 40:52-5+ D '89
Fuel systems
See Motorcycle engines—Fuel feeding
History
CBX: one from the heart [Honda] B. Finlayson. il *Cycle*
40:64-7 Ja '89
Nostalgia minus the bump & grunt. G. Jennings. il *Cycle*
40:82-4+ Ap '89
Parilla. J. P. Burns. il *Cycle* 40:70-3+ F '89
Insurance
See Insurance, Motorcycle
Laws and regulations
Hogrolling [helmet law opposition] A. Heard. *The New
Republic* 201:11-12 N 20 '89
Senator introduces national helmet law [John Chafee] *Cycle*
40:22 S '89
Social costs. S. Anderson. il *Cycle* 40:11 Je '89
Lubrication and lubricants
The spectrometric sleuth [oil analysis] T. Van Hooydonk.
il *Cycle* 40:80-2 F '89
Maintenance and repair
See also
Motorcycle mechanics (Persons)
TDC. K. Cameron. See issues of Cycle
Ownership
See Motorcycle ownership
Parts
See Motorcycle parts
Prices
Bargain blasters 1989 [cover story; special section] *Cycle*
40:30-6+ My '89
Prices. S. Anderson. il *Cycle* 40:9 My '89
Seats
The bottom line: cures for saddle sores. T. Van Hooydonk.
il *Cycle* 40:57-9 D '89
Shock absorbers
Progressive Suspension Fork Springs and Magnumatic Air
Shocks. il *Cycle* 40:60-1 Ja '89
Springs and suspension
New suspenders [BMW R100GS, Honda Hawk GT] S. F.
Brown. il *Popular Science* 234:48 Mr '89
One for the road [improving the suspension and tires on
a Yamaha FZR600] T. Van Hooydonk. il *Cycle* 40:57-9+
O '89
Progressive Suspension Fork Springs and Magnumatic Air
Shocks. il *Cycle* 40:60-1 Ja '89
Testing
400 fours: then & now [Honda racer compared with street
versions] K. Vreeke. il *Cycle* 40:64-7+ Je '89
Bike with a trunk [Honda Pacific Coast] S. F. Brown. il
Popular Science 235:30-1 O '89

Bimota YB6 and Yamaha FZR1000 [cover story] il *Cycle*
40:28-36 Ag '89
BMW K1. T. Van Hooydonk. il *Cycle* 40:44-9 Ag '89
BMW K75. il *Cycle* 40:50-5 O '89
Buell RR1200. il *Cycle* 40:44-9+ Ap '89
Ducati 906 Paso. il *Cycle* 40:38-40 N '89
Ducati 906 Paso. B. De Prato. il *Cycle* 40:53-4+ My '89
Ducati Superbike 851 [cover story] il *Cycle* 40:28-34 S '89
The gentrified hog [Harley-Davidson 883 Sportster] M. Marvel.
il *Esquire* 112:22+ Jl '89
Gilera Saturno sets single standard. B. De Prato. il *Cycle*
40:26 Ag '89
Harley Davidson Electra Glide Ultra Classic FLHTC. il
Cycle 40:44-8+ Mr '89
Hogs [Harleys] S. Anderson. il *Cycle* 40:7 O '89
Honda CB-1. il *Cycle* 40:54-8+ Je '89
Honda CBR1000 Hurricane. il *Cycle* 40:34-8+ Ja '89
Honda GB500. il *Cycle* 40:74-8 Ap '89
Honda Pacific Coast [cover story] il *Cycle* 40:30-6+ Je '89
Honda Pacific Coast PC800. R. Grable. il *Motor Trend*
41:96-7+ S '89
Honda XL600V Transalp [cover story] il *Cycle* 40:18-22+
Ja '89
Katana 1100 vs. FJ1200 [Suzuki vs. Yamaha] il *Cycle* 40:50-1
N '89
Kawasaki EX500. il *Cycle* 40:38-42 My '89
Kawasaki KLR250. il *Cycle* 40:59-60+ N '89
Kawasaki Voyager XII. il *Cycle* 40:39-40+ Ag '89
Kawasaki ZG1000 Concours. J. Karr. il *Motor Trend* 41:108
F '89
Kawasaki ZX-7 Ninja [cover story] il *Cycle* 40:32-7+ Ap
'89
Milwaukee magic [Harley-Davidson Softail Springer; cover
story] K. Vreeke. il *Cycle* 40:30-5+ O '89
Moto Guzzi Mille GT. il *Cycle* 40:54-9+ S '89
The rational 750s: Ninja vs Katana [cover story] il *Cycle*
40:32-8+ Mr '89
Sizzling 600s [Honda CBR, Kawasaki Ninja, Suzuki Katana,
and Yamaha FZR600; cover story] il *Cycle* 40:28-34+ Jl
'89
Spaghetti western [riding cross country on a Ducati 906
Paso] J. P. Burns. il *Cycle* 40:34-7+ N '89
Suzuki GS500. il *Cycle* 40:32-6 My '89
Suzuki GSX-R1100. il *Cycle* 40:46-50+ F '89
Suzuki Katana 1100. il *Cycle* 40:44-8+ N '89
Touring first class. N. Mayersohn. il *Popular Mechanics*
166:80-3+ Ap '89
Yamaha FJ1200. il *Cycle* 40:42-4+ Jl '89
Yamaha FZR1000 [cover story] D. Coe. il *Cycle* 40:20-4+
F '89
Yamaha FZR600. il *Cycle* 40:66-70+ My '89
Yamaha FZR600R. il *Cycle* 40:44-7+ D '89
Yamaha TW200. il *Cycle* 40:69-72 S '89
Yamaha Virago 1100. il *Cycle* 40:50-3+ Ag '89
Yamaha YX600 Radian. il *Cycle* 40:44-8 My '89
Theft
Ripped off. H. Arnett. il *Cycle* 40:28+ Ap '89
Tires
See Tires, Motorcycle
Wheels
Sbarro introduces the hubless wheel. T. Van Hooydonk.
il por *Cycle* 40:19+ Je '89
MOTORCYCLES, RACING
John Player Special Norton shoots for world F1 title. T.
Van Hooydonk. il *Cycle* 40:21 My '89
Lawson, Kanemoto: adding up victory [E. Lawson's Honda
NSR] K. Cameron. il por *Cycle* 40:20 D '89
Mechanical rhymes minus reason. K. Cameron. il *Cycle*
40:12 Mr '89
Norton at the Isle of Man. C. Fox. il *Cycle* 40:36-41 O
'89
Pipeline. J. Greening. See issues of Cycle
Two-fifties. J. Greening. il *Cycle* 40:82 Ja '89
Design
Anatomy of an Elf. K. Cameron. il *Cycle* 40:74+ Mr '89
Project DTX [dirt track bike built from a motocrosser] il
Cycle 40:67-8 Ag '89
Shifting fortunes [Daytona ProTwins] K. Cameron. il *Cycle*
40:48-51+ Je '89
Subtle speed [Harley-Davidson XR750 dirt track bike] T.
Van Hooydonk. il *Cycle* 40:52-3+ Ja '89
Yamaha and Suzuki build new 750 repli-racers. T. Van
Hooydonk. il *Cycle* 40:22 My '89
Yamaha's Daytona battle plan [FZR600s modified by R.
Muzzy] C. Everitt. il por *Cycle* 40:75-7 My '89
History
History lesson [Yamaha TD2] D. Coe. il *Cycle* 40:63 Ap
'89
Testing
400 fours: then & now [Honda racer compared with street
versions] K. Vreeke. il *Cycle* 40:64-7+ Je '89
Kawasaki ZXR-7. il *Cycle* 40:60-3+ Mr '89
Project DTX: the sequel [racing a dirt track bike built from
a motocrosser] K. Vreeke. il *Cycle* 40:61+ O '89
Riding the Elf. M. Oxley. il *Cycle* 40:71-4+ Mr '89
TD2 to TZ250W: the fittest survive [Yamahas] K. Cameron.
il *Cycle* 40:58-62+ Ap '89

MOTORCYCLES, REMODELED
The outlaw tweak for Ducati's 750 Paso. J. P. Burns. il *Cycle* 40:71-3 Ja '89
Project DTX [dirt track bike built from a motocrosser] il *Cycle* 40:67-8 Ag '89

Testing
Fuel-injected ZX-10 [Kawasaki with experimental engine; cover story] K. Cameron. il *Cycle* 40:30-5+ D '89
Full-tilt Hawk [modified Honda] il *Cycle* 40:69-70+ Ap '89
Project DTX: the sequel [racing a dirt track bike built from a motocrosser] K. Vreeke. il *Cycle* 40:61+ O '89
Special FX [Harley-Davidson Super Glide FXR] T. Van Hooydonk. il *Cycle* 40:73-5+ Je '89
Special FX redux [Harley-Davidson] C. Everitt. il *Cycle* 40:63-5+ Ag '89

MOTORCYCLES, USED
Garage of the living dead. S. Steele. il *Cycle* 40:81 Jl '89
Revival [1982 Suzuki GS1100EZ] T. Van Hooydonk. il *Cycle* 40:54-7+ Ag '89

MOTORCYCLING
See also
Alcohol and motorcyclists
Motorcycle racing
Easy riders. C. Pfouts. il *New Choices for the Best Years* 29:64-9 Je '89
Scenic Byways Study Act may improve U.S. touring. T. Van Hooydonk. il *Cycle* 40:23-4 Je '89
Spaghetti western [riding cross country on a Ducati 906 Paso] J. P. Burns. il *Cycle* 40:34-7+ N '89
Tooling down the Mississippi [M. S. Forbes' motorcycling tour] B. Sipchen. il pors map *Forbes* 144:22-3 O 30 '89
Ups and downs, 1989. S. Anderson. il *Cycle* 40:9 D '89

Accidents and injuries
A cop's homage to a slain pal becomes his own tragic farewell [tape made by accident victim R. Shinholser] il por *People Weekly* 31:43 Ja 30 '89
A hit-and-run crash ends the life of kidnap victim Steven Stayner. J. Stark. il pors *People Weekly* 32:40-1 O 2 '89
A near-fatal motorcycle crash changes an actor's life, but not his refusal to wear a helmet; ed. by Jack Kelley. G. Busey. il pors *People Weekly* 31:65-6+ My 15 '89
Questions [questioning relationship between high performance design and accidents] K. Cameron. il *Cycle* 40:15 Ja '89
Too fast at the turn [New Brunswick politician B. Valcourt in motorcycle accident] P. Kopvillem. il por *Maclean's* 102:14 Jl 17 '89

History
Sermon on old mounts. G. Jennings. il *Cycle* 40:64-8 Mr '89

International aspects
Road to ruin [riding a Honda XL500R around the world] C. Reed. il pors map *Cycle* 40:45-9+ O '89

Philosophy
A motorcycle at Walden. H. Arnett. il *Cycle* 40:16 O '89

Photographs and photography
Cycle savvy! [work of R. Cox] M. Stensvold. il *Petersen's Photographic Magazine* 17:14-17 Ap '89

Study and teaching
See also
Motorcycle racing—Study and teaching

Stunt cycling
Daredevil Robbie Knievel heads for Vegas to show his famous dad he's more than a little Evel. P. Axthelm. il pors *People Weekly* 31:62-3 Ap 10 '89
Returning good for Evel [R. Knievel's water fountain jump at Caesars Palace, Las Vegas] F. Lidz. il pors *Sports Illustrated* 70:26-7 Ap 24 '89

California
Revival. S. Anderson. il *Cycle* 40:8 Jl '89

China
Armand Hammer, 90, who doesn't have time to retire or die [helping M. Forbes get permission for motorcycle and balloon trip] A. Hammer. il por *Forbes* 143:20 Ja 23 '89

Colorado
Lion heart [former fighter pilot R. Cunningham in the Colorado 500] C. Furlong. il pors *Cycle* 40:78-80+ Je '89

Spain
Tapas, bulls and kings [Forbes Friendship Tour] R. Morais. il pors map *Forbes* 144:140-6+ Ag 7 '89

United States
See Motorcycling

MOTORCYCLING CLOTHES *See* Clothing and dress—Sports clothes
MOTORCYCLING GLOVES *See* Gloves
MOTORCYCLISTS
See also
Alcohol and motorcyclists
Gardner, Wayne
Kocinski, John
Lawson, Eddie
Mrazek, Frank
Parker, Scott
Rainey, Wayne
Roberts, Kenny
Schwantz, Kevin
Shobert, Bubba

Spencer, Freddie
Strikes—Motorcyclists
Surtees, John
Easy riders. C. Pfouts. il *New Choices for the Best Years* 29:64-9 Je '89
L.A.'s biking celebs bring a roaring trade to Ed and Vern's [Rock Store, grocery and diner] il por *People Weekly* 31:89 My 15 '89

Attitudes
Works riders [rider-machine partnerships] J. Greening. il *Cycle* 40:30 Mr '89

Psychology
Hardware, software [adjusting to advanced technology] K. Cameron. il *Cycle* 40:10+ N '89
Mental health. K. Cameron. il *Cycle* 40:12 Je '89
MOTORHOMES *See* Campers, Truck
MOTORISTS *See* Automobile drivers
MOTORLET (FIRM)
Czech M602 turboprop engine designed for rugged environment. U. Hradiste. il *Aviation Week & Space Technology* 130:41 Ap 3 '89
MOTOROLA, INC. SEMICONDUCTOR PRODUCTS SECTOR
Down in Phoenix, everything is chip-shape. L. Armstrong. il *Business Week* p121 N 13 '89
MOTOROLA, INC.
80486, 68040 open new season of CPU power. *Byte* 14:13-14+ Je '89
Intel to Motorola: race ya [new 860 chip] O. Port. il *Business Week* p42 Mr 13 '89
Motorola is pounding on Japan's 'open door' [cellular market] N. Gross. il *Business Week* p58 My 8 '89
The rival Japan respects [cover story] L. Therrien. il pors *Business Week* p108-10+ N 13 '89
A sanctions scare finally makes the Japanese jump [cellular phone deal] P. Magnusson. *Business Week* p28-9 Jl 10 '89
What Motorola learns from Japan. R. Henkoff. il *Fortune* 119:157+ Ap 24 '89
MOTORSPORTS HALL OF FAME *See* International Motorsports Hall of Fame
MOTOWN PRODUCTIONS
The golden dove [S. de Passe and Motown's investment in TV series Lonesome dove] G. Button. il por *Forbes* 143:58-9 Ja 23 '89
Hitsville goes Hollywood [S. de Passe] J. Castro. il por *Time* 133:51 Ja 30 '89
Motown soars with "Dove". S. Herbert. il por *Black Enterprise* 19:40 My '89
Motown's 'Lonesome dove' ignites CBS-TV ratings. il *Jet* 75:58 Mr 6 '89
MOTOWN RECORDS
Motown deal sounds sweet [joining forces with Apollo Theatre] P. Sharif. il *Black Enterprise* 20:24 N '89
Motown sues Rick James. S. Assael. *Rolling Stone* p30 My 18 '89
MOTT, WILLIAM PENN, JR.
National parks: year 2000. il *National Parks* 63:18-19 Ja/F '89
MOTTAHEDEH, MILDRED
about
Museum pieces for everyday living. C. Brown. il por *Forbes* 144:100 Ag 21 '89
MOTTESI, ALBERTO
about
Evangelist offers advice to Nicaraguan president [interview] R. Frame. il pors *Christianity Today* 33:41-2 N 3 '89
MOTTOES
Collectors and collecting
The joy of motto collecting. D. Stewart. il *Antiques & Collecting Hobbies* 93:60-2 Ja '89
MOTT'S APPLE AWARDS
Books: 'better than ice cream'. il *National Geographic World* 171:24 N '89
MOTYL, ALEXANDER J.
Identity crisis in the Soviet west. map *The Bulletin of the Atomic Scientists* 45:21-4 Mr '89
MOTZKIN, ELHANAN
Artificial intelligence and the Chinese Room: an exchange. il *The New York Review of Books* 36:44-5 F 16 '89
MOULD, BOB
about
Bob Mould works it all out on solo debut. D. Browne. il *Rolling Stone* p165+ My 18 '89
Down to a dull roar. D. Gates. il pors *Newsweek* 113:62+ Je 19 '89
New day rising. D. Fricke. por *Rolling Stone* p78-80+ Je 15 '89
MOULDER, BOB V.
Sounds of home. il *Reader's Digest* 135:143-4 Jl '89
MOULINS, MAURICE
(jt. auth) *See* Hooper, Scott L., and Moulins, Maurice
MOULTON, DAVE
about
Fuso Lux. J. Kukoda. il *Bicycling* 30:188+ Je '89
MOUNT ALLISON UNIVERSITY
A model mission [fund-raising] G. Allen. il *Maclean's* 102:59+ S 18 '89

MOUNT BACHELOR (OR.: RESORT) *See* Resorts—Oregon

MOUNT CASHEL ORPHANAGE (ST. JOHN'S, NFLD.)
Charges of a coverup [sexual and physical abuse] N. Underwood. *Maclean's* 102:66+ D 4 '89
A Church in crisis [sex scandals involving priests] G. Allen. il *Maclean's* 102:66 N 27 '89
Scandal on the Rock [inquiry into sexual abuse involving Christian Brothers] N. Underwood. il *Maclean's* 102:61 O 2 '89
Sex and scandal [former resident S. Earle testifies about sexual abuse] N. Underwood. il por *Maclean's* 102:84 O 30 '89

MOUNT DESERT ISLAND (ME.)
Description and travel
Maine stay. F. FitzGerald. il *Vogue* 179:236-8+ Ag '89

MOUNT DIABLO STATE PARK (CALIF.)
Outflanking Mt. Diablo's foes. M. Mardon. il *Sierra* 74:56-8 Jl/Ag '89

MOUNT EVEREST (CHINA AND NEPAL)
Cold courage [team attempts new route without oxygen or Sherpas] E. Webster. il pors *Sports Illustrated* 70:62-6+ Ja 16 '89
Everest Environmental Expedition: E³. L. Nichol and B. McConnell. il *Focus (New York, N.Y.: 1950)* 39:30-1 Fall '89
High and mighty: the first American women reach Everest's peak. A. Dappen. il *Women's Sports & Fitness* 11:51 Ja/F '89
What it takes to reach the summit [women climbers S. Allison and P. Luce] J. Skow. il pors *Time* 133:14-15+ Mr 6 '89

MOUNT GRAHAM OBSERVATORY (ARIZ.: PROPOSED)
See Astronomical observatories

MOUNT HOOD (OR.: RESORT) *See* Resorts—Oregon

MOUNT HOOD NATIONAL FOREST (OR.)
Mt. Hood Resort expansion. *Wilderness* 52:11-12 Summ '89

MOUNT KILIMANJARO (TANZANIA)
Puffing to Hemingway's peak [tourist route] D. Brand. il *Time* 133:80+ Je 5 '89

MOUNT MAGAZINE (ARK.)
The mount called Magazine. il *Southern Living* 24:43 Ja '89

MOUNT MARCY (N.Y.)
A view from Marcy. R. Loos. il *The Conservationist* 43:20-3 My/Je '89

MOUNT MARION (N.Y.)
Crime
Heigh-ho, heigh-ho, it's far, far off we go; or, Grumpynappers give a cement dwarf a joyride [pranksters steal lawn ornament from the home of C. Horne] il *People Weekly* 31:100-1 Je 26 '89

MOUNT MCKINLEY (ALASKA)
Have slide rule, will climb [scientists climb Mount McKinley to measure height via satellite] *U.S. News & World Report* 106:14 Je 12 '89

MOUNT MCKINLEY NATIONAL PARK (ALASKA) *See* Denali National Park and Preserve (Alaska)

MOUNT MITCHELL (N.C.)
Trouble on the wind [research by Robert I. Bruck] H. Middleton. il *Southern Living* 24:42+ Je '89

MOUNT RORAIMA
Venezuela's islands in time. U. George. il maps *National Geographic* 175:526-61 My '89

MOUNT RUSHMORE NATIONAL MEMORIAL (S.D.)
Reagan on the rock reactions [discussion of July 1989 article, Ron on the rock] D. Shanahan. il por *The American Spectator* 22:43 S '89
Ron on the rock [campaign to add likeness of R. Reagan] D. Shanahan. il por *The American Spectator* 22:26-7 Jl '89

MOUNT SAINT HELENS (WASH.)
Volcano exhibit to travel U.S. il *Earth Science* 42:5-6 Summ '89

MOUNT SAINT MARY'S COLLEGE (MD.)
Transforming general education from remedy to reality. A. Levine. il *Change* 21:4 Jl/Ag '89

MOUNT SHASTA (CALIF.)
High and mighty. S. Kasper. il *Sierra* 74:60 My/Je '89

MOUNT SHASTA SKI PARK (CALIF.) *See* Resorts—California

MOUNT ST. MARY'S COLLEGE
Minority and disadvantaged students [address, February 2, 1989] M. Coughlin. *Vital Speeches of the Day* 55:569-72 Jl 1 '89

MOUNT STEWART (NORTHERN IRELAND: HISTORIC HOUSE) *See* Historic houses, sites, etc.—Northern Ireland

MOUNT VERNON (VA.: ESTATE)
Ancestral seat. *The New Yorker* 65:34-5 Ap 10 '89
Mount Vernon [cover story; special issue; with editorial comment by Wendell Garrett] il *Antiques* 135:452-531 F '89
Gardens
The gardens. D. Nevins. bibl f il *Antiques* 135:524-31 F '89
George Washington's garden. M. Filler. il *House & Garden* 161:140-9 My '89

MOUNT VERNON LADIES' ASSOCIATION OF THE UNION
The Mount Vernon Ladies' Association of the Union. N. W. Horstman. il pors *Antiques* 135:454-61 F '89

MOUNTAIN BICYCLE RACING *See* Bicycle racing

MOUNTAIN BICYCLES *See* Bicycles

MOUNTAIN CLIMBING *See* Mountaineering

MOUNTAIN CYCLING
7 off-road tips. F. Zahradnik. il *Bicycling* 30:116 My '89
Fat fests [U.S. festivals] C. Kelly. il *Bicycling* 30:142-4+ Je '89
Head over wheels [Crested Butte, Colo.] K. Castle. il *Travel Holiday* 171:18-21 Ja '89
I love hills. F. Matheny. il *Bicycling* 30:138 D '89
King of the hill. J. Servin. il *Gentlemen's Quarterly* 59:161+ My '89
Mountain biking just gets better and better. P. Mooney. il por *Women's Sports & Fitness* 11:74 My '89
Mountain biking turns 10. S. Martin. il *Bicycling* 30:39-42+ O/N '89
Sunday outings into the Palm Springs mountains . . . join with fellow cyclists. il *Sunset (Central West edition)* 182:48 Ja '89
The urban jungle [off-road areas near cities; special section] il *Bicycling* 30:80-2+ O/N '89

MOUNTAIN FLYING *See* Aviation—Mountain flying

MOUNTAIN GOATS *See* Rocky Mountain goats

MOUNTAIN LANGUAGE [drama] *See* Pinter, Harold, 1930-

MOUNTAIN LIONS *See* Pumas

MOUNTAIN RUNNING
Mountain running: the peak justifies the means. A. Tinsley. il por *Women's Sports & Fitness* 11:66 N/D '89
Swiss Ms. [Swiss Alpine Marathon] C. Negron. il *Runner's World* 24:60-2 S '89

MOUNTAIN SICKNESS
Big bag theory [body bag invented by Igor Gamow to combat altitude sickness] il *Discover* 10:19 Jl '89
High anxiety. D. Noland. il *American Health* 8:44 My '89

MOUNTAINEERING
See also
    Mount Everest (China and Nepal)
    Ski mountaineering
    Snow and ice climbing
Cliffhanger [woman rock climber L. Hill; cover story] T. Gabriel. il pors *The New York Times Magazine* p20-5+ D 31 '89
Climb every mountain, before lunch [indoor facilities] B. Barol. il *Newsweek* 114:102 N 13 '89
Grit and a granite will conquer El Capitan [paraplegic M. Wellman makes climb assisted by M. Corbett] M. Brower. il pors *People Weekly* 32:36-9 Ag 14 '89
Have slide rule, will climb [scientists climb Mount McKinley to measure height via satellite] *U.S. News & World Report* 106:14 Je 12 '89
High and mighty: the first American women reach Everest's peak. A. Dappen. il *Women's Sports & Fitness* 11:51 Ja/F '89
High Tripping [Sierra Club High Trips] il *Sierra* 74:52-6 Ja/F '89
The mechanics of rock climbing, or Surviving the ultimate physics exam. J. Walker. il *Scientific American* 260:118-21 Je '89
A message in a bottle: or, Honeymoon on Cannon Mountain [1901 climb of Montana peak by newlyweds W. B. and C. J. Cannon] M. C. Schlesinger. il pors map *American Heritage* 40:106-9 Ap '89
The pastures of Class-L heaven [climbing Clark Mountain in the East Mojave Scenic Area] D. Darlington. il *Sierra* 74:70-3+ S/O '89
Puffing to Hemingway's peak [tourist route up Mt. Kilimanjaro] D. Brand. il *Time* 133:80+ Je 5 '89
Sheer delight. J. Scandura. il *American Health* 8:40+ My '89
What's California's easiest 14,000-footer? Try White Mountain Peak. il map *Sunset (Central West edition)* 183:16-17 S '89
Accidents
Injured in a climbing accident, a doctor tests his will in the mountains again [amputee J. Donlou] D. Chu. il pors *People Weekly* 31:93-4+ Mr 20 '89
Left for dead on a Peruvian peak, Joe Simpson survives to write movingly about the climbers' code [Andes climb] S. K. Reed. il pors *People Weekly* 31:151-2 My 1 '89
Economic aspects
Upward mobility [woman rock climber L. Hill] il pors *Life* 12:104-5 Ag '89
Equipment
Big bag theory [body bag invented by Igor Gamow to combat altitude sickness] il *Discover* 10:19 Jl '89
Psychological aspects
Blazing the lonesome trail [stress of mountaineering as a model for interplanetary missions; research by Barbara Kanki and others] S. Kaiser. il *Ad Astra* 1:32-4+ O '89
The challenge of rock climbing: to find an inner resolve more unyielding than stone. J. Scandura. il *Vogue* 179:68+ Jl '89

MOUNTAINEERING VIDEO GAMES See Video games
MOUNTAINS
        See also
    Adirondack Mountains (N.Y.)
    Cannon Mountain (Mont.)
    Clark Mountain (Calif.)
    El Capitan (Calif.)
    Mount Magazine (Ark.)
    Mount Marcy (N.Y.)
    Mount Mitchell (N.C.)
    Mount Shasta (Calif.)
    Ruby Mountains (Nev.)
    Seamounts
    Shawangunk Mountains (N.Y.)
    Thunderhead Mountain (S.D.)
    Tiger Mountain (Wash.)
    Volcanoes
    White Mountain Peak (Calif.)
    Yucca Mountain (Nev.)
            Photographs and photography
How to shoot scenics [work of G. A. Rowell; cover story]
    D. Brockway. il pors Popular Photography 96:48-59+ N
    '89
                Alaska
        See also
    Chugach Mountains (Alaska)
    Mount McKinley (Alaska)
                Canada
        See also
    Canadian Rockies (B.C. and Alta.)
Origins and movement of fluids during deformation and
    metamorphism in the Canadian Cordillera [gold deposits]
    B. E. Nesbitt and K. Muehlenbachs. bibl f il map Science
    245:733-6 Ag 18 '89
Where mountains once stood [research by Frederick A. Cook]
    R. Monastersky. Science News 135:319 My 20 '89
                China
        See also
    Mount Everest (China and Nepal)
                Europe
        See also
    Alps
                Nepal
        See also
    Mount Everest (China and Nepal)
                South America
        See also
    Mount Roraima
                Tanzania
        See also
    Mount Kilimanjaro (Tanzania)
                Venezuela
Venezuela's islands in time [tepuis] U. George. il maps
    National Geographic 175:526-61 My '89
MOUNTAINS AND PLAINS BOOKSELLERS ASSOCIA-
    TION
MPBA meets in Denver. J. Mutter. il Publishers Weekly
    236:34-5+ N 10 '89
MOUNTAINVILLE (N.Y.)
                Galleries and museums
        See also
    Storm King Art Center
MOUNTED ANIMALS See Hunting trophies
MOUNTINGS, TELESCOPE See Telescopes—Mounting
MOURA, VASCO GRAÇA
Luís de Camões: the eventful life and times of Portugal's
    great epic poet. il maps The Courier (Unesco) 42:17-25
    Ap '89
MOURNING See Grief
MOURNING DOVE SHOOTING
Dove hunting with a difference [dove farming] G. Reiger.
    il Field & Stream 94:50-1+ S '89
MOUSE See Mice
MOUSE (COMPUTER EQUIPMENT)
Mouse-ability for 1-2-3 users [MarqNavigator release 2.01,
    version 1.30] M. Antonoff. il Personal Computing 13:206
    Mr '89
PowerMouse courts 1-2-3 users. M. Wiggins. il Byte 14:290+
    N '89
Smarter than your average mouse [Mitsubishi Smart Mouse]
    R. Malloy. il Byte 14:92+ Jl '89
The stationary mouse [TrackMan Stationary Mouse] N. Baran.
    il Byte 14:84 D '89
MOUSE EAR CRESS
A big role for a small weed [Arabidopsis thaliana] il BioScience
    39:761-2 D '89
A dwarf mutant of Arabidopsis generated by T-DNA insertion
    mutagenesis [cover story] K. A. Feldmann and others.
    bibl f il Science 243:1351-4 Mr 10 '89
Genome projects are growing like weeds [National Science
    Foundation plans to map Arabidopsis] J. Palca. il Science
    245:131 Jl 14 '89
MOUSETRAPS
Mouse in the house. R. Kimber. il Country Journal 16:72-4+
    Ja '89
On the rodent again. J. Stone. il Discover 10:38+ N '89

MOUSSE See Desserts
MOUSSE CAKE See Cake
MOUSTACHES See Mustaches
MOUSTIERS-SAINTE-MARIE (FRANCE)
                Description
Moustiers. T. Weeks. il map Gourmet 49:96-101+ O '89
MOUTET, ANNE-ELISABETH
Art lovers. il pors Vogue 179:498-503+ Mr '89
MOUTH
        See also
    Gums
    Teeth
    Tongue
The mouth as body's mirror [clue to illness] J. Folkenberg.
    il FDA Consumer 23:22-4 D '89/Ja '90
                Cancer
                Causes
Oral cancer on rise [smokeless tobacco] J. Folkenberg. il
    FDA Consumer 23:24-5 D '89/Ja '90
Smoking, drinking and oral cancer. il FDA Consumer 23:40
    F '89
                Care and hygiene
        See also
    Halitosis
    Mouthwashes
                Diseases
        See also
    Leukoplakia, Oral
                Microbiology
Where the bad bugs are [role of bacteria in gum disease
    and tooth decay] C. Sears. il American Health 8:50 Ap
    '89
                Transplantation
Need new tissue?—Grow your own [replacing damaged tissue
    in the mouth; work of Stephen Feinberg] il USA Today
    (Periodical) 118:8 O '89
                Wounds and injuries
        See also
    Teeth—Wounds and injuries
MOUTHWASHES
One claim you can brush off [Plax mouthwash] il Consumer
    Reports 54:507 Ag '89
MOVE (ORGANIZATION)
Journey of a cult child [A. Ward helps son M. Ward make
    transition from MOVE] M. Capuzzo. il pors Reader's Digest
    134:109-14 My '89
MOVEMENT, CREATIVE See Dance
MOVEMENT, PSYCHOLOGY OF
        See also
    Communication, Nonverbal
    Motion perception
    Motor ability
MOVEMENT DISORDERS
        See also
    Paralysis
    Tardive dyskinesia
MOVEMENT NOTATION See Dance notation
MOVEMENT OF ALGERIAN JOURNALISTS
Algerian journalists rebel. V. Brittain. il World Press Review
    36:58 Ag '89
MOVEMENT OF ANIMALS See Animal locomotion
MOVEMENT OF CELLS See Cells—Motility
MOVEMENTS OF MAN See Biomechanics
MOVIE MAGAZINES See Motion pictures—Periodicals
MOVIE THEATERS See Motion picture theaters
MOVIES See Motion pictures
MOVING
        See also
    Black executives—Relocation
    Change of address
    Executives—Relocation
    Migration, Internal
A moving experience. G. Rosenblum. il New Choices for
    the Best Years 29:84+ Mr '89
On the move with your cat. A. R. Marder. il Prevention
    (Emmaus, Pa.) 41:110+ S '89
Reader's digest guide to moving. P. Skalka. il Reader's Digest
    134:M1-M12 Mr '89
                Psychological aspects
Facing transformation: the great American house move. W.
    E. Halal. The Futurist 23:60 S/O '89
Moving without misery. L. G. Katz. il Parents 64:210 Je
    '89
MOVING OF STRUCTURES, ETC.
The 200-year-old house that moved [Fall River, Mass. house
    transported to New York] il Good Housekeeping 208:140-3
    Je '89
The barn collectors [S. Spillane's and R. Leech's Connecticut
    house contructed of reassembled barns] M. Cantwell. il
    pors House & Garden 161:126-35 F '89
A minka revival: Japanese farmhouse traditions reinterpreted
    in Hawaii. M. Webb. il Architectural Digest 46:198-204
    Ag '89
Moving a piece of history [pre-Civil War Greenville, Miss.
    house] J. O'Hagan. il Southern Living 24:150-2 S '89
A new kind of moving day [houses relocated for the poor
    by MadCAAP in Canton, Miss.] D. S. Levy. il Time
    134:25-7 O 30 '89

MOVING OF STRUCTURES, ETC.—*cont.*
Old house moving. B. Vila. il *Popular Mechanics* 166:46+ N '89
MOVING PICTURES *See* Motion pictures
MOWATT, PAUL
about
The Queen's cousin, pregnant and unwed, cozies up to the press but gets the big chill from the palace. C. Sanz and L. S. Healy. il pors *People Weekly* 32:47-8 O 30 '89
MOWBRAY, MALCOLM
about
Out cold [film] Reviews
The New Yorker 65:95 Mr 6 '89. P. Kael
People Weekly il 31:19 Mr 20 '89. R. Novak
MOWERY, DAVID C.
(jt. auth) *See* Cyert, Richard Michael, 1921-, and Mowery, David C.
MOWING MACHINES
See also
Lawn mowers
MOWING OF LAWNS *See* Lawns
MOYER, JENNIFER
Calendars for kids. il *Parents* 64:254+ D '89
MOYER, KIM R.
National award honors students who make a difference. il *Change* 21:12-13 S/O '89
MOYERS, BILL
Isaac Asimov speaks [interview; cover story] il pors *The Humanist* 49:5-13+ Ja/F '89
about
Bill Moyers. D. Zurawik. por *Esquire* 112:138-40+ O '89
Bill Moyers angrily defends Joseph Campbell against charges that his wisdom was only a myth. A. Chambers. il pors *People Weekly* 32:64+ N 27 '89
The world according to Moyers [cover story] T. Lindberg. il *National Review* 41:22-5 Mr 10 '89
MOYNIHAN, DANIEL P. (DANIEL PATRICK), 1927-
The coming of age of American social policy. il *USA Today (Periodical)* 118:76-8 N '89
End of the Marxist epoch. il *The New Leader* 72:9-11 Ja 23 '89
How to lose: the story of maglev. *Scientific American* 261:130 N '89
about
Beat the devil. A. Cockburn. il *The Nation* 249:113-14 Jl 24-31 '89
Help for the poorest Americans [interview] il por *Scholastic Update (Teachers' edition)* 121:16 F 24 '89
It's déjà vu all over again. *U.S. News & World Report* 106:15 Ap 3 '89
The Moynihan rip-off. M. Schifrin. il *Forbes* 144:38-9 D 11 '89
MOYNIHAN, MAURA
Tibet's agony. *The New Republic* 201:10-11 N 20 '89
MOZAMBICAN REFUGEES *See* Refugees, Mozambican
MOZAMBIQUE
See also
Americans—Mozambique
Children—Mozambique
Foreign relations
United States
See United States—Foreign relations—Mozambique
Zimbabwe
'Serious disruptions' in Zimbabwe [Renamo activities] J. L. Phillips. *The Christian Century* 106:1038-9 N 15 '89
Politics and government
The emergency (I). W. Finnegan. map *The New Yorker* 65:43-4+ My 22 '89
The emergency (II). W. Finnegan. map *The New Yorker* 65:69-96 My 29 '89
The hidden war in Mozambique. Kalamu ya Salaam. il *Utne Reader* p27 N/D '89
Supporting the enemy in Mozambique [cover story] J. Wheeler. il *Conservative Digest* 15:34-5+ Mr/Ap '89
MOZAMBIQUE NATIONAL RESISTANCE MOVEMENT
The emergency (I). W. Finnegan. map *The New Yorker* 65:43-4+ My 22 '89
The emergency (II). W. Finnegan. map *The New Yorker* 65:69-96 My 29 '89
The hidden war in Mozambique. Kalamu ya Salaam. il *Utne Reader* p27 N/D '89
Rescue in Mozambique [English journalist N. della Casa freed from Renamo through efforts of Freedom Inc.; with editorial comment by James R. Whelan] R. MacKenzie. il pors map *Conservative Digest* 15:39+, 70 Mr/Ap '89
'Serious disruptions' in Zimbabwe. J. L. Phillips. *The Christian Century* 106:1038-9 N 15 '89
A small war's moving targets. E. Ransdell. il *U.S. News & World Report* 107:41 O 23 '89
Supporting the enemy in Mozambique [cover story] J. Wheeler. il *Conservative Digest* 15:34-5+ Mr/Ap '89
MOZART, JOHANN CHRYSOSTOM WOLFGANG AMADEUS *See* Mozart, Wolfgang Amadeus, 1756-1791
MOZART, WOLFGANG AMADEUS, 1756-1791
about
Così fan tutte [opera] Reviews
New York il 22:48-9 Ag 7 '89. P. G. Davis

Don Giovanni [opera] Reviews
The Nation 249:254-5 S 4-11 '89. T. M. Disch
New York il 22:58-9 Jl 24 '89. P. G. Davis
Opera News il 54:62 O '89
Time il 134:63 Ag 7 '89. O. Friedrich
Grand finale [P. Sellars' cycle of Mozart operas at PepsiCo Summerfare] R. Marx. il *Opera News* 54:14-16+ Jl '89
Idomeneo [opera] Reviews
New York il 22:144 F 27 '89. P. G. Davis
The New Yorker 65:72-4 Jl 3 '89. A. Porter
Opera News il 53:28-31 F 18 '89
Mozart à la mode. J. Kerman. bibl f il *The New York Review of Books* 36:50-2 My 18 '89
Musical events:
Mozart operas performed at PepsiCo Summerfare and elsewhere. A. Porter. *The New Yorker* 65:70+ Ag 21 '89
Performance of revised Mozart Requiem. A. Porter. *The New Yorker* 65:115-16+ Ap 10 '89
Le nozze di Figaro [opera] Reviews
New York il 22:48-9 Ag 7 '89. P. G. Davis
Opera News il 54:53 O '89. N. Goodwin
Peter Sellars's Mozart. E. W. Said. *The Nation* 249:289-91 S 18 '89
A time for Mozart. J. Ardoin. il *National Review* 41:49-50 Ap 21 '89
Viewpoint. J. W. Freeman. *Opera News* 53:4 F 4 '89
MOZZARELLA CHEESE *See* Cheese
MPAA *See* Motion Picture Association of America
MPBA *See* Mountains and Plains Booksellers Association
MPC AIRCRAFT GMBH
Managers chosen for German/Chinese MPC-75 transport aircraft program. *Aviation Week & Space Technology* 130:101 My 8 '89
MPD (MYOFACIAL PAIN DYSFUNCTION) SYNDROME *See* TMJ syndrome
MPI HOMEVIDEO (FIRM)
'War' remembered on MPI video [Herman Wouk's War and remembrance] P. Sweeting. *Publishers Weekly* 235:62 Ja 6 '89
MPRI SPECTROSCOPY *See* Multiphoton resonance ionization spectroscopy
MPTP (DRUG)
Role for excitatory amino acids in methamphetamine-induced nigrostriatal dopaminergic toxicity. P. K. Sonsalla and others. bibl f il *Science* 243:398-40 Ja 20 '89
MR. BLACKWELL *See* Blackwell, Richard
MR. MAX CORPORATION
A careful clone of K Mart captivates Japan. T. Holden. il por *Business Week* p115 My 22 '89
MR. T
about
Drink to me only with thy $23,000 goblet. L. Eisenberg. il por *TV Guide* 37:24-5 Ap 22-28 '89
MRAZEK, FRANK
about
The courage of the bike rider. B. Amiel. il *Maclean's* 102:9 Jl 31 '89
MRI *See* Magnetic resonance imaging
MRKVICKA, EDWARD F.
about
A banker tells the secrets of the vault [interview] E. M. MacDonald. il pors *Money* 18:95-6+ Je '89
MRNA *See* Messenger RNA
MRS. FIELDS COOKIES
Tough cookies? S. J. Madden. il *Fortune* 119:112 F 13 '89
MRS. WILKES' BOARDING HOUSE RESTAURANT (SAVANNAH, GA.) *See* Savannah (Ga.)—Restaurants, nightclubs, bars, etc.
MS. (PERIODICAL)
Editor's essay. A. Summers. *See* issues of Ms. beginning February 1988 though November 1989
Women of the Year [cover story; special section] il *Ms.* 17:67-91+ Ja/F '89
MS-DOS OPERATING SYSTEM
Anatomy of a LAN operating system. M. L. Van Name and B. Catchings. il *Byte* 14:157-8+ Je '89
Building an OmniView application. M. Toutonghi. il *Radio-Electronics* 60 ComputerDigest:80-4 Ag '89
DOSTALK [natural language interface] S. Anzovin. *Compute!* 11:132+ D '89
Macintosh vs. MS-DOS: which system is better for page layout? S. Morgenstern. il *Home Office Computing* 7:32+ F '89
An MS-DOS user eyes the Mac. N. Sullivan. il *Home Office Computing* 7:80 Jl '89
MS-DOS word processors for desktop publishing [Microsoft Word, WordPerfect, and WordStar Plus 2000] J. Latimer. il *Home Office Computing* 7:24+ Mr '89
A new face on DOS. D. Gookin. il *Compute!* 11:76-8+ O '89
OmniView and a 386 [DOS multitasking operating environment] M. Toutonghi. il *Radio-Electronics* 60 ComputerDigest:73 Jl '89
One man's experience [switching to Unix] J. Unger. il *Byte* 14:237-8+ My '89

MS-DOS OPERATING SYSTEM—*cont.*

Run MS-DOS on the PT-68K. M. Henry. il *Radio-Electronics* 60 ComputerDigest:96-102 Ja '89

Talk to me, DOS, talk to me [DOSTALK natural language interface] K. Sheldon. *Byte* 14:104 Ap '89

Three assemblers for MS-DOS [Microsoft Macro Assembler; Borland Turbo Assembler; SLR Systems OPTASM] M. Blaszczak. il *Byte* 14:205-9 F '89

Unix tools for DOS [MKS Make and MKS Lex and Yacc] B. Smith. *Byte* 14:97-8 F '89

MSG NETWORK *See* Madison Square Garden Network

MTA *See* Metropolitan Transportation Authority

MTEL (FIRM) *See* Mobile Telecommunications Technologies (Firm)

MTM ENTERTAINMENT INC.

Why MTM isn't the cat's meow [aftermath of TVS takeover] R. A. Melcher and R. Grover. il por *Business Week* p49 S 25 '89

MTV NETWORKS INC.

1989: MTV. B. Barol. il *Newsweek* 114:50-1 Jl 3 '89

Bob Pittman: on creating all-music MTV and all-mouth Morton Downey Jr. B. Pittman. por *People Weekly* 31 Special Issue:152-3 Summ '89

Born to run at the mouth. And dance. And flash her $200 purple lingerie [J. Brown] H. Polskin. il por *TV Guide* 37:20-1 Jl 15-21 '89

Into the groove [cover story] J. M. Robins. il pors *Channels (New York, N.Y.: 1986)* 9:22-3+ My '89

Jon Bon Jovi gives his home to non-Jovi Judy Frappier [winner of Sayreville, N.J. boyhood home in MTV contest] il pors *People Weekly* 31:135 Ap 17 '89

MTV rocks (and rolls) American youth. J. L. Hall. il *USA Today (Periodical)* 118:87-8 N '89

Slouching toward networkhood. S. Fried. il *Gentlemen's Quarterly* 59:96+ F '89

Top hip-hop [Yo! MTV raps] J. Malanowski. il por *Rolling Stone* p77-8 Jl 13-27 '89

MTV VIDEO MUSIC AWARDS

Random notes. il *Rolling Stone* p8 O 19 '89

MUBARAK, HOSNI

Visit of Egyptian president [remarks, April 3, 1989] il por *Department of State Bulletin* 89:40-1 Je '89

about

Contemplating the next step. S. MacLeod. il pors *Time* 133:32-3 Ja 23 '89

A defeated compromise. J. Bierman. il por *Maclean's* 102:31 O 16 '89

The folly of absent-minded imperialism. F. Ajami. il *U.S. News & World Report* 106:44 Ap 10 '89

Islam and democracy in Egypt. R. Bianchi. bibl f *Current History* 88:93-5+ F '89

Mubarak moves to the front lines of the Mideast crisis. B. Slavin and others. il *Business Week* p59 Ja 9 '89

Mubarak's peace plan. il *World Press Review* 36:8 N '89

Waiting for Godot. B. W. Nelan. il por *Time* 134:45 O 16 '89

Visits to the United States, 1989

Visit of Egyptian president [remarks, April 3, 1989] G. Bush; H. Mubarak. il por *Department of State Bulletin* 89:40-1 Je '89

MUCHA, ALPHONSE, 1860-1939

about

Fathers and sons. S. Staggs. il *Art News* 88:83-4+ My '89

MUCHA, JIŘÍ

about

Fathers and sons. S. Staggs. il *Art News* 88:83-4+ My '89

MUCHMUSIC NETWORK

The show moves on [move from pay TV to basic cable] D. Turbide. il *Maclean's* 102:65-6 S 4 '89

MUCHNICK, IRVIN

Joe Montana: state of the art [cover story] il pors *The New York Times Magazine* p26-9+ D 17 '89

Rich makes his pitch. il por *The New York Times Magazine* p18-19+ Jl 30 '89

MUCOSA *See* Mucous membranes

MUCOUS MEMBRANES

Activation of apical chloride channels in the gastric oxyntic cell. J. R. Demarest and others. bibl f il *Science* 245:402-4 Jl 28 '89

MUD

See also

Truck driving—Mud hazards

Mud-line walleyes. D. Nelson. il *Outdoor Life* 183:53-5+ F '89

Therapeutic use

See also

Mud baths

MUD BATHS

My game is mud [Calistoga] P. Mehlman. il *Gentlemen's Quarterly* 59:302-7 O '89

MUDA HASSANAL BOLKIAH *See* Hassanal Bolkiah, Sultan of Brunei, 1946-

MUDGARDS (BICYCLES) *See* Bicycles—Fenders

MUEGGE, KATHRIN, AND OTHERS

Interleukin-1 costimulatory activity on the interleukin-2 promoter via AP-1. bibl f il *Science* 246:249-51 O 13 '89

MUEHLENBACHS, KARLIS

(jt. auth) See Nesbitt, Bruce Edward, and Muehlenbachs, Karlis

MUELLER, C. J.

about

His life is going downhill fast, and C.J. Mueller likes it that way. J. Friedman. il por *People Weekly* 31:81-2 Mr 20 '89

MUELLER, HEINZ

about

Toys are ageless. S. B. Green. il *Antiques & Collecting Hobbies* 94:62-3 My '89

MUELLER, JOHN E.

Enough rope. *The New Republic* 201:14-16 Jl 3 '89

A new Concert of Europe. *Foreign Policy* 77:3-16 Wint '89/'90

about

From atom bombs to Fred Astaire. A. P. Sanoff. il por *U.S. News & World Report* 106:63 My 22 '89

MUELLER, LARRY

Hunting dogs. See issues of Outdoor Life

MUELLER, MICHAEL

Tucker: a man and his car. il pors *American History Illustrated* 23:36-41 Ja '89

MUELLER, PAUL R., AND WOLD, BARBARA

In vivo footprinting of a muscle specific enhancer by ligation mediated PCR. bibl f il *Science* 246:780-6 N 10 '89

MUELLER, RICHARD

about

Selling security for deutschemarks. R. N. Perle. il *U.S. News & World Report* 107:36 Jl 31 '89

MUELLER, ROBERT W.

about

Before you take the plunge . . . [interview] J. H. Ingersoll. il por *Home Mechanix* 85:18+ My '89

MUELLER, STEPHEN

Quadrilateral drift. B. Adams. il *Art in America* 77:188-91 My '89

MUELLER, WILLIAM

K.C.'s Christmas is in the cards. il *The Saturday Evening Post* 261:82-5 N/D '89

Life by the Mississippi. il *The Saturday Evening Post* 261:86-8+ Ap '89

MUENCH, DAVID

about

David Muench: a portfolio. S. Greengard. il por *Sierra* 74:68-76 My/Je '89

MUETZEL, JANICE

about

Winners. L. Rudeen. il por *Motor Boating & Sailing* 163:24 Ap '89

MUFFINS

The big muffin tasting. il *Sunset (Central West edition)* 183:152+ O '89

Down-home muffins & biscuits. il *Good Housekeeping* 208:158-9 Ap '89

How to get kids to love breakfast. il *McCall's* 117:88 N '89

Mad about muffins [microwaving] *Good Housekeeping* 209:212+ N '89

MUFFLERS, AUTOMOBILE *See* Automobile engines—Mufflers

MUFSON, STEVEN

Winnie the shrew. *The New Republic* 200:14-16 Mr 13 '89

MUGGA, RICHARD G.

Safer water for Uganda. il *World Health* p6-7 D '88

MUGGING (CRIME) *See* Assault and battery

MUGHNIYAH, IMAD

about

The man who holds the hostages. il *Time* 133:42 Mr 20 '89

MUGS

See also

Shaving mugs

MUHAMMAD IBN IYĀS *See* Ibn Iyās, 1448-ca. 1524

MUHAMMED, ALIM

about

Muslim dopebusters: the brightest point of light [interview] il *New Perspectives Quarterly* 6:32-6 Summ '89

MUHICH, LISA

about

Woman to watch: cyclocross champion Lisa Muhich. B. Cooper. il por *Women's Sports & Fitness* 11:61 My '89

MUHRCKE, GARY

about

Burning bright. P. Gambaccini. il por *Runner's World* 24:56-7 N '89

MUIR, JOHN, 1838-1914

about

Along the high, wild Sierra. G. A. Rowell. il map *National Geographic* 175:466-93 Ap '89

John Muir. il *Sierra* 74:22-3 Mr/Ap '89

MUIR (JOHN) TRAIL (CALIF.) *See* John Muir Trail (Calif.)

MUIR (JOHN) TRUST *See* John Muir Trust

MUJAHEDIN (AFGHANISTAN) *See* Muslims—Afghanistan

MUJERISTA THEOLOGY

Mujeristas: a name of our own. A. M. Isasi-Díaz. *The Christian Century* 106:560-2 My 24-31 '89

MUKHERJEE, BHARATI
In transit [fiction] *Harper's* 279:40-1 S '89
about
Foreign correspondent. C. McGee. il por *New York* 22:22
Ja 30 '89
PW interviews. S. S. Steinberg. por *Publishers Weekly* 236:46-7
Ag 25 '89
MUKHOPADHYAY, AMITABHA, AND OTHERS
Receptor-mediated drug delivery to macrophages in
chemotherapy of leishmaniasis. bibl f il *Science* 244:705-7
My 12 '89
MULBERRIES
A mulberry success story that's worth sharing [pollarding]
il *Sunset (Central West edition)* 182:126 Ja '89
The mulberry tree. J. Frois. il *Southern Living* 24:108 Je
'89
MULCHING
A guide to mulches. N. Bubel. il *Country Journal* 16:74-8
Mr/Ap '89
Mulch made easy. V. Mattern. il *Organic Gardening* 36:38-42
S '89
MULE DEER HUNTING *See* Deer hunting
MULES
The useful mule. H. Stevens. il *Country Journal* 16:56-60
My/Je '89
MULHOLLAND, WILLIAM D.
about
Stepping aside. P. Chisholm. il pors *Maclean's* 102:40 Ja
30 '89
MULL, KAYLA
about
Hog wild. A. Adato. il pors *Life* 12:86-7 S '89
MULLALY, MARJORIE
Turning a 'dark day' into triumph [ed. by Alexis Lieberman]
il pors *Prevention (Emmaus, Pa.)* 41:100+ D '89
MULLANEY, JOHN J.
Central America and the education president. *America*
160:524-5 Je 3 '89
MULLANY (DESTROYER)
The ship that outsailed time. N. M. Adams. il *Reader's
Digest* 135:117-24+ S '89
MULLEN, BRIAN
about
Hell's angels. S. Kiesling. il pors *Sports Illustrated* 70:82-7+
Mr 27 '89
MULLEN, JOEY
about
Hell's angels. S. Kiesling. il pors *Sports Illustrated* 70:82-7+
Mr 27 '89
MULLEN, ALBRECHT A. C. VON
More to do. *The Bulletin of the Atomic Scientists* 45:43-4
My '89
MULLER, H. J. (HERMANN JOSEPH), 1890-1967
Science fiction as an escape [reprint from November/
December 1957 issue] por *The Humanist* 49:17+ Mr/Ap
'89
MULLER, HERMANN JOSEPH *See* Muller, H. J. (Hermann
Joseph), 1890-1967
MULLER, JERRY Z., 1954-
Anti-Semitism [discussion of August 1988 article, Com-
munism, anti-Semitism & the Jews] *Commentary* 87:11-12+
Ja '89
German historians at war. bibl f *Commentary* 87:33-41 My
'89
MÜLLER, KARL-HEINZ
about
Treasure island. J. Dornberg. il por *Art News* 88:93-4 My
'89
MULLER, MARCIA
Free-form plotting the mystery novel. *The Writer* 102:12-15
S '89
MULLER (JENNIFER)/THE WORKS *See* Jennifer Muller/The
Works
MÜLLER-ULLRICH, BURKHARD
The smallest giant. il por *World Press Review* 36:67 N '89
MULLICAN, MATT, 1951-
about
Sign language. P. Clothier. il por *Art News* 88:142-7 Summ
'89
MULLICH, JOE
Simple holiday stress relievers. il *Reader's Digest* 135:49-50+
D '89
MULLIGAN, BILL, 1942-
"Everything old is new again". il *Flower and Garden* 33:40-4+
Jl/Ag '89
MULLIGAN, GERRY
about
Gerry Mulligan: singing a song of Mulligan. M. Bourne.
il pors *Down Beat* 56:23-5 Ja '89
MULLIGAN, JOSEPH F. (JOSEPH FRANCIS), 1920-
Heinrich Hertz and the development of physics. bibl f il
por *Physics Today* 42:50-7 Mr '89
MULLIGAN, RICHARD
about
Choosing career over marriage, workaholic Richard Mulligan
tries to feather his Empty nest. J. Kaufman. il pors *People
Weekly* 31:55-6 My 29 '89

MULLINS, DAVID W.
about
The Fed gets one of Brady's boys. M. McNamee. por *Business
Week* p102 D 11 '89
MULLOVA, VIKTORIA
about
Mullova and Previn and Shostakovich. R. Freed. il por
Stereo Review 54:123-4 N '89
MULRONEY, BRIAN
President meets with Prime Minister Mulroney [question-and-
answer session, May 4, 1989] *Department of State Bulletin*
89:45-7 Jl '89
President's visit to Canada [news conference, February 10,
1989] il por *Department of State Bulletin* 89:26-8 Ap '89
about
The Canadian election. *World Press Review* 36:12 Ja '89
A Tory game plan. B. Wallace. il por *Maclean's* 102:10-11
S 25 '89
Press relations
Wilful ignorance and lust for page 1 [media distortion of
views on sales tax] G. Bain. il *Maclean's* 102:52 S 25
'89
Staff
Damage control [budget leak controversy] T. Tedesco. il
pors *Maclean's* 102:14-16 Je 12 '89
Anecdotes, facetiae, satire, etc.
Cromwell rules in the nation's capital. A. Fotheringham.
il *Maclean's* 102:68 Ap 3 '89
Travel
Anecdotes, facetiae, satire, etc.
The PM's black, travelling cloud. S. MacLeod. por *Maclean's*
102:68 S 4 '89
Visit to Costa Rica, 1989
A crash course for Mulroney [Nicaragua's decision to cancel
ceasefire overshadows announcement of Canada's intention
to join OAS] H. Mackenzie. il pors *Maclean's* 102:32-3+
N 6 '89
Visit to the Soviet Union, 1989
Catching up. A. Wilson-Smith. il pors *Maclean's* 102:36-8
D 4 '89
Cozying up to the Kremlin [special section] il por map
Maclean's 102:18-22+ N 27 '89
Moscow bound. L. Van Dusen. il por *Maclean's* 102:18-19
N 20 '89
Visits to the United States, 1989
A diplomatic exchange. H. Mackenzie. il por *Maclean's* 102:20
My 15 '89
President meets with Prime Minister Mulroney [question-and-
answer session, May 4, 1989] G. Bush; B. Mulroney.
Department of State Bulletin 89:45-7 Jl '89
A working holiday. H. Mackenzie. il pors *Maclean's* 102:10-11
S 11 '89
MULTI DISC PLAYERS *See* Combination disc players
**MULTICHANNEL MULTIPOINT DISTRIBUTION SER-
VICE**
License to thrive. A. Servetas. il *Channels (New York, N.Y.:
1986)* 9:93 D '89
MULTICULTURAL EDUCATION *See* Intercultural education
MULTICULTURALISM MINISTRY (CANADA) *See* Canada.
Office of the Minister of State for Multiculturalism
MULTIFINDER OPERATING SYSTEM
Software juggler for Macs. J. L. Schefter. *Popular Science*
234:78-9 Ja '89
MULTILINGUALISM
The confusion of tongues [cover story] S. Barańczak. il *The
New Leader* 72:16-18 F 6 '89
MULTIMEDIA
Couch potatoes! Now it's smart TV. B. R. Schlender. il
Fortune 120:111-12+ N 20 '89
It's a PC, it's a TV—it's multimedia. M. Shao and R.
Brandt. il *Business Week* p152-5+ O 9 '89
Multimedia: seeing is deceiving. P. Saffo. il *Personal
Computing* 13:181-2 Ag '89
Why multimedia is multiconfusing. W. M. Hawkins. por
Personal Computing 13:220 O '89
Educational use
NECC's multimedia demos [National Educational Computing
Conference] D. Stanton. il *Compute!* 11:88 O '89
MULTIMEDIA, INC.
The art and advantage of conversation [interview with P.
Lund] il pors *Channels (New York, N.Y.: 1986)* 9:54-5
My '89
MULTIMETERS
B + K Precision Model 388-HD Test Bench. il
Radio-Electronics 60:16-17 Mr '89
Beckman Industrial Model 223 professional digital multimeter.
il *Radio-Electronics* 60:16 Ag '89
Circuitmate DM27 digital multimeter. il *Radio-Electronics*
60:17 O '89
Menu-driven multimeter [Simpson's Model 560] il
Radio-Electronics 60:27-8 F '89
MULTINATIONAL CORPORATIONS *See* Corporations, In-
ternational
**MULTIPHOTON RESONANCE IONIZATION SPEC-
TROSCOPY**
Atom counting at surfaces. D. L. Pappas and others. bibl
f il *Science* 243:64-6 Ja 6 '89

MULTIPHOTON RESONANCE IONIZATION SPECTROSCOPY—*cont.*

Covariance mapping: a correlation method applied to multiphoton multiple ionization. L. J. Frasinski and others. bibl f il *Science* 246:1029-31 N 24 '89

Spatially resolved organic analysis of the Allende meteorite. R. Zenobi and others. bibl f il *Science* 246:1026-9 N 24 '89

MULTIPLE BIRTH *See* Birth, Multiple

MULTIPLE CHEMICAL SENSITIVITY *See* Environmental illness

MULTIPLE EXPOSURE PHOTOGRAPHY *See* Photography, Trick

MULTIPLE JOBHOLDING *See* Supplementary employment

MULTIPLE PERSONALITY

Multiple personalities [result of childhood abuse] B. Wickens. il *Maclean's* 102:60-1 N 27 '89

Three faces of Eve told her story, now Chris Sizemore is battling a major studio over movie rights and wrongs [victim sues Twentieth Century Fox over intellectual property rights] D. Van Biema. il pors *People Weekly* 31:79-80+ Mr 27 '89

MULTIPLE SCLEROSIS

Amplification and molecular cloning of HTLV-I sequences from DNA of multiple sclerosis patients. E. P. Reddy and others. bibl f il *Science* 243:529-33 Ja 27 '89; Correction. 246:10-11 O 6 '89

First since illness: Lola performs onstage with Wayne Newton. il pors *Jet* 76:55-6 Je 26 '89

A game winner [softball player K. Stilwell] L. Rothlein. il por *Women's Sports & Fitness* 11:50 Ja/F '89

Lola Falana: 'I'm back! I'm not cured. But I'm healed!' [cover story] R. E. Johnson. il pors *Jet* 76:54-7 Ag 14 '89

Multiple choice [viral fingerprints in blood of MS patients] T. Beardsley. *Scientific American* 260:34-5 Ap '89

PCR analysis of DNA from multiple sclerosis patients for the presence of HTLV-I [discussion of January 27, 1989 article, Amplification and molecular cloning of HTLV-I sequences from DNA of multiple sclerosis patients] E. P. Reddy and others. il *Science* 246:821-4 N 10 '89

The puzzling picture of multiple sclerosis. M. Patlak. il *FDA Consumer* 23:17-21 Jl/Ag '89

The ups and downs of multiple sclerosis [research by Donald E. Goodkin] K. Fackelmann. *Science News* 135:245 Ap 22 '89

Genetic aspects

MS gene discovery: a piece of the puzzle [T cell receptor gene; research by Stephen L. Hauser] I. Wickelgren. *Science News* 136:21 Jl 8 '89

MULTIPLEXING

I can get it for you wholesale [T1 networks] F. Meeks. il *Forbes* 143:120-1 F 6 '89

MULTIPROCESSORS

See also

Massively parallel supercomputers

Parallel processing (Computers)

The 80486: a hardware perspective. R. Sartore. il *Byte* 14 Special Issue:67-70+ Fall '89

The brains behind the graphics [graphics coprocessor boards] S. Apiki and others. il *Byte* 14:178-82+ N '89

Fax and a whole lot more [Connection coprocessor] C. O'Malley. il *Personal Computing* 13:194-5 Jl '89

A great communicator [Connection CoProcessor PC facsimile board] N. Baran. il *Byte* 14:195-6+ Ja '89

In search of a faster 80287 [IIT-2C87 coprocessor] R. Grehan. *Byte* 14:206 S '89

microExplorer in action! A. Lane. il *Byte* 14:247-8+ N '89

The opposite tack. M. L. Smith and G. White. il *Byte* 14:216-17 Jl '89

Optimizing numeric coprocessing. S. S. Fried. il *Byte* 14 Special Issue:221-4 Fall '89

A PC run circles around a Cray? [coprocessors and transputers] T. J. Byers. il *Radio-Electronics* 60 ComputerDigest:77+ Ap '89

Pixels on the march [8514/A and Artist 10 MC graphics coprocessor boards] B. D. Kliewer. il *Byte* 14:201-2+ Ja '89

Ultra graphics [Ultra Clipper UM1280, bus-mastering coprocessor] B. D. Kliewer. il *Byte* 14:167-9 Ag '89

Update: standout graphics board [Rendition II] S. Apiki. il *Byte* 14:234 D '89

Weitek pushing its own math chip for Intel's 80486. *Byte* 14:26 Jl '89

MULTISKILLING

What flexible workers can do. N. Alster. il *Fortune* 119:62-4+ F 13 '89

MULTITASKING (COMPUTERS)

See also

DESQview (Computer program)

A brave new world? F. Pascal. bibl f il *Byte* 14:247-50+ S '89

Building an OmniView application. M. Toutonghi. il *Radio-Electronics* 60 ComputerDigest:80-4 Ag '89

Getting your priorities straight [use of time slicing with OS/2] M. Minasi. il *Byte* 14:159-60+ N '89

Lisp dialect taps Mac riches [MacScheme + Toolsmith] J. Udell. il *Byte* 14:204 S '89

OmniView and a 386 [DOS multitasking operating environment] M. Toutonghi. il *Radio-Electronics* 60 ComputerDigest:73 Jl '89

OS/2 multitasking revisited. M. Minasi. il *Byte* 14:133-4+ D '89

Software juggler for Macs. J. L. Schefter. *Popular Science* 234:78-9 Ja '89

MULTIUSER SYSTEMS (COMPUTERS) *See* Computers—Multiuser systems

MULTIVIBRATORS

My favorite circuit [Schmitt trigger] D. Lancaster. il *Radio-Electronics* 60:67-71 Jl '89

MUMMICHOGS *See* Killifish

MUMMIES

Entombed beauty provides syphilis clues [mummy of Maria d'Aragona, a Naples Renaissance noblewoman] *Science News* 136:223 S 30 '89

Mummy under glass [preservation with nitrogen] il *Discover* 10:18 Ag '89

MUMPS

Mumps and measles make a comeback. J. Willis. il *Consumers' Research Magazine* 72:23-6 S '89

Mumps makes a comeback. J. Willis. il *FDA Consumer* 23:12-14+ Jl/Ag '89

The office visitor nobody wants. L. C. Cook. il *Health (New York, N.Y.)* 21:78-81 My '89

MUNCH, CHARLES, 1891-1968

about

Encores. R. Freed. pors *Stereo Review* 54:162 D '89

MUNCHAUSEN SYNDROME

Munchausen is more than a movie, it's also the name of a bizarre medical disorder [interview with L. Pankratz] S. Hauser. il pors *People Weekly* 31:95+ My 8 '89

MUNCHKINS (FICTIONAL CHARACTERS)

Now a half century down the yellow brick road, six Munchkins remember Oz. M. Neill. il *People Weekly* 31:38-40 Je 26 '89

MUNCIE (IND.)

Social history

Magic Middletown [excerpt] D. W. Hoover. il *Society* 26:73-7 Mr/Ap '89

MUNDUS, FRANK

about

In the jaws of the law. il por *Sports Illustrated* 71:10 Ag 7 '89

MUNDY, LIZA

The pro bono hustle. *The Washington Monthly* 21:10-14+ S '89

The success story of the war on poverty. *The Washington Monthly* 21:26-31 D '89

(jt. auth) *See* DeParle, Jason, and Mundy, Liza

MUNGAI, EVELYN KARUNGARI

about

A Kenyan tycoon. W. Machua. il por *World Press Review* 36:52 Jl '89

MUNGO, ANTONIO

about

Old Glory. E. H. Gustafson. il *Antiques* 136:728+ O '89

MUNGO, GIUSEPPE

about

Old Glory. E. H. Gustafson. il *Antiques* 136:728+ O '89

MUNGO, RAYMOND, 1946-

Voices from the fringe. il *Utne Reader* p106-7+ S/O '89

MUNICH (GERMANY)

Art

Munich's design for living [Art nouveau in Munich: masters of the Jugendstil] M. Makela. bibl f il *Art in America* 77:144-51 F '89

Description

New Year's in Munich. L. Langseth-Christensen. il *Gourmet* 49:42-3+ Ja '89

Festivals

Photographs and photography

Camera at Oktoberfest. K. Hatfield. il *Petersen's Photographic Magazine* 18:48-51 O '89

Theater

See also

Prinzregenten Theater (Munich, Germany)

MUNICH FOUR-POWER AGREEMENT (1938)

The last lion: alone [excerpt] W. Manchester. il pors *Conservative Digest* 15:63+ Jl/Ag '89

Postscript to Munich [interview with A. Douglas-Home] J. Ranelagh. *National Review* 41:30-1 Je 2 '89

MUNICH PHILHARMONIC

Extreme occasions [S. Celibidache conducts at Carnegie Hall] E. W. Said. *The Nation* 248:898-900 Je 26 '89

MUNICIPAL BOND FUNDS *See* Investment trusts

MUNICIPAL BONDS

After the market shock, munis are standing tall. D. Zigas. il *Business Week* p204 N 6 '89

The beauty of municipal bonds [tax exempt status threatened] J. Mysak. il *The American Spectator* 22:18-20 Je '89

Buy munis while the oversupply lasts. T. Paré. il *Fortune* 120:36 O 23 '89

Buying a boatload of munis for less than the price of one [unit trusts and bond mutual funds] il *Money* 18:201-3 N '89

MUNICIPAL BONDS—cont.

A buying opportunity. B. Weberman. il *Forbes* 144:297 N 27 '89

Medicare tax [municipal bond strategy as way to avoid surtax] B. Weberman. il *Forbes* 143:213 Mr 20 '89

Taking the teeth out of a new tax bite [Medicare surcharge] L. J. Nathans. *Business Week* p156 Mr 13 '89

Tax-free zeros. B. Weberman. il *Forbes* 143:337 My 29 '89

Taxes may take their toll, but not from the superior returns of munis. A. Rock. il *Money* 18:121-2+ Jl '89

Trolling for prizes in 'the backwater of the fixed-income market' [views of S. G. Peabody] L. Light. il por *Business Week* p133 D 25 '89-Ja 1 '90

A warning on muni bonds. M. C. Paulson. il *Changing Times* 43:124 O '89

Whoops: investors may let bygones be bygones [new bond issue] D. Zigas. il *Business Week* p92 S 4 '89

A word to the muni-mad. J. B. Quinn. il *Newsweek* 114:39 S 25 '89

Yield curve strategies. B. Weberman. il *Forbes* 144:337 Jl 24 '89

Default

Caution: downgrade. B. Weberman. il *Forbes* 144:251 O 30 '89

The Moynihan rip-off [municipal bond issues by nonprofit corporations] M. Schifrin. il *Forbes* 144:38-9 D 11 '89

Munis are evolving into more dangerous animals. L. Zinn. *Business Week* p106 Je 19 '89

Laws and regulations

Dirty secrets. B. Weberman. il *Forbes* 143:277 Je 26 '89

MUNICIPAL BUDGET *See* Municipal finance

MUNICIPAL BUILDINGS

See also

City halls

MUNICIPAL CHARTERS

See also

New York (N.Y.)—Charters

MUNICIPAL CONTRACTS

See also

Atlanta (Ga.)—Municipal contracts
Boston (Mass.)—Municipal contracts
New York (N.Y.)—Municipal contracts
Richmond (Va.)—Municipal contracts

NAACP's Gibson urges new tactics to keep set asides. por *Jet* 75:29 Mr 13 '89

Ruling delivers hard blow to set-asides [Supreme Court decision] N. McCall. il *Black Enterprise* 19:17-18 Ap '89

MUNICIPAL FINANCE

See also

Municipal bonds
Municipal contracts
New York (N.Y.)—Finance

Drexel is in the doghouse with cities and states. L. J. Nathans. il *Business Week* p81-2 F 13 '89

More mayors and governors are coming up short. G. Koretz. il *Business Week* p20 S 4 '89

States and cities are facing the budget music. J. L. Sheler. *U.S. News & World Report* 106:29 My 29 '89

MUNICIPAL GOVERNMENT

See also

Decentralization in government
Mayors
Municipal home rule
See also subhead Politics and government under names of cities

It's not just Washington [bureaucratic apathy and incompetence] K. Boo. *The Washington Monthly* 20:37+ Ja '89

Notes and comment [global view in local politics] *The New Yorker* 65:37 O 9 '89

What can a mayor do to save a city? D. Baer. il *U.S. News & World Report* 106:22-3 My 15 '89

MUNICIPAL HOME RULE

D.C. statehood agenda targets 1991 deadline. L. Brown and A. Edmond, Jr. *Black Enterprise* 20:33+ D '89

The sewers of Malibu. M. Beauchamp. il *Forbes* 144:120-1 Ag 7 '89

MUNICIPAL IMPROVEMENT

See also

Business districts
City planning
Detroit (Mich.)—Municipal improvement
New York (N.Y.)—Municipal improvement
Public works
Trees in cities
Waterfronts

Argentina

See also

Mendoza (Argentina)—Municipal improvement

Mexico

See also

Mexico City (Mexico)—Municipal improvement

MUNICIPAL LEASES

Sort-of bonds. B. Weberman. il *Forbes* 143:225 Ap 17 '89

MUNICIPAL LIABILITY *See* Government liability

MUNICIPAL OFFICERS

See also

Mayors

MUNICIPAL ORDINANCES

See also

Cambridge (Mass.)—Ordinances
Gary (Ind.)—Ordinances
New York (N.Y.)—Ordinances
Paris (France)—Ordinances
San Francisco (Calif.)—Ordinances

All they are sayin' is give pigs a chance [cities taking up social causes] *U.S. News & World Report* 106:15 Je 19 '89

Lawsuits, ahoy! [public waterways] D. Fanning. il *Forbes* 143:74-5 Mr 6 '89

MUNICIPAL SERVICES

See also

London (England)—Municipal services

MUNICIPAL SWIMMING POOLS

Aftermath [Coalinga Community Swim Complex, Calif.] J. Fillip. il *Architectural Record* 177:116-19 N '89

MUNICIPAL TRANSIT *See* Local transit

MUNICIPAL UTILITIES *See* Public utilities

MUNITIONS

See also

Aerojet Ordnance Co.
Boeing Co.
Firearms industry
Jaycor (Firm)
Military-industrial complex
Nuclear weapons
Projectiles
Weapons
Westmark Systems, Inc.

Industry observer. See issues of Aviation Week & Space Technology

Acquisitions and mergers

'Pulse power' fuels a bid [Jaycor's bid for Maxwell Labs] E. Schine. il *Business Week* p64 Je 26 '89

Export-import trade

See also

Iran-contra affair

At your service [trade between West Germany and developing countries] M. Brzoska. bibl f *The Bulletin of the Atomic Scientists* 45:34 Jl/Ag '89

Behind the German export scandals. M. Brzoska. bibl f il *The Bulletin of the Atomic Scientists* 45:32-5 Jl/Ag '89

Budget, trade deficits could spur restrictive trade legislation [U.S. military exports and aid] il *Aviation Week & Space Technology* 130:73+ Mr 20 '89

A critical weakness [questions raised about Phalanx warship defense system for Canadian frigates] W. Lowther. il *Maclean's* 102:13 F 13 '89

Dealing arms. J. Cobb and J. M. Zindar. il *Common Cause Magazine* 15:23-7 Mr/Ap '89

Gandhi's Watergate? [Bofors arms sale scandal] *Newsweek* 114:42 O 23 '89

Pentagon purchases Soviet hardware on open market for operational testing. J. D. Morrocco. il *Aviation Week & Space Technology* 130:24-5 Ja 23 '89

Shouldering arms [M. Markus' idea to securitize U.S. armament loans] M. Schifrin. il por *Forbes* 143:208-9 Ap 17 '89

Soviet sale of Su-24 deepens concern about Mideast weapons proliferation. M. Mecham. il *Aviation Week & Space Technology* 130:19-20 Ap 10 '89

U.S. suspends military sales in wake of massacre in China. M. Mecham. il *Aviation Week & Space Technology* 130:69-70+ Je 12 '89

World weapons sales top $1 trillion, paced by South Asia market. il *Aviation Week & Space Technology* 131:34-6 Ag 28 '89

Finance

Aerospace/defense financial report [special section] il *Aviation Week & Space Technology* 130:48-50+ My 29 '89

Aerospace and defense. H. Banks. il *Forbes* 143:82-3 Ja 9 '89

Defense's gravy train nears the end of the line. S. Toy. il *Business Week* p75 Ja 9 '89

Incoming! Incoming! Arms contractors head for the bunkers. E. Schine. il *Business Week* p66+ S 11 '89

U.S. defense industry faces difficult times. B. L. Schwartz. por *Aviation Week & Space Technology* 131:71+ D 4 '89

International aspects

Defense companies seek joint ventures to maintain market share. *Aviation Week & Space Technology* 130:35 Je 19 '89

Maturing NATO could benefit by ending cooperative military procurement barriers. E. H. A. Beckett. por *Aviation Week & Space Technology* 130:73-4 Ap 3 '89

Senate bolsters Commerce Dept.'s authority in reviewing cooperative arms agreements. J. D. Morrocco. *Aviation Week & Space Technology* 131:28 Ag 7 '89

Task force urges overhaul of Pentagon policy on industrial cooperation with Pacific Rim. J. D. Morrocco. *Aviation Week & Space Technology* 131:32 N 13 '89

Management

Defense contractors must change to survive competition in 1990s. W. V. Dee. por *Aviation Week & Space Technology* 131:99+ Jl 17 '89

MUNITIONS—*cont.*

Quality control

Making total quality management work: lessons from industry. C. Leader. por *Aviation Week & Space Technology* 131:65+ O 30 '89

Total quality management will require procurement changes, perseverance. B. A. Smith. il *Aviation Week & Space Technology* 131:59-60 D 18-25 '89

TQM expected to boost productivity, ensure survival of U.S. industry [total quality management] W. B. Scott. il *Aviation Week & Space Technology* 131:64-5+ D 4 '89

Securities

Buy 'em when they're not hot. K. L. Fisher. il *Forbes* 143:338 My 29 '89

Continued defense stock downturn reflects long-term business outlook. N. C. Kernstock. il *Aviation Week & Space Technology* 131:81 N 13 '89

Defense stocks plunge under budget pressure. N. C. Kernstock. *Aviation Week & Space Technology* 131:20-1 N 27 '89

For defense stocks, peace is hell. J. Egan. il *U.S. News & World Report* 106:67 Ja 16 '89

It's bombs away for defense stocks. J. M. Laderman. il *Business Week* p102-3 D 4 '89

Market focus. N. C. Kernstock. See issues of Aviation Week & Space Technology beginning October 3, 1988

Wall Street upbeat on airlines, gloomy about defense stocks. il *Aviation Week & Space Technology* 130:48-50 My 29 '89

Canada

On the defensive. J. Daly. il *Maclean's* 102:36 Jl 10 '89

Developing countries

At your service [munitions trade with West Germany] M. Brzoska. bibl f *The Bulletin of the Atomic Scientists* 45:34 Jl/Ag '89

France

See also
Matra SA

Germany (West)

Behind the German export scandals. M. Brzoska. bibl f il *The Bulletin of the Atomic Scientists* 45:32-5 Jl/Ag '89

Japan

Japan's rising defense industry. C. Rapoport. il *Fortune* 119:257-8+ Ap 24 '89

Tokyo wants its arsenal made in Japan. R. Neff. il *Business Week* p64 S 25 '89

Middle East

Soviet sale of Su-24 deepens concern about Mideast weapons proliferation. M. Mecham. il *Aviation Week & Space Technology* 130:19-20 Ap 10 '89

Pacific region

Task force urges overhaul of Pentagon policy on industrial cooperation with Pacific Rim. J. D. Morrocco. *Aviation Week & Space Technology* 131:32 N 13 '89

Sweden

See also
Bofors Nobel AB

Western Europe

European nations attempt to create single, competitive arms market. il *Aviation Week & Space Technology* 130:87 Je 12 '89

MUNITIONS INDUSTRIES See Munitions

MUNITIONS TRADE See Munitions—Export-import trade

MUNIZ, VIK

about

Vik Muniz at Stux and William Stone at Tom Cugliani. N. Princenthal. *Art in America* 77:266 Ap '89

MUNK, WALTER H., 1917-

about

Geophysical Union salutes excellent work in the field. pors *Physics Today* 42:87-91 D '89

MUNN, GEOFFREY C.

Lost jewels. bibl f il *Antiques* 136:826-33 O '89

MUNRO, ALICE

Differently [story] *The New Yorker* 64:23-36 Ja 2 '89

Goodness and mercy [story] *The New Yorker* 65:38-48 Mr 20 '89

Wigtime [story] *The New Yorker* 65:34-46+ S 4 '89

MUNRO, J. RICHARD

Takeovers [address, February 23, 1989] *Vital Speeches of the Day* 55:470-3 My 15 '89

MUNROE, CHARLES C., III

Estimating your estimates. il por *Architectural Record* 177:44 My '89

MUNSKI, MICHAEL S.

about

Unconventional helicopter tail rotor offers forward thrust advantage. W. B. Scott. il *Aviation Week & Space Technology* 130:49+ F 13 '89

MUNSON, CARRIE

about

Obituary

Jet il por 75:17 Ja 23 '89

MUNVES, JAMES, 1922-

. . . detention. *The Nation* 248:509 Ap 17 '89

MÜNZENBERG, GOTTFRIED

(jt. auth) See Armbruster, Peter, and Münzenberg, Gottfried

MUONS See Particles (Nuclear physics)

MUPPETS

Jim Henson [interview] il por *American Film* 15:18-21 N '89

MURA, DAVID

From the pages of Corriere della sera (Oct. 29, 1975): a Lutheran letter [poem] *The New Republic* 200:32 My 8 '89

MURAL PAINTING AND DECORATION

See also
Cave drawings and paintings
Frescoes

Museum accessions [J. D. Poor murals acquired by Maine State Museum] E. H. Gustafson. il *Antiques* 136:402+ S '89

Painting a portable mural [work of S. Ominski for library in West Salem, Or.] G. Olson. il pors *American Artist* 53:70-5 Ap '89

Roscomural [computerized painting system that produces expanded images] M. S. Eddy. il *Theatre Crafts* 23:90-1 Ja '89

Conservation and restoration

Medical recovery [mural series by W. C. Palmer found] J. Herzfeld. il *Art News* 88:14 Ja '89

MURAL PAINTING AND DECORATION, EXTERIOR

Revolution on the walls [Haiti] A. W. Barnett. il *Art in America* 77:67-9+ Jl '89

Trotsky, whose lively street art became an off-the-wall album cover for Bob Dylan [mural on building in Hell's Kitchen] il por *People Weekly* 32:112 O 23 '89

When Robert Lenkiewicz paints the town in Plymouth, England, some people see only red. R. Wolmuth. il pors *People Weekly* 31:108-11 Ja 23 '89

MURANO GLASS See Glassware

MURAVCHIK, JOSHUA

The Democrats [discussion of February 1989 article, Why the Democrats lost again] *Commentary* 87:2-5 Je '89

Glasnostrums. *The New Republic* 200:16-18 Ja 30 '89

Why the Democrats lost again. *Commentary* 87:13-22 F '89

MURCIA, ANDY

about

"I fear I'm losing my husband". A. Jillian. il pors *Redbook* 173:83-4 Jl '89

MURDER

See also
Assassination
Camarena Salazar, Enrique—Murder case
Capital punishment
Euthanasia
Human sacrifice
Levin, Jennifer Dawn, d. 1986—Murder case
Lynching
Parents of murdered children
Poisons and poisoning
Steinberg, Lisa, d. 1987—Child abuse case
Stuart, Charles—Murder case
Trials (Murder)

The '64 civil rights murders: the struggle continues [honoring J. Chaney, M. Schwerner and A. Goodman; cover story] J. Kornbluth. il pors *The New York Times Magazine* p16-19+ Jl 23 '89

Alleged killer of 'Jet beauty' turns himself in after his crime is aired on TV show [R. Urabez charged with murdering M. Shiferaw] pors *Jet* 77:7 O 16 '89

Anatomy of a racial murder [death of Y. Hawkins in Bensonhurst] J. Derevlany. il pors *Seventeen* 48:108-11+ D '89

Assassination in Brazil [land reform murder] J. F. Alevino] B. Tyson. *The Christian Century* 106:384-7 Ap 12 '89

Back on the bus [events commemorating 25th anniversary of the murder of civil rights workers J. E. Chaney, A. Goodman and M. H. Schwerner] P. Dray. il pors *Mother Jones* 14:37-9+ N '89

The bad mother [M. Tinning kills nine infants in Schenectady, N.Y.] J. Egginton. il pors *Good Housekeeping* 208:119+ Ap '89

Bail is set at $2 mil. for Bridges; faces more charges [T. Bridges] por *Jet* 75:12 Mr 20 '89

The Bandler method [neurolinguistic programming guru R. Bandler acquitted of Santa Cruz, Calif. murder of C. Christensen] F. Clancy and H. Yorkshire. il pors *Mother Jones* 14:22-8+ F/Mr '89

Barbarity in El Salvador [Jesuits murdered] *The Christian Century* 106:1112-13 N 29 '89

Beauty and the beast [case of serial murderer L. G. Bell in South Carolina] E. H. Methvin. il pors *Reader's Digest* 134:132-8 F '89

'Because I was a nobody' [wrongful jailing of R. D. Adams as depicted in The thin blue line] D. Hill. il pors *TV Guide* 37:20-2 My 20-26 '89

Beware of paper tigers [murder of L. Bianco by her ex-husband raises questions about limits of court protection] J. C. Simpson. il pors *Time* 133:104-5 Mr 27 '89

Blind faith [murder of M. Marshall; excerpt] J. McGinniss. il pors *Ladies' Home Journal* 106:62+ Ap '89

Blood circle [author J. E. Wideman haunted by murder convictions of son and brother] C. Brown. il *Esquire* 112:122-8+ Ag '89

MURDER—cont.

Blood on the cross [series of killings in Miramichi River region, New Brunswick] G. W. Taylor. il por *Maclean's* 102:71 N 27 '89

Bridges held on attempted murder charge in L.A. por *Jet* 75:54 F 20 '89

Bridges' mother blames son's problems on drugs [T. Bridges] il por *Jet* 75:52 F 27 '89

Brotherhood week [reaction of D. Dinkins and other mayoral candidates to murder of Y. Hawkins in Bensonhurst] J. Klein. il por *New York* 22:36+ S 11 '89

The business of us all [racial murders of Y. Hawkins and E. Till] *Commonweal* 116:484-5 S 22 '89

Chronicle of a death foretold [murder of environmentalist C. Mendes Filho in Brazil] M. Beck. il por *Newsweek* 113:62 Ja 9 '89

The cop who cared too much [detective B. Grogan's work on Hillside Strangler case] G. Dillow. il por *TV Guide* 37:26-7 Ap 1-7 '89

The 'Cotton Club' murder: cocaine and hit men in Hollywood—a 1980s film noir [B. Evans implicated in murder of R. Radin; cover story] J. Kasindorf. il pors *New York* 22:24-33 Jl 24 '89

Crossing a line that is not thin at all, Randall Dale Adams wins release from a Texas prison. M. Brower. il pors *People Weekly* 31:155-6 Ap 10 '89

Crossing 'The thin blue line' [R. D. Adams sues filmmaker E. Morris] M. Lasswell. il por *Rolling Stone* p30 O 19 '89

D.C. police hunt for suspect in slaying of co-ed and her brother [murder of M. Shiferaw] pors *Jet* 76:52 Jl 24 '89

A dark season of fear [series of murders and assaults in Newcastle, N.B.] G. Allen. il *Maclean's* 102:18-19 N 6 '89

Daughter of Manson victims finds forgiveness [S. LaBerge and inmate C. Watson] J. Shaver. il pors *Christianity Today* 33:50-1 S 22 '89

Death among the innocent [gang related murders in Los Angeles] A. Gregor. il *Maclean's* 102:38 My 22 '89

Death goes to school [P. Purdy's shooting rampage in Stockton, Calif. in January 1989] P. Caputo. il *Esquire* 112:136-8+ D '89

Death in El Salvador [murder of six Jesuit priests] J. Sobrino. il *Commonweal* 116:693-5 D 15 '89

Death in the African bush [murder of lion enthusiast G. Adamson in Kenya] C. S. Manegold. il *Newsweek* 114:32 S 4 '89

Death of a bard [F. Fowle stabbed to death in Forsyth, Ga.] T. Moore. il pors *U.S. News & World Report* 107:20-1+ Jl 31 '89

Death on a mean street [murder of Y. Hawkins in Bensonhurst] F. Trippett. il *Time* 134:28 S 11 '89

Death on the playground [P. Purdy kills children in school yard in Stockton, Calif.] J. N. Baker. il por *Newsweek* 113:35 Ja 30 '89

Deaths in the name of life [R. and J. Lynch accused of murder and kidnapping in Delaware] G. Cerio. il por *Newsweek* 113:29 My 8 '89

Department of amplification [R. D. Adams, wrongly convicted for murder, released from Texas jail] M. Singer. *The New Yorker* 65:119-20 Ap 10 '89

The devil and John Holmes: drugs, porn and the murders on Wonderland Avenue. M. Sager. il pors *Rolling Stone* p50-2+ Je 15 '89

A devoted brother believes he's found little Billy Ruff's killer 31 years after the crime [C. Ruff links cousin R. Ruff to 1957 murder in Colonie, N.Y.] K. Gross. il por *People Weekly* 31:69-70+ Je 5 '89

Diary of a tragedy [L. Dann's shooting spree in Winnetka, Ill. school in 1988] J. Bultman. il por *Parents* 64:105-10 My '89

"Die mother father brother" [teenage Satan worshipper T. Sullivan kills mother then commits suicide in Sparta, N.J.] E. Davidowitz. il por *Redbook* 172:132-4+ Ap '89

The drug-violence nexus [crack-related violence] P. Goldstein and H. Brownstein. *New Perspectives Quarterly* 6:24 Summ '89

The end of a manhunt [capture of A. Legere, suspect in string of murders in Miramichi area, New Brunswick] P. Kopvillem. por *Maclean's* 102:25 D 4 '89

Evolution and family homicide [discussion of October 28, 1988 article, Evolutionary social psychology and family homicide] M. Daly and M. Wilson. *Science* 243:462-4 Ja 27 '89

A fatal obsession with the stars [murder of actress R. Schaeffer and other incidents] A. Toufexis. il por *Time* 134:43-4 Jl 31 '89

A father lifts his "burdens" [L. DeLisle murders his children by driving into the Detroit River] E. Magnuson. il *Time* 134:13 Ag 28 '89

A federal case [murder of DEA agent E. Hatcher] E. Pooley. il por *New York* 22:48-50+ Mr 27 '89

Fighting the power [Bensonhurst racial murder and New York mayoral race] A. Logan. il *The New Yorker* 65:108+ S 11 '89

Final attraction: men who charm women—to death [serial killers] A. Rule. il pors *Redbook* 172:104-6+ F '89

A golf great cut down in her prime [M. Miley murdered in 1941 in Lexington, Ky.] B. K. Bell. il por *Women's Sports & Fitness* 11:60 O '89

Grave thoughts [conversation with Jesuit priest I. Ellacuria nine months before his murder in El Salvador] M. Massing. *The New Republic* 201:12-14 D 11 '89

The Hansel and Gretel syndrome [evolutionary significance of family homicide; research by Martin Daly and Margo Wilson] H. Pringle. il *Omni (New York, N.Y.)* 12:38+ D '89

'Hit Man' Hearns' brother charged in shooting of 'girlfriend' in Michigan. il pors *Jet* 76:51-2 Je 26 '89

Honor trio killed by KKK in Mississippi vote drive [M. Schwerner, J. Chaney and A. Goodman] il pors *Jet* 76:6-7 Jl 10 '89

'I told them I'd be back' [J. T. Wesbecker's murder spree in Louisville] J. N. Baker. il *Newsweek* 114:22 S 25 '89

The impact of Stockton [schoolyard murders gives momentum to gun control] J. Hammer. il *Newsweek* 113:8 F 20 '89

In cold blood [murder of six Jesuit priests in El Salvador] *Time* 134:44 N 27 '89

In hiding for 18 years, a wanted man is caught by the FBI and a TV posse [J. List, alleged murderer, featured on America's most wanted] K. Gross. il pors *People Weekly* 31:69-70+ Je 19 '89

In memory of Chico Mendes [union leader and ecologist slain in Brazil] J. D. Hair. il *International Wildlife* 19:30 Mr/Ap '89

In solidarity with the slain Jesuits of El Salvador [address, November 22, 1989] J. A. O'Hare. *America* 161:443-6 D 16 '89

In the name of God, stop the killing [Jesuit priests in El Salvador] R. A. Hyde. *The Christian Century* 106:1144 D 6 '89

An innocent life, a heartbreaking death [actress R. Schaeffer killed by obsessive fan] P. Axthelm. il por *People Weekly* 32:60-2+ Jl 31 '89

'It must never happen again' [Philadelphia, Miss. relives 1964 murders of Andrew Goodman, James Chaney and Michael Schwerner] A. Murr. il *Newsweek* 113:26-7 Ja 9 '89

The journalist and the murderer (I) [convicted murderer J. MacDonald's suit against author J. McGinniss] J. Malcolm. *The New Yorker* 65:38-42+ Mr 13 '89

The journalist and the murderer (II) [convicted murderer J. MacDonald's suit against author J. McGinniss] J. Malcolm. *The New Yorker* 65:49-50+ Mr 20 '89

Karen Severson swore she'd find her best friend's murderer—now she stands accused of the crime [murder of M. Avila in Arleta, Calif.] K. Kingsbury. il pors *People Weekly* 32:147-8+ S 18 '89

Kids who kill. R. Wright. il *Good Housekeeping* 209:54+ Ag '89

A killing in Maine [K. A. Wood killed by hunter D. Rogerson] J. H. Kunstler. il por *The New York Times Magazine* p58-60+ S 10 '89

Knowing Johnny Jenkins [controversial rare book dealer who was mysteriously murdered in Bastrop County, Tex.] C. Trillin. *The New Yorker* 65:79-97 O 30 '89

Letter from Los Angeles [Cotton Club murder case] J. Didion. *The New Yorker* 65:92-9 S 4 '89

Man in the pink shirt [comparison of Kennedy assassination with witnessing shooting of two security guards] J. Glaeg. *America* 161:370-1 N 25 '89

The man who hated women [M. Lépine murders women at the University of Montreal] W. R. Doerner. il por *Time* 134:30 D 18 '89

Manson. J. Adler. por *Newsweek* 114:54-5 Jl 3 '89

Massacre in Montreal [M. Lépine] B. Turque. il por *Newsweek* 114:39 D 18 '89

Meditating on Bensonhurst [racial murder of Y. Hawkins] *America* 161:131 S 9-16 '89

Montreal massacre [M. Lépine guns down women at Univ. of Montreal; cover story; special section] il *Maclean's* 102:14-19+ D 18 '89

A movie for the defense [R. D. Adams murder case and film The thin blue line] J. N. Baker. il por *Newsweek* 113:27 Mr 13 '89

Murder and the right to die [M. Weaver's right to die protested by criminal N. Pagan in Maine] il por *Newsweek* 113:33 Ap 10 '89

Murder capital [Washington, D.C.] M. Tidwell. il *The Progressive* 53:46 Jl '89

Murder in the Amazon [union leader and ecologist C. Mendes Filho slain] J. Bierman. il por *Maclean's* 102:21 Ja 9 '89

Murder in the game reserve [G. Adamson murdered in Kenya] il *Time* 134:21 S 4 '89

Murder in the safest places [death of Dr. K. Hinnant at Bellevue Hospital] R. Rosenblatt. il *U.S. News & World Report* 106:6-7 Ja 23 '89

Murder most puzzling: can you solve this case? L. Treat. il *The New York Times Book Review* 94:36 O 15 '89

The murder of innocence in Africa [death of lion enthusiast G. Adamson] M. Vollers. il *People Weekly* 32:46-51 S 11 '89

MURDER—*cont.*

Murder on the prairie [Canadian TV show depicts C. Thatcher's 1983 murder of his wife] D. Turbide. il por *Maclean's* 102:45-6 Jl 17 '89

A murder rap at age 10 [C. Kocher of Kunkletown, Pa.] *Newsweek* 114:24 Ag 14 '89

Murder, they broadcast [viewers of America's most wanted identify murderer J. List] T. Jacoby. pors *Newsweek* 113:58 Je 12 '89

Murder wave in the capital [Washington, D.C.] T. Morganthau. il *Newsweek* 113:16-19 Mr 13 '89

The murder—and the mayor [Mayor P. Halat accused of hiring hit man to murder Judge V. Sherry in Biloxi, Miss.] J. N. Baker. il por *Newsweek* 114:32 O 23 '89

"My wife shouldn't have died" [K. A. Wood killed by hunter D. Rogerson in Hermon, Me.] J. Hope. il pors *Good Housekeeping* 209:92+ O '89

N.Y. gunman surrenders in Hawkins slaying; blacks riot on Brooklyn Bridge. il *Jet* 76:7-8 S 18 '89

A nation of certified killers [murderer P. Purdy's firearms transaction record] J. D. McNamara. il *Harper's* 278:58-9 My '89

Nelles's legal gain [Canadian Supreme Court rules in favor of nurse S. Nelles over baby murder mystery at Sick Children's Hospital] B. Wickens. il por *Maclean's* 102:42 Ag 28 '89

New York mother throws two children out of window [M. Abdussalaam] il por *Jet* 77:18 O 23 '89

New York youth killed in racial attack by whites [Bensonhurst] il *Jet* 76:52 S 11 '89

No happy ending [R. Adams denied parole in Texas] J. E. Gallagher. il por *Time* 133:56 Mr 6 '89

Notes and comment [drug murders in Washington, D.C.] *The New Yorker* 65:29-30 Ap 17 '89

Notes and comment [murder of environmentalist C. Mendes Filho in Brazil] il *The New Yorker* 65:27-8 F 20 '89

'Now you be quiet, Oscar' [death squad killings in El Savador] *America* 161:415 D 9 '89

Nowhere to run (I) [R. Linton murdered by her husband in Yonkers, N.Y.] E. Hopkins. il *Rolling Stone* p72-4+ Ap 20 '89

Nowhere to run (II) [R. Linton murdered by her husband in Yonkers, N.Y.] E. Hopkins. il por *Rolling Stone* p74-6+ My 4 '89

Of many things [murder of Jesuits in El Salvador] T. H. Stahel. *America* 161:390 D 2 '89

Park Avenue Gothic: a family feud turns into a fight to the death [death of J. Goodwillie during fight with J. de Sola Mendes] B. Costikyan. il pors *New York* 22:46-50+ Mr 20 '89

Presumed guilty [half brothers E. L. Miller and W. R. Jent released from Florida's death row after new evidence uncovered concerning 1979 murder case] D. Finkel. il pors *Esquire* 111:178-80+ Mr '89

A racist ambush in New York [death of Y. Hawkins in Bensonhurst] J. N. Baker. il por *Newsweek* 114:25 S 4 '89

Recrossing The thin blue line [R. Adams released from jail] M. B. Carlson. il por *Time* 133:23 Ap 3 '89

Reflections on Bundy [T. Bundy links homicidal urges to pornography] *National Review* 41:17-18 F 24 '89

Rural workers face murder [Brazil] W. Steif. il *The Progressive* 53:26 Je '89

Security manager for Guy dead following dispute with New Edition's crew member [murder of A. Bee in Pittsburgh] il *Jet* 76:18 Jl 24 '89

The shots heard 'round the Congress [J. T. Wesbecker's Louisville murder spree with AK-47] il *U.S. News & World Report* 107:15 S 25 '89

Since Mississippi burned [impact of 1964 murder of three civil rights workers on residents of Philadelphia, Miss.] D. McWhorter. il *People Weekly* 31:36-43 Ja 9 '89

Slaughter in a school yard [P. Purdy shoots children in Stockton, Calif.] il *Time* 133:29 Ja 30 '89

A slaughter of innocents [bystanders caught in narcotics trade crossfire] *U.S. News & World Report* 107:12 Jl 10 '89

Special report: . . . till death do us part [cases of April LaSalta, Pamela Dunn, and Lisa Bianco] S. Weller. il *Redbook* 173:112-14+ Ag '89

Stalking the Green River killer [suspect W. J. Stevens] A. Sachs. il por *Time* 134:57 Jl 31 '89

A string of sixty murders [Kansas City] B. Turque. il *Newsweek* 114:64 D 4 '89

Teaching kids how to grieve [program in Watts for children whose lives have been touched by murder] S. Doherty. il *Newsweek* 114:73 N 13 '89

The think tank murder [puzzle to solve] T. Chastain. il *Discover* 10:96+ O '89

A tide of drug killing. L. Martz. il *Newsweek* 113:44-5 Ja 16 '89

To the left of zero [Mexican newspaper editor H. F. Miranda killed in Tijuana] W. Murray. *The New Yorker* 65:57-66 Jl 31 '89

Todd Bridges tells how Hollywood destroyed his life and how God is rebuilding it. il pors *Jet* 76:28-30 Ap 10 '89

The Tokyo chainsaw massacre [accused murderer T. Miyazaki] T. Jackson. *The New Republic* 201:20-1 S 11 '89

Too young to die? [case of H. Wilkins; cover story] R. Rosenbaum. il pors *The New York Times Magazine* p32-5+ Mr 12 '89

Tour rivalry ends in murder: death follows fight between New Edition and Guy. M. Goldberg. *Rolling Stone* p28 Ag 24 '89

The tragedy at Bellevue [murder of Dr. K. Hinnant] E. Salholz. il pors *Newsweek* 113:27 Ja 23 '89

Tribute to a Latin American martyr [L. Espinal, Jesuit missionary murdered in Bolivia in 1980] M. O'Sullivan. *America* 160:8-11+ Ja 7-14 '89

True confession? [excerpt from transcript of police interrogation of murder suspect T. F. Sawyer in Clearwater, Fla.] *Harper's* 279:17-20+ O '89

Two blacks face murder charges in voodoo scheme [charges against J. and L. Ivy in voodoo scheme against judge T. Gardner in Miss.] il pors *Jet* 76:52-3 Jl 17 '89

The two racisms [murder of Y. Hawkins in Bensonhurst] M. E. Dyson. *The Nation* 249:300-1 S 25 '89

An ugly epidemic [Washington D.C. at war with crack] W. Lowther. il *Maclean's* 102:50 Ap 3 '89

Untrue confessions [T. F. Sawyer confesses to Clearwater, Fla. murder after brutal interrogation by police] P. Weiss. il por *Mother Jones* 14:18-20+ S '89

War among Washington's blacks. J. Cassidy. *World Press Review* 36:34 My '89

War is swell? [Soldier of fortune's classifieds held accountable in murder cases] J. Zweig and P. Klebnikov. il por *Forbes* 144:223 S 18 '89

What really happened in Bensonhurst [murder of Y. Hawkins; cover story] M. Stone. il pors map *New York* 22:46-56 N 6 '89

Why did Randall Adams almost die? F. Bruning. il *Maclean's* 102:9 Mr 27 '89

The wild and crazy gangster: Michael Markowitz's twisted American dream. P. Blauner. il pors *New York* 22:52-6+ O 9 '89

Zulu spiritual leader murdered [the Londaukosi Shembe] I. Hexham and K. O. Poewe-Hexham. *Christianity Today* 33:65 Je 16 '89

MURDER IN LITERATURE
> *See also*
> Detective and mystery stories

MURDER MYSTERY STORIES *See* Detective and mystery stories

MURDERERS *See* Murder

MURDERERS AMONG US: THE SIMON WIESENTHAL STORY [television program] *See* Television program reviews—Single works

MURDOCH, RUPERT
> *about*

Craig to head all Murdoch book business; Chapman resigns from Collins; authors' reaction uncertain. por *Publishers Weekly* 235:10+ F 3 '89

Even Rupert Murdoch has his limits. C. Welles. il por *Business Week* p34-5 O 2 '89

Four titans carve up European TV [cover story] W. Fisher and M. Schapiro. il *The Nation* 248:37+ Ja 9-16 '89

"I can think of more important things than being loved by everybody" [interview] W. J. Koschnick. il pors *Forbes* 144:98+ N 27 '89

Keeping up with the Murdochs. D. Lieberman. il *Business Week* p32-4 Mr 20 '89

Murdoch wins Collins, promises autonomy; Craig assesses Harper's new owner. V. Menkes. *Publishers Weekly* 235:16+ Ja 20 '89

Rupert Murdoch. il *The Nation* 248:806 Je 12 '89

A shakeup in books. D. Turbide. *Maclean's* 102:53 F 27 '89

The Sky-watchers. A. Phillips. il *Maclean's* 102:51 F 27 '89

The tarting up of TV guide. R. Zoglin. il por *Time* 133:81 My 29 '89

MURDOUGH, THOMAS G.
> *about*

Why Little Tikes' managers picked up their toys and left. M. Mallory. il *Business Week* p83 N 27 '89

MURILLO, BÁRTOLOMÉ ESTEBAN, 1617 OR 18-1682
> *about*

The portrait of a scandal. C. Dickey. il por *Newsweek* 113:55 Ja 9 '89

MURPHEY-CORB, MICHAEL, AND OTHERS
A formalin-inactivated whole SIV vaccine confers protection in macaques. bibl f il *Science* 246:1293-7 D 8 '89

MURPHY, ANN PLESHETTE
Inside Parents. See issues of Parents beginning September 1988

MURPHY, AUSTIN
All for 1. il *Sports Illustrated* 71:38-44+ S 4 '89
The best and the brightest. il *Sports Illustrated* 70:67-8 Ja 30 '89
Big bad Bear. il pors *Sports Illustrated* 71:56-8+ S 4 '89
Boffo Buffs! il *Sports Illustrated* 71:20-7 N 13 '89
The Cup heats up. il *Sports Illustrated* 70:24-6+ My 22 '89

MURPHY, AUSTIN—*cont.*
Dingdong Cup clash. il *Sports Illustrated* 70:22-3 My 29 '89
A duel in the sun: quarterbacks Troy Aikman and Steve Walsh compete to be the Cowboys' starter [cover story] il pors *Sports Illustrated* 71:30-2+ Ag 21 '89
Dynasty undone. il *Sports Illustrated* 70:18-23 Ap 24 '89
Edmonton gets a wake-up call. il *Sports Illustrated* 70:26-8+ Ap 17 '89
Fanning the Flames. il *Sports Illustrated* 70:38-40 Mr 13 '89
Getting a grip on the Soviets. il *Sports Illustrated* 70:102 Ja 9 '89
High times. il *Sports Illustrated* 71:18-21 O 9 '89
Left out in the cold. il *Sports Illustrated* 70:81 F 20 '89
A lid-lifter in Texas. il pors *Sports Illustrated* 71:56-8+ O 23 '89
A long way from L.A. il pors *Sports Illustrated* 71:44-6+ D 25 '89-Ja 1 '90
Make room for Lemieux [cover story] il pors *Sports Illustrated* 70:28-30+ F 6 '89
Medicine man for Vancouver. il pors *Sports Illustrated* 70:91-2 Ap 3 '89
Minnesota faces were Crimson. il *Sports Illustrated* 70:74+ Ap 10 '89
Montreal goes up in Flames. il *Sports Illustrated* 70:44-7 Je 5 '89
No. 1 no more [cover story] il *Sports Illustrated* 71:24-31 D 4 '89
No. 3 with a bullet. il pors *Sports Illustrated* 70:38-40 Mr 20 '89
Oh, you kids, you. il pors *Sports Illustrated* 70:40-2+ Ja 30 '89
An old habit of the Habs. il *Sports Illustrated* 70:34-5 My 15 '89
The one-two punch [cover story] il *Sports Illustrated* 71:32-6 S 25 '89
Safeties first. il pors *Sports Illustrated* 71:78-80 S 4 '89
Say goodbye to fallball. il *Sports Illustrated* 71:38-40+ O 2 '89
Third-degree Burns. il *Sports Illustrated* 70:50-3 F 27 '89
Toothsome sacrifice. il *Sports Illustrated* 70:24-6+ My 8 '89
A very sorry State. il *Sports Illustrated* 71:48-50+ S 18 '89
Waiting for the call. il pors *Sports Illustrated* 70 Special Issue:179-82+ F '89
Who will bag the prize? [cover story] il *Sports Illustrated* 71:24-6+ N 27 '89

MURPHY, AUSTIN J., 1927-
Should President Bush's minimum wage proposal be adopted? [excerpts from address, March 23, 1989] *Congressional Digest* 68:143+ My '89

MURPHY, BILL
Family reunion vacations. il *Better Homes and Gardens* 67:123-4+ Ag '89

MURPHY, CULLEN
Breakout. il *The Atlantic* 264:14+ Jl '89
Caught in the web of bytes. il *The Atlantic* 263:68-70 F '89
The future of pennies: an exchange. il *The Atlantic* 264:20+ D '89
A grateful nation. il *The Atlantic* 263:16+ Ja '89
The great sandwich caper. il *Reader's Digest* 135:149-50 S '89
"Hey, let me outta here!". il *The Atlantic* 264:62-71 Ag '89
In Galway's fair city. il *The Atlantic* 263:81-3 My '89
Inquisition. il *The Atlantic* 263:14+ Ap '89
They're back. il *The Atlantic* 264:20+ O '89
The tithe. il *The Atlantic* 264:20+ S '89

MURPHY, DENIS
Plenty of nice people. *America* 160:150-2 F 18 '89
Slums then and now. *America* 161:447-9 D 16 '89

MURPHY, EDDIE
about
Bill Cosby's all-stars shock Eddie Murphy's all-stars team 30-18. il pors *Jet* 76:56-8 Jl 3 '89
Comic Eddie Murphy hit with $75 million suit charging sex harassment. pors *Jet* 76:60 My 29 '89
Eddie laughs all way to bank as critics bash 'Harlem nights'. il pors *Jet* 77:56-8 D 11 '89
Eddie Murphy [interview; cover story] B. Zehme. il pors *Rolling Stone* p50-2+ Ag 24 '89
Eddie Murphy comes to prime time. J. D. Stem. il pors *TV Guide* 37:20-1 F 25-Mr 3 '89
Eddie Murphy explains why he's making next movie in Hollywood, not Harlem. *Jet* 76:17 Ap 10 '89
Eddie Murphy turns serious as singer and songwriter on new album, 'So Happy' [cover story] il pors *Jet* 76:62-4 Ag 28 '89
Eddie Murphy's troubled route to America. J. Bernard. il pors *Video* 13:16-17 Je '89
Eddie says he cast Richard in 'Harlem nights' because 'He is my idol' [cover story] R. E. Johnson. il pors *Jet* 77:56-60 N 20 '89
Harlem nights [film] Reviews
American Film il 15:63 N '89. C. Fleming
Jet il pors 77:60-2 D 18 '89. R. E. Johnson
Maclean's il por 102:74 N 27 '89. B. D. Johnson

The New Republic 201:24-5 D 18 '89. S. Kauffmann
Newsweek il por 114:92 N 27 '89. D. Ansen
People Weekly 32:16+ D 18 '89. R. Novak
People Weekly il por 32:76-7 D 4 '89
Time il por 134:88 N 27 '89. R. Schickel
Murphy does $multimillion car commercials in Japan. por *Jet* 77:36 O 23 '89
Pink-slipped by Eddie Murphy, Michael Michele vows their only date will be in court. S. Schindehette. il pors *People Weekly* 31:48-9 My 29 '89
What's Eddie watching? L. Jarvik. il por *American Film* 14:12 Je '89

MURPHY, GERALD
about
Letter from a goddamn Alp. D. Parker. por *Esquire* 112:144-7 Ag '89
Villa America. J. Robinson. il *Gourmet* 49:70+ Jl '89

MURPHY, GREGORY
about
Bittersweet victory. G. W. Taylor. il por *Maclean's* 102:18 Jl 24 '89
A change of heart. A. Walmsley. il por *Maclean's* 102:18-19 Jl 31 '89

MURPHY, HERMANN DUDLEY, 1867-1945
about
The Carrig-Rohane frame. B. Barol. il *American Heritage* 40:30-1 D '89

MURPHY, JACQUELINE
How do you spell "wound," as in gunshot? il *U.S. Catholic* 54:36-9 O '89

MURPHY, JEROME T.
The paradox of decentralizing schools: lessons from business, government, and the Catholic Church. bibl f il *Phi Delta Kappan* 70:808-12 Je '89

MURPHY, JOHN JOSEPH, 1931-
about
Murphy's law. T. Mack. il por *Forbes* 143:174+ Mr 20 '89

MURPHY, JULIE
(ed) See Fageros, Karol, d. 1988. Memoirs of the golden goddess

MURPHY, MARY
Why Robin Givens has rolled with the punches—and still loves Tyson. il pors *TV Guide* 37:6-7+ Jl 1-7 '89
The worries are what to do about love, sex, religion—and where to have pizza Friday night. il por *TV Guide* 37:12-13 F 11-17 '89

MURPHY, MICHAEL E.
What the greenhouse effect portends. *America* 161:470-2 D 23-30 '89

MURPHY, PAT
Scavenger [story] *Omni (New York, N.Y.)* 11:54+ Ap '89

MURPHY, RICHARD W.
Lebanon: at the crossroads [address, October 29, 1988] *Department of State Bulletin* 88:45-7 D '88
The search for Middle East peace [address, December 8, 1988] *Department of State Bulletin* 89:57-9 F '89
Update on the situation in the Middle East [statement, October 13, 1988] *Department of State Bulletin* 88:41-5 D '88
about
Assistant Secretary Murphy's interview on "This week with David Brinkley" [transcript of program, December 18, 1988] *Department of State Bulletin* 89:55-7 F '89

MURPHY, RYAN
Arnold Schwarzenegger: no sweat [cover story] il pors *The Saturday Evening Post* 261:46-9 Mr '89

MURPHY, SARA
about
Letter from a goddamn Alp. D. Parker. por *Esquire* 112:144-7 Ag '89
Villa America. J. Robinson. il *Gourmet* 49:70+ Jl '89

MURPHY, SHIRLEY ROUSSEAU, 1928-
Fantasy for young readers. *The Writer* 102:19-20+ S '89

MURPHY, THOMAS S.
about
The brass at Cap Cities/ABC: rethinking TV [interview] M. Brown and P. Ainslie. il pors *Channels (New York, N.Y.: 1986)* 9:93-5 F '89

MURPHY BEDS
See also
Murphy Door Bed Co., Inc.
The trademark that fell asleep [Murphy bed ruled a generic product] il *U.S. News & World Report* 106:16-17 My 15 '89

MURPHY BROWN (FICTIONAL CHARACTER)
From Mary to Murphy: codependent no more. V. Rebeck. *The Christian Century* 106:948+ O 25 '89
What TV's real newswomen think of Murphy Brown [cover story] J. Elm. il *TV Guide* 37:4-7 D 23-29 '89
MURPHY BROWN [television program] See Television program reviews—Single words

MURPHY DOOR BED CO., INC.
The trademark that fell asleep [Murphy bed ruled a generic product] il *U.S. News & World Report* 106:16-17 My 15 '89

MURRAY, ANDREW W., AND KIRSCHNER, MARC W.
Dominoes and clocks: the union of two views of the cell cycle. bibl f il *Science* 246:614-21 N 3 '89

MURRAY, ANNE, 1947-
about
A milestone in music for a laureate of song. D. Jenish. il por *Maclean's* 102:36-7 D 25 '89
MURRAY, BILL
about
Bill Murray's cynical Xmas. L. Kesten. il por *Video* 13:14 N '89
MURRAY, CHARLES A.
Charles Murray [advice to George Bush] *National Review* 41:21-2 F 10 '89
Functioning communities. *Current (Washington, D.C.)* 311:24-31 Mr/Ap '89
MURRAY, E'LANE CARLISLE
A bird for Miss Alma. il *Southern Living* 24:89 F '89
MURRAY, ELIZABETH
about
Is bigger necessarily better? P. Plagens. il pors *Newsweek* 113:66-7 Ap 17 '89
Shape shifter [cover story] R. Storr. bibl f il *Art in America* 77:210-21+ Ap '89
MURRAY, JO ANNE
about
The woman-managed firm: how big a deal? R. L. Miller. il pors *Architectural Record* 177:47+ Je '89
MURRAY, JOHN
HMS Pandora. il map *Sea Frontiers* 35:328-35 N/D '89
MURRAY, LES A., 1938-
The assimilation of background [poem] *The New Republic* 200:26 F 6 '89
MURRAY, LOWELL
about
The man behind Meech. E. K. Fulton. il por *Maclean's* 102:28 N 20 '89
MURRAY, ROGER F.
about
The guy who helped invent the IRA tells you how to make money in one now. J. Edgerton. il por *Money* 18:195-6 O '89
MURRAY, WILLIAM
Taxation of advertising: a violation of free speech? il *USA Today (Periodical)* 117:23-4 Mr '89
MURRAY, WILLIAM, 1926-
Letter from Cassino. *The New Yorker* 65:112-20 My 15 '89
To the left of zero. *The New Yorker* 65:57-66 Jl 31 '89
MURRAY & ASSOCIATES
The woman-managed firm: how big a deal? R. L. Miller. il pors *Architectural Record* 177:47+ Je '89
MURRAY CHRIS-CRAFT SPORTDECKS INC.
Chris-Craft comes back [acquired by OMC] P. A. Janssen. il *Motor Boating & Sailing* 163:15+ Ap '89
Did Irv Jacobs sandbag Outboard Marine? G. DeGeorge. *Business Week* p38+ F 20 '89
MURRAY LOUIS DANCE COMPANY
See also
Nikolais and Louis Dance
MURRIN, THOMAS J.
about
Washington ins & outs: Graham departs, Murrin to Commerce, top changes at NASA and Pentagon. I. Goodwin. *Physics Today* 42:47-9 Jl '89
MURROW, EDWARD R.
Anecdotes, facetiae, satire, etc.
Blitzed. A. Levine. *The New Republic* 200:16-17 Ja 9-16 '89
MURTAUGH, DANIEL M.
Fathers & their sons. il por *Commonweal* 116:298-302 My 19 '89
MURUROA ATOLL (FRENCH POLYNESIA)
See also
Radioactive pollution—Mururoa Atoll (French Polynesia)
MUSCARINIC RECEPTORS *See* Chemoreceptors
MUSCHAMP, HERBERT
Angels! il *Vogue* 179:278-87 D '89
The good side of bad taste. il *House & Garden* 161:50 Ja '89
Sacred arts. il por *Vogue* 179:420-5 Ap '89
Venturi to order. il por *House & Garden* 161:104-9+ Ag '89
The winds of Windsorism [cover story] *The New Republic* 201:30-5 D 11 '89
With the opening of the first major public building by Peter Eisenman, theory and reality collide. il por *Vogue* 179:272+ O '89
MUSCLE
See also
Heart—Muscle
Lean body mass
Myoblasts
Free calcium at rest during "catch" in single smooth muscle cells [mussels] N. Ishii and others. bibl f il *Science* 243:1367-8 Mr 10 '89
Hyperpolarizing vasodilators activate ATP-sensitive K+ channels in arterial smooth muscle. N. B. Standen and others. bibl f il *Science* 245:177-80 Jl 14 '89

In vivo footprinting of a muscle specific enhancer by ligation mediated PCR. P. R. Mueller and B. Wold. bibl f il *Science* 246:780-6 N 10 '89
The middle-ear muscles. E. Borg and S. A. Counter. bibl il *Scientific American* 261:74-80 Ag '89
Primary structure of the β subunit of the DHP-sensitive calcium channel from skeletal muscle. P. Ruth and others. bibl f il *Science* 245:1115-18 S 8 '89
Regulation of calcium concentration in voltage-clamped smooth muscle cells. P. L. Becker and others. bibl f il *Science* 244:211-14 Ap 14 '89
Transfer of a protein encoded by a single nucleus to nearby nuclei in multinucleated myotubes. E. Ralston and Z. W. Hall. bibl f il *Science* 244:1066-9 Je 2 '89
Vertebrate skeletal muscle: power source for locomotion. O. I. Weeks. bibl f il *BioScience* 39:791-9 D '89
Diseases
See also
Muscular dystrophy
A direct repeat is a hotspot for large-scale deletion of human mitochondrial DNA [neuromuscular disorders characterized by ocular myopathy and ophthalmoplegia] E. A. Schon and others. bibl f il *Science* 244:346-9 Ap 21 '89
Weakness for alcohol borne by muscles [research by Emanuel Rubin] I. Wickelgren. *Science News* 135:117 F 25 '89
Innervation
Couch potatoes' half-baked future [inactivity affects muscle adaptability; research by Gary C. Sieck] il *USA Today (Periodical)* 117:13 Ap '89
Neural control of locomotion. G. E. Loeb. bibl f il *BioScience* 39:800-4 D '89
Proteins
See also
Actin
Myoglobin
MUSCLE CELLS *See* Cells
MUSCLE CONTRACTION
See also
Heart—Muscle—Contraction
Free calcium at rest during "catch" in single smooth muscle cells [mussels] N. Ishii and others. bibl f il *Science* 243:1367-8 Mr 10 '89
Regulation of calcium concentration in voltage-clamped smooth muscle cells. P. L. Becker and others. bibl f il *Science* 244:211-14 Ap 14 '89
MUSCLE POWERED AIRCRAFT *See* Human powered aircraft
MUSCLE STIMULATION (ELECTRICAL) *See* Electrical muscle stimulation
MUSCLE STRENGTH
See also
Bodybuilding
How big a setback is a temporary cutback? [weight training] O. Anderson. il *Women's Sports & Fitness* 11:18 Ap '89
Stimulating athletes [use of electrical muscle stimulation by weight lifter Derrick Crass] il *Discover* 10:14 Mr '89
MUSCLE STRETCH *See* Stretching exercises
MUSCOVY DUCKS *See* Ducks
MUSCULAR DYSTROPHY
Jerry Lewis telethon raises $78.4 million; Sammy Davis performs. il por *Jet* 76:28 S 25 '89
Genetic aspects
Biochemical clues to muscular dystrophy [role of brain dystrophin in Duchenne dystrophy; research by U. Nudel] *Science News* 135:30 Ja 14 '89
Fibroblast growth factor in the extracellular matrix of dystrophic (mdx) mouse muscle. J. DiMario and others. bibl f il *Science* 244:688-90 My 12 '89
The molecular basis of muscular dystrophy in the *mdx* mouse: a point mutation. P. Sicinski and others. bibl f il *Science* 244:1578-80 Je 30 '89
The Quebec phenomenon [high incidence in Saguenay region] S. Strauss. *World Press Review* 36:68 S '89
MUSCULAR POWER *See* Muscle strength
MUSEBECK SHOE COMPANY
U.S. shoe firms thrive in high-quality market. J. E. Bahls. il *Nation's Business* 77:38-40 F '89
MUSÉE CARNAVALET (PARIS, FRANCE)
Musée Carnavalet [French Revolution collection] C. P. Reynolds. il *Gourmet* 49:50+ O '89
MUSÉE D'ART MODERNE DE LA VILLE DE PARIS
The museum as studio [show based on collections] B. Adams. il *Art in America* 77:63+ O '89
MUSÉE DE L'HISTOIRE DE FRANCE
Bicentennial of the French Revolution and the Musée de l'Histoire de France. C. P. Reynolds. il *Gourmet* 49:24+ Ja '89
MUSÉE DES ARTS DÉCORATIFS (STRASBOURG, FRANCE)
Curators in court [P. Rosenberg and J.-D. Ludmann] B. Grauman. il *Art News* 88:72-4 Ap '89
Scandals rock French museums. W. Robinson. il por *Art in America* 77:21+ F '89
MUSÉE DU JEU DE PAUME (PARIS, FRANCE)
Post impressionism [renovation] B. Grauman. il *Art News* 88:58 Ja '89
MUSÉE DU LOUVRE
A castle under the Louvre. P. Miller. il *National Geographic* 176:102-7 Jl '89

MUSÉE DU LOUVRE—cont.
Curators in court [P. Rosenberg and J.-D. Ludmann] B. Grauman. il Art News 88:72-4 Ap '89
'French history, right here' [renovation] R. Marshall. il Newsweek 113:40+ Mr 27 '89
Pei's pyramid—new jewel of the Seine. S. M. Alsop. il Architectural Digest 46:29+ Ap '89
The portrait of a scandal [Louvre implicated in receiving stolen goods in case of Murillo's Gentleman of Seville] C. Dickey. il por Newsweek 113:55 Ja 9 '89
A problematic Poussin [Louvre charged in misattribution of Olympos et Marsyas] G. Danto. il Art News 88:70+ Ap '89
The riddle of the pyramid [I. M. Pei's addition] R. Kimball. il Architectural Record 177:58-61 Ja '89
Scandals rock French museums. W. Robinson. il por Art in America 77:21+ F '89
What becomes a legend most [Mona Lisa; cover story] G. Danto. il Art News 88:148-51 Summ '89
MUSÉE HISTORIQUE DE LA VILLE DE PARIS See Musée Carnavalet (Paris, France)
MUSÉE NISSIM DE CAMONDO (PARIS, FRANCE)
Legacy of splendor. M. Filler. il House & Garden 161:86-91 Jl '89
MUSÉES ROYAUX D'ART ET D'HISTOIRE (BELGIUM)
Belgium's search for sponsors. History Today 39:5 Ja '89
MUSEO DE ARTE ABSTRACTO ESPAÑOL (CUENCA, SPAIN)
Abstraction on the edge. F. Jarque. il por Art News 88:87-8 Mr '89
MUSEO DEL PRADO (MADRID, SPAIN)
Courtship of a collector [Prado to receive major loan of Thyssen-Bornemisza Collection] F. Jarque. il por Art News 88:65+ My '89
MUSEUM DIRECTORS
See also
Fuchs, Rudolf Herman, 1942-
Kennedy, Roger G.
Krens, Thomas
Martin, Jean-Hubert
Oberhuber, Konrad
Serota, Nicholas
Psychology
Gloom at the top [art museum director burnout] P. Failing. il Art News 88:126-31 My '89
MUSEUM EXHIBITS
See also
Paleontological models and exhibits
MUSEUM MODERNER KUNST (VIENNA, AUSTRIA)
Double departure [resignation of directors] F. Protzman. Art News 88:77 O '89
MUSEUM OF ABSTRACT ART (CUENCA, SPAIN) See Museo de Arte Abstracto Español (Cuenca, Spain)
MUSEUM OF AMERICAN FOLK ART
Just folks [director R. Bishop] A. Prud'Homme. il por New York 22:40 Ap 10 '89
Museum accessions. E. H. Gustafson. il Antiques 135:854 Ap '89
MUSEUM OF AMERICAN POLITICAL LIFE
Mementos of politicos. M. E. Neely, Jr. and H. Holzer. il Americana 17:23-7 Jl/Ag '89
MUSEUM OF BROADCASTING (NEW YORK, N.Y.)
Python scholars [Monty Python Marathon] The New Yorker 65:28-9 Mr 13 '89
Thanks for the memories. R. Powers. il Gentlemen's Quarterly 59:170+ O '89
MUSEUM OF DECORATIVE ARTS (STRASBOURG, FRANCE) See Musée des Arts Décoratifs (Strasbourg, France)
MUSEUM OF FINE ARTS (BOSTON, MASS.)
Indecent exposure? [Museum of Fine Arts declines nude photograph of A. Ginsberg by E. Dorfman] C. Giuliano. il pors Art News 88:31 F '89
Starting things [curator of contemporary art K. Halbreich] C. Giuliano. il por Art News 88:32+ Ja '89
MUSEUM OF FLIGHT (SEATTLE, WASH.)
High fliers in a Red Barn. J. E. Stevens. il Americana 17:37-42 Jl/Ag '89
MUSEUM OF FLYING (SANTA MONICA, CALIF.)
Vintage aircraft at a new home in Santa Monica. il Sunset (Central West edition) 183:56-7 Jl '89
MUSEUM OF INTERNATIONAL FOLK ART (SANTA FE, N.M.). HISPANIC HERITAGE WING
Spanish treasures in Santa Fe. il Sunset (Central West edition) 183:70 O '89
MUSEUM OF MODERN ART (NEW YORK, N.Y.)
Market fever at MOMA [sale of seven paintings to obtain van Gogh's Portrait of Joseph Roulin] W. Robinson. il Art in America 77:33 D '89
"Signature piece" [installation by K. Ericson] R. Cembalest. il Art News 88:15 F '89
Unanswered questions [private deal to obtain van Gogh's Portrait of Joseph Roulin] T. McGhee. il Art News 88:56+ O '89
MUSEUM OF MODERN ART (NEW YORK, N.Y.). SCULP-TURE GARDEN
Notes and comment [snow falling on sculptures] The New Yorker 64:23-4 Ja 23 '89

MUSEUM OF MODERN MYTHOLOGY (SAN FRANCISCO, CALIF.)
Snap, crackle, and pop [cover story] R. Rapoport. il Americana 17:36-40 Mr/Ap '89
MUSEUM OF NATURAL HISTORY (NEW YORK, N.Y.)
See American Museum of Natural History
MUSEUM OF NEON ART (LOS ANGELES, CALIF.)
Los Angeles neon, past and present. il Sunset (Central West edition) 183:68-9 N '89
MUSEUM OF THE AMERICAN INDIAN—HEYE FOUNDATION
See also
National Museum of the American Indian (U.S.)
An American legacy. C. Bond. bibl f (p228) il Smithsonian 20:42-55 O '89
MUSEUM OF THE MOVING IMAGE (LONDON, ENGLAND)
Double feature [cover story] D. Dietsch. il Architectural Record 177:110-21 My '89
MUSEUM RIETBERG (ZURICH, SWITZERLAND)
The Rietberg Museum in Zurich. M. Peppiatt. il Architectural Digest 46:74+ Mr '89
MUSEUM STORES
Art chic [Metropolitan Museum of Art] J. Levine. il Forbes 144:94+ Ag 21 '89
The art of shopping. D. P. Marshall. il Travel Holiday 171:86-91 Ap '89
Gift shopping at science museums in the Bay Area. il Sunset (Central West edition) 183:14 D '89
Infinite pattern [museum store at Contemporary Arts Center in Cincinnati designed by T. Brown] D. Dietsch. il Architectural Record 177:94-7 mid-S '89
Stop and shop at a museum [southern art museums] il Southern Living 24:26-7 F '89
MUSEUM VILLAGES See Villages, Restored
MUSEUMS
See also
Art galleries and museums
Children's museums
Historic houses, sites, etc.
Military museums
Science museums
Slavery—Museums
Space museums
See also names of museums; also subhead Galleries and museums under names of cities
Museum news. See issues of Antiques & Collecting Hobbies beginning March 1985 through September 1988
Museums and planetariums. Sky and Telescope 78 Resource Guide:2-6 S '89
Architecture
See also
Art galleries and museums—Architecture
Canada's visionary new museum [Canadian Museum of Civilization] S. Rao. il World Press Review 36:61 Jl '89
Double feature [Museum of the Moving Image and American Museum of the Moving Image; cover story] D. Dietsch. il Architectural Record 177:110-21 My '89
A grand folly in Ottawa [Canadian Museum of Civilization; work of architect D. Cardinal] K. Andersen. il por Time 134:64 Jl 10 '89
How buildings remember [U.S. Holocaust Memorial Museum designed by J. I. Freed] H. Muschamp. The New Republic 201:27-33 Ag 28 '89
Putting on a happy face [Children's Museum of Indianapolis] M. Gaskie. il Architectural Record 177:78-81 Ag '89
Showcasing Canada [Canadian Museum of Civilization] P. Young. il Maclean's 102:38-9 Jl 10 '89
Gifts, legacies, etc.
A pack rat's tale [donating personal items to National Museum of American History] L. Stone. il Americana 17:19-21 My/Je '89
Management
See also
Museum directors
California
See also
California State Railroad Museum
San Francisco Bay Area (Calif.)—Galleries and museums
China
See also
Air Force Museum (China)
Colorado
See also
Tiny Town (Colo.)
France
See also
Paris (France)—Galleries and museums
Beyond the Louvre. G. Rowe. il House & Garden 161:62+ Jl '89
Germany (West)
See also
Hamburg (Germany)—Galleries and museums
Great Britain
See also
Bank of England Museum
British Museum
Eling Tide Mill

MUSEUMS—Great Britain—See also—*cont.*
  Fitzwilliam Museum
  Fort Nelson (Portsmouth, England)
  Museums Association (Great Britain)
  Patrick Collection (Birmingham, England)
  Royal Armouries (Great Britain)
Kenya
  See also
  National Museums of Kenya
Massachusetts
  See also
  Historic Deerfield, Inc.
Ohio
  See also
  Malabar Farm State Park (Lucas, Ohio)
Pennsylvania
  See also
  Philadelphia (Pa.)—Galleries and museums
Soviet Union
  See also
  Moscow (Soviet Union)—Galleries and museums
MUSEUMS AND CHILDREN
  See also
  Children's museums
MUSEUMS AND INDIANS (AMERICAN)
  'Dead Indians out, live Indians in' [museums return artifacts
    to Indian tribes] B. E. Johansen. il *The Progressive* 53:15-16
    D '89
  Returning bones of contention [Smithsonian agrees to return
    Indian remains and burial artifacts] J. Elson. il *Time*
    134:61 S 25 '89
  Skeletons in our museums' closets: Native Americans want
    their ancestors' bones back. D. J. Preston. il *Harper's*
    278:66-70+ F '89
  Skeletons in the attic [Indian remains in museums] C. Spotted
    Elk. il *Scholastic Update (Teachers' edition)* 121:25 My
    26 '89
  Smithsonian, Indian leaders call a truce. E. Marshall. il
    Science 245:1184-6 S 15 '89
  Tribal rights [handling of Canadian Indian artifacts] S. Jen-
    nings. il *Art News* 88:70-1 N '89
  Walter Echo-Hawk fights for his people's right to rest in
    peace—not in museums. M. Brower. il pors *People Weekly*
    32:42-4 S 4 '89
MUSEUMS AND NATIVE PEOPLES
  Museums [native peoples exhibits] E. Chappell. *The Nation*
    249:655-60 N 27 '89
MUSEUMS ASSOCIATION (GREAT BRITAIN)
  Sponsorship and scholarship. R. Burton. il *History Today*
    39:3-4 F '89
MUSEUMSINSEL HOMBROICH (NEUSS, GERMANY)
  Treasure island. J. Dornberg. il por *Art News* 88:93-4 My
    '89
MUSEVENI, YOWERI
                      about
  Starting over in Kampala [with interview] M. S. Serrill.
    il por *Time* 134:54+ N 6 '89
  Uganda: after the terror. R. Kapuściński. il por map *The
    New York Times Magazine* p38-41+ Mr 12 '89
MUSGRAVE, GERALD L.
  Health care cost limitation [address, November 17, 1988]
    Vital Speeches of the Day 55:273-6 F 15 '89
MUSHROOM SAUCES *See* Sauces
MUSHROOMS
  See also
  Cooking—Mushrooms
  New York Mycological Society
  Poisonous mushrooms
  Truffles
  Domesticated mushrooms [hydrazine content linked to cancer]
    B. T. Hunter. il *Consumers' Research Magazine* 72:8-9
    F '89
  On the road with mushrooms [RV camping] B. A. Branson.
    il *Travel Holiday* 171:22-5 F '89
  Wild mushrooms (I). B. T. Hunter. il *Consumers' Research
    Magazine* 72:8-9 Ja '89
MUSHROOMS, CANNED
Contamination
  Cloud over mushrooms. il *FDA Consumer* 23:39 S '89
MUSIC
  See also
  Art and music
  Bands (Music)
  Black music
  Blues music
  Computers—Musical use
  Concerts
  Conductors (Music)
  Copyright—Music
  Country music
  Dance music
  Dining music
  Folk music
  France—History—Revolution, 1789-1799—Music
  Gospel music
  Heavy metal music
  House music
  Improvisation (Music)

  Jazz music
  Melody
  Motion pictures—Music
  Opera
  Oratorio
  Orchestras
  Phonograph records
  Piano music
  Religious music
  Rock music
  Singing
  Tape recordings
  Edward Rothstein on music. E. Rothstein. See occasional
    issues of The New Republic beginning August 27, 1984
  Medley. K. Richardson. See issues of High Fidelity (New
    York, N.Y.) beginning November 1986 through July 1989
Acoustics and physics
  The yellow room. R. Hodges. il *Stereo Review* 54:172 D
    '89
Competitions
  See also
  Singing—Competitions
  Faces in the crowd [Van Cliburn International Piano Com-
    petition] J. Ardoin. il *National Review* 41:48+ Ag 18 '89
History
  Up from Beethoven [nineteenth century] P. Gossett. bibl
    f il *The New York Review of Books* 36:21-2+ O 26 '89
Modes
  See Musical intervals and scales
Performance
  See also
  Improvisation (Music)
Periodicals
  See also
  Musical America (Periodical)
Psychological aspects
  Getting a dose of musical medicine [excerpt from Healthy
    pleasures] R. E. Ornstein and D. S. Sobel. il *Prevention
    (Emmaus, Pa.)* 41:94-5+ Je '89
  Hearing pleasures [excerpt from The five senses] F. Gonzalez-
    Crussi. il *Health (New York, N.Y.)* 21:64-71 Mr '89
  The mind's ear [neuropsychology of music] D. C. Monk.
    bibl f *Design for Arts in Education* 90:17-29 Jl/Ag '89
  Twinkle, twinkle little star: it's more than just a nursery
    song. M. J. Howle. bibl f il *Children Today* 18:18-22
    Jl/Ag '89
  Women: if you like heavy metal, don't tell your date [effect
    of musical preference on perceptions of attractiveness;
    research by Dolf Zillmann and Azra Bhatia] E. Stark.
    il *Psychology Today* 23:14 N '89
Recording and reproducing
  See Sound—Recording and reproducing
Study and teaching
  See also
  Music camps
  Piano—Study and teaching
  Violin—Study and teaching
  Bearding the proverbial lion [use of television commercials
    to teach classical music] W. Greckel. *Design for Arts in
    Education* 90:43-7 Mr/Ap '89
  The mind's ear [neuropsychology of music] D. C. Monk.
    bibl f *Design for Arts in Education* 90:17-29 Jl/Ag '89
  Music lessons. J. Gorka. il *Parents* 64:92 Mr '89
  "Toward civilization" in music education [critique of report
    by the National Endowment for the Arts] P. R. Lehman.
    The Education Digest 54:46-9 My '89
Themes, motives, etc.
  See also
  Environment in music
  Rocks in music
  Weather in music
Theory
  See also
  Melody
  Musical intervals and scales
Africa
  Indestructible beat. C. Sugnet. il *Utne Reader* p12+ Jl/Ag
    '89
California
  See also
  Los Angeles (Calif.)—Music
  San Francisco Bay Area (Calif.)—Music
Illinois
  See also
  Chicago (Ill.)—Music
Italy
  See also
  Fascism and music
Louisiana
  See also
  New Orleans (La.)—Music
Morocco
  See also
  Jahjouka (Morocco)—Music
New Mexico
  See also
  Santa Fe (N.M.)—Music

MUSIC—*cont.*

New York (State)
See also
New York (N.Y.)—Music

Ohio
See also
Cleveland (Ohio)—Music

Ontario
See also
Toronto (Ont.)—Music

Texas
See also
Texas Music Collection

Wisconsin
See also
Milwaukee (Wis.)—Music

MUSIC, AFRICAN
See also
Phonograph records—African music

MUSIC, AMERICAN
See also
Compact discs—American music
Composers, American
Folk music, American
Jazz music
Phonograph records—American music
Texas Music Collection
What's new [American composers commissioned to write for Absolut Concerto] P. G. Davis. il *New York* 22:85 D 18 '89

MUSIC, BALINESE
Bali high, ballet low [Dancers and musicians of Bali at City Center] T. Tobias. il *New York* 22:145 Ap 24 '89
Reviews:
Dancers and musicians of Bali at City Center. D. Hering. il *Dance Magazine* 63:59-60 Ag '89

MUSIC, BAROQUE
See also
Compact discs—Baroque music

MUSIC, BLACK *See* Black music

MUSIC, BRAZILIAN
See also
Bossa nova
Compact discs—Brazilian music
Phonograph records—Brazilian music
Sambas
Crossing the equator. M. Margolis. il *Newsweek* 114:68-9 Jl 10 '89
The old seducer returns. E. M. Gomez. il *Time* 134:81-2 O 16 '89
Som da Gente: Town Hall/New York. S. Stein. il *Down Beat* 56:52 Je '89

MUSIC, CHURCH *See* Religious music

MUSIC, ELECTRONIC
See also
Biomuse system
Compact discs—Electronic music
Computers—Musical use
Musical instruments, Electronic
Television broadcasting—Electronic music
Music-on-hold adapter. S. Sokolowski. il *Radio-Electronics* 60:42-6 Ag '89

MUSIC, EXPERIMENTAL
See also
Compact discs—Experimental music

MUSIC, FRENCH
See also
Compact discs—French music

MUSIC, HAITIAN
See also
Phonograph records—Haitian music

MUSIC, INCIDENTAL
See also
Compact discs—Incidental music

MUSIC, INDIAN (EAST INDIAN)
See also
Phonograph records—Indian music (East Indian)

MUSIC, LATIN AMERICAN
See also
Phonograph records—Latin American music
Music. See issues of *Américas* beginning May/June 1984

MUSIC, MEXICAN
See also
Compact discs—Mexican music

MUSIC, MEXICAN AMERICAN
See also
Phonograph records—Mexican American music

MUSIC, MODERN
See also
Compact discs—Modern music
Composers tune out [serious contemporary music] D. Matthews. *World Press Review* 36:71 N '89
Fiddling in fascist Italy. H. Sachs. il *Opera News* 53:28-30 Mr 4 '89

MUSIC, MOROCCAN
Into the mystic [master musicians of Joujouka] R. Palmer. il *Rolling Stone* p100-3+ Mr 23 '89

MUSIC, POLISH
See also
Songs, Polish

MUSIC, RENAISSANCE
Glorious! [views of P. Phillips, leader of the vocal group Tallis Scholars] *The New Yorker* 65:33-5 D 18 '89
Musical events:
Tallis Scholars' program of Renaissance music. A. Porter. *The New Yorker* 65:70-1 D 25 '89

MUSIC, SOUTH AFRICAN
See also
Compact discs—South African music
Phonograph records—South African music

MUSIC, SPANISH
See also
Zarzuela

MUSIC AND CHILDREN
See also
Children's music
School orchestras
The gift of music. J. Gorka. il *Parents* 64:88+ Mr '89

MUSIC AND LITERATURE
See also
Music in literature

MUSIC AND STATE

Czechoslovakia
Czechoslovakia's most enduring band, The Plastic People, recycles its history-making rock. S. K. Reed. il *People Weekly* 31:116+ My 22 '89
Pulnoc. J. Morley. *The Nation* 248:748-50 My 29 '89
Sound Czech [Pulnoc] D. Fricke. il *Rolling Stone* p70 Jl 13-27 '89

Soviet Union
The door is open [Third International Festival of Music in Leningrad] J. W. Spiegelman. il *High Fidelity (New York, N.Y.)* 39:58-60 Ap '89
The night Stalin died. R. Dubinskiï. il *The New York Times Magazine* p42-3+ Mr 5 '89
The opera and the dictator [D. Shostakovich's Lady Macbeth of Mtsensk] R. Taruskin. il *The New Republic* 200:34-40 Mr 20 '89

MUSIC AND THE BLIND
Bluesman Jeff Healey, the blind gonzo guitarist who puts the musical punch in Road house. il por *People Weekly* 31:85 Je 12 '89

MUSIC AND THE HANDICAPPED
See also
Guitarists, Handicapped
Pianists, Handicapped

MUSIC BEFORE 1800 (MUSICAL GROUP)
Musical events:
Performance of A. Stradella's Santa Pelagia. A. Porter. *The New Yorker* 65:91-2 Mr 20 '89

MUSIC BOXES
See also
San Francisco Music Box Company

MUSIC CAMPS
Camps are for kids??? [jazz camps] D. Helland. il *Down Beat* 56:54-5 Mr '89

MUSIC CONDUCTORS *See* Conductors (Music)

MUSIC CONTESTS *See* Music—Competitions

MUSIC CORPORATION OF AMERICA *See* MCA Inc.

MUSIC CRITICS AND CRITICISM
See also
Jazz critics and criticism
Operetta reviews
Oratorio reviews
Rock critics and criticism

MUSIC DIRECTORS *See* Conductors (Music)

MUSIC EDUCATION *See* Music—Study and teaching

MUSIC FESTIVALS
Calendar. See issues of *Opera News*
Great American music festivals. P. Plawin. il *Changing Times* 43:68-72+ Je '89

International aspects
See also
International Youth and Music Festival
Voices of summer [opera festivals] *Opera News* 53:24-5+ My '89

Austria
Bregenz. H. Koegler. *Opera News* 54:68+ D 9 '89
Cool Noir [Vienna] A. Lange. il por *Down Beat* 56:60 Mr '89

British Columbia
Du Maurier Vancouver Jazz Festival. S. Yanow. il *Down Beat* 56:54 O '89

California
Monterey Jazz Festival. M. Handler. il *Down Beat* 56:52 Ja '89
Wine-and-song festivals at California and Washington wineries. il *Sunset (Central West edition)* 182:26-7+ Ap '89

Caribbean region
S.S. Norway jazz cruise. J. McDonough. il *Down Beat* 56:48+ F '89

Florida
I won't dance, don't ask me [New Music America Festival] S. Fried. il *Gentlemen's Quarterly* 59:165+ Mr '89

MUSIC FESTIVALS—Florida—cont.

The new age of jazz [Palm Beach County] S. Guy. il *Horizon (Tuscaloosa, Ala.)* 32:23-4 Ja/F '89

New Music America Festival. J. Woodard. il *Down Beat* 56:48 Mr '89

Reviews:

Florida choreographers present their work at the New Music America Festival in Miami. L. Horn. il *Dance Magazine* 63:70+ Ap '89

France

Aix-en-Provence [opera] E. Forbes. *Opera News* 54:66-7+ N '89

Musical events:

Purcell's opera The fairy queen at the Aix-en-Provence Festival. A. Porter. *The New Yorker* 65:86-7 Ag 14 '89

Germany (East)

Dresden. J. H. Sutcliffe. il *Opera News* 54:59 S '89

Germany (West)

Bayreuth [Ring directed by Harry Kupfer] J. H. Sutcliffe. il *Opera News* 53:40-1+ F 4 '89

Berlin Jazz Festival. A. Lange. il *Down Beat* 56:51-3 Mr '89

Reviews:

Ludwigsburg Festival performance of opera Einstein on the beach. H. Koegler. *Dance Magazine* 63:26+ Mr '89

Great Britain

Aldeburgh [opera] N. Goodwin. il *Opera News* 53:40 F 18 '89

Buxton. E. Forbes. *Opera News* 53:39 Ja 7 '89

Musical events:

Gluck's opera Alceste at the English Bach Festival. A. Porter. *The New Yorker* 65:85-6 Ag 14 '89

Wexford [opera] E. Forbes. *Opera News* 53:35-6 Ap 15 '89

Idaho

Lionel Hampton/Chevron Jazz Festival. P. De Barros. il por *Down Beat* 56:50 Je '89

Illinois

Chicago Jazz Festival. K. Whitehead. il *Down Beat* 56:57-8 D '89

Chicago: music mecca for '89. il *Ebony* 44:190+ My '89

Italy

Musical events:

Turin's Settembre Musica. A. Porter. *The New Yorker* 65:126-9 N 6 '89

Pesaro [Rossini Opera Festival] W. Weaver. il *Opera News* 54:64+ N '89

Umbria Jazz Festival. G. Santoro. il *Down Beat* 56:52-4 N '89

Louisiana

Jazz by the river [New Orleans Jazz and Heritage Festival] P. Nelson. il *Esquire* 111:44 Ap '89

A New Orleans heritage [Jazz & Heritage Festival] B. Sandmel. il *Down Beat* 56:59-60 My '89

The New Orleans Jazz & Heritage Festival. H. Mandel. il *Down Beat* 56:53-4 Ag '89

Martinique

Martinique's 8th World Crossroads of the Guitar. D. Gordon. il *Down Beat* 56:11-12 My '89

Maryland

Musical events:

Semele performed at the Handel Music Festival. A. Porter. *The New Yorker* 65:146-9 D 4 '89

Massachusetts

See also

Boston Early Music Festival and Exhibition

Jazz and Third Stream Festival: New England Conservatory/Boston. F. Bouchard. il *Down Beat* 56:50-1 Je '89

Matt Glaser's String Fling: Berklee College/Boston [fiddle festival] F. Bouchard. il por *Down Beat* 56:54-5 Ag '89

Netherlands

Northsea Jazz Festival. J. Levenson. il *Down Beat* 56:54-5 N '89

New York (State)

See also

Woodstock Festival, 1969

Glens Falls, N.Y. [Lake George Opera Festival] W. D. West. il *Opera News* 54:63 N '89

JVC Jazz Festival. M. Bourne. il *Down Beat* 56:50-1 O '89

Knitting Factory Festival. K. Whitehead. il *Down Beat* 56:51-2 O '89

New Music America returns to NYC. B. Milkowski. il *Down Beat* 56:13 O '89

New Music Fest marks tenth year; A double dose of Laurie Anderson. F. Goodman. il por *Rolling Stone* p37 N 30 '89

Ushered out [Mostly Mozart] P. G. Davis. il *New York* 22:65-6 Jl 31 '89

Ohio

Tri-C JazzFest '89: Cleveland/Ohio. C. Colombi. il *Down Beat* 56:52-3 Jl '89

Ontario

A choral cornucopia [Toronto festival The Joy of Singing] P. Young. il *Maclean's* 102:59-60 Je 5 '89

Pennsylvania

Central Penn Jazz Friends hold clinics. E. Kehler. il *Down Beat* 56:11 S '89

COTA Cats [high school jazz band featured yearly at Celebration of the Arts festival in the Poconos] J. Cunniff. il *Down Beat* 56:46 Je '89

Poland

Warsaw [opera during the Days of the Great Theatre festival] G. M. Loney. *Opera News* 54:42-3 Ag '89

Québec (Province)

Montreal Jazz Festival. J. Woodard. il *Down Beat* 56:52-4 O '89

Musique Actuelle. A. Lange. il *Down Beat* 56:53-4+ Ja '89

Scotland

See also

Edinburgh International Festival

South Carolina

See also

Spoleto Festival U.S.A.

Soviet Union

The door is open [Third International Festival of Music in Leningrad] J. W. Spiegelman. il *High Fidelity (New York, N.Y.)* 39:58-60 Ap '89

Tell Tchaikovsky the news [Moscow Music Peace Festival] E. Gundersen. il *Rolling Stone* p15-16 O 5 '89

Switzerland

Jammin' in Montreux. D. Brown. il *Black Enterprise* 19:80-2 Ap '89

Texas

Musical events:

M. Tippett's New Year and other productions of the British Opera Festival. A. Porter. *The New Yorker* 65:114-17 N 20 '89

United States

See Music festivals

Washington (State)

Wine-and-song festivals at California and Washington wineries. il *Sunset (Central West edition)* 182:26-7+ Ap '89

Western Europe

Report from Europe: festive dancing [opera ballets included in various festivals] S. Whyte. il *Dance Magazine* 63:50-3 D '89

MUSIC IN ADVERTISING

Bearding the proverbial lion [use of television commercials to teach classical music] W. Greckel. *Design for Arts in Education* 90:43-7 Mr/Ap '89

MUSIC IN ART

Exhibitions

Hannes Brunner: Vera Engelhorn. L. Holst. il *Art News* 88:208-9 Ap '89

MUSIC IN LITERATURE

Developing a specialty in fiction. E. Hunnicutt. *The Writer* 102:9-11+ Jl '89

MUSIC INDUSTRY

See also

AEI Music Network Inc.

MUSIC LOVERS' FOUNDATION *See* Bagby Foundation for the Musical Arts

MUSIC RECITALS

Amazin' Albert (I) [A. Bagby's Musical Mornings recital series from 1891 to 1941] F. Bowers. il pors *Opera News* 53:12-14+ F 4 '89

Amazin' Albert (II) [A. Bagby's Musical Mornings recital series from 1891 to 1941] F. Bowers. il por *Opera News* 53:32-7 F 18 '89

MUSIC RESEARCH *See* Musicology

MUSIC ROOMS

In the music room of Isaac Stern. il por *Esquire* 111:154-5+ Mr '89

Systems [the Duncans of Lincoln, Neb.] R. Day. il *Stereo Review* 54:112-13 N '89

The yellow room. R. Hodges. il *Stereo Review* 54:172 D '89

MUSIC SCHOOLS

See also

California Institute of the Arts

Manhattan School of Music

Mannes College of Music

Music camps

MUSIC SOCIETIES

See also

Da Camera Society

THE MUSIC TEACHER [film] *See* Motion picture reviews—Single works

MUSIC TEACHERS

See also

Singing teachers

MUSICAL ACCOMPANIMENT

Who's that man with Marilyn Horne? B. Jepson. il *The New York Times Magazine* p32-3+ Ap 16 '89

MUSICAL AMERICA (PERIODICAL)

Musical America's 1989 Musician of the Year: Leonard Bernstein. il pors *High Fidelity (New York, N.Y.)* 39:11 Ap '89

MUSICAL ARRANGEMENT

See also

Instrumentation and orchestration

MUSICAL ARRANGEMENT—*cont.*
Big band transcription project begins [Jazz Masterworks Editions] P. Fuller. il *Down Beat* 56:11 Ap '89
Chick Corea's "Folk song"—an exercise in arranging. A. Laverne. il *Down Beat* 56:56-7 Ag '89
MUSICAL COMEDIES, REVUES, ETC. *See* Musicals, revues, etc.
MUSICAL INSTRUMENT DIGITAL INTERFACE *See* MIDI (Musical instrument digital interface)
MUSICAL INSTRUMENTS
    See also
    Keyboard instruments
    Stringed instruments
    See also names of musical instruments
Junkyard music [homemade instruments created by E. Nagler] il *por National Geographic World* 171:12-14 N '89
Maker [B. Hume's folk instruments] *The New Yorker* 65:28-9 Jl 17 '89
Pro shop. See issues of Down Beat
MUSICAL INSTRUMENTS, ELECTRONIC
    See also
    Drum
    Kazoo
    Keyboard instruments
    MIDI (Musical instrument digital interface)
    Saxophone
    Videoharp
MIDI equipment. M. M. Rosenthal. il *Radio-Electronics* 60:34-41 Ag '89
Musical talent. F. Vizard. il *Popular Mechanics* 166:116-17 O '89
Exhibitions
Creative synthesizer technique II—in MIDI Wonderland [West L.A. Music's Keyboard and MIDI Show] A. Holzman. il *Down Beat* 56:59-60 F '89
MUSICAL INSTRUMENTS, MECHANICAL
    See also
    Jukeboxes
    Player piano
MUSICAL INSTRUMENTS INDUSTRY
    See also
    National Association of Music Merchants
Marketing
    See also
    Manny's Musical Instruments & Accessories Inc.
Japan
    See also
    Yamaha International Corp.
MUSICAL INTERVALS AND SCALES
John Scofield's solo on "Best western"—Phrygian voicings. R. Peckham. il *Down Beat* 56:66-7 D '89
MUSICAL PITCH
A matter of imperfect pitch [campaign to lower operatic pitch] W. F. Allman. il *U.S. News & World Report* 106:55-6 Je 26 '89
Musical events [campaign to lower operatic pitch] A. Porter. il *The New Yorker* 65:95-6 My 1 '89
MUSICAL PRODIGIES *See* Children as musicians
MUSICALS, REVUES, ETC.
    See also
    Compact discs—Musicals, revues, etc.
    Floor shows
    Phonograph records—Musicals, revues, etc.
Hopeful highlights [1989-90 Broadway season] K. Grubb. il *Dance Magazine* 63:54-5 O '89
Nearly remarkable [rock singer L. Reed gives concert in Broadway's St. James Theatre, famous for hit musicals] *The New Yorker* 65:29-30 My 22 '89
Auditions
    See Theater—Auditions
Production and direction
Dance man [Jerome Robbins' Broadway] V. Muse. il *Life* 12:122-4+ Mr '89
Drood. M. LaRue. il *Theatre Crafts* 23:52-5+ Ap '89
Jerome Robbins' Broadway. M. Sommers. il *Theatre Crafts* 23:56-63 Ag/S '89
Legs Diamond comes to Broadway: give 'em the old razzle-dazzle [cover story] K. Grubb. il pors *Dance Magazine* 63:40-4 Ja '89
The magic musicals [Les misérables and Phantom of the Opera in Toronto; cover story; special section; with editorial comment by Kevin Doyle] il *Maclean's* 102:2, 40-6+ Mr 27 '89
The 'middlebrow' maestro of megahits [producer C. Mackintosh] E. Behr. il por *Newsweek* 114:68-9 O 2 '89
The Phantom strikes [Phantom of the Opera opens in Toronto] P. Young. il *Maclean's* 102:62-3 O 2 '89
Psychological aspects
After happily ever after [work of S. Sondheim] A. Kohn. il *Psychology Today* 23:66-70 Ja/F '89
Reviews
    See also
    Rock opera reviews
Warmed over and not so hot [Broadway musicals] W. A. Henry. il *Time* 134:87 N 27 '89
Single works
80 days
    Theatre Crafts il 23:56-7+ Ap '89. L. Stevens

Annie 2: Miss Hannigan's revenge
    Life il 12:42-9 N '89. C. Dowling
Black and blue
    America 160:153+ F 18 '89. G. G. Seibert
    Dance Magazine 63:69-70 Je '89. O. Stuart
    Ebony il 44:124-6+ S '89
    Jet il 76:52-3 Ap 10 '89
    Jet il 76:52 My 22 '89
    The Nation 248:281-2 F 27 '89. T. M. Disch
    The New Leader 72:22-3 Mr 6 '89. L. A. Jacobs
    New York il 22:37-40 Ja 2 '89. W. Goodman
    New York il 22:92 F 6 '89. J. Simon
    The New Yorker 64:73-4 F 6 '89. A. Croce
    Time il 133:80 F 6 '89. W. A. Henry
    Vogue il 179:192-3 Ja '89. J. Sherman
Blood brothers
    America 161:145 S 9-16 '89. G. G. Seibert
Buzzsaw Berkeley
    New York 22:56-7 Ag 28 '89. J. Simon
Charlotte's web
    Opera News il 54:38-9 Jl '89. S. Modi
City of Angels
    The New Yorker 65:77 D 25 '89. E. Oliver
    Time il 134:92 D 25 '89. W. A. Henry
Closer than ever
    The New Yorker 65:106 N 13 '89. E. Oliver
Dangerous games
    The Nation 249:611-12 N 20 '89. T. M. Disch
    The New Republic 201:30-1 N 20 '89. R. Brustein
    New York 22:101-2 O 30 '89. J. Simon
Drood
    Theatre Crafts il 23:52-5+ Ap '89. M. LaRue
"Durante" the musical comedy
    Maclean's il 102:55 S 25 '89. H. Quinn
Gala
    Maclean's il 102:60-1 My 15 '89. C. Bell
Grand Hotel
    America 161:453 D 16 '89. T. P. O'Malley
    Harper's Bazaar il 122:180+ O '89. M. Matousek
    New York il 22:99 N 27 '89. J. Simon
    The New Yorker 65:101 N 27 '89. E. Oliver
    Newsweek il 114:79+ D 4 '89. L. Shapiro
Gypsy
    The New Yorker 65:142-3 D 4 '89. M. Kramer
    People Weekly il 32:88-9 Jl 3 '89
Health, the musical
    Maclean's il 102:58-9 Mr 13 '89. J. Bemrose
I do, I do
    People Weekly il 31:89-90 My 1 '89. P. Freeman
In a pig's valise
    New York il 22:138 F 27 '89. J. Simon
    The New Yorker 65:66-7 F 27 '89. M. Kramer
In circles
    The Nation 248:714-15 My 22 '89. T. M. Disch
Jerome Robbins' Broadway
    America 160:330 Ap 8 '89. G. G. Seibert
    Dance Magazine il 63:44-51 Ap '89. D. Hering
    Dance Magazine 63:73-5 Je '89. N. V. Dalva
    Life il pors 12:122-4+ Mr '89. V. Muse
    The Nation 248:713-15 My 22 '89. T. M. Disch
    The New Leader 72:22 Ap 3-17 '89. L. A. Jacobs
    The New Republic 200:28-9 Ap 3 '89. R. Brustein
    New York il 22:72+ Mr 13 '89. J. Simon
    The New Yorker 65:76-7 Mr 13 '89. A. Croce
    Newsweek il por 113:52-4 Mr 6 '89. J. Kroll
    Theatre Crafts il 23:56-63 Ag/S '89. M. Sommers
    Time il por 133:78-9+ Mr 6 '89. R. Corliss
    Vogue il 179:262-3 Mr '89. D. Daniel
Johnny Johnson
    The New Yorker 65:98 O 23 '89. A. Porter
Legs Diamond
    Dance Magazine il 63:40-4 Ja '89. K. Grubb
    New York il 22:56-7 Ja 9 '89. J. Simon
    The New Yorker 64:82-3 Ja 9 '89. M. Kramer
    Time il 133:67 Ja 9 '89. W. A. Henry
Mama I want to sing
    Black Enterprise il 20:66-8+ Ag '89. J. Torrence-Thompson
Meet me in St. Louis
    New York 22:130 N 13 '89. J. Simon
    The New Yorker 65:110-11 N 20 '89. M. Kramer
Les misérables
    Maclean's il 102:40-6+ Mr 27 '89
Miss Saigon
    Newsweek il 114:68-9 O 2 '89. J. Kroll
    Time il 134:94 O 2 '89. W. A. Henry
The pajama game
    New York il 22:66 Mr 27 '89. J. Simon
    The New Yorker 65:87 Mr 20 '89. E. Oliver
The Phantom of the Opera
    Maclean's il 102:11 F 6 '89. D. Francis
    Maclean's il 102:40-4 Mr 27 '89. P. Young
    Maclean's il por 102:62-4 O 2 '89
Prince of Central Park
    The New Yorker 65:111-12 N 20 '89. M. Kramer
Privates on parade
    Commonweal 116:567 O 20 '89. G. C. Weales
    The Nation 249:363-4 O 2 '89. T. M. Disch

MUSICALS, REVUES, ETC. — Reviews — Single works —
Privates on parade—*cont.*
> *New York* il 22:62+ S 4 '89. J. Simon
> *The New Yorker* 65:91 S 4 '89. E. Oliver

Shenandoah
> *New York* il 22:134-5 Ag 21 '89. J. Simon

Show boat
> *The New Yorker* 65:79-94 Jl 3 '89. E. Mordden

Showing off
> *New York* 22:57 Je 26 '89. J. Simon

Songs of paradise
> *The Nation* 248:463 Ap 3 '89. T. M. Disch

Sophisticated ladies
> *Theatre Crafts* il 23:36-8+ My '89. M. Sommers

Starmites
> *The Nation* 248:862-3 Je 19 '89. T. M. Disch
> *New York* il 22:88 My 8 '89. J. Simon

Sweeney Todd
> *Commonweal* 116:566-7 O 20 '89. G. C. Weales
> *New York* il 22:82+ O 2 '89. J. Simon
> *Time* il 134:76 S 25 '89. W. A. Henry

The Taffetas
> *People Weekly* il 31:133 Ap 3 '89

The threepenny opera
> *America* 161:382 N 25 '89. T. P. O'Malley
> *Gentlemen's Quarterly* il 59:280-3+ D '89. J. Greenfield
> *Harper's Bazaar* il 122:180-1+ O '89. C. Worthington
> *Mother Jones* il 14:52-3 N '89. J. Istel
> *The Nation* 249:767-8 D 18 '89. T. M. Disch
> *National Review* il 41:53-4 N 24 '89. R. Grenier
> *The New Republic* 201:29-30 D 11 '89. R. Brustein
> *New York* il 22:126+ N 20 '89. J. Simon
> *New York* il 22:50-1 S 11 '89. R. D. Story
> *The New Yorker* 65:112-13 N 20 '89. M. Kramer
> *People Weekly* il 32:77 N 20 '89
> *Vogue* il 179:424-5 N '89. R. Short

Up against it
> *The New Yorker* 65:108+ D 18 '89. M. Kramer

Welcome to the club
> *New York* il 22:140 Ap 24 '89. J. Simon
> *The New Yorker* 65:82-3 Ap 24 '89. M. Kramer

The Wizard of Oz live!
> *People Weekly* il 31:73-4 My 8 '89. P. Freeman

Wonderful town
> *The Nation* 249:611 N 20 '89. T. M. Disch

Writing
Andy Razaf, the word man of Broadway. M. Evans. il pors
American Visions 4:32-6 O '89

MUSICFEST U.S.A. AWARDS
Musicfest U.S.A. participants strive for success. D. Helland.
il *Down Beat* 56:11 Ja '89
Musicfest U.S.A. swings with education: '89 national finals.
J. Walker. il *Down Beat* 56:28-34 Jl '89

MUSICIANS
See also
> Aged as musicians
> Alcohol and musicians
> Black musicians
> Children as musicians
> Conductors (Music)
> Drugs and musicians
> Jazz musicians
> Pianists
> Rock musicians
> Street music and musicians
> Strikes—Musicians
> Violinists
> Women musicians

Religious life
The practical life of the church musician [cover story] P.
Westermeyer. il *The Christian Century* 106:812-14 S 13-20
'89

MUSICIANS, AMATEUR
Oboe to gamelan . . . want to join a music group? [San
Francisco Bay Area] il *Sunset (Central West edition)* 182:50
F '89

MUSICOLOGY
See also
> Center for Black Music Research
Oft-told tales [search for definitive version of Offenbach's
opera] D. P. Stearns. il *Opera News* 54:14-15+ D 23 '89
Viewpoint. P. J. Smith. *Opera News* 54:4 S '89

MUSK OXEN
Return of the mighty muskox. P. C. Lent. il *Natural History*
p50-9 N '89

MUSKELLUNGE FISHING
The ultimate excuse [Ontario] K. Schultz. il *Field & Stream*
94:30+ Ag '89

Anecdotes, facetiae, satire, etc.
Dating the devil fish. J. M. Vance. il *Outdoor Life* 184:70-1+
Ag '89

MUSKIE, STEPHEN O.
about
Bees, bears, barrens. L. Line. il por *Audubon* 91:6 Jl '89
MUSKIE FISHING *See* Muskellunge fishing
MUSLIM BROTHERHOOD (EGYPT)
A benign Brotherhood? J. Pittaway. il *The Atlantic* 263:25-7+
Ja '89

MUSLIM PAINTING *See* Painting, Islamic
MUSLIM WOMEN
See also
> Women—Afghanistan
France and Islam: veil of tears. il *Newsweek* 114:54 N 6
'89
Going to Cyprus. J. Webb. il pors *Seventeen* 48:166+ Mr
'89
Islam and family planning. M. Mahran. il *World Health*
p22-3 Ap '89
MUSLIMS
See also
> Islam
> Pilgrimages to Mecca
> Rushdie, Salman—Satanic verses case
Middling through. M. Ispahani. *The New Republic* 201:18+
Jl 3 '89

Converts to Christianity
See Converts from Islam
Afghanistan
Afghan follow-through. *National Review* 41:12 My 19 '89
Afghan sitzkrieg. R. Sikorski. il *National Review* 41:37-8
Ap 21 '89
Afghanistan [following Soviet withdrawal; special section]
il *World Press Review* 36:22-5 Ap '89
Afghanistan: "back to feudalism". B. R. Rubin. bibl f *Current
History* 88:421-4+ D '89
Afghanistan: Soviet occupation and withdrawal. il maps
Department of State Bulletin 89:72-90 Mr '89
Afghanistan's uncertain fate. B. R. Rubin. il *The Nation*
248:264-7+ F 27 '89
After the Soviets go. E. MacFarquhar. il map *U.S. News
& World Report* 106:32-4+ F 13 '89
Annals of the freedom fighters [reporting on the mujahadeen]
A. Cockburn. *The Nation* 248:803 Je 12 '89
Another chance for Afghanistan. *National Review* 41:15+ N
10 '89
Bizarre bazaar. P. J. O'Rourke. il *Rolling Stone* p87-8+ Ap
20 '89
A city under siege [Kabul] M. Nemeth. il *Maclean's* 102:22
F 6 '89
A city under siege [Kabul] B. Levin. il *Maclean's* 102:28
F 27 '89
'The end could come any day'. H. Anderson. il map *Newsweek*
113:30-1 F 6 '89
An end game in Afghanistan: the rebel strategy: first Jalalabad,
then Kabul. H. Anderson. il map *Newsweek* 113:38 Mr
27 '89
Fighting for Jalalabad. M. Strmecki. il *The American Spectator*
22:30-2 Je '89
The fragmentation of Afghanistan. B. R. Rubin. *Foreign
Affairs* 68:150-68 Wint '89/'90
Inside a frightened city [Kabul] M. Liu. il *Newsweek* 113:36+
Mr 13 '89
Leaving the quagmire. H. Anderson. il map *Newsweek* 113:32-4
F 13 '89
Legacy of a bloody war. A. Wilson-Smith. il *Maclean's*
102:18-20 F 20 '89
Lessons of Afghanistan. R. Watson. il *Newsweek* 113:26-7
F 20 '89
Liberty, fraternity—disunity [relations between rival
mujahedin factions] il *Time* 134:25 Jl 31 '89
Misplaced optimism [mujahedin gaining little ground] J. Elson.
il *Time* 133:40-1 My 15 '89
Rebels with too many causes: who's who behind the
mujahedin's quarreling factions. W. R. Doerner. il *Time*
133:39 F 27 '89
Rising fear in Kabul. A. Wilson-Smith. il *Maclean's* 102:22-3
F 13 '89
The scent of victory divides Afghan rebels. E. Girardet.
il *U.S. News & World Report* 106:34 F 27 '89
Searching for Soviet MIAs. S. Le Vine. il *Newsweek* 114:28
Jl 10 '89
A Soviet bluff on Afghanistan? F. Coleman. il *Newsweek*
113:38 Ja 23 '89
Stalemate at Jalalabad. E. Ahmad. il *The Nation* 249:384-7
O 9 '89
State of emergency. M. Liu. il *Newsweek* 113:43 F 27 '89
Still-life by shellfire. R. Sikorski. il *National Review* 41:22-3
Ap 7 '89
A surprise turnaround in Afghanistan. map *Newsweek* 114:36
Jl 17 '89
Target: Kabul. D. Lorch. il pors map *The New York Times
Magazine* p32-5+ F 12 '89
A U.S. victory begins to unravel [failure of mujahedin to
oust Communist regime] L. Lief. il *U.S. News & World
Report* 107:38 Jl 24 '89
Victors' justice: danger ahead. W. F. Buckley. *National Review*
41:54 Mr 24 '89
Waiting for the end. E. W. Desmond. il *Time* 133:38-40
F 6 '89
What will follow the pullout? S. R. Galster. il *The Nation*
248:9-10+ Ja 2 '89
When Kabul falls [letter to mujahedin commander] R. Sikor-
ski. *National Review* 41:20 F 24 '89
Why are we in Afghanistan? R. Wright. *The New Republic*
201:23-5 S 4 '89

MUSLIMS—Afghanistan—*cont.*
Without a look back: as the Soviets leave, rebels prepare to strike. J. Smolowe. il *Time* 133:42-3 F 20 '89
Belgium
Murder in the mosque [A. Al Ahdal murdered in Brussels] *Newsweek* 113:41 Ap 10 '89
Egypt
See also
Muslim Brotherhood (Egypt)
Islam and democracy in Egypt. R. Bianchi. bibl f *Current History* 88:93-5+ F '89
France
France and Islam: veil of tears. il *Newsweek* 114:54 N 6 '89
Islam in England and France. J. Valls-Russell. il *The New Leader* 72:5-6 Ag 7-21 '89
Unsettled immigrants. T. J. Abercrombie. il *National Geographic* 176:120-9 Jl '89
Great Britain
Islam in England and France. J. Valls-Russell. il *The New Leader* 72:5-6 Ag 7-21 '89
Iran
See also
Iranian seizure of United States embassy, 1979-1981
Islamic wasteland. B. Crozier. il *National Review* 41:17 Mr 24 '89
Where God sets prices. F. Ajami. il *U.S. News & World Report* 106:47 F 20 '89
Why the Ayatollah is whipping up a new wave of fanaticism. S. Carter and others. il *Business Week* p47 Mr 6 '89
Iraq
Islam in Syria and Iraq. F. Chipaux. *World Press Review* 36:32 Jl '89
Jordan
Jordan votes the Islamic ticket. S. Hubbell. il *The Nation* 249:786+ D 25 '89
Lebanon
See also
Lebanon hostage cases, 1984-
An American soldier's death becomes a pawn in a terrorist power struggle [conflicting accounts of W. R. Higgins' death within Hezbollah factions] D. Halevy and N. C. Livingstone. il *U.S. News & World Report* 107:21 O 23 '89
The deadly Party of God [Hizbollah] H. Jensen. il *Maclean's* 102:28 Ag 14 '89
Hezbollah—sound and futile fury [cover story] K. Seigneurie and T. Nassar. il *The Nation* 249:225+ S 4-11 '89
Inside the mind of a movement [Hezbollah] F. Ajami. il *U.S. News & World Report* 107:28 Ag 14 '89
Middle East
See also
Beirut airplane hijacking, 1985
Health education through religion. A. Aly. il *World Health* p27-8 Jl '89
The march of 'Islamism' [special section] *World Press Review* 36:30-2+ Jl '89
Oman
Oman's benevolent Ibadism. J.-P. Péroncel-Hugoz. *World Press Review* 36:34 Jl '89
Soviet Union
Central Asia: the rise of the Moslems. D. Doder. il map *U.S. News & World Report* 106:48+ Ap 3 '89
Gorbachev's crisis of faith [text of letter] R. Khomeini. *Harper's* 278:21-2 Ap '89
Islam regains its voice. R. N. Ostling. il *Time* 133:98-9 Ap 10 '89
Syria
Islam in Syria and Iraq. F. Chipaux. *World Press Review* 36:32 Jl '89
Turkey
Secular Turkey. M. Farrère. *World Press Review* 36:34 Jl '89
Turkey's identity problem. N. Gelb. il *The New Leader* 72:9-10 My 1 '89
MUSLIMS, BLACK *See* Black Muslims
MUSLIMS AND CHRISTIANS *See* Christianity and other religions
MUSLIMS AND JEWS *See* Islam and Judaism
MUSSELMAN, BILL
about
Wild Bill. N. Karlen. il por *Gentlemen's Quarterly* 59:306-11+ D '89
MUSSELS
See also
Ecomar (Firm)
Zebra mussels
Muscle
See Muscle
MUSSER, THARON
about
Tharon Musser [cover story] M. Sommers. il por *Theatre Crafts* 23:42-9+ O '89
MUSSOLINI, ALESSANDRA
about
Alessandra Mussolini, Benito's granddaughter, acts to erase the shame of the family name. T. Allis. il pors *People Weekly* 32:119-20 S 18 '89

MUSTACHES
Anecdotes, facetiae, satire, etc.
The mustache—man's last bastion of individuality. G. F. Kreyche. il *USA Today (Periodical)* 118:98 S '89
MUSTANG RANCH (NEV.: BROTHEL)
Prostitution goes public [prospectus for public stock offering] *Harper's* 278:21-2 My '89
MUSTANGS *See* Wild horses
MUSTO, MICHAEL, 1955-
Working titles. il *Harper's Bazaar* 122:148-51+ N '89
MUTAGENIC SUBSTANCES
See also
Cancer—Causes
MUTATION
See also
Chromosome abnormalities
Transposons
Tumor suppressor genes
Cancer roadblock on cholesterol pathway [research by William R. Schafer] R. Cowen. *Science News* 136:70-1 Jl 29 '89
Cutting away DNA the mitochondrial way [work of Douglas C. Wallace] P. Young. *Science News* 136:85 Ag 5 '89
Detecting mutations in human genes [use of HPRT gene as an indicator] J. L. Marx. il *Science* 243:737-8 F 10 '89
Direct Brønsted analysis of the restoration of activity to a mutant enzyme by exogenous amines. M. D. Toney and J. F. Kirsch. bibl f il *Science* 243:1485-8 Mr 17 '89
Enhanced activity and altered specificity of phospholipase A_2 by deletion of a surface loop. O. P. Kuipers and others. bibl f il *Science* 244:82-5 Ap 7 '89
A general method for site-specific incorporation of unnatural amino acids into proteins. C. J. Noren and others. bibl f il *Science* 244:182-8 Ap 14 '89
Genetic and pharmacological suppression of oncogenic mutations in *RAS* genes of yeast and humans. W. R. Schafer and others. bibl f il *Science* 245:379-85 Jl 28 '89
Germ-line transmission of a *c-abl* mutation produced by targeted gene disruption in ES cells [cover story] P. L. Schwartzberg and others. bibl f il *Science* 246:799-803 N 10 '89
Hidden thermodynamics of mutant proteins: a molecular dynamics analysis. J. Gao and others. bibl f il *Science* 244:1069-72 Je 2 '89
High-resolution epitope mapping of hGH-receptor interactions by alanine-scanning mutagenesis. B. C. Cunningham and J. A. Wells. bibl f il *Science* 244:1081-5 Je 2 '89
Human diabetes associated with a deletion of the tyrosine kinase domain of the insulin receptor. M. Taira and others. bibl f il *Science* 245:63-6 Jl 7 '89
Human diabetes associated with a mutation in the tyrosine kinase domain of the insulin receptor. M. Odawara and others. bibl f il *Science* 245:66-8 Jl 7 '89
Many gene changes found in cancer [stepwise accumulation of mutations affecting both oncogenes and suppressor genes] J. L. Marx. bibl il *Science* 246:1386-8 D 15 '89
The molecular basis of muscular dystrophy in the *mdx* mouse: a point mutation. P. Sicinski and others. bibl f il *Science* 244:1578-80 Je 30 '89
Mom's legacy [Leber's hereditary optic neuropathy linked to faulty mitochondrial genes; research by Douglas Wallace] J. Spencer. il *American Health* 8:22+ Mr '89
Mutant potassium channels with altered binding of charybdotoxin, a pore-blocking peptide inhibitor. R. MacKinnon and C. Miller. bibl f il *Science* 245:1382-5 S 22 '89
Mutation revealed for adult Tay-Sachs [work of Ruth Navon and Richard L. Proia] I. Wickelgren. *Science News* 135:167 Mr 18 '89
The mutations in Ashkenazi Jews with adult G_{M2} gangliosidosis, the adult form of Tay-Sachs disease. R. Navon and R. L. Proia. bibl f il *Science* 243:1471-4 Mr 17 '89
New insights into Gaucher's tricky course [research by Ari Zimran] R. Weiss. *Science News* 136:135 Ag 26 '89
Point mutational inactivation of the retinoblastoma antioncogene. J. M. Horowitz and others. bibl f il *Science* 243:937-40 F 17 '89
Policy forum:
Are radiation-induced effects hormetic? [low-dose ionizing radiation] S. Wolff. bibl f *Science* 245:575+ Ag 11 '89
On radiation, paradigms, and hormesis [low-dose ionizing radiation] L. A. Sagan. bibl f *Science* 245:574+ Ag 11 '89
Receptor and antibody epitopes in human growth hormone identified by homolog-scanning mutagenesis. B. C. Cunningham and others. bibl f il *Science* 243:1330-6 Mr 10 '89
The role of somatic hypermutation in the generation of antibody diversity. D. L. French and others. bibl f il *Science* 244:1152-7 Je 9 '89
Successful sex [favorable mutation in a sexual population] T. Beardsley. *Scientific American* 261:18 Ag '89
Bacteria
Generation of a catalytic antibody by site-directed mutagenesis. E. Baldwin and P. G. Schultz. bibl f il *Science* 245:1104-7 S 8 '89

MUTATION—Bacteria—*cont.*

Hungry to evolve? [controversy over John Cairns' work with Escherichia coli mutations] J. P. Rennie. *Scientific American* 261:20+ N '89

Structural basis for misaminoacylation by mutant E. coli glutaminyl-tRNA synthetase enzymes. J. J. Perona and others. bibl f il *Science* 246:1152-4 D 1 '89

Triggering of allostery in an enzyme by a point mutation: ornithine transcarbamoylase. L. C. Kuo and others. bibl f il *Science* 245:522-4 Ag 4 '89

Fungi

Clathrin: a role in the intracellular retention of a Golgi membrane protein [yeast] G. S. Payne and R. Schekman. bibl f il *Science* 245:1358-65 S 22 '89

Disruption of the yeast *N*-myristoyl transferase gene causes recessive lethality. R. J. Duronio and others. bibl f il *Science* 243:796-800 F 10 '89

Repeat-induced G-C to A-T mutations in Neurospora. E. B. Cambareri and others. bibl f il *Science* 244:1571-5 Je 30 '89

Insects

Reciprocal effects of hyper- and hypoactivity mutations in the Drosophila pattern gene *torso*. T. R. Strecker and others. bibl f il *Science* 243:1062-6 F 24 '89

Nematodes

Mutations in a protein kinase C homolog confer phorbol ester resistance on Caenorhabditis elegans. Y. Tabuse and others. bibl f il *Science* 243:1713-16 Mr 31 '89

Plants

The Diageotropica mutant of tomato lacks high specific activity auxin binding sites. G. R. Hicks and others. bibl f il *Science* 245:52-4 Jl 7 '89

A dwarf mutant of Arabidopsis generated by T-DNA insertion mutagenesis [cover story] K. A. Feldmann and others. bibl f il *Science* 243:1351-4 Mr 10 '89

Viruses

The fickle virus [HIV mutations] M. Patlak. il *Discover* 10:24+ F '89

Multiple mutations in HIV-1 reverse transcriptase confer high-level resistance to zidovudine (AZT). B. A. Larder and S. D. Kemp. bibl f il *Science* 246:1155-8 D 1 '89

MUTI, RICCARDO

about

Beethoven's nine, times two. E. Salzman. il pors *Stereo Review* 54:128 Ja '89

MUTILATION OF CATTLE See Cattle—Mutilation

MUTINY

See also

Bounty Mutiny, 1789

MUTISM

See also

Elective mutism

MUTO, SUSAN

Integrating faith and functionality [address, January 18, 1989] *Vital Speeches of the Day* 55:370-1 Ap 1 '89

MUTTER, ANNE-SOPHIE, 1963-

about

Anne-Sophie Mutter. H. Kupferberg. il pors *Stereo Review* 54:63-5 Jl '89

MUTTON SNAPPERS See Snappers

MUTTONTOWN (N.Y.)

Historic houses, sites, etc.

Muttontown's King [Knollwood mansion home to Albania's King Zog from 1951 to 1955] *The New Yorker* 65:33-4 S 11 '89

MUTUAL FUND MANAGERS See Investment advisers

MUTUAL FUNDS See Investment trusts

MUTUAL LIFE INSURANCE CO. OF NEW YORK

A copy writer's journey into the age of PCs [J. Lane, manager of electronic publishing] M. Piturro. il por *Personal Computing* 13:146-7 O '89

MUTUAL OF NEW YORK-MONY See Mutual Life Insurance Co. of New York

MUTUALISM (BIOLOGY) See Symbiosis

MUUL, ILLAR

'Use them or lose them'. il *The Courier (Unesco)* 42:29-33 Ja '89

MUWAKKIL, SALIM

New spirit infuses black America. il *Utne Reader* p93-4 S/O '89

MUYBRIDGE, EADWEARD, 1830-1904

about

Time and motion. il pors *American History Illustrated* 24:62-3 S/O '89

MUZZLE-LOADING RIFLES See Rifles

MUZZY, ROB

about

Yamaha's Daytona battle plan. C. Everitt. il por *Cycle* 40:75-7 My '89

MX (MISSILE) See Guided missiles

MX (MISSILE) BASING SYSTEM See Guided missile bases

MY BIG LAND [drama] See Galich, Aleksandr, 1919-1977

MY LAI MASSACRE, 1968

William Calley. C. Unger. il pors *People Weekly* 32:152-8 N 20 '89

MY LEFT FOOT [film] See Motion picture reviews—Single works

MY STEPMOTHER IS AN ALIEN [film] See Motion picture reviews—Single works

MY TWO DADS [television program] See Television program reviews—Single works

MYBASE (DATABASE MANAGEMENT SYSTEM) See Database management

MYCOBACTERIAL DISEASES

See also

Leprosy

Tuberculosis

MYCOBACTERIUM

Activation of γδ T cells in the primary immune response to Mycobacterium tuberculosis. E. M. Janis and others. bibl f il *Science* 244:713-16 My 12 '89

MYCOGEN CORP.

Thank you, Jeremy Rifkin. M. Fritz. il *Forbes* 144:268-9 O 16 '89

MYCOPLASMAS

An AIDS-associated microbe unmasked [Mycoplasma incognita; research by Shyh-Ching Lo] A. McKenzie. *Science News* 136:356 D 2 '89

MYCOSES

See also

Antifungal agents

MYCOTOXINS

Mycotoxins: a significant public health problem. B. T. Hunter. il *Consumers' Research Magazine* 72:8-9 Je '89

Rotting potatoes harbor harmful toxins [trichothecene toxins; research by Anne E. Desjardins and Ronald D. Plattner] *Science News* 135:238 Ap 15 '89

MYDANS, CARL

"The best job in the world". il por *Time* 134 Special Issue:49-50 Fall '89

MYDANS, SETH

An Asian tale: young girls, red roses. il *The New York Times Magazine* p44-7+ Ap 2 '89

MYELOPEROXIDASE

The myeloperoxidase gene in acute promyelocytic leukemia [discussion of May 6, 1988 article, Translocation and rearrangement of myeloperoxidase gene in acute promyelocytic leukemia] S. C. Weil and others. il *Science* 244:823-6 My 19 '89

MYERS, ALAN

(tr) See Zinik, Zinoviĭ. Hooks

MYERS, AMINA CLAUDINE

about

Amina Claudine Myers: invitation to the song. S. Stein. por *Down Beat* 56:27-8 Mr '89

MYERS, DAVID W.

How much home can you afford? [cover story] il *Consumers' Research Magazine* 72:11-15 F '89

MYERS, HANK

about

Captain Tenacious. W. Garvey. il por *Flying* 116:10+ My '89

MYERS, J. P.

Making sense of sexual nonsense. il *Audubon* 91:40-5 Jl '89

MYERS, JOAN ROHR

Blue plates [poem] *Commonweal* 116:348 Je 2 '89

Interiors [poem] *Commonweal* 116:118 F 24 '89

Offertory [poem] *Commonweal* 116:118 F 24 '89

What we wear [poem] *Commonweal* 116:118 F 24 '89

MYERS, JULIAN

Ghost story. il *Flying* 116:70-2+ F '89

MYERS, LARRY

The joy of color printing. il *Astronomy* 17:86-91 N '89

Working against the grain of fast films. il *Astronomy* 17:88-91 F '89

MYERS, MARN G.

Families on welfare foster children with special needs. il *Children Today* 18:6-9+ Jl/Ag '89

MYERS, MARTHA, AND HOROSKO, MARIAN

When classes are not enough: body therapies. il *Dance Magazine* 63:47-51 Jl '89

MYERS, MIKE

about

The basement tapes. B. Flanagan. il *Rolling Stone* p45 N 16 '89

MYERS, NORMAN

Environment and security. *Foreign Policy* 74:23-41 Spr '89

Extinction rates past and present. bibl f *BioScience* 39:39-41 Ja '89

First word. il *Omni (New York, N.Y.)* 11:8 My '89

Making the world work for people. il *International Wildlife* 19:12-14 N/D '89

Reflections on 'Our common future' [interview with G. H. Brundtland] il por *International Wildlife* 19:14-15 N/D '89

Sometimes the graceful flourish. il *International Wildlife* 19:44-51 Ja/F '89

Synergistic interactions and environment. *BioScience* 39:506 S '89

MYERS, RAMON H.

Recent developments in East Asia [address, July 20, 1989] *Vital Speeches of the Day* 55:716-18 S 15 '89

The Republic of Korea [address, March 9, 1989] *Vital Speeches of the Day* 55:418-20 My 1 '89

MYERS, THERESE E.
about
Desqview's different drummer. E. S. Ely. por *Personal Computing* 13:76 Jl '89
Little Quarterdeck throws its weight around. P. Cole. il por *Business Week* p76 Je 19 '89
MYERSON, BESS
about
Bess Myerson: how I survived. C. Adams. il por *Ladies' Home Journal* 106:106-7+ Jl '89
Bess Myerson: the inside story. J. L. Block. il pors *Good Housekeeping* 208:70+ Ap '89
How Bess got out of the mess. J. Kasindorf. il pors *New York* 22:38-48 Ja 16 '89
Miss America wins again. il por *Time* 133:80 Ja 2 '89
Scraping by on $376,000 a year. L. Touby. il pors *Working Woman* 14:99 My '89
MYERSON, RALPH M.
Frederick Albert Cook, M.D. [with editorial comment by Gilbert L. Voss] il por map *Sea Frontiers* 35:3, 8-13 Ja/F '89
MYLAN LABORATORIES INC.
Drug abuse [Mylan Laboratories' suspicions of FDA corruption bear fruit] J. Novack. il *Forbes* 143:42-3 Je 26 '89
Mylan is glad it opened this can of worms. M. Schroeder. il *Business Week* p30-1 S 18 '89
MYLROIE, LAURIE
Iraq's changing role in the Persian Gulf. bibl f *Current History* 88:89-2+ F '89
MYOBLASTS
5-bromo-2'-deoxyuridine blocks myogenesis by extinguishing expression of MyoD1. S. J. Tapscott and others. bibl f il *Science* 245:532-6 Ag 4 '89
Transfer of a protein encoded by a single nucleus to nearby nuclei in multinucleated myotubes. E. Ralston and Z. W. Hall. bibl f il *Science* 244:1066-9 Je 2 '89
MYOCARDIUM *See* Heart—Muscle
MYOFACIAL PAIN DYSFUNCTION SYNDROME *See* TMJ syndrome
MYOGLOBIN
Spectra and spectroscopy
Effects of buried ionizable amino acids on the reduction potential of recombinant myoglobin. R. Varadarajan and others. bibl f il *Science* 243:69-72 Ja 6 '89
MYOPIA
Anecdotes, facetiae, satire, etc.
A pretty girl is like a malady [boy attributes myopia to hours spent reading about sex] P. Freundlich. il *Esquire* 111:122-6 F '89
MYOSIN
Assembly of the native heterodimer of Rana esculenta tropomyosin by chain exchange. S. S. Lehrer and others. bibl f il *Science* 246:926-8 N 17 '89
Expression and characterization of a functional myosin head fragment in Dictyostelium discoideum. D. J. Manstein and others. bibl f il *Science* 246:656-8 N 3 '89
MYRINGOTOMY *See* Ear—Surgery
MYRISTIC ACID
Activation of the cellular proto-oncogene product p21Ras by addition of a myristylation signal. J. E. Buss and others. bibl f il *Science* 243:1600-3 Mr 24 '89
Myristoylated and nonmyristoylated forms of a protein are phosphorylated by protein kinase C. J. M. Graff and others. bibl f il *Science* 246:503-6 O 27 '89
MYRRH
Gifts of the Magi: precious resins. D. Dare. *Earth Science* 41:14 Wint '88
MYRTLE BEACH (S.C.)
Description
Back to the beach. C. F. Wall. il *Southern Living* 24:116+ My '89
MYSAK, JOE
The beauty of municipal bonds. il *The American Spectator* 22:18-20 Je '89
MYSTERY
A mother's manner of looking to the sky [instilling awareness of mystery of life] J. M. Wall. *The Christian Century* 106:99-100 F 1-8 '89
MYSTERY OF THE ROSE BOUQUET [drama] *See* Puig, Manuel
MYSTERY STORIES *See* Detective and mystery stories
MYSTERY TRAIN [film] *See* Motion picture reviews—Single works
MYSTIC (CONN.)
Restaurants, nightclubs, bars, etc.
A hot movie means a bigger piece of the American pie for a Greek immigrant who owns the real Mystic Pizza [S. Zelepos] D. Chun. il pors *People Weekly* 31:98+ Ja 9 '89
MYSTIC FIRE VIDEO, INC.
Making book on video. J. Zinsser. il *Publishers Weekly* 235:32 Ap 14 '89
Video publishers reel in profits with avant-garde offerings. L. Arden. il por *Home Office Computing* 7:45 My '89
MYSTIC PIZZA (MYSTIC, CONN.: RESTAURANT) *See* Mystic (Conn.)—Restaurants, nightclubs, bars, etc.

MYSTIC SEAPORT MUSEUM
Mystic by the sea. R. S. Peffer. il *Travel Holiday* 172:100-2 Jl '89
MYSTICISM
See also
Yoga
The owl in the daylight. L. O. Sanneh. il *The Christian Century* 106:1115 N 29 '89
Catholic Church
See also
Creation spirituality
Judaism
See also
Cabala
MYTHICAL ANIMALS *See* Animals, Mythical
MYTHOLOGY
See also
Gods and goddesses
Weather in mythology
Women in mythology
Bill Moyers angrily defends Joseph Campbell against charges that his wisdom was only a myth. A. Chambers. il pors *People Weekly* 32:64+ N 27 '89
The faces of Joseph Campbell. B. Gill. il *The New York Review of Books* 36:16+ S 28 '89
Joseph Campbell: an exchange [discussion of September 28, 1989 article, The faces of Joseph Campbell] B. Gill. il *The New York Review of Books* 36:57-61 N 9 '89
Mythics: don't take them too literally [excerpt from Imaginary landscape] W. I. Thompson. *Utne Reader* p103 N/D '89
The power of myth: lessons from Joseph Campbell. B. C. Lane. il *The Christian Century* 106:652-4 Jl 5-12 '89
The stories we live by [personal myths; cover story] S. Keen. il *Psychology Today* 22:42-7 D '88
Bibliography
Taking another look at myth. K. Thompson. il *Utne Reader* p102-5+ N/D '89
MYTHOLOGY, GREEK
See also
Argonauts (Greek mythology)
Jason (Greek mythology)
Palamedes (Greek mythology)
The powers of the primeval goddesses. M. R. Lefkowitz. *The American Scholar* 58:586-91 Aut '89
MYTHOLOGY, INDIAN (AMERICAN) *See* Indians of North America—Religion and mythology
MYTHOLOGY, ROMAN
See also
Hercules (Roman mythology)
MYTHOLOGY IN POETRY
Hopkins the mythmaker. J. F. Cotter. *America* 161:106-8 Ag 26-S 2 '89
Poet to poet. D. Dumars. il *The Writer* 102:23-6 Mr '89
MYTHS *See* Mythology

N

N.S. BIENSTOCK INC.
When Leibner calls, the networks listen [agent for newscasters] B. Yagoda. il pors *The New York Times Magazine* p36-8+ Je 18 '89
N.W.A. (MUSICAL GROUP)
N.W.A. cops an attitude. S. Hochman. il *Rolling Stone* p24 Je 29 '89
NAACP *See* National Association for the Advancement of Colored People
NAACP LEGAL DEFENSE AND EDUCATIONAL FUND *See* Legal Defense and Educational Fund
NAAMAN, THE SYRIAN
about
Grateful outcasts. P. J. Ryan. il *America* 161:223 O 7 '89
NÄBAUER, MICHAEL, AND OTHERS
Does voltage affect excitation-contraction coupling in the heart? [discussion of May 19, 1989 article, Regulation of calcium release is gated by calcium current, not gating charge, in cardiac myocytes] bibl f *Science* 246:1640 D 22 '89
Regulation of calcium release is gated by calcium current, not gating charge, in cardiac myocytes. bibl f il *Science* 244:800-3 My 19 '89
NABEL, ELIZABETH G., AND OTHERS
Recombinant gene expression in vivo within endothelial cells of the arterial wall. bibl f il *Science* 244:1342-4 Je 16 '89
NABET *See* National Association of Broadcast Employees and Technicians
NABOKOV, VLADIMIR VLADIMIROVICH, 1899-1977
Nabokov's letters: 'Let me explain a few things' [excerpt from Vladimir Nabokov: selected letters, 1940-1977] il por *The New York Times Book Review* 94:1+ S 17 '89
NABSE *See* National Alliance of Black School Educators
NABUCCO [opera] *See* Verdi, Giuseppe, 1813-1901

NACHMAN, GERALD
Women, pick up the phone! por *Newsweek* 114:8 Jl 31 '89
NACHMAN, JERRY
about
The newest new Post. E. Diamond. il por *New York* 22:28-9 Je 12 '89
NACHTWEY, JAMES, 1948-
Death zone [photographs] il *Life* 12:28-34 Mr '89
about
The eyes of war. il *Life* 12:94-8 My '89
Photography. P. Blauner. il *New York* 22:126-7 S 11 '89
NACK, WILLIAM
The bald eagle. il pors *Sports Illustrated* 70:54-6+ Je 12 '89
Barry breaks away. il pors *Sports Illustrated* 70:24-6+ Ap 10 '89
Blood brothers and bluegrass. il *Sports Illustrated* 71:76-80+ O 30 '89
Echoes of an equine past. il *Sports Illustrated* 71:84-8+ S 18 '89
Fat City for rusty pugs. il pors *Sports Illustrated* 70:36-7 Mr 20 '89
It's a small World. il *Sports Illustrated* 71:60-1+ Jl 24 '89
A life cut short. il pors *Sports Illustrated* 71:136-46 S 4 '89
The longest ride. il pors *Sports Illustrated* 70:116-20+ Mr 20 '89
Nice and easy. il *Sports Illustrated* 70:44-5 Je 19 '89
Rangers risin' [cover story] il pors *Sports Illustrated* 70:16-23 My 1 '89
A Sunday stroll. il *Sports Illustrated* 70:18-25 My 15 '89
Tops at the track. il pors *Sports Illustrated* 70:38-41+ F 6 '89
NACS *See* National Association of College Stores (U.S.)
NADARESKI, CHRISTOPHER A., AND FELLER, MICHAEL J.
The country in the city. il *The Conservationist* 44:12-17 Jl/Ag '89
NADEL, ETHAN
about
Prize flight. A. Burfoot. il pors *Runner's World* 24:28-30 F '89
NADEL, SYBIL
(jt. auth) *See* Cooperman, Saul, and Nadel, Sybil
NADELMAN, CYNTHIA
The shocking blue hair of Elie Nadelman [cover story] il por *American Heritage* 40:80-91 Mr '89
NADELMAN, ELIE, 1882-1946
about
The shocking blue hair of Elie Nadelman [cover story] C. Nadelman. il por *American Heritage* 40:80-91 Mr '89
NADELMANN, ETHAN A.
Drug decriminalization [discussion of September 1, 1989 article, Drug prohibition in the United States: costs, consequences, and alternatives] *Science* 246:1102-5 D 1 '89
Drug prohibition in the United States: costs, consequences, and alternatives. bibl f *Science* 245:939-47 S 1 '89
NADER, RALPH
about
Minority report. C. Hitchens. *The Nation* 249:590 N 20 '89
Ralph Nader reconsidered. J. Rowe. *The Washington Monthly* 21:65+ F '89
Ralph Nader's big mistake. R. J. Samuelson. il *Newsweek* 113:51 Mr 20 '89
The resurrection of Ralph Nader. T. A. Stewart. il pors *Fortune* 119:106-8+ My 22 '89
The second coming of Ralph Nader. D. Harbrecht. il por *Business Week* p28 Mr 6 '89
Should Congress get a 51 percent raise? [interview] J. P. Shapiro. pors *U.S. News & World Report* 106:28 F 13 '89
What risk-free society? [interview] il *New Perspectives Quarterly* 6:32-4 Fall '89
NADIR, ASIL
about
Meet Asil Nadir, the billion-dollar fruit king. M. Maremont. il por *Business Week* p32 S 18 '89
NADIS, STEVEN J.
First light. il *Omni (New York, N.Y.)* 11:94 S '89
Infrared miners. il *Omni (New York, N.Y.)* 11:26 My '89
Mass appeal. il *Omni (New York, N.Y.)* 11:28 Ap '89
Railway to heaven. il *Omni (New York, N.Y.)* 12:30+ N '89
NADLE, MARLENE
What Bush owes. *The Nation* 248:400-1 Mr 27 '89
NADLER, RICHARD, AND DONELSON, TOM
Affirmative reaction. il *National Review* 41:28-9 S 15 '89
NAE *See* National Association of Evangelicals
NAEF, WESTON J., 1942-
Photography discovery and invention. il *Antiques* 135:288-97 Ja '89
NAEP *See* National Assessment of Educational Progress
NAFZGER, SAMUEL H.
America's Lutherans: what they believe. il *Christianity Today* 33:22-5 N 3 '89

NAGAMINE, CLAUDE M., AND OTHERS
Chromosome mapping and expression of a putative testis-determining gene in mouse. bibl f il *Science* 243:80-3 Ja 6 '89
NAGASAKI (JAPAN)
Bombardment, 1945
Study upgrades radiation risks to humans [National Research Council report] J. Raloff. *Science News* 136:404 D 23-30 '89
NAGAWA, FUMIKIYO
(jt. auth) *See* Yoshimatsu, Tadanori, and Nagawa, Fumikiyo
NAGEL, ROBERT F.
The no-bail solution. *The New Republic* 200:13-14 Ap 24 '89
NAGGAR, JEAN
about
How a one-woman show becomes a big-bucks business. E. Prescott. il pors *Working Woman* 14:51-3+ Mr '89
NAGHDI, JAVID
about
Sting operation nabs Iranian counterfeit drug dealer. W. Grigg. il *FDA Consumer* 23:37-8 Ap '89
NAGLER, ERIC
about
Junkyard music. il por *National Geographic World* 171:12-14 N '89
NAGORNO-KARABAKH AUTONOMOUS OBLAST (SOVIET UNION)
Nationalism
Agony and hope in Armenia. R. L. Deats. *The Christian Century* 106:81-2 Ja 25 '89
Fires of nationalism. A. Wilson-Smith. il *Maclean's* 102:43+ O 30 '89
From the rubble. J. Lloyd. il *National Review* 41:31-2 Ja 27 '89
Nightmare of the generals [Soviet generals held captive by Azerbaijanis] *Time* 134:48 S 18 '89
Trouble in the Transcaucasus [dispute between Armenians and Azerbaijanis over Karabakh] M. Saroyan. bibl f il map *The Bulletin of the Atomic Scientists* 45:16-18+ Mr '89
NAGORSKI, ANDREW
Poland: hanging by a thread. il por *Reader's Digest* 135:121-7 N '89
NAGOYA (JAPAN)
Hotels, motels, etc.
Anecdotes, facetiae, satire, etc.
Ye olde inscrutable inn [love hotel] G. Jaynes. il *Life* 12:17 S '89
NAGURSKI, BRONKO, 1908-1990
about
The Bronk and the gazelle. P. Zimmerman. il pors *Sports Illustrated* 71:128-32+ S 11 '89
NAGY, IMRE
Tomb
Catharsis in Hungary. il *Time* 133:38 Je 26 '89
Refolution in Hungary and Poland. T. Garton Ash. bibl f il *The New York Review of Books* 36:9-15 Ag 17 '89
This is the way a world ends. *National Review* 41:11-12 Ag 4 '89
The tumult of the tomb. M. R. Meyer. il *Newsweek* 113:45 Je 26 '89
NAGYVARY, JOSEPH
about
Claiming he can build a better Stradivarius, a Texas biochemist fiddles while violin experts fume. L. Lague. il pors *People Weekly* 31:99-100+ F 13 '89
NAHAS, GABRIEL G., 1920-
about
Dogged crusader against drugs. P. Mann. il por *Reader's Digest* 134:102-6 My '89
NAHAS, NAJI ROBERT
about
Blame it on Nahas. J. Ryser. *Business Week* p40 Jl 3 '89
NAHB *See* National Association of Home Builders (U.S.)
NAIFEH, STEVEN W., 1952-
about
Jackson Pollock bio a milestone for authors. A. Smith. il *Publishers Weekly* 236:39 O 27 '89
NAIL BITING
Confessions of a nail biter. A. Iverson. il *Seventeen* 48:112-15 D '89
NAIL CARE INDUSTRY
Today's products go the distance toward preventing chipping and staining. S. Lord. il *Vogue* 179:344 S '89
NAIL GUNS
Fast but solid fastening. H. Wicks. il *Home Mechanix* 85:22-3+ Ja '89
NAIL POLISH
Spring zing. il *'Teen* 33:82-3 Ap '89
The U.S. nail. il *Mademoiselle* 95:196-7 Je '89
NAIL REMOVERS *See* Nails (Anatomy), Artificial—Removers
NAIL SALONS *See* Beauty shops
NAIL STRENGTHENERS
Formaldehyde caution. *Health (New York, N.Y.)* 21:66 Ag '89

NAILS
Collectors and collecting
Collecting date nails [railroads] R. P. Anjard. il *Antiques & Collecting Hobbies* 94:38 Jl '89
NAILS (ANATOMY)
See also
Manicuring
Nail biting
Nail care industry
Hand signals. il *'Teen* 33:88-9 S '89
Lady fingers. il *Seventeen* 48:246-9 Mr '89
The nail file [special section] L. Daigneault. il *Health (New York, N.Y.)* 21:64-9 Ag '89
NAILS (ANATOMY), ARTIFICIAL
Removers
Artificial nail remover poses poisoning risk [acetonitrile] D. Blumenthal. il *FDA Consumer* 23:22-3 Je '89
NAIM, EDMOND
about
An oasis of sanity. P. Fuhrman. il por *Forbes* 144:100+ O 2 '89
NAIPAUL, V. S. (VIDIADHAR SURAJPRASAD), 1932-
A turn in Atlanta. il *The New York Review of Books* 35:52-7 Ja 19 '89
about
Wanderer of endless curiosity. R. Z. Sheppard. por *Time* 134:58-60 Jl 10 '89
NAIPAUL, VIDIADHAR SURAJPRASAD *See* Naipaul, V. S. (Vidiadhar Surajprasad), 1932-
NAIR, MIRA
about
Salaam Bombay! [film] Reviews
American Film il 14:64 S '89. P. Rainer
Christianity Today il 33:64 F 3 '89. S. Ulstein
Video il 13:80 O '89. R. Gehr
NAIR, N. VIJAYAKRISHNAN
The elderly. il *World Health* p23 N '89
NAISBITT, JOHN, AND ABURDENE, PATRICIA
West by southwest: a Telluride log house with mining camp roots. il pors *Architectural Digest* 46:206-14 Je '89
NAISMITH, JAMES, 1861-1939
about
The basketball man. B. Broeg. il pors *The Saturday Evening Post* 261:59-9+ Ap '89
Ten things you never knew about James Naismith. R. Freiburghouse and R. Freiburghouse. il *Sport (New York, N.Y.)* 80:78 Jl '89
NAISMITH MEMORIAL BASKETBALL HALL OF FAME
Jones, Wilkens, Gates now Basketball Hall of Famers. il *Jet* 76:46 My 29 '89
NAIVETE *See* Innocence (Psychology)
NAJE *See* National Association of Jazz Educators
NAJIMY, KATHY
about
Two good pals laughed together, then shared the joke in a smash comedy, The Kathy & Mo show. J. Cagle. il pors *People Weekly* 31:123-4 My 1 '89
NAKAE, CHŌMIN, 1847-1901
about
Chomin: the Rousseau of the East. S. Ida. il por *The Unesco Courier* 42:40-3 Je '89
NAKAE, TOKUSUKE *See* Nakae, Chōmin, 1847-1901
NAKAJIMA, HIROSHI
A vital role for WHO. *World Health* p3 O '89
about
WHO vs. AIDS [interview] J.-Y. Nau and F. Nouchi. il por *World Press Review* 36:52 Mr '89
NAKAMICHI CORP.
From Nakamichi: DAT at last? [Model 1000] M. Riggs. il *High Fidelity (New York, N.Y.)* 39:5 Mr '89
Pursuing DAT [Nakamichi 1000] K. C. Pohlmann. il *Stereo Review* 54:32 Mr '89
NAKANISHI, DON T.
A quota on excellence? The Asian American admissions debate. il *Change* 21:38-47 N/D '89
NAKANISHI, MARSHA HIRANO- *See* Hirano-Nakanishi, Marsha
NAKASH FAMILY
about
A 'blood war' in the jeans trade. C. Welles. il *Business Week* p74-5+ N 13 '89
The great jeans war. C. Byron. il *New York* 22:13-14 Jl 24 '89
The IRS follies. C. Byron. il *New York* 22:11-12 Ag 7 '89
NAKASHIMA, GEORGE, 1905-
about
Something of a Druid. J. D. Reed. il por *Time* 133:75 Je 26 '89
NAKASONE, YASUHIRO
about
The Recruit scandal bubbles to the top. A. Borrus. por *Business Week* p55 Mr 20 '89
NAKAUCHI, ISAO
about
Japan's master of retailing. S. Wagstyl. por *World Press Review* 36:52 Ja '89

NAKBE (ANCIENT CITY)
The pharaohs of Meso-America. il *U.S. News & World Report* 107:14 N 27 '89
THE NAKED GUN [film] See Motion picture reviews—Single works
NAKED LIE [television program] See Television program reviews—Single works
NAKED TANGO [film] See Motion picture reviews—Single works
NAKEDNESS *See* Nudity
NALLEY, RICHARD
Things that go bump in the mind. *Omni (New York, N.Y.)* 12:33 N '89
NAMATH, JOE
about
The neon nights of Broadway Joe. M. Lupica. il *Esquire* 112:67-8+ O '89
Replaying Super Bowl III, Namath and the '69 Jets meet and beat the Colts again. T. Nugent. il pors *People Weekly* 32:56-7 N 13 '89
NAME DROPPING
Anecdotes, facetiae, satire, etc.
Naming names. D. Blum. il *New York* 22:24 S 4 '89
NAME GAMES
Down and out in a daze and Links: working on the name chain. S. Morris. il *Omni (New York, N.Y.)* 11:96-7 My '89
NAMES
See also
Astronomy—Nomenclature
Ballet—Names
Birds—Nomenclature
Corporations—Names
Drugs—Names
Perfumes—Names
Sandwiches—Names
Wine—Names
NAMES, GEOGRAPHICAL
Bring back Upper Volta. W. Safire. il *The New York Times Magazine* p14+ O 22 '89
Our heritage of Indian names. R. P. Anjard. *Antiques & Collecting Hobbies* 94:22 Jl '89
Playing the name game [countries changing names] il *Time* 133:40 Je 19 '89
NAMES, INDIAN (AMERICAN)
Our heritage of Indian names. R. P. Anjard. *Antiques & Collecting Hobbies* 94:22 Jl '89
NAMES, PERSONAL
See also
Baseball players—Names
Betty Club
Blacks—Names
Name dropping
Nicknames
It hyphened one night [hyphenated surnames] H. G. Chua-Eoan. il *Time* 133:78 Ap 17 '89
Names can hurt [odd names bestowed on black children] C. M. Jackson. por *Essence* 19:134 Ap '89
Remember names better than a computer [mnemonics] A. Roblin. il *Prevention (Emmaus, Pa.)* 41:105-6+ D '89
Anecdotes, facetiae, satire, etc.
Think you've got it bad? [going through life as a G. Steinbrenner soundalike] H. J. Steinbreder. il por *Sports Illustrated* 70:114 Ap 3 '89
What's in a name? M. Royko. *Reader's Digest* 135:195-6 N '89
Pronunciation
Marry-o? Mahr-yo? [M. Cuomo] W. Safire. il *The New York Times Magazine* p10+ Jl 23 '89
Religious aspects
Naming and the act of faith. L. O. Sanneh. *The Christian Century* 106:875 O 4 '89
NAMIAS, JEROME
Written in the winds: the great drought of '88. maps *Weatherwise* 42:85-7 Ap '89
NAMIBIA
See also
Forced labor—Namibia
Government and the press—Namibia
United Nations—Namibia
United Nations Transition Assistance Group in Namibia
Voter registration—Namibia
Wildlife conservation—Namibia
Economic conditions
Africa's next basket case? R. Sikorski. *National Review* 41:21-2+ S 15 '89
Nervous in Namibia. S. C. Saxena. *World Press Review* 36:42-3 Ap '89
Exploring expeditions
Out of Africa [M. Gersi's trek] M. J. Wilcove. il *Omni (New York, N.Y.)* 12:32+ O '89
History
Namibia: 100 years from colony to nation. il *UN Chronicle* 26:47-8 Mr '89
Nationalism
See also
SWAPO

NAMIBIA—cont.
Politics and government
See also
Elections—Namibia
Political campaigns—Namibia

The Angola/Namibia accords. C. W. Freeman. *Foreign Affairs* 68:126-41 Summ '89

Angola/Namibia accords [special section] il maps *Department of State Bulletin* 89:10-23 F '89

As Africa's last colony nears independence [interview with G. Lister] A. Balk. il por *World Press Review* 36:36-8 Jl '89

A bloody road to peace [SWAPO incursion] C. S. Manegold. il map *Newsweek* 113:37 Ap 17 '89

Botching the peace [threat to agreement to bring independence] W. R. Doerner. il map *Time* 133:35 Ap 17 '89

Can Namibia walk alone? Will South Africa let it? E. Girardet. il *U.S. News & World Report* 107:36+ S 11 '89

A crisis for peace [SWAPO incursion inside Namibia] J. Bierman. il *Maclean's* 102:22+ Ap 17 '89

Enter, the Gang of Five? [permanent members of Security Council request cut in funding for supervising Namibian elections] *The Nation* 248:217 F 20 '89

How SWAPO got framed [incursion into Namibia] A. Cockburn. *The Nation* 248:582-3 My 1 '89

Independence process in Namibia [statement, July 20, 1989] H. J. Cohen. *Department of State Bulletin* 89:43-4 N '89

Namibia independence back on track: cease-fire restored after nine-day crisis [special section] il *UN Chronicle* 26:4-17 Je '89

Namibia: independent at last—we hope. S. M. Khalid. map *American Visions* 4:51-2 Je '89

Namibia: peace at last? F. J. Parker. *America* 161:450-2 D 16 '89

The Namibia sting. *National Review* 41:12 My 5 '89

Namibia: the making of a new nation [tripartite agreement among Angola, Cuba, and South Africa; cover story; special section] il map *UN Chronicle* 26:34-48 Mr '89

Namibian independence and troop withdrawal from Angola [statement, March 31, 1989] J. A. Baker, III. *Department of State Bulletin* 89:29 My '89

Namibia's transition to independence. V. C. Knight. bibl f *Current History* 88:225-8+ My '89

A nation in the making. B. Came. map *Maclean's* 102:25+ Mr 27 '89

A new era for Namibia. S. Reiss. il map *Newsweek* 113:30-1 Ap 3 '89

Peace at last in Namibia? G. Lister and M. Verbaan. il *The Nation* 248:18+ Ja 2 '89

Secretary-General in Namibia: the independence process is 'irreversible'; more than 700,000 register to vote [special section] il *UN Chronicle* 26:4-13 D '89

South Africa: a step forward on Namibia, a step backward at home? A. Fine. il *Business Week* p66 Mr 13 '89

SWAPO's witch hunt. S. Reiss. il *Newsweek* 114:33 S 4 '89

Swipe at SWAPO [discussion of May 1, 1989 article, How SWAPO got framed] A. Cockburn. *The Nation* 249:190+ Ag 21-28 '89

Thousands of Namibians return home; UNTAG troops now in place; South African military withdraws [special section] il *UN Chronicle* 26:4-11 S '89

Under specter of Pretoria, Namibia moves to freedom. F. D. Brown. il map *Black Enterprise* 19:52 Je '89

NAMIBIAN (NEWSPAPER)
As Africa's last colony nears independence [interview with G. Lister] A. Balk. il por *World Press Review* 36:36-8 Jl '89

NAMM See National Association of Music Merchants

NANCHANG AIRCRAFT MANUFACTURING COMPANY
Nanchang developing L-8, N-5A aircraft for international civil market. il *Aviation Week & Space Technology* 131:78+ D 11 '89

NANDINA
Nandina news. il *Sunset (Central West edition)* 182:212 Ap '89

NANNIES See Nursemaids

NANOLITHOGRAPHY
Scanning tunneling microscopy and nanolithography on a conducting oxide, $Rb_{0.3}MoO_3$. E. Garfunkel and others. bibl f il *Science* 246:99-100 O 6 '89

NANOTECHNOLOGY
Interview: Eric Drexler. E. Regis. por *Omni (New York, N.Y.)* 11:66-8+ Ja '89

Think small (and mechanical). P. Saffo. il *Personal Computing* 13:219-20 S '89

Conferences
Nonexistent technology gets a hearing. I. Amato. *Science News* 136:295 N 4 '89

NANSAY CORPORATION
It's not even flying yet, and already there's a flap [Discovery Airways' Japanese financing] J. B. Levine and S. Payne. il *Business Week* p36-7 D 4 '89

NAOMI SIMS BEAUTY PRODUCTS LTD.
Battle of the vanities [cover story] A. Edmond, Jr. il por *Black Enterprise* 19:42-3+ Mr '89

NAPA COUNTY (CALIF.)
Race relations
Flower power gives way to firepower [neo-Nazi gathering] il *Newsweek* 113:27 Mr 13 '89

NAPA VALLEY (CALIF.)
Elephants in the vineyard. P. Steinhart. il map *Audubon* 91:68-73 N '89

Wine and dine in the vineyards. B. St. Pierre. il *New Choices for the Best Years* 29:50-1 Ja '89
Architecture, Domestic
See Architecture, Domestic—California
Wine industry
See Wine industry

NAPA VALLEY WINE TRAIN
All aboard? Not so fast . . . K. Courtney. il *Sierra* 74:93-5 Mr/Ap '89

NAPERVILLE (ILL.)
Social conditions
Stressed out in suburbia. N. Lemann. il *The Atlantic* 264:34+ N '89

NAPKIN RINGS, HOLDERS, ETC.
Napkin rings call for a little geometry . . . and not much else. il *Sunset (Central West edition)* 183:94 D '89

Painted napkin holder. il *Workbench* 45:28 S/O '89

NAPOLEON I, EMPEROR OF THE FRENCH, 1769-1821
about
Banished by Napoleon: the American exile of Baron and Baroness Hyde de Neuville. G.-G. Deák. bibl f il pors *Antiques* 136:1148-57 N '89

Building an empire. O. Bernier. il *House & Garden* 161:40+ D '89

The eagle and the sphinx. M. Hussein. il *The Unesco Courier* 42:24-9 Je '89

Liberty, equality, absurdity. R. Darnton. il *The New Republic* 200:29-32 Ap 3 '89

NAPOLEON AND JOSEPHINE: A LOVE STORY [television program] See Television program reviews—Single works

NAPOLEONIC WARS
See also
Austerlitz, Battle of, 1805

NAPPER, GEORGE
about
Should you own a gun for protection? [interview] il *U.S. News & World Report* 106:28 My 8 '89

NAPPI, REBECCA
(ed) See Wilson, Bette. "God made you little and special"

NAPPING (SLEEP)
Great nappers [interview with F. Lebowitz] il por *House & Garden* 161:164-7 My '89

Notes and comment [outdoor napping] *The New Yorker* 65:44-5 N 13 '89
Anecdotes, facetiae, satire, etc.
Sleeping your way to the top (without sex). K. Fury. il *Working Woman* 14:176 O '89

NARA (JAPAN)
Festivals
The Pavilion of the Second Moon [festival celebrated at Buddhist monastery] L. Caillet. il *The Unesco Courier* 42:24-31 D '89

NARAGHI, EHSAN
The Republic's citizens of honour. il *The Unesco Courier* 42:12-17 Je '89

NARAVANE, VISHWANATH S.
5,000 years of Indian culture. il *The Courier (Unesco)* 42:4-9 F '89

NARCISSISM
But enough about you . . . why narcissism is on the rise. S. Goodman. il *Mademoiselle* 95:143 Mr '89

NARCO AVIONICS (FIRM)
Air wave. J. M. McClellan. il *Flying* 116:62-4+ Je '89

NARCOTIC ADDICTS See Drug abuse

NARCOTIC ANTAGONISTS
See also
Buprenorphine

NARCOTICS
See also
Heroin
Stimulants

Brain and immunity: mapping the link [periaqueductal gray matter of mesencephalon mediates opiate-induced immunosuppression; work of Richard J. Weber and Agu Pert] K. Fackelmann. *Science News* 136:36 Jl 15 '89

Doping the immune system [morphine-induced immunosuppression in rats; research by Richard Weber and Agu Pert] *Discover* 10:14 D '89

Narcotics: a primer. J. E. Cohn. il *Current Health 2* 15:11-13 Mr '89

The periaqueductal gray matter mediates opiate-induced immunosuppression [mesencephalon] R. J. Weber and A. Pert. bibl f il *Science* 245:188-90 Jl 14 '89

NARCOTICS LAWS AND REGULATIONS
See also
Airplanes in narcotics regulation
Dogs in narcotics regulation
Drug paraphernalia—Laws and regulations
Helicopters in narcotics regulation
Legalization of narcotics
Marijuana—Laws and regulations

NARCOTICS LAWS AND REGULATIONS—See also—
cont.
Radar in narcotics regulation
United States. Drug Enforcement Administration
Addicted to tough talk. C. W. Colson. il *Christianity Today* 33:88 N 3 '89
Aftermath of a crack article [articles in New republic and Nation stir debate concerning government policy] J. Morley. il *The Nation* 249:592+ N 20 '89
America's domestic quagmire [cover story; special section; with editorial comments by Nathan Gardels and Stanley K. Sheinbaum] il *New Perspectives Quarterly* 6:2-51, 64 Summ '89
Andean strategy [Bush antidrug plan] H. Jensen. il por *Maclean's* 102:26-8 S 18 '89
The annals of permanent war. il *U.S. News & World Report* 107:21 Ag 28-S 4 '89
Apocalypse now: drugs [parallels between drug war and Vietnam War] E. Barnes. il *Life* 12:18-25 S '89
Attitude problem [reactions to J. Morley's article on using crack] *The New Republic* 201:4+ O 9 '89
Back in the bully pulpit [W. J. Bennett named drug czar] H. Sidey. il por *Time* 133:19 Ja 23 '89
Bennett the drug czar: an agenda. F. Barnes. il *The American Spectator* 22:14-15 Ap '89
Bennett's bad job [W. Bennett named "drug czar"] *National Review* 41:14-15 F 10 '89
Bennett's drug war. T. Morganthau. il por *Newsweek* 114:16-18 Ag 21 '89
The big drug bust [Bush program] *America* 161:155 S 23 '89
Bus drivers: dealing while driving [school bus drivers arrested in Chicago] *Newsweek* 114:50 D 11 '89
Busting our mental blocks on drugs and crime. S. Lessard. *The Washington Monthly* 21:70 F '89
Can the drug crisis be solved? il *Jet* 76:12-14 S 18 '89
The case of the conspicuous dealer [Supreme Court upholds use of drug courier profiles] *Newsweek* 113:64 Ap 17 '89
Charles Rangel: the front-line general in the war on drugs. L. Norment. il pors *Ebony* 44:128+ Mr '89
Community. J. P. Shapiro. il *U.S. News & World Report* 107:80-3 S 11 '89
Constitutional rights: a casualty of the drug war? P. Sudo. il *Scholastic Update (Teachers' edition)* 122:17-18 N 17 '89
Contradictions of cocaine capitalism [cover story] J. Morley. il *The Nation* 249:341-7 O 2 '89
The 'Cotton Club' murder: cocaine and hit men in Hollywood—a 1980s film noir [B. Evans implicated in murder of R. Radin; cover story] J. Kasindorf. il pors *New York* 22:24-33 Jl 24 '89
Court orders: dealing with porn and drugs [Supreme Court rules on drug lawyers' fees] *Newsweek* 114:20 Jl 3 '89
Cowboy in the capital: drug czar Bill Bennett. H. Kohn. il *Rolling Stone* p41-2+ N 2 '89
Crack invades the countryside [Martinsburg, W. Va.] M. McConnell. il *Reader's Digest* 134:73-8 F '89
Crackdown [cover story] J. Q. Wilson and J. J. DiIulio. *The New Republic* 201:21-5 Jl 10 '89
Crackmire. *The New Republic* 201:7+ S 11 '89
Czar without a throne? [W. Bennett] J. McLaughlin. *National Review* 41:19 Mr 10 '89
D.C. cracks down on drugs, evicts suspected dealers. il *Jet* 76:52 Je 5 '89
D.C. drug patrol: riding with the 'Adamany Raiders'. D. M. Cheers. il *Ebony* 44:112+ Ag '89
Detective Joe Quantrille quits the losing battle against drugs in D.C. M. Brower. il pors *People Weekly* 31:62-4+ Mr 20 '89
Drug czar in search of a throne [W. Bennett; cover story] W. McGurn. il por *National Review* 41:22-4 Je 16 '89
The drug czar: no "Walter Wallflower". E. Marshall. por *Science* 243:1287 Mr 10 '89
Drug czars we have known. il *The Nation* 248:258 F 27 '89
Drug dealings. R. E. Tyrrell. il *The American Spectator* 22:8 Je '89
Drug decriminalization [discussion of September 1, 1989 article, Drug prohibition in the United States: costs, consequences, and alternatives] E. A. Nadelmann. *Science* 246:1102-5 D 1 '89
Drug frenzy: why the war on drugs misses the real target. B. Ehrenreich. il *Utne Reader* p76-9+ Mr/Ap '89
The drug lawyers. S. Waldman and M. Miller. il *Newsweek* 114:41+ N 13 '89
Drug prohibition in the United States: costs, consequences, and alternatives. E. A. Nadelmann. bibl f *Science* 245:939-47 S 1 '89
The drug warrior [W. J. Bennett; cover story] T. Morganthau and M. Miller. il pors map *Newsweek* 113:20-4 Ap 10 '89
Drugs, Democrats and priorities [call for blacks to fight drug plague] M. Waters. *The Nation* 249:141-4 Jl 24-31 '89
Drugs, lies & TV [G. Bush's televised war on drugs speech] R. Clark. *The Nation* 249:408-9 O 16 '89
Edward I. Koch [advice to George Bush] E. Koch. *National Review* 41:22 F 10 '89

Evicting the drug dealers [J. Kemp's plan for public housing projects] il por *Time* 133:41 My 1 '89
A family business [Washington D.C. drug ring run by R. Edmond] R. Sandza. il *Newsweek* 113:20 Je 26 '89
Fighting back [cover story; special section] il *Time* 134:12-18+ S 11 '89
Fighting on two fronts [W. J. Bennett targets dealers and users] il *Time* 134:29 Ag 14 '89
For states and cities, the Bush drug plan is small consolation [high cost of law enforcement] G. Witkin. *U.S. News & World Report* 107:33 S 18 '89
Fury over an unholy alliance [Cleveland police accused of teaming up with drug dealer A. Feckner] B. Turque. il por *Newsweek* 113:26 My 8 '89
General Bennett. F. Barnes. *The New Republic* 201:14+ S 18-25 '89
Go ask Alice. J. Cummings. *Omni (New York, N.Y.)* 11:42+ S '89
Good place for a test case [W. Bennett to declare war on drugs in Washington, D.C.] il *Time* 133:24 Ap 3 '89
Grabbing the drug bounty. H. Jensen. il *Maclean's* 102:49-50 O 23 '89
How to win the war on drugs: target the users. J. A. Eisenach. il *USA Today (Periodical)* 117:46-8 Ja '89
If women ran the drug war. A. F. Lewis. *Ms.* 18:73 N '89
Jane Fonda's daughter, Vanessa Vadim, is jailed for mouthing off at a drug bust. J. S. Kunen. il pors *People Weekly* 32:44-5 O 23 '89
Johnny-too-bad and the sufferers [Jamaican drug posses; cover story] L. Gunst. *The Nation* 249:549+ N 13 '89
Judging a book by its cover [Supreme Court upholds use of drug courier profiles by federal agents] A. L. Sanders. il *Time* 133:52 Ap 17 '89
Let's get tough with drug users! C. T. Rowan. *Reader's Digest* 135:107-10 Jl '89
Letter from Washington [G. Bush's televised address on war on drugs] E. Drew. *The New Yorker* 65:102-4 O 2 '89
A loose cannon's parting shot [W. Von Raab's comments on U.S. war on drugs] E. Shannon. il por *Time* 134:18-19 Ag 7 '89
A lost cause is a lost cause. W. F. Buckley. *National Review* 41:70-1 S 29 '89
The man who would be czar [W. J. Bennett] G. Witkin and M. Satchell. il pors *U.S. News & World Report* 106:40-1 Mr 6 '89
Manager tied to drug gang [independent record promoter W. Underwood arrested in New York City] W. Bastone. *Rolling Stone* p62 Jl 13-27 '89
Mr. Bennett's war. *National Review* 41:13-14 S 15 '89
National drug control strategy [address, September 5, 1989] G. Bush. *Vital Speeches of the Day* 55:738-40 O 1 '89
The nation's war on drugs [National Guard; address, April 4, 1989] H. R. Temple, Jr. *Vital Speeches of the Day* 55:516-19 Je 15 '89
A note from prison [women convicted of petty drug offenses] K. Kelly. *America* 161:230 O 14 '89
Notes and comment [drug murders in Washington, D.C.] *The New Yorker* 65:29-30 Ap 17 '89
Notes and comment [G. Bush's address on the drug problem] *The New Yorker* 65:33-4 S 18 '89
Now it's Bush's war [televised address] T. Morganthau. il pors *Newsweek* 114:22-4 S 18 '89
On the drug war [discussion of Summer 1989 special section, America's domestic quagmire] *New Perspectives Quarterly* 6:62-3 Fall '89
On the firing line [police and war on drugs] G. Hackett. il *Newsweek* 113:32-4+ My 29 '89
On the front lines [citizens rising up against drug dealers] R. Lacayo. il *Time* 134:14-18 S 11 '89
The paradox of antidrug enforcement [tough enforcement makes drug trade more profitable] J. Cook. il *Forbes* 144:105-6+ N 13 '89
The phony war [Bush administration war on drugs] *Commonweal* 116:515-16 O 6 '89
Phony war on drugs. il *The Progressive* 53:8-9 O '89
A political opiate [war on drugs; cover story] L. H. Lapham. bibl f il *Harper's* 279:43-8 D '89
The president's drug war: is it enough? S. Manning. il *Scholastic Update (Teachers' edition)* 122:15-16 N 17 '89
Putting the heat on dealers. *Newsweek* 114:32 Jl 31 '89
Rangel raps Bush for his snubbing drug czar status. por *Jet* 75:4 Mr 6 '89
Reading the signs of a drug-plagued time [Bush drug program] J. M. Wall. *The Christian Century* 106:803-4 S 13-20 '89
Reps hit Bush plan to fund drug war with money cut from domestic programs. il *Jet* 76:4-5 S 25 '89
Some things you do because they're right [interview with W. J. Bennett] J. Cook. il por *Forbes* 144:118+ N 13 '89
The struggle with ourselves [G. Bush's speech] H. Sidey. il por *Time* 134:32 S 18 '89
Taking drugs—seriously. P. J. O'Rourke. il *Rolling Stone* p57-8+ N 30 '89

NARCOTICS LAWS AND REGULATIONS—*cont.*

"Thank God for people like you" [undercover narcotics officer P. Rosales of Houston, Tex.] M. Siegel. il por *Good Housekeeping* 208:139+ Je '89

A threat to freedom? [civil liberties endangered by war on drugs] R. Lacayo. il *Time* 134:28+ S 18 '89

Thurgood's way [T. Marshall dissents in Supreme Court ruling upholding search of individual fitting drug courier profile] D. Seligman. il *Fortune* 119:165+ My 8 '89

Turf wars in the federal bureaucracy [various agencies fighting war on drugs] S. Waldman. il *Newsweek* 113:24-6 Ap 10 '89

Unveiling Bennett's battle plan [efforts to curb drug trade in Washington, D.C.] M. Miller. il por *Newsweek* 113:6 Ap 24 '89

Waging war without weapons. F. Bruning. il *Maclean's* 102:15 O 9 '89

Walton takes post as top black drug war policymaker [R. B. Walton] por *Jet* 76:6 Je 26 '89

War on what? [Bush proposals] *National Review* 41:14 S 29 '89

The war? program? experiment? on drugs. D. E. Koshland, Jr. *Science* 245:1309 S 22 '89

What must be done [views of J. L. Jackson, C. S. Perry, C. Rangel and K. Schmoke] il pors *Ebony* 44:156+ Ag '89

Where does the anti-drug money come from? W. F. Buckley. *National Review* 41:62 O 13 '89

Why justice can't be done. B. Turque. il *Newsweek* 113:36-7 My 29 '89

Why we're losing the war on drugs. R. Flick. *Reader's Digest* 135:83-8 O '89

Will fear make Americans kick the drug habit? [Bush administration plan] R. Stodghill, II. il *Business Week* p30 S 11 '89

The wrong drug war. *The Nation* 249:297 S 25 '89

Bibliography

Desperate over drugs [cover story] M. Massing. il *The New York Review of Books* 36:22-6 Mr 30 '89

History

From Coca-Cola to the cartels: battling drugs in America. L. Tarshis. il *Scholastic Update (Teachers' edition)* 122:10-11 N 17 '89

International aspects

See also

Convention against Illicit Traffic in Narcotic Drugs and Psychotropic Substances (1988)

United Nations. Commission on Narcotic Drugs

Battling crime through the banks. D. Francis. il *Maclean's* 102:13 My 29 '89

Certification for narcotics source and transit countries [text of letter and statements, March 1-15, 1989] J. A. Baker; A. B. Wrobleski. *Department of State Bulletin* 89:68-72 My '89

The drug-money hunt [money laundering crackdown] P. R. Range. il map *U.S. News & World Report* 107:22-5 Ag 21 '89

From the cold war to the drug war. S. Sabourin. *New Perspectives Quarterly* 6:63 Fall '89

Global narcotics cooperation and presidential certification [statement, April 5, 1989] A. B. Wrobleski. *Department of State Bulletin* 89:49-59 O '89

A global struggle. R. Dolphin. il map *Maclean's* 102:48-9 Ap 3 '89

Heavy flak in the drug war [with editorial comment by David Gergen] B. Duffy and G. Witkin. il *U.S. News & World Report* 107:16-18, 84 D 18 '89

Over there [America's drug war abroad] M. J. McConahay and R. Kirk. il *Mother Jones* 14:36-9+ F/Mr '89

Spies and soldiers enter the drug war. G. Witkin. *U.S. News & World Report* 107:27 Jl 31 '89

Bahamas

Leading a flying posse against cocaine smugglers, Pat Shea is the Batman of the Bahamas [head of Operation BAT] W. Plummer. il pors *People Weekly* 32:99-100 D 18 '89

Bolivia

Choking off the supply [cocaine] J. Madeley. il *World Health* p28-9 Je '89

Playing golf while drugs flow [U.S. in Bolivia] P. Lernoux. il *The Nation* 248:188-90+ F 13 '89

Burma

Dateline drug wars: Burma: the wrong enemy. W. H. Overholt. *Foreign Policy* 77:172-91 Wint '89/'90

Canada

Battle fatigue [drug cases overwhelm courts] P. Kaihla. il *Maclean's* 102:14-16 D 11 '89

A blistering debate [heroin for terminal cancer] R. Dolphin. il *Maclean's* 102:41 F 27 '89

Drugs and guns: is a Colombian assassination team in Canada? G. W. Taylor. il *Maclean's* 102:14 S 25 '89

Hiding the drug money [cover story; special section; with editorial comment by Kevin Doyle] H. Jensen. il *Maclean's* 102:2, 42-4+ O 23 '89

Shuttle to jail [two Colombian pilots sentenced for smuggling cocaine into Canada] P. Kopvillem. il *Maclean's* 102:14-15 N 27 '89

Caribbean region

Rangel leads illegal-drug probe group in Caribbean. por *Jet* 75:25 Ja 16 '89

Colombia

A battle to the death: Colombia versus its cocaine cartels. S. Manning. il map *Scholastic Update (Teachers' edition)* 122:12-14 N 17 '89

Bennett: 'It's their fight right now' [interview with W. J. Bennett] M. Miller. il *Newsweek* 114:32 S 11 '89

Blandishments and bombs. M. S. Serrill. il *Time* 134:23+ S 11 '89

Can the drug lords be dethroned? P. Dwyer. il *Business Week* p28-30 S 11 '89

The chemical connection [Operation Primavera reveals U.S.-manufactured chemicals used in Colombian cocaine production] W. R. Doerner. il *Time* 133:44-5 F 20 '89

The cocaine war: Washington and Bogotá battle the drug lords. M. Nemeth. il *Maclean's* 102:18-19 S 4 '89

Colombia: a drug lord's last shoot-out [death of J. G. Rodríguez Gacha] C. Lane. il *Newsweek* 114:48 D 25 '89

Colombia tries to fight back. *World Press Review* 36:24-5 N '89

Colombia's drug war. il *World Press Review* 36:6 O '89

Dateline drug wars: Colombia: the wrong strategy. B. M. Bagley. *Foreign Policy* 77:154-71 Wint '89/'90

Death of a drug prince [J. G. Rodríguez Gacha] J. Smolowe. por *Time* 134:26 D 25 '89

Emergency package for Colombia's drug flight [statement, August 25, 1989] G. Bush. *Department of State Bulletin* 89:47 O '89

Fighting anarchy in Colombia [cover story] R. Chepesiuk. il *The New Leader* 72:5-8 S 18 '89

Getting banks to just say 'no' [campaign against laundering drug money] P. Dwyer and P. Engardio. il *Business Week* p16-17 Ap 17 '89

Going too far [U.S. and Colombia step up war on drug lords] G. J. Church. il *Time* 134:12-15 S 4 '89

Hitting the drug lords. T. Morganthau. il map *Newsweek* 114:18-23 S 4 '89

Letter from Bogotá. A. Guillermoprieto. *The New Yorker* 65:112-20+ O 16 '89

A mess in the Andes [cocaine cartels] T. Rosenberg. *The New Republic* 201:23-6 S 18-25 '89

A minister under fire [Justice Minister M. de Greiff] A. Bilski. *Maclean's* 102:20 S 11 '89

Most wanted in Medelin. J. Contreras. il pors *Newsweek* 114:30 S 25 '89

Noble battle, terrible toll. J. Moody. il *Time* 134:33-4 D 18 '89

Now, for the real drug war. B. Duffy. il map *U.S. News & World Report* 107:18-20 S 11 '89

'Now the fight is with blood'. T. Morganthau. il *Newsweek* 114:37 Ag 28 '89

Passing the extradition test [Colombian drug lord E. Martínez Romero shipped to the U.S.] M. S. Serrill. il por *Time* 134:48 S 18 '89

Seize the time against cocaine kings [efforts of President V. Barco Vargas] G. F. Gugliotta. il *U.S. News & World Report* 107:21 S 11 '89

'The slaughter has begun' [bomb attacks as response to drug crackdown] il *Newsweek* 114:40 D 18 '89

Truce or consequences? G. D. Garcia. il *Time* 134:38 S 25 '89

'The war on cocaine': an exchange [discussion of December 22, 1988 article] M. Massing. il *The New York Review of Books* 36:40 Mr 2 '89

Cuba

Anatomy of an execution [A. Ochoa Sanchez found guilty in drug trafficking case] A. Cruz, Jr. *Commentary* 88:54-6 N '89

Cuba and narcotics trafficking [statement, July 26, 1989] M. Levitsky. *Department of State Bulletin* 89:46-8 O '89

Death in Havana [execution of Gen. A. Ochoa Sánchez in drug trafficking case] *Newsweek* 114:24 Jl 24 '89

'I have no reason to live' [trial of A. Ochoa Sanchez on drug trading] H. Anderson. il por *Newsweek* 114:25 Jl 10 '89

Reading the coca leaves [Major General A. Ochoa Sanchez convicted of helping drug smugglers] J. Smolowe. il pors *Time* 134:30-1 Jl 10 '89

Revolution doesn't go better with coke [Interior Minister A. Ochoa Sanchez involved in cocaine smuggling] il por *U.S. News & World Report* 107:12 Jl 10 '89

The trial that shook Cuba [drug trafficking case involving A. Ochoa Sanchez and A. de la Guardia; cover story] J. Preston. il pors *The New York Review of Books* 36:24-31 D 7 '89

Great Britain

No quick drug fix. A. Lejeune. *National Review* 41:21-3 Mr 24 '89

Latin America

Attacking the source [proposal to send U.S. military advisers to aid antidrug campaign] E. Shannon. il *Time* 134:10-12 Ag 28 '89

Cocaine countries try to grow straight [America's protectionist policy towards agricultural imports] A. Gabor. il *U.S. News & World Report* 107:57 O 23 '89

NARCOTICS LAWS AND REGULATIONS — Latin America—cont.

Drug war zone [Green Berets] P. Andreas. *The Nation* 249:704-5 D 11 '89

How to fight the drug war [cocaine] G. A. Gorriti. il *The Atlantic* 264:70-2+ Jl '89

Marines aren't the answer to America's drug problem. P. Dwyer. il *Business Week* p30 S 4 '89

Send in the troops? Assessing U.S. military options. E. Salholz. il *Newsweek* 114:20-1 S 4 '89

South American cocaine: why the U.S. can't stop it. R. W. Lee. *Current (Washington, D.C.)* 313:22-31 Je '89

Southern exposure: the view from Peru [cocaine] G. A. Gorriti. il *New Perspectives Quarterly* 6:49-51 Summ '89

Mexico

Every agent's a drug agent [U.S. Border Patrol] F. Gibney, Jr. il *Newsweek* 113:27 My 1 '89

A 'godfather' behind bars in the nick of time [arrest of drug trafficker F. Gallardo] M. Miller. il por *Newsweek* 113:55 Ap 24 '89

Mexico's war on drugs [interview with E. Alvarez del Castillo] il *New Perspectives Quarterly* 6:46-9 Summ '89

Wimp no more [President C. Salinas de Gortari] G. D. Garcia. il por *Time* 133:28-9 Ap 24 '89

Panama

A bungled deal with Panama [DEA money laundering crackdown utilizes M. Noriega's forces] il por *Newsweek* 113:25 Ap 10 '89

Dear Manny [Drug Enforcement Administration's correspondence with M. Noriega] M. Hosenball. *The New Republic* 200:9-10 Je 12 '89

Peru

Coke dusters [U.S. plan to spray Spike on coca plants] M. Massing. *The New Republic* 200:21-3 Ja 30 '89

Soviet Union

The Kremlin's new crackdown. J. Trimble. il *U.S. News & World Report* 106:36 F 20 '89

Switzerland

Crackdown on the Swiss laundry. C. Gorman. il *Time* 133:53 Ap 24 '89

A drug crackdown in the Alps. C. Dickey. il *Newsweek* 113:40 Ap 10 '89

United States

See Narcotics laws and regulations

Western Europe

The drug war—European style [money laundering crackdown] B. Riemer. *Business Week* p31-2 O 2 '89

NARCOTICS PARAPHERNALIA *See* Drug paraphernalia

NARCOTICS SMUGGLING *See* Narcotics trade

NARCOTICS TRADE

See also
Airplanes in narcotics regulation
Airplanes in narcotics trade
Church and narcotics trade
Narcotics laws and regulations
Radar in narcotics regulation
United Nations. Commission on Narcotic Drugs

The blind high [narcotics trade not just a black problem in Cleveland] M. Drexler. *Utne Reader* p99-100 S/O '89

Bright kids, bad business [T. Williams' study of young cocaine dealers in New York's Washington Heights] E. Magnuson. il por *Time* 134:18 S 11 '89

Bring back the Mafia. R. Moran. por *Newsweek* 114:8 Ag 7 '89

Busted [college student arrested for drug trafficking] R. Hamilton. il pors *Seventeen* 48:122+ O '89

City of Angels, indeed [Los Angeles banks involved in laundering drug money] il *U.S. News & World Report* 106:14 Ap 10 '89

Cocaine kids: the underground American dream [teenage drug dealers in New York City's Washington Heights] T. M. Williams. il *New Perspectives Quarterly* 6:21-5 Summ '89

Contradictions of cocaine capitalism [cover story] J. Morley. il *The Nation* 249:341-7 O 2 '89

Crack's destructive sprint across America. M. Massing. il *The New York Times Magazine* p38-41+ O 1 '89

Dead zones [urban crime areas; cover story; special section] T. Moore. il *U.S. News & World Report* 106:20-5+ Ap 10 '89

Dealing death [teenage drug dealers in Hartford, Conn. housing projects] il *Scholastic Update (Teachers' edition)* 122:4-6 N 17 '89

Inside the high-flying pot industry [rise in domestic growers] G. Witkin. il *U.S. News & World Report* 107:27-8+ N 6 '89

Jackson marches against drugs at rally in Boston. il por *Jet* 76:31 Jl 3 '89

Just another night on crack street [drug dealers in East Harlem] P. Bourgois. il *The New York Times Magazine* p52-3+ N 12 '89

No safe place. A. McCarthy. il *Commonweal* 116:72 F 10 '89

Profits in a risky business [Harlem crack trade] R. Sandza. il *Newsweek* 113:37 My 29 '89

A slaughter of innocents [bystanders caught in narcotics trade crossfire] *U.S. News & World Report* 107:12 Jl 10 '89

Street-wise crack research. C. Holden. il *Science* 246:1376-81 D 15 '89

The supply-side scourge [abundance of cocaine] T. McCarroll. il *Time* 134:81 N 13 '89

Tales of the crank trade [southern California] J. Beaty. il *Time* 133:10+ Ap 24 '89

To deal and die in L.A. A. Collier. il *Ebony* 44:106+ Ag '89

Wall-to-wall drug traffickers [smuggling into U.S.] *U.S. News & World Report* 106:14-15 Je 19 '89

International aspects

See also
Convention against Illicit Traffic in Narcotic Drugs and Psychotropic Substances (1988)
Iran-contra affair—Narcotics trade aspects

Coca. P. T. White. il map *National Geographic* 175:2-47 Ja '89

The return of a deadly drug called horse [heroin] G. Witkin. il map *U.S. News & World Report* 107:31-2 Ag 14 '89

Terminology

Drug-war lingo. W. Safire. il *The New York Times Magazine* p20+ S 24 '89

Alaska

Off with their heads [walrus heads traded for illicit drugs by Eskimos] M. Beck. il *Newsweek* 113:78 Je 5 '89

Bulgaria

The Bulgarian connection [drugs and money laundering] P. Fuhrman. il map *Forbes* 143:40-4 Ap 17 '89

Burma

Burma's 'Money Tree' [drug lord Khun Sa] M. Liu. il por map *Newsweek* 113:42-3 My 15 '89

Canada

A deadly plague of drugs [cover story; special section; with editorial comment by Kevin Doyle] il *Maclean's* 102:4, 44-51 Ap 3 '89

China

History

There was a nation . . . [effects of opium trade] P. Harvey. il *Reader's Digest* 134:51-3 Ja '89

Colombia

Anarchy in Colombia [narcoterrorism] J. Contreras. il *Newsweek* 114:30-2 S 11 '89

Cocaine's 'dirty 300' [cover story] T. Morganthau. il map *Newsweek* 114:36-41 N 13 '89

Colombia's search for peace. J. D. Martz. bibl f *Current History* 88:125-8+ Mr '89

Company town [cocaine trade in Medellin] H. Kohn. il *Rolling Stone* p67-8+ Ap 6 '89

A curious retirement [general revealed to be on payroll of drug barons] *Time* 133:44 F 20 '89

The deadliest beat [journalists covering the drug story] W. A. Henry. il *Time* 134:76 N 13 '89

'Good sons' who kill. G. Matthews. il *World Press Review* 36:26-7 N '89

The Israeli connection [mercenaries involved in training Colombian hit squads] E. Magnuson. il *Time* 134:26 S 11 '89

The kingdom of cocaine [cover story] T. Rosenberg. *The New Republic* 201:26-34 N 27 '89

Life styles of the rich and heinous [cocaine kingpins] M. J. Harris. il *Money* 18:70-6 N '89

Pablo Escobar. por *People Weekly* 32:88 D 25 '89-Ja 1 '90

Reporters as targets. J. Contreras. il *Newsweek* 114:59 O 2 '89

Terror in the drug world. H. Jensen. il *Maclean's* 102:18-20 S 11 '89

Viking to publish inside look at Colombian drug-running [story of cocaine dealer K. Wolff] G. Corcoran. *Publishers Weekly* 235:35 Je 9 '89

Jamaica

Johnny-too-bad and the sufferers [Jamaican drug posses; cover story] L. Gunst. *The Nation* 249:549+ N 13 '89

Latin America

Cocaine chemistry [chemicals exported by the U.S. used in cocaine manufacture] P. Andreas. *The New Republic* 201:12+ N 20 '89

Finally, some bad news for drug lords [cocaine trade] C. Poole. il *Forbes* 144:122 Jl 24 '89

The world of narcoterrorism. D. Brock. il *The American Spectator* 22:24-8 Je '89

Mexico

See also
Camarena Salazar, Enrique—Murder case

The believers [M. Kilroy murdered by drug dealers in Matamoros] G. D. Garcia. il *Rolling Stone* p46-9+ Je 29 '89

Cult of the red-haired devil [drug dealers practice human sacrifice in Mexico] R. Woodbury. il map *Time* 133:30 Ap 24 '89

The grisly secrets of a lonely ranch [human sacrifice slaying of M. Kilroy and others by drug smugglers in Matamoros] A. Richman. il por *People Weekly* 31:44-9 My 1 '89

The last time I was in Mexico. R. Kirtland. il *America* 161:7-9 Jl 1-8 '89

Ritual murder [Matamoros] B. Wickens. il *Maclean's* 102:61 Ap 24 '89

NARCOTICS TRADE—Mexico—cont.

Ritual murder in Mexico [human sacrifice practiced by drug dealers] F. Gibney, Jr. il *Newsweek* 113:55 Ap 24 '89

Voodoo in Mexico [human sacrifice practiced by drug dealers] il *U.S. News & World Report* 106:16 Ap 24 '89

Bibliography

Magic! Murder! Mayhem! Drugs! Four new books detail the ritual killings in Matamoros, Mexico. G. Feldman. il *Publishers Weekly* 236:23-4 Ag 18 '89

Netherlands

The Johnny Appleseed of pot [marijuana seed salesman N. Schoenmakers] R. Z. Chesnoff. il *U.S. News & World Report* 107:30 N 6 '89

Nicaragua

See also

Iran-contra affair—Narcotics trade aspects

Panama

The gutsy Panama option [Colombian drug king P. Escobar seeks refuge] pors *U.S. News & World Report* 107:19 S 11 '89

Meanwhile, in Panama. *Time* 134:23 S 11 '89

Why Noriega wins. M. Kempton. il *The New York Review of Books* 36:10 Je 15 '89

United States

See Narcotics trade

Western Europe

The coming cocaine plague in Europe. G. Witkin and S. J. Hedges. il map *U.S. News & World Report* 106:34-6 F 20 '89

NARCOTICS TRADE IN TELEVISION

Guadalajara vice [M. Mann's miniseries The drug wars: Camarena] M. Christensen. il por *Rolling Stone* p53 N 30 '89

NARDIN, ELIZABETH H., AND OTHERS

Conserved repetitive epitope recognized by CD4+ clones from a malaria-immunized volunteer. bibl f il *Science* 246:1603-6 D 22 '89

NARES, JAMES

about

James Nares at Michael Klein. E. Heartney. *Art in America* 77:180 Je '89

NARIN, FRANCIS, 1934-, AND FRAME, J. DAVIDSON

The growth of Japanese science and technology. bibl f il *Science* 245:600-5 Ag 11 '89

NARRAGANSETT BAY (R.I.)

See also

Oil pollution—Narragansett Bay (R.I.)

NARRAGANSETT CAPITAL CORP.

In or out of the game? P. Noglows. il *Channels (New York, N.Y.: 1986)* 9:67 Mr '89

NARRAGANSETT COATED PAPERS (FIRM)

Toward the totally acid-free book. J. P. Frank. il *Publishers Weekly* 236:28-9 Jl 21 '89

NARRATION (RHETORIC)

See also

Fiction—Narration

NARWHALS

Ancient spell of the sea unicorn. F. Bruemmer. il *International Wildlife* 19:38-43 N/D '89

The Arctic hunters [pursuit of narwhals by Inuits in Greenland] C. Dowling. il *Life* 12:140-5 Mr '89

Arctic treasures: what ruler could resist the allure of white falcons, giant moles, and unicorns? F. Bruemmer. il *Natural History* p38-47 Je '89

NASA *See* United States. National Aeronautics and Space Administration

NASA ALUMNI LEAGUE

NASA Alumni League news. See issues of Ad Astra beginning January 1989

NASAL SPRAYS

Blowing hot and cold over Viralizers. il *Newsweek* 113:62 Ja 16 '89

Hot air for sale [Viralizer] il *Consumer Reports* 54:12 Ja '89

NASEBY (ENGLAND), BATTLE OF, 1645

Charles, Cromwell and Channon [highway threatens Naseby battlefield] *History Today* 39:4-5 Ap '89

NASH, ALANNA

Hooked on country [excerpt from Behind closed doors] il *Stereo Review* 54:86-8+ Ja '89

Will women change prime-time TV news? il *Glamour* 87:242-5+ O '89

NASH, DOUGLAS B., AND HOWELL, ROBERT R.

Hydrogen sulfide on Io: evidence from telescopic and laboratory infrared spectra. bibl f il *Science* 244:454-7 Ap 28 '89

NASH, EDDIE

about

The devil and John Holmes: drugs, porn and the murders on Wonderland Avenue. M. Sager. il pors *Rolling Stone* p50-2+ Je 15 '89

NASH, GRAHAM

Woodstock remembered: the artists. il pors *Rolling Stone* p68 Ag 24 '89

NASH, JENNIE

Fear of fruits (or, Waiter, there's a pesticide in my salad). il *Mademoiselle* 95:134 Ag '89

Make love now, babies later. il *Mademoiselle* 95:168-9+ D '89

NASH, JONELL

Fix food fast. See issues of Essence through May 1988

Recipes. See issues of Essence

NASH, STEPHEN

Birth of the dinosaurs [cover story] il *National Parks* 63:16-23 N/D '89

Wolves of Isle Royale. il *National Parks* 63:20-6+ Ja/F '89

NASHER, RAYMOND

about

Thinking big. C. Brown. il por *Forbes* 143:270-1 Je 26 '89

NASHUA CORPORATION

A buyout may ease Nashua's bad news. G. G. Marcial. *Business Week* p150 My 22 '89

NASHVILLE (TENN.)

Architecture

A Republican heritage in the South: Ambassador and Mrs. Guilford Dudley, Jr., in Nashville and Palm Beach. C. T. Buckley. il pors *Architectural Digest* 46:200-9 Ap '89

Auditoriums, convention facilities, etc.

See also

Ryman Auditorium (Nashville, Tenn.)

Description

West Nashville mixes the old and new. J. T. Black. il *Southern Living* 24:84-6 N '89

Historic houses, sites, etc.

For the love of art [addition to 1840 log house] il *Southern Living* 24:130 O '89

Industries

See also

Publishers and publishing

NASSAR, TAREK

(jt. auth) See Seigneurie, Ken, and Nassar, Tarek

NASSAU, ROBERT HAMILL

about

"We were shaking with rage". A. A. Lappen. il pors *Forbes* 144:119+ O 30 '89

NASSAU (BAHAMAS)

Architecture

Nassau via New York [homes of I. and T. A. Kramer decorated by Mark Hampton] Suzy. il *Architectural Digest* 46:142-51 Mr '89

Hotels, motels, etc.

See also

Crystal Palace Resort & Casino (Nassau, Bahamas)

NASSELLA TRICHOTOMA *See* Serrated tussock

NASSY, JOSEF

about

In the shadow of the tower: poignant portrayals of life in a Nazi prison camp. M. C. Rothschild-Boros. il por *USA Today (Periodical)* 118:74-83 S '89

NASTOS, MICHAEL G.

Western Michigan University/Gold Company. *Down Beat* 56:25 O '89

NATALE, RICHARD

The price club. il *American Film* 14:42-4+ Je '89

NATCHER, WILLIAM HUSTON

about

Congressional miracle: Natcher runs, but he won't take the money. J. S. Kunen. il pors *People Weekly* 31:45+ Je 26 '89

NATCHEZ (MISS.)

Description

Natchez. L. J. Lord. il *U.S. News & World Report* 107:67+ D 18 '89

NATCHITOCHES (LA.) IN MOTION PICTURES

Dolled up in Dixie [filming of Steel magnolias] B. D. Johnson. il *Maclean's* 102:84+ N 20 '89

Star bright [filming of R. Harling's play Steel magnolias; special section] L. Hart. il por *Life* 12:82-4+ O '89

NATELCO *See* National Telecommuncations Cos.

NATHAN, AMY

New hope for the bread. il *Esquire* 111:109-12 Ja '89

NATHAN, DEBBIE

Child-abuse evidence debated. *Ms.* 17:81-2 Mr '89

NATHAN, JOAN

All in the family. il *The New York Times Magazine* p71-2 Ap 30 '89

NATHAN, JOE, 1948-

Helping all children, empowering all educators: another view of school choice. bibl f il *Phi Delta Kappan* 71:304-11 D '89

NATHAN, PAUL S.

Rights. See issues of Publishers Weekly

NATHANS, JEREMY

The genes for color vision. bibl il *Scientific American* 260:42-9 F '89

NATHANS, JEREMY, AND OTHERS

Molecular genetics of human blue cone monochromacy. bibl f il *Science* 245:831-8 Ag 25 '89

NATHANSON, JANE

about

The big picture. P. Viladas. il *House & Garden* 161:160-7 S '89

NATHANSON, MARC
about
The big picture. P. Viladas. il *House & Garden* 161:160-7 S '89
Falcon's eye on classic kind of service [interview] il pors *Channels (New York, N.Y.: 1986)* 9:74-5 Jl/Ag '89

NATHER, DAVID
Have one for the runway: how Transportation Department policies add new meaning to the word "red-eye". *The Washington Monthly* 21:12-14+ Ap '89

NATION, CARRY AMELIA MOORE, 1846-1911
about
Carry from Kansas became a Nation all unto herself. R. Day. il pors *Smithsonian* 20:147-8+ Ap '89

NATION (PERIODICAL)
Battle hymns, ancient and modern [former editor F. Kirchwey] A. Cockburn. *The Nation* 249:266-7 S 18 '89
Nation books, 1988. *The Nation* 248:23-4 Ja 2 '89
Anecdotes, facetiae, satire, etc.
Let's do a deal [Nation bids for Time, Inc.] V. S. Navasky. *The Nation* 249:3-4 Jl 3 '89
Time is money [discussion of July 3, 1989 article, Let's do a deal] V. S. Navasky. *The Nation* 249:75-6 Jl 17 '89

NATION OF ISLAM *See* Black Muslims
NATIONAL (NEWSPAPER)
And in this corner coin box: an all-sports daily. S. Baker and D. Lieberman. il pors *Business Week* p30 Ag 21 '89
A fan's notes. E. Diamond. il pors *New York* 22:22-3 Ag 14 '89
Make room in the press box. M. Beck. il pors *Newsweek* 113:53 Je 12 '89

NATIONAL ACADEMY OF ENGINEERING
NAE elects new members. *Science* 243:1432 Mr 17 '89
National Academy of Engineering announces election of new members. *Physics Today* 42:86-7 Jl '89

NATIONAL ACADEMY OF SCIENCES (U.S.)
Biologists elected to NAS. *BioScience* 39:580 S '89
By contrast to last Academy address, Press is hopeful for science . . . if . . . I. Goodwin. *Physics Today* 42:41-2 Je '89
NAS elects new members. *Science* 244:524 My 5 '89
National Academy of Sciences elects new members. *Physics Today* 42:114 S '89
US and Soviet academies reach global ecology agreement. W. Sweet. *Physics Today* 42:101-2 F '89

NATIONAL ACADEMY OF SCIENCES (U.S.). INSTITUTE OF MEDICINE *See* Institute of Medicine (U.S.)
NATIONAL ACADEMY OF SCIENCES (U.S.). NATIONAL ACADEMY OF ENGINEERING *See* National Academy of Engineering
NATIONAL ACTION COMMITTEE ON THE STATUS OF WOMEN (CANADA)
Declining influence. L. Van Dusen. il *Maclean's* 102:23 O 9 '89

NATIONAL ACTION COUNCIL FOR MINORITIES IN ENGINEERING
Engineering growth. W. M. Woodard. *Black Enterprise* 20:22 D '89

NATIONAL ACTION PARTY (MEXICO) *See* Partido Acción Nacional (Mexico)
NATIONAL AERONAUTICS AND SPACE ADMINISTRATION (U.S.) *See* United States. National Aeronautics and Space Administration
NATIONAL AERONAUTICS AND SPACE ADMINISTRATION ALUMNI LEAGUE *See* NASA Alumni League
NATIONAL AFRICAN-AMERICAN HERITAGE MEMORIAL MUSEUM
Fund-raising push on for black memorials in D.C. *Jet* 76:7 Ap 17 '89
The quest for a black museum. M. S. Holmes. il *American Visions* 4:44-8 D '89

NATIONAL AIR AND SPACE MUSEUM
Around the Mall and beyond [Beyond the limits: flight enters the computer age; permanent exhibit] E. Park. il *Smithsonian* 20:16+ Jl '89
Smithsonian initiates effort to salvage space program documents [with editorial comment] *Aviation Week & Space Technology* 131:9, 20 O 16 '89

NATIONAL AIR AND SPACE MUSEUM. PAUL E. GARBER PRESERVATION, RESTORATION AND STORAGE FACILITY *See* Paul E. Garber Preservation, Restoration and Storage Facility
NATIONAL AIR TRAFFIC CONTROLLERS ASSOCIATION
Air traffic controllers, FAA reach tentative agreement on three-year pact. *Aviation Week & Space Technology* 130:66 Ja 23 '89

NATIONAL ALLIANCE OF BLACK SCHOOL EDUCATORS
Black educators cite late Richard Green, elect new officers at Oregon confab. il por *Jet* 77:28 D 18 '89

NATIONAL ARCHIVES AND RECORDS ADMINISTRATION (U.S.) *See* United States. National Archives and Records Administration
NATIONAL ART MATERIALS TRADE ASSOCIATION
Art and Design in Action: show guide [Dearborn, Mich.; special section] il *American Artist* 53:67-8+ N '89

Art and Design in Action: Washington, DC, show guide [special section] il *American Artist* 53:71-2+ Ja '89
NATIONAL ARTS CENTRE ORCHESTRA
Sounds of discord [strike] P. Young. *Maclean's* 102:70 O 16 '89
NATIONAL ASSESSMENT OF EDUCATIONAL PROGRESS
A box full of tools but no blueprint [national goals for schools] A. C. Lewis. *Phi Delta Kappan* 71:180-1 N '89
Mixed review [Crossroads in American Education report] *Time* 133:68 F 27 '89
NATIONAL ASSOCIATION FOR HISPANIC ELDERLY *See* Asociacion Nacional Pro Personas Mayores
NATIONAL ASSOCIATION FOR THE ADVANCEMENT OF COLORED PEOPLE
Freedom Fund gala in Detroit raises $1 million for NAACP. il *Jet* 76:16-17 My 15 '89
NAACP challenges the affirmative action plans of TV, radio stations. *Jet* 76:26 Je 12 '89
NAACP: China's protests will be small to our's. il *Jet* 76:4 Jl 24 '89
NAACP confab ignites blacks to unite against erosion of civil rights. il *Jet* 76:4-8 Jl 31 '89
NAACP: eighty years on freedom road. P. Ruffins. il *Black Enterprise* 19:194-6+ F '89
NAACP march protests 'legal lynching' of civil rights in U.S. il *Jet* 76:4-6 S 11 '89
NAACP proposes new self-help project for blacks. il *Jet* 77:30 D 4 '89
NAACP sues 5 S. Carolina cities over voting systems. il *Jet* 76:32 Jl 24 '89
NAACP to hold silent march in Washington to protest new Supreme Court rulings. il *Jet* 76:6 Ag 21 '89
The NAACP turns 80. L. B. Randolph. il *Ebony* 44:126+ Jl '89
NAACP's Gibson urges new tactics to keep set asides. por *Jet* 75:29 Mr 13 '89
NATIONAL ASSOCIATION OF ATTORNEYS GENERAL
Shut up and show us your rates [proposed guidelines for car rental agencies] G. Eichler. il *Esquire* 111:78 Je '89
Watch out for this new "model" owner/design-professional agreement. A. Kornblut. il por *Architectural Record* 177:29+ F '89
The whole building industry heats up over new contracts for public work. P. Hoffmann. *Architectural Record* 177:31 S '89
NATIONAL ASSOCIATION OF BROADCAST EMPLOYEES AND TECHNICIANS
Unions learn to go with the flow [automation] D. Bollier. il *Channels (New York, N.Y.: 1986)* 9:44-5 My '89
NATIONAL ASSOCIATION OF COLLEGE STORES (U.S.)
College bookstores share the pride in Baltimore [annual meeting] J. Mutter. il *Publishers Weekly* 235:36-9 Je 9 '89
NATIONAL ASSOCIATION OF EVANGELICALS
New and old issues alike fuel the fires of NAE. R. Frame. il *Christianity Today* 33:42-3 Ap 7 '89
NATIONAL ASSOCIATION OF HOME BUILDERS (U.S.)
Cloudy forecast for housing starts doesn't dampen NAHB's Atlanta convention. C. D. W. Koenig. il *Architectural Record* 177:27 Mr '89
NATIONAL ASSOCIATION OF JAZZ EDUCATORS
Grammy fest at NAJE annual. D. Helland. il *Down Beat* 56:12 Ap '89
NATIONAL ASSOCIATION OF MARKET DEVELOPERS
Don't ignore impact of ethnic market on U.S. economy: NAMD prexy. il *Jet* 76:23 Je 26 '89
NATIONAL ASSOCIATION OF MUSIC MERCHANTS
A music educator's look at the summer NAMM show. J. D. Waggoner. il *Down Beat* 56:56-7 O '89
Winter NAMM show sets the pace. J. Woodward. il *Down Beat* 56:10+ Ap '89
NATIONAL ASSOCIATION OF SCHOLARS
Letters [discussion of December 12, 1988 article, Campus voices right and left] J. Wiener. *The Nation* 248:146 F 6 '89
NATIONAL ASSOCIATION OF TELEVISION PROGRAM EXECUTIVES
Lawyers, guns and money. R. Powers. il *Gentlemen's Quarterly* 59:129-30+ Je '89
The more things change . . . [special section] il *Channels (New York, N.Y.: 1986)* 9:43-50 Ja 16 '89
Riding the rumble seat into the '90s [preview of NATPE panel on syndication] A. Butensky. por *Channels (New York, N.Y.: 1986)* 9:88 F '89
Syndication's new strategies [special section] il *Channels (New York, N.Y.: 1986)* 9:59+ F '89
NATIONAL AUDUBON SOCIETY
'Audubon perspectives' gives Wiley new perspective on trade. B. Levine. il *Publishers Weekly* 236:31-2 N 10 '89
Earth angel [policy analyst D. Bolze] P. Pacheco. il pors *Harper's Bazaar* 122:54-7 Jl '89
How the owl drove a wedge between Stroh and Audubon [beer company pulls ads from TV show on Pacific Northwest old growth forests] V. Cahan. *Business Week* p99 S 18 '89

NATIONAL AUDUBON SOCIETY—*cont.*
Intimidation [advertisers cancel sponsorship of television program about Pacific Northwest forests] L. Line. il *Audubon* 91:4 N '89

NATIONAL BALLET OF CANADA
Reviews:
 Performance of Tagore in Toronto. P. Citron. il *Dance Magazine* 63:52 Ag '89
 Triumphant adieu [V. Tennant] P. Young. il pors *Maclean's* 102:50-2 F 20 '89

NATIONAL BALLET SCHOOL (CANADA)
Betty builds bigger. M. Horosko. il *Dance Magazine* 63:62-3 Mr '89

NATIONAL BAPTIST CONVENTION OF THE UNITED STATES OF AMERICA *See* Baptists—United States

NATIONAL BASEBALL HALL OF FAME AND MUSEUM
Baseball and memories in Cooperstown. L. Griffin. il *Car and Driver* 35:187 N '89
Baseball Hall of Fame. H. Holzer. il *American History Illustrated* 24:12+ N/D '89
The 'Belles of the Ball Game' were a hit with their fans [All-American Girls Professional Baseball League commemorated] J. Fincher. il *Smithsonian* 20:88-94+ Jl '89
The creation myths of Cooperstown. S. J. Gould. il *Natural History* p14+ N '89
The keepers of Cooperstown. K. Modesti. il *Sport (New York, N.Y.)* 80:15 F '89
Morals and immortals [urging election of F. Jenkins and G. Perry] P. Gammons. il por *Sports Illustrated* 70:78 Ja 23 '89
Return to Cooperstown. J. Orsini. il *Travel Holiday* 171:76+ F '89
Safe at home [photographs of memorabilia] B. Wills. il *Sports Illustrated* 70:88-99 Je 12 '89
The stuff of legend. S. Wulf. il *Sports Illustrated* 70:100-2+ Je 12 '89
Too good to be left out [J. Jackson, banished for role in 1919 Black Sox scandal, should be elected to Hall of Fame] N. Dawidoff. por *Sports Illustrated* 70:118 Je 12 '89

NATIONAL BASKETBALL ASSOCIATION
A Soviet hoopster in the Promised Land [S. Marciulionis] P. De Jonge. il pors *The New York Times Magazine* p64+ N 5 '89
They're here [Soviet athletes] R. Harvey. il *Sport (New York, N.Y.)* 80:68-72 D '89

NATIONAL BASKETBALL PLAYERS ASSOCIATION
NBA Players Assn. fetes Kareem at benefit dinner. il por *Jet* 77:48-9 O 9 '89

NATIONAL BIPLANE ASSOCIATION
The sport hounds of Bartlesville [Biplane Expo '89] G. Baxter. il *Flying* 116:82-6+ S '89

NATIONAL BISON RANGE (MONT.)
Pronghorns in—and out of—a rut. J. A. Byers. il *Natural History* p38-49 Ap '89

NATIONAL BLACK REPUBLICAN COUNCIL
Leaders offer views on President Bush at Inaugural gala. il *Jet* 75:16+ F 6 '89

NATIONAL BOARD FOR PROFESSIONAL TEACHING STANDARDS (U.S.)
A new dog in town. A. C. Lewis. il *Phi Delta Kappan* 71:100-1 O '89

NATIONAL BOOK AWARDS
Dark horse 'Spartina' wins fiction NBA. J. F. Baker. il *Publishers Weekly* 236:18-19 D 15 '89

NATIONAL BOOK CRITICS CIRCLE AWARDS
Eloquence marks NBCC Awards. J. F. Baker and C. Reid. il *Publishers Weekly* 235:16-17 F 10 '89

NATIONAL BOOK NETWORK INC.
Tentative pact joins Kampmann & Co. with National Book Network. C. Reid. *Publishers Weekly* 235:16 My 26 '89

NATIONAL BOOK WEEK
National Book Week: a burgeoning effort. B. Prete. *Publishers Weekly* 236:40 D 22 '89

NATIONAL BOWLING HALL OF FAME AND MUSEUM
Kegling. *The New Yorker* 64:25-6 Ja 23 '89

NATIONAL BROADCASTING CO., INC.
After Seoul, Barcelona [NBC's J. Gilbert to oversee Olympic coverage] T. Paige. il por *Black Enterprise* 19:16 Ja '89
The ball's in a new court [acquires TV rights to NBA games] H. J. Steinbreder. il *Sports Illustrated* 71:125 N 20 '89
Behind the NBC News blues. J. Alter. il *Newsweek* 114:86-7 O 16 '89
Behind the Peacock throne [NBC News president M. Gartner] E. Diamond. il por *New York* 22:21-2 F 13 '89
Boy wonder gets the boot at NBC [sports producer M. Weisman] S. Smith. il por *Sports Illustrated* 70:82 My 22 '89
Ex-president blues [excerpt from address] F. Silverman. il *Channels (New York, N.Y.: 1986)* 9:87 Ja '89
NBC gets down to business [Consumer News & Business Channel] R. Zoglin. il *Time* 133:69 Ap 17 '89
On a roll with the man from GE [R. Wright; cover story] D. Machan. il por *Forbes* 143:124-7 Ap 17 '89
Playing for the Peacock [pro football broadcaster changes] B. Anderson. il *Sports Illustrated* 71:95 Jl 24 '89
Power failure [NBC News president M. Gartner] E. Diamond. il por *New York* 22:24-5 N 6 '89

Tour! [NBC studio in Manhattan] *The New Yorker* 65:42-3 N 27 '89
With Mary Alice Williams, NBC has a winner in the great anchor sweepstakes. S. K. Reed. il pors *People Weekly* 32:44-6 Ag 7 '89

NATIONAL BROTHERHOOD OF SKIERS
Conquering the slopes. L. Norment. il *Ebony* 44:110+ My '89
Skiers for all seasons. K. Burns. il *Essence* 20:100+ N '89

NATIONAL BUSINESS AIRCRAFT ASSOCIATION
NBAA means business [Atlanta convention] il *Flying* 116:8-10+ D '89
NBAA Show: new, derivative aircraft enhance upbeat atmosphere at exhibition [special section; with editorial comment] il *Aviation Week & Space Technology* 131:19, 36-8 O 9 '89
Unconventional kinda guy [Dallas convention] G. Baxter. il *Flying* 116:86+ F '89

NATIONAL CANCER INSTITUTE (U.S.)
America's top cancer clinics. S. Lally. *Prevention (Emmaus, Pa.)* 41:49-60 My '89
Cancer prevention strategy at the NCI [interview with S. Broder] C. SerVaas. il por *The Saturday Evening Post* 261:50-1+ My/Je '89
Dare to dialogue on cancer [interview with S. Broder] C. SerVaas. il pors *The Saturday Evening Post* 261:42-6+ Jl/Ag '89
A man with a mission [director P. Greenwald] D. Bartley. il pors *The Saturday Evening Post* 261:58-61+ N/D '89

NATIONAL CAPITOL (WASHINGTON, D.C.) *See* Capitol (Washington, D.C.)

NATIONAL CAR RENTAL SYSTEM, INC.
Wheels of fortune [advertising] B. Kanner. il *New York* 22:14+ F 20 '89

NATIONAL CASH REGISTER COMPANY *See* NCR Corp.

NATIONAL CAUCUS AND CENTER ON BLACK AGED
National centers on minority aging. il *Aging* no359:33-4 '89

NATIONAL CEMETERIES
 See also
 Beaufort National Cemetery (S.C.)

NATIONAL CENTER FOR SPACE STUDIES (FRANCE) *See* Centre National d'Etudes Spatiales (France)

NATIONAL CIVIL RIGHTS CENTER (MEMPHIS, TENN.)
Civil Rights Museum to be built in Memphis, where King was killed. il *Jet* 75:22 F 20 '89

NATIONAL COALITION FOR AGRICULTURAL SAFETY AND HEALTH
New ag coalition lobbies for farmer health and safety. C. Tevis. il *Successful Farming* 87:28 Ja '89

NATIONAL COLLEGIATE ATHLETIC ASSOCIATION
Baptists back Thompson in Proposition 42 fight [National Baptist Convention] il por *Jet* 75:50 F 27 '89
Dodging a bullet [Kentucky basketball program put on probation; cover story] C. Kirkpatrick. il *Sports Illustrated* 70:24-6+ My 29 '89
Is Proposition 42 racist? J. B. Johnson; A. Ashe. il *Ebony* 44:138-40 Je '89
National Collegiate Athletic Association [address, January 9, 1989] C. B. Reed. *Vital Speeches of the Day* 55:372-3 Ap 1 '89
A new Proposition [Proposition 42 stiffens rules governing awarding of athletic scholarships] W. F. Reed. il *Sports Illustrated* 70:16-19 Ja 23 '89
Out of bounds [questions regarding the NCAA's Proposition 42 to tighten restrictions on scholarships] *The New Republic* 200:10-11 F 20 '89
Race becomes the game [J. Thompson challenges Proposition 42 which tightens restrictions on athletic scholarships] J. Kroll. il por *Newsweek* 113:56-9 Ja 30 '89
Share the wealth, NCAA [basketball tournament] A. Wolff. por *Sports Illustrated* 71:128 N 20 '89
Thompson's walkout spurs review of Proposition 42. il *Jet* 75:50 F 13 '89
Tightening the rules [Proposition 42 tightens scholarship requirements] il *Newsweek* 113:58 Ja 23 '89
When is the playing field too level? [Proposition 42 tightens restrictions on athletic scholarships] A. P. Sanoff. il *U.S. News & World Report* 106:68-9 Ja 30 '89
"You do it until you get caught" [investigations of various college programs] T. Callahan. il *Time* 133:43 Ja 9 '89

NATIONAL COMMISSION ON LIBRARIES AND INFORMATION SCIENCE (U.S.)
 See also
 White House Conference on Library and Information Services

NATIONAL COMMISSION TO PREVENT INFANT MORTALITY (U.S.)
Putting children before politics [work of former senator L. Chiles] D. Olin. il por *New Choices for the Best Years* 29:16+ Jl '89

NATIONAL COMMITTEE TO PRESERVE SOCIAL SECURITY AND MEDICARE
Some groups are raising funds by raising fears about social security and Medicare. M. C. Paulson. il *Changing Times* 43:124-6 D '89
The torpedo that slammed into catastrophic health care. P. Dwyer. il *Business Week* p70 O 23 '89

NATIONAL COMMITTEES (POLITICAL)
See also
Democratic National Committee
National Republican Congressional Committee
Republican National Committee
NATIONAL CONFERENCE OF CATHOLIC BISHOPS See
Catholic Church. National Conference of Catholic Bishops
NATIONAL CONVENIENCE STORES INC.
A six-pack of Cabernet, please. T. Mack. il por *Forbes*
144:168-9 S 18 '89
NATIONAL CONVENTIONS, DEMOCRATIC
Jackson rules. F. Barnes. *The New Republic* 200:14+ My
1 '89
**NATIONAL COUNCIL FOR ACCREDITATION OF
TEACHER EDUCATION**
NCATE and Texas eyeball to eyeball: who will blink? [interview with C. Parker and H. Gideonse] D. Watts. il *Phi
Delta Kappan* 71:311-18 D '89
**NATIONAL COUNCIL OF ARCHITECTURAL REGISTRA-
TION BOARDS**
NCARB moves on qualification procedures and against
licensing for interior designers and unlicensed architecture.
C. K. Hoyt. il *Architectural Record* 177:33 My '89
NATIONAL COUNCIL OF CHURCHES
The National Council of Churches in crisis. R. Frame. il
Christianity Today 33:49-50 Ag 13 '89
NCC leader stuns board [A. Brouwer attacks critics in speech]
G. Spohn. por *Christianity Today* 33:52 Je 16 '89
NCC moves painfully toward *perestroika*. D. Heim. *The
Christian Century* 106:547-8 My 24-31 '89
NCC: striving to be faithful, not frantic [Governing Board
meeting] J. C. Lyles. *The Christian Century* 106:1142-3
D 6 '89
A streamlined version of the National Council. D. Heim.
The Christian Century 106:519 My 17 '89
NATIONAL COUNCIL OF CHURCHES (PHILIPPINES)
Philippine Council celebrates 25 years. R. M. Brown. *The
Christian Century* 106:69-71 Ja 25 '89
NATIONAL COUNCIL OF JEWISH WOMEN (CANADA)
Dangerous liaisons [B. Stone testifies at Ontario inquiry
into political donations from Tridel Enterprises channeled
through National Council of Jewish Women] P. Kaihla.
il pors *Maclean's* 102:20+ O 16 '89
NATIONAL COUNCIL OF NEGRO WOMEN
Self-help—a black tradition. D. I. Height. il *The Nation*
249:136-8 Jl 24-31 '89
**NATIONAL COUNCIL OF THE CHURCHES OF CHRIST
IN THE UNITED STATES OF AMERICA** See National
Council of Churches
**NATIONAL COUNCIL ON EDUCATION FOR THE
CERAMIC ARTS (U.S.)**
Clay at a crossroads [annual conference] M. Kangas. il
American Craft 49:18-23 Je/Jl '89
NATIONAL DAIRY PROMOTION & RESEARCH BOARD
Her challenge: win new dairy consumers [C. Carson] J. R.
Borcherding and P. Smith. il por *Successful Farming* 87:35
O '89
NATIONAL DANCE ASSOCIATION
At the crossroads: the National Dance Association in the
1990s. D. S. Howe. *Design for Arts in Education* 90:44-7
My/Je '89
NATIONAL DEBT See Debts, Public
NATIONAL DISTILLERS & CHEMICAL CORP.
See also
Quantum Chemical Corp.
NATIONAL ECONOMIC COMMISSION (U.S.)
The deficit: an exchange [discussion of June 1, 1989 article,
A deficit of civic courage] B. M. Friedman. *The New
York Review of Books* 36:73-4 S 28 '89
A deficit of civic courage. B. M. Friedman. il *The New
York Review of Books* 36:23-6 Je 1 '89
The NEC: a success, not a failure. C. W. Weinberger. il
Forbes 143:31 Ap 3 '89
**NATIONAL EDUCATION ASSOCIATION OF THE UNIT-
ED STATES**
A conversation with Mary Hatwood Futrell. M. E. Howard.
por *Black Enterprise* 20:30 O '89
NATIONAL ENDOWMENT FOR DEMOCRACY
Endowment drive. M. Kondracke. *The New Republic* 200:9-11
My 29 '89
Foreign aid for the right. D. Corn. il *The Nation* 249:744-6
D 18 '89
Overt meddling [U.S. plans to fund Nicaraguan elections]
The Nation 249:407-8 O 16 '89
NATIONAL ENDOWMENT FOR THE ARTS
Armey's aesthetic [views of Congressman R. K. Armey] T.
Noah. *The New Republic* 201:14+ S 11 '89
Art and taxpayers. A. C. Danto. *The Nation* 249:192-3 Ag
21-28 '89
Art wars: artists and politicans get worked up about the
NEA. H. Goldstein. il *Utne Reader* p14+ N/D '89
Artistic freedom, public anger. R. Berenson. il *National Review*
41:46 O 13 '89
Arts grants under fire [J. Helms leads Senate vote against
controversial art] C. McGuigan. il por *Newsweek* 114:23
Ag 7 '89
Congress passes compromise NEA bill. H. Fields. il *Publishers
Weekly* 236:10 O 20 '89

Congress rejects Helms amendment. W. Robinson. *Art in
America* 77:41 N '89
Congress votes for new censorship. il *Art in America* 77:33
S '89
Corcoran showdown [aftermath of cancellation of R. Mapple-
thorpe show] C. McGuigan. il pors *Newsweek* 114:111+
O 9 '89
Days of rage [NEA rescinds funding for Witnesses: against
our vanishing] K. Larson. il *New York* 22:80+ N 27 '89
Disaster at the NEA [rescinds funding for AIDS exhibit
Witnesses: against our vanishing] R. Brustein. *The New
Republic* 201:28-30 D 11 '89
A dispute over a photography exhibit raises once again
the relationship of art to conventional standards of taste.
R. M. Adams. il *Smithsonian* 20:12 O '89
Exhibitionism [Corcoran Gallery cancels R. Mapplethorpe
exhibit] *The New Republic* 201:6 Jl 17-24 '89
Fallout from Helms Amendment. B. Wallis. *Art in America*
77:29 O '89
The First Amendment and the NEA. R. Brustein. *The New
Republic* 201:27-9 S 11 '89
Highbrow pork barrel. R. J. Samuelson. il *Newsweek* 114:44
Ag 21 '89
House sets up commission to address Helms NEA proposal.
H. Fields. *Publishers Weekly* 236:10 O 6 '89
Jesse Helms on the meaning of art. F. Bruning. il *Maclean's*
102:9 Ag 14 '89
A loony parody of cultural democracy [J. Helms' attack]
R. Hughes. il *Time* 134:82 Ag 14 '89
Mad about Mapplethorpe [Corcoran Gallery cancels exhibit]
A. Ferguson. *National Review* 41:20-1 Ag 4 '89
Mapplethorpe of my eye [exhibit opens at WPA gallery
after cancellation by the Corcoran] A. Heard. *The New
Republic* 201:10-12 Ag 21 '89
The NEA: looking back, and looking ahead. S. Lipman.
Design for Arts in Education 90:2-9 Ja/F '89
Ol' Jesse's dirty word [amendment prohibiting NEA funding
of obscene art] *The Nation* 249:441 O 23 '89
Recent restrictions on NEA may be unconstitutional. H.
Fields. *Publishers Weekly* 236:11 D 1 '89
Robert Mapplethorpe. il por *People Weekly* 32:100-1 D 25
'89-Ja 1 '90
A "sacrificial lamb"? [aftermath of the Corcoran Gallery's
cancellation of R. Mapplethorpe show] S. Hochfield. il
por *Art News* 88:62 N '89
Sex, politics, religion & art. J. Cobb. *Common Cause
Magazine* 15:22 N/D '89
Shadowboxing with the arts. S. H. Madoff. il *Art News*
88:204 S '89
Shatzkin's report on small press distribution arouses debate.
M. Reuter. *Publishers Weekly* 236:9-10 S 8 '89
Shock art: your tax dollars at work. D. Coran. il *Christianity
Today* 33:69-70 S 8 '89
Should Congress censor art? [Helms Amendment] M. Horn.
il por *U.S. News & World Report* 107:22-4 S 25 '89
Summer, storm [classic drama among artist, patron and
public] M. Greenfield. il *Newsweek* 114:76 S 4 '89
Testing the new arts rules [NEA rescinds funds and later
decides to support AIDS exhibit Witnesses: against our
vanishing] *Newsweek* 114:43 N 27 '89
The war on culture. C. S. Vance. bibl f il *Art in America*
77:39+ S '89
When taxes pay for art. C. McGuigan. il *Newsweek* 114:68
Jl 3 '89
Whose art is it, anyway? [Corcoran Gallery cancels R.
Mapplethorpe exhibit] M. B. Carlson. il *Time* 134:21 Jl
3 '89
NATIONAL ENDOWMENT FOR THE HUMANITIES
Blossom time for the humanities. *America* 160:283-4 Ap
1 '89
NATIONAL ENERGY ASSOCIATES
National Energy Associates. M. Kelly. il *Utne Reader* p78
Ja/F '89
NATIONAL ENERGY BOARD (CANADA)
The value of gas [hearings on proposed export of Canadian
Arctic gas] B. Wickens. il *Maclean's* 102:54-5 My 1 '89
NATIONAL ENQUIRER
Alien beancounters invade the Enquirer [Macfadden Holdings]
A. Fins. il *Business Week* p35 S 11 '89
Bonet sues drugstore over published picture of baby. il por
Jet 76:27 Jl 3 '89
Peter Callahan: an acquiring mind [buyout of National en-
quirer] A. Rothman. il por *Business Week* p139-40 My
15 '89
NATIONAL ENVIRONMENTAL POLICY ACT See Environ-
mental policy
**NATIONAL EXPOSITION OF CONTRACT INTERIOR
FURNISHINGS** See Interior decoration—Exhibitions
NATIONAL FARMS INC.
South Dakota says no to the corporate sow. G. Vincent.
Successful Farming 87:35 F '89
NATIONAL FILM BOARD OF CANADA
Screen shadows. B. D. Johnson. il *Maclean's* 102:42-4 Jl
17 '89
A tale by two cultures [making of The first emperor of
China] T. R. Miller. il *Natural History* p66-9 Jl '89

NATIONAL FILM REGISTRY
Outside and inside the law. S. Kauffmann. *The New Republic* 201:24-6 O 23 '89

NATIONAL FOOTBALL LEAGUE
A happy homecoming [Raiders owner A. Davis now an NFL peacemaker] P. King. por *Sports Illustrated* 71:76 Jl 31 '89

He quit, for Pete's sake [commissioner P. Rozelle] P. Zimmerman. il pors *Sports Illustrated* 70:60-2 Ap 3 '89

A league loses [inability to choose a successor to commissioner Pete Rozelle] P. King. il *Sports Illustrated* 71:86-7 O 23 '89

The NFL's new boss [P. Tagliabue] P. King. il por *Sports Illustrated* 71:19-20 N 6 '89

That head-banging you hear is the NFL owners. B. Bremner. il *Business Week* p36 S 4 '89

Top blacks qualified to replace Pete Rozelle. il por *Jet* 76:51 Ap 10 '89

NATIONAL FOOTBALL LEAGUE PLAYERS ASSOCIATION
The NFL's union could win by committing suicide [gaining free agency by disbanding] A. Bernstein. il por *Business Week* p84 N 27 '89

NATIONAL FOREST TRAILS See Trails

NATIONAL FORESTS
See also
United States. Forest Service
Something in the air [pollution obscuring visibility] L. Kahaner. il *Wilderness* 52:18-27 Wint '88

Alaska
See also
Tongass National Forest (Alaska)

Appalachian region
Biodiversity loss faces the Southern Appalachians. *Wilderness* 52:iii Spr '89

Arizona
See also
Tonto National Forest (Ariz.)

Arkansas
See also
Ouachita National Forest (Ark. and Okla.)

California
See also
Sequoia National Forest (Calif.)

Colorado
See also
Gunnison National Forest (Colo.)
Manti-LaSal National Forest (Utah and Colo.)

Indiana
See also
Hoosier National Forest (Ind.)

Louisiana
See also
Kisatchie National Forest (La.)

Michigan
See also
Huron-Manistee National Forest (Mich.)

Mississippi
See also
Homochitto National Forest (Miss.)

Missouri
See also
Mark Twain National Forest (Mo.)

Montana
See also
Flathead National Forest (Mont.)

New Mexico
See also
Santa Fe National Forest (N.M.)

North Carolina
See also
Pisgah National Forest (N.C.)
A mixed blessing [Forest Service management plan] P. Byrnes. *Wilderness* 53:5-6 Wint '89

Oklahoma
See also
Ouachita National Forest (Ark. and Okla.)

Oregon
See also
Mount Hood National Forest (Or.)

Pacific Northwest
Ancient forests as victims of myth. *Wilderness* 53:3 Fall '89
The ancient ones. il map *Wilderness* 52:44-51 Spr '89
New thinking on old growth. W. Booth. il map *Science* 244:141-3 Ap 14 '89

Puerto Rico
See also
Caribbean National Forest (Puerto Rico)

Tennessee
See also
Cherokee National Forest (Tenn.)

Texas
A clearcutting ban for the birds [red cockaded woodpeckers] P. Larmer. il *Sierra* 74:28-30 Mr/Ap '89

Utah
See also
Manti-LaSal National Forest (Utah and Colo.)

Wyoming
See also
Gallatin National Forest (Mont. and Wyo.)

NATIONAL GALLERY (GREAT BRITAIN)
Picking up the pieces [restoration of damage to L. da Vinci's The Virgin and child with St. Anne and John the Baptist] B. Taylor. il *Art News* 88:43+ F '89

NATIONAL GALLERY OF ART (U.S.)
A $60 million van Gogh? [P. Harriman's donation of Roses] R. W. Walker. il *Art News* 88:31 S '89

NATIONAL GALLERY OF ART (U.S.). EAST BUILDING
The East Building's anniversary of art. il *Southern Living* 24:38-9 D '89
Getting your motor revved up [Twentieth-century art: selections for the tenth anniversary of the East Building] E. M. Gomez. il *Art News* 88:48+ My '89

NATIONAL GALLERY OF CANADA
'Oh, Canada . . .'. P. Johnston. il *History Today* 39:4-5 Ag '89

NATIONAL GEOGRAPHIC SOCIETY (U.S.)
Redrawing the map [Robinson projection] J. Diamond. maps *World Press Review* 36:61 Je '89
Superpowers not so super in geography [1989 projects] G. M. Grosvenor. il map *National Geographic* 176:816-21 D '89

NATIONAL GEOGRAPHIC WORLD PHOTO CONTEST
See Photography—Competitions

NATIONAL GUARD (PA.) See Pennsylvania. National Guard

NATIONAL GUARD (U.S.) See United States. National Guard

NATIONAL HEALTH INSURANCE See Insurance, Health

NATIONAL HEALTH LABORATORIES, INC.
The perils of Perelman. E. Paris. il *Forbes* 144:65+ D 11 '89

NATIONAL HEALTH SERVICE (GREAT BRITAIN) See Great Britain. National Health Service

NATIONAL HIGHWAY TRAFFIC SAFETY ADMINISTRATION (U.S.) See United States. National Highway Traffic Safety Administration

NATIONAL HOCKEY LEAGUE
The honeymooners [Soviet players; cover story] J. Greenberg. il *Sports Illustrated* 71:44-8+ O 9 '89
Is it nyet or not yet? [V. Fetisov of touring Soviets seeks permission to join NHL] E. M. Swift. il pors *Sports Illustrated* 70:30-3 Ja 16 '89
A Red-letter day [Soviet Union's S. Priakin makes NHL debut with Calgary] C. Cotton. il por *Sports Illustrated* 70:38-9 Ap 10 '89
Soviet invasion. J. Howse. il *Maclean's* 102:46-7 O 9 '89
Soviet pretenders to Gretzky's throne [Russian players] il por *U.S. News & World Report* 107:19 O 30 '89
They're here [Soviet athletes] R. Harvey. il *Sport (New York, N.Y.)* 80:68-72 D '89

NATIONAL HUGGING DAY
A concerned Cupidian named Kevin Zaborney squeezes National Hugging Day into the calendar. il por *People Weekly* 31:92 Ja 23 '89

NATIONAL INDIAN COUNCIL ON AGING
National centers on minority aging. il *Aging* no359:33-4 '89

NATIONAL INSTITUTE OF ALLERGY AND INFECTIOUS DISEASES (U.S.)
A research tool in the war against AIDS. P. Honan. il por *Personal Computing* 13:182-4 O '89

NATIONAL INSTITUTE OF MENTAL HEALTH (U.S.)
NIMH assigns blame for tainted studies [Stanford University] M. Barinaga. *Science* 245:812 Ag 25 '89

NATIONAL INSTITUTE ON DRUG ABUSE (U.S.)
NIDA aims to fight drugs with drugs. M. M. Waldrop. *Science* 245:1443-4 S 29 '89

NATIONAL INSTITUTES OF HEALTH (U.S.)
Abortion: litmus test for NIH director. B. J. Culliton. *Science* 246:27 O 6 '89
Baltimore case reopened. *Science News* 135:278 My 6 '89
Baltimore cleared of all fraud charges [disputed Cell paper] B. J. Culliton. il por *Science* 243:727 F 10 '89
Bush goes 0 for 2 with Anthony Fauci. B. J. Culliton. por *Science* 246:880 N 17 '89
The choosing of the NIH director. D. E. Koshland, Jr. *Science* 246:981 N 24 '89
Conduct unbecoming? [D. Baltimore case] P. Weiss. il pors *The New York Times Magazine* p40-3+ O 29 '89
The Dingell probe finally goes public [D. Baltimore case] B. J. Culliton. *Science* 244:643-6+ My 12 '89
Dingell v. Baltimore. B. J. Culliton. pors *Science* 244:412-14 Ap 28 '89
Ethical questions haunt new genetic technologies. L. Roberts. il por *Science* 243:1134-6 Mr 3 '89
Fraud debate aired on Capitol Hill [D. Baltimore case] K. Fackelmann. *Science News* 135:294-5 My 13 '89
Help wanted: director, NIH. B. J. Culliton. *Science* 245:1181 S 15 '89
The lost opportunity in AIDS research. D. Baltimore. il *Technology Review* 92:24-5 F/Mr '89
New round in Dingell v. NIH? [case of C. D. Bridges] J. Palca. *Science* 245:349 Jl 28 '89
NIH: calling all alumni. B. J. Culliton. il *Science* 243:734 F 10 '89

NATIONAL INSTITUTES OF HEALTH (U.S.)—cont.
NIH finds scientific errors but no fraud [D. Baltimore case] K. Fackelmann. *Science News* 135:85 F 11 '89
NIH grapples with conflict of interest. J. Palca. il *Science* 245:23 Jl 7 '89
NIH, Inc.: the CRADA boom [cooperative research and development agreements] B. J. Culliton. il *Science* 245:1034-6 S 8 '89
NIH limits gene experiments done abroad. *Science News* 135:237 Ap 15 '89
NIH offers AZT to exposed workers. W. Booth. *Science* 243:1137 Mr 3 '89
NIH probes researcher's fundraising [case of leukemia researcher R. I. Glazer] C. Holden. *Science* 243:1000 F 24 '89
NIH scientists agonize over technology transfer. W. Booth. *Science* 243:20-1 Ja 6 '89
NIH sees plagiarism in vision paper [case of C. D. Bridges] B. J. Culliton. *Science* 245:120-2 Jl 14 '89
Panel to redesign NIH director's job. B. J. Culliton. il *Science* 246:1244 D 8 '89
Plan for genome centers sparks a controversy. L. Roberts. il *Science* 246:204-5 O 13 '89
Superpay for NIH superstars. B. J. Culliton. *Science* 244:1038 Je 2 '89
Whose notes are they? [proposal to open scientists' personal data books to general scrutiny; Dingell hearings on D. Baltimore case] B. J. Culliton. il *Science* 244:765 My 19 '89
Wyngaarden to leave NIH. B. J. Culliton. por *Science* 244:414 Ap 28 '89

Appropriations and expenditures
Conflict over conflict of interest [research fund recipients] J. Palca. *Science* 245:1440 S 29 '89
Hard times at NIH [research grant problems] J. Palca. il *Science* 246:988-90 N 24 '89
NIH: the good old days [history of the grants program; views of Stephen P. Strickland] B. J. Culliton. *Science* 244:1437 Je 23 '89
Retargeting research on biological weapons. K. R. Yamamoto. il *Technology Review* 92:23-4 Ag/S '89
Who's minding the store? [loss of Bionet funding] P. Wallich. *Scientific American* 261:20+ O 19 '89

NATIONAL INTEREST *See* Nationalism
NATIONAL INTERGROUP INC.
Last chance for Love? G. L. Miles. *Business Week* p31-2 Ap 24 '89
National Intergroup: how Pete Love went wrong. G. L. Miles. il pors *Business Week* p56-7+ Mr 6 '89
NATIONAL LABORATORIES *See* Laboratories, Government
NATIONAL LAMPOON'S CHRISTMAS VACATION [film]
See Motion picture reviews—Single works
NATIONAL LAWYERS GUILD
Another dirty secret [FBI investigation] M. Kempton. *The New York Review of Books* 36:52 D 7 '89
NATIONAL LEAD COMPANY *See* NL Industries, Inc.
NATIONAL LEAD OF OHIO
Dropping a bomb on 'radioactive junkyards' [jury decision against National Lead in Fernald, Ohio pollution case] M. Mallory. il *Business Week* p29-30 Jl 3 '89
Uranium, in moderation [defends radioactive leakage] *Harper's* 278:18+ Ja '89
NATIONAL LEADERSHIP INSTITUTE ON AGING
AoA establishes National Leadership Institute on Aging. il *Aging* no359:36 '89
NATIONAL LIBERATION MOVEMENTS
Playing to the home crowd [Reagan Doctrine] R. H. Johnson. il *The Bulletin of the Atomic Scientists* 45:24-8 Ja/F '89
States, nations, and superpower diplomacy. J. H. Wolfe. il *USA Today (Periodical)* 117:51 My '89
Thesis disPeruvian [third world conflicts] T. Rosenberg. *The New Republic* 201:15-17 O 9 '89
NATIONAL LIBRARIES
See also
Library of Congress
National Library of Medicine (U.S.)
Libraries to the rescue [preserving contemporary manuscripts] G. Cartier. il *The Courier (Unesco)* 42:6-8 My '89
France
See also
Bibliothèque Nationale (France)
NATIONAL LIBRARY OF MEDICINE (U.S.)
A question of information policy [proposed fees] R. C. Atkinson. *Science* 246:33 N 10 '89
NATIONAL LIGHTHOUSE DAY
Tales from the taffrail. H. J. Saxton. *Sea Frontiers* 35:128 Mr/Ap '89
NATIONAL MARINE FISHERIES SERVICE (U.S.) *See* United States. National Marine Fisheries Service
NATIONAL MEDAL OF ARTS
President Bush praises Gillespie and Dunham at White House fete. il pors *Jet* 77:27 D 11 '89
NATIONAL MEDAL OF SCIENCE
Bush awards science, technology medals. *Science* 246:443 O 27 '89
National Medals of Science recognize work in physics. il *Physics Today* 42:91-2+ My '89

NATIONAL MEDAL OF TECHNOLOGY
Bush awards science, technology medals. *Science* 246:443 O 27 '89
National Medals of Technology cite physics research. *Physics Today* 42:98+ Je '89
NATIONAL MEDIATION BOARD (U.S.) *See* United States. National Mediation Board
NATIONAL MONEY MART INC.
A new way for people to beat the banks. P. C. Newman. il *Maclean's* 102:39 Je 19 '89
NATIONAL MONUMENTS
See also
Bandelier National Monument (N.M.)
Custer Battlefield National Monument (Mont.)
Fort Jefferson National Monument (Fla.)
Hovenweep National Monument (Colo. and Utah)
Jewel Cave National Monument (S.D.)
John Day Fossil Beds National Monument (Or.)
Mount Rushmore National Memorial (S.D.)
Organ Pipe Cactus National Monument (Ariz.)
Saguaro National Monument (Ariz.)
NATIONAL MORALE *See* Morale, National
NATIONAL MUSEUM OF AMERICAN ART (U.S.)
Keeping track of sculpture with computers [Inventory of American Sculpture] il *The Futurist* 23:49 Mr/Ap '89
A vision of our nation [photography collection] K. A. Lawson. il *USA Today (Periodical)* 117:52-61 My '89
NATIONAL MUSEUM OF AMERICAN HISTORY (U.S.)
The object at hand [bullet-riddled tree stump from the Spotsylvania battlefield] M. Kernan. il *Smithsonian* 20:24+ My '89
A pack rat's tale [donating personal items] L. Stone. il *Americana* 17:19-21 My/Je '89
The stuff of history. B. Barol. il por *Newsweek* 113:80-1 Ap 24 '89
NATIONAL MUSEUM OF COMMUNICATIONS (IRVING, TEX.)
From smoke signals to satellites. il *Southern Living* 24:28-9 F '89
NATIONAL MUSEUM OF MAN (CANADA)
See also
Canadian Museum of Civilization
NATIONAL MUSEUM OF THE AMERICAN INDIAN (U.S.)
An American legacy. C. Bond. bibl f (p228) il *Smithsonian* 20:42-55 O '89
Ghost riders in the Washington sky. il *U.S. News & World Report* 106:11 My 22 '89
A new national museum may become a cultural rallying point for American Indians and their arts and traditions. R. M. Adams. il *Smithsonian* 20:10 Ag '89
NATIONAL MUSEUMS OF KENYA
Leakey leaves Kenya museums. R. Lewin. il por *Science* 243:473 Ja 27 '89
NATIONAL OCEANIC AND ATMOSPHERIC ADMINISTRATION (U.S.) *See* United States. National Oceanic and Atmospheric Administration
NATIONAL OPTICAL ASTRONOMY OBSERVATORIES
U.S. astronomy's diminished funds. il *Sky and Telescope* 78:244 S '89
NATIONAL ORGANIZATION FOR WOMEN
Can pro-choicers prevail? Feminists squabble over strategy for protecting rights. M. B. Carlson. il *Time* 134:28 Ag 14 '89
NOW proposes new party; black activists respond. il *Jet* 76:14-15 Ag 14 '89
Reconcilable differences [division among women's groups over pro-choice strategies] P. Simpson. *Ms.* 18:70 O '89
Taking issue with NOW. E. Clift. il *Newsweek* 114:21-2 Ag 14 '89
NATIONAL PACIFIC/ASIAN RESOURCE CENTER ON AGING
National centers on minority aging. il *Aging* no359:33-4 '89
NATIONAL PARK PERSONNEL *See* National parks and reserves—Employees
NATIONAL PARK SERVICE (U.S.) *See* United States. National Park Service
NATIONAL PARKS AND CONSERVATION ASSOCIATION
NPCA news. See issues of National Parks
NPCA's seven decades. il *National Parks* 63:26-7 My/Je '89
NATIONAL PARKS AND CONSERVATION ASSOCIATION. COMMISSION ON SCIENCE AND RESOURCE MANAGEMENT POLICY
The scientific method [with editorial comment by Paul C. Pritchard] J. C. Gordon. il *National Parks* 63:5, 16-17 My/Je '89
NATIONAL PARKS AND RESERVES
See also
America in Space National Historical Park (Proposed)
March for Parks
National seashores
United States. National Park Service
Wild and scenic rivers
100th Congress adds new parks. il *National Parks* 63:8-9 Ja/F '89
101st Congress tackles park bills. *National Parks* 63:12-13 My/Je '89

NATIONAL PARKS AND RESERVES—cont.

American beauty. C. Gowdy. il por maps *Popular Mechanics* 166:96-7+ My '89

America's national parks: a special guide for family vacationers [special section] M. Ingebretsen. il *Better Homes and Gardens* 67:167-8+ Ap '89

At city's edge. L. Tuttle. il *National Parks* 63:37-9 N/D '89

Good times: summer of '89: where to go and what to do in the national parks. M. Cronin. il *National Parks* 63:37-41 My/Je '89

The great outdoors [camping] il maps *U.S. News & World Report* 106:65-7+ My 8 '89

The next four national parks. D. R. Wallace. il *Mother Jones* 14:28-31+ Jl/Ag '89

Open letter to President Bush. P. C. Pritchard. il *National Parks* 63:16-17 S/O '89

Parks in bloom. A.-M. Praetzel. il *National Parks* 63:34-6 My/Je '89

A question of degree [evidence of global warming; cover story] J. Page. il map *National Parks* 63:24-9 Jl/Ag '89

The quiet kill [poaching] M. Milstein. il *National Parks* 63:18-25 My/Je '89

Ride the rivers [canoe trips] C. M. Toops. il *National Parks* 63:39-41 Mr/Ap '89

Signs of life: tracking wildlife in the national parks. A.-M. Praetzel. il *National Parks* 63:39-42 Ja/F '89

Something in the air [pollution obscuring visibility] L. Kahaner. il *Wilderness* 52:18-27 Wint '88

Spirits in stone [petroglyphs; cover story] T. Browning. il *National Parks* 63:37-9 S/O '89

U.S. national parks in trouble. L. Lamb. il *Utne Reader* p10-11 N/D '89

Concessions (Food, etc.)

Yosemite national parking lot. K. Ohnuma. il *Sierra* 74:31-2+ N/D '89

Educational use

Using nature as a model [biological diversity in the national parks] D. Hunter. il *National Parks* 63:40-1 S/O '89

Employees

Interior looking to contract out park jobs. *National Parks* 63:11-12 Ja/F '89

International aspects

Exporting park know-how [National Park Service's international programs] D. Drabelle. il *National Parks* 63:32-8 Mr/Ap '89

Photographs and photography

Making portraits of the microcosm [work of K. Givens] K. Sferra. il *National Parks* 63:28-31 Mr/Ap '89

Planning

Guide for transition. P. C. Pritchard. *National Parks* 63:5 Ja/F '89

National parks: year 2000. W. P. Mott, Jr. il *National Parks* 63:18-19 Ja/F '89

Science or scenery? R. W. Sellars. il *Wilderness* 52:28-39 Summ '89

Volunteer workers

Tales from the trail [Sierra Club service vacations] il *Harper's Bazaar* 122:60-1+ Ja '89

Alaska

See also

Denali National Park and Preserve (Alaska)

Grave waters [effect of Exxon Valdez oil spill] J. Kenney. il map *National Parks* 63:18-23+ Jl/Ag '89

Alberta

See also

Banff National Park (Alta.)

Arizona

See also

Grand Canyon National Park (Ariz.)

Organ Pipe Cactus National Monument (Ariz.)

Petrified Forest National Park (Ariz.)

Saguaro National Monument (Ariz.)

Australia

See also

Kakadu National Park (Australia)

Uluru National Park (Australia)

Borneo

See also

Kinabalu National Park (Borneo)

British Columbia

See also

Pacific Rim National Park (B.C.)

California

See also

Golden Gate National Recreation Area (Calif.)

Lassen Volcanic National Park (Calif.)

Redwood National Park (Calif.)

Santa Monica Mountains National Recreation Area (Calif.)

Yosemite National Park (Calif.)

Colombia

See also

Serranía de la Macarena (Colombia)

Colorado

See also

Hovenweep National Monument (Colo. and Utah)

Colorado proposes protecting vistas. *National Parks* 63:13-14 Ja/F '89

Costa Rica

See also

Cocos Island (Costa Rica)

Guanacaste National Park (Costa Rica)

Quetzalandia. D. Bellm. il *Mother Jones* 14:49-50 D '89

Florida

See also

Big Cypress National Preserve (Fla.)

Everglades National Park (Fla.)

Fort Jefferson National Monument (Fla.)

Guatemala

A will to protect. J. P. Cohn. il *Américas* 41 no2:46-51+ '89

Hawaii

See also

Haleakala National Park (Hawaii)

Hawaii Volcanoes National Park (Hawaii)

Italy

See also

Abruzzo National Park (Italy)

Kansas

A prairie park? [Spring Hill Ranch offered for national park status] F. Graham. il *Audubon* 91:20+ S '89

Kentucky

See also

Big South Fork National River and Recreation Area (Tenn. and Ky.)

Kenya

See also

Amboseli National Park (Kenya)

Tsavo National Park (Kenya)

Maine

See also

Acadia National Park (Me.)

Maryland

See also

Antietam National Battlefield (Md.)

Michigan

See also

Isle Royale National Park (Mich.)

Minnesota

See also

Voyageurs National Park (Minn.)

Montana

See also

Custer Battlefield National Monument (Mont.)

Glacier National Park (Mont.)

Grant-Kohrs Ranch National Historic Site (Mont.)

Nepal

See also

Annapurna Conservation Area Project (Nepal)

Royal Chitwan National Park (Nepal)

Netherlands

See also

Hoge Veluwe National Park (Netherlands)

Nevada

See also

Great Basin National Park (Nev.)

New Jersey

See also

Gateway National Recreation Area (N.J. and N.Y.)

New Mexico

See also

Bandelier National Monument (N.M.)

New York (State)

See also

Gateway National Recreation Area (N.J. and N.Y.)

North Carolina

See also

Great Smoky Mountains National Park (N.C. and Tenn.)

North Dakota

See also

Theodore Roosevelt National Park (N.D.)

Oregon

See also

John Day Fossil Beds National Monument (Or.)

Pennsylvania

See also

Gettysburg National Military Park (Pa.)

South Africa

Pay or perish. L. Williamson. il *Outdoor Life* 184:36+ D '89

Tanzania

See also

Serengeti National Park (Tanzania)

Tennessee

See also

Big South Fork National River and Recreation Area (Tenn. and Ky.)

Great Smoky Mountains National Park (N.C. and Tenn.)

Texas

See also

Big Thicket National Preserve (Tex.)

Lyndon B. Johnson National Historical Park (Tex.)

NATIONAL PARKS AND RESERVES—*cont.*
United States
See National parks and reserves
Utah
See also
Bryce Canyon National Park (Utah)
Hovenweep National Monument (Colo. and Utah)
Zion National Park (Utah)
NPCA halts parkland sell-off plan. *National Parks* 63:11
N/D '89
Utah threatens parks with development [planning to sell
stateheld lands] il *National Parks* 63:11 S/O '89
Virginia
See also
Great Falls Park (Va.)
Manassas National Battlefield Park (Va.)
Yorktown Battlefield (Va.)
Washington (State)
See also
Ebey's Landing National Historical Reserve (Wash.)
Olympic National Park (Wash.)
Western States
See also
Yellowstone National Park
Wyoming
See also
Grand Teton National Park (Wyo.)
Yugoslavia
See also
Plitvice National Park (Yugoslavia)
Zambia
See also
South Luangwa National Park (Zambia)
Zimbabwe
See also
Matusadona National Park (Zimbabwe)
NATIONAL PARTY (SOUTH AFRICA)
The end of an era: President Botha bids a resentful goodbye.
A. Bilski. il por *Maclean's* 102:22 Ag 28 '89
Falling apartheid [upcoming elections favor F. W. De Klerk]
M. R. Hoffenberg. *The New Republic* 201:16-17 Jl 31
'89
An heir apparent in the march to Pretoria [F. W. de Klerk]
por *Newsweek* 113:35 F 13 '89
In the teeth of the 'Great Crocodile' [P. W. Botha] S. Reiss.
il pors *Newsweek* 113:39 Mr 27 '89
Return of the Great Crocodile [P. W. Botha] B. W. Nelan.
il por *Time* 133:56 Mr 27 '89
Showdown in Cape Town. M. Nemeth. por *Maclean's* 102:30
Mr 27 '89
South Africa: a step forward on Namibia, a step backward
at home? A. Fine. il *Business Week* p66 Mr 13 '89
NATIONAL PORK PRODUCERS COUNCIL
Pork producers get little from the 'pork barrel'. P. Smith.
il *Successful Farming* 87:52 F '89
NATIONAL PORTRAIT GALLERY (GREAT BRITAIN)
Portraits for the nation [cover story] G. P. Nuding. il *History
Today* 39:30-6 Je '89
NATIONAL POST OFFICE MAIL HANDLERS UNION
Struggling for union democracy. D. Corn. il *The Nation*
248:48-50+ Ja 9-16 '89
NATIONAL PTA (U.S.)
The National PTA's stand on corporal punishment. J. Ball.
The Education Digest 54:23-5 Ap '89
NATIONAL RADIO ASTRONOMY OBSERVATORY (U.S.)
300-foot collapse: the probable cause. il *Sky and Telescope*
78:11-12 Jl '89
A blow to astronomy [collapse of Green Bank radio telescope]
G. L. Verschuur. *Astronomy* 17:8 My '89
Collapse of a legend. A. Fisher. il *Popular Science* 234:8
Mr '89
Cracked plate caused telescope collapse [Green Bank, W.
Va.] *Science News* 135:269 Ap 29 '89
Green Bank's 300-foot radio telescope collapses. *Astronomy*
17:14+ F '89
In memoriam [collapse of Green Bank, W. Va. radio telescope]
T. Rothman. il *Scientific American* 260:17 F '89
Out of the wreckage, a 100-meter radiotelescope is backed
by Congress. C. S. Powell. il *Physics Today* 42 pt1:41-2
Ag '89
Reminiscences of the 300-foot [radio telescope collapses]
G. L. Verschuur. *Sky and Telescope* 77:252-3 Mr '89
Report out on Green Bank collapse; replacement poses
quandary for NSF. P. H. Andersen. il *Physics Today* 42:55-7
Ap '89
Telescope collapse unraveled [Green Bank, W. Va.] C. Nor-
man. il *Science* 244:29 Ap 7 '89
NATIONAL RAILROAD PASSENGER CORP.
Aboard America's favorite train [Zephyr] F. W. Frailey. il
map *Changing Times* 43:84-91 N '89
Amtrak's Florida wasteland [dumping human sewage on the
tracks] B. Turque. il *Newsweek* 114:50 D 11 '89
Another world [Manhattan to Boston ride] *The New Yorker*
65:30-1 Je 5 '89
Is Amtrak turning around? [interview with W. G. Claytor]
H. Gieseking. *Travel Holiday* 171:75-6 Ja '89
Putting Amtrak's best to the test. il *Business Week* p180-1
Jl 17 '89

A train trilogy [riding Amtrak's Coast Starlight from Seattle
to Los Angeles] D. G. Gordon. il map *Travel Holiday*
171:60-6 My '89
Why Amtrak won't stop to let the taxpayer off. S. Payne.
il *Business Week* p90 Ja 30 '89
Working on the railroad. C. C. Williams. il por *Black
Enterprise* 19:62-4 Ap '89
NATIONAL RAINBOW COALITION
Rainbow future. H. Sklar. *The Nation* 248:113-14 Ja 30
'89
Strategies for now—and next time [J. Jackson; cover story]
A. Kopkind. il *The Nation* 249:297+ S 25 '89
Whither the Rainbow? [discussion of September 25, 1989
article, Strategies for now—and next time] A. Kopkind.
The Nation 249:738+ D 18 '89
'Why I'm moving to Washington, D.C.' [cover story] il
por *Jet* 76:4-6 Ag 7 '89
NATIONAL REALTY ADVISORS, INC.
Old dog, old tricks [W. S. Friedman] J. Zweig. il por *Forbes*
144:246+ O 2 '89
NATIONAL REGISTER OF HISTORIC PLACES
All about the National Register. B. Vila. il *Popular Mechanics*
166:36-7 D '89
NATIONAL RELIGIOUS BROADCASTERS
Back to the basics for NRB [annual convention] K. A.
Lawton. il *Christianity Today* 33:46-7 Mr 3 '89
Evangelical broadcasters: preaching to the choir? [annual
convention] M. R. Halton. il *The Christian Century*
106:375-6 Ap 12 '89
Transition time at NRB. il *Christianity Today* 33:38 O 6
'89
**NATIONAL RELIGIOUS BROADCASTERS. ETHICS AND
FINANCIAL INTEGRITY COMMISSION**
EFICOM chugs along. R. Frame. il *Christianity Today* 33:50-1
My 12 '89
**NATIONAL REPUBLICAN CONGRESSIONAL COMMIT-
TEE**
How the Democrats hold on to Congress. S. T. Mandel
and W. McGurn. *National Review* 41:37-40 N 24 '89
How to win an election. W. Allison. *National Review* 41:24
O 13 '89
Off the record. Cato. *National Review* 41:64 O 27 '89
**NATIONAL REPUBLICAN INSTITUTE FOR INTER-
NATIONAL AFFAIRS**
Foreign aid for the right. D. Corn. il *The Nation* 249:744-6
D 18 '89
**NATIONAL RESEARCH INSTITUTE FOR BIOTIC RE-
SOURCES (MEXICO)**
Mexican research center closed. W. Booth. *Science* 243:1654
Mr 31 '89
NATIONAL RESOURCES DEFENSE COUNCIL
Suppressing the office energy appetite [new headquarters]
J. S. Russell. il *Architectural Record* 177:128-33 O '89
NATIONAL RETIREE VOLUNTEER CENTER
National Center helps set up projects to get retirees to
volunteer. il *Aging* no359:31-2 '89
NATIONAL REVIEW
Face the music [attack on rock & roll] K. Loder. il *Rolling
Stone* p57-9+ My 4 '89
Now it can be told. W. A. Rusher. il pors *National Review*
41:36-7+ Ja 27 '89
A toast to Bill Rusher [address, December 9, 1988] W.
F. Buckley. *National Review* 41:19-20 Ja 27 '89
NATIONAL RIFLE ASSOCIATION OF AMERICA
Guns [cover story] D. Baer. il *U.S. News & World Report*
106:20-2+ My 8 '89
How citizens can beat the gun lobby [cover story] R. W.
Bruner. il *The Nation* 248:433+ Ap 3 '89
Is the NRA being shot down? R. F. Drinan. *The Christian
Century* 106:372-3 Ap 12 '89
The meaning of Maryland [gun control] D. E. Petzal. il
Field & Stream 93:24-5 Mr '89
The N.R.A. in a hunter's sights. R. Hughes. il *Time* 133:86
Ap 3 '89
The NRA comes under the gun [on the defensive as opposition
to assault weapons grows] R. Sandza. il *Newsweek* 113:28-30
Mr 27 '89
Secrets behind the gun lobby's staying power. D. Gergen
and T. Gest. il *U.S. News & World Report* 106:26 My
8 '89
Top Gun [president J. Foss] G. Smith. il pors *Sports Illustrated*
71:56-62+ Ag 7 '89
NATIONAL RIGHT TO LIFE COMMITTEE
The advertiser that didn't balk [pressures General Foods
to pull advertising for TV movie Roe vs. Wade] M. Suh.
il *Ms.* 18:75 Jl/Ag '89
NATIONAL SCHOLARS PROGRAM
The National Scholars Program. R. W. Brown. *Ad Astra*
1:30 Je '89
NATIONAL SCIENCE FOUNDATION (U.S.)
See also
NSFnet
Appropriations and expenditures
A fast track for high-risk science [peer review system for
grants] E. Marshall. il *Science* 244:764 My 19 '89
Funding fight over facilities. M. Crawford. *Science* 245:465
Ag 4 '89

NATIONAL SCIENCE FOUNDATION (U.S.) —
Appropriations and expenditures—*cont.*
NSF education head makes risky bid [B. Z. Shakhashiri's public push for big budget increase] J. Walsh. il por *Science* 246:317-19 O 20 '89
NSF peer review under fire from Nader group. E. Marshall. *Science* 245:250 Jl 21 '89
NSF selects 11 science centers as boon to US competitiveness. I. Goodwin. il *Physics Today* 42:57-8 Ja '89
NSF's summer of discontent. J. Palca. *Science* 245:927 S 1 '89
U.S. astronomy's diminished funds. il *Sky and Telescope* 78:244 S '89

NATIONAL SEA PRODUCTS LTD.
Tangled nets. J. DeMont. il por *Maclean's* 102:54-5 S 4 '89

NATIONAL SEASHORES
National seashores [excerpt] C. M. Toops. il *National Parks* 63:46-7 Ja/F '89

California
See also
Point Reyes National Seashore (Calif.)
Massachusetts
See also
Cape Cod National Seashore (Mass.)
New York (State)
See also
Fire Island National Seashore (N.Y.)
North Carolina
See also
Cape Hatteras National Seashore (N.C.)
Southern States
The jewels of southern shores [cover story] D. Young. il map *Southern Living* 24:102-9 Ap '89

NATIONAL SECURITY *See* United States—Defenses
NATIONAL SECURITY COUNCIL (U.S.) *See* United States. National Security Council
NATIONAL SEMICONDUCTOR CORP.
Can Charles Sporck chip out a new niche? R. Brandt. il por *Business Week* p156 Je 26 '89

NATIONAL SERVICE
See also
Points-of-Light Initiative (Program)
Youth Engaged in Service (U.S.)
Can patriotism be legislated? D. J. Boorstin. il *U.S. News & World Report* 106:26 F 13 '89
Four contributions to a checklist. M. A. Kramer. il *Change* 21:16 S/O '89
The gap between will and wallet [S. Nunn's proposal to require national service for college students seeking federal aid] W. Shapiro. il *Time* 133:32 F 6 '89
Learning by doing through public service for students and professors alike [interview with R. Coles] A. Levine. il pors *Change* 21:18-21+ S/O '89
National policies to encourage service [interview with C. Moskos and D. Evans; cover story; with editorial comment by Susan Stroud] F. Newman. il *Change* 21:4, 8-17 S/O '89
National service and the high school. D. J. Eberly. *The Education Digest* 55:54-7 S '89
The push for national service [cover story] J. L. Sheler and D. Whitman. il *U.S. News & World Report* 106:20-3 F 13 '89
Reconstituting America through national service [address, July 19, 1989] J. Duffey. *Vital Speeches of the Day* 56:26-9 O 15 '89
The time for youth service has come. A. C. Lewis. *Phi Delta Kappan* 70:580-1 Ap '89
What President Bush should do about national youth service [address, February 23, 1989] D. J. Eberly. *Vital Speeches of the Day* 55:651-3 Ag 15 '89

NATIONAL SOCIALISM
See also
Anti-Nazi movement
Holocaust, Jewish (1939-1945)
Architect of evil [Adolf Hitler] S. Kanfer. il *Time* 134:48-50 Ag 28 '89
The conversion of Paul [P. H. Nitze's pro-Nazi sentiments] Z. Citron. *The New Republic* 200:33 Ja 30 '89
The Führer's dark legacy. J. Bierman. il pors *Maclean's* 102:32+ My 1 '89
The prince of liars who told the truth [A. Hitler] C. C. Aronsfeld. il *History Today* 39:7-9 Ap '89
Who was Hitler? il *U.S. News & World Report* 107:38+ Ag 28-S 4 '89

Bibliography
Facing up to the Nazis. G. A. Craig. il *The New York Review of Books* 36:10-15 F 2 '89

NATIONAL SOCIALISM AND ART
Chancellor Kohl on "heirless" art [discussion of September 1988 article, The mounting embarrassment of Germany's Nazi treasures] J. Dornberg. il por *Art News* 88:17 Summ '89
Return of the "Bohemian girl" [M. Wolf recovers E. Schiele drawing confiscated by Nazis] A. Decker. il *Art News* 88:74+ Ap '89

Vienna: complexity, contradictions [handling of return of works of art stolen by Nazis] A. Decker. il *Art News* 88:63 My '89

NATIONAL SOCIALISM IN MOTION PICTURES
Double event [A. Hitler and C. Chaplin] H. M. Geduld. il *The Humanist* 49:39-40 Ja/F '89
Nazi film machine [current films] G. Peary. il *American Film* 14:11-12 Jl/Ag '89

NATIONAL SOCIETY OF INTERIOR DESIGNERS *See* American Society of Interior Designers
NATIONAL SOCIETY TO PREVENT BLINDNESS
Dr. Maurice Rabb named new medical director at natl. blindness group. por *Jet* 75:27 F 20 '89
NATIONAL SONGS
See also
Star spangled banner (Song)
NATIONAL SOVEREIGNTY *See* Sovereignty
NATIONAL SPACE COUNCIL (U.S.)
Arms control official leading candidate to head National Space Council staff [H. F. Cooper] *Aviation Week & Space Technology* 130:22 F 27 '89
As his latest flight of fancy goes on sale, novelist Tom Clancy eyes a job in space [offered job as consultant] P. Alson. il pors *People Weekly* 32:86-8 Ag 28 '89
Bush assigns Space Council civil, defense jurisdiction. T. M. Foley. *Aviation Week & Space Technology* 129:24 Mr 6 '89
Do we really need a Space Council? J. M. Logsdon. il *Ad Astra* 1:3 F '89
Quayle denounces U.S. reliance on foreign space launch vehicles. T. M. Foley. il por *Aviation Week & Space Technology* 130:21-2 Ap 10 '89
Rocket man [D. Quayle] B. Reed. *The New Republic* 200:12-13 My 15 '89
Space Council endorses revised NASP schedule [National Aero-Space Plane; with editorial comment] *Aviation Week & Space Technology* 130:7, 18 Jl 10 '89

NATIONAL SPACE INSTITUTE (U.S.)
See also
National Space Society (U.S.)
NATIONAL SPACE SOCIETY (U.S.)
See also
Spacecause
Spacepac
Combatting fear [response to protests against nuclear powered space vehicles] *Ad Astra* 1:48 N '89
Green for go! [Shuttle Launch Tour at Discovery launch] K. McMains. il *Ad Astra* 1:24-7+ Ja '89
President's message. C. D. Walker. See issues of Ad Astra beginning January 1989
Society news. See issues of Ad Astra beginning January 1989
Spreading the word [excerpt from statement, April 5, 1989] C. D. Walker. il por *Ad Astra* 1:31-4 Je '89

NATIONAL SPACE SOCIETY (U.S.). LEGISLATIVE COMMITTEE
The NSS Legislative Committee. S. Pace. *Ad Astra* 1:13 My '89
NATIONAL STEEL CORP.
A stunning blow to cooperation at National Steel [rejection of labor pact] G. L. Miles. *Business Week* p32 Jl 3 '89
NATIONAL TAP DANCE DAY
Tap dancer Bill 'Bojangles' Robinson honored with day. il por *Jet* 77:61 N 27 '89
NATIONAL TASK FORCE ON THE NEXT GENERATION (U.S.)
Sawyer lobbies for U.S. youth on Capitol Hill in final days of term. il por *Jet* 76:13 My 8 '89
NATIONAL TEACHER OF THE YEAR AWARD *See* Teachers—Awards
NATIONAL TECHNICAL SYSTEMS (FIRM)
Firm develops new method to test for delamination. *Aviation Week & Space Technology* 130:52 Ap 17 '89
Independent labs play key role in aerospace testing, verification. W. B. Scott. il *Aviation Week & Space Technology* 130:110-11 My 22 '89
NATIONAL TELECOMMUNCATIONS COS.
Smoke on the line [D. Segress wins cellular licenses for American Indian-owned companies] F. Meeks. il *Forbes* 144:114+ S 4 '89
NATIONAL TENNIS CENTER (U.S.)
No place like home [U.S. Open] S. Hester. il *World Tennis* 37:136 S '89
NATIONAL TEST PILOT SCHOOL
Test-pilot tech. B. Brechner. il *Flying* 116:78-82+ Ag '89
NATIONAL THEATRE (GREAT BRITAIN)
Production: The shaughraun [use of Theta drum revolve stage] M. Sommers. il *Theatre Crafts* 23:10 Ja '89
NATIONAL THEATRE OF LONDON *See* National Theatre (Great Britain)
NATIONAL TRANSPORTATION SAFETY BOARD (U.S.) *See* United States. National Transportation Safety Board
NATIONAL UNION FOR THE TOTAL INDEPENDENCE OF ANGOLA
The end of the affair [J. Savimbi and U.S. support] B. Turque. il por *Newsweek* 114:54 O 16 '89
The last battle? R. Sikorski. *National Review* 41:19-20 Ag 4 '89

NATIONAL UNION FOR THE TOTAL INDEPENDENCE OF ANGOLA—*cont.*
Minority report [J. Savimbi] C. Hitchens. *The Nation* 248:690 My 22 '89
The mystique of Savimbi. R. Sikorski. il por *National Review* 41:34-7 Ag 18 '89
Silencing the guns of Angola. il *Newsweek* 114:31 Jl 3 '89
"We have taken the first step" [President E. Dos Santos and J. Savimbi agree to cease-fire] B. W. Nelan. il pors map *Time* 134:28 Jl 3 '89

NATIONAL URBAN LEAGUE
Major issues facing African-Americans [address, August 6, 1989] J. E. Jacob. *Vital Speeches of the Day* 56:7-12 O 15 '89

NATIONAL WILDLIFE FEDERATION
1988: a year of growth. J. D. Hair. il *National Wildlife* 27:29-32 Ap/My '89
Are Lake Michigan fish dangerous to your health? J. Gibbs. il *Outdoor Life* 184:72-4+ D '89
Report on the 53rd NWF annual meeting. il *National Wildlife* 27:27-8 Je/Jl '89
Wildlife digest. See issues of International Wildlife
Wildlife digest. See issues of National Wildlife

NATIONAL WOMEN IN SPORTS DAY
Women in Sports: a day to celebrate. K. M. Reith. il *Women's Sports & Fitness* 11:72 My '89

NATIONAL WRITERS UNION
What authors want from publishers. J. Tasini. por *Publishers Weekly* 235:46 F 10 '89

NATIONAL ZOOLOGICAL PARK (U.S.)
From back-lot menagerie to nascent biopark in only a hundred years [cover story] J. Page. il *Smithsonian* 20:26-35 Jl '89

NATIONALISM
See also
Arab countries—Nationalism
Armenia (Soviet Union)—Nationalism
Azerbaijan (Soviet Union)—Nationalism
Balkan Peninsula—Nationalism
Baltic States—Nationalism
Canada—Nationalism
Catalonia (Spain)—Nationalism
Communist countries—Nationalism
Estonia—Nationalism
Ethnocentrism
Galicia (Poland and Ukraine)—Nationalism
Georgia (Soviet Union)—Nationalism
Germany—Nationalism
Internationalism
Japan—Nationalism
Latvia—Nationalism
Moldavia (Soviet Union)—Nationalism
Nagorno-Karabakh Autonomous Oblast (Soviet Union)—Nationalism
National liberation movements
Newfoundland—Nationalism
Patriotism
Puerto Rico—Nationalism
Québec (Province)—Nationalism
Regionalism
Serbia (Yugoslavia)—Nationalism
Slovenia (Yugoslavia)—Nationalism
Soviet Union—Nationalism
Tibet—Nationalism
Ukraine—Nationalism
Western Europe—Nationalism
Yugoslavia—Nationalism
Passions that stir in the breeze [flags] M. Horn. il *U.S. News & World Report* 106:54+ My 29 '89

NATIONALITY (CITIZENSHIP) See Citizenship

NATIONS
Scholastic update world almanac 1989-90. il *Scholastic Update (Teachers' edition)* 122:18-28 S 22 '89

NATIVE AMERICAN CHURCH OF NORTH AMERICA
Peyote, wine and the First Amendment [case before Supreme Court on religious use of peyote] D. Laycock. *The Christian Century* 106:876-80 O 4 '89

NATIVE LANGUAGE
Their native tongue [opera singers] D. Hamilton. il *Opera News* 54:18-20+ Ag '89
When women finally got the word [women of medieval Japan and Europe, writing in the vernacular, prefigured modern literature] E. Kolb. il *The New York Times Book Review* 94:1+ Jl 9 '89

NATIVE PEOPLES
See also
Ethnology
Museums and native peoples
See also subhead Native peoples under names of countries
Genocide in our time: 200,000 indigenous people killed last year. J. W. Clay. *Utne Reader* p112-13 N/D '89
Exhibitions
Museums. E. Chappell. *The Nation* 249:655-60 N 27 '89
Land tenure
Radios in the rain forest. J. W. Clay. il *Technology Review* 92:52-7 O '89

Photographs and photography
Native portraiture. C. Rainier. il *Petersen's Photographic Magazine* 17:32-5 Ja '89

NATIVE PEOPLES IN VIDEOTAPES
Close encounters of the third world kind. T. Harrington. il *Video* 13:32+ N '89

NATIVE PLANT GARDENS AND GARDENING
Wildflowers: the case for native plants. N. Diboll. il *Flower and Garden* 33:22-8+ Mr/Ap '89

NATIVITY GROUPS See Christmas cribs

NATIVITY OF CHRIST See Jesus Christ—Nativity

NATKIN, ROBERT, 1930-
about
Color coordinates. L. Campbell. il *Art in America* 77:188-93 S '89

NATO See North Atlantic Treaty Organization

NATRIURETIC FACTOR, ATRIAL See Atrial natriuretic factor

NATURAL AREAS
See also
Wilderness areas
Texas
See also
Enchanted Rock State Natural Area (Tex.)

NATURAL BRIDGES See Bridges, Natural

NATURAL COSMETICS See Cosmetics

NATURAL DISASTERS See Disasters

NATURAL FOOD See Organic food

NATURAL FOOD PRODUCTS (FIRM)
The rocky road to launching a business. M. Bekey. il por *Working Woman* 14:41-2+ Je '89

NATURAL FORMS
Face it! [false faces that appear in plants, animals, and landscapes] il *National Geographic World* 168:11-14 Ag '89

NATURAL GAS
See also
Gas industry
Gas supply
Methane
All fired up [substituting natural gas for coal in a power plant] T. Mack. il *Forbes* 144:266 N 27 '89
Alternative fuels [cars] J. W. Merline. il *Consumers' Research Magazine* 72:38 Ag '89
Changing prospects for natural gas in the United States. W. M. Burnett and S. D. Ban. bibl f il *Science* 244:305-10 Ap 21 '89
Natural gas: for better or for worse? [study by Dean E. Abrahamson] *Science News* 136:127 Ag 19 '89
The wonder fuel for the 1990s. K. R. Sheets. il *U.S. News & World Report* 107:38-9 Jl 31 '89
Leases
See Oil and gas leases
Pipelines
See Gas pipelines
Prices
A fresh start [Patrick Petroleum] J. Cook. por *Forbes* 144:148 N 27 '89
Unrealistic expectations. J. Cook. il *Forbes* 143:72+ Je 12 '89
Why natural gas is burning brighter. M. Ivey. il *Business Week* p68-9 Ag 28 '89
Why you pay too much for natural gas. il *Consumers' Research Magazine* 72:32-5 Mr '89
Rates
See Natural gas—Prices
Well drilling
See Gas well drilling
China
Petroleum and natural gas. R. K. G. Temple. il *The Courier (Unesco)* 41:25 O '88

NATURAL GAS INDUSTRY See Gas industry

NATURAL GAS INVESTMENT TRUSTS
Natural-gas funds could light up your portfolio. L. Zinn. *Business Week* p148 D 11 '89

NATURAL GAS PROSPECTING
See also
Gas well drilling

NATURAL HISTORY
The horn of Triton. S. J. Gould. il *Natural History* p18+ D '89
Gardiners Island (N.Y.)
Day tour [R. Gardiner leads Audubon Society tour] *The New Yorker* 65:26-8 Je 26 '89
Lord of ospreys [R. Gardiner of Gardiners Island] F. Graham. il *Audubon* 91:10+ S '89
Great Britain
Paradise regained [additional journal by Edwardian naturalist E. Holden to be published by Webb & Bower] L. Fleischer. *Publishers Weekly* 235:19 Mr 31 '89
Venezuela
Venezuela's islands in time [tepuis] U. George. il maps *National Geographic* 175:526-61 My '89

NATURAL HISTORY LITERATURE See Nature literature

NATURAL HISTORY MUSEUMS
See also
American Museum of Natural History
Arizona-Sonora Desert Museum

NATURAL HISTORY MUSEUMS—See also—*cont.*
    Field Museum of Natural History
    Grande Galerie de Zoologie (Paris, France)
NATURAL HOUSES See Baubiologie
NATURAL KILLER CELLS See Killer cells
NATURAL LANGUAGE PROCESSING
    DOSTALK [natural language interface] S. Anzovin. *Compute!* 11:132+ D '89
    Talk to me, DOS, talk to me [DOSTALK natural language interface] K. Sheldon. *Byte* 14:104 Ap '89
NATURAL LAW
    See also
    France. Declaration of the Rights of Man and of the Citizen
    Are human rights real? [natural human rights theory] T. R. Machan. por *The Humanist* 49:28-9+ N/D '89
    Demythologizing natural human rights. D. B. McKown. por *The Humanist* 49:21-4+ My/Je '89
    What is conservatism? J. Wadleigh. por *The Humanist* 49:20-6+ N/D '89
NATURAL OVENS OF MANITOWOC INC.
    You are what you eat. J. Harris. il por *Forbes* 144:112+ D 25 '89
NATURAL RESOURCES
    See also
    Conservation of resources
    Forests and forestry
    Holistic resource management
    Mines and mineral resources
    Peat
    Power resources
    Space mineral resources
    United Nations. Committee on Natural Resources
    Water
    Water resources development
        International aspects
    Redefining security. J. T. Mathews. *Foreign Affairs* 68:162-77 Spr '89
    Report on reports: World resources 1988-89. J. A. McNeely. bibl f *Environment* 31:25-8 Ap '89
        Australia
    The natural legacy. R. Slatyer. il *The Courier (Unesco)* 41:16-22 D '88
        Central America
    See also
    Trifinio (Central America)
NATURAL RESOURCES COMMITTEE (UNITED NATIONS) See United Nations. Committee on Natural Resources
NATURAL RESOURCES DEFENSE COUNCIL
    Alar: the numbers game [risk assessment controversy] L. Roberts. *Science* 243:1430 Mr 17 '89
    NRDC on Alar. R. M. Whyatt. bibl f *Science* 245:910-11 S 1 '89
NATURAL SCIENCE See Natural history
NATURAL SELECTION
    See also
    Kin selection
    Variation (Biology)
    Selecting survivors: mother knows best? [selective abortion hypothesis; research by Stephen C. Stearns and Jan Koslowski] D. E. Loupe. *Science News* 136:331 N 18 '89
    Through a lens, darkly. S. J. Gould. il *Natural History* p16+ S '89
NATURALISTS
    See also
    Leopold, Aldo, 1886-1948
    Linné, Carl von, 1707-1778
    Mills, Enos, 1870-1922
    Muir, John, 1838-1914
NATURE
    See also
    Man—Influence of environment
    Man—Influence on nature
    Natural history
    Outdoor life
    Tires to sandals. S. J. Gould. *Natural History* p8+ Ap '89
        Bibliography
    Books. J. Taylor. See issues of The Conservationist
    Reviews. See issues of Natural History
        Religious interpretations
    'May God continue to bless us'. K. Koyama. il *The Christian Century* 106:442 Ap 26 '89
    A new story of creation [theology of ecology] K. L. Woodward. il por *Newsweek* 113:70-2 Je 5 '89
    Thomas Berry and a new creation story [eco-spiritual movement] M. Hope and J. Young. il por *The Christian Century* 106:750-3 Ag 16-23 '89
NATURE, LAW OF See Natural law
NATURE (PERIODICAL)
    Benveniste criticism is diluted [water memory experiment] D. Dickson. *Science* 245:248 Jl 21 '89
    Dilutions of grandeur [investigation of J. Benveniste's water memory experiment] A. C. Revkin. il *Discover* 10:74-5 Ja '89
NATURE AND MAN See Man—Influence of environment; Man—Influence on nature

NATURE AND NURTURE See Heredity and environment
NATURE CENTERS
    See also
    Louisiana Nature and Science Center
NATURE CONSERVATION
    See also
    Forest conservation
    Landscape protection
    Plant conservation
    Shore protection
    Stream conservation
    Wildlife conservation
    Global climate change through the eons [implications for current habitat management; research by George L. Jacobson] J. A. Miller. *BioScience* 39:673-4 N '89
    In defense of outdoorsmen. W. G. Tapply. por *Newsweek* 113:10-11 Ap 10 '89
    Nature under glass. J. R. Udall. il map *Sierra* 74:34-40 Jl/Ag '89
NATURE FORMS See Natural forms
NATURE IN ART
    See also
    Animals in art
    Flowers in art
    Gardens and gardening in art
    Leaves in art
    Plants in art
    No need to be a Rembrandt [drawing from nature] A. Zwinger. il *Reader's Digest* 134:136-8 Ap '89
NATURE IN LITERATURE
    See also
    Animals in literature
NATURE LITERATURE
    See also
    Nature—Bibliography
    Publishers and publishing—Nature literature
    Foxglove laughter, hard listening, and the cut: the winners of Sierra's annual nature writing contest [special section] il *Sierra* 74:68-74+ N/D '89
        Authorship
    The craft of outdoor writing. R. F. Hall. il *The Conservationist* 44:56 Jl/Ag '89
NATURE PHOTOGRAPHY
    See also
    Flowers—Photographs and photography
    Lightning—Photographs and photography
    Photography—Landscapes
    Wildlife—Photographs and photography
    Angel of nature [interview with H. Angel] il *Petersen's Photographic Magazine* 18:48-51+ Ag '89
    David Muench: a portfolio. S. Greengard. il por *Sierra* 74:68-76 My/Je '89
    Eliot Porter. M. Esterow. il por *Art News* 88:158-61 Ap '89
    Eliot Porter: the master eye. M. A. Sandweiss. il *National Wildlife* 27:52-9 F/Mr '89
    The natural moment. See issues of Natural History beginning November 1983
    Nature. J. Shaw. See issues of Popular Photography beginning June 1987
    Photo Contest winners [cover story] il *National Wildlife* 28:50-9 D '89/Ja '90
    Viewpoints: Sierra's tenth annual Photo Contest winners [cover story] il *Sierra* 74:48-57 N/D '89
NATURE PROTECTION See Nature conservation
NATURE SANCTUARIES See Wildlife sanctuaries
NATURE SOUNDS
    Eavesdropping in the wilds. P. Steinhart. il *Audubon* 91:26-9 N '89
NATURE STUDY
    See also
    Bird study
    Computers—Nature study use
    Environmental education
    Nature photography
    Television broadcasting—Nature programs
    Videotapes—Nature study
    Phenomena, comment and notes [nature walks taken with mother] J. P. Wiley, Jr. il *Smithsonian* 20:26+ Ag '89
    Point of view [using binoculars] J. Madson. il *National Wildlife* 27:42-4 O/N '89
NATURE TRAILS See Trails
NATURE'S SUNSHINE PRODUCTS INC.
    The Mary Kay of the herb industry. S. D. Atchison. il por *Business Week* p100 My 22 '89
NATYS, ANNA KASHIA
    Poland's 'lost illusions'. *World Press Review* 36:58 F '89
NAU, JEAN-YVES, AND NOUCHI, FRANCK
    WHO vs. AIDS [interview with H. Nakajima] il por *World Press Review* 36:52 Mr '89
NAUGHTON, BARRY
    Inflation and economic reform in China. bibl f *Current History* 88:269-72+ S '89
NAUSEA
    See also
    Motion sickness

NAUSEA—cont.
Therapy
A portrait of healing [use of imagery to combat side effects of chemotherapy] J. Kaplan. il *Omni (New York, N.Y.)* 11:110-12 F '89
NAUTICAL ARCHEOLOGY *See* Archeology, Submarine
NAUTICAL CHARTS
Notices to boatmen. E. S. Maloney. See issues of Motor Boating & Sailing
NAUTICAL ETIQUETTE *See* Etiquette
NAUTILUS
The paper nautilus. N. Wu. bibl il *Sea Frontiers* 35:94-6 Mr/Ap '89
NAVAHO INDIANS *See* Navajo Indians
NAVAIDS *See* Air navigation—Aids and devices
NAVAILLES, JEAN-PIERRE
Eiffel's Tower. bibl il por *History Today* 39:38-43 D '89
NAVAJO BLANKETS, RUGS, ETC. *See* Indian blankets, rugs, etc. (American)
NAVAJO INDIAN RESERVATION
The Navajo nation. K. Brower. il map *The Atlantic* 263:79-83 Mr '89
NAVAJO INDIANS
Bad day at Window Rock [leader P. MacDonald] S. D. Atchison. il por *Business Week* p32 Mr 6 '89
A canyon, an egret . . . and a mystery [setting for the novel A thief of time] T. Hillerman. il *Audubon* 91:30-4+ Jl '89
Casting a long shadow [leader P. MacDonald under investigation for 1987 land deal] J. N. Baker. por *Newsweek* 113:32 Ja 2 '89
In the heart of Navajo country [books by T. Hillerman] K. Ames. il por *Newsweek* 113:60-1 Je 19 '89
Letting down the tribe [scandal surrounding P. MacDonald, former chairman] J. V. Lamar, Jr. il por *Time* 133:30 Mr 6 '89
Medicine man [elderly Navajo man treated for hypothermia] T. Dajer. il *Discover* 10:47-8+ Jl '89
Navajo cops on the case [T. Hillerman] A. Ward. il pors *The New York Times Magazine* p38-9+ My 14 '89
Showdown at Window Rock [scandal surrounding P. MacDonald; cover story] S. Tolan. il pors *The New York Times Magazine* p28-31+ N 26 '89
NAVAL ARCHITECTURE
See also
Boatbuilding
Hulls (Naval architecture)
Keels
Yachts and yachting—Design
NAVAL BASES *See* Navy yards and naval stations
NAVAL BATTLES
See also
World War, 1939-1945—Naval operations
NAVAL HISTORY
See also
Great Britain—Naval history
Greece—Naval history
Pirates
Portugal—Naval history
United States—Naval history
NAVAL INSTITUTE PRESS
Berkley loses in appeals court over 'Red October' [suit by Naval Institute Press] M. Reuter. *Publishers Weekly* 235:9 Je 9 '89
NAVAL MUSEUMS
See also
Elissa (Ship)
Hawaii Maritime Center
Mariners' Museum (Newport News, Va.)
Maritime Center (Norwalk, Conn.)
Mystic Seaport Museum
Titanic Memorial Museum (Sidney, Ohio)
NAVAL OBSERVATORY (U.S.) *See* United States Naval Observatory
NAVAL RESEARCH
See also
United States. Office of Naval Research
NAVAL RESEARCH OFFICE (U.S.) *See* United States. Office of Naval Research
NAVAL STATIONS *See* Navy yards and naval stations
NAVAL STRIKE WARFARE CENTER (U.S.)
Carrier air wings trained for coordinated strikes. B. M. Greeley, Jr. il *Aviation Week & Space Technology* 130:46-7 F 27 '89
NAVAL WARFARE
See also
Submarine warfare
Arms at sea [discussion of January 1989 article, Troubled waters] W. M. Arkin. il *Technology Review* 92:6-7+ Ag/S '89
Maritime strategy: seapower in a changing world [cover story; special section; with editorial comment] il *Aviation Week & Space Technology* 130:9, 36-9+ F 27 '89
Troubled waters: the Navy's aggressive war strategy. W. M. Arkin. il *Technology Review* 92:54-63 Ja '89

NAVAL WEAPONS CENTER (U.S.)
U.S. Navy tests fiber-optic data links for air-launched weapons. il *Aviation Week & Space Technology* 130:275+ Je 12 '89
NAVEL *See* Umbilical cord
NAVELLIER, LOUIS G.
about
Computers vs. cerebrums. M. Hulbert. il *Forbes* 143:184 Ap 3 '89
NAVIES
See also
Great Britain. Royal Navy
Italy—Navy
Soviet Union—Navy
United States. Navy
NAVIGATION
See also
Air navigation
Automobiles—Navigation systems
Azimuth
Lighthouses
Longitude
Rule of the road at sea
Sailing
Seamanship
Signals and signaling
Boat handling. H. Halsted. See issues of Motor Boating & Sailing
Cruising after dark. H. Halsted. il *Motor Boating & Sailing* 163:42+ Ap '89
Aids and devices
See also
Artificial satellites—Navigational use
Buoys
Depth indicators
Loran
Nautical charts
Navigation [buyer's guide] G. West. il *Motor Boating & Sailing* 164:66-8+ N '89
NAVIGATION SATELLITES *See* Artificial satellites—Navigational use
THE NAVIGATOR [film] *See* Motion picture reviews—Single works
NAVON, RUTH, AND PROIA, RICHARD L.
The mutations in Ashkenazi Jews with adult G$_{M2}$ gangliosidosis, the adult form of Tay-Sachs disease. bibl f il *Science* 243:1471-4 Mr 17 '89
NAVONE, JOHN J.
Italy's re-Renaissance [cover story] *America* 161:417-19 D 9 '89
NAVRATILOVA, MARTINA, 1956-
A great friend and foe. por *Sports Illustrated* 71:88 Ag 28 '89
about
Eight is not enough. K. Moore. il pors *Sports Illustrated* 70:40-2+ Je 12 '89
Martina: crisis or challenge? C. Shmerler. il por *World Tennis* 37:16-17+ Jl '89
NAVSTAR SATELLITES *See* Artificial satellites—Navigational use
NAVY YARDS AND NAVAL STATIONS
Squatters take on the Navy [Vieques Island, Puerto Rico] D. Ramirez. il *The Progressive* 53:36 S '89
NAWROT, MARK, AND BLAKE, RANDOLPH
Neural integration of information specifying structure from stereopsis and motion. bibl f il *Science* 244:716-18 My 12 '89
NAYLOR, GLORIA
about
The women of Brewster Place. il pors *Ebony* 44:122-4+ Mr '89
NAZARENE CHURCH *See* Church of the Nazarene
NAZI ART *See* National socialism and art
NAZI WAR CRIMINALS *See* World War, 1939-1945—War criminals
NAZIS *See* National socialism
NAZIS (NEO-NAZIS) *See* Neo-Nazis
NBA *See* National Basketball Association
NBAA *See* National Business Aircraft Association
NBC *See* National Broadcasting Co., Inc.
NCAA *See* National Collegiate Athletic Association
NCARB *See* National Council of Architectural Registration Boards
NCBA *See* Northern California Booksellers Association
NCC *See* National Council of Churches
NCECA *See* National Council on Education for the Ceramic Arts (U.S.)
NCI *See* National Cancer Institute (U.S.)
NCNB CORP.
Dixie's new superbanks. J. Egan. il map *U.S. News & World Report* 106:43-4 My 15 '89
Getting big fast [H. McColl] J. Huey. il por *Fortune* 119:63 Ja 2 '89
Hugh McColl. D. Foust. il por *Business Week* Special Issue:148 Ap 14 '89
Why Hugh McColl is courting an Atlanta belle [NCNB goes after Citizens & Southern Corp.] D. Foust and S. Ticer. il por *Business Week* p19-20 Ap 17 '89

NCR CORP.
The best-engineered part is no part at all [new cash register] O. Port. il *Business Week* p150 My 8 '89
Cash machine. T. Jaffe. *Forbes* 144:238 S 18 '89
Is AT&T laying the cable for a hookup with NCR? G. G. Marcial. il *Business Week* p92 Ap 3 '89
John Patterson rang up success with the Incorruptible Cashier. M. Bernstein. bibl f (p174) il por *Smithsonian* 20:150-2+ Je '89
NCR is finding out that no strategy works forever. S. Phillips and J. W. Verity. il por *Business Week* p80-1 Ja 30 '89

NDEKI, SIDNEY
Money for health. il *World Health* p11-13 My '89

N'DOUR, YOUSSOU
about
Can Youssou N'Dour score? R. Tannenbaum. por *Rolling Stone* p67 Jl 13-27 '89

NE WIN
about
A rich country gone wrong. S. Sesser. *The New Yorker* 65:55-6+ O 9 '89

NEA *See* National Education Association of the United States

NEAL, JACOB
Give your summer hair a sporting chance. il *Women's Sports & Fitness* 11:20 My '89
Pep up your hair with color enhancers. il *Women's Sports & Fitness* 11:70 Mr '89
Shape up your skin for summer. il *Women's Sports & Fitness* 11:24 Ap '89

NEALON, KEVIN
about
Hans and Franz get pumped. P. Serrani. il pors *Gentlemen's Quarterly* 59:230-5 Ag '89

NEANDERTHAL MAN *See* Man, Prehistoric

NEAR, JAMES W.
about
A new chef lights a flame under Wendy's. S. Phillips. il por *Business Week* p70 My 8 '89

NEAR-DEATH EXPERIENCES
'My brush with death' [black celebrities] il *Ebony* 44:96+ My '89

NEAR WEST SCIENCE CAMPUS *See* Stanford University. Near West Science Campus

NEARSIGHTEDNESS *See* Myopia

NEARY, JOHN, 1937-
The ex-hustler whose pool cues are a fine art. il pors *Smithsonian* 20:158-62+ N '89
Inside high villages. il por *Americana* 17:42-7 Mr/Ap '89

NEATNESS
See also
Messiness

NEBA *See* New England Booksellers Association

NEBRASKA
See also
Agriculture—Nebraska
Organic farming—Nebraska
Paleontology—Nebraska
Platte River (Neb.)
Radioactive waste disposal—Laws and regulations—Nebraska

Capitol
L.A. connection at Nebraska's capitol. il *Sunset (Central West edition)* 183:56 O '89

History
See also
Frontier and pioneer life—Nebraska

NEBULAE
Active young stars in Orion [Herbig-Haro objects] il *Sky and Telescope* 78:7-8 Jl '89
And now for a real Crab Nebula . . . [Southern Crab discovered by Colin Aspin] M. M. Waldrop. il *Science* 243:1140 Mr 3 '89
The art of observing planetaries. D. J. Eicher. il *Astronomy* 17:68-70 Ap '89
The challenge of dusty dark nebulae. D. Higgins. il *Astronomy* 17:86-8 Je '89
The Crab and kin [Crab nebula] il *Sky and Telescope* 77:7-9 Ja '89
The ghostly glow of gaseous nebulae [cover story] D. Higgins. il *Astronomy* 17:93-5 O '89
Inside Orion's stellar nursery. J. Kanipe. il *Astronomy* 17:40-3 Ag '89
The legacy of Edwin Hubble. B. Jones. il pors *Astronomy* 17:38-44 D '89
Making the Southern Crab. il *Sky and Telescope* 78:571 D '89
Mysterious central star identified [NGC 7027; work of George H. Jacoby] il *Astronomy* 17:10 Ja '89
An observer's guide to diffuse nebulae. P. Harrington. il *Sky and Telescope* 78:437-9 O '89
Planetary nebulae. il *Sky and Telescope* 78:131-2 Ag '89
The real Crab nebula [Southern Crab; cover story] il *Sky and Telescope* 77:357-8 Ap '89
'Southern Crab' may be a proto-planetary nebula. il *Astronomy* 17:12 My '89

Photographs and photography
Barnard's 'dark' dilemma. G. L. Verschuur. il pors *Astronomy* 17:30-8 F '89
Crab close up [CCD images by Sidney van den Bergh and Christopher J. Pritchet] il *Sky and Telescope* 77:586 Je '89
Images. il *Sky and Telescope* 77:248-9 Mr '89
Images [NGC 3576 and NGC 3603] il *Sky and Telescope* 78:144-5 Ag '89
Orion and the Swan: new infrared views [work of Mark McCaughrean and Colin Aspin] il *Sky and Telescope* 77:352-3 Ap '89
The Orion Nebula's bright new image. il *Science News* 135:52 Ja 28 '89

Spectra and spectroscopy
The Crab and kin: the helium Crab [Crab nebula research by Alan Uomoto and Gordon M. MacAlpine] il *Sky and Telescope* 77:9 Ja '89
Supernova mystery: cracking the Crab [research by Gordon M. MacAlpine] I. Peterson. il *Science News* 135:391 Je 24 '89

NEC CORP.
The uncertain payoff from Intel's landmark case [microcode copyrights] R. Brandt. il *Business Week* p35 F 20 '89

NECHES, ROBERT
about
Hollywood, just north of Melrose. J. Schwartz. il *Gentlemen's Quarterly* 59:81-2 Jl '89

NECK
Wounds and injuries
Alive & kicking [marathoner J. Welzel's recovery from auto accident] J. Brant. il pors *Runner's World* 24:52-5 F '89
Heads up. P. G. Gill. il *Field & Stream* 94:32+ Jl '89

NECK PAIN
Flying can be a pain in the neck. K. Schaefer. il *Nation's Business* 77:73 S '89

NECKER ISLAND (BRITISH VIRGIN ISLANDS)
Description and travel
Paradise costs. G. Jaynes. il *Life* 12:40-4 Ap '89

NECKLACES
Light or heavy hearts . . . filled with sand or fragrance. il *Sunset (Central West edition)* 182:110 F '89

NECKTIES
A handdog look for dads with the ties that bind. T. H. Wolf. bibl (p164) il *Smithsonian* 20:122-6+ My '89
Taking a tip from a dapper fan, anchorman Don Shelby makes news with the knot in his necktie [Shelby knot created by J. Pratt] il pors *People Weekly* 32:59 O 2 '89
Ties that let it all hang out. T. Segal and D. Castellon. il *Business Week* p118 Ap 3 '89
Where'd you get that tie? The workshop [wooden ties] il *Sunset (Central West edition)* 183:96 D '89

NECROLOGIES *See* Obituaries

NED *See* Oxford English dictionary

NEDVED, PETR
about
Calgary power play. J. Howse. il por *Maclean's* 102:17 Ja 16 '89

NEEDHAM, JOSEPH, 1900-
Precursors of modern science. il *The Courier (Unesco)* 41:6-8 O '88
about
The Chinese scientific genius. R. K. G. Temple. il *The Courier (Unesco)* 41:4-6 O '88

NEEDLEPOINT RUGS *See* Rugs and carpets

NEEDLES (SYRINGES) *See* Syringes

NEEDLEWORK
See also
Appliqué work
Crocheting
Embroidery
Knitting
Lace
Quilts and quilting
Samplers

Collectors and collecting
A new collectible art form: the pau dau. R. P. Anjard. il *Antiques & Collecting Hobbies* 94:69 Jl '89

NEELY, MARK E., JR., AND HOLZER, HAROLD
Mementos of politicos. il *Americana* 17:23-7 Jl/Ag '89

NEELY, RICHARD, 1941-
about
You little tort. D. A. Farber. *The Washington Monthly* 20:49-50+ Ja '89

NEFF, CRAIG
(jt. auth) *See* Lieber, Jill, and Neff, Craig

NEFF, CRAIG, AND LIEBER, JILL
Rose's grim vigil [cover story] il pors *Sports Illustrated* 70:52-4+ Ap 3 '89

NEFF, JOHN B.
about
Early bird got worm. A. Farnham. il por *Fortune* 119:62-3 Ja 2 '89

NEFF, THOMAS J.
about
The new headhunters [cover story] J. A. Byrne. il pors *Business Week* p64-7+ F 6 '89

NEGATIVITY (PSYCHOLOGY)
"Woulda/coulda/shoulda": how to avoid no-win thinking [excerpt] A. M. Freeman. il *Ladies' Home Journal* 106:124+ O '89
NEGEV (ISRAEL)
Desert bloom [runoff agriculture; work of M. Evenari] D. Starr. il *Omni (New York, N.Y.)* 11:28+ Mr '89
NEGLIGENCE
   See also
     Liability (Law)
     Malpractice
     Torts
     Wrongful death
NEGODA, NATALYA
   about
From Russia with sex. J. Kroll. il por *Newsweek* 113:71 Ap 17 '89
Natalya Negoda knocks Soviet cinema reeling. M. Green. il pors *People Weekly* 31:40-2 Mr 27 '89
NEGOTIABLE INSTRUMENTS
   See also
     Certificates of deposit
     Checks
NEGOTIATION
How to improve your negotiation skills. C. Legette. il *Black Enterprise* 20:106-8+ O '89
How to sell and negotiate like a pro. P. Edwards and S. Edwards. il *Home Office Computing* 7:38 Je '89
Turning arguments into agreements. A. L. Matz and M. Matz. *Nation's Business* 77:74 Je '89
NEGOTIATIONS ON CONVENTIONAL ARMED FORCES IN EUROPE *See* Disarmament—Conferences
NEGRO BASEBALL LEAGUES *See* Baseball, Professional—History
NEGROES *See* Blacks
NEGRON, CRISTINA
A show of fans. il *Runner's World* 24:38-9 Jl '89
NEGROPONTE, JOHN
   about
Have savvy, will travel. A. Platt. il por *Newsweek* 113:30 F 20 '89
Mexico. *Business Week* p51 F 20 '89
NEH *See* National Endowment for the Humanities
NEHAMAS, ALEXANDER, 1946-
The attraction of repulsion. *The New Republic* 201:31-6 O 23 '89
NEHEMIAH, FL. CA. 445 B.C.
   about
When the semi-saints come marching in. P. Yancey. il *Christianity Today* 33:64 S 22 '89
NEHRU, JAWAHARLAL, 1889-1964
   about
Makers of modern India. S. Gopal. il pors *The Courier (Unesco)* 42:10-11 F '89
NEIER, ARYEH, 1937-
Cuba: the human rights show. il *The New York Review of Books* 36:33-5 Je 15 '89
NEIFERT, MARIANNE R.
Ask Dr. Mom. See issues of McCall's beginning May 1986
NEIGHBORHOOD CENTERS *See* Community centers
NEIGHBORHOOD DEVELOPMENT *See* Community development
NEIGHBORHOOD ORGANIZATION *See* Community organization
NEIGHBORHOODS
   See also
     NIMBY syndrome
Facing an uncomfortable truth [address, June 15, 1989] J. H. Ross. *Vital Speeches of the Day* 55:690-3 S 1 '89
Growing up in poor neighborhoods: how much does it matter? S. E. Mayer and C. Jencks. bibl f *Science* 243:1441-5 Mr 17 '89
Making neighborhoods safe [community-oriented policing] J. Q. Wilson and G. L. Kelling. il *The Atlantic* 263:46-52 F '89
   Anecdotes, facetiae, satire, etc.
Hot neighborhoods for the nineties [New York City] J. Adler. il *New York* 22:25 Ap 17 '89
NEIGHBORS
A neighborly sort of way [Lincoln, Vt.] C. A. Bohjalian. il *Reader's Digest* 134:71-2 Ja '89
A neighbor's gift. C. De Vinck. il *Reader's Digest* 135:9 N '89
What a neighbor will do [condensed from Out of the Ozarks] W. Childress. il *Reader's Digest* 135:125-7 S '89
NEIKRUG, MARC
   about
Los Alamos [opera] Reviews
   Opera News il 53:40 Mr 4 '89. J. H. Sutcliffe
NEILD, RACHEL
Forgive & forget? *Commonweal* 116:358-60 Je 16 '89
NEILL, D. MONTY, AND MEDINA, NOE J.
Standardized testing: harmful to educational health. bibl f il *Phi Delta Kappan* 70:688-97 My '89
NEIMAN MARCUS
No need to rush. T. Jaffe. *Forbes* 144:348 Jl 24 '89

NEIMAR, JILL
Scared sick! Welcome to the age of hypochondria. il *Mademoiselle* 95:206-7+ N '89
NEIMARK, JILL
Coming clean, staying sober: how good girls kick bad drugs. *Mademoiselle* 95:172-3+ F '89
Violations: the legacy of the Central Park rape. il *Mademoiselle* 95:226-7+ S '89
NEISSER, JUDITH
Chicago vistas. il *Architectural Digest* 46:70-7 Jl '89
Equestrian inspiration. il *Architectural Digest* 46:172-7 Ap '89
NEKOS, STEVE
   about
Candy man. *The New Yorker* 65:34-5 Mr 27 '89
NEKOS PHARMACY
Candy man [S. Nekos makes Easter chocolates in Kingston, N.Y.] *The New Yorker* 65:34-5 Mr 27 '89
NELAN, ROSE
Dance takes hold in South Africa: rewriting the present. il por *Dance Magazine* 63:54-8 F '89
NELKIN, DOROTHY
(jt. auth) See Hanson, Betsy, and Nelkin, Dorothy
NELLENS, ROGER, 1937-
   about
Surreal note in Belgium: artist Roger Nellens' collection at Knokke. E. White. il *Architectural Digest* 46:142-9+ D '89
NELLES, SUSAN
   about
Nelles's legal gain. B. Wickens. il por *Maclean's* 102:42 Ag 28 '89
NELMS, SHERYL LYNNE
North Elm Church [poem] *America* 160:573 Je 17-24 '89
Texas blue norther [poem] *America* 160:270 Mr 25 '89
NELSON, ALAN R.
Humanism and the art of medicine [address, June 21, 1989] *Vital Speeches of the Day* 56:91-3 N 15 '89
NELSON, ANDREW
Threads with a thousand yarns. il *Gentlemen's Quarterly* 59:71+ S '89
NELSON, ANNE GARDNER
   about
The lady is a champ. N. Rabinowitz. il pors *Motor Boating & Sailing* 163:62-5+ F '89
NELSON, ANTONYA
Downstream [story] il *Esquire* 111:178-82+ My '89
NELSON, CALEB
Bring back the old math. il *The American Spectator* 22:36-7 N '89
NELSON, CHRIS
   about
Black U.S. hockey player aims for 1992 Olympics. il por *Jet* 76:47 Ag 21 '89
NELSON, DOUGLAS A., AND MARLER, PETER
Categorical perception of a natural stimulus continuum: birdsong. bibl f il *Science* 244:976-8 My 26 '89
NELSON, HARRY
Pinpointing the culprits. il *World Health* p12-15 Je '89
NELSON, INGRID
Saving kids from the streets. il por *New Choices for the Best Years* 29:14+ Ag '89
Take stock—then fix what you need to. Now. *Working Woman* 14:88+ Je '89
NELSON, JANET
Turning into strength. il *Women's Sports & Fitness* 11:31-3 N/D '89
Women's ski buyer's guide. il *Women's Sports & Fitness* 11:27-8+ O '89
NELSON, JOAN, 1958-
   about
Joan Nelson at Robert Miller. K. Johnson. il *Art in America* 77:144 Mr '89
NELSON, KEVIN, 1953-
San Francisco. il *Sport (New York, N.Y.)* 80:98-100+ O '89
NELSON, LIZA
(jt. auth) See Nelson, Sara, and Nelson, Liza
NELSON, MARION PARKER
   about
About people. V. J. Gallman. il por *Essence* 20:38 N '89
NELSON, MICHAEL A.
Sports, kids, fun, and safety; ed. by Barbara Raymond. il *Good Housekeeping* 209:82+ S '89
NELSON, PAUL
An unapologetic middle ground. *The Christian Century* 106:882-4 O 4 '89
NELSON, PETER, 1953-
A day in the life of a guy's libido. il *Mademoiselle* 95:106-7 Ja '89
Don't blame me, I'm Swedish. il *Esquire* 111:29 F '89
Jazz by the river. il *Esquire* 111:44 Ap '89
Plains? Great! il *Mother Jones* 14:53-4 Je '89
This bier's for me. il por *Esquire* 112:230-3 O '89

NELSON, PHILLIP GILLARD, 1931-, AND OTHERS
Synaptic connections in vitro: modulation of number and efficacy by electrical activity. bibl f il *Science* 244:585-7 My 5 '89

NELSON, PRINCE ROGERS *See* Prince

NELSON, RANDALL W., AND OTHERS
Volatilization of high molecular weight DNA by pulsed laser ablation of frozen aqueous solutions. bibl f il *Science* 246:1585-7 D 22 '89

NELSON, RAYMOND L., JR.
about
Bubba Nelson fights for the dirty jobs. T. Vogel. il por *Business Week* p96 My 22 '89

NELSON, RICHARD A.
Low frequency transmitter. il *Radio-Electronics* 60:43-6+ S '89

NELSON, RICHARD C.
Of robins' eggs, teachers, and education reform. bibl f il *Phi Delta Kappan* 70:632-8 Ap '89

NELSON, RICHARD K.
Coming into clearcut [excerpt from The island within] *Harper's* 279:28+ D '89
A council of trees [excerpt from The island within] il *Life* 12:21-2+ My '89

NELSON, ROBIN
A frog on paper, prince of machines. il *Personal Computing* 13:39-40 O '89

NELSON, SARA
After the fall. il por *Health (New York, N.Y.)* 21:28-9 Mr '89
Amelia's island. il pors *Working Woman* 14:198-202 S '89
Beat the clock. il *Seventeen* 48:145-6+ Ap '89
Can a woman be "too good" in bed? il *Glamour* 87:264-5+ Mr '89
Different strokes: a touch of splash. il pors *Harper's Bazaar* 122:124-7+ F '89
Have you ever shared a look, a touch, a moment of flirtation with a stranger? il *Glamour* 87:222-3+ N '89
I confess: I'm a mess. il *Seventeen* 48:168-9 S '89
Making time for your other life. il por *Working Woman* 14:102-5 Mr '89
Mastering the art of intimacy. *Working Woman* 14:114-16 Je '89
When a woman drives alone. il *Reader's Digest* 134:157-60 Ap '89
When you and your best friend grow apart. il *Seventeen* 48:308-9+ Ag '89
(ed) See Burke, Marian. "My son will always amaze me"

NELSON, SARA, AND NELSON, LIZA
Is married better? il pors *Glamour* 87:274-5+ O '89

NELSON, TODD
(jt. auth) See Evans, Betsy, and Nelson, Todd

NELSON, TRACY
about
"My husband healed me with love". J. Wolf. il pors *Redbook* 173:76+ O '89

NELSON, W. JAMES
(jt. auth) See Rodriguez-Boulan, Enrique, and Nelson, W. James

NELSON, WILLIAM S.
(jt. auth) See Avise, John C., and Nelson, William S.

NELSON (BARTON), INC. *See* Barton Nelson, Inc.

NELSON LEDGES (RACE) *See* Automobile racing

NEMATOCYSTS
Death, where is thy sting? [nudibranch vs. porpita; photograph] K. Atkinson. il *Natural History* p80-1 Ag '89

NEMATODES
See also
Mutation—Nematodes
Nervous system—Nematodes

NEMEC, CORKY
about
Corky Nemec: one cold guy with a hot future. pors *'Teen* 33:54 N '89

NEMEROV, HOWARD
Magnitudes [poem] il *Time* 133:72-3 Ja 2 '89

NEMETH, LANE
about
Spot a problem? Make it your business. L. Washer. il por *Working Woman* 14:100 My '89

NEMY, ENID
Point, shoot, hob, nob. il *Popular Photography* 96:30-1 Ja '89

NEO-NAZIS
See also
Christian Identity (Movement)
Skinheads
Citizens organize against neo-Nazis. A. Sochocky and C. Siegner. il por *The Progressive* 53:15 Ag '89
Flower power gives way to firepower [gathering in Napa County, Calif.] il *Newsweek* 113:27 Mr 13 '89
Let's tear off their hoods. B. Bayh. por *Newsweek* 113:8 Ap 17 '89
Nazi retreat [planned protest march against R. Butler's Aryan Nation in Idaho] B. Reed. *The New Republic* 200:10-11 Ap 3 '89
Tenn. town closes up to shun white racists' rally [Aryan Nation rally in Pulaski] *Jet* 77:30 O 30 '89

Germany (West)
Ausländer raus! T. W. Ryback. *The Nation* 248:590 My 1 '89
Nazi software: the ultimate virus. il *Newsweek* 113:32 Ja 23 '89
One beer-hall putsch is enough [groups gain political influence] *U.S. News & World Report* 106:13-14 F 20 '89
Bibliography
The rising star of the German right [F. Schönhuber] G. A. Craig. il *The New York Review of Books* 36:22-4 Je 15 '89

NEOCLASSICISM (ARCHITECTURE)
Architecture: Quinlan Terry: a Palladian country house in Kentucky [J. Abercrombie's Pin Oak] C. Aslet. il por *Architectural Digest* 46:282-7 O '89

NEOCLASSICISM (ART)
Country neoclassic [L. Krieger's Connecticut cottage] W. B. Logan. il por *House & Garden* 161:216-23+ S '89
Collectors and collecting
The collectors: neoclassical aesthetic: fashion designer Gaston Choron in Wiesbaden. D. H. Minassian. il por *Architectural Digest* 46:240-6+ Ap '89

NEOCON (NATIONAL EXPOSITION OF CONTRACT INTERIOR FURNISHINGS) *See* Interior decoration—Exhibitions

NEOCONSERVATISM *See* Conservatism

NEOLIBERALISM *See* Liberalism

NEOLITHIC PERIOD *See* Stone Age

NEOLOGISMS *See* Words, New

NEON SIGNS
Conservation and restoration
When neon signs were art [L. Davidson's restorations in Philadelphia] J. O'Dwyer. il pors *Americana* 17:50-5 My/Je '89

NEONATOLOGY *See* Infants, Newborn—Hospital care

NEOSHO (MO.)
Poor
Harvest of love [KBTN pitches in to help get food to needy families] A. Winegardner. il por *Good Housekeeping* 209:130+ D '89

NEOSPORA
Lethal look-alike unmasked, examined [Neospora and toxoplasmosis; research by Jitender P. Dubey] J. Raloff. *Science News* 136:71 Jl 29 '89

NEOSTRIATUM *See* Brain

NEOVASCULARIZATION *See* Angiogenesis

NEPA (NATIONAL ENVIRONMENTAL POLICY ACT) *See* Environmental policy

NEPAL
See also
Annapurna Conservation Area Project (Nepal)
Mount Everest (China and Nepal)
Royal Chitwan National Park (Nepal)
Wildlife—Nepal
Wildlife conservation—Nepal
Economic conditions
Nepal: poverty amid soaring peaks. D. O. Relin. il *Scholastic Update (Teachers' edition)* 122:31 S 22 '89
Industries
See also
Tourist trade—Nepal
Photographs and photography
A photographer's guide to the royal kingdom of Nepal. P. Slaughter. il *Petersen's Photographic Magazine* 18:16-18+ N '89
Religious institutions and affairs
See also
Missions—Nepal

NEPHRITIS
Autoimmune target in Heymann nephritis is a glycoprotein with homology to the LDL receptor. R. Raychowdhury and others. bibl f il *Science* 244:1163-5 Je 9 '89

NEPOTISM
Family affairs [cover story] R. Koselka and others. il *Forbes* 144:212-14+ D 11 '89
China
Too much all in the family. J. Greenwald. *Time* 133:23 Je 5 '89

NEPTUNE (PLANET)
Looking ahead to Neptune [cover story] D. J. Stevenson. il *Sky and Telescope* 77:481-3 My '89
Neptune [Voyager 2] J. Kinoshita. il *Scientific American* 261:82-91 N '89
Neptune marvels emerge from data deluge. J. Eberhart. *Science News* 136:391 D 16 '89
Neptune revealed [cover story] R. Berry. il *Astronomy* 17:22-34 D '89
Neptune through the eyepiece. S. J. O'Meara. il *Sky and Telescope* 77:486-7 My '89
Voyager 2 [cover story; special section; with editorial comment by Philip H. Abelson] bibl f il *Science* 246:1369, 1417-1501 D 15 '89
Atmosphere
Another weather report from the outer planets. R. A. Kerr. il *Science* 245:929 S 1 '89
Approaching Neptune. R. Berry. il *Astronomy* 17:30-6 Ag '89

NEPTUNE (PLANET)—Atmosphere—*cont.*

The colors of Neptune. R. Berry. il *Astronomy* 17:34-5 S '89

Energetic charged particles in the magnetosphere of Neptune. E. C. Stone and others. bibl f il *Science* 246:1489-94 D 15 '89

First plasma wave observations at Neptune. D. A. Gurnett and others. bibl f il *Science* 246:1494-8 D 15 '89

Hot plasma and energetic particles in Neptune's magnetosphere. S. M. Krimigis and others. bibl f il *Science* 246:1483-9 D 15 '89

Neptune cloud structure at visible wavelengths. H. B. Hammel. bibl f il *Science* 244:1165-7 Je 9 '89

Neptune's wind speeds obtained by tracking clouds in Voyager images. H. B. Hammel and others. bibl f il *Science* 245:1367-9 S 22 '89

Plasma observations near Neptune: initial results from Voyager 2 [magnetosphere] J. W. Belcher and others. bibl f il *Science* 246:1478-83 D 15 '89

Voyager 2 reveals Neptune's belts, clouds. il *Astronomy* 17:10 Je '89

Magnetic properties

Energetic charged particles in the magnetosphere of Neptune. E. C. Stone and others. bibl f il *Science* 246:1489-94 D 15 '89

Hot plasma and energetic particles in Neptune's magnetosphere. S. M. Krimigis and others. bibl f il *Science* 246:1483-9 D 15 '89

Magnetic fields at Neptune. N. F. Ness and others. bibl f il *Science* 246:1473-8 D 15 '89

Two odd magnetic fields is one too many. R. A. Kerr. *Science* 245:1450-1 S 29 '89

Photographs and photography

Images of Neptune, Triton reveal atmosphere and surface features. il *Aviation Week & Space Technology* 131:60-1+ S 4 '89

Voyager's last picture show [cover story] il *Sky and Telescope* 78:463-70 N '89

Ring system

The baffling ring arcs of Neptune. A. Brahic and W. B. Hubbard. il *Sky and Telescope* 77:606-9 Je '89

Envisioning arcs of moondust at Neptune [debris from collision with Triton; research by Peter Goldreich and Scott Tremaine] J. Eberhart. il *Science News* 136:87 Ag 5 '89

Neptune's forgotten ring [work of W. Lassell] R. Baum and R. W. Smith. il por *Sky and Telescope* 77:610-11 Je '89

Neptune's story. P. Goldreich and others. bibl f il *Science* 245:500-4 Ag 4 '89

Running rings around Neptune [Voyager 2] R. Berry. il *Astronomy* 17:36-40 My '89

Voyager 2 images of Neptune confirm presence of partial rings near moon orbits. il *Aviation Week & Space Technology* 131:21 Ag 21 '89

Voyager finds rings in need of rejuvenation. R. A. Kerr. il *Science* 245:1451 S 29 '89

Voyager sees Neptunian ring-arcs at last. il *Science News* 136:119 Ag 19 '89

Why Neptunian ring sausages? R. A. Kerr. il *Science* 245:930 S 1 '89

Rotation

Neptune's fast spin means trouble for all. R. A. Kerr. *Science* 245:1450 S 29 '89

Satellites

Enigmatic Triton and Nereid. A. M. Thorpe. il *Sky and Telescope* 77:484-5 My '89

Envisioning arcs of moondust at Neptune [debris from collision with Triton; research by Peter Goldreich and Scott Tremaine] J. Eberhart. il *Science News* 136:87 Ag 5 '89

Here's looking at you, Triton—probably [Voyager 2] J. Eberhart. *Science News* 135:191 Mr 25 '89

Neptune's story [Triton] P. Goldreich and others. bibl f il *Science* 245:500-4 Ag 4 '89

The poor man's grand tour of the solar system [Voyager's findings confirm resemblance between Neptune's moon Triton and Pluto] il *Science* 246:998 N 24 '89

Postcards from a distant world [Voyager 2 data from Neptune and Triton] P. Elmer-Dewitt. il *Time* 134:65-6 S 11 '89

Report from the far side of Neptune [Voyager 2 and Triton] il *Newsweek* 114:66 S 11 '89

Searching for the 'real' Triton [Voyager 2] R. Berry. il *Astronomy* 17:20-6 F '89

Triton: do we see to the surface? D. P. Cruikshank and others. bibl f il *Science* 245:283-6 Jl 21 '89

Triton steals Voyager's last show. R. A. Kerr. il *Science* 245:928-30 S 1 '89

Voyager 2 enters home stretch to Neptune. J. Eberhart. *Science News* 136:103 Ag 12 '89

Voyager ends Neptune flyby, yielding historic Triton data [special section] il *Aviation Week & Space Technology* 131:18-22 S 4 '89

'What a way to leave the solar system' [Voyager 2 journey past Neptune and Triton] J. Eberhart. il *Science News* 136:148+ S 2 '89

Geology

Eruption streaks Triton sky. il *Science News* 136:247 O 14 '89

A geologically young Triton after all? R. A. Kerr. *Science* 246:1563 D 22 '89

Neptune's Triton spews a plume. R. A. Kerr. il *Science* 246:313 O 13 '89

Photographs and photography

Images of Neptune, Triton reveal atmosphere and surface features. il *Aviation Week & Space Technology* 131:60-1+ S 4 '89

Spectra and spectroscopy

Ultraviolet spectrometer observations of Neptune and Triton. A. L. Broadfoot and others. bibl f il *Science* 246:1459-66 D 15 '89

NERAD, JACK R.

Roadside. See issues of Motor Trend beginning August 1989

NERCO, INC.

Clean coal. T. Jaffe. *Forbes* 144:266 O 2 '89

NERD (TERM)

The real revenge of the nerds [over-developed frontal lobes; theory by David Forrest] L. Miller. il *Psychology Today* 23:20+ Je '89

NERDRUM, ODD, 1944-

about

Odd Nerdrum at Edward Thorp. B. Adams. il *Art in America* 77:151-2 Mr '89

NEREID (SATELLITE) *See* Neptune (Planet)—Satellites

NERO, ANTHONY V.

Earth, air, radon and home [cover story] bibl f il map *Physics Today* 42:32-9 Ap '89

NERVE CELLS

See also

Astrocytes

Axons

Electrophysiology

Synapses

Addiction and IQ [brain cells conditioned to crave cocaine; research by Larry Stein and James Belluzzi] L. Marsa. il *Omni (New York, N.Y.)* 12:24+ O '89

Amyloid β protein enhances the survival of hippocampal neurons in vitro. J. S. Whitson and others. bibl f il *Science* 243:1488-90 Mr 17 '89

The cholinergic neuronal differentiation factor from heart cells is identical to leukemia inhibitory factor. T. Yamamori and others. bibl f il *Science* 246:1412-16 D 15 '89; Correction. 247:271 Ja 19 '90

Corticosteroid modulation of hippocampal potentials: increased effect with aging. D. S. Kerr and others. bibl f il *Science* 245:1505-9 S 29 '89

Effects of glucocorticoids and norepinephrine on the excitability in the hippocampus. M. Joëls and E. R. de Kloet. bibl f il *Science* 245:1502-5 S 29 '89

Ethanol inhibits NMDA-activated ion current in hippocampal neurons. D. M. Lovinger and others. bibl f il *Science* 243:1721-4 Mr 31 '89

Glial cell diversification in the rat optic nerve. M. C. Raff. bibl f il *Science* 243:1450-5 Mr 17 '89

Localization and mobility of ω-conotoxin-sensitive Ca^{2+} channels in hippocampal CA1 neurons. O. T. Jones and others. bibl f il *Science* 244:1189-93 Je 9 '89

Microcolumn separations and the analysis of single cells [capillary zone electrophoresis and open tubular liquid chromatography] R. T. Kennedy and others. bibl f il *Science* 246:57-63 O 6 '89

Older brains don't fade away [cell shrinkage; research by Robert D. Terry] S. Chollar. il *Psychology Today* 22:22 D '88

Plasticity and differentiation of embryonic retinal cells after terminal mitosis [chick eye] R. Adler and M. Hatlee. bibl f il *Science* 243:391-3 Ja 20 '89

Quisqualate activates a rapidly inactivating high conductance ionic channel in hippocampal neurons. C.-M. Tang and others. bibl f il *Science* 243:1474-7 Mr 17 '89

Role for excitatory amino acids in methamphetamine-induced nigrostriatal dopaminergic toxicity. P. K. Sonsalla and others. bibl f il *Science* 243:398-40 Ja 20 '89

Selective loss of hippocampal granule cells in the mature rat brain after adrenalectomy. R. Sloviter and others. bibl f il *Science* 243:535-8 Ja 27 '89

Spatial buffering of light-evoked potassium increases by retinal Müller (Glial) cells. C. J. Karwoski and others. bibl f il *Science* 244:578-80 My 5 '89

Spatial selectivity of rat hippocampal neurons: dependence on preparedness for movement. T. C. Foster and others. bibl f il *Science* 244:1580-2 Je 30 '89

The stuff memories are made of [role of neural synapses; research by William Greenough] il *U.S. News & World Report* 107:16+ N 13 '89

Subplate neurons pioneer the first axon pathway from the cerebral cortex. S. K. McConnell and others. bibl f il *Science* 245:978-82 S 1 '89

Transient pioneer neurons are essential for formation of an embryonic peripheral nerve [grasshoppers; cover story] M. Klose and D. R. Bentley. bibl f il *Science* 245:982-4 S 1 '89

Culture

Fetal AIDS mimicked in brain-cell culture [research by William D. Lyman] I. Wickelgren. *Science News* 135:199 Ap 1 '89

The infant brain [cell culture pinpoints onset of infection; research by Arye Rubenstein and William Lyman] G. Montgomery. il *Discover* 10:30+ Ag '89

NERVE CELLS—Culture—*cont.*

Perineurium originates from fibroblasts: demonstration in vitro with a retroviral marker. M. B. Bunge and others. bibl f il *Science* 243:229-31 Ja 13 '89

Differentiation

See Differentiation (Biology)

Growth

From bird song to neurogenesis [study of the canary brain] F. Nottebohm. il *Scientific American* 260:74-9 F '89

NERVE CONDUCTION *See* Electrophysiology

NERVE GROWTH FACTOR

Expression of functional nerve growth factor receptors after gene transfer. B. L. Hempstead and others. bibl f il *Science* 243:373-5 Ja 20 '89

Limbic seizures increase neuronal production of messenger RNA for nerve growth factor. C. M. Gall and P. J. Isackson. bibl f il *Science* 245:758-61 Ag 18 '89

NERVE REGENERATION *See* Regeneration (Biology)

NERVE TISSUE

See also
Ependyma

NERVE TRANSMITTER SUBSTANCES *See* Neurotransmitters

NERVES

See also
Nervous system
Olfactory nerves
Optic nerve
Synapses

NERVOUS BREAKDOWN

'I was crying all the time' [suffered by actress K. McNichol; cover story] S. Haller. il pors *People Weekly* 31:88-90+ Ap 3 '89

NERVOUS SYSTEM

See also
Brain
Electrophysiology
Muscle—Innervation
Neural plate
Neural tube
Reflexes
Sensory receptors
Spinal cord
Synapses

Memory storage and neural systems. D. L. Alkon. il *Scientific American* 261:42-50 Jl '89

Nervous energy [excerpt from Neuro; cover story] D. Noonan. il *Health (New York, N.Y.)* 21:58-61 F '89

Annelids

Central synaptic inputs to identified leech neurons determined by peripheral targets. C. M. Loer and W. B. Kristan, Jr. bibl f il *Science* 244:64-6 Ap 7 '89

Birds

Commitment of neural crest cells to the sensory neuron lineage [quail] M. Sieber-Blum. bibl f il *Science* 243:1608-11 Mr 24 '89

Crustaceans

Acetylcholine and GABA mediate opposing actions on neuronal chloride channels in crayfish. C. Pfeiffer-Linn and R. M. Glantz. bibl f il *Science* 245:1249-51 S 15 '89

Switching of a neuron from one network to another by sensory-induced changes in membrane properties [lobsters] S. L. Hooper and M. Moulins. bibl f il *Science* 244:1587-9 Je 30 '89

Diseases

See also
AIDS (Disease)
Amyotrophic lateral sclerosis
Bell's palsy
Brain—Diseases
Encephalomyelitis
Gangliosidosis
Guillain-Barré syndrome
Multiple sclerosis
Tay-Sachs disease

Looking for Lyme in the nervous system [research by John J. Halperin] I. Wickelgren. *Science News* 135:390 Je 24 '89

Unraveling sleep disorders of the aged [sodium experiments point to sympathetic nervous system; work of Michael V. Vitiello] K. Fackelmann. *Science News* 136:7 Jl 1 '89

Growth

See Developmental neurology

Mollusks

Activity-dependent enhancement of presynaptic inhibition in Aplysia sensory neurons. S. A. Small and others. bibl f il *Science* 243:1603-6 Mr 24 '89

Memory in a neuron [associative learning in Hermissenda; work of Daniel L. Alkon] J. Kinoshita. *Scientific American* 260:28+ Ja '89

Molecules of memory [neurobiologist E. R. Kandel's work with Aplysia; cover story] G. Montgomery. il por *Discover* 10:46-50+ D '89

A squid for all seasons [cultured in Texas for axon research] M. Kemp. il *Discover* 10:66-70 Je '89

Nematodes

Genetic control of differentiation of the Caenorhabditis elegans touch receptor neurons. M. Chalfie and M. Au. bibl f il *Science* 243:1027-33 F 24 '89

Rodents

The EGF receptor kinase substrate p35 in the floor plate of the embryonic rat CNS. J. A. McKanna and S. Cohen. bibl f il *Science* 243:1477-9 Mr 17 '89

Wounds and injuries

See also
Carpal tunnel syndrome

NERVOUS TENSION *See* Stress

NERVOUSNESS

See also
Stage fright

NESBIT, E. (EDITH), 1858-1924

about

E. Nesbit's Magic Cities. A. Bahar. il por *Antiques & Collecting Hobbies* 94:64-8 Jl '89

NESBIT, EDITH *See* Nesbit, E. (Edith), 1858-1924

NESBIT, LYNN, 1938-

about

Call my agent! T. Gabriel. il pors *The New York Times Magazine* p44-5+ F 19 '89

Well-read women. D. Lida. il pors *House & Garden* 161:228-31 O '89

NESBITT, BRUCE EDWARD, AND MUEHLENBACHS, KARLIS

Origins and movement of fluids during deformation and metamorphism in the Canadian Cordillera. bibl f il map *Science* 245:733-6 Ag 18 '89

NESBITT, SCOTT

Mini-tiller roundup. il *Flower and Garden* 33:89-93 Ja/F '89

What's new in hoses and nozzles. il *Flower and Garden* 33:56-8 My/Je '89

What's new in lawn mowers. il *Flower and Garden* 33:93-7 Mr/Ap '89

NESS, NORMAN F., AND OTHERS

Magnetic fields at Neptune. bibl f il *Science* 246:1473-8 D 15 '89

NESS, RUTH

My moment of courage. il por *Ladies' Home Journal* 106:28+ N '89

NESSELSON, LISA

20th-century rebels. il pors *Harper's Bazaar* 122:106 Ap '89

NESSEN, ROBERT L.

about

Real estate deals that really work [interview] C. E. Cohen. il pors *Money* 18:115-16+ S '89

NESTEROVA, NATALIA

about

Natalya Nesterova at Hal Bromm. E. Myles. *Art in America* 77:264 Ap '89

NESTING DOLLS *See* Dolls

NESTLE, JOAN, 1940-

about

Lesbian writer fights feminist censors. H. Metz. il por *The Progressive* 53:16-17 Ag '89

NESTLE SA

Nestlé shows how to gobble markets. S. Tully. il por map *Fortune* 119:74-6+ Ja 16 '89

Infant formula boycott case

Corporate cointelpro [confidential report prepared by Ogilvy & Mather Public Relations] *Harper's* 279:24-5 Jl '89

NESTS

See also
Birds—Nests
Dinosaurs—Nests
Wasps—Nests

NET BOOK AGREEMENT (GREAT BRITAIN)

British government decides not to review Net Book Agreement. V. Menkes. *Publishers Weekly* 236:11 Ag 18 '89

Pentos threatens breach of Net Book Agreement. V. Menkes. *Publishers Weekly* 236:11 D 1 '89

NETBIOS (LOCAL AREA NETWORK)

Two tin cans and some string. R. Grehan. il *Byte* 14:427-8+ N '89

Understanding NetBIOS. B. Glass. il *Byte* 14:301-6 Ja '89

NETFRAME SYSTEMS INC.

Teaching PCs how to talk to each other. M. Shao. il por *Business Week* Special Issue:168 Je 16 '89

NETHERLANDS

See also
Amsterdam (Netherlands)
Anti-nuclear movement—Netherlands
Art—Netherlands
Dance festivals—Netherlands
Dikes (Engineering)—Netherlands
Environmental policy—Netherlands
Euthanasia—Netherlands
Flower gardens and gardening—Netherlands
Investments, Dutch
Jews—Netherlands
Legalization of narcotics—Netherlands
Music festivals—Netherlands
Narcotics trade—Netherlands

NETHERLANDS—See also—*cont.*
  Reclamation of land—Netherlands
  Restaurants—Netherlands
  Rotterdam (Netherlands)
  Sculpture gardens and parks—Netherlands
            Commerce
              Canada
    See Canada—Commerce—Netherlands
            United States
    See United States—Commerce—Netherlands
          Foreign relations
            Great Britain
    See Great Britain—Foreign relations—Netherlands
              History
          German occupation, 1940-1945
  Anglo-Dutch relations, 1940-45 [London conference] il *History Today* 39:61 Jl '89
            Industries
      See also
    Fokker BV
    Mail order business—Netherlands
    Philips Industries, NV
    Publishers and publishing—Netherlands
    Royal Dutch/Shell Group
    Unilever NV
          Naval history
      See also
    Anglo-Dutch Wars, 1652-1784
      Religious institutions and affairs
      See also
    Arminianism—Netherlands
NETHERLANDS ANTILLES
      See also
    Aruba
NETI TECHNOLOGIES, INC.
  The man who found himself [L. Brilliant] J. Queenan. *Forbes* 143:138 My 29 '89
NETS, FISHING *See* Fishing nets
NETTER, FRANK H., 1906-
              about
  An atlas for organ country. il por *Newsweek* 114:61 O 2 '89
NETTER, PATRICK, AND CASADY, KERI
  Inside information: our annual home workout equipment guide. il *Women's Sports & Fitness* 11:34-6+ N/D '89
NETTER, THOMAS
  World AIDS Day. il *World Health* p25-7 O '89
NETTLES
  A chitin-binding lectin from stinging nettle rhizomes with antifungal properties. W. F. Broekaert and others. bibl f il *Science* 245:1100-2 S 8 '89
NETWORK EQUIPMENT TECHNOLOGIES INC.
  I can get it for you wholesale [T1 networks] F. Meeks. il *Forbes* 143:120-1 F 6 '89
NETWORK GENERAL CORPORATION
  Is there a doctor in the house? J. Pitta. il *Forbes* 144:254+ N 27 '89
NETWORKING
      See also
    American Business Associates
    Women in Networking (Firm)
  Cutting deals at conventions. M. M. McDowell. il *Black Enterprise* 20:114-16+ O '89
  Getting your name on everyone's lips. D. Cole. il *Working Woman* 14:68-70 Ag '89
  How to succeed in Hollywood. I. Chubbuck. il *TV Guide* 37:14-16 O 28-N 3 '89
  Networking news. See issues of Black Enterprise beginning November 1987
  'Tis the season for new-job networking [business parties] M. M. Kennedy. il *Glamour* 87:94 D '89
  Using contacts to get jobs. P. King. il *Psychology Today* 23:14 Je '89
NETWORKS, COMPUTER *See* Computer networks
NEUHARTH, ALLEN
              about
  Al Neuharth is a tough act to follow. T. Smart. il por *Business Week* p119-20 My 8 '89
  Beauty and the beasts. R. E. Tyrrell. il *The American Spectator* 22:10 O '89
  The Machiavelli of 'McPaper'. J. Hammer. il por *Newsweek* 114:38 S 25 '89
  Media magnate Allen Neuharth's dream house has him up a tree. il por *People Weekly* 31:75 Ja 30 '89
  An SOB's guide to the top. V. S. Sussman. il *U.S. News & World Report* 107:71-2 O 9 '89
NEUHAUS, MAX
              about
  Sounding off . . . safely. D. Stover. il por *Popular Science* 235:36 O '89
NEUHAUS, RICHARD JOHN
  After Roe. il *National Review* 41:38-40 Ap 7 '89
  Pilgrim. See occasional issues of National Review beginning September 12, 1986
  Those turbulent bishops. il *National Review* 41:32-3 D 31 '89
              about
  Unpleasant business. *National Review* 41:12+ Je 16 '89

NEUMAIER, DIANE, 1946-
  (jt. auth) See Cafaro, Terri L., and Neumaier, Diane, 1946-
NEUMANN, FRED C.
              about
  Water witching. C. Kraus. *The New Yorker* 65:97+ O 9 '89
NEUMEIER, JOHN
              about
  Peer Gynt [ballet] Reviews
    Dance Magazine 63:105-7 My '89. H. Koegler
NEURAL CREST *See* Neural plate
NEURAL NETWORK COMPUTERS
  Are neural nets like the human brain? L. Roberts. *Science* 243:481-2 Ja 27 '89
  Brain-style computers. N. J. Freundlich. il *Popular Science* 234:68-72+ F '89
  Caught in the net [bomb detectors; work of Patrick Shea] T. Waters. il *Discover* 10:30 N '89
  Computers that think like people. B. O'Reilly. il *Fortune* 119:90-3 F 27 '89
  First word. L. N. Cooper. il *Omni (New York, N.Y.)* 11:6 Mr '89
  From Descartes to neural networks. P. S. Churchland. *Scientific American* 261:118 Jl '89
  JPL computer researchers develop hardware for neural networks. B. W. Henderson. il *Aviation Week & Space Technology* 131:129+ O 9 '89
  Mead's Silicon Retina points toward brain-like processing. *Byte* 14:11 F '89
  Memory storage and neural systems. D. L. Alkon. il *Scientific American* 261:42-50 Jl '89
  Nets work. T. Beardsley. *Scientific American* 261:79-80 N '89
  Neural-network computers. il *The Futurist* 23:56 S/O '89
  Neural networking [space flight use] C. S. Fuqua. il *Ad Astra* 1:8-13 Ap '89
  Neural networks [special section] bibl il *Byte* 14:214-15+ Ag '89
  Neural networks predict reactions [research by David W. Elrod] J. Raloff. *Science News* 135:271 Ap 29 '89
  Neurobiology gets computational. E. Pennisi. il *BioScience* 39:283-7 My '89
  Snaring hidden explosives with a neural net [research by Patrick M. Shea] R. Cowen. *Science News* 136:6 Jl 1 '89
  Solving the nearly unsolvable [NeuroShell] J. J. Barron. *Byte* 14:102 Je '89
NEURAL PLATE
  Commitment of neural crest cells to the sensory neuron lineage [quail] M. Sieber-Blum. bibl f il *Science* 243:1608-11 Mr 24 '89
NEURAL RECEPTORS *See* Sensory receptors
NEURAL TUBE
            Diseases
      See also
    Spina bifida
  Nutrients and birth defects [taking vitamins before conception may reduce risk] il *Prevention (Emmaus, Pa.)* 41:12+ Mr '89
  Vitamins and moms-to-be [may reduce risk] G. McBride. il *American Health* 8:138 Ap '89
NEURASTHENIA *See* Nervous breakdown
NEUROBIOLOGY
      See also
    Neural network computers
NEUROCHEMISTRY
      See also
    Brain—Analysis and chemistry
    Neurotransmitters
NEUROENDOCRINOLOGY
  To beat stress, don't relax: get tough [research by Richard Dienstbier] L. Miller. il *Psychology Today* 23:62-3 D '89
NEUROFIBROMATOSIS
  "God wouldn't mess with an angry mother!" [case of eight year old K. Alexander] S. Weller. il por *McCall's* 116:130+ My '89
  Physical mapping of a translocation breakpoint in neurofibromatosis. J. W. Fountain and others. bibl f il *Science* 244:1085-7 Je 2 '89
  Two NF1 translocations map within a 600-kilobase segment of 17q11.2. P. O'Connell and others. bibl f il *Science* 244:1087-8 Je 2 '89
NEUROIMMUNOLOGY
      See also
    Psychoneuroimmunology
NEUROLEPTICS *See* Psychopharmacology
NEUROLINGUISTIC PROGRAMMING
  The Bandler method [neurolinguistic programming guru R. Bandler acquitted of Santa Cruz, Calif. murder of C. Christensen] F. Clancy and H. Yorkshire. il pors *Mother Jones* 14:22-8+ F/Mr '89
NEUROLINGUISTICS
  The mind in motion [PET scans by Steven Petersen and Peter T. Fox; cover story] G. Montgomery. il *Discover* 10:58-61+ Mr '89

NEUROLINGUISTICS—cont.

Rhinos in the heart of darkness [language information in the brain stored in various locations; research by Rosaleen A. McCarthy and E. K. Warrington] A. H. Rosenfeld. il *Psychology Today* 23:26 Mr '89

Unbreakable language barriers [English and French processed differently in the brain; research by Anne Cutler and others] *Discover* 10:10+ D '89

NEUROLOGY

See also

Developmental neurology

NEURONS *See* Nerve cells

NEUROPEPTIDES *See* Peptides

NEUROPHYSIOLOGY *See* Nervous system

NEUROPSYCHOLOGY

Mind meets brain [cognitive neuroscience] J. Rubin. il *Technology Review* 92:13-14 Ja '89

NEUROSECRETION

See also

Pituitary hormone releasing factors

NEUROSES

See also

Depression, Mental

Hypochondria

Phobias

Anecdotes, facetiae, satire, etc.

Neuroses are a girl's best friend. E. Hopkins. *Harper's Bazaar* 122:176+ Mr '89

NEUROSPORA

Molecular cloning of genes under control of the circadian clock in Neurospora. J. J. Loros and others. bibl f il *Science* 243:385-8 Ja 20 '89

Repeat-induced G-C to A-T mutations in Neurospora. E. B. Cambareri and others. bibl f il *Science* 244:1571-5 Je 30 '89

NEUROSURGERY *See* Brain—Surgery

NEUROTICISM *See* Neuroses

NEUROTOXINS

Hints of a brain toxin in Alzheimer's [research by Rachael L. Neve] R. Weiss. *Science News* 136:68 Jl 29 '89

Neurotoxicity creates regulatory dilemma [fenfluramine] D. M. Barnes. *Science* 243:29-30 Ja 6 '89

Neurotoxicity of a fragment of the amyloid precursor associated with Alzheimer's disease. B. A. Yankner and others. bibl f il *Science* 245:417-20 Jl 28 '89

Possible role of carbamates in neurotoxicity and neurotransmitter inactivation [discussion of August 19, 1988 article, Beta-N-methylamino-L-alanine neurotoxicity: requirement for bicarbonate as a cofactor] J. H. Weiss and D. W. Choi. *Science* 243:1615 Mr 24 '89

NEUROTRANSMITTERS

See also

Acetylcholine

Aminobutyric acid

Cholecystokinin

Dopamine

Serotonin

The cholinergic neuronal differentiation factor from heart cells is identical to leukemia inhibitory factor. T. Yamamori and others. bibl f il *Science* 246:1412-16 D 15 '89; Correction. 247:271 Ja 19 '90

NEUROTROPHIC FACTORS

See also

Ciliary neurotrophic factor

Nerve growth factor

NEUSCHATZ, MICHAEL

Reaching the critical mass in high school physics. bibl f il *Physics Today* 42 pt1:30-6 Ag '89

NEUSNER, JACOB, 1932-

Polish memories. il *National Review* 41:27-8 O 27 '89

NEUSS (GERMANY)

Galleries and museums

See also

Museumsinsel Hombroich (Neuss, Germany)

NEUTRALITY

See also

Nonalignment

NEUTRINOS

Double-beta decay. M. K. Moe and S. P. Rosen. bibl il *Scientific American* 261:48-52+ N '89

Experiments with high-energy neutrino beams. J. Steinberger. bibl f il *Science* 245:1202-8 S 15 '89

The first high-energy neutrino experiment. M. Schwartz. bibl f il *Science* 243:1445-9 Mr 17 '89

Making sunshine [missing solar neutrinos] I. Peterson. il *Science News* 136:280-1 O 28 '89

Mass appeal [detectors] S. J. Nadis. il *Omni (New York, N.Y.)* 11:28 Ap '89

Neutrino oscillations and solar neutrinos. L. Wolfenstein and E. W. Beier. bibl f il *Physics Today* 42:28-36 Jl '89

Nobel Prize in Physics [L. M. Lederman, M. Schwartz, and J. Steinberger] P. F. Schewe. bibl f *Physics Today* 42:S67 Ja '89

Observations in particle physics from two neutrinos to the standard model [Nobel Prize lecture, December 8, 1988] L. M. Lederman. bibl f il *Science* 244:664-72 My 12 '89

Physics Nobel Prize to Lederman, Schwartz and Steinberger. B. M. Schwarzschild. bibl f il *Physics Today* 42:17-20 Ja '89

Solar neutrinos really are solar. il *Sky and Telescope* 78:568-9 D '89

Stellar collapse rate. il *Sky and Telescope* 78:567-8 D '89

NEUTROGENA CORP.

Neutrogena defends its turf. J. Heins. il por *Forbes* 143:80+ Je 26 '89

NEUTRON IRRADIATION CANCER THERAPY *See* Cancer—Therapy

NEUTRON SOURCES

New probes reveal atomic structures [position sensing atom probe] il *Popular Mechanics* 166:14 My '89

Plea to Bromley: save our neutrons. R. Pool. *Science* 246:1553 D 22 '89

NEUTRONS

A lifetime for neutrons in a bottle. *Science News* 136:159 S 2 '89

NEUTROPHILS *See* Leukocytes

NEUVILLE, ANNE-MARGUERITE-HENRIETTE ROUILLÉ DE MARIGNY HYDE DE *See* Hyde de Neuville, Anne-Marguerite-Henriette Rouillé de Marigny, baronne, 1749?-1849

NEUVILLE, CHARLOTTE

about

Designing woman. V. Woods. il por *Vogue* 179:156-7+ S '89

Fashion. M. Baker. il *New York* 22:150-2 S 11 '89

NEUVILLE, JEAN-GUILLAUME HYDE DE *See* Hyde de Neuville, Jean-Guillaume, baron, 1776-1857

NEUWELT, EDWARD A.

about

Brain man. M. S. Glucksman. il *Omni (New York, N.Y.)* 11:28 My '89

NEUWIRTH, BEBE

about

Why Bebe Neuwirth won't be reading this. J. Marion. il por *TV Guide* 37:21 O 28-N 3 '89

NEVADA

See also

Great Basin National Park (Nev.)

Lake Tahoe (Calif. and Nev.)

Lake Tahoe region (Calif. and Nev.)

Radioactive waste disposal—Nevada

Ranches—Nevada

Ruby Mountains (Nev.)

Sierra Nevada Mountains (Calif. and Nev.)

Strip mining—Nevada

Wilderness areas—Nevada

Yucca Mountain (Nev.)

Description and travel

Basques and buckaroos, meadows and marshes. il maps *Sunset (Central West edition)* 183:20-1+ Jl '89

Industries

See also

Gold mines and mining—Nevada

Moral conditions

See also

Mustang Ranch (Nev.: Brothel)

NEVADA CITY (CALIF.)

Architecture

Reviving a '50s ranch [home of Mike and Nina Snegg] S. Sheetz. il *Better Homes and Gardens* 67:67-77 Ja '89

NEVADA DANCE THEATRE

Reviews:

Performances of Oedipus Rex in Las Vegas. M. Veljkovic. *Dance Magazine* 63:62-3 Jl '89

NEVADA POWER CO.

A smart bet in Vegas. M. Beauchamp. il *Forbes* 144:64 N 27 '89

Utility to trade coal leases near Bryce. *National Parks* 63:11 My/Je '89

NEVAI, LUCIA, 1945-

Creating short fiction from character: five rules. *The Writer* 102:11-13 Ja '89

NEVELSON, LOUISE, 1900-1988

about

The art of the feud: sculptor Louise Nevelson's tangled legal legacy. D. Rabinowitz. il pors *New York* 22:82-8+ S 25 '89

A battle over a legacy pits sculptor Louise Nevelson's son against her loyal aide. P. Freeman. il pors *People Weekly* 32:42-4 Jl 17 '89

NEVELSON, MIKE

about

The art of the feud: sculptor Louise Nevelson's tangled legal legacy. D. Rabinowitz. il pors *New York* 22:82-8+ S 25 '89

A battle over a legacy pits sculptor Louise Nevelson's son against her loyal aide. P. Freeman. il pors *People Weekly* 32:42-4 Jl 17 '89

NEVELSON, MYRON *See* Nevelson, Mike

NEVILL, GUY

Hunt country. il pors *House & Garden* 161:132-9 Mr '89

NEVILLE BROTHERS (MUSICAL GROUP)

Going back to New Orleans. R. Givens. il *Newsweek* 113:62 Mr 6 '89

NEVILLE BROTHERS (MUSICAL GROUP)—*cont.*
The Neville Brothers can take the heat [New Orleans] il
Rolling Stone p43 Jl 13-27 '89
Neville-ry [cover story] J. Woodard. il *Down Beat* 56:16-19
Je '89
New Orleans' Neville Brothers go for the gumbo. S. Dougherty.
il *People Weekly* 31:107-8+ Je 12 '89
NEVINS, DEBORAH, 1947-
The gardens. bibl f il *Antiques* 135:524-31 F '89
about
Hampton classic. K. Whiteside. il *House & Garden* 161:82-9
Ja '89
NEVINSON, CHRISTOPHER RICHARD WYNNE, 1889-1946
about
C. R. W. Nevinson: Kettle's Yard. W. Feaver. il *Art News*
88:164-5 F '89
NEVIS (SAINT KITTS-NEVIS)
Description and travel
Nevis. D. Beal. il map *Gourmet* 49:60-3+ Mr '89
NEVITT, CHUCK
about
Stretch. S. Wulf. il pors *Sports Illustrated* 70:68-74+ Mr
6 '89
NEW, AMY ROFFMANN
As your child grows. il *Better Homes and Gardens* 67:46+
Je '89
A guide to summertime skin care. il *Better Homes and
Gardens* 67:35-6 Je '89
Save your skin: skin care during hot-weather workouts. *Better
Homes and Gardens* 67:33 Ag '89
NEW AGE LITERATURE
See also
Booksellers and bookselling—New Age materials
Publishers and publishing—New Age literature
Still the New Age. M. E. Marty. *The Christian Century*
106:31 Ja 4-11 '89
NEW AGE MOVEMENT
See also
Channelers
Christianity and the New Age movement
Déjà vu: the hidden history of the New Age [excerpt from
The fringes of reason] J. Kinney. il *Utne Reader* p109
S/O '89
New Age loving [cover story] P. Johnson. il *Essence* 19:65-6+
F '89
Shirley MacLaine. B. Darrach. il por *People Weekly* 32
Special Issue:86-7 Fall '89
NEW AGE MOVEMENT AND BUSINESS
Bibliography
Crystal clear. J. Queenan. il *Forbes* 144:52 Ag 7 '89
NEW AGE MOVEMENT AND POLITICS
Agents of the New Age. M. M. Wooster. il *The American
Spectator* 22:38-9 Ag '89
NEW AGE MUSIC
See also
Compact discs—New Age music
Tape recordings—New Age music
NEW AMERICA HIGH INCOME FUND, INC.
True junk. G. Morgenson. il por *Forbes* 144:202 O 2 '89
NEW AMSTERDAM SINGERS
Musical events:
Performance of revised Mozart Requiem. A. Porter.
The New Yorker 65:115-16+ Ap 10 '89
NEW AVANTI MOTOR CORPORATION
Buffing up an old classic. F. Washington. il por *Newsweek*
113:46 Ap 3 '89
The car that won't die. S. Kichen. il pors *Forbes* 144:176+
O 2 '89
NEW BRAUNFELS (TEX.)
See also
Gruene (New Braunfels, Tex.)
Galleries and museums
See also
Sophienburg Museum & Archives Inc.
NEW BRUNSWICK
See also
Acadians—New Brunswick
Civil defense—New Brunswick
Fishing—New Brunswick
Housing—New Brunswick
Miramichi River region (N.B.)
Newcastle (N.B.)
Poor—New Brunswick
Saint John (N.B.)
Description and travel
Tucked away in rural Acadia. W. Scheller. il map *Travel
Holiday* 171:42-8 F '89
Industries
See also
Furniture industry—Canada
Languages
Linguistic backlash [Confederation of Regions Party wages
anti-French campaign] G. Allen. *Maclean's* 102:17 Ag 28
'89
Politics and government
Down but not out [cabinet member B. Valcourt resigns
after crashing his motorcycle while impaired] M. Clark.
il por *Maclean's* 102:14 Ag 14 '89

Too fast at the turn [politician B. Valcourt in motorcycle
accident] P. Kopvillem. il por *Maclean's* 102:14 Jl 17
'89
Under the gun [Meech Lake constitutional accord; with
interview with F. McKenna] il por *Maclean's* 102:10-13
F 27 '89
NEW CANAAN (CONN.)
Architecture
A. Robert Faesy, Jr.: structural drama for a New Canaan
poolhouse. il *Architectural Digest* 46:78-81 Ag '89
NEW CITIES AND TOWNS
See also
Columbia (Md.)
Seaside (Fla.)
NEW DANCE ENSEMBLE
Reviews:
Fall season in St. Paul, Minn. J. Timmis. *Dance Magazine*
63:80-1 Ap '89
NEW DANISH DANCE THEATER
Reviews:
Festival Ny Dans '89 and the New Danish Dance Theater.
E. Aschengreen. il *Dance Magazine* 63:90-2 D '89
NEW DEAL, 1933-1939
The New Deal and the guru [Russian mystic N. Roerich
sent on scientific expedition to North China and Manchuria
by Roosevelt administration's H. A. Wallace] C. J. Errico
and J. S. Walker. il pors *American Heritage* 40:92-5+
Mr '89
NEW DEMOCRACY (GREECE)
Greece adrift. R. C. Carpenter. il *National Review* 41:17-18
D 8 '89
NEW DEMOCRATIC PARTY (CANADA)
Caught in the act: hidden microphones embarrass the NDP.
E. K. Fulton. *Maclean's* 102:23 D 18 '89
Down to the wire [leadership race; special section] il *Maclean's*
102:14-15+ D 4 '89
The NDP drafts a star [D. Barrett] M. Clark. il por *Maclean's*
102:20 O 9 '89
A New Democrat sweep [byelections in British Columbia]
H. Quinn. il *Maclean's* 102:14 Mr 27 '89
The new face of the NDP [A. McLaughlin chosen leader;
cover story; special section; with editorial comment by
Kevin Doyle] il pors *Maclean's* 102:2, 20-4+ D 11 '89
Party politics [expected resignation of party leader E. Broad-
bent] M. Clark. il por *Maclean's* 102:10-11 Ja 23 '89
Passing on the flame; Searching for an heir [E. Broadbent
steps down] M. Clark. il por *Maclean's* 102:10-12 Mr
13 '89
Privatizing the symbols. T. Fennell. il por *Maclean's* 102:28-9
Mr 6 '89
A race without stars [A. McLaughlin joins leadership race]
C. Wood. il por *Maclean's* 102:16-17 Je 5 '89
Reaching for the ring [leadership race] M. Clark. il *Maclean's*
102:14 S 11 '89
A stampede in search of a plum [would-be successors to
Edward Broadbent] A. Fotheringham. il *Maclean's* 102:60
Mr 20 '89
Andecotes, facetiae, satire, etc.
In the corridors of the powerless. A. Fotheringham. il
Maclean's 102:72 D 11 '89
NEW DEMOCRATIC PARTY (QUEBEC) *See* Quebec New
Democratic Party
NEW EDITION (MUSICAL GROUP)
Security manager for Guy dead following dispute with New
Edition's crew member [murder of A. Bee in Pittsburgh]
il *Jet* 76:18 Jl 24 '89
Tour rivalry ends in murder: death follows fight between
New Edition and Guy. M. Goldberg. *Rolling Stone* p28
Ag 24 '89
NEW ENGLAND
See also
Blacks—New England
Forests and forestry—New England
Historic houses, sites, etc.—New England
Resorts—New England
Rural development—New England
Skiing—New England
Wilderness areas—New England
Wildlife—New England
Climate
The siege of New England [hurricanes Carol and Edna]
H. Cobb. il map *Weatherwise* 42:262-6 O '89
Description and travel
See also
Cruising—New England
Another world [Manhattan to Boston ride] *The New Yorker*
65:30-1 Je 5 '89
Autumn in New England [special section] G. S. Bush. il
Better Homes and Gardens 67:162+ S '89
History
See also
Puritans and puritanism
Industries
See also
Paper industry
Religious institutions and affairs
See also
Puritans and puritanism

NEW ENGLAND—Religious institutions and affairs—*cont.*
Will history be repeated in New England? [surge of evangelical piety] T. K. Jones. il *Christianity Today* 33:72+ N 17 '89
NEW ENGLAND AQUARIUM
Operation Rescue [scientists save whales] il *National Geographic World* 162:8-11 F '89
NEW ENGLAND BOOKSELLERS ASSOCIATION
NEBA's trade show. M. J. O'Brien. il *Publishers Weekly* 236:29 N 17 '89
NEW ENGLAND COOKING *See* Cooking, American
NEW ENGLAND CULINARY INSTITUTE
The incredible lightness of cooking. R. A. Barnett. il *American Health* 8:126-8+ Mr '89
NEW ENGLAND FURNITURE *See* Furniture, American
NEW ENGLAND MEDICAL CENTER HOSPITAL
Nursing gets a shot in the arm [case management nurse C. Colburn] D. E. Haupt. il pors *Life* 12:42-5+ O '89
NEW ENGLISH DICTIONARY *See* Oxford English dictionary
NEW ERA PUBLICATIONS
Court splits over fair use language in Hubbard case. M. Reuter. *Publishers Weekly* 236:10 S 22 '89
New Era wins pre-pub review of Hubbard bio [case involving Carol Publishing Group] *Publishers Weekly* 236:332 Ag 11 '89
'Salinger' haunts ruling on Hubbard biography. M. Reuter. *Publishers Weekly* 235:102 My 12 '89
NEW FORUM (GERMANY: EAST)
Calls for reform. D. Jenish. il *Maclean's* 102:42 O 16 '89
NEW FRANCE
Discovery and exploration
'Slaves of one man' [portrayal of American Indians in 17th and 18th century French literature] C. de Grandpré. il *The Unesco Courier* 42:44-7 O '89
NEW GLARUS (WIS.)
Old-World Christmas [chalets modeled after ones in Switzerland] il *Good Housekeeping* 209:162-5 D '89
NEW GUINEA
Exploring expeditions
The price of human folly [comparison of R. F. Scott's Antarctic expedition to author's experiences in New Guinea] J. M. Diamond. il *Discover* 10:72-7 Ap '89
NEW HAMPSHIRE
See also
Agriculture—New Hampshire
Hunting—New Hampshire
Income tax—New Hampshire
Merrimack River (N.H. and Mass.)
Resorts—New Hampshire
Skiing—New Hampshire
Legislature
The political arena [battle over abortion] P. Simpson. *Ms.* 18:46-7 Jl/Ag '89
Politics and government
See also
New Hampshire—Legislature
NEW HAMPSHIRE FOLK ART *See* Folk art
NEW ISRAELI OPERA
Tel Aviv. M. Springer. *Opera News* 54:45 Ag '89
NEW JERSEY
See also
Airports—New Jersey
Architecture, Domestic—New Jersey
Birds—New Jersey
Dance—New Jersey
Educational laws and regulations—New Jersey
Fishing—New Jersey
Gateway National Recreation Area (N.J. and N.Y.)
Hudson River Valley (N.Y. and N.J.)
Palisades (N.J. and N.Y.)
Physics—New Jersey
Pollution—New Jersey
Water pollution—New Jersey
Description and travel
See also
Cycling—New Jersey
Politics and government
Donald Payne: New Jersey's first black congressman. D. M. Cheers. il pors *Ebony* 44:92+ My '89
The mark of Kean [Republican gubernatorial candidates in New Jersey] G. Morris. *National Review* 41:17-18 Je 16 '89
A pair of electoral tests [abortion issue] il *Time* 134:36 O 23 '89
The pollution of politics [negative ads] G. F. Will. il *Newsweek* 114:92 N 6 '89
NEW JERSEY. CASINO CONTROL COMMISSION
No dice for Drexel? [possibly barred from doing business with Bally] J. Crudele. il *New York* 22:22 Ja 23 '89
NEW JERSEY IN ART
Valeri Larko [urban landscapes] R. I. C. Fisher. il por *American Artist* 53:40-1 Ag '89
NEW JERSEY STATE OPERA
Musical events:
Mascagni's Lodoletta. A. Porter. *The New Yorker* 65:80 My 8 '89

NEW KIDS ON THE BLOCK (MUSICAL GROUP)
Awesome! Rad! Live! New Kids take over the teen rock block! S. Dougherty. il *People Weekly* 32:48-50 O 23 '89
Boston's New Kids on the Block, popsters with a smile, work the sunny side of the street. il *People Weekly* 31:146 Je 19 '89
Fresh faces from Beantown. J. Cocks. il *Time* 134:89 N 20 '89
New Kids on the Block. D. McCue. il *Seventeen* 48:70+ S '89
New Kids on the Block. K. Turman. il *Teen* 33:41 Jl '89
Puberty to platinum. D. Wild. il *Rolling Stone* p15-17 N 2 '89
Rockers on a roll. K. Turman. il por *Teen* 33:43 Ja '89
NEW LEADER (PERIODICAL)
Between issues. *The New Leader* 72:2 F 6 '89
Between issues. *The New Leader* 72:2 Ja 9 '89
NEW LEFT (POLITICAL SCIENCE) *See* Radicalism
NEW LINE CINEMA CORP.
"It's great for a date". L. Gubernick. il por *Forbes* 143:110+ F 6 '89
NEW MAN *See* Masculinity (Psychology)
NEW MEXICO
See also
Art—New Mexico
Bandelier National Monument (N.M.)
Booksellers and bookselling—New Mexico
Bosque del Apache National Wildlife Refuge (N.M.)
Geology—New Mexico
Hunting—New Mexico
Paleontology—New Mexico
Pueblo Indians
Radioactive pollution—New Mexico
Resorts—New Mexico
Santa Fe National Forest (N.M.)
Skiing—New Mexico
Wilderness areas—New Mexico
Wildlife sanctuaries—New Mexico
Antiquities
Amateur astroarchaeologists [Tenabo site] il *Astronomy* 17:16-17 Ja '89
Ancient art adds to supernova mystery [American Indian petroglyphs] il *Earth Science* 42:5 Fall '89
Ancient gardeners conserved water [Pueblo Indian settlements] il *Earth Science* 42:5-6 Fall '89
Potluck [Tsiping pueblo ruins] D. J. Preston. il *Omni (New York, N.Y.)* 11:31+ Ja '89
Description and travel
See also
Cycling—New Mexico
Missions
The West's oldest missions . . . in New Mexico. il *Sunset (Central West edition)* 183:179 D '89
Parks and reserves
See also
Rockhound State Park (N.M.)
Photographs and photography
Inside high villages [photographer N. Warren's work among Hispanic communities] J. Neary. il por *Americana* 17:42-7 Mr/Ap '89
NEW MEXICO INSTITUTE OF MINING AND TECHNOLOGY. CENTER FOR EXPLOSIVES TECHNOLOGY RESEARCH
Boomtown. R. Wolkomir. il *Discover* 10:76-81 Ag '89
Dynamite metals. S. Ashley. il *Popular Science* 234:102-4 Mr '89
NEW MEXICO INSTITUTE OF MINING AND TECHNOLOGY. JOINT OBSERVATORY FOR COMETARY RESEARCH *See* Joint Observatory for Cometary Research
NEW MUSIC AMERICA FESTIVAL *See* Music festivals
NEW ORLEANS (LA.)
Architecture
See also
Howard-Tilton Memorial Library. Southeastern Architectural Archive
Art
Party on Julia Street. R. Green. il *Art News* 88:52 Summ '89
Prisoners and piazzas [Prisoner Art Program] R. Green. il *Art News* 88:38+ Mr '89
Banks
See also
Hibernia Corporation
Whitney National Bank
Churches (Buildings)
Keeping the faith in New Orleans. C. Maddox. il *Southern Living* 24:20+ N '89
City planning
Taking care of downtown [Downtown Development District] il *Southern Living* 24:141 Ap '89
Description
Autumn jambalaya. M. Read. il *House & Garden* 161:89+ N '89
The Neville Brothers can take the heat. il *Rolling Stone* p43 Jl 13-27 '89

NEW ORLEANS (LA.)—Description—*cont.*

New Orleans diarist. J. K. Glassman. *The New Republic* 201:42 D 18 '89

New Orleans has it all—and then some! S. Birnbaum. il *Good Housekeeping* 208:44+ My '89

A New Orleans Noel. E. Laborde. il *New Choices for the Best Years* 29:19-24 D '89

Education

New Orleans Jazz Outreach. C. Strictland. il *Down Beat* 56:12 F '89

Galleries and museums

Party on Julia Street. R. Green. il *Art News* 88:52 Summ '89

Gardens and gardening

A jewel in the Japanese style. R. W. Strickland. il *Southern Living* 24:68-9 F '89

One garden, many moods. R. W. Strickland. il *Southern Living* 24:88-90 Je '89

A streetside retreat. R. W. Strickland. il *Southern Living* 24:62-3 Ag '89

Hotels, motels, etc.

The Big Easy getaway [Sheraton New Orleans] M. Di Landro. il *Travel Holiday* 171:76-9 My '89

Housing

Vintage New Orleans: contemporary renovation in the Pontalba Buildings [architecture by Leonard Salvato with interiors by Ann Dupuy and Ann Holden] W. L. Douglas. il *Architectural Digest* 46:158-63+ F '89

Mardi Gras

See Carnival (Pre-Lenten festival)

Markets

See also

French Market (New Orleans, La.)

Music

Big noise from the Big Easy [jazz] il *Southern Living* 24:36+ Je '89

Fats' city. B. Sandmel. il *Mother Jones* 14:40+ N '89

A new beat in Big Easy. N. Jennings. *Maclean's* 102:61-2 My 22 '89

New Orleans Jazz Outreach. C. Strictland. il *Down Beat* 56:12 F '89

New Orleans memories on compact discs. S. M. Stroff. il *Antiques & Collecting Hobbies* 94:68-70 Ap '89

A vibrant legacy [release of A history of New Orleans rhythm & blues] B. Sandmel. il *The Atlantic* 263:88-9+ Ap '89

Wynton Marsalis journeys to the heart of New Orleans. B. Cullman. il por *Vogue* 179:206 Ag '89

Parks and playgrounds

Merrily round and round [carousel in New Orleans' City Park] il *Southern Living* 24:18 Jl '89

Public health

High rate of HTLV-II infection in seropositive IV drug abusers in New Orleans. H. Lee and others. bibl f il *Science* 244:471-5 Ap 28 '89

HTLV-II common among drug abusers [study by Irvin S. Y. Chen] *Science News* 135:284 My 6 '89

Restaurants, nightclubs, bars, etc.

Also on the menu—tradition [Commander's Palace] D. Young. il *Southern Living* 24:110-12+ My '89

Transit systems

Finding your way around New Orleans. il *Southern Living* 24:22 D '89

NEW ORLEANS JAZZ AND HERITAGE FESTIVAL *See* Music festivals—Louisiana

NEW OUTLOOK (PERIODICAL)

An Israeli with a controversial plan for the Palestinians [interview with C. Shur] J. R. Moskin. il por *World Press Review* 36:32-4 Je '89

NEW PEOPLE'S ARMY (PHILIPPINES)

Eenie, meenie, miney, death [purge] R. Vokey. il *Newsweek* 113:47 Je 19 '89

A sense of foreboding in the Philippines [assassination of U.S. Army colonel N. Rowe] B. Duffy. il *U.S. News & World Report* 106:35-6 My 15 '89

Targeting a U.S. hero [claims credit for murdering U.S. Army colonel N. Rowe] D. Waller and R. Vokey. il por *Newsweek* 113:42 My 1 '89

'Total war' in the Philippines. N. Rosca. il *The Nation* 248:839-42 Je 19 '89

NEW PERSPECTIVES QUARTERLY

Just think. S. K. Sheinbaum. See issues of New Perspectives Quarterly

NEW PRODUCTS *See* Products, New

NEW REPUBLIC (PERIODICAL)

75th anniversary [cover story; special section] il *The New Republic* 201:8+ N 6 '89

Notebook. *The New Republic* 200:8 Mr 20 '89

NEW RHYTHM 'N' BLUES QUARTET *See* NRBQ (Musical group)

NEW RIGHT (POLITICAL SCIENCE) *See* Conservatism

NEW RIVER GORGE NATIONAL RIVER (W. VA.)

Dump proposed near New River Gorge. il *National Parks* 63:10 My/Je '89

NEW SCHOOL FOR SOCIAL RESEARCH (NEW YORK, N.Y.)

Arnie Lawrence [director of jazz program] M. Bourne. il por *Down Beat* 56:46-7 O '89

NEW STARS *See* Stars, New

NEW TESTAMENT *See* Bible. N.T.

NEW UNITED MOTOR MFG., INC.

The auto industry enters the 1990s [special section] il *Technology Review* 92:27-34+ Ja '89

The NUMMI plant: revived and renewed. M. DeMere. *Motor Trend* 41:75 Ap '89

This team-up has it all—except sales. R. D. Hof. il *Business Week* p79 Ag 14 '89

NEW WORDS *See* Words, New

NEW WORDS (CAMBRIDGE, MASS.: BOOKSTORE) *See* Booksellers and bookselling—Massachusetts

NEW WORLD ENTERTAINMENT LTD.

Puzzle in Movieland: the case of the mystery moguls [G. Parretti and F. Fiorini] J. Rossant. il pors *Business Week* p80-1+ Mr 13 '89

NEW WORLD MAN *See* Paleo-Indians

NEW YEAR

All about New Year's Eve. M. Calta. il *The New York Times Magazine* p14+ D 31 '89

Oh no, not New Year's Eve! B.-J. Raphael. *Glamour* 87:79 Ja '89

NEW YEAR, JEWISH *See* Rosh Hashanah

NEW YEAR [opera] *See* Tippett, Sir Michael, 1905-

NEW YEAR'S BUFFETS *See* Buffet meals

NEW YEAR'S EVE DINNERS *See* Dinners and dining

NEW YEAR'S EVE SUPPERS *See* Suppers

NEW YEAR'S PARTIES *See* Entertaining

NEW YEAR'S RESOLUTIONS

1989 New Year's resolution: go to heaven. D. E. Koshland, Jr. *Science* 243:9 Ja 6 '89

Great starts! Six simple resolutions for a healthful New Year. P. Krantz. il *Better Homes and Gardens* 67:26+ Ja '89

I resolve . . . [resolutions concerning running] B. Glover. il *Runner's World* 24:22 Ja '89

New Year's resolutions of the stars. J. Marion. il *TV Guide* 37:10 D 30 '89-Ja 5 '90

Anecdotes, facetiae, satire, etc.

Expensive habits: New Year's resolutions. P. Mayle. il *Gentlemen's Quarterly* 59:35+ D '89

Resolutions for 1989. N. Kelton. il *Parents* 64:77-9 Ja '89

NEW YORK (N.Y.)

See also

Bronx (New York, N.Y.)

Brooklyn (New York, N.Y.)

New Yorkers

Queens (New York, N.Y.)

Best bets. C. Pollan. See issues of New York

Fast track. See issues of New York beginning February 13, 1984

Airports

Dangerous traffic. W. Stockton. il *The New York Times Magazine* p40-1+ Je 4 '89

Northeast ATC review cites potential threats to safety. J. T. McKenna. *Aviation Week & Space Technology* 130:66 Ap 3 '89

Review finds no major flaws in LaGuardia water rescue [USAir Flight 5050] J. T. McKenna. *Aviation Week & Space Technology* 131:32 O 9 '89

TNA system at JFK detects 94-99% of explosives in first weeks of test [thermal neutron analysis system] J. T. McKenna. *Aviation Week & Space Technology* 131:143 O 9 '89

Anecdotes, facetiae, satire, etc.

Fun City. See issues of New York beginning January 30, 1989

A letter to the editor. J. Queenan. il *The American Spectator* 22:31 Ja '89

Smart money. D. Blum. il *New York* 22:42 D 4 '89

A survivor's guide to New York City. J. Bohannon. il *The Saturday Evening Post* 261:26+ Ja/F '89

Welcome to Fun City! il *Esquire* 111:96-8 Ja '89

Apartment houses

See New York (N.Y.)—Housing

Architecture

See also

New York (N.Y.)—Buildings

New York (N.Y.)—Historic houses, sites, etc.

Beware the design police. C. Wiseman. il *New York* 22:64-5 My 22 '89

Cityscape. C. Wiseman. See occasional issues of New York

Dollars for density in Manhattan: What is zoning worth? [special section] J. S. Russell. il *Architectural Record* 177:79+ Je '89

Lonely at the top [work of W. K. Harrison] B. Gill. il pors *House & Garden* 161:32+ Ag '89

Residential dilemmas in New York. S. Stephens. il *Architectural Digest* 46:101+ N '89

Art

See also

Art Show (New York, N.Y.)

New York (N.Y.)—Monuments, statues, etc.

Art. A. C. Danto. See issues of The Nation beginning October 20, 1984

Art. K. Larson. See issues of New York

Art in the underground [subway stations] M. Alexander. il *Art in America* 77:35 D '89

NEW YORK (N.Y.)—Art—cont.
The art of the newest [changes in SoHo] K. Larson. il
   New York 22:76-8 D 25 '89-Ja 1 '90
East Side story [end of East Village art scene] P. Taylor.
   il Vogue 179:356-61+ My '89
New York. I. Sischy. il House & Garden 161:196-9+ O
   '89
Notes from the editor . . . M. S. Doherty. American Artist
   53:5 Jl '89
Trotsky, whose lively street art became an off-the-wall album
   cover for Bob Dylan [mural on building in Hell's Kitchen]
   il por People Weekly 32:112 O 23 '89
                        Arts
Cue: a complete entertainment guide for the week. See issues
   of New York
Fall preview [cover story; special section] il New York
   22:49-66+ S 11 '89
Goings on about town. See issues of The New Yorker
Hot line. R. Gilbert. See issues of New York beginning
   October 31, 1988
                        Banks
   See also
   Bowery Savings Bank
   Citibank N.A.
   Federal Reserve Bank of N. Y.
   First Children's Bank
   Greater New York Savings Bank
   Republic New York Corp.
Temples of thrift [bank buildings] The New Yorker 65:27-8
   Mr 6 '89
                        Birds
   See Birds—New York (State)
                        Blacks
   See also
   Harlem (New York, N.Y.)
Three lives [growing up black] M. Stone. il pors New York
   22:35-42 Ja 30 '89
                      Bookstores
   See Booksellers and bookselling—New York (State)
                        Botany
Rose inventory [conducted by S. Scanniello] The New Yorker
   65:49-50 N 6 '89
                        Bridges
   See also
   Brooklyn Bridge (New York, N.Y.)
                        Budget
   See New York (N.Y.)—Finance
                       Buildings
   See also
   Architects & Designers Building (New York, N.Y.)
   Woolworth Building (New York, N.Y.)
   World Financial Center (New York, N.Y.)
The Caligari Club [C. Gifford explores summits of skyscrapers]
   The New Yorker 65:39-41 N 27 '89
Parlor game [favorite buildings] B. Gill. il Architectural Digest
   46:80+ N '89
Pushing the outer limits [real estate developers] J. Taylor.
   il New York 22:84-6+ Ap 10 '89
                        Buses
   See New York (N.Y.)—Transit systems
              Centennial celebrations, etc.
Celebrating a New York inauguration [G. Washington] M.
   Durham. il Americana 17:8 Mr/Ap '89
George Washington and New York City [Changing image
   of George Washington and Celebrating George exhibitions]
   A. E. Ledes. il Antiques 135:392+ F '89
                       Charters
Making New York City safe for plutocracy. R. Fitch. il
   The Nation 249:709-12+ D 11 '89
                     Child welfare
   See also
   Covenant House (New York, N.Y.)
Lives on hold [children in welfare hotels] D. O. Relin.
   il Scholastic Update (Teachers' edition) 121:4-7 F 10 '89
                 Churches (Buildings)
   See also
   Abyssinian Baptist Church (New York, N.Y.)
   Cathedral of St. John the Divine (New York, N.Y.)
   Riverside Church (New York, N.Y.)
                     City planning
   See also
   Columbus Center (New York, N.Y.)
Contrary to previous reports, cities are not dead [views
   of W. H. Whyte] S. Allis. il por Time 134:9-10 Ag 7
   '89
Megacities [studies by Ellen Brennan] A. M. Cunningham.
   il Technology Review 92:12-13 Jl '89
Reconsidering Robert Moses: power vs. paralysis [symposium
   at Columbia University] J. S. Russell. il por Architectural
   Record 177:49+ Ap '89
Robert Moses: the master builder. J. H. Kay. The Nation
   248:569-71 Ap 24 '89
The sky line [views of W. H. Whyte] B. Gill. The New
   Yorker 65:99-104 Mr 6 '89
Standing on those corners, watching all the folks go by
   [W. H. Whyte] S. S. Hall. bibl (p171) il por Smithsonian
   19:119-24+ F '89

                       Climate
Notes and comment [waiting for a snowstorm] The New
   Yorker 65:26-7 Mr 13 '89
              Anecdotes, facetiae, Satire, etc.
Rain, man! W. Geist. il New York 22:30 Je 12 '89
                        Clubs
   See also
   Brooklyn (New York, N.Y.)—Clubs
Buff groups. K. Pryor. il New York 22:56-7 My 1 '89
                 Contracts, Municipal
   See New York (N.Y.)—Municipal contracts
                        Crime
   See also
   Bronx (New York, N.Y.)—Crime
   Brooklyn (New York, N.Y.)—Crime
   Central Park wilding attack, 1989
   Levin, Jennifer Dawn, d. 1986—Murder case
   New York (N.Y.)—Police
   New York (N.Y.)—Prisons and reformatories
   Queens (New York, N.Y.)—Crime
   Staten Island (New York, N.Y.)—Crime
   Steinberg, Lisa, d. 1987—Child abuse case
Bright kids, bad business [T. Williams' study of young cocaine
   dealers] E. Magnuson. il por Time 134:18 S 11 '89
Cocaine kids: the underground American dream [teenage
   drug dealers in Washington Heights] T. M. Williams. il
   New Perspectives Quarterly 6:21-5 Summ '89
Cold-blooded King of a Hill under siege [J. Gotti; cover
   story] K. Gross. il pors People Weekly 31:70-3+ Mr 27
   '89
Fighting back against crack [cover story] E. Pooley. il New
   York 22:30-9 Ja 23 '89
Halloween fright night [street crime] il Newsweek 114:49
   N 13 '89
In Gotti they trust. P. Hamill. il por Esquire 112:63-5 O
   '89
Jane Fonda's daughter, Vanessa Vadim, is jailed for mouthing
   off at a drug bust. J. S. Kunen. il pors People Weekly
   32:44-5 O 23 '89
John Gotti: running the Mob [cover story] S. Raab. il pors
   The New York Times Magazine p30-3+ Ap 2 '89
Just another night on crack street [drug dealers in East
   Harlem] P. Bourgois. il The New York Times Magazine
   p52-3+ N 12 '89
The last Godfather? [arrest of J. Gotti] P. McKillop. il
   pors Newsweek 113:25 F 6 '89
Latest scams. P. Blauner. il New York 22:54-5 My 1 '89
Manager tied to drug gang [independent record promoter
   W. Underwood arrested] W. Bastone. Rolling Stone p62
   Jl 13-27 '89
Murder in the safest places [death of Dr. K. Hinnant at
   Bellevue Hospital] R. Rosenblatt. il U.S. News & World
   Report 106:6-7 Ja 23 '89
N.Y. woman saved by TV cable and plucky tenants [woman
   forced off roof after being raped] il Jet 76:9+ My 1 '89
A nightmare on 42nd Street [Port Authority Bus Terminal]
   G. Hackett and P. McKillop. il Newsweek 113:22-4 F
   27 '89
Park Avenue Gothic: a family feud turns into a fight to
   the death [death of J. Goodwillie during fight with J.
   de Sola Mendes] B. Costikyan. il pors New York 22:46-50+
   Mr 20 '89
Profits in a risky business [Harlem crack trade] R. Sandza.
   il Newsweek 113:37 My 29 '89
Stabs in the dark [racially motivated attacks on women]
   Newsweek 114:49 N 13 '89
The sticks, the slides, and the shaker [shell game con] J.
   P. Zane. il New York 22:36-9 Je 19 '89
Street-wise crack research. C. Holden. il Science 246:1376-81
   D 15 '89
There's crack on my block [neighborhood patrols] C. Buffum.
   il Glamour 87:128 D '89
The tragedy at Bellevue [murder of Dr. K. Hinnant] E.
   Salholz. il pors Newsweek 113:27 Ja 23 '89
                        Dance
Dance [fall preview] R. Gilbert. il New York 22:116+ S
   11 '89
Dance. T. Tobias. See issues of New York
Downtown. R. Sandla. See issues of Dance Magazine beginning
   November 1989
Free dance concerts enliven August in New York City. il
   Dance Magazine 63:16 Ag '89
It's 10:00 a.m.—where are your classes now? [dance studios]
   M. Horosko. il Dance Magazine 63:81 Je '89
                      Description
Downtown [cover story; special issue] il map New York
   22:37-8+ D 25 '89-Ja 1 '90
Inside New York [cover story; special issue] il Architectural
   Digest 46:52+ N '89
Lisa Lisa's West Side story. il por Rolling Stone p31 Jl
   13-27 '89
The new guide to living in New York [cover story; special
   issue] il New York 22:23-4+ My 1 '89
New Yorkers on the move. W. Norwich. il por House
   & Garden 161:214-17 O '89
Notes and comment. The New Yorker 65:47-8 N 6 '89
Notes and comment. The New Yorker 65:37-8 O 16 '89

NEW YORK (N.Y.)—Description—*cont.*
What's better now [cover story] P. Hellman. il *New York* 22:32-9 My 22 '89

Economic conditions
Caught in the eighties: the new debtors. M. Stone. il *New York* 22:40-6 Ap 24 '89
Japan takes Manhattan [study by Barney Warf] *Focus (New York, N.Y.: 1950)* 38:29 Wint '88
New York's future: bright lights, big trouble. M. J. Mandel. il *Business Week* p108-9 N 20 '89
What needs to be done? K. Lipper. il *The New York Times Magazine* p28+ D 31 '89
Will Wall Street fade? J. Cook. il *Forbes* 144:138-9 O 16 '89
A yen for New York: what the Japanese own—what they're after [cover story] D. Burstein. il *New York* 22:26-36 Ja 16 '89

Anecdotes, facetiae, satire, etc.
Funny money. B. Feirstein. *Harper's Bazaar* 122:177+ Mr '89

Education
See also
Arts Partners (Organization)
Brooklyn (New York, N.Y.)—Education
Harvey Milk School (New York, N.Y.)
Literacy Volunteers of New York City
New School for Social Research (New York, N.Y.)
Adult education. M. W. Robbins. il *New York* 22:50-2+ Ag 14 '89
Building unity across a city street [Martin Luther King Jr. High School and Fiorello H. La Guardia High School of the Arts] L. Eskin. il *Scholastic Update (Teachers' edition)* 121:24-5 Ap 7 '89
Convent school [Manhattan's Notre Dame School operated by Sisters of St. Ursula] J. W. Donohue. *America* 160:288-95+ Ap 1 '89
Don't ax the mayor [letter to R. Green on New Yorkese] E. Koch. *Harper's* 278:21-2 Mr '89
From street kids to Royal Knights [B. Hall coaches chess team at J.H.S. 99 in East Harlem] J. Coudert. il por *Reader's Digest* 134:141-6 Je '89
Green: his mission was to serve the children [death of chancellor R. Green] K. Osborne. il *Black Enterprise* 19:14 Jl '89
Hire education [adopt-a-class program at P.S. 175 in Harlem] K. Emmons. il *Omni (New York, N.Y.)* 11:18+ Je '89
Inside a New York City high school: snapshots of hope and hopelessness [Seward Park High School] S. G. Freedman. il *The New York Times Magazine* p58-9+ S 17 '89
New York school system gets first teen trio of valedictorian mothers. il *Jet* 76:13 Jl 17 '89
Real choice [junior high school choice program in Harlem] *National Review* 41:12-13 S 1 '89
The risk keeps rising. L. Weiner. il *The Progressive* 53:50 Mr '89

Finance
See also
New York (N.Y.)—Banks
New York (N.Y.)—Taxation
The bonfire of the fiscal realities. S. Minerbrook. il *U.S. News & World Report* 107:31-2+ N 27 '89

Firefighters
See also
Fire Academy (New York, N.Y.)

Galleries and museums
See also
American Craft Museum (New York, N.Y.)
American Museum of Natural History
Artists Space (New York, N.Y.)
Center for Tapestry Arts (New York, N.Y.)
Chocolate Milk Art Gallery
Cooper-Hewitt Museum
Gagosian Gallery
Galerie St. Etienne
Hirschl & Adler Folk
Mary Boone Gallery
Metropolitan Museum of Art (New York, N.Y.)
Museum of American Folk Art
Museum of Broadcasting (New York, N.Y.)
Museum of Modern Art (New York, N.Y.)
Paula Cooper Gallery
Pierpont Morgan Library
Prisunic Gallery
Ronald Feldman Fine Arts, Inc.
Solomon R. Guggenheim Museum
Songwriters' Hall of Fame and Museum
Sonnabend Gallery Inc.
Whitney Museum of American Art
Best bids. B. Felner. See occassional issues of New York beginning November 14, 1988
Fair warning . . . B. Felner. il *New York* 22:128+ My 1 '89
Galleries [downtown] E. Newhall. il *New York* 22:47+ D 25 '89-Ja 1 '90
Museums; Galleries [fall preview] K. Larson and E. Newhall. il *New York* 22:66+ S 11 '89

The new dealers [gallery owners A. Rosen and C. Burgin] A. Virshup. il pors *Harper's Bazaar* 122:80+ D '89
SoHo ascending. A. Schwartzman. *Harper's Bazaar* 122:84-5+ D '89

Gardens and gardening
See also
Central Park (New York, N.Y.)—Conservatory Garden
Central Park (New York, N.Y.)—Shakespeare Garden

Health facilities
Emergency! J. H. Tanne. il *New York* 22:91-2+ My 1 '89

Highways
See Express highways—New York (State)

Historic houses, sites, etc.
See also
Gracie Mansion (New York, N.Y.)
Old Merchant's House (New York, N.Y.)
House sale [Sotheby auction of only home designed by P. Johnson] *The New Yorker* 65:29-30 My 29 '89
A Manhattan sampler [remodeled brownstone owned by M. Malcé and J. Kelter] S. M. L. Aronson. il pors *Architectural Digest* 46:158-63+ Je '89
Paganizing the plutocrats [S. White] B. Gill. il por *Architectural Digest* 46:58+ D '89

History
Novik and LaGuardia. *The New Yorker* 65:24-6 Ag 28 '89
The sorrow and the city [F. H. La Guardia; cover story] J. Klein. il *The New Republic* 201:24-8 N 13 '89

Hospitals
See also
Bellevue Hospital
Harlem Hospital Center
Memorial Sloan-Kettering Cancer Center
Queens (New York, N.Y.)—Hospitals
AIDS: the numbers game [overwhelmed hospitals] K. Loomis. il map *New York* 22:44-9 Mr 6 '89

Hotels, motels, etc.
See also
Plaza Hotel (New York, N.Y.)
The Algonquin—nights at the Round Table. H. H. Broun. il *Architectural Digest* 46:184+ N '89
Money and the mighty [The Pierre] D. Jenish. il *Maclean's* 102:38+ Je 5 '89
Notes and comment [Hotel Macklowe construction blocks sidewalk] *The New Yorker* 65:26 Je 26 '89
Rags to riches [Royalton Hotel decorated by P. Starck] K. D. Stein. il *Architectural Record* 177:94-5 Mr '89
Rooms at the top [luxury hotels] L. Logan. il *House & Garden* 161:118+ O '89
Royalton flash. il *Vogue* 179:240 Ja '89
The Royalton treatment [decorated by P. Starck] C. K. Gandee. il por *House & Garden* 161:70-7 Ja '89

Housing
See also
Bronx (New York, N.Y.)—Housing
All in the, er, family [ruling on gay couples and rent control] D. Seligman. *Fortune* 120:123-4 Ag 14 '89
The big-city push to fill the housing gap for the poor. S. Minerbrook. il *U.S. News & World Report* 107:28-9 Ag 28-S 4 '89
Co-op quake [shaky limited partnership deals used to finance co-op conversion] C. Byron. il *New York* 22:22+ N 20 '89
Gandee at large [real estate agent L. Stein] C. K. Gandee. il por *House & Garden* 161:146 Ag '89
Hell in a very tall place [public housing projects] C. J. Vergara. il *The Atlantic* 264:72-6+ S '89
Lives on hold [children in welfare hotels] D. O. Relin. il *Scholastic Update (Teachers' edition)* 121:4-7 F 10 '89
Pity the New York landlord [rent control] W. Tucker. il *The American Spectator* 22:19-22 F '89
Residential dilemmas in New York. S. Stephens. il *Architectural Digest* 46:101+ N '89
The rise of the homeless [families in N.Y. welfare hotels; view of J. Kozol] S. M. Halpern. bibl f il *The New York Review of Books* 36:24-7 F 16 '89
Southward ho: moving on down to new spaces and places. E. Pooley. il *New York* 22:80-2+ D 25 '89-Ja 1 '90
Sweet [molasses mysteriously drips from ceiling of SoHo loft] *The New Yorker* 65:24-5 Ag 21 '89

Industries
See also
Motion picture industry
Publishers and publishing

Intellectual life
See also
Algonquin Round Table

Law
See New York (N.Y.)—Ordinances

Libraries
See also
New York Public Library
Pierpont Morgan Library
Book report [specialized libraries] T. Prince. il *New York* 22:78+ My 1 '89

Maps
Small town [Panorama of the City of New York at the Queens Museum] *The New Yorker* 65:33-4 My 8 '89

NEW YORK (N.Y.)—*cont.*

Markets

See also

Fulton Fish Market

Treasure Island [flea markets] J. Molloy. il *New York* 22:84+ My 1 '89

Monuments, statues, etc.

Arc without convenant [R. Serra's Tilted arc] J. Simon. il *National Review* 41:30-2 My 5 '89

Going, going, gone [R. Serra's Tilted arc removed from Federal Plaza] R. Cembalest. il *Art News* 88:50+ Summ '89

Notes and comment [battle over R. Serra's Tilted arc in Federal Plaza] *The New Yorker* 65:33-4 Mr 27 '89

Penny serenade [Adopt-a-Monument program] *The New Yorker* 65:26-7 Jl 17 '89

Smug on Canal Street [T. Smith sculpture installed] il *Art in America* 77:23 Ja '89

"Tilted arc" destroyed [cover story] R. Serra. bibl f il *Art in America* 77:34-7+ My '89

Municipal contracts

N.Y. construction hiring rule voided [minority hiring] K. Osborne. *Black Enterprise* 20:28 D '89

Municipal improvement

Pear trees [street plantings of callery pears] *The New Yorker* 65:31-2 Ap 17 '89

Museums

See New York (N.Y.)—Galleries and museums

Music

See also

Bel Canto Opera (Company)

Carnegie Hall (New York, N.Y.)

Metropolitan Opera (New York, N.Y.)

New York City Opera Company

New York Classical Orchestra

New York Opera Repertory Theatre

New York Philharmonic-Symphony Orchestra

Opera—New York (State)

Opera at the Academy

Opera Ensemble of New York

Opera Orchestra of New York

Orchestra of St. Luke's

Riverside Symphony

Symphony Space (New York, N.Y.)

All that jazz. D. Fagen. il *Harper's Bazaar* 122:178+ Ag '89

Amazin' Albert (I) [A. Bagby's Musical Mornings recital series from 1891 to 1941] F. Bowers. il pors *Opera News* 53:12-14+ F 4 '89

Amazin' Albert (II) [A. Bagby's Musical Mornings recital series from 1891 to 1941] F. Bowers. il por *Opera News* 53:32-7 F 18 '89

Classical jazz at Lincoln Center. K. Whitehead. il *Down Beat* 56:51-2 N '89

Jazz. W. Balliett. See occasional issues of The New Yorker

Knit wits [Knitting Factory] P. Hoban. il *New York* 22:46-9 Jl 31 '89

Knitting a new music scene [Knitting Factory] S. Futterman. il *Rolling Stone* p19 Ap 6 '89

Music. P. G. Davis. See issues of New York

Music [fall preview] F. Fletcher. il *New York* 22:80+ S 11 '89

Musical events. A. Porter. See issues of The New Yorker

New York has something to howl about again—legendary street musician Moondog. M. Small. il pors *People Weekly* 32:109-10 N 27 '89

Nightlife [fall preview] C. Hainer. il *New York* 22:98+ S 11 '89

Sounds and laughs [downtown] C. S. Smith. il *New York* 22:42-4+ D 25 '89-Ja 1 '90

Music festivals

See Music festivals—New York (State)

Newspapers

See also

Amsterdam news (New York, N.Y.)

Daily news (New York, N.Y.)

New York native (Newspaper)

New York post

New York times

The last stand of the tabloids. L. Zuckerman. il *Time* 133:81 Mr 13 '89

The new (land)lords of the press. E. Diamond. il *New York* 22:44-50 F 27 '89

The papers vote [endorsements in New York City mayoral race] E. Diamond. il *New York* 22:24+ S 25 '89

History

See also

New York herald

Ordinances

Mad about guns [proposed ban on assault rifles] M. Kempton. *The New York Review of Books* 36:62 D 21 '89

Paleontology

Big Apple tusks [mastodon fossils] S. Horenstein. il map *Natural History* p96-8+ Mr '89

Parades

See also

Macy's Thanksgiving Day Parade

Details [Lesbian and Gay Big Apple Corps Marching Band participates in bicentennial celebration of George Washington's inauguration] *The New Yorker* 65:28-9 Jl 3 '89

The New York Halloween parade. D. K. Mano. il *National Review* 41:56-8 N 24 '89

Primitive [Greenwich Village Halloween parade] *The New Yorker* 65:48-9 N 6 '89

Scenes from the gay life [Lesbian and Gay Pride Weekend] D. Klinghoffer. *National Review* 41:22-3 Ag 4 '89

Parks and playgrounds

See also

Central Park (New York, N.Y.)

Fort Tryon Park (New York, N.Y.)

New York (N.Y.). Dept. of Parks and Recreation

Tompkins Square Park (New York, N.Y.)

Washington Square (New York, N.Y.)

The country in the city. C. A. Nadareski and M. J. Feller. il *The Conservationist* 44:12-17 Jl/Ag '89

Homeless rights, community wrongs [efforts to keep homeless out of public parks] J. Leo. il *U.S. News & World Report* 107:56 Jl 24 '89

Photographs and photography

Dream streets [downtown] T. Hardin and L. Psihoyos. il *New York* 22:58-67 D 25 '89-Ja 1 '90

Police

Big Ben: has Police Commissioner Ward become a liability to Koch? P. Blauner. il pors *New York* 22:48-50+ Ap 3 '89

To serve and protect [policeman left a paraplegic by gunshot wound; condensed from The Steven McDonald story] ed. by E. J. Kahn. S. McDonald and P. A. McDonald. il pors *Reader's Digest* 135:201-4+ O '89

Politics and government

See also

New York (N.Y.)—Ordinances

Around City Hall (Koch administration). A. Logan. See occasional issues of The New Yorker through December 25, 1989

Been down so long it looks like up to me [E. Koch] J. Klein. il por *New York* 22:34-7 F 20 '89

Bess Myerson: how I survived. C. Adams. il por *Ladies' Home Journal* 106:106-7+ Jl '89

Bess Myerson: the inside story. J. L. Block. il pors *Good Housekeeping* 208:70+ Ap '89

The big spender who would be mayor [R. Lauder] A. Rothman. il por *Business Week* p72-3 S 4 '89

A breakthrough [D. Dinkins elected mayor] H. Mackenzie. il por *Maclean's* 102:38-40 N 20 '89

Brotherhood week [reaction of D. Dinkins and other mayoral candidates to murder of Y. Hawkins in Bensonhurst] J. Klein. il por *New York* 22:36+ S 11 '89

California dreaming [D. Dinkins] J. Klein. il por *New York* 22:24+ O 23 '89

A call for racial harmony [D. Dinkins wins Democratic mayoral primary] E. Salholz. il pors *Newsweek* 114:21-2 S 25 '89

Can Dinkins do it? [cover story] J. Klein. il pors *New York* 22:30-7 Jl 31 '89

The Carter campaign [WLIB reporter D. Carter covers mayoral race] C. S. Smith. il por *New York* 22:36 N 13 '89

Cosby does fund-raiser at Apollo for David Dinkins' N.Y.C. mayoral campaign. il pors *Jet* 77:38-9 O 9 '89

David Dinkins seeks New York mayor's seat. il por *Jet* 75:28 Mr 6 '89

David N. Dinkins: 'I'll bring New York City together' [cover story] D. M. Cheers. il pors *Jet* 77:4-7 N 27 '89

Dinkins readies for N.Y.C. mayoral race after major primary election victory. il pors *Jet* 76:4+ O 2 '89

The Dinkins stock crash [D. Dinkins accused of undervaluation of Inner City Broadcasting stock] C. Byron. il *New York* 22:30+ N 6 '89

Enough already? [E. Koch] J. Klein. il *New York* 22:14+ Je 12 '89

The friends of David Dinkins. J. Klein. il por *New York* 22:14+ O 30 '89

Gandhi vs. Gumby [D. Dinkins vs. R. Giuliani in race for mayor] J. Klein. il pors *New York* 22:42-5 N 6 '89

Gorilla warfare [R. Giuliani takes on M. Cuomo] J. Klein. il pors *New York* 22:24+ Ap 10 '89

Gotham rainbow [D. Dinkins wins Democratic mayoral primary] *The Nation* 249:335-6 O 2 '89

Great-man theory [A. D'Amato's support of mayoral candidate R. Lauder] J. Klein. pors *New York* 22:16+ F 13 '89

The "healer" takes New York: Dinkins wins primary. F. McCoy. il por *Black Enterprise* 20:21-2 N '89

Hope, not fear: New York may be the next city to elect a black mayor [Democratic candidate D. Dinkins] R. Lacayo. il por *Time* 134:20-1 S 25 '89

How Bess got out of the mess [B. Myerson case] J. Kasindorf. il pors *New York* 22:38-48 Ja 16 '89

How'd I do? [letter to D. Dinkins] E. Koch. il pors *The New York Times Magazine* p26-7+ D 31 '89

It's a dirty job—but a lot of people want to do it [mayoral race] H. Collingwood. il por *Business Week* p26 Ap 17 '89

Jackie Mason tries to talk himself out of trouble [effect of racist remarks on R. Giuliani's mayoral campaign; cover story] J. Kasindorf. il pors *New York* 22:36-42 O 16 '89

NEW YORK (N.Y.)—Politics and government—*cont.*

Jackie Mason's racial remarks about Dinkins, Jews' relations with blacks bring backlash. pors *Jet* 77:5 O 16 '89

Koch against Koch. S. Roberts. il pors *The New York Times Magazine* p32-4+ Je 11 '89

Koch lives [mayoral debate] J. Klein. il por *New York* 22:9-10 Ag 7 '89

Last gasps [mayoral campaign] J. Klein. il *New York* 22:19-20 S 18 '89

The last liberal [possibility that Liberal Party leader R. Harding will support R. Giuliani for mayor] J. Klein. il por *New York* 22:14+ Ap 3 '89

The lion in summer: Koch on the comeback trail. J. Klein. il pors *New York* 22:38-42 S 4 '89

London in New York [mayoral candidate H. London] *National Review* 41:16 Ap 21 '89

Mason bombs in New York [comedian's racial slurs hurt R. Giuliani's mayoral campaign] B. Turque. il pors *Newsweek* 114:42 O 9 '89

Mayor culpa [corruption in the Koch administration] J. B. Rose. *The New Republic* 200:18-20+ My 8 '89

Mayor-elect David Dinkins. D. Baer. il pors *U.S. News & World Report* 107:54+ N 20 '89

Mayor Koch's wrinkled brow. W. F. Buckley. *National Review* 41:62-3 Mr 10 '89

The mayor's race: Dinkins vs. Giuliani. F. Barnes. *The New Republic* 201:9-10 O 9 '89

Miss America wins again [B. Myerson acquitted] il por *Time* 133:80 Ja 2 '89

Mr. Softy [possible mayoral candidate D. Dinkins] J. Klein. il por *New York* 22:20-1 Ja 16 '89

The N.Y.C. scandals of Ed Koch [J. Newfield and W. Barrett's *City for sale*; cover story] M. J. Green. *The Nation* 248:397 Mr 27 '89

The new mayor and the crisis of New York [D. Dinkins; cover story] J. Klein. il pors *New York* 22:36-40 N 20 '89

New York's first and last hurrahs [D. Dinkins wins Democratic nomination] D. Baer. il pors *U.S. News & World Report* 107:26-7 S 25 '89

A nice guy finishes first [D. Dinkins elected mayor] J. Attinger. il por *Time* 134:60 N 20 '89

Now, the showdown: Dinkins vs. Giuliani in the void left by Koch. J. Klein. il pors *New York* 22:50-3 S 25 '89

The papers vote [endorsements in New York City mayoral race] E. Diamond. il *New York* 22:24+ S 25 '89

The race for New York: Edward Koch loses a bid for a new term. H. Mackenzie. il pors *Maclean's* 102:32-3 S 25 '89

Ready for Rudy? [R. Giuliani, cover story] J. Klein. il pors *New York* 22:30-7 Mr 6 '89

The real thing [race issue in mayoral campaign] J. Klein. il por *New York* 22:16+ N 13 '89

A Rudy awakening [R. Giuliani's mayoral campaign] J. Klein. il por *New York* 22:16+ O 16 '89

Rudy's fall from grace: can Ailes put Giuliani's campaign back together again? J. Klein. il pors *New York* 22:40-3 Ag 21 '89

So long, Ed [E. Koch] W. F. Buckley. *National Review* 41:63 O 27 '89

War of the sound bites [mayoral race] J. Klein. il *New York* 22:20-1 Ag 14 '89

Zinging Rudy [E. Koch and R. Lauder attack R. Giuliani in mayoral race] J. Klein. por *New York* 22:14-15 Je 5 '89

Anecdotes, facetiae, satire, etc.

The Calphalon candidate [J. McInerney for mayor] D. Blum. por *New York* 22:31 Ap 24 '89

Poor

See also
Emmaus House, Inc.
We Can (Organization)

Autograph [author from Minnesota gives autograph to homeless man] *The New Yorker* 65:30-2 Ag 7 '89

The can people [poor collect aluminum cans] E. Barnes. il *Life* 12:98-102 Ag '89

From Dickens to Beckett in Grand Central [stories created by beggars in New York City] A. Broyard. il *The New York Times Book Review* 94:12 Mr 12 '89

Good neighbors [volunteers assisting poor] H. Evans. il *U.S. News & World Report* 106:76 Ap 10 '89

Homeless rights, community wrongs [efforts to keep homeless out of public parks] J. Leo. il *U.S. News & World Report* 107:56 Jl 24 '89

One heart warms many chilly fingers [M. Greenberg distributes gloves to the homeless] D. Brand. il pors *Time* 133:16+ Ja 2 '89

One point of light [homeless woman M. Davis taken in by S. Braun of Honesdale, Pa.] D. Finkel. il pors *Esquire* 112:123-8+ O '89

Too much, too blindly, too fast. E. Hoagland. il *Harper's* 278:65-8 Je '89

Popular culture

Slaves of New York's fame machine. il *Psychology Today* 22:53 D '88

Prisons and reformatories

Keeper of the keys [J. White, black woman warden at the Manhattan House of Detention] N. A. Nichols. il por *New York* 22:28 F 20 '89

The woman who heads all-male New York jail [warden J. White] D. M. Cheers. il pors *Jet* 76:28-31 Ap 17 '89

Public buildings

Learning curve [new schools being built; special section] E. Posner. il *Architectural Record* 177:106-15 Mr '89

Lease-buy, lease-out, and friendly condemnations: the federal government tries new approaches on its new buildings. P. Hoffmann. il *Architectural Record* 177:29+ Mr '89

Public comfort stations

Hurry calls. B. Ickes and M. Weingarden. il *New York* 22:77-8 My 1 '89

Public health

Thousands may die in the streets [homeless AIDS patients] S. Schulman. il *The Nation* 248:480-2 Ap 10 '89

Yolanda Serrano [work in AIDS prevention] K. Dobie. il pors *Ms.* 17:79-83 Ja/F '89

Race relations

Building unity across a city street [Martin Luther King Jr. High School and Fiorello H. La Guardia High School of the Arts] L. Eskin. il *Scholastic Update (Teachers' edition)* 121:24-5 Ap 7 '89

The fugitive [former black militant H. Ferguson] P. Blauner. il pors *New York* 22:32-7 Ag 7 '89

Jackie Mason tries to talk himself out of trouble [effect of racist remarks on R. Giuliani's mayoral campaign; cover story] J. Kasindorf. il pors *New York* 22:36-42 O 16 '89

Jackie Mason's racial remarks about Dinkins, Jews' relations with blacks bring backlash. pors *Jet* 77:5 O 16 '89

Mason bombs in New York [comedian's racial slurs hurt R. Giuliani's mayoral campaign] B. Turque. il pors *Newsweek* 114:42 O 9 '89

Race: the issue [cover story] J. Klein. il *New York* 22:32-8 My 29 '89

The real thing [race issue in mayoral campaign] J. Klein. il por *New York* 22:16+ N 13 '89

Spike Lee replies: "Say it ain't so, Joe" [discussion of June 26, 1989 article, Spiked?] J. Klein. il por *New York* 22:6 Jl 17 '89

Spiked? [effect of S. Lee's film Do the right thing on D. Dinkins's mayoral campaign] J. Klein. il pors *New York* 22:14-15 Je 26 '89

Stabs in the dark [racially motivated attacks on women] *Newsweek* 114:49 N 13 '89

Tale of two cities. *Time* 134:28 S 11 '89

Recreation

See also
New York (N.Y.). Dept. of Parks and Recreation

Summer pleasures [cover story; special issue] il *New York* 22:19-31+ Jl 3-10 '89

What's free, what's cheap [cover story] V. Frontero. il *New York* 22:38-47 Mr 27 '89

Religious institutions and affairs

See also
Times Square Church
True Church of God

Challenges facing U.S. Catholics. J. J. O'Connor, Cardinal. *Commonweal* 116:619-20 N 17 '89

The great God blackout [Life magazine removes mention of God from cover of copies sold in New York City] M. E. Marty. *The Christian Century* 106:967 O 25 '89

In a rage over AIDS [ACT UP targets Cardinal J. O'Connor] E. Magnuson. il *Time* 134:33 D 25 '89

The view from St. Patrick's [J. Cardinal O'Connor] J. Berger. il pors *The New York Times Magazine* p38-40+ Mr 26 '89

Restaurants, nightclubs, bars, etc.

See also
Brooklyn (New York, N.Y.)—Restaurants, nightclubs, bars, etc.

Ask Gael: new ideas for places to go in '89. G. Greene. il por *New York* 22:20-8 Ja 2 '89

At home on the range [D. Ponzek, chef at Montrachet] J. Freiman. il pors *Harper's Bazaar* 122:216+ Ap '89

Bistro bravura [Park Bistro and Rosolio] G. Greene. il *New York* 22:58+ Mr 6 '89

Borscht Belt [Russian restaurants] J. Freiman. il *Harper's Bazaar* 122:172+ F '89

Brian's body shop [150 Wooster Street] G. Greene. il *New York* 22:44 Jl 17 '89

By the numbers [wine lists] A. Bespaloff. il *New York* 22:100-1 My 1 '89

Circus of the stars [Le Cirque and Brive] G. Greene. il *New York* 22:113-15 Ap 10 '89

Corn meals [Twigs and Bella Luna] J. Freiman. il *New York* 22:80 Mr 13 '89

Cue: a complete entertainment guide for the week. See issues of New York

Dangerous curves [Bolidó designed by M. Iosa Ghini] C. K. Gandee. il por *House & Garden* 161:44 My '89

Deals on meals. J. Freiman. il *New York* 22:48-52 Ja 23 '89

Dessert song [Tirami su and Delia's] G. Greene. il *New York* 22:58+ Ap 17 '89

NEW YORK (N.Y.)—Restaurants, nightclubs, bars, etc.—
cont.

Disco-towing [Dept. of Transportation's program to clear away illegally parked cars near discotheques] il *The New Yorker* 65:30-1 My 22 '89

Eating to the beat: downtown food has attitude, too. G. Greene. il *New York* 22:96-8+ D 25 '89-Ja 1 '90

Endangered species [L. Arpaia, owner of Scarlatti] M. Barrier. il por *Nation's Business* 77:18 O '89

Ever so humble. L. Wells. il *The New York Times Magazine* p35-6 Ja 1 '89

Feasts to go. B. Costikyan. il *New York* 22:109+ My 1 '89

Fine romance [romantic restaurants] G. Greene. il *New York* 22:79-80 F 20 '89

Forbes names New York's 1989 best and special restaurants. il *Forbes* 144:20 D 25 '89

Glad cafés. R. D. Story. il *New York* 22:48-9 My 1 '89

Goings on about town. See issues of The New Yorker

Good taste. L. Wells. il *The New York Times Magazine* p53-4 D 31 '89

Le Grand Orange [Rusty Staub's on 5th] *The New Yorker* 64:18-19 Ja 2 '89

Great new places to have a party (I) [cover story] B. Costikyan. il *New York* 22:58-68+ N 13 '89

Great new places to have a party (II). B. Costikyan. il *New York* 22:48-52+ N 20 '89

Hit lists [wine lists] A. Bespaloff. il *New York* 22:116-17 Ap 10 '89

Hot spots: clubs. M. Berkman. il *New York* 22:38+ D 25 '89-Ja 1 '90

Hotter than hot: why they kill to get into 150 Wooster. G. Greene. il por *New York* 22:44-9 O 30 '89

Julian of the spirits [J. Niccolini of the Four Seasons] A. Richman. il pors *Gentlemen's Quarterly* 59:150-7 Jl '89

Kabobbing along [Bobby Kebobby and Caravan] J. Freiman. il *New York* 22:74 My 29 '89

Kitchen cousins [Sette Mezzo and Bar du Théâtre] G. Greene. il *New York* 22:97-8 Je 5 '89

Knit wits [Knitting Factory] P. Hoban. il *New York* 22:46-9 Jl 31 '89

Knitting a new music scene [Knitting Factory] S. Futterman. il *Rolling Stone* p19 Ap 6 '89

Larry's home cooking [An American Place] G. Greene. il por *New York* 22:72+ Mr 27 '89

Leaner-than-ever Chinese cuisine [recipes of D. Keh, owner of David K's] T. Ney. il por *Prevention (Emmaus, Pa.)* 41:75-8+ F '89

Let's eat out. See issues of Gourmet

The man from Mars [club impresario Rudolf] H. Rubenstein. il por *New York* 22:48-50+ Ap 17 '89

The man upstairs [B. Lamotte's paintings in La Grenouille's private dining room] W. Goodman. il pors *New York* 22:54-9 Je 19 '89

Mars: a visit to a small planet [nightclub designed by Rudolf] il por *Harper's Bazaar* 122:226 Ap '89

Max [death of Village Vanguard owner M. Gordon] W. Balliett. *The New Yorker* 65:69-71 Jl 17 '89

Miso Italian [Duane Park Café and Giorgio Cafe] G. Greene. il *New York* 22:60+ Mr 13 '89

Mixed blessings [Vucciria and Ferrier] G. Greene. il *New York* 22:70-1 O 9 '89

The most happy villa [Malvasia and Le Madri] G. Greene. il *New York* 22:51-2 Je 26 '89

Mothers of invention [P. Luongo's Le Madri] R. D. Story. il por *New York* 22:46-51 Je 5 '89

Mushroom at the top [Chanterelle and Sino] G. Greene. il *New York* 22:66-7 Ap 3 '89

My favorite dishes. G. Greene. il *New York* 22:59-60 My 1 '89

New Foy in town [D. Foy's Mondrian] il por *Harper's Bazaar* 122:228 Mr '89

Night life lives [hot nightclubs] L. Snowden. il *Mademoiselle* 95:242-7+ Ap '89

No trouble with Harry [Harry's at Hanover Square and other locations] J. Zweig. il por *Forbes* 144:122 Jl 10 '89

Nose job [working as a sommelier at Maurice] A. Richman. il *Gentlemen's Quarterly* 59:255-6 Mr '89

Pasta in the piazza [Cafe Bel Canto and Pasta and Dreams] J. Freiman. il *New York* 22:70 Je 19 '89

Personalities plus [Delia's, Darrell's and Trixie's] J. Gruder. il pors *Harper's Bazaar* 122:173-4 Ag '89

Plain and too fancy [Jane's Bar & Grill and Beau Geste] G. Greene. il *New York* 22:106+ My 15 '89

Requiem for a saloonkeeper [B. Cunningham, owner of Bradley's] R. Merkin. il *Gentlemen's Quarterly* 59:48+ Jl '89

Restaurants [fall preview] il *New York* 22:166-8+ S 11 '89

Restaurants—go, consider, stop. M. S. Forbes. *Forbes* 144:20-1 O 30 '89

Restaurants—go, consider, stop. M. S. Forbes. il *Forbes* 143:20 Je 26 '89

Restaurants—go, consider, stop. M. S. Forbes. il *Forbes* 143:20 Mr 20 '89

Restaurants—go, consider, stop. M. S. Forbes. *Forbes* 144:20 S 18 '89

Rising to the top [D. Ponzek's French cuisine at Montrachet] B. Miller and P. Franey. il *The New York Times Magazine* p69-70 F 19 '89

Rock of ages [A. Pepper and S. Snadowsky, co-owners of the Bottom Line] E. Hollreiser. il pors *New York* 22:29 F 6 '89

Romance of the Rose [Sonia Rose] G. Greene. il *New York* 22:139 Ap 24 '89

Royalton flush [44] G. Greene. il *New York* 22:105 N 20 '89

Scenes: looking for young love in all the new places. M. Berkman. il *New York* 22:46-8+ Jl 3-10 '89

Society's café [Mortimer's] M. Filler. il pors *House & Garden* 161:100+ O '89

Sounds and laughs [downtown] C. S. Smith. il *New York* 22:42-4+ D 25 '89-Ja 1 '90

Spécialités de la maison:
Aureole, Da Tommaso, 20 Mott Street Restaurant. A. Birsh. il *Gourmet* 49:70+ N '89
La Caravelle, One Hudson Café, Benny's Burritos. A. Birsh. il *Gourmet* 49:32+ O '89
The Carlyle Restaurant, L'Écluse, Nusantara. A. Birsh. il *Gourmet* 49:24+ F '89
Eze, China Grill, Siracusa. A. Birsh. il *Gourmet* 49:26+ Ja '89
Huberts, J. Sung Dynasty, Jerry's. A. Birsh. il *Gourmet* 49:32+ Ap '89
Metro, Periyali, Darbár. A. Birsh. il *Gourmet* 49:32+ Mr '89
Mondrian, David K's, L'Escale. A. Birsh. il *Gourmet* 49:42+ My '89
Palio, Park Bistro, Luma. A. Birsh. il *Gourmet* 49:44+ D '89
Le Périgord, Le Cheval Blanc, Chez Josephine. A. Birsh. il *Gourmet* 49:32+ Jl '89
San Domenico NY, Canal Bar. A. Birsh. il *Gourmet* 49:32+ Je '89
Toscana Ristorante, The Polo, B. Smith's. A. Birsh. il *Gourmet* 49:22+ Ag '89

Summer in the city: where to dance after you leave the studio. J. Wallace. il *Dance Magazine* 63:16 Je '89

Swan's way [Le Cygne and Mon Cher TonTon] G. Greene. il *New York* 22:76+ O 16 '89

Swiss watch [Adrienne] G. Greene. il *New York* 22:58+ Jl 31 '89

Thai chichi [Sukhothai West] J. Freiman. il *New York* 22:82 Ap 17 '89

Tops underground. J. Freiman. il *New York* 22:74-7 My 1 '89

Tripping the bite fantastic [Alison and Flamingo East] G. Greene. il *New York* 22:73-4 Ag 14 '89

A woman's place [Bar du Theater and Alison on Dominick Street] J. F. Mariani. il por *Harper's Bazaar* 122:190+ N '89

Anecdotes, facetiae, satire, etc.
Alien rations. G. Schwartz. il *New York* 22:34 N 6 '89

Riots
See also
Stonewall Riot, 1969
How to shoot a riot [C. Patterson's video of Tompkins Square Park riot] E. Shawn. il *Video* 13:50+ Ap '89

Sanitary affairs
See also
New York (N.Y.). Dept. of Sanitation
A whiff of things to come [carriage horses to wear canvas bags to catch manure] il *Newsweek* 113:71 Ap 10 '89

Savings and loan associations
See also
Dime Savings Bank of New York
Manhattan Savings Bank

Schools
See New York (N.Y.)—Education

Social conditions
Abortion in New York [cover story] J. Kasindorf. il *New York* 22:32-8+ S 18 '89

East-West relation [escorting a Communist visitor] R. Stone. il *Harper's* 279:63-7 N '89

Mayor Koch and Cardinal O'Connor: a conversation [excerpts from His Eminence and Hizzoner] E. Koch; J. J. O'Connor. il *Good Housekeeping* 208:148+ My '89

The prophet motive [book by E. Koch and J. O'Connor] J. Klein. il pors *New York* 22:12+ Mr 20 '89

Secret lives of New York [cover story] D. Smith. il *New York* 22:34-41 D 11 '89

Too much, too blindly, too fast. E. Hoagland. il *Harper's* 278:65-8 Je '89

Social history
Old hometown. P. Matthiessen. il pors *Architectural Digest* 46:52+ N '89

Social life and customs
Affairs to remember. J. Freiman. il *Harper's Bazaar* 122:132+ Je '89

Attitude [vogueing] *The New Yorker* 64:26-7 Ja 16 '89

Climbing Mt. Manhattan [new money vs. old money] J. Kramer. il *House & Garden* 161:188-9+ O '89

The cutting edge. M. Gross. See issues of New York beginning February 22, 1988

NEW YORK (N.Y.)—Social life and customs—*cont.*

Flower brokers [work of florists Anita Widder, VSF, and Zezé] M. K. Griswold. il *House & Garden* 161:80+ O '89

Hotter than hot: why they kill to get into 150 Wooster. G. Greene. il por *New York* 22:44-9 O 30 '89

Irradiation [visit to Russian Turkish Baths] *The New Yorker* 64:24 Ja 30 '89

Landing front-row seats at fashion shows is a socioeconomic coup. B. Handy. il *Vogue* 179:218-20 Jl '89

Moving from the East to the West, as Claire Scovell found out, doesn't just mean a change of climate. C. Scovell. il *Vogue* 179:162-4 Ag '89

On the town [France-Danse benefit] J. Gruen. il *Dance Magazine* 63:68-71 Jl '89

Party palace: the high life at the gilded Metropolitan Museum [cover story] J. Taylor. il *New York* 22:20-30 Ja 9 '89

Scenes: looking for young love in all the new places. M. Berkman. il *New York* 22:46-8+ Jl 3-10 '89

There's Morton Downey sipping champagne from a loafer . . . Tony Danza singing harmony on 59th Street. C. Adams. il *TV Guide* 37:20-2 Je 17-23 '89

This month, social swell Jerome Zipkin celebrates his seventy-fifth birthday. M. Thomas. il pors *Vogue* 179:369-70+ D '89

To New Yorkers, exercise is a no-frills business. H. Sweet. *Vogue* 179:170+ Ag '89

The wedding [civil ceremony in Municipal Building] *The New Yorker* 65:34-5 S 11 '89

Anecdotes, facetiae, satire, etc.

No swimsuits [reporting on a Sports illustrated preview party] *The New Yorker* 65:31-2 F 20 '89

Not being there. G. Schwartz. il *New York* 22:24 My 22 '89

Wired!! [listening in on private phone conversations; cover story] S. M. L. Aronson and V. Tiger. il *New York* 22:26-33 Ja 30 '89

Caricatures and cartoons

Billy's people. W. Norwich. il *New York* 22:42-6 Ap 3 '89

Social work

Giving teenagers a new view of their future [work of M. Carrera in Harlem] M. Ludtke. il por *Time* 133:12+ My 1 '89

N.Y. trains refugees to be counselors in service agencies. il *Aging* no359:29 '89

Sports

See also

Bronx (New York, N.Y.)—Sports

Courting [tennis courts] J. Seabury. il *New York* 22:124-6 My 1 '89

New York. R. Sears. il *Sport (New York, N.Y.)* 80:42-3+ F '89

Where the pros train. M. Bloom. il *New York* 22:48-57 S 18 '89

Stations

See also

Grand Central Terminal (New York, N.Y.)

Art in the underground [subway stations] M. Alexander. il *Art in America* 77:35 D '89

Statistics

Stats. *The New Yorker* 65:30 Ap 24 '89

Stores

See also

Alaïa (Firm)

B. Altman & Co.

Barney's, New York

Beau Brummel (Firm)

Comme des Garçons SHIRT (Firm)

Emporio Armani (Firm)

Kurland Zabar (Firm)

L'Aquitaine (Firm)

Lexington Gardens (Firm)

Maxilla & Mandible (Firm)

Modern Supply Company

OMO Home (Firm)

Performing Artists Diversified (Firm)

Place des Antiquaires (New York, N.Y.)

R. H. Macy & Co., Inc.

Soup Kitchen International (Firm)

Tender Buttons (Firm)

Tiffany & Co.

Urban Archaeology Ltd.

Urbani Truffles USA

. . . and cheese. R. D. Story. il *New York* 22:67+ My 1 '89

At home on Madison. A. Foxley. il *House & Garden* 161:206+ My '89

Breaking in [elegant boutiques] N. Scovell. il *Vogue* 179:550+ Mr '89

The Christmas table. *The New Yorker* 65:89-94 D 18 '89

Dial-a-dinner party. J. Miller. il *Harper's Bazaar* 122:221+ Mr '89

Fast feasts: for the holidays, take it out—take it all out. B. Costikyan. il *New York* 22:66-8+ D 18 '89

Hard cases [fixing and finding] L. Schnurnberger. il *New York* 22:117-18 My 1 '89

Harvesting antiques in the Big Apple. J. L. Wiltsee. il *Business Week* p150 D 11 '89

HG guide: New York [household furnishings] D. B. Cowin. il *House & Garden* 161:128+ O '89

Hidden treasures [antique shops] D. B. Cowin. il *House & Garden* 161:70+ D '89

The instant office. V. Taylor and A. Berlin. il *New York* 22:104+ My 1 '89

Minding the family store [Korean greengrocers] C. Koehl. il *Newsweek* 114 Special Issue:4 Wint '89/Spr '90

New York designers' favorite shops. J. Simpson. il *Architectural Digest* 46:146-56+ N '89

On and off the avenue [Christmas gifts] *The New Yorker* 65:156-64+ D 4 '89

On and off the avenue [Christmas gifts for children] *The New Yorker* 65:141-53 D 11 '89

On and off the avenue [gifts for the house] *The New Yorker* 65:83-9 D 18 '89

Quick fixes [repair shops] B. Ickes. il *New York* 22:61-3 My 1 '89

Read all about it [magazine stores] P. Eaton. il *New York* 22:58 My 1 '89

Sales & bargains. L. Fleischer. See issues of New York

Saving graces [thrift shops] P. Eaton. il *New York* 22:120-2 My 1 '89

Shopping [fall preview] L. Dyett. il *New York* 22:154-65 S 11 '89

A store is born [Abraham & Straus] B. Kanner. il *New York* 22:24-5 S 18 '89

Takeout. B. Costikyan. il *New York* 22:60-2+ Jl 3-10 '89

Treasure islands [downtown] M. Gross. il *New York* 22:120-4+ D 25 '89-Ja 1 '90

Wine. A. Bespaloff. il *New York* 22:66-7 My 1 '89

Anecdotes, facetiae, satire, etc.

Fear and clothing [boutiques] C. Heimel. il *Vogue* 179:538+ Mr '89

Street trades

Extra-artistic [Times Square street photographers] *The New Yorker* 65:32-3 D 25 '89

Mexico's flower children [flower sellers] R. Miller. il *New York* 22:31 O 16 '89

The plush life [stuffed animal peddler R. Granata] R. Miller. il *New York* 22:25 My 29 '89

Street selling [Senegalese vendors] *The New Yorker* 65:27-8 Jl 3 '89

Street smarts. B. Chant. il *New York* 22:68-9 My 1 '89

Street traffic

See also

New York (N.Y.)—Traffic regulations

A memorable ride. J. Atlas. il *The New York Times Magazine* p14+ F 5 '89

Weekend getaways [getting out of New York City on summer weekends] J. Blyskal and M. Hodge. il *New York* 22:148-9 My 1 '89

Streets

See also

42nd Street (New York, N.Y.)

Madison Avenue (New York, N.Y.)

Prince Street (New York, N.Y.)

Walkman [listening to music while walking] *The New Yorker* 64:19-20 Ja 2 '89

Subways

See also

Metropolitan Transportation Authority

Fade to gray in Gotham [retirement of last graffiti-covered car] il *U.S. News & World Report* 106:12 My 22 '89

Taxation

Anecdotes, facetiae, satire, etc.

Sour tax notes. D. Seligman. il *Fortune* 119:164 Mr 27 '89

Taxicabs

See also

New York (N.Y.). Taxi and Limousine Commission

Taxis in the clutch. M. Berkman. il *New York* 22:50 My 1 '89

Terminals

See New York (N.Y.)—Stations

Theater

See also

AMAS Repertory Theatre, Inc.

Circle Repertory Company

Cirque Grégoire

Mark Hellinger Theater (New York, N.Y.)

New York Shakespeare Festival

St. James Theatre (New York, N.Y.)

Symphony Space (New York, N.Y.)

Act two [A. Holzer charged with investment fraud] J. Kasindorf. il pors *New York* 22:46-52+ Ap 10 '89

Broadway bound [Canadian shows] P. Young. il *Maclean's* 102:54-5 S 25 '89

The Broadway bustle. P. Young. il *Maclean's* 102:58-9 D 11 '89

Broadway's brightest lights. D. H. Dunn. il *Business Week* p105 Je 19 '89

Hopeful highlights [1989-90 Broadway season] K. Grubb. il *Dance Magazine* 63:54-5 O '89

Japanese angels on Broadway. F. H. Katayama. il *Fortune* 119:8 Mr 27 '89

Joe Papp [interview] V. Muse. il pors *Life* 12:23-5 Ap '89

NEW YORK (N.Y.)—Theater—*cont.*
Onstage [Zagat theater ratings] il *New York* 22:56-8 Jl 3-10 '89
Robert Brustein on theater. R. Brustein. See occasional issues of The New Republic
Theater. See occasional issues of The Nation
Theater [fall preview] K. Pryor. il *New York* 22:52-3 S 11 '89
Theater. J. Simon. See issues of New York
The theatre. M. Kramer. See issues of The New Yorker beginning June 8, 1987
The theatre. E. Oliver. See issues of The New Yorker beginning February 16, 1987
Twofer the seesaw [discount tickets] V. Taylor and A. Berlin. il *New York* 22:130+ My 1 '89
Warmed over and not so hot [Broadway musicals] W. A. Henry. il *Time* 134:87 N 27 '89
Traffic regulations
Disco-towing [Dept. of Transportation's program to clear away illegally parked cars near discotheques] il *The New Yorker* 65:30-1 My 22 '89
Transit systems
See also
Metropolitan Transportation Authority
New York (N.Y.)—Subways
Light rail [proposals] T. Hiss. il *The New Yorker* 65:70-4+ Mr 6 '89
Window on the city [interesting bus routes] V. Frontero. il maps *New York* 22:88-9 My 1 '89
Transportation
Anecdotes, facetiae, satire, etc.
I get around. D. Blum. il *New York* 22:15 Jl 24 '89
Underground structures
New York underground. il *National Geographic World* 164:20-1 Ap '89
Zoning
Dollars for density in Manhattan: What is zoning worth? [special section] J. S. Russell. il *Architectural Record* 177:79+ Je '89
Pushing the outer limits [real estate developers] J. Taylor. il *New York* 22:84-6+ Ap 10 '89
Battery Park City
See Battery Park City (New York, N.Y.)
Chelsea
See Chelsea (New York, N.Y.)
Chinatown
See Chinatown (New York, N.Y.)
Gramercy Park
See Gramercy Park (New York, N.Y.)
Greenwich Village
See Greenwich Village (New York, N.Y.)
Harlem
See Harlem (New York, N.Y.)
Hell's Kitchen
See Hell's Kitchen (New York, N.Y.)
Rockefeller Center
See Rockefeller Center
SoHo
See SoHo (New York, N.Y.)
Times Square
See Times Square (New York, N.Y.)
Upper West Side
See Upper West Side (New York, N.Y.)
Wall Street
See Wall Street (New York, N.Y.)
Washington Square
See Washington Square (New York, N.Y.)
Westway (Proposed)
See Express highways—New York (State)
NEW YORK (N.Y.). DEPT. OF PARKS AND RECREATION
The country in the city. C. A. Nadareski and M. J. Feller. il *The Conservationist* 44:12-17 Jl/Ag '89
NEW YORK (N.Y.). DEPT. OF SANITATION
Waste not [M. Ukeles' Flow city art installation at new trash loading facility] P. C. Phillips. il *Art in America* 77:47+ F '89
NEW YORK (N.Y.). DEPT. OF SANITATION. ENVIRON-MENTAL POLICE UNIT *See* New York (N.Y.). Environmental Police Unit
NEW YORK (N.Y.). DEPT. OF THE AGING
English classes open up new opportunities for Hispanic New Yorkers. il *Aging* no359:23 '89
NEW YORK (N.Y.). ENVIRONMENTAL POLICE UNIT
Toxic avengers. J. Stone. il *Discover* 10:40-3+ Ag '89
NEW YORK (N.Y.). GALERIE ST. ETIENNE *See* Galerie St. Etienne
NEW YORK (N.Y.). GRAND CENTRAL TERMINAL *See* Grand Central Terminal (New York, N.Y.)
NEW YORK (N.Y.). METROPOLITAN OPERA *See* Metropolitan Opera (New York, N.Y.)
NEW YORK (N.Y.). RIVERSIDE CHURCH *See* Riverside Church (New York, N.Y.)
NEW YORK (N.Y.). ROCKEFELLER UNIVERSITY *See* Rockefeller University
NEW YORK (N.Y.). SYMPHONY SPACE *See* Symphony Space (New York, N.Y.)

NEW YORK (N.Y.). TAXI AND LIMOUSINE COMMISSION
Fugu, taxis, and Tender Buttons. H. Bridges. il *Gourmet* 49:48+ S '89
T.L.C. *The New Yorker* 65:25-6 Ag 21 '89
NEW YORK (N.Y.). WORLD'S FAIR (1939-1940) *See* New York World's Fair (1939-1940)
NEW YORK (N.Y.). FASHION SHOWS *See* Fashion shows
NEW YORK (N.Y.) IN ART
Art: paintings of New York. M. M. Thomas. il *Architectural Digest* 46:274-9+ N '89
Exhibitions
Ambassador of light [work of J. Button] B. Berkson. il por *Art in America* 77:170-5 N '89
Susanna Heller at Tomoko Liguori. R. Berlind. *Art in America* 77:164 F '89
NEW YORK (N.Y.) IN LITERATURE
The down patrol: the book on downtown fiction. R. Koenig. il *New York* 22:147-8+ D 25 '89-Ja 1 '90
NEW YORK (N.Y.) IN MOTION PICTURES
100 years of filmmaking in New York [special section] il *American Film* 15:57-68+ O '89
Big bad Apple. M. McCreadie. il *Film Comment* 25:3+ Mr/Ap '89
Slaves of New York [production of T. Janowitz's novel] il por *Harper's Bazaar* 122:144-5 F '89
Tales of the Naked City. P. Arthur. il *USA Today (Periodical)* 117:93 Mr '89
NEW YORK (STATE)
See also
Abortion clinics—New York (State)
Adirondack Forest Preserve (N.Y.)
Adirondack Mountains (N.Y.)
Agriculture—New York (State)
Albany County (N.Y.)
Architecture, Domestic—New York (State)
Automobile driving—New York (State)
Ballet—New York (State)
Beaverkill River (N.Y.)
Birds—New York (State)
Blacks—New York (State)
Booksellers and bookselling—New York (State)
Columbia County (N.Y.)
Criminal justice, Administration of—New York (State)
Dance festivals—New York (State)
Drama festivals—New York (State)
Education—New York (State)
Educational laws and regulations—New York (State)
Express highways—New York (State)
Fire Island National Seashore (N.Y.)
Fish—New York (State)
Fishing—New York (State)
Forests and forestry—New York (State)
Gardiners Island (N.Y.)
Gateway National Recreation Area (N.J. and N.Y.)
Groundwater pollution—New York (State)
Health resorts, watering places, etc.—New York (State)
Historic houses, sites, etc.—New York (State)
Hudson River Valley (N.Y. and N.J.)
Hunting—New York (State)
Income tax—New York (State)
Lake George (N.Y.)
Lakes—New York (State)
Land utilization—Laws and regulations—New York (State)
Law—New York (State)
Long Island (N.Y.)
Medical policy—New York (State)
Motion picture festivals—New York (State)
Mount Marcy (N.Y.)
Music festivals—New York (State)
Oil pollution—New York (State)
Opera—New York (State)
Organic gardens and gardening—New York (State)
Paleontology—New York (State)
Palisades (N.J. and N.Y.)
Radon pollution—New York (State)
Roads—New York (State)
Saint Lawrence River
Sculpture gardens and parks—New York (State)
Seneca Lake (N.Y.)
Shawangunk Mountains (N.Y.)
Trapping—New York (State)
Trials—New York (State)
Ulster County (N.Y.)
Water pollution—New York (State)
Water supply—New York (State)
Westchester County (N.Y.)
Wilderness areas—New York (State)
Wildflowers—New York (State)
Wildlife—New York (State)
Wildlife management—New York (State)

NEW YORK REVIEW OF BOOKS
Anecdotes, facetiae, satire, etc.
St. Nicholas: a textual scandal [corrected text of The night before Christmas; cover story] R. R. Lingeman and T. M. Disch. *The Nation* 248:1+ Ja 2 '89

NEW YORK SCHOOL OF DRYCLEANING
Problems [B. Seitz teaches Koreans] *The New Yorker* 65:40-1 O 9 '89

NEW YORK SHAKESPEARE FESTIVAL
Hollywood Shakespeare [cover story] D. Blum. il *New York* 22:28-35 Je 19 '89
Joe Papp [interview] V. Muse. il pors *Life* 12:23-5 Ap '89

NEW YORK STOCK EXCHANGE, INC.
Living off the spread [B. L. Madoff takes advantage of rule that protects specialists] R. L. Stern. il *Forbes* 144:66-7 Jl 10 '89
Seeing double in program trading. G. Weiss. il *Business Week* p31-2 N 20 '89
Why Wall Street is furioso at Raul Gardini [deal to buy out minority holders of Ausimont] J. Rossant and W. Glasgall. il por *Business Week* p48 F 20 '89

NEW YORK STORIES [film] *See* Motion picture reviews—Single works

NEW YORK TIMES
Anthony agonistes [columnist A. Lewis] H. Catto. il *National Review* 41:34-7+ S 1 '89
California dreaming [California edition] E. Diamond. il *New York* 22:16+ My 22 '89
Hello sweetheart, get me mergers and acquisitions [S. Rattner] P. Weiss. *The Washington Monthly* 21:67-8 F '89
Leaning [political labeling] D. Seligman. il *Fortune* 120:135-6 Ag 28 '89
NASA's legal folly [battle to block release of recording of Challenger astronauts' voices] M. Stevens. *Ad Astra* 1:48 My '89
Public opinion and the jogger [coverage of Central Park wilding attack] R. Brookhiser. *Commentary* 88:50-2 Jl '89
Those turbulent bishops [criticism of positions taken by Catholic bishops] R. J. Neuhaus. il *National Review* 41:32-3 D 31 '89
Time + Dallas = ? [coverage of Time Inc. acquisition of Warner Communications] R. Pollak. *The Nation* 248:401 Mr 27 '89

NEW YORK TIMES CABLE
Llewellyn plugs into $420 million NYT cable deal. K. D. Thompson. por *Black Enterprise* 19:17 Mr '89

NEW YORK TIMES COMPANY
There's plenty of life in this old gray lady. G. G. Marcial. il *Business Week* p118 Je 5 '89

NEW YORK TRIBUNE
The Civil War's greatest scoop [account of Battle of Antietam by correspondent G. W. Smalley] J. Weeks. il por *American Heritage* 40:100+ Jl/Ag '89

NEW YORK UNIVERSITY
A preemptive strike for animal research. C. Holden. il *Science* 244:415-16 Ap 28 '89

NEW YORK UNIVERSITY. LABORATORY FOR EXPERIMENTAL MEDICINE AND SURGERY IN PRIMATES *See* Laboratory for Experimental Medicine and Surgery in Primates

NEW YORK UNIVERSITY. TISCH SCHOOL OF THE ARTS
New York University, Tisch School of the Arts, and the Second Avenue Dance Company: a dancer prepares [work of dance dept. chairman L. Rhodes] O. Stuart. il por *Dance Magazine* 63:60-1 Mr '89

NEW YORK WORLD'S FAIR (1939-1940)
Remembering the fairs. il *American History Illustrated* 24:10 Summ '89
Things to come: the 1939 New York World's Fair. B. McIlvaine. il *American History Illustrated* 24:32-47 Summ '89

Collectibles
Remembering a fine fair [collection of J. Riccardelli] G. Turim. il por *Americana* 17:50-4 Jl/Ag '89
Remembering tomorrow. D. Di Costanzo. il *House & Garden* 161:56+ My '89

NEW YORKER (PERIODICAL)
Are journalists basically liars? [J. Malcolm's criticism of J. McGinniss] F. Bruning. il *Maclean's* 102:11 Ap 24 '89
Holier than thou [J. Malcolm's attack on J. McGinniss] J. Taylor. il pors *New York* 22:32-7 Mr 27 '89
The New Yorker lists at this season some books by its contributors published during the year. *The New Yorker* 65:114-15 D 18 '89
PW interviews [former editorial writer J. Schell] C. Deyrup. por *Publishers Weekly* 235:71-2 Ap 21 '89
A reporter isn't a friend [J. Malcolm's piece on J. McGinniss' ethics] J. Alter and G. Cowley. il por *Newsweek* 113:62 Mr 27 '89
The right to fake quotes [J. Masson's suit against J. Malcolm dismissed] W. A. Henry. por *Time* 134:49 Ag 21 '89
The talk of the town [J. Malcolm's piece on J. McGinniss' ethics] *The Nation* 248:469 Ap 10 '89
Talk of the town [literary style] W. Safire. il *The New York Times Magazine* p16+ O 8 '89
Wet verse at the New Yorker. C. Bernstein. *Harper's* 279:28+ N '89

NEW YORKERS
Caught in the eighties: the new debtors. M. Stone. il *New York* 22:40-6 Ap 24 '89
Inside's guide to New York's special places. S. Stephens. il *Architectural Digest* 46:136-45+ N '89
A landscape of people. B. Astor. il por *Architectural Digest* 46:92+ N '89
New Yorkers on New York. W. Norwich. il por *House & Garden* 161:214-17 O '89
O pioneers [downtown] P. Blauner. il *New York* 22:68-70+ D 25 '89-Ja 1 '90

Anecdotes, facetiae, satire, etc.
Women on the verge [special section] il *Harper's Bazaar* 122:176-7+ Mr '89

NEW YORKESE *See* English language—Dialects

NEW ZEALAND
See also
Anti-nuclear movement—New Zealand
Astronomical observatories—New Zealand
Astronomy—New Zealand
Collective bargaining—Airlines—New Zealand
Public health—New Zealand
Skiing—New Zealand
Sports—New Zealand
Traffic accidents—New Zealand
Defenses
See also
Airplanes, Military—New Zealand
Aviation, Military—New Zealand
New Zealand. Royal New Zealand Air Force
Description and travel
New Zealand's magic waters. D. Doubilet. il map *National Geographic* 176:506-29 O '89
Economic policy
Up from Down Under. L. Kraar. il *Fortune* 120 no13 Special Issue:54 Fall '89
Foreign relations
United States
See United States—Foreign relations—New Zealand
Industries
See also
Air New Zealand
Wine industry—New Zealand
Native peoples
See also
Maoris

NEW ZEALAND. DEPT. OF CONSERVATION
Reorganizing conservation efforts in New Zealand. R. Cahn and P. Cahn. bibl f il maps *Environment* 31:18-20+ Ap '89

NEW ZEALAND. ROYAL NEW ZEALAND AIR FORCE
Royal Air Force completing tests of upgraded avionics for A-4s. il *Aviation Week & Space Technology* 130:51 F 6 '89

NEW ZEALAND FLAX
Colorful as marigolds, tough as nails . . . the new New Zealand flax. il *Sunset (Central West edition)* 183:66-7 Jl '89

NEWARK (N.J.)
Education
See also
READY (Program)
Galleries and museums
See also
Newark Museum
Music
See also
New Jersey State Opera

NEWARK MUSEUM
A new Newark Museum. A. E. Ledes. il *Antiques* 136:986+ N '89
Newark Museum: splendid renovation unveiled. il *Americana* 17:24 N/D '89

NEWBORN ANIMALS *See* Animals, Infancy of
NEWBORN INFANTS *See* Infants, Newborn
NEWBURGH (N.Y.)
Social conditions
Our town. P. Hamill. il *Esquire* 112:85-7 S '89

NEWBURY STREET (BOSTON, MASS.)
Common ground. J. Sedgwick. il *Gentlemen's Quarterly* 59:233-4 N '89

NEWBY-FRAZIER, PAULA
about
Enduring greatness. J. Ridge. il por *Women's Sports & Fitness* 11:24-6+ Je '89
Tri-umph! L. Rothlein. il por *Women's Sports & Fitness* 11:50 Ja/F '89

NEWCASTLE (N.B.)
Crime
A dark season of fear [series of murders and assaults] G. Allen. il *Maclean's* 102:18-19 N 6 '89

NEWCASTLE BEACH PARK (BELLEVUE, WASH.)
Natural history. D. Gantenbein. il *Architectural Record* 177:124-7 N '89

NEWELL, REGINALD E., AND OTHERS
Carbon monoxide and the burning earth. bibl il map *Scientific American* 261:82-8 O '89

NEWELL, ROGER D.
about
How to take advantage of fear and greed [interview] T. Paré. il por *Fortune* 119:54 Je 19 '89
NEWELL ASSOCIATES
How to take advantage of fear and greed [relative yield strategy; interview with R. D. Newell] T. Paré. il por *Fortune* 119:54 Je 19 '89
NEWFIELD, JACK
about
The N.Y.C. scandals of Ed Koch [cover story] M. J. Green. *The Nation* 248:397 Mr 27 '89
NEWFOUNDLAND
See also
Agriculture—Newfoundland
Crime and criminals—Newfoundland
Marystown (Nfld.)
Oil pollution—Newfoundland
Saint John's (Nfld.)
Saint Lawrence (Nfld.)
Trials—Newfoundland
Williamsport (Nfld.)
Anniversaries, etc.
Anniversary on the Rock [decision to join Canada; special section] il *Maclean's* 102:16-19+ Ap 3 '89
Fisheries
See Fisheries—Canada
Industries
See also
Petroleum industry—Canada
Whaling—Newfoundland
Nationalism
Anniversary on the Rock [decision to join Canada; special section] il *Maclean's* 102:16-19+ Ap 3 '89
An assault on Meech [interview with premier C. Wells] G. Allen. il por *Maclean's* 102:26 O 16 '89
A Grit stands fast [C. K. Wells' opposition to constitutional accord] G. Allen. il por *Maclean's* 102:25 N 20 '89
Politics and government
Campaign on the Rock. R. Wangersky. il por *Maclean's* 102:17 Ap 17 '89
The newest premier [T. Rideout] P. Kopvillem. il pors *Maclean's* 102:15 Mr 20 '89
Peckford's legacies [B. Peckford announces resignation] M. Clark. il por *Maclean's* 102:12-13 Ja 30 '89
Return of the red tide [Liberals return to power] G. Allen. il por *Maclean's* 102:12-13+ My 1 '89
Religious institutions and affairs
A Church in crisis [sex scandals involving priests] G. Allen. il *Maclean's* 102:66 N 27 '89
NEWFOUNDLAND CONSTABULARY *See* Royal Newfoundland Constabulary
NEWHALL, BEAUMONT, 1908-
about
Beaumont Newhall: photographic memories [interview] M. Esterow. il por *Art News* 88:168-73 Ap '89
NEWHART, TAL
Ski Morocco, fine sir. il pors *Skiing* 42:220-4 O '89
NEWHOUSE, DONALD
about
The trial of Donald and Si Newhouse [cover story] R. Pollak. il *The Nation* 248:325+ Mr 13 '89
NEWHOUSE, JOHN
The abolitionist. *The New Yorker* 64:51-62+ Ja 9 '89
The abolitionist. *The New Yorker* 64:37-52 Ja 2 '89
Changing targets. *The New Yorker* 65:71-82 Jl 10 '89
Eternal severities. *The New Yorker* 65:100-20+ O 23 '89
Profiles [T. S. Foley] il por *The New Yorker* 65:48-50+ Ap 10 '89
NEWHOUSE, SAMUEL I., JR.
about
The Random House shuffle. J. Alter. il pors *Newsweek* 114:74 N 13 '89
S.I. Newhouse and Conde Nast: taking off the white gloves [cover story] G. Mahon. il pors *The New York Times Magazine* p46-51+ S 10 '89
The trial of Donald and Si Newhouse [cover story] R. Pollak. il *The Nation* 248:325+ Mr 13 '89
NEWHOUSE, SAMUEL I., 1895-1979
about
The U.S. Business Hall of Fame. W. Guzzardi. il por *Fortune* 119:135 Mr 13 '89
NEWHOUSE [drama] *See* Rose, Richard
NEWHOUSE BROADCASTING CORPORATION
The trial of Donald and Si Newhouse [cover story] R. Pollak. il *The Nation* 248:325+ Mr 13 '89
NEWMAN, BOBBY
Psychotherapy and science. por *The Humanist* 49:27-8+ Ja/F '89
NEWMAN, BRUCE
Birds of a feather. il pors *Sports Illustrated* 70 Special Issue:139-42 F '89
Hype. il *Sports Illustrated* 70:60-4+ Ja 23 '89
Japan: coming on strong. il *Sports Illustrated* 71:48-54+ Ag 21 '89
Just call it Erickson U. il por *Sports Illustrated* 70:82-3 My 1 '89

Just happy to be here. il pors *Sports Illustrated* 70:34-6+ Ap 17 '89
Keynote Kid. il pors *Sports Illustrated* 71:106-10+ S 4 '89
Man in the slow lane. il pors *Sports Illustrated* 70:28-30+ Je 26 '89
Pushed to the brink. il *Sports Illustrated* 70:22-5 Je 19 '89
Remorse? Not in the NFL. il por *Sports Illustrated* 71:112 O 16 '89
Rich and famous. il pors *Sports Illustrated* 70 Special Issue:161+ F '89
. . . risen again. il *Sports Illustrated* 70:38-41 F 27 '89
Simply perfect [cover story] il *Sports Illustrated* 70:24-9 Je 5 '89
Stonehands rules again. il pors *Sports Illustrated* 70:18-19 Mr 6 '89
This is for you, Sal. il *Sports Illustrated* 71:22-5 O 9 '89
Unstoppable Steffi [cover story] il pors *Sports Illustrated* 70:32-5 Mr 27 '89
Up against the wall. il *Sports Illustrated* 70 Special Issue:222+ F '89
Way above average. il pors *Sports Illustrated* 71:24-6+ S 25 '89
We've grown accustomed to his face. il pors *Sports Illustrated* 70:84-8+ Ap 10 '89
NEWMAN, BRUCE
about
Gandee at large. C. K. Gandee. il por *House & Garden* 161:246 S '89
NEWMAN, CATHY
The fine feathered nest—'la protection sociale'. il *National Geographic* 176:130-1 Jl '89
The Shakers' brief eternity. il map *National Geographic* 176:302-25 S '89
NEWMAN, CONSTANCE BERRY
about
Constance Newman is OK'd for fed. personnel post. il por *Jet* 76:22 Je 26 '89
Constance Newman, new chief of personnel, lauded by Bush. por *Jet* 76:12 Ag 21 '89
NEWMAN, DAVID, 1937-
about
Secrets from the cutting room. R. Rosenbaum. il pors *Mademoiselle* 95:64+ Je '89
NEWMAN, FRANK, 1927-
National policies to encourage service [interview with C. Moskos and D. Evans; cover story; with editorial comment by Susan Stroud] il *Change* 21:4, 8-17 S/O '89
NEWMAN, JAMES L.
What's in a name? il *Focus (New York, N.Y.: 1950)* 38:37 Wint '88
NEWMAN, JOHN HENRY, CARDINAL, 1801-1890
about
Prelude to the making of a saint [cover story] V. F. Blehl. pors *America* 160:213-16 Mr 11 '89
NEWMAN, JUDITH B.
Caviar dreams for couch potatoes. il pors *Channels (New York, N.Y.: 1986)* 9:32-6 Ja 16 '89
NEWMAN, PAUL, 1925-
about
The further adventures of Paul Newman [cover story] R. Scheer. il pors *Esquire* 112:164-6+ O '89
Paul and Joanne—their real life story [excerpt] J. Morella and E. Z. Epstein. pors *Good Housekeeping* 208:72+ Ja '89
Paul Newman: sexy, surprising and almost 65. L. David and I. David. il pors *McCall's* 116:50-2+ Mr '89
NEWMAN, PETER C., 1929-
Business watch. See issues of Maclean's
NEWMAN, RANDY
about
Old Four Eyes is back. H. Gleason. il por *Rolling Stone* p36 My 18 '89
Randy Newman's back. R. Givens. por *Stereo Review* 54:113 Ja '89
NEWPORT (R.I.)
Architecture
Inside Newport. D. Kazanjian. il *House & Garden* 161:54-67+ Ag '89
Galleries and museums
See also
Redwood Library and Athenaeum (Newport, R.I.)
Historic houses, sites, etc.
Newport in winter. C. Davidson. il *American Heritage* 40:33+ D '89
Libraries
See also
Redwood Library and Athenaeum (Newport, R.I.)
Religious institutions and affairs
Apologizing to Anne Hutchinson [United Church of Christ members burn 1638 writ of excommunication] M. P. Nugent. *The Christian Century* 106:304-5 Mr 22-29 '89
Social life and customs
Inside Newport. D. Kazanjian. il *House & Garden* 161:54-67+ Ag '89
Stores
Newport news. D. B. Cowin. il *House & Garden* 161:138-9 Ag '89

NEWPORT BEACH (CALIF.)
Galleries and museums
See also
Newport Harbor Art Museum (Newport Beach, Calif.)
NEWPORT HARBOR ART MUSEUM (NEWPORT BEACH, CALIF.)
Museum roof as flying carpet. il *Architectural Record* 177:53 O '89
NEWPORT NEWS (VA.)
Galleries and museums
See also
Mariners' Museum (Newport News, Va.)
NEWS
See also
Art news
Cable television—News
Current events
Economic news
Educational news
Environmental news
Foreign news
Government and the press
Journalism
Media guide
Medical news
Newsletters
Radio broadcasting—News
Religious news
Reporters and reporting
Science news
Television broadcasting—News
Videotapes—News
Missing from the news. B. Bagdikian. il *The Progressive* 53:32-4 Ag '89
Understanding the news: how the media shapes your world [cover story; special issue] il *Scholastic Update (Teachers' edition)* 122:3-25 S 8 '89
Anecdotes, facetiae, satire, etc.
Searching for a calm summer gin. A. Fotheringham. il *Maclean's* 102:64 Je 12 '89
NEWS AGENCIES
See also
Maturity News Service
Reuters Holdings plc
United Press Intl., Inc.
Reforming the newspaper: how to get the facts straight [alternative news services] H. Cordes. il *Utne Reader* p34 N/D '89
Soviet Union
See also
TASS (Soviet Union)
NEWS BROADCASTS See Radio broadcasting—News; Television broadcasting—News
NEWS COMMENTATORS See Radio broadcasting—News
NEWS CORPORATION LTD.
Even Rupert Murdoch has his limits [financial strains] C. Welles. il por *Business Week* p34-5 O 2 '89
"I can think of more important things than being loved by everybody" [interview with R. Murdoch] W. J. Koschnick. il pors *Forbes* 144:98+ N 27 '89
Rupert Murdoch. il *The Nation* 248:806 Je 12 '89
NEWS DEALERS See Newspaper vendors
NEWS MEDIA See Mass media
NEWS MEDIA ETHICS See Journalistic ethics
NEWS PERIODICALS
See also
Newsweek (Periodical)
Time (Periodical)
U.S. news & world report (Periodical)
God is not providing. F. Meeks. il *Forbes* 144:151+ O 30 '89
What's so special about news magazines? T. Griffith. il *Newsweek* 113:52-3 Je 26 '89
NEWS PHOTOGRAPHS See Current events—Photographs and photography
NEWS PHOTOGRAPHY See Photography, Journalistic
NEWS RELEASES, VIDEOTAPE See Videotapes—Press releases
NEWS SERVICES See News agencies
NEWS SYNDICATES See Newspaper syndicates
NEWS VENDORS See Newspaper vendors
NEWSBOYS
See also
Newspaper carriers
NEWSCASTERS See Radio broadcasting—News; Television broadcasting—News
NEWSCASTS See Radio broadcasting—News; Television broadcasting—News
NEWSLETTERS
See also
Basketball newsletters
Genetic newsletters
House organs
Investment newsletters
Medical newsletters
NewsNet (Information system)
Nutrition newsletters
Physical fitness newsletters

Travel newsletters
Woman's workshop quarterly (Newsletter)
Designed on a desktop [newsletter design using WordPerfect] J. Latimer. il *Compute!* 11:64-6+ D '89
Get info fast from electronic newsletters. A. Glossbrenner. il *Home Office Computing* 7:32 Ap '89
Home truths [ABC home newsletter] D. Blum. il *New York* 22:22 My 29 '89
The inside dope [TV news newsletters The rundown and The Tyndall report] J. M. Robins. *Channels (New York, N.Y.: 1986)* 9:37 F '89
Sell yourself—with a newsletter! [cover story; with editorial comment by Claudia Cohl] R. Raskin. il *Home Office Computing* 7:6, 37-41 Ap '89
To profit from your insights, just get the words out. R. Deigh. il *U.S. News & World Report* 106:68-9 Ja 16 '89
NEWSNET (INFORMATION SYSTEM)
Get info fast from electronic newsletters. A. Glossbrenner. il *Home Office Computing* 7:32 Ap '89
NEWSPAPER ADVERTISING See Advertising, Newspaper
NEWSPAPER AND PERIODICAL LIBRARIES
I read it in the paper [use of newspapers as genealogical resource] C. E. Kraft. il *Antiques & Collecting Hobbies* 94:74-7 Mr '89
NEWSPAPER CARRIERS
Paper boy [excerpt from The good times] R. Baker. il por *Life* 12:17-18+ Ap '89
NEWSPAPER COURT REPORTING
See also
Contempt of court
NEWSPAPER DEALERS See Newspaper vendors
NEWSPAPER ETHICS See Journalistic ethics
NEWSPAPER GUILD
The union-busting Post: labor pains at a liberal paper [cover story] J. Hanrahan. il *The Progressive* 53:18-25 F '89
NEWSPAPER LIBRARIES See Newspaper and periodical libraries
NEWSPAPER PUBLISHERS AND PUBLISHING
See also
Affiliated Publications, Inc.
Brown County Publishing Company
Central Newspapers, Inc.
Collective labor agreements—Newspapers
Computers—Newspaper publishing use
Dow Jones & Co., Inc.
Gannett Co., Inc.
New York Times Company
Newhouse Broadcasting Corporation
Pulitzer Publishing Co.
Tribune Company (Chicago, Ill.)
Washington Post Co.
Women in newspaper publishing
Acquisitions and mergers
Alien beancounters invade the Enquirer [Macfadden Holdings] A. Fins. il *Business Week* p35 S 11 '89
The new (land)lords of the press. E. Diamond. il *New York* 22:44-50 F 27 '89
Peter Callahan: an acquiring mind [buyout of National enquirer] A. Rothman. il por *Business Week* p139-40 My 15 '89
Preserving newspapers or monopoly? [proposed joint operating agreement between Detroit free press and Detroit news; cover story] S. Barnett. *The Nation* 249:513+ N 6 '89
Thinking small [R. Shaw buys American City Business Journals] R. Reiff. il por *Forbes* 144:171+ D 11 '89
International aspects
Media barons are making pilgrimages to Jerusalem [C. M. Black buys Jerusalem post] J. Rossant and N. Sandler. il por *Business Week* p50 My 15 '89
Canada
Buying the Times [Globe and mail takes over Financial times of Canada] D. Todd. il *Maclean's* 102:47-8 D 25 '89
Antitrust cases
Preserving newspapers or monopoly? [proposed joint operating agreement between Detroit free press and Detroit news; cover story] S. Barnett. *The Nation* 249:513+ N 6 '89
Finance
See also
Advertising, Newspaper
Citizen Kane meets Adam Smith [cover story] S. N. Chakravarty. il *Forbes* 143:82-5 F 20 '89
Canada
See also
Hollinger, Inc.
Southam Inc.
Thomson Newspapers Ltd.
In the black. D. Jenish. il *Maclean's* 102:34 Jl 17 '89
Great Britain
The bloke buckled [Britain's union bashing publisher E. Shah] E. McGlinn. il por *Forbes* 143:10 F 6 '89
Israel
Media barons are making pilgrimages to Jerusalem. J. Rossant and N. Sandler. il por *Business Week* p50 My 15 '89
NEWSPAPER READING
ANPA publisher says minorities key to future survival of newspapers [views of David Lawrence Jr.] *Jet* 76:21 My 15 '89

NEWSPAPER SYNDICATES
Free Peanuts! Free Beetle Bailey! E. Schmuckler. il *Forbes* 144:159+ O 30 '89
NEWSPAPER VENDORS
See also
Out of Town News (Firm)
Broadcast newsman [D. Hoffman] J. Hester. il por *New York* 22:26 S 4 '89
NEWSPAPERS
See also
Advertising, Newspaper
Alternative press
Black press
Freedom of the press
Journalism
Journalistic ethics
News agencies
Newsletters
Photography, Journalistic
Stars and stripes (Newspaper)
Tabloid newspapers
TV vs. print: which is best? [research by Ann Crigler] *USA Today (Periodical)* 118:6 Ag '89
Advice columns
Living by the letter [interview with A. Landers] E. Taylor. il pors *Time* 134:62-3 Ag 21 '89
Mr. Lonelyhearts [taking over A. Landers' column] J. Zaslow. il *The New York Times Magazine* p59-60+ O 29 '89
Anecdotes, facetiae, satire, etc.
Devil's stylebook. J. Osburn. *The Nation* 249:705 D 11 '89
Book reviews
See Book reviews and reviewing
Columns
See Newspapers—Advice columns
Comic strips
See Comic books, strips, etc.
Educational news
See Educational news
Employees
See also
Collective labor agreements—Newspapers
Newspaper Guild
Dismissal
Some sackings are more civil than others [Daily telegraph and Toronto Globe and mail] G. Bain. il *Maclean's* 102:46 Ag 28 '89
Financial news
See Journalism, Commercial
Illustration
Pen & ink: drawing for the Wall Street journal. M. S. Doherty. il *American Artist* 53:74-80+ My '89
Letters to the editor
Anecdotes, facetiae, satire, etc.
Vox populi. See issues of World Press Review
Obituaries
See Obituaries
Political news
See Newspapers and politics
Recycling
Does recycling pay? J. McDermott. il *Technology Review* 92:13 N/D '89
The paper chase. S. D. Borowitz. il *Sierra* 74:22 N/D '89
Science news
See Journalism, Scientific
Sections, columns, etc.
See also
Book reviews and reviewing
Gossip columns
Newspapers—Advice columns
Sports news
See Sports journalism
Stock market news
See Journalism, Commercial
Austria
See also
Der Standard (Austria: Newspaper)
Brazil
See also
O Globo (Newspaper)
California
See also
Los Angeles herald examiner
Los Angeles times
California dreaming [California edition of the New York times] E. Diamond. il *New York* 22:16+ My 22 '89
Canada
See also
Financial times of Canada
Czechoslovakia
See also
Lidove noviny (Czechoslovakia: Newspaper)
Great Britain
See also
Daily telegraph (London, England)
Guatemala
See also
La epoca (Guatemala: Newspaper)

Illinois
See also
Chicago sun-times (Newspaper)
Substance (Newspaper)
Iowa
See also
Adair County free press
Massachusetts
See also
Boston globe
Missouri
See also
St. Louis post-dispatch (Newspaper)
St. Louis sun (Newspaper)
Namibia
See also
Namibian (Newspaper)
New York (State)
See also
Amsterdam news (New York, N.Y.)
Daily news (New York, N.Y.)
New York (N.Y.)—Newspapers
New York post
New York times
Nicaragua
See also
La prensa (Nicaragua)
Ontario
See also
Toronto star (Newspaper)
Pennsylvania
See also
Philadelphia inquirer
Soviet Union
See also
Pravda (Moscow, Soviet Union)
Utah
See also
Utah nippo (Newspaper)
Western States
See also
Out West (Newspaper)
Wisconsin
See also
Green Bay news-chronicle
NEWSPAPERS, STUDENT *See* College and school journalism
NEWSPAPERS AND POLITICS
Anthony agonistes [New York times columnist A. Lewis] H. Catto. il *National Review* 41:34-7+ S 1 '89
Leaning [political labeling in New York times] D. Seligman. il *Fortune* 120:135-6 Ag 28 '89
The papers vote [endorsements in New York City mayoral race] E. Diamond. il *New York* 22:24+ S 25 '89
International aspects
Global reach. M. Peretz. *The New Republic* 201:9-11 D 11 '89
NEWSPAPERS IN EDUCATION
See also
College and school journalism
NEWSPAPERS IN LITERATURE
My white whale, or The great newspaper novel. S. Weinberg. il *The New York Times Book Review* 94:1+ Ag 27 '89
NEWSWEEK (PERIODICAL)
God is not providing. F. Meeks. il *Forbes* 144:151+ O 30 '89
NEWSWORLD
The CBC's future [cover story; special section; with editorial comment by Kevin Doyle] il *Maclean's* 102:2, 34-42 Ag 7 '89
Growing pains. H. Jensen. il *Maclean's* 102:52 Ag 14 '89
NEWTON, BEULAH S.
Ice harvesting—the way it was. il *The Conservationist* 43:24-5 Ja/F '89
NEWTON, BOB
about
Great tires, blimp to come. J. Harris. il por *Forbes* 143:288+ My 29 '89
NEWTON, CHRISTOPHER
about
Dramatic delights. J. Bemrose. il por *Maclean's* 102:54-5 Je 5 '89
NEWTON, HELEN
Alan Thicke loves Joanna Kerns—and does he have plans for her! il por *TV Guide* 37:6-7+ Jl 22-28 '89
There she is . . . dethroned Miss America stars as a call girl. il pors *TV Guide* 36:20-3 F 4-10 '89
NEWTON, HELMUT
about
Double exposure [interview] A. Cockburn. il pors *House & Garden* 161:168-73+ S '89
NEWTON, HUEY
about
Obituary
Jet il pors 76:16-17+ S 11 '89
The New Republic 201:10-11 S 18-25 '89. S. Crouch
Newsweek il por 114:27 S 4 '89. B. Turque
NEWTON, JACK, 1942-, AND TEECE, PHILIP
The amateur's universe. *Astronomy* 17:8 Ap '89

NEWTON, JOHN HAYMES
about
Dream Date Sweepstakes: meet the winner! J. Clay. il pors
'Teen 33:46 Jl '89
NEWTON, SALETE M. C., AND OTHERS
Immune response to cholera toxin epitope inserted in Sal-
monella flagellin. bibl f il *Science* 244:70-2 Ap 7 '89
NEWTON, WAYNE
about
First since illness: Lola performs onstage with Wayne Newton.
il pors *Jet* 76:55-6 Je 26 '89
Meet the new Wayne Newton, star of casino and cinema.
J. Park. il pors *People Weekly* 32:74-6 Jl 31 '89
NEWTON-JOHN, OLIVIA
about
Olivia Newton-John. J. Nesin. por *High Fidelity (New York,
N.Y.)* 39:54+ Jl '89
NEWTON'S LAW OF GRAVITY See Gravity and gravitation
NEXT ICE AGE (SKATING COMPANY)
Reviews:
Performances in Columbia, Maryland. G. Jackson. *Dance
Magazine* 63:28+ Ja '89
NEXT INC.
Constant growth is one reward at a start-up [S. K. Barnes]
M. Aaland. il por *Working Woman* 14:61 My '89
How Steve Jobs linked up with IBM [cover story] B. R.
Schlender. il pors *Fortune* 120:48-51+ O 9 '89
A legend's comeback bid. J. Littman. il por *Personal
Computing* 13:70 Jl '89
The Next computer: promises to keep. R. A. Shaffer. il
Personal Computing 13:51-2 Ja '89
Next means business now [agreement with Businessland]
R. A. Shaffer. il *Personal Computing* 13:47-8 Jl '89
The Next step [NextStep object-oriented development environ-
ment] T. Thompson. il *Byte* 14:265-9 Mr '89
Steve Jobs gets the keys to the office PC market [link
with Businessland] R. Brandt. il por *Business Week* p80-1
Ap 10 '89
Steve Jobs: out for revenge. P. Patton. il por *The New
York Times Magazine* p22-3+ Ag 6 '89
Steve Jobs' revolutionary new computer. W. J. Hawkins.
il por *Popular Science* 234:68-70+ Ja '89
Steve Jobs's hard sell [deal with Businessland] *Newsweek*
113:49 Ap 10 '89
What's Next? P. Scisco. il *Compute!* 11:6 Ja '89
NEY, EDWARD N.
about
Men of credentials. H. Mackenzie. il pors *Maclean's* 102:62-3
Jl 3 '89
NEY, NEAL J.
Lightning. il *Bicycling* 30:108 Jl '89
NFL See National Football League
NFL FILMS, INC.
What would happen if . . . 20 of the best-ever NFL teams
played a "Dream season"? S. Smith. il *Sports Illustrated*
71:159 S 11 '89
NFL PLAYERS ASSOCIATION See National Football League
Players Association
NG, FAE MYENNE
Backdaire [story] *Harper's* 278:64-8 Ap '89
NGOR, HAING S.
Journey to freedom [condensed from A Cambodian odyssey];
ed. by Roger Warner. il *Reader's Digest* 134:209-13+ Mr
'89
NGUGI, JOHN
about
John Ngugi. B. Wischnia. il por *Runner's World* 24:48 F
'89
NGUYEN, MARY XINH
about
Mary Nguyen's G.I. dad has never seen her face, but Revlon
thinks it's a winner. M. H. J. Farrell. il pors *People
Weekly* 32:54-5 Ag 7 '89
NHL See National Hockey League
NHTSA See United States. National Highway Traffic Safety
Administration
NI BHRAONIAN, EITHNE See Enya
NIAGARA FALLS (N.Y.)
Pollution
See also
Love Canal case
The next Love Canal? E. Salholz. il *Newsweek* 114:28 Ag
7 '89
NIAGARA RIVER (N.Y. AND ONT.) IN ART
Dan Logé—an artist in touch with the river. H. W. Trimm.
il *The Conservationist* 44:10-15 S/O '89
NIBELUNGENLIED
Hiding in the shadow [nineteenth century adaptations] C.
Abbate. il *Opera News* 53:16+ Ap 1 '89
NICARAGUA
See also
Agriculture—Nicaragua
Americans—Nicaragua
British—Nicaragua
Budget—Nicaragua
Civil rights—Nicaragua
Economic assistance, American—Nicaragua
Environmental policy—Nicaragua

Government and the press—Nicaragua
Hospitals—Nicaragua
Indians of Central America—Nicaragua
Military assistance, American—Nicaragua
Military assistance, Russian—Nicaragua
Motion pictures—Nicaragua
Theater and state—Nicaragua
Commerce
United States
See United States—Commerce—Nicaragua
Defenses
See also
United States. Marine Corps—Forces in Nicaragua
Economic conditions
A troubled revolution. D. Gollob. il *Maclean's* 102:27-8
Jl 31 '89
Foreign relations
Honduras
See Honduras—Foreign relations—Nicaragua
United States
See United States—Foreign relations—Nicaragua
History
The end of a war beginning. R. Jordan. il *The Progressive*
53:29-31 O '89
Filibuster War, 1855-1860
El presidente gringo [W. Walker] R. Bruns and B. Kennedy.
il por map *American History Illustrated* 23:14-21+ F '89
Politics and government
See also
Political campaigns—Nicaragua
Politics, Corruption in—Nicaragua
Are the contras finished? E. Abrams. *National Review* 41:30-1
Mr 10 '89
Blown opportunities in Central America [failure of George
Bush to enact policies] C. A. Robbins. il *U.S. News &
World Report* 106:28 F 27 '89
Catching the administration napping [Nicaragua's pledge of
reforms prompts Central American neighbors to remove
U.S.-backed contras] *Newsweek* 113:43 F 27 '89
Central America. *World Press Review* 36:9-10 Ap '89
Confronting the Sandinistas. R. J. Bresler. il *USA Today
(Periodical)* 118:5 N '89
Contradictions: a decade in documents. P. Kornbluh. il *Mother
Jones* 14:26-7 Jl/Ag '89
A crash course for Mulroney [Nicaragua's decision to cancel
ceasefire overshadows announcement of Canada's intention
to join OAS] H. Mackenzie. il pors *Maclean's* 102:32-3+
N 6 '89
Decade of despair. J. Moody. il *Time* 134:26-8 Jl 24 '89
Disarming the rebels [accord signed by Central American
presidents] M. Nemeth. il *Maclean's* 102:33+ Ag 21 '89
The "disposal problem" [Tela plan to disband contras] J.
Smolowe. il *Time* 134:32 Ag 21 '89
Dithering in Nicaragua. J. Chace. bibl f il *The New York
Review of Books* 36:46-51 Ag 17 '89
The end of a war beginning. R. Jordan. il *The Progressive*
53:29-31 O '89
Enlarging the cloth [Tela agreement disbanding and resettling
the contras] *Commonweal* 116:451-2 S 8 '89
Faith and endurance in eastern Nicaragua. M. D. Wilde.
The Christian Century 106:973-4 N 1 '89
The fight for Nicaragua [Sandinistas break ceasefire] J. Bier-
man. il por *Maclean's* 102:26-8 N 13 '89
Gauging opposition and resources in Nicaragua's 'third war'.
D. M. Rivage-Seul. il *The Christian Century* 106:687-9
Jl 19-26 '89
How to keep pressure on the Sandinistas. J. Bush. il *The
American Spectator* 22:16-17 Jl '89
A kinder, gentler Nicaragua? G. Barrett. *World Press Review*
36:28 Jl '89
The liberty tree [comparison of French and Nicaraguan
revolutions] A. Cockburn. *The Nation* 249:160 Ag 7-14
'89
Look—we've come through. G. Black. il *The Nation*
249:166-8+ Ag 7-14 '89
Nicaragua [cease fire suspension] il *World Press Review* 36:6
D '89
Nicaragua ceases the cease-fire. *Newsweek* 114:53 N 6 '89
Notes and comment [George Bush's reaction to D. Ortega's
announcement ending ceasefire] *The New Yorker* 65:43-4
N 13 '89
Now the Sandinistas can't blame it on the contras. B. Javetski
and S. Baker. il *Business Week* p47 Ag 21 '89
The old gringos [D. Ortega's announcement ending the
cease-fire] A. Kopkind. *The Nation* 249:625 N 27 '89
One Nicaraguan Christian's perspective [interview with G.
Parajón] por *Christianity Today* 33:48 Mr 3 '89
Ortega's ploy [ends cease fire] *The New Republic* 201:9 N
20 '89
Planning for peace [summit of Central American presidents]
A. Bilski. il *Maclean's* 102:29 F 27 '89
Playing politics with peace [D. Ortega cancels cease-fire]
W. R. Doerner. por *Time* 134:49+ N 13 '89
Sending signals—or smoke? [D. Ortega] W. R. Doerner.
il por *Time* 133:46 F 6 '89
A slim hope for freedom in Nicaragua [agreement to disband
contras] C. W. Weinberger. il *Forbes* 144:31 S 18 '89

NICARAGUA—Politics and government—*cont.*
Termination time [move to disband contras] *The Nation*
249:227-8 S 4-11 '89
A troubled revolution. D. Gollob. il *Maclean's* 102:27-8
Jl 31 '89
Religious institutions and affairs
See also
Catholic Church—Nicaragua
Christians—Nicaragua
Evangelical churches—Nicaragua
Evangelistic work—Nicaragua
Moravian Church—Nicaragua
Social conditions
I visited Nicaragua. B. Carey. il por *The Humanist* 49:20-2+
S/O '89
NICARAGUA BOOK FESTIVAL *See* Book fairs
NICARAGUAN MILITARY ASSISTANCE *See* Military assistance, Nicaraguan
NICARAGUAN REFUGEES *See* Refugees, Nicaraguan
NICARAGUANS
United States
Will the contras' next home be Miami? il *Newsweek* 114:29
Ag 21 '89
NICCOLINI, JULIAN
about
Julian of the spirits. A. Richman. il pors *Gentlemen's Quarterly*
59:150-7 Jl '89
NICE (FRANCE)
Historic houses, sites, etc.
On the Côte d'Azur: Martin and Toni Sosnoff's villa above
Nice [1925 house decorated by Timothy Macdonald] J.
Gruen. il *Architectural Digest* 46:88-93 Ja '89
NICENE CREED
Let's cancel the Creed at Sunday Mass [with readers' comments] T. Unsworth. *U.S. Catholic* 54:13-17 Ja '89
NICENESS
The pretzel syndrome: tying yourself in knots to please
others? J. Stone. il *Glamour* 87:156 S '89
Why doesn't he like me when I'm so darned nice? G.
Schwartz. il *Seventeen* 48:76 My '89
Anecdotes, facetiae, satire, etc.
When you kick a liberal. G. Keillor. il *Harper's* 278:72-5
Ja '89
NICHE MARKETING *See* Micro marketing
NICHOL, LIZ, AND MCCONNELL, BOB
Everest Environmental Expedition: E³. il *Focus (New York,
N.Y.: 1950)* 39:30-1 Fall '89
NICHOLAS II, EMPEROR OF RUSSIA, 1868-1918
Tomb
All present and accounted for. il *U.S. News & World Report*
106:20 Ap 24 '89
The last of the czar? [views of Gely Ryabov] *Newsweek*
113:54 Ap 24 '89
NICHOLAS, ALBERT O.
about
The long-distance runner. M. Berss. il por *Forbes* 144:152-3
S 4 '89
NICHOLAS, COLOMBE
about
"Maybe I should have left sooner". D. Machan. il pors
Forbes 143:320+ My 29 '89
NICHOLAS, DENISE
about
Denise Nichols to star in CBN's 'Mother's day'. il por
Jet 76:54 Ap 24 '89
NICHOLAS, JONATHAN
First snow. il *Reader's Digest* 135:7-8 D '89
NICHOLAS, NICHOLAS J., JR.
about
A new media powerhouse. J. DeMont. il por *Maclean's*
102:42-4 Mr 20 '89
NICHOLAS FUND
The long-distance runner. M. Berss. il por *Forbes* 144:152-3
S 4 '89
NICHOLS, CHRISTINA
Trouble at the waterworks. il *The Progressive* 53:33-5 Je
'89
NICHOLS, JIM
The rain barrel [story] *Esquire* 112:120-2 Jl '89
NICHOLS, JOHN TREADWELL, 1883-1958
about
Living legacies. M. Lipske. il por *National Wildlife* 27:14-16
Je/Jl '89
NICHOLS, MIKE
about
Working girl [film] Reviews
The American Spectator 22:38 Ap '89. B. Bawer
Commonweal 116:48-9 Ja 27 '89. T. O'Brien
Fortune il 119:124 F 13 '89. D. Seligman
Glamour il 87:140 F '89. J. G. Boyum
The New Republic 200:28 Ja 30 '89. S. Kauffmann
New York il 22:45-6 Ja 2 '89. D. Denby
The New Yorker 64:80-1 Ja 9 '89. P. Kael
Newsweek il 113:57 Ja 2 '89. D. Ansen
Video il 13:75 N '89. J. Bernard
NICHOLS, ROBERT G.
From footprints to foothold. il *Astronomy* 17:48-53 Jl '89
Showdown at Pad 39-B. il *Ad Astra* 1:8-12+ N '89

Solar Max: 1980-89. il *Sky and Telescope* 78:600-1 D '89
The winged horse. il *Ad Astra* 1:32-6 F '89
NICHOLS (HARVEY) (FIRM) *See* Harvey Nichols (Firm)
NICHOLSON, CHARLES
Evaluating your short story. *The Writer* 102:33-4 Ag '89
NICHOLSON, JACK
about
Jack Nicholson. il por *People Weekly* 32:48-9 D 25 '89-Ja
1 '90
The two Jakes [film] Reviews
New York il por 22:54-5 S 11 '89. D. Denby
NICHOLSON, THOMAS D., 1922-
Celestial events. See issues of Natural History
The longest day. *Natural History* p82-3 Je '89
NICKEL-CADMIUM ELECTRIC BATTERIES *See* Electric
batteries
NICKEL INDUSTRY
Canada
See also
Falconbridge Limited
NICKEL OXIDES
Superconductivity in a nickel oxide [work of Jurgen Honig
and others] R. Pool. *Science* 243:741 F 10 '89
NICKEL SILVER TABLEWARE
Collectors and collecting
Nickel silver. F. T. Andrews. il *Antiques & Collecting Hobbies*
94:27-9 Je '89
NICKERSON, BOB
about
Bob Nickerson, the round man of roundball, shows off his
degree as the Doctor of Dribble. il pors *People Weekly*
31:102-3 Ja 9 '89
NICKERSON, PAT
about
Take charge of your job. R. Thompson. il por *Nation's
Business* 77:36-7 Ap '89
NICKLAUS, JACK
about
18 tips from 18 legends of golf; Jack Nicklaus shows you
the greatest 18 holes of major championship golf. J.
Bessman. il por *Video* 12:90 Ja '89
The glow of the Bear. R. Lewis. il pors *Maclean's* 102:48-50
Ap 10 '89
A golfer's course. il *Maclean's* 102:52 Ap 10 '89
NICKLOS, LEE B., AND BROWN, WILLIAM S.
Recruiting minority teachers. *The Education Digest* 55:28-31
D '89
NICKNAMES
Anecdotes, facetiae, satire, etc.
'He welted the sphere a prodigious biff' [baseball players]
D. D. Jackson. il *Smithsonian* 20:184 Ap '89
NICKOLOFF, BRIAN J., AND GRIFFITHS, CHRISTOPHER
E. M.
Factor XIIIa-expressing dermal dendrocytes in AIDS-associated cutaneous Kaposi's sarcomas. bibl f il *Science*
243:1736-7 Mr 31 '89
NICKS, MIKE
A racer of the purest kind. il pors *Road & Track* 40:74-6+
Je '89
NICLOSAMIDE
New weapon in the war against schistosomiasis. J. Cherfas.
il *Science* 246:1242-3 D 8 '89
NICOLL, PEGGY
The fat firmers. pors *Harper's Bazaar* 122:34+ Ag '89
NICOTINE
Nicotine boosts a busy body's metabolism [research by
Kenneth A. Perkins] R. Weiss. *Science News* 135:214 Ap
8 '89
NICROPHORUS *See* Beetles
NIDAL, ABU *See* Abu Nidal
NIDETCH, JEAN
about
Jean Nidetch knew that Weight Watcher's success hinged
on more than a diet. D. Moreau. il por *Changing Times*
43:88 Ag '89
NIEBERLEIN, NORM
Ryan Vanguard. il por *Bicycling* 30:64-6 Ja/F '89
NIEBUHR, H. RICHARD (HELMUT RICHARD), 1894-1962
The reconstruction of faith [excerpt from Faith on earth]
The Christian Century 106:780-3 Ag 30-S 6 '89
NIEBUHR, HELMUT RICHARD *See* Niebuhr, H. Richard
(Helmut Richard), 1894-1962
NIEDZIALEK, TERRY
about
Terry Niedzialek's hair montages. B. Howard. il *Theatre
Crafts* 23:58+ O '89
NIELSEN, BRIGITTE
about
Murder on the moon—the crimebuster's wearing a strapless
sheath. R. Koenig. il pors *TV Guide* 37:24-6+ Ap 29-My
5 '89
NIELSEN, ERIK, 1924-
about
Caught in the act of rearranging history. P. C. Newman.
il *Maclean's* 102:34 S 11 '89
Hollow accusations from a Holy Ghost. P. C. Newman.
il *Maclean's* 102:56 S 4 '89

NIELSEN, ERIK, 1924—about—cont.
True confessions. L. Van Dusen. il por *Maclean's* 102:15 S 4 '89

Anecdotes, facetiae, satire, etc.
The favor of Erik Nielsen's silence [former Canadian politician's shunning of all interviews about memoirs] S. MacLeod. por *Maclean's* 102:64 S 11 '89

NIELSEN, JOHN
Living on the edge. il pors *National Wildlife* 27:20-3 O/N '89

NIELSEN, LESLIE
about
Ex-sobersides Leslie Nielsen hits a new comic high in The naked gun. J. Kaufman. il pors *People Weekly* 31:70-2 Ja 30 '89

NIELSEN MEDIA RESEARCH
Brother Nielsen is watching. il *Time* 133:61 Je 12 '89
Exploring home video. R. Katz. il *Channels (New York, N.Y.: 1986)* 9:26 S '89

NIELSEN RATINGS SYSTEM *See* Television broadcasting—Ratings

NIEMAN, DAVID C., 1950-
Exercise and the mind. il *Women's Sports & Fitness* 11:54-7 S '89
Exercise: how much is enough; how much is too much? il *Women's Sports & Fitness* 11:30-4 Je '89
The Ten Commandments of sports nutrition. il *Women's Sports & Fitness* 11:58-61 Mr '89

NIEMAN FELLOWSHIPS
The Nieman Foundation at 50: the curator critiques television news [views of H. Simons] P. Ainslie. il por *Channels (New York, N.Y.: 1986)* 9:10 Je '89

NIEMEYER, OSCAR, 1907-
about
The Pritzker Prize winner's landmark house in Rio de Janeiro. B. Gill. il por *Architectural Digest* 46:46+ Jl '89

NIEVES, ORLANDO
about
Hubcap City. *The New Yorker* 65:26-8 My 1 '89

NIEZABITOWSKA, MALGORZATA
about
A spokeswoman with rare flair makes the news in Poland. B. Hewitt. il pors *People Weekly* 32:60-2 N 13 '89

NIGERIA
Description and travel
Nigeria. J. Gray. il *Black Enterprise* 20:121-2 D '89
Economic policy
Economic adjustment and regime creation in Nigeria. J. Kraus. *Current History* 88:233-7+ My '89
Politics and government
Economic adjustment and regime creation in Nigeria. J. Kraus. *Current History* 88:233-7+ My '89

A NIGHT AT THE CHINESE OPERA [opera] *See* Weir, Judith

NIGHT AWAKENING *See* Awakening from sleep
NIGHT BOATING *See* Boats and boating
NIGHT FISHING *See* Fishing
NIGHT FISHING LIGHTS *See* Fishing lights
NIGHT FLYING *See* Aviation—Night flying
NIGHT GAME [film] *See* Motion picture reviews—Single works
THE NIGHT HANK WILLIAMS DIED [drama] *See* King, Larry L.
NIGHT HERONS *See* Herons
NIGHT LAMPS *See* Lamps
NIGHT MUSIC [television program] *See* Television program reviews—Single works
NIGHT PHOTOGRAPHY *See* Photography, Night
NIGHT SKY *See* Sky
NIGHT TRAWLING *See* Trawls and trawling
NIGHT VISION DEVICES
Critics fault U.S. Army helicopter training with night vision goggles. *Aviation Week & Space Technology* 130:23 Mr 27 '89
Flight restrictions prompt U.S. Air Force to reassess Lantirn training in Germany. J. D. Morrocco. map *Aviation Week & Space Technology* 131:26-7 O 16 '89
ITT solves complex problems to produce image intensifiers [night vision goggles] B. D. Nordwall. il *Aviation Week & Space Technology* 130:91+ My 22 '89
New goggles improve night vision but do not match daylight conditions [aviation use] B. D. Nordwall. il *Aviation Week & Space Technology* 130:86-7 Ap 10 '89
NIGHT WORK *See* Hours of labor
NIGHTCLUB DECORATION
Dangerous curves [New York's Bolidó designed by M. Iosa Ghini] C. K. Gandee. il por *House & Garden* 161:44 My '89
NIGHTCLUBS
See also
Comedy nightclubs
Topless nightclubs, bars, etc.
NIGHTGOWNS, PAJAMAS, ETC. *See* Sleepwear
NIGHTINGALES [television program] *See* Television program reviews—Single works
NIGHTMARE CLASSICS [television program] *See* Television program reviews—Single works
A NIGHTMARE ON ELM STREET, PART 4: THE DREAM MASTER [film] *See* Motion picture reviews—Single works

A NIGHTMARE ON ELM STREET, PART 5: THE DREAM CHILD [film] *See* Motion picture reviews—Single works
NIGHTMARES
A child's nightmares. J. Segal and Z. Segal. il *Parents* 64:233 O '89
From out of the past come thundering hoofbeats of the demon 'nightmare'. R. Wernick. il *Smithsonian* 19:72-6+ Mr '89
A midterm night's dream [exam nightmares] il *New Choices for the Best Years* 29:13 Ap '89
Taming our nightmares. R. Wernick. il *Reader's Digest* 135:21-2+ Jl '89
NIGRO, PETER D.
The U.S. role in a changing world economy. il *USA Today (Periodical)* 117:21-2 My '89
NIH *See* National Institutes of Health (U.S.)
NIJINSKA, BRONISLAVA, 1891-1972
about
Choreographer Bronislava Nijinska in revival: the exemplary daughterhood of Irina Nijinska. L. Garafola. il pors *Dance Magazine* 63:43-4 Je '89
Feathers. T. Tobias. il *New York* 22:53 Jl 17 '89
Les noces [ballet] Reviews
The New Yorker 65:86-7 Jl 17 '89. A. Croce
NIJINSKA, IRINA
about
Choreographer Bronislava Nijinska in revival: the exemplary daughterhood of Irina Nijinska. L. Garafola. il pors *Dance Magazine* 63:43-4 Je '89
NIJINSKY, WASLAW, 1890-1950
about
L'après-midi d'un faune [ballet] Reviews
Dance Magazine il 63:32-4 O '89. L. Garafola
NIKKO SECURITIES CO. LTD.
Teaching a Tokyo whiz kid the art of the deal [H. Kondo working for Blackstone Group] J. Friedman. il por *Business Week* p83 Ja 16 '89
Wells Fargo heads for the wild, wild East. M. Shao. il *Business Week* p82 Ag 21 '89
NIKOLAIS, ALWIN
about
Nikolais and Louis discuss their future together. R. Johnson. pors *Dance Magazine* 63:17 O '89
NIKOLAIS AND LOUIS DANCE
Nikolais and Louis discuss their future together. R. Johnson. pors *Dance Magazine* 63:17 O '89
NIKOLAIS DANCE THEATRE
See also
Nikolais and Louis Dance
NIKOLAYEV, VLADIMIR
Life at the local level: a Soviet journalist examines our 'grass-roots' politics. *World Press Review* 36:34-6 N '89
NILE RIVER
Life on the Nile [river trip] J. Eppinger. bibl il map *New Choices for the Best Years* 29:32-9 Ag '89
The Nile in style [cruise] J. Zweig. il map *Forbes* 144:328+ N 13 '89
Delta
The drowning delta. T. Land. *World Press Review* 36:64-5 N '89
NILLO, DAVID
about
They just can't stop dancing. E. Zimmer. il por *Dance Magazine* 63:82-3 Je '89
NILSSON, DAN-E.
Vision optics and evolution [cover story] bibl f il *BioScience* 39:298-307 My '89
NILSSON, ROB
about
Heat and sunlight [film] Reviews
The New Republic 200:31 My 1 '89. S. Kauffmann
NIMAN, MICHAEL I.
Death of a small country. il *The Progressive* 53:24-5 Ag '89
NIMBUS SATELLITES
Ozone hole's reappearance linked to chlorofluorocarbons [data of Total Ozone Mapping Spectrometer on Nimbus 7 satellite] il *Aviation Week & Space Technology* 131:28 O 30 '89
NIMBY SYNDROME
Bringing it all back home. D. Schoonmaker. il *The Mother Earth News* 119:8 S/O '89
Not in my backyard. R. Robotham. il *Omni (New York, N.Y.)* 11:60-2+ S '89
Not in my backyard! The waste-disposal crisis. T. Peters. il *The Christian Century* 106:175-7 F 15 '89
Uncle Sam's NIMBY attack [Justice Dept. suing Chicago Heights for discrimination against mentally disabled] J. P. Shapiro. il *U.S. News & World Report* 107:24 S 18 '89
When the dump is in 'our' backyard [discussion of February 15, 1989 article, Not in my backyard! The waste-disposal crisis] T. Peters. *The Christian Century* 106:660 Jl 5-12 '89
NÎMES (FRANCE)
Roman antiquities
The Roman aqueduct of Nîmes. G. F. W. Hauck. bibl f map *Scientific American* 260:98-100+ Mr '89

NIMODIPINE

Boosting memory in the blink of an eye [use of nimodipine with aging rabbits; work of Richard A. Deyo] B. Bower. *Science News* 135:86 F 11 '89

Nimodipine facilitates associative learning in aging rabbits [could counteract memory loss in the aged] R. A. Deyo and others. bibl f il *Science* 243:809-11 F 10 '89

Rabbit punch [use of nimodipine to boost memory in aging rabbits] il *Discover* 10:12 Je '89

NIMOY, LEONARD

about

The good mother [film] Reviews

The American Spectator 22:36 Ja '89. B. Bawer

Glamour il 87:103 Ja '89. J. G. Boyum

Mademoiselle il 95:46+ Ja '89. R. Rosenbaum

Three men and a baby [film] Reviews

Video 12:59-60 F '89. J. Young

NIMRUD (IRAQ)

See also

Calah (Ancient city)

NIMS, JOHN FREDERICK, 1913-

Poetry workshop (first semester) [poem] *The American Scholar* 58:208-9 Spr '89

NIÑA (SHIP)

Shipshape [replicas of the Niña, Pinta and Santa Maria] il por *Life* 12:26-30 Ap '89

NINETEEN HUNDRED AND EIGHTIES

The '80s [cover story] il *People Weekly* 32 Special Issue:10-13+ Fall '89

The '80s: a look back at the decade [special issue] il *TV Guide* 37:4-6+ D 9-15 '89

The '80s: stop making sense [Los Angeles Museum of Contemporary Art's exhibition A forest of signs; cover story] H. Drohojowska. il *Art News* 88:146-51 O '89

The '80s: the glorious decade [sports; cover story; special section] il *Sport (New York, N.Y.)* 80:46-50+ O '89

The 1980's: a look back. B. Allen. il *Essence* 20:82-4 D '89

The 1980's: where would we be without them? il *Glamour* 87:76 D '89

American film critics poll: the '80s. P. McGilligan and M. Rowland. il *American Film* 15:23-9 N '89

Currents. il *Scholastic Update (Teachers' edition)* 122:16-17 D 15 '89

Decade in review. *Christianity Today* 33:40 D 15 '89

A decade in science: the eight big ideas of the eighties [cover story; special section; with editorial comment by Paul Hoffman] il *Discover* 10:4, 30-3+ O '89

Dollars and change: sport in the '80s was altered for richer and for poorer. R. Telander. por *Sports Illustrated* 71:166 D 25 '89-Ja 1 '90

Don't think twice [cover story] L. Menand. *The New Republic* 201:18-20+ O 9 '89

Dressed for excess [films of the 1980s] D. Edelstein. il *Vogue* 179:186-7+ D '89

The economic myths that the 1980s exploded. A. S. Blinder. il *Business Week* p22 N 27 '89

The eighties [special section] il *Seventeen* 48:68-9 D '89

The eighties: the art. G. Marcus. il *Film Comment* 25:61-4 N/D '89

The eighties: the industry. G. Kilday. il *Film Comment* 25:60+ N/D '89

Epitaph for the eighties. il *Christianity Today* 33:18 D 15 '89

Gonna party like it's 1999. A. Heard. il *Mother Jones* 14:29-31+ N '89

Icons of the '80s [special section] il *U.S. News & World Report* 107:88-90+ D 25 '89-Ja 1 '90

Last look. J. Kaufman. il *Ladies' Home Journal* 106:47-8+ N '89

Masters of the '80s [M. Johnson, W. Gretzky, and J. Montana; cover story] R. Reilly. il pors *Sports Illustrated* 71:44-9 D 18 '89

Miscellaneous ramblings [auto industry] T. L. Bryant. il *Road & Track* 41:43-4 D '89

Movies of the eighties. P. Travers. il *Rolling Stone* p23 D 14-28 '89

Notes and comment. *The New Yorker* 65:37-8 O 16 '89

Now: the nineties [boating in the '80s] P. A. Janssen. il *Motor Boating & Sailing* 164:15 D '89

Of many things [top Catholic news stories] G. W. Hunt. *America* 161:462 D 23-30 '89

Production [best and the worst of farming] G. Johnston. il *Successful Farming* 87:23 N '89

Remember the '80s [tennis events] C. Shmerler. il *World Tennis* 37:34-6 D '89

Technology's hits and misses of the 1980s [cover story] G. T. Pope. il *High Technology Business* 9:16-19+ N/D '89

Ten years after [television in the '80s] H. Rosenberg. il *American Film* 15:18-19 D '89

What a long, strange (shopping) trip it's been: looking back at the 1980s [excerpt from The hunger for more] L. Shames. il *Utne Reader* p66-9+ S/O '89

What was hot [entertainment] L. Jay. il *Ladies' Home Journal* 106:148+ N '89

Anecdotes, facetiae, satire, etc.

The lonely sound of one drum beating [The 1980s: Maclean's chronicles the decade] A. Fotheringham. il *Maclean's* 102:104 N 6 '89

Caricatures and cartoons

Toons. il *Life* 12:89+ Fall '89

Photographs and photography

The 1980s [cover story; special issue] il *Life* 12:12-33+ Fall '89

NINETEEN HUNDRED AND EIGHTY-EIGHT

1988: the year in science [cover story; special section; with editorial comment by Paul Hoffman] il *Discover* 10:4, 15+ Ja '89

America and the world 1988/89 [cover story] bibl f *Foreign Affairs* 68 Special Issue:1-219 ['89]

The best of 1988. il *Business Week* p115-23+ Ja 9 '89

Favorite network news stories [tables] il *Channels (New York, N.Y.: 1986)* 9:56 My '89

Financial bonanzas and bozos of the late, great 1988. il *Money* 18:15-16+ F '89

Jesse Jackson: newsmaker of the year. G. Wills. *The Christian Century* 106:3-4 Ja 4-11 '89

The top 10 news stories of 1988. B. Shelby. il *World Press Review* 36:4-5 F '89

The weather of 1988 [cover story; special issue] il *Weatherwise* 42:8-16+ F '89

The year in review [syndicated TV] M. Burgi. il *Channels (New York, N.Y.: 1986)* 9:13-14 Ja 16 '89

Year of oat bran and ozone. G. F. Will. il *Newsweek* 113:68 Ja 2 '89

Anecdotes, facetiae, satire, etc.

Bless you, Marty. P. Volk. il *The New York Times Magazine* p20-1 Ja 1 '89

Dubious Achievement Awards of 1988 [cover story] il *Esquire* 111:87-90+ Ja '89

Year in review [television] J. Queenan. il *Channels (New York, N.Y.: 1986)* 9:52+ Ja '89

Photographs and photography

'88: the year in pictures [special issue] il *Life* 12:2-3+ Ja '89

NINETEEN HUNDRED AND EIGHTY-NINE

1989 yearbook [cover story; special issue] il *Rolling Stone* p45-9+ D 14-28 '89

Business week's 1989 hip parade. il *Business Week* p37 Ja 16 '89

The early line on 1989 [cover story; special section] il *People Weekly* 31:64-6+ Ja 9 '89

Europe's second Reformation. G. F. Will. il *Newsweek* 114:90 N 20 '89

The Honor Roll [cover story; special section; with editorial comment by Kevin Doyle] D. Jenish. il *Maclean's* 102:4, 15-39 D 25 '89

Images of '89: the year that changed the world [special section; with editorial comment by Kevin Doyle] il *Maclean's* 102:2, 30-2+ D 18 '89

Issues for 1989 [religious stories] il *Christianity Today* 33:44-5 Ja 13 '89

Media: winners and sinners of 1989. E. Diamond. il *New York* 22:20+ D 25 '89-Ja 1 '90

Music's mean season [rock in 1989] A. DeCurtis. il *Rolling Stone* p15-16 D 14-28 '89

Oh, what a year! P. Jennings. il por *TV Guide* 37:20-1 D 30 '89-Ja 5 '90

People of the year [cover story; special section] il *Newsweek* 114:18-26+ D 25 '89

Picks & pans. il *People Weekly* 32:8-10+ D 25 '89-Ja 1 '90

Politics: winners and sinners of 1989. J. Klein. il *New York* 22:17-18 D 25 '89-Ja 1 '90

Religion and revolution: top story of 1989 [cover story] il *The Christian Century* 106:1187-90 D 20-27 '89

A vintage year for greed and stupidity. P. C. Newman. il *Maclean's* 102:46 D 25 '89

Wall St.: winners and sinners of 1989. C. Byron. il *New York* 22:31-2 D 25 '89-Ja 1 '90

Women of the year, 1989. C. Krupp. il *Glamour* 87:154-5 D '89

The year in movies. P. Travers. il *Rolling Stone* p21+ D 14-28 '89

A year of turning points. R. Frame. il *Christianity Today* 33:38-40+ D 15 '89

Anecdotes, facetiae, satire, etc.

1989—slime time live. P. J. O'Rourke. il *Rolling Stone* p36-8+ D 14-28 '89

Field of bad dreams. il *People Weekly* 32:170-1 D 25 '89-Ja 1 '90

I have seen the future . . . W. Jeanes. il *Car and Driver* 34:5 Ja '89

Madison Ave.: winners and sinners of 1989. B. Kanner. il *New York* 22:25-6+ D 25 '89-Ja 1 '90

The political look of 1989. A. Fotheringham. il *Maclean's* 102:48 Ja 16 '89

Photographs and photography

The best photos of 1989. il *Jet* 77:31-4+ D 25 '89-Ja 1 '90

Images '89. il *Time* 134:38-52+ D 25 '89

NINETEEN HUNDRED AND FIFTIES
My summer swing: on the road with a fifties big band. D. Asher. il *Harper's* 278:70-6 Je '89

The way it was, the way it is! J. Romberger and J. K. Davis. il *'Teen* 33:22+ Jl '89

NINETEEN HUNDRED AND FIFTY-FOUR
1954. R. Firmite. il *Sports Illustrated* 71 Special Issue:24-8+ N 15 '89

NINETEEN HUNDRED AND FORTY-NINE
My favorite year [1949 Burgundy and Bordeaux wines] A. Richman. il *Gentlemen's Quarterly* 59:105+ Ja '89

NINETEEN HUNDRED AND FOURTEEN
75th anniversary [cover story; special section] il *The New Republic* 201:8+ N 6 '89

NINETEEN HUNDRED AND NINETIES
10s, 20s, 50s, 100s [anniversary guide] J. Adler. il *Newsweek* 114:78-80 D 18 '89

The 90s [evangelicals; cover story; special section] il *Christianity Today* 33:18-28 N 17 '89

The '90s [sports] R. Sandomir. il *Sport (New York, N.Y.)* 80:91-2+ O '89

The '90s: future tense [special section] il *Film Comment* 25:27-39+ Ja/F '89

1990s key ideas [cover story; special section] il *Fortune* 120:48-51+ Jl 3 '89

Coping with the '90s [U.S. foreign policy] C. W. Maynes. bibl f *Foreign Policy* 74:42-62 Spr '89

Economics for the '90s. D. Pauly. il *Newsweek* 114:58-60 N 27 '89

Fast forward. A. P. Crawford. *Vogue* 179:430-1 N '89

Gonna party like it's 1999. A. Heard. il *Mother Jones* 14:29-31+ N '89

Good-bye to materialism? M. Novak. il *Forbes* 144:108-9 N 27 '89

The gray '90s. il *Psychology Today* 22:8-9 D '88

How to get the jump on the next ten years. M. J. Cetron and O. Davies. il *Glamour* 87:252-7+ O '89

Industry output and employment: a slower trend for the nineties. V. A. Personick. bibl f il *Monthly Labor Review* 112:25-41 N '89

Investing for the 1990s [cover story; special section] il *Business Week* p91-5+ O 16 '89

Moving into the 1990s [cover story; special section] il *World Press Review* 36:11-13+ D '89

The new America [cover story; special section] il maps *Business Week* p90-5+ S 25 '89

Outlook 1990 [cover story; special issue; with editorial comment by Mortimer B. Zuckermam] il *U.S. News & World Report* 107:5+ D 25 '89-Ja 1 '90

Rap for the '90s. il *People Weekly* 32 Special Issue:154 Fall '89

The she decade. L. Langway. il *Ladies' Home Journal* 106:211-14 N '89

Thumbs up for the '90s [cover story; special section] il maps *Changing Times* 43:31-6+ Ja '89

The way we'll be. M. J. Weiss. il *Ladies' Home Journal* 106:220-2+ N '89

What's your wish list for women in the 90's, and what do you want for yourself? [celebrities' opinions] il *Glamour* 87:320-1 Ap '89

Whither policy for the 1990s [special section] bibl *Society* 26:39-82 S/O '89

Women in the '90s [cover story; special section; with editorial comment by Myrna Blyth] il *Ladies' Home Journal* 106:18, 57-8+ N '89

Anecdotes, facetiae, satire, etc.
Divining the nineties. R. Wolkomir. il *New Choices for the Best Years* 29:96 D '89

NINETEEN HUNDRED AND NINETY
Outlook '90 and beyond. il *The Futurist* 23:53-60 N/D '89

NINETEEN HUNDRED AND SEVENTIES
Going home to the '70s [movie sequels] D. Rochester. il *American Film* 14:13 S '89

NBC's "Yesterday" show [Today show's preoccupation with the 1970s] R. E. Tyrrell. *The American Spectator* 22:10-11 Mr '89

NINETEEN HUNDRED AND SIXTIES
See also
Student movement—History

The '60s: when groovy was cool! K. Turman. il *'Teen* 33:52 Ap '89

Blast from the past [1960s and current fashion] il *'Teen* 33:8 F '89

Confessions of a bloodthirsty flower child [contemporary teen discovers the sixties] J. Davidson. il *Seventeen* 48:180 Mr '89

A fury of symbols. J. Agee. il *Harper's* 278:49-52+ Ja '89

Looking for loons [debating 1960s radicalism] R. E. Tyrrell. il *The American Spectator* 22:8-9+ Je '89

Old and in the way. G. Jaynes. il *Life* 12:14 Ag '89

Panthers, contras, and other wars. P. Collier and D. Horowitz. *The New Republic* 200:38-41 Je 26 '89

Those were the days, my friend. P. Yancey. il *Christianity Today* 33:80 N 17 '89

Those weren't the days. J. Garvey. *Commonweal* 116:363-4 Je 16 '89

The way it was, the way it is! J. Romberger and J. K. Davis. il *'Teen* 33:22+ Jl '89

Where is the rage? J. Jordan. il *The Progressive* 53:12-13 O '89

Bibliography
Past tense. L. Wright. il *Vogue* 179:88+ Ja '89

The sixties without metaphor. M. S. Kimmel. *Society* 26:78-84 Mr/Ap '89

NINETEEN HUNDRED AND SIXTIES IN MOTION PICTURES
Flashbacks. il *Vogue* 179:77 Ja '89

NINETEEN HUNDRED AND SIXTIES IN TELEVISION
Sixties-something. C. Schine. il *Vogue* 179:82 Ja '89

Where were you in '68? [Wonder years] D. Blum. il *New York* 22:112-18+ F 27 '89

NINETEEN HUNDRED AND SIXTY-NINE
The summer of 1969 [cover story; special section] il *Newsweek* 114:47-57+ Jl 3 '89

NINETEEN HUNDRED AND THIRTY-NINE
1939: twelve months of magic [motion picture releases] G. Clarke. il *Time* 133:72-4 Mr 13 '89

Hollywood 1939-1989 [cover story; special issue] il *Life* 12:8-14+ Spr '89

NINETEEN HUNDRED AND TWENTIES
Media and morality in the twenties. J. D. Stevens. bibl il *History Today* 39:25-9 N '89

Sex and the automobile in the Jazz Age. P. Ling. bibl il *History Today* 39:18-24 N '89

NINETIES (DECADE) *See* Nineteen hundred and nineties

NINFA'S INC.
Steering safely through setbacks [N. Laurenzo] L. Gite. il pors *Working Woman* 14:39-41+ F '89

NINIVAGGI, DOMINICK
Managing New York's mosquito coast. il por *The Conservationist* 44:26-33 Jl/Ag '89

NINTENDO CO. LTD.
Court games [antitrust suits against Nintendo by Atari and Tengen] G. Keizer. il *Compute!* 11:84 Ap '89

A game of legal punch-out [Atari sues Nintendo] il *Newsweek* 113:50 Ja 2 '89

There's a rumble in the video arcade [Nintendo gets hit with antitrust suits from Tengen and Atari] M. Shao. il *Business Week* p37 F 20 '89

NINTENDO VIDEO GAMES
Court games [antitrust suits against Nintendo by Atari and Tengen] G. Keizer. il *Compute!* 11:84 Ap '89

A game of legal punch-out [Atari sues] il *Newsweek* 113:50 Ja 2 '89

Game wars: new high-tech systems challenge Nintendo's dominance. L. Kesten. il *Video* 13:58-61+ O '89

Nintendo: just kids' play or computer in disguise? K. Ferrell. il *Compute!* 11:28-33 Jl '89

The Nintendo kid. J. Adler. il *Newsweek* 113:64-8 Mr 6 '89

String garlic around your neck, get a wood stake ready—yep, Nintendo's here. G. Keizer. il *Compute!* 11:4 Jl '89

There's a rumble in the video arcade [Nintendo gets hit with antitrust suits from Tengen and Atari] M. Shao. il *Business Week* p37 F 20 '89

NIOS, LAKE (CAMEROON) *See* Lake Nyos (Cameroon)

NIPPON ELECTRIC CO., LTD. *See* NEC Corp.

NIPPON TELEGRAPH & TELEPHONE CORPORATION
Japan's telephone colossus takes its first baby steps overseas. A. Borrus. il *Business Week* p144 Mr 13 '89

NTT test paves way for new chips. *High Technology Business* 9:30-1 Je '89

The Recruit scandal bubbles to the top. A. Borrus. por *Business Week* p55 Mr 20 '89

NIPPON TELEGRAPH & TELEPHONE PUBLIC CORPORATION
See also
Nippon Telegraph & Telephone Corporation

NIRDLINGER, PAUL
about
Easing the pain of a capital gain [interview] M. Henkenius. il por *Home Mechanix* 85:17-19 Ag '89

NISKANEN, WILLIAM, 1933-, AND ENGLAND, CATHERINE
Too little, too late. il *National Review* 41:38-9 My 19 '89

NISSAN (AUTOMOBILE) *See* Automobiles, Foreign; Sports cars

NISSAN MOTOR CO. LTD.
The land of the UAW's setting sun [Nissan votes to keep union out] il *U.S. News & World Report* 107:8 Ag 7 '89

Score another for Japan Inc. [Nissan workers vote to keep out union] L. Reibstein. il *Newsweek* 114:44-5 Ag 7 '89

So where does the UAW go from here? [loss at plant in Smyrna, Tenn.] W. Zellner. il *Business Week* p77 Ag 14 '89

The UAW vs. Japan: it's showdown time in Tennessee [Nissan plant election] D. Foust. il *Business Week* p64-5 Jl 24 '89

NISSAN MOTOR CO. LTD. INFINITI DIVISION
The coming traffic jam in the luxury lane [Toyota Lexus and Nissan Infiniti] W. Zellner. il *Business Week* p78 Ja 30 '89

Consider the urushi tree—is it not like a luxury car? [Hill Holliday's campaign for Nissan's Infiniti] L. Armstrong. il *Business Week* p84+ S 4 '89

NISSAN MOTOR CO. LTD. INFINITI DIVISION—*cont.*
Eastern standard [ads for Infiniti] B. Kanner. il *New York* 22:28+ S 25 '89
From here to Infiniti: Nissan's 'high concept' pitch. il *Newsweek* 114:38 S 25 '89
Infiniti and Lexus: characters in a German nightmare. J. Templeman. il *Business Week* p64 O 9 '89
Infiniti's art of Pacific persuasion [ad campaign] K. R. Sheets. il *U.S. News & World Report* 107:67 N 13 '89
The road to Infiniti [W. Bruce, general manager of Nissan division] S. Kichen. il por *Forbes* 143:104 Ja 23 '89
Taking the classic approach [Toyota Lexus and Nissan Infiniti luxury cars] M. Keller. il *Motor Trend* 41:213 My '89
NISUS (WORD PROCESSOR PROGRAM) *See* Word processors and processing—Programming
NITELLA *See* Stoneworts
NITRIC OXIDE *See* Nitrogen oxides
NITROCHLOROFORM *See* Chloropicrin
NITROGEN
See also
Soils—Nitrogen content
Urea
Mummy under glass [preservation with nitrogen] il *Discover* 10:18 Ag '89
Fixation
See also
Bacteria, Nitrogen fixing
Isotopes
What has caused the secular increase in solar nitrogen-15? J. F. Kerridge. bibl f il *Science* 245:480-6 Ag 4 '89
NITROGEN DIOXIDE
Hazardous gas strikes hockey rink [excess nitrogen dioxide exposure from malfunctioning ice resurfacer; research by Katrina Hedberg and Kristina L. MacDonald] *Science News* 136:396 D 16 '89
NITROGEN FERTILIZERS *See* Fertilizers and manures
NITROGEN OXIDES
Bringing home the bacon [nitric oxide secreted by macrophages; research by Michael Marletta and Dennis Stuehr] S. Vogel. il *Discover* 10:42 Jl '89
New catalysts scavenge NO$_x$ emissions. J. Raloff. *Science News* 135:271 Ap 29 '89
Nitrogen saturation in northern forest ecosystems. J. D. Aber and others. bibl f il *BioScience* 39:378-86 Je '89
NITROGENOUS BASES
See also
Guanine
NITROSAMINES
What's known about the risk [bacon] il *Consumer Reports* 54:648 O '89
NITROUS OXIDE
She who laughs gas conceives last [research by Gerard Kugel and Carlos Letelier] F. Flam. *Science News* 135:182 Mr 25 '89
NITTY GRITTY DIRT BAND (MUSICAL GROUP)
Dirt Band reprises a classic country album. J. Guterman. il *Rolling Stone* p18 Ap 20 '89
NITZE, PAUL H.
Deterrence, parity, stability. *The Bulletin of the Atomic Scientists* 45:37-8 My '89
Security challenges facing NATO in the 1990s [address, February 6, 1989] *Department of State Bulletin* 89:44-8 Ap '89
about
The conversion of Paul. Z. Citron. *The New Republic* 200:33 Ja 30 '89
Government/military: Lord Carrington, Paul H. Nitze, Marshal Sergei Fedorovich Akhromeyev. il pors *Aviation Week & Space Technology* 130:18 Ja 2 '89
The perfect in-and-outer. S. Hoffmann. bibl f il *The New York Review of Books* 36:13-17 N 23 '89
The Silver Fox [cover story] Sir S. Zuckerman. bibl f il *The New York Review of Books* 35:21-5 Ja 19 '89
NITZE, WILLIAM A.
The Intergovernmental Panel on Climate Change. *Environment* 31:44-5 Ja/F '89
NIVEN, FERNANDA
about
Abloom in the city. J. Conlin. il por *House & Garden* 161:168-73+ My '89
NIVEN, JAMES
about
James Niven: bringing London's toniest scents to the states. il por *Business Week* p107 Je 5 '89
NIVENS, BEATRYCE
Work it out! See occasional issues of Essence
NIX, MELINDA
Tropical options. il *House & Garden* 161:186-8 Ap '89
NIXDORF COMPUTER AG
This German company's days of freedom may be numbered. G. E. Schares. il por *Business Week* p51-2 D 4 '89
NIXON, LAURA
(jt. auth) See Dawson, Keith, and Nixon, Laura
NIXON, NICHOLAS, 1947-
about
Nicholas Nixon: Museum of Modern Art; Zabriskie. R. B. Woodward. il por *Art News* 88:132+ Ja '89

NIXON, NORM
about
Debbie Allen and Norman Nixon tell how they mix marriage, business and parenthood [cover story] il pors *Jet* 76:56-8 Jl 31 '89
NIXON, RICHARD M. (RICHARD MILHOUS), 1913-
Advice from a former president. il pors *Time* 134:44+ N 20 '89
American foreign policy: the Bush agenda. *Foreign Affairs* 68 Special Issue:199-219 ['89]
Memo to President Bush: how to use TV—and keep from being abused by it. il pors *TV Guide* 37:26-7+ Ja 14-20 '89
Rapprochement and democracy. *New Perspectives Quarterly* 6:57-8 Summ '89
Should the U.S. help Gorbachev? por *Time* 134:94 D 18 '89
Six (more) crises [excerpt from From: the president; ed. by Bruce Oudes. *Harper's* 278:18-19 Mr '89
about
Comment and correspondence. M. M. Kampelman. *Foreign Affairs* 68:160-2 Summ '89
"Gung ho on O'B". N. Lemann. il *The Atlantic* 263:26+ Je '89
He's back (part 723). H. Hertzberg. *The New Republic* 200:6 F 27 '89
The Hill case. L. Garment. *The New Yorker* 65:90-110 Ap 17 '89
Kissinger vs. Nixon. pors *Time* 134:32 D 25 '89
Nixon visited and revisited. P. Gottfried. il *National Review* 41:41-2 Jl 14 '89
Richard Nixon [discussion of October 1988 article, In praise of Richard Nixon] P. Johnson. *Commentary* 87:6-8+ Mr '89
The unfinished war (II). N. Lemann. il *The Atlantic* 263:52-6+ Ja '89
Archives
Minority report. C. Hitchens. *The Nation* 248:764 Je 5 '89
Homes
Nixon Library and Birthplace being built. *American History Illustrated* 23:6 Ja '89
Resignation
Nixon's penultimate days [TV dramatization of The final days] W. F. Buckley. *National Review* 41:54 D 8 '89
Woodward and Bernstein: what they think of Watergate now [interview] J. Kalter. il pors *TV Guide* 37:6-8 O 28-N 3 '89
Anecdotes, facetiae, satire, etc.
I am not a critic . . . [TV movie The final days] H. Shearer. il *American Film* 15:14+ O '89
Visit to China, 1989
Hard words to hard-liners. S. Burton. il por *Time* 134:37 N 13 '89
'They would not understand'. D. Elliott. il por *Newsweek* 114:61 N 13 '89
NIXON, WILL
Better times for black writers? il *Publishers Weekly* 235:35-40 F 17 '89
Literary cross-pollination. il *Publishers Weekly* 235:30+ Mr 31 '89
New dimensions in remaindering. il *Publishers Weekly* 235:23-4+ Ap 28 '89
University presses: highs & lows. il *Publishers Weekly* 236:18+ S 22 '89
NIXON (RICHARD) LIBRARY AND BIRTHPLACE *See* Richard Nixon Library and Birthplace
NIXON IN CHINA [opera] *See* Adams, John
NIXON IN CHINA [television program] *See* Television program reviews—Single works
NJERI, ITABARI
A new sexuality? il *Essence* 19:66-7+ Ja '89
NJOR, JOHN
The birthday tower. il *World Press Review* 36:62 Mr '89
NK CELLS *See* Killer cells
NL INDUSTRIES, INC.
Harold Simmons is coming out to play again. T. Mason. il por *Business Week* p44+ Ja 9 '89
NLG *See* National Lawyers Guild
NLM *See* National Library of Medicine (U.S.)
NMDA RECEPTORS *See* Chemoreceptors
NMR (NUCLEAR MAGNETIC RESONANCE) *See* Magnetic resonance imaging
NO-FAULT AUTOMOBILE INSURANCE *See* Insurance, Automobile
NO HOLDS BARRED [film] *See* Motion picture reviews—Single works
NO-LOAD MUTUAL FUNDS *See* Investment trusts
NO PLACE LIKE HOME [television program] *See* Television program reviews—Single works
NO SMOKING LAWS AND REGULATIONS *See* Smoking—Laws and regulations
NO-TILLAGE
He gave no-till a second chance. il *Successful Farming* 87:32 Je '89
No-till a blanket of soybeans. R. Fee. il *Successful Farming* 87 no4:28-9 Mr '89
Production [methods of Loren Schuett] J. Walter. il *Successful Farming* 87:19 D '89

NO-TILLAGE—*cont.*

Residue repositioned. R. Fee. il *Successful Farming* 87:36-7 D '89

Ridge-till corn, no-till beans gain acres. R. Fee. *Successful Farming* 87:20 D '89

Trample no-till's toughest weeds. R. Fee. il *Successful Farming* 87 no4:30-1 Mr '89

NO-TOBACCO DAY

Now the world's 2nd No-Tobacco Day. P. Ozorio. il *World Health* p26-7 Ap '89

NOAA *See* United States. National Oceanic and Atmospheric Administration

NOAH, TIMOTHY

Armey's aesthetic. *The New Republic* 201:14+ S 11 '89

Art of the voyeur. por *The New Republic* 201:16+ Ag 7-14 '89

Beverly Hills HUD. *The New Republic* 201:14-16 Ag 21 '89

Born to be mild. por *The Washington Monthly* 21:10-14+ D '89

Feather dusters. *The New Republic* 200:42 F 13 '89

Old bland-dad. *The New Republic* 200:17-19 Ap 3 '89

Rich but dumb. *The New Republic* 201:46 D 25 '89

Shhhhhh! *The New Republic* 201:8-10 O 30 '89

Washington diarist: be happy. *The New Republic* 201:43 Jl 10 '89

Washington diarist: the end of everything. *The New Republic* 201:54 O 16 '89

NOBEL PRIZES

At long last, laurels [Nobel Prize in Economics won by T. Haavelmo] M. J. Mandel. por *Business Week* p66 O 23 '89

A bow to Tibet [Dalai Lama wins Peace Prize] por *Time* 134:44 O 16 '89

Cela vie [C. J. Cela wins Literature Prize] M. Ugarte. *The Nation* 249:646+ N 27 '89

Chauvinism in Nobel nominations [views of Bo G. Malmstrom] C. Holden. *Science* 243:471 Ja 27 '89

Chemistry of life. R. Corelli. il por *Maclean's* 102:58 O 23 '89

China's Nobel rebuke [Peace Prize awarded to Dalai Lama] *Newsweek* 114:54 O 16 '89

Gene-tracking leads to Nobel Prize [oncogenes; work of J. M. Bishop and H. Varmus] A. McKenzie. *Science News* 136:244 O 14 '89

Honoring a god-king [Dalai Lama awarded Peace Prize] R. Corelli. il por *Maclean's* 102:58 O 16 '89

Little things mean a lot [awards in medicine, chemistry, and physics] il *U.S. News & World Report* 107:20 O 23 '89

Nobel chemists shed light on key structure in photosynthesis. B. G. Levi. il por *Physics Today* 42:17-18 F '89

The Nobel pair [G. Elion and G. Hitchings] K. Bouton. il pors *The New York Times Magazine* p28-9+ Ja 29 '89

Nobel Prize for UN peace-keepers accepted in Oslo. il *UN Chronicle* 26:30 Mr '89

Nobel Prize in Physics [L. M. Lederman, M. Schwartz, and J. Steinberger] P. F. Schewe. bibl f *Physics Today* 42:S67 Ja '89

Nobel prizes. J. Horgan. *Scientific American* 261:34-5 D '89

[Nobel prizes] [special section] il *Science* 246:325-8 O 20 '89

Physics Nobel Prize to Lederman, Schwartz and Steinberger. B. M. Schwarzschild. bibl f il *Physics Today* 42:17-20 Ja '89

Ramsey, Dehmelt, Paul win Nobel for helping to set high standards [ion trap techniques] B. G. Levi. il pors *Physics Today* 42:17-19 D '89

A risky life [C. J. Cela wins Literature Prize] por *Time* 134:86 O 30 '89

RNA researchers earn Chemistry Nobel [T. R. Cech and S. Altman] I. Amato. *Science News* 136:262 O 21 '89

Surprise, triumph—and controversy [special section] il *Time* 134:73-4 O 23 '89

Tibet's agony [Dalai Lama awarded Nobel Peace Prize] M. Moynihan. *The New Republic* 201:10-11 N 20 '89

NOBILITY

Employment

Working titles. M. Musto. il *Harper's Bazaar* 122:148-51+ N '89

France

When radical chic courted the guillotine [influence of 18th century French intellectuals] J. H. Huizinga. il *The New York Times Book Review* 94:1+ F 5 '89

Great Britain

Beauty secrets of the elite. P. Barron. il *Harper's Bazaar* 122:50+ S '89

NOBLE, DAVID F.

(jt. auth) *See* Minsky, Leonard, and Noble, David F.

about

Is academic freedom bad for business? K. Hart. il por *The Bulletin of the Atomic Scientists* 45:28-31+ Ap '89

NOBLE, GEORGE

Bad vibrations. il *Flying* 116:142 Jl '89

NOBLE, JENNIFER

about

Facing the future. J. Shields. il *Vogue* 179:206-7 Ja '89

NOBLE, JOHN A.

about

Bayonne. *The New Yorker* 65:32-3 Ap 24 '89

NOBLE, NIGEL

Voices of Sarafina! [film] Reviews

The Nation 248:174-5 F 6 '89. S. Klawans

NOBODY LISTENED [television program] *See* Television program reviews—Single works

NOCERA, JOSEPH

The case against Joe Nocera. *The Washington Monthly* 21:22-4+ F '89

Europe on $233 million a day. *The Washington Monthly* 21:49-50 F '89

Gee, I kind of like fiction. *The Washington Monthly* 21:28-9 Mr '89

Mid-life sax. il *Esquire* 111:52 Ap '89

The profit motive. See issues of Esquire beginning September 1989

about

New boys on the block. L. Eisenberg. il por *Esquire* 112:51 S '89

LES NOCES [ballet] *See* Ballet reviews—Single works

NOCHLIN, LINDA, 1931-

Fragments of a Revolution. bibl f il *Art in America* 77:156-67+ O '89

NOCTILUCENT CLOUDS

Cloudy memories of Krakatau [research by Gary E. Thomas] il *Discover* 10:14 Ag '89

Methane clouding up the twilight [research by Gary E. Thomas] *Science News* 135:255 Ap 22 '89

NODAL SYSTEMS CORPORATION

'I think we can be the next IBM' [work of H. J. Caulfield] D. Foust. il por *Business Week* Special Issue:86 Je 16 '89

NODEN, MERRELL

Beyond the melting pot. il por *Sports Illustrated* 71:46-8 N 13 '89

Big show in Oslo. il *Sports Illustrated* 71:26-8+ Jl 10 '89

A dynamic duo reigns in Spain. il *Sports Illustrated* 71:78+ S 18 '89

Flying at the finish. il por *Sports Illustrated* 70:28 Ap 24 '89

The hares split. il *Sports Illustrated* 70:42+ F 20 '89

He had 'em goggle-eyed. por *Sports Illustrated* 70:82 Ap 10 '89

He has suffered enough. por *Sports Illustrated* 70:98 Je 26 '89

The lady in waiting. il pors *Sports Illustrated* 70:73-4+ Je 5 '89

Much sweeta for Aouita. il por *Sports Illustrated* 70:32-4 F 13 '89

One giant leap. il pors *Sports Illustrated* 71:32-3 Ag 7 '89

A pair of aces. il pors *Sports Illustrated* 71:64-6+ O 16 '89

A peach for the Apple. il *Sports Illustrated* 71:55 Jl 31 '89

A pre-Olympic fling. il *Sports Illustrated* 71:22-4+ Ag 7 '89

Return of the crusher. il pors *Sports Illustrated* 71:78-9 D 4 '89

Smashing! il pors *Sports Illustrated* 71:16-19 Ag 28 '89

Tigers burning bright. il *Sports Illustrated* 70:74+ Je 12 '89

Wendy flew high in Indy. il pors *Sports Illustrated* 70:68+ My 15 '89

(jt. auth) *See* Telander, Rick, and Noden, Merrell

NOE, CLIFFORD DIXON

about

Biggest catch. A. Farnham. il por *Fortune* 119:59 Ja 2 '89

NOËL, GEORGES, 1924-

about

Georges Noël: Arnold Herstand. B. A. MacAdam. il *Art News* 88:146+ F '89

NOEL, VANESSA

about

New talents: Vanessa Noel. N. Malkin. il por *Harper's Bazaar* 122:123 Mr '89

NOGUCHI, ISAMU, 1904-1988

about

Dance. T. Tobias. *New York* 22:109-10 O 30 '89

Frontier of design: Isamu Noguchi 1904-1988. M. U. West. il pors *Dance Magazine* 63:58-60 My '89

Obituary

American Craft il por 49:56-60 Ap/My '89. A. Wardwell

Art News por 88:37-8 Mr '89. A. Wardwell

Talking heads. M. Filler. il por *House & Garden* 161:62 My '89

NOHA, EDWARD J.

Free enterprise and the insurance agency [address, June 9, 1989] *Vital Speeches of the Day* 56:45-9 N 1 '89

NOISE

See also

Airplanes—Noise

Airplanes, Military—Noise

Airplanes, Supersonic—Noise

Amplifiers—Noise

NOISE—See also—*cont.*
  Anechoic chambers
  Audio systems—Noise
  Compact discs—Noise
  Diesel engines, Automotive—Noise
  Fishing—Noise
  Fishing boats—Noise
  Helicopters—Noise
  Radio receivers—Noise
  Silence
  Tape recorders and recording—Noise
  Tinnitus
  Trucks—Noise
  Videotape recorders and recording—Noise

Anecdotes, facetiae, satire, etc.
Your sound and my fury [men and noise] K. Heller. il *Gentlemen's Quarterly* 59:207+ O '89

Physiological effects
Hearing loss. K. K. Gracey. il *Consumers' Research Magazine* 72:2 My '89
How noise can harm you. L. Ponte. il *Reader's Digest* 134:121-5 Mr '89
Modern lifestyles damage ears [views of J. Gail Neely] il *USA Today (Periodical)* 117:9-10 F '89
Ocean creatures resent man's noise [research by Arthur A. Myrberg, Jr.] il *USA Today (Periodical)* 117:7 Je '89

NOISE CONTROL
  See also
  Soundproofing
Fighting noise with antinoise. P. Elmer-Dewitt. il *Time* 134:94+ D 4 '89

Laws and regulations
Noise wars [cover story] A. H. Suter. il *Technology Review* 92:42-9 N/D '89

NOISE REDUCTION SYSTEMS See Tape recorders and recording—Noise

NOLAN, JOHN F.
  about
Why Little Tikes' managers picked up their toys and left. M. Mallory. il *Business Week* p83 N 27 '89

NOLAN, MARTIN
  about
Beat the devil. A. Cockburn. il *The Nation* 249:42-3 Jl 10 '89

NOLAN, PATRICIA
  (ed) See Ann-Margret, 1941-. 'My love is not a burden'
  (ed) See Lemmon, Jack. This Lemmon gets sweeter with age

NOLAN, SARA
  about
SoHo salon. M. Filler. il pors *House & Garden* 161:170-3 O '89

NOLAND, CADY
  about
Cady Noland at American Fine Arts. L. Liebmann. il *Art in America* 77:200-1 N '89

NOLAND, DAVID
Power play. il *Discover* 10:4, 62-8 D '89

NOLES, JANICE
[Month] in the South. See issues of Southern Living beginning February 1987

NOLL, MARK A., 1946-
A tale of two countries. il *Christianity Today* 33:24-5 Jl 14 '89

NOLLEY, BETTY
The planetologists' home. il *Ad Astra* 1:29-30 Mr '89

NOLTE, NICK
  about
The prime of Nick Nolte. C. McGuigan. il pors *Newsweek* 113:66-7 F 27 '89

NOMADS
  See also
  Bedouins

Eurasia
Art—Exhibitions
Ornate treasures from the steppe [at the National Museum of Natural History] K. M. Burke. il *Smithsonian* 20:188 D '89
Three thousand years of civilization. il *Travel Holiday* 171:82 Ja '89

Kenya
Two lives for the Ariaal. E. M. Fratkin. il map *Natural History* p38-49 My '89

Tibet
The remote world of Tibet's nomads. M. C. Goldstein and C. Beall. il map *National Geographic* 175:752-81 Je '89

NOMINATIONS FOR OFFICE
  See also
  Presidents—Nomination

NOMURA SECURITIES CO. LTD.
Nomura seeks a Yankee skipper [M. Chapman] J. Friedman. il por *Business Week* p96 S 4 '89

NOMURA WASSERSTEIN PERELLA COMPANY
The Japanese aren't flocking to this boutique—yet. T. Holden. il *Business Week* p39+ Ag 21 '89

NON-ALIGNED NATIONS See Nonalignment
NON-ALIGNMENT See Nonalignment
NON-SELF GOVERNING TERRITORIES See Colonies
NONALCOHOLIC BARS See Dry bars
NONALIGNMENT

Conferences
Outside the fort [summit in Belgrade] A. W. Singham. *The Nation* 249:337 O 2 '89

NONDESTRUCTIVE TESTING
  See also
  Eddy currents (Electric)
Acoustic emission technique tests aircraft integrity. C. Fotos. *Aviation Week & Space Technology* 131:76 Ag 28 '89
Detecting threats to airplane safety. S. Garfinkel. il *Technology Review* 92:10+ F/Mr '89
Firm develops new method to test for delamination [National Technical Systems] *Aviation Week & Space Technology* 130:52 Ap 17 '89
Update commercial transport inspections. *Aviation Week & Space Technology* 130:7 Jl 10 '89
USAF seeks aerospace applications for innovative X-ray tomography. B. W. Henderson. il *Aviation Week & Space Technology* 131:93+ Jl 31 '89

NONFICTION See Literature
NONFLOWERING PLANTS See Cryptogams
NONGRADED SCHOOLS See Experimental education
NONIMPACT AEROBICS See Aerobics
NONPRESCRIPTION DRUGS See Medicines, Nonprescription
NONPROFIT HOSPITALS See Hospitals
NONPROFIT INSTITUTIONS
  See also
  Charities
Crisis time for the non-profits [address, September 10, 1988] F. W. Wylie. *Vital Speeches of the Day* 55:170-2 Ja 1 '89

Employees
Salaries, pensions, etc.
Rewarding performance that is hard to measure: the private nonprofit sector. B. A. Weisbrod. bibl f *Science* 244:541-6 My 5 '89

Taxation
The Moynihan rip-off [municipal bond issues by nonprofit corporations] M. Schifrin. il *Forbes* 144:38-9 D 11 '89
Nonprofit groups: an unfair edge? D. C. Bacon. il *Nation's Business* 77:33-4 Ap '89
Punitive taxation of science and engineering. P. H. Abelson. *Science* 243:1417 Mr 17 '89

NONPROLIFERATION POLICY See Disarmament
NONVERBAL COMMUNICATION See Communication, Nonverbal
NONVIOLENCE
  See also
  Center for Nonviolent Alternatives
  Hunger strikes
  Martin Luther King, Jr. Center for Nonviolent Social Change
Another way to peace [French Catholics] C. Guicherd. il *Commonweal* 116:704-6 D 15 '89
Building a creative conscience [Catholic ethics]; tr. by Ingrid Knapp. B. Häring. il *Commonweal* 116:433-6 Ag 11 '89
A Christian spirituality of nonviolence [Peru] E. W. Ranly. *America* 161:110-11+ Ag 26-S 2 '89
Daniel: beloved by God & by me [seeing Do the right thing with teenage son] B. B. Morton. *Commonweal* 116:562-3 O 20 '89

NONWAGE PAYMENTS See Fringe benefits
NOOLANDI, JAAN, AND OTHERS
Generalized tube model of biased reptation for gel electrophoresis of DNA. bibl f il *Science* 243:1456-8 Mr 17 '89

NOONAN, DAVID
Nervous energy [excerpt from Neuro; cover story] il *Health (New York, N.Y.)* 21:58-61 F '89

NOONAN, PEGGY
Confessions of a White House speechwriter [excerpt from What I saw at the revolution; cover story] il pors *The New York Times Magazine* p24-7+ O 15 '89
  about
High Noonan. M. Dowd. il por *Vogue* 179:338-41 D '89
Notes & asides. W. F. Buckley. *National Review* 41:15-16 N 24 '89

NOONAN, PEGGY
UFO update. il *Omni (New York, N.Y.)* 12:121 D '89

NOONAN, ROBERT
Mite riders. il *Natural History* p80-1 My '89

NOOR AL-HUSSEIN See Nur el Hussein, Queen, consort of Hussein, King of Jordan
NORA, DOMINIQUE
The corporate 'color bar'. *World Press Review* 36:35 My '89

NORA (NEB.)
Politics and government
Nebraska's new favorite son [H. Kaufman leads opposition to nuclear dump] B. Turque. il por *Newsweek* 114:21 Jl 10 '89

NORAD *See* North American Aerospace Defense Command

NORADRENALINE *See* Norepinephrine

NORANDA INC.

Alfred Powis as corporate superman. D. Francis. il *Maclean's* 102:13 N 27 '89

The final victory [takeover of Falconbridge] J. Daly. il pors *Maclean's* 102:40-1 O 2 '89

Getting the best price [Falconbridge Ltd. favoring AMAX over Noranda in takeover battle; special section] il *Maclean's* 102:34-7 Ag 14 '89

NORCROSS (GA.)

Libraries

Karen Lindsay was overdue at the library; so they threw the book at her [jailed for failure to return books] il pors *People Weekly* 32:113 N 27 '89

NORDBERG, OLIVIA SCHIEFFELIN

Post-vacation blues. il *Parents* 64:112-14 S '89

NORDEN, EDWARD

Behind "Who is a Jew": a letter from Jerusalem. *Commentary* 87:21-33 Ap '89

Oh, Jerusalem! *The New Republic* 200:17-18 Mr 27 '89

"Who is a Jew" [discussion of April 1989 article, Behind "Who is a Jew": a letter from Jerusalem] *Commentary* 88:2-4+ S '89

NORDEN SYSTEMS INC.

Can UTC fix what it can't sell? T. Vogel. *Business Week* p31 Ag 21 '89

Norden develops system to warn controllers of runway incursions [Runway Incursion Management system] B. D. Nordwall. *Aviation Week & Space Technology* 130:28 My 29 '89

NORDIC MACHINES *See* Exercising equipment

NORDSTROM, INC.

Spa-in-store. P. Orenstein. il *Vogue* 179:145-6+ My '89

Watch out Macy's, here comes Nordstrom. R. W. Stevenson. il *The New York Times Magazine* p34+ Ag 27 '89

NOREN, CHRISTOPHER J., AND OTHERS

A general method for site-specific incorporation of unnatural amino acids into proteins. bibl f il *Science* 244:182-8 Ap 14 '89

NORENBERG, MICHAEL D.

(jt. auth) See Kimelberg, Harold K., and Norenberg, Michael D.

NOREPINEPHRINE

Effects of glucocorticoids and norepinephrine on the excitability in the hippocampus. M. Joëls and E. R. de Kloet. bibl f il *Science* 245:1502-5 S 29 '89

NORFOLK (CONN.)

History

Photographs and photography

A town that looked lost so [work of M. Kendall] G. Robinson. il *American Heritage* 40:92-9 Jl/Ag '89

NORFOLK (VA.)

Galleries and museums

See also

Chrysler Museum

Industries

Knocking newspapers [WVEC's campaign for advertising dollar] A. Snyder. il *Channels (New York, N.Y.: 1986)* 9:32-3 F '89

NORGREN, CHRISTIAN

about

An insider caper in Liechtenstein. J. Kapstein. *Business Week* p58-9 D 11 '89

NORIEGA, MANUEL ANTONIO

about

Amateur hour [cover story] C. S. Manegold. il por map *Newsweek* 114:26-31 O 16 '89

Brute politics. A. Bilski. il por *Maclean's* 102:22-4 My 22 '89

A bungled deal with Panama. il por *Newsweek* 113:25 Ap 10 '89

Can we oust Noriega? L. C. Wilson. il *USA Today (Periodical)* 118:15 N '89

Dear Manny. M. Hosenball. *The New Republic* 200:9-10 Je 12 '89

A defiant dictator. B. Levin. il *Maclean's* 102:25 My 29 '89

A dubious ballot. D. Gollob. il por *Maclean's* 102:26 My 1 '89

The Dukakis approach. S. Talbott. il *Time* 133:61 My 29 '89

Dwindling options in Panama. L. S. Robinson. bibl f *Foreign Affairs* 68:187-205 Wint '89/'90

Fiasco in Panama. *The New Republic* 201:5-6 O 30 '89

A fumbled coup. G. W. Taylor. il por *Maclean's* 102:28-30 O 16 '89

The gang that wouldn't shoot. B. Duffy. il por *U.S. News & World Report* 107:26-7, 129 O 16 '89

The gutsy Panama option. pors *U.S. News & World Report* 107:19 S 11 '89

Lead-pipe politics [cover story; special section] il por map *Time* 133:40-4+ My 22 '89

Letter from Washington. E. Drew. *The New Yorker* 65:100-4+ O 30 '89

A man, a plan, an election. K. E. Schuette. il *National Review* 41:18-19 Je 16 '89

Manuel Noriega. il pors *People Weekly* 32:69-70 D 25 '89-Ja 1 '90

Meanwhile, in Panama. *Time* 134:23 S 11 '89

The mothers of intervention. il *The Progressive* 53:8-9 D '89

Noriega celebrates. C. Lane. il *Newsweek* 113:47-8 My 29 '89

Noriega speaks out. S. Calloni. *World Press Review* 36:52-3 D '89

The OAS and the Panama crisis [statements, August 24 and 31, 1989] L. S. Eagleburger. *Department of State Bulletin* 89:67-75 N '89

On Noriega, 'We have failed miserably'. il por *Newsweek* 114:33 S 4 '89

Panama. *Business Week* p51 O 16 '89

Panama. *Business Week* p70 D 25 '89-Ja 1 '90

Panama contras? T. Avirgan. *The Nation* 249:263-5 S 18 '89

Panama elections [statements, April 27-May 18, 1989] G. Bush. *Department of State Bulletin* 89:66-72 Jl '89

Panama: on not being a cowboy. *America* 161:251 O 21 '89

Panama, through Latin eyes. V. A. Palacios. il *World Press Review* 36:24+ Jl '89

The Panamanian mess. W. F. Buckley. il *National Review* 41:70-1 N 10 '89

The perils of Panama. *Commonweal* 116:323-5 Je 2 '89

Playing 'bad cop' in Panama. C. Lane and D. Waller. il por *Newsweek* 113:36-7 My 8 '89

Playing footsie with a dictator. S. J. Hedges and P. Cary. il por *U.S. News & World Report* 106:34 My 22 '89

Prospects dim for Panama. *USA Today (Periodical)* 117:10-11 Ap '89

Sparring (again) with a dictator. J. Smolowe. il por *Time* 133:46 My 8 '89

Standoff in Panama. J. L. Galloway. il por *U.S. News & World Report* 106:28-32 My 22 '89

The stovepipe problem. il por *Time* 134:35 N 6 '89

Surrender, Manny. *The New Republic* 200:9-10 Je 5 '89

T.R.'s invention. G. Black. *The Nation* 248:760-1 Je 5 '89

Taking aim at Noriega. C. A. Robbins. il por *U.S. News & World Report* 106:40-1 My 1 '89

A test of wills. L. Martz. il por map *Newsweek* 112:34-9 My 22 '89

Washington fights the Noriega factor. H. Anderson. il *Newsweek* 114:58 D 11 '89

What next, Noriega? C. S. Manegold. il por *Newsweek* 114:26-8 O 23 '89

When fury turns to foolishness. M. Greenfield. il *Newsweek* 114:92 O 16 '89

Who lost Noriega? D. Goodgame. il por *Time* 134:39-40 O 23 '89

Why Noriega wins. M. Kempton. il *The New York Review of Books* 36:10 Je 15 '89

The widow of a slain rebel leader looks back in anguish after the failed coup in Panama. B. Hewitt. il pors *People Weekly* 32:101-2 O 30 '89

The winds of words. G. F. Will. il *Newsweek* 112:96 My 22 '89

The Yanquis stayed home. J. Smolowe. il por maps *Time* 134:24-8 O 16 '89

NORINCHUKIN BANK

There's no keeping this bank down on the farm. T. Holden. il *Business Week* p59 Jl 24 '89

NORM, SOCIAL *See* Social norm

NORMAN, DAVID A., 1937?-

about

The stubborn maverick of retail. C. O'Malley. por *Personal Computing* 13:76 Jl '89

NORMAN, DONALD A.

about

So you're still having trouble making those Christmas toys work? Don't worry, it's not your fault [interview] K. MacMurran. il pors *People Weekly* 31:91-2+ Ja 9 '89

NORMAN, GEOFFREY

The daily double. il pors *Sports Illustrated* 70:92-6+ Je 5 '89

Harvest of pride. il pors *New Choices for the Best Years* 29:30-5 Jl '89

How I learned to love paradise. il *Esquire* 111:29-30 My '89

The spirit of Christmas South. il *Southern Living* 24:84 D '89

NORMAN, GREG, 1955-

about

Bridesmaid revisited. B. Verdi. il pors *Sports Illustrated* 70:54-7 Ap 24 '89

NORMAN, JEFF

about

Sukhreet's agent man. T. O'Neill. il por *New York* 22:34 Ag 21 '89

NORMAN, JESSYE

about

Glorious live recital from Jessye Norman. R. Freed. il por *Stereo Review* 54:101-2 Ja '89

Jessye Norman. W. Livingstone. il pors *Stereo Review* 54:102-5 O '89

NORMAN, LAURA, AND COWAN, THOMAS DALE
Foot work [excerpt from Feet first] il *Redbook* 173:152-3 S '89

NORMAN, MICHAEL
Coming back to Guffin Bay. il *Gentlemen's Quarterly* 59:199-200+ N '89
Hollywood's uncommon Everyman [cover story] il pors *The New York Times Magazine* p28-31+ Mr 19 '89
Late-night cool [cover story] il pors *The New York Times Magazine* p28-31+ O 1 '89
My affair with fantasy. il *Gentlemen's Quarterly* 59:61+ Mr '89

NORMAN, PETER
Hope for the world economy. *World Press Review* 36:22 D '89

NORMAN, TYLER
Passage. il *Southern Living* 24:98 Ja '89

NORMAN, WILLIAM STANLEY, 1938-
about
Working on the railroad. C. C. Williams. il por *Black Enterprise* 19:62-4 Ap '89

NORMAN KERN & COMPANY
Pit players [P. Kern] D. Sherman. il pors *Ms.* 18:62-4+ N '89

NORMANDY (FRANCE)
Norman retreat [N. Worms' 1823 timbered farmhouse] R. Koenig. il *House & Garden* 161:142-7+ Jl '89
Description and travel
Cruisin' up the river [Seine River] J. Gooding. il *Time* 133:74 Je 26 '89

NORODOM SIHANOUK, PRINCE, 1922-
about
Better times for a ravaged land. W. Stewart. il *Time* 133:42 My 15 '89
Old war, China card & Sihanouk. S. Blaustein. il *The Nation* 249:485-6+ O 30 '89
The progress of peace in Cambodia. E. Becker. bibl f *Current History* 88:169-72+ Ap '89
Sihanouk on the high wire. A. Platt. il pors *Newsweek* 113:45 My 15 '89
Who's the puppet? A. Berlow. *The New Republic* 201:16-18 O 2 '89

NORPLANT (CONTRACEPTIVE) *See* Contraceptives
NORRELL CORPORATION
Temporary assignment. M. Barrier. il pors *Nation's Business* 77:34+ O '89

NORRINGTON, ROGER, 1934-
about
Beethoven lite. P. G. Davis. il por *New York* 22:60-1 Ag 28 '89
A man for all seasons. S. Cantrell. il pors *High Fidelity (New York, N.Y.)* 39:46-8 Mr '89
Music. P. G. Davis. il *New York* 22:78-9 Ap 17 '89
Norrington conducts Berlioz. R. Freed. por *Stereo Review* 54:68 Jl '89
Norrington's exhilarating Beethoven. D. Hall. il por *Stereo Review* 54:126 N '89
Roger Norrington. D. P. Stearns. il pors *Stereo Review* 54:105-7 S '89
Roger Norrington's Beethoven. P. Mattick, Jr. *The Nation* 249:326-8 S 25 '89

NORRIS, CHUCK
about
Chuck Norris' fainting spell. F. Lovece. il por *Video* 12:14-15 Ja '89

NORRIS, KATHLEEN, 1947-
The ignominy of the living [poem] *The New Yorker* 65:42 My 29 '89

NORRIS, PATRICK
about
Costume chief Patrick Norris elevates the look of this season's dressed-up thirtysomething yups. L. Feldon. il pors *People Weekly* 32:115-17 S 25 '89

NORRIS, RUTH, 1952-
The birds and the B&B's. il map *Travel Holiday* 171:55-9 Ap '89

NORTH, OLIVER L., JR.
about
All-black jury ruled in recent Oliver North trial and prayed for guidance. il por *Jet* 76:7 My 22 '89
Case closed. W. Dellinger. *The New Republic* 200:14-16 Ja 9-16 '89
The contratution. *The Nation* 248:723-4 My 29 '89
A convict of conviction, Oliver North takes the fall. il por *People Weekly* 32:30-1 Jl 24 '89
A courtroom endgame for Ollie North. il *U.S. News & World Report* 106:14 Ap 24 '89
Did he lie? E. Magnuson. il por *Time* 133:42 Mr 27 '89
Fallout from the North verdict. B. Duffy and G. Borger. il por *U.S. News & World Report* 106:20-1 My 15 '89
A folk hero on trial. M. McDonald. il por *Maclean's* 102:20 F 13 '89
For Denise Anderson, the jury forewoman, passing judgment on Ollie North was a trial by fire. P. Chin. il pors *People Weekly* 31:49-50 My 22 '89
A forgiving sentence. W. Lowther. il por *Maclean's* 102:23 Jl 17 '89

Getting Ollie North right? It was actor vs. director. M. Leahy. il pors *TV Guide* 37:20-3 Ap 29-My 5 '89
Giving in to "graymail". S. Holmes. il pors *Time* 133:24-5 Ja 16 '89
The guilty parties. il *The Progressive* 53:8-9 Je '89
Hero today, gone tomorrow. *National Review* 41:10-11 My 19 '89
The hero's clay feet. L. Martz. il por *Newsweek* 113:32-3+ My 15 '89
Iran-contra. F. FitzGerald. *The New Yorker* 65:51-4+ O 16 '89
Iran-contra: Reagan's role. il *Newsweek* 113:6 Mr 27 '89
'My bosses made me do it'. *U.S. News & World Report* 106:14 Ap 17 '89
National insecurity. *Commonweal* 116:36-7 Ja 27 '89
New North wind? *The Nation* 248:327-8 Mr 13 '89
The North case. F. FitzGerald. *The Nation* 248:149 F 6 '89
North rains on Bush's parade. *U.S. News & World Report* 106:34-5 Ap 17 '89
Not dumb persons. M. E. Marty. *The Christian Century* 106:575 My 24-31 '89
Oliver North. S. Kanfer. il por *People Weekly* 32 Special Issue:55 Fall '89
Oliver North does time battling drugs in the nation's capital. M. Brower. il pors *People Weekly* 32:52-3 N 27 '89
Ollie North's big jail break. il *U.S. News & World Report* 107:10 Jl 17 '89
Ollie North's eleventh-hour stratagem. T. Morganthau. il pors *Newsweek* 113:24 Ja 9 '89
Ollie North's troubles: the sequel. S. J. Hedges and S. Emerson. il por *U.S. News & World Report* 106:24 F 6 '89
Ollie's cash stash. *Time* 133:18 Ap 24 '89
Ollie's last stand. P. Meyer. il pors *Life* 12:22-6 F '89
Ollie's short-lived victory. R. Parry. il por *Newsweek* 113:33 Ja 16 '89
Ollie's tarnished image. L. Martz. il por *Newsweek* 113:38 Ap 24 '89
Ollie's trial: the Bush factor. L. Martz. il por *Newsweek* 113:20 Ap 17 '89
Ollie's true colors. E. Alterman. *The New Republic* 200:13-14 Mr 13 '89
On & on it goes. W. F. Buckley. *National Review* 41:70 F 10 '89
Pardon Ollie. *The American Spectator* 22:10-11 Ja '89
"A partial vindication". R. Lacayo. il por *Time* 133:34-5 My 15 '89
Pawn among giants. E. Magnuson. il por *Time* 133:22-3 Ap 17 '89
Reagan's role at Ollie's trial. L. Martz. il pors *Newsweek* 113:29 Ap 10 '89
Revelations of the North trial. T. Draper. bibl f il *The New York Review of Books* 36:54-9 Ag 17 '89
Security blanket. *The Nation* 248:111-12 Ja 30 '89
A slap on the wrist for Ollie. L. Martz and R. Parry. il por *Newsweek* 114:28-9 Jl 17 '89
Soliciting for the secret war: a chronicle [summary of classified documents submitted as evidence in O. North's trial] *Harper's* 278:17-19+ Je '89
A tale of two governments. M. Kempton. *The New York Review of Books* 36:43 Mr 30 '89
Top-secret strategy. G. J. Church. il por *Time* 133:16-17 F 27 '89
Verdict by prayer. M. McDonald. il por *Maclean's* 102:18-19 My 15 '89
What Oliver North's trial means to us. W. Greider. il *Rolling Stone* p45-6 Je 1 '89
What Reagan really knew. E. Salholz. il pors *Newsweek* 113:25 Mr 6 '89
Where, oh where have all the scandals gone? il por *U.S. News & World Report* 106:11-12 Ja 16 '89
Whittling away for Ollie. R. Parry. il pors *Newsweek* 113:20 F 20 '89
Who is Ollie's peer? W. F. Buckley. *National Review* 41:62 Mr 10 '89
Winners and losers. *National Review* 41:12 Je 2 '89
Anecdotes, facetiae, satire, etc.
Howls [excerpt from The found poetry of Lt. Col. Oliver L. North] J. W. Hart, III. *Harper's* 279:30 O '89

NORTH (DIRECTION)
Anecdotes, facetiae, satire, etc.
Septentrionalist suicide. M. E. Marty. *The Christian Century* 106:431 Ap 19 '89

NORTH ADAMS (MASS.)
Galleries and museums
See also
Massachusetts Museum of Contemporary Art and Architecture

NORTH AFRICA
See also
Algeria
Droughts—North Africa
Libya
Morocco
Sahara

NORTH AFRICA—*cont.*
Foreign relations
Italy
See Italy—Foreign relations—North Africa
United States
See United States—Foreign relations—North Africa
Politics and government
The Maghreb is ready for reform. *World Press Review* 36:28-30 F '89
Maghreb matters. R. A. Mortimer. *Foreign Policy* 76:160-75 Fall '89

NORTH AMERICA
See also
Acid rain—Laws and regulations—North America
Acid rain—North America
Astronomical observatories—North America
Birds—North America
Canada
Chinese—North America
Drug laws and regulations—North America
Geology—North America
Investments, British—North America
Planetariums—North America
Prairies—North America
Resorts—North America
Russians—North America
Stadiums—North America
United States
Wetlands—North America
Antiquities
See also
Indians of North America—Antiquities
Commerce
Italy
See Italy—Commerce—North America
Western Europe
TWA commitment strengthens Airbus' position in North American market. J. M. Lenorovitz. il *Aviation Week & Space Technology* 130:65 Ap 3 '89
Description and travel
See also
Cycling—North America
Can't afford Europe this summer? il *Glamour* 87:105-6 Jl '89
Industries
Continental destiny. D. Jenish. il *Maclean's* 102:68-70+ Jl 3 '89

NORTH AMERICAN AEROSPACE DEFENSE COMMAND
Software delays NORAD upgrade, increases costs by $207 million. B. D. Nordwall. *Aviation Week & Space Technology* 130:24-5 My 22 '89

NORTH AMERICAN RAYON CORP.
New source expected to prevent shortage of rayon for NASA, defense rockets. *Aviation Week & Space Technology* 131:24 N 27 '89

NORTH ATLANTIC REGION
See also
Air traffic control—North Atlantic region

NORTH ATLANTIC TREATY ORGANIZATION
After the cold war [cover story; special section] il *Newsweek* 113:20-5+ My 15 '89
After the NATO summit: challenges for the West in a changing world [address and excerpts from question-and-answer session, June 8, 1989] J. A. Baker, III. *Department of State Bulletin* 89:55-61 Ag '89
Agreement to disagree [new Soviet proposals during J. Baker visit] A. Wilson-Smith. il pors *Maclean's* 102:25-6 My 22 '89
Allies in dispute [West Germany calls for reducing short-range nuclear weapons] J. Bierman. il *Maclean's* 102:22 My 15 '89
And now it's George's turn [seeking dramatic arms proposal to counter M. Gorbachev's initiatives] H. Anderson. il pors *Newsweek* 113:30-2 Ap 17 '89
Another spy scandal [case of Air Force Capt. J. V. Hirsch] *Newsweek* 114:28 Ag 14 '89
Arms negotiations in Europe. J. Erickson. *Current History* 88:369-72+ N '89
A bad rap for the force de frappe? [views of Richard H. Ullman] C. Dickey. il *Newsweek* 113:35 Je 12 '89
The battle inside NATO. S. Head. bibl f il *The New York Review of Books* 36:41-6 My 18 '89
Britain to get airborne INF. M. Flournoy. *The Bulletin of the Atomic Scientists* 45:4 Jl/Ag '89
Bush and NATO [Brussels summit] il *World Press Review* 36:8 Jl '89
Bush includes combat aircraft cuts in NATO arms proposal [Brussels summit; special section] il map *Aviation Week & Space Technology* 130:16-21 Je 5 '89
Bush makes his mark [peace initiative at NATO summit] J. Bierman. il por *Maclean's* 102:24-5+ Je 12 '89
Bush pulls one out of a hat [arms proposal at NATO summit] B. Javetski. il por *Business Week* p22-3 Je 12 '89
Bush's bold bid to rescue NATO [U.S. troop cuts] H. Trewhitt. il por *U.S. News & World Report* 106:26-9 Je 12 '89
Bush's chintzy offer at Vienna [conventional arms reductions] R. Leavitt. *The Bulletin of the Atomic Scientists* 45:13 O '89

Bush's first foreign crisis [disagreement with West Germany over disarmament] il por *Newsweek* 113:16-18 My 8 '89
Bush's new look for the NATO alliance [troop reduction proposal] H. Anderson. il por *Newsweek* 113:34-5 Je 12 '89
By the numbers [Bush's arms proposals at NATO summit] *The Nation* 248:835-6 Je 19 '89
Calm down [West Germany and NATO] M. S. Forbes, Jr. il *Forbes* 143:27 My 29 '89
Can Moscow play defense? [concerns of NATO negotiators as they begin conventional arms talks with Warsaw Pact] M. B. Zuckerman. il *U.S. News & World Report* 106:76 Mr 13 '89
Can NATO agree on arms control? J. Dean. il *Technology Review* 92:58-62+ O '89
Can NATO survive détente? R. Mauthner. *World Press Review* 36:22-3 F '89
The case for the third zero. H. Beach. *The Bulletin of the Atomic Scientists* 45:14-15 D '89
Central European security. H. Owen and E. C. Meyer. il *Foreign Affairs* 68:22-40 Summ '89
Challenges ahead for NATO and developments in East-West relations [statement, June 20, 1989] J. A. Baker, III. *Department of State Bulletin* 89:61-4 Ag '89
Challenges to NATO in the 1990s [address, September 4, 1989] S. Nunn. *Vital Speeches of the Day* 56:135-40 D 15 '89
Cheney assures allies of U.S.'s continued commitment to NATO. *Aviation Week & Space Technology* 131:24 D 4 '89
The common defense [disproportionate burden shouldered by U.S. compounded by Western loans to Soviet Union] E. Rubenstein. il *National Review* 41:19 Je 30 '89
The conventional balance: a TKO for NATO? [cover story] J. Mendelsohn and T. Halverson. bibl f il *The Bulletin of the Atomic Scientists* 45:30-4+ Mr '89
Conventional talks: a good first round. J. Dean. il *The Bulletin of the Atomic Scientists* 45:26-31 O '89
Converging on peace? Sir S. Zuckerman. bibl f il *The New York Review of Books* 36:26+ S 28 '89
Counterpunching Gorbachev [Bush's policies overshadowed by Soviet arms proposals on eve of NATO summit] S. V. Roberts. il por *U.S. News & World Report* 106:16-17 My 29 '89
The covert French connection [nuclear collaboration with U.S.] R. H. Ullman. *Foreign Policy* 75:3-33 Summ '89
A crisis of confidence [European concerns over Reagan foreign policy] M. Zucconi. bibl f il *The Bulletin of the Atomic Scientists* 45:34-7 Ja/F '89
Crowing before sunrise [G. Bush at NATO summit] *Commonweal* 116:355-6 Je 16 '89
The dangers beyond containment [cover story] P. Glynn. *Commentary* 88:15-22 Ag '89
Dead souls. *The Nation* 248:687-8 My 22 '89
A decision not to decide [NATO response to Soviet arms initiatives] B. Van Voorst. il *Time* 133:46-7 My 1 '89
The defence gap [Canadian budget cuts] M. Clark. il *Maclean's* 102:10-12 My 22 '89
Divorce, alliance-style. A. Tonelson and C. Layne. *The New Republic* 200:23-5 Je 12 '89
Does NATO have middle-age myopia? [reductions in military spending] R. Knight. *U.S. News & World Report* 106:32 Je 5 '89
East bloc political changes add to West's budget battles [with editorial comment by Paul Mann] M. Mecham. il *Aviation Week & Space Technology* 131:19, 28-31 N 20 '89
Effective NATO defenses or none at all. *National Review* 41:11-12 Je 2 '89
European firms told to cut costs of NH-90 by 20% [NATO project] *Aviation Week & Space Technology* 130:31 My 8 '89
Europe's short-range missiles nail their first victim [H. D. Genscher] J. Templeman and G. E. Schares. il por *Business Week* p50 Je 12 '89
The exorbitant anachronism. J. Beatty. il *The Atlantic* 263:40-2+ Je '89
Federal Republic of Germany [address, April 27, 1989] H. Kohl. *Vital Speeches of the Day* 55:482-6 Je 1 '89
The fog of peace: does NATO have a future? J. D. Morrocco. il *Aviation Week & Space Technology* 131:20-1 D 18-25 '89
For a defense that makes sense. J. H. Webb. il *The New York Times Magazine* p38+ My 21 '89
From East Germany: it's NATO's move now [reductions in troops and conventional weapons] M. Schmidt and W. Schwarz. il *The Bulletin of the Atomic Scientists* 45:5-6 S '89
Germany and the alliance [short range nuclear missiles] il *World Press Review* 36:6 Je '89
Germany's burden [flight training in German air space] *Aviation Week & Space Technology* 130:9 F 6 '89
Gorbachev strikes again [plan to reduce short-range nuclear weapons in Europe] H. Anderson. il por *Newsweek* 112:57 My 22 '89

NORTH ATLANTIC TREATY ORGANIZATION—*cont.*
Government/military: Lord Carrington, Paul H. Nitze, Marshal Sergei Fedorovich Akhromeyev [breakthroughs in nuclear arms reduction negotiations; aerospace laureate] il pors *Aviation Week & Space Technology* 130:18 Ja 2 '89

"Here we go, on the offensive" [G. Bush offers troop reduction initiative at NATO meeting] G. J. Church. il por *Time* 133:28-31+ Je 12 '89

The invisible man [G. Bush's lack of foreign policy direction] *Commonweal* 116:291-2 My 19 '89

Is Bush losing the struggle for Europe's hearts and minds? B. Javetski and D. Griffiths. il *Business Week* p61 My 8 '89

It takes two not to tango. J. Tirman. il *The Nation* 248:520-2 Ap 17 '89

Keep the powder dry [interview with J. Galvin] M. Kramer. il por *Time* 133:78-9 My 29 '89

The key to the alliance [West Germany] M. B. Zuckerman. il *U.S. News & World Report* 106:83 Ja 30 '89

Kohl rekindles NATO dispute over upgrading Lance missile. K. F. Mordoff. *Aviation Week & Space Technology* 130:21-2 F 20 '89

The Kohl war [West German opposition to NATO disarmament strategy] *The New Republic* 200:7-8 My 22 '89

Living with the inevitable. H. Kissinger. il *Newsweek* 114:51-2+ D 4 '89

Madison Avenue, Moscow [M. Gorbachev's proposal to J. Baker] G. J. Church. il pors *Time* 133:33-4 My 22 '89

Market unification will expand Europe's influence in NATO. il *Aviation Week & Space Technology* 130:83+ Je 12 '89

Maturing NATO could benefit by ending cooperative military procurement barriers. E. H. A. Beckett. por *Aviation Week & Space Technology* 130:73-4 Ap 3 '89

Military openness proposals tabled at CSBM talks [State Dept. statement, June 9, 1989] *Department of State Bulletin* 89:74 Ag '89

Moves to trim the U.S. role. B. Levin. il *Maclean's* 102:48+ S 4 '89

Moving on double tracks: deterrence and détente. T. Garton Ash. il *World Press Review* 36:28-9 My '89

My life as a NATO collaborator [pacifist computer scientist attends NATO workshop on computer-human interaction in command and control; cover story] N. S. Borenstein. il *The Bulletin of the Atomic Scientists* 45:14-20 Ap '89

A nasty spat among friends [U.S. opposition to West German demand for talks on reduction of short-range nuclear weapons] D. Brand. il *Time* 133:42 My 8 '89

A NATO balancing act [G. Bush's proposals] D. Goodgame. il por *Time* 133:39 Je 5 '89

The NATO compromise: dangerous [G. Bush's proposals] *National Review* 41:12-13 Je 30 '89

NATO Defense Planning Committee meets in Brussels [text of final communique, December 2, 1988] *Department of State Bulletin* 89:42-3 F '89

NATO Defense Planning Committee meets in Brussels [text of final communique, June 9, 1989] *Department of State Bulletin* 89:77-9 Ag '89

NATO disputes Warsaw Pact claim of conventional parity. K. F. Mordoff. *Aviation Week & Space Technology* 130:21-2 F 6 '89

NATO in disarray? This time, reality. D. Gergen. il map *U.S. News & World Report* 106:24-6 Ja 23 '89

NATO nuclear jitters. *The Bulletin of the Atomic Scientists* 45:67 Ja/F '89

NATO Nuclear Planning Group meets in Brussels [text of final communique, April 20, 1989] *Department of State Bulletin* 89:36 Je '89

NATO Nuclear Planning Group meets in The Hague [text of final communique, October 28, 1988] *Department of State Bulletin* 89:28-9 Ja '89

NATO Secretary General stresses West's lead in arms negotiations [conventional arms talks; views of M. Woerner] K. F. Mordoff. *Aviation Week & Space Technology* 130:105 F 20 '89

NATO strategy: back to basics. H. Rühle. *Current (Washington, D.C.)* 312:34-9 My '89

NATO tightens limit on training flights to ease West German concerns. *Aviation Week & Space Technology* 131:30 O 2 '89

NATO weighs air force modernization in light of conventional arms cuts. J. D. Morrocco. il *Aviation Week & Space Technology* 131:29-30 Jl 24 '89

NATO's conventional force reduction proposal [White House fact sheet, July 12, 1989] *Department of State Bulletin* 89:76 S '89

NATO's last mission. R. Steel. *Foreign Policy* 76:83-95 Fall '89

NATO's mid-life crisis. R. K. Betts. bibl f *Foreign Affairs* 68:37-52 Spr '89

NATO's southern flank: bridge or bastion? J. H. Wolfe. *USA Today (Periodical)* 118:15 Jl '89

The naysayer and new détente [J. A. Baker's Soviet visit yields new arms proposals] H. Trewhitt. il pors *U.S. News & World Report* 106:18-19 My 22 '89

Negotiate now, but carefully [West Germany's call for short-range missile negotiations] *America* 160:499 My 27 '89

A new Concert of Europe. J. E. Mueller. *Foreign Policy* 77:3-16 Wint '89/'90

North Atlantic Council session held in Brussels [texts of statement on conventional arms control, final communique, extracts from minutes of meeting, and news conference, December 8-9, 1988] G. P. Shultz. *Department of State Bulletin* 89:43-50 F '89

One for the Gipper [G. Bush's proposals at summit] il *The New Republic* 200:7-8 Je 19 '89

Perception of declining Soviet threat erodes support for NATO modernization. K. F. Mordoff. il *Aviation Week & Space Technology* 130:84-5 Mr 20 '89

President visits Europe; attends North Atlantic Council meeting [cover story; special section] G. Bush. il pors *Department of State Bulletin* 89:11-45 Ag '89

Reagan's radical challenge. L. V. Sigal. il *The Bulletin of the Atomic Scientists* 45:38-41 Ja/F '89

Redefining Europe and the Atlantic link. R. D. Hormats. *Foreign Affairs* 68:71-91 Fall '89

The Russians aren't coming. S. Budiansky. il *U.S. News & World Report* 107:47+ N 27 '89

Secretary meets with NATO allies [remarks, February 11-17, 1989] J. A. Baker, III. *Department of State Bulletin* 89:38-42 Ap '89

Secretary's news conference [May 23, 1989] J. A. Baker, III. *Department of State Bulletin* 89:21-4 Jl '89

Secretary's trip to Moscow and NATO [remarks, news conferences, etc., May 10-12, 1989] J. A. Baker, III. *Department of State Bulletin* 89:29-36 Jl '89

Security challenges facing NATO in the 1990s [address, February 6, 1989] P. H. Nitze. *Department of State Bulletin* 89:44-8 Ap '89

Sharing the U.S. burden: a British view. M. Legge. il *Current (Washington, D.C.)* 313:15-21 Je '89

A short history of NATO. J. E. Miller. il *Department of State Bulletin* 89:1-5 Ag '89

Should Canada bring the boys home? T. Rauf and J. M. Lamb. il *The Bulletin of the Atomic Scientists* 45:36-8 S '89

Superpower disengagement. C. Layne. *Foreign Policy* 77:17-40 Wint '89/'90

Tight budgets, design conflicts undercut NATO weapon projects. J. D. Morrocco. il *Aviation Week & Space Technology* 131:18-19 S 25 '89

The time has come: bring our troops back from Europe. A. Ireland. il *USA Today (Periodical)* 118:16-18 Jl '89

U.S. out of NATO? A French scenario [views of A. Soussan] R. Kaplan. il *The American Spectator* 22:32-3 F '89

U.S. senators threaten troop cutback if West Germany blocks Lance upgrade [with editorial comment] P. A. Gilmartin. *Aviation Week & Space Technology* 130:7, 29 My 8 '89

United States and NATO [address, May 31, 1989] G. Bush. *Vital Speeches of the Day* 55:546-9 Jl 1 '89

Vienna talks trigger NATO air force review [cover story; special section] J. D. Morrocco. il map *Aviation Week & Space Technology* 131:34-7+ O 30 '89

Ein Volk, ein Reich, ein Furor. B. Crozier. il *National Review* 41:26-7 O 27 '89

The war inside NATO [U.S.-German conflict over proposed introduction of new nuclear missiles] D. Johnstone. il *The Progressive* 53:16-18 Ap '89

Western security: the U.S. and its NATO allies. il map *Department of State Bulletin* 89:6-10 Ag '89

When Johnny comes marching home: the pressure for U.S. troops to leave Europe. D. White. map *World Press Review* 36:25-7 S '89

Why Kohl is right [call for U.S. and Soviet Union to negotiate on short-range nuclear weapons] S. Talbott. il por *Time* 133:26 My 15 '89

Will NATO settle for Kohl cuts? T. Risse-Kappen. il *The Bulletin of the Atomic Scientists* 45:9-12 Je '89

Will the allies leave Bush behind? B. Javetski and D. Griffiths. il pors *Business Week* p30-1 My 15 '89

Wither NATO. H. Hertzberg. *The New Republic* 200:4 My 22 '89

Your move again, George [Warsaw Pact proposal on conventional arms] H. Anderson. il *Newsweek* 114:24 Jl 10 '89

Military maneuvers
See Military maneuvers

NORTH AUGUSTA (S.C.)
Race relations
White S.C. restaurateur refuses to admit blacks; state NAACP files lawsuit [B. Salter] *Jet* 76:28 O 2 '89

Restaurants, nightclubs, bars, etc.
White S.C. restaurateur refuses to admit blacks; state NAACP files lawsuit [B. Salter] *Jet* 76:28 O 2 '89

NORTH BEACH LEATHER (FIRM)
Leather soul [work of M. Hoban] A. Kahn. il *Vogue* 179:560+ Mr '89

NORTH BY NORTHWEST [film] *See* Motion picture reviews—Single works

NORTH CAROLINA
See also
Alligator River National Wildlife Refuge (N.C.)
Birds—North Carolina
Blue Ridge Mountains
Cape Hatteras National Seashore (N.C.)
Chattooga River

NORTH CAROLINA—See also—*cont.*
Forests and forestry—North Carolina
Great Smoky Mountains National Park (N.C. and Tenn.)
Jocassee Watershed (N.C.-S.C.)
Mount Mitchell (N.C.)
National forests—North Carolina
Pigeon River (N.C. and Tenn.)
Plantations—North Carolina
Poll tax—North Carolina
Transylvania County (N.C.)
Wake County (N.C.)

NORTH CAROLINA DANCE THEATER
Reviews:
Performances at the Joyce Theater, New York City.
D. Hering. *Dance Magazine* 63:93-5 F '89

NORTH CAROLINA STATE UNIVERSITY AT RALEIGH
Foul play by the book [allegations against basketball coach
J. Valvano] H. F. Waters. por *Newsweek* 114:62 Ag 14
'89
The ordeal of Jim Valvano [allegations against basketball
program] J. Feinstein. il por *Sports Illustrated* 70:34-6
Ja 30 '89

**NORTH CAROLINA STATE UNIVERSITY AT RALEIGH.
ARBORETUM**
Greening the South. D. Young. il pors *Southern Living*
24:125-6+ Je '89

NORTH CAROLINA ZOOLOGICAL PARK
Zoo carts with smarts. il *Southern Living* 24:32 Ap '89

NORTH DAKOTA
See also
Agriculture—North Dakota
Birds—North Dakota
Camps—North Dakota
Theodore Roosevelt National Park (N.D.)
Wetlands—North Dakota

NORTH FORK BANK & TRUST CO.
Better than good. M. Schifrin. il *Forbes* 143:10 Ja 23 '89

NORTH KOREA *See* Korea (North)

NORTH POLE
See also
Arctic exploration
Bittersweet dreams of glory [R. Peary's North Pole claim]
J. M. Diamond. il pors *Natural History* p28-30+ N '89
Peary made it to the Pole after all. *Newsweek* 114:71 D
25 '89
Peary on top. *Time* 134:73 D 25 '89
Peary's North Pole claim reexamined. E. Marshall. il por
Science 243:1131-2 Mr 3 '89
Study puts Admiral Peary at North Pole. il *Science* 246:1564
D 22 '89

NORTH SAILS GROUP, INC.
Sailsmanship [Hood Sailmakers vs. North Sails Group] D.
Churbuck. il por *Forbes* 144:50+ Jl 10 '89

NORTH-SOUTH RELATIONS *See* Developing countries—
Foreign relations

NORTH STAR *See* Polestar

NORTH STONINGTON (CONN.)
Hotels, motels, etc.
Extra Ordinary [B. and C. Clark's Randall's Ordinary] P.
Mandell. il pors map *Americana* 17:26-31+ Mr/Ap '89
The fire's always burning at Randall's Ordinary, a Revolution-
ary inn in Connecticut [proprietors B. and C. Clark] N.
Geeslin. il pors *People Weekly* 32:143-4 N 13 '89

NORTH WIND UNDERSEA INSTITUTE
Seals to the rescue. il *National Geographic World* 161:32-5
Ja '89

NORTH WOODS CLUB
One hundred years in the Adirondack wilderness. L. F.
Wilson. il *The Conservationist* 43:40-5 My/Je '89

NORTH YEMEN *See* Yemen Arab Republic

NORTHEAST RAT AND MOUSE CLUB
Northeast Rat and Mouse Club [founder E. Fucci] *The New
Yorker* 65:35-6 Ap 10 '89

NORTHEASTERN STATES
See also
Finance—Northeastern States
New England

**NORTHEASTERN UNIVERSITY. DEPT. OF THEATRE
AND DANCE**
Northeastern University. il *Theatre Crafts* 23:53+ N '89

**NORTHERN CALIFORNIA BOOKSELLERS ASSOCIA-
TION**
NCBA meets in San Francisco. L. See. *Publishers Weekly*
236:39 N 10 '89

NORTHERN DANCER (RACE HORSE)
The last of a breed [last son sired sold at Keeneland] W.
F. Reed. il *Sports Illustrated* 71:10 Jl 31 '89

NORTHERN ELEPHANT SEALS *See* Seals (Animals)

NORTHERN HEMISPHERE
Climate
Rough justice in the greenhouse. *Newsweek* 114:65 D 18
'89

NORTHERN IRELAND
See also
Aviation and state—Northern Ireland
Government and the press—Northern Ireland
Historic houses, sites, etc.—Northern Ireland
Investments, Canadian—Northern Ireland

Londonderry (Northern Ireland)
Police—Northern Ireland
Terrorism—Northern Ireland
Women—Northern Ireland
Industries
See also
Short Brothers Ltd.
Photographs and photography
A seared land. G. Peress. il *Life* 12:92-100 S '89
Politics and government
See also
Irish unification question
A 20th anniversary with nothing to celebrate. M. Skelton.
il *Christianity Today* 33:36-7 Mr 17 '89
Can Britain ever leave Northern Ireland? C. C. O'Brien.
il *World Press Review* 36:56 O '89
Daughters of Derry [Catholic women] N. McCafferty. il *Ms.*
18:72-7 S '89
The fighting Irish. P. J. O'Rourke. il *Rolling Stone* p99-100+
F 9 '89
Religious institutions and affairs
See also
Catholic Church—Northern Ireland
Catholics—Northern Ireland
Protestants—Northern Ireland
Social conditions
Ireland today: life in the big village. K. McQuaid. il map
Focus (New York, N.Y.: 1950) 39:1-4 Spr '89
Three moves for peace. V. A. Punzo. *Commonweal* 116:422-3
Ag 11 '89

NORTHERN LIGHTS *See* Auroras

NORTHERN PACIFIC RAILWAY
Jacob Schiff and the Northern Pacific corner [1901 battle
with J. P. Morgan for control of company] J. S. Gordon.
il por *American Heritage* 40:86-7 Jl/Ag '89

NORTHERN TELECOM LTD.
A giant cuts costs. P. Chisholm. il *Maclean's* 102:50+ S
18 '89
Is Paul Stern tough enough to toughen up Northern Telecom?
C. Hawkins. il por *Business Week* p84-5 Ag 14 '89
Shooting for the moon [role of chaos in business; address,
April 27, 1989] R. A. Ferchat. *Vital Speeches of the Day*
55:727-31 S 15 '89

NORTHERN TERRITORY (AUSTRALIA)
Slouching through Australia [camel trip] C. J. Hadley. il
The Saturday Evening Post 261:82-5+ Mr '89

NORTHERN TIMBER FRAMING INC.
Building to last. M. King. il por *Nation's Business* 77:17-18
N '89

NORTHROP CORP.
Aeronautics/propulsion [development of Stealth technology;
aerospace laureate] il *Aviation Week & Space Technology*
130:15 Ja 2 '89
Air Force will buy low-rate B-2s under fixed-price incentive
contracts. D. F. Bond. *Aviation Week & Space Technology*
131:26-7 Ag 7 '89
B-2 accounts for 51% of Northrop's revenues during year's
first quarter. *Aviation Week & Space Technology* 130:24
My 22 '89
B-2s built in unique manner. *Aviation Week & Space
Technology* 130:19 Ap 3 '89
Cheney and senior defense aides take firsthand look at B-2
production facilities. W. B. Scott. *Aviation Week & Space
Technology* 130:23 Je 5 '89
The good soldier Kresa steps up at Northrop. E. Schine.
il por *Business Week* p39 My 8 '89
Judge grants motions filed by Northrop [lawsuit involving
production of inertial measurement unit for MX missile]
Aviation Week & Space Technology 130:74 Ja 9 '89
New Northrop Band-3 jammers to be fitted on F-15E in
early 1990. *Aviation Week & Space Technology* 131:67
S 11 '89
Northrop, five employees indicted in fraud case. *Aviation
Week & Space Technology* 130:29 Ap 17 '89
Northrop is flying in a sky full of flak. E. Schine. il *Business
Week* p109-10 Ap 24 '89
Suit claims Northrop wrongfully took $20 billion for Stealth
bomber work. B. A. Smith. *Aviation Week & Space
Technology* 131:26-7 N 13 '89

NORTHSEA JAZZ FESTIVAL *See* Music festivals—Netherlands

NORTHSHIELD, SHAD
about
Sunday mourning. R. Powers. il *Gentlemen's Quarterly* 59:68+
Jl '89

**NORTHSTAR (LAKE TAHOE, CALIF. AND NEV.:
RESORT)** *See* Resorts—Lake Tahoe region (Calif. and
Nev.)

NORTHWEST AIRLINES, INC.
Congress would probe Pan Am-NWA merger's effect on
U.S. competition. J. Ott. *Aviation Week & Space Technology*
130:72-3 My 15 '89
A far-out merger scheme that could just fly [Pan Am-
Northwest deal] C. Power and A. Bernstein. il *Business
Week* p36-7 My 22 '89
A fight for the friendly skies: takeover artists go after Eastern
and Northwest. L. Reibstein. il *Newsweek* 113:50 Ap 10
'89

NORTHWEST AIRLINES, INC.—*cont.*

Foul flying subs [tainted submarine sandwiches served] il *FDA Consumer* 23:34-5 Jl/Ag '89

Front man [A. Checchi fronting for KLM in Northwest takeover] S. Flack. il *Forbes* 144:69 Jl 10 '89

Landing Northwest [A. Checchi] R. Grover and R. Mitchell. il por *Business Week* p24-5 Jl 3 '89

Northwest asks pilots to cooperate in thwarting hostile takeover. *Aviation Week & Space Technology* 130:106 My 1 '89

Northwest pilots warn that talks on new contract near breakdown. *Aviation Week & Space Technology* 131:99 Jl 24 '89

Northwest stockholders weigh options in face of various takeover offers. C. Fotos. map *Aviation Week & Space Technology* 130:103-4 My 22 '89

NWA rejects bids; new date set for proposals. *Aviation Week & Space Technology* 130:315 Je 12 '89

NWA seeks strategy to block Davis' $3.1-billion takeover attempt. *Aviation Week & Space Technology* 130:107 Ap 24 '89

The odd couple chasing Northwest Airlines [A. Checchi and G. L. Wilson] R. Grover. il pors *Business Week* p126 Ap 24 '89

Pan Am considers entering field of Northwest bidders. C. Fotos. *Aviation Week & Space Technology* 130:70-1 My 15 '89

Pan Am Corp., Davis among Northwest bidders. C. Fotos. il *Aviation Week & Space Technology* 130:108-9 Je 5 '89

Pan Am looks Northwest. C. Friday. il *Newsweek* 112:62 My 22 '89

Pilots accuse Northwest of mismanaging hubs. P. Proctor. *Aviation Week & Space Technology* 130:71 Ap 3 '89

Pilots union threatens to seek declaration of impasse in talks with Northwest Airlines. *Aviation Week & Space Technology* 131:97 Jl 17 '89

The power behind Pan Am's bid for Northwest [Airlie Group] C. Power and K. Kelly. il por *Business Week* p29 Je 12 '89

Skinner's limits on NWA buyout fail to dissuade drive for LBO controls. C. Fotos. *Aviation Week & Space Technology* 131:138-9 O 9 '89

A squeeze play at Northwest [M. Davis' bid] C. Power. il *Business Week* p30 My 1 '89

"This will be all-out war" [NWA rebuffs bid by M. Davis] J. Greenwald. il por *Time* 133:46 Ap 17 '89

Two carriers begin using 747-400s in nonstop service to Europe, Asia. M. Mecham. *Aviation Week & Space Technology* 130:316-17 Je 12 '89

U.S. must assess buyout bid's impact on safety at Northwest [KLM's role in Wings Holdings' bid under scrutiny] *Aviation Week & Space Technology* 130:92-3 Je 26 '89

Unions, Minnesota officials vow to fight any break-up of Northwest. *Aviation Week & Space Technology* 130:90 Ap 10 '89

What could stall a run on Northwest. C. Power and R. Mitchell. il *Business Week* p30 Ap 10 '89

Wings Holdings chief pledges to keep Northwest growing [A. A. Checchi] C. Fotos. *Aviation Week & Space Technology* 130:90-1 Je 26 '89

Wings Holdings' purchase of Northwest could become blueprint for future LBOs. *Aviation Week & Space Technology* 131:22 Ag 14 '89

NORTHWEST BALLET

A company without dancers, NorthWest Ballet keeps trying. J. Timmis. il *Dance Magazine* 63:12 Ap '89

NORTHWEST PASSAGE

Braving the Northwest Passage [via catamaran] J. MacInnis. il map *National Geographic* 175:584-601 My '89

NORTHWEST POWER PLANNING COUNCIL

The Columbia River basin [cover story] K. N. Lee. bibl f il map *Environment* 31:6-11+ Jl/Ag '89

Forecasting energy demand in the U.S. Northwest. il *The Futurist* 23:45-6 S/O '89

NORTHWEST TERRITORIES

See also
Back River (N.W.T.)
Geology—Northwest Territories
Pond Inlet (N.W.T.)
Yellowknife (N.W.T.)

Indians

See Indians of North America—Canada

Industries

See also
Gas industry—Canada

NORTHWESTERN STATES

See also
Pacific Northwest

Centennial celebrations, etc.

Birthday parties for the Northwest states. il *Sunset (Central West edition)* 182:275 My '89

Northwest state centennials. *American History Illustrated* 24:6 Mr '89

A Northwestern 100th. J. O'Dwyer. il *Americana* 17:54-9 Mr/Ap '89

History

See also
Oregon Trail

NORTHWESTERN UNIVERSITY (EVANSTON, ILL.)

Daphne Maxwell Reid still bitter over snub as beauty queen at Northwestern U. il pors *Jet* 77:25 N 13 '89

NORTHWESTERN UNIVERSITY PRESS

Northwestern UP looks to the trade. T. Unsworth. *Publishers Weekly* 236:31 O 13 '89

NORTON, ANN

about

Landscaping with sculpture. S. Guy. il *Horizon (Tuscaloosa, Ala.)* 32:29-30 Ja/F '89

NORTON, ARTHUR P.

about

Arthur P. Norton: star atlas maker. I. Ridpath. por *Sky and Telescope* 78:489 N '89

NORTON, AUGUSTUS R., AND WEISS, THOMAS GEORGE

Turning again to UN peacekeepers [cover story] il *The New Leader* 72:12-14 Mr 20 '89

NORTON, BOYD

It's a good thing McNeil's big bears get plenty to eat. il pors *Smithsonian* 20:56-60+ Ap '89

NORTON, CLARK

Taxation hesitation. il *Mother Jones* 14:42-3 Ap '89

NORTON, W. P.

Border crossing. il *The Progressive* 53:46 O '89

Just say moo. il *The Progressive* 53:26-9 N '89

NORTON (ANN) SCULPTURE GARDEN See Ann Norton Sculpture Garden

NORTON MOTORS LTD.

Norton at the Isle of Man. C. Fox. il *Cycle* 40:36-41 O '89

NORVAL, R. A. I., AND OTHERS

Pheromone-mediation of host-selection in bont ticks (Amblyomma hebraeum Koch). bibl f il *Science* 243:364-5 Ja 20 '89

NORVELL, LORA

Ski ya later! il *Women's Sports & Fitness* 11:40-1 Je '89

NORVILLE, DEBORAH

about

All about Deborah. E. Diamond. il pors *New York* 22:28+ O 23 '89

Exit Jane, amid turmoil. R. Zoglin. pors *Time* 134:81 O 23 '89

'Looksism' in TV news. J. Alter. il por *Newsweek* 114:72-3 N 6 '89

Newcomer Deborah Norville stirs the latest tempest in the Today show's coffee cup. J. Kaufman. il pors *People Weekly* 32:48-9 O 9 '89

TV's new golden girl. J. Hoffman. il pors *Gentlemen's Quarterly* 59:232-5+ N '89

Two was company, three a crowd [cover story] il pors *People Weekly* 32:114-16+ N 13 '89

NORWALK (CONN.)

Galleries and museums

See also
Maritime Center (Norwalk, Conn.)

NORWAY

See also
Americans—Norway
Christmas—Norway
Medical care—Norway
Sex education—Norway
Skiing—Norway

Defenses

See also
Guided missiles, Norwegian

Politics and government

Norway's radical daughter [Prime Minister G. H. Brundtland] N. R. Gibbs. il por *Time* 134:42-4 S 25 '89

NORWAY (SHIP)

S.S. Norway jazz cruise. J. McDonough. il *Down Beat* 56:48+ F '89

NORWICH, BILLY See Norwich, William

NORWICH, JOHN JULIUS, 1929-

Royal retreat on the Isle of Wight. il maps *Architectural Digest* 46:160-3 O '89

NORWICH, WILLIAM

Billy's people. il *New York* 22:42-6 Ap 3 '89

For some overbooked social whirlers, sending a stand-in is the next best thing to being there. il *Vogue* 179:286 Je '89

Inside Fergie's dream house. il pors *Redbook* 172:92-5 F '89

New Yorkers on New York. il por *House & Garden* 161:214-17 O '89

NORWOOD, JANET L.

The changing work force [excerpts from address, February 23, 1989] *Monthly Labor Review* 112:2 Mr '89

Statistics and public policy [excerpts from address, August 8, 1989] *Monthly Labor Review* 112:2 S '89

Taking stock [excerpts from address, April 20, 1989] *Monthly Labor Review* 112:2 My '89

NORWOOD, JANET L., AND KLEIN, DEBORAH PISETZ-NER
Developing statistics to meet society's needs. bibl f *Monthly Labor Review* 112:14-19 O '89
NOSE
See also
Smell

Surgery, Plastic
See Surgery, Plastic
NOSSAL, G. J. V. (GUSTAV JOSEPH VICTOR), 1931-
Immunologic tolerance: collaboration between antigen and lymphokines. bibl f il *Science* 245:147-53 Jl 14 '89
NOSSAL, GUSTAV JOSEPH VICTOR See Nossal, G. J. V. (Gustav Joseph Victor), 1931-
NOSSITER, BERNARD D.
The Fed's yo-yo. *The Nation* 249:76-7 Jl 17 '89
Loan sharks. *The Nation* 248:652-3 My 15 '89
NOSTALGIA
See also
Homesickness
Memories for sale [cover story] M. Barrier. il *Nation's Business* 77:18-21+ D '89
Old and in the way. G. Jaynes. il *Life* 12:14 Ag '89
Pass the Indian nuts [language of the recent past] W. Safire. il *The New York Times Magazine* p10+ F 12 '89
A world worth saving [cover story] E. Hoagland. il *Life* 12:50-4+ O '89
NOSTALGIA IN ADVERTISING
Themes like old times. B. Kanner. il *New York* 22:12+ Ja 30 '89
What's it all about, Ralphie? Ralph Lauren and the New Traditionalism. B. Edmondson. il por *Utne Reader* p21-2 Jl/Ag '89
NOSTALGIA IN PHOTOGRAPHY
Creating a nostalgic theme assembly. M. Hammarlund. il *Petersen's Photographic Magazine* 17:84-5 Ap '89
In the mood [work of P. Mach] B. Schwalberg. il *Popular Photography* 96:47-8 Mr '89
NOT IN MY BACKYARD SYNDROME See NIMBY syndrome
NOT OF THIS EARTH [film] See Motion picture reviews—Single works
NOTA BENE (WORD PROCESSOR PROGRAM) See Word processors and processing—Programming
NOTABLES See Black celebrities; Celebrities
NOTCH BABIES
The notchies march on. B. Rosenblatt. il *New Choices for the Best Years* 29:12 F '89
NOTE PAPER See Stationery
NOTEBOOK COMPUTERS See Computers
NOTHOSAURS See Reptiles, Fossil
NOTORANGELO, SUSAN
about
RAAM tough. C. Patterson. il por *Women's Sports & Fitness* 11:57-8 N/D '89
NOTT, JULIAN
about
Balloonist. *The New Yorker* 65:39-40 O 2 '89
NOTTEBOHM, FERNANDO
From bird song to neurogenesis. il *Scientific American* 260:74-9 F '89
LA NOUBA DES FEMMES DU MONT CHENOUA [film]
See Motion picture reviews—Single works
NOUCHI, FRANCK
(jt. auth) See Nau, Jean-Yves, and Nouchi, Franck
NOURSE, ALAN E.
Family doctor. See issues of Good Housekeeping
NOUWEN, HENRI J. M.
Bibliography
A feast of Nouwen. A. Boers. il por *Christianity Today* 33:38-40+ Je 16 '89
NOVA, AN ALBERTA CORPORATION
See also
Nova Corporation of Alberta
NOVA CORPORATION OF ALBERTA
Nova's sell-off. J. DeMont. por *Maclean's* 102:37 Jl 10 '89
Super Nova. A. A. Lappen. il *Forbes* 144:48+ Jl 10 '89
NOVA PHARMACEUTICAL CORP.
What a way to start a company! G. Bylinsky. il *Fortune* 119:141-2+ Je 19 '89
NOVA SCOTIA
See also
Abortion clinics—Nova Scotia
Education—Nova Scotia
Finance—Nova Scotia
Halifax (N.S.)
Halifax County (N.S.)
Oak Island (N.S.)
Public health—Nova Scotia
Public welfare—Nova Scotia
Sable Island (N.S.)
Sales tax—Nova Scotia
Industries
See also
Real estate business—Canada
Race relations
A smouldering race issue [blacks seek school reform] G. Allen. il *Maclean's* 102:14 F 27 '89

NOVÁK, JAN, 1953-
The typewriter made me do it. il por *The New York Times Book Review* 94:1+ Ap 2 '89
NOVAK, MICHAEL
Boredom, virtue, and democratic capitalism. *Commentary* 88:34-7 S '89
In Eastern Europe, little things count. *The Christian Century* 106:1164-5 D 13 '89
The larger context. See issues of Forbes beginning February 6, 1989
Liberals and Catholics: political economy in our time. *Current (Washington, D.C.)* 311:20-3 Mr/Ap '89
Structures of interest, structures of love: a response to Michael Novak [discussion of January 28, 1989 article, Structures of virtue, structures of sin: a theology of natural liberty] *America* 160:369-71 Ap 22 '89
Structures of virtue, structures of sin: a theology of natural liberty [address, May 5, 1988; cover story] *America* 160:54-60 Ja 28 '89
NOVAK, RALPH
As the boys of Zimmer dare to dream, a nostalgic editor returns to his field of futility. il por *People Weekly* 32:52-4 O 9 '89
NOVAK, ROBERT D.
Dining in Moscow. *National Review* 41:30-1 D 8 '89
The shifty Richard Gephardt [cover story] il *The American Spectator* 22:14-16 Ag '89
The unfinished Reagan agenda. il *The American Spectator* 22:14-15 Mr '89
(jt. auth) See Evans, Rowland, and Novak, Robert D.
NOVAK, VIVECA
Hazardous choice. *The Nation* 248:406-8 Mr 27 '89
(jt. auth) See Holland, Max, and Novak, Viveca
NOVAK, WILLIAM
(ed) See Reagan, Nancy, 1923-. My turn
(ed) See Reagan, Nancy, 1923-. My turn: the memoirs of Nancy Reagan
about
The celebs' golden mouthpiece. M. Smilgis. il por *Time* 134:82 N 27 '89
NOVAS See Stars, New
NOVELISTS, AMERICAN
See also
Abbey, Edward, 1927-1989
Ames, Jonathan
Auel, Jean M.
Auster, Paul, 1947-
Banks, Russell, 1940-
Barthelme, Donald
Bayer, William
Bellow, Saul
Blatty, William Peter
Bowles, Paul, 1910-
Braverman, Kate
Brown, Larry, 1951-
Burroughs, William S., 1914-
Caunitz, William J.
Clancy, Tom, 1947-
Cook, Robin, 1940-
Crane, Stephen, 1871-1900
Cunningham, Michael, 1952-
Dillard, Annie
Doctorow, E. L., 1931-
Dreiser, Theodore, 1871-1945
Dunn, Katherine
Dunne, Dominick
Eisenstadt, Jill
Fante, John, 1909-1983
Faulkner, William, 1897-1962
Ford, Richard, 1944-
Gifford, Barry, 1946-
Girzone, Joseph F.
Grafton, Sue
Gurganus, Allan
Harington, Donald
Harrison, Jim, 1937-
Heinlein, Robert A. (Robert Anson), 1907-1988
Helprin, Mark
Hemingway, Ernest, 1899-1961
Hillerman, Tony
Himes, Chester, 1909-1984
Humphrey, William
Irving, John, 1942-
James, Henry, 1843-1916
Janowitz, Tama
Jolley, Elizabeth, 1923-
Jones, James, 1921-1977
Kenan, Randall
Kennedy, William, 1928-
Kesey, Ken
King, Stephen, 1947-
Kingston, Maxine Hong
Kotzwinkle, William
Krantz, Judith
Lawhead, Steve, 1950-
Leimbach, Marti
Leonard, Elmore, 1925-
Maupin, Armistead

NOVELISTS, AMERICAN—See also—*cont.*
McCarthy, Mary, 1912-1989
McCloy, Kristin
McGuane, Thomas, 1939-
McInerney, Jay
McMurtry, Larry
Merritt, Abraham, 1882-1943
Michener, James A. (James Albert), 1907-
Minot, Susan
Mitchell, Margaret, 1900-1949
Morrison, Toni, 1931-
Naylor, Gloria
Parks, Gordon
Percy, Walker
Peretti, Frank E.
Piercy, Marge
Powers, J. F. (James Farl), 1917-
Price, Eugenia
Price, Richard, 1949-
Prose, Francine, 1947-
Rice, Anne, 1941-
Roth, Philip
Saul, John
Schaeffer, Susan Fromberg
Schwamm, Ellen
Schwartz, John Burnham
Spark, Muriel
Spillane, Mickey, 1918-
Steinbeck, John, 1902-1968
Stern, Richard G., 1928-
Styron, William, 1925-
Tarr, Herbert
Turow, Scott
Twain, Mark, 1835-1910
Tyler, Anne, 1941-
Updike, John
Walker, Alice, 1944-
Wharton, William
Wheeler, Charles, 1947-
Wideman, John Edgar
Wiggins, Marianne
    How the other half writes [best-selling authors] il *Esquire* 112:82-9 Jl '89
NOVELISTS, ARGENTINE
    See also
    Puig, Manuel
NOVELISTS, AUSTRALIAN
    See also
    Keneally, Thomas
    McCullough, Colleen, 1937-
NOVELISTS, CANADIAN
    See also
    Atwood, Margaret, 1939-
    Bissoondath, Neil, 1955-
    Davies, Robertson, 1913-
    Major, Kevin, 1949-
    Montgomery, L. M. (Lucy Maud), 1874-1942
    Moore, Brian, 1921-
    Quarrington, Paul
    Richards, David Adams, 1950-
    Richler, Mordecai, 1931-
NOVELISTS, CHINESE AMERICAN
    See also
    Tan, Amy
NOVELISTS, COLOMBIAN
    See also
    García Márquez, Gabriel, 1928-
NOVELISTS, CZECH
    See also
    Mucha, Jiří
NOVELISTS, CZECH AMERICAN
    The typewriter made me do it. J. Novák. il por *The New York Times Book Review* 94:1+ Ap 2 '89
NOVELISTS, DUTCH
    See also
    Haasse, Hella S., 1918-
    Hartog, Jan de, 1914-
NOVELISTS, EGYPTIAN
    See also
    Maḥfūẓ, Najīb, 1912-
NOVELISTS, ENGLISH
    See also
    Aldiss, Brian Wilson, 1925-
    Amis, Kingsley, 1922-
    Baldwin, William, fl. 1547
    Barnes, Julian
    Bragg, Melvyn, 1939-
    Brontë, Charlotte, 1816-1855
    Davis, Lindsay
    Dickens, Charles, 1812-1870
    Fleming, Ian, 1908-1964
    Greene, Graham, 1904-
    James, P. D.
    Le Carré, John, 1931-
    Lodge, David, 1935-
    Potter, Dennis
    Rendell, Ruth, 1930-
    Waugh, Evelyn, 1903-1966

Weldon, Fay
Woolf, Virginia, 1882-1941
NOVELISTS, FRENCH
    See also
    Flaubert, Gustave, 1821-1880
NOVELISTS, INDIAN (EAST INDIAN)
    See also
    Mukherjee, Bharati
    Rushdie, Salman
NOVELISTS, IRISH
    See also
    Joyce, James, 1882-1941
    O'Brien, Edna
NOVELISTS, ISRAELI
    See also
    Kaniuk, Yoram
    Yehoshua, Abraham B.
NOVELISTS, ITALIAN
    See also
    Eco, Umberto
    Ginzburg, Natalia
NOVELISTS, JAPANESE
    See also
    Endō, Shūsaku, 1923-
    Ishiguro, Kazuo, 1954-
NOVELISTS, PERUVIAN
    See also
    Vargas Llosa, Mario, 1936-
NOVELISTS, RUSSIAN
    See also
    Solzhenitsyn, Aleksandr, 1918-
NOVELISTS, SPANISH
    See also
    Cela, Camilo José, 1916-
NOVELISTS, WELSH
    See also
    Follett, Ken, 1949-
NOVELL INC.
    How to lose a lead [3Com Corp. let Novell gain lead in LANs] J. Pitta. il *Forbes* 144:126 Ag 7 '89
NOVELLO, ANTONIA
        about
    Surgeon General: abortion foe. *Newsweek* 114:84 O 30 '89
NOVELS *See* Fiction
NOVELS, COMPUTER *See* Computer novels
NOVELS, GRAPHIC *See* Graphic novels
NOVELTIES
        See also
    Orchids of Hawaii (Firm)
    Russ Berrie & Co., Inc.
NOVEMBER
    The November almanac. il *The Atlantic* 264:22 N '89
NOVICK, NELSON LEE
    The cold and the beautiful. il *Women's Sports & Fitness* 11:56 O '89
NOVIK, MORRIS
        about
    Novik and LaGuardia. *The New Yorker* 65:24-6 Ag 28 '89
NOVIKOFF, ALEX BENJAMIN, 1913-1987
        about
    Pride and perjury. D. M. Oshinsky. por *The New Leader* 72:14-17 S 4 '89
NOVIKOV, ALEKSEI
    'Why the West distrusted us'. *World Press Review* 36:28-30 Je '89
NOVOTNA, JARMILA, 1907-
        about
    The good life [cover story] J. W. Freeman. il pors *Opera News* 54:8-12 D 23 '89
NOVOTNY, MILOS V., 1942-
    Recent developments in analytical chromatography. bibl f il *Science* 246:51-7 O 6 '89
NOVROS, DAVID, 1941-
        about
    David Novros at Fred Hoffman. F. Colpitt. il *Art in America* 77:205 My '89
NOW *See* National Organization for Women
NOWLIN, LINDA
    Revisiting Bonnard: the nudes [poem] *The New Republic* 200:36 Ap 24 '89
NOWPORT, ELISABETH
    Cycle chic. il *American Health* 8:88+ My '89
NOYCE, GAYLORD B.
    Mandate for the mainline. il *The Christian Century* 106:1017-19 N 8 '89
NOYCE, PHILLIP
        about
    Dead calm [film] Reviews
        Newsweek 113:72 Ap 17 '89. D. Ansen
        People Weekly il 31:17+ Ap 17 '89. S. Haller
        Video il 13:79 N '89. J. Silberg
NOYCE, ROBERT, 1927-
    A unique approach against trade violators [address, May 24, 1989] *Vital Speeches of the Day* 55:671-2 Ag 15 '89
        about
    How the U.S. can compete globally [interview] il por *Fortune* 119:248 Je 5 '89

NOYCE, ROBERT, 1927—about—*cont.*

Ignored by the Nobels, engineering and technology are at last being honored by a significant new prize. R. M. Adams. il *Smithsonian* 20:12 D '89

Kilby and Noyce win Draper Prize for developing microchips. I. Goodwin. il *Physics Today* 42:52 N '89

The U.S. Business Hall of Fame. W. Guzzardi. il por *Fortune* 119:132-3 Mr 13 '89

LE NOZZE DI FIGARO [opera] *See* Mozart, Wolfgang Amadeus, 1756-1791

NOZZLES

See also

Airplane engines, Jet—Nozzles
Guided missiles—Nozzles
Space vehicles—Nozzles

NPCA *See* National Parks and Conservation Association

NPT (NON-PROLIFERATION TREATY) *See* Disarmament

NRA *See* National Rifle Association of America

NRBQ (MUSICAL GROUP)

NRBQ. B. Barol. *Newsweek* 114:66 O 16 '89
NRBQ. D. Ouellette. il *Down Beat* 56:42-4 Ap '89

NRC *See* U.S. Nuclear Regulatory Commission

NSC *See* United States. National Security Council

NSFNET

NSF opens high-speed computer network. E. Marshall. map *Science* 243:22-3 Ja 6 '89

NTSB *See* United States. National Transportation Safety Board

NU-WEST INDUSTRIES INC.

History repeats? T. Jaffe. il por *Forbes* 144:127 S 18 '89

NUCABLE RESOURCES CORPORATION

Cable closes in on the classifieds. J. Loftus. il por *Channels (New York, N.Y.: 1986)* 9:52-4 Mr '89

NUCAL DE MEXICO (FIRM)

Death, intrigue and avocados [Mexico accuses Nucal de Mexico of being part of Israeli scheme to control export market] M. A. Lerner. il *Newsweek* 114:37 Ag 14 '89

NUCCI, LEO

about

Overheard in the kitchen, baritone Leo Nucci raised a voice as big as the Met. R. Arias. il pors *People Weekly* 31:66-8 F 20 '89

NUCELL (FIRM)

Soup-can physics [P. M. Brown's nuclear battery] C. Poole. il *Forbes* 143:142 Mr 6 '89

NUCKOLLS, JOHN

about

New directors at Fermilab, Oak Ridge and Lawrence Livermore. W. Sweet. por *Physics Today* 42:63-5 Jl '89

NUCLEAR AIRCRAFT CARRIERS

See also

Dwight D. Eisenhower (Aircraft carrier)

NUCLEAR BATTERIES

Soup-can physics [P. M. Brown's nuclear battery] C. Poole. il *Forbes* 143:142 Mr 6 '89

NUCLEAR BOMBS *See* Atomic bombs; Hydrogen bombs

NUCLEAR ENERGY

See also

Anti-nuclear movement
Nuclear batteries
Nuclear fission
Nuclear fuels
Nuclear fusion
Nuclear reactors
Press and nuclear energy

Cold fusion: is it hot enough to make power? M. Crawford. il *Science* 244:423 Ap 28 '89

Mars? What are the alternatives? W. F. Buckley. *National Review* 41:54 S 1 '89

Awards

See also

Enrico Fermi Award

Economic aspects

See also

Nuclear industry

Environmental aspects

Nuclear energy redux [discussion of October 1988 article, Nuclear energy and the environment: time to think again] W. C. Clark. *Environment* 31:2-3+ Mr '89

International aspects

See also

International Atomic Energy Agency
United Nations. Atomic Energy Commission

Nuclear cooperation with EURATOM [letter to Congress, March 9, 1989] G. Bush. *Department of State Bulletin* 89:44 Je '89

Laws and regulations

See also

Radioactive waste disposal—Laws and regulations
U.S. Nuclear Regulatory Commission

Nuclear sneak attack [executive order on evacuation of civilian nuclear power plants] *The Progressive* 53:7 Ja '89

Argentina

Peronists seek "nuclear greatness". R. A. Kessler. il por *The Bulletin of the Atomic Scientists* 45:13-15 My '89

Brazil

Brazil's nuclear shakeup: military still in control. A. R. Britto de Castro and others. bibl f il *The Bulletin of the Atomic Scientists* 45:22-5 My '89

United States

See Nuclear energy

Western Europe

See also

Euratom

NUCLEAR EXCITED STATES *See* Energy levels (Quantum mechanics)

NUCLEAR EXPLOSIONS *See* Nuclear weapons—Testing

NUCLEAR EXPORTS *See* Nuclear industry—Export-import trade

NUCLEAR FACILITIES

See also

Hanford Nuclear Reservation (Wash.)
Nuclear power plants
Nuclear research laboratories
Nuclear weapons—Manufacture
Radioactive waste disposal

Accidents and explosions

Nuclear bloopers. C. O'Neil and S. Seidenstein. *Utne Reader* p49 Ja/F '89

Soviets admit 1957 nuclear mishap [explosion in tank containing radioactive waste, contaminating south Urals] D. Dickson. map *Science* 244:1435 Je 23 '89

Protests, demonstrations, etc.

See Anti-nuclear movement

Safety devices and measures

Cleaned-up weapons plants may mean fewer weapons. V. Cahan. *Business Week* p57 Ag 14 '89

The costs of cleaning up DOE. *Science News* 135:60 Ja 28 '89

Dangerous mind-set [sloppiness at nuclear weapons plants] *Time* 134:18 Jl 3 '89

Energy czar—and environmental activist? [J. D. Watkins] V. Cahan. il por *Business Week* p54 Jl 24 '89

Fixing the nation's nuclear-weapons plants. J. F. Ahearne. il *Technology Review* 92:24-9 Jl '89

A new scare at Rocky Flats. J. N. Baker. il *Newsweek* 113:60 Je 26 '89

Rocky Flats: a big mistake from day one. B. Abas. bibl f il *The Bulletin of the Atomic Scientists* 45:18-24 D '89

Trouble at Rocky Flats. M. Miller. il *Newsweek* 114:19-20 Ag 14 '89

Soviet Union

Kyshtym visit gives first look at Soviet plutonium production complex. W. Sweet. il map *Physics Today* 42:87-9 N '89

NUCLEAR FALLOUT *See* Radioactive pollution

NUCLEAR FISSION

The discovery of nuclear fission. E. Segrè. bibl f il por *Physics Today* 42:38-43 Jl '89

NUCLEAR FREEZE *See* Disarmament

NUCLEAR FUEL REPROCESSING *See* Reactor fuel reprocessing

NUCLEAR FUELS

See also

Reactor fuel reprocessing

Moon power [helium-3] M. J. Mackowski. il por *Ad Astra* 1:34-9 Jl/Ag '89

Disposal

See Radioactive waste disposal

NUCLEAR FUSION

See also

Cold fusion
Fusion reactors
Laser fusion
Magnetic fusion
Tokamaks

Another kind of fusion? [ion beam fusion; research by Robert J. Beuhler and others] A. Fisher. il *Popular Science* 235:16+ D '89

Big science's fusion race is still at a crawl. il *Business Week* p87 Ap 10 '89

Brookhaven chemists find new fusion method [accelerated ion clusters; work of Lewis Friedman and others] R. Pool. il *Science* 245:1448-9 S 29 '89

Budget squeeze causes fission in fusion labs. M. Crawford. il *Science* 244:138-9 Ap 14 '89

Colliding clusters hint at new fusion route [accelerated ion clusters; research by Robert J. Beuhler and others] I. Amato. *Science News* 136:196 S 23 '89

Divvying up a fusion-fund pie [congressional hearings] *Science News* 136:255 O 14 '89

Fission in the fusion camp. D. Freedman. il *Discover* 10:32-4+ D '89

Fusion redux: new path, warm reaction [accelerated ion clusters; research by Lewis Friedman and others] W. J. Cook. il *U.S. News & World Report* 107:62 O 2 '89

Heavy-ion fusion. J. Horgan. il *Scientific American* 261:30+ O '89

Hot fusion: getting warmer. *High Technology Business* 9:4 Jl/Ag '89

Hot fusion plans get icy reception [congressional hearings] M. Crawford. *Science* 246:207 O 13 '89

Plasma physics. bibl f *Physics Today* 42:S60-S63 Ja '89

NUCLEAR INDUSTRY

See also

Nuclear weapons—Manufacture
Reactor fuel reprocessing
U.S. Committee for Energy Awareness

NUCLEAR POWERED SPACE VEHICLES *See* Space vehicles—Power supply

NUCLEAR REACTIONS
See also
Electroweak interactions

NUCLEAR REACTORS
See also
Fusion reactors
Nuclear power plants
Reactor fuel reprocessing
Clash of the dogmas [tritium shortage] J. D. Isaacs. *The Bulletin of the Atomic Scientists* 45:4 Mr '89

Accidents and explosions
See also
Chernobyl nuclear disaster, 1986
Three Mile Island Nuclear Power Plant (Pa.)—Accident, 1979

Containment
Ka-boom! [impact resistance test at Sandia National Laboratories using an F-4 Phantom jet] J. Kluger. il *Discover* 10:44-5 D '89
Propelled jet [Sandia National Laboratories crash resistance tests of critical structures] A. Fisher. il *Popular Science* 235:14+ D '89

Design
Improved and safer nuclear power. J. J. Taylor. bibl f il *Science* 244:318-25 Ap 21 '89
Nuclear power, act II. W. J. Cook. il *U.S. News & World Report* 106:52-3 My 29 '89

Environmental aspects
Elementary, my dear Watkins. M. Hamilton. il *The Nation* 248:732-4 My 29 '89
Energy czar—and environmental activist? [J. D. Watkins] V. Cahan. il por *Business Week* p54 Jl 24 '89
Reactors redux. M. Philips. il *Sierra* 74:56-61 Mr/Ap '89
Stop Stello [controversial appointment of V. Stello to head national effort to clean up crumbling nuclear weapons facilities] H. Wasserman. *The Nation* 249:372-3 O 9 '89

Fuel
See Nuclear fuels

History
What to do with B Reactor? [old reactors at Hanford] K. D. Steele. il *The Bulletin of the Atomic Scientists* 45:21 O '89

Laws and regulations
See Nuclear energy—Laws and regulations

Maintenance and repair
Hitting the roof [corrupt management practices of E. I. Du Pont de Nemours & Co. at Savannah River nuclear complex] N. Roland. il *Common Cause Magazine* 15:8-9 Jl/Ag '89

Manufacture
See Nuclear industry

Safety devices and measures
See also
Nuclear reactors—Containment
On the nuclear energy front. W. F. Buckley. *National Review* 41:63 F 24 '89
Shortage could force U.S. to curtail tritium sales [consequence of shutdown of Savannah River reactors] *Aviation Week & Space Technology* 130:25 F 27 '89
The tritium follies [debate over restarting Savannah River reactors] D. Albright and J. Beard. bibl f il *The Bulletin of the Atomic Scientists* 45:42-5 N '89
Watkins's decision to restart HFIR heralds new era for DOE reactors [High Flux Isotope Reactor at Oak Ridge National Laboratory] I. Goodwin. il *Physics Today* 42:49-50 My '89

NUCLEAR REGULATORY COMMISSION (U.S.) *See* U.S. Nuclear Regulatory Commission

NUCLEAR RESEARCH

Federal aid
Divvying up a fusion-fund pie [congressional hearings] *Science News* 136:255 O 14 '89
Hot fusion plans get icy reception [congressional hearings] M. Crawford. *Science* 246:207 O 13 '89
Plea to Bromley: save our neutrons. R. Pool. *Science* 246:1553 D 22 '89
Utah looks to Congress for cold fusion cash. M. Crawford. il *Science* 244:522-3 My 5 '89

International aspects
Michigan team to join in first experiment at Soviet accelerator [UNK accelerator] W. Sweet. *Physics Today* 42 pt1:58 Ag '89

Canada
NSAC delays clear decision on Canada's kaon factory. I. Goodwin. *Physics Today* 42:44 Je '89
Subcommittee encourages U.S. to join Canadian kaon factory [TRIUMF cyclotron] B. M. Schwarzschild. il *Physics Today* 42:17-19 My '89

Great Britain
Britain will remain in CERN; management reforms adopted. *Physics Today* 42:65 Ja '89

Japan
Japan and the SSC: Congress raises a flag. M. Crawford. il *Science* 246:577 N 3 '89

Soviet Union
Michigan team to join in first experiment at Soviet accelerator [UNK accelerator] W. Sweet. *Physics Today* 42 pt1:58 Ag '89

Western Europe
See also
Euratom
European Organization for Nuclear Research

NUCLEAR RESEARCH LABORATORIES
See also
Argonne National Laboratory
Fermi National Accelerator Laboratory
Idaho National Engineering Laboratory
Lawrence Livermore National Laboratory
Oak Ridge National Laboratory
Stanford Linear Accelerator Center
At peace with the bomb [nuclear labs and the arms race] H. E. DeWitt. il *The Progressive* 53:26-7 S '89
New directors at Fermilab, Oak Ridge and Lawrence Livermore. W. Sweet. pors *Physics Today* 42:63-5 Jl '89
Weapons labs need new thinking. G. T. Seaborg. *The Bulletin of the Atomic Scientists* 45:10-12 Jl/Ag '89

NUCLEAR SCIENCE ADVISORY COMMITTEE (U.S.) *See* United States. Dept. of Energy. Nuclear Science Advisory Committee

NUCLEAR SHIPS

Accidents and explosions
Nuclear disasters at sea, then and now. W. M. Arkin and J. Handler. bibl f il *The Bulletin of the Atomic Scientists* 45:20-4 Jl/Ag '89
Trouble aboard Red October [Soviet accidents] G. Schoenfeld. il *The Bulletin of the Atomic Scientists* 45:13-15 Je '89

Soviet Union
Trouble aboard Red October [accidents] G. Schoenfeld. il *The Bulletin of the Atomic Scientists* 45:13-15 Je '89

NUCLEAR SPIN
See also
Spin glasses
Proton puzzle puts physicists in a whirl. I. Peterson. *Science News* 135:215 Ap 8 '89

NUCLEAR SUBMARINES
The Navy's 21st-century submarine [Seawolf] R. Kaylor. il *U.S. News & World Report* 106:29-30+ Ap 24 '89

Accidents and explosions
Nuclear disasters at sea, then and now. W. M. Arkin and J. Handler. bibl f il *The Bulletin of the Atomic Scientists* 45:20-4 Jl/Ag '89

Costs
Congress presses treaty objectives on Trident submarine program. D. F. Bond. *Aviation Week & Space Technology* 131:25-6 Ag 21 '89

NUCLEAR SUBMARINES, CANADIAN
An outdated and overpriced policy. A. Fotheringham. il *Maclean's* 102:60 F 6 '89

NUCLEAR SUBMARINES, RUSSIAN
Quiet Soviet subs prompt concern. C. Norman. il *Science* 243:1653-4 Mr 31 '89
Soviets encourage joint research of Arctic areas. R. G. O'Lone. *Aviation Week & Space Technology* 130:83 Ja 30 '89

Accidents and explosions
Danger! Soviet subs at work. D. Benjamin. il *Time* 134:35 Jl 10 '89

Fires and fire prevention
Disaster strikes a Soviet sub [Mike-class sub sinks off the coast of Norway] D. Benjamin. il map *Time* 133:38 Ap 17 '89
Trouble aboard Red October. G. Schoenfeld. il *The Bulletin of the Atomic Scientists* 45:13-15 Je '89
An undersea prize for the taking [Soviet sub sinks in Norwegian Sea] L. Martz. il map *Newsweek* 113:33 Ap 17 '89

NUCLEAR TEST BAN *See* Nuclear weapons—Testing—Suspension

NUCLEAR WARFARE
See also
Anti-nuclear movement
Atomic bomb shelters
Balance of Power (Video game)
Nuclear winter
Space warfare
The Cuban missiles [discussion of March 1989 article, Nuclear revisionism] P. Glynn. *Commentary* 88:9-12 Ag '89
Do nuclear weapons matter? [views of M. Bundy] S. Hoffmann. bibl f il *The New York Review of Books* 36:28-31 F 2 '89
'Do nuclear weapons matter?': an exchange [discussion of February 2, 1989 article] S. Hoffmann. il *The New York Review of Books* 36:57-8 Ap 27 '89
Lobbing one into the Kremlin [U.S. secret war plan] F. Tonello. *The Nation* 249:445-6 O 23 '89
Notes and comment. *The New Yorker* 65:33-4 Mr 20 '89
Nuclear revisionism [views of M. Bundy] P. Glynn. *Commentary* 87:42-7 Mr '89
U.S. missiles on hair trigger? G. E. Marsh. *The Bulletin of the Atomic Scientists* 45:3 My '89
War games [C. J. Johnson sues Defense Dept. over computerized control of nuclear weapons] S. Ditlea. il *Omni (New York, N.Y.)* 11:32+ Mr '89

NUCLEAR WEAPONS—Manufacture—*cont.*

Stop Stello [controversial appointment of V. Stello to head national effort to clean up crumbling nuclear weapons facilities] H. Wasserman. *The Nation* 249:372-3 O 9 '89

The tritium follies [debate over restarting Savannah River reactors] D. Albright and J. Beard. bibl f il *The Bulletin of the Atomic Scientists* 45:42-5 N '89

Tritium puzzle [shipment lost between U.S. and England] P. Elmer-Dewitt. il map *Time* 134:75 N 13 '89

Trouble at Rocky Flats. M. Miller. il *Newsweek* 114:19-20 Ag 14 '89

Uncle Sam's toxic folly. M. Satchell. il *U.S. News & World Report* 106:20-2 Mr 27 '89

Uranium, in moderation [National Lead of Ohio defends radioactive leakage at Fernald plant] *Harper's* 278:18+ Ja '89

Workers welfare [Fernald, Ohio nuclear facility; address, March 22, 1989] R. F. Celeste. *Vital Speeches of the Day* 55:490-2 Je 1 '89

Moral and religious aspects

Another way to peace [French Catholics] C. Guicherd. il *Commonweal* 116:704-6 D 15 '89

Physiological effects

See Radiation—Physiological effects

Protests, demonstrations, etc.

See Anti-nuclear movement

Public opinion

Arms race as sitcom plot [decline of nuclear awareness among college students] P. S. Boyer. il *The Bulletin of the Atomic Scientists* 45:6-8 Je '89

Phantom public haunts nuclear age. J. Rosen. bibl f il *The Bulletin of the Atomic Scientists* 45:16-19 Je '89

Security measures

Navy says no PALs for us [permissive action link] P. D. Zimmerman. bibl f il *The Bulletin of the Atomic Scientists* 45:36-41 N '89

Testing

Earth shaking [Nevada Test Site] B. Weber. il *The New York Times Magazine* p98 Ap 23 '89

Fallout from Pacific tests reaches Congress [Rongelap wants new environmental studies] E. Marshall. map *Science* 245:123-4 Jl 14 '89

The hidden files [1946 accident at Los Alamos Lab; cover story] C. T. Honicker. il *The New York Times Magazine* p38-41+ N 19 '89

Known Chinese nuclear tests, 1964-1988 [table] il *The Bulletin of the Atomic Scientists* 45:48 O '89

Known nuclear tests worldwide, 1945 to December 31, 1988. il *The Bulletin of the Atomic Scientists* 45:48 Ap '89

'No one lives on Rongelap'. D. Goertzen. *The Progressive* 53:18 N '89

Plutonium in paradise [French testing on Mururoa Atoll] A. C. Revkin. il *Discover* 10:38-42 My '89

Testing ground [Nevada Test Site] J. Hanrahan. il *Common Cause Magazine* 15:13-19+ Ja/F '89

Detection

Nevada Test Site's dirty little secrets. R. R. Geary. il *The Bulletin of the Atomic Scientists* 45:35-6+ Ap '89

Nuclear testing talks conclude round three [White House statement, December 15, 1988] *Department of State Bulletin* 89:24 F '89

Nuclear testing talks open round 4 [White House statement, June 26, 1989] *Department of State Bulletin* 89:77 S '89

Public always the last to know [Energy Dept. fighting to avoid giving data on underground nuclear tests to arms control groups] W. J. Lanouette. il *The Bulletin of the Atomic Scientists* 45:11-12 O '89

U.S., Soviets share seismic posts [joint network to collect earthquake and bomb test data] R. J. Smith. il map *Science* 245:807-8 Ag 25 '89

Women at work: Holly Eissler [explosion seismologist with Soviet-American joint effort to monitor compliance with Threshold Test Ban Treaty] L. Dawson-Medina. il pors *Ms.* 18:34-6 O '89

Suspension

How to kill arms control [INF and test ban talks] Sir S. Zuckerman. bibl f il *The New York Review of Books* 36:35-9 O 12 '89

Non-nuclear states move to end testing. W. Epstein and G. T. Seaborg. il *The Bulletin of the Atomic Scientists* 45:36-7 Je '89

Test-ban technical talks of 1958. W. Sweet. bibl f il *Physics Today* 42:43 N '89

Weapons labs need new thinking. G. T. Seaborg. *The Bulletin of the Atomic Scientists* 45:10-12 Jl/Ag '89

Will test ban conference self-destruct? K. P. Clements. bibl f il *The Bulletin of the Atomic Scientists* 45:16-18 Jl/Ag '89

Women at work: Holly Eissler [explosion seismologist with Soviet-American joint effort to monitor compliance with Threshold Test Ban Treaty] L. Dawson-Medina. il pors *Ms.* 18:34-6 O '89

NUCLEAR WEAPONS AND DISARMAMENT *See* Disarmament

NUCLEAR WINTER

Apocalypse again. P. Shaw. *Commentary* 87:50-2 Ap '89

New models confirm nuclear winter. A. Robock. bibl f il *The Bulletin of the Atomic Scientists* 45:32+ S '89

Up in smoke [nuclear winter modeling based on shape of soot particles; work of Jenny Nelson] S. Vogel. il *Discover* 10:26 N '89

NUCLEASES

See also

Ribonucleases

Second cytotoxic pathway of diphtheria toxin suggested by nuclease activity. M. P. Chang and others. bibl f il *Science* 246:1165-8 D 1 '89

NUCLEIC ACIDS

See also

DNA

Nucleotides

RNA

Scanning tunneling microscopy of nucleic acids. G. Lee and others. bibl f il *Science* 244:475-7 Ap 28 '89

Synthesis

Molecular monkeywrench [blocking gene expression] T. Beardsley. *Scientific American* 260:34-5 Je '89

NUCLEOPROTEINS

See also

Cyclin

Interferon

Ribosomes

The RNA processing enzyme RNase MRP is identical to the Th RNP and related to RNase P [autoimmune disease study] H. A. Gold and others. bibl f il *Science* 245:1377-80 S 22 '89

Specific recognition of cruciform DNA by nuclear protein HMG1. M. E. Bianchi and others. bibl f il *Science* 243:1056-9 F 24 '89

NUCLEOSIDES

See also

Thymidine

Prevention of translational frameshifting by the modified nucleoside 1-methylguanosine. G. R. Björk and others. bibl f il *Science* 244:986-9 My 26 '89

NUCLEOSYNTHESIS

The ashes of Supernova 1987A. il *Sky and Telescope* 78:344 O '89

Creating superheavy elements. P. Armbruster and G. Münzenberg. bibl il *Scientific American* 260:66-72 My '89

Pride and prejudice [cosmic lithium abundance and open vs. closed universe; research by Lawrence M. Krauss] T. Rothman. *Scientific American* 261:16-17 Ag '89

NUCLEOTIDE SEQUENCES *See* Genetic code

NUCLEOTIDES

See also

Adenosine monophosphate

Adenosine triphosphate

Guanosine monophosphate

Guanosine triphosphate

Inhibition of DNA binding proteins by oligonucleotide-directed triple helix formation. L. J. Maher, III and others. bibl f il *Science* 245:725-30 Ag 18 '89

Nucleotides in yeast tRNA^{Phe} required for the specific recognition by its cognate synthetase. J. R. Sampson and others. bibl f il *Science* 243:1363-6 Mr 10 '89

Recognition of thymine·adenine base pairs by guanine in a pyrimidine triple helix motif. L. C. Griffin and P. B. Dervan. bibl f il *Science* 245:967-71 S 1 '89

Template-directed oligomerization catalyzed by a polynucleotide analog [polycytidylic acid] J. Visscher and others. bibl f il *Science* 244:329-31 Ap 21 '89

NUCOR CORP.

Nucor's boldest gamble [new flat-roll mill] R. Simon. il *Forbes* 143:122+ Ap 3 '89

NUCOR-YAMATO STEEL COMPANY

Blytheville's bounty [Japanese-U.S. joint steel mill in Arkansas] il *Time* 133:52 Je 5 '89

NUDE IN ART

A conditional paradise [W. Beckman's double portraits of himself and his wife] C. Belz. il pors *Art in America* 77:136-41 Ja '89

Exhibitions

John DeAndrea at Carlo Lamagna. K. Johnson. *Art in America* 77:203 S '89

The naked and the damned [nude art show in Beijing] S. Staggs. il *Art News* 88:24+ Ap '89

NUDE PHOTOGRAPHY *See* Photography of the nude

NUDIBRANCHS

Even for ethereal phantasms, it's a dog-eat-dog world. F. Bavendam. bibl (p135) il *Smithsonian* 20:94-101 Ag '89

Photographs and photography

Death, where is thy sting? [nudibranch vs. porpita] K. Atkinson. il *Natural History* p80-1 Ag '89

NUDING, GERTRUDE PRESCOTT

Portraits for the nation [cover story] il *History Today* 39:30-6 Je '89

NUDITY

See also

Topless nightclubs, bars, etc.

Nudity at home. L. G. Katz. il *Parents* 64:208 My '89

NUDITY IN MOTION PICTURES

The good parts [excerpt from The bare facts video guide 1989] C. Hosoda. *Harper's* 279:32+ D '89

NUGENT, MADELINE PECORA
Apologizing to Anne Hutchinson. *The Christian Century* 106:304-5 Mr 22-29 '89
NUGENT, TED
Call me the hunter. *Harper's* 278:20 Mr '89
NUMBER 10 DOWNING STREET (LONDON, ENGLAND)
Maggie. L. Nickson. il pors *Life* 12:24-8+ O '89
NUMBER THEORY
See also
    Fermat's theorem
    Riemann hypothesis
    Sphere packing
NUMBERS
See also
    Pi
    Sports uniforms—Numbers
Rajan Mahadevan is a memorable master of presto digit-tation [ability to memorize numbers] il por *People Weekly* 32:121 N 6 '89
NUMBERS, PRIME
Computing a prime champion. *Science News* 136:191 S 16 '89
Math team vaults over prime record [work of scientists at Amdahl Corporation] B. A. Cipra. *Science* 245:815 Ag 25 '89
NUMBERS, RANDOM
See also
    Random number generators
NUMBERS, REAL
Computing over the reals. B. A. Cipra. *Science* 243:1142 Mr 3 '89
NUMISMATICS
See also
    Coins as an investment
    Seals (Numismatics)
Numismatics. E. Rochette. See issues of Antiques & Collecting Hobbies beginning March 1985 through July 1989
NUMMI *See* New United Motor Mfg., Inc.
NUNN, MICHAEL
about
The boxer the champs won't fight. J. Stravinsky. il pors *The New York Times Magazine* p32-4+ Ag 13 '89
Middleweight champ Nunn jailed after family feud. il por *Jet* 77:51 O 23 '89
Nunn better. P. Putnam. il pors *Sports Illustrated* 70:40-2+ My 22 '89
Then there was Nunn. J. D. Miller. il pors *Sport (New York, N.Y.)* 80:54-7 S '89
This time Nunn chose not to run. P. Putnam. il pors *Sports Illustrated* 70:80 Ap 3 '89
NUNN, SAM
Challenges to NATO in the 1990s [address, September 4, 1989] *Vital Speeches of the Day* 56:135-40 D 15 '89
about
Born to lead. T. Noah. por *The Washington Monthly* 21:10-14+ D '89
The gap between will and wallet. W. Shapiro. il *Time* 133:32 F 6 '89
Is Sam Nunn Secretary of Defense? G. Borger. il por *U.S. News & World Report* 106:24 F 20 '89
Nunn's SDI two-step. J. D. Isaacs. il por *The Bulletin of the Atomic Scientists* 45:5-6 D '89
Smart, dull and very powerful. M. Kramer. il por *Time* 133:28-30 Mr 13 '89
NUNNERIES *See* Convents
NUNS
See also
    Buddhist nuns
    Carmelites
    Convents
    Society of St. Ursula
        Economic conditions
The little-horse ranch in Texas: miniature thoroughbreds mean big bucks for the nuns of St. Clare. H. Phillips. il *Travel Holiday* 172:106 Jl '89
Of many things [national collection for retirement needs of American religious] G. W. Hunt. *America* 160:258 Mr 25 '89
        History
The "new nuns" of yesteryear. M. S. Thompson. il *USA Today (Periodical)* 117:84-7 Mr '89
        Titles
God's children should be on a first-name basis. R. Tillemans. *U.S. Catholic* 54:37 Ag '89
NUNS AS FARMERS
Agriculture's hell-raising nun [Sister Thomas More Bertels] J. Midgett. il por *Successful Farming* 87:33 F '89
NUNS AS TEACHERS
Teaching orders and the efficacy of school. P. Ellis. *America* 161:262-5 O 21 '89
NUR EL HUSSEIN, QUEEN, CONSORT OF HUSSEIN, KING OF JORDAN
about
In search of peace [interview] J. Howse. il por *Maclean's* 102:48 O 30 '89
NURSE CORPS (ARMY) *See* United States. Army Nurse Corps

NURSEMAIDS
Finding live-in help for your child that is loving, loyal and also legal. R. J. Klein. il *Money* 18:155-6 S '89
He works. She works. What about the kids? [au pairs and nannies] J. Zweig. il *Forbes* 143:317-18 Ja 9 '89
NURSERIES (HORTICULTURE)
See also
    DewKist Plants, Inc.
    Woodlanders, Inc.
Let's go rhododendron crawling [Western States] il *Sunset (Central West edition)* 182:222-3 Ap '89
Where your new rose probably started out [Wasco, Calif.] il *Sunset (Central West edition)* 182:184 F '89
        Ethical aspects
Gentleman scamster [G. Bissell's fraudulent DewKist Plants] R. L. Stern. il por *Forbes* 143:104+ F 20 '89
NURSERY SCHOOLS
See also
    Day care
The little red chair. L. Franks. il *The New York Times Magazine* p28+ Mr 12 '89
Nursery school admissions. F. Roberts. il *Parents* 64:53-4 F '89
NURSES AND NURSING
See also
    AIDS (Disease) and nurses
    Black nurses and nursing
    Collective bargaining—Nurses
    Progressive Nursing Services
    Strikes—Nurses
Looking for a greater voice [Canada] B. Wickens. il *Maclean's* 102:36-7 F 13 '89
Mother-daughter nurses. L. W. Strick. il *Good Housekeeping* 209:65-6+ O '89
The nurses [excerpt from Just a nurse] J. M. Kraegel and M. Kachoyeanos. il *Ladies' Home Journal* 106:62+ Je '89
Nurses and the community [Western Pacific region] K.-S. Lee. il *World Health* p4 N '89
Nursing gets a shot in the arm [case management nurse C. Colburn at New England Medical] D. E. Haupt. il pors *Life* 12:42-5+ O '89
To be or not to be . . . a registered nurse. S. Tise. il *Occupational Outlook Quarterly* 32:8-17 Wint '88
Wartime nurses [World War II] E. E. Rosenbaum. il *New Choices for the Best Years* 29:24+ Jl '89
Weep and you weep alone [nurses unsympathetic to depressed patients; study by Timothy Elliott and Robert Umlaut] H. Hall. *Psychology Today* 23:18 Je '89
        Crime
Nelles's legal gain [Canadian Supreme Court rules in favor of nurse S. Nelles over baby murder mystery at Sick Children's Hospital] B. Wickens. il por *Maclean's* 102:42 Ag 28 '89
        History
Clara Barton: founder of the American Red Cross. C. Schurr. il pors *American History Illustrated* 24:50-8+ N/D '89
Ministering angels [Victorian nursing] A. Summers. bibl il *History Today* 39:31-7 F '89
        Public opinion
Who's to blame for poor image? [survey by Rose and Michael Porter] *USA Today (Periodical)* 118:10-11 O '89
        Recruiting
Seeking an Rx for nurses. A. Miller. il *Newsweek* 114:32-3 Jl 10 '89
        Salaries, pensions, etc.
A nurse's battle with burnout [G. Douglas] S. Seixas. il pors *Money* 18:104-6+ S '89
R.N.s get pay fix: nurses lead way for pay equity in state jobs [Illinois] C. Kleiman. *Ms.* 17:73-4 My '89
        Supply and demand
Code blue [nursing shortage; case of Evanston Hospital] L. Kleinmann. il *Health (New York, N.Y.)* 21:68-71+ F '89
The RCT proposal and the nursing shortage [registered care technologists; address, January 5, 1989] J. H. Sammons. *Vital Speeches of the Day* 55:373-5 Ap 1 '89
Where have all the nurses gone? J. G. Hubbell. il *Reader's Digest* 134:71-6 Je '89
NURSING HOME PATIENT ABUSE
What triggers patient abuse? [research by Karl Pillemer and David Moore] il *USA Today (Periodical)* 117:6 Ap '89
NURSING HOME PATIENT REPRESENTATIVES
Ombudsmen train young doctors [nursing home ombudsmen and Medical College of Ohio program] il *Aging* no359:24-5 '89
NURSING HOME PATIENTS
The perfect Christmas card. J. Elliott. il *The New York Times Magazine* p10+ D 24 '89
NURSING HOMES
See also
    Insurance, Nursing home care
    Manor Care, Inc.
    Motion Picture and Television Country House and Hospital (Woodland Hills, Calif.)
My mother could no longer care for herself. il *Good Housekeeping* 209:40+ Jl '89

NURSING HOMES—*cont.*

Costs

Do only the suckers pay? [Medicaid fraud perpetrated by elderly seeking shelter from nursing home costs] J. B. Quinn. il *Newsweek* 114:52 D 18 '89

Ethical aspects

Is grandma drowsy, or is she drugged? S. Findlay. il *U.S. News & World Report* 106:68 Je 12 '89

NURSS, SALLY

Rough-and-tumble il *Parents* 64:243-4+ N '89

NUSANTARA (NEW YORK, N.Y.: RESTAURANT) *See* New York (N.Y.)—Restaurants, nightclubs, bars, etc.

NUSSAC, SYLVIE DE

The evolution of Pina Bausch [interview] il por *World Press Review* 36:91 O '89

NUSSBAUM, HEDDA, 1942-

Hedda speaks out. por *Ms.* 17:12 My '89

about

Denying his guilt, Joel Steinberg tells how he cared for the child he killed and the lover he beat. K. Gross. il pors *People Weekly* 31:71-2+ Mr 13 '89

Hearing and healing Hedda Nussbaum. L. L. McCloskey. *The Christian Century* 106:178-9 F 15 '89

The Hedda conundrum [special section; with introd. by Anne Summers] il pors *Ms.* 17:54-67 Ap '89

Hedda's secret: what no one understands about abused women [with introduction by Jennifer Farbar] S. A. Feeney. por *Mademoiselle* 95:242-5+ Mr '89

A love betrayed, a brief life lost; ed. by Bonnie Johnson. N. Weiss. il pors *People Weekly* 31:82-4+ F 13 '89

A question of responsibility. R. Lacayo. il pors *Time* 133:68 F 13 '89

The Steinberg file: what the jury didn't hear. E. Wulfhorst and B. Goldberg. il pors *New York* 22:42-6 Ap 17 '89

The Steinberg trial: scenes from a tragedy. P. Volk. il pors *The New York Times Magazine* p22-5 Ja 15 '89

An unnerving tale of domestic abuse. F. Bruning. il *Maclean's* 102:9 F 27 '89

NUSSBAUM, MARTHA CRAVEN, 1947-

Recoiling from reason. bibl f il *The New York Review of Books* 36:36-41 D 7 '89

NUT INDUSTRY

China

Shaking gold from China's treetops [harvesting pine nuts in Manchuria] T. B. Allen. il *International Wildlife* 19:34-6 Jl/Ag '89

THE NUTCRACKER [ballet] See Ballet reviews—Single works

NUTRASWEET *See* Sugar substitutes

NUTRI/SYSTEM, INC.

Living off the fat of the land. M. Schifrin. il por *Forbes* 144:186-7+ N 13 '89

NUTRIENT LABELING OF FOOD *See* Food—Labeling

NUTRITION

See also

Aged—Nutrition
Aging—Nutritional aspects
Antinutrients
Arthritis—Nutritional aspects
Athletes—Nutrition
Black executives—Nutrition
Black women—Nutrition
Blacks—Nutrition
Boron in the body
Breakfasts
Calcium in the body
Cancer—Nutritional aspects
Carbohydrates
Cataracts (Eye defect)—Nutritional aspects
Celebrities—Nutrition
Celiac disease—Nutritional aspects
Children—Nutrition
College students—Nutrition
Cyclists—Nutrition
Dancers—Nutrition
Diabetes—Nutritional aspects
Diet
Dietary supplements
Digestion
Executives—Nutrition
Fashion designers—Nutrition
Fiber in diet
Gallstones—Nutritional aspects
Heart—Diseases—Nutritional aspects
Hispanic Americans—Nutrition
Hypertension—Nutritional aspects
Infants—Nutrition
Infants, Premature—Nutrition
Iron in the body
Magnesium in the body
Malnutrition
Minerals in the body
Plants—Nutrition
Pregnancy—Nutritional aspects
Proteins
Reproduction—Nutritional aspects
Runners—Nutrition
Skiers—Nutrition
Snacks

Television performers—Nutrition
Truck drivers—Nutrition
Tube feeding
Vitamins
Women—Nutrition
Women athletes—Nutrition
Women executives—Nutrition
Youth—Nutrition
Zinc in the body

100 best diet and healing foods. S. Lally. il *Prevention (Emmaus, Pa.)* 41:42-4+ S '89

Appreciating individual differences. B. T. Hunter. il *Consumers' Research Magazine* 72:8-9 D '89

A balancing act. B. T. Hunter. il *Consumers' Research Magazine* 72:8-9 N '89

Diet and your health [report by the National Research Council] il *Consumers' Research Magazine* 72:31-5 Jl '89

Do-it-yourself diet analysis. J. S. Stern and L. Applegate. *Prevention (Emmaus, Pa.)* 41:33-9+ Jl '89

Eat well! Feel great! [lifestyle of the Womacks] B. Goldman. il *Better Homes and Gardens* 67:105-13+ Mr '89

Fast food fare and nutrition. C. Roberts. il *Consumers' Research Magazine* 72:30-3 D '89

First word [trend towards healthier diet] P. Prudhomme. por *Omni (New York, N.Y.)* 12:6 N '89

Food & health. See issues of Organic Gardening beginning April 1988

Food and your health [special section] A. M. Fletcher. il *McCall's* 117:89+ O '89

Food for thought. B. T. Hunter. See issues of Consumers' Research Magazine

Food for thought [quiz] *Women's Sports & Fitness* 11:16 S '89

Good food, good health: 10 things you can do right now for a healthier you. B. Goldman. il *Better Homes and Gardens* 67:36+ Mr '89

The latest word on what to eat [report by the National Research Council] A. Toufexis. il *Time* 133:51+ Mr 13 '89

Making health a family affair. J. Barone. il *Working Woman* 14:179-80+ N '89

NAS weighs in with 7-lb diet guide [work of the National Research Council] B. J. Culliton. *Science* 243:1282-3 Mr 10 '89

A never-drag-again eating plan. L. Applegate. il *Health (New York, N.Y.)* 21:52-3 F '89

New food facts. il *The Mother Earth News* 118:18+ Jl/Ag '89

The nutri-ditionalist. R. L. Duyff. il *Ladies' Home Journal* 106:262-4+ N '89

Nutrition news. See issues of Prevention (Emmaus, Pa.) beginning March 1988

Nutrition news, do's and don'ts. il *Redbook* 174:120-3 N '89

Nutritional importance of pyrroloquinoline quinone. J. Killgore and others. bibl f il *Science* 245:850-2 Ag 25 '89

Pass the veggies [report by the National Research Council] il *U.S. News & World Report* 106:13 Mr 13 '89

The real skinny on bananas and pretzels [food myths] J. Silberner. il *U.S. News & World Report* 106:64+ Ap 10 '89

Rethinking eating out. C. A. Sweet. il *FDA Consumer* 23:8-13 N '89

Variety: for good nutrition. B. T. Hunter. il *Consumers' Research Magazine* 72:8-9 S '89

What's news: nutrition, diet, fitness. See occasional issues of Good Housekeeping beginning May 1985

Anecdotes, facetiae, satire, etc.

Man at the trough. S. Bing. il *Esquire* 112:147-8 S '89

Study and teaching

See Nutrition education

NUTRITION EDUCATION

Learning dietary Spanish [programs for Hispanic Americans] J. Steinberg. il *American Health* 8:140-1 Ap '89

NUTRITION NEWSLETTERS

Nutrition and medical newsletters offer information-hungry readers new food for thought. P. Klass. *Vogue* 179:554+ S '89

NUTRITION POLICY

Five life-extenders [Surgeon General's diet guidelines] L. Applegate. il *Runner's World* 24:18-19 Ja '89

Latest dispatch from the vitamin front [revised recommended daily allowances] S. Findlay. il *U.S. News & World Report* 107:100-1 N 6 '89

Revised RDAs add a few good nutrients. J. Raloff. *Science News* 136:277 O 28 '89

Squaring off over vitamins [debate over nutritional requirements and supplements] S. Findlay. il *U.S. News & World Report* 106:62-4 Ap 10 '89

Vitamins: new RDAs [recommended dietary allowances] il *Newsweek* 114:84 N 6 '89

Europe

Healthy eating in Europe. il *World Health* p30 My '89

NUTRITION POLICY—cont.
United States
See Nutrition policy
NUTRITION PROBLEMS
Developing countries
See also
Nestle SA—Infant formula boycott case
Give them their daily bread [improvements in health result in economic growth; views of Robert Fogel] S. Nasar. *U.S. News & World Report* 107:64 O 30 '89
NUTS
See also
Acorns
Brazil nuts
Cashew nuts
Cooking—Nuts
Pine nuts
Cache economy of the gray squirrel. L. Jacobs. il *Natural History* p40-7 O '89
THE NUTT HOUSE [television program] See Television program reviews—Single works
NUTTING, WALLACE, 1861-1941
about
Wallace Nutting and the colonial revival. A. E. Ledes. il *Antiques* 135:1040+ My '89
NUWER, HANK
A gathering of Eagles. il *Sport (New York, N.Y.)* 80:50-2 Jl '89
Under the volcano. il *Sport (New York, N.Y.)* 80:50-3+ F '89
The world's best woodcutters. il *Country Journal* 16:21-6 F '89
NUYTTEN, BRUNO
about
Camille Claudel [film] Reviews
Vogue il 179:498-503+ Mr '89. A.-E. Moutet
NWA INC.
Front man [A. Checchi fronting for KLM in Northwest takeover] S. Flack. il *Forbes* 144:69 Jl 10 '89
Landing Northwest [A. Checchi] R. Grover and R. Mitchell. il por *Business Week* p24-5 Jl 3 '89
Northwest asks pilots to cooperate in thwarting hostile takeover. *Aviation Week & Space Technology* 130:106 My 1 '89
NWA rejects bids; new date set for proposals. *Aviation Week & Space Technology* 130:315 Je 12 '89
NWA seeks strategy to block Davis' $3.1-billion takeover attempt. *Aviation Week & Space Technology* 130:107 Ap 24 '89
The odd couple chasing Northwest Airlines [A. Checchi and G. L. Wilson] R. Grover. il pors *Business Week* p126 Ap 24 '89
Pan Am Corp., Davis among Northwest bidders. C. Fotos. il *Aviation Week & Space Technology* 130:108-9 Je 5 '89
Pilots union threatens to seek declaration of impasse in talks with Northwest Airlines. *Aviation Week & Space Technology* 131:97 Jl 17 '89
Skinner's limits on NWA buyout fail to dissuade drive for LBO controls. C. Fotos. *Aviation Week & Space Technology* 131:138-9 O 9 '89
"This will be all-out war" [NWA rebuffs bid by M. Davis] J. Greenwald. il por *Time* 133:46 Ap 17 '89
U.S. must assess buyout bid's impact on safety at Northwest [KLM's role in Wings Holdings' bid under scrutiny] *Aviation Week & Space Technology* 130:92-3 Je 26 '89
What could stall a run on Northwest. C. Power and R. Mitchell. il *Business Week* p30 Ap 10 '89
Wings Holdings chief pledges to keep Northwest growing [A. A. Checchi] C. Fotos. *Aviation Week & Space Technology* 130:90-1 Je 26 '89
Wings Holdings' purchase of Northwest could become blueprint for future LBOs. *Aviation Week & Space Technology* 131:22 Ag 14 '89
NYANJA (RESEARCH SHIP)
Snippets from Nyanja chronicles [conducting research on East African lakes] B. Rosendahl. il por map *Sea Frontiers* 35:292-302 S/O '89
NYBORG-ANDERSEN, IRENE, AND O'BRIEN, PAMELA GUTHRIE
The child-care patchwork. il *Ladies' Home Journal* 106:199-200+ N '89
NYCB *See* New York City Ballet
NYE, JOSEPH S., JR.
Arms control after the cold war. bibl f *Foreign Affairs* 68:42-64 Wint '89/'90
The challenges to America—long-term, short-term, or both? [discussion of Summer 1988 article, Short-term folly, not long-term decline] *New Perspectives Quarterly* 5:62-3 Wint '88/'89
Cuban graffiti. *The New Republic* 200:16-18 Mr 13 '89
Don't count on counting. *The Bulletin of the Atomic Scientists* 45:43 My '89
NYE, PETER *See* White, Wallace, 1930-
NYENHUIS, JACQUELYN R.
The right stuff. il *The Saturday Evening Post* 261:106+ Ja/F '89

NYKVIST, SVEN, 1922-
about
Unbearable lightness [interview] A. White. il por *Film Comment* 25:52-3 S/O '89
NYMPHS, ARTIFICIAL *See* Fishing lures, flies, etc.
NYOS, LAKE (CAMEROON) *See* Lake Nyos (Cameroon)
NYRBA *See* New York Regional Booksellers Association
NYSE *See* New York Stock Exchange, Inc.
NYSTROM, LORNE
about
An NDP star is charged. il por *Maclean's* 102:24 D 11 '89
NYSWANER, RON
about
The prince of Pennsylvania [film] Reviews
Video il 13:58+ Ag '89. I. Robbins

O

Ó FIAICH, TOMÁS, CARDINAL
about
Cardinal Ó Fiaich: my vision of a new Ireland [cover story] T. P. O'Mahony. *America* 160:238-40 Mr 18 '89
O VERTIGO DANSE
Reviews:
Performance of Chagall in Montreal. L. Howe-Beck. *Dance Magazine* 63:104-5 My '89
OAK, JUDY
Why writers workshops? *The Writer* 102:26-34 My '89
OAK
See also
Acorns
OAK HILL (ROCHESTER, N.Y.: GOLF COURSE) *See* Golf courses
OAK ISLAND (N.S.)
The secret of Oak Island [Money Pit] il map *National Geographic World* 166:22-5 Je '89
Solving old mysteries. J. Daly. il *Maclean's* 102:45 Mr 20 '89
Writer D'Arcy O'Connor, digging deep into 'Money Pit' lore, unearths a trove of mysteries. P. Freeman. il pors *People Weekly* 31:235-6 Mr 6 '89
OAK PARK (ILL.)
Stores
See also
Boulevard Antique Center (Oak Park, Ill.)
OAK RIDGE NATIONAL LABORATORY
Watkins's decision to restart HFIR heralds new era for DOE reactors [High Flux Isotope Reactor] I. Goodwin. il *Physics Today* 42:49-50 My '89
OAKAR, MARY ROSE
about
Just call me Mary Rose. B. G. Kempton. il pors *New Choices for the Best Years* 29:52-5 D '89
OAKHURST (CALIF.)
Restaurants, nightclubs, bars, etc.
Spécialités de la maison:
Erna's Elderberry House. C. Bates. il *Gourmet* 49:24+ My '89
OAKLAND (CALIF.)
Airports
Oakland prepares to accept traffic from damaged SFO [earthquake] R. G. O'Lone. il *Aviation Week & Space Technology* 131:25+ O 30 '89
Bridges
See also
San Francisco-Oakland Bay Bridge (Calif.)
Education
A program to improve local school site management. B. Barnes and M. Leslie. *The Education Digest* 55:32-4 N '89
Underwriting the future: two women will send 146 kids to college [O. Brown and R. W. Hayre set up funds for black children] R. Brown. il pors *Ebony* 44:74+ Ap '89
Festivals
Art, music, and a boat parade on Oakland's spruced-up waterfront. il *Sunset (Central West edition)* 183:12 S '89
Libraries
See also
Data Center (Oakland, Calif.)
Religious institutions and affairs
Side by side [work of D. Kiteley and J. Alfred Smith at Allen Temple Baptist Church and Shiloh Christian Fellowship] K. H. Sidey. il pors *Christianity Today* 33:33 Mr 3 '89
Restaurants, nightclubs, bars, etc.
Spécialités de la maison:
Oliveto. C. Bates. il *Gourmet* 49:18+ Ja '89
Sports
A fan's view of Bay's ball. R. Fimrite. il *Sports Illustrated* 71:40-1 O 23 '89
Tale of two cities [Oakland vs. San Francisco] R. Corelli. il *Maclean's* 102:61 O 23 '89

OAKLAND (CALIF.)—Sports—*cont.*
Two cities wild for 'Baysball'. H. Caen. il *Newsweek* 114:70 O 23 '89
OAKLAND BALLET
Reviews:
Fall season in the Bay Area. J. Ross. il *Dance Magazine* 63:20-1 F '89
OAKLAND BAY BRIDGE (CALIF.) *See* San Francisco-Oakland Bay Bridge (Calif.)
OAKLAND INTERNATIONAL AIRPORT *See* Oakland (Calif.)—Airports
OAKLEY, FRANCIS
Apocalypse now in U.S. higher education [cover story] *America* 160:286-7+ Ap 1 '89
OAKS, HAROLD R.
Secondary teacher training: the theatre backwater? *Design for Arts in Education* 91:23-6 N/D '89
OARSMANSHIP *See* Rowing
OAS *See* Organization of American States
OASIS LAUNDRIES INC.
Beautiful laundrettes. A. Miller. il *Newsweek* 113:42 Ja 9 '89
OAT BRAN *See* Bran
OAT BRAN COOKING *See* Cooking—Grain
OATES, FREDERIC, 1914-
about
My father, my fiction. J. C. Oates. il pors *The New York Times Magazine* p44-5+ Mr 19 '89
OATES, JOYCE CAROL, 1938-
Family [story] il *Omni (New York, N.Y.)* 12:74-8+ D '89
Home [story] il *Ladies' Home Journal* 106:74+ Ja '89
Kindness [story] il *Ladies' Home Journal* 106:128+ My '89
My father, my fiction. il pors *The New York Times Magazine* p44-5+ Mr 19 '89
Young love, America [poem] il *The Atlantic* 264:60 Jl '89
OATES, WANDA
about
Lady coach shows D.C. high school's boys basketball team its way to victory. il pors *Jet* 75:48-9 Ja 23 '89
OATHS
See also
Loyalty oaths
Physicians' oaths
OATLEY, CHARLES W.
about
Franklin Institute honors Lorenz, Oatley and Madey. M. Siegel. pors *Physics Today* 42:113 S '89
OATMEAL COOKIES *See* Cookies
OATS
See also
Cooking—Grain
Oats: let's grow our own! J. Walter. il *Successful Farming* 87 no4:64V-64W Mr '89
Prices
How I made $812 in the oat bran craze. P. W. Moser. il *Fortune* 120:125+ O 9 '89
OATTS, DICK
about
Dial & Oatts. B. Milkowski. il pors *Down Beat* 56:46-7 N '89
OAXACA (MEXICO)
Description
A movable feast in Mexico. S. Kaye. il *World Press Review* 36:62 Ja '89
Wild about Oaxaca. R. Urquhart. il *Vogue* 179:310+ O '89
OAXACA (MEXICO: STATE)
Description and travel
Mexico's Oaxaca coast. J. Edmondson. il *Harper's Bazaar* 122:58+ Mr '89
O'BARRY, RICHARD, 1939-
about
Flipper's ex-trainer wants his favorite mammals free to swim with the fishes. B. Hewitt. il por *People Weekly* 32:40-1 S 4 '89
OBEID, ABDUL KARIM
Kidnapping
Hostages to terror [cover story; special section; with editorial comment by Kevin Doyle] il pors *Maclean's* 102:2, 20-4+ Ag 14 '89
How the Israelis snatched the sheik. H. Goodman. il por map *U.S. News & World Report* 107:24-5 Ag 14 '89
Inaction is another form of hanging [kidnapping of A. K. Obeid results in murder of W. R. Higgins] R. Rosenblatt. il por *U.S. News & World Report* 107:8-9 Ag 14 '89
Israel snatches a sheik. por *Newsweek* 114:36 Ag 7 '89
Kidnapping and peace. *The New Republic* 201:8-9 Ag 21 '89
Salting the tail of the hostage takers. *U.S. News & World Report* 107:9 Ag 7 '89
O'BEIRNE, BERNARD M.
Coping with Alzheimer's. *America* 161:156-7 S 23 '89

OBERG, ALCESTIS R., 1949-
A cave dweller's chronicle: fifty-six days and counting [interview with S. Follini] il *Omni (New York, N.Y.)* 11:50-2+ Je '89
Cosmic relief. il *Omni (New York, N.Y.)* 11:20 Je '89
NASA's next generation. il *Omni (New York, N.Y.)* 11:26+ Ja '89
OBERG, JAMES E., 1944-
Inside the House of Sputnik. il *Omni (New York, N.Y.)* 11:30 Mr '89
OBERHOFER, THOMAS
Tomorrow? Who cares? *The Futurist* 23:59 My/Je '89
OBERHUBER, KONRAD
about
Palace evolution. F. Protzman. il por *Art News* 88:117-18 Ap '89
OBERLIN (KAN.)
Industries
Looking for a partner. R. J. Margolis. il *The New Leader* 72:12-13 O 2-16 '89
OBERLY, JIM
Spearing fish, playing 'chicken'. il *The Nation* 248:844-5+ Je 19 '89
OBERMAN, KENNETH
about
Stocks that could soar on big trends [interview] E. Schultz. il por *Fortune* 120:39+ D 4 '89
OBERMAYER, ARTHUR
about
Grantsmanship. I. Cithelen. il por *Forbes* 144:310+ N 13 '89
OBEROI, MOHAN SINGH
about
Emperor of India's hotels. R. Saksena. il por *World Press Review* 36:73 O '89
OBERON, MERLE, 1911-1979
about
Wuthering Heights. A. S. Berg. il pors *The New York Times Magazine* p46-8+ F 19 '89
OBERST, ROBERT
Political decay in Sri Lanka. bibl f il *Current History* 88:425-8+ D '89
OBERSTAR, JAMES L.
about
Independent FAA, competition issues top new House chairman's agenda. M. Mecham. il por *Aviation Week & Space Technology* 130:99 F 13 '89
OBERTH, HERMANN
about
The rocket pioneers. M. R. Chartrand. *Ad Astra* 1:38 Mr '89
OBESITY
See also
Prader-Willi syndrome
Weight reducing products
Born to be pudgy? [childhood obesity] B. Livermore. il *Health (New York, N.Y.)* 21:28+ N '89
Childhood obesity. C. Slom. il *McCall's* 117:61 N '89
Couch potato physique [correlation between television watching and obesity; research by Larry Tucker] E. Stark. il *Psychology Today* 23:8 S '89
Heavy viewing [correlation between TV watching and obesity; research by Larry Tucker] il *Prevention (Emmaus, Pa.)* 41:18-19 S '89
Joints feel the weight [osteoarthritis] il *Prevention (Emmaus, Pa.)* 41:10 F '89
"My weight is crushing our marriage". M. D. Rosen. il *Ladies' Home Journal* 106:12+ Ag '89
Shedding pounds through surgery [gastric bypass surgery] C. F. Henderson. pors *McCall's* 116:100+ Je '89
A test of courage [battered wife examines life and obesity after failed suicide] A. M. Gappa. il pors *Ladies' Home Journal* 106:22+ Ja '89
Tubby tubers [correlation between obesity and television watching; research by Larry Tucker] E. Franklin. il *American Health* 8:88 N '89
Genetic aspects
Adipsin and complement factor D activity: an immune-related defect in obesity. B. S. Rosen and others. bibl f il *Science* 244:1483-7 Je 23 '89
Family ties point to recessive 'obesity gene' [study by Trudy L. Burns] K. Fackelmann. *Science News* 136:327 N 18 '89
OBITUARIES
. . . and those who left us [1980s] il *TV Guide* 37:35 D 9-15 '89
Farewell [1989] il *Rolling Stone* p139-40 D 14-28 '89
Farewells. il *Time* 134:64-5 D 25 '89
Final bows. il *Life* 12:141-2+ Ja '89
I read it in the paper [use of newspapers as genealogical resource] C. E. Kraft. il *Antiques & Collecting Hobbies* 94:74-7 Mr '89
Late greats. il *People Weekly* 32:123-4+ D 25 '89-Ja 1 '90
Obituaries [art world] il *Art in America* 77:63 Ag '89
OBJECT ART
Poetic objectives: Curt Marcus. M. E. Haus. il *Art News* 88:169-70 D '89

OBJECT-ORIENTED DATABASES
See also
HyperPad (Database)
A family of models. J. Dawson. bibl f il *Byte* 14:277-8+ S '89
Object-oriented databases make strides. *High Technology Business* 9:33-4 S/O '89

OBJECT-ORIENTED PROGRAMMING
See also
Smalltalk (Computer language)
Clash of the object-oriented Pascals [Quick Pascal and Turbo Pascal 5.5] J. Udell. il *Byte* 14:104-6 Jl '89
Object-oriented Mac windows. J. Amsterdam. il *Byte* 14:277-82+ Jl '89
Object-oriented programming [special section] il *Byte* 14:228-9+ Mr '89
OOP tools designed to make interface building like writing a letter with a word processor [Entryway system] *Byte* 14:18+ S '89
OOPS: building applications with objects. T. Badgett. *Personal Computing* 13:156 D '89
VROOMM: Borland says memory technology will make future programs better, not bigger [Virtual Real-Time Object-Oriented Memory Manager] *Byte* 14:17-18 Ag '89
Testing
Extend [version 1.05] R. Valdés. il *Byte* 14:197-200 Ap '89
FormWorx goes GUI. S. Miastkowski. il *Byte* 14:86+ N '89
Hooked on Smalltalk-80 for the Mac. D. E. Crabb. il *Byte* 14:143+ Ja '89
Lisp dialect taps Mac riches [MacScheme + Toolsmith] J. Udell. il *Byte* 14:204 S '89
Mac modeling in 3-D [Swivel 3D] D. Barker and L. H. Loeb. il *Byte* 14 Mac Special Ed:MAC219-MAC220 Je '89
Modeling the physical world with blocks [Extend 1.05] N. Baran. il *Byte* 14:97 Ja '89
Powerful portable 3-D graphics [HOOPS 2.03] B. D. Kliewer. il *Byte* 14:193-4+ Jl '89
Simulation software for the Macintosh [STELLA and Extend] D. K. Bogen. bibl f il *Science* 246:138-42 O 6 '89
Smalltalk/V comes to the Mac. R. Valdés. il *Byte* 14:201-4 Je '89
Think C goes OOP. T. Thompson. il *Byte* 14:81-2 O '89
VROOMM goes the spreadsheet [Virtual Real-Time Object Oriented Memory Manager for Quattro] R. Malloy. *Byte* 14:111-12 O '89

OBJECTIVITY
Ayn Rand's objectivism: a humanistic interpretation. K. Robinson. por *The Humanist* 49:29-30 Ja/F '89

OBJECTS, MINIATURE *See* Miniature objects

OBRECHT, JACOB, D. 1505
about
Musical events:
Performance of Mass by J. Obrecht. A. Porter. *The New Yorker* 65:69-70 F 27 '89

O'BRIAN, HUGH
about
Though grayer, and wider in the saddle, Gene Barry and Hugh O'Brian ride again. il pors *People Weekly* 32:106-7 Ag 28 '89

O'BRIEN, CONOR CRUISE, 1917-
Can Britain ever leave Northern Ireland? il *World Press Review* 36:56 O '89
A lost chance to save the Jews? il *The New York Review of Books* 36:27-8+ Ap 27 '89

O'BRIEN, DAVID J.
Join it, work it, fight it. il *Commonweal* 116:624-30 N 17 '89
Sex (how about love?) on Catholic campuses [with discussion; cover story] *Commonweal* 116:169-77 Mr 24 '89

O'BRIEN, EDNA
A day out [story] *The New Yorker* 65:39-44 Ap 24 '89
What a sky [story] *The New Yorker* 65:32-7 Jl 10 '89
The widow [story] *The New Yorker* 64:28-33 Ja 23 '89
about
Reveling in heartbreak. R. B. Woodward. il por *The New York Times Magazine* p42+ Mr 12 '89

O'BRIEN, EDWARD
about
A DEA hero is busted. por *Newsweek* 114:32 Ag 28 '89

O'BRIEN, FRANK L., III
about
The profits in hot water. J. Cook. il por *Forbes* 143:88-9 Ap 17 '89

O'BRIEN, GEOFFREY, 1948-
Water music [poem] *The New York Review of Books* 36:7 Jl 20 '89

O'BRIEN, GLENN, 1948-
Long live Andy! il por *House & Garden* 161:32+ F '89

O'BRIEN, JIM
about
The dressmaker [film] Reviews
New York 22:56-7 Mr 6 '89. D. Denby
Newsweek 113:54 Ja 9 '89. D. Ansen

People Weekly 31:20 Ja 16 '89. P. Travers
O'BRIEN, JOHN
about
Dalkey Archive: quarrying for a literary readership. J. Barbato. *Publishers Weekly* 235:38 F 10 '89

O'BRIEN, LAWRENCE F.
about
"Gung ho on O'B". N. Lemann. il *The Atlantic* 263:26+ Je '89

O'BRIEN, MARK, 1950-
Building your own portfolio. il *Nation's Business* 77:30+ Ap '89

O'BRIEN, PAMELA GUTHRIE
(jt. auth) See Nyborg-Andersen, Irene, and O'Brien, Pamela Guthrie

O'BRIEN, THOMAS C.
Some thoughts on treasure-keeping. bibl f il *Phi Delta Kappan* 70:360-4 Ja '89

O'BRIEN, TIM, 1946-
In the field [story] il *Gentlemen's Quarterly* 59:217+ D '89
The lives of the dead [story] il *Esquire* 111:134-8+ Ja '89
Sweetheart of the Song Tra Bong [story] il *Esquire* 112:94-8+ Jl '89

O'BRIEN, TOM
Screen. See occasional issues of Commonweal beginning February 10, 1984

O'BRIEN ENERGY SYSTEMS INC.
The profits in hot water. J. Cook. il por *Forbes* 143:88-9 Ap 17 '89

OBSCENE TELEPHONE CALLS
The unwanted phone call: what to do when a ding-a-ling rings. il *'Teen* 33:91 Je '89

OBSCENITY (LAW)
See also
Trials (Obscenity)
Art for law's sake. R. A. Posner. *The American Scholar* 58:513-20 Aut '89
Bobby Brown's Cruel beguiles fans—but not the cop who nabbed him for dirty dancing [arrested during concert in Columbus, Ga.] S. Dougherty. il pors *People Weekly* 31:108-10 Ap 10 '89
Congress passes compromise NEA bill. H. Fields. il *Publishers Weekly* 236:10 O 20 '89
Congress rejects Helms amendment. W. Robinson. *Art in America* 77:41 N '89
Court to rule on early enforcement of Child Obscenity Act. H. Fields. *Publishers Weekly* 235:106 My 12 '89
Day care, porn cases heard by High Court. *Christianity Today* 33:53 Mr 3 '89
The drive to make America porn-free. T. Gest. il *U.S. News & World Report* 106:26-7 F 6 '89
G-men at the movies [FBI memo on A. Warhol's Lonesome cowboys] *Harper's* 278:26 Je '89
High Court bars pretrial RICO seizure of books [obscene materials in Indiana bookstores] H. Fields. *Publishers Weekly* 235:19 Mr 10 '89
Obscenity: what the Supreme Court says [excerpt from Art law] R. E. Lerner and J. Bresler. il *Art News* 88:144-5 O '89
Ol' Jesse's dirty word [amendment prohibiting NEA funding of obscene art] *The Nation* 249:441 O 23 '89
Pitfalls and penalties lurk in Child Obscenity Act. M. J. Lillienstein. *Publishers Weekly* 235:21+ Ja 20 '89
Record-keeping provisions struck down in porn law [requiring publishers to keep records of models used in depictions of sexual activity] H. Fields. *Publishers Weekly* 235:23-4 Je 2 '89
The sounds of lawsuits: rock lyrics on trial. S. F. Rohde. il *USA Today (Periodical)* 118:86-7 Jl '89
The uphill fight against dial-a-porn. il *Newsweek* 113:42 Ja 9 '89

OBSERVATIONS, ASTRONOMICAL *See* Astronomy—Observations

OBSERVATORIES
See also
Astronomical observatories

OBSERVATORIES OF THE CARNEGIE INSTITUTION OF WASHINGTON
Carnegie makes some changes at its observatories. W. Sweet. *Physics Today* 42:85 S '89

OBSESSION (PSYCHOLOGY) *See* Obsessive-compulsive behavior

OBSESSIVE-COMPULSIVE BEHAVIOR
See also
Hair pulling
Sexual addiction
The biology of obsessions and compulsions. J. L. Rapoport. il *Scientific American* 260:82-9 Mr '89
The chemistry of doubt. P. King. il *Psychology Today* 23:58+ O '89
A fatal obsession with the stars [murder of actress R. Schaeffer and other incidents] A. Toufexis. il por *Time* 134:43-4 Jl 31 '89
Haunted by their habits. D. Gelman. il *Newsweek* 113:71-2+ Mr 27 '89

OBSESSIVE-COMPULSIVE BEHAVIOR—*cont.*

An innocent life, a heartbreaking death [actress R. Schaeffer killed by obsessive fan and other celebrities who have been threatened] P. Axthelm. il por *People Weekly* 32:60-2+ Jl 31 '89

Justine Bateman becomes the latest celebrity to be menaced by an obsessive fan [J. Smetek apprehended by police] B. Hewitt. il por *People Weekly* 32:112-13 S 25 '89

Love gone loco: when breakups go too far! E. Karlsberg. il *'Teen* 33:36-7+ F '89

Messages from a madman [terrorized by former student] P. Rose. il *Glamour* 87:270 Je '89

The obsession of the long-distance runner. B. W. Bloch. il *Gentlemen's Quarterly* 59:312-13+ N '89

A psychiatrist explores the cause—and treatment—of those tormenting, obsessive-compulsive urges [interview with J. Rapoport] K. McMurran. il pors *People Weekly* 31:91-4+ Mr 13 '89

Secret obsessions. E. E. Goode. *Vogue* 179:246+ F '89

The secret world of obsessive-compulsives. S. Pocharski. il *Mademoiselle* 95:138 Ag '89

Thoughts we hate to think [study by D. M. Wegner] E. E. Goode. il *U.S. News & World Report* 107:48-9 Ag 14 '89

Try not to think of a white bear [obsessive thoughts; excerpt from White bears and other unwanted thoughts] D. M. Wegner. il *Psychology Today* 23:64-6 Je '89

OBSTETRICS

See also
Abortion
Cesarean section
Midwives

"I love my doctor!". M. C. Hickey. il *Parents* 64:104-7+ Ap '89

OBUKHOV, ALEXEI

Let's get back to the table. il *The Bulletin of the Atomic Scientists* 45:6 Ap '89

OCCAM (COMPUTER LANGUAGE)

Configuring parallel programs (I) [Occam Transpiler] D. Pountain. il *Byte* 14:349-52 D '89

Occam II. D. Pountain. il *Byte* 14:279-84 O '89

L'OCCASIONE FA IL LADRO [opera] See Rossini, Gioacchino, 1792-1868

OCCHETTO, ACHILLE

about

Achille's gamble. D. Singer. *The Nation* 248:545 Ap 24 '89

OCCIDENT AND ORIENT See East and West

OCCULTATIONS

An afternoon occultation for the south [Regulus] il *Sky and Telescope* 77:407+ Ap '89

A bright-moon Regulus occultation. il maps *Sky and Telescope* 77:73 Ja '89

Crescent moon nicks the Pleiades. D. W. Dunham. il *Sky and Telescope* 77:405-6 Ap '89

European amateurs study Titan [28 Sagittarii occultation] A. J. Hollis and J. Mitton. il *Astronomy* 17:52-4 N '89

First look at the Saturn occultation [28 Sagittarii] D. J. Eicher. il *Astronomy* 17:99+ O '89

Inside the rings of Saturn [28 Sagittarii occultation] R. Irion. il *Astronomy* 17:50-1 N '89

Lunar occultation highlights for 1989. D. W. Dunham. il map *Sky and Telescope* 77:68-9+ Ja '89

El Nath grazing occultation sets records. *Astronomy* 17:94 F '89

Planetary occultations of stars in 1989. D. W. Dunham. il map *Sky and Telescope* 77:70-1 Ja '89

A plethora of lunar occultations. R. Shaffer. il *Astronomy* 17:57-9 Ap '89

A rare occultation by Saturn [28 Sagittarii] R. Shaffer. il *Astronomy* 17:61-2 Jl '89

Regulus occulted. *Astronomy* 17:98-9 My '89

Saturn and 28 Sgr highlights. D. Di Cicco and L. J. Robinson. il *Sky and Telescope* 78:360-5 O '89

Saturn and a winking star [28 Sagittarii] L. J. Robinson. il *Sky and Telescope* 78:259 S '89

Saturn to occult a bright star [28 Sagittarii] D. W. Dunham and others.. il maps *Sky and Telescope* 77:638-9+ Je '89

The seasons of Pluto. N. W. Stauffer. il *Technology Review* 92:9-10 Jl '89

The shot heard round the universe [shooting out light to watch occultation] W. Allen. *Astronomy* 17:110-11 Ja '89

Waning crescent moon in the Pleiades. D. W. Dunham. il *Sky and Telescope* 78:64-5 Jl '89

You can see a star flicker behind Saturn's rings [28 Sagittarii] J. Kanipe. il *Astronomy* 17:80-3 Je '89

OCCULTISM

See also
Astrology
Christianity and occultism
Parapsychology
Satanism
Spiritualism
Theosophy

OCCUPATIONAL APTITUDE TESTS See Aptitude tests

OCCUPATIONAL EDUCATION See Vocational-technical education

OCCUPATIONAL GUIDANCE See Vocational guidance

OCCUPATIONAL HEALTH AND SAFETY

See also
Aerospace industries—Employees—Health and hygiene
AIDS (Disease) and employment
Artists—Health and hygiene
Dental workers—Health and hygiene
Drugs and employment
Farmers—Health and hygiene
Government employees—Health and hygiene
Industrial accidents
Industry—Physical fitness programs
Industry—Prenatal care programs
Insurance, Workers' compensation
Longshore workers—Health and hygiene
Lungs—Dust diseases
Meat industry workers—Health and hygiene
Miners—Health and hygiene
Mobile home industry workers—Health and hygiene
Nuclear power plants—Safety devices and measures
Nuclear power workers—Health and hygiene
Photographers—Health and hygiene
Poisons and poisoning, Industrial
Repetitive strain injuries
Sick building syndrome
Smoking and employment
United States. Occupational Safety and Health Administration
Video display terminals—Health aspects

Bladder cancers: one in four due to jobs [study by Debra T. Silverman] J. Raloff. *Science News* 136:230 O 7 '89

Danger on the job. S. Waldman. il *Newsweek* 114:42-4+ D 11 '89

Danger on the job [job-related deaths; study by J. Paul Leigh] G. Byrne. il *Science* 243:317 Ja 20 '89

Death by science [high incidence of job-related deaths for scientists; study by J. Paul Leigh] *Discover* 10:14 My '89

Job safety in 1987. *Monthly Labor Review* 111:2 D '88

Warning: this job may be hazardous to your health [youth] L. Green. il *Current Health 2* 15:24-5 My '89

Work-related illnesses and injuries. *Congressional Digest* 68:101-2 Ap '89

Laws and regulations

Bias or safety? [appeals court upholds Johnson Controls ban excluding women of childbearing age from hazardous jobs] *Time* 134:61 O 16 '89

Occupational health legislation. *Congressional Digest* 68:98-128 Ap '89

This safety ruling could be hazardous to employers' health [OSHA decision opens business to more criminal charges] S. B. Garland. il *Business Week* p34 F 20 '89

OCCUPATIONAL MOBILITY

See also
Labor turnover

Building a bridge to a new career. A. Edmond, Jr. il *Black Enterprise* 19:96-8+ My '89

Dear Betty Harragan [secretary considers change of career] B. L. Harragan. il *Working Woman* 14:22+ Ag '89

Great transformations [career changes by former teachers] B. G. Kempton. il *Working Woman* 14:88-92 Ja '89

Have law degree, will travel. A. Sachs. il *Time* 134:106 D 11 '89

How to get the job you really want [cover story; special section] il *Working Woman* 14:111-14+ Ap '89

The lure of the classroom [professionals turning to teaching] S. Tifft. il *Time* 133:69 F 13 '89

A new job, a new life [cover story] G. Rosenblum. il *New Choices for the Best Years* 29:27-34 Ja '89

Occupational change: pursuing a different kind of work. J. P. Markey and W. Parks, II. bibl f il *Monthly Labor Review* 112:3-12 S '89

Taking control of career change. D. Cole. *Psychology Today* 23:29 N '89

Those who can, teach [teaching as a second career] C. Reeve. il *New Choices for the Best Years* 29:61-7 N '89

When it's time to change careers [aged] E. McGrath. il *New Choices for the Best Years* 29:45-9 S '89

OCCUPATIONAL SAFETY See Occupational health and safety

OCCUPATIONAL SAFETY AND HEALTH ACT See Occupational health and safety—Laws and regulations

OCCUPATIONAL SAFETY AND HEALTH ADMINISTRATION (U.S.) See United States. Occupational Safety and Health Administration

OCCUPATIONAL STRESS See Job stress

OCCUPATIONAL SUCCESS See Success

OCCUPATIONAL TRAINING See Vocational-technical education

OCCUPATIONS

See also
Aged—Occupations
Blacks—Occupations
Professions
Women—Occupations

Best jobs for the future [cover story; special section] il *U.S. News & World Report* 107:60-2+ S 25 '89

Characteristics of occupational entrants. M. L. Carey. il *Occupational Outlook Quarterly* 33:8-17 Summ '89

OCCUPATIONS—*cont.*
Projections of occupational employment, 1988-2000. G. T. Silvestri and J. M. Lukasiewicz. bibl f il *Monthly Labor Review* 112:42-65 N '89

OCEAN
See also
American Oceans Campaign
Atlantic Ocean
Coasts
Marine biology
Marine fauna
Medical waste disposal in the ocean
Pacific Ocean
Petroleum in submerged lands
Radioactive waste disposal in the ocean
Sea level changes
Sea water
Territorial waters
Waste disposal in the ocean
Wave power
Waves

Comet commotion [theory of L. A. Frank] R. Kunzig. il *Discover* 10:24-5 Ja '89
Down by the sea [running] G. Sheehan. il *Runner's World* 24:16 Ag '89
A snowball's chance [theory of Louis A. Frank] J. Horgan. *Scientific American* 260:21+ Mr '89
The touch of the sea [cover story; special issue] il *Audubon* 91:10-12+ Mr '89

Bibliography
Neptune's bookshelf. F. Graham. il *Audubon* 91:34-40+ Mr '89

Laws and regulations
See Maritime law

OCEAN AND CIVILIZATION
A nation of beachwalkers. P. Steinhart. il *Audubon* 91:10-12 Mr '89
World ocean—the human stake [address, October 13, 1988] G. M. Slonim. *Vital Speeches of the Day* 55:172-6 Ja 1 '89

OCEAN-ATMOSPHERE INTERACTION
See also
El Niño (Ocean current)
La Niña (Ocean current)
Southern Oscillation
Aerosols, cloud microphysics, and fractional cloudiness. B. A. Albrecht. bibl f il *Science* 245:1227-30 S 15 '89
Carbon dioxide transport by ocean currents at 25°N latitude in the Atlantic Ocean. P. Brewer and others. bibl f il *Science* 246:477-9 O 27 '89
Crow's nest. C. G. Harrison. il *Sea Frontiers* 35:195 Jl/Ag '89
Far-off clues to nearby weather [drought research by Kevin Trenberth] B. Carpenter. il map *U.S. News & World Report* 106:56 Ja 16 '89
Pacific plankton outdo land pollution [research by Joseph M. Prospero and Dennis L. Savoie] R. Monastersky. *Science News* 136:7 Jl 1 '89
Secrets of the sea [advances in climate research; cover story] W. J. Cook. il *U.S. News & World Report* 107:48-52+ Ag 21 '89
The summer of '88 [research by Kevin E. Trenberth] L. Burnham. *Scientific American* 260:21 Mr '89

OCEAN BIRDS *See* Sea birds

OCEAN BOTTOM
See also
Marine sediments
Ocean Drilling Program
Seamounts
Subduction (Geology)
Submarine geology
Experiments on hydraulic jumps in turbidity currents near a canyon-fan transition. M. Garcia and G. Parker. bibl f il *Science* 245:393-6 Jl 28 '89
Magma reservoir seen under ocean ridge [study by Mark S. Burnett and others] R. Monastersky. il *Science News* 135:326 My 27 '89
Mid-Atlantic Ridge survey hits bull's-eye. R. Monastersky. il *Science News* 135:295 My 13 '89

Maps
In the trenches [globe of ocean floor relief; work of Pierina R. Nicholson] B. Weber. il *The New York Times Magazine* p110 My 7 '89
Mapping a wet frontier [Sea Beam sonar maps declassified] A. C. Revkin. il *Discover* 10:30 S '89
Navy relents in battle over mapping sea floor. C. Norman. *Science* 244:25 Ap 7 '89
Seafloor maps no longer secret. *Science News* 135:255 Ap 22 '89

OCEAN CATARACTS
Giant ocean cataracts. J. A. Whitehead, Jr. bibl il map *Scientific American* 260:50-7 F '89

OCEAN CIRCULATION
See also
Ocean currents
Clues to an ancient upside-down ocean [research by James P. Kennett and Lowell D. Stott] R. Monastersky. *Science News* 136:71 Jl 29 '89

Did the ocean once run backward? [research by James Kennett and Lowell Stott] R. A. Kerr. *Science* 243:740 F 10 '89
Model simulation of the Cretaceous ocean circulation. E. J. Barron and W. H. Peterson. bibl f il *Science* 244:684-6 My 12 '89
Upside-down oceans [research by James Kennett and Lowell Stott] il *Discover* 10:12 D '89

OCEAN CITY (MD.)
City planning
Only fools build on shifting sands [beach erosion] R. L. Di Silvestro. il map *Audubon* 91:106-12+ Mr '89

OCEAN-CLIMATE INTERACTION *See* Ocean-atmosphere interaction

OCEAN CURRENTS
See also
El Niño (Ocean current)
Gulf Stream
La Niña (Ocean current)
Carbon dioxide transport by ocean currents at 25°N latitude in the Atlantic Ocean. P. Brewer and others. bibl f il *Science* 246:477-9 O 27 '89
Caught in an abyssal storm [sediment upheaval due to benthic current encountered on Alvin mission] R. Gannon. il map *Earth Science* 42:18-20 Spr '89
Experiments on hydraulic jumps in turbidity currents near a canyon-fan transition. M. Garcia and G. Parker. bibl f il *Science* 245:393-6 Jl 28 '89
Remote sensing of ocean currents [synthetic aperture radar] R. M. Goldstein and others. bibl f il *Science* 246:1282-5 D 8 '89

OCEAN DRILLING PROGRAM
Quick flip-flop in the magnetic field [evidence from rocks from ocean floor between the Philippines and Borneo] *Science News* 135:188 Mr 25 '89
Where earth's insides ooze out [Mariana seamount; research by Patricia Fryer] *Science News* 136:15 Jl 1 '89

OCEAN FARMING *See* Aquaculture
OCEAN FISHING *See* Salt water fishing
OCEAN FLOOR *See* Ocean bottom

OCEAN IN ART
See also
Marine painting

OCEAN LIFE *See* Marine biology

OCEAN LINERS
See also
Norway (Ship)
Queen Elizabeth 2 (Ship)
Titanic (Steamship)
Cruising into the 1990s. H. Basch and S. Slater. il *Travel Holiday* 172:30-3 D '89
A cruising winterlude. H. Basch and S. Slater. il *Travel Holiday* 171:62-6 Ja '89
Fitness by sea [cruise ship spas] H. Basch and S. Slater. il *Travel Holiday* 171:79 Ja '89

Accidents
SOS under the midnight sun [rescue of passengers on Soviet cruise liner Maxim Gorky] il *Time* 134:30 Jl 3 '89

OCEAN MINING
See also
Exclusive Economic Zone
United Nations. Preparatory Commission for the International Sea-Bed Authority and the International Tribunal for the Law of the Sea

OCEAN POLLUTION *See* Marine pollution

OCEAN TEMPERATURE
Has the globe really warmed? il *Technology Review* 92:80 N/D '89
Recent ocean warming: are satellites right? [research by Alan E. Strong] R. Monastersky. *Science News* 135:247 Ap 22 '89
Sea surface may follow solar tune [research by Tim P. Barnett] *Science News* 136:159 S 2 '89
We're in hot water [rising ocean temperature] *Newsweek* 113:70 My 1 '89

OCEAN THERMAL POWER PLANTS
Indonesia
Tapping the sea [work of J. Hilbert Anderson] A. C. Revkin. il *Discover* 10:40 Jl '89

OCEAN TRAVEL
See also
Cruising
Ocean liners
Voyages
Voyages around the world

OCEAN WAVE POWER *See* Wave power
OCEAN WAVES *See* Waves

OCEANIA
Politics and government
The unpacified Pacific. B. Crozier. map *National Review* 41:24-5 Ja 27 '89

OCEANIC SOCIETY
Log of the Oceanic Society. See issues of Oceans through March/April 1989

OCEANOGRAPHIC EDUCATION
See also
North Wind Undersea Institute
Seacamp (Fla.)

OCEANOGRAPHIC EDUCATION—cont.
World ocean—the human stake [address, October 13, 1988] G. M. Slonim. *Vital Speeches of the Day* 55:172-6 Ja 1 '89
OCEANOGRAPHIC RESEARCH *See* Oceanography
OCEANOGRAPHIC SUBMERSIBLES
See also
Human powered oceanographic submersible racing
Human powered oceanographic submersibles
Robots—Oceanographic use
Caught in an abyssal storm [sediment upheaval due to benthic current encountered on Alvin mission] R. Gannon. il map *Earth Science* 42:18-20 Spr '89
Monitoring ocean nutrients [Benthic Lander developed by Douglas E. Hammond] il *USA Today (Periodical)* 117:6-7 Je '89
OCEANOGRAPHY
See also
Artificial satellites—Oceanographic use
Closed circuit television—Oceanographic use
Image processing—Oceanographic use
International Oceanographic Foundation
Ocean-atmosphere interaction
Ocean bottom
Ocean circulation
Ocean Drilling Program
Oceanic Society
Oceanographic submersibles
Paleoceanography
Radar in oceanography
Robots—Oceanographic use
Sea water
Tides
United States. National Oceanic and Atmospheric Administration
Low-tech earth observation. E. Marshall. il *Science* 244:1249 Je 16 '89
Profiles [work of S. A. Earle] W. White. il *The New Yorker* 65:41-2+ Jl 3 '89
Sea secrets [questions and answers] F. Schaefer. See issues of Sea Frontiers beginning January/February 1986
Secrets of the sea [advances in climate research; cover story] W. J. Cook. il *U.S. News & World Report* 107:48-52+ Ag 21 '89
Awards
See also
Albatross Award
Bibliography
Books. See issues of Sea Frontiers
Reviews. See issues of Oceans through March/April 1989
Federal aid
Crow's nest. B. Rosendahl. il *Sea Frontiers* 35:259 S/O '89
Study and teaching
See Oceanographic education
OCEANS (PERIODICAL)
Citizen raising Cain. R. Covington. il *Oceans* 22:2 Mr/Ap '89
OCHOA, LAURA G.
(jt. auth) See Peterson, Johnny W., and Ochoa, Laura G.
OCHOA, LAURIE
Behind her blue eyes. il pors *American Film* 15:46-7 O '89
First-time directors. il *American Film* 14:46-51+ Ap '89
OCHOA SÁNCHEZ, ARNALDO
about
Anatomy of an execution. A. Cruz, Jr. *Commentary* 88:54-6 N '89
Death in Havana. *Newsweek* 114:24 Jl 24 '89
'I have no reason to live'. H. Anderson. il por *Newsweek* 114:25 Jl 10 '89
Reading the coca leaves. J. Smolowe. il pors *Time* 134:30-1 Jl 10 '89
Revolution doesn't go better with coke. il por *U.S. News & World Report* 107:12 Jl 10 '89
The trial that shook Cuba [cover story] J. Preston. il pors *The New York Review of Books* 36:24-31 D 7 '89
OCILLA (GA.)
Education
AIDS in America's schoolhouses: learning the hard lessons [cover story; with editorial comment by Pauline B. Gough] D. L. Kirp and S. Epstein. il *Phi Delta Kappan* 70:578, 584-93 Ap '89
OCKELS, WUBBO
Why conduct life science research in space? il *Ad Astra* 1:3+ My '89
OCKENHOUSE, CHRISTIAN F., AND OTHERS
Identification of a platelet membrane glycoprotein as a falciparum malaria sequestration receptor. bibl f il *Science* 243:1469-71 Mr 17 '89
Malaria red cell cytoadherence [discussion of March 17, 1989 article, Identification of a platelet membrane glycoprotein as a falciparum malaria sequestration receptor] *Science* 246:1051 N 24 '89
O'CLEIREACAIN, CAROL
Bailout ripoff. *The Nation* 248:581 My 1 '89

OCOEE (FLA.)
Blacks
History
The Ocoee riot [1920] Z. N. Hurston. il *Essence* 19:61-2+ F '89
Riots
The Ocoee riot [1920] Z. N. Hurston. il *Essence* 19:61-2+ F '89
O'COLLINS, GERALD
Christ's Resurrection and Ascension. *America* 160:262-3 Mr 25 '89
O'CONNELL, PETER, AND OTHERS
Two NF1 translocations map within a 600-kilobase segment of 17q11.2. bibl f il *Science* 244:1087-8 Je 2 '89
O'CONNELL, ROBERT L.
Post haste. il *American Heritage* 40:76-86 S/O '89
O'CONNELL-CAHILL, MICHAEL
The drunk who helped millions get sober. il *U.S. Catholic* 54:10-12 F '89
O'CONNOR, B. WRIGHT
Creating a racquet. il *Black Enterprise* 19:54-5 Jl '89
Leafing through history. il *Black Enterprise* 20:105-6 S '89
What's next for the SBA? *Black Enterprise* 19:137-8 Je '89
O'CONNOR, CARROLL
about
Carroll O'Connor. il pors *People Weekly* 31 Special Issue:40-1 Summ '89
Carroll O'Connor calls it luck. G. Esterly. il pors *The Saturday Evening Post* 261:58-9+ O '89
O'CONNOR, DAGMAR
The most-asked sex questions; ed. by Nelly Edmondson Gupta. *Ladies' Home Journal* 106:72+ F '89
Take 6 steps to better sex. *Redbook* 172:90-1+ F '89
O'CONNOR, D'ARCY
about
Writer D'Arcy O'Connor, digging deep into 'Money Pit' lore, unearths a trove of mysteries. P. Freeman. il pors *People Weekly* 31:235-6 Mr 6 '89
O'CONNOR, JACK, 1902-1978
about
The Jack O'Connor letters (I). il pors *Outdoor Life* 183:66-7+ F '89
The Jack O'Connor letters (II). il pors *Outdoor Life* 183:80-1+ Mr '89
O'CONNOR, JAMES V.
Geoquiz. See issues of Earth Science beginning Summer 1985 through Winter 1988
O'CONNOR, JOHN JOSEPH, CARDINAL, 1920-
Challenges facing U.S. Catholics. *Commonweal* 116:619-20 N 17 '89
Mayor Koch and Cardinal O'Connor: a conversation [excerpts from His Eminence and Hizzoner] il por *Good Housekeeping* 208:148+ My '89
about
In a rage over AIDS. E. Magnuson. il *Time* 134:33 D 25 '89
The prophet motive. J. Klein. il pors *New York* 22:12+ Mr 20 '89
The view from St. Patrick's. J. Berger. il pors *The New York Times Magazine* p38-40+ Mr 26 '89
O'CONNOR, KATHLEEN
Just a little magic [story] il *Good Housekeeping* 209:104-5 Ag '89
O'CONNOR, MICHAEL, AND OTHERS
Construction of large DNA segments in Escherichia coli. bibl f il *Science* 244:1307-12 Je 16 '89
O'CONNOR, PAT
about
The January man [film] Reviews
Maclean's il 102:45 Ja 23 '89. B. D. Johnson
The New Leader 72:23 Ja 23 '89. J. Morrone
Newsweek 113:70 Ja 30 '89. D. Ansen
People Weekly il 31:16 Ja 23 '89. P. Travers
Time il 133:59 Ja 23 '89. R. Schickel
O'CONNOR, PATRICK
Five minutes to midnight. il pors *Opera News* 53:14-16+ Mr 4 '89
Five minutes to midnight [cover story] il pors *Opera News* 53:8-12 Mr 4 '89
O'CONNOR, RICHARD D., 1931-
The future of advertising [address, May 9, 1989] *Vital Speeches of the Day* 55:583-7 Jl 15 '89
O'CONNOR, RORY
Clean vs. dirty. il *Mother Jones* 14:56-7 Je '89
about
Covering news where networks fear to tread. C. Reece. il *Channels (New York, N.Y.: 1986)* 9:17 Ja '89
O'CONNOR, SANDRA DAY
about
All eyes on Justice O'Connor. G. Hackett and A. McDaniel. il pors *Newsweek* 113:34-5 My 1 '89
America's most influential woman. M. C. Williams and A. Kamen. il por *Reader's Digest* 135:71-6 D '89
O'Connor fumbles 'Christian nation' case. E. M. Gaffney, Jr. *The Christian Century* 106:373-5 Ap 12 '89
Sandra Day O'Connor: woman in the middle. M. McLoughlin. por *Ladies' Home Journal* 106:218-19+ N '89

O'CONNOR, SANDRA DAY—about—*cont.*
Sandra's day. H. Schwartz. *The Nation* 249:156-7 Ag 7-14 '89
O'CONNOR, SHIRLEY
about
From art director to rug designer. D. E. Gumpert and D. Davis. il por *New Choices for the Best Years* 29:48-9 O '89
O'CONNOR, THOM
Pro view. See issues of Popular Photography beginning August 1988 through November 1988
OCR (OPTICAL CHARACTER RECOGNITION) DEVICES *See* Optical scanners
OCTAVE, JEAN-NOËL
(jt. auth) *See* De Sauvage, Frédéric, and Octave, Jean-Noël
OCTOBER
The October almanac. il *The Atlantic* 264:18 O '89
OCTOPUSES
Arms and the man [giant Pacific octopus] N. G. McDaniel. il *Oceans* 22:38-45 Mr/Ap '89
Banded octopus: uncommon mimic. il *Sea Frontiers* 35:375 N/D '89
ODA, TATSUYA, AND OTHERS
Oxygen radicals in influenza-induced pathogenesis and treatment with pyran polymer-conjugated SOD. bibl f il *Science* 244:974-6 My 26 '89
ODAWARA, MASATO, AND OTHERS
Human diabetes associated with a mutation in the tyrosine kinase domain of the insulin receptor. bibl f il *Science* 245:66-8 Jl 7 '89
O'DAY, ANITA, 1919-
about
Anita O'Day. D. Hutchings. il pors *People Weekly* 32:93-4+ Ag 14 '89
O'DAY, ROSEMARY
Paperback history. *History Today* 39:51 Mr '89
Retrieved riches: Charles Booth's Life and labour of the people in London. bibl il por map *History Today* 39:29-35 Ap '89
O'DAY CORPORATION
Don't blame me [L. Funston's failed leveraged buyout] A. A. Lappen. il por *Forbes* 144:102-3+ S 4 '89
ODD-LOT FUND
Making odd lots into a silk purse. P. Sellers. il *Fortune* 120:32+ S 11 '89
O'DELL, C. ROBERT
Building the Hubble Space Telescope. il *Sky and Telescope* 78:31-6 Jl '89
ODELL, DAVID, AND BATCHELLER, GORDON
Waterfowl for tomorrow: the North American Waterfowl Management Plan. il map *The Conservationist* 43:6-11 Mr/Ap '89
ODENWALD, STEN
Turning pro: the good, the bad, and the ugly. il *Sky and Telescope* 77:124 F '89
ODOM, A. LEROY, AND RINK, WILLIAM J.
Giant radiation-induced color halos in quartz: solution to a riddle. bibl f il *Science* 246:107-9 O 6 '89
ODOM, WILLIAM E.
Can Gorbachev reform the Soviet military? il *U.S. News & World Report* 107:43 S 11 '89
Has the Soviet Union really changed? il *U.S. News & World Report* 106:55 Ap 3 '89
O'DONNELL, BROPHY
Sweet mystery of life [story] il *Seventeen* 48:116-17+ D '89
O'DONNELL, CORNELIUS
about
Garden swap party. C. A. Rossell. il pors *Organic Gardening* 36:34-7 O '89
O'DONNELL, DONAT *See* O'Brien, Conor Cruise, 1917-
O'DONNELL, KEVIN, JR.
Tomatoes: a tragedy. il por *Organic Gardening* 36:79 S '89
O'DONNELL, MARK
Marred bliss. il *The Atlantic* 263:30-1 Ap '89
O'DONOGHUE, MICHAEL
about
Camping out. Q. Crisp. il por *House & Garden* 161:184-7 O '89
O'DONOVAN, LEO J.
The spring in Spain. *America* 160:510-13 My 27 '89
To find originality. *America* 161:299-300 N 4 '89
ODORS
See also
Aroma therapy
Deodorants
Perfumes
Pheromones
The scent of confidence [body odors] P. Paul. il *Current Health 2* 15:28-9 Mr '89
ODUM, EUGENE PLEASANTS, 1913-
Input management of production systems. bibl f il *Science* 243:177-82 Ja 13 '89
O'DY, SYLVIE
Smashing atom dust. *World Press Review* 36:67 S '89
ODYSSEY BOOK SHOP (SOUTH HADLEY, MASS.) *See* Booksellers and bookselling—Massachusetts

ODYSSEY OF THE MIND
Mind Odyssey [interview with S. Micklus] N. Guccione. il *Omni (New York, N.Y.)* 11:16 Ap '89
Science education: the bright spots. T. H. Cole. il *Popular Mechanics* 166:22 F '89
ODYSSEY PAPERBACKS (FIRM)
HBJ announces new paperback imprint. O. David. *Publishers Weekly* 236:30 S 29 '89
OECD *See* Organisation for Economic Co-operation and Development
OECOPHYLLA SMARAGDINA *See* Ants
OED *See* Oxford English dictionary
OEDIPUS REX [dance] *See* Dance reviews—Single works
OENOTHERA *See* Sundrops
OERI *See* United States. Office of Educational Research and Improvement
OESTERREICHISCHE INDUSTRIEHOLDING AKTIEN-GESELLSCHAFT
Goering's legacy. P. Fuhrman. il map *Forbes* 143:76-7 Ja 23 '89
O'FARRELL, PATRICK H., AND OTHERS
Directing cell division during development. bibl f il *Science* 246:635-40 N 3 '89
OFF-BUDGET PROGRAMS
The $5 trillion shock. S. Waldman. il *Newsweek* 114:26-8 D 18 '89
Burned by the thrifts, Congress looks at other fire hazards. C. Yang. il *Business Week* p57 O 9 '89
Fiscal legerdemain. E. Rubenstein. *National Review* 41:17 Jl 14 '89
A time bomb for U.S. taxpayers. R. E. Norton. il *Fortune* 120:139+ O 23 '89
OFF LIMITS [film] *See* Motion picture reviews—Single works
OFF-ROAD BICYCLES *See* Bicycles
OFF-ROAD CYCLING *See* Mountain cycling
OFF-ROAD DRIVING *See* Motor vehicle driving
OFF-ROAD RACING *See* Motor vehicle racing
OFF-ROAD VEHICLES *See* All terrain vehicles
OFF-TRACK BETTING
Has racing staked its future on a bad pony? [off-track simulcasting's effect on race track attendance] S. Phillips. il *Business Week* p84+ My 8 '89
OFFENBACH, JACQUES, 1819-1880
about
The tales of Hoffmann [opera] Reviews
Opera News il 54:14-15+ D 23 '89. D. P. Stearns
Opera News il 54:24-7 D 23 '89
OFFICE BUILDINGS
See also
Bank buildings
Houston (Tex.)—Buildings
Los Angeles (Calif.)—Buildings
Minneapolis (Minn.)—Buildings
Sick building syndrome
Icons of modernism or machine-age dinosaurs? J. S. Russell. il *Architectural Record* 177:142-7 Je '89
Environmental engineering
See Environmental engineering (Buildings)
Leasing and renting
See Offices—Leasing and renting
OFFICE CHAIRS *See* Chairs
OFFICE CLUB (FIRM)
Seeking big money in paper and pens. S. Caminiti. il *Fortune* 120:173-4 Jl 31 '89
OFFICE DECORATION
Capital gains [office for Capital Research Co. designed by R. A. M. Stern in New York City] P. M. Sachner. il *Architectural Record* 177:98-103 mid-S '89
Coming home [offices for Swid Powell Design by Stephen Sills] H. S. MacIsaac. il *House & Garden* 161:36+ D '89
Habitat [corporate elite] J. H. Dobrzynski. il *Business Week* Special Issue:45-9+ O 20 '89
Imagine this. C. Vogel. il *The New York Times Magazine* p70-3 F 26 '89
My office, my castle. N. Sullivan. il *Home Office Computing* 7:104 O '89
One woman's office. See issues of Working Woman
Playing the angles [office for James Goldstein designed by J. Lautner] D. Dietsch. il *Architectural Record* 177:76-9 mid-S '89
Rational moves [Fernau & Hartman design offices for SBG Partners] K. D. Stein. il *Architectural Record* 177:68-75 mid-S '89
Show offices [special section; with introd. by Karen D. Stein] il *Architectural Record* 177:138-49 My '89
OFFICE DEPOT (FIRM)
Seeking big money in paper and pens. S. Caminiti. il *Fortune* 120:173-4 Jl 31 '89
OFFICE EQUIPMENT
See also
Computers—Business use
Equipping your home office. S. Esters. il *Black Enterprise* 19:76-7 Ap '89
Equipping your home office. D. Lyon and P. Harris. il *Psychology Today* 23:48-9 N '89
Getting the tools to make the office hum. C. Whitmyer and D. Ben-Horin. il *Working Woman* 14:54+ Ja '89

OFFICE EQUIPMENT—*cont.*

Office gear on the go. S. Advokat. il *Nation's Business* 77:56+ N '89

Office machines: more, better, cheaper [special section] J. Pepper. il *Nation's Business* 77:30-2+ F '89

Product reports 1990. il *Architectural Record* 177:26-9+ D '89

Professionals on the go carry office technology in their briefcase. R. E. Barnes. il *Black Enterprise* 20:47 D '89

What's big? What's small. il *Home Office Computing* 7:11 Ag '89

Year-end special: editors' picks 1989: the best and brightest hardware of the year [cover story] il *Home Office Computing* 7:47-51 D '89

Year-end special: great gifts for the home office [cover story] M. Alvich. il *Home Office Computing* 7:56-9 D '89

Your home office [cover story; special section] il *Compute!* 11:23-6+ N '89

OFFICE EQUIPMENT INDUSTRY

    See also
    AM International, Inc.
    Bell & Howell Co.
    Colorocs Corp.
    Datapoint Corp.
    Eldon Industries, Inc.
    General Binding Corp.
    International Business Machines Corp.
    Minnesota Mining & Mfg. Co.
    Nashua Corporation
    Performing Artists Diversified (Firm)
    Quill Corporation
    Savin Corp.
    Smith Corona Corp.
    Stuart Hall Co., Inc.
    Xerox Corp.

Chain and franchise operations

Office services by franchise. N. C. Baker. il *Nation's Business* 77:62-3 My '89

Finance

Industrial and office services. J. Zweig. il *Forbes* 143:158+ Ja 9 '89

Marketing

    See also
    Office Club (Firm)
    Office Depot (Firm)
    Office equipment stores
    Staples (Firm)

Hong Kong

    See also
    Chevalier (OA) Holdings Ltd.

Italy

    See also
    Ing. C. Olivetti & Co., SpA

Japan

    See also
    Canon Inc.

OFFICE EQUIPMENT STORES

The instant office [New York City] V. Taylor and A. Berlin. il *New York* 22:104+ My 1 '89

OFFICE ETIQUETTE *See* Business etiquette

OFFICE FURNITURE

    See also
    Chairs
    Conference tables

Product reports 1990. il *Architectural Record* 177:141-7 D '89

The truly unique executive suite. A. Busch. il *Working Woman* 14:94-7 Mr '89

OFFICE FURNITURE INDUSTRY

    See also
    Herman Miller, Inc.

OFFICE MANAGEMENT

Administrative services managers. A. Gartaganis. il *Occupational Outlook Quarterly* 33:30-1 Summ '89

How to cut the cost of headquarters. T. Paré. il *Fortune* 120:189+ S 11 '89

Managing people and PCs effectively. C. O'Malley. il *Personal Computing* 13:57-8+ Mr '89

Technologizing office work. M. R. Smith. bibl *Society* 26:65-72 My/Je '89

OFFICE OF COMMERCIAL PROGRAMS (U.S.) *See* United States. National Aeronautics and Space Administration. Office of Commercial Programs

OFFICE OF THE SPECIAL COUNSEL (U.S.) *See* United States. Merit Systems Protection Board. Office of the Special Counsel

OFFICE POLITICS *See* Psychology, Industrial

OFFICE ROMANCES *See* Sex in business

OFFICE SUPPLIES *See* Office equipment

OFFICE WORKERS

    See also
    Secretaries

The ominous exporting of U.S. clerical jobs. R. O. Metzger. il *USA Today (Periodical)* 117:30-1 Mr '89

Psychology

    See Psychology, Industrial

OFFICER, MARION E., D. 1989

    about

Obituary

    Jet por 75:16 F 27 '89

OFFICES

    See also
    Architects' offices
    Dental offices
    Home offices
    Lawyers' offices
    Mobile offices
    Offshore offices

Nine to five in a van [fitted out to serve as an office] E. Henry. il *Changing Times* 43:78 Jl '89

Without office. A. Gelb. il *Parents* 64:204 F '89

Automation

    See also
    Datapoint Corp.
    Digital Equipment Corp.
    Harris Corp.
    Ing. C. Olivetti & Co., SpA
    International Business Machines Corp.
    Minnesota Mining & Mfg. Co.
    Northern Telecom Ltd.
    Rolm Corp.
    Voice mail systems
    Wang Laboratories Inc.
    Xerox Corp.

Down to business. W. Rash, Jr. See issues of Byte beginning August 1988

Redefining old jobs, creating new ones. M. Piturro. il *Personal Computing* 13:141+ O '89

Technologizing office work. M. R. Smith. bibl *Society* 26:65-72 My/Je '89

Leasing and renting

My banker wouldn't back my building [futile attempt to obtain mortgage for office space] J. DeParle. il *The Washington Monthly* 20:30-1 Ja '89

So why do they keep on putting up office buildings? G. Koretz. il *Business Week* p22 S 11 '89

Security measures

    See Industry—Security measures

OFFICEVISION SOFTWARE

IBM's Vision for your office. W. Rash, Jr. il *Byte* 14:151-2 O '89

Innovation at Apple and IBM. R. A. Shaffer. il *Personal Computing* 13:45-6 S '89

The software that ties it all together. D. A. Depke. il *Business Week* p74-5 My 29 '89

OFFICIAL SECRETS

    See also
    Classified information
    Executive privilege (Government information)
    Government and the press

At war with the First Amendment [Reagan administration] J. Kalven. *The Bulletin of the Atomic Scientists* 45:56-9 Ja/F '89

Great Britain

Her majesty's censors [M. Thatcher] M. Friedman. il *The Progressive* 53:30-3 F '89

OFFICINE ALFIERI MASERATI SPA

How Chrysler's $30,000 sports car got sideswiped. J. Rossant. il *Business Week* p68+ Ja 23 '89

OFFSHORE BOUNDARIES *See* Territorial waters

OFFSHORE OFFICES

The ominous exporting of U.S. clerical jobs. R. O. Metzger. il *USA Today (Periodical)* 117:30-1 Mr '89

OFFSHORE OIL FIELDS *See* Petroleum in submerged lands

OFFSHORE OIL WELL RIGS *See* Oil well drilling rigs

OFFSHORE POWERBOAT RACING *See* Motor boat racing

O'GARA, GEOFFREY

Beyond the burn. il map *Sierra* 74:40-51 Ja/F '89

OGDEN, SHEPHERD

Lettuce vogue [cover story] il pors *Organic Gardening* 36:30-5 My '89

Pick of the crop. il *Country Journal* 16:29-33 Ja '89

Planting the seed. il *Country Journal* 16:69-73 Mr/Ap '89

OGDEN, SUE

    about

The Mommy doll cues kids on the new reality: mother's place is wherever she wants to be! il *People Weekly* 32:112-13 Ag 7 '89

OGDEN CORP.

It ain't glamorous, but the money sure is good. M. Roman. il *Business Week* p64-5 Ag 28 '89

OGILVY, DAVID JOHN, 1958-

Victorian fantasy. il por *House & Garden* 161:176-81 Mr '89

OGILVY, MARINA

    about

The Queen's cousin, pregnant and unwed, cozies up to the press but gets the big chill from the palace. C. Sanz and L. S. Healy. il pors *People Weekly* 32:47-8 O 30 '89

OGILVY GROUP INC.
Confessions of an advertising man [WPP's M. Sorrell negotiates takeover] R. I. Kirkland, Jr. il por *Fortune* 119:131-2 Je 5 '89
The 'fax attack' that has Ogilvy fuming [WPP Group plc bid] W. Konrad. il por *Business Week* p36 My 15 '89
Machiavelli on Madison Avenue [WPP Group's bid for Ogilvy Group] B. Rudolph. il por *Time* 133:58 My 15 '89
The man who would be king of Madison Ave. [M. Sorrell's WPP Group bids for Ogilvy Group] L. Reibstein. il por *Newsweek* 113:52 My 15 '89
Mediums and messages [WPP buys Ogilvy] A. Walmsley. il por *Maclean's* 102:42 My 29 '89
WPP, the new giant of . . . PR? [WPP buys Ogilvy] W. Konrad. *Business Week* p32 My 29 '89

OGLESBEE, CLAY
The Kemp plan for rebuilding the city. *The Christian Century* 106:340-1 Ap 5 '89

OGONYOK (PERIODICAL)
International Editor of the Year [V. Korotich; with interview] il por *World Press Review* 36:22-6 My '89
A talk with the editor of 'Ogonyok' [interview with V. Korotich; cover story; with editorial comment] M. Mihajlov. il *The New Leader* 72:2, 10-16 F 20 '89
Typing out the fear. V. Korotich. il *Time* 133:124+ Ap 10 '89

O'GRADY, SEAN
The tour of doom. il map *Bicycling* 30:150-4+ My '89

OH, YOUNG BONG
Buddhism in America: can it blend with our philosophy and culture? il *USA Today (Periodical)* 118:84-5 Jl '89

O'HAGAN, DESMOND, 1960-
about
Stirring the viewer's imagination. M. S. Doherty. il *American Artist* 53:54-9 D '89

O'HALLAREN, BILL
It's Dinah vs. the dog—and she's growling. il pors *TV Guide* 37:12-14 Je 24-30 '89
She Snoops to conquer. il pors *TV Guide* 37:10-12 O 28-N 3 '89
Would you let this doctor operate on you? [cover story] il pors *TV Guide* 37:4-5+ D 16-22 '89

OHANIAN, BERNARD
Casey Kasem's flip side. il pors *Mother Jones* 14:21-3+ O '89

OHANIAN, SUSAN
Creating a generation of "aliterates". *The Education Digest* 54:29-32 F '89
Yes, but where are your credits in Recess Management 101? *The Washington Monthly* 21:46-7 F '89

O'HARE, JOSEPH A.
In solidarity with the slain Jesuits of El Salvador [address, November 22, 1989] *America* 161:443-6 D 16 '89
The Vatican and Catholic universities. *America* 160:503-5 My 27 '89

O'HARE INTERNATIONAL AIRPORT *See* Chicago (Ill.)—Airports

O'HEHIR, DIANA, 1929-
Fighting writer's block. *The Writer* 102:12-14+ F '89

O'HIGGINS, MICHAEL B.
about
Where a contrarian finds value in today's blue chips. il por *Money* 18:7-8 My '89

OHIO
See also
Agriculture—Ohio
Athens County (Ohio)
Earthquakes—Ohio
Geology—Ohio
Insurance law—Ohio
Music festivals—Ohio
Sports—Ohio
Description and travel
See also
Automobile touring—Ohio
Parks and reserves
See also
Malabar Farm State Park (Lucas, Ohio)

OHIO BUCKEYE *See* Horse chestnut

OHIO CRANKSHAFT (FIRM)
'Without unions, we'd have nothing' [strike] P. Warloski. il *The Progressive* 53:22 D '89

OHIO STATE UNIVERSITY. WEXNER CENTER FOR THE VISUAL ARTS *See* Wexner Center for the Visual Arts (Columbus, Ohio)

OHIO UNIVERSITY. SCRIPPS SCHOOL OF JOURNALISM *See* Scripps School of Journalism

ÖHLÉN, CLAES, AND OTHERS
Prevention of allogeneic bone marrow graft rejection by H-2 transgene in donor mice. bibl f il *Science* 246:666-8 N 3 '89

OHLHAUSEN, MARILYN M.
(jt. auth) See Ford, Michael P., and Ohlhausen, Marilyn M.

OHM CORPORATION
Down in the dumps. R. Simon. il por *Forbes* 143:104+ My 1 '89

A muddied recycler could still shine. G. G. Marcial. *Business Week* p108 S 18 '89

OHMART, ROBERT D.
"A timid desert creature . . .". il *Natural History* p34-41 S '89

OHNUMA, KEIKO
Yosemite national parking lot. il *Sierra* 74:31-2+ N/D '89

OHR, GEORGE E., 1857-1918
about
Art. K. Larson. *New York* 22:123-4 N 20 '89

OHRBACH, BARBARA MILO
"Look what I found!" [excerpt from Antiques at home] il *Ladies' Home Journal* 106:162-6 S '89
about
Scented rooms. J. Seymore. il por *House & Garden* 161:170-5+ N '89

OIL *See* Petroleum

OIL ANALYSIS
Engine blood test [marine engines] T. P. Banse. il *Motor Boating & Sailing* 164:72 S '89
The spectrometric sleuth [for motorcycles] T. Van Hooydonk. il *Cycle* 40:80-2 F '89

OIL AND GAS LEASES
Adversaries in the Arctic [Arctic National Wildlife Refuge] M. Hager. il map *Newsweek* 113:60 F 27 '89
Arctic National Wildlife Refuge [discussion of May 1989 article, Oil development and the Arctic National Wildlife Refuge] L. Speer. il *Environment* 31:2-4 S '89
Drills across the border [Shell Canada's plans to drill near Waterton-Glacier International Peace Park] K. Van Tighem. il *Wilderness* 52:54-6 Wint '88
Explore no more? [Arctic National Wildlife Refuge] E. F. Cone. il *Forbes* 143:10 My 15 '89
The future of big oil [drilling in Arctic National Wildlife Refuge after Exxon oil spill; cover story] P. Nulty. il map *Fortune* 119:46-9 My 8 '89
Impacts of petroleum development in the Arctic [discussion of November 6, 1987 article, Cumulative impacts of oil fields on northern Alaskan landscapes] D. A. Walker and others. *Science* 245:764-6 Ag 18 '89
Interior paves way for sale of resources. *National Parks* 63:11 Mr/Ap '89
Oil development and the Arctic National Wildlife Refuge. L. Speer. bibl f il *Environment* 31:42-3 My '89
A tale of two villages [natives bordering Arctic National Wildlife Refuge hold opposing viewpoints on oil development] E. Linden. il *Time* 133:62 Ap 17 '89
Tundra plunder [proposed oil exploration in the Arctic National Wildlife Refuge] *The New Republic* 200:8+ My 1 '89
Royalties
British royalty [BP's new royalty trust may signal new takeovers] T. Mack. il *Forbes* 143:92 Ap 3 '89

OIL COMPANIES *See* Petroleum industry
OIL CRISIS *See* Petroleum supply
OIL DRILLING FUNDS *See* Petroleum investment trusts
OIL EXPLORATION *See* Petroleum prospecting
OIL FIELD INVESTMENT TRUSTS *See* Petroleum investment trusts
OIL FILTERS
See also
Automobile engines—Filters
OIL FUTURES *See* Commodity futures
OIL IMPORTS AND EXPORTS *See* Petroleum industry—Export-import trade
OIL LAMPS *See* Lamps
OIL LEASES *See* Oil and gas leases
OIL PAINTING *See* Painting
OIL PASTEL ASSOCIATION
The Oil Pastel Association. il *American Artist* 53:12 N '89
OIL POLLUTION
The legacy of past spills. L. Roberts. *Science* 244:23 Ap 7 '89
Oil in the sea: the big spills and blowouts. L. Ware. il *Audubon* 91:109 S '89
Oilspeak, common sense, and soft science. F. Graham. il *Audubon* 91:102-8+ S '89
An oily blight on the water [Delaware River, Galveston Bay and Rhode Island] L. Martz. il *Newsweek* 114:24 Jl 3 '89
Summer of the spills [accidents off Newport, R.I., Houston and in the Delaware River] F. Trippett. il *Time* 134:18 Jl 3 '89
Control
See also
Airplanes in oil pollution control
Bacteria, Petroleumlytic
Exxon Valdez (Ship) oil spill, 1989—Cleanup
Yankee Companies Inc.
No slick fix. T. Beardsley. *Scientific American* 261:34 S '89
The spill next time: what needs to be done. S. Begley. il *Newsweek* 114:59 S 18 '89
Laws and regulations
To stop spills, punishment must cost more than prevention. V. Cahan. il *Business Week* p26 Jl 10 '89

OIL POLLUTION—Laws and regulations—*cont.*

Whose mess is it? [Congress considers tougher laws in wake of various oil spills] B. Rudolph. il *Time* 134:42-3 Jl 10 '89

Alaska
See also
Exxon Valdez (Ship) oil spill, 1989

Antarctic regions
250,000 gallons of prevention [spill] il *U.S. News & World Report* 106:13 F 20 '89
Stains on the white continent [spill from Argentine ship] D. Thompson. il map *Time* 133:77 F 20 '89

British Columbia
Deadly coastal spills. H. Quinn. il *Maclean's* 102:17 Ja 23 '89

Narragansett Bay (R.I.)
Aground [Greek tanker, World Prodigy, spills oil] *The New Yorker* 65:22-4 Jl 24 '89

New York (State)
On gushes and seeps—what we do about environmental spills. M. Kadlecek. *The Conservationist* 44:52-3 S/O '89

Newfoundland
Deadly coastal spills. H. Quinn. il *Maclean's* 102:17 Ja 23 '89

Panama
Ecological effects of a major oil spill on Panamanian coastal marine communities. J. B. C. Jackson and others. bibl f il map *Science* 243:37-44 Ja 6 '89

Washington (State)
After an oil spill: saving the birds. D. B. Lewis. il *Sea Frontiers* 35:200-5 Jl/Ag '89
Hands against the darkness [cleaning oil-soaked birds after spill] A. E. Simonov. il *The Mother Earth News* 118:8 Jl/Ag '89
Oil spill taints Olympic beaches [Olympic National Park] il *National Parks* 63:8-9 Mr/Ap '89

OIL POLLUTION AND WILDLIFE
After an oil spill: saving the birds [Washington State] D. B. Lewis. il *Sea Frontiers* 35:200-5 Jl/Ag '89
Dead otters, silent ducks [aftermath of oil spill in Alaska] G. Cowley. il *Newsweek* 113:70 Ap 24 '89
A disaster that wasn't [Exxon Valdez oil spill] M. Satchell and B. Carpenter. il map *U.S. News & World Report* 107:60-4+ S 18 '89
Hands against the darkness [cleaning oil-soaked birds after Washington spill] A. E. Simonov. il *The Mother Earth News* 118:8 Jl/Ag '89
Long, slow recovery predicted for Alaska [Exxon Valdez oil spill] L. Roberts. il *Science* 244:22-4 Ap 7 '89
Profiles [work of S. A. Earle] W. White. il *The New Yorker* 65:41-2+ Jl 3 '89
Wreck of the Exxon Valdez [cover story; special section; with editorial comment by Les Line and Peter A. A. Berle] il map *Audubon* 91:4, 6, 10, 73-111 S '89

OIL REFINERIES *See* Petroleum refineries
OIL ROYALTIES *See* Oil and gas leases—Royalties
OIL SANDS
Rise in heavy oil use seen for 21st century. *High Technology Business* 9:34 Ja '89
Spectral reflectance properties of hydrocarbons: remote-sensing implications. E. A. Cloutis. bibl f il *Science* 245:165-8 Jl 14 '89
Tar sands on Iapetus [research by Edward A. Cloutis] *Science News* 136:62 Jl 22 '89

OIL SEEPAGE
The quick recipe for a soup of black gold [research by Bernd R.T. Simoneit] R. Monastersky. *Science News* 136:295 N 4 '89

OIL SHALES
See also
Oil sands

OIL SPILLS *See* Oil pollution
OIL SUPPLY *See* Petroleum supply
OIL TANKERS *See* Tankers
OIL WELL DRILLING
After oil [excerpt from Oil notes] R. Bass. *Harper's* 278:27-8+ My '89
Lateral thinking [horizontal drilling] T. Mack. il *Forbes* 143:130+ My 15 '89
Oil fields of dreams [horizontal oil well drilling] K. R. Sheets. il *U.S. News & World Report* 107:35-6 D 18 '89

Environmental aspects
See Petroleum industry—Environmental aspects

Equipment
See also
Oil well drilling rigs

OIL WELL DRILLING, SUBMARINE

Rigs
See Oil well drilling rigs

OIL WELL DRILLING RIGHTS *See* Oil and gas leases
OIL WELL DRILLING RIGS
Mussel man Bob Meek runs a seafood farm built on mutual shellfishness [harvesting mussels attached to legs of offshore drilling platforms] N. Geeslin. il pors *People Weekly* 31:135-6 My 1 '89

Maintenance and repair
Working underwater [professional divers on an offshore oil rig in the Gulf of Mexico] J. S. McKinna. il *Sea Frontiers* 35:348-55 N/D '89

OILS, ESSENTIAL *See* Essences and essential oils
OILS AND FATS
See also
Soybean oil
OILS AND FATS, EDIBLE
See also
Coconut oil
Fish oil
Food—Fat content
Margarine
Olive oil
Palm oil
Peanut oil
Good food, good health: what's what in vegetable oils. M. Callahan. il *Better Homes and Gardens* 67:45 Je '89
Shopper's guide to oils. *McCall's* 117:96 O '89

OITICICA, HÉLIO, 1937-1980
about
Hélio Oiticica: reverie and revolt [cover story] G. Brett. bibl f il pors *Art in America* 77:110-21+ Ja '89

OJAKANGAS, BEATRICE
Gift breads. il *Ladies' Home Journal* 106:178-80+ D '89
O'JAYS (MUSICAL GROUP)
The O'Jays still turning out hit songs after 32 years [cover story] A. Collier. il *Jet* 76:58-9+ Ag 21 '89
OJEDA, BOB, 1957-
about
Gripping saga. B. Weber. il pors *The New York Times Magazine* p98 F 19 '89
A victim of careless gardening, Bob Ojeda is back in the ball game with the finger he nearly cut off [interview] M. Huzinec. il pors *People Weekly* 31:107-8+ Mr 27 '89
OJEDA RIOS, FILIBERTO
about
Preventive . . . R. A. Falk. *The Nation* 248:508-9 Ap 17 '89

OKADA, MOKICHI, 1882-1955
about
View from the East. R. Rodale. il por *Organic Gardening* 36:19-20 D '89
OKC LIMITED PARTNERSHIP
Third down and long [C. Box maneuvers around dissident partners] E. F. Cone. por *Forbes* 143:10 F 20 '89
O'KEEFE, M. TIMOTHY
Alaska—Northwest passages. il *The Saturday Evening Post* 261:82-4 My/Je '89
O'KEEFE, MICHAEL
Private colleges beating the odds. il *Change* 21:10-19 Mr/Ap '89
O'KEEFE, SUSAN HEYBOER
One hungry monster [story] il *Parents* 64:145-6+ N '89
O'KEEFE, WILLIAM F.
Should the Congress adopt the "Clean Air Act amendments of 1987"? [excerpts from statement, September 28, 1987] *Congressional Digest* 68:49+ F '89
O'KEEFFE, GEORGIA, 1887-1986

Bibliography
The image maker. E. Abrahams. *The New Republic* 200:41-5 Ja 30 '89
O'KEEFFE, ISABEL
Flanders Fields revisited. il *World Press Review* 36:12-13 Mr '89
OKEFENOKEE SWAMP PARK (GA.)
The old swamping grounds of Georgia. il *Southern Living* 24:20 Mr '89
OKIES
Travels with Steinbeck [exploring migrant camps during the Depression]; ed. by Jack Kelly. H. Bristol. il pors *People Weekly* 31:66-8+ My 1 '89
OKIES IN LITERATURE
The grapes of wrath fifty years later. J. H. Timmerman. *The Christian Century* 106:341-3 Ap 5 '89
The grapes of wrath: looking back. L. Owens. il *USA Today (Periodical)* 117:92-3 My '89
OKINAWA, BATTLE OF, 1945
The ship that outsailed time [USS Mullany] N. M. Adams. il *Reader's Digest* 135:117-24+ S '89
ÔKITA, SABURÔ, 1914-
Japan's quiet strength. *Foreign Policy* 75:128-45 Summ '89
OKLAHOMA
See also
Agriculture—Oklahoma
Cimarron County (Okla.)
Flint Hills (Kan. and Okla.)
Ouachita National Forest (Ark. and Okla.)
Prisons—Oklahoma

History
Land Rush, 1889
1889. A. Nielson. il *American Heritage* 40:32 Ap '89
The great Oklahoma Land Rush of 1889. S. Hoig. il map *American History Illustrated* 24:40-50 Mr '89

OKLAHOMA—History—Land Rush, 1889—*cont.*
'Sooners' or 'Goners,' they were hellbent on grabbing free land. R. Day. bibl (p247) il map *Smithsonian* 20:192-4+ N '89
    Land Rush, 1889—Centennial celebrations, etc.
Oklahoma Land Rush. N. McCutchen. il *Americana* 17:32-5 Mr/Ap '89
OKOYE, CHRISTIAN
                    about
Kansas City's gentle giant. por *Time* 134:91-2 D 25 '89
Onward, Christian. P. King. il pors *Sports Illustrated* 71:74-6+ D 11 '89
OKRENT, DANIEL
Brother Harold. por *Esquire* 111:32 Ja '89
Isn't it ironic? il por *Esquire* 112:54 D '89
Oh Mandy. il por *Esquire* 111:40 Ap '89
On the money. il pors *Sports Illustrated* 70:41+ Ap 10 '89
These awards were presented earlier. il *Esquire* 111:52 Mr '89
Thirty years of hard practice. il por *Esquire* 112:28 Jl '89
Who's on third? il *Esquire* 112:41 Ag '89
OKSENBERG, MICHEL, 1938-
Confession of a China watcher. il *Newsweek* 113:30 Je 19 '89
Moscow's Pacific offensive. il *Newsweek* 113:31 Mr 6 '89
OKUBAGZHI, GEBRE SELASSIE
Ethiopia's success story. il *World Health* p21-2 My '89
OKUN, HERBERT S.
Security Council adopts resolution on Central American peace [text of resolution and statement, July 28, 1989] *Department of State Bulletin* 89:73-4 O '89
U.S. reports to United Nations on downing of Libyan planes [letter and statement, January 4-5, 1989] *Department of State Bulletin* 89:90-1 Mr '89
OKUN', L. B. (LEV BORISOVICH)
The concept of mass. bibl f il *Physics Today* 42:31-6 Je '89
OKUN', LEV BORISOVICH See Okun', L. B. (Lev Borisovich)
OKWARE, SAMUEL I.
Giving AIDS a new face. il *World Health* p18-20 O '89
OLAJUWON, AKEEM
                    about
Olajuwon reconciles with mother of his daughter. por *Jet* 75:50 Ja 16 '89
OLANA STATE HISTORIC SITE (HUDSON, N.Y.)
The Hudson River revisited. R. I. C. Fisher. il *American Artist* 53:48-54+ N '89
Olana [home of F. Church; cover story] F. Donegan. il *Americana* 17:26-32 S/O '89
OLANDER, WILLIAM
Material world. il *Art in America* 77:122-9+ Ja '89
OLAUS AND MARGARET MURIE AWARD
Olaus and Margaret Murie Award [J. F. Franklin] *Wilderness* 52:6 Wint '88
OLBERS' PARADOX
Olbers' paradox solved at last [dark night sky] P. S. Wesson. il *Sky and Telescope* 77:594-7 Je '89
OLCOTT-REID, BRENDA
Planning a home fruit garden. il *Flower and Garden* 33:24-9 N/D '89
OLD AGE
            See also
    Aged
    Aging
    Centenarians
    Longevity
    Retirement
            Psychological aspects
    See Aged—Psychology
OLD AGE ASSISTANCE
            See also
    United States. Administration on Aging
A certain species of helplessness [with editorial comment] R. J. Margolis. il *The New Leader* 72:2, 10-12 Ag 7-21 '89
New leaders deal with aging-policy issues [L. Sullivan and D. Pryor] il por *Modern Maturity* 32:85 Ag/S '89
Of capital concern. J. Kosterlitz. il *New Choices for the Best Years* 29:14-15 Mr '89
State and community news. See issues of Aging
What do we owe to the elderly? L. Smith. il *Fortune* 119:54-5+ Mr 27 '89
The young and the old are not enemies. W. R. Hutton. il *USA Today (Periodical)* 117:63-5 Mr '89
OLD AGE CENTERS See Senior centers
OLD AGE HOMES
            See also
    Life care communities
    Nursing homes
    Rest homes
OLD AGE MARKET See Aged market
OLD BELIEVERS
Russia's tenacious Old Believers. J. H. Forest. il *The Christian Century* 106:1121-3 N 29 '89
OLD ERIE CANAL STATE PARK (N.Y.)
The Old Erie Canal State Park. J. Albino. il *The Conservationist* 44:2-7 Jl/Ag '89

OLD EXECUTIVE OFFICE BUILDING (WASHINGTON, D.C.)
Forward to the past [Room 274] il *American Heritage* 40:106-7 Mr '89
OLD FARMER'S ALMANAC See Almanacs
OLD GLORY (FLAG) See American flag
OLD GRINGO [film] See Motion picture reviews—Single works
OLD LYME (CONN.)
                    Art
Two American artists' colonies [En plein air: the art colonies at East Hampton and Old Lyme, 1880-1930] A. E. Ledes. *Antiques* 136:42+ Jl '89
OLD MASTERS PAINTINGS See Painting, European
OLD MERCHANT'S HOUSE (NEW YORK, N.Y.)
No clocks. *The New Yorker* 65:28-9 Je 5 '89
Old Merchants House and Urbani Truffles USA. H. Bridges. il *Gourmet* 49:72+ D '89
OLD SALEM, INC.
Remembering the first Fourth. il *Southern Living* 24:41 Jl '89
OLD SKULL (MUSICAL GROUP)
Prepubescent punk. A. Block. il *Mother Jones* 14:13 O '89
Those precocious young bloods in Old Skull are the only punk rockers with a 9 o'clock bedtime. il *People Weekly* 32:113 S 18 '89
OLD STURBRIDGE VILLAGE
            Photographs and photography
Key in on a theme to help focus your travel shooting [hats] L. Dennis. il *Popular Photography* 96:22-3 Mr '89
OLD TESTAMENT See Bible. O.T.
OLD VIC THEATRE (LONDON, ENGLAND)
Profiles [artistic director J. Miller] P. Gilliatt. il por *The New Yorker* 65:52-6+ Ap 17 '89
OLDER, JULES
High anxiety. il *Skiing* 42:33-4 O '89
OLDFIELD, DUANE M., AND WILDAVSKY, AARON B.
Reconsidering the two presidencies. *Society* 26:54-9 Jl/Ag '89
OLDHAM, JOE
Editor's notes. See issues of Popular Mechanics beginning August 1985
OLDOINYO LENGAI (TANZANIA)
Temperature measurements in carbonatite lava lakes and flows from Oldoinyo Lengai, Tanzania. M. Krafft and J. Keller. bibl f il *Science* 245:168-70 Jl 14 '89
OLDS, JAMES L., AND OTHERS
Imaging of memory-specific changes in the distribution of protein kinase C in the hippocampus. bibl f il *Science* 245:866-9 Ag 25 '89
OLDS, SHARON
The bathrobe [poem] *The New Yorker* 64:36 Ja 23 '89
Outdoor shower [poem] *The Atlantic* 264:110 N '89
OLDSMOBILE DIVISION
Teaching an Oldsmobile new tricks [M. Losh] J. B. Treece. il por *Business Week* p52 S 25 '89
OLDSTONE, MICHAEL B. A.
Viral alteration of cell function. bibl il *Scientific American* 261:42-8 Ag '89
OLDUVAI GORGE (TANZANIA) FOSSILS See Paleontology—Tanzania
OLESTRA See Sucrose polyesters
OLFACTORY NERVES
Odor-induced membrane currents in vertebrate-olfactory receptor neurons. S. Firestein and F. Werblin. bibl f il *Science* 244:79-82 Ap 7 '89
OLFACTORY SENSE See Smell
OLIGOMERIZATION See Polymers
OLIGONUCLEOTIDES See Nucleotides
OLIGOSACCHARIDES
            See also
    Cyclodextrins
OLIN, DIRK
Putting children before politics. il por *New Choices for the Best Years* 29:16+ Jl '89
OLIN, KEN
                    about
thirtysomething's Ken doll. J. Herschel. il por *Mademoiselle* 95:38+ Ja '89
OLIN, LENA
                    about
Not afraid of the dark [cover story] B. Yagoda. il pors *American Film* 15:30-7 N '89
OLIN, MARIAN E.
                    about
Marian E. Olin at Fordham University. L. Campbell. il *Art in America* 77:176-7 Je '89
OLIN, RONALD
                    about
Stocks on sale. J. Clements. il por *Forbes* 144:158+ S 4 '89
OLIPHANT, BETTY
                    about
Betty builds bigger. M. Horosko. il *Dance Magazine* 63:62-3 Mr '89
OLIPHANT, MARK
Three men and the bomb. il pors *The Bulletin of the Atomic Scientists* 45:41-2 Mr '89

OLIPHANT, PATRICK
about
Pat Oliphant. L. Palmer. il por *Gentlemen's Quarterly* 59:290-1 Ap '89
OLIPHANT (BETTY) THEATRE (TORONTO, ONT.) *See* R. A. Laidlaw Center/Betty Oliphant Theatre (Toronto, Ont.)
OLIVE BABOONS *See* Baboons
OLIVE INDUSTRY
See also
Lindsay Olive Growers
Spain
The fruits of Spanish labor. R. Sokolov. il *Natural History* p82+ Mr '89
OLIVE OIL
Diabetic diet [use to lower cholesterol; research by Abhimanyu Garg] il *Prevention (Emmaus, Pa.)* 41:10 Ja '89
Heartfelt splash of olive oil [cholesterol-lowering benefits] il *Prevention (Emmaus, Pa.)* 41:14+ O '89
Olive oil flatters vegetables. il *Southern Living* 24:130 Jl '89
Splash on the olive oil and cut your cholesterol. A. Roblin. il *Prevention (Emmaus, Pa.)* 41:33-7 Ja '89
OLIVER, BILL
about
Troubadours for Mother Nature. C. P. Alexander. il pors *Time* 134:76 N 6 '89
OLIVER, DANIEL
about
Federal Trade Commission: defending the consumer [interview] il por *Consumers' Research Magazine* 72:21-4 O '89
OLIVER, EDITH
The theatre. See issues of The New Yorker beginning February 16, 1987
OLIVER, JOAN DUNCAN
Confessions of a closet clutterer. il por *Health (New York, N.Y.)* 21:38+ S '89
Making sense of scent [cover story; special section] il *Health (New York, N.Y.)* 21:57-62+ N '89
OLIVER, KERMIT
about
A Waco postman designs Hermès scarves with a western flair. il pors *People Weekly* 32:162-3 N 13 '89
OLIVER, LOUIS
about
Look back in anger. D. Scheiber. il pors *Sports Illustrated* 70:42-4+ My 8 '89
OLIVER, MARY, 1935-
Herons in winter in the frozen marsh [poem] *Country Journal* 16:91 Mr/Ap '89
The notebook [poem] *Country Journal* 16:55 Jl/Ag '89
The ponds [poem] *Wilderness* 52:71 Wint '88
White owl flies into and out of the field [poem] *The New Yorker* 64:26 Ja 2 '89
OLIVER, NANCY
Why your service is so primitive. il *Consumers' Research Magazine* 72:14-15 Je '89
OLIVER, PETER
Miracle on 34th Street. il *Travel Holiday* 172:82-7 N '89
The second hundred years. il map *Travel Holiday* 171:62-7 F '89
War and remembrance. il map *Travel Holiday* 172:84-91 Jl '89
OLIVER PEOPLES (FIRM)
The eyes gotta have it. J. Cocks. il *Time* 134:46 Jl 10 '89
OLIVER TWIST (LITERARY CHARACTER)
Love in the lower depths. G. Wills. bibl f il *The New York Review of Books* 36:60-7 O 26 '89
OLIVES
See also
Cooking—Fruit
The thoroughly modern olive. R. Sokolov. il *Natural History* p102-4 Ap '89
Travel notes: cafe olives [Niçoises] M. F. K. Fisher. il *Architectural Digest* 46:70+ Mr '89
OLIVETO (OAKLAND, CALIF.: RESTAURANT) *See* Oakland (Calif.)—Restaurants, nightclubs, bars, etc.
OLIVETTI (ING. C.) & CO., SPA *See* Ing. C. Olivetti & Co., SpA
OLIVIA RECORDS
Olivia turns fifteen. L. Berman. il *High Fidelity (New York, N.Y.)* 39:51 Mr '89
OLIVIER, LAURENCE, 1907-1989
about
Further thoughts on Olivier. R. Brustein. *The New Republic* 201:25-6 O 9 '89
A lunch with Lord Larry. C. P. Andersen. il pors *Ladies' Home Journal* 106:122+ D '89
Obituary
The American Spectator il 22:31-2 S '89. B. Bawer
Film Comment il pors 25:22-4+ S/O '89. R. Schickel
Maclean's il pors 102:48-9 Jl 24 '89. R. Davies
National Review il 41:44-6 Ag 18 '89. J. Sobran
The New Republic 201:28 Ag 21 '89. R. Brustein
New York por 22:52+ Jl 31 '89. J. Simon
New York il por 22:55-6 Jl 31 '89. D. Denby

Newsweek il pors 114:54-6 Jl 24 '89. J. Kroll
People Weekly il pors 32:70-77 Jl 24 '89. B. Darrach
Time por 134:52-3 Jl 24 '89. R. Corliss
U.S. News & World Report il pors 107:16 Jl 24 '89
Vogue il por 179:254+ O '89. S. Callow
Such an actor was this! Laurence Olivier takes his last bow at Westminster Abbey. il por *People Weekly* 32:69-70 N 6 '89
Wuthering Heights. A. S. Berg. il pors *The New York Times Magazine* p46-8+ F 19 '89
OLNEY, JOHN W., AND OTHERS
Pathological changes induced in cerebrocortical neurons by phencyclidine and related drugs. bibl f il *Science* 244:1360-2 Je 16 '89
OLSEN, JOHN W.
about
Stalking the giant ape. J. James. il map *Discover* 10:42-6+ F '89
OLSEN, WILLIAM, 1954-
Big language [poem] *The New Republic* 201:38 Ag 21 '89
OLSHWANGER, RON
about
A lifetime chasing fires and disasters leads to a Pulitzer Prize for a furniture salesman. il por *People Weekly* 31:121-2 Ap 17 '89
OLSON, BRUCE
Kidnapping
Freed missionary tells story of survival. K. H. Sidey. il por *Christianity Today* 33:47 S 22 '89
OLSON, C. G., AND OTHERS
Superconducting gap in Bi-Sr-Ca-Cu-O by high-resolution angle-resolved photoelectron spectroscopy. bibl f il *Science* 245:731-3 Ag 18 '89
OLSON, DONALD E., 1922-
The value of erotica. il por *The Humanist* 49:12-13+ S/O '89
OLSON, DONALD W.
Who first saw the zodiacal light? il *Sky and Telescope* 77:146-8 F '89
OLSON, DONALD W., AND JASINSKI, LAURIE E.
Chaucer and the moon's speed. il *Sky and Telescope* 77:376-7 Ap '89
OLSON, GRETCHEN
Painting a portable mural. il pors *American Artist* 53:70-5 Ap '89
OLSON, MARIAN
Legacy [poem] *America* 161:419 D 9 '89
OLSON, MAYNARD V., AND OTHERS
A common language for physical mapping of the human genome. bibl f *Science* 245:1434-5 S 29 '89
OLSON, RON
A guide to homo religiosus [cover story] *The Christian Century* 106:655-7 Jl 5-12 '89
OLSON, STEVE
Year of the blue-collar guy. por *Newsweek* 114:16 N 6 '89
OLYMPIA & YORK DEVELOPMENTS LTD.
Breathing easier [fallout from Campeau's teetering operations] A. Dunkin and C. Hawkins. il *Business Week* p28-9 O 2 '89
Campeau's big sell-off [proposed sale of Bloomingdale's] P. Chisholm. il por *Maclean's* 102:48 S 18 '89
Campeau's day of reckoning. A. Walmsley. il pors *Maclean's* 102:38-40 S 25 '89
Corporate trophies [New urban landscape exhibit at World Financial Center] A. Schwartzman. il *Art in America* 77:34-7+ F '89
A desperate Campeau grabs a Canadian lifeline [capital infusion by Olympia & York] C. Hawkins. il por *Business Week* p44 S 25 '89
The price of a reprieve [Campeau Corp.] A. Walmsley. il pors *Maclean's* 102:36-9 O 2 '89
A unique monument to urban life [Reichmanns' Yerba Buena Gardens in San Francisco] P. C. Newman. il *Maclean's* 102:33 Mr 13 '89
OLYMPIC ATHLETES *See* Athletes
OLYMPIC ATHLETES, WOMEN *See* Women athletes
OLYMPIC COMMITTEE (U.S.) *See* United States Olympic Committee
OLYMPIC GAMES
See also
United States Olympic Committee
'80s Olympics. M. Kiefer. il *Sport (New York, N.Y.)* 80:82-3 O '89
The Games: Summer Edition [computer game] P. Scisco. il *Compute!* 11:68 F '89
Olympic images [drug use; Maclean's/Decima poll] H. Quinn. il *Maclean's* 102:33 Ja 2 '89
The sportswriters' big drug coverup [government push to improve Canada's Olympics performance] A. Fotheringham. il *Maclean's* 102:68 Ap 24 '89
1924
Summer Olympics
An American coup in Paris [victory over French rugby team for gold medal] M. Jenkins. il *American Heritage* 40:66-71 Jl/Ag '89

OLYMPIC GAMES—*cont.*
1980
Winter Olympics
Hello again III [reunion of U.S. 1980 Olympic hockey team] R. Brofman. il *Life* 12:181-3 Fall '89
1988
Photographs and photography
The Olympics. il *Life* 12:148-54+ Ja '89
Summer Olympics
A day of reckoning [B. Johnson admits he took steroids] il pors *Maclean's* 102:32-3 Je 26 '89
A deepening scandal [physician J. Astaphan testifies on steroid use by B. Johnson] B. Wickens. pors *Maclean's* 102:49-50 Je 5 '89
Did Ria or didn't she? [disqualification of woman marathon runner R. van Landeghem for failing Olympic drug test] *Runner's World* 24:42-3 Ja '89
Missed opportunity [infighting on U.S. men's 4 x 100 relay team] M. Bloom. il por *Runner's World* 24:60-2+ Ja '89
A revealing inquiry [testimony of J. Astaphan on runner B. Johnson's steroid use] M. Noden. il por *Sports Illustrated* 70:19 Je 5 '89
Sabotage at Seoul? [testimony on steroid use by B. Johnson] R. Dolphin. il por *Maclean's* 102:47 Mr 20 '89
Seoul '88 [reports by nine women athletes; cover story] L. Rothlein. il *Women's Sports & Fitness* 11:33-9 Ja/F '89
The 'Seoul searching' begins [poor performance of American cycling team] G. Drake. il *Bicycling* 30:52-6 Ja/F '89
Up where she belongs [high jump gold medalist L. Ritter] K. Moore. il pors *Sports Illustrated* 70:98-101 Ja 9 '89
Winter Olympics—Photographs and photography
Winter sports. il *Petersen's Photographic Magazine* 17:24-7 Ja '89
1992
Summer Olympics
After Seoul, Barcelona [NBC's J. Gilbert to oversee Olympic coverage] T. Paige. il por *Black Enterprise* 19:16 Ja '89
Barcelona's Olympic buildup. J. García. *World Press Review* 36:55 Ap '89
Better way for Barcelona [tennis] J. Feinstein. il *World Tennis* 36:20+ My '89
Welcome to Barcelona. J. Valls-Russell. il *The New Leader* 72:9-10 Ja 9 '89
Winter Olympics
That dammed Hercules [fresco painted on the face of the Tignes Dam in France for 1992 Olympics] B. Weber. il *The New York Times Magazine* p130 N 5 '89
1994
Winter Olympics
How did Lillehammer do it? R. Harvey. il *Sport (New York, N.Y.)* 80:11 My '89
Economic aspects
How to quit losing in the Olympics. D. J. Morrow. il *Fortune* 119:265-6+ Ap 24 '89
OLYMPIC NATIONAL PARK (WASH.)
Oil spill taints Olympic beaches. il *National Parks* 63:8-9 Mr/Ap '89
White glaciers, rain forests and rocky shores. il map *U.S. News & World Report* 106:74+ My 8 '89
OLYMPICS, SENIOR *See* Senior Olympics
OLYMPICS, SPECIAL *See* Special Olympics
OLYMPICS OF THE MIND *See* Odyssey of the Mind
OMAC, INC.
OMAC, Inc., files voluntary petition for bankruptcy. *Aviation Week & Space Technology* 130:25 Mr 13 '89
OMAC to offer two versions of Laser 300. *Aviation Week & Space Technology* 130:31 F 20 '89
OMAHA (NEB.)
Historic houses, sites, etc.
Omaha held hostage [historic district demolished to keep ConAgra from moving] J. Schwab. il *The Progressive* 53:36-9 My '89
Music
See also
Opera/Omaha (Opera company)
OMAHA (NEB.). HOUSING AUTHORITY
As Omaha's tough-talking housing boss, Robert Armstrong helps tenants grab for their bootstraps. M. Brower. il pors *People Weekly* 31:93-4+ My 15 '89
OMAHA BALLET
Reviews:
Performances of Carmina Burana. J. Williams. *Dance Magazine* 63:100-1 F '89
O'MAHONY, T. P.
Cardinal Ó Fiaich: my vision of a new Ireland [cover story] *America* 160:238-40 Mr 18 '89
O'MALLEY, WILLIAM J.
Converting the baptized [cover story] *America* 161:180-2+ S 30 '89
Explaining today to yesterday [cover story] il *America* 161:254-7 O 21 '89
The journey to justice [cover story] *America* 161:28-31 Jl 15-22 '89
A leap in the light: faith, science, & the imagination. il *Commonweal* 116:141-3+ Mr 10 '89
Scripture from scratch [cover story] *America* 160:77-81 F 4 '89

Teen-agers and . . . you know what [cover story] *America* 160:340-4 Ap 15 '89
Teenage spirituality [cover story] *America* 160:390-4 Ap 29 '89
Toward an adult spirituality [cover story] il *America* 161:341-4 N 18 '89
OMAN
Description and travel
A crack in the wall. D. Graff. il map *Travel Holiday* 171:77-81 Mr '89
Religious institutions and affairs
See also
Muslims—Oman
OMARR, SYDNEY
Redbook's astrology guide: month-by-month predictions for 1989. il *Redbook* 172:75-82 Ja '89
OMB *See* United States. Office of Management and Budget
OMBUDSMAN
See also
Nursing home patient representatives
Your friend at the IRS [ombudsman D. Holmes] K. McCormally. il *Changing Times* 43:98 Ja '89
O'MEARA, MARK
about
Oh me, oh my, O'Meara! R. Reilly. il pors *Sports Illustrated* 70:12-19 F 6 '89
O'MEARA, PATRICK
Politics in South Africa. *Current History* 88:217-20+ My '89
O'MEARA, STEPHEN JAMES
Amateur astronomers. See issues of Sky and Telescope
OMEGA (VIDEO GAME)
Compute! choice. K. Ferrell and P. Scisco. il *Compute!* 11:100-2 O '89
OMEGA-3 FATTY ACIDS *See* Acids, Fatty
OMELETS
The age of asparagus [asparagus frittata] E. Sahatjian. il *Esquire* 111:36 My '89
A better omelet [frittata] C. Kummer. il *The Atlantic* 264:99-101 O '89
Get cracking! il *Seventeen* 48:99-100 Ja '89
Summer fresh frittata. il *Redbook* 173:180 My '89
OMESTAD, THOMAS
Selling off America. *Foreign Policy* 76:119-40 Fall '89
Ten-day wonder. *The New Republic* 201:19-20+ D 25 '89
OMICRON CETI (STAR) *See* Stars, Variable
OMINSKI, STEVE, 1952-
about
Painting a portable mural. G. Olson. il pors *American Artist* 53:70-5 Ap '89
OMMEN, JOKE VAN, 1948-1988
about
Obituary
American Craft il por 49:65 F/Mr '89. R. Kuhn
OMNI (PERIODICAL)
Omni's glasnost [Omni magazine to be distributed in the Soviet Union in exchange for Science in the USSR] J. Gilbert. il *Omni (New York, N.Y.)* 11:16 Ag '89
OMNI EXPLORATION INC.
Limited prospects [L. Wexner's oil forays] J. Zweig. il por *Forbes* 144:142 S 4 '89
OMNIUM NORD-AFRICAIN (FIRM)
"My father-in-law is very demanding" [F. Filali] P. Gupte. il por *Forbes* 143:44-5 My 1 '89
OMO HOME (FIRM)
No place like Home. M. Boodro. il por *Vogue* 179:267 F '89
Norma Kamali plays house. il *Seventeen* 48:36 Je '89
OMS, MARCEL
Charlie Chaplin, stranger and brother. il pors *The Unesco Courier* 42:38-43 O '89
OMUNGALA, ROSEMARY OSANYA
A changing society. il *World Health* p11-12 Mr '89
ON CAMERA (FIRM)
Talk-show prep [C. Brown works with author P. Reynolds] L. See. *Publishers Weekly* 236:201 Jl 28 '89
ON DEMAND SYSTEMS, INC.
Software's dirty little secret. D. Churbuck. il *Forbes* 143:128 My 15 '89
ON LINE SEARCHING *See* Online searching
ON-THE-JOB TRAINING *See* Employees—Training
ONASSIS, CHRISTINA
about
Born in fortune's uneasy shadow [cover story] M. Green. il pors *People Weekly* 31:70-4+ F 6 '89
Christina's world. Y. Z. McDonough. il pors *Harper's Bazaar* 122:160-1+ N '89
The richest little girl in the world. M. Hammond. il pors *McCall's* 117:38-40+ N '89
The short, sad life of Christina Onassis. Suzy. il pors *Good Housekeeping* 208:128-9+ Mr '89
Thierry Roussel tells his story—of love for two women and little Athina. M. Green. il pors *People Weekly* 31:52-4 Mr 20 '89
ONASSIS, JACQUELINE KENNEDY
about
Forever Jackie. R. Unger. il pors *Harper's Bazaar* 122:164-5+ My '89

ONASSIS, JACQUELINE KENNEDY—about—cont.
Jackie: a mother's journey. C. Avery. il *Ladies' Home Journal* 106:142-4+ Mr '89
Jackie: beyond the scandal. B. G. Harrison. il pors *McCall's* 116:31-2+ Jl '89
Jackie: her friends finally talk! E. Klein. il pors *Good Housekeeping* 209:60+ N '89

Photographs and photography
Jackie [cover story] il pors *Life* 12:72-8+ Jl '89

ONCHOCERCIASIS
Therapy
Conquering an ancient scourge [West Africa; cover story] E. P. Eckholm. il map *The New York Times Magazine* p20-7+ Ja 8 '89

ONCOGENES See Cancer—Genetic aspects

ONCOGENIC VIRUSES
See also
HIV viruses
HTLV viruses
Human papilloma virus
Leukemia viruses
How DNA viruses may cause cancer. J. L. Marx. il *Science* 243:1012-13 F 24 '89
Induction of mesoderm by a viral oncogene in early Xenopus embryos. M. Whitman and D. A. Melton. bibl f il *Science* 244:803-6 My 19 '89

ONDAATJE, CHRISTOPHER
about
A modern odyssey. J. DeMont. il pors *Maclean's* 102:47-8 O 16 '89

ONDANSETRON
Easing chemo-therapy [antivomiting drug] *Prevention (Emmaus, Pa.)* 41:14 D '89
A kinder cure [combating chemotherapy-induced nausea] *Discover* 10:12 O '89

ONE HUDSON CAFÉ (NEW YORK, N.Y.) See New York (N.Y.)—Restaurants, nightclubs, bars, etc.

ONE PRICE CLOTHING STORES, INC.
Too much at half the price? G. G. Marcial. *Business Week* p134 My 8 '89

ONE THOUSAND (YEAR)
The year 1000 [excerpt from AD 1000] R. Erdoes. il *Psychology Today* 23:44-5 My '89

O'NEAL, GRIFFIN
about
Celebs speak out on addiction. L. E. Brooks. pors *'Teen* 33:30+ S '89
In Vegas, vowing he has changed his wild ways, Griffin O'Neal takes the plunge into marriage. il pors *People Weekly* 32:48 Jl 17 '89
Making up for dues left unpaid, Griffin O'Neal goes to jail. il por *People Weekly* 31:117 F 6 '89

O'NEIL, CAROL, AND SEIDENSTEIN, SHARON
Nuclear bloopers. *Utne Reader* p49 Ja/F '89

O'NEIL, KATRYNA
(jt. auth) See Diamond, Edwin, and O'Neil, Katryna

O'NEILL, DAN
Project Chariot: how Alaska escaped nuclear excavation [cover story] bibl f il maps *The Bulletin of the Atomic Scientists* 45:28-37 D '89

O'NEILL, ED
about
Unlike Al Bundy . . . Ed O'Neill listens to his wife. R. Rense. il pors *TV Guide* 37:25-6 My 27-Je 2 '89

O'NEILL, EUGENE, 1888-1953
Bibliography
The showman cometh. D. Van Leer. il *The New Republic* 201:29-30+ N 13 '89

O'NEILL, GERARD K.
Moon river. il *Omni (New York, N.Y.)* 11:20+ My '89

O'NEILL, HUGH
The gentle art of "I do": advice to the groom. il *Gentlemen's Quarterly* 59:208-9+ Je '89
How to write the ultimate valentine. il *Gentlemen's Quarterly* 59:45+ F '89

O'NEILL, MOLLY
Garden of delights. il *Harper's Bazaar* 122:84-5+ Je '89
Mexican jumping scenes. il *Harper's Bazaar* 122:222+ Ap '89
On the waterfront. il *Harper's Bazaar* 122:126+ Jl '89

O'NEILL, ROSE CECIL, 1875-1944
about
Kewpies: love at first sight. M. Jailer. il *Antiques & Collecting Hobbies* 94:33-4+ My '89

O'NEILL, TERRENCE J., AND OTHERS
Observations of nuclear reactors on satellites with a balloon-borne gamma-ray telescope. bibl f il *Science* 244:451-4 Ap 28 '89

O'NEILL, THOMAS P. See O'Neill, Tip

O'NEILL, TIP
about
Mister spokesman. B. Kanner. il pors *New York* 22:20+ N 6 '89

ONISHI, SEITA
about
Obsessed by James Dean, Japan's Seita Onishi makes a monument to that fallen rebel his cause. il por *People Weekly* 32:66-7 Ag 7 '89

ONLINE DATABASES See Information systems

ONLINE SEARCHING
Searching for new business. J. F. Wasik. il *Home Office Computing* 7:38 F '89

ONLY A BUCK [film] See Motion picture reviews—Single works

ONLY CHILD
It doesn't hurt to be alone. B. Brophy. il *U.S. News & World Report* 106:54-5 Mr 6 '89
Just me. K. Koontz. il pors *Health (New York, N.Y.)* 21:38-9 F '89

ONLY KIDDING [drama] See Geoghan, Jim

ONO, YŌKO
about
The Flux stops here. K. Larson. il *New York* 22:149 F 27 '89
Yoko Ono at the Whitney. K. Johnson. *Art in America* 77:167 Je '89

ONTARIO
See also
Automobile driving—Ontario
Drama festivals—Ontario
Education—Ontario
Educational laws and regulations—Ontario
Finance—Ontario
Fishing—Ontario
Gold mines and mining—Ontario
Lake Saint Clair (Mich. and Ont.)
Motion picture festivals—Ontario
Music festivals—Ontario
Ottawa (Ont.)
Toronto (Ont.)
Trials—Ontario

Commercial policy
Champagne diplomacy [Premier D. Peterson leads business delegation to France] J. Daly. *Maclean's* 102:39+ Ap 17 '89
Words of conciliation [interview with D. Peterson] T. Tedesco. il por *Maclean's* 102:16 Ja 30 '89

Description and travel
'There is no other access' [The Budd two car train runs in northern Ontario] G. W. Taylor. il *Maclean's* 102:25 Ag 21 '89

Industries
See also
Poultry industry—Canada

Languages
A backlash against French. P. Kaihla. *Maclean's* 102:27 Mr 20 '89
Uncertain survival [francophones] G. W. Taylor. il *Maclean's* 102:30 N 6 '89

Politics and government
See also
Politics, Corruption in—Ontario
Combat in Ontario [Peterson government] T. Tedesco. il por *Maclean's* 102:14-15 Ja 30 '89
The rest of the pack [D. Peterson considering race for Liberal Party leadership] T. Tedesco. il por *Maclean's* 102:14-15 Je 26 '89

ONTARIO ASSOCIATION OF ARCHITECTS
Ontario Association of Architects Design Excellence Awards. il *Architectural Record* 177:51 S '89

ONTARIO SCIENCE CENTRE
Games. R. Brody. il *Omni (New York, N.Y.)* 11:94-5 Ja '89

ONTIVEROS, EMILIO
As Spain rushes toward '92. il *The New Leader* 72:10-11 O 2-16 '89

OOCYTES See Ova

OOPS (TERM)
Zsupsz! H. Fairlie. *The New Republic* 200:10-11 F 6 '89

OOPSIE-DAISY DOLLS
Oopsie-Daisy, guess who's tops in Toyland now? M. Roman. il *Business Week* p102 D 18 '89

OORT CLOUDS
Whence come comets? A. H. Delsemme. il *Sky and Telescope* 77:260-4 Mr '89

OP AMPS See Amplifiers

OPAL GLASS
Collectors and collecting
The decorated opal ware of C. F. Monroe. R. V. Simpson. il *Antiques & Collecting Hobbies* 94:36-40 S '89

OPALESCENT GLASS See Opal glass

OPEC See Organization of Petroleum Exporting Countries

OPEL (AUTOMOBILE) See Automobiles, Foreign

OPEN ADOPTION See Adoption and adopted children

OPEN AIR MUSEUMS
See also
Villages, Restored

OPEN ARCHITECTURE TELEVISION RECEIVERS
A modest proposal for an intelligent TV. M. Fleischmann. il *Video* 13:36+ N '89

OPEN DESKTOP OPERATING SYSTEM
Bringing Unix to PCs [D. Michels of Santa Cruz Operation] C. O'Malley. por *Personal Computing* 13:83 Jl '89
Can this small fry put Unix in a million desktops? [Santa Cruz Operation Inc.] R. Brandt. il *Business Week* p116 Mr 27 '89

OPEN-HEART SURGERY *See* Heart—Surgery
OPEN HOUSE [television program] *See* Television program reviews—Single works
OPEN-PIT MINING *See* Strip mining
OPEN SCHOOL (WEST HOLLYWOOD, CALIF.)
PCs for the year 2000 [work of A. Kay] M. Rogers. il por *Newsweek* 114:36 O 2 '89
Where PCs are part of the furniture. C. O'Malley. il *Personal Computing* 13:122-4 O '89
OPEN SOFTWARE FOUNDATION
OSF/Motif [graphical interface] J. Paul. il *Byte* 14:230-1 My '89
OSF seeking shrink-wrapped Unix software. *Byte* 14:22+ S '89
OPEN SYSTEMS (COMPUTERS)
See also
Open Software Foundation
TRON operating systems
EISA sets the stage for open standards. J. Blackford. il *Personal Computing* 13:301-2 Ja '89
EISA under the glass. P. Honan. il *Personal Computing* 13:66-70 Ag '89
The LAN road to OSI. M. L. Van Name and B. Catchings. il *Byte* 14:148-50+ Jl '89
'The Unix war' is over—but the fighting goes on. R. Brandt. il *Business Week* p114+ Mr 27 '89
OPEN UNIVERSITY
Britain's University of the Air [interview with W. Perry of Walton] H. G. Shane. il pors *The Futurist* 23:25-7 Jl/Ag '89
OPENINGS, LITERARY *See* Beginnings, Literary
OPERA
See also
Compact disc video—Opera
Compact discs—Opera
Librettos
Phonograph records—Opera
Radio broadcasting—Opera
Tape recordings—Opera
Television broadcasting—Opera
Videodiscs—Opera
Videotapes—Opera
Broadening the base [U.S. opera survey 1988-89] M. F. Rich. il *Opera News* 54:44+ N '89
Calendar. See issues of Opera News
A new season of regional opera. D. Daniel. *Vogue* 179:266 O '89
Opera news 1989-90 American opera forecast. il *Opera News* 54:35-8+ S '89
The Opera news 1989 American summer opera forecast. il *Opera News* 53:32-6 Je '89
Operascope. See issues of Opera News beginning July 1986
Stages [tracing the progress of the American opera composer from commission to production] B. Kellow. il por *Opera News* 54:18-22 S '89
The trill of it all. M. Gurewitsch. il *Harper's Bazaar* 122:22+ Ja '89
Viewpoint. See issues of Opera News
What makes great performers? [importance of contemporary repertoire] A. Innaurato. il *Opera News* 54:20+ D 9 '89
Appreciation
Viewpoint [on loathing Aida] J. Keates. *Opera News* 53:4 Ja 7 '89
Costume
See Costume, Theatrical
Economic aspects
The business of opera [cover story; special section] il *Opera News* 53:8-12+ Ap 15 '89
Opera for the 'masses'. A. Thorncroft. *World Press Review* 36:61 Ap '89
History
Too strong for fantasias [popularization of tunes through nineteenth century piano transcriptions] B. Ivry. il *Opera News* 53:20-1+ Ja 21 '89
Management
See also
Opera—Trustees, boards, committees, etc.
Production and direction
Bardolator [P. Stein's production of Falstaff] P. Conrad. il pors *Opera News* 53:18-20 F 4 '89
Five minutes to midnight [stage director N. Lehnhoff] P. O'Connor. il pors *Opera News* 53:14-16+ Mr 4 '89
Ghosts [F. Zeffirelli's interpretation of La traviata; cover story] G. Fitzgerald. il por *Opera News* 54:10-11 O '89
Making it at the Met [work of designers and craftspeople] M. Sommers. il *Theatre Crafts* 23:50-5+ O '89
Next stop: Kennedy Center [Wagner's Ring directed by G. Friedrich] M. Swed. il por *Opera News* 53:18-20+ Je '89
Private lives [stage director S. Frisell] B. Paolucci. il por *Opera News* 53:14-15 Ja 7 '89
Psychological aspects
Inner landscape: two American operas probe their characters' thoughts. P. J. Smith. il *Opera News* 54:20-2 Jl '89
Stage lighting
Centerline: Joan Sullivan. M. Sommers. il por *Theatre Crafts* 23:18 Ag/S '89

Stage setting and scenery
Britain's Pavilion Opera. E. Lambert. il por *Architectural Digest* 46:90-5+ Mr '89
Five minutes to midnight [designer J. Rose; cover story] P. O'Connor. il pors *Opera News* 53:8-12 Mr 4 '89
A Ring for the '80s [German Romantic roots of Metropolitan Opera's new production] B. Adams. il *Art in America* 77:222-9 Ap '89
Transported in time [work of set designer G. Quaranta; cover story] C. Battaglia. il por *Opera News* 53:8-10+ Ja 7 '89
Textbooks
Making the grade [Opera America's textbook series] C. B. Fowler. il *Opera News* 54:35-6+ N '89
Themes
See also
Deliverance in opera
Middle East in opera
Politics in opera
Science fiction opera
Trustees, boards, committees, etc.
Board games. W. Price. il *Opera News* 53:8-11+ Ap 15 '89
Alabama
See also
Mobile Opera
Australia
Melbourne [Australian Opera] J. Cargher. *Opera News* 53:40 Ja 7 '89
Austria
Vienna. C. Norton-Welsh. *Opera News* 54:43 Ag '89
California
See also
Los Angeles Music Center Opera
San Francisco Opera
San Francisco Opera Center
Chile
Santiago. E. Berio. il *Opera News* 53:55-6 Ap 1 '89
Colorado
See also
Opera Colorado
Czechoslovakia
Song of the Vltava [Prague opera houses] D. Stevens. il *Opera News* 53:10-13 My '89
Delaware
See also
OperaDelaware (Opera company)
Egypt
History
The cats of Cairo. M. Bauer. il *Opera News* 53:38-9 My '89
France
See also
Opéra de Paris
Aix-en-Provence. E. Forbes. *Opera News* 53:40-1 Mr 4 '89
Paris. D. Sinclair. *Opera News* 54:64 S '89
History
From gods to citizens [changes in opera during the French Revolution] J. Keates. il *Opera News* 54:27-9 Jl '89
Werther's way [difficult road to French premiere of Massenet's opera in 1893] J. W. Hansen. il *Opera News* 53:18-21+ Mr 18 '89
Germany (East)
East Berlin. J. H. Sutcliffe. *Opera News* 53:39-40 Mr 18 '89
Germany (West)
See also
Deutsche Oper Berlin
Hannover. J. H. Sutcliffe. *Opera News* 54:43-4 Jl '89
West Berlin. J. H. Sutcliffe. il *Opera News* 53:38-40 Ja 21 '89
Great Britain
See also
English National Opera
Glyndebourne Festival Opera Company
Opera North
Pavilion Opera
Royal Opera House (London, England)
Cheltenham. N. Goodwin. *Opera News* 54:55-6 O '89
London. N. Goodwin. il *Opera News* 53:48-9 Je '89
London. N. Goodwin. il *Opera News* 54:56-7 O '89
London. N. Goodwin. il *Opera News* 53:38 Ja 7 '89
London. N. Goodwin. *Opera News* 54:69-70 N '89
London. N. Goodwin. *Opera News* 54:41-2 D 23 '89
Opera Britannia. T. Sutcliffe. il *Opera News* 54:36+ O '89
Illinois
See also
Chicago Opera Theater
Lyric Opera Center for American Artists
Lyric Opera of Chicago
Israel
See also
New Israeli Opera
Italy
Kallen Esperian steps in after a raucous night at the opera, and critics sing her praises [La Scala debut] il por *People Weekly* 32:65 Jl 17 '89

OPERA—Italy—*cont.*
Musical events:
Donizetti's Maria Stuarda performed at Bergamo. A.
  Porter. *The New Yorker* 65:117-18 N 13 '89
Wally Toscanini: Milan's first lady of opera [Casa Toscanini]
  C. Aillaud. il pors *Architectural Digest* 46:58+ Mr '89
Minnesota
See also
Minnesota Opera
Missouri
See also
Opera Theatre of Saint Louis
Nebraska
See also
Opera/Omaha (Opera company)
New Jersey
See also
New Jersey State Opera
New Mexico
See also
Santa Fe Opera
New York (State)
See also
Bel Canto Opera (Company)
Chautauqua Opera
Glimmerglass Opera Theater
Manhattan School of Music
Mannes College of Music
Metropolitan Opera (New York, N.Y.)
New York City Opera Company
New York Opera Repertory Theatre
Opera at the Academy
Opera Ensemble of New York
Opera Orchestra of New York
PepsiCo Summerfare
Westchester Opera
New York underground [small companies in New York City]
  S. Zucker. il *Opera News* 53:20-3 Ja 7 '89
Opera blooms in Brooklyn [plans for the Academy of Music]
  O. Friedrich. il *Time* 133:73-4 F 13 '89
Ohio
See also
Cleveland Opera
Ontario
See also
Canadian Opera Company
Pennsylvania
Philadelphia. R. Baxter. *Opera News* 54:55 S '89
Philadelphia. R. Baxter. il *Opera News* 53:35 Mr 18 '89
Scotland
See also
Edinburgh International Festival
Scottish Opera
South Carolina
See also
Spoleto Festival U.S.A.
Soviet Union
The opera and the dictator [D. Shostakovich's Lady Macbeth
  of Mtsensk] R. Taruskin. il *The New Republic* 200:34-40
  Mr 20 '89
History
Vieille Russie [singers of the Imperial Russian Opera; cover
  story] D. Harris. il *Opera News* 54:13-17 S '89
Sweden
Drottningholm. J. W. Freeman. il *Opera News* 54:43 D
  23 '89
Switzerland
Basel. E. Forbes. *Opera News* 53:38-9 Ap 15 '89
Geneva. E. Forbes. *Opera News* 54:44 Ag '89
Zurich. E. Forbes. *Opera News* 53:37-8 Ap 15 '89
Zurich. E. Forbes. *Opera News* 54:43-4 Ag '89
Texas
See also
Dallas Opera
Houston Grand Opera Association
Turkey
History
On the Bosphorus [Istanbul] P. Mansel. il *Opera News* 53:36-7
  My '89
United States
See Opera
Wales
See also
Welsh National Opera
Washington (D.C.)
See also
Washington Opera
Washington (State)
See also
Seattle Opera
Wisconsin
See also
Florentine Opera Company
Skylight Comic Opera Ltd.
OPERA, AMERICAN
See also
Davis, Anthony
Glass, Philip

Thomson, Virgil, 1896-1989
OPERA, FRENCH
See also
Saint-Saëns, Camille, 1835-1921
OPERA, GERMAN
See also
Wagner, Richard, 1813-1883
OPERA, ITALIAN
See also
Monteverdi, Claudio, 1567-1643
Rossini, Gioacchino, 1792-1868
Verdi, Giuseppe, 1813-1901
OPERA, RUSSIAN
See also
Prokofiev, Sergey, 1891-1953
OPERA AMERICA (ORGANIZATION)
Making the grade [textbook series] C. B. Fowler. il *Opera
  News* 54:35-6+ N '89
OPERA AT THE ACADEMY
Sex education [Dido and Aeneas] P. G. Davis. il *New York*
  22:58 S 4 '89
Theater [Dido and Aeneas] T. M. Disch. *The Nation* 249:364
  O 2 '89
OPERA AUDIENCES
Opera for the 'masses'. A. Thorncroft. *World Press Review*
  36:61 Ap '89
OPERA BALLET *See* Ballet
OPÉRA BASTILLE
Clashing egos at the Paris Opera. R. Marshall. il por *Newsweek*
  113:66 Ja 30 '89
Imbroglio at the Bastille. B. Villien. il *Opera News* 54:30-3
  Jl '89
Letter from Europe. J. Kramer. *The New Yorker* 65:81-94
  My 1 '89
A monument to music. B. Janssen. il por *Maclean's* 102:36+
  My 15 '89
Second storming of the Bastille. O. Friedrich. il por *Time*
  133:75 Ja 30 '89
Viewpoint. J. L. Poole. *Opera News* 53:4 Mr 4 '89
Gardens
Green geometry [designed by P. Cribier] M. K. Griswold.
  il por *House & Garden* 161:46+ Jl '89
OPERA BROADCASTS *See* Radio broadcasting—Opera;
  Television broadcasting—Opera
OPERA COLORADO
Denver. G. Giffin. *Opera News* 54:46-7 O '89
Viewpoint. P. J. Smith. *Opera News* 53:4 My '89
OPERA CONDUCTORS *See* Conductors (Music)
OPERA COSTUME *See* Costume, Theatrical
OPERA CRITICS AND CRITICISM
See also
Opera reviews
OPÉRA DE PARIS
Clashing egos at the Paris Opera [P. Bergé fires D. Barenboim]
  R. Marshall. il por *Newsweek* 113:66 Ja 30 '89
Imbroglio at the Bastille. B. Villien. il *Opera News* 54:30-3
  Jl '89
Letter from Europe [controversy surrounding Opéra-Bastille]
  J. Kramer. *The New Yorker* 65:81-94 My 1 '89
A monument to music [Bastille opera house] B. Janssen.
  il por *Maclean's* 102:36+ My 15 '89
Second storming of the Bastille [P. Bergé fires D. Barenboim]
  O. Friedrich. il por *Time* 133:75 Ja 30 '89
Viewpoint [dispute between D. Barenboim and P. Bergé]
  J. L. Poole. *Opera News* 53:4 Mr 4 '89
OPERA DIRECTION *See* Opera—Production and direction
OPERA DIRECTORS
See also
Friedrich, Götz
Frisell, Sonja
Lehnhoff, Nikolaus
Mansouri, Lotfi
Sellars, Peter
Stein, Peter, 1937-
Directions. R. Marx. il *Opera News* 54:28-30+ O '89
OPERA ENSEMBLE OF NEW YORK
Musical events:
Weisgall's The stronger and Will you marry me? A.
  Porter. *The New Yorker* 65:119 Ap 17 '89
New York City [H. Weisgall's Will you marry me?] P. J.
  Smith. il *Opera News* 53:45 My '89
OPERA FESTIVALS *See* Music festivals
OPERA HOUSES
See also
Brooklyn Academy of Music
John F. Kennedy Center for the Performing Arts. Opera
  House
Opéra Bastille
Prinzregenten Theater (Munich, Germany)
A new regime reopens the Teatro Colon in Argentina. C.
  Hardy. il *Dance Magazine* 63:16 O '89
Song of the Vltava [Prague opera houses] D. Stevens. il
  Opera News 53:10-13 My '89
Conservation and restoration
The sleeping Prince [restoration of the Prinzregenten Theater
  in Munich] G. M. Loney. il *Opera News* 53:14+ My '89

OPERA IN ADVERTISING
Viewpoint [TV commercials] G. Fitzgerald. *Opera News* 53:4 Mr 18 '89
OPERA IN LITERATURE
Through dooms of love [opera Lucia di Lammermoor in G. Flaubert's Madame Bovary] S. Willier. por *Opera News* 53:12-14+ F 18 '89
OPERA MAKEUP *See* Makeup, Theatrical
OPERA NORTH
Leeds. N. Goodwin. *Opera News* 54:61-2 S '89
Leeds. N. Goodwin. *Opera News* 53:62 Ap 1 '89
OPERA/OMAHA (OPERA COMPANY)
Omaha. R. G. Ruetz. il *Opera News* 53:34 Ja 21 '89
OPERA ORCHESTRA OF NEW YORK
Musical events:
Bellini's Il pirata. A. Porter. *The New Yorker* 65:97-8 My 1 '89
Fedora. A. Porter. *The New Yorker* 65:103-4 F 20 '89
OPERA REVIEWS
Single works
See name of composer for full entry
L'Africaine. Meyerbeer, Giacomo, 1791-1864
Aida. Verdi, Giuseppe, 1813-1901
Alceste. Gluck, Christoph Willibald, Ritter von, 1714-1787
Arlecchino. Busoni, Ferruccio, 1866-1924
The Aspern papers. Argento, Dominick
Atys. Lully, Jean Baptiste, 1632-1687
The barber of Seville. Rossini, Gioacchino, 1792-1868
Bluebeard's castle. Bartók, Béla, 1881-1945
La bohème. Puccini, Giacomo, 1858-1924
Cosí fan tutte. Mozart, Wolfgang Amadeus, 1756-1791
Desire under the elms. Thomas, Edward
Le devin du village. Rousseau, Jean-Jacques, 1712-1778
Dido and Aeneas. Purcell, Henry, 1659-1695
Don Carlos. Verdi, Giuseppe, 1813-1901
Don Giovanni. Mozart, Wolfgang Amadeus, 1756-1791
Einstein on the beach. Glass, Philip
L'elisir d'amore. Donizetti, Gaetano, 1797-1848
Enrico Leone. Steffani, Agostino
Erwartung. Schoenberg, Arnold, 1874-1951
Eugene Onegin. Tchaikovsky, Peter Ilich, 1840-1893
Euridice. Peri, Jacopo, 1561-1633
The fairy queen. Purcell, Henry, 1659-1695
The fall of the House of Usher. Glass, Philip
Falstaff. Verdi, Giuseppe, 1813-1901
The fan. Goldstein, Lee Scott
Fedora. Giordano, Umberto, 1867-1948
The flying Dutchman. Wagner, Richard, 1813-1883
Die Frau ohne Schatten. Strauss, Richard, 1864-1949
Friedenstag. Strauss, Richard, 1864-1949
Giulio Cesare. Handel, George Frideric, 1685-1759
Giustino. Handel, George Frideric, 1685-1759
Der goldene Topf. Mayer, Eckehard
Hippolyte et Aricie. Rameau, Jean Philippe
Holy blood and crescent moon. Copeland, Stewart
Idomeneo. Mozart, Wolfgang Amadeus, 1756-1791
Iphigénie en Aulide. Gluck, Christoph Willibald, Ritter von, 1714-1787
King Arthur. Purcell, Henry, 1659-1695
Lady Macbeth of Mtsensk. Shostakovich, Dmitriĭ Dmitrievich, 1906-1975
The lay of Cornet Christoph Rilke's love and death. Matthus, Siegfried, 1934-
Lodoletta. Mascagni, Pietro, 1863-1945
Los Alamos. Neikrug, Marc
Lucia di Lammermoor. Donizetti, Gaetano, 1797-1848
The Makropulos affair. Janáček, Leoš, 1854-1928
Maria Stuarda. Donizetti, Gaetano, 1797-1848
Le maschere. Mascagni, Pietro, 1863-1945
Die Meistersinger von Nurnberg. Wagner, Richard, 1813-1883
Nabucco. Verdi, Giuseppe, 1813-1901
New Year. Tippett, Sir Michael, 1905-
A night at the Chinese opera. Weir, Judith
Nixon in China. Adams, John
Le nozze di Figaro. Mozart, Wolfgang Amadeus, 1756-1791
L'occasione fa il ladro. Rossini, Gioacchino, 1792-1868
Il pirata. Bellini, Vincenzo, 1801-1835
Porgy and Bess. Gershwin, George, 1898-1937
Un re in ascolto. Berio, Luciano
Rigoletto. Verdi, Giuseppe, 1813-1901
Der Ring des Nibelungen. Wagner, Richard, 1813-1883
The rise and fall of the city of Mahagonny. Weill, Kurt, 1900-1950
Rita. Donizetti, Gaetano, 1797-1848
Il ritorno d'Ulisse in patria. Monteverdi, Claudio, 1567-1643
Salome. Strauss, Richard, 1864-1949
Siegfried. Wagner, Richard, 1813-1883
Street scene. Weill, Kurt, 1900-1950
The tales of Hoffmann. Offenbach, Jacques, 1819-1880
Telemaco. Gluck, Christoph Willibald, Ritter von, 1714-1787
Tosca. Puccini, Giacomo, 1858-1924
La traviata. Verdi, Giuseppe, 1813-1901
Il trittico. Puccini, Giacomo, 1858-1924
Il Trovatore. Verdi, Giuseppe, 1813-1901
Under the double moon. Davis, Anthony
VALIS. Machover, Tod, 1953-
Die weisse Rose. Zimmermann, Udo, 1943-
Werther. Massenet, Jules, 1842-1912

Will you marry me? Weisgall, Hugo, 1912-
OPERA SINGERS
See also
Bampton, Rose
Beňačkova, Gabriela
Callas, Maria, 1923-1977
Chaliapin, Feodor, 1873-1938
Cuberli, Lella
Danco, Suzanne
Domingo, Placido
Hampson, Thomas
Herbert-Förster, Therese
Krämer, Toni
MacWatters, Virginia
Marc, Alessandra
Mazura, Franz
Melba, Nellie
Merritt, Chris
Milanov, Zinka, 1906-1989
Norman, Jessye
Novotna, Jarmila, 1907-
Nucci, Leo
Schipa, Tito, 1889-1965
Sills, Beverly
Stratas, Teresa
Sutherland, Joan, 1926-
Talvela, Martti, 1935-1989
Toczyska, Stefania
Upshaw, Dawn
A flight of nightingales [coloraturas] M. Springer. il *Opera News* 53:20-3 F 18 '89
Operascope. See issues of Opera News beginning July 1986
Their native tongue. D. Hamilton. il *Opera News* 54:18-20+ Ag '89
Competitions
See Singing—Competitions
Economic conditions
See also
Bagby Foundation for the Musical Arts
Health and hygiene
Viewpoint [weight] J. L. Poole. *Opera News* 53:4 F 18 '89
Photographs and photography
Vieille Russie [singers of the Imperial Russian Opera; cover story] D. Harris. il *Opera News* 54:13-17 S '89
Psychology
"I can't go on" [stage fright] D. G. Winer. il *Opera News* 53:14-16 Je '89
Voice training
See Singing—Study and teaching
OPERA THEATRE OF SAINT LOUIS
Musical events:
King Arthur. A. Porter. *The New Yorker* 65:69 Jl 31 '89
St. Louis. W. Weaver. il *Opera News* 54:53-4 S '89
OPERADELAWARE (OPERA COMPANY)
Wilmington. S. Modi. il *Opera News* 54:38-9 Jl '89
OPERATIC PITCH *See* Musical pitch
OPERATING SYSTEMS (COMPUTERS) *See* Computer operating systems
OPERATION PUSH *See* People United to Serve Humanity (Organization)
OPERATION RESCUE
Abortion clinic obsolescence. C. W. Colson. il *Christianity Today* 33:72 F 3 '89
Abortion foes target clinics and doctors. *Christianity Today* 33:46 Ja 13 '89
Abortion, lies and videotape. T. H. Stahel. *America* 161:288-9 N 4 '89; Correction. 161:313-14 N 11 '89
Abortion: the abusable past. P. Green. *The Nation* 249:177-9 Ag 7-14 '89
Battle of the barricades. B. Turque. il *Newsweek* 113:26 Ap 3 '89
Evangels of abortion. G. Wills. bibl f il por *The New York Review of Books* 36:15+ Je 15 '89
From prison, antiabortion leader Randall Terry says that God, not the law, is his judge. M. Brower. il pors *People Weekly* 32:109+ N 20 '89
The gospel according to Randall Terry. F. Wilkinson. il por *Rolling Stone* p85-6+ O 5 '89
Holy war. P. Tyre. il por *New York* 22:48-51 Ap 24 '89
Operation Rescue. J. M. Connors. il *America* 160:400-2+ Ap 29 '89
Operation Rescue. M. Suh and L. Denworth. il *Ms.* 17:92-4 Ap '89
Operation Rescue. J. Wauch. *National Review* 41:41 Ap 7 '89
Operation Rescue protesters demand trials, clog courts. J. Brazil. il *Christianity Today* 33:44 Mr 17 '89
Rescue theology. R. Frame. il *Christianity Today* 33:46-8 N 17 '89
The right-to-life shock troops. S. Hutchison and J. N. Baker. il *Newsweek* 113:32 My 1 '89
"Save the babies". G. Wills. il *Time* 133:26-8 My 1 '89
What's wrong with Operation Rescue? C. R. DiSalvo. *Commonweal* 116:664-7 D 1 '89
Where did Randy go wrong? [R. Terry; cover story] S. Faludi. il pors *Mother Jones* 14:22-8+ N '89

OPERATIONAL AMPLIFIERS *See* Amplifiers
OPERATIONS, SURGICAL *See* Surgery
OPERETTA
> *See also*
> Compact discs—Operetta
> Phonograph records—Operetta

OPERETTA REVIEWS
Single works
> *See* name of composer for full entry
> Die Fledermaus. Strauss, Johann, 1825-1899

OPHIUCHUS (CONSTELLATION) *See* Constellations
OPHIUROIDS *See* Brittle stars
OPIATES *See* Narcotics
OPINION, PUBLIC *See* Public opinion
OPINION RESEARCH *See* Public opinion polls
OPITZ, EDMUND A.
> What is business? [address, March 17, 1989] *Vital Speeches of the Day* 55:497-500 Je 1 '89

OPIUM TRADE *See* Narcotics trade
OPOSSUMS
> Playing possum is serious business for our only marsupial; ed. by Susan Lumpkin. J. Seidensticker. bibl (p246) il *Smithsonian* 20:108-12+ N '89

OPPÈDE-LE-VIEUX (FRANCE)
Architecture
> In the light of Provence [D. Dumas' house in Oppède-le-Vieux is former café; cover story] D. Kazanjian. il por *House & Garden* 161:98-107+ Ja '89

OPPENHEIM, CAROLYN TOLL
> Middle East peacemakers. *The Progressive* 53:11 Jl '89

OPPENHEIM, DENNIS, 1938-
> *about*
> Dennis Oppenheim at John Gibson, Willoughby Sharp and Anne Plumb. C. Reid. il *Art in America* 77:139-40 Jl '89

OPPENHEIM, JANET, 1948-
> The odyssey of Annie Besant. bibl il pors *History Today* 39:12-18 S '89

OPPENHEIM, JOANNE
> Kids, parents, and homework. il *Good Housekeeping* 209:148+ S '89
> Off to kindergarten! il *Good Housekeeping* 209:134+ S '89

OPPENHEIM, JOSIE A.
> "Mommy, Mommy, I'm scared!". il *Good Housekeeping* 209:108+ S '89

OPPENHEIM, MERET, 1913-1985
> *about*
> Tempest in a fountain. E. Beck. il *Art News* 88:75-6 O '89

OPPENHEIM, MIKE
> How did you catch that? il *Better Homes and Gardens* 67:46+ O '89

OPPENHEIMER, HARRY FREDERICK, 1908-
> *about*
> Harry Oppenheimer's empire: going for the gold. P. Schmeisser. il por *The New York Times Magazine* p32-3+ Mr 19 '89

OPPENHEIMER, J. ROBERT, 1904-1967
> *about*
> Three men and the bomb. M. Oliphant. il pors *The Bulletin of the Atomic Scientists* 45:41-2 Mr '89

OPPENHEIMER, SUZI
> *about*
> Beyond macho: the power of womanly management [excerpt from Tender power] S. S. Cohen. il pors *Working Woman* 14:77-83 F '89

OPPENHEIMER, TODD
> Creative alternatives to urban sprawl: a tale of two cities. il *Utne Reader* p95-8 Mr/Ap '89

OPPENHEIMER GLOBAL FUND
> Stocks that could soar on big trends [interview with K. Oberman] E. Schultz. il por *Fortune* 120:39+ D 4 '89

OPPENHEIMER INDUSTRIES, INC.
> Shangri-La or sun-baked wasteland? G. Weiss. il map *Business Week* p54-6 Ag 7 '89

OPPOLZER, THEODOR EGON VON, 1841-1886
> *about*
> Oppolzer's great canon of eclipses. W. H. C. Carton. il por *Sky and Telescope* 78:475-8 N '89

OPPONENT RUNNERS AVERAGE *See* Baseball, Professional—Statistics
OPPRESSION
> Am I blue? Thoughts on animal feelings, human rights, and justice for all. A. Walker. il *Utne Reader* p98-9+ Ja/F '89

OPRE, TOM
> Sport vehicles. See issues of Outdoor Life

OPRIAN, DANIEL D.
> (jt. auth) See Zhukovsky, Eugene A., and Oprian, Daniel D.

OPTEK TECHNOLOGY (FIRM)
> Infrared has Optek glowing. G. G. Marcial. *Business Week* p79 Ap 10 '89

OPTEX CORPORATION
> Quantum leap. G. F. Gilder. il por *Forbes* 143:138-9 Je 26 '89

OPTIC NERVE
> Glial cell diversification in the rat optic nerve. M. C. Raff. bibl f il *Science* 243:1450-5 Mr 17 '89

OPTICAL CHARACTER RECOGNITION DEVICES *See* Optical scanners
OPTICAL CIRCUITS, INTEGRATED *See* Fiber optics
OPTICAL COMMUNICATION SYSTEMS *See* Light communication systems
OPTICAL COMPUTERS
> 'I think we can be the next IBM' [work of H. J. Caulfield] D. Foust. il por *Business Week* Special Issue:86 Je 16 '89
> Optical broadcast could break access bottleneck [optimul (optical interconnect for multiprocessor systems)] *Byte* 14:17 Jl '89
> Optical technologies [special section; with editorial comment by Jane Morrill Tazelaar] il *Byte* 14:228-9+ O '89
> Optics, electronics become partners. *High Technology Business* 9:32 Mr '89
> Photonics will boost near-term computer processing speeds. B. D. Nordwall. il *Aviation Week & Space Technology* 130:57+ Ap 17 '89

OPTICAL DATA PROCESSING
> *See also*
> Photonics
> Optical technologies [special section; with editorial comment by Jane Morrill Tazelaar] il *Byte* 14:228-9+ O '89
> Optics, electronics become partners. *High Technology Business* 9:32 Mr '89
> Reflected light [lasers] G. T. Forrest. il *Byte* 14:249-54+ O '89

OPTICAL DISCS *See* Optical storage devices
OPTICAL EQUIPMENT
> *See also*
> Binoculars
> Eyeglasses
> Guided missiles—Optical equipment
> Lenses
> Night vision devices
> Submarines—Optical equipment
> Telescopes

OPTICAL FIBERS *See* Fiber optics
OPTICAL ILLUSIONS
> Colored segments of a grid can shed a diffuse glow like the light from a neon tube. J. Walker. bibl il *Scientific American* 261:116-19 N '89
> Illusions. il *National Geographic World* 163:24-8 Mr '89
> Minimal magic: baffling do-as-I-do stunts and other April Foolery. S. Morris. il *Omni (New York, N.Y.)* 11:128-9 Ap '89

OPTICAL INDUSTRY
Marketing
> *See also*
> Eyewear stores
Italy
> *See also*
> Safilo SpA

OPTICAL PATTERN RECOGNITION
> *See also*
> Optical scanners

OPTICAL SCANNERS
> Easy reading [TrueScan and OmniPage] P. R. Robinson. il *Byte* 14:203-4+ My '89
> Fax + scanner [Relisys Tefax Model RA2110P] S. Miller. il *Home Office Computing* 7:62 Ag '89
> Full-spectrum scanners [Sharp JX-450 and Howtek Scanmaster flatbed color scanners] T. Thompson. il *Byte* 14:189-92+ Ap '89
> Give your computer the power to read [Saba Page Reader] J. Latimer. il *Home Office Computing* 7:68-9 Mr '89
> Handy scanners. M. L. Van Name and B. Catchings. il *Byte* 14:187-91 Je '89
> Image power in the palm of your hand. S. Morgenstern. il *Home Office Computing* 7:72+ N '89
> Inconsistency mars budget-priced scanner [Complete Page Scanner] R. L. Mitchell. il *Byte* 14:202-3 S '89
> An inexpensive scanner at its best for line art [Complete PC Page Scanner] R. Lockwood. il *Personal Computing* 13:198 D '89
> More gray for less green [HP ScanJet Plus] C. O'Malley. il *Personal Computing* 13:198 S '89
> Optical character recognition makes gains. *High Technology Business* 9:32-3 My '89
> What's new in scanning. C. O'Malley. il *Personal Computing* 13:103-5+ Mr '89
Grocery trade use
> Thanks to the checkout scanner, marketing is losing some mystery. Z. Schiller. il *Business Week* p57 Ag 28 '89

OPTICAL SOCIETY OF AMERICA
> Howard elected 1989 vice president of Optical Society. por *Physics Today* 42:67 Ja '89
> OSA awards mark achievements in many facets of optical science. *Physics Today* 42:85-6 Jl '89
> OSA recognizes outstanding contributions to optical science. il *Physics Today* 42:145-6+ O '89

OPTICAL STORAGE DEVICES
> *See also*
> 3-D optical storage devices

OPTICAL STORAGE DEVICES—See also—*cont.*
CD-ROM (Compact disc-Read only memory)
Combination disc players
Hypermedia
Optex Corporation
Videodiscs
Write once optical memories
500,000 pages on one erasable disk. M. Alpert. il *Fortune* 119:99-101 Ja 2 '89
Discus Rewritable: the latest in storage technology. A. Reinhardt. il *Byte* 14:102+ Ap '89
The exotic world of optical storage [erasable magneto optics] J. Blackford. il *Personal Computing* 13:277-8 Mr '89
Gigabytes on-line [erasable optical storage devices] J. J. Burke and B. Ryan. il *Byte* 14:259-64 O '89
Holography and computers. il *Byte* 14:234-5 O '89
Just another pretty storage option [erasable optical disks] H. E. H. Aycock. il *Compute!* 11:8 F '89
The optical option [WORM and erasable optical drives] S. Apiki and H. Eglowstein. il *Byte* 14:160-4+ O '89
Quantum leap [J. Lindmayer's Optex device] G. F. Gilder. il por *Forbes* 143:138-9 Je 26 '89
Two digital pies in the sky. D. Ranada. il *High Fidelity (New York, N.Y.)* 39:17 Je '89
What's new in optical storage. P. Honan. il *Personal Computing* 13:111-13+ F '89
OPTICAL WAVE GUIDES
Electron waves could breed new semiconductors. *High Technology Business* 9:33-4 Mr '89
OPTICS
See also
Catastrophe optics
Fiber optics
Light
Meteorological optics
Moth-eye technology
Optical Society of America
Optoelectronics
Reflection (Optics)
Refraction
Refraction, Double
Resolution (Optics)
Spectrum analysis
Optics. bibl f *Physics Today* 42:S57-S59 Ja '89
Synthesis of organic salts with large second-order optical nonlinearities. S. R. Marder and others. bibl f il *Science* 245:626-8 Ag 11 '89
OPTICS, PHYSIOLOGICAL
See also
Optical illusions
Vision
OPTIMISM
See also
Pessimism
Helping students accentuate positive thoughts. C. K. Chandler and C. A. Kolander. *The Education Digest* 54:52-4 Ja '89
The world through rose-colored glasses. A. Ranard. il *Health (New York, N.Y.)* 21:58-61 Ag '89
OPTIMIZATION, MATHEMATICAL See Mathematical optimization
OPTIONS, AUTOMOBILE See Automobiles—Equipment
OPTIONS, BOAT See Boats and boating—Equipment
OPTIONS (CONTRACTS)
See also
Foreign exchange options
Put and call transactions
Stock index options
Stock purchase options
OPTOELECTRONICS
See also
Digitizers (Computers)
Optical wave guides
Optical technologies [special section; with editorial comment by Jane Morrill Tazelaar] il *Byte* 14:228-9+ O '89
Aviation use
Kodak prepares to make larger, cheaper optics for aerospace use. B. D. Nordwall. il *Aviation Week & Space Technology* 131:44-6 Ag 14 '89
Conferences
CLEO-QELS to be held in Baltimore [Conference on Lasers and Electro-Optics and Quantum Electronics and Lasers Science Conference] il *Physics Today* 42:50-2 Ap '89
OPTOELECTRONICS INDUSTRY
See also
Optek Technology (Firm)
OPUS DEI (SOCIETY)
My Opus [discussion of April 10, 1989 article, Opus Dei and the 'perfect society'] P. Lernoux. *The Nation* 249:74+ Jl 17 '89
Opus Dei and the 'perfect society' [cover story] P. Lernoux. il *The Nation* 248:469+ Ap 10 '89
OPUS MCSHANN [dance] See Dance reviews—Single works
ORA (OPPONENT RUNNERS AVERAGE) See Baseball, Professional—Statistics

ORACLE BONES
Dem bones, dem bones [Chinese oracle bone shows evidence of shorter days; work of Kevin D. Pang] A. Fisher. *Popular Science* 235:12 S '89
Oracle bone shows a once-shorter day [work of Kevin D. Pang] I. Peterson. *Science News* 135:374 Je 17 '89
Turtle logic [engraved tortoise shell shows rotation of earth is slowing; research by Kevin Pang] T. Waters. il *Discover* 10:16 D '89
ORACLE SYSTEMS CORP.
Soft dollars. D. Churbuck. il *Forbes* 143:126-7 My 1 '89
ORAL CANCER See Mouth—Cancer
ORAL COMMUNICATION
See also
Listening
Public speaking
ORAL CONTRACEPTIVES See Pill (Contraceptive)
ORAL HISTORY
Harold and Louie [excerpt from Bird, Kansas] T. Parker. *Harper's* 278:35-6+ My '89
Mediawatch. H. David. il *History Today* 39:8-10 Jl '89
Threads of Lancashire history [Young Historians Scheme's History Day in Britain] D. Gregory. il *History Today* 39:4-5 O '89
Voices of the decade [women's history project for the 1990s] il *Ladies' Home Journal* 106:106-9 Ja '89
ORAL LEUKOPLAKIA See Leukoplakia, Oral
ORAL MEDICATION
The opposite of a bitter pill? [Clinical Technologies method to convert certain drugs to oral form] G. G. Marcial. *Business Week* p132 My 15 '89
ORAL MICROBIOLOGY See Mouth—Microbiology
ORAL READING See Reading aloud
ORAL REHYDRATION THERAPY See Diarrhea—Therapy
ORANGE JUICE
Labeling
Orange juice: pure or adulterated [false labeling by Bodine, Inc.] D. Blumenthal and L. Holland. il *FDA Consumer* 23:32-3 D '89/Ja '90
Marketing
Can P&G squeeze profits out of orange juice? Z. Schiller. il *Business Week* p38 Ja 23 '89
ORANGES
See also
Cooking—Fruit
ORANGES, MANDARIN See Mandarin oranges
ORANGUTANS
Braving the hellish jungles of Borneo, Birute Galdikas probes the secrets of one of our oldest relations. J. Friedman. il pors *People Weekly* 31:102-6 Ja 16 '89
ORATORIO
See also
Compact discs—Oratorio
Hallelujah! [Messiah performance in London] P. Yancey. il *Christianity Today* 33:30-3 D 15 '89
ORATORIO REVIEWS
Single works
See name of composer for full entry
Santa Pelagia. Stradella, Alessandro, 1644-1682
Semele. Handel, George Frideric, 1685-1759
ORATORY See Rhetoric
ORBIS (PROJECT) See Project Orbis
ORBISON, ROY, 1936-1988
about
Obituary
High Fidelity (New York, N.Y.) il pors 39:49-50 Mr '89. J. Nesin
Rolling Stone il pors p31-3 Ja 26 '89
Stereo Review il por 54:114 My '89. A. Nash
Roy Orbison: 1936-1988 [interview; cover story] S. Pond. il pors *Rolling Stone* p22-5+ Ja 26 '89
ORBITAL PLATFORMS See Space stations
ORBITAL RENDEZVOUS (SPACE FLIGHT)
Large building-block module docked to Mir following deployment of stuck solar array. J. M. Lenorovitz. *Aviation Week & Space Technology* 131:33-4 D 11 '89
Three companies could build docking system. *High Technology Business* 9:31-2 My '89
ORBITAL SCIENCES CORPORATION
Pegasus air-launched test vehicle is rolled out [cover story] B. A. Smith. il *Aviation Week & Space Technology* 131:36-7+ Ag 14 '89
Pegasus commercial launch project to begin rocket motor test firings. C. Covault. il *Aviation Week & Space Technology* 130:91 F 13 '89
The winged horse [Pegasus booster] R. G. Nichols. il *Ad Astra* 1:32-6 F '89
Winging it into space [Pegasus booster] S. F. Brown. il *Popular Science* 234:126-8+ My '89
ORBITAL TRANSFER VEHICLES See Space vehicles
ORBITS
See also
Artificial satellites—Orbits
Asteroids—Orbits
Comets—Orbits
Planets—Orbits
Space vehicles—Orbits
Stars—Orbits

ORCAS See Killer whales
ORCAS ISLAND (WASH.)
Church leaders support native claim [Lummi Indians vs. development of Madrona Point] J. Magnuson. *The Christian Century* 106:276-7 Mr 15 '89
ORCHARDS
Tending the orchard floor. B. Pleasant. il *Country Journal* 16:40-3 Mr/Ap '89
ORCHARDS (WILLIAMSTOWN, MASS.: HOTEL) See Williamstown (Mass.)—Hotels, motels, etc.
ORCHEM (FIRM)
Big O: he hasn't changed much [O. Robertson] C. Wilson. il pors *American Visions* 4:18+ F '89
ORCHESTRA DIRECTORS See Conductors (Music)
ORCHESTRA OF ST. LUKE'S
Music [Carnegie Hall concert conducted by R. Norrington] P. G. Davis. il *New York* 22:78-9 Ap 17 '89
What's new [American composers commissioned to write for Absolut Concerto] P. G. Davis. il *New York* 22:85 D 18 '89
ORCHESTRAL MUSIC
See also
Compact discs—Orchestral music
Phonograph records—Orchestral music
ORCHESTRAS
See also
Bands (Music)
Berlin Philharmonic Orchestra
Boston Early Music Festival Orchestra
Brooklyn Philharmonic Symphony Orchestra
Classical Band
Cleveland Orchestra
Conductors (Music)
Detroit Symphony Orchestra
Jazz groups
London Classical Players
Los Angeles Philharmonic Orchestra
Milwaukee Symphony Orchestra
Munich Philharmonic
National Arts Centre Orchestra
New York Classical Orchestra
New York Philharmonic-Symphony Orchestra
Opera Orchestra of New York
Orchestra of St. Luke's
Orchestre de Paris
Philadelphia Orchestra
Pro Arte Chorale and Orchestra
Riverside Symphony
School orchestras
Seattle Symphony Orchestra
Vienna Philharmonic
American beauties. T. W. Libbey, Jr. il *High Fidelity (New York, N.Y.)* 39:55 Jl '89

Strikes

See Strikes—Musicians
ORCHESTRATION See Instrumentation and orchestration
ORCHESTRE DE PARIS
Music [New York City concerts with D. Barenboim as conductor] E. W. Said. *The Nation* 248:498-500 Ap 10 '89
Musical events:
New York concerts. A. Porter. *The New Yorker* 65:93-4 Mr 6 '89
ORCHIDS
Bringing orchids down to earth. E. Henke. il *The Saturday Evening Post* 261:46-7 Ap '89
This orchid is easy and outdoorsy [Bletilla] il *Sunset (Central West edition)* 182:158 F '89
ORCHIDS OF HAWAII (FIRM)
Orchids of Hawaii [Bronx firm that deals in novelty tropical items] *The New Yorker* 65:27-8 Jl 10 '89
ORCI, LELIO, AND OTHERS
Localization of the pancreatic beta cell glucose transporter to specific plasma membrane domains. bibl f il *Science* 245:295-7 Jl 21 '89
ORDER-DISORDER TRANSFORMATIONS
Disorder-to-order transition in settling suspensions of colloidal silica: X-ray measurements. K. E. Davis and others. bibl f il *Science* 245:507-10 Ag 4 '89
ORDER OF OUR LADY OF MOUNT CARMEL See Carmelites
ORDER OF SAINT BENEDICT See Benedictines
ORDER PROCESSING
See also
Booksellers and bookselling—Order processing
ORDERS OF PROTECTION
Beware of paper tigers [murder of L. Bianco by her ex-husband raises questions about limits of court protection] J. C. Simpson. il pors *Time* 133:104-5 Mr 27 '89
Special report: . . . till death do us part [cases of April LaSalta, Pamela Dunn, and Lisa Bianco] S. Weller. il *Redbook* 173:112-14+ Ag '89
Thousands of women, fearing for their lives, hear a scary echo in Tracey Thurman's Cry for help. J. Park and S. Schindehette. il por *People Weekly* 32:112-16 O 9 '89

ORDINATION OF HOMOSEXUALS
Keepers of the keys [Port Kells, B.C. congregation refuses to relinquish church building after seceding from United Church over ordination of homosexuals] D. Wolff. *Maclean's* 102:20 My 1 '89
Opposition to gay clergy heating up [United Church of Canada] L. Mackey. *Christianity Today* 33:52-3 Jl 14 '89
When a church supports a lesbian seminarian [United Church of Christ in Carbondale, Ill.] T. A. Braun. *The Christian Century* 106:516-17 My 17 '89
ORDINATION OF WOMEN
Anglican leaders try to preserve unity [meeting in Cyprus] R. Walker. il *Christianity Today* 33:54-5 Je 16 '89
Bishops reach accord on women clergy [Episcopal Church] R. Walker. *Christianity Today* 33:57 N 3 '89
Episcopalian accord [women bishops] il *The Christian Century* 106:977 N 1 '89
John Paul's ecumenical warning [opposition to women priests threatens Anglican-Catholic union] R. N. Ostling. il *Time* 133:96 My 8 '89
LCMS pastor could face heresy charges [D. Bruch] W. Thorkelson. *Christianity Today* 33:43 Ap 21 '89
The Lefebvrite-feminist coalition? M. McGough. il *The American Spectator* 22:28-9 Ag '89
Missouri Synod doctrine [views of Alvin J. Schmidt and Daniel Bruch on women in ministry] *The Christian Century* 106:681 Jl 19-26 '89
Mom, why can't girls be priests? J. G. Hermes. *U.S. Catholic* 54:28-9 Ag '89
ORDNANCE
See also
Carronade (Weapon)
ORDWAY, FREDERICK IRA, 1927-
NSS board members visit Soviet Union. il *Ad Astra* 1:37 Ap '89
ORDWAY, RICHARD W., AND OTHERS
Arachidonic acid and other fatty acids directly activate potassium channels in smooth muscle cells. bibl f il *Science* 244:1176-9 Je 9 '89
ORE DEPOSITS
Origins and movement of fluids during deformation and metamorphism in the Canadian Cordillera [gold deposits] B. E. Nesbitt and K. Muehlenbachs. bibl f il map *Science* 245:733-6 Ag 18 '89
OREGON
See also
Air pollution—Oregon
Columbia River
Country estates—Oregon
Eagle Cap Wilderness (Or.)
Environmental movement—Oregon
Finance—Oregon
Forests and forestry—Oregon
Hunting—Oregon
John Day Fossil Beds National Monument (Or.)
Klamath River (Or. and Calif.)
Medical policy—Oregon
Mount Hood National Forest (Or.)
Paleobotany—Oregon
Resorts—Oregon
Rogue River (Or.)
Skiing—Oregon
South Slough National Estuarine Research Reserve (Or.)
Willamette River Valley (Or.)
Description and travel
See also
Cycling—Oregon
Industries
See also
Lumber industry
OREGON HISTORICAL SOCIETY
The man at OHS [T. Vaughan] M. Durham. il pors *Americana* 17:49-53 Mr/Ap '89
OREGON SHAKESPEAREAN FESTIVAL
Centerline: Jeannie Davidson [resident designer] M. Sommers. por *Theatre Crafts* 23:10 My '89
OREGON TRAIL
On the seacoast of Nebraska. J. G. Mitchell. il map *Audubon* 91:56-77 My '89
OREGON WINES See Wine
O'REILLY, ANTHONY J. F.
about
Heinz ain't broke, but it's doing a lot of fixing. G. L. Miles. il por *Business Week* p84-5+ D 11 '89
O'REILLY, DAVID R., AND MILLER, LOIS K.
A baculovirus blocks insect molting by producing ecdysteroid UDP-glucosyl transferase. bibl f il *Science* 245:1110-12 S 8 '89
O'REILLY, JANE
At last! Women worth watching. il *TV Guide* 37:18-21 My 27-Je 2 '89
Curl up in a country inn. il *New Choices for the Best Years* 29:51-4 Ja '89
Scuba duba do. il *New Choices for the Best Years* 29:44-8 F '89
O'REILLY, KENNETH
A case of misguided good intentions: American Indian policy. il *USA Today (Periodical)* 117:91-3 Ja '89

O'REILLY, TONI
about
Team spirit. il pors *Harper's Bazaar* 122:150-3 My '89
ORENSTEIN, PEGGY
Does father know best? *Vogue* 179:314+ Ap '89
In this age of the fast fix, cosmetic surgery is becoming as common as a visit to the skin salon. *Vogue* 179:192+ O '89
The politics of abortion. *Vogue* 179:250-1 Je '89
Spa-in-store. il *Vogue* 179:145-6+ My '89
Spike's riot [cover story] il pors *Mother Jones* 14:32-5+ S '89
The use of aborted fetal tissue in medical research is as controversial as abortion itself. *Vogue* 179:298+ O '89
Women on the verge of a nervy breakthrough [interview with L. Ellerbee, M. Goldin, A. Rubenstein and M. Vieira; cover story] il pors *Mother Jones* 14:28-31+ Je '89
ORENTAS, RIMAS J.
(jt. auth) See Hildreth, James E. K., and Orentas, Rimas J.
ORESKO, ROBERT
Power and politics in early modern Italy. il *History Today* 39:42-9 S '89
ORFIELD, GARY
Opportunities for minorities: new focus on concern for higher education. il *Change* 21:50-3 My/Je '89
ORGAN, TROY
Dignifying humanity: the humor of Stephen W. Hawking. por *The Humanist* 49:29-30+ Jl/Ag '89
ORGAN DONATION See Donation of organs, tissues, etc.
ORGAN PIPE CACTUS NATIONAL MONUMENT (ARIZ.)
Living in a land of extremes [work of biologist P. Holm] E. Pennisi. il por *National Wildlife* 27:14-21 Ap/My '89
ORGAN PRESERVATION See Preservation of organs, tissues, etc.
ORGAN TRANSPLANTATION See Transplantation of organs, tissues, etc.
ORGANIC COMPOUNDS
See also
Cavitands
Inclusion systems of organic molecules in restacked single-layer molybdenum disulfide. W. M. R. Divigalpitiya and others. bibl f il *Science* 246:369-71 O 20 '89
ORGANIC COSMETICS See Cosmetics
ORGANIC FARMING
Alternatives for US agriculture [National Research Council report] il *BioScience* 39:660 O '89
The attraction is chemical [cooperation between farmers and environmentalists] J. Schwab. *The Nation* 249:416+ O 16 '89
Cultivating alternative agriculture [National Research Council report] *Science News* 136:204 S 23 '89
Farm futures [adaptation of 1987 address] D. Terry. il *Mother Jones* 14:6-8 O '89
Farmers are learning new tricks from Mother Nature [alternative or sustainable agriculture] E. T. Smith. il *Business Week* p76+ N 6 '89
Fields of dreams: old farming is new again. H. Kohn. il *Rolling Stone* p41-2 O 5 '89
Nature vs. nurture on the farm [Alternative agriculture report by the National Research Council] K. R. Sheets. il *U.S. News & World Report* 107:53-4 S 18 '89
New produce pros. R. Rodale. il *Organic Gardening* 36:29-30 Jl/Ag '89
Organic awards [Organic Watch to recognize states that stress alternative agriculture] S. O. Daniels. il *Organic Gardening* 36:5 N '89
Organic for all [pesticide residues] S. O. Daniels. *Organic Gardening* 36:5 Ap '89
Pure produce [discouraging pesticide use] R. Rodale. il *Organic Gardening* 36:25-6 Je '89
Range war [National Research Council report on alternative agriculture] T. Beardsley. *Scientific American* 261:20D+ D '89
"Soil is not a factory" [sustainable agriculture] J. R. Luoma. il *Audubon* 91:61-3 N '89
Sold on organic [cover story; with editorial comment by Stevie O. Daniels] J. Poncavage. il map *Organic Gardening* 36:5, 42-6 Je '89
Suddenly, it's a panic for organic. L. Shapiro. il *Newsweek* 113:24+ Mr 27 '89
Economic aspects
The selling of the O word. P. Stone. il *The Mother Earth News* 119:84-6 S/O '89
There will be no silent spring for these farmers. il *U.S. News & World Report* 106:13 Ap 3 '89
California
A family feud over organic farming pits the Anderson brothers against each other [G. and R. Anderson, almond growers in the San Joaquin Valley] P. Freeman. il pors *People Weekly* 32:47-8 Jl 24 '89
Great Britain
Seeking greener pastures [work of Prince Charles] R. Knight. il por *U.S. News & World Report* 106:54 Je 19 '89
Japan
View from the East [methods of M. Okada] R. Rodale. il por *Organic Gardening* 36:19-20 D '89

Kansas
See also
Land Institute (Kan.)
Nebraska
How livestock make my organic methods possible. J. Bender. il *Successful Farming* 87:17 Ap '89
Texas
Hightower's view. J. Schutze. il pors *Organic Gardening* 36:32-6 D '89
ORGANIC FOOD
A choice for the littlest consumers [baby food] L. Shapiro. il *Newsweek* 113:26 Mr 27 '89
Food & health. See issues of Organic Gardening beginning April 1988
Just what is 'organic' food—and is it good for you? T. Segal. il *Business Week* p232-3 S 25 '89
Wanted: purer food [agricultural research] R. Rodale. il *Prevention (Emmaus, Pa.)* 41:26+ Je '89
Anecdotes, facetiae, satire, etc.
Food fright. W. Geist. il *New York* 22:13 Ag 7 '89
ORGANIC GARDENING (PERIODICAL)
Organic awards [Organic Watch to recognize states that stress alternative agriculture] S. O. Daniels. il *Organic Gardening* 36:5 N '89
Taking stock. S. O. Daniels. il *Organic Gardening* 36:5 Jl/Ag '89
Your first garden. S. O. Daniels. *Organic Gardening* 36:5 D '89
ORGANIC GARDENS AND GARDENING
See also
Compost
Fruit culture
Mulching
Across the land. See issues of Organic Gardening beginning April 1988 through March 1989
Entertaining from your garden [special section; with editorial comment by Stevie O. Daniels] il *Organic Gardening* 36:5, 33-52 O '89
First season. J. Cox. See issues of Organic Gardening beginning April 1988 through November 1989
A new garden era. R. Rodale. il *Organic Gardening* 36:23-4 S '89
New ground. See issues of Organic Gardening beginning April 1988
An organic future. R. Rodale. il *Organic Gardening* 36:23-4 O '89
Organic living. R. Rodale. il *Organic Gardening* 36:23-4 F '89
Preventive gardening. R. Rodale. il *Organic Gardening* 36:23-4 N '89
Solutions. See issues of Organic Gardening beginning April 1988
Periodicals
See also
Organic gardening (Periodical)
Pest control
See Pest control
Florida
Tropical trends. J. Poncavage. il *Organic Gardening* 36:45 N '89
Mexico
Quinta Diana [garden of D. Kennedy; cover story] S. O. Daniels. il pors map *Organic Gardening* 36:40-6 Jl/Ag '89
New York (State)
Garden swap party. C. A. Rossell. il pors *Organic Gardening* 36:34-7 O '89
Pennsylvania
Backyard nursery [D. and M. Keiser's herb garden] K. Martin. il pors *Organic Gardening* 36:48-52 D '89
Southern States
The deep South [cover story; special section] il maps *Organic Gardening* 36:38-52 N '89
Vancouver Island (B.C.)
A rocky start [garden of T. Sewell] V. Mattern. il por *Organic Gardening* 36:60-4 F '89
ORGANIC INSECT CONTROL See Insect control
ORGANIC METALS See Organometallic compounds
ORGANIC PESTICIDES See Pesticides
ORGANIC SALTS See Salts
ORGANISATION FOR ECONOMIC CO-OPERATION AND DEVELOPMENT
Beyond GATT. G. C. Hufbauer. *Foreign Policy* 77:64-76 Wint '89/'90
OECD Council ministerial held in Paris [statement and text of final communique, May 31 and June 1, 1989] N. F. Brady. *Department of State Bulletin* 89:78-83 S '89
OECD social ministers focus on rising pension, health costs. M. Brodsky. bibl f *Monthly Labor Review* 112:47-8 F '89
ORGANIZATION
For the tidy sum of $250 an hour, Jeffrey Mayer does top-drawer desk cleaning. il por *People Weekly* 32:49 Jl 31 '89
How to organize your office [interview with S. Winston] K. Kane. por *Home Office Computing* 7:58 S '89
Morning madness [suggestions by Ronni Eisenberg and Kate Kelly] K. Levine. il *Parents* 64:68+ F '89

ORGANIZATION—*cont.*

Anecdotes, facetiae, satire, etc.

A May-day message about efficiency. K. Fury. il *Working Woman* 14:160 My '89

ORGANIZATION FOR ECONOMIC COOPERATION AND DEVELOPMENT *See* Organisation for Economic Co-operation and Development

ORGANIZATION OF AMERICAN STATES

Can we oust Noriega? L. C. Wilson. il *USA Today (Periodical)* 118:15 N '89

A crash course for Mulroney [Nicaragua's decision to cancel ceasefire overshadows announcement of Canada's intention to join OAS] H. Mackenzie. il pors *Maclean's* 102:32-3+ N 6 '89

The inter-American system: into the next century [statement, November 14, 1988] G. P. Shultz. *Department of State Bulletin* 89:10-13 Ja '89

The OAS and the Panama crisis [statements, August 24 and 31, 1989] L. S. Eagleburger. *Department of State Bulletin* 89:67-75 N '89

On Noriega, 'We have failed miserably' [overthrow attempts] il por *Newsweek* 114:33 S 4 '89

A seat at the table [Canada prepares to join] R. Laver. il *Maclean's* 102:24 O 16 '89

ORGANIZATION OF PETROLEUM EXPORTING COUNTRIES

Coping with the OPEC oil glut. S. J. Fromartz. il *The Nation* 248:692-5 My 22 '89

Gluttons for punishment [U.S. again dependent on OPEC] C. Byron. il *New York* 22:16+ Je 19 '89

It looks as if OPEC may have the last laugh. C. Farrell. il *Business Week* p34 S 25 '89

Conferences

OPEC: which of these men will cheat first? P. Nulty. il *Fortune* 119:10 Ja 2 '89

A storm before the calm? H. Banks. *Forbes* 144:33 Jl 10 '89

Why OPEC's luck may run out. J. Rossant. *Business Week* p48 Je 19 '89

ORGANIZATIONAL BEHAVIOR

See also

Black intrapreneurs

Corporate culture

How the kinder, more cooperative corporation wins [excerpt from When giants learn to dance] R. M. Kanter. *Working Woman* 14:118-20 My '89

In praise of followers. L. Touby. *Working Woman* 14:34+ Ap '89

The new organization man [E. Woolard and others of Du Pont; cover story; special section] J. Buckley. il pors *U.S. News & World Report* 106:40-51 Ja 16 '89

New ways to exercise power. T. A. Stewart. il *Fortune* 120:52-4+ N 6 '89

The secret of life at the limits: cogs become big wheels [research by Todd La Porte and others] J. E. Pfeiffer. il *Smithsonian* 20:38-46+ Jl '89

ORGANIZATIONAL CHANGE

Beyond whistleblowing. S. C. Florman. il *Technology Review* 92:20+ Jl '89

Comeback charisma. J. Ciabattari. *Harper's Bazaar* 122:102+ Ja '89

Facing transformation: the great American house move. W. E. Halal. *The Futurist* 23:60 S/O '89

Making over middle managers. K. Labich. il *Fortune* 119:58-61+ My 8 '89

Shooting for the moon [role of chaos in business; address, April 27, 1989] R. A. Ferchat. *Vital Speeches of the Day* 55:727-31 S 15 '89

Why cowboy management is bad for American business [excerpt from When giants learn to dance] R. M. Kanter. il por *Working Woman* 14:134-6+ Ap '89

ORGANIZATIONAL DEVELOPMENT *See* Organizational change

ORGANIZED CRIME

See also

Mafia

ORGANIZED CRIME IN LITERATURE

The audacious lure of evil [interview with E. L. Doctorow] A. P. Sanoff. il por *U.S. News & World Report* 106:56 Mr 6 '89

ORGANIZED LABOR *See* Labor unions

ORGANOCHLORINE COMPOUNDS

Source Reduction Research Partnership: a unique joint venture [eliminating groundwater pollution caused by chlorinated solvents in California] A. Yazdani. bibl f il *Environment* 31:2-4 N '89

ORGANOMETALLIC COMPOUNDS

See also

Organotin compounds

Polymer synthesis and organotransition metal chemistry. R. H. Grubbs and W. Tumas. bibl f il *Science* 243:907-15 F 17 '89

Preparation of organometallic compounds from highly reactive metal powders. R. D. Rieke. bibl f il *Science* 246:1260-4 D 8 '89

ORGANOTIN COMPOUNDS

Discovering the colorful new world of tin [research by Lawrence R. Sita and Richard D. Bickerstaff] I. Amato. *Science News* 136:23 Jl 8 '89

ORGASM

The extraordinary O: the beauty power of orgasm. il *Mademoiselle* 95:196-7+ Ag '89

ORIENT, JANE M.

Medical preparedness and nuclear war [address, April 23, 1988] *Vital Speeches of the Day* 55:186-90 Ja 1 '89

ORIENT AND OCCIDENT *See* East and West

ORIENT EXPRESS (RAILROAD) *See* Venice Simplon-Orient-Express Ltd.

ORIENTAL (BANGKOK, THAILAND: HOTEL) *See* Bangkok (Thailand)—Hotels, motels, etc.

ORIENTAL AMERICANS *See* Asian Americans

ORIENTAL DOLLS *See* Dolls

ORIENTAL HOUSE DECORATION *See* House decoration, Oriental

ORIENTAL RUGS AND CARPETS *See* Rugs and carpets, Oriental

ORIENTATION

See also

Chemotaxis

Grandpa and the kid [grandfather gets lost while deer hunting] D. Sisson. il *Field & Stream* 94:37+ O '89

Home, sweet-smelling home [homing in black bears] L. L. Rogers. il *Natural History* p60-7 S '89

Show me the way you go home [homing pigeons] C. Walcott. *Natural History* p40+ N '89

ORIENTEERING (SPORT)

Finding your bearings. S. McKee. il *American Health* 8:40 Je '89

Wandering off the beaten path. G. Randall. il *Sierra* 74:88-9 S/O '89

ORIGAMI ARCHITECTURE

Games [contest winners] S. Morris. il *Omni (New York, N.Y.)* 11:112-13 S '89

ORIGEN

about

Ascetic enthusiasm: Origen and the early church. R. Williams. bibl il *History Today* 39:31-7 D '89

ORIGIN OF LANGUAGES *See* Language and languages—Origin

ORIGIN OF LIFE *See* Life (Biology)—Origin

ORIGIN OF MAN *See* Man, Prehistoric

ORIGIN OF SPECIES *See* Evolution

ORIGIN SYSTEMS, INC.

Conversations: Dungeon delving with Richard Garriott. K. Ferrell. il pors *Compute!* 11:16-17 Ja '89

O'RILEY, CHRISTOPHER

about

The call of the wild. D. Daniel. il por *Vogue* 179:295 Mr '89

ORION (CONSTELLATION) *See* Constellations

ORION (NEBULA) *See* Nebulae

ORLANDO (FLA.)

Description

Disney World and the four dwarfs. C. Clark. il *The Saturday Evening Post* 261:86-7 Mr '89

Orlando without Mickey. S. Kaplan. il *Travel Holiday* 172:86-90 S '89

Economic conditions

Coming soon: Hollywood, the sequel. E. Calonius. il *Newsweek* 113:46 F 6 '89

Hotels, motels, etc.

Low-cost hospitality [Tamar Inns] H. Rudnitsky. il por *Forbes* 144:90 S 18 '89

Parks and playgrounds

The playground that Orlando built [All Children's Playground suitable for the handicapped] D. Young. il *Southern Living* 24:159-60 N '89

Restaurants, nightclubs, bars, etc.

Dining out in Disney World. J. Reed. il *Vogue* 179:245-6 D '89

Tourist trade

Mickey is eating my lunch! H. Rudnitsky. il *Forbes* 144:86+ S 18 '89

ORLANDO HELICOPTER AIRWAYS

Orlando Helicopter develops simulated Soviet Hind Es [cover story] E. H. Kolcum. il *Aviation Week & Space Technology* 130:34-5+ Ja 9 '89

ORLANS, HAROLD, 1921-

The politics of minority statistics. *Society* 26:24-5 My/Je '89

The revolution at Gallaudet. il pors *Change* 21:8-18 Ja/F '89

ORLEAN, SUSAN

Fall signals: legs. il *Vogue* 179:164-5 Jl '89

Fit to be tied. il *Vogue* 179:370+ F '89

ORLÉANS, LOUIS PHILIPPE JOSEPH, DUC D', 1747-1793

about

Radical and chic, a duke who courted revolt and doom. R. Wernick. bibl (p122) il *Smithsonian* 20:66-75 Jl '89

ORLICH, DONALD C.

Education reforms: mistakes, misconceptions, miscues. bibl f il *Phi Delta Kappan* 70:512-17 Mr '89

ORLIK, VIKTOR
Spies who come in from the cold war [interview with J. Le Carré] il por *World Press Review* 36:28+ O '89
ORMSBY, ERIC
December [poem] *America* 161:454 D 16 '89
Horseshoe crab [poem] *Wilderness* 52:56 Summ '89
My mother in old age [poem] *The New Yorker* 65:32 Ag 28 '89
Survivors [poem] *America* 161:271 O 21 '89
ORNAMENT *See* Decoration and ornament
ORNAMENTAL COOKING *See* Cooking, Ornamental
ORNAMENTAL GRASSES *See* Grasses
ORNAMENTS, CHRISTMAS TREE *See* Christmas decorations
ORNANO, HUBERT D'
about
Provincial pleasures. C. Petkanas. il pors *Harper's Bazaar* 122:178-85 D '89
ORNANO, ISABELLE D'
about
Provincial pleasures. C. Petkanas. il pors *Harper's Bazaar* 122:178-85 D '89
ORNISH, DEAN
about
Heart disease in retreat. T. G. Harris. il por *Psychology Today* 23:46+ Ja/F '89
Paging Dr. Right. J. Poppy. il *Esquire* 112:49-51 Jl '89
Reversing heart disease [interview] il *The Saturday Evening Post* 261:42-4 O '89
The two essentials of change. J. Davidson. il *Psychology Today* 23:32 S '89
ORNITHINE DECARBOXYLASE *See* Decarboxylases
ORNITHINE TRANSCARBAMYLASE *See* Transferases
ORNITHOLOGY *See* Bird study
ORNITHOPTERS
Like a bird [design by James DeLaurier] S. Strauss. il *Technology Review* 92:8+ Ag/S '89
ORNSTEIN, ALLAN C.
Administrator/student ratios in large school districts. il *Phi Delta Kappan* 70:806-8 Je '89
The irrelevant curriculum. *The Education Digest* 54:21-3 Ja '89
ORNSTEIN, D. S.
Ergodic theory, randomness, and "chaos". bibl f il *Science* 243:182-7 Ja 13 '89
ORNSTEIN, NORMAN J.
What TV news doesn't report about Congress—and should. il *TV Guide* 37:10-13 O 21-27 '89
You get what you pay for. por *Newsweek* 113:10 Ja 16 '89
ORNSTEIN, NORMAN J., AND SCHMITT, MARK
The 1988 election. *Foreign Affairs* 68 Special Issue:39-52 ['89]
ORNSTEIN, ROBERT E. (ROBERT EVAN), 1942-
(jt. auth) See Ehrlich, Paul R., and Ornstein, Robert E. (Robert Evan), 1942-
about
Reeducating America [interview] K. Emmons. il *Omni (New York, N.Y.)* 11:16+ My '89
ORNSTEIN, ROBERT E. (ROBERT EVAN), 1942-, AND SOBEL, DAVID S. (DAVID STUART)
Bare your soul and beat disease. il *Prevention (Emmaus, Pa.)* 41:100+ Jl '89
Getting a dose of musical medicine [excerpt from Healthy pleasures] il *Prevention (Emmaus, Pa.)* 41:94-5+ Je '89
Healthy pleasures [excerpt; with editorial comment by Joel Gurin] il *American Health* 8:53-8+, 116 My '89
OROMO (AFRICAN PEOPLE)
African tribe rears white siblings found after 20 yrs. [H. and T. Gadessa] pors *Jet* 76:25 Ag 21 '89
O'ROURKE, P. J.
How to succeed in business? Here's the secret . . . il *The New York Times Book Review* 94:30 O 29 '89
Let's bring back McCarthyism. *Utne Reader* p118-19 N/D '89
about
Serving up Emily Post with a wicked twist, P. J. O'Rourke takes aim at Modern manners. K. Hubbard. il pors *People Weekly* 32:47-8+ Jl 3 '89
OROVILLE (CALIF.)
Education
The mentor as an expert coach: a model for rural school districts. B. Benoit and J. A. Braun. il *Phi Delta Kappan* 70:488-9 F '89
OROZCO, JOSÉ CLEMENTE, 1883-1949
about
Orozco's American epic. C. Giuliano. il por *Art News* 88:53+ N '89
ORPHAN DRUGS
A plea for 'orphan drugs'. A. E. Ashcraft. por *Newsweek* 114:12 O 30 '89
ORPHANS AND ORPHANAGES
See also
Adoption and adopted children
A reunion revives the bittersweet memories of an age gone by for alumni of an Albany orphanage [Albany Home for Children] S. Carswell. il *People Weekly* 32:159+ D 11 '89

Canada
See also
Mount Cashel Orphanage (St. John's, Nfld.)
Japan
Charlie Smith's second chance [adoption of child] C. Phillips. il *Reader's Digest* 135:29-30+ N '89
ORPHEUS CHAMBER ORCHESTRA
Orpheus Chamber Orchestra [Prokofiev's Classical symphony, Britten's Simple symphony, and Bizet's Symphony in C major] D. Hall. il *Stereo Review* 54:104 My '89
ORPHEUS DESCENDING [drama] *See* Williams, Tennessee, 1911-1983
ORR, JAMES F., 1943-
about
"We understand risk". L. Jereski. il por *Forbes* 143:127+ Mr 20 '89
ORR, ROYAL
about
Quebec fire storm. L. Van Dusen. il por *Maclean's* 102:12-13 F 6 '89
ORR, WILLIAM DAYTON
about
Two first gentlemen. C. Reeve. il pors *New Choices for the Best Years* 29:14-15 F '89
ORR-CAHALL, CHRISTINA, 1947-
about
Corcoran showdown. C. McGuigan. il pors *Newsweek* 114:111+ O 9 '89
A "sacrificial lamb"? S. Hochfield. il por *Art News* 88:62 N '89
ORSI, ROBERT ANTHONY
about
Are Catholics ashamed of their devotions? [interview; cover story] por *U.S. Catholic* 54:6-13 N '89
ORSINI, JOE
Return to Cooperstown. il *Travel Holiday* 171:76+ F '89
St. Martin/St. Barts. il maps *Travel Holiday* 172:48-57 D '89
ORSY, LADISLAS M., 1921-
Profession of faith and the 'oath of fidelity'. *America* 160:345-7+ Ap 15 '89
ORTEGA SAAVEDRA, DANIEL
about
A crash course for Mulroney. H. Mackenzie. il pors *Maclean's* 102:32-3+ N 6 '89
Evangelist offers advice to Nicaraguan president [interview with A. Mottesi] R. Frame. il pors *Christianity Today* 33:41-2 N 3 '89
The fight for Nicaragua. J. Bierman. il por *Maclean's* 102:26-8 N 13 '89
"I felt I had to draw the line". H. Sidey. il por *Time* 134:52 N 13 '89
Nicaragua. il *World Press Review* 36:6 D '89
Nicaragua ceases the cease-fire. *Newsweek* 114:53 N 6 '89
Notes and comment. *The New Yorker* 65:43-4 N 13 '89
The old gringos. A. Kopkind. *The Nation* 249:625 N 27 '89
Ortega's ploy. *The New Republic* 201:9 N 20 '89
Playing politics with peace. W. R. Doerner. por *Time* 134:49+ N 13 '89
Sending signals—or smoke? W. R. Doerner. il por *Time* 133:46 F 6 '89
Turning to the voters in Nicaragua [cover story] F. D. Colburn. il pors *The New Leader* 72:5-7 N 13 '89
When fury turns to foolishness. M. Greenfield. il *Newsweek* 114:92 O 16 '89
ORTH, MAUREEN
Having it all: '60s idealism, $100 haircuts, and a confused conscience. il *Utne Reader* p70 S/O '89
ORTHO PHARMACEUTICAL CORPORATION
A drug that could replace transfusions—if it ever reaches the market [Ortho vs. Amgen in battle over erythropoietin] J. O. Hamilton and J. Weber, Jr. il *Business Week* p60+ Mr 27 '89
The selling of Retin-A. L. N. Vreeland. il *Money* 18:74-80+ Ap '89
ORTHODONTICS
Brace yourself for beauty. il *'Teen* 33:24 Ap '89
Getting straight [braces] R. Vander Schaaf. por *Health (New York, N.Y.)* 21:90+ Je '89
Real men wear braces. C. Sears. il *American Health* 8:52 Ja/F '89
ORTHODOX EASTERN CHURCH
See also
Catholic Church—Relations—Orthodox Eastern Church
Eastern Orthodoxy. J. Garvey. il *The Atlantic* 263:30+ My '89
Greece
Orthodox Greeks clash with evangelicals. B. G. Baker. il *Christianity Today* 33:41 O 6 '89
Yugoslavia
Religious nationalism strains Yugoslavia. J. A. Broun. *The Christian Century* 106:885-8 O 4 '89
ORTHODOX EASTERN CHURCH, RUSSIAN
Keeping the faith in the USSR after a thousand years. J. H. Billington. bibl (p174) il *Smithsonian* 20:130-6+ Ap '89

ORTHODOX EASTERN CHURCH, RUSSIAN—*cont.*
The millennium celebrations [Christianization of Kievan Russia] il *The Courier (Unesco)* 42:34 Ja '89
ORTHOGRAPHY *See* Spelling
ORTHOPEDIA
See also
Ilizarov method
Special report: orthopedic engineering. il *Popular Mechanics* 166:17 S '89
ORTINS, DAVID
about
David Ortins at Pamela Auchincloss. K. Johnson. il *Art in America* 77:173 D '89
ORTIZ, GEORGE
about
On George Ortiz. B. Chatwin. *The New York Review of Books* 36:62 S 28 '89
ORTLEB, CHARLES
about
The outsider. K. Leishman. il por *Rolling Stone* p75-6+ Mr 23 '89
ORTMAYER, ROLAND
about
A most unusual man. D. S. Looney. il pors *Sports Illustrated* 71:118-24+ S 4 '89
ORTOLANI, AL
Where a deer fell [poem] *Wilderness* 52:61 Summ '89
ORTON, JOE
about
What the butler saw [drama] Reviews
America 160:296 Ap 1 '89. G. G. Seibert
The Nation 248:534 Ap 17 '89. M. Hodgson
The New Republic 200:34 Ap 17 '89. R. Brustein
The New Yorker 65:87 Mr 20 '89. E. Oliver
ORWELL, GEORGE, 1903-1950
about
A very partial reclamation project. J. Rodden. il *Commonweal* 116:78-80 F 10 '89
ORZAC, EDWARD S.
Travel health. See alternate issues of Travel Holiday through December 1989
ORZECHOWSKI, WILLIAM
Should the "balanced budget constitutional amendment" be adopted? [excerpts from statement, November 18, 1987] *Congressional Digest* 68:280+ N '89
OS/2 OPERATING SYSTEM
The end of application software? [IBM's Systems Application Architecture] F. Langa. *Byte* 14:6 F '89
Four debuggers in one [MultiScope] M. Heller. il *Byte* 14:195-6 O '89
IBM Operating System/2 Extended Edition Version 1.1. S. S. Ross. *Architectural Record* 177:151+ O '89
Modula-2 and OS/2 join forces. A. Schulman. il *Byte* 14:171-4 Ag '89
MultiBoot brings OS/2 back to earth. S. Miastkowski. *Byte* 14:100+ My '89
OS/2 gets a spreadsheet [Excel for OS/2 with Presentation Manager] A. Reinhardt. il *Byte* 14:81 N '89
OS/2 hits the networks. K. Thurber. il *Byte* 14:285-6+ Ja '89
OS/2 notebook. M. Minasi. See issues of Byte beginning August 1988
OS/2 puts desktop publishing in the fast lane [PageMaker for OS/2 Presentation Manager] H. Eglowstein. il *Byte* 14:81 O '89
OS/3 and Unix's last, best hope [planned enhancements] F. Langa. il *Byte* 14:6 Mr '89
Presentation Manager makes OS/2 attractive. *High Technology Business* 9:31 Mr '89
The state of OS/2. M. Minasi. il *Byte* 14 Special Issue:87-8+ Fall '89
A tale of two operating systems. D. E. Crabb. il *Byte* 14:137-9 D '89
VM under OS/2. J. Anderson. *Byte* 14:344-5 N '89
Word publishing for OS/2 [DeScribe word publisher] S. Miastkowski. il *Byte* 14:82 S '89
OSAGE (IOWA)
Energy policy
The good news: Osage, Iowa, counts kilowatts. *Time* 133:39 Ja 2 '89
OSAKA (JAPAN)
Airports
Island for new international airport rises in Osaka Bay. J. Ott. il *Aviation Week & Space Technology* 130:71-2 My 8 '89
OSBORN, FAIRFIELD, 1887-1969
about
An essay on a pig roast. S. J. Gould. il *Natural History* p14+ Ja '89
OSBORN, FRANK D.
about
"I want to build my own company". R. Bailey. il por *Forbes* 143:68+ Mr 20 '89
OSBORN, HENRY FAIRFIELD *See* Osborn, Fairfield, 1887-1969
OSBORN, NANCY A.
A new look at glasses and contacts. il *Current Health 2* 16:12-13 N '89

OSBORN COMMUNICATIONS CORP.
"I want to build my own company" [F. Osborn] R. Bailey. il por *Forbes* 143:68+ Mr 20 '89
OSBORN ENGINEERING COMPANY
Plans. *The New Yorker* 65:34-5 S 18 '89
OSBORNE, ADAM
about
The fall of Adam? J. Pitta. il por *Forbes* 144:287 O 16 '89
OSBORNE, DAVID
The Kemp cure-all. *The New Republic* 200:21+ Ap 3 '89
A poverty program that works. *The New Republic* 200:22-5 My 8 '89
OSBORNE, HELEN BETTY
about
Unhealed wounds. N. Underwood. il *Maclean's* 102:41 Jl 10 '89
OSBORNE, JEFFREY
about
Jeffrey Osborne's wife Sheri tells how to land and keep man of your dreams [cover story] T. S. Moore. il pors *Jet* 75:56-9 Ja 30 '89
OSBORNE, SHERI
about
Jeffrey Osborne's wife Sheri tells how to land and keep man of your dreams [cover story] T. S. Moore. il pors *Jet* 75:56-9 Ja 30 '89
OSBORNE, THOMAS J., 1942-
The eagle and the arrows: America in the nuclear age. il *USA Today (Periodical)* 118:12-14 Jl '89
OSBORNE HOUSE (ISLE OF WIGHT, ENGLAND)
Royal retreat on the Isle of Wight. J. J. Norwich. il maps *Architectural Digest* 46:160-3 O '89
OSBOURNE, OZZY
about
Life with Ozzy Osbourne, says his wife, Sharon, is a heavy test of mettle. M. Brower. il por *People Weekly* 32:94-5+ Jl 10 '89
OSBOURNE, SALLY
(jt. auth) See Levine, Sarah L., 1946-, and Osbourne, Sally
OSBOURNE, SHARON
about
Life with Ozzy Osbourne, says his wife, Sharon, is a heavy test of mettle. M. Brower. il por *People Weekly* 32:94-5+ Jl 10 '89
OSBURN, JOHN
Devil's stylebook. *The Nation* 249:705 D 11 '89
OSBURN, MARGARET
Kids' museum is second home. il *American Visions* 4:52-4 O '89
OSBY, GREG
about
Greg Osby: open on all sides. D. Helland. il pors *Down Beat* 56:26-8 O '89
OSCAR [ballet] See Ballet reviews—Single works
OSCARS (PRIZES) *See* Academy Awards
OSCILLATIONS
See also
Damping (Mechanics)
Sun—Oscillations
Basic measurements lead to Physics Nobel [N. F. Ramsey for separated oscillatory fields technique] R. Pool. il pors *Science* 246:327-8 O 20 '89
Neutrino oscillations and solar neutrinos. L. Wolfenstein and E. W. Beier. bibl f il *Physics Today* 42:28-36 Jl '89
Physics [Nobel Prize awarded to N. Ramsey for separated oscillatory fields technique and to H. Dehmelt and W. Paul for devising ways of trapping ions] il pors *Time* 134:74 O 23 '89
Physics Nobel: traps, clocks, quantum leaps [to N. F. Ramsey for separated oscillatory fields technique] E. Peterson. *Science News* 136:262 O 21 '89
Ramsey, Dehmelt, Paul win Nobel for helping to set high standards [ion trap techniques] B. G. Levi. il pors *Physics Today* 42:17-19 D '89
Spatial patterns from oscillating microtubules. E. Mandelkow and others. bibl f il *Science* 246:1291-3 D 8 '89
OSCILLATORS
See also
Multivibrators
Op-amp oscillators. R. Marston. il *Radio-Electronics* 60:51-5 Jl '89
OSCILLATORY CHEMICAL REACTIONS *See* Chemical reactions
OSCILLOSCOPES
Getting an oscilloscope. D. Lancaster. il *Radio-Electronics* 60:66-7 Jl '89
Low-capacitance scope probe. H. Friedman. il *Radio-Electronics* 60:52-4 Ja '89
Speed up VCR troubleshooting. J. Emerich. il *Radio-Electronics* 60:65-7 Mr '89
Understanding oscilloscope probes. J. Gordon. il *Radio-Electronics* 60:46-51 Ja '89
VideOsmith Spectrum Probe. il *Radio-Electronics* 60:17-18 Ag '89

OSCILLOSCOPES—*cont.*

Testing

Portable oscilloscope [Createc's SCOUT SC-02] il *Radio-Electronics* 60:28 F '89

Portable oscilloscope [Tektronix 2247A] il *Radio-Electronics* 60:26 Ja '89

Tektronix 222 handheld digital storage oscilloscope. il *Radio-Electronics* 60:20 Jl '89

OSGOOD, AMY

about

Reviews:

Work of J. Erkert and A. Osgood at MoMing Dance and Arts Center. C. Survant. il *Dance Magazine* 63:82-3 D '89

OSGOOD, CHARLES

about

Bard of the airwaves [interview] D. Eviatar. il por *Gentlemen's Quarterly* 59:41-2 Ja '89

OSHA *See* United States. Occupational Safety and Health Administration

O'SHEA, ERIN K., AND OTHERS

Evidence that the leucine zipper is a coiled coil. bibl f il *Science* 243:538-42 Ja 27 '89

Preferential heterodimer formation by isolated leucine zippers from Fos and Jun. bibl f il *Science* 245:646-8 Ag 11 '89

O'SHEA, STEPHEN

A royal pain in La France. il *Mother Jones* 14:39-41+ Jl/Ag '89

OSHIMA, IZUMI

Japan draws a line. *World Press Review* 36:18 N '89

OSHINSKY, DAVID M., 1944-

Pride and perjury. por *The New Leader* 72:14-17 S 4 '89

OSHKOSH FLY-IN *See* Aviation—Exhibitions

OSKI, FRANK A.

Heating up the bottle battle [cover story] *The Nation* 249:665+ D 4 '89

How to raise money for the class of 2000. *The Nation* 248:217+ F 20 '89

OSLIN, K. T.

about

K.T. Oslin. A. Nash. il pors *Stereo Review* 54:67-9 Ag '89

OSMIUM

Isotopes

Rhenium-osmium isotope systematics of carbonaceous chondrites [resonance ionization mass spectrometry] R. J. Walker and J. W. Morgan. bibl f il *Science* 243:519-22 Ja 27 '89

OSMOND, DONNY

about

Donny Osmond gets the last laugh. D. Wild. por *Rolling Stone* p26 Ag 10 '89

OSMOND, MARIE, 1959-

about

Marie Osmond: "I'm beginning a whole new life" [cover story] J. Wolf. il pors *Redbook* 173:132-3+ Jl '89

Marie Osmond's all-out holiday celebration. N. Gittelson. il por *McCall's* 116:23-4+ Ja '89

OSMOSIS

See also

Biological transport

Electroosmosis

OSPREYS

Awesome ospreys [Felix Neck Wildlife Sanctuary] il *National Geographic World* 165:8-11 My '89

Lord of ospreys [R. Gardiner of Gardiners Island] F. Graham. il *Audubon* 91:10+ S '89

OST, DAVID

(tr) *See* Jastrzebowski, Jerzy. Mr. Wujec goes to Warsaw

OSTAR, ALLAN W.

What the future holds for American colleges and universities [address, April 4, 1989] *Vital Speeches of the Day* 55:558-62 Jl 1 '89

OSTEOARTHRITIS *See* Arthritis

OSTEOCALCIN

1,25-dihydroxyvitamin D-responsive element and glucocorticoid repression in the osteocalcin gene. N. A. Morrison and others. bibl f il *Science* 246:1158-61 D 1 '89

OSTEOPOROSIS

Bad to the bone. G. L. Blackburn. il *Prevention (Emmaus, Pa.)* 41:99-100+ Mr '89

The basics of bone [excerpt from Preventing osteoporosis] K. H. Cooper. il *Health (New York, N.Y.)* 21:80-2 Ap '89

Belief in boron: an element of strength [osteoporosis prevention; work of Forrest H. Nielsen] I. Wickelgren. *Science News* 135:204 Ap 1 '89

Beyond calcium. F. Snyder. il *Parents* 64:224+ My '89

Bone booster [sodium fluoride treatment for spinal osteoporosis] *Time* 133:54 Ja 23 '89

Can B-12 prevent bone diseases? *USA Today (Periodical)* 118:18 O '89

Exercising bones. J. Kaplan. il *Vogue* 179:246+ Mr '89

Fluoride-calcium combo builds better bones [research by Charles Y. C. Pak] K. Fackelmann. *Science News* 135:36 Ja 21 '89

New fluoride-calcium treatment for bone loss. *Prevention (Emmaus, Pa.)* 41:14+ Je '89

Osteoporosis: are you at risk? [excerpt from Preventing osteoporosis] K. H. Cooper. il *Ladies' Home Journal* 106:56+ Mr '89

The truth about calcium. P. Mann. il *Reader's Digest* 134:70-4 Mr '89

OSTEOSARCOMA *See* Bone—Cancer

OSTEOSPERMUM

'Whirligig' . . . cousin of freeway daisy. il *Sunset (Central West edition)* 182:240 Je '89

OSTERLUND, PETER

The great right hope [cover story] il *National Review* 41:24-6 Mr 24 '89

The hill climbers. il *Rolling Stone* p116-18+ Mr 23 '89

OSTERMAN, CONSTANCE

about

A Principal toll. J. DeMont. il por *Maclean's* 102:28-9 Ag 7 '89

OSTERMAN, PAUL

Employment policy: rethinking training. *Current (Washington, D.C.)* 312:10-17 My '89

OSTERTAG, BOB

(jt. auth) *See* Miles, Sara, and Ostertag, Bob

OSTLER, SCOTT

Orel in Wonderland. il pors *Sport (New York, N.Y.)* 80:32-4 Mr '89

OSTP *See* United States. Office of Science and Technology Policy

OSTRANDER, PATRICIA

about

True junk. G. Morgenson. il por *Forbes* 144:202 O 2 '89

OSTRICH FARMS

In Oklahoma, Dale Coody sees a day when ostrich wrangling will replace cattle herding. D. Chu. il pors *People Weekly* 32:84+ N 13 '89

OSTRIKER, ALICIA

The circus [poem] *The Nation* 248:424 Mr 27 '89

OSTRO, STEVEN J., AND OTHERS

Radar detection of Phobos. bibl f il *Science* 243:1584-6 Mr 24 '89

OSTROM, HANS A.

The major role of minor characters in fiction. *The Writer* 102:9-11+ F '89

O'SULLIVAN, BOB

Three Samaritans. il *Reader's Digest* 135:55-6+ O '89

O'SULLIVAN, JOHN

Britain: under the iron (high) heel? *Commentary* 88:47-52 S '89

O'SULLIVAN, MAUREEN

The honeymoon's over. il *Commonweal* 116:172-3 Mr 24 '89

O'SULLIVAN, MICHAEL

Tribute to a Latin American martyr. *America* 160:8-11+ Ja 7-14 '89

OSWALD, LEE HARVEY

about

The cross fire over Jack Ruby's gun. il por *U.S. News & World Report* 107:10 D 25 '89-Ja 1 '90

Jack Ruby's family and lawyer battle for possession of the gun that killed Lee Harvey Oswald. W. Plummer. il por *People Weekly* 31:42-3 My 22 '89

Lights and shadows: destiny in Dallas. E. Oxford. bibl f il por *American History Illustrated* 23:12-17+ Ja '89

World of mirrors. E. Oxford. bibl il *American History Illustrated* 23:34-45 F '89

OTC NET INC.

The fugitive king of penny stocks [J. C. Schidlowski] D. Zigas. il pors *Business Week* p124-5+ N 20 '89

OTC TRADING *See* Over-the-counter securities markets

OTCASEK, CHRISTOPHER

about

One to watch: Christopher Otcasek. por *'Teen* 33:57 Ap '89

OTEC (OCEAN THERMAL ENERGY CONVERSION) *See* Ocean thermal power plants

OTHENIN-GIRARD, DOMINIQUE

about

Halloween V [film] Reviews

People Weekly 32:14-15 O 30 '89. R. Novak

OTHER PEOPLE'S MONEY [drama] *See* Sterner, Jerry

OTIS, CARRÉ

about

Facing the future. J. Shields. il *Vogue* 179:206-7 Ja '89

OTIS, ELISHA GRAVES, 1811-1861

about

Elevating thoughts from Elisha Otis and fellow uplifters. D. D. Jackson. bibl (p247) il por *Smithsonian* 20:210-12+ N '89

OTIS, HARRISON GRAY, 1765-1848

about

Behind the Federal facade. A. O. Boulton. il pors *American Heritage* 40:68-75 My/Je '89

OTIS ELEVATOR CO., LTD.

Elevating thoughts from Elisha Otis and fellow uplifters. D. D. Jackson. bibl (p247) il por *Smithsonian* 20:210-12+ N '89

OTITIS EXTERNA (EAR INFECTION) *See* Ear—Diseases

O'TOOLE, LAWRENCE

New faces of '88. il *Film Comment* 25:54-5 Ja/F '89

O'TOOLE, LAWRENCE—cont.
New York story. il *American Film* 15:62-8+ O '89
O'TOOLE, MARGOT
about
Credit for whistle-blower vanishes. B. J. Culliton. por *Science* 244:643 My 12 '89
O'TOOLE, PETER
about
Peter O'Toole's yardstick. por *Time* 133:63 F 6 '89
OTSUKI, TAMAYO
about
Comic Tamayo Otsuki is one Japanese import who comes from the Far-out East. por *People Weekly* 32:168 N 20 '89
OTT, CARLOS
about
A monument to music. B. Janssen. il por *Maclean's* 102:36+ My 15 '89
OTT, JOHN NASH, 1909-
about
A thousand points of light. M. Morse. il *Utne Reader* p12-13 Mr/Ap '89
OTTAWA (ONT.)
Anecdotes, facetiae, satire, etc.
Ottawa's usual air of unreality. A. Fotheringham. il *Maclean's* 102:76 O 16 '89
Why the country is breaking up. A. Fotheringham. il *Maclean's* 102:48 Jl 17 '89
Crime
An NDP star is charged [L. Nystrom charged with shoplifting] il por *Maclean's* 102:24 D 11 '89
Galleries and museums
See also
Canadian Museum of Civilization
National Gallery of Canada
Photographs and photography
Vancouver & Ottawa, beautiful Canada! P. Slaughter. il *Petersen's Photographic Magazine* 18:12-15+ Jl '89
Social life and customs
Anecdotes, facetiae, satire, etc.
'Well-educated, dynamic man seeks . . .'. S. MacLeod. por *Maclean's* 102:64 My 29 '89
Terrorism
See Terrorism—Canada
OTTEN, DAVE
about
Building a better mouse. F. Hapgood. il *Omni (New York, N.Y.)* 12:22+ N '89
OTTERLO (NETHERLANDS)
Galleries and museums
See also
Kröller-Müller National Museum (Otterlo, Netherlands)
OTTERS
See also
Sea otters
The comedian of America's wetlands stages a comeback [river otters] D. M. Schwartz. bibl f (p174) il *Smithsonian* 20:138-42+ Je '89
The otter—northwoods playboy. D. Wharton. il *The Conservationist* 44:22-5 N/D '89
OTTINO, JULIO M.
The mixing of fluids [cover story] il *Scientific American* 260:56-7+ Ja '89
OTTOMANS (FURNITURE)
Rich look—simple steps. il *Southern Living* 24:92-3 D '89
OTTO'S ORIGINAL OAT BRAN BEER *See* Beer
OTWAY BASIN (AUSTRALIA)
The drift of oil. J. Dietzel. il *World Press Review* 36:66 S '89
OUACHITA NATIONAL FOREST (ARK. AND OKLA.)
Watching over the Ouachita. S. McCarthy. il *Sierra* 74:80-1 S/O '89
OUDES, BRUCE
(ed) *See* Nixon, Richard M. (Richard Milhous), 1913-. Six (more) crises
OUÉDRAOGO, ARSÈNE JÉRÔME
The old and the new. il *World Health* p23-4 Mr '89
OULTON, THERESE, 1953-
about
Thérèse Oulton: Hirschl & Adler Modern. J. Higgins. il *Art News* 88:197 Ap '89
OUR COMMON FUTURE CONCERT, 1989
Ecological rock. N. Jennings. il *Maclean's* 102:50-1 Je 12 '89
OUR LADY OF PEACE (CATHEDRAL: YAMOUSSOUKRO, IVORY COAST)
The basilica in the bush. R. N. Ostling. il *Time* 134:38-9 Jl 3 '89
World's largest church. *The Christian Century* 106:106 F 1-8 '89
OUR TOWN [drama] *See* Wilder, Thornton, 1897-1975
OURMAZD, A., AND OTHERS
Quantifying the information content of lattice images. bibl f il *Science* 246:1571-7 D 22 '89
OURSLER, FULTON
My dinner with Groucho. il por *Esquire* 111:130-2+ Je '89
OUT COLD [film] *See* Motion picture reviews—Single works

OUT/LOOK: NATIONAL LESBIAN & GAY QUARTERLY
OUT/LOOK: national lesbian & gay quarterly. K. Walter. *The Nation* 248:640-2 My 8 '89
OUT OF COURT SETTLEMENTS *See* Arbitration and award
OUT OF PRINT BOOKS
OP books: a popular delusion. J. P. Selth. por *Publishers Weekly* 235:78 Ja 6 '89
OUT OF TOWN NEWS (FIRM)
The Hub's hub. J. Sedgwick. il *Gentlemen's Quarterly* 59:93+ S '89
OUT OF WEDLOCK BIRTHS *See* Illegitimacy
OUT WEST (NEWSPAPER)
If it's big news, you won't find it in Chuck Woodbury's sagebrush journal, Out West. S. K. Reed. il pors *People Weekly* 31:61-2 Ja 16 '89
OUTBACK (AUSTRALIA) *See* Australia
OUTBOARD MARINE CORP.
Chris-Craft comes back [acquired by OMC] P. A. Janssen. il *Motor Boating & Sailing* 163:15+ Ap '89
Did Irv Jacobs sandbag Outboard Marine? [auction for assets of Murray Chris-Craft] G. DeGeorge. *Business Week* p38+ F 20 '89
OUTBOARD MOTORS *See* Motor boat engines
OUTCRY (MUSICAL GROUP)
The Outcry: their fans are crying out for more! il *'Teen* 33:54 S '89
OUTDOOR CATALOGS *See* Catalogs, Commercial
OUTDOOR COOKING *See* Cooking, Outdoor
OUTDOOR EDUCATION
See also
Environmental education
National parks and reserves—Educational use
OUTDOOR FIREPLACES *See* Fireplaces, Outdoor
OUTDOOR FURNITURE *See* Furniture, Outdoor
OUTDOOR LIFE
See also
Backpacks and backpacking
Camping
Country life
Fishing
Hiking
Hunting
Mountaineering
Nature
Picnics
Snow and ice climbing
Walking
Wilderness survival
Winter sports
Hill country. G. Hill. See issues of Field & Stream
Outdoors. J. Skorupa. See issues of Popular Mechanics beginning July 1987
Outdoors South. See issues of Southern Living
Tales from the Burma Bridge [adventure outing at Snowbird Ski and Summer Resort] L. J. Sass. il *Health (New York, N.Y.)* 21:40-1+ D '89
Accidents and injuries
Just say don't [outdoor emergency] P. G. Gill. il *Outdoor Life* 184:58+ O '89
The specs on eye care [injuries in the outdoors] P. G. Gill, Jr. il *Outdoor Life* 184:44-5 Jl '89
Anecdotes, facetiae, satire, etc.
PW interviews [humor writer P. F. McManus] W. Brisick. por *Publishers Weekly* 235:42-3 Je 23 '89
Why is it? P. F. McManus. il *Outdoor Life* 184:118+ Ag '89
OUTDOOR LIFE (PERIODICAL)
A sporting competition [invitational clay shoot hosted by Outdoor life at Migdale Estate, N.Y.] R. P. Stuart. il *Outdoor Life* 183:48+ F '89
OUTDOOR LIGHTING *See* Lighting, Outdoor
OUTDOOR LIVING AREAS *See* Decks, patios, terraces, etc.
OUTDOOR MEALS
See also
Barbecue cooking
Picnics
Soup, bread, cheese . . . a summer meal that travels well. il *Sunset (Central West edition)* 182:152-3 Je '89
OUTDOOR ROOMS *See* Decks, patios, terraces, etc.
OUTDOOR SHOWERS *See* Shower baths
OUTDOOR SURVIVAL *See* Wilderness survival
OUTDOOR WIRING *See* Electric wire and wiring
OUTER BANKS (N.C.)
See also
Bars and barrooms—Outer Banks (N.C.)
OUTER SPACE
Exploration
See Space flight; Space research
International aspects
See also
United Nations. Committee on the Peaceful Uses of Outer Space
Assembly reviews outer space issues. *UN Chronicle* 26:63 Mr '89
OUTER SPACE IN ART *See* Astronomy in art; Space flight in art

OUTHOUSES
Muck and its entanglements. J. Berger. *Harper's* 278:60-1 My '89
OUTHWAITE, TONY
A star too soon. *National Review* 41:49-50 D 31 '89
OUTLAW, LOUISE LEE
Family affair [story] il *Good Housekeeping* 208:192-3 My '89
OUTLER, ALBERT COOK
about
Obituary
America 161:204 O 7 '89. D. Toolan
The Christian Century 106:869-70 O 4 '89. M. E. Marty
OUTLET STORES
Cheryl McArthur: discount outlets for mall mavens. P. Y. Hong. il por *Business Week* p117 N 6 '89
OUTLETS, ELECTRIC *See* Electric wire and wiring
OUTLINES (AUTHORSHIP)
Nine steps for outlining nonfiction. S. Bartley. *The Writer* 102:22-4 Ap '89
OUTLINING SOFTWARE
Testing
How to organize work and ideas. D. Barron. il *Home Office Computing* 7:20-1 Jl '89
OUTPLACEMENT CONSULTANT SERVICES
See also
Crystal-Werner Corporation
Women in Networking (Firm)
Headhunters in reverse. D. Machan. il pors *Forbes* 144:238-9 O 30 '89
Look who needs outplacement. J. Main. il *Fortune* 120:85+ O 9 '89
OUTPUT OF WORKERS *See* Productivity, Industrial
OUTRAM, JOHN, 1934-
about
Architecture: John Outram. E. Lambert. il por *Architectural Digest* 46:162-7+ D '89
THE OUTSIDE WOMAN [television program] *See* Television program reviews—Single works
OUTSOURCING CENTERS (DATA PROCESSING)
More companies are chucking their computers. J. Rothfeder. il *Business Week* p72+ Je 19 '89
OUVRY-VIAL, BRIGITTE
Highways in the city. il *The Unesco Courier* 42:34-7 Ag '89
OVA
Block of stretch-activated ion channels in Xenopus oocytes by gadolinium and calcium ions. X.-C. Yang and F. Sachs. bibl f il *Science* 243:1068-71 F 24 '89
Expression of a cloned rat brain potassium channel in Xenopus oocytes. M. J. Christie and others. bibl f il *Science* 244:221-4 Ap 14 '89
The product of the *mos* proto-oncogene as a candidate "initiator" for oocyte maturation [Xenopus] N. Sagata and others. bibl f il *Science* 245:643-6 Ag 11 '89
Translational blockade imposed by cytokine-derived UA-rich sequences [Xenopus oocytes] V. Kruys and others. bibl f il *Science* 245:852-5 Ag 25 '89
Vaccination with a synthetic zona pellucida peptide produces long-term contraception in female mice. S. E. Millar and others. bibl f il *Science* 246:935-8 N 17 '89
Transplantation
See also
Gamete intrafallopian transfer
Zygote intrafallopian transfer
Drilling for fertility [hole made in zona pellucida allows easier passage of sperm; work of Jacques Cohen] M. L. Fuerst. il *Discover* 10:22 O '89
An early-warning system [testing for genetic defects in the human egg] A. Purvis. il *Time* 134:56 N 27 '89
Genetic testing possible before conception [testing unfertilized egg; work of Yury Verlinsky] R. Weiss. *Science News* 136:326 N 18 '89
A technique originally developed for overcoming human infertility may also help endangered species [in vitro fertilization] R. M. Adams. *Smithsonian* 19:12 Ja '89
OVA, FERTILIZED *See* Zygotes
OVARIAN CANCER *See* Ovaries—Cancer
OVARIAN CYSTS *See* Cysts
OVARIES
Cancer
Wish me well. R. Shereff. il *Ms.* 18:26+ O '89
Genetic aspects
Gene signals relapse of breast, ovarian cancers [research by Dennis Slamon] J. L. Marx. il *Science* 244:654-5 My 12 '89
Studies of the HER-2/*neu* proto-oncogene in human breast and ovarian cancer. D. J. Slamon and others. bibl f il *Science* 244:707-12 My 12 '89
Nutritional aspects
Dairy sugar linked to ovarian cancer [research by Daniel W. Cramer] K. Fackelmann. *Science News* 136:52 Jl 22 '89
Therapy
Gilda Radner's love story. J. Powell. il pors *Glamour* 87:112-13 Jl '89

"I have faith my wife will live" [actor P. Brosnan's wife, C. Harris] V. J. Radovsky. il pors *Redbook* 173:36+ My '89
"I've fought so hard to live" [excerpt from It's always something] G. Radner. il pors *Redbook* 173:120-2+ Je '89
OVENS
See also
Convection ovens
Microwave ovens
Stoves
OVER-THE-COUNTER DRUGS *See* Medicines, Nonprescription
OVER-THE-COUNTER SECURITIES MARKETS
See also
OTC Net Inc.
Penny stocks
Computers vs. cerebrums [face off between OTC insight and MPT review] M. Hulbert. il *Forbes* 143:184 Ap 3 '89
Ninth-inning rally [small company stocks] E. Sturza and E. Hardy. il *Forbes* 144:292+ O 16 '89
Searching for small gems [views of D. J. Diamond] R. Simon. il por *Forbes* 143:214-15 Je 26 '89
The wide spread phenomenon [high o-t-c transaction costs] R. L. Stern. il *Forbes* 143:232+ Je 26 '89
Japan
Hidden advantages [decision to allow U.S. over-the-counter stocks onto the Tokyo Stock Exchange] R. Phalon. il *Forbes* 144:40-1 N 13 '89
OVER-THE-HORIZON BACKSCATTER RADAR SYSTEM
See Radar defense networks
OVERALL, PARK
about
Breezy rider. J. Marion. il por *TV Guide* 36:29 F 4-10 '89
OVERCONFIDENCE
The dangers of overconfidence. J. Rubin. il *Technology Review* 92:11-12 Jl '89
OVERDUE LIBRARY BOOKS
Karen Lindsay was overdue at the library; so they threw the book at her [jailed for failure to return books to Norcross, Ga. library] il pors *People Weekly* 32:113 N 27 '89
OVEREATERS ANONYMOUS
Gil Gerard: my weight cost me $1 million in TV roles. G. Esterly. il pors *TV Guide* 37:8-10 N 25-D 1 '89
OVEREATING *See* Eating disorders
OVERHOLT, WILLIAM H.
Dateline drug wars: Burma: the wrong enemy. *Foreign Policy* 77:172-91 Wint '89/'90
OVERLAND JOURNEYS TO THE PACIFIC
See also
Oregon Trail
OVERPOPULATION *See* Population
OVERPROTECTIVE PARENTS
I was an overprotective mother. il *Good Housekeeping* 208:14+ Je '89
OVERSEAS EMPLOYEES *See* Americans—Foreign countries—Employment
OVERSEAS FORCES, AMERICAN *See* United States—Armed Forces—Forces in foreign countries
OVERSIGHT AND INVESTIGATIONS SUBCOMMITTEE (HOUSE COMMITTEE ON ENERGY AND COMMERCE) *See* United States. Congress. House. Committee on Energy and Commerce. Subcommittee on Oversight and Investigations
OVERSTREET, JOY IMBODEN
Strolling under the stars. il *Reader's Digest* 134:111-13 Ja '89
OVERTIME
After-hours homework: managing what, where and when. E. Davidowitz. il *Working Woman* 14:87-8 My '89
OVERWATER FLYING *See* Aviation—Overwater flying
OVERWEIGHT *See* Obesity
OVITZ, MICHAEL
about
Hollywood's most secret agent [cover story] L. J. Davis. il pors *The New York Times Magazine* p24-7+ Jl 9 '89
Movie shogun. S. L. Kirsch. il por *Fortune* 119:50+ Ja 2 '89
Pocketful of stars. J. Castro. il por *Time* 133:58-9 F 13 '89
The scarlet letter. L. Klady. il pors *American Film* 15:15-16 D '89
OVONIC IMAGING SYSTEMS INC.
Breaking away. R. Reiff. il por *Forbes* 144:132+ D 25 '89
Navy chooses LCD technology for new A-12 color displays. B. D. Nordwall. il *Aviation Week & Space Technology* 131:56-7 S 4 '89
OVSHINSKY, STANFORD R.
about
Breaking away. R. Reiff. il por *Forbes* 144:132+ D 25 '89
OVULATION
See also
Estrus

OVULATION—*cont.*
Angiotensin II: does it have a direct obligate role in ovulation? [discussion of June 17, 1988 article, Blockage of ovulation by an angiotensin antagonist] A. Pellicer and others. il *Science* 245:870-1 Ag 25 '89
The involvement of platelet activating factor in ovulation. A. O. Abisogun and others. bibl f il *Science* 243:381-3 Ja 20 '89
OVUM *See* Ova
OWEN, BENNETT
The party at the Wall. il *National Review* 41:20-1 D 22 '89
OWEN, DAVID, 1955-
Are you a difficult person? il *The Atlantic* 264:73-80 O '89
The big question. il *The Atlantic* 263:16 Je '89
Do-it-yourself videotapes. il *The Atlantic* 264:97-100 S '89
How to get rich quick. il *The Atlantic* 263:14+ Mr '89
Washington diarist: outside the Beltway. *The New Republic* 201:54 S 18-25 '89
OWEN, HENRY, AND MEYER, EDWARD C.
Central European security. il *Foreign Affairs* 68:22-40 Summ '89
OWEN, ISABELLA
(tr) *See* Viñes, Benito. The Antilles cyclonoscope
OWEN, JOHN D.
Work-time reduction in the U.S. and Western Europe. bibl f il *Monthly Labor Review* 111:41-5 D '88
OWEN, OLIVER S., 1920-
The heat is on: the greenhouse effect and the earth's future. il por *The Futurist* 23:34-40 S/O '89
OWEN, ROBERT W.
about
A tale of two governments. M. Kempton. *The New York Review of Books* 36:43 Mr 30 '89
OWEN, SARAH
about
Brooding actor James Woods's Immediate family breaks up after four months of marriage. il pors *People Weekly* 32:71 D 18 '89
The wild Woods. V. Muse. il pors *Life* 12:15-16 D '89
OWENS, BUCK, 1929-
about
The finding of a founding father. D. Gates. il pors *Newsweek* 113:56 Ja 9 '89
OWENS, DANIELLE
about
All-American Girl-talk. il pors *'Teen* 33:8 O '89
OWENS, DELIA, AND OWENS, MARK
How meat-eaters rule each other [cover story] il *International Wildlife* 19:4-11 Jl/Ag '89
OWENS, GWINN
A ridiculous addiction. por *Newsweek* 114:7 D 4 '89
OWENS, LOUIS
The grapes of wrath: looking back. il *USA Today (Periodical)* 117:92-3 My '89
OWENS, MACKUBIN THOMAS
DOE's unilateral disarmament. il *National Review* 41:42-3 F 24 '89
OWENS, MARK
(jt. auth) *See* Owens, Delia, and Owens, Mark
OWENS, ORV
about
Rip-off or risky business? *Christianity Today* 33:43 S 22 '89
OWENS, R. MICHAEL
Worm warfare. il *Runner's World* 24:120 O '89
OWENS, TERRI
about
World Vision. B. Brander. il *Petersen's Photographic Magazine* 18:24-6+ Je '89
OWENS, VIRGINIA STEM
A faith that trembles and dances. il *Christianity Today* 33:19-22 Jl 14 '89
Good Friday. il *Christianity Today* 33:21-3 Mr 17 '89
OWENS (R. S.) & COMPANY *See* R. S. Owens & Company
OWENS VALLEY RADIO OBSERVATORY
Owens Valley array upgraded. il *Sky and Telescope* 78:128 Ag '89
OWINGS, DONALD H.
(jt. auth) *See* Coss, Richard G., and Owings, Donald H.
OWLS
Calling the owls. R. Crum. il *Sierra* 74:73-4+ N/D '89
Encounters with great horned owls. C. A. Cubbler. il *The Conservationist* 43:8-9 Ja/F '89
Encounters with great horned owls: how I rescued a great horned owl and saw stars in my eyes [excerpt from A sense of the morning] il *The Conservationist* 43:10-13 Ja/F '89
Lone ranger of the Rockies [boreal owls in Idaho's Frank Church-River of No Return Wilderness] P. H. Hayward and G. D. Hayward. il *Natural History* p78-85 N '89
New thinking on old growth [spotted owl controversy in the Pacific Northwest] W. Booth. il map *Science* 244:141-3 Ap 14 '89
The owl that traded a hoot for a hiss [burrowing owl] M. Rowe. il *Natural History* p32-3 My '89

'The spotted owl could wipe us out' [Northwest lumber industry] J. B. Levine. il *Business Week* p94+ S 18 '89
Still at loggerheads [timber industry vs. conservationists in Oregon] il *Time* 134:24 Jl 10 '89
Hearing
See Hearing—Birds
Photographs and photography
Night stalking the nocturnal barn owl. J. Zuckerman. il *Petersen's Photographic Magazine* 17:34-5 F '89
Vision
See Vision—Birds
OWNBY, CHRIS
about
Chris Ownby. L. Anderson. il por *American Artist* 53:42-3 Ag '89
OXENHORN, HARVEY
Tuning the rig. il *The Atlantic* 264:30+ S '89
OXFORD, EDWARD
The Johnstown flood. il *American History Illustrated* 24:12-25 My '89
Lights and shadows: destiny in Dallas. bibl f il por *American History Illustrated* 23:12-17+ Ja '89
World of mirrors. bibl il *American History Illustrated* 23:34-45 F '89
OXFORD (MISS.)
Description
Faulkner's Mississippi [cover story] W. Morris. il por *National Geographic* 175:312-39 Mr '89
Historic houses, sites, etc.
Warm colors, personal style [restored Victorian house] il *Southern Living* 24:172-3 N '89
OXFORD ENGLISH DICTIONARY
290,500 Oxford words to live by [compiled with help of Univ. of Waterloo software] D. Francis. il *Maclean's* 102:9 F 20 '89
Caught in the web of bytes [electronic version] C. Murphy. il *The Atlantic* 263:68-70 F '89
A celebration of language [second edition] P. S. Prescott. il *Newsweek* 113:69 Mr 27 '89
The dictionary factory. I. Shenker. *The New Yorker* 65:86-100 Ap 3 '89
Electronic Oxford. E. Giguere. il *Byte* 14:371-2+ D '89
It's official: 5,000 new words. A. P. Sanoff. il *U.S. News & World Report* 106:71 Mr 27 '89
A scholarly Everest gets bigger. P. Gray. il *Time* 133:95+ Mr 27 '89
OXFORD UNIVERSITY *See* University of Oxford
OXFORD UNIVERSITY PRESS
The dictionary factory. I. Shenker. *The New Yorker* 65:86-100 Ap 3 '89
OXIDATION, PHYSIOLOGICAL
See also
Cytochromes
Free radicals (Chemistry)
Osteoclastic bone resorption by a polarized vacuolar proton pump. H. C. Blair and others. bibl f il *Science* 245:855-7 Ag 25 '89
OXIDATION REDUCTION REACTION
See also
Reduction, Biochemical
Oxidation-reduction and the molecular mechanism of a regulatory RNA-protein interaction. M. W. Hentze and others. bibl f il *Science* 244:357-9 Ap 21 '89
OXIDES
See also
Ceramic oxides
Copper oxides
Deuterium oxide
Nickel oxides
Nitrogen oxides
Rubidium oxides
Superoxides
OXLEY, DIANA
"House" plans for secondary schools. *The Education Digest* 55:36-9 O '89
OXYGEN
See also
Ozone
Therapeutic use
See Oxygen therapy
OXYGEN EQUIPMENT
See also
Aquanautics Corporation
Gills, Artificial
OXYGEN IN THE BODY
Cellular aging [evidence that mitochondrial DNA damage leads to decrease in cellular respiration; research by Anthony Linnane and others] *Discover* 10:13-14 S '89
VO$_2$ max [cycling] S. Johnson. *Bicycling* 30:130 Ja/F '89
OXYGEN THERAPY
Athlete's oxygen just gas [research by David Winter, Jr.] *Science News* 136:39 Jl 15 '89
Hot air [results of study on oxygen and athletic performance] *Women's Sports & Fitness* 11:10 O '89
OYSTER STEW *See* Stew
OYSTERS
See also
Cooking—Shellfish

OZ, FRANK
about

Dirty rotten scoundrels [film] Reviews
The New Republic 200:28-9 Ja 30 '89. S. Kauffmann
New York 22:60 Ja 16 '89. D. Denby
The New Yorker 64:92-3 Ja 23 '89. P. Kael
Rolling Stone il p44 F 9 '89. A. White
Video il 13:63 Jl '89. J. Walker

OZ VESHALOM (ORGANIZATION)
Blessing both Jew and Palestinian: a religious Zionist view.
Y. Landau. The Christian Century 106:1196-9 D 20-27
'89

OZAL, TURGUT
about

Crossing the straits. M. Viorst. The New Yorker 65:43-4+
Je 5 '89

OZANNE, JULIAN
An Ethiopian success story. World Press Review 36:63 S
'89

OZBEK, RIFAT
about

Hugging the curves. E. MacSweeney. il por Harper's Bazaar
122:62+ S '89
Ozbek: on the fringe. L. Campbell. il por Vogue 179:166-7+
Ja '89
The wizard of Ozbek. M. Gross. il por New York 22:19
Ja 23 '89

ÖZDEMIR, ÖZDEN, AND DUNLOP, DAVID J.
Chemico-viscous remanent magnetization in the Fe_3O_4-γFe_2O_3
system. bibl f il Science 243:1043-7 F 24 '89

OZICK, CYNTHIA
T. S. Eliot at 101. The New Yorker 65:119-28+ N 20 '89
Why I won't go to Germany. Harper's 278:16-19 F '89

OZONE
See also
Trees, Effect of ozone on

And now, the return of the killer trees? [sources of hydrocar-
bons] Newsweek 113:78 Je 5 '89
Antarctic ozone hole unexpectedly severe. R. Monastersky.
il Science News 136:246 O 14 '89
Arctic air primed to destroy ozone [airborne mission] R.
Monastersky. Science News 135:116 F 25 '89
Arctic angst. T. Beardsley. il Scientific American 260:26-7
Ap '89
Arctic ozone is poised for a fall [airborne expedition] R.
A. Kerr. il Science 243:1007-8 F 24 '89
Call for strong ozone protection [Helsinki declaration] Science
News 135:367 Je 10 '89
Can we repair the sky? [chlorofluorocarbons and the ozone
shield] il Consumer Reports 54:322-6 My '89
Changing composition of the global stratosphere. M. McElroy
and R. J. Salawitch. bibl f il Science 243:763-70 F 10
'89
Clean air? Don't hold your breath. E. Marshall. il Science
244:517-20 My 5 '89
Clearing the air of ozone. M. Warren and K. W. Chilton.
bibl Society 26:48-58 Mr/Ap '89
Deadly danger in a spray can [CFCs] M. D. Lemonick.
il Time 133:42 Ja 2 '89
Depleted ring around ozone hole [research by Michael H.
Proffitt] R. Monastersky. Science News 136:324 N 18 '89
Depressed ozone seen in Arctic [study by Michael H. Proffitt]
R. Monastersky. Science News 136:413 D 23-30 '89
Does the ozone hole threaten Antarctic life? [effect of ul-
traviolet radiation on phytoplankton] L. Roberts. il map
Science 244:288-9 Ap 21 '89
Economics of preserving the ozone layer [views of Douglas
G. Cogan] il The Futurist 23:40-1 Ja/F '89
Energetic electrons and ozone loss. R. Monastersky. Science
News 135:335 My 27 '89
Europe recognizes the ozone threat [banning of
chlorofluorocarbons] D. Dickson and E. Marshall. Science
243:1279 Mr 10 '89
Europe to ban CFCs by 2000. Science News 135:148 Mr
11 '89
Fate of Arctic ozone remains up in the air. R. Monastersky.
Science News 135:37 Ja 21 '89
First aid for the ozone layer [European Community agrees
to ban CFCs] M. D. Lemonick. il Time 133:50 Mr 13
'89
Getting by without CFC's. A. Wilson. il The Mother Earth
News 120:110-14+ N/D '89
Highest disregard [use of CFCs by the electronics industry]
D. Hayes. il Mother Jones 14:32-6+ D '89
Just when the ozone war looked winnable . . . V. Cahan.
il Business Week p56 Je 12 '89
Leaves of gas [role of hydrocarbons in urban smog in Atlanta,
Ga.; research by William Chameides] il Discover 10:20
F '89
Low-zone [influence of Antarctic ozone hole] T. Beardsley.
Scientific American 261:26+ O '89
The man who knew too much [S. Rowland] E. Edelson.
il por Popular Science 234:60-5+ Ja '89
My adventures in the ozone layer. S. F. Singer. National
Review 41:34-8 Je 30 '89
Our dirty air [proposed new Clean Air Act; cover story]
M. McLoughlin. il map U.S. News & World Report
106:48-9+ Je 12 '89

Ozone defense [Helsinki accord calls for ban on certain
chlorofluorocarbons] il Time 133:63 My 15 '89
Ozone hits bottom again [Antarctic hole] R. A. Kerr. Science
246:324 O 20 '89
Ozone hole hikes Antarctic ultraviolet [has not caused
significant harm to phytoplankton] R. Monastersky. Science
News 135:228 Ap 15 '89
Ozone hole peril to Antarctic life [research by John Frederick]
il USA Today (Periodical) 117:6 Je '89
The ozone hole that didn't eat the world. R. Bailey. il
Forbes 144:224-5 O 30 '89
Ozone hole threatens polar plankton [research by Sayed
El-Sayed] Science News 136:284 O 28 '89
Ozone hole's reappearance linked to chlorofluorocarbons [data
of Total Ozone Mapping Spectrometer on Nimbus 7
satellite] il Aviation Week & Space Technology 131:28
O 30 '89
Ozone: indoors may offer little protection [research by Charles
J. Weschler] J. Raloff. il Science News 136:198 S 23 '89
Ozone park [research by Alan Teramura] L. Vikhanski. il
Discover 10:32 S '89
The poles in peril. R. Dolphin. Maclean's 102:50 F 27
'89
Potential replacement for ozone killer [development of chemi-
cal blend by Du Pont] Science News 135:94 F 11 '89
Rate of formation of the ClO dimer in the polar stratosphere:
implications for ozone loss. S. P. Sander and others. bibl
f il Science 245:1095-8 S 8 '89
Saving the ozone layer; Ozone depletion worsens. il UN
Chronicle 26:70-1 Je '89
Scientific mission finds potential for ozone destruction in
Arctic. R. G. O'Lone. il Aviation Week & Space Technology
130:33 F 27 '89
The sky is the limit [hole caused by CFCs] J. Bowermaster.
Harper's Bazaar 122:65+ Jl '89
Smog-curbing limits on gas volatility [EPA regulations] Science
News 135:191 Mr 25 '89
Summer smog: not just an urban problem [research by Jennifer
A. Logan] J. Raloff. Science News 136:22 Jl 8 '89
Tackling smog ozone: tougher than thought [Office of Technol-
ogy Assessment report] I. Wickelgren. Science News 136:53
Jl 22 '89
Total ban asked on ozone-killing chemicals [Helsinki
declaration] il UN Chronicle 26:56-7 S '89
Tree pollution [role of hydrocarbons in urban smog; research
by William Chameides] J. W. Merline. il Consumers'
Research Magazine 72:38 Ja '89
The two faces of ozone. R. Monastersky. il Science News
136:154-5 S 2 '89
U.S. scientists, aircraft study ozone depletion above Arctic.
B. W. Henderson. il Aviation Week & Space Technology
130:45+ Ja 16 '89
Ultraviolet levels under sea ice during the Antarctic spring
[discussion of July 22, 1988 article, Ultraviolet radiation
levels during the Antarctic spring] J. E. Frederick and
H. E. Snell. Science 245:194-5 Jl 14 '89
Unpopular packaging [Canadians protest chlorofluorocarbons]
M. Nichols. Maclean's 102:51 D 25 '89
Upstairs, downstairs—the ozone dilemma. B. Hogan and
B. Allen. il The Conservationist 44:16-21 N/D '89
Winter ozone gap detected over the Arctic [research by
David J. Hofmann] R. Monastersky. Science News 136:54
Jl 22 '89
A worse fridge [effect of ban on chlorofluorocarbons] J.
W. Merline. Consumers' Research Magazine 72:38 D '89
Physiological effects
The newest health hazard: breathing. B. Carpenter. il U.S.
News & World Report 106:50-1 Je 12 '89
Why no one's safe [effects of smog on residents in Los
Angeles basin] J. E. Basu. maps American Health 8:64
S '89

OZORIO, PETER
Now the world's 2nd No-Tobacco Day. il World Health
p26-7 Ap '89

P

P. H. GLATFELTER CO.
A niche papermaker undercuts a giant [P. H. Glatfelter vs.
International Paper] il Business Week p88 Mr 27 '89
P.H. Glatfelter Co. R. Abelson. il Fortune 119:176 Je 5
'89

P. MICHAEL MARINO ASSOCIATES
In passing [lobby and facade renovation, Architects &
Designers Building, N.Y.C.] M. Gaskie. il Architectural
Record 177:64-7 mid-S '89

P.O.V. [television program] See Television program reviews—
Single works

P-STAR INDEX See Price indexes

P.T. BARNUM MUSEUM (BRIDGEPORT, CONN.)
Psst! The prince of humbug lives! il U.S. News & World
Report 106:16 Je 19 '89
Under a new top: a museum for Barnum. il Americana
17:17 Jl/Ag '89

PA NDAU (NEEDLEWORK) See Needlework
PACE, SCOTT
The NSS Legislative Committee. *Ad Astra* 1:13 My '89
PACEMAKER, ARTIFICIAL (HEART)
The beat goes on [runner H. Pirie] P. Nye. il por *Women's Sports & Fitness* 11:57 Jl/Ag '89
Tempo of the heart. J. Stone. il *The New York Times Magazine* p81-2 My 21 '89
Defects
Firm pleads guilty to selling faulty pacemakers [Cordis Corporation] D. Farley. il *FDA Consumer* 23:38-9 S '89
PACEMAKER SYSTEMS See Biological rhythms
PACHECO, PATRICK
Earth angel. il pors *Harper's Bazaar* 122:54-7 Jl '89
The sporting life: winning form. il pors *Harper's Bazaar* 122:194-7+ O '89
PACHER, SARA
Cream of the country. See issues of The Mother Earth News beginning September/October 1986
PACIFIC BALLET THEATRE
Reviews:
1988-89 season in Portland, Or. M. U. West. *Dance Magazine* 63:74 O '89
PACIFIC COAST STATES See Pacific States
PACIFIC CONSERVATORY OF THE PERFORMING ARTS
Summer theater in Solvang, Santa Maria. il map *Sunset (Central West edition)* 182:18+ Je '89
PACIFIC CREST NATIONAL SCENIC TRAIL
Trail man [running the length] B. Holtel and B. Darves. il por *Runner's World* 24:66-7 S '89
PACIFIC GAS & ELECTRIC CO.
PG&E: power to the people [computer use] il *Personal Computing* 13:73+ S '89
PACIFIC ISLANDS (TRUST TERRITORY)
See also
Palau
Politics and government
Stranger than paradise. S. L. Malcomson. il map *Mother Jones* 14:19-21+ Ja '89
PACIFIC LUMBER CO.
California's chain-saw massacre [clearcutting of redwood] M. J. Walters. il *Reader's Digest* 135:144-9 N '89
Milken, junk bonds and raping redwoods [C. Hurwitz accelerates logging following takeover] B. McKibben. *Rolling Stone* p39-40 Ag 10 '89
A raider's ruckus in the redwoods [accelerated logging following Maxxam's takeover] E. Schultz. il por *Fortune* 119:172-3+ Ap 24 '89
When the safety net is frayed [takeover of Pacific Lumber by Charles E. Hurwitz causes pension plan termination] J. B. Levine. il *Business Week* p158 N 6 '89
PACIFIC MUTUAL LIFE INSURANCE CO.
Alabama woman wins $1.2 million in insurance case [C. Haslip] *Jet* 77:13 O 23 '89
PACIFIC NORTHWEST
See also
Columbia River Gorge (Or. and Wash.)
Earthquakes—Pacific Northwest
Environmental movement—Pacific Northwest
Environmental policy—Pacific Northwest
Fishing—Pacific Northwest
Forests and forestry—Pacific Northwest
Inside Passage
National forests—Pacific Northwest
Radioactive pollution—Pacific Northwest
Wilderness areas—Pacific Northwest
Wildlife sanctuaries—Pacific Northwest
Description and travel
See also
Cruising—Pacific Northwest
Cycling—Pacific Northwest
America's great Northwest [family vacations] G. S. Bush. il *Better Homes and Gardens* 67:168+ Je '89
PACIFIC NORTHWEST BALLET
The Pacific Northwest Ballet is a shining example of Seattle's cultural prominence. M. Wade. il *Horizon (Tuscaloosa, Ala.)* 32:41-2 Ja/F '89
Seattle strikes gold: Pacific Northwest Ballet's grand pas de deux [artistic directors K. Stowell and F. Russell] M. Hunt. il pors *Dance Magazine* 63:36-41 Mr '89
PACIFIC NORTHWEST ELECTRIC POWER AND CONSERVATION PLANNING COUNCIL See Northwest Power Planning Council
PACIFIC OCEAN
See also
El Niño (Ocean current)
La Niña (Ocean current)
The big picture of the Pacific's undulations [Geosat data] R. A. Kerr. *Science* 243:739-40 F 10 '89
Second megaplume found in Pacific [work of Edward T. Baker] *Science News* 136:239 O 7 '89
PACIFIC PALISADES (LOS ANGELES, CALIF.)
Historic houses, sites, etc.
Architectural digest visits: Steven Spielberg and Amy Irving [cover story] H. Hurt. il *Architectural Digest* 46:196-205+ My '89

PACIFIC REGION
See also
Aged—Pacific region
Air traffic control—Pacific region
Earthquakes—Pacific region
Economic assistance, American—Pacific region
Medicine—Pacific region
Munitions—Pacific region
Oceania
Public health—Pacific region
United Nations—Pacific region
World War, 1939-1945—Campaigns and battles—Pacific
Regional report: Asia/Pacific. A. Giarelli. See issues of World Press Review beginning October 1986
Commerce
Trade in the Pacific Rim [address, October 28, 1988] D. S. Tappan, Jr. *Vital Speeches of the Day* 55:217-20 Ja 15 '89
United States
See United States—Commerce—Pacific region
Defenses
See also
ANZUS Council
Description and travel
Pacific and Asian passages. G. Hesse. il *Travel Holiday* 171:73-4+ Ap '89
Paradise refound. il map *Travel Holiday* 172:80-2 S '89
Economic conditions
East Asia, the Pacific, and the U.S.: an economic partnership. il map *Department of State Bulletin* 89:33-7 Ap '89
A strategic guide to the Rim. R. Rowan. il maps *Fortune* 120 no13 Special Issue:72-4+ Fall '89
Economic relations
See also
Asian Pacific Economic Cooperation (Organization)
United States
See United States—Economic relations—Pacific region
Foreign relations
United States
See United States—Foreign relations—Pacific region
Industries
See also
Airlines—Pacific region
Social life and customs
A matter of custom. E. Devine and N. Braganti. *Travel Holiday* 172:82 S '89
PACIFIC RESOURCES INC.
The price was right [Broken Hill Proprietary acquires Pacific Resources] E. McGlinn. il *Forbes* 143:10 F 20 '89
PACIFIC RIM NATIONAL PARK (B.C.)
A towering fight [proposed logging of Sitka spruce on Vancouver Island] H. Quinn. il *Maclean's* 102:46 Je 5 '89
PACIFIC STATES
See also
Pacific Crest National Scenic Trail
Description and travel
A train trilogy [riding Amtrak's Coast Starlight from Seattle to Los Angeles] D. G. Gordon. il map *Travel Holiday* 171:60-6 My '89
PACIFIC STOCK EXCHANGE
Internationalization of the Pacific Stock Exchange [address, November 2, 1988] M. Mann. *Vital Speeches of the Day* 55:214-17 Ja 15 '89
Pork bellies, move over [chip futures] *Newsweek* 114:70 O 30 '89
PACIFIC TELEPHONE & TELEGRAPH CO. See Pacific Telesis Group
PACIFIC TELESIS GROUP
The Baby Bells toddle toward cable [stake in Group W Cable] R. D. Hof. il *Business Week* p40 My 8 '89
Pacific Telesis: "noon on a sunny day". N. J. Perry. il por *Fortune* 120:76 O 9 '89
PACIFIC THEATRES CORPORATION
"Forman's folly". R. King. il *Forbes* 143:72 Mr 6 '89
PACIFIC TRUST TERRITORY See Pacific Islands (Trust Territory)
PACIFIC WESTERN AIRLINES LTD.
American Airlines, Canadian investors weigh bids for Wardair. C. Fotos. *Aviation Week & Space Technology* 130:108-9 Ap 24 '89
The end of Ward's dream [Wardair sold to Pacific Western Airlines] P. Chisholm. il pors *Maclean's* 102:34-5 Ja 30 '89
PWA Corp. to lay off 1,900 airline personnel [combining Canadian Airlines International and Wardair into one airline] *Aviation Week & Space Technology* 131:45 D 11 '89
Wardair founder agrees to sell airline to PWA Corp. D. Hughes. il *Aviation Week & Space Technology* 130:72-3 Ja 30 '89
PACIFICA FOUNDATION
Pacifica's next wave. M. Fisher. il *Mother Jones* 14:50-2 My '89
PACIFICORP
Power goals [merger of Pacificorp and Utah Power & Light] J. Cook. il map *Forbes* 143:116-17 Ap 3 '89

PACIFISM
    See also
    Conscientious objectors
    Nonviolence
    Vietnamese War, 1957-1975—Protest movements
My life as a NATO collaborator [pacifist computer scientist attends NATO workshop on computer-human interaction in command and control; cover story] N. S. Borenstein. il *The Bulletin of the Atomic Scientists* 45:14-20 Ap '89
No payment enclosed: why I resist war taxes [cover story] A. Ayvazian. il *The Progressive* 53:19-21 Ap '89
Sentence for trespassing [religious pacifist J. Haines given nine months for trespassing at Rocky Flats Plant] *The Christian Century* 106:256 Mr 8 '89

PACIFISTS *See* Pacifism

PACINO, AL
    about
A comeback for Pacino. P. Travers. il *Rolling Stone* p35 O 5 '89

PACK RATS *See* Wood rats

PACK RATS (PERSONS)
Confessions of a closet clutterer [attending workshop conducted by Daralee Schulman] J. D. Oliver. il por *Health (New York, N.Y.)* 21:38+ S '89
A pack rat's tale [donating personal items to National Museum of American History] L. Stone. il *Americana* 17:19-21 My/Je '89
Packrats of America. H. L. Rinker. il *Antiques & Collecting Hobbies* 94:20+ S '89

    Anecdotes, facetiae, satire, etc.
Help! My wife may throw me away! R. Keyes. il *Good Housekeeping* 208:109-10 Mr '89
Saving graces. K. Fury. il *New Choices for the Best Years* 29:88 My '89

    Psychiatric care
Pack rats come out of the closet. il *Newsweek* 113:73 F 13 '89

PACK TRANSPORTATION
    See also
    Backpacks and backpacking

PACK TRIPS *See* Horseback trips

THE PACKAGE [film] *See* Motion picture reviews—Single works

PACKAGED MIXES *See* Food mixes

PACKAGERS, BOOK *See* Book packagers

PACKAGES, WRAPPING OF *See* Wrapping of packages

PACKAGING
    See also
    Candy—Packaging
    Container industry
    Cosmetics—Packaging
    Libby Perszyk Kathman (Firm)
    Phonograph records—Packaging
    Plastics in packaging

    Taxation
A tax jolt by design [package design costs now must be included in inventory] G. W. Padwe. il *Nation's Business* 77:82 Je '89

PACKET SWITCHING (DATA TRANSMISSION)
    See also
    Telenet Communications Corp.
Making waves [packet radio] M. Waller. il *Byte* 14:363-4+ D '89

PACKING OF LUGGAGE
Camp clues: pack these tips! il *'Teen* 33:48+ My '89
Travel without trauma. K. Blouin. il *Essence* 20:102+ D '89
Vacation clothes. W. Gavin and C. DiGrappa. il *Parents* 64:166 Je '89

PACKS
    See also
    Backpacks and backpacking

PACKWOOD, ROBERT
Should the Congress adopt the "Textile and Apparel Trade Act of 1987"? [excerpts from address, September 13, 1988] *Congressional Digest* 68:11+ Ja '89

PACS *See* Political action committees

PACTEL *See* Pacific Telesis Group

PADDLING *See* Canoes and canoeing

PADDOCK, HARRIET KINGSTON
She: 6, he: 3, relationship: 0. il *Glamour* 87:75-6+ Ag '89

PADDOCK, JOE
Black energy [poem] *Organic Gardening* 36:78 F '89

PADDOCK, MARIE-LOUISE
Formal curriculum audits. *The Education Digest* 54:35-6 F '89

PADGETT, MARY ANN
(jt. auth) *See* Heinen, Kay, and Padgett, Mary Ann

PADWE, GERALD W.
For your tax file. *See* issues of Nation's Business beginning July 1983

PAEHLKE, ROBERT
The criteria of net benefit. *Society* 27:13-14 N/D '89

PAGÁN, DARIAN
    about
"We had to kidnap our son from the hospital". J. L. Block. il pors *Good Housekeeping* 209:144-5+ O '89

PAGÁN, DOLLY
    about
"We had to kidnap our son from the hospital". J. L. Block. il pors *Good Housekeeping* 209:144-5+ O '89

PAGAN, NOEL
    about
Murder and the right to die. il por *Newsweek* 113:33 Ap 10 '89

PAGÁN, RAFAEL D., JR.
Framing the public agenda [address, September 29, 1988] *Vital Speeches of the Day* 55:177-80 Ja 1 '89
A new era of activism: who will frame the agenda? il por *The Futurist* 23:12-16 My/Je '89

PAGANELLI, PAOLO
    about
A legend in his spare time. A. Assenza. il *Car and Driver* 34:35 Je '89

PAGANELLI & COMPANY
A legend in his spare time. A. Assenza. il *Car and Driver* 34:35 Je '89

PAGANISM
African, Aztec, and Andean religions draw new worshippers. C. Sugnet. il *Utne Reader* p28+ Mr/Ap '89
Pagan holidays mark earth's yearly cycles. T. Knepher. *Utne Reader* p74-5 N/D '89

    Periodicals
Pagan publications. J. Tedford. il *Utne Reader* p136-8 Jl/Ag '89

PAGANO, PENNY
John Hendricks' big adventure [cover story] il pors *Channels (New York, N.Y.: 1986)* 9:20-3 O '89

PAGE, BENJAMIN I., AND THEOBALD, ROBERT
Creativity in turbulent times. il pors *The Futurist* 23:25-8 S/O '89

PAGE, BETTIE
    about
The case of the vanishing pinup. I. S. Levine. il pors *Rolling Stone* p167+ N 16 '89

PAGE, CLARENCE
    about
Columnist Clarence Page wins Pulitzer at Chicago tribune. por *Jet* 76:23 Ap 17 '89

PAGE, JAKE
Delay for a dump. il *Smithsonian* 20:66 O '89
From back-lot menagerie to nascent biopark in only a hundred years [cover story] il *Smithsonian* 20:26-35 Jl '89
A question of degree [cover story] il map *National Parks* 63:24-9 Jl/Ag '89

PAGE, JAKE, AND HOFFMAN, CARL
On Everest or in the office, it's the tool to have. bibl (p229) il *Smithsonian* 20:106-8+ O '89

PAGE, JOSEPH A.
Brazil: a nation in search of a miracle. *America* 161:273-4 O 28 '89

PAGE, KATHLEEN
    about
The architects of their own success. A. M. Russell. il pors *Working Woman* 14:81-2+ O '89

PAGE, RUSSELL
    about
The flowering of Fort Worth. C. Burden. il por *House & Garden* 161:84-91+ F '89

PAGE, RUTH
Spellbound by seeds. il *Country Journal* 16:34-6 Ja '89

PAGE, SHELLEY
'To remind them that we're here'. *World Press Review* 36:42 F '89

PAGE, TIM
A change of pace. il por *Opera News* 53:24+ Je '89

PAGE-ZEBROWSKI ARCHITECTS
The architects of their own success. A. M. Russell. il pors *Working Woman* 14:81-2+ O '89
Architectural team wins the Helping Hands for Small Business Contest. il *Working Woman* 14:73 Ap '89

PAGEANTS
    See also
    Christmas pageants

PAGEL, AUGUSTA
    about
I'm 109 and guess what . . . I'm a great, great, great, great granny. J. Hayes. il pors *Life* 12:89-92 Ap '89

PAGEL, MARK D., AND HARVEY, PAUL H., 1947-
Taxonomic differences in the scaling of brain on body weight among mammals. bibl f il *Science* 244:1589-93 Je 30 '89

PAGEL FAMILY
    about
I'm 109 and guess what . . . I'm a great, great, great, great granny. J. Hayes. il pors *Life* 12:89-92 Ap '89

PAGELS, HEINZ R., 1939-1988
    about
Obituary
    Physics Today 42:98+ My '89. J. Bernstein and G. Feinberg

PAGEMAKER (DESKTOP PUBLISHING PROGRAM) *See* Desktop publishing—Programming

PAGES (DESKTOP PUBLISHING PROGRAM) *See* Desktop publishing—Programming

PAGING DEVICES
Beepers come of age. N. Santelmann. il *Forbes* 143:170 Je 12 '89

PAGIS, DAN
Ein Leben [poem]; tr. by Stephen Mitchell. *The New Yorker* 65:85 Ap 3 '89
A moment at the Louvre [poem] *The New Yorker* 65:42 My 15 '89

PAGNANELLI, DAVID M.
Light at the end of the carpal tunnel. il *Nation's Business* 77:69 Ag '89

PAHLAVI, MOHAMMED REZA, SHAH OF IRAN *See* Mohammed Reza Pahlavi, Shah of Iran, 1919-1980

PAHLAVI, REZA *See* Reza Pahlavi

PAID VACATIONS *See* Employee vacations

PAIGE, HARRY W., 1922-
Sacred places. il *America* 160:34-5 Ja 21 '89

PAIN
See also
Analgesia and analgesics
Backache
Chest pain
Esophageal pain
Headache
Neck pain
Sadomasochism
Suffering
TMJ syndrome
University of Miami. Comprehensive Pain and Rehabilitation Center
Aches run in the family [study by Kathryn Richard] E. Stark. il *Psychology Today* 23:23 Ap '89
Conquering pain. A. Schechter. il *Modern Maturity* 32:72-4+ Je/Jl '89
Coping with chronic pain. M. Callahan. il *Parents* 64:202+ Ap '89
Listen to your body: little aches and pains that signal trouble. E. Stukane. il *Redbook* 172:104-5+ Ap '89
Pain [dancers] M. Horosko. il *Dance Magazine* 63:62-3 Ja '89
The pain barrier [special section] il *Maclean's* 102:36-42 F 27 '89
Suffering in silence. M. Shuchman and M. S. Wilkes. il *The New York Times Magazine* p36-7 Jl 23 '89
The ten-minute pain transplant [chromaffin cell grafts suppress pain in rats] D. Stein. il *Omni (New York, N.Y.)* 11:22+ Je '89
What can be done when the pain won't go away. E. Weck. il *FDA Consumer* 23:28-31 Jl/Ag '89
When truth doesn't hurt [research by Michael S. Shutty] P. Chance. *Psychology Today* 22:11 D '88
The whys of hard labor [ability to cope during childbirth; research by Nancy K. Lowe] V. Brower. il *American Health* 8:120 Je '89

PAINE, JOHN KNOWLES, 1839-1906
about
New-world symphonies. P. G. Davis. pors *New York* 22:88-9 F 6 '89

PAINE, THOMAS O.
Apollo and Mars. il *Ad Astra* 1:3 Jl/Ag '89
First word. il *Omni (New York, N.Y.)* 11:6 Jl '89

PAINE WEBBER GROUP INC. *See* PaineWebber Group Inc.

PAINEWEBBER GROUP INC.
Lessons in the ledgers [stock picker T. Doerflinger] J. Willoughby. il por *Forbes* 143:104+ My 15 '89
A margin for the electronic broker [R. Baird, futures broker] R. D. R. Hoffmann. il por *Personal Computing* 13:90-2 O '89

PAINT
See also
Lead based paint
Interior semigloss paints. il *Consumer Reports* 54:317-21 My '89
Interior semigloss paints. il *Consumer Reports* 54:381-6 D '89
Pollution produces peeling paint. *USA Today (Periodical)* 118:13 D '89
Technical page [grades and types of artists' paints] R. Mayer. *American Artist* 53:22+ Mr '89
An unusual approach to acrylics [mixed with gel and extruded through syringes] H. J. Drexler. il por *American Artist* 53:44-9 F '89
What makes my paint peel? D. Johnson. il *The Family Handyman* 39:24-8 Mr '89
Whole house painting manual [cover story; special section] A. Rooze and D. Prestly. il *The Family Handyman* 39:31-7 Mr '89

PAINT, PROTECTIVE
The bottom line on bottom paints [marine antifouling paints] B. Gladstone. il *Motor Boating & Sailing* 163:105-8 Ap '89

PAINT AND VARNISH REMOVERS
Safe stripper and more [3M's Safest Stripper] K. Collier. il *The Family Handyman* 39:16 F '89
Super stripper [3M wood refinishing products] A. W. Lees. il *Popular Science* 234:152 Ap '89

Supersafe paint stripper [3M's Safest Stripper] R. Capotosto. il *Popular Mechanics* 166:148 My '89
Take it all off—boatkeeper's guide to paint and varnish removers. B. Gladstone. il *Motor Boating & Sailing* 164:67-9 S '89

PAINT INDUSTRY
See also
Hitox Corporation
PPG Industries, Inc.
Sherwin-Williams Co.

PAINT REMOVERS *See* Paint and varnish removers

PAINT SPRAYING AND SPRAYERS
See also
Airbrush art
Using a paint sprayer. K. Collier. il *The Family Handyman* 39:22-3 Mr '89

PAINT STRIPPERS *See* Paint and varnish removers

PAINTED FURNITURE *See* Furniture, Painted

PAINTER, PAMELA
Feeding the piranha [story] il *The Atlantic* 264:68-70 O '89

PAINTING
See also
Cubism
Expressionism (Art)
Floor painting and decoration
Frescoes
Imitation art
Impressionism (Art)
Landscape painting
Marine painting
Miniature painting
Mural painting and decoration
Mural painting and decoration, Exterior
Portrait painting
Postimpressionism (Art)
Still life painting
Tempera painting
Textile painting
Topographic painting
Watercolor painting
But will it fit over the couch? [spec sheet for custom made paintings] L. Pozzi. *Harper's* 279:35 S '89

Collectors and collecting
See Art—Collectors and collecting

Conservation and restoration
The risk of breaking rules [preservation of Color Field oil paintings] B. Keyser. il *American Artist* 53:20+ O '89
The Ryder cover-up [tampering with paintings of A. P. Ryder] W. I. Homer. il por *Art News* 88:158-61 O '89
Sad tears. C. T. Chieffo. *American Artist* 53:22+ Ap '89

Expertising
See Art—Expertising

Forgeries
See Art—Forgeries

Photographs and photography
See Art—Photographs and photography

Prices
See Art—Prices

Study and teaching
A conversation with Sharon Carson. C. Movalli. il *American Artist* 53:32-7+ N '89

Technique
See also
Airbrush art
Chiaroscuro
An approach to success. L. Garon. il *American Artist* 53:66-71 Jl '89
The evolution of a painting [circus composition] C. Browning. il *American Artist* 53:54-9 Jl '89
Imprimatura. S. G. Sheehan. il *American Artist* 53:26 Ja '89
Leonardo's lessons [excerpt from Leonardo on painting] Leonardo, da Vinci. il *Art News* 88:24 D '89
Painting with oil sticks [Giverny paintings by J. Chesley; cover story] E. Feit. il *American Artist* 53:44-9 Ap '89
Resolving a painting [excerpt from A painterly approach] M. B. McKenzie. il *American Artist* 53:64-9 Ja '89
The risk of breaking rules [preservation of Color Field oil paintings] B. Keyser. il *American Artist* 53:20+ O '89
An unusual approach to acrylics [mixed with gel and extruded through syringes] H. J. Drexler. il por *American Artist* 53:44-9 F '89

Thefts
See Art thefts

Transportation
See Transportation of works of art

PAINTING, ABSTRACT *See* Art, Abstract

PAINTING, AMERICAN
See also
Agrafiotis, Peter
Aiello, Robert
App, Timothy, 1947-
Ault, George C., 1891-1948
Baechler, Donald, 1956-
Baltzell, Jan C.
Bansemer, Roger, 1948-
Barnet, Will, 1911-

PAINTING, AMERICAN—See also—*cont.*
Baron, Hannelore, 1926-1987
Barowitz, Elliott, 1936-
Barrell, Bill, 1932-
Bartlett, Bo
Bartlett, Jennifer, 1941-
Basquiat, Jean-Michel, 1960-1988
Beckman, Stan, 1931-
Beckman, William
Benbridge, Henry, 1743-1812
Benney, Paul
Benton, Thomas Hart, 1889-1975
Berg, Floyd
Berns, Ben, 1936-
Berthot, Jake, 1939-
Bleckner, Ross, 1949-
Bluhm, Norman, 1920-
Brandt, Warren, 1918-
Brega, Doug
Brown, Frederick, 1945-
Brown, John George, 1831-1913
Brown, Roger, 1941-
Buckels, Jim
Button, John, 1929-1982
Cajori, Charles
Carroll, Richard
Carson, Sharon
Carter, Carol
Cartier, Janice
Cassatt, Mary, 1844-1926
Celmins, Vija, 1939-
Chesley, Jacqueline
Church, Frederic Edwin, 1826-1900
Clifford, Howard
Close, Chuck, 1940-
Cole, Thomas, 1801-1848
Colescott, Robert, 1925-
Colson, Jeff, 1956-
Connelly, Chuck, 1956?-
Connor, Russell
Cowan, Ralph Wolfe
Dalglish, Jamie, 1947-
Dassoulas, Mark
De Kooning, Willem, 1904-
Diebenkorn, Richard, 1922-
DiGiorgio, Joseph, 1931-
Dopp, Susan Marie
Du Bois, Guy Pène, 1884-1958
Dunham, Carroll, 1949-
Eubanks, Tony
Fasanella, Ralph, 1914-
Fischl, Eric
Frankenthaler, Helen, 1928-
Frederick, Linden
Friedland, Howard
Friedman, Warner, 1934-
Geiger, Marion
Gilliam, Sam, 1933-
Golub, Leon Albert, 1922-
Gornik, April
Gregor, Harold
Guston, Philip, 1913-
Haas, Richard
Hambleton, Richard
Hannah, Duncan
Harkins, George
Harrison, Allen
Hartley, Marsden, 1877-1943
Haynes, Nancy, 1947-
Held, Al, 1928-
Heller, Susanna
Holden, Donald, 1931-
Hopper, Edward, 1882-1967
Horn, Karen
Hudson River School
Huff, Caroline
Jaffe, Shirley, 1923-
Johns, Jasper
Jonson, Raymond, 1891-1982
Kearns, Jerry
Kelly, Ken, 1955-
Koch, Edwin B., 1937-
La Farge, John, 1835-1910
La Noue, Terence, 1941-
Laffoley, Paul
Larko, Valeri, 1959-
Lewis, Norman, 1909-1979
Lichtenstein, Roy, 1923-
Linden, Ron
Lynch, Michael J.
Marden, Brice, 1938-
Marshall, Neil
Martin, Agnes, 1912-
Matulka, Jan, 1890-1972
Mazur, Michael, 1935-
McCoy, Ann, 1946-
McDermott, David
McGough, Peter

McVicker, Jim
Mendelsohn, John, 1949-
Minter, Marilyn
Moore, John L.
Morley, Malcolm
Morris, Carl A., 1911-
Moskowitz, Robert S., 1935-
Motherwell, Robert
Mueller, Stephen
Murphy, Gerald
Murray, Elizabeth
Nares, James
Nassy, Josef
Natkin, Robert, 1930-
Nelson, Joan, 1958-
Novros, David, 1941-
Olin, Marian E.
Ominski, Steve, 1952-
Ortins, David
Ownby, Chris
Paisley-Jones, Lawley
Palmer, William C., 1906-1987
Panter, Gary, 1950-
Paradise, Phil Herschel, 1905-
Park, David, 1911-1960
Peacock, Cliffton, 1953-
Pekarsky, Mel, 1934-
Pfister, Chris
Pollock, Jackson
Porter, Katherine, 1941-
Portraits, American
Rauschenberg, Robert, 1925-
Register, John, 1939-
Reich, Murray
Remington, Frederic, 1861-1909
Rielle, Nancy
Rivers, Larry
Robertson, Mary
Rockman, Alexis
Row, David
Ruscha, Edward
Ryder, Albert Pinkham, 1847-1917
Ryman, Robert, 1930-
Safranek, Doug
Salle, David
Sampson, Atlanta Constance, 1897-
Saul, Peter, 1934-
Savannah, Sheila
Schlicting, Michael, 1953-
Schnabel, Julian
Scott, Michael, 1952-
Seely, Alice Warder, 1942-
Sennhauser, John, 1907-1978
Shaffer, Richard, 1947-
Shahn, Ben, 1898-1969
Sharrow, Sheba
Shorr, Harriet
Sigler, Hollis, 1948-
Sofer, Ken
Sorman, Steven, 1948-
Steckel, Anita
Steensma, J., 1940-
Stella, Frank
Stroud, Peter, 1921-
Stuart, Gilbert, 1755-1828
Sullivan, Bill, 1942-
Sultan, Donald K., 1951-
Taicher, Richard, 1929-
Tarbell, Edmund Charles, 1862-1938
Traylor, Bill, 1854-1947
Tsiaras, Philip, 1952?-
Tudor, Guy
Twachtman, John Henry, 1853-1902
Twombly, Cy, 1928-
Valadez, John
Van Hook, George
Warhol, Andy, 1928?-1987
West, Benjamin, 1738-1820
Wharton, William
Whittredge, Worthington, 1820-1910
Wiley, William
Williams, Neil, 1934-1988
Wilson, Helen Miranda
Woodruff, Thomas
Wyeth, Andrew, 1917-
Wyeth, Jamie, 1946-
Yanow, Rhoda
Zeldis, Malcah, 1931-
Zerwekh, Robert, 1939-
American painting [cover story; special issue] bibl f il *Antiques*
    136:1108-83 N '89
Art: early California watercolors. T. S. Hines. il *Architectural
    Digest* 46:296-301+ My '89
The winter art show. il *American Heritage* 40:94-103 D
    '89

Collectors and collecting
American paintings in the Manoogian Collection. N. Cikovsky.
    il *Antiques* 136:132-43 Jl '89

PAINTING, AMERICAN—Collectors and collecting—*cont.*
Chacun à son pocketbook [I. R. Koger's collection of paintings and H. Adler's collection of drawings from 1870 to 1930] C. Brown. il pors *Forbes* 144:144-5 D 25 '89

Exhibitions

See also
Whitney Museum of American Art
American art in the Maier Museum of Art, Randolph-Macon Woman's College, Lynchburg, Virginia. D. M. Sokol. il *Antiques* 136:1138-47 N '89
American artists at the 1889 Exposition Universelle in Paris. A. Blaugrund. bibl f il *Antiques* 136:1158-69 N '89
American paintings in the Manoogian Collection. N. Cikovsky. il *Antiques* 136:132-43 Jl '89
American pastels [American pastels in the Metropolitan Museum of Art: 1880-1930] A. E. Ledes. il *Antiques* 136:650+ O '89
The canvas sea [Sounding the depths: 150 years of American seascape] il *Modern Maturity* 32:66-9 D '89/Ja '90
Casting a *glasnost* glow on once-obscured artists [traveling exhibit entitled 10 + 10: contemporary Soviet and American painters] S. Meisler. bibl (p183) il *Smithsonian* 20:130-6+ D '89
Moscow and the Hudson [exhibition of American painting in Moscow] K. Larson. il *New York* 22:79-80 O 16 '89

PAINTING, ARGENTINE
See also
Fontana, Lucio, 1899-1968
Pérez Celis

PAINTING, AUSTRIAN
See also
Klimt, Gustav, 1862-1918
Schiele, Egon, 1890-1918

PAINTING, BELGIAN
See also
Nellens, Roger, 1937-
Art: Belgian impressionism. D. Solomon. il *Architectural Digest* 46:140-5+ F '89

PAINTING, CANADIAN
See also
Grondin, Jean-Luc
Lukacs, Attila Richard

Exhibitions

See also
Thomson Gallery (Toronto, Ont.)

PAINTING, CHILEAN
See also
Matta, 1911-

PAINTING, CHINESE
See also
Wang Yani
Yang, Chihung, 1948-
Zhou Brothers

Exhibitions
Ming and Quing paintings [Metropolitan Museum of Art show] A. C. Danto. *The Nation* 249:469-72 O 23 '89
The naked and the damned [nude art show in Beijing] S. Staggs. il *Art News* 88:24+ Ap '89

PAINTING, CUBAN
See also
Guillén Landrián, Nicolás

PAINTING, CZECH
See also
Kunc, Milan
Mucha, Alphonse, 1860-1939

PAINTING, DUTCH
See also
Gogh, Vincent van, 1853-1890
Hals, Frans, the Elder, ca. 1580-1666
Mondrian, Piet, 1872-1944

Exhibitions
Eloquent bouquets [A prosperous past: the sumptuous still life in the Netherlands, 1600-1700 at the Kimbell Art Museum] R. Bernier. il *House & Garden* 161:96-101+ D '89

PAINTING, ENGLISH
See also
Bacon, Francis, 1909-
Bell, Vanessa, 1879-1961
Coe, Sue, 1951-
Constable, John, 1776-1837
Edmondson, Simon, 1955?-
Hockney, David
Hodgkin, Howard, 1932-
Leighton of Stretton, Frederic Leighton, Baron, 1830-1896
Lenkiewicz, R. O.
Leslie, Charles Robert, 1794-1859
Nevinson, Christopher Richard Wynne, 1889-1946
Oulton, Therese, 1953-
Warrender, Jonathan

Exhibitions
New British painting: Contemporary Arts Center. M. Bloomfield. il *Art News* 88:185 Mr '89

PAINTING, EUROPEAN
See also
Metropolitan Museum of Art (New York, N.Y.). Dept. of European Paintings

Fruit, flowers, and a sweet Madonna [high prices at sales of old masters paintings] G. Barker. il *Art News* 88:44 O '89

PAINTING, FINNISH
See also
Mäkelä, Marika

PAINTING, FLEMISH
See also
Dyck, Sir Anthonie van, 1599-1641

PAINTING, FRENCH
See also
Bonnard, Pierre, 1867-1947
Braque, Georges, 1882-1963
Cézanne, Paul, 1839-1906
Courbet, Gustave, 1819-1877
Courtin, Pierre, 1921-
Degas, Edgar, 1834-1917
Garouste, Gérard
Gauguin, Paul, 1848-1903
Hélion, Jean, 1904-1987
Hyde de Neuville, Anne-Marguerite-Henriette Rouillé de Marigny, baronne, 1749?-1849
Ingres, Jean Auguste Dominique, 1780-1867
Klein, Yves, 1928-1962
Lamotte,, Bernard
Manet, Édouard, 1832-1883
Monet, Claude, 1840-1926
Moreau, Gustave, 1826-1878
Noël, Georges, 1924-
Renoir, Auguste, 1841-1919
Toulouse-Lautrec, Henri de, 1864-1901
Vuillard, Édouard, 1868-1940

Exhibitions

See also
Salon (Exhibition)
Strength of vision [Masterpieces of impressionism and post-impressionism: the Annenberg Collection at the Philadelphia Museum of Art] H. Drohojowska. il *Harper's Bazaar* 122:204-7+ Ap '89

PAINTING, GERMAN
See also
Breder, Hans, 1935-
Ernst, Max, 1891-1976
Herold, Georg, 1947-
Hoehme, Gerhard, 1920-
Kiefer, Anselm, 1945-
A Ring for the '80s [German Romantic roots of Metropolitan Opera's new production] B. Adams. il *Art in America* 77:222-9 Ap '89

Exhibitions
Art [Refigured painting: the German image 1960-88] A. C. Danto. *The Nation* 248:531-4 Ap 17 '89
Blind ambition [Refigured painting: the German image 1960-88] K. Larson. il *New York* 22:63-4 Mr 6 '89
Monstrous mutants, departing souls [Refigured painting: the German image 1960-88] N. Grimes. il *Art News* 88:162 My '89
Some like it hot! [German expressionism in Washington, D.C. and Atlanta, Ga.] G. Sikes. il *Harper's Bazaar* 122:88+ N '89

PAINTING, HUNGARIAN

Exhibitions
Eight Hungarian painters: Gallery Arti et Amicitae. E. Beck. il *Art News* 88:159+ Ja '89

PAINTING, INDUSTRIAL AND PRACTICAL
See also
Airplanes, Jet—Fuselage—Painting
Automobiles—Painting
Boats and boating—Painting
Gilding
House painting
Paint
Paint spraying and sprayers
Varnish and varnishing

Equipment
Paint & Go. M. Thompson. il *The Family Handyman* 39:28 Jl/Ag '89

PAINTING, ISLAMIC

Exhibitions
Islamic paintings at the Sackler enchant the eye [H. Vever collection] C. Bond. il *Smithsonian* 19:122-7 Ja '89

PAINTING, ITALIAN
See also
Canaletto, 1697-1768
Ceccobelli, Bruno, 1952-
Cucchi, Enzo, 1950-
Donati, Enrico, 1909-
Gentileschi, Artemisia, 1597-1651
Guccione, Piero, 1935-
Leonardo, da Vinci, 1452-1519
Magnelli, Alberto, 1888-1971
Michelangelo Buonarroti, 1475-1564
Paladino, Mimmo
Reni, Guido, 1575-1642
Sironi, Mario, 1885-1961
Titian, ca. 1488-1576
Vedova, Emilio, 1919-
Veronese, 1528-1588

PAINTING, ITALIAN—*cont.*
Exhibitions
Art [Painting in Renaissance Siena at the Metropolitan Museum of Art] A. C. Danto. *The Nation* 248:317-20 Mr 6 '89
Magical mystery tour [Painting in Renaissance Siena at the Metropolitan Museum of Art] K. Larson. il *New York* 22:56-7 Ja 16 '89
Painting in Renaissance Siena: 1420-1500: Metropolitan Museum of Art. B. A. MacAdam. il *Art News* 88:159 My '89
The seers of Siena [Metropolitan Museum exhibit] L. Cunningham. il *Commonweal* 116:213-14 Ap 7 '89
PAINTING, JAPANESE
See also
Hirabayashi, Kaoru
Jakuchū, 1716-1800
Takayama, Tatsuo
Teraoka, Masami, 1936-
Collectors and collecting
Buying at the Wright time [Edo painting collection owned by J. Price] C. Brown. il por *Forbes* 143:172 Je 12 '89
PAINTING, LATIN AMERICAN
What's wrong with this painting? [undervaluation of Latin American painting] R. J. Stroessner and T. Dewalt. il *Américas* 41 no2:58-60 '89
PAINTING, MANUSCRIPT *See* Illumination of books and manuscripts
PAINTING, MEXICAN
See also
Orozco, José Clemente, 1883-1949
Villalpando, Cristóbal de
PAINTING, MODERN *See* Art, Modern
PAINTING, NORWEGIAN
See also
Nerdrum, Odd, 1944-
PAINTING, POLISH
Exhibitions
19th-century Polish painting: National Academy of Design. R. Bass. il *Art News* 88:146 Ja '89
PAINTING, PORTUGUESE
See also
Rego, Paula, 1935-
PAINTING, PRE-RAPHAELITE *See* Pre-Raphaelites
PAINTING, PUERTO RICAN
See also
Campeche, José, 1752-1809
PAINTING, RENAISSANCE
Exhibitions
Art [Painting in Renaissance Siena at the Metropolitan Museum of Art] A. C. Danto. *The Nation* 248:317-20 Mr 6 '89
Magical mystery tour [Painting in Renaissance Siena at the Metropolitan Museum of Art] K. Larson. il *New York* 22:56-7 Ja 16 '89
Painting in Renaissance Siena: 1420-1500: Metropolitan Museum of Art. B. A. MacAdam. il *Art News* 88:159 My '89
The seers of Siena [Metropolitan Museum exhibit] L. Cunningham. il *Commonweal* 116:213-14 Ap 7 '89
PAINTING, RUSSIAN
See also
Kandinsky, Wassily, 1866-1944
Komar, Vitali, 1943-
Malevich, Kazimir Severinovich, 1878-1935
Melamid, Aleksandr, 1945-
Mironenko, Vladimir
Nesterova, Natalia
Roerich, Nicholas, 1874-1947
Roiter, Andrei
Zvezdotchetov, Konstantin, 1958-
Exhibitions
Casting a *glasnost* glow on once-obscured artists [traveling exhibit entitled 10 + 10: contemporary Soviet and American painters] S. Meisler. bibl (p183) il *Smithsonian* 20:130-6+ D '89
PAINTING, SCOTTISH
See also
Grant, Duncan James Corrowr, 1885-1978
PAINTING, SPANISH
See also
Dalí, Salvador, 1904-1989
Goya, Francisco, 1746-1828
Murillo, Bartolomé Esteban, 1617 or 18-1682
Picasso, Pablo, 1881-1973
Ribalta, Francisco, 1565?-1628
Sorolla y Bastida, Joaquín, 1863-1923
Velázquez, Diego, 1599-1660
Zobel, Fernando, 1924?-1984
PAINTING, SWEDISH
See also
Klint, Hilma af, 1862-1944
PAINTING, SWISS
See also
Weber, Mili
PAINTING, VICTORIAN
Art: Victorian landscapes. P. Fuller. il *Architectural Digest* 46:160-5+ Ag '89

PAINTING ON GLASS *See* Glass painting and staining
PAINTING ON TEXTILES *See* Textile painting
PAINTING SUPPORTS
Support systems for paintings (I). B. Keyser. il *American Artist* 53:20+ D '89
PAINTON, PATRICIA H.
Trouble on the right in France. il *The New Leader* 72:5-6 My 1 '89
PAINTS *See* Paint
PAIS, ABRAHAM, 1918-
George Uhlenbeck and the discovery of electron spin. bibl f il pors *Physics Today* 42:34-40 D '89
PAISLEY-JONES, LAWLEY
about
Lawley Paisley-Jones at Jones, Troyer, Fitzpatrick. J. W. Mahoney. *Art in America* 77:158 Ja '89
THE PAJAMA GAME [musical] *See* Musicals, revues, etc.—Reviews—Single works
PAJAMA PARTIES *See* Slumber parties
PAKISTAN
See also
Airplanes, Military—Pakistan
Foreign correspondents—Pakistan
Iranians—Pakistan
Medical care—Pakistan
Military assistance, American—Pakistan
Relief work—Pakistan
United Nations—Pakistan
Women—Pakistan
Commerce
United States
See United States—Commerce—Pakistan
Defenses
Debating the Pakistan dilemma. N. Cooper. il *Newsweek* 113:34 F 13 '89
India, Pakistan's nuclear weapons: all the pieces in place [cover story] D. Albright and T. Zamora. bibl f il map *The Bulletin of the Atomic Scientists* 45:20-6 Je '89
Foreign relations
Afghanistan
See Afghanistan—Foreign relations—Pakistan
India
See India—Foreign relations—Pakistan
United States
See United States—Foreign relations—Pakistan
Politics and government
See also
Elections—Pakistan
Bhutto's diplomatic debut. A. Platt. il por *Newsweek* 113:46 Je 19 '89
Can Pakistan's superwoman survive? [B. Bhutto] E. MacFarquhar. il pors *U.S. News & World Report* 106:38-9+ Ap 17 '89
The double life of Benazir Bhutto [cover story] I. Buruma. il *The New York Review of Books* 36:8-11 Mr 2 '89
The education and stormy career of Islam's leading lady [excerpt from Daughter of destiny] B. Bhutto. il pors *People Weekly* 31:218-20+ Mr 6 '89
The Indian subcontinent [cover story; special issue] il maps *Scholastic Update (Teachers' edition)* 121:3-26 Mr 10 '89
A nation divided [B. Bhutto] I. Buruma. il pors *The New York Times Magazine* p26-30+ Ja 15 '89
The new phase in U.S.-Pakistani relations. T. P. Thornton. *Foreign Affairs* 68:142-59 Summ '89
Pakistan under Benazir Bhutto. W. L. Richter. bibl f *Current History* 88:433-6+ D '89
Pakistan's steel magnolia [B. Bhutto] il por *U.S. News & World Report* 106:14 Je 12 '89
The policies of Pakistan [address, June 7, 1989] B. Bhutto. *Vital Speeches of the Day* 55:551-3 Jl 1 '89
Priming the minister [B. Bhutto] K. Starr. il pors *Vogue* 179:416-19+ Ap '89
Was President Zia murdered? J. Barron. *Reader's Digest* 135:59-63 Ag '89
Who killed General Zia? L. Eskin. il por map *Scholastic Update (Teachers' edition)* 121:22-3 Mr 10 '89
Religious institutions and affairs
See also
United Church of Pakistan
PAKULA, ALAN J., 1928-
about
New York state of mind: Hannah and Alan J. Pakula's apartment in the sky. R. Fizdale and A. Gold. il pors *Architectural Digest* 46:270-3 N '89
See you in the morning [film] Reviews
Commonweal 116:302-3 My 19 '89. T. O'Brien
Glamour 87:186 Mr '89. J. G. Boyum
The New Republic 200:28-9 My 15 '89. S. Kauffman
People Weekly il 31:19-20 My 8 '89. R. No...
PAKULA, HANNAH
about
New York state of mind: Hannah a...
apartment in the sky. R. Fizdale...
Architectural Digest 46:270-3 N '89
PALA, GINO N.
about
Better than an M.B.A. F. Meeks. il ...
Je 26 '89

PALACES
See also
Castles

France
See also
Palais-Royal (Paris, France)
The Ideal Palace: Ferdinand Cheval's fantasy in the Rhône Valley. Y. Blumenfeld. il *Architectural Digest* 46:108-13+ Ja '89
The postman's palace [Le Palais Idéal conceived by F. Cheval] B. Weber. il por *The New York Times Magazine* p122 S 10 '89

Germany (East)
See also
Schloss Charlottenhof (Potsdam, Germany)

Italy
Gardens of delight [touring Roman palaces and their gardens] R. Koenig. il *House & Garden* 161:46+ F '89
The Ruspoli legacy in Italy. C. Aillaud. il pors *Architectural Digest* 46:156-64+ Jl '89

Morocco
A Moroccan jewel [residence of B. Willis] C. Aillaud. il *Architectural Digest* 46:126-31+ Jl '89

Soviet Union
Catherine the Great's Chinese jewel box [Chinese Palace near Leningrad] P. Lauritzen. il *Architectural Digest* 46:174-9 O '89
A Russian folly: visiting Catherine the Great's baroque roller coaster near Leningrad. P. Lauritzen. il por *Architectural Digest* 46:146-9+ My '89

Spain
See also
Fundación Casa Ducal de Medinaceli
Iberian weekends [D. Pinto Coelho's Palacio de los Chaves Mendoza in Trujillo] R. Koenig. il pors *House & Garden* 161:142-53+ F '89

Yugoslavia
An Adriatic idyll [Boschi Palace on Korcula] C. Maclean. il *House & Garden* 161:68+ S '89
PALACIO DE LOS CHAVES MENDOZA (TRUJILLO, SPAIN) See Palaces—Spain
PALACIOS, VIRGILIO ANDRADE
Panama, through Latin eyes. il *World Press Review* 36:24+ Jl '89
PALADINO, MIMMO
about
Mimmo Paladino at Sperone Westwater. K. Johnson. il *Art in America* 77:189-90 N '89
PALAIS-ROYAL (PARIS, FRANCE)
The Palais-Royal, garden of the Revolution. C. P. Reynolds. il *Gourmet* 49:62+ Ap '89
PALAMEDES (GREEK MYTHOLOGY)
Who taught Homer his ABC's? [Barry Powell's theory that it was the legendary Palamedes] il *U.S. News & World Report* 106:10 Ja 23 '89
PALAU, LUIS, 1934-
about
Evangelism: the best form of social action [interview] il por *Christianity Today* 33:51-2 F 17 '89
An open-air crusade in the Soviet Union? Believe it! T. C. Muck. il por *Christianity Today* 33:36-7 O 20 '89
Under the eye of the big, red machine [cover story] T. C. Muck. il por *Christianity Today* 33:20-5 D 15 '89
PALAU
See also
United Nations—Palau

Politics and government
Trusteeship Council mission observes conditions in Palau. il *UN Chronicle* 26:66-7 Je '89
Trusteeship Council told 'overwhelming majority' in Palau wants 'free association' status. il *UN Chronicle* 26:28-30 S '89
PALAU DE LA MÚSICA CATALANA (BARCELONA, SPAIN) See Concert halls—Spain
PALAZHCHENKO, PAVEL
about
Pavel Palazhchenko: Gorbachev wouldn't leave home without him. W. Plummer. il pors *People Weekly* 32:187-8 D 4 '89
PALCY, EUZHAN
about
A dry white season [film] Reviews
America 161:353 N 18 '89. R. A. Blake
The Nation 249:507-8 O 30 '89. S. Klawans
National Review il 41:56-8 O 27 '89. J. Simon
The New Republic 201:24-5 O 9 '89. S. Kauffmann
New York 22:75 O 2 '89. D. Denby
The New Yorker 65:101 O 2 '89. P. Kael
People Weekly il 32:16-17 S 25 '89. R. Novak
Rolling Stone il p36 O 5 '89
Time il 134:78 S 25 '89. R. Schickel
Euzhan Palcy has a face the camera loves but finds the view better behind the lens. I. Lacher. il pors *People Weekly* 32:71-2 O 16 '89
...npest [interview] M. Glicksman. il por *Film Comment* ...:64-6+ S/O '89
..., passionate, persuasive. K. McKenna. il por *American* ...14:32-7 S '89

A woman for all seasons. M. Rosen. il por *Ms.* 18:18+ O '89
Women in film. M. Southgate. il pors *Essence* 20:31-2 O '89
PALEO-AMERICANS See Paleo-Indians
PALEO-INDIANS
The bones from Brazil [evidence of earlier New World migration date; work of Maria Beltrão and Niède Guidon] H. Pringle. il *Omni (New York, N.Y.)* 11:26+ Ap '89
Molecular archaeology [mitochondrial DNA sequences from Little Salt Springs, Fla. remains; research by Svante Pääbo] J. Benditt. *Scientific American* 261:25-6 Jl '89
Skepticism fades over pre-Clovis man [Tom Dillehay's Monte Verde excavations] R. Lewin. *Science* 244:1140 Je 9 '89

Food
A grasshopper in every pot. D. B. Madsen. il *Natural History* p22+ Jl '89
PALEOANTHROPOLOGY See Man, Prehistoric
PALEOBIOLOGY
See also
Paleoecology
PALEOBOTANY
See also
Algae, Fossil
Angiosperms, Fossil
Pollen, Fossil
Seeds, Fossil
Trees, Fossil
Land plants' algal roots [research by Charles F. Delwiche] *Science News* 136:70 Jl 29 '89
Lignin-like compounds and sporopollenin in Coleochaete, an algal model for land plant ancestry. C. F. Delwiche and others. bibl f il *Science* 245:399-401 Jl 28 '89

Carboniferous
A novel fossil seed roils botany theory [work of Jean L. Galtier] I. Wickelgren. *Science News* 136:86 Ag 5 '89

Cretaceous
Angiosperm diversification and paleolatitudinal gradients in Cretaceous floristic diversity. P. R. Crane and S. Lidgard. bibl f il *Science* 246:675-8 N 3 '89

Eocene
A 48-million-year-old aphid-host plant association and complex life cycle: biogeographic evidence [aphid subtribe Melaphidina and sumac host plant] N. A. Moran. bibl f il map *Science* 245:173-5 Jl 14 '89
Tom Miner Basin, Montana. R. H. Mohlenbrock. il maps *Natural History* p14-16 D '89

France
A novel fossil seed roils botany theory [work of Jean L. Galtier] I. Wickelgren. *Science News* 136:86 Ag 5 '89

Montana
Tom Miner Basin, Montana. R. H. Mohlenbrock. il maps *Natural History* p14-16 D '89

Oregon
Fossils of Clarno Basin [nuts and seeds at John Day Fossil Beds] C. H. Jones. il *Earth Science* 42:21-3 Spr '89

Wisconsin
Glacial geology [ancient spruce forest] J. M. Moran and others. il map *Earth Science* 41:16-18 Wint '88
PALEOCEANOGRAPHY
Clues to an ancient upside-down ocean [research by James P. Kennett and Lowell D. Stott] R. Monastersky. *Science News* 136:71 Jl 29 '89
Critical depth for the survival of coral islands: effects on the Hawaiian archipelago. R. W. Grigg and D. Epp. bibl f il map *Science* 243:638-41 F 3 '89
Did the ocean once run backward? [research by James Kennett and Lowell Stott] R. A. Kerr. *Science* 243:740 F 10 '89
New way to switch earth between hot and cold [ocean dissolved carbon dioxide; research by Edward Boyle] R. A. Kerr. il *Science* 243:480 Ja 27 '89
Scandinavian, Siberian, and Arctic Ocean glaciation: effect of Holocene atmospheric CO_2 variations. D. R. Lindstrom and D. R. MacAyeal. bibl f il *Science* 245:628-31 Ag 11 '89
Upside-down oceans [research by James Kennett and Lowell Stott] il *Discover* 10:12 D '89
PALEOCLIMATOLOGY
See also
Glacial epochs
Pangaea—Climate
The Arctic: a key to world climate. P. H. Abelson. *Science* 243:873 F 17 '89
Greenland exposed [evidence for melting of ice sheet; research by Roy Koerner] *Discover* 10:14+ N '89
Ice core evidence for extensive melting of the Greenland ice sheet in the last interglacial. R. M. Koerner. bibl f il map *Science* 244:964-8 My 26 '89
The past and future Amazon. P. A. Colinvaux. bibl il maps *Scientific American* 260:102-8 My '89
Pollen provides ancient weather report. *Science News* 135:220 Ap 8 '89
Rivers in the sand [interpretation of shuttle radar imaging in the Sahara] B. Bower. map *Science News* 136:138-9 Ag 26 '89

PALEOCLIMATOLOGY—cont.

Cretaceous

Could a cold heart stand a cold winter? [Australian dinosaurs; research by Thomas H. Rich and Patricia V. Rich] R. Monastersky. *Science News* 136:38 Jl 15 '89

Flowering plants leave earth cold [research by Tyler Volk] *Science News* 135:188 Mr 25 '89

Holocene

Holocene-late Pleistocene climatic ice core records from Qinghai-Tibetan Plateau. L. G. Thompson and others. bibl f il maps *Science* 246:474-7 O 27 '89

Pleistocene

Great Basin calcite vein and the Pleistocene time scale [discussion of December 2, 1988 article, A 250,000-year climatic record from Great Basin vein calcite: implications for Milankovitch theory] I. J. Winograd and others. *Science* 246:262-3 O 13 '89

Ice cycles [findings in Devil's Hole contradict Milankovitch theory; research by Isaac J. Winograd] R. Kunzig. il *Discover* 10:74-9 My '89

Scandinavian, Siberian, and Arctic Ocean glaciation: effect of Holocene atmospheric CO_2 variations. D. R. Lindstrom and D. R. MacAyeal. bibl f il *Science* 245:628-31 Ag 11 '89

Precambrian

Blame it on the moon [Elatina sediment striations tidally induced; George E. Williams overturns his hypothesis] J. Horgan. *Scientific American* 260:18 F '89

It's not the sun, but the moon [tidally induced Australian rock laminations; research by George E. Williams] il *Sky and Telescope* 77:469 My '89

Quaternary

Ancient ice reveals sudden climate shift [Younger Dryas; work of W. Dansgaard] R. Monastersky. *Science News* 135:374 Je 17 '89

Plankton chronicles icy rerun [Younger Dryas cooling] *Science News* 135:335 My 27 '89

PALEOECOLOGY

Burgess Shale faunas and the Cambrian explosion [cover story] S. Conway Morris. bibl f il map *Science* 246:339-46 O 20 '89

PALEOGEOGRAPHY

See also

Continental drift

Model simulation of the Cretaceous ocean circulation. E. J. Barron and W. H. Peterson. bibl f il *Science* 244:684-6 My 12 '89

Origins and movement of fluids during deformation and metamorphism in the Canadian Cordillera [gold deposits] B. E. Nesbitt and K. Muehlenbachs. bibl f il map *Science* 245:733-6 Ag 18 '89

Where mountains once stood [research by Frederick A. Cook] R. Monastersky. *Science News* 135:319 My 20 '89

PALEOMAGNETISM

Quick flip-flop in the magnetic field [Ocean Drilling Program's evidence from rocks from ocean floor between the Philippines and Borneo] *Science News* 135:188 Mr 25 '89

PALEONTOLOGICAL MODELS AND EXHIBITS

See also

Dinamation International Corporation

It's alive! (Or is it?) [robotic dinosaur models] il *National Geographic World* 163:29-33 Mr '89

Mistakes in museum mountings [views of Kenneth Carpenter] R. Monastersky. *Science News* 136:332 N 18 '89

Say 'ah' [Real sea monsters exhibit] B. Weber. il *The New York Times Magazine* p102 O 29 '89

Skinning the dinosaur [work of S. Czerkas; with editorial comment by Paul Hoffman] D. Lessem. il pors *Discover* 10:4, 38-42+ Mr '89

They move, they roar: dinosaurs are here once more [robotic models] W. H. Jordan, Jr. il *Smithsonian* 20:46-52+ Ag '89

PALEONTOLOGISTS

See also

Gould, Stephen Jay, 1941-

PALEONTOLOGY

See also

Arthropods, Fossil
Birds, Fossil
Crocodiles, Fossil
Deer, Fossil
Dinosaurs
Dolphins, Fossil
Eggs, Fossil
Extinct animals
Footprints, Fossil
Invertebrates, Fossil
Man, Prehistoric
Marine fauna, Fossil
Mass extinction of species
Mastodons
Micropaleontology
Paleoecology
Paleontological models and exhibits
Paleopathology
Pinnipedia, Fossil
Plankton, Fossil
Primates, Fossil

Pseudoscorpions, Fossil
Reptiles, Fossil
Rhinoceros, Fossil
Sea birds, Fossil
Sloths, Fossil
Spiders, Fossil
Teeth, Fossil
Tomography—Paleontological use
Trilobites
Whales, Fossil

Superstition to science. W. H. Matthews. il *Earth Science* 42:12-16 Fall '89

Cambrian

See also

Burgess Shale fossils

The early radiation and relationships of the major arthropod groups. D. E. G. Briggs and R. A. Fortey. bibl f il *Science* 246:241-3 O 13 '89

Carboniferous

Record-breaking reptile [found at East Kirkton quarry in Scotland by Timothy R. Smithson] A. McKenzie. *Science News* 136:372 D 9 '89

Collectors and collecting

A new craze for old bones. G. Cerio. il *Newsweek* 114:59 D 25 '89

Cretaceous

Carbon copies [Cretaceous cold-seep communities in the Canadian Arctic; research by Renoit Beauchamp] *Discover* 10:15 Ag '89

Cretaceous cold-seep communities and methane-derived carbonates in the Canadian Arctic. B. Beauchamp and others. bibl f il map *Science* 244:53-6 Ap 7 '89

Giant meteor impacts and great eruptions: dinosaur killers? G. S. Paul. bibl f il *BioScience* 39:162-72 Mr '89

Mammal-like dentition in a Mesozoic crocodylian. J. M. Clark and others. bibl f il *Science* 244:1064-6 Je 2 '89

Methane key to Arctic mystery mounds [research by Benoit Beauchamp] R. Monastersky. *Science News* 135:215 Ap 8 '89

Devonian

A Devonian spinneret: early evidence of spiders and silk use. W. A. Shear and others. bibl f il *Science* 246:479-81 O 27 '89

Old pseudoscorpion had modern features [research by William A. Shear and others] R. Monastersky. *Science News* 136:263 O 21 '89

Ethical aspects

The case of the "misplaced" fossils [V. J. Gupta's Himalayan fossils; views of J. Talent] R. Lewin. il por *Science* 244:277-9 Ap 21 '89

Cooking the paleontological books? [allegations by J. Talent that V. J. Gupta's Himalayan fossils are fake] W. F. Allman. il *U.S. News & World Report* 106:61 My 8 '89

Jurassic

Dinosaur tragedy yields birth clues [research by Karl F. Hirsch] *Science News* 135:220 Ap 8 '89

Sixth find is a feathered friend [Archaeopteryx specimen from West Germany] P. Shipman. il *Discover* 10:63 Ja '89

Upper Jurassic dinosaur egg from Utah. K. F. Hirsch and others. bibl f il *Science* 243:1711-13 Mr 31 '89

Permian

Tracking the early Permian [fossil footprints in Las Cruces, New Mexico discovered by J. P. MacDonald] L. S. Bowlds. il pors *Earth Science* 42:16-19 Summ '89

Pleistocene

Tasmania's earliest settlers [research by Richard Cosgrove] *Science News* 135:223 Ap 8 '89

Thirty thousand years of human colonization in Tasmania: new Pleistocene dates. R. Cosgrove. bibl f il map *Science* 243:1706-8 Mr 31 '89

Precambrian

Cold death questioned for early algae [Pertatataka acritarchs; research by Wen-Long Zang and Malcolm R. Walter] *Science News* 135:126 F 25 '89

Oldest animal fossils may not be so old [Ediacaran fossils from Australia; research by Jeffrey F. Mount] *Earth Science* 41:9 Wint '88

Study and teaching

Small children learn to identify fossils [program developed by Terry Berkland and James M. Cocke in Missouri] il *Earth Science* 41:8 Wint '88

Tertiary

Skeleton of the oldest known pinniped, Enaliarctos mealsi. A. Berta and others. bibl f il *Science* 244:60-2 Ap 7 '89

Triassic

Birth of the dinosaurs [Petrified Forest National Park; cover story] S. Nash. il *National Parks* 63:16-23 N/D '89

The fossils of Monte San Giorgio. T. Bürgin and others. bibl il map *Scientific American* 260:74-81 Je '89

Africa

Human origins. E. L. Simons. bibl f il *Science* 245:1343-50 S 22 '89

Alberta

Dragons and dinosaurs [Dinosaur Project findings in China and Alberta] P. J. Currie. il *Earth Science* 42:10-13 Summ '89

PALEONTOLOGY—cont.

Arctic regions

Carbon copies [Cretaceous cold-seep communities in the Canadian Arctic; research by Renoit Beauchamp] *Discover* 10:15 Ag '89

Cretaceous cold-seep communities and methane-derived carbonates in the Canadian Arctic. B. Beauchamp and others. bibl f il map *Science* 244:53-6 Ap 7 '89

Methane key to Arctic mystery mounds [research by Benoit Beauchamp] R. Monastersky. *Science News* 135:215 Ap 8 '89

Argentina

Oldest dinosaur [Herrerasaurus] il *Time* 134:75 N 13 '89

Arizona

Birth of the dinosaurs [Petrified Forest National Park; cover story] S. Nash. il *National Parks* 63:16-23 N/D '89

Australia

Cold death questioned for early algae [Pertatataka acritarchs; research by Wen-Long Zang and Malcolm R. Walter] *Science News* 135:126 F 25 '89

Could a cold heart stand a cold winter? [Australian dinosaurs; research by Thomas H. Rich and Patricia V. Rich] R. Monastersky. *Science News* 136:38 Jl 15 '89

Migration evolves Down Under [views of Milford H. Wolpoff] B. Bower. *Science News* 136:365 D 2 '89

Oldest animal fossils may not be so old [Ediacaran fossils; research by Jeffrey F. Mount] *Earth Science* 41:9 Wint '88

Brazil

The bones from Brazil [evidence of earlier New World migration date; work of Maria Beltrão and Niède Guidon] H. Pringle. il *Omni (New York, N.Y.)* 11:26+ Ap '89

British Columbia

See also
Burgess Shale fossils

California

Skeleton of the oldest known pinniped, Enaliarctos mealsi. A. Berta and others. bibl f il *Science* 244:60-2 Ap 7 '89

Canada

Secrets of the Gobi Desert [evidence of dinosaur migration from Asia to North America; work of Philip Currie and others] D. Lessem. il map *Discover* 10:40-6 Je '89

China

"Diary in stone" traces extinction [marine fauna extinction evidence found in Changxing quarry; research by David J. Bottjer] *USA Today (Periodical)* 118:10 Ag '89

Dragons and dinosaurs [Dinosaur Project findings in China and Alberta] P. J. Currie. il *Earth Science* 42:10-13 Summ '89

Colorado

Huge dinosaur bones discovered hollow [pelvis of Supersaurus; research by Wade E. Miller] R. Monastersky. il *Science News* 135:261 Ap 29 '89

Supersaurus [hollow pelvis bone; research by Wade E. Miller] il *Discover* 10:8 S '89

East Asia

Bamboo and human evolution. G. G. Pope. il map *Natural History* p48-57 O '89

Florida

Boning up leads to sloth as a student makes a rare find [discovery of ground sloth fossils by D. Delgado] il por *People Weekly* 32:61 Jl 3 '89

Germany (West)

Sixth find is a feathered friend [Archaeopteryx specimen] P. Shipman. il *Discover* 10:63 Ja '89

Greece

Greek contact for humans, Neanderthals? [research by Curtis Runnels] B. Bower. *Science News* 135:39 Ja 21 '89

Hawaii

Critical depth for the survival of coral islands: effects on the Hawaiian archipelago. R. W. Grigg and D. Epp. bibl f il map *Science* 243:638-41 F 3 '89

India

The case of the "misplaced" fossils [V. J. Gupta's Himalayan fossils; views of J. Talent] R. Lewin. il por *Science* 244:277-9 Ap 21 '89

Cooking the paleontological books? [allegations by J. Talent that V. J. Gupta's Himalayan fossils are fake] W. F. Allman. il *U.S. News & World Report* 106:61 My 8 '89

Israel

Modern humans take a spin back in time [electron spin resonance dating of Skhul site; research by Christopher B. Stringer] B. Bower. *Science News* 135:263 Ap 29 '89

Stone tips on ancient hunting [work of John J. Shea] *Science News* 136:13 Jl 1 '89

Talk of ages [Neanderthal hyoid bone from Kebara cave site, Israel; cover story] B. Bower. il *Science News* 136:24-6 Jl 8 '89

Jersey (Channel Islands)

Evolution's rapid shrinkage [dwarf fossil deer on the island of Jersey; research by Adrian M. Lister] R. Monastersky. *Science News* 136:357 D 2 '89

Kenya

The hunt for Proconsul. A. Walker and M. Teaford. il map *Scientific American* 260:76-82 Ja '89

Malawi

Mammal-like dentition in a Mesozoic crocodylian. J. M. Clark and others. bibl f il *Science* 244:1064-6 Je 2 '89

Middle East

Neanderthals get an evolutionary face-lift [evidence for early stage in the Near East] B. Bower. *Science News* 135:229 Ap 15 '89

Mongolia

Secrets of the Gobi Desert [evidence of dinosaur migration from Asia to North America; work of Philip Currie and others] D. Lessem. il map *Discover* 10:40-6 Je '89

Montana

Dinosaur eggs: the inside story [cover story] J. R. Horner and D. B. Weishampel. il *Natural History* p60-7 D '89

A fleet-footed Montana monster [Tyrannosaurus skeleton uncovered] il *U.S. News & World Report* 107:18 N 13 '89

Interview: Jack Horner. J. Gorman. il por *Omni (New York, N.Y.)* 11:72-4+ Mr '89

Nebraska

An essay on a pig roast [role of F. Osborn's erroneous Nebraska Man theory in the creationism debate] S. J. Gould. il *Natural History* p14+ Ja '89

New Mexico

'Earth-shaker' found: seeing is believing this 50-ton monster [Seismosaurus] N. Hickey. il *TV Guide* 36:27-8 F 4-10 '89

Homing in on the longest animal [use of seismic tomography to find Seismosaurus fossils; work of David D. Gillette] R. Monastersky. *Science News* 136:413 D 23-30 '89

Tracking the early Permian [fossil footprints in Las Cruces, New Mexico discovered by J. P. MacDonald] L. S. Bowlds. il pors *Earth Science* 42:16-19 Summ '89

New York (State)

See also
New York (N.Y.)—Paleontology

A Devonian spinneret: early evidence of spiders and silk use. W. A. Shear and others. bibl f il *Science* 246:479-81 O 27 '89

Old pseudoscorpion had modern features [research by William A. Shear and others] R. Monastersky. *Science News* 136:263 O 21 '89

Oregon

See also
John Day Fossil Beds National Monument (Or.)

Scotland

Record-breaking reptile [found at East Kirkton quarry by Timothy R. Smithson] A. McKenzie. *Science News* 136:372 D 9 '89

A soft body of evidence [conodonts] R. J. Aldridge and D. E. G. Briggs. il *Natural History* p6+ My '89

South Africa

The gripping story of Paranthropus [evidence of tool use at Swartkrans site; study by Randall L. Susman] P. Shipman. il *Discover* 10:66-71 Ap '89

Paranthropus yields mosaic arm bone [work of Randall L. Susman and Frederick E. Grine] B. Bower. *Science News* 135:251 Ap 22 '89

Prehistoric barbecue [evidence of fire use at Swartkrans; research by C. K. Brain and Andrew Sillen] *Discover* 10:14-15 Mr '89

Toe-to-toe with Paranthropus [foot bone gives evidence of bipedality at Swartkrans site; research by Randall Susman] il *Discover* 10:16 Ag '89

South Carolina

Largest known flying seabird found in South Carolina [Pseudodontorn fossil; work of Storrs L. Olson] *Earth Science* 41:6-7 Wint '88

Sri Lanka

Human origins recede in southern Asia [research by Kenneth A. R. Kennedy] B. Bower. *Science News* 135:388 Je 24 '89

Switzerland

The fossils of Monte San Giorgio. T. Bürgin and others. bibl il map *Scientific American* 260:74-81 Je '89

Tanzania

The first humans [Homo habilis fossils of Olduvai Gorge; cover story] W. F. Allman. il *U.S. News & World Report* 106:52-9 F 27 '89

A walk back through evolution [study of gaits and footprints of modern people who walk barefooted indicates Laetoli prints are not Australopithecus afarensis; work of Russell H. Tuttle] B. Bower. *Science News* 135:251 Ap 22 '89

Tasmania (Australia)

Tasmania's earliest settlers [research by Richard Cosgrove] *Science News* 135:223 Ap 8 '89

Thirty thousand years of human colonization in Tasmania: new Pleistocene dates. R. Cosgrove. bibl f il map *Science* 243:1706-8 Mr 31 '89

Utah

Dinosaur tragedy yields birth clues [research by Karl F. Hirsch] *Science News* 135:220 Ap 8 '89

Upper Jurassic dinosaur egg from Utah. K. F. Hirsch and others. bibl f il *Science* 243:1711-13 Mr 31 '89

Vietnam

Stalking the giant ape [R. L. Ciochon and J. W. Olsen search for Gigantopithecus remains] J. James. il map *Discover* 10:42-6+ F '89

PALEONTOLOGY—*cont.*

Virginia

Dinosaur tracks found, on exhibit in Virginia [Culpeper quarry; research by Robert Weems] il *Earth Science* 42:8 Fall '89

A walk along the lakeshore, dinosaur-style [footprints in Culpeper, Va. quarry; research by Robert E. Weems] R. Monastersky. il *Science News* 136:21 Jl 8 '89

Washington (State)

The Blue Lake rhinoceros [lava mold found] K. Kaler. il map *Earth Science* 42:22-4 Fall '89

PALEOPATHOLOGY

Entombed beauty provides syphilis clues [mummy of Maria d'Aragona, a Naples Renaissance noblewoman] *Science News* 136:223 S 30 '89

The syphilized world [study by Brenda J. Baker and George J. Armelagos] J. Benditt. *Scientific American* 260:30 Mr '89

PALEOTEMPERATURE *See* Paleoclimatology

PALESTINE

History

See also

Zionism

Jordan/Palestine [discussion of October 1988 article, Is Jordan Palestine?] D. Pipes and A. M. Garfinkle. *Commentary* 87:2+ F '89

Arab rebellion, 1936-1939

The first intifada: rebellion in Palestine, 1936-39. C. Townshend. bibl il *History Today* 39:13-19 Jl '89

PALESTINE LIBERATION ORGANIZATION

Agonizing reappraisal in Israel [cover story] E. Salpeter. *The New Leader* 72:5-6 Ja 9 '89

Altering the formula for Israel's friends. J. M. Wall. *The Christian Century* 106:4-5 Ja 4-11 '89

The Arafat shuffle. il *The New Republic* 200:9-10+ Ja 9-16 '89

Arafat to Israel: pardon my French [statement concerning Palestinian National Charter] il por *Newsweek* 113:48 My 15 '89

Arafat's man in New York [E. Said] D. Smith. il pors *New York* 22:40-6 Ja 23 '89

Arafat's types of ambiguity [interpretation of the Palestinian Declaration of Independence] A. Shammas. *Harper's* 278:60-1 Mr '89

Assembly renews call for Middle East peace conference [Geneva debate keynoted by Y. Arafat] il *UN Chronicle* 26:50-4 Mr '89

At the end of his rope [Y. Arafat] A. Platt. il por *Newsweek* 114:35 S 18 '89

Baker: sheepdog diplomacy? M. G. Warner. il *Newsweek* 113:40 Ap 17 '89

Baker takes a risky step to center stage in the Middle East. S. Reed. il *Business Week* p82 O 23 '89

Beat the devil [U.S. agrees to hold talks with the PLO] A. Cockburn. *The Nation* 248:6-7 Ja 2 '89

Beyond reason. J. Klein. il *New York* 22:16+ Ap 17 '89

Bunker mentality [delegation of American Jewish leaders meets with PLO] S. K. Sheinbaum. *The Nation* 248:77 Ja 23 '89

The challenge to Bush in the Middle East. il *The Progressive* 53:6-7 Ja '89

A chance to seize the moral high ground. J. M. Wall. *The Christian Century* 106:491-2 My 10 '89

Counterforce [conference of Jewish progressives sponsored by Tikkun] M. L. Sifry. *The Nation* 248:112-13 Ja 30 '89

The critical moment for peace. P. Mattar. *Foreign Policy* 76:141-59 Fall '89

Deadly quarantine [proposed amendment to Prevention of Terrorism Act restricting rights of Palestinians] A. Cockburn. *The Nation* 249:338-9 O 2 '89

A defeated compromise [Israel turns down Mubarak plan] J. Bierman. il por *Maclean's* 102:31 O 16 '89

Distrust and dissension in the West Bank and Gaza [Y. Shamir's Palestinian election proposal] R. Z. Chesnoff. il *U.S. News & World Report* 107:38-9 Jl 10 '89

Divisive diplomacy [Canadian cabinet minister J. Clark seeks stronger ties with PLO] M. Nemeth. por *Maclean's* 102:40 Mr 20 '89

Enemies of peace [America's Mideast plan] M. Kondracke. *The New Republic* 201:14-15 Ag 7-14 '89

Finding a response to Arafat's yes. J. B. Miller. *The Christian Century* 106:165-6 F 15 '89

How the PLO was legitimized [cover story] J. J. Kirkpatrick. *Commentary* 88:21-8 Jl '89

The intifada's surreal effect. R. Z. Chesnoff. il *U.S. News & World Report* 106:54-5+ Mr 20 '89

Israel: a chance for peace? il *Scholastic Update (Teachers' edition)* 122:13 N 3 '89

Israel: a lamentation from the future. N. Podhoretz. *Commentary* 87:15-21 Mr '89

Israel and the Palestinians. G. Gottlieb. bibl f *Foreign Affairs* 68:109-26 Fall '89

Israel: some surprising polls [American opinion judged increasingly favorable towards Israel] M. Bard. *Commentary* 88:45-7 Ag '89

An Israeli with a controversial plan for the Palestinians [interview with C. Shur] J. R. Moskin. il por *World Press Review* 36:32-4 Je '89

Israel's dilemma [Palestine question] A. Perlmutter. *Foreign Affairs* 68:119-32 Wint '89/'90

Israel's fateful hour [interview with Y. Harkabi] R. I. Friedman. *Harper's* 279:28+ Jl '89

Israel's prison academies [Palestinians organize while imprisoned by Israelis]; tr. by Ina Friedman. E. Ya'ari. il *The Atlantic* 264:22+ O '89

It's Arab on Arab two years into the intifada [death squads in the occupied territories] R. Z. Chesnoff. il *U.S. News & World Report* 107:15 D 25 '89-Ja 1 '90

Jordan/Palestine [discussion of October 1988 article, Is Jordan Palestine?] D. Pipes and A. M. Garfinkle. *Commentary* 87:2+ F '89

Jordan and reverberations of the uprising. R. Satloff. bibl f *Current History* 88:85-8+ F '89

"Lamentation" [discussion of March 1989 article, Israel: a lamentation from the future] N. Podhoretz. *Commentary* 88:4-8+ Jl '89

A letter to Yasir Arafat. M. Z. Rosensaft. por *Newsweek* 114:14 D 11 '89

Masters of double-talk [reports that Y. Shamir has been talking to the PLO] il pors *Time* 134:30-1 Ag 7 '89

The Middle East [address, April 22, 1989] King Hussein. *Vital Speeches of the Day* 55:486-7 Je 1 '89

The Middle East [Palestinian uprising; special section] il *World Press Review* 36:26-9 Ap '89

Middle East [U.S. opens dialogue with PLO; statements and press conferences, November 26-December 18, 1988; special section] *Department of State Bulletin* 89:51-60 F '89

Middle East peacemakers. C. T. Oppenheim. *The Progressive* 53:11 Jl '89

Mubarak moves to the front lines of the Mideast crisis. B. Slavin and others. il *Business Week* p59 Ja 9 '89

Much has changed [need to negotiate with PLO] *The Nation* 248:435-6 Ap 3 '89

The new PLO? [views of B. A. Sharif] S. MacLeod. bibl f il *The New York Review of Books* 36:44-9 Ap 13 '89

Notes and comment [U.S. meetings with PLO in Tunis] *The New Yorker* 65:33-4 Ap 10 '89

Null and void [Y. Arafat's statement on the 1964 PLO charter] *Time* 133:45 My 15 '89

Old dogs, old tricks. *The New Republic* 200:10-12 Ja 30 '89

The Palestinians [U.S. refusal of visa to Y. Arafat] il *World Press Review* 36:8+ Ja 39

Palestinians and the intifada: one year later. A. D. Miller. bibl f *Current History* 88:73-6+ F '89

Peace later [J. A. Baker's role in Middle East negotiations] M. Kondracke. *The New Republic* 200:10-12 Mr 27 '89

The peace of Saladin [Yitzhak Shamir's Palestinian election proposal] M. B. Zuckerman. il *U.S. News & World Report* 106:78 My 1 '89

The PLO [discussion of July 1989 article, How the PLO was legitimized] J. J. Kirkpatrick. *Commentary* 88:7-8 N '89

The PLO: terrorists or freedom fighters? [interview with M. Awad] por *Christianity Today* 33:62 Ja 13 '89

The politics of health [application to World Health Organization] J. Bierman. il *Maclean's* 102:27 My 22 '89

The politics of peace in the Mideast [cover story] E. Salpeter. il *The New Leader* 72:5-7 O 2-16 '89

Prescriptions for the Middle East. M. Morrison. *The American Spectator* 22:16-18 Ja '89

"Professor of terror" [discussion of August 1989 article] E. Alexander. *Commentary* 88:2-7+ D '89

Professor of terror [views of E. W. Said] E. Alexander. *Commentary* 88:49-50 Ag '89

A profusion of land mines. M. Cohen. il *Commonweal* 116:275-8 My 5 '89

Regrets only [reaction to J. Baker's speech regarding Middle East peace plan] *The New Republic* 200:8 Je 19 '89

Sanctum of the strong. E. W. Said. il *The Nation* 249:48-50 Jl 10 '89

Saying no to Arafat [Y. Shamir forms coalition government and rules out talks with PLO] S. MacLeod. il pors *Time* 133:81-2 Ja 2 '89

Secretary's interview on "This week with David Brinkley" [denial of visa to Y. Arafat; interview with G. P. Shultz; transcript of program, December 4, 1988] *Department of State Bulletin* 89:7-9 F '89

Send in the pols. J. Klein. il por *New York* 22:10-11 Ja 9 '89

Setting Yasser straight [role of American R. E. Hauser in U.S. recognition of PLO] S. Weller. il pors *Ms.* 17:84 Mr '89

Shamir gets set for Washington [cover story] E. Salpeter. il *The New Leader* 72:6-8 Mr 6 '89

Shamir stands his ground [interview with Y. Shamir] R. Rivard and others. il por *Newsweek* 113:42 Ja 2 '89

Shamir under fire [report concludes that Israel must negotiate with the PLO] J. Bierman. il por *Maclean's* 102:24-5 Ap 3 '89

Should we trust Yasir Arafat? D. Reed. por *Reader's Digest* 135:143-8 S '89

PALESTINE LIBERATION ORGANIZATION—*cont.*
Slipping into darkness. H. Goodman. *The New Republic* 201:10-12 Jl 3 '89
Sowing dragons' teeth or talking. *America* 161:228 O 14 '89
Spoilers of peace in the Middle East [radical Palestinian groups supported by Syria] R. Z. Chesnoff. il map *U.S. News & World Report* 107:40-1 Jl 10 '89
Talk to the PLO? More Israelis are thinking about it. N. Sandler and B. Javetski. il *Business Week* p48 Ap 10 '89
A talk with Arafat [cover story] R. O. Freedman. il *The New York Review of Books* 36:8+ Ap 13 '89
Talking to the PLO; A personal triumph. L. Van Dusen. il por *Maclean's* 102:10-12 Ap 10 '89
Tilling the rocky ground of Mideast peacemaking [Y. Shamir's U.S. visit] L. Lief. il por *U.S. News & World Report* 106:43 Ap 10 '89
Turnabout [decision to open talks with PLO] *The Nation* 248:39-40 Ja 9-16 '89
U.S. opposes PLO admission to UN agencies [statement, May 4, 1989] S. L. Vogelgesang. *Department of State Bulletin* 89:65-6 Jl '89
Virtuoso transformations [Y. Arafat and M. Gorbachev] S. Talbott. il *Time* 133:36 Ja 9 '89
Waiting for Godot [Israeli opposition to H. Mubarak's peace plan] B. W. Nelan. il por *Time* 134:45 O 16 '89
West Bank fratricide [violence among the Palestinians] *The New Republic* 201:10-11 S 11 '89
What America should say to Arafat. R. N. Perle. il por *U.S. News & World Report* 106:58-9 Mr 20 '89
Whose Palestine? [cover story; special section] il *World Press Review* 36:13-21 F '89
Why I met with the PLO. M. Z. Rosensaft. por *Newsweek* 113:6 Ja 9 '89
Why should Israel trust the PLO? B. Amiel. il *Maclean's* 102:9 Je 5 '89
Yehoshafat Harkabi [interview] C. Dreifus. il *The Progressive* 53:36-9 Je '89

PALESTINIAN ARAB BUSINESS ENTERPRISES
The big moneymen of Palestine Inc. S. Tully. il *Fortune* 120:176-80+ Jl 31 '89

PALESTINIAN ARAB WOMEN
Women play key role in opposing the occupation. M. Kaye/Kantrowitz. il *Utne Reader* p42-3 S/O '89

PALESTINIAN ARABS
See also
Jewish-Arab relations
Palestine—History—Arab rebellion, 1936-1939
United Nations Relief and Works Agency for Palestine Refugees in the Near East
Abused and confused [discussion of November 21, 1988 column] A. Cockburn. *The Nation* 248:506+ Ap 17 '89
Appeals for Tayseer Aruri [letters] *Physics Today* 42:15+ My '89
Beneath the surface in Israel. E. Salpeter. il *The New Leader* 72:5-6 F 6 '89
Blessing both Jew and Palestinian: a religious Zionist view. Y. Landau. *The Christian Century* 106:1196-9 D 20-27 '89
A crisis of conscience in Israel's Army. R. Watson. il *Newsweek* 113:41 Ja 30 '89
Deadly quarantine [proposed amendment to Prevention of Terrorism Act restricting rights of Palestinians] A. Cockburn. *The Nation* 249:338-9 O 2 '89
Death comes at Ramadan [escalated violence in the West Bank] *Time* 133:36 Ap 24 '89
The diaspora's discontent [American Jews dissatisfied with Israeli handling of occupied territories] L. I. Barrett. il por *Time* 133:18-19 Ap 3 '89
Dissenting opinions about Tayseer Aruri [letters] *Physics Today* 42 pt1:13+ Ag '89
Encounter on the West Bank. G. Corea. il *The Progressive* 53:46 S '89
Fear and loathing in Israel [rising tide of violence in West Bank and Gaza] Z. Chafets. il map *U.S. News & World Report* 107:36-8 Jl 10 '89
Fighting fire with fire [Israeli settlers revolt on the West Bank] J. D. Hull. il *Time* 133:39+ Je 26 '89
Film flam [J. Franklin-Trout's controversial PBS documentary Days of rage] S. Emerson. *The New Republic* 201:29-30+ S 18-25 '89
Four decades of blood vengeance [death of G. Habash's sister in Lydda during 1948 war; tr. by Richard Flantz. A. Kenan. il *The Nation* 248:154-6 F 6 '89
General Assembly asks Security Council to consider ways to protect Palestinian civilians. il *UN Chronicle* 26:16-17 S '89
How to move the immovable [forcing Y. Shamir to negotiate with the Palestinians] S. Talbott. il *Time* 133:20 Ap 3 '89
Inside the intifada [cover story] J. Brinkley. il *The New York Times Magazine* p36-9+ O 29 '89
The internecine war of the West Bank [violence among Palestinians in the occupied territories] R. Z. Chesnoff. il *U.S. News & World Report* 107:38 Ag 21 '89
The intifada's surreal effect. R. Z. Chesnoff. il *U.S. News & World Report* 106:54-5+ Mr 20 '89

Is the intifadeh losing steam? il *Time* 134:21 S 4 '89
Israel and the Palestinians. G. Gottlieb. bibl f *Foreign Affairs* 68:109-26 Fall '89
Israeli physicists, and others, comment on case of Palestinian physicist [T. Aruri] W. Sweet. *Physics Today* 42:83-5 S '89
Israeli policies in occupied territories condemned. il *UN Chronicle* 26:55 Mr '89
An Israeli soldier lives the 'intifada'. D. Langsam. *World Press Review* 36:38-9 D '89
Israelis don't hide from the truth [responses to Palestinian intifada] J. B. Miller. *The Christian Century* 106:552-3 My 24-31 '89
Israel's Arabs. Y. Goell. *The New Republic* 201:16-18 O 23 '89
Israel's blank check [cover story] S. Zunes. il *The Progressive* 53:20-5 N '89
Israel's dilemma [Palestine question] A. Perlmutter. *Foreign Affairs* 68:119-32 Wint '89/'90
Israel's prison academies [Palestinians organize while imprisoned by Israelis]; tr. by Ina Friedman. E. Ya'ari. il *The Atlantic* 264:22+ O '89
Israel's troubled Army. R. Watson. il *Newsweek* 113:44+ My 1 '89
It's Arab on Arab two years into the intifada [death squads in the occupied territories] R. Z. Chesnoff. il *U.S. News & World Report* 107:15 D 25 '89-Ja 1 '90
Justice for the Palestinians. M. Singer. il *National Review* 41:40-2 O 13 '89
Letter from Israel. A. Elon. *The New Yorker* 64:74-80 F 13 '89
Local hero [F. Al-Husseini] *The New Republic* 200:8+ F 20 '89
Massacre in Nahalin [Israeli border police raid on West Bank village] J. Bierman. *Maclean's* 102:26 Ap 24 '89
A moral dilemma [Israeli Army protests conflicting demands of West Bank duty] J. McGeary. il *Time* 133:32-4 Ja 30 '89
Nation-building in an occupied land. J. M. Wall. *The Christian Century* 106:459-60 My 3 '89
Night of the broken clubs [Israeli actions against Palestinians] Y. Sarid. *Harper's* 279:31-2 S '89
No turning back for the Palestinians. J. M. Wall. *The Christian Century* 106:435-6 Ap 26 '89
Palestinian like me: notes from an undercover Jewish journalist [excerpt from My enemy, my self] Y. Binur. il pors *Utne Reader* p34-45 S/O '89
A Palestinian view of Israel's history. E. W. Said. map *Utne Reader* p38-9 S/O '89
Palestinians and the intifada: one year later. A. D. Miller. bibl f *Current History* 88:73-6+ F '89
The peace of Saladin [Yitzhak Shamir's Palestinian election proposal] M. B. Zuckerman. il *U.S. News & World Report* 106:78 My 1 '89
The politicians: avoiding decisions [cover story] T. L. Friedman. il map *The New York Times Magazine* p34-6+ My 7 '89
Power, not peace [Y. Shamir capitulates to A. Sharon on Palestinian issue] J. Smolowe. il por *Time* 134:66-7 Jl 17 '89
'Realism' and human rights [U.S. report criticizes Israel's practices in the occupied territories] H. Anderson. il *Newsweek* 113:28 F 20 '89
Ruckus over Days of rage [controversial PBS documentary] R. Zoglin. il *Time* 134:70 S 4 '89
Running out of answers [Israeli tactics fail to stem intifadeh] J. Bierman. il *Maclean's* 102:24 F 6 '89
Security Council fails to adopt text on Palestinian rights. il *UN Chronicle* 26:18 S '89
A seder for peace in the Mideast. A. Waskow. il *The Nation* 248:557+ Ap 24 '89
The settlers [West Bank] R. I. Friedman. bibl f il *The New York Review of Books* 36:49-56 Je 15 '89
Shamir to school kids: drop dead; No pragmatist at heart. A. Cockburn. *The Nation* 248:150-1 F 6 '89
The soldiers: anger and frustration [cover story] J. Brinkley. il *The New York Times Magazine* p30-3+ My 7 '89
The soul-searchers of the West Bank [Israeli Army] il *U.S. News & World Report* 106:11 Ja 30 '89
State of confusion [consequences of an independent Palestinian state; cover story] S. L. Spiegel. *The New Republic* 200:15-18 Ap 10 '89
Still stuck in the Stone Age [uprising enters third year] J. D. Hull. il *Time* 134:59-60+ D 11 '89
Text deploring Israeli policies in occupied territories vetoed. il *UN Chronicle* 26:31 Je '89
A thin green line [Israeli Arabs in Barta'a] D. L. Kirp. il *Mother Jones* 14:16-17+ My '89
Time check. *The Nation* 249:156 Ag 7-14 '89
'Today's word is revenge' [attack on Israeli bus puts latest peace proposals in jeopardy] A. Platt. il *Newsweek* 114:34 Jl 17 '89
The uprising's hidden toll [comments of Israeli soldiers stationed in the occupied territories]; tr. by Willis Johnson. *Harper's* 279:20-1 Ag '89
The view from the West Bank. E. Salpeter. il *The New Leader* 72:5-6 Je 12-26 '89

PALESTINIAN ARABS—*cont.*

Viewing the intifada stitch by stitch [PBS documentary Days of rage] W. F. Buckley. *National Review* 41:62-3 O 13 '89

Vigilantism on the West Bank: Israeli settlers step up their war against Arabs. T. Stanger. il *Newsweek* 113:41 Je 12 '89

'We can't take chances' [interview with C. Herzog] E. Silver. *Maclean's* 102:23 Je 26 '89

West Bank fratricide [violence among the Palestinians] *The New Republic* 201:10-11 S 11 '89

West Bank story [discussion of June 15, 1989 article, The settlers] R. I. Friedman. *The New York Review of Books* 36:59 N 23 '89

When you can't go home again [Beirut camps] E. Yeranian. il *U.S. News & World Report* 107:45 O 23 '89

Why is this man so glum? [Y. Shamir and S. Peres disagree over peace plan] il por *Time* 134:28 Jl 24 '89

Why Israel needs a gentle intifadeh victory. M. Kramer. il *Time* 134:68 Jl 24 '89

The widening gulf [Palestinian attack on Israeli bus throws peace endeavors into chaos] B. Came. il *Maclean's* 102:21 Jl 17 '89

Zero-plus game: a strategy for the Middle East. J. B. Hehir. *Commonweal* 116:39-40 Ja 27 '89

Economic conditions

The economic underpinnings of the intifada. D. Connell. *Utne Reader* p40-1 S/O '89

Sustainable development an important element of Palestinian uprising. A. Mitchison. *Utne Reader* p44 S/O '89

Education

The plight of Palestinian schools. S. Tifft. il *Time* 134:56 Jl 31 '89

'A real education'. S. Zunes. il *The Progressive* 53:23 N '89

Medical care

The plight of Palestine refugees. R. Cook. il *World Health* p8-10 Jl '89

Religious life

An elusive peace. K. A. Lawton. il *Christianity Today* 33:34-6 Ap 21 '89

No taxation without representation [Palestinian Christians] M. Ward. *America* 161:464-5 D 23-30 '89

Palestinian Christians join intifada tax protest. L. Cryderman. il por *Christianity Today* 33:42 D 15 '89

Taxation

No taxation without representation [Palestinian Christians] M. Ward. *America* 161:464-5 D 23-30 '89

Palestinian Christians join intifada tax protest. L. Cryderman. il por *Christianity Today* 33:42 D 15 '89

PALESTINIAN QUESTION *See* Israel-Arab War, 1948-1949; Israel-Arab Wars, 1967-; Jewish-Arab relations

PALESTINIAN TERRORISTS *See* Terrorists, Arab

PALEY, THOMAS

about

Outrageous fortune? Two guys from D&B cash in. J. Rothfeder. il pors *Business Week* p190 N 27 '89

PALIMONY

Piston's Rodman hit with paternity, palimony suits. il pors *Jet* 76:52 Jl 3 '89

PALINDROMES

Pen palindromes. W. Safire. il *The New York Times Magazine* p16+ Mr 19 '89

PALIO (NEW YORK, N.Y.: RESTAURANT) *See* New York (N.Y.)—Restaurants, nightclubs, bars, etc.

PALIO DI SIENA (ITALY)

The Palio. L. Harris. *The New Yorker* 65:83-6+ Je 5 '89

PALISADES (N.J. AND N.Y.)

Escape from New York [cycling] F. Staub. il *Bicycling* 30:86 O/N '89

PALISADES (N.Y.)

Buildings

An honorable retreat [IBM Palisades Advanced Business Institute] C. Pearson. il *Architectural Record* 177:84-91 S '89

PALISSY, BERNARD, 1510-1589 OR 90

about

Feast of beasts. M. Guralnick. il *House & Garden* 161:98+ S '89

PALL, DAVID B.

about

To catch a particle. G. Slutsker. il por *Forbes* 143:88-9 Ja 23 '89

PALL, ELLEN, 1952-

In the grasp of romance: my life as Fiona Hill. *The New York Times Book Review* 94:1+ Ap 30 '89

PALL CORP.

To catch a particle. G. Slutsker. il por *Forbes* 143:88-9 Ja 23 '89

PALLADIO, ANDREA, 1508-1580

about

Palladio and Veronese at the Villa Barbaro in Maser, Italy. B. L. Brown. bibl f il *Antiques* 135:298-309 Ja '89

PALLADIUM

Analysis of the published calorimetric evidence for electrochemical fusion of deuterium in palladium. G. M. Miskelly and others. bibl f il *Science* 246:793-6 N 10 '89

The great palladium rush [mining asteroids for metal used in cold fusion] H. K. Henson. il *Ad Astra* 1:34-5 N '89

Palladium: the fuel of the future? il *Newsweek* 113:54 My 8 '89

Therapeutic use

New weapon vs. prostate cancer [internal radioactive palladium capsules] *Prevention (Emmaus, Pa.)* 41:16+ Jl '89

PALLADIUM AS AN INVESTMENT

Fusion or not, palladium's hot. T. Segal. il *Business Week* p158 My 15 '89

PALLING, BRUCE

What's cooking on the Coast? il *Vogue* 179:416+ Mr '89

PALLIS, ELFI

Israel's severe censor. *World Press Review* 36:58 Ap '89

PALLONE, JAY

about

Conceptual Cibachromes: techniques inspired by a menu. F. Cameron. il *Petersen's Photographic Magazine* 18:34-7+ Ag '89

PALLRAND, GEORGE

Science, technology, and public knowledge. bibl f il *Phi Delta Kappan* 70:460-4 F '89

PALLY, MARCIA

Closely watched 'train' [cover story] il *Film Comment* 25:19-21 Jl/Ag '89

'Crimes' story. il por *Film Comment* 25:11-12+ N/D '89

Encore, The 400 blows. il *Film Comment* 25:6 Jl/Ag '89

Women's business. il *Film Comment* 25:16-18+ S/O '89

PALM BEACH (FLA.)

Airports

Flights of fantasy [opening celebration for new terminal at Palm Beach International Airport] S. Guy. il *Horizon (Tuscaloosa, Ala.)* 32:25-6 Ja/F '89

Historic houses, sites, etc.

The Palm Beach story [Mar-a-Lago estate bought by D. and I. Trump] C. K. Gandee. il pors *House & Garden* 161:110-19+ D '89

A Republican heritage in the South: Ambassador and Mrs. Guilford Dudley, Jr., in Nashville and Palm Beach. C. T. Buckley. il pors *Architectural Digest* 46:200-9 Ap '89

Restaurants, nightclubs, bars, etc.

Untapped market [kosher restaurant at J. Schlang's Palm Beach Plaza Hotel] *The New Yorker* 64:24-5 Ja 16 '89

Social life and customs

American style! The Palm Beach story. A. Stanley. il *Vogue* 179:274-93 F '89

Anecdotes, facetiae, satire, etc.

On the beach. M. M. Thomas. il *New York* 22:20 Je 19 '89

PALM BEACH COMMUNITY COLLEGE. LANNON GALLERY

Walls without a museum. E. Turner. il *Art News* 88:31-2 Ja '89

PALM BEACH COUNTY (FLA.)

Arts

See also

Palm Beach County Minority Cultural Consortium

Palm Beach [special section] S. Guy. il *Horizon (Tuscaloosa, Ala.)* 32:17-30+ Ja/F '89

PALM BEACH COUNTY MINORITY CULTURAL CONSORTIUM

Celebrating diversity. S. Guy. il *Horizon (Tuscaloosa, Ala.)* 32:20 Ja/F '89

PALM BEACH GARDENS (FLA.)

Stores

Gardens of art [sculpture in The Gardens shopping mall] S. Guy. il *Horizon (Tuscaloosa, Ala.)* 32:27-8 Ja/F '89

PALM BEACH PLAZA HOTEL (PALM BEACH, FLA.: RESTAURANT) *See* Palm Beach (Fla.)—Restaurants, nightclubs, bars, etc.

PALM OIL

Cookies the heart can love [foodmakers replace tropical oils with less saturated fats] A. Toufexis. il *Time* 133:71 Ja 23 '89

Have a heart [P. Sokolof's campaign against products using coconut and palm oils] S. J. Madden. il por *Fortune* 119:117+ Ja 16 '89

A man with a mission—and millions to back it up—takes on brand name cholesterol [P. Sokolof's campaign against products using coconut and palm oils] il por *People Weekly* 31:112 F 6 '89

Putting tropical oils in their place [emphasis should be on reducing total dietary fat] G. L. Blackburn. il *Prevention (Emmaus, Pa.)* 41:30+ Ag '89

The trail of oil [use of dende oil in Bahian cooking] R. Sokolov. il *Natural History* p82-5 My '89

The use of palm and coconut oils in America's food has triggered a debate that is as much about politics as it is about health. L. M. Kase. *Vogue* 179:150+ Je '89

PALM SANDERS *See* Sanding and sanding equipment

PALM SPRINGS (CALIF.)

Architecture

Project: Marc Appleton: plans for a producer's dream estate. il por *Architectural Digest* 46:82-3 Ag '89

A Somers place [home of S. Somers and A. Hamel] P. Viladas. il pors *House & Garden* 161:210-15 S '89

PALM SPRINGS (CALIF.)—cont.

Energy policy
"Turbine renewal" [wind power] E. Paris. il *Forbes* 144:112 Ag 7 '89

Politics and government
Mayor Sonny Bono resists a recall, telling Palm Springs voters, 'You got me, Babe'. T. Gold. il pors *People Weekly* 32:53-4 O 2 '89

Tourist trade
Now Sonny Bono is singing 'I want you, Babe'. R. Grover. il por *Business Week* p44 My 8 '89

PALM SPRINGS INTERNATIONAL FILM FESTIVAL *See* Motion picture festivals—California

PALM SUNDAY
Palm Sunday Christianity. R. S. Chopp. *The Christian Century* 106:277-8 Mr 15 '89

PALM TREES *See* Palms

PALMA GROVE HOMES (RESIDENTIAL DEVELOPMENT) *See* Housing—California

PALMAN, DEBORAH
about
Deer season. F. Graham. *Audubon* 91:18+ N '89

PALME, OLOF, 1927-1986
Assassination
The Swedish version of 'who killed JFK?' [C. Pettersson] por *Newsweek* 114:32 Ag 7 '89

PALMER, AL
10-MHz frequency standard. il *Radio-Electronics* 60:63-9 F '89

PALMER, ALEXANDRA
From Callot Soeurs to Gaultier, Sandy Schreier has it all. il por *Architectural Digest* 46:52+ S '89

PALMER, BEVERLY B., AND COFFMAN, JOE M.
The deadly side of love: the end of the sexual smokescreen. il *USA Today (Periodical)* 117:62-3 My '89

PALMER, DOUGLAS
Object on a complementary background. il *Petersen's Photographic Magazine* 18:48-9 Jl '89

PALMER, E. SAMUEL
Unveiling the hidden Milky Way. il *Astronomy* 17:32-40 N '89

PALMER, GERTRUDE
about
Still hungry for knowledge at 105, Gertrude Palmer is one for the books. il pors *People Weekly* 31:116-17 Mr 20 '89

PALMER, JOE H.
How to observe planets during the day. il *Astronomy* 17:86-7 Mr '89

PALMER, JOHN
about
Why new beepers vibrate. F. Meeks. il por *Forbes* 144:72-3 Ag 21 '89

PALMER, LAURA
Pat Oliphant. il por *Gentlemen's Quarterly* 59:290-1 Ap '89

PALMER, NORMAN D.
United States policy in East Asia. bibl f *Current History* 88:161-4+ Ap '89

PALMER, PHOEBE, 1807-1874
Bibliography
The entire sanctification of an extraordinary ego. G. Wacker. por *Christianity Today* 33:56-9 O 6 '89

PALMER, ROBERT
Hot band. il *Rolling Stone* p97+ My 18 '89
Into the mystic. il *Rolling Stone* p100-3+ Mr 23 '89
Simmer down, son. il pors *American Film* 14:26-33+ Je '89

PALMER, SUSAN J.
AIDS as metaphor. bibl *Society* 26:44-50 Ja/F '89

PALMER, WILLIAM C., 1906-1987
about
Medical recovery. J. Herzfeld. il *Art News* 88:14 Ja '89

PALMERI, DIANE
about
Exploring the dark side of paradise, an American couple takes up misery's gauntlet. M. Green. il pors *People Weekly* 32:93-4+ N 27 '89

PALMERI, TOM
about
Exploring the dark side of paradise, an American couple takes up misery's gauntlet. M. Green. il pors *People Weekly* 32:93-4+ N 27 '89

PALMS
The Arnold Schwarzenegger of palm trees [Chilean wine palm] il *Sunset (Central West edition)* 182:222 Je '89
Lightning rods [caring for palms in the Winter Garden at the World Financial Center] *The New Yorker* 65:36-7 Ap 10 '89

PALO ALTO (CALIF.)
Street traffic
The pedal pusher [cycling enthusiast E. Fletcher] il por *New Choices for the Best Years* 29:12 O '89

PALO ALTO RESEARCH CENTER *See* Xerox Corp. Palo Alto Research Center

PALO MAYOMBE (CULT)
Magic and murder in Matamoros. J. Burnett. *The Christian Century* 106:815-16 S 13-20 '89

PALO MONTE (CULT) *See* Palo Mayombe (Cult)

PALOMA PARTNERS
Hedged bets [views of S. D. Sussman] J. Clements. il por *Forbes* 144 Special Issue:372 O 23 '89

PALOS, DEMETRIUS, AND SOELDNER, TOM
The illusion of reform in South Africa. *The Christian Century* 106:447-50 Ap 26 '89

PALOS VERDES ESTATES (CALIF.)
Gardens and gardening
Mediterranean light [Villa Narcissa; cover story] P. Deitz. il *House & Garden* 161:124-31+ D '89
Historic houses, sites, etc.
Mediterranean light [gardens of the Villa Narcissa; cover story] P. Deitz. il *House & Garden* 161:124-31+ D '89

PALUSZEK, JOHN
Public relations and ethical leadership [address, June 15, 1989] *Vital Speeches of the Day* 55:747-50 O 1 '89
Public relations in the coming global economy [address, July 25, 1989] *Vital Speeches of the Day* 56:22-6 O 15 '89

PAMPHLETS
Booklets. See occasional issues of Health (New York, N.Y.)
Booklets worth writing for [title varies] See issues of Good Housekeeping
Consumer pamphlets. K. K. Gracey and A. W. Simpson. *Consumers' Research Magazine* 72:2 S '89
The cook's corner. il *Southern Living* 24:174-5 O '89
Freebies and almost-freebies [travel brochures] E. McGowan. il *Travel Holiday* 172:30-1 S '89
Freebies and cheapies. il *Teen* 33:14-16 Ja '89
Freebies and cheapies. il *Teen* 33:49-50 Jl '89

PAN *See* Partido Acción Nacional (Mexico)

PAN AM *See* Pan American World Airways, Inc.

PAN AMERICAN FLIGHT 103 DISASTER, 1988
Bomb in forward hold destroyed Pan Am 747, investigators find. *Aviation Week & Space Technology* 130:62 Ja 16 '89
The bombing of Flight 103. A. Phillips. il *Maclean's* 102:18-20 Ja 9 '89
A Christmas tragedy [crash in Lockerbie, Scotland; cover story; special section] il map *Newsweek* 113:14-23 Ja 2 '89
Closing in on the Pan Am bombers [Palestinian-Iranian deal in bombing of Pan Am Flight 103; with interview with A. Jibril] B. Duffy and others. il por *U.S. News & World Report* 106:23-4 My 22 '89
A daunting new quest to secure the skies. il *U.S. News & World Report* 106:9-10 Ja 9 '89
"Diabolically well-planned". E. Magnuson. il *Time* 133:26-8 Ja 9 '89
Did it blow up Flight 103? [bomb possibly made from black market C-4 plastic explosive] D. Corn. il *The Nation* 248:153-4 F 6 '89
A doomed flight home [explosion over Lockerbie, Scotland] A. Phillips. *Maclean's* 102:46 Ja 2 '89
Flight 103. *World Press Review* 36:8+ F '89
A grieving mother turns the horror of Pan Am Flight 103 into a monument to her son [S. Lowenstein creates sculptural work entitled Evolution in memory of A. Lowenstein] D. Grogan. il pors *People Weekly* 32:44-6 S 25 '89
In search of answers. S. MacLeod. il *Time* 133:37 Ja 16 '89
Keeping Lockerbie alive. M. Ludtke. il *Time* 134:33 N 27 '89
Late alarums, failed alerts. J. Smolowe. il *Time* 133:53 Mr 27 '89
Legacy of a grim Christmas past [efforts of V. Cummock and others to make sure tragedy is never repeated] B. Hewitt. il pors *People Weekly* 32:58-64 D 18 '89
Lockerbie disaster [special section; with editorial comment] il *Aviation Week & Space Technology* 130:9, 26-9+ Ja 9 '89
Lockerbie disaster: bomb destroys Pan Am 747 in blast over Scotland [special section] il map *Aviation Week & Space Technology* 130:28-32 Ja 2 '89
On the trail of terror [police in Scotland uncover clues] B. Duffy. il map *U.S. News & World Report* 107:44-6 N 13 '89
Pan Am 103: a Teheran connection? il *Newsweek* 112:58 My 22 '89
Probe focuses on reconstructing container that held bomb used to destroy Pan Am 747. *Aviation Week & Space Technology* 130:64 Ja 23 '89
Safety experts cite similarities between DC-8, 747 crashes [bombing of Pan Am Flight 103 and crash of Arrow Air DC-8 at Gander, Nfld. in 1985; minority report of Canadian Aviation Safety Board] D. Hughes. il *Aviation Week & Space Technology* 130:58-9 F 6 '89
Terror in the night [bomb suspected in crash over Lockerbie, Scotland] W. E. Smith. il *Time* 133:74-8 Ja 2 '89
A trail of terror [special section] il *Newsweek* 113:28-30+ Ja 9 '89
The warnings that weren't. A. Platt. il *Newsweek* 113:42 Mr 27 '89
Legal aspects
Looking for someone to blame. T. Jacoby. il *Newsweek* 113:34 Ja 9 '89

PAN AMERICAN GAMES
Pan Am winter games: for the sport of it [cover story] P. M. Miller. il map *Américas* 41 no2:42-5 '89
Uphill downhill [winter games at Las Leñas] D. Einhorn. il *Américas* 41 no1:3-4 '89

PAN AMERICAN HEALTH ORGANIZATION
Compact disks. C. J. Brito. il *World Health* p18-20 Ag/S '89

PAN AMERICAN HIGHWAY
Another Panamanian headache [to duck highway fees, U.S. truckers are registering and insuring their rigs in Panama] D. Fanning. il *Forbes* 144:80 N 13 '89

PAN AMERICAN SATELLITE CORPORATION
Panamsat files antitrust lawsuit against Comsat. *Aviation Week & Space Technology* 131:28 Jl 31 '89

PAN AMERICAN WORLD AIRWAYS, INC.
The bottom line: he's a better manager [use of computers by T. G. Plaskett] C. O'Malley. il por *Personal Computing* 13:79 Ap '89
Bridging the Atlantic [early transatlantic flights; cover story] R. K. Schrader. il *American History Illustrated* 24:34-47 My '89
Congress would probe Pan Am-NWA merger's effect on U.S. competition. J. Ott. *Aviation Week & Space Technology* 130:72-3 My 15 '89
Effect of crash on Pan Am expected to be minimal. J. T. McKenna. *Aviation Week & Space Technology* 130:27-8 Ja 9 '89
A far-out merger scheme that could just fly [Pan Am-Northwest deal] C. Power and A. Bernstein. il *Business Week* p36-7 My 22 '89
Flying blind [weight standards for female flight attendants ruled illegal] D. Seligman. il *Fortune* 120:204 O 9 '89
The Madman of Mad Ave prepares for takeoff [account goes to Della Femina] W. Konrad. il por *Business Week* p124 F 20 '89
Pan Am considers entering field of Northwest bidders. C. Fotos. *Aviation Week & Space Technology* 130:70-1 My 15 '89
Pan Am Corp., Davis among Northwest bidders. C. Fotos. il *Aviation Week & Space Technology* 130:108-9 Je 5 '89
Pan Am Corp. seeks alternatives after failed Northwest bid. *Aviation Week & Space Technology* 130:91 Je 26 '89
Pan Am Corp. will sell World Services in attempt to give Plaskett more time. J. T. McKenna. il *Aviation Week & Space Technology* 130:68-9 Ja 23 '89
Pan Am intensifies efforts to bail out Airways unit. *Aviation Week & Space Technology* 131:111 D 18-25 '89
Pan Am looks Northwest. C. Friday. il *Newsweek* 112:62 My 22 '89
Pan Am needs a partner, but does anybody need Pan Am? C. Power. il por *Business Week* p92+ Ap 10 '89
Pan Am will use Jetstreams to bolster Miami operations. J. T. McKenna. *Aviation Week & Space Technology* 131:82-3 N 27 '89
Pan American World Airways posts $21.9-million third-quarter loss. *Aviation Week & Space Technology* 131:71 N 13 '89
Pan Am's cupboard is almost bare. T. Pouschine. il *Forbes* 144:74+ D 25 '89
The power behind Pan Am's bid for Northwest [Airlie Group] C. Power and K. Kelly. il por *Business Week* p29 Je 12 '89
Still flying. T. Jaffe. il *Forbes* 143:188 Ap 3 '89
War of the shuttles [Pan Am vs Trump] S. Payne. il *Business Week* p38 F 20 '89

PAN AMERICANISM
See also
Congress of the New World
Organization of American States
United States—Foreign relations—Latin America

PAN DE ZUCCHERO
Pan de zucchero: a new one. W. E. Wooldridge. il *Flower and Garden* 33:108 Ja/F '89

PANAIT, CONSTANTIN
about
Gymnast Nadia Comaneci leaps for freedom—and lands in the arms of a married father of four. il pors *People Weekly* 32:116 D 18 '89

PANAMA
See also
Civil rights—Panama
Colombians—Panama
Insurance, Truck—Panama
Military assistance, American—Panama
Narcotics laws and regulations—Panama
Narcotics trade—Panama
Oil pollution—Panama
Panama Canal
Rain forests—Panama
Trucks—Registration—Panama
United Nations—Panama

Commerce
United States
See United States—Commerce—Panama
Defenses
See also
United States—Armed Forces—Forces in Panama
Economic relations
United States
See United States—Economic relations—Panama
Foreign relations
United States
See United States—Foreign relations—Panama
Politics and government
See also
Elections—Panama
Political campaigns—Panama
Politics, Corruption in—Panama

Amateur hour [failed coup attempt against M. Noriega; cover story] C. S. Manegold. il por map *Newsweek* 114:26-31 O 16 '89
Can we oust Noriega? [involvement of the Organization of American States] L. C. Wilson. il *USA Today (Periodical)* 118:15 N '89
Dwindling options in Panama. L. S. Robinson. bibl f *Foreign Affairs* 68:187-205 Wint '89/'90
Fiasco in Panama [failed coup attempt against M. Noriega] *The New Republic* 201:5-6 O 30 '89
A fumbled coup. G. W. Taylor. il por *Maclean's* 102:28-30 O 16 '89
The gang that wouldn't shoot [failed coup attempt against M. Noriega; with editorial comment by David Gergen] B. Duffy. il por *U.S. News & World Report* 107:26-7, 129 O 16 '89
Letter from Washington [failed coup against M. Noriega] E. Drew. *The New Yorker* 65:100-4+ O 30 '89
Manuel Noriega. il pors *People Weekly* 32:69-70 D 25 '89-Ja 1 '90
The mothers of intervention [failed coup attempt against M. Noriega] il *The Progressive* 53:8-9 D '89
National emergency in Panama [message to Congress, October 14, 1988] R. Reagan. *Department of State Bulletin* 88:57 D '88
Noriega celebrates. C. Lane. il *Newsweek* 113:47-8 My 29 '89
Noriega speaks out. S. Calloni. *World Press Review* 36:52-3 D '89
On Noriega, 'We have failed miserably' [overthrow attempts] il por *Newsweek* 114:33 S 4 '89
Panama [failed coup attempt] *Business Week* p51 O 16 '89
Panama: on not being a cowboy [failed coup] *America* 161:251 O 21 '89
The Panamanian mess [failed coup] W. F. Buckley. il *National Review* 41:70-1 N 10 '89
Prospects dim for Panama. *USA Today (Periodical)* 117:10-11 Ap '89
The stovepipe problem [G. Bush's role in failed coup against M. Noriega] il por *Time* 134:35 N 6 '89
Washington fights the Noriega factor [successful Philippines intervention contrasted with failed Panama coup attempt] H. Anderson. il *Newsweek* 114:58 D 11 '89
What next, Noriega? [aftermath of failed coup] C. S. Manegold. il por *Newsweek* 114:26-8 O 23 '89
Who lost Noriega? D. Goodgame. il por *Time* 134:39-40 O 23 '89
The widow of a slain rebel leader looks back in anguish after the failed coup in Panama [A. Bonilla de Giroldi flees to U.S. after death of M. Giroldi Vega] B. Hewitt. il pors *People Weekly* 32:101-2 O 30 '89
The Yanquis stayed home [U.S. involvement in failed coup against M. Noriega] J. Smolowe. il por maps *Time* 134:24-8 O 16 '89

PANAMA CANAL
The canal's declining importance. map *U.S. News & World Report* 106:32 My 22 '89
History
Panama: made in U.S.A. B. A. Weisberger. il *American Heritage* 40:24-5 N '89

PANAMA CANAL TREATIES (1977)
Panama. *Business Week* p70 D 25 '89-Ja 1 '90

PANASONIC COMPANY
Panasonic gets zapped, too [price fixing case] *Newsweek* 113:54 Ja 30 '89

PANAVIA AIRCRAFT GMBH
Deficit woes prompt Jordan to postpone Tornado purchase. M. Mecham. *Aviation Week & Space Technology* 130:32-3 Ap 3 '89

PANCAKES, WAFFLES, ETC.
See also
Crêpes
Latkes
Brunch: better with berries [blueberry pancakes] H. Titman. il *Working Woman* 14:129 Je '89
Cornmeal. J. Nash. il *Essence* 19:88 Ja '89

PANCREAS
Localization of the pancreatic beta cell glucose transporter to specific plasma membrane domains. L. Orci and others. bibl f il *Science* 245:295-7 Jl 21 '89

PANCREAS—cont.

Transgenic mice with I-A on islet cells are normoglycemic but immunologically intolerant. J. Böhme and others. bibl f il *Science* 244:1179-83 Je 9 '89

Cancer

The final days of Howard Simons. J. Adler. il por *Newsweek* 112:76 My 22 '89

Diseases

See also
Diabetes
Hypoglycemia

Transplantation

A ray of hope for diabetics [transplanting insulin-producing cells] *Maclean's* 102:62 S 18 '89

PANDAS

Panda paradox. E. Dolnick. il map *Discover* 10:70-4+ S '89
Poaching the pandas [China] L. Branson. *World Press Review* 36:53 Mr '89

Training

Panda pumps iron. il *National Geographic World* 163:22-3 Mr '89

PANDAY, SHREEKANT

about

No place like home. E. Giltenan. il por *Forbes* 144:247+ O 30 '89

PANDORA (SHIP)

HMS Pandora. J. Murray. il map *Sea Frontiers* 35:328-35 N/D '89

PANE E VINO (MONTECITO, CALIF.: RESTAURANT)
See Montecito (Calif.)—Restaurants, nightclubs, bars, etc.

PANELING

Two ways to wainscot. il *The Mother Earth News* 115:66-9 Ja/F '89
Wood interiors [installing oak and country paneling; cover story] D. Johnson. il *The Family Handyman* 39:29-37 N/D '89

PANETTONE *See* Bread

PANFISH FISHING

Down-under panfish. J. Dean. il *Outdoor Life* 183:78-9+ Mr '89
Open-water icefishing [spring] D. Zutz. il *Outdoor Life* 183:88-9+ Ap '89

PANG, WING NING

Out of Chinatown and back again. il *Christianity Today* 33:29-31 Mr 3 '89

PANGAEA

Climate

Hot spot [research by Thomas J. Crowley] J. Horgan. il *Scientific American* 261:20+ S '89

PANGAEA RECORDS (FIRM)

Pangaea hits hard times. F. Goodman. *Rolling Stone* p22 Mr 9 '89

PANHANDLE EASTERN CORPORATION

The list nobody wants to be on [L. Iacocca and R. Hunsucker head list of executives returning least value for most pay] T. Vogel and W. Zellner. il pors *Business Week* p50 My 1 '89

PANHANDLING *See* Begging and beggars

PANIC ATTACKS *See* Panic disorder

PANIC DISORDER

An early start for panic [research by James C. Ballenger] *Science News* 136:61 Jl 22 '89
Getting to the heart of panic disorder. K. Fackelmann. *Science News* 135:39 Ja 21 '89
Going public about panic. B. G. Harrison. *Mademoiselle* 95:126 N '89
How to handle a panic attack. B. Hersey. il *Ladies' Home Journal* 106:92 O '89
Panic attacks increase suicide attempts [research by Myrna M. Weissman] B. Bower. *Science News* 136:293 N 4 '89
Panic by the cupful [effect of caffeine; research by Michael F. Breslow] L. Schroepfer. il *American Health* 8:46 Je '89
When panic strikes . . . don't panic. W. LeGro. il *Prevention (Emmaus, Pa.)* 41:40-7+ Ap '89

PANIC OF 1901 *See* Business depression, 1901

PANIKKAR, RAIMUNDO, 1918-

about

Raimundo Panikkar: pluralism without relativism. P. Gorday. il por *The Christian Century* 106:1147-50 D 6 '89

PANISH, LARRY

about

Chef's special. H. S. MacIsaac. il por *House & Garden* 161:90-3 Ja '89

PANKEY, ERIC

When the wood is green [poem] *The New Yorker* 65:40 Je 26 '89

PANKRATZ, DAVID B.

Policies, agendas, and arts education research. bibl f *Design for Arts in Education* 90:2-13 My/Je '89

PANKRATZ, LOREN

about

Munchausen is more than a movie, it's also the name of a bizarre medical disorder [interview] S. Hauser. il pors *People Weekly* 31:95+ My 8 '89

PANORAMIC PHOTOGRAPHY *See* Photography, Panoramic

PANTER, GARY, 1950-

about

Gary Panter at Gracie Mansion. K. Johnson. il *Art in America* 77:208-9 S '89

PANTEV, C., AND OTHERS

Tonotopic organization of the auditory cortex: pitch versus frequency representation. bibl f il *Science* 246:486-8 O 27 '89

PANTHERS

See also
Pumas

PANTHERS, FLORIDA *See* Pumas

PANTRIES

Corner pantry. il *Better Homes and Gardens* 67:104 My '89

PANTRY *See* Pantries

PANTS

See also
Jeans (Clothing)
Knickers

"Is there help for my hips?". il *Ladies' Home Journal* 106:142-3 Je '89
Wearing the pants. il *Harper's Bazaar* 122:178 F '89
Wearing the pants. C. Clifford and S. Farganis. il *Health (New York, N.Y.)* 21:68-73+ Ap '89

PANTYHOSE *See* Hosiery

PANTYHOSE INDUSTRY *See* Hosiery industry

PAOLO, VERONESE *See* Veronese, 1528-1588

PAOLUCCI, BRIDGET

Private lives. il por *Opera News* 53:14-15 Ja 7 '89

PAP TEST

The controversial Pap test. E. Hale. il *FDA Consumer* 23:20-3 S '89
'I love you perfect': a show that could save your life [TV movie depicts life story of V. Williams] D. Hudson. il por *TV Guide* 37:30-1 O 7-13 '89
Is the Pap test valid? R. M. Henig. il *The New York Times Magazine* p37-8 My 28 '89
New test may replace Pap smear [quantitative fluorescent image analysis developed by Jeffrey Smith and George Hemstreet] il *USA Today (Periodical)* 117:7 F '89
The problem with Pap tests. *McCall's* 116:89-90 F '89
Smart planning for the Pap smear. S. Montgomery. *Working Woman* 14:160 Ap '89

PAPACY

See also
Popes

An interview with the author of The papacy and the Church [J. R. Dionne] il *America* 160:12-13+ Ja 7-14 '89

PAPAL INFALLIBILITY *See* Popes—Infallibility

PAPANDREOU, ANDREAS

about

Caught in the labyrinth. il por *Time* 134:29 Jl 3 '89
Greek farce. Taki. il *National Review* 41:25-6 O 27 '89
The looting of Greece. R. Ajemian. il pors *Time* 133:32-5 Mr 13 '89
"No mud touches me". W. R. Doerner. il por *Time* 133:37 Mr 20 '89
Out of office, into the dock? por *Time* 134:38 S 25 '89
Scandal and stalemate. J. Bierman. por *Maclean's* 102:17 Jl 3 '89
When a First Lady's husband leaves her for a younger woman. M. Cohen. il pors *Good Housekeeping* 208:82+ My '89

Anecdotes, facetiae, satire, etc.

The quest of lion-browed Andreas [seeks re-election] D. Lawday. il *U.S. News & World Report* 106:37 Je 19 '89

PAPANDREOU, MARGARET

about

When a First Lady's husband leaves her for a younger woman. M. Cohen. il pors *Good Housekeeping* 208:82+ My '89

PAPARAZZI

The paparazzi have long been considered the foot soldiers of photography. B. Houston-Montgomery. il *Vogue* 179:274-5 Je '89

PAPAZIAN, ED

Who are your heroes? *Working Woman* 14:72 Mr '89

PAPER

See also
Fax paper
Photographic paper

Preservation

Paper progress. J. I. Mattill. il *Technology Review* 92:11 Ap '89
The watchful eye in paper conservation. V. B. Hill. il *American Artist* 53:22+ Ag '89

Anecdotes, facetiae, satire, etc.

Dry. R. Cohen. *The New Yorker* 65:34-5 Ap 3 '89

Recycling

Save the trees—and you may save a bundle. C. McAllister. il *Business Week* p118 S 4 '89
Talking trash. P. Klebnikov and G. Burks. il *Forbes* 143:10 Je 12 '89

Standards

AAUP-ARL survey finds strong university press commitment to acid-free paper. *Publishers Weekly* 235:68+ Mr 17 '89

PAPER—Standards—cont.
An end to the yellowing pages [publishers agree to first printings of quality hard cover trade books on acid-free paper] il *Newsweek* 113:80 Mr 20 '89
House unit hears testimony on availability of acid-free paper. H. Fields. *Publishers Weekly* 235:17 My 26 '89
Public drive for alkaline paper inspires new action in the mills. J. P. Frank. *Publishers Weekly* 236:30+ Jl 21 '89
Top firms pledge use of acid-free paper in hardcover first printings. il *Publishers Weekly* 235:12 Mr 31 '89
PAPER, HANDMADE *See* Paper making
PAPER DOLLS
Collectors and collecting
Personality paper dolls. M. Jailer. il *Antiques & Collecting Hobbies* 93:51-3 F '89
PAPER HOLDERS, ETC.
Notepad caddy. il *Workbench* 45:56-7 Mr/Ap '89
PAPER INDUSTRY
See also
Champion International Corp.
International Paper Co.
Jefferson Smurfit Corp.
Kimberly-Clark Corp.
P. H. Glatfelter Co.
Paper mills
Pope & Talbot, Inc.
Stone Container Corp.
Union Camp Corporation
Weyerhaeuser Company
Happy days for paper mills seen continuing. J. P. Frank. il *Publishers Weekly* 235:110+ Ap 7 '89
Midwest merchants look forward to a continuing strong 1990 market [book industry demand] J. P. Frank. il *Publishers Weekly* 236:32+ O 20 '89
New England competition heats up in a smaller educational market. J. P. Frank. *Publishers Weekly* 235:61-2+ Ap 21 '89
Paper panic subsides but publishers still build inventories. J. P. Frank. il *Publishers Weekly* 235:68+ Ja 6 '89
Public drive for alkaline paper inspires new action in the mills. J. P. Frank. *Publishers Weekly* 236:30+ Jl 21 '89
Acquisitions and mergers
International aspects
Merger wave rolls on [Canada's Consolidated-Bathurst acquired by Stone Container Corp.] D. Jenish. il *Maclean's* 102:28-30 F 6 '89
Great Britain
Jimmy Goldsmith's gun bearer goes gunning [R. A. E. Franklin's hostile bid for DRG plc] P. Finch. il por *Business Week* p63+ O 16 '89
Finance
Paper. S. B. Weiner. il *Forbes* 143:184-5 Ja 9 '89
Papermakers will be as busy as beavers. J. B. Levine. il *Business Week* p101 Ja 9 '89
Turn out the lights, paper's long party is over. T. Vogel. il *Business Week* p47-8 N 6 '89
Canada
See also
Consolidated-Bathurst Inc.
Great Britain
See also
DRG plc
PAPER INDUSTRY WORKERS
See also
Collective labor agreements—Paper industry
United Paperworkers International Union
Salaries, pensions, etc.
Wages and benefits in pulp, paper, and paperboard mills. bibl f il *Monthly Labor Review* 112:33-5 Je '89
PAPER MAKING
India
In search of India's papermaking tradition. A. Soteriou. il *American Craft* 49:32-7 F/Mr '89
PAPER MILLS
Environmental aspects
Confronting the Irvings [paper mill threatened with shutdown in Saint John, N.B.] P. Chisholm. il *Maclean's* 102:50 O 16 '89
Dangerous waters: pollution shuts down B.C. shellfish areas. H. Quinn. il *Maclean's* 102:64 D 4 '89
Dioxin-in-paper update. *Science News* 136:94 Ag 5 '89
Dioxin: paper's trace. J. Raloff. il *Science News* 135:104-6 F 18 '89
Fight for Pigeon River [conflict between Champion International Corp. in Canton, N.C. and Tennessee environmentalists over pollution control] M. Satchell. il map *U.S. News & World Report* 107:27-8+ D 4 '89
The forest fight [environmental concerns over proposed pulp mill on Athabasca River in Alberta] R. Corelli. il *Maclean's* 102:60 N 13 '89
How do you say 'tim-ber' in Japanese? [investment in Alberta-Pacific Forest Industries] T. Mason. il *Business Week* p52 D 4 '89
Of time and the river [Kalamazoo River] B. Gilbert. il *Sports Illustrated* 71:76-80+ Jl 24 '89
Trans-border pollution [pulp mills in British Columbia and Washington State] H. Quinn. il *Maclean's* 102:44-5 Jl 3 '89

PAPER MODELS, ARCHITECTURAL *See* Architectural models
PAPER MONEY
See also
United States. Bureau of Engraving and Printing
The buck starts here, and may stop here, at the nation's money mills. D. Stewart. bibl (p163) il *Smithsonian* 20:36-45 My '89
Mutilation, defacement, etc.
No money in the microwave, please [replacing damaged currency at U.S. Bureau of Engraving and Printing] B. Weber. il *The New York Times Magazine* p126 D 10 '89
Canada
A 'loonie' revolt [opposition to replacing dollar bill with loonie coin] N. Underwood. il *Maclean's* 102:44-5 Je 5 '89
China
Paper money [ancient China] R. K. G. Temple. *The Courier (Unesco)* 41:28 O '88
PAPER NAUTILUS *See* Nautilus
PAPER PRODUCTS
See also
Facial tissues
Paper towels
Toilet paper
Contamination
Dioxin-in-paper update. *Science News* 136:94 Ag 5 '89
Dioxin: paper's trace. J. Raloff. il *Science News* 135:104-6 F 18 '89
PAPER TOWELS
Paper power [microwaving] J. B. Hurley. il *Prevention (Emmaus, Pa.)* 41:85 Ja '89
PAPER WASPS *See* Wasps
PAPER WORK (ART)
See also
Decoupage
Origami architecture
Papier-mâché
PAPERBACK BOOK COVERS *See* Book covers
PAPERBACK BOOK DISTRIBUTORS *See* Book wholesalers and distributors
PAPERBACK BOOKS
See also
Publishers and publishing—Paperback books
Bibliography
See also
Best sellers
Forecasts. See issues of Publishers Weekly
Notable paperbacks. *The New York Times Book Review* 94:78-80 D 3 '89
Paperbacks: new and noteworthy. See issues of The New York Times Book Review
Reads: paperbacks by the sack for when the pressure's off. R. Koenig. il *New York* 22:138+ Jl 3-10 '89
Trade paperbacks; Mass market paperbacks. B. Levine. il *Publishers Weekly* 235:379-82+ Ja 27 '89
Marketing
Bell to use market research for Harper's new paperback line. M. Reuter. por *Publishers Weekly* 235:15 F 10 '89
Reading between the lines [self-licensing of paperback rights can institutionalize half-royalties] L. Chu. il *Publishers Weekly* 235:48 F 17 '89
PAPERBACK SOFTWARE INTERNATIONAL INC.
The fall of Adam? [A. Osborne] J. Pitta. il por *Forbes* 144:287 O 16 '89
PAPERBOARD INDUSTRY
See also
Federal Paper Board Co., Inc.
PAPERHANGING *See* Wallpaper and wallpapering
PAPERHOUSE [film] See Motion picture reviews—Single works
PAPERWEIGHTS
Collectors and collecting
The paperweight chase. D. V. Gast. il *New Choices for the Best Years* 29:72+ Jl '89
PAPIER-MÂCHÉ
Paper chase [Victorian papier-mâché pieces] M. Guralnick. il *House & Garden* 161:62+ Mr '89
PAPILLOMA VIRUSES
See also
Human papilloma virus
PAPILLOTE COOKING
Chicken en papillote. il *Good Housekeeping* 208:34 Je '89
Seafood and pasta in parchment is effortless? All it takes is a good sense of timing. il *Sunset (Central West edition)* 182:192-3 Ap '89
PAPP, JOSEPH
about
Hollywood Shakespeare [cover story] D. Blum. il *New York* 22:28-35 Je 19 '89
Joe Papp [interview] V. Muse. il pors *Life* 12:23-5 Ap '89
PAPPAS, DAVID L., AND OTHERS
Atom counting at surfaces. bibl f il *Science* 243:64-6 Ja 6 '89
PAPPAS, THEODORE
Making the grade: memoirs of a Harvard grader. *The American Scholar* 58:415-19 Summ '89

PAPUA NEW GUINEA
See also
Birds—Papua New Guinea
Public health—Papua New Guinea
Rural development—Papua New Guinea
Native peoples
See also
Fore (Papua New Guinea people)
PAQUIN, ETHEL
Christmas at our house [story] il *McCall's* 117:29+
D '89
PAQUIN, PAT
The virtues of solitude. il *Utne Reader* p68-9 Mr/Ap '89
PARABLES
See also
Jesus Christ—Parables
PARACHUTES
USAF, Sandia developing new parachute system for F-111
crew escape module. il *Aviation Week & Space Technology*
129:54-5 Mr 6 '89
PARACHUTES IN SPACE FLIGHT *See* Space vehicles—
Propulsion systems—Recovery
PARACHUTING
See also
Parasailing
When James Bond jumps, super skydiver B.J. Worth gives
007 an airborne Licence to thrill [motion picture parachute
stunt coordinator] N. Geeslin. il pors *People Weekly* 32:95+
S 4 '89
Accidents and injuries
The fall and rise of Terry Vares. T. Slear. il por *Women's
Sports & Fitness* 11:70 My '89
PARADE FLOATS
Larger than life [B. Kern's floats for New Orleans Mardi
Gras parade] B. Weber. il *The New York Times Magazine*
p70 Ja 22 '89
Presidential Inaugural Parade includes only black builder
of float who participated. il por *Jet* 75:57 F 6 '89
PARADES
France
See also
Paris (France)—Parades
New York (State)
See also
New York (N.Y.)—Parades
Washington (D.C.)
See Washington (D.C.)—Parades
Wisconsin
See also
Milwaukee (Wis.)—Parades
PARADISE, PHIL HERSCHEL, 1905-
about
Paradise revisited. J. Lovoos. il por *American Artist* 53:64-7+
Ag '89
PARADISE [television program] *See* Television program
reviews—Single works
PARADISE BIRDS *See* Birds of paradise
PARADISE GUEST RANCH (BUFFALO, WYO.) *See*
Ranches—Wyoming
PARADJANOV, SERGEI
about
Prisoner. A. Williamson. il pors *Film Comment* 25:57-60+
My/Je '89
PARADOX
See also
Banach-Tarski paradox
Olbers' paradox
PARADOX (DATABASE MANAGEMENT SYSTEM) *See*
Relational databases
PARAGUAY
See also
Civil rights—Paraguay
Government and the press—Paraguay
Political prisoners—Paraguay
Foreign relations
United States
See United States—Foreign relations—Paraguay
Languages
A choice of words. D. Einhorn and S. O. Einhorn. il *Américas*
41 no1:42-7 '89
Politics and government
See also
Political campaigns—Paraguay
Church leaders greet coup with hope, prayer. A. L. Sherman.
il *Christianity Today* 33:48 Mr 17 '89
An extinction in Paraguay [A. Stroessner overthrown by
A. Rodríguez] J. Schwartz and J. Contreras. il por map
Newsweek 113:38-9 F 13 '89
The extinction of a dinosaur [General A. Rodríguez leads
coup to depose A. Stroessner] J. Smolowe. il pors *Time*
133:48 F 13 '89
The last tango in Paraguay [A. Rodríguez overthrows A.
Stroessner] il pors *U.S. News & World Report* 106:14
F 13 '89
Paraguay after Stroessner. R. Roett. *Foreign Affairs* 68:124-42
Spr '89
Revolt in a fiefdom [coup topples A. Stroessner] A. Bilski.
Maclean's 102:21 F 13 '89

Religious institutions and affairs
See also
Christians—Paraguay
PARAJON, GUSTAVO
about
One Nicaraguan Christian's perspective [interview] por
Christianity Today 33:48 Mr 3 '89
PARALLEL PROCESSING (COMPUTERS)
See also
Massively parallel supercomputers
Multiprocessors
Multitasking (Computers)
Configuring parallel programs (I) [Occam Transpiler] D.
Pountain. il *Byte* 14:349-52 D '89
Hands-on parallel processing [hypercube system using Macs
and AppleTalk] G. C. Fox and others. bibl f il *Byte*
14:287-93 O '89
Many hands make light work. J. Heins. il *Forbes* 143:275+
My 29 '89
The metamorphosis of information management. D. Gelernter.
bibl il *Scientific American* 261:66-73 Ag '89
Occam II. D. Pountain. il *Byte* 14:279-84 O '89
A PC run circles around a Cray? [coprocessors and transputers]
T. J. Byers. il *Radio-Electronics* 60 ComputerDigest:77+
Ap '89
PARALYSIS
See also
Cerebral palsy
Parkinson's disease
Poliomyelitis
Therapy
See also
Therapeutic Technologies Inc.
Waiting for the bionic man. R. Simon. il *Forbes* 144:204-5+
S 18 '89
PARALYTICS
Almost charmed [publication of cartoonist J. Callahan's
autobiography] L. Fleischer. *Publishers Weekly* 235:66 Mr
17 '89
The amazing Andertons [quadraplegic couple] L. Gourse.
il pors *McCall's* 116:92+ Ja '89
A boy's best friend [paraplegic T. Berberian's assistance dog]
M. Clary. il por *McCall's* 116:75-6 Je '89
Courage on wheels. D. Gosch. il por *The Mother Earth
News* 119:38-9 S/O '89
Death wish [quadriplegic L. McAfee wins right to refuse
medical treatment] *Time* 134:67 S 18 '89
Grit and a granite will conquer El Capitan [paraplegic M.
Wellman makes climb assisted by M. Corbett] M. Brower.
il pors *People Weekly* 32:36-9 Ag 14 '89
Hell on wheels [excerpt from Don't worry, he won't get
far on foot] J. Callahan. il por *Mother Jones* 14:38-40+
My '89
"I have to save my baby!" [paraplegic C. Stuller rescues
daughter from swimming pool] J. Stuller. il *Reader's Digest*
134:65-70 Ap '89
Last rights [right to die cases of N. Cruzan and L. McAfee]
M. G. Maudlin. *Christianity Today* 33:15 N 3 '89
The life my mother chose [coping with paralysis] M. Ragghian-
ti. il *Reader's Digest* 134:7-9+ My '89
Paralyzed at 21, cartoonist John Callahan finds laughter
the best medicine for his rage. R. Arias. il pors *People
Weekly* 31:102+ Je 12 '89
Sat down for life by fate, former basketball star Landon
Turner rebounds with a gritty comeback. P. Axthelm.
il por *People Weekly* 31:61-2 F 13 '89
Tiring of life without freedom, quadriplegic David Rivlin
chooses to die among friends [wins right to refuse treatment]
M. Dougherty. il pors *People Weekly* 32:56-8 Ag 7 '89
To serve and protect [policeman left a paraplegic by gunshot
wound; condensed from The Steven McDonald story];
ed. by E. J. Kahn. S. McDonald and P. A. McDonald.
il pors *Reader's Digest* 135:201-4+ O '89
PARAMEDICAL CAMOUFLAGE
Help for the beauty disabled. S. Young. *Glamour* 87:66-7
S '89
PARAMEDICS *See* Health workers
PARAMOUNT COMMUNICATIONS INC.
All hitched up and ready to go [Delaware court OKs Time
Warner] J. Greenwald. *Time* 134:39 Ag 7 '89
Banking on Time [role of Toronto Dominion and Bank
of Nova Scotia in Paramount Communications' hostile
bid for Time Inc.] P. Chisholm and J. DeMont. il *Maclean's*
102:34-5 Jl 10 '89
Clash of the titans [Paramount challenges merger of Time
and Warner Communications] J. Greenwald. il *Time*
133:42-5 Je 19 '89
The counterattack [Time Inc. moves to buy Warner in
countermove against Paramount; cover story] J. Schwartz.
il *Newsweek* 113:48-53 Je 26 '89
Feeding frenzy [Paramount's hostile bid to stop Time-Warner
merger] C. Byron. il *New York* 22:24-8 Je 26 '89
First salvos in the fight for Time. B. Saporito. il *Fortune*
120:12 Jl 3 '89
Heading for D-Day in Delaware [court to decide whether
Time Inc. up for sale] J. Castro. il *Time* 134:44 Jl 10
'89

PARAMOUNT COMMUNICATIONS INC.—cont.

How to drive off a raider [battle over Time Inc.] J. Schwartz. il *Newsweek* 114:43 Ag 7 '89

The inside story of Time Warner. B. Saporito. il *Fortune* 120:164-6+ N 20 '89

Is there a line around the block for Paramount? G. G. Marcial. il *Business Week* p122 O 16 '89

A legal battle that could kill off friendly mergers [court to decide if Time-Warner stock swap put Time in play] M. Galen. il *Business Week* p27 Jl 3 '89

A legal victory for the long term [Delaware court allows Time Inc. to buy Warner and repel Paramount's hostile bid] B. Saporito. il *Fortune* 120:56-9 Ag 14 '89

A new march on Time. P. Chisholm. il *Maclean's* 102:37 Je 19 '89

A nice, simple Time-Warner deal was too good to last. D. Lieberman. il *Business Week* p38-9 Je 19 '89

One for the books [Delaware court rejects Paramount's challenge to Time-Warner deal] J. Greenwald. il *Time* 134:34-6 Jl 24 '89

Paramount bid for Time launches all-out battle. *Publishers Weekly* 235:8 Je 23 '89

Paramount raises its ante [increases hostile bid for Time] J. Greenwald. il *Time* 134:42 Jl 3 '89

Paramount takes $140 million write-off on publishing units. C. Reid. *Publishers Weekly* 236:8+ D 1 '89

Return to sender [Paramount's hostile bid for Time] J. Greenwald. il *Time* 133:54-5 Je 26 '89

Time Inc. gets a green light [Delaware judge OKs Warner bid] J. Schwartz and C. Friday. il *Newsweek* 114:50 Jl 24 '89

Time Inc. will have to pull a Houdini [Paramount's hostile bid] D. Lieberman. il *Business Week* p62 Je 26 '89

Time rejects Paramount's sweetened $12 billion bid. *Publishers Weekly* 236:8 Jl 7 '89

Time vs. its shareholders [Paramount's hostile bid to stop merger with Warner] J. Egan. il *U.S. News & World Report* 107:38-40 Jl 3 '89

Time-Warner: this close to victory [Delaware court decision; special section] il *Business Week* p26-9 Jl 31 '89

Time's bad fortune with money people [bid for Time Inc.] *U.S. News & World Report* 106:14 Je 19 '89

Time's counterattack is drawing acid reviews [Warner bid] D. Lieberman. il *Business Week* p26 Jl 3 '89

Upping the ante for Time [Paramount's new bid] J. Schwartz. il *Newsweek* 114:42 Jl 3 '89

The war over Time Inc. [Paramount's hostile bid threatens Warner merger] J. Schwartz. il *Newsweek* 113:48-9+ Je 19 '89

PARAMOUNT HOME VIDEO (FIRM)

Paramount confronts quality issue in summer promotion. il *Publishers Weekly* 235:56 Je 2 '89

S & S to handle Paramount video line. P. Sweeting. il *Publishers Weekly* 235:31+ F 3 '89

PARAMOUNT PICTURES CORP. FAMOUS MUSIC PUBLISHING

Paramount's publishing arm purchases Ellington catalog. pors *Jet* 76:62 My 29 '89

PARAMOUNT PICTURES CORP. TELEVISION GROUP

How Paramount is blitzing the networks [deal to run independent stations owned by TVX Broadcast Group] R. Grover and D. Lieberman. il *Business Week* p94-5 Ja 30 '89

The Paramount challenge: make hits new ways [cover story] N. Koch. il *Channels (New York, N.Y.: 1986)* 9:44-6+ F '89

PARANOIA

LBJ's alter ego [memoir by R. Goodwin] G. C. Ward. il *American Heritage* 40:14+ F '89

Paranoia: fearful delusions. W. Herbert. il *The New York Times Magazine* p62-3 Mr 19 '89

PARANTHROPUS See Man, Prehistoric

PARAPLEGICS See Paralytics

PARAPSYCHOLOGY

See also
Channelers
Extrasensory perception
Psychics
Psychokinesis
Spiritualism
Teleportation

Antimatter. See issues of Omni (New York, N.Y.)

Ghost busters at work. J. Wolkomir and R. Wolkomir. il *McCall's* 116:104+ Jl '89

Looking quickly to the side: the other world of psychic phenomena. M. Ventura. il *Utne Reader* p98-101 N/D '89

Mythics: don't take them too literally [excerpt from Imaginary landscape] W. I. Thompson. *Utne Reader* p103 N/D '89

Soviet Union

Elvis spotted in Estonia! H. G. Chua-Eoan. il *Time* 134:52 O 23 '89

PARAPSYCHOLOGY AND CRIMINAL INVESTIGATION

Psych out! The woman who catches killers with her mind [N. Czetli] il por *Redbook* 173:140-2+ My '89

PARAPSYCHOLOGY AND SCIENCE

Pathological science [address, December 18, 1953] I. Langmuir. bibl f il por *Physics Today* 42:36-48 O '89

Questions for the cosmos [work of R. G. Jahn] S. Fishman. il por *The New York Times Magazine* p50+ N 26 '89

PARASAILING

The Zen of parasailing. C. Cooper. il *Skiing* 42:22+ O '89

PARASITE-HOST RELATIONSHIPS See Host-parasite relationships

PARASITES

See also
Anilocra
Fleas
Host-parasite relationships
Lice
Plasmodium (Parasite)
Protozoa, Pathogenic
Wasps
Worms, Intestinal and parasitic

PARASITIC DISEASES

See also
Coccidiosis
Giardiasis
Leishmaniasis
Onchocerciasis
Q fever
Schistosomiasis
Toxoplasmosis
Trichinosis

PARASKEVIN-YOUNG, CONNIE

about

She goes round in circles. T. D'Ottavio. il por *American Health* 8:86 My '89

PARC DE LA VILLETTE See La Villette (Paris, France)

PARCE, J. WALLACE, AND OTHERS

Detection of cell-affecting agents with a silicon biosensor. bibl f il *Science* 246:243-7 O 13 '89

PARCEL POST

See also
Air freight service
Purolator Courier Corp.
Roadway Package System Inc.

PARCHMENT PAPER IN COOKING See Papillote cooking

PARDAL, INES

The rub in the dubbing. *Américas* 41 no2:64 '89

PARDEE, ARTHUR BECK, 1921-

G_1 events and regulations of cell proliferation. bibl f il *Science* 246:603-8 N 3 '89

PARDON

See also
Amnesty
Forgiveness

Pardon Ollie. *The American Spectator* 22:10-11 Ja '89

The teflon tycoon [George Bush grants A. Hammer pardon for campaign finance law violations] S. Weinberg. il pors *Common Cause Magazine* 15:17-21 N/D '89

PARELES, JON

Music. See issues of Mademoiselle

PARENT AND CHILD (LAW)

See also
Adoption and adopted children
Custody of children
Paternity
Support (Domestic relations)
Visitation rights (Parents)

Abortion: sparring on the bench [Supreme Court hears arguments in cases involving mandatory notification of parents of teenagers seeking abortions] il *Newsweek* 114:49 D 11 '89

Crimes of faith? [denial of medical care to children] D. Neff. *Christianity Today* 33:17 Je 16 '89

Does father know best? [fathers' rights and abortion] P. Orenstein. *Vogue* 179:314+ Ap '89

Equal rights: not for women only [fathers' rights and abortion] M. J. Weiss. il *Glamour* 87:276-7+ Mr '89

Father's rights case declined by High Court. *Christianity Today* 33:53 Ja 13 '89

God's will vs. doctor's orders. C. Levine. il *Parents* 64:220+ Mr '89

Is it fair to punish parents for crimes of their children? il *Jet* 76:12-14 My 29 '89

Just because your kids are 18 doesn't mean you are free and clear. D. W. Englander. il *Money* 18:141-2 Ag '89

Now, parents on trial. B. Kantrowitz. il *Newsweek* 114:54-5 O 2 '89

When parents pay for their kids' sins [parental liability laws] J. P. Shapiro. il *U.S. News & World Report* 107:26 Jl 24 '89

When pregnant girls face mom and dad [Supreme Court hearing on Minnesota law requiring parental notification in teenage abortions] D. Whitman. il *U.S. News & World Report* 107:25-6 D 4 '89

Whose rights are we protecting, anyway? [victims of child abuse; with discussion] K. Dorros and P. Dorsey. il *Children Today* 18:6-11+ My/Je '89

Canada

Abortion agony [Supreme Court okays abortion sought by C. Daigle over objections of former boyfriend] B. Wallace and L. Van Dusen. il por *Maclean's* 102:12-14 Ag 21 '89

PARENT AND CHILD (LAW)—Canada—*cont.*

Abortion in the courts [Quebec court upholds injunction obtained by former boyfriend preventing C. Daigle from getting abortion] B. Wallace. il por *Maclean's* 102:14-16 Ag 7 '89

Abortion on trial [cases of two women seeking abortions over objections of former boyfriends; cover story; special section; with editorial comment by Kevin Doyle] il pors *Maclean's* 102:2, 14-16+ Jl 31 '89

Bittersweet victory [Ontario court decides abortion case in favor of woman B. Dodd] G. W. Taylor. il por *Maclean's* 102:18 Jl 24 '89

Court fails to block abortion [case of C. Daigle] L. Mackey. *Christianity Today* 33:65 S 8 '89

The final appeal [C. Daigle's fight for an abortion to go before Supreme Court] L. Van Dusen. il por *Maclean's* 102:10-11 Ag 14 '89

A unanimous view [Supreme Court ruling in C. Daigle case denying partner's right to prevent an abortion] L. Van Dusen. il por *Maclean's* 102:16 N 27 '89

PARENT-CHILD RELATIONSHIP

See also

Adoption and adopted children
Aged—Family relationships
Cancer patients—Family relationships
Child abuse
Children—Management and training
Children of alcoholics
Children of baby boomers
Children of celebrities
Children of clergymen
Children of divorced parents
Children of executives
Children of Holocaust survivors
Children of prisoners
Children of servicemen
Children of the rich
Children of working parents
Handicapped—Family relationships
Love, Maternal
Maternal deprivation
Mentally ill—Family relationships
Overprotective parents
Parents of divorcees
Sick—Family relationships
Stepparents and stepchildren
Youth—Management and training

Aches run in the family [study by Kathryn Richard] E. Stark. il *Psychology Today* 23:23 Ap '89

"All I ever wanted was my mother's love": the sad life of a child star [television performer on Father knows best]; ed. by Ace Collins. L. Chapin. il pors *Redbook* 173:28+ Ag '89

As the boys of Zimmer dare to dream, a nostalgic editor returns to his field of futility [takes father and son to watch Chicago Cubs game] R. Novak. il por *People Weekly* 32:52-4 O 9 '89

Baby boom [new babies in families with teenagers] D. Kent. il *Seventeen* 48:117-18+ Je '89

Balancing the family act [quiz] K. Hinchman. il *'Teen* 33:34-5 D '89

Baseball diamonds are a girl's best friend [taking daughter to watch Mets games] R. Schoenstein. il *New Choices for the Best Years* 29:80+ O '89

The benefits of fatherhood [research by John Snarey and others] M. Roberts. il *Psychology Today* 23:76 Mr '89

Bonding for life [between parent and infant] K. Karlsrud and D. Schultz. il *Parents* 64:155 Jl '89

Bonus baby [older mother] E. Klein. il *The New York Times Magazine* p22+ Ag 27 '89

The boy in the photograph. D. I. Fine. il por *The New York Times Magazine* p28+ Ap 2 '89

Bricklayer's boy. A. Lubrano. il *Gentlemen's Quarterly* 59:171-2+ Je '89

Can children & parents be adults together? A. Quindlen. il *New Choices for the Best Years* 29:89-90 Ja '89

Can parents be sexist? D. Elkind. il *Parents* 64:218 My '89

Catch of a lifetime [son learns about ethics from fishing with father] J. P. Lenfestey. il *Reader's Digest* 134:111-12 F '89

The Daddy Prize [condensed from It was on fire when I lay down on it] R. Fulghum. il *Reader's Digest* 135:67-9 O '89

The daddy trap [effects of close relationships between fathers and daughters] D. Kent. il *Mademoiselle* 95:182-3+ D '89

Daniel: beloved by God & by me [seeing Do the right thing with teenage son] B. B. Morton. *Commonweal* 116:562-3 O 20 '89

A death in the family 1989 [cover story] H. Epstein. il pors *New York* 22:34-43 N 27 '89

A dog's tale [adolescent daughter relinquishes stuffed animal] E. Berg. il *Ladies' Home Journal* 106:42+ Ja '89

Dr. Mom [teenager's mother attends medical school] C. Parkhurst. il *Seventeen* 48:140+ Ap '89

Father and son [watching sports events in Baltimore, Md.] W. Gildea. *Reader's Digest* 134:127-30 Ja '89

The father-daughter connection. P. Theroux. il *Parents* 64:61-3 S '89

Father love. H. Gold. il por *American Health* 8:72-3 Ja/F '89

Father to daughter [fishing] B. Journey. il *Outdoor Life* 184:94-5+ N '89

First snow [father and infant daughter] J. Nicholas. il *Reader's Digest* 135:7-8 D '89

Getting to know my dad . . . again. G. Hochman. il *New Choices for the Best Years* 29:82+ Je '89

Gifts from children. E. Berg. il *Parents* 64:132-3 N '89

"Good-bye, daddy" [reflections on father's death] M. Mayo. il *Parents* 64:114-15 Je '89

Graduation day [18 year old son about to leave home] R. Hawkley. il *Reader's Digest* 134:9-10 Je '89

The great sleep-out [backyard camping] D. Kennedy. il *Parents* 64:170 Ag '89

Growing pains [trip to airshow revives daughter's interest in airplanes] G. Baxter. il *Flying* 116:122+ S '89

Growing up with Trux [author and his father bound by love of sports] R. Fimrite. por *Sports Illustrated* 71:72 Jl 3 '89

The heat is on [parental pressure and applying to college] P. Goldsmith. il *Seventeen* 48:152-3+ O '89

Holiday visits: home is where the guilt is [adult daughters] E. Welty. *Mademoiselle* 95:102 D '89

Honor thy children. J. Segal. il *Parents* 64:87-90+ D '89

How 3-year-olds learn best. J. Marzollo. il *Parents* 64:124-6+ Mr '89

How much should we tell our kids? L. Salk. il *McCall's* 116:53 Jl '89

How not to turn into your mother: for your child to grow up free, you have to remember all the ways in which you didn't. N. Eberle. il *Glamour* 87:160+ My '89

How to talk to your teenager. M. S. Miller. il *Good Housekeeping* 209:251 O '89

Impalpable dust [author explores father M. Montgomery's role in construction of Fort Peck Dam, Montana] M. R. Montgomery. il *The New Yorker* 65:94-111 Mr 27 '89

The importance of hugging [link between absence of childhood affection and violence in Bedouin society; excerpt from The Lucifer principle] H. Bloom. il *Omni (New York, N.Y.)* 11:30+ F '89

Journey of a cult child [A. Ward helps son M. Ward make transition from MOVE] M. Capuzzo. il pors *Reader's Digest* 134:109-14 My '89

The last farmer [condensation] H. Kohn. il *Reader's Digest* 134:115-20 Mr '89

The life my mother chose [coping with paralysis] M. Ragghianti. il *Reader's Digest* 134:7-9+ My '89

Like father, like daughter. L. B. Randolph. il *Ebony* 44:152+ Je '89

Like mother, like daughter: these Rockettes get their kicks by staying in step with their moms. il *People Weekly* 32:113 D 18 '89

The little red chair. L. Franks. il *The New York Times Magazine* p28+ Mr 12 '89

Mama and Miss Jordan [relationships with mother and high school teacher] M. H. Futrell. il *Reader's Digest* 135:75-80 Jl '89

Methinks I see my father. A. Meyer. il *American Health* 8:66-7 Ja/F '89

Mother-daughter nurses. L. W. Strick. il *Good Housekeeping* 209:65-6+ O '89

Mother hate [symptom of girl's adolescence] P. Theroux. il *Parents* 64:46+ Ag '89

Mother of a pearl (IV) [7-year-old tennis player A. Stevenson] S. Stevenson. il pors *World Tennis* 36:16 Ap '89

Mothers & daughters [special section] il *Harper's Bazaar* 122:154-65+ O '89

Mother's days [mother who has been running since birth of ten year old son] P. L. Potts. il *Runner's World* 24:104 My '89

A mother's manner of looking to the sky [instilling awareness of mystery of life] J. M. Wall. *The Christian Century* 106:99-100 F 1-8 '89

Moving back home [adult children] E. C. Ray. il *Essence* 20:90-1+ Je '89

My dream house and my boy [near drowning of son causes author to realize what is important in life]; ed. by Linda Lawrence. F. E. Baird. il *Reader's Digest* 135:9-10+ O '89

My father's autobiography. D. Cole. il *Psychology Today* 22:56-7 D '88

My mother died too soon. J. Kaufman. il por *Glamour* 87:144+ N '89

My secret valentine [condensed from All I really need to know I learned in kindergarten] R. Fulghum. il *Reader's Digest* 134:9 F '89

Notes and comment [father nervously awaits son's air flight into England] *The New Yorker* 65:47-8 S 25 '89

Notes from a 'king' lovingly deposed [fathers and sons] H. Gold. il *American Health* 8:68-9 Ja/F '89

One mother's story [reaction to teenage son's Mohawk haircut] J. A. Reimer. il *Ladies' Home Journal* 106:90+ Ap '89

PARENT-CHILD RELATIONSHIP—cont.

Our dinner table university [father's use of dinner time to teach children; condensed from Papa, my father] L. F. Buscaglia. il *Reader's Digest* 135:78-80 S '89

Out with dad—and guess who's paying for dinner? [adult children and parents] S. Mansfield. *Mademoiselle* 95:122 My '89

"Papa was so proud" [excerpt from Papa, my father] L. F. Buscaglia. il pors *Redbook* 173:24+ Je '89

Parents and kids: the ESP connection. C. Jones. *McCall's* 116:64+ My '89

Parents: what you can teach them (I) [children's dance education] M. Horosko. il *Dance Magazine* 63:70-1 F '89

Parents: what you can teach them (II) [children's dance education] M. Horosko. il *Dance Magazine* 63:64-5 Ap '89

Phenomena, comment and notes [nature walks taken with mother] J. P. Wiley, Jr. il *Smithsonian* 20:26+ Ag '89

A prayer for July Fourth [mother's hope for son] E. Harrington. il *Reader's Digest* 135:121-2 Jl '89

The roots of my ambition [inspiration of mother; condensed from The good times] R. Baker. il por *Reader's Digest* 135:115-18 N '89

Shining star daughters and their amazing moms. il pors *'Teen* 33:46-7 D '89

Shower your kids with love [excerpt from 101 ways to tell your child "I love you"] V. Lansky. il *Redbook* 172:28+ F '89

Signing off. P. Theroux. il *Parents* 64:51-2 N '89

A skateboarder's guide to unstoked parents. B. Blouin. *Harper's* 279:22+ Ag '89

Snow days. E. Berg. il *Parents* 64:102-4 F '89

Sounds of home [sending son in Korea tape recording of thunderstorm to ward off homesickness] B. V. Moulder. il *Reader's Digest* 135:143-4 Jl '89

Strolling under the stars [mother's intimate moments with children] J. I. Overstreet. il *Reader's Digest* 134:111-13 Ja '89

Surviving family blues [ability of teens to cope with depressed parents; research by William R. Beardslee and Dona Podorefsky] J. Folkenberg. *American Health* 8:119 Mr '89

Taking a lesson from dad. L. Levinger. il *New Choices for the Best Years* 29:79-80 N '89

A talk with my dad. L. Thomas. por *Essence* 20:9 Je '89

Things my children never told me [mother and daughter talk over old wounds] P. Theroux. il *Parents* 64:59-60+ O '89

The ultimate decision [mother's death; cover story] A. H. Malcolm. il pors *The New York Times Magazine* p38-41+ D 3 '89

Upscale girls: a generation outgrows its parents. K. A. Samon. il *Mademoiselle* 95:206-7+ Mr '89

The waiting has finally ended [Russian-Jewish mother and daughter reunited in America] N. Zundelevich. il *The New York Times Magazine* p10+ Ja 1 '89

When a parent dies. J. Segal. il *Parents* 64:112-13+ Je '89

When Johnny comes marching home [adult children] G. Rosenblum. il *New Choices for the Best Years* 29:54-7 O '89

When old men went out of my life [father's death; excerpt from Sweet summer] B. M. Campbell. il pors *Essence* 20:58-60+ Je '89

When they hate the one you love [parents don't like boyfriend] L. Frank. il *Seventeen* 48:96+ N '89

When your child intermarries [Jewish-gentile marriage] G. Rosenblum. il *New Choices for the Best Years* 29:54-8 Jl '89

The woman in the kitchen [mother's sacrifices] G. Sledge. il *Reader's Digest* 135:85-90 S '89

Anecdotes, facetiae, satire, etc.

My son the tour guide [family trip to Europe with adult son] J. Koslow. il *New Choices for the Best Years* 29:77+ Jl '89

PARENT-CHILD RELATIONSHIP IN LITERATURE

Fathers & their sons [novels of W. Kennedy] D. M. Murtaugh. il por *Commonweal* 116:298-302 My 19 '89

PARENT-CHILD RELATIONSHIP IN MOTION PICTURES

Make room for daddy [fathers and sons] G. Kilday. il *American Film* 15:16 N '89

PARENT EDUCATION

See also

Publishers and publishing—Parent education literature

Educators can promote involvement of fathers. B. A. McBride. *The Education Digest* 55:43-5 N '89

If you want to be a better parent . . . here are the TV moms and dads you should learn from. J. Brothers. il *TV Guide* 37:22-5 Mr 4-10 '89

PARENT-TEACHER CONFERENCES See School and the home

PARENT-TEACHER COOPERATION See School and the home

PARENTAGE

See also
Paternity

DNA typing and parentage. L. Levine and L. Kobilinsky. *BioScience* 39:588-9 O '89

PARENTAL BEHAVIOR IN ANIMALS

Easy does it! [mothers and infant chimps] il *National Geographic World* 171:16-17 N '89

Photographs and photography

Animal babies on the go [mothers and offspring] il *National Geographic World* 169:12-15 S '89

PARENTAL BEHAVIOR IN BIRDS

Tricks of the egg trade [common cuckoo] M. Brooke. il *Natural History* p50-4 Ap '89

PARENTAL BEHAVIOR IN INSECTS

Guardians of the underworld [burying beetles] M. P. Scott and J. F. A. Traniello. il *Natural History* p32-7 Je '89

PARENTAL DEPRIVATION

See also
Maternal deprivation

PARENTAL LEAVES

Employer provisions for parental leave. J. R. Meisenheimer, II. bibl f il *Monthly Labor Review* 112:20-4 O '89

Laws and regulations

Parental leave cries to be born. B. Kantrowitz. il *Newsweek* 113:65+ Je 5 '89

PARENTHOOD [film] See Motion picture reviews—Single works

PARENTI, MICHAEL, 1933-

What role do advertisers play in deciding the news? [excerpt from Inventing reality] *Utne Reader* p66 N/D '89

PARENTS

See also
Children
Family
Fathers
Mothers
Overprotective parents
Parent education
Parental leaves
School and the home
School management and organization—Parent participation
Single parent families
Stepparents and stepchildren

Happy parents, happy kids. D. F. Bjorklund and B. Bjorklund. il *Parents* 64:128 Ja '89

How to be a good (not perfect) parent [excerpt from Living beautifully together] A. Stoddard. il por *McCall's* 116:60+ F '89

When parents make mistakes. P. Colman. *Ladies' Home Journal* 106:106 O '89

Psychology

The new intimacy: rediscovering each other after the kids leave home [cover story] S. Levitt. il *New Choices for the Best Years* 29:38-43 S '89

Recreation

Anecdotes, facetiae, satire, etc.

Post-baby beach days. J. Leonard. il *Parents* 64:90-2 Jl '89

PARENTS, HANDICAPPED

"Blindness isn't a handicap—it's a nuisance" [blind couple, M. and P. Maurer, raising children] D. Scoblionkov. il pors *McCall's* 117:49-52 O '89

PARENTS (PERIODICAL)

Inside Parents. A. P. Murphy. See issues of Parents beginning September 1988

PARENTS [film] See Motion picture reviews—Single works

PARENTS' AND TEACHERS' ASSOCIATIONS

See also
National PTA (U.S.)

Parents take action. F. Roberts. *Parents* 64:54+ F '89

PARENTS' GRIEF See Grief

PARENTS IN LITERATURE

Summer reading. L. Yelin. il *Parents* 64:176+ Jl '89

PARENTS IN TELEVISION

If you want to be a better parent . . . here are the TV moms and dads you should learn from. J. Brothers. il *TV Guide* 37:22-5 Mr 4-10 '89

PARENTS OF DIVORCEES

When the kids call it quits [excerpt from What to do when your son or daughter divorces] D. W. Gottlieb and others. il *Modern Maturity* 32:68-70 Je/Jl '89

PARENTS OF MURDERED CHILDREN

'I am still devastated' [J. Walsh, host of America's most wanted] J. Marion. il pors *TV Guide* 37:22-4 Mr 18-24 '89

PARENTS OF PROBLEM CHILDREN

"We're afraid of our son" [mentally ill adoptee was abused by natural parents] B. Harlow. il pors *Ladies' Home Journal* 106:18+ Mr '89

PARENTS OF THE HANDICAPPED

What a beautiful baby. K. H. Avelino. il por *Parents* 64:132-4+ O '89

Economic conditions

Baby makes three: a May-December couple cope with paying for an unexpected child [John and Robyn McCaughan] L. Luciano. il *Money* 18:195-6 N '89

PARENTS OF THE MENTALLY HANDICAPPED

Spilled milk [father and mentally retarded son] D. W. French. il por *Parents* 64:232 Mr '89

PARENTS OF WATTS (ORGANIZATION)

"Sweet Alice" Harris. J. Malveaux. il pors *Ms.* 17:72-5 Ja/F '89

PARENTS' QUARRELS *See* Quarrels

PARFIT, MICHAEL
Antarctic meltdown. il *Discover* 10:38-40+ S '89
The Dust Bowl. bibl (p174) il *Smithsonian* 20:44-54+ Je '89
Whose hands will shape the future of the Amazon's green mansions? [cover story] bibl (p245) il maps *Smithsonian* 20:58-68+ N '89

PARHAM, ROBERT
Walking the edge [poem] *America* 160:40 Ja 21 '89

PARIETARIA
Special bonus tip! [source of allergy] *Prevention (Emmaus, Pa.)* 41:39 Ag '89

PARINGAUX, ROLAND-PIERRE
Boat people, go home. *World Press Review* 36:35-6 Je '89

PARINI, JAY
The more they write, the more they write. il *The New York Times Book Review* 94:1+ Jl 30 '89

PARIS, BARRY
Maximum expression [cover story] il pors *American Film* 15:30-7+ O '89
Our wild Miss Brooks [excerpt from Louise Brooks] il pors *American Film* 15:38-41+ N '89
Profiles [L. Basquette] il por *The New Yorker* 64:54-73 F 13 '89

PARIS, CHERYL
about
Playing Sweet bird of youth's abandoned lover, Cheryl Paris draws on her own unhappy past. J. Park. il pors *People Weekly* 32:48-9+ O 2 '89

PARIS, MICA
about
A new generation of black beauties. il pors *Ebony* 44:152+ S '89

PARIS (FRANCE)
Antiquities
A castle under the Louvre. P. Miller. il *National Geographic* 176:102-7 Jl '89
Architecture
See also
Paris (France)—Public buildings
Starck modern [Bruno Le Moult's house designed by P. Starck] C. K. Gandee. il por *House & Garden* 161:78-85+ Jl '89
Art
SoHo-sur-Seine [Bastille quarter] J. De Lacy. il *House & Garden* 161:36+ Jl '89
Under the pyramid. G. Danto. il *Art News* 88:41-2 F '89
Buildings
See also
Paris (France)—Public buildings
Churches (Buildings)
The domes of Paris. C. Marriott. il map *Gourmet* 49:52-9+ Jl '89
Clubs
See also
Cercle de l'Union Interalliée
Crime
A secret cache [art stolen by F. Fielder] B. Grauman. il *Art News* 88:59-60 Summ '89
Description
Celebrate Paris. S. Birnbaum. il *Good Housekeeping* 209:64+ Ag '89
Liberte, egalite—and one hell of a party. P. Farrell. il *Business Week* p162-3 Je 26 '89
Long live the Revolution! D. Lawday. il *U.S. News & World Report* 106:67-8+ My 22 '89
Paris/London: the chic beat. J. M. Adams. il *Seventeen* 48:172+ Ap '89
Paris. il *Esquire* 111:93+ Je '89
Paris journal. C. P. Reynolds. See occasional issues of Gourmet
Paris: remembering the Revolution [cover story; special issue] il *Travel Holiday* 172:36-73 Jl '89
Anecdotes, facetiae, satire, etc.
It pays to get clipped [travel tips for the American] N. Fein. il *Ms.* 18:28-30 N '89
Galleries and museums
See also
Grande Galerie de Zoologie (Paris, France)
Hermès Museum
Musée Carnavalet (Paris, France)
Musée d'Art Moderne de la Ville de Paris
Musée de l'Histoire de France
Musée du Jeu de Paume (Paris, France)
Musée du Louvre
Musée Nissim de Camondo (Paris, France)
An art market for the '90s? T. Godfrey. il *Art in America* 77:44-5+ O '89
Small museums, big cachet. N. Frey. il *Harper's Bazaar* 122:86+ Ap '89
Gardens and gardening
See also
Jardin des Plantes (Paris, France)
Opéra Bastille—Gardens
Floral decorum. J. Kramer. il *House & Garden* 161:112+ S '89

Historic houses, sites, etc.
See also
Palais-Royal (Paris, France)
Hôtel de Cavoye: a Paris house appointed by antiquarian Bernard Steinitz. C. Styles-McLeod. il *Architectural Digest* 46:234-41 O '89
My Le Corbusier home [Villa Jeanneret] H. McNulty. il *Gourmet* 49:140+ N '89
A Parisian bijou: glittering prizes in a designer's Louis XVI pavilion [designed by Valerian Rybar and J. F. Daigre; cover story] Suzy. il *Architectural Digest* 46:204-11+ O '89
History
Commune, 1871
An exercise in terror? The Paris Commune, 1871. G. Dallas. bibl il *History Today* 39:38-44 F '89
Hotels, motels, etc.
The Hôtel Ritz: Paris' resplendent landmark on the Place Vendôme. C. Aillaud. il *Architectural Digest* 46:120-5+ Ja '89
The king of hospitality [F. Cozzo, general manager of Plaza Athénée] R. Levio. il por *Harper's Bazaar* 122:52 Ap '89
Intellectual life
When radical chic courted the guillotine [influence of 18th century French intellectuals] J. H. Huizinga. il *The New York Times Book Review* 94:1+ F 5 '89
Monuments, statues, etc.
See also
Arche de la Défense (Paris, France)
Eiffel Tower (Paris, France)
Museums
See Paris (France)—Galleries and museums
Music
See also
Opera—France
Opéra de Paris
Orchestre de Paris
Ordinances
Once more, the barricades! [public safety plan announced in Paris to cope with bicentennial festivities] il *Newsweek* 113:45 Je 26 '89
Parades
Moonwalk on the Champs-Elysées [parade to celebrate bicentennial of French Revolution] B. Weber. il *The New York Times Magazine* p130 My 21 '89
Photographs and photography
The new, the enduring Paris. il *National Geographic* 176:6-17 Jl '89
Photo Paris: still a movable feast. P. Slaughter. il *Petersen's Photographic Magazine* 18:40-5 D '89
Prisons and reformatories
See also
Bastille (Prison)
Public buildings
New sizzle for a City of Light. il *U.S. News & World Report* 106:14 Ap 10 '89
Paris à la Mitterrand. R. Hughes. il *Time* 134:88-90+ S 18 '89
What price glory [Grands Projets] M. Filler. il *House & Garden* 161:118-25+ Jl '89
Restaurants, nightclubs, bars, etc.
City of Bites. D. Shaw. il *Gentlemen's Quarterly* 59:157-8+ Je '89
Cooking up profits in Europe [A. Conway's eateries] A. McKenzie. por *Black Enterprise* 20:79-80 N '89
Hautes Boîtes [La Poste and China Club] N. Frey. il *Harper's Bazaar* 122:202+ D '89
Hemingway Bar, the Ritz Hotel, Paris. P. Mayle. il *Gentlemen's Quarterly* 59:286-7 N '89
The hot boîtes: see and be scene. F. Nadine. il *Harper's Bazaar* 122:74 Ap '89
Paris by night. S. McBride. il *Travel Holiday* 172:60-9 Jl '89
Paris when it fizzles. A. Richman. il *Gentlemen's Quarterly* 59:335+ S '89
The real thing [new bistros] G. Greene. il *New York* 22:50-2+ N 27 '89
SoHo-sur-Seine [Bastille quarter] J. De Lacy. il *House & Garden* 161:36+ Jl '89
Stepping out and dining well [La Coupole, Lucas-Carton and Le Paquebot] C. Petkanas. il *Harper's Bazaar* 122:64 Ap '89
Vive la France—and her cuisine. P. Wells. il *Travel Holiday* 172:48-57 Jl '89
Western Europe: the Tex-Mex invasion. A. Bogart. il *Harper's Bazaar* 122:48+ F '89
Social history
Fleeting impressionism [life in 19th century Paris shown through paintings] J. D. Flam. bibl f il *The New York Review of Books* 36:20-5 S 28 '89
Paris: La Belle Époque. E. J. Weber. il *National Geographic* 176:158-74 Jl '89
Social life and customs
A long way from the Rue de la Paix [culture shock experienced by journalist transferred to Los Angeles from Paris] J. Bonfante. il *Time* 133:70 Je 19 '89

PARIS (FRANCE)—Social life and customs—cont.
Soirées on the Seine [S. and J. Yturbe] A. Bogart. il pors *Harper's Bazaar* 122:199+ D '89

Stores

See also

Charvet (Firm)

La Maison du Chocolat (Firm)

Beauty's power elite [salons] A. Bogart. il *Harper's Bazaar* 122:118-19+ Ja '89

Breaking in [elegant boutiques] N. Scovell. il *Vogue* 179:550+ Mr '89

The fall and rise of French bread [B. Ganachaud's bakery] N. Barry. il por *Gourmet* 49:56-9+ Mr '89

The latest crop of shops. C. Petkanas. il *Harper's Bazaar* 122:92+ Ap '89

Tunnel visions [arcades] P. S. Green. il *House & Garden* 161:164-5 Jl '89

Streets

Under the roofs of Paris. A.-M. Châtelet. il *The Unesco Courier* 42:42-5 Ag '89

PARIS (FRANCE). EIFFEL TOWER See Eiffel Tower (Paris, France)

PARIS (FRANCE). LA VILLETTE See La Villette (Paris, France)

PARIS (FRANCE) FASHION SHOWS See Fashion shows

PARIS AUTO SHOW See Automobiles—Exhibitions

PARIS INTERNATIONAL AIR SHOW See Aviation—Exhibitions

PARIS OLYMPICS, 1924 See Olympic Games—1924—Summer Olympics

PARIS OPÉRA See Opéra de Paris

PARIS OPÉRA BALLET

Reviews:

Mid-February program in Paris. F. Pitt. il *Dance Magazine* 63:64-5+ My '89

PARIS REVIEW

The Paris review is a movable feast. M. Richler. il *Gentlemen's Quarterly* 59:183+ O '89

PARIS SUMMIT, 1989 See Economic conferences

PARISH, RALPH, AND OTHERS

Knock at any school. bibl f il *Phi Delta Kappan* 70:386-94 Ja '89

PARISH, SISTER

about

Inside Fergie's dream house. W. Norwich. il pors *Redbook* 172:92-5 F '89

A very private collection. J. Richardson. il *House & Garden* 161:154-61 O '89

PARISHES

The Church: looking to the future [cover story] J. H. Fichter. *America* 160:189-92 Mr 4 '89

Educating the congregation. S. E. Schreiner. il *The Christian Century* 106:985-7 N 1 '89

Never underestimate the power of a parish [Catholic parishes] R. E. Burns. *U.S. Catholic* 54:2 O '89

Parish Bible study: how to learn your faith by the book. T. Unsworth. il *U.S. Catholic* 54:21-5 S '89

Parishes should learn to fight fair [Catholic Church] T. Unsworth. *U.S. Catholic* 54:29-31 F '89

Teaching theology in the church [cover story] A. B. Robinson. *The Christian Century* 106:980-2 N 1 '89

You and your parish deserve more from each other [interview with C. Thero] por *U.S. Catholic* 54:20-7 Ag '89

PARIZEAU, JACQUES, 1930-

about

An independent voice. B. Wallace. il por *Maclean's* 102:21-2 O 23 '89

Storm clouds over Quebec [cover story; special section; with editorial comment by Kevin Doyle] il pors *Maclean's* 102:2, 16-22+ S 25 '89

PARK, DAPHNE MARGARET SYBIL DÉSIRÉE, 1921-

about

Profiles. C. Alexander. il por *The New Yorker* 64:57-71 Ja 30 '89

PARK, DARRAGH

about

Darragh Park at Tibor de Nagy. J. Schuyler. il *Art in America* 77:140-1 Jl '89

PARK, DAVID, 1911-1960

about

David Park: Whitney Museum of American Art. N. Grimes. il *Art News* 88:167 Mr '89

Ethiopia. B. Berkson. il por *Art News* 88:105-6 D '89

PARK, EDWARDS

Around the Mall and beyond. See issues of Smithsonian

PARK, PHILIP

Churches and the emperor. *The Christian Century* 106:6 Ja 4-11 '89

PARK AVENUE BAPTIST CHURCH (NEW YORK, N.Y.) See Riverside Church (New York, N.Y.)

PARK BISTRO (NEW YORK, N.Y.) See New York (N.Y.)—Restaurants, nightclubs, bars, etc.

PARK EMPLOYEES

See also

National parks and reserves—Employees

PARK PLANNING

See also

National parks and reserves—Planning

PARK RANGERS

Fire, then ice [D. Sholly, head ranger at Yellowstone National Park] M. Brower. il pors *People Weekly* 31:42-7 Ja 16 '89

Salaries, pensions, etc.

Backcountry wealth builders [Yellowstone rangers Dick and Mona Divine] C. E. Cohen. il *Money* 18:98-102+ Mr '89

Ranger association reports lean times [report by Association of National Park Rangers] P. Callanan. *National Parks* 63:10-11 S/O '89

PARK SLOPE (NEW YORK, N.Y.)

Moonwalking. *The New Yorker* 65:45-6 N 13 '89

PARKE, RACHEL

Letting go. por *The Humanist* 49:25 Mr/Ap '89

PARKER, ALAN, 1944-

about

Mississippi burning [film] Reviews

Commonweal 116:20 Ja 13 '89. T. O'Brien

Essence il 19:32 Mr '89. D. Bogle

Glamour il 87:140+ F '89. J. G. Boyum

Mademoiselle 95:92 F '89. R. Rosenbaum

Mother Jones il 14:37-9+ N '89. P. Dray

The Nation 248:26 Ja 2 '89. S. Klawans

National Review 41:55-6 Mr 10 '89. J. Simon

The New Republic 200:24 Ja 9-16 '89. S. Kauffmann

People Weekly il 31:36-43 Ja 9 '89. D. McWhorter

Time il 133:56-62 Ja 9 '89. R. Corliss

USA Today (Periodical) 117:35 My '89. P. Arthur

Video il 13:57 Ag '89. S. L. Siegel

PARKER, ALAN MICHAEL

Alchemy [poem] *The New Yorker* 65:38 My 8 '89

PARKER, CARL

about

NCATE and Texas eyeball to eyeball: who will blink? [interview] D. Watts. il *Phi Delta Kappan* 71:311-18 D '89

PARKER, CHARLIE, 1920-1955

about

Bird land [cover story] S. Crouch. il por *The New Republic* 200:25-31 F 27 '89

Charlie Parker's solo on Dewey Square—a piano arrangement [excerpt from Charlie Parker for piano book two] P. Smith. il *Down Beat* 56:56-7 Ap '89

Messy life, perfect art. K. Whitehead. il por *Down Beat* 56:6 F '89

Ornithology. K. Whitehead. il *Down Beat* 56:37-9 Mr '89

Parker postage. D. Helland. il *Down Beat* 56:6 Mr '89

Parker's brood. R. C. Walls. il pors *High Fidelity (New York, N.Y.)* 39:52-5 F '89

The real Charlie Parker: what the movie didn't tell you. M. Marshall. il pors *Ebony* 44:128+ Ja '89

PARKER, DAVE, 1951-

about

Parker: double standard in his, Pete Rose cases. il pors *Jet* 76:48 Jl 24 '89

PARKER, DENISE

about

Finding 'the zone'. L. Shainberg. il pors *The New York Times Magazine* p34-6+ Ap 9 '89

PARKER, DONALD C., 1939-, AND OTHERS

Mars' grand finale. il *Sky and Telescope* 77:369-72 Ap '89

PARKER, DOROTHY, 1893-1967

Letter from a goddamn Alp. por *Esquire* 112:144-7 Ag '89

PARKER, EVERETT C.

about

A telco-cable survey sparks controversy. J. Stilson. il por *Channels (New York, N.Y.: 1986)* 9:17+ S '89

PARKER, FESS

about

King of the mild frontier. M. Barrier. il pors *Nation's Business* 77:10+ Jl '89

PARKER, FRANK J., 1940-

Books on Africa. *America* 161:117-21 Ag 26-S 2 '89

Namibia: peace at last? *America* 161:450-2 D 16 '89

PARKER, GARY

(jt. auth) See Garcia, Marcelo, and Parker, Gary

PARKER, GRAHAM

about

Alone but alive. J. Ressner. il por *Rolling Stone* p29 Je 1 '89

Dodging hippies with Graham Parker. il por *Rolling Stone* p46 Jl 13-27 '89

Graham Parker's acoustic acid. M. Schapiro. por *Mother Jones* 14:53 Jl/Ag '89

PARKER, JACKSON

(jt. auth) See Moir, Rob, and Parker, Jackson

PARKER, JAMES CLINTON

about

After 20 years, an abandoned wife makes her ex pay his due. D. Chu. il pors *People Weekly* 31:79-82 F 20 '89

PARKER, KRIS See KRS-ONE

PARKER, PETER, 1954-

Cousins once removed. il pors *History Today* 39:7-8 S '89

PARKER, RICHARD

Gorbanomics. *The New Republic* 200:18-20 F 27 '89

PARKER, ROBERT K.

(jt. auth) See Freund, Henry P., and Parker, Robert K.

PARKER, ROBERT M., JR.
about
When Robert Parker sips, the wine world shudders. A. Richman. il por *Gentlemen's Quarterly* 59:282+ My '89
PARKER, SCOTT
about
The art of losing. K. Vreeke. il por *Cycle* 40:16 Ja '89
PARKER, TONY
Harold and Louie [excerpt from Bird, Kansas] *Harper's* 278:35-6+ My '89
PARKER HANNIFIN CORP.
Cliff dodger. R. T. Grieves. il por *Forbes* 143:322+ Ja 9 '89
PARKER PEN PLC
Penmanship with a flourish. J. Marcom, Jr. il por *Forbes* 143:152+ Ap 3 '89
PARKHURST, CAROLYN
Dr. Mom. il *Seventeen* 48:140+ Ap '89
In love with the boy next dorm. il *Seventeen* 48:199 S '89
PARKING (SECURITIES)
The feds finger an upstart raider, too [P. Bilzerian] D. Pauly. il por *Newsweek* 113:48 Ja 2 '89
Five years of hard putting [B. L. Jefferies] J. Nocera. il por *Esquire* 112:67-8+ D '89
Is getting rich quick becoming a crime? [case of P. Bilzerian] C. Byron. il por *New York* 22:25-6 Je 12 '89
Just how corrupt is Wall Street? C. Welles. il *Business Week* p34-6 Ja 9 '89
Life after Boyd? And how [Jefferies Group] E. Schine. il por *Business Week* p143 Mr 20 '89
Parking fine: 280 years in jail [J. Regan of Princeton/Newport Partners] W. Baldwin. il por *Forbes* 144:222 O 2 '89
A raider's days of reckoning [SEC files suit against P. Bilzerian] il por *Time* 134:45 Jl 10 '89
Too much firepower to fit the crime? [RICO law used in Princeton/Newport case] A. P. Tobias. il *Time* 134:74 N 20 '89
A verdict that Mike Milken hopes is no warm-up [Princeton/Newport Partners] M. Galen. por *Business Week* p46 Ag 14 '89
Wall Street is glued to the Bilzerian trial. M. Galen. il por *Business Week* p33 My 15 '89
Welcome to the world of sleaze [Princeton/Newport Partners] il *Time* 134:52 Ag 14 '89
PARKING METERS, REMODELED
Lovely cheetahs, meter-saved [California zoos use old parking meters to raise money to fund Guanacaste National Park project in Costa Rica] J. Howard. il *Sierra* 74:26 Mr/Ap '89
PARKINSON, C. NORTHCOTE (CYRIL NORTHCOTE), 1909-
about
How do you cure injelitance? P. Brimelow. il por *Forbes* 144:42-4 Ag 7 '89
PARKINSON, CYRIL NORTHCOTE *See* Parkinson, C. Northcote (Cyril Northcote), 1909-
PARKINSON'S DISEASE
Diagnosis
The case of the shaky diagnosis [D. Carlin] A. Roblin. il *Prevention (Emmaus, Pa.)* 41:103-4+ Mr '89
Therapy
An advance on Parkinson's. N. Underwood. *Maclean's* 102:69 N 27 '89
At last, a better drug for Parkinson's [deprenyl] *U.S. News & World Report* 107:14 N 27 '89
Big first scored with nerve diseases [results of deprenyl trials; research by James Tetrud and William Langston] R. Lewin. il *Science* 245:467-8 Ag 4 '89
Brain defender [use of deprenyl] *Time* 134:56 N 27 '89
Brain repair [adrenal gland transplants] A. Hollister. il *Life* 12:76-80+ My '89
Drug delays Parkinson's progression [deprenyl; research by Caroline M. Tanner] *Science News* 136:365 D 2 '89
Drug slows Parkinson's progression [deprenyl; research by James W. Tetrud and J. William Langston] K. Fackelmann. *Science News* 136:84 Ag 5 '89
The effect of deprenyl (selegiline) on the natural history of Parkinson's disease. J. W. Tetrud and J. W. Langston. bibl f il *Science* 245:519-22 Ag 4 '89
New trial evaluates Parkinsonian therapy [transplantation of adrenal tissue] R. Lewin. *Science* 243:892 F 17 '89
Parkinson's breakthrough [deprenyl] G. Cowley. il *Newsweek* 114:78 N 27 '89
Shock therapy's Parkinsonian potential [work of Richard Douyon] *Science News* 136:381 D 9 '89
Transplants offer promise [adrenal medulla transplants as treatment for Parkinson] *USA Today (Periodical)* 118:11-12 O '89
PARKINSON'S LAW
How do you cure injelitance? P. Brimelow. il por *Forbes* 144:42-4 Ag 7 '89
PARKMAN, PAUL D.
about
Great expectations: is the U.S. doing its best to beat AIDS? [interview] D. C. McLearn. il pors *FDA Consumer* 23:36-8 F '89

PARKS, GORDON
about
'Martin'. D. Moore. il *American Visions* 4:34-9 D '89
A passion for living. A. Berman. il por *Modern Maturity* 32:56-61+ Je/Jl '89
Shooting straight: the many worlds of Gordon Parks. D. Moore. bibl (p174) il pors *Smithsonian* 20:66-72+ Ap '89
PARKS, HENRY G., 1916-1989
about
Obituary
Jet por 76:20 My 15 '89
PARKS
See also
Amusement parks
National parks and reserves
Playgrounds
Sculpture gardens and parks
See also subhead Parks and playgrounds under names of cities; *also* subhead Parks and reserves under names of states
Federal aid
See also
Land and Water Conservation Fund Grant Assistance Program (U.S.)
Interpretive programs
The Adirondacks in microcosm [visitor interpretive centers for Adirondack Park] M. Storey. il *The Conservationist* 43:14-19 My/Je '89
PARKS AND RECREATION DEPT. (NEW YORK, N.Y.) *See* New York (N.Y.). Dept. of Parks and Recreation
PARKS COLLEGE OF SAINT LOUIS UNIVERSITY
Parks College: educating the aviating. A. Laboda. il *Flying* 116:36 S '89
PARLIAMENTARIANS GLOBAL ACTION FOR DISARMAMENT, DEVELOPMENT, AND WORLD REFORM (ORGANIZATION)
How Global Action got action. M. Friedman. *The Bulletin of the Atomic Scientists* 45:17 Jl/Ag '89
PARLIAMENTARY BLACK CAUCUS
Black U.S. leaders join those in England to start Parliament's Black Caucus. D. M. Cheers. il *Jet* 76:28-31 Ap 24 '89
PARLIAMENTS
See also
Canada. Parliament
Great Britain. Parliament
PARLORS *See* Living rooms
PARMA, ZITA VON BOURBON- *See* Zita, Empress, consort of Charles I, Emperor of Austria, 1892-1989
PARMENTIER, DAVID
Mississippi of the North. il por *The Humanist* 49:17-19+ S/O '89
PARMENTIER, MARC, AND OTHERS
Molecular cloning of the thyrotropin receptor. bibl f il *Science* 246:1620-2 D 22 '89
PARNASSUS FUND
Clean vs. dirty [J. Dodson of Parnassus Fund vs. K. Roberts of Shearson Fundamental Value] R. O'Connor. il *Mother Jones* 14:56-7 Je '89
PARNELL, KENNETH EUGENE
about
17 years later, a TV miniseries forces Steven Stayner to relive the horror of his childhood. S. Schindehette. il pors *People Weekly* 31:65-6+ My 22 '89
PARNELL, PETER
about
Hyde in Hollywood [drama] Reviews
New York 22:105-6 D 18 '89. J. Simon
PAROCHIAL SCHOOLS *See* Church schools
PAROCHIAL SCHOOLS, CATHOLIC *See* Catholic schools
PARODY (LITERATURE)
Court removes ban on 'Spy notes' parody. il *Publishers Weekly* 236:10 O 6 '89
Doubleday fights block of 'Spy notes' parody. *Publishers Weekly* 236:9 Ag 18 '89
PARODY (MUSIC)
See also
Phonograph records—Parody (Music)
PAROLE
Jailbird odds. D. Seligman. il *Fortune* 119:136 Ja 16 '89
No happy ending [R. Adams denied parole in Texas] J. E. Gallagher. il por *Time* 133:56 Mr 6 '89
Vicious crime, double jeopardy [parole of A. R. Jackson, attacker of actress T. Saldana] D. Bacon. il pors *People Weekly* 31:44-9 Je 5 '89
PARRETT, WILLIAM H., AND CALKINS, ANNIE
Pacific Rim partnerships: Alaska's bold initiative. il *Phi Delta Kappan* 70:550-2 Mr '89
PARRETTI, GIANCARLO
about
The man who would be mogul trips up in Tinseltown. R. Grover and J. Rossant. *Business Week* p31-2 My 1 '89
Puzzle in Movieland: the case of the mystery moguls. J. Rossant. il pors *Business Week* p80-1+ Mr 13 '89
PARRIOTT, SARA
Party strategies. il *Mademoiselle* 95:128+ D '89

PARRIS ISLAND (S.C.: RECRUIT DEPOT)
Witch hunt at Parris Island: the Marine Corps targets lesbians.
J. Lynch. il *The Progressive* 53:24-7 Mr '89
PARROTS
Polly wants to be saved [work of P. Butler in the Caribbean]
S. Begley. il *Newsweek* 114:65 D 18 '89
PARRSBORO (N.S.)
Theater
See also
Ship's Company Theatre
PARRY, ROBERT T.
Issues shaping the U.S. economic outlook in 1989 [address, December 6, 1988] *Vital Speeches of the Day* 55:197-9 Ja 15 '89
PARSIMONY *See* Stinginess
PARSONAGE, CHRIS
about
A survivor of the Sheffield soccer disaster struggles to live with the memory. D. Grogan. il por *People Weekly* 31:69-70 My 8 '89
PARSONS, JAN
about
Rob Lowe's girl trouble. M. Sager. il por *Rolling Stone* p92-3+ Ag 24 '89
A video romp in the buff gives heartbreaker Rob Lowe a little too much southern exposure. S. Dougherty. il pors *People Weekly* 31:79-80 Je 5 '89
PARSONS, RICHARD D.
about
Turning on a Dime [interview] K. D. Thompson. il pors *Black Enterprise* 19:144-6+ F '89
PARSONS, TALCOTT, 1902-1979
about
Bringing Nazi sympathizers to the U.S. [cover story] J. Wiener. *The Nation* 248:289+ Mr 6 '89
PART TIME EMPLOYMENT
See also
Job sharing
Supplementary employment
Dear Betty Harragan. B. L. Harragan. il *Working Woman* 14:31+ D '89
Does part-time pay off? S. McHenry and L. L. Small. il *Ms.* 17:88-94 Mr '89
Mommy tracks that lead somewhere good [women lawyers] L. Dusky. il *Working Woman* 14:132-4 N '89
PARTEE, CECIL A.
about
Cecil A. Partee becomes Cook County state's atty.: first black to hold post. por *Jet* 76:14-15 My 8 '89
PARTEMI (PORTO ERCOLE, ITALY: HISTORIC HOUSE)
See Porto Ercole (Italy)—Historic houses, sites, etc.
PARTHENON (ATHENS, GREECE)
See also
Elgin marbles
PARTHENOPOULOS, DIMITRI A., AND RENTZEPIS, PETER M., 1934-
Three-dimensional optical storage memory. bibl f il *Science* 245:843-5 Ag 25 '89
PARTI QUÉBÉCOIS
An independent voice [J. Parizeau] B. Wallace. il por *Maclean's* 102:21-2 O 23 '89
Separate futures [interview with Jacques Parizeau] il *Maclean's* 102:24 S 25 '89
PARTICIPATIVE MANAGEMENT
See also
Employee ownership
Team work in industry
Advice to bosses: try a little kindness [views of M. De Pree] J. Greenwald. il por *Time* 134:56 S 11 '89
Business sure would like to retire this bill [worker participation in pension management] S. B. Garland. il *Business Week* p204 S 25 '89
Competing by cooperating [address, May 9, 1989] A. H. Magazine. *Vital Speeches of the Day* 55:604-8 Jl 15 '89
Employee representation on U.S., German boards. E. M. Kassalow. bibl f *Monthly Labor Review* 112:39-42 S '89
Hot company, warm culture [Herman Miller Inc.] K. Labich. il *Fortune* 119:74-6+ F 27 '89
Want to boost productivity? Try giving workers a say. A. S. Blinder. il *Business Week* p10 Ap 17 '89
Worker dignity on the job [address, March 3, 1989] T. R. Donahue. *Vital Speeches of the Day* 55:423-6 My 1 '89
Germany (West)
Employee representation on U.S., German boards. E. M. Kassalow. bibl f *Monthly Labor Review* 112:39-42 S '89
PARTICLE ACCELERATORS *See* Accelerators (Electrons, etc.)
PARTICLE BEAM WEAPONS
Energy Dept. plans to cut spending on nuclear directed-energy weapons. T. M. Foley. *Aviation Week & Space Technology* 130:132-3 F 20 '89
Report says U.S. space power programs inadequate to meet long-term SDI goals [National Research Council report] il *Aviation Week & Space Technology* 130:47+ F 20 '89
Testing
Successful neutral particle beam firing paves way for more ambitious SDI test. il *Aviation Week & Space Technology* 131:31-2 Jl 24 '89

U.S. prepares for first test of neutral particle beam in space. T. M. Foley. il *Aviation Week & Space Technology* 130:56-8 My 15 '89
PARTICLE BEAMS
See also
Atomic beams
Electron beams
Ion bombardment
Neutron sources
PARTICLES
See also
Colloids
Dust
Granular materials
Light—Scattering
Micelles
The liquid state of solid gold particles [research by Laurence D. Marks] I. Peterson. il *Science News* 136:70 Jl 29 '89
PARTICLES (NUCLEAR PHYSICS)
See also
Antiprotons
Anyons
Charged massive particles
Cosmic rays
Cosmic strings
Electrons
Neutrinos
Neutrons
Polarization (Elementary particles)
Positrons
Protons
Scattering (Physics)
Supersymmetry (Physics)
Tachyons
Tunneling (Physics)
University of California, Berkeley. Center for Particle Astrophysics
Z particles
Ambidextrous universe [distinction blurred between fermions and bosons; work of Tom D. Imbo and others] T. Rothman. *Scientific American* 260:26 My '89
Armies of physicists struggle to discover proof of a Scot's brainchild [search for Higgs boson at CERN and Stanford] C. C. Mann. bibl (p191) il *Smithsonian* 19:106-10+ Mr '89
Building matter from a dozen blocks [evidence that there are only three types of fundamental particles] I. Peterson. *Science News* 136:260 O 21 '89
The case of cosmic rays [new Utah observatory to study muons from Cygnus X-3 and Hercules X-1; cover story] G. Taubes. il *Discover* 10:52-8+ S '89
Closing the circle [studying the universe through particle physics] S. L. Glashow. il *Discover* 10:66-70+ O '89
A colossal collision course [CERN's large electron-positron collider] M. D. Lemonick. il *Time* 134:72 Jl 17 '89
Elementary particle physics. bibl f *Physics Today* 42:S37-S40 Ja '89
Feynman and partons. J. D. Bjorken. bibl f il por *Physics Today* 42:56-9 F '89
The heliosphere as an astrophysical laboratory for particle acceleration. T. Terasawa and M. Scholer. bibl f il *Science* 244:1050-7 Je 2 '89
Interview: Leon Lederman. D. Teresi. pors *Omni (New York, N.Y.)* 12:98-100+ O '89
Laboratory limits on dark matter. il *Sky and Telescope* 77:131-2 F '89
The lost generation [evidence that there are no more than three generations of elementary particles] J. Kinoshita. *Scientific American* 261:22 D '89
Observations in particle physics from two neutrinos to the standard model [Nobel Prize lecture, December 8, 1988] L. M. Lederman. bibl f il *Science* 244:664-72 My 12 '89
Optimum chemical sites and techniques for searches for negatively charged rare particles. R. N. Boyd and others. bibl f il *Science* 244:1450-7 Je 23 '89
A quest to fill in the cosmic puzzle [researchers at Stanford determine that the universe has only three types of matter] il *U.S. News & World Report* 107:17 O 23 '89
The search for truth [top quark] J. S. Trefil. il *Discover* 10:56-61 D '89
Searching for strange matter [study of quarks] I. Peterson. il *Science News* 135:138-9 Mr 4 '89
Strange matter [quarks; cover story] S. Vogel. il *Discover* 10:62-7 N '89
A trinity of families [evidence of only three types of fundamental particles] P. Elmer-Dewitt. il *Time* 134:116 O 23 '89
Accelerators
See Accelerators (Electrons, etc.)
Measurement
High-precision tests in particle physics. I. Peterson. *Science News* 135:38 Ja 21 '89
PARTICULATE EMISSION STANDARDS *See* Automobiles—Environmental aspects
PARTIDO ACCIÓN NACIONAL (MEXICO)
Democracy wins a round [P. R. I. concedes gubernatorial race in Baja California Norte] G. D. Garcia. il *Time* 134:67 Jl 17 '89

PARTIDO ACCIÓN NACIONAL (MEXICO)—cont.
Mexico: true concessions [PRI loses to PAN in Baja] S. McGuire. il *Newsweek* 114:36 Jl 17 '89
PARTIES *See* Balls (Parties); Entertaining
PARTIES, BIRTHDAY *See* Birthday parties
PARTIES, CHILDREN'S *See* Children's parties
PARTIES, CHRISTMAS *See* Christmas entertaining
PARTIES, HALLOWEEN *See* Halloween parties
PARTIES, POLITICAL *See* Political parties
PARTITIONS
    See also
      Room dividers
PARTNERSHIP
    See also
      Commodity partnership
      Joint ventures
      Limited partnership
      Master limited partnership
Creative chemistry. A. Tapert. il *Working Woman* 14:106-8+ Mr '89
Entrepreneurial couples [views of Frank and Sharan Barnett] il *The Futurist* 23:50 My/Je '89
How entrepreneurial couples work together. F. Barnett and S. Barnett. il pors *Working Woman* 14:77-80 Ap '89
Partners in entrepreneurship [married couples; research by Frank and Sharan Barnett] S. Nelton. il *Nation's Business* 77:38-9 Mr '89
Wedded to their work [entreprenurial couples; views of Frank and Sharan Barnett] S. Brewer. il *New Choices for the Best Years* 29:13 Jl '89
PARTNERSHIP FOR IMPROVED AIR TRAVEL
Aviation economic impact study begins campaign for more airport capacity. J. Ott. il *Aviation Week & Space Technology* 131:68 Jl 3 '89
Industry alliance will expand efforts to boost capacity. *Aviation Week & Space Technology* 130:67 Ja 23 '89
PARTON, DOLLY
    about
Dolly Parton: feeling good again. L. Gross. por *McCall's* 116:87-8+ S '89
Dolly Parton: here I come again [cover story] H. Gleason. il pors *The Saturday Evening Post* 261:46-9 O '89
The quotable Dolly. K. Jaehne. il pors *Film Comment* 25:62-3 S/O '89
Straight from the heart [cover story] S. Dworkin. pors *Redbook* 174:20+ D '89
PARTONS *See* Particles (Nuclear physics)
PARTRIDGE, DIXIE
Watermark: the reservoir [poem] *Commonweal* 116:118 F 24 '89
PARTRIDGE, JONATHAN
Electric brain waves: acid test. il *Omni (New York, N.Y.)* 12:34+ D '89
PARTRIDGE SHOOTING
Space and time. D. C. Proper. il *Field & Stream* 94:46-7+ O '89
PARTURITION *See* Childbirth
PARTY DINNERS *See* Dinners and dining
PARTY LINES (TELEPHONE)
Dialing for dollies. R. Mead. il *New York* 22:38 N 13 '89
PARZYCH, MARILYN
Two years and 216 pounds lighter; ed. by Cathy Perlmutter. il pors *Prevention (Emmaus, Pa.)* 41:74+ Ja '89
PAS *See* Publishers Association of the South
PAS, INC.
House of the specialty. C. Csere. il por *Car and Driver* 34:109 Je '89
PASADENA (CALIF.)
    Historic houses, sites, etc.
The California bungalow. il *Esquire* 112:132 S '89
PASAYTEN WILDERNESS (WASH.)
The sights and smells of the mountains come vividly alive for the Deaf-Blind Trailblazers [horseback trip] H. Shapiro. il *People Weekly* 32:99+ O 23 '89
PASCAL (COMPUTER LANGUAGE)
Clash of the object-oriented Pascals [Quick Pascal and Turbo Pascal 5.5] J. Udell. il *Byte* 14:104-6 Jl '89
Pascal on the Mac [Just Enough Pascal tutorial] A. F. Lent and L. H. Loeb. *Byte* 14 Mac Special Ed:MAC5-MAC6 Mr '89
Turbo Pascal windowing system. C. J. Butler. il *Byte* 14:283-6+ F '89
Unix filenames for Turbo Pascal. J. Kerr. il *Byte* 14 Special Issue:185-6+ Fall '89
PASCUALETE (EXTREMADURA, SPAIN: HISTORIC HOUSE) *See* Historic houses, sites, etc.—Spain
PASDAR, ADRIAN
    about
Adrian Pasdar: a cookie with a bite. L. Morice. il por *Mademoiselle* 95:102+ Mr '89
PASQUERILLA, FRANK JAMES, 1926-
    about
Look who wants to try Bloomie's on for size. M. Schroeder. il por *Business Week* p30 O 2 '89
PASQUIER, SYLVAINE
Creative progress in Taiwan. *World Press Review* 36:86 O '89

PASSALACQUA, CONNIE
The hottest love stories on daytime soaps [cover story] il *TV Guide* 37:2-5 Je 24-30 '89
PASSE MURAILLE (THEATER COMPANY) *See* Theatre Passe Muraille (Theater company)
PASSELL, PETER
Economics: reading your way out of chaos. il *The New York Times Book Review* 94:1+ O 29 '89
PASSENGER FARES, AIRLINE *See* Airlines—Fares
PASSENGER PIGEONS
In memory of Martha and her kind. D. S. Wilcove. il *Audubon* 91:52-5 S '89
PASSENGER SERVICE ON AIRLINES *See* Airlines—Passenger service
PASSENGER TRAINS *See* Railroads—Trains
PASSENGERS, AIRLINE *See* Air travel
PASSING (FOOTBALL)
Ye shall pass [pro football] A. Barra. il *Sport (New York, N.Y.)* 80:58-60+ S '89
PASSION AND PARADISE [television program] See Television program reviews—Single works
PASSION MUSIC
    See also
      Compact discs—Passion music
PASSION OF CHRIST *See* Jesus Christ—Passion
THE PASSION OF NARCISSE MONDOUX [drama] See Gélinas, Gratien
PASSIVE-AGGRESSIVE PERSONALITY
The passive-aggressive male. L. Grunwald. il *Esquire* 111:105-8+ Ap '89
PASSIVE SAFETY RESTRAINTS *See* Automobiles—Safety devices and measures
PASSIVE SMOKING
Cigarettes: the low-tar irony [research by Orestes T. Chortyk] *Science News* 136:398 D 16 '89
More cervical cancer in passive smokers [research by Martha L. Slattery] K. Fackelmann. *Science News* 135:166 Mr 18 '89
PASSMORE, GEORGE
    See also
      Gilbert and George
PASSOVER
    See also
      Seder
Spring holiday helper. P. Schiller. il *McCall's* 116:37+ Mr '89
PASSOVER COOKING *See* Cooking, Jewish
PASSPORTS
If the camera never lies, then passport photos always tell the truth. Here, the real identities of the rich and famous. G. Doppelt. il *Vogue* 179:447 N '89
McMurtry and others decry continuing use of McCarran Act. H. Fields. *Publishers Weekly* 235:15 My 26 '89
Nonimmigrant visa waiver pilot program with Japan [State Dept. announcement, October 19, 1988] *Department of State Bulletin* 88:23 D '88
The Palestinians [U.S. refusal of visa to Y. Arafat] il *World Press Review* 36:8+ Ja '89
The paper chase: passports made easy. H. Gieseking. il *Travel Holiday* 172:8-10+ O '89
Secretary's interview on "This week with David Brinkley" [denial of visa to Y. Arafat; interview with G. P. Shultz; transcript of program, December 4, 1988] *Department of State Bulletin* 89:7-9 F '89
U.S. denies visa to PLO leader Arafat [State Dept. statement, November 26, 1988] *Department of State Bulletin* 89:53 F '89
U.S. restricts entry of Nicaraguan officials, employees [proclamation, October 22, 1988] R. Reagan. *Department of State Bulletin* 89:47 Ja '89
What Chinese students want to know about visas. *Physics Today* 42 pt1:40 Ag '89
    France
Waiting [visa line outside French consulate in New York City] *The New Yorker* 65:28-9 Je 19 '89
    Japan
Nonimmigrant visa waiver pilot program with Japan [State Dept. announcement, October 19, 1988] *Department of State Bulletin* 88:23 D '88
    Soviet Union
Soviet travel: cutting the red tape. H. Gieseking. il *Travel Holiday* 172:12-13 N '89
    United States
    See Passports
PAST
    See also
      Nostalgia
Reading life backwards. T. K. Jones. il *Christianity Today* 33:28-31 S 22 '89
Son of man [sic], will you judge? [judging by current standards] M. E. Marty. *The Christian Century* 106:1103 N 22 '89
PASTA
    See also
      Couscous
Name that pasta! il *Good Housekeeping* 208:154 Ap '89
Too pretty to eat? [ribbon pasta] il *Sunset (Central West edition)* 183:100-1 N '89

PASTA—*cont.*
Photographs and photography
Noodle doodles. O. Kasper. il *Life* 12:122-4 F '89
PASTA AND DREAMS (NEW YORK, N.Y.: RESTAURANT)
See New York (N.Y.)—Restaurants, nightclubs, bars, etc.
PASTA COOKING *See* Cooking—Pasta
PASTA LOVERS TRATTORIAS
Full plate. F. Meeks. il por *Forbes* 144:286-7 N 27 '89
PASTA SALADS *See* Salads
PASTA SAUCES *See* Sauces
PASTAN, LINDA, 1932-
Crocuses [poem] *The Atlantic* 263:66 My '89
PASTEL (BEVERLY HILLS, CALIF.: RESTAURANT) *See*
Beverly Hills (Calif.)—Restaurants, nightclubs, bars, etc.
PASTEL DRAWING
See also
Oil Pastel Association
Americo DiFranza. E. Agar. il por *American Artist* 53:48-53
Ag '89
Depicting urban landscapes with pastels [Brooklyn, N.Y.]
M. Wickes. il por *American Artist* 53:60-3 Mr '89
A directory of pastel societies. M. E. Stegmaier. il *American
Artist* 53:30-5 Jl '89
Expressing the figure in pastel [work of R. Yanow] M. C.
Nelson. il *American Artist* 53:60-3 F '89
One artist's experience. U. C. Tarbet. il por *American Artist*
53:36-7 Jl '89
Stirring the viewer's imagination [paintings by D. O'Hagan]
M. S. Doherty. il *American Artist* 53:54-9 D '89
Technical page. C. T. Chieffo. *American Artist* 53:26+ My
'89
Exhibitions
American pastels [American pastels in the Metropolitan
Museum of Art: 1880-1930] A. E. Ledes. il *Antiques*
136:650+ O '89
PASTEL PAINTING *See* Pastel drawing
PASTERNAK, BORIS LEONIDOVICH, 1890-1960
about
Doctor Zhivago; tr. by Barry J. Rubin. D. S. Likhachev.
il *The New Republic* 200:30+ F 20 '89
PASTEUR INSTITUTE (PARIS, FRANCE) *See* Institut
Pasteur (Paris, France)
PASTORAL PEOPLES *See* Nomads
PASTORELLI, ROBERT
about
Murphy Brown's Michelangelo, Robert Pastorelli, paints him-
self into a comic corner. T. Allis. il pors *People Weekly*
31:94-5 Je 26 '89
PASTRICK, ROBERT A.
about
The last city machine in America. P. Glastris. il por *U.S.
News & World Report* 107:29-30 Ag 21 '89
PASTRY
See also
Petits fours
Pie
Tarts
Breads and pastries from our ancestors. D. A. Campbell.
il *Southern Living* 24:192-4 N '89
Fancy phyllo cups. il *Good Housekeeping* 208:54 My '89
Profiterole glacée. il *Good Housekeeping* 208:38 Ja '89
Vegetable strudel. il *Good Housekeeping* 208:88 Mr '89
PASTURES
See also
Grazing
Livestock ranges
PAT METHENY GROUP
Pat Metheny: the interview from home [cover story; interview]
J. Roberts. il pors *Down Beat* 56:16-19 Ag '89
THE PAT SAJAK SHOW [television program] *See* Television
program reviews—Single works
PATAGONIA INC.
The man is the message [Y. Chouinard] F. Meeks. il por
Forbes 143:148+ Ap 17 '89
PATCHING MATERIALS
How to repair holes in drywall. R. Capotosto. il *Popular
Mechanics* 166:97-8 Jl '89
PÂTÉ
Pâté animal. B. Shacochis. il *Gentlemen's Quarterly* 59:323-4
N '89
PATEK PHILIPPE (FIRM)
150 years of the watchmaker's art. C. Aillaud. il *Architectural
Digest* 46:54+ Ap '89
High-tick [Calibre '89] B. Weber. il *The New York Times
Magazine* p74 Ja 15 '89
La mystique Philippe. J. Marcom, Jr. il *Forbes* 143:46+
Ap 17 '89
PATENT DEPOSITORY LIBRARY PROGRAM
Microfilm thieves hit university libraries. J. Palca. *Science*
245:248 Jl 21 '89
PATENT ENFORCEMENT INSURANCE *See* Insurance, Pa-
tent enforcement
PATENT INFRINGEMENT
Proactive patent protection. F. H. Colen. il *High Technology
Business* 9:14 S/O '89

PATENT LAWYERS *See* Lawyers
PATENT LIBRARIES
See also
Patent Depository Library Program
PATENTS
See also
Computer programming—Patents
Cookies—Patents
DESQview (Computer program)—Patents
Drugs—Patents
Electric batteries—Patents
Erythropoietin—Patents
Fiber optic television—Patents
Genetic research—Patents
Spreadsheets (Computer programs)—Patents
Superconductors and superconductivity—Patents
Telescopes—Patents
Videotape recorders and recording—Patents
The growth of Japanese science and technology [rising share
of U.S. patents] F. Narin and J. D. Frame. bibl f il
Science 245:600-5 Ag 11 '89
How to protect your bright idea. D. Moreau. il *Changing
Times* 43:63-4+ Ag '89
Laws and regulations
Bars to obtaining patents. N. E. Carte. il *High Technology
Business* 9:16 Ap '89
Cold fusion and property rights. E. Rubenstein. il *National
Review* 41:14 Je 16 '89
Revenge of the nerds: patent lawyers grab the spotlight.
P. Dwyer. il *Business Week* p82 My 22 '89
Western Europe
See also
European Patent Office
PATERNITY
Blood test results validate claim of paternity against Detroit
mayor Coleman Young. il por *Jet* 76:6 My 29 '89
Court papers say Bond denies fathering baby [J. Bond] por
Jet 77:55 N 27 '89
Detroit mayor Coleman Young admits fathering of boy,
6. il por *Jet* 76:7 Je 5 '89
Detroit mayor Young hit with paternity suit by a former
city employee. por *Jet* 75:51 F 13 '89
DNA test says Ali isn't father of Houston girl [B. Mensah's
suit] il pors *Jet* 75:52 F 20 '89
Every parent's nightmare: a hospital nursery swap throws
two Florida families into disarray [A. Twigg and K. Mays
switched at birth in Hardee Memorial Hospital in
Wauchula] M. Green. il pors *People Weekly* 32:77-8+ D
11 '89
Giving birth to a scandal [A. Calvert investigated by police
after winning paternity suit against Detroit mayor C. Young]
por *Time* 133:23 Je 26 '89
"I'll always believe she's my daughter" [U.S. government
wants blood test to prove paternity of Tuyet Mai]; ed.
by Laura Huntoon. B. Huntoon. il pors *Redbook* 174:79-80+
D '89
Mom of Detroit mayor's son wants FBI probe of police
[A. Calvert vs. C. Young] por *Jet* 76:8 Jl 10 '89
Photos, baptism of child revealed in Detroit mayor Young's
paternity case. il por *Jet* 75:36-7 Mr 13 '89
Piston's Rodman hit with paternity, palimony suits. il pors
Jet 76:52 Jl 3 '89
Richard Pryor hit with paternity suit. il por *Jet* 75:55 Ja
16 '89
Whose little girl is Kimberly? [A. Twigg and K. Mays switched
at birth in Hardee Memorial Hospital, Wauchula, Fla.]
M. Jacobbi. il pors *Good Housekeeping* 208:122-3+ Mr
'89
PATERNITY LEAVES
Paternity leave as church praxis [experience of United
Methodist Church minister] B. Schofield-Bodt. il *The
Christian Century* 106:463-4 My 3 '89
Why men don't take paternity leaves. A. Curran. *Health
(New York, N.Y.)* 21:49+ Ja '89
PATERNO, JOE
The man who said no to $1 million [condensed from Paterno];
ed. by Bernard Asbell. il por *Reader's Digest* 135:19-22+
D '89
PATERNO, SUSAN
Immigrant workers fight for wages. il *The Progressive* 53:13-14
Je '89
PATERSON, KATHY
To hug or not to hug. *The Education Digest* 54:58-60 Mr
'89
PATERSON (N.J.)
Education
The blackboard jungle revisited. G. Morris. *National Review*
41:18-19 My 5 '89
Eastside story [views of principal J. Clark] Y. Kramer and
R. Kramer. il *The American Spectator* 22:21-4 Ag '89
His pupils want someone to lean on, but Joe Clark may
simply want out [considering resignation after reaction
to striptease show at Eastside High] D. Van Biema and
G. Moses. il pors *People Weekly* 31:51-3 Mr 27 '89
The make-believe world of "Lean on me" [methods of
principal J. Clark] I. A. Hyman. *The Education Digest*
55:20-2 N '89

PATERSON (N.J.)—Education—*cont.*

Morgan Freeman stars as tough principal Joe Clark in hit movie, 'Lean on me' [cover story] T. S. Moore. il pors *Jet* 75:24-6 Mr 6 '89

Principal Joe Clark leaving school for lecture circuit. por *Jet* 76:22 Jl 31 '89

PATERSON (WILLIAM) COLLEGE OF NEW JERSEY *See* William Paterson College of New Jersey

PATHE COMMUNICATIONS CORP.

Puzzle in Movieland: the case of the mystery moguls [G. Parretti and F. Fiorini] J. Rossant. il pors *Business Week* p80-1+ Mr 13 '89

PATHOLOGY

See also
Forensic pathology
Paleopathology

PATHS *See* Walks (Paths)

PATIENCE

How to be a patient person. J. Coudert. il *Reader's Digest* 135:45-6+ N '89

Patience. T. Leeson. il *Field & Stream* 93:26+ Mr '89

PATIENT REPRESENTATIVES *See* Nursing home patient representatives

PATIENTS *See* Hospital patients

PATIENTS AND PHYSICIANS *See* Physicians and patients

PATIENTS AND PSYCHOTHERAPISTS *See* Psychotherapists and patients

PATIENTS' RECORDS *See* Medical records

PATIENTS' RIGHTS *See* Cancer patients—Civil rights; Hospital patients—Civil rights; Sick—Civil rights

PATINA (LOS ANGELES, CALIF.: RESTAURANT) *See* Los Angeles (Calif.)—Restaurants, nightclubs, bars, etc.

PATINKIN, MANDY, 1953?-

about

Actor Mandy Patinkin battles his perfectionist tendencies—with a solo album of scorching heat. J. Stark. il pors *People Weekly* 31:145-6+ My 8 '89

The hollow croon. J. Simon. por *New York* 22:77-8 Ag 14 '89

Moonlight serenade. C. McGuigan. il por *Newsweek* 113:67-8 F 20 '89

Oh Mandy. D. Okrent. il por *Esquire* 111:40 Ap '89

Two new sides where Sondheim shines. R. Hoffman. il por *Business Week* p120 Mr 27 '89

PATIÑO, BEATRIZ

about

A Victorian Paris: Beatriz Patiño's Plaine Monceau pied-à-terre. C. Aillaud. il *Architectural Digest* 46:100-7 Ja '89

PATIOS *See* Decks, patios, terraces, etc.

PATKIN, IZHAR

about

Izhar Patkin at Holly Solomon. N. Princenthal. il *Art in America* 77:169-70 D '89

PATLAK, MARGIE

The puzzling picture of multiple sclerosis. il *FDA Consumer* 23:17-21 Jl/Ag '89

PATRELLE, FRANCIS

about

Dance. T. Tobias. il *New York* 22:145 Ap 24 '89

PATRICK, BRENNAN

My girlfriend dreams about other men. il por *Glamour* 87:230 D '89

PATRICK, BUTCH

about

Once a little Munster, Butch Patrick grew up to battle scarier demons. T. Allis. il pors *People Weekly* 32:85-6 Jl 10 '89

PATRICK, DAVID

about

A pair of aces. M. Noden. il pors *Sports Illustrated* 71:64-6+ O 16 '89

World-class speed, family style. il pors *Ebony* 45:116+ D '89

PATRICK, DICK

about

The write stuff. B. Wischnia. il pors *Runner's World* 24:34-5+ Mr '89

PATRICK, JANE GASSNER

Don't let these sex myths ruin your marriage. *Reader's Digest* 135:211-12 N '89

PATRICK, JUDY

Successful family farm. il *Successful Farming* 87:54-6 N '89

PATRICK, MARIE

about

How to manage a grand project. A. M. Russell. il pors *Working Woman* 14:73-7 D '89

PATRICK, MICHELLE

Packing for trouble. il *Essence* 20:19-21 Je '89

PATRICK, SANDRA FARMER- *See* Farmer-Patrick, Sandra

PATRICK, UEAL EUGENE

about

A fresh start. J. Cook. por *Forbes* 144:148 N 27 '89

PATRICK COLLECTION (BIRMINGHAM, ENGLAND)

The Patrick Collection. P. Bingham. il *Motor Trend* 41:112-15+ F '89

PATRICK PETROLEUM CO.

A fresh start. J. Cook. por *Forbes* 144:148 N 27 '89

PATRIOTISM

Bertrand Du Guesclin—careerist in arms? [Hundred Years War] K. Fowler. bibl il pors *History Today* 39:37-43 Je '89

My country, right or wrong? [results of poll] I. Groller. il *Parents* 64:28 Jl '89

The new historians recapture the flag. M. Kazin. il *The New York Times Book Review* 94:1+ Jl 2 '89

Reagan and historical memory [final televised remarks] *National Review* 41:11+ F 10 '89

Two cheers for patriotism. J. Buell. il *Utne Reader* p96-7 S/O '89

PATROL AIRPLANES *See* Airplanes in patrol work

PATROL AIRPLANES, MILITARY *See* Airplanes, Military

PATROL CARS *See* Automobiles, Police

PATTEE, DAILEY

about

Continental calm on high. Suzy. il por *Architectural Digest* 46:220-7+ N '89

PATTEE, GORDON

about

Continental calm on high. Suzy. il por *Architectural Digest* 46:220-7+ N '89

PATTEN, PATRICIA

Healthy nails for a polished look. il *Women's Sports & Fitness* 11:22 Je '89

Stubble, stubble, toil and trouble. il *Women's Sports & Fitness* 11:60 Jl/Ag '89

PATTERN (BIOLOGY)

Inferring process from pattern in natural communities. W. G. Cale and others. bibl f il *BioScience* 39:600-5 O '89

PATTERN BOOKS

Exhibitions

Pattern books [Furniture in print: pattern books from the Redwood Library at the Rhode Island School of Design] A. E. Ledes. il *Antiques* 136:662+ O '89

PATTERN STAMPING (CONCRETE WORK) *See* Concrete work

PATTERSON, CASEY

Bicycle buyer's bible. il *Women's Sports & Fitness* 11:46-8+ Ap '89

More power to you with interval training. il por *Women's Sports & Fitness* 11:18-19 S '89

PATTERSON, CHANDRA

Why not? *Essence* 20:83-4+ S '89

PATTERSON, CLAYTON, 1948-

about

The discreet charm of the ball cap. R. Merkin. il *Gentlemen's Quarterly* 59:143+ O '89

How to shoot a riot. E. Shawn. il *Video* 13:50+ Ap '89

PATTERSON, FREDERICK D.

about

Frederick D. Patterson, founder of UNCF leaves entire estate to widow. il por *Jet* 76:5 Ag 14 '89

PATTERSON, FREEMAN, 1937-

Re:vision. See occasional issues of Petersen's Photographic Magazine beginning March 1987

PATTERSON, JAMES

about

Madison Avenue's mystery guy. S. J. Madden. il por *Fortune* 119:192 Ja 30 '89

PATTERSON, JOHN HENRY, 1844-1922

about

John Patterson rang up success with the Incorruptible Cashier. M. Bernstein. bibl f (p174) il por *Smithsonian* 20:150-2+ Je '89

PATTERSON, RODNEY S.

about

Vermont: 'whitest state in America' gets first black church. C. Waldron. il pors *Jet* 75:14-15+ Mr 13 '89

PATTERSON, TRACY

about

Patterson's son captures first pro boxing title. il por *Jet* 76:50 My 8 '89

PATTERSON, WILLIAM

about

The medium is not the message. E. Agar. il pors *American Artist* 53:44-9+ O '89

PATTI, SANDI

about

Supermom Sandi Patti [cover story] H. G. Miller. il pors *The Saturday Evening Post* 261:44-5+ Ja/F '89

PATTISON, JAMES A.

about

A raider from the north blows into the Windy City. B. Bremner. il por *Business Week* p34-5 Ja 16 '89

PATTISON, JIM *See* Pattison, James A.

PATTISON (JIM) GROUP *See* Jim Pattison Group

PATTON, CHRIS

about

High, wide and handsome. J. Garrity. il por *Sports Illustrated* 71:169 S 4 '89

PATTON, GEORGE S. (GEORGE SMITH), 1885-1945

about

Where Patton prepared for North Africa in southern California. il *Sunset (Central West edition)* 182:63 F '89

PATTON, PHIL
'Arader is up again!' and his galleries are in full bloom.
il pors *Smithsonian* 20:86-92+ D '89
Jeans in the genes. il por *New York* 22:40-4+ My 22 '89
Living quarters. See issues of Esquire
Steve Jobs: out for revenge. il por *The New York Times Magazine* p22-3+ Ag 6 '89
PAU DAU (NEEDLEWORK) *See* Needlework
PAUL, DAVID L., 1939-
about
CenTrust's offbeat plan to be a plain old thrift. G. DeGeorge. il por *Business Week* p36 S 18 '89
Even for a go-go banker, there are certain no-nos. G. De-George. il por *Business Week* p140-1 My 22 '89
A spendthrift thrift gets its ears boxed. G. DeGeorge. *Business Week* p46 D 25 '89-Ja 1 '90
PAUL, GREGORY S.
Giant meteor impacts and great eruptions: dinosaur killers? bibl f il *BioScience* 39:162-72 Mr '89
PAUL, JAMES R.
about
Working for Wyatt is the next best thing to throwing beanballs. M. Ivey. il por *Business Week* p137 N 6 '89
PAUL, PAULA
Childhood diseases aren't just kids' stuff. il *Current Health 2* 15:26-7 My '89
The scent of confidence. il *Current Health 2* 15:28-9 Mr '89
PAUL, SUDHIR, AND OTHERS
Catalytic hydrolysis of vasoactive intestinal peptide by human autoantibody. bibl f il *Science* 244:1158-62 Je 9 '89
PAUL, WOLFGANG
about
Basic measurements lead to Physics Nobel. R. Pool. il pors *Science* 246:327-8 O 20 '89
Physics. il pors *Time* 134:74 O 23 '89
Physics Nobel: traps, clocks, quantum leaps. E. Peterson. *Science News* 136:262 O 21 '89
Ramsey, Dehmelt, Paul win Nobel for helping to set high standards. B. G. Levi. il pors *Physics Today* 42:17-19 D '89
PAUL, EPISTLES OF *See* Bible. N.T. Epistles of Paul
PAUL E. GARBER PRESERVATION, RESTORATION AND STORAGE FACILITY
Silver Hill. P. Scott. il *Flying* 116:66-8+ N '89
PAUL TAYLOR DANCE COMPANY
Dancing:
Speaking in tongues and other works presented at City Center. A. Croce. *The New Yorker* 65:78-80 My 1 '89
Dogged dualists [performances at City Center] L. A. Jacobs. por *The New Leader* 72:22-3 Je 12-26 '89
Men and angels [performances at City Center] T. Tobias. il *New York* 22:81-2 My 8 '89
Paul Taylor: ominous and sprightly [1989 season at City Center] G. G. Seibert. *America* 160:430 My 6 '89
Paul Taylor, Santo Loquasto and Speaking in tongues: the right mix. N. V. Dalva. il *Dance Magazine* 63:36-8 Ap '89
Reviews:
Performances at City Center, New York City. G. Solomons. *Dance Magazine* 63:89-90 S '89
PAULA COOPER GALLERY
Quite contrary [cover story] J. Howell. il pors *Art News* 88:152-7 Mr '89
PAULEY, JANE
about
All about Deborah. E. Diamond. il pors *New York* 22:28+ O 23 '89
Exit Jane, amid turmoil. R. Zoglin. pors *Time* 134:81 O 23 '89
Goodbye Today, hello tomorrow [cover story] B. Darrach. il pors *Life* 12:46-8+ D '89
Newcomer Deborah Norville stirs the latest tempest in the Today show's coffee cup. J. Kaufman. il pors *People Weekly* 32:48-9 O 9 '89
Two was company, three a crowd [cover story] il pors *People Weekly* 32:114-16+ N 13 '89
PAULEY PETROLEUM INC.
Pauley hits more red ink than black gold. R. Grover. il por *Business Week* p81 S 11 '89
PAULIST PRESS
Paulist progress: the enterprising Catholic house has flourished in a religious climate that killed off a number of its competitors. W. Griffin. il *Publishers Weekly* 235:34-6 Mr 3 '89
PAULOS, JOHN ALLEN
The odds are you're innumerate. il *The New York Times Book Review* 94:1+ Ja 1 '89
about
Are you an innumerate? K. Bartlett. il por *The Saturday Evening Post* 261:36 S '89
Big numbers for innumeracy: Hill & Wang's first bestseller heralds a new direction. C. Goodrich. il por *Publishers Weekly* 235:46-8 Je 2 '89
An eminent math professor says "innumeracy" rivals illiteracy as a cause for concern in America [interview] D. Chu. il pors *People Weekly* 31:95-6+ My 29 '89

To conquer fear of counting. S. Kanfer. il *Time* 133:66 Ja 30 '89
PAULSEN, PHILIP K.
I was an atheist in a foxhole. *The Humanist* 49:28-30 S/O '89
PAULSON, ALLEN E.
about
"You got to look out for yourself". W. P. Barrett. il *Forbes* 143:43-4+ Ja 23 '89
PAULSON, JEANETTE
about
Interview with Jeannette Paulson. *American Film* 15:63 D '89
PAULSON, MORTON C.
Unclaimed cash: could some be yours? il *Reader's Digest* 134:37-8+ Mr '89
PAULSON INVESTMENT COMPANY
Brokers in the boondocks. M. Schifrin. il pors *Forbes* 143:228+ Je 26 '89
PAULU, NANCY
The superintendent's role in reform. *The Education Digest* 55:31-3 S '89
PAULUCCI, JENO F.
about
Full plate. F. Meeks. il por *Forbes* 144:286-7 N 27 '89
PAVE PAWS *See* Radar defense networks
PAVEMENTS
See also
Roads
Sidewalks
Brick at its easiest. il *Southern Living* 24:77 Ap '89
Concrete results. M. Chotiner. il *Home Mechanix* 85:52-4+ S '89
Soft pavers. il *Popular Science* 235:67-8 Ag '89
PAVILION OPERA
Britain's Pavilion Opera. E. Lambert. il por *Architectural Digest* 46:90-5+ Mr '89
PAVILIONS
A Parisian bijou: glittering prizes in a designer's Louis XVI pavilion [designed by Valerian Rybar and J. F. Daigre; cover story] Suzy. il *Architectural Digest* 46:204-11+ O '89
Return to splendor [Oriental Pavilion Prospect Park] S. Gutterman. il *Architectural Record* 177:110-13 Jl '89
A Russian folly: visiting Catherine the Great's baroque roller coaster near Leningrad. P. Lauritzen. il por *Architectural Digest* 46:146-9+ My '89
PAVLICH, WALTER
Flying to the fire with the doors off [poem] *Commonweal* 116:501 S 22 '89
The hand beginning to burn [poem] *Commonweal* 116:501 S 22 '89
Hardhat pillow [poem] *Commonweal* 116:501 S 22 '89
PAVLOV, VALENTIN
about
Yes . . . but [interview] P. Dragadze. il por *Forbes* 144:94 O 16 '89
PAVLOVIAN CONDITIONING *See* Conditioned responses
PAWLICK, THOMAS
House calls in the wild. il *International Wildlife* 19:12-17 Mr/Ap '89
PAWLIKOWSKI, JOHN T.
A sign of contradiction. il *Commonweal* 116:485-8 S 22 '89
PAWNBROKING
See also
Cash America Investments (Firm)
PAY DIFFERENTIALS *See* Wage differentials
PAY FOR PERFORMANCE *See* Merit pay
PAY-IN-KIND SECURITIES
'Payment-in-kind' paper: when it's good . . . S. Weiss. *Business Week* p100 Ap 17 '89
PAY-PER-VIEW CABLE TELEVISION *See* Cable television
PAY STUBS
What your pay stub tells you. il *Consumer Reports* 54:18 Ja '89
PAY TELEPHONES
See also
Alternative operator services
Calling from the road shouldn't be highway robbery. F. Seghers. il *Business Week* p40 Ap 3 '89
Pay phones pay off. A. A. Layne. il *High Technology Business* 9:24-7 N/D '89
PAY TELEVISION, CABLE *See* Cable television; Cable television, Black
PAYCHEX, INC.
Tom Golisano and the red tape factory. F. Meeks. il por *Forbes* 143:80+ My 15 '89
PAYER, LYNN
Hell week. il *Ms.* 17:28+ Mr '89
PAYLOAD SYSTEMS, INC.
First U.S. commercial cargo for Mir set to lift off Dec. 20 [protein crystal growth experiments] J. M. Lenorovitz. *Aviation Week & Space Technology* 131:34 D 11 '89
Payload's payload [protein crystal experiments on Mir space station] W. H. Ganoe. *Ad Astra* 1:38 Je '89

17:40-2

PAYLOAD SYSTEMS, INC.—*cont.*
U.S. firm's use of Mir faces probable delay [protein crystal experiment] *Aviation Week & Space Technology* 130:21 Ap 17 '89
PAYMENT OF ACCOUNTS
See also
Home banking services
Anecdotes, facetiae, satire, etc.
Check$ and balance$. K. Fury. il *New Choices for the Best Years* 29:96 Ap '89
PAYMENTS, BALANCE OF *See* Balance of payments
PAYNE, CARL
about
Katy duster. G. Baxter. il por *Flying* 116:138-9 Jl '89
PAYNE, CARLA
about
Katy duster. G. Baxter. il por *Flying* 116:138-9 Jl '89
PAYNE, DONALD M.
about
Donald Payne: New Jersey's first black congressman. D. M. Cheers. il pors *Ebony* 44:92+ My '89
PAYNE, GARY
A chemical war on water. *Sierra* 74:40-2 My/Je '89
PAYNE, GREGORY S., AND SCHEKMAN, RANDY
Clathrin: a role in the intracellular retention of a Golgi membrane protein. bibl f il *Science* 245:1358-65 S 22 '89
PAYNE, KATHARINE
Elephant talk [cover story] il maps *National Geographic* 176:264-77 Ag '89
PAYOLA
Payola probe back on track [R. Tashjian indicted] M. Goldberg. *Rolling Stone* p22 Je 15 '89
PAYOT, TURIA MAU
about
Life without a problem. K. Moore. il pors *Sports Illustrated* 70 Special Issue:83-5 F '89
PAYROLL DEDUCTIONS
See also
Savings bonds—Payroll deductions
PAYROLL WITHHOLDING TAXES *See* Withholding tax
PAYROLLS
See also
Paychex, Inc.
PAYSON, PARKER
Why your phone bills keep going up [cover story] il *Consumers' Research Magazine* 72:10-14 Je '89
PAYTON, ROBERT L.
On discovering philanthropy: an informal guide to the core literature. il *Change* 20:32-7 N/D '88
PAYTON, WALTER, 1954-
about
Payton seeks ownership of St. Louis NFL team. il por *Jet* 77:46 D 11 '89
PAZ, OCTAVIO, 1914-
Time's voice; tr. by Edith Grossman. *The New Republic* 201:90+ N 6 '89
PAZ DE ARAUJO, CARLOS A.
(jt. auth) See Scott, J. F., and Paz de Araujo, Carlos A.
PAZZIA (BEVERLY HILLS, CALIF.: RESTAURANT) *See* Beverly Hills (Calif.)—Restaurants, nightclubs, bars, etc.
PBS *See* Public Broadcasting Service
PC DOS OPERATING SYSTEM
DOS 4.0. P. Scisco. il *Compute!* 11:86-7 Ja '89
DOS Power Tools. P. Scisco. il *Compute!* 11:66-8 Ag '89
PC-DOS: pulling out the stops. F. Chen. il *Byte* 14:294-9 Je '89
PC-LINK (DATABASE)
PC-Link. D. Stanton. il *Compute!* 11:74+ Ap '89
PC-WRITE (WORD PROCESSOR PROGRAM) *See* Word processors and processing—Programming
PCBS *See* Polychlorinated biphenyls
PCL (COMPUTER LANGUAGE)
The language of lasers. K. Quirk. il *Byte* 14 Special Issue:203-6+ Fall '89
PCNA *See* Cyclin
PCP
Pathological changes induced in cerebrocortical neurons by phencyclidine and related drugs. J. W. Olney and others. bibl f il *Science* 244:1360-2 Je 16 '89
PC'S LTD.
See also
Dell Computer Corporation
PDGF *See* Platelet-derived growth factor
PEABODY, SUSAN G.
about
Trolling for prizes in 'the backwater of the fixed-income market'. L. Light. il por *Business Week* p133 D 25 '89-Ja 1 '90
PEACE
See also
International security
League of Nations
Pacifism
Religion and peace
United Nations
Credit where credit is due [global boom in peacemaking] S. Talbott. il *Time* 133:33 Ja 23 '89

Diplomacy in an election year and beyond [address, October 7, 1988] M. M. Kampelman. *Department of State Bulletin* 88:38-40 D '88
Peace breaks out around the world [cover story; special issue] il map *Scholastic Update (Teachers' edition)* 121:2-13 Mr 24 '89
Peace (I). L. Wright. il *Rolling Stone* p143-6+ Jl 13-27 '89
Peace (II). L. Wright. il *Rolling Stone* p54-5+ S 7 '89
Peace (III). L. Wright. il *Rolling Stone* p152-3+ N 16 '89
Slow progress. D. Schorr. *The New Leader* 72:3-4 Ja 9 '89
PEACE MOVEMENT
See also
1% for Peace (Program)
Anti-nuclear movement
Center for Nonviolent Alternatives
Children as the Peacemakers Foundation
Grandmothers for Peace (Organization)
Trade for Peace, Inc.
America's last peacenik [interview with W. S. Coffin] F. Ungeheuer. il por *Time* 133:76-7 Je 5 '89
Doves' golden silence [reticence of peace movement in failed nomination of J. Tower as Defense Secretary] J. D. Isaacs. *The Bulletin of the Atomic Scientists* 45:4 Je '89
Marines hit the beaches in Minnesota [recruitment drive meets with antiwar protest] M. Helmberger. il *The Progressive* 53:17 O '89
Peace crusade [peace recruiters visit high schools to provide alternative to military recruiters] S. Tifft. il *Time* 133:68 F 27 '89
Peace (III). L. Wright. il *Rolling Stone* p152-3+ N 16 '89
War and peace in the White Mountains [Army's Firestorm '88 guerrilla exercises in N.H.] A. Alpert. il *The Progressive* 53:13-14 Mr '89
What next for the peace movement? [cover story; special section] il *The Progressive* 53:14-22 Ja '89
History
See also
Vietnamese War, 1957-1975—Protest movements
Eastern Europe
Independent activists challenge the status quo across Eastern Europe. B. Morton and J. Landy. il *Utne Reader* p81-3+ Ja/F '89
Germany (East)
Fighting Honecker's stagnation. D. R. Shanor. il *The New Leader* 72:8-9 Mr 20 '89
Israel
See also
Oz veShalom (Organization)
Yesh G'vul (Organization)
The walls are crumbling down [peace demonstration in the Negev against Israeli occupation of West Bank] D. Hurwitz. *The Progressive* 53:12 Je '89
Switzerland
See also
Group for Switzerland Without an Army
Ukraine
Ukrainian odyssey [American-Soviet International Peace Walk] V. B. Browback. il map *Modern Maturity* 32:58-9+ Ag/S '89
Western Europe
Where the peace movement goes when it disappears. P. P. Everts. bibl f il *The Bulletin of the Atomic Scientists* 45:26-30 N '89
PEACE STUDIES
Conflict over peace education. M. Spencer. il *Scholastic Update (Teachers' edition)* 121:10-11 Mr 24 '89
The politics of cold blood. R. J. Rummel. bibl *Society* 27:32-40 N/D '89
PEACEABLE KINGDOM [television program] See Television program reviews—Single works
PEACEKEEPER (MISSILE) *See* Guided missiles
PEACEMAKING BEHAVIOR OF ANIMALS *See* Animals—Habits and behavior
PEACH DESSERTS *See* Desserts
PEACH TREES
Peach tree planting and care. il *Organic Gardening* 36:43 Mr '89
PEACHES
Peach heaven [cover story] W. B. Logan. il *Organic Gardening* 36:40-5 Mr '89
PEACOCK, CLIFFTON, 1953-
about
Clifton Peacock: Germans van Eck. L. Holst. il *Art News* 88:167-8 My '89
PEACOCKS
Living with your neighbors' fowl habits. W. Maus. *Flower and Garden* 33:64+ Mr/Ap '89
PEALE, MARTHA
Beating the drum for caribou. il *Sierra* 74:32+ My/Je '89
PEALE, NORMAN VINCENT
A different breed of hero. il *Good Housekeeping* 209:66 Jl '89
Who says it's too late? *Reader's Digest* 134:23-4 My '89
PEANUT BUTTER
A most favored food. A. M. Geffen and C. Berglie. il *Americana* 17:40-2 My/Je '89

PEANUT OIL
  Breast implants: a safer method. *Newsweek* 114:52 S 25 '89
PEANUTS (COMIC STRIP)
  Charles Schulz. D. Waggoner and R. Wolmuth. il pors *People Weekly* 32:81-2+ O 30 '89
  He's a howling success at bringing comics to life [B. Melendez] M. Barrier. il por *Nation's Business* 77:16+ O '89
PEAR DESSERTS *See* Desserts
PEAR TARTS *See* Tarts
PEAR TREES
  Bradford callery pear. S. D. Garber. il *Focus (New York, N.Y.: 1950)* 39:33-6 Fall '89
  Pear trees [street plantings of callery pears] *The New Yorker* 65:31-2 Ap 17 '89
PEARCE, JOHN ED
  In praise of sidewalks. il *Reader's Digest* 134:100-1 My '89
PEARCE, NICK
  A Rubens crucifixion on a Chinese export porcelain dish. bibl f il *Antiques* 136:844-7 O '89
PEARCE, SIMON
          about
  Pleasures of the table: Simon Pearce. Z. E. Zakroff. il por *Gourmet* 49:56-61+ Ag '89
PEARL HARBOR (HAWAII), ATTACK ON, 1941
  Yesterday, December 7, 1941 [with editorial comment by Byron Dobell] R. M. Ketchum. il *American Heritage* 40:5, 52-6+ N '89
PEARLMAN, BARBARA
  Are you a sloucher? [excerpt from Workouts that work for women who work] il *Redbook* 172:18 Mr '89
          about
  Personal best [interview] C. Moekle. il *American Health* 8:32 O '89
PEARLMAN, JERRY KENT
          about
  Making software work the way he does. C. O'Malley. il por *Personal Computing* 13:77 Ap '89
  Why Jerry Pearlman gave up his brainchild. L. Therrien. il por *Business Week* p35 O 16 '89
  Zenith's Jerry Pearlman sure is persistent. L. Therrien. il por *Business Week* p67+ O 2 '89
  Zenith's TV picture is getting brighter—for now. L. Therrien. il *Business Week* p41 F 27 '89
PEARLMAN, JILL
  Isn't it romantic? il *Harper's Bazaar* 122:189+ N '89
  Mistress of fright. il por *Harper's Bazaar* 122:52+ F '89
PEARLS
  Pearl crazy. R. Urquhart. il *Vogue* 179:398-401 Ap '89
PEARS
          See also
       Cooking—Fruit
       Pear trees
PEARSON, BRUCE
          about
  Heads you lose, tails you lose even more. R. L. Stern. *Forbes* 144:90-1 O 2 '89
PEARSON, HUGH
  No Jim Crow. por *Essence* 20:8 D '89
PEARSON, JEAN
  In the glades [poem] *Organic Gardening* 36:64 Ap '89
PEARSON, JUDITH
  Myths of choice: the governor's new clothes? *Phi Delta Kappan* 70:821-3 Je '89
  A response to Joe Nathan. il *Phi Delta Kappan* 71:308-10 D '89
PEARSON, SUSIE
  Diana's double life [cover story] il pors *Ladies' Home Journal* 106:115-17+ Ag '89
  The Fergie follies [cover story] il pors *Ladies' Home Journal* 106:180-1+ My '89
PEARSON, SYBILLE
          about
  Phantasie [drama] Reviews
       New York 22:56-7 Ja 23 '89. J. Simon
PEARSON-DAVIS, SUSAN
  Drama in the curriculum for troubled young people: is it worth the fight? bibl f *Design for Arts in Education* 90:25-32 N/D '88
PEARSON PLC
  Pearson half-year results show Penguin loss, Longman advance. V. Menkes. *Publishers Weekly* 236:54 S 15 '89
PEARY, GERALD
  Akira Kurosawa. il pors *American Film* 14:80-2 Ap '89
PEARY, ROBERT EDWIN, 1856-1920
          about
  Bittersweet dreams of glory. J. M. Diamond. il pors *Natural History* p28-30+ N '89
  Frederick Albert Cook, M.D. [with editorial comment by Gilbert L. Voss] R. M. Myerson. il por map *Sea Frontiers* 35:3, 8-13 Ja/F '89
  Peary made it to the Pole after all. *Newsweek* 114:71 D 25 '89
  Peary on top. *Time* 134:73 D 25 '89
  Peary's North Pole claim reexamined. E. Marshall. il por *Science* 243:1131-2 Mr 3 '89
  Study puts Admiral Peary at North Pole. il *Science* 246:1564 D 22 '89

PEARY EXPEDITIONS (1886-1909)
  Bittersweet dreams of glory [R. Peary's North Pole claim] J. M. Diamond. il pors *Natural History* p28-30+ N '89
  Frederick Albert Cook, M.D. [with editorial comment by Gilbert L. Voss] R. M. Myerson. il por map *Sea Frontiers* 35:3, 8-13 Ja/F '89
  Peary made it to the Pole after all. *Newsweek* 114:71 D 25 '89
  Peary on top. *Time* 134:73 D 25 '89
  Peary's North Pole claim reexamined. E. Marshall. il por *Science* 243:1131-2 Mr 3 '89
  Study puts Admiral Peary at North Pole. il *Science* 246:1564 D 22 '89
PEAS
  Well-engineered pea trellis. il *Sunset (Central West edition)* 183:214 N '89
          Diseases and pests
  One enzyme makes a fungal pathogen, but not a saprophyte, virulent on a new host plant. W. Schäfer and others. bibl f il *Science* 246:247-9 O 13 '89
PEASANTRY
          France
  The peasants' revolt? [role in the Revolution] P. M. Jones. bibl il *History Today* 39:15-19 My '89
          Honduras
  Campesina fights hunger and its causes [organizer E. Alvarado] M. C. Turck. por *The Progressive* 53:14 My '89
          Soviet Union
  Hearth, home and rural community [nineteenth century] H. Yvert-Jalu. il *The Unesco Courier* 42:10-15 Jl '89
PEASE AIR FORCE BASE (N.H.) *See* Air bases
PEAT
  Peatlands: a global warming threat? [research by Joseph B. Yavitt and R. Kelman Wieder] J. Raloff. *Science News* 136:143 Ag 26 '89
  Peatlands as source of acid rain [study by Lee F. Klinger] R. Monastersky. *Science News* 136:413 D 23-30 '89
  The world's oldest road [Sweet Track of England: a 6,000-year-old wooden walkway discovered in a peat bog] J. Coles. il maps *Scientific American* 261:100-6 N '89
PECCI (LUIGI) CENTER FOR CONTEMPORARY ART (PRATO, ITALY) *See* Centro per l'Arte Contemporaneo Luigi Pecci (Prato, Italy)
PECHINEY (FIRM)
  Insider-trading shock rocks the Elysee [Triangle affair] B. Riemer. il *Business Week* p54 Ja 23 '89
  The Socialists dodge one bullet—but the next? [insider trading Triangle probe] B. Riemer and F. J. Comes. il *Business Week* p46 F 13 '89
PECK, GREGORY, 1916-
          about
  He's the man [interview] R. Haver. il pors *American Film* 14:26-30+ Mr '89
  Impeccable Gregory Peck. R. Holusha. il pors *The Saturday Evening Post* 261:66-8+ Ja/F '89
  The question of the night: who wasn't at the A.F.I. party honoring Gregory Peck? il pors *People Weekly* 31:38-9 Mr 27 '89
PECK, KATHY
          about
  After Live Aid and Farm Aid, hearing aid may be next for unwary victims of rock. N. Geeslin. il pors *People Weekly* 31:95-6 Ja 23 '89
PECK, ROBERT MCCRACKEN, 1952-
  Seasons of the Canadian soul. il *International Wildlife* 19:44-51 My/Je '89
PECKFORD, BRIAN
          about
  The cucumber scandal. C. White. *Maclean's* 102:16 Ja 23 '89
  The newest premier. P. Kopvillem. il pors *Maclean's* 102:15 Mr 20 '89
  Peckford's legacies. M. Clark. il por *Maclean's* 102:12-13 Ja 30 '89
PECKHAM, RICK
  John Scofield's solo on "Best western"—Phrygian voicings. il *Down Beat* 56:66-7 D '89
PECKINPAH, SAM, 1925-1984
          about
  The wild bunch [film] Reviews
       American Film il 14:18+ Ap '89. R. Shelton
PECK'S LAKE (ARIZ.)
  A peck of trouble at Peck's Lake. J. Bishop. il *Sierra* 74:58-9 Jl/Ag '89
PECTINASES
  Death to albedo [use of pectinase aids grapefruit peeling] *Discover* 10:14 Ap '89
PECTINS
  Canned produce: mush no more [work of Malcolm Bourne] J. Raloff. *Science News* 136:206 S 23 '89
  Overeating remedy [use of pectin to treat eating disorders] il *Prevention (Emmaus, Pa.)* 41:10 My '89

PEDAGOGY See College teaching; Teaching
PEDAL POWERED AIRCRAFT See Human powered aircraft
PEDALS, BICYCLE See Bicycles—Pedals
PEDERSEN, BABILL STRAY- See Stray-Pedersen, Babill
PEDERSEN, WILLIAM
    about
Architecture. C. Wiseman. il por *New York* 22:146-7 S 11 '89
PEDERSON, TAGE
Are you injury-prone? il por *Skiing* 42:67-8+ O '89
PEDESTAL TABLES See Tables
PEDESTRIAN SKYWAYS See Skyways (Architecture)
PEDIATRIC AIDS FOUNDATION
For a star-studded gala against children's AIDS, some politicians will even cross party lines. il *People Weekly* 32:104-5 Jl 10 '89
Hollywood helps a brave couple raise money for children dying of AIDS [P. and E. Glaser host premiere of Immediate family] il pors *People Weekly* 32:58-9 N 13 '89
PEDIATRIC CLINICS See Health facilities
PEDIATRICIANS
    See also
    Women pediatricians
Pediatricians answer 20 nagging questions. L. Yarrow. il *Parents* 64:82-4+ Ja '89
PEDICURE
A perfect 10. L. Daigneault. il *Health (New York, N.Y.)* 21:69 Ag '89
Treat your feet. H. E. Lee. il *Vogue* 179:152 My '89
PEEL, QUENTIN
First GASP. *World Press Review* 36:53 Jl '89
PEELE, GILLIAN, 1949-
History tomorrow. il *History Today* 39:14-15 Je '89
PEELING OF GRAPEFRUITS See Grapefruits—Peeling
PEENO, LARRY N.
Art education: a curriculum dilemma. bibl f *Design for Arts in Education* 90:41-3 N/D '88
PEEPLES, EDWIN A.
Branch libraries. bibl il *Country Journal* 16:30-1 Jl/Ag '89
Flowering locusts. il *Country Journal* 16:13-14 N/D '89
Hickory—the American tree. il *Country Journal* 16:35-8 My/Je '89
PEER COUNSELING
    See also
    Long Distance Love (Organization)
A school-change paradigm [use of peer programs] F. Riessman. *The Education Digest* 54:10-12 My '89
PEER GROUPS
    See also
    Cliques
Back to basics [peer pressure and student achievement] D. Ravitch. *The New Republic* 200:13-15 Mr 6 '89
Following the crowd. D. F. Bjorklund and B. Bjorklund. il *Parents* 64:197 Mr '89
Going along with the crowd: should you? M. Conroy. il *Teen* 33:46+ Ag '89
Peer pressure. N. Rubin. il *Parents* 64:97-100+ My '89
Pressure peer style! [quiz] il *Teen* 33:66-7 Ap '89
Wrong crowd? il *Teen* 33:10-11 Ja '89
PEER GYNT [ballet] See Ballet reviews—Single works
PEER GYNT [drama] See Ibsen, Henrik, 1828-1906
PEER REVIEW
Does peer review have a place in child custody evaluations? S. P. Herman and A. M. Levy. il *Children Today* 18:15-18 My/Je '89
The epilepsy "cure": bold claims, weak data [controversy over peer-reviewed article by Phodios A. Anninos and N. Tsagas in International journal of neuroscience] R. P. Crease. il *Science* 245:1444-5 S 29 '89
A fast track for high-risk science [National Science Foundation peer review system for grants] E. Marshall. il *Science* 244:764 My 19 '89
In defense of confidentiality. D. Lazarus. *Physics Today* 42:57-9 O '89
NSF peer review under fire from Nader group. E. Marshall. *Science* 245:250 Jl 21 '89
Peer review comes under peer review [biomedical publishing] M. Sun. il *Science* 244:910-12 My 26 '89
Public science for public policy. S. Jasanoff. il *Technology Review* 92:26+ F/Mr '89
PEER TUTORING See Tutors and tutoring
PEERCE, LARRY
    about
Wired [film] Reviews
    The Humanist il 49:45-6 N/D '89. H. M. Geduld
    Maclean's il 102:52-3 Ag 28 '89. P. Young
    Newsweek 114:68 S 4 '89. D. Ansen
    People Weekly il 32:17-18 S 11 '89. R. Novak
    Rolling Stone il p32 S 7 '89. P. Travers
    Time il 133:90 Ap 24 '89. R. Zoglin
    Time il 134:64 Ag 28 '89. R. Corliss
PEET, WILLIAM
    about
Altimeter man. *The New Yorker* 65:48-50 S 25 '89
PEEVES
What bugs you about boys? [advice on getting guys to change] il *Seventeen* 48:70-1 Jl '89

Anecdotes, facetiae, satire, etc.
A grateful nation [small problems and annoyances that G. Bush should solve] C. Murphy. il *The Atlantic* 263:16+ Ja '89
It gripes me to say this. R. Blount. il *The New York Times Magazine* p40+ Ap 16 '89
PEFFER, RANDALL S.
"Féliz Navidad". il *Travel Holiday* 172:90+ D '89
Mystic by the sea. il *Travel Holiday* 172:100-2 Jl '89
On Malay Peninsula picking coconuts is monkey business. bibl (p147) il *Smithsonian* 19:110-12+ Ja '89
Pausing in Woods Hole. il *Travel Holiday* 171:35-8 Ja '89
Rite of passage [cover story] il map *Travel Holiday* 172:40-51 Ag '89
PEGASUS (LAUNCH VEHICLE) See Space vehicles—Propulsion systems
PEGS
Repairing pegged furniture. M. Varese. il *Workbench* 45:10-11 S/O '89
PEHE, JIRI
Post-totalitarianism. il *New Perspectives Quarterly* 5:37-41 Wint '88/'89
PEHOSKI, JOSEPH
'Expressive Iron' at Penland. il *American Craft* 49:72 Ag/S '89
PEI, I. M., 1917-
    about
Pei's pyramid—new jewel of the Seine. S. M. Alsop. il *Architectural Digest* 46:29+ Ap '89
The perfectionist. C. McGuigan. il por *Newsweek* 114:60-1+ S 25 '89
The riddle of the pyramid. R. Kimball. il *Architectural Record* 177:58-61 Ja '89
PEIHUI GUO
    about
Dancescape. H. Ostlere. por *Dance Magazine* 63:9 Ag '89
PEKARSKY, MEL, 1934-
    about
Mel Pekarsky. L. K. Petrich. il pors *American Artist* 53:50-5 Ap '89
PEKIN (ILL.)
    Education
Whitest city in Illinois graduates only black teen from high school. il por *Jet* 76:14 Je 26 '89
PEKING (CHINA) See Beijing (China)
THE PEKING OPERA BLUES [film] See Motion picture reviews—Single works
PEKKANEN, JOHN, 1939-
Are we closing in on AIDS? *Reader's Digest* 135:79-85 D '89
I am Joe's aching back. il *Reader's Digest* 135:131-6 N '89
I am Joe's new heart. il *Reader's Digest* 134:89-95 Je '89
The mounting toll of Lyme disease. il *Reader's Digest* 134:88-92 Ap '89
    about
The unhappiest part of medicine, says author John Pekkanen, may be the physicians who practice it. M. Brower. il pors *People Weekly* 31:85+ Ja 9 '89
PÉLADEAU, PIERRE
    about
The acquisitor. J. Daly. il pors *Maclean's* 102:38-9 N 13 '89
PELICANS
    Anecdotes, facetiae, satire, etc.
Noble notes [pelicans in St. James Park] F. Graham. il *Audubon* 91:14 Jl '89
PELIKAN, JAROSLAV JAN, 1923-
    about
Christianity as an enfolding circle [interview] J. Carey. por *U.S. News & World Report* 106:57 Je 26 '89
PELKA, HEIKE
(jt. auth) See Schulman, LaDonne H., and Pelka, Heike
PELL, CLAIBORNE
    about
Mr. Superliberal. D. Seligman. il *Fortune* 119:195-6 Je 19 '89
PELL, EVE
The backbone of hidden government [cover story] *The Nation* 248:833+ Je 19 '89
Chilly draft. *The Nation* 248:400 Mr 27 '89
Judge orders INS to stop the delays. il *The Progressive* 53:13-14 S '89
A new way to intimidate activists. *Utne Reader* p115 N/D '89
PELLÉ, MARIE-PAULE
    about
On the Rue de Rivoli. C. K. Gandee. il por *House & Garden* 161:68-77 Jl '89
PELLE THE CONQUEROR [film] See Motion picture reviews—Single works
PELLICER, ANTONIO, AND OTHERS
Angiotensin II: does it have a direct obligate role in ovulation? [discussion of June 17, 1988 article, Blockage of ovulation by an angiotensin antagonist] il *Science* 245:870-1 Ag 25 '89

PELTIER, W. R., AND TUSHINGHAM, A. M.
Global sea level rise and the greenhouse effect: might they be connected? bibl f il maps *Science* 244:806-10 My 19 '89

PELTON, JOSEPH N.
Telepower: the emerging global brain. il por *The Futurist* 23:9-14 S/O '89

PELTS *See* Hides and skins

PELTZ, NELSON
about
Nelson Peltz: shopping to chase the blues. K. Deveny. il pors *Business Week* p143 Je 26 '89

PELTZER, GILLES, AND OTHERS
Magnitude of late Quaternary left-lateral displacements along the north edge of Tibet. bibl f il maps *Science* 246:1285-9 D 8 '89

PELULLO, LEONARD A.
about
Lenny Pelullo's checkered past—and present. G. DeGeorge. il por *Business Week* p84+ O 23 '89
Victor Posner may soon taste his own medicine. G. DeGeorge. il pors *Business Week* p34+ Ap 10 '89

PEMBERTON, DIXIE ANN
A national network for environmental education. *The Education Digest* 54:42-5 My '89

PEMBERTON, ROBERT
about
Hitch your wagon to the right IBM model. D. Churbuck. il por *Forbes* 144:119+ S 4 '89

PEMBRIDGE INVESTMENTS LTD.
Jimmy Goldsmith's gun bearer goes gunning [R. A. E. Franklin's hostile bid for DRG plc] P. Finch. il por *Business Week* p63+ O 16 '89

PEMEX *See* Petroleos Mexicanos

PEN
Writers and rights [Toronto-Montreal congress] P. Young. il *Maclean's* 102:64+ O 9 '89

PEN AND INK DRAWING *See* Pen drawing

PEN-BASED COMPUTERS
Testing
True notebook computing arrives [GRiDPad] F. Hayes. il *Byte* 14:94-5 D '89

PEN DRAWING
Pen & ink: drawing for the Wall Street journal. M. S. Doherty. il *American Artist* 53:74-80+ My '89
Perfect penmanship [penwork on 18th and 19th century furniture] G. Harrell. il *House & Garden* 161:68 D '89
Collectors and collecting
Fine lines [calligraphy drawings] M. Guralnick. il *House & Garden* 161:50+ Je '89

PEN PALS
Pen pals: our babies' first year. P. Abrams and L. Rosenberg. il pors *Parents* 64:90-4+ N '89
Sharing astronomy across the Atlantic. D. Abbou. *Astronomy* 17:99 F '89
Starmate match-ups. *Teen* 33:63-4 N '89

PENAL INSTITUTIONS *See* Prisons

PENAL LAW *See* Criminal law

PENALTIES (LAW) *See* Fines (Penalties)

PENANCE
Confession, anyone? H. Fehren. *U.S. Catholic* 54:40-2 O '89
Have Catholics found better ways to go to Confession? [cover story] D. Grippo. il *U.S. Catholic* 54:6-12 Ag '89
The rites of sinners. K. L. Woodward. il *Newsweek* 113:62 Mr 13 '89

PENCIL DRAWING
Applying colored pencil over an acrylic wash. D. Dooley. il *American Artist* 53:66-9 D '89
Skip Steinworth. B. S. Goldman. il pors *American Artist* 53:46-51+ Je '89

PENCILS
See also
Dixon Ticonderoga Co.
Collectors and collecting
Pencils: a sharp collecting hobby. D. Stewart. il *Antiques & Collecting Hobbies* 94:28-9+ D '89

PENDANTS (JEWELRY)
The Holly Oak shell [discussion of December 2, 1988 article, Mammoth fraud exposed] R. Lewin. *Science* 243:151-2 Ja 13 '89

PENDERGRASS, KAREN
about
Love conquers all. M. Marshall. il pors *Ebony* 44:152-4+ F '89

PENDERGRASS, TEDDY
about
Love conquers all. M. Marshall. il pors *Ebony* 44:152-4+ F '89

PENDLETON, MICHAELENE
Sardines [story] *Omni (New York, N.Y.)* 11:53-4 Ap '89

PENDLETON, STEVE
Heritage of the Bounty: collectibles from Pitcairn Island. il *Antiques & Collecting Hobbies* 94:41-4 Jl '89

PENDOLINO (TRAIN) *See* Railroads—Trains

PENDULUM CLOCKS *See* Clocks

PÈNE DU BOIS, FELIX, 1957-
about
Felix Pène du Bois at 56 Bleecker. L. Campbell. il *Art in America* 77:177-8 Je '89

PENFIELD (N.Y.)
Education
Penfield Music Commission Project [jazz studies] C. Strickland. il *Down Beat* 56:24 Je '89

PENGUIN BOOKS LTD.
A Rushdie paperback? J. F. Baker. *Publishers Weekly* 236:6 O 13 '89

PENGUIN GROUP
Heads of Hamish Hamilton and Michael Joseph resign. V. Menkes. *Publishers Weekly* 236:13 Jl 14 '89
Penguin Group posts unchanged profits, touts international strength. *Publishers Weekly* 235:102 My 12 '89
Penguin Group sells Sphere to Maxwell's Macdonald Publishing. V. Menkes. *Publishers Weekly* 235:40 Ap 7 '89

PENGUIN USA (FIRM)
Dutton becomes Penguin imprint; 20 of adult trade staff are fired. *Publishers Weekly* 236:10 N 10 '89
Major changes at Penguin: Mint is new CEO, Diforio out at NAL. il *Publishers Weekly* 236:9 N 17 '89
Penguin USA to acquire W. H. Smith Publishers. il *Publishers Weekly* 236:10 S 29 '89

PENGUINS
Penguins. D. Ackerman. il *The New Yorker* 65:38-42+ Jl 10 '89
Food and feeding
Antarctica's well-bred penguins. S. G. Trivelpiece and W. Z. Trivelpiece. il map *Natural History* p28-37 D '89

PENITENTIARIES *See* Prisons

PENMANSHIP
See also
Calligraphy
Dysgraphia

PENN, ARTHUR, 1922-
about
Penn & Teller get killed [film] Reviews
The New Republic 201:25 O 30 '89. S. Kauffmann
The New Yorker 65:100-1 O 2 '89. P. Kael
People Weekly il 32:17+ O 9 '89. R. Novak
Rolling Stone il por p38 N 2 '89. N. Scovell

PENN, IRVING
about
Angels! H. Muschamp. il *Vogue* 179:278-87 D '89

PENN, SEAN
about
Showing dedication and talent, not temper, Sean Penn helps revive David Rabe's Hurlyburly. S. K. Reed. il por *People Weekly* 31:54-5 Ja 9 '89
Surprise! It's splits, fits and quits again for Sean and Madonna. J. S. Kunen. il pors *People Weekly* 31:44-6 Ja 23 '89

PENN & TELLER
about
A daring debut. N. Scovell. il *Rolling Stone* p38 N 2 '89
Profiles. C. Trillin. il *The New Yorker* 65:58+ My 15 '89

PENN & TELLER GET KILLED [film] *See* Motion picture reviews—Single works

PENN CENTER OF THE SEA ISLANDS (SAINT HELENA ISLAND, S.C.)
Treasures on an island. N. L. Mohr. il *American Visions* 4:29-31 O '89

PENNEBAKER, D. A.
about
Depeche Mode 101 [film] Reviews
Rolling Stone il p36 My 18 '89. J. Farber

PENNEFATHER, PETER S.
(jt. auth) *See* Goh, Joanne W., and Pennefather, Peter S.

PENNEY, ALEXANDRA
How to keep your man monogamous [excerpt] il por *Ladies' Home Journal* 106:70+ Jl '89
What men want in bed [excerpt from How to keep your man monogamous] il *Ladies' Home Journal* 106:80+ Ag '89
Will he cheat? Men tell why they do—or don't [excerpt from How to keep your man monogamous] il *Glamour* 87:220-3+ Ag '89

PENNEY (J. C.) COMPANY, INC. *See* J. C. Penney Company, Inc.

PENNIES *See* Coins

PENNING, TIM
Christian school racism. *The Education Digest* 55:40-2 N '89

PENNINGTON, SAMUEL
Old glories. il *House & Garden* 161:140-1 Ja '89

PENNINGTON (N.J.)
Social life and customs
Sweating and sharing [aerobics class serves as women's socializing center] J. D. Reed. il *Time* 134:12-13 Jl 10 '89

PENNISI, ELIZABETH
All things bright & bitter [cover story] il *International Wildlife* 19:46-51 N/D '89
Biology versus astronomy: the battle for Mount Graham. il *BioScience* 39:10-13 Ja '89

PENNISI, ELIZABETH—*cont.*
Living in a land of extremes. il por *National Wildlife* 27:14-21 Ap/My '89
Much ado about eels. il map *BioScience* 39:594-8 O '89
Neurobiology gets computational. il *BioScience* 39:283-7 My '89

PENNOYER, PETER
about
Love nest. M. Baker. il pors *New York* 22:56-9 O 2 '89

PENNSYLVANIA
See also
Agriculture—Pennsylvania
Architecture, Domestic—Pennsylvania
Botany—Pennsylvania
Courts—Pennsylvania
Geology—Pennsylvania
Gettysburg National Military Park (Pa.)
Historic houses, sites, etc.—Pennsylvania
Lakes—Pennsylvania
Lancaster County (Pa.)
Law—Pennsylvania
Montgomery County (Pa.)
Music festivals—Pennsylvania
Opera—Pennsylvania
Organic gardens and gardening—Pennsylvania
Spruce Creek (Pa.)
Water pollution—Pennsylvania
Economic conditions
See also
Unemployment—Pennsylvania
Industries
See also
Strip mining—Pennsylvania
Legislature
Loony legislation [prolife legislators' proposal to ban abortion on basis of gender selection] P. Simpson. *Ms.* 18:72 N '89
Parks and reserves
See also
Black Moshannon State Park (Pa.)
Politics and government
See also
Pennsylvania—Legislature
Stacking the deck [advantages of incumbent in congressional race] E. Howard. il por *Common Cause Magazine* 15:24-6 Ja/F '89

PENNSYLVANIA. NATIONAL GUARD
Whirlybirds not welcome [helicopters near Black Moshannon State Park] S. D. Borowitz. il *Sierra* 74:90-1 N/D '89

PENNSYLVANIA ACADEMY OF THE FINE ARTS
Museum accessions [The Gordon family by H. Benbridge acquired] E. H. Gustafson. il *Antiques* 136:1022 N '89
Two masterworks of American architecture [work of F. Furness] A. Berman. il por *Architectural Digest* 46:314+ O '89

PENNSYLVANIA AND MILWAUKEE BALLET
Reviews:
Debut performances at Kennedy Center. G. Jackson. *Dance Magazine* 63:53+ Jl '89

PENNSYLVANIA BALLET
See also
Pennsylvania and Milwaukee Ballet

PENNSYLVANIA DUTCH *See* Pennsylvania Germans
PENNSYLVANIA FURNITURE *See* Furniture, American
PENNSYLVANIA GERMANS
See also
Fraktur
Antiques: Pennsylvania German chests. R. Conniff. il *Architectural Digest* 46:276-81+ O '89
For a yellow color [saffron] A. Arndt. il por *Americana* 17:34-7 S/O '89

PENNWALT CORP.
Background check [A. J. Butler's offer for Pennwalt] L. Gubernick. *Forbes* 143:14-15 F 20 '89

PENNY STOCKS
Beware of penny stocks [excerpt from Investor alert!] il *Consumers' Research Magazine* 72:26-8 Ap '89
The final frenzy of a penny stock shop [Investors Center] D. Zigas. il por *Business Week* p128 Mr 13 '89
The fugitive king of penny stocks [J. C. Schidlowski] D. Zigas. il pors *Business Week* p124-5+ N 20 '89
Have the penny stock police caught a live one? [Power Securities] P. Engardio. il por *Business Week* p132 F 20 '89
"How did I know the guy was calling from jail?" [J. Darder implicated in penny stock fraud over disposable razor] R. L. Stern. il por *Forbes* 143:120+ My 29 '89
"Like a slaughter-house for hogs" [Mafia manipulation of penny stocks] R. L. Stern and C. Poole. il *Forbes* 144:42-4 D 25 '89
The many incarnations of Barry Davis. L. J. Nathans and D. Zigas. il por *Business Week* p94 My 29 '89
Meyer, meet RICO [penny stock swindler M. Blinder] J. Zweig. il por *Forbes* 143:168 Je 26 '89
The most brazen of the penny hustlers? [Power Securities] P. Engardio. il por *Business Week* p130+ N 20 '89
A penny-stock scam [Haas Securities] C. Friday and J. Hammer. il por *Newsweek* 113:51 My 1 '89

The penny stock scandal [cover story] P. Engardio and G. DeGeorge. il *Business Week* p74-7+ Ja 23 '89
The sad saga of a penny-stock company [Sequential Information Systems Inc.] G. Weiss. il por *Business Week* p124-6+ My 15 '89
The SEC casts a net at penny stocks' biggest fish [Stuart-James] S. D. Atchison. il *Business Week* p128 Ap 24 '89
This penny-stock scam packs a one-two punch [brokers cross investors into another favorite stock] D. Zigas. *Business Week* p154 My 8 '89
The war on penny stocks. J. B. Quinn. il *Newsweek* 113:52 Ap 10 '89
You can run—but maybe you can't hide in Cuba [penny stock fraud scam by L. Zrnic of International Swiss Investments] G. DeGeorge. il por *Business Week* p27 Mr 6 '89

PENNZOIL COMPANY
Does Pennzoil see a gusher in Kerr-McGee? G. G. Marcial. il *Business Week* p134 My 8 '89
Randal McDonald. il por *Business Week* Special Issue:160 Ap 14 '89
What does Liedtke want? [Pennzoil's stake in Chevron] M. Ivey and M. Shao. il por *Business Week* p42-3 D 25 '89-Ja 1 '90

PENROSE, LEE MILLER *See* Miller, Lee, 1907-1977
PENROSE, ROGER
about
A Pandora's box of minds, machines and metaphysics. A. K. Dewdney. il *Scientific American* 261:140+ D '89
Quantum consciousness. J. Horgan. il por *Scientific American* 261:30+ N '89
Wolf Foundation honors Hawking and Penrose for work on relativity. M. Siegel. il por *Physics Today* 42:97-8 Ja '89

PENS
See also
Pen-based computers
Making your mark beautifully. J. Van Milligen. il *American Artist* 53:80-2+ Ja '89
Mightier than the ballpoint [fountain pens] E. Calonius. il *Newsweek* 114:63 Jl 3 '89
Romancing the pen [rebirth of fountain pens] D. Moreau. il *Changing Times* 43:48-52 N '89
Collectors and collecting
Fountain pens sign in as attractive collectibles. L. Rosenkrantz. *Antiques & Collecting Hobbies* 94:24 Je '89
Return of the fountain pen. il *Sunset (Central West edition)* 183:116+ N '89
When one isn't enough [fountain pens] il *Changing Times* 43:51 N '89
Manufacture
See also
Magic Marker Industries Inc.
Parker Pen plc
Pentech Intl. Inc.
Marketing
Brand-new start [Magic Markers to be marketed by Binney & Smith] E. F. Cone. il *Forbes* 143:10 Mr 6 '89
Penmanship with a flourish [Parker Pen] J. Marcom, Jr. il por *Forbes* 143:152+ Ap 3 '89

PENS, LIGHT *See* Light pens
PENSACOLA (FLA.)
Health facilities
America's holy war [Ladies Center abortion clinic] P. Hamill. il por *Esquire* 112:61-4 N '89

PENSHURST PLACE (ENGLAND)
'Not built to envious show'. F. Barker. il por *History Today* 39:3-4 Ap '89

PENSION BENEFIT GUARANTY CORPORATION
The government's golden handshake. E. Clift. il *Newsweek* 114:27 D 18 '89

PENSION FUND MANAGERS
Adios, city hall [H. Cisneros] T. Vogel. il por *Business Week* p40 F 20 '89
Fund managers play 'me too' and fail. D. LeBaron. por *Fortune* 120:148 Jl 3 '89
Pension fund managers get queasy [investing in LBOs] R. Jacob. il *Fortune* 119:68 Ja 2 '89
They make sure the kitty keeps purring. L. J. Nathans. il *Business Week* p166-7 N 6 '89
Wall Street's new musclemen. D. Pauly. il *Newsweek* 113:46-7 Je 5 '89

PENSION FUNDS AND FUNDING *See* Pensions
PENSIONS
See also
401(k) plan
403(b) plan
Civil service pensions
Defined contribution pension plans
Individual retirement accounts
Keogh plans
Pension fund managers
Simplified employee pensions
Social security
The comparative value of pensions in the public and private sectors. L. M. Lovejoy. bibl f il *Monthly Labor Review* 111:18-26 D '88

PENSIONS—*cont.*

The long strings on pension plans [payout methods] N. Santelmann. il *Forbes* 143:145+ My 1 '89

Pensions: off balance [women] F. Leonard. il *Modern Maturity* 32:78+ O/N '89

The power of the pension funds [cover story; special section] il *Business Week* p154-8+ N 6 '89

Laws and regulations

See also

Pension Benefit Guaranty Corporation

The battle over pension surpluses. R. Thompson. il *Nation's Business* 77:66-7 Ag '89

Business sure would like to retire this bill [worker participation in pension management] S. B. Garland. il *Business Week* p204 S 25 '89

Button down your vesting rights. M. C. Paulson. *Changing Times* 43:103-4 Ja '89

Congress has that lean and hungry look. S. B. Garland. il *Business Week* p160+ N 6 '89

The fury over pension funds [terminations] S. B. Garland. il *Business Week* p31 Jl 3 '89

The Hill has fund managers squirming. D. Harbrecht. *Business Week* p45 Ja 30 '89

New strings on private pensions? H. Banks. *Forbes* 144:33 O 16 '89

A warning signal about the safety of your pension. B. Kobliner. il *Money* 18:11+ O '89

Why Washington is worried about your pension. S. V. Roberts. *U.S. News & World Report* 107:42 N 13 '89

Taxation

New rules may force rewriting of pension plans. D. C. Bacon. *Nation's Business* 77:24 F '89

Now you see it . . . [future health benefits for retired employees] J. Novack. il *Forbes* 144:57 Ag 21 '89

Taking—and keeping—your lump sum. E. Schurenberg. il *Money* 18 Money Guide:46-7 Fall '89

Tax on pensions: save time and money. K. McCormally. *Changing Times* 43:118 Mr '89

This new pension tax could feast on your nest egg. R. Wool. il *Money* 18:157-8 F '89

Termination

The battle over pension surpluses. R. Thompson. il *Nation's Business* 77:66-7 Ag '89

The fury over pension funds. S. B. Garland. il *Business Week* p31 Jl 3 '89

Is your pension in peril? M. Hodge. il *New Choices for the Best Years* 29:50-3 Ag '89

What you should know if your pension plan gets shut down. D. M. Topolnicki. il *Money* 18:187-8 Je '89

When the safety net is frayed [takeover of Pacific Lumber by Charles E. Hurwitz causes pension plan termination] J. B. Levine. il *Business Week* p158 N 6 '89

Great Britain

See also

British Rail Pension Fund

PENSIONS, MILITARY

Court limits sharing of Army pension in divorce; Marshall pens decision [Supreme Court] por *Jet* 76:8 Je 19 '89

A pension for trouble. M. Cooper. il *The Washington Monthly* 21:24-9 Jl/Ag '89

PENSKE, ROGER

about

Roger Penske: Detroit Diesel's dynamo. E. Dennis. il por *Motor Boating & Sailing* 164:78-80 Jl '89

PENTAGON *See* United States. Dept. of Defense

PENTAGON (ARLINGTON, VA.: BUILDING)

One day in the life of the Pentagon. T. Brewster. il *Life* 12:61-6+ D '89

PENTAGON PROCUREMENT SCANDAL

FBI alleges illegal payoffs for insider defense data. B. M. Greeley, Jr. *Aviation Week & Space Technology* 130:33-4 Ja 2 '89

FBI charges consultants bribed Navy officials to influence contract awards. J. D. Morrocco. *Aviation Week & Space Technology* 130:22 Ja 9 '89

First gusts from an Ill Wind. *Time* 133:25 Ja 16 '89

GAO advises Air Force to cancel Loral's advanced radar warning receiver contract [allegations of illegally receiving information about competing Litton system] *Aviation Week & Space Technology* 130:23 My 22 '89

'Ill Wind' guilty pleas show pattern of basic corruption. M. Mecham. *Aviation Week & Space Technology* 130:24-5 Ap 3 '89

Judges sentence four to prison for roles in bribery scandal. *Aviation Week & Space Technology* 130:76 Je 12 '89

Litton gets share of ALR-56M program in Ill Wind plea agreement by Loral. D. F. Bond. *Aviation Week & Space Technology* 131:115 D 18-25 '89

Litton protest raises questions about new Loral operation [USAF award for F-16 radar warning receivers] P. J. Klass. *Aviation Week & Space Technology* 130:57 F 6 '89

Marine official pleads guilty to U.S. bribery, fraud charges [J. A. Sherman] M. Mecham. *Aviation Week & Space Technology* 130:26 F 6 '89

Nobody's laughing at Ill Wind now. P. Dwyer. por *Business Week* p34-5 Ja 23 '89

Operation Ill Wind has Cubic fighting for air. E. Schine. il por *Business Week* p90 D 11 '89

Operation Ill Wind may have scared up a canary [Unisys-Pentagon connection] P. Dwyer. il pors *Business Week* p37 F 6 '89

Operation Ill Wind whips through Loral. M. D. Oneal. il *Business Week* p68 Je 12 '89

Pentagon suspends Hazeltine, Teledyne following federal charges of fraud. *Aviation Week & Space Technology* 130:23-4 Ja 16 '89

USAF urges GAO to reconsider criticism of Loral contract award [Litton protest of contract] B. W. Henderson. *Aviation Week & Space Technology* 130:31 Je 5 '89

Where, oh where have all the scandals gone? il por *U.S. News & World Report* 106:11-12 Ja 16 '89

PENTAMIDINE

Help on the way [FDA approval] *Time* 133:65 F 13 '89

Lyphomed's vital signs are stabilizing. J. F. Siler. il *Business Week* p46 Jl 3 '89

Wider use of pneumonia drug approved. il *FDA Consumer* 23:4 Ap '89

Prices

AIDS: the high cost of hope. il *Scholastic Update (Teachers' edition)* 122:12 N 3 '89

PENTECH INTL. INC.

This penmaker's ink is all black. G. G. Marcial. *Business Week* p62 Jl 24 '89

PENTECOST

Spirit and spirits. P. J. Ryan. il *America* 160:439 My 6 '89

Works of God in our tongues. P. Perkins. *The Christian Century* 106:498 My 10 '89

PENTECOSTAL CHURCHES

See also

Assemblies of God

Church of God

Vineyard (Church)

South Africa

Charismatic churches and the struggle against apartheid: a dispute [discussion of August 17-24, 1988 article, Charismatics and change in South Africa] I. Hexham and K. O. Poewe-Hexham. *The Christian Century* 106:16+ Ja 4-11 '89

Soviet Union

Soviet exodus strains church resources. K. A. Lawton. il *Christianity Today* 33:50 Je 16 '89

PENTECOSTAL MOVEMENT *See* Pentecostalism

PENTECOSTALISM

Piety on fire. J. I. Packer. il *Christianity Today* 33:18-23 My 12 '89

about

PENTHOUSE (PERIODICAL)

Centerfold follies [revelations concerning J. Swaggart] L. Cryderman. *Christianity Today* 33:17 Mr 17 '89

PENTHOUSE INTERNATIONAL LTD.

How Trump plays monopoly [D. Trump's lease deal with B. Guccione freezes out Pratt Hotel as Atlantic City competitor] H. Rudnitsky. il *Forbes* 143:128 Ap 17 '89

PENTHOUSES *See* Apartments

PENTOS PLC

Pentos threatens breach of Net Book Agreement. V. Menkes. *Publishers Weekly* 236:11 D 1 '89

PENYCATE, JOHN

Of piracy and payoffs. *World Press Review* 36:53 My '89

PENZIAS, ARNO ALLAN

Teaching statistics to engineers. *Science* 244:1025 Je 2 '89

about

Astrophysicist Arno Penzias on making R&D pay off [interview] E. Warner. il por *High Technology Business* 9:24-7 Jl/Ag '89

"The Japanese are not superhuman" [interview] G. F. Gilder. il por *Forbes* 143:122+ Mr 20 '89

PEOPLE, SINGLE *See* Single people

PEOPLE EXPRESS INC.

Donald Burr may be ready to take to the skies again. J. A. Byrne. il por *Business Week* p74-5 Ja 16 '89

PEOPLE FOR THE ETHICAL TREATMENT OF ANIMALS

Call me the hunter. T. L. Gibbs; T. Nugent. *Harper's* 278:20 Mr '89

Monkey euthanasia stalled by activists. C. Holden. *Science* 244:1437 Je 23 '89

The next big cause. D. Seligman. il *Fortune* 119:163 Mr 27 '89

No longer dismissed as weirdos, animal-rights groups are now threatening medical research. F. Barnes. *Vogue* 179:542 S '89

PEOPLE METERS (TV AUDIENCE RESEARCH)

Brother Nielsen is watching. il *Time* 133:61 Je 12 '89

Demos do the talking [Fox targets under 34 age group] M. Couzens. il *Channels (New York, N.Y.: 1986)* 9:20 Mr '89

Man the lifeboats. M. Couzens. il *Channels (New York, N.Y.: 1986)* 9:22 Ap '89

The verdict—so far—on people meters. N. Hickey. il *TV Guide* 37:6-7 Ag 5-11 '89

Want a local meter? [Arbitron's ScanAmerica] M. Couzens. il *Channels (New York, N.Y.: 1986)* 9:26 Ja '89

THE PEOPLE NEXT DOOR [television program] *See* Television program reviews—Single works

PEOPLE UNITED TO SERVE HUMANITY (ORGANIZA-TION)
Ford and PUSH sign $2.5 billion deal. H. Manly. il *Black Enterprise* 19:18 Mr '89
Ford and PUSH sign affirmative action pact. il *Jet* 75:8+ Ja 9 '89
PUSH convention addresses economic dilemmas; cites major black achievers. il *Jet* 76:10-13 Jl 31 '89

PEOPLE WEEKLY
Our first 15 years! il *People Weekly* 31:1-4+ Mr 6 '89

PEOPLES, JAMES J.
about
Peoples forms firm to publish for students at risk. *Publishers Weekly* 236:11 Ag 4 '89

PEOPLES, JOHN
about
New directors at Fermilab, Oak Ridge and Lawrence Livermore. W. Sweet. pors *Physics Today* 42:63-5 Jl '89

PEOPLE'S BANK
The shape of thrifts to come? R. W. King. il *Business Week* p102 S 18 '89

PEOPLE'S CHOICE AWARDS
Cosby, Phylicia Rashad take Peoples' Choice honors. il *Jet* 75:52-3 Mr 27 '89

THE PEOPLE'S COURT [television program] See Television program reviews—Single works

PEOPLES GAS LIGHT & COKE CO.
A sour scam in Chicago [employees accused in stolen gas meter scam] T. Padgett. il *Newsweek* 114:84 N 6 '89

PEOPLES PUBLISHING GROUP
Peoples forms firm to publish for students at risk. *Publishers Weekly* 236:11 Ag 4 '89

PÉPIN, JACQUES
Coming home to roast. il *The New York Times Magazine* p99-100 S 17 '89

PEPIN, M. BARLOW
Recording the sky on videotape [interview with D. Brewer] il *Astronomy* 17:86-9 S '89

PEPPER, ALLAN
about
Rock of ages. E. Hollreiser. il pors *New York* 22:29 F 6 '89

PEPPER, CLAUDE
about
Obituary
Modern Maturity il 32:11 O/N '89. C. F. Brickfield
U.S. News & World Report por 106:23 Je 12 '89. M. Barone
The score on Claude. D. Seligman. *Fortune* 120:117-18 Jl 17 '89

PEPPER, JANE G.
about
How to manage a grand project. A. M. Russell. il pors *Working Woman* 14:73-7 D '89

PEPPER, JON
How to pick the right printer. il *Working Woman* 14:54+ D '89
Software that battles chaos. il *Working Woman* 14:67-8 Ap '89
Sweet success in sales automation. il *Working Woman* 14:59-60+ Ap '89

PEPPERIDGE FARM, INC.
Pepperidge Farm's doughboy [cookie developer H. Tolmich] D. Machan. il por *Forbes* 143:198-9 Mr 20 '89

PEPPERIDGE FARM BAKERIES See Pepperidge Farm, Inc.

PEPPERS
See also
Cooking—Vegetables
Chili strings pronto. il *Sunset (Central West edition)* 183:64-5 S '89
Chilies. B. Karoff. il *Gourmet* 49:114-17+ O '89
Here comes the hot stuff [chili peppers] N. Vietmeyer. il *International Wildlife* 19:14-19 Jl/Ag '89
Red-hot peppers. H. Hylton. il *New Choices for the Best Years* 29:76-8+ Mr '89

PEPPIATT, MICHAEL
Artist's dialogue: Cesar. il por *Architectural Digest* 46:27+ F '89
The Rietberg Museum in Zurich. il *Architectural Digest* 46:74+ Mr '89
Sicilian perspectives. il por *Architectural Digest* 46:254+ Mr '89
Turin's most surprising museum. il *Architectural Digest* 46:124+ My '89

PEPSI-COLA COMPANY See PepsiCo, Inc.

PEPSICO, INC.
The cola superpowers' outrageous new arsenals. S. Ticer. il *Business Week* p162+ Mr 20 '89
Giving choices to a new generation [internship program] C. A. Rhodes. il *Black Enterprise* 19:184 F '89
How Pepsi broke into India. S. N. Chakravarty. il *Forbes* 144:43-4 N 27 '89
Peddle power [mountain biking used in television ad for Mountain Dew] S. Martin. il *Bicycling* 30:41 O/N '89
Those highflying Pepsico managers. B. Dumaine. il por *Fortune* 119:78-80+ Ap 10 '89
"We can't let Pepsi outflesh us!" [Coke-Pepsi war] J. Levine. il *Forbes* 144:270+ N 27 '89

PEPSICO SUMMERFARE
Beethoven lite [performances by R. Norrington and the London Classical Players] P. G. Davis. il por *New York* 22:60-1 Ag 28 '89
The camping up of Mozart [opera Don Giovanni] O. Friedrich. il *Time* 134:63 Ag 7 '89
Dark victory [P. Sellars' productions of Mozart's operas] P. G. Davis. il *New York* 22:48-9 Ag 7 '89
Don Juan, anybody? [Don Giovanni] P. G. Davis. il *New York* 22:58-9 Jl 24 '89
Grand finale [P. Sellars' cycle of Mozart operas] R. Marx. il *Opera News* 54:14-16+ Jl '89
Musical events:
Mozart operas performed at PepsiCo Summerfare and elsewhere. A. Porter. *The New Yorker* 65:70+ Ag 21 '89
Peter Sellars's Mozart. E. W. Said. *The Nation* 249:289-91 S 18 '89
Roger Norrington's Beethoven. P. Mattick, Jr. *The Nation* 249:326-8 S 25 '89
Theater [Don Giovanni and The dybbuk] T. M. Disch. *The Nation* 249:254-6 S 4-11 '89

PEPTIC ULCERS
Ulcers: screaming or silent, watch them with care [cover story] V. Modeland. il *FDA Consumer* 23:14-17 Je '89
Causes
Increasing evidence links ulcers and NSAIDs [nonsteroidal anti-inflammatory drugs] il *Prevention (Emmaus, Pa.)* 41:16+ Je '89
Psychological aspects
Brain may be the villain [stress ulcers; research by Daniel Hernandez] *USA Today (Periodical)* 117:16 F '89
Ulcers and stress: the missing link? [research by Pamela Walker and Mark Feldman] J. Folkenberg. *Psychology Today* 23:24-5 N '89
Therapy
Overactive machinery. W. I. Bennett. il *The New York Times Magazine* p59-60 My 7 '89

PEPTIDES
See also
Amino acid sequence
Angiotensin
Atrial natriuretic factor
Charybdotoxin
Cholecystokinin
Glutathione
Vasoactive intestinal polypeptide
Brain region and gene specificity of neuropeptide gene expression in cultured astrocytes. H. Shinoda and others. bibl f il *Science* 245:415-17 Jl 28 '89
Identification of a neuropeptide hormone that regulates sex pheromone production in female moths. A. K. Raina and others. bibl f il *Science* 244:796-8 My 19 '89
Identification of an allatotropin from adult Manduca sexta. H. Kataoka and others. bibl f il *Science* 243:1481-3 Mr 17 '89
Modulation of calcium channels in cardiac and neuronal cells by an endogenous peptide. G. Callewaert and others. bibl f il *Science* 243:663-6 F 3 '89
A novel vasodilatory peptide from the salivary glands of the sand fly Lutzomyia longipalpis. J. M. C. Ribeiro and others. bibl f il *Science* 243:212-14 Ja 13 '89
Sequence-specific peptide cleavage catalyzed by an antibody. B. L. Iverson and R. A. Lerner. bibl f il *Science* 243:1184-8 Mr 3 '89
Signal peptide for protein secretion directing glycophospholipid membrane anchor attachment. I. W. Caras and G. N. Weddell. bibl f il *Science* 243:1196-8 Mr 3 '89
Unity in function in the absence of consensus in sequence: role of leader peptides in export [protein export] L. L. Randall and S. J. S. Hardy. bibl f il *Science* 243:1156-9 Mr 3 '89
Synthesis
Peptide and protein synthesis by segment synthesis-condensation. E. T. Kaiser and others. bibl f il *Science* 243:187-92 Ja 13 '89

PERAHIA, MURRAY, 1947-
about
Extreme occasions. E. W. Said. *The Nation* 248:898-900 Je 26 '89

PERAZIO, PETER
Paris a la Perazio [photographs] il *Dance Magazine* 63:30-1 F '89

PERCEPTION
See also
Body image
Cognition
Consciousness
Extrasensory perception
Form perception
Human information processing
Intuition
Motion perception
Self perception
Sound perception
Space perception
Speech perception
Subliminal projection

PERCEPTION—See also—*cont.*
    Synesthesia
    Time perception
    Visual perception
Bigger plates, smaller portions [anorexia linked to distorted perceptions of food; research by Kay Walker] P. McCarthy. il *American Health* 8:50 My '89
The perception of intention [study of preschool children] V. Dasser and others. bibl f *Science* 243:365-7 Ja 20 '89
Pitfalls of perception. A. G. Wheeler. *Utne Reader* p100 N/D '89
Sensory perception and reading disability. R. M. Casbergue and J. F. Greene. *The Education Digest* 54:33-5 Mr '89
PERCIER, CHARLES, 1764-1838
    about
Building an empire. O. Bernier. il *House & Garden* 161:40+ D '89
PERCIVAL, MARILYN TINDALL
    about
A wallflower blossomed. R. Fimrite. il pors *Sports Illustrated* 70 Special Issue:77-9 F '89
PERCIVAL, RAY
Malthus and his ghost. *National Review* 41:30-3 Ag 18 '89
PERCUSSION INSTRUMENTS
    See also
    Drum
    Percussive Arts Society
PERCUSSIVE ARTS SOCIETY
Percussive potpourri. D. Helland. il *Down Beat* 56:11 F '89
PERCUTANEOUS TRANSLUMINAL CORONARY ANGIO-PLASTY *See* Arteries—Diseases—Therapy
PERCY, CHARLES H., 1919-
My toughest campaign: hearing loss. il por *Modern Maturity* 32:88-91 Ap/My '89
PERCY, SUSAN
23 years of outrageous water bills spur two sisters to fight city hall. (P.S.: they won!). il pors *Good Housekeeping* 209:52+ O '89
PERCY, WALKER, 1916-
    about
Thoughts on the genesis of Walker Percy's The thanatos syndrome. P. H. Samway. *America* 161:37-9+ Jl 15-22 '89
PERDUE FARMS INC.
Pressuring Perdue [animal rights activist H. Spira] B. Feder. il por *The New York Times Magazine* p32+ N 26 '89
PERE UBU (MUSICAL GROUP)
Pere Ubu's sunny "Cloudland". S. Simels. il *Stereo Review* 54:72-3 Ag '89
PEREGRINE ENTERTAINMENT LIMITED
Picking on the little guys. A. B. Block. il *Channels (New York, N.Y.: 1986)* 9:76-9 F '89
PEREGRINE FALCONS *See* Falcons
PEREGRINE SMITH BOOKS
Gibbs Smith: 20 years of activist publishing. J. Barbato. *Publishers Weekly* 236:48 S 8 '89
PEREIRA, JOSEPH
Love blooms in the aisles. il *The Saturday Evening Post* 261:54-5+ S '89
PERELLA, JOSEPH R.
    about
The wizards of 'Wasserella'. J. Schwartz and C. Friday. il pors *Newsweek* 114:30-1 Jl 10 '89
PERELMAN, RONALD OWEN, 1943-
    about
The changes at Revlon are more than just cosmetic. M. Roman. il por *Business Week* p74+ N 20 '89
The incredible Perelman. T. Jaffe. il *Forbes* 143:164 My 15 '89
It's end of an era for S&L rescues—but what an end. C. Yang. il por *Business Week* p40 Ja 9 '89
The Perelman papers. il por *Forbes* 144 Special Issue:360 O 23 '89
The perils of Perelman. E. Paris. il *Forbes* 144:65+ D 11 '89
Ron Perelman's $640 million unsure thing. R. King. il por *Forbes* 144:42-4+ O 30 '89
Sam, make way for Ron. il por *Time* 133:87 My 22 '89
The screwiest S&L bailout ever. B. D. Fromson. il por *Fortune* 119:114-15+ Je 19 '89
The smart money in S&L's. L. Reibstein. il por *Newsweek* 113:40 Ja 9 '89
PERENNIALS (PLANTS)
Best perennials for the South. il *Organic Gardening* 36:44 N '89
Bloom time and shopping time for these perennials. il *Sunset (Central West edition)* 183:116 Ag '89
Gardener-at-large [hardiness] F. McGourty. il *Flower and Garden* 33:64 S/O '89
Keys to a classic perennial garden [flower borders; excerpt from The perennial gardener] F. McGourty. il *Country Journal* 16:32-8 S/O '89
Multiplying favorite perennials with stem cuttings. il *Sunset (Central West edition)* 182:250 My '89
Perennial partnerships [cover story] J. A. McKeon. il *Better Homes and Gardens* 67:111-16 My '89

Perennials in pots. il *Sunset (Central West edition)* 183:196 N '89
Spire plants [garden borders] J. Glattstein. il *Flower and Garden* 33:34-9 My/Je '89
What can you expect from sixpack perennials. il *Sunset (Central West edition)* 182:202+ Mr '89
    Prices
Why do flowers cost so blooming much? il *Money* 18:17 Mr '89
PERERA, VICTOR, 1934-
A forest dies in Guatemala. *The Nation* 249:521-2+ N 6 '89
War of words. il por *Mother Jones* 14:19-21 F/Mr '89
PERES, SHIMON, 1923-
    about
Why is this man so glum? il por *Time* 134:28 Jl 24 '89
PERESS, GILLES
A seared land [photographs] il *Life* 12:92-100 S '89
PERETTI, FRANK E.
    about
Christianity today talks to Frank Peretti. M. G. Maudlin. por *Christianity Today* 33:58-9 D 15 '89
PÉREZ, ALAN GARCÍA *See* García Pérez, Alan
PEREZ, ANNA
    about
Anna Perez boards Bush administration as First Lady's press secretary. por *Jet* 75:12 F 6 '89
Women who go for it! B. M. Campbell. il pors *Essence* 20:48-50+ Ag '89
PÉREZ, CARLOS ANDRÉS
    about
The next liberator? M. Collett. il *The Atlantic* 263:29+ F '89
On drugs, debt and poverty [interview] J. Moody and S. Talbott. il por *Time* 134:12-14 N 27 '89
Péreztroika. S. Talbott. il por *Time* 134:50 O 23 '89
Venezuelans voted for reform—and got more than they bargained for. G. DeGeorge. il por *Business Week* p54 S 4 '89
PEREZ, HUGO
    about
Huge move, Hugo. C. Gammon. il por *Sports Illustrated* 71:22-3 S 25 '89
PÉREZ CELIS
    about
Perez Celis: Anita Shapolsky. L. Malen. il *Art News* 88:150 F '89
PÉREZ DE CUELLAR, JAVIER
The 38th floor. See issues of UN Chronicle
    about
Negotiating peace—at a price [interview] H. Sada. il por *World Press Review* 36:50 My '89
Secretary-General in Namibia: the independence process is 'irreversible'; more than 700,000 register to vote [special section] il *UN Chronicle* 26:4-13 D '89
PÉREZ SILLER, JAVIER
Skeletons at the feast. il *The Unesco Courier* 42:19-24 D '89
PERFECTION
    See also
    Utopias
PERFECTION (PSYCHOLOGY)
How to do your best without driving yourself (and others) crazy. K. Crump. *McCall's* 116:58+ Je '89
PERFLUORO COMPOUNDS
The (liquid) breath of life [perfluorocarbon] M. M. Waldrop. il *Science* 245:1043-5 S 8 '89
PERFORMANCE APPRAISAL *See* Employees—Rating; Women executives—Rating
PERFORMANCE ART
    See also
    Anderson, Laurie, 1947-
    Bogosian, Eric
    Byars, James Lee, 1932-
Bill Irwin and the rest of the New Vaudevillians are rescuing performance art from a decade of pretension. R. Short. il por *Vogue* 179:202+ Ag '89
Pacific HIGHWAYS [alternative performance space for Los Angeles area dancers and artists] E. Zimmer. il *Dance Magazine* 63:52-3 S '89
    Reviews:
    A. Carlson's site specific piece at the Minneapolis Sculpture Garden. C. LeFevre. il *Dance Magazine* 63:78 D '89
    Out There, festival in Minneapolis. J. Timmis. *Dance Magazine* 63:118-19 My '89
Riding the apocalypse [R. Longo's Dream jumbo: working the absolutes] J. Kroll. *Newsweek* 114:80 O 23 '89
    Anecdotes, facetiae, satire, etc.
The performance artist's training manual. L. Montano. *Harper's* 279:36-7 Jl '89
PERFORMANCE PAY *See* Merit pay
PERFORMERS *See* Actors and actresses
PERFORMING ARTISTS DIVERSIFIED (FIRM)
A blast from the past. M. Barrier. il por *Nation's Business* 77:79 Ap '89

PERFORMING ARTS
    See also
      Ballet
      Dance
      Entertainment industry
      Motion pictures
      Music
      Opera
      Performance art
      Theater
      Theatrical agencies and agents
      Vaudeville
Cross country. See issues of Horizon (Tuscaloosa, Ala.)
John Cristi, who sees 300 plays and concerts a year, may
be the greatest show man on earth. S. Dougherty. il pors
People Weekly 32:81+ O 2 '89
      Study and teaching
    See also
      Dillard School of Performing Arts
PERFUME BOTTLES
Message in a bottle [designer P. Dinand] E. Stern. il por
Gentlemen's Quarterly 59:329-32 D '89
PERFUME INDUSTRY
    See also
      International Flavors & Fragrances Inc.
      Royal Essence Ltd.
California perfume boom. P. Calistro. il *Harper's Bazaar*
122:30+ My '89
      Acquisitions and mergers
Bob Taylor wants to walk away from his Obsession [shopping
perfume marketer Minnetonka] M. J. Pitzer. il por *Business
Week* p44 Mr 20 '89
      Advertising
Celebrity scents. il *Vogue* 179:352 S '89
The smell of success [celebrity perfumes] R. Dolphin. il
Maclean's 102:46 Mr 6 '89
      Marketing
Soul searching [Samsara fragrance by Guerlain] R. Wiest.
il *American Health* 8:20 N '89
      France
    See also
      Guerlain SA
      Great Britain
    See also
      J. Floris Ltd.
PERFUMES
    See also
      Potpourri
      Sachets
Check your scent-sory perception [quiz] il *'Teen* 33:56-7
D '89
Flowers [Asoluto fragrance by A. Bellanca] R. West. il
American Health 8:28 Je '89
Fragrance burnout. il *Glamour* 87:32 Ja '89
Fragrance now! il *Essence* 20:84-6 My '89
Making sense of scent [cover story; special section] J. D.
Oliver. il *Health (New York, N.Y.)* 21:57-62+ N '89
Monday's child is full of play . . . [choosing a scent based
on birth chart] il *Seventeen* 48:98-103 D '89
Night heat. il *Mademoiselle* 95:210-13 My '89
Nose job [scent research by B. D. Mookherjee] B. Weber.
il pors *The New York Times Magazine* p78 F 5 '89
Scent allergy alert. l *Essence* 20:46 D '89
Scent and sensuality. il *Glamour* 87:288-9 S '89
Scent-sational ideas [with favorite perfumes of celebrities]
il *Redbook* 173:10 Ag '89
Scent-sible workout [wearing fragrance while exercising] L.
A. Mark. il *American Health* 8:22 N '89
Scented & overheard. il *Harper's Bazaar* 122:30+ O '89
Selecting a perfect scent. P. Boyer. il *Prevention (Emmaus,
Pa.)* 41:88+ F '89
Sniff and tell. C. Heimel and L. Grossberger. il *Vogue*
179:312-13 My '89
Suitable scents: a user's guide to fragrance at the office.
J. Resnick. il *Working Woman* 14:120+ D '89
Thoroughly modern. il *Mademoiselle* 95:160-1 D '89
To Diana and Ivana, a nose by any other name than 'Aphelion'
wouldn't smell as sweet [master parfumeur who creates
personalized scents] D. Marlow. il pors *People Weekly*
32:78-80 Jl 24 '89
Understanding dollars and scents [quiz] il *Essence* 20:56
My '89
Your scents of smell. L. A. Mark. il *American Health* 8:18-19
N '89
      Advertising
    See Perfume industry—Advertising
      Anecdotes, facetiae, satire, etc.
Life is often full of unexpected challenges, as William Geist
quickly discovers when he innocently sets out to buy
his wife a new fragrance. W. Geist. il *Vogue* 179:198+
N '89
      History
The fragrance chronicles. il *Health (New York, N.Y.)* 21:64-5
N '89
      Exhibitions
Even pharaohs had facials [Perfumes and cosmetics in the
ancient world at the Israel Museum] il *Newsweek* 114:79
D 11 '89

The Roman nose [perfumes of ancient Rome at Emory
University] il *U.S. News & World Report* 106:14-15 Ap
3 '89
      Names
What's in a name. J. Shields. il *Vogue* 179:196-7 N '89
PERFUMES FOR MEN
Bottled up. il *Esquire* 111:162-5 My '89
Desirée under the elms [4711] H. Sterne. il *Gentlemen's
Quarterly* 59:84 Je '89
Men's bazaar. L. Parker. il *Harper's Bazaar* 122:41 O '89
Oh, boy! Some common sense about men's scents. il
Mademoiselle 95:46 N '89
On the scent of the '90s guy. il *Mademoiselle* 95:22 Je
'89
Smell-shocked. A. Tardio. il *Gentlemen's Quarterly* 59:326-8
D '89
PERI, CAMILLE
Witch craft. il pors *Mother Jones* 14:28-31+ Ap '89
PERI, JACOPO, 1561-1633
      about
Euridice [opera] Reviews
    The New Yorker 65:77 My 8 '89. A. Porter
LE PERIGORD (NEW YORK, N.Y.: RESTAURANT) *See*
New York (N.Y.)—Restaurants, nightclubs, bars, etc.
PERIOD ROOMS, AMERICAN *See* House decoration, Ameri-
can
PERIODIC TABLE
Mapping the periodic landscape of elements [3-D periodic
table proposed by Leland C. Allen] I. Amato. il *Science
News* 136:390 D 16 '89
PERIODICAL ADVERTISING *See* Advertising, Magazine
PERIODICAL ARTICLES
Articles for the rural and country market. R. Matthews.
The Writer 102:28-9 N '89
Computing for dollars [selling articles to computer magazines]
C. Walnum. il *The Writer* 102:20-2 Mr '89
Creating articles for the crafts market. M. Flathers. *The
Writer* 102:24-6 Ag '89
How to write a how-to that sells. G. Luttmann. *The Writer*
102:19-20+ Jl '89
Making article ideas happen. J. Stocker. *The Writer* 102:32-3
Ag '89
Market newsletter. See issues of The Writer
Nine steps for outlining nonfiction. S. Bartley. *The Writer*
102:22-4 Ap '89
Sell your hidden gold with a query [query letters] T. Jenkins.
The Writer 102:18-20+ Ag '89
A specialist in many fields [freelance writers] G. Stern. *The
Writer* 102:17-19 My '89
Spring training for writers [freelancers] J. McCollister. *The
Writer* 102:7-8 Ap '89
This month's special market lists. See issues of The Writer
Three surefire ways to write and sell nonfiction. S. S. Baker.
The Writer 102:11-13 Mr '89
Tips on writing the how-to article. H. J. Pratt. *The Writer*
102:31-2 S '89
Titles can sell articles. C. Robinson. *The Writer* 102:20-1+
Ja '89
Travel writing: a primer. R. W. Anderson. *The Writer*
102:14-16 Je '89
Where to sell manuscripts. See issues of The Writer
Writing for life style magazines (II). il *The Writer* 102:28-30
Ja '89
Writing for Mother Jones. J. A. Cabello. il *The Writer*
102:28 O '89
Writing for the trades. H. Scott. *The Writer* 102:22-5 F
'89
Writing for Vegetarian times. L. Moll. il *The Writer* 102:25-6
Ap '89
You may be an expert and not know it. C. A. Smith.
The Writer 102:26-7 Ja '89
PERIODICAL COVERS
The Christmas cover story [special effects used to create
New York times magazine cover photo; work of Elliot
Erwitt and Bran Ferren] B. Weber. il *The New York
Times Magazine* p34 D 24 '89
PERIODICAL DESIGN
Around the Mall and beyond [graphic artist B. Thompson]
E. Park. il *Smithsonian* 20:22-4+ S '89
The Russian revolutionary [A. Brodovitch, former art director
at Harper's bazaar] E. Hartney. il *Harper's Bazaar*
122:324-5+ S '89
PERIODICAL LIBRARIES *See* Newspaper and periodical
libraries
PERIODICAL VENDORS
    See also
      Booksellers and bookselling—Periodical selling
Read all about it [magazine stores in New York City] P.
Eaton. il *New York* 22:58 My 1 '89
PERIODICALS
    See also
      Alternative press
      Booksellers and bookselling—Periodical selling
      Children's periodicals
      House organs
      Jewish periodicals
      Journalism
      Libraries—Periodical collections

PERIODICALS—See also—*cont.*
News periodicals
See also names of periodicals; *also* subhead Periodicals under various subjects
Ragtime. R. Rosenblatt. *The New Republic* 201:130 N 6 '89
Recommended reading. See issues of Utne Reader
Trying to pick winners among new publications. M. S. Forbes. il *Forbes* 143:20 F 6 '89
Illustration
See Illustration
Letters to the editor
Letters and more letters [Sports illustrated's swimsuit issue] L. Montville. il *Sports Illustrated* 70 Special Issue:276+ F '89
Letters of the '80s. R. J. Ames. il *U.S. News & World Report* 107:6-7 D 25 '89-Ja 1 '90
What Time readers said in '88. il *Time* 133:13 F 20 '89
Prices
Combating high journal costs. P. H. Abelson. *Science* 244:1125 Je 9 '89
The serials pricing controversy. G. Feldman. il *Publishers Weekly* 235:68-70 Ja 13 '89
Subscriptions
Magazine telephone scams. il *Consumers' Research Magazine* 72:36-7 Mr '89
Africa
Providing journals [AAAS program for sub-Saharan Africa] L. A. Levey. il map *Science* 245:538 Ag 4 '89
Canada
See also
Canadian lawyer (Periodical)
Maclean's (Periodical)
Saturday night (Periodical)
Great Britain
See also
Nature (Periodical)
Private eye (Periodical)
Punch (Periodical)
Hong Kong
See also
Far Eastern economic review
Hungary
See also
Interpress expo 4/1988 (Periodical)
Reform (Periodical)
Israel
See also
New outlook (Periodical)
Soviet Union
See also
Kvant (Periodical)
Ogonyok (Periodical)
Science in the USSR (Periodical)
Soviet life (Periodical)
PERIODICALS, PUBLISHING OF *See* Publishers and publishing—Periodicals
PERIODICALS FOR MEN
See also
Gentlemen's quarterly
Penthouse (Periodical)
Playboy (Periodical)
PERIODICALS FOR WOMEN
See also
Essence (Periodical)
Feminism—Periodicals
Glamour (Periodical)
Imagen (Periodical)
Lear's (Periodical)
Mirabella (Periodical)
Ms. (Periodical)
Vogue (Periodical)
Women's sports & fitness (Periodical)
Working woman (Periodical)
PERIODICALS ON VIDEOTAPES
Magazines on cassette hit fast forward. M. Pierson. il *Video* 13:16 Ap '89
PERIODICITY *See* Biological rhythms; Cycles
PERIODONTAL DISEASE *See* Gums—Diseases
PERIPHERAL EQUIPMENT (COMPUTERS) *See* Computers—Equipment
PERISCOPES
Fiber-optic periscope could alter sub design. *High Technology Business* 9:35 Je '89
PERIWINKLE
Diffusible factors essential for epidermal cell redifferentiation in Catharanthus roseus. B. A. Siegel and J. A. Verbeke. bibl f il *Science* 244:580-2 My 5 '89
PERIYALI (NEW YORK, N.Y.: RESTAURANT) *See* New York (N.Y.)—Restaurants, nightclubs, bars, etc.
PERKIN-ELMER CORP.
About to start perkin'? T. Jaffe. *Forbes* 144:304-5 N 27 '89
The big glass [Hubble Space Telescope mirror; cover story] T. Dunkle. il *Discover* 10:68-81 Jl '89
Perkin-Elmer: in fighting trim? J. M. Laderman. *Business Week* p59 Ag 7 '89

Possible Japanese buyout of U.S. chip equipment manufacturer draws fire [with editorial comment] B. D. Nordwall. il *Aviation Week & Space Technology* 131:9, 26-7 D 4 '89
PERKINS, CARL C.
Crossroads: the journey to a permanent presence. *Ad Astra* 1:14 O '89
PERKINS, EDWARD J.
Review of U.S.-South Africa relations [address, June 6, 1989] *Department of State Bulletin* 89:69-73 S '89
The seedlings of hope: U.S. policy in Africa [address, June 11, 1989] *Department of State Bulletin* 89:69-72 Ag '89
about
Perkins installed as new U.S. Foreign Service head. il por *Jet* 77:8 O 23 '89
Todman is Argentina envoy, Perkins is named director of U.S. Foreign Service. il pors *Jet* 76:36-7 My 22 '89
PERKINS, ELIZABETH
about
Elizabeth Perkins. J. Guare. il pors *Esquire* 111:142-3 Ap '89
PERKINS, FRANCES, 1882-1965
about
Frances Perkins and the flowering of economic and social policies. G. Berg. *Monthly Labor Review* 112:28-32 Je '89
PERKINS, JIM C.
about
Chevrolet tries to get the lead out. J. B. Treece. il por *Business Week* p39 My 22 '89
PERKINS, PHEME
Beside the Lord. *The Christian Century* 106:522 My 17 '89
Fit for the reign of God. il *The Christian Century* 106:618 Je 21-28 '89
God's gift of righteousness. il *The Christian Century* 106:954 O 25 '89
How do we live with dying? il *The Christian Century* 106:979 N 1 '89
The Magic Kingdom. il *The Christian Century* 106:1083 N 22 '89
Not through the law. *The Christian Century* 106:587 Je 7-14 '89
'The power of sin is the law'. il *The Christian Century* 106:1044 N 15 '89
Understanding faith and miracle. *The Christian Century* 106:555 My 24-31 '89
Weariness in well-doing. il *The Christian Century* 106:1011 N 8 '89
Works of God in our tongues. *The Christian Century* 106:498 My 10 '89
PERKINS, RAYMOND K.
Nuclear abolition: would cheaters count? *The Bulletin of the Atomic Scientists* 45:16-17 D '89
PERKINS, ROBERT
about
Follow your bliss [interview] P. Edidin. il pors *Psychology Today* 23:62-4 My '89
PERKINS, SPENCER
The prolife credibility gap. il por *Christianity Today* 33:21-2 Ap 21 '89
PERKINS, ABBY (FICTIONAL CHARACTER) *See* Abby Perkins (Fictional character)
PERKINS FAMILY RESTAURANTS LP
Perkins Family Restaurants LP. R. Abelson. il *Fortune* 120:112 Jl 3 '89
PERKINS GEDDIS EASTMAN (FIRM)
The woman-managed firm: how big a deal? R. L. Miller. il pors *Architectural Record* 177:47+ Je '89
PERKO, MARGARET
My Aunt Metka [story] il *Good Housekeeping* 209:78+ O '89
PERKS (EXECUTIVES' BENEFITS) *See* Executives—Salaries, pensions, etc.
PERL, JED, 1951-
Kitsch in synch. il *Vogue* 179:326-7+ F '89
PERLE, RICHARD N.
[Column] See issues of U.S. News & World Report beginning May 25, 1987
PERLMAN, LAWRENCE, 1938-
about
Control Data may finally have the right stuff. R. Mitchell. *Business Week* p30 Ap 24 '89
Fine job, Larry—but don't get too settled. R. Mitchell. il por *Business Week* p34 O 16 '89
PERLMAN, PHILIP S., AND BUTOW, RONALD A.
Mobile introns and intron-encoded proteins. bibl f il *Science* 246:1106-9 D 1 '89
PERLMAN, AMOS
Israel's dilemma. *Foreign Affairs* 68:119-32 Wint '89/'90
PERLMUTTER, CATHY
Greenhouse gold. il pors *Organic Gardening* 36:56-60 O '89
PERLMUTTER, ROGER M.
T cell signaling. bibl f il *Science* 245:344 Jl 28 '89
PERMANENT COURT OF INTERNATIONAL JUSTICE
See also
International Court of Justice

PERMANENT WAVES *See* Hairstyling
PERMEABILITY (BIOLOGY)
    See also
    Vascular permeability factor
PERMIAN PERIOD *See* Paleontology—Permian
PERMIT FISHING *See* Pompano fishing
PERONA, JOHN J., AND OTHERS
    Structural basis for misaminoacylation by mutant E. coli glutaminyl-tRNA synthetase enzymes. bibl f il *Science* 246:1152-4 D 1 '89
PÉRONCEL-HUGOZ, JEAN-PIERRE, 1940-
    Oman's benevolent Ibadism. *World Press Review* 36:34 Jl '89
PERONISM
    Argentina's return to Peronism [C. Menem] R. Graham and G. Mead. *World Press Review* 36:23-4 Jl '89
    A Peronist triumph [C. Menem wins] M. Nemeth. il por *Maclean's* 102:24 My 29 '89
    Peronists seek "nuclear greatness". R. A. Kessler. il por *The Bulletin of the Atomic Scientists* 45:13-15 My '89
    Peron's latest hurrah [election of C. S. Menem] E. Ehrmann. *National Review* 41:20-1 Je 16 '89
    Return of the Peronists? J. Contreras. il por *Newsweek* 113:48 My 15 '89
PEROT, H. ROSS, 1930-
        about
    Airport '89. E. Buckberg. *The New Republic* 201:12-13 Ag 21 '89
    Breaking up is hard to do. D. P. Levin. il pors *The New York Times Magazine* p36-7+ Mr 26 '89
    The Ross Perot riddle. L. Reibstein. il por *Newsweek* 113:38-9 Ja 9 '89
PEROT SYSTEMS CORPORATION
    Breaking up is hard to do [G.M. vs. R. Perot] D. P. Levin. il pors *The New York Times Magazine* p36-7+ Mr 26 '89
    The Ross Perot riddle. L. Reibstein. il por *Newsweek* 113:38-9 Ja 9 '89
PEROVSKITE
    Elasticity of MgSiO$_3$ in the perovskite structure. A. Yeganeh-Haeri and others. bibl f il *Science* 243:787-9 F 10 '89
PEROXIDASES
    See also
    Myeloperoxidase
    Identification by ENDOR of Trp[191] as the free-radical site in cytochrome c peroxidase compound ES. M. Sivaraja and others. bibl f il *Science* 245:738-40 Ag 18 '89
PEROXISOMES
    Clues to a new class of liver carcinogens [peroxisome-proliferating chemicals; research by Janardan Reddy] J. Raloff. *Science News* 135:119 F 25 '89
PERRAULT, DOMINIQUE, 1953-
        about
    An architect for Mitterrand's new library. N. Marmer. il *Art in America* 77:31 O '89
PERREAULT, JOHN, 1937-
    Turning point. il *American Craft* 49:24-31 F/Mr '89
PERREAULT, ROBERT, AND LAURENDEAU, MARIE-CLAIRE
    Tele-Health. il *World Health* p6-7 Mr '89
PERRELLA, JAMES ELBERT, 1935-
    The right way [address, January 19, 1989] *Vital Speeches of the Day* 55:375-6 Ap 1 '89
PERRIER, SOURCE SA *See* Source Perrier SA
PERRIN, NOEL
    Science fiction: imaginary worlds and real-life questions. il *The New York Times Book Review* 94:37-8 Ap 9 '89
    The ten great wants of 1989. il *Country Journal* 16:17-19 Jl/Ag '89
PERRIN LONG INC.
    Perrin Long: the loner everybody listens to. J. Friedman. il por *Business Week* p58 Jl 24 '89
PERRINE, DOUG
    Reef fish feedings: amusement or nuisance? il *Sea Frontiers* 35:272-9 S/O '89
    Reef shark attack! bibl il *Sea Frontiers* 35:31-41 Ja/F '89
PERRITT, GERALD W.
        about
    Beware those high-cost mutual funds [interview] E. Schultz. il por *Fortune* 119:34-5 Mr 13 '89
PERRITT, HENRY H.
    Government information goes on-line. il *Technology Review* 92:60-5+ N/D '89
PERRONE, JEFF
        about
    Jeff Perrone at Charles Cowles. B. Adams. il *Art in America* 77:207-8 S '89
PERRY, CARRIE SAXON
        about
    What must be done. il pors *Ebony* 44:156+ Ag '89
PERRY, CHANA
        about
    Driving on bad wheels. J. Garrity. il por *Sports Illustrated* 70:62-3 F 20 '89
PERRY, CHARLEEN
        about
    A passion for herbs. J. A. McKeon. il pors *Better Homes and Gardens* 67:50-4 Ag '89

PERRY, D. A., AND OTHERS
    Bootstrapping in ecosystems. bibl f il *BioScience* 39:230-7 Ap '89
PERRY, DAVID
    Do the Rice thing. il *Omni (New York, N.Y.)* 12:26+ O '89
    Fantasies of the opera. il *Omni (New York, N.Y.)* 11:24+ My '89
PERRY, EGBERT
        about
    Taking charge [cover story] K. D. Thompson and others. il pors *Black Enterprise* 20:42-4+ Ag '89
PERRY, ELISABETH ISRAELS
    Cleaning up the dance halls. bibl il *History Today* 39:20-6 O '89
PERRY, FRANK
        about
    Diary of a duplex: Barbara Goldsmith and Frank Perry on Park. B. Goldsmith. il pors *Architectural Digest* 46:310-15 N '89
PERRY, GAYLORD
        about
    Morals and immortals. P. Gammons. il por *Sports Illustrated* 70:78 Ja 23 '89
PERRY, JAMES A., AND OTHERS
    X-ray microanalysis of leaf-litter decomposition in lakes. bibl f il *BioScience* 39:260-3 Ap '89
PERRY, KENT W.
    Cops: we're losing the war. por *Newsweek* 113:6-7 Mr 13 '89
PERRY, NANCY J.
    Saving the schools: how business can help. *Current (Washington, D.C.)* 310:20-6 F '89
PERRY, WALTER *See* Perry of Walton, Walter Laing Macdonald Perry, Baron, 1921-
PERRY, WILLIAM JAMES, 1927-
    Defense investment strategy. *Foreign Affairs* 68:72-92 Spr '89
PERRY (ANTOINETTE) AWARDS *See* Tony Awards
PERRY ELLIS SPORTSWEAR INC.
    Life after Perry Ellis [M. Jacobs named head designer] N. Darnton. il por *Newsweek* 113:67 Ja 2 '89
    On the Marc [designer M. Jacobs] C. Heimel. il por *Vogue* 179:84-5+ F '89
PERRY MASON (FICTIONAL CHARACTER)
    Morrow to release first new Perry Mason novel in 15 years [authored by T. Chastain] *Publishers Weekly* 235:66+ F 3 '89
PERRY NUCLEAR POWER PLANT (OHIO) *See* Nuclear power plants
PERRY OF WALTON, WALTER LAING MACDONALD PERRY, BARON, 1921-
        about
    Britain's University of the Air [interview] H. G. Shane. il pors *The Futurist* 23:25-7 Jl/Ag '89
PERRYMAN, ELIZABETH K.
    Folliculo-stellate cells of the pituitary gland. bibl f il *BioScience* 39:81-8 F '89
PERSECUTION
    See also
    Genocide
    'I am Jesus, whom you persecute'. K. Koyama. *The Christian Century* 106:347 Ap 5 '89
PERSEIDS (METEORS) *See* Meteors
PERSIAN AUB ZAM ZAM (SAN FRANCISCO, CALIF.: BAR) *See* San Francisco (Calif.)—Restaurants, nightclubs, bars, etc.
PERSIAN GULF REGION
            Foreign relations
            Iraq
        See Iraq—Foreign relations—Persian Gulf region
            United States
        See United States—Foreign relations—Persian Gulf region
            Industries
    See also
    Aerospace industries—Persian Gulf region
PERSIAN POETRY
    See also
    Epic poetry, Persian
PERSIANS *See* Iranians
PERSKY, BILL
    Conan and me. il *Esquire* 111:34+ My '89
PERSONAL BANKRUPTCY *See* Bankruptcy
PERSONAL BEAUTY *See* Beauty, Personal
PERSONAL CARE APPLIANCES
    Electrical devices for everything from hair removal to facial steaming are proliferating, and other "plugged in" beauty ideas are on the way. L. F. McCarthy. *Vogue* 179:166 D '89
PERSONAL CARE PRODUCTS
    See also
    Cosmetics
    Deodorants
    Feminine hygiene products
    Hair care products
            Storage
    The great beauty clean-up. il *Teen* 33:12 Jl '89

PERSONAL CARE PRODUCTS INDUSTRY
See also
Alberto-Culver Co.
American Health and Beauty Aids Institute
Amway Corp.
Avon Products, Inc.
Bristol-Myers Co.
Colgate-Palmolive Co. (Delaware)
Cosmetics industry
EPI Products Inc.
Gillette Co.
Johnson & Johnson
Mennen Company
Minnetonka Inc.
Procter & Gamble Co.
Shaklee Corp.
Tom's of Maine, Inc.
Windmere Corp.

Acquisitions and mergers
How d'ya say "liquidator" in Japanese? [I. Jacobs plays Tokyo-New York arbitrage in raids on Shaklee and Avon] S. Flack. il por *Forbes* 143:39-40 Je 12 '89
A takeover of Avon could mean a makeover for Amway. W. Zellner. il *Business Week* p38-9 My 22 '89
Warren Buffett makes money by making nice [friendly stake in Gillette] L. Jereski. il por *Business Week* p58 Ag 7 '89

Finance
Consumer products. C. Palmeri. il *Forbes* 143:126-7 Ja 9 '89

PERSONAL COMPUTER INDUSTRY See Computer industry
PERSONAL COMPUTERS See Computers
PERSONAL CRITICISM See Criticism, Personal
PERSONAL EXEMPTION DEDUCTIONS See Income tax— Deductions
PERSONAL FINANCE See Finance, Personal
PERSONAL FINANCIAL PLANNING See Investment advisers
PERSONAL FLOTATION DEVICES See Life preservers
PERSONAL HOLDING COMPANIES
Taxation
New trick for greenmailers [Transtech Industries use of personal holding company loophole] J. Zweig. il *Forbes* 144:110 O 30 '89
PERSONAL INFORMATION MANAGEMENT SOFTWARE
Software that battles chaos. J. Pepper. il *Working Woman* 14:67-8 Ap '89
What's new in personal information managers. C. O'Malley. *Personal Computing* 13:105-7+ Jl '89
Testing
Arriba: the painless PIM. L. Wood. il *Byte* 14:197-8+ S '89
Compute! Choice [Arriba] K. Ferrell. il *Compute!* 11:58-60 D '89
Instant Recall: a pop-up PIM. M. Young. *Personal Computing* 13:206 N '89
Let your computer be your date book. W. C. Symonds and M. Shao. il *Business Week* p81 Ag 7 '89
Lotus Agenda reviewed. R. Gehorsam. il *Home Office Computing* 7:30-1 Mr '89
Organization man, late 1980's style [using Lotus Agenda] N. Sullivan. il *Home Office Computing* 7:96 Mr '89
Personal information made easy [Arriba] B. Krasnoff. il *Personal Computing* 13:196 S '89
PERSONAL LIBERTY See Liberty
PERSONAL LOANS See Loans, Personal
PERSONAL NAMES See Names, Personal
PERSONAL PORTFOLIO MANAGER (NEWSLETTER) See Investment newsletters
PERSONAL PROPERTY See Property
PERSONAL RIGHTS See Civil rights
PERSONAL SECRETS
See also
Self disclosure
Do you keep too many secrets? B. Benson. il *Nation's Business* 77:42+ Ag '89
Don't tell me secrets. C. H. Caplin. *Glamour* 87:168-9 Mr '89
Loose lips sink friendships. S. Mansfield. *Mademoiselle* 95:56 Ja '89
The truth about lying to a lover. D. Heyn. *Mademoiselle* 95:118 F '89
What guys wish women wouldn't tell. W. D. Leight. *Mademoiselle* 95:136 S '89
PERSONAL SPACE
The woman in the yellow hat [encounter with a stranger in Oregon's Eagle Cap Wilderness] P. G. Quinnett. il *Audubon* 91:46-8 S '89
PERSONAL STYLE See Fashion
PERSONAL TRAINERS
The agony and the exercise. J. Green. il *Gentlemen's Quarterly* 59:176-9+ Ja '89
Basic training. P. Lee. il *Black Enterprise* 19:52-3 Jl '89
In search of the perfect trainer. A. Tardio. il *Gentlemen's Quarterly* 59:180-3 Ja '89
One-on-one wonder? I. Borger. il *Vogue* 179:108+ Ja '89
Personal best [interview with B. Pearlman] C. Moekle. il *American Health* 8:32 O '89

Private enterprise. il *Harper's Bazaar* 122:136-7+ My '89
PERSONALITY
See also
Body image
Character
Charisma
Identity (Psychology)
Individuality
Innocence (Psychology)
Leadership
Minnesota Multiphasic Personality Inventory
Moods
Resilience (Psychology)
Self
Typology (Psychology)
The character of controversy [link between disease and personality; work of R. Grossarth-Maticek] J. Fischman. il *Psychology Today* 22:27 D '88
Health's character [link between personality and disease; research by R. Grossarth-Maticek] H. J. Eysenck. il pors *Psychology Today* 22:28-32+ D '88
How to make a good impression [condensed from You are the message]; ed. by Jon Kraushar. R. Ailes. il *Reader's Digest* 135:139-42 S '89
Who stays fit [lifelong link between personality and exercise habits; research by Paula Schnurr and others] E. Stark. *Psychology Today* 23:73 N '89
You are what you play [perceived character traits of sports participants; research by Darwyn Linder and others] V. Bozzi. il *Psychology Today* 23:69 O '89
Your brand of sweat [choosing a sport that suits your personality] J. Gavin. il *Psychology Today* 23:50-3+ Mr '89
Disorders
See also
Alexithymia
Borderline personality disorder
Multiple personality
Narcissism
Schizophrenia
Genetic aspects
What a child is given. D. Franklin. il *The New York Times Magazine* p36-41+ S 3 '89
PERSONALITY TESTS See Psychological tests
PERSONALS
The kids are fine [personals in alumni magazines] J. Atlas. *The New Republic* 201:13-14 S 4 '89
Anecdotes, facetiae, satire, etc.
Desperately seeking . . . anyone [excerpt from My life as a gal] A. Kahn. il *Utne Reader* p67 Mr/Ap '89
'Well-educated, dynamic man seeks . . .'. S. MacLeod. por *Maclean's* 102:64 My 29 '89
PERSONICS CORPORATION
Electronic disc jockeys: a new hit. il *Newsweek* 114:47 Ag 28 '89
Personics offers customer programmed cassettes. E. Kehler. il *Down Beat* 56:11 N '89
Personics steps to the fore. J. Ressner. il *Rolling Stone* p24 O 19 '89
PERSONNEL MANAGEMENT
See also
AIDS (Disease) and employment
Alcohol and employment
Communication in management
Drugs and employment
Employee counseling
Employees—Dismissal
Employees—Rating
Employees—Recruiting
Employees—Training
Employment tests
Factory management
Incentives in industry
Job satisfaction
Labor discipline
Labor turnover
Layoffs
Nepotism
Profit sharing
Promotions
Psychology, Industrial
Seniority, Employee
Smoking and employment
13 ways to re-energize your staff. A. J. Bernstein and S. C. Rozen. il *Working Woman* 14:45-6 Ap '89
The best way to get a new employee up to speed. S. Mardenfeld. *Working Woman* 14:34 N '89
Business secrets of Tommy Lasorda [interview] B. Dumaine. il pors *Fortune* 120:130-2+ Jl 3 '89
Cultivating the gray [managing seniors at Days Inns] D. Machan. il pors *Forbes* 144:126+ S 11 '89
Handling good employees who are lousy time managers. S. Schlenger and R. Roesch. *Working Woman* 14:21 Je '89
How delegation can lead your team to victory. J. Calano and J. Salzman. *Working Woman* 14:86-7+ Ag '89

PERSONNEL MANAGEMENT—cont.

How human resource systems adjust to the shift toward contingent workers. R. S. Belous. bibl f il *Monthly Labor Review* 112:7-12 Mr '89

How to get procrastinators up to speed [excerpt from The now habit] N. A. Fiore. il *Working Woman* 14:38+ Mr '89

Making over middle managers. K. Labich. il *Fortune* 119:58-61+ My 8 '89

Managing your intellectuals [excerpt from Right places, right times] H. Donovan. il pors *Fortune* 120:177-8+ O 23 '89

New hope for handling old-pro procrastinators. S. Chan. *Working Woman* 14:30+ O '89

One minute management [interview with K. H. Blanchard] S. F. Edwards. por *Home Office Computing* 7:62 S '89

Read this article immediately. E. M. Collier. il *Nation's Business* 77:68+ O '89

The special art of managing creative people. M. R. Feinberg. *Working Woman* 14:40 My '89

When you're bullish on two employees but can promote only one. M. R. Feinberg. il *Working Woman* 14:30 O '89

Japan

Help wanted, room to advance—out the door [American managers quit at Mazda's U.S. plant] W. Zellner. il *Business Week* p42 O 30 '89

PERSONS, WALLACE R.

about

The U.S. Business Hall of Fame. W. Guzzardi. il por *Fortune* 119:133-4 Mr 13 '89

PERSPIRATION

Sweat: how sweet it is. il *Mademoiselle* 95:224-5 My '89

PERSUASION (PSYCHOLOGY)

Friendly persuasion: how to help your husband help himself. J. Bailey. *Redbook* 172:110-11+ Ap '89

PERT, AGU

(jt. auth) See Weber, Richard J., and Pert, Agu

PERTSCHUK, MICHAEL, 1933-, AND SCHAETZEL, WENDY

The remaking of Robert Bork. il *The Nation* 249:750-2 D 18 '89

PERTUSSIS See Whooping cough

PERTUSSIS TOXIN

Mutants of pertussis toxin suitable for vaccine development. M. Pizza and others. bibl f il *Science* 246:497-500 O 27 '89

A pertussis toxin-sensitive G protein in hippocampal long-term potentiation. J. W. Goh and P. S. Pennefather. bibl f il *Science* 244:980-3 My 26 '89

Vaccine confers pertussis protection. K. Fackelmann. *Science News* 136:276 O 28 '89

PERU

See also

Arequipa (Peru)

Cultural property—Protection—Peru

Lima (Peru)

Narcotics laws and regulations—Peru

Privatization—Peru

Rain forests—Peru

Antiquities

See also

Machu Picchu (Peru)

Tombs—Peru

Corn and culture in central Andean prehistory. S. Johannessen and C. A. Hastorf. bibl f il *Science* 244:690-2 My 12 '89

Long before the Inca. R. L. Burger. il map *Natural History* p66-73 F '89

Now you see it, now you don't [Cahuachi excavations; work of Helaine Silverman] *Science News* 136:13 Jl 1 '89

Economic conditions

See also

Underground economy—Peru

Economic policy

A tale of two countries: why Chile booms as Peru swoons. C. Roberts. il *Business Week* p18 My 29 '89

Industries

See also

Banco de Credito del Peru

Native peoples

See Indians of South America—Peru

Photographs and photography

Descendants of the Incas. V. Revilla. il *Society* 26:77-80 Jl/Ag '89

Politics and government

See also

Political campaigns—Peru

A Christian spirituality of nonviolence. E. W. Ranly. *America* 161:110-11+ Ag 26-S 2 '89

Cocaine, communism and crisis in Peru. C. A. Robbins. il *U.S. News & World Report* 107:45-9 S 18 '89

Has God forgotten Peru? R. A. Schroth. il *Commonweal* 116:459-61 S 8 '89

Lurching toward anarchy. G. D. Garcia. il *Time* 133:54 Mr 27 '89

Peru fights to overcome its past. A. Riding. il por *The New York Times Magazine* p40+ My 14 '89

Peru in peril. E. W. Ranly. il *The Christian Century* 106:657-9 Jl 5-12 '89

Terrorism, inflation, and debt threaten democracy in Peru [interview with E. Zileri] A. Balk. il por *World Press Review* 36:33-5 Ja '89

Thesis disPeruvian. T. Rosenberg. *The New Republic* 201:15-17 O 9 '89

With the Shining Path. J. Contreras. il map *Newsweek* 113:44-5+ Ap 24 '89

Religious institutions and affairs

See also

Church and narcotics trade—Peru

Church and social problems—Peru

Convents—Peru

PERU AMATEUR CIRCUS (IND.)

Circusmania. H. G. Miller. il *The Saturday Evening Post* 261:40 Jl/Ag '89

PERUGIA (ITALY)

Description

Perugia. N. Stancioff. il map *Gourmet* 49:70-5+ My '89

PERUTZ, MAX, 1914-

Is Britain 'befouled'? bibl f il *The New York Review of Books* 36:51-7 N 23 '89

PERUVIAN COOKING See Cooking, Peruvian

PESAPALLO (GAME)

Ten things you never knew about pesapallo. T. R. Kovach. il *Sport (New York, N.Y.)* 80:15 O '89

PESARO (ITALY)

Music festivals

See Music festivals—Italy

PESKY CRITTERS RELOCATION (FIRM)

Trapper Todd Hardwick tackles the ultimate varmint, a monster python who won't leave home. M. Neill. il pors *People Weekly* 32:179-80+ D 4 '89

PESMEN, CURTIS

Diabetes: the silent partner. il *Seventeen* 48:86-7+ Ja '89

The greenhouse effect. il *Seventeen* 48:162-3+ Je '89

PESSEN, EDWARD, 1920-

On social position and political achievement. *Society* 26:10-12 Mr/Ap '89

PESSIMISM

See also

Catastrophic thinking

Are you a negaholic? [excerpt] C. Carter-Scott. *Harper's Bazaar* 122:103+ Ja '89

Putting pessimism in its place. L. B. Morris. il *Health (New York, N.Y.)* 21:62-3 Ag '89

PESSOA, FERNANDO, 1888-1935

Tabacaria ('the tobacconist's') [poem] *The Courier (Unesco)* 41:32 N '88

about

Fernando Pessoa and the spirit of discovery. J. A. Seabra. il *The Courier (Unesco)* 42:37-8 Ap '89

Fernando Pessoa: many poets in one. J. A. Seabra. il pors *The Courier (Unesco)* 41:30-4 N '88

PEST CONTROL

See also

Insect control

Pesticides

Ultrasonic waves—Pest control use

The biological future of pest control [address, November 15, 1988] D. A. Miller. *Vital Speeches of the Day* 55:337-40 Mr 15 '89

Selected southern pest profiles [garden pests] il *Organic Gardening* 36:48-9 N '89

PEST CONTROL SERVICES

See also

Pesky Critters Relocation (Firm)

PESTICIDE POLLUTION See Pesticides—Environmental aspects

PESTICIDE RESIDUES IN FOOD

The American paradox [address, October 31, 1989] D. A. Miller. *Vital Speeches of the Day* 56:150-3 D 15 '89

Americans, frightened and confused by recent media reports on pesticides, have turned to experts for guidance—and learned there are no easy answers. L. M. Kase. *Vogue* 179:112 Jl '89

Consumers won't sacrifice food appearance. *Successful Farming* 87:40I Ag '89

Dangers in the vegetable patch. S. Begley. il *Newsweek* 113:74-5 Ja 30 '89

Dining with invisible danger [cover story; special section] A. Toufexis. il *Time* 133:28-30+ Mr 27 '89

Fear of fruits (or, Waiter, there's a pesticide in my salad). J. Nash. il *Mademoiselle* 95:134 Ag '89

Food safety is no fad! N. Byal. il *Successful Farming* 87:12-13 D '89

The foods that are poisoning your child. A. Fischer. *Redbook* 173:116-18+ My '89

High cost vs. low risk [pesticide ban will increase food prices] J. W. Merline. il *Consumers' Research Magazine* 72:38 Je '89

Intolerable risk. S. O. Daniels. *Organic Gardening* 36:5 Mr '89

Is our food safe? il *The Mother Earth News* 119:87 S/O '89

Monitoring pesticides in our food. B. T. Hunter. il *Consumers' Research Magazine* 72:34-5+ Je '89

PESTICIDE RESIDUES IN FOOD—cont.

A mother's crusade [M. Streep's campaign against residues in children's food; cover story] J. C. McCullagh. il pors *Organic Gardening* 36:32-7 Ap '89

Ms. Streep goes to Washington to stop a bitter harvest [children's food; interview] B. Johnson. il pors *People Weekly* 31:50-1 Mr 20 '89

Organic for all. S. O. Daniels. *Organic Gardening* 36:5 Ap '89

Pesticide/food risk greatest under age 6. J. Raloff. *Science News* 135:133 Mr 4 '89

Pesticide residues safe for children, too. *FDA Consumer* 23:2 My '89

Pesticides & fruit: ways to lower your risks. S. Nielsen. il *Good Housekeeping* 208:241-2 Je '89

Pesticides and kids. L. Roberts. il *Science* 243:1280-1 Mr 10 '89

Pesticides, risk, and applesauce [discussion of March 10, 1989 article, Pesticides and kids, and March 24, 1989 article, Is risk assessment conservative?] L. Roberts. il *Science* 244:755-7 My 19 '89

Please don't pass the pesticides. S. Squires. *Ladies' Home Journal* 106:56 Jl '89

Protecting against one bad apple. J. Silberner. il *U.S. News & World Report* 106:59 Mr 27 '89

Pure produce [discouraging pesticide use] R. Rodale. il *Organic Gardening* 36:25-6 Je '89

There will be no silent spring for these farmers [trend towards organic farming in wake of pesticide scare] il *U.S. News & World Report* 106:13 Ap 3 '89

This is what you thought: 70% say the government should do more to protect us from dangerous foods and drugs [survey results] il *Glamour* 87:161 O '89

Too much fuss about pesticides? il *Consumer Reports* 54:655-8 O '89

Watch those vegetables, Ma [danger to children] A. Toufexis. il *Time* 133:57 Mr 6 '89

Weighing food safety risks. F. E. Young. il *FDA Consumer* 23:8-13 S '89

Why are rats and actresses dictating U.S. food policy? R. Krumme. *Successful Farming* 87:18-19 Je '89

Why the great grape scare missed the point [focus on pesticide rather than on microbial contamination] N. J. Freundlich. il *Business Week* p107 Ap 3 '89

PESTICIDES

See also

Dibromochloropropane

Herbicides

Baculovirus for biocontrol and biotech. R. Lewis. il *BioScience* 39:431-4 Jl/Ag '89

Biologicals: chemicals of the '90s. B. Freese. il *Successful Farming* 87:64Q-64Q Ap '89

Chemical weapons for plants. I. S. Abrams. il *Current Health 2* 15:28-9 Ap '89

A family feud over organic farming pits the Anderson brothers against each other [G. and R. Anderson, almond growers in the San Joaquin Valley] P. Freeman. il pors *People Weekly* 32:47-8 Jl 24 '89

Nature vs. nurture on the farm [Alternative agriculture report by the National Research Council] K. R. Sheets. il *U.S. News & World Report* 107:53-4 S 18 '89

The nifty nematode and those bug-eating bugs [biopesticides] L. Armstrong. il *Business Week* p80 N 6 '89

Our over-reliance on pesticides. P. Crowley. il *Country Journal* 16:15 N/D '89

The pathway of infection of Autographa californica nuclear polyhedrosis virus in an insect host [pesticide potential] B. A. Keddie and others. bibl f il *Science* 243:1728-30 Mr 31 '89

Two years in bin, no bugs [use of low-cost insecticide treatment protects stored corn] M. Lane. il *Successful Farming* 87:48G O '89

Uninvited guests [gardens pests] S. O. Daniels. il *Organic Gardening* 36:38-42 Ap '89

Decomposition

New generation of chemicals will disappear quicker. *Successful Farming* 87:33 N '89

Disposal

Leftovers for sale [clearinghouse for unused pesticides] G. W. Hansen. il *Successful Farming* 87:16-17 S '89

Environmental aspects

A chemical war on water [pesticides and lake pollution] G. Payne. il *Sierra* 74:40-2 My/Je '89

Fields of dreams: old farming is new again. H. Kohn. il *Rolling Stone* p41-2 O 5 '89

Microbes to aid plants from within [corn field trials of genetically altered Clavibacter xyli] J. A. Miller. *BioScience* 39:227-8 Ap '89

New era for insecticides. B. Freese. il *Successful Farming* 87 no4:64S Mr '89

Export-import trade

A few bugs in the system. P. C. Montgomery. il *Common Cause Magazine* 15:10 Jl/Ag '89

Injurious effects

Be most wary of nature's own pesticides. B. N. Ames. *Consumers' Research Magazine* 72:13-14 My '89

A few bugs in the system [exported pesticides] P. C. Montgomery. il *Common Cause Magazine* 15:10 Jl/Ag '89

Human genotoxicity: pesticide applicators and phosphine. V. F. Garry and others. bibl f il *Science* 246:251-5 O 13 '89

Testing toxins at $100 a day [testing of banned pesticides on humans in California] J. H. Kay. il *The Nation* 248:300-2 Mr 6 '89

Laws and regulations

Action on pesticides [revision of Federal Insecticides, Fungicide and Rodenticide Act] J. S. Weis. *BioScience* 39:14 Ja '89

High cost vs. low risk [ban will increase food prices] J. W. Merline. il *Consumers' Research Magazine* 72:38 Je '89

Monitoring pesticides in our food. B. T. Hunter. il *Consumers' Research Magazine* 72:34-5+ Je '89

New era for insecticides. B. Freese. il *Successful Farming* 87 no4:64S Mr '89

Pesticidal plants face legal hurdle. I. Wickelgren. *Science News* 135:300 My 13 '89

This is what you thought: 70% say the government should do more to protect us from dangerous foods and drugs [survey results] il *Glamour* 87:161 O '89

Why are rats and actresses dictating U.S. food policy? R. Krumme. *Successful Farming* 87:18-19 Je '89

Prices

Chemical prices up; rebates down. B. Freese. il *Successful Farming* 87:50M Ja '89

Safety devices and measures

Caution: pests and pesticides. W. Giese. *Changing Times* 43:24-5 Mr '89

Pesticide safety is on the minds of farmers, too. M. Holmberg. *Successful Farming* 87:4 S '89

Students study ABC's of bean-bar safety. C. Tevis. il *Successful Farming* 87:42 Je '89

What's the shelf life of garden chemicals? [safe storage and disposal] il *Sunset (Central West edition)* 182:244-5 My '89

PESTRONG, RAY

It's about time. il *Earth Science* 42:14-15 Summ '89

PESTS

Control

See Pest control

PET (POSITRON EMISSION TOMOGRAPHY) *See* Tomography

PET FOOD

See also

Cats—Food and feeding

Dogs—Food and feeding

Healing diets. A. R. Marder. il *Prevention (Emmaus, Pa.)* 41:94+ D '89

Is your pet too plump? A. R. Marder. il *Prevention (Emmaus, Pa.)* 41:97-9 Ap '89

The pet food dilemma. G. Hoeppner. il *The Saturday Evening Post* 261:26+ O '89

PET INDUSTRIES

See also

Quaker Oats Co.

PET SEMATARY [film] *See* Motion picture reviews—Single works

PET SITTERS

Home sweet pet sitters [views of Joe Abbate] P. J. Kizilos. il *American Health* 8:110 Jl/Ag '89

PET STORES

Laws and regulations

"Lemon" laws [pet lemon laws] P. J. Kizilos. il *American Health* 8:92 O '89

PET STUNTS

Is your pet a star? D. C. Arkins and A. H. Klein. il *Better Homes and Gardens* 67:132 Ag '89

PET THERAPY *See* Pets—Therapeutic use

PET TRICKS *See* Pet stunts

PETA *See* People for the Ethical Treatment of Animals

PETALUMA (CALIF.)

Public buildings

Holding the center. D. Canty. il *Architectural Record* 177:120-3 N '89

PETER B. CANNELL & COMPANY

The thin file strategy [views of P. Cannell] R. Phalon. il por *Forbes* 143:221-2 Je 26 '89

PETER LUGER (BROOKLYN, N.Y.: RESTAURANT) *See* Brooklyn (New York, N.Y.)—Restaurants, nightclubs, bars, etc.

PETER PAN [film] *See* Motion picture reviews—Single works

PETER PAN [television program] *See* Television program reviews—Single works

PETERS, CHARLES, 1926-

Community [excerpt from Tilting at windmills] *The Washington Monthly* 21:32-3 F '89

Firemen first, or, How to beat a budget cut. il *The Washington Monthly* 21:42-3 F '89

A kind word for the spoils system. *The Washington Monthly* 21:37-8 F '89

Putting yourself on the line. *The Washington Monthly* 21:64-5 F '89

Tilting at windmills. See issues of The Washington Monthly

Et tu, Keisling? *The Washington Monthly* 21:52-4 Mr '89

(jt. auth) See Baker, Russell, 1925-, and Peters, Charles, 1926-

PETERS, DIDI, D. 1989
about
Obituary
Jet il por 75:54 Ap 3 '89
PETERS, JOAN, 1938-
The long march of Alan Bolt. *The Nation* 248:855-8 Je 19 '89
PETERS, JON
about
An American classic [cover story] R. Reilly. il pors *Sports Illustrated* 70:16-21 My 8 '89
In the heart of Texas, Jon Peters is a pitcher of perfection. il por *People Weekly* 31:128 My 15 '89
PETERS, JON
about
Dynamic duos don't come cheap. C. Gorman. il pors *Time* 134:71 N 6 '89
Making up, Hollywood style. il pors *Time* 134:74 N 27 '89
The producers [cover story] D. K. Shah. il pors *The New York Times Magazine* p26-9+ O 22 '89
Walter Yetnikoff's $300 million mistake. L. Gubernick. il pors *Forbes* 144:108+ D 11 '89
PETERS, RON
about
The case against Pete Rose [cover story] J. Lieber and C. Neff. il pors *Sports Illustrated* 71:10-20+ Jl 3 '89
PETERS, TED
Not in my backyard! The waste-disposal crisis. il *The Christian Century* 106:175-7 F 15 '89
When the dump is in 'our' backyard [discussion of February 15, 1989 article, Not in my backyard! The waste-disposal crisis] *The Christian Century* 106:660 Jl 5-12 '89
PETERS, TONI
Christmas in July. il *The Mother Earth News* 120:10 N/D '89
PETERSEN, CAROLYN COLLINS
There's no place like dome. il *Sky and Telescope* 78:255-6+ S '89
PETERSEN, DONALD E.
about
Caution: bumps ahead at Ford. A. L. Taylor, III. il pors *Fortune* 120:93+ D 18 '89
The Ford family wants to take the wheel again. J. B. Treece. il pors *Business Week* p32 Ja 16 '89
From the top. il pors *Car and Driver* 35:93-6+ O '89
PETERSEN, PAT
about
Pat Petersen. S. Littwin. por *TV Guide* 37:12 S 23-29 '89
PETERSEN, PAULANN
Work [poem] *Wilderness* 53:71 Fall '89
PETERSON, AMANDA
about
Amanda Peterson: down to earth star. il pors *'Teen* 33:55 N '89
PETERSON, CASS
Don't seek refuge here. il *Sierra* 74:26+ S/O '89
How do you spell relief? il *National Wildlife* 27:40-3 Ap/My '89
PETERSON, DAVID ROBERT
In defense of the 'L' word [address, March 15, 1989] *Vital Speeches of the Day* 55:420-3 My 1 '89
about
Caught in Starr wars. P. Kaihla. il pors *Maclean's* 102:12-13 Jl 3 '89
Champagne diplomacy. J. Daly. *Maclean's* 102:39+ Ap 17 '89
Combat in Ontario. T. Tedesco. il por *Maclean's* 102:14-15 Ja 30 '89
A flurry of scandals. R. Corelli. il pors *Maclean's* 102:12-13 Jl 10 '89
Liberal controversies. P. Kaihla. il por *Maclean's* 102:17 Je 19 '89
The rest of the pack. T. Tedesco. il por *Maclean's* 102:14-15 Je 26 '89
Words of conciliation [interview] T. Tedesco. il por *Maclean's* 102:16 Ja 30 '89
PETERSON, DUWAYNE J., 1932-
about
The $1.2 billion-dollar man. E. S. Ely. por *Personal Computing* 13:72 Jl '89
PETERSON, ED
about
Centerline: Ed Peterson. M. Sommers. il por *Theatre Crafts* 23:18 D '89
PETERSON, ESTHER
about
The Peterson principle. M. Sinclair. il por *New Choices for the Best Years* 29:16+ Je '89
PETERSON, EUGENE H., 1932-
Holy Saturday. il *Christianity Today* 33:23-5 Mr 17 '89
PETERSON, JOHNNY W., AND OCHOA, LAURA G.
Role of prostaglandins and cAMP in the secretory effects of cholera toxin. bibl f il *Science* 245:857-9 Ag 25 '89
PETERSON, MICHAEL L.
The Church cryptogram: to catch a Tory spy. il *American History Illustrated* 24:36-43 N/D '89

PETERSON, NORMA
Reducing the risk of breast cancer. il *McCall's* 116:101-2+ S '89
PETERSON, PETER G.
What is the 'right' amount of saving? il *National Review* 41:30-1 Je 16 '89
PETERSON, ROBERT A.
Home schooling. il *Conservative Digest* 15:54-7 My/Je '89
PETERSON, ROGER TORY, 1908-
about
Roger Tory Peterson: keeping watch on the needs of wildlife [interview] G. H. Harrison. il por *National Wildlife* 27:7 Ap/My '89
PETERSON, SUE
about
From Baja with love. S. Ballard. il pors *Sports Illustrated* 70 Special Issue:65-7 F '89
PETERSON, WAYNE J.
(jt. auth) See Thee, T. William, and Peterson, Wayne J.
PETERSON, WILLIAM H.
(jt. auth) See Barron, Eric J., and Peterson, William H.
PETERSON/VINE ASSOCIATES
Centerline: Ed Peterson [Las Vegas show room designer] M. Sommers. il por *Theatre Crafts* 23:18 D '89
PETIPA, MARIUS, 1822-1910
about
The sleeping beauty [ballet] Reviews
The New Yorker 65:89-92 Ag 7 '89. A. Croce
PETITION, RIGHT OF *See* Right of petition
PETITS FOURS
Making petits fours at Ritz-Escoffier. A. Touchet. il *Gourmet* 49:102-5+ N '89
PETKANAS, CHRISTOPHER
Castle cast-offs. il *House & Garden* 161:96+ My '89
French independent. il pors *Harper's Bazaar* 122:106-9+ Ag '89
The French touch. il *House & Garden* 161:156+ Jl '89
A harvest of ceramics. il pors *House & Garden* 161:28+ Ag '89
Haut Catroux. il *House & Garden* 161:160-7+ Ap '89
Provincial pleasures. il pors *Harper's Bazaar* 122:178-85 D '89
Romeo, Romeo. il por *Harper's Bazaar* 122:148-9+ Ag '89
Stepping out and dining well. il *Harper's Bazaar* 122:64 Ap '89
Swedish fantasies. il por *House & Garden* 161:126-33+ Ag '89
PETRA (ANCIENT CITY)
Etched in stone. F. Gebhart. il *Travel Holiday* 172:44-51 O '89
PETRASH, OSYP
The mermaid of the Dniester. il *The Courier (Unesco)* 42:23 Mr '89
PETRELS
A seabird in the house of the sun [dark-rumped petrels on Maui] T. Simons and G. C. Whittow. il *Natural History* p50-3 Mr '89
PETRICH, LYNN KARI
Mel Pekarsky. il pors *American Artist* 53:50-5 Ap '89
PETRIE, DANIEL
about
Cocoon: the return [film] Reviews
Video 13:60+ Ag '89. J. Walker
PETRIFIED FOREST NATIONAL PARK (ARIZ.)
Birth of the dinosaurs [cover story] S. Nash. il *National Parks* 63:16-23 N/D '89
PETRIFIED WOOD *See* Trees, Fossil
PETRIK, PAULA EVANS
Desk-top publishing. bibl il *History Today* 39:12-26 O '89
PETRIRENA, MARIO
about
Mario Petrirena at Sandler Hudson. A. Jinkner-Lloyd. *Art in America* 77:219 O '89
PETRO-CANADA INC.
The energy that drives a national success story [B. Hopper] D. Jenish. il por *Maclean's* 102:32-3 D 25 '89
PETROCHEMICAL INDUSTRY
See also
Phillips Petroleum Company
Canada
See also
Nova Corporation of Alberta
Siberia (Soviet Union)
Cold feet in Siberia [joint venture petrochemical projects] P. Galuszka. il *Business Week* p48 Mr 27 '89
Taiwan
Taiwan's U.S. strategy. R. Simon. il *Forbes* 143:43-4 My 29 '89
PETROCHEMICALS
See also
Benzene
PETROGLYPHS
See also
Cave drawings and paintings
Amateur astroarchaeologists [Tenabo site] il *Astronomy* 17:16-17 Ja '89

PETROGLYPHS—*cont.*

Ancient art adds to supernova mystery [American Indian petroglyphs in New Mexico] il *Earth Science* 42:5 Fall '89

Spirits in stone [national parks; cover story] T. Browning. il *National Parks* 63:37-9 S/O '89

Sun dagger misses its mark [Anasazi petroglyphs in Chaco Canyon] J. Palca. il *Science* 244:1538 Je 30 '89

PETROLEOS MEXICANOS

Bald man on a horse [C. Salinas de Gortari takes action against head of oil workers' union] G. B. Lake. il *National Review* 41:38-9 Mr 10 '89

Salinas declares war on 'the maximum chief' of oil [union strongman J. Hernández Galicia] S. Baker. il *Business Week* p52 Ja 23 '89

Touching the 'untouchable' [C. Salinas de Gortari arrests head of oil workers' union] S. McGuire. il por *Newsweek* 113:30-1 Ja 23 '89

PETROLEUM

See also
Oil sands

Conferences

See also
Organization of Petroleum Exporting Countries—Conferences

Export-import trade

See Petroleum industry—Export-import trade

Geology

See also
Oil seepage

Plankton to petroleum [origin of oil and gas] W. W. Dickinson. il *Earth Science* 41:21-3 Wint '88

International aspects

See also
Organization of Petroleum Exporting Countries
Petroleum industry—Export-import trade

Pipelines

See Petroleum pipelines

Prices

See also
Gasoline—Prices

America's oil-chill factor [rising imports increase trade deficit] K. R. Sheets. il *U.S. News & World Report* 106:54-5 Mr 27 '89

Coping with the OPEC oil glut. S. J. Fromartz. il *The Nation* 248:692-5 My 22 '89

Gluttons for punishment [U.S. again dependent on OPEC] C. Byron. il *New York* 22:16+ Je 19 '89

Higher oil prices are casting an ominous shadow. G. Koretz. il *Business Week* p24 Ap 3 '89

Hydrocarbon energy revisited. P. H. Abelson. *Science* 245:1433 S 29 '89

Oil imports are setting an ambush for the economy. G. Koretz. il *Business Week* p26 Mr 13 '89

OPEC: which of these men will cheat first? P. Nulty. il *Fortune* 119:10 Ja 2 '89

Refined profits. T. Mack. il *Forbes* 143:110-11 My 15 '89

Step on the gas, pay the price [increase in imports] B. Rudolph. il *Time* 133:40 Ap 3 '89

A storm before the calm? H. Banks. *Forbes* 144:33 Jl 10 '89

The strong demand for oil means only one thing . . . S. Miller. il *Business Week* p28 Ap 10 '89

Why OPEC's luck may run out. J. Rossant. *Business Week* p48 Je 19 '89

Production methods

See Petroleum engineering

Recovery methods

See Petroleum engineering

Transportation

See also
Petroleum pipelines
Tankers

Moving Alaskan crude: who's in charge? J. R. Gilliland. il *Audubon* 91:87 S '89

Well drilling

See Oil well drilling

Alaska

See also
Petroleum pipelines—Alaska

Adversaries in the Arctic [Arctic National Wildlife Refuge] M. Hager. il map *Newsweek* 113:60 F 27 '89

Arctic National Wildlife Refuge [discussion of May 1989 article, Oil development and the Arctic National Wildlife Refuge] L. Speer. il *Environment* 31:2-4 S '89

Beating the drum for caribou [Gwich'in people bordering Arctic National Wildlife Refuge oppose oil development] M. Peale. il *Sierra* 74:32+ My/Je '89

Explore no more? [Arctic National Wildlife Refuge] E. F. Cone. il *Forbes* 143:10 My 15 '89

The future of big oil [drilling in Arctic National Wildlife Refuge after Exxon oil spill; cover story] P. Nulty. il map *Fortune* 119:46-9 My 8 '89

Impacts of petroleum development in the Arctic [discussion of November 6, 1987 article, Cumulative impacts of oil fields on northern Alaskan landscapes] D. A. Walker and others. *Science* 245:764-6 Ag 18 '89

Oil development and the Arctic National Wildlife Refuge. L. Speer. bibl f il *Environment* 31:42-3 My '89

Protecting Alaskan wildlife [work of Jonathan Bart] *USA Today (Periodical)* 117:5-6 Je '89

Shadow over an ancient land [T. Gilbert, member of Gwich'in tribe opposing oil development] S. K. Reed. il pors *People Weekly* 32:48-53 S 18 '89

A tale of two villages [natives bordering Arctic National Wildlife Refuge hold opposing viewpoints on oil development] E. Linden. il *Time* 133:62 Ap 17 '89

Tundra plunder [proposed oil exploration in the Arctic National Wildlife Refuge] *The New Republic* 200:8+ My 1 '89

Arctic regions

See also
Petroleum—Alaska

Atlantic Ocean

Hibernia postponed [oilfields off Newfoundland] J. Daly. il *Maclean's* 102:31+ Jl 24 '89

Australia

The drift of oil [Otway Basin] J. Dietzel. il *World Press Review* 36:66 S '89

Gulf of Mexico

Working underwater [professional divers on an offshore oil rig] J. S. McKinna. il *Sea Frontiers* 35:348-55 N/D '89

United States

See Petroleum

Zimbabwe

Double jeopardy [proposed oil exploration in Zambezi Valley by Mobil] M. L. Knox. il *Sierra* 74:66-7 N/D '89

PETROLEUM ENGINEERING

See also
Oil sands
Oil well drilling

High tech frontiers in the energy industry [address, November 30, 1988] R. F. Tucker. *Vital Speeches of the Day* 55:437-41 My 1 '89

Oil wells cause earthquakes [research by Paul Segall] A. McKenzie. *Science News* 136:279 O 28 '89

PETROLEUM EQUIPMENT INDUSTRY

See also
Dresser Industries, Inc.
Global Marine Inc.
NL Industries, Inc.
Tidewater Inc.

Oil. T. Mack. il *Forbes* 143:178-80 Ja 9 '89

Acquisitions and mergers

Rig bidders. T. Mack. il *Forbes* 143:114-15 Ap 3 '89

Why Irv Jacobs wants to land Tidewater. R. Mitchell. il *Business Week* p31-2 Ja 30 '89

PETROLEUM FUTURES *See* Commodity futures

PETROLEUM GEOLOGY *See* Petroleum—Geology

PETROLEUM IN SUBMERGED LANDS

Inner space. C. T. Feazel. il *Sea Frontiers* 35:49-52 Ja/F '89

PETROLEUM INCOME FUNDS *See* Petroleum investment trusts

PETROLEUM INDUSTRY

See also
American Exploration Co.
Amoco Corporation
Atlantic Richfield Co.
Chevron Corporation
Crown Central Petroleum Corp.
Crystal Oil Co.
Diamond Shamrock R&M Inc.
Energy Service Company, Inc.
Exxon Corporation
Global Marine Inc.
Mesa Limited Partnership
Mobil Corporation
Omni Exploration Inc.
Patrick Petroleum Co.
Pauley Petroleum Inc.
Pennzoil Company
Petrochemical industry
Petroleum refineries
Phillips Petroleum Company
Pittston Company
Quaker State Corporation
Shell Oil Company
Texaco Inc.
Union Texas Petroleum Holdings, Inc.
Unocal Corp.
Wolverine Exploration Company
Zapata Corporation

High tech frontiers in the energy industry [address, November 30, 1988] R. F. Tucker. *Vital Speeches of the Day* 55:437-41 My 1 '89

Acquisitions and mergers

Does Pennzoil see a gusher in Kerr-McGee? G. G. Marcial. il *Business Week* p134 My 8 '89

What does Liedtke want? [Pennzoil's stake in Chevron] M. Ivey and M. Shao. il por *Business Week* p42-3 D 25 '89-Ja 1 '90

Who's in charge at Texaco now? S. P. Sherman. il pors *Fortune* 119:68-70+ Ja 16 '89

PETROLEUM INDUSTRY — Acquisitions and mergers — cont.

International aspects

BP: making the best of it [buys back half of Kuwait's shares] M. Maremont. *Business Week* p48 Ja 16 '89

British royalty [BP's new royalty trust may signal new takeovers] T. Mack. il *Forbes* 143:92 Ap 3 '89

The price was right [Broken Hill Proprietary acquires Pacific Resources] E. McGlinn. il *Forbes* 143:10 F 20 '89

Canada

Texaco Canada says goodbye [sold to Imperial Oil] J. DeMont. *Maclean's* 102:33 Ja 30 '89

Environmental aspects

Double jeopardy [proposed oil exploration in Zambezi Valley, Zimbabwe by Mobil] M. L. Knox. il *Sierra* 74:66-7 N/D '89

Gaining the environmental initiative [address, July 13, 1989] C. J. Silas. *Vital Speeches of the Day* 56:14-16 O 15 '89

The greening of the energy world [address, September 8, 1989] A. C. Decrane. *Vital Speeches of the Day* 56:117-21 D 1 '89

NPCA wins appeal on Hovenweep drilling. *National Parks* 63:15 Jl/Ag '89

Oilspeak, common sense, and soft science. F. Graham. il *Audubon* 91:102-8+ S '89

What worries Arco's chief the most [interview with L. Cook] il por *Fortune* 120:102 O 9 '89

Export-import trade

See also

Organization of Petroleum Exporting Countries

America's oil-chill factor [rising imports increase trade deficit] K. R. Sheets. il *U.S. News & World Report* 106:54-5 Mr 27 '89

A microchip in hand beats oil in the ground [interview with J. Lichtblau] T. Mack. il por *Forbes* 144:150 O 30 '89

Oil imports are setting an ambush for the economy. G. Koretz. il *Business Week* p26 Mr 13 '89

Step on the gas, pay the price [increase in imports] B. Rudolph. il *Time* 133:40 Ap 3 '89

Finance

See also

Petroleum investment trusts

Big Oil faces a big squeeze. P. Nulty. il *Fortune* 120:94-5+ O 9 '89

The big spill's big chill [aftermath of Alaskan spill] T. Vogel and M. Ivey. il *Business Week* p102-3 My 1 '89

Fill 'er up. H. Rudnitsky. il *Forbes* 143:64+ Ja 9 '89

For the oil companies, 'downstream is mainstream'. T. Vogel. il *Business Week* p100 Ja 9 '89

Oil. T. Mack. il *Forbes* 143:178-80 Ja 9 '89

Oil fields of dreams. K. R. Sheets. il *U.S. News & World Report* 107:35-6 D 18 '89

Refined profits. T. Mack. il *Forbes* 143:110-11 My 15 '89

History

Self-made and self-unmade [G. McCarthy] S. G. Sheehy. il pors *Forbes* 144 Special Issue:72-3 O 23 '89

Marketing

It's not just a fill-up anymore—it's an event. M. Ivey. il *Business Week* p90+ Je 19 '89

Public relations

Who's that screaming at Exxon? Not the environmentalists [Alaska oil spill] A. Rothman. il *Business Week* p31 My 1 '89

Securities

See also

Petroleum investment trusts

Bad days for Exxon, good times for the other major oils. A. E. Serwer. il *Fortune* 119:33-4 My 8 '89

Diamonds in his own backyard [deals made by R. E. Rainwater] J. H. Taylor. il *Forbes* 143:49-50+ Mr 6 '89

Look at the crack spreads [energy securities analyst B. Sahgal checks spread between gasoline and crude oil futures prices] S. N. Chakravarty. il por *Forbes* 143:86+ My 29 '89

Alaska

Moving Alaskan crude: who's in charge? J. R. Gilliland. il *Audubon* 91:87 S '89

The spills and spoils of big oil [cover story] J. Greely. il *The Nation* 248:721+ My 29 '89

Canada

See also

Imperial Oil Limited

Irving Oil Company

Petro-Canada Inc.

Shell Canada Ltd.

Texaco Canada Inc.

Exodus of an industry [Canadian oil explorers look abroad] J. DeMont. il *Maclean's* 102:50+ N 6 '89

Hibernia postponed [oilfields off Newfoundland] J. Daly. il *Maclean's* 102:31+ Jl 24 '89

Great Britain

See also

British Petroleum Co. plc

Hawaii

See also

Pacific Resources Inc.

Japan

Now Japan is plunging into oil. C. Rapoport. il map *Fortune* 119:124-6 Mr 13 '89

World's worst oil policy? A. Tanzer. il *Forbes* 144:245+ Jl 24 '89

Libya

U.S. oil companies authorized to resume operations in Libya [White House statement, January 19, 1989] *Department of State Bulletin* 89:71 Mr '89

Mexico

See also

Petroleos Mexicanos

Netherlands

See also

Royal Dutch/Shell Group

Spain

See also

Repsol SA

United States

See Petroleum industry

PETROLEUM INVESTMENT TRUSTS

See also

OKC Limited Partnership

San Juan Basin Royalty Trust

British royalty [BP's new royalty trust may signal new takeovers] T. Mack. il *Forbes* 143:92 Ap 3 '89

Petro-vulture [M. Andrews] J. R. Hayes. il por *Forbes* 143:96+ F 20 '89

PETROLEUM LAWS AND REGULATIONS

See also

Oil and gas leases

PETROLEUM PIPELINES

Alaska

That's oil, folks [Exxon Valdez spill] H. Hertzberg. *The New Republic* 200:4 Ap 24 '89

PETROLEUM POLLUTION *See* Oil pollution

PETROLEUM PROSPECTING

See also

Oil well drilling

Pennzoil Company

Shell Oil Company

Exodus of an industry [Canadian oil explorers look abroad] J. DeMont. il *Maclean's* 102:50+ N 6 '89

The quest for oil. F. Hapgood. il *National Geographic* 176:226-59 Ag '89

PETROLEUM REFINERIES

Fill 'er up. H. Rudnitsky. il *Forbes* 143:64+ Ja 9 '89

For the oil companies, 'downstream is mainstream'. T. Vogel. il *Business Week* p100 Ja 9 '89

Look at the crack spreads [energy securities analyst B. Sahgal checks spread between gasoline and crude oil futures prices] S. N. Chakravarty. il por *Forbes* 143:86+ My 29 '89

Refined profits. T. Mack. il *Forbes* 143:110-11 My 15 '89

Environmental aspects

Pollution prevention: the Chevron story [Richmond, Calif. refinery] G. Karras. bibl f *Environment* 31:4-5+ O '89

Photographs and photography

Dusk/dark double exposures. M. A. Johnson. il *Petersen's Photographic Magazine* 18:84-5 Ag '89

PETROLEUM SEEPAGE *See* Oil seepage

PETROLEUM SUPPLY

See also

Gasoline supply

Big Oil faces a big squeeze. P. Nulty. il *Fortune* 120:94-5+ O 9 '89

Coping with the OPEC oil glut. S. J. Fromartz. il *The Nation* 248:692-5 My 22 '89

Gluttons for punishment [U.S. again dependent on OPEC] C. Byron. il *New York* 22:16+ Je 19 '89

Hydrocarbon energy revisited. P. H. Abelson. *Science* 245:1433 S 29 '89

It looks as if OPEC may have the last laugh. C. Farrell. il *Business Week* p34 S 25 '89

A microchip in hand beats oil in the ground [interview with J. Lichtblau] T. Mack. il por *Forbes* 144:150 O 30 '89

Oil and gas estimates plummet. R. A. Kerr. *Science* 245:1330-1 S 22 '89

A storm before the calm? H. Banks. *Forbes* 144:33 Jl 10 '89

The strong demand for oil means only one thing . . . S. Miller. il *Business Week* p28 Ap 10 '89

A vulnerable energy supply. J. DeMont. il *Maclean's* 102:77 Ap 10 '89

Why OPEC's luck may run out. J. Rossant. *Business Week* p48 Je 19 '89

PETROLEUM WORKERS

See also

Labor unions—Petroleum workers

PETROLEUMLYTIC BACTERIA *See* Bacteria, Petroleumlytic

PETROSSIAN, VAHE

A new Iranian revolution. *World Press Review* 36:60 F '89

PETROWSKI, ELAINE

Closets! From messy to marvelous. il *Good Housekeeping* 208:188+ Ap '89

PETRUCCI, JUDY
about
The unlikely tamer of Lyons. P. Alson. il por *Life* 12:29-30 N '89
PETRUSHKA [ballet] See Ballet reviews—Single works
PETS
See also
    Birds
    Bush, George, 1924——Pets
    Cats
    Celebrities—Pets
    Dogs
    Lost pets
    Pet stores
    Rabbits
    Rats
    Seals (Animals)
    Swine
    Travel with pets
After Fido dies . . . a support group. *Newsweek* 113:74 Mr 20 '89
Animal love. J. Glass. See alternate issues of Glamour beginning July 1987
The card that says 'charge it' . . . to Fido [Pet Lover's Visa Card] il *Newsweek* 114:63 N 27 '89
Choosing the right pet. A. R. Marder. il *Prevention (Emmaus, Pa.)* 41:96-8 Mr '89
Getting a second pet. B. Devine. il *Better Homes and Gardens* 67:206+ N '89
Personal beast [exotic pets] J. Stone. il *Discover* 10:78+ Ap '89
Pet concerns. See issues of The Mother Earth News beginning September/October 1986
Pet news. See occasional issues of Ladies' Home Journal
Pet set. S. L. Gerstenfeld. See occasional issues of Parents
Pets. See occasional issues of Better Homes and Gardens
Vets on pets. H. E. Whiteley. See issues of The Saturday Evening Post beginning January/February 1984
Accidents and hazards
Pet-proofing your home. S. L. Gerstenfeld. il *Parents* 64:255 N '89
A walk on the wild side [unleashed pets] S. L. Gerstenfeld. il *Parents* 64:216 Ap '89
Anecdotes, facetiae, satire, etc.
Last word [excerpt from The eat a pet cookbook] R. Jones. por *Omni (New York, N.Y.)* 12:128 N '89
Care
See also
    First aid for animals
    Kennels
    Pet sitters
Caring for the older pet. A. R. Marder. il *Prevention (Emmaus, Pa.)* 41:103+ My '89
How to tame a jealous pet. A. R. Marder. il *Prevention (Emmaus, Pa.)* 41:97-9 Ag '89
Play it safe—don't play doctor. D. Calkins. *American Health* 8:124-5 Mr '89
Preparing pets for winter. il *USA Today (Periodical)* 118:14-15 D '89
Summer care for pets [views of Michael Garvey] S. Berkman. il *Good Housekeeping* 208:80 Je '89
Vets on pets [views of Sheldon Gerstenfeld] M. Behen. *American Health* 8:125 Mr '89
Who will care for my pets? A. Winter. *Modern Maturity* 32:18+ D '89/Ja '90
Your aging pet. D. C. Arkins. il *Better Homes and Gardens* 67:168 O '89
Your healthy pet. A. R. Marder. See issues of Prevention (Emmaus, Pa.) beginning July 1987
Diseases and pests
See also
    Fleas
Getting to the root of an itch [skin diseases] A. R. Marder. il *Prevention (Emmaus, Pa.)* 41:97+ F '89
Healing diets. A. R. Marder. il *Prevention (Emmaus, Pa.)* 41:94+ D '89
Help for the allergic pet. A. R. Marder. il *Prevention (Emmaus, Pa.)* 41:97-100+ N '89
How sweet it's not [diabetes] M. Rosenfeld. il *American Health* 8:80 D '89
"Lemon" laws [pet lemon laws] P. J. Kizilos. il *American Health* 8:92 O '89
Equipment
See also
    Christmas gifts for pets
Euthanasia
See Euthanasia—Animals
First aid
See First aid for animals
Food and feeding
See Pet food
Housing
See also
    Kennels
Identification
When pets stray. M. Behen. il *American Health* 8:102 My '89

Photographs and photography
Pet Photography 101. D. C. Arkins. il *Better Homes and Gardens* 67:158 Ap '89
Preservation
See also
    Jeff's Preservation Specialties, Inc.
Therapeutic use
Four-legged medicine [pet visits to help hospital patients; work of Jackie McCurdy] B. Portnow. il *American Health* 8:122 Mr '89
The pet prescription. M.-L. Kamberg. il *Current Health 2* 15:10-12 My '89
PETS AND CHILDREN See Children and animals
PETTERSSON, CHRISTER
about
The Swedish version of 'who killed JFK?'. por *Newsweek* 114:32 Ag 7 '89
PETTINGELL, PHOEBE
Writers & writing. See occasional issues of The New Leader
PETTINGER-GUILEY OBSERVATORY
Washington public observatory expands. A. D. George. il *Sky and Telescope* 77:657-8 Je '89
PETTY, TOM
about
Tom Petty goes it alone. J. Ressner. il por *Rolling Stone* p16 Ap 20 '89
Tom Petty on his own. S. Simels. por *Stereo Review* 54:73 Jl '89
Tom Petty's solo effort: an infectious 'Fever'. J. Guterman. il *Rolling Stone* p85-7 My 4 '89
PETTY, TOM, AND HOCHMAN, STEVE
On the road with Tom Petty and the Heartbreakers: if it's Monday, this must be Miami. il pors *Rolling Stone* p74-5+ O 5 '89
PETTY (TOM) AND THE HEARTBREAKERS (MUSICAL GROUP) See Tom Petty and the Heartbreakers (Musical group)
PETZAL, DAVID E.
Endangered tradition. See issues of Field & Stream beginning March 1985
PEUGEOT (AUTOMOBILE) See Automobiles, Foreign
PEUGEOT SA
Apres Peugeot, le deluge? [strike] S. Toy. *Business Week* p54 O 2 '89
PEURIFOY-GREEN, BEVERLY
Cruising with a cause. il *Black Enterprise* 19:61-2 Jl '89
PEW CHARITABLE TRUSTS
How to borrow a Rodin [Museum Loan Program will fund inter-museum loans in Philadelphia] S. Staggs. il *Art News* 88:50+ Ap '89
PEYOTE
See also
    Peyotism
PEYOTISM
Peyote, wine and the First Amendment [case before Supreme Court on religious use of peyote] D. Laycock. *The Christian Century* 106:876-80 O 4 '89
PEYRELEVADE, JEAN
about
A marriage of giants to defend French finance. B. Riemer. il por *Business Week* p46 Ap 10 '89
PEZIM, MURRAY
about
Gold fever strikes again. H. Quinn. il por *Maclean's* 102:33 S 11 '89
The Lions in winter. J. Queenan. il por *Forbes* 144:286 O 16 '89
The Pez is golden. J. DeMont. il por *Maclean's* 102:39 Ag 21 '89
PFAFF, JUDY
about
Judy Pfaff: Holly Solomon. E. Heartney. il *Art News* 88:136+ F '89
PFAFF, WILLIAM
The fallen hero. *The New Yorker* 65:105-15 My 8 '89
Romania: breaking the silence. il *The New York Review of Books* 36:8-9 Ap 27 '89
Romania: defying the tyrant. il *The New York Review of Books* 36:43 Ag 17 '89
PFANSTIEL, J. F., AND OTHERS
A rotationally resolved fluorescence excitation spectrum of *all-trans*-1,4-diphenyl-1,3-butadiene. bibl f il *Science* 245:736-8 Ag 18 '89
PFATTEICHER, PHILIP H.
A fixed date for Easter? *The Christian Century* 106:300-1 Mr 22-29 '89
PFEIFER, GERD P., AND OTHERS
Genomic sequencing and methylation analysis by ligation mediated PCR. bibl f il *Science* 246:810-13 N 10 '89
PFEIFFER, ECKHARD
about
The power behind Compaq's European powerhouse. T. Peterson. il por *Business Week* p150 Je 26 '89
PFEIFFER, JOHN E., 1915-
The secret of life at the limits: cogs become big wheels. il *Smithsonian* 20:38-46+ Jl '89

PFEIFFER, MICHELLE
about
Fabulous Pfeiffer [cover story] D. Ansen. il pors *Newsweek* 114:64-8+ N 6 '89
Michelle Pfeiffer. il por *People Weekly* 32:94-5 D 25 '89-Ja 1 '90
Starface. E. G. Carter. il pors *Vogue* 179:416-19+ O '89
PFEIFFER-LINN, CINDY, AND GLANTZ, RAYMON M.
Acetylcholine and GABA mediate opposing actions on neuronal chloride channels in crayfish. bibl f il *Science* 245:1249-51 S 15 '89
PFISTER, CHRIS
about
Chris Pfister at Bess Cutler. J. Ash. *Art in America* 77:195 N '89
PFITZINGER, PETE
Pick up the paces. il *American Health* 8:80 Je '89
PFIZER INC.
Pfizer's pipeline is full, but will the drugs flow fast enough? M. Roman. il por *Business Week* p74+ S 11 '89
PFLEGER, MICHAEL
about
In Chicago, two angry priests declare a holy war on drugs. W. Plummer. il pors *People Weekly* 32:102-3 S 4 '89
PFOTENHAUER, PAUL
Steroids: the power drugs. il *USA Today (Periodical)* 117:88-90 Mr '89
PFOUTS, CHRIS
Easy riders. il *New Choices for the Best Years* 29:64-9 Je '89
PGA TOUR INC.
Driving PGA Inc. H. Quinn. il *Maclean's* 102:60-1 Ap 10 '89
Will Europe take a divot out of the PGA Tour? W. C. Symonds. il *Business Week* p188-9 S 25 '89
PHAEDRA BRITANNICA [drama] See Harrison, Tony, 1937-
PHAGES See Bacteriophages
PHAGOCYTES AND PHAGOCYTOSIS
See also
Macrophages
A Salmonella locus that controls resistance to microbicidal proteins from phagocytic cells. P. I. Fields and others. bibl f il *Science* 243:1059-62 F 24 '89
PHALANX WEAPONS SYSTEM See Warships—Armaments
PHAM-VAN-DIEP, G., AND OTHERS
Nonequilibrium molecular motion in a hypersonic shock wave. bibl f il *Science* 245:624-6 Ag 11 '89
PHANTASIE [drama] See Pearson, Sybille
PHANTOM OF THE OPERA (FICTIONAL CHARACTER)
Quick take: whose is that masked musical? M. McCloud. il *Theatre Crafts* 23:23 D '89
THE PHANTOM OF THE OPERA [musical] See Musicals, revues, etc.—Reviews—Single works
PHARAOHS
Weather of the pharaohs. R. S. Cerveny. il *Weatherwise* 42:307-14 D '89
PHARMACEUTICAL INDUSTRY See Drug industry
PHARMACEUTICAL RESEARCH
See also
Information systems—Pharmaceutical use
United States. Food and Drug Administration
The bitter pill [lack of contraceptive research in the U.S.] C. Djerassi. bibl f *Science* 245:356-61 Jl 28 '89
The body's master controls: unraveling proteins to tackle disease at its roots. B. Carpenter. il *U.S. News & World Report* 106:57-9 My 8 '89
A culture that just keeps dishing up success [Merck] J. Weber, Jr. il *Business Week* Special Issue:120 Je 16 '89
Desperation drugs [AIDS drugs] S. Begley. il *Newsweek* 114:48-51 Ag 7 '89
Drug profits seem to be on steroids. J. H. Cutaia. il *Business Week* p97 Ja 9 '89
Drugs from emasculated hormones: the principle of syntopic antagonism [Nobel lecture, December 8, 1988] Sir J. W. Black. bibl f il *Science* 245:486-93 Ag 4 '89
Du Pont's 'drug hunter' stalks his next big trophy [P. B. Timmermans] J. Weber, Jr. il por *Business Week* p174+ N 27 '89
The heart attack business. C. Messina. il *High Technology Business* 9:22-5 Mr '89
Here's one drug war we're winning [views of P. R. Vagelos] M. Magnet. por *Fortune* 120:74 Jl 3 '89
The Nobel pair [G. Elion and G. Hitchings] K. Bouton. il pors *The New York Times Magazine* p28-9+ Ja 29 '89
The purine path of chemotherapy [Nobel Prize lecture, December 8, 1988] G. B. Elion. bibl f il *Science* 244:41-7 Ap 7 '89
Two pluses and a minus [recent developments in AIDS, Parkinson's disease, and estrogen replacement] M. Hager. *Newsweek* 114:63 Ag 14 '89
Ethical aspects
Biggest drug research fraud case in FDA history [case of R. Fogari] J. Folkenberg. il *FDA Consumer* 23:25-6 Je '89
Hospital faulted for dry eye study [Harvard-affiliated Massachusetts Eye and Ear Infirmary] W. Booth. *Science* 243:1000 F 24 '89

Research group forswears financial ties to firms whose drugs it tests. C. Holden. il *Science* 244:282 Ap 21 '89
Study details misconduct in drug research [work of Martin F. Shapiro and Robert P. Charrow] K. Fackelmann. *Science News* 135:278 My 6 '89
Experimentation on man
See Pharmaceutical research—Human experimentation
Human experimentation
Affirmative action [need for more minorities in clinical trials] J. Horgan. *Scientific American* 261:34 D '89
AIDS drug trials enter new age. J. Palca. il *Science* 246:19-21 O 6 '89
AIDS research comes to patients' home towns [FDA program] F. E. Young. il *FDA Consumer* 23:6-7 My '89
Drug testing on trial [problems of human testing] S. Vogel. il *Discover* 10:28-9 Je '89
Government DDI trials on trial. J. Palca. *Science* 246:1244 D 8 '89
Great expectations: is the U.S. doing its best to beat AIDS? [interview with P. Parkman] D. C. McLearn. il pors *FDA Consumer* 23:36-8 F '89
The trials of conducting AIDS drugs trials. J. L. Marx. il *Science* 244:916-18 My 26 '89
The underground test of Compound Q. D. Wyss. il *Time* 134:18+ O 9 '89
PHARMACIES See Drugstores
PHARMACISTS
10 questions to ask your pharmacist [taking medications correctly] C. Slom. *McCall's* 116:96 F '89
PHARMACOLOGY
See also
Drug receptors
Drug resistance
Psychopharmacology
Research
See Pharmaceutical research
PHARMACOPOEIAS
See also
Information systems—Pharmaceutical use
PHARRISS, JOYCE
Better business writing that gets results. il *Working Woman* 14:128+ D '89
PHASE RULE AND EQUILIBRIUM
The liquid state of solid gold particles [research by Laurence D. Marks] I. Peterson. il *Science News* 136:70 Jl 29 '89
PHASE TRANSITIONS
The footprints of chaos [phase space plots] R. Pool. il *Science* 243:605 F 3 '89
From fireball to galaxies: making late waves [late phase transitions in astronomical models of the universe] I. Peterson. *Science News* 135:262 Ap 29 '89
Rearranging oxygen for superconductivity [yttrium-barium-copper oxide; work of Robert B. Beyers] I. Peterson. *Science News* 136:133 Ag 26 '89
A smooth transition to a lumpy universe [theory of David N. Schramm] *Astronomy* 17:14+ S '89
Toward protein tertiary structure recognition by means of associative memory Hamiltonians. M. S. Friedrichs and P. G. Wolynes. bibl f il *Science* 246:371-3 O 20 '89
Ultrafast dynamics at semiconductor and metal surfaces [laser experiments] J. Bokor. bibl f il *Science* 246:1130-4 D 1 '89
PHASED ARRAY ANTENNAS
New type of phased-array antenna could cut cost, weight of airborne systems [Sedco Systems] il *Aviation Week & Space Technology* 131:105+ S 18 '89
Sanders develops MMIC for phased array systems [monolithic microwave integrated circuit device] *Aviation Week & Space Technology* 130:291 Je 12 '89
USAF studies linking phased array radar with fiber-optic cable. *Aviation Week & Space Technology* 130:61+ Ja 30 '89
Westinghouse mounts effort to build entire jammer on single Ga-As wafer. il *Aviation Week & Space Technology* 131:102 S 18 '89
PHASES OF THE MOON See Moon—Phases
PHEASANT SHOOTING
Chinese checker ringnecks. T. Huggler. il *Outdoor Life* 184:66-7+ D '89
Field of pheasant dreams. M. Pearce. il *Outdoor Life* 184:66-7+ O '89
The shooting party [Golden Pheasant Inn, Clwyd County, Wales] P. Davies. il *Gentlemen's Quarterly* 59:330-4+ O '89
Anecdotes, facetiae, satire, etc.
The chase at pheasants. D. C. Proper. il *Field & Stream* 93:28-9 F '89
PHEASANTS
See also
Cooking—Game
PHELAN, JIM
Entertainment news and hints. See issues of Home Office Computing beginning September 1988 through June 1989
PHELPS, BETSY
What every mother fears. il por *Ladies' Home Journal* 106:20+ Jl '89

PHELPS, BRIAN
How to repair CD players. il *Radio-Electronics* 60:52-3+ N '89
PHELPS, DEANNA
Foster home recruitment and retention: a success story. il *Children Today* 18:7-9+ Mr/Ap '89
PHELPS DODGE CORPORATION
Phelps Dodge's treasures may lie below the copper. G. G. Marcial. il *Business Week* p94 Mr 6 '89
PHENCYCLIDINE See PCP
PHENOLOGY
See also
Plants, Effect of climate on
PHENOTYPE See Genotype and phenotype
PHEROMONES

Insects
Hormone triggers moth mating [research by Michel Cusson and Jeremy N. McNeil] *Science News* 135:46 Ja 21 '89
Identification of a neuropeptide hormone that regulates sex pheromone production in female moths. A. K. Raina and others. bibl f il *Science* 244:796-8 My 19 '89
Involvement of juvenile hormone in the regulation of pheromone release activities in a moth. M. Cusson and J. N. McNeil. bibl f il *Science* 243:210-12 Ja 13 '89
Pheromone-mediation of host-selection in bont ticks (Amblyomma hebraeum Koch) [carriers of heartwater disease] R. A. I. Norval and others. bibl f il *Science* 243:364-5 Ja 20 '89
Ticks follow fellows to tastiest cows [carriers of heartwater disease; research by Conrad E. Yunker and others] *Science News* 135:123 F 25 '89

Reptiles
Garter snakes yield sexual chemistry [research by Robert T. Mason] B. Bower. *Science News* 136:55 Jl 22 '89
Sex pheromones in snakes [garter snakes] R. T. Mason and others. bibl f il *Science* 245:290-3 Jl 21 '89
PHI DELTA KAPPAN (PERIODICAL)
The editor's page. P. B. Gough. See issues of Phi Delta Kappan beginning February 1988
PHIBRO ENERGY, INC.
Phibro: Salomon's ace in the oil patch. M. Ivey. *Business Week* p38-9 My 8 '89
PHILADELPHIA (MISS.)

Motion picture theaters
Mississippi theater won't show controversial movie [Mississippi burning] il *Jet* 75:51 Ja 23 '89

Race relations
The '64 civil rights murders: the struggle continues [honoring J. Chaney, M. Schwerner and A. Goodman; cover story] J. Kornbluth. il pors *The New York Times Magazine* p16-19+ Jl 23 '89
Back on the bus [events commemorating 25th anniversary of the murder of civil rights workers J. E. Chaney, A. Goodman and M. H. Schwerner] P. Dray. il pors *Mother Jones* 14:37-9+ N '89
Honor trio killed by KKK in Mississippi vote drive [M. Schwerner, J. Chaney and A. Goodman] il pors *Jet* 76:6-7 Jl 10 '89
'It must never happen again' [relives 1964 murders of Andrew Goodman, James Chaney and Michael Schwerner] A. Murr. il *Newsweek* 113:26-7 Ja 9 '89
Since Mississippi burned [impact of 1964 murder of three civil rights workers on residents] D. McWhorter. il *People Weekly* 31:36-43 Ja 9 '89
PHILADELPHIA (PA.)

Airports
Skinner calls USAir bid for more Philadelphia gates anticompetitive [Eastern gates] *Aviation Week & Space Technology* 130:110 Je 5 '89

Blacks
Children of the underclass [cover story] il *Newsweek* 114:16-20+ S 11 '89

Education
Underwriting the future: two women will send 146 kids to college [O. Brown and R. W. Hayre set up funds for black children] R. Brown. il pors *Ebony* 44:74+ Ap '89

Galleries and museums
See also
Pennsylvania Academy of the Fine Arts
How to borrow a Rodin [Museum Loan Program from Pew Charitable Trusts will fund inter-museum loans] S. Staggs. il *Art News* 88:50+ Ap '89

Historic houses, sites, etc.
Victorian revival [Philadelphia 1857 townhouse decorated by R. Denning] B. Adams. il *House & Garden* 161:102-9 D '89
When neon signs were art [L. Davidson's restorations] J. O'Dwyer. il pors *Americana* 17:50-5 My/Je '89

Hospitals
Fray erupts when white woman wills estate worth $476,000 to black man [Giuffre Medical Center makes claim on M. Barnett's estate] *Jet* 76:4 My 22 '89

Libraries
See also
Furness Building

Music
See also
Opera—Pennsylvania
Philadelphia Orchestra

Newspapers
See also
Philadelphia inquirer

Politics and government
Frank Rizzo without prejudice. J. Lombardi. il por *Esquire* 112:114-17 Ag '89
The worst city government. D. Meyers. *The Washington Monthly* 21:37 S '89

Poor
One teen's campaign for the homeless [work of T. Ferrell] P. W. Cohen. il pors *Scholastic Update (Teachers' edition)* 121:20-2 F 10 '89

Prisons and reformatories
Condoms in the cells. A. Hornblum. *The Progressive* 53:12 F '89

Savings and loan associations
See also
Berean Savings Association

Schools
See Philadelphia (Pa.)—Education

Social work
See also
Project LEIF
Wee Care: reaching teenage mothers and changing their lives. P. R. Rosenwald and G. Porter. *Children Today* 18:28-30 My/Je '89

Sports
Philadelphia. T. Whitaker. il *Sport (New York, N.Y.)* 80:60-4 Ap '89

Stores
Cherchez la store [France's Carrefour opens hypermarket] D. Fong. il *Forbes* 143:311+ Ja 9 '89
PHILADELPHIA COLLEGE OF BIBLE
Profs resign when women named to board. C. Lehmann. il *Christianity Today* 33:46 O 6 '89
PHILADELPHIA INQUIRER
Two reporters you don't want on your tail [D. L. Barlett and J. B. Steele receive Pulitzer Prize for articles on tax loopholes] J. Alter. il pors *Newsweek* 113:71+ Ap 24 '89
PHILADELPHIA INTERNATIONAL AIRPORT See Philadelphia (Pa.)—Airports
PHILADELPHIA INTERNATIONAL RECORDS
Bought and souled. S. Fried. il *Gentlemen's Quarterly* 59:109+ Je '89
PHILADELPHIA ORCHESTRA
Party girl [concert performance of Nabucco] P. G. Davis. il *New York* 22:101-2 Mr 6 '89
PHILADELPHIA SOCIETY
The past as prologue [conference on Reagan years] L. Bridges. *National Review* 41:22-3 Je 2 '89
PHILADELPHIA STOCK EXCHANGE, INC.
Will the Amex and Philly team up against Chicago? [merge options trading] L. J. Nathans. il *Business Week* p78 Jl 31 '89
PHILANTHROPY See Charities; Giving
PHILATELY AND PHILATELISTS See Postage stamps—Collectors and collecting
PHILBIN, TOM
The lawyer and the punk. *Reader's Digest* 135:7-8+ Ag '89
PHILBY, KIM, 1912-1988

about
Mask of treachery [excerpt] J. Costello. il por *Conservative Digest* 15:59+ Ja/F '89
PHILHARMONIC SYMPHONY ORCHESTRA OF NEW YORK See New York Philharmonic-Symphony Orchestra
PHILIP MORRIS, INC.
From soup to nuts [CEO H. Maxwell] A. Farnham. il por *Fortune* 119:43 Ja 2 '89
Hidden values for 1989. B. D. Fromson. il *Fortune* 119:28 Ja 2 '89
How Philip Morris diversified right [acquiring Kraft] S. P. Sherman. il por *Fortune* 120:120-2+ O 23 '89
Is bigger better for Philip Morris? [interview with H. Maxwell] C. Leinster. il por *Fortune* 119:66-71 My 8 '89
Michael Miles. L. Therrien. il por *Business Week* Special Issue:126 Ap 14 '89
The money magician at Philip Morris [H. Storr] L. J. Nathans. il por *Business Week* p78 Ap 10 '89
Philip Morris's big bite [cover story] L. J. Davis. il por *The New York Times Magazine* p30-3+ Ap 9 '89
A smokeless cigarette ad? [Bill of Rights ad campaign stirs controversy] *Newsweek* 114:64 N 13 '89
Smoking gun [C. Yeutter's efforts on behalf of cigarette industry while U.S. Trade Representative] S. Hornik. il *Common Cause Magazine* 15:9 Mr/Ap '89
PHILIPPE, DUC D'ORLÉANS See Orléans, Louis Philippe Joseph, duc d', 1747-1793
PHILIPPINE AIRLINES INC.
Philippine Airlines readies itself for privatization. P. Proctor. il map *Aviation Week & Space Technology* 131:99+ Ag 21 '89

PHILIPPINES
See also
AIDS (Disease)—Philippines
Americans—Philippines
Anti-Communist movements—Philippines
Aviation and state—Philippines
Birth control—Philippines
Children—Employment—Philippines
Civil rights—Philippines
Economic assistance, American—Philippines
Funeral rites and ceremonies—Philippines
Ilocos Norte (Philippines)
Investments, American—Philippines
Labor unions—Philippines
Manila (Philippines)
Military assistance, American—Philippines
Plantations—Philippines
Pollution—Philippines
Relief work—Philippines
Terrorism—Philippines
Youth—Philippines

Defenses
See also
United States—Armed Forces—Forces in the Philippines
United States. Army—Forces in the Philippines
United States. Navy—Forces in the Philippines

Economic conditions
The Philippine rebels aimed for Aquino—but hit the economy. K. S. Barnes and D. J. Yang. por *Business Week* p68 D 18 '89

Economic policy
Aquino's new economic agenda. M. Feria. *World Press Review* 36:54 My '89

Foreign relations
United States
See United States—Foreign relations—Philippines

History
Insurrection, 1899-1901
Manifest Destiny's man of the hour: Frederick Funston. D. H. Bain. bibl (p164) il pors *Smithsonian* 20:134-6+ My '89

Industries
See also
Aboitiz Air Transport
Aerolift (Firm)
Airlines—Philippines
Philippine Airlines Inc.

Native peoples
See also
Tasaday (Philippine people)

Politics and government
See also
Politics, Corruption in—Philippines
Civilians caught in Philippine 'total war'. D. Cunningham. *The Christian Century* 106:1036-7 N 15 '89
Cory's coup. W. S. Thompson. il *National Review* 41:18-19 D 31 '89
Democracies, yes; justice, not yet. *America* 161:463 D 23-30 '89
Democracy in peril [coup attempt] M. Nemeth. il *Maclean's* 102:39 D 11 '89
Democracy in the Philippines. B. A. Aquino. bibl f *Current History* 88:181-4+ Ap '89
Future prospects for the Philippines [statement, March 7, 1989] D. F. Lambertson. *Department of State Bulletin* 89:43-9 My '89
George Bush's thriller in Manila [aid given to C. Aquino during coup attempt] il por *U.S. News & World Report* 107:14-15 D 11 '89
A hard-fought victory [failed coup] M. Nemeth. il *Maclean's* 102:26+ D 18 '89
Letter from the Philippines [coup attempt against C. Aquino] S. Blaustein. *The New Yorker* 65:95-106 D 18 '89
The Philippine rebels aimed for Aquino—but hit the economy. K. S. Barnes and D. J. Yang. por *Business Week* p68 D 18 '89
Plenty of nice people. D. Murphy. *America* 160:150-2 F 18 '89
Setting Marcos adrift. S. Karnow. il pors *The New York Times Magazine* p50+ Mr 19 '89
Shoot-out in Manila [attempted coup against C. Aquino] C. S. Manegold. il map por *Newsweek* 114:56-8 D 11 '89
So much for people power. C. S. Manegold. il por *Newsweek* 114:38-9 D 18 '89
Soldier power [coup attempt against C. Aquino] H. G. Chua-Eoan. il map por *Time* 134:50-2 D 11 '89
There is always a next time. H. G. Chua-Eoan. il por *Time* 134:28-9 D 18 '89
'Total war' in the Philippines. N. Rosca. il *The Nation* 248:839-42 Je 19 '89
Vigilante justice. J. Ross. *The New Republic* 201:9-21 N 27 '89

Religious institutions and affairs
See also
Catholic Church—Philippines
Church and social problems—Philippines
National Council of Churches (Philippines)

Religious conferences—Philippines
PHILIPS, MICHAEL
Reactors redux. il *Sierra* 74:56-61 Mr/Ap '89
PHILIPS INDUSTRIES, NV
The making of a CD player. W. Wolfe. il *Stereo Review* 54:55-61 Ag '89
PHILLABAUM, L. E.
The university press and suitable priorities. il por *Publishers Weekly* 235:39 My 26 '89
PHILLIPS, CHRISTOPHER
Charlie Smith's second chance. il *Reader's Digest* 135:29-30+ N '89
Homage to a phantom avant-garde: the Situationist International. bibl f il *Art in America* 77:182-91+ O '89
PHILLIPS, CHYNNA
about
Mama was a rebel . . . papa was an addict . . . S. Littwin. il pors *TV Guide* 37:6-8+ O 14-20 '89
PHILLIPS, DOUG
about
Years after a crash that killed 248 soldiers, families still seek answers. C. E. Cohen. il pors *People Weekly* 32:65-7 D 18 '89
PHILLIPS, FLIP, 1915-
about
Flip Phillips. M. Bourne. il por *Down Beat* 56:14 Mr '89
PHILLIPS, GLENN S.
Choctaw with a mission. il por *The Progressive* 53:14-15 Jl '89
PHILLIPS, HARVEY E.
Accentuate the positive. il pors *Opera News* 54:26+ D 9 '89
Son of the forest. il por *Opera News* 53:51-2 Ap 1 '89
(jt. auth) See Eckert, Thor, Jr., and Phillips, Harvey E.
PHILLIPS, HERB
The little-horse ranch in Texas: miniature thoroughbreds mean big bucks for the nuns of St. Clare. il *Travel Holiday* 172:106 Jl '89
Look who's talking. il *Travel Holiday* 171:18-19+ My '89
Playing soldier. il *Travel Holiday* 172:106 Ag '89
PHILLIPS, JEFFREY L.
'Serious disruptions' in Zimbabwe. *The Christian Century* 106:1038-9 N 15 '89
PHILLIPS, JOHN F.
about
Black gen. heads computer systems at Ohio air base. il por *Jet* 75:36 Ja 30 '89
PHILLIPS, KEN
about
Living in sin? Not in her apartments, vows Christian landlady Evelyn Smith. M. Brower. il pors *People Weekly* 32:113-14 D 11 '89
PHILLIPS, LESLIE *See* Phillips, Sam
PHILLIPS, LISA
about
Image maker. B. Smith. il por *Harper's Bazaar* 122:88+ D '89
PHILLIPS, LOU DIAMOND
about
Lou Diamond Phillips: more than a Diamond in the rough! il pors *Teen* 33:49 S '89
PHILLIPS, LOUIS
Answering Faulkner. il *America* 160:452-3 My 13 '89
PHILLIPS, LYNN
In the fashion no! il *Ms.* 17:42-3 Mr '89
Media mates: role model marriages. *Harper's Bazaar* 122:119+ F '89
"Move over, Phil". il *Ms.* 17:44+ Ja/F '89
Spreedom, now! il *Ms.* 18:30+ Jl/Ag '89
PHILLIPS, MARK
Growing pains. il *The New York Times Magazine* p22+ S 3 '89
PHILLIPS, MARK, 1948-
about
A crisis rocks a royal marriage [cover story] J. Kaufman. il pors *People Weekly* 31:66-8+ Ap 24 '89
No fairy-tale ending. A. Phillips. il pors *Maclean's* 102:61 S 11 '89
With no hope for a happy ending, Princess Anne brings her storybook marriage to a close. M. H. J. Farrell. il pors *People Weekly* 32:114-17 S 18 '89
PHILLIPS, MARY JO
Homegrown [cover story] il *Flower and Garden* 33:20-1 My/Je '89
PHILLIPS, MICHAEL, 1938-
The door is shut [excerpt from Mental snacks] *The Humanist* 49:11 My/Je '89
PHILLIPS, MICHAEL, 1938-, AND OTHERS
Living grandly on less. il *Utne Reader* p85-6 S/O '89
PHILLIPS, MICHELLE
about
Mama was a rebel . . . papa was an addict . . . S. Littwin. il pors *TV Guide* 37:6-8+ O 14-20 '89
PHILLIPS, PATRICIA C.
Waste not. il *Art in America* 77:47+ F '89
PHILLIPS, PETER
about
Glorious! *The New Yorker* 65:33-5 D 18 '89

PHILLIPS, RODERICK
about
The road to polygamy. L. Stone. bibl f il *The New York Review of Books* 36:12-15 Mr 2 '89
PHILLIPS, SAM
about
Sam Phillips plays the name game. D. Wild. il por *Rolling Stone* p30 My 18 '89
PHILLIPS, SIMON
about
Simon Phillips. B. Milkowski. il por *Down Beat* 56:28-9 D '89
PHILLIPS, WAYNE, 1947-
about
A different drummer. C. Poole. il por *Forbes* 143:166 Ap 3 '89
PHILLIPS PETROLEUM COMPANY
Phillips climbs up from the bottom of the barrel. T. Vogel. il por *Business Week* p76+ Ja 16 '89
Plastics? R. T. Grieves. il por *Forbes* 143:104 Ja 23 '89
Profiting from disaster [explosion at polyethylene plant outside Houston] A. A. Lappen. il *Forbes* 144:203+ N 27 '89
Will Phillips be a gusher? [views of Warren Greene] G. G. Marcial. *Business Week* p78 Ag 28 '89
PHILLIPS-VAN HEUSEN CORP.
How to restructure [views of stock analyst Dennis Rosenberg] T. Jaffe. *Forbes* 143:220-1 Mr 20 '89
Sea change. il *Forbes* 143:87 Ja 9 '89
PHILOSOPHY
See also
Absolute
Atheism
Biology—Philosophy
Civilization
College education—Philosophy
Consciousness
Education—Philosophy
Evolution
Existentialism
Geography—Philosophy
History—Philosophy
Humanism
Idealism
Ideology
Knowledge, Theory of
Law—Philosophy
Materialism
Meaning (Philosophy)
Mind and body
Motorcycling—Philosophy
Mysticism
Pessimism
Pragmatism
Quality (Philosophy)
Science—Philosophy
Self (Philosophy)
Sports—Philosophy
Style (Philosophy)
Theosophy
Truth

Study and teaching
Poland
Where philosophy matters. J. L. Auspitz. *Commentary* 87:54-60 Je '89
PHILOSOPHY, AMERICAN
See also
Croly, Herbert David, 1869-1930
PHILOSOPHY, DANISH
See also
Kierkegaard, Søren, 1813-1855
PHILOSOPHY, FRENCH
See also
Foucault, Michel, 1926-1984
Lévy, Bernard Henri
Ideas and ideologies [philosophers of the French Enlightenment and the French Revolution] M. Cranston. bibl il *History Today* 39:10-14 My '89
PHILOSOPHY, GERMAN
See also
Herder, Johann Gottfried, 1744-1803
PHILOSOPHY, GREEK
See also
Aristotle, 384-322 B.C.
Socrates
PHILOSOPHY, HINDU
See also
Yoga
PHILOSOPHY, INDIAN (EAST INDIAN)
The philosophical tradition. V. S. Naravane. il *The Courier (Unesco)* 42:28-30 F '89
PHILOSOPHY, JEWISH
A (Jewish) double helix. C. Raphael. *Commentary* 87:56-8 My '89
PHILOSOPHY, MEDIEVAL
Alcuin and the 'new Athens'. M. Alberi. il por *History Today* 39:35-41 S '89

PHILOSOPHY, POLISH
Where philosophy matters. J. L. Auspitz. *Commentary* 87:54-60 Je '89
PHILOSOPHY, THAI
Eastern cultures experts on "self". R. Williams. *The Humanist* 49:40 N/D '89
PHILP, RICHARD
Kickoff. See issues of Dance Magazine beginning May 1989
PHIPPS, WILLIAM E., 1930-
Health technology vs. death: should we prolong the inevitable? il *USA Today (Periodical)* 117:71-2 Ja '89
PHLOX
Blue phlox: one of nature's best. L. A. Weathers. il *Southern Living* 24:66-7 Mr '89
PHM CORP.
Sweet deal [acquisitions of Texas thrifts coincide with federal bailout] J. Drummond. il *Forbes* 144:96+ S 18 '89
PHOBIAS
See also
Acrophobia
Dental phobia
Fear of automobile driving
Fear of blood
Fear of flying
Fear of the dark
Homophobia
Phobias: the facts about fears. S. Perrine. il *Parents* 64:208+ S '89
Social phobia. D. Sobel. il *The New York Times Magazine* p24-5 Ja 1 '89
PHOBOS (SATELLITE) *See* Mars (Planet)—Satellites
PHOBOS (SPACE VEHICLES) *See* Space vehicles, Russian
PHOENIX (ARIZ.)
Climate
How hot is it? J. Toobin. *The New Republic* 201:12-14 Ag 7-14 '89
Description
Alice Cooper: healthy, wealthy and dry. D. Koen. por *Rolling Stone* p49 Jl 13-27 '89
Sports
Fast lane for Phoenix [Iceberg U.S.A. Grand Prix] S. Moses. il *Sports Illustrated* 70:28-9 Je 12 '89
PHOENIX AIRLINE SERVICES INC.
Phoenix Airlines may get its wings clipped. D. Foust. il por *Business Week* p114 Mr 13 '89
PHOENIX TECHNOLOGIES LTD.
The sincerest form of flattery. D. Churbuck. il *Forbes* 143:116+ F 20 '89
PHONICS METHOD *See* Reading—Study and teaching
PHONOGRAPH
Pickup
Audio-Technica AT-ML170 phono cartridge. J. D. Hirsch. il *Stereo Review* 54:29-30 Jl '89
Ortofon 540 phono cartridge. R. Long. il *High Fidelity (New York, N.Y.)* 39:28+ Ja '89
Ortofon Model 540 phono cartridge. J. D. Hirsch. il *Stereo Review* 54:42+ Ap '89
The (record) dust settles [moving-magnet or moving coil] R. Hodges. il *Stereo Review* 54:144 Ja '89
Sight and sound: is LP obsolete? H. Fantel. il *Opera News* 54:26 Ag '89
Turntables & cartridges. I. Masters. il *Stereo Review* 54:79-83 Ja '89
Record changers
See Phonograph—Turntables
Testing
Thorens TD280 MkII record player. J. D. Hirsch. il *Stereo Review* 54:42+ Ag '89
Turntables
Ariston Icon Turntable. R. Long. il *High Fidelity (New York, N.Y.)* 39:23-5 My '89
The optical turntable [developed by Finial Technology] R. Hodges. il *Stereo Review* 54:136 Mr '89
Sight and sound: is LP obsolete? H. Fantel. il *Opera News* 54:26 Ag '89
Turntables. il *Stereo Review* 54:110-13 F '89
Turntables & cartridges. I. Masters. il *Stereo Review* 54:79-83 Ja '89
PHONOGRAPH RECORD COVERS
Trotsky, whose lively street art became an off-the-wall album cover for Bob Dylan [mural on building in Hell's Kitchen] il por *People Weekly* 32:112 O 23 '89
PHONOGRAPH RECORD INDUSTRY
See also
A&M Records (Firm)
Apollo Theatre Records
AsianImprov Records (Firm)
Blacks in the phonograph record industry
CBS Records Inc.
Elektra/Asylum Records
Geffen Company
Hollywood Records (Firm)
IRS Records (Firm)
Island Records
Motown Productions
Olivia Records
Pangaea Records (Firm)
Philadelphia International Records

PHONOGRAPH RECORD INDUSTRY—See also—cont.
Phonograph records—Recording
RCA Records
Recording Industry Association of America
Rhino Records
Rykodisc Inc.
Warner Bros. Inc.
Labels back down on DAT. M. Goldberg. *Rolling Stone* p26 S 21 '89

Acquisitions and mergers
International aspects
"I don't loon off all the time" [C. Blackwell sells Island Records to PolyGram] P. Newcomb. il por *Forbes* 144:344+ N 13 '89
Now it's Chris Blackwell, corporate hipster [Island Records surrenders to PolyGram] R. A. Melcher and D. Lieberman. il por *Business Week* p49 Ag 14 '89
Revenge of the antisuits [Sony's takeover of CBS Records] S. N. Chakravarty. il *Forbes* 144:49+ D 11 '89
They're playing whose song? [record companies buy independent publishers] D. Lieberman. il *Business Week* p42 Ja 23 '89

Ethical aspects
See also
Payola
Manager tied to drug gang [independent record promoter W. Underwood arrested in New York City] W. Bastone. *Rolling Stone* p62 Jl 13-27 '89

Finance
Going, going, gone? [demise of vinyl LPs] J. Ressner. il *Rolling Stone* p15-16 Ap 20 '89

History
See also
Starr Piano Company. Gennett Record Division
Phil Spector. K. Hubbard. il pors *People Weekly* 31:84-8 F 6 '89

International aspects
Silver rush. N. Lebrecht. il *Opera News* 54:8-10 Ag '89

Marketing
See Phonograph records—Marketing

Great Britain
See also
Apple Corps Ltd.
Virgin Classics (Firm)

PHONOGRAPH RECORD INDUSTRY IN TELEVISION
Hooks and crooks [Wiseguy episodes] D. Rensin. il *Rolling Stone* p35-6+ Ap 20 '89

PHONOGRAPH RECORD STORES
See also
Spec's Music, Inc.
Electronic disc jockeys: a new hit [Personics system] il *Newsweek* 114:47 Ag 28 '89
Personics offers customer programmed cassettes. E. Kehler. il *Down Beat* 56:11 N '89
Personics steps to the fore [custom-made audiocassettes] J. Ressner. il *Rolling Stone* p24 O 19 '89

Laws and regulations
A rap album in the dock [obscenity case against Alexander, Ala. record store selling The 2 Live Crew] N. Zeman. il *Newsweek* 114:72 O 16 '89

PHONOGRAPH RECORDS
See also
Compact discs
Best of '88. il *Time* 133:100 Ja 2 '89
For the record. See occasional issues of Maclean's
People picks & pans. See issues of People Weekly
The pick of 1988. il *Maclean's* 102:60-1+ Ja 2 '89
Recorded music in review. W. F. Grueninger. See issues of Consumers' Research Magazine
Records. J. W. Freeman. See issues of Opera News
Sight and sound: is LP obsolete? H. Fantel. il *Opera News* 54:26 Ag '89
Sound on disc. R. De Toledano. See occasional issues of National Review
Spotlight. E. Miller. See issues of Seventeen through March 1989
What do phonograph records have in common with windshield wipers? [reflection optics] J. Walker. il *Scientific American* 261:106-9 Jl '89

Advertising jingles
Mad, mad, Mad. Ave. [TeeVee toons: the commercials] S. Simels. il *Stereo Review* 54:140 S '89

African music
Afro-reggae revival. L. Birnbaum. il *Down Beat* 56:41-4 Ag '89
Salif Keita [release of Ko-yan] R. Givens. por *Stereo Review* 54:150 N '89

American music
Dawn Upshaw's American music. R. Freed. por *Stereo Review* 54:152 S '89

Animal sounds
Laying down animal tracks [composer B. Krause's Gorillas in the mix] D. Glick. il por *Newsweek* 114:62 Jl 31 '89
Pet shop boy [B. Krause] E. Smith. il *Omni (New York, N.Y.)* 12:20+ D '89
With an ear to the ground, sea, and sky [B. Krause] D. Glick. il por *Sierra* 74:82-6+ N/D '89

Arias
Singers recycled. P. G. Davis. il *New York* 22:130+ Ag 21 '89

Asian American music
See also
AsianImprov Records (Firm)

Awards
See also
American Music Awards
Grammy Awards
International Rock Awards
Soul Train Music Awards
Stereo Review's Record of the Year Awards for 1988. C. Barter. il *Stereo Review* 54:59-62 F '89

Ballet music
Christmas dream work [The Nutcracker] P. Kennicott. il *Dance Magazine* 63:67 D '89

Black music
See also
Apollo Theatre Records
Philadelphia International Records
Soul Train Music Awards
Anita Baker on love [Giving you the best that I got] P. Garland. por *Stereo Review* 54:108 Mr '89
Black music's new hit doctors [T. Riley, A. Reid, and K. Edmonds] S. Bloom. il pors *Rolling Stone* p32 My 18 '89
Control [Janet Jackson's 1986 album] il *Rolling Stone* p86 N 16 '89
Crossroads for Tracy Chapman. P. Garland. por *Stereo Review* 54:129 D '89
D'Arby's strange soul search [release of Neither fish nor flesh] M. Coleman. il *Rolling Stone* p109-10 N 30 '89
Janet Jackson's 'Nation' under a groove. V. Aletti. il por *Rolling Stone* p81+ O 19 '89
Jet's top 20 albums; Singles. See issues of Jet
L.A. & Babyface [black producers A. Reid and K. Edmonds] il pors *Ebony* 44:134+ Je '89
Marc V. [release of Too true] P. Garland. il por *Stereo Review* 54:80 Jl '89
Midnight love [Marvin Gaye's 1982 album] il *Rolling Stone* p96 N 16 '89
The night I fell in love [Luther Vandross' 1985 album] il *Rolling Stone* p143 N 16 '89
Private dancer [Tina Turner's 1984 album] il *Rolling Stone* p103 N 16 '89
Rapture [Anita Baker's 1986 album] il *Rolling Stone* p94 N 16 '89
Thriller [Michael Jackson's 1982 album] il *Rolling Stone* p67 N 16 '89
The timeless Mavis Staples [release of Time waits for no one] P. Garland. por *Stereo Review* 54:116 O '89
Tracy Chapman. il *Rolling Stone* p72 N 16 '89
Tracy Chapman at the 'Crossroads'. F. Goodman. il *Rolling Stone* p135-6 O 5 '89
A vibrant legacy [release of A history of New Orleans rhythm & blues] B. Sandmel. il *The Atlantic* 263:88-9+ Ap '89
Who's zoomin' who? [Aretha Franklin's 1985 album] il *Rolling Stone* p140 N 16 '89

Blues music
Asking for water [releases by R. Cray, J. L. Walker, and E. James] M. Moses. *The New Yorker* 64:83+ F 13 '89
Generations of blues [J. L. Hooker's The healer] A. DeCurtis. il por *Rolling Stone* p28 N 2 '89
The healer [release by John Lee Hooker] J. Matthews. il *Rolling Stone* p88 O 19 '89
Ray Anderson: Blues bred in the bone. F.-J. Hadley. il *Down Beat* 56:34+ Ap '89
Stevie Ray Vaughan: In step. B. Milkowski. il *Down Beat* 56:29 N '89
Stevie Ray Vaughan is "In step". P. Puterbaugh. il por *Stereo Review* 54:124 D '89
Strong persuader [release by Robert Cray Band] il *Rolling Stone* p100 N 16 '89
Two Chess mates at their very best [The Chess box by W. Dixon] D. Fricke. il pors *Rolling Stone* p40-1 Ja 26 '89

Brazilian music
Brazilian beat. L. Birnbaum. *Down Beat* 56:38-40 N '89
Byrne compiles Brazil LP. M. Goldberg. il por *Rolling Stone* p16 Ja 12 '89
David Byrne's Brazil [Beleza tropical] S. Stein. il por *Down Beat* 56:13 Jl '89

Bulgarian folk music
Voices from another time [release of Le mystère de voix bulgares] J. Cocks. il *Time* 133:100 Ja 2 '89

Christmas music
Anecdotes, facetiae, satire, etc.
A visit from St. Hank. H. Bordowitz. il *High Fidelity (New York, N.Y.)* 39:55 Ja '89

Classical music
Beethoven, Bach, Tallis, & others. R. De Toledano. il *National Review* 41:53+ Jl 14 '89
Classical music. See issues of Stereo Review
Classical reviews. See issues of High Fidelity (New York, N.Y.) through July 1989
Classical sounds. P. Williams-Jones. il *American Visions* 4:58-9 D '89

PHONOGRAPH RECORDS—cont.

Collectors and collecting

Music memorabilia. S. M. Stroff. See issues of Antiques & Collecting Hobbies beginning February 1986

Country music

Billy Hill [release of I am just a rebel] A. Nash. il *Stereo Review* 54:136 D '89

Copperhead Road [release by Steve Earle] R. Tannenbaum. il *Rolling Stone* p41-2 Ja 26 '89

Cowboy Junkies: Trinity session. A. Nash. *Stereo Review* 54:95-6 Ap '89

Garth Brooks. A. Nash. *Stereo Review* 54:131 D '89

George Jones [release of One woman man] D. Gates. *Newsweek* 113:68 Mr 13 '89

Guitar town [Steve Earle's 1986 album] il *Rolling Stone* p130 N 16 '89

Guy Clark and friends [release of Old friends] A. Nash. il por *Stereo Review* 54:102 Je '89

Hillbilly music . . . thank God! volume 1. D. Browne. il *Rolling Stone* p103 Ap 20 '89

K.D. Lang [release of Absolute torch and twang] A. Nash. il por *Stereo Review* 54:75 Ag '89

Lyle Lovett. il *Rolling Stone* p142 N 16 '89

Lyle Lovett's large band [release of Lyle Lovett and his large band] A. Nash. il por *Stereo Review* 54:104+ My '89

Music [release of Trinity session] G. Santoro. *The Nation* 248:67-8 Ja 9-16 '89

Patsy Cline: Her first recordings. J. Morthland. *High Fidelity (New York, N.Y.)* 39:81-2 Je '89

The power of Emmylou Harris [release of Bluebird] A. Nash. por *Stereo Review* 54:81 Ap '89

Smile when you call 'em that, son [release of Hillbilly music . . . thank God] D. Gates. il *Newsweek* 113:81 Mr 20 '89

Steve Earle: Copperhead Road. A. Nash. il *Stereo Review* 54:106 Mr '89

Suzy Bogguss [release of Somewhere between] A. Nash. por *Stereo Review* 54:76 Jl '89

Tammy Wynette [release of Next to you] D. Gates. il *Newsweek* 113:68 Mr 13 '89

Trust in the Tashians [release of Trust in me] A. Nash. pors *Stereo Review* 54:128 O '89

The unbroken circle [release of Will the circle be unbroken, volume two] A. Nash. il *Stereo Review* 54:82 Ag '89

Dance music

See also

Phonograph records—Ballet music

Double bass music

Bass hits [jazz] J. Roberts. il *Down Beat* 56:32-3 Ap '89

Drum music

Michael Shrieve [release of Stiletto and Leaving time] R. Tolleson. il *Down Beat* 56:31-2 Ag '89

Folk music

Crossroads for Tracy Chapman. P. Garland. por *Stereo Review* 54:129 D '89

Library of Congress recordings and Dust Bowl ballads [releases by W. Guthrie] A. DeCurtis. pors *Rolling Stone* p87-8 My 4 '89

Michelle Shocked: mesmerizing [release of Short, sharp, Shocked] A. Nash. il *Stereo Review* 54:104 Mr '89

Suzanne Vega. il *Rolling Stone* p130 N 16 '89

Tracy Chapman. il *Rolling Stone* p72 N 16 '89

Tracy Chapman at the 'Crossroads'. F. Goodman. il *Rolling Stone* p135-6 O 5 '89

Woody Guthrie's enduring vision. J. Walljasper. *Utne Reader* p21 Mr/Ap '89

Guitar music

Play guitar [rock] il *High Fidelity (New York, N.Y.)* 39:70-1+ F '89

Return of the G-men. R. Tolleson. *Down Beat* 56:34-9 My '89

Gypsy music

Voices from another time [release of The Gipsy Kings] J. Cocks. il *Time* 133:100 Ja 2 '89

Haitian music

Something wilder [J. Demme compiles Konbit] J. Farber. il *Rolling Stone* p23 N 2 '89

Indian music (East Indian)

Trilok Gurtu: Usfret. K. Whitehead. il *Down Beat* 56:30-1 Je '89

Jazz music

See also

Phonograph records—Blues music

Starr Piano Company. Gennett Record Division

Reviews

Bebop's children. W. A. Brower. il *American Visions* 4:44+ O '89

Blindfold test. See issues of Down Beat

Bootin' jazz [Italian albums issued by Splasc(h) Records] A. Lange. *Down Beat* 56:36-9 D '89

From Hoagy to Nancy. R. De Toledano. *National Review* 41:62-3 F 10 '89

Fusion renegades. B. Milkowski. *Down Beat* 56:39-42 O '89

Jazz without fear [basic collection] S. Fried. il *Gentlemen's Quarterly* 59:129+ Ap '89

Menage a trois. A. Lange. il *Down Beat* 56:34-5 Mr '89

Out of the mouths of babes . . . sometimes [school bands] J. Sohmer. *Down Beat* 56:34 O '89

Record reviews. See issues of Down Beat

Waxing on. See issues of Down Beat

Reviews—Single works

Anderson, Ray: Blues bred in the bone
Down Beat il 56:34+ Ap '89. F.-J. Hadley

Battaglia, Stefano: Auryn
Down Beat il 56:34 Je '89. J. Ephland

Bert Wilson & Rebirth: Next Rebirth
Down Beat il 56:30+ F '89. R. Welburn

Bobby Watson and Horizon: No question about it
Down Beat il 56:38 Jl '89. A. Lange
High Fidelity (New York, N.Y.) il 39:77+ F '89. J. W. Poses

Bobby Watson Quartet: Love remains
High Fidelity (New York, N.Y.) il 39:77+ F '89. J. W. Poses

Braxton, Anthony: Quartet (London) 1985
Down Beat il 56:29 Je '89. B. Shoemaker

Burton, Gary: Times like these
Stereo Review il 54:116 Mr '89. R. Givens

Chick Corea Akoustic Band: Chick Corea Akoustic Band
Down Beat il 56:35 Jl '89. R. Tolleson

Complete Commodore jazz recordings, vol. 1
High Fidelity (New York, N.Y.) il 39:79-81 Ja '89. M. Ullman

Dave Holland Trio: Triplicate
Down Beat 56:30+ Ja '89. B. Shoemaker

Davis, Miles: Columbia years 1955-1985
Down Beat il 56:30-1 Ap '89. J. Ephland

Dirty Dozen Brass Band: Voodoo
Down Beat il 56:35 Jl '89. O. Cordle
Rolling Stone il p97-8 Ap 20 '89. J. Hannusch

Elements: Liberal arts
Down Beat il 56:34 N '89. B. Milkowski

Fairground Attraction: First of a million kisses
Stereo Review il 54:107 Mr '89. R. Givens

Frisell, Bill: Before we were born
Down Beat il 56:29 Je '89. G. Santoro

Gurtu, Trilok: Usfret
Down Beat il 56:30-1 Je '89. K. Whitehead

Harrell, Tom: Stories
Down Beat il 56:32+ My '89. F.-J. Hadley

Hodges, Johnny: Complete Johnny Hodges sessions: 1951-1955
Down Beat il 56:35-7 Jl '89. J. Sohmer

Hollyday, Christopher: Reverence
Down Beat il 56:29-30 F '89. J. Robert

Jack DeJohnette's Special Edition: Audio visualscapes
Down Beat il 56:29 Ja '89. F. Bouchard

Kenny Wheeler Quintet: Flutter by, butterfly
Down Beat 56:30+ Ja '89. B. Shoemaker

Leaders: Out here like this . . .
Down Beat il 56:29 Ja '89. K. Whitehead

Marsalis, Branford: Trio jeepy
Down Beat il 56:35-6 O '89. A. Lange

New New Orleans music: Jump jazz
American Visions il 4:44-6 Je '89. W. A. Brower
Down Beat il 56:31 My '89. A. Lange

New New Orleans music: New music jazz
American Visions il 4:44-6 Je '89. W. A. Brower
Down Beat il 56:31 My '89. A. Lange

New New Orleans music: Vocal jazz
American Visions il 4:44-6 Je '89. W. A. Brower
Down Beat il 56:31 My '89. A. Lange

Ponty, Jean-Luc: Storytelling
Down Beat il 56:32 D '89. R. Tolleson

Previte, Bobby: Claude's late morning
Down Beat il 56:29 Mr '89. J. Ephland

Roberts, Marcus: Truth is spoken here
Stereo Review il 54:68+ Jl '89. C. Albertson

Robinson, Scott: Winds of change
Down Beat 56:37-8 Ag '89. O. Cordle

Rouse, Charlie: Epistrophy
Down Beat il 56:33-4 N '89. A. Lange

Rova Saxophone Quartet: Beat kennel
Down Beat il 56:29 F '89. B. Shoemaker

Sample, Joe: Spellbound
Down Beat il 56:30 Ag '89. R. Tolleson

Schuur, Diane: Talkin' 'bout you
Stereo Review il 54:144+ F '89. A. Nash

Shrieve, Michael/Roach, Steve: Leaving time
Down Beat 56:32 Ag '89. R. Tolleson

Smith, Marvin "Smitty": Road less traveled
Down Beat il 56:31 D '89. K. Whitehead

Smith, Tommy: Step by step
Down Beat il 56:37-8 Ag '89. O. Cordle

Steps Ahead: N.Y.C.
Down Beat il 56:30 Ap '89. B. Milkowski

Stiletto: Stiletto
Down Beat il 56:31-2 Ag '89. R. Tolleson

Tribute to John Coltrane—live under the sky
Stereo Review il 54:124+ S '89. C. Albertson

Ulmer, James Blood: Original Phalanx
Down Beat il 56:29+ Mr '89. J. Brinsfield

Ulmer, James Blood: Revelation Music Ensemble
Down Beat 56:29 Mr '89. J. Brinsfield

PHONOGRAPH RECORDS—Jazz music—Reviews—Single works—*cont.*

Williams, James: Magical trio 2
  Down Beat il 56:37-8 Jl '89. R. Welburn
Williams, Tony: Angel Street
  Down Beat il 56:29 F '89. J. Ephland
Yellowjackets: Politics
  Down Beat il 56:34 Ja '89. F. Bouchard
Zawinul Syndicate: Black water
  Down Beat il 56:39-40 D '89. F.-J. Hadley

Latin American music
Rei Momo [release by David Byrne] A. DeCurtis. il *Rolling Stone* p111+ N 30 '89

Marketing
See also
Handleman Co.
Phonograph record stores
As the 45-rpm single fades. M. Meyer. *Rolling Stone* p24 O 19 '89
Charts. See issues of Rolling Stone
Motown deal sounds sweet [joining forces with Apollo Theatre] P. Sharif. il *Black Enterprise* 20:24 N '89
The same old songs [rock music remakes for sure-fire hits] D. Handelman. il *Rolling Stone* p11 Ja 26 '89
The top 100 albums of 1989. il *Rolling Stone* p239 D 14-28 '89

Mexican American music
Santana: Viva Santana! P. Puterbaugh. *Stereo Review* 54:153-4 F '89

Motion picture music
How to sell a soundtrack. M. Mabry. il *Newsweek* 114:47 Ag 28 '89
Prince scores Batman film. M. Goldberg. il por *Rolling Stone* p21 Je 29 '89
Prince's personal purple soundtrack side trip [Batman] J. Pareles. il *Rolling Stone* p121-3 Ag 24 '89
Stay awake! Disney for grownups. S. Simels. il *Stereo Review* 54:160 F '89
Stay awake: various interpretations of music from vintage Disney films. J. D. Considine. il *Rolling Stone* p47 Ja 26 '89

Musicals, revues, etc.
"Show boat" crosses over. E. Mordden. *The New Yorker* 65:79-94 Jl 3 '89

Opera
See also
Phonograph records—Arias
Reviews
Music [works of P. Mascagni] P. G. Davis. il *New York* 22:58-9 S 4 '89
Reviews—Single works
Bizet, Georges: Carmen
  New York il 22:105-6 O 16 '89. P. G. Davis
Frumerie, Gunnar de: Singoalla
  Opera News 54:34 Jl '89. J. W. Freeman
Puccini, Giacomo: Madama Butterfly
  Opera News il 53:44 Je '89. J. W. Freeman
Rossini, Gioacchino: La Cenerentola
  Opera News il 53:42 F 4 '89. J. W. Freeman
Szymanowski, Karol: King Roger
  Opera News il 53:45 Je '89. J. W. Freeman
Wagner, Richard: Tannhäuser
  New York il 22:105-6 O 16 '89. P. G. Davis
Wagner, Richard: Die Walküre
  Stereo Review il 54:134 Ja '89. D. P. Stearns

Operetta
Strauss, Johann: Die Fledermaus. J. W. Freeman. il *Opera News* 53:42 Ja 7 '89

Orchestral music
Recording American. W. Livingstone. il *Stereo Review* 54:32 S '89

Packaging
Boxer shorts [boxed collections] J. Ephland. *Down Beat* 56:5 Ap '89

Parody (Music)
Chuckle and hum. K. Richardson. il *High Fidelity (New York, N.Y.)* 39:57 My '89
Cover and duck. K. Richardson. il *High Fidelity (New York, N.Y.)* 39:60 Je '89

Piano music
Horszowski. R. Freed. il por *Stereo Review* 54:126 Mr '89
Richard Goode's late Beethoven [sonatas] R. Freed. il por *Stereo Review* 54:110 O '89

Popular music
See also
Phonograph records—Black music
Phonograph records—Blues music
Phonograph records—Country music
Phonograph records—Jazz music
Phonograph records—Motion picture music
Phonograph records—Musicals, revues, etc.
Phonograph records—Rock music
Popular music. See issues of Stereo Review
Reviews
Backbeat. See issues of High Fidelity (New York, N.Y.) through July 1989
The early line on 1989: music. il *People Weekly* 31:74-5+ Ja 9 '89

In short order. See issues of High Fidelity (New York, N.Y.) through July 1989
International roots roundup. G. Santoro. *The Nation* 249:578-80 N 13 '89
A new beat in Big Easy. N. Jennings. *Maclean's* 102:61-2 My 22 '89
The pick of the fall's pop crop. il *Newsweek* 114:64-6 O 16 '89
Records. See issues of Rolling Stone
Song. il *People Weekly* 32:84 S 4 '89
The ten best records of 1989. S. Fried. il *Gentlemen's Quarterly* 59:139+ D '89
Reviews—Single works
Carmichael, Hoagy: Classic Hoagy Carmichael
  Down Beat 56:30 Je '89. J. McDonough
Patinkin, Mandy: Mandy Patinkin
  Esquire il 111:40 Ap '89. D. Okrent
  Newsweek il 113:67-8 F 20 '89. C. McGuigan

Rap music
The Beasties: def, not dumb [release of Paul's Boutique] D. Handelman. il *Rolling Stone* p89-90 Ag 10 '89
Ghetto music: the blueprint of hip hop. D. Fricke. il *Rolling Stone* p144 O 5 '89
It takes a nation of millions to hold us back [release by Public Enemy] il *Rolling Stone* p75 N 16 '89
Radio [release by L.L. Cool J] il *Rolling Stone* p120 N 16 '89
Raw like sushi [release by Neneh Cherry] R. Tannenbaum. il *Rolling Stone* p92 Ag 10 '89
Run-D.M.C. il *Rolling Stone* p104 N 16 '89
Walking with a panther [release by L. L. Cool J] D. Browne. il *Rolling Stone* p76 S 7 '89

Recording
Recording American. W. Livingstone. il *Stereo Review* 54:32 S '89

Reggae music
Afro-reggae revival. L. Birnbaum. il *Down Beat* 56:41-4 Ag '89
Red [release by Black Uhuru] il *Rolling Stone* p84 N 16 '89
Wailer, Bunny: Liberation. L. Jaffee. il *High Fidelity (New York, N.Y.)* 39:73-4 My '89

Reissues
Boxer shorts [boxed collections] J. Ephland. *Down Beat* 56:5 Ap '89
Old masters. T. Teachout. See alternate issues of High Fidelity (New York, N.Y.) beginning April 1989 through July 1989
Tales from the crypt [rock reissues for CD] J. Ressner. il *Rolling Stone* p13-14 F 23 '89

Rock music
The same old songs [rock music remakes for sure-fire hits] D. Handelman. il *Rolling Stone* p11 Ja 26 '89
Summer's hot music forecast. J. Ressner. il *Rolling Stone* p17 Je 29 '89
Reviews
The 100 best albums of the eighties [cover story; special section] il *Rolling Stone* p53-6+ N 16 '89
Attack of the giant brundlefly. S. Fried. il *Gentlemen's Quarterly* 59:114+ My '89
Music. J. Pareles. See issues of Mademoiselle
Play guitar. il *High Fidelity (New York, N.Y.)* 39:70-1+ F '89
Records. See issues of Rolling Stone
Tributes [tributes to Buddy Holly, the Byrds, Led Zeppelin and Neil Young performed by obscure bands] S. Simels. il *Stereo Review* 54:138 O '89
The year in records [1989] D. Fricke. il *Rolling Stone* p203+ D 14-28 '89
Reviews—Single works
10,000 Maniacs: In my tribe
  Rolling Stone il p119 N 16 '89
AC/DC: Back in black
  Rolling Stone il p86 N 16 '89
Aerosmith: Pump
  Rolling Stone il p83 O 19 '89. K. Neely
Allman Brothers Band: Dreams
  Rolling Stone il p161-2 Jl 13-27 '89. J. Guterman
Artists United Against Apartheid: Sun City
  Rolling Stone il p148-9 N 16 '89
Baker, Anita: Giving you the best that I got
  The New Yorker 65:84-5 Mr 20 '89. M. Moses
  Stereo Review il 54:108 Mr '89. P. Garland
Baker, Anita: Rapture
  Rolling Stone il p94 N 16 '89
Beastie Boys: Paul's Boutique
  Rolling Stone il p89-90 Ag 10 '89. D. Handelman
Beck, Jeff: Jeff Beck's guitar shop
  Rolling Stone il p136 O 5 '89. D. Fricke
Berry, Chuck: Chess box
  Rolling Stone il p40-1 Ja 26 '89. D. Fricke
Berry, Chuck: Chuck Berry
  Down Beat il 56:33-4 Ap '89. G. Santoro
Bobs: Songs for tomorrow morning
  The Nation 248:571 Ap 24 '89. G. Santoro
BoDeans: Home
  Rolling Stone il p123-4 Ag 24 '89. F. Goodman
  Stereo Review il 54:124+ N '89. R. Givens

PHONOGRAPH RECORDS—Rock music—Reviews—Single works—*cont.*

Bowie, David: Let's dance
  Rolling Stone il p135 N 16 '89
Browne, Jackson: Lives in the balance
  Rolling Stone il p140 N 16 '89
Browne, Jackson: World in motion
  Rolling Stone il p162 Jl 13-27 '89. D. Fricke
  Stereo Review il 54:113 O '89. R. Givens
Bruce, Jack: Willpower
  Rolling Stone il p98-9 Ap 20 '89. D. Fricke
Captain Beefheart and the Magic Band: Doc at the radar station
  Rolling Stone il p114 N 16 '89
Case, Peter: Man with the blue postmodern fragmented neo-traditional guitar
  Stereo Review il 54:71 Ag '89. P. Puterbaugh
Clapton, Eric: Journeyman
  Rolling Stone il p113-14 N 30 '89. J. D. Considine
Clash: London calling
  Rolling Stone il p54-6 N 16 '89
Clinton, George: Computer games
  Rolling Stone il p114 N 16 '89
Costello, Elvis: Spike
  High Fidelity (New York, N.Y.) il 39:71+ My '89. R. C. Walls
  The New Yorker 65:84-5 Ap 24 '89. M. Moses
  Newsweek il 113:68 Mr 13 '89. J. Miller
  Rolling Stone il p103-4 Mr 9 '89. D. Wild
  Stereo Review il 54:103 My '89. S. Simels
Crenshaw, Marshall: Good evening
  Stereo Review il 54:123 S '89. S. Simels
Crenshaw, Marshall: Marshall Crenshaw
  Rolling Stone il p124 N 16 '89
Crosby, Stills, Nash and Young: American dream
  Rolling Stone il p64 Ja 12 '89. A. DeCurtis
Crowded House: Crowded House
  Rolling Stone il p124 N 16 '89
Culture Club: Colour by numbers
  Rolling Stone il p145 N 16 '89
Cure: Disintegration
  Rolling Stone il p162+ Jl 13-27 '89. M. Azerrad
D'Arby, Terence Trent: Neither fish nor flesh: a soundtrack of love, faith, hope & destruction
  New York il 22:140 D 4 '89. E. Wurtzel
  Rolling Stone il p109-10 N 30 '89. M. Coleman
Dash Rip Rock: Ace of clubs
  Stereo Review il 54:123 N '89. P. Puterbaugh
Def Leppard: Pyromania
  Rolling Stone il p116 N 16 '89
Dion: Yo Frankie
  Rolling Stone il p140 Je 15 '89. D. Browne
Dire Straits: Making movies
  Rolling Stone il p106 N 16 '89
Dylan, Bob, and the Grateful Dead: Dylan & The Dead
  Down Beat il 56:32 My '89. B. Winters
  Newsweek il 113:67 Mr 13 '89. D. Gates
  Rolling Stone il p61-2 F 23 '89. D. Fricke
Dylan, Bob: Oh mercy
  Rolling Stone il p102 N 16 '89
  Rolling Stone il p115-16 S 21 '89. A. DeCurtis
Earle, Steve: Copperhead Road
  Rolling Stone il p41-2 Ja 26 '89. R. Tannenbaum
  Stereo Review il 54:106 Mr '89. A. Nash
Earle, Steve: Guitar town
  Rolling Stone il p130 N 16 '89
Elvis Costello and the Attractions: Get happy!!
  Rolling Stone il p75 N 16 '89
Elvis Costello and the Attractions: Imperial bedroom
  Rolling Stone il p96 N 16 '89
Feelies: Crazy rhythms
  Rolling Stone il p104 N 16 '89
Fine Young Cannibals: The raw & the cooked
  Time il 133:87 My 29 '89. J. Cocks
Fogerty, John: Centerfield
  Rolling Stone il p108-9 N 16 '89
Fordham, Julia: Julia Fordham
  Stereo Review 54:151-2 F '89. A. Nash
Franklin, Aretha: Who's zoomin' who?
  Rolling Stone il p140 N 16 '89
Gabriel, Peter: Peter Gabriel
  Rolling Stone il p103 N 16 '89
Gabriel, Peter: So
  Rolling Stone il p76 N 16 '89
Gang of Four: Entertainment!
  Rolling Stone il p116+ N 16 '89
Gaye, Marvin: Midnight love
  Rolling Stone il p96 N 16 '89
Get hot or go home
  Rolling Stone il p166 Jl 13-27 '89. D. Fricke
Guns n' Roses: Appetite for destruction
  Rolling Stone il p86 N 16 '89
Guns n' Roses: G n' R lies
  Rolling Stone il p41 Ja 26 '89. K. Neely
Henley, Don: Building the perfect beast
  Rolling Stone il p124 N 16 '89
Henley, Don: End of the innocence
  Rolling Stone il p123 Ag 24 '89. A. DeCurtis

Stereo Review il 54:132 N '89. P. Puterbaugh
Hiatt, John: Bring the family
  Rolling Stone il p106-7 N 16 '89
A history of New Orleans rhythm & blues, volumes 1-3
  The Atlantic il 263:88-9+ Ap '89. B. Sandmel
Human League: Dare
  Rolling Stone il p128-9 N 16 '89
Hüsker Dü: Zen arcade
  Rolling Stone il p91 N 16 '89
Jackson, Janet: Control
  Rolling Stone il p86 N 16 '89
Jackson, Janet: Janet Jackson's rhythm nation 1814
  Rolling Stone il p81+ O 19 '89. V. Aletti
Jackson, Joe: Blaze of glory
  Rolling Stone il p167-8 My 18 '89. P. Puterbaugh
Jackson, Michael: Thriller
  Rolling Stone il p67 N 16 '89
Jason and the Scorchers: Thunder and fire
  Stereo Review il 54:107 O '89. R. Givens
Jimi Hendrix Experience: Radio one
  Rolling Stone il p61 F 23 '89. D. Fricke
Joel, Billy: Storm front
  Rolling Stone il p111 N 30 '89. J. McAlley
Jones, Rickie Lee: Flying cowboys
  New York 22:140+ D 4 '89. E. Wurtzel
  Rolling Stone il p93-4 N 2 '89. A. DeCurtis
  Time il 134:110 O 23 '89. J. Cocks
Joy Division: Closer
  Rolling Stone il p111 N 16 '89
Keita, Salif: Ko-yan
  Stereo Review il 54:150 N '89. R. Givens
Khan, Chaka: C.K.
  The New Yorker 65:83-4 Mr 20 '89. M. Moses
King, Carole: City streets
  Rolling Stone il p171 My 18 '89. R. Hoerburger
Kravitz, Lenny: Let love rule
  Rolling Stone il p75-6 S 7 '89. A. DeCurtis
Lauper, Cyndi: A night to remember
  Rolling Stone il p139 Je 15 '89. J. Guterman
Lauper, Cyndi: She's so unusual
  Rolling Stone il p127 N 16 '89
Lennon, John, and Ono, Yoko: Double fantasy
  Rolling Stone il p88 N 16 '89
Lennon, Julian: Mr. Jordan
  Rolling Stone il p88-9 Je 1 '89. D. Kissinger
Lindley, David and El Rayo-X: Very greasy
  High Fidelity (New York, N.Y.) il 39:70-1 F '89. B. Altman
Living Colour: Vivid
  Rolling Stone il p117 N 16 '89
Los Lobos: How will the wolf survive?
  Rolling Stone il p88+ N 16 '89
Madonna: Like a prayer
  Rolling Stone il p79-80 Ap 6 '89. J. D. Considine
  Stereo Review il 54:67 Jl '89. P. Puterbaugh
Madonna: Madonna
  Rolling Stone il p104 N 16 '89
Marc V.: Too true
  Stereo Review il 54:80 Jl '89. P. Garland
McCartney, Paul: Back in the USSR
  Newsweek il 113:67 Mr 13 '89. B. Barol
McCartney, Paul: Flowers in the dirt
  Rolling Stone il p52-3 Je 29 '89. A. DeCurtis
Mellencamp, John Cougar: Big Daddy
  Rolling Stone il p85-7 Je 1 '89. S. Pond
Mellencamp, John Cougar: Scarecrow
  Rolling Stone il p145 N 16 '89
Mellencamp, John Cougar: Uh-huh
  Rolling Stone il p91 N 16 '89
Metallica: Kill 'em all
  Rolling Stone il p94 N 16 '89
Michael, George: Faith
  Rolling Stone il p135 N 16 '89
Midnight Oil: Diesel and dust
  Rolling Stone il p75 N 16 '89
Mould, Bob: Workbook
  Rolling Stone il p165+ My 18 '89. D. Browne
Neville Brothers: Fiyo on the bayou
  Rolling Stone il p119 N 16 '89
Neville Brothers: Yellow moon
  The Nation 248:571-2 Ap 24 '89. G. Santoro
  Rolling Stone il p97-8 Ap 20 '89. J. Hannusch
New Order Factory: Power, corruption & lies
  Rolling Stone il p145 N 16 '89
Newman, Randy: Land of dreams
  High Fidelity (New York, N.Y.) 39:73+ F '89. M. Moses
  Stereo Review il 54:113 Ja '89. R. Givens
Newman, Randy: Trouble in paradise
  Rolling Stone il p119 N 16 '89
Orbison, Roy: For the lonely: a Roy Orbison anthology, 1956-1965
  Down Beat il 56:29-30 Je '89. G. Santoro
Orbison, Roy: Mystery girl
  Down Beat il 56:29-30 Je '89. G. Santoro
  Rolling Stone il p171-2 Mr 23 '89. M. Azerrad
  Stereo Review il 54:114 My '89. A. Nash
Parker, Graham: Live! Alone in America
  Rolling Stone il p177 Mr 23 '89. D. Handelman

PHONOGRAPH RECORDS—Rock music—Reviews—Single
works—*cont.*
  Parker, Graham: Mona Lisa's sister
    Rolling Stone il p146 N 16 '89
  Pere Ubu: Cloudland
    Stereo Review il 54:72-3 Ag '89. S. Simels
  Petty, Tom: Full moon fever
    Rolling Stone il p142-3 N 16 '89
    Rolling Stone il p85-6 My 4 '89. J. Guterman
    Stereo Review il 54:73 Jl '89. S. Simels
  Phillips, Sam: Indescribable wow
    High Fidelity (New York, N.Y.) il 39:73 F '89. J. Nesin
  Pogues: Peace & love
    Rolling Stone il p85 O 19 '89. C. Mundy
  Poi Dog Pondering: Poi Dog Pondering
    New York il 22:114 N 13 '89. E. Wurtzel
    Rolling Stone il p75-6 S 7 '89. A. DeCurtis
  Police: Synchronicity
    Rolling Stone il p77 N 16 '89
  Pretenders: Pretenders
    Rolling Stone il p80 N 16 '89
  Prince: 1999
    Rolling Stone p76 N 16 '89
  Prince: Dirty mind
    Rolling Stone il p77 N 16 '89
  Prince: Purple rain
    Rolling Stone il p56 N 16 '89
  Prince: Sign o' the times
    Rolling Stone il p127 N 16 '89
  Proclaimers: Sunshine on Leith
    Stereo Review il 54:99 Je '89. P. Puterbaugh
  Public Image Ltd.: Second edition
    Rolling Stone il p127 N 16 '89
  Pursuit of Happiness: Love junk
    Stereo Review il 54:143 F '89. S. Simels
  R.E.M.: Document
    Rolling Stone il p100 N 16 '89
  R.E.M.: Green
    Rolling Stone il p63-4 Ja 12 '89. M. Azerrad
    Time il 133:94-5 Mr 27 '89. J. Cocks
  R.E.M.: Murmur
    Rolling Stone il p68 N 16 '89
  Radiators: Zigzagging through ghostland
    Rolling Stone il p97-8 Ap 20 '89. J. Hannusch
  Rainbow warriors
    Rolling Stone il p17 Ap 20 '89. L. Rotcage
  Raitt, Bonnie: Nick of time
    Newsweek il 113:66 Mr 13 '89. R. Givens
    Stereo Review il 54:93 Je '89. A. Nash
  Reed, Lou: Blue mask
    Rolling Stone il p114 N 16 '89
  Reed, Lou: New York
    The Nation 248:282-4 F 27 '89. G. Santoro
    The New Yorker 65:85-7 Ap 24 '89. M. Moses
    Newsweek il 113:68 Ja 30 '89. D. Gates
    Rolling Stone il p77 N 16 '89
    Rolling Stone il p57+ F 23 '89. A. DeCurtis
    Stereo Review il 54:82 Ap '89. S. Simels
  Replacements: Don't tell a soul
    Rolling Stone il p117-18 F 9 '89. I. Robbins
  Replacements: Let it be
    Rolling Stone il p76 N 16 '89
  Richards, Keith: Talk is cheap
    Down Beat il 56:29-30 Ja '89. G. Santoro
    High Fidelity (New York, N.Y.) il 39:70 F '89. R. C.
      Walls
    Stereo Review il 54:109 Ja '89. S. Simels
  Robertson, Robbie: Robbie Robertson
    Rolling Stone il p128 N 16 '89
  Robyn Hitchcock and the Egyptians: Queen Elvis
    Rolling Stone il p103 Ap 20 '89. D. Fricke
  Rock City Angels: Young man's blues
    Rolling Stone il 54:151 F '89. P. Puterbaugh
  Rolling Stones: Steel wheels
    Rolling Stone il p136 N 16 '89
    Rolling Stone il p115-16 S 21 '89. A. DeCurtis
    Stereo Review il 54:132 D '89. S. Simels
  Rolling Stones: Tattoo you
    Rolling Stone il p94 N 16 '89
  Ronstadt, Linda: Cry like a rainstorm, howl like the wind
    Stereo Review il 54:123 D '89. R. Givens
  Roxy Music: Avalon
    Rolling Stone il p91 N 16 '89
  Rundgren, Todd: Anthology (1968-1985)
    Rolling Stone il p51-2 Je 29 '89. D. Fricke
  Rundgren, Todd: Nearly human
    Rolling Stone il p51-2 Je 29 '89. D. Fricke
  Santana, Carlos: Viva Santana!
    Stereo Review 54:153-4 F '89. P. Puterbaugh
  Scott Morgan Band: Rock action
    Rolling Stone il p116 S 21 '89. D. Fricke
  Simon, Paul: Graceland
    Rolling Stone il p62 N 16 '89
  Siouxsie and the Banshees: Peep show
    Stereo Review il 54:101 Ja '89. P. Puterbaugh
  Smiths: Smiths
    Rolling Stone il p80 N 16 '89

  Snow, Phoebe: Something real
    Stereo Review il 54:84 Jl '89. A. Nash
    Time il 133:74 My 1 '89. J. Cocks
  Sonic Youth: Daydream nation
    The Nation 248:68 Ja 9-16 '89. G. Santoro
    Rolling Stone il p102 N 16 '89
  Soundgarden: Louder than love
    Rolling Stone il p84-5 O 19 '89. J. D. Considine
  Specials: Specials
    Rolling Stone il p120 N 16 '89
  Springsteen, Bruce: Born in the U.S.A.
    Rolling Stone il p64-5 N 16 '89
  Springsteen, Bruce: Nebraska
    Rolling Stone il p102 N 16 '89
  Springsteen, Bruce: River
    Rolling Stone il p136 N 16 '89
  Springsteen, Bruce: Tunnel of love
    Rolling Stone il p84 N 16 '89
  Squeeze: East Side story
    Rolling Stone il p135 N 16 '89
  Staples, Mavis: Time waits for no one
    Stereo Review il 54:116 O '89. P. Garland
  Stevie Ray Vaughan and Double Trouble: In step
    Down Beat il 56:29 N '89. B. Milkowski
    Stereo Review il 54:124 D '89. P. Puterbaugh
  Sting: . . . Nothing like the sun
    Rolling Stone il p140 N 16 '89
  Straw, Syd: Surprise
    Stereo Review il 54:129 N '89. R. Givens
  Talking Heads: Remain in light
    Rolling Stone il p60 N 16 '89
  Talking Heads: Speaking in tongues
    Rolling Stone il p108 N 16 '89
  Tears for Fears: Seeds of love
    Rolling Stone il p95 N 2 '89. M. Azerrad
  They Might Be Giants: Lincoln
    Stereo Review il 54:110 Mr '89. S. Simels
  Thieves: Seduced by money
    Stereo Review il 54:94+ Je '89. S. Simels
  Thompson, Richard/Thompson, Linda: Shoot out the lights
    Rolling Stone il p71 N 16 '89
  Thompson, Richard: Amnesia
    Stereo Review il 54:102+ Ja '89. R. Givens
  Throwing Muses: Hunkpapa
    Stereo Review il 54:109 My '89. P. Puterbaugh
  'til Tuesday: Everything's different now
    Stereo Review il 54:96 Ap '89. P. Puterbaugh
  Tin Machine: Tin Machine
    Rolling Stone il p137-9 Je 15 '89. D. Fricke
    Stereo Review il 54:129 S '89. P. Puterbaugh
  Townshend, Pete: Empty glass
    Rolling Stone il p111 N 16 '89
  Townshend, Pete: Iron man
    Rolling Stone p91 Ag 10 '89. D. Fricke
    Stereo Review il 54:108+ O '89. S. Simels
  Traveling Wilburys: Traveling Wilburys: volume one
    Rolling Stone il p120 N 16 '89
  Turner, Tina: Private dancer
    Rolling Stone il p103 N 16 '89
  U2: Joshua tree
    Rolling Stone il p58-9 N 16 '89
  U2: War
    Rolling Stone il p100 N 16 '89
  UB40: Labour of love
    Rolling Stone il p146 N 16 '89
  Van Halen: 1984
    Rolling Stone il p130 N 16 '89
  Vandross, Luther: Night I fell in love
    Rolling Stone il p143 N 16 '89
  Waits, Tom: Rain dogs
    Rolling Stone il p80 N 16 '89
  Was (Not Was): What up, dog?
    Rolling Stone il p146 N 16 '89
  Waterboys: Fisherman's blues
    Stereo Review il 54:95 Ap '89. P. Puterbaugh
  White, Karyn: Karyn White
    The New Yorker 65:83 Mr 20 '89. M. Moses
  Williams, Lucinda: Lucinda Williams
    Stereo Review il 54:103 Mr '89. S. Simels
  X: Los Angeles
    Rolling Stone il p84 N 16 '89
  XTC: Oranges and lemons
    Rolling Stone il p167-8 Mr 23 '89. M. Azerrad
    Stereo Review il 54:108 Je '89. S. Simels
  XTC: Skylarking
    Rolling Stone il p103 N 16 '89
  Young, Neil: Freedom
    New York 22:140 D 4 '89. E. Wurtzel
    Rolling Stone il p136 N 16 '89
    Rolling Stone il p91-3 N 2 '89. D. Fricke
  ZZ Top: Eliminator
    Rolling Stone il p96-7 N 16 '89
      Saxophone music
  Rova: Beat kennel. B. Shoemaker. il *Down Beat* 56:29 F
    '89

      Sonatas
    See also
  Phonograph records—Piano music

PHONOGRAPH RECORDS—*cont.*

Songs

See also

Phonograph records—Arias

Music [recordings by Jan DeGaetani] P. G. Davis. *New York* 22:152+ O 23 '89

Soul music

See Phonograph records—Black music

South African music

Indestructible beat of Soweto. il *Rolling Stone* p111 N 16 '89

String ensemble music

Breaking strings [jazz] K. Whitehead. *Down Beat* 56:61 Je '89

Symphonies

Barber Down Under [S. Barber's Symphony no 2. recorded in New Zealand] T. W. Libbey, Jr. il *High Fidelity (New York, N.Y.)* 39:56 F '89

Bernstein's Mahler [Symphony no. 1] R. Freed. il por *Stereo Review* 54:145 S '89

Classical music [Brahms symphony cycle by Neeme Järvi] D. Hall. il *Stereo Review* 54:86-7 Ag '89

Mackerras's Schubert ninth. R. Freed. il por *Stereo Review* 54:144 F '89

Solti's thoughtful Beethoven [Symphony nos. 4 and 5] D. Hall. por *Stereo Review* 54:104 Ja '89

Trios, Instrumental

Menage a trois [jazz] A. Lange. il *Down Beat* 56:34-5 Mr '89

Trombone music

Four trombones [jazz] B. Shoemaker. *Down Beat* 56:31-2 Ja '89

Unauthorized recording

Labels back down on DAT. M. Goldberg. *Rolling Stone* p26 S 21 '89

Vibraphone music

Good vibes. O. Cordle. il *Down Beat* 56:30-1 Mr '89

Vocal music

See also

Phonograph records—Arias

Phonograph records—Opera

Phonograph records—Songs

Dawn Upshaw's American music. R. Freed. por *Stereo Review* 54:152 S '89

Singers recycled. P. G. Davis. il *New York* 22:130+ Ag 21 '89

PHONOGRAPH RECORDS AS GIFTS

Holiday gifts [audiophiles] W. Livingstone. il *Stereo Review* 54:113-16+ D '89

Music [Christmas gifts] G. Santoro. *The Nation* 248:28-32 Ja 2 '89

PHONOGRAPH RECORDS IN ART

Walter Bramwell Young's high-stylus jewelry is music to fashionable ears [vinyl jewelry created from melted phonograph records] il por *People Weekly* 32:67 S 18 '89

PHORBOL ESTERS

AP1/*jun* function is differentially induced in promotion-sensitive and resistant JB6 cells [activation by tetradecanoyl-phorbol acetate] L. R. Bernstein and N. H. Colburn. bibl f il *Science* 244:566-9 My 5 '89

Mutations in a protein kinase C homolog confer phorbol ester resistance on Caenorhabditis elegans. Y. Tabuse and others. bibl f il *Science* 243:1713-16 Mr 31 '89

PHORMIUM TENAX *See* New Zealand flax

PHOSPHATASES

See also

Adenosine triphosphatase

Guanosine triphosphatase

PHOSPHATES

See also

Adenosine triphosphate

Cytidine monophosphate

Guanosine triphosphate

Molybdenum phosphate

Phosphorylation

PHOSPHATIDES

See also

Phosphatidylethanol

Phosphatidylinositol

Phosphoinositides

Molecular dynamics simulation of a phospholipid micelle. J. J. Wendoloski and others. bibl f il *Science* 243:636-8 F 3 '89

Potassium channels in cardiac cells activated by arachidonic acid and phospholipids. D. Kim and D. E. Clapham. bibl f il *Science* 244:1174-6 Je 9 '89

PHOSPHATIDYLCHOLINE *See* Lecithin

PHOSPHATIDYLETHANOL

Blood test linked to alcoholism risk [work of Gerald C. Mueller] *Science News* 135:13 Ja 7 '89

PHOSPHATIDYLINOSITOL

Fibroblasts transformed with v-*src* show enhanced formation of an inositol tetrakisphosphate. R. M. Johnson and others. bibl f il *Science* 246:121-4 O 6 '89

Mechanism of membrane anchoring affects polarized expression of two proteins in MDCK cells. D. A. Brown and others. bibl f il *Science* 245:1499-501 S 29 '89

Mechanisms for regulating expression of membrane isoforms of FcγRIII (CD16). M. L. Hibbs and others. bibl f il *Science* 246:1608-11 D 22 '89

Membrane anchoring of a human IgG Fc receptor (CD16) determined by a single amino acid. L. L. Lanier and others. bibl f il *Science* 246:1611-13 D 22 '89

Role of phosphatidylinositol kinase in PDGF receptor signal transduction. S. R. Coughlin and others. bibl f il *Science* 243:1191-4 Mr 3 '89

Studies of inositol phospholipid-specific phospholipase C. S. G. Rhee and others. bibl f *Science* 244:546-50 My 5 '89

PHOSPHINE

Human genotoxicity: pesticide applicators and phosphine. V. F. Garry and others. bibl f il *Science* 246:251-5 O 13 '89

PHOSPHOGLYCOLIPIDS *See* Glycolipids

PHOSPHOINOSITIDES

A biochemical correlate of the critical period for synaptic modification in the visual cortex. S. M. Dudek and M. F. Bear. bibl f il *Science* 246:673-5 N 3 '89

PHOSPHOLIPASES *See* Lipases

PHOSPHOLIPIDS *See* Phosphatides

PHOSPHONATES

Inhibition of a class C β-lactamase by a specific phosphonate monoester. R. F. Pratt. bibl f il *Science* 246:917-19 N 17 '89

PHOSPHORESCENCE

See also

Bioluminescence

PHOSPHORYLASES

Domain separation in the activation of glycogen phosphorylase α. E. J. Goldsmith and others. bibl f il *Science* 245:528-32 Ag 4 '89

PHOSPHORYLATION

Cell cycle-dependent regulation of phosphorylation of the human retinoblastoma gene product. K. Mihara and others. bibl f il *Science* 246:1300-3 D 8 '89

Myristoylated and nonmyristoylated forms of a protein are phosphorylated by protein kinase C. J. M. Graff and others. bibl f il *Science* 246:503-6 O 27 '89

PHOTO MARKETING ASSOCIATION SHOW *See* Photography—Exhibitions

PHOTO-REALISM

Color Close-ups [work of C. Close] C. Finch. il *Art in America* 77:112-19+ Mr '89

PHOTOANALYSIS *See* Photography—Psychological aspects

PHOTOBIOLOGY *See* Light—Physiological effects

PHOTOCHEMISTRY

See also

Photosynthesis

A light meal at sea [study of carbon cycle by Kenneth Mopper] *Science News* 136:284 O 28 '89

Light ways of making a future fuel [work of John M. White] *Science News* 135:123 F 25 '89

Mr. Clean [solar reaction process to destroy toxic chemicals] T. Beardsley. il *Scientific American* 260:83-4 Je '89

New polymers harvest light to do chemistry [work of James E. Guillet in development of photozyme PSSS-VN] I. Amato. *Science News* 135:7 Ja 7 '89

Soaking up the rays to make fuel [liberating hydrogen bound in sea water; work of H. Ti Tien] *Science News* 135:366 Je 10 '89

PHOTOCOPYING

Business use

Texaco photocopy suit moves toward trials. C. Reid. *Publishers Weekly* 235:22 Je 30 '89

Educational use

Eight publishers sue photocopying chain [Kinko's Graphics Corp.] C. Reid. *Publishers Weekly* 235:100 My 12 '89

Unauthorized use

Eight publishers sue photocopying chain [Kinko's Graphics Corp.] C. Reid. *Publishers Weekly* 235:100 My 12 '89

Texaco photocopy suit moves toward trials. C. Reid. *Publishers Weekly* 235:22 Je 30 '89

PHOTOCOPYING EQUIPMENT

See also

AM International, Inc.

Canon Inc.

Colorocs Corp.

Minnesota Mining & Mfg. Co.

Nashua Corporation

Savin Corp.

Xerox Corp.

Copiers: featuring the best they have to offer. S. Esters. *Black Enterprise* 19:28-9 Jl '89

Desktop copiers. S. Usdin. il *Home Office Computing* 7:53-7 Ap '89

Desktop duping. F. Vizard. il *Popular Mechanics* 166:125-7 My '89

Everything imaginable in office copiers. J. Pepper. il *Nation's Business* 77:30 F '89

Full-featured, high-quality Canon copier [PC-7] C. Pierce. il *Home Office Computing* 7:66+ Ja '89

How to choose a personal copier. R. Calem. il *Home Office Computing* 7:39 Ja '89

Low-cost copier [Mita CC-20] R. Cullen. il *Home Office Computing* 7:61-2 Ag '89

PHOTOCOPYING EQUIPMENT—*cont.*
Small copier with a big future [Sharp Z-75 desktop copier] S. Usdin. il *Home Office Computing* 7:80 N '89
PHOTODETECTORS *See* Light detectors
PHOTOELECTRIC CELLS
See also
Solar cells
PHOTOELECTRIC EFFECT
Heinrich Hertz and the development of physics. J. F. Mulligan. bibl f il por *Physics Today* 42:50-7 Mr '89
PHOTOELECTRON HOLOGRAPHY *See* Holography
PHOTOELECTRON SPECTROSCOPY *See* Spectrum analysis
PHOTOEMISSION SPECTROSCOPY *See* Spectrum analysis
PHOTOENGRAVING
See also
Halftone process (Photography)
PHOTOFRIN
New frontiers [cancer research in Canada] A. Steacy. il *Maclean's* 102:45-6 Jl 24 '89
Shedding light on cancer. I. Wickelgren. il *Science News* 135:26-8 Ja 14 '89
A shiny new weapon in the war on cancer: light. S. Yanchinski and N. J. Freundlich. il *Business Week* p106-7 My 29 '89
PHOTOGRAMS
Ask the sun to help you [blueprinted fabric] il *Sunset (Central West edition)* 183:122+ N '89
Blueprint your photos [Sun-Fun Squares and Quilt Squares kits] K. Geller-Shinn. il *Petersen's Photographic Magazine* 17:10 Mr '89
PHOTOGRAPH ALBUMS
Hardwood photo album. D. Bayard. il *Workbench* 45:52-3 N/D '89
PHOTOGRAPHERS
See also
Authors as photographers
Children as photographers
Cinematographers
Paparazzi
Street photographers
Health and hygiene
Pollution solution. il *Popular Photography* 96:52-3+ O '89
PHOTOGRAPHERS, AMERICAN
See also
Begleiter, Steven
Bloom, Barbara
Brady, Mathew B., ca. 1823-1896
Bubley, Esther
Cameron, Betsy
Dorfman, Elsa, 1937-
Dunning, John S., 1905-
Erwitt, Elliott, 1928-
Evans, Walker, 1903-1975
Frankel, Tracy
Friedlander, Lee, 1934-
Geesaman, Lynn
Golden, Judith, 1934-
Greenfield, Lois
Hawes, Josiah Johnson, 1808-1901
Hine, Lewis Wickes, 1874-1940
Jackson, William Henry, 1843-1942
Kane, Bill, 1951-
Kendall, Marie
Kruger, Barbara
Lee, Russell
Maisel, Jay, 1931-
Mapplethorpe, Robert
Mark, Mary Ellen, 1940-
Metzner, Sheila
Michals, Duane, 1932-
Muench, David
Muskie, Stephen O.
Nachtwey, James, 1948-
Nixon, Nicholas, 1947-
Olshwanger, Ron
Parks, Gordon
Porter, Eliot, 1901-
Skoglund, Sandy, 1946-
Smith, W. Eugene, 1918-1978
Southworth, Albert Sands, 1811-1894
Spagna, Ted
Steichen, Edward, 1879-1973
Stieglitz, Alfred, 1864-1946
Swift, W. Arthur
Taylor, Jana
Vachon, John, 1914-1975
Weiner, Dan, 1919-1959
Welling, James
White, Minor, 1908-1976
PHOTOGRAPHERS, AUSTRIAN
See also
Kempinger, Herwig
PHOTOGRAPHERS, BRAZILIAN
See also
Salgado, Sebastiao

PHOTOGRAPHERS, BRITISH
The 150th anniversary of photography [The formative decades: photography in Great Britain, 1839-1920] A. E. Ledes. il *Antiques* 135:54+ Ja '89
Photography discovery and invention [early British and French photographers] W. J. Naef. il *Antiques* 135:288-97 Ja '89
PHOTOGRAPHERS, CANADIAN
See also
Karsh, Yousuf, 1908-
PHOTOGRAPHERS, ENGLISH
See also
Angel, Heather, 1941-
Füss, Adam, 1961-
Talbot, William Henry Fox, 1800-1877
Webb, Boyd, 1947-
PHOTOGRAPHERS, FRENCH
See also
Calle, Sophie
Cartier-Bresson, Henri, 1908-
Kern, Pascal
Photography discovery and invention [early British and French photographers] W. J. Naef. il *Antiques* 135:288-97 Ja '89
PHOTOGRAPHERS, GERMAN
See also
Horst, 1906-
Newton, Helmut
Ruff, Thomas, 1958-
PHOTOGRAPHERS, JAPANESE
See also
Morimura, Yasumasa
PHOTOGRAPHERS, RUSSIAN
Kandid kamera [Soviet photography at San Diego's Museum of Photographic Arts] il *U.S. News & World Report* 107:16 N 13 '89
PHOTOGRAPHERS' MARKETS *See* Photographs—Marketing
PHOTOGRAPHERS' VESTS *See* Vests
PHOTOGRAPHIC BATTERIES *See* Electric batteries
PHOTOGRAPHIC BOOKS *See* Picture books
PHOTOGRAPHIC BUSINESS CARDS *See* Business cards
PHOTOGRAPHIC CHEMISTRY
See also
Photography—Developing and developers
Photography—Processing
Jobo photo technology chemicals. il *Petersen's Photographic Magazine* 18:74 N '89
New Heico chemicals. R. E. Mayer. il *Petersen's Photographic Magazine* 17:46-7 Ja '89
Pollution solution. il *Popular Photography* 96:52-3+ O '89
Refilling SX cartridges [toner cartridges for copiers and laser printers] D. Lancaster. il *Radio-Electronics* 60:27+ Ap '89
Toner refilling tools. D. Lancaster. *Radio-Electronics* 60:71-2 Jl '89
PHOTOGRAPHIC ENLARGERS *See* Photography—Enlargers and enlarging
PHOTOGRAPHIC EQUIPMENT *See* Photography—Equipment
PHOTOGRAPHIC EXHIBITIONS *See* Photography—Exhibitions
PHOTOGRAPHIC FILMS *See* Photography—Films
PHOTOGRAPHIC FILTERS *See* Light filters
PHOTOGRAPHIC INDUSTRY
See also
Bell & Howell Co.
Eastman Kodak Co.
Photographic laboratories
Polaroid Corp.
Traditional Industries, Inc.
Accounting
The facts behind the figures [Traditional Industries] R. L. Stern and M. Beauchamp. il por *Forbes* 144:41-2 Ag 21 '89
Acquisitions and mergers
Kodak and Polaroid? Or GE? How about Disney? G. G. Marcial. il *Business Week* p84 Je 19 '89
Round two for Polaroid and Shamrock [stock buyback] K. H. Hammonds. il *Business Week* p32 F 13 '89
Marketing
See also
Camera stores
Byzantine puzzle: when is a discontinued camera a discontinued camera? H. Keppler. il *Popular Photography* 96:22+ O '89
Is shopping by mail safe? [photographic equipment] J. Augustine. il *Petersen's Photographic Magazine* 18:6 N '89
Sure you can get bargains when you order by mail, but you've got to know how to do it. H. Keppler. il *Popular Photography* 96:75-7 Mr '89
There are good dealers like good car salesmen, but the rotters can spoil it for everyone. H. Keppler. il *Popular Photography* 96:42+ Jl '89
Japan
See also
Canon Inc.
Fuji Photo Film Co., Ltd.
PHOTOGRAPHIC LABORATORIES
See also
Qualex Inc.

PHOTOGRAPHIC LABORATORIES—*cont.*
10 great photo labs. il *Petersen's Photographic Magazine* 18:53-8 S '89
Are your prints off-color? Tell your printer to tune to the right channel! G. Schaub. il *Popular Photography* 96:36+ D '89
The battle of the research labs [color print film technology] B. Schwalberg. il *Popular Photography* 96:46-9 F '89
Great astrophotos in less than an hour. R. Bunge. il *Astronomy* 17:78-83 Ag '89
Popular photography's state-of-the-art super lab. L. White. il *Popular Photography* 96:56-64+ Ag '89
What's a Kodalux? [Kodalux Processing Services] G. Schaub. il *Popular Photography* 96:40 Ap '89
What's new? M. Grimm and T. Grimm. il *Travel Holiday* 171:16-19 Mr '89
PHOTOGRAPHIC LENSES *See* Lenses, Photographic
PHOTOGRAPHIC LITERATURE
    See also
    Photography—Bibliography
PHOTOGRAPHIC METERS
    See also
    Exposure meters
PHOTOGRAPHIC OPTICS
    See also
    Lenses, Photographic
PHOTOGRAPHIC PAPER
    See also
    Fax paper
For the darkroom it's b&w variable-contrast paper, simple color-print processor. il *Popular Photography* 96:104+ Ja '89
Ilford Multigrade III RC Deluxe [tray-process B&W paper] D. Brooks. il *Petersen's Photographic Magazine* 18:72-4 Jl '89
Kodak Polycontrast III paper. il *Petersen's Photographic Magazine* 18:62 My '89
Kodak Polycontrast III RC. D. Brooks. il *Petersen's Photographic Magazine* 17:28+ Ap '89
Oriental Seagull Select VC [fiber-based variable-contrast paper] D. Brooks. il *Petersen's Photographic Magazine* 17:70-1 Mr '89
PHOTOGRAPHIC POSTCARDS *See* Postcards
PHOTOGRAPHIC POSTERS *See* Posters
PHOTOGRAPHIC PROCESSING *See* Photography—Processing
PHOTOGRAPHIC PRODUCTS GROUPS *See* Eastman Kodak Co. Photographic Products Groups
PHOTOGRAPHIC SLIDES *See* Slides (Photography)
PHOTOGRAPHIC SUPPLIES *See* Photography—Equipment
PHOTOGRAPHS
    See also
    Carte de visite photographs
    Daguerreotypes
    Slides (Photography)
      See also subhead Photographs and photography under various subjects
Are these the 15 greatest pictures ever made? A. Goldsmith. il *Popular Photography* 96:52-61 S '89
          Collectors and collecting
    See Photography—Collectors and collecting
          Coloring
Airbrush artistry. S. A. Rafiq. il *Petersen's Photographic Magazine* 18:90-3 D '89
          Evaluation
    See Photography—Criticism, interpretation, etc.
          Exhibitions
    See Photography—Exhibitions
          Framing
    See Photographs—Trimming, mounting, etc.
          Judging
    See Photography—Criticism, interpretation, etc.
          Marketing
Sell your photos at festivals. K. Geller-Shinn. il *Petersen's Photographic Magazine* 17:28 Ja '89
          Prices
20th-century photography. F. Donegan. il *Americana* 17:60-2 N/D '89
Man Ray: undervalued, and still an enigma. il *Art News* 88:39 D '89
Photo opportunities. C. Brown. il *Forbes* 144:280-1 N 27 '89
          Trimming, mounting, etc.
Displaying photos with style. il *Southern Living* 24:116 O '89
Presentation masters [Original Woodcraft frames] K. Geller-Shinn. il *Petersen's Photographic Magazine* 18:44 O '89
Seal's creative display products. K. Geller-Shinn. il *Petersen's Photographic Magazine* 18:12 Ag '89
PHOTOGRAPHS ON CLOTH
Ask the sun to help you [blueprinted fabric] il *Sunset (Central West edition)* 183:122+ N '89
Blueprint your photos [Sun-Fun Squares and Quilt Squares kits] K. Geller-Shinn. il *Petersen's Photographic Magazine* 17:10 Mr '89
PHOTOGRAPHY
    See also
    Ambrotypes

Art and photography
Astronomical photography
Calotypes
Candid photography
Computers—Photographic use
Daguerreotypes
Domestic photography
Erotic photography
Humorous photography
Macrophotography
Motion picture photography
Motion pictures and photography
Nature photography
Nostalgia in photography
Photograms
Photographs
Photomicrography
Photomontage
Radiography
Reflections (Photography)
Slides (Photography)
Stereographs
Tintypes
Travel photography
Underwater photography
Colorvision: seeing the true character of color. J. Marvullo. il *Petersen's Photographic Magazine* 18:40-3 O '89
Critical focus. B. Schwalberg. *See* issues of Popular Photography beginning March 1988 through September 1989
Jay Maisel directs the compacts [Kodak S100EF camera and others] il *Petersen's Photographic Magazine* 17:56-7 Mr '89
One to one [questions and answers] B. Hurter. *See* issues of Petersen's Photographic Magazine
Photography. S. A. Booth. *See* issues of Popular Mechanics beginning January 1986
Re:vision. F. Patterson. *See* occasional issues of Petersen's Photographic Magazine beginning March 1987
Shooting color. G. Schaub. *See* issues of Popular Photography beginning March 1988
SLR world. H. Keppler. *See* issues of Popular Photography beginning September 1987
Snapshots. *See* issues of Popular Photography beginning November 1986
Tools & techniques. C. W. Kennedy. *See* issues of Popular Photography through August 1989
Viewfinder. *See* issues of Petersen's Photographic Magazine beginning April 1987
          Bibliography
Books. *See* occasional issues of Popular Photography
Photography. A. Grundberg. il *The New York Times Book Review* 94:20+ D 3 '89
          Censorship
Corcoran showdown [aftermath of cancellation of R. Mapplethorpe show] C. McGuigan. il pors *Newsweek* 114:111+ O 9 '89
A dispute over a photography exhibit raises once again the relationship of art to conventional standards of taste. R. M. Adams. il *Smithsonian* 20:12 O '89
Exhibitionism [Corcoran Gallery cancels R. Mapplethorpe exhibit] *The New Republic* 201:6 Jl 17-24 '89
Mad about Mapplethorpe [Corcoran Gallery cancels exhibit] A. Ferguson. *National Review* 41:20-1 Ag 4 '89
Mapplethorpe of my eye [exhibit opens at WPA gallery after cancellation by the Corcoran] A. Heard. *The New Republic* 201:10-12 Ag 21 '89
Robert Mapplethorpe. il por *People Weekly* 32:100-1 D 25 '89-Ja 1 '90
A "sacrificial lamb"? [aftermath of the Corcoran Gallery's cancellation of R. Mapplethorpe show] S. Hochfield. il por *Art News* 88:62 N '89
Whose art is it, anyway? [Corcoran Gallery cancels R. Mapplethorpe exhibit] M. B. Carlson. il *Time* 134:21 Jl 3 '89
          Cold weather conditions
Cold hands, bright snow, dead batteries: challenges of cold-weather photography. il *Sunset (Central West edition)* 181:54 D '88
Picture winter. J. Adams. il *Petersen's Photographic Magazine* 17:16-18+ F '89
Prepare your gear—and yourself—for the rigors of frigid-weather photography. J. Shaw. il *Popular Photography* 96:38+ Ja '89
          Collectors and collecting
    See also
    Cameras—Collectors and collecting
20th-century photography. F. Donegan. il *Americana* 17:60-2 N/D '89
The Hallmark Photographic Collection: a commitment to fine photography. K. F. Davis. il *USA Today (Periodical)* 117:54-63 Ja '89
Photo opportunities. C. Brown. il *Forbes* 144:280-1 N 27 '89
A vision of our nation [collection of National Museum of American Art] K. A. Lawson. il *USA Today (Periodical)* 117:52-61 My '89

PHOTOGRAPHY—*cont.*

Competitions

1989 Photo Contest winners [Weatherwise Contest; cover story] il *Weatherwise* 42:197-204 Ag '89

Maclean's fourth national Photo Contest winners. il *Maclean's* 102:75-8 N 27 '89

Olympus VisionAge '88 international contest winners [cover story] il *Petersen's Photographic Magazine* 18:6-7+ O '89

Photo Contest winners [cover story] il *National Wildlife* 28:50-9 D '89/Ja '90

Pictures of the year [contest sponsored by the National Press Photographers Association and the University of Missouri School of Journalism] L. Downes. il *Petersen's Photographic Magazine* 18:14-16 S '89

Viewpoints: Sierra's tenth annual Photo Contest winners [cover story] il *Sierra* 74:48-57 N/D '89

World Photo Contest winners. il *National Geographic World* 162:12-16 F '89

Your Best Shot. See issues of Popular Photography beginning August 1988

Composition

See Composition (Photography)

Contrast

See Photography—Light and lighting

Copying

See also

Slides (Photography)—Copying

Criticism, interpretation, etc.

Indelible images [favorite photos of four curators] R. Cembalest. il pors *Art News* 88:174-9 Ap '89

Marvin Heiferman's all-encompassing eye has redefined photography. R. B. Woodward. il por *Vogue* 179:284+ N '89

Darkrooms

See Photography—Studios and darkrooms

Developing and developers

Develop T-Max by inspection? Kodak says it's a no-no, but you can do it if you really need to. A. Kramer. il *Popular Photography* 96:38+ Ag '89

RT Process 440 [T-Max developer] D. Brooks. il *Petersen's Photographic Magazine* 18:71-2 Ag '89

See also

Camera shutters—Control

Photography—Flash equipment

Nikon MF-21 back. J. Drafahl and S. Drafahl. il *Petersen's Photographic Magazine* 18:68-71 Je '89

Photo-electronics. J. Bailey. See issues of Popular Photography beginning July 1988

Enlargers and enlarging

Beseler 45V-XL enlarger. J. Drafahl and S. Drafahl. il *Petersen's Photographic Magazine* 18:52-3 O '89

Beseler Cadet 35. S. Drafahl and J. Drafahl. il *Petersen's Photographic Magazine* 18:85+ D '89

Daylab 300 enlarger. R. E. Mayer. il *Petersen's Photographic Magazine* 17:70-2 F '89

Daylab 300 enlarger; Saunders/LPL 4500-II enlarger. il *Petersen's Photographic Magazine* 18:70-1 My '89

Hot rod for big enlargements. il *Popular Photography* 96:40 N '89

Saunders salon easels. G. Lewis. il *Petersen's Photographic Magazine* 17:66 Ja '89

Equipment

See also

Astronomical photography—Equipment

Camera bags, cases, etc.

Camera supports

Camera tripods

Cameras

Exposure meters

Foam boards (Photography)

Lenses, Photographic

Light filters

Photography—Flash equipment

Photography—Processing—Equipment

Ideas! See issues of Popular Photography beginning September 1988

Is shopping by mail safe? J. Augustine. il *Petersen's Photographic Magazine* 18:6 N '89

Just out. See issues of Popular Photography beginning July 1988

The little window that could but doesn't—a tale of a good idea gone wrong [film-identification in camera backs] H. Keppler. il *Popular Photography* 96:34-5 My '89

Mamiya motorized winder II. il *Petersen's Photographic Magazine* 18:54 N '89

Proof sheet. See issues of Petersen's Photographic Magazine beginning November 1985

SLR finders are from heaven; point-and-shoot finders are for the birds. H. Keppler. il *Popular Photography* 96:88+ F '89

Sure you can get bargains when you order by mail, but you've got to know how to do it. H. Keppler. il *Popular Photography* 96:75-7 Mr '89

There are good dealers like good car salesmen, but the rotters can spoil it for everyone. H. Keppler. il *Popular Photography* 96:42+ Jl '89

To wind the leader in or leave it out? Now, there's a forked tongue! [Hama leader retriever] H. Keppler. il *Popular Photography* 96:72-3 Ja '89

Tools & techniques. C. W. Kennedy. See issues of Popular Photography through August 1989

Tools of the trade. K. Geller-Shinn. See issues of Petersen's Photographic Magazine

What's new: photography. A. Fisher. See alternate issues of Popular Science beginning January 1986

Exhibitions

See Photography—Exhibitions

Testing

Photographic 1989 pro buyer's guide [special section] A. Stone. il *Petersen's Photographic Magazine* 18:53-4+ N '89

Photographic 1989 pro buyer's guide [special section; with editorial comment by Jackie Augustine] A. Stone. il *Petersen's Photographic Magazine* 18:8, 47-8+ My '89

Popular photography's state-of-the-art super lab. L. White. il *Popular Photography* 96:56-64+ Ag '89

Exhibitions

150 years of photography. *Art in America* 77:51 Ag '89

The 150th anniversary of photography [The formative decades: photography in Great Britain, 1839-1920] A. E. Ledes. il *Antiques* 135:54+ Ja '89

The big show (II) [Photokina; special section] il *Popular Photography* 96:70-1+ Ja '89

Capturing an image: a century and a half of fine photography. il *USA Today (Periodical)* 118:52-61 N '89

Great products at Photokina. J. Augustine. il *Petersen's Photographic Magazine* 17:6 Ja '89

It took a heap of walkin', but we found something new for almost every darkroom [Dallas PMA Show] P. Kolonia. il *Popular Photography* 96:92-3+ My '89

Kandid kamera [Soviet photography at San Diego's Museum of Photographic Arts] il *U.S. News & World Report* 107:16 N 13 '89

Photography [New York City; fall preview] B. Ickes. il *New York* 22:128+ S 11 '89

Photography discovery and invention [early British and French photographers] W. J. Naef. il *Antiques* 135:288-97 Ja '89

Photography on exhibit. il *American History Illustrated* 24:10 S/O '89

Picture perfect [On the art of fixing a shadow: 150 years of photography at the National Gallery of Art] D. Solomon. il *Harper's Bazaar* 122:166-7+ My '89

Sell your photos at festivals. K. Geller-Shinn. il *Petersen's Photographic Magazine* 17:28 Ja '89

Texas point-and-shootout [Photo Marketing Association Show in Dallas] il *Popular Photography* 96:56-63+ My '89

Exposure

See also

Exposure meters

Critical focus [one-way bracketing] B. Schwalberg. il *Popular Photography* 96:84+ Mr '89

Funlights [time exposure] N. Ballenger and J. Tulley. il *Petersen's Photographic Magazine* 17:58-60 Ap '89

Heavenly shades of long exposures [twilight images] D. Skernick. il *Petersen's Photographic Magazine* 18:40-2 Je '89

Just how accurate is your exposure system? The simple answers are based on complex tests. L. White. il *Popular Photography* 96:76+ S '89

Magical world B [special section; cover story] il *Popular Photography* 96:31-2+ Mr '89

Matrix metering: simple solution or dire delusion??? H. Keppler. il *Popular Photography* 96:20-1+ Mr '89

Overriding your exposure meter for precise results. F. Patterson. il *Petersen's Photographic Magazine* 17:26-7 Ap '89

The time machine. A. Goldsmith. il *Popular Photography* 96:42-9 O '89

Zone system protagonists go for the jugular; it's the eye matchers vs. the sensitometrists. A. Kramer. il *Popular Photography* 96:26-7+ Mr '89

Films

See also

Microfilms

Beauty is in the grain [high-speed films] Romé. il *Petersen's Photographic Magazine* 17:24-5+ Ap '89

Bubble film [Mead Corp.'s Cycolor film] J. Free. il *Popular Science* 234:78-9 Ja '89

Film [Dallas PMA Show] il *Popular Photography* 96:58-9 My '89

The great film race. J. Augustine. il *Petersen's Photographic Magazine* 17:4 Ap '89

Konica SR-G series films. il *Petersen's Photographic Magazine* 18:9 O '89

Physics of the photographic latent image [silver halide film] T. Tani. bibl f il *Physics Today* 42:36-41 S '89

Secrets of city astrophotography. K. R. Brasch. il *Astronomy* 17:90-5 Ja '89

Temperature control of a hypering tank. D. C. Cole. il *Sky and Telescope* 78:658-61+ D '89

What's new? M. Grimm and T. Grimm. il *Travel Holiday* 171:16-19 Mr '89

You're shooting in artificial light. Which would you reach for: color-negative or tungsten-balanced slide film? G. Schaub. il *Popular Photography* 96:32+ Ja '89

PHOTOGRAPHY—Films—cont.
Identification
The little window that could but doesn't—a tale of a good idea gone wrong [film-identification in camera backs] H. Keppler. il *Popular Photography* 96:34-5 My '89
Labeling
Should you take a chance on out-of-date color film? G. Schaub. il *Popular Photography* 96:28-9 O '89
Prices
Those little yellow boxes are looking a little paler [Kodak] K. H. Hammonds. il *Business Week* p26 Ag 7 '89
Testing
2 new Agfa films: Agfachrome CT-100 & Agfacolor XRC-100. D. Brooks. il *Petersen's Photographic Magazine* 17:48-51 Ap '89
2 new Kodak films: Kodachrome 200 & Ektachrome 100 HC "amateur" slide films. D. Brooks. il *Petersen's Photographic Magazine* 17:44-5+ F '89
4 new Agfachrome pro films [RS 50, 100, 200, 1000] D. Brooks. il *Petersen's Photographic Magazine* 18:52-5 Ag '89
5 new Fuji colors. il *Popular Photography* 96:52-5+ My '89
Agfa's professional slide film lineup gets a revamp. Are the improvements real? G. Schaub. il *Popular Photography* 96:34+ Ag '89
Any speed is okay for all-around color-print film shooting—as long as it's ISO 400! B. Schwalberg. il *Popular Photography* 96:20-1 F '89
Don't feel left out, slide lovers. There are three new films just for you. G. Schaub. il *Popular Photography* 96:16+ Mr '89
Fast or slow, Ektar can take it. S. A. Booth. *Rolling Stone* p114 Mr 9 '89
Film wars! [cover story; special section] il *Popular Photography* 96:31-49+ F '89; Correction. 96:40-1 May '89
Fuji Super HG 200 & 400. J. Drafahl and S. Drafahl. il *Petersen's Photographic Magazine* 18:88-90 N '89
Fuji Super HR II 100 & 1600. J. Drafahl and S. Drafahl. il *Petersen's Photographic Magazine* 18:92-4 N '89
Fujicolor Reala. D. Brooks. il *Petersen's Photographic Magazine* 18:54-6 Jl '89
Fuji's fastest black-and-white [Neopan 1600] T. Keenan. il *Popular Photography* 96:60-3 Ja '89
Heightened colors, finer grain, improved sharpness mark eight new color-print films. G. Schaub. il *Popular Photography* 96:24+ F '89
Idyllic infra-red [Konica Infrared 750] J. M. Reynolds. il *Petersen's Photographic Magazine* 18:22-7 D '89
Ilford XPI 400 B&W film. il *Petersen's Photographic Magazine* 18:68-9 My '89
In search of the perfect film. il *Consumer Reports* 54:687 N '89
Infrared fantasies [Kodak High Speed Infrared, 2481] J. Zuckerman. il *Petersen's Photographic Magazine* 17:18+ Ap '89
Is One Film enough? [Polaroid OneFilm] J. Augustine. il *Petersen's Photographic Magazine* 18:4 Jl '89
Kodacolor Gold films. J. Drafahl and S. Drafahl. il *Petersen's Photographic Magazine* 18:78-9+ S '89
Kodak Ektapress Gold. J. Drafahl and S. Drafahl. il *Petersen's Photographic Magazine* 18:74-7 My '89
Kodak Ektar 1000 [with editorial comment by Jackie Augustine; cover story] A. Stone and M. Stensvold. il *Petersen's Photographic Magazine* 17:50-1 Mr '89
Kodak Ektar 125; Kodak Ektar 25 Professional. J. Drafahl and S. Drafahl. il *Petersen's Photographic Magazine* 18:80-2 S '89
Kodak Ektar 125 vs. Fujicolor Reala. J. Drafahl and S. Drafahl. il *Petersen's Photographic Magazine* 18:82-4 D '89
Kodak Ektar 25 [with editorial comment by Jackie Augustine] J. Drafahl and S. Drafahl. il *Petersen's Photographic Magazine* 17:4, 48-9 Mr '89
Kodak strikes back. J. Schneider. il *Popular Photography* 96:46-51+ Jl '89
New Fuji Neopan 1600 film. D. Brooks. il *Petersen's Photographic Magazine* 18:58-63 Je '89
Now that Panatomic-X has bitten the dust, what's a fine-grain fanatic to do? Test the other contenders! P. Kolonia. il *Popular Photography* 96:36+ S '89
Polaroid OneFilm. J. Drafahl and S. Drafahl. il *Petersen's Photographic Magazine* 18:38-9 O '89
Scotch Chrome 400 film. D. Brooks. il *Petersen's Photographic Magazine* 18:54-5 O '89
Sharp shooting. S. A. Booth. il *Popular Mechanics* 166:54-5 Ag '89
This is not a test! [new Kodak color negative films] J. Schneider. il *Popular Photography* 96:52 Ja '89
Universal print film??? [Polaroid OneFilm] G. Schaub and H. Keppler. il *Popular Photography* 96:26+ Je '89
Flash equipment
Electronic flash [Dallas PMA Show] il *Popular Photography* 96:59-60 My '89
Flash: the light fantastic [cover story; special section] il *Popular Photography* 96:63-85+ Ap '89
Hurrah, bounce flash for Maxxum 7000i! H. Keppler. il *Popular Photography* 96:31 D '89

Strobe-assist—the order of the day [fashion ad featuring J. and J. Montana] G. Bernstein. il pors *Petersen's Photographic Magazine* 18:12 S '89
Super strobo basketball: bringing light to the pros who shoot the NBA. D. Mazzapica. il *Petersen's Photographic Magazine* 18:20-3+ Je '89
Testing
10 top flash units! il *Petersen's Photographic Magazine* 18:39-44 Jl '89
Bowens Prolites: new compact studio electronic flash system. D. Brooks. il *Petersen's Photographic Magazine* 18:64-5 Jl '89
Courtenay Solaflashes [studio flash units] D. Brooks. il *Petersen's Photographic Magazine* 18:49-51 Je '89
Flash testing: is your flash doing what the instruction book says? Here's how to check it. J. Bailey. il *Popular Photography* 96:56+ Ap '89
Is this bye-bye to red-eye? [Olympus Infinity Zoom 200 preflash system] D. Richards. il *Popular Photography* 96:30 N '89
Point & flatter: the P/S studio [Morris Mini Slave] D. Richards. il *Popular Photography* 96:28+ N '89
Speedotron accelerator [rechargeable battery pack for portable flash systems] il *Petersen's Photographic Magazine* 18:66 My '89
"The studio doctor" [Rokunar Studio Pro multistrobe system] J. Drafahl and S. Drafahl. il *Petersen's Photographic Magazine* 18:36-7 O '89
Sunpak auto 622 pro flash system. il *Petersen's Photographic Magazine* 18:68 N '89
White Lightning Ultras & RC-1 remote control unit. il *Petersen's Photographic Magazine* 18:64 N '89
Focusing
Autofocus too slow? It may be your fault and not your camera's. H. Keppler. il *Popular Photography* 96:28+ D '89
Deep space [adding depth] A. Goldsmith. il *Popular Photography* 96:54-9+ Ja '89
Does your new AF camera focus faster than a speeding bullet? L. White. il *Popular Photography* 96:70 N '89
Don't let autofocus become another step backward in controlling your camera. H. Keppler. il *Popular Photography* 96:28-9+ Ja '89
How well does your P/S "zone in" on subjects? [focusing zones] D. Richards. il *Popular Photography* 96:30 N '89
Lens-scapes: how to put more depth into your scenics. R. N. J. Hostin. il *Petersen's Photographic Magazine* 17:60-1+ Mr '89
Negative and positive aspects of choosing the right depth on field. F. Patterson. il *Petersen's Photographic Magazine* 17:30-1 Ja '89
Only the human eye focuses faster, but how long does your AF SLR take to trip the shutter? B. Schwalberg. il *Popular Photography* 96:75+ Jl '89
What can you do when autofocus doesn't work? Switch to manual as fast as you can! H. Keppler. il *Popular Photography* 96:24+ Ag '89
Grain
Beauty is in the grain [high-speed films] Romé. il *Petersen's Photographic Magazine* 17:24-5+ Ap '89
Working against the grain of fast films [composite prints] L. Myers. il *Astronomy* 17:88-91 F '89
History
See also
Daguerreotypes
150 years of photography. *Art in America* 77:51 Ag '89
150 years of photography [cover story; special section] il *Art News* 88:143-79 Ap '89
150 years of photography [cover story; special section; with editorial comment by Kevin Doyle] il *Maclean's* 102:2, 36-46+ Ap 24 '89
150 years of photography [with editorial comment by Jackie Augustine] F. Cameron. il *Petersen's Photographic Magazine* 18:4, 66-8+ D '89
Are these the 15 greatest pictures ever made? A. Goldsmith. il *Popular Photography* 96:52-61 S '89
Capturing an image: a century and a half of fine photography. il *USA Today (Periodical)* 118:52-61 N '89
The first color photographs. G. B. Romer and J. Delamoir. bibl il *Scientific American* 261:88-96 D '89
The influence of the pictorialists on the art of photography [On the art of fixing a shadow: 150 years of photography] M. Fox. il *Antiques* 136:120-31 Jl '89
Photography discovery and invention [early British and French photographers] W. J. Naef. il *Antiques* 135:288-97 Ja '89
Photography: mirror of the past [cover story; special issue; with editorial comment by Ed Holm] il *American History Illustrated* 24:4, 20-30+ S/O '89
Picture perfect [On the art of fixing a shadow: 150 years of photography at the National Gallery of Art] D. Solomon. il *Harper's Bazaar* 122:166-7+ My '89
Portraits. S. A. Booth. il *Popular Mechanics* 166:58-61+ Ja '89
Seizing the light: photography's first fifty years. E. Zwingle. il *National Geographic* 176:530-47 O '89
Sesquicentennial be damned! This stuff is more important! B. Schwalberg. il *Popular Photography* 96:28+ S '89

PHOTOGRAPHY—History—*cont.*
Bibliography
Books on photography. *American History Illustrated* 24:12 S/O '89

Landscapes
Designer landscapes. M. Van Hesemans. il *Petersen's Photographic Magazine* 18:24-9 O '89
How to shoot scenics [work of G. A. Rowell; cover story] D. Brockway. il pors *Popular Photography* 96:48-59+ N '89
Lens-scapes: how to put more depth into your scenics. R. N. J. Hostin. il *Petersen's Photographic Magazine* 17:60-1+ Mr '89
Reflections. M. Van Hesemans. il *Petersen's Photographic Magazine* 18:16-18+ Jl '89
Uncommon perceptions. R. Solnit. il *Sierra* 74:42-9 Jl/Ag '89

Light and lighting
See also
Photography—Exposure
Photography—Flash equipment
Photography, Flashlight
Bounce lighting. D. Gresch. il *Petersen's Photographic Magazine* 18:24-6+ N '89
Collins on basics. D. Collins. See occasional issues of Petersen's Photographic Magazine beginning July 1983
Cross-polarization of light. J. Bartsch. il *Petersen's Photographic Magazine* 17:58-9 F '89
Dark-field illumination [industrial glassware] K. Collavo. il *Petersen's Photographic Magazine* 18:88-9 My '89
Kathy Smith and the basic 3-light setup. G. Bernstein. il por *Petersen's Photographic Magazine* 18:8 Jl '89
Morris Deluxe Studio Kit. A. Stone. il *Petersen's Photographic Magazine* 18:76-7 Ag '89
Object on a complementary background [hunting knife against black reflective background] D. Palmer. il *Petersen's Photographic Magazine* 18:48-9 Jl '89
On becoming a short-order chef of lighting. J. Fruchtman. il por *Petersen's Photographic Magazine* 18:28-9 S '89
Photographing the deep sky amid city lights [increasing contrast] H. A. Entrop. il *Sky and Telescope* 77:108-10 Ja '89
Pure light [photo of studio lights] J. Frunchtman. il *Petersen's Photographic Magazine* 17:58-9 Mr '89
Pure light: classic light, or, the hurry-up-and-wait syndrome. J. Fruchtman. il *Petersen's Photographic Magazine* 18:28-9 D '89
Pure light: deciding when and if the client is "always right". J. Fruchtman. il *Petersen's Photographic Magazine* 18:52-3 Je '89
Reflective art—a new system paints with light [Gamma One transparencies capture full tonal range] J. P. Frank. il *Publishers Weekly* 235:69 Mr 3 '89
You're shooting in artificial light. Which would you reach for: color-negative or tungsten-balanced slide film? G. Schaub. il *Popular Photography* 96:32+ Ja '89

Masking
Darkroom magic: using multiple printing to make the images you couldn't take. S. Schneiderman. il *Petersen's Photographic Magazine* 18:22-6 S '89

Periodicals
See also
Popular photography (Periodical)

Portraits
See also
Artists, American—Photographs and photography
Black women—Photographs and photography
Carte de visite photographs
Celebrities—Photographs and photography
Children—Photographs and photography
Motion picture actors and actresses—Photographs and photography
Women—Photographs and photography
The 3-minute portrait [photos by George Rose] il *Petersen's Photographic Magazine* 18:20 Ag '89
Native portraiture. C. Rainier. il *Petersen's Photographic Magazine* 17:32-5 Ja '89
Point & flatter: the P/S studio [Morris Mini Slave] D. Richards. il *Popular Photography* 96:28+ N '89
Portraits by the millions [daguerreotypes] il *American History Illustrated* 24:26-7 S/O '89
Portraits like movie stills. R. James. il *Petersen's Photographic Magazine* 18:40-3 N '89
Thomas Ruff. J. Dornberg. il por *Art News* 88:164-5 Ap '89

Printing processes
See Photography—Processing

Processing
See also
Collodion process (Photography)
Halftone process (Photography)
Photographic laboratories
Photography—Developing and developers
Enhanced-color astrophotography [cover story] T. Hallas and D. Mount. il *Sky and Telescope* 78:216-18 Ag '89
Improving color prints. J. Riffle. il *Sky and Telescope* 78:326-7 S '89

In the dark. P. Kolonia. See issues of Popular Photography beginning April 1989
The joy of color printing. L. Myers. il *Astronomy* 17:86-91 N '89
Local color [dodging and burning-in] J. Dow. il *Popular Photography* 96:64-9 Ja '89
Nitty gritty posterization. B. Snowman. il *Petersen's Photographic Magazine* 17:42-5+ Ja '89
Print solarization. W. L. Jolly. il *Petersen's Photographic Magazine* 17:28-33 F '89

Equipment
See also
Photography—Enlargers and enlarging
For the darkroom it's b&w variable-contrast paper, simple color-print processor. il *Popular Photography* 96:104+ Ja '89
It took a heap of walkin', but we found something new for almost every darkroom [Dallas PMA Show] P. Kolonia. il *Popular Photography* 96:92-3+ My '89
Jobo CPP-2 color processor. il *Petersen's Photographic Magazine* 18:67 My '89
Temperature control of a hypering tank. D. C. Cole. il *Sky and Telescope* 78:658-61+ D '89

Psychological aspects
A room with a view [seeing photos of outdoor scenes helps reduce stress; study by Richard G. Coss] il *Harper's Bazaar* 122:62-3 Ja '89

Scientific use
See also
Photomicrography

Setting and scenery
Building a set with two walls. C. Zsarnay and V. Summerhays. il *Petersen's Photographic Magazine* 17:54-5 Ja '89
End studio clutter with support from above [backdrop support] il *Popular Photography* 96:46+ Ja '89
Portable, packable backgrounds [Photek Backgrounds in a Bag] K. Geller-Shinn. il *Petersen's Photographic Magazine* 18:10 S '89

Still life
Pure light: classic light, or, the hurry-up-and-wait syndrome. J. Fruchtman. il *Petersen's Photographic Magazine* 18:28-9 D '89

Studios and darkrooms
See also
CPI Corporation

Equipment
See Photography—Processing—Equipment
Heating and ventilation
Hot darkroom? Try these chilling suggestions. il *Popular Photography* 96:46 Ja '89

Study and teaching
Comp book. See issues of Petersen's Photographic Magazine
Jana Taylor gives new focus to the lives of inner-city kids [teaching photography in Los Angeles] S. Schindehette. il pors *People Weekly* 31:126-7+ Ap 3 '89
Know before you go. M. Grimm and T. Grimm. il *Travel Holiday* 171:6+ My '89
Photo tours & workshops. See issues of Petersen's Photographic Magazine beginning October 1988
Workshops. See issues of Popular Photography beginning June 1986 through June 1989
Aids and devices
Photo videotapes: can they really teach you something? E. Stecker. il *Popular Photography* 96:50-5+ F '89

PHOTOGRAPHY, ADVERTISING
The ad says, "hair" [photography for hairstyling salon] U. Puga. il *Petersen's Photographic Magazine* 18:80-1 Je '89
Lighting for depth, form, and dimension—and softness, as well! [shooting an ad for Coors] T. L. Corbell. il *Petersen's Photographic Magazine* 17:76-7 Ja '89

PHOTOGRAPHY, AERIAL
See also
Aerial reconnaissance
Artificial satellites—Military use
Above China. L. Kohl. il maps *National Geographic* 175:278-311 Mr '89
Above Kenya. Y. Arthus-Bertrand. il *Life* 12:90-5 Ag '89

PHOTOGRAPHY, ARTISTIC
See also
Photography of the nude
American monument [L. Friedlander] R. B. Woodward. il por *Art News* 88:140-5 N '89
Artistic vision—and an artistic visionary [A. Stieglitz] il *American History Illustrated* 24:68-9 S/O '89
Body doubles [work of H. Kempinger] M. Haus. il por *Art News* 88:107-8 S '89
Boyd Webb. B. Taylor. il por *Art News* 88:154-5 Ap '89
Conceptual Cibachromes: techniques inspired by a menu [work of J. Pallone] F. Cameron. il *Petersen's Photographic Magazine* 18:34-7+ Ag '89
Into the fun house. P. Plagens. il *Newsweek* 114:52-7 Ag 21 '89
James Welling. M. E. Haus. il por *Art News* 88:162-3 Ap '89
Sheila Metzner. P. Haldeman. il por *Art News* 88:166-7 Ap '89

PHOTOGRAPHY, ARTISTIC—cont.
Exhibitions
Adam Füss at Massimo Audiello. H. Cotter. *Art in America* 77:175-6 Je '89

Boyd Webb: Sonnabend. E. Heartney. il *Art News* 88:157 D '89

Corcoran showdown [aftermath of cancellation of R. Mapplethorpe show] C. McGuigan. il pors *Newsweek* 114:111+ O 9 '89

David LaChapelle at Trabia-MacAfee. J. Ash. *Art in America* 77:173 Je '89

Drawn by nature's pencil [The art of photography: 1839-1989 at the Museum of Fine Arts in Houston] R. Lacayo. il *Time* 133:64-7 F 27 '89

Exhibitionism [Corcoran Gallery cancels R. Mapplethorpe exhibit] *The New Republic* 201:6 Jl 17-24 '89

Francisco Infante: International Images. H. Schwalb. il *Art News* 88:186 S '89

The Hallmark Photographic Collection: a commitment to fine photography. K. F. Davis. il *USA Today (Periodical)* 117:54-63 Ja '89

The influence of the pictorialists on the art of photography [On the art of fixing a shadow: 150 years of photography] M. Fox. il *Antiques* 136:120-31 Jl '89

Judith Golden at the MCP. J. Frueh. *Art in America* 77:173 F '89

Love the concept [California photography: remaking make-believe and Invention and continuity in contemporary photographs] K. Larson. il *New York* 22:53 Jl 24 '89

Lynn Geesaman: Thomas Barry Fine Arts. M. A. Martin. il *Art News* 88:161 F '89

Mad about Mapplethorpe [Corcoran Gallery cancels exhibit] A. Ferguson. *National Review* 41:20-1 Ag 4 '89

Mapplethorpe of my eye [exhibit opens at WPA gallery after cancellation by the Corcoran] A. Heard. *The New Republic* 201:10-12 Ag 21 '89

Outfoxing the viewer [Fox games; work of S. Skoglund] B. Weber. il por *The New York Times Magazine* p94 O 8 '89

Pascal Kern: Galerie Zabriskie. G. Danto. il *Art News* 88:164 F '89

Robert Mapplethorpe. il por *People Weekly* 32:100-1 D 25 '89-Ja 1 '90

Robert Mapplethorpe at Robert Miller. B. Berkson. il *Art in America* 77:258 Ap '89

Robert Mapplethorpe: Washington Project for the Arts. A. D. Coleman. il *Art News* 88:213 O '89

A "sacrificial lamb"? [aftermath of the Corcoran Gallery's cancellation of R. Mapplethorpe show] S. Hochfield. il por *Art News* 88:62 N '89

Sandy Skoglund: Damon Brandt; Lorence Monk. M. E. Haus. il *Art News* 88:135-6 F '89

Seeing and believing [work of M. White at the Museum of Modern Art] K. Larson. il *New York* 22:62-3 My 22 '89

Surreal to real [work of L. Miller] C. Squiers. il por *Vogue* 179:214+ F '89

White and black [work of M. White and R. Mapplethorpe] I. Sischy. *The New Yorker* 65:124+ N 13 '89

Whose art is it, anyway? [Corcoran Gallery cancels R. Mapplethorpe exhibit] M. B. Carlson. il *Time* 134:21 Jl 3 '89

Yasumasa Morimura at NW House. J. Koplos. il por *Art in America* 77:189 Je '89

PHOTOGRAPHY, CLOSE-UP
See also
Macrophotography

Making portraits of the microcosm [work of K. Givens] K. Sferra. il *National Parks* 63:28-31 Mr/Ap '89

On a camera walkabout across the forest floor [work of K. Givens] P. Skinner. il *Petersen's Photographic Magazine* 17:56-8 Ja '89

Spring has sprung, the flowers are abloom; I wonder where's my macro zoom? G. Schaub. il *Popular Photography* 96:28+ My '89

PHOTOGRAPHY, COLD WEATHER *See* Photography—Cold weather conditions

PHOTOGRAPHY, COMMERCIAL
See also
Photography, Advertising
Photography, Fashion
Photography, Journalistic

Pro talk. G. Bernstein. See issues of Petersen's Photographic Magazine

PHOTOGRAPHY, COMPOSITE *See* Photomontage

PHOTOGRAPHY, DOCUMENTARY
Exhibitions
Walker Evans: American photographs. L. Kirstein. il *USA Today (Periodical)* 117:54-9 Mr '89

Walker Evans: Museum of Modern Art. R. B. Woodward. il *Art News* 88:206 Ap '89

History
An awakening social conscience [work of J. Riis] il *American History Illustrated* 24:70-1 S/O '89

PHOTOGRAPHY, FASHION
Black (leather) on white. G. Bernstein. il *Petersen's Photographic Magazine* 17:12 Mr '89

Strobe-assist—the order of the day [fashion ad featuring J. and J. Montana] G. Bernstein. il pors *Petersen's Photographic Magazine* 18:12 S '89

Collectors and collecting
The designer's eye for timeless fashion photography [collection of J. Banks] J. Gruen. il por *Architectural Digest* 46:78+ S '89

Exhibitions
Horst at Holly Solomon. A. F. Collins. *Art in America* 77:201 N '89

PHOTOGRAPHY, FLASHLIGHT
Bounce lighting. D. Gresch. il *Petersen's Photographic Magazine* 18:24-6+ N '89

Flash: the light fantastic [cover story; special section] il *Popular Photography* 96:63-85+ Ap '89

Getting red-eye in your flash shots? Yes, you can get rid of it. H. Keppler. il *Popular Photography* 96:44-6+ Ap '89

Equipment
See Photography—Flash equipment

PHOTOGRAPHY, HIGH SPEED
See also
Photography of moving objects

The time machine. A. Goldsmith. il *Popular Photography* 96:42-9 O '89

PHOTOGRAPHY, HUMOROUS *See* Humorous photography
PHOTOGRAPHY, INDUSTRIAL *See* Industrial photography

PHOTOGRAPHY, JOURNALISTIC
See also
War—Photographs and photography

A lifetime chasing fires and disasters leads to a Pulitzer Prize for a furniture salesman [R. Olshwanger wins prize for photo appearing in St. Louis post-dispatch] il por *People Weekly* 31:121-2 Ap 17 '89

Mary Ellen Mark. M. Moorman. il por *Art News* 88:152-3 Ap '89

Pictures of the year [contest sponsored by the National Press Photographers Association and the University of Missouri School of Journalism] L. Downes. il *Petersen's Photographic Magazine* 18:14-16 S '89

Rolling stone: the photographs [excerpt] il *Rolling Stone* p57-62 O 19 '89

So, you want to be a news photographer? D. Mazzapica. il *Petersen's Photographic Magazine* 17:60-2+ F '89

Ethical aspects
Spies are us [unauthorized photos published in Aviation week & space technology] il *Discover* 10:10 Mr '89

Exhibitions
Margaret Bourke-White: new vistas in photojournalism. W. M. Barrett. il por *USA Today (Periodical)* 118:54-63 S '89

History
150 years of photojournalism. il *Time* 134 Special Issue:1-10+ Fall '89

Candid cameraman [working for the New York post]; ed. by Joyce Wadler. L. Liotta. il pors *People Weekly* 32:171+ D 11 '89

PHOTOGRAPHY, MEDICAL
See also
Radiography, Medical

PHOTOGRAPHY, METEOROLOGICAL *See* Meteorological photography

PHOTOGRAPHY, MILITARY
See also
Aerial reconnaissance
Artificial satellites—Military use

PHOTOGRAPHY, NIGHT
Dusk/dark double exposures. M. A. Johnson. il *Petersen's Photographic Magazine* 18:84-5 Ag '89

Heavenly shades of long exposures [twilight images] D. Skernick. il *Petersen's Photographic Magazine* 18:40-2 Je '89

Lake Powell's Rainbow Bridge by moonlight with a 3-minute exposure, in wind, on water. J. Zuckerman. il *Petersen's Photographic Magazine* 18:22-3 My '89

Night stalking the nocturnal barn owl. J. Zuckerman. il *Petersen's Photographic Magazine* 17:34-5 F '89

PHOTOGRAPHY, PANORAMIC
Spaced out [multiple-frame composite panoramas] J. Stoliar and A. Stoliar. il *Popular Photography* 96:42-3+ Mr '89

PHOTOGRAPHY, TABLE TOP
Creating the pot of gold. R. Barnhardt. il *Petersen's Photographic Magazine* 18:98-9 N '89

PHOTOGRAPHY, TIME-LAPSE
The time machine. A. Goldsmith. il *Popular Photography* 96:42-9 O '89

PHOTOGRAPHY, TRICK
The Christmas cover story [special effects used to create New York times magazine cover photo; work of Elliot Erwitt and Bran Ferren] B. Weber. il *The New York Times Magazine* p34 D 24 '89

Darkroom magic: using multiple printing to make the images you couldn't take. S. Schneiderman. il *Petersen's Photographic Magazine* 18:22-6 S '89

A dry-ice fogger: how to make the moodiest prop of all. A. B. Smith. il *Petersen's Photographic Magazine* 17:46-8 F '89

PHOTOGRAPHY, TRICK—*cont.*

Earthscapes [cover story] J. Zuckerman. il *Petersen's Photographic Magazine* 17:12-15 Ja '89

Kitchen color [use of food coloring in photos] J. Van Horne. il *Petersen's Photographic Magazine* 17:46-7 Ap '89

A singular system for multiple exposures. il *Popular Photography* 96:38 Ap '89

Special effects flash. B. Schwalberg. il *Popular Photography* 96:75-7 Ap '89

The synthetic kitchen [work of T. Trengove] B. Lobron. il *Popular Photography* 96:63+ O '89

PHOTOGRAPHY, UNDERWATER *See* Underwater photography

PHOTOGRAPHY BY CHILDREN *See* Children as photographers

PHOTOGRAPHY GALLERIES AND MUSEUMS

California

See also

Fraenkel Gallery

New York (State)

See also

International Museum of Photography at George Eastman House

PHOTOGRAPHY IN INDUSTRY *See* Industrial photography

PHOTOGRAPHY IN TRAFFIC CONTROL

Giving Big Brother the birdie [photo radar fails to catch on] S. C. Smith. il *Car and Driver* 35:103-5+ Ag '89

PHOTOGRAPHY OF ART *See* Art—Photographs and photography

PHOTOGRAPHY OF MOVING OBJECTS

See also

Fireworks—Photographs and photography

Time and motion. il pors *American History Illustrated* 24:62-3 S/O '89

PHOTOGRAPHY OF THE NUDE

Indecent exposure? [Museum of Fine Arts declines nude photograph of A. Ginsberg by E. Dorfman] C. Giuliano. il pors *Art News* 88:31 F '89

It's a good nudes, bad nudes game. A. Meisler. il *TV Guide* 37:16-18 Ag 26-S 1 '89

PHOTOGRAPHY OF WORKS OF ART *See* Art—Photographs and photography

PHOTOGRAPHY TRADE *See* Photographs—Marketing

PHOTOJOURNALISM *See* Photography, Journalistic

PHOTOKINA *See* Photography—Exhibitions

PHOTOMACROGRAPHY *See* Macrophotography

PHOTOMETRY, ASTRONOMICAL

Photometry from Voyager 2: initial results from the Neptunian atmosphere, satellites, and rings. A. L. Lane and others. bibl f il *Science* 246:1450-4 D 15 '89

Pluto is red, Charon is gray [work of Richard Binzel] *Astronomy* 17:10+ Ja '89

PHOTOMICROGRAPHY

Sizing up a small world [scanning electron microscope] il *National Geographic World* 162:24-9 F '89

Slide show. N. Guccione. il *Omni (New York, N.Y.)* 11:58-61 F '89

PHOTOMONTAGE

Spaced out [multiple-frame composite panoramas] J. Stoliar and A. Stoliar. il *Popular Photography* 96:42-3+ Mr '89

Working against the grain of fast films [composite prints] L. Myers. il *Astronomy* 17:88-91 F '89

PHOTONICS

A bright future for photonics. *The Futurist* 23:53-4 Mr/Ap '89

Levels of light. J. W. Goodman. il *Byte* 14:240-2 O '89

Photonics shed light on diverse uses. il *Popular Mechanics* 166:17 F '89

Photonics will boost near-term computer processing speeds. B. D. Nordwall. il *Aviation Week & Space Technology* 130:57+ Ap 17 '89

Military use

Air Force pursues photonics research [special section] il *Aviation Week & Space Technology* 130:54-8+ Ja 30 '89

PHOTONS

Can you help the Mets by watching on TV? [Strong Baseball Principal; work of N. D. Mermin] R. Pool. il por *Science* 244:773-4 My 19 '89

Catching a light ride on a plasma wave [photon accelerator; research by John M. Dawson and Scott C. Wilks] I. Peterson. *Science News* 135:358 Je 10 '89

Physics' unseen hand [theory that observing an event can influence outcome; work of D. N. Mermin] W. F. Allman. il *U.S. News & World Report* 107:65 O 23 '89

Quantum baseball [Strong Baseball Principle; work of N. D. Mermin; cover story] I. Peterson. il por *Science News* 136:88-9 Ag 5 '89

PHOTOPERIODISM

Carbohydrates and depression. R. J. Wurtman and J. J. Wurtman. il map *Scientific American* 260:68-75 Ja '89

PHOTORECEPTOR CELLS *See* Rods and cones

PHOTORECEPTORS

The natural roots of fiber optics. I. Amato. il *Science News* 136:414-15 D 23-30 '89

Ubiquitous expression of *sevenless*: position-dependent specification of cell fate. K. Basler and E. Hafen. bibl f il *Science* 243:931-4 F 17 '89

PHOTOSYNTHESIS

See also

Chloroplasts

Dispersed polaron simulations of electron transfer in photosynthetic reaction centers. A. Warshel and others. bibl f il *Science* 246:112-16 O 6 '89

Mimicking photosynthesis. D. Gust and T. A. Moore. bibl f il *Science* 244:35-41 Ap 7 '89

Nobel chemists shed light on key structure in photosynthesis. B. G. Levi. il por *Physics Today* 42:17-18 F '89

Ozone needles loblolly pines . . . and saps sequoia seedlings. *Science News* 136:189 S 16 '89

Reexamination of the three-dimensional structure of the small subunit of RuBisCo from higher plants. S. Knight and others. bibl f il *Science* 244:702-5 My 12 '89

PHOTOSYNTHETIC BACTERIA *See* Bacteria, Photosynthetic

PHOTOTHERAPY

See also

Photofrin

Fighting the winter blues with bright light. M. Terman and M. Link. il *Psychology Today* 23:18+ Ja/F '89

Shedding light on cancer. I. Wickelgren. il *Science News* 135:26-8 Ja 14 '89

A shiny new weapon in the war on cancer: light [light-activated drugs] S. Yanchinski and N. J. Freundlich. il *Business Week* p106-7 My 29 '89

PHOTOVOLTAICS *See* Solar cells

PHRANC

about

A phemale pholkie named Phranc, who hopes to laugh all the way to the bank. il por *People Weekly* 32:62 Ag 14 '89

PHRASES *See* English language—Terms and phrases

PHYLLO PASTRY *See* Pastry

PHYLLOBATES *See* Frogs

PHYLLOTAXIS

Spiral effect [shapes occuring in nature] J. Carey. il *National Wildlife* 27:52-9 Ap/My '89

PHYLOGENY

See also

Homology (Biology)

All in the family [evidence for common pinniped ancestor; research by Andre Wyss] P. Shipman. il *Discover* 10:44 Jl '89

Fungal duo teaches evolutionary lesson [research by Jeffrey D. Palmer] B. Bower. *Science News* 135:318 My 20 '89

How old is the genetic code? Statistical geometry of tRNA provides an answer. M. Eigen and others. bibl f il *Science* 244:673-9 My 12 '89

Phylogenetic meaning of the kingdom concept: an unusual ribosomal RNA from Giardia lamblia. M. L. Sogin and others. bibl f il *Science* 243:75-7 Ja 6 '89

Phylogenetic stains: ribosomal RNA-based probes for the identification of single cells. E. F. DeLong and others. bibl f il *Science* 243:1360-3 Mr 10 '89

Phylogeny and molecular data [discussion of February 12, 1988 article, Molecular phylogeny of the animal kingdom] K. G. Field and others. *Science* 243:548-51 Ja 27 '89

Time bomb [DNA clock; work of Charles G. Sibley and Jon E. Ahlquist] J. Horgan. *Scientific American* 260:24+ Mr '89

PHYSICAL ACOUSTICS CORP.

When he hears, others listen [S. J. Vahaviolos] B. E. Thornbury. il por *Nation's Business* 77:18+ N '89

PHYSICAL ASTRONOMY *See* Astrophysics

PHYSICAL CONSTANTS

See also

Fine structure constant

Hubble constant

Planck's constant

Cosmological constant conundrum. *Sky and Telescope* 78:132-3 Ag '89

The fundamental physical constants. E. R. Cohen and B. N. Taylor. il *Physics Today* 42 pt2:BG8-BG8D Ag '89

Why is the cosmological constant so very small? B. M. Schwarzschild. bibl f il *Physics Today* 42:21-4 Mr '89

PHYSICAL EDUCATION AND TRAINING

Coordinating curriculum in physical education. G. E. Webster. *The Education Digest* 54:48-50 Mr '89

Is gym necessary? F. Roberts. il *Parents* 64:51-2 Je '89

PHYSICAL EQUIPMENT

New products. See issues of Physics Today

Sixth annual Physics today buyers' guide. il *Physics Today* 42 pt2:BG3+ Ag '89

PHYSICAL EVIDENCE [film] *See* Motion picture reviews—Single works

PHYSICAL EXAMINATIONS

The endangered physical. S. M. Halpern. il *Ms.* 18:18+ N '89

The first physical. K. Karlsrud and D. Schultz. il *Parents* 64:120 Ja '89

Hey, look me over [cover story] E. Gofen. il *Current Health 2* 15:3-8 Ja '89

Is the annual physical obsolete? E. Rosenthal. il *Glamour* 87:37-9 Jl '89

Medical checkups. F. Simon. il *Essence* 19:18+ Ja '89

PHYSICAL EXAMINATIONS—*cont.*
More talking, less testing [U.S. Preventive Services Task Force report] J. Carey. il *U.S. News & World Report* 106:62-3+ My 15 '89
Rethinking the annual check-up. *USA Today (Periodical)* 118:12 O '89

PHYSICAL FITNESS
See also
Aged—Care and hygiene
Children—Care and hygiene
Congressmen—Health and hygiene
Endurance
Executives—Health and hygiene
Exercise
Fishermen—Health and hygiene
Health clubs
Homeless—Health and hygiene
Hunters—Health and hygiene
Industry—Physical fitness programs
Muscle strength
Physical education and training
Vitality
Youth—Health and hygiene
1989 fitness guide [cover story; special section] bibl il *U.S. News & World Report* 106:60-2+ My 29 '89
Body be beautiful/89 [special section] il *Good Housekeeping* 208:89+ My '89
Fitness. See issues of Vogue
Fitness matters. G. Legwold. See issues of Better Homes and Gardens beginning October 1987
Ken Cooper made fitness a fad. But that wasn't good enough for him. D. Moreau. il por *Changing Times* 43:100 Je '89
Making health a family affair. J. Barone. il *Working Woman* 14:179-80+ N '89
The mid-life fitness peak [study by Charles A. Garfield] M. Rozak. il *Psychology Today* 23:32-3 Jl/Ag '89
On the West Coast, fitness has moved beyond the pursuit of the perfect body. H. Hansen. il *Vogue* 179:166+ Ag '89
Sex and other pleasures [cover story; special section] G. B. Leonard. il *Esquire* 111:129-32+ My '89
The shape of the Union [views of Krys Spain] D. Raskin. il *American Health* 8:31 O '89
Shape-up. L. Gordon. See issues of Glamour
Special section on health and fitness. il *Ebony* 44:102+ Jl '89
Thirty years of fortitude [staying active to offset physical decline] J. Poppy. il *Esquire* 112:83-5 D '89
What's news: nutrition, diet, fitness. See occasional issues of Good Housekeeping beginning May 1985
What's your fitness quotient? [quiz] J. Wood. *Modern Maturity* 32:28 Je/Jl '89

Testing
Test of a champion [tennis player J. Capriati] J. E. Loehr. il pors *World Tennis* 37:30+ S '89

Soviet Union
Here come the trainers. A. Blackman. il *Time* 133:102 Ap 10 '89
Perestroika, part two [aerobics] M. Madsen. *Women's Sports & Fitness* 11:58-9 O '89

PHYSICAL FITNESS CRUISES *See* Cruising
PHYSICAL FITNESS NEWSLETTERS
Fitness news: read it and sweat. C. Schaeffer. *Changing Times* 43:96+ My '89

PHYSICAL GEOGRAPHY
See also
Climate
Islands
Paleogeography
Volcanoes

PHYSICAL MEASUREMENTS
A passion for precision. D. Kleppner. il por *Physics Today* 42:9+ N '89

PHYSICAL REVIEW
What's wrong with this prose? N. D. Mermin. por *Physics Today* 42:9+ My '89

PHYSICAL THERAPY
See also
Massage

PHYSICALLY HANDICAPPED *See* Handicapped
PHYSICIANS
See also
American Medical Association
Anesthesiologists
Black physicians
Dermatologists
Drugs and physicians
House calls (Medical care)
Medical care
Medical examiners (Law)
Medicine
Pediatricians
Residents (Medicine)
Surgeons
Women physicians

See also names of physicians
Inside track to a specialist. C. Schaeffer. il *Changing Times* 43:96 My '89
To be a physician [address, March 4, 1989] R. E. McAfee. *Vital Speeches of the Day* 55:697-700 S 1 '89

Advertising
Paper medicine [physicians' personalized newsletters] E. Paris. il *Forbes* 143:92 Ja 23 '89

Age
Advice to real-life Doogies: get your first kiss—then apply to med school. D. Hudson. il *TV Guide* 37:7 D 16-22 '89

Antitrust cases
Physician, beware. R. Coorsh. *Consumers' Research Magazine* 72:4 F '89

Evaluation
See Physicians—Rating

Health and hygiene
See also
AIDS (Disease) and physicians
True grit [doctors working while sick] P. Klass. il *Discover* 10:30+ Mr '89

Malpractice
See Malpractice

Political activities
A doctor's dilemma [Cuban-trained doctor T. Marryshow not permitted to practice in Grenada] W. Steif. il por *The Progressive* 53:10 Ja '89

Professional ethics
See Medical ethics

Psychology
Prosecuting the patient. P. Klass. il *Discover* 10:12+ Ja '89

Rating
The 184 best breast cancer doctors [surgeons and oncologists] M. Abrams. *Good Housekeeping* 208:77-80+ Ap '89

Salaries, fees, etc.
Afraid to ask your doctor about money? That's a costly fear. L. Luciano. il *Money* 18:173-4 Ap '89
Applying a scalpel to doctors' wallets [Congress lowers Medicare reimbursements] il *U.S. News & World Report* 107:11 D 4 '89
How doctors boost the cost of Medicare. il *Consumer Reports* 54:377 Je '89
Shopping for surgery. M. Teich. il *Health (New York, N.Y.)* 21:94-5 Je '89
What'll it cost, doc? [fairer price scale for Medicare payment; study by William Hsiao] J. Hamilton. il *American Health* 8:15-16 Ap '89

PHYSICIANS, RURAL *See* Medical care, Rural
PHYSICIANS AND PATIENTS
See also
Physical examinations
Second opinion (Medical consultation)
Afraid to ask your doctor about money? That's a costly fear. L. Luciano. il *Money* 18:173-4 Ap '89
. . . and be the perfect patient [aged] A. Levin. *Modern Maturity* 32:73-4 Ag/S '89
Asking—and telling. M. Shuchman and M. S. Wilkes. il *The New York Times Magazine* p45-6 F 12 '89
Doctors and patients must talk [condensed from Head first] N. Cousins. *Reader's Digest* 135:133-4+ O '89
First word. N. Cousins. por *Omni (New York, N.Y.)* 12:6 D '89
Hands-on healing. E. E. Rosenbaum. il *New Choices for the Best Years* 29:36+ N '89
How to find the perfect doctor . . . W. H. Jones. bibl il *Modern Maturity* 32:72-4+ Ag/S '89
How to talk to your doctor. K. McCoy. *Seventeen* 48:126+ Je '89
Humanism and the art of medicine [address, June 21, 1989] A. R. Nelson. *Vital Speeches of the Day* 56:91-3 N 15 '89
"I love my doctor!". M. C. Hickey. il *Parents* 64:104-7+ Ap '89
I love my doctor, but . . . [survey results] C. Perlmutter. il *Prevention (Emmaus, Pa.)* 41:52-9 Ag '89
Know your legal rights. *McCall's* 116:112 S '89
My holiday memories [former patients] E. E. Rosenbaum. il *New Choices for the Best Years* 29:90+ D '89
"My right to be there" [mother's role in child's medical care] J. Gaylin. il *Parents* 64:74-6 N '89
Paging Dr. Right [work of D. Ornish] J. Poppy. il *Esquire* 112:49-51 Jl '89
Prosecuting the patient. P. Klass. il *Discover* 10:12+ Ja '89
Sick and tired [cover story] N. R. Gibbs. il *Time* 134:48-53 Jl 31 '89
This is what you thought: 59% say they've changed doctors over questions of competence [survey results] il *Glamour* 87:183 S '89
What children teach doctors. il *Reader's Digest* 134:153-6 Ap '89
What's up, doc? [study by Suzanne C. Thompson] B. Fischman. *Psychology Today* 23:75 Ja/F '89
When and how to fire your doctor. S. Berkman. il *Good Housekeeping* 209:269-70 N '89
Why doctors mistreat women: special medical report. R. Baron-Faust. *Redbook* 173:114-15+ My '89

PHYSICIANS AND PATIENTS IN ART
Rockwell's model doc, Donald Campbell, gives his last shot and retires. il por *People Weekly* 31:114-15 Mr 27 '89
PHYSICIANS AS AUTHORS
Doctor fear [interview with R. Cook] M. Segell. il *American Health* 8:82-4+ S '89
PHYSICIANS AS COMEDIANS
Paging Dr. Funny Bone: comedy doc leaves 'em in stitches [work of B. Miller] S. Carrell. il *American Health* 8:22 My '89
PHYSICIANS' OATHS
The Hippocratic oath. il *World Health* p16 Ap '89
PHYSICIANS' RECORDS *See* Medical records
PHYSICISTS
See also
Bloembergen, Nicolaas, 1920-
Bohren, Craig F., 1940-
Bromley, D. Allan (David Allan), 1926-
Einstein, Albert, 1879-1955
Feynman, Richard Phillips
Gray, Henry F.
Hawking, S. W. (Stephen W.)
Hertz, Heinrich Rudolf, 1857-1894
Jones, Steven E.
Landau, Lev Davidovich, 1908-1968
Lederman, Leon M.
Minority physicists
Pagels, Heinz R., 1939-1988
Penzias, Arno Allan
Saha, Meghnad, 1893-1956
Teller, Edward, 1908-
Uhlenbeck, George Eugene, 1900-1988
Women physicists
The physics community. See issues of Physics Today
We hear that. See issues of Physics Today
Supply and demand
AIP survey anticipates shortages of physicists in the 1990s. P. Janowski. *Physics Today* 42:65 Jl '89
APS-AIP survey of faculties finds shortages in two physics subfields. W. Sweet. *Physics Today* 42:101 F '89
Employment news in AIP survey bodes well for physics PhDs. P. Janowski. *Physics Today* 42:93 Mr '89
PHYSICISTS IN GOVERNMENT *See* Scientists in government
PHYSICS
See also
Acoustical Society of America
American Institute of Physics
American Physical Society
American Vacuum Society
Astrophysics
Biophysics
Cluster theory (Physics)
Computers—Physics use
Electricity
Entropy
Field theory (Physics)
Fifth force (Physics)
Fluid dynamics
Fluids
Geophysics
Gravity and gravitation
Lasers—Physics use
Light
Magnetism
Mass (Physics)
Mathematical physics
Matter
Medical physics
Mesoscopic physics
Nuclear physics
Quantum theory
Relativity (Physics)
Relaxation time (Physics)
Rockets—Physics use
Sound
Statistical mechanics
Thermodynamics
Viscosity
The game teachers play [R. Watt's scientific baseball research] S. A. Booth. il por *Rolling Stone* p152-6 Mr 23 '89
Physics lite [beer; studies by C. F. Bohren] W. Sones. il por *Discover* 10:56-60 Ag '89
Awards
See also
Apker Award
International Physics Olympiad
Wolf prizes
AAPT top honors awarded to French and Birgeneau. pors *Physics Today* 42:126-8 Mr '89
ACA honors excellence in research, public service and student work. *Physics Today* 42:113 N '89
AIP awards made to Amaldi, Holton, Redington and Littmann. J. Kumagai. il *Physics Today* 42:57-8 D '89
APS presents a host of awards at spring meeting in Baltimore. il *Physics Today* 42:95-8 Je '89
Franklin Institute honors Lorenz, Oatley and Madey. M. Siegel. pors *Physics Today* 42:113 S '89

OSA awards mark achievements in many facets of optical science. *Physics Today* 42:85-6 Jl '89
OSA recognizes outstanding contributions to optical science. il *Physics Today* 42:145-6+ O '89
Prizes and their problems [discussion of January 1989 article, What's wrong with these prizes?] N. D. Mermin. *Physics Today* 42:97-102 D '89
What's wrong with these prizes? N. D. Mermin. il por *Physics Today* 42:9+ Ja '89
Bibliography
Books. See issues of Physics Today
Conferences
See also
American Physical Society—Meetings
Calendar. See alternate issues of Physics Today
Equipment
See Physical equipment
Experiments
The amateur scientist. J. Walker. See issues of Scientific American
Can you help the Mets by watching on TV? [Strong Baseball Principal; work of N. D. Mermin] R. Pool. il por *Science* 244:773-4 My 19 '89
Quantum baseball [Strong Baseball Principle; work of N. D. Mermin; cover story] I. Peterson. il por *Science News* 136:88-9 Ag 5 '89
Anecdotes, facetiae, satire, etc.
Physics 101, the sequel [experiments involving cars] M. Anson. il *Motor Trend* 41:8 Jl '89
Federal aid
High energy physics crunch foreseen [views of David Berley and David Garelick] M. Crawford. *Science* 243:888 F 17 '89
Numbers game: Bush's 1990 R&D budget uses Reagan's figures in making deals. I. Goodwin. il *Physics Today* 42:43-9 My '89
History
Heinrich Hertz and the development of physics. J. F. Mulligan. bibl f il por *Physics Today* 42:50-7 Mr '89
Periodicals
See also
Kvant (Periodical)
Quantum (Periodical)
Philosophy
Magic on the mind: physicists' use of metaphor. A. P. Lightman. *The American Scholar* 58:97-101 Wint '89
Research
See also
Franklin Institute (Philadelphia, Pa.)
Physics news in 1988 [special section] P. F. Schewe. il *Physics Today* 42:S1-S67 Ja '89
Search & discovery. See issues of Physics Today
Federal aid
See Physics—Federal aid
Scholarships and fellowships
MacArthur Foundation confers five physics-related fellowships. M. Siegel. il *Physics Today* 42:123-4+ Mr '89
Study and teaching
See also
Colleges and universities—Departments of physics
Columbia University. Dept. of Physics
Physics teachers
Discontent with PhD programs voiced at AAPT-APS conference. I. Goodwin. *Physics Today* 42:62-3 Jl '89
Education in physics. J. M. Wilson. bibl f *Physics Today* 42:S35-S36 Ja '89
Reaching the critical mass in high school physics. M. Neuschatz. bibl f il *Physics Today* 42 pt1:30-6 Ag '89
Richard P. Feynman, teacher. D. L. Goodstein. il *Physics Today* 42:70-5 F '89
Summer industrial intern program in tenth year. il *Physics Today* 42:110 S '89
Aids and devices
Using computers in teaching physics [cover story] J. M. Wilson and E. F. Redish. bibl f il *Physics Today* 42:34-41 Ja '89
Brazil
See also
Brazilian Physical Society
New Jersey
Central Jersey strengthens its position as a 'pole' of US physics [special section] W. Sweet. il *Physics Today* 42:61-7 Je '89
Soviet Union
History
Reminiscences of Landau. I. M. Khalatnikov. il pors *Physics Today* 42:34-41 My '89
Western Europe
See also
European Organization for Nuclear Research
PHYSICS AND ECONOMICS
Physics for economists [computer simulations of economic scenarios conducted at Santa Fe Institute] E. Dyson. il *Forbes* 144:266 O 16 '89
Strange bedfellows [physicists and economists at the Santa Fe Institute] R. Pool. il *Science* 245:700-3 Ag 18 '89

PICASSO, PABLO, 1881-1973—about—cont.

Married . . . with cubism. S. Schwartz. *The New Republic* 201:28-30 D 25 '89

Painting by numbers. L. Black. il *Maclean's* 102:80 N 27 '89

Picasso, Braque, and an art revolution. J. Perl. il pors *Vogue* 179:722-7 S '89

Poisoned genius. J. Garvey. il *Commonweal* 116:40-1 Ja 27 '89

Portrait of Picasso's tailor. D. H. Minassian. il pors *Architectural Digest* 46:62+ F '89

Present at the creation. P. Plagens. il *Newsweek* 114:73 O 2 '89

Rubin's cube. K. Larson. il *New York* 22:77-8 O 9 '89

To find originality. L. J. O'Donovan. *America* 161:299-300 N 4 '89

PICASSO, PALOMA
about
Design of the dove. P. Hoban. il pors *Harper's Bazaar* 122:144-7+ D '89

PICCIGALLO, PHILIP R.
In search of exports: the states' new agenda. il *USA Today (Periodical)* 118:20-2 S '89

Renovating urban schools is fundamental to improving them. bibl f il *Phi Delta Kappan* 70:402-6 Ja '89

Thinking globally: educating Americans for the 21st century. il *USA Today (Periodical)* 118:29-31 N '89

PICCOLOMINI, MANFREDI
See Italy before it's too late. il *Art News* 88:190 N '89

PICHUL, VASILY
about
Little Vera [film] Reviews

America 161:116+ Ag 26-S 2 '89. R. A. Blake
The American Spectator 22:43 Je '89. B. Bawer
Film Comment il 25:23-4+ Ja/F '89. A. Williamson
Maclean's 102:54 Je 12 '89. B. D. Johnson
The Nation 248:675-6 My 15 '89. S. Klawans
The New Republic 200:30-1 My 1 '89. S. Kauffmann
New York il 22:61-2 Ap 17 '89. D. Denby
Newsweek il 113:71 Ap 17 '89. J. Kroll

PICK, CHUCK
about
When valet king Chuck Pick parks their wheels, Hollywood heavies count it a lucky brake. T. Allis. il pors *People Weekly* 31:116-17 Ap 24 '89

PICK UP COMPANY See David Gordon/Pick Up Company
PICKENS, T. BOONE, III See Pickens, Tom
PICKENS, T. BOONE, JR.
about
A back burner for T. Boone stake. *U.S. News & World Report* 107:16 Jl 10 '89

Beware the gaijin raider. *Newsweek* 113:48 Ap 17 '89

Boone Pickens, samurai warrior. M. Ivey. il por *Business Week* p90+ My 8 '89

Kamikaze capitalism. M. Lewis. *The New Republic* 200:19-20 My 1 '89

Look what restructuring can do. M. Magnet. por *Fortune* 120:72-3 Jl 3 '89

T. Boone for governor? T. Vogel. il por *Business Week* p43 F 27 '89

T. Boone's declaration of yen-dependence. M. Tharp. il por *U.S. News & World Report* 106:51 My 1 '89

T. Boone's Tokyo campaign. K. Makihara. il por *Time* 134:45 Jl 10 '89

A Texas raider rocks Club Japan. *U.S. News & World Report* 106:15 Ap 17 '89

PICKENS, TOM
about
The Japanese connection. R. Phalon. il pors *Forbes* 143:172+ Ap 3 '89

PICKENS, WILLIAM H.
California perspectives: three viewpoints. bibl il *Change* 21:42-51 S/O '89

PICKFAIR (BEVERLY HILLS, CALIF.: HISTORIC HOUSE)
Pia's Pickfair [house of P. Zadora and M. Riklis] L. Arbus. il pors *Life* 12:59-61 Spr '89

PICKLES AND RELISHES
Pickles and relishes with flair. il *Southern Living* 24:100-1 Ag '89

Pickling pointers [pickled fish] S. Bashline. il *Field & Stream* 93:82 Mr '89

PICKPOCKETS See Stealing
PICKS, GUITAR See Guitar picks
PICKUP CAMPERS See Campers, Truck
PICKUP TRUCKS See Trucks
PICKUP TRUCKS, RESTORED See Trucks, Restored
PICNIC TABLES See Tables
PICNICS
See also
Clambakes

All-Idaho picnic. il *Sunset (Central West edition)* 182:146+ Je '89

Cold soup to football cookies . . . before-the-game picnic [tailgating] il *Sunset (Central West edition)* 183:164-6 O '89

Dejeuners sur l'herbe. N. Hazelton. il *National Review* 41:51-2 S 1 '89

Great American picnics. M. Ungerer. il *Harper's Bazaar* 122:120+ Jl '89

Let them eat brie! Bastille Day picnic. il *Seventeen* 48:106-9 Jl '89

Out of doors, in comfort. N. Hazelton. il *National Review* 41:66-7 S 29 '89

Picnic totables. il *Better Homes and Gardens* 67:130-1+ Jl '89

A picnic under the apple tree. il *Gourmet* 49:126-8+ O '89

Picnics past. M. E. Kirby. il *Gourmet* 49:94+ Je '89

Un pique-nique sur mer [cover story] il *Gourmet* 49:64-6+ Jl '89

Some other picnics. M. F. K. Fisher. il por *Architectural Digest* 46:34+ Jl '89

Star-spangled summer picnic. il *Redbook* 173:101-5+ Jl '89

Take-it-anywhere spring feast. il *Sunset (Central West edition)* 182:124-5 My '89

The ubiquitous picnic. G. Hovis. il *House & Garden* 161:54+ Je '89

PICTURE BOARDS See Dummy board figures
PICTURE BOOKS
Bibliography
10 best photo books of 1989. il *Petersen's Photographic Magazine* 18:74-7 D '89

Coffeetable books: a passion for pictures. il *The New York Times Book Review* 94:44-5 D 3 '89

Deck the shelves. P. S. Prescott. il *Newsweek* 114:82-4+ D 11 '89

Pages of pleasure [holiday gifts] il *Maclean's* 102:60-2 D 18 '89

Season's readings: gifts to delight and instruct. J. H. Dobrzynski. il *Business Week* p160 D 18 '89

Tidings of color and joy [Christmas gifts] il *Time* 134:88-9 D 18 '89

PICTURE BOOKS FOR CHILDREN
See also
Computer picture books for children

Children's books: coming home to print? J. P. Frank. il *Publishers Weekly* 235:199-200+ F 24 '89
Authorship
Picture books from A to Z. J. Giblin. *The Writer* 102:18-21 N '89
Awards
The year's best illustrated books [N Y times book review choices] il *The New York Times Book Review* 94:30-1 N 12 '89
Bibliography
10 best new picturebooks for kids. C. Weston. il *Redbook* 174:32+ D '89

PICTURE ENLARGERS, TELEVISION See Television projection
PICTURE FRAMES AND FRAMING
And here we are at Yellowstone [frameless frames] P. Patton. il *Esquire* 111:52 Je '89

Presentation masters [Original Woodcraft frames] K. Geller-Shinn. il *Petersen's Photographic Magazine* 18:44 O '89

Saving graces. K. Oberrecht. il *Popular Mechanics* 166:73-4 F '89
Collectors and collecting
American picture frames of the arts and crafts period, 1870-1920. S. Smeaton. bibl f il *Antiques* 136:1124-37 N '89

The Carrig-Rohane frame. B. Barol. il *American Heritage* 40:30-1 D '89

PICTURE POSTCARDS See Postcards
PICTURE PROCESSING See Image processing
PICTURE WRITING
See also
Mayas—Writing

PICTUREPHONES See Videophones
PICTURES
See also
Illustration
Photographs
Framing
See Picture frames and framing
Hanging
Hang-ups: creating eye-pleasing picture groupings. il *Better Homes and Gardens* 67:80 S '89

Posters as art. il *Southern Living* 24:78 Ag '89
Trimming, mounting, etc.
Matting for greater impact (I). E. V. Cohen. il *American Artist* 53:102-4 S '89

Saving graces. K. Oberrecht. il *Popular Mechanics* 166:73-4 F '89

PIDDINGTON, KENNETH
Sovereignty and the environment. il *Environment* 31:18-20+ S '89

Who bears the burden of sustainability? il *New Perspectives Quarterly* 6:8-11 Spr '89

PIE
See also
Pot pies

Bring on the pies! il *Redbook* 174:108-11+ N '89

Country kitchen [blueberry custard and Amish sugar-cream pie] M. Adams. il por *McCall's* 116:104 Ag '89

Down East blues [blueberry pie] L. Land. il *Life* 12:41-2 S '89

PIE—cont.

The great American pie expedition [small town restaurants]
S. Hubbell. *The New Yorker* 65:75-6+ Mr 27 '89

Key West's key lime pie. V. Gladstone. il *Americana* 16:36-8+
Ja/F '89

Prizewinning pies. il *Good Housekeeping* 209:186+ O '89

Quick! A pie for dessert. il *Southern Living* 24:162 O '89

Savory pies. J. Nash. il *Essence* 20:95-6+ S '89

Serve a slice of summer [pies and cobblers] D. A. Campbell.
il *Southern Living* 24:80-1 Je '89

Anecdotes, facetiae, satire, etc.

Flour children. B. Shacochis. il *Gentlemen's Quarterly* 59:262+
Ag '89

PIE, SAUSAGE *See* Cooking—Sausage

PIEDMONT AVIATION, INC.

Final integration of Piedmont into USAir completed smoothly.
Aviation Week & Space Technology 131:58 Ag 14 '89

A promising flight plan—if no raiders show [USAir-Piedmont
deal] S. Payne. il *Business Week* p81-2 Ag 14 '89

USAir prepares to complete acquisition of Piedmont. J. Ott.
il *Aviation Week & Space Technology* 131:94-5 Jl 17 '89

PIEPER, RUDOLF *See* Rudolf

PIER TABLES *See* Tables

**PIERANGELO (MONTECATINI TERME, ITALY:
RESTAURANT)** *See* Montecatini Terme (Italy)—
Restaurants, nightclubs, bars, etc.

PIERARD, RICHARD V., 1934-

Lausanne II: reshaping world evangelicalism. *The Christian
Century* 106:740-2 Ag 16-23 '89

Wanted: consensus on abortion. por *Christianity Today* 33:8
O 6 '89

PIERCE, BARBARA HANSON

Ghosts of kitchens past. il *Gourmet* 49:144+ N '89

PIERCE, DEBORAH

In Aroostook [poem] *Commonweal* 116:348 Je 2 '89

PIERCE, DUSTIN

about

A Kentucky boy's wild cry for help. W. Plummer. il pors
People Weekly 32:44-7 O 9 '89

PIERCE, GREGORY F.

Preachers need to spend a day on the job [with readers'
comments] *U.S. Catholic* 54:14-19 D '89

PIERCE, LEE

about

Black family wins $22 million in Illinois lottery. il pors
Jet 76:24-6 Jl 31 '89

PIERCE, PONCHITTA

The prime time of her life. il pors *Ladies' Home Journal*
106:42+ O '89

PIERCE, SAMUEL R., JR.

about

The housing hustle. N. Traver. il por *Time* 133:18-19 Je
26 '89

The HUD scandal hits a stone wall. il por *U.S. News &
World Report* 107:11 O 9 '89

HUD under Reagan: 'close to obscene'. R. Thomas. il por
Newsweek 113:18 Je 12 '89

Moscow on the HUD [cover story] M. Hosenball. il *The
New Republic* 201:18-21 O 23 '89

Poking into HUD's swamp. L. Martz. il por *Newsweek* 113:19
Je 26 '89

Sam Pierce's "turkey farm" [with interview] N. Traver. il
pors *Time* 134:20-4+ S 18 '89

Sam plays it again. *The Nation* 249:405 O 16 '89

Sam stays silent. *National Review* 41:19-20 O 27 '89

Samuel Pierce, House panel clash over housing issue. il
por *Jet* 76:37 Je 19 '89

'Somebody is not telling the truth'. D. Harbrecht. il por
Business Week p21-2 Jl 24 '89

The undoing of Silent Sam Pierce. S. V. Roberts. il *U.S.
News & World Report* 107:29+ S 18 '89

PIERCING OF EARS *See* Ear piercing

PIERCY, MARGE

Bite into the onion [poem] *Organic Gardening* 36:78
Ja '89

Runt vigor [poem] il *Organic Gardening* 36:60 O '89

A writer's garden. il por *Organic Gardening* 36:72 Je '89

about

A turning of the critical tide? C. Iannone. *Commentary*
88:57-9 N '89

PIERPONT MORGAN LIBRARY

New chapter for Morgan Library [expansion] M. Alexander.
il *Art in America* 77:37 Je '89

PIERRARD, JEAN

Paris' new arch. il *World Press Review* 36:73 N '89

PIERRE (NEW YORK, N.Y.: HOTEL) *See* New York (N.Y.)—
Hotels, motels, etc.

PIERRE BELFOND EDITIONS *See* Editions Pierre Belfond

PIERREPONT, PEGGY

about

In the West Village: Peggy Pierrepont's New York apartment.
S. M. Alsop. il por *Architectural Digest* 46:152-7 F '89

PIERRET, JEAN-MARIE

about

That dammed Hercules. B. Weber. il *The New York Times
Magazine* p130 N 5 '89

PIERS *See* Docks, wharves, etc.

PIERSANTI, SILVIO

Monaco's royal family: who will inherit the throne? il *McCall's*
116:14-16+ Mr '89

PIERSON, FRANK

Fellini's magical '8½'. il por *American Film* 14:16-17 Je '89

PIES *See* Pie

PIETERBUREN SEAL SANCTUARY (NETHERLANDS)

Foster mother to Holland's seals [L. 't Hart] B. Krist. il
por map *International Wildlife* 19:20-4 Jl/Ag '89

PIETRANTONI, MICHAEL

Viruses that infect computers. il *USA Today (Periodical)*
117:64-6 Ja '89

PIETRASANTA (ITALY)

Monuments, statues, etc.

A sculptor's heaven on earth is Italy's city of holy stone.
I. Shenker. il *Smithsonian* 19:106-12+ F '89

PIEZOELECTRIC EQUIPMENT

See also

Surface acoustic wave devices

Fantastic plastic [Kynar; cover story] I. Amato. il *Science
News* 136:328-9 N 18 '89

Kynar and gentler streets [traffic-sensing devices] I. Amato.
Science News 135:79 F 4 '89

PIGEON RIVER (N.C. AND TENN.)

Fight for Pigeon River [conflict between Champion International Corp. in Canton, N.C. and Tennessee environmentalists over pollution control] M. Satchell. il map *U.S.
News & World Report* 107:27-8+ D 4 '89

PIGEON SHOOTING

See also

Mourning dove shooting

PIGEONS

See also

Passenger pigeons

Birdmen of Harlem [raising pigeons on tenement roofs] J.
W. Miller. il *The New York Times Magazine* p48-9+ N
19 '89

Show me the way you go home [homing pigeons] C. Walcott.
Natural History p40+ N '89

PIGFORD, ARETHA BUTLER

An administrator training program for minorities. *Phi Delta
Kappan* 70:650-1 Ap '89

PIGG, R. MORGAN

Needs and concerns for school health education. *The
Education Digest* 54:33-7 My '89

PIGGY BANKS *See* Banks, Coin

PIGLIA, PAOLA

The Christmas box [story] il *Life* 12:144-5 D '89

PIGMENTS (BIOLOGY)

See also

Bilirubin

Carotene

Carotenoids

Cytochromes

Phytochrome

Visual pigments

The photosynthetic reaction center from the purple bacterium
Rhodopseudomonas viridis. J. Deisenhofer and H. Michel.
bibl f il *Science* 245:1463-73 S 29 '89

PIGS *See* Swine

PIGS, WILD *See* Wild boars

PIGWEED *See* Purslane

PIKE, DAG

Shipwrecked. il *Motor Boating & Sailing* 164:54-7+ Jl '89

PIKE, JOHN

Qaddafi goes ballistic. *The New Republic* 200:14-16 Mr 20
'89

PIKE

The pike of New York. E. Stegemann. il *The Conservationist*
44:26-33 N/D '89

PIKE FISHING

Manitoba's new pike and walleye hotspot. K. Schultz. il
Field & Stream 93:56+ Mr '89

PIKES PEAK AUTO HILL CLIMB *See* Automobile racing

PIKUL, JOSEPH

about

Justice, at last. S. Weller. *Ms.* 17:75 Je '89

PILAF *See* Cooking—Rice

PILATE, PONTIUS, 1ST CENT.

about

Alliances. P. J. Ryan. il *America* 160:231 Mr 11 '89

PILATUS AIRCRAFT

A Swiss to watch. N. Moll. il *Flying* 116:80-4 N '89

Switzerland's Pilatus unveils PC-12 aircraft at NBAA convention. D. A. Brown. il *Aviation Week & Space Technology*
131:31 O 2 '89

PILCHER, EDITH, 1928-

A winter day in the life of a 19th century farmstead. il
The Conservationist 43:34-9 Ja/F '89

PILCHER, ROSAMUNDE, 1924-

Emotion in fiction. il *The Writer* 102:9-11 S '89

The skates [story] il *Ladies' Home Journal* 106:68+
D '89

PILE, JOHN F.

The language of wood. il *American Craft* 49:56-63 Ag/S
'89

PILGRIM, DIANNE H., 1941-
about
Around the Mall and beyond. E. Park. il *Smithsonian* 20:24-6+ O '89
Pilgrim's progress. K. Pryor. il por *Art News* 88:87-8 Ap '89

PILGRIM FATHERS
See also
Plimoth Plantation, Inc.

PILGRIM PRIME RATE TRUST
A fund that lets you smile as the prime rate soars. L. Zinn. *Business Week* p154 Ap 24 '89

PILGRIMAGES TO MECCA
Annual Moslem pilgrimage to Mecca spurs surge in Malaysia Airline traffic. il *Aviation Week & Space Technology* 131:63 O 30 '89
Inside Mecca. R. Favret. il *Mother Jones* 14:16+ Jl/Ag '89
Pilgrims and politics at Mecca. il *U.S. News & World Report* 107:14 Jl 24 '89

Health aspects
The well-being of pilgrims. J. Aashi. il map *World Health* p4-7 Jl '89

PILGRIMS AND PILGRIMAGES
See also
Pilgrimages to Mecca

PILL (CONTRACEPTIVE)
The absolutely, positively last word on the pill (for now). C. Marks. il *Mademoiselle* 95:170+ D '89
Birth-control pills and breast cancer. A. B. Eagan. il *Ms.* 17:41 Ap '89
Does the pill cause breast cancer? il *Consumer Reports* 54:498-9+ Ag '89
Keys to women's fulfillment. il *USA Today (Periodical)* 117:11 Ja '89
New perils of the pill? [link to breast cancer] A. Toufexis. il *Time* 133:73 Ja 16 '89
Ovarian cysts [linked to oral contraceptives; research by James Caillouette] *Prevention (Emmaus, Pa.)* 41:16 Ja '89
The pill and breast cancer: what doctors say now. L. Holland. il *Good Housekeeping* 208:245-6 My '89
A scare for pill users [breast cancer link] G. Cowley. il *Newsweek* 113:62 Ja 16 '89
Update on the pill. K. McCoy. il *Seventeen* 48:52+ O '89
Who should stop using the pill? [linked to breast cancer] G. Kolata. *Glamour* 87:250-1+ My '89

PILLAGE
The antiquities boom: who pays the price? [cover story] W. Grimes. il pors *The New York Times Magazine* p16-19+ Jl 16 '89
The plunder of the past [Native American artifacts] G. Cowley. il *Newsweek* 113:58-60 Je 26 '89
Potluck [pueblo ruins] D. J. Preston. il *Omni (New York, N.Y.)* 11:31+ Ja '89
Walking on ancestral gods [Mayan ruins damaged by modern Mayas in Yucatan] T. Padgett. il *Newsweek* 114:83 O 9 '89
Who owns our past? [pillage of Indian artifacts on Slack Farm excavation site, Ky.] H. Arden. il map *National Geographic* 175:376-93 Mr '89

PILLAI, THAKAZHI S.
Anger of the sea-goddess [fiction] il *The Courier (Unesco)* 42:37-8 F '89

PILLOW CASES
Sweet dreams. A. Foxley. il *House & Garden* 161:230 S '89

PILLOWS
The pillow chase. N. Hild and B. Livermore. il *Health (New York, N.Y.)* 21:70-1+ Jl '89

PILLS
Don't crush these pills! L. Holland. il *Good Housekeeping* 208:249 My '89

PILLSBURY, EDMUND P.
about
Portrait: Ted Pillsbury. B. Gill. il por *Architectural Digest* 46:72+ O '89

PILLSBURY, SARAH
about
Midge Sanford & Sarah Pillsbury [interview] il pors *American Film* 15:26-9 O '89

PILLSBURY CO.
Grand Met's recipe for Pillsbury. R. I. Kirkland, Jr. il *Fortune* 119:61+ Mr 13 '89

PILOBOLUS DANCE THEATRE
Carnal knowledge [New York City performances] T. Tobias. il *New York* 22:54-5 Ja 2 '89
Reviews:
Performances at the Joyce Theater, New York City. G. Solomons. *Dance Magazine* 63:90-2 Ap '89

PILOT EJECTION SEATS, CAPSULES, ETC. See Airplanes, Military—Escape devices

PILOT EXECUTIVE SOFTWARE (FIRM)
Next time, think big. D. Churbuck. il *Forbes* 143:155-6 Je 12 '89

PILOT FIELD (BUFFALO, N.Y.)
Field of dreams. P. M. Sachner. il *Architectural Record* 177:88-91 N '89

PILOT TRAINING See Aviation—Study and teaching

PILOTING OF AIRPLANES See Airplanes—Piloting; Airplanes, Business—Piloting; Airplanes, Light—Piloting; Airplanes, Training—Piloting; Seaplanes—Piloting

PILOTING OF HELICOPTERS See Helicopters—Piloting

PILOTS, AVIATION See Air pilots

PILOTS, HELICOPTER See Helicopter pilots

PILPEL, HARRIET F.
Combating censorship in the U.S. il *USA Today (Periodical)* 117:84-6 Ja '89

PILSON, NEAL H.
about
Pilson's progress. A. Snyder. il por *Channels (New York, N.Y.: 1986)* 9:58-62 Jl/Ag '89

PIMENTEL, DAVID, 1925-, AND OTHERS
Benefits and risks of genetic engineering in agriculture. bibl f il *BioScience* 39:606-14 O '89

PIN [film] See Motion picture reviews—Single works

PINACATE MOUNTAINS REGION (MEXICO)
The importance of being nothing. C. Bowden. il *National Parks* 63:26-31 S/O '89

PINCHING (PLANT PRUNING)
When and how to pinch. il *Sunset (Central West edition)* 182:238 My '89

PINCHOT, BRONSON
about
Bronson Pinchot's perfect strangeness. L. Morice. il pors *Mademoiselle* 95:78+ My '89

PINCHOT, GIFFORD, 1865-1946
about
Natural cycles. B. W. Walsh. il por *Wilderness* 53:16-17+ Wint '89

PINCKNEY, DARRYL
The last New Negro. il por *The New York Review of Books* 36:14-16 Mr 16 '89
Suitcase in Harlem. bibl f il *The New York Review of Books* 36:38-43 F 16 '89
Trickster tales. il *The New York Review of Books* 36:20+ O 12 '89

PINCUS, ROBERT L.
Sophie Calle: the prying eye. il *Art in America* 77:192-7 O '89

PINCUSHIONS
Light or heavy hearts . . . filled with sand or fragrance. il *Sunset (Central West edition)* 182:110 F '89

PINE, BARBARA
about
Works on paper by contemporary architects. P. Goldberger. il por *Architectural Digest* 46:198+ N '89

PINE, DEVERA
Big help for little ailments. il *Ladies' Home Journal* 106:112+ Ap '89

PINE, RACHAEL
Roe on the brink. *The Nation* 249:112 Jl 24-31 '89

PINE
Ozone needles loblolly pines . . . and saps sequoia seedlings. *Science News* 136:189 S 16 '89

PINE CONES
This tree won't drop a needle [pine cone tree] il *Southern Living* 24:53 D '89

PINE MOUNTAIN (GA.)
Description
Hunkered down on Pine Mountain. M. Bishop. il por *The Mother Earth News* 115:75-7 Ja/F '89

PINE NUTS
See also
Cooking—Nuts
Shaking gold from China's treetops [harvesting in Manchuria] T. B. Allen. il *International Wildlife* 19:34-6 Jl/Ag '89

PINEHURST (N.C.)
Hotels, motels, etc.
The Pinehurst tradition. J. Y. Bartlett. il *Travel Holiday* 172:50-7 N '89

PINELLAS COUNTY (FLA.)
Education
Business, home, and school: cooperating to develop lifelong readers. A. R. Bellack and C. K. Hallin. il *Phi Delta Kappan* 70:415 Ja '89

PINES, A.
(jt. auth) See Chmelka, B. F., and Pines, A.

PINES, BURTON YALE
The ten legacies of Ronald Reagan [address, October 1988] *Vital Speeches of the Day* 55:243-7 F 1 '89

PINES, DAVID, 1924-
Richard Feynman and condensed matter physics. bibl f il *Physics Today* 42:61-6 F '89

PINES See Pine

PINGER, CAROL
about
Gardens: Portland trailblazer. M. Rozek. il *Architectural Digest* 46:208-13 Mr '89

PINK, DANIEL
Law school lite. *The Washington Monthly* 21:20-3 N '89

PINK CADILLAC [film] See Motion picture reviews—Single works

PINK SHEET SECURITIES *See* Under-the-counter securities
PINKERTON, C. F.
A short walk in the garden [poem] *The New Republic*
200:43 Je 19 '89
PINKERTON, RONALD
You and the wind. il *Reader's Digest* 135:105-6 Jl '89
PINKNEY, JERRY, 1939-
about
Pinkney: illustrating the point. A. R. Davis. il por *American Visions* 4:46-9 Ap '89
PINKNEY, JUNETTE A.
Independent black publishing. bibl *American Visions* 4:50-4 Ap '89
PINNA, KATHRYN, AND RATTO, TRISHA
Sports nutrition '89: sugar's in, caffeine's out. il *American Health* 8:74+ Je '89
PINNACLE WEST CAPITAL CORPORATION
A bundle of bad deals has Pinnacle West reeling. R. Grover and T. Carson. il *Business Week* p34 Ja 30 '89
PINNIPEDIA
See also
Seals (Animals)
Walruses
All in the family [evidence for common pinniped ancestor; research by Andre Wyss] P. Shipman. il *Discover* 10:44 Jl '89
PINNIPEDIA, FOSSIL
Skeleton of the oldest known pinniped, Enaliarctos mealsi. A. Berta and others. bibl f il *Science* 244:60-2 Ap 7 '89
PINO, EUGENIA M. DEL
Marsupial frogs. il *Scientific American* 260:110-18 My '89
PINOCHET UGARTE, AUGUSTO
about
¡Adios, General! [cover story] M. Morrison. il *The American Spectator* 22:16-20 My '89
Adiós, General: saying good-bye to Pinochet. A. Dorfman. il *Harper's* 279:72-6 D '89
The Chilean plebiscite: defeat of a dictator. A. Valenzuela and P. Constable. bibl f *Current History* 88:129-32+ Mr '89
Chile's return to democracy. P. Constable and A. Valenzuela. *Foreign Affairs* 68:169-86 Wint '89/'90
Democracy on the slow track. P. Politzer. il *The Nation* 249:781-2+ D 25 '89
Fall of the patriarch. T. Rosenberg. il *The New Republic* 201:20-3 D 18 '89
Sixteen years under Pinochet. M. Montecino. il por *The Progressive* 53:34-7 D '89
A vote for change in Chile. J. Contreras. il por *Newsweek* 114:40 D 18 '89
PINOT NOIR WINES *See* Wine
PINS
Stuck on pins. il *'Teen* 33:26 Ja '89
PINSENT, GORDON, 1930-
about
Brass rubbings [drama] Reviews
Maclean's il 102:62 Ap 3 '89. J. Bemrose
PINSKER, SANFORD
Getting students to think. *Current (Washington, D.C.)* 318:18-21 D '89
Teaching in a litigious time. il *Change* 21:50-4 Jl/Ag '89
PINSKY, MARK A.
VDT radiation. *The Nation* 248:41 Ja 9-16 '89
PINSKY, ROBERT
Dreamer [poem] *The New Republic* 201:36 S 11 '89
Shirt [poem] *The New Yorker* 65:34 Je 5 '89
PINSON, C. WRIGHT
about
Transplant emergency! J. Fincher. il *Reader's Digest* 135:43-8 Jl '89
PINTA (SHIP)
Shipshape [replicas of the Niña, Pinta and Santa María] il por *Life* 12:26-30 Ap '89
PINTAURO, JOSEPH
about
Beside herself [drama] Reviews
Commonweal 116:643 N 17 '89. G. C. Weales
New York il 22:101 O 30 '89. J. Simon
The New Yorker 65:130-2 N 6 '89. M. Kramer
PINTER, HAROLD, 1930-
Mountain language [excerpt from drama] il *Harper's* 278:44-6 F '89
about
Mountain language [drama] Reviews
New York 22:128-9 N 20 '89. J. Simon
Visually speaking [interview] M. Ciment. il por *Film Comment* 25:20-2 My/Je '89
PINTO COELHO, DUARTE
about
Iberian weekends. R. Koenig. il pors *House & Garden* 161:142-53+ F '89
PINUP ART
The case of the vanishing pinup [B. Page in the 1950s] I. S. Levine. il pors *Rolling Stone* p167+ N 16 '89
Collectors and collecting
American pin-up, calendar and glamour art. C. Martignette. il por *Antiques & Collecting Hobbies* 94:44-5+ N '89

PIONEER AEROSPACE (FIRM)
Spacecraft recovery concept embodies parafoil, new reefing techniques [High Glide Recovery System] E. H. Kolcum. il *Aviation Week & Space Technology* 130:101-2 My 1 '89
PIONEER ELECTRONIC CORP.
Pioneer's pioneering is finally paying off. N. Gross. il *Business Week* p89 D 18 '89
PIONEER FLIGHTS *See* Space flight—Pioneer flights
PIONEER GROUP, INC.
More than mutual funds fuel this find [views of J. David Mills] G. G. Marcial. *Business Week* p88 F 13 '89
PIONEER HI-BRED INTERNATIONAL, INC.
Husked. C. Siler. il *Forbes* 144:10 N 27 '89
Seeds of a turnaround. il *Forbes* 143:144 Ja 9 '89
PIONEER LIFE *See* Frontier and pioneer life
PIOTROWSKI, JOHN L.
The geostrategy of space [address, November 17, 1988] *Vital Speeches of the Day* 55:162-4 Ja 1 '89
PIPELINE COMPANIES
See also
Coastal Corporation
Columbia Gas System, Inc.
Enron Corp.
Panhandle Eastern Corporation
Tenneco Inc.
Texas Eastern Corp.
Texas Oil & Gas Corp.
Transco Energy Co.
Valero Energy Corp.
Acquisitions and mergers
Coastal warning [rumor of takeover of Columbia Gas by Coastal Corp.] T. Jaffe. *Forbes* 144:140-1 Jl 10 '89
The lasso is tightening around Texas Eastern [Coastal's bid] M. Ivey. il por *Business Week* p30-1 Ja 30 '89
The man who strikes fear in the heart of the oil patch [O. Wyatt] M. Ivey. il por *Business Week* p120-1+ N 6 '89
Oscar Wyatt. M. Ivey. il por *Business Week* Special Issue:120 Ap 14 '89
Laws and regulations
Good-bye to take-or-pay [Transco Energy] T. Mack. il por *Forbes* 143:120+ Je 12 '89
Canada
See also
TransCanada PipeLines Limited
PIPELINES
See also
Gas pipelines
Petroleum pipelines
Water pipes
PIPER AIRCRAFT CORP.
Father knows best [Piper Training Center courses] N. Moll. il *Flying* 116:100 Ag '89
Piper may still be carrying excess baggage. G. DeGeorge. il por *Business Week* p76 Je 12 '89
Piper upgrades Commanche, Globe Swift for general aviation, military markets. E. H. Phillips. il *Aviation Week & Space Technology* 130:79+ My 22 '89
Piper's big-buck backlog. *Flying* 116:14+ Ja '89
Piper's Continental-powered Malibu is beached again [emergency airworthiness directive] il *Flying* 116:18 S '89
Piper's Malibu Mirage [cover story] J. M. McClellan. il *Flying* 116:32-6+ Ap '89
Piper's new Cadet. N. Moll. il *Flying* 116:42-6 Ja '89
Upgraded engine, systems increase Malibu reliability [Malibu Mirage; cover story] E. H. Phillips. il *Aviation Week & Space Technology* 130:36-9+ Mr 27 '89
PIPES, DANIEL, 1949-
The Ayatollah, the novelist, and the West [cover story] *Commentary* 87:9-17 Je '89
Is the West Bank a vital American interest? [cover story] *Commentary* 88:19-24 N '89
The Rushdie affair [discussion of June 1989 article, The Ayatollah, the novelist, and the West] *Commentary* 88:11-12+ O '89
Whodunit? il *The Atlantic* 263:18+ My '89
PIPES, DANIEL, 1949-, AND GARFINKLE, ADAM M., 1951-
Jordan/Palestine [discussion of October 1988 article, Is Jordan Palestine?] *Commentary* 87:2+ F '89
PIPES, RICHARD
Russia's shuddering empire. il *The New Republic* 201:52+ N 6 '89
PIPES
See also
Steam pipes
Water pipes
PIPES, TOBACCO *See* Tobacco pipes
PIPES LAKE (MISS.)
Pipes Lake, Mississippi. R. H. Mohlenbrock. il map *Natural History* p74-6 My '89
PIPHO, CHRIS
Stateline. See issues of Phi Delta Kappan

PIRACY See Pirates
PIRANDELLO, LUIGI, 1867-1936
about
Enrico IV [drama] Reviews
The Nation 248:246-7 F 20 '89. T. M. Disch
New York il 22:52 Ja 30 '89. J. Simon
The New Yorker 64:97 F 6 '89. E. Oliver
IL PIRATA [opera] See Bellini, Vincenzo, 1801-1835
PIRATEBUSH
Paint Rock, North Carolina. R. H. Mohlenbrock. il maps
Natural History p64-7 Ag '89
PIRATES
See also
Blackbeard, 1680?-1718
Of piracy and payoffs [ships diverted into Lebanese ports]
J. Penycate. World Press Review 36:53 My '89
PIRATING OF BOOKS See Copyright infringement
PIRATING OF COMPUTER SOFTWARE See Computer
programming—Unauthorized use
PIRATING OF PHONOGRAPH RECORDS See Phonograph
records—Unauthorized recording
PIRATING OF RADIO BROADCASTS See Radio broadcast-
ing—Unauthorized use
PIRIE, HIDEKO
about
The beat goes on. P. Nye. il por Women's Sports & Fitness
11:57 Jl/Ag '89
PISA (ITALY)
Historic houses, sites, etc.
See also
Leaning Tower of Pisa
PISATIN
One enzyme makes a fungal pathogen, but not a saprophyte,
virulent on a new host plant. W. Schäfer and others.
bibl f il Science 246:247-9 O 13 '89
PISGAH NATIONAL FOREST (N.C.)
Paint Rock, North Carolina. R. H. Mohlenbrock. il maps
Natural History p64-7 Ag '89
PISTACHIOS
See also
Cooking—Nuts
PISTOLS
See also
Revolvers
Electronic pistol. D. Scott. il Popular Science 234:70 My
'89
PISTONS
Productivity in the carburetors, pistons, and valves industry.
J. W. Ferris and V. L. Klarquist. bibl f il Monthly Labor
Review 112:43-6 F '89
PIT AND FISSURE SEALANTS (DENTAL MATERIALS)
See Dental materials
PIT BULL TERRIERS
Attacked by pit bulls! [Tuskegee, Ala. mayor J. Ford] A.
Rankin. il Reader's Digest 135:105-10 S '89
PITCAIRN, FEODOR
Underseascapes. il Audubon 91:48-55 Mr '89
PITCAIRN ISLAND
Trouble in Christian's paradise. H. Shapiro. il por map
People Weekly 31:42-9 Ap 17 '89
PITCAIRN ISLAND POSTAGE STAMPS See Postage stamps
PITCH, MUSICAL See Musical pitch
PITCH TRIM (JET AIRPLANES) See Airplanes, Jet—Stability
and stabilizers
PITCHERS (BASEBALL PLAYERS) See Baseball players
PITCHERS (POTTERY, GLASS, ETC.)
See also
Toby jugs
PITCHING (BASEBALL)
See also
Strikeouts (Baseball)
Are their days numbered? [using BFS statistics to predict
pitchers' longevity; research by Craig Wright] A. Kim.
il Sports Illustrated 70:46-8+ My 22 '89
By any name, it's hard to hit [splitfingered fastball] P.
Gammons. il Sports Illustrated 71:38 O 23 '89
Calling a game [O. Hershiser pitching in Game 2 of 1988
World Series]; ed. by Peter Gammons. M. Scioscia. il
Sports Illustrated 70 Special Issue:34-9 Ap '89
Gripping saga [P. Ojeda regains pitching grip] B. Weber.
il pors The New York Times Magazine p98 F 19 '89
Move over, ERA [opponent runners average considered more
reliable pitching yardstick than earned run average] T.
Singer. il Sport (New York, N.Y.) 80:14 My '89
Oh-and-two: when the count goes to two strikes, the pitcher-
hitter battle really gets interesting. D. Knobler. il Sport
(New York, N.Y.) 80:98-100+ Je '89
The staff of a lifetime [N.Y. Mets pitchers] H. Hewes. il
Sport (New York, N.Y.) 80:44-5+ Je '89
Tommy Lasorda's "Sermon on the mound" [condensed from
Out of the blue]; ed. by Jerry B. Jenkins. O. Hershiser.
il por Reader's Digest 135:63-5 S '89
A victim of careless gardening, Bob Ojeda is back in the
ball game with the finger he nearly cut off [interview]
M. Huzinec. il pors People Weekly 31:107-8+ Mr 27 '89

Accidents and injuries
See Baseball, Professional—Accidents and injuries
Records
See Baseball records
PITINO, RICK
about
The bluegrass isn't so blue. C. Kirkpatrick. il pors Sports
Illustrated 71:54-6+ D 11 '89
The power of the press [cover story] J. McCallum. il por
Sports Illustrated 70:22-6 F 13 '89
PITRE, LOUISE
about
Doubling up on a dream. G. Hayden. por Maclean's 102:43
Mr 27 '89
PITT, DEBORAH BARTLETT
Out back in Australia. il por House & Garden 161:126-31+
Ja '89
PITTAWAY, JAMES
A benign Brotherhood? il The Atlantic 263:25-7+ Ja '89
PITTMAN, BOB
Bob Pittman: on creating all-music MTV and all-mouth
Morton Downey Jr. por People Weekly 31 Special
Issue:152-3 Summ '89
about
The cool, dark telegenius of Robert Pittman. R. Powers.
il pors Gentlemen's Quarterly 59:324-7+ Mr '89
Fast forward. D. Kazanjian. il pors House & Garden
161:76-83+ F '89
PITTMAN, FRANK S. (FRANK SMITH), 1935-
Secrets of staying together [condensed from Private lies]
il Reader's Digest 134:151-4 Mr '89
PITTMAN, SANDY HILL
about
Fast forward. D. Kazanjian. il pors House & Garden
161:76-83+ F '89
PITTS, DAVID
To be young, British and black. il Black Enterprise 20:86-8+
D '89
PITTS, LEWIS
about
Love takes you a long way. W. H. Willimon. The Christian
Century 106:460-1 My 3 '89
PITTS, OTIS
about
Building on rock, not sand. il por Time 133:22 Ja 9 '89
PITTS, WILLIAM
about
UFO update. V. Cooper. il Omni (New York, N.Y.) 11:81
Mr '89
PITTSBURGH (PA.)
Airports
Pittsburgh expanding capacity with midfield terminal project.
C. Fotos. Aviation Week & Space Technology 130:329+
Je 12 '89
Crime
Security manager for Guy dead following dispute with New
Edition's crew member [murder of A. Bee] il Jet 76:18
Jl 24 '89
Tour rivalry ends in murder: death follows fight between
New Edition and Guy. M. Goldberg. Rolling Stone p28
Ag 24 '89
Description
Pittsburgh cleans up its act. V. Rause. il The New York
Times Magazine p44-7+ N 26 '89
Education
Paddle tales [whitewater rafting trip for Pittsburgh, Pa. physical
education students] il National Geographic World 164:23-7
Ap '89
Recruiting minority teachers. L. B. Nicklos and W. S. Brown.
The Education Digest 55:28-31 D '89
Sink or swim in the mainstream [placement of hearing-
impaired students R. and J. Visco] P. A. Zirkel. bibl
f il Phi Delta Kappan 70:411-13 Ja '89
Stores
See also
Golden Calf (Firm)
PITTSBURGH BALLET THEATRE
Pittsburgh Ballet Theatre forges ahead: the future is now
[cover story] E. Kline. il Dance Magazine 63:37-42 O
'89
Reviews:
Performances in Pittsburgh. K. Dacko. il Dance Magazine
63:25 Mr '89
PITTSBURGH CONFERENCE ON ANALYTICAL
CHEMISTRY AND APPLIED SPECTROSCOPY See
Chemistry—Conferences
PITTSTON COMPANY
A bitter deadlock [strike] W. Lowther. il Maclean's 102:72
N 20 '89
Christians and the coalfield conflict [Episcopalian involvement
in strike] L. Johnson. The Christian Century 106:868-9
O 4 '89
Coal country's war with itself [strike] R. A. Taylor. il U.S.
News & World Report 107:45 Jl 24 '89
Coal wars again [UMW strike] J. Motavalli. il The Progressive
53:24-7 Jl '89
John L., you'd be amazed [nonviolent tactics used in coal
miners' strike] J. Birnbaum. il Time 133:38 My 15 '89

PITTSTON COMPANY—*cont.*
'The Mine Workers must win this fight to survive' [strike] J. P. Hoerr. il *Business Week* p144+ O 9 '89
Miscalculated risk? [strike] R. Phalon. il por *Forbes* 143:41-2 Je 12 '89
Pittston power [United Mine Workers' takeover of the Moss 3 plant] P. Kwik. *The Nation* 249:409 O 16 '89
Solidarity in Appalachia [strike against Pittston Co.] D. Giardina. il *The Nation* 249:12-14 Jl 3 '89
Their miners and ours (I) [contrasting Soviet and Pittston strikes] A. Cockburn. *The Nation* 249:195 Ag 21-28 '89
Their miners and ours (II) [poll indicating more people know about the Soviet coal miners strike than the Pittston strike] A. Cockburn. *The Nation* 249:410-11 O 16 '89
Twilight for the UMW? [strike] M. Schroeder. il *Business Week* p32 Jl 3 '89
PITUITARY BODY
Folliculo-stellate cells of the pituitary gland. E. K. Perryman. bibl f il *BioScience* 39:81-8 F '89
Identification of a thyroid hormone receptor that is pituitary-specific. R. A. Hodin and others. bibl f il *Science* 244:76-9 Ap 7 '89
PITUITARY CELLS *See* Cells
PITUITARY HORMONE RELEASING FACTORS
See also
   Gonadotropin releasing hormone
Pediatric peptide spurs growth hormone [research by Arthur Felix] I. Amato and J. Raloff. *Science News* 135:252 Ap 22 '89
PITUITARY HORMONES
High-resolution epitope mapping of hGH-receptor interactions by alanine-scanning mutagenesis. B. C. Cunningham and J. A. Wells. bibl f il *Science* 244:1081-5 Je 2 '89
Purification of growth hormone-specific transcription factor GHF-1 containing homeobox. J.-L. Castrillo and others. bibl f il *Science* 243:814-17 F 10 '89
Pygmy paradox prompts a short answer [shortage of growth hormone receptors] K. Fackelmann. *Science News* 136:22 Jl 8 '89
Pygmy puzzle [defective growth hormone receptor; research by Gerhard Baumann] il *Discover* 10:14 D '89
Receptor and antibody epitopes in human growth hormone identified by homolog-scanning mutagenesis. B. C. Cunningham and others. bibl f il *Science* 243:1330-6 Mr 10 '89
Short-answer question [defective growth hormone receptor in pygmies; research by Gerhard Baumann] J. Benditt. *Scientific American* 261:32-3 S '89
PITUITARY HORMONES, SYNTHETIC
Bill Eftink [EEC hormone ban on U.S. beef imports] B. Eftink. il *Successful Farming* 87:19 mid-Mr '89
Europe bans boeuf's à l'estradiol. E. Marshall. *Science* 243:161-2 Ja 13 '89
A food fight as big as the Atlantic [EEC threatens ban on U.S. meat] *Newsweek* 113:41 Ja 9 '89
A furious battle over milk [furor over use of bovine somatotropin to increase milk production] D. Wyss. il *Time* 133:77 My 29 '89
Is the beef flap a taste of trade wars to come? [U.S. vs. European Community] F. J. Comes and P. Magnusson. il *Business Week* p47 Ja 16 '89
Just say moo [backlash against use of bovine growth hormone] W. P. Norton. il *The Progressive* 53:26-9 N '89
Market sours on milk hormone [bovine somatotropin] M. Sun. il *Science* 246:876-7 N 17 '89
Milking Bossy for all she's worth [bovine somatotropin] il *FDA Consumer* 23:23 Ap '89
PST-treated hogs need lysine—lots of lysine [porcine somatotropin] il *Successful Farming* 87:50 F '89
What's the beef? [European Community's ban on imports of beef injected with growth hormones] W. E. Sheeline. il *Fortune* 119:8 Ja 30 '89
Why the beef over hormones? [European Community bans import of U.S. meat from animals treated with hormones] J. Castro. il *Time* 133:44 Ja 16 '89
PITY *See* Sympathy
PITZRICK, VIVIAN MILLS
about
Nesting instincts. R. E. Bonney. il *National Wildlife* 27:28 Ap/My '89
PIVA, PAOLO
about
Zest for living. C. Petkanas. il pors *Harper's Bazaar* 122:80-1+ Ja '89
PIVAR, STUART
about
Flesh and spirit. M. E. Haus. il por *Art News* 88:75-6+ Ja '89
THE PIXIE LED [drama] *See* Harris, Christopher
PIXIES (MUSICAL GROUP)
Pixies cast their spell. D. Fricke. il *Rolling Stone* p20 Je 15 '89
The Pixies, who mock their cute name and cast their winning spell with lean, mean rock. il *People Weekly* 32:87+ O 2 '89
PIZZA, MARIGRAZIA, AND OTHERS
Mutants of pertussis toxin suitable for vaccine development. bibl f il *Science* 246:497-500 O 27 '89

PIZZA
Crispy crust pizza. il *Good Housekeeping* 209:38 Jl '89
A different pizza [vegetable pizza] il *Southern Living* 24:209 Mr '89
Easy skillet pizza. il *Redbook* 173:20 S '89
The pizza connection. R. Sokolov. il *Natural History* p102-5 F '89
Pizza for vegetable lovers. il *Southern Living* 24:178 S '89
Pizza pizzazz. C. Lyons. il *Ebony* 44:60-2+ O '89
Pizza with barbecue sauce? [barbecue chicken pie] il *Sunset (Central West edition)* 182:128 F '89
Pizzas with pizzazz. il *McCall's* 116:136 Mr '89
Pizza—the real American pie. il *Glamour* 87:292-5 Mr '89
Speedy microwave pizza starts with a flour tortilla. il *Sunset (Central West edition)* 182:194 Ap '89
PIZZA RESTAURANTS
See also
   California Pizza Kitchen
   Domino's Pizza Inc.
   Saucy's Pizza Franchises Inc.
Two Big Macs, large fries—and a pepperoni pizza, please [McDonald's experiments with pizza sales] B. Bremner. il *Business Week* p33 Ag 7 '89
You deserve a pizza today? [McDonald's] J. Schwartz. il *Newsweek* 114:46 S 11 '89
PIZZA RESTAURANTS IN MOTION PICTURES
A hot movie means a bigger piece of the American pie for a Greek immigrant who owns the real Mystic Pizza [S. Zelepos] D. Chun. il pors *People Weekly* 31:98+ Ja 9 '89
PIZZARELLI, BUCKY, 1926-
about
Bucky Pizzarelli. M. Bourne. il por *Down Beat* 56:47-8 O '89
PK *See* Psychokinesis
PLAATJES, MARK
about
A pilgrim's progress. J. Brant. il pors *Runner's World* 24:66-71 D '89
PLACE, CHUCK
Color gels. il *Petersen's Photographic Magazine* 17:64-7 Ap '89
PLACE DES ANTIQUAIRES (NEW YORK, N.Y.)
Place des Antiquaires. D. P. Marshall. il *Travel Holiday* 171:72-4 Je '89
PLACE NAMES *See* Names, Geographical
PLACEBOS
Placebo effect: the power of suggestion. G. Gregory. il *Current Health 2* 15:23-5 Ap '89
PLACEK, DAVID
In search of a name. il *High Technology Business* 9:10 My '89
PLACENTA
See also
   Maternally acquired immunity
PLACES OF RETIREMENT *See* Retirement, Places of
PLACHER, WILLIAM C. (WILLIAM CARL), 1948-
Hans Frei and the meaning of biblical narrative [cover story] *The Christian Century* 106:556-9 My 24-31 '89
about
An unapologetic middle ground. P. Nelson. *The Christian Century* 106:882-4 O 4 '89
PLAGEMANN, BENTZ, 1913-
The wedding [story] il *Good Housekeeping* 209:172-3 N '89
PLAGENS, PETER, 1941-
German exchange. il *Art in America* 77:42-5+ Ap '89
Under Western eyes. bibl f il *Art in America* 77:32-7+ Ja '89
PLAGIARISM
Back with the wind [M. Mitchell's heirs sue European authors for plagiarizing Gone with the wind] il por *Time* 134:51 O 9 '89
Did the penalty fit the crime? [S. Frazier accused of plagiarism] M. M. Hunt. il por *The New York Times Magazine* p36-7+ My 14 '89
Fogerty wins unusual self-plagiarism suit. M. Goldberg. il por *Rolling Stone* p15 Ja 12 '89
New round in Dingell v. NIH? [case of C. D. Bridges] J. Palca. *Science* 245:349 Jl 28 '89
NIH sees plagiarism in vision paper [case of C. D. Bridges] B. J. Culliton. *Science* 245:120-2 Jl 14 '89
PLAIN, BELVA
What love really means. *Reader's Digest* 134:62-4 F '89
PLAINS
See also
   Great Plains
PLAINSBORO (N.J.)
Stores
Suburban village [Princeton Forrestal Village] G. Anderson. il *Architectural Record* 177:104-5 S '89
PLAMS (PRICE LEVEL ADJUSTED MORTGAGES) *See* Mortgages
PLANCK'S CONSTANT
Can we scale the Planck scale? D. J. Gross. il por *Physics Today* 42:9+ Je '89

PLANERS See Planes and planing

PLANES AND PLANING

See also

Shapers (Machinery)

Joinery and shaping. R. Capotosto. il *Popular Mechanics* 166:81-2+ N '89

Using hand planes with success. B. Kinghorn. il *The Family Handyman* 39:14-16 My '89

Collectors and collecting

Plowing along [antique wooden planes] il *Workbench* 45:88 Ja/F '89

Finishes and finishing

Restoring old wooden planes. M. Varese. il *Workbench* 45:10 Ja/F '89

PLANETARIUMS

See also

Adler Planetarium

Museums and planetariums. *Sky and Telescope* 78 Resource Guide:2-6 S '89

There's no place like dome. C. C. Petersen. il *Sky and Telescope* 78:255-6+ S '89

China

See also

Beijing Planetarium

North America

1989 directory of observatories, planetariums, and museums. il *Astronomy* 17:50-7 My '89

PLANETARY NEBULAE See Nebulae

PLANETARY POLES

Which way is north? Ask right-handed astronomers [controversial International Astronomical Union standard] R. A. Kerr. *Science* 246:999 N 24 '89

PLANETARY SYSTEMS See Solar system

PLANETARY WAVES See Atmospheric waves

PLANETESIMAL HYPOTHESIS

Birth of the moon [cover story] W. K. Hartmann. il *Natural History* p68-77 N '89

Iron planet [theory that Mercury was formed due to impacts with other planets] R. Kunzig. il *Discover* 10:66-9 F '89

Making the moon, remaking earth [giant impact theory] R. A. Kerr. il *Science* 243:1433-5 Mr 17 '89

Piecing together earth's early history. W. K. Hartmann. il *Astronomy* 17:24-34 Je '89

PLANETS

See also

Earth

Jupiter (Planet)

Life on other planets

Mars (Planet)

Mercury (Planet)

Neptune (Planet)

Occultations

Planetesimal hypothesis

Pluto (Planet)

Satellites

Saturn (Planet)

Solar system

Uranus (Planet)

Venus (Planet)

A 1989 planet preview. A. MacRobert. il *Sky and Telescope* 77:66-7 Ja '89

A cosmic unveiling [T Tauri stars and planet formation; research by Karen M. Strom] C. S. Powell. *Scientific American* 261:26-7 D '89

How to observe planets during the day [polar alignment] J. H. Palmer. il *Astronomy* 17:86-7 Mr '89

Outer planets. T. D. Nicholson. il *Natural History* p72-3 S '89

Stalking the extrasolar planet. S. P. Maran. *Natural History* p70+ My '89

The sun, moon, and planets this month. A. MacRobert. See issues of Sky and Telescope beginning April 1988

Twilight stars. T. D. Nicholson. il *Natural History* p74-5 Jl '89

Alignment

See Conjunctions (Astronomy)

Atmosphere

Arsenic in the gas giants [research by Keith S. Noll] *Sky and Telescope* 78:133 Ag '89

Interview: Verner Suomi. P. Bagne. por *Omni (New York, N.Y.)* 11:60-4+ Jl '89

Origin and evolution of outer solar system atmospheres. J. I. Lunine. bibl f il *Science* 245:141-7 Jl 14 '89

Conferences

A passion for the little things among the planets [annual meeting of the Division of Planetary Science of the American Astronomical Society; special section] *Science* 246:998-9 N 24 '89

Planetary scientists focus on impact geology [Lunar and Planetary Science Conference] *Astronomy* 17:14+ Ag '89

Conjunctions

See Conjunctions (Astronomy)

Exploration

See also

Space flight—Mariner Mark II missions

Space flight to Jupiter

Space flight to Mars

Space flight to Saturn

Space flight to Venus

Beyond Washington boundaries. L. David. il *Ad Astra* 1:31-5 Ap '89

Bon Voyager. S. Fritz. il *Omni (New York, N.Y.)* 12:67-71 N '89

The greatest show off earth [viewing images of the planets at the Jet Propulsion Laboratory] F. Pohl. il *Omni (New York, N.Y.)* 12:14+ N '89

Latest Soviet planetary mission plans reflect shift to conservative outlook. M. A. Dornheim. *Aviation Week & Space Technology* 131:21-2 Ag 28 '89

A new Soviet plan for exploring the planets. M. M. Waldrop. il *Science* 246:211-12 O 13 '89

Scoping the solar system. P. Jones. il *Ad Astra* 1:14-18 Mr '89

The struggle for the outer planets [failed Grand Tour mission] C. B. Waff. il *Astronomy* 17:44-52 S '89

There's more to come. il *Newsweek* 114:55 S 4 '89

U.S. planetary launch surge [cover story; special section; with editorial comment] il *Aviation Week & Space Technology* 131:19, 44-5+ O 9 '89

The unknown solar system. I. Asimov. il *Discover* 10:38-43 O '89

Magnetic properties

The planets' magnetic environments. L. J. Lanzerotti and C. Uberoi. il *Sky and Telescope* 77:149-52 F '89

Magnitudes

Planet brightnesses. G. Lovi. il *Sky and Telescope* 77:629-30 Je '89

Orbits

Does chaos permeate the solar system? R. A. Kerr. il *Science* 244:144-5 Ap 14 '89

Where is Planet X? M. Littmann. il *Sky and Telescope* 78:596-9 D '89

PLANETS, MINOR See Asteroids

PLANKTON

See also

Coccolithophores

Phytoplankton

Prochlorophytes

Water bloom

Ozone hole peril to Antarctic life [research by John Frederick] il *USA Today (Periodical)* 117:6 Je '89

Ozone hole threatens polar plankton [research by Sayed El-Sayed] *Science News* 136:284 O 28 '89

Pacific plankton outdo land pollution [research by Joseph M. Prospero and Dennis L. Savoie] R. Monastersky. *Science News* 136:7 Jl 1 '89

PLANKTON, FOSSIL

Plankton chronicles icy rerun [Younger Dryas cooling] *Science News* 135:335 My 27 '89

Plankton to petroleum [origin of oil and gas] W. W. Dickinson. il *Earth Science* 41:21-3 Wint '88

PLANNED PARENTHOOD FEDERATION OF AMERICA

Anne Archer. B. Allen. il por *Ms.* 17:76-8 Ja/F '89

Calm, cool and beleaguered [F. Wattleton; cover story] M. Szegedy-Maszak. il pors *The New York Times Magazine* p16-19+ Ag 6 '89

'Cosby' kid releases safe sex campaign spots [M.-J. Warner] il por *Jet* 75:18 Mr 6 '89

Friend of the family [New York chapter president D. Gurieva] C. S. Smith. il por *New York* 22:26 Ap 17 '89

Kenneth Edelin named chair of Planned Parenthood bd. por *Jet* 77:8 N 13 '89

Nothing less than perfect [F. Wattleton] R. Stengel. il por *Time* 134:82-4 D 11 '89

Planned Parenthood didn't plan on this: abortion foes are attacking the agency's corporate sponsors. B. Tierney. il *Business Week* p34 Jl 3 '89

PLANNING, AGRICULTURAL See Farm management

PLANNING, BUSINESS See Business planning

PLANNING, CITY See City planning

PLANNING, ECONOMIC See Economic policy

PLANNING, EDUCATIONAL See Educational planning

PLANNING, LAND See Land utilization

PLANNING, PRODUCT See Product planning

PLANNING, REGIONAL See Regional planning

PLANNING, SOCIAL See Social policy

PLANS (ARCHITECTURE) See Architecture—Designs and plans; Architecture, Domestic—Designs and plans

PLANT, DAVID F.

Fax Mate [cover story] il *Radio-Electronics* 60:33-6 O '89

PLANT, MIKE

about

Alone against the sea, American sailor Mike Plant braces for a dangerous race around the world. H. Shapiro. il pors *People Weekly* 32:54-6 N 27 '89

PLANT BOXES See Flower boxes, planters, etc.

PLANT CELL MEMBRANES See Membranes (Biology)

PLANT CELLS AND TISSUES

See also

Chloroplasts

Plasmodesmata

Diffusible factors essential for epidermal cell redifferentiation in Catharanthus roseus. B. A. Siegel and J. A. Verbeke. bibl f il *Science* 244:580-2 My 5 '89

PLANT CELLS AND TISSUES—cont.
Culture
See also
Clones (Botany)
PLANT CONSERVATION
See also
Forest conservation
Rare plants
How to get plants into the conservationists' ark. R. Lewin. il *Science* 244:32-3 Ap 7 '89
Plant rescue operation. J. C. Duran. *Flower and Garden* 33:30 Mr/Ap '89
PLANT EATING ANIMALS See Herbivores
PLANT ECOLOGY See Botany—Ecology
PLANT ENZYMES See Enzymes, Plant
PLANT EXPLORATION See Botanical exploration
PLANT FOODS See Plants—Nutrition
PLANT GENETICS
See also
Agracetus Inc.
Clones (Botany)
Germplasm resources—Plants
Mutation—Plants
Population genetics—Plants
Tree genetics
Anticancer tobacco? [transient gene expression system developed by Biosource Genetics] J. E. Rodgers. il *American Health* 8:16 S '89
Benefits and risks of genetic engineering in agriculture. D. Pimentel and others. bibl f il *BioScience* 39:606-14 O '89
The best banana bred [hybrid banana resistant to black sigatoka disease; work of P. Rowe] S. Brownlee. il *The Atlantic* 264:22+ S '89
The biological future of pest control [address, November 15, 1988] D. A. Miller. *Vital Speeches of the Day* 55:337-40 Mr 15 '89
Biotechnically improved seeds to be marketed. *High Technology Business* 9:34 N/D '89
Biotechnology and agriculture [address, November 3, 1989] R. McGuire. *Vital Speeches of the Day* 56:147-50 D 15 '89
Biotech's bust and bloom. R. Rodale. il *Organic Gardening* 36:31-2 Ja '89
Breaking biotech barriers in botany [work of W. J. Brill] L. Therrien. il por *Business Week* Special Issue:78 Je 16 '89
Budding plant genome projects. C. Strange. *BioScience* 39:760-2 D '89
Cancer-fighting tobacco plants? [transient gene expression system developed at Biosource Genetics Corp.] K. Fackelmann. *Science News* 135:238 Ap 15 '89
Ethylene gene control: research ripens [gene for ACC synthase cloned; work of Takahide Sato and Athanasios Theologis] *Science News* 136:188 S 16 '89
The fruits of summer testing. G. Vincent. il *Successful Farming* 87:50X-50Y Ja '89
Genetic design. C. Fenyvesi. il *Organic Gardening* 36:76-8+ Ja '89
Genetically engineering plants for crop improvement. C. S. Gasser and R. T. Fraley. bibl f il *Science* 244:1293-9 Je 16 '89
Genome projects are growing like weeds [National Science Foundation plans to map Arabidopsis] J. Palca. il *Science* 245:131 Jl 14 '89
Pesticidal plants face legal hurdle. I. Wickelgren. *Science News* 135:300 My 13 '89
Plant ion-pump gene cloned, sequenced [work of Michael R. Sussman] I. Wickelgren. *Science News* 135:135 Mr 4 '89
Please pass the genes [cover story] I. Wickelgren. il *Science News* 136:120-2+ Ag 19 '89
Regulated genes in transgenic plants. P. N. Benfey and N.-H. Chua. bibl f il *Science* 244:174-81 Ap 14 '89
Restriction fragment length polymorphisms associated with water use efficiency in tomato. B. Martin and others. bibl f il *Science* 243:1725-8 Mr 31 '89
The revolution will not be fertilized. R. Weiss. *Science News* 135:59 Ja 28 '89
RNA editing in plant mitochondria [Oenothera] R. Hiesel and others. bibl f il *Science* 246:1632-4 D 22 '89
Super weeds. R. Twombly. il *Technology Review* 92:15-16 Ag/S '89
Thank you, Jeremy Rifkin. M. Fritz. il *Forbes* 144:268-9 O 16 '89
Turning plants into antibody factories [work of Andrew Hiatt] *Science News* 136:334 N 18 '89
Visual detection of transposition of the maize element Activator (Ac) in tobacco seedlings. J. D. G. Jones and others. bibl f il *Science* 244:204-7 Ap 14 '89
Yeutter backs plan to map crop genes. M. Crawford. *Science* 243:1137 Mr 3 '89
PLANT HOLDERS See Flower boxes, planters, etc.
PLANT HUNTING See Botanical exploration
PLANT LABELS
Labels to keep track of your plants and planting. il *Sunset (Central West edition)* 182:168+ F '89

PLANT LICE See Aphids
PLANT LITTER DECOMPOSITION See Biodegradation
PLANT LORE
See also
Trees in religion, folklore, etc.
Christmas legends. J. Rapp. il *Redbook* 174:114-15+ D '89
Christmas plant legends. M. Brown. il *Flower and Garden* 33:47-9 N/D '89
PLANT MEMBRANES See Membranes (Biology)
PLANT MITOCHONDRIA See Mitochondria
PLANT NUTRITION See Plants—Nutrition
PLANT POPULATIONS
See also
Population genetics—Plants
PLANT PROPAGATION
See also
Clones (Botany)
Grafting
Seeds
Hardwood cuttings [roses] L. J. Rombough. il *Flower and Garden* 33:68-9 My/Je '89
House plant make-over: gaunt to chubby [air-layering and repotting] il *Sunset (Central West edition)* 182:130-1 Ja '89
Multiplying favorite perennials with stem cuttings. il *Sunset (Central West edition)* 182:250 My '89
Propagating scheffleras: which parts to use? il *Sunset (Central West edition)* 182:236 Je '89
Self-sowers. S. V. Thompson. il *Organic Gardening* 36:53-5 D '89
Taking hardwood cuttings. C. Shirley. il *Organic Gardening* 36:26-7 N '89
Time to divide Shastas. il *Southern Living* 24:70 Ap '89
PLANT PROTEINS
See also
Lectins
New genes for complete-protein beans [research by Samuel Sun] I. Wickelgren. *Science News* 135:300 My 13 '89
A protein that binds to a cis-acting element of wheat histone genes has a leucine zipper motif. T. Tabata and others. bibl f il *Science* 245:965-7 S 1 '89
PLANT RESEARCH See Agricultural research; Botanical research; Horticultural research
PLANT ROOTS See Roots
PLANT SUCCESSION
Forest succession. S. Curtis. il *Field & Stream* 93:30 Ap '89
PLANT SUPPORTS
See also
Trellises
The English call them pea sticks. il *Sunset (Central West edition)* 182:173 F '89
High-rise plantings. S. Sides. il *The Mother Earth News* 118:84+ Jl/Ag '89
Staking options. il *Flower and Garden* 33:38 My/Je '89
"Telephone pole" system gets sprawly tomatoes off the ground. il *Sunset (Central West edition)* 182:232 Je '89
PLANT THERAPY See Gardens and gardening—Therapeutic use
PLANT TISSUES See Plant cells and tissues
PLANT VIRUSES See Viruses, Plant
PLANTAIN BANANAS
See also
Cooking—Fruit
PLANTAR FASCIITIS
Heal your sore heel. S. Lally. il *Prevention (Emmaus, Pa.)* 41:46-9+ Je '89
PLANTATIONS
Louisiana
See also
LSU Rural Life Museum and Burden Research Plantation
Coincoin: plantation owner before the nation was born. P. S. Prather. il *American Visions* 4:46-7 F '89
Mint julep memoirs. D. Darvishian. il *Travel Holiday* 171:14-18 Je '89
Spring in plantation country. il *Southern Living* 24:63 Ap '89
North Carolina
See also
Hope Plantation (Windsor, N.C.)
Somerset Place State Historic Site (Creswell, N.C.)
Ayr Mount on the Eno River, near Hillsborough, North Carolina. J. L. Sanders. bibl f il por *Antiques* 135:1190-201 My '89
Philippines
Land-grab in the Philippines [American corporations displace native farmers] B. Miller. il *The Progressive* 53:30-3 N '89
Virginia
See also
Shirley Plantation (Hopewell, Va.)
PLANTE, ELLEN M.
Ice cream collectibles. il *Antiques & Collecting Hobbies* 94:68-70 Ag '89
PLANTERS (FARM MACHINES)
The blue monster. C. Finck. il *Successful Farming* 87 no4:64L Mr '89

PLANTERS (FARM MACHINES)—*cont.*
Row-squeezing planters. D. Mowitz. il *Successful Farming* 87:20-1 Ap '89

Equipment
Beyond starter to full-feed planters. D. Mowitz. il *Successful Farming* 87:20-3 F '89
Iron to run on ridges. C. Finck and D. Mowitz. il *Successful Farming* 87:34H-34I mid-F '89
No-till a blanket of soybeans. R. Fee. il *Successful Farming* 87 no4:28-9 Mr '89
Residue repositioned. R. Fee. il *Successful Farming* 87:36-7 D '89
Triple-action spray caddy. M. Holmberg. il *Successful Farming* 87:48T N '89
Water wagons [planter tank caddies] D. Mowitz. il *Successful Farming* 87 no4:64AG Mr '89

PLANTERS (FLOWER BOXES) See Flower boxes, planters, etc.
PLANTING See Flower gardens and gardening; Gardens and gardening; Landscape gardening; Seeding; Vegetable gardens and gardening
PLANTING MACHINERY See Planters (Farm machines)
PLANTING OF TREES See Tree planting
PLANTS
    See also
    Angiosperms
    Annuals (Plants)
    Biomass energy
    Botany
    Bulbs
    Climbing plants
    Cryptogams
    Flowers
    Forage plants
    Forcing (Plants)
    Forest vegetation
    Ground cover plants
    Herbs
    Invasive plants
    Leaves
    Mutation—Plants
    Perennials (Plants)
    Poisonous plants
    Pollen
    Rare plants
    Roots
    Seeds
    Shrubs
    Urban flora
    Watering of plants
    Weeds
30 double-duty plants. A. C. Mallozzi. il *Good Housekeeping* 208:247 Je '89
Chi-chi plants. F. McGourty. il *Flower and Garden* 33:80 My/Je '89
[Month] in your garden. See issues of Sunset (Central West edition)
My favorite plant. See issues of Flower and Garden beginning January/February 1989
New plants '89. il *Flower and Garden* 33:45-9 Mr/Ap '89
Plant trek. B. Yinger. See issues of Flower and Garden beginning January/February 1989

All-America Selections
A big year in All-America Selections [flowers] il *Flower and Garden* 33:68+ Ja/F '89
No 1989 AAS vegetable awards. il *Country Journal* 16:15 Ja '89
Our picks for '89: the best new flowers and roses. D. A. Jimerson and J. A. McKeon. il *Better Homes and Gardens* 67:105-8 Ja '89

Breeding
    See also
    Germplasm resources—Plants
    Plant genetics

Classification
    See Botany—Classification
Disease and pest resistance
Deer don't help your garden. il *Southern Living* 24:67 My '89
Pesticidal plants face legal hurdle. I. Wickelgren. *Science News* 135:300 My 13 '89

Diseases and pests
    See also
    Anthracnose
    Aphids
    Chlorosis (Plants)
    Fungi, Pathogenic
    Viruses, Plant
Bugged by drought. B. Freese. il *Successful Farming* 87 no4:64AI Mr '89
Quarantine and the exchange of crop genetic resources. D. L. Plucknett and N. J. H. Smith. bibl f il *BioScience* 39:16-23 Ja '89
What's the diagnosis? W. S. Moore. See issues of Flower and Garden beginning February/March 1984

Evolution
Angiosperm diversification and paleolatitudinal gradients in Cretaceous floristic diversity. P. R. Crane and S. Lidgard. bibl f il *Science* 246:675-8 N 3 '89
Cellulose and the evolution of plant life [plant cell walls] L. C. Duchesne and D. W. Larson. bibl f il *BioScience* 39:238-41 Ap '89
Knotty evolutionary tree in plant world [Prochlorothrix] R. Monastersky. *Science News* 135:71 F 4 '89
A novel fossil seed roils botany theory [work of Jean L. Galtier] I. Wickelgren. *Science News* 136:86 Ag 5 '89

Export-import trade
    See also
    Convention on International Trade in Endangered Species of Wild Fauna and Flora (1973)
Fertilization
    See Fertilization of plants
Folklore
    See Plant lore
Genetics
    See Plant genetics
Hardiness
Gardener-at-large [hardiness of perennials] F. McGourty. il *Flower and Garden* 33:64 S/O '89
In pursuit of a hardy camellia [South Korea] B. Yinger. il map *Flower and Garden* 33:104-6 Mr/Ap '89
On site with hardy camellias: Sochong Island, Korea. B. Yinger. il *Flower and Garden* 33:62-6 My/Je '89
Plant hardiness zone map. il map *Flower and Garden* 33:28 Ja/F '89

Irritability and movements
    See also
    Geotropism

Mercury content
Pot peril [smokers of marijuana risk mercury poisoning; work of Barbara and Sanford Siegel] P. McCarthy. il *American Health* 8:16 D '89

Metabolism
Plant metabolic responses to iron-deficiency stress. J. C. Brown and V. D. Jolley. bibl f il *BioScience* 39:546-51 S '89

Nutrition
Vitamins for vegetables [use as plant foods] R. Williams, III. il por *The Mother Earth News* 117:38+ My/Je '89

Protection
    See also
    Mulching
    Scarecrows
Keeping your late spring crops from bolting [use of lattice shade] il *Sunset (Central West edition)* 182:224 Je '89
Winterize your yard. J. Hudak. il *Organic Gardening* 36:50-2 S '89

Protein content
    See Plant proteins
Reproduction
    See also
    Plants, Sex in
Resistance to disease and pests
    See Plants—Disease and pest resistance
Soilless culture
    See Hydroponics
Temperature
    See also
    Plants, Effect of temperature on
Blazing blossoms [thermogenic plants; cover story] R. Weiss. il *Science News* 135:392-4 Je 24 '89

Training
Standards of beauty [houseplants] J. Rapp. il *Redbook* 172:124-5+ Mr '89

Water requirements
    See also
    Xeriscaping
Can you grow tomatoes where water is short? Yes. il *Sunset (Central West edition)* 182:230 My '89
A little thirst can aid plant defenses [soybeans and Mexican bean beetle larvae; research by Edward F. Connor and Grant McQuate] J. Raloff. *Science News* 136:37 Jl 15 '89
Restriction fragment length polymorphisms associated with water use efficiency in tomato. B. Martin and others. bibl f il *Science* 243:1725-8 Mr 31 '89
PLANTS, ARTIFICIAL
Artificial nature: the synthetic landscape of the future [cover story] R. Vick. il por *The Futurist* 23:29-32 Jl/Ag '89
PLANTS, EDIBLE
    See also
    Cattails
    Flowers as food
    Greens, Edible
    Nettles
    Vegetables
Rabbit-food Rambos [edible plants in diet better for survivalists; research by Stephen Källman] P. McCarthy. il *American Health* 8:144-6 Ap '89
PLANTS, EFFECT OF AIR POLLUTION ON
Flora for the worst neighborhoods [Canada; research by Thomas C. Hutchinson] *BioScience* 39:675-6 N '89

PLANTS, EFFECT OF AIR POLLUTION ON—*cont.*
Greenery filters out indoor air pollution. J. Raloff. *Science News* 136:212 S 30 '89
Ill winds: air pollution's toll on trees and crops. J. J. MacKenzie and M. T. El-Ashry. il map *Technology Review* 92:64-71 Ap '89

PLANTS, EFFECT OF CARBON DIOXIDE ON
Carbon dioxide may spur plant predation. J. Raloff. *Science News* 136:143 Ag 26 '89
The effects of enriched carbon dioxide atmospheres on plant-insect herbivore interactions. E. D. Fajer and others. bibl f il *Science* 243:1198-200 Mr 3 '89
Not all plants will thrive in 'greenhouse' [research by Chantal D. Reid and Boyd R. Strain] J. Raloff. *Science News* 136:134 Ag 26 '89

PLANTS, EFFECT OF CLIMATE ON
Greenhouse effect? [viticulture] H. J. De Blij. *Focus (New York, N.Y.: 1950)* 39:37 Spr '89
Preparing for the greenhouse effect [agriculture] *USA Today (Periodical)* 117:15 Je '89

PLANTS, EFFECT OF DROUGHT ON
Bugged by drought. B. Freese. il *Successful Farming* 87 no4:64AI Mr '89
Mold on corn tough on dairies hit by drought. J. R. Borcherding. *Successful Farming* 87:54 F '89
Restore your lawn. B. Pleasant. il *Organic Gardening* 36:74-8 Ap '89
Some plants slept [Illinois drought] R. H. Mohlenbrock. il *Natural History* p58-60 Ja '89
A springtime drought with a silver lining [low wheat yield] L. W. Adkins. il *U.S. News & World Report* 106:48 My 15 '89
This is the year to scout for a scout. B. Freese. il *Successful Farming* 87:50AC Ja '89
Wintertime—and the farmers aren't easy. K. A. Behof. il *Business Week* p24-5 Mr 6 '89

PLANTS, EFFECT OF GRAVITY ON See Geotropism
PLANTS, EFFECT OF HERBICIDES ON See Herbicides
PLANTS, EFFECT OF LIGHT ON
See also
Artificial light gardening
Photoperiodism
Tomato tumors: red light means grow [research by Theodore W. Tibbitts] I. Wickelgren. il *Science News* 135:23 Ja 14 '89

PLANTS, EFFECT OF TEMPERATURE ON
See also
Plants—Hardiness
Surviving and thriving—plants and animals in winter. P. S. Busch. il *The Conservationist* 43:26-33 Ja/F '89
Wintertime—and the farmers aren't easy. K. A. Behof. il *Business Week* p24-5 Mr 6 '89

PLANTS, EFFECT OF ULTRAVIOLET RAYS ON
Ozone park [research by Alan Teramura] L. Vikhanski. il *Discover* 10:32 S '89

PLANTS, EFFECT OF WEIGHTLESSNESS ON
Garden of unearthly delight. H. Smith. il *Technology Review* 92:16 N/D '89

PLANTS, EXTINCT
See also
Mass extinction of species
PLANTS, FOSSIL See Paleobotany
PLANTS, GEOGRAPHICAL DISTRIBUTION OF See Biogeography
PLANTS, HANGING See Hanging plants
PLANTS, INDUSTRIAL See Factories
PLANTS, MEDICINAL See Botany, Medical
PLANTS, ORNAMENTAL
See also
Caladiums
Hanging plants
House plants
PLANTS, POTTED
See also
Flower boxes, planters, etc.
House plants
Soils, Potting
Watering of plants
Perennials in pots. il *Sunset (Central West edition)* 183:196 N '89
Repotting rootbound plants can save water and work. il *Sunset (Central West edition)* 183:146-7 Jl '89
PLANTS, SEX IN
Where the wild things grow [C. Linne's plant classification system] J. Bosveld. il *Omni (New York, N.Y.)* 11:56-61 Ap '89
PLANTS AND CIVILIZATION
See also
Ethnobotany
The accidental conqueror [importance of animal and plant domestication in the European colonization of the New World] J. M. Diamond. il *Discover* 10:70-6 D '89
PLANTS AS ENERGY SOURCES See Biomass energy
PLANTS AS GIFTS
Five-year-olds have a bulb-planting party. They make Christmas gifts. il *Sunset (Central West edition)* 183:156 D '89

PLANTS IN ART
See also
Leaves in art
Extracting art from nature [work of A. Dürer] J. Kastner. il *Natural History* p76+ S '89
PLANTS IN HOUSE DECORATION
White flowers for the holidays [lilies and spider mums] il *Southern Living* 24:60-1 D '89
PLANTS IN RELIGION, FOLKLORE, ETC. See Plant lore
PLANTZ, MARGARET C., AND OTHERS
Indian Child Welfare: a status report. il *Children Today* 18:24-9 Ja/F '89
PLAQUE, DENTAL See Dental plaque
PLAS, JEANNE M., AND HOOVER-DEMPSEY, KATHLEEN V.
Will you cry on the job? [excerpt from Working up a storm] il *Glamour* 87:286-7+ Mr '89
PLASKETT, THOMAS G., 1943-
about
The bottom line: he's a better manager. C. O'Malley. il por *Personal Computing* 13:79 Ap '89
Pan Am Corp. will sell World Services in attempt to give Plaskett more time. J. T. McKenna. il *Aviation Week & Space Technology* 130:68-9 Ja 23 '89
Pan Am needs a partner, but does anybody need Pan Am? C. Power. il por *Business Week* p92+ Ap 10 '89
PLASMA (IONIZED GASES)
See also
Cosmic jets
Plasma waves
Solar wind
Tokamaks
Cold traps for ion crystals, solid plasmas [research by David J. Wineland] I. Peterson. *Science News* 135:279 My 6 '89
Diagnosing the state of an unruly plasma [research by Yitzhak Maron on pulsed-power diodes] I. Peterson. *Science News* 136:247 O 14 '89
Hot plasma and energetic particles in Neptune's magnetosphere. S. M. Krimigis and others. bibl f il *Science* 246:1483-9 D 15 '89
Penned-in positrons [first antimatter plasma] F. Flam. *Science News* 135:154 Mr 11 '89
Plasma observations near Neptune: initial results from Voyager 2 [magnetosphere] J. W. Belcher and others. bibl f il *Science* 246:1478-83 D 15 '89
Plasma particle accelerators. J. M. Dawson. bibl il *Scientific American* 260:54-61 Mr '89
Plasma physics. bibl f *Physics Today* 42:S60-S63 Ja '89
PLASMA CONFINEMENT
See also
Magnetic fusion
Tokamaks
Toroidal plasma
PLASMA DISPLAY SYSTEMS
Plasma display globe. J. C. Caudill. il *Radio-Electronics* 60:62-4 Ja '89
PLASMA MEMBRANES See Membranes (Biology)
PLASMA WAVES
Catching a light ride on a plasma wave [photon accelerator; research by John M. Dawson and Scott C. Wilks] I. Peterson. *Science News* 135:358 Je 10 '89
First plasma wave observations at Neptune. D. A. Gurnett and others. bibl f il *Science* 246:1494-8 D 15 '89
Nonlinear mixing of electromagnetic waves in plasmas. V. Stefan and others. bibl f il *Science* 243:494-500 Ja 27 '89
PLASMIDS
See also
Transposons
PLASMINOGEN
Lipoprotein(a)'s role in heart attacks explored [research by Richard Lawn] J. L. Marx. *Science* 243:316 Ja 20 '89
PLASMINOGEN ACTIVATORS
See also
TPA (Drug)
Innovative approaches to plasminogen activator therapy. E. Haber and others. bibl f il *Science* 243:51-6 Ja 6 '89
PLASMODESMATA
Movement protein of tobacco mosaic virus modifies plasmodesmatal size exclusion limit. S. Wolf and others. bibl f il *Science* 246:377-9 O 20 '89
PLASMODIUM (PARASITE)
Amplification of a gene related to mammalian mdr genes in drug-resistant Plasmodium falciparum. C. M. Wilson and others. bibl f il *Science* 244:1184-6 Je 9 '89
Circumsporozoite protein heterogeneity in the human malaria parasite Plasmodium vivax. R. Rosenberg and others. bibl f il *Science* 245:973-6 S 1 '89
PLASTER AND PLASTERING
See also
Stucco
Getting plastered [work by Art In Construction] H. S. MacIsaac. il *House & Garden* 161:56 Ja '89
PLASTER BOARD See Wallboard
PLASTER CREEK (IND.)
Plaster Creek, Indiana [seep springs] R. H. Mohlenbrock. il maps *Natural History* p98-100 N '89

PLASTI-LINE, INC.
Will Plasti-Line's party go private? G. G. Marcial. *Business Week* p124 My 1 '89
PLASTIC BONDS *See* Certificates of credit card receivables
PLASTIC EXPLOSIVES
Bombers' choice. G. Slutsker. il *Forbes* 143:121 F 20 '89
British, Czechs push for tighter controls on plastic explosives [proposal at International Civil Aviation Organization assembly] D. Hughes. *Aviation Week & Space Technology* 131:26 S 25 '89
Did it blow up Flight 103? [bomb possibly made from black market C-4 plastic explosive] D. Corn. il *The Nation* 248:153-4 F 6 '89
Easier detection of plastic explosives urged by Security Council. *UN Chronicle* 26:19 S '89
The technology of terror [terrorists' bombs] W. J. Cook. il *U.S. News & World Report* 106:24 Mr 6 '89
PLASTIC FLOORING *See* Flooring, Plastic
PLASTIC HOUSES
Foam-core panels. J. A. Hufnagel. il *Better Homes and Gardens* 67:90+ Mr '89
PLASTIC PRODUCTS INDUSTRY *See* Plastics industry
PLASTIC SURGEONS *See* Surgeons
PLASTIC SURGERY *See* Surgery, Plastic
PLASTIC TRASH BAGS *See* Trash bags
PLASTICITY (PHYSIOLOGY) *See* Adaptation (Biology)
PLASTICS
See also
Conductive polymers
Laminated plastics
Polypropylene
Thermoplastics
Japan's RS plastics [rapid solidification] H. Okada. *High Technology Business* 9:30 My '89
Making plastics visible to X-rays [use of additive triphenyl bismuth] I. Amato and J. Raloff. *Science News* 135:252 Ap 22 '89
Collectors and collecting
Antiques and collectibles: classic plastics! W. C. Ketchum. il *Better Homes and Gardens* 67:129 Ag '89
Degradability
Additive may curb litter [LitterLess plastic film] il *USA Today (Periodical)* 117:4 Je '89
A bag battle pits Big Oil vs. Big Ag [Archer-Daniels-Midland Co.'s biodegradable trash bags threaten conventional bag manufacturers] P. Sherrid. il *U.S. News & World Report* 106:52 Ap 24 '89
Biodegradable plastics fit a changing world. R. Fee. il *Successful Farming* 87:17-19 O '89
Degradable plastics. M. Morse. il *Utne Reader* p10-11 My/Je '89
Helping plastics waste away. J. Raloff. il *Science News* 135:282-3 My 6 '89
Making plastics that biodegrade. A. Gibbons. il *Technology Review* 92:69-73 F/Mr '89
Missouri's capital using trash bags made from corn. il *Successful Farming* 87:30 Ja '89
Obstacles slow degradable uses for cornstarch. *Successful Farming* 87:48N mid-Mr '89
The plastics problem. T. Waters. il *Discover* 10:22-3 F '89
Talking trash. P. Klebnikov and G. Burks. il *Forbes* 143:10 Je 12 '89
Recycling
A Mac attack on plastic wrapping [McDonald's restaurants to recycle food containers] il *U.S. News & World Report* 107:15 N 6 '89
Persistent peril [dealing with plastics pollution] P. Wittig. il map *Organic Gardening* 36:66-72 F '89
The plastics problem. T. Waters. il *Discover* 10:22-3 F '89
Second life for styrofoam. B. Rudolph. il *Time* 133:84 My 22 '89
Trashing a $150 billion business. S. P. Sherman. il *Fortune* 120:90-1+ Ag 28 '89
A word of advice, Benjamin: stay out of plastics. R. Mitchell. il *Business Week* p23 Ap 17 '89
PLASTICS IN AUTOMOBILES *See* Automobiles—Materials
PLASTICS IN MEDICINE *See* Polymers in medicine
PLASTICS IN PACKAGING
Can Reynolds wrap up the kitchen market? M. Schroeder. il *Business Week* p68+ My 29 '89
Unpopular packaging [Canadians protest chlorofluorocarbons] M. Nichols. *Maclean's* 102:51 D 25 '89
Laws and regulations
A word of advice, Benjamin: stay out of plastics. R. Mitchell. il *Business Week* p23 Ap 17 '89
PLASTICS IN VANS *See* Vans—Materials
PLASTICS INDUSTRY
See also
Envirodyne Industries, Inc.
Himont Inc.
Phillips Petroleum Company
Plasti-Line, Inc.
Finance
A bag battle pits Big Oil vs. Big Ag [Archer-Daniels-Midland Co.'s biodegradable trash bags threaten conventional bag manufacturers] P. Sherrid. il *U.S. News & World Report* 106:52 Ap 24 '89

Taiwan
See also
China General Plastics Corp.
Formosa Plastics Corp.
PLASTICS POLLUTION
American myopia. E. Kunes. *Omni (New York, N.Y.)* 11:33 Mr '89
At the beaches this summer, the dirty word is plastics. M. Satchell. *U.S. News & World Report* 107:30 Jl 17 '89
Eliminating plastics. L. Lamb. *Utne Reader* p30 N/D '89
Persistent peril. P. Wittig. il map *Organic Gardening* 36:66-72 F '89
Sea of trouble. K. Brower. il *Omni (New York, N.Y.)* 11:20+ Ap '89
Trashing a $150 billion business. S. P. Sherman. il *Fortune* 120:90-1+ Ag 28 '89
PLATE, ANDREA DARVI
Attention, kids: Sesame Street wants you . . . if you've got the right stuff. il *TV Guide* 37:16-18 Jl 15-21 '89
PLATE
See also
Silverware
PLATE HOLDERS
Dining room duo. B. Kieffer. il *The Family Handyman* 39:66-8+ S '89
PLATE TECTONICS *See* Geology
PLATEAUS, CAREER *See* Career plateaus
PLATELET ACTIVATING FACTOR *See* Blood—Coagulation
PLATELET AGGREGATION *See* Blood cell aggregation
PLATELET-DERIVED GROWTH FACTOR
Interleukin-1 mitogenic activity of fibroblasts and smooth muscle cells is due to PDGF-AA. E. W. Raines and others. bibl f il *Science* 243:393-6 Ja 20 '89
Isolation of a novel receptor cDNA establishes the existence of two PDGF receptor genes. T. Matsui and others. bibl f il *Science* 243:800-4 F 10 '89
Role of phosphatidylinositol kinase in PDGF receptor signal transduction. S. R. Coughlin and others. bibl f il *Science* 243:1191-4 Mr 3 '89
Signal transduction by the platelet-derived growth factor receptor. L. T. Williams. bibl f il *Science* 243:1564-70 Mr 24 '89
Transformation by v-sis occurs by an internal autoactivation mechanism. B. E. Bejcek and others. bibl f il *Science* 245:1496-9 S 29 '89
Vascular permeability factor, an endothelial cell mitogen related to PDGF. P. J. Keck and others. bibl f il *Science* 246:1309-12 D 8 '89
PLATFORMS
See also
Telescopic seating platforms
PLATH, SYLVIA
about
'The dark forces of lust': Plath at Cambridge [excerpt from *Bitter fame*] A. Stevenson. il pors *The New York Times Book Review* 94:1+ Ag 13 '89
Frieda Hughes escapes the shadow of mom Sylvia Plath. F. Hauptfuhrer. il pors *People Weekly* 32:99+ D 4 '89
A poet and her myths. A. Alvarez. il por *The New York Review of Books* 36:34-6 S 28 '89
Sylvia Plath: an exchange [discussion of September 28, 1989 article, A poet and her myths] A. Alvarez. *The New York Review of Books* 36:68 O 26 '89
PLATINUM
Atomic resolution imaging of adsorbates on metal surfaces in air: iodine adsorption on pt(111) [use of scanning tunneling microscope] B. C. Schardt and others. bibl f il *Science* 243:1050-3 F 24 '89
PLATINUM METALS
See also
Palladium
Rhenium-osmium and samarium-neodymium isotopic systematics of the Stillwater Complex. D. D. Lambert and others. bibl f il *Science* 244:1169-74 Je 9 '89
PLATINUM MINES AND MINING
Montana
Digging a mile deep [Stillwater mine] L. J. Fisher. il map *Earth Science* 42:12-13 Spr '89
PLATINUM SILICIDE
Infrared detector technology [platinum silicide detectors; special section] il *Aviation Week & Space Technology* 130:51+ Mr 27 '89
PLATONOV, YURI
about
Gateway to a new detente. M. F. Schmertz. *Architectural Record* 177:9 Je '89
PLATT, ADAM
(ed) See Alsop, Joseph, 1910-1989. The WASP ascendancy
PLATT, HARTY
Spa splurge. il *Seventeen* 48:92-8 Ja '89
PLATTE RIVER (NEB.)
The Platte pretzel [proposed water projects; with editorial comment by Peter A. A. Berle] S. Winckler. il map *Audubon* 91:8, 86-102+ My '89
The Platte River [special issue; with editorial comment by Les Line] il *Audubon* 91:6, 39-102+ My '89

PLATTE RIVER (NEB.)—*cont.*
Where will the cranes go? [Two Forks dam planned by Denver may threaten sandhill crane habitat] J. Adler. il map *Newsweek* 113:62-3 Ap 3 '89

PLAY
See also
Games
Playgrounds
Toys
Child's play. J. Segal and Z. Segal. il *Parents* 64:126 Ja '89
It's playtime [three and four year-olds] L. G. Katz. il *Parents* 64:160 Jl '89
Play's the thing [one year olds] K. Karlsrud and D. Schultz. il *Parents* 64:138 Ag '89
Rough-and-tumble play. S. Nurss. il *Parents* 64:243-4+ N '89

PLAY GROUPS
And the babies had fun, too. L. Ferriss. il *The New York Times Magazine* p16+ My 21 '89

PLAY PRODUCTION AND DIRECTION *See* Theater— Production and direction

PLAYAS
See also
Willcox Playa (Ariz.)
Playa lakes: prairie wetlands of the Southern High Plains. E. G. Bolen and others. bibl f il map *BioScience* 39:615-23 O '89

PLAYBOY (PERIODICAL)
Growing pains's Julie McCullough tries to bury her bare-all past [former cover girl] J. Kaufman. il pors *People Weekly* 32:57+ O 30 '89
It's a good nudes, bad nudes game. A. Meisler. il *TV Guide* 37:16-18 Ag 26-S 1 '89

PLAYER PIANO
The player piano makes a comeback. G. Slutsker. il por *Forbes* 144:124 S 4 '89

PLAYERS CLUB INTERNATIONAL INC.
This casino club is on a roll. G. G. Marcial. *Business Week* p94 O 2 '89

PLAYGROUNDS
Equipment
See also
Swings
Safety devices and measures
Making playgrounds safer. J. Clayton. il *Essence* 20:97 Je '89

PLAYGROUPS *See* Play groups

PLAYHOUSES
See also
Tree houses

PLAYMATES *See* Friendship

PLAYS *See* Drama

PLAYS, FILMED *See* Motion picture adaptations

PLAYTEN, ALICE
Alice Playten: on becoming famous for saying "Poached oysters!". il por *People Weekly* 31 Special Issue:125 Summ '89

PLAYWRITING *See* Drama—Technique

PLAZA ATHÉNÉE (PARIS, FRANCE: HOTEL) *See* Paris (France)—Hotels, motels, etc.

PLAZA HOTEL (NEW YORK, N.Y.)
The Plaza suite. C. Vogel. il por *The New York Times Magazine* p50-2+ Ja 15 '89

PLEAS (LEGAL PROCEDURE)
See also
Insanity defense

PLEASANT, BARBARA
Tending the orchard floor. il *Country Journal* 16:40-3 Mr/Ap '89

PLEASURE
See also
Comfort
Fun
Happiness
Healthy pleasures [excerpt; with editorial comment by Joel Gurin] R. E. Ornstein and D. S. Sobel. il *American Health* 8:53-8+, 116 My '89
No pleasure for lawyers [New York State rules against hedonic damages] *Newsweek* 113:48 Mr 6 '89
The pleasure principle [lawyers sue for hedonic damages] T. Jacoby. *Newsweek* 113:61 F 27 '89
The pleasure principle [views of Robert Ornstein and David Sobel] S. Thompson. il *Health (New York, N.Y.)* 21:28-9 Ag '89
Sex and other pleasures [cover story; special section] G. B. Leonard. il *Esquire* 111:129-32+ My '89
What is life worth? [hedonic damages] H. Smith. il *Christianity Today* 33:14-15 Mr 3 '89

PLEDGE OF ALLEGIANCE
The Pledge of Allegiance in public schools. C. Seefeldt. *The Education Digest* 55:62-3 S '89

PLEIADES
Crescent moon nicks the Pleiades. D. W. Dunham. il *Sky and Telescope* 77:405-6 Ap '89
Waning crescent moon in the Pleiades. D. W. Dunham. il *Sky and Telescope* 78:64-5 Jl '89

PLEISTOCENE PERIOD *See* Paleoclimatology—Pleistocene; Paleontology—Pleistocene

PLESSEY CO. PLC
British-French bid to buy GEC fails after AT&T refuses to join. *Aviation Week & Space Technology* 130:30 Ja 23 '89
British Monopolies panel approves GEC/Siemens offer for Plessey. *Aviation Week & Space Technology* 130:39 My 1 '89
Electronics firms maneuver to gain from GEC, Plessey takeover bids. D. A. Brown. *Aviation Week & Space Technology* 130:25+ Ja 16 '89
For Plessey, a gutsy offense may be its best defense [bid for predator GEC] M. Maremont. *Business Week* p52+ Ja 23 '89
GEC, Siemens renew their bid to buy Plessey. *Aviation Week & Space Technology* 131:34 Ag 14 '89
GEC, Siemens win bid to take over Plessey. *Aviation Week & Space Technology* 131:31 S 18 '89
R & D work in low observables shifts emphasis from coatings to structures. il *Aviation Week & Space Technology* 131:109+ S 18 '89

PLIERS
Pliers. T. Klenck. il *Popular Mechanics* 166:71-4 S '89
Vise squad [locking pliers] P. McCafferty. il *Popular Science* 234:134-6 Je '89

PLIMOTH PLANTATION, INC.
Details, details, details. P. Mandell. il map *Americana* 17:48-54 N/D '89

PLIMPTON, GEORGE
Across the river and into Harry's Bar [excerpt from The best of bad Hemingway] *The New York Times Book Review* 94:1+ Ap 16 '89
American thrills. il por maps *Popular Mechanics* 166:40-3+ My '89
The unlucky seven. il *Sports Illustrated* 71:28-9 S 18 '89
The wild blue yonder. il *Sports Illustrated* 70:64-6+ Ap 3 '89

about
Across the river and into Harry's Bar [excerpt from The best of bad Hemingway] G. Plimpton. *The New York Times Book Review* 94:1+ Ap 16 '89

PLIMPTON, MARTHA
about
For Martha Plimpton style means commitment. J. Sherman. il pors *Vogue* 179:38 Ja '89

PLIMSOLL, SAMUEL, 1824-1898
about
Drawing the line at safety. A. Thomas. il por map *History Today* 39:5-7 F '89

PLITVICE NATIONAL PARK (YUGOSLAVIA)
Yugoslavian discovery: lakes and waterfalls of Plitvice. il map *Sunset (Central West edition)* 182:64-5 Ap '89

PLO *See* Palestine Liberation Organization

THE PLOT AGAINST HARRY [film] *See* Motion picture reviews—Single works

PLOTKIN, MARK
about
Just another day in paradise. D. D. Jackson. il *Reader's Digest* 134:166-8+ Ap '89
Searching for medicinal wealth in Amazonia. D. D. Jackson. bibl (p171) il pors *Smithsonian* 19:94-103 F '89

PLOTKIN, STEVEN E.
The road to fuel efficiency in the passenger vehicle fleet. bibl f il *Environment* 31:18-20+ Jl/Ag '89

PLOTNICK, ROBERT D.
How much poverty is reduced by state income transfers? bibl f il *Monthly Labor Review* 112:21-6 Jl '89

PLOTS (DRAMA, NOVEL, ETC.)
See also
Television broadcasting—Plots, themes, etc.
Free-form plotting the mystery novel. M. Muller. *The Writer* 102:12-15 S '89
Plot and character in suspense fiction. J. Aiken. *The Writer* 102:9-13 My '89
What if . . . ? [mystery novel plots] W. G. Tapply. *The Writer* 102:17-19 Ja '89

PLOTTERS (COMPUTER PRINTERS)
Update: plotter redux [Mural 8000] S. Diehl. il *Byte* 14:235 D '89
What's new in color printers and plotters. P. Honan. il *Personal Computing* 13:107-11+ Ap '89

PLOTTING SYSTEMS (COMPUTER PRINTERS) *See* Plotters (Computer printers)

PLOWDEN, DAVID
The land in between [photographs] il *Americana* 16:39-43 Ja/F '89

PLOWING *See* Tillage

PLUCKNETT, DONALD L., 1931-, AND SMITH, NIGEL J. H., 1949-
Quarantine and the exchange of crop genetic resources. bibl f il *BioScience* 39:16-23 Ja '89

PLUGS, ELECTRIC *See* Electric wire and wiring

PLUHAR, ANNA M.
The need to forget. il *America* 160:134-7 F 18 '89

PLUM, SAMUEL

about

From the Mekong to Motown. M. Schifrin. il por *Forbes* 143:324+ My 29 '89

PLUM BROOK FIELD STATION

NASA reactivating facilities to support research efforts. S. W. Kandebo. il *Aviation Week & Space Technology* 130:93+ My 1 '89

PLUM CREEK TIMBER COMPANY, INC.

Railroaded [clearcutting by Plum Creek Timber Company spurred on by LBO fever] A. Porterfield. il *Common Cause Magazine* 15:21-3 S/O '89

PLUMAGE, COLOR OF *See* Color of birds

PLUMBING

See also
Boats and boating—Water supply
Sinks
Toilets
Water pipes

How to install a freeze-proof sillcock. M. Henkenius. il *Popular Mechanics* 166:87-8 S '89

Just add water [German designed faucets] P. Patton. il *Esquire* 111:21 Ja '89

New products: kitchen and bath. il *Architectural Record* 177:116-17+ mid-Ap '89

Unwanted plumbing [bathroom] il *Popular Mechanics* 166:109-11 Ap '89

Laws and regulations

Uncle Sam may regulate your plumbing. W. Giese. *Changing Times* 43:26-7 O '89

Maintenance and repair

Clogged plumbing? Here's what to do. K. Collier. il *The Family Handyman* 39:70-3 O '89

Help! My bathroom's flooded! D. Johnson. il *The Family Handyman* 39:24+ Ap '89

Leaky faucets. il *The Family Handyman* 39:72-4+ My '89

Single-handle faucet repair. M. Henkenius. il *Popular Mechanics* 166:90-1 Jl '89

Tub drain tuneup. M. Henkenius. il *Home Mechanix* 85:32+ O '89

PLUMBING CODES *See* Plumbing—Laws and regulations

PLUMBING INDUSTRY

See also
Kohler Co.
Roto-Rooter, Inc.

PLUMLY, STANLEY

Coming into LaGuardia late at night [poem] *The New Yorker* 64:30 Ja 23 '89

Four appaloosas [poem] *The New Yorker* 65:91 Jl 10 '89

PLUMMER, JOSEPH T.

Changing values: the new emphasis on self-actualization [cover story] il por *The Futurist* 23:8-13 Ja/F '89

PLUMS

See also
Cooking—Fruit

Hybrids

Apricot crossed with a plum? [apriums, pluots, and plumcots] il *Sunset (Central West edition)* 182:140 Ja '89

PLUMWOOD, VAL

about

Crocodile attack! H. Edwards. il *Reader's Digest* 135:70-5 O '89

PLUNDERING *See* Pillage

PLURALISM (RELIGION) *See* Religious pluralism

PLURALISM (SOCIAL SCIENCES)

The inventor of 'pluralism' [H. J. Laski] L. S. Feuer. por *The New Leader* 72:12-13 S 4 '89

PLUTO, TERRY, 1955-

Into the deep: at playoff time, an NBA team's bench warrants special attention. il *Sport (New York, N.Y.)* 80:54-6+ Je '89

PLUTO (PLANET)

Get ready for Pluto at its best. R. Talcott. il *Astronomy* 17:84-6 My '89

The poor man's grand tour of the solar system [Voyager's findings confirm resemblance between Neptune's moon Triton and Pluto] il *Science* 246:998 N 24 '89

Atmosphere

Pluto at perihelion: summertime atmosphere. il *Sky and Telescope* 78:346-7 O '89

Pluto's atmosphere: more than methane [research by Roger V. Yelle and Jonathan I. Lunine] J. Eberhart. *Science News* 135:326 My 27 '89

The seasons of Pluto. N. W. Stauffer. il *Technology Review* 92:9-10 Jl '89

Satellites

Discovery of Pluto's moon an accident? il *Astronomy* 17:14 Mr '89

Pluto at perihelion: mutual events continue [Charon] il *Sky and Telescope* 78:347 O '89

Pluto is red, Charon is gray [work of Richard Binzel] *Astronomy* 17:10+ Ja '89

Surface

Pluto at perihelion: mapping a mottled surface. il *Sky and Telescope* 78:347-8 O '89

The seasons of Pluto. N. W. Stauffer. il *Technology Review* 92:9-10 Jl '89

PLUTONIUM METALLURGY

Kyshtym visit gives first look at Soviet plutonium production complex. W. Sweet. il map *Physics Today* 42:87-9 N '89

Plutonium—no supply, no demand? W. J. Lanouette. il *The Bulletin of the Atomic Scientists* 45:42-5 D '89

Safeguards controversy, continued [discussion of December 1988 article, Plutonium for all: leaks in global safeguards] R. Bolt. il *The Bulletin of the Atomic Scientists* 45:38-40 Je '89

PLUTONIUM POLLUTION *See* Radioactive pollution

PLUTONIUM REACTORS *See* Nuclear reactors

PLUTONIUM RECYCLING *See* Reactor fuel reprocessing

PLY-GEM INDUSTRIES, INC.

Ply Gem Industries. A. Ramirez. il *Fortune* 120:76 Ag 14 '89

PLYMOUTH (ENGLAND)

Art

When Robert Lenkiewicz paints the town in Plymouth, England, some people see only red. R. Wolmuth. il pors *People Weekly* 31:108-11 Ja 23 '89

PLYMOUTH (MASS.)

Historic houses, sites, etc.

See also
Plimoth Plantation, Inc.

PLYMOUTH (VT.)

Hotels, motels, etc.

A friendly respite at Hawk Inn. C. Mac Connie. il *Travel Holiday* 171:100 Mr '89

PLYMOUTH DIVISION *See* Chrysler Corp. Chrysler-Plymouth Division

PLYOMETRICS

Energy explosion! il *Mademoiselle* 95:230-3 My '89

A new twist on aerobics. J. A. Werman. il *Working Woman* 14:108 Jl '89

PMS *See* Premenstrual syndrome

PNEUMATIC CONVEYING

Plumb around problems [pneumatic grain conveyors] D. Mowitz. il *Successful Farming* 87:42-3 D '89

PNEUMATIC EQUIPMENT

Air power gets the job done. D. Mowitz. il *Successful Farming* 87:22-3 mid-Mr '89

PNEUMATIC TOOLS

TFH tool report: air power. K. Collier. il *The Family Handyman* 39:84+ Ap '89

PNEUMONIA

See also
Q fever

An enigma named Gloria [woman with cytomegalovirus pneumonia] T. Dajer. il *Discover* 10:86-9 N '89

Here comes the flu—again [risk of pneumococcal pneumonia] il *USA Today (Periodical)* 118:10-11 O '89

Pneumonia: everything you must know. F. Snyder. *Ladies' Home Journal* 106:94+ Ja '89

Therapy

Controlling pneumonia in children [Western Pacific region] A. Shimouchi. il *World Health* p18-19 N '89

Help on the way [FDA approval of pentamidine] *Time* 133:65 F 13 '89

Wider use of pneumonia drug approved [pentamidine] il *FDA Consumer* 23:4 Ap '89

PO YI

about

Star-spangled style! il pors *'Teen* 33:64-8 Jl '89

POACHING

Africa is becoming an elephant graveyard. W. Booth. il *Science* 243:732 F 10 '89

A ban on ivory. M. Nichols. il *Maclean's* 102:86 O 30 '89

Big-game forensics [use of DNA fingerprinting to discourage elephant poaching] J. Horgan. il *Scientific American* 261:27+ D '89

Clamscam [B. Hodgson of Washington King Clam prosecuted for geoduck theft] F. Graham. *Audubon* 91:8+ N '89

Decision time on African ivory trade. J. Cherfas. il *Science* 246:26-7 O 6 '89

Deconstructivist rhinos [thwarting poachers by removing horns in Namibia] il *Discover* 10:12 O '89

Elephants in Alaska [handicrafts made from poached African ivory] F. Graham. *Audubon* 91:27-9 S '89

Elephants look best in ivory [ban on imports] L. Troiano. il *American Health* 8:92 O '89

Endangered species: can they be saved? [African elephants; cover story] W. F. Allman. il map *U.S. News & World Report* 107:52-8 O 2 '89

Fishy arguments [Seattle bottom fishermen blame Japanese poaching in Alaskan waters for lower prices] M. Beauchamp. il *Forbes* 143:130+ Mr 20 '89

Game agents foil a gross gros bec feast [night heron massacre in Louisiana] il *Audubon* 91:14 Ja '89

Global ban sought on ivory trade [to save elephants] R. Lewin. il *Science* 244:1135 Je 9 '89

The great bear aphrodisiac caper [animal parts mixed into nostrums] il *U.S. News & World Report* 106:14 F 6 '89

Gunning for bald eagles [Alaska Chilkat Bald Eagle Preserve] il *Newsweek* 113:33 F 27 '89

Heavy artillery for horns of plenty [Kenya's war on ivory poachers] E. Ransdell. il *U.S. News & World Report* 106:61+ F 20 '89

POACHING—cont.

Horns of a dilemma [rhino poaching in Zimbabwe] M. L. Knox. il *Sierra* 74:58-67 N/D '89

How to save the African elephant [economic incentives] M. S. Forbes, Jr. *Forbes* 144:29 N 13 '89

Hunting's most wanted. L. Williamson. il *Outdoor Life* 184:40+ Jl '89

In the African interior, the ivory trade and the slave trade helped each other become paying propositions. R. M. Adams. il *Smithsonian* 19:14 Mr '89

International tusk politics. *Science News* 136:94 Ag 5 '89

The ivory dispute [African countries in opposition to trade ban] F. Bridgland. *World Press Review* 36:69 S '89

Kenya burns $3 mil. in ivory to stop its trade. il *Jet* 76:18 Ag 7 '89

Last stand for Africa's elephants [ivory poaching] E. Linden. il *Time* 133:76-7 F 20 '89

The Louisiana story. G. Reiger. il *Field & Stream* 94:50-1+ O '89

Off with their heads [walrus heads traded for illicit drugs by Eskimos in Alaska] M. Beck. il *Newsweek* 113:78 Je 5 '89

Outlawing ivory [U.S. ban in order to save elephants] il *Time* 133:62 Je 19 '89

Pachyderm policy [elephant herds growing in African countries that permit ivory trading] D. Seligman. il *Fortune* 120:235+ N 20 '89

Poaching the pandas [China] L. Branson. *World Press Review* 36:53 Mr '89

The quiet kill [national parks] M. Milstein. il *National Parks* 63:18-25 My/Je '89

Reprieve for the giant of beasts [efforts to save the elephant] T. Gup. il *Time* 134:77 O 30 '89

The rhino's last stand [battle against poachers in Zimbabwe] A. Linklater. il *Reader's Digest* 134:106-10 F '89

Saving the African elephant. il *The Futurist* 23:49 S/O '89

Science gives ivory a sense of identity [DNA fingerprinting and isotope analyses] J. Cherfas. il *Science* 246:1120-1 D 1 '89

The shrinking roots of heaven [efforts to stop illegal poaching of elephants by restricting ivory trade] *U.S. News & World Report* 106:11-12 My 22 '89

Symbolic flames [proposed ban on ivory sales] A. Steacy. il *Maclean's* 102:37 Jl 31 '89

Threatened animals. D. Jenish. il *Maclean's* 102:44-5 Ag 7 '89

Trail of shame [elephants endangered by ivory poachers; cover story] T. Gup. il map *Time* 134:66-9+ O 16 '89

Tusk, tusk [Sotheby's removes elephant tusks from market to alleviate poaching] il *Time* 133:56 My 1 '89

A tussle over tusks [African nations debate ban on ivory trade] J. Bartholet. il *Newsweek* 114:25 Jl 24 '89

Up front [waterfowl sting operation in Texas] D. Barnes. il *Field & Stream* 93:7 Mr '89

POACHING (COOKING) See Cooking

POAGE, JANET

Wild Basin of Bee Creek. il map *Earth Science* 42:14-17 Spr '89

POBEREZNY, PAUL

about

Poberezny and son [interview] W. Garvey. il pors *Flying* 116:40-5 Ap '89

POBEREZNY, TOM

about

Poberezny and son [interview] W. Garvey. il pors *Flying* 116:40-5 Ap '89

POCHARSKI, SUSAN

The secret world of obsessive-compulsives. il *Mademoiselle* 95:138 Ag '89

POCHIVALOV, LEONID

'Mother Russia' and her exiles. il *World Press Review* 36:30-2 Mr '89

POCHOIR See Stencil work

POCKET BILLIARDS See Pool (Game)

POCKET BOOKS

Pocket acquires book by Notre Dame football coach Lou Holtz. *Publishers Weekly* 235:61 Ja 13 '89

Pocket and Warner announce retail incentive plans [end of antitrust campaign by independent bookstores] J. Mutter. *Publishers Weekly* 235:19-20 Ja 6 '89

Pocket pockets sales brochures. J. Mutter. *Publishers Weekly* 236:28 N 17 '89

POCKET COMPUTERS See Computers

POCKET TELEVISION RECEIVERS See Television receivers

POCKLINGTON, PETER

about

Fighting new battles. J. DeMont. il por *Maclean's* 102:40+ Ag 14 '89

POCONO MOUNTAINS REGION (PA.)

See also

Architecture, Domestic—Pocono Mountains region (Pa.)

PODELL, RICHARD N.

Too tired too often? Vitamins can work wonders. il *Redbook* 172:108-9+ Ja '89

PODELL, RICHARD N., AND FISCHER, ARLENE

The low blood sugar blues: do you have the symptoms? *Redbook* 172:100-1+ Mr '89

PODEWELL, CATHY

about

If J.R. is grinning this year, here's why. S. Littwin. por *TV Guide* 37:28-9 O 7-13 '89

PODGURSKY, MICHAEL

(jt. auth) See Swaim, Paul, and Podgursky, Michael

PODHORETZ, JOHN

She lost it at the movies. *The American Scholar* 58:117-22 Wint '89

PODHORETZ, NORMAN

Israel: a lamentation from the future. *Commentary* 87:15-21 Mr '89

"Lamentation" [discussion of March 1989 article, Israel: a lamentation from the future] *Commentary* 88:4-8+ Jl '89

New vistas for neoconservatives. *Conservative Digest* 15:56-7 Ja/F '89

On being a Jew [interview with S. Hook] *Commentary* 88:28-36 O '89

PODLES, LEON J.

(jt. auth) See Podles, Mary Smith, and Podles, Leon J.

PODLES, MARY SMITH, AND PODLES, LEON J.

The emasculation of God. il *America* 161:372-4 N 25 '89

POE, EDGAR ALLAN, 1809-1849

about

In pursuit of pure horror [cover story] il *Harper's* 279:45-53 O '89

A Poe man's Edgar Allan, actor Norman George evermore plays a haunting, telltale part. il por *People Weekly* 31:66 F 6 '89

POE (EDGAR ALLAN) MUSEUM (RICHMOND, VA.) See Edgar Allan Poe Museum (Richmond, Va.)

POEMS

Single works

See also

Christmas poems—Single works

See name of author for full entry

524. Beum, Robert

1815. Mazzocco, Robert

Abandon in biology class. Estes, Yvonne Baron

Acceptance. De Vinck, Christopher, 1951-

Accessible tombs. Worley, James

African American woman. Kinamore, Angela

After reading Wang Wei, I go outside to the full moon. Wright, Charles, 1935-

After Rilke. Corn, Alfred, 1943-

After the reunion. Baker, David, 1954-

The afterbirth. Harris, Doris

Afterglow. Carver, Raymond

Afternoon of a McGrath. McGrath, Thomas, 1916-

Age. Haroutunian, Saghatel

Air show. Aleshire, Joan

Alchemy. Parker, Alan Michael

All souls'. Gioia, Dana

All Souls' Day. Lee, G.

An allowance of sentiment. Cope, Steven R.

Almost autumn. Lyon, Rick

Aloft. Grennan, Eamon

Ambition. Carson, Ciarán, 1948-

Amusement park. Crooker, Barbara

An anchorite's lament. Hodges, Gregg

An ancient glass medallion. McCurdy, Harold

Angela. Knuckles, Jeffrey

The annulment. Cole, Henri

Apples. Glaser, Michael S., 1943-

The artists. Trudell, Dennis

As I step down from the train. Kraft, Eugene

Assata. Jennings, Regina

The assimilation of background. Murray, Les A., 1938-

At the dime store. Kenyon, Jane

At the Public Market Museum: Charleston, South Carolina. Kenyon, Jane

Au premier coup. Ludvigson, Susan

Aubade. Mazzocco, Robert

Autobiographer. Davison, Peter

Balance brought forward. Taylor, Eleanor Ross, 1920-

Barbed wire. Burns, Ralph, 1949-

The bathrobe. Olds, Sharon

Bedtime story. Carson, Ciarán, 1948-

Being the mother of a black child. Jones, Mona

Believe me. Ratushinskaya, Irina

Bells on Taiwan. Carter, Anne Babson

Better none. Tapscott, Stephen, 1948-

Big fine woman from Ruleville (for Fannie Lou Hamer). Cortez, Jayne

Big language. Olsen, William, 1954-

The birds and Columbus. Stanford, Ann

Bite into the onion. Piercy, Marge

Black energy. Paddock, Joe

Black star line. Dumas, Henry, 1934-1968

Blood, nest, stars. Grennan, Eamon

Blue plates. Myers, Joan Rohr

The blues. Matthews, William, 1942-

Blues children [for Bessie Smith]. Kaliba, Layding Lumumba

Borders. Calderwood, James L.

Boy's life. Cole, Henri

Brown babies—for Brooke and Evan. Williams-Garner, Debra

Brushstrokes. Cannon, Maureen

Cans. Reed, Lou

POEMS—Single works—*cont.*

Medea in Tokyo. McClatchy, J. D., 1945-
The meditation of Sarah. Harr, Barbara
Mediterranean. McGrath, Thomas, 1916-
Memorandums. Hirsch, Edward
A memorial: son Bret. Stafford, William Edgar, 1914-
Milk the mouse. Ryan, Michael
Mine/all mine. Russell, Beverly A.
Mirror. Gonzalez, Mildred
Mississippi song. Dumas, Henry, 1934-1968
A moment at the Louvre. Pagis, Dan
Monarch butterfly. Worley, James
Mood indigo. Matthews, William, 1942-
Moon clock. Hall, Donald, 1928-
Moonlight sonata. Ferris, Mary C.
The morning train. Merwin, W. S. (William Stanley), 1927-
Mountains at St. Remy. Mapp, Erica
Moves. McFall, Gardner
Moving. Grennan, Eamon
Moving into light. Schauble, Virginia
The mummy viewed. Cairns, Scott
Mushrooms. Merwin, W. S. (William Stanley), 1927-
A music. Hodges, Gregg
My congressman. Dennis, Carl
My cousin going blind. Smith-Bowers, Cathy
My cousin Muriel. Clampitt, Amy
My daughter's house. Cannon, Maureen
My father almost ascending. Bergman, David, 1950-
My grandmother's quilt. Schier, Tracy
My mother in old age. Ormsby, Eric
My uncle's canary. Mayhall, Jane
Naming the animals. Hecht, Anthony, 1923-
Native sons. Curtis, Jeannette
Necklace. Bogen, Don
The needle: for a friend who disappeared. Wright, Franz, 1953-
Neighbor. Lilburne, Geoffrey R.
Neither here nor there. Worley, James
New Year's at the methodists. Logan, William, 1950-
The news. Houston, Beth
Next summer. Jacobsen, Josephine
Night piece. McClatchy, J. D., 1945-
Nine cities. Christopher, Nicholas
North Elm Church. Nelms, Sheryl Lynne
Nostalgie de la boue. Bradley, George, 1953-
A note from Leiden. Clampitt, Amy
The notebook. Oliver, Mary, 1935-
Notes from the air. Ashbery, John
Nothing stays put. Clampitt, Amy
October. Worley, James
Offertory. Myers, Joan Rohr
An old counting-game. Hollander, John
Old country recipes. Waters, Michael, 1949-
An old-fashioned song. Hollander, John
An old joke: Christ and the woman take in adultery. Hudgins, Andrew
Old man cleaning bluegills. Quinn, John Robert
An old trembling. Bell, Marvin, 1937-
Old weary one. Curtis, Jeannette
On reading that William Butler Yeats lies forgotten in a pauper's grave. McNamee, Gregory
On refusing to prune an ancient lilac. Worley, James
On the death of a colleague. Dunn, Stephen, 1939-
One size fits all: a critical essay. Lehman, David, 1948-
One story. Merwin, W. S. (William Stanley), 1927-
Only Alice. Jacobsen, Josephine
Oppenheimer ate breakfast on August 6, 1945. Prodans, Richard
Orchestrion. Kleinschmidt, Edward
Orpheus alone. Strand, Mark, 1934-
Orthodontia. Updike, John
The orthodox waltz. Fulton, Alice, 1952-
Our fall. Macklin, Elizabeth
Outdoor shower. Olds, Sharon
Overdue pilgrimage to Nova Scotia. Merrill, James Ingram
Overtime. Levine, Philip, 1928-
Owl flight. Jones, Robert, 1934-
Painted faces. Drury, Michael
Paris in the summer of 1988. Gold, Arthur Ralph, d. 1988
Party per pale. Prospere, Susan
The passing of Thistle. Davison, Peter
Patrick, according to his autobiographer. Shea, J. T.
Paying respects. Hammond, Mary Stewart
Pearls. Glaser, Michael S., 1943-
Pedagogy. Sutton, Jim
Pedestrian, walk! Schendler, Revan
Pennsylvania January. Roberts, Len
Perennials. Levine, Philip, 1928-
Pied beauty. Hopkins, Gerard Manley, 1844-1889
Pigeons. Wormser, Baron
Pink. Svoboda, Terese
A place to stand. Weiss, R., and Weiss, T.
Playing the parts. Fasel, Ida
A poem. Karriem, Jallelah
Poem with 2 lines from a catalogue. Goldbarth, Albert
Poetry. Cassian, Nina, 1924-
Poetry workshop (first semester). Nims, John Frederick, 1913-
Polonaise. Walcott, Derek

The ponds. Oliver, Mary, 1935-
The poor. Mangan, Margaret
Portrait of Aunt Ellen. Rea, Susan
Postmodern love. Drury, John
Powder compact. Lasdun, James
Praise poem. Holmes, Darryl
Prayer for a sick friend. Sutzkever, Abraham
Preparation. Rubin, Larry
The price of perspiration. Ghigna, Charles
The promised land. Higgins, Paul E.
Proposal. Carver, Raymond
A quarter for your thoughts. Karriem, Jallelah
Quatrains for Pegasus. Merrill, James Ingram
Quick bright things. Wallace, Ronald, 1945-
Rain & snow. Leithauser, Brad
Rain years. Beum, Robert
Reading on the beach. Jacobsen, Josephine
Reassurance in a hot summer. Macklin, Elizabeth
Red cat near old snow. Uschuk, Pamela
Red poppy. Gallagher, Tess
Reductio. Dufault, Peter Kane
Redwing blackbirds. Dings, Fred
Remembering. Cherry, Kelly
Reparations of spring. Schendler, Revan
Reports from the front. Grennan, Eamon
Requiescat, for my father. Barker, Wendy
Rereading Jane Austen's novels. Pollitt, Katha
Retirement. Raine, Craig
Revisiting Bonnard: the nudes. Nowlin, Linda
Rhubarb. Bence, Evelyn, 1952-
Rimbaud. Mazzocco, Robert
The river. Rawlins, C. L.
The Rockettes. Digges, Deborah
The romance of American communism. Hirsch, Edward
A romance of widows. Westerfield, Nancy G.
Room and sun. Grennan, Eamon
Runt vigor. Piercy, Marge
Russian still-life. Pow, Tom
Ruth cleaves again to Naomi. Worley, James
Sails. Zagajewski, Adam, 1945-
Salting the oatmeal. Taylor, Eleanor Ross, 1920-
Salutation. Hardy, Dorothy C.
Sarah Orne Jewett. Struthers, Ann
Savannah. Clampitt, Amy
Savannah rising. Jones, Charles, 1932-
Saving memory. Hammond, Mary Stewart
Saviors. Young, Reggie
Schola Latina Bostonienses, O. Sutton, Jim
The scholar in the hospital. Cole, James
Schools/prisons are a mind of state. Sutton, Jim
Schuylkill navy. Dugan, Lawrence
The seagulls. Seifert, Edward
Service. Stemle, Laura
The shadow-line. Logan, William, 1950-
Shadow picture. De Vito, E. B.
The shakers. Bierds, Linda
Shattering the silence. Wagner, Audrey Teare
The shed. Kinzie, Mary
Sheet of ice. Harrison, Jeffrey
Shirt. Pinsky, Robert
A short walk in the garden. Pinkerton, C. F.
Sign language. Grennan, Eamon
Six naps in one day. Hall, Donald, 1928-
Skeletal. Lohmann, Jeanne
Sketch of a young woman picking fruit. Sundahl, Daniel James
Sledding. Grossman, Florence
Slippery elm. Hiestand, Emily
Small birthday poem. Kinzie, Mary
Small talk. Hammond, Mary Stewart
Snails. Levine, Philip, 1928-
Soldiers with green leggings. Meinke, Peter
Solidarity. Jordan, June, 1936-
Something like a sonnet for Phillis Miracle Wheatley. Jordan, June, 1936-
Somewhere in the dark. Holmes, Darryl
A song. Brodsky, Joseph, 1940-
Sorting Mother's things. Boe, Marilyn J.
Soweto song. Baraka, Amina
Spelling lesson. Cantwell, Kevin
Spenser's tower. McClatchy, J. D., 1945-
Spinoza. Mitchell, Stephen
The spirit of Malcolm. Halliburton, Karen J.
Squirrels mating. Updike, John
A star in my street. Blandiana, Ana
Star time. Boyd, John D.
Stars. Karp, Vickie
The status quo. Kaufman, Shirley
Still-life with stranger. Ashbery, John
Still waiting. Cairns, Scott
Stone fig. Stevenson, Anne, 1933-
The stones. Gardinier, Suzanne
Stonework. Awad, Joseph
Strown bliss, scattering bright. Rogoff, Jay
Summer day. Hollander, John
The summer was not long enough. Valentine, Jean
Sunday drive. Friman, Alice
Sunday in November. Kleinzahler, August

POEMS—Single works—*cont.*
Surface tension. Macklin, Elizabeth
Survivors. Ormsby, Eric
Sycamores. Dings, Fred
Tabacaria ('the tobacconist's'). Pessoa, Fernando, 1888-1935
Tabard and terrace. Revell, Donald
Tao-chi. Mitchell, Stephen
Tapestries in Spain. Moore, Mary Rosalie
Tarascon diligence. Mapp, Erica
Tea time. Boyd, John D.
Temple cleansing. Shepherd, J. Barrie
Terrestrial navigation. Crooker, Barbara
The testing. Cochran, Leonard
Texas blue norther. Nelms, Sheryl Lynne
Thanksgiving ritual. Glaser, Michael S., 1943-
That ocean. Grennan, Eamon
There are reasons. Ludvigson, Susan
These friends. Cohen, Rhea L.
This has nothing to do with April. Woods, Alfred L.
The thistle, the nettle. Miłosz, Czesław
Thrasher. Di Piero, W. S.
Three poems. Boland, Eavan
Thus. Hudgins, Andrew
Tightening clotheslines. Westerfield, Nancy G.
Time out. Barnes, Kate
To a box turtle. Updike, John
To hold and to have. Reith, Alma Carmichael
To those of my sisters who kept their naturals. Brooks, Gwendolyn
The tree of knowledge. Graham, Jorie, 1951-
Tribute. Kaliba, Layding Lumumba
Triple toe loop. Berke, Judith
The truth. Quinta, Christine
Turkeys. Wallace, Ronald, 1945-
Turning. Roe, Margie McCreless
The turning point. Hathaway, Jeanine
Twelve words on a windy day. Allen, Gilbert, 1951-
The two cities. Hodges, Gregg
Two poems. Macklin, Elizabeth
The ultimate barricade. Worley, James
Under the nine trees in January. Wright, Charles, 1935-
Up the dark valley. McGrath, Thomas, 1916-
The upper story. Salter, Mary Jo
Used. Dove, Rita
Velocity meadows. Strand, Mark, 1934-
Victim of himself. Bell, Marvin, 1937-
A village walk under snow. Corn, Alfred, 1943-
Visitation. Berger, Bruce, 1938-
Vitale. Sonnenberg, Ben
Volcanoes. Rea, Susan
Waiting patiently. Wishner, Ina
Walking the edge. Parham, Robert
A wall in the woods: Cummington. Wilbur, Richard, 1921-
War crimes. Ramke, Bin, 1947-
The wardrobe. Wilson, Joyce
Warm embrace. Robinson, Jennifer Denise
The warrior spirit. Kinamore, Angela
Water music. O'Brien, Geoffrey, 1948-
Watermark: the reservoir. Partridge, Dixie
We have no need. Anos, Joanna
We need poets. Quinta, Christine
Weatherman. Swanger, David
Webs. Aldrich, Barbara
Weeds. McClatchy, J. D., 1945-
West Street. Feldman, Irving, 1928-
What I forgot to mention. Raab, Lawrence
What they ate; What they drank. Tilghman, Christopher
What we wear. Myers, Joan Rohr
When nights were full of sex and churches. Calbert, Cathleen
When one has lived a long time alone. Kinnell, Galway, 1927-
When she danced. Hunt, Cheryl Yvette
When the wood is green. Pankey, Eric
Where a deer fell. Ortolani, Al
White boat, blue boat. Schuyler, James
White hawthorn in the west of Ireland. Boland, Eavan
White on green. Bowie, Robert
White owl flies into and out of the field. Oliver, Mary, 1935-
Whitman. Shapiro, Karl Jay, 1913-
Windmill (Nebraska 1982). Gillett, Stacy
The wing dike at low water. Santos, Sherod, 1948-
Winslow Homer, "Mink Pond," 1891. Bellinger, Daniel
Winter primitive. Howard, Dorothy R.
The witch hazel wood. Hiestand, Emily
With no other witness. Root, William Pitt, 1941-
With tenure. Lehman, David, 1948-
Wolf. Zahniser, Ed
Women. Hall, Jim, 1947-
Words for my daughter. Balaban, John, 1943-
Work. Petersen, Paulann
Worshipfully. Fasel, Ida
Yellow flowers. Schuyler, James
Young love, America. Oates, Joyce Carol, 1938-
Young lovers. Gilbert, Zack, 1925-
Your natural history. Leithauser, Brad

POETICS *See* Poetry
POETRY
   See also
   Art and poetry
   Brazilian poetry
   Christmas poems
   Computers—Poetry use
   Cowboy poetry
   Epic poetry
   Humorous poetry
   Language poetry
   Limericks
   Love poetry
   Publishers and publishing—Poetry
   Russian poetry
   Sonnets
   Sufi poetry
Writers & writing. P. Pettingell. See occasional issues of The New Leader
   Appreciation and interpretation
Death to the death of poetry. D. Hall. il *Harper's* 279:72-6 S '89
   Authorship
The poet within you. D. K. Kirby. *The Writer* 102:19-21 F '89
Rhymes and reasons [S. Glenn] M. Long. il por *Gentlemen's Quarterly* 59:202-3 F '89
What makes a poet? What makes a poem? P. H. Thompson. *The Writer* 102:22-4 N '89
   Awards
   See also
   Lenore Marshall/Nation Poetry Prize
   Bibliography
Recent poetry. D. M. Epstein. *America* 160:592-4 Je 17-24 '89
   Competitions
Prizewinning poets-1989 [winners of Discovery—The Nation '89] *The Nation* 248:706-8 My 22 '89
   Study and teaching
Ear culture. H. Kenner. *Harper's* 278:26-7+ Mr '89
   Technique
Poet to poet. D. Dumars. *The Writer* 102:24-6+ D '89
The portable poetry workshop. J. Juskie-Nellis and Y. Higgins. *The Writer* 102:21-2 O '89
The writer as starling: advice to a young poet. R. Dana. *The Writer* 102:14-16+ My '89
   Themes
   See also
   Acadians in poetry
   Animals in poetry
   Anti-Semitism in poetry
   Astronomy in poetry
   Jesus Christ in poetry
   Meteors in poetry
   Mythology in poetry
   Quantum theory in poetry
   Religion in poetry
   Time in poetry
   Water in poetry
POETRY AND ART *See* Art and poetry
POETRY AND REVOLUTIONS
Time's voice; tr. by Edith Grossman. O. Paz. *The New Republic* 201:90+ N 6 '89
POETRY AND STATE
   Romania
Ceaușescu: no Little prince [banning poems by A. Blandiana] *Harper's* 279:16+ D '89
   Soviet Union
In a haunting new memoir, poet Irina Ratushinskaya recalls the agonies of a Soviet labor camp. S. K. Reed. il pors *People Weekly* 31:87-8 Ja 16 '89
In solitary cells on winter nights [interview with I. Ratushinskaya and I. Geraschenko] E. S. Vaughn. il pors *Christianity Today* 33:26-9 D 15 '89
POETRY READINGS
Poetry out loud. R. Brookhiser. il *The Atlantic* 263:43-5 F '89
POETS
   See also
   Celebrities as poets
POETS, AMERICAN
   See also
   Braverman, Kate
   Brown, Sterling Allen, 1901-1989
   Dickinson, Emily, 1830-1886
   Harrison, Jim, 1937-
   Hughes, Langston, 1902-1967
   Longfellow, Henry Wadsworth, 1807-1882
   Mahony, Phillip, 1955-
   McGrath, Thomas, 1916-
   Moore, Clement Clarke, 1779-1863
   Plath, Sylvia
   Ransom, John Crowe, 1888-1974
   Warren, Robert Penn, 1905-1989
   Whitman, Walt, 1819-1892
POETS, AUSTRIAN
   See also
   Hofmannsthal, Hugo von, 1874-1929

POETS, CHILEAN
See also
Mistral, Gabriela, 1889-1957
POETS, ENGLISH
See also
Eliot, T. S. (Thomas Stearns), 1888-1965
Hardy, Thomas, 1840-1928
Hopkins, Gerard Manley, 1844-1889
Morris, William, 1834-1896
Shakespeare, William, 1564-1616
Wordsworth, William, 1770-1850
POETS, FRENCH
See also
Cocteau, Jean, 1889-1963
POETS, IRANIAN
See also
Hāfiz, 14th cent.
POETS, IRISH
See also
Yeats, W. B. (William Butler), 1865-1939
POETS, POLISH
See also
Miłosz, Czesław
POETS, PORTUGUESE
See also
Camões, Luís de, 1524?-1580
Pessoa, Fernando, 1888-1935
POETS, ROMANIAN
See also
Eminescu, Mihai, 1850-1889
POETS, RUSSIAN
See also
Ratushinskaya, Irina
Serge, Victor, 1890-1947
POETS, SPANISH
See also
Machado, Antonio, 1875-1939
POETS LAUREATE, AMERICAN
American bards. P. Pettingell. *The New Leader* 72:19-20
My 15-29 '89
POEWE-HEXHAM, KARLA O.
(jt. auth) See Hexham, Irving, and Poewe-Hexham, Karla
O.
POGO (COMIC STRIP)
Discrimination isn't comic [Chicago tribune replaces Kudzu
with Pogo] M. E. Marty. *The Christian Century* 106:215
F 22 '89
Pogo lives! A.-M. Stan. il *New Choices for the Best Years*
29:11 Ja '89
POGREBIN, LETTY COTTIN
Boys will be boys? il *Ms.* 18:24 S '89
Cruel and unusual punishment. por *Ms.* 18:36-7 N '89
Feeling out 50. il por *Ms.* 17:26 Je '89
A fine romance. il *Ms.* 17:21 My '89
It started with a lunch. il *Ms.* 17:50 Ja/F '89
It still takes a bride and groom. il *The New York Times
Magazine* p12+ Jl 2 '89
The Jerusalem agenda [conference] il *Ms.* 17:23-5 Mr '89
Me and my phobia. por *Ms.* 18:16 O '89
The Rushdie riddle. il *Ms.* 18:28 Jl/Ag '89
Twofers. il *Ms.* 17:23 Ap '89
What happened to Marlene Sanders? il pors *New Choices
for the Best Years* 29:67-71+ Mr '89
POGUES (MUSICAL GROUP)
Eight lads putting on airs. J. Cocks. il *Time* 134:56 Ag
21 '89
Under the influence. D. Handelman. il *Rolling Stone* p175-6+
N 16 '89
POHL, FREDERIK, 1919-
Astounding story [cover story] il *American Heritage* 40:42-8+
S/O '89
The greatest show off earth. il *Omni (New York, N.Y.)* 12:14+
N '89
POI DOG PONDERING (MUSICAL GROUP)
New kids chip off the old block. A. DeCurtis. il *Rolling
Stone* p75-6 S 7 '89
POINSETT, ALEX
Paving the path to 8(a) contracts. il *Black Enterprise* 19:160
F '89
POINSETTIAS
How does Sunset get poinsettias to hang? il *Sunset (Central
West edition)* 183:158-9 D '89
Poinsettia and the men in her life. J. F. Lopez. il *Flower
and Garden* 33:41-2 N/D '89
POINT LOBOS STATE RESERVE (CALIF.)
Salty history at Point Lobos. il *Sunset (Central West edition)*
183:20 O '89
POINT-OF-SALE SYSTEMS
The best-engineered part is no part at all [NCR's new cash
register] O. Port. il *Business Week* p150 My 8 '89
Quick checks [verifying checks and credit cards] J. Wynn.
il *Nation's Business* 77:45-6 D '89
POINT OF VIEW (FICTION) See Fiction—Narration
POINT REYES NATIONAL SEASHORE (CALIF.)
Point Reyes. L. Alexander. il *Gourmet* 49:100-7+ D '89
POINTERS (DOGS)
See also
German short-haired pointers

A dog in the hand [bird dog trainer J. Thompson of Rosanky,
Tex.] R. Bass. il pors *Esquire* 112:150-4+ O '89
POINTS-OF-LIGHT INITIATIVE (PROGRAM)
The elusive '1,000 Points'. il *Newsweek* 114:49 D 11 '89
POIRET, PAUL, 1879-1944
about
Fabrics of being. R. E. Slavin, III. il por *Horizon (Tuscaloosa,
Ala.)* 32:49-51 Mr/Ap '89
POIRIER, ANNE
about
Anne and Patrick Poirier at Sonnabend. D. B. Kuspit. il
Art in America 77:152-3 Mr '89
Loose marbles. K. Larson. il *New York* 22:64 Ag 28 '89
POIRIER, PATRICK
about
Anne and Patrick Poirier at Sonnabend. D. B. Kuspit. il
Art in America 77:152-3 Mr '89
Loose marbles. K. Larson. il *New York* 22:64 Ag 28 '89
POISON ARROW FROGS See Frogs
POISON CONTROL CENTERS
Poison control centers: where emergencies are the routine.
V. Modeland. il *FDA Consumer* 23:20-3 Mr '89
POISON IVY
The itch and you. T. Krautwurst. il *The Mother Earth
News* 117:118-23+ My/Je '89
A walk on the wild side can land you in ivy hell. J. Silberner.
il *U.S. News & World Report* 106:76 F 20 '89
When scratchin' don't help. H. Middleton. il *Southern Living*
24:42+ Mr '89
POISON SUMAC
A walk on the wild side can land you in ivy hell. J. Silberner.
il *U.S. News & World Report* 106:76 F 20 '89
POISONING See Poisons and poisoning
POISONOUS ANIMALS
All things bright & bitter [cover story] E. Pennisi. il
International Wildlife 19:46-51 N/D '89
POISONOUS FROGS See Frogs
POISONOUS GASES
See also
Bhopal poisonous gas disaster, India, 1984
Carbon monoxide
Chemical and biological weapons
Gas masks
Hydrogen sulfide
Nyos, the killer lake, may be coming back. R. A. Kerr.
il *Science* 244:1541-2 Je 30 '89
POISONOUS MUSHROOMS
Transplant emergency! [victims of amanita poisoning receive
liver transplants; work of C. W. Pinson] J. Fincher. il
Reader's Digest 135:43-8 Jl '89
Wild mushrooms (I). B. T. Hunter. il *Consumers' Research
Magazine* 72:8-9 Ja '89
POISONOUS PLANTS
See also
Poison ivy
Poison sumac
The toxic four. il maps *The Mother Earth News* 117:124-5
My/Je '89
POISONS AND POISONING
See also
Arsenic
Botulism
Cadmium poisoning
Carbon monoxide
Ciguatera
Cyanide poisoning
Food poisoning
Lead poisoning
Mercury poisoning
Scombroid poisoning
Snake venom
Toxins and antitoxins
Convicted of murdering one of his children, James Richardson
hopes the truth will set him free [Florida man imprisoned
for 1967 poisonings] P. Chin. il pors *People Weekly*
31:191-2+ Mr 6 '89
From tragedy to travesty [questioning the guilt of J. Richard-
son who served 21 years in Florida for poisoning his
children] J. N. Baker. il por *Newsweek* 113:68 Ap 24
'89
A good idea in bad taste [L. Tylczak pushes for the addition
of Bitrex to household products to reduce risk of childhood
poisoning] M. G. Stoddard. il por *The Saturday Evening
Post* 261:38-9 S '89
Poison checklist. C. Loomis. *Parents* 64:23 Mr '89
POISONS AND POISONING, INDUSTRIAL
See also
Bhopal poisonous gas disaster, India, 1984
Trade waste
Deals that smell bad [toxic waste undoing takeovers] R.
Simon. il *Forbes* 143:49+ My 15 '89
POITIER, SIDNEY
about
Poitier's stellar career saluted in New York City. il pors
Jet 75:62-3 Mr 20 '89
POKER (GAME)
Chan is bluffing (we think) [pro J. Chan] P. Alson. il por
Esquire 111:166-8+ My '89

POKER (GAME)—cont.

Dish 'n' deal [women's poker game] D. Raskin. il *Ms.* 18:32-3 S '89

How to host the perfect poker party. S. Wyler. il *New Choices for the Best Years* 29:70-5 Ap '89

POL POT

about

Killing fields II. E. Becker. *The New Republic* 200:10+ Ja 2 '89

Our pal Pol Pot? J. J. Green and B. Whitmore. *Commonweal* 116:668-9 D 1 '89

Stop Pol Pot. il *The New Republic* 200:7-9 Ap 3 '89

POLAK, CHRIS

about

"I like to get the bad guys". W. Urbanska. il pors *McCall's* 116:134+ F '89

POLAND, JOHN LINDSAY- *See* Lindsay-Poland, John

POLAND

See also

Agricultural administration—Poland
Alternative press—Poland
Business schools—Poland
Catholic Church—Relations (Diplomatic)—Poland
Censorship—Poland
Economic assistance—Poland
Economic assistance, American—Poland
Food supply—Poland
Galicia (Poland and Ukraine)
Gdańsk (Poland)
Investments, American—Poland
Jews—Poland
Minorities—Poland
Music festivals—Poland
Philosophy—Study and teaching—Poland
Poles
Student movement—Poland
Warsaw (Poland)
Youth—Poland

Boundaries

Lebensraum all over again [German claims on Polish territory] map *Newsweek* 114:25 Jl 24 '89

Commerce

United States

See United States—Commerce—Poland

Economic conditions

Nobody here but us Democrats. R. Sikorski. il *National Review* 41:40-2 S 29 '89

Economic policy

Back to the drawing board. D. Stanglin. il *U.S. News & World Report* 107:34-5 S 18 '89

The best assistance. M. S. Forbes, Jr. il *Forbes* 144:27 O 2 '89

Can Poland save itself? R. J. Samuelson. il *Newsweek* 114:49 S 18 '89

Capitalist liberation. M. Novak. il *Forbes* 144:102 S 18 '89

Dawn in Poland [non-Communist prime minister T. Mazowiecki] D. Singer. il *The Nation* 249:265 S 18 '89

Glasnost's twin crucibles. G. E. Schares. il *Business Week* p72-3+ Je 5 '89

A grand experiment. L. Weschler. il *The New Yorker* 65:59-60+ N 13 '89

Harsh medicine. A. Bilski. il *Maclean's* 102:32-3 O 23 '89

More help is on the way [with interview with T. Mazowiecki] H. Anderson. il *Newsweek* 114:46-7 O 9 '89

Poland: the long road ahead. S. Sullivan. il *Newsweek* 114:31 S 4 '89

Poland's reforms make *glasnost* look like window dressing. W. Echikson and others. il *Business Week* p35-6 Ap 17 '89

Poland's trial-and-error transition. G. E. Schares. il *Business Week* p62 Jl 17 '89

Solidarity in power. A. Nagorski. il *Newsweek* 114:34-5 N 27 '89

To the brink—and back again [problems confronting Prime Minister C. Kiszczak] J. Smolowe. il por *Time* 134:38-9 Ag 14 '89

Why Solidarity must play point man for economic reform. G. S. Becker. il *Business Week* p18 Jl 31 '89

Economic relations

United States

See United States—Economic relations—Poland

Foreign opinion

Canadian

A matter of trust [views of Polish Canadians on political reforms] A. Bilski. il *Maclean's* 102:32 Ap 17 '89

Foreign relations

Germany (West)

See Germany (West)—Foreign relations—Poland

Great Britain

See Great Britain—Foreign relations—Poland

Soviet Union

See Soviet Union—Foreign relations—Poland

History

Occupation, 1939-1945

See also

World War, 1939-1945—Campaigns and battles—Poland
World War, 1939-1945—Poland

Industries

See also

Promotor (Firm)
Small business—Poland

Photographs and photography

Scenes from a hard land. il *Newsweek* 114:26-7 Ag 28 '89

Politics and government

See also

Communist Party (Poland)
Elections—Poland
Political campaigns—Poland

After the party's over [Solidarity's influence on reform movements in Eastern Europe] D. Stanglin. il *U.S. News & World Report* 107:76-7 Ag 28-S 4 '89

Bloc busters [cover story] J. Rupnik. *The New Republic* 200:18+ My 22 '89

Call to freedom [recognition of Solidarity and promise of open elections; cover story; special section; with editorial comment by Kevin Doyle] il *Maclean's* 102:2, 26-8+ Ap 17 '89

Can Poland ever be free? A. Besançon. *Commentary* 87:15-20 Ap '89

Crisis in Poland. M. Nemeth. il por *Maclean's* 102:16-17 Ag 14 '89

Encouraging political and economic reforms in Poland [address, April 17, 1989] G. Bush. *Department of State Bulletin* 89:3-5 Je '89

An epochal shift [Solidarity to head government] M. Johnson. il por *Time* 134:16-18 Ag 28 '89

Freedom's turn [cover story; special section] il pors *Newsweek* 114:16-23+ Ag 28 '89

A freer, but messier, order. W. Isaacson. il *Time* 134:38-40 Jl 10 '89

From Polonia with love [reaction of Poles in Chicago to events in Poland] J. M. Nash. il *Time* 134:22-3 N 27 '89

The general's sudden retreat [W. Jaruzelski declines to run for president] por *U.S. News & World Report* 107:14 Jl 10 '89

Getting to know you, part 2 [U.S. support for reform] G. D. Garcia. il *Time* 133:46 My 1 '89

A grand experiment. L. Weschler. il *The New Yorker* 65:59-60+ N 13 '89

Historic moment [meeting between Solidarity and government] D. Singer. *The Nation* 248:220 F 20 '89

Instead of revolution. M. J. Wolnicki. il *Commonweal* 116:293-4 My 19 '89

Lech Walesa digs in. N. Zeman. il por *Newsweek* 114:6 N 20 '89

Liberalization in Poland has put Bush in a bind over aid. B. Javetski and others. il *Business Week* p47 Ap 24 '89

Mr. Wujec goes to Warsaw [interview]; tr. by David Ost. J. Jastrzebowski. *Harper's* 279:13-15 D '89

Never say never [proposed legalization of Solidarity] il *Time* 133:38 Ja 30 '89

A new style of socialism? [legalization of Solidarity] M. R. Meyer. il *Newsweek* 113:36-7 Ap 10 '89

Nobody here but us Democrats. R. Sikorski. il *National Review* 41:40-2 S 29 '89

Notes and comment [Chinese and Polish democracy movements] *The New Yorker* 65:25-7 Je 19 '89

An offer you can't refuse [T. Mazowiecki chosen prime minister] *America* 161:99 Ag 26-S 2 '89

Out of misery, a flicker of hope [negotiations between Solidarity and government] S. Bialer. il *U.S. News & World Report* 106:42 Mr 27 '89

Out of the political desert [government cedes power to opposition] il *Time* 133:37 Mr 20 '89

"People are impatient" [interview with T. Mazowiecki] por *Time* 134:35 S 11 '89

Playing the political odds in Poland. A. Platt. il por *Newsweek* 114:30-1 Ag 7 '89

Poland [address, November 15, 1989] L. Wałęsa. *Vital Speeches of the Day* 56:132-5 D 15 '89

Poland: hanging by a thread. A. Nagorski. il por *Reader's Digest* 135:121-7 N '89

Poland: renewal or stagnation? R. F. Staar. bibl f il *Current History* 88:373-6+ N '89

Poland turns to the polls; tr. by Anna Husarska. E. Skalski. il *The New Leader* 72:5-7 Ap 3-17 '89

Poland's good old days (now). R. Sikorski. il *National Review* 41:23-4 D 22 '89

Poland's precipice. *Commonweal* 116:483-4 S 22 '89

Poland's reforms make *glasnost* look like window dressing. W. Echikson and others. il *Business Week* p35-6 Ap 17 '89

President's remarks at Solidarity workers' monument, Gdansk, July 11, 1989. G. Bush. il *Department of State Bulletin* 89:33-6 S '89

Refolution: the springtime of two nations [cover story] T. Garton Ash. bibl f il *The New York Review of Books* 36:3-4+ Je 15 '89

Rehabilitation for Solidarity. *Newsweek* 113:43 Ja 30 '89

Retreat from communism [cover story; special section] il *World Press Review* 36:13-18+ O '89

Seize the day. L. Goodwyn. *The Nation* 249:777 D 25 '89

POLAND—Politics and government—*cont.*

Solidarity in power [appointment of non-Communist T. Mazowiecki as prime minister] J. Bugajski. *The New Republic* 201:12-14 S 11 '89

Solidarity makes a choice [T. Mazowiecki; cover story] D. Warszawski. il *The New Leader* 72:3-4 S 4 '89

Solidarity on the high wire. G. E. Schares and J. Templeman. il *Business Week* p26-7 S 4 '89

Solidarity's glorious game [T. Mazowiecki named prime minister] *National Review* 41:12-13 S 15 '89

Solidarity—the road to power. D. Singer. il *The Nation* 249:376-80 O 9 '89

A spokeswoman with rare flair makes the news in Poland [M. Niezabitowska] B. Hewitt. il pors *People Weekly* 32:60-2 N 13 '89

A symbol of hope [L. Walesa] P. Sudo. il por *Scholastic Update (Teachers' edition)* 122:3-4 O 20 '89

A talk with Adam Michnik [cover story] A. Husarska. pors *The New Leader* 72:8-10 Ap 3-17 '89

Thanks a lot, but no thanks [L. Walesa turns down invitation to join coalition government] M. Johnson. il por *Time* 134:30 Ag 7 '89

To join or not to join: Solidarity debates power sharing in Poland. M. R. Meyer. il *Newsweek* 114:33 Jl 17 '89

To market [negotiations between Solidarity and government] D. Singer. *The Nation* 248:472-3 Ap 10 '89

To the brink—and back again [problems confronting Prime Minister C. Kiszczak] J. Smolowe. il por *Time* 134:38-9 Ag 14 '89

A vote for Jaruzelski [presidency] H. Jensen. il por *Maclean's* 102:26 Jl 31 '89

Walesa's revolution [selection of non-Communist T. Mazowiecki as prime minister; cover story; special section; with editorial comment by Kevin Doyle] il pors *Maclean's* 102:2, 24-30 Ag 28 '89

Warsaw is suddenly banking on Solidarity. R. Brady. il *Business Week* p51 F 6 '89

Warsaw scenes: a burned-out light bulb and other tragedies; tr. by Michael Kott. J. Głowacki. il *The New York Times Magazine* p20-2 Jl 30 '89

Watershed in Warsaw [pact between government and Solidarity] il *Newsweek* 113:36 Ap 17 '89

Will success ruin Solidarity's party? D. Stanglin. il *U.S. News & World Report* 107:34-5 Ag 14 '89

Religious institutions and affairs
See also
    Catholic Church—Poland
    Convents—Poland

POLAND AND THE UNITED STATES
See also
    United States—Foreign opinion—Polish

POLAR BEARS

Sleeping giants [excerpt from Polar bears; cover story] I. Stirling. il *Natural History* p34-9 Ja '89

Migration
Diary of a bear-watcher [Manitoba] F. Bruemmer. il *International Wildlife* 19:46-51 S/O '89

POLAR ESKIMOS *See* Eskimos

POLAR EXPLORATION
See also
    Antarctic exploration
    Arctic exploration

POLAR REGIONS
See also
    Antarctic regions
    Arctic regions
    Ice—Polar regions

POLAR RESEARCH
See also
    Antarctic research
    Arctic research

POLAR WANDER

Wherefore the world's wobble? [Chandler wobble; research by Sultan Hameed and Robert G. Currie] *Science News* 135:220 Ap 8 '89

Wobbling world [theory that Chandler wobble is caused by atmospheric oscillation; research by Sultan Hameed and Robert Currie] S. Vogel. il *Discover* 10:24 Ag '89

POLARITY

Polar solvent dynamics and electron-transfer reactions. M. Maroncelli and others. bibl f il *Science* 243:1674-81 Mr 31 '89

POLARIZATION (ELEMENTARY PARTICLES)

Siberian snake. J. Horgan. *Scientific American* 261:24+ N '89

A snake-in-the-ring keeps spins aligned [Siberian snake device] R. Cowen. *Science News* 136:118 Ag 19 '89

POLARIZATION (LIGHT)

Critical focus. B. Schwalberg. il *Popular Photography* 96:84+ Mr '89

Cross-polarization of light. J. Bartsch. il *Petersen's Photographic Magazine* 17:58-9 F '89

POLARIZATION (SOUND)

Is polarity audible? J. D. Hirsch. il *Stereo Review* 54:28+ My '89

Polarity revisited. J. D. Hirsch. il *Stereo Review* 54:48 O '89

POLAROID CORP.

A new way to keep raiders at bay [ESOP defense gets court O.K.] K. H. Hammonds. il *Business Week* p39 Ja 23 '89

Round two for Polaroid and Shamrock [stock buyback] K. H. Hammonds. il *Business Week* p32 F 13 '89

POLE HOUSES

Hawaiian H. il *Sunset (Central West edition)* 182:158-9 My '89

Lively cottage for the weekend [Lake Pontchartrain; cover story] L. Hallam. il *Southern Living* 24:106-7 Jl '89

POLE STAR *See* Polestar

POLENTA COOKING *See* Cooking—Cornmeal

POLES

Canada
Political activities
A matter of trust [views on political reforms in Poland] A. Bilski. il *Maclean's* 102:32 Ap 17 '89

Germany (West)
West Berlin: a cheerfully irrelevant outpost [Polish flea market] P. R. Range. il *U.S. News & World Report* 107:48 N 6 '89

United States
Ameryka my America; tr. by Anna Husarska. E. Skalski. il *The New Leader* 72:8-9 N 13 '89

The high price of reforms [L. Walesa's visit] *Maclean's* 102:30 N 27 '89

It was shake-the-world time for Lech Walesa in Poland, but polka time for his son in America [S. Walesa tours with Jan Lewan band] il pors *People Weekly* 32:81 S 11 '89

The next generation [S. Walesa] il por *Scholastic Update (Teachers' edition)* 122:5 O 20 '89

One of the great men of our time [visit to U.S. by L. Walesa] M. S. Forbes, Jr. il pors *Forbes* 144:27 D 25 '89

Sighing to God [L. Walesa] *America* 161:416 D 9 '89
Political activities
From Polonia with love [reaction of Poles in Chicago to events in Poland] J. M. Nash. il *Time* 134:22-3 N 27 '89

I'm a Pole watcher. T. R. Swick. il *The American Spectator* 22:24-5 S '89

POLES, FISHING *See* Fishing tackle

POLES, PLANETARY *See* Planetary poles

POLES, SKI *See* Ski poles

POLESTAR

The double polestar of the past [computer program] A. Kammerer. il *Sky and Telescope* 77:531-3 My '89

POLGAR FAMILY
about
Chairwomen of the chessboard. R. Givens. il *Newsweek* 113:63+ Mr 27 '89

POLHEMUS, GUY
about
Can do. R. Flippen. il por *American Health* 8:70 S '89

POLI, GUIDO, AND OTHERS

Interferon-α but not AZT suppresses HIV expression in chronically infected cell lines. bibl f il *Science* 244:575-7 My 5 '89

POLIANOVSKY, E.

(jt. auth) *See* Kovalenko, Y., and Polianovsky, E.

POLICE
See also
    Black police
    Computers—Police use
    Labor unions—Police
    Police dogs
    Policewomen

Cops: we're losing the war. K. W. Perry. por *Newsweek* 113:6-7 Mr 13 '89

On the firing line [police and war on drugs] G. Hackett. il *Newsweek* 113:32-4+ My 29 '89

Stopped by the cops? Roadside advice for you and your kids. M. W. Clark. *Better Homes and Gardens* 67:148 D '89

Equipment
See also
    Police weapons

Public relations
Making neighborhoods safe [community-oriented policing] J. Q. Wilson and G. L. Kelling. il *The Atlantic* 263:46-52 F '89

Salaries, pensions, etc.
The .44-caliber mouthpiece [San Antonio, Tex. police union head H. Flammia] W. P. Barrett. il *Forbes* 144:166 S 18 '89

Songs and music
A cop's homage to a slain pal becomes his own tragic farewell [tape made by accident victim R. Shinholser] il por *People Weekly* 31:43 Ja 30 '89

Surveillance operations
Big Brother was watching [surveillance of demonstrators in China] il *Time* 133:34 Je 26 '89

Training
See also
    Law Enforcement Television Network

POLICE—cont.

Travel

Next year, the Khmer Rouge [excerpts from brochure describing police tour] M. E. Marty. *The Christian Century* 106:895 O 4 '89

Arizona

See also

Mesa (Ariz.)—Police

High-speed heat! [cars used] D. C. Ross. il *Motor Trend* 41:64-8+ Je '89

Brazil

Partners against crime: Brazil's police work with women to fight domestic violence. E. Station. il *Ms.* 18:69-70 N '89

California

See also

Los Angeles (Calif.)—Police

Los Angeles County (Calif.)—Police

Canada

See also

Royal Canadian Mounted Police

Police under fire [cover story; special section; with editorial comment by Kevin Doyle] il *Maclean's* 102:4, 30-8 Ja 9 '89

China

Big Brother was watching [surveillance of demonstrators] il *Time* 133:34 Je 26 '89

Colombia

A curious retirement [general revealed to be on payroll of drug barons] *Time* 133:44 F 20 '89

Florida

See also

Broward County (Fla.)—Police

Jacksonville (Fla.)—Police

Miami (Fla.)—Police

Israel

Forgive us our press passes [Israeli police masquerading as press in the occupied territories] L. Zuckerman. il *Time* 133:65 My 8 '89

Massacre in Nahalin [Israeli border police raid on West Bank village] J. Bierman. *Maclean's* 102:26 Ap 24 '89

Manitoba

See also

Winnipeg (Man.)—Police

Maryland

See also

Prince Georges County (Md.)—Police

Michigan

See also

Detroit (Mich.)—Police

New Jersey

See also

Vineland (N.J.)—Police

New York (State)

See also

New York (N.Y.)—Police

Newfoundland

See also

Royal Newfoundland Constabulary

Northern Ireland

Northern Ireland hit-squad scandal [leak of lists of IRA sympathizers triggers loyalist terrorism] L. Flanders. il *The Nation* 249:491-4 O 30 '89

Ohio

See also

Cincinnati (Ohio)—Police

Cleveland (Ohio)—Police

Ontario

See also

Toronto (Ont.)—Police

Puerto Rico

Island of repression. B. A. Kane. il *The Progressive* 53:35 S '89

Scotland

On the trail of terror [police uncover clues in the Pan Am Flight 103 bombing] B. Duffy. il map *U.S. News & World Report* 107:44-6 N 13 '89

South Africa

Next year, the Khmer Rouge [excerpts from brochure describing police tour] M. E. Marty. *The Christian Century* 106:895 O 4 '89

A South African cop breaks ranks over police violence [G. Rockman reports brutality during student demonstration near Cape Town] B. Hewitt. il pors *People Weekly* 32:44-6 O 16 '89

Texas

See also

Houston (Tex.)—Police

San Antonio (Tex.)—Police

Virginia

See also

Virginia Beach (Va.)—Police

Washington (D.C.)

See Washington (D.C.)—Police

Washington (State)

See also

Seattle (Wash.)—Police

Western States

Seniors as police volunteers. il *Sunset (Central West edition)* 183:138-9 N '89

POLICE, MOUNTED

See also

Royal Canadian Mounted Police

POLICE (MUSICAL GROUP)

Police report. S. Fried. il pors *Gentlemen's Quarterly* 59:151+ O '89

POLICE AUTOMOBILES *See* Automobiles, Police

POLICE BICYCLES *See* Bicycles—Police use

POLICE BRUTALITY *See* Police cruelty

POLICE COMMUNICATION SYSTEMS

See also

Computers—Police use

POLICE-COMMUNITY RELATIONS *See* Police—Public relations

POLICE CORRUPTION

A Detroit police corruption probe. *Newsweek* 114:30 D 18 '89

Fury over an unholy alliance [Cleveland police accused of teaming up with drug dealer A. Feckner] B. Turque. il por *Newsweek* 113:26 My 8 '89

POLICE CRUELTY

Police brutality charges probed after Va. Beach riot; students fault city. il *Jet* 76:6-7 S 25 '89

A private Mod Squad sets out to prove police harassment—and stirs a fight over its tactics [Jackson Lynn Travers detective agency] G. Stone. il *People Weekly* 32:83-4+ D 11 '89

A South African cop breaks ranks over police violence [G. Rockman reports brutality during student demonstration near Cape Town] B. Hewitt. il pors *People Weekly* 32:44-6 O 16 '89

POLICE DOGS

The smell of fine art [combating theft by spraying paintings with scents detectible only by dogs] il *Discover* 10:12 Ag '89

POLICE ETHICS

See also

Police corruption

POLICE FAMILIES

A difficult job to take home [Canada] B. Came. il *Maclean's* 102:36-7 Ja 9 '89

POLICE HELICOPTERS *See* Helicopters in police work

POLICE IN TELEVISION

Too close for comfort [news show Eye on crime shows Miami police in action] J. M. Robins. il *Channels (New York, N.Y.: 1986)* 9:24+ Mr '89

True grit [Cops] D. Friedman. il *Rolling Stone* p26 Ap 6 '89

TV's crime wave gets real [Cops] H. F. Waters. il *Newsweek* 113:72 My 15 '89

Watch the Farrah lookalike make a real drug bust [Cops] J. Weisman. il *TV Guide* 37:18-19 Je 17-23 '89

Anecdotes, facetiae, satire, etc.

Last word [Dragnet vs. killer bees] K. Thornock. il *Omni (New York, N.Y.)* 11:124 Mr '89

POLICE INSIGNIA

Collectors and collecting

Police uniform buttons. B. Manas. il *Antiques & Collecting Hobbies* 94:52-3 My '89

POLICE INTELLIGENCE UNITS

See also

Law Enforcement Intelligence Unit

Police—Surveillance operations

POLICE INTERROGATION *See* Police questioning

POLICE MUSEUMS

See also

Houston Police Museum

POLICE QUESTIONING

True confession? [excerpt from transcript of police interrogation of murder suspect T. F. Sawyer in Clearwater, Fla.] *Harper's* 279:17-20+ O '89

Untrue confessions [T. F. Sawyer confesses to Clearwater, Fla. murder after brutal interrogation by police] P. Weiss. il por *Mother Jones* 14:18-20+ S '89

POLICE RADAR *See* Radar in traffic control

POLICE SHOOTINGS

'All of us are in trouble' [Miami's riots] G. Hackett. il *Newsweek* 113:36-7 Ja 30 '89

Black-and-white issues [Toronto police officers arrested in connection with deaths of two blacks] B. Came. il *Maclean's* 102:13 Ja 23 '89

A brightly colored tinderbox [riots following police shooting of motorcyclist in Overtown] J. V. Lamar, Jr. il *Time* 133:28-9 Ja 30 '89

A city waiting for an explosion [police shooting trial in Miami could spark riots] A. M. Arrarte. il *U.S. News & World Report* 107:37 N 27 '89

Commission seeks answers to the violence in Miami. *Jet* 75:16 F 13 '89

A death in Winnipeg [policeman R. Cross testifies on role in shooting death of native leader J. J. Harper] P. Kaihla. il por *Maclean's* 102:16 S 11 '89

Miami cop who killed two blacks and incited riot guilty of manslaughter [W. Lozano] il por *Jet* 77:4-5 D 25 '89-Ja 1 '90

POLICE SHOOTINGS—*cont.*
Miami: 'We got justice' [policeman W. Lozano found guilty for shootings that resulted in race violence] G. Hackett. il por *Newsweek* 114:30 D 18 '89
Miami's racial fires [police shooting sparks riots] A. Bilski. il *Maclean's* 102:23-5 Ja 30 '89
Police shooting sparks violence in New Jersey [Vineland] il *Jet* 76:6 S 18 '89
Police under fire [Canada; cover story; special section; with editorial comment by Kevin Doyle] il *Maclean's* 102:4, 30-8 Ja 9 '89
Police under fire [shootings involving blacks in Toronto] B. Bergman. il *Maclean's* 102:21-2 N 13 '89
An unfolding tragedy [suicide of Winnipeg, Man. police inspector K. Dowson disrupts inquiry into shooting death of native leader J. J. Harper] P. Kopvillem. il por *Maclean's* 102:23 O 2 '89

POLICE WEAPONS
Furore over firearms [Canadian police push for deadlier weapons] R. Dolphin. il *Maclean's* 102:38 Ja 9 '89

POLICEWOMEN
"I like to get the bad guys" [detective C. Polak of Los Angeles] W. Urbanska. il pors *McCall's* 116:134+ F '89
My sister, the cop. F. Harris, III. por *Essence* 20:6-7 Jl '89
Partners against crime: Brazil's police work with women to fight domestic violence. E. Station. il *Ms.* 18:69-70 N '89
"Thank God for people like you" [undercover narcotics officer P. Rosales of Houston, Tex.] M. Siegel. il por *Good Housekeeping* 208:139+ Je '89

POLICEWOMEN IN TELEVISION
Making an arresting TV debut, deputy sheriff Linda Canada puts the cuffs on fame in Fox's Cops [Broward County, Fla.] P. Jordan. il pors *People Weekly* 31:89-90 Ap 24 '89

POLICIES, INSURANCE *See* Insurance
POLICOFF, STEPHEN PHILLIP
Bottle babies. il *Ladies' Home Journal* 106:182-3+ My '89
POLICY ANALYSIS *See* Policy sciences
POLICY LOANS *See* Insurance, Life—Policy loans
POLICY SCIENCES
    See also
    Cato Institute
    Institute for Public Policy Leadership
    Progressive Policy Institute
    Rockford Institute
Whither policy for the 1990s [special section] bibl *Society* 26:39-82 S/O '89

POLIKOFF, DOROTHY
Testimony of Dorothy L. Polikoff before the Presidential Commission on the HIV Epidemic, May 18, 1988. *The Humanist* 49:18-19 My/Je '89

POLING, HAROLD A.
                    about
Caution: bumps ahead at Ford. A. L. Taylor, III. il pors *Fortune* 120:93+ D 18 '89
Red Poling sure won't have it easy. J. B. Treece. il por *Business Week* p132-3+ N 27 '89

POLIOMYELITIS
                Vaccines and vaccination
Forgotten but not gone [occurrence of polio in developing countries] P. Radetsky. il *Discover* 10:22+ S '89
The hidden dangers of vaccines. S. Saetre. il *Utne Reader* p26 Ja/F '89

POLIS, GARY A.
The unkindest sting of all. il *Natural History* p34-9 Jl '89

POLISARIO FRONT
Efforts continue to solve Western Sahara problem. il *UN Chronicle* 26:29 Je '89
New commission for Western Sahara to advance peace process. *UN Chronicle* 26:25 S '89

POLISH PAINTING *See* Painting, Polish
POLISH PEOPLE *See* Poles
POLISH PHILOSOPHY *See* Philosophy, Polish
POLISH SONGS *See* Songs, Polish
POLISHES *See* Polishing materials
POLISHING MATERIALS
Auto polishes. il *Consumer Reports* 54:142-5 D '89
POLISTES *See* Wasps
POLITENESS *See* Courtesy
POLITICAL ACTION COMMITTEES
    See also
    Harris Corp.-Federal Political Action Committee
    JustLife (Organization)
    Spacepac
Influence for sale [business PACs] J. Novack. il *Forbes* 143:108-9 F 20 '89
Money matters. B. Phillips. il *Scholastic Update (Teachers' edition)* 121:20-1 F 24 '89
PACs: farmers' $8-million muscle man. P. Smith. il *Successful Farming* 87:8-9 Ap '89
Shilling in the Senate. D. Corn. il *The Nation* 249:84-7 Jl 17 '89
                Laws and regulations
Demand-side reform. *The New Republic* 201:7-8 Ag 7-14 '89

Let's make a deal [corporations match employee contributions to PACs with donations to charities] W. Montague. *Common Cause Magazine* 15:9 S/O '89
POLITICAL ADVERTISING *See* Advertising, Political
POLITICAL AND SECURITY COMMITTEE (UNITED NATIONS) *See* United Nations. Political and Security Committee
POLITICAL ASYLUM *See* Asylum, Right of
POLITICAL ATTITUDES
    See also
    Aged—Political activities
    Anti-nuclear movement
    Asian Americans—Political activities
    Baby boom generation—Political activities
    Blacks—Political activities
    Bush, George, 1924—Public relations
    Business—Political aspects
    Chinese Americans—Political activities
    College students—Political activities
    College teachers—Political activities
    Cuban Americans—Political activities
    Disarmament—Public opinion
    Farmers—Political activities
    Iran-contra affair—Public opinion
    Jews—Political activities
    Jews—United States—Political activities
    Korean Americans—Political activities
    Nuclear weapons—Public opinion
    Public opinion polls
    Reagan, Ronald, 1911——Public relations
    Rich—Political activities
    Rock musicians—Political activities
    Scientists—Political activities
    Women—Political activities
    Youth—Political activities
    Yuppies—Political activities
1989 CC issues poll. il *Common Cause Magazine* 15:42 Jl/Ag '89
Bush's lukewarm welcome [results of survey] L. I. Barrett. il *Time* 133:18 Ja 23 '89
Business week/Harris poll. See occasional issues of Business Week
Conservative genes [political attitudes biologically inherited; research by David T. Lykken] D. Seligman. il *Fortune* 120:123 Ag 14 '89
The end of economics? [values issues begin to consume politics] R. J. Samuelson. il *Newsweek* 114:53 Jl 24 '89
Giving the public what it wants [results of Time poll] L. I. Barrett. il *Time* 134:34 O 23 '89
Honey, we shrunk the issues. G. F. Will. il *Newsweek* 114:76 Jl 31 '89
Just think . . . [need to bring Americans back into the political process] S. K. Sheinbaum. *New Perspectives Quarterly* 5:64 Wint '88/'89
Kinder, gentler Soviets [U.S. national public opinion poll] il *Society* 26:3-4 Jl/Ag '89
Political flip-flops. M. Greenfield. il *Newsweek* 114:88 O 30 '89
Twelve ways to make it through the Bush era. S. Smith. il *Utne Reader* p110-11 N/D '89
Who cares? [film Talk radio triggers reflections on the body politic] R. Corliss. il *Film Comment* 25:64-70 Ja/F '89
                International aspects
    See also
    Israel-Arab Wars, 1967- —Public opinion
                Canada
    See also
    Poles—Canada—Political activities
Cheap shots at half . the price [letters to author] A. Fotheringham. il *Maclean's* 102:98 My 1 '89
Fickle voters, new loyalties [Maclean's/Decima poll] R. Laver. il *Maclean's* 102:14-17 Ja 2 '89
                France
A meeting of motherlands. W. Jäger. *World Press Review* 36:24+ Je '89
                Germany (West)
Courage to face the truth of the Holocaust [special section] *Society* 26:4-9 Mr/Ap '89
The Führer's dark legacy. J. Bierman. il pors *Maclean's* 102:32+ My 1 '89
A new German nationalism in the age of Gorbachev. R. Knight. il *U.S. News & World Report* 106:26-7 Ja 23 '89
                Great Britain
The enemies she makes [M. Thatcher] A. Lejeune. *National Review* 41:24 My 19 '89
My girl [M. Thatcher] M. Elliott. *The New Republic* 200:15-16 My 29 '89
                Israel
Israel's Arabs. Y. Goell. *The New Republic* 201:16-18 O 23 '89
                Soviet Union
The buttons of *glasnost*. K. Vanden Heuvel. il *The Nation* 249:45-6+ Jl 10 '89
The me generation in Moscow. A. Izyumov. il *Newsweek* 114:47 D 4 '89
What the comrades say. V. Marinov. il *Time* 133:62-3 Ap 10 '89

POLITICAL ATTITUDES—cont.
United States
See Political attitudes
POLITICAL CAMPAIGN CONSULTANTS See Campaign management
POLITICAL CAMPAIGNS
See also
Advertising, Political
Campaign buttons, posters, etc.
Campaign funds
Campaign management
Campaign workers
Political candidates
Political ethics
Presidential campaigns
See also subhead Politics and government under names of states and cities
Avoiding the Burtonmander [Republicans must win state elections so as to avoid gerrymandering] S. T. Mandel. *National Review* 41:17 D 22 '89
Crossing the color line [black leaders campaign for white votes] G. Borger. il *U.S. News & World Report* 107:22-4 N 6 '89
The dawn of karate-chop Republican politics [Wyoming congressional race] S. V. Roberts. il *U.S. News & World Report* 106:28 My 1 '89
How the Democrats hold on to Congress. S. T. Mandel and W. McGurn. *National Review* 41:37-40 N 24 '89
How to win an election [Republicans in 1990 congressional elections] W. Allison. *National Review* 41:24 O 13 '89
The politics of race [New York City, Virginia, and Cleveland] H. Fineman. il *Newsweek* 114:32-4 N 6 '89
International aspects
America's dubious export [U.S. consultants manipulating foreign elections] W. Shapiro. il *Time* 134:72 S 4 '89
Argentina
Campaigning for president in Argentina. G. W. Wynia. bibl f *Current History* 88:133-6+ Mr '89
Liberty on the line. M. Nemeth. il map *Maclean's* 102:28 My 1 '89
Peronists seek "nuclear greatness". R. A. Kessler. il por *The Bulletin of the Atomic Scientists* 45:13-15 My '89
Privatizing Argentina. A. M. Shapiro. il *The New Leader* 72:7-8 Ja 23 '89
Return of the Peronists? J. Contreras. il por *Newsweek* 113:48 My 15 '89
A test for Latin democracy. G. D. Garcia. il por *Time* 133:46 My 15 '89
The voice of Argentine voters will echo through Latin America. R. A. Kessler and J. Ryser. il por *Business Week* p60 Mr 20 '89
Why the left runs last in Argentina. A. M. Shapiro. il *The New Leader* 72:10-12 F 6 '89
Bolivia
Liberty on the line. M. Nemeth. il map *Maclean's* 102:28 My 1 '89
Brazil
Beat the devil [coverage of presidential candidate F. Collor de Mello] A. Cockburn. *The Nation* 249:232-3 S 4-11 '89
Brazil: a nation in search of a miracle. J. A. Page. *America* 161:273-4 O 28 '89
Brazil finally catches free-market fever. J. Ryser. il *Business Week* p51 O 16 '89
Brazil on the tightrope toward democracy. J. De Onis. *Foreign Affairs* 68:127-43 Fall '89
Brazil turns left. W. Steif. il *The Progressive* 53:24-5+ Je '89
The fiery socialist who could soon be running Brazil [L. I. da Silva] J. Ryser. il por *Business Week* p48 Ja 16 '89
A political free-for-all in Brazil. G. Smith. il *U.S. News & World Report* 107:52 N 13 '89
Chile
Democracy on the slow track. P. Politzer. il *The Nation* 249:781-2+ D 25 '89
Fall of the patriarch. T. Rosenberg. il *The New Republic* 201:20-3 D 18 '89
A vote for change in Chile. J. Contreras. il por *Newsweek* 114:40 D 18 '89
El Salvador
'Absolute, diabolical terror'. S. Miles and B. Ostertag. il *Mother Jones* 14:22-7+ Ap '89
Bush wades into his first quagmire [election proposal from Marxist rebels] il *U.S. News & World Report* 106:12 F 6 '89
El Salvador's hard right in search of a soft image [ARENA party] D. Farah and C. A. Robbins. il *U.S. News & World Report* 106:30-1 Ja 23 '89
Guerrilla tactics [FMLN offers to participate in electoral process] S. MacLeod. il *Time* 133:47 F 6 '89
In Salvador time waits for no one [cover story] R. Zamora. *The Nation* 248:253+ F 27 '89
The return of the right. C. Lane. il por *Newsweek* 113:38+ Mr 20 '89
A Salvadoran peace 'trap'? [offer to support elections] C. Lane. il *Newsweek* 113:40 F 6 '89

Salvador's silver lining [FMLN offer to participate in electoral process] M. Kondracke. *The New Republic* 200:23-5 Mr 13 '89
A slow dying in El Salvador. D. France. il *Rolling Stone* p63-4+ Mr 23 '89
Greece
Anecdotes, facetiae, satire, etc.
The quest of lion-browed Andreas [A. Papandreou seeks re-election] D. Lawday. il *U.S. News & World Report* 106:37 Je 19 '89
Hungary
Danube fever [Hungarian opposition party leaders study Virginia governor's race] A. Heard. *The New Republic* 201:16-18 D 4 '89
India
A dynasty in doubt. A. Phillips. il por *Maclean's* 102:36-8+ N 27 '89
Pilot error [R. Gandhi] J. C. Hollick. *The New Republic* 201:13-14 D 4 '89
A referendum on Rajiv. C. S. Manegold. por *Newsweek* 114:56 N 27 '89
Jamaica
Polling in paradise. J. Bierman. il pors *Maclean's* 102:20 F 6 '89
Japan
The road warriors of Japan's politics [Liberal-Democratic Party candidate S. Sato] M. Tharp. il pors map *U.S. News & World Report* 107:28-30 Jl 24 '89
Namibia
Farce in Namibia. *The Nation* 249:191-2 Ag 21-28 '89
Fix in Namibia? M. Verbaan. *The Nation* 249:516-17 N 6 '89
Namibia holds its breath. S. Reiss. il *Newsweek* 114:31 S 25 '89
Namibia on edge. M. Baumann. il *Mother Jones* 14:18+ O '89
Self-rule in Namibia won't break South Africa's stranglehold. J. Kapstein. il *Business Week* p56 O 2 '89
A test of will. M. Nemeth. il map *Maclean's* 102:40 S 18 '89
Nicaragua
Ballot blocks. R. Kagan. *The New Republic* 200:21-2 Je 12 '89
Civics, Nicaragua-style. H. Hertzberg. *The New Republic* 201:23-5 D 25 '89
Defeat without agony. T. Gjelten. *The New Republic* 201:16-17 Ag 28 '89
Election nearing. H. Belli. il *The New Republic* 201:16-19 N 27 '89
If not the Sandinistas . . . [candidate V. Chamorro] il por *Time* 134:49 N 13 '89
Minority report. C. Hitchens. *The Nation* 249:671 D 4 '89
Minority report [U.S. funding of Nicaraguan elections] C. Hitchens. *The Nation* 249:590 N 20 '89
Money isn't everything [U.S. funding of V. Chamorro's campaign] R. Watson. il por *Newsweek* 114:47 O 9 '89
Overt meddling [U.S. plans to fund Nicaraguan elections] *The Nation* 249:407-8 O 16 '89
Turning to the voters in Nicaragua [cover story] F. D. Colburn. il pors *The New Leader* 72:5-7 N 13 '89
Upcoming elections in Nicaragua [statement, July 19, 1989] G. Bush. *Department of State Bulletin* 89:92 S '89
A vote of confidence. *Commonweal* 116:516-17 O 6 '89
Panama
A dubious ballot. D. Gollob. il por *Maclean's* 102:26 My 1 '89
Playing 'bad cop' in Panama [U.S. policy] C. Lane and D. Waller. il por *Newsweek* 113:36-7 My 8 '89
Sparring (again) with a dictator [U.S. policy] J. Smolowe. il por *Time* 133:46 My 8 '89
Taking aim at Noriega [U.S. policy in upcoming election] C. A. Robbins. il por *U.S. News & World Report* 106:40-1 My 1 '89
Paraguay
Liberty on the line. M. Nemeth. il map *Maclean's* 102:28 My 1 '89
Peru
Can a novelist save Peru? [M. Vargas Llosa; cover story] G. Marzorati. il pors *The New York Times Magazine* p44-7+ N 5 '89
Have typewriter, will run [presidential candidate M. Vargas Llosa] R. Grenier. *National Review* 41:33-4 Mr 24 '89
Latin America's "best-looking great novelist," Mario Vargas Llosa may also be, as Gene Lyons reports, the next president of Peru. G. Lyons. il por *Vogue* 179:272+ N '89
The temptation of Mario [M. Vargas Llosa's presidential candidacy] E. Farnsworth. il por *Mother Jones* 14:22-6+ Ja '89
Poland
Poland turns to the polls; tr. by Anna Husarska. E. Skalski. il *The New Leader* 72:5-7 Ap 3-17 '89
A talk with Adam Michnik [cover story] A. Husarska. pors *The New Leader* 72:8-10 Ap 3-17 '89
South Africa
Choices. R. Bonner. *The New Yorker* 65:43-8+ D 25 '89
Diplomacy and dissent: black protests grow on the eve of an election. J. Bierman. il *Maclean's* 102:22+ S 11 '89

POLITICAL CAMPAIGNS—South Africa—*cont.*

Falling apartheid [upcoming elections favor F. W. De Klerk] M. R. Hoffenberg. *The New Republic* 201:16-17 Jl 31 '89

South Africa: the squeeze is on. J. Kapstein. il por *Business Week* p44-5+ S 11 '89

Upstaging South Africa's elections [black protests] S. Reiss. il *Newsweek* 114:34 S 11 '89

Soviet Union

Gorbachev gets out the vote. F. Coleman. il por *Newsweek* 113:36-7 Mr 27 '89

Gorbachev's not-so-secret weapon: the ballot box. P. Galuszka. il *Business Week* p51 Mr 27 '89

Heading into the homestretch. P. Hofheinz. il *Time* 133:45 Mr 6 '89

New Soviet democracy. A. Wilson-Smith. il *Maclean's* 102:18-19 Mr 27 '89

One man, one vote, one mess [first contested elections] P. Hofheinz. il *Time* 133:48 F 6 '89

United States

See Political campaigns

POLITICAL CANDIDATES

See also

Black political candidates
Political campaigns
Presidential candidates
Vice-presidential candidates

My life as a congressional candidate. M. G. Michaelsen. *The American Spectator* 22:24-5 N '89

Ethics

See Political ethics

Expenditures

See Campaign funds

Brazil

And now, Brazil: Heeeeere's Silvio! [S. Santos] il por *Newsweek* 114:57 N 13 '89

Canada

Reaching for the ring [NDP leadership race] M. Clark. il *Maclean's* 102:14 S 11 '89

A stampede in search of a plum [would-be successors to Edward Broadbent] A. Fotheringham. il *Maclean's* 102:60 Mr 20 '89

Testing the waters [Liberal hopefuls] B. Wallace. il *Maclean's* 102:12-13 Ag 14 '89

Japan

Japan's quest for Mr. Clean [M. Ito declines to run for prime minister] B. Martin and H. Takayama. il por *Newsweek* 112:58 My 22 '89

Soviet Union

Candidate Sakharov. A. Wilson-Smith. il por *Maclean's* 102:26 F 6 '89

Election turmoil at Soviet Academy. D. Dickson. *Science* 243:1659 Mr 31 '89

Marchuk admits flaws in election. D. Dickson. *Science* 243:1548 Mr 24 '89

Moscow subversive chic [Academy of Sciences chooses candidates] T. Rothman. *Scientific American* 261:16+ Jl '89

Sakharov declines to run for Moscow seat. D. Dickson. *Science* 243:1001 F 24 '89

United States

See Political candidates

POLITICAL CARTOONS

Feiffer at sixty. D. K. Mano. por *National Review* 41:58-60 S 15 '89

Pat Oliphant. L. Palmer. il por *Gentlemen's Quarterly* 59:290-1 Ap '89

Poison pens. R. Brookhiser. il *National Review* 41:30-3 S 1 '89

Toons. il *Life* 12:89+ Fall '89

Collectors and collecting

Nast and other nasties [D. Ryan's collection] C. Brown. il por *Forbes* 144:216+ S 18 '89

POLITICAL CHANGE

Don't bet on a 'sure thing'. M. Greenfield. il *Newsweek* 113:78 Ap 3 '89

Political flip-flops. M. Greenfield. il *Newsweek* 114:88 O 30 '89

POLITICAL CLUBS AND ASSOCIATIONS

See also

Philadelphia Society

Soviet Union

The buttons of *glasnost.* K. Vanden Heuvel. il *The Nation* 249:45-6+ Jl 10 '89

Notes from the former underground. A. Hochschild. il *Mother Jones* 14:23-6 My '89

Party animals. S. F. Starr. *The New Republic* 200:18-21 Je 26 '89

POLITICAL CONSULTANTS

See also

Campaign management
Kissinger Associates Inc.

America's dubious export [U.S. consultants manipulating foreign elections] W. Shapiro. il *Time* 133:72 S 4 '89

Roger Ailes: 'I have to take the heat'. H. Fineman and P. McKillop. por *Newsweek* 114:34 N 6 '89

Rudy's fall from grace: can Ailes put Giuliani's campaign back together again? J. Klein. il por *New York* 22:40-3 Ag 21 '89

Willie Ailes [R. Ailes' tactics become campaign issue] J. Klein. il por *New York* 22:38+ D 4 '89

POLITICAL CONTRIBUTIONS *See* Campaign funds

POLITICAL CONVENTIONS

See also

National conventions, Democratic

POLITICAL CORRUPTION *See* Politics, Corruption in

POLITICAL CRIMES AND OFFENSES

See also

Assassination
Impeachments
Terrorism

POLITICAL DEFECTORS *See* Defectors

POLITICAL EDUCATION *See* Political science—Study and teaching

POLITICAL ETHICS

See also

Conflict of interests (Public office)
Government, Resistance to
Politics, Corruption in

1989: ethics. H. Fineman. il *Newsweek* 114:53 Jl 3 '89

Anatomy of a smear [Speaker of the House T. Foley denies rumors of homosexuality] G. Borger. il pors *U.S. News & World Report* 106:40-1 Je 19 '89

Atwatergate [Republican smear campaign against House Speaker T. Foley] H. Hertzberg. *The New Republic* 201:4 Jl 3 '89

Bush's plans to defeat the forces of sleaze. K. T. Walsh. il *U.S. News & World Report* 106:16-17 Ja 23 '89

Congressional miracle: Natcher runs, but he won't take the money. J. S. Kunen. il pors *People Weekly* 31:45+ Je 26 '89

Congressmen for life: the incumbency scandal. R. Evans and R. D. Novak. *Reader's Digest* 134:79-83 Je '89

Deep in the ethics bog. M. Greenfield. il *Newsweek* 113:78 F 6 '89

Dirtball politics [homosexual smear perpetrated by Republican National Committee against Speaker of the House T. Foley] T. Morganthau. il pors *Newsweek* 113:32-3 Je 19 '89

Drawing the line. W. Shapiro. il *Time* 133:18-19 Mr 13 '89

Electioneering etiquette. M. Kinsley. *The New Republic* 201:4 N 13 '89

Fear and trembling [mood of Congress] E. Clift. il *Newsweek* 114:52 D 25 '89

Former Gray aide denies she's object of FBI probe [W. H. Gray staffer L. Baskerville] por *Jet* 76:6 Je 19 '89

Got those old Beltway blues. E. Clift. il *Newsweek* 113:38 My 29 '89

Gray matter [leak to press concerning allegations against Congressman W. H. Gray] T. Eastland. il *The American Spectator* 22:26-7 S '89

Holier than everyone [J. Tower nomination as Secretary of Defense reviewed in the Senate] L. Martz. il por *Newsweek* 113:22-3 Mr 13 '89

House Foleys [rumor of homosexuality of House Speaker T. Foley spread by Republicans and Democrats] T. Eastland. il *The American Spectator* 22:32-3 Ag '89

How reliable are the FBI's reports? [background checks on political nominees] S. J. Hedges. il *U.S. News & World Report* 106:46 Mr 13 '89

How to spread a smear [Republican attack on Speaker of the House T. Foley] M. B. Carlson. il pors *Time* 133:33 Je 19 '89

Lost horizons [lack of ethics in 1988 presidential campaign; effect on women's political participation] L. Carpenter. il *Ms.* 17:86-7 Mr '89

Manipulating the media and America: the negative 1988 presidential campaign. R. L. Fischer. il *USA Today (Periodical)* 117:20-2 Mr '89

Master of disaster [minority whip N. Gingrich; cover story] D. Beers. il porn *Mother Jones* 14:28-9+ O '89

Measuring character in the headlines. J. M. Wall. *The Christian Century* 106:275-6 Mr 15 '89

Mission accomplished [Republican National Committee chairman L. Atwater's involvement in smear campaign against Speaker T. Foley] F. Barnes. il *The New Republic* 201:8-10 Jl 3 '89

Morality vs. moralism [address, January 26, 1989] P. B. Henry. *Vital Speeches of the Day* 55:295-7 Mr 1 '89

The nation's closets [homosexual smear attack against House Speaker T. Foley] *Commonweal* 116:388-9 Jl 14 '89

New club rules [congressmen] A. F. Lewis. il *Ms.* 17:78-9 My '89

On the point [allegations about House minority whip N. Gingrich] *National Review* 41:12-13 Ap 21 '89

Partisanship fuels 'ethics' investigation. J. M. Wall. *The Christian Century* 106:579-80 Je 7-14 '89

The pollution of politics [negative ads] G. F. Will. il *Newsweek* 114:92 N 6 '89

A providential lesson on the need for rules. J. M. Wall. *The Christian Century* 106:611-12 Je 21-28 '89

The reign of the accusers. G. F. Will. il *Newsweek* 113:76 Mr 13 '89

Roger Ailes: 'I have to take the heat'. H. Fineman and P. McKillop. por *Newsweek* 114:34 N 6 '89

POLITICAL ETHICS—cont.

Should public officials' private lives matter? [interviews with G. L. Bauer and L. Sabato] il *U.S. News & World Report* 107:23 S 11 '89

That memo [Republican National Committee attack on House Speaker T. Foley] W. McGurn. por *National Review* 41:22-3 N 10 '89

Wallowing in the fine print. G. F. Will. il *Newsweek* 113:82 F 27 '89

Washington diarist: be happy [congressmen] T. Noah. *The New Republic* 201:43 Jl 10 '89

Washington notebook. D. Schorr. il *The New Leader* 72:3-4 Mr 6 '89

Washington rules. J. Alter. il *Newsweek* 113:16-18 F 20 '89

Who's lying now? D. Baldwin. il *Common Cause Magazine* 15:32-7 My/Je '89

Willie Ailes [R. Ailes' tactics become campaign issue] J. Klein. il por *New York* 22:38+ D 4 '89

Anecdotes, facetiae, satire, etc.

A Modest Proposal for Cleansing our Publick Life of Impurities and Transgressions. H. Fairlie. il *The New Republic* 200:14-16 Mr 27 '89

History

Whangdoodling [political campaigns] B. A. Weisberger. il *American Heritage* 40:24+ F '89

Laws and regulations

See also
  Ethics in Government Act
  United States. Congress. House. Committee on Standards of Official Conduct

Cashing in on ethics [congressional pay raise in exchange for reforms] *Time* 134:16 Jl 3 '89

Congress gropes to reform. L. Martz. il *Newsweek* 113:19-21 Je 12 '89

Congress may finally order a new broom. D. Harbrecht. il *Business Week* p31 S 11 '89

Cutting Congress down to size. M. B. Zuckerman. il *U.S. News & World Report* 107:64 Jl 3 '89

Ethics embarrassments may kick Congress into action. P. Dwyer. il *Business Week* p43 F 20 '89

The ethics issue heats up. F. Wertheimer. *Common Cause Magazine* 15:45-6 My/Je '89

Ethics reform: the trick is to know when to stop. D. Harbrecht and P. Dwyer. il *Business Week* p36 Ap 3 '89

Frenzy on the Hill [ethics battles] T. Morganthau. il pors *Newsweek* 113:14-18 Je 12 '89

Give a little, get a little [pay raise and revision of ethics rules] N. Traver. il *Time* 134:24 N 27 '89

The GOP feeding frenzy is far from over [ethics turmoil in the House] D. Harbrecht. il por *Business Week* p36-7 Je 19 '89

Have we gone too far? [Congress] M. B. Carlson. il *Time* 133:18-22 Je 12 '89

Money, ethics and Congress. *The Nation* 248:833 Je 19 '89

The packaging of a pay raise [in exchange for congressional ethics reforms] M. Barone. *U.S. News & World Report* 107:24 N 27 '89

Pay dirt [congressional pay raise in the guise of ethics reform] C. Hanson. *The New Republic* 201:10-11 D 25 '89

A raise by any other name [congressional pay raise in the guise of ethics reform] J. N. Baker. il *Newsweek* 114:43 N 27 '89

The real ethics debate. D. Beers. il *Mother Jones* 14:30-1 O '89

Rough justice [Congress] M. Kondracke. *The New Republic* 200:8-10 Je 26 '89

Santa and his reindeer could fit through the holes in this ethics bill. P. Dwyer. *Business Week* p59 D 18 '89

Too righteous? [ethics rules discourage prospective public servants] J. Cramer. il *Time* 133:32 My 29 '89

Watchdogs that purr [Bush's ethics commission] Z. Citron. *The New Republic* 200:10-11 Mr 6 '89

Where Angelenos fear to tread [proposed ethics code for city officials] S. Tifft. *Time* 134:70-1 D 4 '89

Who won the ethics war? [Congress] G. Borger and S. V. Roberts. il *U.S. News & World Report* 106:18-20 Je 12 '89

Will Congress come clean? J. Denny. il *Common Cause Magazine* 15:39-40 Jl/Ag '89

Window of opportunity. F. Wertheimer. il *Common Cause Magazine* 15:44-5 Jl/Ag '89

Canada

Caught in the act: hidden microphones embarrass the NDP. E. K. Fulton. *Maclean's* 102:23 D 18 '89

POLITICAL EXECUTIONS See Executions and executioners
POLITICAL FILMS See Politics in motion pictures
POLITICAL FORECASTING

See also
  Congressional Clearinghouse on the Future
  Public opinion polls

2010: a new great powers lineup? *Society* 27:3 N/D '89

The age of indifference. M. Barone. il *U.S. News & World Report* 107:30+ D 25 '89-Ja 1 '90

Coping with the '90s [U.S. foreign policy] C. W. Maynes. bibl f *Foreign Policy* 74:42-62 Spr '89

Escalating tensions. G. Allen. il *Maclean's* 102:48-9 S 11 '89

Foresight: addressing tomorrow's problems today. L. Grant. por *The Futurist* 23:14-17 Ja/F '89

Helping Congress look ahead [interview with R. McCord] T. Willard and D. M. Fields. il pors *The Futurist* 23:23-7 My/Je '89

I didn't tell you so. M. Greenfield. il *Newsweek* 114:104 N 27 '89

Leading the way to tomorrow [seminar, Government with Foresight: Successes and Challenges in Preparing for the 21st Century] C. G. Wagner and B. M. Cornish. il *The Futurist* 23:34-8 Jl/Ag '89

New century, new players [interview with P. M. Kennedy] il *Life* 12:76 F '89

Three scenarios for Mexico's future. S. Galico. il por *The Futurist* 23:17-19 Jl/Ag '89

Toward the 21st century [special 75th anniversary issue; cover story] bibl f *Current History* 88:1-59+ Ja '89

The twentieth century and beyond [address, May 8, 1989] P. W. Williams. *Vital Speeches of the Day* 55:624-6 Ag 1 '89

Whither policy for the 1990s [special section] bibl *Society* 26:39-82 S/O '89

Anecdotes, facetiae, satire, etc.

Gore Vidal on where we're headed. J. Bailey. por *Mother Jones* 14:13 My '89

Bibliography

Can the US remain number one? [cover story] P. M. Kennedy. il *The New York Review of Books* 36:36-42 Mr 16 '89

POLITICAL HUMOR

Politics, late-night style [TV talk show hosts] R. Zoglin. il *Time* 133:66 Je 12 '89

POLITICAL INTEREST GROUPS See Special interest groups
POLITICAL JOURNALISM See Press and politics
POLITICAL LEADERS See Politicians
POLITICAL LEADERSHIP See Leadership
POLITICAL PARTICIPATION

See also
  Lobbyists and lobbying
  Voting

POLITICAL PARTIES

See also
  Communist Party (U.S.)
  Democratic Party (U.S.)
  Green parties (Politics)
  Green Party (U.S.)
  Republican Party (U.S.)

Third-party fever. A. K. Arnove. il *Mother Jones* 14:20 N '89

Third party time? [cover story] M. Rothschild. il *The Progressive* 53:20-5 O '89

Austria

See also
  Socialist Party (Austria)

Canada

See also
  Co-operative Commonwealth Federation
  Confederation of Regions Party (Canada)
  Conservative Party (Canada)
  Liberal Party (Canada)
  New Democratic Party (Canada)
  Parti québécois
  Quebec New Democratic Party
  Reform Party of Canada
  Social Credit Party (B.C.)

China

See also
  Communist Party (China)

Czechoslovakia

See also
  Communist Party (Czechoslovakia)

France

See also
  Socialist Party (France)

Germany (East)

See also
  Communist Party (Germany: East)

Germany (West)

See also
  Christian Democratic Union (Germany: West)
  Green Party (Germany: West)

Great Britain

See also
  Conservative Party (Great Britain)
  Green Party (Great Britain)
  Labour Party (Great Britain)

Greece

See also
  New Democracy (Greece)
  Socialist Party (Greece)

Hungary

See also
  Communist Party (Hungary)
  Socialist Party (Hungary)

India

See also
  Indian National Congress

POLITICAL PARTIES—cont.
Israel
See also
Likud Party (Israel)
Italy
See also
Christian Democratic Party (Italy)
Communist Party (Italy)
Japan
See also
Liberal-Democratic Party (Japan)
Socialist Party (Japan)
Mexico
See also
Institutional Revolutionary Party (Mexico)
Partido Acción Nacional (Mexico)
Poland
See also
Communist Party (Poland)
South Africa
See also
National Party (South Africa)
Soviet Union
See also
Communist Party (Soviet Union)
Spain
See also
Socialist Party (Spain)
United States
See Political parties
Western Europe
See also
Green Party (Western Europe)

POLITICAL PATRONAGE
See also
Nepotism
A kind word for the spoils system. C. Peters. The Washington Monthly 21:37-8 F '89
Canada
The cost of patronage [privatizing public prosecutors] P. Kaihla. il Maclean's 102:17 D 11 '89
Hollow accusations from a Holy Ghost [memoirs of former Tory MP E. Nielsen] P. C. Newman. il Maclean's 102:56 S 4 '89

POLITICAL PHILOSOPHY
See also
Communism
Conservatism
Democracy
Liberalism
Political ethics
Radicalism
Right and left (Political science)
Socialism

POLITICAL POLLS See Public opinion polls
POLITICAL PRISONERS
See also
Amnesty International
Concentration camps
The bloody war in Belfast spills into the U.S. courts [IRA member J. Doherty in U.S. prison] T. Clifton. il por Newsweek 114:96+ D 11 '89
They condone torture [physicians' work with political prisoners] C. A. Chelala. il World Health p24-5 Ap '89
Angola
SWAPO's witch hunt. S. Reiss. il Newsweek 114:33 S 4 '89
Cuba
Cuba: the human rights show. A. Neier. il The New York Review of Books 36:33-5 Je 15 '89
Czechoslovakia
Act of artistic unfreedom [V. Havel jailed] por Time 133:45 Mr 6 '89
A challenge from Citizen Havel. V. Havel. il por World Press Review 36:40-1 My '89
The devil in Eastern Europe [V. Havel] L. Shapiro. il por Newsweek 113:77-8 Ap 24 '89
Fighting back in Prague. J. Laber. il The New York Review of Books 36:39-41 Ap 27 '89
Fueling demands for Czech reform [imprisonment of V. Havel] H. Schwartz. The Nation 248:660-3 My 15 '89
A statement to the court. V. Havel. il The New York Review of Books 36:41 Ap 27 '89
El Salvador
Fear in the midst of war [army detains church workers] M. Nemeth. il Maclean's 102:48 D 4 '89
Home for the holidays—from El Salvador [church worker J. J. Casolo] por Newsweek 114:52 D 25 '89
Under suspicion [Canadian human rights activist K. Ridd] A. Bilski. il por Maclean's 102:52 D 4 '89
Grenada
In Grenada, victors' justice. The Progressive 53:15-16 Mr '89
Israel
Appeals for Tayseer Aruri [letters] Physics Today 42:15+ My '89
Dissenting opinions about Tayseer Aruri [letters] Physics Today 42 pt1:13+ Ag '89

Israeli physicists, and others, comment on case of Palestinian physicist [T. Aruri] W. Sweet. Physics Today 42:83-5 S '89
Israel's prison academies [Palestinians organize while imprisoned by Israelis]; tr. by Ina Friedman. E. Ya'ari. il The Atlantic 264:22+ O '89
Paraguay
The dictator and the journalists. W. Steif. il por The Progressive 53:16-17 O '89
South Africa
Black leaders: free at last. S. Reiss. il Newsweek 114:58 O 30 '89
Ex-ANC leader talks about 26 years of imprisonment [W. Sisulu] il por Jet 77:30 N 6 '89
Freedom at last [eight activists released] M. Nemeth. il Maclean's 102:34-5 O 23 '89
A glimmer of peace [meeting between N. Mandela and P. Botha] C. Erasmus. il por Maclean's 102:26 Jl 24 '89
Meeting of different minds [F. W. De Klerk and N. Mandela] S. MacLeod. il pors Time 134:28 D 25 '89
New steps in a freedom walk [F. W. De Klerk frees eight black leaders] il U.S. News & World Report 107:17 O 23 '89
Teatime in Pretoria [N. Mandela meets with P. W. Botha] C. S. Manegold. il Newsweek 114:24 Jl 24 '89
Then there was one [release of all political prisoners except N. Mandela] S. MacLeod. il Time 134:49-50 O 23 '89
An unlikely tea for two [N. Mandela meets with P. Botha] B. W. Nelan. il pors Time 134:29 Jl 24 '89
Word from South Africa [interview with Z. M. Dlamini] S. L. Taylor and E. B. Washington. il por Essence 20:42-4+ Jl '89
Soviet Union
Glasnost in Perm 35? K. A. Lawton. il Christianity Today 33:37-8 O 20 '89
In a haunting new memoir, poet Irina Ratushinskaya recalls the agonies of a Soviet labor camp. S. K. Reed. il pors People Weekly 31:87-8 Ja 16 '89
In solitary cells on winter nights [interview with I. Ratushinskaya and I. Geraschenko] E. S. Vaughn. il pors Christianity Today 33:26-9 D 15 '89
Into the heart of the gulag [Perm 35] A. M. Rosenthal. il Reader's Digest 134:71-5 Ap '89
A lost prisoner of the gulag still holds Moscow hostage [R. Wallenberg case] D. Stanglin. il pors U.S. News & World Report 106:34-6 Je 26 '89
A pain-filled mystery [Holocaust hero R. Wallenberg] J. Bierman. por Maclean's 102:47 O 30 '89
A profession under stress [abuses by psychiatrists] J. Langone. il Time 133:94-5 Ap 10 '89
Psychiatrists examine Soviet system. C. Holden. Science 243:1547 Mr 24 '89
Should world psychiatry readmit the Soviets? P. Reddaway. bibl f il The New York Review of Books 36:54-8 O 12 '89
Soviet psychiatry: an exchange [discussion of October 12, 1989 article, Should world psychiatry readmit the Soviets?] P. Reddaway. il The New York Review of Books 36:65-6 D 21 '89
Soviet psychiatry: real progress or just PR? C. Holden. il Science 245:348 Jl 28 '89
The triumph of Natan Sharansky [condensed from Fear no evil] N. Sharansky. il por Reader's Digest 134:75-80 Ja '89
The wasted years [labor camp survivor A. Sandler] A. Wilson-Smith. il por Maclean's 102:24 My 15 '89
Why my grandfather Leon Trotsky must be turning in his grave. Y. Akselrod. Commentary 87:39-43 Ap '89
Turkey
Cruel and usual punishment. J. Laber. il The New York Review of Books 36:34-5 Jl 20 '89
United States
The crime of politics. M. Rothschild. il The Progressive 53:28-30 My '89
Uruguay
The great exception (I) [abuses under military dictatorship, 1973-1985] L. Weschler. il The New Yorker 65:43-6+ Ap 3 '89
Vietnam
U.S., Vietnam agree on emigration of detainees [joint statement, July 30, 1989] Department of State Bulletin 89:63 N '89

POLITICAL PROTESTS, DEMONSTRATIONS, ETC. See Protests, demonstrations, etc.
POLITICAL PSYCHOLOGY
See also
Propaganda
Experienced, qualified—and stupid; tr. by Joel Agee. E. Vilar. Harper's 278:28+ Ja '89
Indignation on demand [politicians' use of indignation] M. Greenfield. il Newsweek 114:78 Jl 10 '89
Notes and comment [global view in local politics] The New Yorker 65:37 O 9 '89
The timid are in bed early. M. Greenfield. il Newsweek 114:106 N 13 '89
Why we all love to hate. D. Gelman. il Newsweek 114:62-4 Ag 28 '89

POLITICAL PUBLICITY *See* Advertising, Political
POLITICAL REFUGEES *See* Refugees
POLITICAL REPORTING *See* Press and politics
POLITICAL RHETORIC *See* Rhetoric
POLITICAL SATIRE *See* Political humor
POLITICAL SCANDALS *See* Politics, Corruption in
POLITICAL SCIENCE
> *See also*
> Citizenship
> Communism
> Decentralization in government
> Democracy
> Despotism
> Fascism
> Geopolitics
> Law
> Liberalism
> Liberty
> Local government
> Nations
> Policy sciences
> Populism
> Radicalism
> Revolutions
> Right and left (Political science)
> Separation of powers
> Socialism
> Sovereignty
> Totalitarianism
> Utopias

Study and teaching
> *See also*
> John F. Kennedy School of Government

The case for the case study. S. Goldsmith and K. Boo. *The Washington Monthly* 21:18-20+ Je '89
The games they play in D.C. N. Santelmann. il *Forbes* 143:128 F 20 '89

POLITICAL TERMINOLOGY *See* Politics—Terminology
POLITICIANS
> *See also*
> Alcohol and politicians
> Drugs and politicians
> Public officers

Experienced, qualified—and stupid; tr. by Joel Agee. E. Vilar. *Harper's* 278:28+ Ja '89

Ethics
> *See* Political ethics

Sexual behavior
Fit for the Cabinet? [womanizing charges against J. Tower] D. R. Carlin, Jr. il *Commonweal* 116:136-7 Mr 10 '89
Privates on parade [reporting on private lives of politicians] *The New Republic* 201:7-9 N 13 '89
Wine, women and irony [J. Tower's behavior] M. Greenfield. il *Newsweek* 113:72 F 20 '89

POLITICIANS' WIVES
> *See also*
> Congressmen's wives

Psychology
Politicians Anonymous. P. Theiler. il *Common Cause Magazine* 15:10-11 My/Je '89

POLITICS
> *See also*
> Cable television and politics
> Comic books, strips, etc.—Political aspects
> Computers—Political use
> Conservatism
> Economics and politics
> Elections
> Fax machines—Political use
> Geopolitics
> Liberalism
> Mass media—Political aspects
> New Age movement and politics
> Newspapers and politics
> Political science
> Press and politics
> Radio and politics
> Recall (Politics)
> Religion and politics
> Tape recordings and politics
> Television and politics
> Videotapes and politics
> Voting
> Weather and politics
> World politics
> > *See also* subhead Politics and government under names of continents, countries, states, cities

Anecdotes, facetiae, satire, etc.
> *See* Political humor

Bibliography
Political booknotes. See issues of The Washington Monthly
The Washington monthly annual Political Book Award. il *The Washington Monthly* 21:23 Mr '89

Terminology
In nine little words [modified limited photo op cum statement sans questions] W. Safire. il *The New York Times Magazine* p16+ Mr 26 '89

POLITICS, CORRUPTION IN
> *See also*
> Campaign funds
> Conflict of interests (Public office)
> Watergate case

The abuse of power: misuse of the I.R.S. [cover story] D. Burnham. il *The New York Times Magazine* p24-7+ S 3 '89
The anatomy of corruption. W. F. Buckley. *National Review* 41:54-5 D 22 '89
Can Jack Kemp clean up the HUD mess? S. V. Roberts. il por *U.S. News & World Report* 107:26-7 Jl 3 '89
Cleaning house at HUD—and then some. H. Gleckman and others. il por *Business Week* p72-4 Jl 10 '89
Deborah Gore Dean [executive assistant at Dept. of Housing and Urban Development] il por *People Weekly* 32:84-5 D 25 '89-Ja 1 '90
Delinquent taxmen [Internal Revenue Service] R. Behar. il *Time* 133:66-7 My 29 '89
The disgrace at HUD. M. Greenfield. il *Newsweek* 114:60 Jl 24 '89
Fear and cover-ups in the IRS. R. Behar. il *Time* 134:40 Ag 7 '89
Grow up [HUD scandal] W. F. Buckley. *National Review* 41:54-5 S 1 '89
Hip-deep at HUD. L. Martz. il *Newsweek* 114:16-18 Jl 10 '89
The housing hustle [HUD scandal] N. Traver. il por *Time* 133:18-19 Je 26 '89
How politics is making it tough to clean up HUD. J. P. Shapiro. *U.S. News & World Report* 107:39 D 11 '89
How to end Washington corruption. T. Van Dyk. il por *Fortune* 120:213+ D 18 '89
The howl of congressional watchdogs [oversight probes] S. V. Roberts. il *U.S. News & World Report* 107:24-6 S 11 '89
The HUD party, the party of patronage. *National Review* 41:10 S 1 '89
The HUD ripoff [cover story] S. Waldman. il *Newsweek* 114:16-22 Ag 7 '89
The HUD scandal hits a stone wall [S. R. Pierce takes the Fifth Amendment] il por *U.S. News & World Report* 107:11 O 9 '89
HUD under Reagan: 'close to obscene' [charges against S. Pierce] R. Thomas. il por *Newsweek* 113:18 Je 12 '89
HUD without politics? S. Waldman and C. Bingham. il *Newsweek* 114:38 O 9 '89
HUDscam revisited [grants to Massachusetts during Carter administration] il *National Review* 41:18-19 O 13 '89
Inside job [HUD scandal] P. C. Montgomery. il *Common Cause Magazine* 15:16-20 Jl/Ag '89
Jack be nimble, Jack be quick [HUD scandal] E. Magnuson. il por *Time* 134:20 Jl 24 '89
The lessons of the HUD scandal. D. Gergen. il *U.S. News & World Report* 107:64 Ag 7 '89
Looking beyond the HUD scandal. B. Cohn. il por *Newsweek* 114:19 Ag 21 '89
Poking into HUD's swamp. L. Martz. il por *Newsweek* 113:19 Je 26 '89
The price of influence [HUD scandal] H. Mackenzie. il *Maclean's* 102:29-30 Jl 10 '89
The problem at HUD. S. T. Mandel. il *National Review* 41:21-2 Ag 4 '89
Raising the roof on corruption at HUD. *U.S. News & World Report* 106:11 Je 26 '89
Sam Pierce's "turkey farm" [Dept. of Housing and Urban Development; with interview with S. R. Pierce] N. Traver. il pors *Time* 134:20-4+ S 18 '89
Sam plays it again [S. Pierce takes Fifth Amendment in HUD scandal probe] *The Nation* 249:405 O 16 '89
Sam stays silent [S. Pierce and HUD scandal] *National Review* 41:19-20 O 27 '89
Samuel Pierce, House panel clash over housing issue. il por *Jet* 76:37 Je 19 '89
'Somebody is not telling the truth' [HUD scandal] D. Harbrecht. il por *Business Week* p21-2 Jl 24 '89
Still more scandals at HUD. L. Martz. il *Newsweek* 114:21 Jl 3 '89
The undoing of Silent Sam Pierce [Dept. of Housing and Urban Development] S. V. Roberts. il *U.S. News & World Report* 107:29+ S 18 '89
What Jack Kemp loves about the HUD scandal. R. Stodghill, II and D. Harbrecht. il por *Business Week* p41 Jl 31 '89
What Reagan hath wrought is bedeviling Bush. R. Fly. il *Business Week* p37 Jl 3 '89
Where were the media on HUD? M. Riley. il *Time* 134:48 Jl 24 '89

Anecdotes, facetiae, satire, etc.
Chain of fools. J. Queenan. *The New Republic* 201:8 Jl 17-24 '89

History
The wrongdoers. B. A. Weisberger. il *American Heritage* 40:26+ D '89

Alabama
> *See also*
> Birmingham (Ala.)—Politics and government

POLITICS, CORRUPTION IN—*cont.*

Alberta

Day of reckoning [report on Principal Group collapse; special section] J. DeMont. il por *Maclean's* 102:30-4 Jl 31 '89

A Principal toll [Alberta agrees to compensate investors in failed company] J. DeMont. il por *Maclean's* 102:28-9 Ag 7 '89

The Principal vote [Principal Group scandal at center of election campaign] J. Howse. il *Maclean's* 102:12-13 Mr 20 '89

Austria

Social climber's guide to Vienna [Socialist Party officials linked to U. Proksch and deliberate sinking of the Lucona] E. von Kuehnelt-Leddihn. *National Review* 41:42 Mr 10 '89

California

See also

Los Angeles (Calif.)—Politics and government

Canada

Anecdotes, facetiae, satire, etc.

Watergate envy: it's a scandal [furor over budget leaks couched in Watergate terminology] C. Gordon. il *Maclean's* 102:9 Je 26 '89

China

The economic root of the problem. E. Ellis. il *World Press Review* 36:16-17 Jl '89

Too much all in the family [nepotism] J. Greenwald. *Time* 133:23 Je 5 '89

Cuba

Anatomy of an execution [A. Ochoa Sanchez found guilty in drug trafficking case] A. Cruz, Jr. *Commentary* 88:54-6 N '89

Death in Havana [execution of Gen. A. Ochoa Sánchez in drug trafficking case] *Newsweek* 114:24 Jl 24 '89

'I have no reason to live' [trial of A. Ochoa Sanchez on drug trading] H. Anderson. il por *Newsweek* 114:25 Jl 10 '89

Reading the coca leaves [Major General A. Ochoa Sanchez convicted of helping drug smugglers] J. Smolowe. il pors *Time* 134:30-1 Jl 10 '89

Revolution doesn't go better with coke [Interior Minister A. Ochoa Sanchez involved in cocaine smuggling] il por *U.S. News & World Report* 107:12 Jl 10 '89

The trial that shook Cuba [drug trafficking case involving A. Ochoa Sanchez and A. de la Guardia; cover story] J. Preston. il pors *The New York Review of Books* 36:24-31 D 7 '89

France

Insider-trading shock rocks the Elysee [Triangle affair] B. Riemer. il *Business Week* p54 Ja 23 '89

The Socialists dodge one bullet—but the next? [insider trading Triangle probe] B. Riemer and F. J. Comes. il *Business Week* p46 F 13 '89

Germany (East)

Filling the void. J. Bierman. il *Maclean's* 102:24+ D 18 '89

Life in the golden ghetto. il *Time* 134:17 D 18 '89

To each according to his greed? R. Knight. il por *U.S. News & World Report* 107:26 D 18 '89

Germany (West)

A self-inflicted wound [West Germany's role in Libyan poison gas scandal] M. R. Meyer. il *Newsweek* 113:42 Ja 30 '89

Great Britain

See also

Profumo, John D.—Political scandal

Greece

Greek farce. Taki. il *National Review* 41:25-6 O 27 '89

The looting of Greece [G. Koskotas implicates government in Bank of Crete scandal] R. Ajemian. il pors *Time* 133:32-5 Mr 13 '89

"No mud touches me" [A. Papandreou denies corruption charges leveled by G. Koskotas] W. R. Doerner. il por *Time* 133:37 Mr 20 '89

Out of office, into the dock? [A. Papandreou implicated by G. Koskotas in Bank of Crete scandal] por *Time* 134:38 S 25 '89

Scandal and stalemate. J. Bierman. por *Maclean's* 102:17 Jl 3 '89

India

Gandhi's Watergate? [Bofors arms sale scandal] *Newsweek* 114:42 O 23 '89

Italy

See also

Irpinia (Italy)—Politics and government

Japan

The dark side of Japan Inc. [Recruit insider trading scandal] J. Hammer. il *Newsweek* 113:41 Ja 9 '89

A fatal money scandal [resignation of N. Takeshita] M. Nemeth. il por *Maclean's* 102:25 My 8 '89

The fine art of kinmyaku [contributions to N. Takeshita from Recruit Company] il por *U.S. News & World Report* 106:18 Ap 24 '89

Insider trading. G. Ellwand. il *Maclean's* 102:22-3 Ja 9 '89

The Japanese scandal [Recruit scandal] il *World Press Review* 36:8 Je '89

Japan's quest for Mr. Clean [M. Ito declines to run for prime minister] B. Martin and H. Takayama. il por *Newsweek* 112:58 My 22 '89

Japan's scandal: who's next? S. Solo. il *Fortune* 119:24 Ap 10 '89

'Money politics' makes Tokyo's world go around [Recruit insider trading scandal] M. Tharp. il *U.S. News & World Report* 106:48 Ja 9 '89

Now Takeshita really feels the flames of scandal [Recruit insider trading scandal] T. Holden. por *Business Week* p55 F 27 '89

A pinball empire greased by graft? [charges that Socialist Party took bribes from pachinko parlor owners] il por *U.S. News & World Report* 107:18 O 30 '89

A question of ethics [N. Takeshita admits to receiving political donations from Recruit] A. Bilski. *Maclean's* 102:27 Ap 24 '89

Real reform in Japan? Don't hold your breath. T. Holden. il *Business Week* p51 My 29 '89

The Recruit scandal bubbles to the top. A. Borrus. por *Business Week* p55 Mr 20 '89

Sand in a well-oiled machine [N. Takeshita forced to resign in wake of Recruit scandal] S. MacLeod. por *Time* 133:44 My 8 '89

Scandal, scandal everywhere. I. Rodger. *World Press Review* 36:18 Ap '89

A scandal that will not die [Recruit scandal] W. R. Doerner. il por *Time* 133:37+ Ap 24 '89

Sex, lies, and Japanese politics. M. Sayle. *The New Republic* 201:18-22 S 11 '89

Sinking in a sea of yen [Recruit scandal threatens to topple Prime Minister Takeshita] H. Anderson. il por *Newsweek* 113:49-50 Ap 24 '89

Takeshita bows out. B. Martin and others. il *Newsweek* 113:35 My 8 '89

Takeshita talks political reform—but doesn't sound convincing. A. Borrus. il *Business Week* p57 Ja 23 '89

Uniqueness and sleaze [Recruit scandal] W. M. Stern. *National Review* 41:23-4 Je 2 '89

Why time may be running out for Takeshita [Recruit scandal] T. Holden. por *Business Week* p43 Ap 24 '89

Will the Recruit scandal just go away? A. Borrus and N. Gross. il por *Business Week* p40-1 Je 12 '89

You scratch my back . . . [Recruit insider trading scandal] J. Greenwald. il *Time* 133:47 Ja 9 '89

Latin America

Will democracy in Latin America simply mean plunder? P. C. Roberts. il *Business Week* p18 S 18 '89

Mexico

Wimp no more [President C. Salinas de Gortari] G. D. Garcia. il por *Time* 133:28-9 Ap 24 '89

New Jersey

See also

Atlantic City (N.J.)—Politics and government

New York (State)

See also

New York (N.Y.)—Politics and government

Al's pals [illegal dealings of Sen. A. D'Amato] M. J. Green. il *The New Republic* 201:16-20 O 30 '89

Everybody's pal [controversies surrounding A. D'Amato] il por *Time* 134:28 N 6 '89

Fonzie on the spot: the HUD revelations tarnish the 'new' D'Amato. P. Blauner. il pors *New York* 22:42-8 N 13 '89

Winners and sinners: the D'Amato and Frank dossiers. J. Klein. il por *New York* 22:23-4 O 9 '89

Nicaragua

Ballot blocks. R. Kagan. *The New Republic* 200:21-2 Je 12 '89

Ontario

Caught in Starr wars [scandal in Ontario claims D. Peterson aides P. Starr and G. Ashworth] P. Kaihla. il pors *Maclean's* 102:12-13 Jl 3 '89

Dangerous liaisons [B. Stone testifies at inquiry into political donations from Tridel Enterprises channeled through National Council of Jewish Women] P. Kaihla. il pors *Maclean's* 102:20+ O 16 '89

A flurry of scandals. R. Corelli. il pors *Maclean's* 102:12-13 Jl 10 '89

Liberal controversies [three high-profile resignations] P. Kaihla. il por *Maclean's* 102:17 Je 19 '89

Questions of privilege [H. R. Argue faces charges of misused Senate funds] B. Wallace and D. Jenish. il por *Maclean's* 102:17 N 27 '89

Anecdotes, facetiae, satire, etc.

The real meaning of scandal. A. Fotheringham. il *Maclean's* 102:48 Jl 10 '89

Panama

Brute politics [U.S. dispatches additional troops following disputed election] A. Bilski. il por *Maclean's* 102:22-4 My 22 '89

Dear Manny [Drug Enforcement Administration's correspondence with M. Noriega] M. Hosenball. *The New Republic* 200:9-10 Je 12 '89

A defiant dictator. B. Levin. il *Maclean's* 102:25 My 29 '89

A dubious ballot. D. Gollob. il por *Maclean's* 102:26 My 1 '89

POLITICS, CORRUPTION IN—Panama—*cont.*

The gutsy Panama option [Colombian drug king P. Escobar seeks refuge] pors *U.S. News & World Report* 107:19 S 11 '89

Lead-pipe politics [U.S. sends troops to Panama in wake of election fraud; cover story; special section] il por map *Time* 133:40-4+ My 22 '89

A man, a plan, an election. K. E. Schuette. il *National Review* 41:18-19 Je 16 '89

Meanwhile, in Panama [drug trade] *Time* 134:23 S 11 '89

Mr. Ex-President [J. Carter's visit] H. Hertzberg. *The New Republic* 200:4 Je 5 '89

The OAS and the Panama crisis [statements, August 24 and 31, 1989] L. S. Eagleburger. *Department of State Bulletin* 89:67-75 N '89

Panama elections [statements, April 27-May 18, 1989] G. Bush. *Department of State Bulletin* 89:66-72 Jl '89

Playing 'bad cop' in Panama [U.S. policy] C. Lane and D. Waller. il por *Newsweek* 113:36-7 My 8 '89

Sparring (again) with a dictator [U.S. policy] J. Smolowe. il por *Time* 133:46 My 8 '89

Standoff in Panama [M. A. Noriega vs U.S. after fraudulent election] J. L. Galloway. il por *U.S. News & World Report* 106:28-32 My 22 '89

Surrender, Manny [M. A. Noriega] *The New Republic* 200:9-10 Je 5 '89

T.R.'s invention [M. A. Noriega's election fraud] G. Black. *The Nation* 248:760-1 Je 5 '89

Taking aim at Noriega [U.S. policy in upcoming election] C. A. Robbins. il por *U.S. News & World Report* 106:40-1 My 1 '89

A test of wills [U.S. vs. Noriega government] L. Martz. il por map *Newsweek* 112:34-9 My 22 '89

Why Noriega wins. M. Kempton. il *The New York Review of Books* 36:10 Je 15 '89

Philippines

From jet set to jail cell [U.S. asks for extradition of A. Khashoggi, jailed in Switzerland in connection with alleged looting of Philippine treasure by F. Marcos] C. Dickey. il por *Newsweek* 113:10 My 1 '89

Imelda's 'hell in paradise'. T. Clifton. il por *Newsweek* 113:38 My 8 '89

Stepping out [A. Khashoggi's involvement with the Marcoses] J. Kasindorf. il pors *New York* 22:36-44 D 18 '89

Québec (Province)

Hi-tech disagreements [Senator M. Cogger named in Japanese businessman T. Tsuru's lawsuit against entrepreneur G. Montpetit over misspent loans] P. Kaihla. il por *Maclean's* 102:16-17 Je 26 '89

Politics and policing [Royal Canadian Mounted Police accused of delaying raid on offices of Tory MP R. Grisé] B. Wallace. il *Maclean's* 102:24 D 4 '89

Questions of ethics [business activities of Canadian Senator M. Cogger] B. Wallace. il por *Maclean's* 102:18+ N 13 '89

Soviet Union

Back-alley politics in the Kremlin [charges against Y. Ligachev] D. Brand. il por *Time* 133:48 My 29 '89

Texas

Texas-style ethics. M. Ivins. il *The Progressive* 53:41 Je '89

Anecdotes, facetiae, satire, etc.

Just say no, fellas. M. Ivins. por *Ms.* 18:17 S '89

United States

See Politics, Corruption in

Venezuela

A crackdown in Caracas sends foreign executives fleeing [currency scheme] G. DeGeorge. il *Business Week* p46 Jl 31 '89

West Virginia

A mountainous loss in West Virginia [investment fund fraud] G. L. Miles. il *Business Week* p42 Ap 3 '89

Zaire

'Peacemaker' Mobutu is under fire. S. Askin and B. Javetski. il por *Business Week* p42 Jl 10 '89

POLITICS AND BLACKS *See* Blacks—Political activities

POLITICS AND BUSINESS *See* Business—Political aspects

POLITICS AND EDUCATION

See also

College students—Political activities

College teachers—Political activities

Political science—Study and teaching

Civilization and its malcontents [politicization of humanities; cover story] S. Hook. il *National Review* 41:30-3 O 13 '89

Elections and efficiency. C. Pipho. il *Phi Delta Kappan* 70:350-1 Ja '89

Peace plan for the canon wars. G. Graff and W. E. Cain. *The Nation* 248:310-13 Mr 6 '89

The Pledge of Allegiance in public schools. C. Seefeldt. *The Education Digest* 55:62-3 S '89

Scaring our children. M. Novak. il *Forbes* 144:167 O 30 '89

What culture should mean. L. S. Robinson. *The Nation* 249:319-21 S 25 '89

POLITICS AND INDUSTRY *See* Industry and state

POLITICS AND LITERATURE

See also

Literature and state

Poetry and state

POLITICS AND SCIENCE *See* Science and state

POLITICS AND WAR

The politics of cold blood. R. J. Rummel. bibl *Society* 27:32-40 N/D '89

POLITICS IN ART

Cultural kamikaze [work of R. Conal] J. Diamond. il por *Vogue* 179:350+ Mr '89

Facing the nation [work of R. Conal] il *Mother Jones* 14:56 F/Mr '89

Exhibitions

Group Material at Dia (Wooster St.). E. Heartney. *Art in America* 77:145 Ja '89

Material world [work of Group Material] W. Olander. il *Art in America* 77:122-9+ Ja '89

POLITICS IN LITERATURE

See also

Booksellers and bookselling—Political literature

Compromising positions [novelist W. Just] D. Baldwin. il por *Common Cause Magazine* 15:34-8 Mr/Ap '89

Inside-the-Beltway intrigue [interview with W. S. Just] A. P. Sanoff. por *U.S. News & World Report* 106:60 F 20 '89

A turning of the critical tide? [works of A. Walker and M. Piercy] C. Iannone. *Commentary* 88:57-9 N '89

Walter Karp, 1934-1989 [interview] J. Karp. il por *American Heritage* 40:166-7 N '89

POLITICS IN MOTION PICTURES

America's underculture [interview with Costa-Gavras] il *New Perspectives Quarterly* 5:53-6 Wint '88/'89

Cinema of rage [Toronto's Festival of Festivals] B. D. Johnson. il *Maclean's* 102:58+ S 25 '89

Would Batman vote Republican? M. Sieff. *National Review* 41:55-7 S 15 '89

POLITICS IN OPERA

Viewpoint [works of W. A. Mozart] J. W. Freeman. *Opera News* 53:4 F 4 '89

POLITZER, GENEVA B.

A presidential gazetteer. il *American History Illustrated* 24:43-52 Ap '89

POLITZER, PATRICIA

Democracy on the slow track. il *The Nation* 249:781-2+ D 25 '89

POLIVANOV, MIKHAIL

Memoirs; tr. by Barry J. Rubin. il *The New Republic* 200:34-7 F 20 '89

POLKA

In praise of the polka. R. P. Crease. il *The Atlantic* 264:78-83 Ag '89

POLKA BANDS

It was shake-the-world time for Lech Walesa in Poland, but polka time for his son in America [S. Walesa tours with Jan Lewan band] il pors *People Weekly* 32:81 S 11 '89

The next generation [S. Walesa] il por *Scholastic Update (Teachers' edition)* 122:5 O 20 '89

POLL TAX

North Carolina

N.C. students get state to outlaw its poll tax. *Jet* 76:8 Je 19 '89

POLLACK, STEPHANIE

Solving the lead dilemma. il *Technology Review* 92:22-31 O '89

POLLACK, STEPHANIE, AND SHULMAN, SETH

Toxic responsibility. il *The Atlantic* 263:26+ Mr '89

POLLAK, RICHARD

The trial of Donald and Si Newhouse [cover story] il *The Nation* 248:325+ Mr 13 '89

POLLAN, CORKY

Best bets. See issues of New York

Christmas gifts [cover story] il *New York* 22:59-74+ D 4 '89

POLLAN, MICHAEL

Weeds are us. il *The New York Times Magazine* p48-9+ N 5 '89

Why mow? The case against lawns [cover story] il *The New York Times Magazine* p22-7+ My 28 '89

(jt. auth) See Fox, Michael J., and Pollan, Michael

POLLAN, STEPHEN M., AND LEVINE, MARK, 1958-

How to read the fine print in contracts. il *Money* 18:111-12+ Je '89

'I do'-ing it right. il *New York* 22:38-50 Ja 9 '89

POLLARD, ALFRED H.

My bicentenary message [address, December 2, 1988] *Vital Speeches of the Day* 55:346-9 Mr 15 '89

POLLARD, ANNE

about

Cruel and unusual punishment. L. C. Pogrebin. por *Ms.* 18:36-7 N '89

POLLARD, GAYLE

(jt. auth) See Jackson, Maga E., and Pollard, Gayle

POLLARD, JONATHAN
about
Cruel and unusual punishment. L. C. Pogrebin. por *Ms.* 18:36-7 N '89
POLLARD, TITUS DAVID
about
New music lesson method can have students playing piano within one month. il por *Jet* 76:14 Ag 28 '89
POLLARDING *See* Pruning
POLLEN
Sneeze calendar [chart listing types of pollen by geographic location] il *American Health* 8:16 Jl/Ag '89
POLLEN, FOSSIL
Angiosperm diversification and paleolatitudinal gradients in Cretaceous floristic diversity. P. R. Crane and S. Lidgard. bibl f il *Science* 246:675-8 N 3 '89
Pollen provides ancient weather report. *Science News* 135:220 Ap 8 '89
POLLINATION *See* Fertilization of plants
POLLINI, MAURIZIO
about
Extreme occasions. E. W. Said. *The Nation* 248:898-900 Je 26 '89
POLLITT, KATHA
Collectibles [poem] *The New Yorker* 65:32 Je 19 '89
Rereading Jane Austen's novels [poem] *The New Republic* 201:35 Ag 7-14 '89
Violence in a man's world. il *The New York Times Magazine* p18+ Je 18 '89
POLLOCK, JACKSON, 1912-1956
about
American frontiers. D. Solomon. il pors *House & Garden* 161:124-7 Je '89
Jackson Pollock bio a milestone for authors. A. Smith. il *Publishers Weekly* 236:39 O 27 '89
POLLOCK, LINDA A.
Younger sons in Tudor and Stuart England. bibl il *History Today* 39:23-9 Je '89
POLLOCK, PAUL JACKSON *See* Pollock, Jackson, 1912-1956
POLLOCK, SARAH
The charge of the brook brigades. il *Sierra* 74:24-6+ N/D '89
POLLOCK, TOM
about
Universal pulls out a plum . . . R. Grover. il *Business Week* p51-2 N 13 '89
POLLOCK-KRASNER FOUNDATION
The Pollock-Krasner Foundation: special assistance for needy artists. M. Mathews-Berenson. il *American Artist* 53:80-3 Je '89
POLLS, COLLEGE FOOTBALL *See* Football, College—Polls
POLLUTION
See also
Acid rain
Air pollution
Chemical plants—Environmental aspects
Electric plants—Environmental aspects
Forest products industry—Environmental aspects
Marine pollution
Oil pollution
Pesticides—Environmental aspects
Plastics pollution
Radioactive pollution
Radon pollution
Resorts—Environmental aspects
Soil pollution
Space debris
Trade waste—Disposal
Uranium industry—Environmental aspects
Water pollution
Pollution produces peeling paint. *USA Today (Periodical)* 118:13 D '89
A risk worth worrying about? [views of Bruce Ames]. L. Roberts. *Science* 243:307 Ja 20 '89
Why is the environmental crisis happening? [address, September 13, 1989] B. H. Alexander. *Vital Speeches of the Day* 56:124-8 D 1 '89
Control
See also
Environmental movement
Industry and the environment
Pollution control industries
United States. Environmental Protection Agency
Ailing Australian youth inspires pollution solution [Jonathan Wilson-Fuller] *The Futurist* 23:36 N/D '89
Cleaning up [cover story; special section] G. Easterbrook. il *Newsweek* 114:26-9+ Jl 24 '89
Grime and punishment. *The New Republic* 200:7-8 F 20 '89
Input management of production systems. E. P. Odum. bibl f il *Science* 243:177-82 Ja 13 '89
Pollutant recovery techniques ready for use. il *Popular Mechanics* 166:14 S '89
Pollution prevention. S. K. Friedlander. bibl f il maps *Environment* 31:10-15+ My '89
Will changing your light bulb save the world? C. A. Moore. il *International Wildlife* 19:18-23 My/Je '89

International aspects
A failed initiative [conference at The Hague] B. Wallace. *Maclean's* 102:14 Mr 20 '89
Exhibitions
Pollution parable [T. J. Thordarson designs pollution monster for Big Bang Schtroumpfs theme park in France] B. Weber. il *The New York Times Magazine* p86 F 26 '89
International aspects
See also
United Nations Environment Programme. Global Environmental Monitoring System
Pollution unlimited. F. Bequette. il *The Courier (Unesco)* 42:24-30 N '89
Warning: planet in peril [cover story; special issue] il maps *Scholastic Update (Teachers' edition)* 121:2-8+ Ap 21 '89
Laws and regulations
Prosecuting environmental crimes [address, July 17, 1989] S. Harshbarger. *Vital Speeches of the Day* 55:760-3 O 1 '89

Anecdotes, facetiae, satire, etc.
Pollute the market. B. Ehrenreich. il *Mother Jones* 14:9-10 O '89

Measurement
See also
United Nations Environment Programme. Global Environmental Monitoring System
Antarctic regions
Antarctic pollution. il *Sea Frontiers* 35:133 My/Je '89
California
See also
Richmond (Calif.)—Pollution
Santa Clara County (Calif.)—Pollution
Canada
Flora for the worst neighborhoods [research by Thomas C. Hutchinson] *BioScience* 39:675-6 N '89
Eastern Europe
Eastern Europe faces crisis [views of Hilary F. French] *USA Today (Periodical)* 117:8-9 Ap '89
Perestroika may be both good and bad for Eastern Europe's severe ecological crisis. A. Hittle and D. Malakoff. il *Utne Reader* p86-7 Ja/F '89
Hungary
Will the sun ever shine on Budapest? D. Hinrichsen. il *International Wildlife* 19:18-23 S/O '89
See also
Morgan City (La.)—Pollution
Louisiana
New Jersey
Untouchable [toxic dumping by Transtech Industries] J. Zweig. il *Forbes* 144:10 Jl 24 '89
New York (State)
See also
Love Canal case
Niagara Falls (N.Y.)—Pollution
Philippines
Poverty, negligence, ignorance. M. C. Vidanes. il *World Health* p22 Mr '89
South Carolina
See also
Sumter County (S.C.)—Pollution
Soviet Union
The greening of the U.S.S.R. D. Thompson. il *Time* 133:68-9 Ja 2 '89
United States
See Pollution
POLLUTION, OUTDOOR LIGHT *See* Lighting, Outdoor
POLLUTION AND WILDLIFE
Land of death . . . and life [wildlife thrive on contaminated grounds of the Rocky Mountain Arsenal] G. Gerhardt. il map *National Wildlife* 28:34-40 D '89/Ja '90
POLLUTION CONTROL INDUSTRIES
See also
American Toxxic Control Inc.
Environmental Field Services Inc.
OHM Corporation
Roy F. Weston, Inc.
Yankee Companies Inc.
Dirty business [waste management] E. Corcoran. il *Scientific American* 261:98+ S '89
Would you believe $16.67 an hour to scrub rocks? [cleanup of Alaskan oil spill] K. R. Sheets. il *U.S. News & World Report* 106:48 Ap 17 '89
Securities
Cleaning up on the coming cleanup. E. T. Smith. il *Business Week* p98+ O 16 '89
Danger: hazardous stocks. R. Simon. il *Forbes* 144:41-2 O 16 '89
Roses among the environmental ashes. T. Paré. il *Fortune* 120:36 O 9 '89
You just might clean up with pollution stocks. L. J. Nathans. il *Business Week* p106-7 Je 12 '89
Canada
Profiting from waste. D. Jenish. il *Maclean's* 102:38-40 Ja 23 '89
POLLUTION LIABILITY
Deals that smell bad [toxic waste undoing takeovers] R. Simon. il *Forbes* 143:49+ My 15 '89

POLLUTION POLICY *See* Environmental policy
POLLUTION PROBE FOUNDATION
A divisive alliance [Pollution Probe and Friends of the Earth endorse Loblaw's environmentally friendly line of products] *Maclean's* 102:40 Jl 17 '89
POLLUTION RIGHTS *See* Emission reduction credits
POLLUX (SHIP)
Heroes of the frozen cliff [rescue of crew from wreck by Newfoundlanders in World War II] H. Strauss. il *Reader's Digest* 134:102-7 Ap '89
POLLY [television program] See Television program reviews— Single works
POLLY PECK INTERNATIONAL PLC
Meet Asil Nadir, the billion-dollar fruit king [Polly Peck to buy Del Monte fresh fruit operations] M. Maremont. il por *Business Week* p32 S 18 '89
Polly Peck International plc. J. Slovak. il *Fortune* 119:76 F 13 '89
POLO, ROBERTO, 1950-
                        about
A taste for art and money. C. Dickey. il por *Newsweek* 113:68 My 29 '89
POLO
                Economic aspects
Why more companies are ponying up for polo. G. DeGeorge. il *Business Week* p148+ Mr 13 '89
POLO RESTAURANT (NEW YORK, N.Y.) *See* New York (N.Y.)—Restaurants, nightclubs, bars, etc.
POLSKY, ROSE
                        about
Reviews:
    Performances in Los Angeles. D. Perlmutter. *Dance Magazine* 63:32+ Ja '89
POLSKY (ROSE) AND DANCERS *See* Rose Polsky and Dancers
POLT, RENATA
The Queen of Budapest. il map *Travel Holiday* 171:82-7 Mr '89
POLUNIN, NICHOLAS
Foundation for Environmental Conservation. *Environment* 31:44-5 My '89
POLYCHLORINATED BIPHENYLS
Are Great Lakes fish safe to eat? W. A. Schmidt. il map *National Wildlife* 27:16-19 Ag/S '89
Are Lake Michigan fish dangerous to your health? J. Gibbs. il *Outdoor Life* 184:72-4+ D '89
A campaign setback [uproar over disposal of PCBs in Quebec] M. Rose. il *Maclean's* 102:12-13 S 4 '89
Contaminant Cove: where polluters defile Mohawk land [New York State] J. E. Milich. il *The Progressive* 53:23-5 Ja '89
Dangerous cargo [PCB-contaminated wastes from Quebec turned away by British ports] M. Rose. il *Maclean's* 102:10-12 Ag 28 '89
An industry's mania for nightmares [press inflames concerns over storage of PCBs in Canada] G. Bain. il *Maclean's* 102:60 O 23 '89
Striped bass [effects of Westway decision and PCBs on New York's commercial fisheries] S. D. Garber. il *Focus (New York, N.Y.: 1950)* 39:34-6 Summ '89
Unwanted garbage: British port blocks ship with Canadian PCBs. A. Phillips. il *Maclean's* 102:43 Ag 21 '89
POLYCONOMICS (FIRM)
Here is a pebble of a project [study of Mexico] M. S. Forbes, Jr. il *Forbes* 144:27 Jl 10 '89
POLYESTERS, SUCROSE *See* Sucrose polyesters
POLYETHYLENE
                Prices
Profiting from disaster [explosion at Phillips Petroleum polyethylene plant outside Houston] A. A. Lappen. il *Forbes* 144:203+ N 27 '89
POLYETHYLENE GLYCOLS
All-weather sportswear. il *USA Today (Periodical)* 118:15 D '89
Also worth noting [Enzon's development of polyethylene glycol that attaches to enzymes and some biopharmaceuticals] *High Technology Business* 9:6 Jl/Ag '89
POLYGRAM RECORDS
"I don't loon off all the time" [C. Blackwell sells Island Records to PolyGram] P. Newcomb. il por *Forbes* 144:344+ N 13 '89
Now it's Chris Blackwell, corporate hipster [Island Records surrenders to PolyGram] R. A. Melcher and D. Lieberman. il por *Business Week* p49 Ag 14 '89
POLYMERASE CHAIN REACTION
Access to a messenger RNA sequence or its protein product is not limited by tissue or species specificity. G. Sarkar and S. S. Sommer. bibl f il *Science* 244:331-4 Ap 21 '89
Accounting made easy for gene mappers [sequence tagged sites] R. Weiss. *Science News* 136:230 O 7 '89
Are tissues a patch quilt of ectopic gene expression? [discussion of April 21, 1989 article, Access to a messenger RNA sequence or its protein product is not limited by tissue or species specificity] G. Sarkar and S. S. Sommer. *Science* 246:261 O 13 '89

A common language for physical mapping of the human genome [sequence-tagged sites] M. V. Olson and others. bibl f *Science* 245:1434-5 S 29 '89
Genomic sequencing and methylation analysis by ligation mediated PCR. G. P. Pfeifer and others. bibl f il *Science* 246:810-13 N 10 '89
High rate of HTLV-II infection in seropositive IV drug abusers in New Orleans. H. Lee and others. bibl f il *Science* 244:471-5 Ap 28 '89
In vivo footprinting of a muscle specific enhancer by ligation mediated PCR. P. R. Mueller and B. Wold. bibl f il *Science* 246:780-6 N 10 '89
Molecular cloning of the thyrotropin receptor. M. Parmentier and others. bibl f il *Science* 246:1620-2 D 22 '89
The molecule of the year [cover story; with editorial comment by D. E. Koshland] R. L. Guyer and D. E. Koshland, Jr. il *Science* 246:1543-6 D 22 '89
New game plan for genome mapping [sequence tagged site approach proposed by Maynard V. Olson] L. Roberts. il *Science* 245:1438-40 S 29 '89
New test homes in on evasive Lyme disease [research by Patricia A. Rosa and Tom G. Schwan] K. Fackelmann. *Science News* 136:374 D 9 '89
Polymerase chain reaction with single-sided specificity: analysis of T cell receptor δ chain. E. Y. Loh and others. bibl f il *Science* 243:217-20 Ja 13 '89
Selective amplification and cloning of four new members of the G protein-coupled receptor family. F. Libert and others. bibl f il *Science* 244:569-72 My 5 '89
Test diagnoses AIDS in newborns [work of Chin-Yih Ou] I. Wickelgren. *Science News* 135:389 Je 24 '89
Test screens live 'test tube' embryos. R. Weiss. *Science News* 135:132 Mr 4 '89
                Archeological use
Molecular archaeology [mitochondrial DNA sequences from Little Salt Springs, Fla. remains; research by Svante Pääbo] J. Benditt. *Scientific American* 261:25-6 Jl '89
POLYMERASES
Chromosomal rearrangement generating a composite gene for a developmental transcription factor [Bacillus subtilis] P. Stragier and others. bibl f il *Science* 243:507-12 Ja 27 '89
Enhancement of bacteriophage T4 late transcription by components of the T4 DNA replication apparatus. D. R. Herendeen and others. bibl f il *Science* 245:952-8 S 1 '89
Function of a bacterial activator protein that binds to transcriptional enhancers. D. L. Popham and others. bibl f il *Science* 243:629-35 F 3 '89
Initiation by yeast RNA polymerase II at the adenoviral major late promoter in vitro. N. F. Lue and others. bibl f il *Science* 246:661-4 N 3 '89
Switch protein alters specificity of RNA polymerase containing a compartment-specific sigma factor [Bacillus subtilis] L. Kroos and others. bibl f il *Science* 243:526-9 Ja 27 '89
Transcriptional regulation in mammalian cells by sequence-specific DNA binding proteins [RNA polymerase II transcription initiation] P. J. Mitchell and R. Tjian. bibl f il *Science* 245:371-8 Jl 28 '89
POLYMERS
                See also
                Biopolymers
                Chitin
                Conductive polymers
                Macromolecules
                Plastics
                Polyethylene
                Stereolithography
Chemists probe new crystalline vistas [work of Richard Robson and Bernard F. Hoskins] I. Amato. *Science News* 136:86 Ag 5 '89
Japan's RS plastics [rapid solidification] H. Okada. *High Technology Business* 9:30 N/D '89
Making plastics in Galileo's shadow [space shuttle polymer morphology experiment] *Science News* 136:286 O 28 '89
Polymer synthesis and organotransition metal chemistry. R. H. Grubbs and W. Tumas. bibl f il *Science* 243:907-15 F 17 '89
Polymers, fractals, and ceramic materials. D. W. Schaefer. bibl f il *Science* 243:1023-7 F 24 '89
Strong polymer composites. M. Mandell. *High Technology Business* 9:10-11 Ap '89
Template-directed oligomerization catalyzed by a polynucleotide analog [polycytidylic acid] J. Visscher and others. bibl f il *Science* 244:329-31 Ap 21 '89
POLYMERS IN MEDICINE
The power of plastics [use in transplantation of liver cells; work of Joseph Vacanti] L. Oliwenstein. il *Discover* 10:18 D '89
POLYMORPHISM (BIOLOGY)
                See also
                Restriction fragment length polymorphisms
Caterpillar disguise: you are what you eat [work of Erick Greene with Nemoria arizonaria] I. Wickelgren. il *Science News* 135:70 F 4 '89
Caterpillars and polymorphisms [discussion of February 3, 1989 article, A diet-induced developmental polymorphism in a caterpillar] E. Greene. bibl f *Science* 246:1639-40 D 22 '89

POLYMORPHISM (BIOLOGY)—*cont.*

A diet-induced developmental polymorphism in a caterpillar [Nemoria arizonaria; cover story] E. Greene. bibl f il *Science* 243:643-6 F 3 '89

Duplication, deletion, and polymorphism in the sex-determining region of the mouse Y chromosome. G. Mardon and others. bibl f il *Science* 243:78-80 Ja 6 '89

Is diet destiny? [developmental polymorphism in caterpillars; research by Erick Greene] *Newsweek* 113:62 F 13 '89

Murine MHC polymorphism and T cell specificities. S. Roy and others. bibl f il *Science* 244:572-5 My 5 '89

POLYNESIA

See also
Cook Islands
Hawaii
Pitcairn Island

POLYNESIAN COOKING *See* Cooking, Polynesian

POLYNESIANS

See also
Hawaiians

POLYNUCLEOTIDES *See* Nucleotides

POLYPLOIDY

Temperature and sperm incorporation in polyploid salamanders. J. P. Bogart and others. bibl f il *Science* 246:1032-4 N 24 '89

POLYPROPYLENE

Defying the law of gravity [Himont Inc.] A. A. Lappen. il por *Forbes* 143:76-7 Ap 3 '89

Polypropylene strikes back [stain resistant carpet fiber] J. Harris. il *Forbes* 144:122 Ag 7 '89

POLYSACCHARIDES

See also
Cellulose
Glucans
Hyaluronic acid

Sweet semiconductor snags bacteria [Mark D. Bednarski] I. Amato. *Science News* 136:398 D 16 '89

POLYVINYLIDENE FLUORIDE

Fantastic plastic [Kynar; cover story] I. Amato. il *Science News* 136:328-9 N 18 '89

Kynar and gentler streets [traffic-sensing devices] I. Amato. *Science News* 135:79 F 4 '89

POMEGRANATES

See also
Cooking—Fruit

POMER, MARSHALL

(jt. auth) See Henry, James S., and Pomer, Marshall

POMERANTZ, MARVIN

about

The Marvin and Warren act. R. Reiff. il por *Forbes* 144:52+ S 18 '89

POMPANO FISHING

Permit me this [Florida Keys] H. Middleton. il *Southern Living* 24:36+ S '89

POMPEII (ANCIENT CITY)

The fall and rise of a doomed city: Pompeii. il map *National Geographic World* 165:22-5 My '89

The nuts of Pompeii [work of Frederick Meyer] il *Discover* 10:14 N '89

POMPEU DE TOLEDO, ROBERTO

The road to 1992. *World Press Review* 36:15-16 Ja '89

PONCE, ADOLFO, JR.

about

Midnight race for freedom. S. Kelly. il pors *Reader's Digest* 135:198-202+ S '89

PONCE, ADOLFO, SR.

about

Midnight race for freedom. S. Kelly. il pors *Reader's Digest* 135:198-202+ S '89

PONCE DE LEÓN, JUANA

Gay & lesbian publishing. il *Publishers Weekly* 236:14-16+ D 8 '89

Reflections on a growing market. *Publishers Weekly* 236:24 D 8 '89

Third Latin American Fair focuses on new writers. il *Publishers Weekly* 235:18 My 26 '89

PONCET, SALLY

Wildlife quest to the icy seas of South Georgia. il map *National Geographic* 175:340-75 Mr '89

POND, MIMI

A groom of one's own. il *Gentlemen's Quarterly* 59:125+ F '89

POND, STEVE

Facing the future [cover story] il pors *Gentlemen's Quarterly* 59:266-71+ N '89

POND ECOLOGY

Photographs and photography

Secrets of a small pond. D. Kuhn. il *Country Journal* 16:53-5 My/Je '89

POND INLET (N.W.T.)

Climate

Eskimo spring. il map *National Geographic World* 166:26-31 Je '89

Crime

Mounties forever, but these days rarely on horseback. R. Wolkomir. bibl (p170) il *Smithsonian* 19:78-84+ F '89

PONDS

See also
Walden Pond (Mass.)
Water gardens and gardening

Fantailed fantasies and other fauna for the pond [ornamental fish] D. Hufford. il *Flower and Garden* 33:26-30 Jl/Ag '89

Milk a farm pond for all it's worth. *Successful Farming* 87:68 N '89

PONRATTANAWANAROM, PHISEK

Health is development. il *World Health* p21 Mr '89

PONS, ANNE

The complete Anne Frank. *World Press Review* 36:73 D '89

PONS, PHILIPPE

The Japanese and the Soviets. *World Press Review* 36:15 Ap '89

PONS, STANLEY

about

Cold fusion confusion. R. P. Crease and N. P. Samios. il pors *The New York Times Magazine* p34-6+ S 24 '89

Fusion followup: confusion abounds. R. Pool. il por *Science* 244:27-9 Ap 7 '89

Fusion illusion? [cover story] M. D. Lemonick. il pors *Time* 133:72-6+ My 8 '89

Fusion in a bottle: miracle or mistake? [cover story] J. Carey and W. D. Marbach. il pors *Business Week* p100-3+ My 8 '89

How cold fusion happened—twice! R. Pool. il pors *Science* 244:420-3 Ap 28 '89

Stanley Pons lays claim to table top fusion—but don't sell your oil stocks just yet. P. Chin. il pors *People Weekly* 31:59-60+ My 8 '89

PONTALBAS (NEW ORLEANS, LA.: APARTMENT HOUSES) *See* New Orleans (La.)—Housing

PONTE, LOWELL

How noise can harm you. il *Reader's Digest* 134:121-5 Mr '89

Nature's incredible night show. il *Reader's Digest* 135:86-91 D '89

PONTIKES, KENNETH NICHOLAS, 1940-

about

Arb no more. J. Zweig. il por *Forbes* 144:348 N 13 '89

PONTIUS PILATE *See* Pilate, Pontius, 1st cent.

PONZEK, DEBRA

about

At home on the range. J. Freiman. il pors *Harper's Bazaar* 122:216+ Ap '89

Rising to the top. B. Miller and P. Franey. il *The New York Times Magazine* p69-70 F 19 '89

PONZI SCHEMES

Old name, new game [H. Schreiber] E. Giltenan. por *Forbes* 144:10 Jl 24 '89

POOL, MARY JANE

about

Green secrets of Venice. D. Brenner. il *House & Garden* 161:114 N '89

POOL (GAME)

Rack 'em up. Y. R. Lamb. il *Black Enterprise* 20:115-16+ D '89

Equipment

See also
Pool cues
Pool tables

POOL CUES

The ex-hustler whose pool cues are a fine art [B. Stroud] J. Neary. il pors *Smithsonian* 20:158-62+ N '89

POOL HOUSES

A. Robert Faesy, Jr.: structural drama for a New Canaan poolhouse. il *Architectural Digest* 46:78-81 Ag '89

Cottage industry: a versatile poolhouse near San Francisco [decorated by Ronald Crosetti] J. Chatfield-Taylor. il *Architectural Digest* 46:302-7 My '89

Living the casual life [pool house/guest suite] L. Hallam. il *Southern Living* 24:56-7 Ag '89

Made in the shade. E. Wood. il *Southern Living* 24:114-15 Jl '89

POOL TABLES

Rack 'em up. N. Barrett, Jr. il *Popular Mechanics* 166:74-81 D '89

Rack 'em—in the comfort of your own home. D. H. Dunn. il *Business Week* p104 F 13 '89

Why did Steve Karpa build this humongous pool table? Chalk it up to whimsy. il por *People Weekly* 31:74 Ap 3 '89

POOLE, ROBERT M.

A bygone century comes to light. il pors *National Geographic* 176:366-9 S '89

POOLE, WILLIAM T.

How big business bankrolls the left. il *National Review* 41:34-7 Mr 10 '89

POOLEY, ERIC

The education of Reverend Butts. il pors *New York* 22:42-9 Je 26 '89

A federal case. il por *New York* 22:48-50+ Mr 27 '89

Fighting back against crack [cover story] il *New York* 22:30-9 Ja 23 '89

POOLEY, ERIC—*cont.*

Grins, gore, and videotape: the trouble with local TV news [cover story] il *New York* 22:36-44 O 9 '89

High anxiety. il *New York* 22:60-4+ My 8 '89

Ruptured lives: how the Gramercy Park steam-pipe blast spewed misery with the asbestos. il *New York* 22:50-4+ O 30 '89

Sex, lies, and Andie MacDowell. il pors *New York* 22:38-42 Jl 17 '89

Southward ho: moving on down to new spaces and places. il *New York* 22:80-2+ D 25 '89-Ja 1 '90

This boy's life. il pors *New York* 22:38-43 F 13 '89

POOLS, GARDEN *See* Garden pools

POOLS, MUNICIPAL *See* Municipal swimming pools

POOLS, SWIMMING *See* Swimming pools

POON, DICKSON

about

Keep the calculators out of sight. A. Tanzer. il *Forbes* 143:96+ Mr 20 '89

POOR, JONATHAN D., D. 1845

about

Museum accessions. E. H. Gustafson. il *Antiques* 136:402+ S '89

POOR

See also
Hunger
Public welfare
Underclass
United States. Office of Economic Opportunity

Alcohol abuse grows among pregnant poor [study by Bertis B. Little] B. Bower. *Science News* 136:230 O 7 '89

America's income gap: the closer you look, the worse it gets. A. Bernstein. il *Business Week* p78-9 Ap 17 '89

As the world turns [global economy and U.S. income inequality] R. B. Reich. *The New Republic* 200:23+ My 1 '89

The clay moves awry . . . S. Callery. il *Commonweal* 116:519-21 O 6 '89

The coming of age of American social policy. D. P. Moynihan. il *USA Today (Periodical)* 118:76-8 N '89

A conservative war on poverty [HUD Secretary J. Kemp] J. P. Shapiro. il por *U.S. News & World Report* 106:20-3 F 27 '89

The debate over how to count the poor [Census Bureau report] B. J. Wattenberg. *U.S. News & World Report* 107:47 O 30 '89

Fighting poverty after Reagan. J. Walsh. il *The Nation* 248:336-9 Mr 13 '89

The free market has triumphed, but what about the losers? K. Pennar. il *Business Week* p178-9 S 25 '89

How much poverty is reduced by state income transfers? R. D. Plotnick. bibl f il *Monthly Labor Review* 112:21-6 Jl '89

How we can win the war on poverty. J. Huey. il *Fortune* 119:124-8+ Ap 10 '89

Losing more ground. E. Rubenstein. il *National Review* 41:13 My 19 '89

New permanence of poverty. *Society* 26:2-4 Ja/F '89

The other suburbia [poverty] J. McCormick and P. McKillop. il *Newsweek* 113:22-4 Je 26 '89

Poor women: the sacrificial lambs [abortion issue] C. Kocol. por *The Humanist* 49:37+ Jl/Ag '89

Poverty in the 1980's: are the poor getting poorer? M. S. Littman. bibl f il *Monthly Labor Review* 112:13-18 Je '89

The poverty thing [J. Kemp's program] F. Barnes. *The New Republic* 200:13-15 Ja 30 '89

Razing the liberal plantation [cover story; special section] *National Review* 41:27-32 N 10 '89

Rise of rural poverty [views of William P. O'Hare] il *The Futurist* 23:45 Ja/F '89

The rising tide. E. Rubenstein. il *National Review* 41:20 D 8 '89

Social security should benefit only the elderly poor. G. S. Becker. il *Business Week* p20 Ja 16 '89

Taking stock [excerpts from address, April 20, 1989] J. L. Norwood. *Monthly Labor Review* 112:2 My '89

Targeting the poor: new policy for the new poverty. R. H. Haveman. *Current (Washington, D.C.)* 310:11-19 F '89

The truth about poverty. M. Novak. il *Forbes* 144:82 D 11 '89

The unfinished war (II) [L. Johnson, R. Nixon and the War on Poverty] N. Lemann. il *The Atlantic* 263:52-6+ Ja '89

Why isn't the wealth trickling down? K. Pennar. il *Business Week* p112 My 1 '89

Will the poor always be with us? [interview with M. Cuomo] N. Gardels. il *New Perspectives Quarterly* 6:28-32 Fall '89

With a Republican in office, a recession may be lurking . . . and if it comes, the poor will really take a hit. M. J. Mandel. il *Business Week* p20 Ap 10 '89

Civil rights

Defending the poor: a harder task [cover story] G. M. Anderson. il *America* 160:4-7 Ja 7-14 '89

Employment

The next battle in the war on poverty [proposed minimum wage increase] D. Whitman. il *U.S. News & World Report* 106:18 My 29 '89

A pay hike for the poor. R. Lacayo. il *Time* 134:36 N 13 '89

A profile of the working poor. B. W. Klein and P. L. Rones. bibl f il *Monthly Labor Review* 112:3-13 O '89

Reasons for not working: poor and nonpoor householders. M. S. Littman. bibl f il *Monthly Labor Review* 112:16-21 Ag '89

Housing

See also
Enterprise Foundation
Habitat for Humanity Inc.
Housing vouchers
MadCAAP (Organization)
Slums
United Nations. Commission on Human Settlements

An Atlanta prison gets converted [R. Scott's GlenCastle conversion for the working poor] B. Spring. il por *Christianity Today* 33:53-4 Ap 7 '89

Behind the housing crisis: private-sector forces, not Reagan, killed off affordable rentals [comments on demonstration in Washington] D. Whitman. il *U.S. News & World Report* 107:28+ O 16 '89

The big-city push to fill the housing gap for the poor [New York City] S. Minerbrook. il *U.S. News & World Report* 107:28-9 Ag 28-S 4 '89

Communities, not carpetbaggers [need for government support of nonprofit housing movement] P. Dreier. il *The Nation* 249:198-200+ Ag 21-28 '89

The economies of public housing. W. Tucker. il *The American Spectator* 22:26-9 N '89

Fannie Mae helps put a roof over the nation's poor. C. Yang. il por *Business Week* p113 Je 5 '89

Fresh ideas on affordable housing. R. Kuttner. il *Utne Reader* p73-5 My/Je '89

Help house the poor—and cut your taxes [real estate limited partnerships] T. Segal. *Business Week* p126 D 4 '89

Housing policy needs a rehab. L. S. Richman. il *Fortune* 119:84-7+ Mr 27 '89

A housing program that really works [Community Reinvestment Act] P. Glastris. il *U.S. News & World Report* 106:26-7 F 27 '89

Landlord, beware [real estate partnerships in low income housing] H. Rudnitsky. il *Forbes* 144:44-5 Jl 24 '89

Poor paying more for their shelter. *Society* 26:4 S/O '89

International aspects

Identifying the world's poor [International Labour Organisation project] il *UN Chronicle* 26:60-1 S '89

Legal aid

See Legal aid

Medical care

See also
Medicaid

Status symbol: affluent women have cesareans more often than poor women do. J. Horgan. *Scientific American* 261:36 O '89

Political activities

End of the rainbow [voting patterns of poor and minorities] R. A. Teixeira. il *The New Republic* 200:11-12+ Ap 3 '89

Taxation

Filing for dollars [earned income tax credit] P. Simpson. *Ms.* 17:74 My '89

Help the working poor [earned income tax credit] R. J. Samuelson. il *Newsweek* 113:52 My 1 '89

Higher 'sin' taxes: a low blow to the poor. G. S. Becker. il *Business Week* p23 Je 5 '89

How to help the working poor [dependent care tax credits] B. Cohn. il *Newsweek* 114:26 Ag 7 '89

The rich aren't the only ones who may get a tax break. S. B. Garland and H. Gleckman. il *Business Week* p37 Ag 21 '89

Transportation

Mass transit and the poor. G. M. Anderson. il *America* 161:399-402 D 2 '89

Alabama

The long journey home [excerpt from And their children after them] D. Maharidge and M. Williamson. il *Rolling Stone* p87-96 Mr 23 '89

Brazil

Old friends and new problems. J. B. Malley. *America* 161:275-6 O 28 '89

California

See also
Santa Monica (Calif.)—Poor

Europe

History

Bread of dreams [effects of malnutrition and adulterated bread on the poor of medieval Europe; cover story] P. Camporesi. il *History Today* 39:14-21 Ap '89

Illinois

See also
Chicago (Ill.)—Poor
East Saint Louis (Ill.)—Poor

POOR—*cont.*

Jamaica
See also
Kingston (Jamaica)—Poor

Latin America
A chasm of misery [gap between rich and poor] F. Ungeheuer. il *Time* 134:64-6 N 6 '89

Massachusetts
See also
Boston (Mass.)—Poor
Braintree (Mass.)—Poor

Mexico
See also
Ciudad Juarez (Mexico)—Poor

Missouri
See also
Neosho (Mo.)—Poor

New Brunswick
The 'twilight zone'. G. Allen. il *Maclean's* 102:16 Mr 6 '89

New York (State)
See also
New York (N.Y.)—Poor

Ohio
See also
Portsmouth (Ohio)—Poor

Pennsylvania
See also
Philadelphia (Pa.)—Poor

Peru
See also
Lima (Peru)—Poor

Texas
See also
Austin (Tex.)—Poor

United States
See Poor

Virginia
See also
Reston (Va.)—Poor

Washington (D.C.)
See Washington (D.C.)—Poor
POOR AND THE CHURCH *See* Church and social problems
POOR CHILDREN *See* Socially handicapped children
POOR CLARES
The little-horse ranch in Texas: miniature thoroughbreds mean big bucks for the nuns of St. Clare. H. Phillips. il *Travel Holiday* 172:106 Jl '89
POOR IN LITERATURE
It's so much easier to write about the rich [children's books] M. J. Harris. il *The New York Times Book Review* 94:46 N 12 '89
POOR IN THE BIBLE
The peculiar blessings of poverty. P. Yancey. il *Christianity Today* 33:72 Je 16 '89
POOR RELIEF *See* Public welfare
POP ART
The Warhol impact [special section] il por *Vogue* 179:320-7+ F '89

Exhibitions
The work of Roy Lichtenstein in the age of Walter Benjamin's and Jean Baudrillard's popularity [cover story] C. Ratcliff. il *Art in America* 77:110-23+ F '89
POP MUSIC *See* Popular music
POPCORN
See also
Annie's All-Natural Popcorn (Firm)
Cracker Jack
Golden Valley Microwave Foods Inc.
Popcorn. il *Consumer Reports* 54:242-5 D '89
Popcorn and popcorn poppers. il *Consumer Reports* 54:355-62 Je '89

Marketing
A feud that's really popping [Smartfoods vs. Annie's All-Natural Popcorn] A. Miller. il por *Newsweek* 114:52 Jl 24 '89
POPCORN POPPERS
Popcorn and popcorn poppers. il *Consumer Reports* 54:355-62 Je '89
Popcorn poppers. il *Consumer Reports* 54:265-7 D '89
POPE, GEOFFREY G.
Bamboo and human evolution. il map *Natural History* p48-57 O '89
POPE, GREGORY T.
Machine vision focuses on profits [cover story] il *High Technology Business* 9:14-17 Ja '89
U.S.-Canada free trade: how high tech will benefit [cover story] il *High Technology Business* 9:18-21 Mr '89
POPE, LAWRENCE, D. 1989
about
The banker who robbed banks. J. Morgenstern. il pors *The New York Times Magazine* p54-6+ N 12 '89
POPE, STERETT
Regional report: the Middle East. See issues of World Press Review beginning June 1986
POPE & TALBOT, INC.
Mistaken identity? M. Beauchamp. il *Forbes* 143:43 F 6 '89

POPE-HENNESSY, SIR JOHN
The fall of a great museum [cover story] il *The New York Review of Books* 36:10-14 Ap 27 '89
POPES
See also
John Paul I, Pope, 1912-1978
John Paul II, Pope, 1920-
Papacy

Infallibility
An interview with the author of The papacy and the Church [J. R. Dionne] il *America* 160:12-13+ Ja 7-14 '89
POPEYES FAMOUS FRIED CHICKEN & BISCUITS INC.
Chicken that packs a punch [A. Copeland] M. Barrier. il pors *Nation's Business* 77:52+ Jl '89
POPHAM, DAVID L., AND OTHERS
Function of a bacterial activator protein that binds to transcriptional enhancers. bibl f il *Science* 243:629-35 F 3 '89
POPLAR
See also
Aspen
Cottonwood
POPOV, NICOLAS
Crawfishing in the Bahamas. il *Sea Frontiers* 35:222-30 Jl/Ag '89
POPPE, N. N. (NIKOLAĬ NIKOLAEVICH), 1897-
about
Bringing Nazi sympathizers to the U.S. [cover story] J. Wiener. *The Nation* 248:289+ Mr 6 '89
POPPE, NIKOLAĬ NIKOLAEVICH *See* Poppe, N. N. (Nikolaĭ Nikolaevich), 1897-
POPPER, DAVID, 1843-1913
about
The romantic cello. R. Freed. il por *Stereo Review* 54:147 D '89
POPPERS, POPCORN *See* Popcorn poppers
POPPINS, MARY (FICTIONAL CHARACTER) *See* Mary Poppins (Fictional character)
POPPY, JOHN
Active health. See issues of Esquire beginning June 1988
The paunch line. il *Reader's Digest* 135:133-5 Ag '89
POPPY SEEDS
See also
Cooking—Seeds
POPULAR CULTURE
See also
Cyberpunk culture
Fads
Hip-hop
London (England)—Popular culture
Los Angeles (Calif.)—Popular culture
New York (N.Y.)—Popular culture
United States—Popular culture

Study and teaching
Pop goes the curriculum [college courses] J. Heilemann. *The Washington Monthly* 21:34-5 O '89
POPULAR FRONT FOR THE LIBERATION OF SAGUIA EL HAMRA AND RIO DE ORO *See* Polisario Front
POPULAR MUSIC
See also
Blues music
Body and soul (Song)
Christian contemporary music
Compact discs—Popular music
Country music
Don't worry 'bout me (Song)
Gospel music
House music
Phonograph records—Popular music
Publishers and publishing—Popular music
Rock music
Television broadcasting—Popular music
Videotapes—Popular music
Backbeat. See issues of High Fidelity (New York, N.Y.) through July 1989
Pop-pourri. P. Dell. il *'Teen* 33:68-9 Ag '89
Popular music. M. Moses. See occasional issues of The New Yorker beginning February 1, 1988 through April 24, 1989

Bibliography
Under cover: books in review. il *Rolling Stone* p26 Ap 20 '89

History
Bibliography
History through song. I. C. Bradley. *History Today* 39:56 D '89

International aspects
The global beat. B. Cullman. il *Vogue* 179:192-3+ My '89
International music on videotape. G. Santoro. *The Nation* 249:101-2 Jl 17 '89
International roots roundup. G. Santoro. *The Nation* 249:578-80 N 13 '89
It's zouk to me. C. Eddy. il *High Fidelity (New York, N.Y.)* 39:56 F '89

Brazil
See also
Bossa nova

POPULAR MUSIC—cont.

South Africa
Warrior against racism [J. Clegg] K. McKenna. il por *Scholastic Update (Teachers' edition)* 121:16 Ja 27 '89

POPULAR PHOTOGRAPHY (PERIODICAL)
Popular photography's state-of-the-art super lab. L. White. il *Popular Photography* 96:56-64+ Ag '89
What are all those charts and graphs, and where do they come from? L. White. il *Popular Photography* 96:66 Jl '89

POPULAR SCIENCE (PERIODICAL)
Looking back . . . il *Popular Science* 234:28 Ja '89

POPULARITY
Liking an unlikely guy. il *'Teen* 33:22+ Mr '89

POPULATION
See also
Birth control
Birth rate
Computers—Demographic use
Households
United Nations. Population Commission
United Nations Fund for Population Activities
See also subhead Population under names of continents, countries, states, cities, etc.
The growing human population. N. Keyfitz. il map *Scientific American* 261:118-26 S '89
Population update. M. Morain. See issues of The Humanist beginning July/August 1986
Too many mouths [overpopulation] A. Toufexis. il *Time* 133:48-9 Ja 2 '89

POPULATION BIOLOGY
See also
Fish populations
Ecologists flirt with chaos. R. Pool. il *Science* 243:310-13 Ja 20 '89

POPULATION COMMISSION (UNITED NATIONS) See
United Nations. Population Commission

POPULATION CONTROL See Birth control

POPULATION FORECASTING
America in the 21st century [Population Reference Bureau report] *Children Today* 18:2-3 S/O '89
America's looming shortage. M. S. Forbes, Jr. il *Forbes* 143:27 Mr 20 '89
The big shift [investment strategy tied to population trends] J. Crudele. il *New York* 22:21 Mr 27 '89
The biggest secret of race relations: the new white minority. il *Ebony* 44:84+ Ap '89
The birth dearth confirmed. E. Rubenstein. *National Review* 41:13 My 5 '89
Demographics of the 90s [U.S.; address, April 12, 1989] R. S. Fosler. *Vital Speeches of the Day* 55:572-6 Jl 1 '89
Future shock [population trends point to labor shortage and increase in minority birth rate; cover story] D. E. Bloom and N. G. Bennett. *The New Republic* 200:18-20+ Je 19 '89
IPSS [Interactive Population Statistical System] J. Pournelle. il *Byte* 14:110+ D '89
Malthus and his ghost. R. Percival. *National Review* 41:30-3 Ag 18 '89
World population trends. P. Demeny. bibl f *Current History* 88:17-19+ Ja '89

POPULATION GENETICS
Asian human-origin theory gets new teeth [research by Christy G. Turner] B. Bower. *Science News* 136:100 Ag 12 '89
Man's family tree rooted in Africa [research by Luigi Cavalli-Sforza] il *USA Today (Periodical)* 118:10-11 Ag '89
Teeth and prehistory in Asia [reconstructing the great migrations] C. G. Turner, II. bibl il map *Scientific American* 260:88-91+ F '89

Animals
Limits to DNA fingerprinting. R. Lewin. il *Science* 243:1549-51 Mr 24 '89

Birds
Dusky legacy [mitochondrial DNA of extinct dusky seaside sparrow; research by John Avise] L. Oliwenstein. il *Discover* 10:38 Jl '89
Molecular genetic relationships of the extinct dusky seaside sparrow. J. C. Avise and W. S. Nelson. bibl f il map *Science* 243:646-8 F 3 '89
Reaction norms in genetical ecology [variation in great tits] A. J. Van Noordwijk. bibl f il *BioScience* 39:453-8 Jl/Ag '89
A sparrow's fall [DNA of the dusky seaside sparrow; research by John C. Avise and William S. Nelson] T. Appenzeller. *Scientific American* 260:32+ Ap '89

Fish
Fitness differences among remnant populations of the endangered Sonoran topminnow. J. M. Quattro and R. C. Vrijenhoek. bibl f il *Science* 245:976-8 S 1 '89

Insects
A breed apart [sympatric speciation in apple fruit flies; study by Guy L. Bush] K. Wright. il *Scientific American* 260:22+ F '89
Developmental and physiological aspects of reaction norms [Drosophila] W. Scharloo. bibl f il *BioScience* 39:465-71 Jl/Ag '89

Plants
How to get plants into the conservationists' ark. R. Lewin. il *Science* 244:32-3 Ap 7 '89

POPULATION INSTITUTE
The Population Institute. M. Morain. il *The Humanist* 49:31-2 Mr/Ap '89

POPULATION POLICY
See also
Birth control
Immigration and emigration
Redefining security. J. T. Mathews. *Foreign Affairs* 68:162-77 Spr '89
There is no global population problem [cover story] G. J. Hardin. il por *The Humanist* 49:11-13+ Jl/Ag '89

POPULATIONS, FISH See Fish populations

POPULISM
The future of rural populism. B. W. Hargrove. bibl *Society* 26:39-44 Ja/F '89
'A party within a party': Jim Hightower proposes a populist alliance. D. A. Denison. il *The Progressive* 53:22-3 Mr '89
Populism offers a progressive alternative to liberalism. L. MacAdams. il *Utne Reader* p72 Mr/Ap '89
Raising issues, hope and hell. J. Hightower. il *The Nation* 248:160+ F 6 '89

Burkina Faso
Populism in Ghana and Burkina Faso. D. S. Rothchild and E. Gyimah-Boadi. bibl f *Current History* 88:221-4+ My '89

Ghana
Populism in Ghana and Burkina Faso. D. S. Rothchild and E. Gyimah-Boadi. bibl f *Current History* 88:221-4+ My '89

Latin America
Latin populism at a dead end. *World Press Review* 36:80 N '89

POPULOUS (VIDEO GAME)
Deluged by brilliant world-creation. O. S. Card. *Compute!* 11:88 N '89
Disasters and diversions. J. Pournelle. *Byte* 14:115-16 O '89
Grow up! D. Atkin. il *Compute!* 11:94-6+ D '89

PORCELAIN See Pottery

PORCELAIN CONTAINERS
Collectors and collecting
Keeping things cool in Hall China. L. Rosenkrantz. il *Antiques & Collecting Hobbies* 94:22 My '89

PORCH BENCHES See Benches
PORCH ROOMS See Rooms
PORCHES
Dress-up details [special section] K. Collier. il *The Family Handyman* 39:30-7 Ja '89
A new porch with a history. il *Southern Living* 24:108-9 Jl '89
A porch and a passage [covered walkway] il *Southern Living* 24:159 S '89
The screening process. il *Home Mechanix* 85:46-8+ My '89
A view from the back porch. A. Fitzgibbon. il *Southern Living* 24:146 Mr '89
Maintenance and repair
Replace a rotting porch. D. A. Warren. il *Workbench* 45:24-30 My/Je '89

PORCINE GROWTH HORMONE, SYNTHETIC See Pituitary hormones, Synthetic
PORCINE STRESS SYNDROME See Swine—Diseases and pests
PORCINO, JANE
Homing options in the '80s—and beyond. il *New Choices for the Best Years* 29:34-5 My '89

PORGES, MARIA
Coat tales. il por *American Craft* 49:46-51 O/N '89

PORGY AND BESS [opera] See Gershwin, George, 1898-1937

PORIN
Activation of bacterial porin gene expression by a chimeric signal transducer in response to aspartate. R. Utsumi and others. bibl f il *Science* 245:1246-9 S 15 '89

PORIZKOVA, ANNA
about
Model's role model. il pors *Harper's Bazaar* 122:158-9+ O '89

PORIZKOVA, PAULINA
about
Model's role model. il pors *Harper's Bazaar* 122:158-9+ O '89
Paulina, the $6 million model, tries cashing in on the movies—and she doesn't need an Alibi. P. Axthelm. il pors *People Weekly* 31:104-5+ F 27 '89
The pearls of Paulina. D. S. Looney. il pors *Sports Illustrated* 70 Special Issue:191+ F '89

PORK
See also
Cooking—Meat
Trichinosis
Contented pigs? [Tyson Food's drive to popularize pork] M. Fritz. il *Forbes* 144:118-19 Ag 7 '89

PORK BARREL LEGISLATION
Debate at $3 billion a minute [Senate Defense Appropriations Subcommittee] J. D. Isaacs. il *The Bulletin of the Atomic Scientists* 45:3-4 N '89
House trims off academic pork. C. Norman. *Science* 246:990 N 24 '89
Porkmeisters on parade. J. Klein. il *New York* 22:14+ D 18 '89
Return of the untouchables. R. Thomas. il *Newsweek* 113:42 Mr 6 '89
Universities reach into pork barrel with help from friends in Congress. I. Goodwin. il *Physics Today* 42:43-5 Ap '89
PORK INDUSTRY *See* Meat industry
PORK STEW *See* Stew
PORNOGRAPHY
See also
Obscenity (Law)
Religious Alliance Against Pornography
Telephone pornography
Bundy told Dobson, "It was pornography". *Christianity Today* 33:43 F 17 '89
The devil and John Holmes: drugs, porn and the murders on Wonderland Avenue. M. Sager. il pors *Rolling Stone* p50-2+ Je 15 '89
The drive to make America porn-free. T. Gest. il *U.S. News & World Report* 106:26-7 F 6 '89
Feminist moralism, "pornography", and censorship. B. Dority. il *The Humanist* 49:8-9+ N/D '89
'I come here just to read the articles' [designated pornography areas in Iowa prisons] *Newsweek* 113:76 Ja 30 '89
Reflections on Bundy [T. Bundy links homicidal urges to pornography] *National Review* 41:17-18 F 24 '89
A smut buster battles sin in the city [D. Hurlbut in Houston] R. Woodbury. il pors *Time* 133:22-3+ My 29 '89
What is pornography? [symposium] il *Art News* 88:138-43 O '89
POROUS CONCRETE
Holey concrete! G. Davis. il *Popular Science* 234:25 Ap '89
POROUS MATERIALS
Superfluid transition in porous media shows puzzling features. A. Khurana. bibl f il *Physics Today* 42:21-5 Jl '89
A tight squeeze for mobile water [research by William P. Halperin] *Science News* 136:47 Jl 15 '89
PORPITAS *See* Jellyfish
PORPOISES *See* Dolphins
PORRETTO, DENISE
A married woman's crush. *Glamour* 87:114 F '89
PORRITT, JONATHON, 1950-
Seeing Green: how we can create a more satisfying society. il *Utne Reader* p70-5+ N/D '89
PORSCHE (AUTOMOBILE) *See* Sports cars
PORSCHE AG
Porsche's racing plans. P. Frère. il *Road & Track* 40:163 F '89
What price perfection? J. Levine. il *Forbes* 144:228-9 O 30 '89
PORSCHE DESIGN
Porsche's new speedboat. M. Benson. il *Motor Boating & Sailing* 163:70-1 Ja '89
PORT, SIDNEY LAWRENCE
about
A fresh start after 40. R. Thompson. il pors *Nation's Business* 77:62+ Ap '89
PORT AUTHORITY OF NEW YORK AND NEW JERSEY. BUS TERMINAL
A nightmare on 42nd Street [Port Authority Bus Terminal] G. Hackett and P. McKillop. il *Newsweek* 113:22-4 F 27 '89
PORT BLAKELY (WASH.)
Architecture
All natural [guest house in Seattle and speculative house in Port Blakely designed by J. Cutler] P. M. Sachner. il *Architectural Record* 177:60-7 mid-Ap '89
PORT KELLS (B.C.)
Religious institutions and affairs
Keepers of the keys [congregation refuses to relinquish church building after seceding from United Church over ordination of homosexuals] D. Wolff. *Maclean's* 102:20 My 1 '89
PORT LIBERTÉ PARTNERS
On the waterfront. S. J. Madden. il por *Fortune* 119:112 F 13 '89
PORT SAINT LUCIE (FLA.)
Mets magic (or Anatomy of a deal) [Mets spring training facility centerpiece of St. Lucie West development project] H. J. Steinbreder. il *Sports Illustrated* 70:62-3 Mr 27 '89
PORT WINE *See* Wine
PORT WINE STAINS *See* Birthmarks
PORTABLE ASTRONOMICAL OBSERVATORIES *See* Astronomical observatories
PORTABLE CASSETTE DECKS *See* Tape recorders and recording
PORTABLE COMPUTERS *See* Computers
PORTABLE COMPUTERS AND AIR TRAVEL *See* Computers and air travel
PORTABLE ELECTRIC GENERATORS *See* Electric generators

PORTABLE FAX MACHINES *See* Fax machines
PORTABLE RADIO-CASSETTE PLAYERS *See* Radio receivers—Tape recorder combination
PORTABLE SAWMILLS *See* Sawmills
PORTABLE TELEVISION RECEIVERS *See* Television receivers
PORTABLE THEATER BUILDINGS *See* Theater buildings, Portable
PORTAGES
Portages into the past. J. Kulpa. il *Field & Stream* 93:48-9 Mr '89
PORTALS *See* Doorways
PORTELL, MARIO RÓDOLFO
about
DEA Don Juan. J. Carney. il por *Time* 133:24 Ap 3 '89
PORTER, ANDREW, 1928-
Details! Details! il *Opera News* 54:18-20+ N '89
Musical events. See issues of The New Yorker
PORTER, ANNE
In Chartres [poem] *Commonweal* 116:88 F 10 '89
In storm-watch season [poem] *Commonweal* 116:640 N 17 '89
Living things [poem] *Commonweal* 116:297 My 19 '89
PORTER, BERNARD
Political spying in 20th-century Britain. il *History Today* 39:7-9 O '89
PORTER, CHRIS VIELER- *See* Vieler-Porter, Chris
PORTER, ELIOT, 1901-
about
Eliot Porter. M. Esterow. il por *Art News* 88:158-61 Ap '89
Eliot Porter: the master eye. M. A. Sandweiss. il *National Wildlife* 27:52-9 F/Mr '89
PORTER, GWEN
(jt. auth) See Rosenwald, Priscilla R., and Porter, Gwen
PORTER, HAL, AND RICHMOND, SUZAN
Home insurance: what you need to know. il *Reader's Digest* 134:133-6 Ja '89
PORTER, JANET STREET- *See* Street-Porter, Janet
PORTER, KATHERINE, 1941-
about
Katherine Porter: André Emmerich. E. Hayt-Atkins. il *Art News* 88:130 Ja '89
Katherine Porter at Andre Emmerich. N. Princenthal. il *Art in America* 77:161-2 F '89
PORTER, MIKE
Guide, slice, and glide; ed. by Doug Smith. il *Skiing* 41:134-8 Mr '89
PORTER, PAT, 1960?-
about
Return of the crusher. M. Noden. il pors *Sports Illustrated* 71:78-9 D 4 '89
PORTER, ROGER B.
about
The man with six in boxes. por *Time* 134:20 Ag 21 '89
PORTER, WILLIAM SYDNEY *See* Henry, O., 1862-1910
PORTERFIELD, ANDREW
Railroaded. il *Common Cause Magazine* 15:21-3 S/O '89
Toxic fuel. il *Common Cause Magazine* 15:6-7 Jl/Ag '89
PORTERFIELD, JEANNE
Windows of the world [photographs] il por *Modern Maturity* 32:51-6 Ap/My '89
PORTERFIELD, KAY MARIE
Drug abuse: gambling with infection. il *Current Health 2* 15:17-19 My '89
Marijuana and learning: grass gets an F. il *Current Health 2* 15:20-2 Ja '89
Teen drug rehab: the inside story. il *Current Health 2* 15:19-21 F '89
PORTFOLIOS, INVESTMENT *See* Investments
PORTLAND (ME.)
Stores
See also
Joseph's (Firm)
PORTLAND (OR.)
Architecture
David Rockwood: a steel-and-glass bay-front house in Portland. D. Gantenbein. il por *Architectural Digest* 46:72-7 Ag '89
Less room and more space to spread out [house] il *Sunset (Central West edition)* 182:139+ Ap '89
They started with a Portland pump house and a "passed-over" site. il *Sunset (Central West edition)* 183:130-2 N '89
City planning
Creative alternatives to urban sprawl: a tale of two cities. T. Oppenheimer. il *Utne Reader* p95-8 Mr/Ap '89
Dance
Reviews:
Pulse & impulse, showcase for local choreographers. M. U. West. *Dance Magazine* 63:66+ My '89
Economic conditions
The riches of good citizens. T. Clifton. il *Newsweek* 113:44-5 F 6 '89
Gardens and gardening
Gardens: Portland trailblazer [C. Pinger's garden] M. Rozek. il *Architectural Digest* 46:208-13 Mr '89

PORTLAND (OR.)—*cont.*
Restaurants, nightclubs, bars, etc.
Lunch is being served at the world's smallest restaurant; reservations available in 1990 [Table for Two, owned by N. Briggs and J. Crampton] il pors *People Weekly* 32:150 N 20 '89

Taxicabs
Portland taxis: on hailing and healing. E. E. Rosenbaum. il *New Choices for the Best Years* 29:22+ Ja '89
PORTO ERCOLE (ITALY)
Historic houses, sites, etc.
The pleasures of Partemi: restoring a ruined castellino on the Tuscan coast [home of D. Burn] I. Borger. il por *Architectural Digest* 46:178-85 Ap '89
PORTRAIT DRAWING
Expressing the figure in pastel [work of R. Yanow] M. C. Nelson. il *American Artist* 53:60-3 F '89
Looking at art [Mrs. Charles Badham by Ingres; reprint of December 1982 article] H. Brown. bibl f il *American Artist* 53:34+ Ap '89
PORTRAIT PAINTING
Color Close-ups [work of C. Close] C. Finch. il *Art in America* 77:112-19+ Mr '89
The watercolor page [cover story] J. Fettingis. il por *American Artist* 53:40-3 My '89
Exhibitions
The painted face. J. Brown. il *Vogue* 179:420-5 O '89
PORTRAIT SCULPTURE
Lest they forget. C. Torcellini. il *Forbes* 143:158+ Je 26 '89
Exhibitions
Hank Murta Adams/Dorothy Weiss Gallery. C. White. il *American Craft* 49:80-1 O/N '89
Talking heads [work of I. Noguchi at the National Portrait Gallery] M. Filler. il por *House & Garden* 161:62 My '89
PORTRAITS
See also
Photography—Portraits
PORTRAITS, AMERICAN
The polite lady: portraits of American schoolgirls and their accomplishments, 1725-1830. D. T. Deutsch. bibl f il *Antiques* 135:742-53 Mr '89
Exhibitions
Museum accessions [The Gordon family by H. Benbridge acquired by the Pennsylvania Academy of the Fine Arts] E. H. Gustafson. il *Antiques* 136:1022 N '89
Museum accessions [portraits by G. Stuart and E. Tarbell acquired by Boston Athenaeum] E. H. Gustafson. il *Antiques* 136:240 Ag '89
Portraits by Benjamin West. A. Staley. bibl f il *Antiques* 135:1456-65 Je '89
Portraits in miniature [permanent gallery at the Worcester Art Museum] A. E. Ledes. il *Antiques* 136:1242+ D '89
PORTRAITS, ENGLISH
Exhibitions
See also
National Portrait Gallery (Great Britain)
PORTREE, DAVID S. F.
A planetary comeback: Magellan heads for Venus. il *Astronomy* 17:38-42 S '89
PORTS
See also
Boston (Mass.)—Harbor
Free ports and zones
Houston (Tex.)—Harbor
PORTSMOUTH (ENGLAND)
Fortification
See also
Fort Nelson (Portsmouth, England)
PORTSMOUTH (N.H.)
Airports
Pease AFB could become major commercial airport. *Aviation Week & Space Technology* 130:69 Ja 23 '89
PORTSMOUTH (OHIO)
Child welfare
Children of poverty [C. E. Copas and C. Riley] P. Meyer. il *Life* 12:56-62+ S '89
Poor
Children of poverty [C. E. Copas and C. Riley] P. Meyer. il *Life* 12:56-62+ S '89
PORTUGAL
See also
Automobile racing—Portugal
Cartography—Portugal
Madeira (Madeira Islands)
Portuguese
Cultural relations
Brazil
See Brazil—Cultural relations—Portugal
History
Period of discoveries, 1385-1580
Camões and the Portuguese voyages of discovery [cover story; special issue] il maps *The Courier (Unesco)* 42:3-38 Ap '89
Naval history
Of caravels and cartographers . . . L. de Albuquerque. il *The Courier (Unesco)* 42:10-13 Ap '89

Rivalry in the Red Sea: Portugal's impact on the fortunes of Mamluk Egypt. Ibn Iyās. il *The Courier (Unesco)* 42:30-2 Ap '89
PORTUGUESE
India
History
'Christians and spices': the Portuguese in India. J. Correia-Afonso. il map *The Courier (Unesco)* 42:33-4 Ap '89
PORTUGUESE AMERICANS
Join the Portuguese for a festa. il *Sunset (Central West edition)* 182:20+ My '89
PORTUGUESE ART *See* Art, Portuguese
PORTUGUESE EXPLORERS *See* Explorers, Portuguese
PORTUGUESE GRAND PRIX *See* Automobile racing—Portugal
PORTUGUESE POETRY
See also
Epic poetry, Portuguese
PORTZ-SHOVLIN, EILEEN
(jt. auth) *See* Wischnia, Bob, 1950-, and Portz-Shovlin, Eileen
PORZIO, GIOVANNI
Relighting the Balkan powder keg. *World Press Review* 36:17-18 Je '89
POSES, JONATHAN W.
Beers with . . . David Cone [interview] il pors *Sport (New York, N.Y.)* 80:16+ My '89
The once and future champs. il *Sport (New York, N.Y.)* 80:64-7 Ag '89
POSITION SENSORS
New probes reveal atomic structures [position sensing atom probe] il *Popular Mechanics* 166:14 My '89
POSITIONS, APPLICATIONS FOR *See* Job applications
POSITIONS, SLEEP *See* Sleep positions
POSITIVE THINKING *See* Optimism
POSITRON EMISSION TOMOGRAPHY *See* Tomography
POSITRONS
Distribution and detection of positrons from an orbiting nuclear reactor [observations by Solar Maximum Mission satellite] E. W. Hones and P. R. Higbie. bibl f il *Science* 244:448-51 Ap 28 '89
Penned-in positrons [first antimatter plasma] F. Flam. *Science News* 135:154 Mr 11 '89
POSNER, ELLEN
Learning curve [special section] il *Architectural Record* 177:106-15 Mr '89
POSNER, JAMES
about
The computer option. E. Sturza. il por *Forbes* 143:250 Je 26 '89
POSNER, RICHARD A., 1939-
Art for law's sake. *The American Scholar* 58:513-20 Aut '89
POSNER, VICTOR
about
Fed-up franchisees: they're mad as hell and . . . G. DeGeorge. il por *Business Week* p83+ N 13 '89
He's back! K. Hannon. por *Forbes* 144 Special Issue:8+ O 23 '89
Lenny Pelullo's checkered past—and present. G. DeGeorge. il por *Business Week* p84+ O 23 '89
Reading Posner the riot act. G. DeGeorge. il por *Business Week* p48 D 18 '89
Victor Posner and the case of the mystery financier. G. DeGeorge and R. A. Melcher. il por *Business Week* p34 Ag 28 '89
Victor Posner may soon taste his own medicine. G. DeGeorge. il pors *Business Week* p34+ Ap 10 '89
POSSESSION (LAW)
See also
Adverse possession
POSSESSIONS *See* Property
POSSLQ (PARTNERS OF OPPOSITE SEX SHARING LIVING QUARTERS) *See* Unmarried couples
POSSUMS *See* Opossums
POST, ELIZABETH L.
Etiquette for every day. See issues of Good Housekeeping
Etiquette for the '90s. il *Good Housekeeping* 209:70+ Jl '89
POST, MARTY, 1951-
(jt. auth) *See* Will-Weber, Mark, and Post, Marty, 1951-
POST (NEW YORK, N.Y.) *See* New York post
POST CARDS *See* Postcards
POSTAGE STAMPS
Oceanographic ships [stamps depicting HMS Challenger] A. L. Rice. bibl il *Sea Frontiers* 35:14-17 Ja/F '89
Parker postage [urging stamps honoring C. Parker and other jazz musicians] D. Helland. il *Down Beat* 56:6 Mr '89
A stamp for Staehle. M. G. Stoddard. il por *The Saturday Evening Post* 261:28 Ap '89
Collectors and collecting
Heritage of the Bounty: collectibles from Pitcairn Island. S. Pendleton. il *Antiques & Collecting Hobbies* 94:41-4 Jl '89
POSTAL ADDRESSES, CHANGE OF *See* Change of address
POSTAL EMPLOYEES
See also
National Post Office Mail Handlers Union
Bar Harbor, RFD. R. Sassaman. il por *Country Journal* 16:76-80 S/O '89

POSTAL EMPLOYEES—cont.
Why America loves letter carriers and hates postal clerks [cover story] J. DeParle. il *The Washington Monthly* 21:40-6+ Jl/Ag '89
POSTAL SERVICE
See also
Air freight service
United States Postal Service
Employees
See Postal employees
History
Post haste. R. L. O'Connell. il *American Heritage* 40:76-86 S/O '89
Canada
See also
Canada Post Corporation
POSTAL SERVICE (U.S.) *See* United States Postal Service
POSTAL WORKERS *See* Postal employees
POSTCARDS
Collectors and collecting
In the cards. E. Gwathmey and J. Margolies. il *New York* 22:25 Ag 14 '89
Old postcards featuring famous people: Hoot Gibson. C. Thompson. por *Antiques & Collecting Hobbies* 94:68 Mr '89
Postcards. S. S. Carver. See issues of Antiques & Collecting Hobbies beginning March 1985 through May 1989
POSTCARDS AS AN INVESTMENT
Reviewing postcards as investments. S. S. Carver. il *Antiques & Collecting Hobbies* 93:38-9+ F '89
LA POSTE (PARIS, FRANCE: RESTAURANT) *See* Paris (France)—Restaurants, nightclubs, bars, etc.
POSTEL, SANDRA
Halting land degradation. il *Focus (New York, N.Y.: 1950)* 39:5-12 Spr '89
Regaining land productivity. il *Focus (New York, N.Y.: 1950)* 39:13-18 Summ '89
POSTEL, SANDRA, AND HEISE, LORI
The fragile forest. il *The Courier (Unesco)* 42:12-23 Ja '89
POSTEMA, PAM
about
Call to glory. R. Brown. il pors *Ms.* 17:34 Ap '89
POSTEN, WILLIAM
about
Minneapolis judge lets victim set punishment. por *Jet* 75:24 Ja 30 '89
POSTER STAMPS
Collectors and collecting
Sold with a stamp [collection of H. T. Steele] G. Turim. il *Americana* 17:45-7 N/D '89
POSTERIZATION *See* Photography—Processing
POSTERS
See also
Poster stamps
Assignment: poster [L.A. Zoo fund raising poster] B. Hurter. il *Petersen's Photographic Magazine* 17:24-7 Mr '89
Jim McMahon and the art of the celebrity poster. T. L. Corbell. il por *Petersen's Photographic Magazine* 17:64-5 Mr '89
A paper army that helped pull America into World War I. S. Crawford. il *Smithsonian* 20:122-7 N '89
Collectors and collecting
The art of the reel [movie posters] P. Sikowitz. il *Harper's Bazaar* 122:68+ Mr '89
Old wine in new bottles [M. Shanken's collection of old advertising posters] C. Brown. il por *Forbes* 144:279-80 O 16 '89
Competitions
"And the winners are . . ." [running T-shirt and poster contests] K. Kleppert. il *Runner's World* 24:68-9 F '89
Exhibitions
The modern poster [Colorado International Invitational Poster Exhibition] L. Sandell. il *American Artist* 53:28+ S '89
Hanging
See Pictures—Hanging
POSTHYSTERECTOMY SYNDROME
"Doctor, please help me!". R. Gagnon. il por *Ladies' Home Journal* 106:26+ Ap '89
POSTIMPRESSIONISM (ART)
Exhibitions
Strength of vision [Masterpieces of impressionism and post-impressionism: the Annenberg Collection at the Philadelphia Museum of Art] H. Drohojowska. il *Harper's Bazaar* 122:204-7+ Ap '89
POSTING OF LAND *See* Trespass
POSTMAN, NEIL
Learning by story. il *The Atlantic* 264:119-24 D '89
What is a conservative? (And why Reagan is not one). *Utne Reader* p75 Mr/Ap '89
POSTMODERNISM
Post-modernism: the stenography of surfaces. T. Gitlin. il *New Perspectives Quarterly* 6:56-9 Spr '89
Postmodernism and beyond . . . [cover story; special section; with editorial comment by Eric Utne] il *Utne Reader* p2, 50-76 Jl/Ag '89
POSTMODERNISM (ARCHITECTURE)
Architects' dialogue [views of H. Hollein and C. Jencks] H. Hollein. il pors *Architectural Digest* 46:72+ Ap '89

Postmodernism [discussion of January 1989 article, Postmodernist blues] J. Gardner. *Commentary* 87:11-12 My '89
Postmodernist blues. J. Gardner. *Commentary* 87:55-61 Ja '89
POSTMODERNISM (ART)
The global issue: a symposium [cover story] il *Art in America* 77:86-9+ Jl '89
Postmodern painting. il *Utne Reader* p62-3 Jl/Ag '89
Postmodernism [discussion of January 1989 article, Postmodernist blues] J. Gardner. *Commentary* 87:11-12 My '89
Postmodernist blues. J. Gardner. *Commentary* 87:55-61 Ja '89
POSTMODERNISM (LITERATURE)
Prophet of a new postmodernism: the greater challenge of Salman Rushdie. M. Edmundson. il *Harper's* 279:62-6+ D '89
POSTMORTEMS *See* Autopsies
POSTNATAL EXERCISES *See* Pregnancy exercises
POSTON, GRETCHEN
about
"Why I kept my cancer a secret". M. F. Hoyt. il pors *Good Housekeeping* 208:154-5+ Je '89
POSTPARTUM DEPRESSION
Postpartum depression. P. A. Hillard. il *Parents* 64:202+ D '89
POSTPARTUM EXERCISES *See* Pregnancy exercises
POSTRIO (SAN FRANCISCO, CALIF.: RESTAURANT) *See* San Francisco (Calif.)—Restaurants, nightclubs, bars, etc.
POSTS, FENCE *See* Fence posts
POSTSCRIPT (COMPUTER LANGUAGE)
Adobe's vision for PostScript. M. Antonoff. il *Personal Computing* 13:265-6 Ap '89
Color by numbers [Tektronix Phaser CP] K. Quirk. il *Byte* 14:177-9 Jl '89
A giant leap for small footprints [Fortis DP600P page printer] R. Nelson. il *Personal Computing* 13:190 D '89
The language of lasers. K. Quirk. il *Byte* 14 Special Issue:203-6+ Fall '89
A man of characters [J. Warnock of Adobe Systems] M. Antonoff. por *Personal Computing* 13:86 Jl '89
Plug and play PostScript [PacificPage PostScript emulation cartridge] M. Antonoff. il *Personal Computing* 13:206 D '89
Postscript power with a Canon engine [QMS PS-820] J. Pepper. il *Personal Computing* 13:190-1 Jl '89
What price color PostScript? [QMS Colorscript 100 Model 10] H. Eglowstein. il *Byte* 14:229-30+ D '89
POSTSECONDARY EDUCATION *See* Adult education
POSTTRAUMATIC STRESS DISORDER
And now, emotional aftershocks [effect of earthquake on Bay Area residents] A. Toufexis. il *Time* 134:46 O 30 '89
Coping with quake fear [San Francisco Bay quake, 1989] D. Gelman. il *Newsweek* 114:42+ O 30 '89
A hurricane's haunting legacy [wake of Hugo] D. Gelman. il *Newsweek* 114:68-9 O 23 '89
Marcus Welby, J.D. [mental illness diagnosis and legal defense; cover story] W. Saletan and N. Watzman. *The New Republic* 200:19-22+ Ap 17 '89
POSTURE
See also
Sleep positions
Standing position
Are you a sloucher? [excerpt from Workouts that work for women who work] B. Pearlman. il *Redbook* 172:18 Mr '89
The case for grace: how to move sleek and sensuous. il *Mademoiselle* 95:232-5 S '89
Scaling body support in mammals: limb posture and muscle mechanics. A. A. Biewener. bibl f il *Science* 245:45-8 Jl 7 '89
Slouch no more! K. Anderson. il *Prevention (Emmaus, Pa.)* 41:123-6 D '89
Spines like us. J. Shields. il *Vogue* 179:228-9 Ja '89
Walking tall. B. Kevles. il *Women's Sports & Fitness* 11:26 Ap '89
POT, POL *See* Pol Pot
POT *See* Marijuana
POT HOLES *See* Potholes
POT PIES
Sausage-and-pepper potpies. il *Good Housekeeping* 208:34 F '89
POT RACKS *See* Shelves and racks
POT ROASTING *See* Cooking—Meat
POTAMKIN, MEYER P.
about
The Potamkin Collection of American art. L. Bantel. il *Antiques* 136:292-301 Ag '89
POTAMKIN, VIVIAN
about
The Potamkin Collection of American art. L. Bantel. il *Antiques* 136:292-301 Ag '89
POTASH
Origin of ancient potash evaporites: clues from the modern nonmarine Qaidam basin of western China. T. K. Lowenstein and others. bibl f il map *Science* 245:1090-2 S 8 '89

POTASH CORPORATION OF SASKATCHEWAN
A prairie deadlock [plan to privatize] P. Kopvillem. il *Maclean's* 102:20 Ag 7 '89
Privatizing the symbols. T. Fennell. il por *Maclean's* 102:28-9 Mr 6 '89

POTASH INDUSTRY
Canada
See also
Potash Corporation of Saskatchewan

POTASSIUM
The moon's atmosphere [work of Andrew E. Potter and Thomas H. Morgan] *Sky and Telescope* 77:589 Je '89

POTASSIUM CHANNELS
Arachidonic acid and other fatty acids directly activate potassium channels in smooth muscle cells. R. W. Ordway and others. bibl f il *Science* 244:1176-9 Je 9 '89
Expression of a cloned rat brain potassium channel in Xenopus oocytes. M. J. Christie and others. bibl f il *Science* 244:221-4 Ap 14 '89
A family of putative potassium channel genes in Drosophila. A. Butler and others. bibl f il *Science* 243:943-7 F 17 '89
Hyperpolarizing vasodilators activate ATP-sensitive K^+ channels in arterial smooth muscle. N. B. Standen and others. bibl f il *Science* 245:177-80 Jl 14 '89
Muscarinic modulation of cardiac rate at low acetylcholine concentrations. D. DiFrancesco and others. bibl f il *Science* 243:669-71 F 3 '89
Mutant potassium channels with altered binding of charybdotoxin, a pore-blocking peptide inhibitor. R. MacKinnon and C. Miller. bibl f il *Science* 245:1382-5 S 22 '89
Potassium channels in cardiac cells activated by arachidonic acid and phospholipids. D. Kim and D. E. Clapham. bibl f il *Science* 244:1174-6 Je 9 '89
Spatial buffering of light-evoked potassium increases by retinal Müller (Glial) cells. C. J. Karwoski and others. bibl f il *Science* 244:578-80 My 5 '89

POTASSIUM IN THE BODY
Potassium and high blood pressure [research by Gopal Krishna] il *Prevention (Emmaus, Pa.)* 41:12+ S '89

POTATO SALADS *See* Salads

POTATOES
See also
Cooking—Potatoes
Hot potatoes. J. Cook. il *Organic Gardening* 36:30-2+ Je '89
Potato surprises: new colors, shapes, flavors. il *Sunset (Central West edition)* 182:64-5 Ja '89
Potatoes. J. Reed. il *Vogue* 179:68 Ja '89
Advertising
Hot potatoes. B. Kanner. il *New York* 22:22+ F 6 '89
Contamination
Rotting potatoes harbor harmful toxins [trichothecene toxins; research by Anne E. Desjardins and Ronald D. Plattner] *Science News* 135:238 Ap 15 '89
History
Books you may have missed [R. N. Salaman's The history and social influence of the potato] E. N. Luttwak. il *The American Spectator* 22:46-7 Mr '89

POTEMKIN [ballet] *See* Ballet reviews—Single works

POTENTIOMETERS
See also
Silicon microphysiometers

POTHOLES
Dimples on a black desert [wetland conservation efforts hampered by North Dakota farmers] T. Williams. il *Audubon* 91:36-8+ S '89

POTLATCH CORP.
Computerized geography boosts profits at Potlatch. il *Fortune* 119:238-9 Ap 24 '89

POTOK, ANDREW
Dash leads the way. il pors *Reader's Digest* 134:44-8 Ja '89

POTPOURRI
The pleasures of potpourri. il *Southern Living* 24:64-5 S '89

POTS AND PANS *See* Kitchen utensils and appliances

POTSDAM (GERMANY)
Historic houses, sites, etc.
See also
Schloss Charlottenhof (Potsdam, Germany)

POTTED PLANTS *See* Plants, Potted

POTTER, BEATRIX, 1866-1943
about
A tale of some tails, and the story of their shy creator. T. Foote. bibl (p146-7) il pors *Smithsonian* 19:80-4+ Ja '89

POTTER, CLARE
about
A harvest of ceramics. C. Petkanas. il pors *House & Garden* 161:28+ Ag '89

POTTER, DENNIS
about
Dennis Potter. G. Fuller. il por *American Film* 14:31-3+ Mr '89

POTTER, JOHN
Liminal man. il *Opera News* 53:22+ Ap 1 '89

POTTERIES
See also
Mill (Quechee, Vt.)
Royal Doulton Ltd.
History
See also
Hall China Co.
Red Wing Potteries
Great Britain
From the villages of Stoke-on-Trent, a river of china. I. Shenker. bibl (p191) il *Smithsonian* 19:130-4+ Mr '89
Spain
See also
Lladro, SA

POTTERS
See also
Cowan, R. Guy, 1884-1957
Farrell, David
Farrell, Mary
Gordon, Anne
Israel, Margaret, 1930-1987
MacKenzie, Warren, 1924-
Martz, Karl
Ohr, George E., 1857-1918
Palissy, Bernard, 1510-1589 or 90
Petrirena, Mario
Potter, Clare
Staffel, Rudolf, 1911-

POTTERY
See also
Ceramic sculpture
Figurines
Majolica
Potteries
In the nature of things. il *Gourmet* 49:86-8 My '89
Lead in ceramic dishes. A. W. Simpson. il *Consumers' Research Magazine* 72:2 O '89
The pottery problem: some dishes cause lead poisoning. il *Better Homes and Gardens* 67:156 O '89
An unwanted souvenir: lead in ceramic ware. D. Blumenthal. il *FDA Consumer* 23:18-21 D '89/Ja '90
Collectors and collecting
Classics in china. S. Bagdade and A. Bagdade. See occasional issues of Antiques & Collecting Hobbies beginning March 1985 through May 1989
Decoration
Antiques: topographical porcelains. S. Drummond. il *Architectural Digest* 46:228-33+ Ap '89
Exhibitions
The ceramics [Mount Vernon] S. G. Detweiler. il *Antiques* 135:496-501 F '89
Expertising
Antique or junque. J. G. McCollam. il *Antiques & Collecting Hobbies* 94:21+ Ap '89
Marketing
China and crystal—not for brides only. M. Rowland. il *Working Woman* 14:102-4+ F '89
Philosophy
Comment. W. Higby. *American Craft* 49:16-17 F/Mr '89
Reproductions
Museum pieces for everyday living [M. Mottahedeh] C. Brown. il por *Forbes* 144:100 Ag 21 '89
Study and teaching
See also
Greenwich House Pottery
National Council on Education for the Ceramic Arts (U.S.)

POTTERY, AMERICAN
See also
Potteries
Teco ware
Crack pots. D. Gimelson. il *Harper's Bazaar* 122:80 O '89
Down-to-earth idealist [W. MacKenzie] R. Silberman. bibl f il por *American Craft* 49:32-9 Je/Jl '89
Collectors and collecting
American stoneware in the collection of Arthur and Esther Goldberg. A. C. Frelinghuysen. bibl f il *Antiques* 136:568-81 S '89
Grueby pottery. B. E. Johnson. bibl f il *Antiques & Collecting Hobbies* 94:52-4 O '89
Mr. Cowan's pottery: how one man's vision shaped a generation of potters [R. G. Cowan] E. Beal. il por *Antiques & Collecting Hobbies* 94:55-7+ O '89
Red Wing stoneware soars. M. Leitzke. il *Antiques & Collecting Hobbies* 93:26-7+ F '89
Tucker porcelain. B. Barol. il *American Heritage* 40:28-9 My/Je '89
Exhibitions
Art [work of G. Ohr] K. Larson. *New York* 22:123-4 N 20 '89
Common clay: a Soviet sojourn brings *glasnost* to ceramic art. J. Tognini. il *American Craft* 49:10-11 O/N '89
The first moderns [American studio ceramics: 1920-1950] R. Silberman. il *American Craft* 49:46-53+ F/Mr '89
In the American mold [porcelain at the Metropolitan Museum of Art] M. B. Caldwell. il *House & Garden* 161:174-7+ My '89

POTTERY, AMERICAN—Exhibitions—cont.
Rudolf Staffel/Temple Gallery. R. Barnard. il *American Craft* 49:72-3 D '89/Ja '90
Tucker porcelain, Philadelphia, 1826-1838 [cover story] A. C. Frelinghuysen. il *Antiques* 135:918-29 Ap '89

POTTERY, CHINESE
See also
China trade porcelain
Imari porcelain
Porcelain [ancient China] R. K. G. Temple. il *The Courier (Unesco)* 41:22 O '88

Collectors and collecting
Museum pieces for everyday living [M. Mottahedeh] C. Brown. il por *Forbes* 144:100 Ag 21 '89

POTTERY, ENGLISH
See also
Delft ware
Royal Doulton Ltd.
From the villages of Stoke-on-Trent, a river of china. I. Shenker. bibl (p191) il *Smithsonian* 19:130-4+ Mr '89
Glaze of glory [creamware] D. B. Cowin. il *House & Garden* 161:78 Ap '89

Collectors and collecting
Chelsea porcelain, 1744-1769 [cover story] S. Spero. bibl f il *Antiques* 135:260-71 Ja '89
The collecting life [Doulton pottery; interview with L. Irvine] il por *Antiques & Collecting Hobbies* 94:50-3+ N '89
The joy of Jasper: Wedgwood's finest legacy. E. Baroody. il *Antiques & Collecting Hobbies* 94:30-2 Je '89
The many faces of Royal Doulton [Toby jugs] il *USA Today (Periodical)* 118:71-5 N '89

Exhibitions
A case of the Wedgwood blues [Beeson collection at the Birmingham Museum of Art] il *Southern Living* 24:30 F '89

POTTERY, EUROPEAN
Collectors and collecting
Antiques: topographical porcelains. S. Drummond. il *Architectural Digest* 46:228-33+ Ap '89

POTTERY, FRENCH
Feast of beasts [pottery of B. Palissy] M. Guralnick. il *House & Garden* 161:98+ S '89

Collectors and collecting
Remarkable Sèvres [cover story] M. Forrest. il *Antiques & Collecting Hobbies* 94:31-4+ D '89

POTTERY, JAPANESE
See also
Imari porcelain

POTTERY, MORAVIAN
As the wheel turns [work of D. and M. Farrell] D. B. Cowin. il por *House & Garden* 161:76 Je '89

POTTERY, PREHISTORIC
The origins of ceramic technology at Dolni Věstonice, Czechoslovakia. P. B. Vandiver and others. bibl f il *Science* 246:1002-8 N 24 '89

POTTERY, RUSSIAN
Common clay: a Soviet sojourn brings *glasnost* to ceramic art. J. Tognini. il *American Craft* 49:10-11 O/N '89

POTTERY, SPANISH
Collectors and collecting
Lladro: the art of Spanish porcelain. il *USA Today (Periodical)* 117:78-83 Ja '89

POTTERY IN HOUSE DECORATION
Mix blue and white with books. il *Southern Living* 24:31 My '89

POTTERY INDUSTRY *See* Potteries
POTTING BENCHES
Planting center. M. Ferrara. il *Organic Gardening* 36:84+ Ja '89

POTTING SHEDS *See* Sheds
POTTING SOILS *See* Soils, Potting
POTTS, PAULA LEE
Mother's days. il *Runner's World* 24:104 My '89
Woman of the century. il pors *Runner's World* 24:34-6 Je '89

POTVIN, RAYMOND H.
Setting the record straight. *Commonweal* 116:271+ My 5 '89

POUCHES, FOOD *See* Food pouches
POUILLY-FUISSÉ (WINE) *See* Wine
POULAKAKOS, HARRY
about
No trouble with Harry. J. Zweig. il por *Forbes* 144:122 Jl 10 '89

POULIN, JEANNE
Coming of age in Quebec. il *Publishers Weekly* 235:28-31 My 19 '89

POULIOT, STEPHEN
about
Grandma Moses [drama] Reviews
People Weekly il 31:112-13 My 22 '89. K. Hubbard

POULTRY
See also
Carving (Meat, etc.)
Cooking—Poultry
Ducks
Eggs

Freezer birds [raising chickens] C. Canine. il *The Atlantic* 263:18+ F '89
Fresh chicken. il *Consumer Reports* 54:75-7 F '89
Share your garden with a few chickens? W. D. Adams. il *Flower and Garden* 33:62-4+ Mr/Ap '89

Care
The chicks that stayed home in the range [use of an AGA coal stove to save sick chicks] M. Kernan. il *Smithsonian* 20:214 S '89

Treatment
Pressuring Perdue [animal rights activist H. Spira] B. Feder. il por *The New York Times Magazine* p32+ N 26 '89

POULTRY CONTAMINATION
Sweet solution to tainted poultry [use of lactose in drinking water; research by John R. DeLoach] *Science News* 135:349 Je 3 '89

POULTRY INDUSTRY
See also
Holly Farms Foods, Inc.
Perdue Farms Inc.
Seaboard Corp.
Tyson Foods, Inc.

Acquisitions and mergers
Don Tyson wins Holly Farms, but his debts aren't chicken feed. K. Kelly. il por *Business Week* p29-30 Jl 10 '89
Flying feathers in the coop [Holly Farms makes lockup deal with ConAgra to prevent takeover by Tyson Foods] il *Time* 133:52 F 6 '89

Canada
Chicken wars in the Great White North [L. and P. Trottier fight Ontario marketing board over right to raise chickens] D. Francis. il *Maclean's* 102:11 Ja 9 '89

POUND, EZRA, 1885-1972
Bibliography
Putting Pound together. H. Levin. il *The New York Review of Books* 36:45-7 N 9 '89

POUNTAIN, DICK
Focus on algorithms. See issues of Byte beginning June 1987 through March 1988

POURNELLE, JERRY, 1933-
Computing at Chaos Manor. See issues of Byte beginning June 1984

POUSSIN, NICOLAS, 1594?-1665
about
A problematic Poussin. G. Danto. il *Art News* 88:70+ Ap '89

POVERTY *See* Poor
POVICH, MAURY
about
Two hearts, beating in prime time [cover story] K. McMurran. il pors *People Weekly* 31:116-17+ Ap 10 '89

POW, TOM
Galloway tale [poem] *The New Yorker* 64:81 Ja 9 '89
Russian still-life [poem] *The New Yorker* 65:105 S 4 '89

POWASKI, RONALD E.
Missile madness. il *America* 161:319-20 N 11 '89

POWDER (FACE, TOILET, ETC.)
8 fine reasons to wear powder. il *Mademoiselle* 95:32 D '89
Face it. il *'Teen* 33:88-9 N '89
Great skin: 27 new ways to fake it [foundations and powders] il *Glamour* 87:202-5 D '89
Powder plays. il *'Teen* 33:80-1 Mr '89
Powders only. il *Redbook* 173:98-9 Ag '89

POWDER METALLURGY
See also
Rapid solidification technology
Powder play. P. Klebnikov. il *Forbes* 143:144+ Je 26 '89

POWDER RIVER VALLEY (WYO. AND MONT.)
Description and travel
Powder River country. O. M. Hall. il map *American Heritage* 40:43-51 Ap '89

POWDER ROOMS
Spruce up the powder room. il *Southern Living* 24:164 Ap '89

POWDERED METAL *See* Metal powders
POWEL, NICK
Courts of appeal. See issues of World Tennis
POWELL, ALAN
about
Acoustical Society elects Powell president. il por *Physics Today* 42 pt1:58-9 Ag '89

POWELL, COLIN L.
Economics and national security [address, December 12, 1988] *Vital Speeches of the Day* 55:194-7 Ja 15 '89
U.S. foreign policy in a time of transition [address, October 27, 1988] *Department of State Bulletin* 89:30-2 Ja '89
about
Breaking barriers in the barracks. P. Cary. il pors *U.S. News & World Report* 107:26-7 Ag 21 '89
Called to service: the Colin Powell story. C. T. Rowan. por *Reader's Digest* 135:121-6 D '89
Colin Powell gets fourth star and Georgia command. il pors *Jet* 76:4 Ap 17 '89
Colin Powell named first black and youngest chair of Joint Chiefs of Staff. il pors *Jet* 76:5-7 Ag 28 '89

POWELL, COLIN L.—about—cont.
A "complete soldier" makes it. B. Seaman. por *Time* 134:24 Ag 21 '89
Gen. Colin Powell OK'd by full Senate for chair of Joint Chiefs of Staff. il por *Jet* 77:4 O 9 '89
Gen. Colin Powell takes seat as chair of Joint Chiefs at the Pentagon. il pors *Jet* 77:4-5 O 23 '89
Gen. Colin Powell's advice to young blacks today: prepare and be ready [cover story] il pors *Jet* 76:12-15 S 11 '89
Powell reaches the pinnacle of Pentagon power. M. Brown. il por *Black Enterprise* 20:22 O '89
Pragmatist at the Pentagon. E. Salholz. por *Newsweek* 114:20 Ag 21 '89
POWELL, EARL A., 1943-
    about
LACMA revisited. H. Drohojowska. il por *Architectural Digest* 46:172+ My '89
POWELL, GARETH
Bangkok by day and night. il *World Press Review* 36:62 Ag '89
POWELL, JERRY S., AND OTHERS
Inhibitors of angiotensin-converting enzyme prevent myointimal proliferation after vascular injury. bibl f il *Science* 245:186-8 Jl 14 '89
POWELL, JOHN
What the third world can handle. *The Bulletin of the Atomic Scientists* 45:8 My '89
POWELL, LEWIS F., JR.
Stare decisis and judicial restraint [address, October 17, 1989] *Vital Speeches of the Day* 56:70-3 N 15 '89
POWELL, PADGETT
Dr. Ordinary [story] *Harper's* 279:42 O '89
POWELSON, STEPHEN
    about
Homer's greatest hits. J. Stone. il *Discover* 10:78-80+ S '89
POWER, CHARLES
    about
The cucumber scandal. C. White. *Maclean's* 102:16 Ja 23 '89
POWER, HARRY
Bluebirds liked it hot. maps *Natural History* p61 Ja '89
POWER, ROSS
    about
The patina from the deep. V. Gladstone. il *Art News* 88:15 S '89
POWER (CONGRESSIONAL) *See* United States. Congress—Powers and duties
POWER (JUDICIAL) *See* Judicial power
POWER (MECHANICS)
    See also
    Horsepower (Mechanics)
    Wind power
POWER (SOCIAL SCIENCES)
    See also
    Elite (Social sciences)
Abortion as insurrection. W. M. Hern. por *The Humanist* 49:18-20+ Mr/Ap '89
Beyond macho: the power of womanly management [excerpt from Tender power] S. S. Cohen. il pors *Working Woman* 14:77-83 F '89
CEOs see clout shifting [Fortune poll] T. A. Stewart. il *Fortune* 120:66 N 6 '89
Imagine a river: understanding the balance between power and morality. R. C. Demerle. por *The Humanist* 49:27-8 Mr/Ap '89
New ways to exercise power. T. A. Stewart. il *Fortune* 120:52-4+ N 6 '89
The politics of power [address, April 1, 1989] P. F. Mancini. *Vital Speeches of the Day* 55:657-62 Ag 15 '89
The power and the pay: the 800 best paid executives in America [cover story; special section] il *Forbes* 143:159-65+ My 29 '89
Power babies [influential women under 30] L. Romano. il *Mademoiselle* 95:198-201+ My '89
Power fun. R. Urquhart. il *Mademoiselle* 95:188-9+ D '89
"Power" revisited [views of M. Korda] O. Edwards. il *Gentlemen's Quarterly* 59:164+ Je '89
POWER AMPLIFIERS *See* Amplifiers
POWER BOATS *See* Motor boats
POWER CORDS *See* Electric cords
POWER FAILURES *See* Electric power failures
THE POWER GAME [television program] See Television program reviews—Single works
POWER LAWN MOWERS *See* Lawn mowers
POWER LINES *See* Electric lines
POWER OF ATTORNEY
Wielding the power of attorney. B. M. Stephens. il *Black Enterprise* 20:31-2 Ag '89
POWER PLANTS
    See also
    Electric plants
    Hydroelectric plants
    Nuclear power plants
    Ocean thermal power plants

POWER PLANTS, SOLAR *See* Solar energy
POWER POLICY *See* Energy policy
POWER POOLS *See* Interconnected electric power systems
POWER RESOURCES
    See also
    Biomass energy
    Coal
    Electricity supply
    Electronic equipment—Energy usage
    Energy policy
    Gasoline supply
    Geothermal resources
    Hydroelectric power
    Ice power
    Lunar power resources
    Natural gas
    Nuclear energy
    Ocean thermal power plants
    Peat
    Petroleum
    Solar energy
    Tennessee Valley Authority
    Wave power
    Wind power
Reducing need for foreign oil [study by the Safe Energy Communication Council] il *USA Today (Periodical)* 118:4 Ag '89
    Anecdotes, facetiae, satire, etc.
Last word. S. Kennedy. por *Omni (New York, N.Y.)* 12:168 O '89
    Conservation
    See Energy conservation
    Economic aspects
    See also
    Fuel—Prices
    Petroleum—Prices
    International aspects
    See also
    International Energy Agency
Renewable energy: power for tomorrow. R. L. San Martin. il por *The Futurist* 23:37-40 My/Je '89
    Laws and regulations
    See Energy policy
    Research
Global warming: an energy technology R&D challenge. W. Fulkerson and others. bibl f il *Science* 246:868-9 N 17 '89
High-energy management stirs up energy research [Dept. of Energy's R. O. Hunter] M. Crawford. il por *Science* 245:1182-3 S 15 '89
Our energy future: time horizons and instability. R. S. Berry. *Environment* 31:5+ Jl/Ag '89
Trends in energy technology [cover story; special section; with editorial comment by Philip H. Abelson] bibl f il *Science* 244:273, 297-325 Ap 21 '89
    Asia
The growing strain on Asia's muscular economies [energy shortages] K. R. Sheets. il *U.S. News & World Report* 107:69-70 N 6 '89
    Canada
    See also
    National Energy Board (Canada)
    Developing countries
The fuelwood crisis. S. Postel and L. Heise. il *The Courier (Unesco)* 42:19-23 Ja '89
    Pacific Northwest
    See also
    Northwest Power Planning Council
POWER RESOURCES POLICY *See* Energy policy
POWER SECURITIES CORPORATION
Have the penny stock police caught a live one? P. Engardio. il por *Business Week* p132 F 20 '89
The most brazen of the penny hustlers? P. Engardio. il por *Business Week* p130+ N 20 '89
POWER STEERING (AUTOMOBILES) *See* Automobiles—Steering gear
POWER STEERING (BOATS) *See* Boats and boating—Steering gear
POWER SUPPLY *See* Power resources
POWER SUPPLY, ELECTRIC *See* Electricity supply
POWER TOOLS *See* Tools
POWER WASHERS *See* Pressure washers
POWERBOAT RACING *See* Motor boat racing
POWERS, ALICE L.
Abby's folk art. il *Americana* 16:62-5 Ja/F '89
Powerwear!! il *Americana* 17:17-20 S/O '89
POWERS, DENNIS A.
Fish as model systems. bibl f il *Science* 246:352-8 O 20 '89
POWERS, J. F. (JAMES FARL), 1917-
    about
The second coming of J.F. Powers. C. Iannone. *Commentary* 87:62-4 Ja '89
POWERS, JAMES FARL *See* Powers, J. F. (James Farl), 1917-
POWERS, RETHA
Fat is a black women's issue. il *Essence* 20:75+ O '89
Student power! por *Essence* 20:122 Ag '89

POWERS, RON
The cool, dark telegenius of Robert Pittman. il pors *Gentlemen's Quarterly* 59:324-7+ Mr '89
TV. See issues of Gentlemen's Quarterly
Where television is headed: the next 50 years. il *TV Guide* 37:45-6 My 6-12 '89
POWERS, SEPARATION OF *See* Separation of powers
POWIS, ALFRED
about
Alfred Powis as corporate superman. D. Francis. il *Maclean's* 102:13 N 27 '89
The final victory. J. Daly. il pors *Maclean's* 102:40-1 O 2 '89
POWLEDGE, FRED
Yuppies and microwaves. il *The Progressive* 53:46 D '89
POWWOW HIGHWAY [film] See Motion picture reviews—Single works
POX VIRUSES
Protection against streptococcal pharyngeal colonization with a vaccinia: M protein recombinant. V. A. Fischetti and others. bibl f il *Science* 244:1487-90 Je 23 '89
POZSGAY, IMRE
about
Astonishing reforms [interview] M. Nemeth. por *Maclean's* 102:29+ N 13 '89
Hungary's heir apparent gambles on radical change. R. Knight. il por map *U.S. News & World Report* 107:32-3 Jl 17 '89
Hungary's quiet revolution. J. Rupnik. *The New Republic* 201:18-20+ N 20 '89
Now you see it . . . J. Borrell. il por *Time* 134:46+ O 23 '89
A talk with Hungary's Imre Pozsgay [interview] R. L. Tőkés. por *The New Leader* 72:9-12 Je 12-26 '89
POZZI, LUCIO, 1935-
But will it fit over the couch? *Harper's* 279:35 S '89
PPG INDUSTRIES, INC.
PPG: shiny, not dull. B. Saporito. il *Fortune* 120:107 Jl 17 '89
PPOS *See* Preferred provider organizations
PQQ (PYRROLOQUINOLINE QUINONE) *See* Methoxatin
PR *See* Public relations
PRACTICAL ARTS *See* Home economics; Industrial arts
PRACTICAL JOKES
Getting even . . . Hollywood-style. M. Beck. il *TV Guide* 37:4-6+ Je 10-16 '89
Joe Magrane strikes back [St. Louis Cardinals have baseball player pose for phony GQ fashion layout] G. Collins. il pors *Gentlemen's Quarterly* 59:260-3 Ap '89
Time out for fun & games. il *'Teen* 33:93 S '89
PRADER-WILLI SYNDROME
Prader lacks fader; Angelman misses mom? [research by Robert D. Nicholls] R. Weiss. *Science News* 136:324 N 18 '89
PRADO, DANDA
(jt. auth) See Figueiredo, Mariza de Athayde, and Prado, Danda
PRADO MUSEUM *See* Museo del Prado (Madrid, Spain)
PRADOS, JOHN
China's "new thinking" on nuclear arms. bibl f il *The Bulletin of the Atomic Scientists* 45:32-5 Je '89
PRAEMIUM IMPERIALE
A yen for the arts. il *U.S. News & World Report* 107:18 S 25 '89
PRAGER, DENNIS, 1948-
The secret of true happiness. *Reader's Digest* 134:177-8 Je '89
What makes a happy person? *Redbook* 172:76-7+ F '89
PRAGMATISM
The pragmeologues [J. A. Baker's pragmatism] D. Seligman. il *Fortune* 119:165 My 8 '89
PRAGUE (CZECHOSLOVAKIA)
The magic flute; tr. by Peter Kussi. B. Hrabal. *The New York Review of Books* 36:39 My 18 '89
Description
Prague diarist. M. Peretz. *The New Republic* 200:43 Je 26 '89
Historic houses, sites, etc.
Fathers and sons [house of J. Mucha] S. Staggs. il *Art News* 88:83-4+ My '89
Music
See also
Opera—Czechoslovakia
Riots
Actions speak louder [police crackdown on demonstrators] il *Time* 133:38 Ja 30 '89
PRAIRIE (CHICAGO, ILL.: RESTAURANT) *See* Chicago (Ill.)—Restaurants, nightclubs, bars, etc.
PRAIRIE DOGS
The incredible odyssey of the president's beasts [transporting live specimens from the Lewis and Clark Expedition to T. Jefferson] B. Gilbert. il por *Audubon* 91:100-2+ Ja '89
Starting over [reintroduction of prairie dogs in Utah] J. L. Ferrara. il *National Wildlife* 27:18-21 F/Mr '89
PRAIRIE GRASSES *See* Grasses
PRAIRIE LIGHTS BOOKS (IOWA CITY, IOWA) *See* Booksellers and bookselling—Iowa

PRAIRIE SCHOONER TRIPS *See* Wagon trains
PRAIRIES
Illinois
Prairie in flower [Ragdale estate in Lake Forest designed by H. Shaw] D. G. Lowe. il *House & Garden* 161:68-75+ Ag '89
Kansas
Back to Eden [work of W. Jackson; cover story; with editorial comment] E. Eisenberg. il por *The Atlantic* 264:6, 57-9+ N '89
A prairie park? [Spring Hill Ranch offered for national park status] F. Graham. il *Audubon* 91:20+ S '89
Prophet of the prairie [work of W. Jackson at the Land Institute] J. R. Luoma. il pors map *Audubon* 91:54-60 N '89
North America
The last watering holes on the prairie [loss of wetland habitat for waterfowl] G. L. Krapu. il *Natural History* p66-9 Ja '89
PRAISE
Can you praise a child too much? F. B. Maynard. il *Parents* 64:93-6 S '89
How do we love you? Rudely [rude compliments] G. Schwartz. *Seventeen* 48:56 S '89
Words that can warm up your marriage [paying compliments] D. R. Hales. il *McCall's* 116:70+ Ap '89
PRALINE DESSERTS *See* Desserts
PRAN DITH *See* Dith, Pran
PRANCER [film] See Motion picture reviews—Single works
PRANKS *See* Practical jokes
PRATER, DAVE, 1937-1988
about
Widow of 'Sam & Dave' star, Dave Prater, to administer his estate. por *Jet* 75:17 Mr 27 '89
PRATER, ROSEMARY E.
about
Widow of 'Sam & Dave' star, Dave Prater, to administer his estate. por *Jet* 75:17 Mr 27 '89
PRATHER, PATRICIA SMITH
Coincoin: plantation owner before the nation was born. il *American Visions* 4:46-7 F '89
Watermelon king remembered. il por *American Visions* 4:38-9 Ag '89
PRATHER, WILLIAM E., JR.
about
Burger woes. R. T. Grieves. il por *Forbes* 143:102 Ja 23 '89
PRATO, LOU
Group therapy. il *Channels (New York, N.Y.: 1986)* 9:48-50 Ap '89
PRATO (ITALY)
Galleries and museums
See also
Centro per l'Arte Contemporaneo Luigi Pecci (Prato, Italy)
PRATT, C. DUDLEY, JR.
about
"Having a mother who loves us". M. Beauchamp. il por *Forbes* 144:117+ O 2 '89
PRATT, CHARLES W.
Graduation speech for Tim, who turned out OK [poem] *Commonweal* 116:327 Je 2 '89
Grave for the cat [poem] *Country Journal* 16:95 Mr/Ap '89
PRATT, EDMUND T., JR.
about
Pfizer's pipeline is full, but will the drugs flow fast enough? M. Roman. il por *Business Week* p74+ S 11 '89
PRATT, HENRY J.
Tips on writing the how-to article. *The Writer* 102:31-2 S '89
PRATT, JERRY
about
Taking a tip from a dapper fan, anchorman Don Shelby makes news with the knot in his necktie. il pors *People Weekly* 32:59 O 2 '89
PRATT, JOANNE H.
Shoptalk. See issues of Home Office Computing beginning September 1988
PRATT, R. F.
Inhibition of a class C β-lactamase by a specific phosphonate monoester. bibl f il *Science* 246:917-19 N 17 '89
PRATT & WHITNEY AIRCRAFT GROUP
Douglas prepares to flight test PW-Allison propfan powerplant. il *Aviation Week & Space Technology* 130:35 Ja 2 '89
NASP program office retains two propulsion contractors [National Aerospace Plane] S. W. Kandebo. *Aviation Week & Space Technology* 130:19 My 8 '89
Navy selects GE for future F404 turbofan orders, drops Pratt as second source. *Aviation Week & Space Technology* 131:26 Ag 28 '89
Pratt & Whitney engine turbopumps could fly on space shuttle in 1992. E. H. Kolcum. *Aviation Week & Space Technology* 130:67 F 27 '89
Pratt & Whitney offers RL10 upgrades for Centaur users. E. H. Kolcum. il *Aviation Week & Space Technology* 130:52 F 20 '89

PRATT & WHITNEY AIRCRAFT GROUP—cont.
Pratt & Whitney scramjet design for NASP tested in NASA-Langley facility at Mach 8 [National Aero-Space Plane] il *Aviation Week & Space Technology* 131:26 O 16 '89
Pratt & Whitney to supply 60% of Air Force's fighter engines. *Aviation Week & Space Technology* 130:32 Mr 13 '89
Pratt demonstrates low-speed propulsion concept for National Aero-Space Plane. S. W. Kandebo. il *Aviation Week & Space Technology* 130:79 Je 26 '89
Pratt, General Electric to deliver ATF engines to Air Force by year-end [advanced tactical fighter] il *Aviation Week & Space Technology* 131:21 D 4 '89
Pratt ground tests thrust-reversing, 2D nozzle for STOL demonstrator. il *Aviation Week & Space Technology* 131:29 S 25 '89
Thai International to equip three Airbus A300-600Rs with PW4158 engines. P. Proctor. *Aviation Week & Space Technology* 131:76 Ag 7 '89
Where 1990s-style management is already hard at work. T. Vogel. il por *Business Week* p92-3+ O 23 '89
PRATT & WHITNEY AIRCRAFT OF CANADA LTD.
Leader of the Pratts [PW305] N. Moll. *Flying* 116:105 N '89
Sundstrand, Pratt & Whitney Canada make inroads in APU marketplace [auxiliary power units] il *Aviation Week & Space Technology* 130:78-80 Ap 10 '89
PRATT HOTEL CORPORATION
How Trump plays monopoly [D. Trump's lease deal with B. Guccione freezes out Pratt Hotel as Atlantic City competitor] H. Rudnitsky. il *Forbes* 143:128 Ap 17 '89
PRAVDA (MOSCOW, SOVIET UNION)
Dear editor: You're fired. Signed, Mikhail Gorbachev [V. Afanasev] W. R. Doerner. il pors *Time* 134:62-3 O 30 '89
Gorbachev's one-two punch [scolding the media] A. Deming. il *Newsweek* 114:54-5 O 30 '89
PRAYER
See also
Faith cure
Meditation
Prayers
Badgering God. P. J. Ryan. *America* 161:47 Jl 15-22 '89
Contemplative prayer: taking time to hang out with God [interview with T. Keating; cover story] il por *U.S. Catholic* 54:6-13 Mr '89
Doctors agree: prayer works. T. C. Muck. *Christianity Today* 33:17 Mr 17 '89
How seven spiritual sluggers can help you improve your prayer life [cover story; special section] il *U.S. Catholic* 54:6-15 F '89
I wondered if I would pass the test. S. H. Johnson. il *Commonweal* 116:208-10 Ap 7 '89
Knockin' on heaven's door: how U.S. Catholic readers pray [cover story] T. Unsworth. il *U.S. Catholic* 54:6-15 My '89
Persistence. P. J. Ryan. il *America* 161:247 O 14 '89
Phony and non-phony prayer. P. J. Ryan. il *America* 161:279 O 21 '89
The prayer war [relaxation response theories of H. Benson] S. Kiesling and T. G. Harris. *Psychology Today* 23:65-6 O '89
Prayer—when? how? why? [cover story; special section] il *Commonweal* 116:73-8 F 10 '89
Praying with trees. L. V. Ham. il *The Christian Century* 106:839-40 S 27 '89
The Truman doctrine [statement by H. S. Truman] M. E. Marty. il *The Christian Century* 106:271 Mr 8 '89
What Bush forgot. T. K. Jones. *Christianity Today* 33:17 N 17 '89
PRAYER BOOKS
See also
Catholic Church—Prayer books and devotions
PRAYER IN THE SCHOOLS *See* Public schools and religion
PRAYERS
Of thee (and thy, and thou) I sing. M. Finley. *America* 160:76 F 4 '89
PRE-COLUMBIAN ART *See* Art, Pre-Columbian
PRE-RAPHAELITES
Lost jewels [pieces designed by Pre-Raphaelites] G. C. Munn. bibl f il *Antiques* 136:826-33 O '89
PREACHING
See also
Sermons
Challenges facing U.S. Catholics. A. M. Greeley. *Commonweal* 116:620 N 17 '89
Guidelines for preaching by the laity: another step backward? [Catholic Church] J. A. Wallace. *America* 161:139-41 S 9-16 '89
Martin Luther King: the preacher as virtuoso [cover story] M. E. Marty. *The Christian Century* 106:348-50 Ap 5 '89
Preachers need to spend a day on the job [with readers' comments] G. F. Pierce. *U.S. Catholic* 54:14-19 D '89
PREAKNESS (RACE) *See* Horse racing
PREAMPLIFIERS *See* Amplifiers
PRECAMBRIAN PERIOD *See* Geology, Stratigraphic—Precambrian; Paleoclimatology—Precambrian; Paleontology—Precambrian

PRECANCEROUS CONDITIONS
Lasers vs. skin cancer [removal of precancerous patches; work of William Dobes] *USA Today (Periodical)* 118:13-14 O '89
PRECEDENTS (LAW)
See also
Stare decisis
PRECESSION
The double polestar of the past [computer program] A. Kammerer. il *Sky and Telescope* 77:531-3 My '89
PRECIOUS METALS
See also
Gold
Platinum
Silver
PRECIOUS METALS AS AN INVESTMENT
The latest on precious metals and collectibles. il *Black Enterprise* 20:60 O '89
Will gold shine? Yes, but not enough to blind anybody. T. Segal. il *Business Week* p144 D 25 '89-Ja 1 '90
PRECIOUS STONES
See also
Diamonds
Garnets
Gems
PRECIPITATION (METEOROLOGY)
See also
Rain and rainfall
Snow
Recent decades saw wetter continents [research by Henry F. Diaz] R. Monastersky. *Science News* 135:52-3 Ja 28 '89
PRECISION CASTPARTS CORP.
Smooth flying. M. Beauchamp. il por *Forbes* 144:94+ S 18 '89
PRECOGNITION *See* Extrasensory perception
PRÉDAL, RENÉ
Germans screened through French eyes. il *The Unesco Courier* 42:18-23 O '89
PREDATION (BIOLOGY)
Arms race on the grass flats [mollusks and their predators] E. S. Iversen and D. E. Jory. il *Sea Frontiers* 35:304-11 S/O '89
Attack of the killer cats [study by Peter Churcher and John Lawton on predatory habits of cats] L. Jaroff. il *Time* 134:46 Jl 31 '89
Beware of well-fed felines. P. B. Churcher and J. H. Lawton. il *Natural History* p40-7 Jl '89
Cnidocyte mechanoreceptors are tuned to the movements of swimming prey by chemoreceptors [cover story] G. M. Watson and D. A. Hessinger. bibl f il *Science* 243:1589-91 Mr 24 '89
Crown-of-thorns no Johnny-come-lately [Great Barrier Reef; research by A. J. Timothy Jull] S. Hart. *Science News* 136:133 Ag 26 '89
Evidence from sediments of long-term Acanthaster planci predation on corals of the Great Barrier Reef [crown of thorns starfish; cover story] P. D. Walbran and others. bibl f il map *Science* 245:847-50 Ag 25 '89
Ice sponging off the Antarctic shelf [research by Paul K. Dayton] il *Science News* 136:255 O 14 '89
Interdecadal variation in an Antarctic sponge and its predators from oceanographic climate shifts. P. K. Dayton. bibl f il *Science* 245:1484-6 S 29 '89
The lemming phenomenon. L. Hansson. il *Natural History* p38-43 D '89
Not by grass alone [carnivory by herbivores] R. W. Furness. il *Natural History* p8+ D '89
Predator-induced reaction norms [cyclomorphosis] S. I. Dodson. bibl f il *BioScience* 39:447-52 Jl/Ag '89
Samurai aphids: survival under siege [Japan] M. W. Moffett. il *National Geographic* 176:406-22 S '89
Starry blight [destruction of reefs by crown of thorns starfish] K. Brower. il *Omni (New York, N.Y.)* 11:22+ My '89
The unkindest sting of all [scorpion-scorpion predation] G. A. Polis. il *Natural History* p34-9 Jl '89
What tells anemones to kill their enemies? [research by Glen M. Watson and David A. Hessinger] R. Weiss. *Science News* 135:182 Mr 25 '89
Why bite the right of a trilobite? [research by Loren E. Babcock] R. Monastersky. il *Science News* 136:78 Jl 29 '89
PREDATOR CALLING *See* Animal calling
PREDATOR CONTROL *See* Animals, Predatory—Control
PREDATORY ANIMALS *See* Animals, Predatory
PREDATORY BIRDS *See* Birds of prey
PREDICTION *See* Forecasting
PREDICTION THEORY
Prediction and theory evaluation: the case of light bending. S. G. Brush. bibl f *Science* 246:1124-9 D 1 '89
PREFABRICATED FIREPLACES *See* Fireplaces
PREFABRICATION
See also
Houses, Prefabricated
School buildings, Prefabricated

PREFERRED PROVIDER ORGANIZATIONS

Are companies cutting too close to the bone? [malpractice claims may arise from new insurance plans designed to trim costs] M. Galen. il *Business Week* p141+ O 30 '89
Ouch! The squeeze on your health benefits [cover story] il *Business Week* p110-13+ N 20 '89

PREFERRED STOCKS
See also
Pay-in-kind securities

Great Britain
A sexy new tax shelter from across the Atlantic. L. Jereski. *Business Week* p108 Je 12 '89

PREGNANCY
See also
Abortion
Amniotic fluid
Artificial insemination, Human
Childbirth
Fetus
Industry—Prenatal care programs
Maternally acquired immunity
Maternity leaves
Obstetrics
Prenatal care
Prenatal influences
Teenage pregnancy

As they grow/pregnancy and birth. P. A. Hillard. See issues of Parents
Baby boom II: delayed pregnancies mean more twins. C. Moekle. il *American Health* 8:107 Ap '89
Bonus baby [older mother] E. Klein. il *The New York Times Magazine* p22+ Ag 27 '89
The last 3 months of pregnancy/the first 3 months of parenting. J. Yager. bibl *McCall's* 116:49-50+ Ja '89
Mommy oldest: having babies at 45 and beyond [cover story] J. Kasindorf. il *New York* 22:22-9 Jl 17 '89
The politics of pregnancy. C. Tavris. *Vogue* 179:572-3+ S '89
Sex during pregnancy. K. B. Fader. il *Glamour* 87:64+ F '89
Sixteen—the third time around. I. Davis. il *The New York Times Magazine* p22+ D 17 '89
Sorting out the myths [views of J. Chris Carey] il *USA Today (Periodical)* 118:12 O '89
When you're very possibly pregnant [unmarried couples] D. Heyn. *Mademoiselle* 95:98 D '89
Your pregnancy. L. MacCallum. See issues of Glamour

Complications
See also
Fetus, Effect of drugs on the
Miscarriage

Awakening from a coma, a Washington woman meets her miraculous baby boy [B. Blodgett gives birth] M. Green. il pors *People Weekly* 31:38-40+ F 27 '89
Bias or safety? [appeals court upholds Johnson Controls ban excluding women of childbearing age from hazardous jobs] *Time* 134:61 O 16 '89
Ectopic pregnancy. P. A. Hillard. il *Parents* 64:117-18 Ja '89
Fighting for two lives [contracting synovial sarcoma during pregnancy] M. L. Edwards. il por *Ladies' Home Journal* 106:18+ S '89
Having a baby [lupus patients] D. Stehlin. il *FDA Consumer* 23:11 D '89/Ja '90
Hypertension in pregnancy cuts cancer risk [role of alpha fetoprotein; research by Herbert I. Jacobson] J. Raloff. *Science News* 136:263 O 21 '89
Miracle babies. il *Redbook* 174:136-8+ D '89
Pregnancy raises risk of type II diabetes [research by Donna Kritz-Silverstein] K. Fackelmann. *Science News* 136:294-5 N 4 '89
The silent danger of toxoplasmosis. S. Mahler. *McCall's* 116:109-10 My '89
Tracing the cat connection [danger of toxoplasmosis; views of Robert McCabe] D. Groves. il *American Health* 8:102 Ja/F '89
Unexpected drips and leaks: bladder surprises during pregnancy. S. Young. *Glamour* 87:79 S '89
When you need a helping hand. P. A. Hillard. il *Parents* 64:196+ My '89
When your baby is late. L. MacCallum. il *Glamour* 87:109 Ap '89
When your water breaks. P. A. Hillard. il *Parents* 64:135-6 Ag '89

Nutritional aspects
Eating for two. J. Taylor. il *Better Homes and Gardens* 68:44 F '89
The gastrointestinal tract in growth and reproduction. K. Uvnäs-Moberg. bibl il *Scientific American* 261:78-83 Jl '89
Magnesium for moms-to-be. il *Prevention (Emmaus, Pa.)* 41:8+ Ja '89
Nutrients and birth defects [taking vitamins before conception may reduce risk] il *Prevention (Emmaus, Pa.)* 41:12+ Mr '89
Vitamins and moms-to-be [may reduce risk of neural tube defects; research by Joseph Mullinare] G. McBride. il *American Health* 8:138 Ap '89

Psychological aspects
In the family way [husbands share pregnancy with the Empathy Belly developed by L. Ware] il *Good Housekeeping* 209:76 S '89
Mom, meet your baby [effect of utrasound exams on pregnant women; research by Tiffany Field] B. Py-Lieberman. *Psychology Today* 23:18 Je '89
My husband was afraid to be a father. il *Good Housekeeping* 209:34+ S '89

Signs and diagnosis
All pregnancy tests are not created equal. C. Hacinli. *Mademoiselle* 95:142 Mr '89

PREGNANCY, IMAGINARY *See* Pseudocyesis

PREGNANCY EXERCISES
Biking & baby. M. Drake. il pors *Bicycling* 30:82+ My '89
Finding fitness after baby [resuming running] C. L. Otis. il *Women's Sports & Fitness* 11:10 N/D '89
Fitness boom vs. baby boom. J. Seligmann. il *Newsweek* 114:79 D 11 '89
Pregnant and fit. K. Davis. bibl il pors *Women's Sports & Fitness* 11:50-5 Je '89
Tone up in the pool. L. MacCallum. il *Glamour* 87:59 Ag '89

PREGNANCY IN ANIMALS
Care for pregnant dogs. M. W. Fox. il *McCall's* 117:158 O '89

PREGNANCY IN TELEVISION
Birth day on 'Sesame Street' [Maria's pregnancy] J. Seligmann. il *Newsweek* 113:71 My 15 '89
From Little Ricky to L.A. Law . . . TV's great expectations. A. Waldman. il *TV Guide* 37:6-7+ D 30 '89-Ja 5 '90
Pregnant men on 'Cosby' highlights special episode. il *Jet* 77:58-9 N 27 '89

PREGNANCY KITS *See* Pregnancy—Signs and diagnosis
PREGNANCY TERMINATING DRUGS *See* Abortifacients
PREGNANCY TESTS *See* Pregnancy—Signs and diagnosis
PREGNANT SCHOOLGIRLS *See* Teenage pregnancy
PREHISTORIC AGRICULTURE *See* Agriculture, Prehistoric
PREHISTORIC ANIMALS *See* Extinct animals
PREHISTORIC ART *See* Art, Prehistoric
PREHISTORIC ASTRONOMY *See* Astronomy, Ancient
PREHISTORIC MAN *See* Man, Prehistoric
PREHISTORIC MONUMENTS *See* Megalithic monuments
PREHISTORIC POTTERY *See* Pottery, Prehistoric

PREJUDICE
See also
Anti-Catholicism
Anti-Semitism
Ethnocentrism
Hate crimes
Race discrimination

Are you prejudiced? D. O. Relin. il *Scholastic Update (Teachers' edition)* 121:10-11+ Ap 7 '89
Attacking prejudice [National Parent-Teacher Association brochure] *Children Today* 18:4-5 S/O '89
How bigotry affects all our lives. S. Jacoby. il *Glamour* 87:250-1+ N '89
"Mommy, why is she different?" [answers to sensitive questions children ask] L. Derman-Sparks and others. il *Parents* 64:120-3 D '89
Prejudice, conflict, and ethnoviolence: a national dilemma. J. C. Weiss. il *USA Today (Periodical)* 117:27-9 My '89
Pride and prejudice. D. F. Bjorklund and B. Bjorklund. il *Parents* 64:180 F '89
Two cheers for heterogeneity [Christopher Ricks' T. S. Eliot and prejudice] M. E. Marty. *The Christian Century* 106:837 S 27 '89

PRELINGER, RICK
about
Gems. *The New Yorker* 65:32-3 S 11 '89
PRELUDE ROSES *See* Roses

PREMADASA, RANASINGHE
about
Voting for peace. M. Nemeth. il por *Maclean's* 102:44-5 Ja 2 '89

PREMATURE INFANTS *See* Infants, Premature
PREMATURE LABOR *See* Childbirth—Complications

PREMENSTRUAL SYNDROME
Breaking attitude stereotypes [survey by Stephanie L. Hanson] *USA Today (Periodical)* 117:10 F '89
Hell week. L. Payer. il *Ms.* 17:28+ Mr '89
How do you know if it's PMS? P. Dranov. il *American Health* 8:54-8 D '89
PMS update. K. McCoy. *Seventeen* 48:144+ My '89

Anecdotes, facetiae, satire, etc.
A pathetic bid for sympathy from a long-suffering significant other. K. Gross. *Ms.* 17:30 Mr '89

Therapy
PMS pill [doxycycline] il *Prevention (Emmaus, Pa.)* 41:14+ F '89

PREMIERES, MOTION PICTURE *See* Motion picture premieres

PREMINGER, OTTO, 1906-1986
about
Otto Preminger. A. Sarris. il por *American Film* 14:69-71 Je '89

PREMIUMS
See also
Compass International, Inc.
Holly Driscoll had a fine idea, but it left her in the soup [collecting Campbell Soup labels to obtain van for school in Washburn, Wis.] il por *People Weekly* 31:97 My 22 '89

PREMIUMS, INSURANCE *See* Insurance—Rates and tables
PRENATAL CARE
See also
Claretian Medical Center
National Commission to Prevent Infant Mortality (U.S.)
A case for preplanning [excerpt from Preconceptions] J. T. Queenan and K. K. Leslie. il *Health (New York, N.Y.)* 21:38-9+ D '89
Fighting infant mortality [Momma Mobile] C. SerVaas. il *The Saturday Evening Post* 261:94+ O '89
The pregnancy police, on patrol [enforcing fetal rights by jailing negligent mothers] T. Gest. il *U.S. News & World Report* 106:50 F 6 '89
Prenatal alert [healthy women may need less care; Public Health Service report] *Time* 134:79 O 16 '89
Preventing infant mortality: an investment in the nation's future [study by the National Commission to Prevent Infant Mortality] P. Rowe. il *Children Today* 18:16-20 Ja/F '89
Saving America's babies [high mortality rate] A. Hulbert. *The New Republic* 201:19-21 N 13 '89
The Sikasso project [maternal and child health program in Mali] A. Rougemont and others. il *World Health* p6-8 Je '89
With prenatal care, less may be better [Public Health Service report] S. Findlay. il *U.S. News & World Report* 107:76 O 30 '89

PRENATAL DIAGNOSIS *See* Fetus—Diseases—Diagnosis
PRENATAL INFLUENCES
Preschool? [fetal learning; cover story] P. Weintraub. il *Omni (New York, N.Y.)* 11:34-8+ Ag '89
LA PRENSA (NICARAGUA)
Don't call her comrade [publisher V. Chamorro] J. Moody. il por *Time* 133:62-4 Je 12 '89
PRENTICE, THOMSON
Slowing down the march of time. *World Press Review* 36:31-2 F '89
PRENTICE HALL PRESS
Prentice Hall Press travels to new 'Destinations'. il *Publishers Weekly* 236:32 N 10 '89
PRENUPTIAL CONTRACTS *See* Marriage contracts
PREPAID LEGAL SERVICES
Prepaid legal plans come on strong. C. F. Black. il *Consumers' Research Magazine* 72:19-22 Jl '89
PREPARATION OF MANUSCRIPTS *See* Authorship—Copy preparation
PREPAREDNESS, MILITARY *See* United States—Military policy
PREPAYMENT OF MORTGAGES *See* Mortgages—Prepayment
THE PREPPIE MURDER [television program] *See* Television program reviews—Single works
LES PRÉS D'EUGÉNIE (FRANCE: RESORT) *See* Resorts—France
PRESBYOPIA
The heartbreak of presbyopia. G. Waggoner. *Esquire* 111:158-9 Mr '89
PRESBYTERIAN CHURCH
United States
See also
Presbyterians for Renewal
Evangelicals in the PCUSA consolidate their ranks. R. Frame. il *Christianity Today* 33:48-9 Je 16 '89
First black woman to head merged Presbyterian Church [Rev. J. SalmonCampbell the Presbyterian Church U.S.A.] A. Bradford. il pors *Ebony* 45:100+ N '89
PCUSA and sex issues [meeting in Philadelphia] *The Christian Century* 106:648 Jl 5-12 '89
PCUSA puts hottest issues on hold [Philadelphia assembly] R. Frame. il *Christianity Today* 33:48 Jl 14 '89
Presbyterians consider four views on abortion. R. Frame. *Christianity Today* 33:52-3 D 15 '89
PRESBYTERIAN CHURCH (U.S.A.) *See* Presbyterian Church—United States
PRESBYTERIANS FOR RENEWAL
Evangelicals in the PCUSA consolidate their ranks. R. Frame. il *Christianity Today* 33:48-9 Je 16 '89
PRESCHOOL EDUCATION
See also
Center for Successful Childhood Development (Chicago, Ill.)
Kindergarten
Nursery schools
Project Head Start (U.S.)
Smart Start (U.S.)
University of California, Los Angeles. Child Care Center
As the twig is bent? [special issue of Elementary school journal] G. W. Bracey. il *Phi Delta Kappan* 70:562-3 Mr '89
Building bridges for at-risk children. L. F. Cavazos. *The Education Digest* 55:16-19 N '89

The case for preschool education [views of David P. Weikart] *Children Today* 18:3-4 S/O '89
The color of learning [influence of ethnicity upon learning styles of black children; work of Janice Hale-Benson] L. Troiano. il *American Health* 8:76 D '89
"Curriculum" for preschool [role of the principal] S. G. Sava. *The Education Digest* 54:51-2 Mr '89
Early care and education: reflecting on options and opportunities [cover story; special section; with introd. by Sharon L. Kagan] bibl f il *Phi Delta Kappan* 71:104-41 O '89
Early care and education: tackling the tough issues. S. L. Kagan. *The Education Digest* 54:17-20 My '89
Early care and education: tackling the tough issues [cover story] S. L. Kagan. bibl f il *Phi Delta Kappan* 70:432-9 F '89
Handle with care: educating young children. D. Elkind. il *USA Today (Periodical)* 117:66-8 Mr '89
Issues on four-year-olds and public schooling. S. Lubeck. *The Education Digest* 55:21-4 O '89
Learning all the time. J. C. Holt. il *Parents* 64:112-14+ N '89
Now, which kind of preschool? E. R. Shell. il *Psychology Today* 23:52-3+ D '89
Old baggage, new visions: shaping policy for early childhood programs [cover story; with editorial comment by Pauline B. Gough] A. W. Mitchell. bibl f il *Phi Delta Kappan* 70:658, 664-72 My '89
Parent-teacher communication techniques. E. L. Morgan. *The Education Digest* 55:32-5 O '89
Preschool and your child. B. Brenner. il *Good Housekeeping* 209:98+ S '89
Reflecting on priorities in preschool teaching. G. Heiss. *The Education Digest* 55:48-51 S '89
Restructuring early childhood education [report of the National Association of State Boards of Education Task Force on Early Childhood Education] il *Children Today* 18:2-3 Ja/F '89
Which program is best [for three-year-olds] F. Roberts. *Parents* 64:52+ Je '89
Who meets the standards for early childhood teachers? C. Seefeldt. *The Education Digest* 54:21-4 My '89
Anecdotes, facetiae, satire, etc.
Rebel without a preschool [nonconformist attitude of toddler] J. Hope. il *Parents* 64:222+ S '89
Europe
An international overview of preschool programs. S. B. Kamerman. bibl f il *Phi Delta Kappan* 71:135-41 O '89
PRESCHOOL TEACHERS *See* Teachers
PRESCOTT, EILEEN
How a one-woman show becomes a big-bucks business. il pors *Working Woman* 14:51-3+ Mr '89
PRESCOTT, WILLIAM H., AND OTHERS
Global Positioning System measurements for crustal deformation: precision and accuracy. bibl f il *Science* 244:1337-40 Je 16 '89
PRESCOTT INVESTORS
Rocking the recliners [proxy fight for La-Z-Boy] M. Schifrin. il por *Forbes* 144:194+ O 16 '89
PRESCRIBED BURNING *See* Forest fires—Controlled fires
PRESCRIPTION DRUG ABUSE *See* Drug abuse
PRESCRIPTION DRUG ADVERTISING *See* Drug industry—Advertising
PRESCRIPTION DRUGS *See* Drugs
PRESENILE DEMENTIA *See* Alzheimer's disease
PRESENTATION FOOD *See* Food styling
PRESENTATION MANAGER (COMPUTER PROGRAM)
DTP under Presentation Manager. M. Antonoff. il *Personal Computing* 13:63-4+ Je '89
Figuring out CONFIG. SYS. M. Minasi. il *Byte* 14:129-30+ Jl '89
Graphic Presentation Manager revealed. R. Lockwood. *Personal Computing* 13:31 Ja '89
PM: only a starting point. R. A. Shaffer. il *Personal Computing* 13:45-6 F '89
Presentation Manager makes OS/2 attractive. *High Technology Business* 9:31 Mr '89
Windows on the world [Microsoft's Presentation Manager strategy in conflict with Micrografx' Windows business] D. Churbuck. il pors *Forbes* 144:123+ D 25 '89
Testing
OS/2 gets a spreadsheet [Excel for OS/2 with Presentation Manager] A. Reinhardt. il *Byte* 14:81 N '89
OS/2 puts desktop publishing in the fast lane [PageMaker for OS/2 Presentation Manager] H. Eglowstein. il *Byte* 14:81 O '89
PM, Sun View, and the Mac [early benchmarks] F. Langa. *Byte* 14:6 Ja '89
Presentation Manager. J. Holtzman. il *Radio-Electronics* 60 ComputerDigest:77-8 Ap '89
Reaching critical mass: the arrival of Windows and Presentation Manager applications. R. Lockwood. il *Personal Computing* 13:109-11+ S '89
SideKick for PM: more than just a pretty face [SideKick for Presentation Manager] S. Miastkowski. il *Byte* 14:97 Ap '89
Sidekick revs up for OS/2 [Sidekick for Presentation Manager] R. Lockwood. *Personal Computing* 13:162 Ag '89

PRESENTATIONS (BUSINESS) *See* Business presentations
PRESENTS *See* Gifts
PRESERVATION OF BOOKS *See* Books—Conservation and restoration
PRESERVATION OF HISTORIC SITES *See* Historic houses, sites, etc.
PRESERVATION OF ORGANS, TISSUES, ETC.
Life extension [research by Sufan Chien and Peter Oeltgen] A. C. Revkin. il *Discover* 10:24-5 Jl '89
New way of keeping donor livers healthy [Belzer's solution] K. Fackelmann. *Science News* 135:69 F 4 '89
PRESERVATION OF PAPER *See* Paper—Preservation
PRESERVATION OF WOOD *See* Wood—Preservation and preservatives
PRESERVES, SHOOTING *See* Shooting preserves
PRESERVING *See* Canning and preserving
PRESIDENT (MUSICAL GROUP)
Wayne Horvitz/The President: Park West/Chicago. E. Guregian. il *Down Beat* 56:54 Ag '89
PRESIDENTIAL ADVISERS
See also
Black presidential advisers
Council of Economic Advisers (U.S.)
Bush's farmer in the White House [C. Evans] G. Vincent. il por *Successful Farming* 87:34AF mid-F '89
Bibliography
Getting FDR's ear. A. M. Schlesinger. il *The New York Review of Books* 36:20-3 F 16 '89
PRESIDENTIAL AIRPLANES *See* Airplanes, Government
PRESIDENTIAL AIRWAYS, INC.
Presidential Airways' woes show code sharing no guarantee of success. C. Fotos. *Aviation Week & Space Technology* 131:43-4 D 11 '89
PRESIDENTIAL CAMPAIGNS
See also
Advertising, Political
Campaign management
Campaign workers
Presidential candidates
Press and politics
Television and politics
1964
Extremists in the mainstream [B. Goldwater] V. Gold. il *The American Spectator* 22:34-5 Jl '89
1980
Minority report [link between Iranian hostage case, Reagan's 1980 campaign and contragate] C. Hitchens. *The Nation* 249:78 Jl 17 '89
1988
The 1988 election. N. J. Ornstein and M. Schmitt. *Foreign Affairs* 68 Special Issue:39-52 ['89]
Campaign revelations [book The quest for the presidency 1988] P. L. Goldman and T. Mathews. il *Newsweek* 114:10 O 23 '89
Choosing presidential candidates: why the best man doesn't necessarily win. D. G. Stephenson, Jr. il *USA Today (Periodical)* 117:15-18 Mr '89
"Even the TV people don't understand" [Ripon College conference] T. H. Stahel. *America* 161:354-5 N 18 '89
George Bush's dirty big secrets [stories ignored by the establishment press during the presidential campaign] il *Utne Reader* p59-60 S/O '89
Just think . . . [need to bring Americans back into the political process] S. K. Sheinbaum. *New Perspectives Quarterly* 5:64 Wint '88/'89
Lessons of campaign '88. F. Barnes. il *The American Spectator* 22:14-16 Ja '89
Manipulating the media and America: the negative 1988 presidential campaign. R. L. Fischer. il *USA Today (Periodical)* 117:20-2 Mr '89
Nouns and pronouns [G. Bush's campaign] L. H. Lapham. *Harper's* 278:8-9 Ja '89
A season in hell [D. Brazile, staff member during M. Dukakis campaign] G. E. Curry. il pors *Ms.* 18:58-60+ O '89
Winners. il *Life* 12:20-4 Ja '89
Economic aspects
See also
Campaign funds
Ethical aspects
See Political ethics
PRESIDENTIAL CANDIDATES
See also
Campaign management
Presidential campaigns
Press and politics
Television and politics
1988
See also
Bush, George, 1924-
Dukakis, Michael
Bowing out: a tough choice [P. Schroeder] B. G. Kempton. por *New Choices for the Best Years* 29:20+ O '89
1992
How the Democrats can win in '92. D. R. Mayhew and B. Russett. *The New Leader* 72:13 Ja 9 '89
The iceman goeth [M. Dukakis] H. Hertzberg. *The New Republic* 200:6 Ja 30 '89

Lloyd Bentsen is having a ball bashing George Bush. D. Harbrecht and H. Gleckman. il por *Business Week* p57 O 23 '89
Advertising
See Advertising, Political
Ethics
See Political ethics
Expenditures
See Campaign funds
Psychology
The wimp factor [cover story] B. Curtis. il *American Heritage* 40:40-4+ N '89
PRESIDENTIAL ELECTIONS *See* Presidents—Election
PRESIDENTIAL ENTERTAINING *See* Government entertaining
PRESIDENTIAL LIBRARIES
See also
Franklin D. Roosevelt Library
Ronald Reagan Presidential Library and Center for Public Affairs
A presidential gazetteer. G. B. Politzer. il *American History Illustrated* 24:43-52 Ap '89
PRESIDENTIAL POWER *See* Presidents—Powers and duties
PRESIDENTIAL PRESS CORPS *See* Bush, George, 1924— Press relations; Presidents—Press relations; Reagan, Ronald, 1911—Press relations
PRESIDENTS
See also
Adams, John, 1735-1826
Bush, George, 1924-
Carter, Jimmy, 1924-
Coolidge, Calvin, 1872-1933
Eisenhower, Dwight D. (Dwight David), 1890-1969
Fillmore, Millard, 1800-1874
Jackson, Andrew, 1767-1845
Jefferson, Thomas, 1743-1826
Johnson, Lyndon B. (Lyndon Baines), 1908-1973
Kennedy, John F. (John Fitzgerald), 1917-1963
Lincoln, Abraham, 1809-1865
Madison, James, 1751-1836
Nixon, Richard M. (Richard Milhous), 1913-
Reagan, Ronald, 1911-
Roosevelt, Franklin D. (Franklin Delano), 1882-1945
Truman, Harry S., 1884-1972
Vice-presidents
Washington, George, 1732-1799
Wilson, Woodrow, 1856-1924
Women presidents
200 years of the American presidency [cover story; special issue] il *American History Illustrated* 24:12-18+ Ap '89
Cycles of history. F. Barnes. *The New Republic* 200:10-12 My 22 '89
Mistakes new presidents make. F. Barnes. il *Reader's Digest* 134:38-43 Ja '89
The presidency: from George Washington to George Bush, 200 years of leadership [cover story; special issue] il *Scholastic Update (Teachers' edition)* 121:2-24 Ja 13 '89
Social class in the Oval Office [discussion of September/October 1988 article] E. D. Baltzell and H. G. Schneiderman. *Society* 26:10-15 Mr/Ap '89
Where the founder fits in the picture [place of G. Washington among presidents] R. Brookhiser. il *Time* 133:110 F 20 '89
Will your kid be president? C. Sugarman. il *Parents* 64:65-7 Ja '89
Addresses, messages, etc.
See also
Bush, George, 1924—Addresses, messages, etc.
Kennedy, John F. (John Fitzgerald), 1917-1963—Addresses, messages, etc.
Lincoln, Abraham, 1809-1865—Addresses, messages, etc.
Advisers
See Presidential advisers
Archives
See also
Nixon, Richard M. (Richard Milhous), 1913—Archives
Presidential libraries
Biography
Of many things [H. Brandon's book Special relationships: a foreign correspondent's memoirs from Roosevelt to Reagan] G. W. Hunt. *America* 160:210 Mr 11 '89
Collectibles
See also
Reagan, Ronald, 1911—Collectibles
Correspondence
See also
Bush, George, 1924—Correspondence
Lincoln, Abraham, 1809-1865—Correspondence
Election
See also
Electoral College
Presidential campaigns
Presidential candidates
Voting
The 1988 election. N. J. Ornstein and M. Schmitt. *Foreign Affairs* 68 Special Issue:39-52 ['89]
Act II, winning an election [reviving the Democratic Party] N. Lemann. *The Washington Monthly* 21:30+ Mr '89

PRESIDENTS—Election—*cont.*

The Democrats [discussion of February 1989 article, Why the Democrats lost again] J. Muravchik. *Commentary* 87:2-5 Je '89

Divided we fell: race and the '88 election. J. Williams. il pors *American Visions* 4:31+ F '89

The Duke did his best. R. E. Tyrrell. *The American Spectator* 22:10 Ja '89

Election '88: where do we go from here? J. Walljasper. il *Utne Reader* p126-7 Ja/F '89

JFK's children: the class of '74 [neoliberal Democrats; cover story] W. Schneider. il por *The Atlantic* 263:35-40+ Mr '89

Lessons of campaign '88. F. Barnes. il *The American Spectator* 22:14-16 Ja '89

The road to 1992 [blacks and the election of G. Bush] E. G. Graves. il *Black Enterprise* 19:7 Ja '89

What liberals haven't learned & why. F. F. Siegel. il *Commonweal* 116:16-20 Ja 13 '89

Why the Democrats lost again. J. Muravchik. *Commentary* 87:13-22 F '89

History

With a Republican in office, a recession may be lurking . . . and if it comes, the poor will really take a hit. M. J. Mandel. il *Business Week* p20 Ap 10 '89

Homes

See also

Bush, George, 1924—Homes

Eisenhower, Dwight D. (Dwight David), 1890-1969—Homes

Lincoln, Abraham, 1809-1865—Homes

Washington, George, 1732-1799—Homes

A presidential gazetteer. G. B. Politzer. il *American History Illustrated* 24:43-52 Ap '89

Inaugural addresses

See also

Bush, George, 1924—Inaugural address

Inaugurations

See also

Bush, George, 1924—Inauguration

Washington, George, 1732-1799—Inauguration

Once the election's over, why hold an inauguration? P. M. Jones. il *Scholastic Update (Teachers' edition)* 121:22 Ja 13 '89

Our only American ritual. D. J. Boorstin. il *U.S. News & World Report* 106:35 Ja 30 '89

Language

See also

Bush, George, 1924—Language

Libraries

See Presidential libraries

Museums

A presidential gazetteer. G. B. Politzer. il *American History Illustrated* 24:43-52 Ap '89

Nomination

Choosing presidential candidates: why the best man doesn't necessarily win. D. G. Stephenson, Jr. il *USA Today (Periodical)* 117:15-18 Mr '89

Jackson rules [rules of the Democratic Party] F. Barnes. *The New Republic* 200:14+ My 1 '89

Ron Brown's first test [Democratic presidential nomination rules] il por *Newsweek* 113:7 F 20 '89

Tough talk for Democrats. J. A. Califano. il *The New York Times Magazine* p28-9+ Ja 8 '89

Pets

See also

Bush, George, 1924—Pets

Powers and duties

See also

Pardon

Veto

War and emergency powers

Are presidents too powerful? P. M. Jones. il *Scholastic Update (Teachers' edition)* 121:14-15 Ja 13 '89

The backbone of hidden government [National Security Decision Directives; cover story] E. Pell. *The Nation* 248:833+ Je 19 '89

The evolving presidency. J. E. Ferling. il *American History Illustrated* 24:12-18+ Ap '89

Fifteen presidential decisions that shaped America. P. E. Arnold. il *American History Illustrated* 24:36-42 Ap '89

Hail to the chief [teens say what they would do if they were president] *Seventeen* 48:140+ N '89

Imperial conservatives? [stressing presidential powers in foreign affairs] S. T. Francis. *National Review* 41:37-8 Ag 4 '89

Presidents: the power and the mediocrity [differing views of J. Bryce and H. Laski] S. R. Graubard. il *The New York Times Book Review* 94:1+ Ja 15 '89

Reconsidering the two presidencies. D. M. Oldfield and A. B. Wildavsky. *Society* 26:54-9 Jl/Ag '89

Press conferences

See also

Coolidge, Calvin, 1872-1933—Press conferences

Press relations

See also

Bush, George, 1924—Press relations

Reagan, Ronald, 1911—Press relations

Kennedy was America's best TV president—Johnson the worst. T. E. Cronin. il *TV Guide* 37:22-3 O 14-20 '89

Loud and clear (as ever) . . . Sam Donaldson's parting shot: how TV can cover the White House a whole lot better. S. Donaldson. il pors *TV Guide* 37:36-8 Ja 28-F 3 '89

The press and power [interviewing the president] D. O. Relin. il *Scholastic Update (Teachers' edition)* 122:18+ S 8 '89

Privileges and immunities

See also

Executive privilege (Government information)

Psychology

LBJ's alter ego [memoir by R. Goodwin] G. C. Ward. il *American Heritage* 40:14+ F '89

The wimp factor [cover story] B. Curtis. il *American Heritage* 40:40-4+ N '89

Public relations

See also

Bush, George, 1924—Public relations

Reagan, Ronald, 1911—Public relations

The art of presidential persuasion. M. L. Whicker and T. W. Areson. il *USA Today (Periodical)* 117:12-14 My '89

Reading

See also

Bush, George, 1924—Reading

Relations with Congress

See also

Bush, George, 1924—Relations with Congress

Jackson, Andrew, 1767-1845—Relations with Congress

Wright turn [J. Wright postpones House action on covert operations legislation] *The Nation* 248:255-6 F 27 '89

Religion

See also

Bush, George, 1924—Religion

Carter, Jimmy, 1924—Religion

Jefferson, Thomas, 1743-1826—Religion

Madison, James, 1751-1836—Religion

Truman, Harry S., 1884-1972—Religion

Salaries, allowances, etc.

Expensive ex-presidents. B. A. Weisberger. il *American Heritage* 40:22+ My/Je '89

How to be an ex-president: balancing dignity, diplomacy and dollars. G. Hackett. il *Newsweek* 112:40 My 22 '89

The yen to stay onstage [former presidents] H. Sidey. il *Time* 134:30 N 6 '89

Speechwriters and speechwriting

See also

Reagan, Ronald, 1911—Speechwriters and speechwriting

Sports

See also

Bush, George, 1924—Sports

Staff

See also

Bush, George, 1924—Staff

Reagan, Ronald, 1911—Staff

Staffing a new president. C. M. Brauer. *Current (Washington, D.C.)* 310:28-35 F '89

Statues, portraits, etc.

See also

Lincoln, Abraham, 1809-1865—Statues, portraits, etc.

Reagan, Ronald, 1911—Statues, portraits, etc.

Washington, George, 1732-1799—Statues, portraits, etc.

200 years of the presidency. il *Horizon (Tuscaloosa, Ala.)* 32:33-48 Mr/Ap '89

Taxes

See also

Reagan, Ronald, 1911—Taxes

Term

The civility of American politics. D. J. Boorstin. il *U.S. News & World Report* 106:68 Ja 23 '89

Transition periods

George Bush moves in. J. D. Isaacs. il *The Bulletin of the Atomic Scientists* 45:3-4 Ja/F '89

George Bush's balky start. D. Gergen. il *U.S. News & World Report* 106:34 Ja 30 '89

The 'liberation' of George Bush [with interview] T. Morganthau. il pors *Newsweek* 113:28-9 Ja 16 '89

Staffing a new president. C. M. Brauer. *Current (Washington, D.C.)* 310:28-35 F '89

Transportation

See also

Airplanes, Government

Wives

America's First Ladies. B. B. Caroli. il *American History Illustrated* 24:26-31+ My '89

Fascinating First Ladies [quiz] K. N. Humphrey. il *Good Housekeeping* 209:176 Jl '89

What's a First Lady to do? An open letter to Barbara Bush. A. Hornaday. *Ms.* 17:98 Ja/F '89

PRESIDENTS—cont.

United States

See Presidents
PRESIDENTS, COLLEGE See College presidents
PRESIDENT'S COMMISSION ON THE ASSASSINATION OF PRESIDENT KENNEDY See Warren Commission
PRESIDENTS IN ADVERTISING
This one spells o-o-p-s [Kellogg Co.'s presidents puzzle wrongly includes name of J. Davis] il *Newsweek* 113:50 My 1 '89
Washington sold here. il pors *U.S. News & World Report* 106:14 F 27 '89
PRESIDENT'S PRIVATE SECTOR SURVEY ON COST CONTROL (U.S.)
The deficit time bomb [address, March 13, 1989] J. P. Grace. *Vital Speeches of the Day* 55:390-4 Ap 15 '89
PRESIDENT'S SELECT COMMITTEE ON AUTOMOTIVE REGULATION AND ECONOMICS
What's that? Uncle Sam wants car enthusiasts? W. Jeanes. il *Car and Driver* 34:6 Je '89
PRESIDENT'S TASK FORCE ON COMPETITIVENESS
Introducing Dan Quayle, competitiveness czar. R. Fly. il por *Business Week* p37 F 27 '89
The President's Council on Competitiveness. W. T. Brookes. il *Nation's Business* 77:32 My '89
PRESIDIO (SAN FRANCISCO, CALIF.: ARMY BASE) See Military bases
THE PRESIDIO [film] See Motion picture reviews—Single works
PRESLEY, ELVIS, 1935-1977
about
Brando's back—and better than ever. R. Rosenbaum. il pors *Mademoiselle* 95:102+ O '89
Elvis's prom date remembers a shy guy in blue suede shoes. S. Dougherty. il pors *People Weekly* 32:99-100 Jl 17 '89
Remembering the King; ed. by Kent Demaret. R. Stanley. il pors *People Weekly* 32:32-9 Ag 21 '89
Rock stars on TV: the greatest ever? Forget Springsteen, Jackson and Madonna. Elvis is still King! [cover story] D. Hiltbrand. il pors *TV Guide* 37:4-5+ Ja 21-27 '89
The secret Elvis diary [excerpt from If I can dream]; ed. by Patricia Romanowski. L. Geller and J. Spector. il pors *Good Housekeeping* 208:100-1+ F '89
A Sikh singer who gives Elvis fans a Singh-King feeling. il por *People Weekly* 31:87 My 1 '89
The Vicksburg ghost. S. Hubbell. *The New Yorker* 65:106-17 S 25 '89
Anecdotes, facetiae, satire, etc.
In search of historic Elvis. A. D. Maislen. il *Rolling Stone* p196-201 D 14-28 '89
PRESLEY, LISA MARIE
about
The Presleys' newest star [cover story] M. Green. il pors *People Weekly* 31:108-10+ Je 19 '89
Princess Presley: Elvis' little girl grows up. R. L. Smith. il pors *Ladies' Home Journal* 106:44+ F '89
PRESLEY, PRISCILLA BEAULIEU
about
Priscilla Presley: never better than now. J. Grant. il pors *McCall's* 116:12-13+ Jl '89
PRESS, BEN
A lesson to be learned. il por *World Tennis* 36:142 Ap '89
PRESS, CLIFFORD
about
A little cash and a lot of moxie. L. J. Nathans. il pors *Business Week* p74 Ja 30 '89
PRESS, FRANK
about
By contrast to last Academy address, Press is hopeful for science . . . if . . . I. Goodwin. *Physics Today* 42:41-2 Je '89
PRESS, GARY
about
Funniest accountant in America. il por *Changing Times* 43:29 F '89
PRESS, WILLIAM H., AND SPERGEL, DAVID N.
Cosmic strings: topological fossils of the hot Big Bang [cover story] bibl f il *Physics Today* 42:29-35 Mr '89
PRESS
See also
AIDS (Disease) and the press
Alternative press
Black press
Blacks and the press
Catholic press
Celebrities—Press relations
Church and the press
Confidential communications—Press
Crime and the press
Drugs and the press
Football players—Press relations
Foreign news
Freedom of the press
Government and the press
Journalistic ethics
Labor unions and the press
Newspapers

Race relations and the press
Terrorism and the press
Is there any hope for the mainstream press? [issue of alternative viewpoints] J. Walljasper. il *Utne Reader* p126-7 My/Je '89
Media. E. Diamond. See issues of New York beginning January 28, 1985
Newswatch. T. Griffith. See issues of Time through April 18, 1988
PRESS AGENCIES See News agencies
PRESS AND ABORTION
To march or not to march [reporters' beliefs become an issue] L. Zuckerman. il *Time* 134:45 Ag 14 '89
PRESS AND ART See Art news
PRESS AND AVIATION
Crash course in Denver [TV newsrooms cover Sioux City air crash, July 1989] J. M. Robins. il *Channels (New York, N.Y.: 1986)* 9:16 O '89
Pain behind the camera [covering crash of Pan Am 103 on local TV] K. Frankola. por *Newsweek* 113:9 F 6 '89
Reporters as stunt men [French journalists test airport security] J. Alter. il *Newsweek* 113:47+ Ja 16 '89
PRESS AND ECONOMICS See Economic news
PRESS AND GUN CONTROL
Clark Kent, please call your office [G. Bush asks press to do something about crime] il *Newsweek* 113:28 F 27 '89
Media fallout. D. E. Petzal. il *Field & Stream* 94:18+ Jl '89
PRESS AND IMMIGRATION
Substance versus fabricated fury [press coverage of Canadian refugee policy] G. Bain. il *Maclean's* 102:37 Ja 23 '89
PRESS AND LABOR UNIONS See Labor unions and the press
PRESS AND NUCLEAR ENERGY
Yo-yo journalism and nuclear power. F. Jerome. il *Technology Review* 92:73-4 Ap '89
PRESS AND POLITICS
See also
Bush, George, 1924-—Press relations
Journalists in government
Newspapers and politics
Presidents—Press relations
Reagan, Ronald, 1911-—Press relations
Beat the devil. A. Cockburn. See issues of The Nation
Diarist [trying to get stories on R. Brown and R. Strauss] J. Bennet. *The New Republic* 200:50 Je 19 '89
The gospel reconsidered [neoliberal philosophy of the Washington monthly; cover story; special section] *The Washington Monthly* 21:26-30+ Mr '89
Henry Luce, call your medium [Time's new liberal agenda] L. B. Bozell, III and B. Baker. *National Review* 41:37 S 15 '89
The intimidated press [coverage of presidential campaign] A. Lewis. il *The New York Review of Books* 35:26-8 Ja 19 '89
Is it right to publish rumors? W. Shapiro. il *Time* 134:53 Jl 10 '89
Malice toward none. M. Newman. il *The New Republic* 200:16-17 F 20 '89
Media's liberal slant on the news. B. Baker. il *USA Today (Periodical)* 118:64-6 Jl '89
Minority report [discussion of A. Cockburn's Stalinist leanings] C. Hitchens. *The Nation* 249:375 O 9 '89
Presswatch. T. Eastland. See issues of The American Spectator beginning February 1989
Privates on parade [reporting on private lives of politicians] *The New Republic* 201:7-9 N 13 '89
Pssst [Washington's rumor mill] M. Hosenball and M. Isikoff. *The New Republic* 200:16+ Ja 2 '89
Reporters are members in good standing of Washington high society. C. Hays and J. Rowe. *Utne Reader* p64 N/D '89
Taking the First [presidential campaign] R. W. Wilkins. il *Mother Jones* 14:43-4 F/Mr '89
To march or not to march [reporters' beliefs become an issue] L. Zuckerman. il *Time* 134:45 Ag 14 '89
Viewpoints. See issues of World Press Review
Writing about American politics [presidential campaigns] R. Brookhiser. *The American Scholar* 58:257-64 Spr '89

Afghanistan
Annals of the freedom fighters [reporting on the mujahadeen] A. Cockburn. *The Nation* 248:803 Je 12 '89

Brazil
Beat the devil [coverage of presidential candidate F. Collor de Mello] A. Cockburn. *The Nation* 249:232-3 S 4-11 '89

Canada
Anecdotes, facetiae, satire, etc.
Ever so humble, but no place like home. A. Fotheringham. il *Maclean's* 102:56 F 13 '89
No news, please, summer is here. C. Gordon. il *Maclean's* 102:11 Jl 24 '89

Great Britain
More sex please, we're British [sex scandal involving P. Bordes and various government officials and newspaper editors] A. Stanley. il pors *Time* 133:31 Ap 3 '89

PRESS AND POLITICS—*cont.*
Israel
Forgive us our press passes [Israeli police masquerading as press in the occupied territories] L. Zuckerman. il *Time* 133:65 My 8 '89
United States
See Press and politics
PRESS AND RADICALISM
Confessions of a closet leftist [A. K. MacDougall] L. Zuckerman. il por *Time* 133:58 F 6 '89
PRESS AND SPACE FLIGHT *See* Space flight—Reporters and reporting
PRESS AND THE ENVIRONMENT *See* Environmental news
PRESS AND THE JUDICIARY *See* Government and the press
PRESS LAW
    See also
    Confidential communications—Press
    Libel and slander
PRESS PHOTOGRAPHY *See* Photography, Journalistic
PRESS RELEASES
    See also
    Government and the press
    Videotapes—Press releases
PRESSES
    See also
    Printing presses
PRESSES DE LA CITÉ
    See also
    Groupe de la Cité
PRESSMAN, EDWARD
    about
The quiet man. K. Turan. il por *Gentlemen's Quarterly* 59:50+ Ja '89
PRESSURE
    See also
    Compression
    High pressure (Science)
Putting the squeeze on liquid films [research by Steve Granick and John Van Alsten] I. Peterson. *Science News* 135:207 Ap 1 '89
PRESSURE (ATMOSPHERIC) *See* Atmospheric pressure
PRESSURE (PSYCHOLOGY) *See* Stress
PRESSURE COOKERS
Getting steamed. L. Seymour. il *Health (New York, N.Y.)* 21:34+ S '89
PRESSURE COOKING
The good old pressure cooker. il *Sunset (Central West edition)* 183:140+ D '89
Wild game under pressure. J. Weiss. il *Outdoor Life* 183:92-3+ Ap '89
PRESSURE GROUPS *See* Special interest groups
PRESSURE TREATMENT OF WOOD *See* Wood—Preservation and preservatives
PRESSURE WASHERS
High-pressure washers. B. Eftink. il *Successful Farming* 87 no4:22-4+ Mr '89
PRESSURIZED AIRPLANES *See* Airplanes—Pressurization
PRESTIGE
America's true power. J. Lukacs. il *American Heritage* 40:74-9 Mr '89
PRESTON, DOUGLAS J.
Building with mud signifies success in the Southwest. il *Smithsonian* 20:144-8+ N '89
Potluck. il *Omni (New York, N.Y.)* 11:31+ Ja '89
Skeletons in our museums' closets: Native Americans want their ancestors' bones back. il *Harper's* 278:66-70+ F '89
PRESTON, ELIZABETH, 1950-
The ABC's of copyright. *The Writer* 102:21-3 D '89
PRESTON, JAMES EDWARD, 1933-
    about
Can Avon get Wall Street to answer the door? K. Deveny. il por *Business Week* p123-4 Mr 20 '89
PRESTON, JULIA
The trial that shook Cuba [cover story] il pors *The New York Review of Books* 36:24-31 D 7 '89
PRESTON, KELLY
    about
When Twins' Kelly Preston needs a lift, she gets it from Roseanne's George Clooney. S. Haller. il pors *People Weekly* 31:113-14+ F 13 '89
PRESTON, PAUL
Revenge and reconciliation. il *History Today* 39:28-33 Mr '89
PRESTON, YVONNE
Rising demands in the Baltics. *World Press Review* 36:13-16 Je '89
PRESTOWITZ, CLYDE
    about
Rewriting the book on how to deal with Japan. R. Neff. il pors *Business Week* p49 Ag 7 '89
PRETE, BARBARA
Baltimore, the city that reads. *Publishers Weekly* 236:71-2 Ag 4 '89
Business defines its role. il *Publishers Weekly* 235:20-1 My 26 '89
National Book Week: a burgeoning effort. *Publishers Weekly* 236:40 D 22 '89

What companies can do. *Publishers Weekly* 236:47-8 O 27 '89
PRETRIAL DETENTION *See* Preventive detention
PREUSCH, DEB
(jt. auth) *See* Barry, Tom, 1950-, and Preusch, Deb
PREVENTION (PERIODICAL)
40-something is something special. M. Bricklin. il *Prevention (Emmaus, Pa.)* 41:144+ Je '89
Looking for the good stories. M. Bricklin. il *Prevention (Emmaus, Pa.)* 41:144+ S '89
Prevention and you: together, into the next century. R. Rodale. il *Prevention (Emmaus, Pa.)* 41:22+ D '89
What kind of person reads Prevention? M. Bricklin. il *Prevention (Emmaus, Pa.)* 41:144+ Mr '89
PREVENTION OF ACCIDENTS *See* Accidents—Prevention
PREVENTION OF CRIME *See* Crime prevention
PREVENTION OF CRUELTY TO ANIMALS *See* Animal rights movement
PREVENTION OF SUICIDE *See* Suicide—Prevention
PREVENTIVE DETENTION
The no-bail solution. R. F. Nagel. *The New Republic* 200:13-14 Ap 24 '89
Preventive . . . [Puerto Rican independence activist F. Ojeda Rios held without bail in U.S.] R. A. Falk. *The Nation* 248:508-9 Ap 17 '89
Japan
Forcing confessions in Japan. Y. Takagi. *World Press Review* 36:57 Je '89
PREVENTIVE MEDICINE *See* Medicine, Preventive
PREVIN, ANDRÉ, 1929-
    about
Now, a grab for new chairs. M. Walsh. il pors *Time* 133:90-1 My 8 '89
PREVITE, BOBBY
    about
Blindfold test. G. Santoro. por *Down Beat* 56:53 D '89
PRIAKIN, SERGEI
    about
A Red-letter day. C. Cotton. il por *Sports Illustrated* 70:38-9 Ap 10 '89
PRIAL, FRANK J.
Freeze! You're on TV. il *Reader's Digest* 134:189-92 Mr '89
Guessing games. il *The New York Times Magazine* p43 My 28 '89
Wine. See occasional issues of The New York Times Magazine
PRICE, ALISON
    about
A woman's place. J. F. Mariani. il por *Harper's Bazaar* 122:190+ N '89
PRICE, DAVID
    about
The F.B.I. man who cried libel. M. Garbus. il *The Nation* 249:564+ N 13 '89
Viking, Matthiessen win in Price libel suit. *Publishers Weekly* 236:8 S 1 '89
PRICE, EUGENIA
    about
PW interviews. B. Summer. por *Publishers Weekly* 235:57-8 My 5 '89
PRICE, FREDERICK
    about
FaithDome: 'a grand-slam homer for Jesus'. A. Collier. il pors *Ebony* 45:40-2+ D '89
TV's Rev. Fred Price opens $9 million FaithDome in L.A. il pors *Jet* 77:32-3 O 16 '89
PRICE, JOE D.
    about
Buying at the Wright time. C. Brown. il por *Forbes* 143:172 Je 12 '89
PRICE, JOSEPH L., 1949-
The ultimate and the ordinary: a profile of Langdon Gilkey [cover story] il por *The Christian Century* 106:380-3 Ap 12 '89
PRICE, MARTIN F.
Global change: defining the ill-defined. bibl f il *Environment* 31:18-20+ O '89
PRICE, PETER
    about
And in this corner coin box: an all-sports daily. S. Baker and D. Lieberman. il pors *Business Week* p30 Ag 21 '89
A fan's notes. E. Diamond. il pors *New York* 22:22-3 Ag 14 '89
Make room in the press box. M. Beck. il pors *Newsweek* 113:53 Je 12 '89
PRICE, RICHARD, 1949-
    about
With Sea of love, novelist Richard Price drops anchor among Hollywood's writer elite. T. Allis. il pors *People Weekly* 32:68+ N 27 '89
PRICE, ROBERT, 1932-
    about
Heavy, heavy hangs the debt. J. H. Taylor. il por *Forbes* 144:52+ O 2 '89

PRICE, ROBERT M.
about
Control Data struggles to get back in control. R. Mitchell. il por *Business Week* p130-1 My 1 '89
PRICE, SUSAN
Angela Lansbury: "It's always just beginning!". il pors *McCall's* 116:76-7+ Ap '89
PRICE, TONY
about
A heavy metal message. J. Neary. il por *Life* 12:146-8 Mr '89
PRICE, WALTER
Board games. il *Opera News* 53:8-11+ Ap 15 '89
PRICE COMMUNICATIONS CORP.
Heavy, heavy hangs the debt. J. H. Taylor. il por *Forbes* 144:52+ O 2 '89
PRICE CUTTING
Attention, discount shoppers! [new price policy at Sears] P. Sherrid. il *U.S. News & World Report* 106:54-5 Mr 13 '89
Get down [Sears' new policy] *Time* 133:47 Mr 13 '89
Little prices are looking good to big retailers [Sears' switch] A. Dunkin. il *Business Week* p42+ Jl 3 '89
Price is the object. S. B. Weiner. il *Forbes* 143:123-4 F 20 '89
Sale days at Sears. *Newsweek* 113:43 Mr 6 '89
Will the big markdown get the big store moving again? [Sears] J. E. Ellis and B. Bremner. il *Business Week* p110+ Mr 13 '89
PRICE-EARNINGS RATIOS *See* Stocks—Price-earnings ratios
PRICE FIXING
See also
Electronic equipment—Prices
Japan
And now, another form of Japanese hardball: lowball pricing. R. Neff. il *Business Week* p50 N 20 '89
PRICE INDEXES
BLS to produce monthly indexes of export and import prices. W. Alterman. bibl f il *Monthly Labor Review* 111:36-40 D '88
Bringing inflation home [Consumer Price Index] il *Changing Times* 43:65 Ja '89
The CPI should measure inflation. Your mileage may vary. P. Wallich and E. Corcoran. il *Scientific American* 261:76-7 Jl '89
Experimental cost-of-living indexes: a summary of current research. M. F. Kokoski. bibl f il *Monthly Labor Review* 112:34-9 Jl '89
Is inflation getting better or worse? [conflicting signals of the Producer Price Index vs. the Consumer Price Index] D. Pauly. il *Newsweek* 113:44 Ap 3 '89
Milestones in Producer Price Index methodology and presentation. A. Clem. *Monthly Labor Review* 112:41-2 Ag '89
New methodology reduces importance of used cars in the revised CPI [Consumer Price Index] J. H. Kellar. il *Monthly Labor Review* 111:34-6 D '88
The P-star factor [equation for forecasting inflation rates] P. Chisholm. il *Maclean's* 102:28 Je 26 '89
Price data. See issues of Monthly Labor Review
Price highlights of 1988: rising pressures on consumer prices. C. Howell and others. il *Monthly Labor Review* 112:3-10 My '89
Putting 'Keynes's head on Milton Friedman's body' [P-star] M. McNamee. il *Business Week* p66 Jl 31 '89
The Reserve's silly new equation [P-star index] G. P. Brockway. il *The New Leader* 72:15-16 Je 12-26 '89
U.S. import and export prices continued to register sizable gains in 1988. L. A. Livingston and S. Richards. bibl f il *Monthly Labor Review* 112:11-33 My '89
Why have import and export prices marched in lockstep? K. Pennar. il *Business Week* p24 O 16 '89
PRICE LEVEL ADJUSTED MORTGAGES *See* Mortgages
PRICE MAINTENANCE BY INDUSTRY *See* Price fixing
PRICE POLICIES
See also
Discount, Trade
Price cutting
Price fixing
Price and prejudice. B. Kanner. il *New York* 22:18+ Je 12 '89
The right way to set prices. P. Amend and L. Touby. il *Working Woman* 14:30+ Ag '89
PRICE REGULATION BY GOVERNMENT
France
Traditional booksellers suffer by French price-fix law, study shows. H. R. Lottman. *Publishers Weekly* 235:16 Mr 24 '89
PRICE-SALES RATIOS *See* Stocks—Price-sales ratios
PRICE/STERN/SLOAN, INC.
"Thank God we didn't understand the business". E. Paris. il por *Forbes* 143:64+ Je 12 '89
PRICE SUPPORTS, AGRICULTURAL *See* Agricultural administration
PRICE WATERHOUSE COMPANY
Myth America in the workplace [Supreme Court rules against sex stereotyping in case of A. Hopkins v. Price Waterhouse] por *U.S. News & World Report* 106:14 My 15 '89

A slap at sex stereotypes [Supreme Court decision in favor of A. Hopkins in suit] A. Sachs. il por *Time* 133:66 My 15 '89
Smile when you say that, partner [discrimination suit by employee A. Hopkins before the Supreme Court] D. L. Jacobs. il por *Ms.* 17:137 Ja/F '89
Why Andersen dumped Price. D. Greising. *Business Week* p47 O 9 '89
Wrestling with bias [Supreme Court ruling against sex stereotyping in case of A. Hopkins] D. Seligman. il *Fortune* 119:339 Je 5 '89
PRICES
See also
Cost and standard of living
Deflation (Finance)
Inflation (Finance)
Supply and demand
See also subhead Prices under various subjects
Afraid of 'commodities shock'? Well, relax. M. J. Mandel. il *Business Week* p90+ Jl 17 '89
Falling materials prices are flashing a warning [commodity prices] G. Koretz. il *Business Week* p34 D 25 '89-Ja 1 '90
January's price surge seems more than a flash in the pan. G. Koretz. il *Business Week* p20 Mr 20 '89
Looking back won't tell you where prices are going. K. Pennar. il *Business Week* p37 Mr 13 '89
Southern bargains: Canadians cash in on U.S. prices. A. Walmsley. il *Maclean's* 102:54 D 18 '89
Why inflation gazers are sending up flares [commodity prices] G. Koretz. il *Business Week* p22 F 13 '89
With the economy gathering steam, prices are in a pressure cooker. J. C. Cooper and K. Madigan. il *Business Week* p19-20 Mr 6 '89
Canada
Southern bargains: Canadians cash in on U.S. prices. A. Walmsley. il *Maclean's* 102:54 D 18 '89
Japan
Tokyo's tallest skyscrapers: prices. il *U.S. News & World Report* 107:13 N 20 '89
United States
See Prices
PRICHARD, BOB
Screen test. il *Bicycling* 30:136-8+ Ap '89
about
Stretching your limits. M. Bloom. il *Skiing* 41:36+ Ja '89
PRICING *See* Price policies
PRICKETT, GLENN T., AND WIRTH, DAVID A.
Environmental impact statements and climate change. bibl f *Environment* 31:44-inside back cover Mr '89
PRIDE
Male pride: a pain in the ego. W. D. Leight. *Mademoiselle* 95:60 Ja '89
PRIEST, GEORGE L., 1947-
How to control liability costs. il por *Fortune* 119:323-4 Ap 24 '89
PRIESTHOOD *See* Priests
PRIESTS
See also
Black priests
Marriage of priests
Fifty years of changing minds & structures [priest D. Cantwell of Chicago] T. Unsworth. il *Commonweal* 116:365-7 Je 16 '89
Great expectations: what Catholics want from their priests. R. T. Reilly. il *U.S. Catholic* 54:22-8 F '89
Never underestimate the power of a parish. R. E. Burns. *U.S. Catholic* 54:2 O '89
Crime
A breach of faith [sex charges against Newfoundland priests] G. Allen. il *Maclean's* 102:16-17 Mr 13 '89
A Church in crisis [sex scandals involving priests in Newfoundland] G. Allen. il *Maclean's* 102:66 N 27 '89
Sins of the flesh [priests and sex crimes in Newfoundland] G. W. Taylor. il *Maclean's* 102:10-12 Jl 17 '89
Political activities
Exalted violence [J.-B. Aristide expelled by Salesians for work in Haiti] *The Nation* 248:76-7 Ja 23 '89
Little priest, big general [Haiti's J.-B. Aristide and P. Avril] S. Rodman. il *National Review* 41:24-5 S 29 '89
Mass appeal [A. Giron in Guatemala] M. Cooper. il por *Mother Jones* 14:14 D '89
Psychology
Of many things [Reflections on the morale of priests] G. W. Hunt. *America* 160:26 Ja 21 '89
Recruiting
Help wanted: a few good fishers of men [TV ad campaign for priests in Boston] *Newsweek* 113:61 Je 26 '89
Why some men still want to be priests. M. J. Cook. il *U.S. Catholic* 54:31-8 Ap '89
Sexual behavior
Crisis at Covenant House [charges against Father B. Ritter] J. N. Baker. il por *Newsweek* 114:82 D 25 '89
Supply and demand
Catholics won't settle for half a Mass [priestless liturgies; with readers' comments] T. Unsworth. *U.S. Catholic* 54:13-19 Je '89

PRIESTS—Supply and demand—*cont.*
Challenges facing U.S. Catholics [lack of priests] J. Deedy. *Commonweal* 116:622-3 N 17 '89
A Church without priests [San Patricio's, Throckmorton, Tex.] A. G. Mojtabai. il *The New York Times Magazine* p16-17+ D 24 '89
Priestless rites: Catholic bishops okay services led by nuns and lay people. il *Time* 134:98 N 20 '89
When laity lead. J. Figueroa. *Commonweal* 116:470-1 S 8 '89
PRIESTS IN LITERATURE
The second coming of J.F. Powers. C. Iannone. *Commentary* 87:62-4 Ja '89
PRIMACK, JOEL R.
Gamma-ray observations of orbiting nuclear reactors [cover story] bibl f *Science* 244:407-8 Ap 28 '89
Let's ban nuclear reactors from orbit. il *Technology Review* 92:27-8 My/Je '89
PRIMARY EDUCATION See Elementary education
PRIMATES
See also
Baboons
Chimpanzees
Gorillas
Laboratory for Experimental Medicine and Surgery in Primates
Man
Monkeys
Orangutans
A 'handy' guide to primate evolution. B. Bower. il *Science News* 135:10-12 Ja 7 '89
Is peace as natural as violence? [reconciliation in primates; work of Frans de Waal] B. L. Benderly. *Psychology Today* 23:70 D '89
Time bomb [DNA clock; work of Charles G. Sibley and Jon E. Ahlquist] J. Horgan. *Scientific American* 260:24+ Mr '89
PRIMATES, FOSSIL
Stalking the giant ape [R. L. Ciochon and J. W. Olsen search for Gigantopithecus remains in Vietnam] J. James. il map *Discover* 10:42-6+ F '89
PRIME COMPUTER, INC.
Caveat raider [MAI Basic Four's battle for Prime Computer sours customer relations] K. K. Wiegner. il *Forbes* 143:160 Je 12 '89
The company they couldn't sell. G. Slutsker. il *Forbes* 144:227-9 O 2 '89
The Prime buyout is tough to compute [J. H. Whitney's leveraged buyout] L. Helm. il *Business Week* p28 Jl 10 '89
PRIME MINISTERS
Sexual behavior
An affair to remember [S. Uno's affair with geisha] B. Hillenbrand. il por *Time* 134:33 Jl 10 '89
The dirt on 'Mr. Clean' [S. Uno] M. Nemeth. il por *Maclean's* 102:32 Jl 10 '89
The end of the affair? [S. Uno's affair with geisha triggers women's opposition] B. Powell. il por *Newsweek* 114:22-3 Jl 10 '89
The geisha who knew too much [charges against S. Uno] il *U.S. News & World Report* 106:15-16 Je 19 '89
Japan's geisha scandal [concerning S. Uno] *World Press Review* 36:6+ Ag '89
The premier and the geisha [S. Uno] *Newsweek* 113:46 Je 19 '89
When a First Lady's husband leaves her for a younger woman [M. Papandreou copes] M. Cohen. il pors *Good Housekeeping* 208:82+ My '89
PRIME MOTOR INNS, INC.
Prime Motor Inns restarts its engine. il *Money* 18:8 Jl '89
PRIME NUMBERS See Numbers, Prime
PRIME RATE See Interest (Economics)
PRIME RESOURCES CORPORATION
Gold fever strikes again [Eskay Creek gold find in Northern B.C. sends stocks soaring] H. Quinn. il por *Maclean's* 102:33 S 11 '89
PRIMERICA CORP.
Primerica adds another feather to its cap [BarclaysAmerican/Financial Inc.] J. Friedman. il *Business Week* p98 D 11 '89
Sandy Weill roars back [cover story] J. Friedman. il pors *Business Week* p88-91+ D 4 '89
Tiger by the tail? [cleaning up the A. L. Williams insurance group] H. Rudnitsky. il pors *Forbes* 144:40-1 Ag 7 '89
Turnaround at Primerica. T. Paré. il por *Fortune* 120:120 D 18 '89
PRIMES (SECURITIES)
Blue-chip quality and junk-bond yields [Americus Trusts] D. P. Wiener. il *U.S. News & World Report* 107:107 N 6 '89
How to get bigger dividends or bigger price gains—from the same blue-chip stock [Americus Trusts] M. Schiffres. il *Changing Times* 43:98 F '89
PRIMETIME LIVE [television program] See Television program reviews—Single works
PRIMITIVE AND EARLY CHURCH See Church history—Primitive and early church

PRIMITIVES (MUSICAL GROUP)
Wanted: male singer. C. Connors. il *Seventeen* 48:127 Mr '89
PRIMITIVISM IN ART
Going native [Gauguin] A. Solomon-Godeau. bibl f il *Art in America* 77:118-29+ Jl '89
PRIMITIVISM IN RELIGION
Sophisticated primitives then, primitive sophisticates now [adaptation of address; cover story] M. E. Marty. il *The Christian Century* 106:588-91 Je 7-14 '89
PRIMM, BENY
about
Medic with a mission. R. E. McKinney. il pors *Ebony* 44:134 Ag '89
PRIMUS VENTURE PARTNERS
Diamonds in the Rust Belt. R. Simon. il *Forbes* 144:134+ N 13 '89
PRINCE
about
The Lovesexy lord of flick and funk. J. Milward. il por *TV Guide* 37:24-5 D 16-22 '89
Prince fires managers and his legal team. por *Jet* 75:62 Ja 23 '89
Prince of the City. A. White. il pors *Film Comment* 25:76+ N/D '89
Prince scores Batman film. M. Goldberg. il por *Rolling Stone* p21 Je 29 '89
Prince's personal purple soundtrack side trip. J. Pareles. il *Rolling Stone* p121-3 Ag 24 '89
PRINCE, CLAYTON
about
Soap star Clayton Prince moonlights on Manhattan's mean streets as a Guardian Angel. J. Kaufman. il pors *People Weekly* 32:195-6 D 4 '89
PRINCE, TOM
Mouth of the South. il por *New York* 22:110-14+ Ag 21 '89
PRINCE [drama] See Fuller, Charles
PRINCE EDWARD COUNTY (VA.)
Education
Prince Edward and the past [recovery of public school system after closing to avoid integration in 1959] L. Morrow. il *Time* 134:58 N 20 '89
Race relations
Prince Edward and the past [recovery of public school system after closing to avoid integration in 1959] L. Morrow. il *Time* 134:58 N 20 '89
PRINCE EDWARD ISLAND
See also
Arts and crafts—Prince Edward Island
Shore protection—Prince Edward Island
Industries
See also
Real estate business—Canada
Politics and government
The Island campaign [J. Ghiz calls election] B. MacAndrew. il por *Maclean's* 102:20 My 22 '89
A Liberal landslide. G. Allen. il por *Maclean's* 102:17 Je 12 '89
PRINCE GEORGES COUNTY (MD.)
Child welfare
Foster home recruitment and retention: a success story. D. Phelps. il *Children Today* 18:7-9+ Mr/Ap '89
Police
Black elected FOP prexy in Prince Georges County [D. Jones] por *Jet* 77:14 D 25 '89-Ja 1 '90
PRINCE OF CENTRAL PARK [musical] See Musicals, revues, etc.—Reviews—Single works
THE PRINCE OF PENNSYLVANIA [film] See Motion picture reviews—Single works
PRINCE STREET (NEW YORK, N.Y.)
Prince of the city. H. Sterne. il *Gentlemen's Quarterly* 59:195-6 My '89
PRINCE WILLIAM SOUND (ALASKA)
See also
Birds—Prince William Sound (Alaska)
Exxon Valdez (Ship) oil spill, 1989
Deep water, high peaks. C. Noble. il *Sierra* 74:59 My/Je '89
Just the facts: Prince William Sound. C. A. Dold and G. Soucie. il *Audubon* 91:80 S '89
PRINCETON (N.J.)
Architecture
Kevin Wilkes: double life of a Princeton prefab. S. Stephens. il por *Architectural Digest* 46:102-6+ Ap '89
PRINCETON ENGINEERING ANOMALIES RESEARCH LABORATORY
Questions for the cosmos [work of R. G. Jahn] S. Fishman. il por *The New York Times Magazine* p50+ N 26 '89
PRINCETON/NEWPORT PARTNERS
Parking fine: 280 years in jail [J. Regan] W. Baldwin. il por *Forbes* 144:222 O 2 '89
Too much firepower to fit the crime? [RICO law] A. P. Tobias. il *Time* 134:74 N 20 '89
A verdict that Mike Milken hopes is no warm-up [conviction of five officials of Princeton/Newport Partners and former Drexel Burnham trader] M. Galen. por *Business Week* p46 Ag 14 '89

PRINCETON/NEWPORT PARTNERS—cont.
Welcome to the world of sleaze. il *Time* 134:52 Ag 14 '89
You just can't keep Ed Thorp down. E. Schine. il por *Business Week* p83 Ag 21 '89
PRINCETON REVIEW, LTD.
Cram scam [cover story] J. Hammer. il *The New Republic* 200:15-18 Ap 24 '89
PRINCETON UNIVERSITY
Arms and the man: a sex scandal rocks Princeton [English professor T. McFarland forced to retire] D. Rabinowitz. il pors *New York* 22:30-6 Jl 17 '89
Double identity [Class of 1927/Clapp Hall; dormitory] C. Pearson. il *Architectural Record* 177:118-21 O '89
PRINCIPAL, VICTORIA
about
The girl who has everything: Victoria Principal [cover story] V. Scott. il pors *Good Housekeeping* 208:112+ Je '89
Victoria Principal faces her greatest TV test—playing a blind murder witness [cover story] B. Bruns. il pors *TV Guide* 37:2-3+ N 25-D 1 '89
Yesterday, a mistress—today, a lawyer [cover story] S. Littwin. il pors *TV Guide* 37:12-14 F 25-Mr 3 '89
PRINCIPAL GROUP LTD.
Day of reckoning [report on collapse; special section] J. DeMont. il por *Maclean's* 102:30-4 Jl 31 '89
A Principal toll [Alberta agrees to compensate investors in failed company] J. DeMont. il por *Maclean's* 102:28-9 Ag 7 '89
The Principal vote [scandal at center of Alberta election campaign] J. Howse. il *Maclean's* 102:12-13 Mr 20 '89
PRINCIPALS, SCHOOL *See* School superintendents and principals
PRINGLE, COLOMBE
about
Undone in Paris. E. White. il por *House & Garden* 161:24+ Ja '89
PRINGLE, HEATHER
The bones from Brazil. il *Omni (New York, N.Y.)* 11:26+ Ap '89
The Hansel and Gretel syndrome. il *Omni (New York, N.Y.)* 12:38+ D '89
PRINGLE, PETER
Talking dirty. *The New Republic* 201:42 O 30 '89
PRINTED CIRCUITS
Developing and etching a PC board. R. Grossblatt. il *Radio-Electronics* 60:77-8 D '89
Make your own etching tank. T. Lewis. il *Radio-Electronics* 60:45-50 D '89
PC service. See issues of Radio-Electronics beginning July 1985
Design
Laying out a PC board. R. Grossblatt. il *Radio-Electronics* 60:80-2 O '89
PC-board breakthrough. D. Lancaster. il *Radio-Electronics* 60:68-76 D '89
PC boards. R. Grossblatt. il *Radio-Electronics* 60:73-4+ Ag '89
PC photography. R. Grossblatt. il *Radio-Electronics* 60:78-80 N '89
Photographs and photography
PC photography. R. Grossblatt. il *Radio-Electronics* 60:78-80 N '89
PRINTER PLOTTING SYSTEMS *See* Plotters (Computer printers)
PRINTERS
See also
Labor unions—Printers
PRINTERS (COMPUTERS) *See* Computer printers
PRINTING
See also
Color printing
Computers—Printing use
Photography—Processing
Type and typefounding
PRINTING INDUSTRY
See also
Arcata Graphics Co.
Arion Press
Banta Corporation
Bowne & Co., Inc.
John H. Harland Co.
U.S. Banknote Company L. P.
Acquisitions and mergers
International aspects
The acquisitor [Quebecor chairman P. Péladeau acquires control of U.S. printing plants owned by R. Maxwell] J. Daly. il pors *Maclean's* 102:38-9 N 13 '89
International aspects
Children's books: coming home to print? [increase in U.S. vs. overseas printing of picture books] J. P. Frank. il *Publishers Weekly* 235:199-200+ F 24 '89
Canada
Canadian printers report increasing U.S. business. J. P. Frank. il *Publishers Weekly* 235:56+ My 19 '89
East Asia
Printing in Southeast Asia [special section] S. A. Taylor. il *Publishers Weekly* 236:S1-S2+ S 22 '89

Hong Kong
The changing face of Hong Kong. il *Publishers Weekly* 236:S2+ S 22 '89
Tight schedules haunt Pacific Rim printers. S. A. Taylor. *Publishers Weekly* 235:80 F 3 '89
Singapore
Singapore: a small but fierce competitor. il *Publishers Weekly* 236:S12+ S 22 '89
Tight schedules haunt Pacific Rim printers. S. A. Taylor. *Publishers Weekly* 235:80 F 3 '89
Thailand
In Thailand, a nascent export industry. il *Publishers Weekly* 236:S24+ S 22 '89
PRINTING INK
See also
Soybean ink
PRINTING PAPER (PHOTOGRAPHY) *See* Photographic paper
PRINTING PRESSES
World's fastest press runs Cosby title at three copies a second [Bertelsmann's integrated book manufacturing machine] J. P. Frank. il *Publishers Weekly* 235:67-8 Mr 17 '89
PRINTMAKING *See* Prints—Technique
PRINTS
See also
Collotypes
Etching
Lithographs
Photograms
Collectors and collecting
Art: sporting prints [19th century] A. Berman. il *Architectural Digest* 46:210-15+ Ap '89
Black-and-white fever [collection of D. and R. Williams] C. Brown. il pors *Forbes* 143:197 Mr 20 '89
Exhibitions
See also
San Juan Biennial
Burning bridges [Brücke: German expressionist prints from the Granvil and Marcia Specks Collection] C. Moser. il *Art in America* 77:64-5+ N '89
Long-lasting impressions [Mary Cassatt: the color prints at the National Gallery of Art] J. A. Lewis. il *Harper's Bazaar* 122:48+ Je '89
Mary Cassatt in the 1890's: the color prints in context. N. M. Mathews. bibl f il *Antiques* 136:860-71 O '89
The prints [Mount Vernon] W. W. Reaves. bibl f il *Antiques* 135:502-11 F '89
Robert Motherwell: forty-five years of printmaking: Associated American Artists. C. Lyon. il *Art News* 88:173-4 Mr '89
Prices
See Art—Prices
Technique
Beatrice Berlin. K. Haber. il pors *American Artist* 53:64-7 My '89
Pochoir printing [work of J. DeWoody] R. Williams. il pors *American Artist* 53:70-5 S '89
PRINZREGENTEN THEATER (MUNICH, GERMANY)
The sleeping Prince. G. M. Loney. il *Opera News* 53:14+ My '89
PRIONS
Prions linked to nerve regulation [research by Gerald D. Fischbach] R. Weiss. *Science News* 136:308 N 11 '89
Slow viruses. T. Kiely. il *Technology Review* 92:11-12 O '89
PRIOR, DAVID B., AND OTHERS
Evidence for sediment eruption on deep sea floor, Gulf of Mexico. bibl f il *Science* 243:517-19 Ja 27 '89
PRISO, MANGA BEKOMBO
Lines of descent. il *The Unesco Courier* 42:22-7 Jl '89
PRISON ESCAPES *See* Escapes
PRISON ETHICS
Snitches on snitching [study of inmates in Swedish prisons] M. Åkerström. bibl *Society* 26:22-6 Ja/F '89
PRISON FELLOWSHIP MINISTRIES
A way of escape at San Quentin. C. W. Colson. il *Christianity Today* 33:72 Mr 3 '89
PRISON INDUSTRIES *See* Convict labor
PRISON LABOR *See* Convict labor
PRISON MIRROR (NEWSPAPER)
A free press flourishes behind bars [editor R. Taliaferro] D. Arnold. il pors *Time* 133:12+ Mr 13 '89
PRISON PSYCHOLOGY
The arrogance of predicting dangerousness. R. E. Vatz and L. S. Weinberg. il *USA Today (Periodical)* 118:62-3 N '89
PRISON PUBLICATIONS
See also
Prison mirror (Newspaper)
PRISON REFORM
The banker who robbed banks [L. Pope] J. Morgenstern. il pors *The New York Times Magazine* p54-6+ N 12 '89
The search for ways to break out of the prison crisis. S. Ticer. il *Business Week* p80-1 My 8 '89
PRISON WARDENS
See also
Women prison wardens

PRISONERS

See also
Aged prisoners
Children of prisoners
Convict labor
Escapes
Indians of North America—Imprisonment
Juvenile delinquents and delinquency—Imprisonment
Parole
Political prisoners
Prisons
Refugee children—Imprisonment
Women prisoners

Death-row murderers could be lifesavers [proposal by J. Kevorkian to harvest organs from executed prisoners] *Newsweek* 113:49 Ja 9 '89

My dad's on death row. S. Laney. il *Seventeen* 48:68+ My '89

Employment

See Convict labor

Ethics

See Prison ethics

Health and hygiene

See also
AIDS (Disease) and prisoners

Psychology

See Prison psychology

Reading

'I come here just to read the articles' [designated pornography areas in Iowa prisons] *Newsweek* 113:76 Ja 30 '89

Print in prison. E. Knoll. *The Progressive* 53:4 Jl '89

Recreation

Modern dancers reach out to prisoners and to homeless men [New York City] R. Johnson. il *Dance Magazine* 63:15 S '89

Rehabilitation

See also
Delancey Street Foundation

Religious life

See also
Church work with prisoners

Transportation

The involuntary tourist. M. Rothschild. il *The Progressive* 53:22-3 My '89

Treatment

See also
Torture

Cast into the black hole of Brazil [São Paulo] *Newsweek* 113:30 F 20 '89

To live and die [São Paulo, Brazil] il *U.S. News & World Report* 106:14 F 20 '89

PRISONERS AS ARTISTS

Prisoners and piazzas [Prisoner Art Program, New Orleans] R. Green. il *Art News* 88:38+ Mr '89

PRISONERS AS AUTHORS

Despite 35 years in the big house, real-life Drugstore cowboy James Fogle steals the big screen. C. Sanz. il pors *People Weekly* 32:87+ N 20 '89

PRISONERS OF WAR

See also
United States—History—Civil War, 1861-1865—Prisoners and prisons
Vietnamese War, 1957-1975—Prisoners and prisons
World War, 1939-1945—Prisoners and prisons

PRISONS

See also
Art in prisons
Juvenile delinquents and delinquency—Imprisonment
Parole
Preventive detention
Prison reform
Prisoners
Women prisoners

Dungeons wanted [shortage of prison space] D. Seligman. il *Fortune* 119:208 Ja 30 '89

Governing prisons. J. J. DiIulio; H. Toch. *Society* 26:81-4 Jl/Ag '89

Housing shortage. D. Seligman. il *Fortune* 120:238 N 20 '89

Our bulging prisons. R. Lacayo. il *Time* 133:28-31 My 29 '89

The search for ways to break out of the prison crisis. S. Ticer. il *Business Week* p80-1 My 8 '89

Why George Bush should break his promise [more prisons vs. restitution] C. W. Colson. il *Christianity Today* 33:64 Ap 7 '89

Water supply

Toxins on tap? [contaminated water supply at Marion Federal Penitentiary] L. Rocawich. il *The Progressive* 53:24-7 My '89

Australia

A cry of desperation [deaths of aborigines in police custody] W. E. Smith. il *Time* 133:34 Ja 9 '89

Brazil

See also
São Paulo (Brazil)—Prisons and reformatories

California

The costly business of warehousing violent criminals [study of U.S. Penitentiary at Lompoc] M. S. Fleisher. il *USA Today (Periodical)* 117:60-2 Mr '89

The transformation of Ivan Boesky. A. Miller. il pors *Newsweek* 114:60 N 27 '89

A way of escape at San Quentin [Prison Fellowship] C. W. Colson. il *Christianity Today* 33:72 Mr 3 '89

Illinois

See also
Chicago (Ill.)—Prisons and reformatories
Marion (Ill.)—Prisons and reformatories

Iowa

'I come here just to read the articles' [designated pornography areas] *Newsweek* 113:76 Ja 30 '89

Massachusetts

Build a jail, buy some art [sculpture on grounds of Massachusetts prisons] M. Starr. il *Newsweek* 113:35 Mr 20 '89

Mexico

When jailbirds are also fat cats [luxurious treatment of suspects in the E. Camarena Salazar murder case] *U.S. News & World Report* 107:13 Jl 31 '89

New York (State)

See also
New York (N.Y.)—Prisons and reformatories

Oklahoma

Choctaw with a mission [activist B. Carnes] G. S. Phillips. il por *The Progressive* 53:14-15 Jl '89

Pennsylvania

See also
Philadelphia (Pa.)—Prisons and reformatories

Soviet Union

See also
Concentration camps—Soviet Union
Anecdotes, facetiae, satire, etc.
Gulag capitalism [sending convicts to the Soviet Union] R. Lourie. *The New Republic* 201:18-19 O 16 '89

Sweden

Snitches on snitching. M. Åkerström. bibl *Society* 26:22-6 Ja/F '89

Texas

The banker who robbed banks [L. Pope] J. Morgenstern. il pors *The New York Times Magazine* p54-6+ N 12 '89

United States

See Prisons

PRISUNIC GALLERY

Family business [artists' demonstration for the media] *The New Yorker* 65:31-2 Ap 3 '89

PRITCHARD, AMBROSE EVANS- *See* Evans-Pritchard, Ambrose

PRITCHARD, DAVID E.

about

Building on Nobel research. R. Pool. *Science* 246:328 O 20 '89

PRITCHARD, WILLIAM H.

Nasty reviews: easy to give, hard to take. *The New York Times Book Review* 94:1+ My 7 '89

PRITCHETT, DOLAN B., AND OTHERS

Type I and type II $GABA_A$-benzodiazepine receptors produced in transfected cells. bibl f il *Science* 245:1389-92 S 22 '89

PRITCHETT, V. S. (VICTOR SAWDON), 1900-

A change of policy [story] *The New Yorker* 65:36-46+ Ap 17 '89

PRITCHETT, VICTOR SAWDON *See* Pritchett, V. S. (Victor Sawdon), 1900-

PRITIKIN, ROBERT, AND KENNEY, JAMES J.

The Pritikin plan for better health. il pors *The Humanist* 49:14-16+ Ja/F '89

PRITIKIN LONGEVITY CENTERS

Learning to practice what Pritikin preaches. R. Mitchell. il *Business Week* p102-3 F 13 '89

Rejuvenation vacation. D. Sobel. *Health (New York, N.Y.)* 21:68-9+ O '89

PRITIKIN PROGRAM DIET *See* Diet

PRITZKER, PENNY

about

Penny's ante. J. Zweig. il por *Forbes* 144:352 N 13 '89

PRITZKER ARCHITECTURE PRIZE

A renegade takes the prize [F. Gehry] C. McGuigan. il por *Newsweek* 112:84-6 My 22 '89

PRIVACY

He spies/she spies: why we snoop in the name of love. L. Mosedale. il *Glamour* 87:162-3+ Jl '89

Private time. See issues of Glamour

That's private! C. L. Mithers. *Glamour* 87:362 Ap '89

PRIVACY, RIGHT OF *See* Right of privacy

PRIVATE BANKING

Bankers step back into the future. C. Torcellini. il *Forbes* 144:108+ Jl 10 '89

Your very own banker? It could be time. L. Zinn. *Business Week* p120 Mr 27 '89

PRIVATE BRANDS

The chill wind from Canada [Loblaw's store brands] J. Levine. il *Forbes* 143:308+ My 29 '89

PRIVATE BRANDS—*cont.*
Who makes it? G. Williams. il *Home Mechanix* 85:72-3+ F '89
PRIVATE CLUBS *See* Clubs
PRIVATE COLLEGES AND UNIVERSITIES *See* Colleges and universities
PRIVATE CORPORATIONS *See* Closely held corporations
PRIVATE CURRENCIES *See* Free banking
PRIVATE ENTERPRISE *See* Free enterprise
PRIVATE EYE (DISPLAY SYSTEM)
Eyeball to eyeball [Reflection Technology's invention] P. Scisco. il *Compute!* 11:10 Mr '89
The eyes have it. L. Kesten. il *Video* 13:58 S '89
Peek a view [Reflection Technology's invention] W. J. Hawkins. il *Popular Science* 234:28 F '89
Private screening [Reflection Technology's invention] J. Kluger. il *Discover* 10:32+ Je '89
PRIVATE EYE (PERIODICAL)
A reprieve for the Eye [court of appeal reduces libel award] B. Wickens. *Maclean's* 102:86 O 30 '89
The troubled Eye [libel costs] A. Phillips. il *Maclean's* 102:44 Je 19 '89
PRIVATE FLYING
See also
Airplanes—Private ownership
FAA expands Mode C transponder use to all aircraft near major airports. *Aviation Week & Space Technology* 131:66 Jl 3 '89
Sweet Liberty. W. Garvey. il *Flying* 116:8 F '89
PRIVATE INSTITUTIONS, NONPROFIT *See* Nonprofit institutions
PRIVATE INVESTIGATORS *See* Detectives
PRIVATE LIBRARIES *See* Libraries, Private
PRIVATE NETWORKS (TELECOMMUNICATION)
Why business is glued to the tube. K. Kelly. il *Business Week* p160 Mr 20 '89
PRIVATE PLACEMENTS (SECURITIES)
Another wall comes down [law permitting institutional investors to trade unregistered securities] C. Byron. il *New York* 22:16+ N 27 '89
The best new stocks may never hit the Street [revised SEC rules] D. Foust. il *Business Week* p47 D 25 '89-Ja 1 '90
PRIVATE PROPERTY *See* Property
PRIVATE SCHOOLS
See also
Church schools
Deerfield Academy (Mass.)
Passage [attending Chatham Hall boarding school in Virginia] T. Norman. il *Southern Living* 24:98 Ja '89
Transmitting a vision: religion in independent schools. D. R. Heischman. *The Christian Century* 106:417-9 Ap 19 '89
Curriculum
See also
Arts—Study and teaching
Great Britain
See also
Eton College
PRIVATE SCHOOLS, BLACK *See* Blacks—Education
PRIVATE SECTOR SURVEY ON COST CONTROL IN THE FEDERAL GOVERNMENT *See* President's Private Sector Survey on Cost Control (U.S.)
PRIVATE SECURITY GUARDS *See* Security guards
PRIVATES ON PARADE [musical] *See* Musicals, revues, etc.—Reviews—Single works
PRIVATIZATION
See also
Free banking
And the latest great housing hope is . . . [public-private partnerships] C. Yang. il *Business Week* p74-5 Jl 10 '89
Buyers are starting to circle the airports [new era in privatization] S. Payne and E. Schine. il *Business Week* p38 O 2 '89
Debunking the privatization myth: restoring government to its proper role. R. K. Armey. *USA Today (Periodical)* 117:33-5 Ja '89
FAA rejects two proposals to privatize Albany airport. J. Ott. *Aviation Week & Space Technology* 131:44-5 D 11 '89
False profit. R. Kuttner. *The New Republic* 200:21-3 F 6 '89
Fifteen miles—that'll be $1.50 [for-profit roads] R. Stodghill, II. il *Business Week* p54 Ag 14 '89
The growing interest in privatization. C. O. Ronk. il *USA Today (Periodical)* 117:30-2 Ja '89
HUD Sec. Kemp visits as Chicago gives control of housing unit to tenants. il por *Jet* 76:26 My 29 '89
Interior looking to contract out park jobs. *National Parks* 63:11-12 Ja/F '89
Interior paves way for sale of resources. *National Parks* 63:11 Mr/Ap '89
Keeping the market in its place. R. Kuttner. *Utne Reader* p67 Ja/F '89
McHighways [private toll roads] H. Ullman. *The New Republic* 201:18-19 S 4 '89
The private path to new highways. D. J. Ward. il *Nation's Business* 77:19 Ag '89

The privatization potential. E. Rubenstein. *National Review* 41:24 N 10 '89
Privatizing government. il *The Futurist* 23:55-6 Mr/Ap '89
Raise money, not taxes. E. Rubenstein. *National Review* 41:15 Ap 7 '89
"The tenants could do a better job of managing" [Chicago housing project] M. M. McDowell. il *Black Enterprise* 19:16 Jl '89
When tenants take charge [J. Kemp's plan] B. Turque. il por *Newsweek* 114:44 N 27 '89

Argentina
Argentina gets ready for 'surgery without anesthetic' [with interview with C. Menem] J. Ryser and R. A. Kessler. il por *Business Week* p46+ O 2 '89
Privatizing Argentina. A. M. Shapiro. il *The New Leader* 72:7-8 Ja 23 '89

Brazil
Brazil finally catches free-market fever. J. Ryser. il *Business Week* p51 O 16 '89

Canada
The cost of patronage [privatizing public prosecutors] P. Kaihla. il *Maclean's* 102:17 D 11 '89
The power of Canada Post. G. W. Taylor. il *Maclean's* 102:32-4 O 9 '89
Tories who act like Conservatives. C. Gordon. il *Maclean's* 102:13 N 13 '89

Great Britain
Thatcher's new revolution. R. A. Melcher. il por *Business Week* p42-3 My 1 '89

Israel
"If I were a rich man . . . ". M. Schifrin. *Forbes* 143:56+ Ap 17 '89

Mexico
Bienvenidos to a fire sale. C. P. Work and J. Bussey. il por *U.S. News & World Report* 107:96+ O 16 '89
Mexico's move to the market [interview with F. Solana Morales] N. Gardels. il *New Perspectives Quarterly* 6:41-5 Fall '89

Peru
Privatizing Peru [interview with M. Vargas Llosa] E. Farnsworth. il *New Perspectives Quarterly* 6:38-41 Fall '89

Saskatchewan
A prairie deadlock [Potash Corp. of Saskatchewan] P. Kopvillem. il *Maclean's* 102:20 Ag 7 '89
Privatizing the symbols. T. Fennell. il por *Maclean's* 102:28-9 Mr 6 '89

Soviet Union
Russia's embryonic capitalists. P. Dragadze. il *Forbes* 144:90-4+ O 16 '89
Supply-side theory is alive and well—in Moscow. P. C. Roberts. il *Business Week* p10 Jl 24 '89

United States
See Privatization
PRIVILEGED COMMUNICATIONS *See* Confidential communications
PRIVILEGES AND IMMUNITIES
See also
United States. Congress—Privileges and immunities
PRIX DE LAUSANNE
Prix de Lausanne-san. M. Horosko. il *Dance Magazine* 63:96 Ap '89
PRIZE CONTESTS
How worthy are these causes? [charity sweepstakes] *Modern Maturity* 32:12 F/Mr '89
Is your pet a star? D. C. Arkins and A. H. Klein. il *Better Homes and Gardens* 67:132 Ag '89
Jon Bon Jovi gives his home to non-Jovi Judy Frappier [winner of Sayreville, N.J. boyhood home in MTV contest] il pors *People Weekly* 31:135 Ap 17 '89
Administration
See also
D. L. Blair Inc.
Suits and claims
Treasure hunters denounce concealment of book's solution [case against D. L. Blair, administrator of contest contained in book Treasure in search of the golden horse] C. Reid. *Publishers Weekly* 236:10-11 Ag 25 '89
PRIZE FIGHTING *See* Boxing
PRO ARTE CHORALE AND ORCHESTRA
Musical events:
Gluck's Telemaco. A. Porter. *The New Yorker* 65:117-18 Ap 17 '89
PRO-CHOICE MOVEMENT *See* Prochoice movement
PRO FOOTBALL HALL OF FAME
Blount, Shell and Wood welcomed into NFL Hall. il pors *Jet* 76:57 Ag 21 '89
Blount, Wood and Shell join NFL Hall of Fame. il *Jet* 75:46 F 13 '89
Home of the pigskin. B. McBride and B. McBride. il *Travel Holiday* 172:56-7 Ag '89
PRO-LIFE MOVEMENT *See* Prolife movement
PROBABILITIES
See also
Distribution (Probability theory)
Risk
20 surprising facts on love, marriage, sex and divorce [excerpt from What are the chances?] B. R. Siskin and others. il *Glamour* 87:310-11 S '89

PROBATE LAW AND PRACTICE
See also
Wills
PROBENECID
Gout drug might cut AZT dosage by half [research by David M. Kornhauser] S. Hart. *Science News* 136:167 S 9 '89
PROBES, SPACE See Space vehicles
PROBES, TESTING See Testing equipment
PROBIOTICS
The 'life force' food factor. G. McVeigh. *Prevention (Emmaus, Pa.)* 41:47-51 Ag '89
PROBLEM CHILDREN
See also
Bullying
Hyperactivity
Juvenile delinquents and delinquency
Parents of problem children
Runaways
Fostering intergenerational relationships for at-risk youth. M. Freedman. il *Children Today* 18:10-15 Mr/Ap '89
My daughter was running wild. il *Good Housekeeping* 209:44+ O '89
Youth in transition [need for more services for those moving from foster care to independent living] il *Children Today* 18:2-3 Mr/Ap '89
Education
Curbing teen violence [Barron Assessment and Counseling Center in Boston, Mass.] R. Levine. il *American Health* 8:108 Ap '89
Drama in the curriculum for troubled young people: is it worth the fight? S. Pearson-Davis. bibl f *Design for Arts in Education* 90:25-32 N/D '88
No more teacher's dirty looks [how prospective teachers perceive problem behavior; research by Bruce Cunningham and Alan Sugawara] G. W. Bracey. il *Phi Delta Kappan* 70:561 Mr '89
Ritalin: education's fix-it drug? D. Divoky. bibl f il *Phi Delta Kappan* 70:599-605 Ap '89
"We have a problem" [child claims teacher hates her] J. Marks. il *Parents* 64:68+ O '89
PROBLEM SOLVING
See also
Crisis management (Psychology)
An old idea makes a comeback [apprenticeship method] E. Linden. il *Time* 133:71 Je 12 '89
Turn group input into stellar output [brainstorming; excerpt from Innovation, Inc.] S. R. Grossman and others. il *Working Woman* 14:36+ O '89
Why it pays to know what your employees are thinking. L. Touby. *Working Woman* 14:21-2 Je '89
PROCEDURE (LAW) See Legal procedure
PROCESS CONTROL EQUIPMENT INDUSTRY
Tiny sensors pay off big. G. T. Pope. il *High Technology Business* 9:28-31 S/O '89
PROCESSING, SIGNAL See Signal processing
PROCESSIONS
Belgium
See also
Bruges (Belgium)—Processions
PROCESSORS, FOOD (APPLIANCES) See Food processors (Appliances)
PROCHLOROPHYTES
Knotty evolutionary tree in plant world [Prochlorothrix] R. Monastersky. *Science News* 135:71 F 4 '89
PROCHLOROTHRIX See Prochlorophytes
PROCHNAU, WILLIAM W., 1937-
The last resort. *Vogue* 179:346-7 F '89
PROCHOICE MOVEMENT
Abortion's dividing line [GOP feels impact of activists] E. Salholz. il *Newsweek* 114:31 O 23 '89
Barred from Communion [prochoice assemblywoman L. Killea of San Diego] *The Christian Century* 106:1193-4 D 20-27 '89
Black women's plight cited at pro-choice rally in D.C. [right to abortion march] il *Jet* 76:13 Ap 24 '89
Can pro-choicers prevail? Feminists squabble over strategy for protecting rights. M. B. Carlson. il *Time* 134:28 Ag 14 '89
The Church strikes back [Catholic Church on the offensive against prochoice movement] J. N. Baker. il *Newsweek* 114:28 D 18 '89
A clear majority [rally in Washington, D.C.] *The Nation* 248:579-80 My 1 '89
The first march [march in Washington, D.C.] *National Review* 41:9-10 My 5 '89
If pro-choice is mainstream, now's the time to prove it. E. Ehrlich. il *Business Week* p64 Jl 17 '89
Jane Hodgson's odyssey. *U.S. News & World Report* 107:26 D 4 '89
March on Washington. E. J. Bader. il *The Humanist* 49:26-8+ Jl/Ag '89
A mistake in San Diego [Bishop L. T. Maher bars Assemblywoman L. Killea from receiving Communion because of pro-choice stand on abortion] *America* 161:416 D 9 '89
The moral complexity of choice. J. Leo. il *U.S. News & World Report* 107:64 D 11 '89
Notes and comment [Mobilize for Women's Lives rally in Washington, D.C.] *The New Yorker* 65:42-3 D 4 '89

People's choice [march in Washington, D.C.] H. Hertzberg. *The New Republic* 200:4+ My 1 '89
The politics of abortion: New York's pro-choice mood may mean trouble for the GOP. J. Kasindorf. il *New York* 22:39 S 18 '89
Pols feel the heat: candidates scramble for pro-choice votes. M. Suh. il *Ms.* 18:72-3 N '89
Pro-choice: 'a sleeping giant' awakes [Washington, D.C. demonstration to oppose reversal of Roe v. Wade] E. Salholz. il *Newsweek* 113:39-40 Ap 24 '89
Pro-choice politicking. H. Fineman. il *Newsweek* 114:34-6 O 9 '89
Pro-choicers gird for battle. S. Holmes. il *Time* 133:55 Ja 23 '89
Prochoice forces claim momentum in Washington. il *Christianity Today* 33:59 My 12 '89
Reconcilable differences [division among women's groups over pro-choice strategies] P. Simpson. *Ms.* 18:70 O '89
Silent majority for choice. *The Progressive* 53:9 D '89
PROCLAIMERS (MUSICAL GROUP)
The Proclaimers. P. Puterbaugh. il *Stereo Review* 54:99 Je '89
Proclaimers take on America. S. Rogers. il *Rolling Stone* p22 Ap 20 '89
PROCONSUL AFRICANUS See Man, Prehistoric
PROCOPE, JOHN L.
about
Procope sells interest in N.Y. Amsterdam news. por *Jet* 76:18 Jl 17 '89
PROCRASTINATION
Conquer procrastination. P. Edwards and S. Edwards. il *Home Office Computing* 7:34 Ap '89
How to get procrastinators up to speed [excerpt from The now habit] N. A. Fiore. il *Working Woman* 14:38+ Mr '89
New hope for handling old-pro procrastinators. S. Chan. *Working Woman* 14:30+ O '89
Read this article immediately. E. M. Collier. il *Nation's Business* 77:68+ O '89
PROCTER & GAMBLE CO.
Can P&G commandeer more shelves in the medicine chest? [prescription drug marketing] Z. Schiller. il *Business Week* p64+ Ap 10 '89
Can P&G squeeze profits out of orange juice? Z. Schiller. il *Business Week* p38 Ja 23 '89
Change agents [inventor V. Mills] D. Moreau. il por *Changing Times* 43:108 My '89
The cookie war and how it crumbled [settlement reached in chewy cookie patent dispute] il *U.S. News & World Report* 107:18-19 S 25 '89
Does this cereal belong in the medicine cabinet? [P&G claims that General Mills' cholesterol-reducing Benefit is a drug; Metamucil also contains psyllium] R. Mitchell and others. il *Business Week* p22-3 Jl 24 '89
It's diaper city at the landfill [recycling disposable diapers] *U.S. News & World Report* 107:12 Jl 3 '89
Nothing to sink your teeth into [olestra] J. Gorman. il *The New York Times Magazine* p40+ Je 11 '89
P&G rewrites the marketing rules [cover story] B. Dumaine. il *Fortune* 120:34-6+ N 6 '89
P&G's worldly new boss wants a more worldly company [E. Artzt] Z. Schiller. il por *Business Week* p40-1 O 30 '89
Stalking the new consumer [cover story] Z. Schiller. il *Business Week* p54-8+ Ag 28 '89
PROCUREMENT, MILITARY See United States. Air Force—Procurement; United States. Army—Procurement; United States. Coast Guard—Procurement; United States. Dept. of Defense—Procurement; United States. Navy—Procurement
PRODANS, RICHARD
Oppenheimer ate breakfast on August 6, 1945 [poem] *America* 161:14 Jl 1-8 '89
PRODIGIES, MUSICAL See Children as musicians
PRODIGY (DATABASE)
The Prodigy promise [with editorial comment by Fred Abatemarco] M. Antonoff. il *Personal Computing* 13:5, 66-9+ My '89
"This thing has to change people's habits". S. N. Chakravarty and E. McGlinn. il *Forbes* 143:118+ Je 26 '89
PRODUCE, FARM See Farm produce
PRODUCE TRADE
See also
Avocado industry—Export-import trade
Fruit industry—Export-import trade
Grain trade
Soybean industry—Export-import trade
Wheat trade
The agricultural swamp. J. Bovard. il *National Review* 41:46-8 F 10 '89
Economist tells danger of totally free markets [views of Daryll Ray] *Successful Farming* 87:48E N '89
PRODUCER PRICE INDEX See Price indexes
PRODUCERS, MOTION PICTURE See Motion picture producers

PRODUCERS, TELEVISION See Television producers
PRODUCT CODING See Bar coding
PRODUCT DEVELOPMENT See Product planning
PRODUCT LIABILITY See Liability (Law)
PRODUCT PLACEMENT (MOTION PICTURE) See Motion picture product placement
PRODUCT PLANNING
How high-tech products can achieve profitable longevity. B. Krasnoff and M. Mandell. il *High Technology Business* 9:18-21 Ja '89
Masters of innovation: how 3M keeps its new products coming [cover story] R. Mitchell. il *Business Week* p58-63 Ap 10 '89
PRODUCT STANDARDIZATION See Standardization
PRODUCTION, AGRICULTURAL
The American paradox [address, October 31, 1989] D. A. Miller. *Vital Speeches of the Day* 56:150-3 D 15 '89
Bill Eftink. B. Eftink. il *Successful Farming* 87 no4:17 Mr '89
PRODUCTION, INDUSTRIAL See Productivity, Industrial
PRODUCTION, THEATRICAL See Theater—Production and direction
PRODUCTION CONTROL
See also
Quality control
PRODUCTIVITY, BIOLOGICAL
Magnification of secondary production by kelp detritus in coastal marine ecosystems. D. O. Duggins and others. bibl f il *Science* 245:170-3 Jl 14 '89
Surveys slash away at forest estimates. J. Raloff. *Science News* 136:124 Ag 19 '89
PRODUCTIVITY, INDUSTRIAL
See also
Gross national product
Supply and demand
Are the economy's real problems being overlooked? [views of Peter L. Bernstein] G. Koretz. *Business Week* p26 Ja 9 '89
A fresh look at productivity [service industries; research by Gerald Faulhaber and others] C. G. Burck. il *Fortune* 119:28 F 13 '89
How America can triumph [cover story] L. S. Richman. il *Fortune* 120:52-4+ D 18 '89
How important is morale, really? W. Kiechel. il *Fortune* 119:121-2 F 13 '89
How to regain the productive edge [excerpts from MIT report Made in America] il *Fortune* 119:92-4+ My 22 '89
How well does money motivate? S. Nasar. il *U.S. News & World Report* 107:68 N 13 '89
In search of productivity. N. Sullivan. il *Home Office Computing* 7:96 S '89
Industry output and employment: a slower trend for the nineties. V. A. Personick. bibl f il *Monthly Labor Review* 112:25-41 N '89
Is America working smarter? [study by Council of Economic Advisers] R. Thomas. il *Newsweek* 113:42 Ja 23 '89
Is our eye on the wrong ball? [preoccupation with deficit] D. A. Levy. il por *Forbes* 143:232 Ap 17 '89
Is there a U.S. productivity crisis? W. J. Baumol. bibl f il *Science* 243:611-15 F 3 '89
MIT study confirms productivity slipping in key U.S. industries [Made in America report] *Aviation Week & Space Technology* 131:69-70 D 4 '89
Multifactor productivity advances in the tires and inner tubes industry. D. Litz and L. Moore. bibl f il *Monthly Labor Review* 112:19-27 Je '89
Multifactor productivity slips in the nonrubber footwear industry. J. Duke and L. Usher. il *Monthly Labor Review* 112:32-8 Ap '89
The new look of capital spending. K. Ballen. il *Fortune* 119:115-16+ Mr 13 '89
Notes from underground [coal mines] P. F. Gray. il *The Washington Monthly* 21:19-25 D '89
The password is 'flexible'. il *Business Week* p152+ S 25 '89
Pie-slicers vs. pie-enlargers. R. B. Reich. *The Washington Monthly* 21:60 F '89
Productivity [cover story; special section; with editorial comment by Jonathan Schlefer] il *Technology Review* 92:2, 27-40+ Ag/S '89
Productivity continued to rise in many industries during 1987. A. S. Herman. bibl f il *Monthly Labor Review* 112:13-20 Mr '89
The productivity fetish. *National Review* 41:14 Je 2 '89
Productivity in the carburetors, pistons, and valves industry. J. W. Ferris and V. L. Klarquist. bibl f il *Monthly Labor Review* 112:43-6 F '89
Productivity in the retail auto and home supply store industry. P. S. Wilder. bibl f il *Monthly Labor Review* 112:36-40 Ag '89
Productivity: key to growth. W. T. Brookes. il *Nation's Business* 77:99 N '89
The productivity paradox [service sector] H. Banks. *Forbes* 144:35 Jl 24 '89
Productivity trends in agricultural chemicals. H. Brand and K. Bryant. bibl f il *Monthly Labor Review* 112:21-8 Mr '89

Regaining the productive edge (I). C. W. Weinberger. il *Forbes* 144:31 O 2 '89
Regaining the productive edge (II). C. W. Weinberger. il *Forbes* 144:31 O 16 '89
Smart approaches to productivity. W. T. Brookes. il *Nation's Business* 77:97 O '89
Stuffing nest eggs with ESOPs [use as catalyst for improving productivity] C. Farrell. il *Business Week* p124-5 Ap 24 '89
Toward a new industrial America [views of the M.I.T. Commission on Industrial Productivity] S. Berger and others. il map *Scientific American* 260:39-47 Je '89
Want to boost productivity? Try giving workers a say. A. S. Blinder. il *Business Week* p10 Ap 17 '89
What's dragging productivity down? Women's low wages. A. Bernstein. il *Business Week* p171 N 27 '89
Will our kids live as well as we do? il *Changing Times* 43:38-9 Mr '89
Work smarter, not harder [cover story; special section; with introd. by T George Harris and Robert J. Trotter] il *Psychology Today* 23:33-6+ Mr '89
International aspects
International comparisons of productivity and unit labor cost trends in manufacturing. A. Neef and J. Thomas. bibl f il *Monthly Labor Review* 111:27-33 D '88
Productivity in services is not a problem abroad . . . and higher wages could spur its growth in the U.S. G. Koretz. il *Business Week* p28 My 22 '89
Japan
Why Japan won't slow down. M. Whitaker. il *Newsweek* 113:56 My 15 '89
PRODUCTIVITY, LABOR See Productivity, Industrial
PRODUCTS, ANIMAL See Animal products
PRODUCTS, COMMERCIAL See Commercial products
PRODUCTS, NEW
See also
Product planning
2nd annual best of what's new [cover story; special section] il *Popular Science* 235:49-61+ D '89
12 innovative home shop products. T. Sweeney. il *Home Mechanix* 86:82-4+ Mr '89
12 of the best new products you'll find at home centers in the coming year. il *Home Mechanix* 85:67-71 D '89
1989's hottest new products. il *Workbench* 45:18-22 Ja/F '89
Anticavity pills, edible pet spoons, and other future stuff [excerpt] M. Abrams and H. Bernstein. il *Parents* 64:141-4 O '89
The best of new products [1988] il *Business Week* p118-21 Ja 9 '89
Buy better. See issues of Home Mechanix beginning January 1985
Change agents [inventor V. Mills] D. Moreau. il por *Changing Times* 43:108 My '89
Growing pains—and gains [established brand names used on new products] B. Kanner. il *New York* 22:22+ Mr 13 '89
Home & shop improvements. See issues of The Family Handyman beginning September 1986
Innovations. See issues of Essence beginning August 1987 through January 1989
Just out. See occasional issues of Better Homes and Gardens
New products. See issues of High Technology Business through November/December 1989
New products (including an impostor). F. H. Katayama. il *Fortune* 119:12 Mr 27 '89
New tech. C. Begole. See occasional issues of Glamour
Product reports 1990 [cover story; special issue; with editorial comment by Joan F. Blatterman] il *Architectural Record* 177:25-9+ D '89
Products of the year. E. C. Baig. il *Fortune* 120:162-4+ D 4 '89
Star tech. See issues of Omni (New York, N.Y.) beginning October 1986
What's in store for you [new food products] M. Friedman. See issues of Good Housekeeping beginning December 1989
What's new. D. Stover. See issues of Popular Science beginning January 1987
Will next year's hot gift be an insect orchestra? [test marketing new products in Japan] N. Gross. il *Business Week* p67-8 D 25 '89-Ja 1 '90
Anecdotes, facetiae, satire, etc.
Not available in any store. R. Rosen. il *New York* 22:42-6 N 20 '89
PRODUCTS, QUALITY OF See Quality of products
PROENKEPHALIN
Regulation of proenkephalin by Fos and Jun. J. L. Sonnenberg and others. bibl f il *Science* 246:1622-5 D 22 '89
PROESCH, GILBERT
See also
Gilbert and George
PROFESSIONAL ASSOCIATIONS
Professional association publishing. T. Weyr. il *Publishers Weekly* 235:34+ Je 16 '89

PROFESSIONAL EDUCATION
How schools must change [preparing knowledge workers for the post-business society] P. F. Drucker. il *Psychology Today* 23:18-20 My '89
PROFESSIONAL ETHICS
See also
Business ethics
College teachers—Professional ethics
Comedians—Professional ethics
Journalistic ethics
Legal ethics
Literary ethics
Medical ethics
Psychologists—Professional ethics
Public relations consultants—Professional ethics
School superintendents and principals—Professional ethics
Teachers—Professional ethics
Is professional life just a game? [address, May 12, 1989] J. B. Wyatt. *Vital Speeches of the Day* 55:702-4 S 1 '89
Sex in the forbidden zone [professional men who have illicit affairs with clients; excerpt] P. Rutter. il pors *Psychology Today* 23:34-8+ O '89
PROFESSIONAL LITERATURE
See also
Booksellers and bookselling—Professional literature
Publishers and publishing—Professional literature
PROFESSIONAL SHOW MANAGER'S ASSOCIATION
PSMA: tangible improvements in shows for dealers and collectors. D. V. Trout. il *Antiques & Collecting Hobbies* 94:24-6+ Ag '89
PROFESSIONALS
See also
Black professionals
Yuppies
The lure of the classroom [professionals turning to teaching] S. Tifft. il *Time* 133:69 F 13 '89
Opening the schoolhouse doors [alternative teaching certification] J. Rachlin. il *U.S. News & World Report* 106:62 My 8 '89
Religious life
Integrating faith and functionality [address, January 18, 1989] S. Muto. *Vital Speeches of the Day* 55:370-1 Ap 1 '89
Sexual behavior
Sex in the forbidden zone [professional men who have illicit affairs with clients; excerpt] P. Rutter. il pors *Psychology Today* 23:34-8+ O '89
PROFESSIONS
See also
Blacks—Occupations
Collective bargaining—Professions
Occupations
Women—Occupations
Who business bosses hate most. T. Paré. il *Fortune* 120:107-9 D 4 '89
PROFESSOR GRIFF
about
Public Enemy number one. M. Horowitz. il por *American Film* 14:15 S '89
PROFESSORS *See* College teachers
PROFIT
See also
Capitalism
Corporations—Finance
PROFIT SHARING
The changing basis for pay. R. M. Kanter. bibl *Society* 26:54-65 S/O '89
PROFITEERING
See also
Black markets
PROFITEROLES *See* Pastry
PROFUMO, JOHN D.
Political scandal
The faded flower of a great British scandal, Christine Keeler heeds a last call to the limelight. M. Green. il pors *People Weekly* 31:76-7+ Ap 24 '89
Party-girl Scandal. B. D. Johnson. il pors *Maclean's* 102:58-9 My 22 '89
Scandal: more sex please, we're British. A. Waugh. il *Vogue* 179:507-9 Mr '89
Undercovers [film entitled Scandal] G. Fuller. il por *Film Comment* 25:56-8+ Mr/Ap '89
PROGERIA
"My baby will grow old—but she'll never grow up" [case of M. Schulz]; ed. by LindaCarol Graham. L. D. Schulz. il pors *Redbook* 172:44+ F '89
'Who I really am' [case of J. Ellison] J. Mason. il pors *Life* 12:74-8 O '89
PROGESTATIONAL HORMONES, SYNTHETIC *See* Progestin
PROGESTERONE
Do you have a hormone shortage? L. Graham. *Redbook* 172:16 F '89
Lead upsets menstrual cycle in monkeys [research by Nellie K. Laughlin] A. McKenzie. *Science News* 136:373 D 9 '89

PROGESTIN
See also
Medroxyprogesterone
Birth control goes skin deep [Norplant] D. Carr. il *Ms.* 18:77 Jl/Ag '89
Estrogen effects assessed [risk of breast cancer in post-menopausal women] *Science News* 136:86 Ag 5 '89
Estrogen use linked to breast cancer. J. L. Marx. *Science* 245:593 Ag 11 '89
The five-year contraceptive [Norplant releases continuous dose of levonorgestrel] D. M. Podolsky. il *American Health* 8:16 S '89
Hard looks at hormones [estrogen and progestin may increase risk of breast cancer] J. Langone. il *Time* 134:56 Ag 14 '89
Hormone replacement therapy: is it for you? S. Mahler. *McCall's* 117:149 O '89
The miracles and misfires of medicine [progestin and estrogen increase risk of breast cancer in postmenopausal women] *U.S. News & World Report* 107:16+ Ag 14 '89
Should you take estrogen? [hormone replacement therapy] C. Perlmutter. il *Prevention (Emmaus, Pa.)* 41:42-51 N '89
PROGRAM TRADING (SECURITIES)
See also
Index frontrunning (Securities)
Basket case [Friday the 13th stock market plunge] J. J. Cramer. *The New Republic* 201:12-14 N 13 '89
A bum rap for program trading. S. E. Kuhn. il *Fortune* 120:10-11 D 4 '89
Computer crunch. C. Byron. il *New York* 22:33-4 N 13 '89
The false furor over program trading. J. Egan. il *U.S. News & World Report* 107:85 N 13 '89
Is program trading a threat again? J. Egan. il *U.S. News & World Report* 107:76 S 18 '89
Is program trading the target of a 'witch-hunt'? G. Weiss. il *Business Week* p122-3 N 13 '89
It's an ill wind . . . M. Hulbert. il *Forbes* 144:166 D 25 '89
A "Neanderthal" speaking. D. N. Dreman. il *Forbes* 144:164 D 25 '89
Program trading. M. S. Forbes, Jr. il *Forbes* 144:27 N 27 '89
The villain in the volatility. L. Reibstein. il *Newsweek* 114:58 N 6 '89
We told you so. il *Forbes* 144:10 N 27 '89
Why program traders are like drunken sailors [views of Ralph Wanger] T. Jaffe. *Forbes* 144:304 N 27 '89
Yes, the stock market's risky. Why look for a scapegoat? G. Weiss. il *Business Week* p158 N 27 '89
Statistics
Seeing double in program trading [New York Stock Exchange statistics] G. Weiss. il *Business Week* p31-2 N 20 '89
Japan
An onslaught from the West: foreign traders and methods are rocking Japan's stock markets. T. Holden. il *Business Week* p140-1 Mr 20 '89
PROGRAMMABLE LOGIC DEVICES
Jameco Electronics JE680 universal IC programmer. il *Radio-Electronics* 60:16-17 Je '89
Now engineers don't have to order out for chips. R. Brandt. il *Business Week* p56+ Ap 17 '89
Programmable architectures: the next breakthrough? A. Reeve. il *Radio-Electronics* 60 ComputerDigest:77+ S '89
PROGRAMME ON MAN AND THE BIOSPHERE *See* Man and the Biosphere Programme
PROGRAMMERS, COMPUTER *See* Computer personnel
PROGRAMMING (CABLE TELEVISION) *See* Cable television—Programming
PROGRAMMING (COMPUTERS) *See* Computer programming
PROGRAMMING (TELEVISION) *See* Television broadcasting—Programming
PROGRAMMING (WORD PROCESSORS) *See* Word processors and processing—Programming
PROGRAMMING LANGUAGES (COMPUTERS) *See* Computer languages
PROGRAPH (COMPUTER PROGRAM)
Pictorial programming on the Mac [Prograph 1.2] J. Udell. *Byte* 14:82+ N '89
PROGRESS
See also
Social change
Technological innovations
100 years of attitude [end-of-century effect in creative endeavors; excerpt from American renaissance] M. J. Cetron and O. Davies. il *Omni (New York, N.Y.)* 12:18+ O '89
Tires to sandals. S. J. Gould. *Natural History* p8+ Ap '89
The wheel of fortune and the wedge of progress. S. J. Gould. *Natural History* p14+ Mr '89
PROGRESS ENGINE DESIGN BUREAU (SOVIET UNION)
Progress Engine Design Bureau responsible for wide product line. il *Aviation Week & Space Technology* 130:48 Je 5 '89
PROGRESSIONS, ARITHMETIC *See* Series (Mathematics)
PROGRESSIVE (PERIODICAL)
Memo. E. Knoll. See issues of The Progressive

PROGRESSIVE CONSERVATIVE PARTY (CANADA) *See*
Conservative Party (Canada)
PROGRESSIVE NURSING SERVICES
David Kessler: home nursing for AIDS patients. D. Castellon.
il por *Business Week* p117 N 6 '89
PROGRESSIVE POLICY INSTITUTE
Disclaimer. E. Knoll. *The Progressive* 53:4 S '89
PROGRESSIVE VENTURES INC.
Is this a blow-off? [M. Leibovit of Volume reversal survey
and G. Cutler of Market mania form Progressive Ventures
Inc.] M. Hulbert. il *Forbes* 143:191 Je 12 '89
PROGRESSIVISM (UNITED STATES POLITICS)
Herbert Croly's promise. J. B. Judis. por *The New Republic*
201:84-7 N 6 '89
PROHIBITION
Carry from Kansas became a Nation all unto herself. R.
Day. il pors *Smithsonian* 20:147-8+ Ap '89
Wanted: consensus on abortion. R. V. Pierard. por *Christianity
Today* 33:8 O 6 '89
United States
See Prohibition
PROIA, RICHARD L.
(jt. auth) See Navon, Ruth, and Proia, Richard L.
PROJECT APOLLO *See* Space flight to the moon
PROJECT BLUE BOOK
UFO update. V. Cooper. il *Omni (New York, N.Y.)* 11:81
Mr '89
PROJECT CHARIOT
Project Chariot: how Alaska escaped nuclear excavation [1958
plan to create a harbor by detonating thermonuclear bombs;
cover story] D. O'Neill. bibl f il maps *The Bulletin of
the Atomic Scientists* 45:28-37 D '89
PROJECT EXCELLENCE AWARDS
Making excellence popular [programs sponsored by V. Jarrett
and C. Rowan] il pors *Ebony* 44:90+ S '89
PROJECT FAMILY INDEPENDENCE
Model homes for welfare families. M. Suh. il *Ms.* 18:73-4
Jl/Ag '89
PROJECT HEAD START (U.S.)
Computers and preschoolers: Head Start/IBM Partnership.
L. Tsantis and others. il *Children Today* 18:21-3 Ja/F
'89
Everybody likes Head Start. C. Leslie. il *Newsweek* 113:49-50
F 20 '89
Is Head Start a false start? il *USA Today (Periodical)* 118:10
D '89
A Native American CDA: my personal story [Child Develop-
ment Associate] J. Loretto. il pors *Children Today* 18:26-7
Mr/Ap '89
Serving refugee children and families in Head Start [Spokane,
Wash.; cover story] C. Broughton. il *Children Today* 18:6-10
S/O '89
Storytelling and Native American CDAs [Child Development
Associate credential] C. D. Beers. il *Children Today* 18:24-5
Mr/Ap '89
The success story of the war on poverty. L. Mundy. *The
Washington Monthly* 21:26-31 D '89
PROJECT LEAN
Good food, good health: Project LEAN. N. Byal. il *Better
Homes and Gardens* 67:46+ S '89
**PROJECT LEARNING ENGLISH THROUGH INTER-
GENERATIONAL FRIENDSHIP** *See* Project LEIF
PROJECT LEIF
College students tutor older refugees in English. N. Z. Henkin
and G. Weinstein-Shr. il *Aging* no359:17-19 '89
PROJECT LIGHTHAWK
Lighthawk. D. Wood. il por *National Parks* 63:27-31 Ja/F
'89
Rain forest reconnaissance. M. DiLeo. il por *Mother Jones*
14:18 N '89
The wings of conservation. J. Christensen. il *Sierra* 74:32-5
Ja/F '89
PROJECT LOW-FAT EATING FOR AMERICA NOW *See*
Project LEAN
PROJECT MANAGEMENT SOFTWARE *See* Computers—
Business use—Programming
PROJECT OPEN HAND
Open heart, Open Hand [work of R. Brinker] il por *Time*
133:21 Ja 9 '89
PROJECT ORBIS
Sight and soul. W. Garvey. il *Flying* 116:10 Ja '89
PROJECT PLOWSHARE
See also
Project Chariot
PROJECT PROBE
Snippets from Nyanja chronicles. B. Rosendahl. il por map
Sea Frontiers 35:292-302 S/O '89
PROJECT SAFE RUN
It's 10 p.m. Do you know where your Doberman is? [work
of S. Reecher] C. Gockley. il *American Health* 8:32+ N
'89
PROJECT SELF-HELP AND AWARENESS
Rural exchange program makes links. J. Miller. il por *The
Progressive* 53:12-13 Ap '89
PROJECT STAR
Lessons from on high. S. Allis. il *Time* 133:65-6 Ja 9 '89

PROJECTILES
See also
Bullets
Rockets
Testing
Short-pulse thrusters for SDI require new instrumentation
[magnetic suspension test stand for Lightweight Exoat-
mospheric Projectile] M. A. Dornheim. il *Aviation Week
& Space Technology* 131:53+ Ag 28 '89
PROJECTION TELEVISION *See* Television projection
PROJECTIONS, MAP *See* Cartography
PROJECTORS
See also
Television projection
Video projectors
PROKOFIEV, SERGEY, 1891-1953
about
A new look at Prokofiev. S. Lipman. *Commentary* 87:53-8
Ap '89
PROKSCH, UDO
about
Social climber's guide to Vienna. E. von Kuehnelt-Leddihn.
National Review 41:42 Mr 10 '89
PROLER, HERMAN
about
Scrapman. W. P. Barrett. il por *Forbes* 144:205-6 O 30
'89
PROLER INTERNATIONAL CORP.
Scrapman. W. P. Barrett. il por *Forbes* 144:205-6 O 30
'89
PROLIFE MOVEMENT
See also
Feminists for Life of America
JustLife (Organization)
Operation Rescue
Abolition revisited. J. N. Akers. il *Christianity Today* 33:13
Mr 3 '89
Confrontation's stage is set [Supreme Court decision] K.
A. Lawton. il *Christianity Today* 33:36-8 Ag 18 '89
How prolife protest has backfired. C. W. Colson. il *Christianity
Today* 33:72 D 15 '89
Loony legislation [prolife legislators' proposal to ban abortion
on basis of gender selection in Pennsylvania] P. Simpson.
Ms. 18:72 N '89
Mr. Fast explains [views of H. Fast] W. F. Buckley. *National
Review* 41:62-3 F 24 '89
Planned Parenthood didn't plan on this: abortion foes are
attacking the agency's corporate sponsors. B. Tierney. il
Business Week p34 Jl 3 '89
The politics of abortion. P. Orenstein. *Vogue* 179:250-1 Je
'89
The prolife credibility gap [alienation of black support] S.
Perkins. il por *Christianity Today* 33:21-2 Ap 21 '89
"Prolife": what does it really mean? [cover story; special
section] il *Christianity Today* 33:27-38 Jl 14 '89
Promises to keep [appointment of L. Sullivan as Health
and Human Services Secretary disappoints prolife support-
ers] K. A. Lawton. il por *Christianity Today* 33:44-5 F
3 '89
Scanning the prolife battlefields. K. A. Lawton. *Christianity
Today* 33:52-4 Je 16 '89
Taking it to the states. K. A. Lawton. il *Christianity Today*
33:36-8 N 3 '89
Tar baby [opposition to appointment of L. W. Sullivan
as Health and Human Services Secretary] F. Barnes. *The
New Republic* 200:12-13 F 13 '89
A winning prolife strategy. K. S. Kantzer. *Christianity Today*
33:19 D 15 '89
Winning Webster v. Reproductive Health Services: the crisis
of the pro-life movement. J. R. Kelly. *America* 161:79-83
Ag 12-19 '89
You don't have to believe in God to be prolife. N. Hentoff.
U.S. Catholic 54:28-30 Mr '89
Canada
Defiance in Vancouver [abortion clinic protesters] P. Kopvil-
lem. *Maclean's* 102:17 Jl 31 '89
PROLIFERATING CELL NUCLEAR ANTIGEN *See* Cyclin
PROLOG (COMPUTER LANGUAGE)
An end to dueling rules [Spot] A. Lane. il *Byte* 14:303-6+
Je '89
PROMOTERS AND PROMOTING
See also
Abercrombie, Josephine
Theatrical agencies and agents
PROMOTION, SALES *See* Sales promotion
PROMOTION (SCHOOL)
See also
Grade repetition (Education)
PROMOTION OF MOTION PICTURES *See* Motion picture
industry—Advertising
PROMOTIONS
See also
Air pilots—Promotion
Black executives—Promotion
Career plateaus
Executives—Promotion
Firefighters—Promotion
Women executives—Promotion

PROMOTIONS—cont.

How to know whom to promote. il *Working Woman* 14:14 Jl '89

When you're bullish on two employees but can promote only one. M. R. Feinberg. il *Working Woman* 14:30 O '89

PROMOTOR (FIRM)

Have I got a deal for you. K. Wandycz. il por *Forbes* 144:44-5 O 2 '89

PROMS (DANCES)

Elvis's prom date remembers a shy guy in blue suede shoes [recollections of R. Vaughn] S. Dougherty. il pors *People Weekly* 32:99-100 Jl 17 '89

Girl who sued prom date gets $81.28 in settlement [case of T. Mangrum] il por *Jet* 76:29 Jl 10 '89

Giving courtship a new meaning, a Florida teen sues the date who stood her up for the school prom [T. Mangrum files small claims suit against M. Shadd] il por *People Weekly* 31:101 My 29 '89

Prom previews . . . [special section] il *'Teen* 33:65-75+ Mr '89

PRONGHORN HUNTING

Boomerang bucks. J. Haviland. il *Outdoor Life* 184:80-1+ S '89

Following in my footsteps [father and son hunt antelope] D. Small. il *Outdoor Life* 183:62-3+ F '89

More than numbers. J. Barsness. il *Field & Stream* 94:52-3+ S '89

PRONGHORNS

Sexual behavior

See Sexual behavior—Animals

PRONOUNS *See* English language—Pronouns

PRONUNCIATION

See also

English language—Pronunciation

Names, Personal—Pronunciation

PROOF (LAW) *See* Evidence (Law)

PROOF OF GOD *See* God—Proof

PROOF THEORY

Beyond understanding? [finite projective plane of order 10; work of Clement Lam] P. Wallich. *Scientific American* 260:24 Mr '89

The circle can be squared! [proof by Miklós Laczkovich] B. A. Cipra. *Science* 244:528 My 5 '89

Do mathematicians still do math? [computer-assisted proofs] B. A. Cipra. il *Science* 244:769-70 My 19 '89

How the Grinch stole mathematics [computer-generated combinatorial proof; work of Herb Wilf and Down Zeilberger] B. A. Cipra. *Science* 245:595 Ag 11 '89

Search me and know me [religious reflections on computer search into existence of finite projective plane of order 10] M. E. Marty. *The Christian Century* 106:247 Mr 1 '89

Squaring the circle [proof by Miklós Laczkovich] R. Ruthen. *Scientific American* 261:22+ Jl '89

The straight side of sliced circles [work of Miklós Laczkovich] *Science News* 136:31 Jl 8 '89

PROOFREADING

What's wrong with this prose? N. D. Mermin. por *Physics Today* 42:9+ My '89

PROPAGANDA

See also

United States. Information Agency

Minority report [Reagan era misinformation] C. Hitchens. *The Nation* 248:42 Ja 9-16 '89

PROPAGANDA, AMERICAN *See* Propaganda

PROPAGANDA, CHINESE

Dealing death with a big lie [denial of Tiananmen Square massacre; special section] il *Newsweek* 113:26-9 Je 26 '89

Deng's big lie [denial of Tiananmen Square massacre] J. Smolowe. il *Time* 133:32-4 Je 26 '89

In Beijing, Big Brother is the anchorman. J. Wallace. il *U.S. News & World Report* 106:37-8 Je 26 '89

PROPAGANDA FILMS (FIRM)

Mythic proportions [Los Angeles offices of Propaganda Films designed by Franklin Israel] il *Architectural Record* 177:68-71 Ap '89

PROPANE TORCHES *See* Torches

PROPELLANES

Synthesis

Discovering the colorful new world of tin [organotin; research by Lawrence R. Sita and Richard D. Bickerstaff] I. Amato. *Science News* 136:23 Jl 8 '89

PROPELLERS

See also

Airplanes—Propellers

Airplanes, Jet—Propellers

Airplanes, Racing—Propellers

Boats and boating—Propellers

PROPERTY

See also

Estates, Decedents'

Intellectual property

Joint ownership

Land tenure

Pack rats (Persons)

Real property

Trespass

Wills

Anecdotes, facetiae, satire, etc.

Stuff it! M. Ivins. il *Ms.* 17:46 Mr '89

Too much stuff! Our accumulating crisis. M. Ivins. il *Utne Reader* p77-9 Jl/Ag '89

Taxation

See also

Real property—Taxation

PROPERTY, UNCLAIMED *See* Estates, Unclaimed

PROPERTY APPRAISAL *See* Real property—Valuation

PROPERTY IN LITERATURE

Storied objects [writing at home surrounded by personal possessions] A. Gurganus. il pors *House & Garden* 161:46+ My '89

PROPERTY MANAGEMENT *See* Real estate management

PROPERTY RIGHTS *See* Land tenure

PROPFAN PROPELLERS *See* Airplanes, Jet—Propellers

PROPHECIES

See also

Astrology

Forecasting

Prophets

PROPHECY (CHRISTIANITY)

Blending salt and spice, joining wisdom and prophecy [Latin American Christians; cover story] B. C. Lane. il *The Christian Century* 106:499-502 My 10 '89

Not-sa-pos-ta. M. E. Marty. *The Christian Century* 106:63 Ja 18 '89

Speak my word faithfully. K. Koyama. *The Christian Century* 106:716 Ag 2-9 '89

PROPHET, ELIZABETH CLARE

about

Paradise under siege. M. P. Harris. il por *Time* 134:61 Ag 28 '89

PROPHETS

Prophetic destiny. P. J. Ryan. il *America* 160:47 Ja 21 '89

PROPP, MICHAEL V., AND TARASOV, VITALY G.

Caldron in the sea. il maps *Natural History* p28-33 Ag '89

PROPRANOLOL

Antifitness medication [propranolol takes the good out of exercise] il *Prevention (Emmaus, Pa.)* 41:20 Mr '89

Drugs from emasculated hormones: the principle of syntopic antagonism [Nobel lecture, December 8, 1988] Sir J. W. Black. bibl f il *Science* 245:486-93 Ag 4 '89

Getting to the heart of the Chinese [Chinese men more sensitive than Caucasian men] *Science News* 135:156 Mr 11 '89

PROPRIETARY HOSPITALS *See* Hospital management industry

PROPRIETARY RIGHTS *See* Intellectual property

PROPS, ADVERTISING *See* Advertising properties

PROPS, THEATER *See* Theater properties

PROPULSION, ELECTROMAGNETIC *See* Electromagnetic propulsion

PROSE, FRANCINE, 1947-

The brothers Wolff. il pors *The New York Times Magazine* p22-3+ F 5 '89

Let me entertain you. il *Gentlemen's Quarterly* 59:231+ Mr '89

Living with choices. il *Parents* 64:130-3 My '89

about

Between issues. *The New Leader* 72:2 S 4 '89

PROSECUTORS, PUBLIC *See* Public prosecutors

PROSER, CHIP

about

The Coast. G. Stone. il *Gentlemen's Quarterly* 59:118 F '89

PROSERV INC.

In search of a net gain [Soviet tennis player N. Zvereva signs with ProServ and demands right to control earnings] D. Scheiber. il pors *Sports Illustrated* 70:24-6 My 1 '89

PROSPECT GROUP INC.

Ivy League street fighters [hostile bid for Illinois Central Transportation] B. Bremner. il *Business Week* p34 F 13 '89

An LBO outfit that goes for the long pull. M. Berss. il por *Forbes* 143:94+ Ap 17 '89

PROSPECT PARK (NEW YORK, N.Y.)

Return to splendor [Oriental Pavilion] S. Gutterman. il *Architectural Record* 177:110-13 Jl '89

PROSPECT PARK FINANCIAL

A diamond in the S&L dustheap. G. G. Marcial. *Business Week* p87 Ja 16 '89

PROSPECTING

See also

Computers—Prospecting use

Gold mines and mining

Petroleum prospecting

PROSPECTUSES *See* Securities—Prospectuses

PROSPERE, SUSAN

Party per pale [poem] *The New Yorker* 65:40 Ag 7 '89

PROSPERETTI, ANDREA

about

The fascinating physics of fizz. W. F. Allman. il por *U.S. News & World Report* 107:77 N 20 '89

PROSPERITY
Attacking the deficits now will bring years of prosperity. C. F. Bergsten. il por *Fortune* 119:19+ Ja 2 '89
The key to the dream: prosperity. il *Changing Times* 43:42-5 Mr '89

PROST, ALAIN
about
Alain alone. R. Walker. il por *Road & Track* 41:112-13+ N '89
Down to the wire. R. Walker. il por *Road & Track* 40:126-8 F '89
Just desert. R. Walker. il *Road & Track* 41:82-5 S '89
New beginnings. R. Walker. il por *Road & Track* 40:110-11+ Ja '89
Textbook Prost. I. Ireland. il pors *Road & Track* 41:120-1+ O '89
Winners & losers. I. Ireland. il por *Road & Track* 40:106-8+ Mr '89

PROSTAGLANDINS
Role of prostaglandins and cAMP in the secretory effects of cholera toxin. J. W. Peterson and L. G. Ochoa. bibl f il *Science* 245:857-9 Ag 25 '89

PROSTATE GLAND
Cancer
Intoxicated by my illness. A. Broyard. il *The New York Times Magazine* p32+ N 12 '89
Therapy
Conquering prostate cancer. J. Silberner. il *U.S. News & World Report* 107:55-7 Jl 10 '89
New weapon vs. prostate cancer [internal radioactive palladium capsules] *Prevention (Emmaus, Pa.)* 41:16+ Jl '89
Scientists see new hope for old drug [use of suramin for advanced prostate cancer] *Science News* 135:366 Je 10 '89
Surgery
The imperfect art of healing [surgery increases risk of heart attack] *U.S. News & World Report* 106:10-11 My 8 '89

PROSTHESIS
See also
Bone, Artificial
Foot, Artificial
Heart, Artificial
Hip joint, Artificial
Joints, Artificial
Leg, Artificial
Andy Goose steps out [G. Fleming fits footless goose with sneakers] J. Coudert. il *Reader's Digest* 135:169-70+ Jl '89
Artificial organs: living with risk. P. M. Galletti. *Current (Washington, D.C.)* 311:16-19 Mr/Ap '89
A footless goose becomes a footloose goose—in sneaks [G. Fleming fits gander with sneakers] il *People Weekly* 31:66 Ja 30 '89
Gore Tex organoids and genetic drugs. B. J. Culliton. il *Science* 246:747-9 N 10 '89

PROSTITUTION
See also
Church work with prostitutes
Genesis House
Male prostitution
Mustang Ranch (Nev.: Brothel)
A string of sixty murders [Kansas City] B. Turque. il *Newsweek* 114:64 D 4 '89
Austria
More secrets from the life of Felix Bloch [revelations by Austrian prostitute] il *Newsweek* 114:40 O 23 '89
Great Britain
Hookers aren't the only ones for sale [P. Bordes prostitution scandal] B. Amiel. il *Maclean's* 102:9 My 8 '89
More sex please, we're British [sex scandal involving P. Bordes and various government officials and newspaper editors] A. Stanley. il pors *Time* 133:31 Ap 3 '89
Raising an uncommon furor in the Commons, powerful Brits heed an Indian love call [role of P. Bordes in sex scandal] P. Chin. il pors *People Weekly* 31:52-3 Ap 3 '89
Strange bedfellows [P. Bordes sparks sex and politics scandal] A. Phillips. il por *Maclean's* 102:31+ Ap 3 '89
Hong Kong
The brave new world of Suzie Wong [hostess clubs] W. McGurn. il *Esquire* 111:45 Je '89

PROTEASES
See also
Adipsin
Cathepsin
Renin
Conserved folding in retroviral proteases: crystal structure of a synthetic HIV-1 protease. A. Wlodawer and others. bibl f il *Science* 245:616-21 Ag 11 '89
Crystal versus solution structures of enzymes: NMR spectroscopy of a crystalline serine protease. S. O. Smith and others. bibl f il *Science* 244:961-4 My 26 '89
First 3-D image of AIDS virus protein [work of Manuel A. Navia] R. Weiss. *Science News* 135:100 F 18 '89
Intracellular targeting and structural conservation of a prohormone-processing endoprotease [Saccharomyces] R. S. Fuller and others. bibl f il *Science* 246:482-6 O 27 '89

Molecular modeling of the HIV-1 protease and its substrate binding site. I. T. Weber and others. bibl f il *Science* 243:928-31 F 17 '89
NCI team remodels key AIDS virus enzyme. J. L. Marx. il *Science* 245:598 Ag 11 '89
Pavlovian conditioning of rat mucosal mast cells to secrete rat mast cell protease II. G. MacQueen and others. bibl f il *Science* 243:83-5 Ja 6 '89
Structure of complex of synthetic HIV-1 protease with a substrate-based inhibitor at 2.3 Å resolution. M. Miller and others. bibl f il *Science* 246:1149-52 D 1 '89

PROTECTION (TRADE) *See* Free trade and protection
PROTECTION AGAINST BURGLARY *See* Burglary protection
PROTECTION FROM LIGHTNING *See* Lightning protection
PROTECTION OF CULTURAL PROPERTY *See* Cultural property—Protection
PROTECTION OF MISSIONARIES *See* Missionaries—Protection
PROTECTION OF PLANTS *See* Plants—Protection
PROTECTION ORDERS *See* Orders of protection

PROTECTIVE COATINGS
See also
Airplane engines—Cylinders—Coatings
RPM Inc. (Ohio)
PROTECTIVE MECHANISMS (BIOLOGY) *See* Defense mechanisms (Biology)
PROTECTIVE MIMICRY *See* Mimicry (Biology)
PROTEIN DIETS (LIQUID) *See* Liquid diets

PROTEIN FOLDING
Correct folding of circularly permuted variants of a βα barrel enzyme in vivo. K. Luger and others. bibl f il *Science* 243:206-10 Ja 13 '89
Peptide binding and release by proteins implicated as catalysts of protein assembly. G. C. Flynn and others. bibl f il *Science* 245:385-90 Jl 28 '89
Toward protein tertiary structure recognition by means of associative memory Hamiltonians. M. S. Friedrichs and P. G. Wolynes. bibl f il *Science* 246:371-3 O 20 '89
Water-inserted α-helical segments implicate reverse turns as folding intermediates. M. Sundaralingam and Y. C. Sekharudu. bibl f il *Science* 244:1333-7 Je 16 '89

PROTEIN KINASE
Activators of protein kinase C induce dissociation of CD4, but not CD8, from p56^{lck}. T. R. Hurley and others. bibl f il *Science* 245:407-9 Jl 28 '89
β-adrenergic receptor kinase: primary structure delineates a multigene family. J. L. Benovic and others. bibl f il *Science* 246:235-40 O 13 '89
Cl⁻ channels in CF: lack of activation by protein kinase C and cAMP-dependent protein kinase. T.-C. Hwang and others. bibl f il *Science* 244:1351-3 Je 16 '89
Imaging of memory-specific changes in the distribution of protein kinase C in the hippocampus [associative learning experiment] J. L. Olds and others. bibl f il *Science* 245:866-9 Ag 25 '89
Inhibition of postsynaptic PKC or CaMKII blocks induction but not expression of LTP. R. Malinow and others. bibl f il *Science* 245:862-6 Ag 25 '89
Mutations in a protein kinase C homolog confer phorbol ester resistance on Caenorhabditis elegans. Y. Tabuse and others. bibl f il *Science* 243:1713-16 Mr 31 '89
Myristoylated and nonmyristoylated forms of a protein are phosphorylated by protein kinase C. J. M. Graff and others. bibl f il *Science* 246:503-6 O 27 '89
The protein kinase domain of the ANP receptor is required for signaling. M. Chinkers and D. L. Garbers. bibl f il *Science* 245:1392-4 S 22 '89
Regulation of chloride channels by protein kinase C in normal and cystic fibrosis airway epithelia. M. Li and others. bibl f il *Science* 244:1353-6 Je 16 '89
T cell signaling. R. M. Perlmutter. bibl f il *Science* 245:344 Jl 28 '89

PROTEIN PHOSPHORYLATION *See* Phosphorylation
PROTEIN RECEPTORS
See also
Cadherins
CD4 proteins
T cell receptors
Activation of γδ T cells in the primary immune response to Mycobacterium tuberculosis. E. M. Janis and others. bibl f il *Science* 244:713-16 My 12 '89
Allergy-triggering receptor made en masse [work of Jean Pierre Kinet] R. Weiss. *Science News* 135:246 Ap 22 '89
Antigen-specific helper function of cell-free T cell products bearing TCR V$_\beta$8 determinants. R. Guy and others. bibl f il *Science* 244:1477-80 Je 23 '89
Autoimmune target in Heymann nephritis is a glycoprotein with homology to the LDL receptor. R. Raychowdhury and others. bibl f il *Science* 244:1163-5 Je 9 '89
Contingent genetic regulatory events in T lymphocyte activation. G. R. Crabtree. bibl f il *Science* 243:355-61 Ja 20 '89
Endothelial leukocyte adhesion molecule 1: an inducible receptor for neutrophils related to complement regulatory proteins and lectins. M. P. Bevilacqua and others. bibl f il *Science* 243:1160-5 Mr 3 '89

PROTEIN RECEPTORS—*cont.*

Expression of functional nerve growth factor receptors after gene transfer. B. L. Hempstead and others. bibl f il *Science* 243:373-5 Ja 20 '89

Expression of high-affinity binding of human immunoglobulin E by transfected cells. L. Miller and others. bibl f il *Science* 244:334-7 Ap 21 '89

The Fc and not CD4 receptor mediates antibody enhancement of HIV infection in human cells. J. Homsy and others. bibl f il *Science* 244:1357-60 Je 16 '89

Functionally distinct NF-κB binding sites in the immunoglobulin κ and IL-2 receptor α chain genes. S. L. Cross and others. bibl f il *Science* 244:466-9 Ap 28 '89

Fusion factor in AIDS cells identified [role of leukocyte adhesion receptor LFA-1 in syncytium formation; research by James E. K. Hildreth and Rimas J. Orentas] *Science News* 135:366 Je 10 '89

In vivo modulation of cytolytic activity and thy-1 expression in TCR-γδ⁺ intraepithelial lymphocytes. L. Lefrancois and T. Goodman. bibl f il *Science* 243:1716-18 Mr 31 '89

Interleukin-2 receptor β chain gene: generation of three receptor forms by cloned human α and β chain cDNA's. M. Hatakeyama and others. bibl f il *Science* 244:551-6 My 5 '89

Involvement of a leukocyte adhesion receptor (LFA-1) in HIV-induced syncytium formation. J. E. K. Hildreth and R. J. Orentas. bibl f il *Science* 244:1075-8 Je 2 '89

Isolation and expression of functional high-affinity Fc receptor complementary DNAs. J. M. Allen and B. Seed. bibl f il *Science* 243:378-81 Ja 20 '89

Isolation of a novel receptor cDNA establishes the existence of two PDGF receptor genes. T. Matsui and others. bibl f il *Science* 243:800-4 F 10 '89

Kappa B-specific DNA binding proteins: role in the regulation of human interleukin-2 gene expression. B. Hoyos and others. bibl f il *Science* 244:457-60 Ap 28 '89

Maternal immunity via molecular ferry [research on FcRn by Neil E. Simister and Keith E. Mostov] R. Weiss. *Science News* 135:20 Ja 14 '89

Mechanism of interleukin-2 signaling: mediation of different outcomes by a single receptor and transduction pathway. M. A. Tigges and others. bibl f il *Science* 243:781-6 F 10 '89

Mechanisms for regulating expression of membrane isoforms of FcγRIII (CD16). M. L. Hibbs and others. bibl f il *Science* 246:1608-11 D 22 '89

Membrane anchoring of a human IgG Fc receptor (CD16) determined by a single amino acid. L. L. Lanier and others. bibl f il *Science* 246:1611-13 D 22 '89

Mouse lymph node homing receptor cDNA clone encodes a glycoprotein revealing tandem interaction domains. M. H. Siegelman and others. bibl f il *Science* 243:1165-72 Mr 3 '89

MS gene discovery: a piece of the puzzle [T cell receptor gene; research by Stephen L. Hauser] I. Wickelgren. *Science News* 136:21 Jl 8 '89

New family of adhesion proteins discovered. J. L. Marx. *Science* 243:1144 Mr 3 '89

Purification and complementary DNA cloning of a receptor for basic fibroblast growth factor. P. L. Lee and others. bibl f il *Science* 245:57-60 Jl 7 '89

Role of phosphatidylinositol kinase in PDGF receptor signal transduction. S. R. Coughlin and others. bibl f il *Science* 243:1191-4 Mr 3 '89

Selective amplification and cloning of four new members of the G protein-coupled receptor family. F. Libert and others. bibl f il *Science* 244:569-72 My 5 '89

Signal transduction by the platelet-derived growth factor receptor. L. T. Williams. bibl f il *Science* 243:1564-70 Mr 24 '89

Transformation by v-sis occurs by an internal autoactivation mechanism. B. E. Bejcek and others. bibl f il *Science* 245:1496-9 S 29 '89

PROTEIN TRANSPORT

Clathrin: a role in the intracellular retention of a Golgi membrane protein [yeast] G. S. Payne and R. Schekman. bibl f il *Science* 245:1358-65 S 22 '89

Unity in function in the absence of consensus in sequence: role of leader peptides in export. L. L. Randall and S. J. S. Hardy. bibl f il *Science* 243:1156-9 Mr 3 '89

PROTEINASES

See also

Cathepsin

PROTEINS

See also

Actin
Albumins
Amelogenin
Amino acid sequence
Amino acids
Amyloid
Anti-freeze proteins
Apolipoproteins
Bacterial proteins
Blood—Proteins
Clathrin
Collagen
Cytochromes

Dystrophin
Ferritin
Fetoprotein
G proteins
Glycoproteins
H-Y antigen
Haptoglobin-related protein
Heat shock proteins
Histones
Insulin
Interferon
Interleukin
Lipoproteins
Myoglobin
Myosin
Nucleoproteins
Osteocalcin
Peptides
Plant proteins
Prions
Proteoglycans
Proteolysis
Tryptophan
Ubiquitin
Visual purple

Activation of the cellular proto-oncogene product p21Ras by addition of a myristylation signal. J. E. Buss and others. bibl f il *Science* 243:1600-3 Mr 24 '89

Autocrine induction of collagenase by serum amyloid A-like and β₂-microglobulin-like proteins. C. E. Brinckerhoff and others. bibl f il *Science* 243:655-7 F 3 '89

Brefeldin A specifically inhibits presentation of protein antigens to cytotoxic T lymphocytes. J. W. Yewdell and J. R. Bennink. bibl f il *Science* 244:1072-5 Je 2 '89

Circumsporozoite protein heterogeneity in the human malaria parasite Plasmodium vivax. R. Rosenberg and others. bibl f il *Science* 245:973-6 S 1 '89

Cognate DNA binding specificity retained after leucine zipper exchange between GCN4 and C/EBP. P. Agre and others. bibl f il *Science* 246:922-6 N 17 '89

Crystal clear [Intospace protein crystallization experiment] W. H. Ganoe. *Ad Astra* 1:47 Ja '89

Crystals in zero-G [growing protein crystals in space] J. Kluger. il *Discover* 10:16 Ap '89

Differential effects of *nef* on HIV replication: implications for viral pathogenesis in the host. C. Cheng-Mayer and others. bibl f il *Science* 246:1629-32 D 22 '89

The DNA binding domain of the rat liver nuclear protein C/EBP is bipartite [support for leucine zipper hypothesis] W. H. Landschulz and others. bibl f il *Science* 243:1681-8 Mr 31 '89

Does protein build muscles? [athletes; research by Peter Lemon] P. McCarthy. il *American Health* 8:96 N '89

Evidence that the leucine zipper is a coiled coil. E. K. O'Shea and others. bibl f il *Science* 243:538-42 Ja 27 '89

First U.S. commercial cargo for Mir set to lift off Dec. 20 [Payload Systems protein crystal growth experiments] J. M. Lenorovitz. *Aviation Week & Space Technology* 131:34 D 11 '89

Gene control research gets a boost [TATA protein gene cloned; work of Leonard Guarente] J. L. Marx. il *Science* 245:1329-30 S 22 '89

Identification of a zinc finger protein that binds to the sterol regulatory element. T. B. Rajavashisth and others. bibl f il *Science* 245:640-3 Ag 11 '89

Increased expression of DNA cointroduced with nuclear protein in adult rat liver. Y. Kaneda and others. bibl f il *Science* 243:375-8 Ja 20 '89

Inhibition of antigen-induced lymphocyte proliferation by Tat protein from HIV-1. R. P. Viscidi and others. bibl f il *Science* 246:1606-8 D 22 '89

Inhibition of DNA binding proteins by oligonucleotide-directed triple helix formation. L. J. Maher, III and others. bibl f il *Science* 245:725-30 Ag 18 '89

Kappa B-specific DNA binding proteins: role in the regulation of human interleukin-2 gene expression. B. Hoyos and others. bibl f il *Science* 244:457-60 Ap 28 '89

Leucine repeats and an adjacent DNA binding domain mediate the formation of functional cFos-cJun heterodimers [proposed function of the leucine zipper] R. Turner and R. Tjian. bibl f il *Science* 243:1689-94 Mr 31 '89

Making bigger, better crystals . . . [work of Charles E. Bugg] *Science News* 136:349 N 25 '89

Mechanism of membrane anchoring affects polarized expression of two proteins in MDCK cells. D. A. Brown and others. bibl f il *Science* 245:1499-501 S 29 '89

Molecular sorting in the secretory pathway. K.-N. Chung and others. bibl f il *Science* 243:192-7 Ja 13 '89

Movement protein of tobacco mosaic virus modifies plasmodesmatal size exclusion limit. S. Wolf and others. bibl f il *Science* 246:377-9 O 20 '89

The neuronal growth-associated protein GAP-43 induces filopodia in non-neuronal cells. M. X. Zuber and others. bibl f il *Science* 244:1193-5 Je 9 '89

The neutrophil-activating protein (NAP-1) is also chemotactic for T lymphocytes. C. G. Larsen and others. bibl f il *Science* 243:1464-6 Mr 17 '89

PROTEINS—cont.

New family of adhesion proteins discovered. J. L. Marx. *Science* 243:1144 Mr 3 '89

Parallel association of Fos and Jun leucine zippers juxtaposes DNA binding domains. R. Gentz and others. bibl f il *Science* 243:1695-9 Mr 31 '89

Payload's payload [protein crystal experiments on Mir space station] W. H. Ganoe. *Ad Astra* 1:38 Je '89

Preferential heterodimer formation by isolated leucine zippers from Fos and Jun. E. K. O'Shea and others. bibl f il *Science* 245:646-8 Ag 11 '89

Protein crystal growth in microgravity. L. J. DeLucas and others. bibl f il *Science* 246:651-4 N 3 '89

Regulation of proenkephalin by Fos and Jun. J. L. Sonnenberg and others. bibl f il *Science* 246:1622-5 D 22 '89

Scissors-grip model for DNA recognition by a family of leucine zipper proteins. C. R. Vinson and others. bibl f il *Science* 246:911-16 N 17 '89

Substances found to promote bone growth. *High Technology Business* 9:30 My '89

tat's surprising [HIV protein may derange functioning of cells] R. Rusting. *Scientific American* 260:30+ Mr '89

Transcriptional regulation in mammalian cells by sequence-specific DNA binding proteins [RNA polymerase II transcription initiation] P. J. Mitchell and R. Tjian. bibl f il *Science* 245:371-8 Jl 28 '89

Transfer of a protein encoded by a single nucleus to nearby nuclei in multinucleated myotubes. E. Ralston and Z. W. Hall. bibl f il *Science* 244:1066-9 Je 2 '89

U.S. firm's use of Mir faces probable delay [Payload Systems' protein crystal experiment] *Aviation Week & Space Technology* 130:21 Ap 17 '89

Why less is more. V. Moran and S. S. Lang. il *American Health* 8:130+ Ap '89

A yeast actin-binding protein is encoded by *SAC6*, a gene found by suppression of an actin mutation. A. E. M. Adams and others. bibl f il *Science* 243:231-3 Ja 13 '89

Zero gravity produces weighty improvement [protein crystals grown on the space shuttle] R. Pool. *Science* 246:580 N 3 '89

Analysis

The body's master controls: unraveling proteins to tackle disease at its roots. B. Carpenter. il *U.S. News & World Report* 106:57-9 My 8 '89

The effect of GTPase activating protein upon Ras is inhibited by mitogenically responsive lipids. M.-H. Tsai and others. bibl f il *Science* 243:522-6 Ja 27 '89

A G protein gamma subunit shares homology with *ras* proteins. N. Gautam and others. bibl f il *Science* 244:971-4 My 26 '89

Hidden thermodynamics of mutant proteins: a molecular dynamics analysis. J. Gao and others. bibl f il *Science* 244:1069-72 Je 2 '89

Influence of interior packing and hydrophobicity on the stability of a protein. W. S. Sandberg and T. C. Terwilliger. bibl f il *Science* 245:54-7 Jl 7 '89

Macromolecular crystals. A. McPherson. bibl il *Scientific American* 260:62-9 Mr '89

Protein chemists gain a new analytical tool [mass spectrometry] M. Barinaga. il *Science* 246:32-3 O 6 '89

Protein structure determination in solution by nuclear magnetic resonance spectroscopy. K. Wüthrich. bibl f il *Science* 243:45-50 Ja 6 '89

Thymotaxin, a chemotactic protein, is identical to β_2-microglobulin. C. Dargemont and others. bibl f il *Science* 246:803-6 N 10 '89

Turning cancer off [*ras* protein structure; work of Sung-Hou Kim] G. Montgomery. il *Discover* 10:66-7 Ja '89

Degradation

See Proteolysis

Metabolism

Oxidation-reduction and the molecular mechanism of a regulatory RNA-protein interaction. M. W. Hentze and others. bibl f il *Science* 244:357-9 Ap 21 '89

RNA-protein interactions in 30S ribosomal subunits: folding and function of 16S rRNA. S. Stern and others. bibl f il *Science* 244:783-90 My 19 '89

The turnover of messenger RNA. J. Ross. bibl il *Scientific American* 260:48-55 Ap '89

Synthesis

Building new proteins with odd parts [work of A. Richard Chamberlin] I. Amato. *Science News* 136:246 O 14 '89

Fortifying a protein through family ties [altered form of TPA; work of Joseph F. Sambrook] R. Cowen. *Science News* 136:23 Jl 8 '89

A general method for site-specific incorporation of unnatural amino acids into proteins. C. J. Noren and others. bibl f il *Science* 244:182-8 Ap 14 '89

Hybrid protein may help fight cancer [product of gene for interferon and gene for tumor necrosis factor] *High Technology Business* 9:33 Ja '89

Lab-made proteins stretch like life [work of Dan W. Urry] I. Amato. *Science News* 136:398 D 16 '89

On the trail of transfer RNA identity. C. Mlot. il *BioScience* 39:756-9 D '89

Peptide and protein synthesis by segment synthesis-condensation. E. T. Kaiser and others. bibl f il *Science* 243:187-92 Ja 13 '89

Protein design, a minimalist approach. W. F. DeGrado and others. bibl f il *Science* 243:622-8 F 3 '89

PROTEOGLYCANS

Relation of the amyloid β protein precursor to heparan sulfate proteoglycans [discussion of July 8, 1988 article, Amyloid β protein precursor is possibly a heparan sulfate proteoglycan core protein] D. Schubert and others. *Science* 244:826-8 My 19 '89

PROTEOLYSIS

Degradation of proteins with acetylated amino termini by the ubiquitin system. A. Mayer and others. bibl f il *Science* 244:1480-3 Je 23 '89

Prevention of rapid intracellular degradation of ODC by a carboxyl-terminal truncation. L. Ghoda and others. bibl f il *Science* 243:1493-5 Mr 17 '89

A role for a 70-kilodaton heat shock protein in lysosomal degradation of intracellular proteins. H.-L. Chiang and others. bibl f il *Science* 246:382-5 O 20 '89

PROTEOLYTIC ENZYMES *See* Proteases

PROTESTANT-CATHOLIC MARRIAGE *See* Interfaith marriage

PROTESTANT CHURCHES

> *See also*
> Catholic Church—Relations—Protestant churches
> Consultation on Church Union
> Lutheran Church

Clergy

> *See* Clergy

Education

> *See also*
> Theological seminaries

Canada

> *See also*
> United Church of Canada

China

> *See also*
> Three-Self Movement (China)

Bishop at center of Chinese church debate [K. H. Ting] W. W. Conard. por *Christianity Today* 33:52-3 My 12 '89

Germany

Angel of light [church's reaction to Hitler] T. Stafford. il *Christianity Today* 33:16-19 S 8 '89

Germany (East)

Church in East Germany helps create die Wende. J. P. Burgess. *The Christian Century* 106:1140-2 D 6 '89

Must walls of hostility continue to divide? J. E. Will. il *The Christian Century* 106:1191-2 D 20-27 '89

Pleas from GDR churches. *The Christian Century* 106:905 O 11 '89

Questions for the East German church [Dresden conference] J. C. Erlick. *The Christian Century* 106:791-5 Ag 30-S 6 '89

Schooling for democracy. G. Stassen. *The Christian Century* 106:1199-1201 D 20-27 '89

Germany (West)

The German church is not dead. H. Schwarz. *The Christian Century* 106:196-7 F 22 '89

The German past and unusable churches. A. G. Roeber. *The Christian Century* 106:407-8 Ap 19 '89

Japan

A second look at Japan's churches [discussion of November 2, 1988 article, The inertia of Japan's churches] W. L. Sachs. *The Christian Century* 106:139-41 F 1-8 '89

Latin America

> *See also*
> Latin American Council of Churches

Philippines

> *See also*
> National Council of Churches (Philippines)

United States

> *See also*
> Assemblies of God
> Episcopal Church—United States
> Lutheran Church—United States
> National Council of Churches
> Presbyterian Church—United States
> United Church of Christ
> United Methodist Church

American ecumenism: separatism, separation and schism [adaptation of address] M. E. Marty. *The Christian Century* 106:958-61 O 25 '89

Assemblies of God celebrates 75 years [denominational meetings] R. Frame. il *Christianity Today* 33:45 S 22 '89

The business of the church. R. C. Wood. *The Christian Century* 106:221-2 Mr 1 '89

Missouri Synod Lutherans seek harmony [denominational meetings] R. Frame. il *Christianity Today* 33:45 Ag 18 '89

Nazarenes break ground in social/moral concern [denominational meetings] R. Frame. il *Christianity Today* 33:48+ S 8 '89

Sophisticated primitives then, primitive sophisticates now [adaptation of address; cover story] M. E. Marty. il *The Christian Century* 106:588-91 Je 7-14 '89

Those mainline blues [decline in membership] R. N. Ostling. il *Time* 133:94-6 My 22 '89

PROTESTANT CHURCHES—United States—*cont.*
The underground ecumenist. K. A. Marlin. See issues of The Christian Century beginning October 25, 1989
Where is the 'mainline' headed? [cover story; special section] il *The Christian Century* 106:1012-20+ N 8 '89
History
The establishment that was [Between the times: the travail of the Protestant establishment in America, 1900-1960] M. E. Marty. *The Christian Century* 106:1045-7 N 15 '89

PROTESTANT CHURCHES AND ABORTION See Abortion—Moral and religious aspects

PROTESTANT REFORMATION See Reformation

PROTESTANT THEOLOGY See Theology

PROTESTANTISM
See also
Evangelicalism
Fundamentalism
Protestant churches
Reformation

PROTESTANTS
France
French Protestants: an endangered species? [views of Jean Baubérot] F. Quinn. *The Christian Century* 106:439-40 Ap 26 '89
Northern Ireland
A 20th anniversary with nothing to celebrate. M. Skelton. il *Christianity Today* 33:36-7 Mr 17 '89
United States
See also
WASPs (Persons)

PROTESTS, DEMONSTRATIONS, ETC.
See also
Animal experimentation—Protests, demonstrations, etc.
Anti-nuclear movement
Hunger strikes
Student protests, demonstrations, etc.
Vietnamese War, 1957-1975—Protest movements
Today's uncivil disobedience. J. Leo. il *U.S. News & World Report* 106:64 Ap 17 '89
International aspects
The medium is the message [use of English signs by demonstrators around the world] il *Time* 133:64-5 Je 5 '89
British Columbia
See also
Vancouver (B.C.)—Protests, demonstrations, etc.
Germany (East)
See also
Leipzig (Germany)—Protests, demonstrations, etc.
Calls for reform. D. Jenish. il *Maclean's* 102:42 O 16 '89
Turmoil behind the wall. J. Altman. il *U.S. News & World Report* 107:38-9 O 16 '89
Idaho
See also
Coeur d'Alene (Idaho)—Protests, demonstrations, etc.
Korea (South)
Protests threaten to cripple USAF training operations [Koon-Ni gunnery range] J. D. Morrocco. il *Aviation Week & Space Technology* 130:239+ Je 12 '89
Massachusetts
See also
Boston (Mass.)—Protests, demonstrations, etc.
Minnesota
See also
Duluth (Minn.)—Protests, demonstrations, etc.
Turkey
See also
Istanbul (Turkey)—Protests, demonstrations, etc.
Washington (D.C.)
See Washington (D.C.)—Protests, demonstrations, etc.

PROTO-RIFTS AND OCEAN BASIN EVOLUTION PROJECT See Project PROBE

PROTOCOLS, COMPUTER NETWORK See Computer network protocols

PROTON (LAUNCH VEHICLE) See Space vehicles—Propulsion systems

PROTON THERAPY
Accelerated medicine. G. Levoy. il *Omni (New York, N.Y.)* 11:26+ Mr '89
Chiseling away at tumors with protons [work of James M. Slater] *Science News* 135:46 Ja 21 '89

PROTONS
See also
Antiprotons
Osteoclastic bone resorption by a polarized vacuolar proton pump. H. C. Blair and others. bibl f il *Science* 245:855-7 Ag 25 '89
Proton motive force involved in protein transport across the outer membrane of Aeromonas salmonicida. K. R. Wong and J. T. Buckley. bibl f il *Science* 246:654-6 N 3 '89
Proton puzzle puts physicists in a whirl. I. Peterson. *Science News* 135:215 Ap 8 '89

PROTOTYPER (COMPUTER PROGRAM)
Ease into Mac programming. R. Valdés. il *Byte* 14:241-2+ N '89

PROTOTYPING (COMPUTERS)
Instant gratification. G. T. Pope. il *High Technology Business* 9:24-7 Je '89

PROTOZOA
See also
Amebas
Tetrahymena

PROTOZOA, PATHOGENIC
See also
Amebas
Leptomonas
Neospora
Plasmodium (Parasite)
Parasitic protozoa and helminths: biological and immunological challenges. A. A. F. Mahmoud. bibl f il *Science* 246:1015-22 N 24 '89
Phylogenetic meaning of the kingdom concept: an unusual ribosomal RNA from Giardia lamblia. M. L. Sogin and others. bibl f il *Science* 243:75-7 Ja 6 '89
Resistance and sensitivity
Amplification of a gene related to mammalian mdr genes in drug-resistant Plasmodium falciparum. C. M. Wilson and others. bibl f il *Science* 244:1184-6 Je 9 '89

PROTTI, DENIS
A need for information professionals. il *World Health* p26-7 Ag/S '89

PROTZMAN, CHARLES
about
A lesson learned and a lesson forgotten. R. C. Wood. il pors *Forbes* 143:70-2+ F 6 '89

PROULX, ANNIE
Our vanishing forests. il *Organic Gardening* 36:60-4+ Mr '89

PROVENCE (FRANCE)
The essence of Provence [home of J. and I. Amic] C. Carter. il por *House & Garden* 161:126-31+ Jl '89
A Provençal tale: the house and vineyards of Richeaume [H. Hoesch's estate] D. H. Minassian. il *Architectural Digest* 46:136-41 Ja '89
Description and travel
Christmas in Provence. E. Jones. il *Gourmet* 49:108-9+ D '89
Gourmet holidays: a corner of Provence. D. Beal. il map *Gourmet* 49:44-9+ Jl '89
Provence: a walk in the sun. H. McGrew. il map *Gourmet* 49:96-8+ My '89
Social life and customs
Provence Pilgrims [Thanksgiving dinner] P. Wells. il *The New York Times Magazine* p93-4 N 5 '89
Some other picnics. M. F. K. Fisher. il por *Architectural Digest* 46:34+ Jl '89

PROVENZO, EUGENE F.
Time exposures. il *Society* 26:87-9 S/O '89

PROVERA See Medroxyprogesterone

PROVERBS
See also
Maxims
Love proverbs are universal, says an expert—and like love itself, they can bite [compiler W. Meider] il por *People Weekly* 31:112-13 F 20 '89
Proverbs and place [weather] R. E. Spencer. il *Weatherwise* 42:208-11 Ag '89

PROVIDENCE (R.I.)
Economic conditions
A small miracle on Interstate 95. S. Hutchison. il *Newsweek* 113:47 F 6 '89

PROVIDENT LIFE AND ACCIDENT INSURANCE CO.
Feeling better, thank you. il *Forbes* 143:165 Ja 9 '89

PROVINCIALISM See Regionalism

PROVING GROUNDS
See also
Bombing and gunnery ranges
Naval Weapons Center (U.S.)
Plum Brook Field Station
United States. Air Force. Utah Test and Training Range
Wallops Flight Facility

PROVOST, JAMES H.
Hard cases make bad law. *Commonweal* 116:270+ My 5 '89

PROXIES
Miss Marple meets the modern proxy. S. Chin. il *Forbes* 143:159-61 My 29 '89
Moneymen may stop deep-sixing proxies. J. M. Laderman. il *Business Week* p142 Mr 20 '89
A raider tries to beat Asher Edelman at his own game [M. Ackerman's proxy fight for Datapoint] G. Lewis. il pors *Business Week* p50 S 25 '89
Resolved: shareholders need to take more drastic action. J. H. Dobrzynski. il *Business Week* p32 Ag 7 '89
Rocking the recliners [proxy fight for La-Z-Boy] M. Schifrin. il por *Forbes* 144:194+ O 16 '89
Still trying to land UAL [Coniston Partners' proxy fight] J. E. Ellis. il *Business Week* p28-9 N 20 '89
Take the mystery out of CEO pay [dollars concealed in proxy statements] G. S. Crystal and F. T. Vincent, Jr. il *Fortune* 119:217+ Ap 24 '89

PROXMIRE, WILLIAM
Should the Congress adopt the "Tender Offer Disclosure and Fairness Act of 1987"? [excerpts from address, June 17, 1988] *Congressional Digest* 68:74+ Mr '89
PROZAC *See* Fluoxetine
PRPIC, VERONICA, AND OTHERS
Role of Na$^+$/H$^+$ exchange by interferon-γ in enhanced expression of JE and I-A$_\beta$ genes. bibl f il *Science* 244:469-71 Ap 28 '89
PRUDENT SPECULATOR (NEWSLETTER)
Marty Zweig? Or Al Frank? [aftermath of Friday the 13th stock market plunge] M. Hulbert. il *Forbes* 144:368 N 13 '89
PRUDENTIAL-BACHE SECURITIES INC.
The captains who didn't go down with the ship [Prudential-Bache takes over Thomson McKinnon] G. Morgenson. il *Forbes* 144:39-41 Ag 21 '89
PRUDENTIAL-BACHE UTILITY FUND
A utility fund's shocking profits. M. Schiffres. il *Changing Times* 43:18 F '89
PRUDHOMME, PAUL
First word. por *Omni (New York, N.Y.)* 12:6 N '89
PRUESS, JOANNA
Cool comfort. il *The New York Times Magazine* p53-4 Je 18 '89
Uppity beans. il *The New York Times Magazine* p107-8 N 19 '89
PRUNING
See also
Pinching (Plant pruning)
A mulberry success story that's worth sharing [pollarding] il *Sunset (Central West edition)* 182:126 Ja '89
Pruning camellias. il *Organic Gardening* 36:28-9 Ja '89
Pruning clematis. J. Glattstein. il *Organic Gardening* 36:30-1 Ap '89
Pruning climbing roses. il *Southern Living* 24:60 Je '89
TFH guide to shade tree pruning. D. Prestly. il *The Family Handyman* 39:54-7 S '89
PRUNING EQUIPMENT
Maintenance and repair
How to keep your pruning tools happy. il *Sunset (Central West edition)* 182:134+ Ja '89
PRUNTY, WYATT
Learning the bicycle [poem] *The American Scholar* 58:122 Wint '89
PRYCE-JONES, DAVID
Self-determination, Arab style. *Commentary* 87:39-46 Ja '89
PRYKE, IAN
ESA's next decade. il *Ad Astra* 1:16-19+ My '89
PRYMAK, THOMAS
Hrushevsky and the Ukraine's 'lost' history. bibl il por map *History Today* 39:42-6 Ja '89
PRYOR, DAVID
about
New leaders deal with aging-policy issues. il por *Modern Maturity* 32:85 Ag/S '89
PRYOR, KELLI
The story of her life. il pors *New York* 22:52-5 Je 12 '89
PRYOR, RAIN
about
Richard Pryor's funny girl, Rain, shines in TV's Head of the class. M. Dougherty. il pors *People Weekly* 31:131-2 Ap 17 '89
PRYOR, RICHARD
about
Eddie says he cast Richard in 'Harlem nights' because 'He is my idol' [cover story] R. E. Johnson. il pors *Jet* 77:56-60 N 20 '89
Richard Pryor, Gene Wilder: together again in new movie comedy [cover story] il pors *Jet* 76:36-8 Je 5 '89
Richard Pryor hit with paternity suit. il por *Jet* 75:55 Ja 16 '89
Richard Pryor's funny girl, Rain, shines in TV's Head of the class. M. Dougherty. il pors *People Weekly* 31:131-2 Ap 17 '89
PSALMS, BOOK OF *See* Bible. O.T. Psalms
PSEUDO-INTELLECTUALISM
Get smart. C. Peacock. il *Utne Reader* p16+ My/Je '89
Makeovers of the mind: L.A.'s new intellectuals [celebrities] D. Denicolo. il *Glamour* 87:164 Ag '89
PSEUDOCYESIS
Babies were Linda German's obsession—was she crazy or just madly in love? [charged with baby snatching in Huntington, W. Va.] G. Stone. il pors *People Weekly* 31:84-8 Mr 20 '89
PSEUDOMONAS
Bacterial blight of soybean: regulation of a pathogen gene determining host cultivar specificity. T. V. Huynh and others. bibl f il *Science* 245:1374-7 S 22 '89
Microbial census hints at biotech hurdles [study by Michael H. Smith] R. Weiss. *Science News* 135:4 Ja 7 '89
Sneaky bacteria. G. Devery. il *Outdoor Life* 183:32-3 F '89
PSEUDOSCORPIONS, FOSSIL
Old pseudoscorpion had modern features [research by William A. Shear and others] R. Monastersky. *Science News* 136:263 O 21 '89

PSI PHENOMENA *See* Parapsychology
PSICOR INC.
Out front in the blood business. G. Weiss. *Business Week* p59 Ag 7 '89
PSIHOYOS, LOUIS
(jt. auth) *See* Hardin, Ted, and Psihoyos, Louis
PSORALENS
Psoralen's activity comes to the surface. I. Wickelgren. *Science News* 136:5 Jl 1 '89
PSORIASIS
Overexpression of transforming growth factor α in psoriatic epidermis. J. T. Elder and others. bibl f il *Science* 243:811-14 F 10 '89
Psoriasis—still breaking hearts [views of Mark A. Everett] *USA Today (Periodical)* 118:13 O '89
PSS (PORCINE STRESS SYNDROME) *See* Swine—Diseases and pests
PSYCHIATRIC CLINICS
See also
Community Psychiatric Centers
PSYCHIATRIC DIAGNOSIS *See* Mental illness—Diagnosis
PSYCHIATRIC ETHICS
See also
Psychiatric research—Ethical aspects
PSYCHIATRIC HOSPITALS *See* Hospitals, Psychiatric
PSYCHIATRIC RESEARCH
See also
National Institute of Mental Health (U.S.)
Ethical aspects
NIMH assigns blame for tainted studies [Stanford University case] M. Barinaga. *Science* 245:812 Ag 25 '89
PSYCHIATRISTS
See also
World Psychiatric Association
Yalom, Irvin D., 1931-
Vive la différence [psychologists and psychiatrists] R. D. Fowler. il por *Psychology Today* 22:78 D '88
PSYCHIATRY
See also
Adolescent psychiatry
Aged—Psychiatric care
American Psychiatric Association
Child psychiatry
Forensic psychiatry
Hispanic Americans—Psychiatric care
Indochinese—United States—Psychiatric care
Pack rats (Persons)—Psychiatric care
Psychoanalysis
Psychotherapy
Public officers—Psychiatric care
International aspects
See also
World Psychiatric Association
Soviet Union
Here come the Russian shrinks! G. Garelik. il *Time* 134:78-9 O 30 '89
A profession under stress. J. Langone. il *Time* 133:94-5 Ap 10 '89
Psychiatrists examine Soviet system. C. Holden. *Science* 243:1547 Mr 24 '89
Should world psychiatry readmit the Soviets? P. Reddaway. bibl f il *The New York Review of Books* 36:54-8 O 12 '89
Soviet psychiatry: an exchange [discussion of October 12, 1989 article, Should world psychiatry readmit the Soviets?] P. Reddaway. il *The New York Review of Books* 36:65-6 D 21 '89
Soviet psychiatry: real progress or just PR? C. Holden. il *Science* 245:348 Jl 28 '89
Soviets reenter world psychiatric society. B. Bower. *Science News* 136:278 O 28 '89
PSYCHIATRY AND SOCIETY
The anti-shrinks [views of S. Zinman, J. M. Masson and P. R. Breggin] M. DiLeo. pors *Mother Jones* 14:13 Jl/Ag '89
Order on the couch [treatments of psychiatric disorders] J. Alper. il *The Atlantic* 263:24-7+ My '89
PSYCHIC HEALING *See* Mental healing
PSYCHIC PHENOMENA *See* Parapsychology
PSYCHICAL RESEARCH *See* Parapsychology
PSYCHICS
See also
Czetli, Nancy
Fonte, Morris
Extra-ordinary perception [interview with M. T. Browne] O. J. Lipstein. il pors *American Health* 8:60-5 D '89
A well-lighted place. O. Lipstein. il *American Health* 8:63-4 D '89
PSYCHICS AND CRIMINAL INVESTIGATION *See* Parapsychology and criminal investigation
PSYCHICS IN CABLE TELEVISION
Nice psychic [M. Temple, host of Tele-psychic] *The New Yorker* 65:27-8 Mr 13 '89
PSYCHOACOUSTICS
Beyond stereo [Sound Retrieval System] L. Feldman. il *Radio-Electronics* 60:51-4 S '89
Hearing pleasures [excerpt from The five senses] F. Gonzalez-Crussi. il *Health (New York, N.Y.)* 21:64-71 Mr '89

PSYCHOACOUSTICS—cont.
How loud is real? L. Klein. il *Radio-Electronics* 60:8-9+ Jl '89
Psycho-what? K. C. Pohlmann. il *Stereo Review* 54:116-18+ S '89
Spaced-out stereo [Sound Retrieval System] L. Feldman. il *Popular Science* 234:130-2 Je '89
PSYCHOACTIVE DRUGS *See* Psychopharmacology
PSYCHOANALYSIS
Confessions of a head case. P. Freundlich. il *Esquire* 112:231-4+ S '89
Dreams on the couch. D. Gelman. il *Newsweek* 114:45-7 Ag 14 '89

Anecdotes, facetiae, satire, etc.
McFreud's. M. Feder. *Harper's* 279:32 Ag '89
PSYCHOANALYSIS AND ART
Van Gogh and Gauguin on the couch [symposium] B. Collins. bibl f il *Art in America* 77:57+ D '89
PSYCHOANALYSTS
See also
Freud, Sigmund, 1856-1939
Isay, Richard A.
PSYCHOGRAPHICS *See* Market research
PSYCHOKINESIS
Questions for the cosmos [work of R. G. Jahn] S. Fishman. il por *The New York Times Magazine* p50+ N 26 '89
PSYCHOLOGICAL EQUIPMENT
Brain stretches [special section] J. Hooper and D. Teresi. il *Health (New York, N.Y.)* 21:55-67 Ap '89
Exercise your mind. R. Flippin. il *Working Woman* 14:122+ F '89
Pumping intellect: can mind machines build up our brains? C. H. Otis. il *Utne Reader* p32-3 Ja/F '89
Sound-and-light wars [Synchro-Energizer] J. Hooper. il *Omni (New York, N.Y.)* 12:26+ N '89

Anecdotes, facetiae, satire, etc.
The other 90% [increasing brain power] P. Chance. il *Psychology Today* 23:20-1 N '89
PSYCHOLOGICAL GAMES
Tools for thought. il *Health (New York, N.Y.)* 21:64-5 Ap '89
PSYCHOLOGICAL TESTS
See also
Aptitude tests
Intelligence tests
Lie detectors and detection
Minnesota Multiphasic Personality Inventory
Identifying psychopaths [test based on the Missouri Descriptive Index; work of James M. A. Weiss] il *USA Today (Periodical)* 118:12 Ag '89
A true test of skill for your employees. M.-P. Royer. *Working Woman* 14:32+ N '89
PSYCHOLOGICAL TYPES *See* Typology (Psychology)
PSYCHOLOGICAL WARFARE
See also
Terrorism
PSYCHOLOGISTS
See also
Boothby, Neil
Vive la différence [psychologists and psychiatrists] R. D. Fowler. il por *Psychology Today* 22:78 D '88

Attitudes
Bibliotherapy [self help titles recommended by psychologists; survey by Steven Starker] S. McKee. bibl il *American Health* 8:42 D '89
Re-examining Freud. il *Psychology Today* 23:48-50+ S '89
Rx: 2 self-help books and call me in the morning. E. Stark. bibl il *Psychology Today* 23:26 Je '89

Professional ethics
Free advice [Massachusetts psychologists investigated for speculating about K. Dukakis in the press] por *Time* 134:71 D 4 '89
PSYCHOLOGY
See also
Behavior (Psychology)
Behavior modification
Child psychology
Cognition
Computers—Psychological use
Consciousness
Criminal psychology
Environmental psychology
Escalation (Psychology)
Ethnopsychology
Helplessness (Psychology)
Infant psychology
Mental illness
Mind
Negativity (Psychology)
Parapsychology
Political psychology
Prison psychology
Psychiatry
Psychoanalysis
Psychotherapy

Periodicals
See also
Good spirit (Periodical)

PSYCHOLOGY, EDUCATIONAL
See also
College teachers—Psychology
Learning, Psychology of
Students—Psychology
Teachers—Psychology
Developmentally appropriate practice: philosophical and practical implications [contrasted with psychometric educational psychology] D. Elkind. bibl f il *Phi Delta Kappan* 71:113-17 O '89
PSYCHOLOGY, INDUSTRIAL
See also
Business etiquette
Employee counseling
Employee morale
Entrepreneurs—Psychology
Executives—Psychology
Job satisfaction
Job stress
Motivation (Psychology)
Success
Women executives—Psychology
Workaholics
The "absent boss" syndrome. L. Henry. il *Psychology Today* 23:24-5 Jl/Ag '89
Are you a difficult person? [seminar offered by CareerTrack] D. Owen. il *The Atlantic* 264:73-80 O '89
Are you teaching your staff to be helpless? D. W. Ray. *Working Woman* 14:32 Mr '89
The bad boss contest. il *Glamour* 87:122 O '89
Bosses ignore worker concerns [automation; views of Ann Majchrzak] il *USA Today (Periodical)* 118:4-5 Ag '89
Criticizing your boss—tactfully. J. Weber, Jr. il *Business Week* p98 Ag 28 '89
Dear Betty Harragan. B. L. Harragan. il *Working Woman* 14:31-2 Jl '89
Do you work for a difficult boss? M. M. Kennedy. il *Glamour* 87:57-8 Jl '89
Firing: there's (almost) always a better way. A. Jaffe. il *Psychology Today* 23:68-9 Jl/Ag '89
Hard work (alone) gets you . . . nowhere: the awful truth about office politics. L. Dusky. il *Mademoiselle* 95:138+ F '89
How layoffs affect survivors. M. Chinnici. *Psychology Today* 23:20 O '89
How not to give criticism [excerpt from The critical edge] H. Weisinger. il *Glamour* 87:126+ Mr '89
How to say no and make it stick. M. M. Kennedy. il *Glamour* 87:93 D '89
How tough critics may be mentors in disguise [excerpt from The critical edge] H. Weisinger. il *Working Woman* 14:102-4 Je '89
I see, I want, I get—maybe [views of Albert J. Bernstein and Sydney Craft Rozen in book Dinosaur brains] J. Castro. il *Time* 133:69 My 8 '89
In defense of elitism. O. Edwards. il *Gentlemen's Quarterly* 59:147+ F '89
Leak soup [interpreting the grapevine] O. Edwards. il *Gentlemen's Quarterly* 59:224+ Ap '89
Managing old-timers when you're the young kid on the block. *Working Woman* 14:28 My '89
Office politics: the top 10 potential traps. M. M. Kennedy. il *Glamour* 87:109-10 My '89
Pigs in sheep's clothing: how to spot a secret sexist. S. Beauvais. il *Glamour* 87:116+ Je '89
"Power" revisited [views of M. Korda] O. Edwards. il *Gentlemen's Quarterly* 59:164+ Je '89
Social class in the workplace: the United States versus Japan [study by Keiko Nakao] *Society* 26:2 Ja/F '89
Surviving organizational death [study by Robert Sutton] E. Stark. *Psychology Today* 23:15 Je '89
Taking the edge off competition. H. McCandless. il *Working Woman* 14:110 S '89
What does your boss really want from you? M. M. Kennedy. *Glamour* 87:124 N '89
What mothers know and managers must learn. L. Leritz. il *Working Woman* 14:32+ My '89
When bad bosses happen to good people. J. Ciabattari. il *Working Woman* 14:88-91+ Jl '89
When the boss becomes pregnant. B. Hamer. il *Psychology Today* 23:14+ Ja/F '89
When to listen to the office grapevine. B. Nivens. il *Essence* 19:102 Mr '89
When you should be an office gossip. M. M. Kennedy. il *Working Woman* 14:34 Ap '89
Where did the gung-ho go? [ebbing corporate loyalty] J. Castro. il *Time* 134:52-4+ S 11 '89
Why it pays to know what your employees are thinking. L. Touby. *Working Woman* 14:21-2 Je '89
Will you cry on the job? [excerpt from Working up a storm] J. M. Plas and K. V. Hoover-Dempsey. il *Glamour* 87:286-7+ Mr '89
Work smarter, not harder [cover story; special section; with introd. by T George Harris and Robert J. Trotter] il *Psychology Today* 23:33-6+ Mr '89

Anecdotes, facetiae, satire, etc.
Pachydermic personnel prediction. P. C. Olsen. il *Byte* 14:404 S '89

PSYCHOLOGY, INDUSTRIAL—Anecdotes, facetiae, satire, etc.—*cont.*
Take my heart . . . please! S. Bing. il *Esquire* 111:72 F '89

Japan
Social class in the workplace: the United States versus Japan [study by Keiko Nakao] *Society* 26:2 Ja/F '89
PSYCHOLOGY, PATHOLOGICAL *See* Psychopathology
PSYCHOLOGY, PHYSIOLOGICAL
See also
Body image
Brain—Localization of functions
Conditioned responses
Eating—Psychological aspects
Emotions
Facial expression
Laterality
Left- and right-handedness
Medicine, Psychosomatic
Memory
Mental healing
Mind and body
Neuropsychology
Optical illusions
Pain
Reaction time
Reflexes
Reinforcement (Psychology)
Senses and sensation
Sleep
Space perception
Time perception
The medical side of anxiety [study by Kenneth B. Wells] *Science News* 136:381 D 9 '89
PSYCHOLOGY, RELIGIOUS
See also
Clergy—Psychology
Priests—Psychology
Christians can be good and angry [with readers' comments] R. M. Brown. *U.S. Catholic* 54:14-15 N '89
Do religious people help more? Not so you'd notice. A. Kohn. il *Psychology Today* 23:66+ D '89
Feeling saved. R. A. Fowler. il *Christianity Today* 33:26-7 Ap 7 '89
Parishes should learn to fight fair [Catholic Church] T. Unsworth. *U.S. Catholic* 54:29-31 F '89
When bad things happen to good religion [views of H. Kushner] R. J. Neuhaus. il *National Review* 41:52-4 N 10 '89

Bibliography
Book reviews. A. L. Laffey. *America* 160:403-5 Ap 29 '89
PSYCHOLOGY GAMES *See* Psychological games
PSYCHONEUROIMMUNOLOGY
The chemistry of love. J. Poppy. il *Esquire* 111:130-2+ My '89
The dance of healing [views of C. A. Hammerschlag] C. Perlmutter. *Prevention (Emmaus, Pa.)* 41:69-72 S '89
Do negative emotions cause disease? C. Tavris. *Vogue* 179:228+ Ag '89
Emotions and allergies: the Pavlov connection [research by Glenda MacQueen] B. L. Benderly. *Psychology Today* 23:17 Je '89
A molecular code links emotions, mind and health. S. S. Hall. il *Smithsonian* 20:62-71 Je '89
Pavlov's rats [allergic reaction produced by Pavlovian conditioning] il *Discover* 10:14 My '89
Pictures of health [positive imagery techniques; cover story] A. A. Sheikh. il *Omni (New York, N.Y.)* 11:104-10 F '89
Press the button, depress immunity [research by Carol S. Weisse] B. Bower. *Science News* 136:141 Ag 26 '89
Setting the stage for infection [lowered response rate of natural killer cells; research by Sandra M. Levy] B. Bower. *Science News* 136:141 Ag 26 '89
Stimulating rats [small amounts of stress may be beneficial; research by Jay Weiss] *Discover* 10:10 S '89
Stress' effect on immune system [research by Ronald Glaser] *USA Today (Periodical)* 117:4 Je '89
Your mind's healing powers. *Reader's Digest* 135:5-6+ S '89
PSYCHOPATHOLOGY
See also
Alexithymia
Autism
Catatonia
Codependence (Psychology)
Cyclothymia
Depression, Mental
Erotomania
Hypochondria
Mental illness
Narcissism
Neuroses
Panic disorder
Paranoia
Schizophrenia
Stendhal syndrome

Identifying psychopaths [test based on the Missouri Descriptive Index; work of James M. A. Weiss] il *USA Today (Periodical)* 118:12 Ag '89
PSYCHOPHARMACOLOGY
See also
LSD
Tranquilizing drugs
At 90, the zombie shuffle. H. Willard. por *Newsweek* 113:10 F 20 '89
The biology of obsessions and compulsions. J. L. Rapoport. il *Scientific American* 260:82-9 Mr '89
Flipping the main switch in the central reward system? [cocaine and the brain] C. Holden. il *Science* 246:1378-9 D 15 '89
Is grandma drowsy, or is she drugged? [nursing home care] S. Findlay. il *U.S. News & World Report* 106:68 Je 12 '89
Kids talk about the 'good pill' [psychological side effects of stimulants administered to hyperactive children; research by Peter S. Jensen] B. Bower. *Science News* 135:332 My 27 '89
Medication concerns in rest homes. *Science News* 135:88 F 11 '89
On medication: a call for caution [elderly] M. Masterson. *New Choices for the Best Years* 29:12-13 Jl '89
A poor rest home remedy: drugs in place of care. L. Drew. *Newsweek* 113:56 F 6 '89
A question of time for neuroleptics [research by Paul E. Keck Jr.] *Science News* 136:302 N 4 '89
PSYCHOSES
See also
Depression, Mental
Paranoia
Schizophrenia
PSYCHOSOMATIC MEDICINE *See* Medicine, Psychosomatic
PSYCHOTHERAPISTS
Licenses
Brian Wilson's Svengali has his wings clipped as he gives up his license to shrink [E. Landy] il pors *People Weekly* 31:97 Ap 17 '89
Landy loses license [E. Landy] M. Goldberg. pors *Rolling Stone* p27 My 18 '89
Malpractice
See Malpractice
Psychology
Wounded healers [cover story] T. Maeder. il *The Atlantic* 263:37-47 Ja '89
PSYCHOTHERAPISTS AND PATIENTS
Sex on the couch: Maybe later? B. Fischman. *Psychology Today* 23:26 Je '89
PSYCHOTHERAPISTS AS AUTHORS
Does your analyst read Henry James? A. Broyard. il *The New York Times Book Review* 94:14-15 Ap 16 '89
PSYCHOTHERAPY
See also
Arts therapy
Behavior modification
Biofeedback training
Cognitive therapy
Computers—Psychotherapeutic use
Crisis intervention
Family psychotherapy
Group psychotherapy
Neurolinguistic programming
Psychoanalysis
Psychopharmacology
Self help groups
Shock therapy
Brief encounter. M. Kaplan. il *Gentlemen's Quarterly* 59:204+ Mr '89
Choosing Dr. Right. N. Weber. *Harper's Bazaar* 122:187+ Mr '89
Exploring psychic interiors [interview with I. D. Yalom] E. E. Goode. por *U.S. News & World Report* 107:67 O 30 '89
Facing down the ghosts of the past [flooding therapy for sexual abuse victims] C. Senders. il *Psychology Today* 23:70-1 S '89
Getting off the couch for good [interview with C. Johnson] E. E. Goode. il por *U.S. News & World Report* 106:62 Ja 23 '89
A guide to psychotherapy [special section] il *Essence* 20:49-52+ Je '89
Healthy love [excerpt from Lifemates; ed. by Robert B. Kory. H. H. Bloomfield and S. Vettese. il *Health (New York, N.Y.)* 21:24+ F '89
Is your job driving you crazy? [matching therapy to profession] R. Sandroff. il *Psychology Today* 23:41-5 Jl/Ag '89
The key to successful therapy. P. G. Quinnett. il *Psychology Today* 23:46-7 Ap '89
Kind ears help some depressed patients [comparison of interpersonal psychotherapy with cognitive behavior therapy; work of Irene Elkin] *Science News* 136:365 D 2 '89
More than McTherapy [short term therapy] T. De Angelis. il *Psychology Today* 23:20+ Mr '89
Psychotherapy and science. B. Newman. por *The Humanist* 49:27-8+ Ja/F '89

PSYCHOTHERAPY—cont.

Short-term therapy: less can be more. B. Andrews. il *Working Woman* 14:71-2 F '89

When therapists talk crazy [use of paradoxical techniques] A. Rosenfeld. il *Psychology Today* 22:24-6 D '88

Why psychotherapy must be, and cannot be, a science. W. L. Trotta. por *The Humanist* 49:23-5+ S/O '89

PSYCHOTROPIC DRUGS *See* Psychopharmacology

PSYLLIUM

The breakfast drug [FDA reviews use of psyllim in cereal to determine if it is a food or drug] J. Newman. *American Health* 8:82+ D '89

Does this cereal belong in the medicine cabinet? [P&G claims that General Mills' cholesterol-reducing Benefit is a drug; Metamucil also contains psyllium] R. Mitchell and others. il *Business Week* p22-3 Jl 24 '89

Our thresh-hold to health. M. G. Stoddard. il *The Saturday Evening Post* 261:28-9 N/D '89

Psyllium beats cholesterol. il *Prevention (Emmaus, Pa.)* 41:9-10 D '89

PTA *See* Parents' and teachers' associations

PTARMIGANS

Tough little turncoat. G. Turbak. il *National Wildlife* 28:14-19 D '89/Ja '90

PTASHNE, MARK

How gene activators work. bibl il *Scientific American* 260:40-7 Ja '89

PTCA (PERCUTANEOUS TRANSLUMINAL CORONARY ANGIOPLASTY) *See* Arteries—Diseases—Therapy

PTEROSAURS

Standing pterosaurs on two feet [research by Christopher S. Bennett] R. Monastersky. *Science News* 136:318 N 11 '89

PTL NETWORK

The day of reckoning delayed [J. Bakker's bizarre behavior forces suspension of fraud trial] R. N. Ostling. il por *Time* 134:76-7 S 11 '89

A guilty evangelist [J. Bakker] B. Wickens. il por *Maclean's* 102:55-6 O 16 '89

Having a devil of a time [J. Bakker's trial] il por *Newsweek* 114:61 S 11 '89

Healing the church—after Bakker. T. C. Muck. il *Christianity Today* 33:16 N 17 '89

Jim & Tammy Faye Bakker. D. Barry. il pors *People Weekly* 32 Special Issue:70-1 Fall '89

Jim Bakker and the Eternal Revenue Service. G. Wacker. il pors *The Christian Century* 106:1053-5 N 15 '89

Judgment day [J. Bakker convicted of fraud] il por *Time* 134:65 O 16 '89

The living legacy of Jim Bakker [effects of PTL scandal on TV ministries] il por *U.S. News & World Report* 107:14 N 6 '89

New home for former PTL ministry. *Christianity Today* 33:60 My 12 '89

The remnants of PTL. K. A. Lawton. il por *Christianity Today* 33:36-8 O 6 '89

Trial and tribulation [J. Bakker] N. Underwood. il por *Maclean's* 102:63 S 11 '89

Unholy roller coaster [J. Bakker trial; cover story] M. Brower. il pors *People Weekly* 32:98-100+ S 18 '89

The wrath of "Maximum Bob" [J. Bakker's punishment raises questions over sentencing] A. L. Sanders. il por *Time* 134:62 N 6 '89

PTSD *See* Posttraumatic stress disorder

PU YI, 1906-1967

about

Postmodern tours. J. Krich. il por *Mother Jones* 14:42-4 Jl/Ag '89

PUBERTY

Beat the body blues: a personal primer. E. Karlsberg. il *'Teen* 33:32+ Ag '89

PUBLIC ACCESS CABLE TELEVISION *See* Cable television

PUBLIC ADJUSTERS *See* Insurance adjusters

PUBLIC ADMINISTRATION

See also

Bureaucracy

Crisis management in government

Decentralization in government

Local government

PUBLIC ART

See also

Art in Embassies (Program)

Mural painting and decoration, Exterior

1988 in review: public art. il *Art in America* 77:58-9 Ag '89

The great outdoors. M. Malone. il *Newsweek* 114:76+ O 23 '89

Of rusted walls and flying pigs. M. Horn. il *U.S. News & World Report* 106:57-8 Ap 10 '89

Our most notorious sculptor [R. Serra] D. Solomon. il *The New York Times Magazine* p38-41+ O 8 '89

The problems of going public. D. Hellekson. il *Utne Reader* p24-5 Mr/Ap '89

Public art and its inherent problems. D. Grant. *American Artist* 53:78-9+ O '89

Public rights and critics' failures. A. E. Elsen. il *Art News* 88:174 F '89

Space exploration [work of M. Miss] A. Berman. il pors *Art News* 88:130-5 N '89

Conservation and restoration

Public art and its inherent problems. D. Grant. *American Artist* 53:30+ N '89

Exhibitions

Street scenes [work of D. Adams] E. Heartney. bibl f il *Art in America* 77:230-7+ Ap '89

PUBLIC BATHS

Irradiation [visit to Russian Turkish Baths in New York City] *The New Yorker* 64:24 Ja 30 '89

PUBLIC BROADCASTING SERVICE

Beyond Masterpiece theater [independent productions] E. Hedegaard. il *Mother Jones* 14:49 O '89

Civil rights movement led Lawson to her PBS career [J. Lawson] *Jet* 77:38 D 18 '89

Film flam [J. Franklin-Trout's controversial PBS documentary Days of rage] S. Emerson. *The New Republic* 201:29-30+ S 18-25 '89

Public TV. il *TV Guide* 37:78-81 S 9-15 '89

PUBLIC BUILDINGS

See also

Library architecture

New York (N.Y.)—Public buildings

Petaluma (Calif.)—Public buildings

School buildings

Washington (D.C.)—Public buildings

Contracts and specifications

Lease-buy, lease-out, and friendly condemnations: the federal government tries new approaches on its new buildings. P. Hoffmann. il *Architectural Record* 177:29+ Mr '89

PUBLIC CITIZEN, INC.

NSF peer review under fire from Nader group. E. Marshall. *Science* 245:250 Jl 21 '89

PUBLIC COMFORT STATIONS

See also

Advertising mediums—Public comfort stations

New York (N.Y.)—Public comfort stations

Don't blame the toilet seat [views of Leonard Slater] il *USA Today (Periodical)* 118:16 O '89

PUBLIC DEBT *See* Debts, Public

PUBLIC DOCUMENTS *See* Government publications

PUBLIC ELECTRONIC NETWORK (SANTA MONICA, CALIF.: DATABASE)

Fighting city hall at 2400 baud. M. Antonoff. il *Personal Computing* 13:170-2 O '89

PUBLIC EMPLOYEES *See* Government employees

PUBLIC EMPLOYEES' RETIREMENT SYSTEM (CALIF.) *See* California. Public Employees' Retirement System

PUBLIC ENEMY (MUSICAL GROUP)

Def or dumb? L. Cole. il *Rolling Stone* p47-8+ O 19 '89

Loose cannon guns down Public Enemy. L. Cole. il *Rolling Stone* p24 Ag 10 '89

Public Enemy number one [S. Lee's reaction to anti-Semitic remarks made by Professor Griff] M. Horowitz. il por *American Film* 14:15 S '89

Unbelievable hype. M. DiLeo. il *Mother Jones* 14:10 F/Mr '89

PUBLIC FIGURES *See* Celebrities

PUBLIC FIGURES (LAW) *See* Publicity (Law)

PUBLIC FINANCE *See* Finance

PUBLIC HEALTH

See also

Artificial satellites—Public health use

Environmental health

Epidemics

Epidemiology

Food inspection

Health facilities

Infant mortality

Mass media and public health

Medical care

Medical policy

Medicine, Preventive

Mortality

Nutrition problems

Occupational health and safety

Public comfort stations

Quarantine

Railroads—Sanitation

Sexually transmitted diseases

Telephone in public health

At risk. P. C. Montgomery. il *Common Cause Magazine* 15:28-33 Mr/Ap '89

Better health through the fun factor [concept of civic health] R. Rodale. il *Prevention (Emmaus, Pa.)* 41:25-7 Jl '89

U.S. health: the good and the bad. *Science News* 135:188 Mr 25 '89

Conferences

See also

World Health Assembly

International aspects

See also

World Health Organization

Africa

Health in Africa: a pioneer's point of view [views of J. N. Togba] P. Stroot. il por *World Health* p30 Ap '89

PUBLIC OFFICERS—See also—*cont.*
  Children as public officers
  Conflict of interests (Public office)
  Congressmen
  Drugs and politicians
  Executives as public officers
  Politicians
  Senators
  United States—Executive departments
  United States. Cabinet
  Women public officers
Public service in America [address, January 9, 1989] G. P. Shultz. *Department of State Bulletin* 89:1-4 Mr '89
Appointment, qualifications, etc.
Bush makes some science appointments. B. J. Culliton and E. Marshall. il por *Science* 243:24 Ja 6 '89
Experienced conservatives for Bush. E. J. Feulner. il *The American Spectator* 22:28-9 Ja '89
Help wanted: 3,000 appointees. Right-wing purity not required. R. Fly. *Business Week* p49 Ja 23 '89
How Bush is keeping the radical right inside the tent. R. Fly. il *Business Week* p45 Je 19 '89
How to spread Potomac fever [Fortune poll] A. Deutschman. il *Fortune* 120:84-5 Ag 14 '89
Seeing Crimson [Harvard graduates as Bush appointees] D. Wisenberg. il *Common Cause Magazine* 15:7 S/O '89
Staffing a new president. C. M. Brauer. *Current (Washington, D.C.)* 310:28-35 F '89
Who wants to work in Washington? R. E. Norton. il *Fortune* 120:77-80+ Ag 14 '89
Who's who in the administration. See issues of The Washington Monthly
Anecdotes, facetiae, satire, etc.
Jockey, scheme and pray. S. Waldman. il *Newsweek* 113:24 Ap 3 '89
So you want to be a deputy assistant secretary. S. Sturtivant, III. *National Review* 41:45 F 10 '89
Biography
Cashing in on kiss-and-tell. M. Greenfield. il *Newsweek* 113:70 Ja 23 '89
Ethics
See Political ethics
Psychiatric care
High anxiety [Washington, D.C. psychiatrists treat politicians] D. Baldwin. il *Common Cause Magazine* 15:34-8 Jl/Ag '89
Religious life
Inside the Bible Beltway [political figures active in prayer groups] R. N. Ostling. il *Time* 133:56-7 F 6 '89
Nurturing faith in the nation's capital. T. Eastland. il por *Christianity Today* 33:27-8 Ja 13 '89
Serving God and man in the nation's capital [interview with F. E. Young] il por *Christianity Today* 33:45 S 8 '89
Resignation
The revolving door. S. Waldman. il *Newsweek* 113:16-18 F 6 '89
Salaries, allowances, etc.
Federal pay: only top-to-bottom reform will do. G. S. Becker. il *Business Week* p19 F 13 '89
Just say no. *The New Republic* 200:7-9 F 6 '89
Ralph Nader's big mistake [views on underpaying top career officials] R. J. Samuelson. il *Newsweek* 113:51 Mr 20 '89
Sitting pretty [chairs of government officials] V. Novak. il *Common Cause Magazine* 15:7 Mr/Ap '89
What Lloyd Cutler could learn from Acme Widget: target pay increases to jobs that are hard to fill. B. Frye. *The Washington Monthly* 21:18-22 Jl/Ag '89
Sexual behavior
Hookers aren't the only ones for sale [P. Bordes prostitution scandal in Great Britain] B. Amiel. il *Maclean's* 102:9 My 8 '89
More sex please, we're British [sex scandal involving P. Bordes and various government officials and newspaper editors] A. Stanley. il pors *Time* 133:31 Ap 3 '89
Raising an uncommon furor in the Commons, powerful Brits heed an Indian love call [role of P. Bordes in sex scandal] P. Chin. il pors *People Weekly* 31:52-3 Ap 3 '89
Should public officials' private lives matter? [interviews with G. L. Bauer and L. Sabato] il *U.S. News & World Report* 107:23 S 11 '89
Strange bedfellows [P. Bordes sparks sex and politics scandal in Britain] A. Phillips. il por *Maclean's* 102:31+ Ap 3 '89
Canada
See also
Canada. Cabinet
Great Britain
Hookers aren't the only ones for sale [P. Bordes prostitution scandal] B. Amiel. il *Maclean's* 102:9 My 8 '89
More sex please, we're British [sex scandal involving P. Bordes and various government officials and newspaper editors] A. Stanley. il pors *Time* 133:31 Ap 3 '89

Raising an uncommon furor in the Commons, powerful Brits heed an Indian love call [role of P. Bordes in sex scandal] P. Chin. il pors *People Weekly* 31:52-3 Ap 3 '89
Strange bedfellows [P. Bordes sparks sex and politics scandal] A. Phillips. il por *Maclean's* 102:31+ Ap 3 '89
United States
See Public officers

PUBLIC OPINION
See also
  Abortion—Public opinion
  Afghanistan—Russian invasion, 1979-1989—Public opinion
  Alzheimer's disease—Public opinion
  Canada—Foreign opinion—American
  Child welfare—Public opinion
  Chiropractic—Public opinion
  Crime and criminals—Public opinion
  Disarmament—Public opinion
  Environmental policy—Public opinion
  Exxon Valdez (Ship) oil spill, 1989—Public opinion
  Family—Public opinion
  Genetic research—Public opinion
  Germany—Foreign opinion—American
  Great Britain—Foreign opinion—American
  Iran-contra affair—Public opinion
  Israel—Foreign opinion—American
  Israel-Arab Wars, 1967- —Public opinion
  Japan—Foreign opinion—American
  Lebanon hostage cases, 1984- —Public opinion
  Legalization of narcotics—Public opinion
  Nuclear weapons—Public opinion
  Nurses and nursing—Public opinion
  Political attitudes
  Public opinion polls
  Radioactive waste disposal—Public opinion
  Rumor
  Soviet Union—Foreign opinion—American
  Space research—Public opinion
  Tiananmen Square (China) student occupation, 1989—Public opinion
  United States—Foreign opinion
  Vietnamese War, 1957-1975—Public opinion
The 21st annual Gallup poll of the public's attitudes toward the public schools. S. M. Elam and A. Gallup. il *Phi Delta Kappan* 71:41-54 S '89
The attitudes behind American exceptionalism. B. J. Wattenberg. il *U.S. News & World Report* 107:25 Ag 7 '89
Business week/Harris poll. See occasional issues of Business Week
Economic predictions: personal future seems brightest [Gallup poll] B. Fischman. il *Psychology Today* 23:16 O '89
The new American dream [survey results; cover story] D. Yankelovich and J. Gurin. il *American Health* 8:63-7 Mr '89
New race relations poll reveals widely varying views of blacks, whites. *Jet* 77:12-13 N 13 '89
Personal satisfaction rises [Gallup poll] *Society* 26:2-3 Mr/Ap '89
The ten great wants of 1989 [survey of readers] N. Perrin. il *Country Journal* 16:17-19 Jl/Ag '89
Tracking America's soul [interview with G. Gallup] T. K. Jones. il pors *Christianity Today* 33:22-5 N 17 '89
Canada
See also
Poland—Foreign opinion—Canadian
United States—Foreign opinion—Canadian
A spotlight on Canadians [Maclean's/Decima poll; cover story; special section; with introd. by Allan R. Gregg and editorial comment by Kevin Doyle] il *Maclean's* 102:2, 8-20+ Ja 2 '89
Chile
See also
United States—Foreign opinion—Chilean
France
See also
Algeria—Foreign opinion—French
Germany (West)
See also
United States—Foreign opinion—German
Great Britain
See also
Soviet Union—Foreign opinion—British
United States—Foreign opinion—British
Japan
See also
United States—Foreign opinion—Japanese
Poland
See also
United States—Foreign opinion—Polish
Soviet Union
See also
United States—Foreign opinion—Russian
United States
See Public opinion
Western Europe
See also
United States—Foreign opinion—European

PUBLIC OPINION POLLS
Combining cognitive and statistical approaches to survey design. S. E. Fienberg and J. M. Tanur. bibl f il *Science* 243:1017-22 F 24 '89
Reporting what we think: the pollsters. M. Stanton. il *Occupational Outlook Quarterly* 33:12-19 Spr '89
White lies, bad polls [white voters misinforming pollsters concerning black candidates] *Time* 134:56 N 20 '89
PUBLIC POLICY ANALYSIS *See* Policy sciences
PUBLIC PROSECUTORS
    See also
    Attorneys general
    Giuliani, Rudolph W.
    Hudson, Henry E.
    Valukas, Anton
Prosecuting environmental crimes [address, July 17, 1989] S. Harshbarger. *Vital Speeches of the Day* 55:760-3 O 1 '89
Canada
The cost of patronage [privatizing public prosecutors] P. Kaihla. il *Maclean's* 102:17 D 11 '89
PUBLIC RELATIONS
    See also
    Agriculture—Public relations
    Art galleries and museums—Public relations
    Business—Public relations
    Drug industry—Public relations
    Farmers—Public relations
    Fur industry—Public relations
    Home-based business—Public relations
    Petroleum industry—Public relations
    Publicity
    Railroads—Public relations
    School and the community
    Sports—Public relations
    Tobacco industry—Public relations
    Videotapes—Press releases
    Women in public relations
Anecdotes, facetiae, satire, etc.
He's back!!! [public relations consultants offer advice for the Second Coming of Jesus Christ; cover story] il *Harper's* 278:47-55 Ap '89
Of many things [public relations for Christ's Second Coming] G. W. Hunt. *America* 160:282 Ap 1 '89
International aspects
Public relations in the coming global economy [address, July 25, 1989] J. Paluszek. *Vital Speeches of the Day* 56:22-6 O 15 '89
PUBLIC RELATIONS AND POLITICS
    See also
    Advertising, Political
    Government publicity
    Presidents—Public relations
PUBLIC RELATIONS CONSULTANTS
    See also
    Roberta Greene & Associates, Inc.
Professional ethics
Public relations and ethical leadership [address, June 15, 1989] J. Paluszek. *Vital Speeches of the Day* 55:747-50 O 1 '89
Great Britain
    See also
    Shandwick plc
PUBLIC SCHOOL AND COLLEGE COOPERATION *See* Educational cooperation
PUBLIC SCHOOL CHOICE *See* School choice
PUBLIC SCHOOLS
    See also
    Education
    Education and state
    High schools
    Junior high schools
    Magnet schools
    Middle schools
    Satellite learning centers
    School districts
    Voucher plan in education
The 21st annual Gallup poll of the public's attitudes toward the public schools. S. M. Elam and A. Gallup. il *Phi Delta Kappan* 71:41-54 S '89
The blackboard jungle revisited. G. Morris. *National Review* 41:18-19 My 5 '89
The case against Joe Nocera [exodus of white middle class from public schools] J. Nocera. *The Washington Monthly* 21:22-4+ F '89
How to help America's schools [Fortune's second education summit] N. J. Perry. il *Fortune* 120:137-40+ D 4 '89
Institutional democracy in the public schools. M. A. Raywid. *The Education Digest* 55:8-10 D '89
Issues on four-year-olds and public schooling. S. Lubeck. *The Education Digest* 55:21-4 O '89
Multiple choice. L. H. Lapham. *Harper's* 278:12-15 Mr '89
Saving the schools: how business can help. N. J. Perry. *Current (Washington, D.C.)* 310:20-6 F '89
The second Gallup/Phi Delta Kappa poll of teachers' attitudes toward the public schools [with editorial comment by Pauline B. Gough] S. M. Elam. il *Phi Delta Kappan* 70:746, 785-98 Je '89

Sizing up your local school. N. Henderson. il *Changing Times* 43:101-2+ N '89
We can educate all our children [urban public schools] C. Clayton. *The Nation* 249:132-5 Jl 24-31 '89
Censorship
    See Censorship
Desegregation
    See also
    Busing for school integration
    Magnet schools
Affirmative reaction [dissatisfaction with desegregation plan in Kansas City, Mo.] R. Nadler and T. Donelson. il *National Review* 41:28-9 S 15 '89
After busing: education and choice. D. J. Armor. *Current (Washington, D.C.)* 316:14-20 O '89
Brown plus 35 [Brown v. Board of Education] R. Kennedy. *The Nation* 248:725 My 29 '89
A star shines from Alabama [successful integration in Demopolis] A. Waldron. il *The Nation* 248:664-6 My 15 '89
When desegregation backfires [black parents sue the state to pay for private schools because magnet plan is not working; Kansas City, Mo.] P. King. il *Newsweek* 114:56 Jl 31 '89
Finance
    See Education—Finance
Segregation
Ark. to pay $118 mil. in school bias settlement. *Jet* 75:10 Mr 20 '89
Uniforms
    See School uniforms
PUBLIC SCHOOLS, CHOICE OF *See* School choice
PUBLIC SCHOOLS AND BUSINESS *See* Business and education
PUBLIC SCHOOLS AND POLITICS *See* Politics and education
PUBLIC SCHOOLS AND RELIGION
An apple for the parents [Christian involvement] T. K. Jones. il *Christianity Today* 33:14 S 22 '89
Candlemess. M. E. Marty. *The Christian Century* 106:95 Ja 25 '89
The child becomes the victim. J. R. Joelson. *The Humanist* 49:35-6 N/D '89
Even in high school [freedom of religious speech] N. Hentoff. il *The Progressive* 53:13-14 Ag '89
The "Good Book" gets a bad rap in school. K. Blomquist. il *Christianity Today* 33:52 F 3 '89
Holiday guidelines [brochure Religious holidays in the public schools: questions and answers] *Christianity Today* 33:70 N 17 '89
Prayers ignore court ban [prayers before football games] B. Wilburn. il *Christianity Today* 33:38 N 3 '89
Public schools and the road to religious neutrality. D. A. Spiro. bibl f il *Phi Delta Kappan* 70:759-63 Je '89
Religion goes back to school. T. C. Muck. *Christianity Today* 33:17 My 12 '89
School prayer [results of poll] I. Groller. il *Parents* 64:28 S '89
Teaching religious liberty—the wrong way [Williamsburg Charter curriculum supplements for U.S. history courses] E. Doerr. il *The Humanist* 49:41-2 N/D '89
Throwing God for a loss [prayer ban at high school football games] F. Trippett. il *Time* 134:34 S 18 '89
Upholding students' religious freedom [Supreme Court to hear arguments on access of student religious groups to public school facilities] S. Levicoff. *The Christian Century* 106:1108-9 N 29 '89
Where to draw the line. D. Robinson. *The Humanist* 49:35 Ja/F '89
PUBLIC SCHOOLS AND SOCIAL AND ECONOMIC PROBLEMS *See* School and social and economic problems
PUBLIC SERVICE ADVERTISING *See* Advertising, Public service
PUBLIC SERVICE CO. OF N. H.
Back from the dead. il *Forbes* 143:134 Ja 9 '89
PSNH: down to the last lines in Chapter 11. L. Jereski. il *Business Week* p36 O 2 '89
PUBLIC SERVICE TELEVISION PROGRAMS *See* Television broadcasting—Public service programs
PUBLIC SPEAKING
    See also
    Rhetoric
How to be sure your speech is a success [excerpt from Powerspeak] D. Leeds. *Working Woman* 14:98-9 Mr '89
How to grab—and hold—an audience. D. H. Dunn. il *Business Week* p118 Ap 3 '89
How to stay cool under fire [excerpt from Get to the point] K. Berg and A. Gilman. il *Working Woman* 14:41+ N '89
Leave them laughing [humorous speeches] M. B. Marklein. il *Nation's Business* 77:49 O '89
Putting your best self forward [views of L. Brown] S. Nelton. il pors *Nation's Business* 77:46-7 Ag '89
Scared speechless? How to conquer your fear of the podium. E. J. Belzer. *Working Woman* 14:17+ F '89
Speaking at length [presentations that run too long] J. Cairns. *BioScience* 39:632-3 O '89
Speaking up! B. Nievens. il *Essence* 19:120 F '89

PUBLIC SPEAKING—cont.

Anecdotes, facetiae, satire, etc.
Public freaking. B. Ehrenreich. por *Ms.* 18:40-1 S '89

Fees
Fast money on the rubber chicken circuit. W. E. Sheeline. il *Fortune* 119:8 Mr 13 '89

Study and teaching
Aid for improving public-speaking skills. F. Roberts. *Parents* 64:60-1 Ap '89

PUBLIC TELEVISION *See* Television broadcasting, Public
PUBLIC TRANSPORTATION *See* Local transit
PUBLIC UTILITIES
See also
   Electric utilities
   Gas utilities
   Pacific Gas & Electric Co.

Laws and regulations
Public utilities in transition [address, November 8, 1988] S. W. Hulett. *Vital Speeches of the Day* 55:211-14 Ja 15 '89

Securities
See also
   Prudential-Bache Utility Fund
Good as gold isn't so good these days. T. Segal and G. Weiss. il *Business Week* p116 Je 5 '89
Investors can hook up with utilities for a low-risk total return of 11% or more. M. Sivy. il *Money* 18:59+ O '89

Taxation
Urge your senators to act on campaign finance reform [House Ways and Means Committee vetoes proposal for consumer rebates from utilities] *Common Cause Magazine* 15:31 N/D '89
PUBLIC WELFARE
See also
   Child welfare
   Day care—Federal aid
   Domicile in public welfare
   Income maintenance programs
   Legal Services Corporation
   Old age assistance
   United States. Office of Economic Opportunity
   Welfare hotels
   Workfare
Fighting poverty after Reagan. J. Walsh. il *The Nation* 248:336-9 Mr 13 '89
Getting on with it [welfare reform and education] A. C. Lewis. il *Phi Delta Kappan* 70:428-9 F '89
Hell on wheels [excerpt from Don't worry, he won't get far on foot] J. Callahan. il por *Mother Jones* 14:38-40+ My '89
How one bill became law [welfare-reform bill] S. Manning. il *Scholastic Update (Teachers' edition)* 121:15-16 F 24 '89
Losing more ground. E. Rubenstein. il *National Review* 41:13 My 19 '89
The new welfare bill: when more isn't enough. R. D. Hylton. *Black Enterprise* 19:21 Ja '89
Of many things [Ford Foundation's report entitled The common good: social welfare and the American future] J. W. Donohue. *America* 161:26 Jl 15-22 '89
The powers that free [single mother gets off welfare]; ed. by Bebe Moore Campbell. I. Vanzant. il por *Essence* 20:80-2+ O '89
The racialization of poverty. M. B. Wilkerson and J. H. Gresham. il *The Nation* 249:126-30+ Jl 24-31 '89
Reforming social welfare policy [Ford Foundation report] il *Children Today* 18:2-3 Jl/Ag '89
Revenge of the softheads. M. Kaus. *The New Republic* 200:24+ Je 19 '89
The unfinished war (II) [L. Johnson, R. Nixon and the War on Poverty] N. Lemann. il *The Atlantic* 263:52-6+ Ja '89
Watch what you call welfare. M. Kaus. *The Washington Monthly* 21:45-6 Mr '89
Welfare and workfare: a dispute [discussion of December 14, 1988 article, Blinded by metaphor: churches and welfare reform] R. S. Bachelder. *The Christian Century* 106:419-21 Ap 19 '89

Anecdotes, facetiae, satire, etc.
Those welfare bankers. N. Folbre. por *Newsweek* 114:17 O 16 '89

International aspects
Analyzing the welfare system [address, October 29, 1988] W. Block. *Vital Speeches of the Day* 55:333-7 Mr 15 '89

British Columbia
Analyzing the welfare system [address, October 29, 1988] W. Block. *Vital Speeches of the Day* 55:333-7 Mr 15 '89

California
See also
   Los Angeles (Calif.)—Public welfare
Denmark
When the bough breaks. M. Rose. il *Maclean's* 102:42 Ja 9 '89

Maine
The pain of poverty [contrasting single mothers on welfare in Maine and Nova Scotia] G. Allen. il *Maclean's* 102:38-9 Jl 3 '89

Michigan
See also
   LIFE Program

Minnesota
See also
   Minnesota. Dept. of Human Services
Nova Scotia
The pain of poverty [contrasting single mothers on welfare in Maine and Nova Scotia] G. Allen. il *Maclean's* 102:38-9 Jl 3 '89

Wisconsin
Welfare migrants: getting a cold shoulder in Wisconsin. J. N. Baker. il *Newsweek* 114:23 Ag 14 '89
PUBLIC WORKS
See also
   Dams
   Water resources development
Crumbling roads and bridges: their heavy toll on the economy. G. Koretz. il *Business Week* p18 Ag 7 '89
Good news about infrastructure. N. J. Perry. il *Fortune* 119:94-6+ Ap 10 '89
New streets, paved with gold [investing in public works] J. M. Laderman. il *Business Week* p92-3 O 16 '89
Our crumbling infrastructure [cover story] J. C. Szabo. il *Nation's Business* 77:16-18+ Ag '89
Seeking a solid payoff in crumbling public works. J. Friedman. *Business Week* p116 S 4 '89

Contracts and specifications
Watch out for this new "model" owner/design-professional agreement. A. Kornblut. il por *Architectural Record* 177:29+ F '89
The whole building industry heats up over new contracts for public work. P. Hoffmann. *Architectural Record* 177:31 S '89

Federal aid
Defense savings could help rescue our crumbling bridges [views of Richard B. Du Boff] G. Koretz. *Business Week* p26 N 27 '89

Arizona
See also
   Central Arizona Project

Japan
U.S. contractors finally break ground in Tokyo. N. Usui and N. Gross. il *Business Week* p56 Ap 3 '89
PUBLICATION DATE (BOOKS)
Berkley loses in appeals court over 'Red October' [suit by Naval Institute Press] M. Reuter. *Publishers Weekly* 235:9 Je 9 '89
PUBLICISTS, PUBLISHING *See* Books—Advertising
PUBLICITY
See also
   Advertising
   Government publicity
The art of the deals. J. Alter. il *Newsweek* 113:58-9 Ja 9 '89
PUBLICITY (LAW)
They are hip, hot—and dead [late celebrities used in advertising] J. Hammer and K. Springen. il *Newsweek* 114:34 Jl 10 '89
PUBLICITY (POLITICAL) *See* Advertising, Political
PUBLICKER INDUSTRIES INC.
Liquid assets [Drexel Burnham's backing] M. Schifrin. il *Forbes* 143:48 F 20 '89
PUBLISH IT! (DESKTOP PUBLISHING PROGRAM) *See* Desktop publishing—Programming
PUBLISHERS AND AUTHORS *See* Authors and publishers
PUBLISHERS AND BOOKSELLERS *See* Booksellers and publishers
PUBLISHERS AND COLLEGE TEACHERS *See* College teachers and publishers
PUBLISHERS AND LIBRARIES *See* Libraries and publishers
PUBLISHERS AND PUBLISHING
See also
   Alternative press
   Andrews & McMeel
   Atlantic Monthly Press
   Authors and publishers
   Ballantine Books, Inc.
   Bantam Doubleday Dell Publishing Group Inc.
   Best sellers
   Black Sparrow Press
   Blacks in publishing
   Book packagers
   Books—Marketing
   Books—Prices
   Carol Publishing Group
   Catalogs, Publishers'
   Catbird Press
   Chronicle Books
   Chronicle Publications Inc.
   College teachers—Publications
   College teachers and publishers
   Computers—Publishing use
   Consumer Reports Books (Firm)

PUBLISHERS AND PUBLISHING—See also—*cont.*

Contemporary Books, Inc.
Cornelia & Michael Bessie Books
Dalkey Archive Press
Delacorte Press
Dodd, Mead & Co.
Donald I. Fine, Inc.
Doubleday & Company, Inc.
Dow Jones & Co., Inc.
E. P. Dutton & Company, Inc.
Editors and editing
Facts on File, Inc.
Farrar Straus & Giroux, Inc.
Four Walls Eight Windows (Firm)
Graywolf Press
Grove Weidenfeld (Firm)
GuildAmerica Books
Gulf & Western, Inc.
Harcourt Brace Jovanovich, Inc.
Harper & Row Publishers, Inc.
Hay House (Firm)
Hearst Trade Book Group
Henry Holt and Company
Hill & Wang, Inc.
Houghton Mifflin Co.
Information systems—Publishing use
John F. Blair, Publisher
John Wiley & Sons, Inc.
Kodansha International USA Ltd.
Libraries and publishers
Literary agencies and agents
Macfadden Holdings, Inc.
Macmillan, Inc.
MasterMedia Ltd.
McGraw-Hill, Inc.
Naval Institute Press
New Era Publications
New York Times Company
Penguin USA (Firm)
Peregrine Smith Books
Pocket Books
Prentice Hall Press
Price/Stern/Sloan, Inc.
Printing industry
Publication date (Books)
Random House Inc.
Reader's Digest Association, Inc.
Real Comet Press
Regnery Gateway, Inc.
Riverrun Press Inc.
Rodale Press, Inc.
Routledge, Chapman & Hall
Scholarly publishing
Scribner Book Companies, Inc.
Self publishing
Serial publication of books
Shaw Publishing
Simon & Schuster Inc.
Soho Press Inc.
Spirit That Moves Us Press
Stein & Day
Summit Books
Thunder's Mouth Press Inc.
Time Inc.
Time Warner Trade Publishing
Times Books
Turner Publishing Inc.
University presses
Venture Lifestyles Publishing Company
Videotapes—Publishing use
Viking Penguin Inc.
Viking Press Inc.
Villard Books
W. H. Smith Publishers Inc.
Warner Books Inc.
Washington Post Co.
Watermark Press
Western Publishing Group, Inc.
Whittle Communications Limited Partnership
William Morrow & Co., Inc.
Windgate Press
Women in publishing
Youth as publishers

1988: the year in review [special section] il *Publishers Weekly* 235:23-30+ Mr 10 '89
Avoiding New York publishers: why some West Coast authors do it. L. See. *Publishers Weekly* 235:55 Ap 28 '89
Independent publishing. J. Barbato. See occasional issues of Publishers Weekly beginning October 23, 1987
Letter from the Midwest. T. Unsworth. See occasional issues of Publishers Weekly beginning March 21, 1986
Looking back on '88 [special section] il *Publishers Weekly* 235:37-55 Ja 6 '89
Mistah Perkins—he dead: publishing today. G. Howard. *The American Scholar* 58:355-69 Summ '89
Nashville: the South's booming book city. B. Summer. il *Publishers Weekly* 236:26+ D 15 '89

The new! improved! trade book crisis. G. Van der Leun. por *Publishers Weekly* 236:42-3 D 15 '89
News of the week. M. Reuter and M. Yen. See issues of Publishers Weekly
On writing: let there be less. A. Krystal. il *The New York Times Book Review* 94:1+ Mr 26 '89
Scaling the small press hurdle: getting titles onto the shelves. M. Jones. il *Publishers Weekly* 235:37-41 Ap 14 '89
Small has never looked so beautiful. E. Pomice. il *U.S. News & World Report* 106:49+ Ja 9 '89
Southern spotlight. B. Summer. See occasional issues of Publishers Weekly beginning January 20, 1984
State of the business [views of senior executives] M. Reuter and C. Reid. *Publishers Weekly* 236:14-16 S 29 '89
Struggles of small publishers [special section] il *Publishers Weekly* 235:23-4+ Ap 14 '89
Talk of the trade. L. Fleischer. See issues of Publishers Weekly
Trade news. See issues of Publishers Weekly
West watch. L. See. See occasional issues of Publishers Weekly beginning September 2, 1983

Acquisitions and mergers

Fitting into the conglomerate picture [children's imprints] R. Burroughs. il *Publishers Weekly* 236:138-40 Jl 28 '89
Green leaves as Grove, Weidenfeld merge. *Publishers Weekly* 235:14 My 19 '89
Harper & Row buys Scott, Foresman for $455 million. C. Reid. *Publishers Weekly* 236:8 D 8 '89
KKR to buy Macmillan Book Clubs and Intertec for $310 million. *Publishers Weekly* 235:16 Je 16 '89
Living out every manager's dream [buying and then selling off former CBS magazine group] P. G. Diamandis. il por *Fortune* 120:109+ O 9 '89
Mead tries a new-fangled medium: print [acquisition of Michie Co.] M. Mallory. il *Business Week* p81-2 Ap 10 '89
Penguin USA to acquire W. H. Smith Publishers. il *Publishers Weekly* 236:10 S 29 '89
Time-Warner link pleases book principals. *Publishers Weekly* 235:10+ Mr 17 '89

International aspects

Craig to head all Murdoch book business; Chapman resigns from Collins; authors' reaction uncertain. por *Publishers Weekly* 235:10+ F 3 '89
Houghton Mifflin to acquire Gollancz. M. Reuter and V. Menkes. *Publishers Weekly* 236:10 O 13 '89
Murdoch wins Collins, promises autonomy; Craig assesses Harper's new owner. V. Menkes. *Publishers Weekly* 235:16+ Ja 20 '89
RH-Century deal creates major U.K. trade group. V. Menkes. *Publishers Weekly* 235:9 Je 23 '89

International aspects—Anecdotes, facetiae, satire, etc.

1988: everybody's going global. R. Curtis. *Publishers Weekly* 235:41 Ja 6 '89

France

French trade publisher Belfond joins Masson medical group. H. R. Lottman. *Publishers Weekly* 236:11 N 17 '89

Great Britain

Loss of Bodley Head fuels U.K. disquiet over conglomeration. V. Menkes. *Publishers Weekly* 236:8 Jl 7 '89
Penguin Group sells Sphere to Maxwell's Macdonald Publishing. V. Menkes. *Publishers Weekly* 235:40 Ap 7 '89
With a lineup like this, who needs charisma? [Reed International buys Travel Information Group] M. Maremont. il por *Business Week* p59 My 22 '89

Italy

A firestorm scorches De Benedetti's media empire [Arnoldo Mondadori Editore] J. Rossant. il pors *Business Week* p68 D 25 '89-Ja 1 '90

Adventure stories

Action! Adventure! Sales! [men's adventure series] D. E. Showalter. il *Publishers Weekly* 235:20-2+ My 5 '89

Advertising

See Books—Advertising

American literature

See also
Library of America (Firm)

Antitrust cases

Chain reaction [FTC charges that bookstore chains get preferential treatment from publishers] C. Goodrich. *The Nation* 248:596-8 My 1 '89
Pocket and Warner announce retail incentive plans [end of antitrust campaign by independent bookstores] J. Mutter. *Publishers Weekly* 235:19-20 Ja 6 '89
Six houses win one point in first FTC skirmish [charge that chains get preferential treatment not accorded independent bookstores] H. Fields. *Publishers Weekly* 235:14 Ap 21 '89
Six publishers charged with price bias by FTC [policies favoring bookstore chains over independents] *Publishers Weekly* 235:19 Ja 6 '89

Art

Reflective art—a new system paints with light [Gamma One transparencies capture full tonal range] J. P. Frank. il *Publishers Weekly* 235:69 Mr 3 '89

Art literature

See also
Abbeville Press Inc.

PUBLISHERS AND PUBLISHING—Art literature—*cont.*
Art books—from accordian-fold to electronic imaging. J. P. Frank. il *Publishers Weekly* 236:54+ S 1 '89
The new look in art books. B. Braun. il *Publishers Weekly* 236:12-14+ S 1 '89

Associations
See also
British Publishers Association
Evangelical Christian Publishers Association
Publishers Association of the South

Australian literature
See also
Australian Book Source (Firm)
Australian books in the U.S.: two small companies find success. il *Publishers Weekly* 235:38-40 Mr 24 '89

Automobile literature
See also
Brooklands Books (Firm)

Awards
See also
Carey-Thomas Awards

Backlist books
Hidden supersellers: backlist books whose annual sales rival frontlist topsellers. J. Appelbaum. *Publishers Weekly* 235:53-5 Mr 10 '89
Hidden supersellers II: more backlist books with annual sales rivaling frontlist topsellers. J. Appelbaum. il *Publishers Weekly* 236:36-7 D 22 '89
Tentative pact gives BookCrafters control of Stein & Day backlist. C. Reid. *Publishers Weekly* 235:12 F 17 '89

Bibliography
Writers and the market—II. C. Goodrich. *The Nation* 249:24-6+ Jl 3 '89

Biography
Library of America considers publication of biographies. J. P. Frank. *Publishers Weekly* 235:15 My 19 '89

Biological literature
Why a book? Changes in biology-book publishing. J. A. Miller. bibl f il *BioScience* 39:180-3 Mr '89

Black literature
See also
Black Classic Press
Better times for black writers? W. Nixon. il *Publishers Weekly* 235:35-40 F 17 '89
Book marks. P. Giddings. il *Essence* 19:26 Mr '89

Business literature
See also
American City Business Journals, Inc.
Currency (Firm)
The buying binge in business books. C. Knowlton. il *Fortune* 119:101-3 F 13 '89
Ross Perot as literary critic. J. Queenan. il *Forbes* 143:90+ Ap 17 '89

Children's literature
See also
Green Tiger Press
Just-Us-Books
Kane/Miller Book Publishers
Kar-Ben Copies Inc.
Odyssey Paperbacks (Firm)
Sports Illustrated for Kids Books
Children's book publishing in Australia: a lively business. R. Sessions. il *Publishers Weekly* 235:35-7 Mr 24 '89
Children's books: flourishing [Quebec] M. Colin. *Publishers Weekly* 235:30 My 19 '89
Fall 1989 children's books [special section] D. E. Roback and K. O. Fakih. il *Publishers Weekly* 236:131-43+ Jl 28 '89
Spring 1989 children's books [special section] D. E. Roback and K. O. Fakih. il *Publishers Weekly* 235:132-43+ F 24 '89
Tying up the talent: exclusivity deals and brand name publishing [illustrator contracts] K. O. Fakih. *Publishers Weekly* 235:39+ My 19 '89

Chinese literature
Ballantine's new translations of Chinese classics. M. Wu. *Publishers Weekly* 236:58-9 O 6 '89

Computer literature
The volatile world of computer books. C. T. Anthony. il *Publishers Weekly* 236:17-18+ N 24 '89

Condensed books
See also
Reader's Digest Condensed Books
Time-Life Book Digest

Conferences
Aspen Forum: looking toward 2000. J. R. Moskin. *Publishers Weekly* 235:28-9 Ap 21 '89
Vitale assails chain returns, mega-advances, over-production; U.K. speaker warns of EEC conflicts. J. F. Baker and D. Maryles. *Publishers Weekly* 236:15-16 Jl 14 '89

Cookbooks
The changing style in cookbooks. M. Jones. il *Publishers Weekly* 236:15-16+ S 8 '89
The flavor of a place [community and regional cookbooks] L. Saunders. il *Publishers Weekly* 236:26+ S 8 '89
How the classics shape up for the '90s. C. T. Anthony. il *Publishers Weekly* 236:20+ S 8 '89

Medici culinary Renaissance comes to Fawcett. il *Publishers Weekly* 236:43-4 S 8 '89
Reading food: there's a mythological construct in my soup [university presses] B. H. Fussell. il *The New York Times Book Review* 94:36 S 24 '89
Sampling a cookbook manuscript [authors of The simple secrets of Vietnamese cooking invite prospective publishers to a buffet] D. Brainard. *Publishers Weekly* 236:33 S 8 '89
Workman storms the culinary Bastille [P. Well's Bistro cooking] M. Simson. *Publishers Weekly* 236:44 S 8 '89

Cooperation
Berkley, First and CMG join to revive Classics illustrated. B. Levine. il *Publishers Weekly* 236:48 N 24 '89
Four houses join forces to publicize the plight of the world's refugees [Forced out by C. Kismaric] il *Publishers Weekly* 235:42-3 Mr 24 '89
PSP cooperative ventures. G. Feldman. *Publishers Weekly* 236:30 O 13 '89

Detective and mystery stories
Dutton hopes to make a killing with Spillane's latest Mike Hammer. il *Publishers Weekly* 236:59 O 6 '89
Morrow to release first new Perry Mason novel in 15 years [authored by T. Chastain] *Publishers Weekly* 235:66+ F 3 '89
The sisterhood of sleuths [mysteries by and about women] E. Gibson. il *Publishers Weekly* 235:37-9 My 5 '89

Dictionaries
The dictionary factory [Oxford University Press] I. Shenker. *The New Yorker* 65:86-100 Ap 3 '89

Educational literature
See also
Macmillan/McGraw-Hill School Publishing Company
Peoples Publishing Group
Publishers and publishing—Textbooks
'Eclectic' AAP/West seminar on information publishing. K. Richardson. il *Publishers Weekly* 236:15 N 24 '89

Employees
See also
Blacks in publishing
Collective labor agreements—Publishers and publishing
About new brooms and musical chairs. V. Cobb. por *Publishers Weekly* 236:36 D 8 '89
Felicitations [job changes] il *Publishers Weekly* 235:40-1 Ja 6 '89
Have laser gun, Ballantine reps will travel—faster and smarter [speeding inventory and ordering] J. Mutter. il *Publishers Weekly* 235:53-5 F 17 '89
Saul Gilman: his own salesman [Simon & Schuster vp/sales rep] J. Rosen. por *Publishers Weekly* 235:108+ Ja 20 '89
Salaries, pensions, etc.
Where the money is [salary survey] J. F. Baker. il *Publishers Weekly* 236:17-21 S 29 '89

Encyclopedias
See also
F.E. Compton Company
Grolier Incorporated

Ethical aspects
Kickbacks in university textbook adoptions. R. B. McKenzie. *BioScience* 39:326-7 My '89

Finance
1988 revenue growth for public firms sinks to five-year low. *Publishers Weekly* 236:8-9 D 8 '89
Big books, big bucks. P. Painton. il *Time* 133:44-6 Je 12 '89
Budget aids education, hampers libraries [effects on publishers] H. Fields. *Publishers Weekly* 235:330 Ja 27 '89
Communications media. L. Gubernick. il *Forbes* 143:111-12 Ja 9 '89
Let's keep—and use—our heads. J. F. Baker. *Publishers Weekly* 236:12 D 15 '89
Money: the curse of the publishing class. J. F. Baker. *Publishers Weekly* 235:6 Je 9 '89

Garden literature
The gardening passion. B. Stander. il *Publishers Weekly* 235:23-6+ F 10 '89

Guidebooks
The crowded world of travel books [special section] J. Crichton. il *Publishers Weekly* 235:36-8+ Ja 20 '89

History
A history of book marketing [1940s and 1950s] R. A. Carter. il *Publishers Weekly* 235:54-6 Ja 13 '89
A history of book marketing [1960s through the 1980s] R. A. Carter. il *Publishers Weekly* 235:34-7 My 26 '89

Home economics literature
Self-publishers print 100,000 copies (and survive!) [work of P. Young and P. Jones] J. Barbato. *Publishers Weekly* 236:42 N 10 '89

Home improvement literature
Feathering the nest. D. Joe. il *Publishers Weekly* 235:20+ Je 23 '89

Homosexual literature
Gay & lesbian publishing. J. Ponce de León. il *Publishers Weekly* 236:14-16+ D 8 '89

Illustrated books
Illustrated books—lovely to look at, tough to produce. J. P. Frank. il *Publishers Weekly* 235:109-10 Ap 7 '89

PUBLISHERS AND PUBLISHING—*cont.*
International aspects
See also
Association of American Publishers. International Trade Group
Books—Export-import trade
1992 and all that [round table discussion on the implications for American publishers of the European Economic Community] il *Publishers Weekly* 235:21-8 F 3 '89
International front. H. R. Lottman. See occasional issues of Publishers Weekly beginning May 27, 1983
London's Verso to form joint venture with Soviet house. G. Feldman. *Publishers Weekly* 235:14 Je 16 '89
Talking about 1992 [implications of the consolidation of the European Economic Community] H. R. Lottman. *Publishers Weekly* 235:58 Je 30 '89
Japanese literature
Kodansha brings new Japanese fiction to the U.S. il *Publishers Weekly* 236:57 O 6 '89
Jazz music
See also
Jazz Masterworks Editions
Jewish literature
See also
Kar-Ben Copies Inc.
UAHC Press
'Other lands, other cultures': Jewish Book Council discusses children's books in translation. B. List. il *Publishers Weekly* 235:142-3 F 24 '89
People of the book. W. Wollheim and R. S. Frank. il *Publishers Weekly* 236:21-7 O 6 '89
Korean literature
Soho launches Korean novelist in the U.S. [Ahn Junghyo] il por *Publishers Weekly* 236:57-8 O 6 '89
Large print books
Easy on the eyes. J. Crichton. il *Publishers Weekly* 236:14+ Jl 7 '89
Large print publishers turn to new technology and new designs. J. P. Frank. il *Publishers Weekly* 236:30-2 Jl 7 '89
Latin American literature
See also
Arte Publico Press
The Archives Collection, a laboratory for the future. A. Segala. il *The Courier (Unesco)* 42:18-20 My '89
Laws and regulations
See also
Copyright
Capital doings. H. Fields. *Publishers Weekly* 235:45 Ja 6 '89
Impish role-players ask: can you say that in 1989? [Association of American Publishers panel] C. Reid. il *Publishers Weekly* 235:28+ Je 2 '89
Record-keeping provisions struck down in porn law [requiring publishers to keep records of models used in depictions of sexual activity] H. Fields. *Publishers Weekly* 235:23-4 Je 2 '89
Veliotes gives high marks—and low—to Reagan administration. H. Fields. *Publishers Weekly* 235:18 F 3 '89
Ireland
Irish publishers attempt to reform libel laws. *Publishers Weekly* 236:336 Ag 11 '89
Legal literature
See also
Bowker's legal publishing preview (Newsletter)
Matthew Bender & Co.
Michie Company
Limited editions
See also
Arion Press
Genre [collaboration on My pretty pony by writer S. King and artist B. Kruger] *The New Yorker* 65:27 F 27 '89
Stephen King: limited edition for a bestselling author [collaboration on My pretty pony by writer S. King and artist B. Kruger] C. Reid. il *Publishers Weekly* 235:37-8 Mr 31 '89
Medical literature
See also
Knightsbridge Medical Publishing (Firm)
Masson Editeur
Books with a bedside manner. J. Bethune. il *Publishers Weekly* 235:35-6+ Ap 21 '89
Medical publishers enlist expert advice on the future [American Medical Publishers Association management seminar] C. Kerr. il *Publishers Weekly* 235:43-4 Ap 14 '89
Motion picture literature
Citadel Press celebrates 30 years in film. il *Publishers Weekly* 236:26 O 13 '89
Music
See also
Paramount Pictures Corp. Famous Music Publishing
Nature literature
'Audubon perspectives' gives Wiley new perspective on trade. B. Levine. il *Publishers Weekly* 236:31-2 N 10 '89
New Age literature
Here's to the end of "New Age" publishing. J. P. Tarcher. por *Publishers Weekly* 236:36 N 3 '89
New Age on the brink. M. Jones. il *Publishers Weekly* 236:14-16+ N 3 '89

Sorting out the strata. M. Jones. il *Publishers Weekly* 236:20+ N 3 '89
Paperback books
See also
Avon Books (Firm)
Bantam Books, Inc.
Berkley Publishing Group
Citadel Press
Dell Publishing Co., Inc.
Harper Paperbacks (Firm)
Mandarin Paperbacks (Firm)
Odyssey Paperbacks (Firm)
Paperback books—Marketing
Penguin Books Ltd.
Pocket Books
Spectra Books (Firm)
Sphere Books Ltd.
50 years of paperbacks [special section] il *Publishers Weekly* 235:S4+ My 26 '89
At 73, Nobel laureate Saul Bellow decides he wants to be a paperback writer. A. Chambers. il pors *People Weekly* 31:65-6+ Mr 27 '89
From the two-bit beginning. I. Ballantine and B. Ballantine. il *The New York Times Book Review* 94:25+ Ap 30 '89
Parent education literature
Bringing up baby. R. M. Gilinsky. il *Publishers Weekly* 235:20+ Je 9 '89
Periodicals
See also
American City Business Journals, Inc.
American Express Publishing Corp.
CBS Inc. Magazines Division
Conde Nast Publications Inc.
Johnson Publishing Company, Inc.
Newhouse Broadcasting Corporation
Penthouse International Ltd.
PW international (Periodical)
Time Inc.
A golden age for magazines. P. Chisholm. il *Maclean's* 102:30-1 Jl 17 '89
Tapping a market [swimsuit magazines] J. DeMont. il *Maclean's* 102:28 F 20 '89
Photographic literature
See also
Eastman Kodak Co. Photographic Products Groups
Poetry
Publishing language poets. J. Barbato. *Publishers Weekly* 235:60 Ja 13 '89
Popular music
See also
SBK Entertainment World Inc.
Last laugh [SBK sells former CBS music publishing division to Thorn EMI] L. Gubernick. il por *Forbes* 143:41-2 F 20 '89
They're playing whose song? [record companies buy independent publishers] D. Lieberman. il *Business Week* p42 Ja 23 '89
Professional literature
See also
Scott, Foresman & Company. Professional Books Group
AAP-PSP market-driven publishing strategies. L. Conley. *Publishers Weekly* 235:47-8 F 10 '89
Graphics changes/cost-savings liven professional books. J. P. Frank. il *Publishers Weekly* 235:40+ Je 16 '89
The international PSP market: an update. F. Kobrak. *Publishers Weekly* 236:44-5 N 10 '89
Looking back on the professional year [symposium] G. Feldman. il *Publishers Weekly* 235:22-4 Je 16 '89
Professional association publishing. T. Weyr. il *Publishers Weekly* 235:34+ Je 16 '89
PSP cooperative ventures. G. Feldman. *Publishers Weekly* 236:30 O 13 '89
Reaching the trade: advice from two publishers turned booksellers. J. Kapitan and B. Szabo. il pors *Publishers Weekly* 235:26+ Je 16 '89
Reference books
Looking it up. K. Dawson and L. Nixon. il *Publishers Weekly* 236:18+ Jl 14 '89
NYPL and S & S cooperate on Desk reference. G. Corcoran. il *Publishers Weekly* 235:34 Ap 28 '89
Regional literature
Creating big books for limited areas [independent publishers in California] L. See. *Publishers Weekly* 236:21 O 20 '89
From the campuses: adventures in publishing [university presses] R. Reed. il *The New York Times Book Review* 94:1+ S 24 '89
Going to market [wholesalers' commitment to regional publishing] M. Raymond. il *Publishers Weekly* 236:22-3 O 20 '89
Tending your garden. T. Unsworth. il *Publishers Weekly* 236:17-18 O 20 '89
Religious literature
See also
Bible—Publication and distribution
Crossway Books (Firm)
Evangelical Christian Publishers Association
Paulist Press

PUBLISHERS AND PUBLISHING—Religious literature—
cont.
Creative marketing [Christian Booksellers Association convention] W. Griffin. *Publishers Weekly* 236:18 Ag 18 '89
Religious books. W. Griffin. See occasional issues of Publishers Weekly beginning July 29, 1983
Religious publishing. W. Griffin. See occasional issues of Publishers Weekly beginning July 18, 1986
Spring religious books [special section] il *Publishers Weekly* 235:31-58 Mr 3 '89
Science fiction
Science fiction's outer limits? R. Herbert. il *Publishers Weekly* 236:18-20+ N 10 '89
Scientific literature
See also
Spectra Books (Firm)
A brief history of A brief history. S. W. Hawking. il pors *Popular Science* 235:70-2 Ag '89
Self help literature
On the road to recovery with Prentice Hall, Ballantine et al. J. Crichton. il *Publishers Weekly* 236:52-3 N 3 '89
Sports literature
See also
Sports Illustrated for Kids Books
Sports by the book. T. Weyr. il *Publishers Weekly* 235:21-2+ F 17 '89
Statistics
1988 sales finish strongly. J. P. Dessauer. il *Publishers Weekly* 235:47 Mr 10 '89
1989 sales to rise 4%, says Commerce official. H. Fields. *Publishers Weekly* 235:25 Ja 13 '89
America's biggest publishers [ranking the top 20] il *Publishers Weekly* 236:24-5 D 15 '89
Book sales rise 8.5% to $13 billion in 1988. il *Publishers Weekly* 236:13 S 29 '89
Spending on books to reach $29.4 billion in 1993, study shows. il *Publishers Weekly* 235:24 Je 30 '89
Title output and prices. C. B. Grannis. il *Publishers Weekly* 235:36-9 Mr 10 '89
Titles and prices, 1988; final figures. C. B. Grannis. il *Publishers Weekly* 236:24-7 S 29 '89
Study and teaching
Learning the business. M. Lodge. il *Publishers Weekly* 235:19-23 Mr 24 '89
Study guides
See also
Cliff's Notes Inc.
Taxation
Paramount takes $140 million write-off on publishing units. C. Reid. *Publishers Weekly* 236:8+ D 1 '89
Textbooks
See also
D. C. Heath and Company. School Division
Scott, Foresman & Company
California urges teaching of evolution in science textbooks. M. Colin. il *Publishers Weekly* 235:14 F 3 '89
Kickbacks in university textbook adoptions. R. B. McKenzie. *BioScience* 39:326-7 My '89
A revolutionary new system customizes textbooks [introduced by McGraw-Hill Inc.] J. P. Frank. il *Publishers Weekly* 236:63-4 N 3 '89
Textbook publishers and authors clash over comp copy proposals. C. Reid. il *Publishers Weekly* 236:12 O 20 '89
Theatrical literature
See also
Applause Theatre Books
Travel literature
See also
Travel Information Group
Prentice Hall Press travels to new 'Destinations'. il *Publishers Weekly* 236:32 N 10 '89
Western stories
Bringing back the western. D. E. Showalter. il *Publishers Weekly* 235:25-7 My 5 '89
Australia
Children's book publishing in Australia: a lively business. R. Sessions. il *Publishers Weekly* 235:35-7 Mr 24 '89
An open market for Australia? L. Vardey. por *Publishers Weekly* 236:100 S 15 '89
Canada
See also
Harlequin Enterprises Ltd.
Harper & Collins Publishers Ltd.
Maclean Hunter Ltd.
Quebecor Inc.
Closing the book on government [publishing industry] D. Francis. il *Maclean's* 102:13 Je 12 '89
Coming of age in Quebec [French language publishers] J. Poulin. il *Publishers Weekly* 235:28-31 My 19 '89
A time of change in Canada. B. Slopen. il *Publishers Weekly* 235:22-3+ My 19 '89
China
L. Ron Hubbard inside the Great Wall [Dianetics published in Chinese] il *Publishers Weekly* 235:36 Ap 28 '89
East Asia
Transpacific. S. A. Taylor. See occasional issues of Publishers Weekly beginning February 17, 1989

France
See also
Editions Pierre Belfond
Groupe de la Cité
Hachette SA
Masson Editeur
Germany (West)
See also
Bertelsmann AG
Springer-Verlag GmbH & Co. KG
Great Britain
See also
Bodley Head Ltd.
British Publishers Association
Brooklands Books (Firm)
Century Hutchinson Ltd.
Doubleday U.K. (Firm)
Faber & Faber Inc.
Hamish Hamilton Ltd.
John Calder Ltd.
Longman Group Ltd.
Macdonald Group
Mandarin Paperbacks (Firm)
Michael Joseph Ltd.
Pearson plc
Penguin Books Ltd.
Penguin Group
Random House U.K. Ltd.
Reed International plc
Simon & Schuster Ltd.
Sphere Books Ltd.
Verso (Firm)
Victor Gollancz Ltd.
Webb & Bower
William Collins plc
Senior British publishers form three new companies. V. Menkes. *Publishers Weekly* 236:17 O 27 '89
Italy
See also
Arnoldo Mondadori Editore, SpA
A new Milan. H. R. Lottman. il *Publishers Weekly* 235:34-6+ Je 2 '89
Netherlands
The new shape of Dutch publishing. H. R. Lottman. il *Publishers Weekly* 236:15-16+ N 17 '89
Soviet Union
See also
International Relations Publishing House
Spain
Madrid for its own sake. H. R. Lottman. il *Publishers Weekly* 236:82-7 S 15 '89
United States
See Publishers and publishing
PUBLISHERS ASSOCIATION OF THE SOUTH
Southern publishers shift into high gear [annual meeting] B. Summer. *Publishers Weekly* 236:61 O 6 '89
PUBLISHERS GROUP WEST
Publishers Group West: small press distributor hits the big time. L. See. il *Publishers Weekly* 235:40-3 My 26 '89
PUBLISHING See Publishers and publishing
PUBS (GREAT BRITAIN) See Bars and barrooms—Great Britain
PUCCINI, GIACOMO, 1858-1924
about
La bohème [opera] Reviews
  Opera News il 53:32-5 Mr 4 '89
Tosca [opera] Reviews
  Maclean's il 102:59 F 6 '89. J. Pearce
Il trittico [opera] Reviews
  Opera News il 54:46-9 D 9 '89
PUCK, WOLFGANG
about
Talk of the town. D. P. Marshall. il *Travel Holiday* 172:102-3 Ag '89
PUCKETT, KIRBY
about
Twins' Kirby Puckett cracks $3 million mark. il por *Jet* 77:52 D 11 '89
PUDDINGS
Coffee with cream [Joan Winters's biscotti pudding] B. Costikyan. il *New York* 22:53 Je 5 '89
Perfect puddings [low calorie] il *McCall's* 116:132 Ap '89
PUDDINGTON, ARCH
Life under communism today. *Commentary* 87:32-8 F '89
Those were the days: the SDS revisited. il *The American Spectator* 22:18-20 Mr '89
The wounds of glasnost. il *National Review* 41:26-8 N 24 '89
PUEBLO ARCHITECTURE
Potluck [Tsiping pueblo ruins] D. J. Preston. il *Omni (New York, N.Y.)* 11:31+ Ja '89
PUEBLO INCIDENT, 1968
21 years after losing the Pueblo, Lloyd Bucher wins honors for its crew. M. Brower. il pors *People Weekly* 32:26-7 Jl 31 '89
PUEBLO INDIANS
See also
Indian Pueblo Cultural Center (Albuquerque, N.M.)

PUEBLO INDIANS—*cont.*
Ancient gardeners conserved water. il *Earth Science* 42:5-6 Fall '89
The dark side of the Anasazi [evidence of a cannibalistic ritual at Yellow Jacket, Colo. site; work of John Cater] il *Discover* 10:12 Ap '89
Fall of the Garden of Eden [prehistoric man and the environment] M. Kiefer. il *International Wildlife* 19:38-43 Jl/Ag '89
Sun dagger misses its mark [Anasazi petroglyphs in Chaco Canyon] J. Palca. il *Science* 244:1538 Je 30 '89
PUELMA, HERNAN L. FUENZALIDA- *See* Fuenzalida-Puelma, Hernan L.
PUENZO, LUIS
                                 about
Old gringo [film] Reviews
    Maclean's il 102:60-1 O 16 '89. B. D. Johnson
    People Weekly il 32:17 O 23 '89. R. Novak
    Theatre Crafts il 23:56-7 O '89. J. Calhoun
PUERTO RICANS
                           United States
Black and Latino. R. Santiago. por *Essence* 20:12 N '89
Walter and the raffle [migrant workers send boss W. Jansen to Puerto Rico] P. Kelly. *Reader's Digest* 134:26 Mr '89
                         Political activities
Preventive . . . [Puerto Rican independence activist F. Ojeda Rios held without bail in U.S.] R. A. Falk. *The Nation* 248:508-9 Ap 17 '89
PUERTO RICO
    See also
    Agricultural administration—Puerto Rico
    Astronomical observatories—Puerto Rico
    Caribbean National Forest (Puerto Rico)
    Civil rights—Puerto Rico
    Hotels, motels, etc.—Puerto Rico
    Motion picture festivals—Puerto Rico
    Police—Puerto Rico
    Puerto Ricans
                      Description and travel
Puerto Rico. il *Better Homes and Gardens* 67:212+ N '89
                       Economic history
Puerto Rico: growth, change, progress, development. B. Wallach. il maps *Focus (New York, N.Y.: 1950)* 39:27-33 Summ '89
                          Nationalism
The dilemma in Puerto Rico. S. Rodman. il *The New Leader* 72:3-5 Mr 20 '89
Preventive . . . [Puerto Rican independence activist F. Ojeda Rios held without bail in U.S.] R. A. Falk. *The Nation* 248:508-9 Ap 17 '89
Puerto Rico: nation or state? B. A. Kane and R. Bernard. il *The Progressive* 53:32-5 S '89
                      Politics and government
Political crossroads for islands of enchantment. J. F. Talbot. *America* 161:142-4 S 9-16 '89
Puerto Rico might become the 51st state. M. Barone. *U.S. News & World Report* 107:27 Jl 24 '89
                 Religious institutions and affairs
    See also
    Catholic Church—Puerto Rico
PUERTO VALLARTA (MEXICO)
                          Description
Puerto Vallarta [cover story] R. Bruns. il map *Travel Holiday* 172:38-49 N '89
PUFF PASTRY *See* Pastry
PUFFERS (FISH)
Fugu, taxis, and Tender Buttons. H. Bridges. il *Gourmet* 49:48+ S '89
PUFFINS
Man to puffins: please come back and stay [work of Steve Kress on Seal Island, Me.] M. Satchell. il *U.S. News & World Report* 107:51-2 Ag 7 '89
PUFFS, BOOK *See* Books—Advertising
PUGA, URSULA
The ad says, "hair". il *Petersen's Photographic Magazine* 18:80-1 Je '89
PUGET SOUND (WASH.)
In pursuit of the suburban squid. R. C. Anderson and J. E. Vanderwerff. il *Sea Frontiers* 35:165-9 My/Je '89
PUGH, JIM
                                 about
The dream team. S. Stevenson. il pors *World Tennis* 37:53-4+ Jl '89
PUGWASH MOVEMENT
Pugwash: euphoria marks meeting as *perestroika* lowers tensions. I. Goodwin. il *Physics Today* 42:81-3 S '89
PUIG, MANUEL
                                 about
Mystery of the rose bouquet [drama] Reviews
    Time il 134:109 D 11 '89. W. A. Henry
A novelist copes with the critics [interview] R. Montero. por *World Press Review* 36:60 Mr '89
PULASKI (N.Y.)
                           Tourist trade
A report from salmon run [controversial fishing practices] C. Robohm. il *Country Journal* 16:72-3 S/O '89

The snag in Pulaski [controversial salmon fishing practices] D. W. Hollis. il map *Country Journal* 16:68-71+ S/O '89
PULASKI (TENN.)
                         Race relations
Tenn. town closes up to shun white racists' rally [Aryan Nation rally] *Jet* 77:30 O 30 '89
PULITZER PRIZES
Columnist Clarence Page wins Pulitzer at Chicago tribune. por *Jet* 76:23 Ap 17 '89
A lifetime chasing fires and disasters leads to a Pulitzer Prize for a furniture salesman [R. Olshwanger wins prize for photo appearing in St. Louis post-dispatch] il por *People Weekly* 31:121-2 Ap 17 '89
Plenty of Pulitzers to go around. *Newsweek* 113:60 Ap 10 '89
Two reporters you don't want on your tail [D. L. Barlett and J. B. Steele receive Pulitzer Prize for articles on tax loopholes] J. Alter. il pors *Newsweek* 113:71+ Ap 24 '89
PULITZER PUBLISHING CO.
Why Ingersoll picked St. Louis [Sun to compete with Post-dispatch] J. Heins. il por *Forbes* 144:52+ Jl 24 '89
PULL YOUR HEAD TO THE MOON [dance] See Dance reviews—Single works
PULLEN, DON
                                 about
Blindfold test. H. Mandel. il por *Down Beat* 56:43 N '89
Don Pullen: reconciling opposites. K. Whitehead. il pors *Down Beat* 56:26-8 N '89
PULLER MORTGAGE ASSOCIATES, INC.
Another financial mess [defaults in HUD's program that deputizes firms to issue and underwrite mortgages] M. Schifrin. il *Forbes* 144:10 Jl 10 '89
Come and get it. M. Schifrin. il *Forbes* 143:41-2 My 15 '89
PULLIAM, KESHIA KNIGHT
                                 about
Phylicia, Debbie and Keshia head all-star cast in TV musical, Polly [cover story] il pors *Jet* 77:58-60 N 13 '89
PULLIAM, RUSS
The vice president's Bible. il por *The Saturday Evening Post* 261:26 Ap '89
PULLIAM FAMILY
                                 about
The Quayle family newspapers: black, white—and green all over. J. F. Siler. il por *Business Week* p29 Ag 28 '89
The vice president's Bible. R. Pulliam. il por *The Saturday Evening Post* 261:26 Ap '89
PULMONARY EMBOLISM
Pulmonary embolism: difficult but crucial diagnosis [cover story] E. Zamula. il *FDA Consumer* 23:22-7 N '89
PULMONARY EMPHYSEMA See Emphysema
PULNOC (MUSICAL GROUP)
Czechoslovakia's most enduring band, The Plastic People, recycles its history-making rock. S. K. Reed. il *People Weekly* 31:116+ My 22 '89
Pulnoc. J. Morley. *The Nation* 248:748-50 My 29 '89
Sound Czech. D. Fricke. il *Rolling Stone* p70 Jl 13-27 '89
PULP MILLS *See* Paper mills
PULSARS
Astronomers glimpse birth of a pulsar [spawned by Supernova 1987A] I. Peterson. *Science News* 135:100 F 18 '89
Birth of a pulsar [spawned by Supernova 1987A] S. Flamsteed. il *Discover* 10:26 My '89
Black widow in shock. *Discover* 10:12 Je '89
'Black widow' pulsar shocks neighborhood [1957+20; research by Andrew Fruchter and Jeff Hester] il *Astronomy* 17:10 Ap '89
Cosmic birth [detection of pulsar emerging from Supernova 1987A's dust cloud] *Time* 133:81 F 20 '89
Mysterious pulsar found in Supernova 1987A. *Astronomy* 17:10 My '89
New life for old supernovae [CTB 80] il *Sky and Telescope* 78:350 O '89
On the trail of the black widow pulsar [PSR 1957+20] il *Sky and Telescope* 77:128-9 F '89
The peculiar pulsar in Supernova 1987A [cover story] G. L. Verschuur. il *Astronomy* 17:20-6 S '89
Plenty of pulsars yet to be discovered. *Astronomy* 17:10+ Ag '89
Pulsar eroding companion star [PSR 1957+20; research by Andrew Fruchter] *Astronomy* 17:10 F '89
Pulsar, pulsar, where art thou, pulsar? [Supernova 1987A] M. M. Waldrop. *Science* 243:1553 Mr 24 '89
Pulsars in a crowd [millisecond pulsars] il *Sky and Telescope* 77:127-8 F '89
Pulsars shed new light on evolution of binary stars. P. H. Andersen. *Physics Today* 42:20 Ja '89
Puzzling pulses from a star cluster's core [PSR 2127+11, located near center of M15; work of Alexander Wolszczan] I. Peterson. *Science News* 135:86 F 11 '89
SN 1987A and its ultrafast pulsar. R. A. Schorn. il *Sky and Telescope* 77:480 My '89
Struggling to understand the Supernova 1987A pulsar. *Astronomy* 17:10+ Jl '89
The Supernova 1987A pulsar: found? M. M. Waldrop. *Science* 243:892 F 17 '89

PULSARS—cont.

A surfeit of millisecond pulsars [research by Ramesh Narayan] I. Peterson. *Science News* 135:303 My 13 '89

The Vela pulsar: maybe not a mystery. *Sky and Telescope* 78:458 N '89

PULSE

Pulse-taking the old-fashioned way. il *Health (New York, N.Y.)* 21:46 Ag '89

PULSE CODE MODULATION

MASH to the rescue. R. Hodges. il *Stereo Review* 54:164 S '89

PULSE MONITORS

Fitness toys or tools? L. Kleinmann. il *Health (New York, N.Y.)* 21:42+ Ag '89

Timing your ticker's workout. S. Woolley. il *Business Week* p162 O 23 '89

PULSE TECHNIQUES (ELECTRONICS)

See also

Pulse code modulation

Beating the spread [energy beams that stay in focus indefinitely; research by Richard W. Ziolkowski] R. Ruthen. il *Scientific American* 260:28-9 Ap '89

Making waves that travel like beams [acoustic directed-energy pulse trains; research by Richard W. Ziolkowski] I. Amato. *Science News* 135:38 Ja 21 '89

PULSES, SOLITARY WAVE *See* Solitons

PULTE HOME CORP.

See also

PHM Corp.

PUMAS

Big guy [Florida panthers] F. Graham. il *Audubon* 91:16+ S '89

Searching for the one true cat [Florida panthers] C. Flowers. il *National Wildlife* 27:24-8 O/N '89

PUMPKIN FACES

Pumpkin cutups. il *National Geographic World* 170:10-11 O '89

PUMPKINS

See also

Cooking—Vegetables

PUMPS

See also

Air pumps

Heat pumps

Vacuum pumps

Water pumps

PUNCH (BEVERAGE)

Dip into watermelon punch. il *Southern Living* 24:114 Ag '89

Holiday punches. il *Gourmet* 49:292 D '89

Mimosa punch. il *Good Housekeeping* 208:92 Ja '89

Party-pretty punches that start with fresh fruit. il *Sunset (Central West edition)* 182:204 My '89

PUNCH (PERIODICAL)

Putting pep into Punch. S. Seibert. il por *Newsweek* 113:39 Mr 6 '89

PUNCHED CARD SYSTEMS

The history of census tabulation. K. S. Reid-Green. bibl il *Scientific American* 260:98-103 F '89

PUNCHLINE [film] *See* Motion picture reviews—Single works

PUNISHMENT

See also

Amnesty

Capital punishment

Corporal punishment

Fines (Penalties)

Lynching

Pardon

Parole

Preventive detention

Prisons

School discipline

Torture

The crime of punishment. R. A. Blume and D. Blume. il pors *The Humanist* 49:12-15+ N/D '89

Make the punishment fit the corporate crime. G. S. Becker. il *Business Week* p22 Mr 13 '89

PUNITIVE DAMAGES *See* Damages

PUNK CULTURE

See also

Autonomen

Cyberpunk culture

Skinheads

PUNS AND PUNNING

Giving bad puns the business [corporate names] il *Newsweek* 114:71 D 11 '89

Of many things [Richard Lederer's Get thee to a punnery] G. W. Hunt. *America* 161:50 Jl 29-Ag 5 '89

Title search follow-up. W. Safire. il *The New York Times Magazine* p24+ Ap 2 '89

PUNZO, VINCENT A.

Three moves for peace. *Commonweal* 116:422-3 Ag 11 '89

PUPIL-TEACHER RELATIONSHIP *See* Teachers and students

PUPILS, SCHOOL *See* Students

PUPPETS AND PUPPET PLAYS

See also

Kermit (Muppet)

Muppets

PUPPIES *See* Dogs

PUPPIS A SUPERNOVA *See* Supernovas

PURCELL, EDWARD M.

about

Ewen and Purcell win Tinsley Prize. P. H. Andersen. *Physics Today* 42:92+ Ap '89

PURCELL, HENRY, 1659-1695

about

Dido and Aeneas [opera] Reviews

The Nation 249:364 O 2 '89. T. M. Disch

New York il 22:58 S 4 '89. P. G. Davis

The fairy queen [opera] Reviews

The New Yorker 65:86-7 Ag 14 '89. A. Porter

King Arthur [opera] Reviews

The New Yorker 65:69 Jl 31 '89. A. Porter

PURCELL, JOHN

The specular and the transparent combined. il *Petersen's Photographic Magazine* 18:92-3 S '89

PURCHASE, DAVE

about

Trading good needles for bad. R. Givens. il por *Newsweek* 113:49 Ja 9 '89

PURCHASING

See also

Boats and boating—Purchasing

Bulk buying

Buyers (Retail trade)

Compulsive shopping

Consumption (Economics)

Instalment plan

Sales

Shopping

PURCHASING, GOVERNMENT *See* Contracts, Government

PURCHASING, HOUSEHOLD

See also

Electronic shopping

Ethical shopping [Shopping for a better world, a guide to supermarket shopping] J. Queenan. il *Forbes* 143:80+ Ap 17 '89

Shopping for a better world [guide to socially responsible supermarket shopping] il *USA Today (Periodical)* 117:4-5 Ap '89

Shopping in the year 2000. il *The Futurist* 23:44 N/D '89

PURCHASING, MILITARY *See* United States. Army—Procurement; United States. Dept. of Defense—Procurement

PURDY, CANDY

Think before you (baby)sit. il *Current Health 2* 16:22-3 N '89

PURDY, PATRICK, D. 1989

about

Death goes to school. P. Caputo. il *Esquire* 112:136-8+ D '89

Death on the playground. J. N. Baker. il por *Newsweek* 113:35 Ja 30 '89

A nation of certified killers. J. D. McNamara. il *Harper's* 278:58-9 My '89

Slaughter in a school yard. il *Time* 133:29 Ja 30 '89

PUREES

A rich fat-free puree [microwaving butternut squash] J. B. Hurley. *Prevention (Emmaus, Pa.)* 41:118 N '89

PURIFICATION OF WATER *See* Water purification

PURIFIERS, AIR *See* Air filters

PURINES

The purine path of chemotherapy [Nobel Prize lecture, December 8, 1988] G. B. Elion. bibl f il *Science* 244:41-7 Ap 7 '89

Was adenine the first purine? A. W. Schwartz and C. G. Bakker. bibl f il *Science* 245:1102-4 S 8 '89

PURITAN REVOLUTION, 1642-1660 *See* Great Britain—History—Puritan Revolution, 1642-1660

PURITANS AND PURITANISM

Apologizing to Anne Hutchinson [United Church of Christ members burn 1638 writ of excommunication] M. P. Nugent. *The Christian Century* 106:304-5 Mr 22-29 '89

The troubled voyage of the Rainbow [Massachusetts colony confronts issue of slave trade] L. Gragg. bibl il maps *History Today* 39:36-41 Ag '89

Anecdotes, facetiae, satire, etc.

The dangerous New Puritans. A. Fotheringham. il *Maclean's* 102:80 Ap 10 '89

Bibliography

Struggle over the Puritans. G. S. Wood. il *The New York Review of Books* 36:26-31+ N 9 '89

PURMORT, LOU

about

A curiosity wrapped in a mystery. E. Paris. il por *Forbes* 143:116+ Mr 6 '89

PUROLATOR COURIER CORP.

Brady, buyouts, and Purolator [Nicholas Brady's role in thwarted buyout bid] il *Fortune* 119:66 My 22 '89

PURPLE-STRIPED JELLYFISH *See* Jellyfish

PURSEL, VERNON G., AND OTHERS

Genetic engineering of livestock. bibl f il *Science* 244:1281-8 Je 16 '89

PURSLANE

Eggs naturally rich in 'fish oils' [omega-3 fatty acids from purslane] *Science News* 136:351 N 25 '89

PURSLANE—*cont.*

Purslane: so common it's forgotten. W. E. Woolridge. il *Flower and Garden* 33:55 Jl/Ag '89

PURSUIT OF HAPPINESS *See* Happiness

PURSUIT OF HAPPINESS (MUSICAL GROUP)

Sex and the Pursuit of Happiness [release of Love junk] S. Simels. il *Stereo Review* 54:143 F '89

TPOH declares its independence. D. Wild. il *Rolling Stone* p14 F 23 '89

PURVES, WILLIAM

about

The Bank. A. Tanzer. il por *Forbes* 144:43-4 D 11 '89

PUSEY, ALLEN

Fast money and fraud. il pors *The New York Times Magazine* p30-2+ Ap 23 '89

PUSH *See* People United to Serve Humanity (Organization)

PUSHKAR (INDIA)

Festivals

Photographs and photography

Camel Fair. J. Hunter. il *Petersen's Photographic Magazine* 18:20-3 O '89

To get better people pictures, you've got to conquer your own fear and inertia. L. Dennis. il *Popular Photography* 96:44-5 Ja '89

PUSHKIN MUSEUM OF FINE ARTS (MOSCOW, SOVIET UNION)

Leaps and boundaries [director I. Antonova] D. Matlock. il por *Art News* 88:69-70 Ja '89

PUSZH (DAVID) DANCE COMPANY *See* David Puszh Dance Company

PUT AND CALL TRANSACTIONS

See also

Foreign exchange options

Stock index options

The computer option. E. Sturza. il por *Forbes* 143:250 Je 26 '89

Investors are developing a taste for this poison [poison put insurance] L. Light. il *Business Week* p78 Jl 10 '89

Playing for real [bridge masters M. Becker and R. Rubin become options traders] N. Hass. il pors *New York* 22:60-2+ D 11 '89

Putting a little more punch into your portfolio. D. Greising. il *Business Week* p138 D 25 '89-Ja 1 '90

Take the money and run [stock that becomes target of acquisition or leveraged buyout] M. J. Williams. il *Fortune* 119:26 Ja 2 '89

When stock prices seem to be going nowhere, maybe it's time for a call. M. Schiffres. il *Changing Times* 43:88 Je '89

Taxation

The "wash sale" rule gets scrubbed behind the ears. G. W. Padwe. il *Nation's Business* 77:72 Ja '89

PUTMAN, ANDRÉE

about

Gandee at large. C. K. Gandee. il por *House & Garden* 161:172 Jl '89

PUTNAM, PAT

Another classic [cover story] il pors *Sports Illustrated* 70:18-21 Je 19 '89

Beast from Down East. il *Sports Illustrated* 71:54-5 O 30 '89

The beatings go on. pors *Sports Illustrated* 71:18-19 Jl 31 '89

'Belt the body'. il pors *Sports Illustrated* 70:44-5 F 27 '89

In your face, José Luis. il pors *Sports Illustrated* 71:66-7 Ag 28 '89

Lean and mean. il pors *Sports Illustrated* 71:24-6+ Jl 24 '89

Nunn better. il pors *Sports Illustrated* 70:40-2+ My 22 '89

One angry man. il pors *Sports Illustrated* 71:38-9 N 13 '89

One for the ages. il pors *Sports Illustrated* 71:24-5 D 18 '89

Smashing! il pors *Sports Illustrated* 70:14-17 Mr 6 '89

Stop meeting like this. il pors *Sports Illustrated* 70:75 My 22 '89

Terrific Whitewater journey. il *Sports Illustrated* 70:74+ Mr 27 '89

This time Nunn chose not to run. il pors *Sports Illustrated* 70:80 Ap 3 '89

You're next, Tyson. il pors *Sports Illustrated* 70:34-5 Mr 20 '89

PUTTING (GOLF)

Perils of putting [PGA study] J. Diaz. il *Sports Illustrated* 70:76-8+ Ap 3 '89

PUTTNAM, DAVID, 1941-

about

A man who hates Rambo. E. Linden. il por *Time* 133:62-3 My 1 '89

PUZZLES

See also

Crossword puzzles

Jigsaw puzzles

Palindromes

Riddles

Word games

Brain bogglers. M. Carver. See issues of Discover beginning November 1987

An executive turns puzzle maker [W. Harms] D. E. Gumpert and D. Davis. il por *New Choices for the Best Years* 29:50-1 O '89

Murder most puzzling: can you solve this case? L. Treat. il *The New York Times Book Review* 94:36 O 15 '89

People puzzles: theme and variations. A. K. Dewdney. il *Scientific American* 260:106-9 Ja '89

This one spells o-o-p-s [Kellogg Co.'s presidents puzzle wrongly includes name of J. Davis] il *Newsweek* 113:50 My 1 '89

PW INTERNATIONAL (PERIODICAL)

'PW international' bimonthly to be launched in January. *Publishers Weekly* 236:12 O 13 '89

PYE, MICHAEL, 1946-

Low tales of the highborn. il *The New York Times Magazine* p44+ N 12 '89

PYEATT, MADELYN

about

Reaching out from the inner city. B. Fuller. il por *Sierra* 74:50-4 Jl/Ag '89

PYGMALION [drama] *See* Shaw, Bernard, 1856-1950

PYGMIES

Pygmy paradox prompts a short answer [shortage of growth hormone receptors] K. Fackelmann. *Science News* 136:22 Jl 8 '89

Pygmy puzzle [defective growth hormone receptor; research by Gerhard Baumann] il *Discover* 10:14 D '89

Short-answer question [defective growth hormone receptor in pygmies; research by Gerhard Baumann] J. Benditt. *Scientific American* 261:32-3 S '89

Hunting

The Efe: archers of the African rain forest. R. C. Bailey. il maps *National Geographic* 176:664-86 N '89

Zaire

See also

Efe (African people)

PYLE, ROBERT MICHAEL

Spineless wonders. il *International Wildlife* 19:14-17 S/O '89

PYLON (MUSICAL GROUP)

You can even dance. K. Richardson. il *High Fidelity (New York, N.Y.)* 39:79+ Je '89

PYNE, STEPHEN J., 1949-

The summer we let wild fire loose. il *Natural History* p44-51 Ag '89

PYRAMID HOUSES

21st century pyramid [energy-efficient home of B. Rutan in the Mojave Desert; cover story] J. L. Schefter. il por *Popular Science* 235:65-9 N '89

PYRAMIDS

Egypt

Perilous times for the pyramids. M. D. Lemonick. il *Time* 133:60-2 My 15 '89

PYRANS

Oxygen radicals in influenza-induced pathogenesis and treatment with pyran polymer-conjugated SOD. T. Oda and others. bibl f il *Science* 244:974-6 My 26 '89

PYRIDINE COMPOUNDS

See also

Dihydropyridines

MPTP (Drug)

PYRIMIDINE NUCLEOTIDES *See* Nucleotides

PYROGENS

Macrophage inflammatory protein-1: a prostaglandin-independent endogenous pyrogen. G. Davatelis and others. bibl f il *Science* 243:1066-8 F 24 '89

PYROGRAPHY

Balsa burning [Christmas cards and wrapping paper] il *Sunset (Central West edition)* 181:102-3 D '88

PYROTECHNIC DEVICES

See also

Fireworks

PYROXENITE

Evidence for a heterogeneous upper mantle in the Cabo Ortegal Complex, Spain. J. Girardeau and others. bibl f il map *Science* 245:1231-3 S 15 '89

PYRROLOQUINOLINE QUINONE *See* Methoxatin

PYTHONS

Trapper Todd Hardwick tackles the ultimate varmint, a monster python who won't leave home. M. Neill. il pors *People Weekly* 32:179-80+ D 4 '89

Q

Q, STACEY

about

Shining star daughters and their amazing moms. il pors *'Teen* 33:46-7 D '89

Q FEVER

Annals of medicine [cat-related outbreak in Nova Scotia] B. Roueché. *The New Yorker* 65:100-5 S 4 '89

Q RATINGS

Blacks again dominate top marketing Q-ratings [sports stars] il *Jet* 76:50 My 22 '89

QADDAFI, MUAMMAR AL-, 1942-
about
Chemical reaction. E. Magnuson. il por *Time* 133:18-21 Ja 16 '89
How Qadaffi built his deadly chemical plant. J. Templeman and D. Lee. il *Business Week* p50-1 Ja 23 '89
Libya's 'green *perestroika*'. C. Wallace. *World Press Review* 36:30 F '89
Qaddafi's revolution. P. G. Coy. *Commonweal* 116:552-3 O 20 '89
Showdown with Libya [cover story; special section] il por *Newsweek* 113:16-25 Ja 16 '89
A war of nerves. H. Evans. il *U.S. News & World Report* 106:72 Ja 16 '89

QANTAS AIRWAYS LTD.
Australia eases landing rights policy, putting more pressure on Qantas. P. Proctor. il *Aviation Week & Space Technology* 130:97 Je 26 '89
Qantas, American, JAL gain shares in Air New Zealand. *Aviation Week & Space Technology* 130:108 Ja 2 '89
Qantas security chief seeks new tools to detect terrorists [views of Ronald Armstrong] D. A. Brown. *Aviation Week & Space Technology* 130:125 F 20 '89

QE 2 *See* Queen Elizabeth 2 (Ship)

QI YANFEN
The empire of the ancestors. il *The Unesco Courier* 42:16-21 Jl '89

QING HAO *See* Artemisinin

QINGHAI PROVINCE (CHINA)
Description
The Chinese view of Tibet [Tibetans successfully integrated] Cheng Gang. map *Utne Reader* p36 Mr/Ap '89

QINTEX AUSTRALIA LTD.
Fast fade for Chris Skase. R. Grover and S. Hutcheon. il por *Business Week* p76-7 D 11 '89
Leo the Lion is on the loose again [C. Skase's deal to buy MGM/UA falls apart] R. Grover. il por *Business Week* p60 O 23 '89
Stranger in a strange land [C. Skase of Qintex buys MGM/UA Communications] L. Gubernick. il por *Forbes* 144:164+ O 2 '89
These days, they don't call it 'Down Under' for nothing. S. Hutcheon. il por *Business Week* p66+ N 6 '89

QUACKS AND QUACKERY
Australian convicted in 'Cho Low' fraud [P. Foster's mail order scheme selling Chinese tea to lower cholesterol] il por *FDA Consumer* 23:35 D '89/Ja '90
Bald-faced hair scam [indictment against Philip P. West and Wayne P. Kreklewich] il *FDA Consumer* 23:34-5 Mr '89
Beware the health hucksters. P. Michelmore. *Reader's Digest* 134:114-18 Ja '89
Big fat lies: the new weight-loss scams. N. B. Cardozo. il *Mademoiselle* 95:128-9+ Ja '89
Body Toddy [mineral water claimed to be health cure] il *FDA Consumer* 23:33-4 D '89/Ja '90
Dentist's device [Amalgameter to measure mercury vapor emitted from fillings] il *FDA Consumer* 23:35-6 O '89
Top 10 health frauds. il *FDA Consumer* 23:28-31 O '89
A well-lighted place [visiting a psychic] O. Lipstein. il *American Health* 8:63-4 D '89
Your health: exposing fraud isn't magic. J. Randi. *Modern Maturity* 32:22 Je/Jl '89

QUADE, QUENTIN L.
A university perspective on the 'oath of fidelity'. *America* 160:348-9 Ap 15 '89

QUADRANTIDS (METEORS) *See* Meteors
QUADRIPLEGICS *See* Paralytics

QUAID, DENNIS
about
Dennis Quaid on Big Easy Street. D. Lamanna. pors *Ladies' Home Journal* 106:96+ F '89
Dennis Quaid stokes rock's Fire. I. Robbins. il pors *Video* 13:16-17 D '89
Goodness gracious! [cover story] J. E. Bradley. il pors *Esquire* 111:136-42+ Mr '89
Playing the Killer. N. Tosches. il pors *Vogue* 179:182-5 Jl '89
Simmer down, son [cover story] R. Palmer. il pors *American Film* 14:26-33+ Je '89
Whole lot of shakin' going on. S. Pond. il pors *Rolling Stone* p118-21+ Jl 13-27 '89

QUAID, RANDY, 1953-
about
Big brother and his 'Parents'. J. Kaplan. il por *Rolling Stone* p32+ Mr 9 '89
Randy Quaid, back from his Vacation, finds peace at home. C. Sanz. il pors *People Weekly* 32:153+ D 18 '89

QUAIL SHOOTING
Quail hunting as good as it gets [south Texas] B. Brister. il map *Field & Stream* 93:28-9+ Ja '89
Skyrockets [flight pen design] B. Tarrant. il *Field & Stream* 93:110+ F '89
Anecdotes, facetiae, satire, etc.
The longest day [bobwhite shooting] J. M. Vance. il *Field & Stream* 94:21+ D '89

QUAILS
He's on wild path in CRP. J. Walter. il *Successful Farming* 87:72 S '89
Brain
See Brain
Flight
Skyrockets [flight pen design] B. Tarrant. il *Field & Stream* 93:110+ F '89

QUAKER OATS CO.
Locking up the weekend warriors [marketing of Gatorade] J. Levine. il *Forbes* 144:234-5 O 2 '89
Quaker Oats' pet peeve [Gaines dog food line slips] L. Therrien. *Business Week* p32-3 Jl 31 '89

QUAKER STATE CORPORATION
Quaker State switches into a quick-change artist. M. Schroeder. il por *Business Week* p126-7 O 16 '89

QUALEX INC.
What's a Kodalux? [Kodalux Processing Services] G. Schaub. il *Popular Photography* 96:40 Ap '89

QUALITY (PHILOSOPHY)
Quality is the key to the disciplines. W. Glasser. *The Education Digest* 55:24-7 S '89

QUALITY CONTROL
See also
Aerospace industries—Quality control
Audio equipment industry—Quality control
Automobile industry—Quality control
Electronic industries—Quality control
Guided missile industries—Quality control
Malcolm Baldrige National Quality Award
Munitions—Quality control
Shoe industry—Quality control
The front lines of quality [firms scrutinizing vendors] A. Gabor. il *U.S. News & World Report* 107:57-9 N 27 '89
W. Edwards Deming is the American who taught the Japanese how to compete. D. Moreau. il por *Changing Times* 43:132 S '89
Japan
Quality conscious [Taguchi method] E. Corcoran. *Scientific American* 261:75-6 Jl '89
Zen and the art of being a stickler for perfection. M. Tharp. il *U.S. News & World Report* 107:58-9 N 27 '89

QUALITY CROUTONS INC.
Crunch time. L. Gite. il pors *Black Enterprise* 20:74-6+ S '89

QUALITY OF LIFE
Heartland vs. Sunbelt [study by Dowell Myers] il *USA Today (Periodical)* 118:4-5 D '89
Measuring the quality of life. M. S. Miller. il *Technology Review* 92:13-14 O '89
Quality of life [Environmental Quality Index] il *National Wildlife* 27:40 F/Mr '89

QUALITY OF PRODUCTS
See also
Malcolm Baldrige National Quality Award
Quality control
Standardization
1990 buying guide issue. il *Consumer Reports* 54:1-396 D '89
Classics. R. Keyes. il *Gentlemen's Quarterly* 59:146-51 Ja '89
Counterparts [using cars to judge quality in other products] P. Egan. il *Road & Track* 40:26+ Ap '89
The greatest values in America. C. E. Cohen. il *Money* 18:150-4+ N '89
Making it better [American companies] J. Castro. il *Time* 134:78-81 N 13 '89
Speaker for the house/The Heloise helpline. Heloise. See issues of Good Housekeeping beginning November 1988

QUALITY SERVICE INSTITUTE
Coffee, tea, and the power of positive thinking: seminars teach Continental's workers that good service 'feels' better. C. Power. il *Business Week* p36 Jl 31 '89

QUANTRILLE, JOE
about
Detective Joe Quantrille quits the losing battle against drugs in D.C. M. Brower. il pors *People Weekly* 31:62-4+ Mr 20 '89

QUANTUM (PERIODICAL)
Soviet magazine for high schoolers to appear in English. P. Janowski. *Physics Today* 42:116-17 O '89

QUANTUM CHEMICAL CORP.
Saddled with debt but still able to grow. R. Simon. il por *Forbes* 143:100+ Mr 6 '89

QUANTUM ELECTRODYNAMICS
Cavity quantum electrodynamics. S. Haroche and D. Kleppner. bibl f il *Physics Today* 42:24-30 Ja '89
A path to quantum electrodynamics [work of Richard Feynman] J. Schwinger. il *Physics Today* 42:42-8 F '89
The unification of electromagnetism with the weak force. P. Langacker and A. K. Mann. bibl f il *Physics Today* 42:22-31 D '89

QUANTUM FUND
Was George Soros sheared by Shearson? [futures loss] D. Greising. il por *Business Week* p45 N 6 '89

QUANTUM LEAP [television program] See Television program reviews—Single works

QUANTUM MECHANICS See Quantum theory
QUANTUM MEDIA, INC.
The cool, dark telegenius of Robert Pittman. R. Powers. il pors *Gentlemen's Quarterly* 59:324-7+ Mr '89
QUANTUM THEORY
See also
Aharonov-Bohm effect
Aharonov-Casher effect
Energy levels (Quantum mechanics)
Relativity (Physics)
Statistical mechanics
Thermodynamics
Tunneling (Physics)
Wormholes (Astrophysics)
Can you help the Mets by watching on TV? [Strong Baseball Principal; work of N. D. Mermin] R. Pool. il por *Science* 244:773-4 My 19 '89
Dick Feynman—the guy in the office down the hall. M. Gell-Mann. il por *Physics Today* 42:50-4 F '89
Does quantum mechanics have nonlinear terms? [work of Steven Weinberg] B. G. Levi. bibl f il *Physics Today* 42:20-1 O '89
Electrons may shed light for X-ray lasers [research by David B. Chang and James C. McDaniel] R. Cowen. *Science News* 136:183 S 16 '89
Getting a grip on rubbing bodies. R. Pool. il *Science* 246:445 O 27 '89
Knot physics. I. Peterson. *Science News* 135:174 Mr 18 '89
Mind over matter [G. Gilder's Microcosm] T. Bethell. *The American Spectator* 22:11-13 N '89
The origin of the universe [Big Bang] V. F. Weisskopf. il *The New York Review of Books* 36:10-14 F 16 '89
Physics' unseen hand [theory that observing an event can influence outcome; work of D. N. Mermin] W. F. Allman. il *U.S. News & World Report* 107:65 O 23 '89
Putting quantum theory to a nuclear test [work of Steven Weinberg] I. Peterson. *Science News* 136:181 S 16 '89
Quantum baseball [Strong Baseball Principle; work of N. D. Mermin; cover story] I. Peterson. il por *Science News* 136:88-9 Ag 5 '89
Quantum chaos: enigma wrapped in a mystery. R. Pool. *Science* 243:893-5 F 17 '89
Quantum consciousness [views of R. Penrose] J. Horgan. il por *Scientific American* 261:30+ N '89
Quantum cryptography [research by Charles H. Bennett] P. Wallich. *Scientific American* 260:28+ My '89
Quantum interference. I. Peterson. *Science News* 136:363 D 2 '89
Should quantum physics go unquestioned [discussion of October 1988 article, Ask a foolish question . . .] H. Feshbach and V. F. Weisskopf. il *Physics Today* 42:13+ Ap '89
What's wrong with this pillow? N. D. Mermin. il *Physics Today* 42:9+ Ap '89
The world's next source of wealth [excerpt from Microcosm] G. F. Gilder. il por *Fortune* 120:116-20 Ag 28 '89
The young Feynman. J. A. Wheeler. bibl f il *Physics Today* 42:24-8 F '89
QUANTUM THEORY IN POETRY
Anecdotes, facetiae, satire, etc.
Mr. Eliot's guide to quantum theory. J. Lowell. il *Physics Today* 42:46-7 Ap '89
QUANTUM WELL DEVICES
AT&T "microscopic parallel processor" hits 24 GHz [quantum effect transistor] *Byte* 14:17 Ag '89
Can we switch by control of quantum mechanical transmission? R. Landauer. bibl f *Physics Today* 42:119+ O '89
A growing force in the shrinking business [R. T. Bate's quantum-effect transistor] W. C. Symonds. il por *Business Week* Special Issue:75 Je 16 '89
Laying-on of atoms: quantum-well wires [research by Pierre M. Petroff] I. Amato. il *Science News* 135:69 F 4 '89
Quantum effect chips. O. Port. il *Business Week* p70+ Mr 13 '89
A quantum leap in electronics. G. Bylinsky. il *Fortune* 119:113-14+ Ja 30 '89
The quantum transistor. M. Reed. il *Byte* 14:275-81 My '89
TI's prototype transistor takes a quantum leap. *Byte* 14:11 Mr '89
QUARANTA, GIANNI
about
Transported in time [cover story] C. Battaglia. il por *Opera News* 53:8-10+ Ja 7 '89
QUARANTINE
Quarantine and the exchange of crop genetic resources. D. L. Plucknett and N. J. H. Smith. bibl f il *BioScience* 39:16-23 Ja '89
QUARKS See Particles (Nuclear physics)
QUARLES, JOHN
Should the Congress adopt the "Acid Deposition Control Act of 1987"? [excerpts from statement, July 9, 1987] *Congressional Digest* 68:61+ F '89
QUARRELS
All in the family: resolving disputes [views of Rebecca Bloomgarden and Jacque Cook] il *USA Today (Periodical)* 117:10 Mr '89

Fighting the good fight. M. M. Hunt. il *New Choices for the Best Years* 29:71-3 Ag '89
How to handle family fights [excerpt from When families fight] J. Rubin and C. Rubin. il *Ladies' Home Journal* 106:70+ Ja '89
I hate you; kiss me. C. L. Mithers. *Glamour* 87:278 Je '89
"My get-along gang" [overcoming sibling rivalry] J. Abbott. il *Parents* 64:114-18 Ap '89
When kids see you fight [parents' quarrels] N. Rubin. il *Parents* 64:73-6+ Jl '89
When your spouse wants to argue [condensed from Love is never enough] A. T. Beck. il *Reader's Digest* 135:101-4 S '89
QUARRINGTON, PAUL
about
Loony tunes. J. Gault. il por *Maclean's* 102:61 My 29 '89
QUARTERBACKS (FOOTBALL PLAYERS) See Football players
QUARTERDECK OFFICE SYSTEMS
Desqview's different drummer [T. Myers] E. S. Ely. por *Personal Computing* 13:76 Jl '89
Little Quarterdeck throws its weight around [patent on Desqview] P. Cole. il por *Business Week* p76 Je 19 '89
QUARTETS, STRING See String quartets
QUARTZ
Giant radiation-induced color halos in quartz: solution to a riddle. A. L. Odom and W. J. Rink. bibl f il *Science* 246:107-9 O 6 '89
QUARTZSITE (ARIZ.)
Parked in the middle of nowhere [retirees with RVs migrate to Quartzsite, Ariz. for the winter] J. Ackermann-Blount. il map *Time* 133:108-9 My 22 '89
QUASAR FUND
A big-gain hunter in small stocks [interview with P. Jenkel] T. Paré. il por *Fortune* 120:40+ O 23 '89
QUASARS
Cloud links quasars to Seyfert galaxies [hydrogen cloud; work of Kimiaki Kawara] A. McKenzie. *Science News* 136:215 S 30 '89
A cosmic trip in the time machine [discovery of quasar near the Big Dipper] il *U.S. News & World Report* 107:14-15 D 4 '89
Points of view [quasars and radio galaxies; research by Peter Barthel] J. Horgan. il *Scientific American* 260:20+ Ap '89
Quasars and radio galaxies: in the eye of the beholder [work of Peter D. Barthel] il *Sky and Telescope* 77:463-4 My '89
Starry lens puts a twinkle in quasar's eye [QSO 2237 + 0305; research by M. J. Irwin] I. Peterson. *Science News* 136:375 D 9 '89
Spectra and spectroscopy
The guts of a quasar. il *Sky and Telescope* 78:567 D '89
Quasar-galaxy bridge? [work of Christopher L. Carilli] il *Sky and Telescope* 78:349 O '89
Quasar illuminates the most distant past [research by Donald P. Schneider and others] I. Peterson. *Science News* 136:340 N 25 '89
QUASI-BIENNIAL OSCILLATION
Stratospheric winds alter day's length [research by B. Fong Chao] R. Monastersky. *Science News* 135:102 F 18 '89
QUASI-GOVERNMENT AGENCIES
Burned by the thrifts, Congress looks at other fire hazards. C. Yang. il *Business Week* p57 O 9 '89
A time bomb for U.S. taxpayers. R. E. Norton. il *Fortune* 120:139+ O 23 '89
QUASICRYSTALS
Taking the fuzziness out of quasicrystals. I. Peterson. *Science News* 135:149 Mr 11 '89
QUATERNARY PERIOD See Geology, Stratigraphic—Quaternary; Paleoclimatology—Quaternary
QUATTRO, J. M., AND VRIJENHOEK, ROBERT C.
Fitness differences among remnant populations of the endangered Sonoran topminnow. bibl f il *Science* 245:976-8 S 1 '89
QUATTRO (COMPUTER PROGRAM) See Spreadsheets (Computer programs)
QUATTROCHI, JAMES J., AND OTHERS
Mapping neuronal inputs to REM sleep induction sites with carbachol-fluorescent microspheres. bibl f il *Science* 245:984-6 S 1 '89
QUAYLE, CORINNE
about
Her son: the vice president. P. Stackhouse. il por *The Saturday Evening Post* 261:28+ My/Je '89
QUAYLE, DAN
American leadership in the Pacific [address, May 3, 1989] *Department of State Bulletin* 89:52-5 Ag '89
Dan, you're no Strunk or White [exchange of letters] *Harper's* 278:24-6 Je '89
Sense and etymology in settlers' English. *Harper's* 278:19-20 My '89
U.S. policy in Asia [address, June 22, 1989] *Vital Speeches of the Day* 55:610-13 Ag 1 '89
Vice president visits Venezuela and El Salvador [remarks and statement, February 1 and 3, 1989] il pors *Department of State Bulletin* 89:7 Ap '89

QUAYLE, DAN—cont.

about

Can this VP get respect? S. Manning. il por *Scholastic Update (Teachers' edition)* 121:6 Ja 13 '89

Covert campaigns. P. Montgomery. *Common Cause Magazine* 15:7-8 My/Je '89

Dan Quayle's salvage strategy. L. I. Barrett. il por *Time* 133:22 Je 26 '89

Danny gets his gun. F. Barnes. *The New Republic* 200:10-11 Je 26 '89

The education of a standby. G. J. Church. il por *Time* 133:27 Ja 30 '89

The education of Dan Quayle [cover story] M. Dowd. il pors *The New York Times Magazine* p18-21+ Je 25 '89

The exquisite imprisonment of Dan Quayle. L. Rosellini. il por *U.S. News & World Report* 106:26-7 My 29 '89

Her son: the vice president. P. Stackhouse. il por *The Saturday Evening Post* 261:28+ My/Je '89

Introducing Dan Quayle, competitiveness czar. R. Fly. il por *Business Week* p37 F 27 '89

Quayle denounces U.S. reliance on foreign space launch vehicles. T. M. Foley. il por *Aviation Week & Space Technology* 130:21-2 Ap 10 '89

The Quayle family newspapers: black, white—and green all over. J. F. Siler. il por *Business Week* p29 Ag 28 '89

Rocket man. B. Reed. *The New Republic* 200:12-13 My 15 '89

Sparring partners. M. Kondracke. *The New Republic* 201:14-16 N 13 '89

Talking to Dan Quayle—seriously. L. Weymouth. il pors *New York* 22:44-9 Mr 13 '89

Vice-presidential keepstakes. il por *U.S. News & World Report* 107:12-13 N 20 '89

The vice president's Bible. R. Pulliam. il por *The Saturday Evening Post* 261:26 Ap '89

Will TV give Dan Quayle a fair chance? What he can do to improve his image. E. Diamond and J. Maroe. por *TV Guide* 37:16-19 F 11-17 '89

Anecdotes, facetiae, satire, etc.

A Danny Quayle reader [cover story] il *The American Spectator* 22:13 Je '89

Deconstructing the Danny Quayle reader [discussion of June 1989 article] il *The American Spectator* 22:26-7 Ag '89

Veepers, creepers, where'd ya get those ties? il *Gentlemen's Quarterly* 59:212-13 F '89

Caricatures and cartoons

The adventures of J. Danforth. E. Sorel. See issues of Gentlemen's Quarterly beginning March 1989

From CIA to KGB (kinder, gentler Bush) [cover story] M. Ivins. il por *Mother Jones* 14:32-7 Ap '89

Visit to El Salvador, 1989

Quayle shooting. il por *Newsweek* 113:46 Je 26 '89

Visit to Latin America, 1989

Dan Quayle hits the road. E. Salholz. il por *Newsweek* 113:18 F 13 '89

Dan Quayle's diplomatic debut. D. Goodgame. il por *Time* 133:37 F 13 '89

Giving diplomacy a chance. *America* 160:163 F 25 '89

Vice president visits Venezuela and El Salvador [remarks and statement, February 1 and 3, 1989] D. Quayle. il pors *Department of State Bulletin* 89:7 Ap '89

Visit to Singapore, 1989

American leadership in the Pacific [address, May 3, 1989] D. Quayle. *Department of State Bulletin* 89:52-5 Ag '89

QUAYLE, MARILYN

Marilyn Quayle's first months as the country's Second Lady. il pors *Life* 12:89-90+ My '89

about

Marilyn Quayle: the woman nobody knows. J. Farrell and B. B. Gray. il pors *Ladies' Home Journal* 106:84+ O '89

A new Second Lady who is no second fiddle. A. Stanley. il por *Time* 133:27 Ja 23 '89

QUÉBEC (PROVINCE)

See also
Environmental policy—Québec (Province)
Family—Québec (Province)
Finance—Québec (Province)
Fishing—Québec (Province)
George River (Québec)
Montreal (Québec)
Motion picture festivals—Québec (Province)
Music festivals—Québec (Province)
Québec (Québec)
Saguenay County (Québec)
Water pollution—Québec (Province)
Wildlife conservation—Québec (Province)

Description and travel

Quebec. R. Howell. il *Black Enterprise* 20:123-4 N '89

Industries

See also
Publishers and publishing—Canada

The color of money [francophone business community] G. W. Taylor. il *Maclean's* 102:25-6 S 25 '89

Languages

An Anglo rebellion [English-speaking Quebecers consider alternatives in upcoming provincial election] M. Rose. il *Maclean's* 102:13 Ag 28 '89

The failures of Robert Bourassa. J. Stewart. por *Maclean's* 102:64 Ja 2 '89

Quebec fire storm [language disputes and arson] L. Van Dusen. il por *Maclean's* 102:12-13 F 6 '89

Quebec's challenge [immigrants who shun French] D. Burke. il *Maclean's* 102:25 Jl 10 '89

The return to two solitudes [bilingualism] B. Bergman. il *Maclean's* 102:26+ N 6 '89

War over words [move to restrict use of English signs; special section] il por *Maclean's* 102:38-42 Ja 2 '89

Anecdotes, facetiae, satire, etc.

We're number 1 in language debates. C. Gordon. il *Maclean's* 102:39 Ja 9 '89

Nationalism

A battle joined [P. Trudeau enters debate over constitutional accord; cover story; special section] il pors *Maclean's* 102:20-2+ N 6 '89

The divided nation [Meech Lake constitutional accord in Canada; cover story; special section; with editorial comment by Kevin Doyle] il *Maclean's* 102:4, 18-23+ Mr 20 '89

An independent voice [J. Parizeau] B. Wallace. il por *Maclean's* 102:21-2 O 23 '89

The re-election of a barefaced opportunist [R. Bourassa] P. C. Newman. il *Maclean's* 102:44 O 9 '89

Storm clouds over Quebec [separatism issue in provincial election campaign; cover story; special section; with editorial comment by Kevin Doyle] il pors *Maclean's* 102:2, 16-22+ S 25 '89

Trouble on the Quebec front [R. Bourassa vs. J. Chrétien on constitutional accord] B. Wallace. *Maclean's* 102:12 Je 26 '89

Politics and government

See also
Parti québécois
Politics, Corruption in—Québec (Province)
Quebec New Democratic Party

An Anglo rebellion [English-speaking Quebecers consider alternatives in upcoming provincial election] M. Rose. il *Maclean's* 102:13 Ag 28 '89

Campaigning in Quebec [R. Bourassa calls election] M. Rose. il por *Maclean's* 102:14-15 Ag 21 '89

Heading for the polls [R. Bourassa] B. Wallace. il por *Maclean's* 102:14-15 Je 19 '89

Qualified victory [R. Bourassa re-elected] M. Rose. il por *Maclean's* 102:16-18 O 9 '89

The re-election of a barefaced opportunist [R. Bourassa] P. C. Newman. il *Maclean's* 102:44 O 9 '89

Storm clouds over Quebec [separatism issue in provincial election campaign; cover story; special section; with editorial comment by Kevin Doyle] il pors *Maclean's* 102:2, 16-22+ S 25 '89

Population

Quebec's challenge [immigrants who shun French] D. Burke. il *Maclean's* 102:25 Jl 10 '89

Religious institutions and affairs

See also
Reformed Church of Quebec

Strikes

See also
Strikes—Nurses—Canada

QUÉBEC (PROVINCE). CAISSE DE DÉPÔT ET PLACE-MENT DU QUÉBEC See Caisse de dépôt et placement du Québec

QUÉBEC (QUÉBEC)

Stores

The birthplace of shopping—Quebec. D. P. Marshall. il *Travel Holiday* 171:24+ My '89

QUEBEC AIR SERVICE

Fighting fires from the air: Quebec will upgrade CL-215 waterbomber fleet [cover story; special section] D. Hughes. il *Aviation Week & Space Technology* 131:36-7+ Ag 21 '89

QUÉBEC DEPOSIT AND INVESTMENT FUND See Caisse de dépôt et placement du Québec

QUEBEC NEW DEMOCRATIC PARTY

A declaration of independence. D. Burke. il *Maclean's* 102:17 Je 5 '89

QUEBECOR INC.

The acquisitor [P. Péladeau acquires control of U.S. printing plants owned by R. Maxwell] J. Daly. il pors *Maclean's* 102:38-9 N 13 '89

QUECHEE (VT.)

Restaurants, nightclubs, bars, etc.

See also
Mill (Quechee, Vt.)

QUEEN (MUSICAL GROUP)

Queen. R. C. Walls. il *High Fidelity (New York, N.Y.)* 39:71+ Jl '89

QUEEN ANNE FURNITURE See Furniture, English

QUEEN ELIZABETH 2 (SHIP)

The Queen and I [trip across the Atlantic and back] B. Greene. il *Esquire* 111:47+ My '89

QUEEN OF HEARTS [film] See Motion picture reviews—Single works

QUEEN STREET (TORONTO, ONT.)

Queen for a day. J. Schneller. il *Gentlemen's Quarterly* 59:181-2 Je '89

QUEENAN, JOE
Chain of fools. *The New Republic* 201:8 Jl 17-24 '89
Dead and breakfast. *The New Republic* 200:12+ Mr 20 '89
Drawing on the dark side. il *The New York Times Magazine* p32-4+ Ap 30 '89
Fore play. il *Gentlemen's Quarterly* 59:248-57 Je '89
Japun, Inc. *The New Republic* 201:14-15 O 16 '89
A letter to the editor. il *The American Spectator* 22:31 Ja '89
Nice day for a black wedding. *The American Spectator* 22:18-19 F '89
No dunkin'. No dough. Just nuts. il *Gentlemen's Quarterly* 59:207-8+ N '89
Quark bites. il *The American Spectator* 22:25-6 Mr '89
Ronald Reagan is full of bologna. il *Gentlemen's Quarterly* 59:161-2 Ag '89
Straight men. il *Rolling Stone* p72-3+ N 2 '89
Year in review. il *Channels (New York, N.Y.: 1986)* 9:52+ Ja '89

about
Oy, Canada. M. Richler. il *Gentlemen's Quarterly* 59:181+ Mr '89
QUEENAN, JOHN T., AND LESLIE, KIMBERLY K.
A case for preplanning [excerpt from Preconceptions] il *Health (New York, N.Y.)* 21:38-9+ D '89
QUEENS
Medieval queenship. L. Huneycutt. bibl il *History Today* 39:16-22 Je '89
QUEENS (NEW YORK, N.Y.)
Crime
New York mother throws two children out of window [M. Abdussalaam] il por *Jet* 77:18 O 23 '89
The sad tale of Sweet Pea [basketball player L. Daniels shot during reported drug dispute] il por *Sports Illustrated* 70:12 My 22 '89
Galleries and museums
See also
American Museum of the Moving Image (New York, N.Y.)
New York Hall of Science
Queens Museum
Hospitals
Family doesn't know father died in N.Y. hospital till daughter finds its bill [T. Bennett dies at Jamaica Hospital] il por *Jet* 75:19 F 13 '89
Parks and playgrounds
See also
Jacob Riis Park (New York, N.Y.)
QUEENS MUSEUM
Small town [Panorama of the City of New York] *The New Yorker* 65:33-4 My 8 '89
QUEENSLAND (AUSTRALIA)
Description and travel
Down Under and way up north. il map *Sunset (Central West edition)* 183:60-3 O '89
Gourmet holidays: islands off the Great Barrier Reef. P. J. Wade and K. Wade. il map *Gourmet* 49:46-51+ Mr '89
QUERY LETTERS (AUTHORS TO PUBLISHERS) *See* Authors and publishers
QUESTION OF SCRUPLES (GAME) *See* Scruples (Game)
QUESTIONING
See also
Children's questions and answers
Police questioning
Developing thinking skills through questioning. D. B. Strother. bibl f *Phi Delta Kappan* 71:324-7 D '89
QUESTIONS AND ANSWERS
Anecdotes, facetiae, satire, etc.
Having all the answers is a hard row to hoe. J. Skow. il *Smithsonian* 19:154 Ja '89
QUEUES (WAITING LINES)
Great Britain
Falling in line with the British. R. Johnson. il *World Press Review* 36:71 D '89
QUEZADA, ABEL
about
Touché for a Mexican Lampooner. J. Budd. il por *Américas* 41 no1:38-41 '89
QUICHE
Pie to cry for [Alsatian onion tart] E. Sahatjian. il *Esquire* 111:28 Ja '89
QUICK, RICHARD
about
Once more, with feeling. J. E. Vader. il por *Sports Illustrated* 70:71+ Mr 27 '89
QUIETNESS *See* Quietude
QUIETUDE
Quietude. P. V. Fossel. il *Country Journal* 16:8+ N/D '89
QUIGLEY, LINNEA
about
A real scream, Linnea Quigley gets sliced, diced and chomped on as the new cult queen of the B's. S. K. Reed. il pors *People Weekly* 32:191-2 D 4 '89
QUIGLEY, PAXTON
Women and crime: is this the answer? [excerpt from Armed and female] il *Glamour* 87:344-5+ Ap '89

QUIKSILVER, INC.
Hey, dude, check out these boardshorts. L. Armstrong. il por *Business Week* p96 My 22 '89
QUILL CORPORATION
Brother act. M. Barrier. il *Nation's Business* 77:41-2 Ja '89
QUILLEN, JAMES H.
Should the Congress adopt the "Textile and Apparel Trade Act of 1987"? [excerpts from address, September 16, 1987] *Congressional Digest* 68:16+ Ja '89
QUILLER, STEPHEN, 1946-
Watercolor page: using harmonious color relationships. il por *American Artist* 53:40-3 O '89
QUILTING *See* Quilts and quilting
QUILTS AND QUILTING
See also
AIDS Quilt
Freedom Quilting Bee (Organization)
4 stencil quilts to make. il *Good Housekeeping* 208:126-9+ Ap '89
Comforters. il *Consumer Reports* 54:706-10 N '89
Helping homeless families [quilt made by Long Island women] M. Daly. il *Better Homes and Gardens* 67:35-6 Ap '89
Collectors and collecting
Cozying up to quilts. B. Keating. il *New Choices for the Best Years* 29:84+ O '89
Double wedding ring quilts. R. C. Bishop. il *Antiques* 135:732-41 Mr '89
An old quilt can be a mighty comfy investment. S. D. Atchison. il *Business Week* p106 Mr 6 '89
Quilt crazy. B. Sherman. il *Harper's Bazaar* 122:56+ F '89
Exhibitions
Faith Ringgold/Bernice Steinbaum Gallery. P. Scheinman. il *American Craft* 49:72-3 F/Mr '89
Slave quilts [Stitched from the soul: slave quilts from the ante-bellum South at the Museum of American Folk Art] *The New Yorker* 65:32-3 Ag 7 '89
Susan McCord's quilts: a farmwife's legacy at Henry Ford Museum. il *Antiques & Collecting Hobbies* 94:37-8 Ap '89
Textiles made by southern slaves [Stitched from the soul: slave quilts from the ante-bellum South] A. E. Ledes. il *Antiques* 136:222+ Ag '89
Through her quilts, one women's life unfolds [Susan McCord's quilts: a farmwife's legacy at Henry Ford Museum] il *Americana* 17:26 N/D '89
QUINBY'S (FIRM)
What next for Quinby's? L. See. il *Publishers Weekly* 236:32+ S 29 '89
QUINCY (FLA.)
Architecture
Enriched by tradition [home of Beth and Fount May] il *Southern Living* 24:132 O '89
QUINDLEN, ANNA
Can children & parents be adults together? il *New Choices for the Best Years* 29:89-90 Ja '89
The tree that came to stay [story] il *The New York Times Magazine* p18-19 D 24 '89
QUINE, JUDY
about
Such good friends. il pors *Harper's Bazaar* 122:110-11+ Je '89
QUININE
He gave quinine to the world [C. Ledger] J. Bland. il *World Health* p28-9 D '88
QUINLAN, ALICE
Easing the cost of catastrophe. il *New Choices for the Best Years* 29:45-7 Ap '89
QUINLAN, MICHAEL R.
about
The burger wars were just a warmup for McDonald's. B. Bremner. il *Business Week* p67+ My 8 '89
QUINLAN, NOELLE M.
Icy waters [poem] *America* 161:477 D 23-30 '89
QUINN, AIDAN
about
Where has Aidan Quinn been? L. VanSickle. por *Mademoiselle* 95:96 Ap '89
QUINN, COLIN
about
The mighty Quinn. M. Berkman. il por *New York* 22:26 O 30 '89
QUINN, FREDERICK
French Protestants: an endangered species? *The Christian Century* 106:439-40 Ap 26 '89
QUINN, JANE BRYANT
[Column] *See* occasional issues of Newsweek
QUINN, JOHN R.
Abortion: the axe at the root of human rights. *America* 160:284-5 Ap 1 '89
QUINN, JOHN ROBERT
Old man cleaning bluegills [poem] *America* 160:322 Ap 8 '89
QUINN, KATHRYN
about
Two partners, one floor plan. L. Rosch. il por *Working Woman* 14:69 Ja '89

QUINN, LONGWORTH M., D. 1989
about
Obituary
Jet por 75:54 F 13 '89
QUINN AND SEARL, ARCHITECTS
Two partners, one floor plan [office of K. Quinn and L. Searl] L. Rosch. il por *Working Woman* 14:69 Ja '89
QUINNETT, PAUL G., 1939-
Birding, southern style. il *Audubon* 91:34-7 My '89
The key to successful therapy. il *Psychology Today* 23:46-7 Ap '89
The woman in the yellow hat. il *Audubon* 91:46-8 S '89
QUINONES
See also
Methoxatin
QUINT, BARBARA GILDER
5 super-safe places to save. *Glamour* 87:120+ F '89
More for your money. See issues of Glamour
QUINTA, CHRISTINE
The truth [poem] *Essence* 20:128 N '89
We need poets [poem] *Essence* 20:126 N '89
QUINTANILLA, MARIA ALINE GRIFFITHS Y DEXTER
See Aline, Countess of Romanones
THE QUINTESSENTIAL IMAGE [drama] *See* Chambers, Jane, 1937-1983
QUINTUPLETS
For a gang of five, one for the road [L'Esperance quintuplets celebrate first birthday] M. Brower. il *People Weekly* 31:30-5 Ja 30 '89
QUISQUALATE *See* Quisqualic acid
QUISQUALIC ACID
Quisqualate activates a rapidly inactivating high conductance ionic channel in hippocampal neurons. C.-M. Tang and others. bibl f il *Science* 243:1474-7 Mr 17 '89
QUITTING OF JOBS *See* Employees—Resignation
QUIZ SHOWS *See* Television broadcasting—Quiz shows
QUMRAN SCROLLS *See* Dead Sea scrolls
QUOIREZ, FRANÇOISE *See* Sagan, Françoise, 1935-
QUOTAS, IMPORT (U.S.) *See* United States—Commercial policy
QUOTATIONS
See also
Bartlett's familiar quotations
Maxims
Medicine—Quotations
Money—Quotations
'88: the year in pictures [special issue] il *Life* 12:2-3+ Ja '89
The 128 best things anyone ever said in People. il *People Weekly* 31:25+ Mr 6 '89
"Bon mots". G. F. Kreyche. il *USA Today (Periodical)* 118:98 Jl '89
A heritage of faux mots [Library of Congress' Respectfully quoted] il *U.S. News & World Report* 106:16 Ap 10 '89
Of many things [excerpts from The third and possibly the best 637 best things anybody ever said] G. W. Hunt. *America* 161:262 O 28 '89
Points to ponder. See issues of Reader's Digest
Quotable quotes. See issues of Reader's Digest
Quote quiz. *The Humanist* 49:34 Jl/Ag '89
Thoughts on the business of life. See issues of Forbes
Toward more picturesque speech. See issues of Reader's Digest
Anecdotes, facetiae, satire, etc.
Lines from our times. M. B. Zuckerman. il *U.S. News & World Report* 106:67 Ja 9 '89
QUOTATIONS, STOCK *See* Stock quotations
QUOTRON SYSTEMS, INC.
Rich prospects, poor technology [ADP taking stock quote market away from Quotron] F. Meeks. il *Forbes* 143:72+ Ap 3 '89
QVC NETWORK INC.
QVC Network. R. Abelson. il *Fortune* 120:108 Jl 17 '89

R

R & B COMPACT DISCS *See* Compact discs—Rock music
R. A. LAIDLAW CENTER/BETTY OLIPHANT THEATRE (TORONTO, ONT.)
Betty builds bigger. M. Horosko. il *Dance Magazine* 63:62-3 Mr '89
R.E.M. (MUSICAL GROUP)
Dreaming at the wheel. J. Cocks. il *Time* 133:94-5 Mr 27 '89
The greening of R.E.M. [release of Green] M. Azerrad. il *Rolling Stone* p63-4 Ja 12 '89
Greenpeace gets boost from R.E.M. K. Terry. *Rolling Stone* p67 Jl 13-27 '89
R.E.M.'s brave new world [cover story] A. DeCurtis. il *Rolling Stone* p48-50+ Ap 20 '89
R.F. SCHIFFMANN ASSOCIATES
Doughnut detonator. J. Zweig. il por *Forbes* 143:154+ My 1 '89

R. H. MACY & CO., INC.
The benefits of leverage. S. N. Chakravarty. il por *Forbes* 143:42 My 1 '89
R. J. REYNOLDS INDUSTRIES, INC.
See also
RJR Nabisco Inc.
R. J. REYNOLDS TOBACCO CO.
Patrick Reynolds fumes about his tobacco-rich clan in a tangy, tell-all book. P. Freeman. il pors *People Weekly* 31:46-7 Ap 24 '89
Tobacco road's dirty ashtrays [book by P. Reynolds] J. Castro. il por *Time* 133:52 Ap 24 '89
R. S. OWENS & COMPANY
The prize is right [O. Siegel casts the Oscar statuettes] E. Stern. il por *Gentlemen's Quarterly* 59:49+ Mr '89
R&D (RESEARCH AND DEVELOPMENT) *See* Industrial research; Research
RAAB, LAWRENCE
What I forgot to mention [poem] *The New Yorker* 65:124 S 18 '89
RAAB, SELWYN
John Gotti: running the Mob [cover story] il pors *The New York Times Magazine* p30-3+ Ap 2 '89
RAAB COOKING *See* Cooking—Vegetables
RAABE, TOM
The ultimate church [cover story] *The Christian Century* 106:717-21 Ag 2-9 '89
RABB, MAURICE F.
about
Dr. Maurice Rabb named new medical director at natl. blindness group. por *Jet* 75:27 F 20 '89
RABBIT HUNTING
See also
Basseting (Sport)
Littlebit's first hunt [cottontails] B. Tarrant. il *Field & Stream* 94:110+ N '89
Winter rabbit hunting [New York State] E. S. Feldmann. il *The Conservationist* 43:14-17 Ja/F '89
RABBIT MEAT
Bunnyburgers. J. Zweig. il *Forbes* 143:42-3 Mr 20 '89
RABBITS
See also
Cooking—Game
British rabbits: scholarship down [plan to build facilities on site of rabbit warren being studied by Diana Bell and Nicola Webb at the University of East Anglia] J. Cherfas. *Science* 246:1384 D 15 '89
Real rabbits [pets] *The New Yorker* 65:35-7 Mr 27 '89
Woody and Ed [animal occupants of Illinois garden] R. M. Lerner. il *Organic Gardening* 36:104 Ja '89
RABBITT, EDDIE, 1944-
about
Still grieving after the death of his young son, Eddie Rabbitt finds solace in country music. T. Allis. il pors *People Weekly* 31:83-4 Ap 17 '89
RABE, DAVID
about
Body count. G. Smith. il *Film Comment* 25:49-52 Jl/Ag '89
Hurlyburly [drama] Reviews
People Weekly il 31:54-5 Ja 9 '89. S. K. Reed
RABE COOKING *See* Cooking—Vegetables
LA RABIDA CHILDREN'S HOSPITAL AND RESEARCH CENTER (CHICAGO, ILL.) *See* Children—Hospitals
RABIES
Pets and rabies: cause for concern in the Midwest [dogs and cats] il *Better Homes and Gardens* 67:175 My '89
Vaccines and vaccination
South Carolina blocks test of rabies vaccine [proposed use of genetically engineered virus on wild raccoons] M. Sun. il *Science* 244:1535 Je 30 '89
Virginia OKs rabies vaccine test [use of genetically engineered virus on raccoons] M. Sun. *Science* 245:126 Jl 14 '89
RABIN, ELLIOTT
(tr) *See* Adelmann von Adelmannsfelden, Rainer Rene. Count Dracula makes an offer
RABINOVE, SAMUEL
Finding out who counts. il *Commonweal* 116:360-1 Je 16 '89
RABINOVICH, ABRAHAM
'Bridge' building in Jerusalem. il por *World Press Review* 36:73 S '89
RABINOVICH, ITAMAR, 1942-
Syria and Lebanon in 1988. bibl f *Current History* 88:77-80+ F '89
RABINOVITZ, FRANCINE F.
What should be done? *Society* 26:12-13 My/Je '89
RABINOWITCH, DAVID, 1943-
about
Luminous circles. H. Cotter. il *Art in America* 77:194-5 S '89
RABINOWITZ, DOROTHY
Arms and the man: a sex scandal rocks Princeton. il pors *New York* 22:30-6 Jl 17 '89
The art of the feud: sculptor Louise Nevelson's tangled legal legacy. il pors *New York* 22:82-8+ S 25 '89
Slotnick's law. il pors *New York* 22:30-4 Ja 2 '89

RABINOWITZ, NEIL
Showdown in Seattle. il *Women's Sports & Fitness* 11:22-5 Jl/Ag '89
RABITZ, HERSCHEL
Systems analysis at the molecular scale. bibl f il *Science* 246:221-6 O 13 '89
RABOTEAU, ALBERT
Preaching the word & doing it: black Catholics in America. il *Commonweal* 116:631-2+ N 17 '89
RABUN COUNTY (GA.)
Description and travel
Rabun County, Georgia. L. Harrison. map *New Choices for the Best Years* 29:13 Je '89
RABUSHKA, ALVIN, AND BERNSTAM, MIKHAIL S.
To keep the tax promise, try a lottery. pors *Fortune* 119:126 F 27 '89
RACAMIER, HENRY
about
Avant le deluge at Moet Hennessy Louis Vuitton. S. Toy. il *Business Week* p44 Ap 24 '89
A luxury fight to the finish. S. Greenhouse. il pors *The New York Times Magazine* p38-9+ D 17 '89
RACCOON HUNTING
A hound's start in life [J. Wick's training suggestions] L. Mueller. il por *Outdoor Life* 183:43-4 F '89
Listening in the dark [coon hounds] B. Tarrant. il *Field & Stream* 93:94+ Ja '89
Anecdotes, facetiae, satire, etc.
Jimmy Kimmery and the saddle horse. B. Tarrant. il por *Field & Stream* 94:102-3 D '89
RACCOONS
Anecdotes, facetiae, satire, etc.
The raccoon and the hummingbird. L. Eisenberg. il *Esquire* 112:43 O '89
Diseases and pests
South Carolina blocks test of rabies vaccine [proposed use of genetically engineered virus on wild raccoons] M. Sun. il *Science* 244:1535 Je 30 '89
Virginia OKs rabies vaccine test [use of genetically engineered virus on raccoons] M. Sun. *Science* 245:126 Jl 14 '89
RACE *See* Ethnology
RACE ACROSS AMERICA *See* Bicycle racing
RACE DIFFERENCES
Getting to the heart of the Chinese [Chinese men more sensitive than Caucasian men to propranolol] *Science News* 135:156 Mr 11 '89
Race and behavior [controversy over J. P. Rushton's correlation of race to intelligence and behavior] R. Dolphin. il por *Maclean's* 102:44 F 13 '89
Racial differences in heart rate [research by Lars G. Ekelund] K. Fackelmann. *Science News* 136:15 Jl 1 '89
Tasting the passing favorite flavors [fuss over racial theories of J. P. Rushton] A. Fotheringham. il *Maclean's* 102:56 F 20 '89
RACE DISCRIMINATION
See also
Apartheid
Blacks—Segregation
Discrimination in education
Discrimination in employment
Discrimination in sports
United Nations. Sub-commission on Prevention of Discrimination and Protection of Minorities
The new racism is the old power grab [cover story] W. B. Allen. il por *Conservative Digest* 15:16-21 Jl/Ag '89
Passages: 1989-2000 [address, January 30, 1989] V. Jordan. *Vital Speeches of the Day* 55:406-8 Ap 15 '89
Racism: can we heal the wounds? [cover story; special issue] il *Scholastic Update (Teachers' edition)* 121:2-12+ Ap 7 '89
RACE HORSES
See also
Northern Dancer (Race horse)
Secretariat (Race horse)
A tale of two horses [Kentucky Derby contenders Houston and Easy Goer] D. Stathoplos. il *Sports Illustrated* 70:78-81+ My 8 '89
Well-groomed or well-bred? [thoroughbred breeding in England] N. Russell. il *History Today* 39:10-12 Ja '89
Auctions
See Horse auctions
Breeding
See Horses—Breeding
Handicapping
See Horse race betting
Insurance
High stakes [Lloyd's of London insures race horses] K. Hannon. il por *Forbes* 143:326+ My 29 '89
Training
The bald eagle [Sunday Silence trainer C. Whittingham] W. Nack. il pors *Sports Illustrated* 70:54-6+ Je 12 '89
Tops at the track [C. McGaughey of Phipps Stable] W. Nack. il pors *Sports Illustrated* 70:38-41+ F 6 '89

RACE HORSES, EFFECT OF ULTRASONIC WAVES ON
See Animals, Effect of ultrasonic waves on
RACE IMPROVEMENT *See* Eugenics
RACE PREJUDICE *See* Race discrimination
RACE RELATIONS
See also
Alabama—Race relations
Arizona—Race relations
Atlanta (Ga.)—Race relations
Bensonhurst (New York, N.Y.)—Race relations
Birmingham (Ala.)—Race relations
Boston (Mass.)—Race relations
Brazil—Race relations
Cambridge (Mass.)—Race relations
Canada—Race relations
Chicago (Ill.)—Race relations
China—Race relations
Church and race relations
Church schools—Race relations
Colleges and universities—Race relations
Columbia (Mo.)—Race relations
Conway (S.C.)—Race relations
Cranston (R.I.)—Race relations
Dallas (Tex.)—Race relations
Denver (Colo.)—Race relations
Forsyth County (Ga.)—Race relations
Georgia—Race relations
Halifax County (N.S.)—Race relations
High schools—Race relations
Interracial marriage
Japan—Race relations
Ku Klux Klan
Lansdowne (Pa.)—Race relations
Martin Luther King, Jr. Center for Nonviolent Social Change
Miami (Fla.)—Race relations
Mississippi—Race relations
Mobile (Ala.)—Race relations
Montreal (Québec)—Race relations
Napa County (Calif.)—Race relations
New York (N.Y.)—Race relations
North Augusta (S.C.)—Race relations
Nova Scotia—Race relations
Philadelphia (Miss.)—Race relations
Prince Edward County (Va.)—Race relations
Pulaski (Tenn.)—Race relations
Race discrimination
Racial slurs
Richmond (Va.)—Race relations
Southern States—Race relations
Soviet Union—Race relations
Toronto (Ont.)—Race relations
United States—Race relations
Vancouver (B.C.)—Race relations
Wisconsin—Race relations
Waiting for a taxi [adaptation of address, April 1989] J. Jordan. il *The Progressive* 53:16-18 Je '89
RACE RELATIONS AND THE PRESS
Yellow-peril journalism: is latent racism coloring business coverage of Japan? E. Cose. il *Time* 134:79 N 27 '89
RACE RELATIONS IN MOTION PICTURES
Daniel: beloved by God & by me [seeing Do the right thing with teenage son] B. B. Morton. *Commonweal* 116:562-3 O 20 '89
Do the right thing: a jarring look at racism. J. M. Wall. *The Christian Century* 106:739-40 Ag 16-23 '89
Doing the controversial thing [S. Lee's film Do the right thing] A. P. Sanoff. por *U.S. News & World Report* 107:51 Jl 10 '89
Fire this time [Mississippi burning; cover story] R. Corliss. il *Time* 133:56-62 Ja 9 '89
Hollywood and civil rights [shortcomings of Mississippi burning] D. Bogle. il *Essence* 19:32 Mr '89
Hollywood: the dustbin of history [Mississippi burning] P. Arthur. il *USA Today (Periodical)* 117:35 My '89
How hot is too hot? [S. Lee's Do the right thing; special section] il *Newsweek* 114:64-6 Jl 3 '89
Insight to riot [S. Lee's Do the right thing] D. Handelman. il por *Rolling Stone* p104-5+ Jl 13-27 '89
Mississippi theater won't show controversial movie [Philadelphia, Miss. theater won't show Mississippi burning] il *Jet* 75:51 Ja 23 '89
Spike Lee explores racial conflict in 'Do the right thing' [cover story] T. S. Moore. il pors *Jet* 76:36-9 Jl 10 '89
Spike Lee inflames the critics with a film he swears is The right thing. J. S. Kunen. il pors *People Weekly* 32:67-8 Jl 10 '89
Spike Lee replies: "Say it ain't so, Joe" [discussion of June 26, 1989 article, Spiked?] J. Klein. il por *New York* 22:6 Jl 17 '89
Spike Lee's Bed-Stuy BBQ [Do the right thing; interview] M. Glicksman. il pors *Film Comment* 25:12-16+ Jl/Ag '89
Spiked? [effect of S. Lee's film Do the right thing on D. Dinkins's mayoral campaign] J. Klein. il pors *New York* 22:14-15 Je 26 '89
Spike's riot [S. Lee; cover story] P. Orenstein. il pors *Mother Jones* 14:32-5+ S '89

RACE RELATIONS IN MOTION PICTURES—cont.
What no one will admit about race in America. R. Rosenbaum. il *Mademoiselle* 95:94+ Ag '89
The world according to Spike Lee [Do the right thing; cover story] M. Morrison. por *National Review* 41:24-5 Ag 4 '89

RACE RELATIONS IN TELEVISION
Outcast to hero [R. Flowers Jr.] J. Wooten. il pors *TV Guide* 37:36-8 Ja 14-20 '89
A soap for us: Generations. D. Donloe. il *Essence* 20:32 Je '89
A soap goes black and white [interracial theme on Generations] J. Birnbaum. il *Time* 133:85 Mr 27 '89

RACE RELATIONS IN VIDEOTAPES
What no one will admit about race in America [Madonna's Like a prayer] R. Rosenbaum. il *Mademoiselle* 95:94+ Ag '89

RACE TRACKS
See also
Arlington International Racecourse (Ill.)
Dog tracks
Hollywood Park (Inglewood, Calif.: Race track)
Economic aspects
Has racing staked its future on a bad pony? [off-track simulcasting's effect on race track attendance] S. Phillips. il *Business Week* p84+ My 8 '89
An oil heiress looks for pay dirt at the track [fight promoter and race horse breeder J. Abercrombie] T. Vogel. il por *Business Week* p162 My 22 '89
History
See also
Arlington Park (Ill.: Racetrack)
RACE TRACKS, AUTOMOBILE *See* Speedways
RACE WALKING
An aerobic walkout. L. E. Koszuta. il *Current Health 2* 15:20-1 My '89
From the hip [racewalker M. Torrellas] S. Christenson. il por *American Health* 8:50 Mr '89
Take your walking to the max. M. Spilner. il *Women's Sports & Fitness* 11:12 O '89
RACES OF MAN *See* Ethnology
THE RACHEL PAPERS [film] *See* Motion picture reviews—Single works
RACHEL RIVER [television program] *See* Television program reviews—Single works
RACHLIN, JILL
(jt. auth) *See* Calio, Jim, and Rachlin, Jill
RACHLIN, JILL, AND ROVIN, JEFF
The Steel magnolias scrapbook. il *Ladies' Home Journal* 106:126+ N '89
RACHWALD, ARTHUR R.
Soviet-East European relations. bibl f *Current History* 88:377-80+ N '89
RACIAL DIFFERENCES *See* Race differences
RACIAL DISCRIMINATION *See* Race discrimination
RACIAL SLURS
Banning ethnic slurs on campus [University of Wisconsin] *Newsweek* 113:68 Ap 24 '89
RACINE, FRANCOIS-NICOLAS-HENRI *See* Monville, Francois-Nicolas-Henri Racine, baron de, 1737-1794
RACING
See also
Airplane model racing
Airplane racing
Automobile racing
Balloon racing
Bicycle racing
Boat racing
Camel racing
Harness racing
Horse racing
Human powered oceanographic submersible racing
Human powered vehicle racing
Hurdle racing
Hydroplane racing
Midget automobile racing
Motor boat racing
Motor vehicle racing
Motorcycle racing
Sailboat racing
Ski racing
Sled dog racing
Wheelchair racing
Yacht racing
RACING AIRPLANES *See* Airplanes, Racing
RACING BICYCLES *See* Bicycles
RACING BOAT ENGINES *See* Motor boat engines
RACING CAR MODELS *See* Automobile models
RACING CARS *See* Automobiles, Racing
RACING MOTORCYCLES *See* Motorcycles, Racing
RACING TIRES, AUTOMOBILE *See* Tires, Automobile
RACISM *See* Race discrimination
RACK JOBBERS
See also
Handleman Co.
RACKET SPORTS
See also
Racquetball

RACKETEER INFLUENCED AND CORRUPT ORGANIZATIONS ACT OF 1970
Business may have found a way to defang RICO. P. Dwyer. il *Business Week* p26 Ag 28 '89
Charges against Teamsters resolved. *Monthly Labor Review* 112:58 My '89
Don't let them gut RICO. M. Waldman and P. Gilbert. il *USA Today (Periodical)* 118:50-1 N '89
The feds rein in RICO. il *Newsweek* 114:58 N 6 '89
G. Robert Blakey versus Michael Milken [author of RICO statute] J. Queenan. il por *Forbes* 143:57+ My 1 '89
High Court bars pretrial RICO seizure of books [obscene materials in Indiana bookstores] H. Fields. *Publishers Weekly* 235:19 Mr 10 '89
In defense of RICO. *The New Republic* 201:4+ O 16 '89
Overhauling the Teamsters. A. Bernstein. *Business Week* p35-6 Mr 27 '89
RICO: a racketeering law run amok. R. Boucher. il *USA Today (Periodical)* 118:48-9 N '89
RICO is bad law. *National Review* 41:14 Ap 21 '89
The RICO squeeze. C. Byron. il *New York* 22:10-11 Jl 17 '89
The RICO weapon: too harsh for Wall Street? il *Newsweek* 113:44-5 Ja 2 '89
Round up the usual brokers. J. O'Sullivan. *National Review* 41:11 N 10 '89
Showdown at Gucci Gulch. A. L. Sanders. il *Time* 134:48 Ag 21 '89
Supreme Court upholds broad use of RICO. H. Fields. *Publishers Weekly* 236:7 Jl 7 '89
Too much firepower to fit the crime? [RICO law used in Princeton/Newport case] A. P. Tobias. il *Time* 134:74 N 20 '89
White-collar crime. il *Nation's Business* 77:91 Je '89
RACKETEERING
See also
Mafia
Racketeer Influenced and Corrupt Organizations Act of 1970
RACKETS, TENNIS *See* Tennis rackets
RACKS, CAR-TOP *See* Automobiles—Equipment
RACKS, TOWEL *See* Towel racks, rings, etc.
RACKS AND SHELVES *See* Shelves and racks
RACQUETBALL
Innerviews [interview with C. McKinney] il por *Women's Sports & Fitness* 11:57 N/D '89
Racquetball: grace, grit, and greatness. L. Mojer. il por *Women's Sports & Fitness* 11:72 Mr '89
RADAR
See also
Ground penetrating radar
Transponders
Ultra-wideband radar
Antennas
See also
Phased array antennas
Interference
See Radar interference
Meteorological use
See Radar meteorology
Military use
See also
Airplanes, Military—Radar equipment
Guided missiles—Radar equipment
Radar defense networks
Radar in aviation
Remotely piloted vehicles—Radar equipment
Stealth technology
HEMT devices could speed work on next-generation radar systems [high electron mobility transistors] B. D. Nordwall. il *Aviation Week & Space Technology* 130:65+ My 15 '89
Threats to the old magic. B. Van Voorst. il *Time* 134:83 N 6 '89
RADAR ASTRONOMY *See* Radar in astronomy
RADAR DEFENSE NETWORKS
Arms and the woman [Soviet admission that Krasnoyarsk radar violates ABM Treaty] J. O'Sullivan. *National Review* 41:9 N 24 '89
Boeing told to solve Peace Shield problems [system for Saudi Arabia] D. Hughes. *Aviation Week & Space Technology* 131:114 D 18-25 '89
The costs of secrecy [Krasnoyarsk radar] M. Bundy. il *The New York Times Magazine* p71 Ag 20 '89
The hazards of electromagnetic fields (II) [Pave Paws radar] P. Brodeur. *The New Yorker* 65:47-9+ Je 19 '89
Krasnoyarsk radar discussions [element of ABM Treaty; State Dept. statement, November 2, 1988] *Department of State Bulletin* 89:16 Ja '89
Navy installs ROTHR system in Alaska to protect battle groups in Pacific [relocatable over-the-horizon radar] D. Hughes. il map *Aviation Week & Space Technology* 131:69+ N 27 '89
Radar networks, computing advances seen as keys to counter Stealth technologies [views of Robert W. Selden] D. F. Bond. *Aviation Week & Space Technology* 131:41 D 4 '89

RADAR DEFENSE NETWORKS—*cont.*

USAF study asserts that Soviet defenses would be ineffective against B-2 bomber. D. F. Bond. il *Aviation Week & Space Technology* 131:29-30 O 30 '89

USAF to buy used Boeing 707s for use as Joint STARS platforms [Surveillance Target Attack Radar System] P. A. Gilmartin. *Aviation Week & Space Technology* 131:25 N 13 '89

Virginia ROTHR system covers Caribbean drug smuggling routes [Navy relocatable over-the-horizon radar] il map *Aviation Week & Space Technology* 131:76+ N 27 '89

Costs

Cost of building OTH-B radar in Alaska doubles. *Aviation Week & Space Technology* 131:27 N 13 '89

RADAR DETECTORS

See also

Group United Against Radar Detectors

Darth Radar. il *Time* 133:55 Mr 13 '89

Geico versus the DAKonians [anti-radar detector campaign] B. Visnic. *Car and Driver* 35:32-3 N '89

Laser thwarts auto radar detectors. il *Popular Mechanics* 166:11 S '89

Pocket protectors [compact radar detectors] C. Csere and N. Bissoon Dath. il *Car and Driver* 35:105-7+ O '89

Target [Geico targets Cycle in anti-radar detector campaign] P. Schilling. il *Cycle* 40:9+ Ja '89

RADAR IN ASTRONOMY

A different view of Mars [radar map by Duane O. Muhleman] J. Eberhart. il *Science News* 135:75 F 4 '89

Feeling the face of Venus [Magellan radar mapping; cover story] J. Eberhart. il *Science News* 135:248-9 Ap 22 '89

Largest radar detects dumbbell in space [Steven Ostro detects fused asteroid] *Science* 246:999 N 24 '89

Magellan's radar images of Venus to unmask cloud-shrouded planet. il *Aviation Week & Space Technology* 131:113+ O 9 '89

The planet next door [Venus] A. T. Bazilevskiy. il *Sky and Telescope* 77:360-6+ Ap '89

Radar detection of Phobos. S. J. Ostro and others. bibl f il *Science* 243:1584-6 Mr 24 '89

Radar reveals an asteroid's strange shape [research by Steven J. Ostro] J. Eberhart. il *Science News* 136:343 N 25 '89

Rivers in the sand [interpretation of shuttle radar imaging in the Sahara] B. Bower. map *Science News* 136:138-9 Ag 26 '89

Sighting comets with radar. *Sky and Telescope* 77:239 Mr '89

Styles of volcanism on Venus: new Arecibo high resolution radar data. D. B. Campbell and others. bibl f il *Science* 246:373-7 O 20 '89

Titan: continents in a hydrocarbon sea. M. M. Waldrop. il *Science* 245:129-30 Jl 14 '89

Venus unveiled [Magellan mission] S. D. Wall. il *Astronomy* 17:26-32 Ap '89

Watching meteors by radar [work of Graham Poole and David Roux] il *Sky and Telescope* 78:244-5 S '89

RADAR IN AVIATION

See also

Airplanes—Collision avoidance systems

Airplanes, Military—Radar equipment

Guided missiles—Radar equipment

Helicopters—Radar equipment

Radar meteorology

Remotely piloted vehicles—Radar equipment

Airspace, ARSA and you [airport radar service areas] J. M. McClellan. il *Flying* 116:74-5 Mr '89

Britain's Rediffusion Simulation offers microcomputer-based ATC trainer. C. A. Shifrin. il *Aviation Week & Space Technology* 131:83+ Ag 21 '89

FAA expands Mode C transponder use to all aircraft near major airports. *Aviation Week & Space Technology* 131:66 Jl 3 '89

First improved terminal radar installed at Huntsville Airport [ASR-9] J. Ott. *Aviation Week & Space Technology* 130:61 Jl 10 '89

NTSB report says safety diminished at Coast Tracon [southern California] *Aviation Week & Space Technology* 130:42 My 29 '89

Smarter radar can tell friend or foe [aftermath of Iranian air disaster, 1988] G. Davis. il *Popular Science* 235:78-82 Jl '89

Unisys wins $44.9-million contract to upgrade airport radar systems. il *Aviation Week & Space Technology* 131:57 N 6 '89

RADAR IN METEOROLOGY *See* Radar meteorology

RADAR IN NARCOTICS REGULATION

Virginia ROTHR system covers Caribbean drug smuggling routes [Navy relocatable over-the-horizon radar] il map *Aviation Week & Space Technology* 131:76+ N 27 '89

RADAR IN OCEANOGRAPHY

Remote sensing of ocean currents [synthetic aperture radar] R. M. Goldstein and others. bibl f il *Science* 246:1282-5 D 8 '89

RADAR IN RESCUE WORK

Life detector. G. Davis. il *Popular Science* 235:59 Ag '89

RADAR IN TRAFFIC CONTROL

See also

Radar detectors

Darth Radar. il *Time* 133:55 Mr 13 '89

Giving Big Brother the birdie [photo radar fails to catch on] S. C. Smith. il *Car and Driver* 35:103-5+ Ag '89

RADAR INTERFERENCE

See also

Stealth technology

Eaton to propose $600 million modification to ALQ-161 system [B-1B] *Aviation Week & Space Technology* 130:75+ Je 26 '89

GAO cites faulty test equipment for hampering EW system readiness [Air Force's electronic warfare systems] B. D. Nordwall. il *Aviation Week & Space Technology* 131:133+ O 9 '89

Grumman prepares for flight tests of advanced capability EA-6B. S. W. Kandebo. il *Aviation Week & Space Technology* 131:41+ S 25 '89

Grumman using visual simulations to improve electronic warfare capabilities of U.S. Navy. il *Aviation Week & Space Technology* 131:123-4 S 11 '89

Hercules concentrates EW effort on small, low-cost jammers. il *Aviation Week & Space Technology* 131:115+ S 11 '89

ITT Avionics emphasizes development of software, improves electronic system. B. D. Nordwall. il *Aviation Week & Space Technology* 131:83+ Jl 17 '89

More capable IR-guided weapons prompting improved jammers, decoys. il *Aviation Week & Space Technology* 131:50+ S 11 '89

The Navy: that blip on the screen may be a blooper [Airborne Self-Protection Jammer] D. Griffiths. *Business Week* p43 O 2 '89

Navy, USAF to award contracts for limited ALQ-165 production [airborne self-protection jamming systems] il *Aviation Week & Space Technology* 131:89+ S 11 '89

Need to detect signals instantly spurs call for digital components. il *Aviation Week & Space Technology* 131:104-5 S 18 '89

New Northrop Band-3 jammers to be fitted on F-15E in early 1990. *Aviation Week & Space Technology* 131:67 S 11 '89

New type of phased-array antenna could cut cost, weight of airborne systems [Sedco Systems] il *Aviation Week & Space Technology* 131:105+ S 18 '89

Pentagon awards production contracts for ALQ-165 to ITT, Westinghouse [airborne self-protection jammer] P. J. Klass. il *Aviation Week & Space Technology* 131:59+ O 16 '89

R & D work in low observables shifts emphasis from coatings to structures. il *Aviation Week & Space Technology* 131:109+ S 18 '89

USAF says F-15E integration problems may delay initial operating capability [ALQ-135 jammer] P. A. Gilmartin. *Aviation Week & Space Technology* 130:21 My 15 '89

USAF will use stand-alone radar warning system to shore up B-1B's EW capabilities. *Aviation Week & Space Technology* 130:101 Ja 2 '89

Westinghouse mounts effort to build entire jammer on single Ga-As wafer. il *Aviation Week & Space Technology* 131:102 S 18 '89

RADAR METEOROLOGY

Microburst radar may spur review of tower's role in aborting landings [Doppler radar tested at Denver] P. J. Klass. il *Aviation Week & Space Technology* 130:79+ My 1 '89

NOWrad now [WSI computer briefing services for pilots] A. Laboda. il *Flying* 116:30 S '89

Storm seers [Honeywell Primus 870 and Rockwell/Collins TWR-850 Doppler turbulence radars] F. George. il *Flying* 116:42-3 Ag '89

RADCLIFFE, DONNIE

Welcome to the Bushes'. il pors *The Saturday Evening Post* 261:42+ N/D '89

RADER, DOTSON

Tennessee fever. il *Harper's Bazaar* 122:364-5+ S '89

RADER, DOUG

about

He's an Angel now. P. Gammons. il pors *Sports Illustrated* 71:34-9 Ag 7 '89

RADETSKY, PETER

Forgotten but not gone. il *Discover* 10:22+ S '89

Taming the wily rhinovirus. il *Discover* 10:38-43 Ap '89

The ultimate parasite. il *Discover* 10:20-1 Ag '89

RADHAKRISHNAN, S. (SARVEPALLI), 1888-1975

about

Makers of modern India. S. Gopal. il pors *The Courier (Unesco)* 42:10-11 F '89

RADHAKRISHNAN, SARVEPALLI *See* Radhakrishnan, S. (Sarvepalli), 1888-1975

RADIAL SAWS *See* Saws and sawing

RADIAL TIRES *See* Tires, Automobile

RADIAL TIRES, MOTORCYCLE *See* Tires, Motorcycle

RADIATION

See also

Artificial satellites, Effect of radiation on

Cosmic background radiation

Cosmic rays

Doppler effect

Electromagnetic waves

Light

Luminescence

Masers, Celestial

RADIATION—See also—*cont.*
Minerals, Effect of radiation on
Scattering (Physics)
Solar radiation
Stars—Radiation
Synchrotron radiation
Ultraviolet rays
X rays
Channeling effects
See Channeling (Physics)
Measurement
See also
Geiger counters
Measurements of radiation from a Soviet warhead [cruise missile] S. Fetter and F. Von Hippel. il *Physics Today* 42:45 N '89
Physiological effects
See also
Electromagnetic waves—Physiological effects
Light—Physiological effects
Microwaves—Physiological effects
Ultraviolet rays—Physiological effects
Video display terminals—Health aspects
X rays—Physiological effects
Bone marrow transplants approved [radiation victims] J. L. Marx. il *Science* 244:768 My 19 '89
Chernobyl fallout. S. Shulman. il *Technology Review* 92:12-13 F/Mr '89
Effect of antisense c-*raf*-1 on tumorigenicity and radiation sensitivity of a human squamous carcinoma. U. Kasid and others. bibl f il *Science* 243:1354-6 Mr 10 '89
The hidden files [1946 accident at Los Alamos Lab; cover story] C. T. Honicker. il *The New York Times Magazine* p38-41+ N 19 '89
Living with radiation. C. E. Cobb. il maps *National Geographic* 175:402-37 Ap '89
Medical preparedness and nuclear war [address, April 23, 1988] J. M. Orient. *Vital Speeches of the Day* 55:186-90 Ja 1 '89
Policy forum:
Are radiation-induced effects hormetic? [low-dose ionizing radiation] S. Wolff. bibl f *Science* 245:575+ Ag 11 '89
On radiation, paradigms, and hormesis [low-dose ionizing radiation] L. A. Sagan. bibl f *Science* 245:574+ Ag 11 '89
Rad risks in young breasts. *Science News* 136:311 N 11 '89
The residue of nuclear hubris [possible link between waste disposal from weapons plants and cancer] J. Kluger. il *Discover* 10:10-11 Ja '89
Study upgrades radiation risks to humans [National Research Council report] J. Raloff. *Science News* 136:404 D 23-30 '89
Testing ground [Nevada Test Site] J. Hanrahan. il *Common Cause Magazine* 15:13-19+ Ja/F '89
Ukraine fallout debate [new Soviet standard for radiation exposure following Chernobyl accident] D. R. Marples. bibl f il *The Bulletin of the Atomic Scientists* 45:9-11 D '89
Safety devices and measures
See also
Nuclear facilities—Safety devices and measures
Nuclear power plants—Safety devices and measures
Nuclear reactors—Safety devices and measures
Radioactive waste disposal
RADIATORS
See also
Automobiles—Radiators
RADICAL LEFT (POLITICAL SCIENCE) *See* Radicalism
RADICALISM
See also
Black militants
Neo-Nazis
Press and radicalism
Students for a Democratic Society
Youth movement
Academic jackboots [leftists; cover story] S. L. M. Huck. il *Conservative Digest* 15:16-21 My/Je '89
Looking for loons [debating 1960s radicalism] R. E. Tyrrell. il *The American Spectator* 22:8-9+ Je '89
The new left vigilantes [academic discourse] J. P. Roche. il *National Review* 41:34-5 D 8 '89
Panthers, contras, and other wars. P. Collier and D. Horowitz. *The New Republic* 200:38-41 Je 26 '89
The young have to be there. A. Hoffman. il *The Progressive* 53:15 Je '89
Anecdotes, facetiae, satire, etc.
Brunch [radical couples] S. L. Wisenberg. *The New Yorker* 64:24-5 Ja 9 '89
Germany (West)
See also
Autonomen
RADICALS (CHEMISTRY)
See also
Free radicals (Chemistry)
Hydroxyl group

THE RADICALS [film] *See* Motion picture reviews—Single works
RADICALS AND RADICALISM *See* Radicalism
RADIN, ROY, 1950-1983
about
The 'Cotton Club' murder: cocaine and hit men in Hollywood—a 1980s film noir [cover story] J. Kasindorf. il pors *New York* 22:24-33 Jl 24 '89
Letter from Los Angeles. J. Didion. *The New Yorker* 65:92-9 S 4 '89
RADIN, VICTORIA
The Bard stripped bare. il *Vogue* 179:248-51 Ap '89
RADIO
See also
Ham radio
Interference
See Radio interference
RADIO, AMATEUR *See* Ham radio
RADIO, SHORTWAVE *See* Shortwave radio
RADIO, SINGLE SIDEBAND
See also
Radiotelephone on ships, boats, etc.
RADIO AMPLIFIERS *See* Amplifiers
RADIO AND POLITICS
Bugle boys of the airwaves [influence of talk show hosts] R. Zoglin. il *Time* 133:88-9 My 15 '89
The Carter campaign [WLIB reporter D. Carter covers New York City's mayoral race] C. S. Smith. il por *New York* 22:36 N 13 '89
O.K., caller, you're on the air [influence of talk show hosts] il *U.S. News & World Report* 106:12-13 F 20 '89
Planning ahead? [Washington, D.C. radio station WNTR purchased by Christian Broadcasting Network] V. Novak. il *Common Cause Magazine* 15:6 S/O '89
Talk politics [campaign against congressional pay raise] J. Klein. il *New York* 22:28+ F 27 '89
RADIO ANTENNAS
See also
Radio telescopes
Active antenna. R. A. Kreuter. il *Radio-Electronics* 60:51-2+ F '89
Antennas do make a difference [auto antenna] B. C. Fishkind. il *High Fidelity (New York, N.Y.)* 39:21 Mr '89
Choosing the right shortwave antenna. J. J. Carr. il *Radio-Electronics* 60:61-5 Jl '89
Testing
Better FM reception [Parsec's LS-4 and Terk's π antenna] F. Vizard. il *Popular Mechanics* 166:68 Ap '89
Tuning
Tunable preselectors. H. Friedman. il *Radio-Electronics* 60:82-3 Ja '89
RADIO ASTRONOMY
See also
Cosmic background radiation
Interstellar communication
Meteor burst communication
National Radio Astronomy Observatory (U.S.)
Owens Valley Radio Observatory
Radio sources (Astronomy)
Radio telescopes
Astronomers find evidence of galaxies still forming [interstellar hydrogen cloud found by Riccardo Giovanelli and Martha Haynes] *Earth Science* 42:9-10 Fall '89
Ball will build radio astronomy payload for Submillimeter Wave Satellite. il *Aviation Week & Space Technology* 131:50 S 18 '89
Einstein's ring and a galaxy's mass [MG 1654 + 1346] il *Sky and Telescope* 77:465-6 My '89
Galactic birth? [intergalactic hydrogen cloud discovered by Riccardo Giovanelli and Martha Haynes] *Time* 134:66 S 11 '89
How a star is born [Submillimeter Wave Astronomy Satellite project by Gary Melnick] K. Hartley. il *Astronomy* 17:14 D '89
In the beginning was a cloud [intergalactic hydrogen cloud discovered by Riccardo Giovanelli and Martha Haynes] S. Begley. *Newsweek* 114:66 S 11 '89
Island gas cloud may be protogalaxy [intergalactic hydrogen cloud discovered by Martha P. Haynes and Riccardo Giovanelli] il *Astronomy* 17:10 D '89
Jupiter on your shortwave. D. A. Rosenthal. il *Sky and Telescope* 78:628 D '89
Listening for hints of the sun's heliopause [research by Ralph L. McNutt] J. Eberhart. *Science News* 136:231 O 7 '89
Noisy cosmic neighbors [electromagnetic interference from Soviet Glonass satellite] S. Vogel. il *Discover* 10:28 Ap '89
Radio twinkling in Venusian ionosphere. J. Eberhart. *Science News* 135:119 F 25 '89
Reshaping views of how young stars evolve [AS431; research by Richard J. Davis] R. Cowen. *Science News* 136:102 Ag 12 '89
A star is born. *Sky and Telescope* 77:588-9 Je '89
Starlight shadows protogalaxy finding [intergalactic hydrogen cloud discovered by Martha P. Haynes and Riccardo Giovanelli] R. Cowen. il *Science News* 136:164 S 9 '89

RADIO ASTRONOMY—*cont.*

Stillborn [interstellar hydrogen cloud found by Riccardo Giovanelli and Martha P. Haynes] J. Horgan. *Scientific American* 261:28 N '89

A surprise near Virgo [intergalactic hydrogen cloud discovered by Riccardo Giovanelli and Martha Haynes] J. Palca. *Science* 245:933 S 1 '89

Unveiling the hidden Milky Way [molecular cloud mapping] E. S. Palmer. il *Astronomy* 17:32-40 N '89

Uranus' signature in a radio signal [work of Michael D. Desch and others] R. Monastersky. *Science News* 135:319 My 20 '89

Voyager planetary radio astronomy at Neptune. J. W. Warwick and others. bibl f il *Science* 246:1498-1501 D 15 '89

Voyager radio science observations of Neptune and Triton. G. L. Tyler and others. bibl f il *Science* 246:1466-73 D 15 '89

RADIO BROADCASTING

See also

Cable radio

Radio industry

Radio program reviews

Radio stations

Tape recordings—Radio programs

Hi-fi AM radio. J. D. Hirsch. il *Stereo Review* 54:20 Jl '89

Archives

See also

Museum of Broadcasting (New York, N.Y.)

Automobile repair programs

Motor mouths [R. and T. Magliozzi's Car talk] E. Yoffe. il pors *Rolling Stone* p163-4+ N 16 '89

Ray and Tom Magliozzi get stalled auto owners in gear with nuts-and-bolts Car talk. A. Schulman. il pors *People Weekly* 32:93-4+ Ag 7 '89

Black programs

Coors 'Inside black America' begins 5th broadcasting year. il *Jet* 75:9 Ja 30 '89

Cajun music

From offices of excellence [Rendez-vous des Cajuns begun by C. Joubert] D. Young. il pors *Southern Living* 24:142+ Ap '89

Comedy programs

Radio days [F. Allen] M. Richler. il por *Gentlemen's Quarterly* 59:122+ Je '89

Conversation programs

Bugle boys of the airwaves [influence of talk show hosts] R. Zoglin. il *Time* 133:88-9 My 15 '89

Frank Rizzo without prejudice. J. Lombardi. il por *Esquire* 112:114-17 Ag '89

Night callers. J. Schwartz. il *Gentlemen's Quarterly* 59:121-2+ Ag '89

O.K., caller, you're on the air [political influence of talk show hosts] il *U.S. News & World Report* 106:12-13 F 20 '89

Radio guru Bruce Williams offers soothing advice on-air. A. Abrahams. il pors *People Weekly* 32:119+ O 9 '89

Sally Jessy Raphaël on the move. R. Beach. il pors *The Saturday Evening Post* 261:58-9+ S '89

Sound bites from Never-never Land. P. Yancey. il *Christianity Today* 33:56 Ap 21 '89

Talk politics [campaign against congressional pay raise] J. Klein. il *New York* 22:28+ F 27 '89

Who cares? [film Talk radio triggers reflections on the body politic] R. Corliss. il *Film Comment* 25:64-70 Ja/F '89

Frequency allocation

See Radio frequency allocation

Frequency modulation

See Radio frequency modulation

Government use

See also

Voice of America

Music

See also

Satellite Music Network

News

See also

CKO Inc.

John Wingate's hard fall: a onetime radio star ends up broke and homeless. E. Tivnan. il pors *New York* 22:50-5 Mr 13 '89

Opera

Chicago on the air (I). il *Opera News* 53:41-4 My '89

Chicago on the air (II). il *Opera News* 53:37-40 Je '89

Star power [fiftieth anniversary of Texaco sponsorship of Metropolitan Opera broadcasts; cover story] bibl il *Opera News* 54:10-12+ N '89

Texaco-Metropolitan Opera radio network: 1989-90 season. il *Opera News* 54:50 D 9 '89

Viewpoint. P. J. Smith. *Opera News* 54:6 D 9 '89

Payola scandals

See Payola

Political programs

See Radio and politics

Propaganda

See also

Radio Free Europe

Radio Liberty

Voice of America

Religious programs

See also

Christian Broadcasting Network, Inc.

National Religious Broadcasters

Father Coughlin and the Jews: a broadcast remembered [justifying Kristallnacht] R. Modras. *America* 160:219-22 Mr 11 '89

Questions raised about Bob Larson campaign [evangelical radio programs] L. Cryderman. il *Christianity Today* 33:47-8 Mr 3 '89

Rock music

Casey Kasem's flip side. B. Ohanian. il pors *Mother Jones* 14:21-3+ O '89

Lee Abrams: out to fill the air with heavy-metal fare. D. Foust. il por *Business Week* p107 Je 5 '89

Magna cum loud [favorite rock bands of college radio programmers] il *Rolling Stone* p127-8+ Mr 23 '89

Metal romances radio. J. Ressner. il *Rolling Stone* p22 F 9 '89

New waves [college stations] K. Miller. il *Seventeen* 48:114+ My '89

Radio's rock of ages [effect of classic rock format on new acts] M. Goldberg. il *Rolling Stone* p19-20 Je 1 '89

The top 40 times two [C. Kasem and S. Stevens] B. Barol. il por *Newsweek* 113:56 F 6 '89

Social aspects

See also

Dating (Social customs) in radio

Sports

Holy cow! It's Harry Caray [Chicago Cubs broadcaster] C. P. Miller. il pors *The Saturday Evening Post* 261:54-5+ O '89

LA voices. D. McLean and K. Garrett. il *Sport (New York, N.Y.)* 80:28-9 Ja '89

Unauthorized use

The silencing of 'Radio Sarah' [FCC shutdown of Radio New York International] D. Kuipers. il *The Nation* 248:559+ Ap 24 '89

Bolivia

Tin miners' radio on the ropes. J. Slaughter. il *The Progressive* 53:11 F '89

Canada

See also

Canadian Broadcasting Corporation

Canadian Radio-Television and Telecommunications Commission

Eastern Europe

See also

Radio Free Europe

RADIO BROADCASTING, PUBLIC

See also

Pacifica Foundation

RADIO BROADCASTING, SHORTWAVE *See* Shortwave radio

RADIO-CANADA *See* Canadian Broadcasting Corporation

RADIO CITY MUSIC HALL PRODUCTIONS

Taking it on the road. P. Newcomb. il por *Forbes* 144:275 Jl 24 '89

RADIO CONTROL

See also

Automobile models—Control

Garage doors—Control

RADIO CRITICS AND CRITICISM

See also

Radio program reviews

RADIO DETECTORS

Bug detector [cover story] L. K. Ross. il *Radio-Electronics* 60:42-4+ Je '89

RADIO EQUIPMENT

See also

Paging devices

Transponders

RADIO FREE EUROPE

Too many Voices of America. K. A. Elliott. *Foreign Policy* 77:113-31 Wint '89/'90

RADIO FREQUENCY ALLOCATION

See also

International Frequency Coordinating Committee

Noisy cosmic neighbors [electromagnetic interference from Soviet Glonass satellite] S. Vogel. il *Discover* 10:28 Ap '89

RADIO FREQUENCY CONVERTERS *See* Frequency changers

RADIO FREQUENCY INTERFERENCE *See* Radio interference

RADIO FREQUENCY MODULATION

FMX: is it good for FM? L. Feldman. il *Radio-Electronics* 60:52-5+ O '89

FMX noise. J. D. Hirsch. il *Stereo Review* 54:30+ Ap '89

The noise about FMX. R. Warren. il *Stereo Review* 54:113-15 S '89

Noise over radio reception [views of Amar Bose on FMX technology] D. P. Hamilton. *Technology Review* 92:79 My/Je '89

Taping off of FM: why bother? R. Long. il *High Fidelity (New York, N.Y.)* 39:19 Ja '89

RADIO FREQUENCY WAVES *See* Electromagnetic waves
RADIO GALAXIES *See* Radio sources (Astronomy)
RADIO IN ASTRONOMY *See* Radio astronomy
RADIO IN AVIATION
> *See also*
> Airplanes—Radio equipment
RADIO IN NAVIGATION
> *See also*
> Loran
RADIO INDUSTRY
> *See also*
> American Broadcasting Companies, Inc.
> Blacks in the radio industry
> Cable radio
> Cook Inlet Communications Inc.
> DIR Broadcasting Corporation
> Great American Communications Corp.
> Inner City Broadcasting Corporation
> National Broadcasting Co., Inc.
> Osborn Communications Corp.
> Radio stations
> Radio Vision International Inc.
> Radio. il *Channels (New York, N.Y.: 1986)* 9:47 Jl/Ag '89
> ### Canada
> *See also*
> CKO Inc.
> ### Great Britain
> *See also*
> Crown Communications Group plc
RADIO INTERFERENCE
> Jamming: the end of an era? [Soviet Union] S. Leinwoll. il *Radio-Electronics* 60:75-7 Je '89
> The Soviet jamming system and the future of jamming. S. Leinwoll. il *Radio-Electronics* 60:78-9 O '89
RADIO LAWS AND REGULATIONS
> *See also*
> Fairness Doctrine (Broadcasting)
> Radio frequency allocation
> ### Canada
> *See also*
> Canadian Radio-Television and Telecommunications Commission
RADIO LIBERTY
> Too many Voices of America. K. A. Elliott. *Foreign Policy* 77:113-31 Wint '89/'90
RADIO NEW YORK INTERNATIONAL
> The silencing of 'Radio Sarah' [FCC shutdown] D. Kuipers. il *The Nation* 248:559+ Ap 24 '89
RADIO NEWS *See* Radio broadcasting—News
RADIO OBSERVATORIES *See* Astronomical observatories
RADIO PROGRAM REVIEWS
> #### Single works
> American Radio Company of the air
> > *Time* il 134:109 D 11 '89. J. Skow
> American top 40
> > *Newsweek* il 113:56 F 6 '89. B. Barol
> Car talk
> > *People Weekly* il 32:93-4+ Ag 7 '89. A. Schulman
> > *Rolling Stone* il p163-4+ N 16 '89. E. Yoffe
> Casey's top 40
> > *Newsweek* il 113:56 F 6 '89. B. Barol
> Desperate and dateless
> > *People Weekly* il 32:59 Jl 24 '89
> Inside black America
> > *Jet* 75:9 Ja 30 '89
> Rendez-vouz des Cajuns
> > *Southern Living* il 24:142+ Ap '89. D. Young
RADIO PROGRAMS *See* Radio broadcasting
RADIO RECEIVERS
> *See also*
> Automobiles—Radio equipment
> Clock radios
> Shortwave radio—Equipment
> Television receivers—Radio receiver combination
> Carrier current receiver. W. Sheets and R. F. Graf. il *Radio-Electronics* 60:55+ F '89
> Made in Japan [RX-530 receiver by Yamaha] B. Harrell. il *Stereo Review* 54:49-55 Jl '89
> Receivers. il *Stereo Review* 54:68-70+ F '89
> #### Collectors and collecting
> Antique radios. R. D. Fitch. See issues of Radio-Electronics beginning February 1985 through May 1989
> Radios: over 70 years of technology. G. E. Zook. il *Antiques & Collecting Hobbies* 94:48-51 My '89
> #### Maintenance and repair
> New radios, new problems, new solutions (I). G. McClellan. il *Radio-Electronics* 60:57-60 Jl '89
> New radios, new problems, new solutions (II). G. McClellan. il *Radio-Electronics* 60:60-3 Ag '89
> #### Noise
> FMX: is it good for FM? L. Feldman. il *Radio-Electronics* 60:52-5+ O '89
> FMX noise. J. D. Hirsch. il *Stereo Review* 54:30+ Ap '89
> The noise about FMX. R. Warren. il *Stereo Review* 54:113-15 S '89
> Noise over radio reception [views of Amar Bose on FMX technology] D. P. Hamilton. *Technology Review* 92:79 My/Je '89

> #### Tape recorder combination
> Walkman [listening to music while walking in New York City] *The New Yorker* 64:19-20 Ja 2 '89
> #### Testing
> ACE Communications AOR AR-2515 communications receiver. il *Radio-Electronics* 60:24+ N '89
> Brain—with some brawn [Sansui's RZ-3000 receiver] F. Vizard. il *Popular Mechanics* 166:46 Ja '89
> Carver Model 6250 AM/FM receiver. J. D. Hirsch. il *Stereo Review* 54:50+ Mr '89
> Low-priced stereo receivers. il *Consumer Reports* 54:89-4 D '89
> NAD 7100 AM/FM receiver. R. Long. il *High Fidelity (New York, N.Y.)* 39:29-31 Ap '89
> Nakamichi TA-4A AM/FM receiver. J. D. Hirsch. il *Stereo Review* 54:68+ N '89
> Onkyo TX-890 AM/FM receiver. J. D. Hirsch. il *Stereo Review* 54:57-8+ D '89
> Receivers: heart of the system [stereo receivers] il *Consumer Reports* 54:156-9 Mr '89
> Sansui RZ-7000 receiver. J. D. Hirsch. il *Stereo Review* 54:37-9 F '89
> Tandberg TPR-3080A FM receiver. R. Long. il *High Fidelity (New York, N.Y.)* 39:19+ My '89
> #### Tuning
> Blaupunkt New York SCD-08 car tuner/CD player. R. Long. il *High Fidelity (New York, N.Y.)* 39:30-3 Jl '89
> Blaupunkt New York SCD 08 CD tuner [car stereo] K. C. Pohlmann. il *Stereo Review* 54:24-5 N '89
> Dual CT-5040 AM/FM tuner. J. D. Hirsch. il *Stereo Review* 54:34+ Ag '89
> Luxman TP-117 tuner/preamplifier and multiroom system controller. J. D. Hirsch. il *Stereo Review* 54:64+ S '89
> Onkyo T-G10 FM tuner. R. Long. il *High Fidelity (New York, N.Y.)* 39:36-8 Ap '89
> Progress in FM tuners? M. Riggs. il *High Fidelity (New York, N.Y.)* 39:5 My '89
> Rotel RTC-850 tuner/preamplifier. R. Long. il *High Fidelity (New York, N.Y.)* 39:26-7+ Jl '89
> Sony CDX-R77 car tuner/CD player. R. Long. il *High Fidelity (New York, N.Y.)* 39:33-5 Jl '89
> Technics ST-G70 AM/FM tuner. R. Long. il *High Fidelity (New York, N.Y.)* 39:25-6+ Ja '89
> Tuners. il *Stereo Review* 54:106-9 F '89
RADIO SHACK *See* Tandy Corp.
RADIO SOURCES (ASTRONOMY)
> *See also*
> Pulsars
> Quasars
> Milky Way's youngest supernova? [G25.5 + 0.2 discovered by John J. Cowan] il *Sky and Telescope* 78:348-9 O '89
> Points of view [quasars and radio galaxies; research by Peter Barthel] J. Horgan. il *Scientific American* 260:20+ Ap '89
> Quasars and radio galaxies: in the eye of the beholder [work of Peter D. Barthel] il *Sky and Telescope* 77:463-4 My '89
> Radio noise from colliding galaxies [Markarian 266; research by Joseph M. Mazzarella] il *Sky and Telescope* 77:241-2 Mr '89
> Supernova aftermath [Cassiopeia A gas shell; cover story] L. A. Marschall. il *Astronomy* 17:40-2 F '89
> Swirls and threads at the Milky Way's core. il *Science News* 136:279 O 28 '89
RADIO SPECTRUM ALLOCATION *See* Radio frequency allocation
RADIO STATIONS
> *See also*
> College radio stations
> Harvest of love [KBTN pitches in to help get food to needy families in Neosho, Mo.] A. Winegardner. il por *Good Housekeeping* 209:130+ D '89
> The Johnson years: buying and selling [L. B. Johnson's involvement with radio station KTBC] R. A. Caro. *The New Yorker* 65:43-8+ D 18 '89
> Little Ricky Rocko, the world's youngest deejay, proves you're never too small to rock and roll [9 year old S. Rogoway at KKRZ-FM in Portland, Or.] S. K. Reed. il pors *People Weekly* 31:91-2 Ja 16 '89
> M.M. [Mama Montego broadcast on WRKS in New York City] *The New Yorker* 65:36-7 O 30 '89
> The magic mating-call letters for Desperate and dateless singles are WKRC in Cincinnati [phone in program hosted by deejay J. B. Miller] il por *People Weekly* 32:59 Jl 24 '89
> Planning ahead? [Washington, D.C. radio station WNTR purchased by Christian Broadcasting Network] V. Novak. il *Common Cause Magazine* 15:6 S/O '89
> Spinning off his Partridge past, Danny Bonaduce rocks Philly as a raunchy midnight deejay [WEGX-FM] T. Cunneff. il pors *People Weekly* 31:97-9 F 27 '89
RADIO STATIONS, BLACK
> *See also*
> Inner City Broadcasting Corporation
> Broadcast news [B. Lamont, B. A. Mayo and F. Melton] L. Gite. il pors *Black Enterprise* 20:100-3+ D '89
> The Carter campaign [WLIB reporter D. Carter covers New York City's mayoral race] C. S. Smith. il por *New York* 22:36 N 13 '89

RADIO STATIONS, PIRATE *See* Radio broadcasting—Unauthorized use

RADIO TELEPHONE *See* Radiotelephone

RADIO TELESCOPES

Improvements for Arecibo. il *Sky and Telescope* 77:467-8 My '89

A new window on star birth [submillimeter astronomy] K. Hartley. il *Astronomy* 17:32-6 Mr '89

Owens Valley array upgraded. il *Sky and Telescope* 78:128 Ag '89

Probing the heliosphere from India. S. K. Alurkar and R. V. Bhonsle. il map *Sky and Telescope* 78:151 Ag '89

Accidents

300-foot collapse: the probable cause. il *Sky and Telescope* 78:11-12 Jl '89

A blow to astronomy [collapse of Green Bank radio telescope] G. L. Verschuur. *Astronomy* 17:8 My '89

Collapse of a legend [National Radio Astronomy Observatory] A. Fisher. il *Popular Science* 234:8 Mr '89

Cracked plate caused telescope collapse [Green Bank, W. Va.] *Science News* 135:269 Ap 29 '89

Green Bank's 300-foot radio telescope collapses. *Astronomy* 17:14+ F '89

In memoriam [collapse of Green Bank, W. Va. radio telescope] T. Rothman. il *Scientific American* 260:17 F '89

Out of the wreckage, a 100-meter radiotelescope is backed by Congress. C. S. Powell. il *Physics Today* 42 pt1:41-2 Ag '89

Reminiscences of the 300-foot. G. L. Verschuur. *Sky and Telescope* 77:252-3 Mr '89

Report out on Green Bank collapse; replacement poses quandary for NSF. P. H. Andersen. il *Physics Today* 42:55-7 Ap '89

Telescope collapse unraveled [National Radio Astronomy Observatory at Green Bank, W. Va.] C. Norman. il *Science* 244:29 Ap 7 '89

RADIO TRACKING, BIOLOGICAL *See* Biotelemetry

RADIO TRANSMITTERS

Low frequency transmitter. R. A. Nelson. il *Radio-Electronics* 60:43-6+ S '89

Wireless FM microphone. M. Spiwak. il *Radio-Electronics* 60:43-5 Mr '89

RADIO TUBES

Condensers and tubes. R. D. Fitch. il *Radio-Electronics* 60:84-5 Ja '89

RADIO TUNERS *See* Radio receivers—Tuning

RADIO VISION INTERNATIONAL INC.

These Walls have ears for music and business [K. and K. Wall] P. Cole. il pors *Business Week* p91 Je 26 '89

RADIO WAVES *See* Electromagnetic waves

RADIO WORKERS

See also

Strikes—Radio workers

RADIOACTIVE DATING

See also

Radiocarbon dating

^{40}Ar-^{39}Ar dating of the Manson impact structure: a Cretaceous-Tertiary boundary crater candidate [north-central Iowa] M. J. Kunk and others. bibl f il *Science* 244:1565-8 Je 30 '89

Dating craters [beryllium-aluminum dating of rocks from Meteor Crater, Ariz.; work of James Arnold] J. A. Yeaple. *Popular Science* 235:128 N '89

History of meteorites from the moon collected in Antarctica. O. Eugster. bibl f il *Science* 245:1197-1202 S 15 '89

Manson, Iowa: where the 'big one' struck? [crater; research by M. J. Kunk] *Astronomy* 17:10-11 O '89

New record for world's oldest rocks [work of Samuel A. Bowring] R. Monastersky. il *Science News* 136:228 O 7 '89

Rates of tectonometamorphic processes from rubidium and strontium isotopes in garnet [southeast Vermont] J. N. Christensen and others. bibl f il *Science* 244:1465-9 Je 23 '89

Uranium-series dated authigenic carbonates and Acheulian sites in southern Egypt. B. J. Szabo and others. bibl f il maps *Science* 243:1053-6 F 24 '89

RADIOACTIVE DECAY

See also

Double-beta decay

RADIOACTIVE DRUGS *See* Nuclear medicine

RADIOACTIVE FALLOUT *See* Radioactive pollution

RADIOACTIVE POLLUTION

See also

Nuclear power plants—Environmental aspects

Nuclear reactors—Environmental aspects

Radioactive space pollution

Radioactive waste disposal

Radon pollution

Uranium industry—Environmental aspects

Nuclear bloopers. C. O'Neil and S. Seidenstein. *Utne Reader* p49 Ja/F '89

Laws and regulations

Dropping a bomb on 'radioactive junkyards' [jury decision against National Lead in Fernald, Ohio pollution case and Rocky Flats plant under criminal investigation] M. Mallory. il *Business Week* p29-30 Jl 3 '89

Physiological effects

See Radiation—Physiological effects

California

'Real nasty stuff' [radioactive pollution from Rockwell International's Santa Susana Field Laboratory] A. L. Huebner. il *The Progressive* 53:26-8 O '89

Colorado

Rocky Flats radiation remains unexplained. R. Cowen. *Science News* 135:391 Je 24 '89

Great Britain

Is Britain 'befouled'? [pollution from the Sellafield power plants] M. Perutz. bibl f il *The New York Review of Books* 36:51-7 N 23 '89

Sheepfarming after Chernobyl. B. Wynne. bibl f il maps *Environment* 31:10-15+ Mr '89

Idaho

Necessary defense or technological toy? [protest against proposed Special Isotope Separation project at Idaho National Engineering Laboratory] S. Cline. *Sierra* 74:95-6 Mr/Ap '89

Mururoa Atoll (French Polynesia)

Plutonium in paradise [French weapons testing] A. C. Revkin. il *Discover* 10:38-42 My '89

New Mexico

The hidden files [1946 accident at Los Alamos Lab; cover story] C. T. Honicker. il *The New York Times Magazine* p38-41+ N 19 '89

Ohio

See also

Fernald (Ohio)—Radioactive pollution

Pacific Northwest

Hanford: America's nuclear graveyard. K. D. Steele. bibl f il *The Bulletin of the Atomic Scientists* 45:14-20+ O '89

Rongelap Atoll (Marshall Islands)

Fallout from Pacific tests reaches Congress. E. Marshall. map *Science* 245:123-4 Jl 14 '89

'No one lives on Rongelap'. D. Goertzen. *The Progressive* 53:18 N '89

Soviet Union

A dosimeter for every dacha. G. Schoenfeld. bibl f il *The Bulletin of the Atomic Scientists* 45:13-15 Jl/Ag '89

Soviets admit 1957 nuclear mishap [explosion in tank containing radioactive waste, contaminating south Urals] D. Dickson. map *Science* 244:1435 Je 23 '89

Sweden

Swedish moose a la cesium 137 [high concentration of radiation in muscle tissue following Chernobyl accident] il *Environment* 31:22-3 My '89

Ukraine

See also

Chernobyl nuclear disaster, 1986

United States

See Radioactive pollution

Western States

Testing ground [Nevada Test Site] J. Hanrahan. il *Common Cause Magazine* 15:13-19+ Ja/F '89

RADIOACTIVE SPACE POLLUTION

Court rejects activists' bid to halt Galileo/shuttle launch [nuclear powered spacecraft] *Aviation Week & Space Technology* 131:21 O 16 '89

Gamma-ray observations of orbiting nuclear reactors [cover story] J. R. Primack. bibl f *Science* 244:407-8 Ap 28 '89

Geomagnetic origin for transient particle events from nuclear reactor-powered satellites [experiment on Solar Maximum Mission satellite] G. H. Share and others. bibl f il *Science* 244:444-8 Ap 28 '89

Let's ban nuclear reactors from orbit. J. R. Primack. il *Technology Review* 92:27-8 My/Je '89

Man-made transients observed by the gamma-ray spectrometer on the Solar Maximum Mission satellite. E. Rieger and others. bibl f il *Science* 244:441-4 Ap 28 '89

NASA prepares for protests over nuclear system launch on shuttle in October [Galileo mission to Jupiter] T. M. Foley. *Aviation Week & Space Technology* 130:83+ Je 26 '89

Nuclear fears about Galileo. A. Toufexis. il *Time* 134:76 O 16 '89

Project Galileo: the risk of a nuclear disaster in space. *Utne Reader* p60 S/O '89

Rifkin tries to stop Galileo launch [nuclear fears] M. M. Waldrop. il *Science* 246:30 O 6 '89

Scientists call for policy on space nuclear reactors. R. G. O'Lone. il *Aviation Week & Space Technology* 130:23 Ja 23 '89

Showdown at Pad 39-B [nuclear powered space vehicles] R. G. Nichols. il *Ad Astra* 1:8-12+ N '89

Stable orbit [space reactors] T. Beardsley. *Scientific American* 260:14+ F '89

"Stop the plutonium shuttle!" [Galileo mission to Jupiter] M. M. Waldrop. *Science* 245:1328 S 22 '89

RADIOACTIVE SUBSTANCES

See also

Radon

Tritium

RADIOACTIVE SUBSTANCES—*cont.*
Transportation
A trash can for the nuclear age [Trupact II container developed by the DOE to transport nuclear waste] il *Discover* 10:18 My '89
RADIOACTIVE TRACERS
See also
Nuclear medicine
RADIOACTIVE WASTE DISPOSAL
Cleaning up after the Pentagon: the dangers of nuclear weapons waste. R. Alvarez and A. Makhijani. il *Utne Reader* p50-2 Ja/F '89
Dirty business [Dept. of Energy weapons-production facilities] T. Beardsley. il *Scientific American* 260:27-8 Ap '89
DOE calls in the labs for defense waste cleanup. M. Crawford. il *Science* 246:24-5 O 6 '89
Doing something about high-level nuclear waste. G. G. Wicks and D. Bickford. il *Technology Review* 92:50-8 N/D '89
Fusing dangerous weapons refuse into glass [in situ vitrification of contaminated soil] il *Popular Mechanics* 166:17 Jl '89
The nuclear waste dilemma. M. Hamilton. il *USA Today (Periodical)* 117:44-6 Mr '89
The residue of nuclear hubris [possible link between waste disposal from weapons plants and cancer] J. Kluger. il *Discover* 10:10-11 Ja '89
Special report: managing America's nuclear waste. il *Popular Mechanics* 166:17 Je '89
A trash can for the nuclear age [Trupact II container developed by the DOE to transport nuclear waste] il *Discover* 10:18 My '89
Uncle Sam's toxic folly. M. Satchell. il *U.S. News & World Report* 106:20-2 Mr 27 '89
Laws and regulations
Admiral Watkins's toughest command [cleanup of nuclear weapons plants] S. J. Hedges. il pors *U.S. News & World Report* 107:29-30 Ag 14 '89
Not in my backyard! The waste-disposal crisis. T. Peters. il *The Christian Century* 106:175-7 F 15 '89
Stop Stello [controversial appointment of V. Stello to head national effort to clean up crumbling nuclear weapons facilities] H. Wasserman. *The Nation* 249:372-3 O 9 '89
When the dump is in 'our' backyard [discussion of February 15, 1989 article, Not in my backyard! The waste-disposal crisis] T. Peters. *The Christian Century* 106:660 Jl 5-12 '89
Colorado
Dropping a bomb on 'radioactive junkyards' [Rocky Flats plant under criminal investigation] M. Mallory. il *Business Week* p29-30 Jl 3 '89
A new scare at Rocky Flats. J. N. Baker. il *Newsweek* 113:60 Je 26 '89
Rocky Flats: a big mistake from day one. B. Abas. bibl f il *The Bulletin of the Atomic Scientists* 45:18-24 D '89
Trouble at Rocky Flats. M. Miller. il *Newsweek* 114:19-20 Ag 14 '89
Germany (West)
Germans tighten export rules amid spreading scandals. W. Sweet. *Physics Today* 42:58-9 Ap '89
The Transnuklear affair. D. Charles. *The Bulletin of the Atomic Scientists* 45:23 Ap '89
Nebraska
Nebraska's new favorite son [H. Kaufman leads opposition to nuclear dump in Nora] B. Turque. il por *Newsweek* 114:21 Jl 10 '89
Public opinion
Disposal is a political problem. *USA Today (Periodical)* 117:3-4 Je '89
Nevada
No home for hot trash [Yucca Mountain dump delayed] *Time* 134:81 D 11 '89
A nuclear dump: the experiment begins [Yucca Mountain] D. Grossman and S. Shulman. il map *Discover* 10:48-51+ Mr '89
Showdown at Yucca Mountain: the high stakes of a nuclear waste dump. W. Kittredge. il *Utne Reader* p44-9 Ja/F '89
Something dead that can't be buried [Yucca Mountain] il map *U.S. News & World Report* 107:17 D 11 '89
New Mexico
See also
Waste Isolation Pilot Plant (N.M.)
Scotland
Waste plan bestirs Scots Nationalists [Dounreay site] D. Dickson. *Science* 243:1660 Mr 31 '89
Soviet Union
Soviets admit 1957 nuclear mishap [explosion in tank containing radioactive waste, contaminating south Urals] D. Dickson. map *Science* 244:1435 Je 23 '89
Washington (State)
Hanford: America's nuclear graveyard. K. D. Steele. bibl f il *The Bulletin of the Atomic Scientists* 45:14-20+ O '89
When a nuclear reactor dies, $98 million is a cheap funeral [Shippingport shutdown] S. Shulman. bibl (p228) il *Smithsonian* 20:56-62+ O '89

RADIOACTIVE WASTE DISPOSAL IN THE OCEAN
Is Britain 'befouled'? [pollution from the Sellafield power plants] M. Perutz. bibl f il *The New York Review of Books* 36:51-7 N 23 '89
RADIOACTIVE WASTE REPROCESSING *See* Reactor fuel reprocessing
RADIOACTIVE WASTES
Transportation
See Radioactive substances—Transportation
RADIOACTIVITY
See also
Autoradiography
Physiological effects
See Radiation—Physiological effects
RADIOAUTOGRAPHY *See* Autoradiography
RADIOCARBON DATING
Tasmania's earliest settlers [research by Richard Cosgrove] *Science News* 135:223 Ap 8 '89
Thirty thousand years of human colonization in Tasmania: new Pleistocene dates. R. Cosgrove. bibl f il map *Science* 243:1706-8 Mr 31 '89
RADIOGRAPHY
See also
Autoradiography
Tomography
X-ray movies reveal sand flow patterns [research by Robert P. Behringer] I. Peterson. il *Science News* 135:293 My 13 '89
An X-ray peek into electrochemistry [work of Owen R. Melroy] I. Peterson. *Science News* 135:77 F 4 '89
RADIOGRAPHY, DENTAL *See* Radiography, Medical
RADIOGRAPHY, INDUSTRIAL
See also
X ray lithography
RADIOGRAPHY, MEDICAL
See also
Magnetic resonance imaging—Medical use
Mammography
Tomography—Medical use
Are you safe from X-rays? [views of B. Wally Ahluwalia] il *USA Today (Periodical)* 117:11 Ap '89
Lead toxicity: bones tell the real story [children] *Science News* 135:111 F 18 '89
Medical physics. bibl f *Physics Today* 42:S49-S52 Ja '89
Need those X-rays? [dental X-rays] V. Brower. il *American Health* 8:42 Je '89
A primer on medical imaging. E. Weck. il *FDA Consumer* 23:24-7 Ap '89
When X-rays are too costly [Basic Radiological System used in Middle East] A. Modjtabai. il *World Health* p29 Jl '89
RADIOISOTOPES
See also
Tritium
RADIOISOTOPES IN MEDICINE *See* Nuclear medicine
RADIOISOTOPIC THERMOELECTRIC GENERATORS *See* Nuclear batteries
RADIONUCLIDE DATING *See* Radioactive dating
RADIOS *See* Radio receivers
RADIOTELEPHONE
See also
Cellular radio
Communications satellites—Radiotelephone use
Cordless telephone
International Mobile Machines Corp.
Telepoint communications
Testing
Hand-held with care [Sporty's A300 transceiver] J. M. McClellan. il *Flying* 116:24 Ap '89
RADIOTELEPHONE ON AIRPLANES
Carriers, manufacturers assess aerosat communication systems. P. J. Klass. il map *Aviation Week & Space Technology* 130:54-5 Ja 9 '89
Carry-along navcoms [Narco's HT 870] J. M. McClellan. il *Flying* 116:26 Ag '89
Hand-held with care [Sporty's A300 transceiver] J. M. McClellan. il *Flying* 116:24 Ap '89
Satcom calling [air ambulance equipped with Aerosat communications system] il *Flying* 116:19 F '89
Tests demonstrate potential benefits of satellites in air-ground communications. P. J. Klass. il *Aviation Week & Space Technology* 130:57+ Jl 10 '89
Touchtone Flitefone [Global-Wulfsberg's automated air-ground radio service and Flitefone VI] J. M. McClellan. il *Flying* 116:32 My '89
RADIOTELEPHONE ON SHIPS, BOATS, ETC.
See also
Cellular radio on ships, boats, etc.
1990 buyer's guide: communications [VHFs, SSBs, and cellular phones] G. West. il *Motor Boating & Sailing* 164:70-2+ O '89
VHF range factors. S. Stapleton. *Motor Boating & Sailing* 163:94 Ap '89
RADIOTHERAPY
See also
Cancer—Therapy
Prostate gland—Cancer—Therapy
Proton therapy

RADIOTHERAPY—See also—*cont.*
Thyroid gland—Cancer—Therapy
RADIUS, INC.
Radius: facing growth challenges. R. A. Shaffer. il *Personal Computing* 13:41-2 Mr '89
RADKAI, KAREN
Consuming Rome. il *Gentlemen's Quarterly* 59:366-9 Mr '89
RADKE, LAWRENCE F., AND OTHERS
Direct and remote sensing observations of the effects of ships on clouds. bibl f il *Science* 246:1146-9 D 1 '89
RADLOFF, MAX
Autumn's galaxies: the best and the brightest. il *Astronomy* 17:78-84 S '89
RADNER, EPHRAIM
From 'liberation' to 'exile': a new image for church mission. *The Christian Century* 106:931-4 O 18 '89
RADNER, GILDA, 1946-1989
"I've fought so hard to live" [excerpt from It's always something] il pors *Redbook* 173:120-2+ Je '89
about
Gilda Radner's love story. J. Powell. il pors *Glamour* 87:112-13 Jl '89
Obituary
The Nation 249:215-17 Ag 21-28 '89. E. P. Frank
People Weekly il pors 31:98-9+ Je 5 '89. S. Schindehette
Rolling Stone il pors p133-4+ Jl 13-27 '89. H. Johnson
RADON
Therapeutic use
Folk belief in deep-down relief [arthritis] J. Adler. il *Newsweek* 113:70 Mr 20 '89
RADON DETECTORS
More data than you need? [Survivor 2 Continuous Radon Monitor and Honeywell At Ease Radon Monitor] il *Consumer Reports* 54:624 O '89
Radon? Don't panic. il *Parents* 64:26 Ja '89
Radon test kits. C. Tevis. il *Successful Farming* 87:64-5 N '89
Radon-testing problems. W. Giese. il *Changing Times* 43:28-9 Ap '89
Radon—some common sense, please! D. Johnson. il *The Family Handyman* 39:20+ Ja '89
The trouble with radon detectors: it's in the quacks. B. Kobliner. il *Money* 18:147-8 Ja '89
RADON POLLUTION
See also
Radon detectors
Change agents [R. Guimond] D. Moreau. il por *Changing Times* 43:104 F '89
Earth, air, radon and home [cover story] A. V. Nero. bibl f il map *Physics Today* 42:32-9 Ap '89
Geoquiz. J. V. O'Connor. il *Earth Science* 41:35 Wint '88
Help in reducing radon. W. Giese. il *Changing Times* 43:26 Ja '89
How to control radon gas. D. W. Moeller. il *Consumers' Research Magazine* 72:19-23 F '89
Iowa ranked no. 1 in radon survey. *Science News* 136:317 N 11 '89
Keep risky rocks under wraps [radon levels in homes displaying minerals] *Science News* 136:317 N 11 '89
Menace of Whispering Hills. J. Egginton. il *Audubon* 91:28+ Ja '89
Radon is threat to healthy home. C. Tevis. il *Successful Farming* 87:62 N '89
The radon menace: and update. J. Egginton. il *Reader's Digest* 134:141-4+ My '89
The radon that came in from the cold [home testing] M. Elias. *American Health* 8:15 Mr '89
Radon: the problem no one wants to face. il *Consumer Reports* 54:623-5 O '89
Radon venting system. S. Willson. il *Popular Mechanics* 166:95 S '89
Radon zapper [No-Rad fan] D. W. Moeller. il map *Popular Science* 235:78-80 O '89
Schools flunk the radon test. *U.S. News & World Report* 106:18+ My 1 '89
What we know now about radon. A. C. Mallozzi. *Good Housekeeping* 209:272 N '89
New York (State)
Righting the risk of radon. P. Barnes-Svarney. il map *Earth Science* 42:17-18 Fall '89
RADOVSKY, VICKI JO
Don Johnson: "Relationships are difficult for me". il pors *Redbook* 172:24+ Ja '89
"Getting married is the best thing that's ever happened to me!". il pors *Redbook* 173:30+ S '89
"I didn't know how to be a mom". il pors *Redbook* 172:44+ Ap '89
"I have faith my wife will live". il pors *Redbook* 173:36+ My '89
"I nearly lost my marriage". il pors *Redbook* 173:46+ Je '89
Tony Danza: "I tried, but I wasn't a good father" [interview] il por *Redbook* 172:54+ Mr '89
RADTKE, H. HELMUT
about
Helmut Radtke: no grind at selling coffee. il por *Business Week* p68 S 18 '89

RAE, STEPHEN
The agony of Ecstasy. il *Mademoiselle* 95:158-61+ Je '89
RAELIN, JOSEPH A., 1948-
Teacher autonomy and managerial control. *The Education Digest* 54:16-18 Ap '89
RAFELSON, BOB
about
Five easy pieces [film] Reviews
Video il 12:84-5 Ja '89. F. Lovece
RAFF, MARTIN C.
Glial cell diversification in the rat optic nerve. bibl f il *Science* 243:1450-5 Mr 17 '89
RAFFA, CHARLES, D. 1988
about
All-star family feud. P. Blauner. il pors *New York* 22:34-7 F 13 '89
RAFFA, KENNETH F.
Genetic engineering of trees to enhance resistance to insects [cover story] bibl f il *BioScience* 39:524-34 S '89
RAFFA, SAM
about
All-star family feud. P. Blauner. il pors *New York* 22:34-7 F 13 '89
RAFFERTY, MAGGIE
Fearless flying. il *Ms.* 17:51+ My '89
RAFFERTY DAM (SASK.) See Dams—Canada
RAFFI
about
The electronic baby sitter. M. Meyer. il por *Video* 12:91-2 Ja '89
Raffi. C. Ricci. il pors *Parents* 64:134-6+ N '89
RAFFLES See Lotteries
RAFIQ, SEKANDAR A.
Airbrush artistry. il *Petersen's Photographic Magazine* 18:90-3 D '89
RAFSANJANI, ALI AKBAR See Rafsanjani, Hashemi
RAFSANJANI, HASHEMI
about
Burying the passions Khomeini inflamed. B. Hewitt. il por *Newsweek* 113:44-5 Je 19 '89
'Moderate' is no longer a dirty word in Iran. S. Reed and others. il por *Business Week* p54 S 11 '89
A new Iran? [cover story; special section] il pors *World Press Review* 36:11-14+ Ag '89
A new 'king' for Iran? A. Platt. il por *Newsweek* 114:31 Jl 3 '89
Post-Khomeini Iran. S. T. Hunter. *Foreign Affairs* 68:133-49 Wint '89/'90
Rafsanjani's no moderate. M. Farhang. il *The Nation* 249:560+ N 13 '89
A standoff in Iran: Rafsanjani is too weak for a deal on the hostages. R. Watson. il por *Newsweek* 114:51-2 N 6 '89
Visit to the Soviet Union, 1989
Good neighbors again. A. Wilson-Smith. il por *Maclean's* 102:19 Jl 3 '89
Just a little like home. *Time* 134:32 Jl 3 '89
RAFT TRIPS
See also
Running rapids
Floating down from Hoover Dam. il *Sunset (Central West edition)* 182:66 Je '89
Most reliable rafter's river? Perhaps the Klamath. il map *Sunset (Central West edition)* 182:38-40 My '89
Anecdotes, facetiae, satire, etc.
Deep ecology [taking a raft trip on the San Juan River; excerpt from Outposts of Eden] P. Stegner. il *Sierra* 74:68-73+ Mr/Ap '89
RAFTERS
Rafter layout with a framing square. R. Capotosto. il *Popular Mechanics* 166:69-70 F '89
RAFTING COMPETITIONS See Running rapids—Competitions
RAGDALE (LAKE FOREST, ILL.: HISTORIC HOUSE) See Lake Forest (Ill.)—Historic houses, sites, etc.
RAGE See Anger
RAGER, LES
How to expand by franchising. *Nation's Business* 77:33-6 Je '89
RAGGHIANTI, MARIE
The life my mother chose. il *Reader's Digest* 134:7-9+ My '89
RAGTIME MUSIC
See also
Compact discs—Ragtime music
RAHM, DAVE
about
The stunt pilot. A. Dillard. il *Esquire* 111:118-23 Ja '89
RAHMAN, SADIQ ABDUL See El Mahdi, Sadiq, 1936-
RAHMOUNI, A. RACHID, AND WELLS, R. D. (ROBERT D.)
Stabilization of Z DNA in vivo by localized supercoiling. bibl f il *Science* 246:358-63 O 20 '89
RAIA, JAMES M.
Cool awakening. il *Runner's World* 24:112 Je '89

RAIATEA (FRENCH POLYNESIA)
Description and travel
Gourmet holidays: Society Islands. C. Bates. il map *Gourmet* 49:58-63+ F '89
RAIFORD, IRIS
about
The kids win one in Harlem as, 20 years later, the Little League returns—on drug dealers' turf. il por *People Weekly* 31:64 Je 19 '89
RAIL CAR LEASING *See* Railroads—Cars—Leasing and renting
RAILEY, PEGGY
about
The victim of a savage attack, a minister's wife is condemned to a long death in life. J. Young. il pors *People Weekly* 31:50-2+ Ja 16 '89
RAILEY, WALKER
about
The victim of a savage attack, a minister's wife is condemned to a long death in life. J. Young. il pors *People Weekly* 31:50-2+ Ja 16 '89
RAILGUNS
Electric rockets. T. L. Metzgar. il *Discover* 10:18+ Mr '89
RAILINGS *See* Hand railings
RAILROAD ACCIDENTS *See* Railroads—Accidents
RAILROAD CARS *See* Railroads—Cars
RAILROAD EQUIPMENT INDUSTRY
See also
Railroads—Cars—Leasing and renting
Canada
See also
Bombardier Inc.
RAILROAD HOLDING COMPANIES
See also
CNW Corp.
CSX Corporation
Kansas City Southern Industries, Inc.
Santa Fe Southern Pacific Corporation
RAILROAD MODELS
See also
Lionel Trains Inc.
His garden is a railway. il *Sunset (Central West edition)* 183:142 Jl '89
RAILROAD MUSEUMS
See also
California State Railroad Museum
RAILROAD TRAINS *See* Railroads—Trains
RAILROAD TRAMPS *See* Hoboes
RAILROAD TRAVEL
See also
American-European Express
Venice Simplon-Orient-Express Ltd.
Aboard America's favorite train [Zephyr] F. W. Frailey. il map *Changing Times* 43:84-91 N '89
Along the Eel and through the redwoods [North Coast Daylight train] il map *Sunset (Central West edition)* 182:28+ My '89
Another world [Manhattan to Boston ride] *The New Yorker* 65:30-1 Je 5 '89
Let's make tracks [cover story; special section] il *New Choices for the Best Years* 29:48-59 Ap '89
One of the world's best train rides [Chihuahua al Pacifico] L. Sutherland. il map *New Choices for the Best Years* 29:34-9 O '89
Putting Amtrak's best to the test. il *Business Week* p180-1 Jl 17 '89
See you in Kisumu [Kenya Railways' Mombasa to Kisumu service] D. Boyles. il *Esquire* 112:34+ Ag '89
A train trilogy [riding Amtrak's Coast Starlight from Seattle to Los Angeles] D. G. Gordon. il map *Travel Holiday* 171:60-6 My '89
RAILROAD TUNNELS
Canada
Taming a mountain [opening of Canadian Pacific tunnel through Rogers Pass] J. DeMont. *Maclean's* 102:45+ My 15 '89
RAILROAD WORKERS
See also
United Transportation Union
Rail transportation workers. H. Dillon. il *Occupational Outlook Quarterly* 33:24-8 Spr '89
Health and hygiene
Is this liability law a gravy train? [Federal Employers' Liability Act] R. Stodghill, II. il *Business Week* p93+ N 6 '89
Salaries, pensions, etc.
See also
British Rail Pension Fund
RAILROADS
See also
Burlington Northern Inc.
Collective labor agreements—Railroads
Consolidated Rail Corporation
Eureka Southern Railroad
Grand Canyon Railway
Illinois Central Transportation Company
Light rail systems
National Railroad Passenger Corp.
Union Pacific Rr.

Born again [steam trains; cover story] W. Hoffer. il *Popular Mechanics* 166:117-19+ My '89
Accidents
A deadly explosion [pipeline leak causes train disaster in Soviet Union] B. Wickens. il *Maclean's* 102:46-7 Je 19 '89
Faster than a speeding bullet, Anthony Falzo saved two tots from a powerful locomotive [conductor rescues Todd and Scott Pritchard] il por *People Weekly* 31:159 My 22 '89
Acquisitions and mergers
Countdown [Conrail as takeover target] T. Pouschine. il *Forbes* 144:95 D 25 '89
Is there a 'buyout' sign on this railroad's route? [Kansas City Southern Industries] G. G. Marcial. il *Business Week* p206 S 25 '89
Ivy League street fighters [Prospect Group's hostile bid for Illinois Central Transportation] B. Bremner. il *Business Week* p34 F 13 '89
An LBO outfit that goes for the long pull [Prospect Group buys Illinois Central] M. Berss. il por *Forbes* 143:94+ Ap 17 '89
Railroaded [clearcutting by Plum Creek Timber Company spurred on by LBO fever] A. Porterfield. il *Common Cause Magazine* 15:21-3 S/O '89
Will Japonica bag a railroad—or get derailed? [attack on CNW] G. G. Marcial. il *Business Week* p79 Ap 10 '89
International aspects
A confused agenda for selling the country [Canadian Pacific rumored takeover target of Britain's Hanson Trust] A. Fotheringham. il *Maclean's* 102:56 Ag 14 '89
Automation
The Iron Horse enters the space age [cover story] G. T. Pope. il *High Technology Business* 9:18-22 Ap '89
Cars
Leasing and renting
"Private varnish". N. Santelmann. il *Forbes* 144:238-9 O 2 '89
Collectibles
Collecting date nails. R. P. Anjard. il *Antiques & Collecting Hobbies* 94:38 Jl '89
Employees
See Railroad workers
Federal aid
See Railroads and state
Finance
Reregulation dead ahead? J. Cook. il *Forbes* 144:82+ Jl 10 '89
Surface transportation. J. Clements. il *Forbes* 143:192-3 Ja 9 '89
History
See also
Northern Pacific Railway
Jacob Schiff and the Northern Pacific corner [1901 battle with J. P. Morgan for control of company] J. S. Gordon. il por *American Heritage* 40:86-7 Jl/Ag '89
"The public be damned" [statement uttered by W. H. Vanderbilt in 1882] J. S. Gordon. il *American Heritage* 40:18+ S/O '89
Photographs and photography
The Pacific Railroad [completion of the transcontinental railroad] il *American History Illustrated* 24:52-3 S/O '89
Locomotives
See Locomotives
Models
See Railroad models
Public relations
"The public be damned" [statement uttered by W. H. Vanderbilt in 1882] J. S. Gordon. il *American Heritage* 40:18+ S/O '89
Rates
Stormy Heather [chairman H. Gradison of the ICC] J. Cook. il por *Forbes* 143:168+ Je 26 '89
Right of way
See also
Rails-to-Trails Conservancy
Sanitation
Amtrak's Florida wasteland [dumping human sewage on the tracks] B. Turque. il *Newsweek* 114:50 D 11 '89
Securities
A few rails that could. T. Paré. il *Fortune* 119:50 Je 19 '89
Stations
See also
Grand Central Terminal (New York, N.Y.)
Victoria Terminus (Bombay, India)
Suits and claims
Is this liability law a gravy train? [Federal Employers' Liability Act] R. Stodghill, II. il *Business Week* p93+ N 6 '89
Trains
See also
American-European Express
Maglev trains
Napa Valley Wine Train
Aboard America's favorite train [Zephyr] F. W. Frailey. il map *Changing Times* 43:84-91 N '89

RAILROADS—Trains—*cont.*

Along the Eel and through the redwoods [North Coast Daylight train] il map *Sunset (Central West edition)* 182:28+ My '89

Full throttle toward a new era [Europe] S. Tully. il maps *Fortune* 120:131-2+ N 20 '89

Let's make tracks [cover story; special section] il *New Choices for the Best Years* 29:48-59 Ap '89

The new supertrains [Western Europe] S. Sullivan. il map *Newsweek* 114:46-8 Jl 31 '89

Presto Pendolino! [Italy] D. Scott. il *Popular Science* 234:68 My '89

Putting Amtrak's best to the test. il *Business Week* p180-1 Jl 17 '89

Speeding into the future [Europe] P. Lewis. il *Maclean's* 102:26 Ag 21 '89

Splendor on the Andalusian Express. il map *Sunset (Central West edition)* 182:28-30 Mr '89

Supertrain: a solution to U.S. transportation woes. J. Miller and M. Miller. il *USA Today (Periodical)* 118:27-9 S '89

'There is no other access' [The Budd two car train runs in northern Ontario] G. W. Taylor. il *Maclean's* 102:25 Ag 21 '89

A train trilogy [riding Amtrak's Coast Starlight from Seattle to Los Angeles] D. G. Gordon. il map *Travel Holiday* 171:60-6 My '89

Why the fuss? Just ask the Japanese [bullet trains] M. Mabry. il *Newsweek* 114:48 Jl 31 '89

You can't get there from here [end of Canadian transcontinental train] N. R. Gibbs. il *Time* 134:61 O 16 '89

Waste disposal operations

"Urban ore". R. Simon. il *Forbes* 144:84-5 Ag 21 '89

Canada

See also

Canadian National Railway Company
Canadian Pacific Limited
Via Rail Canada Inc.

History

The golden age of steel. P. Berton. il *Maclean's* 102:18-19 Ag 21 '89

Europe

See also

Venice Simplon-Orient-Express Ltd.

Italy

Presto Pendolino! D. Scott. il *Popular Science* 234:68 My '89

See also

Seibu Railway Co. Ltd.

Japan

Why the fuss? Just ask the Japanese [bullet trains] M. Mabry. il *Newsweek* 114:48 Jl 31 '89

Kenya

See you in Kisumu [Kenya Railways' Mombasa to Kisumu service] D. Boyles. il *Esquire* 112:34+ Ag '89

Mexico

One of the world's best train rides [Chihuahua al Pacifico] L. Sutherland. il map *New Choices for the Best Years* 29:34-9 O '89

Soviet Union

A deadly explosion [pipeline leak causes train disaster] B. Wickens. il *Maclean's* 102:46-7 Je 19 '89

Spain

Splendor on the Andalusian Express. il map *Sunset (Central West edition)* 182:28-30 Mr '89

United States

See Railroads

Western Europe

Full throttle toward a new era. S. Tully. il maps *Fortune* 120:131-2+ N 20 '89

The new supertrains. S. Sullivan. il map *Newsweek* 114:46-8 Jl 31 '89

Speeding into the future. P. Lewis. il *Maclean's* 102:26 Ag 21 '89

RAILROADS AND STATE

See also

Consolidated Rail Corporation
National Railroad Passenger Corp.

Reregulation dead ahead? J. Cook. il *Forbes* 144:82+ Jl 10 '89

Canada

See also

Via Rail Canada Inc.

Western Europe

Europe tries to stay on track. B. Behrens and U. Schulte-Döinghaus. *World Press Review* 36:56 Ap '89

RAILS-TO-TRAILS CONSERVANCY

From rails to trails. il *Country Journal* 16:23 Mr/Ap '89

RAIMON, LOUIS ALEXANDRE *See* Alexandre, 1922-

RAIN AND RAINFALL

See also

Acid rain
Aviation—Storm hazards
Cycling—Storm hazards
Droughts
Floods
Runoff
Tennis—Storm hazards

Herring from heaven [showers of marine creatures] M. Reed. il *Weatherwise* 42:156-8 Je '89

The rain maps [U.S.] T. Klingler and J. Klingler. maps *Bicycling* 30:134 Ap '89

The rains return to the tropics [1988] D. LeComte. il *Weatherwise* 42:8-12 F '89

What makes a rainy day. D. Albers. il *Sierra* 74:104-5 N/D '89

RAIN CLOTHING *See* Clothing, Waterproof
RAIN FOREST CROWN CANOPY *See* Forest crown canopy
RAIN FORESTS

Bungle in the jungle [deforestation] C. Spencer. *Omni (New York, N.Y.)* 11:48-9 S '89

The fate of the earth depends on the fate of the trees. M. N. Mead and others. il *Utne Reader* p49-57 My/Je '89

Fire at the equator [tropical deforestation] R. Wild. il por map *Organic Gardening* 36:54-9 My '89

The fragile forest [cover story; special section] il *The Courier (Unesco)* 42:3-33 Ja '89

Gal pals Sandra Bernhard and Madonna monkey around to save the jungle [benefit at the Brooklyn Academy of Music] il pors *People Weekly* 31:54-6 Je 12 '89

John Seed and the Council of All Beings [interview] P. Stone. il por *The Mother Earth News* 117:58-63 My/Je '89

Our vanishing forests [special section] il *World Press Review* 36:40-1+ O '89

Radios in the rain forest. J. W. Clay. il *Technology Review* 92:52-7 O '89

Saving the rain forests. il *Scholastic Update (Teachers' edition)* 122:11 N 3 '89

Threats to biodiversity. E. O. Wilson. bibl il *Scientific American* 261:108-12+ S '89

Tropical chic [saving the rain forests] P. Swire. *The New Republic* 200:18+ Ja 30 '89

The tropical equation [cover story; special section; with introd. by T. H. Watkins] il *Wilderness* 53:18-51 Wint '89

Tropical forests: an endangered species. il *World Press Review* 36:36-8 My '89

A world in crisis. P. H. Raven. il *USA Today (Periodical)* 117:48-50 My '89

Exhibitions

Jungle cries in Milwaukee [Rain forest: exploring life on earth] D. Einhorn. il *Américas* 41 no1:3 '89

Valuation

Have your rain forest and eat it, too [estimated value of Peruvian forest; research by Charles Peters] *Science News* 136:47 Jl 15 '89

Bolivia

Debt deal stacked against Indians [debt for nature swap] M. Collett. *The Progressive* 53:17-18 Ag '89

Borneo

Interdependence [work of M. Leighton in Gunung Palung Nature Reserve] F. Graham. il *Audubon* 91:14+ My '89

Our vanishing forests . . . it's not just the Amazon. il *World Press Review* 36:40-1 O '89

Brazil

A catbird's seat on Amazon destruction [monitoring of illegal agricultural burning by remote sensing satellites] F. Golden. il *Science* 246:201-2 O 13 '89

Chronicle of a death foretold [murder of environmentalist C. Mendes Filho] M. Beck. il por *Newsweek* 113:62 Ja 9 '89

Defenders of the Amazon [rubber tappers; cover story] S. Hecht and A. Cockburn. il *The Nation* 248:695-6+ My 22 '89

Deforestation in Amazonia. P. M. Fearnside. bibl f il map *Environment* 31:16-20+ My '89

Deforestation in the Amazon [discussion of May 1989 article, Deforestation in Amazonia] P. M. Fearnside. *Environment* 31:4-5 S '89

A dubious plan for the Amazon. M. S. Serrill. il *Time* 133:67 Ap 17 '89

Extractive reserves in Brazilian Amazonia [rubber workers' proposal to fight deforestation] P. M. Fearnside. bibl f il map *BioScience* 39:387-93 Je '89

Fall of the rain forest. T. Waters. il *Discover* 10:40 Ja '89

Hegel and the Amazon Basin [environmental cost of hydroelectric dams] S. C. Florman. il *Technology Review* 92:19 O '89

'Hug a tree' kiss an herb [making money saving Brazil's forests] S. Seibert. il *Newsweek* 113:50 My 1 '89

In memory of Chico Mendes [union leader and ecologist slain] J. D. Hair. il *International Wildlife* 19:30 Mr/Ap '89

The mote & the beam. *Commonweal* 116:260-1 My 5 '89

Murder in the Amazon [union leader and ecologist C. Mendes Filho slain] J. Bierman. il por *Maclean's* 102:21 Ja 9 '89

Notes and comment [murder of environmentalist C. Mendes Filho] il *The New Yorker* 65:27-8 F 20 '89

Our vanishing rain forests. S. McCabe. il *Scholastic Update (Teachers' edition)* 121:13-14 Ap 21 '89

The past and future Amazon. P. A. Colinvaux. bibl il maps *Scientific American* 260:102-8 My '89

Playing with fire [destruction; cover story] E. Linden. il map *Time* 134:76-80+ S 18 '89

RAIN FORESTS—Brazil—*cont.*
Rain forest politics [discussion of May 22, 1989 article, Defenders of the Amazon] S. Hecht and A. Cockburn. *The Nation* 249:262+ S 18 '89
The scorched earth. A. DeCurtis. il *Rolling Stone* p40-9 F 23 '89
A tale of two forests [Amazon] *World Press Review* 36:40+ S '89
Tom Lovejoy and the last crusade. R. Migler. il pors *Gentlemen's Quarterly* 59:286-9+ O '89
Using red ink to keep tropical forests green [debt-for-nature swaps] C. P. Work and G. Smith. il map *U.S. News & World Report* 106:48-9 Mr 6 '89
Whose hands will shape the future of the Amazon's green mansions? [plight of the rubber tappers; cover story] M. Parfit. bibl (p245) il maps *Smithsonian* 20:58-68+ N '89
The world puts the heat on Brazil [forgiving part of debt in exchange for help in protecting nature] *World Press Review* 36:38 My '89

Central Africa
Slime time [reduced numbers of slime molds; research by James Cavender] il *Discover* 10:10 O '89

Central America
See also
La Ruta Maya

Costa Rica
Capital conservation [debt for nature swaps] J. Zweig. por *Forbes* 143:208 Ap 17 '89
Quetzalandia. D. Bellm. il *Mother Jones* 14:49-50 D '89

French Guiana
Photogenic science [studying the tropical forest canopy by hot air balloon; work of Francis Hallé] J. Horgan. il *Scientific American* 261:20+ D '89
Treed [exploring the tropical forest canopy by hot air balloon; work of Francis Halle and others] B. Weber. il *The New York Times Magazine* p86 D 17 '89

Guatemala
A forest dies in Guatemala [conservation initiatives] V. Perera. *The Nation* 249:521-2+ N 6 '89
Treasures of the Guatemala rain forest. A. Wade. il *The New Leader* 72:11-13 Ap 3-17 '89

Hawaii
Losing paradise. K. Brower. il map *Wilderness* 53:20-8 Wint '89

Latin America
Bear of the clouds [effects of deforestation on the spectacled bear] P. Steinhart. il map *Audubon* 91:92-4+ Jl '89

Mexico
A plea for Mexico [open letter to Carlos Salinas de Gortari from the Group of 100] *World Press Review* 36:45+ O '89

Panama
Tropical forest gardening: an alternative to destruction. il *The Futurist* 23:53 My/Je '89

Peru
Have your rain forest and eat it, too [estimated value of forest; research by Charles Peters] *Science News* 136:47 Jl 15 '89

Puerto Rico
See also
Caribbean National Forest (Puerto Rico)

Tanzania
Tracing the roots of the world's favorite houseplant [African violets] J. Lovett. il *International Wildlife* 19:34-7 Mr/Ap '89

Zaire
The Efe: archers of the African rain forest. R. C. Bailey. il maps *National Geographic* 176:664-86 N '89
RAIN HAZARDS (AVIATION) *See* Aviation—Storm hazards
RAIN MAN [film] *See* Motion picture reviews—Single works
RAINA, ASHOK K., AND OTHERS
Identification of a neuropeptide hormone that regulates sex pheromone production in female moths. bibl f il *Science* 244:796-8 My 19 '89
RAINBOW (SHIP)
The troubled voyage of the Rainbow [Massachusetts colony confronts issue of slave trade] L. Gragg. bibl il maps *History Today* 39:36-41 Ag '89
THE RAINBOW [film] *See* Motion picture reviews—Single works
RAINBOW BRIDGE (UTAH AND ARIZ.)
Photographs and photography
Lake Powell's Rainbow Bridge by moonlight with a 3-minute exposure, in wind, on water. J. Zuckerman. il *Petersen's Photographic Magazine* 18:22-3 My '89
RAINBOW COALITION *See* National Rainbow Coalition
RAINBOW IN ART
Glass, steel and sunlight [works by D. Eldred] B. Kantrowitz. il *Newsweek* 113:69 My 15 '89
RAINBOW TECHNOLOGIES INC.
This could be the key to keeping computer intruders out. L. Armstrong. il *Business Week* p54 Jl 31 '89
RAINE, CRAIG
Retirement [poem] *The New Yorker* 65:72 D 4 '89
RAINER, PETER
The new Gary Cooper? Yup. il pors *The New York Times Magazine* p38-9+ Ap 23 '89
(jt. auth) See Edwards, Henry, and Rainer, Peter

RAINES, ELAINE W., AND OTHERS
Interleukin-1 mitogenic activity of fibroblasts and smooth muscle cells is due to PDGF-AA. bibl f il *Science* 243:393-6 Ja 20 '89
RAINES, HOWELL
Getting to the heart of Dixie. il *The New York Times Book Review* 94:3+ S 17 '89
RAINEY, WAYNE
about
Lawson closes on Rainey in 500 GPs. M. Oxley. il por *Cycle* 40:24+ O '89
Schwantz and Rainey top Euro Grands Prix. M. Oxley. il *Cycle* 40:24 S '89
RAINIER III, PRINCE OF MONACO, 1923-
about
Prince Rainier marks his 40-year reign with a Monaco gala. D. Bacon. il por *People Weekly* 32:96-9 Jl 24 '89
RAINIER, CHRIS
Native portraiture. il *Petersen's Photographic Magazine* 17:32-5 Ja '89
RAINS-WEBER, MARY
Who'll take these family treasures? [story] il *Redbook* 172:38+ Ja '89
RAINSFORD, BETTIS C.
about
Iconoclasts. R. Addis. il pors *Forbes* 143:49+ Ap 17 '89
RAINWATER, RICHARD E.
about
Diamonds in his own backyard. J. H. Taylor. il *Forbes* 143:49-50+ Mr 6 '89
RAINWEAR *See* Clothing, Waterproof
RAISED BED VEGETABLE GARDENING *See* Vegetable gardens and gardening
RAISIN BREAD *See* Bread
A RAISIN IN THE SUN [television program] *See* Television program reviews—Single works
RAISTRICK, I. D.
(jt. auth) *See* Conradson, S. D., and Raistrick, I. D.
RAITT, BONNIE
about
Bonnie Raitt: still nobody's girl. M. McCormick. il por *Rolling Stone* p24 Je 29 '89
Bonnie Raitt works her magic again. A. Nash. il por *Stereo Review* 54:93 Je '89
Getting back on track. R. Givens. il pors *Newsweek* 113:66 Mr 13 '89
It's Bonnie Raitt's 'Time'. S. Rogers. il por *Rolling Stone* p19 O 19 '89
Time is on her side. M. Segell. il pors *American Health* 8:60-1 Jl/Ag '89
Veteran rocker Bonnie Raitt gets back on track in the Nick of time. K. Hubbard. il pors *People Weekly* 31:85-6 Ap 24 '89
RAIZEN, SENTA A., AND KASER, JOYCE S.
Assessing science learning in elementary school: why, what, and how? bibl f il *Phi Delta Kappan* 70:718-22 My '89
RAJAGOPAL, JAYARAJ, AND OTHERS
Stereochemical course of catalysis by the Tetrahymena ribozyme. bibl f il *Science* 244:692-4 My 12 '89
RAJANEESH, ACHARYA *See* Rajneesh, Bhagwan Shree, 1931-1990
RAJAVASHISTH, TRIPATHI B., AND OTHERS
Identification of a zinc finger protein that binds to the sterol regulatory element. bibl f il *Science* 245:640-3 Ag 11 '89
RAJNEESH, BHAGWAN SHREE, 1931-1990
about
The cult leader: how absolute power corrupts [excerpt from The golden guru] J. S. Gordon. il por *Utne Reader* p136-7 Mr/Ap '89
Anecdotes, facetiae, satire, etc.
Dinner on Rajneesh. D. K. Mano. *National Review* 41:56-7 Ap 7 '89
RAJNEESHPURAM (OR.)
The cult leader: how absolute power corrupts [excerpt from The golden guru] J. S. Gordon. il por *Utne Reader* p136-7 Mr/Ap '89
RAKING OF LEAVES *See* Lawns
RALEIGH (N.C.)
City planning
Landscaping blooms in Raleigh. il *Southern Living* 24:122 My '89
RALLIES, AUTOMOBILE *See* Automobile rallies
RALLIES, BICYCLE *See* Bicycle rallies
RALLIES, BOAT *See* Boat rallies
RALLIES, MOTOR VEHICLE *See* Motor vehicle rallies
RALLS, KATHERINE, AND BROWNELL, ROBERT L., JR.
Protected species—research permits and the value of basic research. bibl f il *BioScience* 39:394-6 Je '89
RALLY CARS *See* Automobiles, Racing
RALPH, ELAINE
about
Fish carvings at Creel Creek. D. W. Hollis. il pors *The Conservationist* 43:36-9 My/Je '89
RALPH, FRITZ
about
Fish carvings at Creel Creek. D. W. Hollis. il pors *The Conservationist* 43:36-9 My/Je '89

RALPH, JOHN H.
Improving education for the disadvantaged: do we know whom to help? bibl f il *Phi Delta Kappan* 70:395-401 Ja '89

RALPH, SHERYL LEE
about
Black stars shine in murder mystery 'The Mighty Quinn'. il pors *Jet* 75:46-8 F 20 '89
Star quality. M. Southgate. il por *Essence* 19:24 Mr '89

RALSTON, ARTHUR
She's not having a baby. il *Gentlemen's Quarterly* 59:281+ S '89

RALSTON, DENNIS
Backhand return. il por *World Tennis* 37:74 N '89
Direct the ball. il por *World Tennis* 37:106 S '89
Don't lean. il por *World Tennis* 36:93 Mr '89
A heel up. il por *World Tennis* 36:19 Ja '89
Help your partner. il por *World Tennis* 37:74 Jl '89
Keep you hips still. il por *World Tennis* 36:26 My '89
Keep your head back. il por *World Tennis* 37:54 Ag '89
Keep your heels up. il *World Tennis* 37:73 Je '89
Volley position. il por *World Tennis* 37:53 D '89
Weigh your options. il *World Tennis* 36:91 Ap '89
Work your way in. il por *World Tennis* 36:79 F '89

RALSTON, EVELYN, AND HALL, ZACH W.
Transfer of a protein encoded by a single nucleus to nearby nuclei in multinucleated myotubes. bibl f il *Science* 244:1066-9 Je 2 '89

RALSTON, JEANNIE
Coal miner's doctor. il pors *McCall's* 116:70+ S '89
The comeback of Phyllis George. il pors *McCall's* 116:12-14+ S '89
One big, happy family has a grand reunion. il *McCall's* 116:62+ Jl '89
Women against toxic waste. il *McCall's* 117:132+ O '89

RALSTON, RICHARD D.
South Africa: between history and the handwriting on the wall (III). il *American Visions* 4:38-45 Ap '89

RALSTON PURINA CO.
Chow down. G. Morgenson. il *Forbes* 144:78-9 Ag 21 '89

RAM, ERIC R.
Information is power. il *World Health* p8-9 Ja/F '89
RAM *See* Random access memory

RAM (FIRM)
Blueprinters [custom overhauls] F. George. il *Flying* 116:66-8+ Ag '89
Liquid-cooled engine mod for 414A. il *Flying* 116:18 F '89
Wolf in RAM's clothing [converted Cessna 414A with liquid-cooled engines] J. M. McClellan. il *Flying* 116:70-6 D '89

RAM DASS
Parents: sixties hippies, eighties babies. il *American Health* 8:54 O '89

RAMAN SPECTROSCOPY
Optical studies of hydrogen above 200 gigapascals: evidence for metallization by band overlap. H. K. Mao and R. J. Hemley. bibl f il *Science* 244:1462-5 Je 23 '89

RAMANATHAN, V., AND OTHERS
Climate and the earth's radiation budget [cover story] bibl f il *Physics Today* 42:22-7+ My '89
Cloud-radiative forcing and climate: results from the Earth Radiation Budget Experiment. bibl f il maps *Science* 243:57-63 Ja 6 '89

RAMANUJAN, S. R.
An 'eloquent brush' in India. il *World Press Review* 36:58-9 Mr '89

RAMANUJAN AIYANGAR, SRINIVASA, 1887-1920
about
The master of math. G. Williams. il *Omni (New York, N.Y.)* 11:58-60+ Mr '89
Srinivasa Ramanujan. B. C. Berndt. *The American Scholar* 58:234-44 Spr '89

RAMAT, CHARLES S.
about
Can't get no respect. T. Jaffe. *Forbes* 144:316-17 S 4 '89

RAMEAU, JEAN PHILIPPE
about
Hippolyte et Aricie [opera] Reviews
The New Yorker 65:71-2 D 25 '89. A. Porter

RAMET, PEDRO, 1949-
Catholics under communism: the case of Czechoslovakia [cover story] il *The Christian Century* 106:202-5 F 22 '89

RAMIREZ, BENJI
about
The death of an athlete. R. Telander and M. Noden. il pors *Sports Illustrated* 70:68-72+ F 20 '89

RAMIREZ, DEBORAH
Squatters take on the Navy. il *The Progressive* 53:36 S '89

RAMIREZ, JOSE LUIS
about
In your face, José Luis. P. Putnam. il pors *Sports Illustrated* 71:66-7 Ag 28 '89

RAMKE, BIN, 1947-
War crimes [poem] *The New Republic* 201:34 O 9 '89

RAMO, SIMON
How we can regain our competitive edge. *Scientific American* 260:148 My '89
RAMPLING, ANNE *See* Rice, Anne, 1941-

RAMSDELL, FRED, AND OTHERS
A nondeletional mechanism of thymic self tolerance. bibl f il *Science* 246:1038-41 N 24 '89

RAMSEY, NORMAN FOSTER, 1915-
about
Basic measurements lead to Physics Nobel. R. Pool. il pors *Science* 246:327-8 O 20 '89
Physics. il pors *Time* 134:74 O 23 '89
Physics Nobel: traps, clocks, quantum leaps. E. Peterson. *Science News* 136:262 O 21 '89
Ramsey, Dehmelt, Paul win Nobel for helping to set high standards. B. G. Levi. il pors *Physics Today* 42:17-19 D '89

RAMSEY, VAN BROUGHTON
about
The clothes make the cowboy . . . and even the Indian. il *Theatre Crafts* 23:44-6+ F '89

RAMSLAND, KATHERINE M., 1953-
Hunger for the marvelous: the vampire craze in the computer age [cover story] il *Psychology Today* 23:31-5 N '89

RANADA, DAVID
Bits & pieces. See alternate issues of High Fidelity (New York, N.Y.) beginning January 1986 through July 1989
Scan lines. See alternate issues of High Fidelity (New York, N.Y.) beginning April 1986 through July 1989

RANCH HOUSES
The rambling ranch idea . . . updated in the wine country. il *Sunset (Central West edition)* 183:116-17 O '89
Ranch house with a veranda that invites you to slow down [Napa Valley] il *Sunset (Central West edition)* 183:102 O '89

RANCH HOUSES, REMODELED *See* Houses, Remodeled
RANCH LIFE
See also
Cowboys
Journal of a woman rancher [South Dakota cattle ranch] L. M. Hasselstrom. il *Life* 12:88-92+ Jl '89

RANCHES
See also
Ranch life

California
See also
Valley Teen Ranch (Madera, Calif.)

Kansas
A prairie park? [Spring Hill Ranch offered for national park status] F. Graham. il *Audubon* 91:20+ S '89

Montana
See also
Grant-Kohrs Ranch National Historic Site (Mont.)

Nevada
Saga of the urban buckarettes [horseback trip from Cottonwood Ranch through the Jarbidge wilderness] C. J. Hadley. il *The Saturday Evening Post* 261:70-1 Jl/Ag '89

New Mexico
See also
Armendaris Ranch (N.M.)

New York (State)
See also
Lucky Star Ranch

South Dakota
Journal of a woman rancher [cattle ranch] L. M. Hasselstrom. il *Life* 12:88-92+ Jl '89

Western States
Rounding up the best of the true West: great guest ranches from Wyoming to California. A. Dana. il *Vogue* 179:170 Je '89

Wyoming
Cattle driving for fun. S. Cohen. il map *Travel Holiday* 171:68-71 F '89
Heaven can wait [Paradise Guest Ranch] N. Giustina. il *Travel Holiday* 171:80-2 My '89
Queen of the range [cattle rancher D. Chastain] B. Eftink. il por *Successful Farming* 87:46-7 Ja '89

RANCHO LA PUERTA (MEXICO: RESORT) *See* Health resorts, watering places, etc.—Mexico
RANCHO SECO NUCLEAR POWER PLANT (CALIF.) *See* Nuclear power plants
RANCIDITY
Crab-shell derivative retards rancidity [chitosan compound, NCMC, developed by John R. Vercellotti and Allen J. St. Angelo] J. Raloff. *Science News* 136:189 S 16 '89

RAND, ABBY
Is Europe worth the big price? il map *New Choices for the Best Years* 29:38-40+ F '89

RAND, AYN, 1905-1982
about
Ayn Rand's objectivism: a humanistic interpretation. K. Robinson. por *The Humanist* 49:29-30 Ja/F '89
Mussolini shrugged. J. Sobran. *National Review* 41:52-3 Ja 27 '89

RAND, MAN, JR.
about
Let's not forget. B. Tarrant. il por *Field & Stream* 94:136-8 O '89

RAND, ROBERT
Perestroika up close. il *Reader's Digest* 135:115-19 Ag '89
RANDALL, GAIL

about

Living in sin? Not in her apartments, vows Christian landlady Evelyn Smith. M. Brower. il pors *People Weekly* 32:113-14 D 11 '89
RANDALL, GLENN, 1957-
Wandering off the beaten path. il *Sierra* 74:88-9 S/O '89
RANDALL, L. L., AND HARDY, S. J. S.
Unity in function in the absence of consensus in sequence: role of leader peptides in export. bibl f il *Science* 243:1156-9 Mr 3 '89
RANDALL, MARGARET, 1936-

about

Author wins citizenship battle. L. Stapleton. il por *Ms.* 18:71 N '89
RANDALL, RICKY

about

The last Olympian. C. Gammon. il pors *Sports Illustrated* 70:42-4+ My 15 '89
RANDALL'S ORDINARY (NORTH STONINGTON, CONN.: INN) *See* North Stonington (Conn.)—Hotels, motels, etc.
RANDI, JAMES
Your health: exposing fraud isn't magic. *Modern Maturity* 32:22 Je/Jl '89
RANDO (DOG) *See* Dogs in motion pictures
RANDOLPH, BERNARD P.
The B-2 bomber [address, April 29, 1989] *Vital Speeches of the Day* 55:494-7 Je 1 '89
Total quality management [address, November 29, 1988] *Vital Speeches of the Day* 55:322-4 Mr 15 '89
RANDOM ACCESS MEMORY
Almost-magic EMS emulation [Turbo EMS] S. Miastkowski. il *Byte* 14:97-8 Mr '89
America's gambling chips [U.S. Memories Inc. to make dynamic random access memory chips] *Newsweek* 114:44 Jl 3 '89
Better than cache in the bank? [Western Digital Speedkit caching controller] H. Eglowstein. il *Byte* 14:204+ S '89
Big Blue's chip club [U.S. Memories Inc. formed to manufacture dynamic random access memory chips] il *Time* 134:44 Jl 3 '89
Caching in on memory systems. B. Glass. il *Byte* 14:281-5 Mr '89
Cold cache for your hard disk [hyperStore-816 and Smart Cache PM3011] S. Miastkowski. *Byte* 14:86+ O '89
EMS with a cache [Elite 16 Plus HyperCache] J. Holtzman. il *Byte* 14:181-2+ Jl '89
Ferroelectric memories. J. F. Scott and C. A. Paz de Araujo. bibl f il *Science* 246:1400-5 D 15 '89
Futuristic markets [proposed futures markets for dynamic random access memory chips] E. Corcoran. il *Scientific American* 261:62-3 Ag '89
Hands across the chipmaking chasm [U.S. Memories and Sematech to work with JESSI Project] O. Port. *Business Week* p28-9 Jl 3 '89
Memory expansion boards [tables] C. D. Hanlon. il *Compute!* 11:42+ S '89
More Mac RAM for less [Virtual from Connectix] T. Thompson. il *Byte* 14:98+ My '89
Nonvolatile memory advances reduce avionics weight, power requirements. W. B. Scott. il *Aviation Week & Space Technology* 131:79+ Jl 17 '89
PC-Kwik Power Pak. D. English. il *Compute!* 11:134-5 D '89
Please feed the PC. D. Gookin. il *Compute!* 11:76-8+ N '89
PopDrop [TSR memory manager] D. English. il *Compute!* 11:62+ S '89
Seeking a wide berth [dynamic random access memory] R. Sartore. il *Byte* 14:307-8+ N '89
The silicon chip race advances into X-rays. M. Crawford. il *Science* 246:1382-3 D 15 '89
Teletek X-Bandit EMS 4.0 memory board. J. Holtzman. il *Radio-Electronics* 60 ComputerDigest:79-80 Je '89
Three ways to improve your memory [expanded memory boards for XTs and ATs] H. F. Beechhold and E. P. Stevenson. il *Home Office Computing* 7:74+ D '89
Turbo EMS. J. B. Lambert. il *Compute!* 11:116+ D '89
U.S. chips are down [dynamic random access memory] M. Mandell. il *High Technology Business* 9:12 Mr '89
Using expanded memory. D. M. Yancich. il *Byte* 14 Special Issue:123-4+ Fall '89
A virtual crowd [special section] il *Byte* 14:341-50+ N '89
Virtual memory, "hot links" coming to the Mac OS. *Byte* 14:17-18+ Jl '89
VROOMM: Borland says memory technology will make future programs better, not bigger [Virtual Real-Time Object-Oriented Memory Manager] *Byte* 14:17-18 Ag '89
VROOMM goes the spreadsheet [Virtual Real-Time Object Oriented Memory Manager for Quattro] R. Malloy. *Byte* 14:111-12 O '89
What's behind the Texas Instruments-Hitachi deal. O. Port and T. Mason. il *Business Week* p93+ Ja 16 '89

Prices

First wave of 4-megabit memory chips arriving, but at what cost to users? [dynamic random access memory] *Byte* 14:17-18 S '89
I usually don't do this, but . . . A. R. Levitan. il *Compute!* 11:88+ Mr '89
Trade protection comes to Silicon Valley. A. T. Denzau. *Society* 26:38-42 Mr/Ap '89
Why Apple went sour. M. Shao. il *Business Week* p30-1 F 13 '89
RANDOM ACCESS MEMORY FUTURES
Pork bellies, move over. *Newsweek* 114:70 O 30 '89
RANDOM HOUSE AUDIOBOOKS
Random, Bantam to distribute audiotapes through video stores. *Publishers Weekly* 236:27 D 1 '89
RANDOM HOUSE INC.
Bernstein retiring from Random; Vitale is new chairman. C. Reid and J. F. Baker. pors *Publishers Weekly* 236:8 N 17 '89
Cerf to Newhouse [departure of R. L. Bernstein] *The Nation* 249:62-4 N 27 '89
The Random House shuffle [R. L. Bernstein leaves] J. Alter. il pors *Newsweek* 114:74 N 13 '89
RH-Century deal creates major U.K. trade group. V. Menkes. *Publishers Weekly* 235:9 Je 23 '89
RANDOM HOUSE U.K. LTD.
Loss of Bodley Head fuels U.K. disquiet over conglomeration. V. Menkes. *Publishers Weekly* 236:8 Jl 7 '89
RANDOM NUMBER GENERATORS
Pseudo-random sequences. D. Lancaster. il *Radio-Electronics* 60:79-82+ F '89
RANELAGH, JOHN
Postscript to Munich [interview with A. Douglas-Home] *National Review* 41:30-1 Je 2 '89
RANGEFINDER CAMERAS *See* Cameras
RANGEL, CHARLES B.

about

Charles Rangel: the front-line general in the war on drugs. L. Norment. il pors *Ebony* 44:128+ Mr '89
Rangel-backed tax law pushes Mobil Oil to sell its S. African holdings. por *Jet* 76:5 My 15 '89
Rangel leads illegal-drug probe group in Caribbean. por *Jet* 75:25 Ja 16 '89
Rangel raps Bush for his snubbing drug czar status. por *Jet* 75:4 Mr 6 '89
What must be done. il pors *Ebony* 44:156+ Ag '89
RANGEL, LYLE
(jt. auth) *See* Watson, Dan, and Rangel, Lyle
RANGERS, PARK *See* Park rangers
RANGES, KITCHEN *See* Stoves
RANGES, LIVESTOCK *See* Livestock ranges
RANGOON RACQUET CLUB (LOS ANGELES, CALIF.: RESTAURANT) *See* Los Angeles (Calif.)—Restaurants, nightclubs, bars, etc.
RANGOS, JOHN

about

Talking trash. E. F. Cone. il por *Forbes* 143:14 Ap 17 '89
RANKIN, ALLEN
Attacked by pit bulls! il *Reader's Digest* 135:105-10 S '89
(ed) *See* Totzauer, Josef. Love at first sound
RANKIN, DEBORAH M.
Inside moves. *Harper's Bazaar* 122:28+ Je '89
Live-in losers: staying out of the ring. *Harper's Bazaar* 122:44-5+ Ja '89
RANKIN, JEANNETTE

about

The first woman in Congress. D. O. Relin. il por *Scholastic Update (Teachers' edition)* 121:19 F 24 '89
RANKING OF COLLEGES AND UNIVERSITIES *See* Colleges and universities—Evaluation
RANLY, ERNEST W.
A Christian spirituality of nonviolence. *America* 161:110-11+ Ag 26-S 2 '89
Peru in peril. il *The Christian Century* 106:657-9 Jl 5-12 '89
RANNEY, JONATHAN
A ghost outside the fence. il *The Progressive* 53:50 Ap '89
RANSOM, JOHN CROWE, 1888-1974

about

John Crowe Ransom: as I remember him. C. Brooks. *The American Scholar* 58:211-33 Spr '89
RAO, SATISH
Canada's visionary new museum. il *World Press Review* 36:61 Jl '89
RAO, VEENA N., AND OTHERS
elk, tissue-specific *ets*-related genes on chromosomes X and 14 near translocation breakpoints. bibl f il *Science* 244:66-70 Ap 7 '89
RAOUL, NINAJ
Shop talk. *Black Enterprise* 20:139 O '89
RAP MUSIC

See also

Cable television—Rap music
Phonograph records—Rap music
Girls ain't nothin' but trouble? [women rap artists] C. Cooper. *Essence* 19:80+ Ap '89
Hip-hop madness. H. Allen. il *Essence* 19:78-80+ Ap '89

RAP MUSIC—*cont.*

Kris Parker, who came home from life on the streets to become gold record rapper 'KRS-ONE'. S. Dougherty. il pors *People Weekly* 31:101+ F 27 '89

N.W.A. cops an attitude. S. Hochman. il *Rolling Stone* p24 Je 29 '89

Rap as a second language [Mother Fussin' Rappers] G. Collins. il *Ms.* 17:56-8 Ja/F '89

Rap roundup [1989] il *Rolling Stone* p73-5 D 14-28 '89

Rapping about the 'Wild thing,' Tone-Lōc crashes the pop party. il por *People Weekly* 31:115 Mr 20 '89

Unbelievable hype [Public Enemy] M. DiLeo. il *Mother Jones* 14:10 F/Mr '89

What's behind the rise of rap? R. E. McKinney. il *Ebony* 44:66-8+ Ja '89

Women who rap—Salt-n-Pepa. D. DeNicolo. il *Glamour* 87:204 My '89

Anecdotes, facetiae, satire, etc.

I still remember English. R. Schoenstein. il *New Choices for the Best Years* 29:96 Mr '89

Moral and religious aspects

A rap album in the dock [obscenity case against Alexander, Ala. record store selling The 2 Live Crew] N. Zeman. il *Newsweek* 114:72 O 16 '89

RAPAPORT, BEN

More than just blowin' smoke! Collecting antique tobacco pipes [cover story] il *Antiques & Collecting Hobbies* 93:40-1+ Ja '89

RAPE

See also

Brawley, Tawana—Assault case

Central Park wilding attack, 1989

Child molesting

Date rape

Trials (Rape)

Abortion and the rapee. W. F. Buckley. *National Review* 41:53-4 D 8 '89

Darkness at the heart of town [high school boys arrested for sexually assaulting a retarded girl in Glen Ridge, N.J.] P. Wilkinson. il *Rolling Stone* p55-6+ O 5 '89

Fetal position [G. Bush states he would veto abortions in cases of rape or incest] Z. R. Eisenstein. *The Nation* 249:588-9 N 20 '89

Gang rape in the suburbs [attack on retarded girl in Glen Ridge, N.J.] B. Turque. il *Newsweek* 113:26 Je 5 '89

Jailed for a rape that never happened, Gary Dotson has his name cleared at last. M. Brower. il pors *People Weekly* 32:80-1 Ag 28 '89

Minneapolis judge lets victim set punishment [W. Posten lets rape victim decide sentence] por *Jet* 75:24 Ja 30 '89

A mother's revenge [R. Baldridge catches man who raped her daughter in Columbus, Ohio] M. Cohen. il por *Ladies' Home Journal* 106:140-1+ S '89

N.Y. woman saved by TV cable and plucky tenants [woman forced off roof after being raped] il *Jet* 76:9+ My 1 '89

New reasons to report a rape. L. Holland. il *Good Housekeeping* 209:167 Ag '89

Rape: a woman's worst nightmare. R. Distelheim. *McCall's* 116:60+ S '89

Rape on campus. A. Rule. il *Good Housekeeping* 209:189+ S '89

Sexual violence and its aftermath [special section] il *Psychology Today* 23:70-3 S '89

Society loves a good victim. L. Jackson. por *Newsweek* 114:8 Jl 24 '89

Speaking of the unspeakable. A. Sebold. il *The New York Times Magazine* p16+ F 26 '89

You can talk your way out of a rape. L. Jack. il *Mademoiselle* 95:98 Je '89

RAPE COUNSELING

Support for partners [male response to rape] D. Burden. *Psychology Today* 23:72-3 S '89

RAPE IN MOTION PICTURES

Jodie Foster takes a stand in 'The accused'. S. Roman. il pors *Video* 13:14 My '89

RAPE IN TELEVISION

A plea to the soaps: let's stop turning rapists into heroes. G. J. Waggett. il *TV Guide* 37:10-11 My 27-Je 2 '89

RAPESEED OIL

See also

Canola oil

RAPHAEL, BETTE-JANE

Can this be love? See issues of Glamour through January 1989

RAPHAEL, CHAIM

A (Jewish) double helix. *Commentary* 87:56-8 My '89

RAPHAËL, SALLY JESSY

about

Sally Jessy Raphaël driven? You'd be too—if you were fired 18 times and lived on food stamps. D. Hill. il por *TV Guide* 37:17-19 Jl 8-14 '89

Sally Jessy Raphaël on the move. R. Beach. il pors *The Saturday Evening Post* 261:58-9+ S '89

RAPHIOLEPIS INDICA *See* Indian hawthorn

RAPID-AMERICAN CORP.

Riklis' fancy footwork may be tripping him up. A. Rothman. il por *Business Week* p86-8 Je 19 '89

RAPID CITY (S.D.)

Social work

Tiospaye Teca: working with young Native American families in the Dakotas [problems associated with teenage pregnancy] A. Floden. il *Children Today* 18:28-32 S/O '89

RAPID READING *See* Speed reading

RAPID SOLIDIFICATION TECHNOLOGY

Boomtown [Center for Explosives Technology Research] R. Wolkomir. il *Discover* 10:76-81 Ag '89

Dynamite metals [Center for Explosives Technology Research] S. Ashley. il *Popular Science* 234:102-4 Mr '89

Rapidly solidified materials. T. Abraham and G. T. Pope. il *High Technology Business* 9:28-32 N/D '89

Japan

Japan's RS plastics. H. Okada. *High Technology Business* 9:30 N/D '89

RAPIDS, RUNNING OF *See* Running rapids

RAPINI COOKING *See* Cooking—Vegetables

RAPOPORT, ANATOL, 1911-

War without hatred. il por *The Humanist* 49:14-17+ Jl/Ag '89

RAPOPORT, JUDITH L., 1933-

The biology of obsessions and compulsions. il *Scientific American* 260:82-9 Mr '89

about

A psychiatrist explores the cause—and treatment—of those tormenting, obsessive-compulsive urges [interview] K. McMurran. il pors *People Weekly* 31:91-4+ Mr 13 '89

RAPOPORT, ROGER

Snap, crackle, and pop [cover story] il *Americana* 17:36-40 Mr/Ap '89

RAPOPORT, RON

With all due respect: some guys don't get it, no matter how much they win. il *Sport (New York, N.Y.)* 80:46-50 Mr '89

RAPOZA, RITA S., AND LANCASTER, LYNNE C.

Straight talk from key employees. il *Nation's Business* 77:40 N '89

RAPP, JOEL

The 10 most rewarding houseplants [excerpt from Mr. Mother Earth's most rewarding houseplants] il *Redbook* 172:126-7+ Ap '89

Christmas legends. il *Redbook* 174:114-15+ D '89

Standards of beauty. il *Redbook* 172:124-5+ Mr '89

Step into our edible garden. il *Redbook* 173:75-7+ Je '89

RAPP, JOHN P., AND OTHERS

A genetic polymorphism in the renin gene of Dahl rats cosegregates with blood pressure. bibl f il *Science* 243:542-4 Ja 27 '89

RAPPING (MUSIC) *See* Rap music

RAPPOPORT, SOLOMON *See* Ansky, S., 1863-1920

RAPTORS *See* Birds of prey

RAQUE, SALLY

Golf guide: the whole in one [cover story] il *Women's Sports & Fitness* 11:44-8+ Jl/Ag '89

RARE (RARE ANIMAL RESCUE EFFORT) CENTER

Polly wants to be saved [work of P. Butler] S. Begley. il *Newsweek* 114:65 D 18 '89

RARE ANIMALS

See also

Bison, American

Bobcats

Caribou

Cheetahs

Convention on International Trade in Endangered Species of Wild Fauna and Flora (1973)

Crocodiles

Elephants

Endangered Species Act (1973)

Gorillas

Leopards

Manatees

Otters

Pandas

RARE (Rare Animal Rescue Effort) Center

Rhinoceros

Sea otters

Seals (Animals)

Tigers

Turtles

Whales

Wolves

Ark de triomphe [saving endangered species in Yellowstone] C. Spencer. il *Omni (New York, N.Y.)* 11:48-50+ Ja '89

Doling out DNA [DNA fingerprinting for captive breeding programs; cover story] R. Weiss. il *Science News* 135:72-4 F 4 '89

Endangered species. A. Hollister. il *Life* 12:60-1+ Ap '89

Endangered species: can they be saved? [cover story] W. F. Allman. il map *U.S. News & World Report* 107:52-8 O 2 '89

Evolution and extinction [species preservers trying to stop the clock; with reply by N. Meyers] N. D. Levine. *BioScience* 39:38-40 Ja '89

Glass menageries [use of cryopreservation in captive breeding] T. Beardsley. il *Scientific American* 261:36+ O '89

RARE ANIMALS—*cont.*
Protected species—research permits and the value of basic research. K. Ralls and R. L. Brownell, Jr. bibl f il *BioScience* 39:394-6 Je '89
Reintroduction of captive mammals for conservation [cover story] D. G. Kleiman. bibl f il *BioScience* 39:152-61 Mr '89
Return of the natives [rare species reintroduction] D. E. Brown. il *Wilderness* 52:40-52 Wint '88
The science of saving endangered species: directions for research in conservation biology. C. Mlot. il *BioScience* 39:68-70 F '89
A technique originally developed for overcoming human infertility may also help endangered species [in vitro fertilization] R. M. Adams. *Smithsonian* 19:12 Ja '89
Why save endangered species? G. Reiger. il *Field & Stream* 93:15 Ja '89

RARE BIRDS
See also
Bluebirds
Condors
Cracids (Birds)
Eagles
Falcons
Ibises
Parrots
Pelicans
Sparrows
Woodpeckers
In the struggle to protect our planet, ornithologists and their grass-roots flock have insights worth following. J. P. Wiley, Jr. il *Smithsonian* 20:34+ D '89
Protection
See Bird sanctuaries

RARE BOOKS
See also
Manuscripts
Can onions prevent baldness? [medical book collection of C. C. Tandy] C. Brown. il por *Forbes* 144:135 Ag 7 '89
How to be an old book's latest lover. K. M. Hafner. il *Business Week* p182 My 22 '89

RARE COINS AS AN INVESTMENT *See* Coins as an investment

RARE EARTH METALS
See also
Cesium

RARE FISH
See also
Topminnows

RARE PLANTS
See also
Cactus
Convention on International Trade in Endangered Species of Wild Fauna and Flora (1973)
Endangered Species Act (1973)
Piratebush
Blueprint for conserving plant diversity. C. Mlot. il *BioScience* 39:364-8 Je '89
Endangered species [bulbs] il *Flower and Garden* 33:33 S/O '89
Extinction countdown for US plants [survey by Center for Plant Conservation] il *BioScience* 39:276 Ap '89
How to get plants into the conservationists' ark. R. Lewin. il *Science* 244:32-3 Ap 7 '89

RASA ISLAND (MEXICO)
New tensions for a rough crowd [nesting space battles for terns and gulls] E. Velarde. il *International Wildlife* 19:20-4 N/D '89

RASCANO FAMILY
about
An Asian tale: young girls, red roses. S. Mydans. il *The New York Times Magazine* p44-7+ Ap 2 '89

RASH, WAYNE, JR.
Down to business. See issues of Byte beginning August 1988

RASHAD, PHYLICIA
about
Phylicia and Philip are lovers and lawyers in thriller, 'False witness'. A. Collier. il pors *Jet* 77:60-2 O 30 '89
Phylicia, Debbie and Keshia head all-star cast in TV musical, Polly [cover story] il pors *Jet* 77:58-60 N 13 '89

RASHED, ROSHDI
about
Where geometry and algebra intersect [interview] il *The Unesco Courier* 42:36-41 N '89

RASHES *See* Skin—Diseases

RASHI, 1040-1105
about
A (Jewish) double helix. C. Raphael. *Commentary* 87:56-8 My '89

RASKIN, A. H.
Cyrus S. Ching: pioneer in industrial peacemaking. il *Monthly Labor Review* 112:22-35 Ag '89

RASKIN, DONNA
Dish 'n' deal. il *Ms.* 18:32-3 S '89

RASKIN, JULIE
(jt. auth) See Males, Carolyn, and Raskin, Julie

RASKOLNIKS *See* Old Believers

RASMUSSEN, HOWARD
The cycling of calcium as an intracellular messenger. bibl il *Scientific American* 261:66-73 O '89

RASPBERRIES
See also
Cooking—Fruit
Berries for fall. B. Pleasant. il *Organic Gardening* 36:44-8 S '89

RASPBERRY, WILLIAM
There is no black agenda. *American Visions* 4:36 F '89
Too good for manual labor. il *Reader's Digest* 135:155-6 N '89

RASPS *See* Files and rasps

RASTOGI, RADHA
Back to the veil? *World Press Review* 36:60 My '89

RAT CONTROL *See* Rats—Control

RATATOUILLE
Lean and easy ratatouille [microwaved] J. B. Hurley. il *Prevention (Emmaus, Pa.)* 41:80 Ag '89

RATCHET WRENCHES *See* Wrenches

RATCLIFF, CARTER
Enrico Donati: Manhattan transfer. bibl f il pors *Art in America* 77:174-81 My '89
Folk, or art? il *Antiques* 135:281 Ja '89
Framing America. il pors *Harper's Bazaar* 122:114+ Ap '89
Reginato's improvisations. bibl f il *Art in America* 77:146-51 D '89
Swamp things. il *Vogue* 179:282+ Ap '89
The work of Roy Lichtenstein in the age of Walter Benjamin's and Jean Baudrillard's popularity [cover story] il *Art in America* 77:110-23+ F '89

RATES, INTEREST *See* Interest (Economics)
RATES, RAILROAD *See* Railroads—Rates
RATES, TELEPHONE *See* Telephone—Rates
RATES, WATER *See* Water rates

RATHER, DAN
The threat to foreign news. por *Newsweek* 114:9 Jl 17 '89
about
Dan Rather's difficult days. J. Rovin. il pors *Ladies' Home Journal* 106:80+ Ja '89
A day in the life of the evening news. D. O. Relin. il por *Scholastic Update (Teachers' edition)* 122:7-9 S 8 '89
Rather strange: behind Dan's odd behavior. R. Townley. il pors *TV Guide* 37:4-7 F 25-Mr 3 '89
Truth and consequences. il *Time* 134:98 O 9 '89

RATHJE, WILLIAM L.
Rubbish! il *The Atlantic* 264:99-106+ D '89

RATHJENS, GEORGE W.
Global security: approaching the year 2000. bibl f *Current History* 88:1-4+ Ja '89

RATICAN, PETER
about
Even heroic measures may not save Maxicare. P. Cole. il por *Business Week* p96+ Mr 27 '89

RATING OF AIR PILOTS *See* Air pilots—Rating
RATING OF BONDS *See* Bonds—Rating
RATING OF CABLE TELEVISION PROGRAMS *See* Cable television—Ratings
RATING OF COLLEGES AND UNIVERSITIES *See* Colleges and universities—Evaluation
RATING OF CONGRESSMEN *See* Congressmen—Rating
RATING OF EMPLOYEES *See* Employees—Rating
RATING OF EXECUTIVES *See* Executives—Rating
RATING OF JUDGES *See* Judges—Rating
RATING OF MOTION PICTURES *See* Motion pictures—Ratings
RATING OF PHYSICIANS *See* Physicians—Rating
RATING OF SENATORS *See* Senators—Rating
RATING OF TEACHERS *See* Teachers—Rating
RATING OF TELEVISION PROGRAMS *See* Television broadcasting—Ratings
RATING OF VIDEOTAPES *See* Videotapes—Ratings
RATING OF WOMEN EXECUTIVES *See* Women executives—Rating

RATIONALISM
See also
Faith and reason
Paleo right and natural right [views of C. R. Kesler] P. J. Stanlis. *National Review* 41:44 O 27 '89

RATKAI, STEPHEN JOSEPH
about
Catching a spy. G. Allen. il por *Maclean's* 102:13 F 20 '89

RATNER, MEGAN
How to watch a cycling race. il *Women's Sports & Fitness* 11:18-19 My '89

RATNY, RUTH L.
The state that shoots straight. il *American Film* 15:56-8+ N '89

RATS
See also
Kangaroo rats
An economic animal [use of rats to test economic theories; work of John H. Kagel and Raymond C. Battalio] E. Corcoran. *Scientific American* 260:73 Mr '89
Northeast Rat and Mouse Club [founder E. Fucci] *The New Yorker* 65:35-6 Ap 10 '89

RATS—cont.

The rat as an experimental animal. T. J. Gill and others. bibl f il *Science* 245:269-76 Jl 21 '89

Brain

See Brain

Control

The rats are coming [effect of Central Artery project in Boston] S. Allis. il *Time* 133:63 F 27 '89

Embryology

See Embryology—Rodents

Nervous system

See Nervous system—Rodents

Optic nerve

See Optic nerve

RATS, WOOD *See* Wood rats

RATS AS CARRIERS OF INFECTION

Rat-borne virus may take secret toll [Hantaan virus; research by James W. Le Duc] R. Weiss. *Science News* 135:292 My 13 '89

RATTAZZI, PRISCILLA

Best friends [excerpt] il *Good Housekeeping* 209:48 Ag '89

RATTLE, SIMON

about

A vivid "Firebird" from Rattle. D. Hall. por *Stereo Review* 54:73 Ag '89

RATTLESNAKES

Rattler battlers [California ground squirrels] R. G. Coss and D. H. Owings. il *Natural History* p30-5 My '89

Rattlesnake: fact and folklore. J. Merritt. il *Field & Stream* 93:74-5+ Ap '89

Trappers and rattlers. G. Reiger. il *Field & Stream* 94:15-16 Jl '89

RATTNER, ROBERT

Point and splash. il *Popular Photography* 96:62-7 S '89

RATTNER, STEVEN

about

Hello sweetheart, get me mergers and acquisitions. P. Weiss. *The Washington Monthly* 21:67-8 F '89

The Rattner years. P. Noglows. il por *Channels (New York, N.Y.: 1986)* 9:73 Jl/Ag '89

RATTO, TRISHA

(jt. auth) *See* Pinna, Kathryn, and Ratto, Trisha

RATUSHINSKAYA, IRINA

Believe me [poem] *Christianity Today* 33:27 D 15 '89

about

In a haunting new memoir, poet Irina Ratushinskaya recalls the agonies of a Soviet labor camp. S. K. Reed. il pors *People Weekly* 31:87-8 Ja 16 '89

In solitary cells on winter nights [interview] E. S. Vaughn. il pors *Christianity Today* 33:26-9 D 15 '89

RAUCH, JONATHAN

The future of pennies: an exchange. il *The Atlantic* 264:20+ D '89

Is the deficit really so bad? [cover story] il *The Atlantic* 263:36-42 F '89

Kids as capital. il *The Atlantic* 264:56-61 Ag '89

RAUDSEPP, EUGENE

Taking a chance on life. *Harper's Bazaar* 122:163+ My '89

RAUF, TARIQ, AND LAMB, JOHN M.

Should Canada bring the boys home? il *The Bulletin of the Atomic Scientists* 45:36-8 S '89

RAULSTON, J. C.

about

Greening the South. D. Young. il pors *Southern Living* 24:125-6+ Je '89

RAUSCH, THOMAS P.

Ethical issues and ecumenism. *America* 160:30-3 Ja 21 '89

RAUSCHENBERG, ROBERT, 1925-

about

Rauschenberg goes to Moscow. A. Wallach. il por *Art in America* 77:21+ Mr '89

The ROCI road show. M. L. Kotz. il por *Art News* 88:48+ Summ '89

RAUSCHENBERG OVERSEAS CULTURE INTERCHANGE (EXHIBITION) *See* ROCI (Exhibition)

RAUSCHENBUSCH, WALTER, 1861-1918

about

Rauschenbusch today: the legacy of a loving prophet [cover story] M. L. Stackhouse. *The Christian Century* 106:75-8 Ja 25 '89

RAUSE, VINCE

Pittsburgh cleans up its act. il *The New York Times Magazine* p44-7+ N 26 '89

RAVEN, PETER H.

A world in crisis. il *USA Today (Periodical)* 117:48-50 My '89

RAVENS

Food and feeding

The ravens' feast. B. Heinrich. il *Natural History* p44-51 F '89

RAVER, ANNE

My secret garden. il *Reader's Digest* 135:39-40 Jl '89

Pocketful of spring. il *Reader's Digest* 134:83-4 Mr '89

RAVIN, NEIL

Mere mortals [fiction] il por *Good Housekeeping* 209:249-52+ S '89

RAVITCH, DIANE

Back to basics. *The New Republic* 200:13-15 Mr 6 '89

RAVITCH, RICHARD

about

Bowery follies. C. Byron. il por *New York* 22:14+ My 29 '89

RAW FISH *See* Fish, Raw

RAW FOOD *See* Food, Raw

RAW MATERIALS

See also

Commodity control

Mines and mineral resources

Falling materials prices are flashing a warning [commodity prices] G. Koretz. il *Business Week* p34 D 25 '89-Ja 1 '90

RAWL, LAWRENCE G.

about

In ten years you'll see 'nothing' [interview] il por *Fortune* 119:50-1+ My 8 '89

Nowhere to run or to hide. B. Rudolph. il *Time* 133:69 My 29 '89

RAWLINS, C. L.

Lines on the land. il *Sierra* 74:66-9+ S/O '89

The river [poem] *Wilderness* 52:64 Summ '89

RAWLS, LOU

about

Chicago names street for Lou Rawls; brother dies before ceremony. il pors *Jet* 76:61 Je 26 '89

RAWSTHORN, ALICE

The rise of Jindo. *World Press Review* 36:51 Je '89

RAY, ELAINE C.

Going places. il *Essence* 19:19+ Mr '89

RAY, MAN, 1890-1976

about

Man Ray: National Museum of American Art. V. H. Winner. il *Art News* 88:216 Ap '89

Man Ray: undervalued, and still an enigma. il *Art News* 88:39 D '89

Man Ray: Zabriskie. R. B. Woodward. il *Art News* 88:174 Mr '89

RAY, MICHAEL

about

Escape to Normandy [cover story] C. K. Gandee. il pors *House & Garden* 161:96-105+ F '89

The gilded and the grand. N. Frey. il pors *Harper's Bazaar* 122:110+ Ap '89

RAY, THOMAS WILLARD

about

A father's homecoming. C. M. Turtle. il *Reader's Digest* 134:57-61 F '89

RAYBON, PATRICIA

A case of 'severe bias'. por *Newsweek* 114:11 O 2 '89

RAYCHEM CORP.

"We've heard that all before". J. Heins. il por *Forbes* 143:40-1 F 6 '89

RAYCHOWDHURY, RAKTIMA, AND OTHERS

Autoimmune target in Heymann nephritis is a glycoprotein with homology to the LDL receptor. bibl f il *Science* 244:1163-5 Je 9 '89

RAYL, A. J. S.

Dr. Database. il *Omni (New York, N.Y.)* 11:100 F '89

Encyclopedia psychedelia. il *Omni (New York, N.Y.)* 11:30+ Je '89

Interview: James Schaefer. il pors *Omni (New York, N.Y.)* 12:106-8+ D '89

The second coming [excerpt from Beatles '64] il *Rolling Stone* p110-17 Jl 13-27 '89

War . . . hhuuuuh . . . what is it good for? *Omni (New York, N.Y.)* 11:49+ S '89

RAYLEIGH SCATTERING

The colors seen in the sky offer lessons in optical scattering. J. Walker. il bibl *Scientific American* 260:102-5 Ja '89

RAYMOND, BARBARA

(ed) *See* Nelson, Michael A. Sports, kids, fun, and safety

RAYMOND, CHRIS

A miracle goes sour. il *Discover* 10:72 Ja '89

RAYMOND, ILENE

Daniel [story] il *Ladies' Home Journal* 106:86+ Je '89

RAYMOND, MICHAEL

Going to market. il *Publishers Weekly* 236:22-3 O 20 '89

RAYMOND JAMES & ASSOCIATES, INC.

Brokers in the boondocks. M. Schifrin. il pors *Forbes* 143:228+ Je 26 '89

RAYNAUD, PATRICK, 1946-

about

Patrick Raynaud at Andre Zarre. K. Johnson. *Art in America* 77:188 N '89

RAYNAUD'S DISEASE

Shiver no more: about Raynaud's. *Prevention (Emmaus, Pa.)* 41:104 F '89

Why some hands get so cold. J. Stone. il *The New York Times Magazine* p62+ Mr 12 '89

RAYNER, CHESSY

about

Island of calm. B. Howar. il *House & Garden* 161:140-5 D '89

RAYNER, WILLIAM P.

By any other name. il *House & Garden* 161:70+ My '89

Foreigner affair. il pors *House & Garden* 161:72+ O '89

RAYON
New source expected to prevent shortage of rayon for NASA, defense rockets [North American Rayon Corp.] *Aviation Week & Space Technology* 131:24 N 27 '89

RAYS (FISH)
See also
Stingrays (Fish)

RAYTHEON CO.
Raytheon/TI aim at high-volume MMIC chip production capacity. il *Aviation Week & Space Technology* 131:92-3 S 18 '89
Raytheon adapts color workstations to meet requirements of military users. D. Hughes. il *Aviation Week & Space Technology* 130:104-5 Ap 24 '89
Raytheon delivers production AMRAAM; competition expected to reduce costs [advanced medium-range air-to-air missile] *Aviation Week & Space Technology* 130:30 F 27 '89
Raytheon team selected to develop ground-launched Tacit Rainbow. J. D. Morrocco. il *Aviation Week & Space Technology* 131:24-5 S 18 '89

RAYWID, MARY ANNE
Institutional democracy in the public schools. *The Education Digest* 55:8-10 D '89

RAZAF, ANDY, 1895-1973
about
Andy Razaf, the word man of Broadway. M. Evans. il pors *American Visions* 4:32-6 O '89

RAZORS
A $200 million close shave [twin blade Gillette Sensor] il *U.S. News & World Report* 107:24 O 16 '89
A better blade [Gillette's Sensor razor] J. W. Merline. il *Consumers' Research Magazine* 72:38 D '89
"How did I know the guy was calling from jail?" [J. Darder implicated in penny stock fraud over disposable razor] R. L. Stern. il por *Forbes* 143:120+ My 29 '89
Men's shavers: foil or rotary. il *Consumer Reports* 54:718-21 N '89
Razors & blades. il *Consumer Reports* 54:300-4 My '89
Razors & blades. il *Consumer Reports* 54:42-5 D '89
Advertising
At Gillette, disposable is a dirty word. K. H. Hammonds. il por *Business Week* p54+ My 29 '89

RCA CORP.
Is it TV's 50th birthday or not? F. Lovece. il *Channels (New York, N.Y.: 1986)* 9:9 Je '89

RCA RECORDS
New regime at RCA. T. W. Libbey, Jr. il *High Fidelity (New York, N.Y.)* 39:60 Je '89
Restoring harmony [country and blues material for RCA's Heritage Series] B. Altman. il *High Fidelity (New York, N.Y.)* 39:54-6 My '89

RCAF *See* Canada. Royal Canadian Air Force
RDAS (RECOMMENDED DIETARY ALLOWANCES) *See* Nutrition policy
RE-ENACTMENTS OF EVENTS (TELEVISION) *See* Television broadcasting—Re-enactments of events
UN RE IN ASCOLTO [opera] See Berio, Luciano

REA, DAN
Sociology 101 in a shoe box. por *Newsweek* 113:8 Mr 27 '89

REA, KELLEY V.
Your firm may need a "legal checkup". *Nation's Business* 77:20 Jl '89

REA, SUSAN
Portrait of Aunt Ellen [poem] *The American Scholar* 58:543-4 Aut '89
Volcanoes [poem] *The American Scholar* 58:542-3 Aut '89

REACTION TIME
Stand up for clearer thoughts [research by Max Vercruyssen] il *USA Today (Periodical)* 117:12 Ap '89
REACTIONS, CHEMICAL *See* Chemical reactions
REACTOR FUEL *See* Nuclear fuels
REACTOR FUEL REPROCESSING
Is Britain 'befouled'? [radioactive pollution from the Sellafield power plants] M. Perutz. bibl f il *The New York Review of Books* 36:51-7 N 23 '89
REACTORS, NUCLEAR *See* Nuclear reactors
READ, ALLEN WALKER
about
Profiles. M. Stacey. por *The New Yorker* 65:51-3+ S 4 '89
READ, GERALD HOWARD
Education in the Soviet Union: has *perestroika* met its match? bibl f il *Phi Delta Kappan* 70:606-13 Ap '89
READ, KEN
Grand slam for the Bomb. il *Skiing* 42:250-5+ S '89
'Snake, rattle, and roll. il *Skiing* 41:76-80 Ja '89
READ, MIMI
Autumn jambalaya. il *House & Garden* 161:89+ N '89
READ ONLY MEMORY
See also
CD-ROM (Compact disc-Read only memory)
A complete circuit [character generator] R. Grossblatt. il *Radio-Electronics* 60:28-9+ Jl '89
The contest is over [EPROM contest] R. Grossblatt. il *Radio-Electronics* 60:72-3 S '89

A custom-character generator [EPROM character sets for LED displays] R. Grossblatt. il *Radio-Electronics* 60:80-2+ Mr '89
"Custom" EPROM decoders. R. Grossblatt. il *Radio-Electronics* 60:80-1 Ja '89
The IBM PC BIOS. B. Glass. il *Byte* 14:303-10 Ap '89
Jameco Electronics JE680 universal IC programmer. il *Radio-Electronics* 60:16-17 Je '89
Let's start programming! [EPROM character sets for LED displays] R. Grossblatt. il *Radio-Electronics* 60:72-3+ My '89
OOP tools designed to make interface building like writing a letter with a word processor [Entryway system] *Byte* 14:18+ S '89
READER, TRISTAN
No sanctuary. *The Nation* 249:193 Ag 21-28 '89
READERS AND AUTHORS *See* Authors and readers
READER'S CATALOG *See* Catalogs, Booksellers'
READER'S DIGEST
Working with Reader's digest [article illustration] il *American Artist* 53:42-3+ S '89
READER'S DIGEST ASSOCIATION, INC.
Integrating public relations into the marketing mix [address, August 7, 1989] C. Howard. *Vital Speeches of the Day* 56:93-6 N 15 '89
Reader's Digest launching direct-mail nonfiction series [Today's best nonfiction] D. Brainard. il *Publishers Weekly* 235:37-8 My 26 '89
READER'S DIGEST CONDENSED BOOKS
Time-Life to challenge Reader's Digest in condensed books market. *Publishers Weekly* 236:14 S 22 '89
READINESS FOR SCHOOL
Delaying kindergarten. F. Roberts. *Parents* 64:66+ Mr '89
The kindergarten wars [holding children back to ensure academic success] B. Brophy. il *U.S. News & World Report* 106:53-4 Ap 10 '89
The redshirt solution [delaying kindergarten] J. Elson. il *Time* 134:102 N 13 '89
READING, BRIAN
Doomsayer. *National Review* 41:50-1 Ja 27 '89
READING
See also
Authors—Reading
Black authors—Reading
Books and reading
Children's reading
College students—Reading
Executives—Reading
Men—Reading
Minorities—Reading
Prisoners—Reading
Speed reading
Television and reading
Study and teaching
See also
Literacy education
Reading comprehension
Reading research
Does phonics cure reading problems? F. Roberts. il *Parents* 64:49 Ja '89
An evaluation of Jeanne Chall's response to 'Debunking the great phonics myth' [discussion of November 1988 and March 1989 articles] M. Carbo. bibl f il *Phi Delta Kappan* 71:152-7 O '89
The 'great' debate—can both Carbo and Chall be right? [phonics method] R. L. Turner. bibl f il *Phi Delta Kappan* 71:276-83 D '89
Helping disabled readers in the regular classroom. M. P. Ford and M. M. Ohlhausen. *The Education Digest* 54:48-51 Ja '89
Learning to read and write [four year study of children from low income families by Connie Juel] G. W. Bracey. il *Phi Delta Kappan* 70:559-60 Mr '89
Learning to read: the great debate 20 years later—a response to 'Debunking the great phonics myth' [discussion of November 1988 article; with editorial comment by Pauline B. Gough] M. Carbo. bibl f il *Phi Delta Kappan* 70:498, 521-38 Mr '89
Taking the drill out of reading [whole language instruction] F. P. Hodge. il *Publishers Weekly* 235:99-100 Ja 20 '89
Thirty-one reasons to stop the school reading machine. M. Haberman. bibl f il *Phi Delta Kappan* 71:284-8 D '89
Aids and devices
Give your child's reading skills a big boost—turn on the computer. D. Stanton. il *Compute!* 11:15 Mr '89
Joshua's Reading Machine. M. J. W. Ratcliff. il *Home Office Computing* 7:87 O '89
Testing
SAT bashing [research by Stuart Katz] T. Waters. il *Discover* 10:28 Ag '89
READING ABILITY
Time out of school [correlation between out-of-school activities and reading proficiency; research by Richard Anderson and others] G. W. Bracey. il *Phi Delta Kappan* 70:408-9 Ja '89
READING ALCOVES, ETC.
Curl up and read. il *Southern Living* 24:182 N '89

READING ALOUD
See also
Poetry readings
Short story readings

Debby Boone and family send you . . . hugs, laughter, love: "Mommy, read me a story". D. Boone and G. Ferrer. il pors *Redbook* 173:28 My '89

Listening and learning [effect of reading stories aloud on children's vocabulary; research by Warwick Elley] G. W. Bracey. il *Phi Delta Kappan* 71:77 S '89

Read my lips: on the joys—and the necessity—of reading aloud [excerpt from Dancing at the edge of the world] U. K. Le Guin. il *Utne Reader* p126-7 Jl/Ag '89

Spell of a storyteller [reading stories to children; condensed from Wordstruck] R. MacNeil. bibl *Reader's Digest* 135:181-2+ O '89

What do you read to your children? [famous parents share their children's most cherished books] T. Reinhold. bibl il *Redbook* 173:20 Jl '89

READING COMPREHENSION
A shift in theory in reading research. J. F. Savage. *The Education Digest* 54:49-53 Ap '89

Testing
See Reading—Testing

READING DISABILITY
See also
Dyslexia

Helping disabled readers in the regular classroom. M. P. Ford and M. M. Ohlhausen. *The Education Digest* 54:48-51 Ja '89

Sensory perception and reading disability. R. M. Casbergue and J. F. Greene. *The Education Digest* 54:33-5 Mr '89

READING LISTS
See also
Best sellers
Books and reading—Best books
Children's literature—Bibliography

Creating a generation of "aliterates" [criticism of W. Bennett's list] S. Ohanian. *The Education Digest* 54:29-32 F '89

READING OF NEWSPAPERS See Newspaper reading

READING RAINBOW [television program] See Television program reviews—Single works

READING RESEARCH
An evaluation of Jeanne Chall's response to 'Debunking the great phonics myth' [discussion of November 1988 and March 1989 articles] M. Carbo. bibl f il *Phi Delta Kappan* 71:152-7 O '89

The 'great' debate—can both Carbo and Chall be right? [phonics method] R. L. Turner. bibl f il *Phi Delta Kappan* 71:276-83 D '89

Learning to read: the great debate 20 years later—a response to 'Debunking the great phonics myth' [discussion of November 1988 article; with editorial comment by Pauline B. Gough] M. Carbo. bibl f il *Phi Delta Kappan* 70:498, 521-38 Mr '89

A shift in theory in reading research. J. F. Savage. *The Education Digest* 54:49-53 Ap '89

READY (PROGRAM)
Ready to roll. R. King. il por *Forbes* 144 Special Issue:118-19+ O 23 '89

REAGAN, MAUREEN
In a dark and fearful place [excerpt from First Father, First Daughter] il pors *People Weekly* 31:94-6+ Ap 10 '89

REAGAN, NANCY, 1923-
My turn [excerpts; cover story]; ed. by William Novak. il pors *Newsweek* 114:52-6+ O 23 '89

My turn: the memoirs of Nancy Reagan [excerpts]; ed. by William Novak. il pors *Ladies' Home Journal* 106:136-40+ D '89

about
After the end, a beginning [cover story] M. Green. il pors *People Weekly* 31:70-2+ F 20 '89

A cute number for the taxman. il por *Time* 134:42 D 18 '89

Eight days in Japan earn Ron and Nancy $2 million—now that's Reaganomics. il pors *People Weekly* 32:52-3 N 6 '89

'I really tried not to be mean' [interview] T. Fuller. il por *Newsweek* 114:50-1 O 23 '89

S & S, Random House to release Reagan titles on audio. J. Tangorra. il pors *Publishers Weekly* 236:63 O 6 '89

Tennis, anyone? Sporting a new 'do, Ronald Reagan joins Nancy at courtside. il pors *People Weekly* 32:46-7 O 23 '89

Anecdotes, facetiae, satire, etc.
Seeing red. il por *People Weekly* 32 Special Issue:146-7 Fall '89

Bibliography
Life at court [R. Reagan administration] J. Didion. il *The New York Review of Books* 36:3-4+ D 21 '89

REAGAN, RONALD, 1911-
39th report on Cyprus [message to Congress, October 3, 1988] *Department of State Bulletin* 88:37 D '88

40th report on Cyprus. *Department of State Bulletin* 89:50 F '89

Berne Convention Implementation Act of 1988 [statement, October 31, 1988] *Department of State Bulletin* 89:35 Ja '89

Chancellor Kohl's visit [remarks, November 15, 1988] il por *Department of State Bulletin* 89:56 Mr '89

Genocide Convention Implementation Act of 1987 [remarks and fact sheet, November 4, 1988] *Department of State Bulletin* 89:38-9 Ja '89

Margaret Thatcher and the revival of the West [cover story] il *National Review* 41:21-2 My 19 '89

The month in Congress [excerpts from message to Congress, January 9, 1989] il *Congressional Digest* 68:33-4 F '89

National emergency in Panama [message to Congress, October 14, 1988] *Department of State Bulletin* 88:57 D '88

Ninth anniversary of Soviet invasion of Afghanistan [statement, December 27, 1988] *Department of State Bulletin* 89:89 Mr '89

Nuclear and space arms talks conclude round 10 [statement, November 16, 1988] *Department of State Bulletin* 89:10 Mr '89

President Reagan and President Gorbachev meet in New York [remarks, addresses, and news conference, December 3-10, 1988; cover story; special section] il pors *Department of State Bulletin* 89:1-7 F '89

President Reagan declares Martin Luther King, Jr. Day. il por *Jet* 75:6+ Ja 23 '89

President's farewell address to the American people [address, January 11, 1989] *Vital Speeches of the Day* 55:226-9 F 1 '89

Prime Minister Thatcher's visit [remarks, November 16, 1988] il por *Department of State Bulletin* 89:57-8 Mr '89

Territorial sea of the United States [proclamation, December 27, 1988] *Department of State Bulletin* 89:72 Mr '89

U.S.-Canada sign free trade agreement [remarks, September 28, 1988] *Department of State Bulletin* 88:22-3 D '88

U.S. import duties increase for certain Brazilian products [proclamation, October 20, 1988] *Department of State Bulletin* 89:49 Ja '89

U.S. opens dialogue with PLO [statements and press conference, December 14, 1988] *Department of State Bulletin* 89:51-3 F '89

U.S. restricts entry of Nicaraguan officials, employees [proclamation, October 22, 1988] *Department of State Bulletin* 89:47 Ja '89

U.S., Soviet Union exchange New Year's messages [remarks, January 1, 1989] *Department of State Bulletin* 89:54-5 Mr '89

Visit of Hungarian premier [remarks, July 27, 1988] il por *Department of State Bulletin* 88:36 D '88

Visit of Mali president [remarks and exchange of toasts, October 6, 1988] il por *Department of State Bulletin* 89:14-15 Ja '89

World Food Day, 1988 [proclamation, September 28, 1988] *Department of State Bulletin* 88:37 D '88

about
The abolitionist. J. Newhouse. *The New Yorker* 64:51-62+ Ja 9 '89

The abolitionist. J. Newhouse. *The New Yorker* 64:37-52 Ja 2 '89

After the end, a beginning [cover story] M. Green. il pors *People Weekly* 31:70-2+ F 20 '89

Beat the devil. A. Cockburn. *The Nation* 248:78-9 Ja 23 '89

Bless me, father. D. Goodgame. il pors *Time* 133:22-3 My 8 '89

Bush's shovel brigade. S. V. Roberts. il *U.S. News & World Report* 107:14-16 Ag 7 '89

Did he lie? E. Magnuson. il por *Time* 133:42 Mr 27 '89

The end [cover story; special issue] il *The New Republic* 200:6, 17-18+ Ja 9-16 '89

Europe and the Reagan years. P. Johnson. *Foreign Affairs* 68 Special Issue:28-38 ['89]

Farewell and hail. *National Review* 41:11 F 10 '89

A farewell to the Reagans. W. F. Buckley. *National Review* 41:62 F 24 '89

Feather dusters. T. Noah. *The New Republic* 200:42 F 13 '89

The Gipper says goodbye. H. Sidey. il pors *Time* 133:24-5 Ja 30 '89

Going home a winner. L. I. Barrett. il *Time* 133:14-16+ Ja 23 '89

Gone with the wind. *Commonweal* 116:68-9 F 10 '89

Good-bye to all that. A. J. Glass. il *The New Leader* 72:3-4 Ja 23 '89

The guilty parties. il *The Progressive* 53:8-9 Je '89

How Reagan changed America [cover story] G. F. Will. il pors *Newsweek* 113:12-17 Ja 9 '89

Iran-contra: Reagan's role. il *Newsweek* 113:6 Mr 27 '89

The lessons of the Reagan era [cover story] M. Ruby. il pors *U.S. News & World Report* 106:18-24+ Ja 9 '89

The memory lingers on. M. Ivins. il *Ms.* 17:26-7 Ja/F '89

Minority report. C. Hitchens. *The Nation* 248:42 Ja 9-16 '89

Misha and Ron. T. Brewster. il pors *Life* 12:52-4+ Fall '89

My turn [excerpts; cover story]; ed. by William Novak. N. Reagan. il pors *Newsweek* 114:52-6+ O 23 '89

My turn: the memoirs of Nancy Reagan [excerpts]; ed. by William Novak. N. Reagan. il pors *Ladies' Home Journal* 106:136-40+ D '89

REAGAN, RONALD, 1911——about——cont.

Ollie North's eleventh-hour stratagem. T. Morganthau. il pors *Newsweek* 113:24 Ja 9 '89

One for the Gypper. F. Barnes. *The New Republic* 200:14-15 F 27 '89

The past as prologue. L. Bridges. *National Review* 41:22-3 Je 2 '89

Reagan, Bush, and the liberal revolution [address, December 8, 1988] E. H. Crane. *Vital Speeches of the Day* 55:265-8 F 15 '89

Reagan foreign policy: a mixed legacy. T. L. Deibel. *Current (Washington, D.C.)* 317:16-24 N '89

The Reagan presidency [special section] il *World Press Review* 36:26-9 Ja '89

Reagan revisited. A. R. Dolan. por *National Review* 41:45+ N 24 '89

Reagan's budget, Bush's battle. H. Gleckman. il *Business Week* p32-4 Ja 23 '89

Reagan's foreign policy. R. W. Tucker. *Foreign Affairs* 68 Special Issue:1-27 ['89]

Reagan's gift. J. Beatty. il *The Atlantic* 263:58-62+ F '89

Reagan's mixed legacy. T. L. Deibel. *Foreign Policy* 75:34-55 Summ '89

Reagan's role at Ollie's trial. L. Martz. il pors *Newsweek* 113:29 Ap 10 '89

Reagan's security legacy [cover story; special issue; with editorial comment by Len Ackland] bibl f il pors *The Bulletin of the Atomic Scientists* 45:2, 5-32+ Ja/F '89

Ronald Reagan. il pors *People Weekly* 31 Special Issue:76-7 Summ '89

Ronald Reagan & Mikhail Gorbachev. B. Darrach. il pors *People Weekly* 32 Special Issue:44-6 Fall '89

Ronald Reagan's most important legacy. D. Gergen. il por *U.S. News & World Report* 106:28 Ja 9 '89

S & S, Janklow, negotiate two-book Reagan deal. *Publishers Weekly* 235:34 F 10 '89

S & S, Random House to release Reagan titles on audio. J. Tangorra. il pors *Publishers Weekly* 236:63 O 6 '89

The sayings of Ronald Reagan. il por *Life* 12:128 F '89

Setting Marcos adrift. S. Karnow. il pors *The New York Times Magazine* p50+ Mr 19 '89

The ten legacies of Ronald Reagan [address, October 1988] B. Y. Pines. *Vital Speeches of the Day* 55:243-7 F 1 '89

Tennis, anyone? Sporting a new 'do, Ronald Reagan joins Nancy at courtside. il pors *People Weekly* 32:46-7 O 23 '89

A valentine for Ron [resignation letter, November 9, 1988] J. S. Herrington. *Harper's* 278:20+ F '89

The warm reverie of Reagan's retirement. H. Sidey. il por *Time* 133:23 Je 26 '89

What is a conservative? (And why Reagan is not one). N. Postman. *Utne Reader* p75 Mr/Ap '89

What Reagan hath wrought is bedeviling Bush. R. Fly. il *Business Week* p37 Jl 3 '89

What Reagan really knew. E. Salholz. il pors *Newsweek* 113:25 Mr 6 '89

Why I am not Ronald Reagan, by G. Bush. E. Clift. il por *Newsweek* 113:18 F 20 '89

Why military spending pays off. R. N. Perle. il por *U.S. News & World Report* 106:23-4 Ja 16 '89

With friends like these . . . [criticism of former president by G. Bush staff] B. Turque. il por *Newsweek* 113:40 Ap 24 '89

Addresses, messages, etc.

I had a dream. H. Hertzberg. *The New Republic* 200:4 F 6 '89

A new age of world peace . . . breaking the wall of suspicion . . . [R. Reagan and M. Gorbachev address the United Nations] pors *UN Chronicle* 26:31-3 Mr '89

Reagan and historical memory [final televised remarks] *National Review* 41:11+ F 10 '89

Anecdotes, facetiae, satire, etc.

A brief history of the Reagan years [excerpt from index to The clothes have no emperor] P. Slansky. *Harper's* 279:30-2 O '89

Uncivil liberties. C. Trillin. il *The Nation* 248:186 F 13 '89

Bibliography

The faking of the president. D. Gates. il por *Newsweek* 114:84-5 N 27 '89

Life at court [R. Reagan administration] J. Didion. il *The New York Review of Books* 36:3-4+ D 21 '89

Collectibles

A shrine to the Gipper [memorabilia at Eureka College] B. Turque. il *Newsweek* 113:28 My 8 '89

Photographs and photography

Goodbye to the Gipper. il pors *Newsweek* 113:18-23 Ja 9 '89

Press relations

Printheads vs. pictureheads. T. Eastland. il *The American Spectator* 22:40-1 D '89

Stupefying imbeciles. R. E. Tyrrell. il *The American Spectator* 22:10 Mr '89

Public relations

F.D.R., anyone? T. Ferguson. il *The Nation* 248:689 My 22 '89

Speechwriters and speechwriting

Confessions of a White House speechwriter [excerpt from What I saw at the revolution; cover story] P. Noonan. il pors *The New York Times Magazine* p24-7+ O 15 '89

High Noonan. M. Dowd. il por *Vogue* 179:338-41 D '89

Notes & asides [P. Noonan] W. F. Buckley. *National Review* 41:15-16 N 24 '89

Staff

Memoirs of the Reagan era. F. FitzGerald. il *The New Yorker* 64:71-83+ Ja 16 '89

Some of the president's men. N. Reagan. il *Newsweek* 114:58-9 O 23 '89

Washington memoirs: bombshell or bust [books by former staffers] C. T. Buckley. il *The New York Times Book Review* 94:1+ O 1 '89

Who's who in the administration. See issues of The Washington Monthly

Statues, portraits, etc.

Portrait, portrait on the wall . . . il pors *U.S. News & World Report* 107:12-13 N 27 '89

Reagan on the rock reactions [discussion of July 1989 article, Ron on the rock] D. Shanahan. il por *The American Spectator* 22:43 S '89

Ron on the rock [campaign to add likeness to Mount Rushmore] D. Shanahan. il por *The American Spectator* 22:26-7 Jl '89

Taxes

A cute number for the taxman [IRS investigates N. Reagan's borrowing of designer clothes] il por *Time* 134:42 D 18 '89

Visit to Japan, 1989

'A big fuss of a visit'. il por *Newsweek* 114:54 N 6 '89

Eight days in Japan earn Ron and Nancy $2 million—now that's Reaganomics. il pors *People Weekly* 32:52-3 N 6 '89

Elder $tatesman. *The Nation* 249:552-3 N 13 '89

One hand clapping. D. Sneider. il *The New Republic* 201:16-17 N 20 '89

Western stars shine in the East. il por *U.S. News & World Report* 107:15 N 6 '89

REAGAN (RONALD) PRESIDENTIAL LIBRARY AND CENTER FOR PUBLIC AFFAIRS *See* Ronald Reagan Presidential Library and Center for Public Affairs

REAGAN FAMILY

about

Books, bucks. il *U.S. News & World Report* 106:14 F 6 '89

A family album. N. Reagan. il *Newsweek* 114:64-5 O 23 '89

REAGANOMICS *See* United States—Economic policy

REAL COMET PRESS

Real Comet Press: breaking down categories. J. Barbato. *Publishers Weekly* 236:46 Jl 14 '89

REAL ESTATE AGENCIES AND AGENTS

See also

Douglas Elliman Gibbons & Ives Inc.

Grubb & Ellis Co.

Women real estate agents

Bringing real-estate profits home [cover story] P. G. Miller. il *Home Office Computing* 7:31-6 Jl '89

Gandee at large [New York City real estate agent L. Stein] C. K. Gandee. il por *House & Garden* 161:146 Ag '89

In a soft market, buyers and sellers may get a better deal by using a broker. H. Weil. il *Money* 18:187-8 My '89

Real estate brokers. K. K. Gracey. *Consumers' Research Magazine* 72:2 Jl '89

Ethical aspects

Your broker must tell all. W. Giese. il *Changing Times* 43:28 Ap '89

Fees

Playing percentages with those flat-fee real estate brokers. B. Hager. il *Money* 18:19-20 O '89

REAL ESTATE AUCTIONS *See* Auctions

REAL ESTATE BUSINESS

See also

American Continental Corp.

Banks and banking—Real estate operations

Calmark Financial Corporation

Computers—Real estate use

Corporations—Real estate operations

Crown American Corporation

Del E. Webb Corp.

Donald T. Sterling Corporation

Fractional ownership (Real estate)

General Development Corp.

House buying

House selling

Irvine Co.

Lincoln Property Company

Maguire Thomas Partners

McArthur/Glen Group

Melvin Simon & Associates, Inc.

Port Liberté Partners

Real estate agencies and agents

Real estate management

Rouse Co.

Royale Group Ltd.

REAL ESTATE INVESTMENT TRUSTS—*cont.*
At 20% yields, these CMO REITS make junk bonds look safe. il *Money* 18:16+ Ap '89
Carving up mortgages [collateralized mortgage obligation residuals] B. Weberman. il *Forbes* 143:165 Mr 6 '89
Real estate: finding buys in the ruins. J. J. Curran. il *Fortune* 120 no10 Special Issue:24 Fall '89
The right REITs: they deliver high yields without betting the ranch. E. Schultz. il *Fortune* 120:41-2 Ag 28 '89
The top real estate play may be on the Street. T. Segal. il *Business Week* p143 D 25 '89-Ja 1 '90
Top yields and prospects of gains make REITS right. A. Rock. il *Money* 18:159-60+ Je '89

Acquisitions and mergers
From the Mekong to Motown [S. Plum of Charterhouse Inc. bids on Income Opportunity Realty Trust] M. Schifrin. il por *Forbes* 143:324+ My 29 '89

REAL ESTATE MANAGEMENT
See also
Condominium associations
Grubb & Ellis Co.
National Realty Advisors, Inc.
Managing your ski country home. K. Brizzolara. il *Skiing* 41:20+ Ja '89

REAL ESTATE MORTGAGE INVESTMENT CONDUITS
Ginnie's and Freddie's more predictable cousins [collateralized mortgage obligations] D. H. Dunn. *Business Week* p104 F 13 '89

REAL ESTATE TAX *See* Real property—Taxation
REAL NUMBERS *See* Numbers, Real
REAL PROPERTY
See also
Adverse possession
Building sites
Deeds
Joint ownership
Land
Land tenure
Land trusts
Mortgages
Real estate business
Real estate investment
Trespass

Taxation
See also
Mortgages—Taxation
Real estate exchanges—Taxation
Charity stops at home [tax consequences of donating rental time at vacation house to a charity] G. W. Padwe. il *Nation's Business* 77:76 S '89
Death and taxes. G. Reiger. il *Field & Stream* 93:18+ Ap '89
Down but not out. C. E. Babin. il por *Forbes* 144:235 S 18 '89
George on my mind [H. George] M. Kinsley. *The New Republic* 201:8+ N 6 '89
Home is where the shelter is [taxation rules on house sales] G. W. Padwe. il *Nation's Business* 77:67 Mr '89
Investing in that home away from home. G. J. Gallagher. il *Black Enterprise* 20:31-2 S '89
IRS traps for the unwary home seller [tax exclusion on profits for those over age 55] L. Wiener. il *U.S. News & World Report* 106:80 My 22 '89
Of ski huts and beach houses. L. Saunders. il *Forbes* 144:258 O 16 '89
Real estate legal advice. W. Giese. *Changing Times* 43:29 Ap '89
Selling rental real estate: ways to sweeten the deal. il *Changing Times* 43:71-2+ Jl '89
Trimming the IRS' cut on a second home. D. H. Dunn. il *Business Week* p184 Jl 17 '89
Uncle Sam will subsidize your Shangri-La. *Changing Times* 43:42 Je '89
Uncle Sam's retirement gift [tax exclusion on house sale profits for seniors] M. C. Paulson. *Changing Times* 43:104 Ja '89
Use it, rent it, write it off [vacation place] H. Wheelwright. il *Money* 18:112 Jl '89
Your house's hidden problem [estate tax] R. Wool. il *Money* 18:177-8 N '89

Taxation for education
See Education—Finance

Valuation
Do you have enough property insurance? [guide developed by American Appraisal Associates] il *Consumers' Research Magazine* 72:27-32 Ag '89
George on my mind [H. George] M. Kinsley. *The New Republic* 201:8+ N 6 '89
Investors will find that a home is not so sweet. L. Wiener. il *U.S. News & World Report* 107:80+ D 4 '89
Real estate appraisals. S. J. Ackerman. il *Consumers' Research Magazine* 72:16-18 F '89
Remodeling: hard truths in soft markets. E. Schurenberg. il *Money* 18:76 Je '89
Unhappy anniversary. A. Bladen. il *Forbes* 144:258 O 2 '89

REAL PROPERTY EXCHANGES *See* Real estate exchanges
REAL-TIME DATA PROCESSING
See also
TRON operating systems
REALISM IN ART
See also
Figurative art
Photo-realism
Trompe-l'oeil
Classical realism: the other 20th century. R. Lack. il *Utne Reader* p59 Jl/Ag '89
John Register. M. E. Stegmaier. il *American Artist* 53:64-7+ F '89
Pix: commercial applications of realist art [special section] il *American Artist* 53:21+ S '89

Exhibitions
Competition winners revisited [Realism today: American Artist Competition winners] V. R. Rivers. il *American Artist* 53:58-60 Je '89

REALISM IN LITERATURE
Stalking the billion-footed beast [abandonment of tradition by American novelists; cover story] T. Wolfe. il *Harper's* 279:45-56 N '89
Wolfe among the pigeons [T. Wolfe criticizes American novelists for departing from realistic tradition] D. Aikman. il por *Time* 134:78 N 27 '89

REALISM IN TELEVISION
See also
Tabloid television
Truth? It's in TV's fiction . . . not the reality shows. T. J. Fleming. il *TV Guide* 37:24-6 F 25-Mr 3 '89
When anchors meet actors [news shows to use re-enactments] J. Alter. il *Newsweek* 114:44-5 Jl 24 '89
Where is the Goober? [effects of reality-based programming] K. Rickenbaker. por *Newsweek* 113:12 My 1 '89

REALITY
See also
Knowledge, Theory of
Objectivity
Relativity
REALTORS *See* Real estate agencies and agents
REAMS, RICHARD
about
Little girl, big trouble. D. Grogan. il pors *People Weekly* 31:36-41 F 20 '89
REAPPORTIONMENT *See* Apportionment (Election law)
REAR WHEEL DRIVE AUTOMOBILES *See* Automobiles—Rear wheel drive; Automobiles, Foreign—Rear wheel drive
REASENBERG, PAUL A., AND JONES, LUCILE M.
Earthquake hazard after a mainshock in California. bibl f il *Science* 243:1173-6 Mr 3 '89
REASON
See also
Faith and reason
Rationalism
Wisdom
Recoiling from reason [views of A. MacIntyre] M. C. Nussbaum. bibl f il *The New York Review of Books* 36:36-41 D 7 '89
REASONING
See also
Analogy
Problem solving
Thought and thinking
REAVES, WENDY WICK, 1950-
The prints. bibl f il *Antiques* 135:502-11 F '89
REBATES
Cheap loans vs. rebates [automobiles] J. Goldwasser. il *Changing Times* 43:53-4 Mr '89
REBECCA HOWE (FICTIONAL CHARACTER)
Cheers free-for-all! Rebecca commits memo-cide [cover story] il *TV Guide* 37:2-5 My 27-Je 2 '89
REBECK, VICTORIA
From Mary to Murphy: codependent no more. *The Christian Century* 106:948+ O 25 '89
REBELLIONS *See* Revolutions
REBODIED AUTOMOBILES *See* Automobiles, Remodeled
REBOUNDING (BASKETBALL)
Guru of the glass [Auburn coach S. Smith's ability to develop rebounders] T. Kertes. il por *Sport (New York, N.Y.)* 80:68-71 Mr '89
RECALL (POLITICS)
Mayor Sonny Bono resists a recall, telling Palm Springs voters, 'You got me, Babe'. T. Gold. il pors *People Weekly* 32:53-4 O 2 '89
RECALL (PSYCHOLOGY) *See* Memory
RECALL OF AUTOMOBILES *See* Automobiles—Recall; Automobiles, Foreign—Recall
RECALL OF COMMERCIAL PRODUCTS *See* Commercial products—Recall
RECAPITALIZATION
A drug wholesaler that looks as if it's on steroids [Bergen Brunswig] G. G. Marcial. il *Business Week* p88 F 6 '89
Even heroic measures may not save Maxicare. P. Cole. il por *Business Week* p96+ Mr 27 '89
If you crave more thrills, try 'stubs'. P. Sellers. il *Fortune* 120:56+ N 20 '89

RECAPITALIZATION—*cont.*

KKR tiptoes into Texas [Kohlberg Kravis Roberts pumps capital into MCorp] T. Mason. il *Business Week* p33 Ja 16 '89

Saddled with debt but still able to grow [Quantum Chemical] R. Simon. il *por Forbes* 143:100+ Mr 6 '89

Stubs revisited. M. Schifrin. *Forbes* 144:378 N 13 '89

Yet another company pulls a raid on itself [Service Merchandise] S. Flack. il *Forbes* 143:107-8 Je 26 '89

RECEIVERS (MICROWAVE) *See* Microwave receivers

RECEIVING STOLEN GOODS

Hot retailing. S. B. Weiner and J. Harris. il *Forbes* 144:105-10 Ag 7 '89

RECEPTIONS, WEDDING *See* Wedding receptions

RECEPTOR SITES (BIOCHEMISTRY) *See* Binding sites (Biochemistry)

RECEPTORS, CHEMICAL *See* Chemoreceptors

RECEPTORS, DRUG *See* Drug receptors

RECEPTORS, HORMONE *See* Hormone receptors

RECEPTORS, NEURAL *See* Sensory receptors

RECEPTORS, PROTEIN *See* Protein receptors

RECEPTORS, SENSORY *See* Sensory receptors

RECEPTORS, VISUAL *See* Rods and cones

RECESSION, BUSINESS *See* Business depression

RECIDIVISTS

A criminal lack of common sense [career criminal W. Bland finally sentenced to life imprisonment in California] J. Leo. il *U.S. News & World Report* 107:56 Ag 21 '89

"I won't kill, I'll just maim" [career criminal W. Bosket] R. Behar. il *por Time* 133:30-1 My 29 '89

Jailbird odds. D. Seligman. il *Fortune* 119:136 Ja 16 '89

RECIPE TESTING *See* Cooking—Testing

RECIPES *See* Cooking

RECITALS (MUSIC) *See* Music recitals

RECLAMA (TERM)

Rethinking reclama. W. Safire. il *The New York Times Magazine* p18+ Je 11 '89

RECLAMATION OF LAND

See also
Dikes (Engineering)
Irrigation

Netherlands

The reclamation of Holland. P. Canova. il map *Sea Frontiers* 35:154-64 My/Je '89

RECLAMATION OF WASTE WATER *See* Water reuse

RECOGNITION (PSYCHOLOGY)

R.T.'s topsy-turvy world [role of mental rotation in recognition of common objects; research by Martha Farah and Katherine Hammond] J. Rubin. il *Psychology Today* 22:20 D '88

Recognizing faces and expressions [research by Michael Hasselmo] J. Rubin. *Psychology Today* 23:22 My '89

Why a man may mistake his wife for a cat [study of cognitive disabilities by Antonio R. Damasio] R. Weiss. *Science News* 136:309 N 11 '89

RECOMBINANT DNA RESEARCH *See* Genetic research

RECOMBINASE

Key piece found for immunology puzzle? [gene encoding recombinase; work of David Schatz and others] J. L. Marx. il *Science* 246:1561 D 22 '89

RECOMMENDED DIETARY ALLOWANCES *See* Nutrition policy

RECONCILIATION

Who says it's too late? [rectifying past mistakes] N. V. Peale. *Reader's Digest* 134:23-4 My '89

RECONCILIATION IN ANIMALS *See* Animals—Habits and behavior

RECONNAISSANCE, AERIAL *See* Aerial reconnaissance

RECONNAISSANCE AIRPLANES *See* Airplanes, Military

RECONNAISSANCE SATELLITES *See* Artificial satellites—Military use

RECONSTRUCTION (1939-1951)

Western Europe

See also
Marshall Plan

RECORD CHANGERS *See* Phonograph—Turntables

RECORD HOUSES AWARDS *See* Architecture—Awards

RECORD INDUSTRY *See* Phonograph record industry

RECORD INTERIORS AWARDS *See* Interior decoration—Awards

RECORD PLAYERS *See* Phonograph

RECORDERS, FLIGHT *See* Flight recorders

RECORDING INDUSTRY ASSOCIATION OF AMERICA

Calling the RIAA's bluff [threat to sue any company trying to sell a DAT recorder] R. Long. il *High Fidelity (New York, N.Y.)* 39:18 Ap '89

RECORDING OF MUSIC *See* Sound—Recording and reproducing

RECORDING STUDIOS *See* Sound—Recording and reproducing

RECORDS

See also
Automobile speed records
Criminal records
Household records
Medical records
School reports and records
Tax records

Truck speed records
Weather records
World records

Here's a hot tip with a guaranteed payoff: keep good records [investments] M. T. Smith. *Money* 18:145 Ja '89

Preservation

See Archives

RECOVERY OF PETROLEUM *See* Petroleum engineering

RECREATION

See also
Aged—Recreation
Boats and boating
Children—Recreation
City children—Recreation
College students—Recreation
Executives—Recreation
Handicapped—Recreation
Hobbies
Homeless—Recreation
Industry—Recreation programs
Leisure
Outdoor life
Parents—Recreation
Play
Playgrounds
Prisoners—Recreation
Socially handicapped children—Recreation
Sports
Women executives—Recreation
Youth—Recreation

Private time. See issues of Glamour

Equipment

What's new: recreation. S. F. Brown. See occasional issues of Popular Science beginning December 1985

Fees

The OMB octopus. L. Williamson. il *Outdoor Life* 183:62+ My '89

New York (State)

See also
New York (N.Y.)—Recreation

United States

See Recreation

RECREATION AREAS

Arizona

See also
Glen Canyon National Recreation Area (Ariz. and Utah)

California

See also
Golden Gate National Recreation Area (Calif.)
Santa Monica Mountains National Recreation Area (Calif.)

Kentucky

See also
Big South Fork National River and Recreation Area (Tenn. and Ky.)

Tennessee

See also
Big South Fork National River and Recreation Area (Tenn. and Ky.)

Utah

See also
Glen Canyon National Recreation Area (Ariz. and Utah)

RECREATION BUILDINGS *See* Recreation centers

RECREATION CENTERS

See also
Coalinga (Calif.)—Recreation centers
Commerce City (Colo.)—Recreation centers
Sports facilities
Westminster (Colo.)—Recreation centers

In this issue [In the Public Interest Award; special issue] il *Architectural Record* 177:83-137 N '89

RECREATION ROOMS

See also
Media rooms

RECREATIONAL VEHICLE CAMPING *See* Camping

RECREATIONAL VEHICLE INDUSTRY

See also
Fleetwood Enterprises, Inc.
Skyline Corp.
Winnebago Industries, Inc.

RECREATIONAL VEHICLES

See also
All terrain vehicles
Automobile trailers
Campers, Truck
Snowmobiles and snowmobiling
Vans

Sport vehicles. T. Opre. See issues of Outdoor Life

Vehicles. See issues of Field & Stream

Equipment

Creating the ideal home—on wheels. M. Rogers. il *New Choices for the Best Years* 29:87-8 Ja '89

RECREATIONAL VEHICLES IN ADVERTISING

Giving new meaning to direct marketing, three filmmakers hit the bricks to sell their own movie [Brickmobile tours U.S. to sell Only a buck video] il *People Weekly* 31:107 Ap 10 '89

RECRUIT COMPANY
The dark side of Japan Inc. [insider trading scandal] J. Hammer. il *Newsweek* 113:41 Ja 9 '89
A fatal money scandal [resignation of N. Takeshita] M. Nemeth. il por *Maclean's* 102:25 My 8 '89
The fine art of kinmyaku [contributions to N. Takeshita from Recruit Company] il por *U.S. News & World Report* 106:18 Ap 24 '89
Insider trading. G. Ellwand. il *Maclean's* 102:22-3 Ja 9 '89
The Japanese scandal. il *World Press Review* 36:8 Je '89
Japan's scandal: who's next? S. Solo. il *Fortune* 119:24 Ap 10 '89
'Money politics' makes Tokyo's world go around [insider trading scandal] M. Tharp. il *U.S. News & World Report* 106:48 Ja 9 '89
Now Takeshita really feels the flames of scandal [insider trading scandal] T. Holden. por *Business Week* p55 F 27 '89
A question of ethics [N. Takeshita admits to receiving political donations from Recruit] A. Bilski. *Maclean's* 102:27 Ap 24 '89
The Recruit scandal bubbles to the top. A. Borrus. por *Business Week* p55 Mr 20 '89
Sand in a well-oiled machine [N. Takeshita forced to resign in wake of Recruit scandal] S. MacLeod. por *Time* 133:44 My 8 '89
A scandal that will not die. W. R. Doerner. il por *Time* 133:37+ Ap 24 '89
Sinking in a sea of yen. H. Anderson. il por *Newsweek* 113:49-50 Ap 24 '89
Takeshita talks political reform—but doesn't sound convincing. A. Borrus. il *Business Week* p57 Ja 23 '89
Uniqueness and sleaze. W. M. Stern. *National Review* 41:23-4 Je 2 '89
Unwelcome Recruit [Recruit Co. forces out G. Chichilnisky from management of Financial Telecommunications Inc.] J. Zweig. il por *Forbes* 143:149 My 15 '89
Why time may be running out for Takeshita. T. Holden. por *Business Week* p43 Ap 24 '89
Will the Recruit scandal just go away? A. Borrus and N. Gross. il por *Business Week* p40-1 Je 12 '89
You scratch my back . . . [insider trading scandal] J. Greenwald. il *Time* 133:47 Ja 9 '89
RECRUIT USA
'White people, black people' not wanted here? [Japanese employment agencies in U.S. charged with discrimination] M. Galen and L. J. Nathans. il *Business Week* p31 Jl 10 '89
RECRUITING
See also
Bankers—Recruiting
Basketball, College—Recruiting
Brokers—Recruiting
College sororities—Recruiting
College teachers—Recruiting
Colleges and universities—Student recruiting
Draft
Employees—Recruiting
Football, College—Recruiting
Government employees—Recruiting
Minority teachers—Recruiting
Nurses and nursing—Recruiting
Priests—Recruiting
Teachers—Recruiting
United States—Armed Forces—Recruiting, enlistment, etc.
RECTOR, LIAM, 1949-
Hans reading, Hans smoking [poem] *The New Republic* 201:126 N 6 '89
RECTUM

Cancer
See also
Colorectal cancer
RECUSE (TERM)
Recuse, J'accuse! W. Safire. il *The New York Times Magazine* p22+ Mr 12 '89
RECYCLED BUILDINGS See Buildings, Remodeled
RECYCLING (WASTE, ETC.)
See also
Automobile junkyards
Cans—Recycling
Diapers—Recycling
Hazardous substances—Recycling
Junkyards
Leaves—Recycling
Newspapers—Recycling
Paper—Recycling
Plastics—Recycling
Refuse as fuel
Water reuse
Wellman, Inc.
Alchemy, 1990s style. R. Simon. il *Forbes* 144:92+ Jl 24 '89
Dirty business [waste management] E. Corcoran. il *Scientific American* 261:98+ S '89
Facing up to the garbage challenge. il *Sunset (Central West edition)* 182:220 Mr '89

Getting started in recycling. T. Jackson. il *Better Homes and Gardens* 67:26 O '89
A lot of rubbish. W. J. Cook. il *U.S. News & World Report* 107:60-1 D 25 '89-Ja 1 '90
Mass burn is dying. N. Seldman. bibl f *Environment* 31:42-4 S '89
Our garbage crisis. S. O. Daniels. il *Organic Gardening* 36:5 Ja '89
Stop the trashing of America [views of Richard England] il *USA Today (Periodical)* 117:3 Je '89
Strategies for manufacturing. R. A. Frosch and N. E. Gallopoulos. bibl il *Scientific American* 261:144-52 S '89
Talkin' trash, talkin' cash. H. Cordes. il *Utne Reader* p19-20 Ja/F '89
Use it up—wear it out—make it do. il *The Conservationist* 43:40-3 Ja/F '89
Waste not, want not? Not necessarily. V. Cahan. il *Business Week* p116-17 Jl 17 '89
A 'waste not, want not' solution to help clean up rural America by recycling. il *Successful Farming* 87:34 O '89
Developing countries
Recycling in third world cities. il *The Futurist* 23:50-1 Mr/Ap '89
Japan
The good news: Japan gives trash a second chance. *Time* 133:47 Ja 2 '89
RED APPLE COMPANIES
"They hated me" [J. Catsimatidis] J. Flint. il por *Forbes* 144:240-1 O 30 '89
RED ARMY (JAPAN) See Japanese Red Army
RED ARMY CHORUS
From Russia with schmaltz. L. Shapiro. il *Newsweek* 114:71+ O 23 '89
RED ARMY FACTION
The bloody return of the Red Army Faction [killing of A. Herrhausen] il *Newsweek* 114:62 D 11 '89
Target for the Red Army Faction [murder of A. Herrhausen] D. Brand. il por *Time* 134:54 D 11 '89
RED BLOOD CELLS See Erythrocytes
RED COCKADED WOODPECKERS See Woodpeckers
RED CRABS See Crabs
RED CROSS
See also
International Museum of the Red Cross
RED GIANT STARS See Stars, Giant
RED HAIR See Hair
RED HEAT [film] See Motion picture reviews—Single works
RED HOUSE (KENT, ENGLAND) See Historic houses, sites, etc.—Great Britain
RED KING, WHITE KNIGHT [television program] See Television program reviews—Single works
RED SEA
See also
Gulf of Aqaba
RED SEA CORAL REEFS See Coral reefs and islands
RED SHIFT
Expanding a theory for shifting starlight [work of Emil Wolf] I. Amato. *Science News* 136:326 N 18 '89
Quasar-galaxy bridge? [work of Christopher L. Carilli] il *Sky and Telescope* 78:349 O '89
Quasar illuminates the most distant past [research by Donald P. Schneider and others] I. Peterson. *Science News* 136:340 N 25 '89
RED SQUIRRELS See Squirrels
RED TAPE See Bureaucracy
RED TIDE
Red tidings. M. Root. il *Technology Review* 92:13-14 Jl '89
Why the dolphins died. S. Hersh. il *Sea Frontiers* 35:246-7 Jl/Ag '89
RED WINES See Wine
RED WING POTTERIES
Red Wing stoneware soars. M. Leitzke. il *Antiques & Collecting Hobbies* 93:26-7+ F '89
RED WOLVES See Wolves
REDDAWAY, PETER
Should world psychiatry readmit the Soviets? bibl f il *The New York Review of Books* 36:54-8 O 12 '89
Soviet psychiatry: an exchange [discussion of October 12, 1989 article, Should world psychiatry readmit the Soviets?] il *The New York Review of Books* 36:65-6 D 21 '89
The threat to Gorbachev. bibl f il *The New York Review of Books* 36:19-24 Ag 17 '89
REDDING (CALIF.)
Architecture
Think of it as a house with an outdoor and indoor courtyard. il *Sunset (Central West edition)* 182:112-14 F '89
REDDY, E. PREMKUMAR, AND OTHERS
Amplification and molecular cloning of HTLV-I sequences from DNA of multiple sclerosis patients. bibl f il *Science* 243:529-33 Ja 27 '89; Correction. 246:10-11 O 6 '89
PCR analysis of DNA from multiple sclerosis patients for the presence of HTLV-I [discussion of January 27, 1989 article, Amplification and molecular cloning of HTLV-I sequences from DNA of multiple sclerosis patients] il *Science* 246:821-4 N 10 '89

REDECORATING See House decoration
REDEMPTION See Salvation
REDEMPTION OF BONDS See Bonds—Redemption
REDFISH FISHING
The fertile crescent [lower Texas coast] J. Doggett. il *Field & Stream* 93:36-7+ Ja '89
REDFORD, DOROTHY SPRUILL
about
Dot Redford found her roots at Somerset. D. Young. il pors *Southern Living* 24:92+ Ja '89
Plantation home. R. Mashburn. il pors map *Americana* 16:50-4 Ja/F '89
REDFORD, KENT H., AND SHAW, PAMELA
The terror bird still screams. il *International Wildlife* 19:14-16 My/Je '89
REDFORD, ROBERT, 1936-
about
Architectural digest visits: Robert Redford at Sundance [cover story] J. Thurman. il *Architectural Digest* 46:162-71+ Ap '89
REDGRAVE, VANESSA, 1937-
about
Vanessa ascending. W. A. Henry. il pors *Time* 134:109+ O 9 '89
REDIFFUSION SIMULATION LTD.
Britain's Rediffusion Simulation offers microcomputer-based ATC trainer. C. A. Shifrin. il *Aviation Week & Space Technology* 131:83+ Ag 21 '89
REDIG, PATRICK, 1948-
about
Minnesotans struggle to save their poisoned swans. M. Nelson. il *People Weekly* 31:103-5 Mr 13 '89
REDISH, EDWARD F.
(jt. auth) See Wilson, Jack M., and Redish, Edward F.
REDISTRICTING See Apportionment (Election law)
REDMAN, JOE
about
Down East chic. C. Hacinli. il *Gentlemen's Quarterly* 59:114+ S '89
REDMONT, JANE
When the Spirit leads. il por *Commonweal* 116:133-5 Mr 10 '89
REDONDO BEACH (CALIF.)
Photographs and photography
Hometown photo essay. D. Mazzapica. il *Petersen's Photographic Magazine* 18:34-7 S '89
REDOUBT VOLCANO (ALASKA)
A perilous passage through volcanic ash [KLM Royal Dutch Airlines' loss of engine power] R. Monastersky. *Science News* 136:407 D 23-30 '89
REDOX See Oxidation reduction reaction
REDSHIFT See Red shift
REDSTONE, SUMNER
about
Is Viacom ready to channel the world? D. Lieberman. il pors *Business Week* p72-4 D 18 '89
REDUCED INSTRUCTION SET COMPUTERS
The battle royal in chips. G. Lewis. il *Business Week* p192-6+ N 27 '89
DEC's RISC powerhouse [DECstation] B. Smith and R. L. Mitchell. il *Byte* 14:201-2+ N '89
DOS at RISC. C. B. Hunter and J. Banning. il *Byte* 14:361-2+ N '89
The Intel 80860. N. Margulis. il *Byte* 14:333-4+ D '89
Intel to Motorola: race ya [new 860 chip] O. Port. il *Business Week* p42 Mr 13 '89
Intel's Cray-on-a-chip [80860 RISC microprocessor] F. Hayes. il *Byte* 14:113-14 My '89
Intel's new 80860 CPU aims to be a Cray on a chip. *Byte* 14:11 Ap '89
Intel's plan for staying on top. C. Gottlieb. il *Fortune* 119:98-100 Mr 27 '89
A look at what's ahead. *High Technology Business* 9:37 Je '89
RISC chip acceleration. R. Bel Bruno. *Personal Computing* 13:107 Ag '89
RISC to eclipse CISC PDQ? R. Lockwood. il *Personal Computing* 13:25 My '89
RISCs: unsafe at any speed. D. Nelson. il *Byte* 14:488 N '89
Worth the RISC [workstation technology] T. G. Marshall and J. M. Tazelaar. il *Byte* 14:245-9 F '89
REDUCING DIET See Diet
REDUCING PRODUCTS See Weight reducing products
REDUCTION, BIOCHEMICAL
Effects of buried ionizable amino acids on the reduction potential of recombinant myoglobin. R. Varadarajan and others. bibl f il *Science* 243:69-72 Ja 6 '89
REDUCTION, CHEMICAL
See also
Oxidation reduction reaction
REDWOOD
California's chain-saw massacre [clearcutting by Pacific Lumber] M. J. Walters. il *Reader's Digest* 135:144-9 N '89
Milken, junk bonds and raping redwoods [C. Hurwitz accelerates logging following takeover] B. McKibben. *Rolling Stone* p39-40 Ag 10 '89

Monarchs of the mist [excerpt] J. E. Brown. il *National Parks* 63:46-7 S/O '89
Notes and comment [felling of Discovery Tree redwood in 1853 at Calaveras Big Trees State Park, Calif.] *The New Yorker* 64:23-4 F 13 '89
Ozone needles loblolly pines . . . and saps sequoia seedlings. *Science News* 136:189 S 16 '89
Park-quality sequoias logged [Sequoia National Forest] il *National Parks* 63:8-9 My/Je '89
A raider's ruckus in the redwoods [accelerated logging following Maxxam's takeover of Pacific Lumber] E. Schultz. il por *Fortune* 119:172-3+ Ap 24 '89
These woods are made for burning [fire studies of giant sequoia groves] R. Kunzig. il map *Discover* 10:86-7+ Mr '89
Unsung sequoias [Sequoia National Forest] il map *Sunset (Central West edition)* 183:42-3 Ag '89
REDWOOD LIBRARY AND ATHENAEUM (NEWPORT, R.I.)
Pattern books [Furniture in print: pattern books from the Redwood Library at the Rhode Island School of Design] A. E. Ledes. il *Antiques* 136:662+ O '89
REDWOOD NATIONAL PARK (CALIF.)
Monarchs of the mist [excerpt] J. E. Brown. il *National Parks* 63:46-7 S/O '89
REEBOK INTERNATIONAL LTD.
Paul Fireman pulls on his old running shoes [founder is back in control] L. Jereski. il por *Business Week* p46-7 N 6 '89
Reebok on the rebound. B. Kanner. il *New York* 22:26+ O 16 '89
REECE, GABRIELLE
about
Volleyball, anyone? Model Gabrielle Reece's favorite spikes are not on her heels. S. K. Reed. il pors *People Weekly* 32:97-9 O 16 '89
REECHER, SHELLEY
about
It's 10 p.m. Do you know where your Doberman is? C. Gockley. il *American Health* 8:32+ N '89
REED, ALAINA
about
Alaina Reed, Kevin Peter Hall tie knot in Los Angeles rites. il por *Jet* 76:61 My 29 '89
REED, BARBARA
about
Shining star daughters and their amazing moms. il pors *'Teen* 33:46-7 D '89
REED, BILLY See Reed, William F.
REED, BRUCE
Half Watt. il *The New Republic* 201:20-2 O 16 '89
Nazi retreat. *The New Republic* 200:10-11 Ap 3 '89
Rocket man. *The New Republic* 200:12-13 My 15 '89
REED, CHARLES B.
National Collegiate Athletic Association [address, January 9, 1989] *Vital Speeches of the Day* 55:372-3 Ap 1 '89
REED, CHRIS
Road to ruin. il pors map *Cycle* 40:45-9+ O '89
REED, CHRISTOPHER G.
What makes a good teacher? il *BioScience* 39:555-7 S '89
REED, DAVID
Do South African sanctions make sense? il *Reader's Digest* 134:51-6 F '89
Should we trust Yasir Arafat? por *Reader's Digest* 135:143-8 S '89
REED, DAVID
Adequate supply of electricity [address, May 22, 1989] *Vital Speeches of the Day* 55:687-90 S 1 '89
REED, ERIN
about
Shining star daughters and their amazing moms. il pors *'Teen* 33:46-7 D '89
REED, ISHMAEL, 1938-
The black pathology biz. il *The Nation* 249:597-8 N 20 '89
What's American about America? Toward claiming our multicultural heritage [excerpt from Writin' is fightin'] il *Utne Reader* p100-3+ Mr/Ap '89
Bibliography
Trickster tales. D. Pinckney. il *The New York Review of Books* 36:20+ O 12 '89
REED, JOHN
Cold war on ice. *National Review* 41:18-19 Ag 18 '89
REED, JOHN SHELTON
Informed consent. *Society* 27:25-7 N/D '89
REED, JULIA
Little big man. il *Vogue* 179:444-6 Ap '89
REED, LOU
Cans [poem] *Life* 12:102 Ag '89
about
Lou Reed: back on the streets. D. Fricke. por *Rolling Stone* p26 Mr 9 '89
Lou Reed's angry "New York". S. Simels. il por *Stereo Review* 54:82 Ap '89
Lou Reed's New York state of mind. A. DeCurtis. il *Rolling Stone* p57+ F 23 '89
Music. G. Santoro. *The Nation* 248:282-4 F 27 '89
Nearly remarkable. *The New Yorker* 65:29-30 My 22 '89

REED, LOU—about—cont.

Lou Reed: the Rolling stone interview [cover story] D. Fricke. il pors *Rolling Stone* p36-8+ My 4 '89

Reed to New York: drop dead. D. Gates. il pors *Newsweek* 113:68 Ja 30 '89

Rock noir: Lou Reed reckons with Andy Warhol in 'Songs for 'Drella'. P. Blauner. il pors *New York* 22:44-9 N 27 '89

Wise guys. M. Moses. *The New Yorker* 65:84-7 Ap 24 '89

REED, MARY

Weather talk. See issues of Weatherwise beginning December 1986

REED, RANDALL R.

(jt. auth) See Jones, David T., and Reed, Randall R.

REED, ROBERT

The collectibles of Oz. il *Antiques & Collecting Hobbies* 94:32-4 Jl '89

Hot collectibles of the Old West. il *Antiques & Collecting Hobbies* 94:42-5 Je '89

REED, ROY, 1930-

From the campuses: adventures in publishing. il *The New York Times Book Review* 94:1+ S 24 '89

REED, SANDRA R.

View from the Valley. See issues of Personal Computing beginning June 1987 through November 1989

REED, WILLIAM F.

'Bama roars back. il *Sports Illustrated* 71:46-8+ O 30 '89

College football top 20. il *Sports Illustrated* 71:64-9+ S 4 '89

Kentucky Derby: the Ultimate Derby. il *Sports Illustrated* 70:47+ My 1 '89

A new Proposition. il *Sports Illustrated* 70:16-19 Ja 23 '89

On the brink again. il *Sports Illustrated* 70:42-5 Mr 13 '89

This coach did it right. il por *Sports Illustrated* 71:126 D 11 '89

REED, WILLIS

about

Mountains of men. T. Loverro. il pors *Sport (New York, N.Y.)* 80:58-62 F '89

REED INTERNATIONAL PLC

Reed Book Group posts big profits in half-year earnings. V. Menkes. *Publishers Weekly* 236:12 D 8 '89

With a lineup like this, who needs charisma? [Reed International buys Travel Information Group] M. Maremont. il por *Business Week* p59 My 22 '89

REEFS, ARTIFICIAL

Mussel man Bob Meek runs a seafood farm built on mutual shellfishness [harvesting mussels attached to legs of offshore drilling platforms] N. Geeslin. il pors *People Weekly* 31:135-6 My 1 '89

The patina from the deep [work of R. Power] V. Gladstone. il *Art News* 88:15 S '89

REELS, FISHING See Fishing tackle

REES, D. C., AND OTHERS

Hydrophobic organization of membrane proteins. bibl f il *Science* 245:510-13 Ag 4 '89

REES, GROVER

Scourge or plot? *National Review* 41:34-5 Ag 4 '89

REES, JOHN R.

The Stanford Linear Collider [cover story] il *Scientific American* 261:58-65 O '89

REES, MARTIN J., 1942-

(jt. auth) See Jasani, Bhupendra, and Rees, Martin J., 1942-

REESE, CHARLEY

America on the rise: our people get it done. il *Reader's Digest* 135:129-30 Ag '89

REESE, COREY A.

Just the facts please. il *Current Health 2* 15:12-13 F '89

REESE, FRED

A view to a thrill. il *Runner's World* 24:120 Ap '89

REESE, THOMAS J.

The archbishops go to Rome. *America* 160:187-8 Mr 4 '89

Bishops and theologians. *America* 161:4-6 Jl 1-8 '89

Bishops meet in Baltimore. *America* 161:369 N 25 '89

Bishops on bishops. *America* 161:290-3 N 4 '89

Discussions in Rome. *America* 160:260-1 Mr 25 '89

REEVES, DIANNE

about

Dianne Reeves. P. Johnson. por *Essence* 19:55-6 Ja '89

REEVES, KEANU

about

Peaking in the valley. L. Snowden. por *Rolling Stone* p31 Mr 9 '89

REEVES, RICHARD

What's right with America? il *New Choices for the Best Years* 29:64-9 Ap '89

REEVES, ROBERT

Astronomy tests the Northern Lites cold camera. il *Astronomy* 17:86-9 Jl '89

Astrophotos the easy way. il *Astronomy* 17:70-5 S '89

(ed) See Evans, Robert O. Supernova hunter

REEVES (LONDON, ENGLAND: HOTEL) See London (England)—Hotels, motels, etc.

REFCO GROUP LTD.

Did Refco help take Uncle Sam to the cleaners? [dodging taxes through phony London trading] D. Greising. il *Business Week* p33-4 O 2 '89

REFEREEING OF SCIENTIFIC LITERATURE See Scientific literature—Refereeing

REFEREES AND REFEREEING (SPORTS) See Football, Professional—Officiating

REFERENCE BOOKS

See also

CD-ROM (Compact disc-Read only memory)—Reference books

Information systems—Reference books

Publishers and publishing—Reference books

Bibliography

In short/reference. il *The New York Times Book Review* 94:10-11 O 8 '89

REFERENCE FILE (DATABASE MANAGEMENT SYSTEM) See Database management

REFERENCES, EMPLOYMENT See Employment references

REFERENDUM

The changing nature of initiative campaigns. A. E. Young. *Common Cause Magazine* 15:43 Jl/Ag '89

Is this any way to run a state? [government by initiative in California] M. Reese. *Newsweek* 114:27 Jl 31 '89

Canada

The call for a referendum [Maclean's/Decima poll on free trade agreement with the U.S.] *Maclean's* 102:13 Ja 2 '89

Switzerland

The Swiss debate their Army's future. A. Schalk. il *Commonweal* 116:331-3 Je 2 '89

Uruguay

Department of amplification [amnesty law sustained] L. Weschler. *The New Yorker* 65:92-3 My 22 '89

Forgive & forget? [referendum to uphold or overturn law giving amnesty to military responsible for violations of human rights] R. Neild. *Commonweal* 116:358-60 Je 16 '89

The great exception (II) [drive for referendum to overturn amnesty for military civil rights abusers] L. Weschler. *The New Yorker* 65:85-102+ Ap 10 '89

Sign on the invisible line; tr. by Tracey Hill. E. H. Galeano. *The Nation* 248:411-12 Mr 27 '89

Torture, memory and justice. C. G. Brown and R. K. Goldman. il *The Nation* 248:408+ Mr 27 '89

Uruguay confronts its torturers [amnesty law referendum] il *U.S. News & World Report* 106:36-7 Ap 17 '89

REFERRAL, MEDICAL See Medical referral

REFINANCING OF MORTGAGES See Mortgages—Refinancing

REFINERIES, PETROLEUM See Petroleum refineries

REFINERIES, SPACE FUEL See Space fuel refineries

REFINISHING OF FURNITURE See Furniture—Finishes and finishing

REFLECTION (OPTICS)

See also

Light—Scattering

Mirages

Light reflection models for computer graphics. D. Greenberg. bibl f il *Science* 244:166-73 Ap 14 '89

What do phonograph records have in common with windshield wipers? J. Walker. il *Scientific American* 261:106-9 Jl '89

REFLECTIONS (PHOTOGRAPHY)

Object on a complementary background [hunting knife against black reflective background] D. Palmer. il *Petersen's Photographic Magazine* 18:48-9 Jl '89

Reflections. M. Van Hesemans. il *Petersen's Photographic Magazine* 18:16-18+ Jl '89

The specular and the transparent combined. J. Purcell. il *Petersen's Photographic Magazine* 18:92-3 S '89

REFLECTORS (PHOTOGRAPHY) See Photography—Light and lighting

REFLECTORS (SAFETY DEVICES)

Lighten up [cycling safety] J. Kukoda. il *Bicycling* 30:128-9 Ja/F '89

REFLEX (COMPUTER PROGRAM)

Perfect compromise between complex and weak-kneed databases [Borland's Reflex 2.0] T. A. Summers. il *Home Office Computing* 7:34+ D '89

Reflex: a new view of data [Borland's Reflex 2.0] J. Pepper. il *Personal Computing* 13:192 N '89

REFLEXES

See also

Conditioned responses

Ocular responses to linear motion are inversely proportional to viewing distance. U. Schwarz and others. bibl f il *Science* 245:1394-6 S 22 '89

Reflex reactions [infants] K. Karlsrud and D. Schultz. il *Parents* 64:185 Ap '89

REFLEXOLOGY

Best foot forward. il *Seventeen* 48:352 Ag '89

Foot work [excerpt from Feet first] L. Norman and T. D. Cowan. il *Redbook* 173:152-3 S '89

Hands on—reflexology: putting a little pressure on stress. il *Mademoiselle* 95:240-1 Ap '89

REFORESTATION

Earth needs 'Releaf' [tree planting to counter greenhouse effect] T. Jackson. il *Better Homes and Gardens* 67:28 N '89

REFORESTATION—*cont.*
First word. N. Myers. il *Omni (New York, N.Y.)* 11:8 My '89
Forests: a tool to moderate global warming? R. A. Sedjo. bibl f il map *Environment* 31:14-20 Ja/F '89
Towards a Green Revolution in forestry. S. Postel and L. Heise. il *The Courier (Unesco)* 42:18 Ja '89
Trees' new role [countering the greenhouse effect] R. Rodale. il *Organic Gardening* 36:27-8 Ap '89
Tropical forest gardening: an alternative to destruction [Panama] il *The Futurist* 23:53 My/Je '89

REFORM (PERIODICAL)
Hungary: Red tabloid bares all. il *Newsweek* 113:36 Ap 17 '89

REFORM PARTY OF CANADA
From Alberta with ire. J. Howse. il *Maclean's* 102:24-5 N 13 '89
Upset in the West [D. Grey wins byelection in Alberta] J. Howse. il por *Maclean's* 102:12-13 Mr 27 '89

REFORMATION
Anecdotes, facetiae, satire, etc.
Cowboys and clerics. M. E. Marty. *The Christian Century* 106:543 My 17 '89
Bibliography
Paperback history. R. O'Day. *History Today* 39:51 Mr '89

REFORMATION DAY
God's gift of righteousness. P. Perkins. il *The Christian Century* 106:954 O 25 '89

REFORMED CHURCH OF QUEBEC
Quebec Reformed Church. *The Christian Century* 106:170 F 15 '89

REFORMERS
See also
Besant, Annie, 1847-1933

REFRACTING TELESCOPES *See* Telescopes
REFRACTION
See also
Light—Scattering
Refraction by earth's atmosphere [computer program] B. E. Schaefer. il *Sky and Telescope* 77:311-13 Mr '89

REFRACTION, DOUBLE
Cross-polarization of light. J. Bartsch. il *Petersen's Photographic Magazine* 17:58-9 F '89

REFRIGERATED DINNERS
Supermarket dinners come in from the cold. il *Consumer Reports* 54:73 F '89

REFRIGERATOR FOOD CONTAINERS, PORCELAIN *See* Porcelain containers
REFRIGERATOR-FREEZERS *See* Refrigerators
REFRIGERATOR MAGNETS
Collectors and collecting
New kitsch in the kitchen. J. Schwartz. il *Newsweek* 114:74 S 18 '89

REFRIGERATORS
See also
Magnetic refrigeration
The big chill. il *Home Mechanix* 86:68+ Ap '89
How to choose a top-freezer refrigerator. il *Consumer Reports* 54:729-37 N '89
Top-freezer refrigerators. il *Consumer Reports* 54:299-303 D '89
A worse fridge [effect of ban on chlorofluorocarbons] J. W. Merline. *Consumers' Research Magazine* 72:38 D '89
Defects
This 'glitch' may cost GE $350 million [rotary compressor refrigerators] Z. Schiller. *Business Week* p28-9 Ja 30 '89

REFUELING OF JET AIRPLANES *See* Airplane engines, Jet—Refueling
REFUGEE CHILDREN
The children who come alone [refugees sent by parents from third world countries to West Germany] M. Fisher. *World Press Review* 36:14+ N '89
Ticket to loneliness [refugee children in West Germany] N. Darnton. il *Newsweek* 114:43 Ag 28 '89
Education
Serving refugee children and families in Head Start [Spokane, Wash.; cover story] C. Broughton. il *Children Today* 18:6-10 S/O '89
Imprisonment
Plight of the 'border orphans' [Central Americans] J. N. Baker. il *Newsweek* 114:18-19 Jl 24 '89

REFUGEES
See also
Aged refugees
Asylum, Right of
Environmental refugees
Exiles
Refugee children
United Nations. High Commissioner for Refugees
United Nations Relief and Works Agency for Palestine Refugees in the Near East
United States. Dept. of State. Bureau for Refugee Programs
Clearing the logjam [Canada's overwhelmed refugee determination system] P. Kaihla. il *Maclean's* 102:16 Ja 9 '89
Closing the doors. J. Smolowe. il *Time* 134:24-6 Jl 3 '89

Confronting realities of refugee assistance [address, May 26, 1989] J. Moore. *Department of State Bulletin* 89:85-6 Ag '89
Cooling the welcome [Canada's refugee policy] R. Laver. il *Maclean's* 102:17-18 Jl 10 '89
Forced out: the tragic plight of the world's refugees [excerpts] C. Kismaric. il *People Weekly* 31:98-102+ Ap 17 '89
Four houses join forces to publicize the plight of the world's refugees [Forced out by C. Kismaric] il *Publishers Weekly* 235:42-3 Mr 24 '89
FY 1990 assistance request for refugee programs [statement, March 22, 1989] J. Moore. *Department of State Bulletin* 89:72-3 My '89
Knock knock [U.S. policy] *The New Republic* 201:7-8 O 2 '89
The new refugees [cover story; special section] il *World Press Review* 36:11-14+ N '89
The new refugees [cover story; special section] il *U.S. News & World Report* 107:34-7+ O 23 '89
Recent trends in U.S. refugee policy. W. P. Fuller. *America* 161:238-40 O 14 '89
Refugee reality and the U.N. High Commission. S. E. Smith. *America* 161:10-12+ Jl 1-8 '89
Substance versus fabricated fury [press coverage of Canadian refugee policy] G. Bain. il *Maclean's* 102:37 Ja 23 '89
Update on immigration and refugee issues [statement, April 6, 1989] J. Moore. *Department of State Bulletin* 89:59-62 Jl '89
A world awash in refugees [U.S. policy] D. Waller. il map *Newsweek* 114:44-5 O 9 '89
Education
Serving refugee children and families in Head Start [Spokane, Wash.; cover story] C. Broughton. il *Children Today* 18:6-10 S/O '89
Photographs and photography
Refugees. E. Bazan. il *Life* 12:94-100 Ap '89
Refugees. P. Turnley. il maps *Newsweek* 113:36-41 Ja 2 '89

REFUGEES, AFGHAN
Afghanistan after the turmoil. M. Hussein. il *World Health* p11-12 Jl '89
The next Afghan war [women refugees in Pakistan] D. Lorch. il *Ms.* 17:84 Ap '89

REFUGEES, AFRICAN
See also
Bishop Desmond Tutu Southern African Refugee Scholarship Fund

REFUGEES, ARAB
See also
Palestinian Arabs
United Nations Relief and Works Agency for Palestine Refugees in the Near East

REFUGEES, ASIAN
Japan draws a line. I. Oshima. *World Press Review* 36:18 N '89
Let's let Asians in. K. Labich. il *Fortune* 120:89-90 Jl 17 '89

REFUGEES, CAMBODIAN
See also
Cambodians—United States
Cambodia's violent border camps. L. Williams. *World Press Review* 36:20 N '89
A ghost outside the fence [Khao I Dang Holding Center on the Thai-Kampuchean border] J. Ranney. il *The Progressive* 53:50 Ap '89
Killing time [Cambodian refugee camp in Thailand] M. Drabble. il *Harper's* 278:69-72 Ap '89
A life of war and waiting. N. Cumming-Bruce. il *U.S. News & World Report* 107:44-5 O 23 '89
The return of the Khmer Rouge [cover story] S. Erlanger. il map *The New York Times Magazine* p24-7+ Mr 5 '89

REFUGEES, CENTRAL AMERICAN
As the huddled masses roll across El Norte [U.S. policy] il *U.S. News & World Report* 106:10-11 Ja 30 '89
The battering ram at the golden door. A. Fins. il *Business Week* p52-3+ F 6 '89
Developing solutions for Central American refugee problems [address, May 30, 1989] J. Moore. *Department of State Bulletin* 89:87-8 Ag '89
Guatemala City conference. il *UN Chronicle* 26:14-15 S '89
The immigration mess. J. V. Lamar, Jr. il *Time* 133:14-15 F 27 '89
The journey to the Rio Grande [undocumented Central Americans cross Mexico] J. Reyes Estrada. il *World Press Review* 36:30-1 Ap '89
No sanctuary. T. Reader. *The Nation* 249:193 Ag 21-28 '89
Plight of the 'border orphans'. J. N. Baker. il *Newsweek* 114:18-19 Jl 24 '89
Refugees find little refuge in U.S. D. Moul. il *Christianity Today* 33:40-1 Ap 21 '89
Roundup on the Rio Grande. J. Juffer. il *The Progressive* 53:32-3 Ap '89
Texas pitches a 'tent city' [Port Isabel detention center holds refugees for deportation] E. Salholz. il *Newsweek* 113:27 Mr 6 '89

REFUGEES, CHINESE
Computer engineer turns entrepreneur-in-exile [Wan Runnan] M. Sun. *Science* 245:592 Ag 11 '89
REFUGEES, CUBAN
  See also
  Cubans—United States
REFUGEES, EAST EUROPEAN
Come one—but not all. E. Steen. il *World Press Review* 36:11-12 N '89
Holes in the Iron Curtain. H. Anderson. il map *Newsweek* 114:22 Ag 28 '89
A mixed welcome for returning Germans. G. Epp. *The Christian Century* 106:902-3 O 11 '89
Welcome, East bloc refugees! Well, sort of. J. Templeman. il *Business Week* p50 S 18 '89
REFUGEES, EAST GERMAN
Borderline Marxists. *The Nation* 249:333 O 2 '89
Breaching the wall. W. R. Doerner. il maps *Time* 134:32-4 S 11 '89
East Germans go west. *Commonweal* 116:580-1 N 3 '89
Exchanging a prison for a maze [East German refugees and A. de Tocqueville's views on democracy] R. Rosenblatt. il *U.S. News & World Report* 107:10-11 S 25 '89
A 'fall to freedom'. il *World Press Review* 36:13-14 N '89
The flight to freedom. H. Anderson. il por *Newsweek* 114:40-3+ O 16 '89
Flight to freedom [M. Dürer and family] M. Ryan. il pors *People Weekly* 32:36-9 O 2 '89
Freedom train. W. R. Doerner. il *Time* 134:38-41+ O 16 '89
The gift that blessed the giver [Wohlfahrt family's chain of Christmas stores in West Germany] S. Wilding. il *Good Housekeeping* 209:234+ D '89
The great escape [cover story; special section; with editorial comment by Kevin Doyle] il *Maclean's* 102:8, 32-6+ O 16 '89
The great escape [Hungary grants East Germans passage across Austrian border] J. Smolowe. il map *Time* 134:30-2 S 25 '89
Help definitely wanted [views of Norbert Walter] P. Fuhrman. il *Forbes* 144:241 O 30 '89
How to bleed a Red nation white [fleeing to West Germany] il *U.S. News & World Report* 107:14 S 25 '89
Is a new economic juggernaut on the way? J. Templeman. il *Business Week* p72+ O 23 '89
A last mile to freedom [refugee A. Rudolf's escape route to Austria] R. Nordland. il por map *Newsweek* 114:34 S 18 '89
A mass exodus. J. Bierman. il map *Maclean's* 102:28-30 S 25 '89
A mixed blessing for Bonn. H. Anderson. il *Newsweek* 114:33-4 N 27 '89
Old Volk's home [German refugees in West Germany] K. Breslau. *The New Republic* 200:16+ My 1 '89
One people still divided [ramifications of East Germans' flight into West Germany] H. Anderson. il *Newsweek* 114:27 S 25 '89
Pleas from GDR churches. *The Christian Century* 106:905 O 11 '89
A quick leap into a new life [Balzer family] D. Lawday. il *U.S. News & World Report* 107:37+ O 23 '89
A strange new place called home [List family and S. Schulz] M. Ryan. il pors *Life* 12:34-9 N '89
Turmoil behind the wall. J. Altman. il *U.S. News & World Report* 107:38-9 O 16 '89
Uber alles? *National Review* 41:16+ O 13 '89
The welcome can wear thin. P. Clough. *World Press Review* 36:12 N '89
Where vacations can last forever [East German refugees reaching Austria via Hungary] map *U.S. News & World Report* 107:16 Ag 14 '89
REFUGEES, ETHIOPIAN
A man in orbit [Eritrean refugee W. Ahmed] *Time* 134:26 Jl 3 '89
REFUGEES, GERMAN
A mixed welcome for returning Germans [emigration out of East Europe] G. Epp. *The Christian Century* 106:902-3 O 11 '89
REFUGEES, INDOCHINESE
  See also
  Indochinese—United States
Indochinese refugees conference held in Geneva [statement, June 18, 1989; texts of draft declaration and comprehensive plan of action, June 14, 1989] L. S. Eagleburger. *Department of State Bulletin* 89:69-73 O '89
International Conference adopts plan to solve Indochinese refugee problem. *UN Chronicle* 26:23 S '89
REFUGEES, IRANIAN
Iranian Christians flee persecution [refuge in Pakistan] H. Martyn. *The Christian Century* 106:461-2 My 3 '89
REFUGEES, LAOTIAN
  See also
  Hmong (Asian people)—United States
REFUGEES, LEBANESE
Escape from danger: Lebanese refugees seek safety in Canada. J. Bierman. il *Maclean's* 102:35 O 2 '89

REFUGEES, MOZAMBICAN
A small war's moving targets [victims of Renamo] E. Ransdell. il *U.S. News & World Report* 107:41 O 23 '89
REFUGEES, NICARAGUAN
  See also
  Nicaraguans—United States
A new life on Block B. A. M. Arrarte. il *U.S. News & World Report* 107:43 O 23 '89
Newcomers meet hard hearts [Nicaraguans seek U.S. asylum] *America* 160:131 F 18 '89
REFUGEES, POLISH
  See also
  Poles—Canada
REFUGEES, RUSSIAN
New U.S. policy may stem flow of Soviet Christians. il *Christianity Today* 33:52+ N 3 '89
Soviet exodus strains church resources. K. A. Lawton. il *Christianity Today* 33:50 Je 16 '89
U.S. denies refugee status to Soviets. il *Christianity Today* 33:58 Mr 3 '89
REFUGEES, SALVADORAN
A community of remembrance. S. Hutchinson. *The Christian Century* 106:853-6 S 27 '89
Salvadoran refugees come home [village of Copapayo] R. R. Ruether. il *The Christian Century* 106:851-3 S 27 '89
Unwelcome in El Salvador [treatment of volunteers assisting refugees] J. Lindsay-Poland. il *The Progressive* 53:32-5 My '89
REFUGEES, TURKISH
A modern Balkan exodus. R. Flamini. il *Time* 134:39 Ag 14 '89
REFUGEES, VIETNAMESE
  See also
  Vietnamese—Canada
  Vietnamese—United States
Boat people, go home. R.-P. Paringaux. *World Press Review* 36:35-6 Je '89
The boat people in peril [Hong Kong] W. Shawcross. il *The New York Review of Books* 36:58-9 N 23 '89
Compassion fatigue: Hong Kong and the boat people [cover story] D. L. Kirp. il *The American Spectator* 22:16-19 Ap '89
Dashing their dreams [Britain forces repatriation of Vietnamese boat people] W. Stewart. il *Time* 134:26 D 25 '89
Don't keelhaul the boat people [returning Vietnamese boat people from Hong Kong to Vietnam] *National Review* 41:14 D 22 '89
The exodus continues. B. Came. *Maclean's* 102:24 Jl 10 '89
Hypocrisy in Hong Kong [forced repatriation of boat people] B. Amiel. il *Maclean's* 102:17 N 20 '89
The limits of mercy [Hong Kong] J. L. Du Sablon. *World Press Review* 36:17-18 N '89
The long goodbye [Hong Kong residents who wish to leave and boat people who have arrived] R. Brookhiser. il *National Review* 41:18-19 N 24 '89
No room at the inn. W. McGurn. *National Review* 41:26 Je 30 '89
U.S., Vietnam agree on emigration of detainees [joint statement, July 30, 1989] *Department of State Bulletin* 89:63 N '89
What will the next favorable wind bring? [boat people entering Hong Kong] F. Moan. il *America* 160:86-7 F 4 '89
REFUGEES AND THE CHURCH *See* Church and social problems
REFUGES, WILDLIFE *See* Wildlife sanctuaries
REFUGIO (TEX.)
                    Social life and customs
Refugio [reunion of high school class of 1959] J. L. Galloway. il *U.S. News & World Report* 107:51+ D 18 '89
REFUSE AND REFUSE DISPOSAL
  See also
  Arcata (Calif.)—Sanitary affairs
  Asbestos—Disposal
  Beaches—Sanitation
  Benton (Ky.)—Sanitary affairs
  Boston (Mass.)—Sanitary affairs
  Chambers Development Company
  Florida—Sanitary affairs
  Hazardous substances—Disposal
  Incineration and incinerators
  Jefferson City (Mo.)—Sanitary affairs
  Malibu (Calif.)—Sanitary affairs
  New York (N.Y.)—Sanitary affairs
  Pollution control industries
  Radioactive waste disposal
  Railroads—Waste disposal operations
  San Diego (Calif.)—Sanitary affairs
  Sanitary landfills
  Toronto (Ont.)—Sanitary affairs
  Trade waste—Disposal
  Transtech Industries Inc.
  Waste disposal in the ocean
  Waste Management, Inc.
  Wheelabrator Technologies Inc.
American myopia. E. Kunes. *Omni (New York, N.Y.)* 11:33 Mr '89

REFUSE AND REFUSE DISPOSAL—*cont.*

America's waste crisis: how you can help solve it! S. Nielsen. il *Good Housekeeping* 209:272 S '89

Buried alive [cover story] M. Beck. il map *Newsweek* 114:66-71+ N 27 '89

The continuing diaper debate [disposables are a serious solid waste problem] J. Brooks. il *Utne Reader* p24-5 Jl/Ag '89

Environmental costs of keeping baby dry [disposable diapers] *Science News* 135:141 Mr 4 '89

A lot of rubbish. W. J. Cook. il *U.S. News & World Report* 107:60-1 D 25 '89-Ja 1 '90

Our garbage crisis. S. O. Daniels. il *Organic Gardening* 36:5 Ja '89

Rubbish! W. L. Rathje. il *The Atlantic* 264:99-106+ D '89

Rural America laid to waste. C. Tevis. il *Successful Farming* 87:32-4 O '89

A stinking mess. J. Langone. il *Time* 133:44-5+ Ja 2 '89

Swamp gas. A. Meyer. il *The Mother Earth News* 120:48+ N/D '89

Thinking twice about trash. il *Glamour* 87:122 S '89

Anecdotes, facetiae, satire, etc.

Talking dirty. P. Pringle. *The New Republic* 201:42 O 30 '89

Equipment

See also
Allwaste Inc.

Japan

Land of plenty [sodai gomi nights] J. M. Fallows. il *The Atlantic* 263:29-31 Je '89

Teeing off on Japan's garbage. S. Begley. il *Newsweek* 114:70 N 27 '89

Western Europe

Europe's garbage smells sweet to Waste Management. B. Bremner. il *Business Week* p33 My 29 '89

REFUSE AND REFUSE DISPOSAL IN ART

Exhibitions

Waste not [M. Ukeles' Flow city art installation at New York City's new trash loading facility] P. C. Phillips. il *Art in America* 77:47+ F '89

REFUSE AS FUEL

Assessing the benefits of biogas [China] R. Hamburg. bibl f il *Environment* 30:31-2 D '88

Cofiring troubles prompt guidelines. *High Technology Business* 9:36 My '89

National Energy Associates [use of cow manure] M. Kelly. il *Utne Reader* p78 Ja/F '89

Skygas promises clean fuel from wastes. *High Technology Business* 9:37 N/D '89

REFUSE CONTAINERS

See also
Trash bags
Wastebaskets

REFUSE RECYCLING *See* Recycling (Waste, etc.)

REFUSE TRUCKS

See also
Allwaste Inc.

REFUSENIKS *See* Immigration and emigration—Soviet Union

REGAN, DONALD T.

Donald T. Regan [advice to George Bush] *National Review* 41:23-4 F 10 '89

about

Now it's broke. J. R. Adams. *The New Republic* 201:16-18 N 13 '89

REGAN, JAMES

about

Parking fine: 280 years in jail. W. Baldwin. il por *Forbes* 144:222 O 2 '89

Too much firepower to fit the crime? A. P. Tobias. il *Time* 134:74 N 20 '89

REGATTAS

See also
Rowing—Competitions

REGENCY ROMANCE FICTION *See* Romance fiction

REGENERATION (BIOLOGY)

Another fish tale [ependymal cells in knifefish spinal cord responsible for tissue regeneration; research by Marilyn Anderson] il *Discover* 10:15 Ag '89

Electrophysiologic responses in hamster superior colliculus evoked by regenerating retinal axons. S. A. Keirstead and others. bibl f il *Science* 246:255-7 O 13 '89

Regenerated nerves send first messages. R. Weiss. il *Science News* 136:244 O 14 '89

REGENS, JAMES L., AND OTHERS

Greenhouse gases, climate change, and U.S. forest markets. bibl f il *Environment* 31:4-5+ My '89

REGENT INTERNATIONAL HOTELS

Steep sleep. M. Beauchamp. il por *Forbes* 143:209 Ap 17 '89

REGENTS BOARD (N.Y.) *See* University of the State of New York. Board of Regents

REGGAE MUSIC

See also
Phonograph records—Reggae music
Tape recordings—Reggae music

REGIER, GAIL

Users, like me. il *Harper's* 278:51-4 My '89

REGINA (SASK.)

Crime

Murder on the prairie [Canadian TV show depicts C. Thatcher's 1983 murder of his wife] D. Turbide. il por *Maclean's* 102:45-6 Jl 17 '89

REGINATO, JAMES

Above it all. il por *House & Garden* 161:152-9+ Je '89

Earning his stripes [cover story] il pors *House & Garden* 161:224-7+ O '89

Island shelter. il por *House & Garden* 161:98-107 Ap '89

Paris on Park: Countess Eugenia de Serigny's Manhattan apartment. il por *Architectural Digest* 46:156-61 Ap '89

REGINATO, PETER, 1945-

about

Reginato's improvisations. C. Ratcliff. bibl f il *Art in America* 77:146-51 D '89

Timely obsessions. M. Guralnick. il pors *House & Garden* 161:94+ S '89

REGIONAL ADVERTISING

Playing to the home crowd. D. Tsiantar and A. Miller. il *Newsweek* 114:45 Ag 7 '89

REGIONAL AIRLINES *See* Airlines—Local service

REGIONAL HISTORY *See* Local history

REGIONAL LITERATURE

See also
Booksellers and bookselling—Regional literature
Publishers and publishing—Regional literature

REGIONAL PLANNING

See also
Bioregionalism
City planning
Shopping centers
Suburbs
Tennessee Valley Authority

Encountering the countryside (I). T. Hiss. il *The New Yorker* 65:40-2+ Ag 21 '89

Encountering the countryside (II). T. Hiss. il *The New Yorker* 65:37-40+ Ag 28 '89

Central America

See also
La Ruta Maya
Trifinio (Central America)

REGIONAL THEATER *See* Theater

REGIONALISM

Mapping the real geography. B. H. Lopez. *Harper's* 279:19-21+ N '89

History

Editorial [question of colonial regionalism] W. Garrett. *Antiques* 136:1319 D '89

Remapping American culture [D. H. Fischer traces regionalism back to early English settlers] A. P. Sanoff. il maps *U.S. News & World Report* 107:60-4 D 4 '89

United States

See Regionalism

REGISTER, JOHN, 1939-

about

John Register. M. E. Stegmaier. il *American Artist* 53:64-7+ F '89

REGISTERED CARE TECHNOLOGISTS *See* Health workers

REGISTERED NURSES *See* Nurses and nursing

REGISTERS OF BIRTHS, ETC.

Birth certificate says she's white, but woman gets a judge to declare her black [M. C. Walker] por *Jet* 76:36 S 18 '89

REGISTRATION OF ARCHITECTS *See* Architects—Licenses and registration

REGISTRATION OF SECURITIES *See* Securities—Registration

REGISTRATION OF TRUCKS *See* Trucks—Registration

REGISTRATION OF VOTERS *See* Voter registration

REGNERY, HENRY

about

Henry Regnery: a public private man. J. R. Coyne, Jr. il *National Review* 41:40-2 Je 16 '89

REGNERY GATEWAY, INC.

Henry Regnery: a public private man. J. R. Coyne, Jr. il *National Review* 41:40-2 Je 16 '89

REGO, PAULA, 1935-

about

Rego's girls. S. Kent. il *Art in America* 77:158-63+ Je '89

REGULATION OF BODY TEMPERATURE *See* Temperature, Animal and human

REGULATION OF INDUSTRY BY GOVERNMENT *See* Industry and state

REGULATORY AGENCIES

Watching the watchdogs [work of the Office of Management and Budget] S. Waldman. il *Newsweek* 113:34 F 20 '89

REHABILITATION

See also
Amputees—Rehabilitation
Drug abuse—Rehabilitation
Handicapped and animals
Mentally handicapped—Rehabilitation
Mentally ill—Rehabilitation
United States. Rehabilitation Services Administration

REHABILITATION CENTERS

See also
Delancey Street Foundation

REHABILITATION CENTERS—See also—*cont.*
  Drug abuse—Rehabilitation
REHEARSALS, DANCE *See* Dance production
REHEARSALS, TELEVISION *See* Television production and direction
REIBSTEIN, LARRY, AND FRIDAY, CAROLYN
  Warning: con men want to manage your money. il *Reader's Digest* 134:169-70+ My '89
REICH, CHARLES
  Lisa: betrayed by the law. por *Glamour* 87:195 Ap '89
REICH, MURRAY
      about
  Shirley Jaffe and Murray Reich at Artists Space. L. Campbell. il *Art in America* 77:199-200 N '89
REICH, ROBERT B.
  America pays the price. il *The New York Times Magazine* p32-3+ Ja 29 '89
  The future of work. *Harper's* 278:26+ Ap '89
  Pie-slicers vs. pie-enlargers. *The Washington Monthly* 21:60 F '89
  The quiet path to technological preeminence. bibl il *Scientific American* 261:41-7 O '89
  Wake-up call. il *Ms.* 18:32-3 O '89
REICHARDT, CARL E.
      about
  What are you going to do for us tomorrow? J. Heins. il por *Forbes* 143:51 F 6 '89
REICHERT, JACK FRANK
      about
  Has Brunswick gone overboard in powerboats? J. F. Siler. il *Business Week* p27 Ag 7 '89
REICHMANN BROTHERS
      about
  A unique monument to urban life [Reichmanns' Yerba Buena Gardens in San Francisco] P. C. Newman. il *Maclean's* 102:33 Mr 13 '89
REICK, FRANK
      about
  Super (conductor) man. A. Fisher. il por *Popular Science* 235:76-7 D '89
REID, ANTONIO
      about
  Black music's new hit doctors. S. Bloom. il pors *Rolling Stone* p32 My 18 '89
  L.A. & Babyface. il pors *Ebony* 44:134+ Je '89
REID, BILL, 1920-
      about
  Haidas on the Seine. N. Jennings. il por *Maclean's* 102:67-8 O 16 '89
REID, BRENDA OLCOTT- *See* Olcott-Reid, Brenda
REID, BRIAN HOLDEN
  Paperback history. *History Today* 39:51 Ap '89
  Theory from practice—Major General J.F.C. Fuller. bibl il pors *History Today* 39:44-9 Je '89
REID, CATHERINE
  Candice Bergen: finally getting it all together at 42. il pors *Good Housekeeping* 208:72+ Mr '89
REID, DAPHNE MAXWELL
      about
  Daphne Maxwell Reid still bitter over snub as beauty queen at Northwestern U. il pors *Jet* 77:25 N 13 '89
  She Snoops to conquer. B. O'Hallaren. il pors *TV Guide* 37:10-12 O 28-N 3 '89
  Tim Reid and Daphne Maxwell Reid return in new TV series 'Snoops' [cover story] pors *Jet* 76:58-60 S 18 '89
REID, FRANK M., D. 1989
      about
  Obituary
    Jet por 76:54 S 18 '89
REID, JAMES EARL
      about
  "The art case of the decade". S. Staggs. il *Art News* 88:49-50 Ap '89
  Copyright ruling favors artists. il *Art in America* 77:240 S '89
  Court aids freelancers in work-for-hire ruling. H. Fields. *Publishers Weekly* 235:11 Je 16 '89
  Professional page. D. Grant. *American Artist* 53:10+ Jl '89
  Sculpture clash. il *Time* 133:63 Ja 30 '89
  Supreme Court hears work-for-hire arguments. H. Fields. *Publishers Weekly* 235:14 Ap 14 '89
REID, JEFF
  Media watchdogs. il *Utne Reader* p110-12 My/Je '89
REID, JIM
      about
  Thar's gold, white gold, in them thar ponds, and golf ball hunter Jim Reid is diving to claim it. A. Abrahams. il *People Weekly* 31:67-8 Je 12 '89
REID, JOHN
      about
  Party hearty Elton John lights 40 candles in the wind for his manager's birthday. il pors *People Weekly* 32:40-1 S 25 '89
REID, JOSEPH
      about
  Bagging the Albatross. G. Byrne. il *Science* 243:32 Ja 6 '89

REID, L.A. *See* Reid, Antonio
REID, MIKE
      about
  Putting on the style. E. M. Swift. il pors *Sports Illustrated* 71:28-9 Ag 21 '89
REID, PEDRITO U. MAYNARD- *See* Maynard-Reid, Pedrito U.
REID, PETER C.
  How Harley beat back the Japanese [excerpt from Well-made in America] il *Fortune* 120:155+ S 25 '89
REID, RON, 1949-
  Quietly by canoe. il *Sierra* 74:112-13 My/Je '89
REID, TIM
      about
  Tim Reid and Daphne Maxwell Reid return in new TV series 'Snoops' [cover story] pors *Jet* 76:58-60 S 18 '89
  Tim Reid has a dream. R. Powers. il por *Gentlemen's Quarterly* 59:151-2+ N '89
REID, VERNON
      about
  One of rock's liveliest new bands comes to you in Living Colour. D. Grogan. il por *People Weekly* 32:84-5 Ag 21 '89
  Vernon Reid. B. Milkowski. il por *Down Beat* 56:26-7 My '89
REID, WALTER V. C.
  Sustainable development: lessons from success [cover story] bibl f il *Environment* 31:6-9+ My '89
REID BANKS, LYNNE, 1929-
      about
  Lynne Reid Banks. A. Smith. il por *Publishers Weekly* 236:30+ O 27 '89
REID-GREEN, KEITH S.
  The history of census tabulation. bibl il *Scientific American* 260:98-103 F '89
REIGER, GEORGE, 1939-
  Conservation. See issues of Field & Stream
REILLY, PETER
  Randy Travis. por *Stereo Review* 54:90-1 Je '89
REILLY, RICK
  2054: a sports odyssey. il *Sports Illustrated* 71 Special Issue:226-8+ N 15 '89
  An American classic [cover story] il pors *Sports Illustrated* 70:16-21 My 8 '89
  America's sweetheart. il pors *Sports Illustrated* 71:92-6+ N 27 '89
  Back in the groove. il *Sports Illustrated* 70:36-9 Ja 9 '89
  Captain Marvel. il pors *Sports Illustrated* 71:60-2+ S 18 '89
  Dash and flash. il pors *Sports Illustrated* 70:50-4 Ja 23 '89
  Dog days. il pors *Sports Illustrated* 71:58-60+ D 4 '89
  Give this plan an 'F'. por *Sports Illustrated* 71:100 S 18 '89
  The heavenly hundred: which numbers should be retired in whose honor. por *Sports Illustrated* 70:104 My 22 '89
  Here today, gone today. por *Sports Illustrated* 70:102 Mr 27 '89
  High noon at Troon. il por *Sports Illustrated* 71:20-2+ Jl 31 '89
  Hoch as in choke. il pors *Sports Illustrated* 70:62-4+ Je 12 '89
  ¡Hola! ¡Gracias! ¡Destapador! il *Sports Illustrated* 70 Special Issue:258-62+ F '89
  How cheap can you get? por *Sports Illustrated* 71:160 N 6 '89
  'I'm about to suffocate'. il pors *Sports Illustrated* 71:34-6+ N 6 '89
  It's time for a tune-up. il *Sports Illustrated* 70:80 Ja 16 '89
  King of the hill [cover story] il pors *Sports Illustrated* 70:20-5 Je 26 '89
  KJ! il pors *Sports Illustrated* 70:60+ Ap 24 '89
  Love that golf. il *Sports Illustrated* 71:70-6+ Ag 21 '89
  Masters of the '80s [cover story] il pors *Sports Illustrated* 71:44-9 D 18 '89
  No trick, just treat [cover story] il pors *Sports Illustrated* 70:14-17 Ja 16 '89
  Oh me, oh my, O'Meara! il pors *Sports Illustrated* 70:12-19 F 6 '89
  Seniority run rampant. por *Sports Illustrated* 71:80 Jl 17 '89
  Tannia and me. por *Sports Illustrated* 70 Special Issue:282 F '89
  West is best. il *Sports Illustrated* 70 Special Issue:8-14 Ap '89
  What price glory? il *Sports Illustrated* 70:32-4 F 27 '89
  Whoa, whippersnapper! [discussion of July 17, 1989 article, Seniority run rampant] il *Sports Illustrated* 71:90 Ag 14 '89
  You can count them out. il *Sports Illustrated* 71:86-96+ O 16 '89
REILLY, ROBERT T.
  Great expectations: what Catholics want from their priests. il *U.S. Catholic* 54:22-8 F '89
  How interfaith couples make the most of their differences. il *U.S. Catholic* 54:23-8 My '89

REILLY, WILLIAM K., 1940-
about
Can the EPA chief clean up Bush's image? V. Cahan. il pors *Business Week* p135-6 D 11 '89
EPA should clean up its own act. A. Ramirez. il por *Fortune* 120:139-40+ N 6 '89
Greening the White House [cover story] T. Gabriel. il pors *The New York Times Magazine* p24-7+ Ag 13 '89
Hazardous choice. V. Novak. *The Nation* 248:406-8 Mr 27 '89
Is Bill Reilly too nice to run the EPA? V. Cahan. il por *Business Week* p61 Ap 3 '89
Reilly vows environmental activism. L. Roberts. il por *Science* 243:731 F 10 '89
REIMAN, ERIC M., AND OTHERS
Neuroanatomical correlates of anticipatory anxiety. bibl f il *Science* 243:1071-4 F 24 '89
REIMER, BENNETT
A comprehensive arts curriculum model. il *Design for Arts in Education* 90:2-16 Jl/Ag '89
REIMER, JUDITH A.
One mother's story. il *Ladies' Home Journal* 106:90+ Ap '89
REIMS (FRANCE)
Description
Reims remembered. I. Ireland. il *Road & Track* 40:90-2+ Mr '89
REINDEER
See also
Caribou
REINDERS, JIM
about
In a Nebraska wheat field stands Carhenge, attracting a bumper crop of tourists—and trouble. M. Neill. il por *People Weekly* 32:196-7 D 11 '89
REINER, CARL, 1922-
about
Bert Rigby, you're a fool [film] Reviews
Time il 133:82 F 27 '89. R. Schickel
REINER, FRITZ, 1888-1963
about
Encores. R. Freed. pors *Stereo Review* 54:162 D '89
REINER, ROB
about
Pals. R. Lloyd. il pors *American Film* 14:28-33+ Jl/Ag '89
When Harry met Sally . . . [film] Reviews
The American Spectator 22:38-40 O '89. B. Bawer
Commonweal 116:472 S 8 '89. P. D. Baumann
Maclean's il 102:51 Jl 24 '89. B. D. Johnson
The New Republic 201:26-8 Ag 21 '89. S. Kauffmann
New York il 22:50+ Jl 24 '89. D. Denby
The New Yorker 65:74-5 Ag 7 '89. T. Rafferty
Newsweek il 114:52 Jl 17 '89. D. Ansen
People Weekly il 32:13-14 Jl 24 '89. R. Novak
Rolling Stone il p32 Ag 10 '89
Time il 134:65 Jl 31 '89. R. Corliss
REINFORCEMENT (PSYCHOLOGY)
Addiction and IQ [brain cells conditioned to crave cocaine; research by Larry Stein and James Belluzzi] L. Marsa. il *Omni (New York, N.Y.)* 12:24+ O '89
REINGANUM, MARC
about
This professor majors in finding stocks that double in value. B. Hager. il por *Money* 18:153-4 F '89
REINHARDT, RICHARD, 1927-
Careless love. il *Wilderness* 52:16-27 Summ '89
The other fair. il *American Heritage* 40:42-7+ My/Je '89
REINISCH, JUNE
about
Sex (research) scandals! E. E. Goode. il pors *U.S. News & World Report* 106:54-5 Ja 9 '89
REINVESTMENT OF DIVIDENDS *See* Dividend reinvestment
REIS, RICARDO *See* Pessoa, Fernando, 1888-1935
REISS, RICHARD
about
Richard Reiss. P. Noglows. il por *Channels (New York, N.Y.: 1986)* 9:54 Jl/Ag '89
REISS, WINOLD, 1886-1953
about
An eye on ethnicity [cover story] B. Jacob. il por *American Visions* 4:14-19 O '89
An immigrant artist captured the faces of the New World. J. H. Heminway. il pors *Smithsonian* 20:172-8+ N '89
REISSUES OF PHONOGRAPH RECORDS *See* Phonograph records—Reissues
REIT, SEYMOUR
When siblings are different. il *Good Housekeeping* 209:126+ S '89
REITER-SOFFER, DOMY
about
Lady of the camellias [ballet] Reviews
Dance Magazine il 63:26 Mr '89. R. Libermann
Oscar [ballet] Reviews
Dance Magazine 63:100+ My '89. C. Swift
REITH, ALMA CARMICHAEL
To hold and to have [poem] il *Good Housekeeping* 208:262 My '89

REITH, KATHRYN M.
Attack the gender gap in amateur sports. il *Women's Sports & Fitness* 11:64 Je '89
Coaches wanted, unlimited benefits. il *Women's Sports & Fitness* 11:64 Jl/Ag '89
Four of the best join the greatest. il *Women's Sports & Fitness* 11:56-7 Ja/F '89
Make a move on the media. il *Women's Sports & Fitness* 11:70 S '89
A mixed report about high school sports. il *Women's Sports & Fitness* 11:64 N/D '89
Title IX is back in action! il *Women's Sports & Fitness* 11:74 Mr '89
Tomorrow's stars: the 1989 Secret Up & Coming Award winners. il *Women's Sports & Fitness* 11:64-5 O '89
Women in Sports: a day to celebrate. il *Women's Sports & Fitness* 11:72 My '89
REITMAN, IVAN
about
Ghostbusters II [film] Reviews
New York il 22:46 Jl 17 '89. D. Denby
The New Yorker 65:85 Jl 10 '89. P. Kael
Newsweek il 113:68 Je 26 '89. D. Ansen
People Weekly il 32:14-15 Jl 3 '89. R. Novak
Rolling Stone il por p52-4+ Je 1 '89. P. Goldstein
Time il 133:89 Je 26 '89. R. Schickel
Video il 13:87 D '89. J. Young
Raising 'Twins' [interview] L. Snowden. il por *Rolling Stone* p20 Ja 26 '89
Twins [film] Reviews
The Humanist il 49:39 Mr/Ap '89. H. M. Geduld
Video il 13:61 Jl '89. J. Bernard
REITSEMA, H. J., AND OTHERS
Active polar region on the nucleus of Comet Halley. bibl f il *Science* 243:198-200 Ja 13 '89
REJECTION (ORGANS, TISSUES, ETC.) *See* Immunological tolerance
REJECTION (PSYCHOLOGY)
Don't say no! C. Marberry. por *Essence* 19:12 Ap '89
Don't take no for an answer. P. Edwards and S. Edwards. il *Home Office Computing* 7:46 O '89
It's 10 p.m. Why haven't you been rejected yet? E. Welty. il *Mademoiselle* 95:172-3+ Ag '89
Kids without friends. P. Chance. il *Psychology Today* 23:28-31 Ja/F '89
Rejection in Hollywood: how the stars cope. I. Chubbuck. il *TV Guide* 37:16-18 O 7-13 '89
Rejection protection: landing on your feet [special section] *Harper's Bazaar* 122:102-3+ Ja '89
RELATIONAL DATABASES
See also
Interactive marketing
Reflex (Computer program)
A brave new world? F. Pascal. bibl f il *Byte* 14:247-50+ S '89
dBase IV is a godsend—to the competition [glitches] P. Cole. il *Business Week* p102 N 13 '89
dBugs in dBase IV spread to the bottom line [Ashton-Tate] P. Cole. il *Business Week* p135-6 Jl 17 '89
A family of models. J. Dawson. bibl f il *Byte* 14:277-8+ S '89
If we could talk to the database . . . [SQL] M. Bryan. il *Personal Computing* 13:51-2+ Mr '89
Is Ashton-Tate born again? [with editorial comment by Fred Abatemarco] C. Strehlo. il *Personal Computing* 13:5, 66-9+ Mr '89
Keys to dBase IV programming. M. Liskin. il *Personal Computing* 13:51-2+ Ap '89
The spotlight turns to database servers. M. Liskin. il *Personal Computing* 13:53-6 N '89
SQL: a database language sequel to dBASE. M. L. Van Name and B. Catchings. *Byte* 14 Special Issue:175-8+ Fall '89
Testing
Alpha Four: no programming required. M. Rubel. il *Byte* 14:265-6+ N '89
Borland's new Paradox [version 3.0] B. Krasnoff. il *Personal Computing* 13:29 F '89
Clipper applications get SQL. M. Schnapp. *Byte* 14:211-12+ D '89
Customize without programming [Alpha Four] C. O'Malley. il *Personal Computing* 13:200 D '89
Database managers. il *Personal Computing* 13:151-6+ D '89
Database power with a graphical interface [Superbase 4] M. Liskin. il *Personal Computing* 13:176+ Je '89
dBase IV arrives. M. Rubel. il *Byte* 14:217-18+ F '89
dBase IV faces the competition. M. Liskin. il *Personal Computing* 13:79-81+ Mr '89
dBase IV: setting the new standard? A. F. Lent and M. Rubel. *Byte* 14:102+ Ja '89
A pair of Paradox helpers [DataFinder and ScriptView] S. Miastkowski. il *Byte* 14:100 Je '89
Paradox 3.0: new features, same basics. J. Devlin. il *Personal Computing* 13:195-6 Mr '89
Paradox 3: neither enigma nor riddle. S. Miastkowski and N. Baran. *Byte* 14:109-11 F '89
Serving business [SQL database server products] W. Rash, Jr. il *Byte* 14:147-8+ N '89

RELATIONAL DATABASES—Testing—*cont.*
Superbase 4. N. Baran. il *Byte* 14:221-2+ Mr '89
Superbase 4: bringing the power of windows to databases.
M. Bryan. il *Personal Computing* 13:154-5 D '89
RELATIVES *See* Family
RELATIVISM *See* Relativity
RELATIVITY
    See also
       Subjectivity
The opening of the American mind [case for relativism
over absolutes] A. M. Schlesinger. *The New York Times
Book Review* 94:1+ Jl 23 '89
RELATIVITY (PHYSICS)
    See also
       Field theory (Physics)
       Gravity and gravitation
       Quantum theory
       Space and time
The concept of mass. L. B. Okun'. bibl f il *Physics Today*
42:31-6 Je '89
Cosmological constant conundrum. *Sky and Telescope*
78:132-3 Ag '89
DI Herculis explained? *Sky and Telescope* 78:14 Jl '89
Did Einstein espouse his spouse's ideas? [discussion of May
1987 article, Einstein and ether drift experiments] J. Stachel.
il *Physics Today* 42:9+ F '89
Why is the cosmological constant so very small? B. M.
Schwarzschild. bibl f il *Physics Today* 42:21-4 Mr '89
RELAXATION
6 natural tranquilizers and how to use them. J. Mullich.
il *Prevention (Emmaus, Pa.)* 41:41-6 Ag '89
Diabetes? Relax! [after meals] il *Prevention (Emmaus, Pa.)*
41:10+ N '89
Life is but a dream [alert relaxation techniques for experiencing
waking dreams; cover story] K. Harary and P. Weintraub.
il *Omni (New York, N.Y.)* 12:42-4+ N '89
Mental matchplay: how to relax between points. J. E. Loehr.
il *World Tennis* 37:54-5 D '89
The prayer war [relaxation response theories of H. Benson]
S. Kiesling and T. G. Harris. *Psychology Today* 23:65-6
O '89
Relax to the max [running] J. Lynch. il *Runner's World*
24:38-40 Mr '89
A shortcut to mellow [instant calming sequence] M. Madsen.
il *Women's Sports & Fitness* 11:14 Ap '89
Simple holiday stress relievers. J. Mullich. il *Reader's Digest*
135:49-50+ D '89
Trash is good for you. K. Robinson. il *Glamour* 87:133
My '89
RELAXATION TIME (PHYSICS)
Time to relax [fractal time; cover story] I. Peterson. il *Science
News* 135:157-9 Mr 11 '89
RELAY MIRROR EXPERIMENT (ARTIFICIAL SATEL-
LITE)
Relay Mirror Experiment spacecraft completes environmental,
optical tests. il *Aviation Week & Space Technology* 131:51+
N 13 '89
SDI experiments set for launch in January. P. A. Gilmartin.
il *Aviation Week & Space Technology* 131:35 S 11 '89
RELAYS, ELECTRIC *See* Electric relays
RELENTLESS [film] *See* Motion picture reviews—Single works
RELIABILITY
Tests to target dependability [employment tests] T. J. Burns.
il *Nation's Business* 77:26+ Mr '89
RELIABILITY (ENGINEERING)
    See also
       Quality control
Reliability of electric service. P. H. Abelson. *Science* 245:689
Ag 18 '89
The secret of life at the limits: cogs become big wheels
[research by Todd La Porte and others] J. E. Pfeiffer.
il *Smithsonian* 20:38-46+ Jl '89
RELIANCE ELECTRIC CO.
What LBOs really do to R&D spending. A. Ramirez. il
Fortune 119:98 Mr 13 '89
RELIANCE GROUP HOLDINGS, INC.
Birthday present. T. Jaffe. il por *Forbes* 144:42-3 S 4 '89
RELIEF PITCHERS (BASEBALL PLAYERS) *See* Baseball
players
RELIEF WORK
    See also
       Evacuation of civilians
       Food banks
       United States. Federal Emergency Management Agency
Filling the gaps [helping the homeless] E. Whitford. il
Scholastic Update (Teachers' edition) 121:18-19 F 10 '89
Good neighbors [volunteers assisting New York City poor]
H. Evans. il *U.S. News & World Report* 106:76 Ap 10
'89
Harvest of love [KBTN pitches in to help get food to needy
families in Neosho, Mo.] A. Winegardner. il por *Good
Housekeeping* 209:130+ D '89
Help for the homeless. R. R. Roha. il *Changing Times*
43:100+ Ja '89
Ministries come to aid of quake victims [San Francisco
Bay area] il *Christianity Today* 33:74-5 N 17 '89

One teen's campaign for the homeless [work of T. Ferrell]
P. W. Cohen. il pors *Scholastic Update (Teachers' edition)*
121:20-2 F 10 '89
Shut in but not shut off, actor Dick York gives the time
he has left to the homeless. T. Allis. il pors *People Weekly*
31:209-10+ Mr 6 '89
The storm after Hugo. J. N. Baker. il *Newsweek* 114:40
O 9 '89
What it's like to aid the homeless [Washington, D.C.] R.
R. Roha. il *Changing Times* 43:80-1 Jl '89
                     International aspects
    See also
       Missions, Medical
       Salvation Army
       UNICEF
         Photographs and photography
World Vision [work of photographers E. Mooneyham and
T. Owens and D. Ward] B. Brander. ii *Petersen's
Photographic Magazine* 18:24-6+ Je '89
                   Afghanistan
After the Soviets go. E. MacFarquhar. il map *U.S. News
& World Report* 106:32-4+ F 13 '89
                    Africa
Africa better prepared to deal with catastrophes [WHO opens
Regional Centre for Emergency Preparedness and Response]
il *World Health* p30-1 Mr '89
Before death, Leland wrote in Ebony about starvation in
Africa. il pors *Jet* 76:16-18+ Ag 28 '89
Hunger in Africa: why it persists, why we must care [cover
story; special section] il map *Scholastic Update (Teachers'
edition)* 121:2-15 Ja 27 '89
What African-Americans can do about starvation in Africa.
M. Leland. il *Ebony* 44:80-2+ O '89
Who will step forward to fulfill Leland's agenda? S. Jones.
il *Black Enterprise* 20:21 O '89
           Armenia (Soviet Union)
Anguish in Armenia. il *Reader's Digest* 134:140-6 Mr '89
Armenia: what U.S. companies did. F. H. Katayama. il
Fortune 119:10-11 Ja 16 '89
Armenian earthquakes and Soviet tremors. G. J. Libaridian.
Society 26:59-63 Mr/Ap '89
Christians send aid to Armenian quake victims. *Christianity
Today* 33:62-3 Ja 13 '89
Gorbachev in Armenia. M. Kempton. il *The New York
Review of Books* 35:58 Ja 19 '89
A struggle for new life. A. Wilson-Smith. il *Maclean's* 102:20-2
Ap 24 '89
            Developing countries
    See also
       Food for the Poor (Organization)
101 uses for a T-shirt [donating running T-shirts] R. Rodale.
il por *Runner's World* 24:26 Ag '89
                 El Salvador
Unwelcome in El Salvador [treatment of volunteers assisting
refugees] J. Lindsay-Poland. il *The Progressive* 53:32-5 My
'89
                   Ethiopia
Congressman Leland dies in plane crash during mission
to feed the hungry. il *Jet* 76:10-13+ Ag 28 '89
Five years after the famine. R. Wilson. il *Christianity Today*
33:50-1 O 6 '89
The nonstory of the year. H. Smith. *Christianity Today*
33:15 F 17 '89
One teen's struggle to end hunger [student M. Varilla raises
funds for Ethiopian relief] L. Eskin. il por *Scholastic Update
(Teachers' edition)* 121:12-13 Ja 27 '89
                   Honduras
A Hobson's choice for Miskito refugees. M. D. Wilde. il
The Christian Century 106:726-8 Ag 2-9 '89
                   Jamaica
Blessings from and for the poor [work of Food for the
Poor in Kingston, Jamaica] M. G. Harter. il *America*
161:395-8 D 2 '89
                   Kenya
Two lives for the Ariaal. E. M. Fratkin. il map *Natural
History* p38-49 My '89
                  Middle East
    See also
       United Nations Relief and Works Agency for Palestine
       Refugees in the Near East
                   Nicaragua
    See also
       Evangelical Committee for Aid and Development in
       Nicaragua
                   Pakistan
Afghanistan after the turmoil. M. Hussein. il *World Health*
p11-12 Jl '89
                   Philippines
Exploring the dark side of paradise, an American couple
takes up misery's gauntlet [work of D. and T. Palmeri]
M. Green. il pors *People Weekly* 32:93-4+ N 27 '89
                   Sudan
Desperate hunger. D. Jones. il *Maclean's* 102:29+ Je 12
'89
Famine. R. Bonner. map *The New Yorker* 65:85-96+ Mr
13 '89
'Operation Lifeline Sudan' launched; 100,000 lives at stake.
il *UN Chronicle* 26:35 Je '89

RELIEF WORK—Sudan—*cont.*
Peace and relief in Sudan. *Department of State Bulletin* 89:24-6 Ap '89
Politics block relief efforts to Sudan. K. Blomquist. il map *Christianity Today* 33:40-1 Ap 7 '89
Starvation as a political weapon. L. Lief. il map *U.S. News & World Report* 106:34-5+ F 6 '89
United States
See Relief work
Virgin Islands of the United States
Hurricane Hugo aftermath: train Caribbean victims in skills needed to rebuild their homes, Jackson says. D. M. Cheers. il pors *Jet* 77:22-3+ O 23 '89

RELIGION
See also
AIDS (Disease)—Religious aspects
Alcohol and religion
Animals—Religious aspects
Art and religion
Artists—Religious life
Arts and religion
Atheism
Authors—Religious life
Baby boom generation—Religious life
Baseball fans—Religious life
Baseball players—Religious life
Black celebrities—Religious life
Black children—Religious life
Blacks—Religious life
Catholic Church
Children of divorced parents—Religious life
Chinese—North America—Religious life
Chinese Americans—Religious life
Christianity
Christianity and other religions
Church
College students—Religious life
Comic books, strips, etc.—Religious use
Computers—Religious use
Conductors (Music)—Religious life
Cults
Dance—Moral and religious aspects
Death—Religious aspects
Direct broadcast satellite services—Religious programs
Evangelicalism
Faith
Family—Religious life
Football players—Religious life
Fundamentalism
God
Gods and goddesses
Hispanic Americans—Religious life
Humanism
Indians of Central America—Religion and mythology
Indians of North America—Religion and mythology
Indians of South America—Religion and mythology
Interfaith marriage
Islam
Japanese Americans—Religious life
Jesus Christ
Judaism
Korean Americans—Religious life
Lawyers—Religious life
Liberalism (Religion)
Literature—Moral and religious aspects
Mass media in religion
Medicine and religion
Men—Religious life
Minorities—Religious life
Mithraism
Mothers—Religious life
Motion picture actors and actresses—Religious life
Motion pictures—Moral and religious aspects
Musicians—Religious life
Mysticism
Mythology
Nuclear weapons—Moral and religious aspects
Paganism
Palestinian Arabs—Religious life
Prayer
Preaching
Primitivism in religion
Professionals—Religious life
Protestant churches
Public schools and religion
Radio broadcasting—Religious programs
Religious education
Religious liberty
Religious pluralism
Revivals
Revolutions and religion
Sects
Secularism
Servicemen—Religious life
Sex and religion
Shamans and shamanism
Sick—Religious life
Sin

Spiritual life
Spirituality
Sunday
Television broadcasting—Moral and religious aspects
Television broadcasting—Religious programs
Theism
Theology
Theosophy
Transcendental meditation
Trees in religion, folklore, etc.
Veterans—Religious life
Videotapes—Religious use
War and religion
Women—Religious life
Women and religion
Worship
Youth—Religious life
Two from the heart [interviews with E. Bombeck and H. Kushner] M. Lodge. il pors *Ladies' Home Journal* 106:78+ D '89
Anecdotes, facetiae, satire, etc.
How to start a religion. O. Johnson. por *The Humanist* 49:16-17+ N/D '89
Awards
See also
Templeton Foundation Prize for Progress in Religion
Bibliography
Book briefs. W. Griffin. il *Christianity Today* 33:32-3 Ap 7 '89
Book reviews. A. L. Laffey. *America* 160:403-5 Ap 29 '89
Books. See issues of The Christian Century
Books. See issues of Christianity Today
[Column] G. M. Costello. See issues of U.S. Catholic beginning January 1985
Experience & the claims of faith. L. Cunningham. *Commonweal* 116:379-80 Je 16 '89
Religious Book Week: critics' choices. il *Commonweal* 116:148-58 Mr 10 '89
Religious books: fall 1989. W. Griffin. il *Publishers Weekly* 236:34+ O 6 '89
Religious books: spring 1989. il *Publishers Weekly* 235:40-57 Mr 3 '89
Encyclopedias
A guide to homo religiosus [Encyclopedia of religion; cover story] P. Olson. *The Christian Century* 106:655-7 Jl 5-12 '89
Study and teaching
See also
American Academy of Religion
The high priest of scholarship [R. W. Lynn] K. L. Woodward. il por *Newsweek* 114:52 Ag 7 '89
RELIGION, PRIMITIVE
See also
Voodooism
RELIGION AND AGRICULTURE
Church exchange strengthens urban/rural ties [Brooklyn's Zion Lutheran Church and Elstad-Highland Prairie Churches, Minn.] B. Heidtke. *Successful Farming* 87:F4 D '89
The future of rural populism. B. W. Hargrove. bibl *Society* 26:39-44 Ja/F '89
RELIGION AND CULTURE
See also
Christianity and culture
RELIGION AND EDUCATION See Church schools; Public schools and religion
RELIGION AND GEOGRAPHY
See also
Sacred space
RELIGION AND JUSTICE
Faith and justice: a delicate balance [care for the poor] A. DiIanni. il *America* 161:32-4+ Jl 15-22 '89
The journey to justice [cover story] W. J. O'Malley. *America* 161:28-31 Jl 15-22 '89
RELIGION AND LABOR See Church and labor
RELIGION AND LAW
Love takes you a long way [activist lawyer L. Pitts] W. H. Willimon. *The Christian Century* 106:460-1 My 3 '89
Not dumb persons [jurors in trial of O. L. North] M. E. Marty. *The Christian Century* 106:575 My 24-31 '89
RELIGION AND LITERATURE See Literature—Moral and religious aspects
RELIGION AND MUSIC
See also
Christian contemporary music
Rock music—Moral and religious aspects
RELIGION AND PEACE
See also
Church and disarmament
A prayer of hope: religion as a key to cooperation. K. Henderson. por *The Humanist* 49:23-4+ Mr/Ap '89
Shalom! P. J. Ryan. *America* 161:22 Jl 1-8 '89
RELIGION AND POLITICS
See also
Bishops—Political activities
Black clergy—Political activities
Catholics—United States—Political activities
Christianity and democracy
Communism and religion

RELIGION AND POLITICS—See also—*cont.*
  Congressmen—Religious life
  International Christian Embassy Jerusalem (Organization)
  Jews—United States—Political activities
  Moral Majority
  Priests—Political activities
  Public officers—Religious life
  Religion and peace
  Socialism and religion
The battle for the Catholic Church [P. Lernoux's People of God] P. Berryman. por *The Christian Century* 106:523-6 My 17 '89
Can we be good without God? [political meaning of Christianity; cover story] G. Tinder. il *The Atlantic* 264:68-72+ D '89
Filling in the gaps of liberal culture [Robert Booth Fowler's Unconventional partners: religion and liberal culture in the United States] M. E. Marty. *The Christian Century* 106:1019-20+ N 8 '89
Focus bids farewell to EPA [Evangelical Press Association] il *Christianity Today* 33:40 Mr 17 '89
If you don't swing, you can't zing [evangelical Republicans] il *U.S. News & World Report* 106:12 Je 26 '89
Jews and Christians: striving to shape America's future. R. F. Thiemann. il *USA Today (Periodical)* 118:84-7 S '89
Join it, work it, fight it [public Catholicism] D. J. O'Brien. il *Commonweal* 116:624-30 N 17 '89
Measuring character in the headlines. J. M. Wall. *The Christian Century* 106:275-6 Mr 15 '89
The new coalitions [evangelicals and others] C. F. H. Henry. il *Christianity Today* 33:26-8 N 17 '89
Politics: not the dirty word it used to be [Christian perspectives: issues facing the new administration conference] M. L. Chandler. il *Christianity Today* 33:50-1 Mr 3 '89
Religion and power in the American experience. N. J. Demerath and R. H. Williams. bibl il *Society* 26:29-38 Ja/F '89
Religion in the Bush White House. R. G. Hutcheson. *The Christian Century* 106:37-8 Ja 18 '89
Rev. Moon's rising political influence [American Freedom Coalition] J. B. Judis. il *U.S. News & World Report* 106:27-9+ Mr 27 '89
A reverence for fundamentalism [Catholic Church] P. Lernoux. il *The Nation* 248:513-16 Ap 17 '89
Right-wing activists take aim at Bush. J. M. Wall. *The Christian Century* 106:163-4 F 15 '89
Seeking humility in political debate. P. B. Henry. *The Christian Century* 106:303 Mr 22-29 '89
Should religion concern itself with political and social questions? [views of J. Macmurray] W. A. Barry. *America* 161:61-2+ Jl 29-Ag 5 '89
Were Christians courted for their votes or beliefs? R. Frame. il *Christianity Today* 33:38-9 F 17 '89
Whatever happened to the religious right? K. A. Lawton. il *Christianity Today* 33:44+ D 15 '89
Whither the Christian right? K. Fahey. il *Utne Reader* p22 Ja/F '89
RELIGION AND PSYCHOLOGY See Psychology, Religious
RELIGION AND SCIENCE
  See also
  Creation
  Evolution
  Nature—Religious interpretations
  Religion and space research
  Religion and technology
A common quest for understanding [letter by John Paul II] E. McMullin. il *America* 160:100-2+ F 11 '89
A leap in the light: faith, science, & the imagination. W. J. O'Malley. il *Commonweal* 116:141-3+ Mr 10 '89
The love of randomness. D. K. Mano. *National Review* 41:58-9 O 13 '89
Physics and Christmas. *National Review* 41:15 D 31 '89
RELIGION AND SOCIAL PROBLEMS See Church and social problems
RELIGION AND SOCIOLOGY
  See also
  Sociology, Christian
RELIGION AND SPACE RESEARCH
Religion and space technology. M. Gordon. il *The Futurist* 23:60 Jl/Ag '89
RELIGION AND SPORTS
  See also
  Football, College—Religious aspects
  Football, High school—Religious aspects
RELIGION AND STATE See Church and state; Religious liberty
RELIGION AND TECHNOLOGY
Capitalism and technology in global perspective: a dispute [discussion of May 3, 1989 article, The theological challenge of globalization] M. L. Stackhouse. *The Christian Century* 106:690-3 Jl 19-26 '89
RELIGION AND THE ENVIRONMENT
  See also
  AuSable Institute of Environmental Studies
Christian ecology. P. Stone. il *The Mother Earth News* 115:58-61 Ja/F '89
Christian ecology: a growing force in the environmental movement. P. Stone. *Utne Reader* p78-9 N/D '89

Crabgrass wars: my father's surrender. W. French. il *Commonweal* 116:421-2 Ag 11 '89
The earth groans, and Christians are listening. K. G. Streiffert. il *Christianity Today* 33:38+ S 22 '89
The earth, its body is my body. *America* 161:368 N 25 '89
Environmental crisis: put Christian virtues at your disposal [interview with F. W. Krueger] por *U.S. Catholic* 54:25-30 O '89
The greening of the church. B. Carpenter. il *U.S. News & World Report* 107:66-7 N 27 '89
Human folly on a grand scale. L. O. Sanneh. il *The Christian Century* 106:843 S 27 '89
The management of the biosphere [address, July 19, 1989] P. C. Cato. *Vital Speeches of the Day* 56:53-5 N 1 '89
A new story of creation [theology of ecology] K. L. Woodward. il por *Newsweek* 113:70-2 Je 5 '89
Renewing the earth. A. McCarthy. il *Commonweal* 116:586 N 3 '89
Theology not ecology [interview] N. Gardels. il *New Perspectives Quarterly* 6:36-9 Spr '89
'This precious home for all us earthlings'. *America* 160:363 Ap 22 '89
Thomas Berry and a new creation story [eco-spiritual movement] M. Hope and J. Young. il por *The Christian Century* 106:750-3 Ag 16-23 '89
RELIGION IN LITERATURE
  See also
  Priests in literature
America's moral landscape in the fiction of Richard Ford. R. A. Schroth. por *The Christian Century* 106:227-30 Mr 1 '89
And now, a word from our Creator [God as a subject in fiction] D. Wakefield. il *The New York Times Book Review* 94:1+ F 12 '89
Annie Dillard: pilgrim at midstream. P. S. Hawkins. *The Christian Century* 106:592-5 Je 7-14 '89
The battle for the imagination [need for Christianity to be portrayed sympathetically] J. N. Akers. il *Christianity Today* 33:13 Je 16 '89
Fathers & their sons [novels of W. Kennedy] D. M. Murtaugh. il por *Commonweal* 116:298-302 My 19 '89
A literary roundup. J. P. Baumgaertner. il *The Christian Century* 106:1048-50 N 15 '89
The message the Japanese have missed [views of S. Endo] P. Yancey. il *Christianity Today* 33:56 Mr 17 '89
Never a question of easy grace [Catholicism in the novels of T. Keneally] P. D. Baumann. il por *Commonweal* 116:395-400 Jl 14 '89
Owen Meany and the presence of God [novel by J. Irving] J. M. Wall. *The Christian Century* 106:299-300 Mr 22-29 '89
A silence that is not hollow [works of S. Endo] E. Beverly. il por *Commonweal* 116:491-4 S 22 '89
Updike's song of himself [Self-consciousness] R. C. Wood. il por *The Christian Century* 106:526-8 My 17 '89
Walking the tightrope of mystery [works of B. Moore] J. V. Long. il por *Commonweal* 116:555-8 O 20 '89
Writing with intent [Catholicism in the novels of M. Spark; cover story] R. E. Hosmer. il pors *Commonweal* 116:233-41 Ap 21 '89
RELIGION IN POETRY
  See also
  Jesus Christ in poetry
Gerard Manley Hopkins [cover story; special section; with editorial comment by George W. Hunt] *America* 161:98, 102-9 Ag 26-S 2 '89
RELIGION IN PUBLIC SCHOOLS See Public schools and religion
RELIGIONS See Religion
RELIGIOUS (CATHOLIC CHURCH) See Catholic Church—Clergy
RELIGIOUS ADVERTISING
Help wanted: a few good fishers of men [TV ad campaign for priests in Boston] *Newsweek* 113:61 Je 26 '89
RELIGIOUS ALLIANCE AGAINST PORNOGRAPHY
Pornography foes urge renewed awareness. il *Christianity Today* 33:48-9 D 15 '89
RELIGIOUS ARCHITECTURE See Churches (Buildings)
RELIGIOUS ART, CHRISTIAN See Christian art and symbolism
RELIGIOUS CANDLES See Votive candles
RELIGIOUS CONFERENCES
  See also
  Catholic Church. National Conference of Catholic Bishops
  Consultation on Church Union
  Synod of Bishops (1987)
The ivory tower comes to the Windy City [1988 meeting of American Academy of Religion and Society of Biblical Literature; cover story] R. Clapp. il *Christianity Today* 33:16-21 Ap 7 '89
Rattling the dry bones of the student Christian movement [denominational conferences] D. G. Shockley. *The Christian Century* 106:1087-9 N 22 '89
Trying to hold on to the Medellín legacy [Notre Dame conference marks 20th anniversary of Latin American Bishops' Conference] D. G. Peerman. *The Christian Century* 106:403-4 Ap 19 '89

RELIGIOUS CONFERENCES—*cont.*

What does it mean to be evangelical? [conference at Trinity Evangelical Divinity School] il *Christianity Today* 33:60+ Je 16 '89

Brazil

A new Pentecost: hope in solidarity [Latin American Council of Churches assembly in Indaiatuba, Brazil] J. H. Sinclair. il *The Christian Century* 106:83-4 Ja 25 '89

Philippines

Global camp meeting [Lausanne II in Manila] L. Cryderman. il *Christianity Today* 33:39-41 Ag 18 '89

High hopes for Lausanne II [Manila] W. Conard. il *Christianity Today* 33:44 F 17 '89

Lausanne II: reshaping world evangelicalism. R. V. Pierard. *The Christian Century* 106:740-2 Ag 16-23 '89

Lausanne lives on. *Christianity Today* 33:15 S 8 '89

Manila Manifesto to undergo further study [Lausanne II] L. Cryderman. il *Christianity Today* 33:62-3 S 8 '89

The Prayboy Club [attending Lausanne II] J. I. Packer. il *Christianity Today* 33:11 O 20 '89

Singapore

AD 2000: eleven years to reach the world [Global Consultation on World Evangelization by AD 2000 and beyond] A. Toalston. il *Christianity Today* 33:48+ F 3 '89

Switzerland

See also

Lausanne Committee for World Evangelization

RELIGIOUS COOPERATION

See also

Ecumenical movement

Unity and community. P. J. Ryan. *America* 160:407 Ap 29 '89

RELIGIOUS DANCE *See* Dance in religion, folklore, etc.

RELIGIOUS DISCRIMINATION IN EMPLOYMENT *See* Discrimination in employment

RELIGIOUS EDUCATION

See also

Bible—Study and teaching
Catholic Church—Education
Church colleges and universities
Church schools
Jesuits—Education
Religion—Study and teaching
Sunday schools
Theology—Study and teaching

Candlemess. M. E. Marty. *The Christian Century* 106:95 Ja 25 '89

Transmitting a vision: religion in independent schools. D. R. Heischman. *The Christian Century* 106:417-9 Ap 19 '89

RELIGIOUS FAITH *See* Faith

RELIGIOUS FREEDOM *See* Religious liberty

RELIGIOUS HISTORY *See* Church history

RELIGIOUS HOLIDAYS *See* Holidays

RELIGIOUS INVESTMENT FRAUD

Cashing in on conversions [B. Dintino accused of conning churches by claiming to be a disenchanted Mormon missionary] por *Christianity Today* Je 16 '89

The land of bilk and money. D. Alexander. il *The Humanist* 49:43-4 N/D '89

Let us prey: false prophets con believers. il *Consumers' Research Magazine* 72:17-19 O '89

Swindlers prey on trust of believers. K. A. Lawton. il *Christianity Today* 33:42-3 S 22 '89

RELIGIOUS LIBERTY

See also

Church and state
Persecution
Sunday—Laws and regulations
Taxation, Exemption from
Williamsburg charter

Brainwashed or converted? [suit against Unification Church by former members] L. D. Streiker. *The Christian Century* 106:721-3 Ag 2-9 '89

Peyote, wine and the First Amendment [case before Supreme Court on religious use of peyote] D. Laycock. *The Christian Century* 106:876-80 O 4 '89

Teaching religious liberty—the wrong way [Williamsburg Charter curriculum supplements for U.S. history courses] E. Doerr. il *The Humanist* 49:41-2 N/D '89

Two centuries of Virginia's Act for Religious Freedom. E. Turner. il *USA Today (Periodical)* 117:73-5 Mr '89

Bulgaria

No *glasnost* yet for religion in Bulgaria. J. A. Broun. *The Christian Century* 106:1124-5 N 29 '89

Soviet Union

New freedoms for old faiths. il *Time* 133:100-1 Ap 10 '89

Religious liberties long denied [Washington, D.C. conference] T. P. O'Malley. *America* 161:229 O 14 '89

RELIGIOUS LIFE *See* Christian life; Spiritual life

RELIGIOUS LITERATURE

See also

Christian literature
Publishers and publishing—Religious literature
Religion—Bibliography

RELIGIOUS MEDITATION *See* Meditation

RELIGIOUS MUSIC

See also

Choirs
Gospel music
Hymns
Oratorio

The practical life of the church musician [cover story] P. Westermeyer. il *The Christian Century* 106:812-14 S 13-20 '89

Robert Shaw's ministry of music. H. Ziegenhals. il por *The Christian Century* 106:311-13 Mr 22-29 '89

To found traditions of Catholic Church music. J. P. Swain. il *America* 161:186-9 S 30 '89

RELIGIOUS NEWS

See also

Church and the press

Bad-news bearers [news stories on clergy scandals] L. Cryderman. il *Christianity Today* 33:12 Ap 21 '89

Events and people. See issues of The Christian Century Issues for 1989. il *Christianity Today* 33:44-5 Ja 13 '89

Jesse Jackson: newsmaker of the year. G. Wills. *The Christian Century* 106:3-4 Ja 4-11 '89

Of many things [top Catholic news stories of 1980s] G. W. Hunt. *America* 161:462 D 23-30 '89

Religion and revolution: top story of 1989 [cover story] il *The Christian Century* 106:1187-90 D 20-27 '89

The underground ecumenist. K. A. Marlin. See issues of The Christian Century beginning October 25, 1989

A year of turning points [1989] R. Frame. il *Christianity Today* 33:38-40+ D 15 '89

RELIGIOUS NEWSPAPERS AND PERIODICALS

See also

Catholic press
Christian Science monitor
Christianity today (Periodical)
Image (Periodical)

RELIGIOUS ORDERS

See also

Christian Brothers
Dominicans (Religious order)
Jesuits
Salesians
Society of the Divine Word

RELIGIOUS PERSECUTION *See* Persecution

RELIGIOUS PLURALISM

Capitalism and technology in global perspective: a dispute [discussion of May 3, 1989 article, The theological challenge of globalization] M. L. Stackhouse. *The Christian Century* 106:690-3 Jl 19-26 '89

The Catholic experience at taming pluralism [cover story] J. M. McShane. il *The Christian Century* 106:443-6 Ap 26 '89

Christian claims in a pluralistic society. A. M. Watts. *The Christian Century* 106:222-3 Mr 1 '89

Raimundo Panikkar: pluralism without relativism. P. Gorday. il por *The Christian Century* 106:1147-50 D 6 '89

The theological challenge of globalization [cover story] M. L. Stackhouse. il *The Christian Century* 106:468-71 My 3 '89

RELIGIOUS PSYCHOLOGY *See* Psychology, Religious

RELIGIOUS RADIO PROGRAMS *See* Radio broadcasting—Religious programs

RELIGIOUS SCHOOLS *See* Church schools

RELIGIOUS SOCIETIES

See also

Campus Crusade for Christ

RELIGIOUS TELEVISION PROGRAMS *See* Television broadcasting—Religious programs

RELIGIOUS TOLERANCE *See* Religious liberty

RELIGIOUS VOCATION *See* Vocation in religion

RELISHES *See* Pickles and relishes

RELLIM, FRANCESCA

Have a nice day! il *World Press Review* 36:56 Ag '89

RELMAN, ARNOLD

Fraud in science: causes and remedies. il *Scientific American* 260:126 Ap '89

about

Confronting the crisis in health care: an interview with Arnold Relman [cover story] S. Hackman and R. Howard. il pors *Technology Review* 92:30-8+ Jl '89

Health care: confronting the crisis [interview] S. Hackman and R. Howard. *Current (Washington, D.C.)* 317:10-15 N '89

REM (RAPID EYE MOVEMENT) SLEEP *See* Sleep

REMAINDERS (BOOKS)

See also

Booksellers and bookselling—Remainders

REMAKES, MOTION PICTURE *See* Motion picture remakes

REMARRIAGE

See also

Stepparents and stepchildren

The CEO's second wife [cover story] J. Connelly. il *Fortune* 120:52-7+ Ag 28 '89

I do, I do, I do. B. Astor. il por *House & Garden* 161:78-80 Je '89

Secrets of women who marry over and over . . . (and over) again. il *Ebony* 44:142+ S '89

REMARRIAGE—*cont.*
To make a harvest honeymoon last, first decide what's yours, mine and ours. D. M. Topolnicki. il *Money* 18:145-6 S '89
REMEDIAL TEACHING
Classroom dialogues [high school class] S. Gibson. il *Phi Delta Kappan* 70:553-5 Mr '89
REMEIKA, JOSEPH P.
about
Obituary
Physics Today por 42:114+ N '89. D. B. McWhan and others
REMICS *See* Real estate mortgage investment conduits
REMINGTON, DEBORAH, 1935-
about
A lot of dealers. il *American Artist* 53:53 D '89
REMINGTON, FREDERIC, 1861-1909
about
Frederic Remington: masterworks of Western art. P. H. Hassrick. il por *USA Today (Periodical)* 117:76-83 Mr '89
REMISSION, SPONTANEOUS *See* Spontaneous remission
REMLER, EMILY
about
Emily Remler. B. Milkowski. il por *Down Beat* 56:26 My '89
REMMES, BRENDA BEVAN
Why kids drop out. por *Newsweek* 113:10-11 Mr 6 '89
REMODELED ATTICS *See* Attics, Remodeled
REMODELED AUTOMOBILES *See* Automobiles, Remodeled
REMODELED BASEMENTS *See* Basements, Remodeled
REMODELED FOUR WHEEL DRIVE VEHICLES *See* Four wheel drive vehicles, Remodeled
REMODELED GARAGES *See* Garages, Remodeled
REMODELED HELICOPTERS *See* Helicopters, Remodeled
REMODELED MOTORCYCLES *See* Motorcycles, Remodeled
REMODELED PARKING METERS *See* Parking meters, Remodeled
REMODELED TRUCKS *See* Trucks, Remodeled
REMODELING (ARCHITECTURE)
See also
Apartments, Remodeled
Buildings, Remodeled
Houses, Remodeled
School buildings, Remodeled
REMOTE CONTROL
See also
Audio systems—Control
Audiovisual equipment—Control
Camera shutters—Control
Computers—Control use
Garage doors—Control
Remote procedure calls (Computers)
Remotely piloted vehicles
Television receivers—Control
Videotape recorders and recording—Control
Better remote control. K. McManus and W. Giese. il *Changing Times* 43:22 My '89
Boosting your home's IQ [wiring standard called Consumer Electronics Bus] P. Elmer-Dewitt. il *Time* 133:70-1 Ja 23 '89
A dream come true: homes that care for themselves—and you. S. Esters. il *Black Enterprise* 19:29+ Ja '89
Houses of the future today [smart houses] P. Carroll. il *Working Woman* 14:82+ N '89
Phonlink II (I). J. McNabb and G. Roseth. il *Radio-Electronics* 60:44-9 F '89
Phonlink II (II). J. McNabb and G. Roseth. il *Radio-Electronics* 60:46-9 Mr '89
Remote A/B switch. R. A. Heil. il *Radio-Electronics* 60:37+ O '89
Remote controls. J. D. Hirsch. il *Stereo Review* 54:26+ Ag '89
Secrets of the universals. I. Berger. il *Video* 12:44-7+ F '89
Super remotes. W. J. Hawkins. il *Popular Science* 234:76-7 F '89
REMOTE CONTROL [television program] *See* Television program reviews—Single works
REMOTE CONTROL MANIPULATORS *See* Manipulators (Mechanism)
REMOTE METER READING *See* Meter reading
REMOTE PROCEDURE CALLS (COMPUTERS)
Remote control. C. Manson and K. J. Thurber. il *Byte* 14:235-8+ Jl '89
REMOTE SENSING
See also
Artificial satellites—Earth sciences use
Remote sensing of the earth: a synoptic view. J. R. Schott. bibl f il *Physics Today* 42:72-9 S '89
Revealing the ancient world through high technology. V. Lightfoot and D. Lightfoot. il *Technology Review* 92:54-61 My/Je '89
Spectral reflectance properties of hydrocarbons: remote-sensing implications. E. A. Cloutis. bibl f il *Science* 245:165-8 Jl 14 '89

REMOTELY PILOTED VEHICLE MODELS
Manufacturers unveil models of new remotely piloted vehicles [Paris Air Show] J. D. Morrocco. il *Aviation Week & Space Technology* 131:48-9+ Jl 3 '89
REMOTELY PILOTED VEHICLES
International RPVs and drones [tables] il *Aviation Week & Space Technology* 130:164-5 Mr 20 '89
Pentagon will select two contractors to demonstrate unmanned aerial vehicles. P. J. Klass. il *Aviation Week & Space Technology* 131:34-5 Jl 31 '89
U.S. RPVs & drones [tables] il *Aviation Week & Space Technology* 130:162-3 Mr 20 '89
Costs
Pentagon considers buying additional Pioneer RPVs. J. D. Morrocco. *Aviation Week & Space Technology* 131:81+ Jl 31 '89
U.S. panel acts to simplify purchase of short-range UAV. il *Aviation Week & Space Technology* 130:57 Ja 23 '89
Radar equipment
Radar-equipped UAVs may aid all-weather reconnaissance [unmanned aerial vehicles] B. D. Nordwall. il *Aviation Week & Space Technology* 130:69+ F 13 '89
Testing
Joint-services Amber RPV testing to begin this spring. *Aviation Week & Space Technology* 130:100 F 20 '89
Canada
Canadair to resume CL-227 flights after completing technical review [remotely piloted vehicle] il *Aviation Week & Space Technology* 130:78-9 My 15 '89
Egypt
Egypt begins using unmanned aircraft for reconnaissance. M. A. Dornheim. il *Aviation Week & Space Technology* 130:56-7 Ja 23 '89
REMSBERG, BONNIE
"I wish I could hold you more". il *Reader's Digest* 134:147-52 Je '89
REMY, JACQUELINE
Woman = man? il *World Press Review* 36:54 Ap '89
REMY, RICHARD C.
(jt. auth) *See* Woyack, Robert B., and Remy, Richard C.
RÉMY MARTIN ET COMPAGNIE SA
The feuding families of fine goods. C. Dickey. il *Newsweek* 114:42 Ag 7 '89
RENAISSANCE
See also
Painting, Renaissance
Bibliography
Paperback history. R. O'Day. *History Today* 39:51 Mr '89
RENAISSANCE, HARLEM *See* Harlem renaissance
RENAL DISEASES *See* Kidneys—Diseases
RENAMO *See* Mozambique National Resistance Movement
RENAN, ERNEST, 1823-1892
about
Remembering Renan. W. Fowlie. *The American Scholar* 58:245-56 Spr '89
RENAN, NOÉMI
about
Remembering Renan. W. Fowlie. *The American Scholar* 58:245-56 Spr '89
RENAULT (REGIE NATIONALE DES USINES RENAULT)
Is Renault's new engine built for the long haul? S. Toy. il por *Business Week* p38-9 Ag 21 '89
RENCH, J. FREDERICK
about
Cleaning stain-resistant carpet [interview] il por *Home Mechanix* 86:20+ Ap '89
RENDELL, RUTH, 1930-
about
Murderous secrets. D. Turbide. por *Maclean's* 102:94+ N 6 '89
PW interviews. M. Field. por *Publishers Weekly* 235:46+ My 26 '89
RENDERING, ARCHITECTURAL *See* Architectural drawing
RENDERING INDUSTRY
See also
Darling-Delaware Co., Inc.
RENDEZ-VOUZ DES CAJUNS [radio program] *See* Radio program reviews—Single works
RENDEZVOUS (SPACE) *See* Orbital rendezvous (Space flight)
RENDILE (AFRICAN PEOPLE)
Two lives for the Ariaal. E. M. Fratkin. il map *Natural History* p38-49 My '89
RENDU, MARC AMBROISE- *See* Ambroise-Rendu, Marc
RENEGADES [film] *See* Motion picture reviews—Single works
RENEWAL OF PROGRAMS *See* Television broadcasting—Renewal of programs
RENEWAL OF THE CHURCH *See* Church renewal
RENFREW, COLIN, 1937-
The origins of Indo-European languages. bibl il maps *Scientific American* 261:106-14 O '89
RENFRO, JULIE
The girl who loved cat sailing. il por *Women's Sports & Fitness* 11:42-3 Je '89
RENFRO, SANDRA
about
Houston jury decides Winfield already wed. il pors *Jet* 76:28-9 Jl 17 '89

RENFRO, SANDRA—about—*cont.*
An uncommon marriage. il pors *People Weekly* 32:79 Ag 7 '89
Winfield must pay support, plans appeal of decision. pors *Jet* 76:50 Jl 31 '89
RENI, GUIDO, 1575-1642
about
The partial comeback of a fallen angel. R. Hughes. il *Time* 133:95-6 My 8 '89
RENIER, JAMES J.
about
Butt kicking at Honeywell. R. Henkoff. il por *Fortune* 119:141 My 22 '89
RENIN
A genetic polymorphism in the renin gene of Dahl rats cosegregates with blood pressure. J. P. Rapp and others. bibl f il *Science* 243:542-4 Ja 27 '89
Structure of recombinant human renin, a target for cardiovascular-active drugs, at 2.5 Å resolution. A. R. Sielecki and others. bibl f il *Science* 243:1346-51 Mr 10 '89
RENKERS POSSE (GANG)
Johnny-too-bad and the sufferers [Jamaican drug posses; cover story] L. Gunst. *The Nation* 249:549+ N 13 '89
RENNER, MICHAEL
Cars and pollution: rethinking transportation. *Current (Washington, D.C.)* 313:32-40 Je '89
The drain of a permanent war economy. il *USA Today (Periodical)* 118:19-21 Jl '89
Rethinking the auto: blueprints for a cleaner, greener future. il *Utne Reader* p82-9 Mr/Ap '89
Rethinking the future of global transportation. il *USA Today (Periodical)* 118:23-6 S '89
Transportation tomorrow. il por *The Futurist* 23:14-16+ Mr/Ap '89
RENNIE, J. C.
Ethical choice in food systems [address, October 26, 1989] *Vital Speeches of the Day* 56:143-7 D 15 '89
RENO
about
Hot prospect. R. Buchanan. il por *Rolling Stone* p124-5+ My 18 '89
RENO, JAMIE
Dying AIDS victim calls for safe sex and understanding. il pors *Ebony* 44:148+ Mr '89
RENOIR, AUGUSTE, 1841-1919
about
Museum accessions. E. H. Gustafson. il *Antiques* 136:76+ Jl '89
Renoir's gifts. V. H. Winner. il *Art News* 88:25 Summ '89
Scholarly sleuth. E. Beck. il por *Art News* 88:83-4 O '89
RENOUF, DEANE
Sensory function in the harbor seal. bibl il map *Scientific American* 260:90-5 Ap '89
RENOUNCE (TERM)
The big renouncement. W. Safire. il *The New York Times Magazine* p6+ Ja 1 '89
RENSE, PAIGE
about
Professional space, personal grace. L. Rosch. il pors *Working Woman* 14:94-5 Je '89
RENSE, RIP
Fred Savage says . . . acting's easy—except for the kissing [cover story] il pors *TV Guide* 37:10-11 Je 10-16 '89
Unlike Al Bundy . . . Ed O'Neill listens to his wife. il pors *TV Guide* 37:25-6 My 27-Je 2 '89
RENT
See also
Farm rents
Houses—Leasing and renting
Landlord and tenant
RENT CONTROL *See* Rent laws
RENT LAWS
All in the, er, family [New York ruling on gay couples and rent control] D. Seligman. *Fortune* 120:123-4 Ag 14 '89
Bankrupt landlords in Wonderland [rent control in Santa Monica] M. Beauchamp. il *Forbes* 143:105-7 Mr 20 '89
The economies of public housing. W. Tucker. il *The American Spectator* 22:26-9 N '89
The phony case against rent control. J. Atlas and P. Dreier. il *The Progressive* 53:26-7+ Ap '89
Pity the New York landlord [rent control] W. Tucker. il *The American Spectator* 22:19-22 F '89
Thoughts on homelessness today. E. Van den Haag. *The American Spectator* 22:36-7 Ap '89
RENT STABILIZATION LAWS *See* Rent laws
RENTING OF AUTOMOBILES *See* Automobiles—Leasing and renting
RENTING OF DANCE STUDIOS *See* Dance studios—Leasing and renting
RENTON (WASH.)
Education
Bad Astra: the other side of the Spectrum [court rules against predistribution review policy in case of high school underground newspaper] P. A. Zirkel. bibl f il *Phi Delta Kappan* 70:734-5+ My '89

RENTZEPIS, PETER M., 1934-
(jt. auth) See Parthenopoulos, Dimitri A., and Rentzepis, Peter M., 1934-
REORGANIZATION OF CORPORATIONS *See* Corporations—Reorganization
REPAIR SHOPS
See also
Automobile service stations
Quick fixes [New York City] B. Ickes. il *New York* 22:61-3 My 1 '89
REPAIRING
See also
Houses—Maintenance and repair
Patching materials
Anecdotes, facetiae, satire, etc.
If it's broke, I can't fix it [men who aren't mechanically inclined] W. D. Leight. *Mademoiselle* 95:82 Jl '89
REPAIRMEN
Anecdotes, facetiae, satire, etc.
Be my handy man. J. Ackermann-Blount. il *Gentlemen's Quarterly* 59:307+ S '89
REPARATION
Why George Bush should break his promise [more prisons vs. restitution] C. W. Colson. il *Christianity Today* 33:64 Ap 7 '89
REPARATIONS
See also
Slavery—Reparations
REPATRIATION
El Salvador
Salvadoran refugees come home [village of Copapayo] R. R. Ruether. il *The Christian Century* 106:851-3 S 27 '89
Vietnam
Dashing their dreams [Britain forces repatriation of Vietnamese boat people] W. Stewart. il *Time* 134:26 D 25 '89
REPELLENTS, DEER *See* Deer repellents
REPELLENTS, INSECT *See* Insect repellents
REPELLENTS, TICK *See* Tick repellents
REPELLENTS, WILDLIFE *See* Wildlife repellents
REPENTANCE
See also
Penance
REPERTORY-WEST (DANCE COMPANY)
Reviews:
Performances at the University of California at Santa Barbara. J. O. McLeod. *Dance Magazine* 63:121-2 My '89
REPETITIVE STRAIN INJURIES
An invisible workplace hazard gets harder to ignore. M. Mallory and H. Bradford. il *Business Week* p92-3 Ja 30 '89
REPLACEMENTS (MUSICAL GROUP)
Down to a dull roar. D. Gates. il pors *Newsweek* 113:62+ Je 19 '89
The growing pains and pleasures of the Replacements. S. Pond. il *Rolling Stone* p79-80+ Je 1 '89
The Replacements' adult entertainment [release of Don't tell a soul] I. Robbins. il *Rolling Stone* p117-18 F 9 '89
REPLICA BOATS *See* Boats and boating
REPLICA SPORTS CARS *See* Sports cars
REPORT CARDS *See* School reports and records
THE REPORTERS [television program] See Television program reviews—Single works
REPORTERS AND REPORTING
See also
Afghanistan—Russian invasion, 1979-1989—Reporters and reporting
AIDS (Disease) and the press
Berlin Wall, 1961-1989—Reporters and reporting
Black journalists
Brawley, Tawana—Assault case—Reporters and reporting
Bush, George, 1924—Visit to Poland, 1989—Reporters and reporting
Cable television—News
Cambodia—History—Civil War, 1970-1975—Reporters and reporting
Challenger (Space shuttle) explosion, 1986—Reporters and reporting
Confidential communications—Press
Crime and the press
El Salvador—Civil War, 1980- —Reporters and reporting
Environmental news
Foreign correspondents
Gorbachev, Mikhail—Visit to Cuba, 1989—Reporters and reporting
Government and the press
Holocaust, Jewish (1939-1945)—Reporters and reporting
Hurricane Hugo, 1989—Reporters and reporting
Interviewing
Journalists
Kennedy, John F. (John Fitzgerald), 1917-1963—Assassination—Reporters and reporting
Lebanon hostage cases, 1984- —Reporters and reporting
News
Press and abortion
Press and nuclear energy

REPORTERS AND REPORTING—See also—*cont.*
Press and politics
Radio broadcasting—News
San Francisco Bay Area (Calif.)—Earthquake, 1989—Reporters and reporting
Space flight—Reporters and reporting
Sports journalism
Stock market crash, 1987—Reporters and reporting
Television broadcasting—News
Terrorism and the press
Tiananmen Square (China) student occupation, 1989—Reporters and reporting
UFOs—Reporters and reporting
United States—History—Civil War, 1861-1865—Reporters and reporting
Vietnamese War, 1957-1975—Reporters and reporting
World War, 1939-1945—Reporters and reporting
See also names of reporters
What's going on? L. Eskin. il *Scholastic Update (Teachers' edition)* 122:5 S 8 '89
Anecdotes, facetiae, satire, etc.
No swimsuits [reporting on a Sports illustrated preview party] *The New Yorker* 65:31-2 F 20 '89
REPORTS
See also
Corporation reports
Financial statements
REPPY, JUDITH
More for the military. bibl f il *The Bulletin of the Atomic Scientists* 45:46-8 Ja/F '89
REPRESENTATIVE GOVERNMENT AND REPRESENTATION
See also
Democracy
REPRESENTATIVES, CONGRESSIONAL *See* Congressmen; Congresswomen
REPRESSION (PSYCHOLOGY)
The repressed road to trauma recovery [lack of dream recall in Holocaust survivors; research by Peretz Lavie] B. Bower. *Science News* 136:4 Jl 1 '89
REPRINTS, UNAUTHORIZED *See* Copyright infringement
REPRODUCTION
See also
Amphibia—Reproduction
Artificial insemination, Human
Conjugation (Biology)
Embryology
Estrus
Fertility (Biology)
Fertilization in vitro
Fetus
Gamete intrafallopian transfer
Infertility
Menstruation
Rodents—Reproduction
Salamanders—Reproduction
Sea urchins—Reproduction
Sex determination and control
Spawning
Spermatophores
Thrips—Reproduction
Tuataras—Reproduction
Zygote intrafallopian transfer
Go forth & multiply? [reproduction in space] L. Frazer. il *Ad Astra* 1:24-9 Je '89
Playing demigod [limits to tinkering with reproduction] K. Wright. *Scientific American* 260:30-1 My '89
Research in human reproduction [WHO's Special Programme of Research, Development and Research Training in Human Reproduction] J. Barzelatto. il *World Health* p18-21 Ap '89
Technology as destiny: the new eugenics challenges feminism [cover story] J. B. Elshtain. il *The Progressive* 53:19-23 Je '89
Moral and religious aspects
The religious response to reproductive technology. A. L. Greil. *The Christian Century* 106:11-14 Ja 4-11 '89
Sex, law and ethics [Canadian commission formed to examine questions raised by new reproductive technologies] L. Van Dusen. il *Maclean's* 102:16 N 13 '89
There's no such thing as a right to bear children [with readers' comments] D. DeMarco. *U.S. Catholic* 54:13-19 Ag '89
The Vatican heresy [Instruction on respect for human life in its origins and on the dignity of procreation] W. Michalsky. il *The Humanist* 49:27+ N/D '89
Bibliography
Books on ethical issues [Catholic views] il *America* 161:241-5 O 14 '89
Nutritional aspects
Availability of metabolic fuels controls estrous cyclicity of Syrian hamsters. J. E. Schneider and G. N. Wade. bibl f il *Science* 244:1326-8 Je 16 '89
REPRODUCTION, ASEXUAL *See* Asexual reproduction
REPRODUCTIONS OF AMERICAN FURNITURE *See* Furniture, American—Reproductions
REPRODUCTIONS OF FURNITURE *See* Furniture—Reproductions

REPRODUCTIONS OF WORKS OF ART *See* Art—Reproductions
REPRODUCTIVE ORGANS
See also
Fallopian tubes
Ovaries
Testicles
Uterus
Vagina
Child-abuse evidence debated [variations in girls' genitals] D. Nathan. *Ms.* 17:81-2 Mr '89
Diseases
15 reasons to say 'no' to hysterectomy. C. Perlmutter. bibl il *Prevention (Emmaus, Pa.)* 41:50-9 Je '89
The bacteria that hate women. M. Beck. il *Ladies' Home Journal* 106:118-19+ Ag '89
Surgery
See also
Vasectomy
James Burt's 'love surgery' was supposed to boost pleasure, but some patients say it brought pain [faces malpractice suits for experimental gynecological surgery] M. Brower. il por *People Weekly* 31:97-6+ Mr 27 '89
The love surgeon [experimental gynecological surgery performed by J. Burt] J. A. Hennessee. il *Mademoiselle* 95:206-7+ Ag '89
Maverick doctor: martyr or fraud? [V. Hufnagel loses medical license] K. Moloney. por *Ms.* 18:69-70 N '89
"My gynecologist butchered me!" [J. Burt performs experimental reconstructive surgery]; ed. by Judith Kelman. G. Harness. il por *Redbook* 173:22+ Jl '89
REPRODUCTIVE TECHNOLOGY *See* Reproduction
REPSOL SA
. . . and a surprise gusher in Spain. G. G. Marcial. *Business Week* p142 O 9 '89
REPTILE SKINS *See* Hides and skins
REPTILES
See also
Alligators
Crocodiles
Herpetologists
Iguanas
Lizards
Pheromones—Reptiles
Skin—Reptiles
Snakes
Tuataras
Turtles
Classification
A lizard foretold [search for Gymnophthalmus species by chromosome comparison] C. J. Cole and others. map *Natural History* p12+ My '89
REPTILES, FOSSIL
See also
Dinosaurs
Pterosaurs
Fossil babies or little adults? [ichthyosaurs and nothosaurs] il *Natural History* p62-3 D '89
A nose for combat [mosasaurs] R. Monastersky. *Science News* 136:318 N 11 '89
Record-breaking reptile [found at East Kirkton quarry in Scotland by Timothy R. Smithson] A. McKenzie. *Science News* 136:372 D 9 '89
REPUBLIC NEW YORK CORP.
American Express slings mud—and gets splattered [smear campaign against financier E. Safra] W. Glasgall and J. Meehan. il por *Business Week* p102+ Ag 14 '89
Bank shot: Edmond Safra turns the tables on American Express. J. Taylor. il pors *New York* 22:42-7 S 18 '89
REPUBLIC PICTURES CORPORATION
Betting on Republic's bonanza. A. B. Block. il por *Channels (New York, N.Y.: 1986)* 9:48-51 Ja '89
REPUBLICAN CONGRESSIONAL COMMITTEE *See* National Republican Congressional Committee
REPUBLICAN NATIONAL COMMITTEE
Ambitious visions for a GOP majority [attracting minorities] G. Borger. il por *U.S. News & World Report* 106:18-19 Ja 23 '89
Anatomy of a smear [Speaker of the House T. Foley denies rumors of homosexuality] G. Borger. il pors *U.S. News & World Report* 106:40-1 Je 19 '89
Atwater to the rescue. J. McLaughlin. *National Review* 41:54 Ja 27 '89
Atwatergate [smear campaign against House Speaker T. Foley] H. Hertzberg. *The New Republic* 201:4 Jl 3 '89
Dirtball politics [homosexual smear perpetrated against Speaker of the House T. Foley] T. Morganthau. il pors *Newsweek* 113:32-3 Je 19 '89
From two new party chairmen: plans to woo and keep the black vote. R. Brown; L. Atwater. il *American Visions* 4:16-18 Je '89
The GOP blues [L. Atwater] M. Kempton. il *The New York Review of Books* 36:4 Mr 16 '89
How to spread a smear [attack on Speaker of the House T. Foley] M. B. Carlson. il pors *Time* 133:33 Je 19 '89
Lee Atwater's GOP offensive is off and stumbling. R. Fly. por *Business Week* p31 Ap 17 '89

REPUBLICAN NATIONAL COMMITTEE—*cont.*

Mission accomplished [chairman L. Atwater's involvement in smear campaign against Speaker T. Foley] F. Barnes. il *The New Republic* 201:8-10 Jl 3 '89

The nation's closets [homosexual smear attack against House Speaker T. Foley] *Commonweal* 116:388-9 Jl 14 '89

Playing hardball [L. Atwater] E. Alterman. il pors *The New York Times Magazine* p30-1+ Ap 30 '89

"Ten steps, then we shoot," says Ron Brown. "I've got my AK-47," replies Lee Atwater. "What've you got?". M. Kelly. il pors *Gentlemen's Quarterly* 59:142-7+ Jl '89

That memo [attack on House Speaker T. Foley] W. McGurn. por *National Review* 41:22-3 N 10 '89

REPUBLICAN PARTY (U.S.)

See also
National Black Republican Council
National Republican Congressional Committee
Republican Senatorial Inner Circle

Abortion's dividing line [GOP feels impact of prochoice activists] E. Salholz. il *Newsweek* 114:31 O 23 '89

Abortive issue. F. Barnes. *The New Republic* 201:10-11 D 4 '89

An attack dog, not a lapdog [election of Republican whip N. Gingrich] J. V. Lamar, Jr. il por *Time* 133:22 Ap 3 '89

Avoiding the Burtonmander [must win state elections so as to avoid gerrymandering] S. T. Mandel. *National Review* 41:17 D 22 '89

Blacks and Republicans. W. A. Keyes. il *Conservative Digest* 15:47-9 Jl/Ag '89

A 'Christian nation' in the Far West [declaration by E. Mecham supporters] *U.S. News & World Report* 106:14 Mr 27 '89

Congress's $113 million junk-mail habit [target of reform] G. Borger. il *U.S. News & World Report* 107:17-18 Ag 7 '89

Cracking the whip [minority whip N. Gingrich; cover story] T. Bethell. il *The American Spectator* 22:9-11 Ag '89

The dawn of karate-chop Republican politics [Wyoming congressional race] S. V. Roberts. il *U.S. News & World Report* 106:28 My 1 '89

Dennis the Menace comes in from the cold [N. Gingrich enters race for House Speaker] G. Borger. il pors *U.S. News & World Report* 106:25-6 Mr 27 '89

The disgrace at HUD. M. Greenfield. il *Newsweek* 114:60 Jl 24 '89

Ditch the cheerleaders, Lee. A. F. Lewis. il por *Ms.* 17:86 Ap '89

Dream on [realignment quest] F. Barnes. *The New Republic* 200:9-10 Ja 23 '89

Eyeing the prize: GOP sets sights on blacks. K. D. Thompson. il *Black Enterprise* 19:35 My '89

Fellow Republicans [Progressive readers receive fund raising letters] E. Knoll. *The Progressive* 53:4 D '89

For the Son of C-SPAN, exposure = power [N. Gingrich elected House minority whip] H. Fineman. il por *Newsweek* 113:22-3 Ap 3 '89

Getting serious about blacks. P. Weyrich. il *Conservative Digest* 15:11-14 Jl/Ag '89

Golden State opportunity [gubernatorial race in Calif.] T. Bethell. il *National Review* 41:34+ N 10 '89

Goodbye to the 'yellow dogs' [GOP's new recruits in the South] J. N. Baker. il *Newsweek* 113:32 Ap 10 '89

The GOP feeding frenzy is far from over [ethics turmoil in the House] D. Harbrecht. il por *Business Week* p36-7 Je 19 '89

The GOP's new whip really knows how to lash out [N. Gingrich] D. Harbrecht. *Business Week* p47 Ap 3 '89

The GOP's plan for Jesse. il por *Newsweek* 113:6 F 13 '89

Guess who's (not) coming to dinner [rejected civil rights nominee W. Lucas and other black Republicans undercut by White House] W. McGurn. il *National Review* 41:18-19 S 1 '89

High noon for Newt [minority whip N. Gingrich; cover story] W. McGurn. il pors *National Review* 41:21-3 Ag 18 '89

House Republicans may be a House divided. D. Harbrecht. *Business Week* p43 Mr 27 '89

How the Democrats hold on to Congress. S. T. Mandel and W. McGurn. *National Review* 41:37-40 N 24 '89

How to win an election [Republicans in 1990 congressional elections] W. Allison. *National Review* 41:24 O 13 '89

If you don't swing, you can't zing [evangelical Republicans] il *U.S. News & World Report* 106:12 Je 26 '89

Let the great gerrymander war begin [effects of reapportionment after 1990 census] P. R. Range. il map *U.S. News & World Report* 106:29-30 D 4 '89

Letter from Washington [House Republicans] Cato. *National Review* 41:8 My 5 '89

Losing well is the best revenge. W. McGurn. *National Review* 41:16 D 8 '89

The mark of Kean [gubernatorial candidates in New Jersey] G. Morris. *National Review* 41:17-18 Je 16 '89

Master of disaster [minority whip N. Gingrich; cover story] D. Beers. il pors *Mother Jones* 14:28-9+ O '89

O'Connor fumbles 'Christian nation' case [Justice S. D. O'Connor's letter in support of Arizona Republican Party resolution] E. M. Gaffney, Jr. *The Christian Century* 106:373-5 Ap 12 '89

On the point [allegations about House minority whip N. Gingrich] *National Review* 41:12-13 Ap 21 '89

One-man/one-vote Gingrich. W. F. Buckley. *National Review* 41:62 My 5 '89

Party of Lincoln [seeks black support] F. Barnes. *The New Republic* 200:10-12 Mr 20 '89

Playing the politics of race [R. Brown to be Democratic Party chairman while Republicans woo blacks] H. Fineman. il por *Newsweek* 113:20 F 6 '89

Ready for Wright: a GOP grudge match. E. Salholz. il por *Newsweek* 113:28 Mr 20 '89

Republican racist [D. Duke of Louisiana] L. Cohler. *The New Republic* 201:11-14 S 18-25 '89

'Republicans are thirsting for blood' [hard feelings over J. Tower nomination] R. Fly and D. Harbrecht. il por *Business Week* p39 Mr 20 '89

Republicans for Jackson [J. L. Jackson proposed as mayor of Washington, D.C.] W. Schneider. il *The Atlantic* 264:48 N '89

The resurrection of Evan Mecham. K. V. Smith. il por *National Review* 41:42-3 My 19 '89

Right-wing activists take aim at Bush. J. M. Wall. *The Christian Century* 106:163-4 F 15 '89

Slim GOP pickin's in Dixie. H. Wyman. il *The American Spectator* 22:30-1 Ag '89

Timidity [address, April 6, 1989] T. H. Kean. *Vital Speeches of the Day* 55:488-90 Je 1 '89

Unanswered letters [Progressive editor receives fund raising letter] E. Knoll. *The Progressive* 53:4 N '89

What the people really say [abortion issue] W. McGurn. il *National Review* 41:26-9 D 22 '89

Will the GOP trip itself as it backpedals on abortion? D. Harbrecht. il *Business Week* p47 D 4 '89

With a Republican in office, a recession may be lurking . . . and if it comes, the poor will really take a hit. M. J. Mandel. il *Business Week* p20 Ap 10 '89

With friends like Bob Martinez, the GOP doesn't need . . . G. DeGeorge and R. Fly. il por *Business Week* p47 O 30 '89

REPUBLICAN SENATORIAL INNER CIRCLE

Anecdotes, facetiae, satire, etc.

Dan, you're no Strunk or White [exchange of letters] D. Quayle. *Harper's* 278:24-6 Je '89

REPUBLICANS (GERMANY: WEST) *See* Republikaner (Germany: West)

REPUBLIKANER (GERMANY: WEST)

One beer-hall putsch is enough. *U.S. News & World Report* 106:13-14 F 20 '89

The rising star of the German right [F. Schönhuber] G. A. Craig. il *The New York Review of Books* 36:22-4 Je 15 '89

REPURCHASE OF STOCKS *See* Stocks—Repurchase

REQUIEMS

See also
Compact discs—Requiems

Music [Messa per Rossini] P. G. Davis. il *New York* 22:107-8 O 30 '89

Musical events:
Performance of revised Mozart Requiem. A. Porter. *The New Yorker* 65:115-16+ Ap 10 '89
Requiem for Rossini. A. Porter. *The New Yorker* 65:114-17 N 13 '89

REREGULATION OF INDUSTRY *See* Industry and state

RERIKH, NIKOLAĬ KONSTANTINOVICH *See* Roerich, Nicholas, 1874-1947

REROOFING *See* Roofs and roofing—Maintenance and repair

RERUNS, SYNDICATED *See* Television broadcasting—Syndicated programs

RESALE TRADE *See* Secondhand trade

RESCISSION (LAW)

Anecdotes, facetiae, satire, etc.

Let's rake a deal [reverse bankruptcy and fraternal equalization rescission] B. Stein. il *The American Spectator* 22:37 O '89

RESCUE 911 [television program] See Television program reviews—Single works

RESCUE OF WILDLIFE *See* Wildlife conservation

RESCUE WORK

See also
First aid in illness and injury
Helicopters in rescue work
Radar in rescue work
Seals (Animals) in rescue work
United States. Coast Guard

A deadly struggle against the sea [adrift in rubber dinghy after shipwreck of Anaulis; cover story]; ed. by Ron Arias. J. Culver. il pors *People Weekly* 32:62-6+ Ag 21 '89

"Don't let my father die!" [C. Cooke saves father's life after he is seriously injured by horse] P. O. D'Aulaire and E. D'Aulaire. il *Reader's Digest* 134:115-20 Je '89

Faster than a speeding bullet, Anthony Falzo saved two tots from a powerful locomotive [conductor rescues Todd and Scott Pritchard] il por *People Weekly* 31:159 My 22 '89

RESCUE WORK—*cont.*

Heroes of the frozen cliff [rescue of crew from USS Pollux wreck by Newfoundlanders in World War II] H. Strauss. il *Reader's Digest* 134:102-7 Ap '89

High school grad thanks retired firefighter who rescued her 14 years ago [L. Greene thanks M. Bunch, former Brooklyn fireman] il pors *Jet* 76:23 Jl 17 '89

"I have to save my baby!" [paraplegic C. Dunlop rescues daughter from swimming pool] J. Stuller. il *Reader's Digest* 134:65-70 Ap '89

Man overboard maneuvers. S. Stapleton. il *Motor Boating & Sailing* 163:38+ Ap '89

Message of the pond [rescue of horse trapped in ice helps families cope with grief] P. Michelmore. il *Reader's Digest* 135:106-10 D '89

"My son is under the ice—find him!" [rescue and revival of drowning victim]; ed. by Elaine Fein. M. H. Garza. il por *Redbook* 172:44+ Mr '89

N.Y. woman saved by TV cable and plucky tenants [woman forced off roof after being raped] il *Jet* 76:9+ My 1 '89

Ocean stations [work of Coast Guard cutters] R. L. Scheina. il *Sea Frontiers* 35:53-5 Ja/F '89

"Pull me out" [K. Rodriguez rescued from machine in chemical plant] P. Michelmore. il *Reader's Digest* 135:120-5 Ag '89

Rescue coordination, drills helped speed evacuation of survivors [United Airlines DC-10 crash at Sioux City, Iowa] D. Hughes. *Aviation Week & Space Technology* 131:31+ Jl 31 '89

Review finds no major flaws in LaGuardia water rescue [USAir Flight 5050] J. T. McKenna. *Aviation Week & Space Technology* 131:32 O 9 '89

The search for Lauren [mother reclaims kidnapped child from ex-husband in daring rescue in Jordan] N. C. Livingstone and D. Halevy. il pors *Reader's Digest* 135:77-84 Ag '89

SOS under the midnight sun [rescue of passengers on Soviet cruise liner Maxim Gorky] il *Time* 134:30 Jl 3 '89

"That car is going to explode!" [D. Maher saves N. Feagley's infant daughter after traffic accident] S. Kelly. il pors *Reader's Digest* 134:96-100 Ja '89

To the rescue [runner and paramedic S. Forbes, who carried J. McClure from Texas well] R. MacInnis. il pors *Runner's World* 24:36-8 Ag '89

When Joe Ross rescued little Maura Handren, he didn't know he was really a wife-saver [future bride rescued from drowning in Charles River] il pors *People Weekly* 31:94 Ap 17 '89

THE RESCUERS [film] See Motion picture reviews—Single works

RESEARCH

See also

Advertising research

Agricultural research

Animal experimentation

Arctic research

Astronomical research

Atmospheric research

Aviation research

Biological research

Botanical research

CD-ROM (Compact disc-Read only memory)—Scientific use

Chemical research

Communication in science

Computers—Scientific use

Educational research

Environmental research

Genetic research industry

Geological research

Horticultural research

Industrial research

Market research

Materials research

Medical research

Military research

Nuclear research

Pharmaceutical research

Psychiatric research

Reading research

Social science research

See also subhead Research under various subjects

America's technology trump cards [hidden strengths of research system] B. Carpenter. il *U.S. News & World Report* 107:46-7 Jl 10 '89

Ethical aspects

Another congressional look at fraud [Roe hearings] B. J. Culliton. *Science* 244:1538 Je 30 '89

A clash of cultures at meeting on misconduct. W. Booth. il *Science* 243:598 F 3 '89

Conflict of interest in science. D. Runkle. *Science* 246:1177 D 1 '89

Conflict over conflict of interest [research fund recipients; guidelines drafted by the National Institutes of Health] J. Palca. *Science* 245:1440 S 29 '89

Fraud in science: causes and remedies. A. Relman. il *Scientific American* 260:126 Ap '89

Government and quality in science. B. D. Davis. *Science* 246:736 N 10 '89

The government's role in investigating scientific misconduct. N. Bell. *BioScience* 39:79 F '89

Interview: Walter Stewart. D. Stewart. por *Omni (New York, N.Y.)* 11:64-6+ F '89

New rules on misconduct [issued by Dept. of Health and Human Services] C. Holden. *Science* 245:593 Ag 11 '89

The process of publication [Science magazine's attempts to avert fraud] D. E. Koshland, Jr. *Science* 245:573 Ag 11 '89

Professional ethics for research biologists. A. G. Heath. bibl f *BioScience* 39:472-4 Jl/Ag '89

Public policy issues in scientific fraud and misconduct. R. M. Rosenzweig. *BioScience* 39:552-4 S '89

Representative Roe rides to the rescue. B. J. Culliton. il por *Science* 245:24 Jl 7 '89

Self-regulation of science: reflections on a day spent testifying at a congressional hearing. D. Baltimore. il por *Technology Review* 92:20+ Ag/S '89

Federal aid

See also

Colleges and universities—Research—Federal aid

Research grants

Bush adopts Reagan's R&D budget. C. Norman. il *Science* 243:881-2 F 17 '89

Bush's first budget: still very Reaganesque. J. Raloff. *Science News* 135:103 F 18 '89

By contrast to last Academy address, Press is hopeful for science . . . if . . . I. Goodwin. *Physics Today* 42:41-2 Je '89

CBO lists options for cutting R&D. M. Crawford. *Science* 243:1001 F 24 '89

Days of reckoning: deficit woes weigh heavily on science budgets. I. Goodwin. il *Physics Today* 42:49-50 N '89

Defense cut savings should be pumped into civilian research & development. C. Covault. *Aviation Week & Space Technology* 131:48 D 18-25 '89

Deficit woes cloud research funding. M. Crawford. *Science* 245:1441-2 S 29 '89

FY 1990 budget: Bush's words, Reagan's numbers. N. Bell. il *BioScience* 39:292-6 My '89

Gramm-Rudman avoided, for now. C. Norman. *Science* 244:281 Ap 21 '89

More for the military [Reagan administration] J. Reppy. bibl f il *The Bulletin of the Atomic Scientists* 45:46-8 Ja/F '89

Numbers game: Bush's 1990 R&D budget uses Reagan's figures in making deals. I. Goodwin. il *Physics Today* 42:43-9 My '89

Public science for public policy. S. Jasanoff. il *Technology Review* 92:26+ F/Mr '89

Reagan's last budget: modest R&D hikes. J. Raloff. il *Science News* 135:22 Ja 14 '89

Science and the lame-duck budget. C. Norman. il *Science* 243:159-61 Ja 13 '89

Science as a national priority. L. Friedman and T. B. Lynch. il *USA Today (Periodical)* 118:47-8 S '89

Science lights a bunsen burner under Washington. F. Seghers. il *Business Week* p94+ Ja 23 '89

Scientists and politicians: can they work together? B. Adams. *USA Today (Periodical)* 117:32-3 Mr '89

Talking tall. T. Beardsley. *Scientific American* 260:20 Ap '89

Canada

Big science, big thinking [address, June 27, 1989] A. W. May. *Vital Speeches of the Day* 56:114-17 D 1 '89

Seeking the best [Networks of Centres of Excellence] B. Wickens. il *Maclean's* 102:68+ N 20 '89

Why Canada could be the new Manchuria. P. C. Newman. il *Maclean's* 102:31 Je 26 '89

Great Britain

New U.K. science initiatives backed. D. Dickson. *Science* 243:882 F 17 '89

Searching for researchers. B. Holland. il *World Press Review* 36:54 Ja '89

Greece

See also

Research Center of Crete

Japan

The growth of Japanese science and technology. F. Narin and J. D. Frame. bibl f il *Science* 245:600-5 Ag 11 '89

Japan faces big task in improving basic science. M. Sun. il *Science* 243:1285-7 Mr 10 '89

Japan lays out welcome mat for U.S. scientists. M. Sun. *Science* 243:1546-7 Mr 24 '89

An open door the U.S. isn't using [few American researchers in Japan's labs] A. Borrus. il *Business Week* p59+ My 15 '89

Where Japan is second-best. Y. Hirayama. *World Press Review* 36:55 Ja '89

United States

See Research

RESEARCH, FREEDOM OF See Science, Freedom of

RESEARCH AIRPLANES See Airplanes, Experimental

RESEARCH AND DEVELOPMENT See Industrial research; Research

RESEARCH AND STATE See Research—Federal aid; Science and state
RESEARCH CENTER OF CRETE
If it's Tuesday, this must be . . . Heraklion? D. Dickson. il *Science* 243:470-1 Ja 27 '89
RESEARCH GRANTS
See also
 National Institutes of Health (U.S.)—Appropriations and expenditures
 National Science Foundation (U.S.)—Appropriations and expenditures
 United States. Dept. of Defense—Appropriations and expenditures
AIDS research gets the grants. M. Beck. il *Newsweek* 113:46-7 Mr 6 '89
Budget fix hits research grants. M. Crawford. *Science* 246:1115 D 1 '89
Grantsmanship [career of A. Obermayer] I. Cithelen. il por *Forbes* 144:310+ N 13 '89
Publish or perish [scientists] J. M. Diamond. il *Discover* 10:96-101 Jl '89
RESEARCH INSTITUTIONS
See also
 Battelle Memorial Institute
 Franklin Institute (Philadelphia, Pa.)
 Institute for Advanced Study (Princeton, N.J.)
 Institute for Public Policy Leadership
 Rockford Institute
 Santa Fe Institute (N.M.)
 SEI Center for Advanced Studies in Management
 Xerox Corp. Palo Alto Research Center
Germany (West)
See also
 Wissenschaftszentrum Berlin für Sozialforschung
RESEARCH LABORATORIES See Laboratories
RESEARCH LABORATORIES, GOVERNMENT See Laboratories, Government
RESEARCH LIBRARIES
Crumbling books. P. M. Battin. il *Change* 21:6+ S/O '89
Automation
The electronic library: changing the character of research. T. C. Weiskel. il *Change* 20:38-47 N/D '88
RESEARCH PAPERS, SCIENTIFIC See Scientific literature
RESEARCH PARKS
America's technopolis complex. A. Holmes. il *U.S. News & World Report* 107:66 N 13 '89
R&D clusters: what makes them happen? *The Futurist* 23:55-6 Jl/Ag '89
RESEARCH SHIPS
See also
 Challenger (Research ship)
 Project PROBE
RESERVATIONS, AIRLINE See Airlines—Reservation systems
RESERVATIONS, INDIAN (AMERICAN) See Indians of North America—Reservations
RESERVATIONS, MILITARY See Military reservations
RESERVES (ARMY) See United States. Army Reserve
RESERVES (BANK) See Banks and banking—Reserves
RESIDENCE IN PUBLIC WELFARE See Domicile in public welfare
RESIDENCE IN TAXATION See Domicile in taxation
RESIDENT THEATER See Theater
RESIDENTIAL ENERGY CONSERVATION See Energy conservation
RESIDENTIAL MOBILITY See Migration, Internal
RESIDENTIAL RESOURCES MORTGAGE INVESTMENTS CORPORATION
How a real estate highflier flamed out. D. Zigas. il *Business Week* p90 Mr 6 '89
RESIDENTS (MEDICINE)
No longer my brother's keeper. M. Frank. il *The New York Times Magazine* p30+ S 17 '89
RESIDUALS (ACTORS' PAYMENTS)
Residuals woes plague ESPN, CNN [advertisements beamed into Latin America] J. Loftus. il *Channels (New York, N.Y.: 1986)* 9:8 Jl/Ag '89
RESIDUES, CROP See Crop residues
RESIGNATION
See also
 Alfonsín, Raúl—Resignation
 Congressmen—Resignation
 Employees—Resignation
 Executives—Resignation
 Nixon, Richard M. (Richard Milhous), 1913—Resignation
 Public officers—Resignation
 Takeshita, Noboru—Resignation
 Teachers—Resignation
RESILIENCE (PSYCHOLOGY)
Children of the Garden Island [30-year study of Kauai children] E. E. Werner. bibl il map *Scientific American* 260:106-8+ Ap '89
Kids who beat the odds. C. Safran. il *Reader's Digest* 134:197-8+ Mr '89
Secrets of survivors. A. Whitman. il *Reader's Digest* 135:113-16 Jl '89

Surviving family blues [ability of teens to cope with depressed parents; research by William R. Beardslee and Dona Podorefsky] J. Folkenberg. *American Health* 8:119 Mr '89
Turning loss into growth. S. Dundon. il por *Working Woman* 14:92-4 Ag '89
RESISTANCE TO DRUGS See Drug resistance
RESISTANCE TO GOVERNMENT See Government, Resistance to
RESISTANCE TO INFECTION See Immunity
RESISTANCE TRAINERS (BICYCLE EQUIPMENT) See Bicycles—Equipment
RESISTORS, ELECTRIC See Electric resistors
RESNICK, JILL
Suitable scents: a user's guide to fragrance at the office. il *Working Woman* 14:120+ D '89
RESOLUTION (OPTICS)
How faint can you see? B. E. Schaefer. il *Sky and Telescope* 77:332-3+ Mr '89
Your telescope's limiting magnitude [computer program] B. E. Schaefer. il *Sky and Telescope* 78:522-5 N '89
RESOLUTION TRUST CORPORATION (U.S.)
At the 'El Dorado of impaired assets,' everything must go. C. Yang and D. Zigas. il *Business Week* p176+ N 6 '89
Delays, not deals. J. Drummond. il *Forbes* 144:212 N 27 '89
For sale by owner: junk real estate. M. W. Karmin. il *U.S. News & World Report* 107:54-5 D 11 '89
Silver lining. B. Weberman. il *Forbes* 143:179 Ap 3 '89
RESOLUTIONS
See also
 New Year's resolutions
RESOLVING POWER (OPTICS) See Resolution (Optics)
RESORT FRACTIONAL OWNERSHIP (REAL ESTATE) See Fractional ownership (Real estate)
RESORT TIMESHARING (REAL ESTATE) See Timesharing (Real estate)
RESORTS
See also
 Health resorts, watering places, etc.
50 favorite family resorts. G. S. Bush. il *Better Homes and Gardens* 67:179-80+ My '89
The best places to go for fun in the snow. R. J. Christmas. *Black Enterprise* 19:64 Ja '89
Call of the wild [luxury lodges in the wilderness; survey by T. Zagat] N. M. Better. il *House & Garden* 161:46+ Je '89
A coast-to-coast guide for cross-country skiers. S. Woolley. il *Business Week* p147 D 11 '89
Coastal getaways [tennis resorts] P. M. Coan. il *World Tennis* 37:63-6 Ag '89
Out-of-the-way, out-of-the-ordinary golf vacations. il *Women's Sports & Fitness* 11:51 Jl/Ag '89
A potent pick of ski resorts. il *Women's Sports & Fitness* 11:41 O '89
Resorts for a splurge—or just for skiing. W. C. Symonds. il *Business Week* p206-7 N 27 '89
Ski resorts that go beyond the slopes. W. C. Symonds. il *Business Week* p106-7 Ja 16 '89
Where the skiing's best. A. H. Greenberg. *Skiing* 41:10+ Ja '89
Economic aspects
Managing your ski country home. K. Brizzolara. il *Skiing* 41:20+ Ja '89
Vacation homes: it's a buyer's market. M. C. Paulson. il *Changing Times* 43:37-8+ Je '89
White sales [ski resort condominium investments] M. Lukens. il *House & Garden* 161:142+ Ja '89
Environmental aspects
Environmentalism and skiing. A. H. Greenberg. il *Skiing* 42:20+ D '89
An identity crisis [debate over expansion of skiing operation in Banff] J. Howse. il *Maclean's* 102:48 F 27 '89
Mt. Hood Resort expansion. *Wilderness* 52:11-12 Summ '89
History
Monuments to millions. H. Chipkin. il *Harper's Bazaar* 122:104+ O '89
Worship by-the-sea; camp-meetings and seaside resorts in 19th century America. S. E. Demars. bibl il maps *Focus (New York, N.Y.: 1950)* 38:15-20 Wint '88
Information services
Ski info, PC-style. C. Walter. il *Skiing* 42:14 O '89
International aspects
See also
 Club Méditerranée SA
Family travel [tennis resorts] P. M. Coan. il *World Tennis* 37:81-4 Jl '89
My favorite touring centers [cross country skiing] B. Koch. il *Skiing* 42:28+ D '89
World tennis travel annual [tennis resorts] P. M. Coan and B. Stambler. il *World Tennis* 37:61+ D '89
Marketing
"I am sorry, we have changed" [family image for Club Med] J. Levine. il *Forbes* 144:136-7 S 4 '89
Alberta
See also
 Lake Louise (Alta.)

RESORTS—Alberta—*cont.*

An identity crisis [debate over expansion of skiing operation in Banff] J. Howse. il *Maclean's* 102:48 F 27 '89

Anguilla

Heaven can wait—for now, try Anguilla [Mallihouana] T. Segal. il *Business Week* p116 Ap 3 '89

Argentina

Uphill downhill [Pan American winter games at Las Leñas] D. Einhorn. il *Américas* 41 no1:3-4 '89

Austria

See also
Lech (Austria)

Bahamas

See also
Crystal Palace Resort & Casino (Nassau, Bahamas)

California

See also
Calistoga (Calif.)
Palm Springs (Calif.)

California dreamin' [tennis resorts] P. M. Coan. il *World Tennis* 36:119-26 Ap '89

Palm Springs ploy [movie companies sue La Mancha Private Club & Villas over royalties from videotapes shown in hotel rooms] P. Newcomb. il *Forbes* 143:100 Mr 20 '89

Shasta snow fun. il maps *Sunset (Central West edition)* 183:20-3 D '89

Wine and dine in the vineyards [Napa Valley's Meadowood] B. St. Pierre. il *New Choices for the Best Years* 29:50-1 Ja '89

Caribbean region

Caribbean hideaways. S. Birnbaum. il *Good Housekeeping* 209:146+ N '89

Island travel. L. Wolfe and J. Cecil. il *New York* 22:66-70+ N 6 '89

Plunge right in. B. Wallraff. il *The Atlantic* 264:111-14 D '89

The secret Caribbean [special section] il map *Vogue* 179:304-5+ N '89

Travel guide. P. M. Coan. il *World Tennis* 37:75-80 O '89

Chile

A midsummer ski vacation? [Valle Nevado] J. W. Michaels. il *Forbes* 143:200-1 Ap 17 '89

Colorado

See also
Aspen (Colo.)
Crested Butte (Colo.)
Telluride (Colo.)
Vail (Colo.)

Back-country skiing is back at Berthoud Pass, near Denver. il *Sunset (Central West edition)* 183:62 N '89

Peak moments [Beaver Creek] J. Bowermaster. il *Harper's Bazaar* 122:90+ F '89

Florida

See also
Miami Beach (Fla.)

Florida [tennis resorts] P. M. Coan. il *World Tennis* 37:116-18+ S '89

Florida bound [tennis resorts] P. M. Coan. il *World Tennis* 36:73-8 F '89

Fore play [Grand Cypress golf resort in Orlando] J. Queenan. il *Gentlemen's Quarterly* 59:248-57 Je '89

France

See also
Cap d'Antibes (France)
Chamonix (France)

Du créateur de la cuisine minceur . . . à la châtelaine d'un restaurant célèbre [M. Guérard's Les Prés d'Eugénie] F. Ferretti. il *Gourmet* 49:42+ Jl '89

Georgia

Down Willow Way [tennis resorts] P. M. Coan. il *World Tennis* 36:82-7 Mr '89

Hawaii

See also
Waikiki Beach (Honolulu, Hawaii)

Hawaii [tennis resorts] P. M. Coan. il *World Tennis* 37:76-9 N '89

How I learned to love paradise [Kona Village] G. Norman. il *Esquire* 111:29-30 My '89

Wait'll we tell the folks back home [Hyatt Regency Waikoloa] N. R. Gibbs. il *Time* 133:71-2 F 27 '89

Idaho

See also
Sun Valley (Idaho)

Italy

See also
Courmayeur (Italy)
Porto Ercole (Italy)

Jamaica

Jamaica, no problem. C. Hoogendorn. il *Black Enterprise* 19:111 My '89

Lake Tahoe region (Calif. and Nev.)

Fast times at Tahoe [ski resorts] P. Oliver. il *Skiing* 42:114-22+ N '89

The skier's edge [ski school at Northstar resort] M. Behen. il *American Health* 8:79-80 N '89

Massachusetts

See also
Revere Beach (Mass.)

Mexico

See also
Cancún (Mexico)
Cozumel Island (Mexico)

Middle Western States

Hills alive! [ski resorts] E. Hanson. il map *Skiing* 41:122-4+ Ja '89

Montana

Glide through a 'snow forest' [cross country skiing at Lone Mountain Ranch] G. Lichtenstein. il *New Choices for the Best Years* 29:54-5 Ja '89

Mosquito Island (British Virgin Islands)

Mosquito Island: barefoot luxury in the British Virgins [Drake's Anchorage] R. Alleman. il *Vogue* 179:320 N '89

New England

The new New England [ski resorts] A. H. Greenberg. il *Skiing* 42:224-7+ D '89

Verdant vistas [tennis resorts] P. M. Coan. il *World Tennis* 37:70-2 Je '89

New Hampshire

Attaway, Attitash [ski resort] C. Walter. il *Skiing* 41:50-3+ Ja '89

Loon rising [ski resort] N. Howe. il *Skiing* 41:90-3+ Mr '89

New Mexico

Taos [Taos Ski Valley resort] N. Howe. il *Skiing* 41:42-8 F '89

New York (State)

See also
Hunter Mountain (N.Y.)

North America

Pre-season scouting report [ski resorts; cover story] il *Skiing* 42:81-8+ O '89

Oregon

Mt. Hood Resort expansion. *Wilderness* 52:11-12 Summ '89

Oregon's delectable Alp [skiing Mt. Bachelor] D. Ford. il *Skiing* 41:42-8+ Mr '89

Saint Croix (Virgin Islands of the U.S.)

Trouble in paradise [W. Bregman tries resort management] D. Machan. il pors *Forbes* 143:144+ My 15 '89

Saint Lucia

La Toc: a St. Lucian sojourn. S. Rothenberg and R. S. Rothenberg. il *USA Today (Periodical)* 117:38-43 Mr '89

Sea Island (Ga.)

The other Georgia [cover story] H. Leifermann. il map *New Choices for the Best Years* 29:46-52 Jl '89

South Carolina

See also
Myrtle Beach (S.C.)

Down Willow Way [tennis resorts] P. M. Coan. il *World Tennis* 36:82-7 Mr '89

Switzerland

See also
Saint Moritz (Switzerland)

United States

See Resorts

Utah

A tale of Deer Valley [ski resort] E. Hanson. il *Skiing* 42:206-8+ O '89

Tales from the Burma Bridge [adventure outing at Snowbird Ski and Summer Resort] L. J. Sass. il *Health (New York, N.Y.)* 21:40-1+ D '89

Vermont

See also
Stratton (Vt.)

The many faces of Killington. K. Brizzolara. il *Skiing* 42:218-24+ N '89

Western Europe

Pre-season scouting report [ski resorts] il *Skiing* 42:122-4+ O '89

Western States

Cross-country getaways. il map *Sunset (Central West edition)* 182:54-9 Ja '89

Southwest skiing: lodes of fun [ski resorts] D. Chaney. il *The Saturday Evening Post* 261:86-7+ N/D '89

Taking a powder late in the season [ski resorts] L. J. Moore. il *U.S. News & World Report* 106:72 F 27 '89

RESORTS INTERNATIONAL INC.

The Merv and Don boardwalk game [financial difficulties] il por *U.S. News & World Report* 107:17 N 27 '89

Merv Griffin may ground the seaplanes Miami Vice made famous [Chalk's International Airlines] A. Fins. il *Business Week* p36 D 4 '89

Merv Griffin's last Resort may be bankruptcy. R. Grover. il *Business Week* p34 N 20 '89

The new Merv Griffin show [Resorts deal sours] K. Hannon. il *Forbes* 144:10 Ag 21 '89

The Wheel of Fortune turns badly for Merv Griffin. L. Reibstein. il por *Newsweek* 114:62 N 27 '89

The wheel of misfortune? [M. Griffin's deal for Resorts turns sour] R. Grover. il *Business Week* p35-6 Ja 16 '89

RESOURCE ALLOCATION

Exxon and squatter economics. G. P. Brockway. *The New Leader* 72:13-14 Ag 7-21 '89

RESOURCE CENTERS
Resource centers for science teachers. R. F. Brinckerhoff. *The Education Digest* 54:36-9 Mr '89
RESOURCE MANAGEMENT *See* Conservation of resources
RESOURCE RECOVERY *See* Recycling (Waste, etc.)
RESOURCES, CONSERVATION OF *See* Conservation of resources
RESOURCES, NATURAL *See* Natural resources
RESPECT
Honor thy children. J. Segal. il *Parents* 64:87-90+ D '89
Should you quit if you're not getting respect? [results of survey on tactics of television character Roseanne] il *Glamour* 87:123 N '89
RESPIRATION
See also
Breathing exercises
Hyperventilation
Air ventilation by recoil aspiration in polypterid fishes. E. L. Brainerd and others. bibl f il *Science* 246:1593-5 D 22 '89
Breathing space [labored breathing, brought on by anxiety, cured by visiting garden] S. Safransky. il por *Organic Gardening* 36:83-4 O '89
Breathless seals [cessation of breathing by Weddell and elephant seals while diving and sleeping] *Discover* 10:16 Jl '89
The (liquid) breath of life [perfluorocarbon] M. M. Waldrop. il *Science* 245:1043-5 S 8 '89
Lung power [use of ketoconazole to prevent respiratory failure from fluid in the lungs] *Prevention (Emmaus, Pa.)* 41:16+ Ag '89
RESPIRATORS
See also
Gas masks
Selecting a respirator. D. Lane. il *Workbench* 45:68-9 Ja/F '89
RESPIRATORY ORGANS
See also
Lungs
Respiratory system [cover story] M.-L. Kamberg. bibl il *Current Health 2* 16:4-9 N '89
Diseases
See also
Asthma
Cold (Disease)
Emphysema
Influenza
Lungs—Diseases
Pneumonia
Sinusitis
Smallest aerosol pollutants linked to disease [research by C. A. Pope] J. Raloff. *Science News* 135:277 My 6 '89
Viral infections cause spasms [development of asthma from respiratory infections; views of William Busse] *USA Today (Periodical)* 118:2-3 O '89
RESPIRATORY SYNCYTIAL VIRUS
Vaccines and vaccination
Deadly RSV may fall to improved vaccines. R. Weiss. *Science News* 136:38 Jl 15 '89
RESPONSE, FREQUENCY (ELECTRIC ENGINEERING) *See* Frequency response (Electric engineering)
RESPONSIBILITY
See also
Assistance in emergencies
Crime and responsibility [rape of woman by teenagers in New York City] C. Krauthammer. il *Time* 133:104 My 8 '89
Don't blame "society" [rape of woman jogger in New York City] C. Krauthammer. *Reader's Digest* 135:54-5 Ag '89
Hearing what we ought to hear [address, May 8, 1989] W. F. Eadie. *Vital Speeches of the Day* 55:587-8 Jl 15 '89
Pavlov lives: who's to blame for educational failures? G. Keller. il *Change* 21:54 My/Je '89
Teaching children responsibility. L. Salk. il *McCall's* 117:29 O '89
RESPONSIBILITY (CORPORATE) *See* Business—Social aspects
RESPONSIBILITY (LAW) *See* Liability (Law)
RESSNER, JEFFREY
The passion of Theresa [cover story] il pors *American Film* 14:34-7+ Ap '89
REST
See also
Relaxation
Sleep
REST HOMES
Medication concerns in rest homes. *Science News* 135:88 F 11 '89
A poor rest home remedy: drugs in place of care. L. Drew. *Newsweek* 113:56 F 6 '89
RESTAURANT CRITICS AND CRITICISM *See* Food critics and criticism
RESTAURANT DECORATION
On the go [America restaurant in Washington, D.C. designed by MGS Architects] C. Pearson. il *Architectural Record* 177:80-5 mid-S '89

RESTAURANT DELIVERY SERVICE *See* Food delivery service
RESTAURANT EMPLOYEES
See also
Fast food restaurant employees
Hotel Employees and Restaurant Employees International Union
Waiters and waitresses
RESTAURANT ENTERPRISES GROUP, INC.
When the honeymoon's over: how to tell how you're really doing [J. Colson and J. Simon] J. Ciabattari. il pors *Working Woman* 14:82-6+ Je '89
RESTAURANT MANAGEMENT
See also
Women in restaurant management
RESTAURANT MATISSE (SANTA ROSA, CALIF.) *See* Santa Rosa (Calif.)—Restaurants, nightclubs, bars, etc.
RESTAURANT SHIRO (SOUTH PASADENA, CALIF.) *See* South Pasadena (Calif.)—Restaurants, nightclubs, bars, etc.
RESTAURANT TIPPING *See* Tipping
RESTAURANTS
See also
Airports—Restaurants, nightclubs, bars, etc.
Art in restaurants
Barbecue restaurants
Cabarets
Delicatessens
Diners (Restaurants)
Fast food restaurants
Kosher restaurants
Pizza restaurants
Best restaurants' best recipes. il *Ladies' Home Journal* 106:198-9+ S '89
Beyond egg roll: great Chinese food [Chinese American restaurants] il *Glamour* 87:293 O '89
Cheers! The best new restaurants of 1989. J. F. Mariani. il *Esquire* 112:187-8+ N '89
The cooks who can't be fired [restaurants at U.S. cooking schools] J. D. Reed. il *Time* 133:99-100 My 8 '89
Dining for the masses [megarestaurants] M. Starr. il *Newsweek* 114:75 S 18 '89
Eating ethnic and lean [tips for eating out; excerpt from International cuisines calorie counter] D. Webb. il *Health (New York, N.Y.)* 21:46+ N '89
The game is up! [U.S. restaurants serving more game] N. S. Mehta. il *Time* 134:63 N 6 '89
The great American pie expedition. S. Hubbell. *The New Yorker* 65:75-6+ Mr 27 '89
Lost in America [regional cooking] L. Wells. il *The New York Times Magazine* p115-16 D 3 '89
Mexican jumping scenes. M. O'Neill. il *Harper's Bazaar* 122:222+ Ap '89
Palate polls [Zagat surveys] J. Elson. il por *Time* 134:65-6 Ag 28 '89
"The Paris restaurant diet" [developed by Pierre Azam] il *Glamour* 87:265 Ag '89
Rethinking eating out. C. A. Sweet. il *FDA Consumer* 23:8-13 N '89
So there, Thomas Wolfe [cooking at home vs. dining out] B. Kafka. il *Gourmet* 49:60 S '89
Acquisitions and mergers
International aspects
An English suitor for Max & Erma's? [Mercury Asset Management] G. G. Marcial. *Business Week* p166 N 27 '89
Chain and franchise operations
See also
Benihana National Corporation
Fast food restaurants
Horn & Hardart Co.
Howard Johnson Co.
Max & Erma's Restaurants
Ninfa's Inc.
Pasta Lovers Trattorias
Perkins Family Restaurants LP
Pillsbury Co.
Restaurant Enterprises Group, Inc.
Shoney's Inc.
Wendy's International Inc.
Dinner's on the drawing board [new themes for chains of the future] M. Sheraton. il *Time* 133:108-9 F 20 '89
The good-times places. il *Glamour* 87:348-51 Ap '89
Directories
Let's eat out. See issues of Gourmet
Finance
Among restaurateurs, it's dog eat dog. B. Bremner. il *Business Week* p86 Ja 9 '89
Couch potatoes don't dine out. R. Phalon. il *Forbes* 144:209+ O 30 '89
History
"Everybody likes Italian food". J. F. Mariani. il *American Heritage* 40:122-31 D '89
Interior decoration
See Restaurant decoration
International aspects
On the waterfront [off-shore island restaurants] M. O'Neill. il *Harper's Bazaar* 122:126+ Jl '89

RESTAURANTS—cont.

Prices
Food critics pick the biggest rip-offs. il *Glamour* 87:336 S '89

Sanitation
Is this restaurant safe? il *Glamour* 87:298 Mr '89

Wine lists
See Wine lists

Wine service
See Wine service

Alaska
See also
Girdwood (Alaska)—Restaurants, nightclubs, bars, etc.

Belgium
See also
Brussels (Belgium)—Restaurants, nightclubs, bars, etc.

Brazil
See also
Rio de Janeiro (Brazil)—Restaurants, nightclubs, bars, etc.

British Columbia
See also
Victoria (B.C.)—Restaurants, nightclubs, bars, etc.

California
See also
Albany (Calif.)—Restaurants, nightclubs, bars, etc.
Beverly Hills (Calif.)—Restaurants, nightclubs, bars, etc.
Brentwood (Los Angeles, Calif.)—Restaurants, nightclubs, bars, etc.
Century City (Los Angeles, Calif.)—Restaurants, nightclubs, bars, etc.
Fresno (Calif.)—Restaurants, nightclubs, bars, etc.
Los Angeles (Calif.)—Restaurants, nightclubs, bars, etc.
Los Olivos (Calif.)—Restaurants, nightclubs, bars, etc.
Manhattan Beach (Calif.)—Restaurants, nightclubs, bars, etc.
Mendocino (Calif.)—Restaurants, nightclubs, bars, etc.
Montecito (Calif.)—Restaurants, nightclubs, bars, etc.
Oakhurst (Calif.)—Restaurants, nightclubs, bars, etc.
Oakland (Calif.)—Restaurants, nightclubs, bars, etc.
Rock Store (Calif.)
Sacramento (Calif.)—Restaurants, nightclubs, bars, etc.
Saint Helena (Calif.)—Restaurants, nightclubs, bars, etc.
San Francisco (Calif.)—Restaurants, nightclubs, bars, etc.
Santa Barbara (Calif.)—Restaurants, nightclubs, bars, etc.
Santa Monica (Calif.)—Restaurants, nightclubs, bars, etc.
Santa Rosa (Calif.)—Restaurants, nightclubs, bars, etc.
South Pasadena (Calif.)—Restaurants, nightclubs, bars, etc.
Walnut Creek (Calif.)—Restaurants, nightclubs, bars, etc.
West Hollywood (Calif.)—Restaurants, nightclubs, bars, etc.
What's cooking on the Coast? B. Palling. il *Vogue* 179:416+ Mr '89

China
See also
Shanghai (China)—Restaurants, nightclubs, bars, etc.

Connecticut
See also
Mystic (Conn.)—Restaurants, nightclubs, bars, etc.

Florida
See also
Key West (Fla.)—Restaurants, nightclubs, bars, etc.
Miami (Fla.)—Restaurants, nightclubs, bars, etc.
Miami Beach (Fla.)—Restaurants, nightclubs, bars, etc.
Orlando (Fla.)—Restaurants, nightclubs, bars, etc.
Palm Beach (Fla.)—Restaurants, nightclubs, bars, etc.

France
See also
Paris (France)—Restaurants, nightclubs, bars, etc.
New French fare: vive la revolution. P. Farrell. il *Business Week* p110 Je 12 '89
Taste of the provinces. P. Wells. il *House & Garden* 161:58+ Jl '89

Georgia
See also
Savannah (Ga.)—Restaurants, nightclubs, bars, etc.

Great Britain
See also
London (England)—Restaurants, nightclubs, bars, etc.

Illinois
See also
Chicago (Ill.)—Restaurants, nightclubs, bars, etc.

Italy
See also
Albaretto della Torre (Italy)—Restaurants, nightclubs, bars, etc.
Milan (Italy)—Restaurants, nightclubs, bars, etc.
Montecatini Terme (Italy)—Restaurants, nightclubs, bars, etc.

Louisiana
See also
New Orleans (La.)—Restaurants, nightclubs, bars, etc.

Massachusetts
See also
Saugus (Mass.)—Restaurants, nightclubs, bars, etc.

Middle Western States
Going haute in the heartland. J. F. Siler. il *Business Week* p80 Ag 7 '89

Minnesota
See also
Minneapolis (Minn.)—Restaurants, nightclubs, bars, etc.

Netherlands
Beyond tulips and windmills. R. L. Balzer. il *Travel Holiday* 171:22-5 Ja '89

New Jersey
See also
Edgewater (N.J.)—Restaurants, nightclubs, bars, etc.

New Mexico
See also
Santa Fe (N.M.)—Restaurants, nightclubs, bars, etc.

New York (State)
See also
Brooklyn (New York, N.Y.)—Restaurants, nightclubs, bars, etc.
New York (N.Y.)—Restaurants, nightclubs, bars, etc.

Oregon
See also
Portland (Or.)—Restaurants, nightclubs, bars, etc.

South Carolina
See also
North Augusta (S.C.)—Restaurants, nightclubs, bars, etc.

Soviet Union
See also
Leningrad (Soviet Union)—Restaurants, nightclubs, bars, etc.
Moscow (Soviet Union)—Restaurants, nightclubs, bars, etc.

Spain
See also
Madrid (Spain)—Restaurants, nightclubs, bars, etc.
Sizzling Spain. G. Greene. il *New York* 22:34-41 Jl 24 '89

Switzerland
See also
Crissier (Switzerland)—Restaurants, nightclubs, bars, etc.

Texas
See also
Fort Worth (Tex.)—Restaurants, nightclubs, bars, etc.

Thailand
See also
Bangkok (Thailand)—Restaurants, nightclubs, bars, etc.

United States
See Restaurants

Washington (D.C.)
See Washington (D.C.)—Restaurants, nightclubs, bars, etc.

Washington (State)
See also
Seattle (Wash.)—Restaurants, nightclubs, bars, etc.

Wyoming
See also
Alpine (Wyo.)—Restaurants, nightclubs, bars, etc.

RESTITUTION, CORRECTIONAL *See* Reparation

RESTON (VA.)

Housing
A town with pity [Embry Rucker Shelter] M. J. Weiss. il *Ladies' Home Journal* 106:48-9+ D '89

Poor
A town with pity [Embry Rucker Shelter] M. J. Weiss. il *Ladies' Home Journal* 106:48-9+ D '89

RESTORATION ECOLOGY
See also
Society for Ecological Restoration and Management

Aruba
Phenomena, comment and notes. J. P. Wiley, Jr. il *Smithsonian* 20:30+ My '89

RESTORATION OF BOOKS *See* Books—Conservation and restoration

RESTORATION OF DRAWING *See* Drawing—Conservation and restoration

RESTORATION OF FRESCOES *See* Frescoes—Conservation and restoration

RESTORATION OF MURAL PAINTING AND DECORATION *See* Mural painting and decoration—Conservation and restoration

RESTORATION OF PAINTING *See* Painting—Conservation and restoration

RESTORATION OF SCULPTURE *See* Sculpture—Conservation and restoration

RESTORATION OF WORKS OF ART *See* Art—Conservation and restoration

RESTORED AUTOMOBILES *See* Automobiles, Restored
RESTORED BICYCLES *See* Bicycles, Restored
RESTORED HOUSES *See* Houses, Restored
RESTORED TRUCKS *See* Trucks, Restored
RESTORED VILLAGES *See* Villages, Restored

RESTRAINT OF TRADE
See also
Boycott
Price fixing

RESTRICTED STOCK GRANTS
Incentive pay that doesn't work. G. S. Crystal. il *Fortune* 120:101+ Ag 28 '89

RESTRICTION FRAGMENT LENGTH POLYMORPHISMS
See also
 DNA fingerprints
DNA analysis in forensic science. M. D. Moody. bibl f il *BioScience* 39:31-6 Ja '89
A genetic polymorphism in the renin gene of Dahl rats cosegregates with blood pressure. J. P. Rapp and others. bibl f il *Science* 243:542-4 Ja 27 '89
New look at turtle migration mystery [restriction mapping of mitochondrial DNA; research by Brian W. Bowen] R. Lewin. *Science* 243:1009 F 24 '89
Restriction fragment length polymorphisms associated with water use efficiency in tomato. B. Martin and others. bibl f il *Science* 243:1725-8 Mr 31 '89
RESTROOMS *See* Public comfort stations
RESTRUCTURING (EDUCATION) *See* Education
RESURRECTION
See also
 Jesus Christ—Resurrection and Ascension
Death threats. P. J. Ryan. il *America* 161:307 N 4 '89
Easter meditation:
 The resurrection of the body. J. P. Baumgaertner. *The Christian Century* 106:302-3 Mr 22-29 '89
RESUSCITATION
CPR: 4 steps to save a life. A. C. Mallozzi. il *Good Housekeeping* 208:211 Mr '89
Problems reported with two heart rescues. S. Hart. *Science News* 136:85 Ag 5 '89
RETAIL TRADE
See also
 Allied Stores Corp.
 American Stores Co.
 Blacks in retail trade
 Bloomingdale's
 Christmas business
 Claire's Stores Inc.
 Clothing industry—Marketing
 CML Group, Inc.
 Collective labor agreements—Retail trade
 Dayton-Hudson Corp.
 Department stores
 Designs, Inc.
 Edison Brothers Stores, Inc.
 F. W. Woolworth Co.
 Franchise system
 Goldblatt's Department Stores
 J. C. Penney Company, Inc.
 K Mart Corp.
 Lands' End, Inc.
 Limited, Inc.
 Mail order business
 Melville Corporation
 Nordstrom, Inc.
 Outlet stores
 R. H. Macy & Co., Inc.
 Rose's Stores, Inc.
 Sales
 Sales personnel
 Sears, Roebuck and Co.
 Secondhand trade
 Shopping centers
 Stores
 Supermarkets
 Thrift shops and rummage sales
 Wal-Mart Stores, Inc.
 Women in retail trade
Pressures reshaping retailing in the '90's [address, January 27, 1989] J. F. Coates. *Vital Speeches of the Day* 55:356-60 Ap 1 '89
The shape of 1990: a new projection. *Nation's Business* 77:8 O '89
Acquisitions and mergers
How Ames is digesting its 'whale' [Zayre stores] C. Tucher. il *Business Week* p62 S 11 '89
International aspects
Fast break at Tiffany's [Mitsukoshi's stake] M. Roman. il por *Business Week* p102+ O 9 '89
Great Britain
Another bloody nose for Asher? [stakes in Storehouse plc owned by A. Edelman and D. Rowland] J. Ferry. il por *Forbes* 144:184+ N 27 '89
Advertising
See also
 In-store advertising
As price tags shrink, so will the daily newspaper. W. Konrad. il *Business Week* p44 Jl 3 '89
Finance
Little prices are looking good to big retailers [Sears' switch] A. Dunkin. il *Business Week* p42+ Jl 3 '89
Retailing. J. A. Trachtenberg. il *Forbes* 143:188-90 Ja 9 '89
A storekeeper's caveat: let the seller beware. A. Dunkin. il *Business Week* p84 Ja 9 '89
Laws and regulations
Japan
Japan's master of retailing [I. Nakauchi] S. Wagstyl. por *World Press Review* 36:52 Ja '89

A land of papa-mama shops [complex marketing regulations deter foreign retailers] J. Impoco. il *U.S. News & World Report* 106:47-8 Ap 24 '89
Management
Retailing's winners & losers. B. Saporito. il *Fortune* 120:69+ D 18 '89
What ails retailing. S. Caminiti. il *Fortune* 119:61+ Ja 30 '89
Securities
Big fish in small ponds. K. L. Fisher. il *Forbes* 143:278 Je 26 '89
Security measures
See also
 Checkpoint Systems, Inc.
 Shoplifting—Security measures
Her eyes see all, her face reveals nothing: Anne Droid is the shoplifter's nemesis [mannequin with built-in surveillance system; developed by F. J. Gutierrez] il por *People Weekly* 32:97 O 23 '89
Quick checks [point-of-sale systems that verify checks and credit cards] J. Wynn. il *Nation's Business* 77:45-6 D '89
Great Britain
See also
 B A T Industries plc
 House of Fraser plc
 Isosceles plc
 Marks & Spencer plc
 Storehouse plc
Japan
See also
 Mitsukoshi Ltd.
 Mr. Max Corporation
 Seibu Group
 Yaohan Department Store Co. Ltd.
Ready, set, sell—Japan is buying. C. Rapoport. il *Fortune* 120:159-60+ S 11 '89
Sweden
See also
 IKEA Svenska Forsaljnings AB
RETAIL TRADE CATALOGS *See* Catalogs, Commercial
RETAINING WALLS
3 easy holdups [interlocking concrete blocks] T. O. Bakke. il *Popular Science* 235:90-1 Jl '89
Build a dry stone retaining wall. A. Rooze. il *The Family Handyman* 39:62-4+ Je '89
Building with native material [stone and concrete wall] M. Landis. il *Workbench* 45:46-8 My/Je '89
A stone wall for a steep slope. il *Southern Living* 24:69 Je '89
RETALIATION AGAINST TERRORISTS *See* Terrorism—Retaliation
RETALLICK, MARTHA J.
Terry Chröm. il por *Bicycling* 30:62-3 Ja/F '89
RETARDED CHILDREN *See* Mentally handicapped children
RETARDED PERSONS *See* Mentally handicapped
RETIN-A *See* Tretinoin
RETINA
See also
 Rods and cones
 Visual purple
Electrophysiologic responses in hamster superior colliculus evoked by regenerating retinal axons. S. A. Keirstead and others. bibl f il *Science* 246:255-7 O 13 '89
Gating of retinal transmission by afferent eye position and movement signals [cats] R. Lal and M. J. Friedlander. bibl f il *Science* 243:93-6 Ja 6 '89
Plasticity and differentiation of embryonic retinal cells after terminal mitosis. R. Adler and M. Hatlee. bibl f il *Science* 243:391-3 Ja 20 '89
Spatial buffering of light-evoked potassium increases by retinal Müller (Glial) cells. C. J. Karwoski and others. bibl f il *Science* 244:578-80 My 5 '89
Transplantation
Transplanting the light fantastic [cover story] R. Weiss. il *Science News* 136:297+ N 4 '89
RETINOBLASTOMA *See* Eye—Cancer
RETINOIC ACID
See also
 Isotretinoin
 Tretinoin
From wrinkle cream to cancer cure? N. J. Freundlich. il *Business Week* p146 F 20 '89
RETINOL *See* Vitamin A
RETINOPATHY, DIABETIC *See* Diabetic retinopathy
RETINOPATHY OF PREMATURITY
Trouble in the nursery [hospital lights] G. Cowley. il *Newsweek* 114:52 Ag 28 '89
RETIREES *See* Aged
RETIREMENT
See also
 Air pilots—Retirement
 American Association of Retired Persons
 Athletes—Retirement
 Blacks—Retirement
 Executives—Retirement
 Farmers—Retirement
 Football players—Retirement

RETIREMENT—See also—*cont.*
   Senators—Retirement
   Social security
Are Americans retiring too early? D. Cordtz. il *Reader's Digest* 135:103-5 N '89
"Golden years" are costly to U.S. [views of Kingsley Davis] il *USA Today (Periodical)* 117:16 Ap '89
Jobs that will keep you working happily ever after. T. Thompson. il *U.S. News & World Report* 107:64-6+ Ag 14 '89
A new job, a new life [cover story] G. Rosenblum. il *New Choices for the Best Years* 29:27-34 Ja '89
No reason to force retirement [views of Martin Lyon Levine] il *USA Today (Periodical)* 118:7 Ag '89
The retiring kind. A. A. Ettinger. il *The New York Times Magazine* p18+ My 28 '89
Services to get your head ready for life without work. D. M. Topolnicki. il *Money* 18:161 Ja '89
The trend toward earlier retirement [views of Michael D. Packard and Virginia P. Reno] *The Futurist* 23:52-3 Jl/Ag '89
Two of us is one too many [husband takes early retirement] H. Bennett. il *The New York Times Magazine* p22+ O 22 '89
Working late: the railroad to retirement. R. Hoopes. il *Modern Maturity* 32:34-7+ F/Mr '89

RETIREMENT, PLACES OF
   See also
   Retirement communities
Fort Myers, Fla. il map *New Choices for the Best Years* 29:12 Mr '89
Hot Springs, Ark. il *New Choices for the Best Years* 29:13 My '89
Is Europe worth the big price? A. Rand. il map *New Choices for the Best Years* 29:38-40+ F '89
Move or stay put? M. C. Paulson. *Changing Times* 43:126-7 O '89
Rabun County, Georgia. L. Harrison. map *New Choices for the Best Years* 29:13 Je '89
Recruiting retirees can help turn a bust into a boomtown. S. R. Gregg. il *U.S. News & World Report* 106:46-7 Mr 6 '89
Roswell, N.M. map *New Choices for the Best Years* 29:14 F '89
San Antonio, Texas. il map *New Choices for the Best Years* 29:12 Ap '89
Santa Rosa, Calif. map *New Choices for the Best Years* 29:10 Ja '89
Where the living is easy and taxes are low. T. Tritch. il *Money* 18 Money Guide:84 Fall '89
Winter in the Texas tropics [Rio Grande Valley; cover story] N. Cornell. il *New Choices for the Best Years* 29:22-6 N '89

RETIREMENT BENEFITS
Before the well runs dry: cutting the cost of retiree health benefits. C. A. Hanks. *USA Today (Periodical)* 117:86-8 My '89
How to finance a comfortable retirement [cover story; special issue; with editorial comment by Frank B. Merrick] il *Money* 18 Money Guide:4, 8-18+ Fall '89
Saying the big goodbye [early retirement offers] J. B. Quinn. il *Newsweek* 114:74 O 9 '89

   Accounting
The killer cost stalking business [health benefits] C. J. Loomis. il *Fortune* 119:58-9+ F 27 '89
Retiree benefits: this footnote doesn't have to become a nightmare. J. R. Norman. il *Business Week* p39 F 27 '89
Soothing the sting of an accounting rule [employee health benefits] L. J. Nathans. il *Business Week* p106 S 18 '89

   Taxation
Avoiding the IRS penalty box. E. Schurenberg. il *Money* 18 Money Guide:44 Fall '89
Now you see it . . . [future health benefits for retired employees] J. Novack. il *Forbes* 144:57 Ag 21 '89

RETIREMENT COMMUNITIES
   See also
   Life care communities
   Quartzsite (Ariz.)
Joey Dee, past master of twist, plans a refuge for those caught between rock and a hard place [for former recording stars] P. Freeman. il pors *People Weekly* 32:131-2+ N 20 '89

   Segregation
A welcome mat for minorities? A. Winter. *Modern Maturity* 32:14 Ag/S '89

RETIREMENT INCOME
   See also
   401(k) plan
   403(b) plan
   Individual retirement accounts
   Pensions
   Simplified employee pensions
   Social security
Age 70: a duo comfortably retired. M. B. Front. il por *Fortune* 120 no10 Special Issue:142 Fall '89
The baby-boomer retirement blues. il *Black Enterprise* 20:51 O '89

Early retirees look to boost income and cope with inflation [Ken and Dessa Dunn] L. Luciano. il *Money* 18:145-6 Ag '89
Early retirement: it pays to plan early. D. H. Dunn. il *Business Week* p134-5 F 27 '89
Financial security: what every woman must know [results of survey] C. L. Hayes. *McCall's* 117:124+ O '89
Five sins to avoid when investing for retirement [experience of Virginia Kinet] E. Schultz. il *Fortune* 119:24+ Mr 27 '89
Growing old frugally. J. B. Quinn. il *Newsweek* 114 Special Issue:102-5 Wint '89/Spr '90
How to afford retirement [cover story; special section] il *U.S. News & World Report* 107:55-7+ Ag 14 '89
How to finance a comfortable retirement [cover story; special issue; with editorial comment by Frank B. Merrick] il *Money* 18 Money Guide:4, 8-18+ Fall '89
How to plan now for your retirement. R. J. Klein. il *Fortune* 120 no10 Special Issue:28-9+ Fall '89
How we will live [baby boomers] S. Dentzer. il *U.S. News & World Report* 107:62-4 D 25 '89-Ja 1 '90
The pre-retiree: a supersaver, a positive thinker, a terrible planner. D. M. Topolnicki. il *Money* 18:195-6 Ap '89
Six mistakes retirees make and how to avoid them. M. C. Paulson. *Changing Times* 43:100-1 F '89
What nest for your egg? P. N. Strassels. il *Nation's Business* 77:80-1 Je '89
Will you be able to retire? [cover story] D. Kirkpatrick. il *Fortune* 120:56-9+ Jl 31 '89
Wrap session [retirement income strategy for millionaires] B. Weberman. il *Forbes* 144 Special Issue:395 O 23 '89

RETIX (FIRM)
Let your modem do the walking. D. Churbuck. il *Forbes* 143:280 My 29 '89

RETRIEVERS
   See also
   Golden retrievers
   Labrador retrievers
A good retriever conserves wildlife. S. Z. Miller. il *The Conservationist* 43:26-33 Mr/Ap '89
Grandpa and the kid [hunting for Christmas goose with Chesapeake Bay retriever] D. Sisson. il *Field & Stream* 94:43+ D '89

   Anecdotes, facetiae, satire, etc.
A fetching story. P. Stone. il *The Mother Earth News* 120:144 N/D '89

RETROVIR See Azidothymidine
RETROVIRUSES
   See also
   HIV viruses
   HTLV viruses
   Leukemia viruses
A genetic shield to prevent emphysema? [work of Ronald G. Crystal with antitrypsin gene-carrying retrovirus] B. J. Culliton. il *Science* 246:750-1 N 10 '89
Germline transmission of exogenous genes in the chicken. R. A. Bosselman and others. bibl f il *Science* 243:533-5 Ja 27 '89
High-level recombinant gene expression in rabbit endothelial cells transduced by retroviral vectors. J. A. Zwiebel and others. bibl f il *Science* 243:220-2 Ja 13 '89
Immunodeficiency and clonal growth of target cells induced by helper-free defective retrovirus. M. Huang and others. bibl f il *Science* 246:1614-17 D 22 '89
Perineurium originates from fibroblasts: demonstration in vitro with a retroviral marker. M. B. Bunge and others. bibl f il *Science* 243:229-31 Ja 13 '89
Retrovirus vectors: promise and reality. H. M. Temin. bibl f *Science* 246:983 N 24 '89
Two new approaches to genetic emphysema [antitrypsin gene-carrying retrovirus; work of Ronald G. Crystal] S. Hart and A. McKenzie. *Science News* 136:233 O 7 '89

RETTON, MARY LOU
   about
Return of the pixies. L. Montville. il pors *Sports Illustrated* 71:34-6+ N 27 '89

RETURN OF THE KILLER TOMATOES: THE SEQUEL [film] See Motion picture reviews—Single works

REUBEN, CAROLYN, 1947-
How healthy is your home? Ways to eliminate indoor pollution. il *Utne Reader* p76-9 My/Je '89
On the cuspid. il *Ms.* 17:16+ Je '89

REUBEN, DAVID R.
Cigarette face—another reason not to smoke. il *Good Housekeeping* 208:70 Mr '89

REUBENS, BEATRICE G.
Unemployment insurance in the United States and Europe, 1973-83. bibl f il *Monthly Labor Review* 112:22-31 Ap '89

REULAND, TIMOTHY J.
God is my client. il *Commonweal* 116:527-9 O 6 '89

REUNION [film] See Motion picture reviews—Single works
REUNIONS
   See also
   College reunions
   Family reunions
   High school reunions

REUNIONS—cont.
A reunion revives the bittersweet memories of an age gone
by for alumni of an Albany orphanage [Albany Home
for Children] S. Carswell. il *People Weekly* 32:159+ D
11 '89
REUSCHEL, RICK
                    about
On the stick [cover story] R. Fimrite. il pors *Sports Illustrated*
71:18-23 Jl 10 '89
REUTER, EDZARD
                    about
The even-bigger shadow Daimler could cast. J. Templeman.
il por *Business Week* p54-5 My 22 '89
Herr Reuter takes to the skies. P. Fuhrman. il por *Forbes*
143:88+ Mr 20 '89
REUTER, MADALYNNE, AND YEN, MARIANNE
News of the week. See issues of Publishers Weekly
REUTERS HOLDINGS PLC
Welcome to Hauppauge, the world's next financial capital
[cover story] J. Marcom, Jr. il *Forbes* 144:143-9 O 30
'89
REUTHER, VICTOR
                    about
Victor Reuther [interview] B. Koeppel. il *The Progressive*
53:25-8 D '89
REUTTEN, PAM
                    about
Audiotape business reels in profits. R. Gunnerson. il pors
Home Office Computing 7:63-4 N '89
REUTTEN, TERRY
                    about
Audiotape business reels in profits. R. Gunnerson. il pors
Home Office Computing 7:63-4 N '89
REVCO D.S., INC.
Chain of troubles: the LBO that went bust. E. Pomice.
U.S. News & World Report 106:69 F 13 '89
REVEGETATION
                    Australia
How to stop the desert's march. J. Cribb. *World Press Review*
36:32 Ap '89
REVEL, JEAN-FRANÇOIS
Hastening the death of communism. *Commentary* 88:19-23
O '89
Is communism reversible? [cover story] *Commentary* 87:17-24
Ja '89
REVELATION
                    See also
Mystery
REVELL, DONALD
Tabard and terrace [poem] *The New Republic* 200:34
Mr 6 '89
REVENGE
Getting even . . . . Hollywood-style. M. Beck. il *TV Guide*
37:4-6+ Je 10-16 '89
REVENUE CANADA *See* Canada. Revenue Canada
REVENUE SHARING *See* Intergovernmental tax relations
REVENUE STAMPS
New York State migratory bird print and stamp program.
il *The Conservationist* 43:56 Mr/Ap '89
REVERE BEACH (MASS.)
Revere Beach: a peculiarly American seaside resort. M.
Berman. bibl il map *Focus (New York, N.Y.: 1950)* 39:4-8
Fall '89
REVERSE MORTGAGES *See* Home equity conversion
REVERSE TRANSCRIPTASE *See* Transcriptases
REVIEWS OF BALLET *See* Ballet reviews
REVIEWS OF BOOKS *See* Book reviews and reviewing
REVIEWS OF DANCE *See* Dance reviews
REVIEWS OF MOTION PICTURES *See* Motion picture
reviews
REVIEWS OF MUSICALS, REVUES, ETC. *See* Musicals,
revues, etc.—Reviews
REVIEWS OF OPERA *See* Opera reviews
REVIEWS OF OPERETTA *See* Operetta reviews
REVIEWS OF ORATORIOS *See* Oratorio reviews
REVIEWS OF PLAYS *See* Theater reviews
REVIEWS OF RADIO PROGRAMS *See* Radio program
reviews
REVIEWS OF ROCK OPERAS *See* Rock opera reviews
REVIEWS OF TELEVISION PROGRAMS *See* Television
program reviews
REVIEWS OF VIDEODISCS *See* Videodisc reviews
REVIEWS OF VIDEOTAPES *See* Videotape reviews
REVILLA, VICENTE
Descendants of the Incas. il *Society* 26:77-80 Jl/Ag '89
REVISED STANDARD VERSION OF THE BIBLE *See*
Bible—Versions
REVISION OF MANUSCRIPTS *See* Authorship—Copy
preparation
REVIVALS
Worship by-the-sea; camp-meetings and seaside resorts in
19th century America. S. E. Demars. bibl il maps *Focus
(New York, N.Y.: 1950)* 38:15-20 Wint '88
REVKIN, ANDREW C.
Endless summer. *Current (Washington, D.C.)* 310:4-10 F
'89

REVLON INC.
The changes at Revlon are more than just cosmetic. M.
Roman. il por *Business Week* p74+ N 20 '89
Do it yourself [D. Tarlow appointed executive vice president
of advertising] B. Kanner. il por *New York* 22:26+ Ag
21 '89
The inimitable Halston. N. Darnton. il pors *Newsweek*
114:64-6 Ag 7 '89
Mary Nguyen's G.I. dad has never seen her face, but Revlon
thinks it's a winner [Most Unforgettable Woman of the
Year] M. H. J. Farrell. il pors *People Weekly* 32:54-5
Ag 7 '89
REVOLUTION, INDUSTRIAL *See* Industrial revolution
REVOLUTIONARY WAR (U.S.) *See* United States—History—
Revolution, 1775-1783
REVOLUTIONS
                    See also
Coups d'etat
France—History—Revolution, 1789-1799
France—History—February Revolution, 1848
Haiti—History—Revolution, 1791-1804
Mexico—History—Revolution, 1910-1920
National liberation movements
Poetry and revolutions
United States—History—Revolution, 1775-1783
In Europe, history repeats itself [parallels between 1989 and
1848] M. Mandelbaum. il *Time* 134:80 D 25 '89
People power. R. A. Falk. *The Nation* 248:801 Je 12 '89
You say you want a revolution. E. Selbin. il *Utne Reader*
p20+ N/D '89
REVOLUTIONS AND RELIGION
What are the rules for revolution? A. L. Sherman. il
Christianity Today 33:54-5 Ja 13 '89
REVOLVERS
The cross fire over Jack Ruby's gun. il por *U.S. News
& World Report* 107:10 D 25 '89-Ja 1 '90
Jack Ruby's family and lawyer battle for possession of the
gun that killed Lee Harvey Oswald. W. Plummer. il por
People Weekly 31:42-3 My 22 '89
                    Anecdotes, facetiae, satire, etc.
Beretta versus Beretta [car vs. gun] B. McCall. il *Car and
Driver* 34:86-9 F '89
REVOLVING DOORS
New products [Cirkel-Line multifunction revolving door] il
Architectural Record 177:148 Je '89
REVUES (FLOOR SHOWS) *See* Floor shows
REWARD (PSYCHOLOGY)
                    See also
Delay of gratification
REWARDS, PRIZES, ETC.
                    See also
American Black Achievement Awards
Certificates of merit
Literary prizes
Nobel prizes
                    Anecdotes, facetiae, satire, etc.
Dubious Achievement Awards of 1988 [cover story] il *Esquire*
111:87-90+ Ja '89
REX
                    about
Best face forward. D. Guerre. il pors *Harper's Bazaar* 122:28+
Ag '89
REX (LOS ANGELES, CALIF.: RESTAURANT) *See* Los
Angeles (Calif.)—Restaurants, nightclubs, bars, etc.
REYBURN, ELVA KLING
                    about
There's still hope, Elva. R. Telander. por *Sports Illustrated*
71:128 O 9 '89
REYER, H.-U.
(jt. auth) See Isack, H. A., and Reyer, H.-U.
REYES, ANGELITA
In the flower garden. il *America* 160:138-40+ F 18 '89
REYES, WALFREDO, JR.
                    about
Walfredo Reyes, Jr. S. Yanow. il por *Down Beat* 56:27-8
D '89
REYES ESTRADA, JORGE
The journey to the Rio Grande. il *World Press Review*
36:30-1 Ap '89
REYKJAVIK (ICELAND)
                    Social conditions
President Vigdís [helps Americans free car from a snowdrift]
The New Yorker 65:36-7 Mr 20 '89
REYKOWSKI, JANUSZ
                    about
Time of chaos [interview] il *Maclean's* 102:33 Ap 17 '89
REYNOLDS, A. H.
Herman [poem] *Essence* 19:145 F '89
REYNOLDS, BURT
                    about
Breaking in to family life. il pors *People Weekly* 32:98-9+
N 6 '89
Burt Reynolds on the skids . . . will B. L. Stryker be
his deliverance? P. Jordan. il pors *TV Guide* 37:26-9 Mr
4-10 '89
REYNOLDS, C. P.
Paris journal. See occasional issues of Gourmet

REYNOLDS, CAROLYN
about
At MIPCOM: a buyer's life. P. Ainslie. il pors *Channels (New York, N.Y.: 1986)* 9:36-40 Mr '89
REYNOLDS, GLENN H.
A guide to budget politics. *Ad Astra* 1:21 Je '89
REYNOLDS, JEFFREY M.
Idyllic infra-red. il *Petersen's Photographic Magazine* 18:22-7 D '89
REYNOLDS, NANCY, 1938-
East meets West in Amsterdam: student days in Holland. il *Dance Magazine* 63:52-5 N '89
REYNOLDS, PATRICK
about
Patrick Reynolds fumes about his tobacco-rich clan in a tangy, tell-all book. P. Freeman. il pors *People Weekly* 31:46-7 Ap 24 '89
RJR dearest. M. Alpert. il por *Fortune* 119:142 Ap 10 '89
Talk-show prep. L. See. *Publishers Weekly* 236:201 Jl 28 '89
Tobacco road's dirty ashtrays. J. Castro. il por *Time* 133:52 Ap 24 '89
REYNOLDS, PATRICK T.
An art of conflict. il por *Americana* 17:22-5 Mr/Ap '89
REYNOLDS, QUINTON
about
Breaking in to family life. il pors *People Weekly* 32:98-9+ N 6 '89
REYNOLDS, RENNY
about
Bloom service deluxe. E. Louie. il por *Harper's Bazaar* 122:134+ Je '89
REYNOLDS, SIÂN
High flyers: women aviators in pre-war France. bibl il *History Today* 39:36-41 Ap '89
REYNOLDS (R. J.) TOBACCO CO. See R. J. Reynolds Tobacco Co.
REYNOLDS FAMILY
about
Patrick Reynolds fumes about his tobacco-rich clan in a tangy, tell-all book. P. Freeman. il pors *People Weekly* 31:46-7 Ap 24 '89
RJR dearest. M. Alpert. il por *Fortune* 119:142 Ap 10 '89
Tobacco road's dirty ashtrays. J. Castro. il por *Time* 133:52 Ap 24 '89
REYNOLDS METALS CO.
Can Reynolds wrap up the kitchen market? [plastic packaging] M. Schroeder. il *Business Week* p68+ My 29 '89
REZA PAHLAVI
about
Battle of the heirs: son of Ayatollah vs. son of Shah. E. Flores. il pors *World Press Review* 36:16 Ag '89
The man who would be Shah. P. Axthelm. il pors *People Weekly* 31:46-51 Ap 3 '89
RF WAVES See Electromagnetic waves
RFLPS See Restriction fragment length polymorphisms
RHAGOLETIS See Fruit flies
RHEE, SUE GOO, AND OTHERS
Studies of inositol phospholipid-specific phospholipase C. bibl f *Science* 244:546-50 My 5 '89
RHEINEISEN CHEMICAL PRODUCTS
More German dealing in the poison trade [selling chemical weapons to Iran] *Newsweek* 114:28 Jl 10 '89
RHEINSTEIN, SUZANNE
about
Los-Anglophile. B. Goodwin. il pors *House & Garden* 161:82-9+ Ag '89
RHENIUM
Isotopes
Rhenium-osmium isotope systematics of carbonaceous chondrites [resonance ionization mass spectrometry] R. J. Walker and J. W. Morgan. bibl f il *Science* 243:519-22 Ja 27 '89
RHEOLOGY
See also
Electrorheological fluids
RHESUS MONKEYS See Monkeys
RHETORIC
See also
Hyperbole
Irony
Oratory in the modern Senate [J. Tower nomination] A. Heard. il *The American Spectator* 22:14-15 My '89
RHEUMATISM
See also
Arthritis
Fibrositis
RHEUMATOID ARTHRITIS See Arthritis
RHINE RIVER
Cruising down or up the Rhine. il map *Sunset (Central West edition)* 182:92-3 My '89
RHINEBECK (N.Y.)
Historic houses, sites, etc.
See also
Wilderstein (Historic house: Rhinebeck, N.Y.)

RHINITIS, ALLERGIC See Hay fever
RHINO RECORDS
The gold in oldies. F. Meeks. il pors *Forbes* 143:68+ My 1 '89
RHINOCEROS
Deconstructivist rhinos [thwarting poachers by removing horns in Namibia] il *Discover* 10:12 O '89
Heavy artillery for horns of plenty [Kenya's war on ivory poachers] E. Ransdell. il *U.S. News & World Report* 106:61+ F 20 '89
Horns of a dilemma [rhino poaching in Zimbabwe] M. L. Knox. il *Sierra* 74:58-67 N/D '89
King of the marsh [tracking rhinoceros in Royal Chitwan National Park, Nepal; cover story] E. Dinerstein. il *International Wildlife* 19:4-11 Mr/Ap '89
Rhino warrior [conservation efforts in Royal Chitwan National Park] D. Starr. il *Omni (New York, N.Y.)* 11:17+ S '89
The rhino's last stand [battle against poachers in Zimbabwe] A. Linklater. il *Reader's Digest* 134:106-10 F '89
Breeding
Oh, give me a home where wild rhinos roam [C. Bentsen's breeding farm for black rhinos in McAllen, Tex.] M. Vollers. il por *Time* 133:12+ Je 26 '89
Texas rancher Calvin Bentsen, a former big-game hunter, takes his best shot at saving the rhinos [breeding farm for black rhinos in McAllen, Tex.] K. Demaret. il pors *People Weekly* 32:103-4 D 11 '89
RHINOCEROS, FOSSIL
The Blue Lake rhinoceros [lava mold found in Washington State] K. Kaler. il map *Earth Science* 42:22-4 Fall '89
RHINOPLASTY See Surgery, Plastic
RHINOVIRUSES
Inactivation
A cold remedy not to be sneezed at [identification of ICAM-1, rhinovirus receptor site] il *U.S. News & World Report* 106:14 Mr 20 '89
The cold war heats up [identification of rhinovirus receptor site] R. Trubo. il *American Health* 8:12 N '89
Coming closer to a common-cold cure [rhinovirus receptor molecule ICAM-1] il *Newsweek* 113:60 Mr 20 '89
Rhinovirus receptor found; colds carry on [identification of ICAM-1] R. Weiss. *Science News* 135:165 Mr 18 '89
Snuffed sniffles [discovery of ICAM-1 receptor site] *Time* 133:61 Mr 20 '89
Taming the wily rhinovirus [work of Michael Rossmann and Richard Colonno] P. Radetsky. il *Discover* 10:38-43 Ap '89
RHIZOMES See Stems (Plants)
RHOADS, ROSS, 1932-
about
Fatigue fatigue. M. E. Marty. *The Christian Century* 106:767 Ag 16-23 '89
RHODE ISLAND
See also
Birds—Rhode Island
Block Island (R.I.)
Politics and government
The failure of success. D. R. Carlin, Jr. *Commonweal* 116:8 Ja 13 '89
New talents: Patrick J. Kennedy. il por *Harper's Bazaar* 122:118 Mr '89
Religious institutions and affairs
The tax-exempt witch [coven of witches deserves tax-exempt status as a legitimate religious group] T. K. Jones. *Christianity Today* 33:15 O 6 '89
RHODES, DANIEL, 1911-1989
about
Obituary
American Craft il por 49:74 O/N '89. W. D. Parry
RHODES, FRANK H. T., 1926-
The mission and ministry of Jesuits in higher education [address, June 5, 1989; cover story] *America* 161:54-60 Jl 29-Ag 5 '89
RHODES, JOHN J.
Should the "balanced budget constitutional amendment" be adopted? [excerpts from statement, October 15, 1987] *Congressional Digest* 68:281+ N '89
RHODES, LAWRENCE
about
New York University, Tisch School of the Arts, and the Second Avenue Dance Company: a dancer prepares. O. Stuart. il por *Dance Magazine* 63:60-1 Mr '89
RHODES, MAURA
Beware the new tick invasion! il *Redbook* 173:14 Jl '89
Countering the chemistry of fatigue. il *Health (New York, N.Y.)* 21:48-9 F '89
For less stress—breathe right. il *Redbook* 173:14 Je '89
RHODES, MILTON
ACA: a view from the field. See issues of Horizon (Tuscaloosa, Ala.)
RHODES, RICHARD
about
PW interviews. M. McQuade. il por *Publishers Weekly* 236:39-40 O 20 '89
RHODES, WILLIAM REGINALD
about
Rhodes to Latin America. J. Zweig. il por *Forbes* 144:142+ S 4 '89

RHODES SCHOLARS AND SCHOLARSHIPS
Black South African, 26, wins Rhodes scholarship [I. Shongwe] *Jet* 75:23 Ja 9 '89
RHODOBACTER
Hydrophobic organization of membrane proteins. D. C. Rees and others. bibl f il *Science* 245:510-13 Ag 4 '89
RHODODENDRONS
Let's go rhododendron crawling [Western States] il *Sunset (Central West edition)* 182:222-3 Ap '89
Wild rhododendrons on their home turf. il *Sunset (Central West edition)* 182:24 My '89
RHODOPSEUDOMONAS
Dispersed polaron simulations of electron transfer in photosynthetic reaction centers. A. Warshel and others. bibl f il *Science* 246:112-16 O 6 '89
The photosynthetic reaction center from the purple bacterium Rhodopseudomonas viridis. J. Deisenhofer and H. Michel. bibl f il *Science* 245:1463-73 S 29 '89
RHODOPSIN *See* Visual purple
RHODOPSIN, BACTERIAL *See* Pigments (Biology)
RHONE-POULENC SA
On the prowl in America. J. Zweig. il por *Forbes* 143:154 My 1 '89
RHUBARB
See also
Cooking—Rhubarb
About rhubarb. S. Pacher. il *The Mother Earth News* 116:28-32 Mr/Ap '89
RHUBARB DESSERTS *See* Desserts
RHUS *See* Sumac
RHYTHM
See also
Cycles
Psychological aspects
Just say yes to rhythms [path to altered consciousness and spiritual exploration] J. Tibbetts. il *Utne Reader* p32+ N/D '89
RHYTHM, BIOLOGICAL *See* Biological rhythms
RHYTHM AND BLUES COMPACT DISCS *See* Compact discs—Rock music
RHYTHMIC GYMNASTICS
Great lengths. il *Mademoiselle* 95:146-9 Jl '89
RIBALTA, FRANCISCO, 1565?-1628
about
The man from Valencia. A. F. Collins. il *Art in America* 77:71-3 Ap '89
RIBBS, WILLY T.
about
Cosbys backing race car driver Willy T. Ribbs in championship auto racing. il pors *Jet* 77:16-17 D 4 '89
RIBEIRO, JOSÉ M. C., AND OTHERS
A novel vasodilatory peptide from the salivary glands of the sand fly Lutzomyia longipalpis. bibl f il *Science* 243:212-14 Ja 13 '89
RIBES, JACQUELINE DE
about
Regal air. A. Bogart. il pors *Harper's Bazaar* 122:378-9 S '89
RIBOFLAVIN *See* Vitamin B₂
RIBONUCLEASES
The design and catalytic properties of a simplified ribonuclease P RNA. D. S. Waugh and others. bibl f il *Science* 244:1569-71 Je 30 '89
Double-stranded ribonuclease coinduced with interferon. J. M. Meegan and P. I. Marcus. bibl f il *Science* 244:1089-91 Je 2 '89
The RNA processing enzyme RNase MRP is identical to the Th RNP and related to RNase P [autoimmune disease study] H. A. Gold and others. bibl f il *Science* 245:1377-80 S 22 '89
Specific interactions in RNA enzyme-substrate complexes. C. Guerrier-Takada and others. bibl f il *Science* 246:1578-84 D 22 '89
RIBONUCLEIC ACID *See* RNA
RIBONUCLEOPROTEINS *See* Nucleoproteins
RIBOSOMAL RNA
Phylogenetic meaning of the kingdom concept: an unusual ribosomal RNA from Giardia lamblia. M. L. Sogin and others. bibl f il *Science* 243:75-7 Ja 6 '89
Phylogenetic stains: ribosomal RNA-based probes for the identification of single cells. E. F. DeLong and others. bibl f il *Science* 243:1360-3 Mr 10 '89
RNA-protein interactions in 30S ribosomal subunits: folding and function of 16S rRNA. S. Stern and others. bibl f il *Science* 244:783-90 My 19 '89
RIBOSOMES
The tails of ubiquitin [linked to both protein decay and synthesis; research by Daniel Finley and others] J. Kinoshita. *Scientific American* 260:33-4 Je '89
RIBOT, MARC
about
Leapin' Lizard. D. Handelman. il por *Rolling Stone* p25 S 7 '89
RIBOUD, ANTOINE
about
Is BSN's stomach as big as its eyes? F. J. Comes. il por *Business Week* p55+ Ja 9 '89

RIBOUD, BARBARA CHASE- *See* Chase-Riboud, Barbara, 1936-
RIBOZYMES
Catalytic RNA wins Chemistry Nobel [T. R. Cech and S. Altman] M. M. Waldrop. il pors *Science* 246:325 O 20 '89
Chemistry [S. Altman and T. R. Cech awarded Nobel Prize] il pors *Time* 134:73 O 23 '89
Chemistry of life [work of S. Altman] R. Corelli. il por *Maclean's* 102:58 O 23 '89
Defining the inside and outside of a catalytic RNA molecule [structure of Tetrahymena ribozyme] J. A. Latham and T. R. Cech. bibl f il *Science* 245:276-82 Jl 21 '89
How do you read from the palimpsest of life? M. M. Waldrop. il *Science* 246:578-9 N 3 '89
In the beginning [work of Jack W. Szostak and Jennifer Doudna] J. P. Rennie. *Scientific American* 261:28+ S '89
RNA offers clue to life's start [work of Jack W. Szostak and Jennifer A. Doudna] I. Amato. *Science News* 135:372 Je 17 '89
RNA researchers earn Chemistry Nobel [T. R. Cech and S. Altman] I. Amato. *Science News* 136:262 O 21 '89
Stereochemical course of catalysis by the Tetrahymena ribozyme. J. Rajagopal and others. bibl f il *Science* 244:692-4 My 12 '89
Stereochemistry of RNA cleavage by the Tetrahymena ribozyme and evidence that the chemical step is not rate-limiting. J. A. McSwiggen and T. R. Cech. bibl f il *Science* 244:679-83 My 12 '89
RICCARDELLI, JOHN
about
Remembering a fine fair. G. Turim. il por *Americana* 17:50-4 Jl/Ag '89
I RICCHI (WASHINGTON, D.C.: RESTAURANT) *See* Washington (D.C.)—Restaurants, nightclubs, bars, etc.
RICCI, CLAUDIA
Raffi. il pors *Parents* 64:134-6+ N '89
RICCI, ROBERT, 1905-1988
about
Gardens: a philosophy of fragrance: Robert Ricci's floral domain in the Île-de-France. C. Styles-McLeod. il por *Architectural Digest* 46:142-7 Ja '89
RICE, ANNE, 1941-
Do the Rice thing. D. Perry. il *Omni (New York, N.Y.)* 12:26+ O '89
Interview with the vampire writer. K. M. Ramsland. il por *Psychology Today* 23:34 N '89
RICE, ANTHONY L.
Oceanographic ships. bibl il *Sea Frontiers* 35:14-17 Ja/F '89
RICE, CHARLES EDWARD
about
"Do we know how to run something like this?". J. H. Taylor. il por *Forbes* 144:79-80 N 27 '89
RICE, G. EDGAR, AND BEVILACQUA, MICHAEL P.
An inducible endothelial cell surface glycoprotein mediates melanoma adhesion. bibl f il *Science* 246:1303-6 D 8 '89
RICE, GEORGE P.
On the origins of speech [address, February 1, 1989] *Vital Speeches of the Day* 55:400-3 Ap 15 '89
RICE, JACKSON *See* Lish, Gordon
RICE, JERRY
about
The 1989 Sport Super Bowl MVP. il pors *Sport (New York, N.Y.)* 80:46 My '89
Beers with . . . Jerry Rice [interview] G. Dickey. il pors *Sport (New York, N.Y.)* 80:19-20 N '89
The hero as huckster. R. Fimrite. por *Sports Illustrated* 70:92 F 13 '89
The San Francisco treat [interview] S. Kettmann. il pors *Gentlemen's Quarterly* 59:121+ O '89
A step above 'em all. R. Wiley. il *Sports Illustrated* 70:30-1 Ja 30 '89
RICE, MATTHEW
about
The Viscount Linley: at home with a royal entrepreneur. E. Lambert. il por *Architectural Digest* 46:50+ F '89
RICE, ROBERT A.
A casualty of war: the Nicaraguan environment. il map *Technology Review* 92:62-71 My/Je '89
RICE, TONY
about
Throwing Rice. H. Gould. il por *Sport (New York, N.Y.)* 80:32 S '89
RICE
See also
Cooking—Rice
Breeding
See also
International Rice Research Institute
Yield
Fading miracle. B. Johnstone. *World Press Review* 36:48 Mr '89

RICE BRAN *See* Bran
RICE PAPER
Japanese glow lamps. il *Sunset (Central West edition)* 182:74-5
F '89
RICE TABLE *See* Rijsttafel
RICH, ANITA
Retirement benefits. il por *World Tennis* 37:22 O '89
RICH, BRUCE
Conservation woes at the World Bank. il *The Nation* 248:73+
Ja 23 '89
RICH, JOHN MARTIN
Self-renewal as faculty development. *The Education Digest*
55:54-7 D '89
RICH, MARC
about
A first world fugitive dabbles in the third world. J. Zweig.
por *Forbes* 144:12 N 13 '89
Letters from home. J. Willoughby. il por *Forbes* 143:38-9
Je 12 '89
RICH, MARIA F.
Broadening the base. il *Opera News* 54:44+ N '89
RICH, ROBERT E.
about
Buffalo's Rich baseball legacy. G. Macnow. il por *Nation's
Business* 77:42-5 F '89
Rich makes his pitch. I. Muchnick. il por *The New York
Times Magazine* p18-19+ Jl 30 '89
RICH
See also
Billionaires
Billionaires' wives
Children of the rich
Millionaires
Wealth
Age 50: rich, with three teenagers [investment portfolio]
R. H. Dillon, Jr. il por *Fortune* 120 no10 Special Issue:136
Fall '89
America's income gap: the closer you look, the worse it
gets. A. Bernstein. il *Business Week* p78-9 Ap 17 '89
Are you watching, Chairman Greenspan? [Forbes four hundred
cost of living extremely well index] M. Kripalani. il *Forbes*
144 Special Issue:388-9 O 23 '89
Chic savages [excerpt] J. Fairchild. il por *New York* 22:44-54
O 16 '89
Climbing Mt. Manhattan [new money vs. old money] J.
Kramer. il *House & Garden* 161:188-9+ O '89
Dating for dollars: the gold diggers of 1989. C. Bushnell.
il *Mademoiselle* 95:176-7 N '89
The Forbes four hundred [cover story] il *Forbes* 144 Special
Issue:145-50+ O 23 '89
Gift list [Forbes four hundred contributors to charities] il
Forbes 144 Special Issue:124-5 O 23 '89
Hard times. *The Nation* 248:544 Ap 24 '89
In defence of the freedom to spend. B. Amiel. il *Maclean's*
102:17 O 23 '89
Mistakes rich investors make. A. C. Brown. il *Forbes* 144
Special Issue:397 O 23 '89
Rich but dumb. T. Noah. *The New Republic* 201:46 D
25 '89
Rich for a day. J. S. Gordon. il *American Heritage* 40:16+
Ap '89
Tracking the rich and famous [R. Leach] H. G. Miller.
por *The Saturday Evening Post* 261:30-1 My/Je '89
Welfare for the rich. A. Etzioni. il *The New Leader* 72:13-14
My 1 '89

Anecdotes, facetiae, satire, etc.
How to get rich quick. D. Owen. il *The Atlantic* 263:14+
Mr '89

Attitudes
What good are the rich? [exhibiting greater concern for the
public good] T. G. Harris and D. Yankelovich. il *Psychology
Today* 23:36-9 Ap '89

Medical care
Status symbol: affluent women have cesareans more often
than poor women do. J. Horgan. *Scientific American* 261:36
O '89

Political activities
Income and ideology: the new nexus [liberalism] D. Seligman.
il *Fortune* 120:185-6 D 4 '89

Psychology
Drowning in wealth. P. Edidin. il *Psychology Today* 23:32-5+
Ap '89
When having everything isn't enough [cover story] A. Landi.
il *Psychology Today* 23:27-30 Ap '89

Taxation
The 1 percent solution [consumption tax] J. S. Henry and
M. Pomer. *The New Republic* 200:12-13 F 6 '89
The Capitol gains of the well-to-do [Democratic Congress
addresses tax cuts] M. Barone. il *U.S. News & World
Report* 107:26-7+ O 2 '89
On the Hill, class war over taxes [Democratic plan to raise
top rate] E. Clift and R. Thomas. il *Newsweek* 114:24
O 2 '89
A rich man's tax? [capital gains] E. Rubenstein. *National
Review* 41:15 Ap 21 '89
Them's the breaks [George Bush's tax proposals] *The New
Republic* 200:7-8 F 27 '89
Who cheats? D. Seligman. il *Fortune* 120:203 O 9 '89

Why Bush's trickle-up theory is sailing through Congress.
H. Gleckman and D. Harbrecht. il *Business Week* p47
O 16 '89
Australia
Dallas Down Under. M. Lewis. *The New Republic* 200:14+
My 22 '89
Colombia
Life styles of the rich and heinous [cocaine kingpins] M.
J. Harris. il *Money* 18:70-6 N '89
Latin America
A chasm of misery [gap between rich and poor] F. Ungeheuer.
il *Time* 134:64-6 N 6 '89
RICH PRODUCTS CORPORATION
Buffalo's Rich baseball legacy [Bisons owner R. Rich] G.
Macnow. il por *Nation's Business* 77:42-5 F '89
RICHA, JEAN, AND LO, CECILIA W.
Introduction of human DNA into mouse eggs by injection
of dissected chromosome fragments. bibl f il *Science*
245:175-7 Jl 14 '89
RICHARD, ELLIS
Lassen Volcanic [excerpt] il *National Parks* 63:46-7 Mr/Ap
'89
RICHARD, JEROME
The $5,347 rock. *The Washington Monthly* 21:26-7 Je '89
RICHARD, MARK, 1955-
The theory of man [story] il *Esquire* 111:146-8+ F
'89
RICHARD C. BLUM & ASSOCIATES
"How do you put a lien on an elephant?". M. Berss. il
por *Forbes* 144:114+ O 30 '89
RICHARD NIXON LIBRARY AND BIRTHPLACE
Nixon Library and Birthplace being built. *American History
Illustrated* 23:6 Ja '89
RICHARDS, ANN
about
The way we are. L. Wyse. il por *Good Housekeeping* 208:202
F '89
RICHARDS, DAVID ADAMS, 1950-
about
Exploring the dignity in downtrodden lives. D. Jenish. il
por *Maclean's* 102:34-5 D 25 '89
A world in one town. D. Turbide. por *Maclean's* 102:59
Mr 13 '89
RICHARDS, ELIZABETH
Never marry a millionaire [story] il *Mademoiselle*
95:150+ N '89
RICHARDS, EUGENE, 1944-
The knife and gun club [photographs] il *Life* 12:48-53+ Ap
'89
RICHARDS, KEITH
about
Keith Richards: Beacon Theatre/New York. B. Milkowski.
il por *Down Beat* 56:49 Ap '89
Keith Richards solo. S. Simels. il por *Stereo Review* 54:109
Ja '89
Raw, raunchy and middle-aged. B. Spitz. il pors *The New
York Times Magazine* p30-2+ Je 4 '89
A Stone rolls alone. A. DeCurtis. il por *Rolling Stone* p23
Ja 12 '89
RICHARDS, LOUISE
Giving the gift of life. il *Ladies' Home Journal* 106:22+
F '89
RICHARDS, MARK A., AND OTHERS
Flood basalts and hot-spot tracks: plume heads and tails.
bibl f il map *Science* 246:103-7 O 6 '89
RICHARDS, REUBEN FRANCIS, 1929-
about
Improvised resources? R. Simon. il por *Forbes* 143:88-9
F 20 '89
RICHARDS, MARY (FICTIONAL CHARACTER) *See* Mary
Richards (Fictional character)
RICHARDSON, DOUG
about
Growin' bananas. L. Hollenhorst. il por *Organic Gardening*
36:54-6+ S '89
RICHARDSON, GARY
Guess how I became rich without working. il *Utne Reader*
p74-5 S/O '89
RICHARDSON, JACQUES
Mapping the human genome. il *The Unesco Courier* 42:54-5
S '89
RICHARDSON, JAMES
about
Convicted of murdering one of his children, James Richardson
hopes the truth will set him free. P. Chin. il pors *People
Weekly* 31:191-2+ Mr 6 '89
From tragedy to travesty. J. N. Baker. il por *Newsweek*
113:68 Ap 24 '89
RICHARDSON, JOHN, 1924-
The dark side of Goya. il *House & Garden* 161:106-11+
F '89
A very private collection. il *House & Garden* 161:154-61
O '89
RICHARDSON, KAREN
'Eclectic' AAP/West seminar on information publishing. il
Publishers Weekly 236:15 N 24 '89

RICHARDSON, KEN
Medley. See issues of High Fidelity (New York, N.Y.) beginning November 1986 through July 1989
RICHARDSON, KYM
Prime-time jobs. il *Essence* 19:108+ Ja '89
RICHARDSON, NANCY D.
The Women's Theological Center: learning and acting for justice. *The Christian Century* 106:130+ F 1-8 '89
RICHARDSON, NATASHA
about
Natasha Richardson does the right thing. L. Morice. il pors *Mademoiselle* 95:62+ D '89
RICHARDSON, PATRICE
It's okay to ask for help: one woman's story. il *Essence* 20:50-1+ Je '89
RICHARDSON, PEGGY A., AND ADLER, BILL
Psychological momentum. il *World Tennis* 36:46-7+ Ja '89
RICHARDSON, PETER
about
Eat the rich [film] Reviews
Video 12:85 Ja '89. I. Robbins
RICHARDSON, RICHARD
about
Lost stove art [cover story] A. Meyer. il *The Mother Earth News* 115:62-5 Ja/F '89
RICHARDSON, SAMANTHA
Guest work: the good (business) guest's guide to being wined and dined. il *Working Woman* 14:114+ D '89
RICHARDSON, TONY
about
Tom Jones [film] Reviews
Gentlemen's Quarterly il 59:93+ Ag '89. K. Turan
People Weekly il 32:11 O 2 '89. R. Novak
RICHARDSON, WILLIAM J.
Golden cup and silver bag [address, September 24, 1989] *America* 161:315-16+ N 11 '89
RICHCO GRAIN (FIRM)
Letters from home [tax fugitive M. Rich gets U.S. export subsidies on wheat deals with the Soviets] J. Willoughby. il por *Forbes* 143:38-9 Je 12 '89
RICHE, MARTHA FARNSWORTH
The postmarital society: Americans now spend more of their lives single. il *Utne Reader* p50-1 Mr/Ap '89
RICHEAUME (FRANCE: HISTORIC HOUSE) *See* Historic houses, sites, etc.—France
RICHELSON, JEFFREY
Military intelligence—SPOT is not enough. bibl f il *The Bulletin of the Atomic Scientists* 45:26-7 S '89
RICHER, JASON
about
A young driver humbles the car. C. Gordon. il *Maclean's* 102:50 My 29 '89
RICHER, STÉPHANE
about
The new Flying Frenchman. C. Warner. il pors *Sport (New York, N.Y.)* 80:56-8+ Mr '89
RICHEY, JEFFREY E., AND OTHERS
Amazon River discharge and climate variability: 1903 to 1985. bibl f il map *Science* 246:101-3 O 6 '89
RICHLAND (WASH.)
Education
Reading, 'riting & running [J. Deatherage incorporates running into his high school English class] R. Blount. il pors *Runner's World* 24:26-8 Ja '89
RICHLER, MORDECAI, 1931-
Books & things. See issues of Gentlemen's Quarterly
Catch-and-release [fiction] il *Gentlemen's Quarterly* 59:288-93+ N '89
Overbite Halburton's revenge [story] il *Gentlemen's Quarterly* 59:165-6+ Ag '89
about
Witness to his time. M. Ritts. il pors *Maclean's* 102:64-7 N 13 '89
RICHMAN, ADAM, AND HAYDAY, ADRIAN
Normal expression of a rearranged and mutated *c-myc* oncogene after transfection into fibroblasts. bibl f il *Science* 246:494-7 O 27 '89
RICHMAN, ALAN
Wine & spirits. See issues of Gentlemen's Quarterly
RICHMAN, LOUIS S.
Income growth: are we better off? il *Current (Washington, D.C.)* 312:4-9 My '89
RICHMAN, ROBERT
The fossil [poem] *The American Scholar* 58:585 Aut '89
Reclaiming Yeats. *Commentary* 88:57-9 D '89
RICHMOND, GEORGE
The future school: is Lowell pointing us toward a revolution in education? il *Phi Delta Kappan* 71:232-6 N '89
RICHMOND, MITCH
about
Rock of a rook. H. Hersch. il pors *Sports Illustrated* 70:20-2+ F 6 '89
RICHMOND, SANDRA M.
A Christmas letter to myself. il *Ladies' Home Journal* 106:94 D '89
RICHMOND, SUZAN
(jt. auth) See Porter, Hal, and Richmond, Suzan

RICHMOND, TONY, 1942-
about
Architectural digest visits: Jaclyn Smith and Tony Richmond [cover story] J. Giovannini. il pors *Architectural Digest* 46:180-5+ Ag '89
RICHMOND, YALE
To Russia, with books. por *Publishers Weekly* 235:76 F 3 '89
RICHMOND (CALIF.)
Pollution
Pollution prevention: the Chevron story. G. Karras. bibl f *Environment* 31:4-5+ O '89
RICHMOND (VA.)
Description
Richmond: the renaissance city. K. Lingo. il *Southern Living* 24:72-9 Je '89
Galleries and museums
See also
Edgar Allan Poe Museum (Richmond, Va.)
Virginia Museum of Fine Arts
Gardens and gardening
See also
Agecroft Hall (Richmond, Va.)—Gardens
Historic houses, sites, etc.
See also
Agecroft Hall (Richmond, Va.)
White House of the Confederacy
The best of Georgian [Westover] A. O. Boulton. il por *American Heritage* 40:110-17 F '89
Monuments, statues, etc.
Richmond's dancin' man [Bill "Bojangles" Robinson] il *Southern Living* 24:59 My '89
Municipal contracts
A blow to affirmative action [Supreme Court strikes down minority set-aside law] A. Sachs. il *Time* 133:60 F 6 '89
A build-down for black contractors [Supreme Court ruling against minority set-aside program] *U.S. News & World Report* 106:13 F 6 '89
Court in the middle [Supreme Court strikes down set-aside program for minority firms] *National Review* 41:14 F 24 '89
A negative on affirmative action [Supreme Court ruling on minority set-aside law] R. Stodghill, II and P. Dwyer. *Business Week* p40 F 6 '89
'Now we're on our own' [Supreme Court strikes down minority set-aside law] T. Jacoby. il *Newsweek* 113:64-5 F 6 '89
Racial preference in court (again) [Supreme Court to decide legality of minority set-asides] T. Eastland. *Commentary* 87:32-8 Ja '89
Ruling delivers hard blow to set-asides [Supreme Court decision] N. McCall. il *Black Enterprise* 19:17-18 Ap '89
'Stigmatic harm' [Supreme Court's nullification of the minority set-aside program] *The Nation* 248:183-4 F 13 '89
Supreme Court set aside ruling not 'devastating' blow to black businesses. il *Jet* 75:4 F 13 '89
Race relations
Valentine Museum's Jim Crow [Racism and reaction in the New South, Richmond, 1865-1940] E. Chappell. *The Nation* 249:102-4 Jl 17 '89
Religious institutions and affairs
Va. priest fired after announcing plans to join separatist Catholic Church [B. Greening] pors *Jet* 76:26 Ag 21 '89
RICHMOND COLLEGE (LONDON, ENGLAND)
Run Richmond graduates, run [address, May 11, 1989] R. E. Leestamper. *Vital Speeches of the Day* 56:156-7 D 15 '89
RICHTER, GERHARD
about
The "Melancholist of virtuosity". M. Hübl. il por *Art News* 88:120-5 F '89
RICHTER, SVIATOSLAV, 1915-
about
Richter live. R. Freed. il por *Stereo Review* 54:89 Jl '89
RICHTER, THOMAS
about
Brokers in the boondocks. M. Schifrin. il pors *Forbes* 143:228+ Je 26 '89
RICHTER, WILLIAM L. (WILLIAM LEE), 1942-
Pakistan under Benazir Bhutto. bibl f *Current History* 88:433-6+ D '89
RICKENBACKER, WILLIAM F.
about
A hero's heir aims for 15% a year the old-fashioned way. G. Anrig, Jr. il por *Money* 18:149-50 Ag '89
RICKENBAKER, KELLEY
Where is the Goober? por *Newsweek* 113:12 My 1 '89
RICKETTSIA
See also
Q fever
RICO *See* Racketeer Influenced and Corrupt Organizations Act of 1970
RIDD, KAREN
about
Under suspicion. A. Bilski. il por *Maclean's* 102:52 D 4 '89

RIDDELL, JANICE BERGMANN
The education reform movement and its critics: implications for arts education. bibl f *Design for Arts in Education* 90:2-13 N/D '88
RIDDER, KATIE
about
Love nest. M. Baker. il pors *New York* 22:56-9 O 2 '89
RIDDICK, JANE
Taking charge [story] il *'Teen* 33:60+ O '89
RIDDICK, LINDA
about
Woman pleads guilty to theft after swallowing $2500 worth of jewelry. il por *Jet* 76:18 Jl 10 '89
RIDDLES
Noble riddles and surrealist fruits [riddles by G. García Márquez accompany Matta paintings] I. Stavans. il *Art News* 88:29 N '89
RIDE, SALLY K.
(jt. auth) See Banks, Peter M., and Ride, Sally K.
RIDEOUT, THOMAS
about
Campaign on the Rock. R. Wangersky. il por *Maclean's* 102:17 Ap 17 '89
The newest premier. P. Kopvillem. il pors *Maclean's* 102:15 Mr 20 '89
RIDEOUT, THOMAS P.
For tomorrow's bank managers [address, August 25, 1989] *Vital Speeches of the Day* 56:153-5 D 15 '89
RIDERS IN THE SKY (MUSICAL GROUP)
Riders in the Sky lasso listeners by poking fun at cowpokes while singing sweetly of the prairie. S. Dougherty. il *People Weekly* 31:69-70 F 27 '89
RIDES, AMUSEMENT See Amusement parks—Equipment
RIDGE, JULIE
Enduring greatness. il por *Women's Sports & Fitness* 11:24-6+ Je '89
RIDGED FIELDS See Terraces (Agriculture)
RIDGES, OCEAN See Ocean bottom
RIDGEWAY, CHARLES
about
The hunt for Charles Ridgeway. J. Shannon. il *Reader's Digest* 135:40-2+ D '89
RIDING, ALAN
Peru fights to overcome its past. il por *The New York Times Magazine* p40+ My 14 '89
RIDING, PETER
Save a Life. il *World Health* p29 Ja/F '89
RIDING See Horsemanship
RIDING MOWERS See Lawn mowers
RIDLEY, SCOTT
The hidden menace: indoor pollution. il *USA Today (Periodical)* 118:44-6 S '89
RIDLEY TURTLES See Turtles
RIDLON, JIM
about
The second time around. R. Fimrite. il pors *Sports Illustrated* 70:110-14+ Ja 9 '89
RIEDEL, MICHAEL
The right combination [story] il *'Teen* 33:74-6+ Ag '89
RIEDL, JOACHIM
'King of the mountain'. il por *World Press Review* 36:61 My '89
RIEGER, ERICH, AND OTHERS
Man-made transients observed by the gamma-ray spectrometer on the Solar Maximum Mission satellite. bibl f il *Science* 244:441-4 Ap 28 '89
RIEGLE, DONALD W., JR.
Should the Congress adopt the "Financial Institutions Reform, Recovery, and Enforcement Act of 1989"? [excerpts from address, April 17, 1989] *Congressional Digest* 68:172+ Je/Jl '89
RIEKE, REUBEN D.
Preparation of organometallic compounds from highly reactive metal powders. bibl f il *Science* 246:1260-4 D 8 '89
RIELLE, NANCY
about
Artistry in makeup. M. Gazzaniga. il pors *Harper's Bazaar* 122:26+ D '89
RIEMANN HYPOTHESIS
Zeta zero update. B. A. Cipra. *Science* 243:1143 Mr 3 '89
RIESLING WINES See Wine
RIESMAN, DAVID, 1909-
(jt. auth) See McLaughlin, Judith, and Riesman, David, 1909-
David Riesman's Freud. S. Weiland. *Society* 26:73-7 My/Je '89
RIESSMAN, FRANK, 1924-
A school-change paradigm. *The Education Digest* 54:10-12 My '89
RIETI, VITTORIO
about
Profiles. S. Lessard. il por *The New Yorker* 64:32-6+ Ja 9 '89
RIETVELD, GERRIT
about
Rietveld's geometry. E. Silberman. il *Vogue* 179:100 Ja '89

RIFKIN, JEREMY
about
Ethical questions haunt new genetic technologies. L. Roberts. il por *Science* 243:1134-6 Mr 3 '89
The most hated man in science. D. Thompson. il por *Time* 134:102-4 D 4 '89
Rifkin tries to stop Galileo launch. M. M. Waldrop. il *Science* 246:30 O 6 '89
Thank you, Jeremy Rifkin. M. Fritz. il *Forbes* 144:268-9 O 16 '89
RIFLE CARTRIDGES See Cartridges
RIFLE SIGHTS See Firearms—Sights
RIFLES
See also
Assault rifles
National Rifle Association of America
Accuracy unraveled. D. E. Petzal. il *Field & Stream* 94:58-9 Ag '89
The big boom in big bores (I). J. Carmichel. il *Outdoor Life* 184:38+ O '89
The big boom in big bores (II). J. Carmichel. il *Outdoor Life* 184:34+ N '89
Is it necessarily so? J. Carmichel. il *Outdoor Life* 183:36+ My '89
A lethal choice for a murderer [Ruger Mini-14 semiautomatic rifle used in massacre of women at Univ. of Montreal] P. Kaihla. il *Maclean's* 102:16 D 18 '89
Second-season turkeys. J. Bashline. il *Field & Stream* 94:50+ N '89
The serious elk rifle. J. Carmichel. il *Outdoor Life* 184:28+ S '89
Success secrets for front loaders. R. Hacker. il *Field & Stream* 94:70-1+ N '89
The time for the double deuce. D. E. Petzal. il *Field & Stream* 93:121-2 Ap '89
Cleaning
The latest in accuracy improvement. J. Carmichel. il *Outdoor Life* 184:24+ D '89
RIFTS (GEOLOGY) See Faults (Geology)
RIGBY, MARK T.
Cape York update. *Ad Astra* 1:42 F '89
RIGBY & PELLER (FIRM)
Fit for a queen. M. Killen. il *Vogue* 179:406 My '89
RIGBY-LEATHER, ELA MILOSZEWSKI
about
Block Island light. J. Kaplan. il pors *House & Garden* 161:84-91 Je '89
RIGBY-LEATHER, GEOFFREY
about
Block Island light. J. Kaplan. il pors *House & Garden* 161:84-91 Je '89
RIGER, ROBERT
about
BOMC's Riger is president of Doubleday Clubs. M. Reuter. por *Publishers Weekly* 235:34-5 Ap 7 '89
RIGGIO, LEONARD
about
Riggio foresees 'golden age' in bookselling. J. Mutter. *Publishers Weekly* 236:8+ N 24 '89
Why B. Dalton had second thoughts. J. F. Baker. *Publishers Weekly* 235:14-15 Mr 10 '89
RIGGS, BOBBY
The Queen and I. il por *World Tennis* 37:98 Jl '89
RIGGS, MICHAEL
Front lines. See issues of High Fidelity (New York, N.Y.) beginning March 1987 through July 1989
RIGHT (POLITICAL SCIENCE) See Conservatism; Fascism
RIGHT AND LEFT (POLITICAL SCIENCE)
See also
Communism
Conservatism
Fascism
Liberalism
Radicalism
Socialism
Panthers, contras, and other wars. P. Collier and D. Horowitz. *The New Republic* 200:38-41 Je 26 '89
The prodigal son [former radical reconciles with terminally ill father] P. Collier. il *Reader's Digest* 135:64-8 Ag '89
Radical transformations [D. Horowitz and P. Collier] S. Churcher. il pors *The New York Times Magazine* p30-1+ Jl 16 '89
RIGHT- AND LEFT-HANDEDNESS See Left- and right-handedness
RIGHT OF ASYLUM See Asylum, Right of
RIGHT OF ENTRY FEES (IMMIGRATION) See Immigration and emigration—Right of entry fees
RIGHT OF PETITION
Around the Mall and beyond [National Archives exhibit American voices: 200 years of speaking out] E. Park. il *Smithsonian* 19:28+ F '89
RIGHT OF PRIVACY
See also
Confidential communications
Trade secrets
Wiretapping

RIGHT OF PRIVACY—cont.

The Court and the right to privacy [right to die case impacts indirectly on privacy rights underlying abortion ruling; Supreme Court cases] A. McDaniel. il *Newsweek* 114:36 O 9 '89

Disclosing genetic information: who should know? D. C. Wertz and J. C. Fletcher. il *Technology Review* 92:22-3 Jl '89

The Hill case [impact of 1967 Time Inc. v. Hill privacy case, argued by R. Nixon, on freedom of the press] L. Garment. *The New Yorker* 65:90-110 Ap 17 '89

Is nothing private? [cover story] J. Rothfeder. il *Business Week* p74-7+ S 4 '89

Knocking on death's door [journalists covering tragedies] L. Zuckerman. il *Time* 133:49 F 27 '89

The law criminals love [controversy over confidentiality of criminal records] R. J. Bidinotto. *Reader's Digest* 135:57-62 S '89

The privacy invaders: who knows what about you? S. Nielsen. il *Good Housekeeping* 209:275 N '89

The right to privacy. D. Elkind. il *Parents* 64:135 Ja '89

A right to privacy? [with reply by Joseph Sobran] H. V. Jaffa. *National Review* 41:51-2 Mr 24 '89

Unwilling players in the name game [sale of credit and medical information to direct marketing companies] A. Mundy. il *U.S. News & World Report* 106:52+ My 1 '89

Where does a writer's family draw the line? J. M. Smith. il *por The New York Times Book Review* 94:1+ N 5 '89

RIGHT OF PUBLICITY *See* Publicity (Law)

RIGHT TO COUNSEL

Defending the poor: a harder task [cover story] G. M. Anderson. il *America* 160:4-7 Ja 7-14 '89

RIGHT TO DIE

See also
Euthanasia
Living wills

The amicus curiae brief: public policy versus personal freedom [brief filed by New Jersey Catholic Conference in case of brain-damaged woman] R. J. Devine. *America* 160:323-6+ Ap 8 '89

The Court and the right to privacy [right to die case impacts indirectly on privacy rights underlying abortion ruling; Supreme Court cases] A. McDaniel. il *Newsweek* 114:36 O 9 '89

The Cruzan decision: refusing treatment [Missouri Supreme Court decision in N. Cruzan case] J. M. Swomley. *The Christian Century* 106:1110-11 N 29 '89

A death in the family 1989 [cover story] H. Epstein. il pors *New York* 22:34-43 N 27 '89

Death wish [quadriplegic L. McAfee wins right to refuse medical treatment] *Time* 134:67 S 18 '89

The extraordinary case of the woman who couldn't die [coma patient N. Jobes kept alive because she had no living will] B. D. Colen. il por *Redbook* 172:126-9+ Mr '89

Feeling no pain. *The New Republic* 201:9-10 N 27 '89

Health technology vs. death: should we prolong the inevitable? W. E. Phipps. il *USA Today (Periodical)* 117:71-2 Ja '89

Is there a right to die? [Supreme Court to hear N. Cruzan case] T. Gest. il por *U.S. News & World Report* 107:35-7 D 11 '89

Last rights [cases of N. Cruzan and L. McAfee] M. G. Maudlin. *Christianity Today* 33:15 N 3 '89

Murder and the right to die [M. Weaver's right to die protested by criminal N. Pagan in Maine] il por *Newsweek* 113:33 Ap 10 '89

Nancy Cruzan's parents want to let her die—and are taking the case to the Supreme Court. M. Brower. il pors *People Weekly* 32:135-6+ D 4 '89

To be or not to be [case of N. Cruzan] M. Kinsley. *The New Republic* 201:6+ N 27 '89

The ultimate decision [cover story] A. H. Malcolm. il pors *The New York Times Magazine* p38-41+ D 3 '89

Whose death is it, anyway? [case of C. Coons] J. Seligmann. *Newsweek* 113:69 Ap 24 '89

Whose right to die? [case of N. Cruzan before the Supreme Court] A. L. Sanders. il *Time* 134:80 D 11 '89

RIGHT TO LIFE MOVEMENT *See* Prolife movement

RIGHTEOUSNESS

For the sake of ten. K. Koyama. *The Christian Century* 106:683 Jl 19-26 '89

God's gift of righteousness. P. Perkins. il *The Christian Century* 106:954 O 25 '89

RIGHTS, CIVIL *See* Civil rights

RIGHTS OF ARTISTS *See* Artists' rights

RIGHTS OF EMPLOYEES *See* Employees—Civil rights

RIGHTS OF WOMEN *See* Women—Equal rights

RIGOLETTO [opera] *See* Verdi, Giuseppe, 1813-1901

RIGOROUS EDUCATIONAL ASSISTANCE FOR DESERVING YOUTH (PROGRAM) *See* READY (Program)

RIIS, JACOB A. (JACOB AUGUST), 1849-1914

about

An awakening social conscience. il *American History Illustrated* 24:70-1 S/O '89

RIJKSMUSEUM (NETHERLANDS)

From a Rijksmuseum buffet. F. Ferretti. il *Gourmet* 49:82+ O '89

RIJSTTAFEL

A simple but still spectacular Indonesian rice table. il *Sunset (Central West edition)* 182:86-7 Je '89

RIKLIS, MESHULAM

about

Riklis' fancy footwork may be tripping him up. A. Rothman. il por *Business Week* p86-8 Je 19 '89

RIKLIS FAMILY CORPORATION

Riklis' fancy footwork may be tripping him up. A. Rothman. il por *Business Week* p86-8 Je 19 '89

RILES, ANNELISE

The Chinese student movement moves to America. il *The Progressive* 53:28-30 S '89

RILEY, CHERYL

about

Grand designs. D. Sapolin. il pors *Essence* 20:80-1+ Jl '89

RILEY, CHUCK

about

Children of poverty. P. Meyer. il *Life* 12:56-62+ S '89

RILEY, PAT

about

The transformation of Pat Riley [cover story] D. K. Shah. il pors *Gentlemen's Quarterly* 59:136-41+ Ja '89

RILEY, TEDDY

about

Black music's new hit doctors. S. Bloom. il pors *Rolling Stone* p32 My 18 '89

Star quality. B. M. Cooper. il por *Essence* 19:29 F '89

RILEY AIRCRAFT MODIFICATION (FIRM) *See* RAM (Firm)

RILL, JAMES F.

about

Putting the 'anti' back in the Antitrust Div. P. Dwyer. il por *Business Week* p64+ Je 19 '89

THE RIMERS OF ELDRITCH [drama] *See* Wilson, Lanford, 1937-

RINALDO PIAGGIO (FIRM)

Drag eraser [Avanti; cover story] J. M. McClellan. il *Flying* 116:28-32+ Ja '89

Piaggio picks AMR for Avanti [North American sales and support organization] *Flying* 116:14+ Ap '89

Piaggio selects AMR Services to market P. 180 in North America [business aircraft] *Aviation Week & Space Technology* 130:27 Ja 30 '89

Piaggio will select U.S. site for Avanti airframe production. E. H. Phillips. il *Aviation Week & Space Technology* 130:101 My 22 '89

RINCKER, WILLIAM

about

Birth of a salesman. J. Zweig. il por *Forbes* 143:149 My 15 '89

RINDT, JOCHEN, 1942-1970

about

The trinity. C. Fox. il pors *Car and Driver* 34:139-40+ Mr '89

RINEHART, MARY ROBERTS, 1876-1958

The young visitor [story] il *The Saturday Evening Post* 261:32-4+ My/Je '89

The young visitor [story] il *The Saturday Evening Post* 261:54-7+ Ap '89

RINEHART, PAULA

The pivotal generation. il *Christianity Today* 33:21-6 O 6 '89

RINELLA, SAL D., AND KOPECKY, ROBERT J.

Tuition payments cut job turnover. il por *Nation's Business* 77:25-6 Ag '89

RING, SEAN

Students unite for a better society. por *The Humanist* 49:26-7+ S/O '89

RING (PERIODICAL)

Back for another fight [new owner S. Weston] R. O'Brien. il por *Sports Illustrated* 71:18 O 30 '89

DER RING DES NIBELUNGEN [opera] *See* Wagner, Richard, 1813-1883

RING GALAXIES *See* Galaxies

RING SYSTEMS (ASTRONOMY)

See also
Neptune (Planet)—Ring system
Saturn (Planet)—Ring system

RINGERS, TELEPHONE *See* Telephone ringers

RINGGOLD, FAITH

about

Faith Ringgold/Bernice Steinbaum Gallery. P. Scheinman. il *American Craft* 49:72-3 F/Mr '89

RINGLE, KEN

A victim's story. pors *Reader's Digest* 135:49-54 Ag '89

RINGNECKED PHEASANT SHOOTING *See* Pheasant shooting

RINGS

See also
Engagement rings

RINGS, NAPKIN *See* Napkin rings, holders, etc.

RINGWOOD, BOB

about

Designer. L. Nickson and N. Le Quesne. il pors *Life* 12:84-6 Spr '89

RINK, WILLIAM J.

(jt. auth) *See* Odom, A. Leroy, and Rink, William J.

RINKER, HARRY L.
Rinker on collectibles. See issues of Antiques & Collecting Hobbies beginning October 1988
RINKS, ICE SKATING *See* Ice skating rinks
RINZLER, CAROL EISEN
Print pursuit. il *House & Garden* 161:68+ Ap '89
RIO DE JANEIRO (BRAZIL)
Carnival (Pre-Lenten festival)
See Carnival (Pre-Lenten festival)—Brazil
Description
The ultimate fast lane [Brazilian Grand Prix] S. McBride. il *Travel Holiday* 171:72-6 Mr '89
Historic houses, sites, etc.
The Pritzker Prize winner's landmark house in Rio de Janeiro [O. Niemeyer's classic 1953 house] B. Gill. il por *Architectural Digest* 46:46+ Jl '89
Restaurants, nightclubs, bars, etc.
Rio! From companheiros . . . to cariocas. F. Ferretti. il *Gourmet* 49:94+ N '89
Social conditions
Rio: Is the carnival over? A. Shoumatoff. il *The New York Times Magazine* p46-8+ Mr 19 '89
RIO DE JANEIRO (SHIP) *See* City of Rio de Janeiro (Ship)
RIO DE JANEIRO STOCK EXCHANGE *See* Bolsa de Valores do Rio de Janeiro
RIO GRANDE VALLEY
A corridor in peril. C. A. Douglis. il map *Wilderness* 53:32-7 Wint '89
Winter in the Texas tropics [retirees; cover story] N. Cornell. il *New Choices for the Best Years* 29:22-6 N '89
RIORDAN, JOHN R., AND OTHERS
Identification of the cystic fibrosis gene: cloning and characterization of complementary DNA. bibl f il *Science* 245:1066-73 S 8 '89
RIORDAN, TERESA
Miller guy life. *The New Republic* 200:16-17 Mr 27 '89
RIOS, FILIBERTO OJEDA *See* Ojeda Rios, Filiberto
RIOTS
Algeria
Letter from Europe. J. Kramer. *The New Yorker* 64:72-4+ Ja 30 '89
Arkansas
See also
Little Rock (Ark.)—Riots
Czechoslovakia
See also
Prague (Czechoslovakia)—Riots
Florida
See also
Miami (Fla.)—Riots
Ocoee (Fla.)—Riots
New Jersey
See also
Vineland (N.J.)—Riots
New York (State)
See also
New York (N.Y.)—Riots
South Africa
A South African cop breaks ranks over police violence [G. Rockman reports brutality during student demonstration near Cape Town] B. Hewitt. il pors *People Weekly* 32:44-6 O 16 '89
South Africa's violent rage [election violence; cover story; special section; with editorial comment by Kevin Doyle] il pors *Maclean's* 102:4, 32-6+ S 18 '89
Squeezed left, squeezed right. B. W. Nelan. il por *Time* 134:46-7 S 18 '89
Two cheers for moderation. S. Reiss. il *Newsweek* 114:31 S 18 '89
Soviet Union
See also
Tbilisi (Soviet Union)—Riots
Tibet
A firestorm in Shangri-La. H. Anderson. il *Newsweek* 113:36-8 Mr 20 '89
Massacre in the Forbidden Kingdom [riot in Lhasa] C. Meindersma. il *Reader's Digest* 135:126-30 O '89
Tibet. *Business Week* p60 Mr 20 '89
Witness to repression. B. Kerr and J. Ackerly. il *Utne Reader* p42-3 Mr/Ap '89
Venezuela
Crackdown in Caracas [austerity measures trigger rioting throughout country] L. Beyer. il *Time* 133:36 Mr 13 '89
Fires of discontent [austerity plan creates rioting] M. Nemeth. il *Maclean's* 102:28 Mr 13 '89
A volcano in Venezuela. A. Platt. il *Newsweek* 113:35 Mr 13 '89
Virginia
See also
Virginia Beach (Va.)—Riots
Yugoslavia
See also
Kosovo (Yugoslavia)—Riots

RIPENING OF FRUIT *See* Fruit—Ripening
RIPENING OF MELONS *See* Melons—Ripening
RIPENING OF TOMATOES *See* Tomatoes—Ripening
RIPOFFS *See* Fraud
RIPPE, JAMES M.
CEO fitness: the performance plus [excerpt from Dr. James M. Rippe's Fit for success] il *Psychology Today* 23:50-3 My '89
RIPPE, JAMES M., AND GROVES, DAVID
Cross training: more than just the sum of its parts. il *American Health* 8:92-4+ S '89
RISC *See* Reduced instruction set computers
THE RISE AND FALL OF THE CITY OF MAHAGONNY [opera] See Weill, Kurt, 1900-1950
RISHER, CAROL, AND BAUMGARTEN, JON A.
Two views of electrocopying: the American experience. por *Publishers Weekly* 236:52 Jl 14 '89
RISK
See also
Hedging (Finance)
Alar in apples [discussion of April 7, 1989 article, Scare of the week] D. E. Koshland, Jr. *Science* 244:755 My 19 '89
Alar: the numbers game [risk assessment controversy between the Natural Resources Defense Council and the Environmental Protection Agency] L. Roberts. *Science* 243:1430 Mr 17 '89
Epidemiologic investigation [discussion of December 2, 1988 article, Scientific standards in epidemiologic studies of the menace of daily life] A. R. Feinstein. *Science* 243:1255-6 Mr 10 '89
Gene Johnston [risk management in farming] G. Johnston. il *Successful Farming* 87:7 mid-Mr '89
How the Japanese manage risk. B. Harrison. il *Technology Review* 92:16 Ja '89
Is risk assessment conservative? L. Roberts. *Science* 243:1553 Mr 24 '89
Life's little gambles. B. Bryson. il *Reader's Digest* 135:61-2+ D '89
NRDC on Alar. R. M. Whyatt. bibl f *Science* 245:910-11 S 1 '89
Opening doors: making risk communication agency reality [environmental protection agencies] C. Chess and B. J. Hance. bibl f il *Environment* 31:10-15+ Je '89
Optimistic biases about personal risks. N. D. Weinstein. bibl f *Science* 246:1232-3 D 8 '89
Pesticides, risk, and applesauce [discussion of March 10, 1989 article, Pesticides and kids, and March 24, 1989 article, Is risk assessment conservative?] L. Roberts. il *Science* 244:755-7 My 19 '89
Risk, safety and capitalism [special section] bibl *Society* 27:4-31 N/D '89
Risky business [Alar and cancer] T. Beardsley. *Scientific American* 260:35-6 My '89
Scare of the week [Alar-treated apples and cyanide in Chilean grapes] D. E. Koshland, Jr. *Science* 244:9 Ap 7 '89
What risk-free society? [interview with R. Nader] il *New Perspectives Quarterly* 6:32-4 Fall '89
When risk analysis confronts faith. J. M. Wall. *The Christian Century* 106:1139-40 D 6 '89
Anecdotes, facetiae, satire, etc.
Interview with a risk expert. D. E. Koshland, Jr. *Science* 244:1529 Je 30 '89
RISK BENEFIT ANALYSIS *See* Risk
RISK TAKING (PSYCHOLOGY)
See also
Type T behavior
Fear of living [cover story] H. Fairlie. *The New Republic* 200:14+ Ja 23 '89
"Go for it, lady!". J. Coudert. il *Reader's Digest* 134:121-3 Ja '89
The joy of risk. J. Etra. *Harper's Bazaar* 122:162-3+ My '89
Risk phobia: Europe's disease? [business startups] D. Dickson. il *Science* 245:1038-9 S 8 '89
Taking a chance on life [quiz] E. Raudsepp. *Harper's Bazaar* 122:163+ My '89
Teens who take risks. D. Elkind. il *Parents* 64:218 Je '89
Where have all the risk takers gone? [address, March 29, 1989] C. J. Silas. *Vital Speeches of the Day* 55:530-3 Je 15 '89
RISKIN, LEONARD L., 1942-
Unsportsmanlike conduct. il *The New York Times Magazine* p14+ Ja 22 '89
RISOTTO *See* Cooking—Rice
RISSE-KAPPEN, THOMAS
Will NATO settle for Kohl cuts? il *The Bulletin of the Atomic Scientists* 45:9-12 Je '89
RIST, DARRELL YATES
Darrell Yates Rist replies [discussion of February 13, 1989 article, The deadly costs of an obsession] *The Nation* 248:834+ Je 19 '89
The deadly costs of an obsession [cover story] il *The Nation* 248:181+ F 13 '89
Exchange [discussion of February 13, 1989 article, The deadly costs of an obsession] *The Nation* 248:578+ My 1 '89

RIST, DARRELL YATES—*cont.*
Gay politics and AIDS [discussion of February 13, 1989 article, The deadly costs of an obsession] *The Nation* 248:362+ Mr 20 '89
RIST, MARILEE C.
Should parents choose their child's school? *The Education Digest* 55:3-6 S '89
RIST, RAY C.
Declining options/increasing needs. *Society* 26:39-45 S/O '89
RISTORANTE MILANO (SAN FRANCISCO, CALIF.) *See* San Francisco (Calif.)—Restaurants, nightclubs, bars, etc.
RISTORI, AL
Bluefish—a great marine resource. il *The Conservationist* 44:18-21 Jl/Ag '89
RITA [opera] *See* Donizetti, Gaetano, 1797-1848
RITALIN *See* Methylphenidate
RITCHIE, JOSEPH
about
GAO will review Ritchie, Lorenzo plans for Eastern. J. T. McKenna. *Aviation Week & Space Technology* 131:100-1 Jl 31 '89
RITCHIE, MICHAEL
about
Fletch lives [film] Reviews
Newsweek il 113:83 Mr 20 '89. D. Ansen
People Weekly il 31:11-12 Mr 27 '89. R. Novak
RITCHIE, TOM
Marine crocodiles [cover story] bibl il *Sea Frontiers* 35:212-19 Jl/Ag '89
RITE AID CORP.
Are raiders right behind Rite Aid? G. G. Marcial. *Business Week* p94 Mr 6 '89
RITENOUR, LEE
about
Lee Ritenour. B. Milkowski. il por *Down Beat* 56:27 My '89
RITES AND CEREMONIES
See also
Circumcision
Festivals
Hazing
Initiation rites
Seeking meaning [lapsed Catholic creates own rituals] J. Callahan. il *Glamour* 87:326 S '89
Great Britain
See also
Trooping the Color
IL RITORNO D'ULISSE IN PATRIA [opera] *See* Monteverdi, Claudio, 1567-1643
RITT, MARTIN
about
True Ritt. J. Cameron. il pors *American Film* 15:42-8 N '89
RITTER, BRUCE, 1927-
about
Crisis at Covenant House. J. N. Baker. il por *Newsweek* 114:82 D 25 '89
Saving kids from the streets. I. Nelson. il por *New Choices for the Best Years* 29:14+ Ag '89
RITTER, DONALD
Unshackle scientists from stifling government regulations. il *USA Today (Periodical)* 118:66-7 N '89
RITTER, JAMES
Prime numbers. il *The Unesco Courier* 42:12-17 N '89
RITTER, LOUISE
about
Up where she belongs. K. Moore. il pors *Sports Illustrated* 70:98-101 Ja 9 '89
RITUAL *See* Rites and ceremonies
RITZ, CÉSAR
about
The Hôtel Ritz: Paris' resplendent landmark on the Place Vendôme. C. Aillaud. il *Architectural Digest* 46:120-5+ Ja '89
RITZ (PARIS, FRANCE: HOTEL) *See* Paris (France)—Hotels, motels, etc.
RITZ-CARLTON HOTEL COMPANY
Puttin' on the Ritz—in New York, Washington, Aspen . . . [M. Hadid's deals] T. Smart. il por *Business Week* p32+ Ap 24 '89
RIVAGE-SEUL, D. MICHAEL
Gauging opposition and resources in Nicaragua's 'third war'. il *The Christian Century* 106:687-9 Jl 19-26 '89
RIVALRY *See* Competition (Psychology)
RIVALRY, SIBLING *See* Siblings
RIVER BLINDNESS *See* Onchocerciasis
RIVER BOATS *See* Steamships and steamboats
RIVER CAFÉ (BROOKLYN, N.Y.) *See* Brooklyn (New York, N.Y.)—Restaurants, nightclubs, bars, etc.
RIVER CAFE (LONDON, ENGLAND) *See* London (England)—Restaurants, nightclubs, bars, etc.
RIVER CONSERVATION *See* Stream conservation
RIVER CROSSING
Crossing rivers safely. B. Tilton. il *Field & Stream* 93:56 Ap '89

RIVER OTTERS *See* Otters
RIVER TRIPS
See also
Canoes and canoeing
Raft trips
Running rapids
Another week on the Concord and Merrimack [H. D. Thoreau's trip] R. Crum. *Wilderness* 53:11-12+ Fall '89
Cruisin' up the river [Seine River] J. Gooding. il *Time* 133:74 Je 26 '89
Cruising down or up the Rhine. il map *Sunset (Central West edition)* 182:92-3 My '89
Joe Kane ran the mighty Amazon and lived to tell the tale. K. McMurran. il pors *People Weekly* 32:83+ Jl 17 '89
Life on the Nile. J. Eppinger. bibl il map *New Choices for the Best Years* 29:32-9 Ag '89
The Nile in style. J. Zweig. il map *Forbes* 144:328+ N 13 '89
Rafting piano, floating opera . . . here are musical river trips. il *Sunset (Central West edition)* 183:50-1 Jl '89
RIVERA, GERALDO
about
Geraldo's compromising tattoo. J. Marion. il por *TV Guide* 37:21 My 13-19 '89
Is Geraldo Rivera running out of control? D. Hill. il pors *TV Guide* 37:28-31 Ja 28-F 3 '89
Anecdotes, facetiae, satire, etc.
Blitzed. A. Levine. *The New Republic* 200:16-17 Ja 9-16 '89
RIVERCENTER (SAN ANTONIO, TEX.)
Just add water. M. Gaskie. il *Architectural Record* 177:100-5 Mr '89
RIVERRUN PRESS INC.
John Calder: a sturdy survivor. J. Barbato. *Publishers Weekly* 235:254 My 12 '89
RIVERS, JOAN, 1937-
about
Architectural digest visits: Joan Rivers. J. Allen. il pors *Architectural Digest* 46:134-9+ F '89
The Joan Rivers show. R. MacKenzie. il por *TV Guide* 37:32 O 28-N 3 '89
A triumph of spirit. D. De Dubovay. il pors *Ladies' Home Journal* 106:62+ S '89
RIVERS, LARRY
about
Larry Rivers at Marlborough. B. Adams. *Art in America* 77:262 Ap '89
RIVERS, LINDA
A family's legacy. *Reader's Digest* 134:159-60 Mr '89
RIVERS, VALERIE R.
Robert Wisnewski. il por *American Artist* 53:58-63 My '89
RIVERS
See also
Columbia River
Mississippi River
Saint Lawrence River
Wild and scenic rivers
Cleaning
See Cleaning of lakes, rivers, etc.
Crossing
See River crossing
Regulation
See also
Dams
Wandering river [bank armor and Iowa vanes prevent meandering] R. Kunzig. il *Discover* 10:68-71 N '89
Wading
See Wading
Africa
See also
Zambezi River
River basin projects in Africa [cover story] T. Scudder. bibl f il map *Environment* 31:4-9+ Mr '89
Alaska
See also
Yukon River (Yukon and Alaska)
Alberta
See also
Athabasca River (Alta.)
California
See also
Big Sur River (Calif.)
Sacramento River (Calif.)
Winter madness on northern California rivers [rafting] il *Sunset (Central West edition)* 181:56+ D '88
Canada
See also
Back River (N.W.T.)
George River (Québec)
Yukon River (Yukon and Alaska)
China
See also
Amur River (China and Soviet Union)
Egypt
See also
Nile River

RIVERS—Egypt—cont.
Rivers in the sand [interpretation of shuttle radar imaging in the Sahara] B. Bower. map *Science News* 136:138-9 Ag 26 '89

India
See also
Ganges River (India and Bangladesh)
Zanskar River (India)

Maine
See also
Kennebec River (Me.)

Massachusetts
See also
Concord River (Mass.)
Merrimack River (N.H. and Mass.)

Michigan
See also
Kalamazoo River (Mich.)

Mississippi
See also
Yazoo River (Miss.)

Montana
See also
Bighorn River (Wyo. and Mont.)

Nebraska
See also
Platte River (Neb.)

New Hampshire
See also
Merrimack River (N.H. and Mass.)

New York (State)
See also
Beaverkill River (N.Y.)

North America
See also
Souris River

Oregon
See also
Rogue River (Or.)

Soviet Union
See also
Amur River (China and Soviet Union)

Washington (State)
Rivers flow toward showdown [additions to wild river designations] J. Stiak. il *Sierra* 74:78-80 S/O '89

West Virginia
See also
Gauley River (W. Va.)
New River Gorge National River (W. Va.)

Western Europe
See also
Rhine River

Wyoming
See also
Bighorn River (Wyo. and Mont.)

RIVERS IN ART
See also
Russian River (Calif.) in art

RIVERSIDE CHURCH (NEW YORK, N.Y.)
Riverside Church in N.Y. gets 1st black sr. pastor [J. Forbes] por *Jet* 75:23 F 20 '89

RIVERSIDE RESORT HOTEL & CASINO
A desert fox [D. Laughlin] G. Buchalter. il pors map *Forbes* 144:244+ O 16 '89

RIVERSIDE SYMPHONY
Musical events:
Alice Tully Hall concert. A. Porter. *The New Yorker* 65:90-1 My 22 '89
D. Martino's Concerto for alto saxophone. A. Porter. *The New Yorker* 65:92-3 Mr 6 '89

RIVERSIDE TELESCOPE MAKERS CONFERENCE *See* Astronomy—Conferences

RIVETS AND RIVETING
Riveting repairs. M. Morris. il *Home Mechanix* 85:20-1 Ja '89

Antitrust cases
Rivets and revelation [Textron's acquisition of Avdel prompts FTC antitrust case concerning blind rivets] H. Banks. *Forbes* 143:153 Je 12 '89

RIVIERA (FRANCE AND ITALY)
See also
Cap Martin (France)
Saint-Tropez (France)

RIVIÈRE, JEAN-PIERRE MARCIE- *See* Marcie-Rivière, Jean-Pierre

RIVIÈRE, ROSEMARIE MARCIE- *See* Marcie-Rivière, Rosemarie

RIVLIN, DAVID
about
Tiring of life without freedom, quadriplegic David Rivlin chooses to die among friends. M. Dougherty. il pors *People Weekly* 32:56-8 Ag 7 '89

RIVOLI CASTELLO (TURIN, ITALY) *See* Castello di Rivoli (Turin, Italy)

RIVULUS
Room without a view [rivulus living in land crab burrows] D. S. Taylor. il *Natural History* p26+ S '89

RIX, TIM
about
Rix to retire as Longman plans further global expansion. V. Menkes. *Publishers Weekly* 236:336 Ag 11 '89

RIXFORD, ELLEN
Making dimensional illustration. il *American Artist* 53:70-2+ N '89

RIZZO, FRANK LAZARRO
about
Frank Rizzo without prejudice. J. Lombardi. il por *Esquire* 112:114-17 Ag '89

RIZZO, PAUL J., 1928-
about
Why angels are flocking to Chapel Hill's B-school. M. Roman. il por *Business Week* p110+ O 2 '89

RJR NABISCO INC.
The $600 million cigarette scam [bogus profits through trade loading] C. J. Loomis. il *Fortune* 120:89+ D 4 '89
Biggest bidders, wildest auction. B. Saporito. il pors *Fortune* 119:34-5 Ja 2 '89
The biggest buy-out in history means hard decisions for a chemist and his wife [RJR Nabisco stockholders Don and Nancy Roberts] H. Wheelwright. il *Money* 18:129-30 F '89
Bonds that bind [Swiss court intervention in Kohlberg Kravis Roberts' bid for RJR Nabisco] D. Fanning. il *Forbes* 143:48 My 1 '89
'Greed really turns me off' [buyout; interview with H. Kravis] C. Leinster. il por *Fortune* 119:69-71 Ja 2 '89
How Ross Johnson blew the buyout. B. Saporito. il por *Fortune* 119:296-8+ Ap 24 '89
It's fun to fight a fettered foe. M. J. Williams. il *Fortune* 120:126 O 23 '89
Lou Gerstner is girding for a long, hard campaign. S. Ticer. il por *Business Week* p32-3 Mr 27 '89
Louis Gerstner. S. Ticer. il por *Business Week* Special Issue:96 Ap 14 '89
The race to stock Europe's common supermarket [BSN buys European operations of RJR Nabisco with more food deals to follow] S. Toy and R. A. Melcher. il *Business Week* p80+ Je 26 '89
RJR dearest [effect of book by P. Reynolds] M. Alpert. il por *Fortune* 119:142 Ap 10 '89
Running the biggest LBO [L. Gerstner; cover story] J. H. Dobrzynski. il pors *Business Week* p72-5+ O 2 '89
'They cleaned our clock' [buyout; interview with F. R. Johnson] B. Saporito. il por *Fortune* 119:72-4 Ja 2 '89
When the smoke clears [junk bonds] B. Weberman. il *Forbes* 144:131 Jl 10 '89

RNA
See also
Genetic code
Genetic transcription
Messenger RNA
Ribosomal RNA
Ribozymes
Transfer RNA
Antisense RNA-induced reduction in murine TIMP levels confers oncogenicity on Swiss 3T3 cells. R. Khokha and others. bibl f il *Science* 243:947-50 F 17 '89
The design and catalytic properties of a simplified ribonuclease P RNA. D. S. Waugh and others. bibl f il *Science* 244:1569-71 Je 30 '89
Did life really start out in an RNA world? M. M. Waldrop. il *Science* 246:1248-9 D 8 '89
Double-stranded ribonuclease coinduced with interferon. J. M. Meegan and P. I. Marcus. bibl f il *Science* 244:1089-91 Je 2 '89
Functional analysis of CAR, the target sequence for the Rev protein of HIV-1. E. T. Dayton and others. bibl f il *Science* 246:1625-9 D 22 '89
On finding all suboptimal foldings of an RNA molecule. M. Zuker. bibl f il *Science* 244:48-52 Ap 7 '89
Protein-RNA interactions in an icosahedral virus at 3.0 Å resolution [bean-pod mottle virus] Z. Chen and others. bibl f il *Science* 245:154-9 Jl 14 '89
Rapid redistribution of auxin-regulated RNAs during gravitropism. B. A. McClure and T. Guilfoyle. bibl f il *Science* 243:91-3 Ja 6 '89
Reversible cleavage and ligation of hepatitis delta virus RNA. H.-N. Wu and M. M. C. Lai. bibl f il *Science* 243:652-4 F 3 '89
Specific interactions in RNA enzyme-substrate complexes. C. Guerrier-Takada and others. bibl f il *Science* 246:1578-84 D 22 '89
The ultimate parasite [hepatitis delta virus] P. Radetsky. il *Discover* 10:20-1 Ag '89
An ultraviolet-sensitive RNA structural element in a viroid-like domain of the hepatitis delta virus. A. D. Branch and others. bibl f il *Science* 243:649-52 F 3 '89

RNA POLYMERASE *See* Polymerases

ROACH, JOHN V.
The pace of change in corporate America. por *Personal Computing* 13:240 O '89

ROACH, MAX
about
Max Roach [reprint] D. Gold. il por *Down Beat* 56:42 S '89

ROACH, VIRGINIA
Home schooling in times of educational reform. *The Education Digest* 54:58-61 F '89
ROACHFORD, ANDREW
about
Roachford puts it all together. J. Ressner. il por *Rolling Stone* p18 Je 29 '89
Star quality. M. Southgate. il por *Essence* 20:27 S '89
ROAD & TRACK (PERIODICAL)
Miscellaneous ramblings [redesign] T. L. Bryant. il *Road & Track* 40:33 Ja '89
Years ago. See issues of Road & Track
ROAD BICYCLES *See* Bicycles
ROAD HOUSE [film] See Motion picture reviews—Single works
ROAD MAPS, GUIDES, ETC.
Are we there yet? [maps for cycling] G. D. MacFadden. map *Bicycling* 30:152 Je '89
Cars that know where they're going [cover story] R. L. French. il por *The Futurist* 23:29-36 My/Je '89
Just what we need. Automatic roads [onboard navigation systems] B. W. Yates. il *Car and Driver* 34:19 F '89
ROAD RUNNERS (BIRDS) *See* Roadrunners (Birds)
ROAD RUNNING *See* Running
ROAD SHOWS *See* Theater, Traveling
ROAD SIGNS *See* Billboards
ROAD TRAFFIC
See also
Traffic engineering
ROADRUNNERS (BIRDS)
"A timid desert creature . . .". R. D. Ohmart. il *Natural History* p34-41 S '89
ROADS
See also
Express highways
Great River Road
Pan American Highway
Portages
Wilderness areas—Roads
All-American highways. R. Mears. il por maps *Popular Mechanics* 166:66-8+ My '89
Finance
See also
Toll roads
California
The road least traveled [Highway 1] D. M. Roth. il map *Travel Holiday* 172:62-3 O '89
A road still good as gold [California 49] L. Griffin. il *Car and Driver* 34:154 Mr '89
Germany (West)
Germany's Fairy-tale Road. S. Wilding and A. Del Balso. il map *Gourmet* 49:52-5+ Mr '89
Great Britain
The world's oldest road [Sweet Track of England: a 6,000-year-old wooden walkway discovered in a peat bog] J. Coles. il maps *Scientific American* 261:100-6 N '89
New York (State)
Scenic roads. M. Barylski. il *The Conservationist* 44:16-21 S/O '89
United States
See Roads
ROADSIDE ART
Roadside fantasies. S. Kaplan. il *Travel Holiday* 172:98 N '89
ROADSIDE IMPROVEMENT
Scenic roads [New York State] M. Barylski. il *The Conservationist* 44:16-21 S/O '89
Laws and regulations
Open roads: keeping America's scenic roads free of billboard blight. E. T. McMahon. il *National Parks* 63:14-15 N/D '89
Scenic Byways Study Act may improve U.S. touring. T. Van Hooydonk. il *Cycle* 40:23-4 Je '89
ROADSIDE MARKETING
The Wickham family holds fast. S. Wick. il *Country Journal* 16:61-6 My/Je '89
ROADSIDE STANDS *See* Roadside marketing
ROADWAY PACKAGE SYSTEM INC.
Shifting gears. K. Hannon. il *Forbes* 144:124+ D 11 '89
ROANE, SUSAN, 1948-
Mingling successfully for fun and profit [excerpt from How to work a room] il *Glamour* 87:111 Mr '89
ROANOKE (VA.)
Education
A high school play helps suicidal teenagers [Empty chairs written and performed by students] P. Feinour. *The Education Digest* 54:50-1 My '89
ROASTING *See* Cooking—Meat; Cooking—Poultry
ROAZEN, PAUL, 1936-
Encountering Freud. *Society* 26:77-82 My/Je '89
ROBB, LYNDA BIRD JOHNSON, 1943-
about
Catching up with the Johnson women. L. Carpenter. il pors *Good Housekeeping* 208:88+ Ja '89
ROBBERIES AND ASSAULTS
See also
Bank robberies
Pillage

ROBBERSON, KAY
Where there's a wind, there's a way. il *Women's Sports & Fitness* 11:36-7 Je '89
ROBBIE, JOE, 1916-1990
about
A Super Sunday victory for Joe Robbie. A. Fins. il por *Business Week* p62 Ja 23 '89
ROBBIE (JOE) STADIUM (MIAMI, FLA.) *See* Joe Robbie Stadium (Miami, Fla.)
ROBBINS, ANTHONY
How to control U.S. health costs. *Scientific American* 261:158 D '89
ROBBINS, FRED
Bruce Willis: from "wild man" to family man [interview] il por *McCall's* 116:82+ Je '89
The ever-lovin' Dinah Shore [interview; cover story] il pors *New Choices for the Best Years* 29:32-7 F '89
Roseanne: no-holds-Barred [interview] il por *Ladies' Home Journal* 106:102+ F '89
ROBBINS, JEROME
about
Dancing through life. J. Kroll. il pors *Newsweek* 113:56 Mr 6 '89
Jerome Robbins' Broadway: Jerry's legacy [cover story] D. Hering. il *Dance Magazine* 63:44-51 Ap '89
ROBBINS, JUDY FLOYD
"Broadcast English" for nonstandard dialect speakers. *The Education Digest* 54:52-3 F '89
ROBBINS, MATTHEW
about
Batteries not included [film] Reviews
Video il 12:89 Ja '89. M. Coyle
ROBBINS, MICHAEL W.
Adult education. il *New York* 22:50-2+ Ag 14 '89
(jt. auth) See Cecil, Jennifer, and Robbins, Michael W.
ROBBINS, PAUL
Heading for an 'off' year. il *Skiing* 42:42+ S '89
ROBBINS, RICHARD
The east shore [poem] *The Christian Century* 106:1006 N 8 '89
ROBBINS, THOMAS, 1943-
From private identity to public power. bibl *Society* 26:27-8 Ja/F '89
ROBBINS, TIM
about
Tim Robbins comes to off-Broadway, via Hollywood. K. Dieckmann. por *Vogue* 179:258 O '89
Tim Robbins does what he has to (so he can do what he wants). L. Morice. il pors *Mademoiselle* 95:80 F '89
ROBERSON, PHYLLIS
about
Phyllis Roberson gets promotion at Supreme Beauty Products Co. por *Jet* 75:14+ Ja 23 '89
ROBERT I, KING OF SCOTLAND, 1274-1329
about
A patriot for whom? Wallace & Bruce: Scotland's uneasy heroes. A. Fisher. bibl il *History Today* 39:18-23 F '89
ROBERT, JOSEPH
about
An odd sort of takeover play. J. R. Hayes. il por *Forbes* 143:142 F 6 '89
ROBERT (J. E.) COS. *See* J. E. Robert Cos.
THE ROBERT GUILLAUME SHOW [television program]
See Television program reviews—Single works
ROBERT M. BASS GROUP INC.
Bob Bass may have to settle for a quick profit on this one [disappointing results of Bell & Howell leveraged buyout] J. F. Siler. il por *Business Week* p48+ O 9 '89
Help your country and help yourself [takeover of the American Savings and Loan Assn.] S. C. Gwynne. il *Time* 133:72 F 20 '89
Secret agent [R. M. Bass] J. P. Newport, Jr. il por *Fortune* 119:50 Ja 2 '89
ROBERT THE BRUCE *See* Robert I, King of Scotland, 1274-1329
ROBERTA GREENE & ASSOCIATES, INC.
High-profile creativity from a brownstone base [office of R. Greene] L. Rosch. il por *Working Woman* 14:89 My '89
ROBERTS, CHRISTOPHER M.
Restoration along the Delaware. il *The Conservationist* 43:2-9 My/Je '89
ROBERTS, CONNIE
Fast food fare and nutrition. il *Consumers' Research Magazine* 72:30-3 D '89
ROBERTS, DARRYL
about
Black man overcomes frostbite to become youngest American to walk to the North Pole. D. M. Cheers. il pors map *Jet* 76:12-14 Je 12 '89
ROBERTS, DAVID, 1943-
Architectural digest visits: Julie Harris. il por *Architectural Digest* 46:140-5+ Je '89
Architectural digest visits: Liv Ullmann. il por *Architectural Digest* 46:208-14+ D '89
Back Bay Victorian. il *Architectural Digest* 46:152-9 Mr '89
Rock steady. il *Mother Jones* 14:49-51 Ap '89

ROBERTS, DAVID, 1943—cont.
Tantalizing to scholars and tourists, Carnac's megaliths remain an enigma. il *Smithsonian* 20:146-54+ S '89

ROBERTS, ERIC
about
Scene three. D. Garr. il pors *Harper's Bazaar* 122:162-5+ F '89

ROBERTS, FRANCESCA
about
Heart of Dixie. J. E. Fitch. il por *American Film* 14:58 S '89

ROBERTS, FRANCIS
School days. See issues of Parents beginning January 1983

ROBERTS, H. EDWARD
about
Even his banker didn't know that Ed Roberts had spawned a huge industry. D. Moreau. il por *Changing Times* 43:128 Ap '89

ROBERTS, JIM
Pat Metheny: the interview from home [cover story; interview] il pors *Down Beat* 56:16-19 Ag '89

ROBERTS, JULIA
about
America's 10 most beautiful women. J. Etra. il pors *Harper's Bazaar* 122:174+ S '89
Answered prayers. A. Richman. il por *Gentlemen's Quarterly* 59:298-9 D '89
Julia Roberts. il pors *Esquire* 111:152-3 Mr '89
Scene three. D. Garr. il pors *Harper's Bazaar* 122:162-5+ F '89
A starlet is born. J. Kaplan. il por *Rolling Stone* p29-30 Ja 12 '89

ROBERTS, KEN
about
Clean vs. dirty. R. O'Connor. il *Mother Jones* 14:56-7 Je '89

ROBERTS, KENNY
about
Hickman Haul-Ass Club (II). K. Vreeke. il pors *Cycle* 40:45-8+ Ja '89

ROBERTS, LEN
Pennsylvania January [poem] *Country Journal* 16:22 Ja '89

ROBERTS, LISA
about
Scene three. D. Garr. il pors *Harper's Bazaar* 122:162-5+ F '89

ROBERTS, MARCUS
about
Cooking at the keys. J. Cocks. il por *Time* 134:85 Jl 17 '89
Jazz pianist Marcus Roberts. C. Albertson. il por *Stereo Review* 54:68+ Jl '89

ROBERTS, MAUREEN Y.
The importance of community-based art education programs for adults. bibl f *Design for Arts in Education* 90:43-8 Jl/Ag '89

ROBERTS, MEADE
Tennessee rising. il pors *Vogue* 179:706-9+ S '89

ROBERTS, ORAL
about
How the others are faring. pors *Time* 134:76 S 11 '89

ROBERTS, PAUL CRAIG
Economic viewpoint. See issues of Business Week beginning September 5, 1983
Pinball wizard at the flippers. il *National Review* 41:24+ F 24 '89
Stop panicking over inflation. *The Washington Monthly* 21:26-30 My '89
Supply-side economics and the future [address, December 8, 1988] *Vital Speeches of the Day* 55:307-9 Mr 1 '89

ROBERTS, SAM
Koch against Koch. il pors *The New York Times Magazine* p32-4+ Je 11 '89

ROBERTSON, ANNE
about
Obituary
Commonweal 116:452-3 S 8 '89

ROBERTSON, GRAY
about
Caution: an ill wind may be blowing in your office, warns building doctor Gray Robertson [interview] M. J. Weiss. il pors *People Weekly* 31:89+ F 20 '89

ROBERTSON, J. L., AND OTHERS
Epitaxial growth of diamond films on Si(111) at room temperature by mass-selected low-energy C^+ beams. bibl f il *Science* 243:1047-50 F 24 '89

ROBERTSON, JAQUELIN TAYLOR
about
Cottage classic. M. Filler. il *House & Garden* 161:192-9+ My '89

ROBERTSON, JULIAN
about
Why growth stocks look good [interview] J. Mendes. il por *Fortune* 119:41-3 My 8 '89

ROBERTSON, MARY
about
Mary Robertson. K. Turcotte. il por *American Artist* 53:52-7 My '89

ROBERTSON, OSCAR
about
Big O: he hasn't changed much. C. Wilson. il pors *American Visions* 4:18+ F '89

ROBERTSON, PAT
about
How the others are faring. pors *Time* 134:76 S 11 '89
Planning ahead? V. Novak. il *Common Cause Magazine* 15:6 S/O '89
Where's Pat? for *Christianity Today* 33:46-7 D 15 '89

ROBERTSON, ROBBIE
Woodstock remembered: the artists. il pors *Rolling Stone* p80 Ag 24 '89

ROBERTSON (H. H.) CO. See H. H. Robertson Co.

ROBESON, PAUL, 1898-1976
about
PW interviews [biographer M. Duberman] S. Staggs. por *Publishers Weekly* 235:72-3 Ja 13 '89
The Robeson record. B. Gewen. *The New Leader* 72:17-18 F 20 '89
Robeson's choice. G. C. Ward. il *American Heritage* 40:12+ Ap '89

ROBEY
about
Topless photos, African pigs and psychics—that's Robey. J. Marion. il por *TV Guide* 37:34-5 Je 10-16 '89

ROBINS, ANTHONY
Theater preservation update: London 1989. il *Architectural Record* 177:79 N '89

ROBINS, C. RICHARD
Nature's one-upmanship. il *Sea Frontiers* 35:192 My/Je '89

ROBINS (A. H.) COMPANY, INC. See A. H. Robins Company, Inc.

ROBINSON, ANDREA
about
The beauty elite. il pors *Harper's Bazaar* 122:40+ Ag '89

ROBINSON, ANDREA, AND SCHEFER, DOROTHY
Beautystyle. See issues of Vogue beginning July 1985 through July 1988

ROBINSON, ANTHONY B.
Teaching theology in the church [cover story] *The Christian Century* 106:980-2 N 1 '89

ROBINSON, BILL, 1878-1949
about
Tap dancer Bill 'Bojangles' Robinson honored with day. il por *Jet* 77:61 N 27 '89
Statues, portraits, etc.
Richmond's dancin' man. il *Southern Living* 24:59 My '89

ROBINSON, BILL, 1949-
about
Designing men. il pors *Gentlemen's Quarterly* 59:120-5 Jl '89

ROBINSON, BONNIE
Why did America's funniest housewife leave home? il pors *Redbook* 174:54+ N '89

ROBINSON, BROOKS, 1937-
about
Baseball lives [excerpt] M. Bryan. il por *Sports Illustrated* 70:78+ Ap 24 '89

ROBINSON, BRUCE
about
How to get ahead in advertising [film] Reviews
The Nation 248:676-7 My 15 '89. S. Klawans
The New Leader 72:21 My 1 '89. J. Morrone
The New Republic 200:28-9 Je 5 '89. S. Kauffmann
New York il 22:71-2 My 22 '89. D. Denby
People Weekly il 31:16+ Je 26 '89. R. Novak
Time il 133:110 My 22 '89. R. Schickel
Vogue il 179:204 My '89
Withnail and I [film] Reviews
Video 12:86 Ja '89. I. Robbins

ROBINSON, CHARLIE
about
'You learn . . . about pain and humility and failing'. T. Carlson. il pors *TV Guide* 37:42-5 Ja 7-13 '89

ROBINSON, CHRIS
Titles can sell articles. *The Writer* 102:20-1+ Ja '89

ROBINSON, DARRELL
about
Drugs and track. C. Neff. il pors *Sports Illustrated* 71:25-6 O 2 '89
Flo Jo confronts accuser on drug use allegations. il por *Jet* 77:46 O 9 '89

ROBINSON, DAVID
about
David is Goliath. P. Boivin. il por *Sport (New York, N.Y.)* 80:62-3 N '89
He's the Spur of the moment. J. McCallum. il por *Sports Illustrated* 71:72-3 N 13 '89

ROBINSON, DAVID A., AND LUDLUM, DAVID M., 1910-
The weather where you live. *Weatherwise* 42:328-9 D '89

ROBINSON, DENISE GARY
about
Women who go for it! B. M. Campbell. il pors *Essence* 20:48-50+ Ag '89
ROBINSON, DINDY
Where to draw the line. *The Humanist* 49:35 Ja/F '89
ROBINSON, EDNA MAE
about
Remembering Sugar Ray. il pors *Ebony* 45:74+ D '89
ROBINSON, FRANK
about
Orioles, Blue Jays, put black managers on spot. il pors *Jet* 77:51 O 16 '89
Toronto, Baltimore game pits two black managers. il pors *Jet* 76:46 Jl 17 '89
ROBINSON, FRANKLIN
about
Robinson's millenium. *Flying* 116:30 Je '89
ROBINSON, GENE E., AND OTHERS
Hormonal and genetic control of behavioral integration in honey bee colonies. bibl f il *Science* 246:109-12 O 6 '89
ROBINSON, GLYNNE
A town that looked just so. il *American Heritage* 40:92-9 Jl/Ag '89
ROBINSON, JAMES D., III
about
American Express: service that sells [cover story] J. P. Newport, Jr. il pors *Fortune* 120:80-2+ N 20 '89
American Express slings mud—and gets splattered. W. Glasgall and J. Meehan. il por *Business Week* p102+ Ag 14 '89
Bank shot: Edmond Safra turns the tables on American Express. J. Taylor. il pors *New York* 22:42-7 S 18 '89
ROBINSON, JAMES G.
about
From cars to stars. P. Newcomb. il pors *Forbes* 143:60-1 Ja 23 '89
ROBINSON, JEFFREY
London's Sunday antiques fairs. il *Gourmet* 49:66-9+ Je '89
Villa America. il *Gourmet* 49:70+ Jl '89
ROBINSON, JENNIFER DENISE
Warm embrace [poem] *Essence* 19:118 Ja '89
ROBINSON, JOAN, 1903-1983
about
In praise of Joan Robinson: economics as social control. W. J. Samuels. *Society* 26:73-6 Ja/F '89
ROBINSON, JOHN P.
The shopping days of our lives. il *Utne Reader* p68 S/O '89
ROBINSON, KATHRYN
Trash is good for you. il *Glamour* 87:133 My '89
ROBINSON, KRISTIN
Ayn Rand's objectivism: a humanistic interpretation. por *The Humanist* 49:29-30 Ja/F '89
ROBINSON, LILLIAN S.
What culture should mean. *The Nation* 249:319-21 S 25 '89
ROBINSON, LINDA GOSDEN, 1953-
about
The perfect power couple's perfect power marriage. il por *Fortune* 120:86 N 20 '89
ROBINSON, LINDA S.
Dwindling options in Panama. bibl f *Foreign Affairs* 68:187-205 Wint '89/'90
Hanging in the balance: El Salvador's future & the limits of U.S. power. il *Commonweal* 116:242-5 Ap 21 '89
ROBINSON, MAGGIE GREENWOOD- *See* Greenwood-Robinson, Maggie
ROBINSON, MARGARET A.
Marry for life [story] il *Redbook* 173:42+ Jl '89
ROBINSON, MARK S.
Surveying the scars of ancient Martian floods. il *Astronomy* 17:38-45 O '89
ROBINSON, MAX, 1939-1988
about
Obituary
  Jet il por 75:14-15 Ja 9 '89
  Newsweek il por 113:65 Ja 2 '89
ROBINSON, PHIL ALDEN
about
Field of dreams [film] Reviews
  American Film 14:62 My '89. J. E. Fitch
  The Christian Century 106:515-16 My 17 '89. J. M. Wall
  Commonweal 116:303 My 19 '89. T. O'Brien
  Film Comment il 25:78-9 My/Je '89. H. Jacobson
  Maclean's il 102:66 My 1 '89. B. D. Johnson
  Mademoiselle il 95:66+ Jl '89. R. Rosenbaum
  The Nation 248:678 My 15 '89. S. Klawans
  The New Republic 200:26+ My 8 '89. S. Kauffmann
  New York il 22:96+ Ap 24 '89. D. Denby
  The New Yorker 65:76-7 My 1 '89. P. Kael
  Newsweek il 113:72-3 Ap 24 '89. D. Ansen
  People Weekly il 31:13-14 My 15 '89. R. Novak
  People Weekly il 32:120-1 O 23 '89. M. Donovan
  Sports Illustrated il 70:81 My 1 '89. S. Wulf
  Time 133:78 Ap 24 '89. R. Corliss
  Vogue il 179:204 My '89

ROBINSON, RICHARD
about
A limit to affirmative action? J. Blanton. *Commentary* 87:28-32 Je '89
ROBINSON, ROGER
Better late than never. il pors *Runner's World* 24:62-5 Ag '89
ROBINSON, RUMEAL
about
Special delivery. L. Montville. il pors *Sports Illustrated* 71:64-9 N 20 '89
ROBINSON, SHAWNA
about
A little hugging's okay, but race driver Shawna Robinson sees red when you ask her to wear pink. P. Jordan. il pors *People Weekly* 31:55-6 F 20 '89
ROBINSON, SMOKEY
Smokey Robinson reveals: how infidelity and drugs destroyed his marriage. il pors *Ebony* 44:148+ My '89
about
Smokey Robinson cited as 'Living Legend' at gala tribute held in Hollywood. il pors *Jet* 77:22 D 18 '89
Smokey Robinson's book tells how drugs and other woman almost ruined life and career [cover story] il pors *Jet* 75:58-60 Mr 13 '89
Tracing the tracks of his tears in a new book, Smokey Robinson says crack nearly killed him. S. Dougherty. il pors *People Weekly* 31:79-80+ Ap 3 '89
ROBINSON, SUGAR RAY
about
Obituary
  Jet il por 76:52-5 My 8 '89
  Jet il pors 76:16-17+ My 1 '89
  Newsweek il por 113:64 Ap 24 '89
  People Weekly il pors 31:155-7 My 1 '89
  Sports Illustrated il 70:96 Ap 24 '89. G. L. Rogin
  Time il por 133:89 Ap 24 '89. R. Lacayo
Remembering Sugar Ray. il pors *Ebony* 45:74+ D '89
ROBINSON HUMPHREY COMPANY INC.
Brokers in the boondocks. M. Schifrin. il pors *Forbes* 143:228+ Je 26 '89
ROBINSON, LAKE, LERER & MONTGOMERY
The perfect power couple's perfect power marriage [L. G. Robinson] il por *Fortune* 120:86 N 20 '89
ROBOCK, ALAN
New models confirm nuclear winter. bibl f il *The Bulletin of the Atomic Scientists* 45:32+ S '89
ROBOHM, CATHY
A report from salmon run. il *Country Journal* 16:72-3 S/O '89
ROBOT ARMS *See* Manipulators (Mechanism)
ROBOTHAM, ROSEMARIE
Islands of genius. il *Omni (New York, N.Y.)* 11:18+ S '89
Not in my backyard. il *Omni (New York, N.Y.)* 11:60-2+ S '89
ROBOTS
See also
  Manipulators (Mechanism)
  Micromice
  Microrobots
  Telerobots
Homebody [J. F. Engelberger] E. Corcoran. il por *Scientific American* 261:77-8 O '89
Interview: Hans Moravec. E. Regis. por *Omni (New York, N.Y.)* 11:74-6+ Ag '89
Robots with human intelligence. il *The Futurist* 23:52-3 Mr/Ap '89
The well-tempered robot. K. Black. il *House & Garden* 161:146-9+ D '89
Biological use
Disco-bee [robot bee designed by Wolfgang H. Kirchner and Axel Michelsen] J. Horgan. *Scientific American* 260:31-2 Je '89
New dancer in the hive [robot honeybee; cover story] R. Weiss. il *Science News* 136:282-3 O 28 '89
Industrial use
See also
  Honeybee Robotics (Firm)
The automation generation [work of David Bourne and Paul Wright] A. Kozlov. il *Omni (New York, N.Y.)* 11:18+ Mr '89
The finishing touch [use of robots in making Steinway pianos; cover story] I. Amato. il *Science News* 135:108-9 F 18 '89
Lawn care use
Robo-mower [Lawn Ranger] il *The Futurist* 23:39 Ja/F '89
Medical use
See also
  Telesurgery
Will your doctor be a robot? *USA Today (Periodical)* 117:9 F '89
Military use
USAF expects robotic inspection facility to cut maintenance costs. B. W. Henderson. il *Aviation Week & Space Technology* 130:53-5+ Mr 13 '89
Oceanographic use
Submersible acrobat [Scorpio Scout mine hunting vehicle] P. Britton. il *Popular Science* 234:96 Ap '89

ROBOTS—*cont.*

Space flight use

Commercialization policy threatens space station's robotic contract [OMB decision requiring private financing] T. M. Foley. il *Aviation Week & Space Technology* 130:30-1 F 6 '89

The debris collector [University of Arizona's Autonomous Space Processor for Orbital Debris program] W. H. Ganoe. il *Ad Astra* 1:35-7 Je '89

Desperately seeking Cyborg [Flight Telerobotic Servicer for space station assembly designed by Honeybee Robotics] J. Goldberg. il *Omni (New York, N.Y.)* 11:12+ Ag '89

Martin Marietta robotic device will aid in space station assembly [Flight Telerobotic Servicer] B. D. Nordwall. il *Aviation Week & Space Technology* 130:53 My 15 '89

NASA robot to have private-sector spinoffs. *High Technology Business* 9:37 Mr '89

Orbital mechanic [Flight Telerobotic Servicer] G. R. Graf. il *Ad Astra* 1:5-6 O '89

A robot-built lunar observatory. B. D. Gibson. il *Astronomy* 17:14 Jl '89

Robotic microscope could allow R&D in space. *High Technology Business* 9:36-7 F '89

ROCAWICH, LINDA

Toxins on tap? il *The Progressive* 53:24-7 My '89

ROCCO, ALEX

about

Alex Rocco. E. Warren. por *TV Guide* 37:7 S 23-29 '89

ROCHA, MARCO ANTONIO, AND RODRIGUES ALVES, MARCIA

Flying in the fast lane. il *Américas* 41 no2:16-21 '89

ROCHE, JOHN PEARSON, 1923-

The Cuban Missile Crisis revisited. *The New Leader* 72:5 Mr 6 '89

The great Mafia wedding [cover story] il *National Review* 41:23-4 S 1 '89

Guilty of what? il *National Review* 41:47-8 S 29 '89

The new left vigilantes. il *National Review* 41:34-5 D 8 '89

ROCHE, LISSA

(jt. auth) See Davis, Bernard David, and Roche, Lissa

ROCHE, LUIS ARMANDO

about

The secret [film] Reviews

Américas il 41 no1:63 '89. J. Mosier

ROCHE-KELLY, DELIA

about

Personalities plus. J. Gruder. il pors *Harper's Bazaar* 122:173-4 Ag '89

ROCHESTER, DESMOND

Compelling evidence. il *American Film* 15:72 D '89

ROCHESTER (N.Y.)

Education

Fixing the teaching, not the kids [reducing special education classes in Rochester, N.Y. middle school] J. Buckley. il *U.S. News & World Report* 106:61-2 Mr 13 '89

The hard lessons of school reform. J. Buckley. il *U.S. News & World Report* 106:58-60 Je 26 '89

A local business invests in the kids [work-study program offered by Wegmans' supermarkets] il *U.S. News & World Report* 106:60 Je 26 '89

Upgrading education in local public schools [Nathaniel Rochester Community School] B. Delatiner. *The Education Digest* 55:28-30 S '89

Galleries and museums

See also

International Museum of Photography at George Eastman House

Industries

Norman Lear, meet Adam Smith [Greater Rochester Cablevision owned by Time Warner competes with Act III Broadcasting's independent station in syndicated market] P. Newcomb. il *Forbes* 144:206+ N 27 '89

ROCHETTE, ED, 1927-

Numismatics. See issues of Antiques & Collecting Hobbies beginning March 1985 through July 1989

ROCHLIN, MARGY

Lords of the ring. il pors *Harper's Bazaar* 122:103 D '89

ROCHLIN, SHELDON

about

Video publishers reel in profits with avant-garde offerings. L. Arden. il por *Home Office Computing* 7:45 My '89

ROCHON, DONALD

about

Black FBI agent loses case at Justice Dept. *Jet* 76:7 Jl 24 '89

ROCI (EXHIBITION)

Rauschenberg goes to Moscow. A. Wallach. il por *Art in America* 77:21+ Mr '89

The ROCI road show [R. Rauschenberg show in Moscow] M. L. Kotz. il por *Art News* 88:48+ Summ '89

ROCK & ROLL HALL OF FAME

Age displays its virtues as the Stones, Stevie and Dion join rock's Hall of Fame. S. Dougherty. il *People Weekly* 31:52-4 F 6 '89

Cleveland affirms Rock Hall of Fame deal. M. Goldberg. *Rolling Stone* p25 Ag 10 '89

Cleveland may finally get some satisfaction. S. Phillips. il *Business Week* p60 O 2 '89

January. il *Rolling Stone* p46 D 14-28 '89

Rock & Roll Hall of Fame. P. Puterbaugh. il *Rolling Stone* p75-82+ F 9 '89

Rock and Roll Hall of Fame [induction dinner] D. Fricke and S. Rogers. il *Rolling Stone* p8-9+ Mr 9 '89

Wonder and Temptations among new inductees into Rock 'n' Roll Hall of Fame. il por *Jet* 75:60+ F 6 '89

ROCK BANDS See Rock groups

ROCK CARVINGS See Petroglyphs

ROCK CITY ANGELS (MUSICAL GROUP)

Rock City Angels [release of Young man's blues] P. Puterbaugh. il *Stereo Review* 54:151 F '89

ROCK CLIMBING See Mountaineering

ROCK CONCERTS

See also

Concert Productions International

Alternative bands make their stand. il *Rolling Stone* p22+ Ag 24 '89

Attaché case full of blues [L. Atwater's participation in R&B inaugural jam] G. Hirshey. il pors *Rolling Stone* p19-20 Mr 9 '89

Blasts from the past [summer 1989] M. Goldberg. il *Rolling Stone* p21-3 My 18 '89

Bush rhythm & blues bash headlined by black stars [final concert of the Bush inauguration] il *Jet* 75:59 F 6 '89

Designstyle: plenty of hot air [oversized inflatable women designed by R. Harries for Rolling Stones' Steel wheels tour] D. L. Umansky. il *Theatre Crafts* 23:20 D '89

It's a musical marathon as rock meets country for a Motown hoedown [This country's rockin' concert at Detroit's Silverdome] il *People Weekly* 31:53-4 My 22 '89

Revivals [1989] il *Rolling Stone* p104-5 D 14-28 '89

Welcome back, Grace Slick [aging rock groups] P. Newcomb. il *Forbes* 143:56+ My 15 '89

When dinosaurs roamed the earth! [aging rock groups on tour] il *People Weekly* 32:72-5 Ag 28 '89

Benefit performances

See also

Earthquake Relief concert, 1989

Our Common Future concert, 1989

AIDS benefits planned. J. Ressner. *Rolling Stone* p16 Ap 6 '89

Whirlwind worldwide touring: Amnesty International's Human Rights Now tour. M. Loeffler. il *Theatre Crafts* 23:50-4 My '89

Photographs and photography

Rock tour [work of G. Rose] F. Cameron. il *Petersen's Photographic Magazine* 18:18-20+ Ag '89

Security measures

Heavy mettle. S. Fried. il *Gentlemen's Quarterly* 59:117-18 Ag '89

ROCK CORNISH GAME HEN COOKING See Cooking—Poultry

ROCK CRITICS AND CRITICISM

See also

Rock opera reviews

Explore: adopt a critic. P. Doskoch. *High Fidelity (New York, N.Y.)* 39:55 Jl '89

ROCK DEFORMATION

Deep earthquakes. C. Frohlich. bibl il maps *Scientific American* 260:48-55 Ja '89

Dynamic pore-pressure fluctuations in rapidly shearing granular materials. R. M. Iverson and R. G. LaHusen. bibl f il *Science* 246:796-9 N 10 '89

ROCK DRAWINGS See Cave drawings and paintings

ROCK FESTIVALS See Music festivals

ROCK GARDENS AND GARDENING

The riverbed look . . . without water. il *Sunset (Central West edition)* 182:246+ My '89

ROCK GROUPS

See also

Groupies

Phonograph records—Rock music

Rock musicians

See also names of rock groups

Hard-rock roundup. K. Turman. il *'Teen* 33:54-5 Mr '89

Magna cum loud [favorite rock bands of college radio programmers] il *Rolling Stone* p127-8+ Mr 23 '89

Random notes. S. Rogers. See issues of Rolling Stone

Roll them bones [veteran bands return; cover story] J. Cocks. il *Time* 134:58-62 S 4 '89

Ten best bands [1980s] A. Schwartz. il *Seventeen* 48:68-9 D '89

Today's rock of all ages [appeal of 1960s groups to today's youth] il *U.S. News & World Report* 107:11 Jl 31 '89

Up-and-coming bands to watch. il *Rolling Stone* p34 Ag 24 '89

Welcome back, Grace Slick [aging rock groups] P. Newcomb. il *Forbes* 143:56+ My 15 '89

When dinosaurs roamed the earth! [aging rock groups on tour] il *People Weekly* 32:72-5 Ag 28 '89

ROCK GROUPS—cont.

Agencies and agents
See Theatrical agencies and agents
ROCK HUNTING *See* Rocks—Collectors and collecting
ROCK MUSIC
See also
Cable television—Rock music
Compact disc video—Rock music
Compact discs—Rock music
Heavy metal music
House music
MTV Networks Inc.
MuchMusic Network
Phonograph records—Rock music
Radio broadcasting—Rock music
Rock groups
Rock musicians
Television broadcasting—Rock music
Video Jukebox Network, Inc.
Videotapes—Rock music
1989 yearbook [cover story; special issue] il *Rolling Stone* p45-9+ D 14-28 '89
New directions for the next decade. J. Cocks. il *Time* 134:63 S 4 '89
Rock & roll summer [special section] il *Rolling Stone* p14-15+ Jl 13-27 '89
Rockin' thunder [rock songs with references to weather; cover story] R. E. Schmid. il *Weatherwise* 42:192-6 Ag '89

Archives
Tales from the crypt [rock reissues for CD] J. Ressner. il *Rolling Stone* p13-14 F 23 '89

Awards
See also
International Rock Awards
1988 Music Awards [Rolling Stone Readers and Critics Poll; special section] il *Rolling Stone* p61-3+ Mr 9 '89

Bibliography
Book reports. il *Rolling Stone* p122-3 D 14-28 '89

Economic aspects
See also
BCL Entertainment Corporation
Concert Productions International
Radio Vision International Inc.
Bringing it all back home. J. Queenan. il *Forbes* 144:152-3 O 2 '89
Finding fame without fortune. L. Silverman. il *Rolling Stone* p33 S 21 '89
Welcome back, Grace Slick [aging rock groups] P. Newcomb. il *Forbes* 143:56+ My 15 '89

History
Fusion: jazz-rock-classical [reprint] M. Bourne. il *Down Beat* 56:79-80 S '89
Joey Dee, past master of twist, plans a refuge for those caught between rock and a hard place. P. Freeman. il pors *People Weekly* 32:131-2+ N 20 '89
Rock of ages [A. Pepper and S. Snadowsky, co-owners of the Bottom Line] E. Hollreiser. il pors *New York* 22:29 F 6 '89

Information services
Rock's 900 lines: a hot number? J. Ressner. il *Rolling Stone* p24 Mr 23 '89

Moral and religious aspects
See also
Christian contemporary music
The blooming of rock 'n' roll [discussion of February 24, 1989 article, That old devil music] S. Goldman. il *National Review* 41:44-5 My 5 '89
Face the music [National review's attack] K. Loder. il *Rolling Stone* p57-9+ My 4 '89
Music's mean season [rock in 1989] A. DeCurtis. il *Rolling Stone* p15-16 D 14-28 '89
Pop stars blast evangelists. P. Crescenti. il *Christianity Today* 33:63 Mr 3 '89
The sounds of lawsuits: rock lyrics on trial. S. F. Rohde. il *USA Today (Periodical)* 118:86-7 Jl '89
That old devil music [cover story] S. Goldman. il *National Review* 41:28-31+ F 24 '89

Physiological effects
After Live Aid and Farm Aid, hearing aid may be next for unwary victims of rock [work of K. Peck and F. Gordon] N. Geeslin. il pors *People Weekly* 31:95-6 Ja 23 '89
Into the plug zone [effects of noise on rock musicians] T. Imbimbo. il *Seventeen* 48:65 F '89
Townshend, tinnitus and rock & roll. E. Murphy. *Rolling Stone* p101 Jl 13-27 '89

Psychological aspects
Old and in the way. G. Jaynes. il *Life* 12:14 Ag '89

Czechoslovakia
Czechoslovakia's most enduring band, The Plastic People, recycles its history-making rock. S. K. Reed. il *People Weekly* 31:116+ My 22 '89
Pulnoc. J. Morley. *The Nation* 248:748-50 My 29 '89
Sound Czech [Pulnoc] D. Fricke. il *Rolling Stone* p70 Jl 13-27 '89

Louisiana
See also
New Orleans (La.)—Music

South Africa
S. Africa tour furor basis for Milan Williams firing from 'Commodores' group. il por *Jet* 76:17 Ag 14 '89

Soviet Union
Bon voyage [tour by Bon Jovi; cover story] R. Tannenbaum. il *Rolling Stone* p52-4+ F 9 '89
Glasnost rock. il *Rolling Stone* p58-9 D 14-28 '89
Glasnost rock [B. Grebenshikov] F. Rose. il pors *New York* 22:56-60+ Mr 20 '89
Hot, hot, hot: Brigada S. P. Hofheinz. il *Time* 133:110-11 Ap 10 '89
Red suede shoes. T. W. Ryback. *The New Republic* 200:13-14 Ja 9-16 '89
Tell Tchaikovsky the news [Moscow Music Peace Festival] E. Gundersen. il *Rolling Stone* p15-16 O 5 '89
U.S.S.R. welcomes Greenpeace [debut of benefit album Rainbow warriors] L. Rotcage. il *Rolling Stone* p17 Ap 20 '89

ROCK MUSICIANS
See also
Clothing and dress—Rock musicians
Groupies
Phonograph records—Rock music
Rock & Roll Hall of Fame
Rock groups
Teachers as rock musicians
Women rock musicians
See also names of rock musicians
Are white singers taking over blues and soul? il *Jet* 75:60-2+ Mr 6 '89
Are whites taking over rhythm & blues? D. Narine. il *Ebony* 44:90+ Jl '89
Joey Dee, past master of twist, plans a refuge for those caught between rock and a hard place [retirement community for former recording stars] P. Freeman. il pors *People Weekly* 32:131-2+ N 20 '89
Making it in Metal Mecca [heavy metal rockers in Los Angeles] J. Foote. il *Newsweek* 114:56-8 Ag 7 '89
New faces. il *Rolling Stone* p83-4+ D 14-28 '89
Random notes. S. Rogers. See issues of Rolling Stone
Stereos of the stars. il *Rolling Stone* p123+ Je 15 '89
Where are they now? il *Rolling Stone* p51-2+ Ag 10 '89

Health and hygiene
See also
Hearing Education and Awareness for Rockers (Organization)
Into the plug zone [effects of noise] T. Imbimbo. il *Seventeen* 48:65 F '89
Townshend, tinnitus and rock & roll. E. Murphy. *Rolling Stone* p101 Jl 13-27 '89

Photographs and photography
Rock & roll photo album [cover story; special section] il *Rolling Stone* p53+ S 21 '89

Political activities
See also
Rock concerts—Benefit performances
Billy Bragg: of Labour and love. D. Fricke. por *Rolling Stone* p18 Ja 12 '89
U.S.S.R. welcomes Greenpeace [debut of benefit album Rainbow warriors] L. Rotcage. il *Rolling Stone* p17 Ap 20 '89

Protection
Stand by me: inside the world of rock & roll bodyguards. J. Ressner. il *Rolling Stone* p56-60+ Ap 6 '89
ROCK MUSICIANS AND THE ENVIRONMENT
See also
Our Common Future concert, 1989
Ecological rock. N. Jennings. il *Maclean's* 102:50-1 Je 12 '89
Save the earth. il *Rolling Stone* p65 D 14-28 '89
ROCK OPERA REVIEWS

Single works
See name of composer for full entry
Tommy. Townshend, Pete
ROCK PAINTINGS *See* Cave drawings and paintings; Petroglyphs
ROCK SONGS *See* Rock music
ROCK STORE (CALIF.)
L.A.'s biking celebs bring a roaring trade to Ed and Vern's [grocery and diner] il por *People Weekly* 31:89 My 15 '89
ROCKCASTLE, GARTH
Franklin D. Israel subject of first exhibition in Walker series. il *Architectural Record* 177:69 F '89
ROCKEFELLER, DAVID, 1915-
about
The Rockefeller Congress. E. A. Finn, Jr. il pors *Forbes* 144:74+ O 30 '89
ROCKEFELLER, WINTHROP, 1948-
about
Winners. L. Rudeen. il por *Motor Boating & Sailing* 163:30 My '89
ROCKEFELLER (ABBY ALDRICH) FOLK ART CENTER
See Abby Aldrich Rockefeller Folk Art Center
ROCKEFELLER (WINTHROP) FOUNDATION *See* Winthrop Rockefeller Foundation

ROCKEFELLER CENTER

Architecture [Rockefeller Plaza West designed by W. Pedersen] C. Wiseman. il por *New York* 22:146-7 S 11 '89

Big tree for the Big Apple [Christmas tree] J. Grossmann. il pors *National Wildlife* 28:10-13 D '89/Ja '90

The Japs capture Rockefeller Center. W. F. Buckley. il *National Review* 41:53 D 8 '89

Mitsubishi's gamble on a Manhattan jewel. L. Light. il *Business Week* p124 N 13 '89

'Now they're just rich' [sale to Mitsubishi Estate Co.] C. Friday and J. Hammer. il *Newsweek* 114:62-3 N 13 '89

Pa-rum-pum-pum-pum [Christmas cadets used as decorations] B. Weber. il *The New York Times Magazine* p130 N 19 '89

The Rockefeller generation gap [sold to Japan's Mitsubishi Estate Co.] *U.S. News & World Report* 107:14+ N 13 '89

Sure, we'll take Manhattan [sale to Mitsubishi] J. Greenwald. il *Time* 134:83 N 13 '89

ROCKEFELLER FAMILY

about

'Now they're just rich' [sale of Rockefeller Center to Mitsubishi Estate Co.] C. Friday and J. Hammer. il *Newsweek* 114:62-3 N 13 '89

The Rockefeller generation gap [Rockefeller Center sold to Mitsubishi Estate Co.] *U.S. News & World Report* 107:14+ N 13 '89

ROCKEFELLER INSTITUTE FOR MEDICAL RESEARCH

See Rockefeller University

ROCKEFELLER UNIVERSITY

Baltimore to succeed Lederberg? B. J. Culliton. il por *Science* 245:1441 S 29 '89

ROCKET ENGINES

See also
Guided missiles—Propulsion systems
Space vehicles—Propulsion systems

ROCKET MODELS

Competitions

Comrades in rocketry [Soviet and U.S. amateur rocketeers compete at Wallops Station, Va.] A. Jackson. il *Ad Astra* 1:29-31 F '89

ROCKETDYNE (FIRM)

NASP program office retains two propulsion contractors [National Aerospace Plane] S. W. Kandebo. *Aviation Week & Space Technology* 130:19 My 8 '89

Preliminary tests bolster Rocketdyne's confidence in NASP propulsion system [National Aero-Space Plane] B. A. Smith. il *Aviation Week & Space Technology* 130:98-9 My 22 '89

Rocketdyne developing facility for hypersonic propulsion tests. W. B. Scott. il *Aviation Week & Space Technology* 130:65 Ja 30 '89

Rocketdyne to use simple designs, production efficiency to trim ALS costs [advanced launch system] B. A. Smith. il *Aviation Week & Space Technology* 130:299+ Je 12 '89

ROCKETS

See also
Guided missiles

History

"The dream of yesterday is the reality of tomorrow" [R. Goddard] R. Bruns and B. Kennedy. il pors *American History Illustrated* 24:24-9+ Summ '89

Robert Goddard and his rocket were lonely pioneers of man's thrust into the limitlessness of space. M. Kernan. il pors *Smithsonian* 20:46+ N '89

The rocket pioneers. M. R. Chartrand. *Ad Astra* 1:38 Mr '89

Meteorological use

Little missions, big returns. S. P. Maran. il *Astronomy* 17:34-40 Ja '89

Physics use

Seeing is believing! [Echo 7 sounding rocket experiment photographs electrons spiraling around earth's magnetic field lines] il *Sky and Telescope* 77:130-1 F '89

ROCKETTES

Like mother, like daughter: these Rockettes get their kicks by staying in step with their moms. il *People Weekly* 32:113 D 18 '89

ROCKFORD (ILL.)

Politics and government

Charles Box elected first black Rockford, Il., mayor. il por *Jet* 76:25 Ap 24 '89

ROCKFORD INSTITUTE

Unpleasant business [locks out R. J. Neuhaus] *National Review* 41:12+ Je 16 '89

ROCKFORD INSTITUTE. CENTER ON RELIGION & SOCIETY *See* Center on Religion & Society (New York, N.Y.)

ROCKHOUND STATE PARK (N.M.)

New Mexico's Rockhound Park. il *Sunset (Central West edition)* 183:56 N '89

ROCKHOUNDS *See* Rocks—Collectors and collecting
ROCKING CHAIRS *See* Chairs
ROCKING HORSES, ETC.

The rocking moose. P. Butler and M. Butler. il *Outdoor Life* 184:48-9 D '89

A running, jumping, rocking horse. il *The Family Handyman* 39:48-9 N/D '89

ROCKMAN, ALEXIS

about

Alexis Rockman at Jay Gorney. K. Johnson. il *Art in America* 77:168-9 Je '89

ROCKMAN, GREGORY

about

A South African cop breaks ranks over police violence. B. Hewitt. il pors *People Weekly* 32:44-6 O 16 '89

ROCK'N FLOWERS

With cool shades and hot moves, Rock'n Flowers plant their claim as the year's silliest sensation. il *People Weekly* 32:84 Ag 28 '89

ROCKS

See also
Amphibolites
Geology

Age

See Geological time

Collectors and collecting

Keep risky rocks under wraps [radon levels in homes displaying minerals] *Science News* 136:317 N 11 '89

Deformation

See Rock deformation

ROCKS, IGNEOUS

See also
Basalt
Carbonatites
Lava
Magma
Pyroxenite
Volcanic ash, tuff, etc.

ROCKS, SEDIMENTARY

See also
Evaporites

ROCKS IN ART

The watercolor page: Sheila Savannah. M. N. Balcomb. il por *American Artist* 53:76-9+ S '89

ROCKS IN MUSIC

Rock music. R. V. Dietrich. il *Earth Science* 42:24-5 Summ '89

ROCKWELL, NORMAN, 1894-1978

about

The market for Norman Rockwell's work. D. Grant. *American Artist* 53:10+ F '89

Rockwell's model doc, Donald Campbell, gives his last shot and retires. il por *People Weekly* 31:114-15 Mr 27 '89

ROCKWELL, PAUL

Fighting the fires of racism. il *The Nation* 249:714-16+ D 11 '89

ROCKWELL INTERNATIONAL CORP.

Aeronautical engineering [National Aero-Space Plane; special section] il *Aviation Week & Space Technology* 131:50-1+ O 23 '89

Commander lawsuit settled. il *Flying* 116:10 Ag '89

Consolidation of orbiter logistics speeds repairs, reduces delays. E. H. Kolcum. il *Aviation Week & Space Technology* 131:45+ Jl 31 '89

Electronics increase in importance at Rockwell as B-1B winds down. B. A. Smith. il *Aviation Week & Space Technology* 130:65-7 F 6 '89

Judge fines Rockwell $5.5 million for concealing Navstar double-billing. M. A. Dornheim. *Aviation Week & Space Technology* 130:24-5 Mr 13 '89

Pentagon tests new Hellfire platforms as contractors analyze improvements [surface launches] D. F. Bond. il *Aviation Week & Space Technology* 131:32-3 N 6 '89

'Real nasty stuff' [radioactive pollution from Santa Susana Field Laboratory] A. L. Huebner. il *The Progressive* 53:26-8 O '89

Rockwell declines AIL deal due to plan's complexity [plan to acquire AIL subsidiary of Eaton Corp. to expedite fixes to B-1B bomber's ALQ-161 system] *Aviation Week & Space Technology* 130:67 F 6 '89

Rockwell working with AIL to develop B-1B avionics fix. *Aviation Week & Space Technology* 130:101+ Ja 2 '89

Rockwell's loss on AC-130U estimated at $81 million [gunship program] *Aviation Week & Space Technology* 130:265 Mr 20 '89

ROCKWELL INTERNATIONAL CORP. AVIONICS GROUP

Collins demonstrates first hand-held Global Positioning System receiver. il *Aviation Week & Space Technology* 130:153 Je 19 '89

ROCKWOOD, DAVID

about

David Rockwood: a steel-and-glass bay-front house in Portland. D. Gantenbein. il por *Architectural Digest* 46:72-7 Ag '89

ROCKY FLATS NUCLEAR WEAPONS FACILITY *See* Nuclear weapons—Manufacture

ROCKY MOUNTAIN ARSENAL (COLO.)

Land of death . . . and life [wildlife thrive on contaminated grounds] G. Gerhardt. il map *National Wildlife* 28:34-40 D '89/Ja '90

The toxic morass in Denver's backyard. S. D. Atchison. il *Business Week* p46 Ja 9 '89

ROCKY MOUNTAIN GOATS
Sky-high acrobats [cover story] il map *National Geographic World* 163:4-9 Mr '89
ROCKY MOUNTAINS
See also
Canadian Rockies (B.C. and Alta.)
ROCKY MOUNTAINS REGION
See also
Health resorts, watering places, etc.—Rocky Mountains region
Description and travel
My West. A. B. Guthrie. il por *The Mother Earth News* 118:48-53 Jl/Ag '89
ROCOCO ARCHITECTURE *See* Architecture, Rococo
ROCOCO DECORATION AND ORNAMENT *See* Decoration and ornament, Rococo
ROCOCO FURNITURE *See* Furniture, Rococo
RODALE, ROBERT
101 uses for a T-shirt. il por *Runner's World* 24:26 Ag '89
Focal point. See issues of Organic Gardening beginning April 1988
Running from drugs. il por *Runner's World* 24:24 F '89
With the editor. See issues of Prevention (Emmaus, Pa.)
RODALE PRESS, INC.
Rodale Press bails out St. Mark's Bookstore in Manhattan. C. Reid. il *Publishers Weekly* 236:12 S 22 '89
RODALE RESEARCH CENTER
A garden visit. R. Rodale. il *Organic Gardening* 36:25-6 My '89
RODALE'S ORGANIC GARDENING (PERIODICAL) *See* Organic gardening (Periodical)
RODCHENKO, ALEKSANDR MIKHAĬLOVICH, 1891-1956
about
Rodchenko in Moscow: miraculous survival of the constructivist's historic studio. M. Ruthven. il pors *Architectural Digest* 46:53+ O '89
RODDEN, JOHN
A very partial reclamation project. il *Commonweal* 116:78-80 F 10 '89
RODDICK, ANITA
about
The Body Shop. M. Kelly. por *Utne Reader* p76 Ja/F '89
The naked truth. il pors *Seventeen* 48:138-43 O '89
RODEGHIER, KATHERINE
Wandering along Michigan's golden shoreline. il *Travel Holiday* 171:10+ My '89
RODENTS
See also
Beavers
Chipmunks
Embryology—Rodents
Hamsters
Mice
Nervous system—Rodents
Northeast Rat and Mouse Club
Prairie dogs
Rats
Sexual behavior—Rodents
Squirrels
Woodchucks
Food and feeding
Availability of metabolic fuels controls estrous cyclicity of Syrian hamsters. J. E. Schneider and G. N. Wade. bibl f il *Science* 244:1326-8 Je 16 '89
Migration
The lemming phenomenon. L. Hansson. il *Natural History* p38-43 D '89
Reproduction
Specific expression of nuclear proto-oncogenes before entry into meiotic prophase of spermatogenesis [mice] H. Wolfes and others. bibl f il *Science* 245:740-3 Ag 18 '89
RODEO DRIVE (BEVERLY HILLS, CALIF.)
Dressing the part [relationship between film industry and clothing stores on Rodeo Drive] C. Fleming. il *American Film* 14:48-51 S '89
RODEOS
Talk rodeo [rider R. Rodriguez] il pors *Seventeen* 48:74 My '89
Photographs and photography
Shooting rodeo! M. Epstein. il *Petersen's Photographic Magazine* 18:56-8 O '89
RODERICK, KYLE
Chronic fatigue syndrome: solving a medical mystery. il *Glamour* 87:80 N '89
Pumping iron. il *Harper's Bazaar* 122:134-5+ My '89
RODEWALD, KATE
about
William Wharton, author of Dad, seeks to avenge his daughter's horrible death. M. Green. il pors *People Weekly* 32:122-4 N 27 '89
RODGER, IAN
Scandal, scandal everywhere. *World Press Review* 36:18 Ap '89
RODGERS, BILL, 1947-
about
Bill Rodgers. A. Burfoot. il por *Runner's World* 24:51 F '89

RODGERS, MARY AUGUSTA
Keep those Christmas cards coming! il *McCall's* 117:105 D '89
RODGERS DAIRY FARM
Land of milk and maple syrup. C. H. Crowley. il *The Saturday Evening Post* 261:68-9 Jl/Ag '89
RODHOUSE, PAUL G.
Squid. il map *Sea Frontiers* 35:206-11 Jl/Ag '89
RODIN, AUGUSTE, 1840-1917
about
Art lovers. A.-E. Moutet. il pors *Vogue* 179:498-503+ Mr '89
RODMAN, DENNIS
about
Piston's Rodman hit with paternity, palimony suits. il pors *Jet* 76:52 Jl 3 '89
Rebounding into court. il pors *People Weekly* 32:75 Ag 7 '89
RODMAN, HOWARD A.
The five nominees and how they grew. *Film Comment* 25:8+ Mr/Ap '89
They shoot comic books, don't they? il *American Film* 14:34-9 My '89
RODMAN, SELDEN, 1909-
The dilemma in Puerto Rico. il *The New Leader* 72:3-5 Mr 20 '89
Haiti's prospects under Prosper Avril. il por *The New Leader* 72:5-7 S 4 '89
Little priest, big general. il *National Review* 41:24-5 S 29 '89
RODOREDA, GEOFF
Inside with the INS. il *The Progressive* 53:50 My '89
RODRIGUES, ADILSON
about
Lean and mean. P. Putnam. il pors *Sports Illustrated* 71:24-6+ Jl 24 '89
RODRIGUES, CHARLES
about
Rodrigues Cartoon Caption Contest. il *Stereo Review* 54:27 Ja '89
The winner of the Rodrigues Caption Contest. W. Livingstone. il *Stereo Review* 54:18 Jl '89
RODRIGUES ALVES, MARCIA
(jt. auth) See Rocha, Marco Antonio, and Rodrigues Alves, Marcia
RODRíGUEZ, ANDRÉS
about
An extinction in Paraguay. J. Schwartz and J. Contreras. il por map *Newsweek* 113:38-9 F 13 '89
The extinction of a dinosaur. J. Smolowe. il pors *Time* 133:48 F 13 '89
The last tango in Paraguay. il pors *U.S. News & World Report* 106:14 F 13 '89
Paraguay after Stroessner. R. Roett. *Foreign Affairs* 68:124-42 Spr '89
RODRIGUEZ, BEATRIZ
about
The "steady strengthening" of a ballerina [cover story] S. Anawalt. il pors *Dance Magazine* 63:34-9 N '89
RODRIGUEZ, CHI CHI
about
Chi Chi's children. S. Cronkite. il *Life* 12:48-50+ Ag '89
Golf's clown prince. I. Wolfman. il pors *New Choices for the Best Years* 29:40-3+ Je '89
Golf's Good Samaritan. D. L. McCoy. il por *The Saturday Evening Post* 261:52-3 Mr '89
RODRIGUEZ, DIONICIO
about
Looks like wood. T. Kazas. il pors *Americana* 17:54-8 S/O '89
RODRIGUEZ, FREDDI
about
M.M. *The New Yorker* 65:36-7 O 30 '89
RODRIGUEZ, KENNETH
about
"Pull me out". P. Michelmore. il *Reader's Digest* 135:120-5 Ag '89
RODRíGUEZ, OSMARINO AMANCIO
about
A 2 percent chance to live. S. Hecht and A. Cockburn. *The Nation* 248:700-1 My 22 '89
RODRIGUEZ, PAUL
about
He names his cars after old girlfriends. J. Marion. il por *TV Guide* 37:19 Jl 1-7 '89
RODRIGUEZ, RACHEL
about
Talk rodeo. il pors *Seventeen* 48:74 My '89
RODRIGUEZ, RICHARD
To the border. il *Harper's* 278:31-2+ Ap '89
RODRIGUEZ, ROCIO
about
Rocio Rodriguez at McIntosh and the Arts Exchange. A. Jinkner-Lloyd. il *Art in America* 77:217 S '89
RODRIGUEZ (CHI CHI) YOUTH FOUNDATION *See* Chi Chi Rodriguez Youth Foundation

RODRIGUEZ-BOULAN, ENRIQUE, AND NELSON, W. JAMES
Morphogenesis of the polarized epithelial cell phenotype. bibl f il *Science* 245:718-25 Ag 18 '89
RODRíGUEZ GACHA, JOSÉ GONZALO
about
Colombia: a drug lord's last shoot-out. C. Lane. il *Newsweek* 114:48 D 25 '89
Death of a drug prince. J. Smolowe. por *Time* 134:26 D 25 '89
Most wanted in Medelin. J. Contreras. il pors *Newsweek* 114:30 S 25 '89
RODS, FISHING *See* Fishing tackle
RODS AND CONES
The incremental threshold of the rod visual system and Weber's law. L. T. Sharpe and others. bibl f il *Science* 244:354-6 Ap 21 '89
Light adaptation in cat retinal rods. T. Tamura and others. bibl f il *Science* 245:755-8 Ag 18 '89
Modulation of rod-cone coupling by light. X.-L. Yang and S. M. Wu. bibl f il *Science* 244:352-4 Ap 21 '89
Molecular genetics of human blue cone monochromacy. J. Nathans and others. bibl f il *Science* 245:831-8 Ag 25 '89
ROE, DAVID
about
Miracle baby. S. M. Halpern. il pors *Ms.* 18:56-60+ S '89
ROE, ISABELLE
about
Miracle baby. S. M. Halpern. il pors *Ms.* 18:56-60+ S '89
ROE, MARGIE MCCRELESS
Turning [poem] *The Christian Century* 106:686 Jl 19-26 '89
ROE, ROBERT A.
Keeping partners. *Ad Astra* 1:3 N '89
about
Representative Roe rides to the rescue. B. J. Culliton. il por *Science* 245:24 Jl 7 '89
ROE V. WADE DECISION *See* United States. Supreme Court—Decisions—Abortion decisions
ROE VS. WADE [television program] *See* Television program reviews—Single works
ROEBER, A. G.
The German past and unusable churches. *The Christian Century* 106:407-8 Ap 19 '89
ROEBLING'S (JOHN A.) SONS (FIRM) *See* John A. Roebling's Sons (Firm)
ROEHM, CAROLYNE
about
And she makes her own clothes. il por *Fortune* 120:60 Ag 28 '89
Can you ever be too rich, too thin, or too driven? V. Woods. il *Vogue* 179:356+ Ag '89
Carolyne Roehm: an opulent aesthetic for the designer's Manhattan residence. Suzy. il por *Architectural Digest* 46:112-19 S '89
Mover and shaper. il pors *Harper's Bazaar* 122:374-7 S '89
ROELOFSMA, DERK KINNANE- *See* Kinnane-Roelofsma, Derk
ROEMER, BUDDY
about
'I feel like a dentist pulling teeth'. M. Ivey. il *Business Week* p64 F 27 '89
St. Buddy. M. Lewis. il *The New Republic* 200:16+ Mr 20 '89
ROEMER, CHARLES E. *See* Roemer, Buddy
ROEMER, MICHAEL
about
The plot against Harry [film] Reviews
American Film il 15:16-17 D '89. R. Seidenberg
New York 22:82 O 9 '89. D. Denby
ROENKE, H. MERRILL, JR.
(jt. auth) See Lanmon, Lorraine Welling, 1932-, and Roenke, H. Merrill, Jr.
ROEPER, ANNEMARIE
Ethics education for the gifted. *The Education Digest* 54:37-9 F '89
ROERICH, NICHOLAS, 1874-1947
about
The New Deal and the guru. C. J. Errico and J. S. Walker. il pors *American Heritage* 40:92-5+ Mr '89
ROETHLISBERGER, DORIS
about
Obituary
Christianity Today il 33:13 F 3 '89. K. S. Kantzer
ROETT, RIORDAN, 1938-
Brazil's transition to democracy. bibl f *Current History* 88:117-20+ Mr '89
Paraguay after Stroessner. *Foreign Affairs* 68:124-42 Spr '89
ROEVER, DAVE
about
Me and the Preacher Man [condensed from Before the dawn]; ed. by William R. Kimball. M. Block. *Reader's Digest* 134:33-7 Ja '89
ROFFMAN, FREDERICK S.
Egyptian love song. il pors *Opera News* 53:32-3+ Ja 7 '89

ROFIHE, RICK
Elevator neighbors [story] *The New Yorker* 65:32-5 My 22 '89
Read Chinese [story] *The New Yorker* 65:29 Ag 21 '89
Satellite dish [story] *The New Yorker* 65:30-1 Mr 13 '89
ROGAK, LISA
Endless summer. il *Runner's World* 24:66-8 Ja '89
ROGER & ME [film] See Motion picture reviews—Single works
ROGERS, BRIAN
Wet respite [photograph] il *Natural History* p104-5 Mr '89
ROGERS, BUDDY
about
Nature Boy. B. Greene. il pors *Esquire* 111:59-60+ Ap '89
ROGERS, EDWARD S.
about
Let the Second Force be with you. P. C. Newman. il *Maclean's* 102:46 Mr 20 '89
ROGERS, ELAINE
How low-impact can you go? il *Women's Sports & Fitness* 11:20-1 Ap '89
ROGERS, EVERETT M., AND DEARING, JAMES W.
The delayed reporting of the AIDS epidemic. *USA Today (Periodical)* 117:64-5 My '89
ROGERS, FRED
about
Mister Rogers: everybody's neighbor. M. J. Bandler. il pors *Parents* 64:118-20+ Mr '89
ROGERS, JACKIE
about
Metropolitan flair: telling details for Jackie Rogers in Manhattan. C. R. Milbank. il por *Architectural Digest* 46:286-9 N '89
ROGERS, JOHN W.
about
UPS isn't about to be left holding the parcel. R. W. King. il por *Business Week* p69 F 13 '89
ROGERS, LINDA
Regional report: Latin America. See issues of World Press Review beginning September 1986 through March 1989
ROGERS, LYNN L.
Home, sweet-smelling home. il *Natural History* p60-7 S '89
ROGERS, MICHAEL, 1950-
Creating the ideal home—on wheels. il *New Choices for the Best Years* 29:87-8 Ja '89
Valley culture in the Age of Accretion. il *Personal Computing* 13:27-8 O '89
ROGERS, PATTIANN, 1940-
In my time [poem] *Wilderness* 53:71 Fall '89
ROGERS, PETER
about
Pared down penthouse. A. Virshup. il por *House & Garden* 161:186-91 S '89
ROGERS, PHIL
How can a student 'fail' to be educated? *Phi Delta Kappan* 70:478-9 F '89
ROGERS, RICHARD, 1933-
about
Heroic transformations. D. Dietsch. il *Architectural Record* 177:72-83 S '89
ROGERS, RUSS
about
Missed opportunity. M. Bloom. il por *Runner's World* 24:60-2+ Ja '89
ROGERS, SHARON
about
Bombs across the ocean? E. Magnuson. il *Time* 133:26 Mr 20 '89
The exile of Sharon Rogers. J. V. Lamar, Jr. il por *Time* 133:27 Ap 17 '89
An Iranian message to the U.S. Navy? *U.S. News & World Report* 106:10+ Mr 20 '89
A terrorist retaliation? R. Sandza. il por *Newsweek* 113:34 Mr 20 '89
ROGERS, SHEILA
Random notes. See issues of Rolling Stone
ROGERS, THOMAS F.
Space settlements: sooner than we think? il *Ad Astra* 1:30-4 Ja '89
ROGERS, VINCENT ROBERT, 1926-
Assessing the curriculum experienced by children. bibl f il *Phi Delta Kappan* 70:714-17 My '89
School texts: the outlook of teachers. *The Education Digest* 54:24-6 Ja '89
ROGERS, WILL, 1879-1935
about
On the triumph of memories. J. M. Wall. *The Christian Century* 106:899-900 O 11 '89
ROGERS, WILL C., III
about
Bombs across the ocean? E. Magnuson. il *Time* 133:26 Mr 20 '89
An Iranian message to the U.S. Navy? *U.S. News & World Report* 106:10+ Mr 20 '89
A terrorist retaliation? R. Sandza. il por *Newsweek* 113:34 Mr 20 '89

ROGERS COMMUNICATIONS INC.
Let the Second Force be with you [E. S. Rogers] P. C. Newman. il *Maclean's* 102:46 Mr 20 '89
ROGERS PASS (B.C.)
Taming a mountain [opening of Canadian Pacific tunnel] J. DeMont. *Maclean's* 102:45+ My 15 '89
ROGERSON, DONALD
about
A killing in Maine. J. H. Kunstler. il por *The New York Times Magazine* p58-60+ S 10 '89
"My wife shouldn't have died". J. Hope. il pors *Good Housekeeping* 209:92+ O '89
ROGICH, SIG
about
The moment-maker. F. Barnes. *The New Republic* 201:11-12 D 11 '89
ROGO, D. SCOTT
UFO update. il *Omni (New York, N.Y.)* 12:121 O '89
ROGOFF, JAY
Strown bliss, scattering bright [poem] *The New Republic* 200:34 Ap 17 '89
ROGOV, SERGEY M.
Detente is not enough. *Foreign Policy* 74:86-102 Spr '89
ROGOWAY, SAM
about
Little Ricky Rocko, the world's youngest deejay, proves you're never too small to rock and roll. S. K. Reed. il pors *People Weekly* 31:91-2 Ja 16 '89
ROGOZNICA, JUNE
Stamina smart. il *Health (New York, N.Y.)* 21:41-7 F '89
ROGUE RIVER (OR.)
Give us your tires, your Coors cans . . . [cleanup trips] T. Bielefeldt. il *Sierra* 74:74-7 Mr/Ap '89
ROH, TAE WOO
about
Has Bush helped paint Roh into a corner? L. Nakarmi. il pors *Business Week* p61-2 Mr 13 '89
It's time for the main bout: Roh vs. labor. L. Nakarmi. il *Business Week* p45-6 Ap 10 '89
Roh on Korea's referendum: no go. *Newsweek* 113:33 Ap 3 '89
Visit to the United States, 1989
Punish the ambassador! D. Bank and P. Leyden. il *Newsweek* 114:40 O 23 '89
South Korea. *Business Week* p82 O 23 '89
ROHATYN, FELIX G., 1928-
America's economic dependence. *Foreign Affairs* 68 Special Issue:53-65 ['89]
The debt addiction. il *The New York Review of Books* 36:39-42 Ap 13 '89
about
Preparing for a different world. P. Mann. il *Aviation Week & Space Technology* 130:17 Mr 20 '89
ROHDE, STEPHEN F.
The sounds of lawsuits: rock lyrics on trial. il *USA Today (Periodical)* 118:86-7 Jl '89
ROHLFING, CARLA
Do the new liquid diets really work? il *Reader's Digest* 134:15-18 Je '89
ROHM & HAAS CO.
'Big buying' at Rohm & Haas? G. G. Marcial. *Business Week* p118 Je 5 '89
Fungicides, emulsions and more. T. Jaffe. il *Forbes* 143:196 Je 12 '89
ROHMER, ERIC
about
Four adventures of Reinette and Mirabelle [film] Reviews *The New Republic* 201:26-7 Ag 28 '89. S. Kauffmann *People Weekly* 32:18 Ag 14 '89. R. Novak
ROHR, WENDY JOI
Be a working girl! il *'Teen* 33:36-7+ My '89
ROHRER, TRISH DEITCH
Married to the mod. il pors *Gentlemen's Quarterly* 59:167+ S '89
ROITER, ANDREI
about
"In a neutral zone". S. Hochfield. il pors *Art News* 88:47-8 D '89
ROLAND, ANDRE, D. 1989
about
Blacks demand probe in death of Missouri youth found hanging from tree. por *Jet* 76:52 Ap 24 '89
ROLAND, NEIL
Affairs of State. *Common Cause Magazine* 15:7-8 Mr/Ap '89
Hitting the roof. il *Common Cause Magazine* 15:8-9 Jl/Ag '89
ROLBEIN, SETH
Bizarre sleep disorders. il *Good Housekeeping* 208:69-72 My '89
(ed) See Weinstein, Louis, 1909-. Help! The stuffy nose, watery eyes, aches and pain, chills and fever, sore throat, colds and flu book
ROLE, SEX *See* Sex role
ROLE MODELS
Bouncing back from dead-end situations [black role models] D. Narine. il *Ebony* 44:40+ O '89
Down with role models. il *Glamour* 87:79 Mr '89

A dubious call to arms [call for athletes to become role models in war against drugs] R. Telander. il por *Sports Illustrated* 70:116 Je 5 '89
Jill Eikenberry: role model [excerpts from address] J. Eikenberry. il por *Ladies' Home Journal* 106:68 N '89
ROLE PLAYING
Role-playing tedium transcends the computer age [fantasy games] O. S. Card. *Compute!* 11:92 D '89
ROLFE, JOHN
New York, New York . . . New Jersey. il *Sport (New York, N.Y.)* 80:34-8 Ja '89
ROLLAND, SOLANGE CHAPUT- *See* Chaput-Rolland, Solange
ROLLE, ESTHER
about
Black actors are still ignored: Esther Rolle. por *Jet* 76:22 S 11 '89
ROLLER COASTERS
See also
Arrow Dynamics, Inc.
American thrills. G. Plimpton. il por maps *Popular Mechanics* 166:40-3+ My '89
Coasters used to be scary, now they're downright weird. R. Conniff. bibl (p135) il *Smithsonian* 20:82-6+ Ag '89
Coasting through summer. S. Wernick. il *Parents* 64:164+ Ag '89
Mystery trains. M. T. Smith. il *Money* 18:54-7+ Ag '89
Wheeeee! D. C. Craig. il *Life* 12:34-7 Jl '89
History
A Russian folly: visiting Catherine the Great's baroque roller coaster near Leningrad. P. Lauritzen. il por *Architectural Digest* 46:146-9+ My '89
ROLLER SKATING
You just have to smile when you roller-skate. C. R. Wolpert. il *Women's Sports & Fitness* 11:90 Ap '89
ROLLERGAMES [television program] See Television program reviews—Single works
ROLLIER, ANNE-MARIE DOURLEN- *See* Dourlen-Rollier, Anne-Marie
ROLLING STONE (PERIODICAL)
1988 Music Awards [Rolling Stone Readers and Critics Poll; special section] il *Rolling Stone* p61-3+ Mr 9 '89
Rolling stone: the photographs [excerpt] il *Rolling Stone* p57-62 O 19 '89
ROLLING STONES
Back on tour, rock's old men are rolling with a hot new video. H. Polskin. il *TV Guide* 37:18-20+ N 18-24 '89
Designstyle: plenty of hot air [oversized inflatable women designed by R. Harries for Steel wheels tour] D. L. Umansky. il *Theatre Crafts* 23:20 D '89
Dylan and the Stones: the shock of the old. A. DeCurtis. il *Rolling Stone* p115-16 S 21 '89
The music man [promoter of tour M. Cohl] T. Powis. il por *Maclean's* 102:53+ S 11 '89
Nightlife. M. Gross. il *New York* 22:96-7 S 11 '89
Raw, raunchy and middle-aged [K. Richards] B. Spitz. il pors *The New York Times Magazine* p30-2+ Je 4 '89
The really, really big stars come out to spend the night together with Mick Jagger and the Stones. il *People Weekly* 32:56 N 6 '89
Rock of ages [North American tour] N. Jennings. il *Maclean's* 102:50-2 S 11 '89
Roll them bones [cover story] J. Cocks. il *Time* 134:58-62 S 4 '89
Satisfaction? [cover story] D. Fricke. il *Rolling Stone* p36-8+ S 7 '89
Satisfaction guaranteed. P. Newcomb. il *Forbes* 144:154-6+ O 2 '89
'Steel wheels' spawns new deals. M. Goldberg. *Rolling Stone* p16 O 19 '89
'Steel wheels' tour rolls. A. DeCurtis. il *Rolling Stone* p11+ O 19 '89
Still rolling [release of Steel wheels] S. Simels. il *Stereo Review* 54:132 D '89
Stones complete album. D. Fricke. il *Rolling Stone* p20 Ag 10 '89
Stones plan club dates. M. Goldberg. *Rolling Stone* p28 Je 15 '89
Stones set tour dates. S. Rogers. il *Rolling Stone* p19 Ag 24 '89
The Stones start it up. D. Gates. il *Newsweek* 114:50-2 S 11 '89
Stones tour: money talks. M. Goldberg. il *Rolling Stone* p17 My 4 '89
Stony Rolls. J. Sobran. il *National Review* 41:55-6 O 27 '89
Their rockin' uncorrupted by money or age, the Stones roll toward a Steel wheels TV spectacular. S. Dougherty. il *People Weekly* 32:168-9 D 18 '89
Washington diarist: outside the Beltway [summer in Washington, Conn.] D. Owen. *The New Republic* 201:54 S 18-25 '89

Anecdotes, facetiae, satire, etc.
Golden oldies. W. Geist. il *New York* 22:26 N 27 '89
ROLLINS, TIMOTHY
about
Art from the heart. J. M. Adams. il por *Seventeen* 48:70+ Mr '89

ROLLINS, TIMOTHY—about—*cont.*
Coming to Amerika. K. Larson. il *New York* 22:123-4 N 20 '89
ROLLINS (TIM) + K.O.S. (GROUP) *See* Tim Rollins + K.O.S. (Group)
ROLLS *See* Bread
ROLLS ROYCE (AUTOMOBILE) *See* Automobiles, Foreign
ROLLS-ROYCE LTD.
Rolls assessing market interest in RB580 engine. il *Aviation Week & Space Technology* 130:24 Jl 10 '89
Rolls-Royce completes initial testing of improved Pegasus engine for Harrier. C. A. Shifrin. il *Aviation Week & Space Technology* 131:28-9 Ag 21 '89
Rolls-Royce developing more powerful version of Pegasus engine for third-generation Harrier. *Aviation Week & Space Technology* 130:30 My 29 '89
Williams, Rolls plan to certify 1,900-lb.-thrust FJ44 in 1992 [business jet engine] S. W. Kandebo. il *Aviation Week & Space Technology* 131:47 N 6 '89
ROLLWAGEN, JOHN AUGUST
about
Cray versus Japan Inc. [interview] D. Churbuck. il por *Forbes* 144:118-19 S 4 '89
Now Cray faces life without Cray. R. Mitchell. il por *Business Week* p31 My 29 '89
ROLM CORP.
Behind the scenes at the fall of Rolm. R. D. Hof. il *Business Week* p82-4 Jl 10 '89
Telecomputing lives [IBM's deal with Siemens for Rolm] G. Slutsker and F. Meeks. il *Forbes* 143:51 Ja 9 '89
ROM *See* Read only memory
ROMAN, KENNETH
The neo-prohibitionists [address, February 8, 1989] *Vital Speeches of the Day* 55:441-4 My 1 '89
ROMAN, MARK B.
The little waves that could. il *Discover* 10:54-8+ N '89
Tornado tracker. il por *Discover* 10:50-6 Je '89
ROMAN ANTIQUITIES
See also
Nîmes (France)—Roman antiquities
Exhibitions
The Roman nose [perfumes of ancient Rome at Emory University] il *U.S. News & World Report* 106:14-15 Ap 3 '89
ROMAN AQUEDUCTS *See* Aqueducts
ROMAN ASTRONOMY *See* Astronomy, Roman
ROMAN CATHOLIC CHURCH *See* Catholic Church
ROMAN CATHOLICS *See* Catholics
ROMAN EMPIRE *See* Rome
ROMAN VASES *See* Vases, Roman
ROMANCE
See also
Dating (Social customs)
Are Americans romantic? [results of survey] I. Groller. il *Parents* 64:37 F '89
A fine romance [special section] il *Harper's Bazaar* 122:200-1+ Ap '89
Isn't it romantic? [LHJ Roper poll] il *Ladies' Home Journal* 106:86 F '89
Lovers' weekend: a stay-at-home guide to romance. il *Glamour* 87:190-3+ F '89
Modern romance: a lesson in appetite control. M. Gaitskill. il por *Ms.* 17:55-6 My '89
Places in the heart: the most romantic thing a girl's ever done: boys' true tales. A. Elliot. il *Seventeen* 48:90-1 F '89
Romance away from home. S. R. Hamilton. il *Essence* 19:23+ F '89
Anecdotes, facetiae, satire, etc.
A kinder, gentler marriage. M. G. Stoddard. il *The Saturday Evening Post* 261:56-7+ S '89
ROMANCE FICTION
See also
Harlequin Enterprises Ltd.
In the grasp of romance: my life as Fiona Hill [writing Regency romances] E. Pall. *The New York Times Book Review* 94:1+ Ap 30 '89
Passion's promise. J. Yglesias. il *Publishers Weekly* 236:13-14+ Ag 25 '89
When Elaine Duillo paints it, a romance novel's cover is worth a thousand steamy words. M. Neill. il pors *People Weekly* 31:141+ My 15 '89
Writing successful proposals for the romance market. T. Carter. *The Writer* 102:23-5 My '89
Writing the romantic novel you'd like to read. M. Chittenden. *The Writer* 102:19-21 Ap '89
Anecdotes, facetiae, satire, etc.
Fiction can be hazardous to your health. J. Weger. *The Writer* 102:7-8 S '89
Bibliography
Ravished by romances. J. Maynard. il *Mademoiselle* 95:98+ Ag '89
Conferences
Lust at sea [Caribbean cruise conference] S. Anthony. il *Ms.* 17:128-9 Ja/F '89

ROMANENKO, YURI, 1944-
about
Space travelers rendezvous in Chicago. J. Liss. *Ad Astra* 1:41-4 D '89
ROMANESQUE ART *See* Art, Romanesque
ROMANIA
See also
Civil rights—Romania
Hungarians—Romania
Poetry and state—Romania
Romanians
Politics and government
Curtain still down. A. Daniels. por *National Review* 41:21-3 D 22 '89
The last great Stalinist [N. Ceausescu] M. R. Meyer. il por *Newsweek* 114:30+ Ag 21 '89
Romania: breaking the silence. W. Pfaff. il *The New York Review of Books* 36:8-9 Ap 27 '89
Romania: defying the tyrant. W. Pfaff. il *The New York Review of Books* 36:43 Ag 17 '89
Romania, Romania. T. R. Swick. *Commonweal* 116:263-4 My 5 '89
Romania's reign of terror. il *Reader's Digest* 134:91-5 F '89
Solving the Rumanian problem. C. Davies. *National Review* 41:37 D 31 '89
The three holdouts against change. J. Borrell. il *Time* 134:51 N 6 '89
Where Stalinism still thrives. R. Knight. por *U.S. News & World Report* 107:35 D 4 '89
ROMANIAN DEFECTORS *See* Defectors
ROMANIANS
United States
Gymnast Nadia Comaneci leaps for freedom—and lands in the arms of a married father of four. il pors *People Weekly* 32:116 D 18 '89
Leap to the West [gymnast N. Comaneci] W. O. Johnson and A. Verschoth. il pors *Sports Illustrated* 71:40-1 D 11 '89
Crime
The wild and crazy gangster: Michael Markowitz's twisted American dream. P. Blauner. il pors *New York* 22:52-6+ O 9 '89
ROMANO, ANDROMEDA
Girls play guitar. il *Seventeen* 48:146-7+ My '89
ROMANO, ANTONIO
about
Born to paint. *The New Yorker* 64:24-6 F 6 '89
ROMANO, GIULIO *See* Giulio, Romano, 1499?-1546
ROMANO, LOIS
Power babies. il *Mademoiselle* 95:198-201+ My '89
Washington watch: will we follow the new leaders? *Mademoiselle* 95:236 Ag '89
Winning is the best revenge. il pors *Good Housekeeping* 208:46+ Ap '89
ROMANONES, ALINE GRIFFITH *See* Aline, Countess of Romanones
ROMANOV, NIKOLAI *See* Nicholas II, Emperor of Russia, 1868-1918
ROMANOWSKI, PATRICIA
(ed) *See* Geller, Larry, 1937-, and Spector, Joel. The secret Elvis diary
ROMANTICISM
Germany
Universality and national identity. A. Finkielkraut. bibl f il pors *The Unesco Courier* 42:30-3 Je '89
ROMANTICISM IN ART
A Ring for the '80s [German Romantic roots of Metropolitan Opera's new production] B. Adams. il *Art in America* 77:222-9 Ap '89
Exhibitions
The romantic spirit: Pierpont Morgan Library. M. Moorman. il *Art News* 88:153 F '89
Tracing God's fingerprint [The romantic spirit: German drawings, 1780-1850] R. Hughes. il *Time* 133:62 Ja 23 '89
ROMBOUGH, LON J.
Hardwood cuttings. il *Flower and Garden* 33:68-9 My/Je '89
ROMÉ
Beauty is in the grain. il *Petersen's Photographic Magazine* 17:24-5+ Ap '89
ROME
Bibliography
Greeks, Romans, Jews & others. J. Griffin. il *The New York Review of Books* 36:6+ Mr 16 '89
Paperback history [late Roman empire] S. E. Cleary. *History Today* 39:58-9 N '89
Church history
See Church history—Primitive and early church
Historiography
Herodotus, Alexander, and Rome. G. W. Bowersock. *The American Scholar* 58:407-14 Summ '89
ROME (ITALY)
Airports
Avanti [stretch of track that will connect Leonardo da Vinci Airport with Ostiense station] B. Weber. il *The New York Times Magazine* p94 S 24 '89

ROME (ITALY)—*cont.*

Antiquities

Early Rome: surprises below the surface. B. Bower. *Science News* 135:20 Ja 14 '89

Climate

A cool Roman holiday. L. Inturrisi. il *Travel Holiday* 172:98 S '89

Crime

Roman holiday? [pickpockets] R. Phalon. il *Forbes* 144:132-4 Ag 7 '89

Gardens and gardening

Gardens of delight [touring Roman palaces and their gardens] R. Koenig. il *House & Garden* 161:46+ F '89

Photographs and photography

Consuming Rome. K. Radkai. il *Gentlemen's Quarterly* 59:366-9 Mr '89

Transit systems

Avanti [stretch of track that will connect Leonardo da Vinci Airport with Ostiense station] B. Weber. il *The New York Times Magazine* p94 S 24 '89

ROME AIR DEVELOPMENT CENTER

Air Force pursues photonics research [special section] il *Aviation Week & Space Technology* 130:54-8+ Ja 30 '89

Platinum silicide detectors incorporated into new generation of missile seekers. D. Hughes. il *Aviation Week & Space Technology* 130:51+ Mr 27 '89

ROME IN LITERATURE

Sam Spade in ancient Rome [work of L. Davis] S. J. Evans. il *History Today* 39:4-5 Jl '89

ROMEDENNE, PATRICE

Rainy—but proud—Vancouver. il *World Press Review* 36:94 O '89

ROMEO, BERESFORD *See* Jazzie B.

ROMEO AND JULIET (LEGEND)

Romeo & Juliet and . . . suicide [teen suicide; views of Ed Beckham] il *USA Today (Periodical)* 118:15 D '89

ROMER, GRANT B., AND DELAMOIR, JEANNETTE

The first color photographs. bibl il *Scientific American* 261:88-96 D '89

ROMERO, EDUARDO MARTÍNEZ *See* Martínez Romero, Eduardo

ROMERO, OSCAR A. (OSCAR ARNULFO), 1917-1980

Assassination

Celluloid evangelism [motion picture Romero] S. Ulstein. il por *Christianity Today* 33:77-8 N 3 '89

Demonizing D'Aubuisson. J. Morley. il *The Nation* 248:624-6 My 8 '89

Romero: evolution of a martyr [motion picture] D. G. Peerman. il *The Christian Century* 106:870-2 O 4 '89

ROMERO [film] *See* Motion picture reviews—Single works

ROMME, WILLIAM H., AND DESPAIN, DON G.

Historical perspective on the Yellowstone fires of 1988. bibl f il map *BioScience* 39:695-9 N '89

The Yellowstone fires. bibl il map *Scientific American* 261:36-44+ N '89

ROMMENS, JOHANNA M., AND OTHERS

Identification of the cystic fibrosis gene: chromosome walking and jumping. bibl f il *Science* 245:1059-65 S 8 '89

ROMO (DENMARK)

Description and travel

Romo: sandy island 6 miles by causeway from mainland Denmark. il map *Sunset (Central West edition)* 182:68-9 Je '89

ROMUALDEZ MARCOS, IMELDA *See* Marcos, Imelda

RÔNA, PETER

Shareholders have too much power. il *Fortune* 120:125-6 Ag 28 '89

RONALD FELDMAN FINE ARTS, INC.

Price-tag update: court test due [New York dealer R. Feldman refuses to post prices] W. Robinson. *Art in America* 77:23 Ja '89

RONALD REAGAN PRESIDENTIAL LIBRARY AND CENTER FOR PUBLIC AFFAIRS

Gandee at large [exhibit designer N. Green] C. K. Gandee. il *House & Garden* 161:218 My '89

RONDEL, STEPHEN A.

On the front lines in the trade war. il *Nation's Business* 77:10 Je '89

about

The accidental tourist. M. Barrier. il por *Nation's Business* 77:78 Ap '89

Instant spoken translation. W. J. Hawkins. il por *Popular Science* 234:78+ My '89

RONDÔNIA (BRAZIL)

The scorched earth. A. DeCurtis. il *Rolling Stone* p40-9 F 23 '89

RONGELAP ATOLL (MARSHALL ISLANDS)

See also

Radioactive pollution—Rongelap Atoll (Marshall Islands)

RONK, CHERYL O.

The growing interest in privatization. il *USA Today (Periodical)* 117:30-2 Ja '89

RONSTADT, LINDA

about

Linda Ronstadt: rock with a pop flavor. R. Givens. por *Stereo Review* 54:123 D '89

ROOF, WADE CLARK

The church in the centrifuge. *The Christian Century* 106:1012-14 N 8 '89

ROOF DECKS *See* Decks, patios, terraces, etc.

ROOF GARDENS *See* Balcony gardens, roof gardens, etc.

ROOF VENTS *See* Vents (Architecture)

ROOFS AND ROOFING

See also

Domes

Rafters

Shells (Structural engineering)

Shingles and shingling

Metal roofing: new versatility. J. S. Russell. il *Architectural Record* 177:120-3 F '89

Metal roofs. J. Vara. *Country Journal* 16:94-6+ S/O '89

Roofing. il *Popular Science* 235:63-5 Ag '89

To weather or not [copper roof] *Southern Living* 24:158 S '89

Maintenance and repair

Replace your roof [cover story] D. A. Warren. il *Workbench* 45:36-40 Jl/Ag '89

Reroofing a landmark [restoration of tin roofs at University of Virginia] D. Rastorfer. il *Architectural Record* 177:124-7 F '89

Restoring slate and tile roofs. B. Vila. il *Popular Mechanics* 166:34-5 Ag '89

Time for a new roof? K. Childers and A. Rooze. il *The Family Handyman* 39:56-9 Jl/Ag '89

ROOKER, MICHAEL

about

Not your average serial killer. C. S. Smith. il por *New York* 22:30 O 16 '89

ROOKIES, BASEBALL *See* Baseball players

ROOM AIR CONDITIONERS *See* Air conditioning equipment

ROOM DIVIDERS

Build a multipurpose room divider. S. Scull. il *The Family Handyman* 39:57-61 Ap '89

Divider and three-level cabinet. il *Sunset (Central West edition)* 182:161 Ap '89

Mini-wall with lights and bookshelves. il *Sunset (Central West edition)* 182:118 F '89

ROOM FURNISHINGS *See* Household furnishings

ROOM MODELS

Exhibitions

Big job on little rooms [Thorne Miniature Rooms at the Art Institute of Chicago] B. Lau. il *Americana* 17:30-3 My/Je '89

ROOM OF ONE'S OWN (MADISON, WIS.: BOOKSTORE)

See Booksellers and bookselling—Wisconsin

ROOM PAINTING *See* House painting

ROOMS

See also

Bathrooms

Bedrooms

Children's rooms

Dens (Rooms)

Dining rooms

Dormers

Dressing rooms

Editing rooms

Family rooms

Furniture arrangement

Garden rooms

Garrets

Guest rooms

House decoration

Kitchens

Living rooms

Media rooms

Music rooms

Powder rooms

Sitting rooms

Studies (Rooms)

Sun rooms

Where the living is easy [enclosed porch] C. Engle. il *Southern Living* 24:112-13 Ap '89

Terminology

The name of the room. E. Hopkins. il *House & Garden* 161:62+ D '89

ROOMS, CLEAN *See* Clean rooms

ROOMS, MINIATURE *See* Room models

ROOMS, OUTDOOR *See* Decks, patios, terraces, etc.

ROOMS, REMODELED *See* Houses, Remodeled

ROOMS IN ART

The art of the interior [collecting paintings of interiors] M. Guralnick. il *House & Garden* 161:158 F '89

Some sources for the paintings of C. R. Leslie. G. Jackson-Stops. bibl f il *Antiques* 135:310-21 Ja '89

ROONEY, ANDREW A.

53 more cranky opinions from Andy Rooney [excerpt from Not that you asked . . .] il *TV Guide* 37:24-6 Mr 11-17 '89

ROONEY, ANDY *See* Rooney, Andrew A.

ROONEY, ART, 1901-1988

about

Unforgettable Art Rooney. R. Bleier. il por *Reader's Digest* 135:15-16+ N '89

ROONEY, MICKEY
The value of villains. por *Newsweek* 114:12 N 27 '89
ROOS, DAVID
about
Eccentricities. C. Vogel. il *The New York Times Magazine* p98-9 Mr 5 '89
Restoration drama. S. Calloway. il por *House & Garden* 161:120-3+ D '89
ROOSEN, MIA WESTERLUND *See* Westerlund Roosen, Mia, 1942-
ROOSEVELT, ANNA CURTENIUS
Lost civilizations of the lower Amazon. il map *Natural History* p74-83 F '89
ROOSEVELT, ELEANOR, 1884-1962
about
The wonderful husband. G. C. Ward. il pors *American Heritage* 40:57-8+ S/O '89
ROOSEVELT, FRANKLIN D. (FRANKLIN DELANO), 1882-1945
about
First encounters. E. Sorel and N. C. Sorel. il *The Atlantic* 263:67 Mr '89
The New Deal and the guru. C. J. Errico and J. S. Walker. il pors *American Heritage* 40:92-5+ Mr '89
The United States and Russia in World War II [reprint from November and December 1950 issues] R. W. Van Alstyne. *Current History* 88:26-9+ Ja '89
A war for others to fight. il *U.S. News & World Report* 107:57 Ag 28-S 4 '89
The wonderful husband. G. C. Ward. il pors *American Heritage* 40:57-8+ S/O '89
Bibliography
Getting FDR's ear. A. M. Schlesinger. il *The New York Review of Books* 36:20-3 F 16 '89
ROOSEVELT (FRANKLIN D.) LIBRARY *See* Franklin D. Roosevelt Library
ROOSEVELT (THEODORE) NATIONAL PARK (N.D.) *See* Theodore Roosevelt National Park (N.D.)
ROOT, ALAN
about
Presenting crazy Alan Root. M. McRae. il pors *International Wildlife* 19:30-5 N/D '89
ROOT, JUDITH
Good Friday [poem] *Commonweal* 116:348 Je 2 '89
ROOT, MICHAEL
Almost human? Marine animal models. il *BioScience* 39:520-1 S '89
ROOT, THOMAS L.
about
A bizarre and suspicious flight. G. J. Church. il por map *Time* 134:21 Jl 24 '89
Flying straight into trouble. J. S. Kunen. il por *People Weekly* 32:20-3 Jl 31 '89
A mysterious plane crash. A. Miller. il por *Newsweek* 114:19 Jl 24 '89
ROOT, WILLIAM PITT, 1941-
With no other witness [poem] *Commonweal* 116:15 Ja 13 '89
ROOT CANAL THERAPY
Tooth troubles? Consider a root canal before having a tooth pulled [views of Joseph D. Maggio] *Prevention (Emmaus, Pa.)* 41:20 O '89
ROOT VEGETABLES
See also
Cooking—Vegetables
ROOT WEEVILS *See* Weevils
ROOTS
Control
Biobarrier inhibits root growth [Rootguard] C. M. Fiorillo. *Popular Science* 234:38 F '89
ROOTSTEIN, ADEL
about
Adel Rootstein knows the fanciest dummies in fashion. H. Shapiro. il pors *People Weekly* 32:123-4 S 18 '89
ROOTSTEIN (ADEL) INC. *See* Adel Rootstein Inc.
ROOTWORMS, CORN *See* Corn rootworms
ROP *See* Retinopathy of prematurity
ROPE
The long rode to success [rope and anchor techniques] B. Stearns. il *Field & Stream* 94:68+ O '89
ROPE JUMPING
Jump for joy. il *Seventeen* 48:222 Mr '89
These girls know the ropes [Double Dutch champs] il *National Geographic World* 166:16-18 Je '89
ROPER, H. R. TREVOR- *See* Trevor-Roper, H. R. (Hugh Redwald), 1914-
ROPER, JIM
MIDI and the theatre: a guide to music software applications. *Theatre Crafts* 23:70+ O '89
RORAIMA, MOUNT *See* Mount Roraima
ROREM, NED, 1923-
Cries in the dark. il *Opera News* 53:8-14 Ja 21 '89
about
Musical events:
Messiaen's Et exspecto, Lutoslawski's Piano concerto, and Rorem's Violin concerto. A. Porter. *The New Yorker* 64:65-6 Ja 16 '89

RORER GROUP INC.
Has Rorer found a friend? G. G. Marcial. *Business Week* p88 Ag 21 '89
Please pass the Maalox. J. Novack. il por *Forbes* 144:114-15 Ag 7 '89
RORTY, RICHARD
The opening of American minds [adaptation of address, January 1989] *Harper's* 279:18-20+ Jl '89
ROS-LEHTINEN, ILEANA
about
Miami advice. W. McGurn. *National Review* 41:39 N 24 '89
Off-key notes in an ethnic symphony. il por *U.S. News & World Report* 107:10 S 11 '89
ROSALES, PAT
about
"Thank God for people like you". M. Siegel. il por *Good Housekeeping* 208:139+ Je '89
ROSAND, DAVID
Brush fire. il *The New Republic* 200:38-41 Ja 23 '89
ROSARIO, LOUISE DO
The law bends to party needs. *World Press Review* 36:23-4 Ag '89
Quick step backward. *World Press Review* 36:60-1 D '89
ROSAS, VICTOR
World soccer prodigy: the U.S. il *World Press Review* 36:92 O '89
ROSCA, NINOTCHKA
The arts and the Asian American community. il *Change* 21:52-5 N/D '89
'Total war' in the Philippines. il *The Nation* 248:839-42 Je 19 '89
ROSCIOLI, BOB
about
Debut in paradise. J. Clemans. il *Motor Boating & Sailing* 164:36-41+ S '89
ROSCOE, SHEILA
about
No prima donna. J. Diaz. il pors *Sports Illustrated* 70 Special Issue:115-17 F '89
ROSE, ALBERT, AND WEIMER, PAUL K.
Physical limits to the performance of imaging systems. bibl f il *Physics Today* 42:24-32 S '89
ROSE, AXL
about
The Rolling stone interview: Axl Rose [cover story] D. James. il pors *Rolling Stone* p42-4+ Ag 10 '89
ROSE, BERNARD
about
Paperhouse [film] Reviews
Newsweek 113:65 F 20 '89. D. Ansen
ROSE, DANIEL ASA
Those wacky Finns. il *Esquire* 111:47-8 Mr '89
ROSE, EDWARD W., III
about
Rusty the Mortician. J. H. Taylor. il por *Forbes* 144:60+ Jl 24 '89
ROSE, FRANK
Celebrity victims: crime casualties are turning into stars on tabloid TV. il *New York* 22:38-44 Jl 31 '89
Glasnost rock. il pors *New York* 22:56-60+ Mr 20 '89
ROSE, GEORGE
about
Rock tour. F. Cameron. il *Petersen's Photographic Magazine* 18:18-20+ Ag '89
ROSE, JAMES T.
about
Building better partnerships. W. H. Ganoe. *Ad Astra* 1:31 O '89
ROSE, JOSEPH B.
Mayor culpa. *The New Republic* 200:18-20+ My 8 '89
ROSE, JULIE
The impossible life of a college president. *The Washington Monthly* 21:18-22+ Mr '89
ROSE, JÜRGEN, 1937-
about
Five minutes to midnight [cover story] P. O'Connor. il pors *Opera News* 53:8-12 Mr 4 '89
ROSE, PETE, 1941-
about
All the odds against him. C. Leerhsen. il por *Newsweek* 114:74-5 Jl 10 '89
The case against Pete Rose [cover story] J. Lieber and C. Neff. il pors *Sports Illustrated* 71:10-20+ Jl 3 '89
Charlie Hustle's final play. M. B. Carlson. il por *Time* 134:64 S 4 '89
Closing in on Charlie Hustle. C. Leerhsen. il por *Newsweek* 114:23 Jl 3 '89
The darkening cloud over Pete. T. Callahan. por *Time* 134:57 Jl 3 '89
The end of the affair. C. Leerhsen. il por *Newsweek* 114:58-9 S 4 '89
A game of chance. R. Dolphin. il por *Maclean's* 102:52-3 Ap 17 '89
An idol banned. J. Lieber and C. Neff. il pors *Sports Illustrated* 71:29-30 S 4 '89
Parker: double standard in his, Pete Rose cases. il pors *Jet* 76:48 Jl 24 '89

ROSE, PETE, 1941-—about—*cont.*
Pete Rose. il por *People Weekly* 32:86-7 D 25 '89-Ja 1 '90
Pete Rose can't lose. E. Asinof. il pors *Sport (New York, N.Y.)* 80:54-6 Ap '89
The Rose probe. C. Neff. il por *Sports Illustrated* 70:13 Mr 27 '89
Rose probe (cont.). C. Neff. il por *Sports Illustrated* 70:11-12 My 8 '89
Rose probe (cont.). C. Neff. il por *Sports Illustrated* 70:13+ Ap 17 '89
Rose's grim vigil [cover story] C. Neff and J. Lieber. il pors *Sports Illustrated* 70:52-4+ Ap 3 '89
The sad ordeal of Mr. Baseball. T. Callahan. il por *Time* 133:85 Ap 3 '89
Troubled times. M. Nichols. il por *Maclean's* 102:42 Jl 10 '89
Up to speed. R. Wright. *The New Republic* 201:42 Jl 31 '89
Waiting for the final chapter. C. Leerhsen. il pors *Newsweek* 113:71 Ap 10 '89
War of the Roses. P. Jordan. il pors *Gentlemen's Quarterly* 59:274-9+ Ap '89
Why pick on Pete? [cover story] G. J. Church. il por *Time* 134:16-21 Jl 10 '89

Anecdotes, facetiae, satire, etc.
Baseball: not the movie. J. Leo. il *U.S. News & World Report* 107:54 Jl 10 '89
Rose lives! M. Lupica. il *Esquire* 112:63-4 D '89

ROSE, PETEY
about
War of the Roses. P. Jordan. il pors *Gentlemen's Quarterly* 59:274-9+ Ap '89

ROSE, PHYLLIS, 1942-
Cut down by the hairdresser. il *The New York Times Magazine* p12+ Ja 15 '89
Josephine Baker's war on racism [excerpt from Jazz Cleopatra] il pors *American Visions* 4:25-8 O '89
Messages from a madman. il *Glamour* 87:270 Je '89
Monk's House—the author's country retreat in Sussex. il *Architectural Digest* 46:62+ Jl '89
about
The lives of women. T. Mathews and L. Beachy. il por *Newsweek* 114:78-9+ N 6 '89
PW interviews. K. Weber. por *Publishers Weekly* 236:36-7 S 22 '89

ROSE, RICHARD
about
Drama's daredevil. J. Bemrose. il por *Maclean's* 102:62-3 My 1 '89
Newhouse [drama] Reviews
Maclean's il 102:63 My 1 '89. J. Bemrose

ROSE, SUSAN
about
A big surprise in Boston: everything's coming up (Susan) Rose. I. M. Fanger. il pors *Dance Magazine* 63:42-3 My '89

ROSE, SUSAN D.
Gender, education and the new Christian right. bibl *Society* 26:59-66 Ja/F '89

ROSE HILL MANSION (GENEVA, N.Y.)
Rose Hill near Geneva, New York. L. W. Lanmon and H. M. Roenke, Jr. il *Antiques* 136:144-53 Jl '89

ROSE OF SHARON
Rose of Sharon. M. Fink. il por *Organic Gardening* 36:72 D '89

ROSE POLSKY AND DANCERS
Reviews:
Performances in Los Angeles. D. Perlmutter. *Dance Magazine* 63:32+ Ja '89

ROSE THEATRE (LONDON, ENGLAND)
Coming up roses? D. Gregory. il *History Today* 39:3-4 Jl '89

ROSEANNE [television program] See Television program reviews—Single works

ROSEANNE CONNERS (FICTIONAL CHARACTER)
Should you quit if you're not getting respect? [results of survey on tactics of television character] il *Glamour* 87:123 N '89

ROSELAND COTTAGE *See* Bowen House, Roseland Cottage (Woodstock, Conn.)

ROSEMARY
Rosemary: a culinary herb with holiday history. W. E. Wooldridge. il *Flower and Garden* 33:33 N/D '89

ROSEMOND, JOHN K.
Parenting. See issues of Better Homes and Gardens beginning June 1985

ROSEN, ANDREA
about
The new dealers. A. Virshup. il pors *Harper's Bazaar* 122:80+ D '89

ROSEN, ANNE
Sweet sorrow. il *Ms.* 18:24-5 N '89

ROSEN, BARRY S., AND OTHERS
Adipsin and complement factor D activity: an immune-related defect in obesity. bibl f il *Science* 244:1483-7 Je 23 '89

ROSEN, BENJAMIN M.
about
The biggest dealmaker of all. E. S. Ely. por *Personal Computing* 13:74 Jl '89

ROSEN, HARRIS
about
Low-cost hospitality. H. Rudnitsky. il por *Forbes* 144:90 S 18 '89

ROSEN, JAY
Don't need a weatherman? *Harper's* 278:34-6 Ap '89
Phantom public haunts nuclear age. bibl f il *The Bulletin of the Atomic Scientists* 45:16-19 Je '89

ROSEN, JUDITH
New Words: the collective works. il *Publishers Weekly* 235:56-9 Ap 21 '89
Saul Gilman: his own salesman. por *Publishers Weekly* 235:108+ Ja 20 '89

ROSEN, MARGERY D.
(jt. auth) See Mohler, Mary, and Rosen, Margery D.

ROSEN, MARJORIE
Bankable Bette [cover story] il pors *Ms.* 17:52-7 Mr '89
Fast food. il *Ms.* 17:36+ Ja/F '89
The Hurd instinct [cover story] il pors *Ms.* 18:66-71 S '89
A woman for all seasons. il por *Ms.* 18:18+ O '89

ROSEN, RICHARD
Bullcrit. il *New York* 22:44-7 F 6 '89
Not available in any store. il *New York* 22:42-6 N 20 '89

ROSEN, ROY
Dear doctor. See issues of 'Teen beginning June 1984

ROSEN, RUDIGER VON
The future of the European stock exchange system approaching 1992 [address, April 29, 1989] *Vital Speeches of the Day* 56:49-53 N 1 '89

ROSEN, SIMON PETER
(jt. auth) See Moe, Michael K., and Rosen, Simon Peter

ROSENBAUM, ANDREW
Fortress Europe for 1992. il *The Nation* 249:748-50 D 18 '89

ROSENBAUM, LEE
The anxious acquisitors. il *Art News* 88:144-51 Mr '89

ROSENBAUM, MAJ-BRITT
Body and soul. See issues of Mademoiselle

ROSENBAUM, MARYHELÉNE
Death of a secular humanist. *The Christian Century* 106:167-8 F 15 '89

ROSENBAUM, RON
Movies. See issues of Mademoiselle
Too young to die? [cover story] il pors *The New York Times Magazine* p32-5+ Mr 12 '89

ROSENBERG, ALISON
FY 1990 assistance request for Sub-Saharan Africa [statement, April 14, 1989] *Department of State Bulletin* 89:39-42 Jl '89

ROSENBERG, BELLA
How do we balance public school choice? *The Education Digest* 55:7-11 N '89

ROSENBERG, EDGAR
about
A triumph of spirit. D. De Dubovay. il pors *Ladies' Home Journal* 106:62+ S '89

ROSENBERG, EVELYN
about
First impressions. R. Ruthen. il *Scientific American* 260:18+ F '89

ROSENBERG, HOWARD
Ten years after. il *American Film* 15:18-19 D '89

ROSENBERG, KAREN
How Soviet cinema went Hollywood. il *Technology Review* 92:76-7 Ap '89
In the eye of the beholder: poetic documentaries about technology. il *Technology Review* 92:62-8 F/Mr '89

ROSENBERG, LIZ
It's all right to be innocent again. il *The New York Times Book Review* 94:46 My 21 '89
(jt. auth) See Abrams, Pamela, and Rosenberg, Liz

ROSENBERG, MERRI
"No, I won't!". il *Parents* 64:68-70+ Ja '89

ROSENBERG, NORMAN J., 1930-
(jt. auth) See Crosson, Pierre R., and Rosenberg, Norman J., 1930-

ROSENBERG, NORMAN J., 1930-, AND OTHERS
Climate change. il *Environment* 31:2-3+ Ja/F '89

ROSENBERG, PIERRE
about
Curators in court. B. Grauman. il *Art News* 88:72-4 Ap '89
The portrait of a scandal. C. Dickey. il por *Newsweek* 113:55 Ja 9 '89
Scandals rock French museums. W. Robinson. il por *Art in America* 77:21+ F '89

ROSENBERG, RICHARD M.
about
Watch out: here comes Bank of America again. J. B. Levine. il por *Business Week* p129-30 F 20 '89

ROSENBERG, RONALD, AND OTHERS
Circumsporozoite protein heterogeneity in the human malaria parasite Plasmodium vivax. bibl f il *Science* 245:973-6 S 1 '89

ROSENBERG, STEVE, 1948-
The sea lions of Monterey. bibl il map *Sea Frontiers* 35:97-103 Mr/Ap '89
ROSENBERG, STEVEN A.
about
Fighting cancer with designer cells. B. J. Culliton. il por *Science* 244:1430-3 Je 23 '89
Immunology's designer genes. S. Brownlee. il por *U.S. News & World Report* 107:65-6 O 30 '89
ROSENBERG, TED
about
Basic training for value investors [interview] E. Schultz. il por *Fortune* 119:29-31 Ja 2 '89
ROSENBERG, TINA
Fall of the patriarch. il *The New Republic* 201:20-3 D 18 '89
Farm workers don't have to be poor. *The Washington Monthly* 21:22-4+ Ap '89
The kingdom of cocaine [cover story] *The New Republic* 201:26-34 N 27 '89
A mess in the Andes. *The New Republic* 201:23-6 S 18-25 '89
Thesis disPeruvian. *The New Republic* 201:15-17 O 9 '89
ROSENBERG (JULIUS AND ETHEL) CASE
Echoes of the Rosenberg case: an autobiographical postscript [Judge I. Kaufman] S. Hook. il *The American Spectator* 22:18-20 Ja '89
ROSENBLATT, JAY
about
A Chicago grad student strikes a career high note, finding a long-lost Liszt. il por *People Weekly* 31:113 Ap 10 '89
ROSENBLATT, ROGER
Ragtime. *The New Republic* 201:130 N 6 '89
ROSENBLUM, GAIL
A moving experience. il *New Choices for the Best Years* 29:84+ Mr '89
My brother, my twin. il pors *New Choices for the Best Years* 29:83-5 Ap '89
A new job, a new life [cover story] il *New Choices for the Best Years* 29:27-34 Ja '89
New ways to live together. il *New Choices for the Best Years* 29:29-35 My '89
A sobering story. il *New Choices for the Best Years* 29:62-9 My '89
When Johnny comes marching home. il *New Choices for the Best Years* 29:54-7 O '89
When your child intermarries. il *New Choices for the Best Years* 29:54-8 Jl '89
ROSENBLUM, ROBERT
Art: artists by artists. il *Architectural Digest* 46:132-7+ Jl '89
Gilbert & George: the AIDS pictures [cover story] il *Art in America* 77:152-5 N '89
ROSENBLUM, VICTOR G.
Letting the states set abortion policy. *The Christian Century* 106:252-3 Mr 8 '89
ROSENDAHL, BRUCE
Snippets from Nyanja chronicles. il por map *Sea Frontiers* 35:292-302 S/O '89
ROSENFELD, ALBERT
Tough cases, hard choices. il pors *New York* 22:32-7 Ja 9 '89
ROSENFELD, ISAAC, 1918-1956
about
Golden boy. J. Atlas. bibl f il *The New York Review of Books* 36:42-6 Je 29 '89
ROSENFELD, ISADORE
The stories nails can tell [excerpt from Symptoms] il *Health (New York, N.Y.)* 21:68-9+ Ag '89
ROSENFIELD, HARVEY
about
The flamboyant force behind California's auto insurance revolt. G. Anrig, Jr. il por *Money* 18:145-6 Jl '89
ROSENFIELD, JAMES H.
about
Bringing Blair back to life. K. Haley. il por *Channels (New York, N.Y.: 1986)* 9:38-40+ Je '89
ROSENFIELD, RICHARD L.
about
Flax and Rosenfield: taking pizza way past pepperoni. P. Cole. il pors *Business Week* p98 My 8 '89
ROSENGARTEN, THEODORE
about
All God's dangers [drama] Reviews
The New Yorker 65:110 O 30 '89. E. Oliver
ROSENKRANTZ, LINDA
Bough wows. il *House & Garden* 161:53-4 D '89
Contemporary collectibles. See issues of Antiques & Collecting Hobbies beginning October 1988
ROSENSAFT, MENACHEM Z.
A letter to Yasir Arafat. por *Newsweek* 114:14 D 11 '89
Why I met with the PLO. por *Newsweek* 113:6 Ja 9 '89
ROSENSHINE, ILAN, AND OTHERS
The mechanism of DNA transfer in the mating system of an archaebacterium. bibl f il *Science* 245:1387-9 S 22 '89

ROSENSTEIN, BARBARA
Inflammatory bowel disease: incurable and difficult to diagnose. il por *USA Today (Periodical)* 117:91-2 Mr '89
ROSENTHAL, A. M.
From China with contempt. *Reader's Digest* 135:197-8 N '89
Into the heart of the gulag. il *Reader's Digest* 134:71-5 Ap '89
ROSENTHAL, DAVID H.
Thriving without a state. il *The Atlantic* 263:20+ Je '89
ROSENTHAL, ELISABETH
Backward protection. il *The New York Times Magazine* p27-8 Jl 2 '89
Different but deadly. il *The New York Times Magazine* p60+ S 17 '89
Is the annual physical obsolete? il *Glamour* 87:37-9 Jl '89
The unsung hero. il *The New York Times Magazine* p53-4 Ap 30 '89
Vital signs. See alternate issues of Discover beginning December 1987
When your immune system panics. il *The Saturday Evening Post* 261:60-1 O '89
ROSENTHAL, HERMA M.
(ed) See King, Billie Jean. The best shots in tennis
ROSENTHAL, LESLIE
about
A blast from the past for the Chicago Board of Trade? D. Greising. il por *Business Week* p137 D 25 '89-Ja 1 '90
ROSENTHAL, MARSHAL M.
MIDI equipment. il *Radio-Electronics* 60:34-41 Ag '89
ROSENTHAL, PEGGY
Challenges facing U.S. Catholics. *Commonweal* 116:617-18 N 17 '89
ROSENTHAL, RAYMOND
(tr) See Levi, Primo, 1919-1987. Beetlemania
(tr) See Levi, Primo, 1919-1987. The mark of the chemist
(tr) See Levi, Primo, 1919-1987. My house
ROSENTHAL, ROBERT
about
How do you build a luxury image? J. Flint. il pors *Forbes* 143:60-3 Ap 3 '89
ROSENWACH TANK COMPANY
Keeping up the pressure. B. Weber. il *The New York Times Magazine* p62 S 3 '89
ROSENWALD, PRISCILLA R., AND PORTER, GWEN
Wee Care: reaching teenage mothers and changing their lives. *Children Today* 18:28-30 My/Je '89
ROSENZWEIG, ROBERT M.
Public policy issues in scientific fraud and misconduct. *BioScience* 39:552-4 S '89
Thatcherism and higher education: California, here she comes. il *Change* 21:40-1 S/O '89
ROSES
The 25 best cut roses. M. E. Guffey. il *Flower and Garden* 33:26-8+ My/Je '89
Hardwood cuttings. L. J. Rombough. il *Flower and Garden* 33:68-9 My/Je '89
New Elizabeth Park [rose garden restored in Hartford, Conn.] G. Morris. il *Americana* 17:61-3 Mr/Ap '89
Pruning climbing roses. il *Southern Living* 24:60 Je '89
A rose for the nose [Prelude variety developed in France] il *Life* 12:102-3 Je '89
Rose inventory [conducted in New York City by S. Scanniello] *The New Yorker* 65:49-50 N 6 '89
Roses and annuals together. il *Sunset (Central West edition)* 182:156 F '89
Roses for hedges, edges, ground covers. il *Sunset (Central West edition)* 182:128 Ja '89
Roses in miniature. il *Southern Living* 24:52 F '89
Where your new rose probably started out [Wasco, Calif. nurseries] il *Sunset (Central West edition)* 182:184 F '89
All-America Selections
See Plants—All-America Selections
ROSES IN ART
Exhibitions
Museum accessions [Roses by Renoir acquired by Virginia Musuem of Fine Arts] E. H. Gustafson. il *Antiques* 136:76+ Jl '89
Renoir's gifts. V. H. Winner. il *Art News* 88:25 Summ '89
ROSE'S STORES, INC.
Don't discount this discounter. G. G. Marcial. *Business Week* p130 O 23 '89
ROSETH, GENE
(jt. auth) See McNabb, Janet, and Roseth, Gene
ROSETTA STONE
Champollion, a hero of the Enlightenment [interview with J. Lacouture] il por *The Unesco Courier* 42:4-9 O '89
ROSEVEARE, HELEN
about
The cost of loving Jesus [interview] por *Christianity Today* 33:45 My 12 '89
ROSEWALL, KEN
about
Forever young. N. Amdur. il pors *World Tennis* 37:29-30 N '89

ROSEWOMAN, MICHELE
about
Michele Rosewoman. S. Stein. il por *Down Beat* 56:15 S '89
ROSH HASHANAH
Intention [services in Santa Fe] *The New Yorker* 65:38-9 O 16 '89
ROSIN, MARK BRUCE
The other father. il *Parents* 64:252+ My '89
ROSINSKI, JEANNE
about
Living proof that walking changes walkers. M. Spilner. il pors *Prevention (Emmaus, Pa.)* 41:84+ Jl '89
ROSKAM, SWEDE
about
The business of making dreams come true. C. Lutes. il por *Christianity Today* 33:12-13 Ag 18 '89
ROSKENS, RONALD W.
Integrity [address, March 13, 1989] *Vital Speeches of the Day* 55:511-12 Je 1 '89
ROSLER, MARTHA, 1943-
about
Martha Rosler at Dia. E. Heartney. *Art in America* 77:186 N '89
ROSMERSHOLM [drama] See Ibsen, Henrik, 1828-1906
ROSOLIO (NEW YORK, N.Y.: RESTAURANT) *See* New York (N.Y.)—Restaurants, nightclubs, bars, etc.
ROSOW, LA VERGNE
Arthur: a tale of disempowerment. bibl f il *Phi Delta Kappan* 71:194-9 N '89
ROSS, ALAN
Greenwich House Pottery at 80. il *American Craft* 49:44-7 Ap/My '89
ROSS, DANIEL CHARLES
Detroit report. See issues of Motor Trend
ROSS, DENNIS B.
about
Foggy Bottom's new bright light. B. Javetski. il por *Business Week* p66+ F 20 '89
ROSS, DIANA
about
Diana: down-to-earth [cover story] P. Cleage. il pors *Essence* 20:70-2+ O '89
ROSS, HERBERT
about
Steel magnolias [film] Reviews
American Film il 15:62 N '89. J. E. Fitch
Ladies' Home Journal il 106:126+ N '89. J. Rachlin
Life il 12:82-4+ O '89
Maclean's il 102:84+ N 20 '89. B. D. Johnson
New York 22:78 N 27 '89. D. Denby
Newsweek il 114:90 N 27 '89. D. Ansen
People Weekly il 32:21-2 D 4 '89. R. Novak
Time il 134:92 N 20 '89. R. Schickel
ROSS, JAMES
Vigilante justice. *The New Republic* 201:9-21 N 27 '89
ROSS, JAMES H.
Facing an uncomfortable truth [address, June 15, 1989] *Vital Speeches of the Day* 55:690-3 S 1 '89
ROSS, JANICE
San Francisco's ethnic dance festival: the new melting pot. il *Dance Magazine* 63:36-8 Je '89
San Francisco's Joe Goode: working hard to be the bad boy of modern dance. il pors *Dance Magazine* 63:46-50 Ja '89
ROSS, JEFFREY
The turnover of messenger RNA. bibl il *Scientific American* 260:48-55 Ap '89
ROSS, JERRY
(jt. auth) See Staw, Barry M., and Ross, Jerry
ROSS, JOE
about
When Joe Ross rescued little Maura Handren, he didn't know he was really a wife-saver. il pors *People Weekly* 31:94 Ap 17 '89
ROSS, JOHN, 1921-, AND OTHERS
Technical page [excerpt from The complete printmaker] il *American Artist* 53:56 S '89
ROSS, KEVIN
about
Former basketball player sues Creighton University. por *Jet* 76:50 Ag 14 '89
ROSS, L. K.
Bug detector [cover story] il *Radio-Electronics* 60:42-4+ Je '89
ROSS, L. K., AND WATTS, AMP
High-power hi-fi audio amp for your home or car. il *Radio-Electronics* 60:51-5+ Mr '89
ROSS, MARC HANSEN
Improving the efficiency of electricity use in manufacturing. bibl f il *Science* 244:311-17 Ap 21 '89
ROSS, MARION
Go, oh thoughts, on wings of gold [address, October 7, 1988] *Vital Speeches of the Day* 55:282-4 F 15 '89
ROSS, MICHAEL
Disarmament at sea. *Foreign Policy* 77:94-112 Wint '89/'90
Trident II misfires in Congress. il *The Bulletin of the Atomic Scientists* 45:11-12 D '89

ROSS, MICHAEL E.
Coming to terms with the j-jitters. il *The New York Times Magazine* p26+ My 14 '89
ROSS, PAT
Formal country [excerpt] il *Redbook* 173:146-51 O '89
ROSS, STEVEN J.
about
Steve Ross' big sweet deal. G. Morgenson. il por *Forbes* 143:14 Ap 3 '89
The thorn in Steve Ross's side. R. Grover. il por *Business Week* p51 Ag 14 '89
ROSS, STEVEN S.
Green groceries. il *Mother Jones* 14:48-52 F/Mr '89
IBM Operating System/2 Extended Edition Version 1.1. *Architectural Record* 177:151+ O '89
Software reviews for architects. See issues of Architectural Record beginning October 1987
ROSSANT, COLETTE
America entertains. See issues of McCall's beginning February 1987
ROSSELLINI, ISABELLA
about
Mother and daughter. *The New Yorker* 65:44-6 O 23 '89
Unique star quality. Y. Z. McDonough. il pors *Harper's Bazaar* 122:208-15+ Ap '89
ROSSI PRIZE
Rashid Sunyaev wins 1988 Rossi Prize. P. H. Andersen. il por *Physics Today* 42:90+ Ap '89
ROSSINI, GIOACCHINO, 1792-1868
about
The barber of Seville [opera] Reviews
Opera News il 53:28-31 F 4 '89
L'occasione fa il ladro [opera] Reviews
The New Yorker 65:118-19 Ap 17 '89. A. Porter
A superb new "Cenerentola" from Marriner. R. Ackart. il *Stereo Review* 54:146 F '89
ROSSINI OPERA FESTIVAL (PESARO, ITALY) *See* Music festivals—Italy
ROSSMAN, CHARLES
The new 'Ulysses': grave matters [discussion of December 8, 1988 article, The new 'Ulysses': the hidden controversy] il *The New York Review of Books* 36:43-5 Mr 30 '89
The new 'Ulysses': unanswered questions [discussion of December 8, 1988 article, The new 'Ulysses': the hidden controversy] *The New York Review of Books* 35:58-9 Ja 19 '89
ROSSO, MEDARDO, 1858-1928
about
Medardo Rosso: radical anti-classicist. H. Cotter. bibl f il *Art in America* 77:182-7 My '89
ROSTAND, EDMOND, 1868-1918
about
Cyrano de Bergerac [drama] Reviews
America il 161:65 Jl 29-Ag 5 '89. G. G. Seibert
ROSTENKOWSKI, DAN
about
Rostenkowski adds a twist to the tax tango. H. Gleckman. il *Business Week* p61 Je 26 '89
Rostenkowski: 'My head is bloodied, but I'm not bowed'. D. Harbrecht. il por *Business Week* p31-2 S 18 '89
Ways without means. *National Review* 41:11 Ag 18 '89
What will the folks back in Chicago think? *Newsweek* 113:54 Je 19 '89
ROSTOV-ON-DON (SOVIET UNION)
Description
Letter from Rostov-on-Don [effects of *perestroika*] R. B. Cullen. *The New Yorker* 65:107-20 Je 12 '89
ROSTOW, EUGENE VICTOR, 1913-
A false start in the Middle East. *Commentary* 88:24-7 O '89
Letters. *Foreign Policy* 75:182-9 Summ '89
Now, about those Baltic Republics. map *The New Leader* 72:8-9 O 30 '89
ROSWELL (N.M.)
Description
Roswell, N.M. map *New Choices for the Best Years* 29:14 F '89
ROTARY ENGINES
Laughing stock and beyond [success of Norton-Wankel in World TT Formula One] J. Greening. il *Cycle* 40:12 F '89
Mazda 3-rotor RX-7. D. Fuller. il *Motor Trend* 41:122-4 F '89
Rotary engine gets airborne. F. Mackerodt. il *Popular Mechanics* 166:44-5 F '89
Rotary-mill renaissance [aviation] N. Moll. *Flying* 116:23 Ap '89
ROTARY TILLERS *See* Cultivators
ROTATION
See also
Earth—Rotation
Neptune (Planet)—Rotation
Precession
Saturn (Planet)—Satellites—Rotation
How to get the playground swing going: a first lesson in the mechanics of rotation. J. Walker. il *Scientific American* 260:106-9 Mr '89

ROTATION DIET See Diet
ROTE ARMEE FRAKTION See Red Army Faction
ROTH, CHRISTIAN FRANCIS
about
A New York upstart puts a smile on the face of fashion. il por *People Weekly* 32:122-3 O 30 '89
ROTH, DAVID M.
The road least traveled. il map *Travel Holiday* 172:62-3 O '89
ROTH, GUENTHER
Remembrance and responsibility. *Society* 26:4-5 Mr/Ap '89
ROTH, JOE
about
From cars to stars. P. Newcomb. il pors *Forbes* 143:60-1 Ja 23 '89
ROTH, PHILIP
Goodbye, Newark: Roth remembers his beginnings. por *The New York Times Book Review* 94:14 O 1 '89
Pro-life pro. il *The New York Review of Books* 36:5 Ag 17 '89
about
Philip Roth and Bill Cosby move houses for high stakes. pors *Publishers Weekly* 236:42-3 S 8 '89
ROTH, ROBERT A.
The teacher education program: an endangered species? bibl f il *Phi Delta Kappan* 71:319-23 D '89
ROTH, WILLIAM V., JR.
about
Ansel Adams Awards. il pors *Wilderness* 52:9 Summ '89
ROTHBARD, MURRAY NEWTON, 1926-
about
"No water" economics. P. Brimelow. por *Forbes* 143:86+ Mr 6 '89
ROTHCHILD, DONALD S., AND GYIMAH-BOADI, E.
Populism in Ghana and Burkina Faso. bibl f *Current History* 88:221-4+ My '89
ROTHCHILD, JOHN, 1945-
I'm irresponsible! il *Mother Jones* 14:42-3 S '89
(ed) See Lynch, Peter. One up on Wall Street
(ed) See Lynch, Peter. The power of common knowledge
ROTHE, JOHN PETER, 1948-
Regulating the deregulated. *Society* 27:11-12 N/D '89
ROTHENBERG, RANDALL
Brits buy up the ad business [cover story] il por *The New York Times Magazine* p14-19+ Jl 2 '89
ROTHENBERG, ROBERT S.
Videos. See issues of USA Today (Periodical) beginning May 1988
(jt. auth) See Rothenberg, Sheila, and Rothenberg, Robert S.
ROTHENBERG, SHEILA, AND ROTHENBERG, ROBERT S.
La Toc: a St. Lucian sojourn. il *USA Today (Periodical)* 117:38-43 Mr '89
ROTHENBERG, STUART
The invisible success story. il *National Review* 41:43-4+ S 15 '89
ROTHER, STANLEY, 1935-1981
about
Blood bond: where Oklahoma and Guatemala meet. D. Thomson. *America* 161:277-8 O 28 '89
ROTHFEDER, JEFFREY
Quieting electrical storms of the heart [excerpt from Heart rhythms] il *Prevention (Emmaus, Pa.)* 41:62-8 S '89
Transplants in demand. il *The Saturday Evening Post* 261:12-13 N/D '89
ROTHKO, MARK, 1903-1970
about
Rothko's legacy. A. Decker. il por *Art News* 88:41+ S '89
ROTHKO (MARK) FOUNDATION See Mark Rothko Foundation
ROTHLEIN, LEWIS
Editorial. See issues of Women's Sports & Fitness beginning December 1988 through March 1990
ROTHMAN, HOWARD
Wellness works for small firms. il *Nation's Business* 77:42+ D '89
ROTHMAN, STANLEY, 1927-, AND LERNER, ROBERT
Politics and the media: a TV revolution. *Current (Washington, D.C.)* 311:4-11 Mr/Ap '89
ROTHSCHILD, MATTHEW
The crime of politics. il *The Progressive* 53:28-30 My '89
The involuntary tourist. il *The Progressive* 53:22-3 My '89
Third party time? [cover story] il *The Progressive* 53:20-5 O '89
ROTHSCHILD (L.F.) HOLDINGS INC. See L.F. Rothschild Holdings Inc.
ROTHSCHILD-BOROS, MONICA C.
In the shadow of the tower: poignant portrayals of life in a Nazi prison camp. il por *USA Today (Periodical)* 118:74-83 S '89
ROTHSCHILD FAMILY
about
Big scam on campus. F. Trippett. il por *Time* 134:25 S 25 '89
ROTHSTEIN, EDWARD
Edward Rothstein on music. See occasional issues of The New Republic beginning August 27, 1984

ROTHSTEIN, MERVYN
Is there life after 'M*A*S*H'? il por *The New York Times Magazine* p53-6+ O 8 '89
ROTHWAX, HAROLD
about
When the guilty go free. H. Evans. il *U.S. News & World Report* 106:84 My 22 '89
RÔTI (SAN FRANCISCO, CALIF.: RESTAURANT) See San Francisco (Calif.)—Restaurants, nightclubs, bars, etc.
ROTISSERIE LEAGUE BASEBALL
Rotisserie like it oughta be. B. Shapiro. il *Sport (New York, N.Y.)* 80:43-5 Mr '89
Rotisserie revisited. S. Wulf. por *Sports Illustrated* 71:78 Ag 7 '89
ROTO-ROOTER, INC.
Roto-Rooter's new drill. R. Phalon. il *Forbes* 144:176+ D 11 '89
ROTOR AIRCRAFT
FAA awards California grant to study applications for commercial tilt-rotor. *Aviation Week & Space Technology* 131:25 Jl 31 '89
Costs
The B-2: fly before buy [Stealth bomber and V-22 tilt rotor aircraft] *Aviation Week & Space Technology* 131:9 N 6 '89
Bell, Boeing push V-22 flight test program [Osprey tilt-rotor aircraft; cover story] D. A. Brown. il *Aviation Week & Space Technology* 131:38-40 O 16 '89
Congress may ram a chopper down the Pentagon's throat [V-22 Osprey] D. Griffiths. il *Business Week* p92 Je 5 '89
House panel backs plan to cancel V-22, F-14D. P. A. Gilmartin and D. F. Bond. il *Aviation Week & Space Technology* 130:28-9 Je 26 '89
Navy terminates $328.8 million in V-22 advance production contracts [tilt-rotor aircraft] D. F. Bond. il *Aviation Week & Space Technology* 131:38 D 11 '89
Osprey wings clipped in 1990 budget. il *Flying* 116:11 Ag '89
Will the Osprey ever fly? D. Waller. il *Newsweek* 114:16 Jl 24 '89
Export-import trade
European firms agree to join Bell-Boeing in marketing V-22 [tilt-rotor aircraft] *Aviation Week & Space Technology* 130:37 Je 19 '89
Testing
Bell-Boeing accelerates flight testing of No. 1 V-22 tilt-rotor aircraft [Osprey] il *Aviation Week & Space Technology* 131:19 S 25 '89
Bell, Boeing push V-22 flight test program [Osprey tilt-rotor aircraft; cover story] D. A. Brown. il *Aviation Week & Space Technology* 131:38-40 O 16 '89
Bell-Boeing V-22 tilt-rotor prototype makes first flight. C. A. Shifrin. il *Aviation Week & Space Technology* 130:20-1 Mr 27 '89
V-22 flexes its wings [Osprey tilt-rotor] il *Flying* 116:11 Je '89
V-22 prepared for further expansion of flight envelope [Osprey tilt-rotor prototype; cover story] C. A. Shifrin. il *Aviation Week & Space Technology* 130:34-6+ Ap 10 '89
Japan
Japanese foundation plans wind tunnel tests on model of tilt-wing transport this summer [TW-68] il *Aviation Week & Space Technology* 130:70 Je 19 '89
ROTORS (HELICOPTERS) See Helicopters—Rotors
ROTTENBERG, ISAAC C.
Christian fulfillment and Jewish-Christian dialogue. *The Christian Century* 106:387-91 Ap 12 '89
ROTTERDAM (NETHERLANDS)
Theater
Rotterdamse Schouwburg. R. Long. il *Theatre Crafts* 23:74+ Mr '89
ROTTERDAM MARATHON See Marathon running
ROTTERDAMSE SCHOUWBURG (ROTTERDAM, NETHERLANDS) See Rotterdam (Netherlands)—Theater
ROTTIER, BARBARA
(jt. auth) See Stross, Ray, and Rottier, Barbara
ROUD, RICHARD, 1929-1989
about
Obituary
Film Comment por 25:78-9 Mr/Ap '89. R. Corliss
ROUECHÉ, BERTON, 1911-
Annals of medicine. *The New Yorker* 65:100-5 S 4 '89
The thyroid mystery (II). il *The Saturday Evening Post* 261:46-9+ Ja/F '89
ROUFBERG, RUTH B.
A guide for us grandparents. il *New Choices for the Best Years* 29:77-9 D '89
Treasures! 10 top toys. il *Redbook* 174:38 D '89
The well-balanced playroom. il *Essence* 20:90+ N '89
ROUGEMONT, ANDRÉ, AND OTHERS
The Sikasso project. il *World Health* p6-8 Je '89
ROUGHGARDEN, JONATHAN
The United States needs an ecological survey. *BioScience* 39:5 Ja '89

ROULD, MARK A., AND OTHERS
Structure of E. coli glutaminyl-tRNA synthetase complexed with tRNA^{Gln} and ATP at 2.8 Å resolution. bibl f il *Science* 246:1135-42 D 1 '89
ROUND THE WORLD YACHT RACES *See* Yacht racing
ROUNTREE, SUE
about
A miniaturist of (new) Williamsburg. A. Bahar. il *Antiques & Collecting Hobbies* 94:62-5 Je '89
ROUSE, CHARLIE, 1924-1988
about
Obituary
Down Beat il por 56:59-60 Ap '89. P. Keepnews
ROUSE, JAMES W.
about
James Rouse set out to do the impossible—build a city that works. D. Moreau. il por *Changing Times* 43:132 O '89
ROUSE, MEREDITH FRAME- *See* Frame-Rouse, Meredith
ROUSE CO.
Malled. T. Pouschine. il *Forbes* 144:46+ O 30 '89
ROUSH, EDD, 1893-1988
about
A visit to Edd Roush [excerpt from Spring training] W. K. Zinsser. *The American Scholar* 58:113-16 Wint '89
ROUSSEAU, JEAN-JACQUES, 1712-1778
about
Le devin du village [opera] Reviews
New York il 22:62 Je 19 '89. P. G. Davis
The New Yorker 65:74-5 Jl 3 '89. A. Porter
ROUSSEL, ATHINA
about
Athina. il pors *Life* 12:40-1 O '89
Born in fortune's uneasy shadow [cover story] M. Green. il pors *People Weekly* 31:70-4+ F 6 '89
The richest little girl in the world. M. Hammond. il pors *McCall's* 117:38-40+ N '89
Thierry Roussel tells his story—of love for two women and little Athina. M. Green. il pors *People Weekly* 31:52-4 Mr 20 '89
ROUSSEL, THIERRY
about
Born in fortune's uneasy shadow [cover story] M. Green. il pors *People Weekly* 31:70-4+ F 6 '89
Thierry Roussel tells his story—of love for two women and little Athina. M. Green. il pors *People Weekly* 31:52-4 Mr 20 '89
ROUSSEL-UCLAF SA
The case of the reluctant drug maker [will not market RU-486 outside of France] E. MacFarquhar. il *U.S. News & World Report* 106:54 Ja 23 '89
Dispute surfaces over paternity of RU 486. J. Cherfas. *Science* 246:994 N 24 '89
A new pill, a fierce battle [RU-486] S. Greenhouse. il por *The New York Times Magazine* p22-4+ F 12 '89
The pill of choice? [RU-486; cover story] J. Palca. il *Science* 245:1319-23 S 22 '89
ROUSSEVE, DAVID
about
Pull your head to the moon [dance] Reviews
Dance Magazine 63:71-2 Je '89. J. Lewis
ROUTER BITS *See* Bits (Drilling and boring)
ROUTING MACHINES
Floor show [rout-and-stain method] J. Truini. il *Home Mechanix* 85:74-6 D '89
Mastering the router. R. Capotosto. il *Popular Mechanics* 166:75-9+ Ja '89
Router power. H. Wicks. il *Home Mechanix* 86:38-40+ Mr '89
Router tips. H. Wicks. il *Home Mechanix* 85:22-3 F '89
Routing hinge mortises. T. H. Jones. il *Home Mechanix* 85:29-30 O '89
The Workbench guide to routers. P. McCafferty. il *Workbench* 45:62-7 Mr/Ap '89
Equipment
Router jigs to make and buy. il *Workbench* 45:65 Mr/Ap '89
Stands, tables, etc.
See Machinery—Stands, tables, etc.
ROUTLEDGE, CHAPMAN & HALL
Routledge boosts its sales and image in Iowa [book week at University of Iowa bookstore] J. Mutter. il *Publishers Weekly* 235:112-13 Ja 20 '89
ROUVRAY, D. H.
(jt. auth) *See* Duncan, Michael A., and Rouvray, D. H.
ROUX, ANNETTE
about
Safe harbor. K. Weisman. il por *Forbes* 144:58+ S 4 '89
ROUX, MICHEL
about
Absolut marketing. E. McGlinn. il por *Forbes* 144:282+ D 11 '89
Breaking the last taboo. I. Bosch. il *Mother Jones* 14:49 My '89
ROVER (SPACE VEHICLE) *See* Mars vehicles
ROVER GROUP PLC
Rover boy [G. Simpson] J. Flint. il por *Forbes* 143:201 Mr 20 '89

ROVIN, JEFF
Dan Rather's difficult days. il pors *Ladies' Home Journal* 106:80+ Ja '89
Shirley MacLaine: the prime of her lives. il pors *Ladies' Home Journal* 106:74+ Ap '89
(jt. auth) *See* Rachlin, Jill, and Rovin, Jeff
ROW, DAVID
about
David Row: John Good. N. Grimes. il *Art News* 88:176-7 S '89
ROW HOUSES
Fix a fixer-upper [home of Catherine and Peter Van Allen] il *Better Homes and Gardens* 67:42-3 Ag '89
ROWAN, CARL THOMAS, 1925-
Called to service: the Colin Powell story. por *Reader's Digest* 135:121-6 D '89
Let's get tough with drug users! *Reader's Digest* 135:107-10 Jl '89
about
Making excellence popular. il pors *Ebony* 44:90+ S '89
ROWAN, ROY
Two Shanghais. il *Life* 12:78-80+ Je '89
ROWBOTHAM, MICHAEL
about
Leopard: a most dangerous game. J. Carmichel. il *Outdoor Life* 183:58-9+ F '89
ROWE, FREDERICK E.
about
A maverick's forecast: high inflation and a boom in Texas stocks. il por *Money* 18:191-2 My '89
ROWE, GREGORY
Beyond the Louvre. il *House & Garden* 161:62+ Jl '89
ROWE, JONATHAN
Down and out in Washington on $89,500 a year. *The Washington Monthly* 21:12-14+ Jl/Ag '89
Ralph Nader reconsidered. *The Washington Monthly* 21:65+ F '89
(jt. auth) *See* Hays, Charlotte, and Rowe, Jonathan
ROWE, MATTHEW
The owl that traded a hoot for a hiss. il *Natural History* p32-3 My '89
ROWE, NICK, D. 1989
about
Obituary
National Review 41:14 My 19 '89. J. A. Rehyansky
A sense of foreboding in the Philippines. B. Duffy. il *U.S. News & World Report* 106:35-6 My 15 '89
Targeting a U.S. hero. D. Waller and R. Vokey. il por *Newsweek* 113:42 My 1 '89
ROWE, PHILLIP
about
The best banana bred. S. Brownlee. il *The Atlantic* 264:22+ S '89
ROWE, SANDRA
about
Sandra Rowe: practitioner of a healing art [cover story] L. LeFalle-Collins. il pors *American Visions* 4:27-9 Ag '89
ROWELL, GALEN A.
Along the high, wild Sierra. il map *National Geographic* 175:466-93 Ap '89
Annapurna: sanctuary for the Himalaya. il map *National Geographic* 176:390-405 S '89
about
How to shoot scenics [cover story] D. Brockway. il pors *Popular Photography* 96:48-59+ N '89
ROWEN, JOHN
New York's great angling secret. il *The Conservationist* 44:34-9 S/O '89
ROWING
Rowing Antarctica's "most mad seas". N. Gillette. il map *National Geographic* 175:128-38 Ja '89
Competitions
Ho hum, it's Harvard [national championships] D. S. Looney. il *Sports Illustrated* 70:64 Je 26 '89
Showdown in Seattle [Opening Day competition] N. Rabinowitz. il *Women's Sports & Fitness* 11:22-5 Jl/Ag '89
ROWING MACHINES *See* Exercising equipment
ROWLAND, DAVID
about
Another bloody nose for Asher? J. Ferry. il por *Forbes* 144:184+ N 27 '89
ROWLAND, FRANK SHERWOOD
about
Highest disregard. D. Hayes. il *Mother Jones* 14:32-6+ D '89
The man who knew too much. E. Edelson. il por *Popular Science* 234:60-5+ Ja '89
ROWLAND, MARY
A question of money. See issues of New Choices for the Best Years beginning January 1989
ROWLAND, ROLAND W. *See* Rowland, Tiny
ROWLAND, SHERRY *See* Rowland, Frank Sherwood
ROWLAND, TINY
about
Banned in Britain: a new chapter in the Harrods saga. M. Maremont. pors *Business Week* p36 Ap 17 '89

ROWLAND, TINY—about—cont.

Brawling over Harrods. S. Lohr. il pors *The New York Times Magazine* p32-3+ O 8 '89

Tiny Rowland versus Mohamed Al-Fayed (cont.). E. F. Cone. il pors *Forbes* 143:10 My 1 '89

Tit for tat on London's High Street. J. Barnes. il pors *U.S. News & World Report* 106:63 Ja 30 '89

ROWLANDS, GENA

about

Gena. B. Walker. pors *Film Comment* 25:42-3 My/Je '89

ROWLEY, GWYN, 1938-

Lebanon: from change and turmoil to cantonization? il maps *Focus (New York, N.Y.: 1950)* 39:9-16 Fall '89

ROWNY, EDWARD L., 1917-

Vigilance [address, September 7, 1989] *Vital Speeches of the Day* 56:73-6 N 15 '89

ROY, D. H.

Turning ideas into reality [address, February 23, 1989] *Vital Speeches of the Day* 55:662-6 Ag 15 '89

ROY, SANJIT BUNKER

Village wisdom. il *The Courier (Unesco)* 42:25-7 F '89

ROY, SYAMAL, AND OTHERS

Murine MHC polymorphism and T cell specificities. bibl f il *Science* 244:572-5 My 5 '89

ROY F. WESTON, INC.

If you look past the smoke, Weston may shine. G. Weiss and J. M. Laderman. il *Business Week* p106 F 27 '89

ROYAL, JENNIFER

about

The littlest victim [interview] V. Gladstone. il pors *Life* 12:16+ O '89

The littlest witness may testify about her friend's killing. M. Brower. il pors *People Weekly* 31:108-10 Ap 24 '89

ROYAL AGRICULTURAL SOCIETY OF ENGLAND

Royal shows & agricultural progress, 1839-1989. N. Goddard. bibl il *History Today* 39:44-51 Jl '89

ROYAL ARMOURIES (GREAT BRITAIN)

A folly no more [Fort Nelson in Portsmouth being developed into artillery museum] D. Gregory. il *History Today* 39:3-4 Je '89

ROYAL BALLET

Dancing:

Grand pas classique with S. Guillem, The spirit of fugue, and Apollo. A. Croce. *The New Yorker* 64:63-4 Ja 16 '89

Reviews:

Performance of La bayadère. M. E. Willis. il *Dance Magazine* 63:77-8 O '89

ROYAL BALLET OF FLANDERS

Reviews:

Performances at Brooklyn Center for the Performing Arts. C. Hardy. *Dance Magazine* 63:79-80 Mr '89

ROYAL BOTANIC GARDENS (KEW, ENGLAND)

Blooming beauties from Britain [Flowers from the Royal Gardens of Kew at the National Museum of Natural History] K. M. Burke. il *Smithsonian* 19:176 F '89

ROYAL CANADIAN MOUNTED POLICE

Courtroom chaos [Mountie R. Jordan alleges political interference at budget leak trial] M. Clark. il por *Maclean's* 102:20 N 20 '89

Mounties forever, but these days rarely on horseback. R. Wolkomir. bibl (p170) il *Smithsonian* 19:78-84+ F '89

Politics and policing [accused of delaying raid on offices of Tory MP R. Grisé] B. Wallace. il *Maclean's* 102:24 D 4 '89

ROYAL CANADIAN MOUNTED POLICE IN ART

Exhibitions

Maintain the right. R. J. Maturi. il *American History Illustrated* 24:32-9 Mr '89

ROYAL CHITWAN NATIONAL PARK (NEPAL)

Around the Mall and beyond [capture and tracking of a clouded leopard] E. Dinerstein. il *Smithsonian* 20:24+ Ap '89

King of the marsh [tracking rhinoceros; cover story] E. Dinerstein. il *International Wildlife* 19:4-11 Mr/Ap '89

Rhino warrior [conservation efforts] D. Starr. il *Omni (New York, N.Y.)* 11:17+ S '89

ROYAL CRESCENT MOB (MUSICAL GROUP)

Royal Crescent Mob. H. Weinger. il *Rolling Stone* p18 S 7 '89

ROYAL DANISH BALLET

Reviews:

Performance of Don Quixote. E. Aschengreen. *Dance Magazine* 63:86 F '89

Witchcraft [S. Englund in La Sylphide] T. Tobias. il *New York* 22:121-2 S 25 '89

ROYAL DOULTON LTD.

The collecting life [interview with L. Irvine] il por *Antiques & Collecting Hobbies* 94:50-3+ N '89

ROYAL DUTCH/SHELL GROUP

Time, money and patience. T. Mack. il por *Forbes* 144:60-2 Ag 21 '89

ROYAL ESSENCE LTD.

A nose for success. K. Osborne and C. C. Williams. por *Black Enterprise* 19:32 F '89

ROYAL FAMILY OF GREAT BRITAIN *See* Great Britain—Royal family

ROYAL FAMILY OF MONACO *See* Monaco—Royal family

ROYAL INTERNATIONAL OPTICAL CORPORATION

This raider may have beaten 'em by joining 'em [E. Buchanan may sell] G. G. Marcial. il *Business Week* p88 F 13 '89

ROYAL JORDANIAN AIRLINE *See* Alia-The Royal Jordanian Airline

ROYAL NEWFOUNDLAND CONSTABULARY

Charges of a coverup [sexual and physical abuse at Mount Cashel Orphanage] N. Underwood. *Maclean's* 102:66+ D 4 '89

ROYAL ONTARIO MUSEUM. SAMUEL EUROPEAN GALLERIES

A new wing in Canada. A. E. Ledes. il *Antiques* 136:682 O '89

ROYAL OPERA HOUSE (LONDON, ENGLAND)

London. N. Goodwin. *Opera News* 53:41 Mr 4 '89

London. N. Goodwin. il *Opera News* 53:60-1 Ap 1 '89

London [L. Berio's Un re in ascolto] N. Goodwin. il *Opera News* 53:47 My '89

ROYAL PUBLISHING-WALTERS INTERNATIONAL SPEAKERS BUREAU

Small-town woman talks her way through bigger and bigger doors. L. Arden. il por *Home Office Computing* 7:46 My '89

ROYAL SWEDISH BALLET

Reviews:

Performances at the Royal Opera House, Stockholm. L. Svedin. *Dance Magazine* 63:32-3 Mr '89

Performances of N. Makarova's La bayadère. L. Svedin. il *Dance Magazine* 63:76-7 O '89

ROYAL TRUST COMPANY OF CANADA

Canada's growing economic outreach [views of M. Cornelissen] P. C. Newman. il *Maclean's* 102:42 Ja 23 '89

ROYAL TRUSTCO LIMITED

See also

Royal Trust Company of Canada

ROYAL WINNIPEG BALLET

Death palls a Canadian anniversary. D. Campbell. il *Dance Magazine* 63:24 O '89

Heart and sole. P. Young. il *Maclean's* 102:78-9 O 23 '89

Kickoff [artistic director A. Spohr] R. Philp. *Dance Magazine* 63:7 D '89

Slaying the dragons of pain with loyalty and love [E. Hart] D. Jenish. il por *Maclean's* 102:30-1 D 25 '89

ROYALE GROUP LTD.

Lenny Pelullo's checkered past—and present. G. DeGeorge. il por *Business Week* p84+ O 23 '89

ROYALTIES

See also

Public lending rights (of authors)

Making money from the grave [black entertainers] D. Narine. il *Ebony* 44:142+ Je '89

Palm Springs ploy [movie companies sue La Mancha Private Club & Villas over royalties from videotapes shown in hotel rooms] P. Newcomb. il *Forbes* 143:100 Mr 20 '89

Reading between the lines [self-licensing of paperback rights can institutionalize half-royalties] L. Chu. il *Publishers Weekly* 235:48 F 17 '89

Resale royalties for artists: the debate continues. D. Grant. *American Artist* 53:12+ Je '89

Rhythm and blues, on the upbeat [payment of retroactive royalties to singers] A. Levine. il *U.S. News & World Report* 106:59-60 Ja 16 '89

Anecdotes, facetiae, satire, etc.

Uncivil liberties [royalties and J. Wright] C. Trillin. il *The Nation* 248:762 Je 5 '89

ROYALTIES, OIL AND GAS *See* Oil and gas leases—Royalties

ROYALTON HOTEL (NEW YORK, N.Y.) *See* New York (N.Y.)—Hotels, motels, etc.

ROYALTY *See* Nobility; Queens

ROYCE, JOSEPH

about

Avenging years of sexual abuse, twins take their adoptive father to court. C. McCall. il pors *People Weekly* 31:54-6+ Je 26 '89

ROYCE, RACHEL

about

Avenging years of sexual abuse, twins take their adoptive father to court. C. McCall. il pors *People Weekly* 31:54-6+ Je 26 '89

ROYCE, TONI

about

Avenging years of sexual abuse, twins take their adoptive father to court. C. McCall. il pors *People Weekly* 31:54-6+ Je 26 '89

ROYCROFT SHOP

Collecting "fit for a king": defining Roycroft. K. Turgeon and R. C. Rust. il *Antiques & Collecting Hobbies* 94:75-7 O '89

ROYKO, MIKE, 1933-

Confessions of a network dropout. *Reader's Digest* 135:93-4 S '89

What's in a name? *Reader's Digest* 135:195-6 N '89

about

The old man's Irish eyes are smiling. il por *U.S. News & World Report* 106:12-13 Mr 13 '89

ROYTE, ELIZABETH
. . . and the woman who loves him. il *Mademoiselle* 95:190+ My '89
ROZEK, MICHAEL
Gardens: Portland trailblazer. il *Architectural Digest* 46:208-13 Mr '89
ROZELLE, PETE
about
He quit, for Pete's sake. P. Zimmerman. il pors *Sports Illustrated* 70:60-2 Ap 3 '89
Top blacks qualified to replace Pete Rozelle. il por *Jet* 76:51 Ap 10 '89
ROZEN, SYDNEY CRAFT
(jt. auth) See Bernstein, Albert J., and Rozen, Sydney Craft
ROZHDESTVENSKI, GENNADI
about
Rachmaninoff's Second from Rozhdestvensky. R. Freed. por *Stereo Review* 54:93-4 Je '89
ROZINER, FELIX
Purple smoke [story] *Commentary* 87:48-59 Mr '89
RPM INC. (OHIO)
Has this outfit found 'a miracle for oil spills'? [views of J. Siebert] G. G. Marcial. il por *Business Week* p150 My 22 '89
RPVS (REMOTELY PILOTED VEHICLES) *See* Remotely piloted vehicles
RRNA *See* Ribosomal RNA
RSV *See* Respiratory syncytial virus
RTC *See* Resolution Trust Corporation (U.S.)
RU 486 (DRUG)
Abortion clinic obsolescence. C. W. Colson. il *Christianity Today* 33:72 F 3 '89
Abortion in the form of a pill. J. Seligmann. il *Newsweek* 113:61 Ap 17 '89
The abortion pill debate. J. Brooks and L. Lamb. *Utne Reader* p19 N/D '89
The case of the reluctant drug maker [Roussel-Uclaf will not market RU-486 outside of France] E. MacFarquhar. il *U.S. News & World Report* 106:54 Ja 23 '89
Contragestion and other clinical applications of RU 486, an antiprogesterone at the receptor [cover story] E.-E. Baulieu. bibl f il *Science* 245:1351-7 S 22 '89
Dispute surfaces over paternity of RU 486. J. Cherfas. *Science* 246:994 N 24 '89
Etienne-Emile Baulieu: in the eye of the storm. J. Cherfas. il pors *Science* 245:1323-4 S 22 '89
The mysteries of RU-486. C. L. Allen. il *The American Spectator* 22:17-20 O '89
A new pill, a fierce battle. S. Greenhouse. il por *The New York Times Magazine* p22-4+ F 12 '89
The pill of choice? [cover story] J. Palca. il *Science* 245:1319-23 S 22 '89
RU detour [abortion pill] M. Suh. il *Ms.* 17:135-6 Ja/F '89
RUBBER BANDS (EXERCISING EQUIPMENT)
Pumping rubber. il *Vogue* 179:186 F '89
RUBBER CHECKS *See* Checks, Fraudulent
RUBBER FLOORING *See* Flooring, Rubber
RUBBER INDUSTRY
See also
B.F. Goodrich Co.
Firestone Tire & Rubber Co.
Goodyear Tire & Rubber Company
Tire industry
RUBBER INDUSTRY WORKERS
See also
Labor unions—Rubber industry workers
RUBBERMAID INCORPORATED
Profits on everything but the kitchen sink. M. Mallory. il *Business Week* Special Issue:122 Je 16 '89
Why Little Tikes' managers picked up their toys and left. M. Mallory. il *Business Week* p83 N 27 '89
RUBELL, STEVE
about
Obituary
New York il pors 22:44-8 Ag 14 '89. M. Gross
People Weekly il por 32:40-1 Ag 14 '89. M. Neill
Rolling Stone por p24 S 7 '89. M. Goldberg
RUBELLA
Vaccines and vaccination
Suspect vaccine [K. Fox files suit against Merck & Co. after developing rubella vaccine side effects] H. S. Miller. il por *Ms.* 17:81-2 Ap '89
RUBEN, GEORGE
Developments in industrial relations. See issues of Monthly Labor Review
RUBEN, JOE
about
True believer [film] Reviews
Maclean's il 102:55 F 27 '89. B. D. Johnson
The New Republic 200:26-7 F 13 '89. S. Kauffmann
New York il 22:70-1 F 20 '89. D. Denby
The New Yorker 65:95-6 F 20 '89. P. Kael
People Weekly il 31:11 F 27 '89. S. Haller
Time il 133:94 F 20 '89. R. Schickel
Video il 13:58 Ag '89. I. Robbins

RUBENS, SIR PETER PAUL, 1577-1640
about
The House that Rubens built. B. Grauman. il por *Art News* 88:107-8 Ap '89
A Rubens crucifixion on a Chinese export porcelain dish. N. Pearce. bibl f il *Antiques* 136:844-7 O '89
RUBENS' HOUSE (ANTWERP, BELGIUM) See Rubenshuis (Antwerp, Belgium)
RUBENSHUIS (ANTWERP, BELGIUM)
The House that Rubens built. B. Grauman. il por *Art News* 88:107-8 Ap '89
RUBENSTEIN, ANN
about
Women on the verge of a nervy breakthrough [interview] P. Orenstein. il pors *Mother Jones* 14:28-31+ Je '89
RUBENSTEIN, EDWARD
Stages of evolution and their messengers. il *Scientific American* 260:132 Je '89
RUBENSTEIN, EDWIN
Right data. See issues of National Review beginning February 19, 1988
RUBENSTEIN, HAL
The man from Mars. il por *New York* 22:48-50+ Ap 17 '89
RUBENSTEIN, JAMES M.
Baltimore, Maryland, USA: would H.L. Mencken recognize it? bibl il maps *Focus (New York, N.Y.: 1950)* 39:30-2 Spr '89
The changing distribution of U.S. motor vehicle parts suppliers. il maps *Focus (New York, N.Y.: 1950)* 38:10-14+ Wint '88
RUBIANO, TANNIA See Hecht, Tannia Rubiano
RUBICAM, SHANNON
about
Boy Meets Girl: a star-quality couple! D. McCue. il pors *'Teen* 33:45 Jl '89
Boy Meets Girl! Boy loses girl! But now they're back together, and singing in an altared state. il pors *People Weekly* 31:69 Ja 16 '89
RUBIDIUM OXIDES
Scanning tunneling microscopy and nanolithography on a conducting oxide, $Rb_{0.3}MoO_3$. E. Garfunkel and others. bibl f il *Science* 246:99-100 O 6 '89
RUBIDIUM-STRONTIUM DATING See Radioactive dating
RUBIN, BARNETT R.
Afghanistan: "back to feudalism". bibl f *Current History* 88:421-4+ D '89
Afghanistan's uncertain fate. il *The Nation* 248:264-7+ F 27 '89
The fragmentation of Afghanistan. *Foreign Affairs* 68:150-68 Wint '89/'90
RUBIN, BARRY J.
(tr) See Chubinsky, V. Darkness at noon
(tr) See Kovalenko, Y., and Polianovsky, E. Joseph Brodsky's Nobel Prize
(tr) See Likhachev, Dmitrii Sergeevich. Doctor Zhivago
(tr) See Polivanov, Mikhail. Memoirs
RUBIN, CAROL
(jt. auth) See Rubin, Jeff, and Rubin, Carol
RUBIN, CAROL, AND RUBIN, JEFF
'Tis the season to be fighting. il *Psychology Today* 22:36-9 D '88
RUBIN, HANNA
The clean machine. il *Seventeen* 48:122+ My '89
RUBIN, HANNA, AND GRISOLIA, CYNTHIA
Star quality. il *American Film* 15:58-61+ O '89
RUBIN, JAMES P.
START finish. *Foreign Policy* 76:96-118 Fall '89
RUBIN, JEFF
(jt. auth) See Rubin, Carol, and Rubin, Jeff
RUBIN, JEFF, AND RUBIN, CAROL
How to handle family fights [excerpt from When families fight] il *Ladies' Home Journal* 106:70+ Ja '89
RUBIN, JERRY
about
Rebel without a pause. G. Averbuch. il pors *Runner's World* 24:32-4 Ap '89
RUBIN, LARRY
Preparation [poem] *America* 160:368 Ap 22 '89
RUBIN, LILLIAN B.
How we play the game. il *Ms.* 17:40-3 My '89
RUBIN, RON
about
Playing for real. N. Hass. il pors *New York* 22:60-2+ D 11 '89
RUBIN, SAM
Julia Duffy. il pors *McCall's* 116:14-16 My '89
RUBIN, WILLIAM STANLEY
about
The legacy of cubism [interview] M. Horn. il pors *U.S. News & World Report* 107:68 O 23 '89
RUBINOFF, IRA
The Smithsonian Tropical Research Institute. il *Environment* 31:44-5 Je '89
RUBINSTEIN, LESLIE
Risk taker. il pors *Opera News* 54:18-20+ O '89

RUBINSTEIN, ROBERT E., 1943-
Building an atmosphere of success in a middle school. *Phi Delta Kappan* 71:328-9 D '89
RUBISCO *See* Enzymes, Plant
RUBY, JACK
about
The cross fire over Jack Ruby's gun. il por *U.S. News & World Report* 107:10 D 25 '89-Ja 1 '90
Jack Ruby's family and lawyer battle for possession of the gun that killed Lee Harvey Oswald. W. Plummer. il por *People Weekly* 31:42-3 My 22 '89
RUBY MOUNTAINS (NEV.)
Elko to Eden [hiking in the Ruby Mountains; cover story] T. Kizzia. il map *Sierra* 74:46-54 Mr/Ap '89
RUCKELSHAUS, WILLIAM D.
Toward a sustainable world. il map *Scientific American* 261:166-70+ S '89
RUDBECKIA HIRTA *See* Black-eyed Susans
RUDDERS, AIRPLANE *See* Airplanes, Jet—Stability and stabilizers
RUDDICK CORPORATION
Juicy results at an upscale grocer. G. G. Marcial. *Business Week* p104 D 11 '89
RUDE AWAKENING [film] *See* Motion picture reviews—Single works
RUDENESS
America in the '80s was a kinder, gentler nation. R. Lacayo. il *People Weekly* 32 Special Issue:102-7 Fall '89
The decline of civility. R. J. Bresler. il *USA Today (Periodical)* 117:7 Mr '89
Declining civility. D. Schorr. *The New Leader* 72:4 Ja 9 '89
How do we love you? Rudely [rude compliments] G. Schwartz. *Seventeen* 48:56 S '89
RUDLOE, ANNE
(jt. auth) *See* Rudloe, Jack, and Rudloe, Anne
RUDLOE, JACK, AND RUDLOE, ANNE
Shrimpers and lawmakers collide over a move to save the sea turtles. il *Smithsonian* 20:44-55 D '89
RUDMAN, THEO
South Africa's 'dummy' shops. *World Press Review* 36:64 D '89
RUDNER, RUTH
Fire and glory. il *Ms.* 18:34 S '89
RUDNICK, PAUL
Born in the U.S.A. il *Vogue* 179:300-11 F '89
Paul Rudnick is addicted to television's beauty show-and-sell. il *Vogue* 179:364+ S '89
Where John Barrymore once hid from fans, Paul Rudnick has found the actor's ghost—and medieval inspiration. il por *Vogue* 179:130-2 Jl '89
Wings of desire. il *Vogue* 179:384-5 My '89
RUDNICK, PAUL, AND ANDERSEN, KURT, 1954-
The irony epidemic: the dark side of Fiestaware and the Flintstones. il *Utne Reader* p34-40 My/Je '89
RUDNICKY, JAMES L.
The New York Botanical Garden Forest—an urban natural area in the Bronx. il *The Conservationist* 43:46-9 My/Je '89
RUDOLF
about
The man from Mars. H. Rubenstein. il por *New York* 22:48-50+ Ap 17 '89
Mars: a visit to a small planet. il por *Harper's Bazaar* 122:226 Ap '89
RUDOLF, ANDREAS
about
A last mile to freedom. R. Nordland. il por map *Newsweek* 114:34 S 18 '89
RUDOLPH, JOHN
(jt. auth) *See* Gunst, Kathy, and Rudolph, John
RUDOLPH, PAUL, 1918-
about
Resolutely modernist [special section] M. F. Schmertz. il *Architectural Record* 177:74-85 Ja '89
RUDOLPH THE RED-NOSED REINDEER (FICTIONAL CHARACTER)
The story behind Rudolph the Red-Nosed Reindeer. S. A. Frankel. il *Good Housekeeping* 209:126+ D '89
RUETHER, ROSEMARY RADFORD
Salvadoran refugees come home. il *The Christian Century* 106:851-3 S 27 '89
RUFF, BILLY
about
A devoted brother believes he's found little Billy Ruff's killer 31 years after the crime. K. Gross. il pors *People Weekly* 31:69-70+ Je 5 '89
RUFF, CHRISTOPHER
about
A devoted brother believes he's found little Billy Ruff's killer 31 years after the crime. K. Gross. il pors *People Weekly* 31:69-70+ Je 5 '89
RUFF, RICHARD
about
A devoted brother believes he's found little Billy Ruff's killer 31 years after the crime. K. Gross. il pors *People Weekly* 31:69-70+ Je 5 '89

RUFF, THOMAS, 1958-
about
Thomas Ruff. J. Dornberg. il por *Art News* 88:164-5 Ap '89
RUFFINS, PAUL
NAACP: eighty years on freedom road. il *Black Enterprise* 19:194-6+ F '89
Passing the torch. il *Black Enterprise* 19:46-7 Ja '89
RUFUS-ISAACS, ANTONY
about
Casual aristocrats: eclectic charm. C. Seipp. il pors *Harper's Bazaar* 122:198-201+ O '89
RUFUS-ISAACS, HEIDE
about
Casual aristocrats: eclectic charm. C. Seipp. il pors *Harper's Bazaar* 122:198-201+ O '89
RUG AND CARPET INDUSTRY
See also
Interface Inc.
RUGBY
Rugby: a gentlewoman's sport. R. S. Burton. il *Women's Sports & Fitness* 11:66 Je '89
Tournaments
History
An American coup in Paris [victory over French team for gold medal at 1924 Olympics] M. Jenkins. il *American Heritage* 40:66-71 Jl/Ag '89
RUGBY (TENN.)
Galleries and museums
See also
Historic Rugby
RUGGIERO, VINCENT RYAN
The role of business in educational reform [address, December 8, 1988] *Vital Speeches of the Day* 55:286-8 F 15 '89
RUGOFF, RALPH
The last word [cover story] il pors *Art News* 88:120-5 D '89
Liberal arts. il *Vogue* 179:328-33+ Ag '89
RUGS AND CARPETS
See also
American Designer Heirlooms (Firm)
Indian blankets, rugs, etc. (American)
Barbara Bush's hand-made rug [needlepoint project] il por *Good Housekeeping* 209:40+ Ag '89
Captain Hook [hooked rug designer T. Harbison] D. B. Cowin. il por *House & Garden* 161:110 My '89
Needlepoint rugs—bold color and design. il *Southern Living* 24:171 Mr '89
Polypropylene strikes back [stain resistant carpet fiber] J. Harris. il *Forbes* 144:122 Ag 7 '89
Stain resistant carpets. B. Freese. il *Successful Farming* 87:52-3 My '89
Care
See also
ZZZZ Best Company
Cleaning stain-resistant carpet [interview with J. F. Rench] il por *Home Mechanix* 86:20+ Ap '89
RUGS AND CARPETS, ORIENTAL
Oriental rugs: fine art that's affordable. S. Reed. il *Business Week* p128 D 4 '89
RÜHLE, HANS
NATO strategy: back to basics. *Current (Washington, D.C.)* 312:34-9 My '89
RULE, ANN, 1934?-
Final attraction: men who charm women—to death. il pors *Redbook* 172:104-6+ F '89
Have you seen my missing wife? il pors *Good Housekeeping* 208:99+ F '89
Rape on campus. il *Good Housekeeping* 209:189+ S '89
RULE, SHEILA
Africa up close. il *The New York Times Magazine* p36+ Ap 30 '89
RULE OF THE ROAD AT SEA
Rules of the road. H. Halsted. il *Motor Boating & Sailing* 163:44+ F '89
RULERS *See* Queens
RULING, KARL
Making a telephone ring. il *Theatre Crafts* 23:92+ Ap '89
RUM
Rum! il *Better Homes and Gardens* 67:144 Mr '89
Rum drinks with punch. E. Fried. il *Black Enterprise* 19:120 My '89
RUMANIA *See* Romania
RUMER, BORIS, AND SCHOENFELD, GABRIEL
The perils of *perestroika*. il *The New Leader* 72:7-9 Ag 7-21 '89
RUMINANTS
See also
Camels
RUMMEL, R. J. (RUDOLPH J.), 1932-
The politics of cold blood. bibl *Society* 27:32-40 N/D '89
RUMMEL, RUDOLPH J. *See* Rummel, R. J. (Rudolph J.), 1932-
RUMOR
American Express slings mud—and gets splattered [smear campaign against financier E. Safra] W. Glasgall and J. Meehan. il por *Business Week* p102+ Ag 14 '89

RUMOR—*cont.*

Bank shot: Edmond Safra turns the tables on American Express. J. Taylor. il pors *New York* 22:42-7 S 18 '89

Beware of the headhunters [rumors circulating in Malaysia] M. Liu. il map *Newsweek* 114:62 D 11 '89

Is it right to publish rumors? W. Shapiro. il *Time* 134:53 Jl 10 '89

Pssst [Washington's rumor mill] M. Hosenball and M. Isikoff. *The New Republic* 200:16+ Ja 2 '89

RUMORS [drama] See Simon, Neil

RUMRILL, HARRY BARLOW

about

H.B. Rumrill: an amateur's legacy. B. Fried. il por *Sky and Telescope* 77:86-7 Ja '89

RUN FOR YOUR WIFE! [drama] See Cooney, Ray, 1932-

RUNAWAY HUSBANDS

After 20 years, an abandoned wife makes her ex pay his due [case of P. Bennett] D. Chu. il pors *People Weekly* 31:79-82 F 20 '89

When Ed Greer vanished, a myth was born—and a bitter reality for the family he left behind [resurfaces in Houston, Tex. after 7 years] G. Stone. il pors *People Weekly* 31:109+ Je 5 '89

RUNAWAYS

Desperate odds [teenagers] L. Morgan. *Seventeen* 48:257+ Mr '89

Portrait of a runaway [teenager in New York City] L. Ullmann. il *Seventeen* 48:254-7+ Mr '89

Running away: a 50-50 chance to survive? D. Hughes. il *USA Today (Periodical)* 118:64-6 S '89

When you run: the problems that follow [teenagers] W. Woodward. il *Teen* 33:48+ O '89

RUNDGREN, TODD, 1948-

about

Todd looks back in style. D. Fricke. il *Rolling Stone* p51-2 Je 29 '89

RUNDOWN (NEWSLETTER) See Newsletters

RUNNELLS, TOM

about

On deck. il por *Sport (New York, N.Y.)* 80:16 Jl '89

RUNNERS

Color commentary [lack of black distance runners] J. Henderson. il *Runner's World* 24:12 F '89

Lionhearted [1992 Olympic hopefuls in distance running] R. Flippin. il *Runner's World* 24:36-9+ Ap '89

Mark Curp & Lisa Weidenbach top the rankings [road racing] il *Runner's World* 24:56-62 F '89

Top of the charts [all time best distance runners] M. Tymn. il *Runner's World* 24:72-3 Ag '89

Health and hygiene

The beat goes on [runner H. Pirie has a pacemaker] P. Nye. il por *Women's Sports & Fitness* 11:57 Jl/Ag '89

Health watch. K. Delhagen. See issues of Runner's World

Heat success [treating runners with heatstroke] G. Sheehan. il *Runner's World* 24:16 Jl '89

In search of a magic bullet [annual convention of the American College of Sportsmedicine] A. Burfoot. il *Runner's World* 24:73-7 O '89

Medical & training advice. K. Delhagen and M. Will-Weber. See issues of Runner's World

The road to recovery [post-race guidelines] H. Higdon. il *Runner's World* 24:44-6+ N '89

Skin games. H. Higdon. il *Runner's World* 24:70-4+ My '89

Summer running [special section] il *Runner's World* 24:66-76+ Jl '89

Nutrition

Dairy tales. N. Clark. il *Runner's World* 24:44-8+ Je '89

Diet daze. S. Malley. il *Runner's World* 24:86-8 O '89

Drink to your health. J. Stifler. il *Runner's World* 24:72-6+ Jl '89

Fill 'er up [glycogen burning] G. Sheehan. il *Runner's World* 24:16 N '89

Just desserts. K. Anderson. il *Runner's World* 24:40-4 S '89

The last supper [pre-race meal] J. Stifler. il *Runner's World* 24:38-42 N '89

Movers and shakers. L. E. Armstrong and R. H. Lind. il *Runner's World* 24:80-2 Jl '89

Nutrition. L. Applegate. See issues of Runner's World

Sports nutrition '89: sugar's in, caffeine's out. K. Pinna and T. Ratto. il *American Health* 8:74+ Je '89

You lead, I'll swallow [use of dietary supplements] H. Higdon. il *Runner's World* 24:82-5 Ap '89

Training

5-speed transition. M. Tymn. il *Runner's World* 24:26 Je '89

Beat the clock [improving 10K time; cover story] B. Glover. il *Runner's World* 24:46-50 S '89

The flex factor [cover story] B. Anderson. il *Runner's World* 24:38-43 F '89

Great workouts. J. Galloway. il *Runner's World* 24:42-6+ Jl '89

Hill, yes! [training for the St. George Marathon] J. Ullyot. il por *Runner's World* 24:24-5 Ap '89

How to improve your 5K and 10K times. N. Kuscsik. il *Women's Sports & Fitness* 11:30-5 My '89

Medical & training advice. K. Delhagen and M. Will-Weber. See issues of Runner's World

Pick up the paces [tempo training] P. Pfitzinger. il *American Health* 8:80 Je '89

Push it [weight training] K. Anderson. il *Runner's World* 24:40-4 Ag '89

The runner's companion [cover story; special section] K. Delhagen. il *Women's Sports & Fitness* 11:31+ S '89

Spring training [special section] il *Runner's World* 24:57-62+ Mr '89

That first marathon [advice for women] N. Kuscsik. il *Women's Sports & Fitness* 11:20-5 O '89

Total fitness. K. Delhagen. See issues of Runner's World

Training log. M. Will-Weber. See issues of Runner's World

Triple your pleasure [cross training] G. Sheehan. il *Runner's World* 24:16 S '89

Will weight training improve your running? O. Anderson. bibl il *Women's Sports & Fitness* 11:22-3 Ap '89

RUNNER'S WORLD (PERIODICAL)

The inside track. G. A. Hirsch. See issues of Runner's World

RUNNING

See also

 Biathlon (Running and cycling)
 Cross country running
 Desert running
 Fifty-Plus Runners Association
 Hash House Harriers (Organization)
 Hurdle racing
 Marathon running
 Mountain running
 Track and field athletics
 Triathlon
 Ultramarathon running

All in the family [cover story; special section] il *Runner's World* 24:59-66+ Je '89

The best of '88 [special section] il *Runner's World* 24:47-69 F '89

Bookin' in the basement [Swarthmore's McCabe Mile race run in the library] M. Will-Weber. il *Runner's World* 24:94-7 O '89

A day at the races. G. Sheehan. il *Runner's World* 24:14 Ap '89

Do you speak metric? [measuring race distances] J. Henderson. il *Runner's World* 24:12 Ja '89

Double trouble [running as part of football player R. Craig's training] J. Brant. il pors *Runner's World* 24:30-2 O '89

Endless summer [runners' winter vacations] L. Rogak. il *Runner's World* 24:66-8 Ja '89

Feet revenge [running instead of driving] N. L. Howe. il *Runner's World* 24:104 S '89

Freeze Yer Gizzard [10K race in International Falls, Minn.] D. Kardong. il *Runner's World* 24:72-5 D '89

Gore goes for it [senator's views on running] A. Gore, Jr. il por *American Health* 8:42 Ja/F '89

Great races to run in 1989. il *Women's Sports & Fitness* 11:40-3 Ja/F '89

The human race. B. Wischnia and E. Portz-Shovlin. See issues of Runner's World

I love winter running [cover story] H. Higdon. il *Runner's World* 24:52-7 D '89

I resolve . . . [New Year's resolutions] B. Glover. il *Runner's World* 24:22 Ja '89

Just peachy [Atlanta's Peachtree Road Race] D. Kardong. il *Runner's World* 24:34-6+ O '89

Masters running [cover story; special section] il *Runner's World* 24:46-7+ Ag '89

Miles of predawn sky [studying the sky while running] T. B. Hunter. il *Astronomy* 17:90 Ap '89

Morning glory [early morning running] J. Iorillo. il *Runner's World* 24:104 Jl '89

Mother's days [mother who has been running since birth of ten year old son] P. L. Potts. il *Runner's World* 24:104 My '89

Myth adventures [Spokane's Lilac Bloomsday Run] D. Kardong. il *Runner's World* 24:78-82 My '89

Of ice and men [Canadian Arctic] H. Chernovsky. il *Runner's World* 24:96 Ja '89

Pie in the sky [Domino's Pizza president T. Monaghan's devotion to running] K. Shyne. il pors *Runner's World* 24:34-6 N '89

Play it again, Anne [distance runner A. Hannam] K. Williams. il pors *Runner's World* 24:70-5 Ja '89

Racing report. M. Will-Weber and M. Post. See issues of Runner's World

Reading, 'riting & running [J. Deatherage incorporates running into his high school English class in Richland, Wash.] R. Blount. il pors *Runner's World* 24:26-8 Ja '89

Rebel without a pause [J. Rubin] G. Averbuch. il pors *Runner's World* 24:32-4 Ap '89

Rough and ready [races in Alaska] J. Henderson. il *Runner's World* 24:14 N '89

'Round midnight [New Year's Eve Midnight Run in New York City] il *Runner's World* 24:52-5 Mr '89

The runner's roadbook [special section] il *American Health* 8:67-8+ Je '89

Running. il *World Tennis* 36:76 My '89

RUNNING—cont.

Running at age 40 and beyond [masters running for women] G. Averbuch. il *Women's Sports & Fitness* 11:18 N/D '89

Running for our lives [running across U.S. to raise public consciousness about AIDS]; ed. by Gary Smith. B. N. Earle. il pors *People Weekly* 32 Special Issue:134-5+ Fall '89

Running wild [San Francisco's Bay to Breakers race; cover story] il *National Geographic World* 164:4-7 Ap '89

Runs in the family. J. Henderson. il *Runner's World* 24:14 Ag '89

The Russians are here [women runners in New Orleans for the Crescent City Classic] J. Brant. il *Runner's World* 24:78-84 O '89

Short and sweet [5K races] B. Glover. il *Runner's World* 24:24 My '89

Silent night [running on Christmas Eve in home town] J. Atkinson. il *Runner's World* 24:96 D '89

Staying healthy is a daily habit on this farm [Puzey family] C. Tevis. il *Successful Farming* 87:52 Ap '89

Stuck in the middle? [midrace strategy] B. Glover. il *Runner's World* 24:44-6 F '89

Sworn to run [G. Bush] K. Hosler. il por *Runner's World* 24:30-1+ D '89

That old college try [Alamo Alumni Run for college graduates] M. Bloom. il *Runner's World* 24:36-8 S '89

Ticket to stride [running while traveling] J. Henderson. il *Runner's World* 24:14 My '89

To the rescue [runner and paramedic S. Forbes, who carried J. McClure from Texas well] R. MacInnis. il pors *Runner's World* 24:36-8 Ag '89

Trail blazers [Eugene, Or.] J. Henderson. il *Runner's World* 24:14 Jl '89

Trail man [running the length of the Pacific Crest Trail] B. Holtel and B. Darves. il por *Runner's World* 24:66-7 S '89

Trek star [actor G. Takei] J. Harmon. il pors *Runner's World* 24:32-4 S '89

Woman to watch: road runner Anne Hannam. L. Rothlein. il por *Women's Sports & Fitness* 11:49 Ja/F '89

World tour [D. Balhi's 16,000 mile trek] J. Henderson. il por *Runner's World* 24:16 Je '89

Accidents and injuries

Between a sock and a hard place [foot blisters] J. Ellis. il *Runner's World* 24:28 Ag '89

Hell on heels [effects of wearing high heeled shoes] W. Feigel. il *Runner's World* 24:30 N '89

The ice is right. M. Chasnov. il *Runner's World* 24:24 Jl '89

A pain in the knee! [iliotibial band syndrome] D. W. Jackson and P. R. Kurzweil. il *Runner's World* 24:24 D '89

Stressful situation [stress fractures] J. F. Durkin. il *Runner's World* 24:28 O '89

Take care of your knees [views of Dennis Phelps] *USA Today (Periodical)* 117:7-8 F '89

When you haven't got time for the pain [views of Kenneth Meisler] B. Kevles. il *Women's Sports & Fitness* 11:12 Jl/Ag '89

Anecdotes, facetiae, satire, etc.

Cool awakening. J. M. Raia. il *Runner's World* 24:112 Je '89

Bibliography

The self-coached runner. K. Delhagen. il *Women's Sports & Fitness* 11:14-15 Je '89

Economic aspects

Dream jobs. B. Wischnia. il *Runner's World* 24:82-6+ Je '89

Equipment

See also
    Running shoes

The runner's companion [cover story; special section] K. Delhagen. il *Women's Sports & Fitness* 11:31+ S '89

Stroll models [running strollers] M. Cimons. il *Runner's World* 24:74-5 Je '89

Ethical aspects

Users and losers [drug use] J. Henderson. il *Runner's World* 24:14 Mr '89

Periodicals

See also
    Runner's world (Periodical)

Photographs and photography

Those magic moments: photo highlights of the 1980s. il *Runner's World* 24:59-65 D '89

Physiological effects

Burn, baby, burn [effect on weight loss] D. Kardong. il *Runner's World* 24:32-7 F '89

Finding fitness after baby [resuming running] C. L. Otis. il *Women's Sports & Fitness* 11:10 N/D '89

It's Greek to me [listening to your body] G. Sheehan. il *Runner's World* 24:18 Mr '89

Last legs. M. Tymn. il *Runner's World* 24:24 Mr '89

A run a day keeps the doctor away? [boosting immune system] O. Anderson. il *Runner's World* 24:54-7 Ja '89

Run for your life. H. Higdon. il *Runner's World* 24:46-7+ Ag '89

Striking a balance [effect on metabolism] L. Applegate. il *Runner's World* 24:22-3 D '89

Psychological aspects

The best way to tough it out [comparison of distraction methods; research by Vernon Padgett and Angela Hill] J. C. Horn. *Psychology Today* 23:72-3 N '89

Desert son [Marathon Des Sables] K. McKinney. il *Omni (New York, N.Y.)* 12:16+ N '89

Down by the sea. G. Sheehan. il *Runner's World* 24:16 Ag '89

The jitter bug [pre-race nervousness] K. McAlpine. il *Runner's World* 24:24 S '89

Notes from a veteran jogger. D. Goldstrom. il *Health (New York, N.Y.)* 21:32-3 O '89

The obsession of the long-distance runner. B. W. Bloch. il *Gentlemen's Quarterly* 59:312-13+ N '89

Relax to the max. J. Lynch. il *Runner's World* 24:38-40 Mr '89

Running from drugs. R. Rodale. il por *Runner's World* 24:24 F '89

When the saints go running in [comparison between a marathon and a 10K race] G. Sheehan. il *Runner's World* 24:14 O '89

Safety devices and measures

See also
    Project Safe Run

Exercising caution. C. Schaeffer. *Changing Times* 43:94+ F '89

Let's be careful out there [women] J. Ullyot. il por *Runner's World* 24:26 S '89

Never again [attack on woman jogger in Central Park] G. Averbuch. il *Runner's World* 24:10-11 Ag '89

Statistics

Numbers up [increased race participation] J. Henderson. il *Runner's World* 24:14 D '89

Study and teaching

Short strides: a short cut to the finish line. J. Galloway. il *Women's Sports & Fitness* 11:12-13 Mr '89

Summer camp '89 [running camps] il *Runner's World* 24:76-8 Je '89

Television broadcasting

See Television broadcasting—Sports

RUNNING AGROUND (BOATS) See Boats and boating—Accidents

RUNNING CAMPS See Camps

RUNNING CLOTHES See Clothing and dress—Sports clothes

RUNNING POSTERS See Posters

RUNNING RAPIDS

Canoeing our rivers. V. Chambers. il *The Conservationist* 44:8-11 Jl/Ag '89

The Chattooga River: a weekend white-water adventure. il map *Southern Living* 24:30+ S '89

The great raft adventure [motorcycle-powered raft trip up the Yukon River] K. Schubert. il map *Cycle* 40:38-41+ Jl '89

The great white way. J. Seabury. il *New York* 22:101-2 S 25 '89

Into the breach [kayaking in Great Falls Park, Va.; cover story] T. Kilpatrick. il *National Parks* 63:22-7 Mr/Ap '89

Paddle tales [whitewater rafting trip for Pittsburgh, Pa. physical education students] il *National Geographic World* 164:23-7 Ap '89

A raft of fun [white water rafting in Utah; with editorial comment by Donald J. Barr] J. McCallum. il pors *Sports Illustrated* 71:4, 34-7 Jl 10 '89

Rumbling rafters. S. J. Cooke. il *Women's Sports & Fitness* 11:38-9 Je '89

Shoot-out at Gauley Gorge. D. Harbrecht. il *Business Week* p142 O 16 '89

Wet and wild [white-water rafting on the Zambezi River] E. McGowan. il *Travel Holiday* 171:50-1 Ap '89

Winter madness on northern California rivers [rafting] il *Sunset (Central West edition)* 181:56+ D '88

Competitions

Perestroika, part one [American women participate in whitewater kayaking and rafting event in the Soviet Union] S. Norman. il *Women's Sports & Fitness* 11:58 O '89

RUNNING RECORDS

See also
    Marathon running records
    Track and field athletics records

The longest run ever [journey runner S. Fulcher] B. Kevles. il por *Women's Sports & Fitness* 11:67 Mr '89

RUNNING SHOES

1989 fall shoe survey [cover story] il *Runner's World* 24:49-54+ O '89

1989 spring shoe survey [cover story] il *Runner's World* 24:45-50+ Ap '89

Fleet feet. S. R. Hurlburt. il *American Health* 8:70+ Je '89

Just how good are those special insoles? O. Anderson. il *Women's Sports & Fitness* 11:14 Ja/F '89

On the run. il *Women's Sports & Fitness* 11:31-4 Mr '89

The race to make a 'perfect' shoe starts in the laboratory. R. Wolkomir. il *Smithsonian* 20:94-100+ S '89

Steady as you go. B. Wischnia and T. Brunick. il *Runner's World* 24:58-61 Jl '89

RUNNING TIGHTS *See* Tights (Clothing)
RUNOFF
Desert bloom [runoff agriculture in the Negev Desert; work of M. Evenari] D. Starr. il *Omni (New York, N.Y.)* 11:28+ Mr '89
Trout in the spring runoff. J. Gierach. il *Field & Stream* 93:70-1+ Ap '89
RUNTÉ, TERRY
Last word. il *Omni (New York, N.Y.)* 11:132 F '89
Last word. por *Omni (New York, N.Y.)* 11:116 S '89
RUNYAN, JOE
about
Man's best friends. R. F. Jones. il por map *Sports Illustrated* 70:40-2+ Mr 27 '89
RUNYON, LINDA
about
Weed all about it! Linda Runyon, a wild chef, says we should veg out on crabgrass and clover. D. Chu. il pors *People Weekly* 32:85-6 Jl 24 '89
RUPNIK, JACQUES
Bloc busters [cover story] *The New Republic* 200:18+ My 22 '89
The empire breaks up. *The New Republic* 200:20-4 F 20 '89
Hungary's quiet revolution. *The New Republic* 201:18-20+ N 20 '89
RUPP, REBECCA
Treehouses. il *Country Journal* 16:47-50 Jl/Ag '89
RUPPERT, ROBERT
about
Charlie Keating in the Show Me state. G. Morgenson. il por *Forbes* 143:12 My 29 '89
RURAL CHURCHES
Church exchange strengthens urban/rural ties [Brooklyn's Zion Lutheran Church and Elstad-Highland Prairie Churches, Minn.] B. Heidtke. *Successful Farming* 87:F4 D '89
Rural churches remain strong in tough times. *Successful Farming* 87:40L Ag '89
RURAL CRIMES
The newest drug war [crack and crank] J. N. Baker. il *Newsweek* 113:20-2 Ap 3 '89
No safe place. A. McCarthy. il *Commonweal* 116:72 F 10 '89
RURAL DEVELOPMENT
'Declare rural America a third-world country!' [views of V. Bailey] C. Tevis. il por map *Successful Farming* 87:13-14 Ag '89
Thoughts along a country road. S. Pietz. il *Successful Farming* 87:14 Ag '89
Conferences
Farmer ideas to make towns thrive [REDI-Midwest Conference] C. Tevis. il *Successful Farming* 87:14-15 Je '89
Revving up rural America [REDI-Midwest] C. Tevis. *Successful Farming* 87:11 Ag '89
Canada
Fragile roots. G. Allen. il *Maclean's* 102:18-20 O 23 '89
India
Village wisdom. S. B. Roy. il *The Courier (Unesco)* 42:25-7 F '89
New England
New England forests sought by developers [Northern Forest Lands Study] map *National Parks* 63:13-14 Mr/Ap '89
Whose woods these are [cover story; with editorial comment by T. H. Watkins] N. Boucher. il map *Wilderness* 53:16-41 Fall '89
Papua New Guinea
Village development: working together. J. Mills and G. Kila. il *World Health* p5 N '89
Vermont
For sale: rural America. R. M. Ketchum. il *Country Journal* 16:80-3 My/Je '89
RURAL EDUCATION
The mentor as an expert coach: a model for rural school districts [program in Oroville, Calif.] B. Benoit and J. A. Braun. il *Phi Delta Kappan* 70:488-9 F '89
Second grader Brandon Schlund is a standout student in his school—he's also the only one [Bois Blanc Island, Mich.] M. Neill. il pors *People Weekly* 32:111-12 N 6 '89
Ways of being at risk: the case of Billy Charles Barnett [middle school student] T. Barone. il *Phi Delta Kappan* 71:147-51 O '89
RURAL HOMELESS *See* Homeless
RURAL HOSPITALS *See* Hospitals, Rural
RURAL LIFE *See* Country life; Farm life
RURAL MEDICAL CARE *See* Medical care, Rural
RURAL MIGRATION *See* Migration, Internal
RURAL PLANNING *See* Rural development
RURAL POOR *See* Poor
RURAL SCHOOLS *See* Rural education
RURAL TELEPHONE SERVICE
The country connection. T. Barrett. il *Newsweek* 114:47 S 18 '89
The great cellular giveaway [rural cellular licenses] H. Rudnitsky. il *Forbes* 144:40-1 D 25 '89
RURAL WOMEN
Doing home work down on the farm. O. Davidson. il *The Nation* 249:87-8+ Jl 17 '89

RURAL ZONING *See* Zoning
RUSCHA, EDWARD
about
Apocalypse now. K. Larson. il *New York* 22:66-7 My 29 '89
The last word [cover story] R. Rugoff. il pors *Art News* 88:120-5 D '89
RUSH (SORORITIES) *See* College sororities—Recruiting
RUSHDIE, SALMAN
The book burning. il *The New York Review of Books* 36:26 Mr 2 '89
A clash of faiths. il *Maclean's* 102:24 F 27 '89
about
Prophet of a new postmodernism: the greater challenge of Salman Rushdie. M. Edmundson. il *Harper's* 279:62-6+ D '89
Satanic verses case
The Ayatollah, the novelist, and the West [S. Rushdie affair; cover story] D. Pipes. *Commentary* 87:9-17 Je '89
Beat the devil. A. Cockburn. *The Nation* 248:366-7 Mr 20 '89
The book burning. S. Rushdie. il *The New York Review of Books* 36:26 Mr 2 '89
Book world reacts to Khomeini's threats [special section; with editorial comment by John F. Baker] *Publishers Weekly* 235:22, 26-8+ Mr 3 '89
Book world unites to fight threats to Rushdie and free speech [special section] *Publishers Weekly* 235:12+ Mr 10 '89
Deadly defiance [Khomeini's death threat] A. Phillips. il por *Maclean's* 102:18-19 Mr 6 '89
Diagnosis: a severe case of the wobblies [interview with J. Clark] A. Fotheringham. il *Maclean's* 102:56 Mr 27 '89
Ducking the Rushdie challenge [Canadian reaction] A. Fotheringham. il *Maclean's* 102:64 Mr 6 '89
Embroiled Salman. M. Peretz. *The New Republic* 200:50 Mr 20 '89
Fiction's embattled infidel [cover story] G. Marzorati. il pors *The New York Times Magazine* p24-7+ Ja 29 '89
Hunted by an angry faith [death threat against novelist by R. Khomeini; cover story] W. E. Smith. il pors *Time* 133:28-33 F 27 '89
In search of the middle ground [Muslim protest of book occasions thoughts on the need for self-imposed censorship] J. Leo. il *U.S. News & World Report* 106:30 Mr 6 '89
Iran's threats against author [statement, March 8, 1989] A. P. Adams, Jr. *Department of State Bulletin* 89:78-80 My '89
'Islamic sanctities' and the West. *America* 160:235 Mr 18 '89
Islamic wasteland. B. Crozier. il *National Review* 41:17 Mr 24 '89
Khomeini strikes back. J. Bierman. il pors *Maclean's* 102:25 Ap 10 '89
Killing for God. K. Kolenda. il *The Humanist* 49:47 My/Je '89
A life in hiding. A. Phillips. il pors *Maclean's* 102:30 Ag 21 '89
McGraw-Hill and Wiley quit Iran Fair but decry book boycotts. C. Reid. *Publishers Weekly* 235:104 My 12 '89
Minority report. C. Hitchens. *The Nation* 248:332 Mr 13 '89
Murder in the mosque [A. Al Ahdal murdered in Brussels] *Newsweek* 113:41 Ap 10 '89
The new Satans [Western reaction to R. Khomeini's death threat against novelist] W. E. Smith. il por *Time* 133:36-8 Mr 6 '89
Notes and comment. *The New Yorker* 65:27 Mr 6 '89
Offense and counter-offense. E. D. Mallon. il *America* 160:327-9 Ap 8 '89
Offensive defenders: Rushdie's rights & wrongs. J. Garvey. il *Commonweal* 116:166-8 Mr 24 '89
On blasphemy: advice for the Ayatollah. R. Goetz. *The Christian Century* 106:253-5 Mr 8 '89
On protecting the honor of the Koran. W. F. Buckley. *National Review* 41:62-3 Ap 7 '89
Our own ayatollahs. E. Knoll. *The Progressive* 53:4 Ap '89
The power of the printed word. D. O. Relin. il por *Scholastic Update (Teachers' edition)* 121:26 Mr 10 '89
Prosaic justice all around. P. Iyer. il *Time* 133:84 Mr 6 '89
Religious fanatics and censorship. J. R. Joelson. il *The Humanist* 49:33 My/Je '89
The Rushdiad. M. Decter. *Commentary* 87:18-23 Je '89
The Rushdie affair [discussion of June 1989 article, The Ayatollah, the novelist, and the West] D. Pipes. *Commentary* 88:11-12+ O '89
A Rushdie backlash. *Newsweek* 113:47 Mr 20 '89
The Rushdie crisis: a report from the front lines. M. J. O'Brien. il *Publishers Weekly* 236:45-8 S 29 '89
Rushdie furor highlights the nature of Islamic faith [interview with S. Johnson] il pors *Christianity Today* 33:38-9 Ap 7 '89
A Rushdie paperback? J. F. Baker. *Publishers Weekly* 236:6 O 13 '89
The Rushdie riddle. L. C. Pogrebin. il *Ms.* 18:28 Jl/Ag '89

RUSHDIE, SALMAN—Satanic verses case—*cont.*
Rushdie versus the sword of Islam. F. Edwords. il por *The Humanist* 49:5-6+ My/Je '89
The Rushdie watch [special section] il *Publishers Weekly* 235:12-14 Mr 17 '89
Rushdie's moral hegira. L. O. Sanneh. *The Christian Century* 106:622-6 Je 21-28 '89
Sacred truth, novelistic truths. C. Fuentes. *Harper's* 278:17-18 My '89
Salman Rushdie. por *People Weekly* 32:93 D 25 '89-Ja 1 '90
Salman Rushdie: a collage of comment [special section; with introd. by Nathan Gardels] il *New Perspectives Quarterly* 6:48-55 Spr '89
The 'Satanic' furor [cover story; special section; with editorial comment by Kevin Doyle] il pors *Maclean's* 102:2, 16-22+ F 27 '89
A 'Satanic' fury [Khomeini orders murder of novelist; cover story] R. Watson. il pors *Newsweek* 113:34-6+ F 27 '89
'The satanic verses'. il *World Press Review* 36:8-9 Ap '89
The satanic verses and beyond. D. A. Kerr. *The Christian Century* 106:354-8 Ap 5 '89
Secular sermon. H. Hertzberg. *The New Republic* 200:4+ Mr 20 '89
Security [measures taken at American Booksellers Association convention in wake of Rushdie death threat] M. J. O'Brien. il *Publishers Weekly* 235:33-4 Je 30 '89
Senate unit hears testimony on censorship. H. Fields. *Publishers Weekly* 235:10 Mr 24 '89
Separating the man from the cause. B. Amiel. il *Maclean's* 102:9 Mr 13 '89
'Shame' [Britain's slow response to threats against novelist] G. Black. *The Nation* 248:328-9 Mr 13 '89
A shattered deal [release of British hostages in Beirut jeopardized] il *Newsweek* 113:5 Mr 13 '89
The sins of Salman. M. Walzer. *The New Republic* 200:13-15 Ap 10 '89
Two cheers for blasphemy. *The New Republic* 200:7-9 Mr 13 '89
U.K. publishers vote Rushdie support, reject Teheran boycott. V. Menkes. *Publishers Weekly* 235:104 My 12 '89
Unrighteous indignation. T. C. Muck. il *Christianity Today* 33:14 Ap 7 '89
War of the words. *Commonweal* 116:131-2 Mr 10 '89
The West gets tough with Iran—sort of. R. Watson. il *Newsweek* 113:32-3 Mr 6 '89
Why the Ayatollah is whipping up a new wave of fanaticism. S. Carter and others. il *Business Week* p47 Mr 6 '89
Words for Salman Rushdie. il *The New York Times Book Review* 94:1+ Mr 12 '89
Writer Salman Rushdie's life on the run leaves his marriage to Marianne Wiggins on the rocks. il pors *People Weekly* 32:60 S 11 '89
Zealots with fear in their eyes [Muslim protest against book] R. Rosenblatt. il por *U.S. News & World Report* 106:8-11 F 27 '89

Anecdotes, facetiae, satire, etc.
A time to stand. J. Queenan. il *The American Spectator* 22:36 My '89
Write in plain sight. R. Cohen. *The Nation* 248:528-9 Ap 17 '89

Drama
'Iranian nights': but will it play in Teheran? il *Newsweek* 113:43 My 1 '89

RUSHER, WILLIAM A., 1923-
Now it can be told. il pors *National Review* 41:36-7+ Ja 27 '89
about
A toast to Bill Rusher [address, December 9, 1988] W. F. Buckley. *National Review* 41:19-20 Ja 27 '89

RUSHIN, STEVE
about
From the publisher. D. J. Barr. il por *Sports Illustrated* 71:4 N 6 '89

RUSHING RECORDS (FOOTBALL) *See* Football records
RUSHTON, J. PHILIPPE
about
Race and behavior. R. Dolphin. il por *Maclean's* 102:44 F 13 '89

RUSKIN, UZI
about
The incredible shrinking company. A. A. Lappen. il *Forbes* 144:207+ D 11 '89

RUSPOLI, MARIA PIA
about
The Ruspoli legacy in Italy. C. Aillaud. il pors *Architectural Digest* 46:156-64+ Jl '89

RUSPOLI, SFORZA
about
The Ruspoli legacy in Italy. C. Aillaud. il pors *Architectural Digest* 46:156-64+ Jl '89

RUSS BERRIE & CO., INC.
Bullish on Berrie. T. Jaffe. *Forbes* 143:173 Mr 6 '89
RUSSELL, BEVERLY A.
Mine/all mine [poem] *Essence* 19:152 F '89

RUSSELL, CHUCK
about
The blob [film] Reviews
   Video il 12:86+ Ja '89. M. Pierson
RUSSELL, CRISTINE
Forewarned is fairly warned. il *Sierra* 74:36-8+ N/D '89
RUSSELL, DICK
Earth last! *The Nation* 249:77 Jl 17 '89
'We are all losing the war'. il *The Nation* 248:403-8 Mr 27 '89
RUSSELL, EMILY
Why don't you? [story] il *Gentlemen's Quarterly* 59:345-6+ S '89
RUSSELL, FRANCIA
about
Seattle strikes gold: Pacific Northwest Ballet's grand pas de deux. M. Hunt. il pors *Dance Magazine* 63:36-41 Mr '89
RUSSELL, FRANCIS, 1910-1989
about
Obituary
   National Review 41:16-17 Ap 21 '89. W. F. Buckley
RUSSELL, GEORGE
The Japanese challenge. *Commentary* 88:70-2 S '89
RUSSELL, HAROLD
about
Special pursuits: Oscar-winner Harold Russell. S. C. Soman. il por *Home Office Computing* 7:16 D '89
RUSSELL, HELEN ROSS
City backyard. il *The Conservationist* 43:40-5 Mr/Ap '89
RUSSELL, HENRY NORRIS, 1877-1957
about
Henry Norris Russell. D. H. DeVorkin. bibl il por *Scientific American* 260:126-33 My '89
RUSSELL, HERMAN J.
about
Herman J. Russell named to U.S. Chamber board. por *Jet* 76:6 Je 5 '89
RUSSELL, HILARY
The carpenter's wage [poem] *Country Journal* 16:48 S/O '89
Living too close to the road [poem] *Country Journal* 16:59 Jl/Ag '89
RUSSELL, JANICE VALLS- *See* Valls-Russell, Janice
RUSSELL, JOHN, 1919-
Art. il *The New York Times Book Review* 94:9+ D 3 '89
Art books. il *The New York Times Book Review* 94:13+ Je 11 '89
An educated palette. il pors *House & Garden* 161:136-9+ Je '89
RUSSELL, KEN, 1927-
about
The rainbow [film] Reviews
   America 161:40+ Jl 15-22 '89. R. A. Blake
   American Film il 14:11-12 My '89. J. Greenberg
   Commonweal 116:337-8 Je 2 '89. T. O'Brien
   Film Comment 25:2+ My/Je '89. G. Fuller
   Gentlemen's Quarterly il 59:117-19 Je '89. K. Turan
   The New Republic 200:28 My 15 '89. S. Kauffmann
   New York 22:65 My 29 '89. D. Denby
   The New Yorker 65:102-3 My 29 '89. P. Kael
   Newsweek il 113:70 My 8 '89. J. Kroll
   People Weekly il 31:15-16 Je 26 '89. R. Novak
   Rolling Stone il p36 Je 1 '89
   Time il 133:75 My 15 '89. R. Schickel
RUSSELL, LOUISE B.
Some of the tough decisions required by a national health plan. bibl f il *Science* 246:892-6 N 17 '89
RUSSELL, NICHOLAS
Well-groomed or well-bred? il *History Today* 39:10-12 Ja '89
RUSSELL, PAUL
about
Paul Russell leads ballet in Idaho. S. English. il *Dance Magazine* 63:18 O '89
RUSSELL, THERESA
about
The passion of Theresa [cover story] J. Ressner. il pors *American Film* 14:34-7+ Ap '89
RUSSELL, WILLY
about
Shirley Valentine [drama] Reviews
   America 160:272 Mr 25 '89. G. G. Seibert
   The Nation 248:462 Ap 3 '89. T. M. Disch
   The New Republic 200:26 My 29 '89. R. Brustein
   New York il 22:99 Mr 6 '89. J. Simon
   The New Yorker 65:66 F 27 '89. E. Oliver
   Time il 133:80 F 27 '89. W. A. Henry
RUSSETT, BRUCE
No sticks, no aspirins. *Commonweal* 116:336-7 Je 2 '89 (jt. auth) See Mayhew, David R., and Russett, Bruce
RUSSIA *See* Soviet Union
THE RUSSIA HOUSE [film] *See* Motion picture reviews—Single works
RUSSIAN AIRSHIPS *See* Airships, Russian
RUSSIAN-AMERICAN COMPANY
Russia's American adventure. L. Black. il map *Natural History* p46-57 D '89

RUSSIAN ART *See* Art, Russian
RUSSIAN ARTIFICIAL SATELLITES *See* Artificial satellites, Russian
RUSSIAN ARTISTS *See* Artists, Russian
RUSSIAN ASTRONAUTS *See* Astronauts
RUSSIAN ATHLETES *See* Athletes
RUSSIAN AUTHORS *See* Authors, Russian
RUSSIAN COOKING *See* Cooking, Russian
RUSSIAN DEFECTORS *See* Defectors
RUSSIAN DISSENTERS *See* Dissenters
RUSSIAN EXILES *See* Exiles
RUSSIAN FASHION DESIGNERS *See* Fashion designers
RUSSIAN HELICOPTERS *See* Helicopters
RUSSIAN HOUSE DECORATION *See* House decoration, Russian
RUSSIAN HUMOR *See* Humor, Russian
RUSSIAN JEWS *See* Jews—Soviet Union
RUSSIAN LANGUAGE
  See also
  American literature—Translations into Russian
War of the words [controversy over Russian as official language of Moldavia] R. Knight. *U.S. News & World Report* 107:32 Jl 31 '89
RUSSIAN LITERATURE
  See also
  Booksellers and bookselling—Russian literature
    Bibliography
The real thing. H. Gifford. il *The New York Review of Books* 36:3-4+ Je 1 '89
    Translations into English
Why you'll never have fun in Russian [translation as a form of *glasnost*] R. Lourie and A. Mikhalev. *The New York Times Book Review* 94:1+ Je 18 '89
RUSSIAN MILITARY ASSISTANCE *See* Military assistance, Russian
RUSSIAN NUCLEAR SUBMARINES *See* Nuclear submarines, Russian
RUSSIAN ORTHODOX CHURCH *See* Orthodox Eastern Church, Russian
RUSSIAN PAINTING *See* Painting, Russian
RUSSIAN PHOTOGRAPHERS *See* Photographers, Russian
RUSSIAN POETRY
  See also
  Epic poetry, Russian
Poetry, freedom and revolution [influence of the French Revolution] S. S. Averintsev. il *The Unesco Courier* 42:36-9 Je '89
RUSSIAN POTTERY *See* Pottery, Russian
RUSSIAN REFUGEES *See* Refugees, Russian
RUSSIAN RESEARCH CENTER *See* Harvard University. Russian Research Center
RUSSIAN REVOLUTION *See* Soviet Union—History—Revolution, 1917-1921
RUSSIAN RIVER (CALIF.) IN ART
Mary Robertson. K. Turcotte. il por *American Artist* 53:52-7 My '89
RUSSIAN SCIENTISTS *See* Scientists, Russian
RUSSIAN SHUTTLE MISSIONS *See* Space flight—Shuttle missions, Russian
RUSSIAN SPACE STATIONS *See* Space stations, Russian
RUSSIAN SPACE VEHICLES *See* Space vehicles, Russian
RUSSIAN SPACEPLANE *See* Spaceplane, Russian
RUSSIAN STUDENTS IN THE UNITED STATES *See* Foreign students—United States
RUSSIAN STUDIES *See* Soviet studies
RUSSIAN THISTLE *See* Tumbleweeds
RUSSIAN TURKISH BATHS (NEW YORK, N.Y.) *See* Public baths
RUSSIANS
Look who's feeling picked on [Russians who are in the minority in the ethnic republics] G. J. Church. il *Time* 134:36-7 S 25 '89
    Afghanistan
  See also
  Afghanistan—Russian invasion, 1979-1989
    Alaska
      History
Russia's American adventure. L. Black. il map *Natural History* p46-57 D '89
    Canada
A Red-letter day [Soviet Union's S. Priakin makes NHL debut with Calgary] C. Cotton. il por *Sports Illustrated* 70:38-9 Ap 10 '89
    Foreign countries
Unfit for the occasion [showing Russians how to dress when conducting foreign business] C. Bogert. il *Newsweek* 114:71 D 25 '89
    Israel
Free at last [Soviet Jew A. Stolar] il por *Newsweek* 113:6 Mr 27 '89
    North America
The honeymooners [Soviet players in National Hockey League; cover story] J. Greenberg. il *Sports Illustrated* 71:44-8+ O 9 '89
Soviet invasion [National Hockey League] J. Howse. il *Maclean's* 102:46-7 O 9 '89

Soviet pretenders to Gretzky's throne [Russian players in National Hockey League] il por *U.S. News & World Report* 107:19 O 30 '89
    United States
After 58 years in Moscow, prodigal son Abe Stolar comes back to his kind of town [Soviet Jew visits Chicago] W. Plummer. il pors *People Weekly* 32:65-6 Jl 24 '89
A brave Soviet deputy speaks up for a forgotten minority [I. Zaslavskiy tours U.S.] C. Phillips. il pors *People Weekly* 32:109-10 O 9 '89
Can you say "apple pie" in Russian? [Soviet women visit America] E. Sloan-Bubrick. il *McCall's* 116:10 Jl '89
Changing times: Sakharov in the US on human rights and arms control. I. Goodwin. il *Physics Today* 42:91-5 F '89
Flight no. 30 carries the goodies [Soviet visitors returning from the U.S.] *Time* 133:81 Ap 10 '89
From Russia with love [reunion of I. Yershov and exiled son-in-law E. D. Lozansky] il pors *U.S. News & World Report* 107:16 O 2 '89
Gateway to a new detente [architect Y. Platonov's visit to the U.S.] M. F. Schmertz. *Architectural Record* 177:9 Je '89
Here she comes, Miss U.S.S.R.! And Yulia Sukhanova even wins a fight to visit the decadent West. H. Shapiro. il pors *People Weekly* 32:42-3 S 25 '89
If Columbus had a bike [Soviet cycling team's U.S. visit] V. Senatorov. il *Bicycling* 30:164-5 Ap '89
"In a neutral zone" [Soviet artists V. Mironenko, A. Roiter and K. Zvezdochetov visit the U.S.] S. Hochfield. il pors *Art News* 88:47-8 D '89
Red Army vet Vladimir Kuts joins up with his GI pals 44 years after battling the Nazis together. W. Plummer. il por *People Weekly* 32:86-8 Ag 21 '89
The Russians are here [women runners in New Orleans for the Crescent City Classic] J. Brant. il *Runner's World* 24:78-84 O '89
Sergey Kuryokhin: the Russian Martian arrives [improvising pianist] H. Mandel. il pors *Down Beat* 56:26-8 Ap '89
A Soviet hoopster in the Promised Land [S. Marciulionis signs with the NBA] P. De Jonge. il pors *The New York Times Magazine* p64+ N 5 '89
They're here [Soviet athletes] R. Harvey. il *Sport (New York, N.Y.)* 80:68-72 D '89
The waiting has finally ended [Russian-Jewish mother and daughter reunited in America] N. Zundelevich. il *The New York Times Magazine* p10+ Ja 1 '89
'We need yuppies in Moscow' [Soviet managers attend business course in U.S.] C. Leinster. il *Fortune* 120:153+ N 20 '89
When American vets meet Soviet vets [Vietnam and Afghanistan veterans] C. Thibaud. *World Press Review* 36:70 S '89
    Economic conditions
Undertow: LA copes with the flood of Soviet émigrés. E. Schrader. *The New Republic* 201:11-12 D 4 '89
RUSSO, AARON
    about
Rude awakening [film] Reviews
  Newsweek il 114:68 S 4 '89. D. Ansen
RUSSO, JANET
    about
Another Nantucket. G. Harrell. il pors *House & Garden* 161:124-31 Ap '89
RUST, ROBERT C.
  (jt. auth) See Turgeon, Kitty, and Rust, Robert C.
RUST *See* Corrosion and anticorrosives
RUST (AUTOMOBILES) *See* Automobiles—Corrosion and anticorrosives
RUSTLERS, CACTUS *See* Cactus—Theft
RUSTLERS, CATTLE *See* Cattle—Theft
A RUSTLING OF LEAVES: INSIDE THE PHILIPPINE REVOLUTION [film] See Motion picture reviews—Single works
RUSTY STAUB'S ON 5TH (NEW YORK, N.Y.: RESTAURANT) *See* New York (N.Y.)—Restaurants, nightclubs, bars, etc.
RUSZ, JOE
About the sport. See issues of Road & Track
RUTA, SUZANNE
Nouveau hip. il *Utne Reader* p56-7 S/O '89
RUTA MAYA *See* La Ruta Maya
RUTAN, BURT
    about
21st century pyramid [cover story] J. L. Schefter. il por *Popular Science* 235:65-9 N '89
Burt Rutan: a profile. P. Garrison. il pors *Flying* 116:48-50+ F '89
Wanted: business as unusual. W. H. Ganoe. *Ad Astra* 1:47 N '89
RUTAN AIRCRAFT FACTORY
Lawsuit against Rutans could test liability of designers, test pilots [filed by Aviation Composites Co.] *Aviation Week & Space Technology* 130:61 Ja 23 '89
RUTGERS UNIVERSITY
Rutgers builds particle theory, surface science and computation. W. Sweet. *Physics Today* 42:62-3 Je '89

RUTH, BABE, 1895-1948

about

Papa, Satchmo, and the Babe. G. C. Ward. il *American Heritage* 40:14+ My/Je '89

Anecdotes, facetiae, satire, etc.

It's Back to the Bambino [back as free agent] L. Montville. il por *Sports Illustrated* 71:100 D 18 '89

RUTH, GEORGE HERMAN *See* Ruth, Babe, 1895-1948

RUTH, PETER, AND OTHERS

Primary structure of the β subunit of the DHP-sensitive calcium channel from skeletal muscle. bibl f il *Science* 245:1115-18 S 8 '89

RUTHERFORD, JACK DOWD

Ten ways to take the pain out of cost cutting. il *Working Woman* 14:20+ F '89

RUTHERFORD, MIKE

about

An unlikely hit for Mike Rutherford. M. Azerrad. il por *Rolling Stone* p30 Ap 20 '89

RUTHERFORD (CALIF.)

Architecture

Artists' assemblage [home of Helen Berggruen and Mandy Wallace] M. Filler. il *House & Garden* 161:198-205 S '89

Back to basics [Berggruen House] D. Dietsch. il *Architectural Record* 177:50-5 mid-Ap '89

RUTHVEN, MALISE

Gardens: politics of Little Sparta: Ian Hamilton Finlay's statements in stone. il por *Architectural Digest* 46:104-11+ Jl '89

Mlinaric: now and then. il pors *House & Garden* 161:164-73 Mr '89

Rodchenko in Moscow: miraculous survival of the constructivist's historic studio. il pors *Architectural Digest* 46:53+ O '89

RUTIGLIANO, SAM, 1932-

about

The last temptation of price. J. D. Miller. il *Sport (New York, N.Y.)* 80:12 Jl '89

RUTLEDGE, JOHN

about

The sky is rising? P. Brimelow. il pors *Forbes* 144:156+ N 13 '89

RUTTER, CAROL

Colorific [interview with V. Storaro] il por *Film Comment* 25:46-8+ S/O '89

RUTTER, PETER

Sex in the forbidden zone [excerpt] il pors *Psychology Today* 23:34-8+ O '89

RVS *See* Recreational vehicles

RWANDA

See also

Wildlife conservation—Rwanda

RYAN, ALAN

Scholar slip. *The New Republic* 201:14-16 D 4 '89

RYAN, ANNE, 1889-1954

about

Material witness. H. Cotter. bibl f il *Art in America* 77:176-83+ N '89

RYAN, BOB

Boston. il *Sport (New York, N.Y.)* 80:54-8 Jl '89

NBA playoffs: big wins on the way to the title. il *Sports Illustrated* 70:5+ Ap 24 '89

The Sport 1989-90 NBA preview [cover story] il *Sport (New York, N.Y.)* 80:52-6+ N '89

The Sport all-time NBA all-star team. il *Sport (New York, N.Y.)* 80:52-5 Mr '89

RYAN, BUDDY

about

Big Buddy is watching. M. Lupica. il *Esquire* 112:49-50 Ag '89

RYAN, CHEYNEY

about

Actor's son Cheyney Ryan brings migrant workers a theater that could save their lives. A. Chambers. il pors *People Weekly* 32:175-6 D 4 '89

RYAN, DENNIS

about

Nast and other nasties. C. Brown. il por *Forbes* 144:216+ S 18 '89

RYAN, HEATHER KEITH- *See* Keith-Ryan, Heather

RYAN, JAMES T.

What would our children think of us? il *Commonweal* 116:115-17 F 24 '89

RYAN, JEFF

'80s boxing. il *Sport (New York, N.Y.)* 80:76-7 O '89

RYAN, MEG

about

Actress Meg Ryan is on the fast track to movie stardom. il pors *Vogue* 179:46+ Jl '89

Men, women, sex, love and marriage—from the mouths of Billy Crystal and Meg Ryan [interview] D. DeNicolo. il pors *Glamour* 87:205 S '89

Something in the way Meg moves . . . L. Morice. il pors *Mademoiselle* 95:164-5 Jl '89

RYAN, MICHAEL

A strange new place called home. il pors *Life* 12:34-9 N '89

RYAN, MICHAEL

Milk the mouse [poem] *The Nation* 249:99 Jl 17 '89

RYAN, NOLAN

about

The care and feeding of baseball's greatest arm. T. Brewster. il por *Life* 12:86-7 My '89

K. il pors *Sports Illustrated* 71:30-2 Ag 28 '89

Rangers risin' [cover story] W. Nack. il pors *Sports Illustrated* 70:16-23 My 1 '89

Throwing old gracefully. R. Givens. il por *Newsweek* 114:65 Ag 28 '89

RYAN, PATRICK H.

Dialogue [poem] *America* 161:60 Jl 29-Ag 5 '89

RYAN, PATRICK J.

The Word. See issues of America beginning November 21, 1987

RYAN, RICHARD

Animal activists antagonize allies. il *Utne Reader* p50-2 S/O '89

RYAN, ROB

Agatha's murder island. il *Gentlemen's Quarterly* 59:93+ N '89

A birthday at kilometer zero. il por *Gentlemen's Quarterly* 59:49+ N '89

The man who put the grouch into Groucho's. il por *Gentlemen's Quarterly* 59:31+ Ja '89

Return of the Jaguar. il *Gentlemen's Quarterly* 59:92+ O '89

RYAN, TONY

about

A sky-high bet on the plane-leasing business. M. Maremont. il por *Business Week* p120 My 1 '89

RYAN, WILL

Just a bullhead. il *The Conservationist* 44:34-7 Jl/Ag '89

RYAN, WILLIAM F.

Europe '92 [address, April 19, 1989] *Vital Speeches of the Day* 55:492-4 Je 1 '89

THE RYAN WHITE STORY [television program] *See* Television program reviews—Single works

RYANAIR (FIRM)

Dublin trims international, domestic competition between Irish carriers. J. Ott. *Aviation Week & Space Technology* 131:107-8 O 2 '89

Ryanair seeks to strengthen position during reprieve from competition. J. Ott. il map *Aviation Week & Space Technology* 131:58-9 N 6 '89

RYAZANOV, ELDAR

about

A forgotten tune for the flute [film] Reviews *Commonweal* 116:119 F 24 '89. T. O'Brien

RYBACK, TIMOTHY W.

Ausländer raus! *The Nation* 248:590 My 1 '89

Red suede shoes. *The New Republic* 200:13-14 Ja 9-16 '89

RYBCZYNSKI, WITOLD

about

The house that dreams are made of [interview] A. P. Sanoff. il por *U.S. News & World Report* 107:55 Jl 3 '89

RYCKMANS, PIERRE *See* Leys, Simon

RYDELL, CHRIS

about

Bully! for Chris Rydell. S. Pocharski. por *Mademoiselle* 95:56 Je '89

RYDEN, HOPE

The world of Lily Pond [condensation] il *Reader's Digest* 135:189-92+ Ag '89

RYDER, ALBERT PINKHAM, 1847-1917

about

The Ryder cover-up. W. I. Homer. il por *Art News* 88:158-61 O '89

RYDER, JIM

about

What, me quit? D. Wechsler. il pors *Forbes* 143:162+ Ap 3 '89

RYDER, WINONA

about

Catch a rising star. pors *'Teen* 33:67 Ag '89

Hot actress. D. Handelman. il pors *Rolling Stone* p69-70+ My 18 '89

Vamp. il por *Life* 12:106-7 Je '89

View. S. Mansfield. il pors *Vogue* 179:72+ Je '89

Whole lotta shakin' goin' on. D. Ansen. il por *Newsweek* 114:72 Jl 10 '89

RYDER SYSTEM, INC.

Ryder aviation services profits from changes in airline industry. *Aviation Week & Space Technology* 130:56 Ap 17 '89

Ryder expands aviation business with Braniff, Trump contracts. *Aviation Week & Space Technology* 131:52 Jl 3 '89

Suddenly, Ryder's engine is sputtering. P. Engardio. il *Business Week* p56 Je 19 '89

Turning around. T. Jaffe. *Forbes* 143:236 Ap 17 '89

RYKODISC INC.

The wooing of David Bowie. J. Guterman. *Rolling Stone* p28 My 18 '89

RYKWERT, JOSEPH, 1926-

Pioneering the modern movement in Palestine. il por *Architectural Digest* 46:82+ O '89

RYLAND, ROBIN SMITH- *See* Smith-Ryland, Robin
RYLL, DEBRA
Magma force. il *Omni (New York, N.Y.)* 11:66-8+ Ag '89
RYMAN, ROBERT, 1930-
about
Red desert & Arctic dreams. D. B. Kuspit. il *Art in America* 77:120-5 Mr '89
RYMAN AUDITORIUM (NASHVILLE, TENN.)
The Opry's first real home. il *Southern Living* 24:24+ My '89
RYN, CLAES G., 1943-
The democracy boosters. *National Review* 41:30-2+ Mr 24 '89
Hook on democracy [discussion of March 24, 1989 article, The democracy boosters] *National Review* 41:4+ Je 2 '89
RYZHKOV, NIKOLAI, 1929-
about
"Let your readers be reassured there will be no military coup" [interview; with reply by Paul Klebnikov] P. Dragadze. il por *Forbes* 144:82+ O 16 '89
A talk with Nikolai Ryzkhov, economic czar. P. Galuszka. por *Business Week* p62-3 Je 5 '89
RZHEVSKY, NICHOLAS, 1943-
Soviet theater. *The Nation* 249:180-1 Ag 7-14 '89

S

S & B REPORT
It's a jungle out there, so savvy buyers let Elysa Lazar guide them on their shopping safaris. S. Carswell. il por *People Weekly* 32:105-6 O 30 '89
S CORPORATIONS
When an S corp may spell tax relief. C. Yang. il *Business Week* p160 My 15 '89
S&P COMPANY
One last call for fading beer brands [launches antitrust suit against Adolph Coors Co.'s acquisition of Stroh Brewery] L. Armstrong. il *Business Week* p68 O 16 '89
SA, KHUN *See* Khun Sa
SAAB (AUTOMOBILE) *See* Automobiles, Foreign
SAAB-SCANIA AB
Allison engine chosen for Saab 2000; Sweden certifies Saab 340B transport. il *Aviation Week & Space Technology* 131:29 Jl 17 '89
AMR Eagle boosts Saab-Scania with firm order for 50 SF340Bs. C. Fotos. il *Aviation Week & Space Technology* 130:110-11 My 29 '89
A bid for upward mobility [Ford bids on Jaguar and Saab] A. Gabor. il *U.S. News & World Report* 107:46 O 2 '89
Ford is kicking Saab's tires. R. A. Melcher. il *Business Week* p52 S 18 '89
Northwest commuter boosts Saab sales with orders for 340B, 2000 aircraft [Express Airlines 1] C. A. Shifrin. il *Aviation Week & Space Technology* 131:62 N 6 '89
Saab completes definition work, selects contractors for Saab 2000 [regional turboprop transport] C. A. Shifrin. il *Aviation Week & Space Technology* 131:72-3 O 23 '89
Saab story [Saab 2000] il *Flying* 116:13 Mr '89
SAAB-SCANIA OF AMERICA, INC.
Will power [W. South, systems support manager] S. M. Williams. il por *Black Enterprise* 20:71-2 N '89
SAATCHI, DORIS
Fair city. il *House & Garden* 161:74+ My '89
Precious metals. il por *House & Garden* 161:146-51+ Je '89
SAATCHI & SAATCHI COMPANY PLC
Brits buy up the ad business [cover story] R. Rothenberg. il por *The New York Times Magazine* p14-19+ Jl 2 '89
An eroding empire. A. Walmsley. il *Maclean's* 102:30 Ap 10 '89
Gideon Gartner wants his baby back. T. Vogel. il por *Business Week* p108+ D 4 '89
Saatchi & Saatchi: the empire trembles. R. A. Melcher. *Business Week* p38-9 Ap 3 '89
Saatchi beats a retreat back to Mad Ave. [wants out of consulting] W. Konrad and R. A. Melcher. il *Business Week* p70-1 Jl 10 '89
Saatchi says this change is for real [R. Louis-Dreyfus] R. A. Melcher. il por *Business Week* p50 O 30 '89
Sibling setbacks [R. Louis-Dreyfus hired as president] J. Castro. il *Time* 134:66-7 D 25 '89
SAAVEDRA, DANIEL ORTEGA *See* Ortega Saavedra, Daniel
SABAH (MALAYSIA)
See also
Headhunters—Sabah (Malaysia)
SABATINI, GABRIELA
about
Sabatini: a second look [cover story] S. Flink. il pors *World Tennis* 36:10-11 Ja '89
SABATO, LARRY
about
Should public officials' private lives matter? [interview] il *U.S. News & World Report* 107:23 S 11 '89

SABBATH
See also
Sunday
SABBATH LAW, JEWISH *See* Jewish law
SABBATICALS (BUSINESS) *See* Leaves of absence
SABCA *See* Belge de Constructions Aéronautiques SA
SABENA WORLD AIRLINES
Belgium will sell British Airways, KLM 20% stakes in new Sabena. *Aviation Week & Space Technology* 130:95 Je 26 '89
SABER SAWS *See* Saws and sawing
SABICU
Wood you believe? E. H. Gustafson. bibl f il *Antiques* 135:1102+ My '89
SABINE, ELIZABETH
about
Vocal coach Elizabeth Sabine, the heavy metal grandma, teaches speech and screech. S. Dougherty. il pors *People Weekly* 31:137-9 My 15 '89
SABIROV, A.
Missile check. *World Press Review* 36:40 Mr '89
SABLE ISLAND (N.S.)
Description and travel
The devil's work in an ark of sand. H. Thurston. il map *Audubon* 91:82-91 Mr '89
SABLON, JEAN LECLERC DU *See* Leclerc du Sablon, Jean
SABOL, STEVE
about
What would happen if . . . 20 of the best-ever NFL teams played a "Dream season"? S. Smith. il *Sports Illustrated* 71:159 S 11 '89
SABOURIN, SERGE
From the cold war to the drug war. *New Perspectives Quarterly* 6:63 Fall '89
SABRELINER CORPORATION
Sabreliner Corp. seeks partner to resume business jet production. E. H. Phillips. *Aviation Week & Space Technology* 130:27 Mr 27 '89
SAC *See* United States. Air Force. Strategic Air Command
SACCHARIN
See also
Denatonium saccharide
SACCHAROMYCES *See* Yeasts
SACERDOTI, DAVID, AND OTHERS
Treatment with tin prevents the development of hypertension in spontaneously hypertensive rats. bibl f il *Science* 243:388-90 Ja 20 '89
SACHETS
Light or heavy hearts . . . filled with sand or fragrance. il *Sunset (Central West edition)* 182:110 F '89
SACHS, AVIVA
Jane Fonda enters a new era. il pors *McCall's* 116:32-4+ S '89
Michael J. Fox: what's next? il pors *McCall's* 116:71+ Jl '89
Spunky Sally Field. il pors *McCall's* 117:10-13+ N '89
SACHS, FREDERICK
(jt. auth) See Yang, Xian-Cheng, and Sachs, Frederick
SACHS, HARVEY, 1946-
Fiddling in fascist Italy. il *Opera News* 53:28-30 Mr 4 '89
SACHS, JEFFREY D.
Lack of Solidarity [cover story] *The New Republic* 201:20-1 Ag 7-14 '89
Making the Brady plan work. bibl f il *Foreign Affairs* 68:87-104 Summ '89
Robbin' hoods [cover story] il *The New Republic* 200:19-20+ Mr 13 '89
about
The Harvard debt doctor's controversial cure. J. Greenwald. il por *Time* 134:66 N 6 '89
SACHS, WILLIAM L., 1947-
The Episcopal Synod: reinforcing boundaries. *The Christian Century* 106:710-11 Ag 2-9 '89
A second look at Japan's churches [discussion of November 2, 1988 article, The inertia of Japan's churches] *The Christian Century* 106:139-41 F 1-8 '89
Willimon's project: does it make sense? *The Christian Century* 106:412-14 Ap 19 '89
SACHS, WOLFGANG
The virtue of enoughness. il *New Perspectives Quarterly* 6:16-19 Spr '89
SACK, HAROLD
The bombé furniture of Boston and Salem, Massachusetts. bibl f il *Antiques* 135:1178-89 My '89
SACKLER (ARTHUR M.) GALLERY (WASHINGTON, D.C.) *See* Arthur M. Sackler Gallery (Washington, D.C.)
SACKS, DAVID
Manhattan country. il *House & Garden* 161:132-43 Ap '89
SACKS, GLENN
about
"This is like stealing". D. Akst. il *Forbes* 144:142+ N 13 '89
SACKS, OLIVER W.
about
Oliver Sacks journeys into the world of the deaf for title from California. por *Publishers Weekly* 235:28-9 My 26 '89

SACKS, OLIVER W.—about—*cont.*
A strange and marvelous culture. *U.S. News & World Report* 107:88 O 16 '89
SACKS, SUSAN RIEMER
(jt. auth) See Travers, Eva Foldes, and Sacks, Susan Riemer
SACKVILLE, JOHN FREDERICK See Dorset, John Frederick Sackville, 3rd Duke of, 1745-1799
SACRAMENTO (CALIF.)
Economic conditions
The gold rush by Sutter's Mill. L. Wright. il *Newsweek* 113:46-7 F 6 '89
Restaurants, nightclubs, bars, etc.
Spécialités de la maison:
Biba. C. Bates. il *Gourmet* 49:24+ My '89
SACRAMENTO RIVER (CALIF.)
See also
Sacramento-San Joaquin Delta (Calif.)
What's ahead for salmon? Let's look at two vital rivers, the Columbia and the Sacramento. il *Sunset (Central West edition)* 182:96-7 Ap '89
SACRAMENTO-SAN JOAQUIN DELTA (CALIF.)
Biking the Delta. il map *Sunset (Central West edition)* 182:18+ Mr '89
SACRAMENTS
See also
Baptism
Catholic Church—Eucharist
Lord's Supper
Penance
Barriers to the sacraments. J. M. Champlin. il *Commonweal* 116:559-61 O 20 '89
Who owns the sacraments? [cover story] B. Doyle. il *U.S. Catholic* 54:6-12 O '89
SACRED BOOKS
See also
Bible
Talmud
SACRED CONGREGATION FOR CATHOLIC EDUCATION See Catholic Church. Congregation for Catholic Education
SACRED CONGREGATION FOR THE DOCTRINE OF THE FAITH See Catholic Church. Congregation for the Doctrine of the Faith
SACRED MUSIC See Religious music
SACRED SPACE
An adventurer's Baedeker [sacred places located on public lands] J. A. Swan. *American Health* 8:54-5 N '89
Fierce landscapes and the indifference of God [cover story] B. C. Lane. *The Christian Century* 106:907-10 O 11 '89
Sacred places. H. W. Paige. il *America* 160:34-5 Ja 21 '89
Sacred places [vacationing in environments which affect the psyche] W. Gallagher. il *American Health* 8:44-6+ N '89
SACRIFICE
See also
Human sacrifice
SAD See Seasonal affective disorder
SADA, HUGO
Negotiating peace—at a price [interview with J. Pérez de Cuéllar] il por *World Press Review* 36:50 My '89
SADDLE HORSES See Horses
SADDLE SHOES See Footwear
SADDLES (BICYCLE SEATS) See Bicycles—Saddles
SADISM
See also
Sadomasochism
SADNESS
See also
Depression, Mental
SADOMASOCHISM
Out of bounds. J. Simmons. il *Ms.* 17:65-7 Ap '89
SAËNS, CAMILLE SAINT- See Saint-Saëns, Camille, 1835-1921
SAËNS, CHARLES CAMILLE SAINT- See Saint-Saëns, Camille, 1835-1921
SAFDIE, MOSHE, 1938-
about
'Bridge' building in Jerusalem. A. Rabinovich. il por *World Press Review* 36:73 S '89
SAFE See Save America's Future (Organization)
SAFETY, INDUSTRIAL See Occupational health and safety
SAFETY BELTS
See also
Automobiles—Safety belts
SAFETY DEVICES AND MEASURES See Accidents—Prevention
SAFETY EDUCATION
See also
Automobile driving—Study and teaching
Aviation—Safety devices and measures
Boats and boating—Safety devices and measures
Cycling
Alone at home: 10 safety tips for working parents & their kids [excerpt] A. Banks. *Redbook* 173:110+ O '89
Child sexual abuse prevention programs: what makes them effective in protecting children? S. Kraizer and others. bibl f *Children Today* 18:23-7 S/O '89
Modern-day monsters [pretend games may allow children to respond appropriately to real-life violence] J. C. Compton. il *Psychology Today* 23:30-1 Mr '89

Safety training falls short [farm safety] il *Successful Farming* 87:18L-18M mid-F '89
SAFETY GOGGLES See Goggles
SAFETY HELMETS See Helmets
SAFETY-KLEEN CORP.
Safety-Kleen bets on recycling. G. G. Marcial. *Business Week* p120 D 18 '89
SAFETY LAWS AND REGULATIONS
See also
Occupational health and safety—Laws and regulations
Risk, safety and capitalism [special section] bibl *Society* 27:4-31 N/D '89
SAFETY SEATS (AUTOMOBILES) See Automobiles—Safety devices and measures
SAFEWAY STORES, INC.
How Safeway coped with the quake [Bay Area] G. Hector. il map *Fortune* 120:101-2+ N 20 '89
Safeway: it's confounding critics. R. D. Hof. il por *Business Week* p141 Ap 24 '89
SAFFO, PAUL
Desktop publishing. See issues of Personal Computing beginning May 1987 through December 1988
Future tense. See issues of Personal Computing beginning April 1989
SAFFRON
For a yellow color. A. Arndt. il por *Americana* 17:34-7 S/O '89
The fruits of Spanish labor. R. Sokolov. il *Natural History* p82+ Mr '89
SAFFRON BOXES
Collectors and collecting
Just for pretty: Joseph Lehn's boxes. il *Americana* 17:36 S/O '89
SAFILO SPA
An export focus at Italy's farsighted frame company. J. Rossant. il por *Business Week* p114 My 22 '89
SAFINA, CARL
Can overboard! il *Sea Frontiers* 35:384 N/D '89
SAFIRE, WILLIAM
On language. See issues of The New York Times Magazine
Stamp out Congress's "franking" privilege. *Reader's Digest* 135:131-2 O '89
SAFRA, EDMOND J.
about
American Express slings mud—and gets splattered. W. Glasgall and J. Meehan. il por *Business Week* p102+ Ag 14 '89
Bank shot: Edmond Safra turns the tables on American Express. J. Taylor. il pors *New York* 22:42-7 S 18 '89
SAFRAN, CLAIRE
Kids who beat the odds. il *Reader's Digest* 134:197-8+ Mr '89
SAFRANEK, DOUG
about
Douglas Safranek. L. S. Hurwitz. il *American Artist* 53:36-7 Ag '89
SAFRANSKY, SY
Breathing space. il por *Organic Gardening* 36:83-4 O '89
SAG HARBOR (N.Y.)
Historic houses, sites, etc.
The spirit of '76: saving a pre-Revolutionary house in Sag Harbor [J. and R. K. Lewis] R. Fizdale and A. Gold. il por *Architectural Digest* 46:194-9+ Je '89
The Sultans of Sag Harbor [home of D. K. Sultan] D. Kazanjian. il por *House & Garden* 161:192-7+ S '89
SAGALYN, RAPHAEL
about
Washington's Rafe Sagalyn. G. Feldman. il por *Publishers Weekly* 235:246+ My 12 '89
SAGAMORE HOTEL (BOLTON LANDING, N.Y.) See Bolton Landing (N.Y.)—Hotels, motels, etc.
SAGAN, FRANÇOISE, 1935-
The Lot. il por *Architectural Digest* 46:22+ Ja '89
SAGAN, LEONARD A.
On radiation, paradigms, and hormesis. bibl f *Science* 245:574+ Ag 11 '89
SAGATA, NORIYUKI, AND OTHERS
The product of the *mos* proto-oncogene as a candidate "initiator" for oocyte maturation. bibl f il *Science* 245:643-6 Ag 11 '89
SAGDEEV, R. Z. See Sagdeyev, Roald Zinnurovich
SAGDEYEV, ROALD ZINNUROVICH
about
Sakharov elected to presidium of Soviet Academy of Sciences. W. Sweet. il *Physics Today* 42:61-4 Ja '89
Soviet scientists rebel, Sakharov and Sagdeev elected to new Congress. W. Sweet. il *Physics Today* 42:65-6 My '89
SAGE, JEREMY
about
A birthday presence second to none, Jeremy Sage treats his business like child's play. D. Van Biema. il pors *People Weekly* 31:87-8 My 8 '89
SAGE FEDERAL SYSTEMS
Computers programming computers. E. Dyson. il *Forbes* 143:137 Mr 6 '89
SAGEBRUSH
Sagebrush country: America's outback. D. H. Chadwick. il map *National Geographic* 175:52-71+ Ja '89

SAGEBRUSH ECOLOGY
A corridor in peril [Rio Grande Valley] C. A. Douglis. il map *Wilderness* 53:32-7 Wint '89
SAGER, MIKE
The devil and John Holmes: drugs, porn and the murders on Wonderland Avenue. il pors *Rolling Stone* p50-2+ Je 15 '89
SAGER, RUTH
Tumor suppressor genes: the puzzle and the promise. bibl f il *Science* 246:1406-12 D 15 '89
SAGUARO *See* Cactus
SAGUARO NATIONAL MONUMENT (ARIZ.)
The regeneration gap [disappearance of saguaro and long-nosed bats] J. Erickson. il *National Parks* 63:30-3 Jl/Ag '89
SAGUENAY COUNTY (QUÉBEC)
　　　　　Public health
The Quebec phenomenon [high incidence of genetic disorder] S. Strauss. *World Press Review* 36:68 S '89
SAGUIER, RUBÉN BAREIRO *See* Bareiro Saguier, Rubén
SAH, P., AND OTHERS
Tonic activation of NMDA receptors by ambient glutamate enhances excitability of neurons. bibl f il *Science* 246:815-18 N 10 '89
SAHA, MEGHNAD, 1893-1956
　　　　　about
Meghnad N. Saha. por *Scientific American* 260:132 My '89
SAHAG, JOHN
　　　　　about
Mane attraction. il por *Harper's Bazaar* 122:36+ Mr '89
SAHARA
　　　See also
　　Geology—Sahara
Desert son [Marathon Des Sables] K. McKinney. il *Omni (New York, N.Y.)* 12:16+ N '89
. . . or is the desert really moving? B. Forse. *World Press Review* 36:33-5 Ap '89
Sahara marathoners: they're hot to trot [Marathon Des Sables] D. Van Biema. il *People Weekly* 31:56-61 Ap 10 '89
Sand dudes [Marathon Des Sables] J. Loeschhorn. il *Runner's World* 24:58-9 S '89
Some like it hot [Marathon Des Sables] S. Brummell. il *Women's Sports & Fitness* 11:58 N/D '89
SAHATJIAN, ELIZABETH
The age of asparagus. il *Esquire* 111:36 My '89
Business and pleasure: champagne tasting and toasting. il *Working Woman* 14:107-10+ D '89
Five pounds of garlic, please. il *Esquire* 112:56 O '89
Pie to cry for. il *Esquire* 111:28 Ja '89
SAHGAL, BARRY
　　　　　about
Look at the crack spreads. S. N. Chakravarty. il por *Forbes* 143:86+ My 29 '89
SAHLEN, HAROLD F., JR.
　　　　　about
Whodunit. K. Hannon. il *Forbes* 143:40-1 Je 26 '89
SAHLEN & ASSOCIATES INC.
Whodunit. K. Hannon. il *Forbes* 143:40-1 Je 26 '89
SAHLINS, BERNARD
　　　　　about
Onstage in the toddlin' town. J. Kroll. il *Newsweek* 113:64+ Je 19 '89
SAID, EDWARD W.
A Palestinian view of Israel's history. map *Utne Reader* p38-9 S/O '89
Sanctum of the strong. il *The Nation* 249:48-50 Jl 10 '89
　　　　　about
Arafat's man in New York. D. Smith. il pors *New York* 22:40-6 Ja 23 '89
"Professor of terror" [discussion of August 1989 article] E. Alexander. *Commentary* 88:2-7+ D '89
Professor of terror. E. Alexander. *Commentary* 88:49-50 Ag '89
SAIGO, ROY H.
The barriers of racism. il *Change* 21:8+ N/D '89
SAIGON (VIETNAM)
　　　　　Description
Saigon: fourteen years after. P. T. White. il maps *National Geographic* 176:604-21 N '89
　　　　　Hotels, motels, etc.
A venerable haunt returns [Continental Hotel] B. Weber. il *The New York Times Magazine* p70 Ag 13 '89
SAIL ASSISTED SHIPS *See* Windships
SAILBOAT RACING
　　　See also
　　Yacht racing
Getting your feet wet in sailboat racing. L. Zinn. il *Business Week* p84-5 Jl 24 '89
SAILBOATS
　　　See also
　　Cruisers (Pleasure boats)
　　Trimarans
　　Yachts and yachting
Gone with the wind [sailboat owners] J. A. Fishman. il *Motor Boating & Sailing* 163:94-7+ F '89
Sailboats. R. Marshall. il *Motor Boating & Sailing* 164:63-5 S '89

SAILBOATS, MODEL *See* Ship and boat models
SAILFISH FISHING
Go fishing, young man [sailfish fishing off Palm Beach, Fla. in a 32-foot Marlin 28] J. Skorupa. il *Popular Mechanics* 166:28+ Je '89
SAILING
　　　See also
　　Cruising
　　Sailboat racing
　　Voyages
　　Voyages around the world
　　Yachts and yachting
The girl who loved cat sailing. J. Renfro. il por *Women's Sports & Fitness* 11:42-3 Je '89
They call him Captain Blood [B. Dennehy] M. Long. il por *Gentlemen's Quarterly* 59:244-5 My '89
　　　　　Study and teaching
　　　See also
　　Womanship, Inc.
SAILING CRUISERS *See* Cruisers (Pleasure boats)
SAILING SHIPS *See* Sailing vessels
SAILING VESSELS
　　　See also
　　Clipper ships
　　Windships
Abandon ship! A galleon runs aground in a highway wreck [J. Fiondella's replica of Spanish galleon overturns on road] il por *People Weekly* 32:206 D 4 '89
SAILING VESSELS ON POSTAGE STAMPS *See* Postage stamps
SAILING YACHTS *See* Yachts and yachting
SAILPLANES *See* Gliders (Aviation)
SAILS
　　　See also
　　Hood Sailmakers, Inc.
　　North Sails Group, Inc.
SAILS, SOLAR *See* Solar sails
SAINT BARTHÉLEMY (GUADELOUPE)
　　　　　Description and travel
St. Martin/St. Barts. J. Orsini. il maps *Travel Holiday* 172:48-57 D '89
SAINT-BLANQUAT, HENRI DE
Cave man started it. *World Press Review* 36:41 O '89
SAINT CLAIR, LAKE (MICH. AND ONT.) *See* Lake Saint Clair (Mich. and Ont.)
SAINT CLOUD (MINN.)
　　　　　Social work
Networking on a shoestring [Young Parent Program] K. Heinen and M. A. Padgett. il *Children Today* 18:30-2 Ja/F '89
SAINT CROIX (VIRGIN ISLANDS OF THE U.S.)
　　　See also
　　Crime and criminals—Saint Croix (Virgin Islands of the U.S.)
　　Resorts—Saint Croix (Virgin Islands of the U.S.)
　　Women—Saint Croix (Virgin Islands of the U.S.)
　　　　　Description and travel
Destination St. Croix [special section] il *Essence* 19:87-90+ Ap '89
St. Croix. il *Better Homes and Gardens* 67:216 N '89
　　　　　Industries
　　　See also
　　Tourist trade—Saint Croix (Virgin Islands of the U.S.)
SAINT CROIX (VIRGIN ISLANDS OF THE U.S.) COOKING
See Cooking, Crucian
SAINT ESTÈPHE (MANHATTAN BEACH, CALIF.: RESTAURANT) *See* Manhattan Beach (Calif.)— Restaurants, nightclubs, bars, etc.
SAINT-GAUDENS, AUGUSTUS, 1848-1907
　　　　　about
When people cared that Miss Liberty was Irish! E. Rochette. il *Antiques & Collecting Hobbies* 94:55+ Mr '89
SAINT-GENYS, MARQUISE DE
　　　　　about
Château de La Lorie: Marquise de Saint-Genys in the Haut-Anjou. B. D. Colen. il *Architectural Digest* 46:154-8+ Ja '89
SAINT HELENA (CALIF.)
　　　　　Gardens and gardening
Down-to-earth . . . and delicious [entertaining at the home of H. Dake] S. Costner. il por *Working Woman* 14:153-6 N '89
　　　　　Restaurants, nightclubs, bars, etc.
Culinary crossroads [recipes of M. Chiarello from Tra Vigne] D. Welch. il por *Health (New York, N.Y.)* 21:74-9+ Ap '89
SAINT HELENA ISLAND (S.C.)
　　　See also
　　Blacks—Saint Helena Island (S.C.)
SAINT JOHN, BONNIE
　　　　　about
The 1989 Essence Awards [with editorial comment by Susan L. Taylor] il pors *Essence* 20:57-60+, 69 O '89
SAINT JOHN (N.B.)
　　　　　Air pollution
Confronting the Irvings [paper mill threatened with shutdown] P. Chisholm. il *Maclean's* 102:50 O 16 '89

SAINT JOHN (N.B.)—cont.
History
Cabinetmakers of St. John, New Brunswick. D. B. Webster. bibl il *Antiques* 135:942-9 Ap '89
SAINT JOHN (VIRGIN ISLANDS OF THE U.S.)
Description and travel
St. John. il *Better Homes and Gardens* 67:218-19 N '89
SAINT JOHN'S (NFLD.)
Crime
Charges of a coverup [sexual and physical abuse at Mount Cashel Orphanage] N. Underwood. *Maclean's* 102:66+ D 4 '89
Scandal on the Rock [inquiry into sexual abuse involving Christian Brothers at Mount Cashel Orphanage, St. John's] N. Underwood. il *Maclean's* 102:61 O 2 '89
Sex and scandal [former resident S. Earle testifies about sexual abuse at Mount Cashel Orphanage] N. Underwood. il por *Maclean's* 102:84 O 30 '89
Social work
A disquieting mystery: St. John's rallies behind an abandoned girl [known as Christina] G. Allen. il por *Maclean's* 102:18-19 Ag 7 '89
Resolving a riddle [identity of girl known as Christina is discovered] B. Came and H. Quinn. il por *Maclean's* 102:40-2 Ag 21 '89
SAINT JOSEPH (MINN.)
Crime
See also
Wetterling, Jacob—Kidnapping
SAINT KITTS-NEVIS
See also
Nevis (Saint Kitts-Nevis)
SAINT LAURENT, YVES
about
Couture report: the four schools of design. J. J. Buck. il *Vogue* 179:324-5+ O '89
SAINT LAWRENCE (NFLD.)
History
Heroes of the frozen cliff [rescue of crew from USS Pollux wreck by Newfoundlanders in World War II] H. Strauss. il *Reader's Digest* 134:102-7 Ap '89
SAINT LAWRENCE RIVER
Canada's white whales are dying. P. Benesh. *World Press Review* 36:56 Ja '89
Doomed canaries of Tadoussac [P. Béland's work with beluga whales] J. R. Luoma. il por map *Audubon* 91:92-7 Mr '89
SAINT LOUIS (MO.)
Description
St. Louis. W. F. Allman. il *U.S. News & World Report* 107:49-50 D 18 '89
Education
What it really takes to make school choice work. S. Uchitelle. *Phi Delta Kappan* 71:301-3 D '89
Health facilities
Amid a raging debate, one woman chooses abortion [D. Barber at Reproductive Health Services after Supreme Court decision] D. Grogan and others. il *People Weekly* 32:89-90+ Jl 24 '89
Housing
People power transforms a St. Louis housing project [B. Gilkey organizes Cochran Gardens] H. C. Boyte. il por *Utne Reader* p46-7 Jl/Ag '89
Monuments, statues, etc.
See also
Gateway Arch (Saint Louis, Mo.)
Music
See also
Opera Theatre of Saint Louis
Newspapers
See also
St. Louis post-dispatch (Newspaper)
St. Louis sun (Newspaper)
SAINT LOUIS ART MUSEUM
Renovation and expansion in Saint Louis. A. E. Ledes. il *Antiques* 136:220 Ag '89
SAINT LOUIS UNIVERSITY. PARKS COLLEGE *See* Parks College of Saint Louis University
SAINT LUCIA
See also
Resorts—Saint Lucia
Soufrière (Saint Lucia)
Description and travel
Beauty and the beach. R. W. Cox. il map *Travel Holiday* 171:56-61 F '89
Undiscovered paradise: the faces of Saint Lucia. B. Warf. il map *Focus (New York, N.Y.: 1950)* 38:34-6 Wint '88
SAINT MARTIN
Description and travel
St. Martin/St. Barts. J. Orsini. il maps *Travel Holiday* 172:48-57 D '89
SAINT MORITZ (SWITZERLAND)
Historic houses, sites, etc.
Mili Weber's world: the artist's fairy-tale house near St. Moritz. D. Harris. il por *Architectural Digest* 46:174-9 D '89

SAINT NAPA (CYPRUS)
Tourist trade
A town moves out of town. T. Stanger. il *Newsweek* 113:39 Mr 13 '89
SAINT PATRICK'S DAY CUPCAKES *See* Cupcakes
SAINT PAUL (MINN.)
Economic conditions
The Twin Cities' better half. J. McCormick. il *Newsweek* 113:43-4 F 6 '89
Music
See also
Minnesota Opera
Sports
The Twin Cities. D. Barreiro. il *Sport (New York, N.Y.)* 80:76-9 D '89
SAINT REGIS AKWESASNE INDIAN RESERVE
Contaminant Cove: where polluters defile Mohawk land. J. E. Milich. il *The Progressive* 53:23-5 Ja '89
Gambling and guns. M. Clark. il *Maclean's* 102:21+ S 18 '89
SAINT-SAËNS, CAMILLE, 1835-1921
about
Salute to France. W. Livingstone. il *Stereo Review* 54:164 N '89
SAINT-SAËNS, CHARLES CAMILLE *See* Saint-Saëns, Camille, 1835-1921
SAINT THOMAS (VIRGIN ISLANDS OF THE U.S.)
Description and travel
St. Thomas. il *Better Homes and Gardens* 67:220 N '89
SAINT-TROPEZ (FRANCE)
Harbor
Sexy expatriates [American-made yachts] J. Clemans. il *Motor Boating & Sailing* 163:62-5+ Ja '89
Tourist trade
Taking some pity on Brigitte Bardot. B. Amiel. il *Maclean's* 102:9 Ag 28 '89
SAINT VALENTINE'S DAY *See* Valentine's Day
SAINT VINCENT AND THE GRENADINES
See also
Bequia (Saint Vincent and the Grenadines)
SAINTS
See also
Beatification
Benedict, Saint, Abbot of Monte Cassino
Francis, de Sales, Saint, 1567-1622
Ignatius, of Loyola, Saint, 1491-1556
John, the Baptist
Teresa, of Avila, Saint, 1515-1582
Thérèse, de Lisieux, Saint, 1873-1897
Thomas, Aquinas, Saint, 1225?-1274
When the semi-saints come marching in. P. Yancey. il *Christianity Today* 33:64 S 22 '89
SAIVETZ, CAROL R.
"New thinking" and Soviet third world policy. bibl f *Current History* 88:325-8+ O '89
SAJAK, PAT
about
And now, nice-guy talk hosts. R. Zoglin. pors *Time* 133:74 Ja 9 '89
Johnny come lately. N. Scovell. il por *Rolling Stone* p23 F 23 '89
Taking a spin at late-night. B. Barol. il por *Newsweek* 113:63+ Ja 16 '89
SAKAI, NAOKI
about
The man behind the O. H. Gaffin. il pors *Popular Photography* 96:34 D '89
SAKARIS, KAY WATERS
about
Looking into a shared past. D. Young. il pors *Southern Living* 24:79+ D '89
SAKE, PATIENCE
The pursuit of happiness. il *World Health* p13 Mr '89
SAKHALIN (SOVIET UNION)
Politics and government
Where *perestroika* makes strange bedfellows [People's Deputies V. Guliy and A. Kapustin] J. Trimble. il pors map *U.S. News & World Report* 107:77-8+ Ag 28-S 4 '89
SAKHAROV, ANDREI DMITRIEVICH, 1921-1989
The making of an activist [excerpt from Memoirs] *Time* 134:24 D 25 '89
Sakharov's view of Soviet changes [adaptation of remarks, June 20, 1989] il por *World Press Review* 36:32+ Ag '89
A speech to the People's Congress [address, June 9, 1989]; tr. by Edward Kline. il por *The New York Review of Books* 36:25-6 Ag 17 '89
about
Candidate Sakharov. A. Wilson-Smith. il por *Maclean's* 102:26 F 6 '89
Changing times: Sakharov in the US on human rights and arms control. I. Goodwin. il *Physics Today* 42:91-5 F '89
An evening with the Sakharovs [interview] A. W. Bouis and J.-C. Bouis. il pors *Life* 12:96-8+ Jl '89
Face-off on reform. J. Kohan. il pors *Time* 134:20-2 D 25 '89
An interview with Andrei Sakharov. J.-P. Barou. il *The New York Review of Books* 36:6-7 Mr 2 '89

SAKHAROV, ANDREI DMITRIEVICH, 1921-1989—about
—cont.
Obituary
  Maclean's por 102:42 D 25 '89. A. Wilson-Smith
  Newsweek por 114:45 D 25 '89. F. Coleman
  Time il pors 134:23-4 D 25 '89. P. Blake
  U.S. News & World Report il por 107:9 D 25 '89-Ja 1 '90
Sakharov declines to run for Moscow seat. D. Dickson. *Science* 243:1001 F 24 '89
Sakharov elected to presidium of Soviet Academy of Sciences. W. Sweet. il *Physics Today* 42:61-4 Ja '89
Sakharov's bold challenge [with interview] J. Trimble. il por *U.S. News & World Report* 106:49-50 Ja 30 '89
Soviet scientists rebel, Sakharov and Sagdeev elected to new Congress. W. Sweet. il *Physics Today* 42:65-6 My '89
SAKHAROV, ELENA BONNER *See* Bonner, Elena
SAKSENA, RASHMI
  Emperor of India's hotels. il por *World Press Review* 36:73 O '89
SALAAM, KALAMU YA *See* Kalamu ya Salaam, 1947-
SALAAM BOMBAY! [film] *See* Motion picture reviews—Single works
SALAD DRESSINGS
  Pour salt-free freshness on salads. J. P. Day. il *The Saturday Evening Post* 261:18-21 O '89
SALAD GREENS *See* Greens, Edible
SALADS
       See also
    Coleslaw
7 pasta dinner-salads. il *Redbook* 173:139-42+ Jl '89
Chats? [spicy salads from India] il *Sunset (Central West edition)* 182:186+ My '89
Crisp vegetables, warm fish . . . they're main-dish salads. il *Sunset (Central West edition)* 183:160 O '89
Dressed to chill. L. Goldrich. il *Working Woman* 14:88-90 Ag '89
French duck encounters Mexican carnitas [canardita salad] il *Sunset (Central West edition)* 182:184 Ap '89
Fresh summer salads. il *Better Homes and Gardens* 67:153-4 Je '89
Gastronomie sans argent [chicken salads] il *Gourmet* 49:88-9+ Je '89
Gastronomie sans argent [salades françaises] il *Gourmet* 49:62-3+ Jl '89
Good food, good health: salad smarts! B. Goldman. il *Better Homes and Gardens* 67:38 My '89
Here's just the salad you need [gelatin salads] il *Southern Living* 24:114 D '89
Larry Forgione: salad savvy. il *Organic Gardening* 36:45 O '89
Leaf, loaf, and ladle. K. Haedrich. il *Country Journal* 16:60-4 F '89
Lean but "high-powered" salads. il *Sunset (Central West edition)* 181:125 D '88
Light & luscious [fruit salad and pasta stuffed tomatoes] J. Nash. il *Essence* 20:76 Jl '89
Lite eating: late-summer salads. il *McCall's* 116:137 S '89
A perfect salad every time? il *Sunset (Central West edition)* 182:104-5 Ap '89
Quick and cool, these are breakfast salads. il *Sunset (Central West edition)* 183:94 Ag '89
Quick! Toss a salad. il *Southern Living* 24:152 Je '89
Recipe of the week [summer salad] il *Jet* 76:24 Jl 17 '89
Salad days. il *Ladies' Home Journal* 106:159-60+ Je '89
Salad for supper. A. Johnson. il *Parents* 64:187-8+ Je '89
Shipshape salad fixin's [microwaving] J. B. Hurley. il *Prevention (Emmaus, Pa.)* 41:80 Jl '89
Smartly dressed holiday salads. il *Sunset (Central West edition)* 183:110+ D '89
Smash potatoes [Jean-Michel Diot's warm potato salad] B. Costikyan. il *New York* 22:55 S 4 '89
Soulful salads. L. W. Eckhardt. il *Organic Gardening* 36:37-42 My '89
Soup & salad. il *Sunset (Central West edition)* 182:114-15 Ja '89
Southwest salad: it's speedy and simple. il *Sunset (Central West edition)* 183:188-9 N '89
Summer-perfect salads. il *Glamour* 87:184-6 Jl '89
Summer salads cookbook. M. Langan. il *McCall's* 116:95-100+ Ag '89
Sunny summer salads a la heart [Mediterranean cuisine] J. B. Hurley. il *Prevention (Emmaus, Pa.)* 41:68-72+ Je '89
These salads are pretty but not fussy. il *Sunset (Central West edition)* 183:112-13 Jl '89
Those hazy, lazy salad days. J. F. Mariani. il *Motor Boating & Sailing* 164:32-3 Ag '89
Whole-meal salads. K. Haedrich. il *Country Journal* 16:74-7 Jl/Ag '89
A winter salad sampler. P. Y. Cordell. il *Southern Living* 24:86-7 Ja '89
SALAHI, ADIL
  A sporting partnership. il *World Health* p18-19 Jl '89
SALAM, ABDUS, 1926-
  What the third world can handle [discussion of November 1988 article, What the third world really needs] *The Bulletin of the Atomic Scientists* 45:8 My '89

SALAMAN, REDCLIFFE N. (REDCLIFFE NATHAN), 1874-1955
       about
  Books you may have missed. E. N. Luttwak. il *The American Spectator* 22:46-7 Mr '89
SALAMANDERS
  Activation of apical chloride channels in the gastric oxyntic cell. J. R. Demarest and others. bibl f il *Science* 245:402-4 Jl 28 '89
       Reproduction
  Temperature and sperm incorporation in polyploid salamanders. J. P. Bogart and others. bibl f il *Science* 246:1032-4 N 24 '89
SALAMON, ROGER
  Expert systems in medicine. il *World Health* p12-13 Ag/S '89
SALARIES *See* Wages and salaries
SALAWITCH, ROSS J.
  (jt. auth) *See* McElroy, Michael, 1939-, and Salawitch, Ross J.
SALAZAR, ENRIQUE CAMARENA *See* Camarena Salazar, Enrique
SALDANA, THERESA
       about
  Vicious crime, double jeopardy. D. Bacon. il pors *People Weekly* 31:44-9 Je 5 '89
SALEM, ELLEN
  The new Chinese warlords. *World Press Review* 36:50 Ja '89
SALEM (MASS.)
       Galleries and museums
       See also
    Essex Institute
       Historic houses, sites, etc.
  Restoring the restored [Gardner-Pingree House] K. Korieth. il por map *Americana* 17:44-9 S/O '89
       Monuments, statues, etc.
  Witch trial memorial. il *American History Illustrated* 23:6 Ja '89
SALEM (MASS.). ESSEX INSTITUTE *See* Essex Institute
SALERNO, STEVE
  See Spot write. *The Writer* 102:9-10 Ja '89
SALERNO-SONNENBERG, NADJA
       about
  Nadja Salerno-Sonnenberg. T. Robbins. il por *Esquire* 112:172-3 N '89
SALES
       See also
    Auctions
    Billing
    Thrift shops and rummage sales
  Heavy metal [Transit Authority's Auction and Tag Sale] *The New Yorker* 65:46-7 D 11 '89
  Helping homeless families [Great American Yard Sale and National Home Furnishings Sale; with editorial comment by David Jordan] M. Daly. il *Better Homes and Gardens* 67:8, 18+ S '89
  Sales & bargains. L. Fleischer. See issues of New York
       Directories
       See also
    S & B report
SALES CATALOGS *See* Catalogs, Commercial
SALES PERSONNEL
       See also
    Automobile sales personnel
    Booksellers and bookselling
    Marketing
    Telephone selling
  The birth of a saleswoman. B. Brophy. il *U.S. News & World Report* 106:40-2 F 6 '89
  What every manager needs to know about sales. R. Welch. il *Working Woman* 14:96-8+ Ja '89
       Salaries, commissions, pensions, etc.
  Now salespeople really must sell for their supper. A. Dunkin. il *Business Week* p50+ Jl 31 '89
       Training
       Aids and devices
  When theater meets big business [Simulations, Inc.] S. P. Herman. il pors *Home Office Computing* 7:56-7 Mr '89
SALES POLICIES
       See also
    Discount, Cash
SALES PROMOTION
       See also
    Premiums
    Prize contests
    Samples (Merchandising)
    Trading stamps
  Promoting your business on a tight budget. R. Gunnerson. il *Home Office Computing* 7:32 Ag '89
  Stealing the right shoppers [expanding market share] J. Levine. *Forbes* 144:104-5 Jl 10 '89
SALES REPRESENTATIVES, PUBLISHERS' *See* Publishers and publishing—Employees
SALES TAX
       See also
    Value added tax

SALES TAX—*cont.*

Catalog firms bite the hand that squeezes [move to impose state sales tax on mail orders] E. Pomice. il *U.S. News & World Report* 107:44 Jl 31 '89

If you catalog-shop [state sales tax] R. Coorsh. il *Consumers' Research Magazine* 72:4 Jl '89

Tax by mail [mail order business] D. Fanning. il *Forbes* 143:126+ Ap 3 '89

Canada

Canada tackles its deficit. H. M. Waller. il *The New Leader* 72:8-9 O 2-16 '89

Duelling over the tax bite [First Ministers' conference] R. Laver. il *Maclean's* 102:26 N 20 '89

Fighting the opposition [interview with M. Wilson] il por *Maclean's* 102:41 S 25 '89

A looming tax revolt. M. Clark. il *Maclean's* 102:16-17 Ag 21 '89

The nine-percent battle. M. Clark. il *Maclean's* 102:8-10 Jl 3 '89

The tax battle. M. Clark. il *Maclean's* 102:20-1 O 2 '89

Taxing choices [pressure to amend proposed Goods and Services Tax] M. Clark. il *Maclean's* 102:18-19 D 11 '89

Taxing the already overburdened [proposed Goods and Services Tax] P. C. Newman. il *Maclean's* 102:69 N 6 '89

The Tories' new sales tax could be a windfall. D. Francis. il *Maclean's* 102:13 Ag 7 '89

Wilful ignorance and lust for page 1 [media distortion of B. Mulroney's views] G. Bain. il *Maclean's* 102:52 S 25 '89

Nova Scotia

Barking about a budget [charges that Sobeys supermarket chain obtained advance information on budget] G. Allen. il *Maclean's* 102:21 My 22 '89

SALES TRAINING *See* Sales personnel—Training

SALESIANS

Exalted violence [J.-B. Aristide expelled by Salesians for work in Haiti] *The Nation* 248:76-7 Ja 23 '89

SALESMANSHIP *See* Selling

SALESWOMEN *See* Sales personnel

SALETAN, WILLIAM

Genes 'R' Us. *The New Republic* 201:18-20 Jl 17-24 '89

If fetuses are people . . . *The New Republic* 201:18-20 S 18-25 '89

Jar wars. *The New Republic* 201:13-14 O 2 '89

SALETAN, WILLIAM, AND WATZMAN, NANCY

Marcus Welby, J.D. [cover story] *The New Republic* 200:19-22+ Ap 17 '89

SALGADO, SEBASTIAO

Ship breakers [photographs] il *Life* 12:64-8 Ag '89

about

In the rhythms of the tides fishing. il *Life* 12:70-4+ Je '89

SALICK, BERNARD

about

Doing good, getting well. M. Barrier. il pors *Nation's Business* 77:50+ Ag '89

SALICK HEALTH CARE, INC.

Doing good, getting well. M. Barrier. il pors *Nation's Business* 77:50+ Ag '89

SALIN, DOMINIQUE

Education in France: renewal in the secondary schools; tr. by John L. Farrand. *America* 160:587-90 Je 17-24 '89

SALINAS (CALIF.)

Historic houses, sites, etc.

Strolling Steinbeck's Salinas. il map *Sunset (Central West edition)* 183:14 Ag '89

SALINAS DE GORTARI, CARLOS

about

Bald man on a horse. G. B. Lake. il *National Review* 41:38-9 Mr 10 '89

Bienvenidos to a fire sale. C. P. Work and J. Bussey. il por *U.S. News & World Report* 107:96+ O 16 '89

A Gorbo for Mexico. M. Kondracke. *The New Republic* 200:11-12+ F 20 '89

If Washington can learn, Mexico can teach. *America* 160:411 My 6 '89

No more mañana. R. S. Strother. il *National Review* 41:21-2 N 24 '89

One tough hombre. S. Baker and E. Weiner. il pors *Business Week* p50-3 Ap 3 '89

The power politics of Carlos Salinas. C. A. Robbins. il por *U.S. News & World Report* 106:61-2+ Mr 20 '89

Salinas declares war on 'the maximum chief' of oil. S. Baker. il *Business Week* p52 Ja 23 '89

Salinas' flashy new step in the Mexican debt dance. A. Bard. il *Business Week* p28 My 29 '89

Salinas goes after another monster: the phone system. S. Baker. il *Business Week* p42 Mr 6 '89

Salinas strikes before the miners can. S. Baker. il map *Business Week* p50 S 4 '89

Touching the 'untouchable'. S. McGuire. il por *Newsweek* 113:30-1 Ja 23 '89

A vote of confidence. L. Meyer. il *World Press Review* 36:64 Ja '89

Why Salinas must tame the teachers. S. Baker. il *Business Week* p46+ My 15 '89

Wimp no more. G. D. Garcia. il por *Time* 133:28-9 Ap 24 '89

SALINE WATER

See also

Sea water

SALINE WATER CONVERSION

Seawater to drink. R. Friedman. il *Technology Review* 92:14-15 Ag/S '89

A shipwrecked Miami couple owe their lives to a clever gadget that makes seawater drinkable [Survivor-35 pump; case of William and Simone Butler] il *People Weekly* 32:101 O 2 '89

Automation

The soul of a new machine [E. Fredkin's desalinator] G. Cowley. il por *Newsweek* 113:53 My 29 '89

SALIVA

See also

Sputum

SALIVARY GLANDS

Activation of salivary secretion: coupling of cell volume and $[Ca^{2+}]_i$ in single cells. J. K. Foskett and J. E. Melvin. bibl f il *Science* 244:1582-5 Je 30 '89

A novel vasodilatory peptide from the salivary glands of the sand fly Lutzomyia longipalpis. J. M. C. Ribeiro and others. bibl f il *Science* 243:212-14 Ja 13 '89

Diseases

See also

Sjögren's syndrome

SALK, LEE, 1926-

The child psychologist. See issues of McCall's beginning March 1986

Super sitters. il *McCall's* 116:69+ Je '89

SALKELD, ROGER

about

On deck. il por *Sport (New York, N.Y.)* 80:16 N '89

SALLE, DAVID

about

Motivating factors. D. Kazanjian. il pors *Vogue* 179:516-17+ S '89

SALLEY, JOHN

about

Holy cow, what digs! L. Montville. il pors *Sports Illustrated* 71:122-7 N 6 '89

SALLY [drama] *See* Fuller, Charles

SALMI, ERNEST W.

about

Obituary

Physics Today 42:132-3 Mr '89. C. M. Fowler and others

SALMON, ALICE WOOLEDGE

Cookery of the Caucasus. il *Gourmet* 49:132+ O '89

La Maison du Chocolat. il *Gourmet* 49:80-5+ S '89

SALMON, DENA K.

How to outwit your two-year-old. il *Parents* 64:135-6+ D '89

SALMON

See also

Cooking—Fish

Photographs and photography

Leap of faith [brown bear catching sockeye salmon] J. Foott. il *Natural History* p112-13 O '89

SALMON, DRESSING OF *See* Fish, Dressing of

SALMON FISHERIES (COMMERCIAL) *See* Fisheries

SALMON FISHING

Grandpa and the kid. D. Sisson. il *Field & Stream* 94:41+ Ag '89

Helen's Falls [Atlantic salmon fishing on George River] D. Barnes. il *Field & Stream* 94:90+ Je '89

Jousting with river kings [backtrolling for chinook salmon] P. Barrett. il *Field & Stream* 94:57-8+ O '89

Lodges on the run [floating lodges for salmon fishing in British Columbia] J. Gibbs. il *Outdoor Life* 183:86-7+ My '89

The mystery fish. G. Hill. il *Field & Stream* 94:8 Ag '89

A report from salmon run [controversial fishing practices in Pulaski, N.Y.] C. Robohm. il *Country Journal* 16:72-3 S/O '89

Salmon. il map *Sunset (Central West edition)* 182:90-7 Ap '89

Signals [fishing by biological rhythms] M. Hilbert. il *Field & Stream* 94:22+ D '89

The snag in Pulaski [controversial practices] D. W. Hollis. il map *Country Journal* 16:68-71+ S/O '89

SALMONCAMPBELL, JOAN

about

First black woman to head merged Presbyterian Church. A. Bradford. il pors *Ebony* 45:100+ N '89

SALMONELLA

Epithelial cell surfaces induce Salmonella proteins required for bacterial adherence and invasion. B. B. Finlay and others. bibl f il *Science* 243:940-3 F 17 '89

Immune response to cholera toxin epitope inserted in Salmonella flagellin. S. M. C. Newton and others. bibl f il *Science* 244:70-2 Ap 7 '89

A Salmonella locus that controls resistance to microbicidal proteins from phagocytic cells. P. I. Fields and others. bibl f il *Science* 243:1059-62 F 24 '89

SALMONELLA—*cont.*
Sweet solution to tainted poultry [use of lactose in drinking water; research by John R. DeLoach] *Science News* 135:349 Je 3 '89

SALMONELLOSIS
Fear of eggs. il *Consumer Reports* 54:650-2 O '89
From our kitchen to yours [handling eggs safely] K. Adams. il *Southern Living* 24:126 Ja '89
Good food, good health: unscrambling the facts about eggs. B. Goldman. il *Better Homes and Gardens* 67:45-6 Ap '89
Salmonella and food safety. il *Consumers' Research Magazine* 72:29-31 Mr '89
Trojan eggs [eggs and salmonella] A. A. Hanson and W. I. Bennett. il *The New York Times Magazine* p25-6 Jl 30 '89

SALOME (BIBLICAL FIGURE)
about
Born of obsession [nineteenth century depictions] J. Kestner. il *Opera News* 53:24-6+ Mr 4 '89

SALOME [drama] *See* Wilde, Oscar, 1854-1900
SALOME [opera] *See* Strauss, Richard, 1864-1949

SALOMON, GEORGES
about
The slopes are groomed for Salomon's new ski. E. Wallace. il por *Business Week* p94 Ap 10 '89

SALOMON ET FILS FRANÇOIS
The slopes are groomed for Salomon's new ski. E. Wallace. il por *Business Week* p94 Ap 10 '89

SALOMON INC.
Is John Gutfreund dreaming an impossible dream? J. H. Dobrzynski. il por *Business Week* p98-9+ F 27 '89
A kiss-and-tell tale from the trading floor [M. Lewis' book Liar's poker] J. Schwartz. il por *Newsweek* 114:62 N 20 '89
One million dollars, no tears [book by M. Lewis] C. Byron. il por *New York* 22:26+ O 9 '89
Phibro: Salomon's ace in the oil patch. M. Ivey. *Business Week* p38-9 My 8 '89
Playing for keeps when he quit Wall Street, Michael Lewis hits the jackpot with Liar's poker. K. Hubbard. il pors *People Weekly* 32:73-4 D 18 '89
Salomon just can't lose—in Tokyo. T. Holden. il *Business Week* p94 Je 12 '89
There goes the bonus [M. Lewis' book] J. Queenan. il *Forbes* 144:14 O 30 '89
Tokyo's bull has further to run [interview with C. Mitchinson of Salomon Inc.] S. Solo. il por *Fortune* 120:43 Jl 3 '89

SALON (EXHIBITION)
Salon paintings on the rise in New York. D. Gimelson. il *Architectural Digest* 46:360+ N '89

SALÓN INTERNACIONAL DEL LIBRO (BOOK FAIR) *See* Book fairs
SALONE INTERNAZIONALE DEL MOBILE *See* Furniture, Italian—Exhibitions
SALONS, BEAUTY *See* Beauty shops
SALONS, SUNTAN *See* Suntan
SALOONS *See* Bars and barrooms
SALPETER, ELIAHU
Agonizing reappraisal in Israel [cover story] *The New Leader* 72:5-6 Ja 9 '89
Beneath the surface in Israel. il *The New Leader* 72:5-6 F 6 '89
The Mideast on the back burner. il *The New Leader* 72:5-6 N 27 '89
The politics of peace in the Mideast [cover story] il *The New Leader* 72:5-7 O 2-16 '89
Shamir gets set for Washington [cover story] il *The New Leader* 72:6-8 Mr 6 '89
The view from the West Bank. il *The New Leader* 72:5-6 Je 12-26 '89

SALSA *See* Sauces
SALT
See also
Low sodium cooking
Physiological effects
See Salt in the body
SALT AND PEPPER GRINDERS, SHAKERS, ETC.
Collectors and collecting
Colorless glass salts. M. Ginaven. il *Antiques & Collecting Hobbies* 94:34-6 Je '89
SALT COD COOKING *See* Cooking—Fish
SALT DEPOSITS
See also
Evaporites
Salt domes
SALT DISHES *See* Salt and pepper grinders, shakers, etc.
SALT DOMES
New ways to meet off-peak power demands [compressed air storage facilities flushed out of underground salt domes] il *Popular Mechanics* 166:15 Mr '89
SALT IN THE BODY
Diet restores youth to aging vessels [research by Ross D. Feldman and Christine Sinkey] K. Fackelmann. *Science News* 136:367 D 2 '89
Fats and sodium in your diet. T. Mendoza. il *Current Health 2* 16:18-21 O '89

Movers and shakers [runners] L. E. Armstrong and R. H. Lind. il *Runner's World* 24:80-2 Jl '89
The salt alarm. W. I. Bennett. il *The New York Times Magazine* p30-1 Ja 22 '89
Shake salt from your diet. il *McCall's* 116:96 Je '89
Unraveling sleep disorders of the aged [sodium experiments point to sympathetic nervous system; work of Michael V. Vitiello] K. Fackelmann. *Science News* 136:7 Jl 1 '89

SALT LAKE CITY (UTAH)
Buildings
Making a little look like a lot [Delta Air Lines Reservations and Training Center] G. Anderson. il *Architectural Record* 177:128-31 My '89
Education
The children's cleanup crusade [students from Jackson Elementary School lobby to establish state Superfund] B. A. Lewis. il *Sierra* 74:62-6 Mr/Ap '89
Groundwater pollution
The children's cleanup crusade [students from Jackson Elementary School lobby to establish state Superfund] B. A. Lewis. il *Sierra* 74:62-6 Mr/Ap '89
Newspapers
See also
Utah nippo (Newspaper)
Religious institutions and affairs
See also
Mormons and Mormonism
SALT LAKE COUNTY (UTAH)
Social work
Utah increases access to services for the Asian elderly. *Aging* no359:26 '89
SALT 'N PEPA (MUSICAL GROUP)
Women who rap—Salt-n-Pepa. D. DeNicolo. il *Glamour* 87:204 My '89
SALT TALKS *See* Strategic Arms Limitation Talks
SALT WATER *See* Sea water
SALT WATER FISHING
See also
Barracuda fishing
Billfish fishing
Bluefish fishing
Bonefish fishing
Halibut fishing
Marlin fishing
Pompano fishing
Sailfish fishing
Shark fishing
Tarpon fishing
Weakfish fishing
Monsters of the deep—delights for the palate [New York's offshore ocean fisheries; cover story] J. M. Mason and J. G. Casey. il *The Conservationist* 44:2-9+ S/O '89
Saltwater fishing. B. Stearns. See occasional issues of Field & Stream
The silent approach [electric trolling motors] B. Stearns. il *Field & Stream* 94:70+ Je '89
The Wright stuff. P. B. Wright. See issues of Motor Boating & Sailing beginning October 1987
SALTER, BRUCE
about
White S.C. restaurateur refuses to admit blacks; state NAACP files lawsuit. *Jet* 76:28 O 2 '89
SALTER, JAMES
Goddesses. il *Gentlemen's Quarterly* 59:282-5+ O '89
The houses of a French summer. il *Esquire* 111:145-53 Ap '89
Splendid splinters. il *Esquire* 112:118-21 Ag '89
Winter of the lion [with editorial comment by Lee Eisenberg] il pors *Esquire* 112:11, 69-76 Jl '89
SALTER, MARY JO
The upper story [poem] il *The Atlantic* 263:70-1 Ja '89
SALTS
Synthesis of organic salts with large second-order optical nonlinearities. S. R. Marder and others. bibl f il *Science* 245:626-8 Ag 11 '89
SALTS, MARINE *See* Sea water
SALTUS, RICHARD
How we heal. il *Health (New York, N.Y.)* 21:82-3 F '89
SALTWATER CROCODILES *See* Crocodiles
SALTZ, JERRY, 1951-
Playing for keeps. il pors *House & Garden* 161:162-9 O '89
SALTZMAN, JOE
TV news theater. il *USA Today (Periodical)* 118:89 N '89
Women in television are second-class citizens. il *USA Today (Periodical)* 118:51-3 S '89
SALTZMAN, RUSSELL E.
Meeting the quota for church conservatives. *The Christian Century* 106:975 N 1 '89
SALUTATIONS
The Mulvihill perplexity [use of salutations in business writing] W. Safire. il *The New York Times Magazine* p10+ Je 25 '89

SALVADOR See El Salvador
SALVADORAN REFUGEES See Refugees, Salvadoran
SALVAGE (SHIPS)
    See also
    Archeology, Submarine
    Treasure trove
    Millions of dollars on the ocean floor [Navy's management
        of surplus ships] E. Clift. il *Newsweek* 114:30 Ag 28 '89
    An undersea prize for the taking [Soviet sub sinks in Norwe-
        gian Sea] L. Martz. il map *Newsweek* 113:33 Ap 17 '89
        Bangladesh
        Photographs and photography
    Ship breakers. S. Salgado. il *Life* 12:64-8 Ag '89
SALVAGE (WASTE)
    See also
    Automobile junkyards
    Computer junkyards
    Junkyards
    Recycling (Waste, etc.)
SALVATION
    See also
    Justification
    Christian fulfillment and Jewish-Christian dialogue. I. C.
        Rottenberg. *The Christian Century* 106:387-91 Ap 12 '89
    How faith works [Lordship Salvation debate] S. L. Johnson,
        Jr. il *Christianity Today* 33:21-5 S 22 '89
    Old debate finds new life [requirements for salvation] B.
        Bird. il *Christianity Today* 33:38-40 Mr 17 '89
SALVATION ARMY
    A decree went out: humbug to Salvation [banned from many
        shopping centers] S. Budiansky. il *U.S. News & World
        Report* 107:8-9 D 18 '89
SALVINIA MOLESTA See Kariba weeds
SALZBURG (AUSTRIA)
        Description
    The sounds of Salzburg. D. Wickers. il *World Press Review*
        36:62 F '89
SALZMAN, GLEN
        about
    Milk and honey [film] Reviews
        People Weekly il 32:11-12 Jl 17 '89. R. Novak
SALZMAN, JEFF
    (jt. auth) See Calano, James, and Salzman, Jeff
SALZMAN, RANDY
    Something to 'BRAG' about. il *Bicycling* 30:190-1 Mr '89
SAMANA CAY (BAHAMAS)
    Where did Columbus land? [research by Kim Gainer indicates
        San Salvador more likely than Samana Cay] map *USA
        Today (Periodical)* 117:10 Ap '89
SAMARAS, LUCAS, 1936-
        about
    Lucas Samaras at Pace and Pace/MacGill. K. Johnson. il
        Art in America 77:143 Ja '89
    Lucas Samaras: Pace/MacGill; Pace. R. B. Woodward. il
        Art News 88:170-1 Mr '89
SAMBAS
    Samba time! [Rio de Janeiro carnival] S. A. Teixeira. il
        The Unesco Courier 42:38-41 D '89
SAMIOS, CORINNE
        about
    Greek visions. J. P. Gage. il *House & Garden* 161:72 F
        '89
SAMIOS, NICHOLAS P.
    (jt. auth) See Crease, Robert P., and Samios, Nicholas P.
SAMMONS, JAMES HARRIS, 1927-
    The RCT proposal and the nursing shortage [address, January
        5, 1989] *Vital Speeches of the Day* 55:373-5 Ap 1 '89
        about
    Does the AMA need to heal itself? J. F. Siler. il *Business
        Week* p50 N 13 '89
SAMNA WORD (WORD PROCESSOR PROGRAM) See
    Word processors and processing—Programming
SAMOAN ISLANDS
    See also
    American Samoa
SAMON, KATHERINE ANN
    How one woman got back on track. *Mademoiselle* 95:247+
        S '89
    "If you could read my mind . . . you'd probably go home":
        behind the lines of a first date. il *Mademoiselle* 95:142+
        My '89
    Night of the living dud and other . . . dates from hell.
        il *Mademoiselle* 95:162-3+ D '89
    Pale bonding. il *Gentlemen's Quarterly* 59:183-4+ N '89
    Upscale girls: a generation outgrows its parents. il
        Mademoiselle 95:206-7+ Mr '89
SAMPLERS
    Recent discoveries about Philadelphia samplers [18th and
        19th centuries] S. B. Swan. bibl f il *Antiques* 136:1334-43
        D '89
SAMPLES (MERCHANDISING)
    Freebies and cheapies. il *Teen* 33:14-16 Ja '89
    Freebies and cheapies. il *Teen* 33:49-50 Jl '89
SAMPLING (STATISTICS)
    Combining cognitive and statistical approaches to survey
        design. S. E. Fienberg and J. M. Tanur. bibl f il *Science*
        243:1017-22 F 24 '89

SAMPSON, ANTHONY, 1926-
    I've seen the future and it's the fax. *World Press Review*
        36:28+ D '89
SAMPSON, ATLANTA CONSTANCE, 1897-
        about
    Atlanta Constance Sampson at the National Arts Club. L.
        Campbell. il *Art in America* 77:148-9 Ja '89
SAMPSON, DENNIS
    Coming home late and alone [poem] *The American Scholar*
        58:420 Summ '89
SAMPSON, JEFFREY R., AND OTHERS
    Nucleotides in yeast tRNA^{Phe} required for the specific recogni-
        tion by its cognate synthetase. bibl f il *Science* 243:1363-6
        Mr 10 '89
SAMPSON, RALPH
        about
    No legs to stand on. L. Montville. il pors *Sports Illustrated*
        71:44-6+ D 4 '89
SAMS, FERROL, 1922-
    Once upon a Christmas [excerpt from Christmas gift!] il
        Good Housekeeping 209:172-3+ D '89
SAM'S GRILL (SAN FRANCISCO, CALIF.) See San Francisco
    (Calif.)—Restaurants, nightclubs, bars, etc.
SAMSUNG AEROSPACE INDUSTRIES LTD.
    Samsung keys future growth to FX fighter program. J. D.
        Morrocco. il *Aviation Week & Space Technology* 130:215+
        Je 12 '89
SAMUEL, HENRI
        about
    Design dialogue: Henri Samuel. C. Aillaud. il por *Architectural
        Digest* 46:50+ Ja '89
    Master of the house. M. Filler. il por *House & Garden*
        161:42 Jl '89
SAMUEL, RAPHAEL
    Dickens on stage and screen [cover story] il por *History
        Today* 39:44-51 D '89
SAMUEL EUROPEAN GALLERIES See Royal Ontario
    Museum. Samuel European Galleries
SAMUEL SMITH'S (FIRM)
    Beer from a stone. W. Grimes. il *Esquire* 111:30 My '89
SAMUELS, AMY
    (jt. auth) See Altmann, Jeanne, and Samuels, Amy
**SAMUELS, RICHARD J., AND WHIPPLE, BENJAMIN
    C.**
    The FSX and Japan's strategy for aerospace. il *Technology
        Review* 92:42-51 O '89
SAMUELS, WARREN J., 1933-
    In praise of Joan Robinson: economics as social control.
        Society 26:73-6 Ja/F '89
SAMUELSON, ROBERT J.
    America for sale? *The New Republic* 200:31-5 Je 12 '89
    [Column on economic questions] See occasional issues of
        Newsweek beginning February 20, 1984
    The enigma. *The New Republic* 200:21-3 Ja 9-16 '89
SAMUI (THAILAND)
        Description and travel
    Thailand's secluded paradise. J. Lubarsky. il *Travel Holiday*
        171:8-13 Je '89
SAMURAI
    Samurai anthropologist [evidence that samurai were descen-
        dants of the Ainu people; research by C. Loring Brace]
        Discover 10:12-13 S '89
SAMURAI APHIDS See Woolly aphids
SAMWAY, PATRICK H.
    (tr) See Margerie, Emmanuel de. Bicentennial events worth
        commemorating
SAN ANDREAS FAULT See Faults (Geology)
SAN ANTONIO (TEX.)
        City planning
    See also
    Rivercenter (San Antonio, Tex.)
        Description
    Lighting the way to Christmas. il *Southern Living* 24:35
        D '89
    San Antonio, Texas. il map *New Choices for the Best Years*
        29:12 Ap '89
    San Antonio's Mexican charm. L. Moss. il *McCall's* 117:16
        O '89
        Gardens and gardening
    See also
    San Antonio Botanical Gardens
        Historic houses, sites, etc.
    Addition blends with historic home. il *Southern Living*
        24:122-3 O '89
        Monuments, statues, etc.
    In the path of famous Texans [Texas Walk at Sea World]
        il *Southern Living* 24:43 F '89
        Police
    The .44-caliber mouthpiece [police union head H. Flammia]
        W. P. Barrett. il *Forbes* 144:166 S 18 '89
**SAN ANTONIO BOTANICAL GARDENS. LUCILE
    HALSELL CONSERVATORY**
    Reclaiming Eden [work of architect E. Ambasz] E. Edelman.
        il por *Art News* 88:73-4 F '89
    San Antonio gardens under glass. il *Southern Living* 24:30-1
        N '89

SAN CARLOS (CALIF.)

Bookstores
See Booksellers and bookselling—California

SAN DIEGO (CALIF.)

Architecture
Bali in San Diego [house] il *Sunset (Central West edition)* 182:128-30 Je '89

Art
Living on the border. D. Joselit. bibl f il *Art in America* 77:120-9 D '89

Description
Where two Californias meet: San Diego. N. B. Morgan. il map *National Geographic* 176:176-205 Ag '89

Education
The exile of Sharon Rogers [barred from her teaching job after bomb attack on her van] J. V. Lamar, Jr. il por *Time* 133:27 Ap 17 '89
Using research data to shape our schools [interview with R. Carriedo] D. B. Strother. il por *Phi Delta Kappan* 70:480-3 F '89

Monuments, statues, etc.
See also
University of California, San Diego. Stuart Collection

Religious institutions and affairs
Barred from Communion [prochoice assemblywoman L. Killea] *The Christian Century* 106:1193-4 D 20-27 '89
A mistake in San Diego [Bishop L. T. Maher bars Assemblywoman L. Killea from receiving Communion because of pro-choice stand on abortion] *America* 161:416 D 9 '89

Sanitary affairs
Mud-slinging over sewage technology [EPA vs. Boston and San Diego] M. Sun. il *Science* 246:440-3 O 27 '89

SAN DIEGO BAY (CALIF.)
San Diego's great bay. il map *Sunset (Central West edition)* 183:46-51 Ag '89

SAN DIEGO WILD ANIMAL PARK (ESCONDIDO, CALIF.)
Gordy and Schroeder growing up [gorillas] il *National Geographic World* 165:26-9 My '89
Sanctuary. C. J. Hadley. il *The Saturday Evening Post* 261:82-5 S '89

SAN DIEGO ZOO
Sanctuary. C. J. Hadley. il *The Saturday Evening Post* 261:82-5 S '89
Zoo babies. P. Gustke. il *Good Housekeeping* 208:60 F '89

SAN DOMENICO NY (RESTAURANT) *See* New York (N.Y.)—Restaurants, nightclubs, bars, etc.

SAN FRANCISCO (CALIF.)

Airports
Earthquake closes San Francisco airport for 13 hr., damages tower. R. G. O'Lone and B. W. Henderson. *Aviation Week & Space Technology* 131:20 O 23 '89
Oakland prepares to accept traffic from damaged SFO [earthquake] R. G. O'Lone. il *Aviation Week & Space Technology* 131:25+ O 30 '89

Architecture
Ace Architects: historical gamesmanship in San Francisco. J. Chatfield-Taylor. il *Architectural Digest* 46:84-7+ Ag '89
Honor award for a San Francisco remodel. il *Sunset (Central West edition)* 183:88-9 O '89
A lively climb up for a dramatic view. il *Sunset (Central West edition)* 183:115 O '89
Opening up and "zoning" an 1880s Victorian [Russian Hill] il *Sunset (Central West edition)* 183:120+ Je '89
Reach for natural light: mandate for old cabinet shop [converted to single-family residence] il *Sunset (Central West edition)* 182:102+ F '89
Remodeling for light, views, outdoor living. il *Sunset (Central West edition)* 183:98 O '89
Townhouses step back and up from the street. il *Sunset (Central West edition)* 183:126 O '89

Banks
See also
Wells Fargo Bank, National Association

Bridges
See also
San Francisco-Oakland Bay Bridge (Calif.)

Charities
See also
Project Open Hand

City planning
See also
Yerba Buena Gardens (San Francisco, Calif.)

Crime
Fare's fare, but when cabdriver Chuck Hollom goes off the meter, criminals had better look out. W. Plummer. il pors *People Weekly* 32:97-8 S 25 '89

Description
Factory outlets and neighborhood eateries . . . San Francisco's South Park. il map *Sunset (Central West edition)* 183:16+ N '89
Infinite riches in a little room. H. Caen. il por *Architectural Digest* 46:52+ My '89
The other San Francisco. L. Moss. il *McCall's* 117:16 O '89
Sammy Hagar does the wheel thing. por *Rolling Stone* p39 Jl 13-27 '89

Earthquake and fire, 1906
First the shaking, then the flames. F. Trippett. il *Time* 134:50-1 O 30 '89
The original big one. J. London. il *U.S. News & World Report* 107:34 O 30 '89

Festivals
Lively times in Latino San Francisco [Day of the Dead celebration] il map *Sunset (Central West edition)* 183:32-3+ O '89

Galleries and museums
See also
Fraenkel Gallery

Harbor
See also
Fisherman's Wharf (San Francisco, Calif.)

Historic houses, sites, etc.
The 1909 Leon K. Roos house in San Francisco [designed by B. Maybeck] S. B. Woodbridge. il *Architectural Digest* 46:162+ My '89
Fantasies by the Bay: Tony Duquette's San Francisco residence and sculpture pavilion. T. Duquette. il por *Architectural Digest* 46:262-9+ My '89
Golden Gate to get Presidio Army base. il *National Parks* 63:14 Jl/Ag '89
The Presidio: another great park for San Francisco? [cover story] il maps *Sunset (Central West edition)* 183:78-85 N '89
Quake cabin conversion: Chuck Williams' 1906 house in San Francisco. B. D. Colen. il por *Architectural Digest* 46:290-5 My '89

History
See also
San Francisco (Calif.)—Earthquake and fire, 1906

Hotels, motels, etc.
Once and future luxury [restoration of the Sheraton Palace] B. Weber. il *The New York Times Magazine* p94 O 15 '89

Music
See also
San Francisco Opera
San Francisco Opera Center

Ordinances
San Francisco set to define 'family' [referendum on affording legal recognition to unmarried heterosexual and homosexual couples] R. Digitale. il *Christianity Today* 33:44-6 O 20 '89
See also
San Francisco (Calif.)—Ordinances

Politics and government
See also
San Francisco (Calif.)—Ordinances
Art Agnos: scapegoat by the Bay? J. O. Hamilton. il por *Business Week* p46+ Ap 17 '89

Religious institutions and affairs
Forty hours [devotions for end to AIDS at Most Holy Redeemer Catholic Church] T. McGrath. il *U.S. Catholic* 54:20-7 N '89

Restaurants, nightclubs, bars, etc.
Fowl play [Masa's] D. Shaw. il *Gentlemen's Quarterly* 59:476+ S '89
A fresh California cuisine [Postrio, Speedo 690, Roti, and Lark Creek Inn] T. Clifton. il *Newsweek* 113:66+ Je 5 '89
Golden Gate late spots. B. Fong-Torres. il *Harper's Bazaar* 122:178+ My '89
Golden gates [chef B. Tropp of China Moon Cafe] S. H. Loomis. il *The New York Times Magazine* p49-50 F 12 '89
The martini master [bartender B. Mooshei at the Persian Aub Zam Zam] S. Kettmann. il por *Gentlemen's Quarterly* 59:72+ My '89
Slimming summer suppers [work of chef K. Mills at the Clift Hotel] T. Ney. il por *Prevention (Emmaus, Pa.)* 41:66-8+ Ag '89
Spécialités de la maison:
Bix, Angkor Wat. C. Bates. il *Gourmet* 49:18+ Ja '89
Il Fornaio. C. Bates. il *Gourmet* 49:36+ Ag '89
The French Room, Rôti, Lascaux. C. Bates. il *Gourmet* 49:62+ O '89
Postrio, Harbor Village Restaurant, Ristorante Milano. C. Bates. il *Gourmet* 49:64+ D '89
Tadich Grill, Sam's Grill, Corona Bar & Grill. C. Bates. il *Gourmet* 49:26+ Mr '89
Talk of the town [W. Puck's Postrio] D. P. Marshall. il *Travel Holiday* 172:102-3 Ag '89
The taste of the town. J. Wood. il *Harper's Bazaar* 122:176+ My '89

Social life and customs
San Francisco protocol: Charlotte Mailliard Swig in Pacific Heights. H. Junker. il por *Architectural Digest* 46:238-43+ My '89

Sports
A fan's view of Bay's ball. R. Fimrite. il *Sports Illustrated* 71:40-1 O 23 '89
San Francisco. K. Nelson. il *Sport (New York, N.Y.)* 80:98-100+ O '89
Tale of two cities [Oakland vs. San Francisco] R. Corelli. il *Maclean's* 102:61 O 23 '89
Two cities wild for 'Baysball'. H. Caen. il *Newsweek* 114:70 O 23 '89

SAN FRANCISCO (CALIF.)—*cont.*
Stores
See also
Bellini (Firm)
Traveler's market. D. P. Marshall. il *Travel Holiday* 172:34-9 Ag '89
Two on the town [San Francisco Centre] P. M. Sachner. il maps *Architectural Record* 177:122-7 My '89
Taxicabs
Fare's fare, but when cabdriver Chuck Hollom goes off the meter, criminals had better look out. W. Plummer. il pors *People Weekly* 32:97-8 S 25 '89
Theater
See also
American Conservatory Theatre
San Francisco Mime Troupe
SAN FRANCISCO BALLET
Reviews:
January-to-May season in San Francisco. J. Ross. il *Dance Magazine* 63:70+ O '89
SAN FRANCISCO BAY (CALIF.)
Thanks to Boat & Breakfast, Bay Area landlubbers can enjoy the high life on the high seas [owner R. Harris] J. Boudreau. il pors *People Weekly* 32:107-8 O 16 '89
Bridges
Exhibitions
Bridging the Bay, dreams and reality [Oakland Museum exhibit] il *Sunset (Central West edition)* 182:28-9 Je '89
SAN FRANCISCO BAY AREA (CALIF.)
Art
The Bay Area: the persistence of light. M. Schapiro. il *Art News* 88:132-7 D '89
A new exhibition proves that even when abstraction dominates, the figure remains irresistible [Bay Area figurative art, 1950-1965] J. Tarshis. il *Vogue* 179:210+ D '89
Blacks
Black areas in California hit hard by quake. D. M. Cheers. il *Jet* 77:4-7+ N 6 '89
Description and travel
Hiking up for Bay views. il *Sunset (Central West edition)* 182:14-16 Ja '89
Earthquake, 1989
After the great quake of '89 [cover story; special section] il *U.S. News & World Report* 107:28-31+ O 30 '89
After the shock [cover story; special section] il maps *Newsweek* 114:22-32+ O 30 '89
Aftershocks. B. Bradley. *The New Republic* 201:15-16 N 27 '89
Bay Area quake fails to fit textbook model. R. Monastersky. map *Science News* 136:277 O 28 '89
A city trembled, its people held [cover story] il *People Weekly* 32:32-7 O 30 '89
Digging out from under. il pors *People Weekly* 32:46-51 N 6 '89
Earthquake [cover story; special section] il maps *Time* 134:30-40+ O 30 '89
Earthquake closes San Francisco airport for 13 hr., damages tower. R. G. O'Lone and B. W. Henderson. *Aviation Week & Space Technology* 131:20 O 23 '89
Earthquake: four stores face uncertain future. M. Reuter and others. *Publishers Weekly* 236:10-11 N 3 '89
Earthquake leaves Bay Area still vulnerable. R. Monastersky. *Science News* 136:261 O 21 '89
The earthquake: the day the World Series stopped [cover story; special section] il *Sports Illustrated* 71:22-32+ O 30 '89
Hurricane Hugo and the Bay Area earthquake: America responds to disaster [cover story; special issue] il maps *Scholastic Update (Teachers' edition)* 122:1-15 D 15 '89
Julio Berumen. il por *People Weekly* 32:54 D 25 '89-Ja 1 '90
Learning from the big quake, getting ready for the future. il *Sunset (Central West edition)* 183:106-7 D '89
Little big one. L. Bensky. *The Nation* 249:553 N 13 '89
Loma Prieta quake unsettles geophysicists. R. A. Kerr. il *Science* 246:1562-3 D 22 '89
Loma Prieta: saved by a short, sharp shock. M. Barinaga. il map *Science* 246:1390-1 D 15 '89
A loving father eases the recovery of Julio Berumen, the quake's littlest survivor. M. Brower. il pors *People Weekly* 32:74-5 D 4 '89
Magnetic signal preceded October quake. R. Monastersky. *Science News* 136:390 D 16 '89
On earthquakes and aftershocks. R. M. Brown. *The Christian Century* 106:1039-40 N 15 '89
Picking up the pieces. M. Nemeth. il *Maclean's* 102:44-5 N 6 '89
'Preshock' pattern may foretell quakes [research by Karen C. McNally] R. Monastersky. *Science News* 136:374-5 D 9 '89
Reading the future in Loma Prieta. R. A. Kerr. il map *Science* 246:436-9 O 27 '89
Recovery by the Bay. E. Salholz. il *Newsweek* 114:37+ N 6 '89
Resonance implicated in Nimitz tragedy [collapse of Oakland freeway] *Science News* 136:367 D 2 '89
Shakeup. E. Yoffe. *The New Republic* 201:11-12 N 13 '89

Shock and aftershock [cover story; special section; with editorial comment by Kevin Doyle] il maps *Maclean's* 102:2, 52-60+ O 30 '89
Unrecorded agonies. J. Jordan. il *The Progressive* 53:12-14 D '89
'We've been remarkably lucky'. J. B. Levine and R. Barker. il *Business Week* p38-9 O 30 '89
What, when and where next? il *U.S. News & World Report* 107:14-15 N 6 '89
Economic aspects
See also
Earthquake Relief concert, 1989
Beat the devil. A. Cockburn. il *The Nation* 249:628-9 N 27 '89
Black areas in California hit hard by quake. D. M. Cheers. il *Jet* 77:4-7+ N 6 '89
Getting money to fix the roads will take more than an earthquake. P. Dworkin. *U.S. News & World Report* 107:44 N 6 '89
How Safeway coped with the quake. G. Hector. il map *Fortune* 120:101-2+ N 20 '89
Now, the financial aftershocks. G. J. Church. il *Time* 134:21+ N 6 '89
Oakland prepares to accept traffic from damaged SFO. R. G. O'Lone. il *Aviation Week & Space Technology* 131:25+ O 30 '89
Oaklanders rap aid after quake; mayor pushes for his city's fair share. il *Jet* 77:7 N 13 '89
The quake may shake more taxes out of Californians. R. D. Hof and J. B. Levine. il *Business Week* p42 N 6 '89
Quake update: damaged stores reopen; Debt forgiveness asked [bookstores] J. Mutter and M. J. O'Brien. *Publishers Weekly* 236:10 D 1 '89
'Save the books' fund helps quake-damaged bookstores replace children's books. B. Stander. *Publishers Weekly* 236:44-5 N 24 '89
Psychological aspects
And now, emotional aftershocks. A. Toufexis. il *Time* 134:46 O 30 '89
Coping with quake fear. D. Gelman. il *Newsweek* 114:42+ O 30 '89
Religious aspects
Ministries come to aid of quake victims. il *Christianity Today* 33:74-5 N 17 '89
Reporters and reporting
Made for television tragedies. P. Sudo. *Scholastic Update (Teachers' edition)* 122:13 D 15 '89
Perspectives on San Francisco. il *World Press Review* 36:44 D '89
Television in the dark. W. Isaacson. il *Time* 134:47 O 30 '89
"We're having an . . ." [work of ABC sports anchor A. Michaels] S. Smith. il por *Sports Illustrated* 71:35 O 30 '89

Galleries and museums
Gift shopping at science museums in the Bay Area. il *Sunset (Central West edition)* 183:14 D '89
Oddball museums in the Bay Area. il *Sunset (Central West edition)* 183:22-5 O '89
Historic houses, sites, etc.
Bay Area mansions to rent for special occasions. il *Sunset (Central West edition)* 183:20+ N '89
Industries
See also
Coffee industry
Music
Oboe to gamelan . . . want to join a music group? [San Francisco Bay Area] il *Sunset (Central West edition)* 182:50 F '89
Photographs and photography
Vintage San Francisco. il *Sunset (Central West edition)* 183:16 D '89
Stores
A food lover's tour of East Bay "gourmet gulches" [shops in Oakland, Berkeley, Albany] il map *Sunset (Central West edition)* 183:168+ S '89
Santa Fe hits the Bay Area. il *Sunset (Central West edition)* 182:74+ Je '89
SAN FRANCISCO CONSERVATION CORPS
Doing something meaningful. B. Cohn. il *Newsweek* 114:38 Ag 28 '89
SAN FRANCISCO ETHNIC DANCE FESTIVAL *See* Dance festivals—California
SAN FRANCISCO INTERNATIONAL AIRPORT *See* San Francisco (Calif.)—Airports
SAN FRANCISCO MIME TROUPE
Fighting that Bushed feeling. B. Ohanian. il *Mother Jones* 14:49 Ja '89
SAN FRANCISCO MUSIC BOX COMPANY
Music to their ears [J. and M. Lenser] M. Barrier. il pors *Nation's Business* 77:69-70 Mr '89
SAN FRANCISCO-OAKLAND BAY BRIDGE (CALIF.)
A blessing in disguise [partial collapse] M. Barinaga. map *Science* 246:1391 D 15 '89
SAN FRANCISCO OPERA
Detail man [general director L. Mansouri] S. Von Buchau. il pors *Opera News* 54:24-7 S '89

SAN FRANCISCO OPERA—cont.
San Francisco. S. Von Buchau. il *Opera News* 53:36-7 Ja 7 '89
SAN FRANCISCO OPERA CENTER
San Francisco. S. Von Buchau. il *Opera News* 54:52 S '89
SAN GIACOMO, LAURA
about
How Laura San Giacomo got a bad rep. R. Sekoff. il por *Mademoiselle* 95:114+ S '89
No fib—in sex, lies, and videotape newcomer Laura San Giacomo provides plenty of the first. il pors *People Weekly* 32:90-2 S 11 '89
SAN JOAQUIN RIVER (CALIF.)
See also
Sacramento-San Joaquin Delta (Calif.)
SAN JOSE (CALIF.)
Education
Caroline Davis Jr. High [jazz band] R. Tolleson. il *Down Beat* 56:24 O '89
SAN JUAN BASIN ROYALTY TRUST
Coal feat. T. Mack. il *Forbes* 144:198 O 2 '89
SAN JUAN BIENNIAL
San Juan Biennial: Arsenal de la Marina. T. Wall. il *Art News* 88:183 Summ '89
SAN JUAN ISLANDS (WASH.)
See also
Architecture, Domestic—San Juan Islands (Wash.)
Orcas Island (Wash.)
SAN JUAN RIVER (COLO.-UTAH)
A canyon, an egret . . . and a mystery [setting for the novel A thief of time] T. Hillerman. il *Audubon* 91:30-4+ Jl '89
Anecdotes, facetiae, satire, etc.
Deep ecology [taking a raft trip; excerpt from Outposts of Eden] P. Stegner. il *Sierra* 74:68-73+ Mr/Ap '89
SAN MARINO GRAND PRIX *See* Automobile racing—Italy
SAN MARTIN, ROBERT L.
Renewable energy: power for tomorrow. il por *The Futurist* 23:37-40 My/Je '89
SAN PEDRO DE MACORIS (DOMINICAN REPUBLIC)
Japan turns the double play [scouts from Japan in Dominican Republic] G. Black. il *The Nation* 248:370+ Mr 20 '89
SAN QUENTIN PRISON (CALIF.) *See* Prisons—California
SAN RAFAEL (CALIF.)
Historic houses, sites, etc.
See also
St. Vincent's School for Boys (San Rafael, Calif.)
SAN SALVADOR (EL SALVADOR)
Where did Columbus land? [research by Kim Gainer indicates San Salvador more likely than Samana Cay] map *USA Today (Periodical)* 117:10 Ap '89
SANAA (YEMEN ARAB REPUBLIC)
Historic houses, sites, etc.
Helping Ham's hammams. A. Hills. il *History Today* 39:4-5 Ja '89
SANBORN, DAVID
about
David Sanborn beat childhood polio to play in the big time. A. Abrahams. il pors *People Weekly* 32:89-90 D 18 '89
SANBORN, TONIA
about
All-American Girl-talk. il pors *Teen* 33:98 N '89
SANCHEZ, ARANTXA
about
Giant killers. C. Kirkpatrick. il pors *Sports Illustrated* 70:34-6+ Je 19 '89
They reign in Spain. C. Shmerler. il pors *World Tennis* 37:38-41 N '89
Youth will be served. T. Callahan. il pors *Time* 133:90 Je 26 '89
SÁNCHEZ, ARNALDO OCHOA *See* Ochoa Sánchez, Arnaldo
SANCHEZ, FERNANDO
about
Minimalism with a flourish. R. Urquhart. il *Vogue* 179:194-201+ Ja '89
SANCHEZ, JOSE GUILLERMO MEDINA *See* Medina Sanchez, Jose Guillermo
SANCHEZ, OSCAR ARIAS *See* Arias Sanchez, Oscar
SANCHEZ, PONCHO
about
Poncho Sanchez. M. Handler. il por *Down Beat* 56:14 N '89
SANCHEZ-LAVEGA, AGUSTIN
Saturn's great white spots. il *Sky and Telescope* 78:141-2 Ag '89
SANCTIFICATION *See* Holiness
SANCTIONS (INTERNATIONAL LAW)
See also
Embargo
Iranian seizure of United States embassy, 1979-1981—Economic aspects
Libyan-American conflict, 1986—Economic aspects
AAP report hits book embargo of South Africa as 'misguided'. C. Reid. *Publishers Weekly* 236:8+ D 1 '89
Canada in a hot seat [business transactions with South Africa questioned at Commonwealth meeting] M. Nemeth. il por *Maclean's* 102:21 F 20 '89

The challenge to sanctions [South Africa] J. Bierman. il *Maclean's* 102:24+ Mr 13 '89
Do South African sanctions make sense? D. Reed. il *Reader's Digest* 134:51-6 F '89
Family quarrel [British opposition to sanctions against South Africa at Commonwealth summit in Kuala Lumpur, Malaysia] R. Laver. il *Maclean's* 102:40-1 O 30 '89
National emergency in Panama [message to Congress, October 14, 1988] R. Reagan. *Department of State Bulletin* 88:57 D '88
Polling the Israelites: Boesak on sanctions. A. Welsh-Huggins. *The Christian Century* 106:924-5 O 18 '89
Real sanctions [against South Africa] *The Nation* 249:372 O 9 '89
A thorny dispute [Britain refuses to endorse call for sanctions against South Africa at Commonwealth conference in Malaysia] R. Laver. il por *Maclean's* 102:36-7 N 6 '89
SANCTUARIES, BIRD *See* Bird sanctuaries
SANCTUARIES, WILDLIFE *See* Wildlife sanctuaries
SANCTUARY (LAW) *See* Asylum, Right of
SANCTUARY MOVEMENT (REFUGEE AID)
Refugees find little refuge in U.S. D. Moul. il *Christianity Today* 33:40-1 Ap 21 '89
SAND
See also
Oil sands
Digging into sand [sandpile avalanches and self-organized criticality; cover story] I. Peterson. il *Science News* 136:40-2 Jl 15 '89
Dynamics of liquefaction during the 1987 Superstition Hills, California, earthquake [cover story] T. L. Holzer and others. bibl f il map *Science* 244:56-9 Ap 7 '89
Large-scale, low-amplitude bedforms (chevrons) in the Selima sand sheet, Egypt [Landsat images] T. A. Maxwell and C. V. Haynes. bibl f il map *Science* 243:1179-82 Mr 3 '89
X-ray movies reveal sand flow patterns [research by Robert P. Behringer] I. Peterson. il *Science News* 135:293 My 13 '89
SAND FLIES *See* Moth flies
SAND IN LANDSCAPE ARCHITECTURE
The back-yard beach. il *Sunset (Central West edition)* 183:68-9 Jl '89
SAND SCULPTORS INTERNATIONAL
Todd Vander Pluym: making a pile in sand sculpture. D. Castellon. il por *Business Week* p98 My 8 '89
SAND SCULPTURE
See also
Sand Sculptors International
SANDBERG, RYNE
about
Home base. M. Huzinec. il pors *Ladies' Home Journal* 106:130+ S '89
SANDBERG, WARREN S., AND TERWILLIGER, THOMAS C.
Influence of interior packing and hydrophobicity on the stability of a protein. bibl f il *Science* 245:54-7 Jl 7 '89
SANDBOXES
Open or shut sandbox . . . built into the deck. il *Sunset (Central West edition)* 182:126 Ap '89
SANDBULTE, AREND J.
about
Deft management. J. Cook. il por *Forbes* 144:96+ D 11 '89
SANDELL, LAURA
The modern poster. il *American Artist* 53:28+ S '89
SANDEMAN, ROBERT
about
History repeats itself. J. I. Packer. *Christianity Today* 33:22 S 22 '89
SANDER, STANLEY P., AND OTHERS
Rate of formation of the ClO dimer in the polar stratosphere: implications for ozone loss. bibl f il *Science* 245:1095-8 S 8 '89
SANDERS, BARRY
about
Barry breaks away. W. Nack. il pors *Sports Illustrated* 70:24-6+ Ap 10 '89
Heisman winner Sanders hires black agent, lawyer. il por *Jet* 76:47 My 29 '89
Sanders gives his church $1/4 million in tithes. il por *Jet* 76:51 S 25 '89
SANDERS, DEION
about
Decisions, decisions. D. Scheiber. il *Sports Illustrated* 71:30-2+ Jl 3 '89
A double play for Deion? A. Kim. por *Sports Illustrated* 70:26 Je 12 '89
'They don't pay nobody to be humble' [cover story] C. Kirkpatrick. il pors *Sports Illustrated* 71:52-6+ N 13 '89
SANDERS, JOHN L.
Ayr Mount on the Eno River, near Hillsborough, North Carolina. bibl f il por *Antiques* 135:1190-201 My '89
SANDERS, KEN
Emerging trends in architectural CAD software. il *Architectural Record* 177:130-1+ Mr '89

SANDERS, L. C., AND LORD, ELIZABETH M.
Directed movement of latex particles in the gynoecia of three species of flowering plants. bibl f il *Science* 243:1606-8 Mr 24 '89

SANDERS, MARLENE
Are women reporters better than men? il *TV Guide* 37:15-16+ Mr 18-24 '89

about
What happened to Marlene Sanders? L. C. Pogrebin. il pors *New Choices for the Best Years* 29:67-71+ Mr '89

SANDERS, SCOTT
about
Taking it on the road. P. Newcomb. il por *Forbes* 144:275 Jl 24 '89

SANDERS, SCOTT R. (SCOTT RUSSELL), 1945-
Under the influence. il *Harper's* 279:68-75 N '89

SANDERS, TIMOTHY GREENFIELD- *See* Greenfield-Sanders, Timothy

SANDERS, WILLIAM
about
Barry breaks away. W. Nack. il pors *Sports Illustrated* 70:24-6+ Ap 10 '89

SANDERS (MACHINERY) *See* Sanding and sanding equipment

SANDERS ASSOCIATES, INC.
Lockheed establishes military avionics unit in Sanders affiliate. D. Hughes. il *Aviation Week & Space Technology* 130:92-3+ Ap 24 '89
Sanders develops MMIC chips for use in electronic warfare. il *Aviation Week & Space Technology* 131:99+ S 18 '89
Sanders develops MMIC for phased array systems [monolithic microwave integrated circuit device] *Aviation Week & Space Technology* 130:291 Je 12 '89
Sanders upgrades IR countermeasures, explores techniques for future systems [coverage against infrared guided missiles] il *Aviation Week & Space Technology* 131:118-19+ S 11 '89

SANDERSON, MICHAEL
about
Revolution at Merrill Lynch. P. C. Newman. il *Maclean's* 102:66 N 20 '89

SANDES, FLORA
about
Flora Sandes—military maid. J. Wheelwright. bibl f il pors map *History Today* 39:42-8 Mr '89

SANDHILL CRANES *See* Cranes (Birds)

SANDIA NATIONAL LABORATORIES
Ka-boom! [impact resistance test using an F-4 Phantom jet] J. Kluger. il *Discover* 10:44-5 D '89
Propelled jet [crash resistance tests of critical structures] A. Fisher. il *Popular Science* 235:14+ D '89
USAF, Sandia developing new parachute system for F-111 crew escape module. il *Aviation Week & Space Technology* 129:54-5 Mr 6 '89

SANDIEGO, CARMEN (VIDEO GAMES) *See* Carmen Sandiego (Video games)

SANDING AND SANDING EQUIPMENT
Finishing sanders. H. Wicks. il *Home Mechanix* 85:24+ My '89
New belt sander [Elu Model 4024] R. Capotosto. il *Popular Mechanics* 166:86 D '89
Sander secrets. R. Capotosto. il *Popular Mechanics* 166:85-9 Jl '89
Sanding on a radial arm saw [Performax S/T attachment] A. R. Gould. il *Workbench* 45:22 S/O '89
Shopmade drum sanders. D. M. Batory. il *Workbench* 45:67 My/Je '89
Shopsmith hits the mark [add-on biscuit joiner and strip sander] J. Truini. il *Popular Mechanics* 166:64 Ap '89
Three's company [Delta's new Sawbuck, belt/disc sander and table saw] J. Truini. il *Popular Mechanics* 166:94 Jl '89
Using a belt sander (without disasters!). K. Collier. il *The Family Handyman* 39:16+ Ja '89

SANDINISTA GOVERNMENT *See* Nicaragua—Politics and government

SANDLA, ROBERT
Downtown. See issues of Dance Magazine beginning November 1989

SANDLER, ASIR
about
The wasted years. A. Wilson-Smith. il por *Maclean's* 102:24 My 15 '89

SANDLER, HARVEY
about
Harvey Sandler. P. Noglows. il por *Channels (New York, N.Y.: 1986)* 9:54 Jl/Ag '89

SANDLER CAPITAL MANAGEMENT
Harvey Sandler. P. Noglows. il por *Channels (New York, N.Y.: 1986)* 9:54 Jl/Ag '89
Station-dealing blues [views of B. Lewis] P. Noglows. il *Channels (New York, N.Y.: 1986)* 9:89 F '89

SANDMAIER, MARIAN
Is there angst after abortion? *Mademoiselle* 95:94+ Jl '89
News. See issues of Mademoiselle
Sex-shy: why we're still squeamish after all these years. il *Mademoiselle* 95:155+ Ap '89

SANDMEL, BEN
Fats' city. il *Mother Jones* 14:40+ N '89
A vibrant legacy. il *The Atlantic* 263:88-9+ Ap '89

SANDOMIR, RICHARD
The '90s. il *Sport (New York, N.Y.)* 80:91-2+ O '89

SANDOVAL, FRANCES
about
Frances Sandoval. S. Kanfer. il por *People Weekly* 32 Special Issue:126 Fall '89

SANDPIPERS
Sexual behavior
See Sexual behavior—Birds

SANDROFF, C. J., AND OTHERS
GaAs clusters in the quantum size regime: growth on high surface area silica by molecular beam epitaxy. bibl f il *Science* 245:391-3 Jl 28 '89

SANDROFF, RONNI
The baby shoppers. *Vogue* 179:246+ My '89
Is your job driving you crazy? il *Psychology Today* 23:41-5 Jl/Ag '89

SANDVED, KJELL BLOCH, 1922-
On the wing [photographs] il *Harper's* 279:43 O '89

SANDWEISS, MARTHA A.
Eliot Porter: the master eye. il *National Wildlife* 27:52-9 F/Mr '89

SANDWICH ISLANDS *See* Hawaii

SANDWICHES
Breakfast sandwiches [microwaved] il *Southern Living* 24:130-1 Ja '89
Heart-smart soups and sandwiches. J. B. Hurley. il *Prevention (Emmaus, Pa.)* 41:70-2+ Mr '89
Hot, hearty sandwich. J. Taylor. il *Better Homes and Gardens* 67:132 Mr '89
New hope for the bread. A. Nathan. il *Esquire* 111:109-12 Ja '89
Piled high and hot off the grill . . . turkey or pork sandwiches. il *Sunset (Central West edition)* 183:110 Jl '89
The sandwich club. S. Costner. il *Working Woman* 14:122-4 My '89
Sandwiches: the moveable feast. J. F. Mariani. il *Motor Boating & Sailing* 163:44-5 Je '89
Soup & sandwich [cran-turkey sandwiches] il *Good Housekeeping* 209:128 O '89
Summer sense in a sandwich. M. S. Boyd. il *American Health* 8:100-2 Jl/Ag '89
Summer sense in a sandwich. M. S. Boyd. il *The Mother Earth News* 118:78+ Jl/Ag '89
Super supper sandwiches. il *Ladies' Home Journal* 106:170-2+ O '89
Tasty chicken sandwiches [microwaving] il *McCall's* 116:135 Ap '89
Teatime sandwiches. il *Good Housekeeping* 209:228 N '89
Anecdotes, facetiae, satire, etc.
The great sandwich caper [memories of frozen sandwiches for school lunches] C. Murphy. il *Reader's Digest* 135:149-50 S '89
Contamination
Foul flying subs [tainted submarine sandwiches served by Northwest Airlines] il *FDA Consumer* 23:34-5 Jl/Ag '89
Names
Ronald Reagan is full of bologna [deli sandwiches named for celebrities] J. Queenan. il *Gentlemen's Quarterly* 59:161-2 Ag '89

SANFORD, MIDGE
about
Midge Sanford & Sarah Pillsbury [interview] il pors *American Film* 15:26-9 O '89

SANFORD, TERRY, 1917-
Should the Congress adopt the "Financial Institutions Reform, Recovery, and Enforcement Act of 1989"? [excerpts from address, April 18, 1989] *Congressional Digest* 68:180+ Je/Jl '89
Should the Senate-passed Immigration Act of 1989 be approved? [excerpts from debate, July 12, 1989] *Congressional Digest* 68:248+ O '89

SANFORD C. BERNSTEIN & CO., INC.
The next waves [interview with M. Stahlman] G. F. Gilder. il por *Forbes* 143:186+ Ap 17 '89

SANIBEL ISLAND (FLA.)
Climate
Nature's one-upmanship [effects of tropical storm on Sanibel Island ecosystem] C. R. Robins. il *Sea Frontiers* 35:192 My/Je '89

SANITARY LANDFILLS
Dump proposed near New River Gorge. il *National Parks* 63:10 My/Je '89
Unexpected leakage through landfill liners [diffusion of chemicals through clay] J. Raloff. *Science News* 135:164 Mr 18 '89
Canada
Profiting from waste [Toronto] D. Jenish. il *Maclean's* 102:38-40 Ja 23 '89

SANITARY NAPKINS, TAMPONS, ETC. *See* Feminine hygiene products

SANITATION
See also
Arcata (Calif.)—Sanitary affairs
Beaches—Sanitation

SANITATION—See also—*cont.*
Benton (Ky.)—Sanitary affairs
Boston (Mass.)—Sanitary affairs
Day care—Sanitation
Florida—Sanitary affairs
Food handling
Jefferson City (Mo.)—Sanitary affairs
Malibu (Calif.)—Sanitary affairs
New York (N.Y.)—Sanitary affairs
Plumbing
Public comfort stations
Railroads—Sanitation
Refuse and refuse disposal
Restaurants—Sanitation
San Diego (Calif.)—Sanitary affairs
Septic tanks
Shellfish industry—Sanitation
Space stations—Sanitation
Swine houses—Sanitation
Toronto (Ont.)—Sanitary affairs
SANITATION DEPT. (NEW YORK, N.Y.) *See* New York
(N.Y.). Dept. of Sanitation
SANJURJO DE CASCIERO, ANNICK
Art in the limelight. il *Américas* 41 no1:52-7 '89
SANNEH, LAMIN O.
A child shall lead us. *The Christian Century* 106:1146 D
6 '89
Dreams and letting God be God. *The Christian Century*
106:1195 D 20-27 '89
Human folly on a grand scale. il *The Christian Century*
106:843 S 27 '89
Naming and the act of faith. *The Christian Century* 106:875
O 4 '89
A 'new moon' sensitivity. *The Christian Century* 106:811
S 13-20 '89
The owl in the daylight. il *The Christian Century* 106:1115
N 29 '89
Rushdie's moral hegira. *The Christian Century* 106:622-6
Je 21-28 '89
The spirit in sound doctrine. *The Christian Century* 106:930
O 18 '89
Tales of miraculous healing. *The Christian Century* 106:906
O 11 '89
Waiting on God. *The Christian Century* 106:1170 D 13
'89
about
Missions and the translatable Gospel [cover story] J. B.
Carman. *The Christian Century* 106:786+ Ag 30-S 6 '89
SANS SOUCI (JAMAICA: RESORT) *See* Health resorts,
watering places, etc.—Jamaica
SANSON, CHARLES-HENRI
about
The heirs of Madame Guillotine. D. Lawday. il por *U.S.
News & World Report* 107:46-8 Jl 17 '89
Patrick Brunet, whose ancestor guillotined Louis XVI, swears
he's no chip off the old block. T. Allis. il pors *People
Weekly* 31:128+ Je 5 '89
SANT' ANGELO, GIORGIO
about
Obituary
Vogue il por 179:162+ N '89
SANTA BARBARA (CALIF.)
Architecture
Western tilt [B. Berkus' Santa Barbara home] P. Clothier.
il por *Art News* 88:95-6+ Summ '89
Art
Artists in residences [installations in private houses] K. Baker.
il *House & Garden* 161:38+ Ja '89
Gardens and gardening
Vegetables all year from their front garden [garden of Stephen
Holbrook] il *Sunset (Central West edition)* 183:190+ O
'89
Water-stingy but colorful slope garden in Santa Barbara.
il *Sunset (Central West edition)* 183:200 O '89
Restaurants, nightclubs, bars, etc.
Spécialités de la maison:
Wine Cask. C. Bates. il *Gourmet* 49:38+ S '89
SANTA BARBARA COUNTY (CALIF.)
Wine industry
See Wine industry
SANTA CATALINA ISLAND (CALIF.)
See also
Fish—Santa Catalina Island (Calif.)
SANTA CLARA COUNTY (CALIF.)
Pollution
From Silicon Valley to 'Death Valley'. M. A. Lerner. il
Newsweek 114:26-7 Jl 31 '89
Social life and customs
Valley culture in the Age of Accretion [Silicon Valley] M.
Rogers. il *Personal Computing* 13:27-8 O '89
SANTA CLAUS
Collectibles
Santa is everything that is Christmas [excerpt from Homes
for the holiday with painted treasures] M. J. Leisure and
M. Wentz. il *Good Housekeeping* 209:166-7 D '89

SANTA CRUZ (CALIF.)
Crime
The Bandler method [neurolinguistic programming guru R.
Bandler acquitted of Santa Cruz, Calif. murder of C.
Christensen] F. Clancy and H. Yorkshire. il pors *Mother
Jones* 14:22-8+ F/Mr '89
Waterfront
Last of the West's beach boardwalks. il *Sunset (Central
West edition)* 183:136 Ag '89
SANTA CRUZ OPERATION INC.
Bringing Unix to PCs [D. Michels] C. O'Malley. por *Personal
Computing* 13:83 Jl '89
Can this small fry put Unix in a million desktops? R.
Brandt. il *Business Week* p116 Mr 27 '89
SANTA FE (N.M.)
Architecture
Contemporary Southwest [adobe home of S. S. Lewis] R.
Morris. il *Architectural Digest* 46:148-55 Ap '89
Art
Artists of different cultures in the New Mexico light. A.
Hines. il *American Artist* 53:60-5+ D '89
Soul of the plains [Native American artists] T. Gold. il
Harper's Bazaar 122:20+ Jl '89
Bookstores
See Booksellers and bookselling—New Mexico
Description
Do you know the way to Sante Fe? P. Johnson. il *Black
Enterprise* 19:335-6+ Je '89
Gourmet holidays: Santa Fe [southwestern cooking] Z. E.
Zakroff. il *Gourmet* 49:86-93+ D '89
Galleries and museums
See also
Museum of International Folk Art (Santa Fe, N.M.)
Gardens and gardening
Living tapestry in Santa Fe. il *Sunset (Central West edition)*
182:90-1 Je '89
Housing
The Santa Fe adobe. il *Esquire* 112:80 D '89
Markets
See also
Indian Market (Santa Fe, N.M.)
Music
See also
Santa Fe Opera
Starlit melodies. M. Wolf. il *Harper's Bazaar* 122:28 Jl '89
Religious institutions and affairs
Intention [Rosh Hashanah services] *The New Yorker* 65:38-9
O 16 '89
Restaurants, nightclubs, bars, etc.
Concerning food and wine. R. L. Balzer. il *Travel Holiday*
171:20+ Ap '89
Coyote cuisine. J. Steingarten. il *Vogue* 179:196-7+ Jl '89
Shopper's sustenance. *Travel Holiday* 171:28-9 Mr '89
Stores
Santa Fe: a desert shopping oasis. D. P. Marshall. il *Travel
Holiday* 171:20+ Mr '89
SANTA FE INSTITUTE (N.M.)
Physics for economists [computer simulations of economic
scenarios] E. Dyson. il *Forbes* 144:266 O 16 '89
Strange bedfellows [physicists and economists] R. Pool. il
Science 245:700-3 Ag 18 '89
SANTA FE NATIONAL FOREST (N.M.)
Logging poses threat to Bandelier. il *National Parks* 63:10
N/D '89
SANTA FE OPERA
Musical events:
A night at the Chinese opera and other works presented
during the summer. A. Porter. *The New Yorker* 65:125-8
S 18 '89
Santa Fe. D. Harris. *Opera News* 54:63-6 D 9 '89
SANTA FE SOUTHERN PACIFIC CORPORATION
Almost everybody wants to break up Santa Fe. B. Bremner
and C. Hawkins. il por *Business Week* p67 Mr 6 '89
Impatient money. T. Jaffe. *Forbes* 143:236 Ap 17 '89
SANTA MARIA (SHIP)
Shipshape [replicas of the Niña, Pinta and Santa Maria]
il por *Life* 12:26-30 Ap '89
The three sisters [replica of Columbus' ship] B. Weber. il
The New York Times Magazine p102 My 14 '89
SANTA MONICA (CALIF.)
Architecture
Domesticated experiment [Whitney House] D. Dietsch. il
Architectural Record 177:88-95 mid-Ap '89
Bookstores
See Booksellers and bookselling—California
Buildings
Main Street [Edgemar Development] K. D. Stein. il
Architectural Record 177:104-9 Jl '89
Galleries and museums
See also
Museum of Flying (Santa Monica, Calif.)
Hospitals
See also
Santa Monica Medical Center (Calif.)
Housing
Bankrupt landlords in Wonderland [rent control] M.
Beauchamp. il *Forbes* 143:105-7 Mr 20 '89

SANTA MONICA (CALIF.)—*cont.*
Politics and government
See also
Public Electronic Network (Santa Monica, Calif.:
Database)
Poor
Aerobic altruism [classes for the homeless; work of Lisa
de Mondesir] D. Groves. *American Health* 8:37 Je '89
Restaurants, nightclubs, bars, etc.
Smooth take-off [B. Marder's DC3 at Santa Monica Airport]
P. Viladas. il por *House & Garden* 161:42 Ap '89
Spécialités de la maison:
Fennel. C. Bates. il *Gourmet* 49:22+ Jl '89
Il Forno. C. Bates. il *Gourmet* 49:38+ F '89
To live and dine in L.A. [Rex, Pazzia and Fennel] D. Shaw.
il por *Gentlemen's Quarterly* 59:161+ Ap '89
Streets
The Main event [Main Street] R. Reed. il *Gentlemen's
Quarterly* 59:367-8 S '89
SANTA MONICA MEDICAL CENTER (CALIF.)
Merle Norman Pavilion, Santa Monica Medical Center. M.
Gaskie. il *Architectural Record* 177:86-9 Ap '89
**SANTA MONICA MOUNTAINS NATIONAL RECREA-
TION AREA (CALIF.)**
Exploring L.A.'s vast island of wilderness amid 11 million
people. il map *Sunset (Central West edition)* 182:22-4
Ap '89
SANTA MONICA PARTNERS
Still in the pinks [L. Goldstein's pink sheet picks] T. Jaffe.
Forbes 143:172-3 F 6 '89
SANTA PELAGIA [oratorio] See Stradella, Alessandro,
1644-1682
SANTA ROSA (CALIF.)
Description
Santa Rosa, Calif. map *New Choices for the Best Years*
29:10 Ja '89
Restaurants, nightclubs, bars, etc.
Spécialités de la maison:
Restaurant Matisse. C. Bates. il *Gourmet* 49:36+ Ag
'89
SANTA TERESA (N.M.)
Charlie Crowder sees utopia, and it's a border town. S.
Baker. il por map *Business Week* p35-6 Jl 31 '89
SANTANA, CARLOS, 1947-
Woodstock remembered: the artists. il pors *Rolling Stone*
p65 Ag 24 '89
about
Devadip Carlos Santana: instrument of light [reprint from
January 1981 issue] L. Underwood. il por *Down Beat*
56:90 S '89
SANTARONE, PAT
about
Baseball lives [excerpt] M. Bryan. il por *Sports Illustrated*
70:84-5 Ap 24 '89
SANTE, LUC
about
From the publisher. D. J. Barr. il por *Sports Illustrated*
71:4 D 4 '89
SANTIAGO, ROBERTO
Black and Latino. por *Essence* 20:12 N '89
SANTIAGO (CHILE)
Music
See also
Opera—Chile
SANTINI, SYLVIE
Spain's strike: a warning signal. *World Press Review* 36:23
Mr '89
SANTORINI (GREECE) See Thera (Greece: Island)
SANTORO, CARMELO J.
about
Thrill a minute. I. Chithelen. por *Forbes* 143:125-6 My
1 '89
SANTORO, GENE
The World Saxophone Quartet: building on a new tradition
[cover story; interview] il *Down Beat* 56:16-19 Jl '89
SANTOS, JOSÉ EDUARDO DOS, 1942-
about
"We have taken the first step". B. W. Nelan. il pors map
Time 134:28 Jl 3 '89
SANTOS, SHEROD, 1948-
The wing date at low water [poem] *The New Yorker*
65:32 Jl 3 '89
SANTOS, SILVIO
about
And now, Brazil: Heeeeere's Silvio! il por *Newsweek* 114:57
N 13 '89
SANUDO, MARIN See Sanuto, Marino, 14th cent.
SANUTO, MARINO, 14TH CENT.
about
Mapping a Crusade. O. A. W. Dilke and M. Dilke. bibl
il maps *History Today* 39:31-5 Ag '89
SÃO PAULO (BRAZIL)
Art
São Paulo diary. E. Leffingwell. il *Art in America* 77:55-7+
Ja '89
Prisons and reformatories
Cast into the black hole of Brazil. *Newsweek* 113:30 F 20
'89

To live and die. il *U.S. News & World Report* 106:14 F
20 '89
Public health
User-friendly videotex. I. Fogelman and E. O. C. Chaves.
il *World Health* p14-15 Ag/S '89
Theater
Curtains up! [restoration of Municipal Theater] il *Américas*
41 no2:3-4 '89
SÃO PAULO STOCK EXCHANGE See Bolsa de Valores
de São Paulo
SAPELO ISLAND (GA.)
Sapelo's seaside feast. S. Pacher. il maps *The Mother Earth
News* 119:80-3 S/O '89
SAPERS, CARL M.
The ability to practice as a corporation gains new impetus.
il *Architectural Record* 177:39 S '89
Who will design buildings for human habitation? (I) [interview
with M. Lunch] pors *Architectural Record* 177:41+ Je '89
Who will design buildings for human habitation? (II) [inter-
view with M. Lunch] il por *Architectural Record* 177:41-2
Jl '89
Workable firm-ownership transitions through ESOPs. por
Architectural Record 177:37+ Ja '89
SAPOCH, BETTY
about
Political pair: a win-win situation. A. L. Ball. il pors *Working
Woman* 14:137-8 O '89
SAPOLSKY, ROBERT M.
Junk food monkeys. il *Discover* 10:48-51 S '89
SAPONE, MICHEL
about
Portrait of Picasso's tailor. D. H. Minassian. il pors
Architectural Digest 46:62+ F '89
SARA LEE CORP.
How do you say L'eggs in French? S. B. Weiner. il *Forbes*
144:73+ N 27 '89
The price was right [Sara Lee acquires Champion Products]
W. Heuslein. il *Forbes* 143:10 My 15 '89
SARACENI, ELYSE
about
Obituary
High Fidelity (New York, N.Y.) il 39:51 Mr '89. T.
W. Libbey, Jr.
SARAH, DUCHESS OF YORK, 1959-
Budgie the little helicopter [story] il *Redbook* 173:128-30
S '89
about
Discordant notes [visit to Canada] M. Nichols. il pors
Maclean's 102:36 Jl 31 '89
Do good friends dress alike? (Di & Fergie do). il pors *Redbook*
173:18+ O '89
Fascinating Fergie facts [cover story] il *Redbook* 173:132
S '89
The Fergie follies [cover story] S. Pearson. il pors *Ladies'
Home Journal* 106:180-1+ My '89
Flowers abroad, flak at home [cover story] il pors *People
Weekly* 32:118-22+ N 20 '89
The furor over Fergie. P. Junor. il por *McCall's* 116:48-50+
F '89
Inside Fergie's dream house. W. Norwich. il pors *Redbook*
172:92-5 F '89
A royal mum writes for children. A. Smith. il por *Publishers
Weekly* 236:34+ S 29 '89
Royal revenge [visits to Canada; cover story; special section;
with editorial comment by Kevin Doyle] il pors *Maclean's*
102:4, 36-42+ Jl 24 '89
SARANDON, SUSAN
about
America's 10 most beautiful women. J. Etra. il pors *Harper's
Bazaar* 122:170+ S '89
Miss Congeniality. J. Queenan. por *Rolling Stone* p39-40
F 9 '89
Sarandon, seriously [cover story] A. L. Ball. pors *Mother
Jones* 14:30-3+ F/Mr '89
Susan Sarandon [interview] C. Dreifus. il *The Progressive*
53:33-6 O '89
SARASOHN, HOMER M.
about
A lesson learned and a lesson forgotten. R. C. Wood. il
pors *Forbes* 143:70-2+ F 6 '89
SARATOGA SPRINGS (N.Y.)
Bookstores
See Booksellers and bookselling—New York (State)
SARBANES, PAUL S.
Should the Congress adopt the "Tender Offer Disclosure
and Fairness Act of 1987"? [excerpts from address, June
20, 1988] *Congressional Digest* 68:84+ Mr '89
SARC See South Asian Association for Regional Cooperation
SARCOMA, KAPOSI'S See Kaposi's sarcoma
SARCOMA, SYNOVIAL See Synovioma
SARDIÑA, ADOLFO F. See Adolfo, 1933-
SARET, ALAN, 1944-
about
Alan Saret at Lorence-Monk. N. Princenthal. il *Art in America*
77:207 O '89
SARID, YOSSI
Night of the broken clubs. *Harper's* 279:31-2 S '89

SARKAR, GOBINDA, AND SOMMER, STEVE S.
Access to a messenger RNA sequence or its protein product is not limited by tissue or species specificity. bibl f il *Science* 244:331-4 Ap 21 '89
Are tissues a patch quilt of ectopic gene expression? [discussion of April 21, 1989 article, Access to a messenger RNA sequence or its protein product is not limited by tissue or species specificity] *Science* 246:261 O 13 '89
SARLOS, ANDY
about
Bay Street comes to the Danube. P. C. Newman. il *Maclean's* 102:44 Ap 17 '89
SARNOFF, ARTHUR
about
Arthur Sarnoff: American artist and illustrator. C. Martignette. il por *Antiques & Collecting Hobbies* 94:40-1+ N '89
SARNOFF, IRVING, AND SARNOFF, SUZANNE
The dialectic of marriage. il *Psychology Today* 23:54-7 O '89
SARNOFF, SUZANNE
(jt. auth) See Sarnoff, Irving, and Sarnoff, Suzanne
SARNOFF (DAVID) RESEARCH CENTER See David Sarnoff Research Center
SAROFIM, FAYEZ
about
Even behind the scenes, the Time-Warner drama has its stars. M. Ivey; J. Friedman. il pors *Business Week* p55-6 Jl 31 '89
SAROYAN, LUCY
Wish-list weekends. il *Working Woman* 14:112-13+ Je '89
SAROYAN, MARK
Trouble in the Transcaucasus. bibl f il map *The Bulletin of the Atomic Scientists* 45:16-18+ Mr '89
SARRIS, ANDREW
Carole Lombard. il pors *American Film* 14:62-4 Mr '89
Otto Preminger. il por *American Film* 14:69-71 Je '89
SARVEPALLI RADHAKRISHNAN See Radhakrishnan, S. (Sarvepalli), 1888-1975
SARVER, CARLETON
A perfect friendship [cover story] il *High Fidelity (New York, N.Y.)* 39:42-8 My '89
SARVIS, SHIRLEY
A passion for pine nuts. il *Gourmet* 49:118-19+ O '89
SAS
Can SAS keep flying with the big birds? J. Kapstein. il por *Business Week* p142+ N 27 '89
Nordic nations face need to find links with European Community. *Aviation Week & Space Technology* 130:118 Je 12 '89
SAS, Airlines of Britain to discuss possible operational merger. *Aviation Week & Space Technology* 130:109 Ja 2 '89
SAS, Swissair agree to cooperate on traffic and travel services system. *Aviation Week & Space Technology* 131:104 O 2 '89
SASKATCHEWAN
See also
Fishing—Saskatchewan
Humboldt (Sask.)
Privatization—Saskatchewan
Regina (Sask.)
Industries
See also
Potash Corporation of Saskatchewan
Politics and government
A prairie deadlock [plan to privatize Potash Corp. of Saskatchewan] P. Kopvillem. il *Maclean's* 102:20 Ag 7 '89
SASS, LORNA J.
Delicious immersions. il *Health (New York, N.Y.)* 21:54-7 Ja '89
Tales from the Burma Bridge. il *Health (New York, N.Y.)* 21:40-1+ D '89
SASSAFRAS
Sassafras: fascinating history, beautiful leaves. S. P. Bender. il *Southern Living* 24:56-7 N '89
SASSAMAN, RICHARD
Bar Harbor, RFD. il por *Country Journal* 16:76-80 S/O '89
The original "Big Cheese". il *American History Illustrated* 23:34-5 Ja '89
SASSER, JAMES R.
Should the Congress adopt the "Tender Offer Disclosure and Fairness Act of 1987"? [excerpts from address, June 20, 1988] *Congressional Digest* 68:92+ Mr '89
about
The Hill has fund managers squirming. D. Harbrecht. *Business Week* p45 Ja 30 '89
SASTRY, M. ANJALI, AND OTHERS
Can the U.S. economy survive a few nuclear weapons? il *Technology Review* 92:22-9 Ap '89
SAT See Scholastic Aptitude Test
SATANIC VERSES CASE See Rushdie, Salman—Satanic verses case
SATANISM
Christianity today talks to Frank Peretti [author of Piercing the darkness] M. G. Maudlin. por *Christianity Today* 33:58-9 D 15 '89

"Die mother father brother" [teenage Satan worshipper T. Sullivan kills mother then commits suicide in Sparta, N.J.] E. Davidowitz. il por *Redbook* 172:132-4+ Ap '89
The horror and the hype. K. H. Sidey. il *Christianity Today* 33:48-50 N 17 '89
Satan. J. Furth and M. Murphy. il *Life* 12:48-51+ Je '89
Anecdotes, facetiae, satire, etc.
Nice day for a black wedding. J. Queenan. *The American Spectator* 22:18-19 F '89
Canada
Questions of Satanism [child abuse] A. Steacy and B. Bethune. il *Maclean's* 102:62 N 27 '89
SATCOMS See Communications satellites
SATELLITE LEARNING CENTERS
A different business school [Dade County, Fla.] C. Leslie. *Newsweek* 113:77 Ja 30 '89
SATELLITE MUSIC NETWORK
Lee Abrams: out to fill the air with heavy-metal fare. D. Foust. il por *Business Week* p107 Je 5 '89
SATELLITES
See also
Artificial satellites
Jupiter (Planet)—Satellites
Mars (Planet)—Satellites
Moon
Neptune (Planet)—Satellites
Pluto (Planet)—Satellites
Saturn (Planet)—Satellites
Uranus (Planet)—Satellites
How many moons can you see? A. MacRobert. il *Sky and Telescope* 78:67+ Jl '89
Observe the moons of the outer planets. R. Talcott. il *Astronomy* 17:74-7 Je '89
SATIETY See Appetite
SATIRE
See also
Irony
Political humor
SATISFACTION
See also
Comfort
Job satisfaction
Personal satisfaction rises [Gallup poll] *Society* 26:2-3 Mr/Ap '89
SATLOFF, ROBERT
Jordan and reverberations of the uprising. bibl f *Current History* 88:85-8+ F '89
SATO, SEIZABURO
Time to accept new responsibility. il *World Press Review* 36:14 Ap '89
SATO, SHIZUO
about
The road warriors of Japan's politics. M. Tharp. il pors map *U.S. News & World Report* 107:28-30 Jl 24 '89
SATRAN, PAMELA REDMOND
The evolution of women's friendships. il *Working Woman* 14:158-60+ N '89
Family crushes. il *Glamour* 87:274-5+ My '89
Makeovers for success: is how you dress your company's business? il por *Glamour* 87:154-5+ Jl '89
SATRIANI, JOE
about
Joe Satriani. B. Milkowski. il por *Down Beat* 56:24-5 My '89
SATTER, DAVID
Why Russia can't feed itself. *Reader's Digest* 135:61-6 O '89
SATTER, ELLYN
Food: the family dinner. il *American Health* 8:58-9 O '89
Rescuing the family meal. il *American Health* 8:93-8 My '89
SATTES, BETH
Parental involvement in student learning. *The Education Digest* 54:37-9 Ja '89
SATURDAY NIGHT (PERIODICAL)
The Saturday night wars [dispute between editor J. Fraser and writer M. Harris over article on Globe and mail] G. Bain. il *Maclean's* 102:72 N 27 '89
SATURDAY NIGHT LIVE [television program] See Television program reviews—Single works
SATURN, BOB
Audio specialists for aurally savvy audiences. *Theatre Crafts* 23:34+ Ap '89
SATURN (PLANET)
See also
Space flight to Saturn
Atmosphere
Hexagon jet around Saturn's northern pole [discovery by David Godfrey] il *Astronomy* 17:10 Mr '89
High-resolution microwave images of Saturn. A. W. Grossman and others. bibl f il *Science* 245:1211-15 S 15 '89
Mapping deeper within Saturn's clouds [microwave images; work of A. W. Grossman and others] J. Eberhart. il *Science News* 136:183 S 16 '89
Saturn's great white spots. A. Sanchez-Lavega. il *Sky and Telescope* 78:141-2 Ag '89

SATURN (PLANET)—cont.
Ring system
First look at the Saturn occultation [28 Sagittarii] D. J. Eicher. il *Astronomy* 17:99+ O '89
High-resolution microwave images of Saturn. A. W. Grossman and others. bibl f il *Science* 245:1211-15 S 15 '89
Inside the rings of Saturn [28 Sagittarii occultation] R. Irion. il *Astronomy* 17:50-1 N '89
Mapping deeper within Saturn's clouds [microwave images; work of A. W. Grossman and others] J. Eberhart. il *Science News* 136:183 S 16 '89
A rare occultation by Saturn [28 Sagittarii] R. Shaffer. il *Astronomy* 17:61-2 Jl '89
Saturn and 28 Sgr highlights. D. Di Cicco and L. J. Robinson. il *Sky and Telescope* 78:360-5 O '89
Saturn and a winking star [28 Sagittarii] L. J. Robinson. il *Sky and Telescope* 78:259 S '89
Saturn to occult a bright star [28 Sagittarii] D. W. Dunham and others. il maps *Sky and Telescope* 77:638-9+ Je '89
Saturn's youthful rings [research by Wing-Huan Ip] il *Sky and Telescope* 78:10-11 Jl '89
You can see a star flicker behind Saturn's rings [28 Sagittarii] J. Kanipe. il *Astronomy* 17:80-3 Je '89
Satellites
Cassini to provide detailed, extended views of Saturn [Titan] il *Aviation Week & Space Technology* 131:109-10 O 9 '89
Finding the moons of Saturn. il *Sky and Telescope* 78:70 Jl '89
Iapetus: Saturn's harlequin moon. il *Astronomy* 17:10+ N '89
Methane rain on Titan? il *Sky and Telescope* 77:246 Mr '89
Tar sands on Iapetus [research by Edward A. Cloutis] *Science News* 136:62 Jl 22 '89
Titan: continents in a hydrocarbon sea. M. M. Waldrop. il *Science* 245:129-30 Jl 14 '89
Titan: no global ocean, maybe some seas. J. Eberhart. il *Science News* 136:5 Jl 1 '89
Atmosphere
European amateurs study Titan [28 Sagittarii occultation] A. J. Hollis and J. Mitton. il *Astronomy* 17:52-4 N '89
Rotation
First direct view of solar system chaos [Hyperion observations by James Klavetter] *Science* 246:998-9 N 24 '89
SATURN CORPORATION
Case of the purloined pix [photos of GM's Saturn sold to Automobile magazine] il *Time* 134:74 N 27 '89
SAUCES
See also
Marinades
Mayonnaise
Tabasco sauce
Worcestershire sauce
Accent vegetables with an easy sauce [asparagus and broccoli] il *Southern Living* 24:202 N '89
Custard sauces. il *Gourmet* 49:244 Ap '89
Dessert sauces [fruit sauces] il *Better Homes and Gardens* 67:181-2 N '89
Fruit sauces. il *Gourmet* 49:202 Je '89
Gastronomie sans argent [winter pasta sauces] il *Gourmet* 49:52-3+ Ja '89
None die of heartburn [S. Bellow's sugo di carni] il por *Esquire* 111:192-3 Je '89
Saucy sauces [barbecue sauces] *Parents* 64:184 Je '89
Simply delicious fruit sauces. il *Parents* 64:142-3 Jl '89
Three-mushroom sauce in crêpes, on asparagus. il *Sunset* (Central West edition) 182:108-9 Ja '89
Vegetable sauces and salsas. R. Haskell. il *Flower and Garden* 33:56-8 Jl/Ag '89
Whetting the appetite [cooking with champagne] B. Miller and P. Franey. il *The New York Times Magazine* p53-4 Ap 16 '89
SAUCY'S PIZZA FRANCHISES INC.
A pizza the action. M. Barrier. il por *Nation's Business* 77:68 My '89
SAUDI ARABIA
See also
Government publicity—Saudi Arabia
Investments, American—Saudi Arabia
Saudi Arabians
Commerce
Great Britain
See Great Britain—Commerce—Saudi Arabia
United States
See United States—Commerce—Saudi Arabia
Defenses
See also
Airplanes, Military—Saudi Arabia
Boeing told to solve Peace Shield problems. D. Hughes. *Aviation Week & Space Technology* 131:114 D 18-25 '89
Foreign opinion
American
Mecca bucks [traveling promotional exhibit] A. Heard. *The New Republic* 201:16-17 S 4 '89

Foreign relations
Lebanon
See Lebanon—Foreign relations—Saudi Arabia
SAUDI ARABIANS
Switzerland
From jet set to jail cell [U.S. asks for extradition of A. Khashoggi, jailed in Switzerland in connection with alleged looting of Philippine treasure by F. Marcos] C. Dickey. il por *Newsweek* 113:10 My 1 '89
Scandal, sex and the stir [A. Khashoggi jailed] S. Slewka and N. Le Quesne. il pors *Life* 12:28-31 Je '89
United States
Stepping out [A. Khashoggi's involvement with the Marcoses] J. Kasindorf. il pors *New York* 22:36-44 D 18 '89
SAUERKRAUT
The quest for a true choucroute leads Jeffrey Steingarten from the inns of Alsace to the meat markets of Harlem. J. Steingarten. il *Vogue* 179:336+ N '89
SAUGERTIES (N.Y.)
Monuments, statues, etc.
Opus 40: a sculptor's obsession in upstate New York [work of H. Fite] B. Gill. il por *Architectural Digest* 46:46+ Mr '89
SAUGUS (MASS.)
Restaurants, nightclubs, bars, etc.
Dining for the masses [Weylu's] M. Starr. il *Newsweek* 114:75 S 18 '89
SAUL, JOHN
about
Careful plotting for success lets thriller writer John Saul enjoy all the 'Creature' comforts. A. Chambers. il pors *People Weekly* 31:79+ Je 26 '89
SAUL, PETER, 1934-
about
Peter Saul at Frumkin/Adams. K. Johnson. *Art in America* 77:140 Jl '89
SAUNDERS, D. ANDREW
The Adirondack Wildlife Program. il *The Conservationist* 43:18-23 Ja/F '89
SAUNDERS, DERO A.
Flashbacks. See issues of Forbes
SAUNDERS, ERNEST WALTER, 1935-
about
Ernest Saunders markets his innocence. M. Maremont. il por *Business Week* p92-3 Ag 14 '89
SAUNDERS, JEAN, 1932-
Writing the historical saga. *The Writer* 102:22-5 Ja '89
SAUNDERS, LUCY
The flavor of a place. il *Publishers Weekly* 236:26+ S 8 '89
SAUNDERS, RICHARD H., 1949-
Collecting the West [cover story] il *American History Illustrated* 23:22-33 Ja '89
SAURO, JOAN
Bookends [story] il *U.S. Catholic* 54:34-7 D '89
SAUSAGE
See also
Cooking—Sausage
Frankfurters
SAUSAGE POT PIE See Pot pies
SAUTÉING
Quick! Sauté an entrée. il *Southern Living* 24:152 My '89
SAUTER, VAN GORDON
In defense of tabloid TV [cover story] il *TV Guide* 37:2-4 Ag 5-11 '89
SAUTERNE (WINE) See Wine
SAUVAGE, PIERRE
about
Weapons of the spirit [film] Reviews
Newsweek il 114:81 S 18 '89. D. Ansen
SAVA, SAMUEL G.
"Curriculum" for preschool. *The Education Digest* 54:51-2 Mr '89
SAVAGE, FRED
about
Fred Savage. T. J. Meyer. il pors *Seventeen* 48:105-6+ Je '89
Fred Savage may be TV's Wonder boy, but when mom says jump . . . S. Schindehette. il pors *People Weekly* 31:68-70+ Ap 17 '89
Fred Savage says . . . acting's easy—except for the kissing [cover story] R. Rense. il pors *TV Guide* 37:10-11 Je 10-16 '89
"My parents never push me". L. Grobel. il pors *Redbook* 174:40+ D '89
SAVAGE, JOHN F., 1938-
A shift in theory in reading research. *The Education Digest* 54:49-53 Ap '89
SAVAGE, LETITIA
Protecting your rural well. il *Country Journal* 16:23-7+ S/O '89
SAVAGE, RANDY
about
Look out, Hulk—'Macho Man' wants revenge. J. Martel. il pors *TV Guide* 37:20-2 Jl 29-Ag 4 '89

SAVALAS, TELLY
about
Telly Savalas surrenders to the TV cop he can't escape—Kojak. J. Park. il pors *People Weekly* 32:169-70+ D 4 '89

SAVAN, LESLIE
Activism in the checkout line: the rising tide of boycotts. il *Utne Reader* p87-9 S/O '89

SAVANNAH, SHEILA
about
The watercolor page: Sheila Savannah. M. N. Balcomb. il por *American Artist* 53:76-9+ S '89

SAVANNAH (GA.)
Description
Seeing Savannah. *Southern Living* 24:43 N '89
Historic houses, sites, etc.
Savannah: a plan preserved. G. D. Ford. il map *Southern Living* 24:78-85 Mr '89
Savannah's amazing grace. C. Davidson. il *American Heritage* 40:32+ F '89
Religious institutions and affairs
In Savannah, First African Baptist Church means first. W. Yancey. il *American Visions* 4:42-3 Ag '89
Restaurants, nightclubs, bars, etc.
When Sema Wilkes puts food on the table, her guests better have a Boardinghouse reach [Mrs. Wilkes' Boarding House Restaurant] D. Chu. il pors *People Weekly* 32:139-40 S 18 '89

SAVANNAH FOODS & INDUSTRIES, INC.
Three yards and a cloud of (sugar) dust. J. Novack. il *Forbes* 144:39-41 S 4 '89

SAVANNAH RIVER PLANT NUCLEAR REACTORS *See* Nuclear reactors

SAVANT, MARILYN MACH VOS *See* Vos Savant, Marilyn Mach

SAVANT SYNDROME
The enigma of autistic savants. J. Adler. il *Newsweek* 113:54-5 Ja 16 '89
Islands of genius [link between savant syndrome and cerebral cortex abnormalities] R. Robotham. il *Omni (New York, N.Y.)* 11:18+ S '89
The piano is Eddie's key [E. Bonafe, savant syndrome pianist] N. Epstein and M. Fay. il pors *Life* 12:102-4 Ap '89

SAVARIN *See* Cake

SAVATH BON
about
Pilgrim. *The New Yorker* 65:47 N 20 '89

SAVE AMERICA'S FUTURE (ORGANIZATION)
Oliver North does time battling drugs in the nation's capital. M. Brower. il pors *People Weekly* 32:52-3 N 27 '89

SAVED BY THE BELL [television program] *See* Television program reviews—Single works

SAVILE ROW TAILORS *See* Tailors—Great Britain

SAVIMBI, JONAS, 1934-
about
The end of the affair. B. Turque. il por *Newsweek* 114:54 O 16 '89
Minority report. C. Hitchens. *The Nation* 248:690 My 22 '89
The mystique of Savimbi. R. Sikorski. il por *National Review* 41:34-7 Ag 18 '89
"We have taken the first step". B. W. Nelan. il pors map *Time* 134:28 Jl 3 '89

SAVIN CORP.
It's alive! il *Forbes* 143:158 Ja 9 '89

SAVING AND SAVINGS
See also
Bank accounts
Finance, Personal
Investments
5 super-safe places to save. B. G. Quint. *Glamour* 87:120+ F '89
The aging of America [economic impact of baby boomers; address, June 21, 1989] R. Christian. *Vital Speeches of the Day* 56:29-32 O 15 '89
America mends its spendthrift ways. S. Nasar. *U.S. News & World Report* 107:108 O 16 '89
Are fatter piggy banks merely an illusion . . . or does the jump in savings reflect a demographic shift? G. Koretz. il *Business Week* p24 My 15 '89
Automatic ways to save or invest. il *Consumer Reports* 54:78+ F '89
Clock power [impact on savings rate of perceived threat of nuclear war; research by Joel Slemrod] L. Ackland. *The Bulletin of the Atomic Scientists* 45:2 Je '89
Cultivating a savings habit. L. Wiener. il *U.S. News & World Report* 107:56-7+ Ag 14 '89
Getting rich $100 at a time [cover story] J. Kosnett. il *Changing Times* 43:20-6 Ag '89
Have you hugged your bankbook today? K. Pennar. il *Business Week* p88-9 My 29 '89
How capital costs cripple America. L. S. Richman. il *Fortune* 120:50-2+ Ag 14 '89
How to pay a $150,000 tuition bill. N. Henderson. il *Changing Times* 43:88-90+ O '89
How to save for what you want (I). M. J. Weiss. il *Ladies' Home Journal* 106:48+ S '89

How to save for what you want (II). M. J. Weiss. il *Ladies' Home Journal* 106:50+ O '89
How to set up a plan that takes the pain out of saving. R. J. Klein. il *Money* 18:129-30 Jl '89
How you can put your rainy-day cash to work and still have it for emergencies. R. J. Klein. il *Money* 18:175-6 My '89
How you gonna pay for baby's B.A.? D. R. Katz. il *Esquire* 112:57-8 Ag '89
Keeping up with Japan [shortage of capital in U.S. due to lack of savings] D. Gergen. il *U.S. News & World Report* 106:68 Mr 6 '89
Lost horizons [cover story] L. H. Summers. *The New Republic* 200:11-13 Je 26 '89
Making those college nest eggs grow. T. Segal. il *Business Week* p146-7 D 11 '89
A nation of savers? E. Rubenstein. *National Review* 41:28 O 27 '89
The "net savings" illusion. A. Reynolds. il *Forbes* 143:169 F 6 '89
The political realities of saving. H. Banks. *Forbes* 143:35 My 29 '89
The "savings crisis" is a caricature. W. T. Brookes. il *Nation's Business* 77:68 D '89
The surge in savings. M. W. Karmin. *U.S. News & World Report* 106:56 My 22 '89
Taking aim at the savings shortfall [American Business Conference paper] T. May, Jr. il *Fortune* 119:26 Ap 24 '89
Tuition shock! [special section] il *Money* 18:60-6+ S '89
Use slow but steady ways to build your cash stash. C. Willis. il *Money* 18:70-2 F '89
What is the 'right' amount of saving? [with discussion] M. Friedman. il *National Review* 41:25-32 Je 16 '89
Why detente may raise the savings rate [imminence of nuclear war] G. Koretz. il *Business Week* p18 Mr 6 '89
Why junk in the first place? Skimpy savings. C. Farrell. il *Business Week* p92 S 11 '89
Will Americans keep buying less and saving more? [views of Robert S. Gay] G. Koretz. il *Business Week* p20 Jl 31 '89

Japan
Japanese thrift? The stereotype suffers a setback. K. Pennar. il *Business Week* p36 Ag 14 '89

Soviet Union
Why Ivan sleeps on his savings. *Business Week* p60+ Je 5 '89

SAVINGS AND LOAN ASSOCIATIONS
See also
Black savings and loan associations
Federal Asset Disposition Association
A coup de grace for savings and loans. M. W. Karmin. *U.S. News & World Report* 106:55 Je 19 '89
Digging their own graves? [adjustable rate mortgages' impact on thrifts] H. Rudnitsky. il *Forbes* 143:44-5 My 29 '89
The latest threat to the thrifts: rising interest rates. F. A. Miller. il *Business Week* p104-5 F 27 '89
Sick CDs. B. Weberman. il *Forbes* 143:165 F 6 '89
Teasing the teasers [adjustable rate mortgage refinancing's impact on shaky thrifts] J. Willoughby. il *Forbes* 143:68 Ap 3 '89
Acquisitions and mergers
Bowery follies [1985 federal bailout of Bowery Savings arranged by R. Ravitch] C. Byron. il por *New York* 22:14+ My 29 '89
The great S&L fire sale. il *U.S. News & World Report* 106:11+ Ja 9 '89
Help your country and help yourself [Robert M. Bass Group's takeover of the American Savings and Loan Assn.] S. C. Gwynne. il *Time* 133:72 F 20 '89
It's the end of an era for S&L rescues—but what an end. C. Yang. il por *Business Week* p40 Ja 9 '89
S&Ls: 219 down, maybe 300 to go. W. E. Sheeline. il *Fortune* 119:9 Ja 30 '89
S&Ls are hot properties by act of Congress. J. Meehan. il *Business Week* p76 Ag 28 '89
The screwiest S&L bailout ever [R. O. Perelman's acquisition of First Texas Gibraltar] B. D. Fromson. il por *Fortune* 119:114-15+ Je 19 '89
The smart money in S&L's. L. Reibstein. il por *Newsweek* 113:40 Ja 9 '89
So you think buying a sick thrift is just a license to print money [W. E. Gibson] K. Kelly. il pors *Business Week* p78-9 Je 19 '89
Sweet deal [PHM Corp.'s acquisitions of Texas thrifts coincide with federal bailout] J. Drummond. il *Forbes* 144:96+ S 18 '89
Federal aid
The $100 billion blunder. A. Bladen. il *Forbes* 143:167 F 6 '89
All you need to know about the S&L bailout. P. Wang. il *Money* 18:21 S '89
At the 'El Dorado of impaired assets,' everything must go [Resolution Trust Corp.] C. Yang and D. Zigas. il *Business Week* p176+ N 6 '89
Bailout ripoff. C. O'Cleireacain. *The Nation* 248:581 My 1 '89

SAVINGS AND LOAN ASSOCIATIONS—Federal aid—
cont.

Bush's S&L plan: full of good intentions—and holes. C.
Yang. il *Business Week* p32 F 20 '89

Bush's sweet and sour S&L recipe. R. E. Norton. il *U.S.
News & World Report* 106:49-51 F 20 '89

The bust of '89 [cover story] T. Moore. il por *U.S. News
& World Report* 106:36-43 Ja 23 '89

Can the thrifts be salvaged? D. Pauly. il *Newsweek* 114:38-9
Ag 21 '89

Delays, not deals. J. Drummond. il *Forbes* 144:212 N 27
'89

Dumb dip at work. M. Ivins. il *The Progressive* 53:37 S
'89

Finally, the bill has come due. B. Rudolph. il *Time* 133:68-9+
F 20 '89

FSLIC fizzles. *National Review* 41:18 Ja 27 '89

Goodbye S&Ls? R. Coorsh. *Consumers' Research Magazine*
72:4 Mr '89

The great S&L fire sale. il *U.S. News & World Report*
106:11+ Ja 9 '89

How taxpayers lost the S&L numbers game. R. Thomas.
il *Newsweek* 113:32-3 F 20 '89

If it's not on the budget this year, it doesn't exist [OMB's
reluctance to address savings and loan crisis] J. Bennet.
The Washington Monthly 21:28-9 N '89

"It's a wonderful lie" [Financial Institutions Reform, Recovery,
and Enforcement Act] T. Miller. il *Consumers' Research
Magazine* 72:24-5 D '89

It's a wonderful life: the sequel. J. Cobb. il *Common Cause
Magazine* 15:26-30 S/O '89

It's the end of an era for S&L rescues—but what an end.
C. Yang. il por *Business Week* p40 Ja 9 '89

The money has already been borrowed. W. Baldwin. il *Forbes*
143:38-9 F 20 '89

The money pit. W. E. Sheeline. il *Fortune* 119:8-9 F 13
'89

More bailouts to come. A. Bladen. il *Forbes* 143:148 F
20 '89

Out of sight, out of mind [bailout plan] il *Time* 134:46
Ag 21 '89

Piggy banks. P. J. O'Rourke. il *Rolling Stone* p43+ Ag 24
'89

A run on the political bank. L. Reibstein. il *Newsweek*
113:51 F 13 '89

S&L bailout a disaster for taxpayers. J. P. Lewis. il *Utne
Reader* p28+ S/O '89

S&Ls: 219 down, maybe 300 to go. W. E. Sheeline. il *Fortune*
119:9 Ja 30 '89

S&L's: after the crackup. J. B. Quinn. il *Newsweek* 113:56
F 27 '89

S&Ls are hot properties by act of Congress. J. Meehan.
il *Business Week* p76 Ag 28 '89

Sale of the century [federal agencies sell real estate seized
from insolvent banks] B. Rudolph. il *Time* 133:54-5 My
1 '89

Saving the thrifts. G. Hector. il *Fortune* 119:8-9 Mr 13
'89

Silver lining [thrift bailout bonds from Resolution Funding
Corp.] B. Weberman. il *Forbes* 143:179 Ap 3 '89

The smart money in S&L's. L. Reibstein. il por *Newsweek*
113:40 Ja 9 '89

A Soviet cure for the S&L mess. J. Mois. il por *Fortune*
120:207+ N 6 '89

Spring cleaning for savings and loans. M. W. Karmin. *U.S.
News & World Report* 107:47 Ag 14 '89

Sticking it to the taxpayers [bailout proposal of J. P. Kennedy
and B. A. Morrison] D. Corn. il *The Nation* 249:238-40
S 4-11 '89

Sweet deal [PHM Corp.'s acquisitions of Texas thrifts coincide
with federal bailout] J. Drummond. il *Forbes* 144:96+
S 18 '89

'This is a dirty business' [interview with FDIC chairman
L. W. Seidman] G. Hector. il pors *Fortune* 119:133-4+
My 22 '89

Too little, too late. W. Niskanen and C. England. il *National
Review* 41:38-9 My 19 '89

Trial by balloon [ways to bail out ailing S&Ls] *National
Review* 41:14-16 F 24 '89

The unending deposit insurance mess. E. J. Kane. bibl f
il *Science* 246:451-6 O 27 '89

Unfinished business [bailout plan] P. C. Montgomery. il
Common Cause Magazine 15:31-3 S/O '89

Warning: further—and maybe bigger—federal bailouts ahead.
J. Greenwald. il *Time* 134:40 D 18 '89

Why Bush's S&L bailout is fundamentally flawed. R. Kuttner.
il *Business Week* p24 F 27 '89

Why our S&Ls are in trouble. il *Reader's Digest* 135:70-4
Jl '89

You owe us $100 billion. J. Edgerton. il *Money* 18:52-3
Mr '89

Anecdotes, facetiae, satire, etc.

How the savings and loans were saved. G. Keillor. *The
New Yorker* 65:42 O 16 '89

Those welfare bankers. N. Folbre. por *Newsweek* 114:17
O 16 '89

Laws and regulations

See also

United States. Office of Thrift Supervision

$1 billion worth of influence [C. Keating's dealings with
five senators in the Lincoln Savings & Loan affair] M.
B. Carlson. il por *Time* 134:27-8 N 6 '89

Asleep at the S&L switch [M. D. Wall and the Lincoln
Savings & Loan scandal] R. Thomas and E. Clift. il por
Newsweek 114:71 D 11 '89

Avoiding another S&L crisis. M. S. Forbes, Jr. il *Forbes*
143:27 My 15 '89

The big fix [cover story] J. R. Adams. il *The American
Spectator* 22:21-4 Mr '89

Black S&Ls and thrift reform: the purge begins. A. Edmond,
Jr. il *Black Enterprise* 20:33+ N '89

Bob Bennett: on the trail of the 'Keating Five' [Senate Ethics
inquiry into Lincoln Savings & Loan scandal] T. Smart.
il por *Business Week* p60 D 11 '89

Breaking the banks. B. Burgower. *Ladies' Home Journal*
106:24 Je '89

Can Bush's thrift doctors find a treatment that will take?
C. Yang and F. A. Miller. il *Business Week* p80-1 F
13 '89

Can the thrifts be salvaged? D. Pauly. il *Newsweek* 114:38-9
Ag 21 '89

Capital crimes. M. B. Zuckerman. il *U.S. News & World
Report* 107:72 O 2 '89

CC calls for ethics inquiry of five senators [dealings with
C. Keating in the Lincoln Savings & Loan affair] J. Denny.
Common Cause Magazine 15:28 N/D '89

Congress and the banking community [address, October 10,
1988] R. L. Clarke. *Vital Speeches of the Day* 55:203-6
Ja 15 '89

Don't touch my bailout. B. Rudolph. il *Time* 133:56-7 Je
26 '89

Financier Charles Keating is the $2 billion man of the
savings and loan crisis [Lincoln Savings & Loan scandal
involving five senators] B. Hewitt. il pors *People Weekly*
32:78-80 D 4 '89

Good timing, Charlie [C. Keating's Lincoln Savings & Loan]
H. Rudnitsky. il por *Forbes* 144:140-2+ N 27 '89

If it's not on the budget this year, it doesn't exist [OMB's
reluctance to address savings and loan crisis] J. Bennet.
The Washington Monthly 21:28-9 N '89

Is Danny Wall on the way out? [tainted by Lincoln Savings
& Loan scandal] C. Yang and P. Dwyer. *Business Week*
p59 N 13 '89

"It's a wonderful lie" [Financial Institutions Reform, Recovery,
and Enforcement Act] T. Miller. il *Consumers' Research
Magazine* 72:24-5 D '89

Keating takes the Fifth [Lincoln Savings & Loan scandal]
M. B. Carlson. il por *Time* 134:46 D 4 '89

"A legal bank robbery" [complicity of federal regulators in
Lincoln Savings and Loan scandal] M. B. Carlson. il pors
Time 134:29 N 27 '89

The man who tried to buy Washington [C. Keating's dealings
with five senators in the Lincoln Savings & Loan affair]
G. Borger and S. J. Hedges. il pors *U.S. News & World
Report* 107:18-21+ N 27 '89

Now it's broke [D. Regan's role in S&L scandal] J. R.
Adams. *The New Republic* 201:16-18 N 13 '89

Only the strong will survive the thrift rescue. C. Yang.
il *Business Week* p122-3 My 8 '89

Out of sight, out of mind [bailout plan] il *Time* 134:46
Ag 21 '89

Piggy banks. P. J. O'Rourke. il *Rolling Stone* p43+ Ag 24
'89

Read their lips: no S&L tax [proposed savers' fee] il *Newsweek*
113:50 F 6 '89

Reformers 3, S&L lobby 1 [House vote] D. Pauly. il *Newsweek*
113:55 Je 26 '89

Responsibility and regulation [address, June 26, 1989] J.
A. Grundfest. *Vital Speeches of the Day* 55:718-22 S 15
'89

S&L bailout a disaster for taxpayers. J. P. Lewis. il *Utne
Reader* p28+ S/O '89

The S&L bailout bust. S. Dentzer. il *U.S. News & World
Report* 106:20-2 Je 26 '89

The S&L scandal's biggest blowout [C. H. Keating's Lincoln
Savings & Loan scandal involves five senators] T. Morganthau. il por *Newsweek* 114:35-6 N 6 '89

S&L time bomb. *The Nation* 248:75-6 Ja 23 '89

The S&Ls' last stand against Congress. C. Yang. il *Business
Week* p30-1 Jl 3 '89

Savings and loan legislation. il *Congressional Digest* 68:163-92
Je/Jl '89

The second S&L scandal: a push to dilute reform. R. Thomas.
il *Newsweek* 113:45 Je 12 '89

The seduction of Senator Alan Cranston [Lincoln Savings
& Loan Assn. scandal] P. Dwyer. il pors *Business Week*
p82-4 D 4 '89

The thrift police [FSLIC files malpractice suit against law
firm Jenkens & Gilchrist over its dealings with State Savings
& Loan Association of Lubbock] D. Fanning. il *Forbes*
143:74 Ja 9 '89

Thrifts on the slide. *Commonweal* 116:3-4 Ja 13 '89

SAVINGS AND LOAN ASSOCIATIONS—Laws and regulations—*cont.*

The tumbling of Danny Wall [Lincoln Savings & Loan scandal] S. J. Hedges. *U.S. News & World Report* 107:55 D 11 '89

The unending deposit insurance mess. E. J. Kane. bibl f il *Science* 246:451-6 O 27 '89

Unfinished business [bailout plan] P. C. Montgomery. il *Common Cause Magazine* 15:31-3 S/O '89

Warning: further—and maybe bigger—federal bailouts ahead. J. Greenwald. il *Time* 134:40 D 18 '89

What's behind the S&L crisis? F. L. Smith. il *Consumers' Research Magazine* 72:24-7 My '89

When hell sleazes over [cover story] K. Day. *The New Republic* 200:26-30 Mr 20 '89

When you're in a hole, stop digging. R. E. Norton. il *U.S. News & World Report* 106:46 Ja 23 '89

Who is to blame for the S&L crisis? D. Seligman. il *Fortune* 119:152 Mr 13 '89

Management

How to succeed in a lousy business. J. F. Lawrence. il *Fortune* 120:125-6+ Jl 3 '89

Real estate operations

Delays, not deals [federal S&L bailout] J. Drummond. il *Forbes* 144:212 N 27 '89

A diamond in the S&L dustheap [Prospect Park Financial] G. G. Marcial. *Business Week* p87 Ja 16 '89

Fast money and fraud [Empire Savings & Loan] A. Pusey. il pors *The New York Times Magazine* p30-2+ Ap 23 '89

Feds: 40 taxpayers: love [FSLIC inherits control of International Tennis Center of Delray Beach, Fla. from failed thrift] R. L. Stern. il *Forbes* 144:43-4 S 4 '89

For sale by owner: junk real estate [acquired by Resolution Trust Corporation] M. W. Karmin. il *U.S. News & World Report* 107:54-5 D 11 '89

Sale of the century [federal agencies sell real estate seized from insolvent banks] B. Rudolph. il *Time* 133:54-5 My 1 '89

The 'toxic waste' of the thrift crisis. C. Yang. il *Business Week* p104-5 Mr 27 '89

Securities

Bailout bulls [A. Cope and N. Adams of First Financial Fund] J. Zweig. il pors *Forbes* 143:167 Ap 3 '89

S&Ls are hot properties by act of Congress. J. Meehan. il *Business Week* p76 Ag 28 '89

Zombie bonds. M. Schifrin. il *Forbes* 143:70 Ap 3 '89

California

See also

American Savings & Loan Assn.

CalFed Inc.

Family Savings & Loan Association (Los Angeles, Calif.)

Founders Savings & Loan Association

Great Western Financial Corp.

Home Savings of America, a Federal Savings & Loan Assn.

Lincoln Savings & Loan Association

Kansas

See also

Franklin Savings Association

New York (State)

See also

Long Island City Financial

Texas

See also

American Federal Bank FSB (Dallas, Tex.)

Empire Savings and Loan Association

First Texas Gibraltar (Firm)

Sunbelt Savings, FSB

Sunbelt Savings Association of Texas

Vernon Savings & Loan Association

The big fix [cover story] J. R. Adams. il *The American Spectator* 22:21-4 Mr '89

Quis custodiet? [J. Wright's efforts on behalf of thrifts] R. C. Kirkwood and T. P. Jeffrey. il *National Review* 41:35-6 Ap 21 '89

The real sleaze [J. Wright's suspected misdeeds in efforts on behalf of Texas S&Ls] *The Nation* 248:615-16 My 8 '89

Sweet deal [PHM Corp.'s acquisitions of Texas thrifts coincide with federal bailout] J. Drummond. il *Forbes* 144:96+ S 18 '89

There is not much chance of getting those billions back. S. J. Hedges. il *U.S. News & World Report* 106:22 Je 26 '89

Wright, Coelho and the S&L fiasco. M. Barone. il pors *U.S. News & World Report* 106:21-2 Je 12 '89

Wright was not wronged [excerpt from report issued by House Ethics Committee] *Harper's* 279:18+ Ag '89

SAVINGS BANKS

See also

Bowery Savings Bank

CenTrust Savings Bank

Dime Savings Bank of New York

Greater New York Savings Bank

Household Bank

Manhattan Savings Bank

People's Bank

Savings and loan associations

Savings Banks Life Insurance Fund

Securities

The shape of thrifts to come? [People's Bank issues stock] R. W. King. il *Business Week* p102 S 18 '89

SAVINGS BANKS LIFE INSURANCE FUND

Birth of a salesman. J. Zweig. il por *Forbes* 143:149 My 15 '89

SAVINGS BONDS

Payroll deductions

Payroll savings pay off in bonds. J. C. Szabo. il *Nation's Business* 77:45-6 My '89

Taxation

A double-E break on tuition costs [tax-free education bonds] L. Wiener. il *U.S. News & World Report* 106:64 Je 12 '89

A gift to savings-bond owners from the IRS [delayed reporting of interest] L. Wiener. il *U.S. News & World Report* 107:72 S 18 '89

Yields

Savings bonds may pay off with high yields for you. N. Dunnan. il *Money* 18:183+ D '89

SAVINGS CERTIFICATES See Certificates of deposit

SAVKO, ED

about

L.A.'s biking celebs bring a roaring trade to Ed and Vern's. il por *People Weekly* 31:89 My 15 '89

SAVOCA, NANCY

about

True love [film] Reviews

Rolling Stone il por p48 S 21 '89. P. Travers

SAVONAROLA, GIROLAMO, 1452-1498

about

Savonarola—preacher and patriot? D. Weinstein. bibl il por *History Today* 39:30-6 N '89

SAVORIES

Nutted savories. il *Gourmet* 49:318 N '89

SAVOY, PAUL

Deregulating political murder. il *The Nation* 248:869+ Je 26 '89

When criminal rights go wrong [cover story] *The Washington Monthly* 21:36-41+ D '89

SAVOY HOTEL PLC

Diana slept here [Trusthouse Forte's pursuit of Savoy Hotel plc] J. Marcom, Jr. il *Forbes* 143:116+ My 15 '89

SAVUKA (MUSICAL GROUP)

Warrior against racism [J. Clegg] K. McKenna. il por *Scholastic Update (Teachers' edition)* 121:16 Ja 27 '89

SAW DEVICES See Surface acoustic wave devices

SAW GUIDES See Saws and sawing—Equipment

SAWBUCKS See Sawhorses

SAWHORSES

Easy-to-build saw-horses. R. Capotosto. il *Popular Mechanics* 166:80 S '89

A tale of two sawbucks [firewood cutting racks] M. Lamphier; H. Mitchell. il *The Mother Earth News* 120:82-3 N/D '89

Two great sawhorses. M. Thompson and D. Stoffel. il *The Family Handyman* 39:72-3 S '89

SAWING See Saws and sawing

SAWMILLS

The Workbench guide to portable sawmills. P. McCafferty. il *Workbench* 45:26-31 Jl/Ag '89

Shutdowns

Sawmills are starting to drop like trees. J. B. Levine. il *Business Week* p42 F 6 '89

SAWS, TOY See Toys

SAWS AND SAWING

See also

Miter boxes, gages, etc.

Wood cutting

Buying the circular saw that's right for you. K. Collier. il *The Family Handyman* 39:50-2 Ja '89

Buying the table saw that's right for you. K. Collier. il *The Family Handyman* 39:53-4+ N/D '89

Chain saws. F. Buckingham. il *Successful Farming* 87:42-3 O '89

Fast-cutting handsaw [Sandvik 252] H. Wicks. il *Workbench* 45:22 N/D '89

Grit-edge blades: tackling the tough cuts. R. Capotosto. il *Popular Mechanics* 166:96 Mr '89

Little big saws [Porter-Cable's Saw Boss and Tiger Cub] J. Truini. il *Popular Mechanics* 166:48 F '89

Sabre saw know-how. H. Wicks. il *Workbench* 45:24+ S/O '89

Sabre saws. T. Klenck. il *Popular Mechanics* 166:79-84 O '89

Table saw basics. H. Wicks. il *Home Mechanix* 86:17-18+ Mr '89

Tackling the table saw. R. Capotosto. il *Popular Mechanics* 166:135-9 My '89

Three stationary power tools [Grizzly Table Saw, Kity K-5, Shopsmith Scroll Saw] L. Okrend. il *Workbench* 45:88-91 Mr/Ap '89

Three's company [Delta's new Sawbuck, belt/disc sander and table saw] J. Truini. il *Popular Mechanics* 166:94 Jl '89

SAWS AND SAWING—*cont.*

Using your circular saw like a pro. K. Collier. il *The Family Handyman* 39:20-1 Je '89

Equipment

Life extension for band saw blades [guide blocks] R. Capotosto. il *Popular Mechanics* 166:101 Je '89

Sanding on a radial arm saw [Performax S/T attachment] A. R. Gould. il *Workbench* 45:22 S/O '89

Table saw pushstick. G. Liberty. il *Workbench* 45:70 My/Je '89

Maintenance and repair

How to maintain your chain saw. S. Willson. il *Popular Mechanics* 166:101-4 Ja '89

Safety devices and measures

Radial arm saw—only as safe as you make it. R. J. DeCristoforo. il *Workbench* 45:12+ My/Je '89

Sharpening

See Sharpeners and sharpening

SAWYER, DIANE

about

If Nixon could possess the soul of this woman, why the hell can't I? F. Exley. il *Esquire* 112:208-10+ D '89

Let's go to the videotape. E. Diamond. il pors *New York* 22:24+ D 4 '89

On the roller coaster with Diane and Sam. E. Diamond. pors *New York* 22:10-12 Jl 24 '89

The prime time of her life. P. Pierce. il pors *Ladies' Home Journal* 106:42+ O '89

The prime times of Diane Sawyer. J. Grant. il pors *Life* 12:72-4+ Ag '89

Star power [cover story] R. Zoglin. il pors *Time* 134:46-51 Ag 7 '89

Star wars at the networks. R. Zoglin. il pors *Time* 133:70-1 Ap 3 '89

Winning Diane: how ABC's Roone Arledge snatched her away from CBS [cover story] E. Klein. il pors *New York* 22:36-43 Mr 13 '89

The wooing of Diane Sawyer sparks a fierce network battle. il pors *People Weekly* 31:124 Ap 10 '89

SAWYER, EUGENE

about

Chicago alderman Evans to run for mayor after Sawyer's primary defeat. il pors *Jet* 75:4-5 Mr 20 '89

Eugene Sawyer faces an Hispanic, two whites, in Chicago mayoral race. por *Jet* 75:26 Ja 23 '89

Jackson backs Sawyer in Chicago mayoral primary. il pors *Jet* 75:6 F 13 '89

Jackson strikes out. J. McCormick. il pors *Newsweek* 113:24 Mr 13 '89

Mayor Sawyer supports Chicago public schools. il por *Jet* 75:8 F 13 '89

Race after Washington. P. Greene. il *Commonweal* 116:199-201 Ap 7 '89

Racial politics—Chicago's raw nerve. D. Johnson. il pors *The New York Times Magazine* p34-8+ F 19 '89

Sawyer lobbies for U.S. youth on Capitol Hill in final days of term. il por *Jet* 76:13 My 8 '89

SAWYER, JUDITH

Channel one. See issues of Video through June 1989

SAWYER, STEVE

about

A blast from the past. M. Barrier. il por *Nation's Business* 77:79 Ap '89

SAWYER, TOM F.

about

True confession? [excerpt from transcript of police interrogation of murder suspect T. F. Sawyer in Clearwater, Fla.] *Harper's* 279:17-20+ O '89

Untrue confessions. P. Weiss. il por *Mother Jones* 14:18-20+ S '89

SAX, RICHARD

Cooking with coffee. il *Gourmet* 49:84-5+ My '89

Easy weekend eating. il *Working Woman* 14:191-4 S '89

High comfort low calorie. il *Working Woman* 14:106-8 F '89

Miami's restaurant scene. il *Gourmet* 49:84+ O '89

SAXENA, POONAM

Shashi Kapoor branches out. il por *World Press Review* 36:75 S '89

SAXENA, S. C.

Nervous in Namibia. *World Press Review* 36:42-3 Ap '89

SAXENA, SATYA P., AND OTHERS

Histamine is an intracellular messenger mediating platelet aggregation. bibl f il *Science* 243:1596-9 Mr 24 '89

SAXHAUG, BRAD

Look up, look down. il *Good Housekeeping* 208:195-7 Ap '89

SAXOPHONE

Michael Brecker: re-charged sax [Akai EWI] R. Tolleson. il por *Down Beat* 56:56-7 N '89

The Sax Doctor rides again; ed. by Fred Bouchard. E. Lyons. il por *Down Beat* 56:61 F '89

SAXOPHONE MUSIC

See also

Compact discs—Saxophone music

World Saxophone Quartet

SAXOPHONE PLAYERS

See also

Brecker, Michael
Breuker, Willem
Carter, Benny
Cartwright, George
Cobb, Arnett Cleophus, 1918-1989
Cole, Richie
Coleman, Ornette
Coltrane, John, 1926-1967
D'Rivera, Paquito
Evans, Bill, 1958-
Getz, Stan, 1927-
Gordon, Dexter
Green, Bunky
Handy, John
Hawkins, Coleman
Hemphill, Julius
Hollyday, Chris
Jacquet, Illinois
Lacy, Steve
Lawrence, Arnie
Liebman, Dave
Marsalis, Branford
Morgan, Frank
Mulligan, Gerry
Oatts, Dick
Osby, Greg
Parker, Charlie, 1920-1955
Phillips, Flip, 1915-
Rouse, Charlie, 1924-1988
Sanborn, David
Scott, Tom
Shorter, Wayne
Wilkerson, Edward
Young, Lester

Anecdotes, facetiae, satire, etc.

Mid-life sax [middle-aged men taking up saxophone] J. Nocera. il *Esquire* 111:52 Ap '89

SAXTON, H. JAMES

Tales from the taffrail. *Sea Frontiers* 35:128 Mr/Ap '89

SAY ANYTHING [film] See Motion picture reviews—Single works

SAYINGS *See* Maxims; Proverbs; Quotations

SAYLE, MURRAY

Axis, Ltd. [cover story] il *The New Republic* 200:22-4+ Je 5 '89

Sex, lies, and Japanese politics. *The New Republic* 201:18-22 S 11 '89

SAYLES, JOHN, 1950-

about

Baby, it's you [film] Reviews

Video il 13:78+ N '89. J. Young

SAYRE, HENRY M., 1948-

The subjective object. il por *American Artist* 53:70-5+ D '89

SAYRES, WILLIAM

The lighter side of lying. il *Parents* 64:131-4 Je '89

SAYREVILLE (N.J.)

Historic houses, sites, etc.

Jon Bon Jovi gives his home to non-Jovi Judy Frappier [winner of boyhood home in MTV contest] il pors *People Weekly* 31:135 Ap 17 '89

SBA *See* United States. Small Business Administration

SBARRO, FRANCO

about

Sbarro introduces the hubless wheel. T. Van Hooydonk. il por *Cycle* 40:19+ Je '89

SBG PARTNERS

Rational moves [Fernau & Hartman design offices for SBG Partners] K. D. Stein. il *Architectural Record* 177:68-75 mid-S '89

SBK ENTERTAINMENT WORLD INC.

Last laugh [SBK sells former CBS music publishing division to Thorn EMI] L. Gubernick. il por *Forbes* 143:41-2 F 20 '89

They're playing whose song? D. Lieberman. il *Business Week* p42 Ja 23 '89

SBLI *See* Savings Banks Life Insurance Fund

SCA SUBCARRIERS *See* Radio frequency modulation

SCAASI, ARNOLD, 1932?-

about

The art of Arnold Scaasi: a colorful collection on eastern Long Island. R. Fizdale and A. Gold. il por *Architectural Digest* 46:174-9 S '89

Little big man. J. Reed. il *Vogue* 179:444-6 Ap '89

SCABS (STRIKEBREAKERS) *See* Strikebreakers

SCALA, JAMES

Nutrition. See issues of Dance Magazine beginning September 1988

SCALDS *See* Burns and scalds

SCALED COMPOSITES, INC.

AT[3] demonstrates feasibility of cargo STOL with long range [advanced technology tactical transport; cover story] W. B. Scott. il *Aviation Week & Space Technology* 131:38-40+ S 4 '89

Burt Rutan: a profile. P. Garrison. il pors *Flying* 116:48-50+ F '89

SCALED COMPOSITES, INC.—*cont.*
Lawsuit against Rutans could test liability of designers, test pilots [filed by Aviation Composites Co.] *Aviation Week & Space Technology* 130:61 Ja 23 '89
Scaled Composites rolls out modified ATTT for DARPA tests [advanced technology tactical transport] il *Aviation Week & Space Technology* 130:30 Ap 17 '89

SCALES (WEIGHING INSTRUMENTS)
Bathroom scales. il *Consumer Reports* 54:461-5 Jl '89
Bathroom scales. il *Consumer Reports* 54:53-6 D '89
Upscale baboons [Kenya's Amboseli National Park] J. Altmann and A. Samuels. il *Natural History* p60-3 My '89
You might even like to step on these scales [bathroom scales] M. Galen. il *Business Week* p176 O 9 '89

SCALIA, JOSEPH E.
The postman didn't ring even once. *The Writer* 102:7-8 My '89

SCALP
See also
Baldness

SCALPING OF TICKETS *See* Ticket selling—Ethical aspects

SCALZO, JOE
about
The flexible engine. S. F. Brown. il *Popular Science* 235:82-4 N '89

SCAMBIO, ELENA J.
about
A case of academic bankruptcy. *Newsweek* 114:74 O 16 '89

SCAMS *See* Fraud
SCANDAL [film] *See* Motion picture reviews—Single works
SCANDALS, POLITICAL *See* Politics, Corruption in
SCANDINAVIA
See also
Art—Scandinavia
Aviation and state—Scandinavia
Finland
Norway
Sweden

Industries
See also
SAS

SCANDINAVIAN AIRLINES SYSTEM *See* SAS
SCANDINAVIAN ART *See* Art, Scandinavian
SCANDURA, JANETTE
Aerobic circuit training—a combination of strength and aerobic exercises—is today's state-of-the-art workout. *Vogue* 179:234+ O '89
The challenge of rock climbing: to find an inner resolve more unyielding than stone. il *Vogue* 179:68+ Jl '89
A leggier look is in fashion for fall, and, luckily, heredity is not destiny: with a focused workout, legs can be reshaped. il *Vogue* 179:402+ S '89

SCANLAN, JAMES P.
Strategic defense can be dangerous. il *The New Leader* 72:13-14 Je 12-26 '89

SCANLON, TERRENCE M., 1939-
All terrain vehicles: a safety success story. il *Consumers' Research Magazine* 72:29-31 Je '89

SCANNIELLO, STEPHEN
about
Rose inventory. *The New Yorker* 65:49-50 N 6 '89

SCANNING ELECTRON MICROSCOPES
Microscopy au naturel. il *High Technology Business* 9:12 N/D '89
Sizing up a small world. il *National Geographic World* 162:24-9 F '89
Spatially resolved observation of supercurrents across grain boundaries in YBaCuO films. J. Mannhart and others. bibl f il *Science* 245:839-41 Ag 25 '89

SCANNING ION-CONDUCTANCE MICROSCOPES
Imaging ionic tides and soft surfaces [developed by Paul K. Hansma] I. Amato. il *Science News* 135:84 F 11 '89
New microscope images ions' ins and outs. R. Pool. il *Science* 243:609 F 3 '89
The scanning ion-conductance microscope. P. K. Hansma and others. bibl f il *Science* 243:641-3 F 3 '89

SCANNING MICROSCOPES *See* Microscopes
SCANNING SYSTEMS
See also
Optical scanners
Tomography

SCANNING TUNNELING MICROSCOPES
Atomic resolution imaging of adsorbates on metal surfaces in air: iodine adsorption on pt(111). B. C. Schardt and others. bibl f il *Science* 243:1050-3 F 24 '89
The coil of life [DNA structure] A. Fisher. il *Popular Science* 234:10+ Je '89
Direct observation of native DNA structures with the scanning tunneling microscope. T. P. Beebe, Jr. and others. bibl f il *Science* 243:370-2 Ja 20 '89
Direct view of DNA. J. A. Miller. il *BioScience* 39:225-6 Ap '89
A dream come true [benzene ring revealed] J. Kluger. il *Discover* 10:56 Ja '89
Fishing for current with an STM rod [tunnel diodes; work of Peter J. Bedrossian] *Science News* 136:351 N 25 '89

Hexagonal domain-like charge density wave phase of TaS_2 determined by scanning tunneling microscopy. X. L. Wu and C. M. Lieber. bibl f il *Science* 243:1703-5 Mr 31 '89
Images of the DNA double helix in water [cover story] S. M. Lindsay and others. bibl f il *Science* 244:1063-4 Je 2 '89
A kinky new look for DNA [work of Stuart Lindsay] il *Discover* 10:18 O '89
Long-range electronic perturbations caused by defects using scanning tunneling microscopy [graphite] H. A. Mizes and J. S. Foster. bibl f il *Science* 244:559-62 My 5 '89
Microscopy au naturel. il *High Technology Business* 9:12 N/D '89
Molecular structure of DNA by scanning tunneling microscopy. A. Cricenti and others. bibl f il *Science* 245:1226-7 S 15 '89
The picture of life [picture of DNA] il *Newsweek* 113:67 F 6 '89
Ripples in a crystalline copper bed [chemisorption process; research by Young Kuk] I. Peterson. *Science News* 135:62 Ja 28 '89
Scanning the surface. I. Peterson. il *Science News* 135:200-1+ Ap 1 '89
Scanning the winding coils of naked DNA [research by Miquel B. Salmeron] I. Peterson. il *Science News* 135:53 Ja 28 '89
Scanning tunneling microscopy and nanolithography on a conducting oxide, $Rb_{0.3}MoO_3$. E. Garfunkel and others. bibl f il *Science* 246:99-100 O 6 '89
Scanning tunneling microscopy of nucleic acids. G. Lee and others. bibl f il *Science* 244:475-7 Ap 28 '89
Scanning tunneling microscopy of uncoated recA-DNA complexes. M. Amrein and others. bibl f il *Science* 243:1708-11 Mr 31 '89
Seeing atoms [cover story] A. Fisher. il *Popular Science* 234:102-7 Ap '89
Sequencing DNA using remote Braille [work of David D. Dunlap and Carlos Bustamante] *Science News* 136:351 N 25 '89
A small, small, very small diode [tunnel diode] R. Pool. il *Science* 246:1251 D 8 '89
Smectic liquid crystal monolayers on graphite observed by scanning tunneling microscopy [cover story] D. P. E. Smith and others. bibl f il *Science* 245:43-5 Jl 7 '89

SCANNING X RAY MICROSCOPES *See* X ray microscopes
SCARBOROUGH, DANNY
about
Dying AIDS victim calls for safe sex and understanding. J. Reno. il pors *Ebony* 44:148+ Mr '89

SCARCITY
Doomsday again. E. Rubenstein. il *National Review* 41:16 Ag 4 '89

SCARDINO, DOROTHY
about
Dividends. *The New Yorker* 65:38-9 O 2 '89

SCARE *See* President's Select Committee on Automotive Regulation and Economics

SCARECROWS
The Great American Scarecrow Contest [winners] il *The Mother Earth News* 118:54-5 Jl/Ag '89

SCARF, FREDERICK L.
about
Obituary
Physics Today por 42:116+ S '89. L. Fisk and others

SCARF, MAGGIE, 1932-
What, me angry? il *The New York Times Magazine* p22+ Ap 23 '89

SCARLATTI (NEW YORK, N.Y.: RESTAURANT) *See* New York (N.Y.)—Restaurants, nightclubs, bars, etc.

SCARLET IBISES *See* Ibises

SCARS
Barely there scar minimizers. P. Boyer. il *Prevention (Emmaus, Pa.)* 41:94-5+ Jl '89
Latest ways to remove scars and birthmarks. L. Holland. il *Good Housekeeping* 209:179 Jl '89

SCARVES
The scarf wrap. K. Heller. il *Vogue* 179:114-15 Mr '89
Tying it up! il *Teen* 33:22 Ap '89
A Waco postman designs Hermès scarves with a western flair [K. Oliver] il pors *People Weekly* 32:162-3 N 13 '89

Exhibitions
Scarves everywhere [show at Hermès Gallery, New York City] *The New Yorker* 64:24-6 Ja 30 '89

SCATTERING (PHYSICS)
See also
Aharonov-Casher effect
Light—Scattering
Macromolecular structure from anomalous dispersion [cover story] J. Karle. bibl f il *Physics Today* 42:22-9 Je '89

SCAVULLO, FRANCESCO, 1929-
about
Rare beauty: fashion & fantasy. il *Harper's Bazaar* 122:132-7 D '89

SCCA *See* Sports Car Club of America
SCENE DESIGNERS *See* Set designers
SCENE DESIGNING *See* Motion pictures—Setting and scenery;
    Opera—Stage setting and scenery; Television broadcasting—
    Setting and scenery; Theater—Stage setting and scenery
SCENERY, PHOTOGRAPHIC *See* Photography—Setting and
    scenery
SCENERY, STAGE *See* Opera—Stage setting and scenery;
    Television broadcasting—Setting and scenery; Theater—
    Stage setting and scenery
SCENES FROM THE CLASS STRUGGLE IN BEVERLY
    HILLS [film] *See* Motion picture reviews—Single works
SCENIC RIVERS *See* Wild and scenic rivers
SCENIC VIEWS *See* Views (Scenery)
SCENT *See* Perfumes
SCENT BOTTLES *See* Perfume bottles
SCENTED GARDENS *See* Fragrant gardens
SCHAAF, FRED
    1989 almanac for skygazers. il *The Mother Earth News*
        115:94-6+ Ja/F '89
    A field guide to atmospheric optics [cover story] bibl il
        Sky and Telescope 77:254-9 Mr '89
    Return of the northern lights. il *The Mother Earth News*
        119:75-7 S/O '89
SCHAAF, RACHELLE VANDER *See* Vander Schaaf, Rachelle
SCHACHT, HENRY B.
    about
    Why Henry Schacht is watching his rearview mirror. J.
        E. Ellis. il por *Business Week* p43 Ja 9 '89
SCHACKNOW, MAX
    about
    Portraits. *The New Yorker* 65:36-7 S 18 '89
SCHAD, GEOFFREY D.
    (jt. auth) *See* Bakshian, Aram, and Schad, Geoffrey D.
SCHAECHER, ROBERT
    Reducing homophobia among educators and students. *The
        Education Digest* 54:58-61 Ap '89
SCHAEFER, BRADLEY E.
    (jt. auth) *See* Doggett, LeRoy E., and Schaefer, Bradley E.
SCHAEFER, DALE W.
    Polymers, fractals, and ceramic materials. bibl f il *Science*
        243:1023-7 F 24 '89
SCHAEFER, DAN
    Should the "balanced budget constitutional amendment" be
        adopted? [excerpts from statement, November 17, 1987]
        Congressional Digest 68:274+ N '89
SCHAEFER, FAITH
    Sea secrets. *See* issues of Sea Frontiers beginning January/
        February 1986
SCHAEFER, GEORGE ANTHONY, 1928-
    about
    Can Caterpillar inch its way back to heftier profits? B.
        Bremner. il *Business Week* p75+ S 25 '89
SCHAEFER, JAMES M.
    about
    Interview: James Schaefer. A. J. S. Rayl. il pors *Omni (New
        York, N.Y.)* 12:106-8+ D '89
    Lookin' for science in all the wrong places. J. Stone. il
        Discover 10:96-9 Mr '89
SCHAEFER, KAY
    Flying can be a pain in the neck. il *Nation's Business* 77:73
        S '89
SCHAEFERS, JIM
    Why boys have more fun. il *Seventeen* 48:68-9 Jl '89
SCHAEFFER, REBECCA
    about
    A fatal obsession with the stars. A. Toufexis. il por *Time*
        134:43-4 Jl 31 '89
    Obituary
        People Weekly il pors 32:60-2+ Jl 31 '89. P. Axthelm
SCHAEFFER, SUSAN FROMBERG
    about
    A soldier's tale. C. McGee. il por *New York* 22:26 My
        22 '89
SCHAETZEL, WENDY
    (jt. auth) *See* Pertschuk, Michael, 1933-, and Schaetzel, Wendy
SCHAFALE, CHRISTIE MARIE, D. 1988
    about
    Scared to death! Terror and tragedy at America's amusement
        parks. E. Davidowitz. il por *Redbook* 173:106-7+ Jl '89
SCHAFER, WILLIAM R., AND OTHERS
    Genetic and pharmacological suppression of oncogenic muta-
        tions in *RAS* genes of yeast and humans. bibl f il *Science*
        245:379-85 Jl 28 '89
SCHÄFER, WOLF, 1942-, AND OTHERS
    One enzyme makes a fungal pathogen, but not a saprophyte,
        virulent on a new host plant. bibl f il *Science* 246:247-9
        O 13 '89
SCHAFFER, TERESITA
    Proposal to sell F-16s to Pakistan [statement, August 2,
        1989] *Department of State Bulletin* 89:65-6 O '89
SCHAFFNER, FRANKLIN J., 1920-1989
    about
    Welcome home [film] Reviews
        People Weekly il 32:22-3 N 27 '89. R. Novak
SCHAFFNER, TIMOTHY
    A good agent is not hard to find—if you know how, when,
        and where to look. *The Writer* 102:14-16 Ja '89

SCHALK, ADOLPH
    The Swiss debate their Army's future. il *Commonweal*
        116:331-3 Je 2 '89
SCHALL, JEFFREY D.
    (jt. auth) *See* Logothetis, Nikos K., and Schall, Jeffrey D.
SCHAMA, SIMON
    The nightmares of reason. il *The New Republic* 201:26-33
        Jl 31 '89
SCHANBERG, SYDNEY
    The risk of being different [address, May 14, 1989] *Vital
        Speeches of the Day* 55:700-2 S 1 '89
SCHAPIRO, MARK
    The Bay Area: the persistence of light. il *Art News* 88:132-7
        D '89
    (jt. auth) *See* Fisher, William, and Schapiro, Mark
SCHAPPELL, ELISSA
    In rehab with the love junkies. *Mademoiselle* 95:217+ O
        '89
SCHAPS, ERIC
    (jt. auth) *See* Streshly, William, and Schaps, Eric
SCHARDT, BRUCE C., AND OTHERS
    Atomic resolution imaging of adsorbates on metal surfaces
        in air: iodine adsorption on pt(111). bibl f il *Science*
        243:1050-3 F 24 '89
SCHARFMAN, HELEN E., AND SCHWARTZKROIN,
    PHILIP A.
    Protection of dentate hilar cells from prolonged stimulation
        by intracellular calcium chelation. bibl f il *Science*
        246:257-60 O 13 '89
SCHARLOO, W.
    Developmental and physiological aspects of reaction norms.
        bibl f il *BioScience* 39:465-71 Jl/Ag '89
SCHATZBERG, JERRY, 1927-
    about
    Expatriate. M. Ciment. il por *Film Comment* 25:16-19 My/Je
        '89
SCHAUB, GEORGE
    The compleat camcorder. il *Video* 12:40-3+ Mr '89
    One-pound wonders. il *Video* 13:44-7 Ap '89
    Shooting color. *See* issues of Popular Photography beginning
        March 1988
SCHAUBLE, VIRGINIA
    Moving into light [poem] *Commonweal* 116:526 O 6
        '89
SCHAUFUSS, PETER
    about
    Bad boy makes good. T. Tobias. il por *New York* 22:16
        Jl 24 '89
SCHAUT, NORMAN F.
    How we put the "antique" in Atlantique City. il por *Antiques
        & Collecting Hobbies* 94:28-9 Ag '89
SCHECHTER, ARNOLD
    Conquering pain. il *Modern Maturity* 32:72-4+ Je/Jl '89
SCHECHTER, BRUCE
    Flux creep. il *Discover* 10:20 O '89
    Suspending disbelief over superconductivity. il *Discover*
        10:59-60 Ja '89
SCHECHTER, SUSAN
    about
    Understanding battered women [interview] M. Suh. il *Ms.*
        17:62 Ap '89
SCHEDULES
    See also
    Airlines—Schedules
SCHEER, ROBERT
    The further adventures of Paul Newman [cover story] il
        pors *Esquire* 112:164-6+ O '89
SCHEER, STEFANIE
    about
    From the publisher. D. J. Barr. il por *Sports Illustrated*
        71:1 S 18 '89
SCHEFER, DOROTHY
    (jt. auth) *See* Robinson, Andrea, and Schefer, Dorothy
SCHEFFER, DAVID J.
    Nouveau law and foreign policy. *Foreign Policy* 76:44-65
        Fall '89
SCHEFFLERA
    Propagating scheffleras: which parts to use? il *Sunset (Central
        West edition)* 182:236 Je '89
SCHEIBER, DAVE
    Decisions, decisions. il *Sports Illustrated* 71:30-2+ Jl 3 '89
    In search of a net gain. il pors *Sports Illustrated* 70:24-6
        My 1 '89
    Look back in anger. il pors *Sports Illustrated* 70:42-4+ My
        8 '89
SCHEIDLINGER, SAUL, 1918-
    about
    Leader of the group. S. Goodman. il por *New York* 22:36
        My 15 '89
SCHEIN, OLIVER
    about
    An eye doctor says wearing contacts for weeks at a time
        can be blindingly shortsighted [interview] D. Mathison.
        il por *People Weekly* 32:65-6 N 6 '89
SCHEINA, ROBERT L.
    Ocean stations. il *Sea Frontiers* 35:53-5 Ja/F '89

SCHEINMAN, PAMELA, 1945-
Faith Ringgold/Bernice Steinbaum Gallery. il *American Craft* 49:72-3 F/Mr '89
Urban tapestry [cover story] il *American Craft* 49:42-7 Ag/S '89
SCHEKMAN, RANDY
(jt. auth) See Payne, Gregory S., and Schekman, Randy
SCHELL, JONATHAN, 1943-
Our fragile earth. il *Discover* 10:44-7+ O '89
Speak loudly, carry a small stick. il *Harper's* 278:39-41+ Mr '89
about
PW interviews. C. Deyrup. por *Publishers Weekly* 235:71-2 Ap 21 '89
SCHELL, ORVILLE
An act of defiance [cover story] il pors *The New York Times Magazine* p26-7+ Ap 16 '89
Children of Tiananmen. il pors *Rolling Stone* p185-8+ D 14-28 '89
China's spring [cover story] il *The New York Review of Books* 36:3-4+ Je 29 '89
Lost chance: how Bush failed the heroes of Tiananmen Square. il *Mother Jones* 14:36-9 S '89
The old China is dead. *New Perspectives Quarterly* 6:56-7 Summ '89
(tr) See Fang Lizhi. Keeping the faith
SCHELLER, WILLIAM
Tucked away in rural Acadia. il map *Travel Holiday* 171:42-8 F '89
about
Under the hood. *The New Yorker* 65:26-7 Ag 14 '89
SCHELLING, THOMAS C., 1921-
From an airport bench. il por *The Bulletin of the Atomic Scientists* 45:29-31 My '89
about
Has arms control worked? [cover story; special section; with introd. by Michael Krepon] bibl f il *The Bulletin of the Atomic Scientists* 45:26-45 My '89
SCHEMBECHLER, BO
about
The right man for the job. A. Wolff. il pors *Sports Illustrated* 70:58-60+ Ap 17 '89
SCHEME (COMPUTER LANGUAGE)
Lisp dialect taps Mac riches [MacScheme + Toolsmith] J. Udell. il *Byte* 14:204 S '89
SCHEMMEL, WILLIAM
Vicksburg revisited. il *Travel Holiday* 171:67-71 Ja '89
SCHENDLER, REVAN
Pedestrian, walk! [poem] *The New Yorker* 65:36 My 1 '89
Reparations of spring [poem] *The New Yorker* 65:46 Mr 27 '89
SCHENECTADY (N.Y.)
Crime
The bad mother [M. Tinning kills nine infants] J. Egginton. il pors *Good Housekeeping* 208:119+ Ap '89
SCHENKEL, CARL
about
The Mighty Quinn [film] Reviews
New York il 22:56 Mr 6 '89. D. Denby
People Weekly 31:11 Mr 27 '89. S. Haller
SCHENKKAN, ROBERT
Heaven on earth [drama] Reviews
The New Yorker 65:110 N 20 '89. E. Oliver
SCHEPER-HUGHES, NANCY
Death without weeping. *Natural History* p8+ O '89
SCHEPISI, FRED
about
A cry in the dark [film] Reviews
American Film il 14:72 Je '89. P. Rainer
Glamour il 87:103-4 Ja '89. J. G. Boyum
Mademoiselle il 95:46+ Ja '89. R. Rosenbaum
Video il 13:62 Jl '89. J. Young
The Russia house [film] Reviews
Newsweek il por 114:66-7 N 6 '89. C. Bogert
SCHER, CAROL
(jt. auth) See Scher, Les, and Scher, Carol
SCHER, JILL
about
All-American Girl-talk. il pors *Teen* 33:12 S '89
SCHER, JON
The farm report. il *Sport (New York, N.Y.)* 80:52-3 Ap '89
SCHER, LES, AND SCHER, CAROL
Country water [excerpt from Finding and buying your place in the country] il *The Mother Earth News* 118:92-6+ Jl/Ag '89
SCHERER, BARRYMORE LAURENCE
Revolving door? (I) [with editorial comment by Jane L. Poole] il *Opera News* 53:4, 22-4 Ja 21 '89
Revolving door? (II). il *Opera News* 53:18-21 Ap 15 '89
Revolving door? (III). il *Opera News* 54:32-4 O '89
SCHERER, ROY See Hudson, Rock, 1925-1985
SCHERING-PLOUGH CORP.
Will takeover fever strike Schering-Plough? G. G. Marcial. il *Business Week* p130 O 23 '89

SCHERR, JIM
about
Scherr determination. B. Anderson. il pors *Sports Illustrated* 70:71+ Ap 10 '89
SCHERRER, HERMANN ARTHUR
about
Gardens: wonders of Scherrer Park. D. H. Minassian. il *Architectural Digest* 46:228-33 O '89
SCHERRER, JEAN-RAOUL, AND BORST, FRANÇOIS
A common standard. il *World Health* p24-5 Ag/S '89
SCHERVISH, HERBERT
about
Tuition payments cut job turnover. S. D. Rinella and R. J. Kopecky. il por *Nation's Business* 77:25-6 Ag '89
SCHEUER, RUTH TANNENBAUM
about
Urban tapestry [cover story] P. Scheinman. il *American Craft* 49:42-7 Ag/S '89
SCHEUER TAPESTRY STUDIO (NEW YORK, N.Y.) See Center for Tapestry Arts (New York, N.Y.)
SCHEWE, PHILLIP F.
Physics news in 1988 [special section] il *Physics Today* 42:S1-S67 Ja '89
SCHICK, JAMES B. M.
John Smith's bill: then & now. il *American Heritage* 40:158-65 N '89
SCHICKEL, RICHARD
Bette [cover story] il pors *Film Comment* 25:20-2+ Mr/Ap '89
SCHIDLOWSKI, JUAN CARLOS
about
The fugitive king of penny stocks. D. Zigas. il pors *Business Week* p124-5+ N 20 '89
SCHIELE, EGON, 1890-1918
about
Return of the "Bohemian girl". A. Decker. il *Art News* 88:74+ Ap '89
SCHIER, PHILIP
about
Electronic retailer makes cash register ring. L. Arden. il por *Home Office Computing* 7:42 My '89
SCHIER, TRACY
My grandmother's quilt [poem] *America* 161:377 N 25 '89
A survey of research on Church life today. *America* 161:351-2 N 18 '89
SCHIFF, ANDRÁS, 1953-
about
Andras Schiff at Carnegie Hall. E. W. Said. *The Nation* 249:802-4 D 25 '89
Schiff's Bach. S. Lincoln. il por *Stereo Review* 54:87 Ag '89
SCHIFF, JACOB HENRY, 1847-1920
about
Jacob Schiff and the Northern Pacific corner. J. S. Gordon. il por *American Heritage* 40:86-7 Jl/Ag '89
SCHIFF, JEFFREY
about
Jeffrey Schiff at the Williams College Museum of Art. K. Johnson. il *Art in America* 77:171+ F '89
SCHIFFER, CLAUDIA
about
Who's that girl? M. Gross. il por *New York* 22:38 S 25 '89
SCHIFFMANN, ROBERT
about
Doughnut detonator. J. Zweig. il por *Forbes* 143:154+ My 1 '89
SCHIFFMANN (R.F.) ASSOCIATES See R.F. Schiffmann Associates
SCHIFTER, RICHARD
Human rights situation in Cuba [statement, August 2, 1989] *Department of State Bulletin* 89:41-3 O '89
SCHILIT, BARRY
[Month] weather. See issues of Southern Living
SCHILLER, BILL
'F.W.' brings cautious hope for reform. *World Press Review* 36:30-1 N '89
SCHILLER, HARVEY
about
'I enjoy stress' [interview] R. Sullivan. il por *Sports Illustrated* 71:16 N 13 '89
SCHILLER, HERBERT I., 1919-
Pitchers at an exhibition [cover story] il *The Nation* 249:37+ Jl 10 '89
SCHILLER, LEWIS S.
about
The sad saga of a penny-stock company. G. Weiss. il por *Business Week* p124-6+ My 15 '89
SCHILLING, DON
about
Tiny terrors. L. Griffin. il *Car and Driver* 35:158-9+ D '89
SCHILLING, PAUL
about
To market, to market. N. C. Baker. il por *Nation's Business* 77:61 Ja '89

SCHILLING, PHIL
Editorial. See issues of Cycle through February 1989
SCHIMMEL, SELMA
about
Young cancer victims. L. Mosedale. il por *Glamour* 87:88 Je '89
SCHINDLER, D. W.
Biotic impoverishment at home and abroad. *BioScience* 39:426 Jl/Ag '89
SCHINE, CATHLEEN
Floor wars. il *The New York Times Magazine* p28-31+ Ag 13 '89
SCHINE, JOAN G.
Adolescents help themselves by helping others. il *Children Today* 18:10-15 Ja/F '89
SCHINKEL, KARL FRIEDRICH, 1781-1841
about
Schloss Charlottenhof in Potsdam: a Karl Friedrich Schinkel masterpiece restored. M. Filler. il *Antiques* 135:930-41 Ap '89
SCHINTZIUS, DWAYNE
about
Much ado about a 'do. C. Kirkpatrick. il pors *Sports Illustrated* 70:52-4+ Ja 16 '89
SCHIPA, TITO, 1889-1965
about
The name is the voice. J. B. Steane. por *Opera News* 54:22+ Ag '89
SCHIRMER, JENNIFER
Waging war to prevent war. il *The Nation* 248:478-9 Ap 10 '89
SCHISM
A black Catholic priest's renegade church stirs up an unholy furor [G. A. Stallings launches the Imani Temple] D. Grogan. il pors *People Weekly* 32:28-30 Jl 31 '89
Black priest in schism? [G. A. Stallings] *The Christian Century* 106:649 Jl 5-12 '89
Cardinal bars black D.C. priest from saying Mass [G. A. Stallings] por *Jet* 76:5 Jl 17 '89
D.C. priest splits from Catholic Church; black bishops decry the act [G. Stallings] *Jet* 76:12 Jl 10 '89
Equal rites [G. A. Stallings' rebellion] M. McGough. *The New Republic* 201:11-12 Ag 28 '89
Father Stallings' choices. *America* 161:75 Ag 12-19 '89
Heretic as hero [G. A. Stallings] T. Bethell. il *The American Spectator* 22:11-13 S '89
Is a separate church the answer to blacks' prayers? [G. A. Stallings] D. Pitts. il por *Black Enterprise* 20:28 O '89
The Lefebvrite-feminist coalition? M. McGough. il *The American Spectator* 22:28-9 Ag '89
Priest seeks to reconcile with Catholic hierarchy; White Chicago priest backs Stallings' stand. il por *Jet* 76:16-17 Jl 24 '89
Va. priest fired after announcing plans to join separatist Catholic Church [B. Greening] pors *Jet* 76:26 Ag 21 '89
What's behind the black rebellion in the Catholic Church? [G. A. Stallings] L. B. Randolph. il pors *Ebony* 45:160-2+ N '89
SCHISTOSOMIASIS
Africa's 'wonder weed' [use of endod] il *The Unesco Courier* 42:48-9 Jl '89
. . . and how it was fought [Brazil] Z. A. Andrade. il *World Health* p26-7 D '88
Mollusks in midstream [study of snails in Zimbabwe] M. Woolhouse. il *Natural History* p6+ Mr '89
New weapon in the war against schistosomiasis [niclosamide prevents infection] J. Cherfas. il *Science* 246:1242-3 D 8 '89
Schisto in Brazil . . . P. L. Tauil. il *World Health* p24-5 D '88
SCHIZOPHRENIA
. . . and among young schizophrenics [drug abuse; study by Mary Ann Test] *Science News* 136:239 O 7 '89
Lost brother. K. King. il pors *Life* 12:94-8+ N '89
Out of the ashes, a family restored [P. Daniluk reunited with mother who is a patient in mental institution after separation of 64 years] M. Dougherty. il pors *People Weekly* 31:46-51 F 13 '89
Return of Marie Balter [former patient helps administer Danvers State Hospital] T. Armbrister. il por *Reader's Digest* 135:123-7 Jl '89
Schizophrenia: fact vs. fantasy. S. R. Arbetter. il *Current Health 2* 16:23-5 S '89
When mental illness hits home [with case study of J. Alexander; cover story; special section] E. E. Goode. il pors *U.S. News & World Report* 106:54-7+ Ap 24 '89
Causes
Explaining the inexplicable. il *U.S. News & World Report* 106:60 Ap 24 '89
Genetic aspects
Schizophrenia gene: a family link fades [research by David St. Clair] B. Bower. *Science News* 135:359 Je 10 '89
Schizophrenic results. R. Rusting. *Scientific American* 260:32 Ja '89
Therapy
Clozaril approved. *FDA Consumer* 23:2 D '89/Ja '90

Schizophrenia drug gains FDA approval [clozapine] B. Bower. *Science News* 136:245 O 14 '89
SCHLAMME, THOMAS
about
Miss Firecracker [film] Reviews
American Film il 14:60-1 My '89. C. Hodenfield
Commonweal 116:338 Je 2 '89. T. O'Brien
Film Comment il 25:9-12+ My/Je '89. K. Jaehne
The Nation 248:677-8 My 15 '89. S. Klawans
The New Republic 200:26-7 Je 12 '89. S. Kauffmann
New York il 22:101-2 My 15 '89. D. Denby
The New Yorker 65:103-4 My 29 '89. P. Kael
Newsweek il 113:75 My 1 '89. J. Kroll
People Weekly 31:15 My 29 '89. S. Haller
Time il 133:68 My 1 '89. R. Corliss
SCHLANG, JOSEPH
about
Untapped market. *The New Yorker* 64:24-5 Ja 16 '89
SCHLATTER, THOMAS
Weather queries. See issues of Weatherwise
SCHLEGEL, SHARON
His brother's keeper. *Reader's Digest* 134:112-14 F '89
SCHLESINGER, ARTHUR M., 1917-
The ages of Jackson. bibl f il *The New York Review of Books* 36:48-51 D 7 '89
Getting FDR's ear. il *The New York Review of Books* 36:20-3 F 16 '89
The opening of the American mind. *The New York Times Book Review* 94:1+ Jl 23 '89
SCHLESINGER, JOHN, 1926-
about
Madame Sousatzka [film] Reviews
Video 13:59 Ag '89. J. Bernard
SCHLESINGER, MARIAN CANNON
A message in a bottle: or, Honeymoon on Cannon Mountain. il pors map *American Heritage* 40:106-9 Ap '89
SCHLICHTING, CARL D.
Phenotypic integration and environmental change. bibl f il *BioScience* 39:460-4 Jl/Ag '89
SCHLICTING, MICHAEL, 1953-
about
The watercolor page: Michael Schlicting. M. Madenski. il pors *American Artist* 53:42-5+ Je '89
SCHLOCK ART *See* Imitation art
SCHLOEMER, PAUL G.
about
Cliff dodger. R. T. Grieves. il por *Forbes* 143:322+ Ja 9 '89
SCHLOSBERG, JEREMY
The start-up blues. *The Washington Monthly* 20:25-30 Ja '89
SCHLOSS CHARLOTTENHOF (POTSDAM, GERMANY)
Schloss Charlottenhof in Potsdam: a Karl Friedrich Schinkel masterpiece restored. M. Filler. il *Antiques* 135:930-41 Ap '89
SCHLOSSBERG, EDWIN
about
The family's first year. L. David. il pors *McCall's* 116:12-14 Ag '89
SCHLOSSBERG, ROSE KENNEDY
about
The family's first year. L. David. il pors *McCall's* 116:12-14 Ag '89
SCHLUND, BRANDON
about
Second grader Brandon Schlund is a standout student in his school—he's also the only one. M. Neill. il pors *People Weekly* 32:111-12 N 6 '89
SCHMANDT, JURGEN
Science and technology: its future in the U.S. *Current (Washington, D.C.)* 309:7-13 Ja '89
SCHMEISSER, PETER
Harry Oppenheimer's empire: going for the gold. il por *The New York Times Magazine* p32-3+ Mr 19 '89
SCHMELING, MAX, 1905-
Collectibles
Mementos of a champ: Max Schmeling, world's heavyweight boxing champion, 1930-1932. D. E. Matter and R. M. Matter. il pors *Antiques & Collecting Hobbies* 94:59-60 Jl '89
SCHMERTZ, MILDRED F.
Editorial. See issues of Architectural Record beginning October 1985
SCHMICH, MARY
Driving. il *Vogue* 179:162 Je '89
SCHMID, PETER, AND OTHERS
Dynamic expression pattern of the *myc* protooncogene in midgestation mouse embryos. bibl f il *Science* 243:226-9 Ja 13 '89
SCHMID, RANDOLPH E.
Rockin' thunder [cover story] il *Weatherwise* 42:192-6 Ag '89
SCHMIDGALL, GARY, 1945-
Sewing down a dream. il pors *Opera News* 53:30-2 Ap 1 '89

SCHMIDT, GEORGE
about
A watchdog guards the public schools. M. Ervin. por *The Progressive* 53:16-17 N '89
SCHMIDT, JAMES
about
Banking on regionals. C. Poole. il *Forbes* 144:190 S 4 '89
SCHMIDT, KARL
The art of healthy living. il *World Health* p26 Ja/F '89
SCHMIDT, MAX, AND SCHWARZ, WOLFGANG
From East Germany: it's NATO's move now. il *The Bulletin of the Atomic Scientists* 45:5-6 S '89
SCHMIDT, STEPHEN
Living with chronic illness: why should I go on? *The Christian Century* 106:475-6+ My 3 '89
SCHMIDT, THOMAS J.
The hard sayings of Jesus. il *Christianity Today* 33:28-30 My 12 '89
SCHMIDT, WAYNE A.
Are Great Lakes fish safe to eat? il map *National Wildlife* 27:16-19 Ag/S '89
SCHMIDT CAMERAS *See* Cameras
SCHMIDT-CASSEGRAIN TELESCOPES *See* Telescopes
SCHMIES, HOWARD
(jt. auth) See Bernier, André, and Schmies, Howard
SCHMITT, MARK
(jt. auth) See Ornstein, Norman J., and Schmitt, Mark
SCHMITT, PETER
Homecoming [poem] *The Nation* 248:861 Je 19 '89
SCHMITT TRIGGER *See* Multivibrators
SCHMOKE, KURT
First word. il *Omni (New York, N.Y.)* 11:8 Ap '89
A war for the Surgeon General, not the Attorney General. il *New Perspectives Quarterly* 6:12-15 Summ '89
about
Baltimore mayor Schmoke cites city's Read-A-Thon. il por *Jet* 76:23-4 Ag 28 '89
What must be done. il pors *Ebony* 44:156+ Ag '89
SCHNAARS, STEVEN P.
about
Sweet technology, sour marketing. R. Bailey. il por *Forbes* 143:140 My 1 '89
SCHNABEL, ARTUR, 1882-1951
about
Schnabel: stylish as ever on CD. T. Teachout. il *High Fidelity (New York, N.Y.)* 39:75 Ap '89
SCHNABEL, JACQUELINE
about
Downtown chic. A. Radakovich. il por *Harper's Bazaar* 122:72 N '89
SCHNABEL, JULIAN
about
Julian Schnabel at CAPC. B. Adams. il *Art in America* 77:205 N '89
Sacred arts. H. Muschamp. il por *Vogue* 179:420-5 Ap '89
SCHNECKLOTH, TIM
Frank Zappa: garni du jour, Lizard King, poetry and slime [interview; reprint] por *Down Beat* 56:84-5 S '89
SCHNEIDER, BRUCE, 1941-, AND OTHERS
Binocular unmasking: an analog to binaural unmasking? bibl f il *Science* 243:1479-81 Mr 17 '89
SCHNEIDER, CLAUDINE
Turning down the heat. il *National Parks* 63:16-17+ Jl/Ag '89
SCHNEIDER, HANNES
about
The Hannes Schneider story. N. Howe. il pors *Skiing* 41:126-9+ Mr '89
SCHNEIDER, JASON
Collecting cameras. See issues of Popular Photography beginning March 1988
SCHNEIDER, JILL E., AND WADE, GEORGE N.
Availability of metabolic fuels controls estrous cyclicity of Syrian hamsters. bibl f il *Science* 244:1326-8 Je 16 '89
SCHNEIDER, PAUL
Casablanca going south. il *Esquire* 111:22+ Ja '89
This blue city. il pors *Esquire* 111:38 F '89
SCHNEIDER, PETER, 1940-
If the Wall came tumbling down. il *The New York Times Magazine* p22-4+ Je 25 '89
SCHNEIDER, PHYLLIS
Dermatology checkup. il *Redbook* 173:152-4+ O '89
SCHNEIDER, RICHARD CHAIM
Marriage, death, and Israel. il por *World Press Review* 36:60 Ag '89
SCHNEIDER, STEPHEN HENRY
The changing climate. bibl il *Scientific American* 261:70-9 S '89
The greenhouse effect: science and policy. bibl f il *Science* 243:771-81 F 10 '89
about
The bold ones. S. Brewer. il pors *New Choices for the Best Years* 29:37-41 Jl '89
SCHNEIDER, WILLIAM, 1944-
JFK's children: the class of '74 [cover story] il por *The Atlantic* 263:35-40+ Mr '89
Republicans for Jackson. il *The Atlantic* 264:48 N '89

SCHNEIDERMAN, HOWARD G.
(jt. auth) See Baltzell, E. Digby (Edward Digby), 1915-, and Schneiderman, Howard G.
SCHNEIDERMAN, RON
Profitable technology from Uncle Sam. il map *High Technology Business* 9:26-30 F '89
SCHNEIDERMAN, STEPHEN
Darkroom magic: using multiple printing to make the images you couldn't take. il *Petersen's Photographic Magazine* 18:22-6 S '89
SCHNELLER, JOHANNA
Braking away. il *Gentlemen's Quarterly* 59:326-9+ O '89
The lust for thin. il *Mademoiselle* 95:222-3+ Mr '89
Married . . . with chicken [cover story] il pors *Gentlemen's Quarterly* 59:222-7+ Je '89
When your best friend's parents get divorced. il *Seventeen* 48:113-14+ Mr '89
SCHNEPPER, JEFF A.
The fantasy of federal tax policy. il *USA Today (Periodical)* 117:29 Ja '89
How fair is the progressive tax? il *USA Today (Periodical)* 118:17 S '89
A long-term solution for social security. il *USA Today (Periodical)* 117:69 Mr '89
Making homes affordable. il *USA Today (Periodical)* 118:25 N '89
SCHNITTMAN, STEVEN M., AND OTHERS
The reservoir for HIV-1 in human peripheral blood is a T cell that maintains expression of CD4. bibl f il *Science* 245:305-8 Jl 21 '89
SCHNOL, JANET
Time Warner trade publishing announces kick-off of Sports Illustrated for Kids Books. il *Publishers Weekly* 236:27+ O 27 '89
SCHNURNBERGER, LYNN
First vacation after the baby. il *Parents* 64:114-18 D '89
"It's for you, Mom!". il *Parents* 64:112-16 Mr '89
Kids: hot or not, keep them busy. il *New York* 22:120+ Jl 3-10 '89
SCHOCH, HENRY
Theodore Roosevelt National Park [excerpt] il *National Parks* 63:46-7 My/Je '89
SCHOELLHORN, ROBERT ALBERT
Challenges, choices and concerns [address, May 8, 1989] *Vital Speeches of the Day* 56:56-9 N 1 '89
about
The slippery ladder at Abbott Labs. J. F. Siler. il por *Business Week* p136-7 O 30 '89
SCHOEN, ALLEN
about
Pet acupuncture. R. H. Loeb. il pors *Good Housekeeping* 209:150+ N '89
SCHOEN, MARTIN, AND OTHERS
Shear forces in molecularly thin films. bibl f il *Science* 245:1223-5 S 15 '89
SCHOENBERG, ARNOLD, 1874-1951
about
Erwartung [opera] Reviews
   The Nation 248:316-17 Mr 6 '89. E. W. Said
   New York il 22:54 Ja 30 '89. P. G. Davis
   The New Yorker 64:98+ F 6 '89. A. Porter
   Newsweek il 113:70 Ja 30 '89. K. Ames
   Opera News il 53:31-3 Ja 21 '89
   Opera News il 53:8-14 Ja 21 '89. N. Rorem
Jews and geniuses. R. Craft. il pors *The New York Review of Books* 36:35-7 F 16 '89
SCHOENFELD, GABRIEL
A dosimeter for every dacha. bibl f il *The Bulletin of the Atomic Scientists* 45:13-15 Jl/Ag '89
Trouble aboard Red October. il *The Bulletin of the Atomic Scientists* 45:13-15 Je '89
(jt. auth) See Rumer, Boris, and Schoenfeld, Gabriel
SCHOENMAKERS, NEVIL
about
The Johnny Appleseed of pot. R. Z. Chesnoff. il *U.S. News & World Report* 107:30 N 6 '89
SCHOENSTEIN, RALPH, 1933-
Baseball diamonds are a girl's best friend. il *New Choices for the Best Years* 29:80+ O '89
Confessions of a cranberry-sauce addict. il *New Choices for the Best Years* 29:96 N '89
I still remember English. il *New Choices for the Best Years* 29:96 Mr '89
SCHOFIELD, MICHAEL
Exercises in diplomacy: simulating future crises. il *The Futurist* 23:8-11 Mr/Ap '89
SCHOFIELD-BODT, BRIAN
Paternity leave as church praxis. il *The Christian Century* 106:463-4 My 3 '89
SCHOLARLY PUBLISHING
See also
Society for Scholarly Publishing (U.S.)
University presses
The international PSP market: an update. F. Kobrak. *Publishers Weekly* 236:44-5 N 10 '89
PSP cooperative ventures. G. Feldman. *Publishers Weekly* 236:30 O 13 '89

SCHOLARLY PUBLISHING—*cont.*
Shatzkin's report on small press distribution arouses debate. M. Reuter. *Publishers Weekly* 236:9-10 S 8 '89

SCHOLARS
See also
Intellectuals and intellectual life

SCHOLARSHIPS AND FELLOWSHIPS
See also
ACT-SO Awards
Agriculture—Scholarships and fellowships
Aviation—Scholarships and fellowships
Bishop Desmond Tutu Southern African Refugee Scholarship Fund
Educational Assistance Limited
Physics—Scholarships and fellowships
Project Excellence Awards
Rhodes scholars and scholarships
Science—Scholarships and fellowships
Sister Thea Bowman Black Catholic Educational Foundation
An accident of birth delivers a most unusual scholarship [J. Lester, born on campus of Lane Community College, receives scholarship] il por *People Weekly* 32:81 O 23 '89
B.E. guide to fellowships and executive training programs. S. S. Harrison. il *Black Enterprise* 19:119-20+ F '89
Central America and the education president [scholarships bring students to U.S. universities] J. J. Mullaney. *America* 160:524-5 Je 3 '89
Coca-Cola USA to award $130,000 in scholarships [Share the Dream Scholarship Sweepstakes] il *Jet* 75:32 Mr 6 '89
Doug Williams Foundation annual benefit awards $100,000 in scholarships. il pors *Jet* 76:28-9 Je 26 '89
Finance your dreams. E. C. Ray. il *Essence* 20:118+ S '89
Is Proposition 42 racist? J. B. Johnson; A. Ashe. il *Ebony* 44:138-40 Je '89
A new Proposition [NCAA's Proposition 42 stiffens rules governing awarding of athletic scholarships] W. F. Reed. il *Sports Illustrated* 70:16-19 Ja 23 '89
Out of bounds [questions regarding the NCAA's Proposition 42 to tighten restrictions on scholarships] *The New Republic* 200:10-11 F 20 '89
Race becomes the game [J. Thompson challenges NCAA's Proposition 42 which tightens restrictions on athletic scholarships] J. Kroll. il por *Newsweek* 113:56-9 Ja 30 '89
Score a $sports $cholarship [women] E. Karlsberg. il *Teen* 33:80-1+ Ap '89
Tightening the rules [NCAA's Proposition 42 tightens athletic scholarship requirements] il *Newsweek* 113:58 Ja 23 '89
Underwriting the future: two women will send 146 kids to college [O. Brown and R. W. Hayre set up funds for black children] R. Brown. il pors *Ebony* 44:74+ Ap '89
When is the playing field too level? [NCAA's Proposition 42 tightens restrictions on athletic scholarships] A. P. Sanoff. il *U.S. News & World Report* 106:68-9 Ja 30 '89

SCHOLASTIC APTITUDE TEST
The $150 million redundancy. G. W. Bracey. bibl f il *Phi Delta Kappan* 70:698-702 My '89
Court ruling rekindles controversy over SATs [question of race and sex bias] C. Holden. il *Science* 243:885-7 F 17 '89
Cram scam [J. Katzman's Princeton Review cram course; cover story] J. Hammer. il *The New Republic* 200:15-18 Ap 24 '89
Ethnic groups' SAT scores rising. *USA Today (Periodical)* 118:15 Ag '89
Fiddling with the ACTs and SATs. B. Diamond. il *Seventeen* 48:44 O '89
Five challenges for the Scholastic Aptitude Test. J. Crouse and D. Trusheim. *The Education Digest* 54:26-8 Ap '89
Further mysteries of the SAT [sex discrimination charges] D. Seligman. il *Fortune* 119:112 Ja 2 '89
A multiple choice of SAT cram courses. R. Wilder. bibl il *U.S. News & World Report* 106:65-6+ F 27 '89
Putting a new SAT to the test. T. Toch. il *U.S. News & World Report* 107:60+ D 11 '89
SAT bashing [research by Stuart Katz] T. Waters. il *Discover* 10:28 Ag '89
The score before the game starts [question of bias against blacks] *Newsweek* 113:58 Ja 30 '89
Stop blaming the tests [question of bias against blacks and women] J. Leo. il *U.S. News & World Report* 106:80 Mr 20 '89
Thinking the unthinkable [address, February 22, 1989] D. M. Stewart. *Vital Speeches of the Day* 55:444-8 My 1 '89
Unacceptable ideas [charge that SATs discriminate against women] D. Seligman. il *Fortune* 119:151-2 Mr 13 '89

SCHOLEM, GERSHOM GERHARD, 1897-1982
about
Jewish mysticism in dispute. R. Alter. *Commentary* 88:53-9 S '89

SCHOLER, M., 1940-
(jt. auth) See Terasawa, T., and Scholer, M., 1940-

SCHOLL, ROCHELLE
about
A disquieting mystery: St. John's rallies behind an abandoned girl. G. Allen. il por *Maclean's* 102:18-19 Ag 7 '89
Resolving a riddle. B. Came and H. Quinn. il por *Maclean's* 102:40-2 Ag 21 '89

SCHOMAKER, ZIMMETH
(jt. auth) See Baier, Sue, and Schomaker, Zimmeth

SCHON, ERIC A., AND OTHERS
A direct repeat is a hotspot for large-scale deletion of human mitochondrial DNA. bibl f il *Science* 244:346-9 Ap 21 '89

SCHÖNBERG, ARNOLD See Schoenberg, Arnold, 1874-1951

SCHÖNHUBER, FRANZ
Bibliography
The rising star of the German right. G. A. Craig. il *The New York Review of Books* 36:22-4 Je 15 '89

SCHOOL, CHOICE OF See School choice

SCHOOL, READINESS FOR See Readiness for school

SCHOOL ACTIVITIES See Student activities

SCHOOL ADMINISTRATION See School management and organization

SCHOOL ADMINISTRATORS
See also
School superintendents and principals
Administrator/student ratios in large school districts. A. C. Ornstein. il *Phi Delta Kappan* 70:806-8 Je '89
Education
See School management and organization—Study and teaching

SCHOOL AGE
See also
Readiness for school
Age and achievement [research by Zvia Breznitz and Tamar Teltsch] G. W. Bracey. il *Phi Delta Kappan* 70:732 My '89

SCHOOL AND SOCIAL AND ECONOMIC PROBLEMS
See also
School children—Social and economic status
Socially handicapped children—Education
The clock is ticking. A. C. Lewis. il *Phi Delta Kappan* 71:4-5 S '89
School prevention of suicide, violence, and abuse. E. Guetzloe. *The Education Digest* 54:46-9 F '89

SCHOOL AND THE COMMUNITY
See also
Colleges and universities—Public relations
School buildings—Extended use
Volunteer service
Arts educators should work with the arts community. G. C. Wenner. *The Education Digest* 54:54-7 F '89
Early care and education: beyond the schoolhouse doors. S. L. Kagan. bibl f il *Phi Delta Kappan* 71:107-12 O '89
School order and safety as community issues [study of Chicago schools] J. Menacker and others. bibl f il *Phi Delta Kappan* 71:39-40+ S '89

SCHOOL AND THE HOME
See also
Home education
Parents' and teachers' associations
School management and organization—Parent participation
Adjusting to changing families [survey by the National Association of Elementary School Principals] il *USA Today (Periodical)* 118:11 D '89
An apple for the parents [Christian involvement in public schools] T. K. Jones. il *Christianity Today* 33:14 S 22 '89
Arthur: a tale of disempowerment. L. V. Rosow. bibl f il *Phi Delta Kappan* 71:194-9 N '89
The business-education link. J. Dawes. il por *Nation's Business* 77:27 Je '89
Business, home, and school: cooperating to develop lifelong readers [project in Pinellas County, Fla.] A. R. Bellack and C. K. Hallin. il *Phi Delta Kappan* 70:415 Ja '89
Dr. Salk talks to parents about kids and school. L. Salk. il *McCall's* 116:53-6 S '89
Early care and education: beyond the schoolhouse doors. S. L. Kagan. bibl f il *Phi Delta Kappan* 71:107-12 O '89
Educators can promote involvement of fathers. B. A. McBride. *The Education Digest* 55:43-5 N '89
The families of gifted underachievers [research by Sylvia Rimm and Barbara Lowe] G. W. Bracey. il *Phi Delta Kappan* 70:563 Mr '89
The homework dilemma. J. Stewart. il *Parents* 64:80+ F '89
How educators can help latchkey children. L. Long. *The Education Digest* 54:53-7 Mr '89
How schools help families. J. A. Levine. il *Good Housekeeping* 209:141-2 S '89
How to be a totally awesome parent. P. Welsh. *Reader's Digest* 135:87-9 N '89
How to improve your child's test scores [standardized tests] E. Kiester and S. V. Kiester. il *Reader's Digest* 134:84-8 My '89

SCHOOL AND THE HOME—*cont.*

Is life too fast for baby boomers' kids? D. Harrington-Lueker. *The Education Digest* 55:29-31 O '89

Kids, parents, and homework. J. Oppenheim. il *Good Housekeeping* 209:148+ S '89

Lesson plans: eleven ways to help your child excel in school. D. C. Williams. il *Essence* 20:100 Ag '89

Making peace with your child's school. K. Levine. il *Parents* 64:73-4+ Ap '89

Parent-teacher communication techniques [preschool] E. L. Morgan. *The Education Digest* 55:32-5 O '89

Parent-teacher conference. J. Cenedella. il *Good Housekeeping* 209:132+ S '89

Parental involvement in student learning. B. Sattes. *The Education Digest* 54:37-9 Ja '89

Report cards can hurt you [poor grades trigger child abuse] A. Toufexis. il *Time* 133:75 My 1 '89

Sizing up your local school. N. Henderson. il *Changing Times* 43:101-2+ N '89

Your child's teacher. J. Segal and Z. Segal. il *Parents* 64:217 N '89

SCHOOL ARCHITECTURE *See* School buildings
SCHOOL ART *See* Art—Study and teaching
SCHOOL ATHLETICS
    See also
    Baseball, High school
    Basketball, High school
    College athletics
    Football, High school
    Physical education and training
    Softball, High school
    Wrestling, High school

Bing saves school sports [D. Bing's work in Detroit] V. Lynn. por *Black Enterprise* 20:34 O '89
    Accidents and injuries

Heavy toll in high schools [studies by the National Athletic Trainers' Association] il *USA Today (Periodical)* 118:13 O '89

High school athletic injuries rated [study by Larry G. McLain] *Science News* 136:188 S 16 '89
    Ethical aspects

Choosing hockey [effects of open enrollment] il *U.S. News & World Report* 107:80 N 6 '89
    Safety devices and measures

Making sports safer for your kids. K. McManus. il *Changing Times* 43:45-6+ F '89

SCHOOL ATTENDANCE
    See also
    Dropouts
    School day

SCHOOL BANDS *See* Bands (Music)
SCHOOL-BASED MANAGEMENT

Can parents save schools? [Chicago] C. Leslie. il *Newsweek* 114:74 O 16 '89

Help for no-hope kids [work of J. P. Comer] C. Leslie. il por *Newsweek* 114:50 O 2 '89

The new apple of teachers' eyes [Los Angeles teachers pushing for school-based management] il *U.S. News & World Report* 106:11 My 29 '89

The quiet revolution: school-based budgeting [Edmonton, Alta.] T. McConaghy. il *Phi Delta Kappan* 70:486-7 F '89

Site-managed schools: the Chicago plan [excerpt from Organizing for learning] J. J. Lane and H. J. Walberg. *The Education Digest* 55:28-31 N '89

SCHOOL BOARDS

Are school boards on the way out? A. Shanker. *The Education Digest* 55:34-6 S '89

SCHOOL BOOKS *See* Textbooks
SCHOOL BREAKFASTS

In-school breakfasts improve test scores [Lawrence, Mass. study] J. Raloff. *Science News* 136:247 O 14 '89

SCHOOL BUILDINGS
    See also
    Classrooms

The case for natural schools. M. Wells. il *Country Journal* 16:34-9 Mr/Ap '89

Learning curve [new schools being built in New York City; special section] E. Posner. il *Architectural Record* 177:106-15 Mr '89

Prefab preschool [UCLA Child Care Center] D. Dietsch. il *Architectural Record* 177:126-9 Je '89

A school of one's own [bidding on vacant high school building] B. Greene. il *Esquire* 111:37-8 Ja '89

Schools flunk the radon test. *U.S. News & World Report* 106:18+ My 1 '89
    Community use
    See School buildings—Extended use
    Extended use
    See also
    After school programs
    School of the 21st Century (Program)

L.A. law helps latchkey pupils; extends hours for after-school play. il *Jet* 75:38 Ja 16 '89
    Laws and regulations

Asbestos makers run out of breathing room. B. Bremner. il *Business Week* p36+ N 20 '89

    Maintenance and repair

Renovating urban schools is fundamental to improving them. P. R. Piccigallo. bibl f il *Phi Delta Kappan* 70:402-6 Ja '89

SCHOOL BUILDINGS, PREFABRICATED

A new look at modular classrooms. B. Gossett. *The Education Digest* 54:64-5 Mr '89

SCHOOL BUILDINGS, REMODELED

New lessons for old schools. il *Southern Living* 24:139 Mr '89

SCHOOL BUS DRIVERS AND DRUGS *See* Drugs and bus drivers
SCHOOL BUSES

When kids sing the school-bus blues. F. Roberts. *Parents* 64:56-7 O '89

SCHOOL BUSING FOR INTEGRATION *See* Busing for school integration
SCHOOL CENSORSHIP *See* Censorship
SCHOOL CHILDREN
    See also
    Children, Gifted
    High school students
    Readiness for school
    Teachers and students

School days. F. Roberts. See issues of Parents beginning January 1983
    Adjustment
    See also
    Students—Transfer
    After school programs
    See After school programs
    Health and hygiene

AIDS in America's schoolhouses: learning the hard lessons [cover story; with editorial comment by Pauline B. Gough] D. L. Kirp and S. Epstein. il *Phi Delta Kappan* 70:578, 584-93 Ap '89

AIDS: infected children have the right to attend school. R. J. Shoop. *USA Today (Periodical)* 117:68-70 My '89

AIDS: students in glass houses? [case of E. Martinez in Tampa, Fla.] P. A. Zirkel. bibl f il *Phi Delta Kappan* 70:646-8 Ap '89

Can a child catch AIDS in school? F. Roberts. il *Parents* 64:51 My '89

Of lice and children: going to the head of the class [head lice] T. A. Young and J. Willis. il *FDA Consumer* 23:28-31 N '89
    Nutrition
    See School breakfasts; School lunches
    Punishment
    See School discipline
    Reading
    See Children's reading
    Recreation
    See Children—Recreation
    Social and economic status

War between the classes [Chicago's South Loop Elementary School] T. Padgett. il *Newsweek* 113:64 My 1 '89
    Transportation for integration
    See Busing for school integration
    Uniforms
    See School uniforms

SCHOOL CHILDREN AND DRUGS *See* Drugs and youth
SCHOOL CHOICE
    See also
    College choice

After busing: education and choice. D. J. Armor. *Current (Washington, D.C.)* 316:14-20 O '89

The choice backlash. C. E. Finn. il *National Review* 41:30-2 N 10 '89

Choice: claims of success, predictions of failure [Minnesota plan] L. W. Finch. *The Education Digest* 55:12-15 N '89

Choice: the hottest education issue of the '90s. A. Atkins. il *Better Homes and Gardens* 67:18+ O '89

Choosing hockey [effects of open enrollment] il *U.S. News & World Report* 107:80 N 6 '89

Family. C. Tevis. il *Successful Farming* 87:45 Ag '89

The fight over school choice. S. Tifft. il *Time* 133:54 Mr 13 '89

Giving parents a choice of schools. J. Fierman. il *Fortune* 120:147+ D 4 '89

Helping all children, empowering all educators: another view of school choice [Minnesota; with reply by J. Pearson] J. Nathan. bibl f il *Phi Delta Kappan* 71:304-11 D '89

High school choice and students at risk. D. R. Moore and S. Davenport. *The Education Digest* 55:7-10 S '89

How do we balance public school choice? B. Rosenberg. *The Education Digest* 55:7-11 N '89

Myths of choice: the governor's new clothes? [Minnesota's open enrollment plan] J. Pearson. *Phi Delta Kappan* 70:821-3 Je '89

President Bush and school choice. *America* 160:99 F 11 '89

Private choices for public schools. J. Hood. il *Conservative Digest* 15:70-3 My/Je '89

Public school choice: absolutely necessary but not wholly sufficient. E. Clinchy. il *Phi Delta Kappan* 71:289-94 D '89

SCHOOL CHOICE—*cont.*
Putting school choice in place. C. L. Glenn. il *Phi Delta Kappan* 71:295-300 D '89
Real choice [junior high school choice program in Harlem] *National Review* 41:12-13 S 1 '89
Restructuring American education through choice [address, May 19, 1989] L. F. Cavazos. *Vital Speeches of the Day* 55:514-16 Je 15 '89
Should parents choose their child's school? [Minnesota plan] M. C. Rist. *The Education Digest* 55:3-6 S '89
The uncertain benefits of school choice [Minnesota's open enrollment policy] P. Glastris and T. Toch. il *U.S. News & World Report* 107:79-80+ N 6 '89
What it really takes to make school choice work [St. Louis, Mo.] S. Uchitelle. *Phi Delta Kappan* 71:301-3 D '89
What our schools need is a healthy dose of competition. G. S. Becker. il *Business Week* p28 D 18 '89
SCHOOL CONTESTS
See also
Odyssey of the Mind
SCHOOL COUNSELING *See* Educational counseling
SCHOOL COUNSELORS *See* Educational counselors
SCHOOL CREDITS
See also
College credits
High school credits
SCHOOL DAY
See also
After school programs
From half day to full day [kindergarten] C. Leslie and P. Wingert. il *Newsweek* 113:62 Je 26 '89
SCHOOL DISCIPLINE
See also
Corporal punishment
Assertive Discipline—more than names on the board and marbles in a jar. L. Canter. bibl f il *Phi Delta Kappan* 71:57-61 S '89
Do school uniforms enforce discipline? F. Roberts. il *Parents* 64:59-60 Ap '89
Eastside story [views of principal J. Clark] Y. Kramer and R. Kramer. il *The American Spectator* 22:21-4 Ag '89
The make-believe world of "Lean on me" [methods of Paterson, N.J. principal J. Clark] I. A. Hyman. *The Education Digest* 55:20-2 N '89
Morgan Freeman stars as tough principal Joe Clark in hit movie, 'Lean on me' [cover story] T. S. Moore. il pors *Jet* 75:24-6 Mr 6 '89
SCHOOL DISTRICTS
Administrator/student ratios in large school districts. A. C. Ornstein. il *Phi Delta Kappan* 70:806-8 Je '89
SCHOOL ENROLLMENT
"House" plans for secondary schools [reducing size by subdivision] D. Oxley. *The Education Digest* 55:36-9 O '89
SCHOOL EVALUATION *See* Education—Evaluation
SCHOOL FINANCE *See* Education—Finance
SCHOOL GRADES *See* Grading and marking (Education)
SCHOOL INSURANCE *See* Insurance, School
SCHOOL JOURNALISM *See* College and school journalism
SCHOOL LAWS AND REGULATIONS *See* Educational laws and regulations
SCHOOL LUNCHES
Let's do lunch [San Diego school system] il *Seventeen* 48:189 S '89
Lunches kids will love. C. Koury. il *Parents* 64:161-4+ S '89
Anecdotes, facetiae, satire, etc.
The great sandwich caper [memories of frozen sandwiches for school lunches] C. Murphy. il *Reader's Digest* 135:149-50 S '89
SCHOOL MAGAZINES *See* College and school journalism
SCHOOL MANAGEMENT AND ORGANIZATION
See also
Class size
Colleges and universities—Administration
School administrators
School-based management
School boards
School discipline
School districts
School superintendents and principals
The 'at-risk' label and the problem of urban school reform [case against graded schools] L. Cuban. bibl f il *Phi Delta Kappan* 70:780-4+ Je '89
Early care and education: beyond the schoolhouse doors. S. L. Kagan. bibl f il *Phi Delta Kappan* 71:107-12 O '89
Education reform in the 1980s: lessons from the states [cover story] T. Timar and D. L. Kirp. bibl f il *Phi Delta Kappan* 70:504-11 Mr '89
Hawaii's school system is one of a kind [centralized system] J. Zulich. bibl f il *Phi Delta Kappan* 70:546-9 Mr '89
Institutional democracy in the public schools. M. A. Raywid. *The Education Digest* 55:8-10 D '89
Lessons from the states about education reform. T. Timar and D. L. Kirp. *The Education Digest* 55:11-14 S '89
The paradox of decentralizing schools: lessons from business, government, and the Catholic Church. J. T. Murphy. bibl f il *Phi Delta Kappan* 70:808-12 Je '89

Reconstructing the nation's worst schools [Chicago] H. J. Walberg and others. il *Phi Delta Kappan* 70:802-5 Je '89
Redistributing work to shrink class size. T. A. Chandler. *The Education Digest* 54:44-5 F '89
Rich schools, poor schools [issue of local control] A. E. Wise and T. Gendler. *The Education Digest* 55:3-7 D '89
Seizing control of school disasters [state takeovers of public schools] T. Toch. il *U.S. News & World Report* 107:69 O 23 '89
Sorting out local control. C. Pipho. il *Phi Delta Kappan* 70:430-1 F '89
Very hostile takeovers: states may step in when local schools fail. C. Leslie. il *Newsweek* 113:63+ Mr 13 '89
Parent participation
Can parents save schools? [Chicago] C. Leslie. il *Newsweek* 114:74 O 16 '89
Chicago parents 1, bureaucrats 0 [community control of schools] J. Rachlin. il *U.S. News & World Report* 106:51-2 F 6 '89
Power to parents [Western Europe] M. G. Bruce. il *Phi Delta Kappan* 70:413-14 Ja '89
Upgrading the schools: a primer for parents. B. Kantrowitz. il *Ladies' Home Journal* 106:70+ S '89
War between the classes [Chicago's South Loop Elementary School] T. Padgett. il *Newsweek* 113:64 My 1 '89
When teachers fail: what parents can do about it. P. Welsh. il *TV Guide* 37:18-20 S 2-8 '89
Study and teaching
See also
Academy for the Advancement of Teaching and Management
An administrator training program for minorities [internship program in South Carolina] A. B. Pigford. *Phi Delta Kappan* 70:650-1 Ap '89
Preparing the 21st-century superintendent [adaptation of address, February 1988] J. Hoyle. bibl f il *Phi Delta Kappan* 70:376-9 Ja '89
A program to improve local school site management [Oakland, Calif.] B. Barnes and M. Leslie. *The Education Digest* 55:32-4 N '89
Troubled kingdoms, restless natives. S. D. Thomson. bibl f il *Phi Delta Kappan* 70:371-5 Ja '89
Teacher participation
Education by charter [restructuring school districts] R. Budde. il *Phi Delta Kappan* 70:518-20 Mr '89
The politics of school restructuring [cover story] T. Timar. bibl f il *Phi Delta Kappan* 71:264-75 D '89
The principles of teacher empowerment. G. I. Maeroff. *The Education Digest* 54:6-9 F '89
School reform: a proposal for change. A. Shanker. il *USA Today (Periodical)* 117:71-3 My '89
Shared decision making for principals and teachers. A. S. Vann. *The Education Digest* 54:17-20 Ja '89
Teacher autonomy and managerial control. J. A. Raelin. *The Education Digest* 54:16-18 Ap '89
SCHOOL NEWSPAPERS *See* College and school journalism
SCHOOL OF AMERICAN BALLET
Ballerina leaves school to coach [A. Danilova] R. Johnson. il pors *Dance Magazine* 63:16 S '89
Bus stop [students prepare to leave for the Holland Festival] *The New Yorker* 65:26-7 Jl 10 '89
East meets West in Amsterdam: student days in Holland. N. Reynolds. il *Dance Magazine* 63:52-5 N '89
Reviews:
Annual workshop performance. C. Hardy. il *Dance Magazine* 63:67-9 N '89
School days [annual workshop performances] T. Tobias. il *New York* 22:70 Je 12 '89
Workshop 25. H. Watts. il *Dance Magazine* 63:38-41 My '89
SCHOOL OF THE 21ST CENTURY (PROGRAM)
21st Century School. R. E. Watson and K. FitzGerald. il *Parents* 64:112-16+ O '89
SCHOOL OF THE ART INSTITUTE OF CHICAGO *See* Art Institute of Chicago. School
SCHOOL ORCHESTRAS
Michael's orchestra. E. Berlin. *Ladies' Home Journal* 106:108 O '89
SCHOOL ORGANIZATION *See* School management and organization
SCHOOL PRAYER *See* Public schools and religion
SCHOOL PRINCIPALS *See* School superintendents and principals
SCHOOL REFORM *See* Education
SCHOOL REPORTS AND RECORDS
See also
Grading and marking (Education)
Report cards can hurt you [poor grades trigger child abuse] A. Toufexis. il *Time* 133:75 My 1 '89
Anecdotes, facetiae, satire, etc.
Your permanent record [condensed from Cheeseburgers] B. Greene. il *Reader's Digest* 134:147-8 Ap '89

SCHOOL SIZE *See* School enrollment
SCHOOL SUBJECTS *See* Curriculum
SCHOOL SUPERINTENDENTS AND PRINCIPALS
    See also
    Black school superintendents and principals
"Curriculum" for preschool [role of the principal] S. G. Sava. *The Education Digest* 54:51-2 Mr '89
Education: the movie [principals J. Clark, G. McKenna, D. Meier; cover story] D. L. Kirp. il pors *Mother Jones* 14:36-45 Ja '89
Shared decision making for principals and teachers. A. S. Vann. *The Education Digest* 54:17-20 Ja '89
The superintendent's role in reform. N. Paulu. *The Education Digest* 55:31-3 S '89
    Education
    See School management and organization—Study and teaching
    Professional ethics
Ethics for principals. R. L. Calabrese. *The Education Digest* 54:16-19 Mr '89
    Qualifications
Must principals have teaching experience? [requirement eliminated in New Jersey] S. Cooperman. *The Education Digest* 54:11-12 Mr '89
Teaching experience: a must for principals. S. D. Thomson. *The Education Digest* 54:11-15 Ap '89
Why principals should first be teachers [critique of New Jersey's decision to remove teaching experience as a qualification] J. W. Guthrie. *The Education Digest* 54:13-15 Mr '89
    Selection and appointment
Hiring a new principal. F. Roberts. *Parents* 64:49+ Ja '89
SCHOOL TAX SYSTEM *See* Education—Finance
SCHOOL TEACHERS *See* Teachers
SCHOOL TEACHING *See* Teaching
SCHOOL UNIFORMS
Do school uniforms enforce discipline? F. Roberts. il *Parents* 64:59-60 Ap '89
New rule: dress like me. W. M. Woodard. il *Black Enterprise* 19:15 Ja '89
SCHOOL VIOLENCE
Battling the school-yard bully. D. F. Bjorklund and B. Bjorklund. il *Parents* 64:195 Ap '89
Curbing teen violence [Barron Assessment and Counseling Center in Boston, Mass.] R. Levine. il *American Health* 8:108 Ap '89
Protecting schools from outside violence. D. Harrington-Lueker. *The Education Digest* 55:46-9 D '89
Robberies push Detroit's school board to propose district-wide dress code. *Jet* 77:29 D 25 '89-Ja 1 '90
School order and safety as community issues [study of Chicago schools] J. Menacker and others. bibl f il *Phi Delta Kappan* 71:39-40+ S '89
School prevention of suicide, violence, and abuse. E. Guetzloe. *The Education Digest* 54:46-9 F '89
Shootouts in the schools. R. N. Ostling. il *Time* 134:116 N 20 '89
A study in fear [school violence in Montreal] D. Burke. il *Maclean's* 102:42 My 22 '89
These perilous halls of learning. T. Gest. il *U.S. News & World Report* 106:68-9 Mr 13 '89
SCHOOL-WORK PLANS *See* Business and education
SCHOOLS
    See also
    Art schools
    Catholic schools
    Church schools
    Correspondence schools and courses
    Education
    High schools
    Private schools
    Public schools
    School buildings
    Summer schools
    Sunday schools
    Traffic schools
    Vocational-technical education
    Security measures
Protecting schools from outside violence. D. Harrington-Lueker. *The Education Digest* 55:46-9 D '89
Shootouts in the schools. R. N. Ostling. il *Time* 134:116 N 20 '89
These perilous halls of learning. T. Gest. il *U.S. News & World Report* 106:68-9 Mr 13 '89
SCHOOLS, RURAL *See* Rural education
SCHOOLS OF EDUCATION *See* Teachers colleges
SCHOOLS OF FISH *See* Fish—Habits and behavior
SCHORE, JACK
Triumphant returns. il pors *World Tennis* 37:70-1 Jl '89
SCHORR, DANIEL, 1916-
How TV helped tear down the Berlin Wall. il *TV Guide* 37:10-11 D 23-29 '89
Washington notebook. See issues of The New Leader
SCHOTT, JOHN R.
Remote sensing of the earth: a synoptic view. bibl f il *Physics Today* 42:72-9 S '89

SCHOUMACHER, STEPHANIE, AND CADDEN, VIVIAN
Preparing your child for the 21st century [special section] il *McCall's* 116:41+ S '89
SCHRADER, ESTHER
Undertow: LA copes with the flood of Soviet émigrés. *The New Republic* 201:11-12 D 4 '89
SCHRADER, PAUL
'Lolita'. il *American Film* 15:18-20+ O '89
    about
Paul Schrader [interview] il pors *American Film* 14:16-21 Jl/Ag '89
SCHRADER, RICHARD K.
Bridging the Atlantic [cover story] il *American History Illustrated* 24:34-47 My '89
SCHRAG, KARL, 1912-
    about
Karl Schrag at Kraushaar. C. Little. *Art in America* 77:153 Mr '89
SCHRAMBLING, REGINA
Beyond expectations. il *The New York Times Magazine* p67-8 D 17 '89
Bluegrass flavor. il *The New York Times Magazine* p39-40 My 28 '89
Campfire cachet. il *The New York Times Magazine* p69-70 O 1 '89
Hot stuff. il *The New York Times Magazine* p39-40 Jl 23 '89
Lucky breaks. il *The New York Times Magazine* p25-6 D 24 '89
Not Mom's beans. il *Esquire* 112:20 Jl '89
Pass the gorditas, pilgrim. il *Esquire* 112:45 N '89
Pure and simple. il *The New York Times Magazine* p65-6 Mr 19 '89
Seeding time. il *The New York Times Magazine* p63-4 O 22 '89
Soup's on! il *McCall's* 117:43+ O '89
Split the difference. il *The New York Times Magazine* p85-6 My 7 '89
SCHRAMM, TEX
    about
Can Tex Schramm make pigskin fashionable in Paris? K. Kelly. il *Business Week* p34-5 Jl 31 '89
SCHREIBER, HARRY
    about
Old name, new game. E. Giltenan. por *Forbes* 144:10 Jl 24 '89
SCHREIBER, JEAN-LOUIS SERVAN- *See* Servan-Schreiber, Jean-Louis
SCHREIBER, NORMAN
Let's take a closer look. il *New Choices for the Best Years* 29:79-81 Ap '89
'Tell about the South. What's it like there. What do they do . . .'. il *Smithsonian* 20:163-4+ S '89
SCHREIBER, WILLIAM F.
    about
Television and the economy [interview] il por *Technology Review* 92:35-7 Ap '89
SCHREIER, SANDY
    about
From Callot Soeurs to Gaultier, Sandy Schreier has it all. A. Palmer. il por *Architectural Digest* 46:52+ S '89
SCHREINER, SUSAN E.
Educating the congregation. il *The Christian Century* 106:985-7 N 1 '89
SCHREIVOGEL, PAUL A.
Dog-eared days. il por *Runner's World* 24:86 F '89
SCHREYER, WILLIAM A.
    about
The remaking of Merrill Lynch. J. Friedman. il por *Business Week* p122-5 Jl 17 '89
SCHROBILGEN, LINDA
    about
At a California toy store, kids play Santa for the homeless. il por *People Weekly* 32:115 D 18 '89
SCHRODER, RICKY
    about
Over the hill at 15? Boy, was Ricky mad! B. Davidson. il pors *TV Guide* 37:18-20 My 13-19 '89
SCHROEDER, JAY, 1961-
    about
Beers with . . . Jay Schroeder [interview] S. Rosenbloom. il pors *Sport (New York, N.Y.)* 80:15-16 Ja '89
SCHROEDER, PATRICIA
    about
Bowing out: a tough choice. B. G. Kempton. por *New Choices for the Best Years* 29:20+ O '89
SCHROTH, RAYMOND A.
America's moral landscape in the fiction of Richard Ford. por *The Christian Century* 106:227-30 Mr 1 '89
Has God forgotten Peru? il *Commonweal* 116:459-61 S 8 '89
SCHUBERT, BERND, AND OTHERS
β-adrenergic inhibition of cardiac sodium channels by dual G-protein pathways. bibl f il *Science* 245:516-19 Ag 4 '89

SCHUBERT, DAVID, 1943-, AND OTHERS
Relation of the amyloid β protein precursor to heparan sulfate proteoglycans [discussion of July 8, 1988 article, Amyloid β protein precursor is possibly a heparan sulfate proteoglycan core protein] *Science* 244:826-8 My 19 '89
SCHUBERT, FRANZ, 1797-1828
about
Musical events:
Schubertiade at the 92nd Street Y. A. Porter. il *The New Yorker* 65:90-1 Mr 27 '89
Schubert's last sonatas. A. Brendel. bibl f il *The New York Review of Books* 36:32-6 F 2 '89
'Schubert's last sonatas': an exchange [discussion of February 2, 1989 article] A. Brendel. il *The New York Review of Books* 36:42-3 Mr 16 '89
The wonder years. P. G. Davis. il *New York* 22:78-9 Mr 13 '89
SCHUBERT, KLAUS
The great raft adventure. il map *Cycle* 40:38-41+ Jl '89
SCHUCKING, E. L. (ENGELBERT L.)
The first Texas Symposium on Relativistic Astrophysics. bibl f il *Physics Today* 42 pt1:46-52 Ag '89
SCHUCKING, ENGELBERT L. *See* Schucking, E. L. (Engelbert L.)
SCHUESSLER, NANCY
A question of rights. il *Seventeen* 48:192-3+ My '89
SCHUETTE, KEITH E.
A man, a plan, an election. il *National Review* 41:18-19 Je 16 '89
SCHULBERG, BUDD
about
Budd Schulberg. K. Gross. il pors *People Weekly* 32:93-5+ D 18 '89
Budd Schulberg in Great Gatsby land. A. Fotheringham. il *Maclean's* 102:56 Ag 28 '89
SCHULER, JACK WILLIAM
about
The slippery ladder at Abbott Labs. J. F. Siler. il por *Business Week* p136-7 O 30 '89
SCHULER, MIKE
about
Is anybody happy here? J. McCallum. il por *Sports Illustrated* 70:22-4+ Ja 16 '89
SCHULHOF, MICHAEL P.
about
The leading man in the Sony-Columbia deal. L. J. Nathans. por *Business Week* p44-5 O 9 '89
SCHULIAN, JOHN, 1945-
Splendor on the grass. il *Gentlemen's Quarterly* 59:142-5+ Ja '89
Virginia real. il pors *Gentlemen's Quarterly* 59:204-7 F '89
SCHULLERY, PAUL
The fires and fire policy. bibl f il maps *BioScience* 39:686-94 N '89
Yellowstone grizzlies: the new breed. il *National Parks* 63:24-9+ N/D '89
(jt. auth) See Barbee, Robert, and Schullery, Paul
SCHULMAN, LADONNE H., AND PELKA, HEIKE
The anticodon contains a major element of the identity of arginine transfer RNAs. bibl f il *Science* 246:1595-7 D 22 '89
SCHULMAN, SARAH, 1958-
Thousands may die in the streets. il *The Nation* 248:480-2 Ap 10 '89
SCHULTE-DÖINGHAUS, ULI
(jt. auth) See Behrens, Bolke, and Schulte-Döinghaus, Uli
SCHULTZ, DODI
(jt. auth) See Karlsrud, Katherine, and Schultz, Dodi
SCHULTZ, DUTCH
about
The audacious lure of evil [interview with E. L. Doctorow] A. P. Sanoff. il por *U.S. News & World Report* 106:56 Mr 6 '89
SCHULTZ, DWIGHT
about
The making of Fat Man and Little Boy [interview] D. K. Mano. il *National Review* 41:63-7 N 10 '89
SCHULTZ, MORTON J.
Car clinic. See issues of Popular Mechanics
SCHULTZ, PETER G.
(jt. auth) See Baldwin, Enoch, and Schultz, Peter G.
SCHULTZ, SHERMAN W.
Make a telescope for $500: model 2. il *Sky and Telescope* 77:26-9 Ja '89
SCHULTZ, TOM
Testing and retention of young children: moving from controversy to reform. bibl f il *Phi Delta Kappan* 71:125-9 O '89
SCHULZ, BRUNO, 1892-1942
about
A few words on Bruno Schulz. C. Miłosz. il *The New Republic* 200:30-1 Ja 2 '89
On Bruno Schulz; tr. by Lillian Vallee. W. Gombrowicz. bibl f il *The New York Review of Books* 36:5-7 Ap 13 '89

SCHULZ, CHARLES M.
about
Charles Schulz. D. Waggoner and R. Wolmuth. il pors *People Weekly* 32:81-2+ O 30 '89
It's a biography, Charlie Brown!!! J. Crichton. il por *Publishers Weekly* 236:57-8 Ag 4 '89
SCHULZ, LESLIE DUNN
"My baby will grow old—but she'll never grow up"; ed. by LindaCarol Graham. il pors *Redbook* 172:44+ F '89
SCHULZ, MORIAH
about
"My baby will grow old—but she'll never grow up"; ed. by LindaCarol Graham. L. D. Schulz. il pors *Redbook* 172:44+ F '89
SCHULZ, SUSANNA
about
A strange new place called home. M. Ryan. il pors *Life* 12:34-9 N '89
SCHULZE, DAVID
Canadian utility threatens Cree. il *The Progressive* 53:18 O '89
SCHULZE, E.-D.
Air pollution and forest decline in a spruce (Picea abies) forest. bibl f il map *Science* 244:776-83 My 19 '89
SCHUMACHER, JOEL
about
Cousins [film] Reviews
Commonweal 116:177-8 Mr 24 '89. T. O'Brien
Glamour il 87:226 Ap '89. D. Denicolo
The New Yorker 65:97-8 Mr 6 '89. P. Kael
Newsweek il 113:65 F 20 '89. D. Ansen
People Weekly 31:17-18 F 20 '89. S. Haller
Video il 13:77+ N '89. J. Walker
Vogue il 179:268 Mr '89. J. Sherman
SCHUMACHER, JULIE
The private life of Robert Schumann [story] il *The Atlantic* 263:65-71 Ap '89
SCHUMACHER (F.) & CO. *See* F. Schumacher & Co.
SCHUMAN, PATRICIA, 1943-
Promise and problems at Guadalajara Book Fair. il *Publishers Weekly* 235:24+ Ja 6 '89
SCHUMER, FRAN
Bye-bye, blues: a new wonder drug for depression [cover story] il *New York* 22:46-50+ D 18 '89
SCHUMPETER, JOSEPH ALOIS, 1883-1950
Creative destruction: the essence of capitalism [excerpts from Capitalism, socialism and democracy] *New Perspectives Quarterly* 6:10-11 Fall '89
about
The coming global boom [cover story; with editorial comment] C. R. Morris. il *The Atlantic* 264:6, 51-8+ O '89
SCHUR, CHRIS
Dramatically diverse globulars. il *Astronomy* 17:90-5 My '89
SCHURENBERG, ERIC
Colleges learn to sell their services. il *Working Woman* 14:65-8 N '89
SCHURR, CATHLEEN
Clara Barton: founder of the American Red Cross. il pors *American History Illustrated* 24:50-8+ N/D '89
SCHUSTER, EDGAR HOWARD, 1930-
In pursuit of cultural literacy. il *Phi Delta Kappan* 70:539-42 Mr '89
SCHUSTER, JOSEPH
. . . and your Super game plan. il *Sport (New York, N.Y.)* 80:37-9 F '89
Beers with . . . Dan Dierdorf [interview with Monday night football broadcaster] il pors *Sport (New York, N.Y.)* 80:17-19 D '89
Beers with . . . Harry Caray [interview] il por *Sport (New York, N.Y.)* 80:19-20 O '89
It's in the cards. il *Sport (New York, N.Y.)* 80:48-52+ My '89
SCHUTT, RUSSELL K.
Objectivity versus outrage. *Society* 26:14-16 My/Je '89
SCHÜTTE, THOMAS
about
Thomas Schütte at Marian Goodman. N. Princenthal. il *Art in America* 77:207-8 O '89
SCHUTZE, JIM
Hightower's view. il pors *Organic Gardening* 36:32-6 D '89
SCHUUR, DIANE
about
Diane Schuur: powerful pop/jazz. A. Nash. il por *Stereo Review* 54:144+ F '89
SCHUYLER, JAMES
Haze [poem] *The New Yorker* 65:28 Jl 31 '89
White boat, blue boat [poem] *The New Yorker* 65:100 N 27 '89
Yellow flowers [poem] *The New Yorker* 65:42 S 11 '89
SCHUYLER, LINDA
about
The greening of Degrassi. K. Beck. il pors *Channels (New York, N.Y.: 1986)* 9:62-4 N '89

SCHWAB, CHARLES
about
After cost cuts, what? J. Heins. il por *Forbes* 143:46 My 1 '89
SCHWAB, GARY
about
Life on a small but fast track. J. McCallum. il pors *Sports Illustrated* 71:58+ Ag 14 '89
SCHWAB, JIM
The attraction is chemical. *The Nation* 249:416+ O 16 '89
Omaha held hostage. il *The Progressive* 53:36-9 My '89
SCHWAB (CHARLES) & CO., INC. *See* Charles Schwab & Co., Inc.
SCHWALBERG, BOB
Critical focus. See issues of Popular Photography beginning March 1988 through September 1989
SCHWAMM, ELLEN
about
America's most-awaited writer profits from an impatient wife. P. Freeman. il pors *People Weekly* 31:56-7+ Ja 9 '89
SCHWAN, MARVIN
about
Schwan's song. M. Fritz. il por *Forbes* 143:42-3 Ap 3 '89
SCHWAN'S SALES ENTERPRISES
Schwan's song. M. Fritz. il por *Forbes* 143:42-3 Ap 3 '89
SCHWANTZ, KEVIN
about
Lawson takes GP point lead as Rainey crashes. M. Oxley. il pors *Cycle* 40:24 N '89
Schwantz and Rainey top Euro Grands Prix. M. Oxley. il *Cycle* 40:24 S '89
Schwantz, Kocinski win at Japanese GP. T. Van Hooydonk. il *Cycle* 40:24 Je '89
SCHWARCZ, SAMUEL
about
Returning home. C. Fenyvesi. por *Organic Gardening* 36:99 Ap '89
SCHWARTZ, ALAN W., AND BAKKER, C. G.
Was adenine the first purine? bibl f il *Science* 245:1102-4 S 8 '89
SCHWARTZ, ANDY
Remembering U2. il *Seventeen* 48:88+ O '89
SCHWARTZ, BERNARD L.
U.S. defense industry faces difficult times. por *Aviation Week & Space Technology* 131:71+ D 4 '89
SCHWARTZ, DAVID M.
The comedian of America's wetlands stages a comeback. bibl f (p174) il *Smithsonian* 20:138-42+ Je '89
It takes more than repellent to make flying pests bug off. il *Smithsonian* 20:76-80+ Jl '89
On the royal road to adventures with 'Daring Dick'. il pors *Smithsonian* 19:159-60+ Mr '89
SCHWARTZ, FELICE N.
Mothers in careers: business makes adjustments. *Current (Washington, D.C.)* 314:4-11 Jl/Ag '89
about
Advocating a 'mommy track'. B. Kantrowitz. il por *Newsweek* 113:45 Mr 13 '89
Blowing the whistle on the "mommy track". B. Ehrenreich and D. English. il *Ms.* 18:56-8 Jl/Ag '89
Reality check for harassed parents. J. Leo. il *U.S. News & World Report* 106:64 Ap 3 '89
The truth about women managers [interview] B. Brophy. il por *U.S. News & World Report* 106:57 Mr 13 '89
SCHWARTZ, FRED
about
R.I.P. Fred the Furrier. J. A. Trachtenberg. il por *Forbes* 143:122-3 F 20 '89
SCHWARTZ, GIL
Him. See issues of Seventeen beginning August 1987
Lube job. il *New York* 22:27 F 13 '89
SCHWARTZ, HARRY
The right medicine. il *National Review* 41:26-9 Mr 10 '89
SCHWARTZ, HERMAN, 1931-
Consolidating the new majority. il *The Nation* 249:380-3 O 9 '89
Fueling demands for Czech reform. *The Nation* 248:660-3 My 15 '89
Illogical force. *The Nation* 249:40-1 Jl 10 '89
SCHWARTZ, JIM
Struggle for the soul of the union. il *The Nation* 249:8-10 Jl 3 '89
SCHWARTZ, JOHN BURNHAM
about
'Am I somebody?'. K. Pryor. il por *New York* 22:32 Ap 24 '89
Brat Pack II. A. Heard. il *The American Spectator* 22:27-9 O '89
SCHWARTZ, JONATHAN
At large. See issues of Gentlemen's Quarterly beginning May 1989
SCHWARTZ, LARRY
Beers with . . . Bob Costas [interview] il pors *Sport (New York, N.Y.)* 80:19-20 Mr '89
SCHWARTZ, LLOYD, 1941-
The voices of Kurt Weill. il *The Atlantic* 264:115-18 D '89

SCHWARTZ, MELVIN, 1932-
The first high-energy neutrino experiment. bibl f il *Science* 243:1445-9 Mr 17 '89
about
Business-minded professor. M. Alpert. il por *Fortune* 119:319 Ap 24 '89
Nobel Prize in Physics. P. F. Schewe. bibl f *Physics Today* 42:S67 Ja '89
Physics Nobel Prize to Lederman, Schwartz and Steinberger. B. M. Schwarzschild. bibl f il *Physics Today* 42:17-20 Ja '89
SCHWARTZ, MICHAEL, 1959-
about
Playing for keeps. J. Saltz. il pors *House & Garden* 161:162-9 O '89
SCHWARTZ, ROBERT S.
HDTV: keeping the rabbit ears alive. il *High Fidelity (New York, N.Y.)* 39:51-2+ Ap '89
SCHWARTZ, SANFORD, 1946-
Andy Warhol the painter. il *The Atlantic* 264:73-7 Ag '89
Married . . . with cubism. *The New Republic* 201:28-30 D 25 '89
Summer nights at Russell's Corners. *The Atlantic* 263:84+ My '89
SCHWARTZ, SEYMOUR I.
about
Caught mapping. C. Brown. il por *Forbes* 144:134 S 4 '89
SCHWARTZ, STEPHEN E. (STEPHEN EUGENE)
Acid deposition: unraveling a regional phenomenon. bibl f il maps *Science* 243:753-63 F 10 '89
SCHWARTZ, TONY, 1952-
Acceleration syndrome: does everyone live in the fast lane nowadays? il *Utne Reader* p36-43 Ja/F '89
The art of the mind: how I learned to draw. il por *New York* 22:42-6+ D 11 '89
Doctor love [cover story] il pors *New York* 22:40-9 Je 12 '89
Obsession [cover story] il pors *New York* 22:30-41 Je 26 '89
SCHWARTZBERG, NEALA S.
That magic touch. il *Parents* 64:87-90+ F '89
SCHWARTZBERG, PAMELA L., AND OTHERS
Germ-line transmission of a *c-abl* mutation produced by targeted gene disruption in ES cells [cover story] bibl f il *Science* 246:799-803 N 10 '89
SCHWARTZKROIN, PHILIP A.
(jt. auth) See Scharfman, Helen E., and Schwartzkroin, Philip A.
SCHWARTZMAN, ALLAN
Corporate trophies. il *Art in America* 77:34-7+ F '89
SoHo ascending. *Harper's Bazaar* 122:84-5+ D '89
SCHWARTZMAN, SUSAN
Magazines: ups and downs. il *Publishers Weekly* 235:21-2+ Mr 31 '89
SCHWARZ, HANS, 1939-
The German church is not dead. *The Christian Century* 106:196-7 F 22 '89
SCHWARZ, JOEL
He fixed it. il pors map *Americana* 16:57-60 Ja/F '89
SCHWARZ, U., AND OTHERS
Ocular responses to linear motion are inversely proportional to viewing distance. bibl f il *Science* 245:1394-6 S 22 '89
SCHWARZ, WOLFGANG
(jt. auth) See Schmidt, Max, and Schwarz, Wolfgang
SCHWARZENEGGER, ARNOLD
about
Arnold Schwarzenegger: no sweat [cover story] R. Murphy. il pors *The Saturday Evening Post* 261:46-9 Mr '89
SCHWARZKOGLER, RUDOLF, 1940-1969
about
Rudolf Schwarzkogler at Burnett Miller. F. Colpitt. il *Art in America* 77:180-1 D '89
SCHWEITZER, GERTRUDE, 1909-
Moment of decision [story] il *Good Housekeeping* 209:112-13 Jl '89
SCHWEIZER AIRCRAFT CORP.
All in the family. N. Moll. il *Flying* 116:64 N '89
Schweizer, Enstrom join teams to bid for Army trainer work [helicopters] il *Aviation Week & Space Technology* 130:18-19 Ja 23 '89
SCHWELIEN, MICHAEL
Are equal rights only a dream? il *World Press Review* 36:32-4 My '89
SCHWEON, CRAIG
(jt. auth) See Hernandez, Andres H., and Schweon, Craig
SCHWERNER, MICHAEL HENRY, 1939-1964
about
The '64 civil rights murders: the struggle continues [cover story] J. Kornbluth. il pors *The New York Times Magazine* p16-19+ Jl 23 '89
Back on the bus. P. Dray. il pors *Mother Jones* 14:37-9+ N '89
Honor trio killed by KKK in Mississippi vote drive. il pors *Jet* 76:6-7 Jl 10 '89
SCHWINGER, JULIAN, 1918-
A path to quantum electrodynamics. il *Physics Today* 42:42-8 F '89

SCI TELEVISION INC.
How KKR stubbed its toe. L. J. Nathans. il *Business Week* p56 Ag 7 '89
SCIASCIA, LEONARDO
about
Letter from Sicily: Mr. Sciascia explains [excerpt from To noto, or Through Europe in a Ford] D. Fallowell. *The American Scholar* 58:581-5 Aut '89
SCID (SEVERE COMBINED IMMUNODEFICIENCY) See Immunologic diseases
SCIENCE
See also
American Association for the Advancement of Science
Art and science
Biology
CD-ROM (Compact disc-Read only memory)—Scientific use
Chaos (Science)
Chemistry
Children and science
Communication in science
Computers—Scientific use
Humor in science
Information systems—Scientific use
Medicine
Natural history
Parapsychology and science
Physics
Religion and science
Scientists
Technology
A decade in science: the eight big ideas of the eighties [cover story; special section; with editorial comment by Paul Hoffman] il *Discover* 10:4, 30-3+ O '89
Science & technology. See issues of Forbes beginning March 10, 1986
Anecdotes, facetiae, satire, etc.
Science Q & A. F. Catapano. il *The Atlantic* 263:32 Mr '89
Awards
See also
National Medal of Science
Awards [presented at AAAS winter meeting] il *Science* 243:672-3 F 3 '89
Bibliography
Book reviews. See issues of Science
Books. See issues of Physics Today
Books. See issues of Science News
Books. P. Morrison. See issues of Scientific American
The worlds of science [special section] il *The New York Times Book Review* 94:23-6+ Ap 9 '89
Collectibles
Science artifacts on the block [London auction arranged by P. Cook] D. Dickson. il por *Science* 244:649 My 12 '89
Conferences
See also
American Association for the Advancement of Science—Meetings
Dahlem Konferenzen
Gordon Research Conferences
Speaking at length [presentations that run too long] J. Cairns. *BioScience* 39:632-3 O '89
Fiction
See Science fiction
History
50 and 100 years ago. See issues of Scientific American
Science and technology: the age of limits [1980s] W. F. Allman. il *U.S. News & World Report* 107:111 D 25 '89-Ja 1 '90
Study and teaching
The "civics" of technology in history textbooks. J. L. Heilbron and D. J. Kevles. *The Education Digest* 55:42-4 S '89
International aspects
See also
Exchanges, Literary and scientific
United Nations. Intergovernmental Committee on Science and Technology for Development
Juvenile literature
See Scientific literature for children
Methodology
See also
Simultaneous replication
Miscellanea
Antimatter. See issues of Omni (New York, N.Y.)
Moral aspects
See Science and ethics
Periodicals
See also
Bulletin of the atomic scientists
Discover (Periodical)
Nature (Periodical)
Omni (Periodical)
Popular science (Periodical)
Science (Periodical)
Science in the USSR (Periodical)

"L'affaire Pasteur" prompts Canadian outcry [decision to publish journals in English] D. Dickson. il *Science* 244:280-1 Ap 21 '89
Combating high journal costs. P. H. Abelson. *Science* 244:1125 Je 9 '89
Providing journals [AAAS program for sub-Saharan Africa] L. A. Levey. il map *Science* 245:538 Ag 4 '89
The serials pricing controversy. G. Feldman. il *Publishers Weekly* 235:68-70 Ja 13 '89
Philosophy
Rethinking physics [scientific orthodoxy called into question] T. Cashman. il *Utne Reader* p24-5 Ja/F '89
Political aspects
See Science and state
Religious aspects
See Religion and science
Research
See Research
Scholarships and fellowships
See also
Science Talent Search
Congressional fellowships for science [proposed legislation] P. H. Abelson. *Science* 243:1649 Mr 31 '89
Social aspects
The chemicals of half-life. N. J. Bolls. *BioScience* 39:138 Mr '89
Science's public persona. C. Norman. il *Science* 243:474-5 Ja 27 '89
Study and teaching
See also
National Scholars Program
Science teachers
Assessing science learning in elementary school: why, what, and how? S. A. Raizen and J. S. Kaser. bibl f il *Phi Delta Kappan* 70:718-22 My '89
Case proved [need for curriculum changes] T. Beardsley. *Scientific American* 260:22 My '89
A crisis looms in science. S. Tifft. il *Time* 134:68-70 S 11 '89
The dinosaur rip-off. S. J. Gould. *Natural History* p14+ Ag '89
Educating John Q. Public. M. Estren. *High Technology Business* 9:3 Je '89
The huge problem in American schools [address, December 6, 1988] L. F. Cavazos. *Vital Speeches of the Day* 55:236-8 F 1 '89
Making science more seductive to women on campus. N. J. Freundlich. il *Business Week* p89 Ag 28 '89
Nowhere are the shortcomings of our educational system more critical than in the area of science and technology. R. M. Adams. bibl f (p122) il *Smithsonian* 20:8 Jl '89
Radical reform for science education [Project 2061 report] C. Holden. *Science* 243:1133 Mr 3 '89
Science education for whom? J. A. Miller. *BioScience* 39:354 Je '89
Science education in the United States: what the scientific community can do [with editorial comment by Richard S. Nicholson] W. E. Massey. bibl f il *Science* 245:905, 915-21 S 1 '89
Science education: the bright spots. T. H. Cole. il *Popular Mechanics* 166:22 F '89
The science of bad science [AAAS Project 2061 report] C. E. Finn. il *The American Spectator* 22:34-5 Ag '89
Scientific competency through fun. D. E. Koshland, Jr. *Science* 243:989 F 24 '89
The sorry state of science education. P. R. Vagelos. *Scientific American* 261:128 O '89
Teach your children. R. Fleming. il *Omni (New York, N.Y.)* 11:36+ S '89
U.S. students flunk math, science [study by the Educational Testing Service] G. Byrne. *Science* 243:729 F 10 '89
University scientists as precollege science curriculum developers [discussion of September 1988 article, The role of universities in developing precollege science curricula] J. D. McInerney. bibl f *BioScience* 39:102-3 F '89
Upgrading a science program. F. Roberts. *Parents* 64:68-9 Mr '89
Writing off our future? M. Estren. *High Technology Business* 9:5 F '89
Aids and devices
Earthling: take me to your teacher [teaching science through science fiction films] G. Byrne. il *Science* 244:919 My 26 '89
Learn on me [Macintosh engineering and scientific courseware] D. E. Crabb. il *Byte* 14:143-4+ Jl '89
Resource centers for science. R. F. Brinckerhoff. *The Education Digest* 54:36-9 Mr '89
Science! [with editorial comment by Gregg Keizer] D. Stanton. il *Compute!* 11:4, 18-24 Je '89
Federal aid
Getting Energy into the schools [J. Watkins' efforts] M. Barinaga. il por *Science* 246:318 O 20 '89
Navy awards $14 million to foster math, science degrees at universities. il *Jet* 77:18 O 16 '89
NSF education head makes risky bid [B. Z. Shakhashiri's public push for big budget increase] J. Walsh. il por *Science* 246:317-19 O 20 '89

SCIENCE—Study and teaching—*cont.*
Soviet Union
U.S. students trail Soviets [views of Marjorie Gardner] *USA Today (Periodical)* 118:14-15 Ag '89
Terminology
Anecdotes, facetiae, satire, etc.
Last word. S. Fox. il *Omni (New York, N.Y.)* 11:124 My '89
Textbooks
California backs evolution education. M. Barinaga. il *Science* 246:881 N 17 '89
California urges teaching of evolution in science textbooks. M. Colin. il *Publishers Weekly* 235:14 F 3 '89
Facts of life [science textbooks support evolution in California] R. N. Ostling. il *Time* 134:118 N 20 '89
Australia
At the frontiers of science and technology. R. Williams. il *The Courier (Unesco)* 41:27-9 D '88
China
History
The Chinese scientific genius [cover story; special issue] R. K. G. Temple. il *The Courier (Unesco)* 41:3-34 O '88
Developing countries
See also
Third World Academy of Sciences
United Nations. Intergovernmental Committee on Science and Technology for Development
Science for developing countries. M. Singham. *Physics Today* 42 pt1:61+ Ag '89
What the third world can handle [discussion of November 1988 article, What the third world really needs] A. Salam. *The Bulletin of the Atomic Scientists* 45:8 My '89
India
History
The scientific legacy. V. S. Naravane. il *The Courier (Unesco)* 42:33-4 F '89
SCIENCE, FREEDOM OF
Doctored data [OMB censors testimony of J. E. Hansen on the greenhouse effect] *Commonweal* 116:325 Je 2 '89
Feeling the heat on the greenhouse [OMB censors J. Hansen's testimony on greenhouse effect] S. Begley. il *Newsweek* 112:79-80 My 22 '89
Hansen and the greenhouse effect [discussion of June 2, 1989 article, Hansen vs. the world on the greenhouse threat] R. A. Kerr. *Science* 245:451-2 Ag 4 '89
Hansen vs. the world on the greenhouse threat. R. A. Kerr. il por *Science* 244:1041-3 Je 2 '89
A hot issue [OMB censors facts on greenhouse effect] D. Lindorff. *The Nation* 248:724-5 My 29 '89
Needed: a free flow of information and ideas. J. H. F. Shattuck and M. M. Spence. *Scientific American* 260:114 Ja '89
Political science. P. A. A. Berle. *Audubon* 91:8 Jl '89
SCIENCE (PERIODICAL)
The process of publication. D. E. Koshland, Jr. *Science* 245:573 Ag 11 '89
The underrepresentation syndrome. D. E. Koshland, Jr. *Science* 245:341 Jl 28 '89
SCIENCE ADVISERS, GOVERNMENTAL *See* Scientists in government
SCIENCE AND ART *See* Art and science
SCIENCE AND BUSINESS *See* Science and industry
SCIENCE AND CHILDREN *See* Children and science
SCIENCE AND ETHICS
See also
Bioethics
Research—Ethical aspects
A Hippocratic oath for scientists. A. Bacard. il *The Humanist* 49:43 Jl/Ag '89
SCIENCE AND INDUSTRY
See also
Industrial research
Corporate Associates meet at GM, focus on competition [American Institute of Physics] W. Sweet. il *Physics Today* 42:55-7 D '89
Million-dollar professors: should the ivory tower be a gold mine? J. F. Siler. il *Business Week* p90-2 Ag 21 '89
NIH, Inc.: the CRADA boom [cooperative research and development agreements] B. J. Culliton. il *Science* 245:1034-6 S 8 '89
NIH scientists agonize over technology transfer. W. Booth. *Science* 243:20-1 Ja 6 '89
SCIENCE AND POLITICS *See* Science and state
SCIENCE AND RELIGION *See* Religion and science
SCIENCE AND SOCIETY *See* Science—Social aspects
SCIENCE AND STATE
See also
Horticultural research—Federal aid
Laboratories, Government
Research—Federal aid
Science, Freedom of
Scientists—Political activities
Scientists in government
Technology and state
United States. Congress. House. Committee on Science, Space, and Technology
United States. Office of Science and Technology Policy

Communism, capitalism, and dissent. D. E. Koshland, Jr. *Science* 245:109 Jl 14 '89
Dear president-elect . . . [special section] il *Science* 243:163-4 Ja 13 '89
Government and quality in science. B. D. Davis. *Science* 246:736 N 10 '89
The government's role in investigating scientific misconduct. N. Bell. *BioScience* 39:79 F '89
New deal? [Bush administration] T. Beardsley. *Scientific American* 260:12+ Ja '89
Protected species—research permits and the value of basic research. K. Ralls and R. L. Brownell, Jr. bibl f il *BioScience* 39:394-6 Je '89
Science and technology: its future in the U.S. J. Schmandt. *Current (Washington, D.C.)* 309:7-13 Ja '89
Scientists and politicians: can they work together? B. Adams. *USA Today (Periodical)* 117:32-3 Mr '89
Self-regulation of science: reflections on a day spent testifying at a congressional hearing. D. Baltimore. il por *Technology Review* 92:20+ Ag/S '89
Unprecedented advice to the new president. J. Raloff. *Science News* 135:23 Ja 14 '89
Washington reports. See issues of Physics Today beginning July 1983
Washington watch. See issues of BioScience beginning April 1983
History
The centennial annual meeting, starring Harry Truman and civil liberties [excerpt from Renewing a scientific society] D. L. Wolfle. il por *Science* 246:130-1 O 6 '89
Canada
Big science, big thinking [address, June 27, 1989] A. W. May. *Vital Speeches of the Day* 56:114-17 D 1 '89
Seeking the best [Networks of Centres of Excellence] B. Wickens. il *Maclean's* 102:68+ N 20 '89
France
French boost support for science amid concern about its status. W. Sweet. il *Physics Today* 42:89-92 Mr '89
Japan
Japan faces big task in improving basic science. M. Sun. il *Science* 243:1285-7 Mr 10 '89
Soviet Union
First word. D. Goldfarb. il *Omni (New York, N.Y.)* 11:8 F '89
Soviet Academy attacked for being undemocratic. D. Dickson. il *Science* 243:728-9 F 10 '89
United States
See Science and state
SCIENCE AND TECHNOLOGY POLICY OFFICE (U.S.)
See United States. Office of Science and Technology Policy
SCIENCE AND THE HUMANITIES
Our human heritage as makers and builders [address, April 11, 1989] R. Kanigel. *Vital Speeches of the Day* 55:681-3 S 1 '89
Sci-humanists unite [address, January 26, 1989] L. W. Cabot. *Vital Speeches of the Day* 55:467-70 My 15 '89
SCIENCE CENTER BERLIN *See* Wissenschaftszentrum Berlin für Sozialforschung
SCIENCE EDUCATION *See* Science—Study and teaching
SCIENCE FELLOWS, CONGRESSIONAL *See* Scientists in government
SCIENCE FICTION
See also
Booksellers and bookselling—Science fiction
Publishers and publishing—Science fiction
Astounding story [tracing the course of science fiction in the U.S.; cover story] F. Pohl. il *American Heritage* 40:42-8+ S/O '89
Biology in science fiction. E. Van Dommelen. bibl f il *BioScience* 39:729-31 N '89
A chat with Brian W. Aldiss. R. Herbert. il por *Publishers Weekly* 236:24 N 10 '89
Cyberpunk. E. Selbin. il *Utne Reader* p28+ Jl/Ag '89
Fatal fiction: a weapon to end all wars [how early science fiction helped shape U.S. conceptions of nuclear weapons; cover story] H. B. Franklin. bibl f il *The Bulletin of the Atomic Scientists* 45:18-25 N '89
Light-years and lasers: science fiction inside your computer [cover story; with editorial comment by Gregg Keizer] O. S. Card. il *Compute!* 11:4, 28-34 Je '89
Science fiction writers speak to the future [cover story; special section; with introd. by Bette Chambers] il *The Humanist* 49:5-17+ Mr/Ap '89
Authorship
Birth of a writer. O. E. Butler. por *Essence* 20:74+ My '89
Dateline 1999 [predictions of science fiction authors] E. Bryant. il *Omni (New York, N.Y.)* 11:22+ Ja '89
Gender & genre: women in science fiction and fantasy. R. Herbert. il *Publishers Weekly* 236:22 N 10 '89
Think of the reader. P. Anthony. *The Writer* 102:11-13+ Ag '89
Bibliography
My favorite dozen science-fiction novels. F. Pohl. *American Heritage* 40:48-9 S/O '89
Science fiction. G. Jonas. *The New York Times Book Review* 94:31 Ja 8 '89

SCIENCE FICTION—Bibliography—*cont.*
Science fiction. G. Jonas. il *The New York Times Book Review* 94:4 D 31 '89
Science fiction. G. Jonas. il *The New York Times Book Review* 94:24 Ag 20 '89
Science fiction. G. Jonas. *The New York Times Book Review* 94:26 My 21 '89
Science fiction. G. Jonas. il *The New York Times Book Review* 94:32 F 26 '89
Science fiction. G. Jonas. il *The New York Times Book Review* 94:32 N 19 '89
Science fiction. G. Jonas. il *The New York Times Book Review* 94:38 Ap 9 '89
Science fiction. G. Jonas. il *The New York Times Book Review* 94:40 O 1 '89

Collectibles
The science-fiction fantasy world of A. Merritt. D. E. Matter and R. M. Matter. il *Antiques & Collecting Hobbies* 93:47-9 F '89

Single works
See name of author for full entry
At the Rialto. Willis, Connie
Baby strange. Maddox, Tom
Becoming Cindy. Kadrey, Richard, 1957-
Egg and chips. Disch, Thomas M.
Faded roses. Fowler, Karen Joy
The gates of Babel. Dunn, J. R.
The gulag on the Rue des Grandes Augustins. Keizer, Gregg
His powder'd wig, his crown of thornes. Laidlaw, Marc
Leviathan. Benford, Gregory, 1941-
Lucky. Dworetzky, Tom
Mod dogs. Bryant, Edward
Reading the silks. Bishop, Michael, 1945-
Shoot the moon. Cadigan, Pat
To the promised land. Silverberg, Robert
Tomorrow's child. Mason, Lisa
Unidentified objects. Blaylock, James P.

Study and teaching
Science fiction: imaginary worlds and real-life questions [teaching at Dartmouth] N. Perrin. il *The New York Times Book Review* 94:37-8 Ap 9 '89

Technique
Writing science fiction. J. Womack. *The Writer* 102:15-17 O '89

SCIENCE FICTION FILMS *See* Motion pictures—Science fiction films
SCIENCE FICTION LIBRARIES
See also
Spaced Out Library (Toronto, Ont.)
SCIENCE FICTION OPERA
Fantasies of the opera. D. Perry. il *Omni (New York, N.Y.)* 11:24+ My '89
Musical events. A. Porter. *The New Yorker* 65:67-9 Jl 31 '89
SCIENCE IN ART
See also
Chaos (Science) in art
SCIENCE IN LITERATURE
See also
Science fiction
SCIENCE IN TELEVISION
See also
Television broadcasting—Science programs
SCIENCE IN THE USSR (PERIODICAL)
Omni's glasnost [Omni magazine to be distributed in the Soviet Union in exchange for Science in the USSR] J. Gilbert. il *Omni (New York, N.Y.)* 11:16 Ag '89
SCIENCE INFORMATION *See* Communication in science
SCIENCE JOURNALISM *See* Journalism, Scientific
SCIENCE LITERACY *See* Scientific literacy
SCIENCE LITERATURE *See* Scientific literature
SCIENCE MUSEUMS
See also
New York Hall of Science
Ontario Science Centre
Southwest Museum of Science and Technology, The Science Place
Tepia (Tokyo, Japan)
1989 directory of observatories, planetariums, and museums. il *Astronomy* 17:50-7 My '89
The atomic museum. P. N. Kirstein. bibl f il *Art in America* 77:44-5+ Je '89
Gift shopping at science museums in the Bay Area. il *Sunset (Central West edition)* 183:14 D '89
Playgrounds for the mind. il *Newsweek* 113:50-2 Je 12 '89
SCIENCE NEWS
See also
Journalism, Scientific
Medical news
Space flight—Reporters and reporting
1988: the year in science [cover story; special section; with editorial comment by Paul Hoffman] il *Discover* 10:4, 15+ Ja '89
Continuum. See issues of Omni (New York, N.Y.)
Hype-energy physics [cold fusion; press reports of University of Utah fusion breakthrough] R. Bazell. *The New Republic* 200:7-8 Ap 24 '89

The molecule of the year [cover story; with editorial comment by D. E. Koshland] R. L. Guyer and D. E. Koshland, Jr. il *Science* 246:1543-6 D 22 '89
News from the world of science. See occasional issues of Reader's Digest
Phenomena, comment and notes. J. P. Wiley, Jr. See issues of Smithsonian
Physics news in 1988 [special section] P. F. Schewe. il *Physics Today* 42:S1-S67 Ja '89
Science. T. H. Cole. See issues of Popular Mechanics beginning July 1987
Science by press conference [cold fusion] F. Jerome. il *Technology Review* 92:72-3 Jl '89
Science news of the year. il *Science News* 136:416-22 D 23-30 '89
Science newsfront. A. Fisher. See issues of Popular Science
Search & discovery. See issues of Physics Today
Up front. See issues of Discover
SCIENCE PLACE (MUSEUM) *See* Southwest Museum of Science and Technology, The Science Place
SCIENCE POLICY *See* Science and state
SCIENCE STUDENTS
See also
Physics students
Science Talent Search
SCIENCE TALENT SEARCH
The mentor chase [many winners worked with professional scientists] il *U.S. News & World Report* 106:14 Mr 20 '89
Talent Search yields young scientists. *Science News* 135:55 Ja 28 '89
Young research scientists win scholarships. il *Science News* 135:151 Mr 11 '89
SCIENCE TEACHERS
Education in service
Mentorships and the perceived educational payoffs [Houston program pairing secondary teachers with mathematicians and scientists] L. M. Miller and others. il *Phi Delta Kappan* 70:465-7 F '89
Science, technology, and public knowledge [having high school teachers spend time in university and industrial research laboratories] G. Pallrand. bibl f il *Phi Delta Kappan* 70:460-4 F '89
Supply and demand
The lost generation [shortage of college professors] M. B. Zuckerman. il *U.S. News & World Report* 107:68 Ag 21 '89
SCIENTIFIC CONFERENCES *See* Science—Conferences
SCIENTIFIC CREATIONISM *See* Creation
SCIENTIFIC EDUCATION *See* Science—Study and teaching
SCIENTIFIC EQUIPMENT
See also
Astronomical equipment
Biological equipment
Chemical equipment
Medical equipment
Perkin-Elmer Corp.
Physical equipment
Psychological equipment
Spectrograph
Advances in instrumentation [cover story; special section; with editorial comment by Philip H. Abelson] bibl f il *Science* 246:9, 51-77 O 6 '89
Products and materials. See issues of Science
SCIENTIFIC ERRORS
An essay on a pig roast [role of F. Osborn's erroneous Nebraska Man theory in the creationism debate] S. J. Gould. il *Natural History* p14+ Ja '89
The follies of science. M. Rogers. il *Newsweek* 113:56 My 8 '89
Full of hot air [Darwin's theory that lungs evolved from swim bladders] S. J. Gould. il *Natural History* p28+ O '89
Fusion, afussin' and afightin' [cold fusion discovery of Stanley Pons found to be product of experimental error] *U.S. News & World Report* 106:13 My 15 '89
Pathological science [address, December 18, 1953] I. Langmuir. bibl f il por *Physics Today* 42:36-48 O '89
PW interviews [S. J. Gould, author of book on the Burgess Shale fossils] W. Smith. por *Publishers Weekly* 236:32-3 O 13 '89
SCIENTIFIC EXCHANGES *See* Exchanges, Literary and scientific
SCIENTIFIC EXPEDITIONS
See also
Antarctic exploration
Arctic exploration
Botanical exploration
The pirate scientist [travels of W. Dampier in the seventeenth century] M. Cherrington. il por *Weatherwise* 42:205-7 Ag '89
SCIENTIFIC FREEDOM *See* Science, Freedom of
SCIENTIFIC HOAXES *See* Hoaxes
SCIENTIFIC ILLUSTRATION
See also
Astronomy in art

SCIENTIFIC ILLUSTRATION—*cont.*

Scientific illustration: a working relationship between the scientist and artist [cover story] E. R. S. Hodges. bibl f il *BioScience* 39:104-11 F '89

SCIENTIFIC INFORMATION *See* Communication in science

SCIENTIFIC INSTRUMENTS *See* Scientific equipment

SCIENTIFIC LITERACY

The dismal state of scientific literacy. B. J. Culliton. *Science* 243:600 F 3 '89

Project 2061: a congressional view. G. E. Brown, Jr. *Science* 245:340 Jl 28 '89

Scientific illiteracy. *Science* 246:214 O 13 '89

What is scientific literacy? *The Education Digest* 55:43-5 D '89

Anecdotes, facetiae, satire, etc.

Ignorance on parade. J. Stone. il *Discover* 10:102 Jl '89

SCIENTIFIC LITERATURE

See also

Publishers and publishing—Scientific literature

Science—Bibliography

Science—Periodicals

Assessing publication impact. M. Bekoff. *BioScience* 39:586 O '89

Publication bias: looking for missing data [survey by Colin B. Begg] I. Peterson. *Science News* 135:5 Ja 7 '89

Two sides to every science story [work of J. D. Watson and F. Crick] G. Johnson. *The New York Times Book Review* 94:1+ Ap 9 '89

Anecdotes, facetiae, satire, etc.

Quark bites. J. Queenan. il *The American Spectator* 22:25-6 Mr '89

Authorship

Did the penalty fit the crime? [S. Frazier accused of plagiarism] M. M. Hunt. il por *The New York Times Magazine* p36-7+ My 14 '89

The missing crystallography data [study by Richard E. Dickerson] M. Barinaga. il *Science* 245:1179-81 S 15 '89

New round in Dingell v. NIH? [case of C. D. Bridges] J. Palca. *Science* 245:349 Jl 28 '89

NIH sees plagiarism in vision paper [case of C. D. Bridges] B. J. Culliton. *Science* 245:120-2 Jl 14 '89

Publish or perish. J. M. Diamond. il *Discover* 10:96-101 Jl '89

Whose notes are they? [proposal to open scientists' personal data books to general scrutiny; Dingell hearings on D. Baltimore case] B. J. Culliton. il *Science* 244:765 My 19 '89

Writing about science. D. Bane. *The Writer* 102:25-7 N '89

Refereeing

In defense of confidentiality. D. Lazarus. *Physics Today* 42:57-9 O '89

Peer review comes under peer review [biomedical publishing] M. Sun. il *Science* 244:910-12 My 26 '89

SCIENTIFIC LITERATURE FOR CHILDREN

Bibliography

Santa Claus bags a varied collection of science books for children. P. Morrison and P. Morrison. il *Scientific American* 261:144-53 D '89

SCIENTIFIC RESEARCH *See* Research

SCIENTIFIC SOCIETIES

See also

Academy of Sciences of the USSR

Acoustical Society of America

American Association for the Advancement of Science

American Crystallographic Association

American Institute of Physics

American Physical Society

American Vacuum Society

Materials Research Society

National Academy of Sciences (U.S.)

Optical Society of America

Third World Academy of Sciences

SCIENTIFIC TERMS *See* Science—Terminology

SCIENTISTS

See also

Biologists

Engineers

Inventors

Physicists

Women scientists

On being a scientist [booklet published by the National Academy of Sciences] R. S. Nicholson. *Science* 246:305 O 20 '89

People [special section] A. Hall. il *Business Week* Special Issue:70-6+ Je 16 '89

Mortality

Danger on the job [job-related deaths; study by J. Paul Leigh] G. Byrne. il *Science* 243:317 Ja 20 '89

Death by science [high incidence of job-related deaths; study by J. Paul Leigh] *Discover* 10:14 My '89

Political activities

See also

Federation of American Scientists

March 4, 1969 [MIT conference on political awareness] J. Schlefer. *Technology Review* 92:2 Ap '89

Taking apart the doomsday machine [adaptation of address, December 1988] F. Von Hippel. il *The Bulletin of the Atomic Scientists* 45:10-12 My '89

Weapons labs need new thinking. G. T. Seaborg. *The Bulletin of the Atomic Scientists* 45:10-12 Jl/Ag '89

Psychology

What produces scientific genius? [views of Dean Keith Simonton] il *USA Today (Periodical)* 117:11 Je '89

Salaries, pensions, etc.

Superpay for NIH superstars. B. J. Culliton. *Science* 244:1038 Je 2 '89

Supply and demand

The hot demand for new scientists. P. Nulty. il *Fortune* 120:155+ Jl 31 '89

Research Council cites flaws in NSF employment statistics. C. S. Powell. *Physics Today* 42:49 Jl '89

Scientist shortage. E. Stark. il *Psychology Today* 23:12 My '89

The scientist shortage and the gender gap. D. W. Freckman. *BioScience* 39:523 S '89

Wanted: 675,000 future scientists and engineers. C. Holden. il *Science* 244:1536-7 Je 30 '89

SCIENTISTS, AMATEUR

See also

Astronomers, Amateur

The amateur scientist. J. Walker. See issues of Scientific American

SCIENTISTS, AMERICAN

See also

Federation of American Scientists

SCIENTISTS, CHINESE AMERICAN

China's turmoil touches U.S. science; U.S.-Chinese scientists see dreams imperiled. M. Sun and E. Marshall. il *Science* 244:1130-2 Je 9 '89

SCIENTISTS, HANDICAPPED

Stephen Hawking shoots for the stars. il por *Home Office Computing* 7:12 S '89

SCIENTISTS, RUSSIAN

Science and scientists for a nuclear-weapon-free world. Y. P. Velikhov. il *Physics Today* 42:32-3+ N '89

SCIENTISTS IN GOVERNMENT

Blahous will be APS Congressional Scientist Fellow in 1989-90. por *Physics Today* 42:109-10 S '89

Bromley in line for science adviser. M. Crawford. por *Science* 244:283 Ap 21 '89

Bush picks science adviser [D. A. Bromley] I. Wickelgren. *Science News* 135:263 Ap 29 '89

A conversation with D. Allan Bromley [president's science adviser] B. J. Culliton. il por *Science* 246:203-4 O 13 '89

CRADAs raise conflict issues. B. J. Culliton. *Science* 245:1035 S 8 '89

Goettel is AIP's Congressional Fellow in 1989-90. P. Janowski. *Physics Today* 42:117 O '89

How can science best serve the president? W. T. Golden. *Scientific American* 260:116 F '89

Is Bush putting science on the back burner? J. Carey. *Business Week* p47 Ap 3 '89

Knapp resigns from URA leadership; Truly to pilot NASA, Fields at DARPA. I. Goodwin. *Physics Today* 42:42-4 Je '89

Meet D. Allan Bromley [interview] J. Carey. il por *Business Week* Special Issue:44 Je 16 '89

On science advice to the president. J. B. Wiesner. bibl il *Scientific American* 260:34-9 Ja '89

A place at the head table [status of presidential science adviser] C. Norman. il *Science* 243:163 Ja 13 '89

President Bush and the world of science. T. H. Cole. il *Popular Mechanics* 166:48 Mr '89

President Bush picks Yale's Bromley for Cabinet-level science adviser. I. Goodwin. il por *Physics Today* 42:39-41 Je '89

Room at the top [problems in filling top posts in the federal science bureaucracy] J. Palca. il *Science* 246:566-8 N 3 '89

Science adviser gets first formal look [D. A. Bromley] B. J. Culliton. por *Science* 245:247-8 Jl 21 '89

Science advisers need advice [toxicologists who served on Environmental Protection Agency advisory panel charged with breaking conflict of interest laws] E. Marshall. il *Science* 245:20-2 Jl 7 '89

Science gains a voice [appointment of D. A. Bromley as science adviser] T. Beardsley. *Scientific American* 261:14 Jl '89

Science regains the White House [science adviser D. A. Bromley] N. Bell. il *BioScience* 39:435 Jl/Ag '89

Senate committee quizzes Bromley. M. Crawford. *Science* 245:349 Jl 28 '89

Senate quiz show: Bromley passes but he faces tougher tests ahead. I. Goodwin. por *Physics Today* 42:65-7 S '89

Washington ins & outs: Graham departs, Murrin to Commerce, top changes at NASA and Pentagon. I. Goodwin. *Physics Today* 42:47-9 Jl '89

Washington ins & outs: moves from House Science Panel; new positions at NSF and SSC. I. Goodwin. *Physics Today* 42:50-1 My '89

While science advice pours in, Bush dawdles on science adviser. I. Goodwin. il *Physics Today* 42:41-3 Ap '89

SCIENTOLOGY
L. Ron Hubbard inside the Great Wall [Dianetics published in Chinese] il *Publishers Weekly* 235:36 Ap 28 '89

SCIGLIANO, ERIC
Doi moi, hold the *glasnost*. map *The Nation* 249:304-6 S 25 '89
Yes. *Utne Reader* p80 Mr/Ap '89

SCIORRA, ANNABELLA
about
Ageless wonder. K. M. Chanko. il por *New York* 22:44 O 23 '89

SCIOSCIA, MIKE
Calling a game; ed. by Peter Gammons. il *Sports Illustrated* 70 Special Issue:34-9 Ap '89

SCIPES, KIM
The AFL-CIO meddles in the Philippines. il *The Progressive* 53:33 N '89

SCLC *See* Southern Christian Leadership Conference

SCLEROSIS, AMYOTROPHIC LATERAL *See* Amyotrophic lateral sclerosis

SCLEROSIS, MULTIPLE *See* Multiple sclerosis

SCLEROTHERAPY
A cure for spider veins. C. Slom. il *McCall's* 116:109 My '89
Leg lifts. N. Weber. *Harper's Bazaar* 122:136+ Ag '89

SCOBEE, DICK *See* Scobee, Francis R., 1939-1986

SCOBEE, FRANCIS R., 1939-1986
about
A thousand days of tears. K. Casey. il pors *Ladies' Home Journal* 106:120-2+ F '89

SCOBEE, JUNE
about
A thousand days of tears. K. Casey. il pors *Ladies' Home Journal* 106:120-2+ F '89

SCOBLIONKOV, DEBORAH
"Blindness isn't a handicap—it's a nuisance". il pors *McCall's* 117:49-52 O '89
The marriage of wine and food. il *American Health* 8:74 N '89

SCOFIELD, JOHN
about
John Scofield: restless guitar player [cover story] H. Mandel. il pors *Down Beat* 56:16-19 Mr '89
John Scofield's solo on "Best western"—Phrygian voicings. R. Peckham. il *Down Beat* 56:66-7 D '89

SCOGGINS, TRACY
about
The truth about Tracy Scoggins—why she's so hard to figure [cover story] E. Warren. il pors *TV Guide* 37:14-17 My 13-19 '89

SCOLARI, PETER
about
Finally on the yupswing, Newhart's preppy Peter Scolari finds love the second time around. M. Dougherty. il pors *People Weekly* 31:85-6 F 20 '89
Tootsie role [interview] G. Collins. il pors *Gentlemen's Quarterly* 59:77+ F '89

SCOMBROID POISONING
Fish poisoning. B. T. Hunter. il *Consumers' Research Magazine* 72:8-9 Mr '89

SCOOTERS, MOTOR *See* Motor scooters

SCOPES FOR FIREARMS *See* Firearms—Sights

SCOPES TRIAL *See* Tennessee evolution controversy

SCOREBOARDS
Scoreboard instant replays can be hazardous to your health. D. Shaw. il *TV Guide* 37:10-12 Mr 18-24 '89

SCORES (SECURITIES)
Blue-chip quality and junk-bond yields [Americus Trusts] D. P. Wiener. il *U.S. News & World Report* 107:107 N 6 '89
How to get bigger dividends or bigger price gains—from the same blue-chip stock [Americus Trusts] M. Schiffres. il *Changing Times* 43:98 F '89
Sure, stocks are flying—but 'Scores' are in orbit. L. Jereski. il *Business Week* p86 Ag 21 '89

SCORPIO, RALPH
Are U.S. Catholic readers hooked on the Book? il *U.S. Catholic* 54:12-17 S '89

SCORPIONS
The unkindest sting of all [scorpion-scorpion predation] G. A. Polis. il *Natural History* p34-9 Jl '89

SCORSESE, MARTIN
about
The art of noncompromise [cover story] C. Hodenfield. il pors *American Film* 14:46-51 Mr '89
The last temptation of Christ [film] Reviews
America 160:199-201 Mr 4 '89. R. A. Blake
American Film il 14:12 Jl/Ag '89. C. Koseluk
Christianity Today il por 33:57 My 12 '89. B. G. Baker
Christianity Today il 33:14 Ap 7 '89. T. C. Muck
Christianity Today 33:36-7 Ap 21 '89. K. H. Sidey
Video il 13:78 O '89. I. Robbins
New York stories [film] Reviews
America 160:353 Ap 15 '89. R. A. Blake
The American Spectator il 22:37-8 My '89. B. Bawer
Commonweal 116:212-13 Ap 7 '89. T. O'Brien
Maclean's il pors 102:62 Mr 13 '89. B. D. Johnson
The Nation 248:426-7 Mr 27 '89. S. Klawans

National Review 41:45+ Je 16 '89. J. Simon
The New Leader il 72:20-1 Mr 6 '89. J. Morrone
The New Republic 200:24-6 Mr 27 '89. S. Kauffmann
New York il 22:63-4 Mr 13 '89. D. Denby
The New Yorker 65:93-6 Mr 20 '89. P. Kael
Newsweek il 113:58 Mr 6 '89. D. Ansen
People Weekly il 31:15-16 Mr 13 '89. S. Haller
Time il 133:68 Mr 6 '89. R. Schickel
Thunder's Mouth, Faber both profiling filmmaker Martin Scorsese. M. Simson. il por *Publishers Weekly* 236:28 S 22 '89

SCOTCH WHISKEY
Expensive habits: single-malt whisky. P. Mayle. il *Gentlemen's Quarterly* 59:69+ Ap '89
Scotch. E. Fried. il *Black Enterprise* 20:124 D '89
Single malt scotch whisky. G. Asher. il *Gourmet* 49:94-9+ D '89
Single malts: back to the future. J. Marcom, Jr. *Forbes* 143:88 Je 12 '89

SCOTIABANK *See* Bank of Nova Scotia

SCOTLAND
See also
Antique dealers—Scotland
Argyll (Scotland)
Gardens and gardening—Scotland
Glasgow (Scotland)
Paleontology—Scotland
Police—Scotland
Radioactive waste disposal—Scotland
Sculpture gardens and parks—Scotland
Description and travel
On the high and low roads of Scotland. G. D. Ford. il *Southern Living* 24:26+ Je '89
History
Wallace's Rising, 1297-1304
A patriot for whom? Wallace & Bruce: Scotland's uneasy heroes. A. Fisher. bibl il *History Today* 39:18-23 F '89
Industries
See also
Liquor industry—Scotland
Kings and rulers
See also
Robert I, King of Scotland, 1274-1329

SCOTSMAN INDUSTRIES
Spinning gold out of spinoffs [M. Gabelli's interest in Household International spinoffs] G. G. Marcial. *Business Week* p80 Jl 31 '89

SCOTT, CHARLES R., 1928-
about
Intermark keeps pressing its luck—and winning. S. Toy. il por *Business Week* p60+ F 6 '89

SCOTT, CHERIE CARTER- *See* Carter-Scott, Cherie

SCOTT, CYNTHIA D.
(jt. auth) *See* Jaffe, Dennis T., and Scott, Cynthia D.

SCOTT, DAVE
Commit to get fit [special section]; ed. by Marc Bloom. il *World Tennis* 36:69-70+ My '89
about
Tips from the super jocks. P. Serrani. il pors *Gentlemen's Quarterly* 59:250-7 My '89

SCOTT, EDGAR
about
A Philadelphia story: Edgar and Hope Scott at Ardrossan Farms. M. Tree. il por *Architectural Digest* 46:164-9 Je '89

SCOTT, ERNIE
about
Wed when the West was wild, Ernie and Maud Scott celebrate 80 years of staying hitched. il pors *People Weekly* 31:99 Je 26 '89

SCOTT, GEOFF
Our planet, our health [cover story] bibl il *Current Health 2* 16:4-7+ D '89

SCOTT, HOPE
about
A Philadelphia story: Edgar and Hope Scott at Ardrossan Farms. M. Tree. il por *Architectural Digest* 46:164-9 Je '89

SCOTT, HOWARD
Writing for the trades. *The Writer* 102:22-5 F '89

SCOTT, J. F., AND PAZ DE ARAUJO, CARLOS A.
Ferroelectric memories. bibl f il *Science* 246:1400-5 D 15 '89

SCOTT, J. MICHAEL, AND OTHERS
Integrated conservation strategy for Hawaiian forest birds [discussion of April 1988 article, Conservation of Hawaii's vanishing avifauna] bibl f *BioScience* 39:475-9 Jl/Ag '89

SCOTT, JACK
about
The saga behind the shame. J. Brant. il pors *Runner's World* 24:78-80 Ap '89

SCOTT, JAY
Dignity in drag [cover story] il pors *Film Comment* 25:9-12+ Ja/F '89
Mirror, mirror . . . il *Film Comment* 25:11-14 S/O '89

SCOTT, JERRY
about
Art, intrigue and human rights. E. Shorris. il *The Nation* 249:14-18 Jl 3 '89
SCOTT, LARY
about
"This global thing is not a fad". M. Beauchamp. il *Forbes* 144:122+ D 11 '89
SCOTT, MARGARET
Hong Kong on borrowed time. il *The New York Times Magazine* p30-2+ O 22 '89
SCOTT, MATTHEW
Doing business on the home front. il *Black Enterprise* 19:68-70 Ap '89
SCOTT, MAUD
about
Wed when the West was wild, Ernie and Maud Scott celebrate 80 years of staying hitched. il pors *People Weekly* 31:99 Je 26 '89
SCOTT, MICHAEL
In harmony. il pors *Opera News* 53:30-2 Ap 15 '89
SCOTT, MICHAEL, 1924-1989
about
Obituary
American Craft por 49:64 D '89/Ja '90. S. Lub
SCOTT, MICHAEL, 1952-
about
Michael Scott. L. S. Hurwitz. il por *American Artist* 53:46-7 Ag '89
SCOTT, MICHELLE PELLISSIER, AND TRANIELLO, JAMES F. A.
Guardians of the underworld. il *Natural History* p32-7 Je '89
SCOTT, PATRICIA REED
about
Interview with Patricia Reed Scott. J. E. Fitch. il por *American Film* 15:90-3 O '89
SCOTT, PETER
about
Great, Scott. K. Hannon. il por *Forbes* 143:172 Mr 6 '89
SCOTT, RACHEL SHIELDS
Alzheimer's: questions children ask. il *Children Today* 18:23-5 Jl/Ag '89
SCOTT, RAY
about
Deer and the bass man. C. Conley. il pors *Outdoor Life* 184:4 Ag '89
SCOTT, RENNY
about
An Atlanta prison gets converted. B. Spring. il por *Christianity Today* 33:53-4 Ap 7 '89
SCOTT, RIDLEY
about
Black rain [film] Reviews
Commonweal 116:565-6 O 20 '89. P. D. Baumann
Maclean's 102:65+ O 2 '89. B. D. Johnson
The New Republic 201:31-2 O 16 '89. S. Kauffmann
New York il 22:66+ O 2 '89. D. Denby
Newsweek il 114:70-1 O 2 '89. D. Ansen
People Weekly il 32:17 O 9 '89. R. Novak
Time 134:90 O 2 '89. R. Corliss
SCOTT, ROBERT FALCON, 1868-1912
about
The price of human folly. J. M. Diamond. il *Discover* 10:72-7 Ap '89
SCOTT, SANDY
(jt. auth) See Hughes, Larry, and Scott, Sandy
SCOTT, TOM
about
Follow the leader. J. Marchese. il por *Rolling Stone* p32-3 Je 15 '89
The musical directions of Tom Scott. S. Yanow. il pors *Down Beat* 56:23-6 Mr '89
SCOTT, VERNON
Cristina Ferrare [cover story] il pors *Good Housekeeping* 209:16+ S '89
Delta Burke: "The man who taught me to love again" [cover story] pors *Good Housekeeping* 208:76+ F '89
The girl who has everything: Victoria Principal [cover story] il pors *Good Housekeeping* 208:112+ Je '89
"I will live . . .": Jill Ireland fights back. il pors *Good Housekeeping* 208:183+ My '89
Tony Danza, my husband, and me. il pors *Good Housekeeping* 208:86+ Ap '89
SCOTT, SIR WALTER, 1771-1832
about
Beyond reason [cover story] J. Kestner. il *Opera News* 53:8-11+ F 18 '89
SCOTT, WILLARD
about
A case of morning sickness. J. Adler. il pors *Newsweek* 113:61 Mr 13 '89
Despite tremors on the set, Today's Willard Scott says: I'm still on solid ground. H. Sterne. por *TV Guide* 37:26-8 N 18-24 '89
Willard Scott is blowing his top. A. Richman. il pors *People Weekly* 31:44-9 Mr 20 '89

SCOTT ANTARCTIC EXPEDITION, 1910-1912 *See* Antarctic exploration
SCOTT AVIATION DIVISION
Casualties of peace [Navy investigates faulty smoke protection gear] *Time* 134:30 N 27 '89
SCOTT BROWN, DENISE, 1931-
about
Blueprint for growth: (not always) an easy alliance. A. L. Ball. il pors *Working Woman* 14:138+ O '89
SCOTT, FORESMAN & COMPANY
Harper & Row buys Scott, Foresman for $455 million. C. Reid. *Publishers Weekly* 236:8 D 8 '89
SCOTT, FORESMAN & COMPANY. PROFESSIONAL BOOKS GROUP
Scott, Foresman: building a trade presence. T. Unsworth. *Publishers Weekly* 236:437 Ag 11 '89
SCOTT-MONTAGU, EDWARD JOHN BARRINGTON DOUGLAS- *See* Montagu of Beaulieu, Edward John Barrington Douglas-Scott-Montagu, Baron, 1926-
SCOTTISH BALLET
Reviews:
Performance of O. Vinogradov's Petrushka. M. E. Willis. il *Dance Magazine* 63:78-9 O '89
SCOTTISH COOKING *See* Cooking, Scottish
SCOTTISH OPERA
Glasgow/Oxford. N. Goodwin. il *Opera News* 54:42 Jl '89
Glasgow. N. Goodwin. *Opera News* 53:47 My '89
Glasgow. N. Goodwin. il *Opera News* 54:45 Ag '89
Glasgow. N. Goodwin. il *Opera News* 54:60-1 S '89
SCOTTSDALE (ARIZ.)
Stores
Shopping in Scottsdale. L. Langseth-Christensen. il *Gourmet* 49:70-5+ F '89
SCOUT (LAUNCH VEHICLE) *See* Space vehicles—Propulsion systems
SCOUTING, BASEBALL *See* Baseball, Professional—Scouting
SCOUTING, FOOTBALL *See* Football, Professional—Super Bowl—Scouting
SCOUTS AND SCOUTING
See also
Boy Scouts of America
Wilderness Scouts of America
SCOVELL, CLAIRE
The Los Angeles man. il *Gentlemen's Quarterly* 59:139-40 Ag '89
Moving from the East to the West, as Claire Scovell found out, doesn't just mean a change of climate. il *Vogue* 179:162-4 Ag '89
SCOVELL, NELL
Breaking in. il *Vogue* 179:550+ Mr '89
Class notes. il *Vogue* 179:400 F '89
SCOWCROFT, BRENT
about
Blind men's bluff [cover story] M. Kondracke. *The New Republic* 200:20+ Mr 6 '89
Can Brent Scowcroft be converted to SDI? J. T. Hackett. por *Conservative Digest* 15:15 Mr/Ap '89
Defense leaders line up with Scowcroft on Midgetman and carry-hard basing. P. Mann. il *Aviation Week & Space Technology* 130:23-4 F 6 '89
The general's little missile. J. D. Isaacs. il *The Bulletin of the Atomic Scientists* 45:3-4 Mr '89
Mr. Inside, Mr. Outside. J. Barry. pors *Newsweek* 113:28 F 27 '89
The quiet sage steering Bush's foreign policy. H. Trewhitt. il por *U.S. News & World Report* 106:22-4 F 20 '89
SCP LTD.
Coakley's clan. H. S. MacIsaac. il por *House & Garden* 161:48 Mr '89
SCRAMBLED TELEPHONES *See* Telephone—Security measures
SCRAP METAL
Recycling
See also
Proler International Corp.
SCRAPBOOKS
Make this guy a scout [C. L. Brannen compiles scrapbooks on athletes] R. Harper. il *Sport (New York, N.Y.)* 80:76 Jl '89
SCRAPERS (TOOLS)
Mortar scraper and shaper [Jointmaster] D. Scott. il *Popular Science* 234:160 Ap '89
Smoothing with scrapers. B. Johnson. il *Home Mechanix* 85:20+ Ag '89
SCREEN HOUSES *See* Garden houses, shelters, etc.
SCREENPLAYS *See* Motion picture scripts
SCREENS (DOORS, WINDOWS, ETC.)
Garage door screens. S. Kingman and P. Kingman. il *The Family Handyman* 39:82-3 Ap '89
Japanese banners as sun screens. il *Sunset (Central West edition)* 182:162 My '89
The screening process. il *Home Mechanix* 85:46-8+ My '89
SCREENS (FENCES) *See* Fences
THE SCREENS [drama] See Genet, Jean, 1910-1986
SCREENWRITING *See* Motion picture authorship
SCREW THREADS
Loctite Form-A-Thread repair kit. il *Cycle* 40:69 Ja '89

SCREWDRIVERS
Cordless screwdrivers. il *Consumer Reports* 54:86-8 D '89
Cordless screwdrivers: a new twist in tools. il *Consumer Reports* 54:535-8 Ag '89
The new age of screwdriving. B. Kinghorn. il *The Family Handyman* 39:12+ O '89
SCREWS
The new age of screwdriving. B. Kinghorn. il *The Family Handyman* 39:12+ O '89
Taming of the screw. K. Cameron. il *Cycle* 40:10 Jl '89
SCRIBNER BOOK COMPANIES, INC.
Some Scribners memories. R. M. Elman. por *Publishers Weekly* 235:439 Ja 27 '89
SCRIBNER BOOKSTORE (NEW YORK, N.Y.) *See* Booksellers and bookselling—New York (State)
SCRIPPS SCHOOL OF JOURNALISM
Yukking it up for credit [M. Helitzer's comedy course] B. Barol. il *Newsweek* 114:83 D 4 '89
SCRIPT WRITING (MOTION PICTURES) *See* Motion picture authorship
SCRIPT WRITING (TELEVISION) *See* Television authorship
SCRIPTS, MOTION PICTURE *See* Motion picture scripts
SCRIPTURE STUDIES *See* Bible—Study and teaching
SCROOGED [film] *See* Motion picture reviews—Single works
SCRUPLES (GAME)
Fun and games—and ethics. S. Nelton. il *Nation's Business* 77:38 N '89
SCSI (COMPUTER BUS)
Mac color by SCSI [ScuzzyGraph II external graphics display] H. Eglowstein. *Byte* 14:235 D '89
SCUBA DIVING *See* Skin diving
SCUDDER, THAYER
River basin projects in Africa [cover story] bibl f il map *Environment* 31:4-9+ Mr '89
SCUDDER CAPITAL GROWTH FUND
A growth-stock fund for value-minded investors. M. Meyer. il *Money* 18:59 Ap '89
Growth stocks with more climb left [interview with S. Aronoff] K. Nickel. il por *Fortune* 120:28+ N 6 '89
SCULLEY, JOHN
The power of ideas and information [address, February 2, 1989] *Vital Speeches of the Day* 55:565-9 Jl 1 '89
Technology is reshaping both work and workers. por *Personal Computing* 13:218 O '89
about
Apple Computer's risky revolution. B. O'Reilly. il por *Fortune* 119:75-6+ My 8 '89
Apple turns from revolution to evolution. M. Shao. il por *Business Week* p90+ Ja 23 '89
John Sculley on sabbatical. B. O'Reilly. il por *Fortune* 119:79-80 Mr 27 '89
SCULLY, SEAN, 1945 OR 6-
about
Earning his stripes. R. Hughes. il por *Time* 134:70 Ag 14 '89
SCULLY, VINCENT JOSEPH, 1920-
A stick style curiosity on the Jersey coast. il por *Architectural Digest* 46:34+ Mr '89
SCULPTURE
See also
Animals in art
Automobiles in art
Birmingham (Ala.)—Monuments, statues, etc.
Bronzes
Butter sculpture
Casting (Sculpture)
Ceramic sculpture
Concrete sculpture
Figurines
Forensic sculpture
Glass sculpture
Horses in art
Ice sculpture
Inflatable art
Junk art
Lava sculpture
Los Angeles (Calif.)—Monuments, statues, etc.
Masks
Metal sculpture
New York (N.Y.)—Monuments, statues, etc.
Portrait sculpture
Salem (Mass.)—Monuments, statues, etc.
Saugerties (N.Y.)—Monuments, statues, etc.
Stone carving
Underwater sculpture
Votive sculpture
Wales (Alaska)—Monuments, statues, etc.
Washington (D.C.)—Monuments, statues, etc.
Wood carving
Collectors and collecting
Thinking big [R. Nasher] C. Brown. il por *Forbes* 143:270-1 Je 26 '89
Conservation and restoration
A dying sculptor fights vandals over Myrna Loy [W. Van Orden restores statue outside Venice High School in Los Angeles] il por *People Weekly* 31:111 My 29 '89
Penny serenade [Adopt-a-Monument program in New York City] *The New Yorker* 65:26-7 Jl 17 '89

Exhibitions
Sculpted essences [modern sculpture] M. Stevens. il *The New Republic* 201:28-30 S 4 '89
Preservation
See Sculpture—Conservation and restoration
SCULPTURE, AMERICAN
See also
Adams, Hank Murta, 1956-
Adams, Phoebe
Ahrens, Hanno, 1954-
Barr, David, 1939-
Brady, Robert, 1946-
Brennan, Thompson
Bruch, Cris
Burke, Selma, 1900-
Butterfield, Deborah, 1949-
Cassilly, Bob
Chamberlain, John Angus, 1927-
Colson, Jeff, 1956-
Coyne, Petah
De Maria, Walter, 1935-
DeStaebler, Stephen, 1933-
Downsbrough, Peter
Drake, James, 1946-
Eldred, Dale, 1934-
Ericson, Kate
Finster, Howard
Fleming, Linda
French, Daniel Chester, 1850-1931
Hawkinson, Tim
Herring, James
Hesse, Eva, 1936-1970
Hunt, Bryan, 1947-
Johnson, Cletus
Judd, Donald, 1928-
Kahn, Ned
Kearney, John
Kienholz, Edward, 1927-
Kienholz, Nancy Reddin
Lang, Stephen
Lehman, Wendy
Lowenstein, Suse
Manship, Paul, 1885-1966
Masters, Deborah
Minkowitz, Norma, 1937-
Miss, Mary, 1944-
Nadelman, Elie, 1882-1946
Nevelson, Louise, 1900-1988
Noguchi, Isamu, 1904-1988
Noland, Cady
Norton, Ann
Oppenheim, Dennis, 1938-
Power, Ross
Price, Tony
Rabinowitch, David, 1943-
Reginato, Peter, 1945-
Reid, James Earl
Rhodes, Daniel, 1911-1989
Rosenberg, Evelyn
Saret, Alan, 1944-
Schiff, Jeffrey
Serra, Richard
Silver, Jonathan
Sonnier, Keith, 1941-
Stone, William
Tadlock, Paul
Taye, John
Tinker, John
Vander Pluym, Todd
Von Schlegell, David, 1920-
Westerlund Roosen, Mia, 1942-
Wilmarth, Christopher, 1943-1987
Ziolkowski, Korczak, 1908-1982
Keeping track of sculpture with computers [Inventory of American Sculpture at the National Museum of American Art] il *The Futurist* 23:49 Mr/Ap '89
Exhibitions
Pilgrims' process [4 Americans at the Brooklyn Museum] K. Larson. il *New York* 22:76-7 Mr 13 '89
SCULPTURE, ARGENTINE
See also
Fontana, Lucio, 1899-1968
SCULPTURE, AUSTRIAN
See also
West, Franz, 1947-
SCULPTURE, BRAZILIAN
See also
Muniz, Vik
Exhibitions
House of miracles [votive sculptures at the Americas Society] K. Canton. il *Art in America* 77:73+ D '89
SCULPTURE, CANADIAN
See also
Reid, Bill, 1920-
SCULPTURE, CUBAN
See also
Brito-Avellana, Maria

SCULPTURE, CZECH
See also
  Jetelova, Magdalena
SCULPTURE, ENGLISH
See also
  Caro, Anthony, 1924-
  Cragg, Tony
  Glen, Robert
  Moore, Henry, 1898-1986
SCULPTURE, FINNISH
Exhibitions
The language of wood [at the American Craft Museum]
  J. F. Pile. il *American Craft* 49:56-63 Ag/S '89
SCULPTURE, FRENCH
See also
  César, 1921-
  Cheval, Ferdinand, 1836-1924
  Claudel, Camille
  Degas, Edgar, 1834-1917
  Lalanne, Claude
  Lalanne, François-Xavier, 1924-
  Poirier, Anne
  Poirier, Patrick
  Raynaud, Patrick, 1946-
  Rodin, Auguste, 1840-1917
In a clash of symbols, Chanel's top model falls from the
  runway [I. de la Fressange selected to be model for bust
  of Marianne] M. H. J. Farrell. il pors *People Weekly*
  32:51+ Ag 14 '89
SCULPTURE, GERMAN
See also
  Hartlieb, Ingrid, 1944-
  Herold, Georg, 1947-
  Schütte, Thomas
SCULPTURE, GREEK
See also
  Elgin marbles
Authenticating ancient marble sculpture. S. V. Margolis. bibl
  il map *Scientific American* 260:104-10 Je '89
SCULPTURE, INDIAN (AMERICAN) *See* Indians of North
  America—Art
SCULPTURE, ITALIAN
See also
  Anselmo, Giovanni
  Merz, Mario, 1925-
  Michelangelo Buonarroti, 1475-1564
  Rosso, Medardo, 1858-1928
SCULPTURE, JAPANESE
See also
  I'ida, Yoshikuni, 1923-
  Uematsu, Keiji
SCULPTURE, MEXICAN *See also*
  Rodriguez, Dionicio
SCULPTURE, SCOTTISH
See also
  Finlay, Ian Hamilton, 1925-
SCULPTURE, SPANISH
See also
  Calatrava, Santiago, 1951-
SCULPTURE, SWISS
See also
  Brunner, Hannes
  Giacometti, Alberto, 1901-1966
SCULPTURE, TIBETAN
Exhibitions
With no margarine for error, eight Buddhist monks practice
  a butter way to honor the gods [butter sculpting at the
  American Museum of Natural History] il *People Weekly*
  31:81 F 27 '89
SCULPTURE, VIETNAMESE
See also
  Vietati
SCULPTURE GARDENS AND PARKS
California
See also
  Duquette Pavilion
  University of California, San Diego. Stuart Collection
Florida
See also
  Ann Norton Sculpture Garden
France
The Ideal Palace: Ferdinand Cheval's fantasy in the Rhône
  Valley. Y. Blumenfeld. il *Architectural Digest* 46:108-13+
  Ja '89
The postman's palace [Le Palais Idéal conceived by F. Cheval]
  B. Weber. il por *The New York Times Magazine* p122
  S 10 '89
Kansas
See also
  Concrete Garden of Eden (Lucas, Kan.)
Missouri
See also
  Henry Moore Sculpture Garden
Netherlands
Country charms [Kroller-Muller Museum's sculpture garden
  in Hoge Veluwe National Park] M. K. Talley, Jr. il *Art
  News* 88:77-8 Summ '89

New York (State)
See also
  Museum of Modern Art (New York, N.Y.). Sculpture
  Garden
  Storm King Art Center
Caro country: the artist's New York State sculpture studio
  and fields [designed by Donald Clinton] K. Wilken. il
  por *Architectural Digest* 46:192-7+ Ag '89
Scotland
Gardens: politics of Little Sparta: Ian Hamilton Finlay's
  statements in stone. M. Ruthven. il por *Architectural Digest*
  46:104-11+ Jl '89
Sir William Keswick's sculptural landscape in Scotland
  [Glenkiln] J. McEwen. il por *Architectural Digest* 46:324+
  O '89
South Carolina
See also
  Brookgreen Gardens
Switzerland
Gardens: wonders of Scherrer Park. D. H. Minassian. il
  Architectural Digest 46:228-33 O '89
SCURVY
Henry VIII—a malnourished king? S. M. Kybett. bibl il
  pors *History Today* 39:19-25 S '89
SDI *See* Strategic Defense Initiative
SDS *See* Students for a Democratic Society
SEA *See* Ocean
SEA-AIR INTERACTION *See* Ocean-atmosphere interaction
SEA ANEMONES
Cnidocyte mechanoreceptors are tuned to the movements
  of swimming prey by chemoreceptors [cover story] G.
  M. Watson and D. A. Hessinger. bibl f il *Science*
  243:1589-91 Mr 24 '89
Sexual stunts of clownfish [cover story] D. G. Fautin. il
  Natural History p42-7 S '89
What tells anemones to kill their enemies? [research by
  Glen M. Watson and David A. Hessinger] R. Weiss. *Science
  News* 135:182 Mr 25 '89
SEA BIRDS
See also
  Albatrosses
  Gulls
  Terns
After an oil spill: saving the birds [Washington State] D.
  B. Lewis. il *Sea Frontiers* 35:200-5 Jl/Ag '89
Hands against the darkness [cleaning oil-soaked birds after
  Washington spill] A. E. Simonov. il *The Mother Earth
  News* 118:8 Jl/Ag '89
SEA BIRDS, FOSSIL
Largest known flying seabird found in South Carolina
  [Pseudodontorn fossil; work of Storrs L. Olson] *Earth
  Science* 41:6-7 Wint '88
SEA BREEZE AWARDS *See* Youth—Awards
SEA CAPTAINS *See* Shipmasters
SEA DRAGONS
Photographs and photography
Father does best. R. Kuiter. il *International Wildlife* 19:12-13
  Ja/F '89
SEA ELEPHANTS *See* Seals (Animals)
SEA FLOOR *See* Ocean bottom
SEA FRONTIERS (PERIODICAL)
Crow's nest. B. Rosendahl. il *Sea Frontiers* 35:323 N/D
  '89
SEA GULLS *See* Gulls
SEA HORSES
Seahorses [cover story] W. Arrigoni. il *Sea Frontiers* 35:358-65
  N/D '89
Unusual pets. S. L. Gerstenfeld. il *Parents* 64:257 O '89
SEA INDUSTRIES LTD.
New brooms against deadly weapons [Manta minehunter]
  P. C. Newman. il *Maclean's* 102:28 Ja 9 '89
SEA ISLAND (GA.)
See also
  Resorts—Sea Island (Ga.)
SEA LAW *See* Maritime law
SEA LEVEL CHANGES
After the deluge [Ice Age floods; research by John Shaw]
  T. Appenzeller. il *Scientific American* 261:22+ D '89
Bringing down the sea level rise. R. A. Kerr. *Science* 246:1563
  D 22 '89
Catastrophe looms as sea levels rise [research by Jodi L.
  Jacobson] il *USA Today (Periodical)* 117:1-2 Je '89
Critical depth for the survival of coral islands: effects on
  the Hawaiian archipelago. R. W. Grigg and D. Epp. bibl
  f il map *Science* 243:638-41 F 3 '89
The drowning delta [Nile River] T. Land. *World Press Review*
  36:64-5 N '89
Global sea level rise and the greenhouse effect: might they
  be connected? W. R. Peltier and A. M. Tushingham. bibl
  f il maps *Science* 244:806-10 My 19 '89
Growth of Greenland ice sheet: interpretation. H. J. Zwally.
  bibl f il map *Science* 246:1589-91 D 22 '89
Hills point to catastrophic Ice Age floods [drumlins; work
  of John Shaw] R. Monastersky. *Science News* 136:213
  S 30 '89
The inundation of our coastlines [effects of rising sea level
  on south Florida] H. R. Wanless. bibl il maps *Sea Frontiers*
  35:264-71 S/O '89

SEA LEVEL CHANGES—*cont.*
Is it time to build another ark? [concern over greenhouse-induced sea level changes in the Netherlands] il *U.S. News & World Report* 107:12 N 20 '89
Predictions drop for future sea-level rise [views of Mark F. Meier] R. Monastersky. *Science News* 136:397 D 16 '89
Rising seas may herald global warming [views of W. Richard Peltier] *Science News* 135:367 Je 10 '89
SEA LIONS *See* Seals (Animals)
SEA OF GALILEE (ISRAEL)
Boat resurfaces at Sea of Galilee. B. Bower. *Science News* 135:44 Ja 21 '89
SEA OF LOVE [film] *See* Motion picture reviews—Single works
SEA OTTERS
Where to watch sea otters, at work and play [California coast] il map *Sunset (Central West edition)* 182:68+ Mr '89
SEA PARROTS *See* Puffins
SEA RESCUES *See* Rescue work
SEA SHELLS *See* Shells (Conchology)
SEA SLUGS
See also
Nudibranchs
SEA STARS *See* Starfish
SEA TROUT FISHING *See* Weakfish fishing
SEA TURTLES *See* Turtles
SEA URCHINS
Embryology
See Embryology—Echinoderms
Reproduction
Direct measurements of sliding between outer doublet microtubules in swimming sperm flagella. C. J. Brokaw. bibl f il *Science* 243:1593-6 Mr 24 '89
SEA WALLS
See also
Dikes (Engineering)
SEA WATER
Carbon dioxide: where does it all go? [research by Pieter P. Tans] R. Monastersky. *Science News* 136:132 Ag 26 '89
A light meal at sea [study of carbon cycle by Kenneth Mopper] *Science News* 136:284 O 28 '89
New way to switch earth between hot and cold [ocean dissolved carbon dioxide; research by Edward Boyle] R. A. Kerr. il *Science* 243:480 Ja 27 '89
Soaking up the rays to make fuel [liberating hydrogen bound in sea water; work of H. Ti Tien] *Science News* 135:366 Je 10 '89
Desalting
See Saline water conversion
Pollution
See Marine pollution
SEA WAVES *See* Waves
SEA WORLD (ORLANDO, FLA.)
Seagate [failure to inform public about ocean pollution] D. Adcroft. *Omni (New York, N.Y.)* 11:33 Je '89
SEA WORLD (SAN ANTONIO, TEX.)
In the path of famous Texans [Texas Walk] il *Southern Living* 24:43 F '89
SEABED TREATY (1972)
Third review conference on operation of Sea-Bed Treaty adopts final declaration. il *UN Chronicle* 26:33 D '89
SEABIRDS *See* Sea birds
SEABOARD CORP.
A poultry bargain may be hatching. J. M. Laderman. *Business Week* p80 Jl 3 '89
SEABORG, ERIC
Finding funding for parks. il *Sierra* 74:30-2 My/Je '89
SEABORG, GLENN THEODORE, 1912-
Weapons labs need new thinking. *The Bulletin of the Atomic Scientists* 45:10-12 Jl/Ag '89
(jt. auth) See Epstein, William, 1912-, and Seaborg, Glenn Theodore, 1912-
SEABRA, JOSE AUGUSTO
Fernando Pessoa and the spirit of discovery. il *The Courier (Unesco)* 42:37-8 Ap '89
Fernando Pessoa: many poets in one. il pors *The Courier (Unesco)* 41:30-4 N '88
SEABROOK, JOHN
Diamond stud. por *Vogue* 179:406-7+ Ap '89
Invisible gold. *The New Yorker* 65:45-6+ Ap 24 '89
SEABROOK NUCLEAR POWER PLANT (N.H.) *See* Nuclear power plants
SEABURY TREADWELL HOUSE (NEW YORK, N.Y.) *See* Old Merchant's House (New York, N.Y.)
SEACAMP (FLA.)
Florida's Seacamp [cover story] il map *National Geographic World* 169:4-9 S '89
SEAFARING LIFE
See also
Voyages
SEAFOOD
See also
Cooking—Seafood
Fish as food
Surimi

Catches with new cachet. M. Starr. il *Newsweek* 113:48 Ja 9 '89
Contamination
Alaskan oil spill: health risks uncovered. M. Barinaga. il *Science* 245:463 Ag 4 '89
SEAFOOD CULTURE *See* Aquaculture
SEAFOOD GATHERING
Sapelo's seaside feast. S. Pacher. il maps *The Mother Earth News* 119:80-3 S/O '89
SEAFOOD HANDLING
Kitchen safety tips for seafood. il *FDA Consumer* 23:25 F '89
SEAGA, EDWARD P. G.
about
A comeback in Jamaica [with interview] E. Calonius. il por *Newsweek* 113:29 F 20 '89
Once more, with moderation. G. D. Garcia. il por *Time* 133:48 F 20 '89
Polling in paradise. J. Bierman. il pors *Maclean's* 102:20 F 6 '89
A sweet victory. A. Bilski. il por *Maclean's* 102:22 F 20 '89
SEAGAMB (FIRM)
Raise the Rio! [work of B. Gibson] J. Grissim. il map *Oceans* 22:30-7+ Mr/Ap '89
SEAGATE TECHNOLOGY
Driven down. il por *Forbes* 143:115 Ja 9 '89
SEAGER, SARAH
about
Sarah Seager at Dennis Anderson. M. Anderson. *Art in America* 77:183 D '89
SEAGRAM COMPANY LTD.
Give me a Chivas and natural soda [E. M. Bronfman, Jr.] P. Sherrid. il pors *U.S. News & World Report* 107:42-3 Jl 17 '89
The maverick boss at Seagram [E. Bronfman Jr., cover story] A. Rothman. il pors *Business Week* p90-3+ D 18 '89
SEAHORSES *See* Sea horses
SEAL ISLAND (ME.)
See also
Birds—Seal Island (Me.)
SEALANTS, PIT AND FISSURE (DENTAL MATERIALS)
See Dental materials
SEALED POWER CORP.
See also
SPX (Firm)
SEALES, SUGAR RAY
about
They never gave up. R. Hoffer. il pors *Sports Illustrated* 71:117-27+ D 25 '89-Ja 1 '90
SEALING COMPOUNDS
See also
Loctite Corp.
SEALS (ANIMALS)
See also
Pieterburen Seal Sanctuary (Netherlands)
Australia's sea lions. il *National Geographic World* 172:26-31 D '89
Breathless seals [cessation of breathing by Weddell and elephant seals while diving and sleeping] *Discover* 10:16 Jl '89
The diving seal [adaptations of harbor seals; research by Ronald W. Millard] S. Kleene. bibl il *Sea Frontiers* 35:370-4 N/D '89
Incredible diving machines [northern elephant seals; cover story] B. J. Le Boeuf. il *Natural History* p34-41 F '89
The sea lions of Monterey. S. Rosenberg. bibl il map *Sea Frontiers* 35:97-103 Mr/Ap '89
Sensory function in the harbor seal. D. Renouf. bibl il map *Scientific American* 260:90-5 Ap '89
The summer of Cecily [pet harbor seal] N. Lincoln. il *Reader's Digest* 134:84-8 Je '89
Vaccination success convicts seal killer [canine distemper virus in harbor seals; research by Alfred D. M. E. Osterhaus] I. Wickelgren. *Science News* 135:39 Ja 21 '89
Care
Foster mother to Holland's seals [L. 't Hart] B. Krist. il por map *International Wildlife* 19:20-4 Jl/Ag '89
Photographs and photography
From here to paternity [fight between two elephant seals] K. Ward. il *Natural History* p84-5 D '89
SEALS (ANIMALS) IN RESCUE WORK
Seals to the rescue [North Wind Undersea Institute] il *National Geographic World* 161:32-5 Ja '89
SEALS (CHRISTMAS) *See* Christmas seals
SEALS (NUMISMATICS)
The eagle and the arrows: America in the nuclear age [Great Seal] T. J. Osborne. il *USA Today (Periodical)* 118:12-14 Jl '89
SEAMAN, CARL
about
Fool's gold? S. Flack. il por *Forbes* 144:150+ D 25 '89
SEAMAN, DICK
about
Miscellaneous ramblings. T. L. Bryant. il *Road & Track* 41:47 N '89

SEAMAN FURNITURE CO., INC.
Fool's gold? [recent investments by C. Seaman] S. Flack. il por *Forbes* 144:150+ D 25 '89
See you in bankruptcy court [leveraged buyout of Seaman Furniture turns into headache for Kohlberg Kravis Roberts] S. Flack. il *Forbes* 144:77+ O 16 '89
What would Grandpa say? K. Hannon. *Forbes* 144:10 S 18 '89

SEAMANSHIP
See also
Boats and boating—Handling
Fishing boats—Handling
Motor boats—Handling
Navigation
Seamanship. See alternate issues of Motor Boating & Sailing

SEAMEN
See also
Alcohol and seamen

SEAMOUNTS
Where earth's insides ooze out [Mariana seamount; research by Patricia Fryer] *Science News* 136:15 Jl 1 '89

SEAPLANES
See also
Chalk's International Airlines
Over Africa. R. Alleman. il *Vogue* 179:320+ Ap '89
Design
Dornier, Aeritalia to use twin-engine design for advanced amphibian concept. il *Aviation Week & Space Technology* 130:64 Je 19 '89
History
Bridging the Atlantic [early transatlantic flights with Pan Am; cover story] R. K. Schrader. il *American History Illustrated* 24:34-47 My '89
Anecdotes, facetiae, satire, etc.
Wings ahoy! [75th anniversary of the flying boat] B. McCall. il *The New Yorker* 65:30-3 My 1 '89
Piloting
Splash party. A. Laboda. il *Flying* 116:104+ My '89
Standards
Orders mounting for Huskys. il *Flying* 116:16 My '89
Testing
Dornier Seastar begins certification tests of CD. 2 amphibious aircraft. K. F. Mordoff. il *Aviation Week & Space Technology* 129:31 Mr 6 '89

SEARCH & RESEARCH (FIRM)
Entrepreneur looks for laws—and finds success. B. Stein. il por *Home Office Computing* 7:52-3 F '89

SEARCH AND RESCUE OPERATIONS *See* Rescue work
SEARCH FOR EXTRATERRESTRIAL INTELLIGENCE *See* Interstellar communication
THE SEARCH FOR NIJINSKY'S RITE OF SPRING [television program] *See* Television program reviews—Single works
THE SEARCH FOR SIGNS OF INTELLIGENT LIFE IN THE UNIVERSE [drama] *See* Wagner, Jane

SEARCHES AND SEIZURES
Boarded [Coast Guard search] P. A. Janssen. il *Motor Boating & Sailing* 164:13 O '89
The case of the conspicuous dealer [Supreme Court upholds use of drug courier profiles] *Newsweek* 113:64 Ap 17 '89
Judging a book by its cover [Supreme Court upholds use of drug courier profiles by federal agents] A. L. Sanders. il *Time* 133:52 Ap 17 '89
Searching and researching [use of sniffer dogs in detecting suspicious student automobiles in Joshua, Tex.] P. A. Zirkel. bibl f *Phi Delta Kappan* 71:330-2 D '89
Thurgood's way [T. Marshall dissents in Supreme Court ruling upholding search of additional fitting drug courier profile] D. Seligman. il *Fortune* 119:165+ My 8 '89

SEARCHING, ONLINE *See* Online searching
SEARING, SUSAN E.
Feminist publications. il *Utne Reader* p134+ N/D '89
SEARL, LINDA
about
Two partners, one floor plan. L. Rosch. il por *Working Woman* 14:69 Ja '89
SEARLE, JOHN R.
about
Artificial intelligence and the Chinese Room: an exchange. E. Motzkin. il *The New York Review of Books* 36:44-5 F 16 '89
SEARS, EVA
Skinheads: a new generation of hate-mongers. il *USA Today (Periodical)* 117:24-6 My '89
SEARS, JOHN F.
about
Sights sacred and profane [interview] A. P. Sanoff. il por *U.S. News & World Report* 107:52 Ag 14 '89
SEARS, RUFUS
New York. il *Sport (New York, N.Y.)* 80:42-3+ F '89
SEARS, STEPHEN W.
The terrible price of freedom. il maps *American Heritage* 40:92-9+ Ap '89
SEARS, ROEBUCK AND CO.
Attention, discount shoppers! [new price policy] P. Sherrid. il *U.S. News & World Report* 106:54-5 Mr 13 '89
The Big Store's big trauma. B. Bremner and M. D. Oneal. il por *Business Week* p50-1+ Jl 10 '89

The Discover Card is no longer a joker. D. Greising. il *Business Week* p138 O 9 '89
Get down [new price policy] *Time* 133:47 Mr 13 '89
Holdup in the Windy City [tax incentives spur Sears' move to suburbs] P. Glastris. il *U.S. News & World Report* 107:40-1 Jl 17 '89
Little prices are looking good to big retailers. A. Dunkin. il *Business Week* p42+ Jl 3 '89
Now Sears has everyday low profits, too. B. Bremner. il *Business Week* p28 Ag 21 '89
Sale days at Sears. *Newsweek* 113:43 Mr 6 '89
Sears changes gears. T. Jaffe. il *Forbes* 144:260 O 30 '89
A season of hope for Sears. P. Glastris. il *U.S. News & World Report* 107:52+ D 11 '89
Will the big markdown get the big store moving again? J. E. Ellis and B. Bremner. il *Business Week* p110+ Mr 13 '89

SEASCAPES *See* Marine painting
SEASHORE
See also
Beaches
National seashores
SEASHORE ECOLOGY
The edge of the sea [excerpt] R. Carson. il *The Conservationist* 44:55 S/O '89
Magnification of secondary production by kelp detritus in coastal marine ecosystems. D. O. Duggins and others. bibl f il *Science* 245:170-3 Jl 14 '89
Nature's one-upmanship [effects of tropical storm on Sanibel Island ecosystem] C. R. Robins. il *Sea Frontiers* 35:192 My/Je '89
SEASHORE PROTECTION *See* Shore protection
SEASICKNESS *See* Motion sickness
SEASIDE (FLA.)
Architecture
Breaking the code [Chatham House; cover story] P. M. Sachner. il *Architectural Record* 177:100-5 mid-Ap '89
Coming of age. B. Dunlop. il map *Architectural Record* 177:96-103 Jl '89
Double standards [Walter Chatham's beach house] C. Vogel. il *The New York Times Magazine* p56-7 Ap 30 '89
Model houses [work of D. Berke] M. Filler. il por *House & Garden* 161:44 Ap '89
Streets
Dreamstreets. H. Leifermann. il *New Choices for the Best Years* 29:14 O '89
SEASIDE BANANA GARDENS
Growin' bananas [techniques of D. Richardson and P. Turner] L. Hollenhorst. il por *Organic Gardening* 36:54-6+ S '89
SEASON TICKETS (SPORTS EVENTS) *See* Sports tickets
SEASON TO TASTE BOOKS (CHICAGO, ILL.) *See* Booksellers and bookselling—Illinois
SEASONAL AFFECTIVE DISORDER
Carbohydrates and depression. R. J. Wurtman and J. J. Wurtman. il map *Scientific American* 260:68-75 Ja '89
Recognize the symptoms. J. Rogoznica. *Working Woman* 14:116 F '89
Red-hot and blue: the new summer depression. S. Diamond. il *Mademoiselle* 95:134 My '89
Shedding light on seasonal affective disorder. *Current Health 2* 16:19 D '89
Sizing up SADness according to latitude [research by Norman E. Rosenthal] B. Bower. *Science News* 136:198 S 23 '89
Therapy
Fighting the winter blues with bright light. M. Terman and M. Link. il *Psychology Today* 23:18+ Ja/F '89
Snowy days and Mondays. S. Kallop. il *Women's Sports & Fitness* 11:12 N/D '89
SEASONAL INDUSTRIES
See also
Construction industry
SEASONAL LABOR
See also
Migrant labor
SEASONINGS
See also
Capers
Celestial Seasonings Inc.
Herbs
Spices
Mexican, Italian, Scandinavian . . . they're handy seasonings to mix and keep. il *Sunset (Central West edition)* 183:150+ N '89
SEASONS
See also
Autumn
Spring
Summer
Winter
Disease of the month [seasonality of childhood illnesses] P. Klass. il *Discover* 10:32+ My '89
SEASTAR AIRPLANES *See* Seaplanes
SEAT BELTS, AUTOMOBILE *See* Automobiles—Safety belts
SEATING
See also
Airlines—Seating policy
Chairs
Corporations—Meetings—Seating

SEATING PLATFORMS, TELESCOPIC See Telescopic seating platforms

SEATS
See also
Airplanes, Jet—Seats
Automobiles—Seats
Bicycles—Saddles
Motorcycles—Seats
Theater seats

SEATTLE (WASH.)
"Seattle fits with my energies," says a booster. M. T. Smith. il *Money* 18:126 S '89
Architecture
All natural [guest house in Seattle and speculative house in Port Blakely designed by J. Cutler] P. M. Sachner. il *Architectural Record* 177:60-7 mid-Ap '89
Art
If Leonardo had driven a Chevy, would The Last Supper have been the first meal on wheels? [artists paint original designs on cars] S. K. Reed. il *People Weekly* 32:57-9 Jl 31 '89
Seattle King County [special section] il *Horizon (Tuscaloosa, Ala.)* 32:41-54+ Ja/F '89
Auditoriums, convention facilities, etc.
See also
Washington State Convention and Trade Center
City planning
Seattle CAPs downtown growth. D. Gantenbein. il *Architectural Record* 177:51 Jl '89
Urban growing pains [Seattle votes for restrictions on building size] G. J. Church. il *Time* 133:33 My 29 '89
Description
Seattle King County [special section] il *Horizon (Tuscaloosa, Ala.)* 32:41-54+ Ja/F '89
Education
Teaching as though life hangs in the balance [Zion Christian School] S. Ulstein. il *Christianity Today* 33:10-11 Ap 21 '89
Galleries and museums
See also
Museum of Flight (Seattle, Wash.)
Seattle Art Museum
Harbor
See also
Fishermen's Terminal (Seattle, Wash.)
Shipshape. M. Beauchamp. il por *Forbes* 143:200 Mr 20 '89
Historic houses, sites, etc.
He fixed it [Seattle street clock restorations by J. Martin] J. Schwarz. il pors map *Americana* 16:57-60 Ja/F '89
Music
See also
Seattle Opera
Seattle Symphony Orchestra
Photographs and photography
Back from the fire. il *American Heritage* 40:120-1 S/O '89
Police
Long leg of the law [bike use] S. Martin. il *Bicycling* 30:42 O/N '89
Population
Californians keep out! J. Bonfante. il *Time* 134:38-9 N 13 '89
Seattle's welcome mat begins to fray. il *U.S. News & World Report* 107:16 N 6 '89
Religious institutions and affairs
Church leaders support native claim [Lummi Indians vs. development of Madrona Point, Orcas Island, Wash.] J. Magnuson. *The Christian Century* 106:276-7 Mr 15 '89
Restaurants, nightclubs, bars, etc.
Seattle crew. B. H. Fussell. il *The New York Times Magazine* p57-8 Ap 9 '89
Theater
Modern storytellers. M. Wade. il *Horizon (Tuscaloosa, Ala.)* 32:44-7 Ja/F '89
Chinatown
See Chinatown (Seattle, Wash.)

SEATTLE ART MUSEUM
An open invitation. K. Simmons. il *Horizon (Tuscaloosa, Ala.)* 32:48 Ja/F '89

SEATTLE CENTRAL COMMUNITY COLLEGE
Maritime maneuvers [Marine technology facility designed by Miller/Hull Partnership] P. M. Sachner. il *Architectural Record* 177:118-19 F '89

SEATTLE OPERA
Making headlines. J. Bultmann. il *Horizon (Tuscaloosa, Ala.)* 32:49 Ja/F '89
Musical events:
Die Meistersinger. A. Porter. *The New Yorker* 65:100+ S 25 '89
Northern Pacific [interview with general manager S. Jenkins] S. Von Buchau. il por *Opera News* 53:14-17 Mr 18 '89

SEATTLE SYMPHONY ORCHESTRA
Symphonic success. K. Simmons. il *Horizon (Tuscaloosa, Ala.)* 32:43 Ja/F '89

SEAVER, PAUL S.
A social contract? Master against servant in the Court of Requests. il *History Today* 39:50-6 S '89

SEAVERS, NAOMI TUTU- See Tutu-Seavers, Naomi
SEAWATER See Sea water
SEAWEED
See also
Kelp
Collecting seaweed by the seashore—nature's natural soother [use in skin care] P. Lister. il *American Health* 8:26-8+ Ap '89

SEAWOLF SUBMARINES See Nuclear submarines
SEBA See Southeast Booksellers Association
SEBASTIAN, JOHN
Woodstock remembered: the artists. il pors *Rolling Stone* p84 Ag 24 '89

SEBOLD, ALICE
Speaking of the unspeakable. il *The New York Times Magazine* p16+ F 26 '89

SEC See United States. Securities and Exchange Commission
SECK, MAMADOU
Mock lion and real heroes. il *The Unesco Courier* 42:16-18 D '89

SECOND ADVENT
See also
Millennium
The year 1000 [excerpt from AD 1000] R. Erdoes. il *Psychology Today* 23:44-5 My '89
Anecdotes, facetiae, satire, etc.
He's back!!! [public relations consultants offer advice for the Second Coming of Jesus Christ; cover story] il *Harper's* 278:47-55 Ap '89
Of many things [public relations for Christ's Second Coming] G. W. Hunt. *America* 160:282 Ap 1 '89

SECOND CHANCE (FIRM)
Thar's gold, white gold, in them thar ponds, and golf ball hunter Jim Reid is diving to claim it. A. Abrahams. il *People Weekly* 31:67-8 Je 12 '89

SECOND COMMITTEE (UNITED NATIONS) See United Nations. Economic and Financial Committee
SECOND HONEYMOON See Honeymoon
SECOND OPINION (MEDICAL CONSULTATION)
Second opinions: first, talk to your insurer. D. H. Dunn. il *Business Week* p142 Je 5 '89
Vital opinions. G. Kolata. il *The New York Times Magazine* p46-7 Ap 16 '89
When once is not enough. E. E. Rosenbaum. il *New Choices for the Best Years* 29:30+ O '89
When they say it's cancer. G. Kolata. *Reader's Digest* 135:151-3 S '89

SECOND SIGHT [film] See Motion picture reviews—Single works
SECONDARY EDUCATION
See also
Coalition of Essential Schools
High schools
Education in France: renewal in the secondary schools; tr. by John L. Farrand. D. Salin. *America* 160:587-90 Je 17-24 '89
Is there a crisis in British secondary schools? H. G. Judge. bibl f *Phi Delta Kappan* 70:813-16 Je '89

SECONDARY INFERTILITY See Infertility
SECONDHAND BICYCLES See Bicycles, Used
SECONDHAND BOOKS
See also
Booksellers and bookselling—Secondhand books
SECONDHAND FURNITURE See Furniture, Used
SECONDHAND TRADE
See also
Flea markets
Thrift shops and rummage sales
Masters of thrift. K. McManus. il *Changing Times* 43:59-63 F '89

SECRECY (LAW)
See also
Confidential communications
Trade secrets
SECRECY IN GOVERNMENT See Classified information; Official secrets
THE SECRET [film] See Motion picture reviews—Single works
SECRET CHAMBERS See Hiding places (Secret chambers, etc.)
SECRET CODES See Cryptography
THE SECRET RAPTURE [drama] See Hare, David
SECRET SERVICE
See also
Intelligence service
United States—History—Revolution, 1775-1783—Secret service
United States. Central Intelligence Agency
United States. Secret Service
Canada
See also
Royal Canadian Mounted Police
Soviet Union
See also
KGB
SECRET SERVICE (U.S.) See United States. Secret Service
SECRET SOCIETIES
See also
Ku Klux Klan

SECRETARIAT (RACE HORSE)
The baron of the bluegrass [death of Triple Crown winner] il *U.S. News & World Report* 107:25 O 16 '89
Big Red (1970-89). W. Nack. il *Sports Illustrated* 71:25-6 O 16 '89
Secretariat leaves the world behind one last time. il *People Weekly* 32:119 O 23 '89

SECRETARIAT OF THE UNITED NATIONS *See* United Nations. Secretariat

SECRETARIES
Dear Betty Harragan [secretary considers change of career] B. L. Harragan. il *Working Woman* 14:22+ Ag '89
Finding—and keeping—the perfect secretary. T. Segal. il *Business Week* p104-5 F 6 '89
Good-bye, Miss Phipps. O. Edwards. il *Gentlemen's Quarterly* 59:229-30+ D '89

Attitudes
Secretaries seek more recognition [Gallup poll] il *USA Today (Periodical)* 118:8 Ag '89

Supply and demand
Anybody take shorthand? M. Mabry. il *Newsweek* 114:42 S 18 '89

SECRETARIES (FURNITURE) *See* Desks

SECRETIONS
See also
Pheromones
Molecular sorting in the secretory pathway. K.-N. Chung and others. bibl f il *Science* 243:192-7a Ja 13 '89

SECRETS, OFFICIAL *See* Official secrets
SECRETS, PERSONAL *See* Personal secrets
SECRETS, TRADE *See* Trade secrets
SECTARIANISM (TERM)
The High Court's "S" word [sectarian used as synonym for religious] R. A. Baer. il *Christianity Today* 33:20-1 S 8 '89

SECTIONALISM *See* Regionalism
SECTS
See also
Amish
Hutterian Brethren
Mormons and Mormonism
Shakers
Unification Church
The success of the sects among Hispanics in the United States. J. J. Diaz Vilar. il *America* 160:174-5+ F 25 '89

SECULAR HUMANISM *See* Humanism
SECULARISM
Secular sermon [Western reaction to Khomeini's death threat against novelist S. Rushdie] H. Hertzberg. *The New Republic* 200:4+ Mr 20 '89

SECURA, ROGER D.
Digital peak detector. il *Radio-Electronics* 60:59-62 Ap '89
SECURE TELEPHONES *See* Telephone—Security measures
SECURITIES
See also
American depositary receipts
Asset-backed financing
Banks and banking—Securities handling
Beta (Securities measurement)
Blind pools (Securities)
Brokers
Certificates of credit card receivables
Certificates of participation
Clearing of securities
Convertible securities
Government securities
Initial public offerings (Securities)
Over-the-counter securities markets
Parking (Securities)
Pay-in-kind securities
Primes (Securities)
Private placements (Securities)
Scores (Securities)
Stock exchanges
Stocks
Stubs (Securities)
Tactical asset allocation (Investments)
Treasury bills and notes
Under-the-counter securities
See also subhead Securities under various subjects
Markets & investments. See issues of Business Week
Statistical spotlight. See issues of Forbes

Guaranty
Just how safe is that guaranteed investment? W. L. Updegrave. il *Money* 18:123-6+ Mr '89
What's a guarantee worth? M. Schifrin. il *Forbes* 144:88+ Jl 24 '89

Laws and regulations
See also
Corporations—Acquisitions and mergers—Laws and regulations
United States. Securities and Exchange Commission
A backlash against business? [special section] il *Business Week* p30-6 F 6 '89
Can we prevent another Black Monday? J. A. Grundfest. il *USA Today (Periodical)* 117:16-18 My '89
Federal securities and merger laws. *Congressional Digest* 68:68-9+ Mr '89

The feds finger an upstart raider, too [P. Bilzerian] D. Pauly. il por *Newsweek* 113:48 Ja 2 '89
Investors say: stop jerking us around! J. Edgerton. il *Money* 18:125-6 D '89
Is getting rich quick becoming a crime? [case of P. Bilzerian] C. Byron. il por *New York* 22:25-6 Je 12 '89
Lessons from the market's plunge [Friday the 13th drop] J. J. Curran. il *Fortune* 120:97-8 N 20 '89
Living off the spread [B. L. Madoff takes advantage of New York Stock Exchange rule that protects specialists] R. L. Stern. il *Forbes* 144:66-7 Jl 10 '89
Make room in prison for market-riggers, too. G. Weiss. il *Business Week* p82 Ja 23 '89
Real victim of the takeover fever [address, April 7, 1989] J. A. Katarincic. *Vital Speeches of the Day* 55:540-4 Je 15 '89
Regulate the Wall Street casino. L. Lowenstein. il por *Fortune* 119:125-6 F 27 '89
Wall Street is glued to the Bilzerian trial. M. Galen. il por *Business Week* p33 My 15 '89

Brazil
Blame it on Nahas [stock market crash] J. Ryser. *Business Week* p40 Jl 3 '89

Costa Rica
Taken to the cleaners in Costa Rica [scam launched by International Swiss Investments Corp.] G. DeGeorge. il por *Business Week* p78 Ja 23 '89
You can run—but maybe you can't hide in Cuba [penny stock fraud scam by L. Zrnic of International Swiss Investments] G. DeGeorge. il por *Business Week* p27 Mr 6 '89

Switzerland
Bonds that bind [Swiss court intervention in Kohlberg Kravis Roberts' bid for RJR Nabisco] D. Fanning. il *Forbes* 143:48 My 1 '89
The three-percent solution. J. Marcom, Jr. il *Forbes* 143:68 My 29 '89

Western Europe
The future of the European stock exchange system approaching 1992 [address, April 29, 1989] R. V. Rosen. *Vital Speeches of the Day* 56:49-53 N 1 '89

Lending
'The business nobody wants to talk about' [stock loan abuses] J. Friedman. il *Business Week* p196+ S 25 '89

Marketing
See also
Specialists (Stock exchange firms)
Deals of the year. R. Henkoff. il *Fortune* 119:162-4+ Ja 30 '89

Mathematical models
Can you beat the Street? D. R. Katz. il *Esquire* 112:81-2 N '89

Prospectuses
Prostitution goes public [prospectus for public stock offering by Mustang Ranch] *Harper's* 278:21-2 My '89
When it sounds too good to be true. G. Slutsker. il *Forbes* 143:256-7 Je 26 '89

Registration
Another wall comes down [law permitting institutional investors to trade unregistered securities] C. Byron. il *New York* 22:16+ N 27 '89

Short selling
Advice to bears: hibernate. F. E. Rowe. il *Forbes* 144:344 Jl 24 '89
Charlie Keating in the Show Me state [American Continental Corp.'s bankruptcy hits broker R. Ruppert] G. Morgenson. il por *Forbes* 143:12 My 29 '89
Clear signs to sell short [Casey's General Stores] G. G. Marcial. *Business Week* p108 Mr 27 '89
Closing credits [C. Bronfman sells stake in Cineplex Odeon] J. Daly. *Maclean's* 102:34 Ap 24 '89
Meet big, bad bear Milton Berg. L. J. Nathans. il por *Business Week* p82 Je 19 '89
Should stocks take a tumble, short sellers could make a bundle. M. Schiffres. il *Changing Times* 43:128 O '89
What the short sellers love to hate now. L. Zinn. *Business Week* p162 O 23 '89
Where did I go wrong, doctor? F. E. Rowe. il por *Forbes* 144:301 O 16 '89

Taxation
Lost horizons [cover story] L. H. Summers. *The New Republic* 200:11-13 Je 26 '89
The silly push to tax stock trading. R. E. Norton. il *Fortune* 120:151+ D 18 '89
Tax the big casino. *The Nation* 249:189 Ag 21-28 '89
These swaps can keep you a step ahead of the taxman. S. Woolley. *Business Week* p180 N 13 '89
This penny-stock scam packs a one-two punch [brokers cross investors into another favorite stock] D. Zigas. *Business Week* p154 My 8 '89

Yields
20 ways to cash in on high yields [cover story] M. Schiffres. il *Changing Times* 43:30-9 Ap '89
Catching the crest of rising yields [cover story; special section] il *Money* 18:90-4+ Ap '89
Playing the highest rates. J. B. Quinn. il *Newsweek* 113:48 Mr 27 '89

SECURITIES—Yields—*cont.*
Putting together a portfolio with a 10% yield. il *Money* 18:7-8+ Jl '89

Austria

See also
Austria Fund

Canada

See also
Brokers—Canada
Government to sell 41.1 million shares of Air Canada stock, finish privatization. N. C. Kernstock. il *Aviation Week & Space Technology* 130:171-2 Je 19 '89
Reshaping an empire [Bronfmans to sell portion of Edper Enterprises to public] D. Jenish. *Maclean's* 102:43 My 29 '89

Developing countries

See also
Investment trusts—Developing countries

East Asia

How to win in Pac Rim stocks. J. J. Curran. il *Fortune* 120 no13 Special Issue:57+ Fall '89

Hong Kong

See also
Hong Kong Stock Exchange

Hungary

See also
Budapest Stock Exchange

Japan

See also
Brokers—Japan
Japan Tilt Fund
Over-the-counter securities markets—Japan
How to ride Japan Inc.'s raging bull. W. Glasgall and T. Holden. il *Business Week* p108 F 6 '89
Japan's investors say the best may be yet to come. T. Holden. il *Business Week* p120+ D 25 '89-Ja 1 '90
Thinking small in Tokyo. R. Phalon. il *Forbes* 143:198+ Je 26 '89
Tokyo's bull has further to run [interview with C. Mitchinson of Salomon Inc.] S. Solo. il por *Fortune* 120:43 Jl 3 '89
A top analyst sees Tokyo stocks soaring before the big bust [M. Ida] J. Ellis. il por *Money* 18:187-8 Mr '89

Soviet Union

See also
Treasury bills and notes—Soviet Union

Switzerland

See also
Swissbar (Firm)
The names of Zurich [views of H. Kaufmann] J. Marcom, Jr. il por *Forbes* 143:206+ Je 26 '89

Taiwan

See also
Taiwan Stock Exchange

Western Europe

Buying a Euro-stake that will thrive on the happenings of 1992. B. Dumaine. il *Fortune* 119:37-8 Ja 30 '89
The coming revival of Europe. M. K. Evans. il *Gentlemen's Quarterly* 59:131-2+ F '89
Europe: it's already 1992 [investing in European securities through mutual funds] J. B. Quinn. il *Newsweek* 114:63 N 20 '89
A European expedition [funds specializing in European stocks] E. Giltenan. il *Forbes* 144:172 S 4 '89
Investors are grabbing their checkbooks—and heading for Europe. B. Riemer. il *Business Week* p118-19 D 25 '89-Ja 1 '90
Two cheers for the new Europe. J. Reid. il *Money* 18:93-4+ Jl '89
The view from abroad: the hottest stocks in Europe for 1990. il *Money* 18:47+ D '89
Young funds with an eye on 1992 [U.S. mutual funds that invest in European stocks] L. J. Nathans. il *Business Week* p116 My 29 '89

SECURITIES, TAX EXEMPT
See also
Mortgage bonds and notes
Municipal bonds
SECURITIES AND EXCHANGE COMMISSION (U.S.) *See* United States. Securities and Exchange Commission
SECURITIES FRAUD *See* Investment fraud
SECURITIES INDUSTRY *See* Brokers
SECURITIZATION *See* Asset-backed financing
SECURITY, INTERNATIONAL *See* International security
SECURITY ANALYSTS *See* Investment advisers
SECURITY AND INSECURITY (PSYCHOLOGY)
Comforting habits [toddlers] J. T. Gibson. il *Parents* 64:208 D '89
"My blankie and me" [with editorial comment by Ann Pleshette Murphy] B. J. Berg. il *Parents* 64:6, 94-8+ Jl '89
Rock-a-bye toddler. J. T. Gibson. il *Parents* 64:210 N '89
Stamp out insecurity (yes, you can!). V. S. Brown. il *'Teen* 33:18+ Ap '89
SECURITY CLASSIFICATION (GOVERNMENT DOCU-MENTS) *See* Classified information
SECURITY COUNCIL (UNITED NATIONS) *See* United Nations. Security Council

SECURITY GUARDS
The new lions who guard the gates [security firms specializing in labor disputes] il *U.S. News & World Report* 107:46 Jl 24 '89
SECURITY SYSTEMS
See also
Air bases—Security measures
Alarms
Automobile boat trailers—Security measures
Automobiles—Security measures
Booksellers and bookselling—Security measures
Checkpoint Systems, Inc.
Chemical and biological weapons—Security measures
Colleges and universities—Security measures
Computers—Security measures
Embassies (Buildings)—Security measures
Industry—Security measures
Information systems—Security measures
Nuclear power plants—Security measures
Retail trade—Security measures
Rock concerts—Security measures
Telephone—Security measures
Putting the finger on security [biometrics] C. Garcia. il *Time* 133:79 Ap 3 '89
SEDATIVES
See also
Hypnotics
Tranquilizing drugs
SEDCO SYSTEMS, INC.
New type of phased-array antenna could cut cost, weight of airborne systems. il *Aviation Week & Space Technology* 131:105+ S 18 '89
SEDER
Between Passovers. R. R. Wisse. *Commentary* 88:42-7 D '89
A seder for peace in the Mideast. A. Waskow. il *The Nation* 248:557+ Ap 24 '89
SEDERBURG, WILLIAM A.
A legislator looks at academe. il *Change* 21:30-8 Ja/F '89
SEDGWICK, JOHN, 1954-
East to Eden. il *Gentlemen's Quarterly* 59:370-4+ Mr '89
The Hub's hub. il *Gentlemen's Quarterly* 59:93+ S '89
Kin ship. il *Gentlemen's Quarterly* 59:48+ Ag '89
The museum that eccentricity built. il *Gentlemen's Quarterly* 59:87+ N '89
SEDIMENTATION AND DEPOSITION
See also
Detritus
Marine sediments
Turbidity
Disorder-to-order transition in settling suspensions of colloidal silica: X-ray measurements. K. E. Davis and others. bibl f il *Science* 245:507-10 Ag 4 '89
Microbial life in deep terrestrial subsurfaces [sediments from Savannah River Plant] C. B. Fliermans and D. L. Balkwill. bibl f il *BioScience* 39:370-7 Je '89
SEDJO, ROGER A.
Forests: a tool to moderate global warming? bibl f il map *Environment* 31:14-20 Ja/F '89
SEE, CAROLYN
Why Australian writers keep their heads down. il *The New York Times Book Review* 94:1+ My 14 '89
SEE, LISA
West watch. See occasional issues of Publishers Weekly beginning September 2, 1983
SEE NO EVIL (MUSICAL GROUP)
See No Evil. I. Robbins. il *Rolling Stone* p32 N 16 '89
SEE NO EVIL, HEAR NO EVIL [film] See Motion picture reviews—Single works
SEE YOU IN THE MORNING [film] See Motion picture reviews—Single works
SEEBOHM, CAROLINE
The vicar's walk [excerpt from Private landscapes] il *House & Garden* 161:174-8 S '89
SEED, BRIAN
(jt. auth) See Allen, Janet M., and Seed, Brian
SEED, JOHN
about
John Seed and the Council of All Beings [interview] P. Stone. il por *The Mother Earth News* 117:58-63 My/Je '89
SEED BANKS *See* Germplasm resources—Plants
SEED CATALOGS *See* Catalogs, Seed and plant
SEED INDUSTRY
See also
Pioneer Hi-Bred International, Inc.
Select Seeds (Firm)
1989 gardeners' choice [cover story] V. Mattern. *Organic Gardening* 36:34-53 Ja '89
Detasselers wooed for big seed harvest [seed corn] il *Successful Farming* 87:57 Ap '89
Seed producers hustle for acres and detasselers [seed corn] *Successful Farming* 87 no4:64C Mr '89
Seeds that fill a niche. M. Lane. il *Successful Farming* 87:12-13 S '89

International aspects

Bad seeds in Nicaragua. B. Weinberg. *The Nation* 249:50+ Jl 10 '89

SEED INDUSTRY—cont.

Marketing

Seed prices up $2-$3 per acre. R. Fee. il *Successful Farming* 87:50AB Ja '89

SEED PRODUCTION *See* Seed industry

SEED SAVERS EXCHANGE

Heirlooms in your garden [cover story] J. R. Luoma. il *Audubon* 91:46-53 N '89

Looking for rare fruits? [Fruit, berry and nut inventory] *Sunset (Central West edition)* 183:196 O '89

SEED STARTING *See* Seeding

SEEDING

See also

Soybeans—Seeding

Get the garden going [bedding plants from seed] il *Southern Living* 24:48-9 Ja '89

Planting the seed. S. Ogden. il *Country Journal* 16:69-73 Mr/Ap '89

SEEDING MACHINERY *See* Planters (Farm machines)

SEEDS

See also

Cooking—Seeds

Corn—Seed

Germplasm resources—Plants

Grasses—Seed

Pine cones

Seed industry

Seed Savers Exchange

Vegetables—Seed

Inside seeds. N. Bubel. il *Country Journal* 16:65-6 F '89

SEEDS, FOSSIL

Fossils of Clarno Basin [nuts and seeds at John Day Fossil Beds in Oregon] C. H. Jones. il *Earth Science* 42:21-3 Spr '89

A novel fossil seed roils botany theory [work of Jean L. Galtier] I. Wickelgren. *Science News* 136:86 Ag 5 '89

SEEFELDT, CAROL

The Pledge of Allegiance in public schools. *The Education Digest* 55:62-3 S '89

Who meets the standards for early childhood teachers? *The Education Digest* 54:21-4 My '89

SEEFELDT, PAULA A.

Great 1990 gift calendars. il *Good Housekeeping* 209:271 N '89

SEEGAL, FREDERIC M.

Inside the market. il por *Channels (New York, N.Y.: 1986)* 9:89 Ja '89

SEEGER, PETE

about

Pete Seeger: keeping the dream. L. Ware. il por *Sierra* 74:82-6+ Mr/Ap '89

SEEING EYE DOGS *See* Guide dogs

SEELEY, DAVID

Anatomy of a breakup: . . . he says "There's nothing left to say". il *Mademoiselle* 95:144-5+ Jl '89

The lies men tell. il *Mademoiselle* 95:172-3+ Je '89

What boys really think about makeup. il *Seventeen* 48:52-3+ Jl '89

Who, him? Worry about his body? il *Mademoiselle* 95:258-9+ Ap '89

Why boys are so bad at breakups. il *Seventeen* 48:150-1+ O '89

SEELY, ALICE WARDER, 1942-

about

Alice Warder Seely. S. Marcus. il por *American Artist* 53:38-9 Ag '89

SEEPAGE

See also

Oil seepage

SEERSUCKER

Seersucker joins the ranks of the chic. T. Segal. il *Business Week* p184 Jl 17 '89

SEEWAGEN, BUTCH

Armed and ready. il *World Tennis* 37:14 D '89

Kids' stuff. il *World Tennis* 36:92-3 Ap '89

SEFTON, NANCY

Seafarers of the Caymans. bibl il map *Sea Frontiers* 35:106-13 Mr/Ap '89

The secret lives of sponges [cover story] bibl il *Sea Frontiers* 35:170-5 My/Je '89

SEGA (FIRM)

The other guys: zap or be zapped. M. Rogers. il *Newsweek* 113:66-7 Mr 6 '89

SEGAL, BARBARA HANDLER

about

As a tiny plastic star turns 30, the real Barbie and Ken reflect on life in the shadow of the dolls. M. Green. il pors *People Weekly* 31:186-7+ Mr 6 '89

SEGAL, JULIUS, 1924-, AND SEGAL, ZELDA

As they grow/5 and 6. See issues of Parents beginning July 1985

SEGAL, LORE GROSZMANN

Money, fame, and beautiful women [story] *The New Yorker* 65:28-36 Ag 28 '89

The reverse bug [story] *The New Yorker* 65:34-40 My 1 '89

SEGAL, ZELDA

(jt. auth) See Segal, Julius, 1924-, and Segal, Zelda

SEGALA, AMOS

The Archives Collection, a laboratory for the future. il *The Courier (Unesco)* 42:18-20 My '89

SEGRÉ, EMILIO

The discovery of nuclear fission. bibl f il por *Physics Today* 42:38-43 Jl '89

SEGREGATION

See also

Apartheid

Blacks—Segregation

Colleges and universities—Segregation

Country clubs—Segregation

Public schools—Segregation

Retirement communities—Segregation

SEGREGATION IN EDUCATION *See* Discrimination in education

SEGRETO, KARA

A college education: is it all in the game? *World Tennis* 36:90+ My '89

SEGUSO, ARCHIMEDE

about

Master of Murano. A. Duncan. il *House & Garden* 161:118 My '89

SEGUSO, ROBERT

(jt. auth) See Flach, Ken, and Seguso, Robert

SEI CENTER FOR ADVANCED STUDIES IN MANAGEMENT

Wharton's think tank. *Omni (New York, N.Y.)* 12:70 O '89

SEIBERT, GARY G.

All the world's a Habima. il *America* 160:395-9 Ap 29 '89

A conversation with Israeli playwright Joshua Sobol. *America* 160:559-62 Je 10 '89

SEIBERT, PETE

about

A vision fulfilled. W. O. Johnson. il pors *Sports Illustrated* 70:70-4+ Ja 30 '89

SEIBU GROUP

Joust of the half brothers [Y. and S. Tsutsumi] S. Kanise. il pors *Time* 133:46 Ja 23 '89

A radical retailer. S. Solo. il por *Fortune* 119:58-9 Ja 2 '89

SEIBU RAILWAY CO. LTD.

Joust of the half brothers [Y. and S. Tsutsumi] S. Kanise. il pors *Time* 133:46 Ja 23 '89

SEIDEL, GEORGE E.

Biotech on the farm: geneticists in the pasture. *Current (Washington, D.C.)* 316:21-6 O '89

Geneticists in the pasture. il *Technology Review* 92:42-50+ Ap '89

SEIDEL, MITCHELL

Benny Carter: a legend in process. il pors *Down Beat* 56:24-6 D '89

SEIDELMAN, RAYMOND

More than just Chinese racism. il *The Nation* 248:195-6 F 13 '89

SEIDELMAN, SUSAN

about

Cookie [film] Reviews

The New Yorker 65:90 S 4 '89. T. Rafferty

Newsweek 114:68 S 4 '89. D. Ansen

People Weekly il 32:17 S 11 '89. R. Novak

Rolling Stone il por p48 S 21 '89. P. Travers

Time il 134:64 Ag 28 '89. R. Corliss

She-devil [film] Reviews

American Film il 14:14 My '89. G. Kilday

American Film il 15:64 D '89. J. Ressner

Maclean's il 102:59 D 18 '89. B. D. Johnson

Newsweek 114:88 D 11 '89. D. Ansen

People Weekly il 32:18 D 18 '89. R. Novak

Time il 134:93 D 11 '89. R. Corliss

She devil [interview] D. DeNicolo. il por *Glamour* 87:158+ D '89

SEIDEN, HENRY M., 1940-

about

How sharing grief can ease the pain [interview] E. E. Goode. il por *U.S. News & World Report* 106:80 Ja 30 '89

SEIDENBERG, ROBERT

At long last, jazz. il pors *American Film* 14:50-4 My '89

Funny as hell [cover story] il pors *American Film* 14:42-7+ S '89

SEIDENSTEIN, SHARON

(jt. auth) See O'Neil, Carol, and Seidenstein, Sharon

SEIDENSTICKER, JOHN

Playing possum is serious business for our only marsupial; ed. by Susan Lumpkin. bibl (p246) il *Smithsonian* 20:108-12+ N '89

SEIDMAN, L. WILLIAM

about

'This is a dirty business' [interview] G. Hector. il pors *Fortune* 119:133-4+ My 22 '89

SEIFERT, EDWARD

The seagulls [poem] *America* 160:509 My 27 '89

SEIGNEURIE, KEN, AND NASSAR, TAREK

Hezbollah—sound and futile fury [cover story] il *The Nation* 249:225+ S 4-11 '89

SEIKO GROUP
The last emperor? G. Eisenstodt. il por *Forbes* 144:92+ O 2 '89

SEINE RIVER (FRANCE)
Cruisin' up the river. J. Gooding. il *Time* 133:74 Je 26 '89

SEINELDIN, MUHAMMAD ALI
about
Argentina after Villa Martelli. A. M. Shapiro. il *The New Leader* 72:11-12 Ja 9 '89

SEINFELD, JOHN H.
Urban air pollution: state of the science. bibl f il *Science* 243:745-52 F 10 '89

SEIPP, CATHERINE
Casual aristocrats: eclectic charm. il pors *Harper's Bazaar* 122:198-201+ O '89
Picture perfect. il pors *Harper's Bazaar* 122:118-21+ Ag '89

SEIPP, WALTER
Post-1992 Europe [address, January 12, 1989] *Vital Speeches of the Day* 55:300-3 Mr 1 '89

SEISMIC DETECTION OF NUCLEAR EXPLOSIONS *See* Nuclear weapons—Testing—Detection

SEISMIC SEA WAVES *See* Tsunamis

SEISMIC WAVES
High-rises rock to shuttle shock [research by Hiroo Kanamori] R. Monastersky. *Science News* 136:396 D 16 '89
Homing in on the longest animal [use of seismic tomography to find Seismosaurus fossils; work of David D. Gillette] R. Monastersky. *Science News* 136:413 D 23-30 '89
Snippets from Nyanja chronicles [conducting research on East African lakes] B. Rosendahl. il por map *Sea Frontiers* 35:292-302 S/O '89
The sound of silent earthquakes [research by Gregory C. Beroza and Thomas H. Jordan] R. Monastersky. *Science News* 135:335 My 27 '89

SEISMOLOGICAL RESEARCH *See* Seismometers and seismometry

SEISMOMETERS AND SEISMOMETRY
See also
Earthquake prediction
Helioseismology
Microearthquake imaging of the Parkfield asperity [San Andreas fault] P. E. Malin and others. bibl f il *Science* 244:557-9 My 5 '89

SEISMOSAURUS *See* Dinosaurs

SEITZ, BILL
about
Problems. *The New Yorker* 65:40-1 O 9 '89

SEITZ, RUSSELL
The Cup that ran amok. il *The American Spectator* 22:21-3 Je '89

SEIXAS, JUDITH S.
(jt. auth) See Youcha, Geraldine, and Seixas, Judith S.

SEIZURE OF VESSELS AND CARGOES
See also
Pirates

SEIZURES (MEDICINE) *See* Convulsions

SEIZURES AND SEARCHES *See* Searches and seizures

SEKHARUDU, Y. C.
(jt. auth) See Sundaralingam, M., and Sekharudu, Y. C.

SEKIGUCHI, RISA
about
Risa Sekiguchi at CompassRose. S. Taylor. *Art in America* 77:221 O '89

SEKO, MOBUTU SESE *See* Mobutu Sese Seko, 1930-

SELBOURNE, DAVID, 1937-
Marx is not quite dead. *World Press Review* 36:20+ O '89

SELDES, GEORGE, 1890-
The FBI and I. il *The Progressive* 53:50 F '89
about
George Seldes, grandfather of the alternative press. J. Walljasper. il por *Utne Reader* p142-3 Jl/Ag '89

SELDMAN, NEIL
Mass burn is dying. bibl f *Environment* 31:42-4 S '89

SELECT SEEDS (FIRM)
Seeds selected from the past [work of M. Barlow] J. Parente. il *Americana* 17:12 Mr/Ap '89

SELECTED AMERICAN SHARES, INC.
There's cash flow, and there's cash flow [views of D. Yacktman] J. Clements. il por *Forbes* 144:138+ S 18 '89

SELECTION, NATURAL *See* Natural selection

SELECTIVE SERVICE *See* Draft

SELECTIVE TERMINATION *See* Fetal reduction

SELEGILINE
An advance on Parkinson's. N. Underwood. *Maclean's* 102:69 N 27 '89
At last, a better drug for Parkinson's [deprenyl] *U.S. News & World Report* 107:14 N 27 '89
Big first scored with nerve diseases [results of deprenyl trials; research by James Tetrud and William Langston] R. Lewin. il *Science* 245:467-8 Ag 4 '89
Brain defender [use of deprenyl to treat Parkinson's disease] *Time* 134:56 N 27 '89
Drug delays Parkinson's progression [deprenyl; research by Caroline M. Tanner] *Science News* 136:365 D 2 '89
Drug slows Parkinson's progression [deprenyl; research by James W. Tetrud and J. William Langston] K. Fackelmann. *Science News* 136:84 Ag 5 '89

The effect of deprenyl (selegiline) on the natural history of Parkinson's disease. J. W. Tetrud and J. W. Langston. bibl f il *Science* 245:519-22 Ag 4 '89
Parkinson's breakthrough [deprenyl] G. Cowley. il *Newsweek* 114:78 N 27 '89

SELENIA INDUSTRIE ELETTRONICHE ASSOCIATE SPA
Selenia developing new version of Aspide multirole missile. J. M. Lenorovitz. il *Aviation Week & Space Technology* 131:51 D 4 '89

SELENIUM IN THE BODY
Nuts about selenium [Brazil nuts] R. A. Barnett. il *American Health* 8:149 Mr '89

SELES, MONIKA
about
Not until she's good and ready. J. E. Loehr. il por *World Tennis* 37:22+ Je '89

SELF, LEE S.
Bednets that kill mosquitos. il *World Health* p20-2 N '89

SELF
See also
Consciousness
Identity (Psychology)
Individuality
Mind and body
Personality
First word [growing up in a troubled family] C. L. Whitfield. por *Omni (New York, N.Y.)* 11:6 Je '89

SELF (PHILOSOPHY)
Eastern cultures experts on "self". R. Williams. *The Humanist* 49:40 N/D '89

SELF ACTUALIZATION *See* Self realization

SELF AWARENESS *See* Self perception; Self realization

SELF CARE, MEDICAL *See* Medical care

SELF CONCEPT *See* Self perception

SELF CONFIDENCE
See also
Overconfidence
Raise your "notice-me-ability" [quiz] il *Teen* 33:50+ Ag '89
Social jitters: from awkward to awesome. il *Teen* 33:26-8 F '89

SELF CONSCIOUSNESS
See also
Bashfulness

SELF CONTROL
Delay of gratification in children. W. Mischel and others. bibl f il *Science* 244:933-8 My 26 '89
No-fault psychology. C. Tavris. *Vogue* 179:116 Ja '89
Preschool self-control and pretzel logic [research by Walter Mischel] B. Bower. *Science News* 135:325 My 27 '89

SELF CRITICISM *See* Criticism, Personal

SELF CULTURE *See* Self improvement

SELF DEFENSE
Do guns save lives? E. Magnuson. il *Time* 134:25-6 Ag 21 '89
Protection [use of firearms in self defense; views of S. D'Andrilli] *The New Yorker* 64:22-3 Ja 9 '89
Should you own a gun for protection? [interviews with D. B. Kates and G. Napper] il *U.S. News & World Report* 106:28 My 8 '89

Anecdotes, facetiae, satire, etc.
Conan and me. B. Persky. il *Esquire* 111:34+ My '89

SELF DEFENSE FOR WOMEN
See also
Model Mugging (Program)
The Central Park rape: has it made us angry? Scared? Or smart? L. Mosedale. il *Glamour* 87:212-13+ Ag '89
Defensive exercising. *Glamour* 87:28+ Jl '89
Defensive moves [safety while exercising] R. Mayer. il *Health (New York, N.Y.)* 21:90-1 S '89
For the ladies, a .38 caliber [Smith & Wesson's gun ads targeted at women] il *Newsweek* 113:48 F 27 '89
For the woman who has everything [dummy called Gregory] il *Newsweek* 112:64 My 22 '89
Guns à la mode [designer handguns] B. G. Harrison. *Mademoiselle* 95:140 Mr '89
How to come to your own defense. S. Pocharski. *Mademoiselle* 95:227+ S '89
Let's be careful out there [runners] J. Ullyot. il por *Runner's World* 24:26 S '89
Pistols for the women of America [Smith & Wesson's Lady Smith revolver targeted at women; cover story] L. C. Pogrebin. *The Nation* 248:649+ My 15 '89
Up in arms [women and gun control] J. Torrey. *Harper's Bazaar* 122:64+ Jl '89
When a woman drives alone. S. Nelson. il *Reader's Digest* 134:157-60 Ap '89
Women and crime: is this the answer? [handgun ownership; excerpt from Armed and female] P. Quigley. il *Glamour* 87:344-5+ Ap '89
You can talk your way out of a rape. L. Jack. il *Mademoiselle* 95:98 Je '89

SELF DEFENSE IN ANIMALS *See* Defense mechanisms (Biology)

SELF DEPENDENCE *See* Self reliance

SELF DESTRUCTION *See* Suicide

SELF DESTRUCTIVE BEHAVIOR
"Just say no" is not enough. J. P. Comer. il *Parents* 64:216 My '89

SELF DIAGNOSIS *See* Diagnosis
SELF DISCIPLINE *See* Self control
SELF DISCLOSURE
Are you tired of turning on TV and being turned off by the new breed confessors? L. Wyse. il *Good Housekeeping* 209:198 Ag '89
Bare your soul and beat disease [excerpt from Healthy pleasures] R. E. Ornstein and D. S. Sobel. il *Prevention (Emmaus, Pa.)* 41:100+ Jl '89
SELF EDUCATION *See* Self improvement
SELF EMPLOYED
See also
Entrepreneurs
Home-based business
Independent contractors
SELF ESTEEM *See* Self respect
SELF EVALUATION
See also
Criticism, Personal
Self perception
SELF EXAMINATION OF THE BREAST *See* Breast—Examination
SELF FULFILLMENT *See* Self realization
SELF HELP GROUPS
Easing the anguish [support groups available to couples choosing to abort a pregnancy] M. Krance. il *American Health* 8:14 Jl/Ag '89
Help yourself to self-help. E. Franklin. il *American Health* 8:22 Ap '89
In rehab with the love junkies. E. Schappell. *Mademoiselle* 95:217+ O '89
Mother to mother. E. Klavan. il *Parents* 64:74+ F '89
A place to belong. G. Levoy. il *Health (New York, N.Y.)* 21:54-7 F '89
When prenatal tests bring bad news [lack of support groups available for couples choosing to abort pregnancies] M. Krance. bibl il *American Health* 8:11-12 Jl/Ag '89
Germany (West)
Support groups spread in West Germany. *The Futurist* 23:44-5 Ja/F '89
SELF HELP LITERATURE
See also
Publishers and publishing—Self help literature
Bibliotherapy [titles recommended by psychologists; survey by Steven Starker] S. McKee. bibl il *American Health* 8:42 D '89
Individualism unbound: reconsidering modern-day romance [popularity of self help books] J. Henkin. il *Utne Reader* p64-6+ Mr/Ap '89
Off-the-shelf salvation. E. Stark. il *Health (New York, N.Y.)* 21:28-30 Jl '89
Rx: 2 self-help books and call me in the morning [views of psychologists] E. Stark. bibl il *Psychology Today* 23:26 Je '89
Stop blaming men for everything! (A guy begs for mercy) A. Heard. il *Mademoiselle* 95:182-3+ Ag '89
When self-help books can help. J. Wasser. bibl il *Mademoiselle* 95:118 D '89
Bibliography
Advice and consent. E. Hopkins. *Harper's Bazaar* 122:201+ Ap '89
SELF IMAGE *See* Self perception
SELF IMPROVEMENT
Anecdotes, facetiae, satire, etc.
I was a flirtatious backwalker for the CIA. J. Harkison. il *Smithsonian* 20:128 Jl '89
SELF IMPROVEMENT LITERATURE *See* Self help literature
SELF INTEREST
Social commitment: beyond self-interest. R. H. Frank. *Current (Washington, D.C.)* 316:4-13 O '89
SELF LOVE *See* Narcissism; Self respect
SELF MUTILATION
See also
Hair pulling
SELF ORGANIZING SYSTEMS
Digging into sand [sandpile avalanches and self-organized criticality; cover story] I. Peterson. il *Science News* 136:40-2 Jl 15 '89
Esoteric borrowing from physics. R. Pool. *Science* 245:702 Ag 18 '89
SELF PERCEPTION
See also
Body image
Getting people to give [concerns over self image; research by Robert Cialdini and others] W. Herbert. il *Psychology Today* 22:66 D '88
To know you is to love you [study by Ann Baumgardner] P. King. *Psychology Today* 23:73 Ja/F '89
SELF PUBLISHING
A rising career for Roger Bansemer [artist who published his own book on ballooning] M. E. Stegmaier. il por *American Artist* 53:58-63+ Ag '89
Savvy marketer learns about publishing . . . and vice versa? [experiences of P. C. Gallagher] M. Reuter. il por *Publishers Weekly* 236:13 Ag 4 '89
Self-publishers print 100,000 copies (and survive!) [work of P. Young and P. Jones] J. Barbato. *Publishers Weekly* 236:42 N 10 '89

SELF REALIZATION
Changing values: the new emphasis on self-actualization [cover story] J. T. Plummer. il por *The Futurist* 23:8-13 Ja/F '89
How to get lucky in life [excerpt from You'll see it when you believe it] W. W. Dyer. *Redbook* 173:120-1+ Jl '89
Self-fulfillment through service to others. T. Malone. *The Humanist* 49:24+ Ja/F '89
SELF RELIANCE
The age of independence [with editorial comment by Ann Pleshette Murphy] F. B. Maynard. il *Parents* 64:6, 122-5+ Ap '89
Are you getting your child's messages? B. Weissbourd. il *Parents* 64:172 F '89
Encouraging independence [children] B. Weissbourd. il *Parents* 64:144 Ag '89
Escape from autonomy. K. Kolenda. il *The Humanist* 49:37 Mr/Ap '89
Letting go [teenagers] D. Elkind. il *Parents* 64:185 F '89
Return to babyhood. L. G. Katz. il *Parents* 64:231 O '89
"You can do it!". S. Isaacs. il *Parents* 64:114-18 F '89
SELF RESPECT
Just the way you are. R. Coles. il *New Choices for the Best Years* 29:92+ Ap '89
Like yourself! 10 ways. W. Woodward. il *'Teen* 33:36+ Jl '89
"My son needed to feel needed" [learning disabled teenage volunteer] M. B. White. il *Parents* 64:84+ Ap '89
To know you is to love you [study by Ann Baumgardner] P. King. *Psychology Today* 23:73 Ja/F '89
SELF REVELATION *See* Self disclosure
SELF SUFFICIENCY *See* Self reliance
SELIG, ALLAN H.
about
A crucial inning for baseball. W. C. Symonds. il por *Business Week* p90 O 23 '89
SELIGER, SUSAN
Ways to reduce holiday stress. il *McCall's* 116:100+ Ja '89
SELIGMAN, DANIEL
The case of Michael Levin. *National Review* 41:38-40 My 5 '89
Keeping up. See issues of Fortune
SELIGMAN (J. & W.) & CO. INC. *See* J. & W. Seligman & Co. Inc.
SELIMUDDIN, ABU K.
The selling of America [cover story] il *USA Today (Periodical)* 117:12-14 Mr '89
Will America become #2? il *USA Today (Periodical)* 118:14-16 S '89
SELKIRK, ANDREW
1988 Archaeological Book of the Year Award. il *History Today* 39:51 Ja '89
SELKIRK COMMUNICATIONS LIMITED
Assuring the regulators [Maclean Hunter Ltd.'s purchase of Selkirk] J. DeMont. il *Maclean's* 102:36 Je 12 '89
SELLARS, PETER
about
Dark victory. P. G. Davis. il *New York* 22:48-9 Ag 7 '89
Grand finale. R. Marx. il *Opera News* 54:14-16+ Jl '89
Parallel bars [Conversations with fear and hope after death] P. G. Davis. il pors *New York* 22:78 Ap 17 '89
Peter Sellars's Mozart. E. W. Said. *The Nation* 249:289-91 S 18 '89
SELLARS, RICHARD WEST
Science or scenery? il *Wilderness* 52:28-39 Summ '89
SELLECCA, CONNIE
about
Can't sing. Can't cook. But she thinks she can make you laugh. G. Esterly. il pors *TV Guide* 37:30-1+ N 18-24 '89
SELLECK, TOM
about
Magnum, P(retty) I(ndecisive) [cover story] P. Jordan. il pors *Gentlemen's Quarterly* 59:278-81+ O '89
Tom Selleck: one man and a baby. P. Leigh. il por *Ladies' Home Journal* 106:38+ Mr '89
Tom Selleck settles down . . . N. Gittelson. il pors *McCall's* 116:83-4+ F '89
SELLING
See also
Direct selling
Marketing
Sales personnel
Fear of selling and 6 ways to overcome it. P. Edwards and S. Edwards. il *Home Office Computing* 7:18 S '89
How to sell and negotiate like a pro. P. Edwards and S. Edwards. il *Home Office Computing* 7:38 Je '89
What every manager needs to know about sales. R. Welch. il *Working Woman* 14:96-8+ Ja '89
Bibliography
Into the heart of selling. M. Estren. il *High Technology Business* 9:9 Jl/Ag '89
SELLING BY TELEPHONE *See* Telephone selling
SELLING OF SMALL BUSINESSES *See* Small business, Sale of

SELLINGS, DAVID
about
Attack from the ocean deep. S. Kelly. il *Reader's Digest* 134:67-72 F '89
SELLNER, EDWARD C.
Lay leadership in the 1990's [cover story] *America* 161:133-8 S 9-16 '89
SELMA (ALA.)
Politics and government
King's dream becomes a reality in Selma [black commissioners sworn in] il *Jet* 75:10-11 F 13 '89
SELTH, JEFFERSON P., 1930-
OP books: a popular delusion. por *Publishers Weekly* 235:78 Ja 6 '89
SELTZER, DAVID
about
Punchline [film] Reviews
Video 12:62-3 Mr '89. R. Granger
SELVIN, PAUL
Graduate students make history. *The Progressive* 53:19 O '89
SELZNICK, DAVID O., 1902-1965
about
Unforgettable Gone with the wind. J. Culhane. il *Reader's Digest* 135:146-51 D '89
SEMATECH
Hands across the chipmaking chasm [U.S. Memories and Sematech to work with JESSI Project] O. Port. *Business Week* p28-9 Jl 3 '89
High tech's fickle helping hand [White House wavers on funding] P. Elmer-Dewitt. il *Time* 134:68 D 4 '89
How the U.S. can compete globally [interview with R. Noyce] il por *Fortune* 119:248 Je 5 '89
Keeping semiconductors safe for democracy. D. Charles. il *The Bulletin of the Atomic Scientists* 45:8-10 N '89
A transatlantic Mexican standoff [exclusion of foreign-owned firms from research consortiums] D. Dickson. il *Science* 245:245-6 Jl 21 '89
Will the White House torpedo America Inc.? J. Carey. il *Business Week* p80 N 27 '89
SEMELE [oratorio] See Handel, George Frideric, 1685-1759
SEMESTER AT SEA (PROGRAM)
My Semester at Sea. M. R. Barnwell. il pors *Essence* 20:23+ Ag '89
SEMI-PRO BASEBALL See Baseball, Semi-pro
SEMI-TECH MICROELECTRONICS (FAR EAST) LTD.
Forging new links [bid for SSMC] T. Fennell. il pors *Maclean's* 102:26-8 F 20 '89
Who is James Ting and what will he buy next? [SSMC] C. Hawkins. il por *Business Week* p33 F 13 '89
SEMIAUTOMATIC WEAPONS See Assault rifles
SEMICONDUCTOR INDUSTRY See Electronic industries
SEMICONDUCTOR MANUFACTURING TECHNOLOGY INSTITUTE See Sematech
SEMICONDUCTOR WAFERS
Manufacture
See Electronic industries
SEMICONDUCTORS
See also
Charge coupled devices (Electronics)
Gallium arsenide semiconductors
Mesoscopic physics
Metal oxide semiconductors
Silicon
Transistors
The chemistry of solid-state electronics. E. Yablonovitch. bibl f il *Science* 246:347-51 O 20 '89
Diamond chips [semiconductor production and doping through carbon in bombardment of silicon; work of Wayne Rabalais] *Discover* 10:12 Jl '89
Electron waves could breed new semiconductors. *High Technology Business* 9:33-4 Mr '89
Semiconductor studies get a rise from yeast. F. Flam. *Science News* 135:231 Ap 15 '89
Ultrafast dynamics at semiconductor and metal surfaces [laser experiments] J. Bokor. bibl f il *Science* 246:1130-4 D 1 '89
USAF stresses development of semiconductor laser. il *Aviation Week & Space Technology* 130:57-8 Ja 30 '89
SEMIGLOSS PAINT See Paint
SEMINARIANS
'Second career' students turn to divinity schools. il *Jet* 75:39 Mr 27 '89
SEMINARIES See Theological seminaries
SEMINARS
See also
Investment seminars
SENATE (CANADA) See Canada. Parliament. Senate
SENATE (U.S.) See United States. Congress. Senate
SENATOROV, VASSILI
If Columbus had a bike. il *Bicycling* 30:164-5 Ap '89
SENATORS
What happens to a senator's day. J. Boyd. *The Washington Monthly* 21:48-9 F '89

Campaign funds
See Campaign funds
Conflict of interests
See Conflict of interests (Public office)
Rating
Mr. Superliberal [C. Pell] D. Seligman. il *Fortune* 119:195-6 Je 19 '89
Portrait of a liberal [highest liberal rankings] D. Seligman. il *Fortune* 119:341 Je 5 '89
Retirement
Putting children before politics [work of former senator L. Chiles] D. Olin. il por *New Choices for the Best Years* 29:16+ Jl '89
Staff
Blacks lacking on staffs of U.S. senators: report. il *Jet* 75:12-13 Mr 27 '89
Meredith readies for post on Sen. Jesse Helms' staff, black leaders bristling [J. Meredith] il pors *Jet* 77:12-13 O 16 '89
SENDAK, MAURICE
about
Taming the Wild Things. M. H. Lystad. bibl f il *Children Today* 18:16-19 Mr/Ap '89
SENDERO LUMINOSO (GUERRILLA GROUP)
Bloody footprints on Peru's Shining Path. il *U.S. News & World Report* 107:49 S 18 '89
A Christian spirituality of nonviolence. E. W. Ranly. *America* 161:110-11+ Ag 26-S 2 '89
Cocaine, communism and crisis in Peru. C. A. Robbins. il *U.S. News & World Report* 107:45-9 S 18 '89
Lurching toward anarchy. G. D. Garcia. il *Time* 133:54 Mr 27 '89
Peru fights to overcome its past. A. Riding. il por *The New York Times Magazine* p40+ My 14 '89
Terrorism, inflation, and debt threaten democracy in Peru [interview with E. Zileri] A. Balk. il por *World Press Review* 36:33-5 Ja '89
With the Shining Path. J. Contreras. il map *Newsweek* 113:44-5+ Ap 24 '89
SENECA LAKE (N.Y.)
Big lakers on Seneca [trout] T. P. Maguire. il *The Conservationist* 43:10-13 My/Je '89
SENEGAL
See also
Festivals—Senegal
Senegalese
SENEGALESE
United States
Street selling [vendors in New York City] *The New Yorker* 65:27-8 Jl 3 '89
SENESCENCE See Aging
SENGHOR, LÉOPOLD SÉDAR, 1906-
The written word . . . il *The Courier (Unesco)* 42:4 My '89
SENIGALLIA, SILVIO F.
How the Italians see Europe. *The New Leader* 72:8 Je 12-26 '89
Italian justice on the run. il *The New Leader* 72:10-11 S 4 '89
Italy watches an empire stumble. il *The New Leader* 72:10-11 O 30 '89
Italy's DC recycles Forlani. il *The New Leader* 72:9-10 Mr 6 '89
One Europe indivisible? il *The New Leader* 72:5-6 Ja 23 '89
SENILE MACULAR DEGENERATION See Macular degeneration
SENILITY
See also
Alzheimer's disease
SENIOR, WALTER
about
The screen wars. J. Daly. il pors *Maclean's* 102:40-1 My 29 '89
SENIOR CENTERS
Starting a senior center latchkey program. *Children Today* 18:5 Jl/Ag '89
SENIOR CITIZENS See Aged
SENIOR OLYMPICS
Silver threads among the gold (medals) [U.S. National Senior Olympics] D. Stathoplos. il *Sports Illustrated* 71:38-41 Jl 3 '89
Photographs and photography
Victories of the spirit. M. E. Mark. il *The New York Times Magazine* p28-31 Ag 27 '89
SENIOR PROFESSIONAL BASEBALL ASSOCIATION
The boys of winter. S. Wulf. il *Sports Illustrated* 71:28-33 N 20 '89
Never having to grow up. R. Corliss. il *Time* 134:76 D 18 '89
The twilight boys. F. Adams. il *Maclean's* 102:58-9 N 13 '89
SENIORITY, EMPLOYEE
See also
Promotions
The numbers game [seniority system and air pilots] L. Morgan. il *Flying* 116:118-19 Je '89

SENNA, AYRTON
about
The 1988 Grand Prix season: setting records. J. Thompson. il por *Road & Track* 40:126-7+ Ap '89
Encore, encore! R. Walker. il pors *Road & Track* 40:108-10+ Ag '89
Original Senna. D. Phipps. il pors *Car and Driver* 34:125+ F '89
Quibbles & bits. I. Ireland. il por *Road & Track* 40:114-16+ Ag '89
Senna's single. R. Walker. il por *Road & Track* 41:78-81 S '89
Senna's surprise. I. Ireland. il pors *Road & Track* 41:120-2+ N '89
Splash & dash. I. Ireland. il *Road & Track* 41:132-5 D '89
Winners & losers. I. Ireland. il por *Road & Track* 40:106-8+ Mr '89

SENNHAUSER, JOHN, 1907-1978
about
John Sennhauser: Struve. S. Taylor. il *Art News* 88:154 Ja '89

SENSATION See Senses and sensation
SENSE OF HUMOR See Humor
SENSE ORGANS
See also
Ear
Eye
Mouth
Photoreceptors
Senses and sensation
Sensory receptors

SENSER, ROBERT A.
How Poland's Solidarity won freedom of association. bibl f *Monthly Labor Review* 112:34-8 S '89

SENSES AND SENSATION
See also
Brain
Hearing
Pain
Perception
Pleasure
Smell
Synesthesia
Taste
Time perception
Touch
Vision
Pitfalls of perception. A. G. Wheeler. *Utne Reader* p100 N/D '89
Sensory function in the harbor seal. D. Renouf. bibl il map *Scientific American* 260:90-5 Ap '89
When our senses grow old . . . L. J. Brown. il *Good Housekeeping* 208:170-1 Ja '89

SENSING, REMOTE See Remote sensing
SENSORS See Detectors
SENSORS, BIOMEDICAL See Biosensors
SENSORS, INFRARED See Detectors, Infrared
SENSORY RECEPTORS
Cnidocyte mechanoreceptors are tuned to the movements of swimming prey by chemoreceptors [cover story] G. M. Watson and D. A. Hessinger. bibl f il *Science* 243:1589-91 Mr 24 '89
Genetic control of differentiation of the Caenorhabditis elegans touch receptor neurons. M. Chalfie and M. Au. bibl f il *Science* 243:1027-33 F 24 '89
Odor-induced membrane currents in vertebrate-olfactory receptor neurons. S. Firestein and F. Werblin. bibl f il *Science* 244:79-82 Ap 7 '89
What tells anemones to kill their enemies? [research by Glen M. Watson and David A. Hessinger] R. Weiss. *Science News* 135:182 Mr 25 '89

SENTENCES (CRIMINAL JUSTICE) See Criminal justice, Administration of
SENTENCING CONSULTANTS
Personalized penalties [alternative sentences arranged by consultants] T. Gest. il *U.S. News & World Report* 107:75-6 N 20 '89

SENZ, LAURIE S.
Juvenile periodontitis: no laughing matter. il *The Saturday Evening Post* 261:76 My/Je '89

SEOUL OLYMPICS, 1988 See Olympic Games—1988—Summer Olympics
SEP See Société Européenne de Propulsion
SEPARATION (PSYCHOLOGY)
See also
Maternal deprivation
First vacation after the baby. L. Schnurnberger. il *Parents* 64:114-18 D '89
Letting go. R. Parke. por *The Humanist* 49:25 Mr/Ap '89
The little red chair. L. Franks. il *The New York Times Magazine* p28+ Mr 12 '89
Time out for busy parents [vacations without children] B. Spock. por *Redbook* 173:30 Je '89
When you can't let go [ending a relationship] G. Schwartz. il *Seventeen* 48:124 Ap '89

SEPARATION (TECHNOLOGY)
See also
Chromatographic analysis
Cytology—Methodology
Electrophoresis
Membranes (Technology)
Sperm sorter ensures sex-linked litters [livestock breeding] *Science News* 136:175 S 9 '89

SEPARATION OF POWERS
See also
Executive privilege (Government information)
Judicial power
Presidents—Powers and duties
United States. Congress—Powers and duties
The godfather of the American Constitution [Montesquieu] R. Wernick. il *Smithsonian* 20:183-4+ S '89
Hamilton made me do it. M. Greenfield. il *Newsweek* 113:88 Mr 20 '89

SEPS See Simplified employee pensions
SEPTEMBER
The September almanac. il *The Atlantic* 264:16 S '89
SEPTIC TANKS
Pumped septics. N. Stuart. il *Popular Science* 234:84 My '89
Secrets of the septic system. R. Freudenberger. il *The Mother Earth News* 116:108-12+ Mr/Ap '89

SÉPTIMA (BOGOTÁ, COLOMBIA: STREET) See Bogotá (Colombia)—Streets
SEPULCHRAL MONUMENTS
Conservation and restoration
See also
Church Monuments Society

SEQUELS (MOTION PICTURES) See Motion picture sequels
SEQUENT COMPUTER SYSTEMS INC.
Many hands make light work. J. Heins. il *Forbes* 143:275+ My 29 '89
SEQUENTIAL INFORMATION SYSTEMS INC.
The sad saga of a penny-stock company. G. Weiss. il por *Business Week* p124-6+ My 15 '89
SEQUESTERING AGENTS
See also
Ethylenediamine tetraacetic acid
SEQUINS
Skin, burnished and smooth, is the perfect foil for the glitter of sequins. L. Cunliffe. il *Vogue* 179:340-5 Ag '89
SEQUOIA NATIONAL FOREST (CALIF.)
Park-quality sequoias logged. il *National Parks* 63:8-9 My/Je '89
These woods are made for burning [fire studies of giant sequoia groves] R. Kunzig. il map *Discover* 10:86-7+ Mr '89
Unsung sequoias. il map *Sunset (Central West edition)* 183:42-3 Ag '89

SEQUOIADENDRON GIGANTEUM See Redwood
SERAGEN INC.
At Boston University, Biotech 101 is no breeze. L. Jereski. *Business Week* p30-1 Ap 10 '89
Letting the losses run [Boston University's investment] D. Wechsler. il *Forbes* 143:116 Ap 17 '89
SERBIA (YUGOSLAVIA)
Nationalism
Nationalist rage [rioting in Kesovo] A. Bilski. il *Maclean's* 102:24 Ap 10 '89
Relighting the Balkan powder keg. G. Porzio. *World Press Review* 36:17-18 Je '89
Religious nationalism strains Yugoslavia. J. A. Broun. *The Christian Century* 106:885-8 O 4 '89
Yugoslavia's new political truth. S. Drakulić. il *The Nation* 248:297-8+ Mr 6 '89

SERED, MIKE
about
Brushed-aside artists have their day. D. Neff. il por *Christianity Today* 33:62 D 15 '89

SEREMETIS, STEPHANIE, AND OTHERS
Transformation and plasmacytoid differentiation of EBV-infected human B lymphoblast by *ras* oncogenes. bibl f il *Science* 243:660-3 F 3 '89
SERENGETI NATIONAL PARK (TANZANIA)
The brotherhood of cheetahs [cover story] T. Caro. il *Natural History* p50-9 Je '89
SERENGETI PLAIN (TANZANIA)
See also
Wildlife—Serengeti Plain (Tanzania)
SERGE, VICTOR, 1890-1947
about
Minority report. C. Hitchens. *The Nation* 249:447 O 23 '89
SERGENT, DENIS
Microwaves that save manuscripts. il *The Courier (Unesco)* 42:9 My '89
SERGERS
Sergers. il *Consumer Reports* 54:83-5 D '89
SERIAL MURDER MYSTERY STORIES See Detective and mystery stories
SERIAL MURDERS See Murder
SERIAL PUBLICATION OF BOOKS
The birth of a series character [detective fiction] G. C. Chesbro. *The Writer* 102:14-16 Mr '89

SERIALS, TELEVISION *See* Television serials
SERIEMAS
The terror bird still screams. K. H. Redford and P. Shaw. il *International Wildlife* 19:14-16 My/Je '89
SERIES (BOOKS) *See* Serial publication of books
SERIES (MATHEMATICS)
Progress in progressions. B. A. Cipra. *Science* 243:1143 Mr 3 '89
SERIGNY, EUGENIA DE
about
Paris on Park: Countess Eugenia de Serigny's Manhattan apartment. J. Reginato. il por *Architectural Digest* 46:156-61 Ap '89
SERINE PROTEASES *See* Proteases
SERIOUS, YAHOO
about
Say who?! il por *Teen* 33:70 Ag '89
Young Einstein [film] Reviews
Gentlemen's Quarterly il 59:93+ Ag '89. K. Turan
Mademoiselle il 95:106 S '89. L. Morice
People Weekly il 32:13-14 Ag 21 '89. R. Novak
SERMADIRAS, GILLES
about
Coup de maître in the Dordogne: a flourish of classical traditions at Eyrignac. Countess Du Saillant. il por *Architectural Digest* 46:132-5 Ja '89
SERMADIRAS, PATRICK
about
Coup de maître in the Dordogne: a flourish of classical traditions at Eyrignac. Countess Du Saillant. il por *Architectural Digest* 46:132-5 Ja '89
SERMONS
See also
Preaching
'In the tongues of men': homilies for women [cover story] K. Coffey. il *America* 161:392-4 D 2 '89
We ask for poor sermons. K. Miller. por *Christianity Today* 33:10 D 15 '89
SEROTA, NICHOLAS
about
Getting the hang of it. E. Beck. il por *Art News* 88:117-18 Mr '89
SEROTONIN
Early alcoholism: crime, depression higher [research by Laure Buydens-Branchey] B. Bower. *Science News* 135:180 Mr 25 '89
Effect of serotonergic afferents on quantal release at central inhibitory synapses. I. Mintz and others. bibl f il *Science* 245:190-2 Jl 14 '89
Sociopaths, suicide and serotonin. R. Cowen. *Science News* 136:250 O 14 '89
SEROTONIN RECEPTORS
Ectopic expression of the serotonin 1c receptor and the triggering of malignant transformation. D. Julius and others. bibl f il *Science* 244:1057-62 Je 2 '89
Receptor encounters: untangling the threads of the serotonin system. R. Cowen. il *Science News* 136:248-50+ O 14 '89
SERPENTINITE
Where earth's insides ooze out [Mariana seamount; research by Patricia Fryer] *Science News* 136:15 Jl 1 '89
SERRA, RICHARD
"Tilted arc" destroyed [cover story] bibl f il *Art in America* 77:34-7+ My '89
about
Arc without convenant. J. Simon. il *National Review* 41:30-2 My 5 '89
Going, going, gone. R. Cembalest. il *Art News* 88:50+ Summ '89
Notes and comment. *The New Yorker* 65:33-4 Mr 27 '89
Our most notorious sculptor. D. Solomon. il *The New York Times Magazine* p38-41+ O 8 '89
Richard Serra: Pace. M. Moorman. il *Art News* 88:157-8 D '89
"Stacks" of complaints. D. Waterman. *Art News* 88:53+ O '89
SERRANÍA DE LA MACARENA (COLOMBIA)
Dangerous days in the Macarena. A. Weisman. il map *The New York Times Magazine* p40-2+ Ap 23 '89
SERRANO, YOLANDA
about
Yolanda Serrano. K. Dobie. il pors *Ms.* 17:79-83 Ja/F '89
SERRATED TUSSOCK
Imported weed called threat to sheep and cattle. S. Christie. *Successful Farming* 87:40A Ag '89
SERRIN, WILLIAM
A great American job machine? il *The Nation* 249:269-70+ S 18 '89
Playing down unemployment. *The Nation* 248:84+ Ja 23 '89
SERUM ALBUMIN
Serum albumin seen in three dimensions [work of Daniel C. Carter] I. Amato. *Science News* 135:359 Je 10 '89
Three-dimensional structure of human serum albumin. D. C. Carter and others. bibl f il *Science* 244:1195-8 Je 9 '89

SERVAAS, BEURT
How to be young at heart. il map *The Saturday Evening Post* 261:90+ My/Je '89
about
Indianapolis intrigue. E. Schmuckler. il por *Forbes* 144:222-3 S 18 '89
SERVAAS, CORY
Medical mailbox. See issues of The Saturday Evening Post
SERVALS
Photographs and photography
Luck and long lenses—tips on photographing young animals in the wild. J. Zuckerman. il *Petersen's Photographic Magazine* 18:32-3 Ag '89
SERVAN-SCHREIBER, JEAN-LOUIS
The art of time [excerpt] il *American Health* 8:80+ Mr '89
SERVANTS *See* Household employees
SERVERS (COMPUTERS) *See* File servers (Computers)
SERVICE, NATIONAL *See* National service
SERVICE, VOLUNTEER *See* Volunteer service
SERVICE CONTRACTS
Choosing the right PC repair option. R. Lockwood. il *Personal Computing* 13:117-19+ N '89
Why the dealer wins [appliance contracts] D. Moreau. il *Changing Times* 43:83-4+ Ja '89
SERVICE CORPORATION INTERNATIONAL
This funeral stock is full of life. G. G. Marcial. *Business Week* p78 Ag 28 '89
SERVICE INDUSTRIES
See also
House cleaning services
Labor unions—Service industries
America still reigns in services. S. Nasar. il *Fortune* 119:64-6+ Je 5 '89
American mirage: a post-industrial economy? L. C. Thurow. *Current History* 88:13-14+ Ja '89
The hired and the mighty [perks of Hollywood] E. Stern. il *Gentlemen's Quarterly* 59:242-7+ Je '89
Employees
Are we becoming a nation of burger flippers? il *Changing Times* 43:32-3 Mr '89
Salaries, pensions, etc.
Productivity in services is not a problem abroad . . . and higher wages could spur its growth in the U.S. G. Koretz. il *Business Week* p28 My 22 '89
What's dragging productivity down? Women's low wages. A. Bernstein. il *Business Week* p171 N 27 '89
Export-import trade
A trade gap worth a smile [U.S. leads competition] C. P. Work. il *U.S. News & World Report* 107:66-7+ N 6 '89
Finance
Industrial and office services. J. Zweig. il *Forbes* 143:158+ Ja 9 '89
Services are supplying the steam for business investment. M. F. Allyn. il *Fortune* 119:37-8 Je 5 '89
Slower growth expected for the service sector. J. C. Szabo. il *Nation's Business* 77:12 Ja '89
Statistics
The service 500 [special section] il *Fortune* 119:351-5+ Je 5 '89
Management
A fresh look at productivity [research by Gerald Faulhaber and others] C. G. Burck. il *Fortune* 119:28 F 13 '89
Productivity in services is not a problem abroad . . . and higher wages could spur its growth in the U.S. G. Koretz. il *Business Week* p28 My 22 '89
The productivity paradox. H. Banks. *Forbes* 144:35 Jl 24 '89
Stars of the service 500 [cover story] C. J. Loomis. il *Fortune* 119:54-8+ Je 5 '89
Securities
Service stocks should continue to serve investors nicely. A. E. Serwer. il *Fortune* 119:41-2 Je 5 '89
SERVICE MERCHANDISE CO., INC.
Yet another company pulls a raid on itself. S. Flack. il *Forbes* 143:107-8 Je 26 '89
SERVICE STATIONS, AIRPLANE *See* Airplane service stations
SERVICE STATIONS, AUTOMOBILE *See* Automobile service stations
SERVICE STATIONS, TRUCK *See* Truck service stations
SERVICEMASTER LIMITED PARTNERSHIP
He doesn't walk on water? [W. Buffett sells stake] J. Zweig. il por *Forbes* 144:144 S 4 '89
SERVICEMEN
See also
AIDS (Disease) and servicemen
Children of servicemen
Unknown soldiers
Accidents and injuries
See United States—Armed Forces—Accidents and injuries; United States. Marine Corps—Accidents and injuries; United States. Navy—Accidents and injuries
Religious life
I was an atheist in a foxhole [Vietnam War] P. K. Paulsen. *The Humanist* 49:28-30 S/O '89
Sexual behavior
Court OKs re-enlistment of homosexual soldier [case of P. Watkins] il por *Jet* 76:18 My 22 '89

SERVICEMEN—Sexual behavior—*cont.*
Forced march in the military [cases challenging regulations banning lesbians and gay men] G. L. Atkins. il *The Nation* 248:16-18 Ja 2 '89
The Pentagon's fight to keep gays away. P. Cary. il *U.S. News & World Report* 107:57+ N 20 '89
Should homosexuals be able to serve? [case of P. Watkins] L. Eskin. por *Scholastic Update (Teachers' edition)* 122:22 O 6 '89

SERVICEMEN, DISCHARGED *See* Veterans

SERVICEMEN'S FAMILIES
Salute to military moms. B. Kanner. il *Parents* 64:130-4+ D '89

SERVICEMEN'S WIVES
Court limits sharing of Army pension in divorce; Marshall pens decision [Supreme Court] por *Jet* 76:8 Je 19 '89

SERVICEWOMEN
See also
Women cadets
Are women the weak link in the military? J. M. Schrof. il *U.S. News & World Report* 107:61 N 20 '89
Breaking barriers [Army] L. Eskin. il *Scholastic Update (Teachers' edition)* 122:20-1 O 6 '89
Help build a memorial to American heroines. J. M. Carter. il *Good Housekeeping* 208:64 My '89
Women in the Armed Forces. F. M. Eckman. il *McCall's* 116:63-4+ Ap '89
Sexual behavior
Forced march in the military [cases challenging regulations banning lesbians and gay men] G. L. Atkins. il *The Nation* 248:16-18 Ja 2 '89
The Pentagon's fight to keep gays away. P. Cary. il *U.S. News & World Report* 107:57+ N 20 '89
Witch hunt at Parris Island: the Marine Corps targets lesbians. J. Lynch. il *The Progressive* 53:24-7 Mr '89
Canada
Canadian women at arms [I. Gauthier wins suit against Canadian Armed Forces over combat duty regulations] M. Suh. il *Ms.* 17:71-2 Je '89
Women in combat. N. Underwood. il *Maclean's* 102:53 Mr 6 '89

SERVING CARTS *See* Carts

SERVOMECHANISMS
See also
Stepping motors

SERVOS, NORBERT
The independent dance scene in West Germany. il *Dance Magazine* 63:60-1 O '89

SESAME STREET [television program] See Television program reviews—Single works

SESSER, STAN
A rich country gone wrong. *The New Yorker* 65:55-6+ O 9 '89

SESSIONS, ROBERT
Children's book publishing in Australia: a lively business. il *Publishers Weekly* 235:35-7 Mr 24 '89

SESSIONS, ROGER
about
Musical events:
Selections from R. Session's Montezuma, Duo for violin and cello, and Waltz. A. Porter. *The New Yorker* 64:94-5 Ja 23 '89

SESSIONS, WILLIAM STEELE
The challenges we face in law enforcement [address, October 17, 1988] *Vital Speeches of the Day* 55:260-2 F 15 '89
about
Can Sessions tame the Bureau? D. R. Gordon. il *The Nation* 249:488-91 O 30 '89

SET DESIGN *See* Motion pictures—Setting and scenery; Opera—Stage setting and scenery; Television advertising—Setting and scenery; Television broadcasting—Setting and scenery; Theater—Stage setting and scenery

SET DESIGNERS
See also
Cinnabar (Firm)
Edwards, Ben
Eigsti, Karl
Larkin, Peter
Quaranta, Gianni
Rose, Jürgen, 1937-
White, Cary
Zea, Kristi
Training
The recruitment trail: my MFA design program's better than yours. J. Dolan. *Theatre Crafts* 23:22+ Ag/S '89
Training facilities in Boston [colleges offering courses in theater design and technology; special section] M. Sommers. il *Theatre Crafts* 23:50-5+ N '89

SET THEORY
See also
Fractals

SETI (SEARCH FOR EXTRATERRESTRIAL INTELLIGENCE) *See* Interstellar communication

SETLOW, RICHARD B.
about
DOE honors Setlow and Weisskopf with Fermi Award. pors *Physics Today* 42:89-90 Ap '89

SETON HALL UNIVERSITY
Seton Hall on the map. P. McKillop. il *Newsweek* 113:63 Ap 17 '89

SETTE MEZZO (NEW YORK, N.Y.: RESTAURANT) *See* New York (N.Y.)—Restaurants, nightclubs, bars, etc.

SETTEES
Sit-a-spell garden settee. W. L. Nolan. il *Better Homes and Gardens* 67:128 Ag '89

SETTEMBRE MUSICA (TURIN, ITALY) *See* Music festivals—Italy

SETTERBERG, FRED
Where to find the facts. il *The Progressive* 53:14 Jl '89

SETTERS (DOGS)
See also
Gordon setters
The price of things. R. L. Hall. il *Field & Stream* 94:68-9+ N '89

SETTLE, MEL
Must we tear them down? [reprint from May/June 1978 issue] il *The Humanist* 49:9 My/Je '89

SETTLEMENTS, SPACE *See* Space colonies

SETTLEMENTS, SQUATTER *See* Squatter settlements

SEUL, D. MICHAEL RIVAGE- *See* Rivage-Seul, D. Michael

SEUSS, DR.
about
A boy sides with Dr. Seuss's Lorax, and puts a town at loggerheads. R. Arias. il pors *People Weekly* 32:67-8 O 23 '89
Dr. Seuss. il pors *Life* 12:104-7 Jl '89

SEVEN DIALS (LONDON, ENGLAND)
Sunrise at Seven Dials [replica of 17th-century column erected] T. Aldous. il *History Today* 39:6 Jl '89

SEVENTIES (DECADE) *See* Nineteen hundred and seventies

SEVERANCE, JOAN
about
Riding high: city-smart jodhpurs. il pors *Harper's Bazaar* 122:146-51 F '89

SEVERE COMBINED IMMUNODEFICIENCY *See* Immunologic diseases

SEVERIN, TIMOTHY
Retracing the First Crusade [cover story] il map *National Geographic* 176:326-65 S '89

SEVERIN WUNDERMAN FOUNDATION MUSEUM
Severin Wunderman's Jean Cocteau obsession is so strong he sometimes feels he's possessed by the artist's spirit. R. Urquhart. il por *Vogue* 179:182-4 Je '89

SEVERINSEN, DOC
about
Doc Severinsen's musical medicine. J. McCollister. il por *The Saturday Evening Post* 261:64-5+ N/D '89
The many facets of Doc Severinsen. S. Yanow. il por *Down Beat* 56:27-8 F '89

SEVERSON, KAREN
about
Karen Severson swore she'd find her best friend's murderer—now she stands accused of the crime. K. Kingsbury. il pors *People Weekly* 32:147-8+ S 18 '89

SEVERY, MERLE
The great Revolution. il map *National Geographic* 176:18-49 Jl '89

SEVILLA-GONZAGA, MARYLIS
Keep your eye on . . . [with editorial comment by Patrick J. Smith] il *Opera News* 54:4, 8-9 Jl '89

SEVILLANO, TRINIDAD
about
Trinidad Sevillano's special promise: straight from the heart. J. Mackrell. il pors *Dance Magazine* 63:24-7 Jl '89

SEVIN ROSEN MANAGEMENT COMPANY
The biggest dealmaker of all [B. J. Rosen] E. S. Ely. por *Personal Computing* 13:74 Jl '89

SÈVRES PORCELAIN *See* Pottery, French

SEWAGE AS FERTILIZER
Recycling our most prolific by-product. J. L. Jacobson. *USA Today (Periodical)* 118:88-9 Jl '89

SEWAGE DISPOSAL
See also
Microwave sewage disposal
Septic tanks
Sewage as fertilizer
Waste disposal in the ocean

SEWAGE PURIFICATION
See also
Water reuse
Mud-slinging over sewage technology [EPA vs. Boston and San Diego] M. Sun. il *Science* 246:440-3 O 27 '89
Biological treatment
See also
Solar waste water treatment
Cleansing waters [artificial wetlands as sewage treatment facility in Benton, Ky.] M. Klockenbrink. il map *American Health* 8:72 S '89
A swamp makes waste to be sweet again. J. Willwerth. il *Time* 133:10+ Mr 20 '89
Washing up with wetlands. il *Country Journal* 16:28 S/O '89

SEWARD, INGRID
The rush-rush routine of Charles and Diana [cover story] il pors *The Saturday Evening Post* 261:42-7 S '89

SEWARD, INGRID—*cont.*
(jt. auth) See Hall, Unity, and Seward, Ingrid
SEWELL, TOM
about
A rocky start. V. Mattern. il por *Organic Gardening* 36:60-4 F '89
SEWING
See also
Tailoring
Tropical tote. il *Sunset (Central West edition)* 183:54-5 Ag '89
Competitions
Sewin' up winning style [winners of Sew 'n Show contest] il *'Teen* 33:32 Ja '89
Equipment
See also
Pincushions
Study and teaching
South Africa
Sticking a needle in apartheid [church sponsored sewing classes] M. S. Van Leeuwen. il *Christianity Today* 33:13 Mr 17 '89
SEWING MACHINES
See also
Sergers
SSMC Inc.
Grandma's sewing machine. J. Leonard. il por *Good Housekeeping* 208:56 Ap '89
Sewing machines. il *Consumer Reports* 54:73-82 D '89
SEX (BIOLOGY)
See also
Conjugation (Biology)
Estrus
Plants, Sex in
Reproduction
The mechanism of DNA transfer in the mating system of an archaebacterium. I. Rosenshine and others. bibl f il *Science* 245:1387-9 S 22 '89
Successful sex [favorable mutation in a sexual population] T. Beardsley. *Scientific American* 261:18 Ag '89
SEX (PSYCHOLOGY) *See* Sexual behavior
SEX AND FASHION
Androgyny is going strong in the streets and salons, promoted by today's hot stars. L. Wolfe. il *Vogue* 179:45-6 Ja '89
Boyish good looks [menswear for women] B. Boehlert. il *Vogue* 179:78-9 F '89
A dash of haberdashery [menswear for women] il *Glamour* 87:251 Ap '89
Menswear: a girl's best friend. A. Holch. il *American Health* 8:34-6 Ja/F '89
Exhibitions
A new Smithsonian exhibit looks at the opportunities and rewards for both genders in American life [Men and women: a history of costume, gender and power at the National Museum of American History] R. M. Adams. il *Smithsonian* 20:10 N '89
Powerwear!! [Men and women: a history of costume, gender, and power at National Museum of American History] A. L. Powers. il *Americana* 17:17-20 S/O '89
SEX AND LAW
See also
Prostitution
Rape
SEX AND RELIGION
See also
Black priests—Sexual behavior
Homosexuality and Christianity
Priests—Sexual behavior
Beyond the stiff upper lip [excerpt from The sexual Christian] T. Stafford. il *Christianity Today* 33:30-4 Ja 13 '89
Like a Catholic: Madonna's challenge to her Church [music video Like a prayer] A. M. Greeley. il *America* 160:447-9 My 13 '89
Parents should teach the joy of sex [Catholics; with readers' comments] M. Finley. *U.S. Catholic* 54:16-21 F '89
PCUSA and sex issues [Presbyterian meeting in Philadelphia] *The Christian Century* 106:648 Jl 5-12 '89
The phallic pulpit. G. Wills. bibl f il *The New York Review of Books* 36:20+ D 21 '89
Sex (how about love?) on Catholic campuses [with discussion; cover story] D. J. O'Brien. *Commonweal* 116:169-77 Mr 24 '89
Sleeping like spoons. J. G. Milhaven. il *Commonweal* 116:205-7 Ap 7 '89
Teen-agers and . . . you know what [cover story] W. J. O'Malley. *America* 160:340-4 Ap 15 '89
SEX ATTRACTANTS
See also
Pheromones
SEX BEHAVIOR *See* Sexual behavior
SEX BUSINESS *See* Sex oriented business
SEX CHANGE *See* Change of sex
SEX CHROMOSOMES *See* Chromosomes
SEX CONTROL *See* Sex determination and control
SEX CRIMES
See also
Child molesting
Incest

Prostitution
Rape
Teenagers and sex crimes. A. Toufexis. il *Time* 133:60 Je 5 '89
The war against women. C. L. Mithers. il *Ladies' Home Journal* 106:137-9+ O '89
SEX DETERMINATION AND CONTROL
See also
Amniocentesis
Chorionic villi sampling
Testis determining factor
Abortion-rights boomerang [femicide] D. Neff. il *Christianity Today* 33:16 Mr 17 '89
Baby boys, to order [use of abortion if fetus is not desired sex] J. Leo. il *U.S. News & World Report* 106:59 Ja 9 '89
Baby shopping: sex selection. *Vogue* 179:255 My '89
Can you choose your baby's sex? [H-Y antigen; research by Kenneth White] il *USA Today (Periodical)* 117:5 Je '89
In India, they abort females. J. McGowan. por *Newsweek* 113:12 Ja 30 '89
Loony legislation [prolife legislators' proposal to ban abortion on basis of gender selection in Pennsylvania] P. Simpson. *Ms.* 18:72 N '89
The men's club [synthetic male hormones induce feminization in catfish] *Discover* 10:18 Ag '89
Sperm sorter ensures sex-linked litters [livestock breeding] *Science News* 136:175 S 9 '89
SEX DIFFERENCES
See also
Androgyny (Psychology)
Dimorphism (Biology)
Are men just born to be mean? B. G. Harrison. *Mademoiselle* 95:102 F '89
Brain and gender: the missing data [discussion of January 4-11, 1989 article, Ways of knowing God: gender and the brain] J. B. Ashbrook. *The Christian Century* 106:263-4 Mr 8 '89
Don't believe everything you read . . . [inaccurate newspaper accounts of sex hormone research by Doreen Kimura and Elizabeth Hampson] B. L. Benderly. il *Psychology Today* 23:67-9 N '89
The gender gap [differences in men's and women's mental skills] C. Tavris. *Vogue* 179:302+ Ap '89
Grief's lessons: his and hers. D. Cole. *Psychology Today* 22:60-1 D '88
How sex hormones boost—or cut—intellectual ability. D. Kimura. il *Psychology Today* 23:62-6 N '89
The longevity gap [men and women] E. Berlow. il *New Choices for the Best Years* 29:10 N '89
The myths of feminism. N. Davidson. il *National Review* 41:44+ My 19 '89
Sexual chemistry. R. Ellis. il *Glamour* 87:322-3+ Ap '89
Ways of knowing God: gender and the brain. J. B. Ashbrook. il *The Christian Century* 106:14-15 Ja 4-11 '89
Why boys have more fun. J. Schaefers. il *Seventeen* 48:68-9 Jl '89
Woman = man? J. Remy. il *World Press Review* 36:54 Ap '89
Anecdotes, facetiae, satire, etc.
Excuse me, there's branches on my dendrites. K. Fury. il *Working Woman* 14:102 Ag '89
Men win a point at bridge [Bridge Battle of the Sexes] M. Starr. il *Newsweek* 113:82 Ap 24 '89
A neat gift idea [cleaning threshold difference between men and women] P. Chance. il *Psychology Today* 22:58-9 D '88
SEX DISCRIMINATION
See also
Black women—Employment
Discrimination in employment
Equal pay for equal work
Women—Employment
Ditch the cheerleaders, Lee [suggestions for Republican Party] A. F. Lewis. il por *Ms.* 17:86 Ap '89
Great explorations [women explorers] J. Mills. bibl il *Ms.* 17:58-62 Je '89
What's a woman worth? [unpaid work should be included in figuring of gross national product; views of M. Waring] Y. Preston. il *Ms.* 18:78 Jl/Ag '89
SEX DISCRIMINATION IN ADVERTISING
See also
Media Watch (Organization)
The sexism watch. il *U.S. News & World Report* 106:12 Mr 27 '89
Television insults men, too. B. R. Goldberg. il *Reader's Digest* 134:185-6 Je '89
SEX DISCRIMINATION IN EDUCATION
Can schools eliminate sexual harassment? R. H. Decker. *The Education Digest* 54:59-62 Ja '89
Court ruling rekindles controversy over SATs [question of bias against women] C. Holden. il *Science* 243:885-7 F 17 '89
Further mysteries of the SAT [sex discrimination charges] D. Seligman. il *Fortune* 119:112 Ja 2 '89

SEX DISCRIMINATION IN EDUCATION—cont.

Here's looking at you, kid [sexual harassment case against Prof. R. Hummel at Univ. of Toronto] B. Amiel. il *Maclean's* 102:9 Ap 10 '89

Opening doors for women in academia [address, 1988] B. D. Webster. bibl f *BioScience* 39:96-8 F '89

Stop blaming the tests [question of SAT's bias against women] J. Leo. il *U.S. News & World Report* 106:80 Mr 20 '89

Title IX is back in action! [effect on women athletes] K. M. Reith. il *Women's Sports & Fitness* 11:74 Mr '89

Unacceptable ideas [charge that SATs discriminate against women] D. Seligman. il *Fortune* 119:151-2 Mr 13 '89

Wake-up call [reaction to wife's denial of tenure] R. B. Reich. il *Ms.* 18:32-3 O '89

Where have all the smart girls gone? [study of female valedictorians seven years after high school graduation; work of Terry Denny] M. Conroy. il *Psychology Today* 23:20 Ap '89

Where the boys are [effect of Title IX on women athletic directors and coaches at the college level] M. Goodman. *The Washington Monthly* 21:18-20 Ap '89

SEX DISCRIMINATION IN LANGUAGE

Doing right by women and the Trinity too. D. A. Helminiak. il *America* 160:110+ F 11 '89

Gender benders. D. Seligman. il *Fortune* 119:154 Ap 10 '89

SEX DISCRIMINATION IN SPORTS

Attack the gender gap in amateur sports [lack of women on National Governing Bodies] K. M. Reith. il *Women's Sports & Fitness* 11:64 Je '89

Champions or cheesecake? [remarks about women athletes made by television sportscasters] il *Glamour* 87:105 Ag '89

For women golfers, life in the rough. A. Engeler. il *The New York Times Magazine* p42+ O 1 '89

More than just a pretty face? [statements about women athletes by television sportscasters; views of Cynthia Hasbrook and Margaret Carlisle Duncan] C. Potera. il *American Health* 8:46 Mr '89

Past echoes, future challenges [adaptation of address, January 1989] C. Mann. il *Women's Sports & Fitness* 11:88 Ap '89

SEX EDUCATION

Beyond the birds and bees. D. F. Bjorklund and B. Bjorklund. il *Parents* 64:235 O '89

The birds and the bees. D. Elkind. il *Parents* 64:200 Mr '89

Girls: just say "Not now" [views of Carol Cassell] L. C. Cook. *Psychology Today* 23:59 Ap '89

Helping our children understand their sexuality. A. R. Davis. il *Essence* 20:76+ D '89

Kids get the message: it's okay to say no [abstinence programs] K. H. Sidey. il *Christianity Today* 33:40 O 6 '89

Parents should teach the joy of sex [Catholics; with readers' comments] M. Finley. *U.S. Catholic* 54:16-21 F '89

Reducing homophobia among educators and students. R. Schaecher. *The Education Digest* 54:58-61 Ap '89

Sex ed: why wait? R. M. Christenson. il *Christianity Today* 33:19-20 S 22 '89

Teen sexuality [Berkeley High School, Calif.] G. H. Colt. il *Life* 12:24-30 Jl '89

Anecdotes, facetiae, satire, etc.

The big question. D. Owen. il *The Atlantic* 263:16 Je '89

Half a century of sex education. N. R. Campion. il *The New York Times Magazine* p22+ Mr 26 '89

China

At last, Birds and Bees 101. *U.S. News & World Report* 106:38 Ap 24 '89

Kenya

A changing society. R. O. Omungala. il *World Health* p11-12 Mr '89

Mexico

Talking to teenagers about sex. A. Monroy de Velasco. il *World Health* p15 Ja/F '89

Norway

"Take care of yourself". B. Stray-Pedersen. il *World Health* p27-8 Ja/F '89

SEX HORMONES *See* Hormones, Sex

SEX IN ADVERTISING

The hot sell [using sex in Canadian TV commercials] J. Daly. il *Maclean's* 102:34-5 Je 12 '89

Pubescent howls, human connections. J. M. Wall. *The Christian Century* 106:771-2 Ag 30-S 6 '89

SEX IN BUSINESS

Comic Eddie Murphy hit with $75 million suit charging sex harassment. pors *Jet* 76:60 My 29 '89

Dear Betty Harragan. B. L. Harragan. il *Working Woman* 14:41-2 O '89

Handling an office crush. P. R. Satran. il *Working Woman* 14:103 N '89

Hot times from 9 to 5: the new social life is strictly an office affair. C. Bushnell. il *Mademoiselle* 95:162-3+ Jl '89

Men at work: is sex on their minds—or what? [survey results] il *Glamour* 87:124-9 Ja '89

Pink-slipped by Eddie Murphy, Michael Michele vows their only date will be in court [charging movie set harassment] S. Schindehette. il pors *People Weekly* 31:48-9 My 29 '89

Sexual harassment. M. O'Koon. *Good Housekeeping* 208:171 Ja '89

Should you outlaw romance in the office? E. Flax. *Working Woman* 14:16 Ag '89

This is what you thought: 62% don't like suggestive comments in the office. il *Glamour* 87:185 Ap '89

Watch that leer, stifle that joke. G. Morgenson. il *Forbes* 143:69-72 My 15 '89

Winning is the best revenge [C. Broderick wins discrimination suit against the Securities and Exchange Commission] L. Romano. il pors *Good Housekeeping* 208:46+ Ap '89

SEX IN CABLE TELEVISION

Locking out sex and violence on cable. M. Meyer. il *Video* 13:61-2 Ap '89

SEX IN COMIC BOOKS, STRIPS, ETC.

Drawing on the dark side. J. Queenan. il *The New York Times Magazine* p32-4+ Ap 30 '89

SEX IN MASS MEDIA

Media and morality in the twenties. J. D. Stevens. bibl il *History Today* 39:25-9 N '89

SEX IN MOTION PICTURES

The many faces of Eve: the changing image of the sex goddess. J. Kristin. il *American Film* 14:38-41+ Ap '89

Pre-Code parlance [risqué dialogue from the early 1930s] F. Thompson. il *American Film* 15:13 N '89

Sex-rated. H. Edwards and P. Rainer. il *Vogue* 179:236-7+ Ap '89

SEX IN RELIGION

See also

Sex in the Bible

SEX IN TELEVISION

See also

Tabloid television

Author Judith Krantz tells: why TV strips the sex out of my novels [cover story] B. Davidson. il por *TV Guide* 37:2-4 N 18-24 '89

Behind TV's passionate love scenes: is it all just acting? E. Warren. il *TV Guide* 37:20-2 S 30-O 6 '89

The boob tube. J. Martel. il *Rolling Stone* p46+ Mr 23 '89

Sex still sells. B. Bird. il *Christianity Today* 33:44-5 Mr 3 '89

There she is . . . dethroned Miss America stars as a call girl [V. Williams in The sex tapes] H. Newton. il pors *TV Guide* 36:20-3 F 4-10 '89

TV's getting sexier . . . how far will it go? H. Polskin. il *TV Guide* 37:16-21 Ja 7-13 '89

SEX IN TELEVISION ADVERTISING *See* Sex in advertising

SEX IN THE BIBLE

Original sin: when sex was clean [views of Elaine Pagels] W. Herbert. il *Psychology Today* 22:67 D '88

SEX IN VIDEOTAPES

Like a Catholic: Madonna's challenge to her Church [music video Like a prayer] A. M. Greeley. il *America* 160:447-9 My 13 '89

MTV rocks (and rolls) American youth. J. L. Hall. il *USA Today (Periodical)* 118:87-8 N '89

Rob Lowe's girl trouble. M. Sager. il por *Rolling Stone* p92-3+ Ag 24 '89

A video romp in the buff gives heartbreaker Rob Lowe a little too much southern exposure. S. Dougherty. il pors *People Weekly* 31:79-80 Je 5 '89

SEX, LIES, AND VIDEOTAPE [film] *See* Motion picture reviews—Single works

SEX ORGANS *See* Reproductive organs

SEX ORIENTED BUSINESS

See also

Pornography

Prostitution

Striptease

'Porndale' sings the red-light blues [zoning for red light district in Ferndale, Mich.] il *Newsweek* 113:28 Ap 3 '89

SEX PHEROMONES *See* Pheromones

SEX RELATIONS *See* Sexual behavior

SEX RESEARCH

See also

Kinsey Institute for Research in Sex, Gender and Reproduction

SEX ROLE

See also

Androgyny (Psychology)

Role models

The American man in transition [cover story; special section] il *American Health* 8:59-73 Ja/F '89

Can parents be sexist? D. Elkind. il *Parents* 64:218 My '89

The man who would be bossy. W. D. Leight. *Mademoiselle* 95:97 D '89

The myths of feminism. N. Davidson. il *National Review* 41:44+ My 19 '89

Sexism and summer camp or: Am I crazy??!! [young girl's appearance anxiety] E. Berg. il *Parents* 64:86-8 Ag '89

SEX ROLE—*cont.*
Sexual stereotypes persist [views of Jane Collier] *USA Today (Periodical)* 117:10 Ja '89
A working wife. D. A. Williams. por *Essence* 20:12-13 Ag '89

Anecdotes, facetiae, satire, etc.
Is that rouge, Son? S. Bing. il *Esquire* 112:45-6 Jl '89
SEX SELECTION *See* Sex determination and control
SEX STEREOTYPES *See* Sex role
SEX SURGERY *See* Reproductive organs—Surgery
SEXISM *See* Sex discrimination
SEXIST LANGUAGE *See* Sex discrimination in language
SEXTANT AVIONIQUE (FIRM)
European aerospace industry enters period of restructuring. J. M. Lenorovitz. il *Aviation Week & Space Technology* 131:34-5 Jl 3 '89
SEXTON, MARK
Dispelling more myths about marketing to libraries. *Publishers Weekly* 236:38 D 22 '89
Replacing the myths about marketing to libraries. *Publishers Weekly* 235:56-7 Mr 10 '89
Springer-Verlag's 25 years in New York. il *Publishers Weekly* 236:434+ Ag 11 '89
SEXUAL ABUSE OF CHILDREN *See* Child molesting
SEXUAL ADDICTION
. . . and the woman who loves him [relationship with a Casanova] E. Royte. il *Mademoiselle* 95:190+ My '89
The man who couldn't be faithful [confessions of a Casanova] P. Trachtenberg. il *Mademoiselle* 95:188-9+ My '89
SEXUAL ATTRACTION *See* Interpersonal attraction
SEXUAL BEHAVIOR
See also
Aged—Sexual behavior
Androgyny (Psychology)
Artists—Sexual behavior
Baseball players—Sexual behavior
Black priests—Sexual behavior
Celibacy
Children—Sexual behavior
Clergy—Sexual behavior
College students—Sexual behavior
College teachers—Sexual behavior
Congressmen—Sexual behavior
Cyclists—Sexual behavior
Flirting
G spot
Homosexuality
Lesbianism
Married couples—Sexual behavior
Masculinity (Psychology)
Masturbation
Monogamy
Orgasm
Pheromones
Politicians—Sexual behavior
Priests—Sexual behavior
Prime ministers—Sexual behavior
Professionals—Sexual behavior
Public officers—Sexual behavior
Sadomasochism
Servicemen—Sexual behavior
Servicewomen—Sexual behavior
Sexual desire
Youth—Sexual behavior
31 facts and tips on sex after 30. C. Perlmutter. bibl il *Prevention (Emmaus, Pa.)* 41:54-64 Jl '89
Are you too inhibited in bed? L. G. Barbach. *Redbook* 172:112-13+ Mr '89
Asking America about its sex life [proposed NIH-sponsored national survey] W. Booth. il *Science* 243:304 Ja 20 '89
Body and soul. M.-B. Rosenbaum. See issues of Mademoiselle
Can a woman be "too good" in bed? S. Nelson. il *Glamour* 87:264-5+ Mr '89
Can exercise make you sexier? P. Whitten and E. J. Whiteside. il *Psychology Today* 23:42-4 Ap '89
Desperately seeking sexual statistics [survey by the National Institute of Child Health and Human Development] R. Weiss. *Science News* 136:28 Jl 8 '89
Don't touch! What makes a guy lose his lust. K. Krajick. il *Mademoiselle* 95:189-90+ N '89
How sexual ghosts can haunt your—and his—love life. H. McCandless. il *Glamour* 87:138-9+ Ja '89
The intelligent woman's guide to sex. D. Heyn. See issues of Mademoiselle beginning December 1986
Love & sex: the book of questions [results of survey] G. Stock. il *Redbook* 173:134-5 O '89
Love, sex and condoms. il *Glamour* 87:146+ O '89
Lust he must: the nature of a man's desire. K. Krajick. por *Mademoiselle* 95:108-9+ Ja '89
My year of loving dangerously: confessions of a non-condom-user. L. Allen. *Mademoiselle* 95:221+ Mr '89
Myths about black female sexuality. B. M. Campbell. il *Essence* 19:71-2+ Ap '89
The new black sexuality. il *Ebony* 44:146+ Je '89
A new sexuality? [black women] I. Njeri. il *Essence* 19:66-7+ Ja '89
Sex & health. S. Zussman. See issues of Glamour beginning November 1986

Sex and other pleasures [cover story; special section] G. B. Leonard. il *Esquire* 111:129-32+ My '89
Sex grows up. D. Sobel. il *Health (New York, N.Y.)* 21:76 O '89
Sex, sex, sex. *Glamour* 87:132 F '89
Sex-shy: why we're still squeamish after all these years. M. Sandmaier. il *Mademoiselle* 95:155+ Ap '89
Sexual chemistry. R. Ellis. il *Glamour* 87:322-3+ Ap '89
Sexual health [questions and answers] L. F. Webb. See issues of Essence
Sexual pursuit [cover story; special section] il *Ms.* 17:39-52+ My '89
The surprising eroticism of sound. B. Hersey. il *Glamour* 87:190-3 D '89
Try a little tenderness. B. De Angelis. *Redbook* 173:98-9+ Je '89
U.S. probe meets resistance [National Institutes of Health survey] W. Booth. il *Science* 244:419 Ap 28 '89
What men really want in bed. J. P. Davis. il *Glamour* 87:256-7+ Je '89
What men want (I). S. Cook. il *Gentlemen's Quarterly* 59:294-301+ O '89
What men want (II). S. Cook. il *Gentlemen's Quarterly* 59:272-7+ N '89
What men want in bed [excerpt from How to keep your man monogamous] A. Penney. il *Ladies' Home Journal* 106:80+ Ag '89
Who's the boss in bed? W. D. Leight. *Mademoiselle* 95:118 N '89

Animals
Nice nitpickers [non-aggressive behavior leads to successful mating in olive baboons; research by Shirley Strum] il *Discover* 10:16 N '89
Pronghorns in—and out of—a rut [National Bison Range] J. A. Byers. il *Natural History* p38-49 Ap '89
Sex and friendship among baboons [research by Shirley C. Strum] B. Bower. *Science News* 135:251 Ap 22 '89

Arthropods
Doing their primal thing [horseshoe crabs mating on the N.J. shore] M. Riley. il *Time* 134:10-11+ Ag 21 '89

Birds
The birds of paradise [diet's influence on sexual behavior; cover story] B. M. Beehler. bibl il map *Scientific American* 261:116-23 D '89
Blackbirds that flock together breed better [study by Gordon H. Orians and Les D. Beletsky] D. E. Loupe. il *Science News* 136:311 N 11 '89
How females entrap males [pied flycatchers; research by Eivin Roskaft] R. Lewin. il *Science* 243:1289 Mr 10 '89
Judging paternity in the hedge sparrow's world [research by Nicholas Davies] R. Lewin. il *Science* 243:1663-4 Mr 31 '89
Looking for Mr. Right [cover story] R. Wolkomir and J. Wolkomir. il *National Wildlife* 27:44-51 Je/Jl '89
Making sense of sexual nonsense [sandpipers] J. P. Myers. il *Audubon* 91:40-5 Jl '89
Sexual deception [pied flycatchers] J. M. Diamond. il *Discover* 10:70-4 Ag '89
Who listens to the mockingbird? R. Breitwisch. il *Natural History* p6+ Je '89

Fish
Grouper sex in Belize. J. Carter. il *Natural History* p60-9 O '89
Sexual stunts of clownfish [cover story] D. G. Fautin. il *Natural History* p42-7 S '89

History
Sex American-style [views of John D'Emilio] L. Gilman. il *American Health* 8:54 Ja/F '89
Sex and the automobile in the Jazz Age. P. Ling. bibl il *History Today* 39:18-24 N '89

Insects
Circadian system controlling release of sperm in the insect testes [gypsy moth] J. M. Giebultowicz and others. bibl f il *Science* 245:1098-100 S 8 '89
Freedom fighters [Sonoran Desert digger bees] J. Alcock. il *Natural History* p68-74 Mr '89
Hormone triggers moth mating [research by Michel Cusson and Jeremy N. McNeil] *Science News* 135:46 Ja 21 '89
Involvement of juvenile hormone in the regulation of pheromone release activities in a moth. M. Cusson and J. N. McNeil. bibl f il *Science* 243:210-12 Ja 13 '89
The mating of tree crickets. D. H. Funk. bibl il *Scientific American* 261:50-5+ Ag '89
Overnight sensation [orange tip butterflies] S. Barbour. il *Natural History* p24+ My '89
Spanish fly's lure: ardor or armor? [aphrodisiac for pyrochroid beetles; research by Jerrold Meinwald] J. Raloff. *Science News* 136:189 S 16 '89

International aspects
WHO seeks global data on sexual practices. W. Booth. *Science* 244:418-19 Ap 28 '89

Rodents
Sex lives of the small and furry [frequent sexual encounters weaken immune system of golden hamsters; research by Nancy Ostrowski] il *Discover* 10:10 D '89

Canada
Sex life in Canada [Maclean's/Decima poll] il *Maclean's* 102:30-1 Ja 2 '89

SEXUAL BEHAVIOR—*cont.*

Japan

Anecdotes, facetiae, satire, etc.

Ye olde inscrutable inn [love hotel in Nagoya] G. Jaynes. il *Life* 12:17 S '89

Soviet Union

Rehabilitating sex. M. D. Lemonick. il *Time* 133:105 Ap 10 '89

SEXUAL DESIRE

See also

Aphrodisiacs

How to feel sexier (in bed and out). D. A. Wilburn. il *Redbook* 173:106-7+ My '89

"Not tonight, dear" [inhibited sexual desire] D. Gelman. il *Reader's Digest* 134:33-4+ Je '89

Rules of attraction: why you're hot—or not. L. F. McCarthy. il *Mademoiselle* 95:125-6 F '89

Sex offenders [prescription drugs can inhibit sexual desire] C. Platt. *Harper's Bazaar* 122:135+ Ag '89

Anecdotes, facetiae, satire, etc.

What's your line? S. Bing. il *Esquire* 112:111-12 O '89

SEXUAL DEVIATION

See also

Sex crimes

SEXUAL DIMORPHISM *See* Dimorphism (Biology)

SEXUAL DISORDERS

See also

Impotence

Sexual addiction

SEXUAL ETHICS

See also

Adultery

Monogamy

Prostitution

Sex and religion

Sex education

Dating, dishonesty and AIDS [study by Susan Cochran] M. Roberts. il *Psychology Today* 22:60 D '88

The deadly side of love: the end of the sexual smokescreen. B. B. Palmer and J. M. Coffman. il *USA Today (Periodical)* 117:62-3 My '89

"Don't! Stop!" or "Don't stop!" [research by Charlene Muehlenhard and Lisa Hollabaugh] V. Bozzi. il *Psychology Today* 23:62 Mr '89

Nice girls do or want to. K. Monagle. il *Ms.* 17:50+ My '89

Sex in the forbidden zone [professional men who have illicit affairs with clients; excerpt] P. Rutter. il pors *Psychology Today* 23:34-8+ O '89

Sex on the couch: Maybe later? [psychotherapists] B. Fischman. *Psychology Today* 23:26 Je '89

Sexual ethics. C. L. Mithers. See issues of Glamour beginning April 1987

Sexual lies: his and yours. L. Dormen. il *Glamour* 87:262-3+ O '89

Sexual morality for young humanists and their parents. D. Carroll. *The Humanist* 49:41-2+ Jl/Ag '89

Should you use a guy for sex? E. Welty. *Mademoiselle* 95:118 O '89

The worst lie of all: what they'll say for sex [lying about having had an AIDS test] L. Sanders. *Mademoiselle* 95:216 Je '89

Ziplash: a sexual libertine recants. E. Jong. por *Ms.* 17:49 My '89

SEXUAL FANTASY

What turns him on. il *Glamour* 87:102 Jl '89

SEXUAL HARASSMENT

See also

Sex discrimination in education

Sex in business

Love gone loco: when breakups go too far! E. Karlsberg. il *'Teen* 33:36-7+ F '89

Watch that leer, stifle that joke. G. Morgenson. il *Forbes* 143:69-72 My 15 '89

When a pastor turns seducer. K. L. Woodward. il *Newsweek* 114:48-9 Ag 28 '89

SEXUAL MATURITY *See* Puberty

SEXUALITY *See* Sexual behavior

SEXUALLY TRANSMITTED DISEASES

See also

AIDS (Disease)

Chlamydia infections

Human papilloma virus

Syphilis

Warts

Contagious fortune. D. Berreby. il *Ms.* 17:30+ My '89

Don't blame the toilet seat [views of Leonard Slater] il *USA Today (Periodical)* 118:16 O '89

Hepatitis C may spread heterosexually. D. E. Loupe. *Science News* 136:151 S 2 '89

The other dangers of close encounters. il *Time* 133:62 Ja 30 '89

Sexually transmitted diseases: are you at risk? R. Baron-Faust. il *McCall's* 116:105-6+ Ap '89

Prevention

Partner tracing [Colorado program] L. M. Kase. *Vogue* 179:258+ My '89

SEYCHELLES

Description and travel

The Seychelles (Treasure) Islands. F. L. Lambrecht and D. Lambrecht. il map *Focus (New York, N.Y.: 1950)* 39:35-6+ Spr '89

SEYFERT GALAXIES *See* Galaxies

SEYMORE, JOYCE

Scented rooms. il por *House & Garden* 161:170-5+ N '89

SEYMOUR, BEVERLY

about

Little girl, big trouble. D. Grogan. il pors *People Weekly* 31:36-41 F 20 '89

SEYMOUR, IAN

The political magic of John Dee. bibl il por *History Today* 39:29-35 Ja '89

SEYMOUR, JANE

about

Jane Seymour: a fairy-tale life [cover story] il pors *Ladies' Home Journal* 106:124-6+ Je '89

Not-so-plain Jane Seymour [cover story] C. Millner. il pors *The Saturday Evening Post* 261:42-3+ My/Je '89

SEYMOUR, LIZ

Getting steamed. il *Health (New York, N.Y.)* 21:34+ S '89

SEYMOUR, PERCY

about

Dr. Zodiac. D. Sobel. il pors *Omni (New York, N.Y.)* 12:60-2+ D '89

SFERRA, KATHY

Making portraits of the microcosm. il *National Parks* 63:28-31 Mr/Ap '89

SHABAD, STEVEN

Regional report: the Soviet Union. See issues of World Press Review beginning October 1986

SHABAZZ, ATTALLAH

about

Their fathers' daughters. E. Hopkins. il pors *Rolling Stone* p76-7+ N 30 '89

SHABBAT LAW *See* Jewish law

SHACKELFORD, GEORGE T. M., 1955-

Behind closed doors. il por *House & Garden* 161:50+ N '89

SHACOCHIS, BOB

Dining in. See issues of Gentlemen's Quarterly beginning December 1988

In deepest Gringolandia [cover story] il *Harper's* 279:42-50 Jl '89

SHAD, JOHN S. R.

about

Securities exchange. *The Nation* 248:613 My 8 '89

Wanted: a Mr. Clean for Drexel Burnham. il por *Newsweek* 113:42 Ja 23 '89

SHAD FISHING

Shad: the perfect fly-rod fish. L. M. Wright. il *Field & Stream* 94:62+ My '89

SHADD, MARLON

about

Girl who sued prom date gets $81.28 in settlement. il por *Jet* 76:29 Jl 10 '89

Giving courtship a new meaning, a Florida teen sues the date who stood her up for the school prom. il por *People Weekly* 31:101 My 29 '89

SHADE GARDENS AND GARDENING

Looking for dependable and compact shade plants? il *Sunset (Central West edition)* 182:188 Mr '89

SHADE TREE PRUNING *See* Pruning

SHADE TREES *See* Trees

SHADES (WINDOW) *See* Window shades

SHADING OF PLANTS *See* Plants—Protection

SHADOW MATTER (ASTRONOMY) *See* Dark matter (Astronomy)

SHAFFER, MARC

Rubén Zamora [interview] pors *The Progressive* 53:32-5 Jl '89

SHAFFER, PAUL

about

Paul Shaffer and the World's Most Dangerous Band [cover story] J. Cunniff. il pors *Down Beat* 56:16-19 O '89

Profiles. J. Kaplan. il *The New Yorker* 64:36-40+ Ja 16 '89

SHAFFER, RICHARD, 1947-

about

Richard Shaffer: Eugene Binder. J. Kutner. il *Art News* 88:172 D '89

SHAFFER, RICHARD A.

Computer stocks vintage 1989. il *Forbes* 143:180+ Ap 17 '89

Industry watch. See issues of Personal Computing beginning January 1985

SHAFFER, RICK

Through the eyepiece. See issues of Astronomy beginning July 1988

SHAG: THE MOVIE [film] See Motion picture reviews—Single works

SHAH, DIANE K.

All together, now: "Sean Connery is an icon!" [cover story] il pors *Gentlemen's Quarterly* 59:126-31+ Jl '89

The producers [cover story] il pors *The New York Times Magazine* p26-9+ O 22 '89

SHAH, DIANE K.—cont.

The transformation of Pat Riley [cover story] il pors *Gentlemen's Quarterly* 59:136-41+ Ja '89

What do you expect for $2.25 million? il por *The New York Times Magazine* p54-6+ S 10 '89

SHAH, EDDIE

about

The bloke buckled. E. McGlinn. il por *Forbes* 143:10 F 6 '89

SHAHN, BEN, 1898-1969

about

Time share. *The New Yorker* 65:26-7 Jl 3 '89

SHAINBERG, LAWRENCE, 1936-

Finding 'the zone'. il pors *The New York Times Magazine* p34-6+ Ap 9 '89

SHAKA *See* Chaka, Zulu Chief, 1787?-1828

SHAKEEL, HADIA DAJANI- *See* Dajani-Shakeel, Hadia

SHAKER FURNITURE

Blanket chest. R. N. Hoffman. il *Workbench* 45:32-3 My/Je '89

Five-board bench [Shaker bench] R. N. Hoffman. il *Workbench* 45:74-6+ S/O '89

Shaker blanket chest. K. Collier. il *The Family Handyman* 39:94-8 Ap '89

Shaker end table. N. Barrett, Jr. il *Popular Mechanics* 166:85-8 O '89

Collectors and collecting

Shaker all over. il *Architectural Digest* 46:190 Jl '89

Shaker chic. F. Donegan. il *Americana* 16:66-8 Ja/F '89

Exhibitions

Forty untouched masterpieces of Shaker design. J. T. Kirk and J. V. Grant. il *Antiques* 135:1226-37 My '89

SHAKER HEIGHTS (OHIO)

Education

Feeling the heat at Shaker High [college admissions] B. Kobliner. il *Money* 18:148 My '89

SHAKER MUSEUM (OLD CHATHAM, N.Y.)

Between issues [story reading by F. Prose] *The New Leader* 72:2 S 4 '89

Forty untouched masterpieces of Shaker design. J. T. Kirk and J. V. Grant. il *Antiques* 135:1226-37 My '89

SHAKERS

The Shakers' brief eternity. C. Newman. il map *National Geographic* 176:302-25 S '89

THE SHAKERS [ballet] See Ballet reviews—Single works

SHAKESPEARE, MARGARET

Fat-finding mission. il *Health (New York, N.Y.)* 21:30-1 Mr '89

SHAKESPEARE, WILLIAM, 1564-1616

about

Coriolanus [drama] Reviews

The New Republic 200:26-7 Ja 2 '89. R. Brustein

The New York Review of Books il 35:46-7 Ja 19 '89. G. Wills

Cymbeline [drama] Reviews

The Nation 249:29-30 Jl 3 '89. M. Hodgson

The New Republic 201:28-30 Jl 10 '89. R. Brustein

New York il 22:86-7 Je 12 '89. J. Simon

The New Yorker 65:89 Je 12 '89. E. Oliver

Doubleday introduces new 20-volume Shakespeare series [GuildAmerica edition] J. P. Frank. il *Publishers Weekly* 235:54-6 My 5 '89

Forsooth, did Shakespeare know best? *USA Today (Periodical)* 117:13 F '89

Julius Caesar [drama] Reviews

The New York Review of Books il 36:40-2 O 12 '89. J. Kott

Left homeless, Irvin Matus preferred the Bard to a bed. K. Gross. il pors *People Weekly* 31:125+ My 22 '89

Love's labor's lost [drama] Reviews

The Nation 248:464 Ap 3 '89. T. M. Disch

New York 22:100 Mr 6 '89. J. Simon

The New Yorker 65:91 Mr 6 '89. E. Oliver

Measure for measure [drama] Reviews

The Nation 248:604 My 1 '89. M. Hodgson

New York il 22:78+ Mr 20 '89. J. Simon

The New Yorker 65:93 Mr 27 '89. M. Kramer

The merchant of Venice [drama] Reviews

National Review 41:57-8 S 15 '89. E. Resnikova

People Weekly il 31:101 Je 19 '89

Vogue il 179:198+ D '89. J. Heilpern

A midsummer night's dream: the sequel. P. Iyer. il *Time* 134:66 Ag 7 '89

Shakespeare in the Park [Shakespeare Garden in Central Park] P. Hagan. il *House & Garden* 161:200-3+ O '89

The tempest [drama] Reviews

New York 22:167-8 D 4 '89. J. Simon

The New Yorker 65:101 N 27 '89. E. Oliver

Titus Andronicus [drama] Reviews

The Nation 249:362-3 O 2 '89. T. M. Disch

New York 22:64 S 4 '89. J. Simon

The New Yorker 65:91 S 4 '89. E. Oliver

Troilus and Cressida [drama] Reviews

The Nation 249:612-13 N 20 '89. T. M. Disch

Twelfth night [drama] Reviews

Jet il 76:63 Jl 17 '89

The New Republic 201:29-30 Ag 21 '89. R. Brustein

New York il 22:28-35 Je 19 '89. D. Blum

New York il 22:54-5 Jl 24 '89. J. Simon

The New Yorker 65:66-7 Jl 24 '89. M. Kramer

Newsweek il 114:50-1 Jl 17 '89. J. Kroll

Time il 134:91 Jl 17 '89. W. A. Henry

The winter's tale [drama] Reviews

The Nation 248:604 My 1 '89. M. Hodgson

The New Republic 200:28-30 My 8 '89. R. Brustein

New York il 22:79-80 Ap 3 '89. J. Simon

The New Yorker 65:101-2 Ap 3 '89. M. Kramer

Newsweek il 113:70 Ap 3 '89. J. Kroll

Staging and acting of plays

King Lear's a woman, Mozart's in a diner [modern renditions of the classics] M. Horn. il *U.S. News & World Report* 107:50-1 Ag 14 '89

SHAKESPEARE & CO. (PARIS, FRANCE: BOOKSTORE) *See* Booksellers and bookselling—France

SHAKESPEARE FESTIVAL (STRATFORD, ONT.) *See* Stratford Festival (Ont.)

SHAKESPEARE FESTIVALS

See also

New York Shakespeare Festival

Oregon Shakespearean Festival

Stratford Festival (Ont.)

Open-air Shakespeare [Western States] il map *Sunset (Central West edition)* 182:80+ My '89

SHAKESPEARE GARDEN (NEW YORK, N.Y.) *See* Central Park (New York, N.Y.)—Shakespeare Garden

SHAKESPEAR'S SISTER (MUSICAL GROUP)

Shakespear's Sister. M. Azerrad. il *Rolling Stone* p43 N 30 '89

SHAKHASHIRI, BASSAM Z.

about

NSF education head makes risky bid. J. Walsh. il por *Science* 246:317-19 O 20 '89

SHAKLEE CORP.

How d'ya say "liquidator" in Japanese? [I. Jacobs plays Tokyo-New York arbitrage in raids on Shaklee and Avon] S. Flack. il por *Forbes* 143:39-40 Je 12 '89

SHALALA, DONNA

about

The indomitable Donna Shalala. L. DePaulo. il por *New Choices for the Best Years* 29:26-30 Ag '89

On changing academic culture from the inside [interview] A. Bernstein and S. Mow. il pors *Change* 21:20-9 Ja/F '89

Taking on the risk of bigger vistas. L. Calvacca. il por *Working Woman* 14:116 O '89

SHALEV, MENACHEM

The worst surprise was no surprise. il *World Press Review* 36:15-16 F '89

SHAMANS AND SHAMANISM

Dark side of the shaman [Aguaruna Indians of Peru] M. F. Brown. *Natural History* p8+ N '89

SHAMASK, RONALDUS

about

Designing men. il pors *Gentlemen's Quarterly* 59:120-5 Jl '89

SHAMBERG, MICHAEL

about

Michael Shamberg [interview] il por *American Film* 14:16-18+ Ja/F '89

SHAME

See also

Guilt

Stigma (Social psychology)

Shame: the secret emotion. M. E. Donovan. *Ladies' Home Journal* 106:70+ My '89

SHAMES, LAURENCE

CBS has won the World Series . . . now it could lose its shirt. il *The New York Times Magazine* p20-4 Jl 23 '89

What a long, strange (shopping) trip it's been: looking back at the 1980s [excerpt from The hunger for more] il *Utne Reader* p66-9+ S/O '89

When an older man chooses a younger woman. il *New Choices for the Best Years* 29:60-1 Ap '89

SHAMIR, YITZHAK

Visit of Israeli prime minister [remarks, April 6, 1989] il por *Department of State Bulletin* 89:42-3 Je '89

about

The diaspora's discontent. L. I. Barrett. il por *Time* 133:18-19 Ap 3 '89

Distrust and dissension in the West Bank and Gaza. R. Z. Chesnoff. il *U.S. News & World Report* 107:38-9 Jl 10 '89

How to move the immovable. S. Talbott. il *Time* 133:20 Ap 3 '89

Masters of double-talk. il pors *Time* 134:30-1 Ag 7 '89

Minority report. C. Hitchens. *The Nation* 249:159 Ag 7-14 '89

Power, not peace. J. Smolowe. il por *Time* 134:66-7 Jl 17 '89

A profusion of land mines. M. Cohen. il *Commonweal* 116:275-8 My 5 '89

Saying no to Arafat. S. MacLeod. il pors *Time* 133:81-2 Ja 2 '89

Shamir molds a peace plan. *Time* 133:53 F 13 '89

SHAMIR, YITZHAK—about—cont.
Shamir stands his ground [interview] R. Rivard and others. il por *Newsweek* 113:42 Ja 2 '89
Shamir to school kids: drop dead; No pragmatist at heart. A. Cockburn. *The Nation* 248:150-1 F 6 '89
Shamir under fire. J. Bierman. il por *Maclean's* 102:24-5 Ap 3 '89
A talk with Dr. No. J. Amalric and A. Frachon. il por *World Press Review* 36:27-8 Ap '89
Why is this man so glum? il por *Time* 134:28 Jl 24 '89
Visit to the United States, 1989
Inch by inch, step by step. S. MacLeod. il por *Time* 133:36+ Ap 17 '89
Peace offering. *The New Republic* 200:7-8 My 1 '89
Shamir gets set for Washington [cover story] E. Salpeter. il *The New Leader* 72:6-8 Mr 6 '89
Shamir's new plan. J. Bierman. il por *Maclean's* 102:20 Ap 17 '89
Tilling the rocky ground of Mideast peacemaking. L. Lief. il por *U.S. News & World Report* 106:43 Ap 10 '89
Visit of Israeli prime minister [remarks, April 6, 1989] G. Bush; Y. Shamir. il por *Department of State Bulletin* 89:42-3 Je '89
SHAMMAS, ANTON
Arafat's types of ambiguity. *Harper's* 278:60-1 Mr '89
The shroud of Mahfouz. il *The New York Review of Books* 36:19-21 F 2 '89
SHAMPOOS
Are all shampoos created equal? L. F. McCarthy. *Vogue* 179:170 D '89
Shampoos. il *Consumer Reports* 54:12-18 D '89
Shampoos [cover story] il *Consumer Reports* 54:95-9 F '89
Smell well. R. Wiest. il *American Health* 8:24 S '89
Surprising chemistry in the shower [mixture of shampoo and soap lathers releases ammonia] il *Consumer Reports* 54:610 O '89
SHAMROCK HOLDINGS, INC.
A new way to keep raiders at bay [ESOP defense gets court O.K.] K. H. Hammonds. il *Business Week* p39 Ja 23 '89
The other Disney in the spotlight [R. Disney] F. Rice. il pors *Fortune* 119:161+ Je 5 '89
Round two for Polaroid and Shamrock [stock buyback] K. H. Hammonds. il *Business Week* p32 F 13 '89
SHANDWICK PLC
Selling the sultan [public relations for Sultan of Brunei] J. Levine. il por *Forbes* 144:264-5 Jl 24 '89
SHANE, HAROLD GRAY, 1914-
Britain's University of the Air [interview with W. Perry of Walton] il pors *The Futurist* 23:25-7 Jl/Ag '89
SHANGHAI (CHINA)
Description
Bright lights fade in China's big city. J. M. Fallows. il *U.S. News & World Report* 107:32-3+ Ag 21 '89
Letter from Beijing. F. C. Shapiro. *The New Yorker* 65:97-103 My 8 '89
Two Shanghais. R. Rowan. il *Life* 12:78-80+ Je '89
Politics and government
China gropes toward a way out [cover story] P. Kwong and D. Mišcevič. il *The Nation* 249:73+ Jl 17 '89
A tale of two cities: Hong Kong & Shanghai. N. R. Clifford. il *Commonweal* 116:453-5 S 8 '89
Restaurants, nightclubs, bars, etc.
Jam's. W. McGurn. il *The American Spectator* 22:36-7 Jl '89
SHANGHAI AVIATION INDUSTRIAL CORPORATION
MD-82 transport assembly accelerates at Shanghai. il *Aviation Week & Space Technology* 131:68-9 D 11 '89
Shanghai will deliver No. 13 MD-82 ahead of schedule. il *Aviation Week & Space Technology* 131:61-2 D 11 '89
SHANK, STEPHEN GEORGE, 1943-
about
Keep on truckin'. S. B. Weiner. il por *Forbes* 144:220-1 O 16 '89
SHANKEN, MARVIN R.
about
Old wine in new bottles. C. Brown. il por *Forbes* 144:279-80 O 16 '89
SHANKER, ALBERT
Are school boards on the way out? *The Education Digest* 55:34-6 S '89
Restructuring leadership. *The Education Digest* 54:3-5 F '89
School reform: a proposal for change. il *USA Today (Periodical)* 117:71-3 My '89
SHANLEY, JOHN PATRICK
about
John Patrick Shanley [interview] il pors *American Film* 14:20-4 S '89
SHANLEY, MARY KAY
Iowa pioneer days. il *Travel Holiday* 171:96-99 Mr '89
SHANNON, JACQUELINE
The hunt for Charles Ridgeway. il *Reader's Digest* 135:40-2+ D '89
SHANNON, MICHAEL
about
Michael Shannon, a California beach boy who's making waves with the Bolshoi Ballet. il por *People Weekly* 32:74 Ag 21 '89

Shannon shines with Soviets. M. E. Willis. por *Dance Magazine* 63:50 Ag '89
SHANNON, PEGGY LEE
about
Former hurler Vida Blue takes a bride on mound. il pors *Jet* 77:56-7 O 9 '89
SHANNON, WILLIAM HENRY, 1917-
Thomas Merton's three gifts: a review essay. *America* 161:267-73+ O 21 '89
SHANNON BOAT COMPANY
All that floats is not equal. C. Brown. il por *Forbes* 143:84+ Ap 3 '89
SHANOR, DONALD R.
The choice for East Germany. il por *The New Leader* 72:3-4 O 30 '89
Fighting Honecker's stagnation. il *The New Leader* 72:8-9 Mr 20 '89
SHAPE, INC.
Charming their bankers. R. Behar. il *Forbes* 143:43-4 F 20 '89
SHAPE PERCEPTION *See* Form perception
SHAPERS (MACHINERY)
Put a shaper in your shop. R. J. DeCristoforo. il *Workbench* 45:23-4 N/D '89
SHAPIRO, A. R.
Anatomy of a breakup: she says "I think we need to talk" . . . il *Mademoiselle* 95:142-3+ Jl '89
Loving an older man. il *Mademoiselle* 95:182-3+ O '89
SHAPIRO, ARTHUR M.
Argentina after Villa Martelli. il *The New Leader* 72:11-12 Ja 9 '89
Carlos Menem in the driver's seat. il *The New Leader* 72:10-11 Jl 10-24 '89
Menem's dangerous maneuvers. il *The New Leader* 72:12-13 N 13 '89
Privatizing Argentina. il *The New Leader* 72:7-8 Ja 23 '89
Why the left runs last in Argentina. il *The New Leader* 72:10-12 F 6 '89
SHAPIRO, BARRY
Rotisserie like it oughta be. il *Sport (New York, N.Y.)* 80:43-5 Mr '89
SHAPIRO, EZRA
Applications plus. See issues of Byte beginning March 1986 through July 1989
SHAPIRO, FRED C.
Letter from Beijing. *The New Yorker* 65:66-71 Jl 3 '89
Letter from Beijing. *The New Yorker* 65:74-9 Ag 14 '89
Letter from Beijing. *The New Yorker* 65:83-7 Je 19 '89
Letter from Beijing. *The New Yorker* 65:73-82 Je 5 '89
Letter from Beijing. *The New Yorker* 65:97-103 My 8 '89
SHAPIRO, KARL JAY, 1913-
Whitman [poem] *The American Scholar* 58:210 Spr '89
SHAPIRO, STEPHEN
about
What do you expect for $2.25 million? D. K. Shah. il por *The New York Times Magazine* p54-6+ S 10 '89
SHAPIRO, SUSIN
Laundry daze. il *Ms.* 17:34+ My '89
Neat tricks. il *Ms.* 18:43-4+ O '89
SHAPIRO, WALTER
Neoliberals in the wilderness. *The Washington Monthly* 21:48+ Mr '89
SHARANSKY, NATAN
The triumph of Natan Sharansky [condensed from Fear no evil] il por *Reader's Digest* 134:75-80 Ja '89
SHARAWADGI (TERM)
Sharawadgi. P. Lubin. *National Review* 41:52-3 O 27 '89
SHARE, G. H., AND OTHERS
Geomagnetic origin for transient particle events from nuclear reactor-powered satellites. bibl f il *Science* 244:444-8 Ap 28 '89
SHARECROPPING
The long journey home [excerpt from And their children after them] D. Maharidge and M. Williamson. il *Rolling Stone* p87-96 Mr 23 '89
SHARED APPRECIATION MORTGAGES *See* Equity sharing mortgages
SHAREHOLDERS *See* Stockholders
SHAREHOLDERS' MEETINGS *See* Stockholders' meetings
SHAREHOLDING SOCIALIST ENTERPRISE (UKRAINE)
First GASP. Q. Peel. *World Press Review* 36:53 Jl '89
SHAREWARE (COMPUTER PROGRAMS)
Cheapware—instant relief for an empty pocket [public domain, freeware, and shareware] D. Stanton. *Compute!* 11:104 Ja '89
Testing
Best of the almost-free software. K. Davis. il *Changing Times* 43:41-4 My '89
Cheapware [shareware and public domain software] D. Stanton. il *Compute!* 11:36-8+ S '89
SHARIF, BASSAM ABU
about
The new PLO? S. MacLeod. bibl f il *The New York Review of Books* 36:44-9 Ap 13 '89
SHARIF, PAMELA
Getting the most out of your bank. il *Black Enterprise* 19:46-8 Jl '89

SHARIF, PAMELA—*cont.*
Teaching your children the financial facts of life [cover story; with editorial comment by Earl G. Graves] il *Black Enterprise* 20:9, 56-8+ D '89
Using your home as an investment. il *Black Enterprise* 19:57-8+ Ap '89
SHARING OF HOMES *See* House sharing
SHARING OF JOBS *See* Job sharing
SHARK FISHING
The remarkable shark. G. Reiger. il *Field & Stream* 94:48-51+ Ag '89
Sharks find a friend in Washington [National Marine Fisheries Service protection plan] il *U.S. News & World Report* 107:16 N 20 '89
SHARKEY, BETSY
Knocking on Hollywood's door [cover story] il pors *American Film* 14:22-7+ Jl/Ag '89
The return of the return of the summer sequel. il *American Film* 14:40-1 Je '89
SHARKEY, RAY
about
Healthy, wealthy and a Wiseguy no longer, rehabbed Ray Sharkey is looking at a bright future. S. Schindehette. il pors *People Weekly* 31:50-2 F 27 '89
SHARKS
The myth of the monster [great white sharks] M. Tennesen. il *National Wildlife* 27:14-17 O/N '89
Reef shark attack! D. Perrine. bibl il *Sea Frontiers* 35:31-41 Ja/F '89
The remarkable shark. G. Reiger. il *Field & Stream* 94:48-51+ Ag '89
Why the hammer head? R. Martin. il *Sea Frontiers* 35:142-5 My/Je '89
SHARMA, KALPANA
Women of Japan. *World Press Review* 36:70 D '89
SHARON, ARIEL
about
Never! Never! Never! [interview] M. J. Gart. por *Time* 133:40-2 Ap 17 '89
Power, not peace. J. Smolowe. il por *Time* 134:66-7 Jl 17 '89
SHARON, NATHAN, AND LIS, HALINA
Lectins as cell recognition molecules. bibl f il *Science* 246:227-34 O 13 '89
SHARON, LOIS & BRAM (MUSICAL GROUP)
Buzz off, Big Bird! Pack it in, Pee-wee! The big names on little lips are Sharon, Lois and Bram. T. Allis. il *People Weekly* 31:127-8 My 1 '89
SHARP, ISADORE
about
Four Seasons heads for the beach. C. Hawkins. il por *Business Week* p111 Ap 24 '89
Sharp's luxury empire [cover story; special section] il por *Maclean's* 102:30-4+ Je 5 '89
SHARP, PAUL M., AND OTHERS
Chromosomal location and evolutionary rate variation in enterobacterial genes. bibl f il *Science* 246:808-10 N 10 '89
SHARP, REBECCA
Your brilliant career. See issues of Mademoiselle beginning May 1987
SHARPE, AVERY
about
Avery Sharpe. J. Roberts. il por *Down Beat* 56:14 Ja '89
SHARPE, ERNEST, JR.
The man who changed his skin. il pors *American Heritage* 40:44-55 F '89
SHARPE, LARRY
about
To get a hold on a pro career, wrestlers pin their hopes on Larry Sharpe's Monster Factory. M. Neill. il pors *People Weekly* 31:131+ My 15 '89
SHARPE, LESLIE T.
Hushing the homeless. il *Psychology Today* 23:64-5 D '89
SHARPE, LINDSAY T., AND OTHERS
The incremental threshold of the rod visual system and Weber's law. bibl f il *Science* 244:354-6 Ap 21 '89
SHARPENERS AND SHARPENING
The cutting edge [woodworking tools] R. Capotosto. il *Popular Mechanics* 166:107-8+ N '89
Diamond-plate knife sharpener [Chef's Choice (model No. 100)] R. Capotosto. il *Popular Mechanics* 166:72 F '89
Expand your sharpening skills. B. Kinghorn. il *The Family Handyman* 39:6+ Jl/Ag '89
How to sharpen a lawnmower blade. R. Capotosto. il *Popular Mechanics* 166:106 Mr '89
How to sharpen spade bits. R. Capotosto. il *Popular Mechanics* 166:58 Mr '89
Saw blade sharpening [circular saw] R. Capotosto. il *Popular Mechanics* 166:86-8 Ag '89
SHARROW, SHEBA
about
Sheba Sharrow at Paula Allen. A. F. Collins. *Art in America* 77:157 Ja '89
SHASTA, MOUNT (CALIF.) *See* Mount Shasta (Calif.)
SHASTA DAISIES
Old reliables: more than a dozen Shasta daisies. il *Sunset (Central West edition)* 182:232 My '89

Time to divide Shastas. il *Southern Living* 24:70 Ap '89
SHATNER, WILLIAM, 1931-
about
Star trek V: the final frontier [film] Reviews
New York il por 22:68 Je 19 '89. D. Denby
Newsweek il 113:63+ Je 19 '89. D. Ansen
People Weekly il por 31:15 Je 26 '89. R. Novak
Rolling Stone il p75 Jl 13-27 '89. P. Travers
Time il 133:89 Je 26 '89. R. Schickel
SHATTOCK, MICHAEL
Thatcherism and British higher education [address, April 1989] il pors *Change* 21:30-9 S/O '89
SHATTUCK, JOHN H. F., AND SPENCE, MURIEL MORISEY
Needed: a free flow of information and ideas. *Scientific American* 260:114 Ja '89
SHAUD, GRANT
about
Grant Shaud's résumé secret: fake it! J. Marion. il por *TV Guide* 37:7 Ag 26-S 1 '89
THE SHAUGHRAUN [drama] *See* Boucicault, Dion, 1820-1890
SHAVERS, BUTCH
about
Black mechanic is among 14 Ohioans splitting 8.25 mil. winning share in Pa. lottery. il por *Jet* 76:6 My 15 '89
SHAVERS, ELECTRIC *See* Razors
SHAVING
See also
Razors
A close shave. il *Mademoiselle* 95:16 Jl '89
The smoothest legs ever. S. Young. il *Glamour* 87:56 My '89
The trouble with hairy. A. Tardio. il *Gentlemen's Quarterly* 59:340-5 Mr '89
SHAVING MUGS
Collectors and collecting
Collecting history. R. F. Snow. il *American Heritage* 40:34-6+ Ap '89
SHAW, BERNARD
about
Vet Bernard Shaw, rookie newcomer, co-anchor CNN's 'The world today' newscast. pors *Jet* 77:23 O 30 '89
SHAW, BERNARD, 1856-1950
about
Arms and the man [drama] Reviews
New York il 22:71-2 Je 19 '89. J. Simon
The New Yorker 65:74 Je 19 '89. E. Oliver
Man and superman [drama] Reviews
Maclean's 102:55 Je 5 '89. J. Bemrose
Pygmalion [drama] Reviews
The New Republic 201 [Reprint v1]:25 N 6 '89 [N 7 '14] F. Hackett
Shaw and super-Shaw. J. J. Gross. il *The New York Review of Books* 36:27-8+ D 21 '89
SHAW, DAVID, 1943-
Scoreboard instant replays can be hazardous to your health. il *TV Guide* 37:10-12 Mr 18-24 '89
Take a number and wait. *The Washington Monthly* 21:28-30+ S '89
SHAW, FIONA
about
Bringing down the house. J. Kavanagh. il pors *Harper's Bazaar* 122:47+ S '89
SHAW, GEORGE BERNARD *See* Shaw, Bernard, 1856-1950
SHAW, HOWARD VAN DOREN, 1869-1926
about
Prairie in flower. D. G. Lowe. il *House & Garden* 161:68-75+ Ag '89
SHAW, IRWIN, 1913-1984
about
Winter of the lion [with editorial comment by Lee Eisenberg] J. Salter. il pors *Esquire* 112:11, 69-76 Jl '89
SHAW, JANE S., AND STROUP, RICHARD (RICHARD L.)
Getting warmer? il *National Review* 41:26-8 Jl 14 '89
SHAW, JOHN, 1944-
Nature. See issues of Popular Photography beginning June 1987
SHAW, PAMELA
(jt. auth) *See* Redford, Kent H., and Shaw, Pamela
SHAW, PETER, 1936-
Apocalypse again. *Commentary* 87:50-2 Ap '89
Feminist literary criticism [discussion of Autumn 1988 article] *The American Scholar* 58:317-19 Spr '89
SHAW, RAY
about
Thinking small. R. Reiff. il por *Forbes* 144:171+ D 11 '89
SHAW, RICHARD, 1941-
about
Richard Shaw at Braunstein/Quay. B. Berkson. *Art in America* 77:157 Mr '89
SHAW, ROBERT
about
Robert Shaw's ministry of music. H. Ziegenhals. il por *The Christian Century* 106:311-13 Mr 22-29 '89

SHAW, ROBERT T.
about
This could be the end of a beautiful friendship. K. Kerwin and Z. Schiller. il pors *Business Week* p33-4 S 4 '89
SHAW, ROS BYAM
Cotswold retreat. il *House & Garden* 161:124-31+ Mr '89
SHAW, YU-MING
Turning quantitative change into qualitative change [address, August 1, 1989] *Vital Speeches of the Day* 55:713-15 S 15 '89
SHAW FESTIVAL (NIAGARA-ON-THE-LAKE, ONT.)
Dramatic delights. J. Bemrose. il por *Maclean's* 102:54-5 Je 5 '89
A radiant revival [Peer Gynt] J. Bemrose. il *Maclean's* 102:50 Jl 24 '89
SHAW PUBLISHING
Thinking small [R. Shaw buys American City Business Journals] R. Reiff. il por *Forbes* 144:171+ D 11 '89
SHAWANGUNK MOUNTAINS (N.Y.)
The Shawangunk Mountains. F. Knight. il *The Conservationist* 44:26-33 S/O '89
SHAWCROSS, WILLIAM
The boat people in peril. il *The New York Review of Books* 36:58-9 N 23 '89
SHAWN, MICHAEL
about
Choreographer charges AIDS discrimination at Legs Diamond. R. Sandla. por *Dance Magazine* 63:18 Je '89
SHAWN, TED, 1891-1972
about
Ted Shawn's summer oasis, 1942: Pillow talk [excerpt from American dancesong] S. T. Underwood. il por *Dance Magazine* 63:28-31 Jl '89
SHAYE, ROBERT
about
"It's great for a date". L. Gubernick. il por *Forbes* 143:110+ F 6 '89
SHAYKIN, LEONARD P.
about
Wanted: ailing companies. Call: Leonard Shaykin. P. Finch. il por *Business Week* p75+ F 27 '89
SHAYON, ROBERT LEWIS
(jt. auth) See Dean, Sidney W., Jr., and Shayon, Robert Lewis
SHCHARANSKY, ANATOLY See Sharansky, Natan
SHE-DEVIL [film] See Motion picture reviews—Single works
SHEA, J. T.
Patrick, according to his autobiographer [poem] il *America* 160:246-7 Mr 18 '89
SHEA, JOHN
Christmas wonders. il *U.S. Catholic* 54:20-5 D '89
Four stories that shape the Christian character. il *U.S. Catholic* 54:39-43 S '89
SHEA, PAT
about
Leading a flying posse against cocaine smugglers, Pat Shea is the Batman of the Bahamas. W. Plummer. il pors *People Weekly* 32:99-100 D 18 '89
SHEA-STONUM, MARILYN, AND SLOAN, DAVID
Technology licenses: new law closes bankruptcy loophole. il *High Technology Business* 9:15 Mr '89
SHEAR, WILLIAM A., AND OTHERS
A Devonian spinneret: early evidence of spiders and silk use. bibl f il *Science* 246:479-81 O 27 '89
SHEAR STRESS See Strains and stresses
SHEARER, HARRY
I am not a critic . . . il *American Film* 15:14+ O '89
SHEARING, GRAHAM
about
Tempted by the past. J. M. Laskas. il por *House & Garden* 161:122 My '89
SHEARSON FUNDAMENTAL VALUE FUND
Clean vs. dirty [J. Dodson of Parnassus Fund vs. K. Roberts of Shearson Fundamental Value] R. O'Connor. il *Mother Jones* 14:56-7 Je '89
SHEARSON LEHMAN HUTTON INC.
Can Shearson regain that old Midas touch? J. Friedman. il *Business Week* p85 Ja 23 '89
For Peter Cohen, it's even lonelier at the top. J. Friedman. il por *Business Week* p90-1 Ap 3 '89
The greatest invention since . . . burnt toast? [unbundled stock unit] J. Friedman. il *Business Week* p88 Mr 6 '89
How the unbundled unit came unbundled. J. Friedman. il *Business Week* p71 Ap 10 '89
Is Shearson no. 1 on Amex' sell list? G. G. Marcial. *Business Week* p130 Mr 13 '89
Musical chairs may not do the trick at Shearson. J. Friedman. il por *Business Week* p59-60 D 11 '89
Peter Cohen. J. Friedman. il por *Business Week* Special Issue:112 Ap 14 '89
The Peter principle [P. Cohen] J. Queenan and T. Pouschine. il por *Forbes* 144:40-3 Jl 10 '89
The slide of Shearson Lehman. L. Reibstein and C. Friday. il por *Newsweek* 114:70 D 11 '89
Unbundled stocks: how they work. W. E. Sheeline. il *Fortune* 119:11-12 Ja 2 '89
Was George Soros sheared by Shearson? [futures loss] D. Greising. il por *Business Week* p45 N 6 '89

What did Boston Co. know and when did it know it? [accounting errors] K. H. Hammonds. por *Business Week* p87 F 6 '89
SHEDDING OF ANIMAL SKIN See Molting
SHEDS
Build the Workbench outdoor storage building. M. Landis. il *Workbench* 45:36-41 My/Je '89
Designing a tool or potting shed. M. Wells. il *Country Journal* 16:32-4 My/Je '89
Garden shed. B. Eden and D. Ware. il *Organic Gardening* 36:56+ D '89
One dandy doghouse packed with style, storage, and fun [combined with storage shed] J. Franck. il *Better Homes and Gardens* 67:124 Jl '89
Outer spaces. J. Truini. il *Home Mechanix* 85:44-51 Ag '89
Space station [stone-sheathed utility shed] W. Winans and D. Winans. il *Popular Mechanics* 166:94-6 Mr '89
Stylish storage [cover story] M. Phair. il *Home Mechanix* 86:28-30+ Mr '89
SHEED, WILFRID
Outside baseball. il *The New York Review of Books* 36:49-53 O 12 '89
Where have you gone, Joe DiMaggio? il pors *Life* 12:94-8+ O '89
SHEEHAN, GEORGE
George Sheehan's viewpoint. See issues of Runner's World
SHEEHAN, JAN
High-altitude health havens. il *Travel Holiday* 171:27-31 Ja '89
SHEEHAN, NEIL
about
Hot writers. A. DeCurtis. il pors *Rolling Stone* p117-18+ My 18 '89
SHEEHY, GAIL
The happiness report. il *Glamour* 87:308-13+ Ap '89
SHEEHY, PATRICK
about
Take that, Jimmy Goldsmith. R. A. Melcher. il *Business Week* p60-1 O 9 '89
SHEEHY, SANDY GRANVILLE
Active minivacations. il *Working Woman* 14:121-2+ Mr '89
Adventure travel. il *Working Woman* 14:204+ S '89
. . . and other rites of passage. il *Working Woman* 14:90-2 Je '89
SHEEN, CHARLIE
about
Fame in the family. il pors *'Teen* 33:51 Ap '89
SHEEP
See also
Lambs
Contamination
Sheepfarming after Chernobyl [Great Britain] B. Wynne. bibl f il maps *Environment* 31:10-15+ Mr '89
SHEEP HERDING
See also
Ganados del Valle (Organization)
SHEEP INDUSTRY
Great Britain
Sheepfarming after Chernobyl. B. Wynne. bibl f il maps *Environment* 31:10-15+ Mr '89
SHEETS, WILLIAM
(jt. auth) See Graf, Rudolf F., and Sheets, William
SHEETS, WILLIAM, AND GRAF, RUDOLF F.
Amateur TV transmitter (II). il *Radio-Electronics* 60:45-50 Jl '89
Carrier current audio transmitter [cover story] il *Radio-Electronics* 60:55+ Ja '89
Carrier current receiver. il *Radio-Electronics* 60:55+ F '89
Low frequency converter. il *Radio-Electronics* 60:47-50+ S '89
Video scene switcher (I) [cover story] il *Radio-Electronics* 60:33-8 N '89
Video scene switcher (II). il *Radio-Electronics* 60:42-4+ D '89
SHEFFER, SUSANNAH
A note on John Holt. il por *Parents* 64:114 N '89
SHEFFIELD, CHARLES
Looking back in 2073. *Ad Astra* 1:48 Mr '89
SHEFFIELD, GARY
about
Street smarts. P. Gammons. il pors *Sports Illustrated* 70 Special Issue:92-6 Ap '89
SHEFFIELD, LEE
about
Obituary
Flying il 116:136-7 N '89. G. Baxter
SHEFFIELD, PAPPY See Sheffield, Lee
SHEFFIELD, RICHARD G.
Entertainment news. See issues of Home Office Computing beginning July 1989
SHEFFIELD SILVERWARE See Silverware
SHEIKH, ANEES A.
Pictures of health [cover story] il *Omni (New York, N.Y.)* 11:104-10 F '89
SHEINBAUM, STANLEY K.
Bunker mentality. *The Nation* 248:77 Ja 23 '89
Just think. See issues of New Perspectives Quarterly

SHEINBAUM, URI
about
The playboy and the 'teddy bear' taking aim at Del Webb. T. Carson. *Business Week* p43-4 Ja 9 '89
SHEINBERG, ZENA
about
The bowling bumper cushion spares frustrated alley cats the indignity of gutter balls. il pors *People Weekly* 32:157 D 11 '89
SHEINFELD, LOIS P.
Dangerous liaisons. il *Film Comment* 25:70-2 S/O '89
SHELBY, BARRY
Regional report: Africa. See issues of World Press Review beginning June 1986
SHELBY, CARROLL, 1923-
about
Cobra revisited: long ago and not so far away. T. C. Browne. il por *Road & Track* 40:54-6 Ap '89
Shelby quits car making. il por *Motor Trend* 41:30 D '89
SHELBY, DON
about
Taking a tip from a dapper fan, anchorman Don Shelby makes news with the knot in his necktie. il pors *People Weekly* 32:59 O 2 '89
SHELBY AUTOMOBILES, INC.
Shelby quits car making. il por *Motor Trend* 41:30 D '89
SHELDON, PETER
about
Phenomena, comment and notes. J. S. Trefil. il por *Smithsonian* 20:34+ Je '89
SHELDON, SIDNEY, 1917-
The professional response. *The Writer* 102:7-8 Jl '89
The professional response. *The Writer* 102:9-10 Mr '89
The professional response. *The Writer* 102:11 D '89
The sands of time [fiction] il pors *Good Housekeeping* 208:185-8+ Mr '89
SHELF SPACE (SUPERMARKETS) *See* Supermarkets—Space allocation
SHELL, ART
about
Black named NFL coach after 7 decades. L. Ransom. il pors *Jet* 77:48-50 O 23 '89
Blount, Shell and Wood welcomed into NFL Hall. il pors *Jet* 76:57 Ag 21 '89
Dreams do come true. J. Lieber. il pors *Sports Illustrated* 71:74-8 O 23 '89
Wins, not race, are the issue for new Raiders coach Art Shell. J. Park. il pors *People Weekly* 32:95-6 D 4 '89
SHELL, ELLEN RUPPEL
Now, which kind of preschool? il *Psychology Today* 23:52-3+ D '89
SHELL CANADA LTD.
Drills across the border [plans to drill near Waterton-Glacier International Peace Park] K. Van Tighem. il *Wilderness* 52:54-6 Wint '88
SHELL GROUP *See* Royal Dutch/Shell Group
SHELL OIL COMPANY
The toxic morass in Denver's backyard [Rocky Mountain Arsenal] S. D. Atchison. il *Business Week* p46 Ja 9 '89
THE SHELL SEEKERS [television program] *See* Television program reviews—Single works
SHELLEY, BRUCE L. (BRUCE LEON), 1927-
Why work? il *Christianity Today* 33:16-18 Jl 14 '89
SHELLFISH
See also
Cooking—Shellfish
Crabs
Krill
Mollusks
Shrimp
SHELLFISH CONTAMINATION
See also
Crabs—Contamination
Shrimp—Contamination
Catching fish in all the wrong places. D. Blumenthal. il *FDA Consumer* 23:22-3 F '89
Dangerous waters: pollution shuts down B.C. shellfish areas [pulp mills] H. Quinn. il *Maclean's* 102:64 D 4 '89
SHELLFISH CULTURE
See also
Abalone culture
Crayfish culture
Ecomar (Firm)
SHELLFISH FISHERIES
See also
Clam fisheries
Seafood is Chesapeake's tradition. S. Dosier. il *Southern Living* 24:58-61 Ag '89
Laws and regulations
Dropping the net on Gulf shrimpers [requiring trapdoor devices on nets to prevent ridley turtle drownings in Gulf of Mexico] il *Newsweek* 114:28 Ag 7 '89
Shrimpers and lawmakers collide over a move to save the sea turtles [Turtle Excluder Devices required on fishing nets] J. Rudloe and A. Rudloe. il *Smithsonian* 20:44-55 D '89

Canada
Dangerous waters: pollution shuts down B.C. shellfish areas [pulp mills] H. Quinn. il *Maclean's* 102:64 D 4 '89
SHELLFISH INDUSTRY
Sanitation
E. coli clue to contamination [crab meat in Louisiana seafood processing plant] il *FDA Consumer* 23:34-5 O '89
SHELLFISH PACKING INDUSTRY *See* Shellfish industry
SHELLFISH PROCESSING INDUSTRY *See* Shellfish industry
SHELLS (CONCHOLOGY)
See also
Nautilus
Mollusk teaches ceramics to scientists [rugged shell of the red abalone; research by Mehmet Sarikaya] I. Amato. *Science News* 136:383 D 9 '89
Some Long Island seashells. H. Foglino and R. Foglino. il *The Conservationist* 44:22-5 Jl/Ag '89
SHELLS (PROJECTILES) *See* Projectiles
SHELLS (STRUCTURAL ENGINEERING)
Archome [owner-built barrel vault structure] G. Carlsen. il por *The Mother Earth News* 119:66-71+ S/O '89
SHELTERS
See also
Garden houses, shelters, etc.
SHELTERS, ATOMIC BOMB *See* Atomic bomb shelters
SHELTERS, TAX *See* Tax shelters
SHELTERS, WOMEN'S *See* Women's shelters
SHELTON, JUDY
The coming Soviet crash [excerpt] il *Conservative Digest* 15:63+ Mr/Ap '89
The Western economic response [address, March 14, 1989] *Vital Speeches of the Day* 55:429-33 My 1 '89
SHELTON, RON
'The wild bunch'. il por *American Film* 14:18+ Ap '89
about
Blaze [film] Reviews
Maclean's il 102:53-4 D 25 '89. B. D. Johnson
The New Yorker 65:136+ D 11 '89. P. Kael
Newsweek il 114:69+ D 18 '89. D. Ansen
Time il 134:93 D 18 '89. R. Corliss
Bull Durham [film] Reviews
Video il 12:16 F '89. L. Kesten
Video il 12:61-2 Mr '89. D. Schweiger
The cockeyed world of Ron Shelton. J. Silverman. il pors *American Film* 15:34-9+ O '89
Ron's rules of order. P. Jordan. il pors *Gentlemen's Quarterly* 59:300-5+ D '89
SHELTON, STEVEN E.
(jt. auth) *See* Kalin, Ned H., and Shelton, Steven E.
SHELVES AND RACKS
See also
Bookcases
Bookends and bookracks
Plate holders
Spice racks
Accessory rack. il *Workbench* 45:20 S/O '89
Bath trio [vanity, linen locker, and mirror-backed shelves] L. M. Dalsgaard. il *Home Mechanix* 85:42-4+ Je '89
Cassette and disk holders . . . easy to make. il *Sunset (Central West edition)* 181:110 D '88
Country shelving. il *Home Mechanix* 85:14 F '89
How does that shelf hang in there? [wall shelf] il *Sunset (Central West edition)* 182:162-3 Ap '89
Off the wall. il *The New York Times Magazine* p78-9 Ap 23 '89
Pot rack with built-in lighting. il *Home Mechanix* 85:50+ F '89
A rack and cleaning board. P. Butler and M. Butler. il *Outdoor Life* 183:32+ Ap '89
Shelf-awareness: getting a fix on fixtures [bookstores] M. Jones. il *Publishers Weekly* 236:18+ Jl 21 '89
Ski storage rack. S. Kingman and P. Kingman. il *The Family Handyman* 39:70-1 Ja '89
SHEMBE, LONDAUKOSI, D. 1989
about
Zulu spiritual leader murdered. I. Hexham and K. O. Poewe-Hexham. *Christianity Today* 33:65 Je 16 '89
SHEN TONG
about
Children of Tiananmen. O. Schell. il pors *Rolling Stone* p185-8+ D 14-28 '89
SHENANDOAH (AIRSHIP)
Shenandoah [cover story] J. W. Wensyel. il *American History Illustrated* 23:24-33+ F '89
SHENANDOAH [musical] *See* Musicals, revues, etc.—Reviews—Single works
SHENKER, ISRAEL
A celebrated Roman vase has become a 20th-century phoenix. bibl (p122) il *Smithsonian* 20:52-4+ Jl '89
The dictionary factory. *The New Yorker* 65:86-100 Ap 3 '89
From the villages of Stoke-on-Trent, a river of china. bibl (p191) il *Smithsonian* 19:130-4+ Mr '89
Profiles [C. de Hamel] il por *The New Yorker* 65:48+ My 29 '89
A sculptor's heaven on earth is Italy's city of holy stone. il *Smithsonian* 19:106-12+ F '89

SHENKER, ISRAEL—*cont.*
Yoicks! Yoicks! and Brolly ho! Rah for the parapluie! bibl (p246) il *Smithsonian* 20:130-2+ N '89

SHENYANG AIRCRAFT CORPORATION
Shenyang focuses on commercial projects as military aircraft requirements shrink. il *Aviation Week & Space Technology* 131:70-5 D 11 '89

SHEPARD, ROY
Great blue heron [poem] *Commonweal* 116:402 Jl 14 '89
Hubris in March [poem] *Commonweal* 116:178 Mr 24 '89
The interloper [poem] *Commonweal* 116:590 N 3 '89
Late snow [poem] *America* 160:263 Mr 25 '89

SHEPARD, SAM, 1943-
about
Far north [film] Reviews
Glamour il 87:104 Ja '89. J. G. Boyum

SHEPHARD, BEN
Vietnam 'vets' & the Soviet experience. il *History Today* 39:10-12 Jl '89

SHEPHERD, CYBILL
about
Cybill from the heart: "I'll have a fourth baby—or adopt" [cover story] A. W. Petrucelli. il pors *Redbook* 172:92-3+ Ja '89
Cybill Shepherd and Bruce Willis are named as prime suspects in Moonlighting's untimely death. M. Dougherty. il pors *People Weekly* 31:112-13 My 29 '89
Cybill Shepherd sounds off. E. Sherman. il pors *Ladies' Home Journal* 106:56+ Ja '89
The Moonlighting mess—behind the feuding that almost killed the show [cover story] L. Farr. il pors *TV Guide* 37:2-4+ Ja 14-20 '89
Why I decided to march for abortion rights [interview] il por *Glamour* 87:96 Jl '89

SHEPHERD, HARVEY
about
Quality shows are the key to net survival [interview] N. Koch. il pors *Channels (New York, N.Y.: 1986)* 9:94-5 Ja '89

SHEPHERD, J. BARRIE
I'm dreaming [poem] *The Christian Century* 106:1141 D 6 '89
Temple cleansing [poem] *The Christian Century* 106:304 Mr 22-29 '89

SHEPHERD, NIKI LEWIS
Caring for holiday cacti. il *Flower and Garden* 33:43-4 N/D '89

SHEPHERDS IN THE BIBLE
Divided flock. P. J. Ryan. il *America* 160:355 Ap 8 '89
Shepherd as lamb. P. J. Ryan. il *America* 160:311 Ap 1 '89

SHEPHERDSON, NANCY
The first 1040. il *American Heritage* 40:101-5 Mr '89

SHEPPARD, ALLEN
about
"We've got a serious problem". J. Marcom, Jr. il por *Forbes* 144:48-9+ D 25 '89

SHER, BARBARA, AND GOTTLIEB, ANNIE
3 ways to make your dreams come true. il *Glamour* 87:87 My '89

SHERATON NEW ORLEANS (NEW ORLEANS, LA.: HOTEL) *See* New Orleans (La.)—Hotels, motels, etc.
SHERATON PALACE (SAN FRANCISCO, CALIF.: HOTEL) *See* San Francisco (Calif.)—Hotels, motels, etc.
SHERBET *See* Ice cream, ices, etc.
SHEREFF, RUTH
How to reward the criminals. *The Nation* 248:192-5 F 13 '89
Wish me well. il *Ms.* 18:26+ O '89

SHERIDAN, DANNY
Autumn madness. il *Sport (New York, N.Y.)* 80:109-10 O '89
Bettin' baseball: the key to diamond dollars: pick your spots. il *Sport (New York, N.Y.)* 80:72-3 Jl '89
College education. il *Sport (New York, N.Y.)* 80:79-80 S '89
A fighting chance. il *Sport (New York, N.Y.)* 80:75-6 Ag '89
Home cookin'. il *Sport (New York, N.Y.)* 80:123-4 Je '89
Playoff payoffs. il *Sport (New York, N.Y.)* 80:82-4 N '89
Turkey weekend wagering. il *Sport (New York, N.Y.)* 80:80 D '89

SHERIDAN, JIM
about
My left foot [film] Reviews
American Film 15:64-5 D '89. A. Insdorf
Harper's Bazaar il 122:84+ N '89
Maclean's il 102:87 N 13 '89. B. D. Johnson
The New Republic 201:25-6 N 27 '89. S. Kauffmann
New York il 22:109-10 N 13 '89. D. Denby
The New Yorker 65:98-100 O 2 '89. P. Kael
Newsweek 114:90 N 27 '89. D. Ansen
Rolling Stone il p38 N 16 '89. P. Travers
Time il 134:84 N 6 '89. R. Corliss

SHERIDAN, THOMAS B.
Merging mind and machine [cover story] il *Technology Review* 92:32-40 O '89

SHERIFFS
See also
Black sheriffs

SHERLOCK HOLMES (FICTIONAL CHARACTER)
Sherlock Holmes and the weather [cover story] R. S. Cerveny and S. W. Brazel. il *Weatherwise* 42:80-4 Ap '89

SHERMAN, BETH
American beauty. il pors *Harper's Bazaar* 122:58-63+ Jl '89
Quilt crazy. il *Harper's Bazaar* 122:56+ F '89
A touch of glass. il *Harper's Bazaar* 122:94+ O '89

SHERMAN, CARL
Body and soul: health. See issues of Gentlemen's Quarterly
The complete summer-safety guide. il *Parents* 64:103-6+ Jl '89
Fighting cancer with carrots. il *New Choices for the Best Years* 29:59-63 O '89

SHERMAN, DEBRA
Pit players. il pors *Ms.* 18:62-4+ N '89

SHERMAN, DON
4WD in demand. *Skiing* 41:12+ F '89

SHERMAN, ERIC
Bette Midler gets serious. il pors *Ladies' Home Journal* 106:58+ Ja '89
Cybill Shepherd sounds off. il pors *Ladies' Home Journal* 106:56+ Ja '89
Roseanne's main squeeze. il pors *Ladies' Home Journal* 106:136+ My '89
Success is the best answer. il pors *Ladies' Home Journal* 106:44 S '89
What's hot. See issues of Ladies' Home Journal beginning March 1987

SHERMAN, JACK A.
about
Marine official pleads guilty to U.S. bribery, fraud charges. M. Mecham. *Aviation Week & Space Technology* 130:26 F 6 '89

SHERMAN, JOE
In the halcyon days when pictures of the land came first. bibl (p229) il por *Smithsonian* 20:88-96+ O '89

SHERMAN, STEVE, 1938-
Trails West rounds up western readers. il *Publishers Weekly* 235:41+ My 5 '89

SHERMAN, WILLIAM T. (WILLIAM TECUMSEH), 1820-1891
about
1864. A. Nielsen. il *American Heritage* 40:36-7 S/O '89

SHERMAN OAKS (CALIF.)
Architecture
Three-level answer for a 45° slope [house] il *Sunset (Central West edition)* 183:84-5 Ag '89

SHERMER, MICHAEL
Are RAAM riders crazy? *Bicycling* 30:108+ Ag '89
Astound yourself! il *Bicycling* 30:36-40 S '89
Master of my fate. il *Bicycling* 30:73-5 Je '89

SHERMETA, MARGO
Norma Minkowitz: shadow boxes. il *American Craft* 49:38-41 D '89/Ja '90

SHERRATT & HUGHES
W. H. Smith merges specialist bookselling chain with Waterstone's. V. Menkes. *Publishers Weekly* 236:14 Ag 4 '89

SHERRY, VINCENT, D. 1987
about
The murder—and the mayor. J. N. Baker. il por *Newsweek* 114:32 O 23 '89

SHERWIN-WILLIAMS CO.
A chemical maker's secret admirer? [interest in Dexter Corp.] G. G. Marcial. *Business Week* p76 Ja 30 '89

SHERWOOD, DOLLY
Chesterwood: a sculptor's studio. il *Gourmet* 49:76-9+ Je '89

SHE'S OUT OF CONTROL [film] See Motion picture reviews—Single works

SHETTERLY, SUSAN HAND
My mother-in-law is for the birds. il *New Choices for the Best Years* 29:89-92 Mr '89

SHEVARDNADZE, EDUARD
about
Agenda for Baker-Shevardnadze. *National Review* 41:11-12 My 5 '89
Aiming for the heights. H. Mackenzie. il pors *Maclean's* 102:31-3 O 2 '89
The boss of Smolensky Square [with interview; cover story] J. Kohan. il pors *Time* 133:29-30+ My 15 '89
Divided together. A. Bilski. il por *Maclean's* 102:26 Mr 6 '89
Fresh air, fresh ideas. G. J. Church. il por *Time* 134:24 O 2 '89
Inching ever closer together. B. Javetski. il *Business Week* p40-1 O 9 '89
Moscow's new role in the Middle East [cover story] F. Halliday. il *The Nation* 248:361+ Mr 20 '89
The politics of diplomacy. H. Anderson. il *Newsweek* 114:20-1 O 2 '89
START deals cut at Jackson Hole. J. Mendelsohn. il pors *The Bulletin of the Atomic Scientists* 45:25-7 D '89

SHEVARDNADZE, EDUARD—about—*cont.*
The Wyoming ministerial [cover story; special section] il pors *Department of State Bulletin* 89:1-26 N '89
SHIDLER (OKLA.)

Description
A wonderful place to live. W. Fields. il *American Heritage* 40:114-17 Ap '89
SHIELDS, BROOKE

about
Model witness. L. Snowden. il pors *Vogue* 179:374-5 D '89
Of many things. G. W. Hunt. *America* 160:162 F 25 '89
SHIELDS, JODY
Facing the future. il *Vogue* 179:206-7 Ja '89
Spines like us. il *Vogue* 179:228-9 Ja '89
SHIELDS, PATRICIA M.
Freud, efficiency and pragmatism. bibl *Society* 26:67-72 Ja/F '89
SHIELDS, STEPHEN
Triumph and tragedy. il por *American Heritage* 40:82-6+ D '89
SHIFERAW, MONA, D. 1989

about
Alleged killer of 'Jet beauty' turns himself in after his crime is aired on TV show. pors *Jet* 77:7 O 16 '89
D.C. police hunt for suspect in slaying of co-ed and her brother. pors *Jet* 76:52 Jl 24 '89
SHIFT WORK *See* Hours of labor
SHIFTING, BICYCLE *See* Bicycles—Gearing
SHIFTING CULTIVATION
A catbird's seat on Amazon destruction [monitoring of illegal agricultural burning by remote sensing satellites] F. Golden. il *Science* 246:201-2 O 13 '89
Farming the forest. M. Hadley. il *The Courier (Unesco)* 42:26-8 Ja '89
SHIITAKE MUSHROOM COOKING *See* Cooking—Mushrooms
SHIITE MUSLIMS *See* Muslims
SHILLING, A. GARY

about
Mirror, mirror, on the wall, will the economy really fall? J. C. Cooper. il por *Business Week* p80 D 25 '89-Ja 1 '90
SHILSTONE SOFTWARE COMPANY
Ma-and-pa engineering. E. Dyson. il *Forbes* 143:122 F 6 '89
SHILTS, RANDY
The era of bad feelings. il *Mother Jones* 14:32-6+ N '89
Talking AIDS to death. por *Esquire* 111:123-6+ Mr '89
SHIMA, MASATOSHI

about
Microprocessor challenge. R. C. Wood. il *High Technology Business* 9:12+ My '89
SHIMOUCHI, AKIRA
Controlling pneumonia in children. il *World Health* p18-19 N '89
SHINGLES AND SHINGLING
Fire-resistant shingles: treatments for cedar. *Better Homes and Gardens* 67:63 Ap '89
Roofing shingle repair. M. Morris. il *Home Mechanix* 86:28-30 Ap '89
Solar shingles. V. E. Gilmore. il *Popular Science* 234:146 Je '89
SHINHOLSER, RAY

about
A cop's homage to a slain pal becomes his own tragic farewell. il por *People Weekly* 31:43 Ja 30 '89
SHINING PATH (GUERRILLA GROUP) *See* Sendero Luminoso (Guerrilla group)
SHINING TIME STATION [television program] See Television program reviews—Single works
SHINKARETSKY, VICTOR

about
Oh, no here comes Joe. A. Blackman. il por *Time* 133:76 Ap 10 '89
SHINKMAN, RON
Boy behavior: what's behind it? il *'Teen* 33:34-5 Jl '89
SHINN, EUGENE A.
What is really killing the corals [cover story] bibl il map *Sea Frontiers* 35:72-81 Mr/Ap '89
SHINN, KAREN GELLER- *See* Geller-Shinn, Karen
SHINODA, HISAHARU, AND OTHERS
Brain region and gene specificity of neuropeptide gene expression in cultured astrocytes. bibl f il *Science* 245:415-17 Jl 28 '89
SHINTO, HISASHI

about
The Recruit scandal bubbles to the top. A. Borrus. por *Business Week* p55 Mr 20 '89
SHINTO

See also
Izanagi and Izanami (Shinto deities)
SHIP AND BOAT MODELS
They moved the holiday regatta to their swimming pool. il *Sunset (Central West edition)* 181:94 D '88

Collectors and collecting
Down to the sea in ship models [dockyard models in R. Kriegstein's collection] C. Brown. il *Forbes* 144:336+ N 13 '89

Exhibitions
The August Crabtree ship model collection [Mariners' Museum] il *Americana* 17:43 S/O '89
SHIP BUILDING *See* Shipbuilding
SHIP CANALS *See* Canals
SHIP HIJACKING
Of piracy and payoffs [ships diverted into Lebanese ports] J. Penycate. *World Press Review* 36:53 My '89
SHIP SIGNALS *See* Signals and signaling
SHIPBUILDING

See also
Avondale Industries Inc.
Collective labor agreements—Shipbuilding
Tenneco Inc.

Federal aid
A kinder, gentler Navy? [address, January 18, 1989] W. E. Haggett. *Vital Speeches of the Day* 55:403-5 Ap 15 '89

Japan

See also
Hitachi Zosen Corp.
The Japanese do it again. A. Tanzer. il *Forbes* 144:40-1 O 16 '89

Poland

See also
Barbara Piasecka Johnson-Gdańsk Shipyard Company
SHIPLER, DAVID K.
Dateline USSR: on the human rights track. *Foreign Policy* 75:164-81 Summ '89
Letter from Budapest. *The New Yorker* 65:74+ N 20 '89
Symbols of sovereignty. *The New Yorker* 65:52+ S 18 '89
SHIPMAN, HARRY L.
Do we have a place in space? *Astronomy* 17:8 S '89
SHIPMAN, PAT
All in the family. il *Discover* 10:44 Jl '89
The gripping story of Paranthropus. il *Discover* 10:66-71 Ap '89
Sixth find is a feathered friend. il *Discover* 10:63 Ja '89
SHIPMASTERS
How smart is your skipper? S. Stapleton. *Motor Boating & Sailing* 164:80-2 D '89
SHIPMENT OF BOOKS *See* Books—Transportation
SHIPMENT OF GOODS

See also
United Parcel Service of America, Inc.
SHIPMENT OF WORKS OF ART *See* Transportation of works of art
SHIPPING

See also
Anangel-American Shipholdings Ltd.
Longshore workers
McLean Industries Inc.
Panama Canal
Tankers

International aspects

See also
Stolt Tankers & Terminals (Holdings)
SHIPPINGPORT NUCLEAR POWER PLANT (PA.) *See* Nuclear power plants
SHIPS

See also
Clipper ships
Cutters (Ships)
Ice breaking vessels
Nuclear ships
Ocean liners
Sailing vessels
Salvage (Ships)
Shipwrecks
Steamships and steamboats
Submarines
Tankers
Tugboats
Warships
Windships
Yachts and yachting
Direct and remote sensing observations of the effects of ships on clouds. L. F. Radke and others. bibl f il *Science* 246:1146-9 D 1 '89

Manufacture

See Shipbuilding

Officers

See Shipmasters

Safety devices and measures
Drawing the line at safety [S. Plimsoll's reform campaign in 19th century Britain] A. Thomas. il por map *History Today* 39:5-7 F '89
SHIPS, MODEL *See* Ship and boat models
SHIPS, RESEARCH

See also
Nyanja (Research ship)
SHIP'S COMPANY THEATRE
A ship of dreams. P. Hluchy. il *Maclean's* 102:50 Ag 21 '89

SHIPS IN ART
Masterpieces [work of M. Keane] A. Shreve. il por *Motor Boating & Sailing* 163:58-61+ Ja '89
SHIPWRECKS
See also
Arabia (Steamship)
Archeology, Submarine
Bermuda Triangle
Bismarck (Battleship)
Central America (Steamship)
City of Rio de Janeiro (Ship)
Dorchester (Ship)
Kronan (Ship)
Lucona (Ship)
Pandora (Ship)
Pollux (Ship)
Salvage (Ships)
Titanic (Steamship)
Attack from the ocean deep [D. Sellings survives attack by whales during the Carlsberg Single-handed Transatlantic Race] S. Kelly. il *Reader's Digest* 134:67-72 F '89
A deadly struggle against the sea [adrift in rubber dinghy after shipwreck of Anaulis; cover story]; ed. by Ron Arias. J. Culver. il pors *People Weekly* 32:62-6+ Ag 21 '89
Heroes [Coast Guard rescues shipwrecked sailors from the Lloyd Bermuda container ship] J. A. Fishman. il *Motor Boating & Sailing* 163:52-7+ Mr '89
Shipwrecked [disastrous effort to set trans-Atlantic speed record] D. Pike. il *Motor Boating & Sailing* 164:54-7+ Jl '89
A shipwrecked Miami couple owe their lives to a clever gadget that makes seawater drinkable [Survivor-35 pump; case of William and Simone Butler] il *People Weekly* 32:101 O 2 '89
Staying alive [B. Butler and his wife survive 66 days on a raft after their boat was sunk by killer whales] S. Stapleton. il pors *Motor Boating & Sailing* 164:48-51+ N '89
Laws and regulations
Is a treasure hunter's gain history's loss? B. Carpenter. il *U.S. News & World Report* 107:54-5 Ag 21 '89
Rescue work
See Rescue work
SHIPYARDS
See also
Shipbuilding
SHIRAS, LEIF
Down and out. il *World Tennis* 37:46-8 O '89
A sign of the times. il *World Tennis* 37:82 Ag '89
SHIRLEY PLANTATION (HOPEWELL, VA.)
Virginia's Shirley Plantation. J. S. Wamsley. il *Architectural Digest* 46:126-31+ Je '89
SHIRLEY VALENTINE (FICTIONAL CHARACTER)
Shirley Valentine's day [views of P. Collins] D. DeNicolo. il por *Glamour* 87:192 O '89
SHIRLEY VALENTINE [drama] *See* Russell, Willy
SHIRLEY VALENTINE [film] *See* Motion picture reviews—Single works
SHIRTS
See also
Phillips-Van Heusen Corp.
T-shirts
The bowling shirt. J. Berendt. il *Esquire* 111:26 Ja '89
Check mate [tattersall shirt] E. Siff. il *Gentlemen's Quarterly* 59:25 Jl '89
The elegant man: white-collar jobs. E. Siff. il *Gentlemen's Quarterly* 59:374-5 S '89
Expensive habits: the Charvet shirt. P. Mayle. il *Gentlemen's Quarterly* 59:53+ Je '89
From eternity to here [Hawaiian shirts] P. Jordan. il *Gentlemen's Quarterly* 59:88+ Mr '89
The madras shirt. J. Berendt. il *Esquire* 111:46 Je '89
My shirt tale. S. Elkin. il *Harper's* 278:73-6 Ap '89
SHISEIDO COMPANY LTD.
Shiseido grant: more than skin deep [Japanese funding of Massachusetts General Hospital-Harvard University's Cutaneous Biology Research Center] M. Sun. *Science* 245:810-11 Ag 25 '89
SHIVANANDAN, MARY
The blessings of fertility. *America* 161:474-7 D 23-30 '89
SHIVELY, CAROL A.
A smoke-scented diary. il *Natural History* p34-43 Ag '89
SHIVERS, STEVE
about
Message of the pond. P. Michelmore. il *Reader's Digest* 135:106-10 D '89
SHLAIM, AVI
about
Charging Israel with original sin. S. Teveth. bibl f *Commentary* 88:24-33 S '89
SHMERLER, CINDY
It ain't all glamour. il *Women's Sports & Fitness* 11:53-7 Mr '89
SHOBERT, BUBBA
about
Fall from grace. K. Cameron. il *Cycle* 40:8 Ag '89
SHOCK
See also
Electric shock

Toxic shock syndrome
Traumatism
SHOCK, ANAPHYLACTIC *See* Anaphylaxis
SHOCK ABSORBERS
See also
All terrain vehicles—Shock absorbers
Automobiles—Shock absorbers
Motorcycles—Shock absorbers
SHOCK THERAPY
Shock therapy's Parkinsonian potential [work of Richard Douyon] *Science News* 136:381 D 9 '89
SHOCK WAVES
See also
Sonic boom
How to analyze the shock waves that sweep through expressway traffic. J. Walker. il *Scientific American* 261:98-100+ Ag '89
Nonequilibrium molecular motion in a hypersonic shock wave. G. Pham-Van-Diep and others. bibl f il *Science* 245:624-6 Ag 11 '89
Medical use
See also
Lithotripsy
SHOCKED, MICHELLE
about
Michelle Shocked: mesmerizing. A. Nash. il *Stereo Review* 54:104 Mr '89
SHOCKER [film] *See* Motion picture reviews—Single works
SHOCKEY, GAYLE
The best quick breakfasts for active women. il *Women's Sports & Fitness* 11:34-5+ Ap '89
The truth about iron. il *Women's Sports & Fitness* 11:20-1 Ja/F '89
SHOCKLEY, DONALD G., 1937-
Rattling the dry bones of the student Christian movement. *The Christian Century* 106:1087-9 N 22 '89
SHOCKLEY, WILLIAM
about
Obituary
U.S. News & World Report il por 107:16 Ag 28-S 4 '89
SHOE INDUSTRY
See also
Allen-Edmonds Shoe Corp.
Brown Group, Inc.
L.A. Gear Inc.
Musebeck Shoe Company
Reebok International Ltd.
Stride Rite Corp.
Timberland Company
Toddler University Inc.
Tony Lama Company
U.S. Shoe Corp.
Acquisitions and mergers
If the shoe fits, sell it? [U.S. Shoe to sell most of its footwear division] S. Phillips. *Business Week* p42+ Mr 13 '89
Advertising
Reebok on the rebound. B. Kanner. il *New York* 22:26+ O 16 '89
Ethical aspects
Has sneaker madness gone too far? [industry accused of exploiting youth] T. Barrett. il *Newsweek* 114:51 D 18 '89
Export-import trade
Party crasher [Allen-Edmonds Shoe Corp.] R. Reiff. il por *Forbes* 143:128+ Je 12 '89
Finance
Apparel, shoes and textiles. G. Eisenstodt. il *Forbes* 143:86-8 Ja 9 '89
Management
Multifactor productivity slips in the nonrubber footwear industry. J. Duke and L. Usher. il *Monthly Labor Review* 112:32-8 Ap '89
Marketing
Foot's paradise [athletic shoes] B. Rudolph. il *Time* 134:54-5 Ag 28 '89
Sneak attacks [athletic shoes] J. Kaplan. il *Vogue* 179:178+ My '89
Quality control
U.S. shoe firms thrive in high-quality market. J. E. Bahls. il *Nation's Business* 77:38-40 F '89
SHOE SHINE BUSINESS *See* Shoeshine business
SHOE STORES
See also
Belgian Shoes Inc.
SHOELESS JOE JACKSON *See* Jackson, Joe, 1887 or 8-1951
SHOEMAKER, BILL
Anthony Braxton: the dynamics of creativity [interview] il pors *Down Beat* 56:20-2 Mr '89
SHOEMAKER, BILL, 1931-
about
Silent Shoe's last ride. S. Crist. il pors *The New York Times Magazine* p42-4+ Je 4 '89
SHOEMAKER, WILLIAM
about
Tribulation at William Tyndale. *Christianity Today* 33:49 My 12 '89

SHOEMAKER, WILLIE *See* Shoemaker, Bill, 1931-
SHOEMAKERS *See* Shoe industry
SHOES *See* Footwear
SHOESHINE BUSINESS
Spit 'n' polish [New York City] R. D. Story. il *New York* 22:57 My 1 '89
SHOLDER, JACK
about
Renegades [film] Reviews
People Weekly il 31:15 Je 19 '89. R. Novak
Rolling Stone p29 Je 29 '89. P. Travers
SHOLLY, DAN
about
Fire, then ice. M. Brower. il pors *People Weekly* 31:42-7 Ja 16 '89
SHOMETTE, DONALD G.
Heyday of the horse ferry. il map *National Geographic* 176:548-56 O '89
SHONEY'S INC.
NAACP/LDEF sues Shoney's. L. Brown. *Black Enterprise* 20:20 Ag '89
Shoney's needs a recipe for succession. W. Konrad. il por *Business Week* p52 D 25 '89-Ja 1 '90
SHONGWE, ISAAC
about
Black South African, 26, wins Rhodes scholarship. *Jet* 75:23 Ja 9 '89
SHOOP, ROBERT J.
AIDS: infected children have the right to attend school. *USA Today (Periodical)* 117:68-70 My '89
SHOOTING
See also
Decoys (Hunting)
Duck shooting
Game bird shooting
Goose shooting
Grouse shooting
Hunting
Mourning dove shooting
National Rifle Association of America
Partridge shooting
Pheasant shooting
Quail shooting
Rifles
Snipe shooting
Target practice
Targets
Trapshooting
Water bird shooting
Woodcock shooting
Shooting. See issues of Field & Stream
Shooting. J. Carmichel. See issues of Outdoor Life
Competitions
See also
Biathlon (Skiing and shooting)
SHOOTING PRESERVES
An appetite for food and sport [privately owned hunting preserves] S. Dosier. il *Southern Living* 24:154+ O '89
Quest for a dream bull [elk] K. Etling. il *Outdoor Life* 183:70-1+ Ja '89
Great Britain
Keepers of the game. B. Alexander. il *International Wildlife* 19:34-40 S/O '89
SHOOTING RANGES
Gun buffs risk loading lungs with lead [handgun hobbyists using indoor firing ranges] *Science News* 136:126 Ag 19 '89
SHOP WINDOWS *See* Show windows
SHOPE RENO WHARTON ASSOCIATES
Shope Reno Wharton: "architectural furniture" revitalizes a Connecticut attic. il *Architectural Digest* 46:92-3 Ap '89
SHOPLIFTING
An NDP star is charged [L. Nystrom charged in Ottawa, Ont.] il por *Maclean's* 102:24 D 11 '89
Security measures
Big Brother at the mall. D. Tsiantar. il *Newsweek* 114:44 Jl 3 '89
SHOPPING
See also
Bargains
Bulk buying
Christmas shopping
Electronic shopping
Mail order business
Purchasing, Household
Sales
Secondhand trade
Stores
Warehouse clubs
All shopped out? [cover story; special section] il *Utne Reader* p65-89 S/O '89
Reflections in a mass eye [women in a communal dressing room at Loehmann's] S. A. Feeney. il *Ms.* 18:30+ N '89
Shopping smart. S. Dresner. il *Essence* 20:42 O '89
The way we were [shopping for back-to-school clothes with children] D. Sobel. il *Ladies' Home Journal* 106:82 S '89

Anecdotes, facetiae, satire, etc.
Clothes klutz. B. Ehrenreich. il *Ms.* 17:24-5 Je '89
Spreedom, now! L. Phillips. il *Ms.* 18:30+ Jl/Ag '89
International aspects
Traveler's market. D. P. Marshall. il *Travel Holiday* 172:24-7 N '89
Psychological aspects
See also
Compulsive shopping
Is consumer frenzy an outlet for people's growing feelings of powerlessness? J. Williamson. *Utne Reader* p78 S/O '89
Swimsuit anxiety. L. F. McCarthy. il *Health (New York, N.Y.)* 21:43+ My '89
Your shopping personality. il *Glamour* 87:30 Ja '89
Statistics
The shopping days of our lives. J. P. Robinson. il *Utne Reader* p68 S/O '89
Canada
The birthplace of shopping—Quebec. D. P. Marshall. il *Travel Holiday* 171:24+ My '89
Soviet Union
'I'll take it. What is it?' The shopping spree in Russia. P. Galuszka. il *Business Week* p41 My 1 '89
Why the Bear's cupboards are bare. W. R. Doerner. il *Time* 133:33+ Ja 16 '89
Western Europe
Getting a good return [value added tax refunds to shoppers] D. P. Marshall. il *Travel Holiday* 171:28+ F '89
SHOPPING BAG LADIES *See* Homeless women
SHOPPING BAGS
Shopping bags imitate art. A. Miller. il *Newsweek* 113:44 Ja 23 '89
SHOPPING CENTERS
See also
Mall of America (Bloomington, Minn.)
Rouse Co.
Underground Atlanta
Cheryl McArthur: discount outlets for mall mavens. P. Y. Hong. il por *Business Week* p117 N 6 '89
A decree went out: humbug to Salvation [Salvation Army banned] S. Budiansky. il *U.S. News & World Report* 107:8-9 D 18 '89
Discipline, discipline, discipline [Weingarten Realty] J. H. Taylor. il por *Forbes* 144:42-3 Jl 24 '89
Downtowns revived [special section] G. Anderson. il *Architectural Record* 177:96-105 S '89
Guys and dolls at the mall [children's fashions] R. La Ferla. il *The New York Times Magazine* p58-61 Jl 9 '89
A Japanese mall in—New Jersey? [Yaohan Plaza] L. J. Nathans. il *Business Week* p100 Ja 30 '89
Love blooms in the aisles [shopping malls used for walking] J. Pereira. il *The Saturday Evening Post* 261:54-5+ S '89
The magic is back in Little Rock [MainStreet] il *Southern Living* 24:33 Mr '89
No more plastic plants [Melvin Simon & Associates] S. B. Weiner. il por *Forbes* 143:107-8 Mr 20 '89
Say g'day to the megamall [Forest Fair in Cincinnati] S. Phillips. il *Business Week* p29 Mr 6 '89
Two on the town [Heritage on the Garden in Boston and San Francisco Centre] P. M. Sachner. il maps *Architectural Record* 177:122-7 My '89
Environmental aspects
The third battle of Manassas [defeat of proposed mall] A. Hills. il *History Today* 39:4-5 Mr '89
Food service
Mall mania: too many temptations [food court] il *Glamour* 87:258-60 Ag '89
International aspects
Will wonders never cease? [Ghermezian brothers] J. Queenan. il *Forbes* 144:72-3+ S 4 '89
Canada
See also
West Edmonton Mall (Alta.)
SHOPPING MALLS *See* Shopping centers
SHORB, MICHAEL
A flower responds to certain criticisms advanced by the cathedral [poem] *Commonweal* 116:273 My 5 '89
SHORE, DINAH, 1920-
about
The ever-lovin' Dinah Shore [interview; cover story] F. Robbins. il pors *New Choices for the Best Years* 29:32-7 F '89
SHORE, IRMA, 1947-
about
Please touch the art works. J. Seligmann. il por *Newsweek* 114:77+ N 6 '89
SHORE, LYS ANN
An uphill battle for comet research. il *Astronomy* 17:46-50 F '89
SHORE BIRDS
See also
Herons
Sea birds
Migration
Standing room only. P. Steinhart. il *National Wildlife* 27:46-51 Ap/My '89

SHORE EROSION *See* Coast changes
SHORE LINE CHANGES *See* Coast changes
SHORE PROTECTION
 See also
  Dikes (Engineering)
  Jetties
                Egypt
The drowning delta [Nile River] T. Land. *World Press Review*
 36:64-5 N '89
                Massachusetts
Tires, trees, terns, terrapins [planting Christmas trees on
 Massachusetts beaches to halt erosion] T. Williams. il
 Audubon 91:26-8+ My '89
              Prince Edward Island
Protecting coastal riches. D. Jenish. il *Maclean's* 102:29 Ja
 16 '89
SHOREBANK CORPORATION (CHICAGO, ILL.)
A poverty program that works. D. Osborne. *The New Republic*
 200:22-5 My 8 '89
Shorebank Corporation: rebuilding a community. J. David
 and K. File. *Working Woman* 14:171+ O '89
SHOREHAM NUCLEAR POWER PLANT (N.Y.) *See* Nuclear
 power plants
SHORR, HARRIET
                about
Harriet Shorr. L. S. Hurwitz. il por *American Artist* 53:34-9+
 O '89
SHORRIS, EARL, 1936-
Art, intrigue and human rights. il *The Nation* 249:14-18
 Jl 3 '89
The priest who loves gangsters [cover story] il *The Nation*
 249:737+ D 18 '89
Raids, racism and the I.N.S. il *The Nation* 248:628-30 My
 8 '89
SHORS, TRACEY J., AND OTHERS
Inescapable versus escapable shock modulates long-term
 potentiation in the rat hippocampus. bibl f il *Science*
 244:224-6 Ap 14 '89
SHORT, KAROL FAGEROS *See* Fageros, Karol, d. 1988
SHORT, RANDALL
Bill Irwin and the rest of the New Vaudevillians are rescuing
 performance art from a decade of pretension. il por *Vogue*
 179:202+ Ag '89
Blair Brown, television's Molly Dodd, returns to the stage—her
 first love. por *Vogue* 179:486+ S '89
SHORT, THOMAS
Homophobiaphobia. *National Review* 41:19-20 Ag 18 '89
SHORT BROTHERS LTD.
Bombardier, GEC-Fokker team lead field of suitors for
 Northern Ireland's Short Brothers. *Aviation Week & Space
 Technology* 130:31 Mr 13 '89
Bombardier of Canada wins competition to buy Short
 Brothers. *Aviation Week & Space Technology* 130:63 Je
 12 '89
Britain to assume Short's debt as step toward sale. *Aviation
 Week & Space Technology* 129:30 Mr 6 '89
Britain will recapitalize Short Brothers prior to sale. *Aviation
 Week & Space Technology* 130:28 Ja 16 '89
SHORT LIST (TERM)
Short grows the list. W. Safire. il *The New York Times
 Magazine* p10+ Ja 22 '89
SHORT PEOPLE *See* Stature
SHORT SELLING *See* Securities—Short selling
SHORT STORIES
        See also
  Children's stories
  Christmas stories
  Detective and mystery stories
  See name of author for full entry
??? !!! Mishveladze, Revaz
6 little love notes. Wilson, Shirley
Accident. Troy, Judy
Ado. Willis, Connie
The adopted baby. Gerber, Merrill Joan
An affair of the hat. Jordan, Eileen Herbert
After the beep. Dixon, Carol
An almost perfect fit. Shyer, Marlene Fanta
Americana. Simpson, Mona
Among the roses. Lessing, Doris May, 1919-
The announcement. Hersey, John, 1914-
Another bad dream. Lott, Bret
Answers. Lipsky, David
Anything for a baby. Barrett, Helen
Backdaire. Ng, Fae Myenne
The beautiful ones. Allen, Edward, 1948-
Berard's luck. Chiarella, Tom
The better to know you. Soman, Florence Jane
Between mother and daughter. Kupfer, Fern
Billie Dyer. Maxwell, William, 1908-
Birthday blessings. Bittle, Camilla R.
The bite. Buchanan, Lisa K.
Bread, butter, and Florrie Ford. Spark, Muriel
A brief fall. Woiwode, Larry
Bringing the family together. Hood, Ann, 1956-
The bullet's flight. Johnson, Denis, 1949-
Call me Cinderella. Blackburn, Taye
Camaro City. Sternberg, Alan
The case of the misplaced faith. Matson, Howard

Chance of a lifetime. Franco, Marjorie
A change of policy. Pritchett, V. S. (Victor Sawdon), 1900-
Chau bandoneón. Contou-Carrère, Enrique Jorge
Choices. Brown, Virginia M.
Closer to God. Wood, Monica
Color blind. Jermyn, Amanda
Cousins. Tester, William
Cutting weight. Bache, Ellyn
Daniel. Raymond, Ilene
A day out. O'Brien, Edna
Devils. Kadohata, Cynthia
Differently. Munro, Alice
Do ye ken Wilbur Pope—. Brooks, Walter R., 1886-1958
Doctor Kamikaze. Armah, Ayi Kwei, 1938-
Dog heaven. Vaughn, Stephanie
Downstream. Nelson, Antonya
Dr. Ordinary. Powell, Padgett
Driving gloves. Dovlatov, Sergeĭ
Eight candles of hope. Goldreich, Gloria
Elevator neighbors. Rofihe, Rick
Esther. Kureishi, Hanif
Everything is green. Wallace, David Foster
Everything that counts. Bodett, Tom
Eyes. Matheson, Richard, 1926-
Fair-weather friend. Anderson, Cristina
Family. Oates, Joyce Carol, 1938-
Family affair. Outlaw, Louise Lee
Fanning an old flame. Hood, Ann, 1956-
Fat people. Lurie, Alison
The feather in the toque. Minot, Susan
Feeding the piranha. Painter, Pamela
Filming the making of the film of the making of 'Fitzcarraldo'.
 Kilworth, Garry
The fireman's wife. Bausch, Richard, 1945-
The foul ball. Irving, John, 1942-
Friends . . . and other creeps. Gourlay, Darlene
Ghost night. Cunningham, Michael, 1952-
A gift of life. Anderson, Colleen
The Goldin boys. Epstein, Joseph
The good fight. Desaulniers, Janet
Good friends. Campbell, Bebe Moore
Goodness and mercy. Munro, Alice
The happily married woman. Martine, Jean Kinkead
Headed for happiness. Yellin, Linda Nell
Here I am. Updike, John
Hippies, Indians, buffalo. Johnson, Wayne
Hold her tightly. Strout, Elizabeth
Hole in the day. Tilghman, Christopher
A Hollywood success story. Mason, Judi Ann
Home. Oates, Joyce Carol, 1938-
Homesick. Glickman, James
Hooks. Zinik, Zinoviĭ
How love goes. Minot, Susan
How sunlight figures in. Kauffman, Janet, 1945-
If you want to see your shoe. Todd, Larrie
The illusionist. Millhauser, Steven
In a war. Gallant, Mavis
In and out. Le Guin, Ursula K., 1929-
In love with Ariadne. Trevor, William, 1928-
In the field. O'Brien, Tim, 1946-
In training to be famous. Lewis, Sara E.
Ind Aff. Weldon, Fay
Insulation. DeMarinis, Rick, 1934-
The Jewish hunter. Moore, Lorrie
Jump. Gordimer, Nadine, 1923-
Jungle video. Lombreglia, Ralph
Just a little magic. O'Connor, Kathleen
Kaplan's big deal. Epstein, Joseph
Kindness. Oates, Joyce Carol, 1938-
The knowing wife. McNeal, Tom
Lassie come home. Knight, Eric
The last generation. Williams, Joy, 1944-
The last leaf. Henry, O., 1862-1910
The last time he saw her. Stanton, Will
Leavings. Wilson, Gahan
Letter to the lady of the house. Bausch, Richard, 1945-
Little boy blue. McAllister, Bruce, 1946-
The lives of the dead. O'Brien, Tim, 1946-
Lobstermen. Franklet, Duane
Look where you're going. Verlaine, M. J.
Love never forgets. Alpha, Karen
Low anxiety. Epstein, Joseph
Making room for baby. Franco, Marjorie
The man nobody remembered. Brandon, William
Many happy returns. Soman, Florence Jane
Mariah. Kincaid, Jamaica
Marry for life. Robinson, Margaret A.
Ma's moving in! Gerber, Merrill Joan
Millions. Wiggins, Marianne
A model world. Chabon, Michael
Molly's baby. Collins, Pat Lowery, 1932-
Moment of decision. Schweitzer, Gertrude, 1909-
Money, fame, and beautiful women. Segal, Lore Groszmann
Monroe's wedding. Holman, John
More than human. Chabon, Michael
The most beautiful place. Corodimas, Peter
Mr. Fiddlehead. Carroll, Jonathan, 1949-
Mr. Reed's house. Bennet, John

SHORT STORIES—*cont.*

Murder. Hempel, Amy
The music room. McFarland, Dennis
My Aunt Metka. Perko, Margaret
The mystery of the bag lady's bundle. Vaughan, Ralph E.
Never marry a millionaire. Richards, Elizabeth
News of the world. Berney, Louis
El Niño. Lee, Don
No regrets. Kupfer, Fern
Not scared of you. Stone, Robert, 1937-
Nothing to ask for. McFarland, Dennis
Now I think I might almost understand. Dronzek, Anna
Ocean Avenue. Chabon, Michael
One of the great seductresses of Irish history. Carroll, Ethna
Oral history. Goodman, Allegra
The other side of innocence. Dionis, Kim
Outcast of the hills. Toland, Stewart
Overbite Halburton's revenge. Richler, Mordecai, 1931-
The overnight letter. Kalpakian, Laura
A passing fancy. Gingher, Marianne
Peace. Apple, Max
Peace of mind. Boyle, T. Coraghessan
Penelope. Brooks, Gertrude
Perfect vision. Hecht, Julie
The photo album. Dovlatov, Sergeĭ
Poor visitor. Kincaid, Jamaica
Precious little time. Kingsolver, Barbara
The private life of Robert Schumann. Schumacher, Julie
The proud rooster. Coles, Rosalind Bradley
Prowler. Tallent, Elizabeth, 1954-
The proximity. Boswell, Robert, 1953-
Purple smoke. Roziner, Felix
Rain. Boswell, Robert, 1953-
The rain barrel. Nichols, Jim
Read Chinese. Rofihe, Rick
Reassurance. Gurganus, Allan
The reverse bug. Segal, Lore Groszmann
The right combination. Riedel, Michael
The right thing. Stark, Stephen
Sardines. Pendleton, Michaelene
Satellite dish. Rofihe, Rick
Scavenger. Murphy, Pat
Scheherazade. Baxter, Charles
The secret of cartwheels. Henley, Patricia
The seducer. Barrett, Andrea
She's not the daughter we wanted. Hood, Ann, 1956-
Ship in a bottle. Dillard, Annie
Shipwreck. Barnes, Julian
Short Easter. Updike, John
A sign of love. Carlson, Ron, 1947-
The size of love. Leyner, Mark
Sleeping arrangements. Cunningham, Laura
Snow angels. Swanwick, Michael
Solace. Dozois, Gardner R.
"Someone is watching me". Cooke, Elizabeth
Someplace like New Jersey. Weiss, Deborah Chanley
Spat. Updike, John
Split ends. Gerber, Merrill Joan
Stand. Kaplan, David Michael
A step & a half. Dagon, Janet
Stone cowboy on the high plains. Jacobs, Mark
A street of bugles. Tyler, Anne, 1941-
The stylist. Egan, Jennifer
Subtotals. Burnham, Gregory
Sudden fever. Walker, Jeanne Murray
A sudden fortune. Bodett, Tom
Summer rental. Thompson, Barbara
The Superman affair. Hood, Ann, 1956-
Surprise ahead. Stanton, Will
Sweet as kisses. Solomon, Pearl Canick
Sweet mystery of life. O'Donnell, Brophy
Sweetheart of the Song Tra Bong. O'Brien, Tim, 1946-
A tail. Wang Zengqi
Taking charge. Riddick, Jane
Taking toll. Wentzien, Marion
Tall, dark & clingy. McWey, Michael
Thawing out. Boyle, T. Coraghessan
The theory of man. Richard, Mark, 1955-
The third child. Franken, Rose, 1895-1988
Tickets. Barthelme, Donald
To die for one's country is glorious. Kiš, Danilo
To love again. Aguallo, Thomaline
The tongue. Kincaid, Jamaica
Too far from Texas. Eisenstein, Sam
Too much women. George, Kathleen
The trick of it. Frayn, Michael
The tunnel. MacInnes, Patricia
Two boys. Moore, Lorrie
Two kinds. Tan, Amy
Two years. Grimm, Mary
Under the 82nd Airborne. Eisenberg, Deborah
The undertow. Dougherty, Shannon
Unfinished business. Kaplan, David Michael
Uno más. Morris, Wright, 1910-
A van for Violet. Havemann, Ernst
Une vie de château. Bedford, Sybille
Waiting. Berle, Milton
The wedding. Ganesan, Indira

The wedding. Plagemann, Bentz, 1913-
A wedge of shade. Erdrich, Louise
A week in the country. McConnell, Jean
What a sky. O'Brien, Edna
What was mine. Beattie, Ann
When I began to understand quantum mechanics. Hamilton, Jane, 1957-
When two hearts meet. Dubus, Elizabeth Nell
Where we all should have been. Desaulniers, Janet
Who'll take these family treasures? Rains-Weber, Mary
Why don't you? Russell, Emily
The widow. O'Brien, Edna
Wigtime. Munro, Alice
A winding stair. Mattison, Alice
The wishes. Cobb, William
With Ray and Judy. Barthelme, Frederick
A woman like a fieldstone house. Tyler, Anne, 1941-
Woodpecker. Kiser, Rosemarie
Yellow stars of Utah. Kirn, Walter
The young visitor. Rinehart, Mary Roberts, 1876-1958
You're ugly, too. Moore, Lorrie

SHORT STORY
See also
Fiction in periodicals and newspapers
Creating short fiction from character: five rules. L. Nevai. *The Writer* 102:11-13 Ja '89
Developing a specialty in fiction. E. Hunnicutt. *The Writer* 102:9-11+ Jl '89
Evaluating your short story. C. Nicholson. *The Writer* 102:33-4 Ag '89
A method that works (for me). L. N. Yellin. *The Writer* 102:18-20+ O '89
The shape that satisfies. R. Twohy. *The Writer* 102:16-17 D '89
Staying with it. M. J. Gerber. il *The Writer* 102:9-11 O '89
Writing the short story: three basic points. M. J. Heffernan. *The Writer* 102:16-18 S '89

Anthologies
'Selected shorts' due from Symphony Space [tapes of actors reading American short stories] *Publishers Weekly* 235:34 F 3 '89

Competitions
Laurie Berry's 252-word story may seem an under-a-Cheever, but it ended up a big winner [World's Best Short Short Story contest] por *People Weekly* 31:107 Je 19 '89

SHORT STORY READINGS
Between issues [story reading by F. Prose at Shaker Museum] *The New Leader* 72:2 S 4 '89
Symphony Space break [Selected shorts: series of readings by actors] M. Kramer. *The New Yorker* 65:74-5 Mr 13 '89

SHORTAGES *See* Scarcity
SHORTBREAD
Lee Bailey's brown-sugar shortbread. il *Redbook* 172:26 Mr '89
Mocha shortbread. il *Better Homes and Gardens* 67:100 Ja '89

SHORTER, WAYNE
about
Wayne Shorter's solo on On Green Dolphin St.—a trombonist's analysis. R. Eubanks. il *Down Beat* 56:58-9 Ja '89

SHORTO, RUSSELL
High tea and hashish. il *Gentlemen's Quarterly* 59:64+ N '89

SHORTS (CLOTHING)
"Please hide my thighs". il *Ladies' Home Journal* 106:140-1 Je '89

SHORTT, TERENCE M.
Pufted tuffins (and other backward birds). il *International Wildlife* 19:12-13 Jl/Ag '89

SHORTWAVE RADIO
See also
International Frequency Coordinating Committee
E-Z listening [eavesdropping on Soviet spacecraft] A. R. Curtis. il *Omni (New York, N.Y.)* 11:22+ F '89
Jupiter on your shortwave. D. A. Rosenthal. il *Sky and Telescope* 78:628 D '89
Shortwave radio. S. Leinwoll. See issues of Radio-Electronics beginning April 1988

Equipment
See also
Radio antennas
One-band shortwave converter. R. F. Graf and W. Sheets. il *Radio-Electronics* 60:49-51 O '89
Time for the news. Where's Radio Norway? A. Comarow. il *U.S. News & World Report* 107:94+ N 20 '89
Tuning in to Beijing—and beyond. D. H. Dunn. il *Business Week* p142 O 16 '89

SHORTWAVE RADIO ANTENNAS *See* Radio antennas
SHOSHONE (CALIF.)
The vultures were circling, but Susan Sorrells wouldn't let her little desert town die. R. Johnson. il pors *People Weekly* 32:79+ Ag 14 '89

SHOSTAKOVICH, DMITRII DMITRIEVICH, 1906-1975
about
Lady Macbeth of Mtsensk [opera] Reviews
   The New Republic il 200:34-40 Mr 20 '89. R. Taruskin
Lost in Crete. P. G. Davis. il *New York* 22:144+ F 27
   '89
SHOT
Cutting our losses (I). B. Brister. il *Field & Stream* 94:74+
   D '89
SHOTGUN SHELLS *See* Cartridges
SHOTGUNS
Is it necessarily so? J. Carmichel. il *Outdoor Life* 183:36+
   My '89
Meet the SP-10 (and other news). B. Brister. il *Field &*
   Stream 93:66+ Mr '89
October slugfest. B. Brister and D. E. Petzal. il *Field &*
   Stream 94:62+ O '89
Shotguns for sporting. R. Hinton. il *Outdoor Life* 183:17+
   Ap '89
      Chokes
New chokes; new names. J. Carmichel. il *Outdoor Life* 184:44+
   Ag '89
The smoking choke [sporting clays] R. Hinton. il *Outdoor*
   Life 184:39-41 Ag '89
SHOTPUTTING
A show of strength [R. Barnes] J. E. Vader. il pors *Sports*
   Illustrated 70:62-4+ My 15 '89
SHOULDER PADS
Shed a tear for shoulder pads. B. Lindsmith. il *Glamour*
   87:148 N '89
SHOUMATOFF, ALEX
Rio: Is the carnival over? il *The New York Times Magazine*
   p46-8+ Mr 19 '89
SHOVELING OF SNOW *See* Snow shoveling
SHOVLIN, EILEEN PORTZ- *See* Portz-Shovlin, Eileen
SHOW BOAT [musical] See Musicals, revues, etc.—Reviews—
   Single works
SHOW BUSINESS *See* Entertainment industry; Performing
   arts
SHOW ROOMS *See* Showrooms
SHOW WINDOWS
Window shopping [clothing stores' display windows] il
   Glamour 87:220 My '89
Windows [S. J. Gerberich's window environments] *The New*
   Yorker 65:40-1 O 2 '89
SHOWALTER, DENNIS E.
Action! Adventure! Sales! il *Publishers Weekly* 235:20-2+
   My 5 '89
Bringing back the western. il *Publishers Weekly* 235:25-7
   My 5 '89
SHOWER BATHS
Install a corner shower enclosure. A. Rooze. il *The Family*
   Handyman 39:61-5 O '89
A solar shower [outdoor] P. Butler and M. Butler. il *Outdoor*
   Life 184:52+ S '89
Working with oversized fixtures. il *Popular Mechanics*
   166:112-13 Ap '89
      Doors
See Doors
SHOWER CURTAINS
Shirred look for shower rod [fabric-covered PVC tubes] il
   Southern Living 24:111 Ja '89
SHOWER DOORS *See* Doors
SHOWERS, MARGI
      about
Saga of a business start-up (I). L. Washer. il pors *Working*
   Woman 14:45-6+ D '89
SHOWERS (PARTIES)
See also
   Bridal showers
SHOWING OFF [musical] See Musicals, revues, etc.—
   Reviews—Single works
SHOWROOMS
Heavy metal [L. Max showroom in Los Angeles designed
   by Morphosis] A. Betsky. il *Architectural Record* 177:86-93
   mid-S '89
Patrick Kelly: exuberant style animates the American
   designer's Paris atelier. M. Gross. il por *Architectural Digest*
   46:218-24 S '89
Spatial craft [Herman Miller showroom, Atlanta, Ga.; cover
   story] K. D. Stein. il *Architectural Record* 177:98-107 Je
   '89
SHOWSCAN FILM CORPORATION
The hottest thing since Cinerama. L. Gubernick. il *Forbes*
   144:70 S 4 '89
SHOWSCAN PROCESS
The hottest thing since Cinerama. L. Gubernick. il *Forbes*
   144:70 S 4 '89
SHOYAB, MOHAMMED, AND OTHERS
Structure and function of human amphiregulin: a member
   of the epidermal growth factor family. bibl f il *Science*
   243:1074-6 F 24 '89
SHRAGIN, BORIS
      about
Will the Soviet Union survive until 1994? [interview; cover
   story] D. Evanier. *National Review* 41:24+ Ap 7 '89

SHREDDERS, GARDEN See Garden equipment
SHRIMP
      See also
   Cooking—Shellfish
      Anecdotes, facetiae, satire, etc.
A shrimp cocktail. P. F. McManus. il *Outdoor Life* 184:112+
   D '89
      Contamination
Minute shrimp [boiling time required to reduce risk of
   listeriosis] D. Blumenthal. il *FDA Consumer* 23:29-30 My
   '89
      Eye
See Eye—Crustaceans
SHRIMP FISHERIES *See* Shellfish fisheries
SHRINES, WAR *See* War memorials
SHRIVER, MARIA
      about
Maria Shriver: you call this a glamour job? C. Krupp. il
   pors *Glamour* 87:172-3 N '89
What makes Maria Shriver run so fast. J. Kalter. il pors
   TV Guide 37:6-10 Jl 29-Ag 4 '89
SHRONTZ, FRANK A.
      about
Frank Shrontz. M. Shao. il por *Business Week* Special
   Issue:129 Ap 14 '89
SHRUBS
      See also
   Rhododendrons
   Sagebrush
   Vitex roundifolia
   Weigela
   Windbreaks
The shrubs that pass for trees [standards] il *Sunset (Central*
   West edition) 182:84-5 Je '89
SHUCHMAN, MIRIAM
(jt. auth) See Wilkes, Michael S., and Shuchman, Miriam
SHUCHMAN, MIRIAM, AND WILKES, MICHAEL S.
Asking—and telling. il *The New York Times Magazine* p45-6
   F 12 '89
Suffering in silence. il *The New York Times Magazine* p36-7
   Jl 23 '89
SHUGART, ALAN F.
      about
Driven down. il por *Forbes* 143:115 Ja 9 '89
SHUGER, SCOTT
How to revolutionize Washington with 140 people [cover
   story] *The Washington Monthly* 21:38-40+ Je '89
The Navy we need and the one we got. il *The Washington*
   Monthly 21:10-14+ Mr '89
What America hasn't learned from its greatest peacekeeping
   disaster. il *The Washington Monthly* 21:40-4+ O '89
SHULMAN, ADAM
(tr) See Sirotkin, Albert. Filling in the blank spots in Soviet
   history
SHULMAN, MARTHA ROSE
      about
Light food. L. Troiano. il *American Health* 8:147-8 Ap '89
SHULMAN, SETH
Not a pretty picture. il *The Progressive* 53:24-5 S '89
When a nuclear reactor dies, $98 million is a cheap funeral.
   bibl (p228) il *Smithsonian* 20:56-62+ O '89
(jt. auth) See Grossman, Daniel, and Shulman, Seth
(jt. auth) See Pollack, Stephanie, and Shulman, Seth
SHULTZ, GEORGE PRATT, 1920-
The ecology of international change [address, October 28,
   1988] *Department of State Bulletin* 89:6-10 Ja '89
Efforts for peace in Africa [remarks, October 4, 1988]
   Department of State Bulletin 88:20-2 D '88
The future agenda in arms control [address, October 31,
   1988] *Department of State Bulletin* 89:1-4 Ja '89
The inter-American system: into the next century [statement,
   November 14, 1988] *Department of State Bulletin* 89:10-13
   Ja '89
Key to the future: enlightened engagement [address, October
   10, 1988] *Department of State Bulletin* 88:16-19 D '88
North Atlantic Council session held in Brussels [texts of
   statement on conventional arms control, final communique,
   extracts from minutes of meeting, and news conference,
   December 8-9, 1988] *Department of State Bulletin* 89:43-50
   F '89
The open society and its friends [address, October 11, 1988]
   Department of State Bulletin 88:13-16 D '88
Prohibition of chemical weapons conference held in Paris
   [address and news conference, January 7-8, 1989]
   Department of State Bulletin 89:4-9 Mr '89
Promoting peace and prosperity in the South Asian region
   [address, October 6, 1988] *Department of State Bulletin*
   88:19-20 D '88
Public service in America [address, January 9, 1989]
   Department of State Bulletin 89:1-4 Mr '89
Secretary meets with EC ministers [text of joint conference,
   December 9, 1988] *Department of State Bulletin* 89:27-30
   F '89
Secretary's news conference [January 17, 1989] *Department*
   of State Bulletin 89:52-4 Mr '89
Secretary's news conference [November 14, 1988] *Department*
   of State Bulletin 89:13 Ja '89

SHULTZ, GEORGE PRATT, 1920—cont.

Security awareness, measures, and management [address, November 2, 1988] *Department of State Bulletin* 89:4-5 Ja '89

U.S., China celebrate decade of diplomatic relations [toast, December 15, 1988] *Department of State Bulletin* 89:25-6 F '89

U.S. opens dialogue with PLO [statements and press conference, December 14, 1988] *Department of State Bulletin* 89:51-3 F '89

about

In his plodding way, Shultz got things done. B. Javetski. por *Business Week* p30 Ja 16 '89

Macmillan/Shultz deal, take two. por *Publishers Weekly* 236:53 N 3 '89

Secretary's interview on "This week with David Brinkley" [transcript of program, December 4, 1988] *Department of State Bulletin* 89:7-9 F '89

Visit to Mexico, 1988

Secretary attends inaugural of Mexico's president [interview] *Department of State Bulletin* 89:71-3 F '89

SHULZ, WALTER

about

All that floats is not equal. C. Brown. il por *Forbes* 143:84+ Ap 3 '89

SHUMATE, PAUL W., JR.

(jt. auth) See Weinstein, Stephen B., and Shumate, Paul W., Jr.

SHUMATE, PAUL W., JR., AND WEINSTEIN, STEPHEN B.

On the cutting edge of tomorrow's technology. il *USA Today (Periodical)* 118:30-2 S '89

SHUPE, ANSON D.

The Reconstructionist Movement on the new Christian right [cover story] *The Christian Century* 106:880-2 O 4 '89

SHUR, CHAIM

about

An Israeli with a controversial plan for the Palestinians [interview] J. R. Moskin. il por *World Press Review* 36:32-4 Je '89

SHUTDOWNS OF AIR BASES See Air bases—Shutdowns

SHUTDOWNS OF FACTORIES See Factories—Shutdowns

SHUTDOWNS OF MILITARY BASES See Military bases—Shutdowns

SHUTDOWNS OF SAWMILLS See Sawmills—Shutdowns

SHUTDOWNS OF STEEL WORKS See Steel works—Shutdowns

SHUTE, NANCY

The trouble with leaves. il *National Wildlife* 27:18-19 O/N '89

SHUTT, STEVE

about

Didn't your used to be . . . W. Ladson. il pors *Sport (New York, N.Y.)* 80:126 Je '89

SHUTTERS, CAMERA See Camera shutters

SHUTTERS, VIDEO CAMERA See Video camera shutters

SHUTTLE, SPACE See Space vehicles

SHUTTLE MISSIONS See Space flight—Shuttle missions

SHUTTLE SERVICE, AIRLINE See Airlines—Shuttle service

SHUTTLE SERVICE, HELICOPTER See Helicopter airlines—Shuttle service

SHWEDER, RICHARD A.

In Paris—miniskirts of the mind. il *The New York Times Book Review* 94:1+ Ja 8 '89

SHY PEOPLE [film] See Motion picture reviews—Single works

SHYER, MARLENE FANTA

An almost perfect fit [story] il *McCall's* 116:52+ Ag '89

Sophia Loren: the private woman. il pors *McCall's* 116:36-7+ My '89

SHYNE, KEVIN

Pie in the sky. il pors *Runner's World* 24:34-6 N '89

Walkabouts! [cover story] il *New Choices for the Best Years* 29:29-32 Mr '89

SHYNESS See Bashfulness

SHYRE, PAUL

about

Hizzoner! [drama] Reviews

America 160:272 Mr 25 '89. G. G. Seibert

The Nation 248:462 Ap 3 '89. T. M. Disch

The New Yorker 65:91 Mr 6 '89. E. Oliver

SIAMESE TWINS

The pure joy of being alive [Cady twins; cover story] M. L. S. Cady. il pors *People Weekly* 32:64-71 Jl 3 '89

Rare Siamese twins, 39, to get own apartment [McCarther twins] il *Jet* 75:51 Ja 16 '89

SIAN KA'AN BIOSPHERE RESERVE (MEXICO)

Where the sky was born. J. Emory. il *Wilderness* 52:55-7 Summ '89

SIAS, JOHN

about

The brass at Cap Cities/ABC: rethinking TV [interview] M. Brown and P. Ainslie. il pors *Channels (New York, N.Y.: 1986)* 9:93-5 F '89

SIBBISON, JIM

Revolving door at the E.P.A. il *The Nation* 249:524-8 N 6 '89

SIBERIA (SOVIET UNION)

See also

Bering Strait

Camping—Siberia (Soviet Union)

Investments, Foreign—Siberia (Soviet Union)

Boundaries

Thaw on the Bering Strait. J. Mettke. il *World Press Review* 36:58 Ja '89

Industries

See also

Petrochemical industry—Siberia (Soviet Union)

SIBERIAN DANCE See Dance, Siberian

SIBERIAN FOLK MUSIC See Folk music, Siberian

SIBERIAN IRISES See Irises

SIBERRY, JANE

about

Bound for glory. N. Jennings. il por *Maclean's* 102:63 O 9 '89

SIBLEY, LOIS

Religious bestsellers. *Publishers Weekly* 235:39 Mr 3 '89

SIBLINGS

See also

Birth order

All-in-the-family birth [sibling-attended birth] L. Mosedale. il *Health (New York, N.Y.)* 21:85-6+ S '89

Baby boom [new babies in families with teenagers] D. Kent. il *Seventeen* 48:117-18+ Je '89

Best friends, all the way [celebrities] L. Stover. il *Mademoiselle* 95:212-17 S '89

Born rivals [identical twins] G. Levoy. il *Psychology Today* 23:67-8 Je '89

Born rivals [identical twins] G. Levoy. *Utne Reader* p101-2 S/O '89

Breaking the news [sibling rivalry; views of Adele Faber] S. Epel. il *Parents* 64:74 Ag '89

A brother's death. B. L. Ascher. il *The New York Times Magazine* p30+ N 19 '89

Is married better? [sisters exchange places] S. Nelson and L. Nelson. il pors *Glamour* 87:274-5+ O '89

Little girl lost [wondering what happened to the sister given up for adoption] B. E. Hall. por *Essence* 20:12 O '89

Lost brother [coping with schizophrenic] K. King. il pors *Life* 12:94-8+ N '89

Memories of Frank [manic-depressive brother who committed suicide] M. K. Blakely. il *Psychology Today* 23:48-50+ O '89

Mom liked you best: how Christians outgrow sibling rivalry [cover story] D. Morris. il *U.S. Catholic* 54:6-12 Ja '89

"My get-along gang" [overcoming sibling rivalry] J. Abbott. il *Parents* 64:114-18 Ap '89

No longer my brother's keeper. M. Frank. il *The New York Times Magazine* p30+ S 17 '89

Number of siblings and educational attainment. J. Blake. bibl f il *Science* 245:32-6 Jl 7 '89

The secret life of siblings. P. La Farge. il *Parents* 64:106-8+ F '89

Sister love. R. Brown. il *Ebony* 44:25-6+ S '89

Sisters. C. Hanauer. il *Seventeen* 48:106-7+ D '89

When siblings are different. S. Reit. il *Good Housekeeping* 209:126+ S '89

When siblings are superstars: you can still shine! E. Karlsberg. il *Teen* 33:12+ Mr '89

Wouldn't you like your kids to be closer? A. Faber and E. Mazlish. il *Redbook* 172:98-9+ F '89

Younger sons in Tudor and Stuart England. L. A. Pollock. bibl il *History Today* 39:23-9 Je '89

Your siblings, yourself. S. Weller. il *Glamour* 87:224-5+ D '89

Anecdotes, facetiae, satire, etc.

Sharing a room with toxic fumes [14 year old little sister] M. Vickers. *Seventeen* 48:165 Mr '89

SICANGU ELDERLY CONCERNS, INC.

Sioux elders organize an advocacy group. il *Aging* no359:25-6 '89

SICILIAN COOKING See Cooking, Italian

SICILIAN MAFIA See Mafia

SICILY

Description and travel

Letter from Sicily: Mr. Sciascia explains [excerpt from To noto, or Through Europe in a Ford] D. Fallowell. *The American Scholar* 58:581-5 Aut '89

SICINSKI, PIOTR, AND OTHERS

The molecular basis of muscular dystrophy in the *mdx* mouse: a point mutation. bibl f il *Science* 244:1578-80 Je 30 '89

SICK

See also

Church work with the sick

Hospital patients

Anecdotes, facetiae, satire, etc.

For better, for worst: why are men such babies when they get sick? M. Kaufman. *Reader's Digest* 134:49-50 F '89

Sick of the sick. B. Ehrenreich. il *Mother Jones* 14:7+ N '89

Civil rights

See also

Cancer patients—Civil rights

Hospital patients—Civil rights

SICK—Civil rights—*cont.*
Patients' rights. M. M. Hunt. il *The New York Times Magazine* p55-6 Mr 5 '89

Family relationships
Caregiving: coping with a chronically ill spouse. M. Blau. *McCall's* 117:108+ N '89
Caring for the caregiver [depression caused by caring for chronically ill family member] D. Burden. il *Psychology Today* 23:22 Jl/Ag '89
When mom's feeling ill. J. T. Gibson. il *Parents* 64:197 S '89

Psychology
See also
Medicine, Psychosomatic

Religious life
Living with chronic illness: why should I go on? S. Schmidt. *The Christian Century* 106:475-6+ My 3 '89

SICK BUILDING SYNDROME
Bake-offs may not cure 'sick buildings' [study by Charlene W. Bayer] J. Raloff. *Science News* 136:206 S 23 '89
Caution: an ill wind may be blowing in your office, warns building doctor Gray Robertson [interview] M. J. Weiss. il pors *People Weekly* 31:89+ F 20 '89
Do you have the working-girl flu? P. S. Derron. il *Mademoiselle* 95:120 D '89
Pollution strikes the EPA. M. Weisskopf. il *Discover* 10:32-3 Ja '89
A sickness in the air. M. B. Marklein. *The Progressive* 53:17 D '89
When each day is a sick day. A. Saltzman and J. Silberner. il *U.S. News & World Report* 106:65-7 Mr 13 '89

SICK CHILDREN
See also
Children—Hospital care
Children—Medical care
Children—Preparation for hospital and medical care
Hole-in-the-Wall Gang Camp
Starlight Foundation
Day care for sick kids. R. Levine. *American Health* 8:108 Ap '89
Fighting for their lives. J. Krementz. il *American Health* 8:62+ N '89
What children teach doctors. il *Reader's Digest* 134:153-6 Ap '89

SICKLE CELL ANEMIA
Blood, genes, and malaria. J. M. Diamond. il maps *Natural History* p8+ F '89
Brain risk seen in sickle cell kids [study by Andrea V. Swift] R. Weiss. *Science News* 136:404 D 23-30 '89
Recombinant rodents, human hemoglobin [work of R. R. Behringer] R. Weiss. *Science News* 136:149 S 2 '89
Synthesis of functional human hemoglobin in transgenic mice. R. R. Behringer and others. bibl f il *Science* 245:971-3 S 1 '89

Therapy
Breaking the sickle cycle [cover story] D. E. Loupe. il *Science News* 136:360-2 D 2 '89
Drug shows promise in sickle cell anemia [hydroxyurea; research by George J. Dover] I. Wickelgren. *Science News* 135:349 Je 3 '89
New hope for children with sickle cell disease. M. Segal. il *FDA Consumer* 23:14-19 Mr '89

SICKMAN, LAURENCE, 1906-1988
about
"Excellent! Excellent! World-honored Sakyamuni!". il por *Art News* 88:32+ F '89

SICKNESS
See also
Diagnosis
Diseases
Sick

SIDDIQUI, WASIM
about
Malaria researcher indicted. E. Marshall. *Science* 245:1326 S 22 '89

SIDDON, TOM
Free trade [address, November 22, 1988] *Vital Speeches of the Day* 55:222-4 Ja 15 '89

SIDE EFFECTS OF DRUGS *See* Drugs—Physiological effects
SIDEBOARDS *See* Buffets, sideboards, etc. (Furniture)
SIDECAR RACING *See* Motorcycle racing
SIDELINES, BOOKSTORE *See* Booksellers and bookselling—Sidelines

SIDER, RONALD J.
Abortion is not the only issue. il *Christianity Today* 33:28-32 Jl 14 '89

SIDERS, HARVEY
Chicago: jazz-rock pioneers [reprint] il *Down Beat* 56:81-2 S '89

SIDEWALK STORIES [film] *See* Motion picture reviews—Single works
SIDEWALKS
See also
Walk of Fame (Hollywood, Calif.)
In praise of sidewalks. J. E. Pearce. il *Reader's Digest* 134:100-1 My '89

SIDEY, HUGH
The presidency (administration of George Bush). See issues of *Time* beginning January 23, 1989

SIDHU, SHIVINDER SINGH
about
ICAO upgrades security unit as part of antiterrorist effort. J. Ott. por *Aviation Week & Space Technology* 130:109+ My 1 '89

SIDLINE, GEORGE
Nathalie & the MG. il *Good Housekeeping* 209:66+ S '89

SIDNEY, WILLIAM PHILIP *See* De L'Isle, William Philip Sidney, Viscount

SIDNEY (OHIO)
Galleries and museums
See also
Titanic Memorial Museum (Sidney, Ohio)

SIDNEY FAMILY
about
'Not built to envious show'. F. Barker. il por *History Today* 39:3-4 Ap '89

SIDNEY KRAMER BOOKS (WASHINGTON, D.C.: BOOKSTORE) *See* Booksellers and bookselling—Washington (D.C.)

SIDRAN, BEN
about
Ben Sidrán. K. Lynch. il por *Down Beat* 56:15 Ag '89

SIDS *See* Sudden infant death syndrome

SIEBER-BLUM, MAYA
Commitment of neural crest cells to the sensory neuron lineage. bibl f il *Science* 243:1608-11 Mr 24 '89

SIEBERT, JEROME
about
Has this outfit found 'a miracle for oil spills'? G. G. Marcial. il por *Business Week* p150 My 22 '89

SIEDEN, LLOYD STEVEN
The birth of the geodesic dome. il pors *The Futurist* 23:14-19 N/D '89

SIEFF, MARTIN
A Duma by any other name. il *National Review* 41:40-1 Je 30 '89
Would Batman vote Republican? *National Review* 41:55-7 S 15 '89

SIEG, THEO. LE *See* Seuss, Dr.

SIEGAL, DIANA LASKIN
about
Celebrating my change of life. R. Loth. il por *New Choices for the Best Years* 29:16+ My '89

SIEGAL, ROSLYN
Dazzling baths [excerpt from Country floors—decorating with tiles] il *Redbook* 173:122-4 Jl '89

SIEGEL, BERNIE S.
How to heal yourself! [excerpt from Peace, love and healing] *Redbook* 173:110-11+ Je '89
about
Doctor love [cover story] T. Schwartz. il pors *New York* 22:40-9 Je 12 '89
Hay House plans Siegel releases. J. Zinsser. *Publishers Weekly* 236:56+ N 3 '89
How to heal yourself [interview] M. Lodge. por *Ladies' Home Journal* 106:108+ Je '89

SIEGEL, BRUCE A., AND VERBEKE, JUDITH A.
Diffusible factors essential for epidermal cell redifferentiation in Catharanthus roseus. bibl f il *Science* 244:580-2 My 5 '89

SIEGEL, FREDERICK F., 1945-
What liberals haven't learned & why. il *Commonweal* 116:16-20 Ja 13 '89

SIEGEL, HENRY HOWARD
about
Mr. Hardball sheds his Grey. J. M. Robins. il pors *Channels (New York, N.Y.: 1986)* 9:62-6 F '89

SIEGEL, HERBERT J.
about
The new Herb Siegel play. T. Jaffe. *Forbes* 144:172 D 25 '89
The thorn in Steve Ross's side. R. Grover. il por *Business Week* p51 Ag 14 '89

SIEGEL, JANIS
about
Janis Siegel & Fred Hersch. M. Bourne. pors *Down Beat* 56:14 O '89

SIEGEL, MARTIN A.
about
The debris in Rudolph Giuliani's wake. C. Welles. pors *Business Week* p36-7 Ja 23 '89

SIEGEL, MICKI
He talks to the animals . . . il por *Good Housekeeping* 209:56+ Jl '89
My mother, the doctor. il *Good Housekeeping* 209:90+ S '89
"Thank God for people like you". il por *Good Housekeeping* 208:139+ Je '89

SIEGEL, OWEN
about
The prize is right. E. Stern. il por *Gentlemen's Quarterly* 59:49+ Mr '89

SIEGEL, RONALD K.
about
Do humans need to get high? J. Beaty. il *Time* 134:58
Ag 21 '89
The 'fourth drive'. N. Underwood. por *Maclean's* 102:45
Ag 28 '89
SIEGEL, STEVE
Animal research is unnecessary and dangerous to human
health. il *Utne Reader* p47-9 S/O '89
SIEGELBAUM, LEWIS H.
Behind the Soviet miners' strike. il *The Nation* 249:451-2+
O 23 '89
SIEGELMAN, MARK H., AND OTHERS
Mouse lymph node homing receptor cDNA clone encodes
a glycoprotein revealing tandem interaction domains. bibl
f il *Science* 243:1165-72 Mr 3 '89
SIEGFRIED [opera] See Wagner, Richard, 1813-1883
SIEGLER, BEN
about
The good coach [drama] Reviews
New York 22:56-7 Je 26 '89. J. Simon
SIEGNER, CATHERINE
(jt. auth) See Sochocky, Anna, and Siegner, Catherine
SIELECKI, ANITA R., AND OTHERS
Structure of recombinant human renin, a target for
cardiovascular-active drugs, at 2.5 Å resolution. bibl f
il *Science* 243:1346-51 Mr 10 '89
SIEMENS AG
British Monopolies panel approves GEC/Siemens offer for
Plessey. *Aviation Week & Space Technology* 130:39 My
1 '89
GEC, Siemens renew their bid to buy Plessey. *Aviation Week
& Space Technology* 131:34 Ag 14 '89
GEC, Siemens win bid to take over Plessey. *Aviation Week
& Space Technology* 131:31 S 18 '89
Siemens: a plodding giant starts to pick up speed. G. E.
Schares. il *Business Week* p136-8 F 20 '89
Telecomputing lives [IBM's deal with Siemens for Rolm]
G. Slutsker and F. Meeks. il *Forbes* 143:51 Ja 9 '89
SIENA (ITALY)
Art
Art [Painting in Renaissance Siena at the Metropolitan
Museum of Art] A. C. Danto. *The Nation* 248:317-20
Mr 6 '89
Magical mystery tour [Painting in Renaissance Siena at the
Metropolitan Museum of Art] K. Larson. il *New York*
22:56-7 Ja 16 '89
Painting in Renaissance Siena: 1420-1500: Metropolitan
Museum of Art. B. A. MacAdam. il *Art News* 88:159
My '89
The seers of Siena [Metropolitan Museum exhibit] L. Cun-
ningham. il *Commonweal* 116:213-14 Ap 7 '89
Social life and customs
See also
Palio di Siena (Italy)
SIENKIEWICZ-MERCER, RUTH
about
Driven by an unquenchable spirit, a Massachusetts woman
writes an impossible book. L. Smith. il pors *People Weekly*
32:107+ S 11 '89
**SIENKIEWICZ-MERCER, RUTH, AND KAPLAN, STEVEN
B.**
I raise my eyes to say yes [excerpts] il *Glamour* 87:280-1+
O '89
SIERRA ACADEMY OF AERONAUTICS
Golden opportunity. F. George. il *Flying* 116:34-5 O '89
SIERRA CLUB
High Tripping. il *Sierra* 74:52-6 Ja/F '89
Lewis & Nathan Clark: friends and brothers. B. Fuller. il
pors *Sierra* 74:148-50+ Ja/F '89
Questions & answers. See issues of Sierra beginning March/
April 1983
Sierra Club financial report. il *Sierra* 74:79-81 Mr/Ap '89
Sierra Club public lands campaigns. il map *Sierra* 74:52-64
S/O '89
The Sierra Club's climate campaign. D. W. Scott. il *Sierra*
74:40 Jl/Ag '89
Sierra notes. See issue of Sierra
Tales from the trail [service vacations] il *Harper's Bazaar*
122:60-1+ Ja '89
Yogurt-eaters for wilderness. J. F. King. il *Sierra* 74:22-3
Ja/F '89
SIERRA LEONE
Description and travel
The land of 'Lion Mountain'. N. Marshall. il *World Press
Review* 36:62 Je '89
SIERRA NEVADA MOUNTAINS (CALIF. AND NEV.)
Carson Pass country: low-key, pure Sierra. il map *Sunset
(Central West edition)* 183:12+ Jl '89
High Tripping [Sierra Club High Trips] il *Sierra* 74:52-6
Ja/F '89
Looking for Sierra gold [fall color tour] il map *Sunset (Central
West edition)* 183:22-5 S '89
SIERRA PHOTO CONTEST See Photography—Competitions
SIETZEN, FRANK, JR.
In search of the Apollo spirit. il *Ad Astra* 1:8-12 Jl/Ag
'89

SIGAL, LEON V.
Reagan's radical challenge. il *The Bulletin of the Atomic
Scientists* 45:38-41 Ja/F '89
SIGATOKA DISEASE, BLACK See Black sigatoka disease
SIGGINS, JEFF
Lunar timekeeper. il *Omni (New York, N.Y.)* 11:96-102 Jl
'89
SIGGRAPH See Association for Computing Machinery. Special
Interest Group on Computer Graphics
SIGHT See Vision
SIGHTS FOR FIREARMS See Firearms—Sights
SIGHTSEEING AIRPLANES See Airplanes in sightseeing
SIGHTSEEING BOATS
In port in Houston [Sam Houston tour boat] il *Southern
Living* 24:49 S '89
SIGHTSEEING HELICOPTERS See Helicopters in sightseeing
SIGLER, HOLLIS, 1948-
about
Hollis Sigler: Printworks. S. Taylor. il *Art News* 88:177 Summ
'89
SIGMA FACTOR See Transcription factors
SIGN LANGUAGE
The indomitable Word. *Commonweal* 116:691-2 D 15 '89
Oliver Sacks journeys into the world of the deaf for title
from California. por *Publishers Weekly* 235:28-9 My 26
'89
The signs of silence [ability of deaf children to learn English
after mastering American Sign Language] S. Brownlee.
il *U.S. News & World Report* 107:86+ O 16 '89
A strange and marvelous culture [O. Sacks' book Seeing
voices] *U.S. News & World Report* 107:88 O 16 '89
SIGN LANGUAGE ASSOCIATES
Fingers of speech. S. Nelton. il por *Nation's Business* 77:12+
Jl '89
SIGN OF PEACE (CATHOLIC LITURGY)
Exchanging peace. P. J. Ryan. il *America* 160:383 Ap 22
'89
SIGNAL COMPANIES, INC.
See also
Allied-Signal Inc.
SIGNAL GENERATORS
See also
Oscillators
Digital sine waves. D. Lancaster. il *Radio-Electronics* 60:36-7
Ja '89
My favorite circuit [Schmitt trigger] D. Lancaster. il
Radio-Electronics 60:67-71 Jl '89
Sibex FG-1 handheld function generator. il *Radio-Electronics*
60:24 S '89
SIGNAL PROCESSING
See also
Charge coupled devices (Electronics)
Surround sound processors
Chips ahoy. K. C. Pohlmann. *Stereo Review* 54:22 My '89
Dealing with a digital world [DSP chips] D. A. Mindell.
il *Byte* 14:246-8+ Ag '89
Digital signal-processing news [DSP chips] D. Ranada. il
High Fidelity (New York, N.Y.) 39:22 Mr '89
JVC audio/video selector [JX-S900U] il *Video* 13:30+ My
'89
Pioneer SP-91D digital sound processor. J. D. Hirsch. il
Stereo Review 54:82+ D '89
Signal processors. D. Simon. il *Stereo Review* 54:107-10 D
'89
Sony TA-E1000ESD digital preamplifier. J. D. Hirsch. il
Stereo Review 54:90-4 O '89
Sony video/audio selector [SB-V1000] il *Video* 12:32+ F '89
Sound and image processing [special section] il *Byte* 14:240-1+
D '89
SIGNALS AND SIGNALING
I scream, you scream [signaling aboard boats] S. Stapleton.
il *Motor Boating & Sailing* 163:42+ Mr '89
SIGNATURES (ART)
"Signature piece" [installation by K. Ericson at MOMA]
R. Cembalest. il *Art News* 88:15 F '89
SIGNS AND SIGNBOARDS
See also
Billboards
Neon signs
Plasti-Line, Inc.
Sunsign Manufacturing Company
The failures of Robert Bourassa [language issue in Quebec]
J. Stewart. por *Maclean's* 102:64 Ja 2 '89
War over words [Quebec's move to restrict use of English
signs; special section] il por *Maclean's* 102:38-42 Ja 2
'89
Collectors and collecting
Advertising art. F. Donegan. bibl il *Americana* 17:62-4 S/O
'89
SIGNS AND WONDERS MOVEMENT
"Signs and wonders" back in school? M. L. Chandler.
Christianity Today 33:56 Ja 13 '89
Bibliography
Fruit of the Vineyard. T. Stafford. il *Christianity Today*
33:35-6 N 17 '89
SIGURDSON, WADE J.
(jt. auth) See Morris, Catherine E., and Sigurdson, Wade
J.

SIHANOUK *See* Norodom Sihanouk, Prince, 1922-
SIHLWALD FOREST (SWITZERLAND)
Natural cycles. B. W. Walsh. il por *Wilderness* 53:16-17+
Wint '89
SIKASSO (MALI)

Public health

The Sikasso project [maternal and child health program]
A. Rougemont and others. il *World Health* p6-8 Je '89
SIKES, ALFRED

about

Will Alfred Sikes fix the power shortage at the FCC? D.
Foust. por *Business Week* p73 Je 26 '89
SIKES, GINI
Some like it hot! il *Harper's Bazaar* 122:88+ N '89
William McNamara. il por *Seventeen* 48:108-9 My '89
SIKHS

Great Britain

A Sikh singer who gives Elvis fans a Singh-King feeling
[impersonator P. Singh] il por *People Weekly* 31:87 My
1 '89
SIKORSKI, GERRY
Should the Congress adopt the "Acid Deposition Control
Act of 1987"? [excerpts from address, June 11, 1987]
Congressional Digest 68:56+ F '89
SIKORSKI, RADEK
Afghan sitzkrieg. il *National Review* 41:37-8 Ap 21 '89
Africa's next basket case? *National Review* 41:21-2+ S 15
'89
Decline or fall? il *National Review* 41:28-30 Ja 27 '89
The last battle? *National Review* 41:19-20 Ag 4 '89
The mystique of Savimbi. il por *National Review* 41:34-7
Ag 18 '89
Nobody here but us Democrats. il *National Review* 41:40-2
S 29 '89
Poland's good old days (now). il *National Review* 41:23-4
D 22 '89
Still-life by shellfire. il *National Review* 41:22-3 Ap 7 '89
When Kabul falls. *National Review* 41:20 F 24 '89
SIKORSKY, ROBERT
Dollar-saving car questions. *Reader's Digest* 135:157-8+ Ag
'89
Where to find a street smart car. *Consumers' Research
Magazine* 72:16 O '89
SIKORSKY AIRCRAFT
Boeing and Sikorsky near completion of U.S. Army special
operations aircraft. S. W. Kandebo. il *Aviation Week &
Space Technology* 131:53+ N 27 '89
Korean Air negotiates agreement to coproduce Sikorsky
UH-60. J. D. Morrocco. il *Aviation Week & Space
Technology* 130:225+ Je 12 '89
SIKOWITZ, PETER
The art of the reel. il *Harper's Bazaar* 122:68+ Mr '89
SILAGE
Combine grain, steal the stalks! il *Successful Farming* 87:48X
N '89
Homegrown approach to least-cost rations. J. R. Borcherding.
il *Successful Farming* 87:31 mid-Mr '89
How to pick and use silage additives. J. R. Borcherding.
il *Successful Farming* 87:26+ Je '89
Spike forage to beat meal prices [anhydrous ammonia] V.
Ehmke. il *Successful Farming* 87:40 My '89
SILAS, CECIL JESSE, 1932-
Gaining the environmental initiative [address, July 13, 1989]
Vital Speeches of the Day 56:14-16 O 15 '89
A question of scruples [address, March 6, 1989] *Vital Speeches
of the Day* 55:473-6 My 15 '89
Where have all the risk takers gone? [address, March 29,
1989] *Vital Speeches of the Day* 55:530-3 Je 15 '89

about

Phillips climbs up from the bottom of the barrel. T. Vogel.
il por *Business Week* p76+ Ja 16 '89
Plastics? R. T. Grieves. il por *Forbes* 143:104 Ja 23 '89
SILBART, LAWRENCE K., AND KEREN, DAVID F.
Reduction of intestinal carcinogen absorption by carcinogen-
specific secretory immunity. bibl f il *Science* 243:1462-4
Mr 17 '89
SILBER, JOHN R.

about

Crusader on the Charles [cover story] H. Epstein. il pors
The New York Times Magazine p26-9+ Ap 23 '89
The ivory tower triggerman. S. Allis. il por *Time* 134:69
Ag 28 '89
Silber bullet. D. P. Hamilton. *The New Republic* 201:18-19
D 4 '89
SILBERMAN, RICHARD T.

about

'He started at the top and worked his way down'. K. Kerwin.
il por *Business Week* p139 My 1 '89
SILBERMAN, ROBERT
Down-to-earth idealist. bibl f il por *American Craft* 49:32-9
Je/Jl '89
The first moderns. il *American Craft* 49:46-53+ F/Mr '89
SILBERT, MIMI

about

Delancey Street's road to success. C. Males and J. Raskin.
il por *Reader's Digest* 134:108-12 Mr '89

SILENCE
See also
Quietude
Say it with silence. S. Isaacs. il *Parents* 64:134-7 Mr '89
Sharpening the silence. C. Anderson. *Commonweal* 116:230
Ap 21 '89
SILENT COMPANIONS *See* Dummy board figures
SILENT FILMS *See* Motion pictures—Silent films
SILENT HEART ATTACKS *See* Heart—Diseases
SILER, CINDA
Indoor gardening. il *Parents* 64:247+ O '89
SILGAN CORPORATION
Count your blessings? [Morgan Stanley involved in dispute
with investors over Silgan Corp. buyout] R. L. Stern.
il *Forbes* 144:14 N 13 '89
SILICA
See also
Stishovite
Disorder-to-order transition in settling suspensions of colloidal
silica: X-ray measurements. K. E. Davis and others. bibl
f il *Science* 245:507-10 Ag 4 '89
SILICATES
See also
Cordierite
Magnesium silicates
Zeolites
An empirical model for predicting diffusion coefficients in
silicate minerals. S. M. Fortier and B. J. Giletti. bibl
f il *Science* 245:1481-4 S 29 '89
Geological and geochemical record of 3400-million-year-old
terrestrial meteorite impacts [South Africa] D. R. Lowe
and others. bibl f il *Science* 245:959-62 S 1 '89
Phyllosilicate absorption features in main-belt and outer-belt
asteroid reflectance spectra. F. Vilas and M. J. Gaffey.
bibl f il *Science* 246:790-2 N 10 '89
Silicon coordination and speciation changes in a silicate
liquid at high pressures. X. Xue and others. bibl f il
Science 245:962-4 S 1 '89
SILICON
Epitaxial growth of diamond films on Si(111) at room
temperature by mass-selected low-energy C^+ beams. J. L.
Robertson and others. bibl f il *Science* 243:1047-50 F
24 '89
SILICON CARBIDE
The making of interstellar grit [research by Michael Frenklach]
Science News 135:351 Je 3 '89
SILICON CHIP COPYRIGHT *See* Copyright—Integrated cir-
cuits
SILICON CHIPS *See* Integrated circuits
SILICON COMPILERS (COMPUTERS)
Mead's Silicon Retina points toward brain-like processing.
Byte 14:11 F '89
SILICON DIOXIDE *See* Silica
SILICON MICROPHYSIOMETERS
Detection of cell-affecting agents with a silicon biosensor.
J. W. Parce and others. bibl f il *Science* 246:243-7 O
13 '89
Listening to the breaths of 1,000 cells. *Science News* 136:286
O 28 '89
SILICON SYSTEMS, INC.
Thrill a minute. I. Chithelen. por *Forbes* 143:125-6 My
1 '89
SILICON VALLEY ELECTRONIC INDUSTRIES *See* Elec-
tronic industries
SILICON WAFER INDUSTRY *See* Electronic industries
SILICONE
Beyond bucks [possible cancer risk linked to breast implants]
D. M. Podolsky. il *American Health* 8:12 D '89
FDA to require safety data on breast implants. *FDA Consumer*
23:2 Mr '89
The new breast-implant scare [possible link to cancer] C.
Marks. *Mademoiselle* 95:124+ F '89
SILK
Spiders of industry [genetically engineered bacteria produce
silk; work of Nick Ashley] il *Discover* 10:8 F '89
SILK, ARTIFICIAL *See* Rayon
SILK INDUSTRY

France
History

Royal orders for Lyons silk, 1730-1800. J. M. Tuchscherer.
il *Antiques* 136:154-65 Jl '89

Italy

The silks of Como. A. M. Zwack. il *Gourmet* 49:54-5+
Ag '89
SILK ROADS *See* Trade routes
SILK WEAVING

Exhibitions

Royal orders for Lyons silk, 1730-1800. J. M. Tuchscherer.
il *Antiques* 136:154-65 Jl '89
SILKA, JOANN
Use it or lose it. *U.S. Catholic* 54:47 S '89
SILKS (JOCKEY'S UNIFORMS) *See* Horse racing—Uniforms
SILLCOCKS *See* Plumbing
SILLER, JAVIER PÉREZ *See* Pérez Siller, Javier
SILLS, BEVERLY

about

Beverly Sills hits all the high notes. J. Kobler. il pors *New
Choices for the Best Years* 29:36-40 Mr '89

SILLS, STEPHEN
about

Earning his stripes [cover story] J. Reginato. il pors *House & Garden* 161:224-7+ O '89

Exotic treasures and secondhand serendipity meet in the coolly eclectic interiors of Stephen Sills. M. Boodro. il por *Vogue* 179:615+ S '89

SILVA, LUIS INÁCIO DA
about

Brazil's election is a watershed no matter who wins. J. Ryser. il pors *Business Week* p61 D 4 '89

The fiery socialist who could soon be running Brazil. J. Ryser. il por *Business Week* p48 Ja 16 '89

Lula's in town. K. Silverstein. *The Nation* 249:776-7 D 25 '89

SILVER, JOAN MICKLIN
about

Crossing Delancey [film] Reviews
Video il 13:75 My '89. J. Bernard

Joan Micklin Silver [interview] il por *American Film* 14:22-4+ My '89

Loverboy [film] Reviews
People Weekly il 31:12 My 22 '89. R. Novak

SILVER, JONATHAN
about

Jonathan Silver: Sculpture Center. L. Holst. il *Art News* 88:169-70 N '89

SILVER, RON, 1946-
about

Quick Silver. P. Hoban. il pors *New York* 22:72-4+ D 11 '89

SILVER, STEPHEN
about

NTSB asserts captain's cocaine use contributed to crash of Continental Express Metro 3. C. Fotos. *Aviation Week & Space Technology* 130:59 F 6 '89

SILVER
See also
Silverware

Silver supports superconducting paste. il *Science News* 136:182 S 16 '89

Advertising

Can Mad Ave. turn silver into gold? S. D. Atchison. il *Business Week* p99 D 11 '89

Prices

Can Mad Ave. turn silver into gold? S. D. Atchison. il *Business Week* p99 D 11 '89

Therapeutic use

Precious metals: sutures with silver . . . [work of Chih-Chang Chu] *Science News* 136:223 S 30 '89

SILVER BAY STATE PARK (MINN.)

A Superior dive is hard to find. *Newsweek* 113:63 Ap 3 '89

SILVER-IRON STORAGE BATTERIES See Storage batteries

SILVER LINING SEAFOOD (FIRM)

To market, to market [P. Schilling of Alaska Gourmet Seafood and B. Woldrop of Silver Lining Seafood] N. C. Baker. il por *Nation's Business* 77:61 Ja 18 '89

SILVERBERG, ROBERT

To the promised land [fiction] il *Omni (New York, N.Y.)* 11:104-12+ My '89

SILVERMAN, FRED

Ex-president blues [excerpt from address] il *Channels (New York, N.Y.: 1986)* 9:87 Ja '89
about

"I'm not rumpled anymore". L. Gubernick. il por *Forbes* 143:84-5 Mr 6 '89

SILVERMAN, JEFF

The cockeyed world of Ron Shelton. il pors *American Film* 15:34-9+ D '89

SILVERMAN, JEFFREY N.
about

At Toddler University, the chairman is getting A's. J. R. Norman. il por *Business Week* p61 Ja 16 '89

SILVERMAN, JOEL

Tough stuff for the masses: mainstreaming the Ironman. il *Health (New York, N.Y.)* 21:86-8 Ag '89

SILVERMAN, JONATHAN
about

Jon Silverman: leaving the Broadway blues behind. S. Pocharski. il por *Mademoiselle* 95:92 Ag '89

Profile. S. Burkat. il por *Seventeen* 48:56+ Jl '89

SILVERMAN, RONALD H.

Discipline-based art education. *The Education Digest* 55:53-6 O '89

SILVERMAN, STEPHEN
about

Abrams buys authorized bio of filmmaker David Lean. B. Levine. il por *Publishers Weekly* 235:43 Mr 24 '89

SILVERMAN (FRED) COMPANY See Fred Silverman Company

SILVERSTEIN, ANDREW See Clay, Andrew Dice

SILVERSTEIN, KEN

Lula's in town. *The Nation* 249:776-7 D 25 '89

SILVERSTEIN, SHEL
about

The devil and Billy Markham [drama] Reviews
New York 22:105 D 18 '89. J. Simon

The New Yorker 65:77-8+ D 25 '89. M. Kramer

Time il 134:78 D 18 '89. W. A. Henry

SILVERWARE
See also
Gorham Manufacturing Company

China's polished art. M. Guralnick. il *House & Garden* 161:78+ My '89

Care

Kits that claim to help restore silver plate. il *Consumer Reports* 54:6 Ja '89

Collectors and collecting

Chantilly [silverware pattern by Gorham] B. Barol. il *American Heritage* 40:26-7 N '89

Nelly Arrieta de Blaquier's South American silver [collection at La Biznaga] J. Gruen. il por *Architectural Digest* 46:102+ O '89

The pleasure of the chase [auction of S. Wagstaff's silver collection] C. McGuigan. il pors *Newsweek* 113:62-3 Ja 30 '89

Sam Wagstaff's silver. I. Sischy. il por *House & Garden* 161:108-13+ Ja '89

The silver of Carlo Bugatti. A. Duncan. bibl f il por *Antiques* 136:1344-55 D '89

Victorian silver. F. Donegan. il *Americana* 17:61-3 Jl/Ag '89

Exhibitions

The Lowry Dale Kirby Collection of old Sheffield plate. J. D. Davis. il *Antiques* 136:848-59 O '89

The silver [Mount Vernon] M. G. Fales. bibl f il *Antiques* 135:518-23 F '89

Silver for the table [Treasures for the table: silver from the Chrysler Museum] A. E. Ledes. il *Antiques* 135:1314+ Je '89

SIMCITY (VIDEO GAME)

Big fun in a small town. B. Barol. il *Newsweek* 113:64 My 29 '89

Deluged by brilliant world-creation. O. S. Card. *Compute!* 11:88 N '89

SimCity. H. E. H. Aycock. il *Compute!* 11:64 Ag '89

SimCity. R. Gehorsam. *Home Office Computing* 7:94 D '89

Video scans. B. Lindstrom. il *Omni (New York, N.Y.)* 11:122 Je '89

SIMENON, GEORGES, 1903-1989
about

Obituary
U.S. News & World Report il por 107:14 S 18 '89

SIMETI, MARY TAYLOR

A taste of Sicily: the gardens of paradise. il *Gourmet* 49:98-9+ S '89

SIMIAN IMMUNODEFICIENCY VIRUSES See SIV viruses

SIMIAN VIRUSES
See also
SIV viruses

Metastatic hibernomas in transgenic mice expressing an α-amylase-SV40 T antigen hybrid gene. N. Fox and others. bibl f il *Science* 244:460-3 Ap 28 '89

Transformation by v-sis occurs by an internal autoactivation mechanism. B. E. Bejcek and others. bibl f il *Science* 245:1496-9 S 29 '89

SIMLA (INDIA)

Description

Simla: remnants of the Raj. A. Weller. il *Gourmet* 49:136+ N '89

SIMLA (INDIA) IN LITERATURE

Kipling's Simla. *Gourmet* 49:232 N '89

SIMMONS, HAROLD C.
about

Harold Simmons is coming out to play again. T. Mason. il por *Business Week* p44+ Ja 9 '89

Simmons' sleeper. T. Jaffe. *Forbes* 143:285 Je 26 '89

Three raging bulls and two restrained ones. R. King. il pors *Forbes* 144 Special Issue:362+ O 23 '89

The whistling billionaire. A. E. Serwer. il pors *Fortune* 119:102+ Ap 10 '89

SIMMONS, JEAN
about

Jean Simmons picks up her career where it started four decades ago—with Great expectations. T. Allis. il pors *People Weekly* 32:70-1 Jl 10 '89

SIMMONS, JEROLD, 1941-
(jt. auth) See Leff, Leonard J., and Simmons, Jerold, 1941-

SIMMONS, JERRY
about

The coach that roared. S. C. Prince. il por *World Tennis* 36:88-9+ My '89

SIMMONS, JUDY

Out of bounds. il *Ms.* 17:65-7 Ap '89

SIMMONS, MARIE

Chicken à la zing. il *New Choices for the Best Years* 29:76-9 O '89

Cucina fresca. il *Working Woman* 14:96-8 Jl '89

Going nuts. il *New Choices for the Best Years* 29:82-5 S '89

Offbeat veggies. il *New Choices for the Best Years* 29:68-72 Ja '89

SIMMONS, RICHARD
    about
Richard Simmons' New Year's revolution. P. Perry. il por *The Saturday Evening Post* 261:58-9+ Ja/F '89
SIMMS, JOANNA
Witness to child abuse. il *Parents* 64:90+ My '89
SIMMS, MARY
    about
Shedding pounds through surgery. C. F. Henderson. pors *McCall's* 116:100+ Je '89
SIMMS, PHIL, 1955-
    about
Simms was Simmsational. il por *Sports Illustrated* 70:80 Ja 9 '89
SIMON, ALLEN
Foods that fight cholesterol. il *The Saturday Evening Post* 261:30-2 Mr '89
SIMON, CARLY
    about
Carly Simon's Vineyard. J. Brackman. il pors *House & Garden* 161:182-7+ N '89
SIMON, CHERYL
The triumphant dieter. il *Psychology Today* 23:48+ Je '89
SIMON, DAVID
Signal processors. il *Stereo Review* 54:107-10 D '89
SIMON, DICK
    about
Indy oldie. J. Zweig. il por *Forbes* 143:178+ Je 12 '89
SIMON, E. JAMES
    about
When the honeymoon's over: how to tell how you're really doing. J. Ciabattari. il pors *Working Woman* 14:82-6+ Je '89
SIMON, EMERY
Pursuing the pirates. *Publishers Weekly* 236:88-9 S 15 '89
SIMON, FRANCESCA
Countering the crises. *American Visions* 4:48+ Je '89
Medical checkups. il *Essence* 19:18+ Ja '89
SIMON, JOHN
Arc without convenant. il *National Review* 41:30-2 My 5 '89
Film. See occasional issues of National Review
Theater. See issues of New York
SIMON, LAURA
A taste of heaven [fiction] il por *Good Housekeeping* 209:233-6+ N '89
SIMON, MARK
    about
Gothic getaway. M. Filler. il *House & Garden* 161:104-9 Je '89
SIMON, MELVIN
    about
No more plastic plants. S. B. Weiner. il por *Forbes* 143:107-8 Mr 20 '89
SIMON, NEIL
    about
Rumors [drama] Reviews
  The Nation 248:102 Ja 23 '89. T. M. Disch
SIMON, NISSA
An update on estrogen-replacement therapy. il *Working Woman* 14:148+ My '89
SIMON, PAUL, 1928-
Should the Senate-passed Immigration Act of 1989 be approved? [excerpts from debate, July 11-12, 1989] *Congressional Digest* 68:244+ O '89
SIMON, ROGER, 1948-
The weather? Funny and wild (and downright incidental). il *TV Guide* 37:12-15 My 27-Je 2 '89
SIMON, SIDNEY B.
Willpower workout [excerpt from Getting unstuck] il *Ladies' Home Journal* 106:64+ Mr '89
SIMON, STEVEN H.
    about
Kuchnir and Simon are co-winners of undergraduate Apker Award. pors *Physics Today* 42:85 D '89
SIMON, WILLIAM E., 1927-
    about
A silver lining in a stormy recession. M. Magnet. il por *Fortune* 120:71-2 Jl 3 '89
Three raging bulls and two restrained ones. R. King. il pors *Forbes* 144 Special Issue:362+ O 23 '89
SIMON (MELVIN) & ASSOCIATES, INC. *See* Melvin Simon & Associates, Inc.
SIMON & SCHUSTER AUDIO
Court enjoins Dove's distribution of 'Lonesome dove' audio. J. Tangorra. *Publishers Weekly* 236:12 S 22 '89
Dueling 'Doves': acrimony clouds copyright issue. P. Sweeting. il *Publishers Weekly* 235:54-6 Je 2 '89
S&S issues unabridged Carnegie [How to win friends & influence people] P. Sweeting. il *Publishers Weekly* 235:62 Ja 6 '89
SIMON & SCHUSTER INC.
Paramount takes $140 million write-off on publishing units. C. Reid. *Publishers Weekly* 236:8+ D 1 '89
S & S, Janklow, negotiate two-book Reagan deal. *Publishers Weekly* 235:34 F 10 '89
S & S to handle Paramount video line. P. Sweeting. il *Publishers Weekly* 235:31+ F 3 '89

Saul Gilman: his own salesman [vp/sales rep] J. Rosen. por *Publishers Weekly* 235:108+ Ja 20 '89
SIMON & SCHUSTER LTD.
Top executive leaves S & S London trade operation. V. Menkes. *Publishers Weekly* 236:8+ S 1 '89
SIMON GREENLEAF SCHOOL OF LAW
Problems derail law school founder [J. W. Montgomery] R. Frame. *Christianity Today* 33:48 Mr 17 '89
SIMONDS, FRANK H.
Has German strategy failed? *The New Republic* 201 [Reprint v1]:13-14 N 6 '89 [N 7 '14]
SIMONDS, NINA
Chinese lessons. il *American Health* 8:114-16+ S '89
SIMONE, LOUISE
    about
Manhattan transformation. J. Giovannini. il *Architectural Digest* 46:182-7+ Mr '89
SIMONOV, ALLA ERICA
Hands against the darkness. il *The Mother Earth News* 118:8 Jl/Ag '89
SIMONS, ELWYN L.
Human origins. bibl f il *Science* 245:1343-50 S 22 '89
SIMONS, HOWARD
    about
The final days of Howard Simons. J. Adler. il por *Newsweek* 112:76 My 22 '89
The Nieman Foundation at 50: the curator critiques television news. P. Ainslie. il por *Channels (New York, N.Y.: 1986)* 9:10 Je '89
SIMONS, MARLISE
The Amazon's savvy Indians. il map *The New York Times Magazine* p36-7+ F 26 '89
SIMONS, TED, AND WHITTOW, G. CAUSEY, 1930-
A seabird in the house of the sun. il *Natural History* p50-3 Mr '89
SIMONTON, ANN
    about
The woman warrior. J. Lieber. il pors *Sports Illustrated* 70 Special Issue:131-4 F '89
SIMONTON, JOHN
Musical Instrument Digital Interface [cover story] il *Radio-Electronics* 60:33-41 Ag '89
THE SIMPLE ACTS OF LIFE [television program] See Television program reviews—Single works
SIMPLE MINDS (MUSICAL GROUP)
Not so Simple. R. G. Karr. il *Stereo Review* 54:103-5 N '89
SIMPLICITY
Does simple living have to be so complicated? L. Jacquet. il *U.S. Catholic* 54:28-35 Jl '89
Finding Christmas. G. Logsdon. il *Country Journal* 16:82-7 N/D '89
SIMPLIFIED EMPLOYEE PENSIONS
Moving your IRA, SEP or Keogh into a new home. M. Meyer. il *Money* 18:59-60 Ap '89
SIMPLOT, JACK
    about
The magic of 'Mr. Spud'. D. Glick. il por *Newsweek* 114:63 N 27 '89
Third down and long. E. F. Cone. por *Forbes* 143:10 F 20 '89
SIMPLOT (J. R.) CO. *See* J. R. Simplot Co.
SIMPSON, ALAN K.
Should the Congress adopt the "High Risk Occupational Disease Notification and Prevention Act of 1987"? [excerpts from address, March 23, 1988] *Congressional Digest* 68:117+ Ap '89
Should the Senate-passed Immigration Act of 1989 be approved? [excerpts from debate, July 11, 1989] *Congressional Digest* 68:240+ O '89
SIMPSON, CLIVE A.
Hotol goes private. il *Ad Astra* 1:27-9 My '89
SIMPSON, GEORGE
    about
Rover boy. J. Flint. il por *Forbes* 143:201 Mr 20 '89
SIMPSON, JACK W.
Competition in the information industry [address, October 31, 1988] *Vital Speeches of the Day* 55:284-6 F 15 '89
SIMPSON, JEFFREY
Antiques: lacca povera furniture. il *Architectural Digest* 46:168-73 F '89
SIMPSON, JOE
    about
Left for dead on a Peruvian peak, Joe Simpson survives to write movingly about the climbers' code. S. K. Reed. il pors *People Weekly* 31:151-2 My 1 '89
SIMPSON, JOEL
Music writing programs for the Macintosh (I). il *Down Beat* 56:54-6 Ap '89
Music writing programs for the Macintosh (II). il *Down Beat* 56:53-6 Je '89
SIMPSON, KEVIN
The best little division in basketball. il *Sport (New York, N.Y.)* 80:48-52 Ja '89
SIMPSON, MONA
Americana [story] il *Harper's* 278:62-76 My '89

SIMPSON, O. J.
about
O.J. Simpson charged with beating his wife. il por *Jet* 75:26 F 20 '89
O.J. Simpson ordered to pay $200 fine by court in wife-beating case. il por *Jet* 76:51 Je 12 '89

SIMPSON, PEGGY
Constitutional crisis. il *Ms.* 18:90+ S '89
The political arena. *Ms.* 18:46-7 Jl/Ag '89
Politics. il *Ms.* 17:88-9 Ap '89

SIMPSON, RICHARD V.
The art of the fire: cloisonné enamels [cover story] bibl il *Antiques & Collecting Hobbies* 94:40-1+ Ap '89
The decorated opal ware of C. F. Monroe. il *Antiques & Collecting Hobbies* 94:36-40 S '89
U.S.A. space mission patches. il *Antiques & Collecting Hobbies* 93:50-3 Ja '89

SIMPSON, WALLIS WARFIELD *See* Windsor, Wallis Warfield, Duchess of, 1896-1986

THE SIMPSONS [television program] *See* Television program reviews—Single works

SIMRELL, DAN
about
The ax falls at Toledo. D. S. Looney. il por *Sports Illustrated* 71:32-3 D 25 '89-Ja 1 '90

SIMS, NAOMI, 1949-
about
Battle of the vanities [cover story] A. Edmond, Jr. il por *Black Enterprise* 19:42-3+ Mr '89

SIMS (NAOMI) BEAUTY PRODUCTS LTD. *See* Naomi Sims Beauty Products Ltd.

SIMULATION, COMPUTER *See* Computer simulation

SIMULATIONS, INC.
When theater meets big business. S. P. Herman. il pors *Home Office Computing* 7:56-7 Mr '89

SIMULATORS
See also
Automobile driving simulators
Flight simulators
Rediffusion Simulation Ltd.
Space flight simulators
Threat simulators

SIMULTANEOUS REPLICATION
Simultaneous replication: a technique for large-scale research. J. R. Frymier and others. bibl f il *Phi Delta Kappan* 71:228-31 N '89

SIN
See also
Fall of man
Penance
'The power of sin is the law'. P. Perkins. il *The Christian Century* 106:1044 N 15 '89
Sin no more? R. E. Burns. *U.S. Catholic* 54:2 D '89
You can't cure the wilding sickness [attack on Central Park jogger] C. W. Colson. il *Christianity Today* 33:80 S 8 '89

SIN NATIONAL SPANISH TELEVISION NETWORK
See also
Univision/Spanish International Network

SIN TAXES *See* Alcoholic beverages—Taxation; Cigarettes—Taxation

SINAI (PENINSULA)
Description and travel
Go down, Moses [exploring reefs near Ras Muhammed off tip of Sinai Peninsula] N. MacFarquhar. il *Esquire* 112:56 D '89

SINAI SUPPORT MISSION *See* United States. Army—Forces in the Middle East

SINATRA, FRANK, 1915-
about
Sinatra. J. Schwartz. il pors *Gentlemen's Quarterly* 59:228-31+ Je '89

SINBERG, STAN
Last word. por *Omni (New York, N.Y.)* 11:104 Ag '89

SINCERITY
Facial clues to deceptive behavior [study by Brian Mullen and Martin Skinner] il *USA Today (Periodical)* 118:8 S '89

SINCLAIR, JAMES E.
about
Gold's new role. R. L. Stern. il por *Forbes* 144:83+ D 25 '89

SINCLAIR, JOHN H.
A new Pentecost: hope in solidarity. il *The Christian Century* 106:83-4 Ja 25 '89

SINCLAIR, MICHAEL J.
about
Michael Sinclair: health care's whirling dervish. R. A. Melcher. il por *Business Week* p69 D 4 '89

SINCLAIR, MOLLY
The Peterson principle. il por *New Choices for the Best Years* 29:16+ Je '89

SINCLAIR, WARD
about
Fields of dreams: old farming is new again. H. Kohn. il *Rolling Stone* p41-2 O 5 '89

SINDBIS VIRUS
Sindbis virus: an efficient, broad host range vector for gene expression in animal cells. C. Xiong and others. bibl f il *Science* 243:1188-91 Mr 3 '89

SINE, TOM
Exchange of values. por *Christianity Today* 33:52 Mr 17 '89
God's will—and a little creativity. il *Christianity Today* 33:24-5 F 17 '89
Shifting into the future tense. il *Christianity Today* 33:18-21 N 17 '89

SINE NOMINE SINGERS
Musical events:
Performance of Mass by J. Obrecht. A. Porter. *The New Yorker* 65:69-70 F 27 '89

SINE WAVE GENERATORS *See* Signal generators

SING [film] *See* Motion picture reviews—Single works

SINGAPORE
See also
Government publicity—Singapore
Defenses
See also
United States—Armed Forces—Forces in Singapore
Foreign relations
United States
See United States—Foreign relations—Singapore
Industries
See also
Aeroleasing Far East (Firm)
Printing industry—Singapore
Singapore Airlines Ltd.
Tradewinds (Firm)
Politics and government
Singapore—an ally we need. C. W. Weinberger. il por *Forbes* 143:31 My 29 '89
Religious institutions and affairs
See also
Evangelical churches—Singapore
Religious conferences—Singapore
Social history
Singapore in the thirties. N. Barber. il map *Gourmet* 49:100+ My '89

SINGAPORE AIRLINES LTD.
Two carriers begin using 747-400s in nonstop service to Europe, Asia. M. Mecham. *Aviation Week & Space Technology* 130:316-17 Je 12 '89

SINGAPORE INTERNATIONAL BOOK FAIR *See* Book fairs

SINGER, BARRY
Buying British. il *House & Garden* 161:198+ Mr '89

SINGER, DANIEL, 1926-
Dancing on the grave of revolution [cover story] *The Nation* 248:145+ F 6 '89
From Balzac to Salvador Dali. il *The Nation* 248:333-4+ Mr 13 '89

SINGER, FRANCIS J., AND OTHERS
Drought, fires, and large mammals. bibl f il maps *BioScience* 39:716-22 N '89

SINGER, IRA D.
AIDS concerns for business. il *Nation's Business* 77:75-7 Je '89

SINGER, MARK
La cabeza de Villa. *The New Yorker* 65:108-12+ N 27 '89
Department of amplification. *The New Yorker* 65:119-20 Ap 10 '89
Profiles [E. Morris] por *The New Yorker* 64:38-40+ F 6 '89

SINGER, MAX, 1931-
Justice for the Palestinians. il *National Review* 41:40-2 O 13 '89

SINGER, PETER
Unkind to animals. bibl f il *The New York Review of Books* 36:36-8 F 2 '89

SINGER, S. FRED
My adventures in the ozone layer. *National Review* 41:34-8 Je 30 '89

SINGER COMPANY. LINK FLIGHT SIMULATION DIVISION
U.S. joins ex-employee in accusing Singer of fraud. *Aviation Week & Space Technology* 130:263 Mr 20 '89

SINGER SEWING MACHINE COMPANY
See also
SSMC Inc.

SINGERS
See also
Black singers
Choirs
Opera singers
Women singers

SINGH, PETER
about
A Sikh singer who gives Elvis fans a Singh-King feeling. il por *People Weekly* 31:87 My 1 '89

SINGH, PRITAM
about
Pritam Singh's strange career. R. Conniff. il por *Time* 134:21-2+ D 11 '89

SINGH, RAHUL
Project Tiger. il *The Courier (Unesco)* 42:35-6 F '89

SINGH, S. NIHAL
From market to community. il *World Press Review* 36:14 Ja '89
UNESCO's second crisis. il *World Press Review* 36:64 Jl '89

SINGH, VISHWANATH PRATAP
about
The end of a dynasty. R. Moreau and S. Mazumdar. il pors *Newsweek* 114:60 D 11 '89
The end of a dynasty: voters reject Prime Minister Rajiv Gandhi. A. Bilski. il pors *Maclean's* 102:40-1 D 11 '89
The fall of the House of Nehru. L. Beyer. il pors *Time* 134:57 D 11 '89
No rerun for the Gandhi-dynasty show. E. MacFarquhar. il pors *U.S. News & World Report* 107:47-8 D 11 '89
A referendum on Rajiv. C. S. Manegold. por *Newsweek* 114:56 N 27 '89

SINGHAM, MANO
Science for developing countries. *Physics Today* 42 pt1:61+ Ag '89

SINGIN' IN THE RAIN [film] See Motion picture reviews—Single works

SINGING
Competitions
See also
International Youth and Music Festival
Revolving door? (I) [Metropolitan Opera National Council Auditions; with editorial comment by Jane L. Poole] B. L. Scherer. il *Opera News* 53:4, 22-4 Ja 21 '89
Revolving door? (II) [international contests for opera singers] B. L. Scherer. il *Opera News* 53:18-21 Ap 15 '89
Revolving door? (III) [competitions for opera singers] B. L. Scherer. il *Opera News* 54:32-4 O '89
Study and teaching
Close encounters [master classes for opera singers] D. G. Winer. il *Opera News* 54:28-31+ S '89
Vocal coach Elizabeth Sabine, the heavy metal grandma, teaches speech and screech. S. Dougherty. il pors *People Weekly* 31:137-9 My 15 '89

SINGING TEACHERS
See also
Garrett, Joyce
Sabine, Elizabeth
Close encounters [master classes for opera singers] D. G. Winer. il *Opera News* 54:28-31+ S '89

SINGLE FATHERS
Crack pushes dads to duty. J. Seligmann. il *Newsweek* 113:64-5 Ap 17 '89

SINGLE-LENS REFLEX CAMERAS See Cameras, Single-lens reflex

SINGLE MALT SCOTCH WHISKEY See Scotch whiskey

SINGLE MEN
See also
Divorced fathers
Divorcees
Widowers
Bachelors for 1989 [black men] il *Ebony* 44:116-18+ Je '89
My two uncles. L. Cunningham. il *The New York Times Magazine* p32+ D 3 '89
No ties to bind [friendships between single men and married men] C. Yearwood. por *Essence* 20:10 S '89
Uncensored: inside seven bachelor pads. B. E. Ellis. il *Mademoiselle* 95:164-71 F '89
Where the men are [six cities with eligible single black men] il *Ebony* 44:98+ F '89
Anecdotes, facetiae, satire, etc.
Bachelor angst. J. Achenbach. il *Utne Reader* p58-9 Mr/Ap '89
Crimes against
The trouble with angels [mail order fraud perpetrated against single men by Church of Love] il *New Choices for the Best Years* 29:13+ Ap '89
Victims of the Church of Love were only the lonely [mail order scam perpetrated by D. S. Lowry] J. Friedman. il por *People Weekly* 31:77-8+ Ja 30 '89
Economic conditions
Millionaire bachelors: the 20 most wanted. S. Bidel. il *Harper's Bazaar* 122:46+ Ja '89
Medical care
"Fast-food" medical care [research by David Stewart] il *USA Today (Periodical)* 118:16 O '89

SINGLE MOTHERS
3 strikes for you [black single mother] S. Henderson. por *Essence* 19:136 Mr '89
A courage born of broken promises. M. Blumenthal. il *The New York Times Magazine* p14+ Jl 23 '89
The lives of teenage mothers [Kingsbridge Heights Community Center, Bronx, N.Y.] E. Marek. il *Harper's* 278:56-8+ Ap '89
One woman's family: the plight of single mothers. S. Weller. *McCall's* 116:75-6+ F '89
Single mothers by choice. J. Seligmann. il *Newsweek* 114 Special Issue:40+ Wint '89/Spr '90
When mom plays the dating game, do you lose? D. Dodds. il *'Teen* 33:68-9 D '89
Why mothers are not getting married. A. Bernstein. il *Business Week* p74-5 My 22 '89

Anecdotes, facetiae, satire, etc.
Dating at forty. N. Kelton. il *Parents* 64:126-8 S '89
Economic conditions
"From welfare mom to millionaire". E. Goudge. il por *Ladies' Home Journal* 106:22+ Ag '89
The pain of poverty [contrasting single mothers on welfare in Maine and Nova Scotia] G. Allen. il *Maclean's* 102:38-9 Jl 3 '89
The racialization of poverty. M. B. Wilkerson and J. H. Gresham. il *The Nation* 249:126-30+ Jl 24-31 '89
A single mom bets it all on herself [Caraway's owner A. Marchette] S. Seixas. il pors *Money* 18:127-32 Ap '89
A single mom must use her energy and ambition to beat a low-pay handicap [Janet Beck] L. Luciano. il *Money* 18:161-2 S '89
Education
New York school system gets first teen trio of valedictorian mothers. il *Jet* 76:13 Jl 17 '89
The powers that free [single mother gets off welfare]; ed. by Bebe Moore Campbell. I. Vanzant. il por *Essence* 20:80-2+ O '89
School paper's story on teen mother who's class valedictorian is barred [C. M. Dixon] il por *Jet* 76:31 My 8 '89
Teen mom tells of 'beating odds' to be valedictorian [C. M. Dixon] il pors *Jet* 76:12 Je 26 '89
Teen mother with straight A's tells how education is changing her life [C. M. Dixon] D. M. Cheers. il pors *Jet* 76:28-30 My 22 '89
The triumph of Bonnie Lovette. L. Marsa. il pors *Good Housekeeping* 209:72+ Ag '89
Valedictorian Carrie Dixon gets top grades in high school— even with a second child on the way [Houston, Tex.] il por *People Weekly* 31:62 My 29 '89

SINGLE PARENT FAMILIES
Solo parenting breeds a keen eye for priorities. B. Kobliner. il *Money* 18:63-4 Mr '89
Spending patterns and income of single and married parents. M. Boyle. bibl f il *Monthly Labor Review* 112:37-41 Mr '89

SINGLE PEOPLE
See also
Cooking by single people
Dating (Social customs)
Divorcees
Unmarried couples
Single jeopardy. B. Ehrenreich. il *Ms.* 17:24-5 My '89
What's so bad about being single? [cover story; special section] il *Utne Reader* p47-69 Mr/Ap '89
When you ain't got nobody. G. Schwartz. *Seventeen* 48:68 Mr '89
Economic conditions
For singles, the trick is knowing when to be a tiger. G. Anrig, Jr. il *Money* 18:70+ Mr '89
Real estate attracts singles [views of Jerry D. Anderson] *USA Today (Periodical)* 118:13-14 Ag '89
Women living alone. A. Quinlan. il *New Choices for the Best Years* 29:13 Ja '89
Housing
Anecdotes, facetiae, satire, etc.
Next summer, I'll be married [house sharing in the Hamptons] P. Mehlman. il *The New York Times Magazine* p44+ My 21 '89
A summer place [taking a summer share in the Hamptons] M. McCully. il *Gentlemen's Quarterly* 59:143-4+ Je '89
Religious life
See also
Church work with single people
Travel
Going solo—sans the supplement. H. Gieseking. *Travel Holiday* 171:101-2 Ap '89
Traveling single [cover story] J. Cecil. il *New York* 22:44-50+ F 13 '89

SINGLE PREMIUM LIFE INSURANCE See Insurance, Life

SINGLE ROOM OCCUPANCY HOTELS
Washington, D.C., contemplates the SRO as affordable housing. B. Black. il *Architectural Record* 177:43 F '89

SINGLE SIDEBAND RADIOTELEPHONE ON BOATS See Radiotelephone on ships, boats, etc.

SINGLE-SOURCE RESEARCH (TV AUDIENCE RE- SEARCH)
Denver does ScanAmerica. M. Couzens. *Channels (New York, N.Y.: 1986)* 9:24 N '89

SINGLE SPIES [drama] See Bennett, Alan, 1934-

SINGLE WOMEN
See also
Divorcees
Widows
1989 bachelorettes: smart, pretty and available [black women] il *Ebony* 44:132-4+ Jl '89
Alone at last [excerpt from Grownups] C. Merser. il *Utne Reader* p62-3 Mr/Ap '89
Beat the no-love-life blues. il *Glamour* 87:154-7 Ja '89
Invasion of the couple people: what's a happily single girl to do? M. McNamara. il *Mademoiselle* 95:206-7+ S '89
Is married better? [sisters exchange places] S. Nelson and L. Nelson. il pors *Glamour* 87:274-5+ O '89
Single women, married women: can we be friends? B. M. Campbell. il *Essence* 20:47-8+ Jl '89

SINGLE WOMEN—*cont.*

A therapist who's been there urges sympathy for the 'other woman' [interview with J. Bitner] S. Adelson. il pors *People Weekly* 32:116+ O 30 '89

Toward a new definition of singleness: building a life with close friends [female friends] R. Kranz. il *Utne Reader* p56-7+ Mr/Ap '89

The virtues of solitude. P. Paquin. il *Utne Reader* p68-9 Mr/Ap '89

Economic conditions

Age 30: single, just getting under way. J. A. Engle. il por *Fortune* 120 no10 Special Issue:128 Fall '89

She's got to have it all now! [media planner K. Crowley] S. Seixas. il pors *Money* 18:86-8+ O '89

You, men and money. A. Edwards. *Essence* 20:55-6+ Ag '89

Travel

Romance away from home. S. R. Hamilton. il *Essence* 19:23+ F '89

SINGLE WOMEN, MARRIED MEN [television program] See Television program reviews—Single works

SINGLEHANDED YACHT RACING *See* Yacht racing

SINKS

New products: kitchen and bath. il *Architectural Record* 177:116-17+ mid-Ap '89

Repair porcelain enamel. il *The Family Handyman* 39:52-3 S '89

SINNOTT, ROGER W.

Astronomical computing. See issues of Sky and Telescope beginning April 1984

Gleanings for ATM's. See issues of Sky and Telescope

SINO (NEW YORK, N.Y.: RESTAURANT) *See* New York (N.Y.)—Restaurants, nightclubs, bars, etc.

SINO-SOVIET RELATIONS *See* Soviet Union—Foreign relations—China

SINT MAARTEN *See* Saint Martin

SINUSITIS

Best tips for beating sinusitis. K. Anderson. il *Prevention (Emmaus, Pa.)* 41:38-43 Ja '89

SINYAVSKY, ANDREY, 1925-

Would I move back? il pors *Time* 133:129-30+ Ap 10 '89

SIOUX CITY (IOWA)

Airports

Rescue coordination, drills helped speed evacuation of survivors [United Airlines DC-10 crash] D. Hughes. *Aviation Week & Space Technology* 131:31+ Jl 31 '89

SIOUX INDIANS *See* Dakota Indians

SIOUXSIE AND THE BANSHEES (MUSICAL GROUP)

Siouxsie and the Banshees: "Peep show". P. Puterbaugh. il *Stereo Review* 54:101 Ja '89

SIPCHEN, BOB

Tooling down the Mississippi. il pors map *Forbes* 144:22-3 O 30 '89

SIR NOEL COWARD'S FIREFLY HILL MUSEUM (JAMAICA)

Coward's Jamaica. D. Butwin. il pors *Oceans* 22:54-7 Mr/Ap '89

SIRACUSA (NEW YORK, N.Y.: RESTAURANT) *See* New York (N.Y.)—Restaurants, nightclubs, bars, etc.

SIRENIA

See also

Manatees

SIRENS

Sounding off . . . safely [work of M. Neuhaus] D. Stover. il por *Popular Science* 235:36 O '89

SIRICO, ROBERT A.

George's story. *Commonweal* 116:464-5 S 8 '89

SIRIUS (STAR) *See* Stars, Double

SIRKIN, ELLIOTT, AND LAMANNA, DEAN

Julie and Carol together again. il pors *Ladies' Home Journal* 106:62+ D '89

SIRONI, MARIO, 1885-1961

about

Mario Sironi: Philippe Daverio. N. Grimes. il *Art News* 88:200+ O '89

SIROTKIN, ALBERT

Filling in the blank spots in Soviet history [interview with Y. Afanasyev; tr. by Vladimir Voronin and Adam Shulman. il *History Today* 39:12-17 F '89

SISCHY, INGRID

Belief. *The New Yorker* 65:79-82 My 22 '89

The hands of time. il *House & Garden* 161:136-41+ Jl '89

New York. il *House & Garden* 161:196-9+ O '89

Sam Wagstaff's silver. il por *House & Garden* 161:108-13+ Ja '89

White and black. *The New Yorker* 65:124+ N 13 '89

SISKEL, GENE

about

Critical success: Gene Siskel and Marlene Iglitzen's art déco Chicago apartment. C. T. Buckley. il pors *Architectural Digest* 46:256-61+ O '89

SISKIN, BERNARD R., 1944-, AND OTHERS

20 surprising facts on love, marriage, sex and divorce [excerpt from What are the chances?] il *Glamour* 87:310-11 S '89

SISKIN, PAUL

about

Pared to perfection. M. Boodro. il *Vogue* 179:282-3+ My '89

SISLER, DICK, 1920-

about

The College of Cardinals. J. Garrity. il pors *Sports Illustrated* 71:64-8+ Ag 14 '89

SISSON, DAN

Grandpa and the kid. See alternate issues of Field & Stream beginning September 1983

SISSON, RICHARD

about

Britain's blue-blood bad boys 'Kit and the Widow' make even their royal targets laugh. J. Wadler. il pors *People Weekly* 31:97-9 Ap 24 '89

SISTER KATE [television program] See Television program reviews—Single works

SISTER THEA BOWMAN BLACK CATHOLIC EDUCATIONAL FOUNDATION

Thea Bowman Foundation launches $150 million college scholarship fund. il *Jet* 77:27 N 6 '89

SISTERS *See* Siblings

SISTERS AND BROTHERS *See* Siblings

SISTERS OF ST. CLARE *See* Poor Clares

SISTINE CHAPEL *See* Vatican. Cappella Sistina

SISULU, ALBERTINA

about

President meets with South African antiapartheid activist [statement, June 30, 1989] G. Bush. il pors *Department of State Bulletin* 89:71 S '89

SISULU, WALTER

about

Ex-ANC leader talks about 26 years of imprisonment. il por *Jet* 77:30 N 6 '89

Sisulu: "We want immediate change" [interview] S. MacLeod. il por *Time* 134:70 O 30 '89

SITBON, MARTINE

about

Paris originals. M. Gross. il por *New York* 22:28+ My 15 '89

SITCOMS (PROGRAMS) *See* Television broadcasting—Comedy programs

SITE PLANNING *See* Building sites

SITES, BUILDING *See* Building sites

SITES, HISTORIC *See* Historic houses, sites, etc.

SITES, INDUSTRIAL *See* Location in business and industry

SITKOVETSKY, DMITRY

about

Sitkovetsky's dazzling Prokofiev. D. Hall. il por *Stereo Review* 54:96 Je '89

SITTING ROOMS

Private sitting room—convenient study. il *Southern Living* 24:175 Ap '89

SITUATION COMEDY PROGRAMS *See* Television broadcasting—Comedy programs

SITUATIONISTS INTERNATIONAL (GROUP)

Homage to a phantom avant-garde: the Situationist International. C. Phillips. bibl f il *Art in America* 77:182-91+ O '89

L'Internationale Situationiste: Centre Pompidou. G. Danto. il *Art News* 88:180 N '89

SIV, SICHAN

about

Escape from the inferno. J. Friedman. il pors *People Weekly* 31:32-7 Mr 27 '89

SIV VIRUSES

A formalin-inactivated whole SIV vaccine confers protection in macaques. M. Murphey-Corb and others. bibl f il *Science* 246:1293-7 D 8 '89

Monkey vaccine prevents AIDS-like disease [research by Ronald C. Desrosiers] K. Fackelmann. *Science News* 136:116 Ag 19 '89

One step closer to an AIDS vaccine [inoculation of monkeys with SIV virus; work of Michael Murphey-Corb and others] *Newsweek* 114:66 D 18 '89

Progress in vaccines against AIDS. D. Bolognesi. bibl f *Science* 246:1233-4 D 8 '89

A simian clue to the prevention of AIDS [vaccine combats SIV virus; research by Michael Murphey-Corb and others] il *U.S. News & World Report* 107:10-11 D 18 '89

SIVA (HINDU DEITY) IN ART

Who owns the Nataraja? [British court rules that Siva bronze bought by Canadian collector belongs to India] S. E. Weil. il *Art News* 88:188 My '89

SIVARAJA, MOHANRAM, AND OTHERS

Identification by ENDOR of Trp[191] as the free-radical site in cytochrome c peroxidase compound ES. bibl f il *Science* 245:738-40 Ag 18 '89

SIXTH COMMITTEE (UNITED NATIONS) *See* United Nations. Legal Committee

SIXTIES (DECADE) *See* Nineteen hundred and sixties

SIZE

See also

Clothing and dress—Size

SIZE OF BODY *See* Body size
SIZEMORE, CHRIS COSTNER
about
Three faces of Eve told her story, now Chris Sizemore is battling a major studio over movie rights and wrongs. D. Van Biema. il pors *People Weekly* 31:79-80+ Mr 27 '89
SJA (FIRM)
Lafayette Jones forms new company. por *Jet* 75:14 Ja 23 '89
SJÖGREN'S SYNDROME
Eyes too dry to cry: how Sjögren's syndrome makes the body a 'desert'. A. Hecht. il *FDA Consumer* 23:26-30 F '89
Sometimes dryness isn't so welcome. J. Wood. il *Modern Maturity* 32:27 D '89/Ja '90
SKAGGS, JOEY
about
Pranks a lot! M. Callum. il por *TV Guide* 37:23 Jl 29-Ag 4 '89
SKALBANIA, NELSON
about
Running hard. P. Chisholm. il por *Maclean's* 102:38-9 Ap 3 '89
SKALKA, PATRICIA
It's not the heat, it's the humidity. il *Reader's Digest* 135:61-4 Jl '89
Kids' diseases doctors miss. il *Ladies' Home Journal* 106:80+ F '89
"No one's born a loser!". *Reader's Digest* 134:21-2+ F '89
Reader's digest guide to moving. il *Reader's Digest* 134:M1-M12 Mr '89
Who lives longer? *McCall's* 116:91+ Ag '89
SKALSKI, ERNEST
Ameryka my America; tr. by Anna Husarska. il *The New Leader* 72:8-9 N 13 '89
Poland turns to the polls; tr. by Anna Husarska. il *The New Leader* 72:5-7 Ap 3-17 '89
SKAPINKER, MICHAEL
Enduring conferences. il *World Press Review* 36:50 Mr '89
SKASE, CHRISTOPHER
about
Fast fade for Chris Skase. R. Grover and S. Hutcheon. il por *Business Week* p76-7 D 11 '89
Leo the Lion is on the loose again. R. Grover. il por *Business Week* p60 O 23 '89
Stranger in a strange land. L. Gubernick. il por *Forbes* 144:164+ O 2 '89
These days, they don't call it 'Down Under' for nothing. S. Hutcheon. il por *Business Week* p66+ N 6 '89
SKATEBOARDING
Rad dog! Rad dog! When it comes to skateboarding, Sidney the bulldog is a wheelie big star. il *People Weekly* 31:80 Je 12 '89
A skateboarder's guide to unstoked parents. B. Blouin. *Harper's* 279:22+ Ag '89
SKATING
See also
Figure skating
Roller skating
Speed skating
SKEET SHOOTING *See* Trapshooting
SKELETAL MUSCLE *See* Muscle
SKELETON
See also
Maxilla & Mandible (Firm)
Skull
Adaptive nature of skeletal design [plasticity to cope with locomotive stress] K. R. Gordon. bibl f il *BioScience* 39:784-90 D '89
SKELETON IN ART
Gogo Fuller's sassy skeletal jewelry is not for the spineless [bone jewelry created from animal skeletons] M. Dougherty. il pors *People Weekly* 32:101+ O 16 '89
SKELLIE FAMILY
about
Successful family farm: deep roots and dairy traditions. J. R. Borcherding. il *Successful Farming* 87:46-8 Ag '89
SKELTON, TOM
about
Tom Skelton [cover story] G. M. Loney. il pors *Theatre Crafts* 23:44-51+ Ap '89
SKEPTICISM
See also
New York Area Skeptics (Organization)
Take a stand, or several. D. R. Carlin, Jr. *Commonweal* 116:457-8 S 8 '89
SKERNICK, DAVID
Heavenly shades of long exposures. il *Petersen's Photographic Magazine* 18:40-2 Je '89
SKEWER COOKING (BARBECUING) *See* Barbecue cooking
SKI BINDINGS
The 3-D looks. C. Ettlinger. il *Skiing* 41:107-8+ F '89
Bindings. C. Ettlinger. il *Skiing* 42:187+ S '89
Bizarre binding for the slopes [Nava ski boot] V. E. Gilmore. il *Popular Science* 234:111 Mr '89
Kids' stuff. C. Ettlinger. il *Skiing* 41:88+ F '89

The Marker Twincam system. C. Ettlinger. il *Skiing* 41:142-4 Ja '89
Marker's new full-spectrum. C. Ettlinger. il *Skiing* 42:159-60+ N '89
The new Tyrolias. C. Ettlinger. il *Skiing* 42:170-4 O '89
Upward release at the toe. C. Ettlinger. il *Skiing* 42:217-18+ D '89
SKI BOOTS
Bizarre binding for the slopes [Nava ski boot] V. E. Gilmore. il *Popular Science* 234:111 Mr '89
Boots. C. Meader. il *Skiing* 42:118-20+ S '89
Bred for racing. C. Meader. il *Skiing* 42:154-6+ O '89
Downhill skiing—with panache. H. King. il *Business Week* p170 O 30 '89
Fit for kids. C. Meader. il *Skiing* 41:113-14+ Ja '89
Four buckle drive. C. Meader. il *Skiing* 42:137-8+ N '89
Intermediary boots. C. Meader. il *Skiing* 41:93-4+ F '89
More choices for sport skiers. C. Meader. il *Skiing* 42:248-50+ D '89
New for '90. I. Devlin. il *Skiing* 41:122-4 Mr '89
Slope yoga and other remedies [heel lift] D. Killham. il *Skiing* 42:40 D '89
SKI CLOTHES *See* Clothing and dress—Sports clothes
SKI CLUBS *See* Sports clubs
SKI COACHES
The endless winter [Vail ski instructors R. Colfer and J. Stanley] P. Mehlman. il pors *Gentlemen's Quarterly* 59:336-9+ Mr '89
SKI HOUSES *See* Vacation houses
SKI JUMPING
Heading for an 'off' year [year without a nordic world championship] P. Robbins. il *Skiing* 42:42+ S '89
SKI LIFTS
High anxiety [fear of riding ski lifts] J. Older. il *Skiing* 42:33-4 O '89
Quadrophenia. A. H. Greenberg. *Skiing* 41:40 F '89
SKI MOUNTAINEERING
U.S. tourers tackle USSR. E. Perlman. il *Skiing* 41:22 F '89
SKI POLES
Poles. J. Chase. il *Skiing* 42:212 S '89
SKI RACING
See also
Biathlon (Skiing and shooting)
Cross country ski racing
Speed skiing
Able disableds. T. Latsis. il *Skiing* 42:286+ S '89
The boys are back! [P. and S. Mahre on pro racing circuit] P. Oliver. il pors *Skiing* 41:38-40 Mr '89
A flight so fancy [Alpine World Championships at Vail] W. O. Johnson. il pors *Sports Illustrated* 70:14-21 F 13 '89
Getting along on skis [first United Airlines Friendship Cup] il *National Geographic World* 162:18-21 F '89
Grand slam for the Bomb [men's World Cup] K. Read. il *Skiing* 42:250-5+ S '89
Inside racing. C. Cooper. See issues of Skiing beginning September 1985 through March 1989
Mountain melodrama [Alpine World Championships in Vail] W. O. Johnson. il *Sports Illustrated* 70:32-5 F 20 '89
Pan Am winter games: for the sport of it [cover story] P. M. Miller. il map *Américas* 41 no2:42-5 '89
Preview: Vail Worlds '89 [special section] il *Skiing* 41:74-80+ Ja '89
Racing's authentic amateurs. C. Walter. il *Skiing* 42:105-6+ D '89
The shrinking World Cup. K. Read. il *Skiing* 42:30+ O '89
Sisterhood of speed [women's pro tour] N. Howe. il *Skiing* 42:232-4+ N '89
Skiing scene. See issues of Skiing
Skiing tip:
Racing for the whole family. H. Kashiwa. il *Skiing* 41:27 Mr '89
Super streak for Vreni [women's World Cup] N. Howe. il *Skiing* 42:268-71+ S '89
Uphill downhill [Pan American winter games at Las Leñas] D. Einhorn. il *Américas* 41 no1:3-4 '89
Year of the rookie [men's pro tour] P. Oliver. il por *Skiing* 42:137+ O '89
Accidents and injuries
After the fall [skier P. Fletcher recovers from leg fracture] S. Nelson. il por *Health (New York, N.Y.)* 21:28-9 Mr '89
Downhill dangers. K. Read. il *Skiing* 42:42-3 N '89
History
'Race Country USA' [Vail, Colo.] B. Kidd. il *Skiing* 41:94-5+ Ja '89
A time to remember [Aspen as World Championships host in 1950] N. Howe. il *Skiing* 41:106-8 Ja '89
SKI RACING COURSES
Designer downhills. K. Read. il *Skiing* 42:56+ D '89
SKI RESORTS *See* Resorts
SKID ROW (MUSICAL GROUP)
Skid Row strike it rich! il *Teen* 33:53 N '89

SKIDDING OF AUTOMOBILES See Automobiles—Skidding
SKIDMORE, JAMES A., JR.
Bring in the leaders. il *USA Today (Periodical)* 118:79-80
  N '89
SKIERS
  See also
  Carmichael, Nelson
  Mahre, Phil
  Mahre, Steve
  Matt, Toni, d. 1989
  McKinney, Tamara
  Mueller, C. J.
Skiing people. See issues of Skiing beginning September 1986
Accidents and injuries
  See Skiing—Accidents and injuries
Health and hygiene
High and dry [dehydration problems] M. Bloom. *Skiing*
  41:16-17 Mr '89
Slim down for better skiing. M. Bloom. *Skiing* 41:24-5 F
  '89
Nutrition
Fuel in your tank. M. Bloom. il *Skiing* 42:46+ N '89
Training
Are you injury-prone? T. Pederson. il por *Skiing* 42:67-8+
  O '89
Get in shape to schuss [views of John Atkins] W. Sturgeon.
  il *American Health* 8:82 N '89
Ski-specific exercise gear. J. Chase. il *Skiing* 42:30+ N '89
The strength to ski. M. Bloom. il *Skiing* 42:12+ S '89
Stretching your limits [work of B. Prichard] M. Bloom.
  il *Skiing* 41:36+ Ja '89
Turning into strength. J. Nelson. il *Women's Sports & Fitness*
  11:31-3 N/D '89
Transportation
4WD in demand. D. Sherman. *Skiing* 41:12+ F '89
Environmentalism and skiing. A. H. Greenberg. il *Skiing*
  42:20+ D '89
Simplifying your options [choosing a car for ski country
  driving] B. Glenne. il *Skiing* 42:50+ N '89
SKIING
  See also
  Cross country skiing
  Freestyle skiing
  National Brotherhood of Skiers
  Parasailing
  Speed skiing
  Upskiing
  Water skiing
A family affair. P. Taylor. il *Black Enterprise* 19:66-7 Ja
  '89
How good are you? [cover story; with editorial comment
  by William Grout] S. Still. il *Skiing* 42:10, 206-15 N
  '89
Inside Skiing. W. Grout. See issues of Skiing beginning
  September 1986
It's all sliding. L. Tejada-Flores. il *Skiing* 42:52-8+ S '89
Mad about moguls. P. Oliver. il *Skiing* 42:60-5 D '89
A question of balance [telemarking] C. Cooper. il *Skiing*
  42:34+ N '89
Ski scene '90 [cover story; special section] il *Women's Sports
  & Fitness* 11:27-8+ O '89
The skier's edge. il *American Health* 8:79-80+ N '89
Skiing scene. See issues of Skiing
Accidents and injuries
  See also
  Ski racing—Accidents and injuries
Are you injury-prone? T. Pederson. il por *Skiing* 42:67-8+
  O '89
How safe is skiing? A. H. Greenberg. il *Skiing* 42:56+ N
  '89
What can be done about knee injuries? [anterior cruciate
  ligament sprains] C. Ettlinger. il *Skiing* 41:85-7+ Mr '89
Aesthetics
New images, old passion: meditations on the romance of
  skiing. L. Tejada-Flores. il *Skiing* 42:74-8 O '89
Anecdotes, facetiae, satire, etc.
Long time no ski. M. G. Stoddard. il *The Saturday Evening
  Post* 261:60-1 Ja/F '89
Clothing and dress
  See Clothing and dress—Sports clothes
Competitions
  See also
  Ski racing
Economic aspects
Savings on short notice [ski trips from travel clubs] S. Russell.
  il *Skiing* 41:10 F '89
A season's sampler. S. Russell. il *Skiing* 42:16+ S '89
Equipment
  See also
  Salomon et Fils François
  Ski bindings
  Ski boots
  Ski poles
  Skis
Eyewear. D. White. il *Skiing* 42:234-7 S '89
Geared up for downhill [skiing gear] il *Health (New York,
  N.Y.)* 21:30+ D '89

Gifts '90: cheap thrills. D. White. il *Skiing* 42:186-9 D
  '89
Glass acts: high-style shades for skiers. D. White. il *Skiing*
  41:28+ F '89
Thrills and chills. M. Porter. il *Gentlemen's Quarterly* 59:193+
  N '89
Women's ski buyer's guide. J. Nelson. il *Women's Sports
  & Fitness* 11:27-8+ O '89
Storage
Ski storage rack. S. Kingman and P. Kingman. il *The Family
  Handyman* 39:70-1 Ja '89
History
The Hannes Schneider story [inventor of modern skiing
  rescued from Nazi Germany and brought to U.S. in 1939]
  N. Howe. il pors *Skiing* 41:126-9+ Mr '89
International aspects
The world's greatest ski runs. il *Skiing* 42:93-6+ N '89
Safety devices and measures
Downhill dangers. K. Read. il *Skiing* 42:42-3 N '89
Is skiing overregulated? A. H. Greenberg. il *Skiing* 41:12+
  Mr '89
Ski trips [avoiding knee injuries] il *Prevention (Emmaus,
  Pa.)* 41:10+ Ja '89
Study and teaching
  See also
  Ski coaches
A beginner's guide to skiing. M. Behen. *American Health*
  8:84-5 N '89
Downhill ski? Who, me? E. Wetschler. il *New Choices for
  the Best Years* 29:34-8 D '89
Getting zee drift [female instructors and all-women classes]
  G. Lichtenstein. il *Ms.* 17:122 Ja/F '89
Guide, slice, and glide [keys to accurate turns]; ed. by Doug
  Smith. M. Porter. il *Skiing* 42:74-8 Mr '89
The skier's edge [ski school at Northstar resort in Lake
  Tahoe region] M. Behen. il *American Health* 8:79-80 N
  '89
Skiing tip for family skiers:
  Free skiing to better technique. H. Kashiwa. il *Skiing*
    41:74 F '89
  Get the racer's edge. H. Kashiwa. il *Skiing* 41:72 Ja
    '89
Strategies for success. S. Still. il *Skiing* 42:138+ D '89
A touch of class: how to go from wide-track to a narrow
  stance. W. Chauner. il *Skiing* 41:137-41 Ja '89
Us & them [moguls] L. Tejada-Flores. il *Skiing* 42:67-71
  D '89
Workshops for better skiers. S. Russell. il *Skiing* 42:14+
  D '89
Aids and devices
Learn from watching the best [use of videotapes] O. Larsson.
  il *Skiing* 41:69-73 F '89
Training
  See Skiers—Training
Alberta
  See also
  Lake Louise (Alta.)
Antarctic regions
Odyssey over ice. A. Steacy. il *Maclean's* 102:55 F 6 '89
South Pole or bust [S. Metz's skiing expedition] B. Sims.
  il por *Skiing* 42:18 O '89
Arctic regions
Polar dare [H. Thayer's expedition to the North Pole] P.
  Turner. il por *Ms.* 17:55-7 Je '89
Austria
  See also
  Lech (Austria)
California
Good reasons to join a ski club [northern California clubs]
  il *Sunset (Central West edition)* 183:27 D '89
Shasta snow fun. il maps *Sunset (Central West edition)*
  183:20-3 D '89
Colorado
  See also
  Aspen (Colo.)
  Crested Butte (Colo.)
  Telluride (Colo.)
  Vail (Colo.)
Back-country skiing is back at Berthoud Pass, near Denver.
  il *Sunset (Central West edition)* 183:62 N '89
Peak moments [Beaver Creek] J. Bowermaster. il *Harper's
  Bazaar* 122:90+ F '89
France
  See also
  Chamonix (France)
Idaho
  See also
  Sun Valley (Idaho)
Italy
  See also
  Courmayeur (Italy)
Lake Tahoe region (Calif. and Nev.)
Fast times at Tahoe. P. Oliver. il *Skiing* 42:114-22+ N '89
Middle Western States
Hills alive! E. Hanson. il map *Skiing* 41:122-4+ Ja '89
Morocco
Ski Morocco, fine sir. T. Newhart. il pors *Skiing* 42:220-4
  O '89

SKIING—cont.

New England
The new New England. A. H. Greenberg. il *Skiing* 42:224-7+ D '89

New Hampshire
Attaway, Attitash [ski resort] C. Walter. il *Skiing* 41:50-3+ Ja '89

Loon rising. N. Howe. il *Skiing* 41:90-3+ Mr '89

New Mexico
Taos [Taos Ski Valley resort] N. Howe. il *Skiing* 41:42-8 F '89

New York (State)
See also
Hunter Mountain (N.Y.)

New Zealand
Off-season in New Zealand. C. Cooper. il *Skiing* 41:28+ Mr '89

Norway
Home of giants. A. Pospisil. il *Skiing* 41:58-64 F '89

Oregon
Oregon's delectable Alp [Mt. Bachelor] D. Ford. il *Skiing* 41:42-8+ Mr '89

Soviet Union
U.S. tourers tackle USSR. E. Perlman. il *Skiing* 41:22 F '89

Switzerland
See also
Saint Moritz (Switzerland)

Utah
A tale of Deer Valley. E. Hanson. il *Skiing* 42:206-8+ O '89

World's greatest runs:
High Rustler, Alta, Utah. E. Bowen. il *Skiing* 42:12 D '89

Vermont
See also
Stratton (Vt.)
The many faces of Killington. K. Brizzolara. il *Skiing* 42:218-24+ N '89

Western States
Skiing in a swimsuit. il *Sunset (Central West edition)* 182:36 My '89

SKIING, CHILDREN'S
A family affair. P. Taylor. il *Black Enterprise* 19:66-7 Ja '89

Fit for kids [boots] C. Meader. il *Skiing* 41:113-14+ Ja '89

Getting along on skis [first United Airlines Friendship Cup] il *National Geographic World* 162:18-21 F '89

Kids on the slopes. M. Behen. il *American Health* 8:83-4 N '89

Kids page. B. Kidd. See issues of Skiing beginning September 1984

Kids' stuff [bindings] C. Ettlinger. il *Skiing* 41:88+ F '89

Starting young. il *Sunset (Central West edition)* 181:72-4 D '88

SKILBECK, MALCOLM
Long-range learning. il *The Courier (Unesco)* 41:32-4 D '88

SKILLED LABOR
See also
Multiskilling
America on the rise: our people get it done. C. Reese. il *Reader's Digest* 135:129-30 Ag '89

The forgotten half [undereducated work force; cover story] D. Whitman. il *U.S. News & World Report* 106:44-9+ Je 26 '89

Roll out America's red carpet for the skilled [immigrants] M. J. Mandel. il *Business Week* p128 O 30 '89

SKILLEN, JAMES W.
How do we solve the global debt crisis? *The Christian Century* 106:1004-6 N 8 '89

SKILLET COOKING
See also
Stir-frying
Dinner in a skillet. A. Johnson. il *Parents* 64:153-4+ F '89

Easy skillet pizza. il *Redbook* 173:20 S '89

Fast skillet stews. il *Redbook* 172:87-91+ Mr '89

Recipe of the week [California cheeseburger skillet] il *Jet* 76:38 S 4 '89

Recipe of the week [chili and rice skillet] il *Jet* 75:38 Mr 20 '89

Recipe of the week [quick skillet meal] il *Jet* 77:38 N 6 '89

Skillet skills. P. Meyers. il *The New York Times Magazine* p31-2 Jl 30 '89

SKIM MILK
Buying milk: what's best for your family? *Better Homes and Gardens* 67:48 S '89

SKIN
See also
Birthmarks
Moles (Dermatology)
Sunburn
Suntan
Cigarette face—another reason not to smoke. D. R. Reuben. il *Good Housekeeping* 208:70 Mr '89

Dioxin via skin: a hazard at low doses? [research by Linda S. Birnbaum] *Science News* 135:141 Mr 4 '89

Freckle face. il *Seventeen* 48:90-1 Ja '89

Cancer
Leg moles? Get out the sunblocker [susceptibility to melanoma; research by Martin A. Weinstock] *Science News* 136:30 Jl 8 '89

Melanoma: can the sun be protective? [research by Neil Dubin] *Science News* 136:30 Jl 8 '89

Causes
See also
Suntan

Diagnosis
Virtually 100 percent cancer cure [early melanoma detection] il *Prevention (Emmaus, Pa.)* 41:14 O '89

Prevention
See also
Suntan products
Lasers vs. skin cancer [removal of precancerous patches; work of William Dobes] *USA Today (Periodical)* 118:13-14 O '89

Melanoma. D. Sobel. il *Good Housekeeping* 209:86+ Jl '89

Care and hygiene
See also
Cosmetics
Paramedical camouflage
5 ways to clean your face [excerpt from Take care of your skin] E. Brumberg. il *Health (New York, N.Y.)* 21:84-5+ Ag '89

A.M. skin care. il *Seventeen* 48:148-51 S '89

About face. J. Logan. *Harper's Bazaar* 122:134+ Ag '89

Accutane survival guide. *Glamour* 87:52-3 Je '89

Act now to age-proof your eyes. il *Glamour* 87:270-3 O '89

Active-duty skin care. S. Lord. il *Vogue* 179:166+ F '89

Baby your body. C. Straley. il *Parents* 64:152-4 Mr '89

Baby your self. il *Redbook* 172:112-13 Ap '89

Beauty's new horizon. P. Lister. il *American Health* 8:78-80+ Ap '89

Between the lines [Retin-A] A. Ranard. il *Health (New York, N.Y.)* 21:66-7+ O '89

The body beautiful. L. J. Johnson. il *Ladies' Home Journal* 106:118-24 Jl '89

Chart your skin skills. il *'Teen* 33:76-9 Mr '89

Clean obsessed. B. Bauer. il *Vogue* 179:180 Ap '89

The cold and the beautiful. N. L. Novick. il *Women's Sports & Fitness* 11:56 O '89

Collecting seaweed by the seashore—nature's natural soother. P. Lister. il *American Health* 8:26-8+ Ap '89

Cosmedics—makeup that's good to your skin. K. C. Engles. il *Redbook* 174:8+ N '89

Dermatology checkup. P. Schneider. il *Redbook* 173:152-4+ O '89

Does your skin look as good as it could? il *Redbook* 172:78-81 F '89

Face [presummer tips] il *Seventeen* 48:190-1 Ap '89

The facts about removing dead skin cells [exfoliation] L. F. McCarthy. *Vogue* 179:226 Mr '89

Fast fixes for winter beauty blahs. il *Glamour* 87:206-9 F '89

Feel the heat: cool looks, hot times. il *Mademoiselle* 95:146-51 Je '89

Five skin sins. S. Inglis. *Harper's Bazaar* 122:133+ Ag '89

For fast, short-term skin firming and toning, there are now a multitude of interesting products to choose from. L. F. McCarthy. *Vogue* 179:154 Ag '89

Fresh & glorious skin. L. Lebowitz. il *Harper's Bazaar* 122:68-9+ Ja '89

From good skin to great skin. il *Glamour* 87:312-15 S '89

Good-bye, dry . . . il *Mademoiselle* 95:14 Ja '89

A guide to summertime skin care. A. R. New. il *Better Homes and Gardens* 67:35-6 Je '89

Here's mud in your eye [skin treatments offered by spas] D. Longstreet. il *American Health* 8:102 Ap '89

How good is Retin-A? il *Consumer Reports* 54:112-13 F '89

Images: skin care [blacks] L. F. McCarthy. *Vogue* 179:110 Je '89

In search of . . . clear skin. il *Seventeen* 48:46 O '89

Is your skin showing signs of stress? [advice from medical experts] il *Redbook* 173:90-3 Jl '89

It's never too late to keep an eye on your eyes. L. George. il *American Health* 8:26-8+ Mr '89

Nature girl. il *Seventeen* 48:160 N '89

Psych out your skin. il *Glamour* 87:328-31 Ap '89

Putting the wrap on wrinkles. P. Lister. il *New Choices for the Best Years* 29:41-6 D '89

Retin-A. S. Lord. *Vogue* 179:346-7+ Ag '89

Retin-A: a buyer's guide [wrinkle treatment] P. Boyer. il *Prevention (Emmaus, Pa.)* 41:95+ Ap '89

Save your skin: skin care during hot-weather workouts [views of Rodney Basler] A. R. New. *Better Homes and Gardens* 67:33 Ag '89

School-day skincare. il *'Teen* 33:108-9 Ag '89

The selling of Retin-A. L. N. Vreeland. il *Money* 18:74-80+ Ap '89

Sensitive subjects. il *'Teen* 33:94-5 O '89

Serious face-saving [anti-aging cosmetics and drugs] D. Sobel. il *Health (New York, N.Y.)* 21:64-5+ O '89

Shape up your skin for summer. J. Neal. il *Women's Sports & Fitness* 11:24 Ap '89

SKIN—Care and hygiene—cont.

Skin and emotion. J. J. Buck. *Vogue* 179:204-5 Ja '89

Skin, burnished and smooth, is the perfect foil for the glitter of sequins. L. Cunliffe. il *Vogue* 179:340-5 Ag '89

Skin care simplified! C. Straley. il *Parents* 64:198-200 O '89

Skin changes during pregnancy. L. MacCallum. il *Glamour* 87:78 My '89

Skin deep (I). M. Horosko. il *Dance Magazine* 63:70 Ag '89

Skin deep (II). M. Horosko. il *Dance Magazine* 63:54-5 S '89

Skin forecast: clear! il *Mademoiselle* 95:242-5 S '89

Skin games [runners] H. Higdon. il *Runner's World* 24:70-4+ My '89

A skin tune-up for summer. il *Mademoiselle* 95:18 Je '89

Summer smoothers. A. Liounis. il *Health (New York, N.Y.)* 21:58-61 Jl '89

Sun-proof skin. il *'Teen* 33:68-9 Je '89

Three steps to fresh: skin care made simple. il *Mademoiselle* 95:230-3 Mr '89

Top 10 summer beauty boosters. il *'Teen* 33:64-5 Je '89

When the sun moves south and the days cool down, it isn't just your wardrobe you need to change. It's time for new beauty habits too. L. F. McCarthy. il *Vogue* 179:177-8 O '89

Winter skin. J. Randal. il *American Health* 8:18-20 D '89

Winter skin and hair repair. P. Kripke. il *Working Woman* 14:108 Ja '89

Winter sun sense. il *Glamour* 87:158-61 Ja '89

Diseases

See also
Acne
Contact dermatitis
Psoriasis
Schistosomiasis
Warts

Getting to the root of an itch [pets] A. R. Marder. il *Prevention (Emmaus, Pa.)* 41:97+ F '89

Remedies for common rashes. K. Karlsrud and D. Schultz. il *Parents* 64:168 F '89

The skin and mind connection. S. Lord. *Vogue* 179:205 Ja '89

Skin symptoms you must not ignore [clues to internal illness] W. Korn. il *Ladies' Home Journal* 106:66+ S '89

Those little brown 'moles' [dermatosis papulosa nigra on black women] J. Clayton. il *Essence* 20:22 My '89

Fish

Not guilty as charged [effect of eel skin wallets on credit card scrambling] il *Discover* 10:12 Mr '89

Reptiles

Skinning the dinosaur [work of S. Czerkas; with editorial comment by Paul Hoffman] D. Lessem. il pors *Discover* 10:4, 38-42+ Mr '89

Wounds and injuries

See also
Burns and scalds

Road rash [cycling abrasions] S. Johnson. *Bicycling* 30:134 Je '89

Saddle sores [cycling] S. Johnson. il *Bicycling* 30:74 O/N '89

SKIN, ARTIFICIAL

Patient, heal thyself—with lab-grown cells. N. J. Freundlich. il *Business Week* p148+ Mr 20 '89

SKIN CARE PRODUCTS *See* Cosmetics

SKIN CARE PRODUCTS INDUSTRY *See* Cosmetics industry

SKIN CARE SALONS *See* Beauty shops

SKIN DEEP [film] *See* Motion picture reviews—Single works

SKIN DIVING

See also
Second Chance (Firm)
Spear fishing

Ballet with stingrays [divers hand-feed stingrays] D. Doubilet. il map *National Geographic* 175:84-95 Ja '89

Dolphins [diver aids wounded baby dolphin] W. Grover. il *Sea Frontiers* 35:28-30 Ja/F '89

Don't leave the dock [exotic marine life off Cayman Kai dock] F. J. Viola. il *Sea Frontiers* 35:336-41 N/D '89

Go down, Moses [exploring reefs near Ras Muhammed off tip of Sinai Peninsula] N. MacFarquhar. il *Esquire* 112:56 D '89

In the depths of a flooded mine, Doug and Cathy Goergens found a Missouri mecca for scuba divers. D. Chu. il pors *People Weekly* 32:81+ N 6 '89

Scuba photography. L. Lipsky. il *Petersen's Photographic Magazine* 17:36-8+ Mr '89

Splash! [scuba diving vacations] K. Castle. il *Travel Holiday* 172:74-81 Jl '89

Take the plunge! [scuba diving] C. S. Black. il por *Women's Sports & Fitness* 11:66 Jl/Ag '89

A truly fresh fish [snorkeling off Santa Catalina Island] N. Vander Velde. il *Sea Frontiers* 35:320 S/O '89

Accidents and injuries

Reef fish feedings: amusement or nuisance? D. Perrine. il *Sea Frontiers* 35:272-9 S/O '89

Too much pressure? [research by Richard E. Moon] K. Wright. *Scientific American* 261:36+ S '89

Costs

Dives. R. Micheli. il *Money* 18:101-4+ Jl '89

Equipment

High fashion meets high tech—underwater. R. Brandt. il *Business Week* p115 S 4 '89

Phenomena, comment and notes [diving mask] J. P. Wiley, Jr. il *Smithsonian* 20:30+ S '89

Study and teaching

Florida's Seacamp [cover story] il map *National Geographic World* 169:4-9 S '89

Plunge right in [Caribbean] B. Wallraff. il *The Atlantic* 264:111-14 D '89

Scuba duba do [Club Med] J. O'Reilly. il *New Choices for the Best Years* 29:44-8 F '89

SKIN GRAFTING

See also
Skin, Artificial

SKIN PATCHES *See* Transdermal patches

SKIN RESEARCH

See also
Cutaneous Biology Research Center (Boston, Mass.)

SKINHEADS

Anti-racist skinheads ready to strike back at neo-Nazis. C. Gunderson. *Utne Reader* p88-9 My/Je '89

A growing menace. B. Came. il *Maclean's* 102:43-4 Ja 23 '89

Harvesting young people's hate. D. O. Relin. il *Scholastic Update (Teachers' edition)* 121:4-6 Ap 7 '89

The roots of skinhead violence: dim economic prospects for young men. il *Utne Reader* p84 My/Je '89

The skinhead reich. J. Coplon. il *Utne Reader* p80-3+ My/Je '89

Skinheads: a new generation of hate-mongers. E. Sears. il *USA Today (Periodical)* 117:24-6 My '89

Skinheads + Klan = trouble. D. J. Dent. il *Black Enterprise* 19:22 Ap '89

SKINHEADS IN ART

Exhibitions

Attila Richard Lukacs at 49th Parallel. K. Johnson. *Art in America* 77:204 S '89

SKINNER, EVA M.

The prolongation of life [address, December 3, 1988] *Vital Speeches of the Day* 55:271-3 F 15 '89

SKINNER, MICHAEL

Easy money [cover story] il *Omni (New York, N.Y.)* 11:42-4+ My '89

SKINNER, SAMUEL K.

about

The heat is on airline deals. S. Payne. il por *Business Week* p32 O 2 '89

How 'Sam the Hammer' could nail the airlines. S. Payne. il por *Business Week* p126-7 Je 26 '89

A master plan from Bush's unlikely star. P. Barry and P. Glastris. il pors *U.S. News & World Report* 107:24-5 Jl 24 '89

Senators press Skinner on civil aviation agenda. M. Mecham. *Aviation Week & Space Technology* 130:70-1 Ja 30 '89

Skinner calls USAir bid for more Philadelphia gates anticompetitive. *Aviation Week & Space Technology* 130:110 Je 5 '89

Skinner speaks. *Flying* 116:22 Je '89

Skinner's limits on NWA buyout fail to dissuade drive for LBO controls. C. Fotos. *Aviation Week & Space Technology* 131:138-9 O 9 '89

Skinner's proposal to expand service by foreign airlines gets mixed response. J. Ott. *Aviation Week & Space Technology* 131:57 O 30 '89

SKINNING OF GAME *See* Game, Dressing of

SKINS *See* Hides and skins

SKIP BARBER RACING SCHOOL *See* Automobile racing—Study and teaching

SKIPPING ROPE *See* Rope jumping

SKIRTS (CLOTHING)

Men hate short hair, love short skirts. True or false? W. Geist. il *Vogue* 179:152 Ag '89

SKIS

See also
Cross country skis

Downhill skiing—with panache. H. King. il *Business Week* p170 O 30 '89

The slopes are groomed for Salomon's new ski. E. Wallace. il por *Business Week* p94 Ap 10 '89

Maintenance and repair

Base repair tools. J. Deines. il *Skiing* 42:44+ D '89

Testing

All-terrain vehicles. W. Grout. il *Skiing* 42:200-4+ D '89

New for '90. I. Devlin. il *Skiing* 41:122-4 Mr '89

The new slalom skis: how quick? W. Grout. il *Skiing* 42:38-40+ O '89

Skis. W. Grout. il *Skiing* 42:90-2+ S '89

Skis for sport. B. Glenne. il *Skiing* 42:188-92 O '89

Sporty skis for women. L. Guerrette. il *Skiing* 42:180-2+ D '89

Versatile performers [sport/racing models] J. Deines. il *Skiing* 42:104-6+ N '89

SKIWEAR *See* Clothing and dress—Sports clothes

SKLAR, HOLLY, 1955-

Rainbow future. *The Nation* 248:113-14 Ja 30 '89

SKLAR, MORTY, 1935-
about
A seat-of-the pants veteran comes home. J. Barbato. *Publishers Weekly* 236:33 D 8 '89
SKLAREWITZ, NORMAN
Touring from Tokyo. il *New Choices for the Best Years* 29:28-35 N '89
SKODA (AUTOMOBILE) *See* Automobiles, Foreign
SKOGLUND, SANDY, 1946-
about
Outfoxing the viewer. B. Weber. il por *The New York Times Magazine* p94 O 8 '89
Sandy Skoglund: Damon Brandt; Lorence Monk. M. E. Haus. il *Art News* 88:135-6 F '89
SKOLNICK, LEE H.
about
An architectural presence in the Manhattan art world. K. Andersen. il por *Architectural Digest* 46:170+ N '89
SKOLNIK, RICHARD
Hit, field and cheat. il *TV Guide* 37:18-19 Je 10-16 '89
SKOLNIKOFF, EUGENE B.
Technology and the world tomorrow. *Current History* 88:5-8+ Ja '89
SKORUPA, JOE
Outdoors. See issues of Popular Mechanics beginning July 1987
SKOW, JOHN
Having all the answers is a hard row to hoe. il *Smithsonian* 19:154 Ja '89
Kick a radio and call me in the morning. il *Smithsonian* 20:256 N '89
SKROCKI, MERRILL ROGERS
Leaving a child in charge. *McCall's* 117:71 N '89
SKULL
La cabeza de Villa [El Paso, Tex. group hounds Yale University's Skull and Bones Society for P. Villa's skull] M. Singer. *The New Yorker* 65:108-12+ N 27 '89
Surgery
3-D maps for surgeons [use of system devised by Michael Vannier for abnormality correction] il *Life* 12:45-6 Je '89
SKULL AND BONES SOCIETY
La cabeza de Villa [El Paso, Tex. group hounds Yale University's Skull and Bones Society for P. Villa's skull] M. Singer. *The New Yorker* 65:108-12+ N 27 '89
SKUNK AT THE GARDEN PARTY (PHRASE)
Garden party whatsit. W. Safire. il *The New York Times Magazine* p22+ N 19 '89
SKUNK CABBAGES
Stalking the stinking hot cabbage. R. Weiss. il *Science News* 135:394 Je 24 '89
SKUNKS
Responsibility for the skunk. P. V. Fossel. il *Country Journal* 16:7-8 Ja '89
Skunk in the cellar! A. B. C. Whipple. il *Reader's Digest* 134:155-8 Mr '89
ŠKVORECKÝ, JOSEF
Czech-out time. *The New Republic* 201:15-17 D 25 '89
Czech writers: politicians in spite of themselves. *The New York Times Book Review* 94:1+ D 10 '89
SKY
See also
Airglow
Constellations
Astronomy's 1989 sky guide. R. Burnham. il map *Astronomy* 17:78-89 Ja '89
Eye on the sky. D. Byrd. See issues of Astronomy beginning July 1988
Miles of predawn sky [studying the sky while running] T. B. Hunter. il *Astronomy* 17:90 Ap '89
Observing among the smokestacks [night sky] G. Coburn. il *Astronomy* 17:104-5 My '89
Olbers' paradox solved at last [dark night sky] P. S. Wesson. il *Sky and Telescope* 77:594-7 Je '89
The southern sky's attic. G. Lovi. il *Sky and Telescope* 77:515-16 My '89
Color
The colors seen in the sky offer lessons in optical scattering. J. Walker. bibl il *Scientific American* 260:102-5 Ja '89
Photographs and photography
Sky photography with just a camera. D. Di Cicco. il *Sky and Telescope* 78:152-4 Ag '89
SKY AND TELESCOPE (PERIODICAL)
StarTrails [advertisements] D. H. Levy. *Sky and Telescope* 77:548-9 My '89
SKY CHARTS *See* Astronomy—Charts, diagrams, etc.
SKY ENDEAVORS (FIRM)
Up, up, & away. A. Reid-Dove. il *Black Enterprise* 20:73-4+ Ag '89
SKY EYE [dance] *See* Dance reviews—Single works
SKY TELEVISION PLC
Hollywood reaps a windfall from television's richest endeavor. K. Pearce. il *Channels (New York, N.Y.: 1986)* 9:9 Mr '89
The Sky-watchers [Great Britain] A. Phillips. il *Maclean's* 102:51 F 27 '89

SKYDIVING *See* Parachuting
SKYDOME (TORONTO, ONT.)
After SkyDome, stadiums will never be the same. C. Hawkins. il *Business Week* p136+ Mr 20 '89
Field of fancy, field of dreams [contrasting SkyDome with plans for Baltimore's new old-fashioned ballpark] J. Adler. il *Newsweek* 113:66-7 Je 19 '89
Open and shut case. J. S. Russell. il *Architectural Record* 177:128-37 N '89
Play ball! [cover story; special section; with editorial comment by Kevin Doyle] il *Maclean's* 102:2, 40-8 Je 12 '89
Raising the roof. S. Wulf. il *Sports Illustrated* 70:48-50+ Je 12 '89
Shutter-dome stadium. C. M. Fiorillo. il *Popular Science* 234:112 Je '89
Anecdotes, facetiae, satire, etc.
Pitying Toronto is not natural. C. Gordon. il *Maclean's* 102:58 Ap 3 '89
SKYE, IONE
about
Ione Skye studies for success. il por *Scholastic Update (Teachers' edition)* 121:12 Ap 21 '89
Skye's the limit. B. Stepko. il pors *Seventeen* 48:108-9+ Ap '89
SKYLIGHT COMIC OPERA LTD.
Milwaukee. J. Koopman. il *Opera News* 53:39 F 4 '89
Musical events:
Monteverdi's Orfeo, L'incoronatione di Poppea, and Il ritorno d'Ulisse. A. Porter. *The New Yorker* 65:78-9 My 8 '89
SKYLIGHTS
How to install a skylight [cover story] D. Johnson. il *The Family Handyman* 39:30-6 My '89
One 12-foot skylight brightens two rooms. il *Sunset (Central West edition)* 182:140 Mr '89
The skylight. J. Vara. il *Country Journal* 16:68-9+ F '89
Skylight installation [bathrooms] il *Popular Mechanics* 166:102+ Ap '89
Skylight savvy. D. Johnson. il *The Family Handyman* 39:18-21+ My '89
A spine of light. il *Sunset (Central West edition)* 182:78-81 F '89
SKYLINE CORP.
This Skyline is drawing crowds. G. G. Marcial. *Business Week* p92 Ap 3 '89
SKYLINE FINANCIAL SERVICES CORPORATION
Epic task. J. Novack. il por *Forbes* 143:142+ F 6 '89
SKYLINE PHOTOGRAPHY *See* Cities and towns—Photographs and photography
SKYSCRAPERS
Able to leap the Sears Tower in a single bound? [125 story skyscraper to be built in Chicago] D. Greising. il *Business Week* p94 Je 5 '89
And, now, another tall story [125 story skyscraper to be built in Chicago] il *U.S. News & World Report* 106:14-15 Je 12 '89
The Caligari Club [C. Gifford explores summits of New York skyscrapers] *The New Yorker* 65:39-41 N 27 '89
Frankfurt builds upward. H. Uniewski. il *World Press Review* 36:59 N '89
The sky line [mania for skyscrapers and growth in American cities] B. Gill. *The New Yorker* 64:73-7 Ja 9 '89
Skyscrapers. W. S. Ellis. il *National Geographic* 175:140-73 F '89
SKYTRADER CORPORATION
STOL Scout begins flight tests with Astazou 16 powerplants. W. B. Scott. il *Aviation Week & Space Technology* 130:64 F 13 '89
SKYWALKS *See* Skyways (Architecture)
SKYWAY FREIGHT SYSTEMS INC.
Go with the flow. M. Barrier. il por *Nation's Business* 77:37-8 My '89
SKYWAYS (ARCHITECTURE)
Sidewalks in the sky [views of Kent Robertson] *The Futurist* 23:46 Ja/F '89
SLAC *See* Stanford Linear Accelerator Center
SLACK FARM EXCAVATION SITE (KY.) *See* Kentucky—Antiquities
SLACKS *See* Pants
SLADEK, JOHN R.
(jt. auth) *See* Hansen, John T., and Sladek, John R.
SLAGLE, JACOB W.
about
Repairing a home-repair firm. B. Belleville. il por *Nation's Business* 77:10+ Ag '89
SLAGLE & SLAGLE
Repairing a home-repair firm. B. Belleville. il por *Nation's Business* 77:10+ Ag '89
SLAIGHT, ANNABEL, 1940-
about
Cultivating a child's garden. D. Turbide. *Maclean's* 102:57 F 6 '89
SLAMON, DENNIS J., AND OTHERS
Studies of the HER-2/*neu* proto-oncogene in human breast and ovarian cancer. bibl f il *Science* 244:707-12 My 12 '89

SLANEY, MARY DECKER
about
What makes Mary run? S. McKee. il por *American Health* 8:68 Je '89
SLANSKY, PAUL
A brief history of the Reagan years [excerpt from index to The clothes have no emperor] *Harper's* 279:30-2 O '89
about
Portrait of the Gippophobe as a young man. il por *Newsweek* 114:85 N 27 '89
SLAPP *See* Strategic lawsuits against public participation
SLASH-AND-BURN AGRICULTURE *See* Shifting cultivation
SLATE ROOFING *See* Roofs and roofing
SLATER, CHRISTIAN
about
The boy can't help it. C. Connors. il pors *Seventeen* 48:58 Jl '89
Hot actor. B. Flanagan. il pors *Rolling Stone* p77-9 My 18 '89
Nice kid no more, Christian Slater turns homicidal in Heathers. J. Stark. il pors *People Weekly* 31:53-4 Ap 24 '89
SLATER, SAMUEL, 1768-1835
about
Samuel Slater: father of the American Industrial Revolution. J. Gustaitis. por *American History Illustrated* 24:32-3 My '89
SLATKIN, EDWARD
about
Two guys sitting around with $100 million. E. Schine. il pors *Business Week* p76+ O 9 '89
SLATKIN, THOMAS
about
Two guys sitting around with $100 million. E. Schine. il pors *Business Week* p76+ O 9 '89
SLATTERY, CHRIS
about
Holy war. P. Tyre. il por *New York* 22:48-51 Ap 24 '89
SLATTERY, DENNIS PATRICK, 1944-
An Orwellian wedding. por *Newsweek* 114:10 N 13 '89
SLATYER, RALPH
The natural legacy. il *The Courier (Unesco)* 41:16-22 D '88
SLAUGHTER, D. FRENCH, JR.
Should the "balanced budget constitutional amendment" be adopted? [excerpts from statement, November 17, 1987] *Congressional Digest* 68:278+ N '89
SLAUGHTER, JANE, 1941-
Is labor ready to break the siege? [cover story] il *The Progressive* 53:20-1+ D '89
Lethal Lordstown: workers fight poison at a GM plant. il *The Progressive* 53:28-9+ Mr '89
Tin miners' radio on the ropes. il *The Progressive* 53:11 F '89
SLAUGHTER, PAUL
A photographer's guide to Hong Kong. il *Petersen's Photographic Magazine* 18:64-7 Je '89
A photographer's guide to Morocco. il *Petersen's Photographic Magazine* 17:76-7 F '89
A photographer's guide to southern India [cover story] il *Petersen's Photographic Magazine* 17:38-44 Ap '89
Vancouver & Ottawa, beautiful Canada! il *Petersen's Photographic Magazine* 18:12-15+ Jl '89
SLAUGHTERING AND SLAUGHTERHOUSES IN ART
Slaughterhouse '89. S. Coe. il *The Progressive* 53:33-9 Mr '89
Exhibitions
Sue Coe: Galerie St. Etienne. E. Heartney. il *Art News* 88:158 D '89
SLAVE LABOR CAMPS *See* Concentration camps
SLAVE TRADE
The troubled voyage of the Rainbow [Massachusetts colony confronts issue of slave trade] L. Gragg. bibl il maps *History Today* 39:36-41 Ag '89
Africa
In the African interior, the ivory trade and the slave trade helped each other become paying propositions. R. M. Adams. il *Smithsonian* 19:14 Mr '89
SLAVERY
See also
Abolitionists
Forced labor
Slave trade
Dot Redford found her roots at Somerset [plantation slave descendants] D. Young. il pors *Southern Living* 24:92+ Ja '89
Plantation home [D. Redford traces descendants of slaves from Somerset Place, N.C.] R. Mashburn. il pors map *Americana* 16:50-4 Ja/F '89
Bibliography
Upward in slavery. M. P. Johnson. il *The New York Review of Books* 36:51-5 D 21 '89
Exhibitions
Slave quilts [Stitched from the soul: slave quilts from the ante-bellum South at the Museum of American Folk Art] *The New Yorker* 65:32-3 Ag 7 '89

Textiles made by southern slaves [Stitched from the soul: slave quilts from the ante-bellum South] A. E. Ledes. il *Antiques* 136:222+ Ag '89
Fugitive slaves
Flight to freedom. il map *American Visions* 4:60-1 F '89
Insurrections, etc.
1739 [rebellion near Stono River, S.C.] A. Nielsen. il *American Heritage* 40:34 S/O '89
Children of the Amistad. E. N. Lawson. il *American Visions* 4:38-41 F '89
Museums
Finding a heritage: museums begin to explore the slave experience. R. Mashburn. il *Americana* 16:55 Ja/F '89
Reparations
Payback time. D. Ellen. *The New Republic* 201:10-11 Jl 31 '89
Paying for sins of the past. E. Salholz. il *Newsweek* 112:44 My 22 '89
Reparation bill for blacks pending in Congress after Japanese get reparation pay. *Jet* 77:10 D 25 '89-Ja 1 '90
United States
See Slavery
SLAVERY AND THE CHURCH
The troubled voyage of the Rainbow [Massachusetts colony confronts issue of slave trade] L. Gragg. bibl il maps *History Today* 39:36-41 Ag '89
SLAVES OF NEW YORK [film] *See* Motion picture reviews—Single works
SLAVIN, RICHARD E., III
F. Schumacher and Company and the art moderne style. il *Antiques* 135:964-73 Ap '89
Fabrics of being. il por *Horizon (Tuscaloosa, Ala.)* 32:49-51 Mr/Ap '89
SLAVIN, ROBERT E.
Cooperative learning and student achievement. *The Education Digest* 54:15-17 F '89
PET and the pendulum: faddism in education and how to stop it [cover story] bibl f il *Phi Delta Kappan* 70:752-8 Je '89
SLEAR, TOM
The fall and rise of Terry Vares. il por *Women's Sports & Fitness* 11:70 My '89
SLED DOG RACING
The dog days of winter [Iditarod Trail Sled Dog Race] K. Castle. il *Travel Holiday* 171:60-1 Ja '89
Go, team, go! [Junior North American Championships; cover story] il *National Geographic World* 172:3-7 D '89
An intense drive [Iditarod champ S. Butcher] C. Szirak. il por *Women's Sports & Fitness* 11:66-7 Mr '89
Man's best friends [J. Runyan wins Iditarod Trail Sled Dog Race] R. F. Jones. il por map *Sports Illustrated* 70:40-2+ Mr 27 '89
SLED DOGS
The 4,000-mile marathon [W. Steger and sled dogs prepare for Antarctic expedition] L. Troiano. il por *American Health* 8:95-7 Jl/Ag '89
SLEDDING
See also
Dog sledding
Anecdotes, facetiae, satire, etc.
A good deed undoes. P. F. McManus. il *Outdoor Life* 183:144+ My '89
SLEDGE, GARY
The grandest art on earth. il *Reader's Digest* 134:178-80 My '89
The woman in the kitchen. il *Reader's Digest* 135:85-90 S '89
SLEDGE, JOANNA
about
The woman in the kitchen. G. Sledge. il *Reader's Digest* 135:85-90 S '89
SLEDGE, LINDA CHING
Why I teach Sunday school. *Reader's Digest* 135:11-12+ Jl '89
SLEDS
See also
Sledding
Icefisherman's sled. P. Butler and M. Butler. il *Outdoor Life* 184:66+ N '89
A pull-along sled for baby. il *Sunset (Central West edition)* 183:29 D '89
SLEEP
See also
Bedtime
Dreams
Napping (Sleep)
Nightmares
Wakening from sleep
Bedtime beauties. il *'Teen* 33:88-9 Ap '89
Do wake the baby [establishing schedules] P. Raeburn. il *American Health* 8:98 Ja/F '89
Everything you wanted to know about sleep [aged] E. Kiester. bibl il *New Choices for the Best Years* 29:62-3+ Ja '89
Fending off AIDS with deep sleep? [research by Suzan E. Norman] K. Fackelmann. *Science News* 136:13 Jl 1 '89
Looking great in bed. il *Essence* 19:78-9+ F '89

SLEEP—cont.

Mapping neuronal inputs to REM sleep induction sites with carbachol-fluorescent microspheres. J. J. Quattrochi and others. bibl f il *Science* 245:984-6 S 1 '89

Routine is key to good rest [older adults; views of Steve Weber] il *USA Today (Periodical)* 117:13-14 F '89

Scientists give the nod to more sleep time [alertness and vigilance testing by Timothy Roehrs and others] K. Fackelmann. *Science News* 136:260 O 21 '89

Sleep: get it while you can [adjusting to infant's sleep schedules] K. Karlsrud and D. Schultz. il *Parents* 64:195 S '89

Sleep researchers awake to possibilities. J. Palca. il *Science* 245:351-2 Jl 28 '89

Snooze news. il *Women's Sports & Fitness* 11:11 Je '89

Summoning the sandman. W. Lowe. il *Better Homes and Gardens* 67:39-40 Je '89

Teaching baby to sleep through the night [research by Amy Wolfson] S. Chollar. il *Psychology Today* 23:58-9 Ap '89

Unraveling sleep disorders of the aged [sodium experiments point to sympathetic nervous system; work of Michael V. Vitiello] K. Fackelmann. *Science News* 136:7 Jl 1 '89

Voyeurs in the kingdom of sleep. L. Lamberg. il *Health (New York, N.Y.)* 21:66-9 Jl '89

Where should baby sleep? M. Konner. il *The New York Times Magazine* p39-40 Ja 8 '89

Anecdotes, facetiae, satire, etc.

Pillow talk. E. Keyishian. il *Glamour* 87:168 Ja '89

SLEEP APNEA

Inspirational obstruction blown away [work of John E. Remmers] S. Hart and A. McKenzie. *Science News* 136:233 O 7 '89

Sleep . . . at last. J. Wilkes. il *Health (New York, N.Y.)* 21:84+ Jl '89

SLEEP DEPRIVATION

The rest is up to you [effect on tennis players] S. Festa. il *World Tennis* 37:18-19 Ag '89

Sleep in and smell the coffee [linked to human error] M. Adessa. *Psychology Today* 22:18 D '88

SLEEP DISORDERS

See also

Insomnia
Sleep apnea
Snoring

Bizarre sleep disorders. S. Rolbein. il *Good Housekeeping* 208:69-72 My '89

Sleep problems send psychiatric signals [research by Daniel E. Ford and Douglas B. Kamerow] B. Bower. *Science News* 136:180 S 16 '89

Sleep researchers awake to possibilities. J. Palca. il *Science* 245:351-2 Jl 28 '89

Sleeping a light fantastic. E. E. Goode. il *U.S. News & World Report* 107:49-50 Jl 10 '89

Unraveling sleep disorders of the aged [sodium experiments point to sympathetic nervous system; work of Michael V. Vitiello] K. Fackelmann. *Science News* 136:7 Jl 1 '89

"We have a problem" [child's fear of going to sleep] J. Marks. il *Parents* 64:65-9 S '89

SLEEP HABITS OF ANIMALS See Animals—Habits and behavior

SLEEP POSITIONS

Photographs and photography

Posing for photographer Ted Spagna? Just say ZZZZ. P. Chin. il pors *People Weekly* 31:97-8+ F 6 '89

Sleep shots [work of T. Spagna] T. Frick. il *Art in America* 77:66-9+ Je '89

SLEEP-WAKE CYCLES See Biological rhythms

SLEEPING BAGS

The key to happy camping. il *Parents* 64:22 Jl '89

THE SLEEPING BEAUTY [ballet] See Ballet reviews—Single works

SLEEPING GARMENTS See Sleepwear
SLEEPING MEDICINES See Hypnotics
SLEEPING PILLS See Hypnotics
SLEEPLESSNESS See Insomnia
SLEEPWEAR

Hot nights, cool clothes. il *Health (New York, N.Y.)* 21:72-5 Jl '89

What they're wearing in bed [designers] C. Donovan. il *The New York Times Magazine* p96-7 N 12 '89

SLEIGHT, ARTHUR W.

about

Superconductivity stars move. R. Pool. pors *Science* 244:1141 Je 9 '89

SLEPAK, ALEXANDER

about

Rules of the road to Red Square. E. Pomice. il *U.S. News & World Report* 107:63 N 27 '89

SLESIN, LOUIS

The danger of ignoring non-ionizing radiation. il *Technology Review* 92:22-3 Ja '89

SLICK, BOB

about

Dry times at Slick's Bar. M. A. Kuharski. il pors *Christianity Today* 33:14-15 Mr 17 '89

SLICK'S ALTERNATIVE BAR (MINNEAPOLIS, MINN.) See Minneapolis (Minn.)—Restaurants, nightclubs, bars, etc.

SLIDE FILMS See Photography—Films
SLIDES (PHOTOGRAPHY)

Photographing your artwork [slides of paintings] S. Marcus. *American Artist* 53:32-3+ F '89

Copying

Beseler Dual Mode slide duplicator. J. Drafahl and S. Drafahl. il *Petersen's Photographic Magazine* 17:36-8+ Ja '89

SLIGER, KEN

(jt. auth) See Tousignant, Doug, and Sliger, Ken

SLIM, GUITAR See Guitar Slim, Jr.

SLIME MOLDS

Dictyostelium discoideum: a model system for cell-cell interactions in development. P. Devreotes. bibl f il *Science* 245:1054-8 S 8 '89

Expression and characterization of a functional myosin head fragment in Dictyostelium discoideum. D. J. Manstein and others. bibl f il *Science* 246:656-8 N 3 '89

Slime time [reduced numbers in Central African rain forests; research by James Cavender] il *Discover* 10:10 O '89

Transfer RNA genes: landmarks for integration of mobile genetic elements in Dictyostelium discoideum. R. Marschalek and others. bibl f il *Science* 244:1493-6 Je 23 '89

SLIPPER CHAIRS See Chairs
SLIPS OF THE TONGUE See Speech errors
SLOAN, DAVID

(jt. auth) See Shea-Stonum, Marilyn, and Sloan, David

SLOAN, JOHN E.

And the music tells of history [address, May 6, 1989] *Vital Speeches of the Day* 55:649-51 Ag 15 '89

SLOAN, L. LAWRENCE

about

"Thank God we didn't understand the business". E. Paris. il por *Forbes* 143:64+ Je 12 '89

SLOAN, LARRY

about

Ubu [drama] Reviews

New York il 22:47-8 Jl 17 '89. J. Simon
The New Yorker il 65:91 Jl 10 '89. E. Oliver

SLOAN-BUBRICK, ELIZABETH

From our editor. See issues of McCall's beginning March 1986 through December 1989

SLOAN-KETTERING CANCER CENTER See Memorial Sloan-Kettering Cancer Center

SLOANE, N. J. A. (NEIL JAMES ALEXANDER), 1939-

about

Interview: Neil Sloane. A. Liversidge. il pors *Omni (New York, N.Y.)* 11:78-80+ S '89

SLOANE, NEIL JAMES ALEXANDER See Sloane, N. J. A. (Neil James Alexander), 1939-

SLOCUM, GEORGE SIGMAN, 1940-

about

Good-bye to take-or-pay. T. Mack. il por *Forbes* 143:120+ Je 12 '89

SLOGANS

Who can pass judgment on the Joneses? R. E. Burns. *U.S. Catholic* 54:2 Je '89

SLONIM, GILVEN M.

World ocean—the human stake [address, October 13, 1988] *Vital Speeches of the Day* 55:172-6 Ja 1 '89

SLOPE PLANTING See Hillside gardens and gardening
SLOPPINESS See Messiness
SLOSS, KERR, ROSENBERG & MOORE [dance] See Dance reviews—Single works

SLOTH See Laziness

SLOTHS

Photographs and photography

Don't hurry, be happy. M. Fogden and P. Fogden. il *Natural History* p92-3 Je '89

SLOTHS, FOSSIL

Boning up leads to sloth as a student makes a rare find [discovery of ground sloth fossils by D. Delgado in Florida] il por *People Weekly* 32:61 Jl 3 '89

SLOTNICK, BARRY IVAN

about

Slotnick's law. D. Rabinowitz. il pors *New York* 22:30-4 Ja 2 '89

SLOVENIA (YUGOSLAVIA)

Nationalism

Slovene model. M. Mihajlov. *The New Leader* 72:3-4 N 27 '89

SLOVICK, MURRAY

Camcorders 2000. il *Video* 13:64-8 S '89
Deluxe decks. il *Video* 13:45-9+ O '89
Power shopping. il *Video* 13:74-5+ O '89

SLOVITER, ROBERT, 1950-, AND OTHERS

Selective loss of hippocampal granule cells in the mature rat brain after adrenalectomy. bibl f il *Science* 243:535-8 Ja 27 '89

SLOW COOKERS See Kitchen utensils and appliances

SLOW LEARNING CHILDREN

See also

Learning disabilities
Reading disability

SLOW VIRUSES *See* Viruses

SLR CAMERAS *See* Cameras, Single-lens reflex

SLUDGE AS FERTILIZER *See* Sewage as fertilizer

SLUGS
They're still slimy, but naked snails are finding new friends. S. McCredie. bibl (p171) il *Smithsonian* 19:134-41 F '89

SLUGS, SHOTGUN *See* Bullets

SLUM CLEARANCE *See* Urban renewal

SLUMBER PARTIES
Adolescence lives at L.A.'s all-gal celeb pajama bash [hosted by A. Willis] P. Lansden. il pors *People Weekly* 32:147-8 N 27 '89
Slumber party pointers. il *'Teen* 33:49 My '89

SLUMS
See also
Squatter settlements
Slums then and now. D. Murphy. *America* 161:447-9 D 16 '89

SLURS, RACIAL *See* Racial slurs

SLUSSER, RICHARD
Who killed Lebanon? A list of culprits. *The Christian Century* 106:900-1 O 11 '89

SLUTSKY, ROBERT
about
Setting the record straight. M. Sun. *Science* 244:911 My 26 '89

SM *See* Sadomasochism

SMALE, JOHN GRAY, 1927-
Corporate takeovers [address, February 7, 1989] *Vital Speeches of the Day* 55:330-2 Mr 15 '89

SMALL, LINDA A.
Blacks enrich modern dance [cover story] il *American Visions* 4:24-9 Je '89

SMALL, LINDA LEE
(jt. auth) *See* McHenry, Susan, and Small, Linda Lee

SMALL, MARY LUINS
Denver's black "bookstore and more". il *American Visions* 4:42-5 F '89

SMALL, MEREDITH F.
Ms. Monkey. il *Natural History* p10+ Ja '89

SMALL, PAMELA
about
One of the boys. M. B. Carlson. *The New Republic* 200:11-13 Je 5 '89
The protégé and the victim. E. Clift. il pors *Newsweek* 113:38 My 15 '89
A victim's story. K. Ringle. pors *Reader's Digest* 135:49-54 Ag '89

SMALL, S. A., AND OTHERS
Activity-dependent enhancement of presynaptic inhibition in Aplysia sensory neurons. bibl f il *Science* 243:1603-6 Mr 24 '89

SMALL BUSINESS
See also
Entrepreneurs
Franchise system
Hispanic American business enterprises
Home-based business
Minority business enterprises
Women entrepreneurs
The 1990 guide to small business [special section] bibl il *U.S. News & World Report* 107:72-3+ O 23 '89
And the music tells of history [address, May 6, 1989] J. E. Sloan. *Vital Speeches of the Day* 55:649-51 Ag 15 '89
The B.E. guide to growing a business [special section] il *Black Enterprise* 19:125-6+ Je '89
Big ideas for your small business. D. M. Kehrer. il *Changing Times* 43:56-60 N '89
Conquering "computer phobia" can pay off for small and mid-size businesses [purchasing decisions] *Black Enterprise* 20:47 N '89
Enterprise. See issues of Business Week beginning July 27, 1987
Enterprise. See issues of Working Woman beginning September 1983
Fitting PCs to small business needs. F. Gibbons. por *Personal Computing* 13:232 O '89
Is your company too big? [cover story] J. A. Byrne. il *Business Week* p84-8+ Mr 27 '89
Small-business update. See issues of Nation's Business beginning January 1988
Software's big guns take aim at small business. D. A. Depke. il *Business Week* p216-18 S 25 '89
Who innovates? [role of small firms in adopting new technologies] B. Harrison. il *Technology Review* 92:15+ Ap '89

Accounting
Choosing your accountant. B. A. McKee. *Nation's Business* 77:28 N '89

Bibliography
A look at new "how-to" books for small business. *Nation's Business* 77:6+ F '89

Directories
The 200 best small companies in America [special section] il *Forbes* 144:185-7+ N 13 '89
Hot growth companies [cover story; special section] il *Business Week* p90-3+ My 22 '89

Export-import trade
Blunders abroad. C. F. Valentine. il *Nation's Business* 77:54+ Mr '89
EC92 [cover story] R. Thompson. il map *Nation's Business* 77:18-24+ Je '89
Keeping up with EC92. A. Holzinger. il *Nation's Business* 77:38-40 D '89
The little guys are making it big overseas. W. J. Holstein and B. Bremner. il *Business Week* p94-6 F 27 '89
A new era in trade [U.S.-Canadian trade] A. Holzinger. il *Nation's Business* 77:67-72 S '89
New service to exporters [Japanese companies set up export promotion offices to help U.S. firms] il *Nation's Business* 77:70 N '89
Oases of opportunity [duty free zones] S. Golob. il *Nation's Business* 77:45-6 Jl '89
On the front lines in the trade war. S. A. Rondel. il *Nation's Business* 77:10 Je '89
Taking your small business global. R. R. Roha. il *Changing Times* 43:103-9 D '89

Federal aid
See also
United States. Small Business Administration
Business' role in war on drugs [federal contractors required to establish antidrug programs] D. C. Bacon. *Nation's Business* 77:5 Ja '89
A mother lode of loans for small businesses. T. Segal. il *Business Week* p104-5 Je 19 '89
Small business briefs Mr. Bush. D. C. Bacon. *Nation's Business* 77:20 Ja '89
Small business seeks "kinder and gentler" treatment from Bush administration. S. Harvey. il *Home Office Computing* 7:10 Ap '89

Finance
See also
Venture capital
How to calculate capital needs. M. Stevens. il *Nation's Business* 77:32 N '89
Maine millionaire David Franklin goes for broke by giving big bucks to people who need it. D. Mathison. il pors *People Weekly* 32:83-4+ D 18 '89
Managing your company's money [interview with B. Michels] N. Sullivan. por *Home Office Computing* 7:60 S '89
Prospecting on the money trail. P. Sharif. il *Black Enterprise* 19:126+ Je '89
Small business: an upbeat '89 [cover story] R. Thompson. il *Nation's Business* 77:10-12+ Ja '89
The start-up blues. J. Schlosberg. *The Washington Monthly* 20:25-30 Ja '89
State funds for start-ups. J. C. Szabo. il *Nation's Business* 77:42+ Je '89
They're small, but they're scrappy. J. Egan. il *U.S. News & World Report* 106:78 My 22 '89
Three ways banks can help your business. M. Stevens. il *Working Woman* 14:34 Ag '89
An upbeat mood suddenly strikes small business. G. Koretz. il *Business Week* p26 N 27 '89

Statistics
The 200 best small companies in America [special section] il *Forbes* 144:185-7+ N 13 '89
Hot growth companies [cover story; special section] il *Business Week* p90-3+ My 22 '89
How to tell an eagle from an Icarus [analysis of 1979 list of Up & Comers] F. Meeks and others. il *Forbes* 144:213-14+ N 13 '89

Laws and regulations
Business: applaud the cooperation, but be prepared for the conflict. *Nation's Business* 77:80 Mr '89
Congress's initiatives seen as threats to small architectural firms and the costs of construction. P. Hoffmann. il *Architectural Record* 177:21 Ap '89
Dateline: Washington. See issues of Nation's Business beginning September 1989
A status report on Congress. D. C. Bacon. il *Nation's Business* 77:6+ Ag '89

Taxation
Changes ahead for Section 89. D. C. Bacon. il *Nation's Business* 77:6 Je '89
Doubts multiply on Section 89 [federal benefits law] R. Thompson. il *Nation's Business* 77:17-18+ My '89
"Government gone crazy" [Section 89 of tax code on employee benefits discrimination; cover story] R. Thompson. il *Nation's Business* 77:20-4+ Jl '89
Health insurance: a tax-reform footnote trips up small business. S. B. Garland. il *Business Week* p45 Ja 30 '89
How tax changes affect business. G. W. Padwe. il *Nation's Business* 77:57 F '89
How the good guys won the battle of Section 89. il *Nation's Business* 77:101 N '89
Look before you leap into a VAT. *Nation's Business* 77:52 Ap '89
Looking beyond Section 89. R. Thompson. il *Nation's Business* 77:27-8 D '89
Nonprofit groups: an unfair edge? D. C. Bacon. il *Nation's Business* 77:33-4 Ap '89
A push to repeal Section 89 [strictures on employee benefits] R. Thompson. il *Nation's Business* 77:6 Mr '89

SMALL BUSINESS—Taxation—*cont.*
Section 89: beyond repair. R. Thompson. il *Nation's Business* 77:65-7 Ap '89
Separating your business from your personal life. L. Wiener. il *U.S. News & World Report* 107:67 O 2 '89
Taxes: don't pay too much [cover story; with editorial comment by Robert T. Gray] J. C. Szabo. il *Nation's Business* 77:22-6+ N '89
There's only one way to clear up this misunderstanding [repeal of Section 89] *Nation's Business* 77:80 Ag '89
Great Britain
History
Enterprise past and present [working class entrepreneurs in late 19th and early 20th century] J. Benson. il *History Today* 39:5-7 Ag '89
Italy
For Italy's entrepreneurs, the figures are bella. C. Haberman. il *The New York Times Magazine* p32-4+ Jl 16 '89
Poland
Capitalist liberation. M. Novak. il *Forbes* 144:102 S 18 '89
Western Europe
An entrepreneurial tree sprouts in Europe [high tech companies] D. Dickson. il *Science* 245:1038-40 S 8 '89
SMALL BUSINESS, SALE OF
Rule no. 1 for selling your company: don't rush. S. Woolley. il *Business Week* p114-15 Ap 3 '89
Selling your firm may hike your pay. M. Stevens. il *Nation's Business* 77:46+ S '89
Shaping up your company [excerpt from Cashing in] L. Berger and others. il *Working Woman* 14:47-8+ My '89
Staying aboard after the sale. S. Nelton. il *Nation's Business* 77:34-5 S '89
When it's time to sell out. T. Thompson. il *U.S. News & World Report* 106:62-4 Je 26 '89
SMALL BUSINESS ADMINISTRATION (U.S.) *See* United States. Small Business Administration
SMALL BUSINESS PERSON OF THE YEAR AWARDS
Folding napkins to ring up sales [T. Bretting wins] M. Barrier. il por *Nation's Business* 77:58-9 Jl '89
SMALL CLAIMS COURTS
See you in court. P. Besson. il *Black Enterprise* 20:74-6 N '89
Small-claims court: winning is just the beginning. D. W. Englander. il *Money* 18:150-1 Ap '89
SMALL COMPUTER SYSTEM INTERFACE *See* SCSI (Computer bus)
SMALL FARMS *See* Farms, Small
SMALL PRESS EXPO *See* Book fairs
SMALL PRESSES *See* Publishers and publishing
SMALL SACRIFICES [television program] *See* Television program reviews—Single works
SMALL SCHOOLS *See* School enrollment
SMALL TOWNS
Small-town America: an endangered species. G. Smith. il map *National Geographic* 175:186-215 F '89
Small-town blues. R. Hornik. il *Time* 133:66-8 Mr 27 '89
SMALLEY, GEORGE WASHBURN, 1833-1916
about
The Civil War's greatest scoop. J. Weeks. il por *American Heritage* 40:100+ Jl/Ag '89
SMALLMOUTH BASS FISHING *See* Bass fishing
SMALLPOX
Virus on ice [preserved in vaults in Atlanta and Moscow] B. Wacker. il *Health (New York, N.Y.)* 21:48-51 D '89
Vaccines and vaccination
Immunology [ancient China] R. K. G. Temple. il *The Courier (Unesco)* 41:34 O '88
SMALLTALK (COMPUTER LANGUAGE)
Hooked on Smalltalk-80 for the Mac. D. E. Crabb. il *Byte* 14:143+ Ja '89
Smalltalk/V comes to the Mac. R. Valdés. il *Byte* 14:201-4 Je '89
Smalltalk can be cheap [Smalltalk/V Mac] D. E. Crabb. il *Byte* 14:141-2+ Ap '89
SMALTZ, AUDREY
about
Ruler of the runway. S. Rae. il por *Harper's Bazaar* 122:80-1 N '89
SMART, JEAN
about
Baby boom! [cover story] A. Meisler. il pors *TV Guide* 37:4-7+ D 30 '89-Ja 5 '90
'People are shocked at my views on certain things'. E. Warren. il pors *TV Guide* 37:10-12 Mr 11-17 '89
SMART CARDS
Not in the cards? P. Wallich. *Scientific American* 260:101 Ja '89
Smart cards: pocket power. M. Rogers. il *Newsweek* 114:54-5 Jl 31 '89
Smart cards will respond to owner's voice. *Radio-Electronics* 60:4 D '89
SMART HOUSES *See* Computers—Home use
SMART MACHINES *See* Computers
SMART MODEMS *See* Modems
SMART START (U.S.)
CEOs for 4-year-olds. J. Lieblich. il *Fortune* 119:8 Mr 27 '89

SMARTFOODS, INC.
A feud that's really popping [Smartfoods vs. Annie's All-Natural Popcorn] A. Miller. il por *Newsweek* 114:52 Jl 24 '89
SMEATON, SUZANNE
American picture frames of the arts and crafts period, 1870-1920. bibl f il *Antiques* 136:1124-37 N '89
SMECTIC LIQUID CRYSTALS *See* Liquid crystals
SMELL
See also
Aroma therapy
Odors
G_{olf}: an olfactory neuron specific-G protein involved in odorant signal transduction. D. T. Jones and R. R. Reed. bibl f il *Science* 244:790-5 My 19 '89
Home, sweet-smelling home [homing in black bears] L. L. Rogers. il *Natural History* p60-7 S '89
Molecular custodians sweep away odorants [research by Doren Lancet] I. Amato. *Science News* 136:374 D 9 '89
Odor-induced membrane currents in vertebrate-olfactory receptor neurons. S. Firestein and F. Werblin. bibl f il *Science* 244:79-82 Ap 7 '89
SMELSER, LYNNE M.
When sadness turns to childhood depression. *The Education Digest* 55:52-3 S '89
SMETEK, JOHN THOMAS
about
Justine Bateman becomes the latest celebrity to be menaced by an obsessive fan. B. Hewitt. il por *People Weekly* 32:112-13 S 25 '89
SMIGIEL, NICOLE
about
Travis comes home. M. Jacobbi. il pors *Good Housekeeping* 209:103+ Jl '89
SMIGIEL, TRAVIS CHRISTIAN
about
Travis comes home. M. Jacobbi. il pors *Good Housekeeping* 209:103+ Jl '89
SMIL, VACLAV
China's environmental morass. bibl f *Current History* 88:277-80+ S '89
Our changing environment. bibl f *Current History* 88:9-12+ Ja '89
SMILES
What makes a show-off smile? A. Ranard. il *Health (New York, N.Y.)* 21:50-3+ Ja '89
SMILEY, STU
about
Smiley's people. V. Ziegel. il por *Gentlemen's Quarterly* 59:240-3+ Ag '89
SMILEY, WALTER V.
about
When it's time to go. M. Barrier. il por *Nation's Business* 77:74+ N '89
SMITH, ADAM, 1723-1790
about
A hero for consumers. S. Nasar. il por *Fortune* 119:63 Ja 2 '89
SMITH, ADAM, 1930-
Unconventional wisdom. See issues of Esquire
SMITH, ALLEN B.
A dry-ice fogger: how to make the moodiest prop of all. il *Petersen's Photographic Magazine* 17:46-8 F '89
SMITH, ALYSSA
about
A family account at the organ bank. il por *U.S. News & World Report* 107:17 D 11 '89
Lifesaving surgery. H. Jensen. il por *Maclean's* 102:54 D 11 '89
Liver-transplant surgeons use living donor. K. Fackelmann. *Science News* 136:358 D 2 '89
A mother's gift of life. B. Dolan. il por *Time* 134:96 D 11 '89
A mother's gift of love and life. M. Beck. il pors *Newsweek* 114:91-2 D 11 '89
SMITH, AMANDA
Lynne Reid Banks. il por *Publishers Weekly* 236:30+ O 27 '89
A royal mum writes for children. il por *Publishers Weekly* 236:34+ S 29 '89
SMITH, ARTHUR E.
about
Long Island symmetry: reworking a designer's 1920s residence in Southampton. P. Warner. il *Architectural Digest* 46:138-43 Jl '89
SMITH, B. A., AND OTHERS
Voyager 2 at Neptune: imaging science results. bibl f il *Science* 246:1422-49 D 15 '89
SMITH, BARBARA
about
My time. V. Yaz. il pors *Essence* 20:83-8 Ag '89
SMITH, BERNARD WILLIAM
The unknown art of Australia. il *The Courier (Unesco)* 41:23-6 D '88
SMITH, BESSIE
about
Bessie Smith. M. Azerrad. por *Rolling Stone* p93 F 9 '89

SMITH, BOB, 1917-
Buffalo Bob Smith: on overnight success and the Howdy-for-
president campaign. il por *People Weekly* 31 Special
Issue:107 Summ '89
SMITH, BONNIE
about
Makeovers for success: is how you dress your company's
business? P. R. Satran. il por *Glamour* 87:154-5+ Jl '89
SMITH, BRIAN
Image maker. il por *Harper's Bazaar* 122:88+ D '89
SMITH, BRUCE D.
Origins of agriculture in eastern North America. bibl f il
map *Science* 246:1566-71 D 22 '89
SMITH, C. R., (CYRUS ROWLETT)
about
Collecting the West [cover story] R. H. Saunders. il *American
History Illustrated* 23:22-33 Ja '89
SMITH, CHARLES
about
Charlie Smith's second chance. C. Phillips. il *Reader's Digest*
135:29-30+ N '89
SMITH, CHARLES
about
Double dose of divinity. R. Brown. il pors *Ebony* 44:52+
Ja '89
SMITH, CHARLOTTE ANNE
You may be an expert and not know it. *The Writer* 102:26-7
Ja '89
SMITH, CHESTER
about
Double dose of divinity. R. Brown. il pors *Ebony* 44:52+
Ja '89
SMITH, CURT
It's going, going, going . . . il por *Sports Illustrated* 70:104
Ap 17 '89
SMITH, CYRUS ROWLETT See Smith, C. R., (Cyrus Rowlett)
SMITH, D. P. E., AND OTHERS
Smectic liquid crystal monolayers on graphite observed by
scanning tunneling microscopy [cover story] bibl f il *Science*
245:43-5 Jl 7 '89
SMITH, DARDEN
about
Boo Hewerdine & Darden Smith. M. McCormick. pors *Rolling
Stone* p30 N 2 '89
SMITH, DEBBI KEMPTON- See Kempton-Smith, Debbi
SMITH, DENNY
Should the House-passed wage proposal be enacted? [excerpts
from address, March 23, 1989] *Congressional Digest* 68:157+
My '89
SMITH, DESMOND
TV news did not just happen—it had to invent itself. il
Smithsonian 20:74-8+ Je '89
SMITH, DIANA KAPPEL- See Kappel-Smith, Diana
SMITH, DICK
Dick Smith: on aging a woman 40 years in five minutes
for live '50s TV. il por *People Weekly* 31 Special Issue:106
Summ '89
SMITH, DINITIA
Arafat's man in New York. il pors *New York* 22:40-6 Ja
23 '89
The book of Jason. il pors *New York* 22:26-31 Ag 7 '89
The Midas curse [cover story] il pors *New York* 22:32-40
Ap 3 '89
Secret lives of New York [cover story] il *New York* 22:34-41
D 11 '89
Wasps' nest [cover story] il pors *New York* 22:30-9 Je 5
'89
SMITH, DOUG
(ed) See Porter, Mike. Guide, slice, and glide
SMITH, EDITH HOLDEN See Holden, Edith, 1871-1920
SMITH, ELEANOR, 1954-
The new moral classroom. il *Psychology Today* 23:32-6 My
'89
Pet shop boy. il *Omni (New York, N.Y.)* 12:20+ D '89
(jt. auth) See Glucksman, Mary S., and Smith, Eleanor,
1954-
SMITH, ELWOOD H., 1941-
about
Elwood Smith. L. S. Hurwitz. il *American Artist* 53:53-5+
S '89
SMITH, ERNEST, JR.
about
Fray erupts when white woman wills estate worth $476,000
to black man. *Jet* 76:4 My 22 '89
SMITH, EVELYN
about
Living in sin? Not in her apartments, vows Christian landlady
Evelyn Smith. M. Brower. il pors *People Weekly* 32:113-14
D 11 '89
SMITH, FRANK, 1928-
Overselling literacy [adaptation of address, May 1988; cover
story; with editorial comment by Pauline B. Gough] bibl
f il *Phi Delta Kappan* 70:346, 352-9 Ja '89
SMITH, FRED L.
What's behind the S&L crisis? il *Consumers' Research
Magazine* 72:24-7 My '89

SMITH, FREDERICK W., 1944-
about
Fred Smith. D. Foust. il por *Business Week* Special Issue:102
Ap 14 '89
Mr. Smith goes global [cover story] D. Foust. il pors map
Business Week p66-8+ F 13 '89
SMITH, GARY
A celebration of Muhammad Ali [cover story] il pors *Sports
Illustrated* 71 Special Issue:214-18+ N 15 '89
Dear Mike . . . il pors *Sports Illustrated* 70:58-64+ F 27
'89
Out of the blue. il *Life* 12:82-4+ N '89
She who laughs last . . . [cover story] il pors *Sports Illustrated*
70:84-8+ My 22 '89
Top Gun. il pors *Sports Illustrated* 71:56-62+ Ag 7 '89
The world according to Ray. il pors *Sports Illustrated* 71:80-6+
D 4 '89
about
From the publisher. D. J. Barr. il por *Sports Illustrated*
70:1 F 27 '89
SMITH, GAVIN
Actors face the truth. il *Film Comment* 25:32-5 Ja/F '89
Actor's fury. il *Film Comment* 25:44-5 My/Je '89
Body count. il *Film Comment* 25:49-52 Jl/Ag '89
Fun with Ben & John [interview with B. Gazzara] il pors
Film Comment 25:46-7 My/Je '89
Hickey [interview] il pors *Film Comment* 25:52-4 N/D '89
The outsider [interview with J. Hurt] il pors *Film Comment*
25:64-7 Mr/Ap '89
SMITH, GEOFFREY M.
Coping with the coming labor shortage [address, May 11,
1989] *Vital Speeches of the Day* 55:669-71 Ag 15 '89
SMITH, GERARD C.
The Gorbachev spin. *The Bulletin of the Atomic Scientists*
45:35+ My '89
SMITH, GERARD C., AND COBBAN, HELENA
A blind eye to nuclear proliferation. bibl f *Foreign Affairs*
68:53-70 Summ '89
SMITH, GIBBS M.
about
Gibbs Smith: 20 years of activist publishing. J. Barbato.
Publishers Weekly 236:48 S 8 '89
SMITH, GREG
about
And now, Hollywood Babble-on. R. Corliss. il *Time* 133:76-7
Ja 16 '89
SMITH, GREGORY WHITE
about
Jackson Pollock bio a milestone for authors. A. Smith. il
Publishers Weekly 236:39 O 27 '89
SMITH, GRIFFIN, 1941-
Small-town America: an endangered species. il map *National
Geographic* 175:186-215 F '89
SMITH, H. ALLEN
Are you a midnight genius? il *The Saturday Evening Post*
261:54-7+ Mr '89
SMITH, HARLAN J.
about
Director of McDonald Observatory honored. il por *Astronomy*
17:12 Ja '89
SMITH, HEDRICK
about
Public TV goes to Washington. H. F. Waters. il por *Newsweek*
113:65 Ja 2 '89
SMITH, HEDY, AND OTHERS
Neonatal thymectomy results in a repertoire enriched in
T cells deleted in adult thymus. bibl f il *Science* 245:749-52
Ag 18 '89
SMITH, J. ALFRED (JAMES ALFRED)
The invisible church. il *Christianity Today* 33:32-4 Mr 3
'89
about
Side by side. K. H. Sidey. il pors *Christianity Today* 33:33
Mr 3 '89
SMITH, JACLYN
about
Architectural digest visits: Jaclyn Smith and Tony Richmond
[cover story] J. Giovannini. il pors *Architectural Digest*
46:180-5+ Ag '89
A salute to the Oscars. il pors *Ladies' Home Journal*
106:131-6+ Ap '89
"Whatever happens to me, I'm going to be happy". M.
J. Bandler. il pors *Redbook* 174:42+ N '89
SMITH, JAMES ALFRED See Smith, J. Alfred (James Alfred)
SMITH, JAMES D.
Fortysomething: Saint Thomas in winter. *U.S. Catholic* 54:35
O '89
SMITH, JANNA MALAMUD
Where does a writer's family draw the line? il por *The
New York Times Book Review* 94:1+ N 5 '89
SMITH, JEFF
Everyday dinners with an Italian, Greek or Chinese twist
[excerpt from The frugal gourmet cooks three ancient
cuisines] il *Redbook* 173:144-9+ S '89
SMITH, JIM
about
If you missed what they said, contact Jim Smith. P. Finch.
il por *Business Week* p89 Mr 13 '89

SMITH, JOAN IRVINE
about
Bleak ranch. E. Schmuckler. il por *Forbes* 144 Special Issue:14 O 23 '89
SMITH, JOAN LIEBMANN- *See* Liebmann-Smith, Joan
SMITH, JOHN, 1580-1631
about
John Smith's bill: then & now. J. B. M. Schick. il *American Heritage* 40:158-65 N '89
SMITH, JOHN W.
Worse for the terns. il *Natural History* p65 Ja '89
SMITH, JOSHUA I.
about
Bush taps Joshua Smith to lead business commission. por *Jet* 76:37 Ag 14 '89
SMITH, KAREN
Cutting through start-up problems. por *Nation's Business* 77:9 Ap '89
SMITH, KATHY
about
Kathy Smith and the basic 3-light setup. G. Bernstein. il por *Petersen's Photographic Magazine* 18:8 Jl '89
SMITH, KATIE R.
Give the homeless a chance. por *Christianity Today* 33:8 Jl 14 '89
SMITH, KENNETH V.
The resurrection of Evan Mecham. il por *National Review* 41:42-3 My 19 '89
SMITH, KIRK R.
Air pollution. bibl f il *Environment* 30:16-20+ D '88
Air pollution [discussion of December 1988 article] il *Environment* 31:2-3 My '89
SMITH, LELAND
about
A buyout guru shares two takeover visions. G. G. Marcial. il por *Business Week* p146 Mr 20 '89
SMITH, LIZ
America's need to read. il por *Harper's Bazaar* 122:70-1 Ja '89
about
Loose lips. C. Jahr. il por *Ladies' Home Journal* 106:110-12+ Ja '89
SMITH, LLOYD P.
about
Obituary
Physics Today por 42 pt1:83-4 Ag '89. H. A. Bethe and others
SMITH, LONNIE
about
Some kind of comeback. R. Demak. il por *Sports Illustrated* 71:52 Ag 7 '89
SMITH, MALIK, D. 1989
about
Actress Beverly Todd's son dies after nightclub brawl. il por *Jet* 76:54 Ap 10 '89
SMITH, MANDY
about
A May-December wedding finally puts a brake on the oldest Rolling Stone. P. Freeman. il pors *People Weekly* 31:54-6 Je 19 '89
SMITH, MAXINE
about
Play of patterns: a designer's vivid realm in Los Angeles. H. Hurt. il por *Architectural Digest* 46:192-7 D '89
SMITH, MICHAEL B., 1936-
about
Smith to Japan: here's the beef. A. Kupfer. il por *Fortune* 119:53 Ja 2 '89
SMITH, MICHAEL K.
Why is Pythagoras following me? bibl f il *Phi Delta Kappan* 70:446-54 F '89
SMITH, MICHAEL R.
Technologizing office work. bibl *Society* 26:65-72 My/Je '89
SMITH, MICHELE
about
All bases covered. M. Kort. il pors *Women's Sports & Fitness* 11:48-51 O '89
SMITH, MIKE
The Triple Crown affair. il *Sport (New York, N.Y.)* 80:104-7 Je '89
SMITH, NIGEL J. H., 1949-
(jt. auth) *See* Plucknett, Donald L., 1931-, and Smith, Nigel J. H., 1949-
SMITH, OLIVER
about
The startling Shelly Prine case. P. Michelmore. *Reader's Digest* 135:179-80+ Jl '89
SMITH, OLIVER, 1918-
about
At American Ballet Theatre—Hermann, Smith, and Taras take up the slack. J. H. Mazo. il pors *Dance Magazine* 63:16-17 D '89
SMITH, PATRICK J., 1932-
Inner landscape: two American operas probe their characters' thoughts. il *Opera News* 54:20-2 Jl '89
Summer idyll [cover story] il pors *Opera News* 53:10-12 Je '89

SMITH, PAUL
about
Designing men. il pors *Gentlemen's Quarterly* 59:120-5 Jl '89
SMITH, PAUL
Charlie Parker's solo on Dewey Square—a piano arrangement [excerpt from Charlie Parker for piano book two] il *Down Beat* 56:56-7 Ap '89
SMITH, PERRY M.
Twenty guidelines for leadership. il *Nation's Business* 77:60-1 S '89
SMITH, PETER J.
Rocker John Hiatt: as good as his words. il por *The New York Times Magazine* p55+ Mr 12 '89
SMITH, PRESTON
Washington report. See issues of Successful Farming beginning April 1987 through January 1989
SMITH, R. J.
Lord's prayer. il por *Film Comment* 25:2+ Jl/Ag '89
SMITH, RAY, 1949-
about
Ray Smith at Sperone Westwater. K. Johnson. *Art in America* 77:203 My '89
SMITH, RICHARD E.
about
Troubled Circle K is turning this way and that. K. Kerwin. il por *Business Week* p78+ N 20 '89
SMITH, ROBERT
about
'Dr. Bob'. R. D. Turner. il pors *Ebony* 44:102+ S '89
SMITH, ROBERT
about
Bailing out of Airbus. S. Toy. il *Business Week* p47 D 18 '89
SMITH, ROBERT P.
Living my childhood dream. il por *Reader's Digest* 134:163-4 Ja '89
SMITH, ROBERT W. (ROBERT WILLIAM), 1952-
The selling of space astronomy. *Astronomy* 17:8 Ja '89
(jt. auth) See Baum, Richard, and Smith, Robert W. (Robert William), 1952-
SMITH, ROBERTA
A shift in perspective. il *Vogue* 179:230+ My '89
SMITH, ROBIN ANN
about
Case of the 'nervous stomach'. A. Roblin. *Prevention (Emmaus, Pa.)* 41:112+ D '89
SMITH, ROGER
about
'My love is not a burden'; ed. by Patricia Nolan. Ann-Margret. por *New Choices for the Best Years* 29:14+ Ja '89
SMITH, ROGER B.
Smart cars and smart policies [address, March 28, 1989] *Vital Speeches of the Day* 55:534-7 Je 15 '89
about
"1990 will be the year of the General". J. Flint. il por *Forbes* 144:40-1 N 27 '89
Breaking up is hard to do. D. P. Levin. il pors *The New York Times Magazine* p36-7+ Mr 26 '89
General Motors reinvents the wheel. A. Gabor. il por *U.S. News & World Report* 107:40-1 Ag 21 '89
'The U.S. must do as GM has done' [interview] C. Leinster. il por *Fortune* 119:70-3 F 13 '89
SMITH, RONALD L.
Princess Presley: Elvis' little girl grows up. il pors *Ladies' Home Journal* 106:44+ F '89
SMITH, RONN
Ethyl Eichelberger. il pors *Theatre Crafts* 23:28-33+ Ja '89
SMITH, SALLY LIBERMAN
Learning-disabled students: the masks they wear. *The Education Digest* 55:50-3 D '89
SMITH, SAM
Twelve ways to make it through the Bush era. il *Utne Reader* p110-11 N/D '89
SMITH, SHARI
about
Beauty and the beast. E. H. Methvin. il pors *Reader's Digest* 134:132-8 F '89
SMITH, SHELLEY
Aim for the stars. il *Sports Illustrated* 71:66-9 Ag 21 '89
Boy wonder gets the boot at NBC. il por *Sports Illustrated* 70:82 My 22 '89
What would happen if . . . 20 of the best-ever NFL teams played a "Dream season"? il *Sports Illustrated* 71:159 S 11 '89
SMITH, SHELLEY TAYLOR- *See* Taylor-Smith, Shelley
SMITH, SIMON E.
Refugee reality and the U.N. High Commission. *America* 161:10-12+ Jl 1-8 '89
SMITH, SONNY
about
Guru of the glass. T. Kertes. il por *Sport (New York, N.Y.)* 80:68-71 Mr '89
SMITH, STACY JENEL
Aaron Henry's dangerous journey. il *Reader's Digest* 135:116-20 D '89

SMITH, STEVE

about

Steve Smith. R. Tolleson. il por *Down Beat* 56:14 My '89

SMITH, STEVEN

about

The tragedy at Bellevue. E. Salholz. il pors *Newsweek* 113:27 Ja 23 '89

SMITH, STEVEN B., AND OTHERS

Observation of individual DNA molecules undergoing gel electrophoresis. bibl f il *Science* 243:203-6 Ja 13 '89

SMITH, STEVEN O., AND OTHERS

Crystal versus solution structures of enzymes: NMR spectroscopy of a crystalline serine protease. bibl f il *Science* 244:961-4 My 26 '89

SMITH, SUSAN MALE

Take five. il *Health (New York, N.Y.)* 21:66-71+ S '89

SMITH, SYBIL

Why the obsession with race? il por *Sports Illustrated* 70:12 My 8 '89

SMITH, TONY, 1912-1981

about

Smug on Canal Street. il *Art in America* 77:23 Ja '89

SMITH, TOUKIE

about

The worst of times are over for 227's red-hot Toukie Smith. J. Stark. il pors *People Weekly* 32:135-6 D 18 '89

SMITH, VERNON L.

about

The economists' new guinea pigs. R. Bailey. il pors *Forbes* 144:148+ N 13 '89

SMITH, W. EUGENE, 1918-1978

about

Through a lens darkly. A. Goldsmith. il por *Popular Photography* 96:60-1+ N '89

SMITH, WILLI

about

'Willi Smith' Day held to aid needy N.Y. groups. il *Jet* 75:14-15 Mr 20 '89

SMITH, WILLIAM JAY, 1918-

(tr) See Cassian, Nina, 1924-. Poetry

SMITH (A. O.) CORP. See A. O. Smith Corp.

SMITH (W. H.) & SON (HOLDINGS) PLC See W. H. Smith & Son (Holdings) plc

SMITH (W. H.) PUBLISHERS INC. See W. H. Smith Publishers Inc.

SMITH & WESSON

For the ladies, a .38 caliber [gun ads targeted at women] il *Newsweek* 113:48 F 27 '89

Pistols for the women of America [Smith & Wesson's Lady Smith revolver targeted at women; cover story] L. C. Pogrebin. *The Nation* 248:649+ My 15 '89

SMITH BARNEY, HARRIS UPHAM & CO. INCORPORATED

Sandy Weill roars back [cover story] J. Friedman. il pors *Business Week* p88-91+ D 4 '89

SMITH-BOWERS, CATHY

My cousin going blind [poem] *America* 161:240 O 14 '89

SMITH-CARTER, CAROL

about

At a California camp where no husbands are allowed, moms get a weekend on chore leave. M. Neill. il por *People Weekly* 32:85-6 Jl 3 '89

No Pampers, pampering. J. Gordon. il por *Newsweek* 114:76 Jl 10 '89

SMITH CORONA CORP.

Did Hanson hide bad news? [Smith Corona spinoff] C. Tucher. *Business Week* p27-8 Ag 28 '89

SMITH FAMILY

about

One big, happy family has a grand reunion [Atlantic Highlands, N.J.] J. Ralston. il *McCall's* 116:62+ Jl '89

SMITH-RYLAND, ROBIN

about

Hunt country. G. Nevill. il pors *House & Garden* 161:132-9 Mr '89

SMITHKLINE BECKMAN CORP.

See also

SmithKline Beecham plc

Henry Wendt. J. Weber, Jr. il por *Business Week* Special Issue:151 Ap 14 '89

SmithKline thinks Beecham can cure what ails it. J. Weber, Jr. and M. Maremont. il *Business Week* p22 Ap 17 '89

Will SmithKline succumb to takeover fever? G. G. Marcial. il *Business Week* p86 Ja 23 '89

SMITHKLINE BEECHAM PLC

Genentech: a David that comes on like Goliath [fighting SmithKline Beecham's Eminase] J. Carey and J. O. Hamilton. il *Business Week* p165 O 30 '89

SMITH'S (SAMUEL) (FIRM) See Samuel Smith's (Firm)

SMITHSONIAN (PERIODICAL)

Around the Mall and beyond [graphic artist B. Thompson] E. Park. il *Smithsonian* 20:22-4+ S '89

SMITHSONIAN CENTER FOR ASTROPHYSICS See Harvard-Smithsonian Center for Astrophysics

SMITHSONIAN INSTITUTION

Around the Mall and beyond. E. Park. See issues of Smithsonian

The quest for a black museum. M. S. Holmes. il *American Visions* 4:44-8 D '89

Returning bones of contention [Smithsonian agrees to return Indian remains and burial artifacts] J. Elson. il *Time* 134:61 S 25 '89

Smithsonian horizons. R. M. Adams. See issues of Smithsonian beginning October 1984

Smithsonian, Indian leaders call a truce. E. Marshall. il *Science* 245:1184-6 S 15 '89

SMITHSONIAN INSTITUTION. ARTHUR M. SACKLER GALLERY See Arthur M. Sackler Gallery (Washington, D.C.)

SMITHSONIAN INSTITUTION. CONSERVATION AND RESEARCH CENTER

Playing possum is serious business for our only marsupial; ed. by Susan Lumpkin. J. Seidensticker. bibl (p246) il *Smithsonian* 20:108-12+ N '89

SMITHSONIAN INSTITUTION. COOPER-HEWITT MUSEUM See Cooper-Hewitt Museum

SMITHSONIAN INSTITUTION. ENID A. HAUPT GARDEN See Enid A. Haupt Garden (Washington, D.C.)

SMITHSONIAN INSTITUTION. HIRSHHORN MUSEUM AND SCULPTURE GARDEN See Hirshhorn Museum and Sculpture Garden

SMITHSONIAN INSTITUTION. INFORMATION CENTER

Around the Mall and beyond. E. Park. il *Smithsonian* 20:28+ N '89

SMITHSONIAN INSTITUTION. NATIONAL AIR AND SPACE MUSEUM See National Air and Space Museum

SMITHSONIAN INSTITUTION. NATIONAL MUSEUM OF AMERICAN ART See National Museum of American Art (U.S.)

SMITHSONIAN INSTITUTION. NATIONAL MUSEUM OF AMERICAN HISTORY See National Museum of American History (U.S.)

SMITHSONIAN INSTITUTION. NATIONAL MUSEUM OF THE AMERICAN INDIAN See National Museum of the American Indian (U.S.)

SMITHSONIAN TROPICAL RESEARCH INSTITUTE

The Smithsonian Tropical Research Institute. I. Rubinoff. il *Environment* 31:44-5 Je '89

Tropical forest gardening: an alternative to destruction [Panama] il *The Futurist* 23:53 My/Je '89

SMITROVICH, BILL

about

His father's proudest moment? The day his son got expelled from school. S. Littwin. por *TV Guide* 37:13 D 23-29 '89

SMITTER, LEILA HADLEY See Hadley, Leila

SMM (SOLAR MAXIMUM MISSION) SATELLITE See Artificial satellites—Astronomical use

SMOG

Air quality: unacceptable [cover story] P. Jaret. il *Health (New York, N.Y.)* 21:48-51 Mr '89

Blueprint for clear skies [Los Angeles] M. Cone. il *Sierra* 74:16+ Jl/Ag '89

A drastic plan to banish smog [Los Angeles] P. Elmer-Dewitt. il *Time* 133:65 Mr 27 '89

Getting a clearer view of smog [supercomputer pollution model developed by G. J. McRae] M. Schroeder. il por *Business Week* Special Issue:73 Je 16 '89

Global smog: newest greenhouse projection [research by David Rind] J. Raloff. *Science News* 135:262-3 Ap 29 '89

Leaves of gas [role of hydrocarbons in urban smog in Atlanta, Ga.; research by William Chameides] il *Discover* 10:20 F '89

Summer smog: not just an urban problem [research by Jennifer A. Logan] J. Raloff. *Science News* 136:22 Jl 8 '89

Tackling smog ozone: tougher than thought [Office of Technology Assessment report] I. Wickelgren. *Science News* 136:53 Jl 22 '89

To live and breathe in L.A. J. E. Basu. il maps *American Health* 8:52-4+ S '89

Tree pollution [role of hydrocarbons in urban smog; research by William Chameides] J. W. Merline. il *Consumers' Research Magazine* 72:38 Ja '89

The two faces of ozone. R. Monastersky. il *Science News* 136:154-5 S 2 '89

Why no one's safe [effects of smog on residents in Los Angeles basin] J. E. Basu. maps *American Health* 8:64 S '89

SMOKE, RICHARD

(jt. auth) See Yankelovich, Daniel, and Smoke, Richard

SMOKE

See also

Soot

William Wharton, author of Dad, seeks to avenge his daughter's horrible death [K. Rodewald killed in automobile crash caused by smoke cloud from grass fires in Oregon's Willamette Valley] M. Green. il pors *People Weekly* 32:122-4 N 27 '89

SMOKE, ARTIFICIAL

Cutting through the fog; Safely navigating the haze [fog and smoke machines] M. S. Eddy. il *Theatre Crafts* 23:26+ O '89

SMOKE DETECTORS *See* Fire detectors
SMOKED FISH *See* Fish, Smoked
SMOKED FOOD *See* Food, Smoked
SMOKELESS CIGARETTES
Burn this [Premier cigarettes] D. Blundy. il *Vogue* 179:65 Ja '89
Smokeless cigarettes under fire [can be used to smoke crack] *Science News* 135:30 Ja 14 '89
SMOKELESS TOBACCO
Oral cancer on rise. J. Folkenberg. il *FDA Consumer* 23:24-5 D '89/Ja '90
SMOKESTACK INDUSTRIES *See* Manufacturing industries
SMOKING

> *See also*
> Cigarettes
> No-Tobacco Day
> Passive smoking

The art of quitting smoking. N. Henderson. il *Changing Times* 43:105-6+ O '89
Cancer Board attacks tobacco. B. J. Culliton. *Science* 243:889 F 17 '89
Cancer prevention strategy at the NCI [interview with S. Broder] C. SerVaas. il por *The Saturday Evening Post* 261:50-1+ My/Je '89
Cigarette face—another reason not to smoke. D. R. Reuben. il *Good Housekeeping* 208:70 Mr '89
The downside of smoking tobacco and marijuana. W. Steele. il *Current Health 2* 16:24-6 N '89
Elasticity, it's wonderful [effect of raising cigarette tax] D. Seligman. *Fortune* 119:123-4 F 13 '89
A financial incentive to quit [lower non-smoker insurance rates] il *USA Today (Periodical)* 117:14 Ap '89
Getting opium to the masses: the political economy of addiction [U.S. cigarette exports to Asia] A. Cockburn. il *The Nation* 249:482-3 O 30 '89
The guilt-free guide to a smoke-free life. T. Ferguson. il *Modern Maturity* 32:76-7+ F/Mr '89
Hazardous to whose health? [U.S. cigarette exports] J. Drummond. il *Forbes* 144:89+ D 11 '89
Kicking a deadly habit [Surgeon General's report] G. Cowley. il *Newsweek* 113:60 Ja 23 '89
Lung cancer—the smoking gun. C. Gloeckner. il *Current Health 2* 15:14-15 Mr '89
Nicotine boosts a busy body's metabolism [research by Kenneth A. Perkins] R. Weiss. *Science News* 135:214 Ap 8 '89
A not-so-happy anniversary [Surgeon General's report] A. Toufexis. il *Time* 133:54 Ja 23 '89
Panel steps up cancer war [recommendations of the National Cancer Advisory Board] *Science News* 135:85 F 11 '89
Phenomena, comment and notes [heart attack brought on by smoking] J. P. Wiley, Jr. *Smithsonian* 20:32+ Ap '89
Pictures show smoking's ill effects on DNA [research by Kurt and Erika Randerath] J. Raloff. il *Science News* 135:151 Mr 11 '89
Psyching up to quit. L. Schroepfer. *American Health* 8:46 Jl/Ag '89
Scared smokeless [undergoing bypass surgery] J. E. Brown. il *Reader's Digest* 134:117-21 My '89
Smoker's "high" [may increase cholesterol levels] J. C. Horn. *American Health* 8:16+ Je '89
Smoking 101 [tax level to maximize federal revenues; research by Michael Grossman] D. Seligman. il *Fortune* 119:134 F 27 '89
Smoking and nutrition. J. Scala. il *Dance Magazine* 63:136-7 My '89
Smoking inhibits lung's immune cells [research by Mohan L. Sopori and George M. Shopp] *Science News* 135:255 Ap 22 '89
Smoking out the best way to quit smoking. B. Bower. *Science News* 136:358 D 2 '89
A stroke alert sounds for smokers [Surgeon General's report] il *U.S. News & World Report* 106:9 Ja 23 '89
The tobacco tradition in India. M. B. Aghee. il *World Health* p23 Ja/F '89
Uncle Sam shouldn't be a traveling salesman for tobacco [cigarette exports to Asia] P. Magnusson. il *Business Week* p61 O 9 '89
Warning: sports stars may be hazardous to your health [cigarette ads; cover story] J. DeParle. il *The Washington Monthly* 21:34-44+ S '89

> **Anecdotes, facetiae, satire, etc.**

A born-again nonsmoker. A. Buchwald. por *The Saturday Evening Post* 261:28 Jl/Ag '89
Smoke gets in your eyes. J. Epstein. *The American Scholar* 58:7-10+ Wint '89
Where there's smoke there's ire . . . G. Keillor. il por *American Health* 8:50-3 D '89

> **History**

In the 1800s, antismoking was a burning issue. C. Tate. bibl f (p122) il *Smithsonian* 20:107-8+ Jl '89

> **Laws and regulations**

Big Tobacco's toughest road [activists and lawmakers launch new attacks on smoking] A. Plattner. il map *U.S. News & World Report* 106:26 Ap 17 '89
How would you vote? il *Scholastic Update (Teachers' edition)* 121:17+ F 24 '89

A new tobacco alliance [smoking industry looks to blacks for support] M. Miller. il *Newsweek* 113:20 F 13 '89

> *Canada*

A smoking issue [laws banning Canadian tobacco advertising] P. Chisholm. il *Maclean's* 102:28 Ja 16 '89

> *Canada—Anecdotes, facetiae, satire, etc.*

The dangerous New Puritans. A. Fotheringham. il *Maclean's* 102:80 Ap 10 '89
Smoking out a burning issue. C. Gordon. il *Maclean's* 102:50 F 6 '89

> *Western Europe*

Planning for a smoke-free Europe. il *World Health* p30 Ja/F '89
SMOKING ACCESSORIES

> *See also*
> Tobacco pipes

SMOKING AND BLACKS
Blackstabbers [special interests pursue black vote] R. Blow. *The New Republic* 200:16-18 My 29 '89
A new tobacco alliance [smoking industry looks to blacks for support] M. Miller. il *Newsweek* 113:20 F 13 '89
SMOKING AND EMPLOYMENT

> *Canada*
> *Anecdotes, facetiae, satire, etc.*

Smoking out a burning issue. C. Gordon. il *Maclean's* 102:50 F 6 '89
SMOKING AND THE AGED
Quitting secrets of older smokers. J. Wood. *Modern Maturity* 32:28 Je/Jl '89
SMOKING AND WOMEN
Kicking the habit [stop-smoking program at the Canyon Ranch Spa] H. Sweet. *Vogue* 179:414-15 O '89
More cervical cancer in passive smokers [research by Martha L. Slattery] K. Fackelmann. *Science News* 135:166 Mr 18 '89
Women & smoking. E. Frank. *Vogue* 179:412-13 O '89
Yet another deadly link [cigarette smoke and cervical cancer] *Time* 133:82 Mr 27 '89
SMOKING AND YOUTH
Grandad learns about smoking. M. Matinyi. il *World Health* p25-6 Mr '89
Non-smoking: begin with kids under age 11. il *World Health* p30 D '88
Smoke signals [Doonesbury mocks cigarette ads that entice teens to smoke] P. Theiler. il *Common Cause Magazine* 15:8 S/O '89
Smoking and schools. F. Roberts. *Parents* 64:54 D '89
Smoking: no butts about it! il *Teen* 33:22+ O '89
Taking the pledge. C. SerVaas. il *The Saturday Evening Post* 261:100 Jl/Ag '89
The tragedy of teenage smoking [cancer victim S. Emerson] il pors *The Saturday Evening Post* 261:52 My/Je '89
We are vending addiction to our children [cigarette vending machines] il *The Saturday Evening Post* 261:14 Jl/Ag '89
SMOKING ON AIRPLANES
Clearing the air: resolving the aircraft ventilation controversy. H. Gieseking. il *Travel Holiday* 172:14-15 N '89
Cruel & unusual punishment. W. F. Buckley. *National Review* 41:62-3 O 27 '89
Quit stalling on the smoking ban. *Aviation Week & Space Technology* 131:11 S 18 '89
Ten-year lobbying effort results in smoking ban on most U.S. flights. *Aviation Week & Space Technology* 131:71 O 23 '89
SMOKY MOUNTAINS NATIONAL PARK (N.C. AND TENN.) *See* Great Smoky Mountains National Park (N.C. and Tenn.)
SMOLER, FREDRIC PAUL
The secret of the soldiers who didn't shoot. il pors *American Heritage* 40:5, 36-45 Mr '89
SMOLICH, TOM

> *about*

A: The Jeopardy! priest; Q: Who is Tom Smolich? Correct for $39,802! il pors *People Weekly* 32:58 O 9 '89
SMOLLA, RODNEY A.
Why does libel law need reform? *Society* 26:67-70 Jl/Ag '89
SMOLYANSKY, MIKE

> *about*

Liquid gold. M. Barrier. il por *Nation's Business* 77:14 Jl '89
SMOOT, OLIVER R.

> *about*

With a campus legend in peril, members of a fraternity vow to save the endangered M.I.T. smoot. N. Geeslin. il pors *People Weekly* 31:93-5 Ap 24 '89
SMOOTH MUSCLE *See* Muscle
SMOTHERS, DICK

> *about*

The Smothers Brothers: a new life for the old team. J. Wolf. il pors *McCall's* 116:103+ My '89
SMOTHERS, TOM

> *about*

The Smothers Brothers: a new life for the old team. J. Wolf. il pors *McCall's* 116:103+ My '89
Tom Smothers' flick of the wrist. F. Lovece. il pors *Video* 12:14 Mr '89

SMPS *See* Society for Marketing Professional Services
SMUCKER (J. M.) CO. *See* J. M. Smucker Co.
SMUCKLER, RALPH, AND SOMMERS, LAWRENCE M.
Internationalizing college curriculum. *The Education Digest* 54:43-7 Mr '89
SMUGGLING
       See also
    Narcotics trade
Off the record [Cuban-Palestinian arms smuggling network] *National Review* 41:18 F 24 '89
Running guns up the interstate. R. Lacayo. *Time* 133:24 F 6 '89
SMULYAN, JEFFREY
       about
If the Mariners don't shape up, they may get shipped out. W. C. Symonds. il por *Business Week* p36 S 11 '89
SMYTH, FRANK
El Salvador: behind the lines with the rebels. il *The Progressive* 53:26-9 F '89
Negotiations or total war. il *The Nation* 249:164-6 Ag 7-14 '89
SMYTH, HENRY DEWOLF, 1898-1986
       about
Obituary
    Physics Today por 42:96+ My '89. R. H. Dicke and others
SNACKS
       See also
    Corn chips
Appetizing alternatives. il *The Saturday Evening Post* 261:16 N/D '89
Backyard snacks. il *Better Homes and Gardens* 67:128-9+ Jl '89
Calorie-crunching snacks. H. A. Dorrough. il *Southern Living* 24:122+ Ja '89
Cookbook for kids: snack attack! il *Redbook* 173:70+ S '89
Fast snacks [microwaving] il *Southern Living* 24:168 My '89
The 'grazing' of America: a guide to healthy snacking [cover story] C. P. Weinstock. il *FDA Consumer* 23:8-13 Mr '89
Microwave snacks. il *Better Homes and Gardens* 67:159-60 S '89
Microwave snacks for kids. M. Cone and T. Snyder. il *Working Woman* 14:224 S '89
Snack-attack cookbook. il *Ladies' Home Journal* 106:163-4+ F '89
Summer snacks for kids [microwaving] il *McCall's* 116:129 Jl '89
       Labeling
Seal of approval [dentists' endorsements for snacks safe for teeth] C. Sears. il *American Health* 8:55 Mr '89
SNADOWSKY, STANLEY
       about
Rock of ages. E. Hollreiser. il pors *New York* 22:29 F 6 '89
SNAIL FEVER *See* Schistosomiasis
SNAILS
       See also
    Slugs
       Control
Africa's 'wonder weed' [use of endod] il *The Unesco Courier* 42:48-9 Jl '89
       Diseases and pests
Mollusks in midstream [study of snails in Zimbabwe] M. Woolhouse. il *Natural History* p6+ Mr '89
SNAKE HANDLING (HOLINESS CHURCHES)
Courting death, Appalachia's old-time religionists praise the Lord and pass the snakes [snake handlers in Jolo, W. Va.] D. Grogan. il pors *People Weekly* 31:79+ My 1 '89
SNAKE VENOM
       Therapeutic use
Viper venom for stroke. il *Prevention (Emmaus, Pa.)* 41:16+ My '89
SNAKES
       See also
    Herpetologists
    Pythons
    Rattlesnakes
Cold-blooded killers [Guam's birds eaten by brown tree snakes] *Discover* 10:16 Ag '89
The far side of paradise [brown tree snakes on Guam] il *U.S. News & World Report* 106:15 F 13 '89
Garter snakes yield sexual chemistry [research by Robert T. Mason] B. Bower. *Science News* 136:55 Jl 22 '89
Pulmonary blood flow regulation in an aquatic snake [diving by Acrochordus granulatus] H. B. Lillywhite and J. A. Donald. bibl f il *Science* 245:293-5 Jl 21 '89
Sex pheromones in snakes [garter snakes] R. T. Mason and others. bibl f il *Science* 245:290-3 Jl 21 '89
       Food and feeding
Nature's way [snake eating a frog] M. Gadomski. il *The Conservationist* 43:56 My/Je '89
SNAKES IN RELIGION, FOLKLORE, ETC.
       See also
    Snake handling (Holiness churches)

SNAPPERS
The unsung hero of the flats [mutton snappers] A. J. McClane. il *Field & Stream* 94:34+ Jl '89
SNCC *See* Student Nonviolent Coordinating Committee
SNEAKERS *See* Footwear
SNEAKERS, RUNNING *See* Running shoes
SNEAKERS, TENNIS *See* Tennis shoes
SNECMA
Snecma to deliver Atar 9K50 powerplants for use in prototypes of upgraded Kfir. il *Aviation Week & Space Technology* 131:19 O 30 '89
SNEDEN, CHRISTOPHER
Reading the colors of the stars. il *Astronomy* 17:36-45 Ap '89
SNEEZING
The anatomy of a sneeze. T. Yulsman. il *American Health* 8:16 My '89
SNEIDER, DANIEL
One hand clapping. il *The New Republic* 201:16-17 N 20 '89
SNELL, HILARY E.
(jt. auth) *See* Frederick, John E., and Snell, Hilary E.
SNELLVILLE (GA.)
       Synagogues
Anti-Semitism in Atlanta [construction of synagogue] *The Christian Century* 106:808 S 13-20 '89
SNIDER, EDWARD MALCOLM
       about
From calamity to conglomerate. G. Macnow. il por *Nation's Business* 77:48-50+ My '89
SNIPE SHOOTING
       Anecdotes, facetiae, satire, etc.
How to shoot snipe (I). E. Zern. il *Field & Stream* 94:144 My '89
SNIPES
Never snicker at a snipe. D. H. Chadwick. il *National Wildlife* 27:12-15 Ag/S '89
SNN *See* Sports News Network (Cable television)
SNOBS AND SNOBBISHNESS
A partiality for lords: Evelyn Waugh and snobbery. D. J. Greene. *The American Scholar* 58:444-5+ Summ '89
Who's a snob and who's not. J. M. Fallows. *The Washington Monthly* 21:34+ F '89
SNODGRASS, MARY ELLEN
Growing up Baptist. il *Ms.* 17:66-7 Mr '89
SNOOPS [television program] *See* Television program reviews—Single works
SNORING
9 bed-tested snore stoppers. P. J. Donahue. il *Prevention (Emmaus, Pa.)* 41:60-4 Mr '89
Facts on snoring: A to ZZZ. C. Schaeffer. il *Changing Times* 43:94 F '89
Fed up with snoring? Here's help! L. Weber. il *Good Housekeeping* 208:169 F '89
Snoring: getting it under control. il *Glamour* 87:306+ Mr '89
Snoring: the midnight serenade. E. Kiester. il *New Choices for the Best Years* 29:67 Ja '89
SNORKELING *See* Skin diving
SNOW, CLYDE, AND OTHERS
Scientists as detectives: investigating human rights. il *Technology Review* 92:42-9+ F/Mr '89
SNOW, PHOEBE
       about
Phoebe Snow drifts back. S. Rogers. por *Rolling Stone* p28 My 18 '89
The real Phoebe Snow. A. Nash. por *Stereo Review* 54:84 Jl '89
Throwing in the crying towel. J. Cocks. il por *Time* 133:74 My 1 '89
SNOW, RICHARD F.
Collecting history. il *American Heritage* 40:34-6+ Ap '89
SNOW
       See also
    Avalanches
    Color of snow and ice
    Snowstorms
Fallen snow. S. Curtis. il *Field & Stream* 94:28 D '89
First snow [father and infant daughter] J. Nicholas. il *Reader's Digest* 135:7-8 D '89
The land of lavish snow [Keweenaw Peninsula] K. Walters. il map *Country Journal* 16:56-9 F '89
Notes and comment [snow falling on sculptures in the garden at the Museum of Modern Art] *The New Yorker* 64:23-4 Ja 23 '89
Snow: a spotty season [1987-1988] D. M. Ludlum. il *Weatherwise* 42:38-41 F '89
SNOW AND ICE CLIMBING
       See also
    Airplanes in snow and ice climbing
Summer snow [special section] il *Sierra* 74:56-61 My/Je '89
SNOW AND ICE REMOVAL
       See also
    Airports—Snow and ice removal
    Snow shoveling
SNOW AVIATION INTERNATIONAL, INC.
Snow Aviation is developing short takeoff, landing aircraft. il *Aviation Week & Space Technology* 130:115 F 20 '89

SNOW BLOWERS, THROWERS, ETC.
7 snow stoppers. B. Markovich. il *Home Mechanix* 85:112-13 N '89
Snow machines [Simplicity 870 ST and Toro Power Curve 1800] S. Willson. il *Popular Mechanics* 166:87 D '89
Snow throwers. il *Consumer Reports* 54:659-63 O '89
Snow throwers. il *Consumer Reports* 54:375-80 D '89

SNOW CRYSTALS
Snow clones [identical crystals found by Nancy Knight] S. Vogel. il *Discover* 10:52-4 F '89

SNOW DEVILS
Snow devils and contrails. T. Schlatter. *Weatherwise* 42:48-9 F '89

SNOW DOMES
Collectors and collecting
Snow domes. H. R. Biederman. il *Antiques & Collecting Hobbies* 93:28-31 Ja '89

SNOW ECOLOGY
Snow season survivors. K. Fadiman. il *Sierra* 74:158-9 Ja/F '89
Surviving and thriving—plants and animals in winter. P. S. Busch. il *The Conservationist* 43:26-33 Ja/F '89

SNOW FENCES
Harvest the snow. B. Eftink. il *Successful Farming* 87:60 F '89

SNOW GEESE *See* Geese, Wild
SNOW LEOPARDS *See* Leopards
SNOW MONKEYS *See* Macaques

SNOW REMOVAL EQUIPMENT
See also
Snow blowers, throwers, etc.

SNOW SHOVELING
Warm up before shoveling out [reducing heart stress; views of Dan Fintel] *Prevention (Emmaus, Pa.)* 41:12+ D '89

SNOW SLIDES *See* Avalanches
SNOW STORMS *See* Snowstorms
SNOW THROWERS *See* Snow blowers, throwers, etc.
SNOW TIRES *See* Tires, Automobile
SNOW TRAILS (ANIMAL TRACKS) *See* Animal tracks and trails

SNOW WHITE (FICTIONAL CHARACTER)
Mondrian in Disneyland. E. Hoek. bibl f il *Art in America* 77:136-43+ F '89

SNOWBALL, EMMA
about
Eyes on Emma. il pors *Seventeen* 48:148-9 O '89

SNOWBIRD (UTAH: RESORT) *See* Resorts—Utah

SNOWBIRDS (FLIGHT SQUADRON)
Two Canadian Snowbirds crash into Lake Ontario. *Aviation Week & Space Technology* 131:34 S 11 '89

SNOWBOARDING
Getting on board. C. Cooper. il *Skiing* 42:25-6 S '89
Hanging ten on the ski slopes. R. Duffy. il *Business Week* p106 F 13 '89
Jake and the Rad Man [J. Burton and B. LaMar] D. White. il pors *Skiing* 42:238-40+ D '89
Photographs and photography
Cowabunga! Snowboarding [cover story] M. Epstein. il *Petersen's Photographic Magazine* 17:22-6 F '89

SNOWBOARDS
See also
Burton Snowboards (Firm)
How they ride. B. Glenne. il *Skiing* 41:62-4+ Ja '89
Snowboards. D. White. il *Skiing* 42:168-70+ S '89
Maintenance and repair
Snowboard maintenance. J. Deines. il *Skiing* 41:76-7 F '89

SNOWDEN, LYNN
Night life lives. il *Mademoiselle* 95:242-7+ Ap '89
Victoria's secret. il por *House & Garden* 161:188-91+ My '89

SNOWFALL *See* Snow
SNOWFLAKES *See* Snow crystals

SNOWMAN, BOB
Nitty gritty posterization. il *Petersen's Photographic Magazine* 17:42-5+ Ja '89

SNOWMOBILES AND SNOWMOBILING
Environmental aspects
Teton, Yellowstone snowmobile issue [proposed trail] il *National Parks* 63:9-10 My/Je '89
Testing
Snowbusters. C. Plueddeman. il *Popular Mechanics* 166:64-7 D '89
Wyoming
Trailblazing Wyoming's white-open spaces. J. Skorupa. il *Popular Mechanics* 166:44 D '89

SNOWSHOES AND SNOWSHOEING
Shoeing through the snow. J. Nelson. il *American Health* 8:36 D '89

SNOWSLIDES *See* Avalanches

SNOWSTORMS
See also
Fishing—Storm conditions
Snow devils
Notes and comment [waiting for a snowstorm in New York City] *The New Yorker* 65:26-7 Mr 13 '89

SNUFFBOXES, BOTTLES, ETC.
Snuff bottles. G. Michael. il *Antiques & Collecting Hobbies* 94:62 S '89

SNYDER, FRAN
Beyond calcium. il *Parents* 64:224+ My '89
Pneumonia: everything you must know. *Ladies' Home Journal* 106:94+ Ja '89

SNYDER, GARY
The etiquette of freedom. il *Sierra* 74:74-7+ S/O '89

SNYDER, JIMMY THE GREEK *See* Jimmy the Greek

SNYDER, RICH
about
Where Bob Hope buys his burgers. E. Paris. il por *Forbes* 144:46+ Jl 24 '89

SNYDER, THELMA
(jt. auth) *See* Cone, Marcia, and Snyder, Thelma

SNYDER, TOM
about
Putting parents in the loop with kids and computers [interview] K. Kane. il por *Home Office Computing* 7:80+ Mr '89

SNYDER (TOM) PRODUCTIONS *See* Tom Snyder Productions

SOAP
Surprising chemistry in the shower [mixture of shampoo and soap lathers releases ammonia] il *Consumer Reports* 54:610 O '89
Photographs and photography
Pure light: deciding when and if the client is "always right". J. Fruchtman. il *Petersen's Photographic Magazine* 18:52-3 Je '89

SOAP BOX DERBIES
Matt's biggest race [epileptic M. Margules wins the All-American Soap Box Derby] S. L. Englebardt. il pors *Reader's Digest* 135:53-8 Jl '89

SOAP BUBBLES AND FILMS
Foam Day! [Westwood, Mass.] il *National Geographic World* 165:4-7 My '89
Frothy physics [cover story] F. Flam. il *Science News* 136:72-3+ Jl 29 '89
Why are the first few puffs the hardest when you blow up a balloon? J. Walker. bibl il *Scientific American* 261:136-9 D '89
Photographs and photography
Bubbles can be beautiful. J. Maxymuik. il *Popular Photography* 96:60-1 Je '89

SOAP INDUSTRY
See also
Colgate-Palmolive Co. (Delaware)
Lever Brothers Company
Minnetonka Inc.
Neutrogena Corp.
Procter & Gamble Co.
Soviet Union
Why there is no soap. C. Bogert. il *Newsweek* 114:46-7 D 4 '89

SOAP OPERAS *See* Television serials
SOARING (AVIATION) *See* Hang gliding

SOBEL, DAVA
Dr. Zodiac. il pors *Omni (New York, N.Y.)* 12:60-2+ D '89
Face to face with the new me. il *The New York Times Magazine* p26+ Ap 9 '89
Melanoma. il *Good Housekeeping* 209:86+ Jl '89
On leaving. il *Ladies' Home Journal* 106:54+ Je '89
Rejuvenation vacation. *Health (New York, N.Y.)* 21:68-9+ O '89
Serious face-saving. il *Health (New York, N.Y.)* 21:64-5+ O '89
Sex grows up. il *Health (New York, N.Y.)* 21:76 O '89
Social phobia. il *The New York Times Magazine* p24-5 Ja 1 '89
The way we were. il *Ladies' Home Journal* 106:82 S '89

SOBEL, DAVA, AND KLEIN, ARTHUR C.
Arthritis: what works [excerpt] il *Good Housekeeping* 209:138-9+ O '89

SOBEL, DAVID S. (DAVID STUART)
(jt. auth) *See* Ornstein, Robert E. (Robert Evan), 1942-, and Sobel, David S. (David Stuart)

SOBERING COMPOUNDS *See* Alcohol antagonists

SOBEYS STORES, LTD.
Barking about a budget [charges that Sobeys obtained advance information on Nova Scotia budget] G. Allen. il *Maclean's* 102:21 My 22 '89

SOBOL, JOSHUA
about
A conversation with Israeli playwright Joshua Sobol. G. Seibert. *America* 160:559-62 Je 10 '89
Ghetto [drama] Reviews
America 160:536 Je 3 '89. G. G. Seibert
America 160:559-62 Je 10 '89. G. G. Seibert
Commonweal 116:370-1 Je 16 '89. G. C. Weales
New York il 22:123-4 My 15 '89. J. Simon

SOBRAN, JOSEPH
Mussolini shrugged. *National Review* 41:52-3 Ja 27 '89
A nation of loners. il *National Review* 41:28-9 S 1 '89
Stony Rolls. il *National Review* 41:55-6 O 27 '89

SOBRINO, JON
Death in El Salvador. il *Commonweal* 116:693-5 D 15 '89

SOCATA
China uses Trinidad TB-20s to replace aging Y-5 biplanes in pilot training. il *Aviation Week & Space Technology* 131:97 Ag 21 '89
Socata, Mooney proceed with TBM 700 production. J. M. Lenorovitz. il *Aviation Week & Space Technology* 130:53-4 Je 26 '89
Tobago from Tarbes [Aerospatiale Tobago; cover story] W. Garvey. il *Flying* 116:30-2+ Mr '89

SOCCER
See also
    Foot tennis
World soccer prodigy: the U.S. V. Rosas. il *World Press Review* 36:92 O '89
Photographs and photography
Shooting soccer strategies. B. Fox. il *Petersen's Photographic Magazine* 18:38-40+ S '89
Tournaments
America's teen [T. Haskins of U.S. under-16 national team] C. Gammon. il pors *Sports Illustrated* 70:68-9+ Je 12 '89
World Cup
America to world: Sock it to us [U.S. qualifies for 1990 competition in Italy] il *U.S. News & World Report* 107:15 D 4 '89
Huge move, Hugo [H. Perez's goal propels U.S. past El Salvador] C. Gammon. il por *Sports Illustrated* 71:22-3 S 25 '89
It's a real kick [U.S. team] C. Gammon. il *Sports Illustrated* 70:64+ Ap 17 '89
Safe at home on a close call [U.S. vs. Costa Rica in qualifying game] C. Gammon. il *Sports Illustrated* 70:89+ My 8 '89
To Italy, feet first [U.S. team] C. Isenhart. il *Sport (New York, N.Y.)* 80:105-8 O '89
A way was found [U.S. defeats Trinidad & Tobago to reach World Cup finals] C. Gammon. il *Sports Illustrated* 71:22-3 N 27 '89
Will the U.S. be ready for its own World Cup? [views of Anson Dorrance] P. Gambaccini. il *Sport (New York, N.Y.)* 80:19 F '89
Germany (West)
Greener fields [coach G. Knappertsbusch] C. Joritz. il por *Women's Sports & Fitness* 11:58-9 N/D '89

SOCCER, COLLEGE
A glue-fingered U.S. goalie keeps opponents' net profits to zero [University of Virginia's T. Meola] R. Arias. il pors *People Weekly* 32:105-6 D 18 '89
Tournaments
Not just for kicks [Santa Clara and Virginia tie in NCAA championship game] C. Gammon. il *Sports Illustrated* 71:96 D 11 '89

SOCCER, PROFESSIONAL
Crowd control
Anger, then death [fans crushed in Sheffield, England] C. Gammon. il *Sports Illustrated* 70:24-5 Ap 24 '89
Death in the stands [Sheffield, England] A. Phillips. il *Maclean's* 102:24 Ap 24 '89
A death trap in Sheffield [soccer stadium disaster in England] R. Watson. il *Newsweek* 113:54 Ap 24 '89
The press of the crowd, the license of the loner [soccer crowd stampede in Sheffield, England] T. Moore. il *U.S. News & World Report* 106:12-13 My 1 '89
A survivor of the Sheffield soccer disaster struggles to live with the memory [C. Parsonage] D. Grogan. il por *People Weekly* 31:69-70 My 8 '89
Ethical aspects
Barring hooligans [British plan] A. Phillips. il *Maclean's* 102:52 F 6 '89
British soccer: the deadly game. L. Hazleton. il *The New York Times Magazine* p40-1+ My 7 '89
Great Britain
Anger, then death [fans crushed in Sheffield, England] C. Gammon. il *Sports Illustrated* 70:24-5 Ap 24 '89
Barring hooligans. A. Phillips. il *Maclean's* 102:52 F 6 '89
British soccer: the deadly game. L. Hazleton. il *The New York Times Magazine* p40-1+ My 7 '89
Death in the stands [Sheffield] A. Phillips. il *Maclean's* 102:24 Ap 24 '89
A death trap in Sheffield [soccer stadium disaster] R. Watson. il *Newsweek* 113:54 Ap 24 '89
The press of the crowd, the license of the loner [soccer crowd stampede in Sheffield] T. Moore. il *U.S. News & World Report* 106:12-13 My 1 '89
A survivor of the Sheffield soccer disaster struggles to live with the memory [C. Parsonage] D. Grogan. il por *People Weekly* 31:69-70 My 8 '89

SOCCER COACHES
See also
    Knappertsbusch, Gerda
SOCCER FANS
Anger, then death [fans crushed in Sheffield, England] C. Gammon. il *Sports Illustrated* 70:24-5 Ap 24 '89
Barring hooligans [British plan] A. Phillips. il *Maclean's* 102:52 F 6 '89
British soccer: the deadly game. L. Hazleton. il *The New York Times Magazine* p40-1+ My 7 '89

Death in the stands [Sheffield, England] A. Phillips. il *Maclean's* 102:24 Ap 24 '89
A death trap in Sheffield [soccer stadium disaster in England] R. Watson. il *Newsweek* 113:54 Ap 24 '89
The press of the crowd, the license of the loner [soccer crowd stampede in Sheffield, England] T. Moore. il *U.S. News & World Report* 106:12-13 My 1 '89
A survivor of the Sheffield soccer disaster struggles to live with the memory [C. Parsonage] D. Grogan. il por *People Weekly* 31:69-70 My 8 '89
SOCCER PLAYERS
See also
    Byrne, Beth
    Haskins, Todd
    Meola, Tony
    Perez, Hugo
SOCCER VIDEO GAMES *See* Video games
SOCHOCKY, ANNA, AND SIEGNER, CATHERINE
Citizens organize against neo-Nazis. il por *The Progressive* 53:15 Ag '89
SOCIAL ACTION
See also
    Church and social problems
    Giraffe Project
All they are sayin' is give pigs a chance [cities taking up social causes] *U.S. News & World Report* 106:15 Je 19 '89
Fighting back. R. Grover. il *Business Week* p34-5 My 22 '89
Framing the public agenda [address, September 29, 1988] R. D. Pagán, Jr. *Vital Speeches of the Day* 55:177-80 Ja 1 '89
Liberalism's future may depend on social movements. M. E. Leary. *Utne Reader* p74 Mr/Ap '89
Listen here, Mr. Big! [emphasis on corporate responsibility by consumers] C. Gorman. il *Time* 134:40-1 Jl 3 '89
Moving to greener pastures [ecological consciousness infusing social movements] B. Ahlberg. il *Utne Reader* p10-11 Mr/Ap '89
A new era of activism: who will frame the agenda? R. D. Pagán, Jr. il por *The Futurist* 23:12-16 My/Je '89
Scorned but not defeated. F. Butler. il *The Progressive* 53:50 Je '89
Self-fulfillment through service to others. T. Malone. *The Humanist* 49:24+ Ja/F '89
Social commitment: beyond self-interest. R. H. Frank. *Current (Washington, D.C.)* 316:4-13 O '89
SOCIAL ACTIVISM *See* Social action
SOCIAL AGENCIES
Cooperation
See also
    AIDS ARMS Network
SOCIAL ANXIETY
Social anxiety. L. B. Morris. il *Health (New York, N.Y.)* 21:50-1+ S '89
SOCIAL BEHAVIOR OF ANIMALS *See* Animals—Habits and behavior
SOCIAL BEHAVIOR OF INSECTS *See* Insects—Habits and behavior
SOCIAL CENTERS *See* Community centers
SOCIAL CHANGE
See also
    Acculturation
    Social mobility
Creativity in turbulent times. B. I. Page and R. Theobald. il pors *The Futurist* 23:25-8 S/O '89
Facing transformation: the great American house move. W. E. Halal. *The Futurist* 23:60 S/O '89
Reactionary rhetoric. A. O. Hirschman. il *The Atlantic* 263:63-6+ My '89
SOCIAL CLASSES
See also
    Caste
    Elite (Social sciences)
    Labor
    Middle classes
    Poor
    Underclass
    Upper classes
Social class in the Oval Office [discussion of September/October 1988 article] E. D. Baltzell and H. G. Schneiderman. *Society* 26:10-15 Mr/Ap '89
Social class in the workplace: the United States versus Japan [study by Keiko Nakao] *Society* 26:2 Ja/F '89
Waiting for a taxi [adaptation of address, April 1989] J. Jordan. il *The Progressive* 53:16-18 Je '89
Great Britain
Just you move over, 'Enry 'Iggins [changes in the class system attributed to M. Thatcher's economic reforms] R. Knight. il *U.S. News & World Report* 106:40 Ap 24 '89
Japan
Social class in the workplace: the United States versus Japan [study by Keiko Nakao] *Society* 26:2 Ja/F '89

SOCIAL CLASSES—*cont.*
United States
See Social classes
SOCIAL CLIMBING See Social mobility
SOCIAL CONDITIONS
See also
Civilization
Peace
Quality of life
Social problems
Women—Social conditions
See also subhead Social conditions under names
of countries, states, cities, etc.
As the last decade of the twentieth century approaches .
. . [excerpts from Report on the world social situation]
il *UN Chronicle* 26:74-5 Je '89
SOCIAL CREDIT PARTY (B.C.)
A New Democrat sweep [byelections] H. Quinn. il *Maclean's*
102:14 Mr 27 '89
A picture of unity: William Vander Zalm survives a show-
down. P. Kopvillem. il por *Maclean's* 102:27 O 16 '89
Vander Zalm besieged [cabinet resignation and byelection
loss in Cariboo] B. Bergman. il por *Maclean's* 102:26-7
O 2 '89
SOCIAL DEMOCRACY See Socialism
SOCIAL DEVELOPMENT COMMISSION (UNITED
NATIONS) See United Nations. Commission for Social
Development
SOCIAL DEVELOPMENT OF CHILDREN See Children—
Growth and development
SOCIAL DISEASES See Sexually transmitted diseases
SOCIAL DRINKING See Drinking customs
SOCIAL ECOLOGY See Human ecology
SOCIAL EDUCATION
See also
Family education
Moral education
Peace studies
Political science—Study and teaching
Social sciences—Study and teaching
"Mommy, are homeless people bad?". J. G. Fitzpatrick.
il *Parents* 64:95-8+ F '89
Raising kids who care. A. Kohn. il *Ladies' Home Journal*
106:112 D '89
SOCIAL EVOLUTION See Social change
SOCIAL FORECASTING
Changing values: the new emphasis on self-actualization [cover
story] J. T. Plummer. il por *The Futurist* 23:8-13 Ja/F
'89
How the next decade will differ [special section] il *Business
Week* p142-5+ S 25 '89
How to get the jump on the next ten years. M. J. Cetron
and O. Davies. il *Glamour* 87:252-7+ O '89
Measures of change. il *U.S. News & World Report* 107:66-7
D 25 '89-Ja 1 '90
On surviving the day after tomorrow. H. M. Hodges, Jr.
The Humanist 49:25-9+ My/Je '89
Selecting priorities for a positive future. A. Tough. il *The
Futurist* 23:59 Mr/Ap '89
The twentieth century and beyond [address, May 8, 1989]
P. W. Williams. *Vital Speeches of the Day* 55:624-6 Ag
1 '89
We are the world. il *Life* 12:74-8+ F '89
SOCIAL GOSPEL
Rauschenbusch today: the legacy of a loving prophet [cover
story] M. L. Stackhouse. *The Christian Century* 106:75-8
Ja 25 '89
SOCIAL HISTORY
See also
Alabama—Social history
Atlanta (Ga.)—Social history
Cooperstown (N.Y.)—Social history
Fort Wayne (Ind.)—Social history
Ireland—Social history
Mclean (Va.)—Social history
Mogadishu (Somalia)—Social history
Muncie (Ind.)—Social history
Paris (France)—Social history
Singapore—Social history
SOCIAL INSURANCE See Social security
SOCIAL INTERACTION
The hug factor [effect of close relationships upon health
and longevity] J. Hooper. il *Health (New York, N.Y.)*
21:72-5 O '89
The ties that heal: how family and friends keep you healthy.
B. Justice. il *Better Homes and Gardens* 67:48+ N '89
Why lovers live longer [effect of close relationships upon
health] L. Moll. il *Mademoiselle* 95:132+ My '89
SOCIAL ISOLATION
See also
Alienation (Social psychology)
Loneliness
Ace in the hole Stefania Follini never caved in [spends
130 days isolated in cave in New Mexico] T. Allis. il
por *People Weekly* 31:52-3 Je 12 '89
A cave dweller's chronicle: fifty-six days and counting [inter-
view with S. Follini] A. R. Oberg. il *Omni (New York,
N.Y.)* 11:50-2+ Je '89

Notes from the underground [S. Follini emerges from New
Mexico cave, ending isolation experiment] S. Begley. il
pors *Newsweek* 113:64 Je 5 '89
Stefania Follini goes down under. L. Morgan. il *Seventeen*
48:34 D '89
The times of your life [effects of long term isolation studied
by S. Follini in New Mexico cave] A. Toufexis. il por
Time 133:66-7 Je 5 '89
Voluntary solitary [S. Follini spends eighteen weeks in New
Mexico cave] M. Heenan. il por *Ad Astra* 1:35 O '89
SOCIAL JUSTICE See Justice
SOCIAL MARKETING See Marketing—Social aspects
SOCIAL MOBILITY
Can your kid become president? M. Magnet. il *Fortune*
119:271+ Je 5 '89
Climbing Mt. Manhattan [new money vs. old money] J.
Kramer. il *House & Garden* 161:188-9+ O '89
SOCIAL NORM
What's normal? J. P. Comer. il *Parents* 64:132 Ja '89
SOCIAL PLANNING See Social policy
SOCIAL POLICY
See also
United States—Social policy
OECD social ministers focus on rising pension, health costs.
M. Brodsky. bibl f *Monthly Labor Review* 112:47-8 F
'89
SOCIAL PRESTIGE See Prestige
SOCIAL PROBLEMS
See also
Alcoholics and alcoholism
Church and social problems
Cost and standard of living
Crime and criminals
Discrimination
Divorce
Drug abuse
Family
Family size
Homeless
Illegitimacy
Juvenile delinquents and delinquency
Migrant labor
Poor
Prejudice
Prostitution
School and social and economic problems
Social action
Social work
Save the planet [cover story; special section] il *Omni (New
York, N.Y.)* 11:34-6+ S '89
SOCIAL PROGRESS See Social change
SOCIAL PSYCHOLOGY
See also
Alienation (Social psychology)
Behavior (Psychology)
Competition (Psychology)
Empathy
Ethnopsychology
Family
Helping behavior
Human relations
Leadership
Morale, National
NIMBY syndrome
Political psychology
Prestige
Prison psychology
Public opinion
Stereotype (Psychology)
Stigma (Social psychology)
Violence
SOCIAL REFORM See Social problems
SOCIAL RESEARCH See Social science research
SOCIAL REVOLUTION
See also
Counterculture
SOCIAL ROLE
See also
Role models
Sex role
SOCIAL SCIENCE RESEARCH
See also
New School for Social Research (New York, N.Y.)
Counting trees as the forest burns: why the experts have
been slow to respond to the crack epidemic. il *Newsweek*
114:26-8 S 11 '89
Deconstructing the social sciences [special section] *Society*
26:49-66 Jl/Ag '89
Street-wise crack research. C. Holden. il *Science* 246:1376-81
D 15 '89
Arctic regions
Environment, culture, and change in the Arctic [National
Academy of Sciences outlines research] C. Holden. map
Science 243:883 F 17 '89
Soviet Union
Liberating Soviet social science. P. C. Stern and J. Husbands.
il *The Bulletin of the Atomic Scientists* 45:28-31 S '89

SOCIAL SCIENCES
See also
Economics
Pluralism (Social sciences)
Policy sciences
Political science
Power (Social sciences)
Sociology
Research
See Social science research
Study and teaching
See also
Intercultural education
Helping students use leisure time effectively. W. W. Crowder. *The Education Digest* 55:54-6 N '89
Social studies in elementary education [report of the National Council for the Social Studies] *The Education Digest* 54:25-8 My '89

SOCIAL SECURITY
See also
National Committee to Preserve Social Security and Medicare
Another catastrophe. D. Seligman. il *Fortune* 120:216 N 6 '89
Autonomy for social security? S. B. Garland. *Business Week* p70 O 23 '89
Gwendolyn King is first black social security chief. il por *Jet* 76:4 Ag 21 '89
The notchies march on. B. Rosenblatt. il *New Choices for the Best Years* 29:12 F '89
Paying to work [report from National Center for Policy Analysis] J. W. Merline. il *Consumers' Research Magazine* 72:38 Ag '89
Smokers may be keeping social security healthy . . . but pricier smokes and drinks may still make economic sense. G. Koretz. il *Business Week* p27 Je 5 '89
Social security. M. Hodge. il *New Choices for the Best Years* 29:49-52 Je '89
Social security bridges income gap. *Society* 26:2 My/Je '89
Social security should benefit only the elderly poor. G. S. Becker. il *Business Week* p20 Ja 16 '89
Social security: the bottom line. E. Giltenan. il *Forbes* 143:96 Ja 23 '89
Some groups are raising funds by raising fears about social security and Medicare. M. C. Paulson. il *Changing Times* 43:124-6 D '89
Watch what you call welfare. M. Kaus. *The Washington Monthly* 21:45-6 Mr '89
Taxation
Are you overpaying social security? P. N. Strassels. il *Nation's Business* 77:63 Jl '89
A long-term solution for social security. J. A. Schnepper. il *USA Today (Periodical)* 117:69 Mr '89
This social security tax hike would actually lose money. H. Gleckman. il *Business Week* p25-6 Ag 7 '89
Canada
Taxing back the pension. T. Tedesco. il *Maclean's* 102:18 My 8 '89
France
The fine feathered nest—'la protection sociale'. C. Newman. il *National Geographic* 176:130-1 Jl '89
United States
See Social security
SOCIAL SECURITY TAXES See Social security—Taxation
SOCIAL STATUS
See also
Prestige
School children—Social and economic status
Social classes
Social mobility
Taste, class, and Mary Tyler Moore. S. Lessard. *The Washington Monthly* 21:33-4 F '89
SOCIAL STRATIFICATION See Social classes
SOCIAL STUDIES See Social sciences
SOCIAL VALUES See Values
SOCIAL WELFARE See Economic assistance, Domestic; Public welfare
SOCIAL WORK
See also
Crisis intervention
Public welfare
Social action
Social workers
Fees
Freud, efficiency and pragmatism [human service fee policy] P. M. Shields. bibl *Society* 26:67-72 Ja/F '89
Minnesota
See also
Saint Cloud (Minn.)—Social work
New York (State)
See also
Bronx (New York, N.Y.)—Social work
New York (N.Y.)—Social work
Pennsylvania
See also
Philadelphia (Pa.)—Social work

South Dakota
See also
Rapid City (S.D.)—Social work
Utah
See also
Salt Lake County (Utah)—Social work
Wisconsin
See also
Project Self-Help and Awareness
SOCIAL WORK WITH YOUTH
See also
Mothers Against Gangs (Organization)
Fighting back [community youth programs across the country] B. W. Baye. il *Essence* 20:59+ N '89
Hands across the ages [aged working with children; cover story] A. Korpivaara. il *New Choices for the Best Years* 29:41-3+ Ag '89
Minotaurs and mentors [address, October 4, 1988] J. C. Cutler. *Vital Speeches of the Day* 55:202-3 Ja 15 '89
Youth in transition [need for more services for those moving from foster care to independent living] il *Children Today* 18:2-3 Mr/Ap '89
SOCIAL WORKERS
Legal status, laws, etc.
Whose responsibility is it, anyway? [child welfare worker liability] J. P. Shapiro. il *U.S. News & World Report* 106:29-30 Ja 9 '89
SOCIALISM
See also
Communism
Utopias
After socialism, what? [reevaluation after Chinese crackdown on demonstrators] M. Novak. il *Forbes* 144:62-3 Jl 10 '89
Beat the devil [interview with P. Sweezy and H. Magdoff] A. Cockburn. il *The Nation* 248:726-7 My 29 '89
The death of radicalism. R. E. Tyrrell. il *The American Spectator* 22:10 Jl '89
A green face instead of a red face? P. Brimelow. il *Forbes* 144:76+ D 11 '89
Socialism then and now [social democracy] M. Walzer. il *The New Republic* 201:75-8 N 6 '89
Testing time for both socialism and capitalism. A. Chambraud. il *World Press Review* 36:11-13 D '89
The triumph of capitalism. R. L. Heilbroner. *The New Yorker* 64:98-109 Ja 23 '89
The triumph of capitalism [cover story; special section; with editorial comments by Nathan Gardels and Stanley K. Sheinbaum] il *New Perspectives Quarterly* 6:2-52, 64 Fall '89
The world turns [views of F. A. Hayek] R. Bailey. il por *Forbes* 143:43-4 My 15 '89
Conferences
Socialists at work and play [Socialist Scholars Conference] M. Cunningham. *National Review* 41:19-21 My 5 '89
Argentina
Socialism fades out of fashion. P. Winn. il *The Nation* 248:882-6 Je 26 '89
Why the left runs last in Argentina. A. M. Shapiro. il *The New Leader* 72:10-12 F 6 '89
Brazil
Brazil turns left. W. Steif. il *The Progressive* 53:24-5+ Je '89
The fiery socialist who could soon be running Brazil [L. I. da Silva] J. Ryser. il por *Business Week* p48 Ja 16 '89
Lula's in town [L. da Silva vs. F. Collor de Mello] K. Silverstein. *The Nation* 249:776-7 D 25 '89
Canada
Canadian conundrums: nationalism, socialism, and free trade. A. Stark. il *The American Spectator* 22:20-2 Ap '89
Chile
Socialism fades out of fashion. P. Winn. il *The Nation* 248:882-6 Je 26 '89
East Asia
The capitalism/socialism debate in East Asia. S. N. G. Davies. bibl *Society* 26:29-37 Mr/Ap '89
Eastern Europe
After the Wall, a new socialism? D. Singer. il *The Nation* 249:790-2 D 25 '89
Goodbye, Stalin hello, marketplace. O. T. Bogomolov. il *World Press Review* 36:13+ D '89
The specter of capitalism. D. Singer. il *The Nation* 249:202-5 Ag 21-28 '89
Upheaval in the East: is the socialist bloc ready for socialism? [cover story] R. Blackburn. *The Progressive* 53:18-22 Jl '89
Europe
Europe in the post-Yalta era [cover story] D. Singer. il *The Nation* 249:701+ D 11 '89
Revolutionary nostalgia. D. Singer. il *The Nation* 249:598-600 N 20 '89
Great Britain
Is there life after Thatcher? G. Black. *The Nation* 248:620-2 My 8 '89
Soviet Union
Gorbachev, freedom fighter. *National Review* 41:9-10 Ag 18 '89

SOCIALISM—Soviet Union—*cont.*

'The need to rethink Leninism' [interview with V. Medvedev] B. Guetta. por *World Press Review* 36:23 S '89

Socialism by the textbook [economics textbooks] T. Bethell. il *National Review* 41:36-8 O 13 '89

The specter of capitalism. D. Singer. il *The Nation* 249:202-5 Ag 21-28 '89

Turning Marx on his head [adaptation of address, October 4, 1988] V. Medvedev. il *New Perspectives Quarterly* 5:4-6 Wint '88/'89

Upheaval in the East: is the socialist bloc ready for socialism? [cover story] R. Blackburn. *The Progressive* 53:18-22 Jl '89

Sweden

Sweden's shining example [social democracy] M. Harvey. il *Utne Reader* p9-10 S/O '89

Uruguay

Socialism fades out of fashion. P. Winn. il *The Nation* 248:882-6 Je 26 '89

SOCIALISM AND EDUCATION

Socialism by the textbook [economics textbooks] T. Bethell. il *National Review* 41:36-8 O 13 '89

SOCIALISM AND RELIGION

Doing the Lord's work: churches energize the left. D. Collum. il *The Progressive* 53:34-7 F '89

The last socialist? [John Paul II; cover story] J. Gray. il *National Review* 41:27-9+ Je 30 '89

SOCIALISM IN ART

Exhibitions

Two lives: ordinary/extraordinary [photomontages of R. Luxemburg and artist M. Stevens' mother, Alice] C. Jacobsen. bibl f il pors *Art in America* 77:152-7+ F '89

SOCIALIST PARTY (AUSTRIA)

Social climber's guide to Vienna [officials linked to U. Proksch and deliberate sinking of the Lucona] E. von Kuehnelt-Leddihn. *National Review* 41:42 Mr 10 '89

SOCIALIST PARTY (FRANCE)

God is a French Socialist. M. Lilla. il *The American Spectator* 22:27-8 My '89

SOCIALIST PARTY (GREECE)

Greece: sanctuary of international terrorism. N. M. Adams. il map *Reader's Digest* 134:199-200+ Je '89

SOCIALIST PARTY (HUNGARY)

'Feeling our way to the future'. R. Watson. il *Newsweek* 114:36-7 O 23 '89

Hungary's hazy future. R. L. Tőkés. il *The New Leader* 72:5-7 O 30 '89

Hungary's quiet revolution. J. Rupnik. *The New Republic* 201:18-20+ N 20 '89

Letter from Budapest [party congress] D. K. Shipler. *The New Yorker* 65:74+ N 20 '89

Now you see it . . . [rejection of communism; with interview with I. Pozsgay] J. Borrell. il por *Time* 134:46+ O 23 '89

SOCIALIST PARTY (JAPAN)

A mountain moves [results of vote for the upper house of parliament] J. Smolowe. il *Time* 134:24-6 Ag 7 '89

A pinball empire greased by graft? [charges that Socialist Party took bribes from pachinko parlor owners] il por *U.S. News & World Report* 107:18 O 30 '89

Sex, lies, and Japanese politics. M. Sayle. *The New Republic* 201:18-22 S 11 '89

Sex, taxes and 'the Madonna factor' [T. Doi's Socialist Party wins parliamentary elections] J. Impoco. il por *U.S. News & World Report* 107:36 Ag 7 '89

The Socialists' stunning win. B. Powell and others. il *Newsweek* 114:33 Ag 7 '89

Takako Doi: an unmarried woman. *Time* 134:26 Ag 7 '89

Upset in Japan [vote for upper house of parliament] H. Jensen. il pors *Maclean's* 102:22-3 Ag 7 '89

Would a socialist Japan be the same old Japan? R. Neff. il *Business Week* p67 Ag 14 '89

SOCIALIST PARTY (SPAIN)

As Spain rushes toward '92. E. Ontiveros. il *The New Leader* 72:10-11 O 2-16 '89

Shifting politics in Spain. J. Valls-Russell. il *The New Leader* 72:9-10 N 27 '89

SOCIALLY HANDICAPPED CHILDREN

Children of the Garden Island [30-year resilience study of Kauai children] E. E. Werner. bibl il map *Scientific American* 260:106-8+ Ap '89

Growing up in poor neighborhoods: how much does it matter? S. E. Mayer and C. Jencks. bibl f *Science* 243:1441-5 Mr 17 '89

The new untouchables. J. Kozol. il *Newsweek* 114 Special Issue:48-9+ Wint '89/Spr '90

One fifth of the nation's children: why are they poor? M. J. Bane and D. T. Ellwood. bibl f il *Science* 245:1047-53 S 8 '89

Programs that can make a difference. J. N. Baker. il *Newsweek* 114:28 S 11 '89

Education

See also

Center for Successful Childhood Development (Chicago, Ill.)

Compensatory education

I Have a Dream Foundation

READY (Program)

The 'at-risk' label and the problem of urban school reform [case against graded schools] L. Cuban. bibl f il *Phi Delta Kappan* 70:780-4+ Je '89

Building bridges for at-risk children. L. F. Cavazos. *The Education Digest* 55:16-19 N '89

Educational disadvantage: a threat from within [research by Aaron Pallas and others] G. W. Bracey. il *Phi Delta Kappan* 71:76-7 S '89

High school choice and students at risk. D. R. Moore and S. Davenport. *The Education Digest* 55:7-10 S '89

Knock at any school. R. Parish and others. bibl f il *Phi Delta Kappan* 70:386-94 Ja '89

Learning to read and write [four year study of children from low income families by Connie Juel] G. W. Bracey. il *Phi Delta Kappan* 70:559-60 Mr '89

Minority and disadvantaged students [address, February 2, 1989] M. Coughlin. *Vital Speeches of the Day* 55:569-72 Jl 1 '89

The Phi Delta Kappa study of students at risk. J. R. Frymier and B. Gansneder. il *Phi Delta Kappan* 71:142-6 O '89

A promise at risk [cover story] S. C. Taylor. il *Modern Maturity* 32:32-6+ Ag/S '89

A report card on schools after 20 years. J. Kozol. *The Education Digest* 54:7-9 Ja '89

Symbol—or substance? [drive for flag burning amendment vs. addressing needs of poor children] P. B. Gough. *Phi Delta Kappan* 71:99 O '89

Time is not on their side [poor sense of time accounts for poor academic performance among poor children] E. Taylor. il *Time* 133:74 F 27 '89

Two faces in a crowd of graduates [Appalachian woman and black boy from inner city Washington, D.C.] J. R. Hacala. *America* 161:190-1 S 30 '89

Ways of being at risk: the case of Billy Charles Barnett [rural middle school student] T. Barone. il *Phi Delta Kappan* 71:147-51 O '89

Recreation

Miracle on Hoe Avenue [Community Tennis Center in the South Bronx helps inner city children] P. M. Coan. il pors *World Tennis* 37:36-41+ O '89

SOCIALLY HANDICAPPED COLLEGE STUDENTS

Broadening community service to include low-income students. K. Bojar. il *Change* 21:22-3 S/O '89

SOCIETÀ AZIONARIA FABBRICA ITALIANA LAVORAZIONE *See* Safilo SpA

SOCIETAS SACERDOTALIS SANCTAE CRUCIS *See* Opus Dei (Society)

SOCIETE ANONYME BELGE DE CONSTRUCTIONS AÉRONAUTIQUES *See* Belge de Constructions Aéronautiques SA

SOCIÉTÉ DE CONSTRUCTION D'AVIATIONS TOURISMES ET D'AFFAIRS *See* SOCATA

SOCIÉTÉ EUROPÉENNE DE PROPULSION

French firm to test fire composite nozzle for use on large, liquid-fueled engines. *Aviation Week & Space Technology* 130:29 Ja 30 '89

SOCIÉTÉ NATIONALE D'ETUDE & DE CONSTRUCTION DE MOTEURS D'AVIATION SA *See* SNECMA

SOCIÉTÉ RADIO-CANADA *See* Canadian Broadcasting Corporation

SOCIETIES

See also

Art clubs and societies

Clubs

SOCIETY, PRIMITIVE

See also

Cannibalism

Headhunters

Hunters and gatherers

Man, Prehistoric

Nomads

Tribes and tribal systems

SOCIETY AND ARCHITECTURE *See* Architecture—Social aspects

SOCIETY AND ART *See* Art—Social aspects

SOCIETY AND COMPUTERS *See* Computers and civilization

SOCIETY AND PSYCHIATRY *See* Psychiatry and society

SOCIETY AND SCIENCE *See* Science—Social aspects

SOCIETY AND THE ARTS *See* Arts—Social aspects

SOCIETY AND THE CHURCH *See* Church and the world

SOCIETY CORP.

Higher Society. T. Jaffe. *Forbes* 144:164 Ag 7 '89

SOCIETY FOR ECOLOGICAL RESTORATION AND MANAGEMENT

Phenomena, comment and notes. J. P. Wiley, Jr. il *Smithsonian* 19:32+ Mr '89

SOCIETY FOR MARKETING PROFESSIONAL SERVICES

Awards program reveals the latest techniques. E. E. Burden. il *Architectural Record* 177:29+ Ja '89

SOCIETY FOR SCHOLARLY PUBLISHING (U.S.)

SSP top management roundtable: whither intellectual property? *Publishers Weekly* 236:34 D 8 '89

SOCIETY FOR THE SOCIAL HISTORY OF MEDICINE

Society for the Social History of Medicine. R. Cavendish. il *History Today* 39:63 D '89

SOCIETY ISLANDS

See also

Bora Bora (French Polynesia)

SOCIETY ISLANDS—See also—*cont.*
  Huahine (French Polynesia)
  Moorea (French Polynesia)
  Raiatea (French Polynesia)
  Tahiti (French Polynesia)
SOCIETY OF BIBLICAL LITERATURE
  The ivory tower comes to the Windy City [1988 meeting; cover story] R. Clapp. il *Christianity Today* 33:16-21 Ap 7 '89
  Serious religious publishers ponder their problems [annual meeting] T. Unsworth. *Publishers Weekly* 235:77 Ja 6 '89
SOCIETY OF JESUS *See* Jesuits
SOCIETY OF NORTH AMERICAN GOLDSMITHS
  Jewelry American style. A. DiNoto. il *American Craft* 49:46-53 Je/Jl '89
SOCIETY OF ST. FRANCIS DE SALES *See* Salesians
SOCIETY OF ST. URSULA
  Convent school [Manhattan's Notre Dame School] J. W. Donohue. *America* 160:288-95+ Ap 1 '89
SOCIETY OF THE DIVINE WORD
  Double dose of divinity [twin Catholic priests C. and C. Smith] R. Brown. il pors *Ebony* 44:52+ Ja '89
SOCIETY OF THE SACRED HEART
  Those were the days [V. V. Harrison's book describing changes since Vatican II in secondary schools operated by Society of the Sacred Heart] J. W. Donohue. il *America* 161:258-61 O 21 '89
SOCIOBIOLOGY
  Evolution and family homicide [discussion of October 28, 1988 article, Evolutionary social psychology and family homicide] M. Daly and M. Wilson. *Science* 243:462-4 Ja 27 '89
  Finite social space, evolutionary pathways, and reconstructing hominid behavior. R. A. Foley and P. C. Lee. bibl f il *Science* 243:901-6 F 17 '89
  The Hansel and Gretel syndrome [evolutionary significance of family homicide; research by Martin Daly and Margo Wilson] H. Pringle. il *Omni (New York, N.Y.)* 12:38+ D '89
  How the mind was designed. G. Cowley. il *Newsweek* 113:56-8 Mr 13 '89
SOCIOECONOMIC STATUS *See* Social status
SOCIOECONOMICS
  Economists really should get out more often. R. Kuttner. il *Business Week* p16 Ap 24 '89
SOCIOLOGICAL SOCIETIES
  See also
  American Sociological Association
SOCIOLOGY
  See also
  Anthropology
  Community
  Educational sociology
  Human ecology
  Human relations
  Individualism
  Intercultural research
  Man—Influence of environment
  Socioeconomics
  Sociology and subjectivism. I. L. Horowitz. *Society* 26:49-54 Jl/Ag '89
  What's in a number? J. Torpey. *The Nation* 249:393-5 O 9 '89

          Soviet Union
  Soviet sociology makes a comeback. C. Holden. il *Science* 246:991-2 N 24 '89
SOCIOLOGY, CHRISTIAN
  See also
  Center on Religion & Society (New York, N.Y.)
  Christianity and economics
  Church and social problems
  Church work
  Liberation theology
  Social gospel
  Habits of the hearth [interview with R. Bellah] R. Clapp. il pors *Christianity Today* 33:20-4 F 3 '89
  Religious revival in American life [cover story; special section] bibl *Society* 26:27-66 Ja/F '89
  Shifting into the future tense [1990s] T. Sine. il *Christianity Today* 33:18-21 N 17 '89
SOCIOLOGY, RURAL
  See also
  Peasantry
  Small towns
SOCIOLOGY, URBAN
  See also
  Urban renewal
  Contrary to previous reports, cities are not dead [views of W. H. Whyte] S. Allis. il por *Time* 134:9-10 Ag 7 '89
  Secret lives of New York [cover story] D. Smith. il *New York* 22:34-41 D 11 '89
  The sky line [views of W. H. Whyte] B. Gill. *The New Yorker* 65:99-104 Mr 6 '89
  Standing on those corners, watching all the folks go by [W. H. Whyte] S. S. Hall. bibl (p171) il por *Smithsonian* 19:119-24+ F '89

SOCK SHOP INTERNATIONAL PLC
  Queen of pantyhose [S. Mirman] D. Fong. il por *Forbes* 143:72+ Mr 20 '89
SOCK STORES *See* Hosiery stores
SOCKET WRENCHES *See* Wrenches
SOCKEYE SALMON *See* Salmon
SOCKS *See* Hosiery
SOCRATES
      Anecdotes, facetiae, satire, etc.
  Our guest tonight is Socrates, himself a noted interviewer. H. Arkes. *National Review* 41:23 Mr 10 '89
SOD
  How to restore your lawn. D. Prestly. il *The Family Handyman* 39:62-6+ Ap '89
SOD (SUPEROXIDE DISMUTASE) *See* Superoxide dismutase
SODEN, JACK
      about
  Elvis lives. F. Meeks. il por *Forbes* 144:104 Ag 21 '89
SODERBERGH, STEVEN
      about
  Hot phenom. T. Minsky. il por *Rolling Stone* p81+ My 18 '89
  sex, lies, and videotape [film] Reviews
    American Film il 14:76-7 Ap '89. R. Seidenberg
    The American Spectator il 22:38-9 N '89. B. Bawer
    Commonweal 116:529-30 O 6 '89. P. D. Baumann
    Maclean's il 102:61 S 25 '89. B. D. Johnson
    The Nation 249:250+ S 4-11 '89. S. Klawans
    National Review 41:62-3 N 10 '89. J. Simon
    The New Leader 72:20-1 O 2-16 '89. J. Morrone
    The New Republic 201:26-7 S 4 '89. S. Kauffmann
    New York il 22:40+ Ag 7 '89. D. Denby
    The New Yorker 65:73-4 Ag 7 '89. T. Rafferty
    Newsweek il 114:61 Ag 7 '89. D. Ansen
    People Weekly il 32:14-15 S 4 '89. R. Novak
    Rolling Stone il p38 Ag 24 '89. P. Travers
    Time il 134:65+ Jl 31 '89. R. Corliss
    Vogue il 179:454-5 S '89. P. Rainer
  Truth or consequences [interview] H. Jacobson. il por *Film Comment* 25:22-4+ Jl/Ag '89
SODIUM
  See also
  Low sodium cooking
  The moon's atmosphere [work of Andrew E. Potter and Thomas H. Morgan] *Sky and Telescope* 77:589 Je '89
SODIUM BICARBONATE
  Problems reported with two heart rescues [sodium bicarbonate injections] S. Hart. *Science News* 136:85 Ag 5 '89
SODIUM CHANNELS
  β-adrenergic inhibition of cardiac sodium channels by dual G-protein pathways. B. Schubert and others. bibl f il *Science* 245:516-19 Ag 4 '89
  Two molecular transitions influence cardiac sodium channel gating. D. T. Yue and others. bibl f il *Science* 244:349-52 Ap 21 '89
SODIUM FLUORIDE
  Bone booster [treatment for spinal osteoporosis] *Time* 133:54 Ja 23 '89
  New fluoride-calcium treatment for bone loss. *Prevention (Emmaus, Pa.)* 41:14+ Je '89
SODOM AND GOMORRAH (BIBLICAL STORY)
  For the sake of ten. K. Koyama. *The Christian Century* 106:683 Jl 19-26 '89
SODOWSKY, ROLAND
  The origins of the cowboy boot. il *The Atlantic* 264:46+ D '89
SOEHARTO, 1921-
      about
  A global leader of a new kind; A part of the fabric of life. M. Morain. il *The Humanist* 49:31 My/Je '89
SOELDNER, TOM
  (jt. auth) See Palos, Demetrius, and Soeldner, Tom
SOFAS
  My sofa beats your couch [K sofa designed by Steven Holl] P. Patton. il *Esquire* 111:40 My '89
SOFER, KEN
      about
  Ken Sofer: M-13. M. Moorman. il *Art News* 88:136 Ja '89
SOFER, RENA
      about
  Loving's Rena Sofer is hot, hot, hot. J. Marion. por *TV Guide* 37:28-9 N 11-17 '89
SOFFER, DOMY REITER- *See* Reiter-Soffer, Domy
SOFT CONTACT LENSES *See* Contact lenses
SOFT DOLLAR BROKERS
      Ethical aspects
  Wall Street falls in love with 'soft dollars'. J. M. Laderman. il *Business Week* p127-8 Ap 24 '89
SOFT DRINK INDUSTRY
  See also
  A&W Brands Inc.
  Coca-Cola Company
  Coca-Cola Enterprises Inc.
  PepsiCo, Inc.
      Advertising
  The cola superpowers' outrageous new arsenals [Coke vs. Pepsi] S. Ticer. il *Business Week* p162+ Mr 20 '89

SOFT DRINK INDUSTRY—Advertising—*cont.*
Peddle power [mountain biking used in television ad for Mountain Dew] S. Martin. il *Bicycling* 30:41 O/N '89
"We can't let Pepsi outflesh us!" [Coke-Pepsi war] J. Levine. il *Forbes* 144:270+ N 27 '89
International aspects
Globalization [address, February 9, 1989] R. C. Goizueta. *Vital Speeches of the Day* 55:360-2 Ap 1 '89
Marketing
Locking up the weekend warriors [marketing of Gatorade] J. Levine. il *Forbes* 144:234-5 O 2 '89
India
How Pepsi broke into India. S. N. Chakravarty. il *Forbes* 144:43-4 N 27 '89
SOFT LANDINGS (TERM)
Happy soft landings. W. Safire. il *The New York Times Magazine* p6 D 24 '89
SOFT MONEY (TERM)
The hard truth about soft money. W. Safire. il *The New York Times Magazine* p12+ F 26 '89
SOFT SHEEN PRODUCTS INC.
Soft Sheen's triangle of trade. D. T. Dingle. il *Black Enterprise* 19:222-6+ Je '89
SOFTBALL
Bill Cosby's all-stars shock Eddie Murphy's all-stars team 30-18. il pors *Jet* 76:56-8 Jl 3 '89
A game winner [player K. Stilwell contracts multiple sclerosis] L. Rothlein. il por *Women's Sports & Fitness* 11:50 Ja/F '89
Accidents and injuries
Safe on base [sliding injuries reduced by use of breakaway bases] *Women's Sports & Fitness* 11:12+ N/D '89
Equipment
See also
Softball bats
Soviet Union
The day we blasted Moscow [American team challenges Soviets] R. Fimrite. il *Sports Illustrated* 70:46-8+ Je 19 '89
SOFTBALL, COLLEGE
All bases covered [M. Smith of Oklahoma State] M. Kort. il pors *Women's Sports & Fitness* 11:48-51 O '89
SOFTBALL, HIGH SCHOOL
Batters know that where there's smoke, there's Jill Klein [pitcher breaks record by notching 104th victory] il pors *People Weekly* 31:60 My 22 '89
SOFTBALL BATS
The new softball bats: great at the plate. S. Linson. il *Women's Sports & Fitness* 11:86 Ap '89
SOFTBALL RECORDS
Batters know that where there's smoke, there's Jill Klein [pitcher breaks high school record by notching 104th victory] il pors *People Weekly* 31:60 My 22 '89
SOFTENING OF WATER *See* Water softening
SOFTWARE *See* Computer programming
SOFTWARE 2000 INC.
Hitch your wagon to the right IBM model. D. Churbuck. il por *Forbes* 144:119+ S 4 '89
SOFTWARE INDUSTRY *See* Computer service industries
SOFTWARE PUBLISHERS ASSOCIATION
Facts on File settles claims in software copyright suit. C. Reid. *Publishers Weekly* 235:9-10 Je 23 '89
SOFTWARE PUBLISHING CORPORATION
Driving a company from the back seat. R. Brandt. il por *Business Week* p96 Ag 21 '89
SOFTWARE TOOLWORKS INC.
Les Crane makes the floppy-disk hit parade. P. Cole. il *Business Week* p93 My 22 '89
SOGIN, MITCHELL L., AND OTHERS
Phylogenetic meaning of the kingdom concept: an unusual ribosomal RNA from Giardia lamblia. bibl f il *Science* 243:75-7 Ja 6 '89
SOHO (NEW YORK, N.Y.)
The art of the newest. K. Larson. il *New York* 22:76-8 D 25 '89-Ja 1 '90
The new dealers [gallery owners A. Rosen and C. Burgin] A. Virshup. il pors *Harper's Bazaar* 122:80+ D '89
SoHo ascending. A. Schwartzman. *Harper's Bazaar* 122:84-5+ D '89
SOHO (NEW YORK, N.Y.) IN MOTION PICTURES
Mondo Longo [R. Longo's Arena brains] C. Lewis. il *Art in America* 77:35+ Mr '89
SOHO PRESS INC.
Soho launches Korean novelist in the U.S. [Ahn Junghyo] il por *Publishers Weekly* 236:57-8 O 6 '89
SOIL *See* Soils
SOIL AMENDMENTS *See* Soil conditioners
SOIL-ATMOSPHERE INTERACTION
Seasonal dust [airborne global dust] map *Sea Frontiers* 35:197 Jl/Ag '89
Soil nitrogen leaves methane up in the air [research by Paul A. Steudler] D. E. Loupe. *Science News* 136:213 S 30 '89
SOIL BIOLOGY
In defense of species [emphasis on ecology in soil research] N. L. Stanton and J. D. Lattin. *BioScience* 39:67 F '89

SOIL COMPACTION
Farming on the fast track [rubber-tracked machines curtail compaction] R. Fee. il *Successful Farming* 87:48E O '89
Heavy load crushes yields 7 years later. il *Successful Farming* 87:24 S '89
SOIL CONDITIONERS
Cyril Hopkins: a voice for the soil [excerpt from Soil fertility and permanent agriculture] C. G. Hopkins. por *Organic Gardening* 36:70 O '89
Living soil [organic amendments] E. Coleman. il por *Organic Gardening* 36:67-8+ O '89
SOIL CONSERVATION
See also
Contour farming
Filter strips (Soil conservation)
Revegetation
Terraces (Agriculture)
Conservation on your own [special section] J. Walter. il *Successful Farming* 87:21-8 D '89
Food, not dust [work of B. A. Stewart] A. Farnham. il *Fortune* 119:37 Ja 2 '89
Soil [Environmental Quality Index] il *National Wildlife* 27:39 F/Mr '89
Laws and regulations
See also
United States. Dept. of Agriculture. Conservation Reserve Program
Most farmers at ease with compliance plans. D. Mowitz. *Successful Farming* 87:10 O '89
SOIL ECOLOGY
Bootstrapping in ecosystems [reciprocal interactions between plants and soils] D. A. Perry and others. bibl f il *BioScience* 39:230-7 Ap '89
SOIL FERTILITY
See also
Gardens and gardening—Soil preparation
Green manuring
Soil conditioners
SOIL MECHANICS
Dynamics of liquefaction during the 1987 Superstition Hills, California, earthquake [cover story] T. L. Holzer and others. bibl f il map *Science* 244:56-9 Ap 7 '89
"We have built our houses on sand" [San Francisco Bay Area earthquake] M. Barinaga. il *Science* 246:437 O 27 '89
SOIL MICROBIOLOGY
Supersolo [cryptogamic soils; research by Tyler Volk and David W. Schwartzman; cover story] R. Monastersky. il *Science News* 136:376-7 D 9 '89
SOIL MOISTURE
See also
Plants—Water requirements
Dynamics of liquefaction during the 1987 Superstition Hills, California, earthquake [cover story] T. L. Holzer and others. bibl f il map *Science* 244:56-9 Ap 7 '89
SOIL POLLUTION
Window-box test for carryover [indoor soil bioassay for herbicide residues] B. Freese. il *Successful Farming* 87:48T mid-Mr '89
SOIL TESTING *See* Soils—Analysis
SOIL TILTH
Tilth! J. Walter. il *Successful Farming* 87:42-3 S '89
SOILLESS GARDENING *See* Hydroponics
SOILS
See also
Clay
Gardens and gardening—Soil preparation
Mud
Sedimentation and deposition
Sod
Loam sweet loam [manufactured soil by Bud and David Bulpitt of Brookside Nurseries] J. Stone. il *Discover* 10:26+ O '89
Analysis
Window-box test for carryover [indoor soil bioassay for herbicide residues] B. Freese. il *Successful Farming* 87:48T mid-Mr '89
Nitrogen content
Nitrogen saturation in northern forest ecosystems. J. D. Aber and others. bibl f il *BioScience* 39:378-86 Je '89
Soil nitrogen leaves methane up in the air [research by Paul A. Steudler] D. E. Loupe. *Science News* 136:213 S 30 '89
Sulfate content
Southeast waterways will face an acid test [research by M. Robbins Church] J. Raloff. *Science News* 136:151 S 2 '89
Testing
See Soils—Analysis
SOILS, POTTING
Soil advice [commercial mixes] J. Cook. il *Organic Gardening* 36:47-50 F '89
SOKOL, DAVID M.
American art in the Maier Museum of Art, Randolph-Macon Woman's College, Lynchburg, Virginia. il *Antiques* 136:1138-47 N '89

SOKOLIN, WILLIAM
about
Murder at Four Seasons. il *U.S. News & World Report* 106:11 My 8 '89
A New York wine merchant turns a 1787 Chateau Margaux into the world's most expensive puddle. A. Richman. il por *People Weekly* 31:155-6 My 15 '89

SOKOLOF, PHIL
about
Have a heart. S. J. Madden. il por *Fortune* 119:117+ Ja 16 '89
A man with a mission—and millions to back it up—takes on brand name cholesterol. il por *People Weekly* 31:112 F 6 '89

SOKOLOV, RAYMOND
A matter of taste. See issues of Natural History

SOKOLOV, VLADIMIR
about
A race against time. N. Underwood. pors *Maclean's* 102:44 Ja 23 '89

SOKOLOWSKI, STEVE
Music-on-hold adapter. il *Radio-Electronics* 60:42-6 Ag '89

SOKUROV, ALEXANDER
about
Sokurov's 'Lonely voice'. A. Vogel. il por *Film Comment* 25:64+ My/Je '89

SOLANA MORALES, FERNANDO
about
Mexico's move to the market [interview] N. Gardels. il *New Perspectives Quarterly* 6:41-5 Fall '89

SOLAR ACTIVITY
See also
Solar flares
Sunspots
Fantastic fortnight of active region 5395. J. Eberhart. il *Science News* 135:212-13 Ap 8 '89
Global warming: blaming the sun [report Scientific perspectives on the greenhouse problem] L. Roberts. il *Science* 246:992-3 N 24 '89
Sun tantrums. F. Harrois-Monin. *World Press Review* 36:82-3 O '89
The sunspot syndrome [with editorial comment by Paul Hoffman] M. Bartusiak. il *Discover* 10:4, 44-8+ N '89

SOLAR AIR CONDITIONING
New light on solar cooling [Desiccant Enhanced Radiative Cooling] M. DiChristina. il *Popular Science* 235:24+ S '89

SOLAR ARRAY
Large building-block module docked to Mir following deployment of stuck solar array. J. M. Lenorovitz. *Aviation Week & Space Technology* 131:33-4 D 11 '89

SOLAR AUTOMOBILES See Automobiles, Solar
SOLAR CELLS
Boeing achieves major advance in space solar cell efficiency. B. W. Henderson. il *Aviation Week & Space Technology* 131:61+ O 23 '89
New life for solar? [cover story] S. Ashley. il *Popular Science* 234:117-21+ My '89
Photovoltaics today and tomorrow. H. M. Hubbard. bibl f il *Science* 244:297-304 Ap 21 '89
Solar cell that works nights [work of Stuart Licht] D. Stover. il *Popular Science* 234:142 Ap '89
Solar power supply. D. Becker. il *Radio-Electronics* 60:47-51 Ag '89
Solar shingles. V. E. Gilmore. il *Popular Science* 234:146 Je '89

SOLAR CHEMISTRY See Photochemistry
SOLAR-CLIMATE RELATIONSHIPS See Sun and meteorology
SOLAR COLLECTORS
See also
Solar water heaters
A bright idea for funneling sunlight [solar concentrator design by Roland Winston] il *Science News* 135:351 Je 3 '89
Bring me sunshine [solar concentrator design by Roland Winston] T. Beardsley. il *Scientific American* 261:20-1 Ag '89
Making concentrated solar juice affordable [photovoltaic concentrator module] I. Amato. il *Science News* 136:44 Jl 15 '89

SOLAR CONSTANT See Solar radiation
SOLAR COOLING See Solar air conditioning
SOLAR CORONA See Sun—Corona
SOLAR CYCLE See Sunspots
SOLAR ECLIPSES See Eclipses, Solar
SOLAR ENERGY
See also
Ocean thermal power plants
Solar cells
Solar Energy Research Institute
Space flight—Solar energy use
Space stations—Solar energy use
Space vehicles—Solar energy use
New life for solar? [cover story] S. Ashley. il *Popular Science* 234:117-21+ My '89
Solar breakthroughs. il *The Futurist* 23:54 Mr/Ap '89
Solar power and priorities. D. E. Koshland, Jr. *Science* 245:805 Ag 25 '89

California
Warming trend [Luz plants] J. Cook. il *Forbes* 143:68+ F 20 '89
SOLAR ENERGY INDUSTRY
See also
Chronar Corp.
Sunsign Manufacturing Company
Acquisitions and mergers
International aspects
ARCO Solar sale raises concerns over potential technology export. M. Crawford. *Science* 244:918 My 26 '89
International aspects
See also
Luz International Ltd.
SOLAR ENERGY RESEARCH INSTITUTE
Solar studies. S. Hassol and T. Flanigan. il *Technology Review* 92:14-15 Ja '89
SOLAR EQUIPMENT INDUSTRY See Solar energy industry
SOLAR FILTERS See Light filters
SOLAR FLARES
Brilliant aurorae produced by solar flare. D. J. Eicher. il *Astronomy* 17:95+ Jl '89
The day the sun cut loose. G. L. Verschuur. il *Astronomy* 17:48-51 Ag '89
Diary of a solar flare. M. M. Waldrop. *Science* 243:1436 Mr 17 '89
Giant solar flare stuns astronomers. il *Astronomy* 17:10 Jl '89
Jupiter-bound Galileo starts with the sun. J. Eberhart. *Science News* 136:325 N 18 '89
Solar Max snaps a big, brilliant flare. il *Science News* 135:164 Mr 18 '89
The ups and downs of solar flares [Solar Maximum Mission satellite data] J. Eberhart. *Science News* 135:391 Je 24 '89
When the sun went wild [flare activity recorded by the Solar Maximum Mission satellite] il *Sky and Telescope* 77:590-1 Je '89
Photographs and photography
A flare-up on the sun. il *Astronomy* 17:91 Jl '89
SOLAR GREENHOUSES See Greenhouses
SOLAR HEATING
See also
Solar collectors
Solar houses
SOLAR HEATING INDUSTRY See Solar energy industry
SOLAR HOUSES
6 summer houses for year-round living. A. W. Lees. il *Popular Science* 234:128-32+ Ap '89
Solar shingles. V. E. Gilmore. il *Popular Science* 234:146 Je '89
SOLAR MAGNETIC FIELD See Sun—Magnetic properties
SOLAR MAXIMUM MISSION SATELLITE See Artificial satellites—Astronomical use
SOLAR MOTION See Solar system—Motion in space
SOLAR NEUTRINOS See Neutrinos
SOLAR POWER See Solar energy
SOLAR POWER PLANTS See Solar energy
SOLAR POWERED SPACE VEHICLES See Space vehicles—Solar energy use
SOLAR PROMINENCES See Sun—Prominences
SOLAR RADIATION
See also
Solar flares
Solar wind
Sunspots
Ultraviolet rays
Climate and the earth's radiation budget [cover story] V. Ramanathan and others. bibl f il *Physics Today* 42:22-7+ My '89
Contribution of ultraviolet irradiance variations to changes in the sun's total irradiance. J. Lean. bibl f il *Science* 244:197-200 Ap 14 '89
Solar declination, altitude, and azimuth [computer program] il *Weatherwise* 42:113 Ap '89
Physiological effects
See Ultraviolet rays—Physiological effects
SOLAR RESEARCH See Sun
SOLAR SAILS
On gossamer wings. E. Corcoran. il *Scientific American* 260:80-1 Ap '89
SOLAR SPECTRA AND SPECTROSCOPY See Sun—Spectra and spectroscopy
SOLAR SYSTEM
See also
Moon
Planetesimal hypothesis
Planets
Sun
Dance of the Planets [computer orrery] J. E. Mosley. il *Sky and Telescope* 78:642 D '89
Origin and evolution of outer solar system atmospheres. J. I. Lunine. bibl f il *Science* 245:141-7 Jl 14 '89
Playing dice with the solar system. A. M. Killian. il *Sky and Telescope* 78:136-8+ Ag '89
Surface discharges on natural dielectrics in the solar system. H. Campins and E. P. Krider. bibl f il *Science* 245:622-4 Ag 11 '89

SOLAR SYSTEM—*cont.*

Exploration

See Space flight

Motion in space

How to observe planets during the day [polar alignment] J. H. Palmer. il *Astronomy* 17:86-7 Mr '89

Portrait of a year. H. J. P. Arnold. *Sky and Telescope* 77:678-9 Je '89

SOLAR WASTE WATER TREATMENT

If you leave it to Mother Nature, says biologist John Todd, sewage doesn't have to go to waste. D. Chu. il pors *People Weekly* 32:133+ N 27 '89

Sun-powered pollution clean up. R. Pool. il *Science* 245:130 Jl 14 '89

This greenhouse effect just might be good for us. L. Jereski. il por *Business Week* p119-20 S 18 '89

SOLAR WATER HEATERS

Solar heat with perks. M. McPhee. il *Popular Science* 235:76-8 Jl '89

SOLAR WIND

See also

Heliopause

Heliosphere

The dynamic aurora [cover story] S.-I. Akasofu. bibl il *Scientific American* 260:90-7 My '89

Sing the asteroid electric [work of Floyd Herbert] il *Sky and Telescope* 77:356-7 Ap '89

What has caused the secular increase in solar nitrogen-15? J. F. Kerridge. bibl f il *Science* 245:480-6 Ag 4 '89

SOLARIUMS *See* Sun rooms

SOLARIZATION (PHOTOGRAPHY) *See* Photography—Processing

SOLDIER OF FORTUNE (PERIODICAL)

War is swell? [classifieds held accountable in murder cases] J. Zweig and P. Klebnikov. il por *Forbes* 144:223 S 18 '89

SOLDIERS, BLACK *See* United States. Army—Blacks

SOLE (FISH)

See also

Cooking—Fish

SOLERI, PAOLO, 1919-

about

Paolo Soleri: man for all futures. L. David. il por *Ad Astra* 1:31 N '89

SOLHEIM, KARSTEN

about

The golf club with a handicap all its own. P. Finch. il por *Business Week* p126+ My 1 '89

SOLICITING DONATIONS *See* Fund raising

SOLICITOR GENERAL (U.S.) *See* United States. Dept. of Justice. Office of the Solicitor General

SOLID STATE DEVICES *See* Semiconductors

SOLIDARITY

Incremental solidarity. K. Kolenda. il *The Humanist* 49:43 S/O '89

SOLIDARITY (LABOR UNION)

After the party's over [influence on reform movements in Eastern Europe] D. Stanglin. il *U.S. News & World Report* 107:76-7 Ag 28-S 4 '89

Between issues [electoral victory] A. Husarska. *The New Leader* 72:2 Je 12-26 '89

Call to freedom [recognition of Solidarity and promise of open elections; cover story; special section; with editorial comment by Kevin Doyle] il *Maclean's* 102:2, 26-8+ Ap 17 '89

Can Poland ever be free? A. Besançon. *Commentary* 87:15-20 Ap '89

Dawn in Poland [non-Communist prime minister T. Mazowiecki] D. Singer. il *The Nation* 249:265 S 18 '89

The defeated party plays for time. J. Baczynski and A. Krzeminski. *World Press Review* 36:29-30 Ag '89

An epochal shift [Solidarity to head government] M. Johnson. il por *Time* 134:16-18 Ag 28 '89

Freedom's turn [cover story; special section] il pors *Newsweek* 114:16-23+ Ag 28 '89

Getting to know you, part 2 [U.S. support for reform] G. D. Garcia. il *Time* 133:46 My 1 '89

A grand experiment. L. Weschler. il *The New Yorker* 65:59-60+ N 13 '89

Historic moment [meeting between Solidarity and government] D. Singer. *The Nation* 248:220 F 20 '89

How Poland's Solidarity won freedom of association. R. A. Senser. bibl f *Monthly Labor Review* 112:34-8 S '89

A humiliation for the party [victory for Solidarity candidates] T. A. Sancton. il *Time* 133:24-6 Je 19 '89

In Poland, if you can't beat them, ask them to join you [victory for Solidarity candidates] D. Stanglin. il *U.S. News & World Report* 106:30 Je 19 '89

Instead of revolution. M. J. Wolnicki. il *Commonweal* 116:293-4 My 19 '89

Lack of Solidarity [cover story] J. D. Sachs. *The New Republic* 201:20-1 Ag 7-14 '89

Lech Walesa digs in. N. Zeman. il por *Newsweek* 114:6 N 20 '89

Lech's American angel [heiress B. Johnson bails out shipyard in Gdańsk, Poland; cover story] D. Margolick. il pors *The New York Times Magazine* p28-31+ O 8 '89

Liberalization in Poland has put Bush in a bind over aid. B. Javetski and others. il *Business Week* p47 Ap 24 '89

Mr. Wujec goes to Warsaw [interview]; tr. by David Ost. J. Jastrzebowski. *Harper's* 279:13-15 D '89

Never say never [proposed legalization] il *Time* 133:38 Ja 30 '89

A new style of socialism? [legalization of Solidarity] M. R. Meyer. il *Newsweek* 113:36-7 Ap 10 '89

An offer you can't refuse [T. Mazowiecki chosen prime minister] *America* 161:99 Ag 26-S 2 '89

Out of misery, a flicker of hope [negotiations between Solidarity and government] S. Bialer. il *U.S. News & World Report* 106:42 Mr 27 '89

Partnership for Poland? [Solidarity's victory] D. Singer. il *The Nation* 248:878-80 Je 26 '89

"People are impatient" [interview with T. Mazowiecki] por *Time* 134:35 S 11 '89

Playing the political odds in Poland. A. Platt. il por *Newsweek* 114:30-1 Ag 7 '89

Poland [address, November 15, 1989] L. Wałęsa. *Vital Speeches of the Day* 56:132-5 D 15 '89

Poland: hanging by a thread. A. Nagorski. il por *Reader's Digest* 135:121-7 N '89

Poland: the long road ahead. S. Sullivan. il *Newsweek* 114:31 S 4 '89

Poland turns to the polls; tr. by Anna Husarska. E. Skalski. il *The New Leader* 72:5-7 Ap 3-17 '89

Poland's elections. *World Press Review* 36:10 Jl '89

Poland's precipice. *Commonweal* 116:483-4 S 22 '89

Poland's reforms make *glasnost* look like window dressing. W. Echikson and others. il *Business Week* p35-6 Ap 17 '89

President's remarks at Solidarity workers' monument, Gdansk, July 11, 1989. G. Bush. il *Department of State Bulletin* 89:33-6 S '89

Refolution in Hungary and Poland. T. Garton Ash. bibl f il *The New York Review of Books* 36:9-15 Ag 17 '89

Rehabilitation for Solidarity. *Newsweek* 113:43 Ja 30 '89

Retreat from communism [cover story; special section] il *World Press Review* 36:13-18+ O '89

Seize the day. L. Goodwyn. *The Nation* 249:777 D 25 '89

Solidarity has no time to celebrate. G. E. Schares. il *Business Week* p46-7 Je 19 '89

Solidarity in power. A. Nagorski. il *Newsweek* 114:34-5 N 27 '89

Solidarity in power [appointment of non-Communist T. Mazowiecki as prime minister] J. Bugajski. *The New Republic* 201:12-14 S 11 '89

Solidarity makes a choice [T. Mazowiecki; cover story] D. Warszawski. il *The New Leader* 72:3-4 S 4 '89

Solidarity on the high wire. G. E. Schares and J. Templeman. il *Business Week* p26-7 S 4 '89

Solidarity's glorious game [T. Mazowiecki named prime minister] *National Review* 41:12-13 S 15 '89

Solidarity's many faces. K. Moore. il *Commonweal* 116:391-2 Jl 14 '89

Solidarity's stunning win. M. R. Meyer. il *Newsweek* 113:42-3 Je 19 '89

Solidarity—the road to power. D. Singer. il *The Nation* 249:376-80 O 9 '89

Something happened [election] C. Kiechel. *National Review* 41:23-4 Jl 14 '89

A spokeswoman with rare flair makes the news in Poland [M. Niezabitowska] B. Hewitt. il pors *People Weekly* 32:60-2 N 13 '89

A stunning victory. A. Wilson-Smith. il *Maclean's* 102:18-19 Je 19 '89

A symbol of hope [L. Walesa] P. Sudo. il por *Scholastic Update (Teachers' edition)* 122:3-4 O 20 '89

A talk with Adam Michnik [cover story] A. Husarska. pors *The New Leader* 72:8-10 Ap 3-17 '89

Thanks a lot, but no thanks [L. Walesa turns down invitation to join coalition government] M. Johnson. il por *Time* 134:30 Ag 7 '89

'This farewell to communism' [election victory] E. Clemente. il *World Press Review* 36:28-9 Ag '89

To join or not to join: Solidarity debates power sharing in Poland. M. R. Meyer. il *Newsweek* 114:33 Jl 17 '89

To market [negotiations between Solidarity and government] D. Singer. *The Nation* 248:472-3 Ap 10 '89

Walesa's revolution [selection of non-Communist T. Mazowiecki as prime minister; cover story; special section; with editorial comment by Kevin Doyle] il pors *Maclean's* 102:2, 24-30 Ag 28 '89

Warsaw is suddenly banking on Solidarity. R. Brady. il *Business Week* p51 F 6 '89

Watershed in Warsaw [pact between government and Solidarity] il *Newsweek* 113:36 Ap 17 '89

Why Solidarity must play point man for economic reform. G. S. Becker. il *Business Week* p18 Jl 31 '89

Will success ruin Solidarity's party? D. Stanglin. il *U.S. News & World Report* 107:34-5 Ag 14 '89

SOLIDS

See also

Rapid solidification technology

SOLIDS—cont.

Bombardment versus quick cooling [relationship between microscopic structure of amorphous material and method used to produce it] I. Peterson. *Science News* 135:207 Ap 1 '89

Dreaming up crystals that outdo diamond [work of Marvin L. Cohen and Amy Y. Liu] I. Amato. il *Science News* 136:134 Ag 26 '89

Prediction of new low compressibility solids. A. Y. Liu and M. L. Cohen. bibl f il *Science* 245:841-2 Ag 25 '89

Some developments in nuclear magnetic resonance of solids [cover story] B. F. Chmelka and A. Pines. bibl f il *Science* 246:71-7 O 6 '89

Fracture
See Fracture mechanics

SOLIMAN, LOTFALLAH

Bibliotheca Alexandrina. il map *The Courier (Unesco)* 41:8-11 N '88

SOLITAIRE (GAME)

Solitaire Royale [computer version] N. Randall. il *Compute!* 11:71-2 Mr '89

SOLITARY WAVE PULSES *See* Solitons

SOLITONS

What goes around comes around [optical solitons; work of Linn Mollenauer] il *Discover* 10:14+ F '89

SOLITUDE

See also
Loneliness

Alone at last [excerpt from Grownups] C. Merser. il *Utne Reader* p62-3 Mr/Ap '89

In my solitude. P. Cleage. por *Essence* 19:56-8+ F '89

Solitude [elk hunting] K. McCafferty. il *Field & Stream* 94:48-9+ D '89

The virtues of solitude. P. Paquin. il *Utne Reader* p68-9 Mr/Ap '89

SOLLEN, ROBERT

A world at war. il *The Nation* 248:46-7 Ja 9-16 '89

SOLNIT, REBECCA

Uncommon perceptions. il *Sierra* 74:42-9 Jl/Ag '89

SOLO, PAM

Rejecting cold war politics. il *The Progressive* 53:18-19 Ja '89

SOLOGNE (FRANCE)

Historic houses, sites, etc.

Provincial pleasures [Christmas at H. and I. Ornano's 18th century house] C. Petkanas. il pors *Harper's Bazaar* 122:178-85 D '89

SOLOMON, ALISA

Breaking away. bibl il *Women's Sports & Fitness* 11:28-32 Ja/F '89

SOLOMON, DANIEL

about

Daniel Solomon: a villa of classical proportions in Oregon. L. Whiteson. il por *Architectural Digest* 46:86-91+ Ap '89

SOLOMON, DEBORAH

Al Held's Catskill pastoral: the artist's studio and house in Woodstock, New York. il por *Architectural Digest* 46:170-3+ Je '89

American frontiers. il pors *House & Garden* 161:124-7 Je '89

Art: Belgian impressionism. il *Architectural Digest* 46:140-5+ F '89

Art: painters of the Bauhaus. il *Architectural Digest* 46:242-7+ O '89

Artful survivor [cover story] il pors *The New York Times Magazine* p30-3+ My 14 '89

Cubism's odd couple. il pors *House & Garden* 161:58+ S '89

A downtown aesthetic: the residence and studio of artist Jennifer Bartlett. il por *Architectural Digest* 46:316-21+ N '89

Our most notorious sculptor. il *The New York Times Magazine* p38-41+ O 8 '89

Picture perfect. il *Harper's Bazaar* 122:166-7+ My '89

Psychological portraits. il *Harper's Bazaar* 122:28+ Ja '89

Sovereign strokes. il por *Harper's Bazaar* 122:360-1+ S '89

Stardust memory. il *Harper's Bazaar* 122:136-7+ F '89

SOLOMON, HARVEY

The meaning of the merger. il *Channels (New York, N.Y.: 1986)* 9:62-3 Je '89

Off-net hours: life after cable? il *Channels (New York, N.Y.: 1986)* 9:48-50 Ja 16 '89

Refranchising: cities fight back. il *Channels (New York, N.Y.: 1986)* 9:46-9 Mr '89

SOLOMON, PEARL CANICK

Sweet as kisses [story] il *Redbook* 172:58+ Ja '89

SOLOMON, RICHARD H., 1937-

An agenda for U.S.-Soviet cooperation [address, November 2, 1988] il *Department of State Bulletin* 89:38-42 F '89

Cambodia and Vietnam: trapped in an eddy of history? [address, September 8, 1989] por *Department of State Bulletin* 89:47-51 N '89

SOLOMON-GODEAU, ABIGAIL

Going native. bibl f il *Art in America* 77:118-29+ Jl '89

SOLOMON R. GUGGENHEIM MUSEUM

Guggenheim lassoes jet-set curator [G. Celant] B. Wallis. *Art in America* 77:25 Ja '89

A megamuseum in a mill town. D. Weisgall. il por *The New York Times Magazine* p32-5+ Mr 5 '89

New talents: Thomas Krens. C. Ratcliff. il por *Harper's Bazaar* 122:108 Mr '89

SOLOMONS, GUS

Graham assoluta. il *Dance Magazine* 63:48-51 Mr '89

SOLOW, ROBERT M.

What is the 'right' amount of saving? *National Review* 41:27-9 Je 16 '89

about

Swan song for laissez-faire? O. Port. il por *Business Week* Special Issue:174 Je 16 '89

SOLOY, JOE

about

Turbine powerhouse [cover story] N. Moll. il por *Flying* 116:44-8+ O '89

SOLOY CONVERSIONS (FIRM)

Turbine powerhouse [cover story] N. Moll. il por *Flying* 116:44-8+ O '89

SOLSTICE, SUMMER *See* Summer solstice

SOLSTICE, WINTER *See* Winter solstice

SOLTI, SIR GEORG, 1912-

about

Solti's thoughtful Beethoven. D. Hall. por *Stereo Review* 54:104 Ja '89

SOLUBILITY

Water-soluble vitamin A shows promise [work of Arun B. Barua, Desiree B. Gunning and James A. Olson] I. Wickelgren. *Science News* 135:204 Ap 1 '89

SOLUNAR THEORY *See* Fishing

SOLUTION (CHEMISTRY)

See also
Colloids
Diffusion
Solvents

SOLVENTS

See also
Cleaning compositions

Polar solvent dynamics and electron-transfer reactions. M. Maroncelli and others. bibl f il *Science* 243:1674-81 Mr 31 '89

Source Reduction Research Partnership: a unique joint venture [eliminating groundwater pollution caused by chlorinated solvents in California] A. Yazdani. bibl f il *Environment* 31:2-4 N '89

SOLVIVA WINTER GARDEN (FIRM)

Greenhouse gold [organic produce] C. Perlmutter. il pors *Organic Gardening* 36:56-60 O '89

SOLZHENITSYN, ALEKSANDR, 1918-

about

Russia's prophet in exile [interview] D. Aikman. il pors *Time* 134:56-60 Jl 24 '89

SOMALIA

See also
Civil rights—Somalia
Mogadishu (Somalia)

SOMAN, FLORENCE JANE

The better to know you [story] il *Good Housekeeping* 208:116-17 F '89

Many happy returns [story] il *Good Housekeeping* 209:204-5 S '89

SOMATIC CELL THERAPY *See* Gene therapy

SOMATOTROPIN *See* Pituitary hormones

SOMATOTYPES

Shape-onomics: adding muscle where it counts [bodyshaping] M. Greenwood-Robinson. il *Women's Sports & Fitness* 11:43-7 O '89

SOME GIRLS [film] *See* Motion picture reviews—Single works

SOMEONE TO LOVE [film] *See* Motion picture reviews—Single works

SOMERS, EMMANUEL

The numbers game. il *World Health* p12-14 D '88

SOMERS, JANE *See* Lessing, Doris May, 1919-

SOMERS, ROBERT G.

Breast cancer: most common, most curable. il *USA Today (Periodical)* 118:49-50 S '89

SOMERS, SUZANNE

about

A Somers place. P. Viladas. il pors *House & Garden* 161:210-15 S '89

SOMERS H. WHITE COMPANY, INC.

Former bank president sells financial know-how for $5,000 an hour [S. H. White] L. Arden. il por *Home Office Computing* 7:43 My '89

SOMERSET (ENGLAND)

Gardens and gardening

Best laid plan [Hestercombe garden designed by G. Jekyll and E. Lutyens] M. R. Van Valkenburgh and C. D. Van Valkenburgh. il *House & Garden* 161:150-7 Mr '89

SOMERSET PLACE STATE HISTORIC SITE (CRESWELL, N.C.)

Dot Redford found her roots at Somerset. D. Young. il pors *Southern Living* 24:92+ Ja '89

Plantation home [D. Redford traces descendants of slaves] R. Mashburn. il pors map *Americana* 16:50-4 Ja/F '89

SOMERVILLE COLLEGE *See* University of Oxford. Somerville College

SORCERY See Witchcraft
SOREL, EDWARD, 1929-
The adventures of J. Danforth. See issues of Gentlemen's Quarterly beginning March 1989
SOREL, EDWARD, 1929-, AND SOREL, NANCY CALDWELL
First encounters. See alternate issues of The Atlantic
SOREL, NANCY CALDWELL
(jt. auth) See Sorel, Edward, 1929-, and Sorel, Nancy Caldwell
SOREL BOOTS See Boots
SØRENSEN, ALLAN H., AND UGGERHØJ, ERIK
The channeling of electrons and positrons. bibl il *Scientific American* 260:96-102 Je '89
SORENSON, LAUREL
(jt. auth) See Ward, John L., and Sorenson, Laurel
SORGHUM SYRUP
See also
Cooking—Sorghum syrup
SORKIN, AARON
about
A few good men [drama] Reviews
America 161:453 D 16 '89. T. P. O'Malley
New York 22:99-100 N 27 '89. J. Simon
New York il pors 22:58-60+ N 6 '89. R. Wetzsteon
The New Yorker 65:101-3 N 27 '89. M. Kramer
Time il 134:88 N 27 '89. W. A. Henry
Young man with a play. R. Wetzsteon. il pors *New York* 22:58-60+ N 6 '89
SORKIN, MICHAEL, 1948-
Exploring space. il *House & Garden* 161:80+ S '89
Solid geometry. il por *House & Garden* 161:62+ O '89
SORMAN, STEVEN, 1948-
about
Steven Sorman at Cantor Lemberg. C. Waddington. *Art in America* 77:145 Jl '89
SOROLLA Y BASTIDA, JOAQUÍN, 1863-1923
about
Notes from the editor . . . M. S. Doherty. il *American Artist* 53:10 Je '89
SORORITIES, COLLEGE See College sororities
SOROS, GEORGE
The Gorbachev prospect. il *The New York Review of Books* 36:16-18 Je 1 '89
about
A clear shot at Crystal Oil. G. G. Marcial. *Business Week* p104 Ag 14 '89
Wall Street philanthropist. M. R. Meyer. il por *Newsweek* 112:64 My 22 '89
Was George Soros sheared by Shearson? D. Greising. il por *Business Week* p45 N 6 '89
SOROS FOUNDATION
Wall Street philanthropist [G. Soros] M. R. Meyer. il por *Newsweek* 112:64 My 22 '89
SORRELL, MARTIN S.
about
Brits buy up the ad business [cover story] R. Rothenberg. il por *The New York Times Magazine* p14-19+ Jl 2 '89
Confessions of an advertising man. R. I. Kirkland, Jr. il por *Fortune* 119:131-2 Je 5 '89
The 'fax attack' that has Ogilvy fuming. W. Konrad. il por *Business Week* p36 My 15 '89
Machiavelli on Madison Avenue. B. Rudolph. il por *Time* 133:58 My 15 '89
The man who would be king of Madison Ave. L. Reibstein. il por *Newsweek* 113:52 My 15 '89
Mediums and messages. A. Walmsley. il por *Maclean's* 102:42 My 29 '89
SORRELL RIDGE (FIRM)
Sorrell Ridge makes Smucker pucker. J. Levine. il *Forbes* 143:166+ Je 12 '89
SORRELLS, SUSAN
about
The vultures were circling, but Susan Sorrells wouldn't let her little desert town die. R. Johnson. il pors *People Weekly* 32:79+ Ag 14 '89
SORROW
See also
Grief
SOSA, MERCEDES
about
Mercedes Sosa. por *Esquire* 111:124-5 My '89
SOSHENSKY, EMANUEL
Are you covered? il *Travel Holiday* 172:10+ Ag '89
SOSKIN, MARK
about
Mark Soskin. B. Milkowski. *Down Beat* 56:48+ Ja '89
SOSNOFF, MARTIN
about
On the Côte d'Azur: Martin and Toni Sosnoff's villa above Nice. J. Gruen. il *Architectural Digest* 46:88-93 Ja '89
SOSNOFF, TONI
about
On the Côte d'Azur: Martin and Toni Sosnoff's villa above Nice. J. Gruen. il *Architectural Digest* 46:88-93 Ja '89
SOTERIOU, ALEXANDRA, 1948-
In search of India's papermaking tradition. il *American Craft* 49:32-7 F/Mr '89

SOTHEBY PARKE BERNET & CO.
See also
Sotheby's (Firm)
SOTHEBY'S (FIRM)
The $430-million week [auctions of contemporary and impressionist paintings] B. B. Stretch. il *Art News* 88:25 Ja '89
The anatomy of a deal [A. Bond's purchase of van Gogh's Irises at auction] R. Hughes. il *Time* 134:66+ N 27 '89
Bullish on Sotheby's. R. W. Walker. il *Art News* 88:27+ Mr '89
From soup to sèvres [auction of works from the estate of J. T. Dorrance] S. Greenspan. il *House & Garden* 161:244+ O '89
House sale [auction of only New York City home designed by P. Johnson] *The New Yorker* 65:29-30 My 29 '89
Painting by numbers [sale of Picasso's Au lapin agile] L. Black. il *Maclean's* 102:80 N 27 '89
Profiles [C. de Hamel, manuscript cataloger at Sotheby's] I. Shenker. il por *The New Yorker* 65:48+ My 29 '89
Sotheby's art market trends. See issues of Forbes beginning November 2, 1987
Tusk, tusk [Sotheby's removes elephant tusks from market to alleviate poaching] il *Time* 133:56 My 1 '89
SOTINEL, THOMAS
David Lean is back [interview] il por *World Press Review* 36:59 Ag '89
SOTO, HERNANDO DE
about
Crusader for Peru's have-nots. E. H. Methvin. il *Reader's Digest* 134:137-40 Ja '89
From mercantilism to markets. T. Bethell. il *The American Spectator* 22:11-13 Ap '89
How to make poor countries rich. J. Main. il por *Fortune* 119:101-2+ Ja 16 '89
The only hope for Latin America. M. Falcoff. *Commentary* 87:34-8 Ap '89
The right path. R. Bailey. il por *Forbes* 143:80-1 Ja 23 '89
Third world economies: a new proposal. J. Main. *Current (Washington, D.C.)* 314:38-40 Jl/Ag '89
SOTO, JOCK
about
Jock Soto: portrait of a young artist [cover story] J. Gruen. il pors *Dance Magazine* 63:32-7 Ag '89
SOTO, TALISA
about
Talisa Soto. M. W. Hirschorn. il pors *Esquire* 112:162-3 O '89
Talisa Soto puts her stock in Bond. J. C. Johnson. por *Mademoiselle* 95:52 Je '89
SOTOMAYOR, JAVIER
about
The eight-foot feat. il por *Newsweek* 114:62 Ag 14 '89
One giant leap. M. Noden. il pors *Sports Illustrated* 71:32-3 Ag 7 '89
SOUFRIÈRE (SAINT LUCIA)
Description
St. Lucia: secret Soufrière. J. Quale. il *Vogue* 179:322+ N '89
SOUKHANOV, ANNE H.
Word watch. See alternate issues of The Atlantic beginning January 1987
SOUL FOOD See Cooking, Black
SOUL II SOUL (MUSICAL GROUP)
From Soul II gold. S. Bloom. il por *Rolling Stone* p15 S 7 '89
SOUL MUSIC See Black music
SOUL MUSIC PHONOGRAPH RECORDS See Phonograph records—Black music
SOUL STIRRERS (MUSICAL GROUP)
Soul Stirrers. M. Azerrad. il *Rolling Stone* p91 F 9 '89
SOUL TRAIN MUSIC AWARDS
Dionne Warwick is not happy with Dick Clark. J. D. Stem. il pors *TV Guide* 37:6-8 Ap 8-14 '89
SOULBEAT ENTERTAINMENT NETWORK
Soulbeat mines inner-city gold. W. J. Drummond. il por *Channels (New York, N.Y.: 1986)* 9:19 S '89
SOUND
See also
Acoustics, Architectural
Animal sounds
Audio engineering
Bioacoustics
Motion picture theaters—Electronic sound control
Nature sounds
Noise
Polarization (Sound)
Psychoacoustics
Television sound
Theater—Electronic sound control
Underwater acoustics
Acoustics. bibl f *Physics Today* 42:S4-S7 Ja '89
Psychological aspects
The surprising eroticism of sound. B. Hersey. il *Glamour* 87:190-3 D '89
Recording and reproducing
See also
Audio systems

SOUND—Recording and reproducing—See also—*cont.*
　　Compact disc players
　　Compact disc recorders and recording
　　Digital audio tape recorders and recording
　　Motion picture sound recording
　　Phonograph records—Recording
　　Pulse code modulation
　　Tape recorders and recording
　　Videotape recorders and recording—Sound quality
The basics: from coding to recording. I. Masters. il *Stereo Review* 54:43-5 O '89
The basics: names and numbers. I. Masters. il *Stereo Review* 54:27-8+ N '89
Bits & pieces. D. Ranada. See alternate issues of High Fidelity (New York, N.Y.) beginning January 1986 through July 1989
Building a MIDI studio [schools] T. Messina. il *Down Beat* 56:56-7 Je '89
Compute! choice [Sound Blaster card] R. C. Leinecker. il *Compute!* 11:88-90 D '89
Innovation Sound Standard. J. Latimer. *Compute!* 11:68 Ag '89
"Just the facts, please". K. C. Pohlmann. *Stereo Review* 54:22 D '89
Magnets and music. I. Masters. il *Stereo Review* 54:39-40+ D '89
The next revolution(s) [digital audio] K. C. Pohlmann. *Stereo Review* 54:28 S '89
One hand clapping [digital audio film sound] K. Wright. *Scientific American* 260:35-7 Je '89
Revamped A&M is L.A.'s hot studio. M. Goldberg. il *Rolling Stone* p29 F 9 '89
Scan lines. D. Ranada. See alternate issues of High Fidelity (New York, N.Y.) beginning April 1986 through July 1989
Sound and image processing [special section] il *Byte* 14:240-1+ D '89
The speaker gap. K. C. Pohlmann. *Stereo Review* 54:24 O '89

　　　　Anecdotes, facetiae, satire, etc.
Audio fetish finalists. il *High Fidelity (New York, N.Y.)* 39:41-3 Je '89

　　　　Equipment
　　See Sound equipment
　　　　History
Technological turkeys [Selectavision] J. S. Gordon. il *American Heritage* 40:18+ My/Je '89
　　　　Study and teaching
Do recording schools have the inside track? K. Neely. il *Rolling Stone* p112-13+ O 5 '89

SOUND CONTRACTORS
Audio specialists for aurally savvy audiences. B. Saturn. *Theatre Crafts* 23:34+ Ap '89

SOUND DESIGNERS
　　See also
　　Kuhn, Hans Peter

SOUND EDITING (MOTION PICTURES) *See* Motion pictures—Sound editing

SOUND EFFECTS
　　See also
　　Compact discs—Sound effects
　　Theater—Sound effects

SOUND ENGINEERING *See* Audio engineering

SOUND EQUIPMENT
　　See also
　　Amplifiers
　　Headphones
　　Loudspeakers
　　Microphones
　　Phonograph
　　Sonar
　　Surround sound processors
　　Tape recorders and recording
Pioneer SP-91D digital sound processor. J. D. Hirsch. il *Stereo Review* 54:82+ D '89
Pro shop. See issues of Down Beat
Signal processors. D. Simon. il *Stereo Review* 54:107-10 D '89

　　　　Exhibitions
AES report [annual convention] R. Heller. *Theatre Crafts* 23:30-3 F '89

SOUND LABORATORIES
　　See also
　　Anechoic chambers

SOUND PERCEPTION
　　See also
　　Psychoacoustics
　　Speech perception
Binocular unmasking: an analog to binaural unmasking? B. Schneider and others. bibl f il *Science* 243:1479-81 Mr 17 '89
Tonotopic organization of the auditory cortex: pitch versus frequency representation. C. Pantev and others. bibl f il *Science* 246:486-8 O 27 '89

SOUND WAVES
　　See also
　　Helioseismology
　　Infrasonic waves
　　Ultrasonic waves

Fighting noise with antinoise. P. Elmer-Dewitt. il *Time* 134:94+ D 4 '89
SOUNDERS *See* Depth indicators
SOUNDING AND SOUNDINGS
　　See also
　　Depth indicators
SOUNDING ROCKETS *See* Rockets—Meteorological use
SOUNDPROOFING
A quiet room. J. Vara. il *Country Journal* 16:69-71 Ja '89
SOUNDS *See* Sound
SOUNDTRACK RECORDINGS *See* Phonograph records—Motion picture music
SOUP KITCHEN INTERNATIONAL (FIRM)
Slave [owner A. Yeganeh] *The New Yorker* 64:24-5 Ja 23 '89
SOUPS
　　See also
　　Campbell Soup Company
　　Chowder
　　Soup Kitchen International (Firm)
6 ingredient soups. C. Koury. il *Parents* 64:173-4+ S '89
Cool two-toners [fruit soup] il *Sunset (Central West edition)* 183:92-3 Ag '89
Festive first-course soups [microwaving] il *McCall's* 116:129 Ja '89
First things first [leak and rice soup and Tuscan vegetable soup] N. Hazelton. *National Review* 41:54-5 N 24 '89
From our kitchen to yours [making broth and stock] K. Adams. *Southern Living* 24:131 F '89
Fruit soups. C. Taylor. il *The Mother Earth News* 117:66-9 My/Je '89
Gastronomie sans argent [hearty soups] il *Gourmet* 49:66-7+ Mr '89
Heart-smart soups and sandwiches. J. B. Hurley. il *Prevention (Emmaus, Pa.)* 41:70-2+ Mr '89
In Sichuan, mild tofu meets aggressive seasoning [hot and sour tofu soup] il *Sunset (Central West edition)* 182:202+ Ap '89
Italian soup, quick and light [vegetable soup with eggs] il *Sunset (Central West edition)* 183:182 O '89
Leaf, loaf, and ladle. K. Haedrich. il *Country Journal* 16:60-4 F '89
Micro-way: super savory soups. il *McCall's* 116:135 S '89
Quick and light soups rely on fresh vegetables. il *Sunset (Central West edition)* 182:206 My '89
Selling your birthright. B. Kafka. il *Gourmet* 49:84 D '89
Soup & salad. il *Sunset (Central West edition)* 182:114-15 Ja '89
Soup & sandwich [leek & potato soup] il *Good Housekeeping* 209:128 O '89
The souper bowl. il *Ladies' Home Journal* 106:126-7+ Ja '89
Soups and stews [vegetable soup and pork stew] il *Better Homes and Gardens* 67:161-2 O '89
Soups of the South. S. Dosier. il *Southern Living* 24:66-7 F '89
Soup's on! il *Good Housekeeping* 208:150 F '89
Soup's on! R. Schrambling. il *McCall's* 117:43+ O '89
Soup's on! [microwaved] il *Good Housekeeping* 209:243-4 D '89
Stir cheese into the soup. il *Southern Living* 24:128 Ja '89
Vegetable soups for winter . . . light but satisfying. il *Sunset (Central West edition)* 182:126 F '89
Warmth and whimsy [M. Katzen's vegetable soup recipes] S. Margolis. il por *Health (New York, N.Y.)* 21:64-7+ Ja '89
SOUPS, CANNED
Quick! Start with soup. il *Southern Living* 24:172 S '89
Soup-er game recipes. S. Bashline. il *Field & Stream* 93:24 Ja '89
　　　　Labeling
Holly Driscoll had a fine idea, but it left her in the soup [collecting Campbell Soup labels to obtain van for school in Washburn, Wis.] il por *People Weekly* 31:97 My 22 '89
SOURCE CAPITAL, INC.
Compound interest machines [G. Michaelis] J. Clements. il por *Forbes* 144:43-4 Ag 21 '89
SOURCE PERRIER SA
Perrier, your bubbles are too big. T. Pouschine. il *Forbes* 143:106+ My 1 '89
SOURDOUGH BREAD *See* Bread
SOURIS RIVER
Rafferty goes on hold. P. Kopvillem. il *Maclean's* 102:14 Ap 24 '89
SOUS-VIDE COOKING *See* Food pouches
SOUSA, JAN HART
Save your family from a fire. il *Parents* 64:82+ O '89
SOUSA, MARIA JOÃO LEAL DE
　　　　about
A touch of magic. H. J. Maier. il pors *Sports Illustrated* 70 Special Issue:153-6 F '89
SOUSSAN, ANDRÉ
　　　　about
U.S. out of NATO? A French scenario. R. Kaplan. il *The American Spectator* 22:32-3 F '89

SOUTH, WILL
about
Will power. S. M. Williams. il por *Black Enterprise* 20:71-2 N '89
SOUTH *See* Southern States
SOUTH AFRICA
See also
Americans—South Africa
Beaches—South Africa
Blacks—South Africa
Capital punishment—South Africa
Civil rights—South Africa
Geology—South Africa
Government and the press—South Africa
Hospitals—South Africa
Investments, American—South Africa
Investments, Foreign—South Africa
Investments, South African
Loans, Bank—South Africa
National parks and reserves—South Africa
Paleontology—South Africa
Police—South Africa
Political prisoners—South Africa
Popular music—South Africa
Riots—South Africa
Rock music—South Africa
Sewing—Study and teaching—South Africa
South Africans
Sports—South Africa
Tennis—South Africa
United Nations—South Africa
Wildlife conservation—South Africa
Women—South Africa
Commerce
The challenge to sanctions. J. Bierman. il *Maclean's* 102:24+ Mr 13 '89
Family quarrel [British opposition to sanctions against South Africa at Commonwealth summit in Kuala Lumpur, Malaysia] R. Laver. il *Maclean's* 102:40-1 O 30 '89
Polling the Israelites: Boesak on sanctions. A. Welsh-Huggins. *The Christian Century* 106:924-5 O 18 '89
Real sanctions. *The Nation* 249:372 O 9 '89
A thorny dispute [Britain refuses to endorse call for sanctions against South Africa at Commonwealth conference in Malaysia] R. Laver. il por *Maclean's* 102:36-7 N 6 '89
Canada
See Canada—Commerce—South Africa
Great Britain
See Great Britain—Commerce—South Africa
Israel
See Israel—Commerce—South Africa
United States
See United States—Commerce—South Africa
Cultural relations
United States
See United States—Cultural relations—South Africa
Defenses
See also
Guided missiles, South African
Description and travel
Next year, the Khmer Rouge [excerpts from brochure describing police tour] M. E. Marty. *The Christian Century* 106:895 O 4 '89
Economic conditions
See also
Underground economy—South Africa
Economic policy
South Africa: the squeeze is on. J. Kapstein. il por *Business Week* p44-5+ S 11 '89
Foreign relations
Angola
The Angola/Namibia accords. C. W. Freeman. *Foreign Affairs* 68:126-41 Summ '89
Angola/Namibia accords [special section] il maps *Department of State Bulletin* 89:10-23 F '89
Namibia: the making of a new nation [tripartite agreement among Angola, Cuba, and South Africa; cover story; special section] il map *UN Chronicle* 26:34-48 Mr '89
Peace at last in Namibia? G. Lister and M. Verbaan. il *The Nation* 248:18+ Ja 2 '89
Peace in Angola? P. M. Martin. bibl f *Current History* 88:229-32+ My '89
Pretoria outflanks the ANC. S. Reiss. il map *Newsweek* 113:37 Ja 23 '89
Soviet Union
See Soviet Union—Foreign relations—South Africa
United States
See United States—Foreign relations—South Africa
History
Bibliography
South Africa: between history and the handwriting on the wall (III). R. D. Ralston. il *American Visions* 4:38-45 Ap '89
Industries
See also
Black business enterprises—South Africa
Gold mines and mining—South Africa

Native peoples
See also
Zulus
Photographs and photography
South Africa: the cordoned heart. il *Society* 26:83-7 My/Je '89
Politics and government
See also
Apartheid
Elections—South Africa
Mass Democratic Movement (South Africa)
National Party (South Africa)
Political campaigns—South Africa
Television and politics—South Africa
The beginning of the end of apartheid? [F. W. De Klerk's reforms] S. V. Roberts. il *U.S. News & World Report* 107:55 O 30 '89
Botha's untimely stroke. M. Nemeth. il por *Maclean's* 102:28 Ja 30 '89
Brother against brother [F. W. and W. De Klerk] S. MacLeod. il pors *Time* 134:49 O 9 '89
The end of an era: President Botha bids a resentful goodbye. A. Bilski. il por *Maclean's* 102:22 Ag 28 '89
The great white hope [F. W. De Klerk] B. W. Nelan. il por *Time* 134:42 S 11 '89
How far will De Klerk go? C. S. Wren. il por *The New York Times Magazine* p42-3+ N 19 '89
Masked by turmoil, apartheid weakens. R. Knight and J. Jones. il *U.S. News & World Report* 107:34-6 S 11 '89
Moving to the next stage. M. Gevisser. il *The Nation* 249:674+ D 4 '89
Peace at the mouth of the water cannon [President F. W. De Klerk's show of moderation] il por *U.S. News & World Report* 107:14 S 25 '89
Poised for change [special section] J. Bierman. il *Maclean's* 102:18-22+ Mr 13 '89
Politics in South Africa. P. O'Meara. *Current History* 88:217-20+ My '89
Pretoria's mixed signals. *Commonweal* 116:692-3 D 15 '89
Time to talk in South Africa. S. Reiss. il *Newsweek* 114:40-1 Ag 28 '89
'We're committed to reform, and we really mean business' [interview with F. W. De Klerk] S. Reiss and W. Claiborne. il por *Newsweek* 114:70 D 4 '89
Race relations
See also
Apartheid
Religious institutions and affairs
See also
African Independent Church (South Africa)
Church and race relations—South Africa
Pentecostal churches—South Africa
Territories and possessions
See also
Namibia
SOUTH AFRICA. ARMY. CIVIL COOPERATION BUREAU
Probing the hit squads. *Time* 134:30 D 18 '89
The secrets of South Africa's hit squad [D. Coetzee tells of attacks on African National Congress] *Newsweek* 114:56 N 27 '89
SOUTH AFRICA. CONSTITUTION
The illusion of reform in South Africa. D. Palos and T. Soeldner. *The Christian Century* 106:447-50 Ap 26 '89
SOUTH AFRICA IN LITERATURE
See also
Apartheid in literature
Can South Africa change? [cover story] G. M. Fredrickson. il *The New York Review of Books* 36:48-55 O 26 '89
South Africa: between history and the handwriting on the wall (III). R. D. Ralston. il *American Visions* 4:38-45 Ap '89
Time stands still. M. Gevisser. *The Nation* 249:390-3 O 9 '89
SOUTH AFRICA IN MOTION PICTURES
See also
Apartheid in motion pictures
SOUTH AFRICA NOW [television program] See Television program reviews—Single works
SOUTH AFRICANS
France
True confessions of an exiled Afrikaner [B. Breytenbach] G. Marzorati. il pors *The New York Times Magazine* p32-3+ Ag 27 '89
United States
A pilgrim's progress [black marathoner M. Plaatjes] J. Brant. il pors *Runner's World* 24:66-71 D '89
SOUTH AMERICA
See also
Agriculture—South America
Amazon River Valley
Argentina
Birds—South America
Brazil
Chile
Colombia
Mount Roraima
Paraguay
Peru

SOUTH AMERICA—See also—cont.
Venezuela
Native peoples
See Indians of South America
Politics and government
See Latin America—Politics and government
SOUTH AMERICAN INDIANS See Indians of South America
SOUTH ASIA
Bibliography
Book reviews. *Current History* 88:441+ D '89
Foreign relations
United States
See United States—Foreign relations—South Asia
Politics and government
A diverse and troubled region. S. Manning. map *Scholastic Update (Teachers' edition)* 121:6-7 Mr 10 '89
Middle East opportunities. G. Kemp. *Foreign Affairs* 68 Special Issue:139-58 ['89]
South Asia [cover story; special issue] bibl f il map (inside back cover) *Current History* 88:417-40+ D '89
SOUTH ASIAN ASSOCIATION FOR REGIONAL COOPERATION
Promoting peace and prosperity in the South Asian region [address, October 6, 1988] G. P. Shultz. *Department of State Bulletin* 88:19-20 D '88
SOUTH BARRINGTON (ILL.)
Religious institutions and affairs
See also
Willow Creek Community Church (South Barrington, Ill.)
SOUTH BRONX (NEW YORK, N.Y.) See Bronx (New York, N.Y.)
SOUTH CAROLINA
See also
Beaches—South Carolina
Chattooga River
Criminal justice, Administration of—South Carolina
Education—South Carolina
Geology—South Carolina
Greenville County (S.C.)
Historic houses, sites, etc.—South Carolina
Housing—South Carolina
Jocassee Watershed (N.C.-S.C.)
Paleontology—South Carolina
Resorts—South Carolina
Sumter County (S.C.)
Climate
The brutal lesson of Hurricane Hugo [problems of coastal development] il *U.S. News & World Report* 107:13 O 2 '89
Politics and government
NAACP sues 5 S. Carolina cities over voting systems. il *Jet* 76:32 Jl 24 '89
SOUTH CAROLINA COOKING See Cooking, American
SOUTH DAKOTA
See also
Agriculture—South Dakota
Black Hills (S.D. and Wyo.)
Jewel Cave National Monument (S.D.)
Mount Rushmore National Memorial (S.D.)
Public health—South Dakota
Ranches—South Dakota
Thunderhead Mountain (S.D.)
How the West was lost. R. J. Margolis. *The New Leader* 72:13-14 N 27 '89
Industries
See also
Swine industry
Politics and government
South Dakota says no to the corporate sow. G. Vincent. *Successful Farming* 87:35 F '89
SOUTH FLORIDA CULTURAL CONSORTIUM
A cultural consortium helps the arts bloom in sunny South Florida. S. Guy. il *Horizon (Tuscaloosa, Ala.)* 32:17-20 Ja/F '89
SOUTH GEORGIA ISLAND
See also
Wildlife—South Georgia Island
Description and travel
See also
Cruising—South Georgia Island
SOUTH HADLEY (MASS.)
Bookstores
See Booksellers and bookselling—Massachusetts
Stores
Small-town village [Village Commons] G. Anderson. il *Architectural Record* 177:102-3 S '89
SOUTH KOREA See Korea (South)
SOUTH LUANGWA NATIONAL PARK (ZAMBIA)
Zambia. E. McGowan. il map *Travel Holiday* 171:42-51 Ap '89
SOUTH PADRE ISLAND (TEX.)
See also
Beaches—South Padre Island (Tex.)
Social life and customs
Spring break at Padre Island: a new kind of tourism. J. Gerlach. bibl il map *Focus (New York, N.Y.: 1950)* 39:13-16+ Spr '89

SOUTH PASADENA (CALIF.)
Restaurants, nightclubs, bars, etc.
Spécialités de la maison:
Restaurant Shiro. C. Bates. *Gourmet* 49:38+ F '89
SOUTH POLE
See also
Antarctic exploration
SOUTH SEA COMPANY
When the Bubble burst, all of England wound up broke [18th century stock swindle] R. Wernick. bibl (p183) il *Smithsonian* 20:155-6+ D '89
SOUTH SEA ISLANDS See Oceania
SOUTH SLOUGH NATIONAL ESTUARINE RESEARCH RESERVE (OR.)
Researching the Slough. M. Hoy. il map *Audubon* 91:98-105 Mr '89
SOUTH WEST AFRICA PEOPLE'S ORGANIZATION See SWAPO
SOUTH YEMEN See Yemen (People's Democratic Republic)
SOUTHAM INC.
Buying the Times [Globe and mail takes over Financial times of Canada] D. Todd. il *Maclean's* 102:47-8 D 25 '89
SOUTHAMPTON (N.Y.)
Gardens and gardening
By any other name [garden of R. de Rose] W. P. Rayner. il *House & Garden* 161:70+ My '89
Hampton classic [L. Mezzacappa's Southampton garden designed by D. Nevins] K. Whiteside. il *House & Garden* 161:82-9 Ja '89
Historic houses, sites, etc.
Clean sweep [remodeled farmhouse by Motif Designs] D. Brenner. il *House & Garden* 161:118-23 Je '89
Long Island symmetry: reworking a designer's 1920s residence in Southampton [home of A. E. Smith] P. Warner. il *Architectural Digest* 46:138-43 Jl '89
SOUTHEAST ASIA
See also
Airlines—Routes—Southeast Asia
Architecture—Southeast Asia
ASEAN
Burma
Cambodia
Drug laws and regulations—Southeast Asia
Thailand
Vietnam
Commerce
Asia's rising export powers. L. Kraar. il *Fortune* 120 no13 Special Issue:43+ Fall '89
Japan
See Japan—Commerce—Southeast Asia
Foreign relations
United States
See United States—Foreign relations—Southeast Asia
SOUTHEAST BOOKSELLERS ASSOCIATION
SEBA meets in Atlanta. J. Mutter. il *Publishers Weekly* 236:60-2 O 6 '89
SOUTHEAST TOYOTA DISTRIBUTORS
Jim Moran, master salesman. G. Button. il pors *Forbes* 144 Special Issue:54-5+ O 23 '89
SOUTHEASTERN ASSET MANAGEMENT INC.
Eyeing companies with lots of cash [interview with M. Hawkins] A. E. Serwer. il por *Fortune* 119:37-9 F 13 '89
SOUTHEASTERN BAPTIST THEOLOGICAL SEMINARY
AAUP censures Southeastern Seminary [academic freedom issues] R. L. Hester. *The Christian Century* 106:742-4 Ag 16-23 '89
SBC seminary accused [alleged infringements of academic freedom] *The Christian Century* 106:41 Ja 18 '89
Seminary given until December to correct hiring policy. M. Wingfield. *Christianity Today* 33:54-5 F 3 '89
SOUTHEASTERN INSURANCE GROUP
Guarantees with nothing behind them. A. A. Lappen. il *Forbes* 144:41-2 Jl 24 '89
Worthless guarantees. A. A. Lappen. il *Forbes* 144:10 S 4 '89
SOUTHEASTERN SPORTS NETWORK
The man of a thousand networks [T. Turner] M. Curriden. il *Sport (New York, N.Y.)* 80:14 S '89
SOUTHEASTERN STATES
See also
Acid rain—Southeastern States
Banks and banking—Southeastern States
SOUTHEND MUSICWORKS, INC.
New oasis for Southend Musicworks. J. Dejong. il *Down Beat* 56:11+ Mr '89
SOUTHER, GLENN MICHAEL, 1957-1989
about
Obituary
People Weekly il pors 32:105-6 Jl 17 '89. W. Plummer
Time por 134:40 Jl 10 '89
SOUTHERN, HUGH
about
New man in charge [interview] P. J. Smith. il por *Opera News* 54:16-17 N '89

SOUTHERN AFRICA
   See also
   Angola
   Malawi
   Namibia
   South Africa
   Wildlife management—Southern Africa
   Zimbabwe
       Foreign relations
       United States
   See United States—Foreign relations—Southern Africa
     Politics and government
Southern Africa: eight years later. C. A. Crocker. bibl f
   Foreign Affairs 68:144-64 Fall '89
SOUTHERN BAPTIST CONVENTION *See* Baptists—United
   States
SOUTHERN CHRISTIAN LEADERSHIP CONFERENCE
SCLC inks a fair share pact; hears pledges of Bush Cabinet
   at confab. il *Jet* 76:4-5 S 4 '89
SOUTHERN COOKING *See* Cooking, American
SOUTHERN FESTIVAL OF BOOKS *See* Book fairs
SOUTHERN FURNITURE MARKET *See* Furniture—Ex-
   hibitions
SOUTHERN HEMISPHERE
       Climate
South stays cooler in greenhouse models. R. Monastersky.
   Science News 136:413 D 23-30 '89
SOUTHERN HIGHLAND HANDICRAFT GUILD
The guild gives crafts a hand. J. T. Black. il *Southern Living*
   24:74-7 S '89
SOUTHERN HOME AWARDS
1989 Southern Home Awards [cover story; special section]
   il *Southern Living* 24:55-65 F '89
SOUTHERN LIVING (PERIODICAL)
Life at Southern living. G. E. McCalla. See issues of Southern
   Living
SOUTHERN OSCILLATION
Deep-rooted disturbance [link between earthquakes and El
   Niño; research by Daniel Walker] S. Vogel. il *Discover*
   10:26+ Jl '89
Length-of-day variations caused by El Niño-Southern Oscilla-
   tion and Quasi-Biennial Oscillation. B. F. Chao. bibl f
   il *Science* 243:923-5 F 17 '89
Stratospheric winds alter day's length [research by B. Fong
   Chao] R. Monastersky. *Science News* 135:102 F 18 '89
SOUTHERN STATES
   See also
   Architecture, Domestic—Southern States
   Art galleries and museums—Southern States
   Birds—Southern States
   Blacks—Southern States
   Child welfare—Southern States
   Education—Southern States
   Festivals—Southern States
   Fishing—Southern States
   Gardens and gardening—Southern States
   Historic houses, sites, etc.—Southern States
   Hotels, motels, etc.—Southern States
   Hunting—Southern States
   National seashores—Southern States
   Organic gardens and gardening—Southern States
Heartland vs. Sunbelt [quality of life; study by Dowell Myers]
   il *USA Today (Periodical)* 118:4-5 D '89
[Month] in the South. J. Noles. See issues of Southern Living
   beginning February 1987
       Bibliography
Books about the South. See issues of Southern Living
       Civilization
       Encyclopedias
Books about antiques [Encyclopedia of Southern culture]
   W. Garrett. il *Antiques* 136:756 O '89
Geophagy explained! [Encyclopedia of southern culture] P.
   Patton. il *Esquire* 112:49 O '89
Getting to the heart of Dixie. H. Raines. il *The New York
   Times Book Review* 94:3+ S 17 '89
The narcissistic South. C. V. Woodward. bibl f il *The New
   York Review of Books* 36:13-14+ O 26 '89
North Carolina to publish southern culture compendium.
   G. Corcoran. il *Publishers Weekly* 235:48-9 My 19 '89
The South rises—to the occasion of an 'Encycloparty'
   [promotional event] M. J. O'Brien. il *Publishers Weekly*
   236:40 Ag 25 '89
'Tell about the South. What's it like there. What do they
   do . . .' [Encyclopedia of southern culture] N. Schreiber.
   il *Smithsonian* 20:163-4+ S '89
       Climate
[Month] weather. B. Schilit. See issues of Southern Living
     Description and travel
   See also
   Automobile touring—Southern States
Call for fall color. il *Southern Living* 24:33 S '89
Travel South. See issues of Southern Living
       History
   See also
   Confederate States of America
   Slavery
   United States—History—Civil War, 1861-1865

Library with a southern accent [Tutwiler Collection of
   Southern History and Literature maintained by the public
   library in Birmingham] il *Southern Living* 24:46 Mr '89
       Industries
Spotting the true belles among southern stocks. J. Edgerton
   and others. il *Money* 18:7-8 Ap '89
     Politics and government
Goodbye to the 'yellow dogs' [GOP's new recruits] J. N.
   Baker. il *Newsweek* 113:32 Ap 10 '89
Slim GOP pickin's in Dixie. H. Wyman. il *The American
   Spectator* 22:30-1 Ag '89
       Race relations
   See also
   Ku Klux Klan
The man who changed his skin [white author J. H. Griffin's
   four weeks as an itinerant southern black in 1959] E.
   Sharpe, Jr. il pors *American Heritage* 40:44-55 F '89
     Social life and customs
Southern journal. See issues of Southern Living
SOUTHERN UNIVERSITY
Southern Univ. fighting fed. desegregation order. *Jet* 77:26
   N 27 '89
SOUTHERNERS
Southerners. See issues of Southern Living
SOUTHERNERS IN MOTION PICTURES
Beth's beauties [Miss Firecracker; cover story] K. Jaehne.
   il pors *Film Comment* 25:9-12+ My/Je '89
Dolled up in Dixie [filming of Steel magnolias] B. D. Johnson.
   il *Maclean's* 102:84+ N 20 '89
Star bright [filming of R. Harling's play Steel magnolias;
   special section] L. Hart. il por *Life* 12:82-4+ O '89
SOUTHFIELD (MICH.)
'Hit Man' Hearns' brother charged in shooting of 'girlfriend'
   in Michigan. il pors *Jet* 76:51-2 Je 26 '89
SOUTHGATE, COLIN
       about
Don't worry, he's happy. L. Gubernick. il por *Forbes* 143:154
   Ap 17 '89
SOUTHLAND CORP.
The Texas chain store massacre [leveraged buyout and
   Cityplace Center] J. H. Taylor. il *Forbes* 143:54+ F 6
   '89
Today, class, we'll learn about soap [7-Eleven store operated
   by students in Union City, Calif. high school] L. Wright.
   Newsweek 113:63 Mr 20 '89
SOUTHWEST AIRLINES CO.
Southwest Airlines: flying high with 'Uncle Herb' [H. Kelleher]
   K. Kelly. il por *Business Week* p53+ Jl 3 '89
SOUTHWEST BANCSHARES, INC.
   See also
   MCorp
**SOUTHWEST MUSEUM OF SCIENCE AND TECHNOLO-
   GY, THE SCIENCE PLACE**
Turning physics into fun. il *Southern Living* 24:36 Ja '89
SOUTHWESTERN COOKING *See* Cooking, American
SOUTHWESTERN STATES
   See also
   Architecture, Domestic—Southwestern States
     Photographs and photography
Southwest! J. Hunter and P. Makaea. il *Petersen's Photographic
   Magazine* 18:30-3+ Je '89
SOUTHWORTH, ALBERT SANDS, 1811-1894
       about
Masters of the daguerreotype. il *American History Illustrated*
   24:32-3 S/O '89
SOUVENIR SPOONS *See* Spoons
SOUVENIRS (KEEPSAKES)
   See also
   Baseball, Professional—Collectibles
   Black collectibles
   Vietnamese War, 1957-1975—Collectibles
Turning point [family memorabilia] C. L. Mithers. il *Ladies'
   Home Journal* 106:94 O '89
SOVEREIGNTY
Sovereignty and the environment. K. Piddington. il
   Environment 31:18-20+ S '89
SOVERN, MICHAEL I.
The real crisis. il *The New York Times Magazine* p24-5+
   Ja 22 '89
SOVEY, L. TERRELL, JR.
       about
Scuffle in the boardroom. A. A. Lappen. pors *Forbes* 144:112+
   O 16 '89
SOVIET ACADEMY OF SCIENCES *See* Academy of Sciences
   of the USSR
SOVIET LIFE (PERIODICAL)
     Anecdotes, facetiae, satire, etc.
Caught red-handed [Progressive caught using Soviet life's
   subscriber list] E. Knoll. *The Progressive* 53:4 My '89
SOVIET STUDIES
   See also
   Harvard University. Russian Research Center
Confessions of a self-made Sovietologist. W. Laqueur. *Society*
   26:5-9 S/O '89
Kremlin watchers: the new guard [women specialists] il *Ms.*
   17:76-7 My '89

SOVIET STUDIES—*cont.*
The Soviet challenge to American education [interpreting policies of M. Gorbachev] B. T. Trout. *The Education Digest* 54:35-7 Ap '89
A surprise for Sovietologists. C. Bogert. il *Newsweek* 113:62 My 15 '89
Understanding the USSR. K. Egan. *The Education Digest* 54:40-2 Mr '89
SOVIET TENNIS FEDERATION
In search of a net gain [Soviet player N. Zvereva signs with ProServ and demands right to control earnings] D. Scheiber. il pors *Sports Illustrated* 70:24-6 My 1 '89
SOVIET UNION
See also
Abortion—Laws and regulations—Soviet Union
Abortion clinics—Soviet Union
Advertising—Soviet Union
Agriculture—Soviet Union
AIDS (Disease)—Soviet Union
Alcoholics and alcoholism—Soviet Union
Americans—Soviet Union
Amur River (China and Soviet Union)
Architecture—Soviet Union
Armenia (Soviet Union)
Art—Soviet Union
Art and state—Soviet Union
Art trade—Soviet Union
Arts—Soviet Union
Astronomical observatories—Soviet Union
Astronomical research—Soviet Union
Astronomy—Soviet Union
Aviation—Soviet Union
Azerbaijan (Soviet Union)
Ballet—Soviet Union
Baltic States
Banks and banking—Soviet Union
Baseball—Soviet Union
Basketball—Soviet Union
Beauty contests—Soviet Union
Blacks—Soviet Union
Blagoveshchensk (Soviet Union)
Booksellers and bookselling—Soviet Union
Budget—Soviet Union
Business management—Soviet Union
Canadians—Soviet Union
Carnival (Pre-Lenten festival)—Soviet Union
Catholic Church—Relations (Diplomatic)—Soviet Union
Celebrities—Soviet Union
Censorship—Soviet Union
Chernobyl nuclear disaster, 1986
Churches (Buildings)—Soviet Union
Civil rights—Soviet Union
Clothing and dress—Soviet Union
Computers—Study and teaching—Soviet Union
Concentration camps—Soviet Union
Conservatism—Soviet Union
Consumer protection—Soviet Union
Consumption (Economics)—Soviet Union
Cooperative associations—Soviet Union
Costume—Soviet Union
Courts—Soviet Union
Criminal justice, Administration of—Soviet Union
Dance—Soviet Union
Drinking customs—Soviet Union
Economic assistance—Soviet Union
Economic assistance, American—Soviet Union
Economic conversion—Soviet Union
Education—Soviet Union
Elite (Social sciences)—Soviet Union
Environmental movement—Soviet Union
Environmental policy—Soviet Union
Estonia
Factory management—Soviet Union
Family—Soviet Union
Finance—Soviet Union
Food supply—Soviet Union
Foreign exchange—Laws and regulations—Soviet Union
Freedom of information—Soviet Union
Gangs—Soviet Union
Gas pipelines—Soviet Union
Georgia (Soviet Union)
Government and the press—Soviet Union
Hackers (Computer enthusiasts)—Soviet Union
Handicapped—Soviet Union
Hockey—Soviet Union
Hospitals, Psychiatric—Soviet Union
Housing—Soviet Union
Hunting—Soviet Union
Immigration and emigration—Soviet Union
Industry and the environment—Soviet Union
Investments, American—Soviet Union
Investments, Canadian—Soviet Union
Investments, Foreign—Soviet Union
Investments, West German—Soviet Union
Jazz music—Soviet Union
Jews—Soviet Union
Kraternaya Bay (Soviet Union)
Labor laws and regulations—Soviet Union

Land reform—Soviet Union
Latvia
Leningrad (Soviet Union)
Literature and state—Soviet Union
Loans, Bank—Soviet Union
Loans, Russian
Military education—Soviet Union
Military research—Soviet Union
Minorities—Soviet Union
Moldavia (Soviet Union)
Money—Soviet Union
Morale, National—Soviet Union
Moscow (Soviet Union)
Motion pictures—Soviet Union
Music and state—Soviet Union
Music festivals—Soviet Union
Nagorno-Karabakh Autonomous Oblast (Soviet Union)
Narcotics laws and regulations—Soviet Union
Nuclear facilities—Soviet Union
Nuclear research—Soviet Union
Nuclear ships—Soviet Union
Opera—Soviet Union
Palaces—Soviet Union
Parapsychology—Soviet Union
Passports—Soviet Union
Peasantry—Soviet Union
Physical fitness—Soviet Union
Physics—Soviet Union
Poetry and state—Soviet Union
Political campaigns—Soviet Union
Political clubs and associations—Soviet Union
Political prisoners—Soviet Union
Pollution—Soviet Union
Privatization—Soviet Union
Psychiatry—Soviet Union
Radioactive pollution—Soviet Union
Radioactive waste disposal—Soviet Union
Railroads—Soviet Union
Real estate investment—Soviet Union
Religious liberty—Soviet Union
Rock music—Soviet Union
Rostov-on-Don (Soviet Union)
Sakhalin (Soviet Union)
Saving and savings—Soviet Union
Science—Study and teaching—Soviet Union
Science and state—Soviet Union
Sexual behavior—Soviet Union
Shopping—Soviet Union
Siberia (Soviet Union)
Skiing—Soviet Union
Social science research—Soviet Union
Sociology—Soviet Union
Softball—Soviet Union
Space centers—Soviet Union
Space research—Soviet Union
Sports and state—Soviet Union
Strikes—Coal miners—Soviet Union
Strikes—Soviet Union
Swedes—Soviet Union
Tambov (Soviet Union)
Tbilisi (Soviet Union)
Technical assistance, American—Soviet Union
Technology—Soviet Union
Television broadcasting—Soviet Union
Textbooks—Soviet Union
Theater—Soviet Union
Treasury bills and notes—Soviet Union
Trials—Soviet Union
Underground literature—Soviet Union
United States—Diplomatic and consular service—Soviet Union
Women—Soviet Union
Youth—Soviet Union
Zhukovka (Soviet Union)
The new U.S.S.R.: special issue. il *Time* 133:3-6+ Ap 10 '89
Regional report: the Soviet Union. S. Shabad. See issues of World Press Review beginning October 1986
The Soviets' uncertain future [views of Henry S. Rowen] *USA Today (Periodical)* 117:9-10 Ap '89
Anecdotes, facetiae, satire, etc.
Last word. S. Sinberg. por *Omni (New York, N.Y.)* 11:104 Ag '89
Appropriations and expenditures
See also
Soviet Union—Armed Forces—Appropriations and expenditures
Armed Forces
See also
Soviet Union—Army
Can Gorbachev reform the Soviet military? W. E. Odom. il *U.S. News & World Report* 107:43 S 11 '89
The Soviet empire: the military [cover story; special section] il maps *U.S. News & World Report* 106:18-21+ Mr 13 '89

SOVIET UNION—Armed Forces—*cont.*
Appropriations and expenditures
CIA sees long-term pressures against Soviet defense budget. P. Mann. *Aviation Week & Space Technology* 130:30 My 1 '89
The common defense [disproportionate burden shouldered by U.S. compounded by Western loans to Soviet Union] E. Rubenstein. il *National Review* 41:19 Je 30 '89
A farewell to arms? The Soviets rethink defense spending. P. Grenier and E. Stubbs. il *USA Today (Periodical)* 118:19-21 N '89
Outflanking Gorbachev. *Aviation Week & Space Technology* 130:7 Ja 23 '89
Forces in Afghanistan
See also
Afghanistan—Russian invasion, 1979-1989
Forces in Eastern Europe
Arms negotiations in Europe. J. Erickson. *Current History* 88:369-72+ N '89
Can we trust this nice Mr. Gorbachev? C. W. Weinberger. il *Forbes* 143:37 Ja 9 '89
Gorba Claus [effects of Soviet troop reduction proposal] *The New Republic* 200:5-7 Ja 2 '89
Gorbachev talks but who listens? W. M. Arkin. il por *The Bulletin of the Atomic Scientists* 45:5-6 Mr '89
A leaner, meaner Soviet military. S. Budiansky. il map *U.S. News & World Report* 107:54+ N 6 '89
Remember Khrushchev. M. Tatu. *World Press Review* 36:24 F '89
Superpower disengagement. C. Layne. *Foreign Policy* 77:17-40 Wint '89/'90
U.S.S.R. arms reduction [address, December 7, 1988] M. Gorbachev. *Vital Speeches of the Day* 55:229-36 F 1 '89
Army
Building a military machine. J. Trimble. il *U.S. News & World Report* 106:31-2+ Mr 13 '89
Here come the '*glasnost* generals'. J. Lloyd. *World Press Review* 36:38-9 Mr '89
Bibliography
Book reviews. *Current History* 88:345-6+ O '89
Civilization
Black and white houses? [contrasting cultures of United States and Soviet Union] P. Dukes. il *History Today* 39:9-11 Ap '89
Commerce
The five-percenters, Moscow's pet capitalists [privileged foreign businessmen acting as go-betweens; cover story] P. Berman. il *Forbes* 143:93-7 F 6 '89
Canada
See also
Canada-U.S.S.R. Business Council
The art of the deal: prying open the Soviet market. M. Gray. il *Maclean's* 102:40 D 4 '89
China
Watermelon diplomacy on the border [Sino-Soviet thaw along Amur River] J. Trimble. il map *U.S. News & World Report* 106:33 My 15 '89
East Asia
Chips for the Soviet bloc? Computers from Asia short-circuit America's export controls. S. Budiansky. il *U.S. News & World Report* 107:28-30 O 9 '89
Germany (West)
Selling security for deutschemarks [R. Mueller gets suspended sentence for selling military technology to the Soviets] R. N. Perle. il *U.S. News & World Report* 107:36 Jl 31 '89
Soviets book new commercial payloads, grant greater access to space facilities [Kayser-Threde microgravity missions] J. M. Lenorovitz. *Aviation Week & Space Technology* 131:121+ O 9 '89
Italy
'Hey! Want a hot little alloy from Shemyakin?' [Soviet sales of high tech] J. Rossant. il *Business Week* p82 Je 26 '89
Libya
Red mischief [Soviet sale of bombers] *The New Republic* 200:10-11 My 1 '89
Soviet sale of Su-24 deepens concern about Mideast weapons proliferation. M. Mecham. il *Aviation Week & Space Technology* 130:19-20 Ap 10 '89
United States
See United States—Commerce—Soviet Union
Western Europe
See also
Coordinating Committee on Multilateral Export Controls
Aeroflot signs letter of intent to purchase five Airbus A310-300s. *Aviation Week & Space Technology* 131:18 N 6 '89
The curtain that still divides Europe. D. Lawday. il maps *U.S. News & World Report* 107:36+ Jl 17 '89
Commercial policy
See also
Soviet Union. Aviaexport
Economic changes in the U.S.S.R. [address, May 23, 1989] A. W. Clausen. *Vital Speeches of the Day* 55:674-7 S 1 '89
Soviet adventures in capitalism. *World Press Review* 36:51 Ja '89

The Supreme Soviet flexes its nyet power. P. Galuszka. il *Business Week* p77+ Jl 17 '89
Cultural policy
Andris Liepa leaps to the U.S., but with *glasnost* the Bolshoi star can go home again [performing with American Ballet Theatre] R. Arias. il pors *People Weekly* 31:50-2 My 29 '89
The red shoes dance modern [Kirov Ballet will perform works of G. Balanchine] il por *U.S. News & World Report* 106:16 F 27 '89
Cultural relations
Germany (West)
Ludwig museums go east. J. Gambrell. *Art in America* 77:35+ Je '89
Great Britain
See Great Britain—Cultural relations—Soviet Union
India
Shashi Kapoor branches out [Indo-Soviet production of film Ajooba] P. Saxena. il por *World Press Review* 36:75 S '89
United States
See United States—Cultural relations—Soviet Union
Defenses
See also
Airplanes, Military—Soviet Union
Disarmament
Guided missiles, Russian
Korean Air Lines Flight 007 disaster, 1983
Nuclear submarines, Russian
Soviet Union—Armed Forces
Soviet Union—Army
Soviet Union—Navy
Strategic Arms Limitation Talks
Strategic Arms Reduction Talks
Warsaw Treaty Organization
Defense Dept. assessment says Soviets deploying improved ICBMs [1989 edition of Soviet military power] D. F. Bond. il *Aviation Week & Space Technology* 131:24-5 O 2 '89
Estimated Soviet nuclear stockpile, July 1989. il *The Bulletin of the Atomic Scientists* 45:56 Jl/Ag '89
Grudging kindness, gentle exaggeration. D. Lockwood. il *The Bulletin of the Atomic Scientists* 45:4-5 D '89
Soviet strategic nuclear forces, end of 1988. il *The Bulletin of the Atomic Scientists* 45:52 Mr '89
Description and travel
Back to the USSR. R. Conquest. il *National Review* 41:24-7 Ag 18 '89
A journey to the U.S.S.R. H. Herman. il map *National Geographic World* 165:12-16 My '89
Economic conditions
See also
Agriculture—Soviet Union
Cost and standard of living—Soviet Union
Food supply—Soviet Union
Inflation (Finance)—Soviet Union
Underground economy—Soviet Union
Empire of the will. P. Brimelow. il *Forbes* 143:53+ Ja 9 '89
The poverty of communism. E. Rubenstein. il *National Review* 41:15 F 24 '89
Economic policy
Adam Smithkichov lives. W. F. Buckley. *National Review* 41:55 Ag 4 '89
Adrift. P. Fuhrman. il *Forbes* 144:44 Ag 7 '89
'At least we now have the will to fight'. D. Elliott. il *Newsweek* 112:49 My 22 '89
At the top of Washington's reading list [A. Aslund's Gorbachev's struggle for economic reform] A. Platt. il *Newsweek* 114:23 O 2 '89
Atari Communists: from hardline to software [effects of *perestroika*; cover story; special section; with editorial comment by Nathan Gardels] il *New Perspectives Quarterly* 5:2-60 Wint '88/'89
The benefits of benign neglect [G. Bush's non-interference in M. Gorbachev's economic reform strategies] M. Ruby. il *U.S. News & World Report* 107:68 Jl 31 '89
Can Gorbachev radicalize *perestroika*? S. Bialer. il *U.S. News & World Report* 107:39-40 Ag 7 '89
Crises around the clock. H. Anderson. il por *Newsweek* 114:30-1 Ag 7 '89
The economic crisis. il *National Review* 41:26-7 Ap 7 '89
For Gorbachev, *perestroika II* may mean survival. R. Brady. il *Business Week* p60+ S 25 '89
The future of Soviet economic reform. M. I. Goldman. bibl f *Current History* 88:329-32+ O '89
The Gorbachev prospect. G. Soros. il *The New York Review of Books* 36:16-18 Je 1 '89
Gorbachev's gamble. A. Wilson-Smith. il por *Maclean's* 102:25-6 Ag 7 '89
Gorbachev's long journey. R. Grenier. il *National Review* 41:27-9 D 31 '89
Gorbachev's reforms: will they work? [special section] il por *Business Week* p52-7+ Je 5 '89
His vision thing [policies of M. Gorbachev] B. W. Nelan. il pors *Time* 134:22-3 O 2 '89
How much longer can Gorbachev keep putting out fires? D. Rinehart. il *Business Week* p41 Ag 7 '89

SOVIET UNION—Economic policy—*cont.*
How to dismantle communism [interview with I. Birman] P. Lubin. il *National Review* 41:29-33 D 8 '89
I was a teenage Communist. A. P. Tobias. il *Time* 134:39 Jl 31 '89
Is Gorbachev's economy doomed to collapse? R. Cornwell. il *World Press Review* 36:20+ S '89
Is the Soviet economy too sick for *perestroika*? R. Brady and M. McNamee. *Business Week* p33 O 16 '89
"Let your readers be reassured there will be no military coup" [interview with N. Ryzhkov; with reply by Paul Klebnikov] P. Dragadze. il por *Forbes* 144:82+ O 16 '89
A long, mighty struggle. W. Isaacson. il por *Time* 133:48-52+ Ap 10 '89
The man behind Gorbachev [A. G. Aganbegian] R. I. Kirkland. por *Fortune* 119:47 Ja 2 '89
New York, New York—it's a wonderful town [excerpts from address] B. Yeltsin. *National Review* 41:19-20 O 13 '89
On the Atari Communists [discussion of Winter 1988-89 special section, Atari Communists: from hardline to software] *New Perspectives Quarterly* 6:60-1 Spr '89
Perestroika [address, September 11, 1989] M. Gorbachev. *Vital Speeches of the Day* 56:5-7 O 15 '89
Perestroika isn't working. F. Coleman and R. Watson. il por *Newsweek* 113:28-31+ Mr 13 '89
Perestroika on ice. R. Brady. il *Business Week* p44 D 25 '89-Ja 1 '90
Reform: Moscow vs. Beijing. S. Bialer. il *U.S. News & World Report* 106:32-3 F 6 '89
Riding a dangerous wave [effects of *perestroika*] B. W. Nelan. il por *Time* 134:27 Ag 7 '89
The Soviet economy in shambles [cover story; special section; with editorial comment by Mortimer B. Zuckerman] S. Dentzer and J. Trimble. il map *U.S. News & World Report* 107:25-9+, 100 N 20 '89
Soviet economy: oxymoron? *National Review* 41:14-15 D 22 '89
The Soviet empire: the society [effects of *glasnost* and *perestroika*; cover story; special section; with editorial comment by Mortimer B. Zuckerman] il por maps *U.S. News & World Report* 106:34-9+, 80 Ap 3 '89
Supply-side theory is alive and well—in Moscow. P. C. Roberts. il *Business Week* p10 Jl 24 '89
'Waiting is death. It cannot be tolerated any longer' [interview with A. G. Aganbegian] por *U.S. News & World Report* 107:35 S 25 '89
Why Russia is still in the red. R. I. Kirkland, Jr. il *Fortune* 119:173-4+ Ja 30 '89
Why the Bear's cupboards are bare. W. R. Doerner. il *Time* 133:33+ Ja 16 '89
Winter's bitter wind. R. Hornik. il *Time* 134:62-5 D 4 '89
Yes . . . but [interview with V. Pavlov] P. Dragadze. il por *Forbes* 144:94 O 16 '89
Anecdotes, facetiae, satire, etc.
The finer points of *perestroika* [imaginary meeting among Gorbachev and his advisers following the Baker mini-summit] R. N. Perle. *U.S. News & World Report* 107:41 O 2 '89
Economic relations
See also
Soviet Union—Commerce
Economic growth and military power: erosion of the superpowers. W. Goldstein. *Current (Washington, D.C.)* 309:23-31 Ja '89
The West should not bankroll *perestroika*. B. Bradley. *USA Today (Periodical)* 118:22-4 Jl '89
East Asia
Challenges and issues for Asia and the Pacific [address, June 7, 1989] W.-C. Kim. *Vital Speeches of the Day* 55:642-4 Ag 15 '89
The Soviet Union and the Asian-Pacific region in the 1990s [address, November 11, 1988] V. Krasnov. *Vital Speeches of the Day* 55:164-6 Ja 1 '89
Germany (West)
Playing the German card. *National Review* 41:16-18 Jl 14 '89
Japan
Will Gorbachev team up with Japan and Korea? P. Galuszka. il *Business Week* p70 Je 5 '89
Korea (South)
Will Gorbachev team up with Japan and Korea? P. Galuszka. il *Business Week* p70 Je 5 '89
United States
See United States—Economic relations—Soviet Union
Western Europe
Two great experiments: 'perestroika' and 1992. *World Press Review* 36:24 Ja '89
Foreign opinion
American
Changing cold war attitudes: America's "new thinking". D. Yankelovich and R. Smoke. il *Current (Washington, D.C.)* 309:32-40 Ja '89
Gorby of Mayberry. R. E. Tyrrell. *The American Spectator* 22:10-11 O '89
How open shall we be to *glasnost*? C. W. Colson. il *Christianity Today* 33:72 My 12 '89

Is *glasnost* genuine? [address, November 6, 1988] M. Warder. *Vital Speeches of the Day* 55:341-4 Mr 15 '89
Kinder, gentler Soviets [U.S. national public opinion poll] il *Society* 26:3-4 Jl/Ag '89
The world turned upside down [post cold war attitudes; cover story] M. Kondracke. il *The New Republic* 201:26-9 S 18-25 '89
The wounds of *glasnost* [apprehension of the American left over changes in Soviet Union] A. Puddington. il *National Review* 41:26-8 N 24 '89
British
Spies who come in from the cold war [interview with J. Le Carré] V. Orlik. il por *World Press Review* 36:28+ O 17 '89
Foreign relations
See also
Espionage, Russian
Military assistance, Russian
As Kabul teeters, Gorbachev lands on his feet. P. Galuszka and others. il *Business Week* p51 F 20 '89
The boss of Smolensky Square [with interview with A. Shevardnadze; cover story] J. Kohan. il pors *Time* 133:29-30+ My 15 '89
The dangers beyond containment [cover story] P. Glynn. *Commentary* 88:15-22 Ag '89
East-West relations. V. Giscard d'Estaing and others. *Foreign Affairs* 68:1-21 Summ '89
Gorbachev's challenge to the West [address, April 11, 1989] E. W. Lefever. *Vital Speeches of the Day* 55:588-91 Jl 15 '89
Gorbachev's new thinking. D. Holloway. bibl f *Foreign Affairs* 68 Special Issue:66-81 ['89]
The new math. R. Wright. *The New Republic* 200:4 Ja 23 '89
Pavel Palazhchenko: Gorbachev wouldn't leave home without him. W. Plummer. il pors *People Weekly* 32:187-8 D 4 '89
Red mischief. *The New Republic* 200:10-11 My 1 '89
The revolution in Soviet foreign policy. R. Legvold. bibl f *Foreign Affairs* 68 Special Issue:82-98 ['89]
History
'Why the West distrusted us'. A. Novikov. *World Press Review* 36:28-30 Je '89
The world war created [World War II] M. B. Zuckerman. il map *U.S. News & World Report* 107:68-9+ Ag 28-S 4 '89
Afghanistan
See also
Afghanistan—Russian invasion, 1979-1989
Asia
Containment's last gasp. P. H. Kreisberg. *Foreign Policy* 75:146-63 Summ '89
When ideology bows to economics. D. Stanglin. il *U.S. News & World Report* 106:30-1 F 6 '89
Canada
See also
Mulroney, Brian—Visit to the Soviet Union, 1989
Hands across the Pole [co-operation between Canada and Soviet Union] B. Bergman. il map *Maclean's* 102:24-5 N 27 '89
Central America
Help out with the Latins, por favor. H. Trewhitt. il *U.S. News & World Report* 106:42-3 Ap 10 '89
China
See also
Gorbachev, Mikhail—Visit to China, 1989
The beat of a dissonant drummer [China's criticism of Soviet reforms] D. Doder and S. V. Lawrence. il *U.S. News & World Report* 107:31 D 18 '89
Comrades again? D. O. Relin. il *Scholastic Update (Teachers' edition)* 121:6-7 My 5 '89
Pacific overtures [cover story; special section] il *World Press Review* 36:11-20 My '89
China—History
Settling a bitter feud. A. Bilski. il *Maclean's* 102:35 My 29 '89
Cuba
See also
Gorbachev, Mikhail—Visit to Cuba, 1989
Castro keeps the faith—but can he keep it alone? A. Fins. il *Business Week* p81 D 11 '89
The graying of a revolution. C. A. Robbins. il pors *U.S. News & World Report* 106:37-41 Ja 9 '89
Minority report [Moscow news and Sputnik banned in Cuba] C. Hitchens. *The Nation* 249:231 S 4-11 '89
Cuba—History
See also
Cuban Missile Crisis, 1962
Czechoslovakia—History
See also
Czechoslovakia—History—Intervention, 1968
Developing countries
"New thinking" and Soviet third world policy. C. R. Saivetz. bibl f *Current History* 88:325-8+ O '89
East Asia
Moscow's Pacific offensive. M. Oksenberg. il *Newsweek* 113:31 Mr 6 '89

SOVIET UNION—Foreign relations—East Asia—*cont.*

Soviet policy in East Asia: a new beginning? D. S. Zagoria. *Foreign Affairs* 68 Special Issue:120-38 ['89]

Eastern Europe

After the party's over [Solidarity's influence on reform movements] D. Stanglin. il *U.S. News & World Report* 107:76-7 Ag 28-S 4 '89

Chips off the old bloc. C. Ogden. il *Time* 133:46-8+ Mr 27 '89

Communism at the crossroads in Eastern Europe. R. F. Staar. il *USA Today (Periodical)* 117:46-7 My '89

East European divides. M. Svec. *Foreign Policy* 77:41-63 Wint '89/'90

Eastern Europe on its own. C. Gati. bibl f *Foreign Affairs* 68 Special Issue:99-119 ['89]

The Gorbachev tease. M. Peretz. *The New Republic* 201:14+ Jl 10 '89

Gorbachev's doctrine. D. Schorr. *The New Leader* 72:4 N 13 '89

Is Stalin dead? Yes—at last. M. B. Zuckerman. il *U.S. News & World Report* 107:88+ D 4 '89

Looking for cracks in the bloc. R. Watson. il *Newsweek* 113:42 Mr 20 '89

Perestroika shakes Eastern Europe. F. S. Larrabee. il por *The Bulletin of the Atomic Scientists* 45:25-9 Mr '89

Prague sprung. *The New Republic* 201:7-8 D 18 '89

Problems in paradigm. G. Flynn. *Foreign Policy* 74:63-84 Spr '89

Satellites do it their way. M. R. Meyer. il *Newsweek* 114:48 N 6 '89

Seize the day. L. Goodwyn. *The Nation* 249:777 D 25 '89

The 'Sinatra Doctrine' [Kremlin's hands-off attitude] J. Bierman. il *Maclean's* 102:40+ N 6 '89

Soviet-East European relations. A. R. Rachwald. bibl f *Current History* 88:377-80+ N '89

The Soviet empire: Eastern Europe [special section] il *U.S. News & World Report* 106:35-6+ Mr 27 '89

Stalin blew it . . . but Gorbachev may not. M. S. Forbes, Jr. il *Forbes* 144:27 D 11 '89

Trying to control a runaway train. D. Stanglin. il *U.S. News & World Report* 107:24-6 D 18 '89

Uncharted waters. J. Smolowe. il *Time* 134:18-20 S 4 '89

Walking a tight-rope. M. Malkasian. il por *Scholastic Update (Teachers' edition)* 122:20-1 O 20 '89

What's behind the 'Sinatra Doctrine' [influence over East European reforms] *U.S. News & World Report* 107:22 N 20 '89

What's wrong with Yalta II [H. Kissinger's proposal] S. Talbott. il *Time* 133:36 Ap 24 '89

The winds of change. S. Manning. il *Scholastic Update (Teachers' edition)* 121:26 My 5 '89

Workers of the world ignite. D. Stanglin. il *U.S. News & World Report* 107:48-9 O 30 '89

Yes, he's for real [M. Gorbachev; cover story; special section] il por *Time* 134:40-2+ N 6 '89

Eastern Europe—History

See also
Yalta Conference (1945)

Europe

Europe in the post-Yalta era [cover story] D. Singer. il *The Nation* 249:701+ D 11 '89

Gorbachev speaks to the Council of Europe [excerpts from address, July 6, 1989] M. Gorbachev. *Current History* 88:347 O '89

The international community and change [address, July 6, 1989] M. Gorbachev. *Vital Speeches of the Day* 55:706-11 S 15 '89

Is the cold war over? R. J. Bresler. *USA Today (Periodical)* 118:7 Jl '89

Securing peace. A. Wilson-Smith. il *Maclean's* 102:46 S 4 '89

France

See also
Gorbachev, Mikhail—Visit to France, 1989

Germany

Dangerous liaisons [German and British alliances with the Soviet Union during World War II] G. A. Craig. bibl f il *The New York Review of Books* 36:15-19 Mr 30 '89

The deal that still lives in infamy [Soviet-Nazi pact] S. Bialer. *U.S. News & World Report* 107:68-9 Ag 28-S 4 '89

The great Mafia wedding [Hitler-Stalin pact; cover story] J. P. Roche. il *National Review* 41:23-4 S 1 '89

The Nazi-Soviet pacts: a half-century later. G. L. Weinberg. bibl f *Foreign Affairs* 68:175-89 Fall '89

Nineteen thirty-nine [German-Soviet non-aggression pact] C. S. Maier. *The New Republic* 201:16-17 S 11 '89

The secret protocols [texts of 1939 pacts] *Maclean's* 102:24 S 4 '89

Germany (East)

See also
Gorbachev, Mikhail—Visit to Germany (East), 1989

Germany (West)

See also
Gorbachev, Mikhail—Visit to Germany (West), 1989

Appeasement in our time [Foreign Minister H. D. Genscher; cover story] H. Walter. il por *National Review* 41:26-8+ Je 2 '89

Dead souls. *The Nation* 248:687-8 My 22 '89

Europe's short-range missiles nail their first victim [H. D. Genscher] J. Templeman and G. E. Schares. il por *Business Week* p50 Je 12 '89

Germany's attention wanders. *National Review* 41:14 Mr 24 '89

A new German nationalism in the age of Gorbachev. R. Knight. il *U.S. News & World Report* 106:26-7 Ja 23 '89

Recentralizing Europe. T. S. Molnar. *National Review* 41:34+ N 24 '89

Great Britain

See Great Britain—Foreign relations—Soviet Union

Hungary—History

See also
Hungary—History—Revolution, 1956

Iran

See also
Rafsanjani, Hashemi—Visit to the Soviet Union, 1989

The Ayatollahs and the Bear. D. Hiro. il *The Nation* 249:414-16 O 16 '89

Gorbachev's crisis of faith [text of letter] R. Khomeini. *Harper's* 278:21-2 Ap '89

The new Iran bows toward Moscow. il *U.S. News & World Report* 107:9 Jl 3 '89

Italy

Italy watches an empire stumble. S. F. Senigallia. il *The New Leader* 72:10-11 O 30 '89

Japan

Japan: from 'Inc.' to superpower? B. Crozier. *National Review* 41:20 S 15 '89

The Japanese and the Soviets. P. Pons. *World Press Review* 36:15 Ap '89

Moscow's latest bid for the Pacific. M. Tharp. *U.S. News & World Report* 107:68 N 20 '89

Now, Gorbachev is building a bridge to Japan. A. Borrus. il *Business Week* p70 D 25 '89-Ja 1 '90

Middle East

Divided together [Soviets press new peace initiative] A. Bilski. il por *Maclean's* 102:26 Mr 6 '89

Enter the Soviet Union. J. Smolowe. il *Time* 133:40 Mr 6 '89

Hands off by the superpowers. R. Fisk. il *World Press Review* 36:26-7 O '89

Moscow's new role in the Middle East [cover story] F. Halliday. il *The Nation* 248:361+ Mr 20 '89

Reach out and touch someone. D. Stanglin. il *U.S. News & World Report* 106:31-2 F 27 '89

Poland

Can Warsaw and Moscow be friends? J. Gray. *World Press Review* 36:17+ O '89

Moscow speaks softly. il *Time* 134:18 Ag 28 '89

To tell the truth. E. K. Valkenier. *The New Republic* 200:20-1 My 22 '89

South Africa

Glasnost meets apartheid [Soviet Union disowns African National Congress] B. Crozier. *National Review* 41:22 My 5 '89

United States

See United States—Foreign relations—Soviet Union

Western Europe

A decision not to decide [NATO response to Soviet arms initiatives] B. Van Voorst. il *Time* 133:46-7 My 1 '89

Perspective from Europe [address, May 23, 1989] Sir J. Goldsmith. *Vital Speeches of the Day* 55:525-8 Je 15 '89

Soviet change and Western security. J. Chirac. *Current (Washington, D.C.)* 315:27-32 S '89

Will the allies leave Bush behind? B. Javetski and D. Griffiths. il pors *Business Week* p30-1 My 15 '89

History

Back to the future. M. S. Forbes, Jr. il por *Forbes* 143:27 Je 26 '89

A usable past [M. Gorbachev's reforms evoke Russia's past liberalism] S. F. Starr. *The New Republic* 200:24+ My 15 '89

Kievan period, 862-1237

The millennium celebrations [Christianization of Kievan Russia] il *The Courier (Unesco)* 42:34 Ja '89

1917-

Truth and consequences [struggle for historical truth in the Soviet bloc] R. Knight. il *U.S. News & World Report* 106:33-4 Je 26 '89

U.S. support for Soviet technology: a lesson from history. T. P. Hughes. *Current (Washington, D.C.)* 315:18-26 S '89

Revolution, 1917-1921

Bolsheviks of the Bastille. L. Steinmetz. *National Review* 41:39 Jl 14 '89

The power of an idea. S. Manning. il por *Scholastic Update (Teachers' edition)* 121:22 My 5 '89

1925-1953

Alexander Cockburn: a voice of moderation [figures for deaths under J. Stalin] A. Puddington. *National Review* 41:27 N 24 '89

SOVIET UNION—History—1925-1953—*cont.*

Coming to terms with the past [Stalin terror] R. Conquest. il *National Review* 41:14-16 Mr 10 '89

Haunted by history's horrors [official discrediting of J. Stalin] G. J. Church. il por *Time* 133:71-2 Ap 10 '89

A million here, a million there [differing figures for deaths under J. Stalin] A. Cockburn. *The Nation* 248:294-5 Mr 6 '89

Stalin takes the stand [proposed posthumous trial] E. Gellner. *The New Republic* 200:20+ Mr 20 '89

Stalin's purge of Soviet astronomers. R. A. McCutcheon. il *Sky and Telescope* 78:352-7 O '89

Stalin's victims [discussion of March 6, 1989 article, A million here, a million there] A. Cockburn. *The Nation* 249:154+ Ag 7-14 '89

The unquiet ghosts of Stalin's victims. E. H. Methvin. *National Review* 41:24-5+ S 1 '89

1925-1953—Historiography

De-Stalinizing the Soviet past [interview with Y. Afanasyev] S. F. Cohen and K. Vanden Heuvel. *Harper's* 279:32+ O '89

Filling in the blank spots in Soviet history [interview with Y. Afanasyev]; tr. by Vladimir Voronin and Adam Shulman. A. Sirotkin. il *History Today* 39:12-17 F '89

Industries

See also

Aeroflot

Aerospace industries—Soviet Union

Airplane industry—Soviet Union

Antonov Design Bureau (Soviet Union)

Aviakompaniya Sverkhdalnykh Avialiniy

Computer industry—Soviet Union

Gold mines and mining—Soviet Union

Ilyushin Design Bureau (Soviet Union)

International Relations Publishing House

M. L. Mil Helicopter Design Bureau (Soviet Union)

Medical care industry—Soviet Union

Mikoyan Design Bureau (Soviet Union)

Motion picture industry—Soviet Union

Progress Engine Design Bureau (Soviet Union)

Soap industry—Soviet Union

Sukhoi Design Bureau (Soviet Union)

Technopribor (Firm)

Trading companies—Soviet Union

Tupolev Design Bureau (Soviet Union)

Voronezh Aircraft Production Association (Soviet Union)

Zaporozhye Motorworks (Soviet Union)

And you think Western capitalists have problems. P. Galuszka. il *Business Week* p50 Ja 30 '89

Soviet profits. A. Wilson-Smith. il *Maclean's* 102:24-5 Jl 17 '89

Turning up the power. J. Greenwald. il *Time* 133:74-6 Ap 10 '89

Intellectual life

The perils of *perestroika*. B. Rumer and G. Schoenfeld. il *The New Leader* 72:7-9 Ag 7-21 '89

What *glasnost* has destroyed. L. Aron. *Commentary* 88:30-4 N '89

Kings and rulers

See also

Nicholas II, Emperor of Russia, 1868-1918

Maps

USSR: mapping the blank spots [cover story] G. J. Demko and W. Hezlep. maps *Focus (New York, N.Y.: 1950)* 39:20-1 Spr '89

Military policy

See also

Soviet Union—Defenses

About face: how the Soviets stopped planning for world war. M. K. MccGwire. il *Technology Review* 92:32-6+ N/D '89

Can Gorbachev reform the Soviet military? W. E. Odom. il *U.S. News & World Report* 107:43 S 11 '89

Can Moscow play defense? M. B. Zuckerman. il *U.S. News & World Report* 106:76 Mr 13 '89

Can we trust this nice Mr. Gorbachev? C. W. Weinberger. il *Forbes* 143:37 Ja 9 '89

Consequences of Soviet decline [views of Kurt M. Campbell] *The Futurist* 23:39-40 Ja/F '89

Economic growth and military power: erosion of the superpowers. W. Goldstein. *Current (Washington, D.C.)* 309:23-31 Ja '89

From cold war to odd couple [friendship of W. J. Crowe and S. Akhromeyev] J. Barry. il pors *Newsweek* 114:42 Jl 31 '89

Global security: approaching the year 2000. G. W. Rathjens. bibl f *Current History* 88:1-4+ Ja '89

Gorba Claus [effects of Soviet troop reduction proposal] *The New Republic* 200:5-7 Ja 2 '89

Gorbachev talks but who listens? W. M. Arkin. il por *The Bulletin of the Atomic Scientists* 45:5-6 Mr '89

Gorbachev's strategy, and ours. E. N. Luttwak. *Commentary* 88:29-36 Jl '89

Gorbachev's triumph. W. F. Buckley. *National Review* 41:70 Ja 27 '89

Is Bush bold enough to answer Gorbachev? W. Greider. il *Rolling Stone* p48+ F 9 '89

A leaner, meaner Soviet military [cut in East European forces] S. Budiansky. il map *U.S. News & World Report* 107:54+ N 6 '89

News and comment [views of Joint Chiefs of Staff] *The New Yorker* 65:24-5 Ag 14 '89

A soldier talks peace [interview with S. Akhromeyev] J. Kohan and K. Prager. il por *Time* 134:58-60 N 13 '89

The soldiers' summit [visit by Joint Chiefs of Staff chairman W. Crowe to Moscow] K. M. Campbell. bibl f *Foreign Policy* 75:76-91 Summ '89

The Soviet empire: the military [cover story; special section] il maps *U.S. News & World Report* 106:18-21+ Mr 13 '89

Soviet military adviser addresses House panel [S. Akhromeyev] *Aviation Week & Space Technology* 131:26 Jl 31 '89

Soviet military policy. M. Kramer. bibl f *Current History* 88:337-40+ O '89

The Soviet threat [discussion of November 1988 article, Is there still a Soviet threat?] A. M. Codevilla. *Commentary* 87:2+ Mr '89

A Soviet view: defense only. S. Blagovolin. *World Press Review* 36:23-4 F '89

'There is little question that real change is afoot' [interview with W. J. Crowe] il por *U.S. News & World Report* 107:80 Ag 28-S 4 '89

Toward better military manners [U.S.-Soviet Agreement on the Prevention of Dangerous Military Activities] W. J. Lanouette. il *The Bulletin of the Atomic Scientists* 45:8-9 D '89

U.S.S.R. arms reduction [address, December 7, 1988] M. Gorbachev. *Vital Speeches of the Day* 55:229-36 F 1 '89

A Yankee in Gorbachev's court [tour by Joint Chiefs of Staff chairman W. J. Crowe] S. Talbott. il por *Time* 134:32 Jl 3 '89

Nationalism

Back in the U.S.S.R. M. Malkasian. il *Scholastic Update (Teachers' edition)* 122:22 O 20 '89

The coming crack-up of communism [cover story; special section] il *National Review* 41:28-32 Ja 27 '89

Crises around the clock. H. Anderson. il por *Newsweek* 114:30-1 Ag 7 '89

Dateline USSR: ethnic tremors. P. Cockburn. *Foreign Policy* 74:168-84 Spr '89

The empire breaks up. J. Rupnik. *The New Republic* 200:20-4 F 20 '89

Gorbachev lays down the law. R. Watson. il map *Newsweek* 113:52+ Ap 24 '89

Gorbachev's crisis of faith; tr. by Michael Davies. R. Debray. *Harper's* 278:22+ Ap '89

Gorbachev's nationalities problem. G. W. Lapidus. bibl f *Foreign Affairs* 68:92-108 Fall '89

Gorby's two Achilles' heels. M. S. Forbes, Jr. il *Forbes* 144:27 Jl 24 '89

Identity crisis in the Soviet west. A. J. Motyl. map *The Bulletin of the Atomic Scientists* 45:21-4 Mr '89

Look who's feeling picked on [Russians who are in the minority in the ethnic republics] G. J. Church. il *Time* 134:36-7 S 25 '89

The nationalities crisis. M. Sieff. *National Review* 41:27 Ap 7 '89

New hopes, old grudges, great dangers. R. Knight. il *U.S. News & World Report* 107:30-2 Jl 31 '89

Post-Communist nationalism. Z. Brzezinski. il map *Foreign Affairs* 68:1-25 Wint '89/'90

Russia's shuddering empire. R. Pipes. il *The New Republic* 201:52+ N 6 '89

The Soviet agony over states' rights. J. Trimble. il map *U.S. News & World Report* 106:34-5 Ap 24 '89

The Soviet empire: the society [effects of *glasnost* and *perestroika*; cover story; special section; with editorial comment by Mortimer B. Zuckerman] il por maps *U.S. News & World Report* 106:34-9+, 80 Ap 3 '89

The Soviet republics. *World Press Review* 36:10 Ja '89

The Soviet Union's nationalities question. S. L. Burg. bibl f map *Current History* 88:341-4+ O '89

Stalin takes the stand. E. Gellner. *The New Republic* 200:20+ Mr 20 '89

Unloosing demons. P. Berman. il *Forbes* 143:86+ F 6 '89

USSR and its ethnics: the desire for autonomy. P. Cockburn. *Current (Washington, D.C.)* 315:33-9 S '89

When God fails, Russia remains. R. Debray. il *New Perspectives Quarterly* 5:30-3 Wint '88/'89

Will the Soviet empire self-destruct? Z. Brzezinski. il *The New York Times Magazine* p38+ F 26 '89

The winter of their discontent. A. Nagorski. il map *Newsweek* 113:34+ Ap 3 '89

Navy

Disarmament at sea. M. Ross. *Foreign Policy* 77:94-112 Wint '89/'90

Soviets building naval strength while pursuing maritime arms control. B. M. Greeley. il *Aviation Week & Space Technology* 130:63 Mr 13 '89

The U.S. Navy today [address, May 16, 1989] C. A. H. Trost. *Vital Speeches of the Day* 55:578-80 Jl 15 '89

Forces in the Arctic

Soviets encourage joint research of Arctic areas. R. G. O'Lone. *Aviation Week & Space Technology* 130:83 Ja 30 '89

SOVIET UNION—*cont.*

Politics and government

See also

Communism—Soviet Union
Communist Party (Soviet Union)
Elections—Soviet Union
Interregional Group (Soviet Union)
Liberalism—Soviet Union
Political attitudes—Soviet Union
Political candidates—Soviet Union
Politics, Corruption in—Soviet Union
Socialism—Soviet Union
Soviet Union. Congress of People's Deputies
Soviet Union. Supreme Soviet

A bargain at twice the price. por *U.S. News & World Report* 106:13 F 13 '89

Boris the trigger-happy [B. Yeltsin] il por *Time* 134:63 O 30 '89

The boss of Smolensky Square [with interview with A. Shevardnadze; cover story] J. Kohan. il pors *Time* 133:29-30+ My 15 '89

Change in the Soviet Union [address, May 12, 1989] G. Bush. *Department of State Bulletin* 89:16-17 Jl '89

China and the U.S.S.R.: the changing face of communism [cover story; special issue] il map *Scholastic Update (Teachers' edition)* 121:2-12+ My 5 '89

The China syndrome [popular unrest in China and its impact on the Soviet Union] F. Coleman. il *Newsweek* 113:36 Je 5 '89

The cold war: a presidential agenda. S. F. Cohen. *Current (Washington, D.C.)* 311:32-8 Mr/Ap '89

Confessions of a self-made Sovietologist. W. Laqueur. *Society* 26:5-9 S/O '89

Dealing warily with a sick Bear. D. Stanglin. il *U.S. News & World Report* 107:32+ S 25 '89

Don't die yet. D. R. Carlin, Jr. *Commonweal* 116:265 My 5 '89

Ending the cold war. M. Mandelbaum. bibl f *Foreign Affairs* 68:16-36 Spr '89

The enlightened patriot [M. Gorbachev] M. Grondona. *World Press Review* 36:64 Ap '89

Fighting off hasty change. M. Nemeth. il *Maclean's* 102:42-3 D 25 '89

Fighting the founders [cover story] S. Talbott. il *Time* 133:16-19 Je 5 '89

Giving Gorbachev a boost: Soviet reform is in the U.S. national interest. R. Holbrooke. il *Newsweek* 114:28 S 25 '89

Glasnost in action. A. Wilson-Smith. il por *Maclean's* 102:20+ Je 5 '89

Glasnostrums. J. Muravchik. *The New Republic* 200:16-18 Ja 30 '89

Gorbachev & the U.S. [discussion of August 1989 article, Gorbachev's cultural revolution] C. H. Fairbanks, Jr. *Commentary* 88:2+ N '89

Gorbachev and the '1946 rules'. G. F. Will. il *Newsweek* 114:70 S 25 '89

The Gorbachev jitters. R. Watson. il *Newsweek* 114:24-6 S 25 '89

The Gorbachev prospect. G. Soros. il *The New York Review of Books* 36:16-18 Je 1 '89

Gorbachev's cultural revolution. C. H. Fairbanks, Jr. *Commentary* 88:23-7 Ag '89

Gorbachev's fate. J. Trimble. il por *U.S. News & World Report* 107:26 D 25 '89-Ja 1 '90

Gorbachev's long journey. R. Grenier. il *National Review* 41:27-9 D 31 '89

Gorbachev's politics. J. F. Hough. bibl f *Foreign Affairs* 68:26-41 Wint '89/'90

Gorbachev's reforms: will they work? [special section] il por *Business Week* p52-7+ Je 5 '89

Gorbie's choice [influence of dissident literature on Soviet reforms] S. Anderson. *The New Republic* 200:11-12 Ap 17 '89

Gorby of Mayberry. R. E. Tyrrell. *The American Spectator* 22:10-11 O '89

Hard lessons and unhappy citizens. W. R. Doerner. il por *Time* 133:28-9 Je 19 '89

How open shall we be to *glasnost*? C. W. Colson. il *Christianity Today* 33:72 My 12 '89

Is *glasnost* genuine? [address, November 6, 1988] M. Warder. *Vital Speeches of the Day* 55:341-4 Mr 15 '89

"Let your readers be reassured there will be no military coup" [interview with N. Ryzhkov; with reply by Paul Klebnikov] P. Dragadze. il por *Forbes* 144:82+ O 16 '89

A letter from Moscow. J. Trimble. il *U.S. News & World Report* 107:32-3 S 25 '89

Letter from Rostov-on-Don [effects of *perestroika*] R. B. Cullen. *The New Yorker* 65:107-20 Je 12 '89

A long, mighty struggle. W. Isaacson. il por *Time* 133:48-52+ Ap 10 '89

Mikhail Gorbachev. il por *People Weekly* 32:58-9 D 25 '89-Ja 1 '90

Moscow subversive chic. T. Rothman. *Scientific American* 261:16+ Jl '89

Moscow: the struggle for reform. A. Brumberg. bibl f il *The New York Review of Books* 36:37-42 Mr 30 '89

Moscow's other mastermind [A. Yakovlev; cover story] B. Keller. il pors *The New York Times Magazine* p30-3+ F 19 '89

New days that shake the world [cover story] D. Singer. il *The Nation* 248:577+ My 1 '89

The new Russian riddles. *America* 160:387 Ap 29 '89

Nikita Gorbachev? F. Coleman. il pors *Newsweek* 114:39 S 11 '89

Notes from the former underground. A. Hochschild. il *Mother Jones* 14:23-6 My '89

One Bear of a Soviet politician [interview with B. Yeltsin] D. Aikman. il por *Time* 133:44-6 Mr 20 '89

Perestroika [address, September 11, 1989] M. Gorbachev. *Vital Speeches of the Day* 56:5-7 O 15 '89

The perils of *perestroika*. B. Rumer and G. Schoenfeld. il *The New Leader* 72:7-9 Ag 7-21 '89

Points of mutual advantage [address, October 16, 1989] J. A. Baker, III. *Vital Speeches of the Day* 56:66-70 N 15 '89

Pondering *perestroika*. J. Train. *The American Spectator* 22:30-1 F '89

Prague sprung. *The New Republic* 201:7-8 D 18 '89

Red storm rising. M. Novak. il *Forbes* 144:136-7 O 16 '89

Reflections of a bourgeois Menshevik [interview with D. Bell] L. Greenfeld. *Society* 26:10-20 S/O '89

Riding the tiger [cover story] R. Watson. il pors *Newsweek* 114:40-2+ D 4 '89

Sakharov's view of Soviet changes [adaptation of remarks, June 20, 1989] A. D. Sakharov. il por *World Press Review* 36:32+ Ag '89

The secret of our success. C. Krauthammer. il *Time* 133:82 Ja 30 '89

Send in the pols. J. Klein. il por *New York* 22:10-11 Ja 9 '89

The shaky fortunes of Gorby Inc. J. Smolowe. il *Time* 133:37 Ja 30 '89

Soviet change and Western security. J. Chirac. *Current (Washington, D.C.)* 315:27-32 S '89

Soviet seduction. P. B. Gemma, Jr. il *Conservative Digest* 15:6-7+ Mr/Ap '89

The Soviet Union, 1989 [cover story; special issue] bibl f map (inside back cover) *Current History* 88:321-44+ O '89

The suave Gorbachev wears no clothes [cover story] M. Ledeen. il *The American Spectator* 22:16-17 F '89

The threat to Gorbachev. P. Reddaway. bibl f il *The New York Review of Books* 36:19-24 Ag 17 '89

A usable past [M. Gorbachev's reforms evoke Russia's past . liberalism] S. F. Starr. *The New Republic* 200:24+ My 15 '89

The view from Moscow. A. Wilson-Smith. il *Maclean's* 102:21-2 N 27 '89

Vindication of a hard-liner [interview with Z. Brzezinski] S. Talbott and R. T. Zintl. il por *Time* 134:10+ D 18 '89

Virtuoso transformations [Y. Arafat and M. Gorbachev] S. Talbott. il *Time* 133:36 Ja 9 '89

Waiting for Wyoming [Bush administration's policy of constructive engagement] P. Glynn. *The New Republic* 201:14-16 O 2 '89

What if the Soviet Union collapses? D. Aikman. il *Time* 134:94 D 25 '89

What the future holds. F. Painton. il *Time* 134:23+ D 18 '89

Will the Soviet empire self-destruct? Z. Brzezinski. il *The New York Times Magazine* p38+ F 26 '89

Will the Soviet Union survive until 1994? [interview with B. Shragin; cover story] D. Evanier. *National Review* 41:24+ Ap 7 '89

The wounds of *glasnost* [apprehension of the American left over changes] A. Puddington. il *National Review* 41:26-8 N 24 '89

Yeltsin. D. K. Mano. por *National Review* 41:48-9 D 8 '89

The young fight for the 'three Ds' [political reform and Komsomol] K. Vanden Heuvel. il *The Nation* 248:729-31 My 29 '89

Bibliography

Gorby fever and the publishing body politic. *Publishers Weekly* 236:42 O 27 '89

Population

See also

Africans—Soviet Union

Race relations

Racism in the Soviet Union [Africans] B. Asoyan. *World Press Review* 36:85 O '89

Religious institutions and affairs

See also

Christians—Soviet Union
Church and state—Soviet Union
Evangelistic work—Soviet Union
Muslims—Soviet Union
Old Believers
Orthodox Eastern Church, Russian
Pentecostal churches—Soviet Union

Religious openings in the U.S.S.R. J. H. Forest. *The Christian Century* 106:848-50 S 27 '89

SOVIET UNION—Religious institutions and affairs—*cont.*

History

The idea of Holy Russia; tr. by J. Crowfoot. S. S. Averintsev. il *History Today* 39:37-44 N '89

Social conditions

See also

Communism—Soviet Union

Women—Soviet Union

Back to the USSR. R. Conquest. il *National Review* 41:24-7 Ag 18 '89

Punk *perestroika* [cover story] M. Walker. il *The New Republic* 201:22+ D 4 '89

Reflections of a bourgeois Menshevik [interview with D. Bell] L. Greenfeld. *Society* 26:10-20 S/O '89

What *glasnost* has destroyed. L. Aron. *Commentary* 88:30-4 N '89

Social life and customs

The hat. A. Meyer. il *The Mother Earth News* 115:50 Ja/F '89

Statistics

When high hopes meet harsh realities. il *U.S. News & World Report* 106:43-4 Ap 3 '89

Study and teaching

See Soviet studies

SOVIET UNION. ACADEMY OF SCIENCES *See* Academy of Sciences of the USSR

SOVIET UNION. AVIAEXPORT

Aviaexport expects surge in foreign orders after release of new transports. il *Aviation Week & Space Technology* 130:38-9 Je 5 '89

Soviets display export version of Mi-24 at helicopter trade show [Helitech '89 in England] il *Aviation Week & Space Technology* 131:30 S 25 '89

SOVIET UNION. CONGRESS OF PEOPLE'S DEPUTIES

An evening with the Sakharovs [interview] A. W. Bouis and J.-C. Bouis. il pors *Life* 12:96-8+ Jl '89

Face-off on reform. J. Kohan. il pors *Time* 134:20-2 D 25 '89

The foes who came in from the cold. il *U.S. News & World Report* 106:10 Je 12 '89

Glasnost in action. A. Wilson-Smith. il por *Maclean's* 102:20+ Je 5 '89

A hearty da! to democratia [first meeting] il por *U.S. News & World Report* 106:12 Je 5 '89

The Kremlin's talkathon. F. Coleman. il *Newsweek* 113:39 Je 12 '89

The new Soviet Congress. il *World Press Review* 36:10 Jl '89

Reform is risky business [first meeting] J. Trimble. il por *U.S. News & World Report* 106:27-8 Je 19 '89

A speech to the People's Congress [address, June 9, 1989]; tr. by Edward Kline. A. D. Sakharov. il por *The New York Review of Books* 36:25-6 Ag 17 '89

USSR [first meeting; cover story] W. R. Doerner. il pors *Time* 133:30-1 Je 5 '89

A volcano of words and wishes. J. Kohan. il *Time* 133:35 Je 12 '89

SOVIET UNION. CONSTITUTION

Chipping away at an icon [Interregional Group wants to debunk V. Lenin and rewrite the Constitution] B. W. Nelan. il pors *Time* 134:34-5 Ag 14 '89

SOVIET UNION. SUPREME SOVIET

Comrade Engver goes to Moscow [cover story] B. Keller. il pors *The New York Times Magazine* p24-7+ Ag 27 '89

A dose of advise and consentski. *U.S. News & World Report* 107:14+ Jl 10 '89

A Duma by any other name. M. Sieff. il *National Review* 41:40-1 Je 30 '89

Is time running out? A. Wilson-Smith. il *Maclean's* 102:30-1 O 9 '89

The Supreme Soviet flexes its nyet power. P. Galuszka. il *Business Week* p77+ Jl 17 '89

SOVIET UNION AND CHINA

The China syndrome [popular unrest in China and its impact on the Soviet Union] F. Coleman. il *Newsweek* 113:36 Je 5 '89

SOVIET UNION AND THE UNITED STATES

See also

Exchanges, Literary and scientific

Soviet Union—Foreign opinion—American

United States—Foreign opinion—Russian

Back in the USSA. G. Martin. *Utne Reader* p97-8 S/O '89

Fighting the bends in the Indian Ocean [joint Soviet-U.S. effort to rescue Soviet researchers] M. Sun. il *Science* 244:1134 Je 9 '89

Notes and comment. *The New Yorker* 65:23-4 Ag 21 '89

West meets East. il pors *Esquire* 111:62-5 Ja '89

SOVIET UNION IN LITERATURE

Spies who come in from the cold war [interview with J. Le Carré] V. Orlik. il por *World Press Review* 36:28+ O '89

The thawing of the old spymaster [interview with J. Le Carré] A. P. Sanoff. il por *U.S. News & World Report* 106:59-61 Je 19 '89

SOVIET UNION IN MOTION PICTURES

In Moscow with 'Fayfer' and 'Oh-Oh-Seven' [shooting The Russia house] C. Bogert. il *Newsweek* 114:66-7 N 6 '89

Mussolini shrugged [film version of A. Rand's We the living] J. Sobran. *National Review* 41:52-3 Ja 27 '89

SOWELL, DAWN

about

Woman to watch. B. Kevles. il por *Women's Sports & Fitness* 11:56 N/D '89

SOWELL, THOMAS, 1930-

"Affirmative action": a worldwide disaster [cover story] *Commentary* 88:21-41 D '89

The economics of academia. por *Conservative Digest* 15:14-15 My/Je '89

The new racism on campus. il por *Fortune* 119:115-16+ F 13 '89

SOWERS, LUTHER

about

A modern armor maker dresses men in knights' clothing. R. Mashburn. bibl (p183) il pors *Smithsonian* 20:116-20+ D '89

SOWING *See* Seeding

SOWS *See* Swine

SOYBEAN FUTURES *See* Commodity futures

SOYBEAN INDUSTRY

Export-import trade

Jungle road to Tokyo [U.S. soybean growers concern over Brazilian highway's impact on trade with Japan] P. Duggan. il map *Forbes* 143:96 My 29 '89

Brazil

Jungle road to Tokyo [U.S. soybean growers concern over Brazilian highway's impact on trade with Japan] P. Duggan. il map *Forbes* 143:96 My 29 '89

SOYBEAN INK

Soy ink makes colorful imprint on publishers. M. Holmberg. il *Successful Farming* 87:30 S '89

SOYBEAN MILK

Not like mother made [illegal sale of soy milk as infant formula by Eden Foods] *FDA Consumer* 23:30-1 My '89

SOYBEAN OIL

Soy oil ready to eat your dust. M. Holmberg. il *Successful Farming* 87:24 O '89

SOYBEAN PRODUCTS

See also

Cooking—Soybean products

Tempeh

SOYBEANS

Rapid redistribution of auxin-regulated RNAs during gravitropism. B. A. McClure and T. Guilfoyle. bibl f il *Science* 243:91-3 Ja 6 '89

Soybeans: old in the field, new in the garden. W. E. Wooldridge. il *Flower and Garden* 33:114 Mr/Ap '89

Cultivation

No-till a blanket of soybeans. R. Fee. il *Successful Farming* 87 no4:28-9 Mr '89

Disease and pest resistance

Bacterial blight of soybean: regulation of a pathogen gene determining host cultivar specificity. T. V. Huynh and others. bibl f il *Science* 245:1374-7 S 22 '89

A little thirst can aid plant defenses [soybeans and Mexican bean beetle larvae; research by Edward F. Connor and Grant McQuate] J. Raloff. *Science News* 136:37 Jl 15 '89

Prices

Ferruzzi trading "illogical" for many months. *Successful Farming* 87:48P N '89

Gene Johnston. G. Johnston. il *Successful Farming* 87 no4:5 Mr '89

An Italian 'peasant' who would be soybean king [Ferruzzi chairman R. Gardini's attempt to corner U.S. soybean market] E. Pomice. il por *U.S. News & World Report* 107:44-5 Ag 7 '89

Why the pits are sick over soybeans [Chicago Board of Trade directive, in response to Ferruzzi Group maneuvers, sends prices tumbling] D. Greising. il *Business Week* p76+ Jl 31 '89

Seeding

Row-squeezing planters. D. Mowitz. il *Successful Farming* 87:20-1 Ap '89

Yield

1989 corn may top 8 billion bushels, beans 1.9 billion. *Successful Farming* 87:63 F '89

Picture-perfect weed control might not pay. B. Freese. il *Successful Farming* 87:27 My '89

SOYINKA, KAYODE

The collapse born of civil war. il *World Press Review* 36:28-9 Mr '89

SOYUZ FLIGHTS *See* Space flight—Soyuz flights

SPA TUBS *See* Hot tubs

SPACE, OUTER *See* Outer space

SPACE, PERSONAL *See* Personal space

SPACE AGENCY (CANADA) *See* Canada. Space Agency

SPACE AND TIME

See also

Hyperspace

Relativity (Physics)

Time travel

Wormholes (Astrophysics)

SPACE AND TIME—*cont.*

Cosmic quarrel [Huw Price questions S. W. Hawking's arrow of time explanation] T. Beardsley. *Scientific American* 261:22+ O '89

SPACE ASTRONOMY

See also

Artificial satellites—Astronomical use

Let Freedom ring! F. D. Martin. il *Sky and Telescope* 77:460-1 My '89

The selling of space astronomy. R. W. Smith. *Astronomy* 17:8 Ja '89

Space astronomy moves forward [special section] il *Astronomy* 17:22-31+ Ja '89

Space station Freedom: bad news for astronomy. R. C. Bless. *Sky and Telescope* 77:460 My '89

SPACE BIOLOGY

See also

Plants, Effect of weightlessness on

Weightlessness

Why conduct life science research in space? W. Ockels. il *Ad Astra* 1:3+ My '89

Will there be life in our space program? N. Y. Mineta. *Ad Astra* 1:20 N '89

SPACE CAMP (HUNTSVILLE, ALA.) *See* U.S. Space Camp (Huntsville, Ala.)

SPACE CENTERS

See also

Space vehicles—Launching pads, sites, etc.

Centers for the Commercial Development of Space. il *Ad Astra* 1:12 D '89

NASA commercial centers gain greater independence. il *Aviation Week & Space Technology* 131:41+ N 20 '89

The South reaches for the stars [Apollo 11 celebrations] J. T. Black. il *Southern Living* 24:52+ Jl '89

Spaceport America. M. Crichton. il por maps *Popular Mechanics* 166:32-6+ My '89

Employees

NASA faces personnel crisis, long-term funding shortage [with editorial comment] C. Covault. il *Aviation Week & Space Technology* 130:7, 23-4 F 20 '89

Australia

Cape York update. M. T. Rigby. *Ad Astra* 1:42 F '89

California

See also

Ames Research Center

Florida

See also

John F. Kennedy Space Center

Governor seeks to set up 'Spaceport Florida' Authority. E. H. Kolcum. *Aviation Week & Space Technology* 130:24-5 F 20 '89

Spaceport 2000. I. Klotz. il map *Ad Astra* 1:39-42 F '89

French Guiana

Propellant mixer delay could stall Ariane 5 program [U.S.-built mixer intended for propellant factory under construction at Guiana Space Center] J. M. Lenorovitz. *Aviation Week & Space Technology* 130:35 Je 26 '89

Work on Ariane 5 launch, assembly facilities proceeds at site in Kourou. il *Aviation Week & Space Technology* 130:175 Je 12 '89

Hawaii

Spaceport 2000. I. Klotz. il map *Ad Astra* 1:39-42 F '89

Ohio

See also

Plum Brook Field Station

Soviet Union

Inside the House of Sputnik [TsUP facility in Moscow] J. E. Oberg. il *Omni (New York, N.Y.)* 11:30 Mr '89

Launch pad used for first Energia flight designed for non-shuttle missions. il *Aviation Week & Space Technology* 130:42-3 Ja 16 '89

Report from Baikonur Cosmodrome: Soviets' vast space launch facility supports manned, unmanned programs [special section] J. M. Lenorovitz. il *Aviation Week & Space Technology* 131:70-3+ O 16 '89

Soviet using Plesetsk site to launch military satellites. il *Aviation Week & Space Technology* 131:22-3 Jl 3 '89

Sweden

Home on the Esrange. M. J. Mackowski. il *Ad Astra* 1:39-40+ My '89

Texas

See also

Kealing Space Center

Lyndon B. Johnson Space Center

Virginia

See also

Langley Research Center (U.S.)

Wallops Flight Facility

SPACE CENTERS, AUSTRALIAN

See also

Cape York Space Agency (Australia)

SPACE CHEMISTRY *See* Astrochemistry

SPACE COLONIES

See also

Lunar bases

Beyond techno-talk. B. Brown. *Ad Astra* 1:3 O '89

Crossroads: the journey to a permanent presence. C. C. Perkins. *Ad Astra* 1:14 O '89

Do we have a place in space? H. L. Shipman. *Astronomy* 17:8 S '89

Life on Mars: cultivating a planet—and ourselves [cover story] F. Turner. il *Harper's* 279:33-40 Ag '89

Paolo Soleri: man for all futures. L. David. il por *Ad Astra* 1:31 N '89

Settling space: the main objective. il *Ad Astra* 1:16-20 O '89

Space settlements: sooner than we think? T. F. Rogers. il *Ad Astra* 1:30-4 Ja '89

Advertising

Selling space [ads of the future promoting life in space] il *Omni (New York, N.Y.)* 11:53-9 Jl '89

SPACE COMMAND (U.S.) *See* United States. Space Command

SPACE COMMERCE CORPORATION

Marketing the Proton [Soviet booster] S. Arenstein. il *Ad Astra* 1:31-4 D '89

Soviets propose using Energia to launch NASA space station. il *Aviation Week & Space Technology* 130:22 My 8 '89

Soviets sign space pact, launch military satellites [joint venture between Space Commerce Corp. and Glavcosmos] C. Covault. il *Aviation Week & Space Technology* 130:24-5 Ja 9 '89

U.S., Soviet firms to develop, market commercial booster based on SS-20 [Start mobile launcher] J. D. Morrocco. il *Aviation Week & Space Technology* 131:21 Ag 7 '89

SPACE COMMUNICATION *See* Interstellar communication

SPACE CONSTRUCTION

Commercialization policy threatens space station's robotic contract [OMB decision requiring private financing] T. M. Foley. il *Aviation Week & Space Technology* 130:30-1 F 6 '89

Desperately seeking Cyborg [Flight Telerobotic Servicer for space station assembly designed by Honeybee Robotics] J. Goldberg. il *Omni (New York, N.Y.)* 11:12+ Ag '89

Martin Marietta robotic device will aid in space station assembly [Flight Telerobotic Servicer] B. D. Nordwall. il *Aviation Week & Space Technology* 130:53 My 15 '89

New cosmonaut crew launched to Mir; station expansion to begin in October. il *Aviation Week & Space Technology* 131:39 S 11 '89

Orbital mechanic [Flight Telerobotic Servicer] G. R. Graf. il *Ad Astra* 1:5-6 O '89

Soviet space: expanding the Mir station [special section] il *Aviation Week & Space Technology* 131:94-6+ S 25 '89

SPACE DEBRIS

See also

Radioactive space pollution

The debris collector [University of Arizona's Autonomous Space Processor for Orbital Debris program] W. H. Ganoe. il *Ad Astra* 1:35-7 Je '89

The junkyard in orbit. B. Jasani and M. J. Rees. bibl f il *The Bulletin of the Atomic Scientists* 45:24-5+ O '89

Reentry of Solar Max satellite to pose falling debris hazard. C. Covault. il *Aviation Week & Space Technology* 131:23-4 O 16 '89

Space pollution obscures night sky. il *Earth Science* 42:9 Spr '89

Anecdotes, facetiae, satire, etc.

Uncivil liberties. C. Trillin. il *The Nation* 248:114 Ja 30 '89

SPACE DIVISION (AIR FORCE) *See* United States. Air Force. Space Division

SPACE FLIGHT

See also

Association of Space Explorers

Astronauts

Computers—Space flight use

Image processing—Space flight use

Information systems—Space flight use

Insurance, Space flight

Microscopes—Space flight use

Orbital rendezvous (Space flight)

Planets—Exploration

Robots—Space flight use

Space stations

United States. National Aeronautics and Space Administration

The edge of infinity [cover story] W. J. Cook. il *U.S. News & World Report* 106:52-6+ My 15 '89

Manned vs. unmanned. il *Popular Science* 235:69 Jl '89

Moonraker [interview with N. Mailer] T. Piazza. por *Omni (New York, N.Y.)* 11:18+ Jl '89

We can outlive our star [interstellar flight] E. F. Mallove and G. L. Matloff. *Astronomy* 17:8 D '89

Accidents

See also

Challenger (Space shuttle) explosion, 1986

Space vehicles—Accidents and explosions

OTA to NASA: accidents will happen. M. M. Waldrop. *Science* 245:697 Ag 18 '89

Asteroid missions

The great palladium rush [mining asteroids for metal used in cold fusion] H. K. Henson. il *Ad Astra* 1:34-5 N '89

Harvesting the near-earthers [cover story] W. Barton and M. Capobianco. il *Ad Astra* 1:24-30+ N '89

SPACE FLIGHT—Asteroid missions—*cont.*
Nonterrestrial materials: a critical resource. il *Ad Astra* 1:16-19 N '89

Cometary missions
CRAF will be first in series of missions using Mariner MK. 2 [Comet Rendezvous Asteroid Flyby for Comet Kopff] il *Aviation Week & Space Technology* 131:99+ O 9 '89
Probing the solar system by PC [XonVu: Voyager and Giotto Space Mission Simulator] J. L. Wilson. *Ad Astra* 1:14 Je '89

Earth sciences use
See also
Mission to Planet Earth (Project)
Economic aspects
See also
American Rocket Company
Astrotech International Corporation
Eosat (Firm)
Hummingbird Launch Systems Inc.
INSCOM (Firm)
Orbital Sciences Corporation
Payload Systems, Inc.
Space Commerce Corporation
Space Industries, Inc.
Space Services, Inc.
Space vouchers
United States. National Aeronautics and Space Administration. Office of Commercial Programs
AIAA report says U.S. needs 'major policy changes' to win substantial share of commercial space markets [American Institute of Aeronautics and Astronautics] *Aviation Week & Space Technology* 131:27 N 6 '89
America's private road to heaven [artificial satellite launchings] il *U.S. News & World Report* 107:11+ S 11 '89
Are we serious about a commercial launch industry? B. Forman. *Ad Astra* 1:3 Je '89
Ariane 4 vehicle to orbit Hughes payloads in 1990. *Aviation Week & Space Technology* 131:35 Jl 24 '89
Ariane to continue key role in launch service market. il *Aviation Week & Space Technology* 130:131 Mr 20 '89
Buggy whips on starships. J. D. Kirwan. *Ad Astra* 1:46 Ap '89
A "buyer's guide" for space vehicles [Office of Technology Assessment report] il *The Futurist* 23:42 Ja/F '89
China agrees to limit marketing of Long March booster in U.S. C. Covault. il *Aviation Week & Space Technology* 130:37 Ja 2 '89
Commercial launches: getting the business? I. Klotz. il *Ad Astra* 1:16-19 Ap '89
Commercial space: lost on the way to Mars? J. P. Allen. *Ad Astra* 1:3 D '89
Commercial space shows long-term promise despite early setbacks. T. M. Foley. il *Aviation Week & Space Technology* 130:118-19 Mr 20 '89
Commercialization policy threatens space station's robotic contract [OMB decision requiring private financing] T. M. Foley. il *Aviation Week & Space Technology* 130:30-1 F 6 '89
Do we have a place in space? H. L. Shipman. *Astronomy* 17:8 S '89
Enterprises. W. H. Ganoe. See issues of Ad Astra beginning January 1989
For sale: commercial space. J. Egan. il *Ad Astra* 1:8-11+ D '89
Forget Mars—the race now should be to commercialize space. S. Payne. il *Business Week* p92 Jl 31 '89
Getting there from here. J. L. Struthers. *Ad Astra* 1:22 Ja '89
Government procurement: friend or foe? [commercial space enterprises] C. D. Ahearn. *Ad Astra* 1:36 S '89
Headline: commercial space dies . . . C. Miller. *Ad Astra* 1:13 F '89
The launch triad. C. Stadd. il *Ad Astra* 1:3 Mr '89
Launches into low-earth orbit should be economical, routine. R. C. Henry. por *Aviation Week & Space Technology* 131:93+ N 27 '89
Marketing the Proton [Soviet booster] S. Arenstein. il *Ad Astra* 1:31-4 D '89
NASA commercial centers gain greater independence. il *Aviation Week & Space Technology* 131:41+ N 20 '89
Need money? Good luck! L. Keesey. il *Ad Astra* 1:17-21 D '89
Opportunity knocking, no one home: educating space entrepreneurs. L. Frazer. *Ad Astra* 1:36-7 D '89
Potential increasing for profitable ventures. C. Covault. *Aviation Week & Space Technology* 130:22 Ap 10 '89
President's message. C. D. Walker. il *Ad Astra* 1:2 D '89
Propellant mixer delay could stall Ariane 5 program [U.S.-built mixer intended for propellant factory under construction at Guiana Space Center] J. M. Lenorovitz. *Aviation Week & Space Technology* 130:35 Je 26 '89
Quayle denounces U.S. reliance on foreign space launch vehicles. T. M. Foley. il por *Aviation Week & Space Technology* 130:21-2 Ap 10 '89
Reach for the stars. R. Jacob. il *Fortune* 120:8 S 25 '89

Soviet space program reflects new policies initiated by Gorbachev. J. M. Lenorovitz. il *Aviation Week & Space Technology* 131:52+ D 18-25 '89
Soviets book new commercial payloads, grant greater access to space facilities [Kayser-Threde microgravity missions] J. M. Lenorovitz. *Aviation Week & Space Technology* 131:121+ O 9 '89
Soviets book new commercial space flights; long-term cooperation with France advances. J. M. Lenorovitz. *Aviation Week & Space Technology* 130:25+ Jl 10 '89
Soviets propose using Energia to launch NASA space station. il *Aviation Week & Space Technology* 130:22 My 8 '89
Soviets sign space pact, launch military satellites [joint venture between Space Commerce Corp. and Glavcosmos] C. Covault. il *Aviation Week & Space Technology* 130:24-5 Ja 9 '89
Soviets will increase efforts to market commercial space flight opportunities. J. M. Lenorovitz. il *Aviation Week & Space Technology* 130:115 Mr 20 '89
Space commerce, Soviet style. J. Goldman. il *Ad Astra* 1:24-30 D '89
Space: more than a program. J. Lewis. *Ad Astra* 1:16 D '89
Space revenues on rise as new birds fly. *High Technology Business* 9:31 My '89
Survival of the fittest [commercial booster industry] *Aviation Week & Space Technology* 130:15 My 29 '89
U.S., China initial agreement on communications satellites [State Dept. statement, December 19, 1988] *Department of State Bulletin* 89:26-7 F '89
U.S. reenters commercial launch arena with private Delta mission [launch of British television relay spacecraft Marcopolo] E. H. Kolcum. il *Aviation Week & Space Technology* 131:24-5 S 4 '89
U.S., Soviet firms to develop, market commercial booster based on SS-20 [Start mobile launcher] J. D. Morrocco. il *Aviation Week & Space Technology* 131:21 Ag 7 '89

Extravehicular activity
Getting a grip on space [gloves] R. Spangenburg and D. Moser. il *Ad Astra* 1:31-4 Mr '89
Soviets will tether maneuvering unit to space station for initial missions. J. M. Lenorovitz. il *Aviation Week & Space Technology* 130:63 Ja 23 '89

Food problems
Garden of unearthly delight. H. Smith. il *Technology Review* 92:16 N/D '89
Ins and outs of astronauts. M. R. Chartrand. *Ad Astra* 1:37 O '89

History
Looking back in 2073. C. Sheffield. *Ad Astra* 1:48 Mr '89
Lunar labors lost [W. Von Braun's original ideas for the space program] B. Forman. il *Omni (New York, N.Y.)* 11:16+ Jl '89
Man in space [preserving relics of the space program] E. Bruske. il *National Parks* 63:32-8 Ja/F '89
The struggle for the outer planets [failed Grand Tour mission] C. B. Waff. il *Astronomy* 17:44-52 S '89
Wernher Von Braun: from Peenemünde to Cape Canaveral. J. Gustaitis. il por *American History Illustrated* 24:30-1 Summ '89

Mariner Mark II missions
CRAF will be first in series of missions using Mariner MK. 2 [Comet Rendezvous Asteroid Flyby for Comet Kopff] il *Aviation Week & Space Technology* 131:99+ O 9 '89

Military use
See also
Air Force Astronautics Laboratory (U.S.)
Artificial satellites—Military use
Space warfare
Spaceplane
Spaceplane, Russian
Strategic Defense Initiative
United States. Space Command
Air Force cannot meet 1989 launch schedule. E. H. Kolcum. il *Aviation Week & Space Technology* 130:21-2 Ja 23 '89
Let common sense prevail in space secrecy. E. H. Kolcum. il *Aviation Week & Space Technology* 131:49-50 D 18-25 '89
Military services assess optimum use of space in era of zero budget growth. E. H. Kolcum. *Aviation Week & Space Technology* 130:87 My 8 '89
Military space capabilities expanding, but excess secrecy limits progress. C. Covault. *Aviation Week & Space Technology* 130:18-19 Ap 17 '89
Military space establishment moves toward major changes. B. A. Smith. il *Aviation Week & Space Technology* 130:121+ Mr 20 '89
NASA mobilizes technical team to ready orbiter Columbia for military launch. E. H. Kolcum. il *Aviation Week & Space Technology* 130:101-2 My 29 '89

Philosophy
Will we have a space age? O. McLean. il *Ad Astra* 1:48 O '89

Physiological aspects
See also
Life support systems (Space environment)

SPACE FLIGHT—Physiological aspects—See also—*cont.*
  Space medicine
  Weightlessness
           Pioneer flights
Are we living in a "bubble"? [Pioneer 10 data; research by Darrell L. Judge] *USA Today (Periodical)* 117:13 Je '89
        Psychological aspects
Blazing the lonesome trail [stress of mountaineering as a model for interplanetary missions; research by Barbara Kanki and others] S. Kaiser. il *Ad Astra* 1:32-4+ O '89
Voyages to the unknown. D. Gelman. il *Newsweek* 113:66-7+ My 15 '89
        Reporters and reporting
   See also
  Challenger (Space shuttle) explosion, 1986—Reporters and reporting
The return of the shuttle syndrome? F. Jerome. il *Technology Review* 92:65-6 Ja '89
          Shuttle missions
   See also
  Challenger (Space shuttle) explosion, 1986
  Space stations—Spacelab missions
Back to the future [meaning of successful Discovery launch] M. D. Lemonick. il *Discover* 10:42-3+ Ja '89
Columbia rolled out; Discovery completes military mission. il *Aviation Week & Space Technology* 131:27 D 4 '89
Crystals in zero-G [growing protein crystals] J. Kluger. il *Discover* 10:16 Ap '89
The decline and fall of LDEF [Long Duration Exposure Facility] P. Jones. il *Ad Astra* 1:36-7 N '89
Discovery crew deploys TDRS, tests space station system. C. Covault. il *Aviation Week & Space Technology* 130:264-5 Mr 20 '89
Discovery's 'cargo of dreams'. J. Kanipe. il *Astronomy* 17:54-9 Ja '89
Final launch preparations under way for signal intelligence satellite mission [shuttle Discovery] il *Aviation Week & Space Technology* 131:24 N 6 '89
Galileo launch to Jupiter by Atlantis culminates difficult effort with shuttle. C. Covault. il *Aviation Week & Space Technology* 131:58+ O 9 '89
Green for go! [National Space Society Shuttle Launch Tour at Discovery launch] K. McMains. il *Ad Astra* 1:24-7+ Ja '89
"It gets better every time". M. D. Lemonick. il *Time* 133:64 Mr 27 '89
LDEF decay sparks move for early retrieval mission [Long-Duration Exposure Facility] E. H. Kolcum. il *Aviation Week & Space Technology* 131:20-1 Ag 21 '89
A lunar cube [artwork by L. Burgess to be on space shuttle] S. Staggs. il *Art News* 88:13-14 Ja '89
Magellan heads toward Venus as U.S. resumes planetary probes [deployed from shuttle Atlantis] E. H. Kolcum. *Aviation Week & Space Technology* 130:23 My 8 '89
Magellan mission to Venus requires precise shuttle launch operations [launch by shuttle Atlantis] C. Covault. il *Aviation Week & Space Technology* 130:42-3+ Ap 24 '89
Magellan prepared for course correction as astronauts land Atlantis in crosswind. C. Covault. il *Aviation Week & Space Technology* 130:25 My 15 '89
Making bigger, better crystals . . . [work of Charles E. Bugg] *Science News* 136:349 N 25 '89
Making plastics in Galileo's shadow [polymer morphology experiment] *Science News* 136:286 O 28 '89
Managers modernize shuttle system to increase efficiency, launch rate [views of Robert L. Crippen] E. H. Kolcum. il *Aviation Week & Space Technology* 131:46-8 D 4 '89
NASA delays launch of space shuttle until mid-March [turbopumps on Discovery engines to be replaced] *Aviation Week & Space Technology* 130:32 F 6 '89
NASA may delay or scrub Mission 29 because of turbopump bearing corrosion [space shuttle Discovery] E. H. Kolcum. il *Aviation Week & Space Technology* 130:31 Ja 30 '89
NASA mobilizes technical team to ready orbiter Columbia for military launch. E. H. Kolcum. il *Aviation Week & Space Technology* 130:101-2 My 29 '89
NASA plans shuttle launch for Feb. 23 despite delay in move to assembly building [orbiter Discovery for Mission 29] *Aviation Week & Space Technology* 130:22 Ja 23 '89
NASA racing the sun to save a satellite [Long-Duration Exposure Facility] R. A. Kerr. il *Science* 244:1443 Je 23 '89
NASA seeks cause of body flap deflection in last Columbia launch. E. H. Kolcum. *Aviation Week & Space Technology* 131:28 S 18 '89
Night launch of Discovery boosts secret military satellite into orbit. E. H. Kolcum. *Aviation Week & Space Technology* 131:29 N 27 '89
The not-so-secret mission of Atlantis. J. Banke. il *Ad Astra* 1:7+ F '89
Orbiter Discovery engine repairs accelerating for shuttle Mission 29. *Aviation Week & Space Technology* 130:25 F 13 '89
Orbiting of advanced imaging satellite bolsters U.S. intelligence capabilities [shuttle mission 28] E. H. Kolcum and C. Covault. il *Aviation Week & Space Technology* 131:30-1 Ag 14 '89

President's message [civilians aboard shuttle] C. D. Walker. il *Ad Astra* 1:2 Ap '89
Protein crystal growth in microgravity. L. J. DeLucas and others. bibl f il *Science* 246:651-4 N 3 '89
Rivers in the sand [interpretation of shuttle radar imaging in the Sahara] B. Bower. map *Science News* 136:138-9 Ag 26 '89
Satellites on a string [Tethered Satellite System] R. G. Nichols. il *Astronomy* 17:18-19 My '89
SDI urges NASA to accelerate satellite retrieval with shuttle [Long-Duration Exposure Facility] C. Covault. il *Aviation Week & Space Technology* 130:80-1 My 8 '89
Shuttle Columbia poised to retrieve LDEF satellite, deploy Navy Syncom [Long-Duration Exposure Facility] C. Covault. il *Aviation Week & Space Technology* 131:35-6 D 11 '89
Shuttle faces tough schedule in 1989. E. Marshall. il *Science* 243:884 F 17 '89
Shuttle glow [cover story] D. E. Hunton. bibl il *Scientific American* 261:92-8 N '89
Shuttle launch of Galileo Jupiter mission highlights U.S. space science renaissance [Atlantis launch] C. Covault. il *Aviation Week & Space Technology* 131:22-4 O 23 '89
Shuttle launch schedule accelerates after Galileo deployment, Atlantis reentry. C. Covault. il *Aviation Week & Space Technology* 131:22-4 O 30 '89
Shuttle Mission 29 set to conduct space station test, deploy TDRS [Tracking and Data Relay Satellite system] C. Covault. il *Aviation Week & Space Technology* 129:48-9 Mr 6 '89
Shuttle orbiter Discovery shows little damage after completing Mission 29. il *Aviation Week & Space Technology* 130:25 Mr 27 '89
Shuttle scan. See issues of Ad Astra beginning January 1989
Shuttle scientists: an endangered species? [astronauts to be given priority over payload specialists] J. Eberhart. *Science News* 135:71 F 4 '89
Shuttle update: new experiments, orbiter. il *Popular Mechanics* 166:25 Ap '89
Space/missiles: NASA/industry shuttle team [aerospace laureate] il por *Aviation Week & Space Technology* 130:14 Ja 2 '89
Space platform consortium seeks NASA shuttle launch [Amica platform] C. Covault. il *Aviation Week & Space Technology* 131:16-17 Jl 3 '89
Space shuttle. il *Popular Science* 235:70-1 Jl '89
Space tethers [Tethered Satellite System] R. Twombly. il *Technology Review* 92:10-11 O '89
Spacecraft on a string [Tethered Satellite System] J. Rennie. *Scientific American* 261:32 O '89
STS-29 mission report [Discovery mission] J. Banke. il *Ad Astra* 1:15+ My '89
STS-30 mission report [Atlantis flight] J. Banke. il *Ad Astra* 1:41-2 S '89
We're back! [Discovery flight] J. Banke. il *Ad Astra* 1:8-12 Ja '89
What killed the chickens? [embryonic chickens on the space shuttle Discovery] *Science News* 135:213 Ap 8 '89
Z biggest or Z best [heavy lift shuttle designed to launch components of Mars spacecraft] G. R. Graf. il *Ad Astra* 1:7 S '89
Zero gravity produces weighty improvement [protein crystals grown on the space shuttle] R. Pool. *Science* 246:580 N 3 '89

          Collectibles
U.S.A. space mission patches [shuttle patches] R. V. Simpson. il *Antiques & Collecting Hobbies* 93:50-3 Ja '89
      Shuttle missions, Russian
Blizzard from Baikonur [shuttle Buran] S. Arenstein. il *Ad Astra* 1:14-18 F '89
Buran inspection shows Soviet shuttle details [Paris Air Show] C. Covault. il *Aviation Week & Space Technology* 130:46-7+ Je 19 '89
Do the Soviets need a shuttle? D. S. F. Portree. il *Astronomy* 17:14+ Ja '89
Government production decision awaited on additional space shuttle orbiters. il *Aviation Week & Space Technology* 130:94-6 Je 5 '89
Ground testing, flight evaluations support Soviet shuttle program. il *Aviation Week & Space Technology* 130:98-9 Je 5 '89
Manned Soviet shuttle flight delayed until 1992 for systems installation. C. Covault. il *Aviation Week & Space Technology* 130:20-1 My 8 '89
Soviet shuttle will appear at Paris show. *Aviation Week & Space Technology* 130:32 My 15 '89
Soviets planning manned shuttle mission for 1989 [cover story] J. M. Lenorovitz. il *Aviation Week & Space Technology* 130:34-6+ Ja 16 '89
Three orbiters to serve as Soviet shuttle fleet. J. M. Lenorovitz. il *Aviation Week & Space Technology* 131:73+ O 16 '89
Winged twins? [Soviet Buran space shuttle and its American counterpart] il *Ad Astra* 1:46 F '89
          Solar energy use
   See also
  Solar array
  Solar sails

SPACE FLIGHT—Solar energy use—*cont.*
Boeing achieves major advance in space solar cell efficiency.
B. W. Henderson. il *Aviation Week & Space Technology*
131:61+ O 23 '89

Soyuz flights
Soviet long-duration cosmonauts readapt rapidly to earth
environment [Mir cosmonauts] J. M. Lenorovitz. il *Aviation
Week & Space Technology* 130:38-9 Ja 2 '89
Soviet Star trek: a year in space. G. Cowley. il *Newsweek*
113:5 Ja 2 '89
Soviets upgrading space transports to support manned station
activities. J. M. Lenorovitz. il *Aviation Week & Space
Technology* 131:49 O 23 '89

Voyager flights
Ad astra per Voyager. A. Fisher. *Popular Science* 235:34-5
N '89
Approaching Neptune. R. Berry. il *Astronomy* 17:30-6 Ag
'89
Bon Voyager. S. Fritz. il *Omni (New York, N.Y.)* 12:67-71
N '89
The colors of Neptune. R. Berry. il *Astronomy* 17:34-5 S
'89
Facing a final exam at Neptune. R. A. Kerr. il *Science*
245:588-9 Ag 11 '89
Fantastic voyage. B. Darrach. il *Life* 12:105-13 N '89
A fantastic voyage to Neptune [Voyager 2] S. Begley and
M. Hager. il *Newsweek* 114:50-6 S 4 '89
A final encounter [Neptune] B. Wickens. il *Maclean's* 102:58+
S 4 '89
First discoveries at Neptune. R. Berry. il *Astronomy* 17:32-4
O '89
The greatest show off earth [viewing images of the planets
at the Jet Propulsion Laboratory] F. Pohl. il *Omni (New
York, N.Y.)* 12:14+ N '89
Hello, Neptune. il *U.S. News & World Report* 107:11 Jl
17 '89
Here's looking at you, Triton—probably [Voyager 2] J. Eber-
hart. *Science News* 135:191 Mr 25 '89
The horn of Triton. S. J. Gould. il *Natural History* p18+
D '89
The human-Voyager 2 collaboration. P. H. Abelson. *Science*
245:1161 S 15 '89
Images of Neptune, Triton reveal atmosphere and surface
features. il *Aviation Week & Space Technology* 131:60-1+
S 4 '89
The last picture show [Neptune] L. Jaroff. il *Time* 134:54-6
S 4 '89
Listening for hints of the sun's heliopause [research by Ralph
L. McNutt] J. Eberhart. *Science News* 136:231 O 7 '89
The little space Voyager that could—and did [journey to
Neptune] S. Budiansky. il *U.S. News & World Report*
107:10-11 Ag 28-S 4 '89
Neptune. J. Kinoshita. il *Scientific American* 261:82-91 N
'89
Neptune: a new page in the book of worlds. J. Eberhart.
Science News 136:300 N 4 '89
Neptune déjà vu [views of Zecharia Sitchin] M. Teich. il
Omni (New York, N.Y.) 12:90-1 N '89
Neptune marvels emerge from data deluge. J. Eberhart. *Science
News* 136:391 D 16 '89
Neptune on the horizon. J. Eberhart. il *Science News* 136:111
Ag 12 '89
Neptune rendezvous will mark final stage of Voyager 2's
mission. B. A. Smith. il *Aviation Week & Space Technology*
131:70-1 Ag 7 '89
Neptune revealed [cover story] R. Berry. il *Astronomy* 17:22-34
D '89
The Neptune system in Voyager's afterglow [special section]
R. A. Kerr. il *Science* 245:1450-1 S 29 '89
Neptune's wind speeds obtained by tracking clouds in Voyager
images. H. B. Hammel and others. bibl f il *Science*
245:1367-9 S 22 '89
Next and final stop: Neptune. M. D. Lemonick. il *Time*
134:44 Ag 7 '89
Next stop: the planet Neptune [Voyager 2] il *Newsweek*
114:66 Ag 21 '89
An open letter to Voyager 2. J. Updike. il *Life* 12:115
N '89
The poor man's grand tour of the solar system [Voyager's
findings confirm resemblance between Neptune's moon
Triton and Pluto] il *Science* 246:998 N 24 '89
Postcards from a distant world [Voyager 2 data from Neptune
and Triton] P. Elmer-Dewitt. il *Time* 134:65-6 S 11 '89
Probing the solar system by PC [XonVu: Voyager and Giotto
Space Mission Simulator] J. L. Wilson. *Ad Astra* 1:14
Je '89
Report from the far side of Neptune [Voyager 2 and Triton]
il *Newsweek* 114:66 S 11 '89
Reprogramming capability proves key to extending Voyager
2's journey. il *Aviation Week & Space Technology* 131:72
Ag 7 '89
Running rings around Neptune [Voyager 2] R. Berry. il
Astronomy 17:36-40 My '89
Searching for the 'real' Triton. R. Berry. il *Astronomy* 17:20-6
F '89
Simple Voyager simulator [XonVu] M. Krochmal. il
Astronomy 17:112-13 My '89

Triton steals Voyager's last show. R. A. Kerr. il *Science*
245:928-30 S 1 '89
Triumph at Neptune [cover story] R. Berry. il *Astronomy*
17:20-8 N '89
The two faces of Nereid. M. D. Lemonick. il *Discover* 10:18-19
Ja '89
The unknown solar system. I. Asimov. il *Discover* 10:38-43
O '89
Uranus' signature in a radio signal [work of Michael D.
Desch and others] R. Monastersky. *Science News* 135:319
My 20 '89
Voyager 2 [cover story; special section; with editorial comment
by Philip H. Abelson] bibl f il *Science* 246:1369, 1417-1501
D 15 '89
Voyager 2 builds suspense for Neptune. J. Eberhart. il *Science
News* 136:36 Jl 15 '89
Voyager 2 enters home stretch to Neptune. J. Eberhart.
Science News 136:103 Ag 12 '89
Voyager 2 images of Neptune confirm presence of partial
rings near moon orbits. il *Aviation Week & Space
Technology* 131:21 Ag 21 '89
Voyager 2: miles to go before it sleeps. L. David. il *Ad
Astra* 1:24-7 O '89
Voyager 2 reveals Neptune's belts, clouds. il *Astronomy* 17:10
Je '89
Voyager ends Neptune flyby, yielding historic Triton data
[special section] il *Aviation Week & Space Technology*
131:18-22 S 4 '89
Voyager sees Neptunian ring-arcs at last. il *Science News*
136:119 Ag 19 '89
Voyager spacecraft beginning new, interstellar part of mission.
il *Aviation Week & Space Technology* 131:117-18 O 9
'89
Voyager's decade of wonder. W. I. McLaughlin. il *Sky and
Telescope* 78:16-20 Jl '89
Voyager's discoveries mount on final rush to Neptune [cover
story; with editorial comment] B. A. Smith. il *Aviation
Week & Space Technology* 131:7, 16-20 Ag 28 '89
Voyager's last close encounter [Neptune] T. H. Cole. il *Popular
Mechanics* 166:51-3+ Ag '89
Voyager's last encounter [Neptune] E. D. Miner. il *Sky and
Telescope* 78:26-9 Jl '89
Voyager's last picture show [cover story] il *Sky and Telescope*
78:463-70 N '89
Voyager's last picture show [Neptune] W. J. Cook. il *U.S.
News & World Report* 107:60-1 S 11 '89
Welcome to Neptune [cover story] J. K. Beatty. il *Sky and
Telescope* 78:358-9 O '89
'What a way to leave the solar system' [Voyager 2 journey
past Neptune and Triton] J. Eberhart. il *Science News*
136:148+ S 2 '89
SPACE FLIGHT CENTERS *See* Space centers
SPACE FLIGHT IN ART
A lunar cube [artwork by L. Burgess to be on space shuttle]
S. Staggs. il *Art News* 88:13-14 Ja '89
Space mailbag [children's drawings] il *National Geographic
World* 171:30-1 N '89
SPACE FLIGHT RECORDERS
NASA's legal folly [battle to block release of recording of
Challenger astronauts' voices] M. Stevens. *Ad Astra* 1:48
My '89
SPACE FLIGHT SIMULATORS
Training for space [U.S. Space Camp] A. Fisher. il *Popular
Science* 234:12 Ja '89
USAF builds facility to study dynamics of lightweight space-
based structures. W. B. Scott. il *Aviation Week & Space
Technology* 130:51 F 20 '89
SPACE FLIGHT TO JUPITER
Can Galileo take the heat? [risky trajectory for space probe]
M. M. Waldrop. il *Science* 245:1327-9 S 22 '89
Combatting fear [National Space Society response to protests
against nuclear powered space vehicles] *Ad Astra* 1:48
N '89
Court rejects activists' bid to halt Galileo/shuttle launch
[nuclear powered spacecraft] *Aviation Week & Space
Technology* 131:21 O 16 '89
Engine controller problem delays launch of Galileo mission
to Jupiter. E. H. Kolcum and C. Covault. *Aviation Week
& Space Technology* 131:20-1 O 16 '89
First Galileo course correction executed; several spacecraft
anomalies uncovered. M. A. Dornheim. *Aviation Week
& Space Technology* 131:43 N 20 '89
Galileo Jupiter orbiter/probe readied for launch by space
shuttle Atlantis. C. Covault. *Aviation Week & Space
Technology* 131:23 S 4 '89
Galileo launch to Jupiter by Atlantis culminates difficult
effort with shuttle. C. Covault. il *Aviation Week & Space
Technology* 131:58+ O 9 '89
Galileo poised for 1995 inspection of Jupiter. il *Popular
Mechanics* 166:14 Je '89
Galileo represents peak in design complexity. *Aviation Week
& Space Technology* 131:77-8 O 9 '89
Galileo thrusters approved for flight but mission plan may
be abbreviated. M. A. Dornheim. *Aviation Week & Space
Technology* 130:23 Ap 10 '89
Galileo to Jupiter [cover story] J. Eberhart. il *Science News*
136:218-19 S 30 '89

SPACE FLIGHT TO JUPITER—*cont.*

Galileo to perform first dedicated study of Jupiter's atmosphere and satellites. M. A. Dornheim. il *Aviation Week & Space Technology* 131:69-70+ O 9 '89

Galileo (whew!) changes course. M. M. Waldrop. *Science* 246:997 N 24 '89

Journey to Jupiter [Galileo] A. Steacy. il *Maclean's* 102:88-90 O 30 '89

Jupiter-bound Galileo starts with the sun. J. Eberhart. *Science News* 136:325 N 18 '89

NASA prepares for protests over nuclear system launch on shuttle in October [Galileo mission to Jupiter] T. M. Foley. *Aviation Week & Space Technology* 130:83+ Je 26 '89

Nuclear fears about Galileo. A. Toufexis. il *Time* 134:76 O 16 '89

Nuclear slingshot [Project Galileo's plutonium] K. Grossman and J. Long. *The Nation* 249:336-7 O 2 '89

Plutonium con [solar energy as an alternative to nuclear powered space probes] K. Grossman and J. Long. *The Nation* 249:589 N 20 '89

Project Galileo: the risk of a nuclear disaster in space. *Utne Reader* p60 S/O '89

A quest to fill in the cosmic puzzle [Galileo flight] il *U.S. News & World Report* 107:17 O 23 '89

Rediscovering Venus and Jupiter [Magellan and Galileo] S. Cole. il *Astronomy* 17:24-31 Ja '89

Repairs completed, Galileo thrusters set to undergo reacceptance tests. M. A. Dornheim. il *Aviation Week & Space Technology* 130:62 Ja 23 '89

Rifkin tries to stop Galileo launch [nuclear fears] M. M. Waldrop. il *Science* 246:30 O 6 '89

Showdown at Pad 39-B [nuclear powered space vehicles] R. G. Nichols. il *Ad Astra* 1:8-12+ N '89

Shuttle launch of Galileo Jupiter mission highlights U.S. space science renaissance [Atlantis launch] C. Covault. il *Aviation Week & Space Technology* 131:22-4 O 23 '89

Shuttle launch schedule accelerates after Galileo deployment, Atlantis reentry. C. Covault. il *Aviation Week & Space Technology* 131:22-4 O 30 '89

"Stop the plutonium shuttle!" [Galileo mission] M. M. Waldrop. *Science* 245:1328 S 22 '89

SPACE FLIGHT TO MARS

Apollo and Mars. T. O. Paine. il *Ad Astra* 1:3 Jl/Ag '89

The art of the possible. G. R. Woodcock. il *Ad Astra* 1:8-13 O '89

A balloonful of earth to help study Mars. *Science News* 135:223 Ap 8 '89

Blazing the lonesome trail [stress of mountaineering as a model for interplanetary missions; research by Barbara Kanki and others] S. Kaiser. il *Ad Astra* 1:32-4+ O '89

Bush: 'the inescapable challenge' [excerpts from address, July 20, 1989] G. Bush. *Aviation Week & Space Technology* 131:13 Jl 31 '89

Chalk talk [Bush space plan] L. David. il *Ad Astra* 1:37 S '89

Commercial space: lost on the way to Mars? J. P. Allen. *Ad Astra* 1:3 D '89

Extending the limits of our frontiers [address, July 20, 1989; with editorial comment by Charles D. Walker] G. Bush. il pors *Ad Astra* 1:2, 38-40 S '89

Forget Mars—the race now should be to commercialize space. S. Payne. il *Business Week* p92 Jl 31 '89

Gassing up on Mars [proposed fuel refinery; work of Robert Ash and Warren Dowler] T. Dollar. il *Discover* 10:22 D '89

'A journey into tomorrow' [G. Bush speech on space program] J. Schwartz and M. Hager. il por *Newsweek* 114:31 Jl 31 '89

Life on Mars: cultivating a planet—and ourselves [cover story] F. Turner. il *Harper's* 279:33-40 Ag '89

Manned lunar base, Mars initiative raised in secret White House review [with editorial comment] C. Covault. il *Aviation Week & Space Technology* 131:7, 24-6 Jl 17 '89

Mars Observer begins new era using proven spacecraft design. M. Mecham. il *Aviation Week & Space Technology* 131:79+ O 9 '89

Mars Observer to aid Soviets. il *Astronomy* 17:16+ Ag '89

Mars? What are the alternatives? W. F. Buckley. *National Review* 41:54 S 1 '89

Martian misgivings [Soviet space program] P. Garrison. il *Omni (New York, N.Y.)* 12:22 D '89

Master plan for Mars [Soviet Union] *Ad Astra* 1:5-6 Ja '89

NASA declares a bold agenda for 21st century. il *Popular Mechanics* 166:11 My '89

NASA offers five alternatives for landing humans on Mars by 2018. J. R. Asker. il *Aviation Week & Space Technology* 131:30-1 N 27 '89

NASA ponders the Mars Rover. il *Astronomy* 17:16 Mr '89

NASA scientists hope Mars Rover will be precursor to manned flight. B. W. Henderson. il *Aviation Week & Space Technology* 131:85-6+ O 9 '89

New views of Mars [Mars the movie and Samara probe] T. H. Cole. il *Popular Mechanics* 166:36 S '89

New views of Mars and Phobos [Phobos mission] R. Burnham. il *Astronomy* 17:28-32 S '89

Phobos 2 asks, "Is Mars magnetic?". il *Sky and Telescope* 77:464 My '89

Phobos at Mars: a dramatic view—and then failure. M. M. Waldrop. il *Science* 245:1044-5 S 8 '89

Planetary partners [cover story] M. A. G. Michaud. il *Ad Astra* 1:24-8 Mr '89

President's message. C. D. Walker. il *Ad Astra* 1:2 N '89

Probing the Mars question. D. S. F. Portree. il *Astronomy* 17:16 Je '89

Soviet failure at Mars a reminder of risks [loss of Phobos 2] R. A. Kerr. il *Science* 244:26 Ap 7 '89

Soviet findings from Phobos and Mars. il *Science News* 136:286 O 28 '89

Soviet Mars probe collects data in preparation for Phobos flyby. il *Aviation Week & Space Technology* 130:26 Mr 27 '89

A Soviet mission to nowhere [loss of Phobos 2 spacecraft] *U.S. News & World Report* 106:16-17 Ap 10 '89

A Soviet perspective [interview with V. L. Barsukov] S. F. Brown. *Popular Science* 235:75 Jl '89

Soviet probe enters Mars orbit; landers to descend on Phobos. C. Covault. il *Aviation Week & Space Technology* 130:24-5 F 13 '89

Soviet space program strife threatens Mars mission plans. C. Covault. il *Aviation Week & Space Technology* 130:18-21 My 22 '89

Soviet space scientists to focus studies on Mars until 2000, seek U.S. cooperation. *Aviation Week & Space Technology* 130:21 My 8 '89

Soviets abandon efforts to regain contact with Phobos 2 [with editorial comment] il *Aviation Week & Space Technology* 130:7, 24-5 Ap 10 '89

Soviets lose contact with Phobos 2 spacecraft. *Aviation Week & Space Technology* 130:22 Ap 3 '89

Soviets revise Mars program; prepare missions to moon. *Aviation Week & Space Technology* 130:39 Ja 2 '89

Taking the next 'giant leap'. *Astronomy* 17:14+ Ap '89

Target: Phobos. K. Croswell. il *Ad Astra* 1:16-21 Ja '89

Time, cost constraints force Soviets to alter 1994 Mars mission. *Aviation Week & Space Technology* 131:22 Ag 28 '89

To the moon or Mars. il *Popular Science* 235:72-4 Jl '89

Viking missions are principal source of scientists' knowledge about Mars. il *Aviation Week & Space Technology* 131:95 O 9 '89

Z biggest or Z best [heavy lift shuttle designed to launch components of Mars spacecraft] G. R. Graf. il *Ad Astra* 1:7 S '89

SPACE FLIGHT TO NEPTUNE
See also
Space flight—Voyager flights

SPACE FLIGHT TO SATURN

Cassini to provide detailed, extended views of Saturn. il *Aviation Week & Space Technology* 131:109-10 O 9 '89

SPACE FLIGHT TO THE MOON

20th anniversary of Apollo 11 [cover story; special section; with editorial comment by Richard Berry] bibl (p108) il *Astronomy* 17:6, 20-35+ Jl '89

Footprints on the moon [Project Apollo flights; cover story] D. MacKinnon and J. Baldanza. il *American History Illustrated* 24:18-23 Summ '89

Lunar prospecting [cover story] W. R. Farrand. il *Ad Astra* 1:8-12 F '89

Lunar reflections [memories of Apollo astronauts] J. Goldberg. il *Omni (New York, N.Y.)* 11:34-6+ Jl '89

Moon river [search for water] G. K. O'Neill. il *Omni (New York, N.Y.)* 11:20+ My '89

Moonrocks [specimens brought back from Apollo missions] L. Hart and others. il *Life* 12:58-9+ Jl '89

Moonstruck. T. Waters. il *Discover* 10:90-5 Jl '89

Soviets revise Mars program; prepare missions to moon. *Aviation Week & Space Technology* 130:39 Ja 2 '89

Apollo 11 flight

20th anniversary of Apollo 11 [cover story; special section; with editorial comment by Richard Berry] bibl (p108) il *Astronomy* 17:6, 20-35+ Jl '89

Apollo 11 [cover story; special issue; with editorial comment by Charles Walker] il *Ad Astra* 1:2, 8-12+ Jl/Ag '89

Getting high. *National Review* 41:11-12 Ag 18 '89

Happy anniversary, man on the moon. il *National Geographic World* 167:22-4 Jl '89

Houston, the Model A has landed [watching the 1969 moon landing on TV while sitting in a 1929 Ford] J. Calabro. il *Road & Track* 40:144+ Jl '89

Men from earth [condensation] B. Aldrin and M. McConnell. il por *Reader's Digest* 135:30-8+ Jl '89

Moonstruck [special section] il *Flying* 116:38-40+ Jl '89

Moonwalk. H. Hurt. il *Newsweek* 114:48-9 Jl 3 '89

Of space and the moon man [astronaut E. E. Aldrin] P. Axthelm. il pors *People Weekly* 32:30-3 Jl 3 '89

Return to Tranquillity Base. S. J. O'Meara. il *Sky and Telescope* 78:84 Jl '89

The South reaches for the stars [Apollo 11 celebrations] J. T. Black. il *Southern Living* 24:52+ Jl '89

A step in time. A. Steacy. il *Maclean's* 102:47 Jl 24 '89

SPACE FLIGHT TO THE MOON—Apollo 11 flight—
cont.

The twentieth anniversary of the first moon landing [cover story; special issue] il *Omni (New York, N.Y.)* 11:6+ Jl '89

An unsung legacy of the first lunar landing [lunar laser ranging] D. C. Morrison. il *Science* 246:447-8 O 27 '89

Where were you in '69? T. H. Cole. il *Popular Mechanics* 166:28-9 Jl '89

Photographs and photography

Images. il *Sky and Telescope* 78:24-5 Jl '89

SPACE FLIGHT TO THE SUN

Ulysses spacecraft prepared for long-delayed mission to sun. il *Aviation Week & Space Technology* 131:25 N 6 '89

SPACE FLIGHT TO URANUS

See also

Space flight—Voyager flights

SPACE FLIGHT TO VENUS

1989: Venus. M. Hager. il *Newsweek* 114:49 Jl 3 '89

Another Magellan. A. Fisher. il *Popular Science* 234:12+ My '89

Feeling the face of Venus [Magellan radar mapping; cover story] J. Eberhart. il *Science News* 135:248-9 Ap 22 '89

Magellan: a fortuitous start to Venus. J. Eberhart. *Science News* 135:292 My 13 '89

Magellan heads toward Venus as U.S. resumes planetary probes [deployed from shuttle Atlantis] E. H. Kolcum. *Aviation Week & Space Technology* 130:23 My 8 '89

Magellan mission to Venus requires precise shuttle launch operations [launch by shuttle Atlantis] C. Covault. il *Aviation Week & Space Technology* 130:42-3+ Ap 24 '89

Magellan prepared for course correction as astronauts land Atlantis in crosswind. C. Covault. il *Aviation Week & Space Technology* 130:25 My 15 '89

Magellan's journey begins. R. G. Nichols. il *Sky and Telescope* 77:367 Ap '89

Magellan's radar images of Venus to unmask cloud-shrouded planet. il *Aviation Week & Space Technology* 131:113+ O 9 '89

One touch of Venus [Magellan mission] il *U.S. News & World Report* 106:11 My 8 '89

The planet next door. A. T. Bazilevskiy. il *Sky and Telescope* 77:360-6+ Ap '89

A planetary comeback: Magellan heads for Venus. D. S. F. Portree. il *Astronomy* 17:38-42 S '89

Rediscovering Venus and Jupiter [Magellan and Galileo] S. Cole. il *Astronomy* 17:24-31 Ja '89

The unveiling of Venus [Magellan flight] M. M. Waldrop. il *Science* 244:526 My 5 '89

Venus unveiled [Magellan mission] S. D. Wall. il *Astronomy* 17:26-32 Ap '89

Voyage to Venus [Magellan flight; cover story] R. Kunzig. il *Discover* 10:54-61 Ap '89

Will earth become another Venus? T. H. Cole. il *Popular Mechanics* 166:18+ Je '89

Photographs and photography

Magellan: Venus bound. il *Sky and Telescope* 78:39 Jl '89

SPACE FUEL REFINERIES

Gassing up on Mars [work of Robert Ash and Warren Dowler] T. Dollar. il *Discover* 10:22 D '89

SPACE GLOVES

Getting a grip on space. R. Spangenburg and D. Moser. il *Ad Astra* 1:31-4 Mr '89

SPACE HEATERS *See* Heaters

SPACE INDUSTRIES, INC.

Forgetting the lesson [National Research Council report on Commercially Developed Space Facility] W. H. Ganoe. il *Ad Astra* 1:59 Jl/Ag '89

NASA advised to drop plan for commercial platform lease. T. M. Foley. il *Aviation Week & Space Technology* 130:20-1 Ap 17 '89

Two studies pan commercial space station. *High Technology Business* 9:35-6 S/O '89

SPACE INSIGNIA *See* Insignia

SPACE LABORATORIES *See* Space stations

SPACE LAW

See also

United Nations. Committee on the Peaceful Uses of Outer Space

SPACE MANUFACTURING *See* Space processing

SPACE MEDICINE

First aid for Freedom. R. Spangenburg and D. Moser. il *Ad Astra* 1:42-5 Ja '89

Surgery in space. il *The Futurist* 23:57-8 S/O '89

Surgery in space. A. Gibbons. il *Technology Review* 92:9-10 Ap '89

SPACE MINERAL RESOURCES

See also

Space mining

Nonterrestrial materials: a critical resource. il *Ad Astra* 1:16-19 N '89

SPACE MINING

See also

Center for Utilization of Local Planetary Resources

The great palladium rush [mining asteroids for metal used in cold fusion] H. K. Henson. il *Ad Astra* 1:34-5 N '89

Harvesting the near-earthers [asteroids; cover story] W. Barton and M. Capobianco. il *Ad Astra* 1:24-30+ N '89

Lunar prospecting [cover story] W. R. Farrand. il *Ad Astra* 1:8-12 F '89

Moon power [helium-3] M. J. Mackowski. il por *Ad Astra* 1:34-9 Jl/Ag '89

SPACE MUSEUMS

See also

National Air and Space Museum

Vacations for the mind. H. A. Butowsky. il *Ad Astra* 1:15-20 Je '89

SPACE PERCEPTION

See also

Orientation

Binocular depth reversals despite familiarity cues. A. van den Enden and H. Spekreijse. bibl f il *Science* 244:959-61 My 26 '89

Neural integration of information specifying structure from stereopsis and motion. M. Nawrot and R. Blake. bibl f il *Science* 244:716-18 My 12 '89

Spatial understanding & universal awareness. C. Twarog. il *Ad Astra* 1:23 S '89

SPACE PHYSICS *See* Astrophysics

SPACE PLANNERS

What space planners do. il *Good Housekeeping* 208:192+ Ap '89

SPACE PLATFORMS *See* Space stations

SPACE POLICY *See* Space research

SPACE POLLUTION *See* Space debris

SPACE PROBES *See* Space vehicles

SPACE PROCESSING

See also

Intospace GmbH

Space fuel refineries

Better crystals? It's a matter of space [research by Charles W. J. Scaife] J. Raloff. il *Science News* 136:206 S 23 '89

Crystal clear [Intospace protein crystallization experiment] W. H. Ganoe. *Ad Astra* 1:47 Ja '89

Crystals in zero-G [growing protein crystals] J. Kluger. il *Discover* 10:16 Ap '89

First U.S. commercial cargo for Mir set to lift off Dec. 20 [Payload Systems protein crystal growth experiments] J. M. Lenorovitz. *Aviation Week & Space Technology* 131:34 D 11 '89

Forgetting the lesson [National Research Council report on Commercially Developed Space Facility] W. H. Ganoe. il *Ad Astra* 1:59 Jl/Ag '89

German microgravity drop capsule approved for operational service [Mikroba balloon-launched system] *Aviation Week & Space Technology* 130:29 Jl 10 '89

Making bigger, better crystals . . . [work of Charles E. Bugg] *Science News* 136:349 N 25 '89

Making plastics in Galileo's shadow [space shuttle polymer morphology experiment] *Science News* 136:286 O 28 '89

Materials processing payloads set for launch [Space Services Inc.] *High Technology Business* 9:33-4 F '89

NASA advised to drop plan for commercial platform lease. T. M. Foley. il *Aviation Week & Space Technology* 130:20-1 Ap 17 '89

No deposit, no return [microgravity research] W. H. Ganoe. il *Ad Astra* 1:47 F '89

Paper trails to contrails [Space Services' Starfire 1 launches suborbital payload] K. Boehler. il *Ad Astra* 1:39-41 Je '89

Payload's payload [protein crystal experiments on Mir space station] W. H. Ganoe. *Ad Astra* 1:38 Je '89

Protein crystal growth in microgravity. L. J. DeLucas and others. bibl f il *Science* 246:651-4 N 3 '89

Soviets book new commercial payloads, grant greater access to space facilities [Kayser-Threde microgravity missions] J. M. Lenorovitz. *Aviation Week & Space Technology* 131:121+ O 9 '89

Space platform consortium seeks NASA shuttle launch [Amica platform] C. Covault. il *Aviation Week & Space Technology* 131:16-17 Jl 3 '89

Starfire [Space Services Inc.] W. H. Ganoe. il *Ad Astra* 1:35 Mr '89

Two studies pan commercial space station. *High Technology Business* 9:35-6 S/O '89

U.S. firm's use of Mir faces probable delay [Payload Systems' protein crystal experiment] *Aviation Week & Space Technology* 130:21 Ap 17 '89

Zero gravity produces weighty improvement [protein crystals grown on the space shuttle] R. Pool. *Science* 246:580 N 3 '89

SPACE PROGRAM (U.S.) *See* United States. National Aeronautics and Space Administration

SPACE PROGRAMS *See* Space research

SPACE PROPULSION *See* Space vehicles—Propulsion systems

SPACE PSYCHOLOGY *See* Space flight—Psychological aspects

SPACE RESCUE WORK

Lifeboat to safer shores. K. Boehler. il *Ad Astra* 1:8-12 Mr '89

Planetary Congress. il *Ad Astra* 1:39 D '89

SPACE RESEARCH

See also

Air Force Astronautics Laboratory (U.S.)

Center for Utilization of Local Planetary Resources

Jet Propulsion Laboratory (U.S.)

SPACE RESEARCH—See also—*cont.*
Lunar and Planetary Institute
National Space Council (U.S.)
Planets—Exploration
Religion and space research
Space flight
Spacecause
Spacepac
United States. Congress. House. Committee on Science, Space, and Technology
United States. National Aeronautics and Space Administration
20 years after Apollo: is the U.S. lost in space? [cover story; special section; with editorial comment by C. P. Gilmore] S. F. Brown. il *Popular Science* 235:4, 63-75 Jl '89
Apollo plus twenty. A. C. Clarke. il *Ad Astra* 1:30-1 Jl/Ag '89
Back to the future [meaning of successful Discovery launch] M. D. Lemonick. il *Discover* 10:42-3+ Ja '89
Buggy whips on starships. J. D. Kirwan. *Ad Astra* 1:46 Ap '89
Bush: 'the inescapable challenge' [excerpts from address, July 20, 1989] G. Bush. *Aviation Week & Space Technology* 131:13 Jl 31 '89
Chalk talk [Bush space plan] L. David. il *Ad Astra* 1:37 S '89
The edge of infinity [cover story] W. J. Cook. il *U.S. News & World Report* 106:52-6+ My 15 '89
Extending the limits of our frontiers [address, July 20, 1989; with editorial comment by Charles D. Walker] G. Bush. il pors *Ad Astra* 1:2, 38-40 S '89
First word [NASA's need for new goals] T. O. Paine. il *Omni (New York, N.Y.)* 11:6 Jl '89
'A journey into tomorrow' [G. Bush speech on space program] J. Schwartz and M. Hager. il por *Newsweek* 114:31 Jl 31 '89
Looking back in 2073. C. Sheffield. *Ad Astra* 1:48 Mr '89
NASA 1989: suddenly it's 1986 [readying postponed science missions] J. Eberhart. il *Science News* 135:15 Ja 7 '89
NASA focuses on station, faces growing budget crisis. C. Covault. il *Aviation Week & Space Technology* 130:109-11 Mr 20 '89
NASA selects 14 scientific experiments to be performed on space station. *Aviation Week & Space Technology* 131:26 Ag 7 '89
"New realities" in space [report of Stever committee] E. Marshall. il *Science* 243:164 Ja 13 '89
The next giant leap for mankind. M. D. Lemonick. il *Time* 134:50-1 Jl 24 '89
Piece by piece [space program hurt by incremental approach] H. E. McCurdy. il *Ad Astra* 1:24-8 F '89
The promise of the 21st century [National Academy of Sciences report] il *Astronomy* 17:44-50 Ja '89
Space: more than a program. J. Lewis. *Ad Astra* 1:16 D '89
Space news. See issues of Astronomy beginning October 1988
Space science on the rebound? M. M. Waldrop. il *Science* 244:525-6 My 5 '89
Spreading the word [excerpt from statement, April 5, 1989] C. D. Walker. il por *Ad Astra* 1:31-4 Je '89
Sweeping changes due for panels that set space policy in Congress. *Aviation Week & Space Technology* 130:83-4 Ja 2 '89
U.S. access to space. J. M. Logsdon and R. A. Williamson. bibl il *Scientific American* 260:34-40 Mr '89
U.S. space leadership in danger [address, January 17, 1989] J. C. Fletcher. *Vital Speeches of the Day* 55:298-300 Mr 1 '89

Archives
Smithsonian initiates effort to salvage space program documents [with editorial comment] *Aviation Week & Space Technology* 131:9, 20 O 16 '89

Ethical aspects
Is space the place to be? J. Marti. il *Utne Reader* p8-9 Ja/F '89

International aspects
See also
Earth Observing System
Inter-Agency Consultative Group
International Astronautical Federation
Mission to Planet Earth (Project)
Space stations—Spacelab missions
United Nations. Committee on the Peaceful Uses of Outer Space
Cooperation in space: the real world. M. A. G. Michaud. il *Sky and Telescope* 77:4 Ja '89
Doing science with the Soviets [Americans and Soviets] R. Burnham. il *Astronomy* 17:106-7 N '89
Europe delays Soho spacecraft work until U.S. approves joint project MOU [solar and heliospheric satellite] J. M. Lenorovitz. il *Aviation Week & Space Technology* 131:31-2 N 13 '89
French reach agreement on Mir mission, seek broader space efforts with U.S. J. M. Lenorovitz. il *Aviation Week & Space Technology* 131:34-5 Jl 24 '89

International co-operation in space. D. Spurgeon. il *The Unesco Courier* 42:48-9 Ag '89
Japanese and Europeans irked by latest space station changes. J. R. Asker. il *Aviation Week & Space Technology* 131:22-3 N 6 '89
Keeping partners [space station] R. A. Roe. *Ad Astra* 1:3 N '89
Mars Observer to aid Soviets. il *Astronomy* 17:16+ Ag '89
Planetary partners [mission to Mars; cover story] M. A. G. Michaud. il *Ad Astra* 1:24-8 Mr '89
President's message [international cooperation] C. D. Walker. il *Ad Astra* 1:2 My '89
The second space revolution. *Aviation Week & Space Technology* 130:19 Je 26 '89
Soviets seek cooperative role in Western hypersonic programs. il *Aviation Week & Space Technology* 130:38 Je 19 '89
Space travelers rendezvous in Chicago [joint lecture by cosmonaut Y. Romanenko and U.S. shuttle mission specialist L. Acton] J. Liss. *Ad Astra* 1:41-4 D '89
Steps toward a real international space station. D. J. Gauthier. il *Ad Astra* 1:28-9 O '89
U.S./Soviet cooperation growing. *Astronomy* 17:16+ F '89
UN space committee notes 1988 achievements by nations. il *UN Chronicle* 26:36-7 Je '89
US, Europeans, Canada and Japan conclude space station agreement. W. Sweet. *Physics Today* 42:64-5 Ja '89

Public opinion
President's message. C. D. Walker. il *Ad Astra* 1:2 N '89
Toward a space ethos and synergy. P. Harris. *Ad Astra* 1:48 Je '89

Australia
See also
Cape York Space Agency (Australia)

Canada
See also
Canada. Space Agency

China
Japan and China consolidate positions as major space powers. C. Covault. il *Aviation Week & Space Technology* 130:127+ Mr 20 '89

France
See also
Centre National d'Études Spatiales (France)
French reach agreement on Mir mission, seek broader space efforts with U.S. J. M. Lenorovitz. il *Aviation Week & Space Technology* 131:34-5 Jl 24 '89
Soviet heavyweight astronomy satellite to be launched with international payload [Granat satellite with French Sigma telescope] J. M. Lenorovitz. il *Aviation Week & Space Technology* 131:31 N 27 '89
Soviets book new commercial space flights; long-term cooperation with France advances. J. M. Lenorovitz. *Aviation Week & Space Technology* 130:25+ Jl 10 '89
Soviets seek French payload for use on large earth observation platforms [Almaz spacecraft] *Aviation Week & Space Technology* 131:41 N 20 '89

Germany (West)
See also
Deutsche Agentur fur Raumfahrtangelegenheiten

Great Britain
Astronaut wanted, no experience needed [selecting British astronaut for Juno mission aboard Soviet Mir space station] C. A. Simpson. il *Ad Astra* 1:5 O '89
Britain reconsiders limited role with France on Ariane 5 program. *Aviation Week & Space Technology* 130:28 Ja 30 '89
Hotol goes private. C. A. Simpson. il *Ad Astra* 1:27-9 My '89

Italy
See also
Agenzia Spaziale Italiana

Japan
See also
Young Astronaut Program (Japan)
David and Goliath in space [views of Daniel Hastings] il *Technology Review* 92:80 Ag/S '89
Great expectations on the Pacific Rim. R. Spangenburg and D. Moser. il *Ad Astra* 1:31-4 My '89
Japan and China consolidate positions as major space powers. C. Covault. il *Aviation Week & Space Technology* 130:127+ Mr 20 '89
Japan as major space power. il *The Futurist* 23:49-50 Mr/Ap '89
Japan showcases maturing space program, manufacturing capabilities [Paris Air Show] il *Aviation Week & Space Technology* 130:66+ Je 19 '89
Japan's moonhouses. A. Brown. il *Omni (New York, N.Y.)* 11:17 Jl '89

Soviet Union
See also
Glavkosmos
Morsviazsputnik
Space flight—Soyuz flights
Doing science with the Soviets [Americans and Soviets] R. Burnham. il *Astronomy* 17:106-7 N '89
Latest Soviet planetary mission plans reflect shift to conservative outlook. M. A. Dornheim. *Aviation Week & Space Technology* 131:21-2 Ag 28 '89

SPACE RESEARCH—Soviet Union—cont.

Mars Observer to aid Soviets. il *Astronomy* 17:16+ Ag '89

Martian misgivings. P. Garrison. il *Omni (New York, N.Y.)* 12:22 D '89

A new Soviet plan for exploring the planets. M. M. Waldrop. il *Science* 246:211-12 O 13 '89

New views of Mars and Phobos [Phobos mission] R. Burnham. il *Astronomy* 17:28-32 S '89

NSS board members visit Soviet Union [International Symposium on the History and Philosophy of Aviation and Cosmonautics] F. I. Ordway. il *Ad Astra* 1:37 Ap '89

Soviet moon base? P. Jackson and L. David. il *Ad Astra* 1:6-7 Jl/Ag '89

A Soviet perspective [interview with V. L. Barsukov] S. F. Brown. *Popular Science* 235:75 Jl '89

Soviet space program [special section] J. M. Lenorovitz. il *Aviation Week & Space Technology* 131:32-4 D 11 '89

Soviet space program reflects new policies initiated by Gorbachev. J. M. Lenorovitz. il *Aviation Week & Space Technology* 131:52+ D 18-25 '89

Soviet space program strife threatens Mars mission plans. C. Covault. il *Aviation Week & Space Technology* 130:18-21 My 22 '89

Soviet space scientists to focus studies on Mars until 2000, seek U.S. cooperation. *Aviation Week & Space Technology* 130:21 My 8 '89

Soviet technology advancing, but unmanned projects falter. il *Aviation Week & Space Technology* 130:111-12 Mr 20 '89

Soviets book new commercial space flights; long-term cooperation with France advances. J. M. Lenorovitz. *Aviation Week & Space Technology* 130:25+ Jl 10 '89

Soviets in space [cover story] P. M. Banks and S. K. Ride. bibl il *Scientific American* 260:32-40 F '89

Soviets revise Mars program; prepare missions to moon. *Aviation Week & Space Technology* 130:39 Ja 2 '89

Soviets will increase efforts to market commercial space flight opportunities. J. M. Lenorovitz. il *Aviation Week & Space Technology* 130:115 Mr 20 '89

Space coloristics [cosmonauts' reporting concerning earth's surface] V. Vasyutin and A. A. Tishchenko. bibl il *Scientific American* 261:84-90 Jl '89

Space commerce, Soviet style. J. Goldman. il *Ad Astra* 1:24-30 D '89

Target: Phobos. K. Croswell. il *Ad Astra* 1:16-21 Ja '89

U.S./Soviet cooperation growing. *Astronomy* 17:16+ F '89

The world's "most active spacefaring nation". N. L. Johnson. il *Ad Astra* 1:8-12 My '89

United States
See Space research

Western Europe
See also
European Space Agency

SPACE SCIENCES
See also
Astronomy
Astrophysics
Videotapes—Space sciences use

Space basics. M. R. Chartrand. See issues of Ad Astra beginning January 1989

Bibliography
Resources. See issues of Ad Astra beginning January 1989
Reviews. See issues of Ad Astra beginning January 1989

Conferences
1989 Space Development Conference. il *Ad Astra* 1:42-4 Ap '89

Activists unite! [International Space Development Conference] M. Guindon. il *Ad Astra* 1:38-40 O '89

Grassroots report [1989 Space Development Conference] D. Fulmer. *Ad Astra* 1:45-6 S '89

NSS board members visit Soviet Union [International Symposium on the History and Philosophy of Aviation and Cosmonautics] F. I. Ordway. il *Ad Astra* 1:37 Ap '89

Rendezvous. See issues of Ad Astra beginning January 1989

SDC '89: a space expo [Space Development Conference] il *Ad Astra* 1:21-2 F '89

Where were you in '69? [Princeton, N.J. conference] T. H. Cole. il *Popular Mechanics* 166:28-9 Jl '89

Study and teaching
See also
International Space University
Kealing Space Center
National Scholars Program
Young Astronaut Program (Japan)

Space ed. See issues of Ad Astra beginning January 1989

Aids and devices
Resources. See issues of Ad Astra beginning January 1989
Reviews. See issues of Ad Astra beginning January 1989

SPACE SCIENCES AS A PROFESSION

Shuttle scientists: an endangered species? [astronauts to be given priority over payload specialists] J. Eberhart. *Science News* 135:71 F 4 '89

Top talent leaving NASA . . . new recruits hard to find [effect of revolving door rules] E. Marshall and M. M. Waldrop. il *Science* 245:251 Jl 21 '89

SPACE SERVICES, INC.

Materials processing payloads set for launch. *High Technology Business* 9:33-4 F '89

Paper trails to contrails [Starfire 1 launches suborbital payload] K. Boehler. il *Ad Astra* 1:39-41 Je '89

Starfire. W. H. Ganoe. il *Ad Astra* 1:35 Mr '89

SPACE SETTLEMENTS *See* Space colonies

SPACE SHUTTLE *See* Space vehicles

SPACE SHUTTLE ASTRONAUTS *See* Astronauts

SPACE SHUTTLE MISSIONS *See* Space flight—Shuttle missions

SPACE SHUTTLE MISSIONS, RUSSIAN *See* Space flight—Shuttle missions, Russian

SPACE SHUTTLE MODELS *See* Space vehicle models

SPACE SOCIETIES
See also
International Astronautical Federation
NASA Alumni League
National Space Society (U.S.)

SPACE STATION MODELS

The cosmic classroom [Kealing Space Center, Texas] J. K. Strickland, Jr. il *Ad Astra* 1:20-3 Mr '89

SPACE STATIONS
See also
Space colonies

External tanks: big dividends [recycling shuttle tanks] D. J. Frederick. il *Ad Astra* 1:5 S '89

Japanese and Europeans irked by latest space station changes. J. R. Asker. il *Aviation Week & Space Technology* 131:22-3 N 6 '89

Let Freedom ring! F. D. Martin. il *Sky and Telescope* 77:460-1 My '89

NASA selects 14 scientific experiments to be performed on space station. *Aviation Week & Space Technology* 131:26 Ag 7 '89

National Academy panel rejects the case for a mini-space station. E. Marshall. il *Science* 244:282-3 Ap 21 '89

Space station. il *Popular Science* 235:71-2 Jl '89

Space station Freedom: bad news for astronomy. R. C. Bless. *Sky and Telescope* 77:460 My '89

The space station program and space development. il *Ad Astra* 1:24-8 S '89

The U.S. space station: a commitment to technological advancement [cover story] F. D. Martin. il *USA Today (Periodical)* 117:30-4 My '89

US, Europeans, Canada and Japan conclude space station agreement. W. Sweet. *Physics Today* 42:64-5 Ja '89

Communication systems

E-Z listening [eavesdropping on Soviet spacecraft using shortwave radio] A. R. Curtis. il *Omni (New York, N.Y.)* 11:22+ F '89

Control

USAF builds facility to study dynamics of lightweight space-based structures. W. B. Scott. il *Aviation Week & Space Technology* 130:51 F 20 '89

Costs

Batteries not included [space station budget crunch] T. Beardsley. *Scientific American* 261:20 O '89

Desperately seeking station. A. Lawler. il *Ad Astra* 1:8-11 Je '89

Europeans urge U.S. to avoid cutting space station funds. il *Aviation Week & Space Technology* 130:39 Je 19 '89

Give space station a dose of reality. *Aviation Week & Space Technology* 131:11 Ag 21 '89

House blocks attempt to slash station funds. M. Mecham. *Aviation Week & Space Technology* 131:32 Jl 24 '89

Keeping partners. R. A. Roe. *Ad Astra* 1:3 N '89

NASA accelerates lunar base planning as station changes draw European fire. C. Covault. il *Aviation Week & Space Technology* 131:26-7 S 18 '89

NASA focuses on station, faces growing budget crisis. C. Covault. il *Aviation Week & Space Technology* 130:109-11 Mr 20 '89

NASA funding cut for X-30, station programs. *Aviation Week & Space Technology* 131:24 O 23 '89

NASA-industry team defines options to salvage space station program. E. H. Kolcum. *Aviation Week & Space Technology* 131:32 Ag 14 '89

NASA space station faces scale-down as budget, technical realities emerge. T. M. Foley. il *Aviation Week & Space Technology* 130:38-40 My 29 '89

NASA to seek space station termination if budget reductions are too severe. T. M. Foley. *Aviation Week & Space Technology* 130:24 My 8 '89

Science as a national priority. L. Friedman and T. B. Lynch. il *USA Today (Periodical)* 118:47-8 S '89

Science fiction [space budget reality and effects of weightlessness] H. Banks. il *Forbes* 143:44+ Mr 6 '89

Space station changes for lunar base would cost NASA more than $1 billion. C. Covault. il *Aviation Week & Space Technology* 131:34-5 O 9 '89

Space station delay planned; management reorganization set. C. Covault. il *Aviation Week & Space Technology* 131:20-1 O 2 '89

Space station faces possible delay or cancellation. T. M. Foley. il *Aviation Week & Space Technology* 130:32-3 My 1 '89

Space station in the balance. S. Cole. il *Astronomy* 17:24-31 My '89

Space station science: up in the air. E. Marshall. il *Science* 246:1110-12 D 1 '89

SPACE STATIONS—*cont.*

Design

First aid for Freedom. R. Spangenburg and D. Moser. il *Ad Astra* 1:42-5 Ja '89

Freedom update: space station systems take shape. il *Popular Mechanics* 166:20 Ag '89

NASA space station faces scale-down as budget, technical realities emerge. T. M. Foley. il *Aviation Week & Space Technology* 130:38-40 My 29 '89

NASA's orbiting dream house [Freedom] J. Kluger. il *Discover* 10:68-72 My '89

On base in space. J. L. Schefter. il *Popular Science* 234:94-9+ Mr '89

Steps toward a real international space station. D. J. Gauthier. il *Ad Astra* 1:28-9 O '89

Surgery in space. il *The Futurist* 23:57-8 S/O '89

Earth sciences use

See also

Earth Observing System

Mission to Planet Earth (Project)

Electronic equipment

Robotic microscope could allow R&D in space. *High Technology Business* 9:36-7 F '89

Soviet station electrical problems force Mir repair mission plan. C. Covault. *Aviation Week & Space Technology* 130:22-3 Ap 17 '89

Escape devices

Lifeboat to safer shores. K. Boehler. il *Ad Astra* 1:8-12 Mr '89

Industrial use

See Space processing

Insulation

Discovery crew deploys TDRS, tests space station system. C. Covault. il *Aviation Week & Space Technology* 130:264-5 Mr 20 '89

Shuttle Mission 29 set to conduct space station test, deploy TDRS [Tracking and Data Relay Satellite system] C. Covault. il *Aviation Week & Space Technology* 129:48-9 Mr 6 '89

Launching

Soviets propose using Energia to launch NASA space station. il *Aviation Week & Space Technology* 130:22 My 8 '89

Space station director urges early launch of first elements [views of William Lenoir] *Aviation Week & Space Technology* 130:41 Je 26 '89

Leasing and renting

Forgetting the lesson [National Research Council report on Commercially Developed Space Facility] W. H. Ganoe. il *Ad Astra* 1:59 Jl/Ag '89

NASA advised to drop plan for commercial platform lease. T. M. Foley. il *Aviation Week & Space Technology* 130:20-1 Ap 17 '89

Two studies pan commercial space station. *High Technology Business* 9:35-6 S/O '89

Maintenance and repair

Commercialization policy threatens space station's robotic contract [OMB decision requiring private financing] T. M. Foley. il *Aviation Week & Space Technology* 130:30-1 F 6 '89

Desperately seeking Cyborg [Flight Telerobotic Servicer for space station assembly designed by Honeybee Robotics] J. Goldberg. il *Omni (New York, N.Y.)* 11:12+ Ag '89

Martin Marietta robotic device will aid in space station assembly [Flight Telerobotic Servicer] B. D. Nordwall. il *Aviation Week & Space Technology* 130:53 My 15 '89

NASA robot to have private-sector spinoffs. *High Technology Business* 9:37 Mr '89

Orbital mechanic [Flight Telerobotic Servicer] G. R. Graf. il *Ad Astra* 1:5-6 O '89

Materials

USAF builds facility to study dynamics of lightweight space-based structures. W. B. Scott. il *Aviation Week & Space Technology* 130:51 F 20 '89

Safety devices and measures

See also

Space stations—Escape devices

Sanitation

Cosmic relief [new toilet designs] A. R. Oberg. il *Omni (New York, N.Y.)* 11:20 Je '89

Solar energy use

NASA considers station design changes, amid funding and cancellation threats [use of solar collector dishes instead of solar arrays] C. Covault. il *Aviation Week & Space Technology* 130:28-9 My 15 '89

Solar power: boosting efficiency, cutting costs. il *Popular Mechanics* 166:13 My '89

Spacelab missions

After Voyager's triumph. il *Popular Mechanics* 166:18 D '89

Telescopes

Looking for a wobble [proposed Astrometric Telescope Facility for space station Freedom; views of David Black] B. Nolley. il *Ad Astra* 1:10-11 S '89

SPACE STATIONS, EUROPEAN

See also

Space stations—Spacelab missions

Columbus—the first step. M. J. Dyson. *Ad Astra* 1:20 My '89

ESA council endorses French Matra design for polar platform [Columbus space station] *Aviation Week & Space Technology* 131:24 O 30 '89

ESA director general selects Matra polar platform design. il *Aviation Week & Space Technology* 130:26 F 27 '89

Europe may barter for external payloads on NASA/international space station. *Aviation Week & Space Technology* 130:29-30 Jl 10 '89

European industry submits proposal for space station design/development [Columbus] J. M. Lenorovitz. il *Aviation Week & Space Technology* 131:22 O 16 '89

Europeans urge U.S. to avoid cutting space station funds. il *Aviation Week & Space Technology* 130:39 Je 19 '89

NASA accelerates lunar base planning as station changes draw European fire. C. Covault. il *Aviation Week & Space Technology* 131:26-7 S 18 '89

Space platform consortium seeks NASA shuttle launch [Amica platform] C. Covault. il *Aviation Week & Space Technology* 131:16-17 Jl 3 '89

SPACE STATIONS, RUSSIAN

Astronaut wanted, no experience needed [selecting British astronaut for Juno mission aboard Mir space station] C. A. Simpson. il *Ad Astra* 1:5 O '89

E-Z listening [eavesdropping on Soviet spacecraft using short-wave radio] A. R. Curtis. il *Omni (New York, N.Y.)* 11:22+ F '89

First U.S. commercial cargo for Mir set to lift off Dec. 20 [Payload Systems protein crystal growth experiments] J. M. Lenorovitz. *Aviation Week & Space Technology* 131:34 D 11 '89

French reach agreement on Mir mission, seek broader space efforts with U.S. J. M. Lenorovitz. il *Aviation Week & Space Technology* 131:34-5 Jl 24 '89

Large building-block module docked to Mir following deployment of stuck solar array. J. M. Lenorovitz. *Aviation Week & Space Technology* 131:33-4 D 11 '89

Mir's pause in permanence. *Science News* 135:245 Ap 22 '89

New cosmonaut crew launched to Mir; station expansion to begin in October. il *Aviation Week & Space Technology* 131:39 S 11 '89

Payload's payload [protein crystal experiments on Mir space station] W. H. Ganoe. *Ad Astra* 1:38 Je '89

Soviet long-duration cosmonauts readapt rapidly to earth environment [Mir cosmonauts] J. M. Lenorovitz. il *Aviation Week & Space Technology* 130:38-9 Ja 2 '89

Soviet modules, money and monkeys. *Ad Astra* 1:45-6 N '89

Soviet space: expanding the Mir station [special section] il *Aviation Week & Space Technology* 131:94-6+ S 25 '89

Soviet Star trek: a year in space. G. Cowley. il *Newsweek* 113:5 Ja 2 '89

Soviet station electrical problems force Mir repair mission plan. C. Covault. *Aviation Week & Space Technology* 130:22-3 Ap 17 '89

Soviet station probes the universe [Mir station] M. Engle. il *Astronomy* 17:16+ S '89

Soviets plan medium-duration missions on board Mir this year. J. M. Lenorovitz. il *Aviation Week & Space Technology* 130:23-4 Ja 9 '89

Soviets reactivate Mir station, prepare for major expansion. *Aviation Week & Space Technology* 131:28 S 18 '89

Soviets seek French payload for use on large earth observation platforms [Almaz spacecraft] *Aviation Week & Space Technology* 131:41 N 20 '89

Soviets to launch two cosmonauts, reestablish presence on board Mir. *Aviation Week & Space Technology* 131:25 S 4 '89

Soviets upgrading space transports to support manned station activities. J. M. Lenorovitz. il *Aviation Week & Space Technology* 131:49 O 23 '89

Soviets will tether maneuvering unit to space station for initial missions. J. M. Lenorovitz. il *Aviation Week & Space Technology* 130:63 Ja 23 '89

Steps toward a real international space station. D. J. Gauthier. il *Ad Astra* 1:28-9 O '89

U.S. firm's use of Mir faces probable delay [Payload Systems' protein crystal experiment] *Aviation Week & Space Technology* 130:21 Ap 17 '89

SPACE TECHNOLOGY

See also

Technology transfer

SPACE TELESCOPE *See* Hubble Space Telescope

SPACE TRAIN *See* Space vehicles—Propulsion systems

SPACE TRAJECTORIES *See* Trajectories

SPACE TRAVEL *See* Space flight

SPACE VEHICLE MODELS

Balloon-launched scale orbiter to gather data for Hermes spaceplane program. *Aviation Week & Space Technology* 131:58 S 18 '89

SPACE VEHICLE PARTS

Consolidation of orbiter logistics speeds repairs, reduces delays. E. H. Kolcum. il *Aviation Week & Space Technology* 131:45+ Jl 31 '89

SPACE VEHICLES

See also

Artificial satellites

SPACE VEHICLES—See also—*cont.*
　Communications satellites
　Mars vehicles
　Space centers
　Space stations
　Spaceplane
Shuttle scan. See issues of Ad Astra beginning January 1989

Accidents and explosions

See also
Challenger (Space shuttle) explosion, 1986
Space vehicles—Fires and fire prevention
Cosmodrome monuments honor victims of 1960s accidents [Soviets killed at Baikonur Cosmodrome] J. M. Lenorovitz. *Aviation Week & Space Technology* 131:72 O 16 '89
NASA evaluates water damage to Columbia. *Aviation Week & Space Technology* 131:22 O 2 '89
Report calls for fifth orbiter, citing probability of accident [Office of Technology Assessment] P. Mann. *Aviation Week & Space Technology* 131:16-17 Ag 7 '89
RTG failures [nuclear powered vehicles] R. G. Nichols. il *Ad Astra* 1:13 N '89

Atmospheric entry

NASA to build 'skipping rock' spacecraft. *High Technology Business* 9:34-5 Ap '89

Communication systems

NSS on the air [Dial-A-Shuttle] P. Jones. il *Ad Astra* 1:28 Ja '89

Control

See also
Computers—Space flight use

Corrosion and anticorrosives

Shuttle glow [cover story] D. E. Hunton. bibl il *Scientific American* 261:92-8 N '89

Crews

See Astronauts

Defects

First Galileo course correction executed; several spacecraft anomalies uncovered. M. A. Dornheim. *Aviation Week & Space Technology* 131:43 N 20 '89
Phobos at Mars: a dramatic view—and then failure. M. M. Waldrop. il *Science* 245:1044-5 S 8 '89
Soviet failure at Mars a reminder of risks [loss of Phobos 2] R. A. Kerr. il *Science* 244:26 Ap 7 '89
A Soviet mission to nowhere [loss of Phobos 2 spacecraft] *U.S. News & World Report* 106:16-17 Ap 10 '89
Soviets abandon efforts to regain contact with Phobos 2 [with editorial comment] il *Aviation Week & Space Technology* 130:7, 24-5 Ap 10 '89
Soviets lose contact with Phobos 2 spacecraft. *Aviation Week & Space Technology* 130:22 Ap 3 '89

Design

Galileo represents peak in design complexity. *Aviation Week & Space Technology* 131:77-8 O 9 '89
Shuttle update: new experiments, orbiter. il *Popular Mechanics* 166:25 Ap '89
Taking full measure [call for building small, simple space probes] S. Morem. *Ad Astra* 1:48 F '89

Electronic equipment

See also
Computers—Space flight use
Ball Aerospace stresses simplicity in space-based motion sensor design [Remote Attitude Measurement Sensor] W. B. Scott. il *Aviation Week & Space Technology* 130:100-2 Je 5 '89

Engines

See Space vehicles—Propulsion systems

Equipment

See also
Life support systems (Space environment)

Fires and fire prevention

Amroc retains key personnel despite cutbacks after pad fire. M. A. Dornheim. *Aviation Week & Space Technology* 131:20 O 30 '89

Flaps

Defects
NASA seeks cause of body flap deflection in last Columbia launch. E. H. Kolcum. *Aviation Week & Space Technology* 131:28 S 18 '89

Fuel systems

See Space vehicles—Propulsion systems

Fuel tanks

Ball Aerospace Systems developing compact toroidal liquid oxygen tank [for orbital transfer vehicles] il *Aviation Week & Space Technology* 130:107 Je 5 '89
External tank talk. W. H. Ganoe. il *Ad Astra* 1:45 Ap '89
External tanks: big dividends [recycling shuttle tanks] D. J. Frederick. il *Ad Astra* 1:5 S '89
External tanks turn into space labs. il *Popular Mechanics* 166:14 F '89
Tanks for the gamma rays [proposals for recycling space shuttle external tanks] T. Waters. il *Discover* 10:34-5 Ag '89

Insulation

Stitch in time [sewing insulation blankets for shuttle Columbia] B. Dickey. il *Ad Astra* 1:40 D '89

Landing and recovery

See also
Space vehicles—Propulsion systems—Recovery

Columbia rolled out; Discovery completes military mission. il *Aviation Week & Space Technology* 131:27 D 4 '89
High-rises rock to shuttle shock [research by Hiroo Kanamori] R. Monastersky. *Science News* 136:396 D 16 '89
Magellan prepared for course correction as astronauts land Atlantis in crosswind. C. Covault. il *Aviation Week & Space Technology* 130:25 My 15 '89
Shuttle launch schedule accelerates after Galileo deployment, Atlantis reentry. C. Covault. il *Aviation Week & Space Technology* 131:22-4 O 30 '89
Shuttle orbiter Discovery shows little damage after completing Mission 29. il *Aviation Week & Space Technology* 130:25 Mr 27 '89

Launchers

See Space vehicles—Propulsion systems

Launching

Engine controller problem delays launch of Galileo mission to Jupiter. E. H. Kolcum and C. Covault. *Aviation Week & Space Technology* 131:20-1 O 16 '89
Final launch preparations under way for signal intelligence satellite mission [shuttle Discovery] il *Aviation Week & Space Technology* 131:24 N 6 '89
Galileo launch to Jupiter by Atlantis culminates difficult effort with shuttle. C. Covault. il *Aviation Week & Space Technology* 131:58+ O 9 '89
Green for go! [National Space Society Shuttle Launch Tour at Discovery launch] K. McMains. il *Ad Astra* 1:24-7+ Ja '89
The little rocket that could [launch of E-Prime's Loft-1 rocket] J. Kluger. il pors *Discover* 10:30+ F '89
Magellan heads toward Venus as U.S. resumes planetary probes [deployed from shuttle Atlantis] E. H. Kolcum. *Aviation Week & Space Technology* 130:23 My 8 '89
Magellan mission to Venus requires precise shuttle launch operations [launch by shuttle Atlantis] C. Covault. il *Aviation Week & Space Technology* 130:42-3+ Ap 24 '89
Managers modernize shuttle system to increase efficiency, launch rate [views of Robert L. Crippen] E. H. Kolcum. il *Aviation Week & Space Technology* 131:46-8 D 4 '89
NASA plans shuttle launch for Feb. 23 despite delay in move to assembly building [orbiter Discovery for Mission 29] *Aviation Week & Space Technology* 130:22 Ja 23 '89
Night launch of Discovery boosts secret military satellite into orbit. E. H. Kolcum. *Aviation Week & Space Technology* 131:29 N 27 '89
Shuttle launch of Galileo Jupiter mission highlights U.S. space science renaissance [Atlantis launch] C. Covault. il *Aviation Week & Space Technology* 131:22-4 O 23 '89

Launching from airplanes

Arianespace weighs marketing satellite launches for Pegasus. *Aviation Week & Space Technology* 130:56 Je 19 '89
Pegasus air-launched test vehicle is rolled out [cover story] B. A. Smith. il *Aviation Week & Space Technology* 131:36-7+ Ag 14 '89
Pegasus, Ball to launch communication satellites into geosynchronous orbit. il *Aviation Week & Space Technology* 130:64 Je 12 '89
Pegasus commercial launch project to begin rocket motor test firings. C. Covault. il *Aviation Week & Space Technology* 130:91 F 13 '89
Pegasus will launch U.S. minisatellite to survey X-rays [Array of Low-Energy X-Ray Imaging Sensors] *Aviation Week & Space Technology* 131:55 S 18 '89
Relay satellite, gas release payload scheduled for Pegasus winged booster. C. Covault. il *Aviation Week & Space Technology* 130:59 Ja 9 '89
The winged horse [Pegasus booster] R. G. Nichols. il *Ad Astra* 1:32-6 F '89
Winging it into space [Pegasus booster] S. F. Brown. il *Popular Science* 234:126-8+ My '89

Launching pads, sites, etc.

Air Force refurbishing Apollo-era test stand for advanced launch system. *Aviation Week & Space Technology* 130:67 F 27 '89

Maintenance and repair

Consolidation of orbiter logistics speeds repairs, reduces delays. E. H. Kolcum. il *Aviation Week & Space Technology* 131:45+ Jl 31 '89
NASA mobilizes technical team to ready orbiter Columbia for military launch. E. H. Kolcum. il *Aviation Week & Space Technology* 130:101-2 My 29 '89

Nozzles

French firm to test fire composite nozzle for use on large, liquid-fueled engines. *Aviation Week & Space Technology* 130:29 Ja 30 '89

Orbits

Can Galileo take the heat? [risky trajectory for space probe] M. M. Waldrop. il *Science* 245:1327-9 S 22 '89
NASA to build 'skipping rock' spacecraft. *High Technology Business* 9:34-5 Ap '89

Parts

See Space vehicle parts

Power supply

Combatting fear [National Space Society response to protests against nuclear powered space vehicles] *Ad Astra* 1:48 N '89

SPACE VEHICLES—Power supply—*cont.*

Court rejects activists' bid to halt Galileo/shuttle launch [nuclear powered spacecraft] *Aviation Week & Space Technology* 131:21 O 16 '89

NASA prepares for protests over nuclear system launch on shuttle in October [Galileo mission to Jupiter] T. M. Foley. *Aviation Week & Space Technology* 130:83+ Je 26 '89

Nuclear fears about Galileo. A. Toufexis. il *Time* 134:76 O 16 '89

Nuclear slingshot [Project Galileo's plutonium] K. Grossman and J. Long. *The Nation* 249:336-7 O 2 '89

Plutonium con [solar energy as an alternative to nuclear powered space probes] K. Grossman and J. Long. *The Nation* 249:589 N 20 '89

Project Galileo: the risk of a nuclear disaster in space. *Utne Reader* p60 S/O '89

Report says U.S. space power programs inadequate to meet long-term SDI goals [National Research Council report] il *Aviation Week & Space Technology* 130:47+ F 20 '89

Rifkin tries to stop Galileo launch [nuclear fears] M. M. Waldrop. il *Science* 246:30 O 6 '89

Showdown at Pad 39-B [nuclear powered space vehicles] R. G. Nichols. il *Ad Astra* 1:8-12+ N '89

Soviets reveal testing in space of thermionic nuclear reactor. T. M. Foley. *Aviation Week & Space Technology* 130:30 Ja 16 '89

"Stop the plutonium shuttle!" [Galileo mission to Jupiter] M. M. Waldrop. *Science* 245:1328 S 22 '89

We need nuclear power in space. J. R. Casani. *Astronomy* 17:8 Je '89

Propulsion systems

See also
    INSCOM (Firm)
    Solar sails
    Space vehicles—Solar energy use

Air Force cannot meet 1989 launch schedule. E. H. Kolcum. il *Aviation Week & Space Technology* 130:21-2 Ja 23 '89

America's private road to heaven [artificial satellite launchings] il *U.S. News & World Report* 107:11+ S 11 '89

Are we serious about a commercial launch industry? B. Forman. *Ad Astra* 1:3 Je '89

Ariane 4 vehicle to orbit Hughes payloads in 1990. *Aviation Week & Space Technology* 131:35 Jl 24 '89

Ariane to continue key role in launch service market. il *Aviation Week & Space Technology* 130:131 Mr 20 '89

Arianespace, European companies sign production contracts for 50 Ariane 4s. J. M. Lenorovitz. *Aviation Week & Space Technology* 130:28 F 20 '89

Arianespace launches JCSAT, Meteosat; nine Ariane missions planned for 1989. J. M. Lenorovitz. il *Aviation Week & Space Technology* 130:29-30 Mr 13 '89

Arianespace plans 1989 launches to clear backlog of payloads. J. M. Lenorovitz. il *Aviation Week & Space Technology* 130:28-9 Ja 30 '89

Britain reconsiders limited role with France on Ariane 5 program. *Aviation Week & Space Technology* 130:28 Ja 30 '89

A "buyer's guide" for space vehicles [Office of Technology Assessment report] il *The Futurist* 23:42 Ja/F '89

China agrees to limit marketing of Long March booster in U.S. C. Covault. il *Aviation Week & Space Technology* 130:37 Ja 2 '89

Commercial launches: getting the business? I. Klotz. il *Ad Astra* 1:16-19 Ap '89

Engine(ering) a propulsion comeback. *Ad Astra* 1:48 Ap '89

First commercial Titan prepared for September launch. il *Aviation Week & Space Technology* 130:97 My 1 '89

First USAF/McDonnell Douglas Delta 2 launch begins new military space era [Navstar launch; with editorial comment] E. H. Kolcum. il *Aviation Week & Space Technology* 130:7, 18-19 F 20 '89

Gassing up on Mars [proposed fuel refinery; work of Robert Ash and Warren Dowler] T. Dollar. il *Discover* 10:22 D '89

General Dynamics will launch first Navy UHF follow-on satellite [Atlas booster] *Aviation Week & Space Technology* 131:22 Ag 21 '89

German, Japanese satellites launched by Ariane 4 version. il *Aviation Week & Space Technology* 130:67 Je 12 '89

Glavcosmos signs Energetics as first U.S. launch customer [Proton rockets] J. R. Asker. il *Aviation Week & Space Technology* 131:40 N 20 '89

Last Titan 34D, Transtage launches classified military spacecraft. E. H. Kolcum. il *Aviation Week & Space Technology* 131:41 S 11 '89

The launch triad. C. Stadd. il *Ad Astra* 1:3 Mr '89

Launches into low-earth orbit should be economical, routine. R. C. Henry. por *Aviation Week & Space Technology* 131:93+ N 27 '89

The little rocket that could [launch of E-Prime's Loft-1 rocket] J. Kluger. il pors *Discover* 10:30+ F '89

Low mission rate planned for Soviet Energia launcher. J. M. Lenorovitz. il *Aviation Week & Space Technology* 131:38 S 11 '89

Marketing the Proton [Soviet booster] S. Arenstein. il *Ad Astra* 1:31-4 D '89

Master plan for Mars [Soviet Union] *Ad Astra* 1:5-6 Ja '89

Materials processing payloads set for launch [Space Services Inc.] *High Technology Business* 9:33-4 F '89

Next Energia mission delayed until early 1991 [Soviet launcher] J. M. Lenorovitz. il *Aviation Week & Space Technology* 131:32-3 D 11 '89

Pegasus will launch U.S. minisatellite to survey X-rays [Array of Low-Energy X-Ray Imaging Sensors] *Aviation Week & Space Technology* 131:55 S 18 '89

Propellant mixer delay could stall Ariane 5 program [U.S.-built mixer intended for propellant factory under construction at Guiana Space Center] J. M. Lenorovitz. *Aviation Week & Space Technology* 130:35 Je 26 '89

Quayle denounces U.S. reliance on foreign space launch vehicles. T. M. Foley. il por *Aviation Week & Space Technology* 130:21-2 Ap 10 '89

Railway to heaven [space train; research by Alvin Marks and Peter H. Diamandis] S. J. Nadis. il *Omni (New York, N.Y.)* 12:30+ N '89

Soviets propose using Energia to launch NASA space station. il *Aviation Week & Space Technology* 130:22 My 8 '89

Starfire [Space Services Inc.] W. H. Ganoe. il *Ad Astra* 1:35 Mr '89

Survival of the fittest [commercial booster industry] *Aviation Week & Space Technology* 130:15 My 29 '89

Technical problems with Japanese satellite could disrupt Ariane's payload launch sequence [traveling wave tube amplifier on Superbird B telecommunications satellite] il *Aviation Week & Space Technology* 131:30 N 13 '89

Titan 4, Delta 2 launches generate confidence in military space operations. E. H. Kolcum. il *Aviation Week & Space Technology* 130:40-1 Je 19 '89

Titan 4 matures [cover story; special section] il *Aviation Week & Space Technology* 131:32-4+ Jl 17 '89

U.S. access to space. J. M. Logsdon and R. A. Williamson. bibl il *Scientific American* 260:34-40 Mr '89

U.S. reenters commercial launch arena with private Delta mission [launch of British television relay spacecraft Marcopolo] E. H. Kolcum. il *Aviation Week & Space Technology* 131:24-5 S 4 '89

U.S. sets insurance minimums for commercial space launches. E. H. Kolcum. *Aviation Week & Space Technology* 130:69 Ja 30 '89

Work on Ariane 5 launch, assembly facilities proceeds at site in Kourou. il *Aviation Week & Space Technology* 130:175 Je 12 '89

Corrosion and anticorrosives

NASA may delay or scrub Mission 29 because of turbopump bearing corrosion [space shuttle Discovery] E. H. Kolcum. il *Aviation Week & Space Technology* 130:31 Ja 30 '89

Orbiter Discovery engine repairs accelerating for shuttle Mission 29. *Aviation Week & Space Technology* 130:25 F 13 '89

Design

ALS cost, efficiency to depend heavily on process improvements [Martin Marietta Advanced Launch System program] W. B. Scott. il *Aviation Week & Space Technology* 131:41+ O 23 '89

Arianespace weighs marketing satellite launches for Pegasus. *Aviation Week & Space Technology* 130:56 Je 19 '89

A blueprint for the '90s—. D. J. Gauthier. il *Ad Astra* 1:24-5 My '89

Decision on Shuttle-C expected after internal NASA review. E. H. Kolcum. il *Aviation Week & Space Technology* 130:123+ Je 19 '89

General Dynamics offers four Atlas-Centaur versions. il *Aviation Week & Space Technology* 130:24 Ap 10 '89

Hummingbird Launch Systems update. T. Holmes. il *Ad Astra* 1:7 My '89

Japan explores liquid air cycle engine for future rocket propulsion needs. *Aviation Week & Space Technology* 130:58 Ap 3 '89

LTV, BPD consider building increased-lift Scout 2 launcher. J. M. Lenorovitz. *Aviation Week & Space Technology* 130:25 Ap 10 '89

Mitsubishi plans to test experimental liquefied air cycle engine based on LE-5. il *Aviation Week & Space Technology* 131:33 Jl 31 '89

NASA selects Lockheed/Aerojet to build shuttle's advanced solid rocket motor. T. M. Foley. il *Aviation Week & Space Technology* 130:31-2 My 1 '89

New SDI surveillance satellite to use upgraded Titan 2 booster [Midcourse Space Experiment spacecraft] C. Covault. il *Aviation Week & Space Technology* 131:31 S 25 '89

Pegasus, Ball to launch communication satellites into geosynchronous orbit. il *Aviation Week & Space Technology* 130:64 Je 12 '89

Pegasus, MX boosters combined for new Defense launch vehicle [Taurus standard small launch vehicle] C. Covault. il *Aviation Week & Space Technology* 131:47+ S 18 '89

Pratt & Whitney offers RL10 upgrades for Centaur users. E. H. Kolcum. il *Aviation Week & Space Technology* 130:52 F 20 '89

Relay satellite, gas release payload scheduled for Pegasus winged booster. C. Covault. il *Aviation Week & Space Technology* 130:59 Ja 9 '89

SPACE VEHICLES—Propulsion systems—Design—*cont.*

Rocketdyne to use simple designs, production efficiency to trim ALS costs [advanced launch system] B. A. Smith. il *Aviation Week & Space Technology* 130:299+ Je 12 '89

Shuttle rocket plan under fire. E. Marshall. il *Science* 244:135-6 Ap 14 '89

Soviets integrate components of Energia heavy-lift vehicle at Cosmodrome site. J. M. Lenorovitz. il *Aviation Week & Space Technology* 131:78-9 O 16 '89

U.S., Soviet firms to develop, market commercial booster based on SS-20 [Start mobile launcher] J. D. Morrocco. il *Aviation Week & Space Technology* 131:21 Ag 7 '89

USAF cuts vehicle design work on advanced launch system. B. A. Smith. *Aviation Week & Space Technology* 131:112 D 18-25 '89

The winged horse [Pegasus booster] R. G. Nichols. il *Ad Astra* 1:32-6 F '89

Winging it into space [Pegasus booster] S. F. Brown. il *Popular Science* 234:126-8+ My '89

Z biggest or Z best [heavy lift shuttle designed to launch components of Mars spacecraft] G. R. Graf. il *Ad Astra* 1:7 S '89

Failure

Amroc retains key personnel despite cutbacks after pad fire. M. A. Dornheim. *Aviation Week & Space Technology* 131:20 O 30 '89

Japan reschedules H-1 mission after launch pad abort. *Aviation Week & Space Technology* 131:23 S 4 '89

USAF assessing liftoff failure of Delta 2 vehicle [Navstar satellite] *Aviation Week & Space Technology* 130:40 My 29 '89

Maintenance and repair

Ariane planning complicated by launcher, payload delays. il *Aviation Week & Space Technology* 131:123 O 9 '89

Repairs completed, Galileo thrusters set to undergo reacceptance tests. M. A. Dornheim. il *Aviation Week & Space Technology* 130:62 Ja 23 '89

Materials

New source expected to prevent shortage of rayon for NASA, defense rockets [North American Rayon Corp.] *Aviation Week & Space Technology* 131:24 N 27 '89

Recovery

Spacecraft recovery concept embodies parafoil, new reefing techniques [High Glide Recovery System designed by Pioneer Aerospace] E. H. Kolcum. il *Aviation Week & Space Technology* 130:101-2 My 1 '89

Safety devices and measures

NASA advised to drop new shuttle motor program. T. M. Foley. *Aviation Week & Space Technology* 130:29+ Ap 3 '89

Specifications

International launch vehicles [tables] il *Aviation Week & Space Technology* 130:174 Mr 20 '89

U.S. launch vehicles [tables] il *Aviation Week & Space Technology* 130:173 Mr 20 '89

Testing

Air Force refurbishing Apollo-era test stand for advanced launch system. *Aviation Week & Space Technology* 130:67 F 27 '89

French firm to test fire composite nozzle for use on large, liquid-fueled engines. *Aviation Week & Space Technology* 130:29 Ja 30 '89

Galileo thrusters approved for flight but mission plan may be abbreviated. M. A. Dornheim. *Aviation Week & Space Technology* 130:23 Ap 10 '89

Initial flight of Japan's H-2 launcher delayed by first-stage engine problems. J. M. Lenorovitz. *Aviation Week & Space Technology* 131:39 N 20 '89

Paper trails to contrails [Space Services' Starfire 1 launches suborbital payload] K. Boehler. il *Ad Astra* 1:39-41 Je '89

Pegasus air-launched test vehicle is rolled out [cover story] B. A. Smith. il *Aviation Week & Space Technology* 131:36-7+ Ag 14 '89

Pegasus commercial launch project to begin rocket motor test firings. C. Covault. il *Aviation Week & Space Technology* 130:91 F 13 '89

Shuttle booster test firing ends redesign process. *Aviation Week & Space Technology* 130:30 Ja 30 '89

Space shuttle meets the wetlands. il *Science* 246:1253 D 8 '89

Turbine pumps

NASA delays launch of space shuttle until mid-March [turbopumps on Discovery engines to be replaced] *Aviation Week & Space Technology* 130:32 F 6 '89

NASA may delay or scrub Mission 29 because of turbopump bearing corrosion. E. H. Kolcum. il *Aviation Week & Space Technology* 130:31 Ja 30 '89

Orbiter Discovery engine repairs accelerating for shuttle Mission 29. *Aviation Week & Space Technology* 130:25 F 13 '89

Pratt & Whitney engine turbopumps could fly on space shuttle in 1992. E. H. Kolcum. *Aviation Week & Space Technology* 130:67 F 27 '89

Radar equipment

See Radar in astronomy

Reentry

See Space vehicles—Atmospheric entry

Safety devices and measures

See also

Space vehicles—Fires and fire prevention

Flying on the edge [space shuttle] P. Hoversten. il map *Discover* 10:20-1 S '89

Solar energy use

Plutonium con [solar energy as an alternative to nuclear powered space probes] K. Grossman and J. Long. *The Nation* 249:589 N 20 '89

USAF funding R&D to design more efficient solar cells. il *Aviation Week & Space Technology* 130:81+ Ap 10 '89

Specifications

International spacecraft [tables] il *Aviation Week & Space Technology* 130:188-9 Mr 20 '89

U.S. spacecraft [tables] il *Aviation Week & Space Technology* 130:187 Mr 20 '89

Testing

Galileo Jupiter orbiter/probe readied for launch by space shuttle Atlantis. C. Covault. *Aviation Week & Space Technology* 131:23 S 4 '89

SPACE VEHICLES, BRITISH

See also

Spaceplane, British

SPACE VEHICLES, CHINESE

China agrees to limit marketing of Long March booster in U.S. C. Covault. il *Aviation Week & Space Technology* 130:37 Ja 2 '89

Crystal clear [Intospace protein crystallization experiment] W. H. Ganoe. *Ad Astra* 1:47 Ja '89

U.S., China initial agreement on communications satellites [State Dept. statement, December 19, 1988] *Department of State Bulletin* 89:26-7 F '89

SPACE VEHICLES, FRENCH

See also

Spaceplane, French

SPACE VEHICLES, GERMAN

See also

Spaceplane, German

German microgravity drop capsule approved for operational service [Mikroba balloon-launched system] *Aviation Week & Space Technology* 130:29 Jl 10 '89

SPACE VEHICLES, JAPANESE

See also

Spaceplane, Japanese

Initial flight of Japan's H-2 launcher delayed by first-stage engine problems. J. M. Lenorovitz. *Aviation Week & Space Technology* 131:39 N 20 '89

Japan reschedules H-1 mission after launch pad abort. *Aviation Week & Space Technology* 131:23 S 4 '89

SPACE VEHICLES, RUSSIAN

See also

Spaceplane, Russian

Buran inspection shows Soviet shuttle details [Paris Air Show] C. Covault. il *Aviation Week & Space Technology* 130:46-7+ Je 19 '89

Do the Soviets need a shuttle? D. S. F. Portree. il *Astronomy* 17:14+ Ja '89

Glavcosmos signs Energetics as first U.S. launch customer [Proton rockets] J. R. Asker. il *Aviation Week & Space Technology* 131:40 N 20 '89

Government production decision awaited on additional space shuttle orbiters. il *Aviation Week & Space Technology* 130:94-6 Je 5 '89

Low mission rate planned for Soviet Energia launcher. J. M. Lenorovitz. il *Aviation Week & Space Technology* 131:38 S 11 '89

Marketing the Proton [Soviet booster] S. Arenstein. il *Ad Astra* 1:31-4 D '89

Martian misgivings. P. Garrison. il *Omni (New York, N.Y.)* 12:22 D '89

Master plan for Mars. *Ad Astra* 1:5-6 Ja '89

Next Energia mission delayed until early 1991. J. M. Lenorovitz. il *Aviation Week & Space Technology* 131:32-3 D 11 '89

Out-of-this-world ads [U.S. companies buying ad space on Soviet space vehicles] il *U.S. News & World Report* 107:10 Jl 24 '89

Phobos 1 images the sun. G. L. Verschuur. il *Astronomy* 17:10-11 Je '89

Phobos at Mars: a dramatic view—and then failure. M. M. Waldrop. il *Science* 245:1044-5 S 8 '89

Report from Baikonur Cosmodrome: Soviets' vast space launch facility supports manned, unmanned programs [special section] J. M. Lenorovitz. il *Aviation Week & Space Technology* 131:70-3+ O 16 '89

Soviet failure at Mars a reminder of risks [loss of Phobos 2] R. A. Kerr. il *Science* 244:26 Ap 7 '89

Soviet Mars probe collects data in preparation for Phobos flyby. il *Aviation Week & Space Technology* 130:26 Mr 27 '89

A Soviet mission to nowhere [loss of Phobos 2 spacecraft] *U.S. News & World Report* 106:16-17 Ap 10 '89

SPACE VEHICLES, RUSSIAN—*cont.*

Soviet probe enters Mars orbit; landers to descend on Phobos. C. Covault. il *Aviation Week & Space Technology* 130:24-5 F 13 '89

Soviet shuttle will appear at Paris show. *Aviation Week & Space Technology* 130:32 My 15 '89

Soviets abandon efforts to regain contact with Phobos 2 [with editorial comment] il *Aviation Week & Space Technology* 130:7, 24-5 Ap 10 '89

Soviets lose contact with Phobos 2 spacecraft. *Aviation Week & Space Technology* 130:22 Ap 3 '89

Soviets propose using Energia to launch NASA space station. il *Aviation Week & Space Technology* 130:22 My 8 '89

Soviets upgrading space transports to support manned station activities. J. M. Lenorovitz. il *Aviation Week & Space Technology* 131:49 O 23 '89

Soviets will bring Su-25 Frogfoot to Paris; orbiter may join it. *Aviation Week & Space Technology* 130:22 Ap 17 '89

Time, cost constraints force Soviets to alter 1994 Mars mission. *Aviation Week & Space Technology* 131:22 Ag 28 '89

Winged twins? [Soviet Buran space shuttle and its American counterpart] il *Ad Astra* 1:46 F '89

Photographs and photography

Soviet manned reusable spacecraft research described at IAF congress. il *Aviation Week & Space Technology* 131:59 N 13 '89

Testing

Ground testing, flight evaluations support Soviet shuttle program. il *Aviation Week & Space Technology* 130:98-9 Je 5 '89

Soviets reveal testing in space of thermionic nuclear reactor. T. M. Foley. *Aviation Week & Space Technology* 130:30 Ja 16 '89

SPACE VEHICLES IN ADVERTISING

Out-of-this-world ads [U.S. companies buying ad space on Soviet space vehicles] il *U.S. News & World Report* 107:10 Jl 24 '89

SPACE VOUCHERS

Ticket to ride [report by Molly K. Macauley] W. H. Ganoe. il *Ad Astra* 1:29 S '89

SPACE WALK INC.

Winning in a walk. M. Fonseca. il *Nation's Business* 77:13-14 D '89

SPACE WALKS *See* Space flight—Extravehicular activity

SPACE WARFARE

See also
Anti-satellite weapons
Brilliant Pebbles (Defense system)
Kinetic kill vehicles
Railguns
Strategic Defense Initiative
United States. Air Force. Space Division
United States. Space Command

The geostrategy of space [address, November 17, 1988] J. L. Piotrowski. *Vital Speeches of the Day* 55:162-4 Ja 1 '89

Monitoring Soviet space weapons adds to demand for U.S. intelligence. T. M. Foley. *Aviation Week & Space Technology* 130:22-3 F 27 '89

SPACE WEAPONS *See* Space warfare

SPACECAUSE

Congressional action teams. C. E. Ward. *Ad Astra* 1:58 Jl/Ag '89

The Spacecause success story. D. Brandt. *Ad Astra* 1:13 Mr '89

SPACECRAFT *See* Space vehicles

SPACED OUT LIBRARY (TORONTO, ONT.)

E.T., phone Toronto. R. Brody. il *Omni (New York, N.Y.)* 12:38 O '89

SPACELAB MISSIONS *See* Space stations—Spacelab missions

SPACEMEN *See* Astronauts

SPACEPAC

Spacepac's election results. D. Brandt. *Ad Astra* 1:15 Ap '89

SPACEPLANE

Aero-Space Plane leading U.S. hypersonic research [X-30 aircraft] C. Covault. il *Aviation Week & Space Technology* 130:18-19 F 27 '89

Aeronautical engineering [National Aero-Space Plane; special section] il *Aviation Week & Space Technology* 131:50-1+ O 23 '89

Los Alamos expands research focus, explores hypersonic flight issues. il *Aviation Week & Space Technology* 130:20-1 F 27 '89

The market for transoceanic airliners. T. A. Heppenheimer. il *High Technology Business* 9:22-5 Ja '89

NASP program officials, contractors optimistic about technology issues. S. W. Kandebo. il *Aviation Week & Space Technology* 131:18-20 Ag 7 '89

NRC committee supports construction of experimental hypersonic X-30 vehicle. S. W. Kandebo. il *Aviation Week & Space Technology* 130:86 My 8 '89

Space plane. J. Kluger. il *Discover* 10:80-4 N '89

The third generation of the space age. G. A. Keyworth and B. Abell. *Science* 245:16 Jl 7 '89

White House acts to reverse Aero-Space Plane cancellation. C. Covault. il *Aviation Week & Space Technology* 130:20-1 Ap 24 '89

Costs

Bush administration speeds NASP review, spurred by Soviet, German competition [National Aero-Space Plane] C. Covault. il *Aviation Week & Space Technology* 130:24-5 Je 5 '89

Controversy over delays in NASP prompts calls for independent technology assessment [with editorial comment] *Aviation Week & Space Technology* 131:7, 18 Ag 7 '89

NASA funding cut for X-30, station programs. *Aviation Week & Space Technology* 131:24 O 23 '89

Preserve the X-30 NASP [National Aero-Space Plane] *Aviation Week & Space Technology* 131:11 O 2 '89

Restore National Aero-Space Plane funds. *Aviation Week & Space Technology* 130:15 My 1 '89

Senate defense panel defers NASP funding, clouding program's future [National Aero-Space Plane] P. A. Gilmartin. *Aviation Week & Space Technology* 131:29 S 18 '89

Space Council endorses revised NASP schedule [National Aero-Space Plane; with editorial comment] *Aviation Week & Space Technology* 130:7, 18 Jl 10 '89

Wanted: business as unusual [views of B. Rutan] W. H. Ganoe. *Ad Astra* 1:47 N '89

Escape devices

Current X-30 design includes escape capsule for pilots. il *Aviation Week & Space Technology* 131:57 O 23 '89

Materials

Contractors pursue NASP technology despite possible funding cutbacks [National Aero-Space Plane] E. H. Kolcum. il *Aviation Week & Space Technology* 130:96-7 My 22 '89

Tires

See Tires, Spaceplane

SPACEPLANE, BRITISH

Hotol goes private. C. A. Simpson. il *Ad Astra* 1:27-9 My '89

SPACEPLANE, FRENCH

Balloon-launched scale orbiter to gather data for Hermes spaceplane program. *Aviation Week & Space Technology* 131:58 S 18 '89

Japan, Europe in hypersonic race. il *Popular Mechanics* 166:16 F '89

SPACEPLANE, GERMAN

Bush administration speeds NASP review, spurred by Soviet, German competition [National Aero-Space Plane] C. Covault. il *Aviation Week & Space Technology* 130:24-5 Je 5 '89

Germany enters hypersonic race. D. Kirk. *Science* 243:1284 Mr 10 '89

Sanger aero-space plane gains increased support in Europe. C. Covault. il *Aviation Week & Space Technology* 130:16-18 Jl 10 '89

SPACEPLANE, JAPANESE

Japan, Europe in hypersonic race. il *Popular Mechanics* 166:16 F '89

Japan showcases maturing space program, manufacturing capabilities [Paris Air Show] il *Aviation Week & Space Technology* 130:66+ Je 19 '89

Japanese refining unmanned HOPE orbiter for planned 1996 launch. S. W. Kandebo. il *Aviation Week & Space Technology* 130:57-8 Ap 3 '89

SPACEPLANE, RUSSIAN

Soviets seek cooperative role in Western hypersonic programs. il *Aviation Week & Space Technology* 130:38 Je 19 '89

SPACEPLANE ENGINES

Design

Contractors pursue NASP technology despite possible funding cutbacks [National Aero-Space Plane] E. H. Kolcum. il *Aviation Week & Space Technology* 130:96-7 My 22 '89

NASP program office retains two propulsion contractors. S. W. Kandebo. *Aviation Week & Space Technology* 130:19 My 8 '89

Fuel

Japan explores liquid air cycle engine for future rocket propulsion needs. *Aviation Week & Space Technology* 130:58 Ap 3 '89

Researchers explore slush hydrogen as fuel for National Aero-Space Plane. S. W. Kandebo. il *Aviation Week & Space Technology* 130:37-8 Je 26 '89

Testing

Aerojet TechSystems facility to test hypersonic engines designed for NASP [National Aero-Space Plane] il *Aviation Week & Space Technology* 130:263 Je 12 '89

Pratt & Whitney scramjet design for NASP tested in NASA-Langley facility at Mach 8 [National Aero-Space Plane] il *Aviation Week & Space Technology* 131:26 O 16 '89

Pratt demonstrates low-speed propulsion concept for National Aero-Space Plane. S. W. Kandebo. il *Aviation Week & Space Technology* 130:79 Je 26 '89

Preliminary tests bolster Rocketdyne's confidence in NASP propulsion system [National Aero-Space Plane] B. A. Smith. il *Aviation Week & Space Technology* 130:98-9 My 22 '89

Rocketdyne developing facility for hypersonic propulsion tests. W. B. Scott. il *Aviation Week & Space Technology* 130:65 Ja 30 '89

SPADAFORA, CORRADO
about
"Dangerous" liaisons in cell biology. D. Dickson. il por *Science* 244:1539-40 Je 30 '89; Correction. 245:252 Jl 21 '89

SPADER, JAMES
about
James Spader. il pors *Esquire* 112:202-3 S '89

SPAETH, MERRIE
Bolstering your high-tech image. il *High Technology Business* 9:26+ Ja '89

SPAETH, ROBERT L.
Educators aren't parents. *Commonweal* 116:174-5 Mr 24 '89

SPAGNA, TED
about
Posing for photographer Ted Spagna? Just say ZZZZ. P. Chin. il pors *People Weekly* 31:97-8+ F 6 '89
Sleep shots. T. Frick. il *Art in America* 77:66-9+ Je '89

SPAIN
See also
Americans—Spain
Andalusia (Spain)
Architecture—Spain
Art—Spain
Automobile racing—Spain
Barcelona (Spain)
British—Spain
Catalonia (Spain)
Concert halls—Spain
Direct broadcast satellite services—Spain
Geology—Spain
Historic houses, sites, etc.—Spain
Madrid (Spain)
Motion pictures—Spain
Motorcycle racing—Spain
Palaces—Spain
Railroads—Spain
Restaurants—Spain
Strikes—Spain
World War, 1914-1918—Spain
Colonies
How Maya culture withstood colonial force [Tipu and Lamanai sites; research by Elizabeth Graham] B. Bower. *Science News* 136:373 D 9 '89
On the fringes of conquest: Maya-Spanish contact in colonial Belize [Tipu and Lamanai sites] E. Graham and others. bibl f il map *Science* 246:1254-9 D 8 '89
Commerce
See also
European Economic Community
France
See France—Commerce—Spain
United States
See United States—Commerce—Spain
Description and travel
See also
Motorcycling—Spain
Spain [via rail] R. Levine. il map *New Choices for the Best Years* 29:50-3 Ap '89
Economic policy
As Spain rushes toward '92. E. Ontiveros. il *The New Leader* 72:10-11 O 2-16 '89
The spark for a new Mediterranean miracle. R. J. Gwyn. il *World Press Review* 36:22-4 Mr '89
Economic relations
See also
European Economic Community
Foreign relations
A two-pronged diplomacy. C. Boudier. *World Press Review* 36:24-5 Mr '89
United States
See United States—Foreign relations—Spain
History
Civil War, 1936-1939
The Spanish Civil War [cover story; special section] bibl il pors map *History Today* 39:13-33 Mr '89
1939-1975
Revenge and reconciliation. P. Preston. il *History Today* 39:28-33 Mr '89
Industries
See also
Aerospace industries—Spain
Fisheries—Spain
Olive industry—Spain
Publishers and publishing—Spain
Repsol SA
Tourist trade—Spain
Naval history
See also
Spanish Armada, 1588
Photographs and photography
Goya: visions of the Spanish soul. il *Life* 12:110-14+ F '89
Politics and government
See also
Elections—Spain
Socialist Party (Spain)

Africa no longer starts at the Pyrenees. D. Lawday. il por *U.S. News & World Report* 107:54 O 30 '89
"I used to have little faith in the U.S." [interview with F. Gonzalez] M. Hornblower and J. Walker. il por *Time* 134:54 O 23 '89
Spain [special section] il *World Press Review* 36:22-5 Mr '89
Spain tightens its European ties. J. Valls-Russell. il *The New Leader* 72:7-8 My 1 '89
The spring in Spain. L. J. O'Donovan. *America* 160:510-13 My 27 '89

SPANIELS
The flush 'n fetchers. L. Mueller. il *Outdoor Life* 184:56+ S '89
Millie's six-pack [G. Bush's springer spaniel has six puppies; cover story] B. Bush. il pors *Life* 12:32-4+ My '89
The sporting springers. L. Mueller. il *Outdoor Life* 184:52+ N '89

SPANISH ARMADA, 1588
Bibliography
1588 and all that. J. R. Hale. il *The New York Review of Books* 36:30-2 F 16 '89

SPANISH ART *See* Art, Spanish
SPANISH CIVIL WAR *See* Spain—History—Civil War, 1936-1939
SPANISH COLONIAL FURNITURE *See* Furniture, Spanish colonial
SPANISH COMMUNICATIONS SATELLITES *See* Communications satellites, Spanish
SPANISH COOKING *See* Cooking, Spanish
SPANISH DANCE *See* Dance, Spanish
SPANISH GRAND PRIX *See* Automobile racing—Spain
SPANISH HOUSE DECORATION *See* House decoration, Spanish
SPANISH LANGUAGE
See also
Motion pictures—Spanish language films
Study and teaching
Abigail y yo. C. Trillin. *The New Yorker* 65:83-8 Je 26 '89
SPANISH LANGUAGE IN ARGENTINA
The rub in the dubbing [films and serials meant for TV screening to be dubbed in Argentina] I. Pardal. *Américas* 41 no2:64 '89
SPANISH LANGUAGE IN LATIN AMERICA
The birth of a language. R. Bareiro Saguier. il *The Courier (Unesco)* 42:24-5 My '89
SPANISH LANGUAGE IN THE UNITED STATES
The language of power. Y. T. De Mola. *America* 160:364-5 Ap 22 '89
SPANISH LANGUAGE PERIODICALS
See also
Imagen (Periodical)
SPANISH LANGUAGE PROGRAMS *See* Television broadcasting—Spanish language programs
SPANISH POTTERY *See* Pottery, Spanish
SPANISH SAHARA CONFLICT, 1975- *See* Western Sahara conflict, 1975-
SPANISH SPEAKING PEOPLE (U.S.) *See* Hispanic Americans
SPANISH WINES *See* Wine
SPANKING *See* Corporal punishment
SPARE TIME *See* Leisure
SPARK, MURIEL
Bread, butter, and Florrie Ford [story] *The New Yorker* 65:36-46 S 11 '89
about
Writing with intent [cover story] R. E. Hosmer. il pors *Commonweal* 116:233-41 Ap 21 '89
SPARK PLUGS
Blue water, green lights, and clean plugs [cleaning plugs on a Morris Minor sedan to avoid installing new rings] M. Anson. il *Motor Trend* 41:8 Ap '89
Marine ignition update. T. P. Banse. il *Motor Boating & Sailing* 164:91 O '89
Collectors and collecting
Spark up your car collection. D. Jordan. il *Popular Mechanics* 166:46 D '89
SPARKLING WATER *See* Bottled water
SPARKS, ALLISTER
South Africa goes black. *World Press Review* 36:64 Je '89
SPARROW, DAVID
Back to basics. il *Health (New York, N.Y.)* 21:30-1+ Ag '89
The racket revolution. il *Health (New York, N.Y.)* 21:51-2+ Je '89
SPARROWS
Dusky legacy [mitochondrial DNA of extinct dusky seaside sparrow; research by John Avise] L. Oliwenstein. il *Discover* 10:38 Jl '89
Molecular genetic relationships of the extinct dusky seaside sparrow. J. C. Avise and W. S. Nelson. bibl f il map *Science* 243:646-8 F 3 '89
A sparrow's fall [DNA of the dusky seaside sparrow; research by John C. Avise and William S. Nelson] T. Appenzeller. *Scientific American* 260:32+ Ap '89

SPARTA (N.J.)
Crime
"Die mother father brother" [teenage Satan worshipper T. Sullivan kills mother then commits suicide] E. Davidowitz. il por *Redbook* 172:132-4+ Ap '89
SPARTAN SCHOOL OF AERONAUTICS
Spartan's big six-oh. N. Moll. *Flying* 116:28+ F '89
SPAS *See* Health resorts, watering places, etc.
SPASMS
See also
Hiccups
SPASTIC COLON *See* Irritable bowel syndrome
SPASTIC DYSPHONIA
A strange ailment left me speechless for 27 years. R. Dempewolff. il *Good Housekeeping* 209:74+ O '89
SPATIAL PERCEPTION *See* Space perception
SPAWN (COMPUTER PROGRAM)
PARC brings Adam Smith to computing. M. M. Waldrop. il *Science* 244:145-6 Ap 14 '89
SPAWNING
Leap of faith [brown bear catching sockeye salmon; photograph] J. Foott. il *Natural History* p112-13 O '89
SPE *See* Sucrose polyesters
SPEAKERS *See* Loudspeakers
SPEAKERS (PERSONS) *See* Public speaking
SPEAKERS OF THE HOUSE OF REPRESENTATIVES *See* United States. Congress. House—Speakers
SPEAKING *See* Speech
SPEAKING, PUBLIC *See* Public speaking
SPEAKING IN TONGUES [dance] See Dance reviews—Single works
SPEAR FISHING
Mississippi of the North [protests over Chippewa fishing rights in Wisconsin] D. Parmentier. il por *The Humanist* 49:17-19+ S/O '89
Spearing fish, playing 'chicken' [confrontation over Chippewa Indian fishing rights in Wisconsin] J. Oberly. il *The Nation* 248:844-5+ Je 19 '89
The Wisconsin fishing war [spearfishing by Chippewa Indians] il *Sports Illustrated* 70:16 My 15 '89
SPEARFISH (S.D.)
Description
A vacation from a vacation. J. McCallum. il *Sports Illustrated* 71:32-4+ Jl 31 '89
SPECIAL EDUCATION
See also
Children, Gifted—Education
Deaf—Education
Handicapped—Education
Mentally handicapped children—Education
Problem children—Education
Special education teachers
Educating students with learning problems. M. Will. *The Education Digest* 54:54-7 Ap '89
Fixing the teaching, not the kids [reducing classes in Rochester, N.Y. middle school] J. Buckley. il *U.S. News & World Report* 106:61-2 Mr 13 '89
Save the baby! A response to 'Integrating the children of the second system' [November 1988 article] M. C. Wang and others. bibl f il *Phi Delta Kappan* 71:61-7 S '89
SPECIAL EDUCATION TEACHERS
Easing the adjustment to mainstreaming programs. H. Margolis and P. P. McCabe. *The Education Digest* 55:58-61 S '89
SPECIAL EFFECTS (MOTION PICTURES) *See* Motion pictures—Special effects
SPECIAL EFFECTS (PHOTOGRAPHY) *See* Photography, Trick
SPECIAL EFFECTS (TELEVISION) *See* Television broadcasting—Special effects
SPECIAL EFFECTS (THEATER) *See* Theater—Special effects
SPECIAL EFFECTS (VIDEOTAPE) *See* Videotape recorders and recording—Special effects
SPECIAL FORCES (U.S. ARMY) *See* United States. Army. Special Forces
SPECIAL INTEREST GROUPS
See also
Anti-nuclear movement
Lobbyists and lobbying
Moral Majority
National Education Association of the United States
National Rifle Association of America
National Right to Life Committee
Political action committees
Blackstabbers [special interests pursue black vote] R. Blow. *The New Republic* 200:16-18 My 29 '89
Courting black power [special interests pursue black vote] V. Novak. il *Common Cause Magazine* 15:17-22 Mr/Ap '89
SPECIAL NEEDS ADOPTION *See* Adoption and adopted children
SPECIAL OLYMPICS
1989 International Winter Special Olympics Games [profiles of top competitors] H. Weiskopf. il *Sports Illustrated* 70:49-50+ Mr 27 '89

SPECIAL PROSECUTORS *See* Government investigations
SPECIALISTS
A specialist in many fields [freelance writers] G. Stern. *The Writer* 102:17-19 My '89
SPECIALISTS (STOCK EXCHANGE FIRMS)
Living off the spread [B. L. Madoff takes advantage of New York Stock Exchange rule that protects specialists] R. L. Stern. il *Forbes* 144:66-7 Jl 10 '89
Yes, the stock market's risky. Why look for a scapegoat? G. Weiss. il *Business Week* p158 N 27 '89
SPECIALTY CLINICS *See* Health facilities
SPECIES
See also
Evolution
Natural selection
Phylogeny
Sympatric speciation
Variation (Biology)
Biotic impoverishment at home and abroad. D. W. Schindler. *BioScience* 39:426 Jl/Ag '89
In defense of species [emphasis on ecology in soil research] N. L. Stanton and J. D. Lattin. *BioScience* 39:67 F '89
Species questions in modern human origins. R. Lewin. il *Science* 243:1666-7 Mr 31 '89
SPECIFICATIONS
See also
Standardization
SPECK, LAWRENCE W.
The shaping of things to come. il por *Omni (New York, N.Y.)* 12:86-95 O '89
SPECKTOR, MORDECAI
The third way: publications bridging the East-West gap. *Utne Reader* p116-19 Ja/F '89
SPEC'S MUSIC, INC.
Singing along with Spec's Music. G. G. Marcial. *Business Week* p130 Mr 13 '89
SPECTACLED BEARS *See* Bears
SPECTACLES *See* Eyeglasses
SPECTACOR (FIRM)
From calamity to conglomerate. G. Macnow. il por *Nation's Business* 77:48-50+ My '89
SPECTER, MICHAEL
Hot tombs [cover story] *The New Republic* 201:22-5 S 11 '89
SPECTER, JOEL
(jt. auth) See Geller, Larry, 1937-, and Spector, Joel
SPECTOR, LEONARD S.
Keep the skies open. il map *The Bulletin of the Atomic Scientists* 45:15-16+ S '89
New players in the nuclear game. il *The Bulletin of the Atomic Scientists* 45:29-32 Ja/F '89
SPECTOR, PHIL
about
Phil Spector. K. Hubbard. il pors *People Weekly* 31:84-8 F 6 '89
Phil Spector. P. Puterbaugh. il por *Rolling Stone* p88 F 9 '89
SPECTOR, REYNOLD, AND JOHANSON, CONRAD E.
The mammalian choroid plexus. bibl il *Scientific American* 261:68-74 N '89
SPECTRA BOOKS (FIRM)
Discovering the 'Microverse' with Bantam Spectra. G. Corcoran. il *Publishers Weekly* 235:47 Je 16 '89
SPECTRA SHIELD
Lightweight armor. J. Free. il *Popular Science* 234:30 Je '89
Step aside, Superman [Kevlar vs. Spectra Shield] A. A. Lappen. il *Forbes* 143:124+ F 6 '89
SPECTROGRAPH
Fiber optics for astronomy. il *Sky and Telescope* 78:569-70 D '89
Spectra galore [UCL Echelle Spectrograph at the Anglo-Australian Telescope] il *Sky and Telescope* 77:585-6 Je '89
SPECTROMETERS
Mass specs move in on protein sequencers. M. Barinaga. il *Science* 246:33 O 6 '89
Ozone hole's reappearance linked to chlorofluorocarbons [data of Total Ozone Mapping Spectrometer on Nimbus 7 satellite] il *Aviation Week & Space Technology* 131:28 O 30 '89
The radial-velocity revolution. R. Griffin. il *Sky and Telescope* 78:263+ S '89
SPECTROMETRY *See* Spectrum analysis
SPECTROSCOPY *See* Spectrum analysis
SPECTRUM (PHILADELPHIA, PA.)
From calamity to conglomerate. G. Macnow. il por *Nation's Business* 77:48-50+ My '89
SPECTRUM ANALYSIS
See also
Accelerator mass spectrometry
Astronomical spectroscopy
Carbon—Spectra and spectroscopy
Galaxies—Spectra and spectroscopy
Hydrocarbons—Spectra and spectroscopy
Magnetic resonance imaging
Microwave spectroscopy
Multiphoton resonance ionization spectroscopy

SPECTRUM ANALYSIS—See also—*cont.*
    Myoglobin—Spectra and spectroscopy
    Nebulae—Spectra and spectroscopy
    Neptune (Planet)—Spectra and spectroscopy
    Quasars—Spectra and spectroscopy
    Raman spectroscopy
    Stars—Spectra and spectroscopy
    Sun—Spectra and spectroscopy
Diode-laser absorption spectroscopy of supersonic carbon cluster beams: the v_3 spectrum of C_5. J. R. Heath and others. bibl f il *Science* 244:564-6 My 5 '89
Electrospray ionization for mass spectrometry of large biomolecules. J. B. Fenn and others. bibl f il *Science* 246:64-71 O 6 '89
Identification by ENDOR of Trp^{191} as the free-radical site in cytochrome c peroxidase compound ES. M. Sivaraja and others. bibl f il *Science* 245:738-40 Ag 18 '89
Ion sits still for sharp 'picture' of its optical transition. B. G. Levi. il *Physics Today* 42:17-18 S '89
Photoemission spectroscopy of the high-temperature superconductivity gap. G. Margaritondo and others. bibl f il *Science* 246:770-5 N 10 '89
Protein chemists gain a new analytical tool [mass spectrometry] M. Barinaga. il *Science* 246:32-3 O 6 '89
Rhenium-osmium isotope systematics of carbonaceous chondrites [resonance ionization mass spectrometry] R. J. Walker and J. W. Morgan. bibl f il *Science* 243:519-22 Ja 27 '89
A rotationally resolved fluorescence excitation spectrum of *all-trans*-1,4-diphenyl-1,3-butadiene. J. F. Pfanstiel and others. bibl f il *Science* 245:736-8 Ag 18 '89
Superconducting gap in Bi-Sr-Ca-Cu-O by high-resolution angle-resolved photoelectron spectroscopy. C. G. Olson and others. bibl f il *Science* 245:731-3 Ag 18 '89
Ultrafast dynamics at semiconductor and metal surfaces [laser experiments] J. Bokor. bibl f il *Science* 246:1130-4 D 1 '89
Volatilization of high molecular weight DNA by pulsed laser ablation of frozen aqueous solutions [mass spectrometry] R. W. Nelson and others. bibl f il *Science* 246:1585-7 D 22 '89

SPECTRUM ANALYZERS
AudioSource EQ Ten equalizer/analyzer. J. D. Hirsch. il *Stereo Review* 54:54+ Mr '89
AVCOM PSA-65A spectrum analyzer. il *Radio-Electronics* 60:25+ N '89
Spectrum monitor (I) [cover story] F. Baumgartner. il *Radio-Electronics* 60:33-6+ S '89
Spectrum monitor (II). F. Baumgartner. il *Radio-Electronics* 60:46-8 O '89
Tracking down bugs using a spectrum analyzer. R. A. Bowen. il *Radio-Electronics* 60:33-7 Je '89
VideOsmith Spectrum Probe. il *Radio-Electronics* 60:17-18 Ag '89

SPECTRUM GROUP
The last fundamentalist? [A. Galef] R. King. il por *Forbes* 144:132+ N 27 '89

SPECULATION
    See also
    Arbitrage
    Commodity futures
    Hedging (Finance)
    Interest rate futures
    Investments
    Parking (Securities)
    Real estate investment
    Risk
    Stocks
A backlash against business? [special section] il *Business Week* p30-6 F 6 '89
The end is nigh. K. L. Fisher. il *Forbes* 144:230 S 18 '89
If you're playing the specs, look hard at the techs. G. G. Marcial. il *Business Week* p96-7 Je 26 '89
Look for lots of bang from small-cap stocks. G. G. Marcial. il *Business Week* p116-17 D 25 '89-Ja 1 '90
The no-P/E stocks [story stocks] R. Simon. il *Forbes* 144:40-1 O 2 '89
The rape of the bondholder. A. Sloan. il *Forbes* 143:67-9 Ja 23 '89
Real victim of the takeover fever [address, April 7, 1989] J. A. Katarincic. *Vital Speeches of the Day* 55:540-4 Je 15 '89
Regulate the Wall Street casino. L. Lowenstein. il por *Fortune* 119:125-6 F 27 '89

SPECULUM MUSICAE (MUSICAL GROUP)
Musical events:
    Merkin Hall concert. A. Porter. *The New Yorker* 65:92 Mr 27 '89

SPEDALLE, SUSAN
Coping with infertility. *Essence* 19:98+ Mr '89
Hyper, not just active? il *Essence* 20:114+ My '89

SPEECH
    See also
    Artists—Language
    Children—Language
    Conversation
    Deaf children—Language

    Diplomats—Language
    Language and languages
    Legislators—Language
    Public speaking
Nac uoy daer siht ecnetnes? David Fuhrer can—dna woh! [backward speech] il por *People Weekly* 31:253 Mr 6 '89
Talk of ages [Neanderthal hyoid bone from Kebara cave site, Israel; cover story] B. Bower. il *Science News* 136:24-6 Jl 8 '89

Origin
    See Language and languages—Origin

SPEECH, FREEDOM OF *See* Freedom of speech

SPEECH DEFECTS
    See also
    Elective mutism
    Stuttering

SPEECH ERRORS
Anecdotes, facetiae, satire, etc.
Of many things [Richard Lederer's Anguished English] G. W. Hunt. *America* 160:186 Mr 4 '89

SPEECH PERCEPTION
Infants show keen ear for speech sounds [research by DiAnne Grieser and Patricia K. Kuhl] B. Bower. *Science News* 136:37 Jl 15 '89
A specialization for speech perception. A. M. Liberman and I. G. Mattingly. bibl f il *Science* 243:489-94 Ja 27 '89
A specialization for speech perception? [discussion of January 27, 1989 article, A specialization for speech perception] A. M. Liberman and I. G. Mattingly. *Science* 244:1530-1 Je 30 '89

SPEECH PROCESSING SYSTEMS
    See also
    Computerphones
The accidental tourist [S. A. Rondel's Voice computer] M. Barrier. il por *Nation's Business* 77:78 Ap '89
Army pursues voice-controlled avionics to improve helicopter pilot performance. B. W. Henderson. il *Aviation Week & Space Technology* 130:43+ My 22 '89
Beyond pattern recognition. R. Kurzweil. il *Byte* 14:277+ D '89
Building blocks for speech [modular neural networks] A. Waibel and J. Hampshire. bibl il *Byte* 14:235-8+ Ag '89
A helping hand [Prab Voice Command workstation] W. Rash, Jr. il *Byte* 14:129-30 D '89
Instant spoken translation [S. A. Rondel's Voice computer] W. J. Hawkins. il por *Popular Science* 234:78+ My '89
Laura Meyers creates software that talks friendly to help disabled kids find their voices [Keytalk] S. Adelson. il por *People Weekly* 32:165-6 D 4 '89
Pepperoni and paperwork. I. Scherr. il *Byte* 14:309-10+ D '89
Smart answering machines. M. Gianturco. il por *Forbes* 143:192 Je 12 '89
Stephen Hawking shoots for the stars. il por *Home Office Computing* 7:12 S '89
Talking to your typewriter [DragonDictate system] *Science News* 135:351 Je 3 '89
Voice recognition becoming feasible. *High Technology Business* 9:38 N/D '89
Voice-system researchers hope to rise above noise. *Byte* 14:11 Ja '89

SPEECH RECOGNITION SYSTEMS *See* Speech processing systems

SPEECH THERAPY
    See also
    Computers—Speech therapy use

SPEECHES, ADDRESSES, ETC.
    See also
    Baccalaureate addresses

SPEECHWRITERS AND SPEECHWRITING
    See also
    Bush, George, 1924-—Speechwriters and speechwriting
    Reagan, Ronald, 1911-—Speechwriters and speechwriting

SPEED, HAROLD
The shock of modern art [excerpt from Oil painting techniques and materials] il *Utne Reader* p68-9 Jl/Ag '89

SPEED
    See also
    Automobiles—Speed
    Automobiles, Police—Speed
    Computers—Speed
    Cruisers (Pleasure boats)—Speed
    Fishing boats—Speed
    Modems—Speed
Is man the fastest animal? N. Myers. il *International Wildlife* 19:33 S/O '89

SPEED (DRUG) *See* Methamphetamine
SPEED BOATS *See* Motor boats
SPEED LIMITS *See* Traffic regulations
SPEED READING
Study and teaching
Aids and devices
Can you read this article in one minute or less? [speed-reading software] T. A. Summers. il *Home Office Computing* 7:73-4 Ag '89

SPEED RECORDS
See also
Airplane speed records
Automobile speed records
Boat speed records
Land speed records
Motorcycle speed records
Truck speed records

SPEED SKATING
Competitions
Bring back Bonnie [B. Blair wins World Sprint Championships] D. S. Looney. il pors *Sports Illustrated* 70:32-3 Mr 6 '89

SPEED SKIING
His life is going downhill fast, and C.J. Mueller likes it that way. J. Friedman. il por *People Weekly* 31:81-2 Mr 20 '89

SPEED TRAPS, RADAR See Radar in traffic control

SPEEDWAYS
See also
Heartland Park Topeka
Food service
Grub. K. Cameron. il *Cycle* 40:12 Ap '89
Safety devices and measures
Riders' strikes [motorcyclists protest unsafe conditions at European tracks] J. Greening. il *Cycle* 40:82 S '89
Western Europe
Riders' strikes [motorcyclists protest unsafe conditions at European tracks] J. Greening. il *Cycle* 40:82 S '89

SPEER, LISA
Arctic National Wildlife Refuge [discussion of May 1989 article, Oil development and the Arctic National Wildlife Refuge] il *Environment* 31:2-4 S '89
Oil development and the Arctic National Wildlife Refuge. bibl f il *Environment* 31:42-3 My '89

SPEKREIJSE, H.
(jt. auth) See Enden, Aad van den, and Spekreijse, H.

SPELLING, AARON
about
Aaron Spelling: on the pitfalls of creating Angels and the threat of dreams. il por *People Weekly* 31 Special Issue:138-9 Summ '89
Is Aaron Spelling still in his prime time? R. Grover. il por *Business Week* p83+ Ap 17 '89

SPELLING
See also
French language in France—Spelling
When spelling—Pow!—wurdz can get you down. J. Kastner. il *Smithsonian* 20:140 Ag '89
Competitions
Spelling champ Scott Isaacs on success [winner of the National Spelling Bee] E. Grinnan. il por *Seventeen* 48:38 N '89

SPELLING BEES See Spelling—Competitions

SPELLING ENTERTAINMENT INC.
Is Aaron Spelling still in his prime time? R. Grover. il por *Business Week* p83+ Ap 17 '89

SPELMAN, JON
Fairy two tales. il *The Mother Earth News* 116:135 Mr/Ap '89

SPELMAN COLLEGE
Bill and Camille Cosby: first family of philanthropy [cover story] R. E. Johnson. il pors *Ebony* 44:25-6+ My '89
Camille Cosby warns Spelman grads about use of sex and money. il por *Jet* 76:4 Je 12 '89
A conversation with Spelman's 'sister president' [J. B. Cole] K. D. Thompson. il por *Black Enterprise* 19:28 F '89
Cosby's $20 million gift: a source of funds—and hope. K. D. Thompson. il por *Black Enterprise* 19:27 F '89
The inspiring leader of scholars (and dollars) [J. B. Cole] A. Edwards. il pors *Working Woman* 14:68-9+ Je '89

SPENCE, CRAIG
about
Art of the voyeur. T. Noah. por *The New Republic* 201:16+ Ag 7-14 '89
The death of a man who disappeared. por *Newsweek* 114:55 N 20 '89
A season of scandal takes its final toll on mysterious lobbyist Craig Spence. il por *People Weekly* 32:103 N 27 '89
Washington's man from nowhere. M. B. Carlson. il por *Time* 134:24 Jl 24 '89

SPENCE, LARRY D.
The soul of the corporation. *Utne Reader* p56-7 Ja/F '89

SPENCE, MURIEL MORISEY
(jt. auth) See Shattuck, John H. F., and Spence, Muriel Morisey

SPENCER, FREDDIE
about
Star search. J. Greening. il *Cycle* 40:82 D '89

SPENCER, HERBERT, 1820-1903
about
Can government outlaw drugs? M. Cranston. pors *National Review* 41:43-5 O 13 '89

SPENCER, R. E.
Proverbs and place. il *Weatherwise* 42:208-11 Ag '89

SPENCER GIFTS, INC.
A Halloween recall [withdraws mask of sheik after Arab American protests] il *Newsweek* 114:61 N 6 '89

SPENCER STUART & ASSOCIATES
The new headhunters [cover story] J. A. Byrne. il pors *Business Week* p64-7+ F 6 '89

SPENDING See Consumption (Economics)

SPERGEL, DAVID N.
(jt. auth) See Press, William H., and Spergel, David N.

SPERM See Spermatozoa

SPERM DONORS See Artificial insemination, Human

SPERMATOPHORES
The mating of tree crickets. D. H. Funk. bibl il *Scientific American* 261:50-5+ Ag '89

SPERMATOZOA
Circadian system controlling release of sperm in the insect testes [gypsy moth] J. M. Giebultowicz and others. bibl f il *Science* 245:1098-100 S 8 '89
"Dangerous" liaisons in cell biology [controversy over work of C. Spadafora] D. Dickson. il por *Science* 244:1539-40 Je 30 '89; Correction. 245:252 Jl 21 '89
Direct measurements of sliding between outer doublet microtubules in swimming sperm flagella [sea urchins] C. J. Brokaw. bibl f il *Science* 243:1593-6 Mr 24 '89
Do sperm spread the AIDS virus? [research by Virginia Scofield] J. L. Marx. il *Science* 245:30 Jl 7 '89
Drilling for fertility [hole made in zona pellucida allows easier passage of sperm; work of Jacques Cohen] M. L. Fuerst. il *Discover* 10:22 O '89
Gene-splicing revolution? [use of sperm cells] *Time* 133:59 Je 12 '89
Gene-transfer method fails test [trying to replicate; work of Corrado Spadafora] M. Barinaga. *Science* 246:446 O 27 '89
Making transgenic mice: is it really that easy? [trying to replicate work of Corrado Spadafora] M. Barinaga. il *Science* 245:590-1 Ag 11 '89
Specific expression of nuclear proto-oncogenes before entry into meiotic prophase of spermatogenesis [mice] H. Wolfes and others. bibl f il *Science* 245:740-3 Ag 18 '89
Sperm capture genes to create new life [research by Corrado Spadafora] I. Wickelgren. *Science News* 135:356 Je 10 '89
Sperm sorter ensures sex-linked litters [livestock breeding] *Science News* 136:175 S 9 '89
Temperature and sperm incorporation in polyploid salamanders. J. P. Bogart and others. bibl f il *Science* 246:1032-4 N 24 '89
Upwardly motile. J. Poppy. il *Esquire* 111:67+ Je '89

SPERO, SIMON
Chelsea porcelain, 1744-1769 [cover story] bibl f il *Antiques* 135:260-71 Ja '89

SPERRY & HUTCHINSON CO.
Green stamps go high tech. il *Newsweek* 113:46 Ap 3 '89

SPERRY CORP.
See also
Unisys Corp.

SPETH, JAMES GUSTAVE
A climate of apocalypse. il *New Perspectives Quarterly* 6:12-15 Spr '89
Energy technology for survival. il *The Bulletin of the Atomic Scientists* 45:9-10 Mr '89

SPHERE BOOKS LTD.
Penguin Group sells Sphere to Maxwell's Macdonald Publishing. V. Menkes. *Publishers Weekly* 235:40 Ap 7 '89

SPHERE PACKING
Interview: Neil Sloane. A. Liversidge. il pors *Omni (New York, N.Y.)* 11:78-80+ S '89

SPHERES
See also
Ceramic spheres
Microspheres
Inside moves [polyhedral sphere eversion; cover story] I. Peterson. il *Science News* 135:299+ My 13 '89

SPHINGOLIPIDS
Functions of sphingolipids and sphingolipid breakdown products in cellular regulation. Y. A. Hannun and R. M. Bell. bibl f il *Science* 243:500-7 Ja 27 '89
Sphingomyelin synthase and PKC activation [discussion of January 27, 1989 article, Functions of sphingolipids and sphingolipid breakdown products in cellular regulation] Y. A. Hannun and R. M. Bell. il *Science* 246:1050 N 24 '89

SPHINXES IN ART
Riddled Sphinxes [paintings of L. Golub] R. Storr. il *Art in America* 77:126-31 Mr '89

SPICE INDUSTRY
See also
Spice 'n Slice (Firm)

SPICE 'N SLICE (FIRM)
Farm girl taps ground beef with magic wand [using Spice 'n Slice] B. Freese. il *Successful Farming* 87:58-9 S '89

SPICE RACKS
Countertop spice rack. il *Workbench* 45:73 Mr/Ap '89

SPICES
See also
Cooking—Herbs and spices
Curry
The search for "living" spices [work of Braja D. Mookherjee] il *USA Today (Periodical)* 117:14 F '89

SPICES [film] See Motion picture reviews—Single works

SPIDER VEINS
A cure for spider veins. C. Slom. il *McCall's* 116:109 My '89
SPIDER WEBS
Spider webs: luring light may be a trap [research by Catherine L. Craig] I. Wickelgren. il *Science News* 135:330 My 27 '89
Spiders of industry [genetically engineered bacteria produce silk; work of Nick Ashley] il *Discover* 10:8 F '89
SPIDERS
See also
Tarantulas
Games spiders play [use of game theory to predict fighting among woodland spiders; research by Susan E. Riechert] J. A. Miller. *BioScience* 39:225 Ap '89
The matriarch [black widow] H. Middleton. il *Southern Living* 24:38+ N '89
Run, arachnids, run! [low stamina of spiders due to anaerobic metabolism; research by Kenneth Prestwich] *Discover* 10:12+ Ag '89
Who needs spiders? N. Vietmeyer. il *Reader's Digest* 134:137-40 Je '89
Eye
See Eye—Arachnids
Photographs and photography
Hanging tough [green lynx spider with babies] R. A. Mendez. il *Natural History* p116-17 N '89
If looks could kill . . . Florida jumping spider. T. Eisner. il *Natural History* p76-7 Jl '89
SPIDERS, FOSSIL
A Devonian spinneret: early evidence of spiders and silk use. W. A. Shear and others. bibl f il *Science* 246:479-81 O 27 '89
SPIEGEL, EMILY
about
Making room for art. J. Giovannini. il *House & Garden* 161:132-9 D '89
SPIEGEL, JERRY
about
Making room for art. J. Giovannini. il *House & Garden* 161:132-9 D '89
SPIEGEL, LAWRENCE D., 1945-
Child abuse hysteria: a warning for educators. *The Education Digest* 54:55-8 Ja '89
SPIEGEL, STEVEN L.
State of confusion [cover story] *The New Republic* 200:15-18 Ap 10 '89
SPIEGEL, THOMAS
about
He who lives by the junk bond . . . K. Kerwin. il por *Business Week* p46-7 D 25 '89-Ja 1 '90
SPIEGEL, INC.
Oldie but goodie. T. Jaffe. il *Forbes* 144:348 Jl 24 '89
SPIEGELMAN, ART
about
Art Spiegelman [interview] C. Dreifus. il *The Progressive* 53:34-7 N '89
SPIEGELMAN, JOEL W.
The door is open. il *High Fidelity (New York, N.Y.)* 39:58-60 Ap '89
SPIEGELMAN, KATHLEEN
about
North of the border. D. Michel. il *House & Garden* 161:92-5 F '89
SPIEGLER, ALLAN
(jt. auth) See Luginbill, Michael, and Spiegler, Allan
SPIELBERG, STEVEN, 1947-
about
Architectural digest visits: Steven Spielberg and Amy Irving [cover story] H. Hurt. il *Architectural Digest* 46:196-205+ My '89
E.T. the extra-terrestrial [film] Reviews
People Weekly il 32 Special Issue:91 Fall '89. B. Darrach
Rolling Stone il p127 F 9 '89. J. B. Meigs
Fear not, Hollywood: golden boy is still golden. R. Grover. il por *Business Week* p64-5 My 29 '89
Indiana Jones and the last crusade [film] Reviews
America 160:591 Je 17-24 '89. R. A. Blake
Commonweal 116:403-4 Jl 14 '89. T. O'Brien
Film Comment il por 25:9-11 Jl/Ag '89. A. White
Maclean's il 102:56 Je 5 '89. B. D. Johnson
The Nation 248:862 Je 19 '89. S. Klawans
The New Republic 200:28-9 Je 19 '89. S. Kauffmann
New York il 22:58-9 Je 5 '89. D. Denby
The New Yorker il 65:103-5 Je 12 '89. P. Kael
Newsweek il 113:69 My 29 '89. D. Ansen
People Weekly il 31:13 Je 5 '89. R. Novak
Rolling Stone il p31 Je 15 '89. P. Travers
Time il 133:82-4 My 29 '89. R. Corliss
The Spielbergs' flop. il pors *People Weekly* 32:70 Ag 7 '89
Steven Spielberg finally suffers a big-budget flop—his marriage. il pors *People Weekly* 31:67 My 8 '89
SPIER, DAVE
Tracks. il *The Conservationist* 44:54-5 N/D '89

SPIERS, RONALD I.
about
The United Nations: 'at the centre of it all' [interview] il por *UN Chronicle* 26:56-7 D '89
SPIES, THOMAS, AND OTHERS
A new cluster of genes within the human major histocompatibility complex. bibl f il *Science* 243:214-17 Ja 13 '89
SPIES, INDUSTRIAL See Business intelligence
SPIKE (HERBICIDE) See Herbicides
SPIKE OF BENSONHURST [film] See Motion picture reviews—Single works
SPILLANE, MICKEY, 1918-
about
Dutton hopes to make a killing with Spillane's latest Mike Hammer. il *Publishers Weekly* 236:59 O 6 '89
SPILLANE, SALLY
about
The barn collectors. M. Cantwell. il pors *House & Garden* 161:126-35 F '89
SPILLER, ROGER J.
The real war [interview with P. Fussell] il por *American Heritage* 40:126-7+ N '89
SPILLMAN, JANE SHADEL
Nineteenth-century White House glassware. bibl f il *Antiques* 135:950-63 Ap '89
SPILNER, MAGGIE
Take your walking to the max. il *Women's Sports & Fitness* 11:12 O '89
SPIN, AIRPLANE See Airplanes—Spinning
SPIN, ELECTRON See Electron spin
SPIN, NUCLEAR See Nuclear spin
SPIN GLASSES
Esoteric borrowing from physics. R. Pool. *Science* 245:702 Ag 18 '89
Spin glass: real power brought to bear. P. W. Anderson. il por *Physics Today* 42:9+ Jl '89
Spin glass: spin glass as cornucopia. P. W. Anderson. por *Physics Today* 42:9+ S '89
Spin glasses. D. L. Stein. bibl il *Scientific American* 261:52-9 Jl '89
SPINA BIFIDA
Spina bifida: paralyzing fluid in the womb? [research by Dan S. Heffez] I. Wickelgren. *Science News* 135:342 Je 3 '89
A White House promise [Health and Human Services nominee R. Fulton's stand on spina bifida and euthanasia] *National Review* 41:15-16 Ap 7 '89
SPINACH
Plant spinach in fall, harvest all winter. L. A. Weathers. il *Southern Living* 24:56 S '89
Reexamination of the three-dimensional structure of the small subunit of RuBisCo from higher plants. S. Knight and others. bibl f il *Science* 244:702-5 My 12 '89
SPINAL CORD
Another fish tale [ependymal cells in knifefish spinal cord responsible for tissue regeneration; research by Marilyn Anderson] il *Discover* 10:15 Ag '89
Visuomotor coordination in reaching and locomotion. A. P. Georgopoulos and S. Grillner. bibl f *Science* 245:1209-10 S 15 '89
Wounds and injuries
The spinal cord: the brain/body connection [cover story] J. E. Cohn. bibl f il *Current Health 2* 15:4-9 My '89
Was it worth the risk? [Arizona State football player M. Tingstad injured after continuing to play despite being warned of paralysis risk] R. Demak. il pors *Sports Illustrated* 71:76-81+ D 18 '89
SPINAL FLUID See Cerebrospinal fluid
SPINAL STENOSIS
Was it worth the risk? [Arizona State football player M. Tingstad injured after continuing to play despite being warned of paralysis risk] R. Demak. il pors *Sports Illustrated* 71:76-81+ D 18 '89
SPINE
See also
Backache
Abnormalities
See also
Spina bifida
Back talk: advice for suffering spines. E. Zamula. il *FDA Consumer* 23:28-35 Ap '89
Diseases
See also
Ankylosing spondylitis
Wounds and injuries
See also
Paralytics
By the skin of his neck [fractured vertebra ends season for Ohio State basketball player J. Burson] H. Hersch. il pors *Sports Illustrated* 70:46-9 Mr 6 '89
SPINELLI, EILEEN, 1942-
About nights [poem] *The Christian Century* 106:1197 D 20-27 '89
SPINKS, LEON
about
Leon Spinks goes from millionaire boxer to bartender. T. S. Moore. il pors *Jet* 75:14-16 Mr 27 '89

SPINKS, LEON—about—*cont.*
The road may not be ready, but Denny McLain and Leon Spinks are getting their acts together. M. Green. il pors *People Weekly* 31:130-1 F 13 '89
SPINNER BAITS *See* Fishing lures, flies, etc.
SPINNING
See also
Yarn
SPINODAL DECOMPOSITION
Japan's RS plastics [rapid solidification] H. Okada. *High Technology Business* 9:30 N/D '89
SPINOFFS (CORPORATE) *See* Corporations—Divestiture
SPINOFFS (TECHNOLOGY) *See* Technology transfer
SPIRA, HENRY
about
Pressuring Perdue. B. Feder. il por *The New York Times Magazine* p32+ N 26 '89
SPIRAL ARRANGEMENT OF LEAVES, ETC. *See* Phyllotaxis
SPIRIT COMMUNICATION *See* Spiritualism
SPIRIT THAT MOVES US PRESS
A seat-of-the pants veteran comes home [M. Sklar returns to N.Y. publishing] J. Barbato. *Publishers Weekly* 236:33 D 8 '89
SPIRITISM *See* Spiritualism
SPIRITUAL GIFTS
See also
Prophecy (Christianity)
SPIRITUAL HEALING *See* Faith cure
SPIRITUAL LIFE
See also
Christian life
Holiness
Meditation
Spirituality
[Column] H. Fehren. See issues of U.S. Catholic
Why Life says we are here [symposium in Life magazine] P. G. Henry. il *The Christian Century* 106:562-3 My 24-31 '89
SPIRITUALISM
See also
Channelers
Salt substitutes. T. C. Muck. il *Christianity Today* 33:14-15 F 3 '89
SPIRITUALITY
See also
Creation spirituality
Mysticism
Teenage spirituality [cover story] W. J. O'Malley. *America* 160:390-4 Ap 29 '89
Toward an adult spirituality [cover story] W. J. O'Malley. il *America* 161:341-4 N 18 '89
Bibliography
Practicing ethics & spirituality. L. Cunningham. *Commonweal* 116:572-4 O 20 '89
SPIRITUALS (SONGS)
Go tell it on the mountain: Christmas and the black spirit. il *Ebony* 45:36-8 D '89
SPIRO, DANIEL A.
Public schools and the road to religious neutrality. bibl f il *Phi Delta Kappan* 70:759-63 Je '89
SPIRO, GIDEON
about
An Israeli draws the line. W. Steif. il por *The Progressive* 53:15 Ap '89
SPIRO, PETER, AND MIRVISH, DANIEL
Whose no-fault is it, anyway? *The Washington Monthly* 21:24-8 O '89
SPIROCHETES
See also
Borrelia
SPIRODELA *See* Duckweeds
SPITTING
Pa-tooey! [spitting by animals] N. Vietmeyer. il *International Wildlife* 19:20-3 Ja/F '89
SPITZ, BOB
Raw, raunchy and middle-aged. il pors *The New York Times Magazine* p30-2+ Je 4 '89
SPITZ, MARK
about
Bionic man. K. Moore. il pors *Sports Illustrated* 71:80-2+ O 23 '89
SPLA *See* Sudan People's Liberation Army
SPLIT BRAIN
Left-brain snow job [research by Michael S. Gazzaniga] *Science News* 136:204 S 23 '89
SPLITFINGERED FASTBALL *See* Pitching (Baseball)
SPLITTING OF STOCKS *See* Stocks—Splitting
SPLITTING OF WOOD *See* Wood cutting
SPOCK, BENJAMIN, 1903-
Circumcision—it's not necessary. por *Redbook* 172:53 Ap '89
Good ways to handle a child's anger. por *Redbook* 174:28+ D '89
How to handle a bossy grandmother. por *Redbook* 172:66 Ja '89
'It's all up to us'. il por *Newsweek* 114 Special Issue:106-7 Wint '89/Spr '90
Time out for busy parents. por *Redbook* 173:30 Je '89

What do you do when your child tells a lie? por *Redbook* 172:36 Mr '89
about
Baby guru Dr. Spock grows up in memoir from Pantheon. J. Crichton. pors *Publishers Weekly* 236:25 O 13 '89
SPOHR, ARNOLD
about
Kickoff. R. Philp. *Dance Magazine* 63:7 D '89
SPOILING OF CHILDREN *See* Children—Management and training
SPOKANE (WASH.)
Arts
See also
Metropolitan Performing Arts Center (Spokane, Wash.)
Education
Serving refugee children and families in Head Start [cover story] C. Broughton. il *Children Today* 18:6-10 S/O '89
SPOKANE BALLET
Its director at odds with its board, Spokane Ballet seeks stability [resignation of artistic director C. Aponte] S. English. por *Dance Magazine* 63:18 Mr '89
SPOLETO FESTIVAL U.S.A.
Charleston, S.C. [opera] C. J. Halperin. il *Opera News* 54:44 O '89
SPONDYLITIS
See also
Ankylosing spondylitis
SPONGES
Ice sponging off the Antarctic shelf [research by Paul K. Dayton] il *Science News* 136:255 O 14 '89
Interdecadal variation in an Antarctic sponge and its predators from oceanographic climate shifts. P. K. Dayton. bibl f il *Science* 245:1484-6 S 29 '89
The secret lives of sponges [cover story] N. Sefton. bibl il *Sea Frontiers* 35:170-5 My/Je '89
The sponge [inadvertently feeding a sponge to a horse] N. Hazelton. *National Review* 41:50+ Ap 21 '89
SPONSORS, ADVERTISING *See* Television advertising
SPONTANEOUS ABORTION *See* Miscarriage
SPONTANEOUS REMISSION
The Lazarus file. H. Straus. il *American Health* 8:67-8+ My '89
SPOONS
How to make wood spoons. R. Capotosto. il *Popular Mechanics* 166:84-5 D '89
Collectors and collecting
Exploring west of the Rockies on souvenir spoons. R. L. Lloyd. il *Antiques & Collecting Hobbies* 94:30-4 S '89
SPOONS (FISHING LURES) *See* Fishing lures, flies, etc.
SPORCK, CHARLES E.
about
Can Charles Sporck chip out a new niche? R. Brandt. il por *Business Week* p156 Je 26 '89
SPORT FISHING *See* Fishing
SPORT FISHING BOATS *See* Fishing boats
SPORTING CLAYS (SHOOTING) *See* Trapshooting
SPORTING GOODS
See also
Aquatic sports—Equipment
Fishing—Equipment
Mountaineering—Equipment
Running—Equipment
Skiing—Equipment
Skin diving—Equipment
Tennis—Equipment
Walking—Equipment
Good sports. il *Harper's Bazaar* 122:40+ My '89
Holiday gift guide: what to buy the sports nut who's seen and played everything. R. Leivenberg. il *Sport (New York, N.Y.)* 80:76-7 Ja '89
Weekend hackers, take heart. T. Barrett. il *Newsweek* 114:41 Jl 17 '89
What's new: recreation. S. F. Brown. See occasional issues of Popular Science beginning December 1985
Exhibitions
A show that has the goods [Super Show in Atlanta] S. Ballard. il *Sports Illustrated* 70:36-40 F 20 '89
What's new? Plenty! [Shooting, Hunting and Outdoor Trade Show] B. Brister. il *Field & Stream* 94:65-6+ My '89
SPORTING GOODS, USED
Anecdotes, facetiae, satire, etc.
Patina, Inc. [with editorial comment by Duncan Barnes] G. Hill. il *Field & Stream* 94:7, 13 My '89
SPORTING GOODS INDUSTRY
See also
Brunswick Corp.
Burton Snowboards (Firm)
Eddie Bauer Inc.
Johnson Worldwide Associates, Inc.
Karsten Manufacturing Corporation
Wilson Sporting Goods Co.
Worth Inc.
France
See also
Salomon et Fils François
Japan
See also
Mizuno Corporation

SPORTS

See also

Aged—Sports
Alcohol and sports
Amateurism (Sports)
Amputees—Sports
Aquatic sports
Arbitration, Sports
Athletes
Baby boom generation—Sports
Black celebrities—Sports
Business and sports
Cable television—Sports
Celebrities—Sports
Children—Sports
Closed circuit television—Sports
Coed sports
College athletics
College graduates—Sports
Computers—Sports use
Deaf—Sports
Discrimination in sports
Drugs and sports
Handicapped—Sports
Industry—Recreation programs
Physical education and training
Radio broadcasting—Sports
Recreation
School athletics
Sex discrimination in sports
Telephone in sports
Television broadcasting—Sports
Time clocks (Sports)
Track and field athletics
Videotapes—Sports
Winter sports
Women—Sports
Women executives—Sports
Yuppies—Sports
    See also names of sports

The '90s. R. Sandomir. il *Sport (New York, N.Y.)* 80:91-2+ O '89
For the record. See issues of Sports Illustrated
Games growup [cover story; special section] il *Health (New York, N.Y.)* 21:55-71 Je '89
Good sports. il *Harper's Bazaar* 122:40+ My '89
Hot fun. il *Rolling Stone* p92-5 My 18 '89
Name that sport [hybrid sports; contest winners] S. Morris. *Omni (New York, N.Y.)* 11:16 S '89
Of Billie Jean and 73-0 [E. D. Hirsch's book on cultural literacy slights the import of sport] F. Deford. il por *Sports Illustrated* 70:70 F 6 '89
Scorecard. See issues of Sports Illustrated
Sport quiz. See issues of Sport (New York, N.Y.)
Sport talk. See issues of Sport (New York, N.Y.)
The sporting life. M. Lupica. See issues of Esquire beginning October 1987
Sports watch. T. Frayne. See occasional issues of Maclean's beginning November 6, 1989

Accidents and injuries

See also

Baseball, Professional—Accidents and injuries
Basketball, College—Accidents and injuries
Basketball, Professional—Accidents and injuries
Football, College—Accidents and injuries
Football, Professional—Accidents and injuries
Horse racing—Accidents and injuries
Motorcycle racing—Accidents and injuries
Parachuting—Accidents and injuries
Running—Accidents and injuries
School athletics—Accidents and injuries
Ski racing—Accidents and injuries
Skiing—Accidents and injuries
Softball—Accidents and injuries
Tennis—Accidents and injuries

Care package for the sports enthusiast. S. Chan. il *Working Woman* 14:100+ Jl '89
Exercise with care—fitness is not risk-free. N. Karkowsky. il *FDA Consumer* 23:24-7 My '89
How safe are vacation sports? H. Gieseking. *Travel Holiday* 171:83-4 F '89
Press on: to reduce swelling, ice is nice but compressed is best. O. Anderson. il *Women's Sports & Fitness* 11:11 Ja/F '89
Sidelined [recovery] J. Mattera. il *Glamour* 87:86 Mr '89
Sight savers [sports goggles] T. Imbimbo. il *Health (New York, N.Y.)* 21:32+ Mr '89
They never gave up. R. Hoffer. il pors *Sports Illustrated* 71:117-27+ D 25 '89-Ja 1 '90
A twist of the wrist [reducing risk of carpal tunnel syndrome] L. Rogak. il *American Health* 8:34 D '89
When to see a sports doc. S. Findlay. bibl il *U.S. News & World Report* 107:56-8 Jl 31 '89

Anecdotes, facetiae, satire, etc.

2054: a sports odyssey. R. Reilly. il *Sports Illustrated* 71 Special Issue:226-8+ N 15 '89
Ask me again, next year. J. McCallum. por *Sports Illustrated* 70:130 Ja 9 '89

Rose lives! M. Lupica. il *Esquire* 112:63-4 D '89

Awards

See also

Football, College—Awards
Hockey, Professional—Awards

The heavenly hundred: which numbers should be retired in whose honor. R. Reilly. por *Sports Illustrated* 70:104 My 22 '89
Tomorrow's stars: the 1989 Secret Up & Coming Award winners [women athletes] K. M. Reith. il *Women's Sports & Fitness* 11:64-5 O '89

Collectibles

Make this guy a scout [C. L. Brannen compiles scrapbooks on athletes] R. Harper. il *Sport (New York, N.Y.)* 80:76 Jl '89

Competitions

See also

Aerobics—Competitions
Diving—Competitions
Figure skating—Competitions
Francophone Games
Olympic Games
Pan American Games
Rowing—Competitions
Senior Olympics
Special Olympics
Speed skating—Competitions
U.S. Olympic Festival
World Veterans Games

Meet the top 24 athletes [finalists in Sportsgirl of the Year contest] il *'Teen* 33:42-3 D '89
Wake me when it's over [J. W. Hershberger's Most Versatile Performer competition] D. Kardong. il por *Runner's World* 24:86-90+ Ap '89

Economic aspects

See also

Athletes—Salaries, pensions, etc.
Boxing—Economic aspects
Football, Professional—Economic aspects
Golf—Economic aspects
Hockey, Professional—Economic aspects
Mountaineering—Economic aspects
Polo—Economic aspects
Race tracks—Economic aspects
Running—Economic aspects
Sports agencies and agents
Wrestling, Professional—Economic aspects

The American sports mania. R. J. Samuelson. il *Newsweek* 114:49 S 4 '89
Betting billions on TV sports. J. Hammer. il *Newsweek* 114:66-8 D 11 '89
Cities get into the game. G. Macnow. il *Nation's Business* 77:48-9+ N '89
How are the owners holding up? Just fine, thank you. T. Mulgannon. il *Sport (New York, N.Y.)* 80:93 Je '89
Japan: coming on strong. B. Newman. il *Sports Illustrated* 71:48-54+ Ag 21 '89

Equipment

See Sporting goods

Ethical aspects

See also

Baseball, Professional—Ethical aspects
Basketball—Ethical aspects
Basketball, College—Ethical aspects
Basketball, High school—Ethical aspects
Basketball, Professional—Ethical aspects
Blood boosting
Boxing—Ethical aspects
College athletics—Ethical aspects
Drugs and sports
Football, College—Ethical aspects
Football, High school—Ethical aspects
Football, Professional—Ethical aspects
Golf—Ethical aspects
Hockey, Professional—Ethical aspects
Horse racing—Ethical aspects
Marathon running—Ethical aspects
Motor boat racing—Ethical aspects
Running—Ethical aspects
School athletics—Ethical aspects
Soccer, Professional—Ethical aspects
Surfing—Ethical aspects
Tennis—Tournaments—Ethical aspects
Track and field athletics—Ethical aspects
Weight lifting—Ethical aspects

The era of the enhanced athlete. L. Winner. il *Technology Review* 92:22 F/Mr '89
A sacrificial rite of spring. P. Iyer. il *Time* 133:106 Mr 27 '89

Exhibitions

Games [Ontario Science Centre] R. Brody. il *Omni (New York, N.Y.)* 11:94-5 Ja '89

History

35th anniversary [Sports illustrated] il *Sports Illustrated* 71 Special Issue:8-10+ N 15 '89
The '80s: the glorious decade [cover story; special section] il *Sport (New York, N.Y.)* 80:46-50+ O '89

SPORTS—History—*cont.*
Blacks in . . . the greatest sports events of all time. il *Ebony* 44:120-2+ O '89
Dollars and change: sport in the '80s was altered for richer and for poorer. R. Telander. por *Sports Illustrated* 71:166 D 25 '89-Ja 1 '90
Masters of the '80s [M. Johnson, W. Gretzky, and J. Montana; cover story] R. Reilly. il pors *Sports Illustrated* 71:44-9 D 18 '89

International aspects
See also
Francophone Games
International Amateur Athletic Federation
Olympic Games
Pan American Games
The global cry: Play ball! T. Callahan. il *Time* 133:87 Je 5 '89
Globe-trotting athletes. W. M. Barrett. il *USA Today (Periodical)* 118:81 N '89
A sporting partnership [health education through sports] A. Salahi. il *World Health* p18-19 Jl '89

Organization and administration
LA owners. S. Ostler. il *Sport (New York, N.Y.)* 80:30-1 Ja '89

Periodicals
See also
Sports illustrated (Periodical)
Women's sports & fitness (Periodical)

Philosophy
Uplifted, gently, by sport. K. Moore. il por *Sports Illustrated* 71 Special Issue:234 N 15 '89

Photographs and photography
Pictures '89. il *Sports Illustrated* 71:86-115 D 25 '89-Ja 1 '90
Tracy Frankel: keeping an eye on the action. C. R. Wolpert. il por *Women's Sports & Fitness* 11:59 Jl/Ag '89

Psychological aspects
See also
Baseball, Professional—Psychological aspects
Boxing—Psychological aspects
Cycling—Psychological aspects
Running—Psychological aspects
Tennis—Psychological aspects
Track and field athletics—Psychological aspects
Coaches preach: win at any cost [views of Edward J. Shea] il *USA Today (Periodical)* 118:9 D '89
Finding 'the zone'. L. Shainberg. il pors *The New York Times Magazine* p34-6+ Ap 9 '89
Head coaches. R. McGarvey. il *Sport (New York, N.Y.)* 80:92-4 F '89
The non-competitive advantage. J. Scandura. *Working Woman* 14:140+ Je '89
Not fan-made [importance of participation] G. Sheehan. il *Runner's World* 24:18 Je '89
Splendor on the grass [sports heroes] J. Schulian. il *Gentlemen's Quarterly* 59:142-5+ Ja '89
Sports shy. J. Bailey. il *Health (New York, N.Y.)* 21:56-61 Je '89
Unsportsmanlike conduct. L. L. Riskin. il *The New York Times Magazine* p14+ Ja 22 '89
Using psychological tools to improve your game. J. R. May. il *Psychology Today* 23:23-5 My '89
Women in sports: what's changed? [negative perception of female high school athletes; research by Mary Jo Kane] V. Bozzi. *Psychology Today* 23:70 O '89
You are what you play [perceived character traits of sports participants; research by Darwyn Linder and others] V. Bozzi. il *Psychology Today* 23:69 O '89
Your brand of sweat [choosing a sport that suits your personality] J. Gavin. il *Psychology Today* 23:50-3+ Mr '89

Public relations
Hype. B. Newman. il *Sports Illustrated* 70:60-4+ Ja 23 '89

Safety devices and measures
Defensive exercising. *Glamour* 87:28+ Jl '89
Sports, kids, fun, and safety; ed. by Barbara Raymond. M. A. Nelson. il *Good Housekeeping* 209:82+ S '89

Social aspects
See also
Baseball, Professional—Social aspects
Football, College—Social aspects
Tennis—Social aspects
Growing up with Trux [author and his father bound by love of sports] R. Fimrite. por *Sports Illustrated* 71:72 Jl 3 '89
She: 6, he: 3, relationship: 0 [couples competing at sports] H. K. Paddock. il *Glamour* 87:75-6+ Ag '89

Africa
Track great Mal Whitfield lauded at USIA retirement. il por *Jet* 77:48 N 20 '89

Arizona
See also
Phoenix (Ariz.)—Sports
The selling of spring [spring training] R. Fimrite. il *Sports Illustrated* 70:58-60+ Mr 27 '89

Australia
See also
Australian rules football

Automobile racing—Australia
Motorcycle racing—Australia

Belgium
See also
Automobile racing—Belgium

Bermuda
A sporting good time in Bermuda. C. Males. il *Travel Holiday* 171:9-10+ F '89

Brazil
See also
Automobile racing—Brazil

California
See also
Los Angeles (Calif.)—Sports
Oakland (Calif.)—Sports
San Francisco (Calif.)—Sports

Canada
See also
Automobile racing—Canada
Football, College—Canada
Golf—Canada
Weight lifting
Sports watch. T. Frayne. See occasional issues of Maclean's beginning November 6, 1989

Cuba
See also
Baseball—Cuba

Dominican Republic
See also
Baseball—Dominican Republic

Finland
See also
Pesapallo (Game)

Florida
The selling of spring [spring training] R. Fimrite. il *Sports Illustrated* 70:58-60+ Mr 27 '89
See also
Automobile racing—France
Bicycle racing—France

France
See also
Automobile racing—France
Bicycle racing—France

Georgia
See also
Atlanta (Ga.)—Sports

Germany (West)
See also
Automobile racing—Germany (West)
Soccer—Germany (West)
Tennis—Germany (West)

Great Britain
See also
Automobile racing—Great Britain
Cricket (Sport)—Great Britain
Motorcycle racing—Great Britain
Soccer, Professional—Great Britain

Hungary
See also
Automobile racing—Hungary

Illinois
See also
Chicago (Ill.)—Sports

Indiana
See also
Indianapolis (Ind.)—Sports

Iowa
The Iowa girl stands tall [1988 six-on-six basketball state tournament] K. Cook. il *Sports Illustrated* 70:76-84+ F 13 '89

Italy
See also
Automobile racing—Italy
Baseball, Professional—Italy
Basketball, Professional—Italy
Bicycle racing—Italy
Motorcycle racing—Italy

Japan
See also
Automobile racing—Japan
Baseball, Professional—Japan
Golf—Japan
Motorcycle racing—Japan
Wrestling
Sports and Japan [special section] il *Sports Illustrated* 71:48-54+ Ag 21 '89

Latin America
See also
Baseball, Professional—Latin America

Maryland
See also
Baltimore (Md.)—Sports

Massachusetts
See also
Boston (Mass.)—Sports

Mexico
See also
Automobile racing—Mexico

Michigan
See also
Detroit (Mich.)—Sports

SPORTS—cont.

Minnesota

See also
Minneapolis (Minn.)—Sports
Saint Paul (Minn.)—Sports

Monaco

See also
Automobile racing—Monaco

Morocco

See also
Skiing—Morocco

New Mexico

See also
Animas (N.M.)—Sports

New York (State)

See also
Bronx (New York, N.Y.)—Sports
Buffalo (N.Y.)—Sports
New York (N.Y.)—Sports

New Zealand

See also
Skiing—New Zealand
Boing! W. P. Barrett. il *Forbes* 144:233+ O 30 '89

Norway

See also
Skiing—Norway

Ohio

Sporting pleasures. G. Logsdon. il *Country Journal* 16:36-41
Jl/Ag '89

Oregon

See also
Eugene (Or.)—Sports

Pennsylvania

See also
Philadelphia (Pa.)—Sports

Portugal

See also
Automobile racing—Portugal

South Africa

See also
Tennis—South Africa
The last wave [surfers boycott competitions] E. Silver. il
Mother Jones 14:12 D '89
South Africa: the saga continues [runners suspended for
attending track meet] A. Burfoot and B. Wischnia. il
Runner's World 24:8-9 F '89

Soviet Union

See also
Baseball—Soviet Union
Basketball—Soviet Union
Hockey—Soviet Union
Skiing—Soviet Union
Softball—Soviet Union

Spain

See also
Automobile racing—Spain
Motorcycle racing—Spain

Sweden

See also
Motorcycle racing—Sweden

Taiwan

See also
Little League baseball—Taiwan

Texas

See also
Dallas (Tex.)—Sports
Houston (Tex.)—Sports

Vietnam

See also
Tennis—Vietnam

Washington (D.C.)

See Washington (D.C.)—Sports

Western Europe

See also
Golf—Western Europe
Motorcycle racing—Western Europe

SPORTS AGENCIES AND AGENTS
See also
ProServ Inc.
He's dialing for dollars [football agent L. Steinberg] il por
Sports Illustrated 71:18-19 Ag 7 '89

Ethical aspects

A bill of wrongs [proposed Ohio legislation to regulate sports
agents] S. Rosenbloom. il *Sport (New York, N.Y.)* 80:19
F '89
A question of fairness [conviction of agents N. Walters and
L. Bloom] R. Telander. por *Sports Illustrated* 70:114 My
1 '89
Tough message [sports agents N. Walters and L. Bloom
found guilty of racketeering, conspiracy, and mail fraud]
il pors *Time* 133:78 Ap 24 '89
SPORTS AND BUSINESS See Business and sports
SPORTS AND DANCE
Choreography on the court. E. Zimmer. il *Dance Magazine*
63:48-9 Ag '89

SPORTS AND GEOGRAPHY
Anecdotes, facetiae, satire, etc.
When East is West. D. Summerford. por *Newsweek* 113:10
Ja 2 '89
SPORTS AND STATE
Canada
A day of reckoning [B. Johnson admits he took steroids]
il pors *Maclean's* 102:32-3 Je 26 '89
A deepening scandal [physician J. Astaphan testifies on steroid
use by B. Johnson] B. Wickens. pors *Maclean's* 102:49-50
Je 5 '89
A dirty coach comes clean [C. Francis testifies on steroid
use by B. Johnson and other Canadian athletes] M. Noden.
il pors *Sports Illustrated* 70:22-3 Mr 13 '89
From dream to nightmare [testimony by track coach C.
Francis during Canadian government inquiry into steroid
use by B. Johnson] A. Burfoot and B. Wischnia. il pors
Runner's World 24:12 Je '89
He has suffered enough [B. Johnson facing lifetime ban
and possible loss of 100 meter world record over steroid
use] M. Noden. por *Sports Illustrated* 70:98 Je 26 '89
A revealing inquiry [testimony of J. Astaphan on runner
B. Johnson's steroid use] M. Noden. il por *Sports Illustrated*
70:19 Je 5 '89
Sabotage at Seoul? [testimony on steroid use by B. Johnson]
R. Dolphin. il por *Maclean's* 102:47 Mr 20 '89
The sportswriters' big drug coverup [government push to
improve Canada's Olympics performance] A. Fotheringham.
il *Maclean's* 102:68 Ap 24 '89
The steroid scandal [weight lifters testify at government
inquiry] D. Burke. il *Maclean's* 102:40 F 20 '89
The steroid scandal [testimony of track coach C. Francis
at Canadian inquiry; cover story; special section; with
editorial comment by Kevin Doyle] il pors *Maclean's*
102:2, 36-42 Mr 13 '89
Whistle blower [track coach C. Francis, testifying during
government inquiry, confirms B. Johnson's steroid use]
por *Time* 133:50 Mr 13 '89
Anecdotes, facetiae, satire, etc.
A community of small communities [demands of Quebec
and New Brunswick for own teams at Francophone Games]
S. MacLeod. por *Maclean's* 102:64 Je 5 '89
Germany (East)
Out of the shadows [effect of opening of Berlin Wall on
East German athletes] W. O. Johnson and A. Verschoth.
il *Sports Illustrated* 71:16-21 N 27 '89
Soviet Union
Rebels with a balance: Soviet artists and athletes want to
keep more of the dollars they earn abroad. D. Rinehart.
il *Maclean's* 102:20-1 Jl 3 '89
SPORTS ARBITRAGE
"This is like stealing" [G. Sacks] D. Akst. il *Forbes* 144:142+
N 13 '89
SPORTS ARENAS See Stadiums
SPORTS BARS
What's a sports bar anyway? [Chicago bars] M. Kiefer. il
Sport (New York, N.Y.) 80:64 Mr '89
SPORTS BETTING
See also
Baseball betting
Basketball betting
Boxing betting
Football betting
Horse race betting
Sports arbitrage
Did Pete do it? What are the odds? T. Callahan. il *Time*
133:92 Je 26 '89
Rose probe (cont.) [alleged sports betting by Cincinnati Reds
manager] C. Neff. il por *Sports Illustrated* 70:13+ Ap 17
'89
Rose's grim vigil [cover story] C. Neff and J. Lieber. il
pors *Sports Illustrated* 70:52-4+ Ap 3 '89
Sports gambling '90s style. R. McGarvey. il *Sport (New
York, N.Y.)* 80:57-9 Ap '89
SPORTS BRAS See Brassieres
SPORTS BROADCASTERS See Cable television—Sports;
Radio broadcasting—Sports; Television broadcasting—
Sports
SPORTS CAR CLUB OF AMERICA
SCCA runoffs: tales of guts and glory. M. DeMere. il *Motor
Trend* 41:127-9 F '89
Sports Car Club of America National Racing School. J.
Karr. il *Motor Trend* 41:118-19+ O '89
SPORTS CARS
See also
Convertibles (Automobiles)
New Avanti Motor Corporation
Sports Car Club of America
Auto exotica [cover story] J. Karr. il *Motor Trend* 41:46-51
D '89
Chevrolet Corvette 1984-1988 [owner survey] P. Bohr. il
Road & Track 40:64+ Je '89
Classy coupes. J. Flint. il *Forbes* 143:156-8 Je 26 '89
The fickle-fingered formula [defining sports cars] P. Bedard.
il *Car and Driver* 34:24 Ap '89
Honda CRX 1984-1988 [owner survey] P. Bohr. il *Road
& Track* 41:75+ O '89

SPORTS CARS—*cont.*

The pussycat that roars [Corvette ZR1] il *Time* 133:69 My 8 '89

The strange case of William Favre [intrigue surrounding Ferrari replica builder] B. W. Yates. il pors *Car and Driver* 35:77+ D '89

Design

Acura NS-X. J. Karr. il *Motor Trend* 41:98 Ap '89

Acura NS-X [cover story] L. Griffin. il *Car and Driver* 34:40-3 Ap '89

Aluminum sports car [Acura NS-X] D. McCosh. il *Popular Science* 234:20 My '89

Aston Martin Virage. R. Hutton. il *Car and Driver* 34:77-8 Mr '89

Buffing up an old classic [Avanti] F. Washington. il por *Newsweek* 113:46 Ap 3 '89

Bugatti super car taking shape. P. Bingham. il *Motor Trend* 41:20-1 Jl '89

Coventry's conceptual cat [Jaguar XJ-220] P. Frère. il *Road & Track* 40:90-1+ F '89

The devil is sighted [Lamborghini Diablo] P. Bingham. il *Motor Trend* 41:18-19 N '89

Jaguar XJ220. R. Hutton. il *Car and Driver* 34:92-3 Mr '89

Japan thinks there's room for vroom in the U.S. D. Woodruff. il *Business Week* p42 F 27 '89

Lamborghini Diablo. D. Hart. il *Road & Track* 41:60-2 N '89

Mid-engine magic [2-seaters from Japan] R. Homan. il *Road & Track* 40:90-1+ My '89

Porsche for 1990. P. Frère. il *Road & Track* 41:174+ N '89

Raymond Loewy's four-door Avanti. S. Kichen. il por *Forbes* 144:180 O 2 '89

Sports car 2010. R. Grable. il *Motor Trend* 41:88-93 Ja '89

Vehement Virage [Aston Martin; cover story] J. Lamm. il *Road & Track* 40:38-43 Ja '89

Virage—Aston Martin of tomorrow. M. Cotton. il *Motor Trend* 41:22 Ja '89

Engines
See Automobile engines

Export-import trade
See Automobiles—Export-import trade

Four wheel drive

Ford RS Cosworth Coupe. G. Perini. il *Car and Driver* 35:30-1 O '89

Porsche 911 Carrera 4. C. Csere. il *Car and Driver* 34:78-81+ F '89

Porsche 911 Carrera 4 [cover story] L. Griffin. il *Car and Driver* 35:36-9+ Ag '89

Porsche 911—with 4WD? [Carrera 4] D. McCosh and T. O. Bakke. il *Popular Science* 234:22 Mr '89

Porsche Carrera 4. J. Karr. il *Motor Trend* 41:73-6 Mr '89

Porsche Carrera 4. J. R. Nerad. il *Motor Trend* 41:106-10 O '89

Porsche refines the right stuff [Carrera 4] D. Woodruff. il *Business Week* p86 Jl 24 '89

Porsches in Provence [Carrera 4, 944 S2 and 911 Turbo; cover story] il *Road & Track* 40:42-53 F '89

World's best cars [Ferrari Testarossa, Mazda MX-5 Miata, Mercedes-Benz 300E, Corvette ZR-1, and Porsche 911 Carrera 4; cover story] il *Road & Track* 40:40-51 Jl '89

History

1950-1965 Porsche 356 Coupes. P. Bohr. il *Road & Track* 41:88-9+ S '89

1968 Bizzarrini 5300 Spyder S.I. R. Thursby. il *Road & Track* 40:134-40 Jl '89

Editors' exotics. il *Motor Trend* 41:115+ My '89

The marque of Zora [original Corvette designer Z. Arkus-Duntov] P. Lyons. il pors *Car and Driver* 34:60-1+ Je '89

Mercedes-Benz 300SL [1957 300SL] C. Csere. il *Car and Driver* 35:92-5+ S '89

My affair with fantasy [1974 MGB] M. Norman. il *Gentlemen's Quarterly* 59:61+ Mr '89

Never again. Until next time [fascination with MGs] A. Assenza. il *Car and Driver* 34:26 Ap '89

Sudden conversions [MG TC buffs] P. Egan. il *Road & Track* 41:26+ D '89

Ten best performance cars of all time. C. Csere. il *Car and Driver* 34:38-41+ Ja '89

Top 10 sports cars of all time [cover story] il *Motor Trend* 41:44-8+ Ap '89

Ownership
See Automobile ownership

Speed

Flat-out fastest American cars II, the sequel [Chevy Camaro IROC-Z and Corvette, Ford Mustang LX and Taurus SHO, Olds Cutlass Calais Quad 4 H.O., Plymouth Laser RS, Dodge Shelby CSX, and Pontiac McLaren Turbo and Trans Am; cover story] R. Grable. il *Motor Trend* 41:42-7+ Je '89

Jaguar XJ220: fastest in the world? il *Motor Trend* 41:19 F '89

The road not taken [driving a Corvette at high speed] R. Grable. il *Motor Trend* 41:132 Ap '89

Testing

Acura NS-X. C. Csere. il *Car and Driver* 35:69-72+ S '89

Acura NS-X [cover story] J. Karr. il *Motor Trend* 41:38-43 S '89

Acura NS-X: birth of an exotic [cover story] J. Dinkel. il *Road & Track* 41:42-50 S '89

Alfa Romeo ES30 [cover story] D. Simanaitis. il *Road & Track* 40:40-7 My '89

Alfa Romeo SZ. G. Perini. il *Car and Driver* 34:40 Je '89

Ambassador of good wheels [Corvette ZR-1] J. Rusz. il *Road & Track* 40:47-9 Je '89

America's supercar [Corvette ZR 1] D. Sherman. il *Popular Science* 234:120-1+ Je '89

Back to the mother lode [old vs. new Alfa Romeos, Corvettes and Porsches; cover story] P. Egan. il *Road & Track* 40:38-49 Ag '89

Bang for the buck! [top 10 performance coupes] J. Karr. il *Motor Trend* 41:42-6+ N '89

Chevrolet Corvette Coupe. J. Miller. il *Motor Trend* 41:180-1+ My '89

Chevrolet Corvette ZR-1. T. Swan. il *Popular Mechanics* 166:78-9+ Je '89

Chevrolet Corvette ZR-1 [cover story] il *Road & Track* 40:40-6 Je '89

Chevrolet Corvette ZR-1 [cover story] W. Jeanes. il *Car and Driver* 34:48-53 Je '89

Cizeta Moroder V16T. S. Cropley and G. Perini. il *Car and Driver* 34:67-9+ Mr '89

Cizeta Moroder V16T [cover story] J. Karr. il *Motor Trend* 41:42-8 Mr '89

Corvette reflections. P. Lyons. il *Car and Driver* 34:56 Je '89

Corvette ZR-1. J. Miller. il *Motor Trend* 41:56-60 Je '89

Coupes de grâce. L. Frank. il *Popular Mechanics* 166:120-4+ My '89

Ferrari 348tb [cover story] C. Csere. il *Car and Driver* 35:32-5+ D '89

Ferrari fun in the Florida sun [driving a Ferrari 328GTS from N.J. to Fla.] J. R. Nerad. il *Motor Trend* 41:70-2+ S '89

Ferrari Mondial T. P. Frère. il *Road & Track* 40:176-7 Jl '89

Ferrari Testarossa. il *Road & Track* 41:66-7+ O '89

Ferrari Testarossa. J. Karr. il *Motor Trend* 41:140-2+ My '89

Four sporty cars [Plymouth Laser, Nissan 240SX, Honda CRX Si, and Subaru XT] il *Consumer Reports* 54:631-7 O '89

Honda CRX Si [long-term test] J. Manfredi. il *Motor Trend* 41:150 My '89

Hot new Z [Datsun 300ZX] D. Sherman. il *Popular Science* 234:112-13 Mr '89

Ital Design Aztec. R. Hutton. il *Car and Driver* 34:87-8 Mr '89

Lamborghini Countach Anniversary. P. Bingham. il *Motor Trend* 41:68-72 F '89

Long-term update [Nissan 240SX SE, Mitsubishi Galant GS and Peugeot 405 Mi16] il *Road & Track* 41:135 O '89

Long-term update [Pontiac Fiero GT] J. Keebler. il *Road & Track* 40:78 Mr '89

Lotus déjà vu [Caterham Super Seven] P. Egan. il *Road & Track* 40:92+ Ap '89

Lotus Esprit Turbo. il *Road & Track* 40:72-4+ My '89

Lotus Esprit Turbo SE. il *Road & Track* 41:142-3+ N '89

Lotus Esprit Turbo SE. J. Karr. il *Motor Trend* 41:64-8+ Jl '89

Lotus Esprit Turbo SE. J. Phillips, III. il *Car and Driver* 35:86-7+ D '89

Matra's little 25th-anniversary bombshell. P. Frère. il *Road & Track* 41:163-4 S '89

Mazda 3-rotor RX-7. D. Fuller. il *Motor Trend* 41:122-4 F '89

Mazda RX-7 GTU[S], il *Road & Track* 40:132-4+ Ag '89

Mazda RX-7s [RX-7 Turbo II and RX-7 Convertible] J. R. Nerad. il *Motor Trend* 41:96-9+ Ag '89

Motown muscle. T. Swan and M. Allen. il *Popular Mechanics* 166:53-7+ Ja '89

MVS Venturi. P. Bedard. il *Car and Driver* 34:85-7+ My '89

MVS Venturi: *oui*, wheee! P. Frère. il *Road & Track* 40:126-30 My '89

Nissan 240SX SE. L. Griffin. il *Car and Driver* 34:93-6+ F '89

Nissan 240SX SE. J. Miller. il *Motor Trend* 41:150 My '89

Nissan 240SX SE [long-term test] D. Kott. il *Road & Track* 40:134 My '89

Nissan 300ZX. il *Road & Track* 40:164-8 My '89

Nissan 300ZX. J. Miller. il *Motor Trend* 41:76-80 S '89

Nissan 300ZX. J. Miller. il *Motor Trend* 41:62-4+ Mr '89

Nissan 300ZX. A. St. Antoine. il *Car and Driver* 35:46-9+ Ag '89

Nissan 300ZX [cover story] L. Griffin. il *Car and Driver* 34:34-7 Mr '89

Nissan 300ZX: the boulevardier stops here [cover story] D. Simanaitis. il *Road & Track* 40:52-9 Mr '89

Nissan 300ZX Turbo. il *Road & Track* 41:68-9+ D '89

SPORTS CARS—Testing—*cont.*

Nissan 300ZX Turbo. C. Csere. il *Car and Driver* 35:46-9+ N '89

Nissan 300ZX Twin Turbo. J. Karr. il *Motor Trend* 41:126-8+ N '89

Nissan 300ZX vs. Porsche 944 S2 [cover story] il *Road & Track* 41:42-9 O '89

Nissan's new 'Z-car' gets an A for acceleration [300ZX] S. Toy. il *Business Week* p100 Ap 10 '89

Nissan's Porsche-chaser [GT-R coupe and Skyline series] J. K. Yamaguchi. *Road & Track* 41:162-3 S '89

Porsche 944. il *Road & Track* 40:58-60 Ap '89

Porsche 944 S2. J. Karr. il *Motor Trend* 41:60-3+ Ag '89

Porsche 944 S2. B. Nagy. il *Motor Trend* 41:82-5 F '89

Porsche 944S2. R. Hutton. il *Car and Driver* 34:28 F '89

Porsche 959. P. Bingham. il *Motor Trend* 41:74-9+ Ja '89

Porsches in Provence [Carrera 4, 944 S2 and 911 Turbo; cover story] il *Road & Track* 40:42-53 F '89

Porsche's performance panoply. L. Griffin. il *Car and Driver* 35:40-1 Ag '89

The rites of spring. T. Swan. il *Popular Mechanics* 166:61-4+ Mr '89

Sizzling performance—without sticker shock [Plymouth Turbo Laser, Nissan 240SX and Mitsubishi Eclipse] S. Toy and W. J. Hampton. il *Business Week* p105 F 6 '89

Ten best cars. W. Jeanes. il *Car and Driver* 34:30-5 Ja '89

Three vintage Vettes [1957, 1965, and 1967 models] P. Lyons. il *Car and Driver* 34:64-5+ Je '89

Two-seat heat [Nissan 300ZX, Mazda RX-7 and Porsche 944 S2] D. Sherman. il *Popular Science* 235:38-40+ S '89

Two times four equals great [Ford Mustang and Probe, Honda Prelude, Mazda MX-6, Mitsubishi Eclipse Turbo, Nissan 240SX, Subaru XT6 and Toyota Celica GT-S; cover story] C. Csere. il *Car and Driver* 35:36-9+ Jl '89

Volkswagen Corrado. P. Bedard. il *Car and Driver* 35:125-7+ N '89

Volkswagen Corrado. F. M. H. Gregory. il *Motor Trend* 41:112-13+ D '89

Volkswagen Corrado. J. R. Nerad. il *Motor Trend* 41:110-12 Mr '89

Volkswagen Corrado G60. il *Road & Track* 41:66-70 N '89

Volkswagen Corrado G60. C. Csere. il *Car and Driver* 34:119-22+ Ja '89

World's best cars [Ferrari Testarossa, Mazda MX-5 Miata, Mercedes-Benz 300E, Corvette ZR-1, and Porsche 911 Carrera 4; cover story] il *Road & Track* 40:40-51 Jl '89

Transmission

Last chance CAFE [purpose of skipshift device in 1989 Corvette] J. R. Nerad. il *Motor Trend* 41:16-17 Ja '89

SPORTS CARS, RACING See Automobiles, Racing

SPORTS CARS, REMODELED See Automobiles, Remodeled

SPORTS CARS, USED See Automobiles, Used

SPORTS CENTER (DATABASE)

Hello, sports fans! P. Scisco. il *Compute!* 11:6 Je '89

SPORTS CLOTHES See Clothing and dress—Sports clothes

SPORTS CLUB. LA See Health clubs

SPORTS CLUBS

See also

Fifty-Plus Runners Association

Hash House Harriers (Organization)

National Brotherhood of Skiers

Creating a racquet [Martha's Vineyard Racquet & Fitness Club] B. W. O'Connor. il *Black Enterprise* 19:54-5 Jl '89

Good reasons to join a ski club [northern California clubs] il *Sunset (Central West edition)* 183:27 D '89

SPORTS DRINKS

Drink to your health [runners] J. Stifler. il *Runner's World* 24:72-6+ Jl '89

Locking up the weekend warriors [marketing of Gatorade] J. Levine. il *Forbes* 144:234-5 O 2 '89

Performance plus? K. McCleary. il *Health (New York, N.Y.)* 21:88-9 Mr '89

Revival of the fittest [cyclists] E. Coleman. *Bicycling* 30:128 Je '89

SPORTS EQUIPMENT See Sporting goods

SPORTS FACILITIES

In the public interest: recreational facilities [Architectural record annual awards program] M. F. Schmertz. *Architectural Record* 177:9 Mr '89

SPORTS FANS

See also

Baseball fans

Basketball fans

Football fans

Hockey fans

Horse racing fans

Soccer fans

Tennis fans

Don't ban the banners. R. Telander. por *Sports Illustrated* 71:100 O 30 '89

A show of fans [Boston Marathon] C. Negron. il *Runner's World* 24:38-9 Jl '89

Anecdotes, facetiae, satire, etc.

A view to a thrill [watching the Boston Marathon] F. Reese. il *Runner's World* 24:120 Ap '89

SPORTS GLOVES See Gloves

SPORTS HALLS OF FAME

See also

International Motorsports Hall of Fame

International Swimming Hall of Fame

Naismith Memorial Basketball Hall of Fame

National Baseball Hall of Fame and Museum

National Bowling Hall of Fame and Museum

Pro Football Hall of Fame

Women's Sports Hall of Fame

Halls of fame. R. Bongartz. il *Americana* 17:56-9 My/Je '89

SPORTS ILLUSTRATED (PERIODICAL)

25th anniversary swimsuit issue. il *Sports Illustrated* 70 Special Issue:20-4+ F '89

35th anniversary. il *Sports Illustrated* 71 Special Issue:8-10+ N 15 '89

The fanciest dive [swimsuit issue] J. Adler. il *Newsweek* 113:53-4 F 13 '89

From the publisher. D. J. Barr. See issues of Sports Illustrated beginning December 9, 1985

No swimsuits [reporting on a Sports illustrated preview party] *The New Yorker* 65:31-2 F 20 '89

SI's swimsuit issue: more than meets the eye. D. Lieberman. il *Business Week* p52 Ja 16 '89

Tapping a market [swimsuit magazines] J. DeMont. il *Maclean's* 102:28 F 20 '89

SPORTS ILLUSTRATED FOR KIDS BOOKS

Time Warner trade publishing announces kick-off of Sports Illustrated for Kids Books. J. Schnol. il *Publishers Weekly* 236:27+ O 27 '89

SPORTS IN ART

See also

Baseball in art

Golf in art

Collectors and collecting

Art: sporting prints [19th century] A. Berman. il *Architectural Digest* 46:210-15+ Ap '89

SPORTS IN LITERATURE

See also

Baseball in literature

Boxing in literature

SPORTS IN MOTION PICTURES

See also

Baseball in motion pictures

SPORTS JOURNALISM

See also

Football players—Press relations

The daily double [turf writers A. Beyer and S. Crist] G. Norman. il pors *Sports Illustrated* 70:92-6+ Je 5 '89

Hazard to your health [columnist excoriated after criticizing Georgia Tech's handling of violent incident involving football players] R. S. Johnson. por *Sports Illustrated* 70:77 F 27 '89

Hype. B. Newman. il *Sports Illustrated* 70:60-4+ Ja 23 '89

Let the words wobble. F. Deford. por *Sports Illustrated* 70:120 My 8 '89

My wife, the sportswriter. M. Winerip. il *Glamour* 87:188 Jl '89

The sportswriters' big drug coverup [government push to improve Canada's Olympics performance] A. Fotheringham. il *Maclean's* 102:68 Ap 24 '89

The write stuff [track columnist D. Patrick] B. Wischnia. il pors *Runner's World* 24:34-5+ Mr '89

SPORTS LITERATURE

See also

Publishers and publishing—Sports literature

SPORTS MANAGEMENT See Sports—Organization and administration

SPORTS MASCOTS See Mascots

SPORTS MEDICINE

See also

American College of Sports Medicine

Running—Accidents and injuries

Skiing—Accidents and injuries

Tennis—Accidents and injuries

Sports medicine. See issues of Outdoor Life

Sports medicine. See issues of Women's Sports & Fitness

When it's all pain and no gain, a sports medicine doctor may help—at a price. B. Hager. il *Money* 18:171-2 S '89

When to see a sports doc. S. Findlay. bibl il *U.S. News & World Report* 107:56-8 Jl 31 '89

Which doctor? G. Sheehan. il *Runner's World* 24:14 F '89

SPORTS NETWORK

The show moves on [move from pay TV to basic cable] D. Turbide. il *Maclean's* 102:65-6 S 4 '89

SPORTS NEWS NETWORK (CABLE TELEVISION)

Piano's latest tune: Sports News Network. J. Stilson. il por *Channels (New York, N.Y.: 1986)* 9:15 S '89

Sports news ad nauseum. B. Shapiro. il *Sport (New York, N.Y.)* 80:11 D '89

SPORTS NEWSLETTERS

See also

Basketball newsletters

SPORTS NEWSPAPERS
See also
National (Newspaper)
SPORTS OFFICIATING
See also
Baseball, Professional—Umpiring
Football, Professional—Officiating
Instant replay (Sports)
SPORTS RECORDS
See also
Baseball records
Basketball records
Boat speed records
Cycling records
Football records
High jumping records
Hockey records
Horse racing records
Hunting records
Hurdle racing records
Marathon running records
Running records
Softball records
Swimming records
Track and field athletics records
Triathlon records
SPORTS SHOE INDUSTRY See Shoe industry
SPORTS SHOES See Footwear
SPORTS SPAS See Health resorts, watering places, etc.
SPORTS TICKETS
You could fill a stadium with some season-ticket waiting
lists. G. Castle. il Sport (New York, N.Y.) 80:13 Ap '89
Prices
Who pays these salaries? You do, of course. T. Mulgannon.
il Sport (New York, N.Y.) 80:94 Je '89
Scalping
See Ticket selling—Ethical aspects
SPORTS TONIGHT [television program] See Television
program reviews—Single works
SPORTS UNIFORMS
See also
Baseball, Professional—Uniforms
Horse racing—Uniforms
Color
Dark forces [impact of black uniforms on temper of a team;
research by Tom Gilovich and Mark G. Frank] S. Boxer.
il Sports Illustrated 70:52-4+ Ap 17 '89
Numbers
The heavenly hundred: which numbers should be retired
in whose honor. R. Reilly. por Sports Illustrated 70:104
My 22 '89
SPORTS VIDEO GAMES See Video games
SPORTS WRITING See Sports journalism
SPORTSCASTERS See Cable television—Sports; Radio broad-
casting—Sports; Television broadcasting—Sports
SPORTSCENTER [television program] See Television program
reviews—Single works
SPORTSCHANNEL AMERICA
Left out in the cold [National Hockey League TV rights]
A. Murphy. il Sports Illustrated 70:81 F 20 '89
SPORTSMANSHIP
See also
Football, Professional—Ethical aspects
Tennis—Tournaments—Ethical aspects
SPORTSMEN See Athletes; Fishermen; Hunters
SPORTSWOMEN See Women athletes
SPORTSWRITING See Sports journalism
SPOT (ARTIFICIAL SATELLITES)
Commercial satellites [used for spying; cover story; special
section] bibl f il map The Bulletin of the Atomic Scientists
45:12-16+ S '89
Decaying orbit [possible Landsat/Spot satellite merger] E.
Corcoran. il Scientific American 260:72-3 Mr '89
French approval of Spot 4 ensures earth imaging services
through 1990s. J. M. Lenorovitz. il Aviation Week &
Space Technology 131:43 Ag 14 '89
Landsat/Spot merger talks spark debate on commercial space
venture [with editorial comment] C. Covault. il Aviation
Week & Space Technology 130:7, 20-1 Ja 23 '89
Magnitude of late Quaternary left-lateral displacements along
the north edge of Tibet [images of the Altyn Tagh fault]
G. Peltzer and others. bibl f il maps Science 246:1285-9
D 8 '89
Space cameras and security risks [use of Spot satellite for
spying; views of Carnegie Endowment for Peace] E. Mar-
shall. Science 243:472-3 Ja 27 '89
SPOT REMOVAL See Stain removal
SPOTNITZ, FRANK
The hottest dead man in Hollywood. il pors American Film
14:40-4+ Jl/Ag '89
Stick it in your ear. il American Film 15:40-5 O '89
What next? il American Film 14:28-35 Ja/F '89
SPOTSYLVANIA, BATTLE OF, 1864
1864. A. Nielsen. il American Heritage 40:34-6 My/Je '89
The object at hand [bullet-riddled tree stump from the
Spotsylvania battlefield at the National Museum of Ameri-
can History] M. Kernan. il Smithsonian 20:24+ My '89

SPOTTED BASS FISHING See Bass fishing
SPOTTED ELK, CLARA
Skeletons in the attic. il Scholastic Update (Teachers' edition)
121:25 My 26 '89
SPOTTED OWLS See Owls
SPOTTISWOODE, ROGER
about
Turner & Hooch [film] Reviews
Newsweek il 114:56 Ag 14 '89. D. Ansen
People Weekly il 32:11 Ag 7 '89. R. Novak
Time il 134:54 Ag 7 '89. R. Schickel
SPRAINS
RICE as a side dish [rest, ice, compression, elevation]
Women's Sports & Fitness 11:54 O '89
What can be done about knee injuries? [skiers' anterior
cruciate ligament sprains] C. Ettlinger. il Skiing 41:85-7+
Mr '89
SPRATT, CHRISTOPHER E.
On the trail of a meteorite. il Astronomy 17:70-6 Ag '89
Return of a bright comet. il Astronomy 17:76-7 Jl '89
SPRATT, JOHN M., JR.
Should the Congress adopt the "Textile and Apparel Trade
Act of 1987"? [excerpts from address, September 16, 1987]
Congressional Digest 68:28+ Ja '89
SPRAY PAINTING See Paint spraying and sprayers
SPRAYING AND DUSTING
See also
Airplanes in agriculture
Herbicides
Pesticides
SPRAYING EQUIPMENT
See also
Glue guns
Paint spraying and sprayers
Pressure washers
Bantamweight sprayers, heavyweight results [ATV sprayers]
D. Mowitz and C. Finck. il Successful Farming 87:66N-66O
F '89
Keep-it-simple sprayer boom. D. Mowitz. il Successful
Farming 87 no4:64AF Mr '89
New idea for Uni's [harvesters become chemical sprayers]
D. Mowitz. il Successful Farming 87:34AC mid-F '89
Sprayer controllers. C. Finck. il Successful Farming 87:14-15
mid-F '89
Sprayer made fancy. D. Mowitz. il Successful Farming
87:64AF Ap '89
Triple-action spray caddy. M. Holmberg. il Successful Farming
87:48T N '89
Workhorse sprayers. D. Mowitz and C. Finck. il Successful
Farming 87:50R-50S Ja '89
SPRAYS, NASAL See Nasal sprays
SPREADS (FOOD)
See also
Butter
Pouring it on for good health [Cheez Whiz spread found
to contain altered fatty acids which may help in cancer
prevention] il Newsweek 113:70 Mr 6 '89
Toasts and spreads, Italian style . . . three combinations.
il Sunset (Central West edition) 183:146 N '89
SPREADSHEETS (COMPUTER PROGRAMS)
See also
VisiCalc (Computer program)
Consultant in a bind [business modeling program Compete!]
D. Churbuck. il por Forbes 144:285-6 N 13 '89
Lotus at war [cover story; with editorial comment by Fred
Abatemarco] J. Schwartz. il Personal Computing 13:5, 70-5+
Je '89
Managing costs with Excel [home-based construction consul-
tant R. West] K. J. Novak. il Home Office Computing
7:32+ N '89
Order from chaos [creating templates] D. McNeill. il Compute!
11:40-5 F '89
The spreadsheet that nearly wore Lotus out [Release 3]
K. H. Hammonds. il por Business Week p62-4 Jl 3 '89
Spreadsheets. See occasional issues of Personal Computing
beginning July 1987
Ten years of rows and columns. T. R. Licklider. il Byte
14:324-5+ D '89
What not doing Windows costs Lotus. K. H. Hammonds.
il Business Week p152 O 30 '89
Patents
Software: in for a patent pounding? M. Galen. Business
Week p30-1 Ag 28 '89
Testing
Excel processes words (as well as numbers). R. Krumm.
il Home Office Computing 7:36-7 F '89
The flying spreadsheet [WingZ] D. E. Crabb. il Byte 14:207-8+
Jl '89
For power users only [Lotus 1-2-3 release 3.0] E. Reno.
il Byte 14:255-6+ N '89
Full Impact. D. Gabaldon. Byte 14:211-12+ F '89
Full Impact for full reports. C. H. Gajeway. il Home Office
Computing 7:22-3 Ag '89
Mouse-ability for 1-2-3 users [MarqNavigator release 2.01,
version 1.30] M. Antonoff. il Personal Computing 13:206
Mr '89
Not quite as simple as 1-2-3 [Lotus 1-2-3 release 3.0] A.
Reinhardt. il Byte 14:90-1 S '89

SPREADSHEETS (COMPUTER PROGRAMS)— Testing — *cont.*

Numbers Up. H. F. Beechhold. *Home Office Computing* 7:70-1 Ap '89

Numbers Up. D. Stanton. il *Compute!* 11:70-1+ Ag '89

OS/2 gets a spreadsheet [Excel for OS/2 with Presentation Manager] A. Reinhardt. il *Byte* 14:81 N '89

PowerMouse courts 1-2-3 users. M. Wiggins. il *Byte* 14:290+ N '89

Software despotism: truth and fiction [Guns & Butter supply and demand video game and Allways utility for Lotus 1-2-3] E. Shapiro. il *Byte* 14:143-4 My '89

Soup up Lotus 1-2-3 with five inexpensive utility programs. R. Kendall. il *Home Office Computing* 7:26+ Ap '89

Spreadsheet-driven presentation tool [Wingz] S. R. Reed. il *Personal Computing* 13:186 S '89

Spreadsheet software. il *Personal Computing* 13:135-40+ N '89

Spreadsheet wars and system wars [Lotus 1-2-3 vs. SuperCalc] J. Pournelle. *Byte* 14:112+ D '89

Sprucing up your Lotus 1-2-3 spread sheets [Allways report generator] H. S. Dashefsky. il *Personal Computing* 13:208+ Mr '89

SuperCalc 5 tries hard to do it all. J. Blackford. il *Personal Computing* 13:182+ Jl '89

VROOMM goes the spreadsheet [Virtual Real-Time Object Oriented Memory Manager for Quattro] R. Malloy. *Byte* 14:111-12 O '89

SPRECHER, PAUL
about
Psycho drama. P. Hoban. il pors *New York* 22:40-2+ Je 19 '89

SPRING
See also
April
June
May
Eskimo spring [Pond Inlet, N.W.T.] il map *National Geographic World* 166:26-31 Je '89
Spring. E. Hoagland. *The Nation* 248:836 Je 19 '89

SPRING BREAK *See* College students—Recreation

SPRING COOKING *See* Cooking

SPRING TRAINING (BASEBALL) *See* Baseball, Professional—Spring training

SPRINGER, DAN
Hill showdown: a year of decision [cover story] il *Channels (New York, N.Y.: 1986)* 9:64-7 Ja '89

SPRINGER, ILENE
Strong-arm tactics. il *Modern Maturity* 32:74-6 O/N '89

SPRINGER, KARL
about
Déco interpretations: Karl Springer on the Upper East Side. J. Thurman. il por *Architectural Digest* 46:228-35 N '89

SPRINGER, MORRIS
A flight of nightingales. il *Opera News* 53:20-3 F 18 '89

SPRINGER SPANIELS *See* Spaniels

SPRINGER-VERLAG GMBH & CO. KG
Springer-Verlag's 25 years in New York. M. Sexton. il *Publishers Weekly* 236:434+ Ag 11 '89

SPRINGFIELD (ILL.)
Historic houses, sites, etc.
See also
Lincoln Home National Historic Site (Ill.)
From the publisher. D. K. Graham. *Antiques & Collecting Hobbies* 94:6 Je '89
"Here I have lived". G. C. Ward. il map *American Heritage* 40:70-1 Ap '89
Mr. Lincoln's Springfield. W. T. Anderson. il *American History Illustrated* 24:26-31 Mr '89

SPRINGS
See also
Hot springs
Plaster Creek, Indiana [seep springs] R. H. Mohlenbrock. il maps *Natural History* p98-100 N '89

SPRINGS (MECHANISM)
See also
Automobiles—Springs and suspension

SPRINGSTEEN, BRUCE
about
The Boss announces a layoff on E Street, but is it a halt or a hiatus? il por *People Weekly* 32:207-8 D 4 '89
Bruce Springsteen. R. Reilly. il por *People Weekly* 32 Special Issue:74-5 Fall '89
Magical tours. J. Cocks. il por *Time* 133:59 Ja 23 '89
My girlfriend dreams about other men. B. Patrick. il por *Glamour* 87:230 D '89
Small-screen Springsteen. L. Meredith. il por *Stereo Review* 54:110 Je '89

SPRINGUT, MILTON
Trademark double-bind eased. il *High Technology Business* 9:4 N/D '89

SPRINT (WORD PROCESSOR PROGRAM) *See* Word processors and processing—Programming

SPRINT COMMUNICATIONS *See* US Sprint Communications Inc.

SPRINTING *See* Track and field athletics

SPROCKETT, DOC
Gone fishing. *Flower and Garden* 33:104-7 Ja/F '89

How to be a good service customer. *Flower and Garden* 33:98-100+ Mr/Ap '89
Organizing Neighborhood Cooperative Machine Maintenance Day. *Flower and Garden* 33:50-1 Jl/Ag '89
Tools for the beginner. il *Flower and Garden* 33:46 N/D '89

SPRUCE
Air pollution and forest decline in a spruce (Picea abies) forest [West Germany] E.-D. Schulze. bibl f il map *Science* 244:776-83 My 19 '89

SPRUCE CREEK (PA.)
Anatomy of a fish kill. J. Bashline. il *Field & Stream* 93:38+ F '89

SPURGEON, DAVID
International co-operation in space. il *The Unesco Courier* 42:48-9 Ag '89

SPUTUM
Fighting cancer [use of monoclonal antibodies to detect lung cancer cells] il *Prevention (Emmaus, Pa.)* 41:16+ Mr '89

SPX (FIRM)
A poison-pill play that may pay off. G. G. Marcial. *Business Week* p86 Ja 23 '89

SPY (PERIODICAL)
Spy anxiety [cover story] J. DeParle. il *The Washington Monthly* 21:10-14+ F '89
Spy anxiety. J. DeParle. il *Utne Reader* p38-9 My/Je '89
Spying on 'Spy' [cover story] D. Blum. il pors *New York* 22:32-41 Ap 17 '89

SPY PLANES *See* Airplanes, Military

SPY SATELLITES *See* Artificial satellites—Military use

SPY STORIES
Merger mystery [book by D. Aaron] B. Van Voorst. il por *Time* 133:54 F 27 '89
Authorship
Spies who come in from the cold war [interview with J. Le Carré] V. Orlik. il por *World Press Review* 36:28+ O '89
The thawing of the old spymaster [interview with J. le Carré] A. P. Sanoff. il por *U.S. News & World Report* 106:59-61 Je 19 '89
Bibliography
Spies & thrillers. N. Callendar. See occasional issues of The New York Times Book Review beginning November 6, 1988

SQL (STRUCTURED QUERY LANGUAGE) *See* Structured Query Language (Computer language)

SQUADRON, HOWARD
Talking back to Jackie. il por *New York* 22:41 O 16 '89

SQUARE D CO.
Blocking, tackling and fumbling. C. Siler. por *Forbes* 143:92 My 29 '89

SQUARES (CARPENTRY EQUIPMENT) *See* Carpenters' squares

SQUARING OF THE CIRCLE *See* Circle-squaring

SQUASH (SPORT)
The short good-bye [career of A. McConnell] C. Shmerler. *Women's Sports & Fitness* 11:56 Jl/Ag '89

SQUASHES
See also
Cooking—Vegetables
About squash. S. Pacher. il *The Mother Earth News* 119:26-30+ S/O '89
Good gosh, winter squash! J. Taylor. il *Better Homes and Gardens* 67:152 O '89
Anecdotes, facetiae, satire, etc.
Tomatoes: a tragedy [planting with zucchini] K. O'Donnell, Jr. il por *Organic Gardening* 36:79 S '89

SQUATTER SETTLEMENTS
Brazil
Death without weeping [mother love in shantytowns of Brazil] N. Scheper-Hughes. *Natural History* p8+ O '89
Vieques Island (Puerto Rico)
Squatters take on the Navy. D. Ramirez. il *The Progressive* 53:36 S '89

SQUATTERS' RIGHTS *See* Adverse possession

SQUATTING (EXERCISE)
Not explainable [A. Furman seeks record for speed squatting] *The New Yorker* 65:25-7 F 27 '89

SQUIBB CORP.
Filling Bristol-Myers' prescription [Squibb merger] J. Weber, Jr. and S. Benway. il pors *Business Week* p80-1 Ag 14 '89
Friendly medicine [merger of Bristol-Myers and Squibb] *Time* 134:39 Ag 7 '89

SQUID
In pursuit of the suburban squid [Puget Sound] R. C. Anderson and J. E. Vanderwerff. il *Sea Frontiers* 35:165-9 My/Je '89
Squid. P. G. Rodhouse. il map *Sea Frontiers* 35:206-11 Jl/Ag '89
Nervous system
See Nervous system—Mollusks

SQUID FISHERIES
Antarctic regions
Squid. P. G. Rodhouse. il map *Sea Frontiers* 35:206-11 Jl/Ag '89

SQUID FISHERIES—*cont.*
Texas
A squid for all seasons [cultured for axon research] M. Kemp. il *Discover* 10:66-70 Je '89
SQUID IN ART
Exhibitions
Armed and fiberglass [B. Cassilly sculpts squid for St. Louis Zoo's Living World pavilion] B. Weber. il por *The New York Times Magazine* p86 Ap 16 '89
SQUIDS (SUPERCONDUCTING QUANTUM INTERFERENCE DEVICES)
Biomagnetism attracts diverse crowd. R. P. Crease. il *Science* 245:1041-3 S 8 '89
Recording and interpretation of cerebral magnetic fields. R. Hari and O. V. Lounasmaa. bibl f il *Science* 244:432-6 Ap 28 '89
SQUIERS, CAROL, 1948-
Surreal to real. il por *Vogue* 179:214+ F '89
SQUIRREL HUNTING
A squirrel call that works. M. Pearce. il *Outdoor Life* 184:76-7+ S '89
SQUIRRELS
See also
Ground squirrels
Biology versus astronomy: the battle for Mount Graham [impact of proposed observatory on red squirrels] E. Pennisi. il *BioScience* 39:10-13 Ja '89
Those high I.Q. squirrels. A. B. C. Whipple. il *Reader's Digest* 135:128-30 N '89
Food and feeding
Cache economy of the gray squirrel. L. Jacobs. il *Natural History* p40-7 O '89
SQUYRES, STEVEN W.
Searching for the waters of Mars [cover story] il *Astronomy* 17:20-8 Ag '89
(jt. auth) See Jankowski, David G., and Squyres, Steven W.
SRA LIFE SCIENCES (FIRM)
Getting in on the biotech revolution. F. Brown, Jr. *American Visions* 4:12+ Je '89
SRAGOW, MICHAEL
Darkness at the edge of Towne. il por *American Film* 14:40-5+ Ja/F '89
When directors get personal. il *American Film* 14:64-6 My '89
SRI LANKA
See also
Forecasting—Study and teaching—Sri Lanka
Foreign correspondents—Sri Lanka
Paleontology—Sri Lanka
Youth—Sri Lanka
Defenses
See also
India—Army—Forces in Sri Lanka
Politics and government
See also
Elections—Sri Lanka
My half year of living dangerously. W. McGowan. il *Gentlemen's Quarterly* 59:152-7+ Ja '89
Political decay in Sri Lanka. R. Oberst. bibl f il *Current History* 88:425-8+ D '89
SRINIVASAN, SEETHA
(jt. auth) See Cole, Hunter, and Srinivasan, Seetha
SROS *See* Single room occupancy hotels
SSANGYONG GROUP
His father's son [Kim Suk-won] A. Tanzer. il por *Forbes* 143:148+ My 29 '89
SSC *See* Superconducting Super Collider
SSC & B: LINTAS
See also
Lintas: Worldwide (Firm)
SSMC INC.
Forging new links [Semi-Tech's bid] T. Fennell. il pors *Maclean's* 102:26-8 F 20 '89
Who is James Ting and what will he buy next? C. Hawkins. il por *Business Week* p33 F 13 '89
SSP *See* Society for Scholarly Publishing (U.S.)
SST (SUPERSONIC TRANSPORT) *See* Airplanes, Supersonic
ST. BARTHÉLEMY (GUADELOUPE) *See* Saint Barthélemy (Guadeloupe)
ST. CROIX (VIRGIN ISLANDS OF THE U.S.) *See* Saint Croix (Virgin Islands of the U.S.)
ST. DOMINIC, ORDER OF *See* Dominicans (Religious order)
ST. ETIENNE GALLERY *See* Galerie St. Etienne
ST. HELENA (CALIF.) *See* Saint Helena (Calif.)
ST. JAMES, LYN
Car smarts. See occasional issues of Seventeen beginning February 1987 through April 1989
about
Driving. M. Schmich. il *Vogue* 179:162 Je '89
In high gear. B. Goodwin. il por *Harper's Bazaar* 122:50-3+ Jl '89
ST. JAMES THEATRE (NEW YORK, N.Y.)
Nearly remarkable [rock singer L. Reed gives concert in Broadway's St. James Theatre, famous for hit musicals] *The New Yorker* 65:29-30 My 22 '89

ST. JOHN, BONNIE *See* Saint John, Bonnie
ST. JOHN (N.B.) *See* Saint John (N.B.)
ST. JOHN (VIRGIN ISLANDS OF THE U.S.) *See* Saint John (Virgin Islands of the U.S.)
ST. JOHN-FOSTER, KEITH EDWARD *See* Aphelion
ST. JOHN'S (NFLD.) *See* Saint John's (Nfld.)
ST. LAURENT, YVES *See* Saint Laurent, Yves
ST. LOUIS (MO.) *See* Saint Louis (Mo.)
ST. LOUIS POST-DISPATCH (NEWSPAPER)
Here comes the Sun, spoiling for a fight in St. Louis. J. E. Ellis. il por *Business Week* p48 S 25 '89
Why Ingersoll picked St. Louis [Sun to compete with Post-dispatch] J. Heins. il por *Forbes* 144:52+ Jl 24 '89
ST. LOUIS SUN (NEWSPAPER)
Here comes the Sun, spoiling for a fight in St. Louis. J. E. Ellis. il por *Business Week* p48 S 25 '89
A media baron's suburban strategy [R. Ingersoll to launch daily paper] A. Gabor. il por map *U.S. News & World Report* 106:49-50 Ap 24 '89
Sun-rise in St. Louis. W. A. Henry. il por *Time* 134:60 S 25 '89
Why Ingersoll picked St. Louis [Sun to compete with Post-dispatch] J. Heins. il por *Forbes* 144:52+ Jl 24 '89
ST. LOUIS ZOO
Armed and fiberglass [B. Cassilly sculpts squid for Living World pavilion] B. Weber. il por *The New York Times Magazine* p86 Ap 16 '89
ST. LUCIA *See* Saint Lucia
ST. MARKS BOOKSTORE (NEW YORK, N.Y.) *See* Booksellers and bookselling—New York (State)
ST. MARTIN *See* Saint Martin
ST. MORITZ (SWITZERLAND) *See* Saint Moritz (Switzerland)
ST. NAPA (CYPRUS) *See* Saint Napa (Cyprus)
ST. PAUL (MINN.) *See* Saint Paul (Minn.)
ST. PIERRE, BRIAN
Wine and dine in the vineyards. il *New Choices for the Best Years* 29:50-1 Ja '89
ST. THOMAS (VIRGIN ISLANDS OF THE U.S.) *See* Saint Thomas (Virgin Islands of the U.S.)
ST. VINCENT, KATHARINE
The year I met Santa. il pors *Good Housekeeping* 209:62+ D '89
ST. VINCENT'S SCHOOL FOR BOYS (SAN RAFAEL, CALIF.)
Architectural discovery just off U.S. 101 in Marin. il *Sunset (Central West edition)* 181:48 D '88
STAAR, RICHARD FELIX, 1923-
Communism at the crossroads in Eastern Europe. il *USA Today (Periodical)* 117:46-7 My '89
Poland: renewal or stagnation? bibl f il *Current History* 88:373-6+ N '89
STAB IN THE BACK (TERM)
Stab in the back. W. Safire. il *The New York Times Magazine* p12+ My 21 '89
STACEY, MICHELLE
Profiles [A. W. Read] por *The New Yorker* 65:51-3+ S 4 '89
STACEY Q *See* Q, Stacey
STACHEL, JOHN
Did Einstein espouse his spouse's ideas? [discussion of May 1987 article, Einstein and ether drift experiments] il *Physics Today* 42:9+ F '89
STACK, ROBERT
about
Is flashing 'the great stone face' such a crime? B. Davidson. il pors *TV Guide* 37:12-14 Ag 26-S 1 '89
STACK, WALT, 1907-
about
Spry energy. J. Brant. il pors *Runner's World* 24:30-2 My '89
STACKHOUSE, JOHN G., JR.
A tour among the evangelicals. *The Christian Century* 106:529-30+ My 17 '89
STACKHOUSE, MAX L.
Capitalism and technology in global perspective: a dispute [discussion of May 3, 1989 article, The theological challenge of globalization] *The Christian Century* 106:690-3 Jl 19-26 '89
Rauschenbusch today: the legacy of a loving prophet [cover story] *The Christian Century* 106:75-8 Ja 25 '89
The theological challenge of globalization [cover story] il *The Christian Century* 106:468-71 My 3 '89
about
Why should anyone believe? Apologetics and theological education. D. M. Campbell. *The Christian Century* 106:136-8 F 1-8 '89
STACKHOUSE, PAT
Her son: the vice president. il por *The Saturday Evening Post* 261:28+ My/Je '89
STADD, COURTNEY
The launch triad. il *Ad Astra* 1:3 Mr '89
STADIUM MODELS
Hockey night in Battle Creek [R. Gibson builds facsimile of Montreal Forum] S. Rushin. il por *Sports Illustrated* 70:14 Mr 27 '89
STADIUMS
See also
Anaheim Stadium

STADIUMS—See also—*cont.*
Candlestick Park (San Francisco, Calif.)
Joe Robbie Stadium (Miami, Fla.)
Kokernot Field (Alpine, Tex.)
Montreal Forum
Pilot Field (Buffalo, N.Y.)
Spectrum (Philadelphia, Pa.)
Tennis stadiums
Wrigley Field (Chicago, Ill.)
Field of fancy, field of dreams [contrasting SkyDome with plans for Baltimore's new old-fashioned ballpark] J. Adler. il *Newsweek* 113:66-7 Je 19 '89
LA stadia. B. Pesta. il *Sport (New York, N.Y.)* 80:24-5 Ja '89
Plans [work of the Osborn Engineering Company] *The New Yorker* 65:34-5 S 18 '89
Play ball—if you don't mind quicksand, the Green Monster or zippers underfoot [ballparks] H. M. Rosenthal. il *TV Guide* 37:8-9 Ap 15-21 '89
Save the Tiger [Detroit stadiums and arenas] J. Lapointe. *Sport (New York, N.Y.)* 80:61 My '89
Concessions (Food, etc.)
Peanuts, popcorn . . . cinnamon rolls? [sold at Anaheim Stadium] E. Cohen. il *Sport (New York, N.Y.)* 80:83 My '89
Maintenance and repair
Baseball lives [Baltimore Orioles head groundskeeper P. Santarone; excerpt] M. Bryan. il por *Sports Illustrated* 70:84-5 Ap 24 '89
Canada
See also
SkyDome (Toronto, Ont.)
The elements of surprise [lack of surprise in domed stadiums] C. Gordon. il *Maclean's* 102:11 Ag 21 '89
North America
Domes of distinction. A. Steacy. il *Maclean's* 102:46-7 Je 12 '89
STAEHLE, ALBERT
about
A stamp for Staehle. M. G. Stoddard. il por *The Saturday Evening Post* 261:28 Ap '89
STAEHLIN, JOHN H.
about
Electronics: John H. Staehlin. il por *Aviation Week & Space Technology* 130:16-17 Ja 2 '89
STAFFEL, RUDOLF, 1911-
about
Rudolf Staffel/Temple Gallery. R. Barnard. il *American Craft* 49:72-3 D '89/Ja '90
STAFFORD, KIM R.
Many pleasures without names. il *Sierra* 74:68-70 N/D '89
STAFFORD, NANCY
about
She's being watched. por *TV Guide* 37:11 Je 24-30 '89
STAFFORD, ROBERT T.
Should the Congress adopt the "High Risk Occupational Disease Notification and Prevention Act of 1987"? [excerpts from address, March 22, 1988] *Congressional Digest* 68:108+ Ap '89
STAFFORD, TIM
Beyond the stiff upper lip [excerpt from The sexual Christian] il *Christianity Today* 33:30-4 Ja 13 '89
STAFFORD, WILLIAM EDGAR, 1914-
Making the best use of a writers' workshop. *The Writer* 102:15-18 Ap '89
A memorial: son Bret [poem] *The American Scholar* 58:370 Summ '89
STAGE *See* Theater
STAGE ADAPTATIONS *See* Theatrical adaptations
STAGE COSTUME *See* Costume, Theatrical
STAGE DESIGNERS *See* Set designers
STAGE FLOORS FOR DANCE *See* Dance floors
STAGE FRIGHT
"I can't go on" [opera singers] D. G. Winer. il *Opera News* 53:14-16 Je '89
Scared speechless? How to conquer your fear of the podium. E. J. Belzer. *Working Woman* 14:17+ F '89
STAGE LIGHTING *See* Opera—Stage lighting; Theater—Stage lighting
STAGE MACHINERY *See* Theater—Stage machinery
STAGE SCENERY *See* Opera—Stage setting and scenery; Television broadcasting—Setting and scenery; Theater—Stage setting and scenery
STAGEBILL
The play's the thing. J. Zweig. il por *Forbes* 144:246 O 2 '89
STAGGERED HOURS OF LABOR *See* Flextime
STAGHORN FERNS *See* Ferns
STAHL, JOE
Into the woods. il por *World Tennis* 37:63 N '89
STAHLMAN, MARK
about
The next waves [interview] G. F. Gilder. il por *Forbes* 143:186+ Ap 17 '89
STAHNKE, WAYNE
about
The player piano makes a comeback. G. Slutsker. il por *Forbes* 144:124 S 4 '89

STAIN REMOVAL
Coping with spills and stains. *McCall's* 116:73 Ja '89
Spot check. M. Mohler and M. D. Rosen. il *Ladies' Home Journal* 106:54 Je '89
STAIN RESISTANT CARPETS *See* Rugs and carpets
STAINED GLASS *See* Glass painting and staining
STAINS, LARRY
Windows open any room. il *Good Housekeeping* 208:202+ Ap '89
STAINS, LAURENCE R. *See* Stains, Larry
STAINS AND STAINING
See also
Gilding
Graining
Floor show [rout-and-stain method] J. Truini. il *Home Mechanix* 85:74-6 D '89
Gel stains. T. O. Bakke. il *Popular Science* 234:84-5+ F '89
STAINS AND STAINING (MICROSCOPY)
See also
Fluorescent indicators in biological research
STAIR MACHINES *See* Exercising equipment
STAIRCASES *See* Stairways
STAIRWAYS
See also
Escalators
Garden steps
Hand railings
Building stairs. A. R. Gould. il *Workbench* 45:80-1 My/Je '89
New steps in the right direction [entrance stairway] il *Southern Living* 24:70 Mr '89
Nifty newel: striking new look for old entry. il *Better Homes and Gardens* 67:120 Je '89
Stair building step by step. R. Freudenberger. il *The Mother Earth News* 118:70-3 Jl/Ag '89
Stair with character. il *Southern Living* 24:109 F '89
View, storage, light . . . the stairwell is the key. il *Sunset (Central West edition)* 182:132 Je '89
Window for the stairwell. il *Sunset (Central West edition)* 182:154 Ap '89
STAKES, WALDO
about
Call me Speedo. B. Weber. il por *The New York Times Magazine* p94 Ap 9 '89
STAKING OF PLANTS *See* Plant supports
STALEY, ALLEN
Portraits by Benjamin West. bibl f il *Antiques* 135:1456-65 Je '89
STALIN, JOSEPH, 1879-1953
about
Alexander Cockburn: a voice of moderation. A. Puddington. *National Review* 41:27 N 24 '89
Coming to terms with the past. R. Conquest. il *National Review* 41:14-16 Mr 10 '89
De-Stalinizing the Soviet past [interview with Y. Afanasyev] S. F. Cohen and K. Vanden Heuvel. *Harper's* 279:32+ O '89
The great Mafia wedding [cover story] J. P. Roche. il *National Review* 41:23-4 S 1 '89
Haunted by history's horrors. G. J. Church. il por *Time* 133:71-2 Ap 10 '89
A million here, a million there. A. Cockburn. *The Nation* 248:294-5 Mr 6 '89
The night Stalin died. R. Dubinskiĭ. il *The New York Times Magazine* p42-3+ Mr 5 '89
The prince and his courtiers: at the White House, the Kremlin, and the Reichschancellery. R. Baker and C. Peters. *The Washington Monthly* 21:38+ F '89
Stalin takes the stand. E. Gellner. *The New Republic* 200:20+ Mr 20 '89
Stalin's purge of Soviet astronomers. R. A. McCutcheon. il *Sky and Telescope* 78:352-7 O '89
Stalin's victims [discussion of March 6, 1989 article, A million here, a million there] A. Cockburn. *The Nation* 249:154+ Ag 7-14 '89
The unquiet ghosts of Stalin's victims. E. H. Methvin. *National Review* 41:24-5+ S 1 '89
STALKING OF GAME *See* Hunting
STALLER, ERIC
about
Camera, lights, action! il por *National Geographic World* 165:30-5 My '89
Twinkle, twinkle, little car. B. Weber. il por *The New York Times Magazine* p82 Mr 26 '89
STALLINGS, GEORGE A., JR.
about
A black Catholic priest's renegade church stirs up an unholy furor. D. Grogan. il pors *People Weekly* 32:28-30 Jl 31 '89
Black Catholics vs. the Church. R. N. Ostling. il por *Time* 134:57 Jl 10 '89
Black priest in schism? *The Christian Century* 106:649 Jl 5-12 '89
Cardinal bars black D.C. priest from saying Mass. por *Jet* 76:5 Jl 17 '89
D.C. priest splits from Catholic Church; black bishops decry the act. *Jet* 76:12 Jl 10 '89

STALLINGS, GEORGE A., JR.—about—cont.
Equal rites. M. McGough. *The New Republic* 201:11-12 Ag 28 '89
Father Stallings' choices. *America* 161:75 Ag 12-19 '89
Heretic as hero. T. Bethell. il *The American Spectator* 22:11-13 S '89
Is a separate church the answer to blacks' prayers? D. Pitts. il por *Black Enterprise* 20:28 O '89
Priest seeks to reconcile with Catholic hierarchy; White Chicago priest backs Stallings' stand. il por *Jet* 76:16-17 Jl 24 '89
Stallings denies charge of a homosexual relationship. por *Jet* 76:38 S 25 '89
Va. priest fired after announcing plans to join separatist Catholic Church. pors *Jet* 76:26 Ag 21 '89
What's behind the black rebellion in the Catholic Church? L. B. Randolph. il pors *Ebony* 45:160-2+ N '89

STALLONE, SYLVESTER
about
Lock up [film] Reviews
People Weekly il 32:13 Ag 21 '89. R. Novak
Sly's progress [cover story] E. Kaye. il pors *Esquire* 111:96-102+ F '89

STALLS, AIRPLANE *See* Airplanes, Jet—Stalling; Airplanes, Light—Stalling; Airplanes, Military—Stalling

STALLWORTH, JOHN
about
Stallworth's time to shine. il por *Sports Illustrated* 70:86 Ja 9 '89

STAMINA *See* Endurance

STAMOS, JOHN
about
Goodbye, long hair—so long, fast times. R. Brantley. il pors *TV Guide* 37:8-10 Ag 5-11 '89

STAMP COLLECTING *See* Postage stamps—Collectors and collecting

STAMPING (CONCRETE WORK) *See* Concrete work

STAMPS, POSTAGE *See* Postage stamps

STAMPS, POSTER *See* Poster stamps

STAMPS, REVENUE *See* Revenue stamps

STAN, SUSAN
Children's book collections. il *Publishers Weekly* 236:26-8+ Ag 25 '89

STAN HERMAN AND ASSOCIATES
What do you expect for $2.25 million? D. K. Shah. il por *The New York Times Magazine* p54-6+ S 10 '89

STANCIOFF, NADIA
Perugia. il map *Gourmet* 49:70-5+ My '89

STAND AND DELIVER [film] *See* Motion picture reviews—Single works

DER STANDARD (AUSTRIA: NEWSPAPER)
A minor revolution in Austria. J. Dempsey. il *World Press Review* 36:60 Ja '89

STANDARD & POOR'S CORP.
Soothing the sting of an accounting rule [employee health benefits] L. J. Nathans. il *Business Week* p106 S 18 '89

STANDARD OF LIVING *See* Cost and standard of living

STANDARD OIL CO. OF CALIFORNIA
See also
Chevron Corporation

STANDARDIZATION
International aspects
Who sets the standards? [product standards] J. R. Hayes. il *Forbes* 143:110+ Ap 17 '89

STANDARDIZED EDUCATIONAL TESTS *See* Educational tests and measurements

STANDARDS, ELECTRIC *See* Electric standards

STANDARDS, FREQUENCY *See* Frequency standards

STANDARDS OF LENGTH
Anecdotes, facetiae, satire, etc.
With a campus legend in peril, members of a fraternity vow to save the endangered M.I.T. smoot [markings spanning the length of the Harvard Bridge created by Lambda Chi Alpha pledges] N. Geeslin. il pors *People Weekly* 31:93-5 Ap 24 '89

STANDEN, N. B., AND OTHERS
Hyperpolarizing vasodilators activate ATP-sensitive K^+ channels in arterial smooth muscle. bibl f il *Science* 245:177-80 Jl 14 '89

STANDEN, NIKA *See* Hazelton, Nika

STANDER, BELLA
The gardening passion. il *Publishers Weekly* 235:23-6+ F 10 '89

STANDIFER, VAN
about
Midnight rescue. B. A. McKee. il por *Nation's Business* 77:86 N '89

STANDING POSITION
Stand up for clearer thoughts [research by Max Vercruyssen] il *USA Today (Periodical)* 117:12 Ap '89

STANDS (FURNITURE)
See also
Valets (Furniture)

STANDS (MACHINE) *See* Machinery—Stands, tables, etc.

STANDS (ROADSIDE) *See* Roadside marketing

STANFORD, ANN
The birds and Columbus [poem] *The Atlantic* 263:46 Je '89

STANFORD, MICHAEL
The Stanford library. *The New Republic* 201:18+ O 2 '89

STANFORD LINEAR ACCELERATOR CENTER
New physics, old rivalries [SLAC vs. CERN] J. Cherfas. il *Science* 246:323-4 O 20 '89
SLAC feels the thrill of the chase [Z particles] M. M. Waldrop. il *Science* 244:771-3 My 19 '89
Zs for two: a critical mass [Fermilab vs. SLAC] M. M. Waldrop. *Science* 245:350 Jl 28 '89

STANFORD LINEAR COLLIDER *See* Accelerators (Electrons, etc.)

STANFORD UNIVERSITY
Bad vibes at Stanford [earthquake damage] C. Norman. il *Science* 246:438 O 27 '89
Black and blue, class of '89. M. Mabry. il *Newsweek* 114:50-1 S 25 '89
NIMH assigns blame for tainted studies. M. Barinaga. *Science* 245:812 Ag 25 '89
The Stanford library. M. Stanford. *The New Republic* 201:18+ O 2 '89
The view from Palo Alto [Stanford orders purging of computer humor file that includes ethnic jokes] D. Seligman. il *Fortune* 119:339+ Ap 24 '89

STANFORD UNIVERSITY. NEAR WEST SCIENCE CAMPUS
Can Stanford build labs for the new millenium? R. Buderi. il *Business Week* p115-16 D 4 '89

STANHOME INC.
Stanhome. J. Slovak. il *Fortune* 119:85 My 8 '89

STANIAR, BURTON BARRINGER, 1942-
about
A bolder Group W. J. Loftus. il por *Channels (New York, N.Y.: 1986)* 9:24-6 O '89

STANKARD, FRANCIS X.
The issue of our environment [address, August 19, 1989] *Vital Speeches of the Day* 56:84-6 N 15 '89

STANKOVIC, CHARLES J., AND OTHERS
Transmembrane channels based on tartaric acid-gramicidin A hybrids. bibl f il *Science* 244:813-17 My 19 '89

STANLEY, ALESSANDRA
All hat and no cows. il *Vogue* 179:462 Ap '89
Capitol gains. il por *Vogue* 179:496-7+ Mr '89

STANLEY, JAMIE
about
The endless winter. P. Mehlman. il pors *Gentlemen's Quarterly* 59:336-9+ Mr '89

STANLEY, LEONARD
about
A rare collection of classic Hollywood costume sketches. J. Chatfield-Taylor. il por *Architectural Digest* 46:250+ S '89

STANLEY, RICK
Remembering the King; ed. by Kent Demaret. il pors *People Weekly* 32:32-9 Ag 21 '89

STANLEY CUP *See* Hockey, Professional

STANLEY HOME PRODUCTS, INC.
See also
Stanhome Inc.

STANLIS, PETER J. (PETER JAMES), 1920-
Paleo right and natural right. *National Review* 41:44 O 27 '89

STANTON, DAVID
Discoveries. See issues of Compute! beginning May 1988

STANTON, NANCY L., AND LATTIN, JOHN D.
In defense of species. *BioScience* 39:67 F '89

STANTON, WILL
The last time he saw her [story] il *Redbook* 172:48+ F '89
Surprise ahead [story] il *McCall's* 116:113-14+ Ag '89

STANWYCK, BARBARA
about
Barbara Stanwyck. G. Peary. il pors *American Film* 14:60-3 Jl/Ag '89

STANYER, FREDERICK W.
Boscobel in Garrison-on-Hudson, New York. bibl f il *Antiques* 136:1356-65 D '89

STAPHYLOCOCCAL DISEASES
See also
Toxic shock syndrome

STAPHYLOCOCCI
Class II MHC molecules are specific receptors for staphylococcus enterotoxin A. J. A. Mollick and others. bibl f il *Science* 244:817-20 My 19 '89
Superantigens [stimulation of T cells by staphylococcal toxins; research by John Kappler and others] T. Beardsley. *Scientific American* 261:19-20 Ag '89
Vβ-specific stimulation of human T cells by staphyloccocal toxins. J. Kappler and others. bibl f il *Science* 244:811-13 My 19 '89

STAPLES, MAVIS
about
The timeless Mavis Staples. P. Garland. por *Stereo Review* 54:116 O '89

STAPLES (FIRM)
Seeking big money in paper and pens. S. Caminiti. il *Fortune* 120:173-4 Jl 31 '89

STAPLES AND STAPLING MACHINES
Fast but solid fastening. H. Wicks. il *Home Mechanix* 85:22-3+ Ja '89
STAPLETON, JOAN M.
Dame at sea. *The New Republic* 200:42 My 22 '89
STAPLETON INTERNATIONAL AIRPORT *See* Denver (Colo.)—Airports
STAPP, MARY
(jt. auth) *See* Achenbach, Joel, and Stapp, Mary
STAR CHARTS *See* Astronomy—Charts, diagrams, etc.
STAR CLUSTERS *See* Stars—Clusters
STAR HUSTLER [television program] *See* Television program reviews—Single works
STAR MAPS *See* Astronomy—Charts, diagrams, etc.
STAR PUBLICATIONS
"How did I know the guy was calling from jail?" [J. Darder implicated in penny stock fraud over disposable razor] R. L. Stern. il por *Forbes* 143:120+ My 29 '89
STAR SPANGLED BANNER (SONG)
Key on display [Maryland Historical Society] J. Nassar. il por *Americana* 17:10 N/D '89
STAR TREK
Paramount's Card Trek [special credit card issued as part of promotional campaign for Star trek] N. Koch. il *Channels (New York, N.Y.: 1986)* 9:52 F '89
Star trek: the continuing saga of a sixties sensation. D. G. Coit. il *USA Today (Periodical)* 117:88-90 Ja '89
STAR TREK V: THE FINAL FRONTIER [film] *See* Motion picture reviews—Single works
STAR WARS DEFENSE PROGRAM *See* Strategic Defense Initiative
STARCH
See also
Cornstarch
STARCK, PHILIPPE, 1950?-
about
Future perfect. B. Grauman. il por *Art News* 88:91-2 Summ '89
Rags to riches. K. D. Stein. il *Architectural Record* 177:94-5 Mr '89
The Royalton treatment. C. K. Gandee. il por *House & Garden* 161:70-7 Ja '89
Starck modern. C. K. Gandee. il por *House & Garden* 161:78-85+ Jl '89
STARDENT (FIRM)
"I love the tumult" [career of A. Michels] J. Pitta. il pors *Forbes* 144:296-8 N 13 '89
STARE DECISIS
Stare decisis and judicial restraint [address, October 17, 1989] L. F. Powell, Jr. *Vital Speeches of the Day* 56:70-3 N 15 '89
STARFISH
Crown-of-thorns no Johnny-come-lately [Great Barrier Reef; research by A. J. Timothy Jull] S. Hart. *Science News* 136:133 Ag 26 '89
Evidence from sediments of long-term Acanthaster planci predation on corals of the Great Barrier Reef [crown of thorns starfish; cover story] P. D. Walbran and others. bibl f il map *Science* 245:847-50 Ag 25 '89
Starry blight [destruction of reefs by crown of thorns starfish] K. Brower. il *Omni (New York, N.Y.)* 11:22+ My '89
STARK, CRAIG
(jt. auth) *See* Hirsch, Julian D., and Stark, Craig
STARK, ELIZABETH
Off-the-shelf salvation. il *Health (New York, N.Y.)* 21:28-30 Jl '89
STARK, H. J. LUTCHER, D. 1965
about
Lutcher Stark's third wife. W. P. Barrett. il por *Forbes* 144:216+ N 27 '89
STARK, NELDA
about
Lutcher Stark's third wife. W. P. Barrett. il por *Forbes* 144:216+ N 27 '89
STARK, STEPHEN
The right thing [story] *The New Yorker* 65:32-6 Je 5 '89
STARK FAMILY
about
Lutcher Stark's third wife. W. P. Barrett. il por *Forbes* 144:216+ N 27 '89
STARKER, JANOS, 1924-
about
The romantic cello. R. Freed. il por *Stereo Review* 54:147 D '89
STARKOV, VLADISLAV
about
Dear editor: You're fired. Signed, Mikhail Gorbachev. W. R. Doerner. il pors *Time* 134:62-3 O 30 '89
STARLIGHT FOUNDATION
Wishing on a star. L. Gross. il *McCall's* 117:64+ N '89
STARLINGS
Starling scourge [red headed woodpeckers] F. Graham. *Audubon* 91:25-7 S '89
Food and feeding
Physiological constraint on feeding behavior: intestinal membrane disaccharidases of the starling. C. Martinez del Rio and B. R. Stevens. bibl f il *Science* 243:794-6 F 10 '89

STARMITES [musical] *See* Musicals, revues, etc.—Reviews—Single works
STARNER, AL
Party animal. il *Flying* 116:100 Mr '89
STARR, BLAZE
Stripper Blaze Starr recalls her affair with the governor; ed. by Margie Bonnett Sellinger. il pors *People Weekly* 32:157+ D 18 '89
about
The cockeyed world of Ron Shelton. J. Silverman. il pors *American Film* 15:34-9+ D '89
Ron's rules of order. P. Jordan. il pors *Gentlemen's Quarterly* 59:300-5+ D '89
STARR, DOUGLAS
Brainstorms: the world's top think tanks predict the future. il *Omni (New York, N.Y.)* 12:66-70+ O '89
Civilizing the hunt. il *International Wildlife* 19:16-19 N/D '89
Desert bloom. il *Omni (New York, N.Y.)* 11:28+ Mr '89
Levitation U. il *Omni (New York, N.Y.)* 11:66-8+ My '89
The lone ranger. il *Omni (New York, N.Y.)* 12:102+ N '89
Rhino warrior. il *Omni (New York, N.Y.)* 11:17+ S '89
STARR, KENNETH W., 1946-
about
Speak softly and carry a big right-wing agenda. T. Smart. il por *Business Week* p115+ N 27 '89
STARR, KEVIN
Priming the minister. il pors *Vogue* 179:416-19+ Ap '89
STARR, PATRICIA
about
Caught in Starr wars. P. Kaihla. il pors *Maclean's* 102:12-13 Jl 3 '89
Dangerous liaisons. P. Kaihla. il pors *Maclean's* 102:20+ O 16 '89
A flurry of scandals. R. Corelli. il pors *Maclean's* 102:12-13 Jl 10 '89
STARR, RINGO
about
Ringo on the rebound [cover story] S. Dougherty. il pors *People Weekly* 32:66-9 Ag 28 '89
A Starr is reborn. D. Wild. il pors *Rolling Stone* p104-6+ Ag 24 '89
STARR, S. FREDERICK
Party animals. *The New Republic* 200:18-21 Je 26 '89
Pooped party. *The New Republic* 201:20-1 D 4 '89
A usable past. *The New Republic* 200:24+ My 15 '89
STARR PIANO COMPANY. GENNETT RECORD DIVISION
Gennett Records. S. M. Stroff. il *Antiques & Collecting Hobbies* 94:66-70 Je '89
STARS
See also
Astrology
Astronomy
Black holes (Astronomy)
Constellations
Galaxies
Herbig-Haro objects
International Star Registry
Occultations
Stellar winds
Sun
Deep-sky wonders. W. S. Houston. *See* issues of Sky and Telescope
Eight out of ten [bright winter stars] T. D. Nicholson. il *Natural History* p72-3 D '89
The magical box of stars. R. Hecker. il *Astronomy* 17:110 Ja '89
The Milky Way's third population [thick-disc stars; research by Bruce W. Carney] *Science News* 135:155 Mr 11 '89
Seeking stellar flares in a deceptive sky [research by Bradley E. Schaefer] F. Flam. *Science News* 135:118 F 25 '89
Age
Great globs of fire [age of globular clusters challenges fast collapse theory of Milky Way's birth; research by Michael Bolte and Peter Stetson] T. Waters. il *Discover* 10:26 S '89
Starburst Milky Way [research by Don C. Barry] il *Sky and Telescope* 77:589-90 Je '89
A young Milky Way? [theory of Harvey Butcher] *Sky and Telescope* 78:349-50 O '89
Atlases
Arthur P. Norton: star atlas maker. I. Ridpath. por *Sky and Telescope* 78:489 N '89
Help for star-atlas fumblers [computer program] R. Job. il *Sky and Telescope* 77:420 Ap '89
More help for star-atlas fumblers [computer program] T. B. Hunter. *Sky and Telescope* 78:298 S '89
Brightness
See Stars—Magnitudes
Charts, diagrams, etc.
See Astronomy—Charts, diagrams, etc.
Clusters
See also
Pleiades
Brown dwarf candidates abound. M. M. Waldrop. il *Science* 245:29-30 Jl 7 '89

STARS—Clusters—*cont.*

Deep-sky wonders [Castor and M35] W. S. Houston. il *Sky and Telescope* 77:338-40 Mr '89

Deep-sky wonders [open clusters] W. S. Houston. il *Sky and Telescope* 78:675-6 D '89

Dramatically diverse globulars. C. Schur. il *Astronomy* 17:90-5 My '89

Great globs of fire [age of globular clusters challenges fast collapse theory of Milky Way's birth; research by Michael Bolte and Peter Stetson] T. Waters. il *Discover* 10:26 S '89

Puzzling pulses from a star cluster's core [PSR 2127+11, located near center of M15; work of Alexander Wolszczan] I. Peterson. *Science News* 135:86 F 11 '89

Rewarding star clusters. A. Ling. il *Astronomy* 17:86-9 Ag '89

A sprinkling of distant star clusters [study of globular clusters by William E. Harris and C. J. Pritchet] I. Peterson. *Science News* 136:12 Jl 1 '89

Standout winter star clusters. A. Ling. il *Astronomy* 17:98-103 Ja '89

Color

Colored stars. J. Mitton and A. MacRobert. il *Sky and Telescope* 77:181-2 F '89

Reading the colors of the stars. C. Sneden. il *Astronomy* 17:36-45 Ap '89

A star that changed its color [HD 38451] A. MacRobert. il *Sky and Telescope* 78:629+ D '89

Distances

Moments of discovery. P. M. Leschak. il *Astronomy* 17:98 F '89

Evolution

See also
Pulsars

Active young stars in Orion [Herbig-Haro objects] il *Sky and Telescope* 78:7-8 Jl '89

'Born-again' red giant baffles astronomers. il *Astronomy* 17:10+ My '89

Gigantic gas jet points to newborn star [within Orion star-formation region; research by Bo Reipurth] I. Peterson. il *Science News* 136:55 Jl 22 '89

The hidden lives of massive stars [role of molecular clouds; research by Edward B. Churchwell and Douglas O. S. Wood] *Science News* 135:88 F 11 '89

How a star is born [Submillimeter Wave Astronomy Satellite project by Gary Melnick] K. Hartley. il *Astronomy* 17:14 D '89

Inside Orion's stellar nursery. J. Kanipe. il *Astronomy* 17:40-3 Ag '89

The Lazarus star [cloud of gas emitted from white dwarf star; research by Howard Bond] il *Discover* 10:10 My '89

A new window on star birth [submillimeter astronomy] K. Hartley. il *Astronomy* 17:32-6 Mr '89

Pride and prejudice [cosmic lithium abundance and open vs. closed universe; research by Lawrence M. Krauss] T. Rothman. *Scientific American* 261:16-17 Ag '89

Reshaping views of how young stars evolve [AS431; research by Richard J. Davis] R. Cowen. *Science News* 136:102 Ag 12 '89

Sing the asteroid electric [work of Floyd Herbert] il *Sky and Telescope* 77:356-7 Ap '89

Star formation in irregular galaxies. D. A. Hunter and J. S. Gallagher. bibl f il *Science* 243:1557-63 Mr 24 '89

A star is born. *Sky and Telescope* 77:588-9 Je '89

Starbirth's soft glow [image of star forming clouds in Cepheus; research by Adair P. Lane] il *Sky and Telescope* 78:239-40 S '89

Throwing tantrums in stellar nurseries. I. Peterson. *Science News* 136:12 Jl 1 '89

Windy setting for a big, young star. il *Science News* 136:20 Jl 8 '89

Witness to creation [computer modeling of star formation; research by Richard Durisen] il *Discover* 10:8+ D '89

Magnitudes

How faint can you see? B. E. Schaefer. il *Sky and Telescope* 77:332-3+ Mr '89

Your telescope's limiting magnitude [computer program] B. E. Schaefer. il *Sky and Telescope* 78:522-5 N '89

Motion

The double polestar of the past [computer program] A. Kammerer. il *Sky and Telescope* 77:531-3 My '89

The radial-velocity revolution. R. Griffin. il *Sky and Telescope* 78:263+ S '89

Nomenclature

See Astronomy—Nomenclature

Orbits

DI Herculis explained? *Sky and Telescope* 78:14 Jl '89

Radiation

Stars that flash [study by Bradley Schaefer] il *Sky and Telescope* 78:133-4 Ag '89

Spectra and spectroscopy

See also
B stars

Our future in the stars? [HK Project; research by Sallie L. Baliunas] M. M. Waldrop. il *Science* 243:890-1 F 17 '89

Reading the colors of the stars. C. Sneden. il *Astronomy* 17:36-45 Ap '89

STARS, DOUBLE

See also
Stars, Eclipsing binary

Binaries with sunlike stars. il *Sky and Telescope* 77:294-5 Mr '89

The case of cosmic rays [new Utah observatory to study muons from Cygnus X-3 and Hercules X-1; cover story] G. Taubes. il *Discover* 10:52-8+ S '89

Deep-sky wonders [Castor and M35] W. S. Houston. il *Sky and Telescope* 77:338-40 Mr '89

Making the Southern Crab. il *Sky and Telescope* 78:571 D '89

The never-ending nova hunt. D. H. Kaiser. *Astronomy* 17:90-1 Ap '89

Pulsars shed new light on evolution of binary stars. P. H. Andersen. *Physics Today* 42:20 Ja '89

Split a star in two. A. Goldstein. il *Astronomy* 17:88-91 D '89

A stellar teaching tool [Sirius] G. Lovi. il *Sky and Telescope* 77:287-8 Mr '89

The ten best double stars. P. Harrington. il *Astronomy* 17:78-83 Jl '89

Vigil for a unique stellar eclipse [Alpha Comae Berenices] il *Sky and Telescope* 77:180 F '89

When two stars become one [W Ursae Majoris contact binaries; research by Edward F. Guinan and David H. Bradstreet] il *Sky and Telescope* 77:239-40 Mr '89

Witness to creation [computer modeling of star formation; research by Richard Durisen] il *Discover* 10:8+ D '89

STARS, DWARF

See also
Stars, Flare

'Born-again' red giant baffles astronomers. il *Astronomy* 17:10+ My '89

Brown dwarf candidates abound. M. M. Waldrop. il *Science* 245:29-30 Jl 7 '89

Brown dwarfs caught in the heat of youth [research by William J. Forrest] I. Peterson. il *Science News* 135:399 Je 24 '89

Brown dwarfs coming and going. R. T. Fienberg. il *Sky and Telescope* 78:482-3 N '89

Brown dwarfs here . . . [research by William J. Forrest] J. Horgan. il *Scientific American* 261:28 S '89

Do brown dwarfs really exist? D. Byrd. il *Astronomy* 17:18-24 Ap '89

Dwarfs galore [brown dwarfs; research by William Forrest] il *Discover* 10:14 O '89

The Lazarus star [cloud of gas emitted from white dwarf star; research by Howard Bond] il *Discover* 10:10 My '89

New brown dwarf evidence looks promising [research by William Forrest] il *Astronomy* 17:10 S '89

Stalking the extrasolar planet [brown dwarfs] S. P. Maran. *Natural History* p70+ My '89

STARS, ECLIPSING BINARY

Black widow in shock [pulsar] *Discover* 10:12 Je '89

'Black widow' pulsar shocks neighborhood [1957+20; research by Andrew Fruchter and Jeff Hester] il *Astronomy* 17:10 Ap '89

DI Herculis explained? *Sky and Telescope* 78:14 Jl '89

Light curves and their secrets [computer program] D. Gossman. il *Sky and Telescope* 78:410-11+ O '89

Now you see it, now you don't [PG 1550 + 131; research by Reinhold Häfner] *Science News* 135:13 Ja 7 '89

On the trail of the black widow pulsar [PSR 1957+20] il *Sky and Telescope* 77:128-9 F '89

Pulsar eroding companion star [PSR 1957+20; research by Andrew Fruchter] *Astronomy* 17:10 F '89

The vanishing star [PG 1550+131; research by Reinhold Häfner] *Astronomy* 17:14+ Mr '89

Vigil for a unique stellar eclipse [Alpha Comae Berenices] il *Sky and Telescope* 77:180 F '89

STARS, FLARE

Stars that flash [study by Bradley Schaefer] il *Sky and Telescope* 78:133-4 Ag '89

STARS, GIANT

See also
Carbon stars

'Born-again' red giant baffles astronomers. il *Astronomy* 17:10+ My '89

Polar winds and excretion disks [B[e] supergiants; research by Franz-Josef Zickgraf and Roberta M. Humphreys] I. Peterson. *Science News* 136:12 Jl 1 '89

When a red giant swallows its planets [theory of Curtis Struck-Marcell] il *Sky and Telescope* 77:7 Ja '89

STARS, NEW

Australian discovers his third LMC nova [Gordon Garradd] il *Astronomy* 17:93-4 F '89

New dwarf nova soon to erupt? [FSV 113211] J. Toone. il *Sky and Telescope* 77:404-5 Ap '89

STARS, VARIABLE

See also
Stars, Flare
Supernovas

STARS, VARIABLE—*cont.*
A cosmic unveiling [T Tauri stars and planet formation; research] by Karen M. Strom] C. S. Powell. *Scientific American* 261:26-7 D '89
An extragalactic Eta Carinae? [Supernova 1961V] il *Sky and Telescope* 77:355 Ap '89
Far-out star. il *Sky and Telescope* 78:573 D '89
Mira nearing maximum [Omicron Ceti] il *Sky and Telescope* 78:400 O '89
R Arietis: a fainter Mira. il *Sky and Telescope* 78:401 O '89
A star that changed its color [HD 38451] A. MacRobert. il *Sky and Telescope* 78:629+ D '89
A trio of Big Dipper variables. il *Sky and Telescope* 77:522-3 My '89
U Orionis: a bright red variable. il *Sky and Telescope* 78:513 N '89
STARS AND STRIPES (FLAG) *See* American flag
STARS AND STRIPES (NEWSPAPER)
Doing it the Army way [charges of censorship] M. Tharp. il *U.S. News & World Report* 107:24 S 25 '89
A mutiny at Stars and stripes [complaints of censorship] *U.S. News & World Report* 106:15 Mr 6 '89
STARSHIP AIRPLANES *See* Airplanes, Business
START TALKS *See* Strategic Arms Reduction Talks
STARTING, AUTOMOBILE *See* Automobiles—Starting
STARTING, LAWN MOWER *See* Lawn mowers—Starting
STARVATION
See also
Anorexia nervosa
Famines
Malnutrition
STARZL, THOMAS E. (THOMAS EARL), 1926-
about
Maverick surgeon. M. Dowie. il pors *American Health* 8:86-9+ Je '89
STASCHAK, JANET L.
about
True confession? [excerpt from transcript of police interrogation of murder suspect T. F. Sawyer in Clearwater, Fla.] *Harper's* 279:17-20+ O '89
Untrue confessions. P. Weiss. il por *Mother Jones* 14:18-20+ S '89
STASHEFF, STEVEN F., AND OTHERS
NMDA antagonists differentiate epileptogenesis from seizure expression in an in vitro model. bibl f il *Science* 245:648-51 Ag 11 '89
STASI, LINDA
Plastic surgery: urban renewal. *Harper's Bazaar* 122:187+ Mr '89
STASIO, MARILYN
Crime. See occasional issues of The New York Times Book Review beginning September 18, 1988
A gastronome, a magician and a First Lady: detectives and their day jobs. *The New York Times Book Review* 94:49 O 15 '89
The homicidal maniac: a novelist's best friend. il *The New York Times Book Review* 94:1+ O 15 '89
STASSEN, GLEN
Schooling for democracy. *The Christian Century* 106:1199-1201 D 20-27 '89
STATE AID TO EDUCATION *See* Education—State aid
STATE AND ART *See* Art and state
STATE AND CHURCH *See* Church and state
STATE AND DANCE *See* Dance and state
STATE AND EDUCATION *See* College education and state; Education and state
STATE AND ENVIRONMENT *See* Environmental policy
STATE AND FEDERAL RELATIONS *See* Federal and state relations
STATE AND INDUSTRY *See* Industry and state
STATE AND LITERATURE *See* Literature and state
STATE AND MEDICINE *See* Medical policy
STATE AND MUSIC *See* Music and state
STATE AND POETRY *See* Poetry and state
STATE AND SCIENCE *See* Science and state
STATE AND SPORTS *See* Sports and state
STATE AND TECHNOLOGY *See* Technology and state
STATE AND THE ARTS *See* Arts and state
STATE AND THE INDIVIDUAL *See* Individual and state
STATE ATTORNEYS GENERAL *See* Attorneys general
STATE BALLET OF MISSOURI
Reviews:
February program in Kansas City. K. LaFave. *Dance Magazine* 63:53 Jl '89
STATE COLLEGES AND UNIVERSITIES *See* Colleges and universities
STATE CONSTITUTIONS
The swing to the left in state courts. T. Gest. il *U.S. News & World Report* 107:32 O 23 '89
STATE COURTS *See* Courts
STATE DEPT. (U.S.) *See* United States. Dept. of State
STATE EMPLOYEES
See also
Collective labor agreements—State employees
Illinois—Employees

STATE FARM MUTUAL AUTOMOBILE INSURANCE CO.
State Farm and Dairyland abolish superbike blacklists. T. Van Hooydonk. *Cycle* 40:23 My '89
State Farm's huge harvest in auto insurance. D. Greising. il *Business Week* p78 Ag 21 '89
STATE-FEDERAL TAX RELATIONS *See* Intergovernmental tax relations
STATE FINANCE
See also
Finance—Massachusetts
Finance—Michigan
Finance—Montana
Finance—Northeastern States
Finance—Oregon
Finance—West Virginia
Taxation, State
Developing healthy state economies: innovation, vision, and strategy. W. S. Edgerly. *USA Today (Periodical)* 118:18-19 S '89
Drexel is in the doghouse with cities and states. L. J. Nathans. il *Business Week* p81-2 F 13 '89
Holding pep rallies for 1992 [states help U.S. firms with export strategy for Western Europe] J. McCormick. il *Newsweek* 114:60 N 6 '89
In search of exports: the states' new agenda. P. R. Piccigallo. il *USA Today (Periodical)* 118:20-2 S '89
More mayors and governors are coming up short. G. Koretz. il *Business Week* p20 S 4 '89
The state and local budget squeeze. H. Banks. *Forbes* 143:35 My 1 '89
States and cities are facing the budget music. J. L. Sheler. *U.S. News & World Report* 106:29 My 29 '89
Stretched thin. H. Gleckman. il *Business Week* p88-9 Je 5 '89
STATE GOVERNMENTS
See also
State constitutions
State legislatures
E pluribus, plures [states set environmental agenda] S. Begley. il *Newsweek* 114:70-2 N 13 '89
More states are telling raiders: not here, you don't. T. Smart. il *Business Week* p28 F 13 '89
Television turns its back on the statehouse. N. Koch. il *Channels (New York, N.Y.: 1986)* 9:12 Ap '89
STATE LEGISLATION *See* Legislation
STATE LEGISLATURES
See also
Louisiana—Legislature
Maine—Legislature
New Hampshire—Legislature
Pennsylvania—Legislature
Texas—Legislature
Dual careers mean potential conflicts for state legislators. A. E. Young. *Common Cause Magazine* 15:40 S/O '89
STATE LOTTERIES *See* Lotteries
STATE OFFICERS
See also
Black state officers
STATE RIGHTS *See* Federal and state relations
STATE SALES TAX *See* Sales tax
STATE SAVINGS & LOAN ASSOCIATION OF LUBBOCK
The thrift police [FSLIC files malpractice suit against law firm Jenkens & Gilchrist over its dealings with State Savings & Loan Association of Lubbock] D. Fanning. il *Forbes* 143:74 Ja 9 '89
STATE SYMBOLS
A nation of symbols. J. Boysen. il *National Wildlife* 28:26-8 D '89/Ja '90
When is a ladybug a matter of state? [designation by state legislatures] W. Ecenbarger. il *Reader's Digest* 135:134-6 D '89
STATE TAXATION *See* Taxation, State
STATE TEACHERS' RETIREMENT SYSTEM (CALIF.) *See* California. State Teachers' Retirement System
STATEN ISLAND (NEW YORK, N.Y.)
Crime
A federal case [murder of DEA agent E. Hatcher] E. Pooley. il por *New York* 22:48-50+ Mr 27 '89
STATEN ISLAND DEVELOPMENTAL CENTER
A home of their own [mentally retarded adults living in group homes at former Willowbrook State School] J. L. McCarthy. il *McCall's* 117:66+ D '89
STATES, IDEAL *See* Utopias
STATES (U.S.)
See also
State governments
STATESMEN
See also
Heads of state
STATESWEST AIRLINES INC.
Is Mesa Airlines facing a dogfight? [stake by StatesWest Airlines] G. G. Marcial. *Business Week* p130 Jl 17 '89
STATHAM (GA.)
Water supply
23 years of outrageous water bills spur two sisters to fight city hall. (P.S.: they won!) [case of C. Freeman and V. Crowe] S. Percy. il pors *Good Housekeeping* 209:52+ O '89

STATHOPLOS, DEMMIE
Auditions for the Derby. il *Sports Illustrated* 70:78+ Ap 17 '89
Loud and clear. il *Sports Illustrated* 71:36-7 O 2 '89
A mystery colt revealed. il *Sports Illustrated* 70:83-4 Ap 3 '89
Nose to nose. il *Sports Illustrated* 70:16-19 My 29 '89
On top of the world. il pors *Sports Illustrated* 70 Special Issue:109-12 F '89
A perfect horse came up flawed. il *Sports Illustrated* 71:75 Jl 24 '89
Silver threads among the gold (medals). il *Sports Illustrated* 71:38-41 Jl 3 '89
Strike up the band. il *Sports Illustrated* 70:48-9 F 27 '89
A tale of two horses. il *Sports Illustrated* 70:78-81+ My 8 '89

STATIC ELECTRICITY
See also
Coulomb's law

STATION WAGONS
Sleek lines and high performance are transforming the station wagon into a new status symbol. D. Barry. il *Vogue* 179:334 N '89
When room for five is not enough. F. Lunzer. il *U.S. News & World Report* 106:64-5 Ja 23 '89
Four wheel drive
See also
Station wagons, Foreign—Four wheel drive
Testing
GMC's Suburban standby. M. Ferrara. il *Organic Gardening* 36:67 S '89
Super Suburban [GMC Suburban with turbocharged diesel engine designed by Gale Banks] L. Frank. il *Popular Mechanics* 166:104+ Ag '89
Versatile vehicles [Chevrolet Suburban] D. Chaikin. il *Home Mechanix* 85:64-70 Jl '89

STATION WAGONS, FOREIGN
Wagon lode [Peugeot 405, Audi 80/90, BMW 5-Series and Volvo 740 GL] B. Hartford. il *Popular Mechanics* 166:36 Je '89
Four wheel drive
Honda Civic 4WD wagon. J. Lamm. il *Road & Track* 40:142 My '89
Honda Civic Wagon Real-Time 4WD. J. Karr. il *Motor Trend* 41:108-10 Ag '89

STATION WAGONS, USED *See* Automobiles, Used

STATIONERY
See also
Barton Nelson, Inc.
Stencil stationery! L. A. Bulow. il *The Mother Earth News* 120:24 N/D '89

STATISTICAL ABSTRACT OF THE UNITED STATES
You can look it up. il *Time* 133:36 My 22 '89

STATISTICAL COMMISSION (UNITED NATIONS) *See* United Nations. Statistical Commission

STATISTICAL MECHANICS
The long chain from Kramers's polymer work [discussion of September 1988 article, Kramers's contributions to statistical mechanics] M. Dresden. bibl *Physics Today* 42:13+ O '89

STATISTICAL METHODS
See also
Correlation (Statistics)
Covariance analysis
Graphic methods
Sampling (Statistics)

STATISTICS
See also
Average
Biometry
Computers—Statistical use
Distribution (Probability theory)
See also subhead Statistics under various subjects
Harper's index. See issues of Harper's
Vital statistics. See issues of U.S. News & World Report beginning August 3, 1987
Study and teaching
Teaching statistics to engineers. A. A. Penzias. *Science* 244:1025 Je 2 '89

STATUES
See also
Douglass, Frederick, 1817?-1895—Statues, portraits, etc.
Irving (Tex.)—Monuments, statues, etc.
Kalamazoo (Mich.)—Monuments, statues, etc.
King, Martin Luther, 1929-1968—Statues, portraits, etc.

STATUETTES *See* Figurines

STATURE
Tall, dark first date [effect of height on perceptions of attractiveness; research by Alan Strathman and James Shepperd] V. Bozzi. il *Psychology Today* 23:67 Jl/Ag '89
Think small, play big [short tennis players] J. E. Loehr. il por *World Tennis* 36:12-13 F '89

STATUS *See* Prestige; Social status

STAUB, FRANK
Chicago's badlands. il *Bicycling* 30:82 O/N '89
Escape from New York. il *Bicycling* 30:86 O/N '89

STAUB, RUSTY, 1944-
about
Le Grand Orange. *The New Yorker* 64:18-19 Ja 2 '89

STAUBACH, ROGER, 1942-
about
Still the Artful Dodger. J. H. Taylor. il por *Forbes* 143:157 Mr 6 '89

STAUBACH COMPANY
Still the Artful Dodger [R. Staubach] J. H. Taylor. il por *Forbes* 143:157 Mr 6 '89

STAUBER, ROBB
about
On deck. il por *Sport (New York, N.Y.)* 80:17 Mr '89

STAUDENMAIER, JOHN M.
The spirituality of Advent. *America* 161:403 D 2 '89

STAUFFER, MICHAEL
CADD for the theatre designer: a comparison of low-cost programs. il *Theatre Crafts* 23:66+ Ja '89

STAUTBERG, SUSAN SCHIFFER
How to choose a distributor. por *Publishers Weekly* 236:429 Ag 11 '89

STAUTH, CAMERON
Big bad Bert [interview with B. Fields] il por *American Film* 15:46-50 D '89

STAVDAL, RICHARD
about
Living legacies. M. Lipske. il por *National Wildlife* 27:14-16 Je/Jl '89

STAVINS, R. N. (ROBERT N.), 1948-
Harnessing market forces to protect the environment [cover story] bibl f il *Environment* 31:4-7+ Ja/F '89

STAVINS, ROBERT N. *See* Stavins, R. N. (Robert N.), 1948-

STAVROPOULOS, GEORGE, 1920-
about
George Stavropoulos: a master of classical line in Manhattan. C. R. Milbank. il pors *Architectural Digest* 46:158-61+ S '89

STAW, BARRY M., AND ROSS, JERRY
Understanding behavior in escalation situations. bibl f il *Science* 246:216-20 O 13 '89

STAYING TOGETHER [film] *See* Motion picture reviews—Single works

STAYNER, KAY
My son was kidnapped for seven years; ed. by Jane Marion. il pors *TV Guide* 37:10-11 My 20-26 '89

STAYNER, STEVEN
about
A hit-and-run crash ends the life of kidnap victim Steven Stayner. J. Stark. il pors *People Weekly* 32:40-1 O 2 '89
Kidnapping
17 years later, a TV miniseries forces Steven Stayner to relive the horror of his childhood [abducted at age 7 by K. E. Parnell] S. Schindehette. il pors *People Weekly* 31:65-6+ My 22 '89
My son was kidnapped for seven years; ed. by Jane Marion. K. Stayner. il pors *TV Guide* 37:10-11 My 20-26 '89

STDS *See* Sexually transmitted diseases

STEAD, DEBORAH
Play me a story: it's tape time. *The New York Times Book Review* 94:48 Je 11 '89

STEAD, JERRE L.
about
Blocking, tackling and fumbling. C. Siler. por *Forbes* 143:92 My 29 '89

STEALING
See also
Art thefts
Automobiles—Theft
Bicycles—Theft
Burglary and burglars
Cactus—Theft
Cattle—Theft
College libraries—Theft
Credit card crimes
Embezzlement
Garden ornaments—Theft
Gas meters—Theft
Jewelry—Theft
Microfilms—Theft
Motorcycles—Theft
Poaching
Receiving stolen goods
Shoplifting
Roman holiday? [pickpockets in Rome] R. Phalon. il *Forbes* 144:132-4 Ag 7 '89
Prevention
How to keep from getting ripped off. D. Fortune. il *Ebony* 44:62+ Mr '89

STEALTH AIRCRAFT
F-117A crash reports cite pilot fatigue, disorientation [Stealth fighter accidents in 1986 and 1987] W. B. Scott. *Aviation Week & Space Technology* 130:22-3 My 15 '89
Irresistible force [Stealth, B-52 and B-1 bombers; cover story] T. H. Cole. il *Popular Mechanics* 166:59-62 O '89
Stealthy strategy. D. Seligman. il *Fortune* 120:136 Ag 28 '89

STEALTH AIRCRAFT—*cont.*

Costs

1990 defense budget [B-2 Stealth bomber; special section] il *Aviation Week & Space Technology* 131:22-4 Jl 31 '89

Air Force will buy low-rate B-2s under fixed-price incentive contracts. D. F. Bond. *Aviation Week & Space Technology* 131:26-7 Ag 7 '89

B-2 accounts for 51% of Northrop's revenues during year's first quarter. *Aviation Week & Space Technology* 130:24 My 22 '89

B-2 first flight [cover story; special section; with editorial comment by Donald E. Fink] il *Aviation Week & Space Technology* 131:13, 22-8 Jl 24 '89

The B-2: fly before buy [Stealth bomber and V-22 tilt rotor aircraft] *Aviation Week & Space Technology* 131:9 N 6 '89

B-2 or not B-2? J. D. Isaacs. il *The Bulletin of the Atomic Scientists* 45:3 S '89

The B-2: winning weapon of the last war. D. A. Hoekema. *The Christian Century* 106:772-3 Ag 30-S 6 '89

The B-2—a low-cost insurance policy. C. W. Weinberger. il *Forbes* 144:31 Ag 21 '89

Bat plane dodges flak at the Capitol [B-2 Stealth bomber] il *U.S. News & World Report* 107:10-11 Jl 31 '89

Bipartisan opposition to B-2 grows despite release of new information. J. D. Morrocco. il *Aviation Week & Space Technology* 131:22-3 Jl 17 '89

Cheney hoists 'red flag' against B-2, orders cost and technical review. P. A. Gilmartin. il *Aviation Week & Space Technology* 130:28-31 My 1 '89

Defense officials weigh B-2 cuts in excess of $8 billion. P. A. Gilmartin. il *Aviation Week & Space Technology* 130:18-20 Ap 3 '89

Don't B-2 sure. *The New Republic* 201:7-8 S 4 '89

Hold tough on the B-2. *Aviation Week & Space Technology* 130:7 My 15 '89

House panel rejects Bush defense budget, signaling trouble for B-2. P. A. Gilmartin. il *Aviation Week & Space Technology* 131:18-19 Jl 3 '89

In search of the elusive Stealth bomber. M. Brower. il *Technology Review* 92:41-5 My/Je '89

Latest B-2 cost data spur mounting Hill opposition. D. F. Bond. il *Aviation Week & Space Technology* 131:20 Jl 3 '89

Sticker shock: the Stealth is a bomb. G. Easterbrook. il *Newsweek* 113:20-2 Ja 23 '89

Suit claims Northrop wrongfully took $20 billion for Stealth bomber work. B. A. Smith. *Aviation Week & Space Technology* 131:26-7 N 13 '89

Why the Stealth bomber should really become invisible [comparison with air launched cruise missiles] D. Griffiths. il *Business Week* p21 Ap 17 '89

Design

Aeronautics/propulsion [development of Stealth technology; aerospace laureate] il *Aviation Week & Space Technology* 130:15 Ja 2 '89

The B-2 bomber [address, April 29, 1989] B. P. Randolph. *Vital Speeches of the Day* 55:494-7 Je 1 '89

Cheney and senior defense aides take firsthand look at B-2 production facilities. W. B. Scott. *Aviation Week & Space Technology* 130:23 Je 5 '89

Initial taxi runs highlight B-2's advanced design details. M. A. Dornheim. il *Aviation Week & Space Technology* 131:16-18 Jl 17 '89

Initial test flight reveals new details about design characteristics of B-2. M. A. Dornheim. il *Aviation Week & Space Technology* 131:85+ Jl 31 '89

It's official: Stealth fighter is operational. il *Popular Mechanics* 166:13 F '89

Now you see it, now you don't. P. Garrison. il *Flying* 116:128+ N '89

Our most secret fighter [cover story] N. Nichols. il *Popular Mechanics* 166:66-9+ Ja '89

Revealed: secret F-117A Stealth fighter. S. Ashley. il *Popular Science* 234:92-3+ Ja '89

Skeleton alleged in the Stealth bomber's closet. W. Biddle. il *Science* 244:650-1 My 12 '89

Stealth at last. C. P. Gilmore. il *Popular Science* 234:57 F '89

Stealth bomber exposed. B. Sweetman. il *Flying* 116:20-1 F '89

The technology of Stealth [cover story] J. H. Goldberg. il *Technology Review* 92:32-40 My/Je '89

Materials

Automated equipment used to maintain close tolerances in B-2 production. il *Aviation Week & Space Technology* 131:125 O 9 '89

Photographs and photography

Photographs reveal relative size of F-117 compared with T-38 [Stealth attack aircraft] M. A. Dornheim. il *Aviation Week & Space Technology* 131:30 S 11 '89

Stealth fighter photographed over Nevada. il *Popular Mechanics* 166:15-18+ Ag '89

Testing

B-2 comes up short. W. Biddle. *Science* 246:322 O 20 '89

B-2 envelope expanded in third test flight. *Aviation Week & Space Technology* 131:31 S 4 '89

B-2 first flight [cover story; special section; with editorial comment by Donald E. Fink] il *Aviation Week & Space Technology* 131:13, 22-8 Jl 24 '89

B-2 flies with gear retracted on shortened second flight. il *Aviation Week & Space Technology* 131:27 Ag 21 '89

B-2 taxi tests [special section] il *Aviation Week & Space Technology* 131:16-23 Jl 17 '89

B-2: what Stealth's first flight reveals [cover story] C. P. Gilmore. il *Popular Science* 235:45-9+ O '89

Initial flight of B-2 to verify aerodynamics. W. B. Scott. *Aviation Week & Space Technology* 130:31 My 8 '89

Initial test flight reveals new details about design characteristics of B-2. M. A. Dornheim. il *Aviation Week & Space Technology* 131:85+ Jl 31 '89

No. 1 B-2 completes first phase of flight envelope expansion tests. il *Aviation Week & Space Technology* 131:30-1 O 2 '89

Pentagon: 0, *glasnost*: 1 [Stealth bomber snafus and Trident II explosion] E. Salholz. il *Newsweek* 114:28-9 Ag 28 '89

Pentagon expected to release more details on F-117A. M. A. Dornheim. il *Aviation Week & Space Technology* 131:42 D 4 '89

Planned Air Force electronic warfare range would be used to test B-2, ATF. il *Aviation Week & Space Technology* 131:58-9 S 11 '89

The Stealth takes wing. B. Van Voorst. il *Time* 134:18 Jl 31 '89

Test pilots describe performance, handling characteristics of B-2. M. A. Dornheim. *Aviation Week & Space Technology* 131:40 O 9 '89

UFO update [theory that Stealth aircraft could be responsible for numerous sitings] P. Huyghe. il *Omni (New York, N.Y.)* 11:89 Ap '89

USAF continues to increase daytime flights of F-117A Stealth aircraft. M. A. Dornheim. il *Aviation Week & Space Technology* 131:24-5 Jl 3 '89

USAF expands use of F-117A, adds more daytime flights [cover story] W. B. Scott. il map *Aviation Week & Space Technology* 131:24-6 My 1 '89

USAF says B-2's range exceeds B-1B's with varied payloads, flight profiles. D. F. Bond. *Aviation Week & Space Technology* 131:30-1 O 23 '89

USAF study asserts that Soviet defenses would be ineffective against B-2 bomber. D. F. Bond. il *Aviation Week & Space Technology* 131:29-30 O 30 '89

Wings

USAF/Lockheed F-117A has high wing sweep but low wing loading. M. A. Dornheim. il *Aviation Week & Space Technology* 130:27 My 1 '89

STEALTH TECHNOLOGY

2D nozzle's Stealth benefits make use on ATF more likely [advanced tactical fighter] D. F. Bond. *Aviation Week & Space Technology* 131:28-9 S 25 '89

Radar networks, computing advances seen as keys to counter Stealth technologies [views of Robert W. Selden] D. F. Bond. *Aviation Week & Space Technology* 131:41 D 4 '89

Stealth/counter-Stealth technologies [cover story; special section] il *Aviation Week & Space Technology* 131:38-42 D 4 '89

STEAM ENGINES

See also

Locomotives

STEAM LOCOMOTIVES See Locomotives

STEAM PIPES

Notes and comment [steam pipe explosion in Gramercy Park section of Manhattan] *The New Yorker* 65:29-30 S 4 '89

Ruptured lives: how the Gramercy Park steam-pipe blast spewed misery with the asbestos. E. Pooley. il *New York* 22:50-4+ O 30 '89

STEAM POWER

See also

Energy cogeneration

STEAM RAILROADS See Railroads

STEAM SHIPS See Steamships and steamboats

STEAMBOATS See Steamships and steamboats

STEAMERS (SHIPS) See Steamships and steamboats

STEAMING (COOKING)

Steaming the French way. G. Usher. il *Gourmet* 49:142+ N '89

STEAMSHIP LINES

See also

Carnival Cruise Lines Inc.

Stormy weather. C. Torcellini. il *Forbes* 143:10 Mr 6 '89

STEAMSHIPS AND STEAMBOATS

See also

Arabia (Steamship)

Central America (Steamship)

Ocean liners

History

To the swiftest [1847 race on Hudson River between C. Vanderbilt and G. Law] J. S. Gordon. il *American Heritage* 40:16+ Mr '89

STEANE, J. B.

The name is the voice. por *Opera News* 54:22+ Ag '89

STEARNS, BOB

Boating. See issues of Field & Stream

STEARNS, BOB—*cont.*
Saltwater fishing. See occasional issues of Field & Stream
STEARNS, DAVID PATRICK
Oft-told tales. il *Opera News* 54:14-15+ D 23 '89
STEARNS, STEPHEN C.
The evolutionary significance of phenotypic plasticity [cover story] bibl f il *BioScience* 39:436-45 Jl/Ag '89
STEBBINS, JONATHAN F., AND FARNAN, IAN
Nuclear magnetic resonance spectroscopy in the earth sciences: structure and dynamics. bibl f il *Science* 245:257-63 Jl 21 '89
STEBEL, S. L.
Rewriting your novel. *The Writer* 102:17-19 Je '89
STECHERT, KATHRYN
Children's museums. il *Better Homes and Gardens* 67:112-13 Ja '89
STECKEL, ANITA
about
Anita Steckel at Underground. E. Heartney. *Art in America* 77:156 Ja '89
STECKER, ELINOR
A few new angles on home videomaking. il *Video* 13:38+ D '89
Video journal. See issues of Popular Photography beginning October 1989
STEEL, DANIELLE
Star [fiction] il pors *Good Housekeeping* 208:143-6+ F '89
STEEL, DAWN
about
Bright as Dawn, strong as Steel. J. Taylor. il pors *New York* 22:40-7 My 29 '89
STEEL, RONALD
Guest of the age. il *The New York Review of Books* 36:3-5 Ag 17 '89
NATO's last mission. *Foreign Policy* 76:83-95 Fall '89
STEEL BEVERAGE CONTAINERS See Beverage containers
STEEL INDUSTRY
See also
Bethlehem Steel Corp.
Birmingham Steel Corp.
Collective bargaining—Steel industry
Collective labor agreements—Steel industry
Independent Steelworkers Union
Lone Star Technologies Inc.
LTV Steel Co.
National Intergroup Inc.
National Steel Corp.
Nucor Corp.
Steel workers
Steel works
United Steelworkers of America
USX Corporation
Weirton Steel Corporation
Sharpening the edge [steel beverage cans vs. aluminum] E. Corcoran. il *Scientific American* 260:72-3 F '89
Export-import trade
Extending America's import restrictions on foreign steel. il *U.S. News & World Report* 106:52 My 8 '89
How George Bush may recast quotas on steel imports. P. Magnusson. il *Business Week* p51 Mr 20 '89
A little tinkering could do wonders for steel quotas. R. Kuttner. il *Business Week* p20 Je 19 '89
Steel trade liberalization program [statement, July 25, 1989] G. Bush. *Department of State Bulletin* 89:35 O '89
Why scrap a steel policy that works? [limiting imports] R. Kuttner. il *Business Week* p24 My 22 '89
Finance
Big steel is red hot again. C. Gorman. il *Time* 133:61 F 13 '89
Metals. R. Reiff. il *Forbes* 143:172-3 Ja 9 '89
Steelmakers are ready to cross swords with anyone. G. L. Miles. il *Business Week* p79 Ja 9 '89
Steel's hollow comeback [Gary, Ind.] P. Glastris. il *U.S. News & World Report* 106:49-50+ My 8 '89
Management
Suddenly, USX is playing Mr. Nice Guy [team work] G. L. Miles. il *Business Week* p151-2 Je 26 '89
Securities
Bearish on steel [views of John Tumazos] T. Jaffe. *Forbes* 143:220 Mr 20 '89
Australia
See also
Broken Hill Proprietary Co., Ltd.
China
History
Steel manufacture [ancient China] R. K. G. Temple. il *The Courier (Unesco)* 41:12-13 O '88
STEEL MAGNOLIAS [film] See Motion picture reviews—Single works
STEEL METALLURGY
Steel manufacture [ancient China] R. K. G. Temple. il *The Courier (Unesco)* 41:12-13 O '88
STEEL MILLS See Steel works
STEEL MINIMILLS
Nucor's boldest gamble [new flat-roll mill] R. Simon. il *Forbes* 143:122+ Ap 3 '89

STEEL SCULPTURE See Metal sculpture
STEEL VALLEY AUTHORITY
When workers become entrepreneurs. B. Harrison. il *Technology Review* 92:19+ Jl '89
STEEL WORKERS
See also
Independent Steelworkers Union
United Steelworkers of America
Education
Blue-collar scholar: a former steelworker hits the books. L. Evans. il *The Progressive* 53:22-5 Ap '89
Salaries, pensions, etc.
Did union leaders sell out the steelworkers? [USX accused of conspiring with negotiators] J. P. Hoerr. il *Business Week* p48-50 D 25 '89-Ja 1 '90
STEEL WORKS
See also
Steel minimills
Shutdowns
Closing up bars and closing up shop on the Monongahela. D. Ignatius. *The Washington Monthly* 21:62 F '89
When workers become entrepreneurs [Monongahela Valley steel mills] B. Harrison. il *Technology Review* 92:19+ Jl '89
STEELE, H. THOMAS
about
Sold with a stamp. G. Turim. il *Americana* 17:45-7 N/D '89
STEELE, JAMES B.
about
Two reporters you don't want on your tail. J. Alter. il pors *Newsweek* 113:71+ Ap 24 '89
STEELE, KAREN DORN
Hanford: America's nuclear graveyard. bibl f il *The Bulletin of the Atomic Scientists* 45:14-20+ O '89
STEELE, SHELBY
Being black and feeling blue. *The American Scholar* 58:497-508 Aut '89
The recoloring of campus life. il *Harper's* 278:47-55 F '89
STEELE, WILLIAM
The downside of smoking tobacco and marijuana. il *Current Health 2* 16:24-6 N '89
STEELHEAD TROUT FISHING See Trout fishing
STEEN, EDWARD
Come one—but not all. il *World Press Review* 36:11-12 N '89
STEEN, LYNN ARTHUR, 1941-
(jt. auth) See Hoffman, Kenneth, 1930-, and Steen, Lynn Arthur, 1941-
STEENBURGEN, MARY
about
After years on the mommy track, Mary Steenburgen knows the full route of Parenthood. M. H. J. Farrell. il pors *People Weekly* 32:77-9 Ag 28 '89
STEENLAND, SALLY
Setting the wrong example [excerpt from Growing up in prime time: an analysis of adolescent girls on television] il *Channels (New York, N.Y.: 1986)* 9:85 F '89
STEENSMA, J., 1940-
about
J. Steensma at Mazey Hickey. M. Kangas. il *Art in America* 77:187 Je '89
STEERE, MIKE
Ferry tales. il map *Travel Holiday* 172:58-67 Ag '89
Hot on the trail. il map *Travel Holiday* 171:55-9 Ja '89
STEERING GEAR
See also
Automobiles—Steering gear
Bicycles—Steering gear
Boats and boating—Steering gear
STEEVES, PHIL
Squeeze play. il *Flying* 116:128-9 S '89
STEFAN, V., AND OTHERS
Nonlinear mixing of electromagnetic waves in plasmas. bibl f il *Science* 243:494-500 Ja 27 '89
STEFFANI, AGOSTINO
about
Enrico Leone [opera] Reviews
Opera News il 54:43-4 Jl '89. J. H. Sutcliffe
STEFFE, CYNTHIA
about
Living a dream. A. Rosenblum. il por *Harper's Bazaar* 122:46 N '89
STEFFEN, LLOYD H., 1951-
The dangerous God: a profile of William Hamilton [cover story] *The Christian Century* 106:844-7 S 27 '89
Diagnosing drinking [discussion of July 19-26, 1989 article, Rethinking drinking: the moral context] il *The Christian Century* 106:987-90 N 1 '89
Rethinking drinking: the moral context [cover story] *The Christian Century* 106:684-6 Jl 19-26 '89
STEGEMANN, EILEEN
The pike of New York. il *The Conservationist* 44:26-33 N/D '89
Some catfishes of New York. il *The Conservationist* 44:38-45 Jl/Ag '89

STEGER, WILL
about
The 4,000-mile marathon. L. Troiano. il por *American Health* 8:95-7 Jl/Ag '89
At last, the South Pole. R. Sullivan. il *Sports Illustrated* 71:14 D 18 '89
The iceman cometh. R. Sullivan. il pors map *Sports Illustrated* 71:40-5+ Jl 31 '89
The last treasure. *The New Yorker* 65:27-8 Jl 17 '89
To the South Pole by sled. A. Toufexis. il map *Time* 134:73 D 25 '89

STEGMAIER, MARK E.
Creating imaginary places. il pors *American Artist* 53:56-9+ O '89
A directory of pastel societies. il *American Artist* 53:30-5 Jl '89
John Register. il *American Artist* 53:64-7+ F '89
A rising career for Roger Bansemer. il por *American Artist* 53:58-63+ Ag '89

STEGNER, PAGE
Deep ecology [excerpt from Outposts of Eden] il *Sierra* 74:68-73+ Mr/Ap '89

STEGNER, WALLACE EARLE, 1909-
Our common domain. il *Sierra* 74:42-7 S/O '89

STEHELIN, DOMINIQUE
about
Controversy over Nobel. J. L. Marx. *Science* 246:326-7 O 20 '89

STEHLIN, DORI
Living with lupus. il *FDA Consumer* 23:8-12 D '89/Ja '90

STEHLING, WENDY
Walk it off! [excerpt from Thin thighs in 30 days] il *Redbook* 173:118-19 Je '89

STEICHEN, EDWARD, 1879-1973
about
The photographer and the banker. J. S. Gordon. il *American Heritage* 40:82-3 Jl/Ag '89

STEIF, WILLIAM
Brazil turns left. il *The Progressive* 53:24-5+ Je '89
Brazilians take on AIDS epidemic. il *The Progressive* 53:17 My '89
The dictator and the journalists. il por *The Progressive* 53:16-17 O '89
A doctor's dilemma. il por *The Progressive* 53:10 Ja '89
Hope for Paraguay. *The Progressive* 53:16-17 Jl '89
An Israeli draws the line. il por *The Progressive* 53:15 Ap '89
Naguib Mahfouz [interview] il *The Progressive* 53:38-9 F '89

STEIN, DANIEL L.
Spin glasses. bibl il *Scientific American* 261:52-9 Jl '89

STEIN, DOUGLAS
The ten-minute pain transplant. il *Omni (New York, N.Y.)* 11:22+ Je '89

STEIN, EDITH, 1891-1942
about
Catholics and Jews: can we bridge the abyss? [adaptation of address, October 16, 1988] S. M. Batzdorff. *America* 160:223-4+ Mr 11 '89

STEIN, GERTRUDE, 1874-1946
about
Words and music. V. Thomson. il *The New York Review of Books* 36:43 Ap 13 '89

STEIN, HARRY
TV's ideal men? il *TV Guide* 37:8-11 Mr 25-31 '89

STEIN, HERBERT, 1916-
My life as a Dee-Cline. il *The American Spectator* 22:23-6 Ap '89
What is the 'right' amount of saving? *National Review* 41:26-7 Je 16 '89

STEIN, LINDA
about
Gandee at large. C. K. Gandee. il por *House & Garden* 161:146 Ag '89

STEIN, PETER, 1937-
about
Bardolator. P. Conrad. il pors *Opera News* 53:18-20 F 4 '89

STEIN, ROSS S., AND YEATS, ROBERT S.
Hidden earthquakes [cover story] bibl il maps *Scientific American* 260:48-57 Je '89

STEIN, STEPHANIE
Amina Claudine Myers: invitation to the song. por *Down Beat* 56:27-8 Mr '89

STEIN & DAY
BookCrafters takes over assets of Stein & Day. *Publishers Weekly* 235:14 Mr 24 '89
BookCrafters to publish Stein & Day titles. C. Reid. il *Publishers Weekly* 236:124 Jl 28 '89
Tentative pact gives BookCrafters control of Stein & Day backlist. C. Reid. *Publishers Weekly* 235:12 F 17 '89

STEINBAUM, ELLEN
"Are you going to love me?" Children with AIDS. il *McCall's* 116:57-9 Jl '89

STEINBECK, JOHN, 1902-1968
about
The grapes of wrath fifty years later. J. H. Timmerman. *The Christian Century* 106:341-3 Ap 5 '89

The grapes of wrath: looking back. L. Owens. il *USA Today (Periodical)* 117:92-3 My '89
Steinbeck country. B. McGinty. il *American History Illustrated* 24:18+ S/O '89
Strolling Steinbeck's Salinas. il map *Sunset (Central West edition)* 183:14 Ag '89
Travels with Steinbeck; ed. by Jack Kelly. H. Bristol. il pors *People Weekly* 31:66-8+ My 1 '89

STEINBERG, DAVID I.
Crisis in Burma. *Current History* 88:185-8+ Ap '89

STEINBERG, JOEL
about
Denying his guilt, Joel Steinberg tells how he cared for the child he killed and the lover he beat. K. Gross. il pors *People Weekly* 31:71-2+ Mr 13 '89
Hearing and healing Hedda Nussbaum. L. L. McCloskey. *The Christian Century* 106:178-9 F 15 '89
The Hedda conundrum [special section; with introd. by Anne Summers] il pors *Ms.* 17:54-67 Ap '89
Hedda speaks out [discussion of April 1989 articles, Madly in love and The Hedda conundrum] S. Brownmiller. il *Ms.* 17:12 My '89
Hedda's secret: what no one understands about abused women [with introduction by Jennifer Farbar] S. A. Feeney. por *Mademoiselle* 95:242-5+ Mr '89
A love betrayed, a brief life lost; ed. by Bonnie Johnson. N. Weiss. il pors *People Weekly* 31:82-4+ F 13 '89
A question of responsibility. R. Lacayo. il pors *Time* 133:68 F 13 '89
The Steinberg file: what the jury didn't hear. E. Wulfhorst and B. Goldberg. il pors *New York* 22:42-6 Ap 17 '89
The Steinberg trial: scenes from a tragedy. P. Volk. il pors *The New York Times Magazine* p22-5 Ja 15 '89
An unnerving tale of domestic abuse. F. Bruning. il *Maclean's* 102:9 F 27 '89

STEINBERG, JON
At debt's door. il *Ms.* 18:74-9 N '89

STEINBERG, LEIGH
about
He's dialing for dollars. il por *Sports Illustrated* 71:18-19 Ag 7 '89

STEINBERG, LISA, D. 1987
Child abuse case
Denying his guilt, Joel Steinberg tells how he cared for the child he killed and the lover he beat. K. Gross. il pors *People Weekly* 31:71-2+ Mr 13 '89
Hearing and healing Hedda Nussbaum. L. L. McCloskey. *The Christian Century* 106:178-9 F 15 '89
The Hedda conundrum [special section; with introd. by Anne Summers] il pors *Ms.* 17:54-67 Ap '89
Hedda speaks out [discussion of April 1989 articles, Madly in love and The Hedda conundrum] S. Brownmiller. il *Ms.* 17:12 My '89
Lisa: betrayed by the law. C. Reich. por *Glamour* 87:195 Ap '89
A love betrayed, a brief life lost; ed. by Bonnie Johnson. N. Weiss. il pors *People Weekly* 31:82-4+ F 13 '89
A question of responsibility [guilty verdict for J. Steinberg] R. Lacayo. il pors *Time* 133:68 F 13 '89
The Steinberg file: what the jury didn't hear. E. Wulfhorst and B. Goldberg. il pors *New York* 22:42-6 Ap 17 '89
Travis comes home [T. Smigiel, child who survived illegal adoption by Joel Steinberg] M. Jacobbi. il pors *Good Housekeeping* 209:103+ Jl '89
An unnerving tale of domestic abuse. F. Bruning. il *Maclean's* 102:9 F 27 '89
Reporters and reporting
The Steinberg trial: scenes from a tragedy. P. Volk. il pors *The New York Times Magazine* p22-5 Ja 15 '89

STEINBERG, SAUL P.
about
Birthday present. T. Jaffe. il por *Forbes* 144:42-3 S 4 '89

STEINBERG INC.
Raising the stakes. P. Chisholm. il *Maclean's* 102:31 Ag 7 '89
A struggle for Steinberg. P. Chisholm. il *Maclean's* 102:30 Jl 24 '89

STEINBERGER, JACK
Experiments with high-energy neutrino beams. bibl f il *Science* 245:1202-8 S 15 '89
about
Nobel Prize in Physics. P. F. Schewe. bibl f *Physics Today* 42:S67 Ja '89
Physics Nobel Prize to Lederman, Schwartz and Steinberger. B. M. Schwarzschild. bibl f il *Physics Today* 42:17-20 Ja '89

STEINBREDER, H. JOHN
The ball's in a new court. il *Sports Illustrated* 71:125 N 20 '89
Baskets full of money. il *Sports Illustrated* 71:66-7 D 4 '89
Think you've got it bad? il por *Sports Illustrated* 70:114 Ap 3 '89

STEINBRENNER, GEORGE M. (GEORGE MICHAEL), 1930-
about
The other kinder, gentler George. *Harper's* 279:26+ Jl '89

STEINBRENNER, GEORGE M. (GEORGE MICHAEL), 1930— *cont.*

Anecdotes, facetiae, satire, etc.

Think you've got it bad? [going through life as a G. Steinbrenner soundalike] H. J. Steinbreder. il por *Sports Illustrated* 70:114 Ap 3 '89

STEINEM, GLORIA

A basic human right. il por *Ms.* 18:38-41 Jl/Ag '89

about

Goals for the future. por *USA Today (Periodical)* 118:3 Ag '89

STEINER, STAN

about

Obituary

Publishers Weekly 235:39 Je 23 '89. L. Fleischer

STEINER PROBLEM

The shortest-network problem. M. W. Bern and R. L. Graham. bibl il map *Scientific American* 260:84-9 Ja '89

STEINFELD, JAKE

about

Tennis body by Jake. S. Stevenson. il pors *World Tennis* 37:33-6 Je '89

STEINFELS, MARGARET O'BRIEN

The Church and its public life [address, May 18, 1989; cover story] *America* 160:550-8 Je 10 '89

about

Of many things. G. W. Hunt. *America* 160:546 Je 10 '89

STEINGARTEN, JEFFREY

Do the mash. il *House & Garden* 161:42+ Ja '89

Into the woods. il *House & Garden* 161:50+ F '89

STEINHARDT, MICHAEL

about

Lights! Cameras! Portfolios! M. Alpert. il por *Fortune* 119:151 Mr 27 '89

STEINHARDT BAER PICTURES COMPANY

Lights! Cameras! Portfolios! M. Alpert. il por *Fortune* 119:151 Mr 27 '89

STEINHARDT CONSERVATORY *See* Brooklyn Botanic Garden. Steinhardt Conservatory

STEINHARDT PARTNERS

USAir takeover unlikely despite SEC filing. *Aviation Week & Space Technology* 131:102 Jl 31 '89

STEINHART, PETER

The enchantment of creeks. il *Reader's Digest* 135:17-19 Ag '89

Essay. See issues of Audubon

Portrait of a deepening crisis. il *National Wildlife* 27:4-13 O/N '89

Snow season. il *Reader's Digest* 134:145-50 Ja '89

Standing room only. il *National Wildlife* 27:46-51 Ap/My '89

Taming our fear of predators [cover story] il *National Wildlife* 27:4-13 F/Mr '89

STEINHART, RONALD GLEN, 1940-

about

The hometown boys. J. H. Taylor. il por *Forbes* 144:253-4 O 16 '89

STEINITZ, BERNARD

about

Château de Cornillon: antiquarian Bernard Steinitz's feudal castle on the Loire [cover story] C. Styles-McLeod. il *Architectural Digest* 46:72-81+ Ja '89

STEINKE, STEVE

about

Weather is for sharing [interview] il pors *Weatherwise* 42:148-50 Je '89

STEINMETZ, LEON

Bolsheviks of the Bastille. *National Review* 41:39 Jl 14 '89

STEINSALTZ, ADIN

about

Thanks to Rabbi Adin Steinsaltz, you don't have to be a Hebrew scholar to enjoy the Talmud. il por *People Weekly* 32:130 D 18 '89

STEINWAY & SONS

Don't shoot the piano. E. Rothstein. *The New Republic* 200:32-5 My 1 '89

The finishing touch [use of robots in making Steinway pianos; cover story] I. Amato. il *Science News* 135:108-9 F 18 '89

STEINWORTH, SKIP

about

Skip Steinworth. B. S. Goldman. il pors *American Artist* 53:46-51+ Je '89

STEITZ, THOMAS A.

about

The structure of the "second genetic code". M. M. Waldrop. il por *Science* 246:1122 D 1 '89

STELE (ARCHEOLOGY)

China

"Excellent! Excellent! World-honored Sakyamuni!" [L. Sickman] il por *Art News* 88:32+ F '89

STELLA, FRANK

about

Frank Stella: Knoedler. M. Moorman. il *Art News* 88:162 Summ '89

Is bigger necessarily better? P. Plagens. il pors *Newsweek* 113:66-7 Ap 17 '89

STELLAFANE CONVENTION *See* Astronomy—Conferences

STELLAR COMPUTER INC.

See also

Stardent (Firm)

"I love the tumult" [career of A. Michels] J. Pitta. il pors *Forbes* 144:296-8 N 13 '89

STELLAR MAGNITUDES *See* Stars—Magnitudes

STELLAR SPECTRA AND SPECTROSCOPY *See* Stars—Spectra and spectroscopy

STELLAR WINDS

Shocks and bubbles around hot stars [IRAS images; research by Dave Van Buren and Richard McCray] il *Sky and Telescope* 77:240-1 Mr '89

STELLMAN, MARTIN

about

For queen and country [film] Reviews

The New Leader 72:21 My 1 '89. J. Morrone

STELLO, VICTOR

about

Stop Stello. H. Wasserman. *The Nation* 249:372-3 O 9 '89

STELZER, IRWIN M.

The business of America. See issues of The American Spectator beginning June 1988

STEM, J. DAVID

Dionne Warwick is not happy with Dick Clark. il pors *TV Guide* 37:6-8 Ap 8-14 '89

Eddie Murphy comes to prime time. il pors *TV Guide* 37:20-1 F 25-Mr 3 '89

STEMLE, LAURA

Service [poem] *America* 161:324 N 11 '89

STEMPEL, ROBERT C.

about

The Big Three's trio of new leaders for the 1990s. *Fortune* 120:112 O 23 '89

From the top. il pors *Car and Driver* 35:93-6+ O '89

STEMS (PLANTS)

A chitin-binding lectin from stinging nettle rhizomes with antifungal properties. W. F. Broekaert and others. bibl f il *Science* 245:1100-2 S 8 '89

STENCIL WORK

4 stencil quilts to make. il *Good Housekeeping* 208:126-9+ Ap '89

Brushing up on stencil basics. il *Better Homes and Gardens* 67:90 Ap '89

Pochoir printing [work of J. DeWoody] R. Williams. il pors *American Artist* 53:70-5 S '89

Stencil stationery! L. A. Bulow. il *The Mother Earth News* 120:24 N/D '89

Technical page [pochoir process; excerpt from The complete printmaker] J. Ross and others. il *American Artist* 53:56 S '89

Transform a wood floor [stenciled border] il *McCall's* 116:96 Ap '89

STENDHAL SYNDROME

The Stendhal syndrome causes museum-goers to make an exhibition of themselves [views of G. Magherini] il *People Weekly* 32:109 Jl 17 '89

That swooning feeling [views of G. Magherini] J. Turner. il por *Art News* 88:150-3 D '89

STENHOLM, CHARLES W.

Should the "balanced budget constitutional amendment" be adopted? [excerpts from statement, November 17, 1987] *Congressional Digest* 68:266+ N '89

STENOSIS OF SPINAL CANAL *See* Spinal stenosis

STEP STOOLS *See* Stools

STEPCHILDREN *See* Stepparents and stepchildren

STEPFATHER II [film] *See* Motion picture reviews—Single works

STEPHANSON, ANDERS

Kennan's lament: American mass culture uncontained. il *New Perspectives Quarterly* 6:54-7 Fall '89

STEPHEN, SIR JAMES FITZJAMES, 1829-1894

about

Can government outlaw drugs? M. Cranston. pors *National Review* 41:43-5 O 13 '89

STEPHEN HAWKING FAN CLUB

Suiting science to a T (shirt), two Chicago bar owners set up a Stephen Hawking Fan Club [Gold Star Sardine Bar] il *People Weekly* 32:111 S 11 '89

STEPHENS, BROOKE M.

Do you really need life insurance? il *Black Enterprise* 20:62-4+ N '89

Higher education, lower debt. il *Black Enterprise* 20:80-2 S '89

STEPHENS, BROOKE M., AND BARNES, ROGER E.

Staying ahead of the IRS. il *Black Enterprise* 20:69-70+ D '89

STEPHENS, DAVID

History at the margins: bagpipers in medieval manuscripts. bibl il *History Today* 39:42-8 Ag '89

STEPHENS, GENE

Future justice: from retribution to reconciliation. il por *The Futurist* 23:21-4 S/O '89

STEPHENS, SUZANNE, 1942-

L'architecture parlante. il *Architectural Record* 177:57+ Ag '89

A page from the past: infusing a Manhattan apartment with period flair. il *Architectural Digest* 46:174-9 F '89

STEPHENS, W. THOMAS
about
Free at last for a second try. C. Leinster. il por *Fortune* 119:36 Ja 2 '89
He won't travel far without his laptop. C. O'Malley. il por *Personal Computing* 13:75 Ap '89
STEPHENSON, ALBERT B.
Secrets of the Model T. il *American Heritage* 40:73-7 Jl/Ag '89
STEPHENSON, D. GRIER, JR.
Choosing presidential candidates: why the best man doesn't necessarily win. il *USA Today (Periodical)* 117:15-18 Mr '89
STEPHENSON, SIR WILLIAM SAMUEL, 1896-1989
about
Obituary
Maclean's il por 102:48 F 13 '89. A. Steacy
STEPPARENTS AND STEPCHILDREN
The double jeopardies of blended families. C. E. Cohen. il *Money* 18:77+ Mr '89
Happy stepfamilies: what are they doing right? A. Morgan. il *Redbook* 173:128-9+ My '89
I was an unwed stepmother. E. Mehren. por *Newsweek* 114:12-13 O 23 '89
The other father. M. B. Rosin. il *Parents* 64:252+ My '89
Step by step. B. Kantrowitz and P. Wingert. il *Newsweek* 114 Special Issue:24-5+ Wint '89/Spr '90
A stepfamily Christmas. K. Barrett and R. Greene. il *Ladies' Home Journal* 106:100+ D '89
Stepparenting: how to make it work. C. Berman. *McCall's* 117:97+ N '89
Successful stepfamilies. J. P. Comer. il *Parents* 64:167 Jl '89
The way it is: the remarried family. S. R. Arbetter. il *Current Health 2* 15:17-19 Mr '89
STEPPING MOTORS
The amazing stepper motor. A. Tardif. il *Sky and Telescope* 77:554-8 My '89
Stepper motors. D. Lancaster. il *Radio-Electronics* 60:64+ N '89
STEPS *See* Stairways
STEPS, GARDEN *See* Garden steps
STEPS AHEAD (MUSICAL GROUP)
Mike Mainieri & Steps Ahead: hitting it heavy. M. Bourne. il pors *Down Beat* 56:20-2 Jl '89
STEPS THEATER COMPANY
Halprin takes STEPS for people with AIDS. J. Ross. il pors *Dance Magazine* 63:9 Ap '89
STEPTOE, JOHN, 1950-1989
about
Obituary
Publishers Weekly por 236:38 S 29 '89
STEREO AMPLIFIERS *See* Amplifiers
STEREO HEADPHONES *See* Headphones
STEREO LOUDSPEAKERS *See* Loudspeakers
STEREO RECEIVERS *See* Radio receivers
STEREO REVIEW'S RECORD OF THE YEAR AWARDS
See Phonograph records—Awards
STEREO SOUND SYSTEMS *See* Audio systems
STEREO TELEVISION SOUND *See* Television sound
STEREOCHEMISTRY
See also
Conformational analysis
Isomerization
Stereochemical course of catalysis by the Tetrahymena ribozyme. J. Rajagopal and others. bibl f il *Science* 244:692-4 My 12 '89
Stereochemistry of RNA cleavage by the Tetrahymena ribozyme and evidence that the chemical step is not rate-limiting. J. A. McSwiggen and T. R. Cech. bibl f il *Science* 244:679-83 My 12 '89
STEREOGRAPHS
The third dimension. il *American History Illustrated* 24:44-5 S/O '89
STEREOLITHOGRAPHY
Instant gratification. G. T. Pope. il *High Technology Business* 9:24-7 Je '89
Presto! "Growing" parts from liquid plastic. S. F. Brown. il *Popular Science* 234:130-1+ My '89
STEREOSCOPES
See also
Stereographs
STEREOTYPE (PSYCHOLOGY)
See also
Jewish American Princess (Term)
Sex role
Stigma (Social psychology)
The 10 biggest myths about the black family [reprint from August 1986 issue] L. Bennett. il *Ebony* 45:114+ N '89
Asian Americans as the "model minority". B. H. Suzuki. il *Change* 21:12-19 N/D '89
Distorted images. N. Fitzgerald. il *Scholastic Update (Teachers' edition)* 121:12 Ap 7 '89
Student voices: breaking the silence [myth of Asian American whiz kids] P. Y. Bagasao. il *Change* 21:28-37 N/D '89

STEREOVIEWS *See* Stereographs
STERILITY IN HUMANS *See* Infertility
STERILIZATION
See also
Surgical equipment—Sterilization
STERILIZATION, SEXUAL
See also
Castration
Vasectomy
STERLING, DONALD T.
about
The L.A. Clippers' full-court mess. P. Cole. il *Business Week* p64 F 13 '89
Poor little rich man. D. Wechsler. il por *Forbes* 144:196+ N 27 '89
STERLING, JOHN
about
An architect of words: Houghton Mifflin's John Sterling. G. Feldman. il por *Publishers Weekly* 235:30-2 Ap 21 '89
STERLING, MARTIE
Computer follies. il *New Choices for the Best Years* 29:104 S '89
A traveler's guide to coming home. il *New Choices for the Best Years* 29:96 O '89
STERLING (AUTOMOBILE) *See* Automobiles, Foreign
STERLING (DONALD T.) CORPORATION *See* Donald T. Sterling Corporation
STERLING DRUG INC.
Kodak may wish it never went to the drugstore. K. H. Hammonds. il *Business Week* p72+ D 4 '89
STERN, A. M.
An architect's impressions of Spain. il por *Architectural Digest* 46:128+ Mr '89
STERN, CINDY
about
The Mommy doll cues kids on the new reality: mother's place is wherever she wants to be! il *People Weekly* 32:112-13 Ag 7 '89
STERN, FRITZ RICHARD, 1926-
The common house of Europe. bibl f il *The New York Review of Books* 36:6+ D 7 '89
STERN, GARY
A specialist in many fields. *The Writer* 102:17-19 My '89
STERN, ISAAC
about
In the music room of Isaac Stern. il por *Esquire* 111:154-5+ Mr '89
STERN, JANE, AND STERN, MICHAEL, 1946-
The 10 winners! America's all-time favorite chicken dinners. il *Redbook* 172:137-42+ Ap '89
Down-home backyard barbecues. il *Redbook* 173:117-22+ Ag '89
STERN, JEROME
What they learn in school. *Harper's* 279:22 Ag '89
STERN, JOHN A.
In the blink of an eye. il *Reader's Digest* 134:99-101 Ap '89
STERN, JUDITH S., AND APPLEGATE, LIZ
Do-it-yourself diet analysis. *Prevention (Emmaus, Pa.)* 41:33-9+ Jl '89
STERN, LEONARD
about
Trump vs. Stern: the unmaking of a documentary [cover story] E. Diamond. il pors *New York* 22:30-7 S 4 '89
STERN, LINDA
How one family spends its money. il *Good Housekeeping* 209:58+ S '89
STERN, MICHAEL, 1946-
(jt. auth) See Stern, Jane, and Stern, Michael, 1946-
STERN, PAUL
about
Is Paul Stern tough enough to toughen up Northern Telecom? C. Hawkins. il por *Business Week* p84-5 Ag 14 '89
STERN, PAUL C., 1944-, AND HUSBANDS, JO
Liberating Soviet social science. il *The Bulletin of the Atomic Scientists* 45:28-31 S '89
STERN, RICHARD G., 1928-
about
PW interviews. M. McQuade. por *Publishers Weekly* 235:126+ Ja 20 '89
STERN, ROBERT A. M., 1939-
Architecture: Stanley Tigerman [cover story] il por *Architectural Digest* 46:146-51+ F '89
about
Capital gains. P. M. Sachner. il *Architectural Record* 177:98-103 mid-S '89
Entertainment architecture [cover story] P. M. Sachner. il *Architectural Record* 177:66-71 S '89
Robert A. M. Stern: new interpretation of the shingle style on Long Island. K. Andersen. il por *Architectural Digest* 46:66-71+ Ag '89
STERN, SANDOR
about
Pin [film] Reviews
Maclean's il 102:55 F 13 '89. B. D. Johnson

STERN, SETH, AND OTHERS
RNA-protein interactions in 30S ribosomal subunits: folding and function of 16S rRNA. bibl f il *Science* 244:783-90 My 19 '89
STERN, WILLIAM
See also
Baby M case
STERN, WILLY MAY
David and Godzilla. *The New Republic* 200:17-18 F 27 '89
Uniqueness and sleaze. *National Review* 41:23-4 Je 2 '89
STERN DRIVE ENGINES *See* Motor boat engines
STERNBERG, ALAN
Camaro City [story] *The New Yorker* 65:42-50 S 18 '89
STERNBERG, MARY ANN
Putting up the Christmas lights, Louisiana-style. il *Smithsonian* 20:146-51 D '89
STERNBERG, RICARDO
For now [poem] *The Nation* 249:693 D 4 '89
STERNE, HILARY
Despite tremors on the set, Today's Willard Scott says: I'm still on solid ground. por *TV Guide* 37:26-8 N 18-24 '89
STERNER, JERRY
about
Burned by the market crash, Jerry Sterner finds another way to make a Wall Street hit. A. Chambers. il pors *People Weekly* 32:123+ D 4 '89
Jerry Sterner: rolling in Other people's money. il por *Business Week* p69 D 4 '89
Other people's money [drama] Reviews
America 160:536 Je 3 '89. G. G. Seibert
Business Week il por p69 D 4 '89
Money il por 18:12 O '89. R. Eisenberg
New York 22:99-100 Mr 6 '89. J. Simon
People Weekly il 32:123+ D 4 '89. A. Chambers
The word from the playwright of Wall Street [interview] R. Eisenberg. il por *Money* 18:12 O '89
STEROIDS
See also
Corticosteroids
Dehydroepiandrosterone
Hormones, Sex
Lipids
Progestin
Testosterone
Aaron Henry's dangerous journey [high school football player who used anabolic steroids] S. J. Smith. il *Reader's Digest* 135:116-20 D '89
A day of reckoning [B. Johnson admits he took steroids] il pors *Maclean's* 102:32-3 Je 26 '89
The death of an athlete [high school steroid user B. Ramirez of Ashtabula, Ohio] R. Telander and M. Noden. il pors *Sports Illustrated* 70:68-72+ F 20 '89
A deepening scandal [physician J. Astaphan testifies on steroid use by B. Johnson] B. Wickens. pors *Maclean's* 102:49-50 Je 5 '89
A dirty coach comes clean [C. Francis testifies on steroid use by B. Johnson and other Canadian athletes] M. Noden. il pors *Sports Illustrated* 70:22-3 Mr 13 '89
Doping for the competitive edge. S. Bressan. il *World Press Review* 36:59 Je '89
From dream to nightmare [testimony by track coach C. Francis during Canadian government inquiry into steroid use by B. Johnson] A. Burfoot and B. Wischnia. il pors *Runner's World* 24:12 Je '89
He has suffered enough [B. Johnson facing lifetime ban and possible loss of 100 meter world record over steroid use] M. Noden. por *Sports Illustrated* 70:98 Je 26 '89
Moses blasts edict to strip Johnson's records. por *Jet* 76:46 O 2 '89
Olympic images [Maclean's/Decima poll] H. Quinn. il *Maclean's* 102:33 Ja 2 '89
Putting pressure on illegal steroid traffic [anabolic steroids] V. Modeland. il *FDA Consumer* 23:33-4 O '89
A revealing inquiry [testimony of J. Astaphan on runner B. Johnson's steroid use] M. Noden. il por *Sports Illustrated* 70:19 Je 5 '89
Sabotage at Seoul? [testimony on steroid use by B. Johnson] R. Dolphin. il por *Maclean's* 102:47 Mr 20 '89
The saga behind the shame [J. Scott describes J. Astaphan's role in B. Johnson's steroid use] J. Brant. il pors *Runner's World* 24:78-80 Ap '89
Shortcut to the Rambo look [use by teenage boys] A. Toufexis. il *Time* 133:78 Ja 30 '89
Starting over [B. Johnson to lose world records in drug use ruling] N. Underwood. il por *Maclean's* 102:66 S 18 '89
Steroid binding at σ-"opioid" receptors [discussion of April 8, 1988 article, Steroid binding at σ receptors suggests a link between endocrine, nervous, and immune systems] T.-P. Su and others. bibl f il *Science* 246:1635-8 D 22 '89
The steroid scandal [Canadian weight lifters testify at government inquiry] D. Burke. il *Maclean's* 102:40 F 20 '89

The steroid scandal [testimony of track coach C. Francis at Canadian inquiry; cover story; special section; with editorial comment by Kevin Doyle] il pors *Maclean's* 102:2, 36-42 Mr 13 '89
Steroids built Mike Keys up; then they tore him down [teen's suicide linked to use of anabolic steroids] M. Brower. il pors *People Weekly* 31:107-8 Mr 20 '89
Steroids: the power drugs. P. Pfotenhauer. il *USA Today (Periodical)* 117:88-90 Mr '89
Teens and steroids. D. Sobel. il *Ladies' Home Journal* 106:110 O '89
The trouble with steroids. G. Legwold. il *Better Homes and Gardens* 67:42 N '89
Users and losers [drug use by runners] J. Henderson. il *Runner's World* 24:14 Mr '89
Was the X factor a factor? [former football player and steroid user S. Courson suffering from cardiomyopathy] por *Sports Illustrated* 70:34 Ap 3 '89
Whistle blower [track coach C. Francis, testifying during Canadian government inquiry, confirms B. Johnson's steroid use] por *Time* 133:50 Mr 13 '89
STEROLS
See also
Cholesterol
STERTZ, BRADLEY A., AND WHITE, JOSEPH B.
Driving into the next decade. il *Consumers' Research Magazine* 72:17-19 S '89
STETHEM, ROBERT DEAN, 1961-1985
about
Portrait of a patriot. H. Hurt. il por *Reader's Digest* 135:65-9 Jl '89
STEVE CANYON (FICTIONAL CHARACTER)
Steve Canyon hangs up his uniform. il *Flying* 116:17 Je '89
STEVENS, ALICE
about
Two lives: ordinary/extraordinary. C. Jacobsen. bibl f il pors *Art in America* 77:152-7+ F '89
STEVENS, BRUCE R.
(jt. auth) See Martinez del Rio, Carlos, and Stevens, Bruce R.
STEVENS, DALTON
about
Well, button my lips if Dalton Stevens hasn't gone and stuck 'em on every ol' thing. il por *People Weekly* 32:141 D 4 '89
STEVENS, DAVID
Song of the Vltava. il *Opera News* 53:10-13 My '89
STEVENS, DAVID LEE
about
The man who would not quit. J. G. Hubbell. il pors *Reader's Digest* 134:115-18 F '89
STEVENS, EDMUND, 1910-
Living the history of modern Russia: Nina and Edmund Stevens in Moscow. il *Architectural Digest* 46:164-7+ F '89
STEVENS, GEOFFREY
about
A new lineup. B. Came. il *Maclean's* 102:46+ F 13 '89
STEVENS, HUGH
The useful mule. il *Country Journal* 16:56-60 My/Je '89
STEVENS, JOHN D.
Media and morality in the twenties. bibl il *History Today* 39:25-9 N '89
STEVENS, JOSEPH E. (JOSEPH EDWARD), 1956-
High fliers in a Red Barn. il *Americana* 17:37-42 Jl/Ag '89
STEVENS, LIANNE
Around the world in 80 days—and 165 masks. il *Theatre Crafts* 23:56-7+ Ap '89
STEVENS, MACK
NASA's legal folly. *Ad Astra* 1:48 My '89
STEVENS, MARK, 1947-
How to calculate capital needs. il *Nation's Business* 77:32 N '89
Learn your firm's inside story. il *Nation's Business* 77:59-60 Ag '89
Selling your firm may hike your pay. il *Nation's Business* 77:46+ S '89
STEVENS, MAY, 1924-
about
Two lives: ordinary/extraordinary. C. Jacobsen. bibl f il pors *Art in America* 77:152-7+ F '89
STEVENS, NINA
about
Living the history of modern Russia: Nina and Edmund Stevens in Moscow. E. Stevens. il *Architectural Digest* 46:164-7+ F '89
STEVENS, ROBIN
Growing up beige. il *Scholastic Update (Teachers' edition)* 121:9 Ap 7 '89
STEVENS, SHADOE
about
The top 40 times two. B. Barol. il por *Newsweek* 113:56 F 6 '89
STEVENS, STUART
Putting on the pigskin. il *Esquire* 112:54 O '89

STEVENS, WILLIAM JAY
about
Stalking the Green River killer. A. Sachs. il por *Time* 134:57
Jl 31 '89
STEVENSON, ADLAI, 1930-, AND FRYE, ALTON
Trading with the Communists. *Foreign Affairs* 68:53-71 Spr
'89
STEVENSON, ADLAI E. (ADLAI EWING), 1900-1965
about
The great hesitator. H. Fairlie. il por *The New Republic*
201:25-30 Jl 17-24 '89
STEVENSON, ALEXANDRA
about
Mother of a pearl (IV). S. Stevenson. il pors *World Tennis*
36:16 Ap '89
STEVENSON, ANNE, 1933-
'The dark forces of lust': Plath at Cambridge [excerpt from
Bitter fame] il pors *The New York Times Book Review*
94:1+ Ag 13 '89
Stone fig [poem] *The Atlantic* 264:40 Ag '89
STEVENSON, DAVID J.
Looking ahead to Neptune [cover story] il *Sky and Telescope*
77:481-3 My '89
STEVENSON, MATTHEW
Fiji: a second Grenada? il *The American Spectator* 22:21-5
Jl '89
STEVENSON, RICHARD W.
Watch out Macy's, here comes Nordstrom. il *The New York
Times Magazine* p34+ Ag 27 '89
STEVENSON, ROBERT
about
Progress in advanced materials. M. Mandell. il *High
Technology Business* 9:12 Jl/Ag '89
STEVENSON, SAMANTHA
Mother of a pearl (IV). il pors *World Tennis* 36:16 Ap
'89
STEVENSON, THOMAS G.
about
Mileposts. J. Kita. il por *Bicycling* 30:88 D '89
STEW
See also
Cassoulet
Ratatouille
Classic stews. J. T. Hazard. il *Ladies' Home Journal*
106:144-6+ F '89
Fast skillet stews. il *Redbook* 172:87-91+ Mr '89
Follow that carbonnade [Bill Lalor's carbonnade de boeuf]
B. Costikyan. il *New York* 22:64 F 13 '89
Garden swap party [serving turkey burgoo] C. A. Rossell.
il pors *Organic Gardening* 36:34-7 O '89
Gastronomie sans argent: winter stews for entertaining. il
Gourmet 49:124-5+ D '89
A great beef stew. il *Glamour* 87:260 N '89
Hearty fisherman's stew. il *Glamour* 87:263 Ag '89
Hearty game stews. S. Bashline. il *Field & Stream* 93:52
F '89
Hot, hearty stews [using winter vegetables] D. Madison.
il *Organic Gardening* 36:38-42 F '89
The LHJ cooking school: beef bourguignon. il *Ladies' Home
Journal* 106:194 O '89
Rosemary: a culinary herb with holiday history [lamb stew]
W. E. Wooldridge. il *Flower and Garden* 33:33 N/D '89
Savory stews. K. Haedrich. il *Country Journal* 16:64+ Ja
'89
She has kitchen in barn [chicken bake and venison stew]
il *Successful Farming* 87:38 Ja '89
Simmered or oven baked, simple but hearty beef stews.
il *Sunset (Central West edition)* 182:156 Mr '89
Soups and stews [vegetable soup and pork stew] il *Better
Homes and Gardens* 67:161-2 O '89
Spain in a stew. P. Casas. il *The New York Times Magazine*
p69-70 O 15 '89
You'll hardly recognize oyster stew. il *Southern Living* 24:178
O '89
STEWARDESSES, AIR *See* Flight attendants
STEWART, ALANA
about
A long goodbye. il pors *People Weekly* 32:77 Ag 7 '89
STEWART, ALDEN
about
On the prowl in big-growth country [interview] A. E. Serwer.
il por *Fortune* 120:48+ D 18 '89
STEWART, ALEX
about
One angry man. P. Putnam. il pors *Sports Illustrated* 71:38-9
N 13 '89
STEWART, ALISON CLARK- *See* Clark-Stewart, Alison
STEWART, B. A. (BOBBY ALTON), 1932-
about
Food, not dust. A. Farnham. il *Fortune* 119:37 Ja 2 '89
STEWART, BOB
about
Bob Stewart. K. Whitehead. il por *Down Beat* 56:14 O
'89
STEWART, BOBBY ALTON *See* Stewart, B. A. (Bobby Alton),
1932-

STEWART, C. JIM, II
about
"We're still harnessing power". J. Cook. il por *Forbes* 143:100+
My 29 '89
STEWART, DAVE
about
A hero lives here. P. Gammons. il pors *Sports Illustrated*
71:28-31 N 6 '89
STEWART, DAVE '89
Rolling garden bench. il *Flower and Garden* 33:90-1 Mr/Ap
'89
STEWART, DON
Collecting advertising thermometers. il *Antiques & Collecting
Hobbies* 94:36-8+ My '89
Collecting campaign buttons: a short losers history. il *Antiques
& Collecting Hobbies* 93:24-6+ Ja '89
The joy of motto collecting. il *Antiques & Collecting Hobbies*
93:60-2 Ja '89
Pencils: a sharp collecting hobby. il *Antiques & Collecting
Hobbies* 94:28-9+ D '89
Treasure Island: the forgotten world's fair. il *Antiques &
Collecting Hobbies* 94:29-31 Jl '89
STEWART, DONALD M.
Thinking the unthinkable [address, February 22, 1989] *Vital
Speeches of the Day* 55:444-8 My 1 '89
STEWART, DOUG
The buck starts here, and may stop here, at the nation's
money mills. bibl (p163) il *Smithsonian* 20:36-45 My '89
Doing the dishes: a TV bonanza is up there in orbit. il
Smithsonian 20:156-60+ O '89
In the cutthroat world of toy sales, child's play is serious
business [cover story] il *Smithsonian* 20:72-6+ D '89
Interview: Walter Stewart. por *Omni (New York, N.Y.)*
11:64-6+ F '89
STEWART, JACKIE
about
The trinity. C. Fox. il pors *Car and Driver* 34:139-40+ Mr
'89
STEWART, JAMES
about
Bard of Beverly Hills. T. Gold. il por *Harper's Bazaar*
122:71+ O '89
A celluloid charm [cover story] N. Dillon. il pors *Modern
Maturity* 32:38-43 D '89/Ja '90
The real thing. B. Bull. il pors *Vogue* 179:232-7 Je '89
STEWART, JAMES
The failures of Robert Bourassa. por *Maclean's* 102:64 Ja
2 '89
STEWART, JAMES E.
about
Home, sweet cement. M. Alpert. il por *Fortune* 119:121
F 27 '89
No pipe dream, Jim Stewart's house is built of bric-a-brac
and mortar. il por *People Weekly* 31:101 Ap 24 '89
STEWART, JIMMY *See* Stewart, James
STEWART, JULIA
The homework dilemma. il *Parents* 64:80+ F '89
STEWART, KATHRYN
Blackberrying. il *Gourmet* 49:62-3+ Ag '89
STEWART, MARTHA
Celebrate and decorate with Martha Stewart [excerpt from
Martha Stewart's Christmas] il *Redbook* 174:101-7 D '89
Martha Stewart's fabulous orange-flavored fried chicken [ex-
cerpt from Martha Stewart's Quick cook menus] il *Redbook*
172:20 Ja '89
about
Alexis' birthday party with Martha Stewart. B. Rodriguez.
il por *Organic Gardening* 36:38-40+ O '89
Lean listening cuisine. K. Ames. il por *Newsweek* 114:62
Ag 7 '89
Anecdotes, facetiae, satire, etc.
Why I haven't invited Martha Stewart to dinner. K. Fury.
il *Working Woman* 14:152 Je '89
STEWART, NORM
about
Tempest at Mizzou. A. Wolff. il pors *Sports Illustrated*
70:24-6+ F 20 '89
STEWART, PAUL, 1925-
about
How Paul Stewart mines lost 'gold' with a tape recorder.
E. C. White. bibl (p135) il pors *Smithsonian* 20:58-64+
Ag '89
STEWART, PAYNE
about
Putting on the style. E. M. Swift. il pors *Sports Illustrated*
71:28-9 Ag 21 '89
STEWART, ROBERT G.
Portraits of George and Martha Washington. bibl f il pors
Antiques 135:474-9 F '89
STEWART, ROD
about
A long goodbye. il pors *People Weekly* 32:77 Ag 7 '89
STEWART, SHERWOOD
about
The man from Goose Creek. S. Stevenson. il pors *World
Tennis* 36:51-2+ Ap '89

STEWART, WALTER
about
Interview: Walter Stewart. D. Stewart. por *Omni (New York, N.Y.)* 11:64-6+ F '89
STEWART & STEVENSON SERVICES, INC.
"We're still harnessing power". J. Cook. il por *Forbes* 143:100+ My 29 '89
STEWART'S DUROC FARM
Successful family farm. G. Johnston. il *Successful Farming* 87:44-6 My '89
STEWARTT, MICHAEL
about
Lighthawk. D. Wood. il por *National Parks* 63:27-31 Ja/F '89
Rain forest reconnaissance. M. DiLeo. il por *Mother Jones* 14:18 N '89
The wings of conservation. J. Christensen. il *Sierra* 74:32-5 Ja/F '89
STEYERT, WILLIAM A.
about
Obituary
Physics Today 42:100 Ja '89. A. C. Anderson and others
STIAK, JIM
Stand up and be sued. *Sierra* 74:28+ N/D '89
The Washington State ferries. il *Travel Holiday* 172:72-9 N '89
STICKERS
Colorful Concepts come to the holidays [personalized photo labels] K. Geller-Shinn. il *Petersen's Photographic Magazine* 18:14 D '89
STICKLEY, GUSTAV, 1858-1942
about
Gustav Stickley and the Craftsman Furniture Workshops. B. E. Johnson. bibl f il *Antiques & Collecting Hobbies* 94:48-9+ O '89
STIEGLITZ, ALFRED, 1864-1946
about
Artistic vision—and an artistic visionary. il *American History Illustrated* 24:68-9 S/O '89
STIFLER, JOHN
Drink to your health. il *Runner's World* 24:72-6+ Jl '89
The last supper. il *Runner's World* 24:38-42 N '89
STIGMA (SOCIAL PSYCHOLOGY)
A pox on all our houses. J. Leo. il *U.S. News & World Report* 106:65 F 20 '89
STILL, STEVE
How good are you? [cover story; with editorial comment by William Grout] il *Skiing* 42:10, 206-15 N '89
Strategies for success. il *Skiing* 42:138+ D '89
STILL LIFE DRAWING
Skip Steinworth. B. S. Goldman. il pors *American Artist* 53:46-51+ Je '89
STILL LIFE PAINTING
Harriet Shorr. L. S. Hurwitz. il por *American Artist* 53:34-9+ O '89
Karen Horn. B. S. Goldman. il por *American Artist* 53:68-73 Ag '89
Warren Brandt [excerpt] N. F. Weber. il *American Artist* 53:48-53+ Mr '89
Exhibitions
Eloquent bouquets [A prosperous past: the sumptuous still life in the Netherlands, 1600-1700 at the Kimbell Art Museum] R. Bernier. il *House & Garden* 161:96-101+ D '89
STILL LIFE PHOTOGRAPHY *See* Photography—Still life
STILL VIDEO CAMERAS
Filmless camera a threat? *High Technology Business* 9:35 My '89
Finally, they're here! il *Popular Photography* 96:53-4 Mr '89
Navy tests near real-time reconnaissance system using commercial magnetic camera. P. J. Klass. il *Aviation Week & Space Technology* 131:98-9+ O 2 '89
One-pound wonders. G. Schaub. il *Video* 13:44-7 Ap '89
Phototechnology: the future is now. E. M. Gomez. il *Art News* 88:151 Ap '89
Profiting from electronic photography. G. Graff. il *High Technology Business* 9:20-3 My '89
Video snaps for grandma? P. Elmer-Dewitt. il *Time* 133:81 F 20 '89
Testing
Cameras for electronic snapshots [Canon Xapshot RC-250 and the Sony Mavica MVC-1] il *Consumer Reports* 54:609 O '89
Canon Xap Shot. S. Sweetow. il *Petersen's Photographic Magazine* 18:78-9 Ag '89
Filmless photography arrives [Canon Xap Shot and Sony Mavica] S. A. Booth. il *Popular Mechanics* 166:34 N '89
Instant pictures through electronics [Canon RC-250] S. A. Booth. il *Popular Mechanics* 166:42-3 Ja '89
Photographs and television. J. W. Merline. il *Consumers' Research Magazine* 72:23 D '89
Pix-on-a-chip camera [Toshiba's IC Card camera] W. J. Hawkins. il *Popular Science* 235:96 N '89
See, no film [Canon Zapshot and Sony Mavica] S. A. Booth. il *Rolling Stone* p113+ Mr 9 '89

Still image video camera [Consumer Mavica] il *Radio-Electronics* 60:22 Mr '89
STILL VIDEO FORMAT (DIGITAL AUDIO TAPE RECORDERS AND RECORDING) *See* Digital audio tape recorders and recording—Still video format
STILLBIRTH IN ANIMALS
Incident at Ossabaw [boaters witness bottlenose dolphin giving birth to stillborn calf] N. McIntosh. il *Reader's Digest* 135:112-14 N '89
STILLE, ALEXANDER
A disturbing echo. il *The Atlantic* 263:20-1+ F '89
STILLER, BEN
about
Jerry's kid. M. Berkman. il por *New York* 22:26 Ap 3 '89
STILLMAN, BRUCE
(jt. auth) *See* Diffley, John F. X., and Stillman, Bruce
STILLWATER MINING COMPANY
Digging a mile deep [platinum mine in Montana] L. J. Fisher. il map *Earth Science* 42:12-13 Spr '89
STILWELL, KATHY
about
A game winner. L. Rothlein. il por *Women's Sports & Fitness* 11:50 Ja/F '89
STIMULANTS
See also
  Amphetamines
  Caffeine
  Cocaine
  Coffee
Kids talk about the 'good pill' [psychological side effects of stimulants administered to hyperactive children; research by Peter S. Jensen] B. Bower. *Science News* 135:332 My 27 '89
STIMULATION (PHYSIOLOGY)
See also
  Brain—Innervation
  Electricity—Physiological effects
  Electrophysiology
STIMULATION OF MUSCLE (ELECTRICAL) *See* Electrical muscle stimulation
STIMULUS AND RESPONSE
See also
  Reaction time
  Reflexes
STINCHECUM, AMANDA MAYER
Hong Kong. il *Travel Holiday* 172:50-9 S '89
STINE, SUSAN B.
(jt. auth) *See* Zemsky, Robert, 1940-, and Stine, Susan B.
STINESPRING, JOHN A., AND KENNEDY, LINDA
Discipline-based art education neglects learning theory: an affirmation of studio art. bibl f *Design for Arts in Education* 90:33-40 N/D '88
STING
about
Big Mack. R. Short. il por *Vogue* 179:424-5 N '89
Big Mack. C. Worthington. il por *Harper's Bazaar* 122:180-1+ O '89
Did our boy do something rash? [cover story] J. Greenfield. il pors *Gentlemen's Quarterly* 59:280-3+ D '89
Police report. S. Fried. il pors *Gentlemen's Quarterly* 59:151+ O '89
Sting speaks [interview; reprint from December 1985 issue] A. Lange. il por *Down Beat* 56:93-4 S '89
Theater. R. D. Story. il por *New York* 22:50-1 S 11 '89
Threepenny opera, critics claim, ain't got a thing if it's still got that Sting. il pors *People Weekly* 32:77 N 20 '89
STINGINESS
Anecdotes, facetiae, satire, etc.
How cheap can you get? [pro athletes] R. Reilly. por *Sports Illustrated* 71:160 N 6 '89
STINGING JELLYFISH *See* Jellyfish
STINGING NETTLES *See* Nettles
STINGRAYS (FISH)
Food and feeding
Ballet with stingrays [divers hand-feed stingrays] D. Doubilet. il map *National Geographic* 175:84-95 Ja '89
STINGS, INSECT *See* Insect bites and stings
STINNETT, CASKIE
In praise of small places. il *Country Journal* 16:72-4 My/Je '89
STINSON, ANDREA
about
Pick of the pack. A. Wolff. il pors *Sports Illustrated* 71:138-9 D 25 '89-Ja 1 '90
STINSON BEACH (CALIF.)
Architecture
It's an easy-going all-year retreat. il *Sunset (Central West edition)* 183:96-7 O '89
On Stinson Beach: Pacific spaces for John and Elinor McGuire [house designed by Joseph Esherick and decorated by Andrew Delfino] J. Chatfield-Taylor. il pors *Architectural Digest* 46:206-13 My '89
STIR-FRYING
Chicken chinoise. il *Good Housekeeping* 208:230 My '89
Sizzling stir-fry creations. il *Southern Living* 24:134 Jl '89

STOCKHOLDERS—*cont.*

The biggest buy-out in history means hard decisions for a chemist and his wife [RJR Nabisco stockholders Don and Nancy Roberts] H. Wheelwright. il *Money* 18:129-30 F '89

Bull market geniuses, revisited [investors profiled in 1987] J. E. Goodman. il *Money* 18:122-3 Ap '89

Courts clamp down on boards. S. C. Bahls and J. E. Bahls. il *Nation's Business* 77:52-3 D '89

The joys of haggling [relations with brokers] E. Giltenan. il *Forbes* 143:236 Je 26 '89

The market rally is getting no respect. G. Weiss. il *Business Week* p84 F 13 '89

Resolved: shareholders need to take more drastic action. J. H. Dobrzynski. il *Business Week* p32 Ag 7 '89

Romantics, radicals and realists [address, April 10, 1989] D. C. Jones. *Vital Speeches of the Day* 55:750-5 O 1 '89

A seat on the board is getting hotter. M. Galen. il *Business Week* p72-3 Jl 3 '89

Shareholders have too much power. P. Róna. il *Fortune* 120:125-6 Ag 28 '89

Small investors tiptoe back to Wall Street. G. Weiss. il *Business Week* p99-100 Ag 14 '89

Time vs. its shareholders [Paramount's hostile bid to stop merger with Warner] J. Egan. il *U.S. News & World Report* 107:38-40 Jl 3 '89

Wall Street's other arbs [stockholders vs. brokers in arbitration] E. Giltenan. il *Forbes* 143:196-7 Mr 20 '89

STOCKHOLDERS' MEETINGS

Exxon's one-act. R. Engler. *The Nation* 248:836-7 Je 19 '89

Nowhere to run or to hide [Exxon meeting confronts oil spill] B. Rudolph. il *Time* 133:69 My 29 '89

Ready for your annual meeting? C. Knowlton. il *Fortune* 119:137-8+ Ap 24 '89

STOCKHOLM (SWEDEN)

History

The spirit of Stockholm [visiting during World War I] Sir H. Walpole. *The New Republic* 201 [Reprint v1]:16 N 6 '89 [N 7 '14]

Hotels, motels, etc.

Bed and Biedermeier [Greenhouse] M. Hampton. il *House & Garden* 161:46+ Ag '89

STOCKING OF STREAMS, LAKES, ETC. *See* Fish culture

STOCKMARKET CYCLES (NEWSLETTER)

Music of the spheres? [views of P. G. Eliades] P. Brimelow. il por *Forbes* 144:192+ O 2 '89

STOCKS

See also
Banks and banking—Securities handling
Brokers
Dividends
Penny stocks
Preferred stocks
Restricted stock grants
Speculation
Stock exchanges
Stockholders
Stubs (Securities)
Television broadcasting—Financial programs
See also subhead Securities under various subjects

100 U.S.-traded foreign stocks. il *Forbes* 144:326+ Jl 24 '89

Inside Wall Street. G. G. Marcial. See issues of Business Week

Seven signals that help you answer the toughest question of all: when to sell. W. L. Updegrave. il *Money* 18:123-4 F '89

Sometimes it's smart to be lazy. F. E. Rowe. il por *Forbes* 144:255 O 30 '89

Streetwalker. See issues of Forbes

Wall Street. See issues of Money beginning January 1988

What's hot in stocks. P. Sharif. *Black Enterprise* 20:54 O '89

The world is an investor's oyster [views of P. Lynch] M. Magnet. por *Fortune* 120:67-8 Jl 3 '89

Buybacks
See Stocks—Repurchase

Certificates

Collectors and collecting

"Worthless" stock. B. B. Figarsky. il *Antiques & Collecting Hobbies* 94:46-8+ Jl '89

Clearing
See Clearing of securities

Insider trading
See Insider trading

Laws and regulations
See Securities—Laws and regulations

Margin buying

Doing well by sitting tight [A. Frank] M. Hulbert. il *Forbes* 144:161 Ag 7 '89

Marketing

See also
Initial public offerings (Securities)
Specialists (Stock exchange firms)
Stocks—Repurchase

Over-the-counter trading
See Over-the-counter securities markets

Price-earnings ratios

Basic training for value investors [interview with T. Rosenberg of Burney Co.] E. Schultz. il por *Fortune* 119:29-31 Ja 2 '89

The bottom line on the bottom line. J. Egan. il *U.S. News & World Report* 106:78 Ja 30 '89

But the client is delighted [new stock issue performance] R. L. Stern and C. M. Bartlett, Jr. il *Forbes* 143:130+ Ap 3 '89

Coincidence versus cause [too rigid computerized investment programs] D. N. Dreman. il *Forbes* 144:158 Ag 7 '89

Companies even better than they look [interview with K. Heebner of Loomis Sayles] P. Sellers. il por *Fortune* 120:28-9 Ag 14 '89

Corporate earnings cast a shadow on the Street. K. Madigan. il *Business Week* p32-3 O 30 '89

Did you miss the bus? D. N. Dreman. *Forbes* 144:132 Jl 10 '89

A discount ticket aboard some first-class growth companies. A. Kupfer. il *Fortune* 119:23-4 Mr 27 '89

Earnings guesstimates. C. Palmeri. il *Forbes* 143:216+ Ap 17 '89

Fortress stocks whose prices won't drive you up the wall. E. Schultz. il *Fortune* 120:35-6 O 23 '89

The golden median [median price-earnings ratios overlooked by computers] M. Gianturco. il *Forbes* 144:342 Jl 24 '89

How to get whipsawed. D. N. Dreman. il *Forbes* 143:146 F 20 '89

Industries that Wall Street expects to shine in 1990. E. Schultz. il *Fortune* 120:39+ D 18 '89

Light-blue chips offer heavy-duty growth. il *Money* 18:12 Je '89

Market doomsayers may be in for some earnings surprises. J. Edgerton and others. il *Money* 18:7 Ap '89

A new kind of arbitrage [discrepancy between Tokyo and New York P/Es] E. Sturza. il *Forbes* 144:128 Jl 10 '89

The new two-tier market. D. N. Dreman. il *Forbes* 144:308 S 4 '89

The no-P/E stocks [story stocks] R. Simon. il *Forbes* 144:40-1 O 2 '89

A peculiar beauty contest [concentration on cash flow vs. earnings in stock valuation as highlighted in Time Inc. merger] D. Wechsler. il *Forbes* 144:43-4+ Jl 10 '89

Safe stocks for an uneasy bull market. J. J. Curran. il *Fortune* 120 no10 Special Issue:12-13+ Fall '89

Stocks for the skittish. E. Schultz. il *Fortune* 120:36 Jl 3 '89

A tale of two crashes. D. N. Dreman. il *Forbes* 143:214 Mr 20 '89

There's gold in that lead [low P/E stocks] D. N. Dreman. il *Forbes* 143:188 Je 12 '89

Price forecasting

See also
Contrarian investments
Efficient market hypothesis

5 ways to find good stocks now [value investing] M. Schiffres. il *Changing Times* 43:64-6+ D '89

10 stocks that top newsletter editors are recommending now. il *Money* 18:39-43 Ag '89

A '90s guide to widows' and orphans' stocks. D. P. Wiener. il *U.S. News & World Report* 107:74-6 D 4 '89

All in a name [brand names] K. L. Fisher. il *Forbes* 143:166 Mr 6 '89

As the economy slows, investors should prepare for rough weather. M. Sivy. il *Money* 18:39-43 S '89

Avner Arbel's crystal ball. M. Schifrin. *Forbes* 144:374 N 13 '89

The bandwagon market keeps on rolling. J. Egan. il *U.S. News & World Report* 107:118 O 16 '89

Better dead than alive [stock picker P. Cundill] J. Clements. il por *Forbes* 143:208-9 Mr 20 '89

A big-gain hunter in small stocks [interview with P. Jenkel of Quasar Fund] T. Paré. il por *Fortune* 120:40+ O 23 '89

Big payoffs from small stocks [interview with R. Wanger of Acorn Fund] J. Mendes. il por *Fortune* 120:35-7 Jl 17 '89

A boomer plays the leisure boom [interview with K. Firestone] K. Nickel. il por *Fortune* 120:63+ N 20 '89

Born-again stocks [former leveraged buyout companies taken public with new offerings] C. Palmeri. il *Forbes* 143:210-11 Mr 20 '89

Bull market geniuses, revisited [investors profiled in 1987] J. E. Goodman. il *Money* 18:122-3 Ap '89

The bull that will not die. J. Egan. il *U.S. News & World Report* 106:59-60 Je 5 '89

Bullish beachcomber [D. Sullivan's Chartist] P. Brimelow. il por *Forbes* 144:118-19 O 30 '89

Bulls, bears and bowls [Super Bowl games and stock market] T. Jaffe. il *Forbes* 143:172 F 6 '89

Buy American [views of R. Leuschel of Banque Bruxelles] P. Fuhrman. il por *Forbes* 144:64 Jl 10 '89

Buying on bad news [purchasing stock of companies in trouble] W. Giese. il *Changing Times* 43:41-2+ Ag '89

Can Lynch live up to his reputation? [Magellan Fund's P. Lynch] J. Clements. il por *Forbes* 143:174+ Ap 3 '89

STOCKS—Price forecasting—*cont.*

Can you beat the Street? D. R. Katz. il *Esquire* 112:81-2 N '89

Capital idea [capital goods stocks] T. Jaffe. il *Forbes* 144:326 D 11 '89

Cash flow can be the investor's best guide to a stock's true worth. A. Rock. *Money* 18:161-2 Mr '89

Cashing in on cash-rich companies. J. Kosnett. il *Changing Times* 43:29-33 Jl '89

Coming home to growth stocks. J. M. Laderman. il *Business Week* p106-7 D 25 '89-Ja 1 '90

Companies should "create capital" [interview with J. Barksdale of Equity Investment] E. Schultz. il por *Fortune* 120:48+ Jl 31 '89

Compound interest machines [G. Michaelis] J. Clements. il por *Forbes* 144:43-4 Ag 21 '89

The contrarian. D. N. Dreman. See alternate issues of Forbes

Count the cash and go home early [strategies of G. Angulo] T. Pouschine. il por *Forbes* 143:124+ My 29 '89

Cut your losses. M. Hulbert. il *Forbes* 144:311 S 4 '89

'Deathwatch' investments. D. Pauly. il por *Newsweek* 113:62 Ap 24 '89

Despite those post-crash highs, be wary of the stock market. J. J. Curran. il *Fortune* 119:25-6+ My 22 '89

A Dow theorist sees stocks falling 400 points only to soar again to beyond 3000 [R. L. Evans of Dow theory forecasts] C. E. Cohen. il por *Money* 18:177-8 S '89

Down-and-out investing. J. B. Quinn. il *Newsweek* 114:46 Jl 3 '89

Down time. J. Crudele. il *New York* 22:16 Ja 16 '89

Early bird got worm [J. B. Neff of Windsor Fund] A. Farnham. il por *Fortune* 119:62-3 Ja 2 '89

Early casualties. K. L. Fisher. il *Forbes* 144:168 D 25 '89

Earnings, schmernings—look at the cash. J. M. Laderman. il *Business Week* p56-7 Jl 24 '89

The end is nigh. K. L. Fisher. il *Forbes* 144:230 S 18 '89

An expert on risk says you can make money in stocks without losing sleep [views of R. Gibson] C. Willis. il por *Money* 18:205-6 N '89

Eyeing companies with lots of cash [interview with M. Hawkins of Southeastern Asset Management] A. E. Serwer. il por *Fortune* 119:37-9 F 13 '89

Fidelity's newest wunderkind runs the fund that may be the next Magellan [T. Sweeney] G. Anrig, Jr. il por *Money* 18:201-2 Ap '89

A forecast for '89: exporters will profit as the dollar declines. J. Edgerton and M. T. Smith. il *Money* 18:7 Ja '89

Getting the lowdown. K. L. Fisher. il *Forbes* 143:334 Ja 9 '89

The gloat factor and other market indicators. A. P. Tobias. il *Time* 134:62-3 S 18 '89

Good buys in bad times for interest-sensitive shares. J. Mendes. il *Fortune* 119:25-6 Ja 2 '89

The "good fund, bad sector" theory [small company funds] J. Clements. il *Forbes* 143:110 Ja 23 '89

Great stock buys [cover story] J. Kosnett and R. J. Maturi. il *Changing Times* 43:28-38 O '89

Growth stocks with more climb left [interview with S. Aronoff of Scudder Capital Growth Fund] K. Nickel. il por *Fortune* 120:28+ N 6 '89

Happy breakups [spinoffs] C. Palmeri. *Forbes* 144:110-11 Ag 21 '89

The hot stocks of 1989. M. K. Evans. il *Gentlemen's Quarterly* 59:94+ Ja '89

How long will the bull run? C. Friday and J. Schwartz. il *Newsweek* 113:44 Je 12 '89

How the Basses caught their billions. C. Palmeri. il *Forbes* 144 Special Issue:404-5 O 23 '89

How to play the market now [dealing with Friday the 13th plunge] J. B. Quinn. il *Newsweek* 114:46 O 23 '89

How to play the takeover game. J. Kosnett. il *Changing Times* 43:69-70+ Ap '89

How to spot trends for fun and profit [interview with E. Antoian of Trend Fund] P. Sellers. il por *Fortune* 120:40-1 S 11 '89

How to take advantage of fear and greed [relative yield strategy; interview with R. D. Newell] T. Paré. il por *Fortune* 119:54 Je 19 '89

I call them "takeaways". K. L. Fisher. il *Forbes* 143:180 Ap 3 '89

If you've money to buy stocks, it's dumb—and costly—not to. M. S. Forbes. *Forbes* 143:19-20 Ja 23 '89

In a soaring market, there's still room at the top. J. M. Laderman. il *Business Week* p94-5 Je 26 '89

In the boss' shadow [E. Bramwell] G. Button. il por *Forbes* 144:238+ N 27 '89

Inside indication? [Market logic newsletter] M. Hulbert. il *Forbes* 143:120 Ja 23 '89

Inside traitor [views of P. Lynch] M. K. Evans. il *Gentlemen's Quarterly* 59:153-4 Je '89

Investing for the 1990s [cover story; special section] il *Business Week* p91-5+ O 16 '89

Investing: how to beat the pros [interview with P. Lynch; cover story] il pors *Changing Times* 43:32-4+ My '89

Is any stock shock-proof? These come close [views of L. Birinyi] G. G. Marcial. il *Business Week* p180 N 6 '89

Is it time, once again, to bail out? D. P. Wiener. il *U.S. News & World Report* 107:60-2 Ag 21 '89

Is the market retracing its 1987 course? No, but use caution. J. J. Curran. il *Fortune* 120:31-2 S 11 '89

Is this a blow-off? [M. Leibovit of Volume reversal survey and G. Cutler of Market mania form Progressive Ventures Inc.] M. Hulbert. il *Forbes* 143:191 Je 12 '89

Is your portfolio weatherproofed? E. Schultz. il *Fortune* 120:30 S 25 '89

A last hurrah for stocks? [interview with B. Biggs of Morgan Stanley] J. Mendes. il por *Fortune* 120:46-8 Ag 28 '89

Lessons in the ledgers [stock picker T. Doerflinger] J. Willoughby. il por *Forbes* 143:104+ My 15 '89

A little advice from Wall Street, in triplicate. D. P. Wiener. il *U.S. News & World Report* 107:61 Jl 3 '89

The long and short of it [C. Allmon's performance] M. Hulbert. il *Forbes* 143:217 Mr 20 '89

Look before you laugh at 'Chapter 11' investments. L. Zinn. il *Business Week* p100 Ap 10 '89

Look for lots of bang from small-cap stocks. G. G. Marcial. il *Business Week* p116-17 D 25 '89-Ja 1 '90

Looking for a few good takeover stocks? J. Friedman. il *Business Week* p108-9 D 25 '89-Ja 1 '90

Low-stress investments for the decade ahead [portfolio tips from investment advisers; cover story] M. Schiffres. il *Changing Times* 43:29-35 N '89

Lynch's law? [record of P. Lynch] M. Hulbert. il *Forbes* 143:230 Ap 17 '89

Making money in unmergers [spinoffs as investments] R. J. Maturi. il *Changing Times* 43:31-2+ Je '89

The market is high but cash is a trap [interview with C. Clough of Merrill Lynch] J. Mendes. il por *Fortune* 120:37 O 9 '89

Market timers and the market march to different drummers. il *Money* 18:17 Je '89

A maverick's forecast: high inflation and a boom in Texas stocks [F. Rowe] il por *Money* 18:191-2 My '89

Meet big, bad bear Milton Berg. L. J. Nathans. il por *Business Week* p82 Je 19 '89

Money's second annual all pro stockbrokers: 1989. J. Ellis. il *Money* 18:112-14+ O '89

Music of the spheres? [views of P. G. Eliades] P. Brimelow. il por *Forbes* 144:192+ O 2 '89

Ninth-inning rally [small company stocks] E. Sturza and E. Hardy. il *Forbes* 144:292+ O 16 '89

Old-fashioned and proud of it [interview with F. Fearington] A. E. Serwer. il por *Fortune* 119:32 My 22 '89

On the prowl in big-growth country [interview with A. Stewart] A. E. Serwer. il por *Fortune* 120:48+ D 18 '89

One up on Wall Street [excerpt; ed. by J. Rothchild. P. Lynch. il pors *Money* 18:128-9+ Ja '89

Peter Lynch's seven rules for making money. il por *Money* 18:74-5 D '89

The power of common knowledge [condensed from One up on Wall Street; ed. by John Rothchild. P. Lynch. *Reader's Digest* 135:85-9 Ag '89

Promising industries for 1990. B. Dumaine. il *Fortune* 120 no10 Special Issue:151-2+ Fall '89

The quiet bear. K. L. Fisher. il *Forbes* 144:298 O 16 '89

Reach out and touch the market's latest fad [telephone investment services] L. J. Nathans. il *Business Week* p144-5 My 22 '89

Ready, aim, fire: acquirers are hunting a new flock of targets. J. Edgerton and others. il *Money* 18:7 Mr '89

Relative strength is absolutely hot. M. Hulbert. il *Forbes* 144:117 Ag 21 '89

A rerun of October 1987? [views of Buzz Zaino and William Ehrman] T. Jaffe. *Forbes* 144:304 O 16 '89

Right under your nose. K. L. Fisher. il *Forbes* 144:338 Jl 24 '89

Risk rewarded. S. Ramos. il *Forbes* 143:330-1 Ja 9 '89

The same . . . but different [contrasting BI research and Market mania newsletters] M. Hulbert. il *Forbes* 143:408 My 1 '89

Searching for value in the stock market [cover story] F. N. Jelks. il *Consumers' Research Magazine* 72:10-13 Mr '89

Security analysis updated. K. L. Fisher. il *Forbes* 143:166 F 6 '89

The shaky refuge of defensive stocks. J. Egan. il *U.S. News & World Report* 107:64 Jl 31 '89

Shock absorbers for small investors [dealing with market fluctuations] D. P. Wiener. il *U.S. News & World Report* 107:63 O 30 '89

The smart way to go global. B. D. Fromson. il *Fortune* 120 no10 Special Issue:103-4+ Fall '89

A soft landing will send the market soaring. J. M. Laderman. il *Business Week* p92-3 My 29 '89

Some stock advice. J. Blyskal and M. Hodge. il *New Choices for the Best Years* 29:65-6+ O '89

Spotting the true belles among southern stocks. J. Edgerton and others. il *Money* 18:7-8 Ap '89

Stock trends. A. C. Brown. See issues of Forbes

Stocks that could soar on big trends [interview with K. Oberman] E. Schultz. il por *Fortune* 120:39+ D 4 '89

Stocks that pass tough tests [interview with A. Greene of David J. Greene] S. Smith. il por *Fortune* 119:36+ Ap 24 '89

STOCKS—Price forecasting—*cont.*

Stocks that seem chancy. R. Henkoff. il *Fortune* 120 no10 Special Issue:179+ Fall '89

Surviving a bear attack. C. Knowlton. il *Fortune* 120 no10 Special Issue:65+ Fall '89

There's cash flow, and there's cash flow [views of D. Yacktman] J. Clements. il por *Forbes* 144:138+ S 18 '89

They're small, but they're scrappy. J. Egan. il *U.S. News & World Report* 106:78 My 22 '89

The thin file strategy [views of P. Cannell] R. Phalon. il por *Forbes* 143:221-2 Je 26 '89

Think like an amateur, profit like a pro [interview with P. Lynch] pors *U.S. News & World Report* 106:86+ Mr 20 '89

This professor majors in finding stocks that double in value [M. Reinganum] B. Hager. il por *Money* 18:153-4 F '89

This pro's advice: hunt down Wall Street's orphans [views of J. Lappin] C. E. Cohen. il por *Money* 18:205-6 Je '89

This top-ranked contrarian predicts stocks will hit their pre-crash highs in '89 [Market mania publisher G. Cutler] J. Ellis. il por *Money* 18:163-4 Ja '89

Three easy steps. K. L. Fisher. il *Forbes* 144:253 O 30 '89

Three raging bulls and two restrained ones [views of I. Jacobs, S. C. Davis, H. Simmons, S. Zell and W. E. Simon] R. King. il pors *Forbes* 144 Special Issue:362+ O 23 '89

Three ways for investors to follow the smart money. D. P. Wiener. il *U.S. News & World Report* 107:61 Ag 7 '89

To all yardsticks there is a season [J. Grantham] D. Churbuck. il por *Forbes* 144:44+ Ag 21 '89

To find tomorrow's hot stocks, go where the big boys aren't. A. E. Serwer. il *Fortune* 119:29-30+ F 27 '89

The top bear [S. Einhorn] R. Henkoff. il por *Fortune* 119:47+ Ja 2 '89

Unhappy New Year? M. Hulbert. il *Forbes* 143:337 Ja 9 '89

Value is where you find it [Fireman's Fund's stock picker B. Bruce] J. Clements. il por *Forbes* 143:62+ Mr 20 '89

Waltzing with the wallflowers [interview with C. Browne of Tweedy Browne] S. Smith. il por *Fortune* 119:43+ Ap 10 '89

We put our finger on six market indicators that still work. D. Harris. il *Money* 18:43-5 N '89

What looks good to Mario Gabelli [interview] J. Mendes. il por *Fortune* 119:32+ Mr 27 '89

What Magellan's man at the top is buying [views of P. Lynch] G. G. Marcial. por *Business Week* p142 O 9 '89

What, me worry about an all-time stock market high? M. Meyer and P. Misra. il *Money* 18:45-6 O '89

What to do when the stock market drops 200 points [dividend discount model] E. Schultz. il *Fortune* 120:53+ N 20 '89

What to do when your broker says 'buy'. D. P. Wiener. il *U.S. News & World Report* 106:62-4 Je 19 '89

What will the market do for an encore? J. M. Laderman. il *Business Week* p98-9 Ag 14 '89

What you're not reading about. K. L. Fisher. il *Forbes* 144:301 N 27 '89

Where a contrarian finds value in today's blue chips [M. O'Higgins] il por *Money* 18:7-8 My '89

Where losses are assets [tax-loss carryforwards] C. Palmeri. il *Forbes* 144:154-5 Ag 7 '89

Where to profit in the coming slowdown. J. Egan and R. F. Black. *U.S. News & World Report* 107:44 Ag 14 '89

While cyclical stocks go begging, the companies are getting rich. J. Mendes. il *Fortune* 119:37-8 Ap 10 '89

Whiplash? [investment newsletters] M. Hulbert. il *Forbes* 143:216+ Je 26 '89

Why 'cash flow' might still be magic words. L. J. Nathans. il *Business Week* p114 D 25 '89-Ja 1 '90

Why growth stocks look good [interview with J. Robertson of Tiger Fund] J. Mendes. il por *Fortune* 119:41-3 My 8 '89

Will 1989's fast start fizzle out? J. Egan. il *U.S. News & World Report* 106:70 F 27 '89

Will the pendulum swing again? [views of F. Friess] J. Clements. il por *Forbes* 144:360+ N 13 '89

Will the real Ben Graham please stand up? [stock pickers E. Kiehne and W. H. Miller] J. Clements. il pors *Forbes* 144:310+ D 11 '89

A word from the wise [predictions for 1989] J. Crudele. il *New York* 22:10 Ja 2 '89

Worldwide trends make him bullish [interview with R. Thompson of United Income Fund] P. Sellers. il por *Fortune* 120:31+ S 25 '89

Yellow lights [views of Susan and Lawrence Sterne] T. Jaffe. *Forbes* 143:284 Je 26 '89

Price indexes and averages

See also

Index frontrunning (Securities)

Index funds

Program trading (Securities)

Stock index futures

Stock index options

Stock market crash, 1987

1988: the year the sun came out again—but too few noticed. E. Schurenberg. il *Money* 18:49-51 F '89

Apples no, whiskey yes [small investors tend to magnify stock market risks] W. Baldwin. il *Forbes* 144:252+ D 11 '89

Basket case [Friday the 13th stock market plunge] J. J. Cramer. *The New Republic* 201:12-14 N 13 '89

Boom, boom, ka-boom! [Friday the 13th drop in stock market] J. Greenwald. il *Time* 134:66-9 O 23 '89

Bull? Or bear? M. Hulbert. il *Forbes* 144:340 Jl 24 '89

The bulls of summer. F. Ungeheuer. il *Time* 134:40-2 Ag 21 '89

The Canadian who sparked the crash [decline in value of R. Campeau's junk bonds before Friday the 13th plunge] P. C. Newman. il *Maclean's* 102:75 O 30 '89

Congress caused the crash [threat to capital gains tax cut responsible for Friday the 13th drop] *National Review* 41:14-15 N 10 '89

The crash—now a faint echo. il *Newsweek* 114:49 Jl 31 '89

Cruel October [Friday the 13th stock plunge] *The Nation* 249:515-16 N 6 '89

Does the market matter? [Friday the 13th plunge, 1989; cover story; special section] il *Business Week* p24-33+ O 30 '89

Don't be lulled [Friday the 13th stock plunge] G. Shilling. il *Forbes* 144:370 N 13 '89

The fabled January effect may come early this year. J. Willoughby. il *Money* 18:17 D '89

The Forbes/Wilshire 5000 review. See issues of Forbes

Holiday blues? Play the 'January effect'. S. Woolley. *Business Week* p208 N 27 '89

How to get the Dow to 3000 [cut capital gains tax and interest rates] M. S. Forbes, Jr. il *Forbes* 144:29 N 13 '89

Investment figures of the week. See issues of Business Week beginning January 25, 1988

Investments: what goes up for bad reasons must come down [recent rise in Dow Jones industrial average] il *Money* 18:38 Mr '89

Is it inflation? Recession? or just spring fever? J. M. Laderman. il *Business Week* p70-1 Ap 10 '89

Lassoing herd instincts for the good of the market. G. S. Becker. il *Business Week* p20 N 20 '89

Lessons from the market's plunge [Friday the 13th drop] J. J. Curran. il *Fortune* 120:97-8 N 20 '89

The market rally is getting no respect. G. Weiss. il *Business Week* p84 F 13 '89

The markets' new optimism. T. Fennell. il *Maclean's* 102:36-7 Ag 21 '89

Marty Zweig? Or Al Frank? [aftermath of Friday the 13th stock market plunge] M. Hulbert. il *Forbes* 144:368 N 13 '89

The message of the market [stock plunges reflect business' response to competition] R. J. Samuelson. il *Newsweek* 114:64-8 O 30 '89

A new high, but many sit tight. il *Newsweek* 114:44 S 4 '89

The nosedive of '89 [Friday the 13th drop] L. Reibstein. il *Newsweek* 114:44-5 O 23 '89

The road to recovery: a market diary [Friday the 13th plunge] C. Friday and R. Thomas. il *Newsweek* 114:67 O 30 '89

A scary reminder [Friday the 13th plunge, 1989] J. DeMont. il *Maclean's* 102:36-7 O 23 '89

Shocks in the markets. J. Daly. il *Maclean's* 102:70-2+ O 30 '89

Small investors tiptoe back to Wall Street. G. Weiss. il *Business Week* p99-100 Ag 14 '89

Soothing the wild beast [market comeback from Friday the 13th plunge] J. Greenwald. il *Time* 134:74 O 30 '89

A startling rally. J. DeMont. il *Maclean's* 102:30 Ag 7 '89

Statistical spotlight. See issues of Forbes

The stock table, simplified. il *Consumer Reports* 54:534 Ag '89

The surging markets. J. DeMont. il *Maclean's* 102:26+ F 13 '89

Up—and down—on Wall Street. J. Egan. il *U.S. News & World Report* 107:58-9+ O 30 '89

Wall Street: on the road to 2700. J. M. Laderman. il *Business Week* p57 Ag 7 '89

Wall Street reels from undone deals [Friday the 13th plunge] il *U.S. News & World Report* 107:19-20 O 23 '89

What to do when the stock market drops 200 points [dividend discount model] E. Schultz. il *Fortune* 120:53+ N 20 '89

Why private investors don't trust the stock market [Friday the 13th plunge] R. Jacob. il *Fortune* 120:8 N 6 '89

Why the bulls are running wild on three continents. J. M. Laderman. il *Business Week* p70-1 Ja 30 '89

Why the Dow's dizzy dancing can be deceptive. D. Zigas. *Business Week* p158 D 18 '89

Yes, the stock market's risky. Why look for a scapegoat? G. Weiss. il *Business Week* p158 N 27 '89

Price-sales ratios

Catching the rebound [views of P. Greco] D. Kortrey. il *Forbes* 144:227 S 18 '89

New, improved version. E. Sturza. il *Forbes* 143:162-3 Mr 6 '89

STOCKS—cont.

Prices

The 100 cheapest foreign stocks. il *Forbes* 144:278-80 Jl 24 '89

A $1990 portfolio. A. C. Brown. il *Forbes* 144:318 D 11 '89

The acquisition boom has lost a lot of its thunder . . . but takeover candidates still thrill Wall Street. G. Koretz. il *Business Week* p18 Je 12 '89

The art of selling shares when a raider is buying. L. Zinn. il *Business Week* p236 S 25 '89

The best and worst stocks of 1988. J. Mendes. il *Fortune* 119:156-9 Ja 30 '89

Get ready to start buying at discount. C. Willis. il *Money* 18:75-6+ D '89

Take the money and run [stock that becomes target of acquisition or leveraged buyout] M. J. Williams. il *Fortune* 119:26 Ja 2 '89

Telltale signs of bargain stocks [interview with T. S. White of the Chicago Group] il por *Fortune* 119:30+ Ja 16 '89

These pros were smiling on Friday the 13th. G. G. Marcial. il *Business Week* p37 O 30 '89

Toys, tobacco, and metals lead a comeback in Fortune 500 stocks. A. E. Serwer. il *Fortune* 119:29-30 Ap 24 '89

When to say goodbye to a stock. E. Henry. il *Changing Times* 43:20 N '89

Repurchase

See also
Greenmail
Unbundled stock units

BP: making the best of it [buys back half of Kuwait's shares] M. Maremont. *Business Week* p48 Ja 16 '89

A buyback backfires [Marriott Corp.] T. Smart. il *Business Week* p29 My 1 '89

Round two for Polaroid and Shamrock. K. H. Hammonds. il *Business Week* p32 F 13 '89

Short selling

See Securities—Short selling

Splitting

See also
Americus Shareowner Service Corporation

Just what the doctor ordered [Hoffmann-La Roche plan to recapitalize] J. Greenwald. il *Time* 133:68 My 8 '89

Why the Dow's dizzy dancing can be deceptive. D. Zigas. *Business Week* p158 D 18 '89

Taxation

See Securities—Taxation

Under-the-counter trading

See Under-the-counter securities

Valuation

See Corporations—Valuation

Yields

Aim for 9% yields with no risk [money market funds] M. Sivy. *Money* 18:85+ D '89

The case for stocks. D. N. Dreman. il *Forbes* 143:156 My 15 '89

Dividends and interest matter a lot more than you think. R. E. Norton. il *Fortune* 120:19+ N 6 '89

Growth yields. E. Sturza. il *Forbes* 143:222 Ap 17 '89

How to take advantage of fear and greed [relative yield strategy; interview with R. D. Newell] T. Paré. il por *Fortune* 119:54 Je 19 '89

More today, more tomorrow. T. Jaffe. *Forbes* 143:164 My 15 '89

The party's over, but there's still fun to be had. J. Friedman. il *Business Week* p110+ D 25 '89-Ja 1 '90

When do 'dividend plays' really pay off? J. Friedman. il *Business Week* p150 N 20 '89

Why stocks get weaker as inflation gets stronger. M. J. Mandel. il *Business Week* p20 Ap 24 '89

STOCKS (COOKING)

From our kitchen to yours [making broth and stock] K. Adams. *Southern Living* 24:131 F '89

Stocks. il *Gourmet* 49:286 O '89

STOCKTON, WILLIAM

Dangerous traffic. il *The New York Times Magazine* p40-1+ Je 4 '89

STOCKTON (CALIF.)

Crime

Death goes to school [P. Purdy's shooting rampage in January 1989] P. Caputo. il *Esquire* 112:136-8+ D '89

Death on the playground [P. Purdy kills children in school yard] J. N. Baker. il por *Newsweek* 113:35 Ja 30 '89

The impact of Stockton [schoolyard murders gives momentum to gun control] J. Hammer. il *Newsweek* 113:8 F 20 '89

A nation of certified killers [murderer P. Purdy's firearms transaction record] J. D. McNamara. il *Harper's* 278:58-9 My '89

Slaughter in a school yard [P. Purdy shoots children] il *Time* 133:29 Ja 30 '89

Education

Teaching students cultural mediation [Amos Alonso Stagg High School] B. Huie. *The Education Digest* 55:50-2 O '89

Housing

Must we tear them down? [low-cost Cougar Apartments; reprint from May/June 1978 issue] M. Settle. il *The Humanist* 49:9 My/Je '89

STOCKWELL, DEAN, 1935-

about

Married to the mod. T. D. Rohrer. il pors *Gentlemen's Quarterly* 59:167+ S '89

A mob hit. P. Brock. il por *Rolling Stone* p29 My 4 '89

STODDARD, ALAN G., AND DIBNER, MARK D. (MARK DOUGLAS)

Europe's HDTV: tuning out Japan. *Technology Review* 92:39 Ap '89

STODDARD, ALEXANDRA

Colors for a happy home [excerpt from Alexandra Stoddard's book of color] il *McCall's* 117:34-6 N '89

How to be a good (not perfect) parent [excerpt from Living beautifully together] il por *McCall's* 116:60+ F '89

Living beautifully. See issues of McCall's beginning March 1989

STODDARD, MAYNARD GOOD

Baseball's closest calls. il *The Saturday Evening Post* 261:30+ Jl/Ag '89

STODDART, VERONICA GOULD

Art. See issues of *Américas* through January/February 1989

STOISICH, ANTHONY J.

about

The final frenzy of a penny stock shop. D. Zigas. il por *Business Week* p128 Mr 13 '89

STOKE-ON-TRENT (ENGLAND)

From the villages of Stoke-on-Trent, a river of china. I. Shenker. bibl (p191) il *Smithsonian* 19:130-4+ Mr '89

STOKELY USA, INC.

Stokely USA. S. L. Kirsch. il *Fortune* 120:134 D 4 '89

STOKES, DEWEY

about

Should more limits be placed on guns? [interview] il *U.S. News & World Report* 106:32 Ap 10 '89

STOLAR, ABE, 1911-

about

After 58 years in Moscow, prodigal son Abe Stolar comes back to his kind of town. W. Plummer. il pors *People Weekly* 32:65-6 Jl 24 '89

Free at last. il por *Newsweek* 113:6 Mr 27 '89

STOLBERG, E. THEODORE

about

History repeats? T. Jaffe. il por *Forbes* 144:127 S 18 '89

STOLEN GOODS, RECEIVING *See* Receiving stolen goods

STOLER, MARGARET G.

Benjamin Church: Son of Liberty, Tory spy. il pors *American History Illustrated* 24:28-35 N/D '89

STOLÉRU, LIONEL

Who swallows the debt? *World Press Review* 36:80 S '89

STOLIAR, ARTHUR

(jt. auth) *See* Stoliar, Joan, and Stoliar, Arthur

STOLIAR, JOAN, AND STOLIAR, ARTHUR

Spaced out. il *Popular Photography* 96:42-3+ Mr '89

STOLL, CLIFFORD

about

Astronomer Cliff Stoll stars in the espionage game, but for him spying doesn't really compute. J. S. Kunen. il pors *People Weekly* 32:118+ D 11 '89

STOLLE, FRED

Complete the shot. il *World Tennis* 36:86 Ap '89

Concentrate on the lines. il *World Tennis* 37:22 Ag '89

Learn to slice. il por *World Tennis* 37:41 S '89

Move back smoothly. il *World Tennis* 36:18 F '89

Play close to the waist. il *World Tennis* 36:28 My '89

Play no patterns. il por *World Tennis* 36:31 Ja '89

Play with pace. il por *World Tennis* 37:26 Jl '89

Release with control. il *World Tennis* 37:46 Je '89

Shorten your swing. il por *World Tennis* 36:77 Mr '89

Stick with rituals. il *World Tennis* 37:68 N '89

STOLLENWERK, JOHN JOSEPH, 1940-

about

Party crasher. R. Reiff. il por *Forbes* 143:128+ Je 12 '89

STOLT TANKERS & TERMINALS (HOLDINGS)

Stolt Tankers & Terminals (Holdings). J. Slovak. il *Fortune* 119:80 F 27 '89

STOLTENBERG, JOHN

Fighting violence against women is a man's job too. *Utne Reader* p44 N/D '89

STOLTZ, CRAIG

D.C. delectables. il *Harper's Bazaar* 122:218+ O '89

STOLTZ, ERIC

about

Eric Stoltz wouldn't hurt a Fly. C. Passalacqua. por *Mademoiselle* 95:84 F '89

STOLZE, WILLIAM J.

A team approach from the start. por *Nation's Business* 77:9 N '89

STOMACH

See also
Digestion

Diseases

See also
Peptic ulcers

Surgery

Shedding pounds through surgery [gastric bypass surgery] C. F. Henderson. pors *McCall's* 116:100+ Je '89

STOMACH EXERCISES See Exercise
STOMACH MUCOSA See Mucous membranes
STOMACH ULCERS See Peptic ulcers
STONE, BETTY
about
Dangerous liaisons. P. Kaihla. il pors *Maclean's* 102:20+ O 16 '89
STONE, DEBORAH
Dartmouth vs. freedom of speech. il *Conservative Digest* 15:24-7 My/Je '89
STONE, E. C., AND MINER, ELLIS D.
The Voyager 2 encounter with the Neptunian system. bibl f il *Science* 246:1417-21 D 15 '89
STONE, E. C., AND OTHERS
Energetic charged particles in the magnetosphere of Neptune. bibl f il *Science* 246:1489-94 D 15 '89
STONE, ELIZABETH, 1946-
My teacher, my friend. il *New Choices for the Best Years* 29:80+ Je '89
Stories worth retelling. il *New Choices for the Best Years* 29:89-90 F '89
STONE, GENE
The Coast. See issues of Gentlemen's Quarterly beginning September 1988
STONE, I. F. (ISIDOR FEINSTEIN), 1907-1989
The rights of Gorbachev [cover story] il *The New York Review of Books* 36:3-4+ F 16 '89
about
Obituary
Maclean's il 102:35 Jl 24 '89. G. Bain
Mother Jones il pors 14:17 S '89. M. Hertsgaard
The Nation 249:37+ Jl 10 '89
The New Republic 201:8+ Jl 10 '89
The New Yorker 65:21-2 Jl 24 '89
The Progressive 53:4 Ag '89. E. Knoll
Utne Reader por p144 S/O '89. T. Coffin
STONE, ISIDOR FEINSTEIN See Stone, I. F. (Isidor Feinstein), 1907-1989
STONE, JOHN, 1936-
Billows in the heart. il *The New York Times Magazine* p44-5 Je 18 '89
Chest pains: what do they mean? il *The New York Times Magazine* p53-4 F 19 '89
Fixing a child's heart. il *The New York Times Magazine* p37-8 Ag 13 '89
The man in green. il *Discover* 10:88-91 O '89
Tempo of the heart. il *The New York Times Magazine* p81-2 My 21 '89
Why some hands get so cold. il *The New York Times Magazine* p62+ Mr 12 '89
STONE, JUDITH
Light elements. See issues of Discover beginning April 1988
On your own. See issues of Glamour beginning February 1987
Priorities. il *Seventeen* 48:116-17+ N '89
STONE, LAWRENCE
The road to polygamy. bibl f il *The New York Review of Books* 36:12-15 Mr 2 '89
STONE, LOIS
A pack rat's tale. il *Americana* 17:19-21 My/Je '89
STONE, MICHAEL
Caught in the eighties: the new debtors. il *New York* 22:40-6 Ap 24 '89
Three lives. il pors *New York* 22:35-42 Ja 30 '89
What really happened in Bensonhurst [cover story] il pors map *New York* 22:46-56 N 6 '89
What really happened in Central Park [cover story] il map *New York* 22:30-43 Ag 14 '89
STONE, MICHAEL
about
Contractor licensing: who benefits? [interview] il *Home Mechanix* 85:22-3+ Je '89
STONE, OLIVER
about
Born on the Fourth of July [film] Reviews
New York il 22:101-2 D 18 '89. D. Denby
Newsweek il 114:74 D 25 '89. D. Ansen
Time il por 134:75-9 D 25 '89. R. Corliss
Talk radio [film] Reviews
The American Spectator 22:32 Mr '89. B. Bawer
Commonweal 116:20-1 Ja 13 '89. T. O'Brien
Film Comment il 25:64-70 Ja/F '89. R. Corliss
The Nation 248:67 Ja 9-16 '89. S. Klawans
National Review 41:46-9 Mr 24 '89. J. Simon
The New Republic 200:26 F 13 '89. S. Kauffmann
Newsweek il 113:54 Ja 9 '89. D. Ansen
People Weekly 31:15 Ja 9 '89. P. Travers
Video il 13:59+ Ag '89. J. Bernard
STONE, PAT
Christian ecology: a growing force in the environmental movement. *Utne Reader* p78-9 N/D '89
STONE, ROBERT, 1937-
East-West relation. il *Harper's* 279:63-7 N '89
Not scared of you [story] il *Gentlemen's Quarterly* 59:259+ Mr '89

STONE, TONY
about
The new Stone age. C. Connors. por *Seventeen* 48:134-5 Mr '89
STONE, WARD
about
Environmental sleuth battles bureaucrats. J. E. Milich. il por *The Progressive* 53:15-16 N '89
STONE, WILLIAM
about
Vik Muniz at Stux and William Stone at Tom Cugliani. N. Princenthal. *Art in America* 77:266 Ap '89
STONE
See also
Building stones
Marble
Rocks
STONE AGE
See also
Stone implements and weapons
America
See Paleo-Indians
Belgium
Conflict enters early European farm life [research by Lawrence H. Keeley] B. Bower. *Science News* 136:165 S 9 '89
Egypt
Uranium-series dated authigenic carbonates and Acheulian sites in southern Egypt. B. J. Szabo and others. bibl f il maps *Science* 243:1053-6 F 24 '89
Europe
European prehistory gets even older. S. Ackerman. il *Science* 246:28-30 O 6 '89
Letters [discussion of July 1989 article, Visual thinking in the Ice Age] R. White. *Scientific American* 261:12+ D '89
New evidence ages modern Europeans [accelerator mass spectrometry dating of Aurignacian remains; work of James L. Bischoff] B. Bower. *Science News* 136:388 D 16 '89
Visual thinking in the Ice Age [Aurignacian period body ornaments] R. White. bibl il *Scientific American* 261:92-9 Jl '89
Great Britain
The world's oldest road [Sweet Track of England: a 6,000-year-old wooden walkway discovered in a peat bog] J. Coles. il maps *Scientific American* 261:100-6 N '89
Israel
Stone blades yield early cultivation clues [research by Romana Unger-Hamilton] B. Bower. *Science News* 135:101 F 18 '89
Turkey
Ritual clues flow from prehistoric blood [analysis of hemoglobin residues from stone slab at Çayönü Tepesi site; work of Andrée R. Wood and Thomas H. Loy] B. Bower. *Science News* 136:405 D 23-30 '89
STONE CARVING
The gospel according to Verity [carving central entryway figures at Cathedral of St. John the Divine] B. Weber. il *The New York Times Magazine* p86 Jl 9 '89
The Ziolkowskis are honoring Chief Crazy Horse, by blasting out a mountain of a sculpture [Thunderhead Mountain] D. Grogan. il pors *People Weekly* 32:105+ D 4 '89
STONE CONSTRUCTION
See also
Stone houses
Building Stone Institute 1989 Tucker Awards. il *Architectural Record* 177:52-3 S '89
STONE CONTAINER CORP.
Merger wave rolls on [Canada's Consolidated-Bathurst acquired] D. Jenish. il *Maclean's* 102:28-30 F 6 '89
STONE GROUP CORPORATION
Computer engineer turns entrepreneur-in-exile [Wan Runnan] M. Sun. *Science* 245:592 Ag 11 '89
STONE HOUSES
A Philadelphia story: Edgar and Hope Scott at Ardrossan Farms. M. Tree. il por *Architectural Digest* 46:164-9 Je '89
STONE IMPLEMENTS AND WEAPONS
Blood from a stone [analysis of hemoglobin residue on tools leads to identification of prehistoric species; work of Thomas Loy] il *Discover* 10:18 N '89
Greek contact for humans, Neanderthals? [research by Curtis Runnels] B. Bower. *Science News* 135:39 Ja 21 '89
The gripping story of Paranthropus [evidence of tool use at Swartkrans site; study by Randall L. Susman] P. Shipman. il *Discover* 10:66-71 Ap '89
Ritual clues flow from prehistoric blood [analysis of hemoglobin residues from stone slab at Çayönü Tepesi site in Turkey; work of Andrée R. Wood and Thomas H. Loy] B. Bower. *Science News* 136:405 D 23-30 '89
Stone blades yield early cultivation clues [research by Romana Unger-Hamilton] B. Bower. *Science News* 135:101 F 18 '89
Stone tips on ancient hunting [work of John J. Shea] *Science News* 136:13 Jl 1 '89
When is a rock an artifact? S. Ackerman. *Science* 246:29 O 6 '89

STORES—cont.

Japan

See also
Tokyo (Japan)—Stores

Massachusetts

See also
Boston (Mass.)—Stores
South Hadley (Mass.)—Stores

New Jersey

See also
Edgewater (N.J.)—Stores
Plainsboro (N.J.)—Stores

New Mexico

See also
Santa Fe (N.M.)—Stores

New York (State)

See also
Indigo (Firm)
New York (N.Y.)—Stores

Ohio

See also
Cincinnati (Ohio)—Stores

Pennsylvania

See also
Philadelphia (Pa.)—Stores

Québec (Province)

See also
Québec (Québec)—Stores

Rhode Island

See also
Newport (R.I.)—Stores

Washington (D.C.)

See Washington (D.C.)—Stores
STORES, SECONDHAND *See* Secondhand trade
STOREY, MIKE
The Adirondacks in microcosm. il *The Conservationist*
43:14-19 My/Je '89
STORIES, CHILDREN'S *See* Children's stories
STORM, JACKIE
Nutrition advice to think twice about. il *Women's Sports
& Fitness* 11:20 N/D '89
Seeing through advertisers' health claims. il *Women's Sports
& Fitness* 11:82 Ap '89
STORM KING ART CENTER
Loose marbles. K. Larson. il *New York* 22:64 Ag 28 '89
STORMS

See also
Aviation—Storm hazards
Boats and boating—Storm hazards
Cycling—Storm hazards
Dust storms
Fishing—Storm conditions
Hunting—Storm conditions
Hurricanes
Snowstorms
Tennis—Storm hazards
Thunderstorms
Tornadoes
Stalking the super storms. R. Lipkin. il *Reader's Digest*
134:76-80 Ap '89
STORR, HANS GEORGE, 1931-
about
The money magician at Philip Morris. L. J. Nathans. il
por *Business Week* p78 Ap 10 '89
STORR, ROBERT
Riddled Sphinxes. il *Art in America* 77:126-31 Mr '89
Shape shifter [cover story] bibl f il *Art in America* 77:210-21+
Ap '89
STORRS, ELEANOR
about
Rising star. J. Watson. il pors *National Wildlife* 27:46-9
O/N '89
STORY, ALISA
about
Hit-and-run: a family's nightmare. D. M. Mazie. il *Reader's
Digest* 135:152-7 D '89
STORY, RICHARD DAVID
Mothers of invention. il por *New York* 22:46-51 Je 5 '89
THE STORY OF KUFUR SHAMMA [drama] *See* Lubeck,
Jackie
STORY OF WOMEN [film] *See* Motion picture reviews—Single
works
STORY TELLING
From Dickens to Beckett in Grand Central [stories created
by beggars in New York City] A. Broyard. il *The New
York Times Book Review* 94:12 Mr 12 '89
Learning by story [work of E. D. Hirsch and A. Bloom]
N. Postman. il *The Atlantic* 264:119-24 D '89
Memory, imagination, and learning: connected by the story
[place of story telling in teaching] K. Egan. bibl f il *Phi
Delta Kappan* 70:455-9 F '89
Stories worth retelling [family tales] E. Stone. il *New Choices
for the Best Years* 29:89-90 F '89
Storytelling and Native American CDAs [Child Development
Associate credential] C. D. Beers. il *Children Today* 18:24-5
Mr/Ap '89

Anecdotes, facetiae, satire, etc.
The way mama tells it. R. Blount. il *The Atlantic* 264:30+
Jl '89
STORYTELLING *See* Story telling
STOTSKI, LEE
about
Little girl, big trouble. D. Grogan. il pors *People Weekly*
31:36-41 F 20 '89
STOUT, JUANITA KIDD
about
A career of firsts. il pors *Ebony* 44:76+ F '89
Juanita Stout forced off Philadelphia high court. il por *Jet*
76:12 Je 5 '89
STOUT (BEVERAGE)
The crowned heads of Britain in a can [new beer can for
Guinness stout works like a keg tap] il *U.S. News &
World Report* 107:19 Ag 21 '89
STOVE BLACK *See* Richardson, Richard
STOVER, ALLAN C.
Automatic test equipment. il *Radio-Electronics* 60:61-4 O
'89
STOVER, DAWN
What's new. See issues of Popular Science beginning January
1987
STOVER, LAREN
Best friends, all the way. il *Mademoiselle* 95:212-17 S '89
STOVES

See also
Convection ovens
Wood stoves
The chicks that stayed home in the range [use of an AGA
coal stove to save sick chicks] M. Kernan. il *Smithsonian*
20:214 S '89
Electric & gas ranges. il *Consumer Reports* 54:80-3 F '89
Electric & gas ranges. il *Consumer Reports* 54:304-7 D '89
The woman in the kitchen [mother's sacrifices] G. Sledge.
il *Reader's Digest* 135:85-90 S '89
Collectors and collecting
Lost stove art [cover story] A. Meyer. il *The Mother Earth
News* 115:62-5 Ja/F '89
Safety devices and measures
Commercial stoves at home: it could be risky business.
il *Sunset (Central West edition)* 182:114 Mr '89
STOWELL, KENT
about
Seattle strikes gold: Pacific Northwest Ballet's grand pas
de deux. M. Hunt. il pors *Dance Magazine* 63:36-41 Mr
'89
STOWELL (LEIGH) & COMPANY *See* Leigh Stowell &
Company
STOWERS, JAMES E.
about
Twentieth Century: a mighty performer for truly small in-
vestors. G. Weiss. il por *Business Week* p130 D 25 '89-Ja
1 '90
STRADELLA, ALESSANDRO, 1644-1682
about
Santa Pelagia [oratorio] Reviews
The New Yorker 65:91-2 Mr 20 '89. A. Porter
STRADIVARIUS VIOLIN *See* Violin
STRAFACE, FRANK J.
about
A luxury supermarket woos its upscale clients with a yuppie
credo—you are what you eat! il por *People Weekly* 32:135-6
D 11 '89
**STRAFFORD, THOMAS WENTWORTH, 1ST EARL OF,
1593-1641**
about
Strafford in Ireland, 1633-40. H. F. Kearney. il por maps
History Today 39:20-5 Jl '89
STRAGIER, PATRICK, AND OTHERS
Chromosomal rearrangement generating a composite gene
for a developmental transcription factor. bibl f il *Science*
243:507-12 Ja 27 '89
STRAIGHT, INC.
Straight. C. Tarpy. il *National Geographic* 175:48-51 Ja '89
STRAIN GAGES
Predicting earthquakes [strainmeter developed by Michael
Gladwin] S. F. Brown. il *Popular Science* 234:124-5 Je
'89
STRAINS AND STRESSES

See also
Strain gages
A relation to describe rate-dependent material failure. B.
Voight. bibl f il *Science* 243:200-3 Ja 13 '89
Shear forces in molecularly thin films. M. Schoen and others.
bibl f il *Science* 245:1223-5 S 15 '89
STRANAHAN HOUSE (FORT LAUDERDALE, FLA.)
Little house on the New River. il *Southern Living* 24:25
Ag '89
STRAND, MARK, 1934-
The continuous life [poem] *The New Yorker* 64:34 Ja
9 '89
The idea [poem] *The New Yorker* 65:120 Je 12 '89
Life in the valley [poem] *The New Yorker* 65:38 Ap
3 '89
Orpheus alone [poem] *The New Yorker* 65:42-3 Mr
6 '89

STRAND, MARK, 1934——cont.
Velocity meadows [poem] *The New Republic* 200:35
My 22 '89
STRANGE, CURTIS   *about*
King of the hill [cover story] R. Reilly. il pors *Sports Illustrated* 70:20-5 Je 26 '89
STRANGE, IAN J.
Albatross alley [cover story] il *Natural History* p26-33 Jl '89
STRANGE, MARTY   *about*
A fighter for family farming. il por *Successful Farming* 87:24-5 Ja '89
STRANGE ATTRACTORS
Where strange attractors lurk. R. Pool. *Science* 243:1292 Mr 10 '89
STRANGE MATTER *See* Matter
STRANGERS
Have you ever shared a look, a touch, a moment of flirtation with a stranger? S. Nelson. il *Glamour* 87:222-3+ N '89
Strangers can enrich your life. A. Whitman. il *Reader's Digest* 134:57-8+ Je '89
The woman in the yellow hat [encounter with a stranger in Oregon's Eagle Cap Wilderness] P. G. Quinnett. il *Audubon* 91:46-8 S '89
STRANGERS IN MOTION PICTURES
Strangers on the screen [cover story; special issue] il *The Unesco Courier* 42:10-43 O '89
STRANGULATION
The victim of a savage attack, a minister's wife is condemned to a long death in life [P. Railey, severely brain damaged after being strangled in Dallas, Tex. home] J. Young. il pors *People Weekly* 31:50-2+ Ja 16 '89
STRASBERG, ANDY
Baseball lives [excerpt] M. Bryan. il por *Sports Illustrated* 70:85+ Ap 24 '89
STRASBOURG (FRANCE)
                    Description
Surprising Strasbourg. A. Furst. il *New Choices for the Best Years* 29:54-7 Je '89
          See also   **Galleries and museums**
Musée des Arts Décoratifs (Strasbourg, France)
STRASSELS, PAUL N.
For your tax file. See issues of Nation's Business beginning April 1988
It's your money. See issues of Nation's Business beginning September 1988
STRATAS, TERESA   *about*
Out of her own way [cover story] M. Mayer. il pors *Opera News* 54:14-16+ D 9 '89
STRATEGIC AIR COMMAND *See* United States. Air Force. Strategic Air Command
STRATEGIC ARMS LIMITATION TALKS
The abolitionist [arms control efforts during R. Reagan's first term] J. Newhouse. *The New Yorker* 64:37-52 Ja 2 '89
STRATEGIC ARMS REDUCTION TALKS
Accords on SDI, cruise missiles, mobile ICBMs aid START process. *Aviation Week & Space Technology* 131:25 O 2 '89
Can mobile missiles give Bush a shot in the arms talks? D. Griffiths and others. il *Business Week* p61 F 27 '89
Chop down the nuclear arsenals. H. A. Bethe. il *The Bulletin of the Atomic Scientists* 45:11-15 Mr '89
Comment and correspondence. M. M. Kampelman. *Foreign Affairs* 68:160-2 Summ '89
Congress presses treaty objectives on Trident submarine program. D. F. Bond. *Aviation Week & Space Technology* 131:25-6 Ag 21 '89
Congressional debate on B-2 turns to arms control impact. D. F. Bond. il *Aviation Week & Space Technology* 131:24 Jl 31 '89
Did anyone tell the Pentagon? [nuclear weapons programs in proposed budget] P. F. Walker. *The Bulletin of the Atomic Scientists* 45:12+ O '89
Getting out of the STARTing block [verification issues] S. N. Graybeal and P. B. McFate. il *Scientific American* 261:61-7 D '89
How to understand the unthinkable. D. Stanglin. il *U.S. News & World Report* 106:32-3+ Je 12 '89
Inching ever closer together [Jackson Hole meeting between J. A. Baker and E. Shevardnadze] B. Javetski. il *Business Week* p40-1 O 9 '89
Jump start. A. Gilchrist and L. Halper. *The Nation* 248:653 My 15 '89
Let's get back to the table. A. Obukhov. il *The Bulletin of the Atomic Scientists* 45:6 Ap '89
Merchants of peace. T. Beardsley. *Scientific American* 260:98+ Ja '89
The muddle on missiles. J. Barry. il *Newsweek* 113:42 F 13 '89
NATO strategy: back to basics. H. Rühle. *Current (Washington, D.C.)* 312:34-9 My '89
Reagan's gift [opportunity for G. Bush to complete strategic arms reduction treaty] J. Beatty. il *The Atlantic* 263:58-62+ F '89

Ripe for revision [limit on number of strategic bombers and proposed ban on mobile missiles] M. Flournoy. il *The Bulletin of the Atomic Scientists* 45:4 My '89
START deals cut at Jackson Hole. J. Mendelsohn. il pors *The Bulletin of the Atomic Scientists* 45:25-7 D '89
START finish. J. P. Rubin. *Foreign Policy* 76:96-118 Fall '89
Status of the Strategic Arms Reduction Talks [statement, August 3, 1989] R. Burt. *Department of State Bulletin* 89:17-19 O '89
Strategic defense in peril again. C. W. Weinberger. il *Forbes* 144:33 O 30 '89
"Swift responses" usually mean bad agreements. C. W. Weinberger. il *Forbes* 144 Special Issue:31 O 23 '89
STRATEGIC DEFENSE INITIATIVE
Accords on SDI, cruise missiles, mobile ICBMs aid START process. *Aviation Week & Space Technology* 131:25 O 2 '89
Advances in induction-type FEL add to its antimissile potential [free electron laser] B. W. Henderson. il *Aviation Week & Space Technology* 130:81+ My 8 '89
Airborne Optical Adjunct program threatened with cancellation. P. A. Gilmartin. *Aviation Week & Space Technology* 131:24 Ag 21 '89
Alpha missile defense laser is fired for first time [Zenith Star project] il *Aviation Week & Space Technology* 130:23-4 Ap 17 '89
Army to broaden effort to develop extended-range interceptor. P. A. Gilmartin. il *Aviation Week & Space Technology* 131:30 O 16 '89
ASATs: Star Wars on the cheap. C. A. Monfort. bibl f il *The Bulletin of the Atomic Scientists* 45:10-13 Ap '89
Ball develops multi-anode microchannel array for Space Telescope, defense uses. W. B. Scott. il *Aviation Week & Space Technology* 130:296-7 Je 12 '89
Boeing Aerospace wins SDI contract for RF-driven free electron laser. P. A. Gilmartin. il *Aviation Week & Space Technology* 131:21 O 23 '89
Brilliant Pebbles: amazing new missile killer [work of L. Wood and G. Canavan] R. K. Bennett. *Reader's Digest* 135:128-33 S '89
Brilliant Pebbles shines in phase one SDI test. il *Popular Mechanics* 166:14 O '89
Budget cuts threaten full-scale development start for SDI. *Aviation Week & Space Technology* 130:22 Ap 24 '89
Bush defense strategy to reshape SDI program. T. M. Foley. *Aviation Week & Space Technology* 130:18-20 Ja 30 '89
Can Brent Scowcroft be converted to SDI? J. T. Hackett. por *Conservative Digest* 15:15 Mr/Ap '89
Courting disaster in orbit [nuclear power] G. E. Brown, Jr. il *The Bulletin of the Atomic Scientists* 45:7-9 Ap '89
Defending people by defending rockets [MX vs. Midgetman] R. N. Perle. il *U.S. News & World Report* 106:39+ Je 26 '89
Defense Dept. postpones decision on Brilliant Pebbles until November. P. A. Gilmartin. *Aviation Week & Space Technology* 131:23-4 Ag 14 '89
Defense Dept. to launch competition for exoatmospheric interceptor design. P. A. Gilmartin. *Aviation Week & Space Technology* 131:27+ N 6 '89
Delay of first HEDI test launch caused by flight destruct system replacement [High Endoatmospheric Defense Interceptor] P. A. Gilmartin. *Aviation Week & Space Technology* 131:21 O 30 '89
A deterrent that deters [special section] *National Review* 41:33-5 My 5 '89
Econo-SDI. J. Horgan. *Scientific American* 260:14 F '89
Energy Dept. plans to cut spending on nuclear directed-energy weapons. T. M. Foley. *Aviation Week & Space Technology* 130:132-3 F 20 '89
Heavenly Pebbles. *Commonweal* 116:292-3 My 19 '89
Interview: Peter Hagelstein [resignation from Lawrence Livermore's X ray laser work] B. Moseley. pors *Omni (New York, N.Y.)* 11:74-6+ My '89
Laser-based communication system eyed. *High Technology Business* 9:35 F '89
Lockheed develops threat warning system for U.S. military satellites [Satellite On-board Attack Warning System] B. W. Henderson. il *Aviation Week & Space Technology* 131:61+ Jl 3 '89
Lockheed integrating components of SDI exoatmospheric interceptor. B. W. Henderson. il *Aviation Week & Space Technology* 130:50 Ja 2 '89
Los Alamos free electron laser altered for higher-power tests. T. M. Foley. il *Aviation Week & Space Technology* 130:88-9 F 13 '89
Medical preparedness and nuclear war [address, April 23, 1988] J. M. Orient. *Vital Speeches of the Day* 55:186-90 Ja 1 '89
New SDI surveillance satellite to use upgraded Titan 2 booster [Midcourse Space Experiment spacecraft] C. Covault. il *Aviation Week & Space Technology* 131:31 S 25 '89
Nonlinear thinking [chaotic theories of G. Mayer-Kress] J. Horgan. *Scientific American* 260:26+ Je '89
Nunn's SDI two-step. J. D. Isaacs. il por *The Bulletin of the Atomic Scientists* 45:5-6 D '89

STRATEGIC DEFENSE INITIATIVE—*cont.*

Pebbles go bam-bam [Brilliant Pebbles] F. Barnes. *The New Republic* 200:12+ Ap 17 '89

Pentagon seeks 50% rise in SDI funding for 1990. P. A. Gilmartin. *Aviation Week & Space Technology* 130:39 Ja 23 '89

Political review, technical tests will set course of SDI research. il *Aviation Week & Space Technology* 130:61+ Mr 20 '89

Promise of Brilliant Pebbles casts doubt on SDI plan. T. M. Foley. il *Aviation Week & Space Technology* 130:260-1 Mr 20 '89

Qaddafi goes ballistic [Accidental Launch Protection System] J. Pike. *The New Republic* 200:14-16 Mr 20 '89

Relay Mirror Experiment spacecraft completes environmental, optical tests. il *Aviation Week & Space Technology* 131:51+ N 13 '89

Report says U.S. space power programs inadequate to meet long-term SDI goals [National Research Council report] il *Aviation Week & Space Technology* 130:47+ F 20 '89

Rings of power [superconducting magnetic energy storage ring] N. J. Freundlich. il *Popular Science* 234:66-7+ Ja '89

Scientists call for policy on space nuclear reactors. R. G. O'Lone. il *Aviation Week & Space Technology* 130:23 Ja 23 '89

SDI budget cutbacks to delay near-term weapons deployment [views of George L. Monahan] *Aviation Week & Space Technology* 130:22-3 My 22 '89

SDI Delta Star satellite readied for targeting research flight. *Aviation Week & Space Technology* 129:32 Mr 6 '89

SDI experiments set for launch in January [Low-power Atmospheric Compensation and Relay Mirror experiments] P. A. Gilmartin. il *Aviation Week & Space Technology* 131:35 S 11 '89

SDI free electron laser faces cut in power, delay. il *Aviation Week & Space Technology* 130:22 My 22 '89

SDI officials plan to boost Brilliant Pebbles funding. P. A. Gilmartin. *Aviation Week & Space Technology* 131:21 N 27 '89

SDI Phase One system will meet Joint Chiefs' minimum defense levels. T. M. Foley. *Aviation Week & Space Technology* 130:30-1 Je 26 '89

SDI technology tests launched as defense budget is assessed. il *Aviation Week & Space Technology* 131:22 O 2 '89

SDI urges NASA to accelerate satellite retrieval with shuttle [Long-Duration Exposure Facility] C. Covault. il *Aviation Week & Space Technology* 130:80-1 My 8 '89

SDI watch. See occasional issues of National Review beginning February 13, 1987

SDIO begins measuring booster plumes with Delta Star sensors. E. H. Kolcum. il *Aviation Week & Space Technology* 130:26-7 Ap 3 '89

Sharp rise in Brilliant Pebbles interceptor funding accompanied by new questions about technical feasibility. T. M. Foley. il *Aviation Week & Space Technology* 130:20-1 My 22 '89

Short-pulse thrusters for SDI require new instrumentation [magnetic suspension test stand for Lightweight Exoatmospheric Projectile] M. A. Dornheim. il *Aviation Week & Space Technology* 131:53+ Ag 28 '89

Smart rocks, Brilliant Pebbles, genius dust? G. Chapman. il *The Bulletin of the Atomic Scientists* 45:10-11+ N '89

Space interceptor model hovers during laboratory tests at Edwards. T. M. Foley. il *Aviation Week & Space Technology* 130:49 Ja 2 '89

Space reactors and arms control. C. Norman. il *Science* 243:476 Ja 27 '89

Star Wars isn't dead yet. T. Pouschine. il *Forbes* 143:76+ My 1 '89

Star Wars won't die. T. Engelhardt. il *The Progressive* 53:22-3 S '89

Stopping killer bees with Star Wars [Africanized honey bees] J. Schlefer. *Technology Review* 92:2 My/Je '89

Strategic defense can be dangerous. J. P. Scanlan. il *The New Leader* 72:13-14 Je 12-26 '89

Strategic defense in peril again. C. W. Weinberger. il *Forbes* 144:33 O 30 '89

Strategic Defense Initiative [special section] il *Aviation Week & Space Technology* 130:45+ Ap 3 '89

Strategic Defense Initiative [weapons developments; special section] il *Aviation Week & Space Technology* 130:56-8+ My 15 '89

Successful neutral particle beam firing paves way for more ambitious SDI test. il *Aviation Week & Space Technology* 131:31-2 Jl 24 '89

Testing weapons in space [problems of Anti-Ballistic Missile Treaty compliance] A. B. Carter. bibl il *Scientific American* 261:33-40 Jl '89

Throwing stones at "Brilliant Pebbles". J. Jacky. il *Technology Review* 92:20-1+ O '89

Too Brilliant by half [Brilliant Pebbles] il *The New Republic* 200:7-9 My 29 '89

Tower supports SDI, citing Soviet antimissile advances [Defense Secretary confirmation hearings] *Aviation Week & Space Technology* 130:20-1 Ja 30 '89

U.S. developing survivable warning/antimissile satellites [Boost Surveillance Tracking System; cover story] T. M. Foley. il *Aviation Week & Space Technology* 130:34-5+ Ja 23 '89

The waning technological glitter of Star Wars [Brilliant Pebbles] S. Budiansky. il *U.S. News & World Report* 107:53-4 Jl 3 '89

We must not give up Strategic Defense. C. W. Weinberger. il *Forbes* 143:31 F 6 '89

Will Star Wars ever fly? B. Van Voorst. il *Time* 133:20 Je 26 '89

STRATEGIC INFORMATION INC.

Boy wonder grows up [W. Berkley] E. F. Cone. il por *Forbes* 143:49+ F 20 '89

STRATEGIC LAWSUITS AGAINST PUBLIC PARTICIPATION

A new way to intimidate activists. E. Pell. *Utne Reader* p115 N/D '89

A SLAPP in the face. J. Zweig. il *Forbes* 143:106 My 29 '89

Stand up and be sued. J. Stiak. *Sierra* 74:28+ N/D '89

STRATFORD FESTIVAL (ONT.)

A summer triumph. J. Bemrose. il *Maclean's* 102:44-5 Jl 10 '89

STRATIGRAPHIC GEOLOGY See Geology, Stratigraphic

STRATOSPHERE See Atmosphere, Upper

STRATTEN, DOROTHY, 1960-1980
about
The passions of Peter Bogdanovich [cover story] J. Wadler. il pors *People Weekly* 31:56-8+ Ja 23 '89

STRATTON (VT.)
The Volvo tournament brings Vermont to the net. R. Duffy. il *Business Week* p82-3 Jl 24 '89

STRAUS, HAL
Freaks of nurture. il por *American Health* 8:70-1 Ja/F '89
The Lazarus file. il *American Health* 8:67-8+ My '89

STRAUSS, ELTON
Aaron: on the mend. il por *World Tennis* 36:12-13 Ja '89

STRAUSS, HENRY
Heroes of the frozen cliff. il *Reader's Digest* 134:102-7 Ap '89

STRAUSS, JOHANN, 1825-1899
about
Die Fledermaus [operetta] Reviews
   Opera News il 53:28-31 Ja 7 '89

STRAUSS, RICHARD, 1864-1949
about
Die Frau ohne Schatten [opera] Reviews
   The New Yorker 65:134 D 11 '89. A. Porter
   Opera News il 54:33+ D 9 '89. R. Markow
   Opera News il 54:38-9+ D 9 '89. S. R. Cerf
   Opera News il 54:42-5 D 9 '89
Friedenstag [opera] Reviews
   The New Yorker 65:134-5 D 11 '89. A. Porter
Salome [opera] Reviews
   New York il 22:101 Mr 6 '89. P. G. Davis
   The New Yorker 65:90 Mr 20 '89. A. Porter
   Opera News il 53:18+ Mr 4 '89
   Opera News il 53:24-6+ Mr 4 '89. J. Kestner
Spirited Strauss from Gerard Schwarz. D. Hall. il *Stereo Review* 54:123-4 D '89
Top of the line. P. G. Davis. il *New York* 22:100+ Ap 24 '89

STRAUSS, ROBERT S.
about
Diarist. J. Bennet. *The New Republic* 200:50 Je 19 '89

STRAUSS, STEPHEN
The Quebec phenomenon. *World Press Review* 36:68 S '89

STRAVINSKY, IGOR, 1882-1971
about
Jews and geniuses. R. Craft. il pors *The New York Review of Books* 36:35-7 F 16 '89
'Jews and geniuses': an exchange [discussion of February 16, 1989 article] R. Craft. il *The New York Review of Books* 36:57-8 Je 15 '89

STRAVINSKY, JOHN
The boxer the champs won't fight. il pors *The New York Times Magazine* p32-4+ Ag 13 '89

STRAW, SYD
about
Surprise! It's Syd Straw! R. Givens. por *Stereo Review* 54:129 N '89
Syd Straw. J. Ressner. por *Rolling Stone* p25 S 21 '89

STRAW
Grasping at straws . . . [fashions] il *'Teen* 33:34 My '89
Straw bargains [accessories] S. Clark. il *Glamour* 87:186 Ag '89

STRAWBERRIES
See also
Cooking—Fruit

STRAWBERRY, DARRYL
about
Pied à Darryl. il pors *Esquire* 111:176-7 Je '89
The week that was. B. Newman. il pors *Sports Illustrated* 70:18-20 Mr 13 '89

STRAWBERRY DESSERTS See Desserts

STRAY-PEDERSEN, BABILL
"Take care of yourself". il *World Health* p27-8 Ja/F '89

STRAYER, BARRY
about
Preparing for 1997. J. Keating. *Maclean's* 102:73-4 N 20 '89

STREAM CONSERVATION
See also
Adopt-a-Stream Foundation
The charge of the brook brigades. S. Pollock. il *Sierra* 74:24-6+ N/D '89

STREAM CROSSING *See* River crossing

STREAM ECOLOGY
Shredders and riparian vegetation [relationship between plant litter and aquatic invertebrate growth] K. W. Cummins and others. bibl f il *BioScience* 39:24-30 Ja '89
Wildfires and Yellowstone's stream ecosystems. G. W. Minshall and others. bibl f il maps *BioScience* 39:707-15 N '89

STREAM IMPROVEMENT *See* Stream conservation

STREAMERS (COMPUTER MEMORY SYSTEMS) *See* Computers—Memory systems

STREAMERS (FISHING FLIES) *See* Fishing lures, flies, etc.

STREAMS *See* Brooks, creeks, etc.

STREBEIGH, FRED
The Chinese intelligentsia: training the new elite. il *Current (Washington, D.C.)* 318:32-40 D '89
Training China's new elite. il *The Atlantic* 263:72-80 Ap '89

STRECKER, TERESA R., AND OTHERS
Reciprocal effects of hyper- and hypoactivity mutations in the Drosophila pattern gene *torso*. bibl f il *Science* 243:1062-6 F 24 '89

STREEP, MERYL
about
Meryl Streep comes calling [cover story; interview] W. Wasserstein. il pors *The Saturday Evening Post* 261:50-3+ Jl/Ag '89
A mother's crusade [cover story] J. C. McCullagh. il pors *Organic Gardening* 36:32-7 Ap '89
Ms. Streep goes to Washington to stop a bitter harvest [interview] B. Johnson. il pors *People Weekly* 31:50-1 Mr 20 '89
Streep vs. Davis. pors *Life* 12:114-15 Spr '89
Unnatural actresses. R. Rosenbaum. il pors *Mademoiselle* 95:46+ Ja '89

STREET ADDRESSES
See also
Address books
Change of address

STREET ART
Building a sidewalk art booth. E. V. Cohen. il *American Artist* 53:68-72+ My '89

STREET CARS *See* Trolleys

STREET CLOCKS *See* Clocks

STREET GANGS *See* Gangs

STREET LIGHTING
See also
Flagstaff (Ariz.)—Lighting
Traverse City (Mich.)—Lighting

STREET MUSIC AND MUSICIANS
New York has something to howl about again—legendary street musician Moondog. M. Small. il pors *People Weekly* 32:109-10 N 27 '89

STREET PHOTOGRAPHERS
Extra-artistic [Times Square street photographers] *The New Yorker* 65:32-3 D 25 '89

STREET-PORTER, JANET
about
Prime time. C. K. Gandee. il por *House & Garden* 161:182-7+ Mr '89

STREET SCENE [opera] *See* Weill, Kurt, 1900-1950

STREET TRADES
See also
New York (N.Y.)—Street trades
Street art

STREET TRAFFIC *See* City traffic

STREET TREES *See* Trees in cities

STREETCARS *See* Trolleys

STREETS
Sprucing up our cities' streets [views of Gary Greenan] *USA Today (Periodical)* 118:5-6 D '89
Streetscapes: impressions of city life [cover story; special issue] il *The Unesco Courier* 42:9-45 Ag '89

STREIKER, LOWELL D.
Brainwashed or converted? *The Christian Century* 106:721-3 Ag 2-9 '89

STREITFELD, DAVID
Capital venture. il por *House & Garden* 161:76-81+ Ag '89

STREITFERDT, THOMAS
about
White Harlem minister convicted of sex abuse. il por *Jet* 76:32 Je 19 '89
White minister called 'wolf in sheep's clothes' gets 7 years in sex cases. il por *Jet* 76:53 Jl 24 '89

STRENGTH OF MATERIALS
See also
Fracture mechanics
Hardness

STRENGTH OF MUSCLES *See* Muscle strength

STREP THROAT
Protection against streptococcal pharyngeal colonization with a vaccinia: M protein recombinant. V. A. Fischetti and others. bibl f il *Science* 244:1487-90 Je 23 '89

STREPTAVIDIN
Structural origins of high-affinity biotin binding to streptavidin. P. C. Weber and others. bibl f il *Science* 243:85-8 Ja 6 '89

STREPTOCOCCAL INFECTIONS
Vaccines and vaccination
Protection against streptococcal pharyngeal colonization with a vaccinia: M protein recombinant. V. A. Fischetti and others. bibl f il *Science* 244:1487-90 Je 23 '89

STREPTOKINASE
Clot-buster's cost-effectiveness questioned [TPA vs. streptokinase] R. Weiss. *Science News* 135:214 Ap 8 '89
Heart teamwork [use of aspirin and streptokinase to reduce heart-attack deaths; research by Samuel Z. Goldhaber] il *Prevention (Emmaus, Pa.)* 41:14 Ja '89

STRESEMANN, GUSTAV, 1878-1929
about
Stresemann and Weimar. J. Wright. bibl il pors *History Today* 39:35-41 O '89

STRESHLY, WILLIAM, AND SCHAPS, ERIC
Teaching character development. *The Education Digest* 54:25-8 Mr '89

STRESS
See also
Anxiety
Crisis management (Psychology)
Job stress
Posttraumatic stress disorder
Time pressure
Time sickness
TMJ syndrome
Traumatism
6 natural tranquilizers and how to use them [relaxation techniques] J. Mullich. il *Prevention (Emmaus, Pa.)* 41:41-6 Ag '89
Avoiding stress [weddings; views of William J. Doherty] C. Slom. il *McCall's* 116:34 My '89
Blazing the lonesome trail [stress of mountaineering as a model for interplanetary missions; research by Barbara Kanki and others] S. Kaiser. il *Ad Astra* 1:32-4+ O '89
Brain may be the villain [stress ulcers; research by Daniel Hernandez] *USA Today (Periodical)* 117:16 F '89
Caution: your stress style may be hazardous to your health. D. Fields. il *Mademoiselle* 95:158 Ap '89
Coping with stress. L. G. Katz. il *Parents* 64:174 F '89
Easy does it [travel stress] R. McGarvey. il *Travel Holiday* 172:28-31 O '89
Energy up—stress-level down! [excerpt from Positive living and health] il *Redbook* 174:126-7+ D '89
The evening rush hour [family stress at day's end] K. Levine. il *Parents* 64:58+ Ag '89
Fame means stress. il *Psychology Today* 22:54-5 D '88
For less stress—breathe right. M. Rhodes. il *Redbook* 173:14 Je '89
Gut emotions [irritable bowel syndrome] M. Adessa. il *Psychology Today* 23:72+ Mr '89
Hidden emotions, high cholesterol [research by Raymond Niaura] S. Chollar. *Psychology Today* 23:24 S '89
Holiday stress [results of poll] I. Groller. il *Parents* 64:33 D '89
How to slow down [setting limits on volunteer work] J. G. Fitzpatrick. il *Parents* 64:97-102 Ap '89
Is your skin showing signs of stress? [advice from medical experts] il *Redbook* 173:90-3 Jl '89
Making health a family affair. J. Barone. il *Working Woman* 14:179-80+ N '89
Making stress work for you [views of Robert J. Kriegel] S. Young. *Glamour* 87:40 Ag '89
Modest treatment yields heartfelt benefits [stress-monitoring program by Nancy Frasure-Smith and Raymond Prince] B. Bower. *Science News* 136:261 O 21 '89
Press the button, depress immunity [research by Carol S. Weisse] B. Bower. *Science News* 136:141 Ag 26 '89
The relaxed tummy [effects upon digestion; research by Donald R. Morse] W. Cole. il *American Health* 8:126-8 Je '89
Setting the stage for infection [lowered response rate of natural killer cells; research by Sandra M. Levy] B. Bower. *Science News* 136:141 Ag 26 '89
Simple holiday stress relievers. J. Mullich. il *Reader's Digest* 135:49-50+ D '89
The state of the kids [special section; with editorial comment by Joel Gurin] il *American Health* 8:43-6+, 110 O '89
Stimulating rats [small amounts of stress may be beneficial; research by Jay Weiss] *Discover* 10:10 S '89
Stress' effect on immune system [research by Ronald Glaser] *USA Today (Periodical)* 117:4 Je '89
Stressbusters. D. Sobel. il *Ladies' Home Journal* 106:74 '89
Stressed tresses [may cause baldness] R. Wiest. il *American Health* 8:20-2 S '89
To beat stress, don't relax: get tough [research by Ric Dienstbier] L. Miller. il *Psychology Today* 23:62-3

STRESS—*cont.*

Type-A tots: when pushing kids leads to stress. A. Atkins. il *Better Homes and Gardens* 67:36+ N '89

Ulcers and stress: the missing link? [research by Pamela Walker and Mark Feldman] J. Folkenberg. *Psychology Today* 23:24-5 N '89

Unsweetened stress [link between stress and desire for sweets; research by Neil Grunberg] B. Fischman. il *Psychology Today* 23:72 Mr '89

Unwind! Relax and enjoy life. A. Mascelli. il *Essence* 19:59-62 Ja '89

Ways to reduce holiday stress. S. Seliger. il *McCall's* 116:100+ Ja '89

What farmers are saying. C. Tevis. il *Successful Farming* 87:49 My '89

When stress is best. E. E. Rosenbaum. il *New Choices for the Best Years* 29:26+ Je '89

Will there be bad fairies at your wedding? L. Dormen. il *Glamour* 87:236-7+ Je '89

Anecdotes, facetiae, satire, etc.

Some great ways to ruin your day [views of Ed Beckham] il *USA Today (Periodical)* 118:3 D '89

STRESS FRACTURES *See* Fractures

STRESS REDUCING EXERCISES

Decompress! This workout battles burnout. il *Mademoiselle* 95:196-9 F '89

Take a breather—take a stress break [with tips from Shirley MacLaine] E. Byron. il *Redbook* 173:87-9 Jl '89

STRESSES *See* Strains and stresses

STRETCHING EXERCISES

The desk stretch: 5 stress stoppers. il *Mademoiselle* 95:30 D '89

Eight minutes to stretch [cover story] B. Anderson. il *Women's Sports & Fitness* 11:46-8+ N/D '89

The flex factor [runners; cover story] B. Anderson. il *Runner's World* 24:38-43 F '89

Must you stretch before exercise? S. Young. il *Glamour* 87:55 Ap '89

Screen test [videotaping yourself to improve cycling form] B. Prichard. il *Bicycling* 30:136-8+ Ap '89

Stretch-and-strengthen exercises [for arthritis] G. Yanker and K. Burton. il *New Choices for the Best Years* 29:64-5 S '89

Stretching. il *World Tennis* 36:72 My '89

Stretching your limits [work of B. Prichard] M. Bloom. il *Skiing* 41:36+ Ja '89

Super muscle stretches [for backache] *Prevention (Emmaus, Pa.)* 41:42-6 Mr '89

The turning point [D. Goldie's stretching routine] P. Stites. il pors *World Tennis* 36:66-9 F '89

STRETTON, FREDERIC LEIGHTON *See* Leighton of Stretton, Frederic Leighton, Baron, 1830-1896

STRICK, DAVID

about

Hometown: Hollywood. M. Kiwak. il *Petersen's Photographic Magazine* 18:27-9 My '89

STRICK, LISA WILSON

Mother-daughter nurses. il *Good Housekeeping* 209:65-6+ O '89

STRICKLAND, CAROL

Penfield Music Commission Project. il *Down Beat* 56:24 Je '89

STRICKLAND, CAROL

Something stinks in Morgan City. il *The Nation* 249:448-51 O 23 '89

STRICKLAND, EDWARD

Pieces of Robin Chandler. il por *American Visions* 4:40-3 D '89

STRICKLAND, JOHN K., JR.

The cosmic classroom. il *Ad Astra* 1:20-3 Mr '89

STRICKLAND, WILLIAM

The future of black men. il *Essence* 20:50-2+ N '89

STRIDE RITE CORP.

Stride Rite may soon be walking taller [stock price] G. G. Marcial. il *Business Week* p96 Je 12 '89

STRIETER, R. M., AND OTHERS

Endothelial cell gene expression of a neutrophil chemotactic factor by TNF-α, LPS, and IL-1β. bibl f il *Science* 243:1467-9 Mr 17 '89

STRIKE-SLIP FAULTS *See* Faults (Geology)

STRIKEBREAKERS

Supreme Court ruling lets airlines assure jobs to strike breakers [case of TWA vs. Independent Federation of Flight Attendants] M. Mecham. *Aviation Week & Space Technology* 129:67 Mr 6 '89

STRIKEOUTS (BASEBALL)

K [list of everyone N. Ryan has fanned] il pors *Sports Illustrated* 71:30-2 Ag 28 '89

STRIKES

See also

Collective labor agreements

Hunger strikes

Strikebreakers

Labor's bark is back, but not its bite. R. A. Taylor. il *U.S. News & World Report* 106:54 My 22 '89

The new lions who guard the gates [security firms specializing in labor disputes] il *U.S. News & World Report* 107:46 Jl 24 '89

The unions strike, again. D. Pauly. il *Newsweek* 114:59 O 16 '89

Aerospace industries

Boeing machinists strike hits economy, airline fleet plans. R. G. O'Lone. il *Aviation Week & Space Technology* 131:126-7 N 20 '89

The Boeing strike: both sides are flying. A. Bernstein and others. il *Business Week* p44 N 6 '89

Grounding a high-flying giant [machinists strike at Boeing] L. Griggs. il *Time* 134:57 O 16 '89

No progress reported in second week of strike [Boeing] R. G. O'Lone. il *Aviation Week & Space Technology* 131:18-19 O 16 '89

Strike at Boeing cripples production of transports. R. G. O'Lone. *Aviation Week & Space Technology* 131:136-7 O 9 '89

Air pilots

Pilots vote to continue Eastern strike, but many decide to cross picket lines. *Aviation Week & Space Technology* 131:59 Ag 14 '89

Australia

Australia struggles to restore air service using military, regional and foreign aircraft. *Aviation Week & Space Technology* 131:70 S 4 '89

Australian carriers expand services without union pilots. *Aviation Week & Space Technology* 131:124 S 18 '89

Foreign aircraft, crews replace flights halted by Australian pilots. *Aviation Week & Space Technology* 131:129 S 11 '89

Grounded, frustrated and angry. J. C. Rubin. il *Time* 134:73 N 20 '89

Airline employees

Advantage, Lorenzo [Chapter 11 strategy at Eastern] G. DeGeorge and S. Payne. il por *Business Week* p24-6 Jl 10 '89

Air sickness [F. Lorenzo] H. Fairlie. *The New Republic* 200:14-16+ Je 5 '89

Beat the devil [coverage of the strike against Eastern and of the struggle in El Salvador] A. Cockburn. *The Nation* 248:438-9 Ap 3 '89

A boss they love to hate [F. Lorenzo and Eastern Air Lines strike] J. Schwartz. il por *Newsweek* 113:20-4 Mr 20 '89

Can Eastern Air Lines survive? D. Pauly. il *Newsweek* 113:42 Mr 13 '89

Caught in Eastern's slipstream [airlines raise fares as a result of strike] il *U.S. News & World Report* 106:10+ Mr 27 '89

Crashing Eastern. il *National Review* 41:12 Ap 7 '89

Eastern Air Lines. *Monthly Labor Review* 112:44 S '89

Eastern building pilot corps amid strike, bankruptcy battles. C. Fotos. il *Aviation Week & Space Technology* 131:101-2 Jl 31 '89

Eastern: does anybody win? W. Woods. il por *Fortune* 119:14 Ap 10 '89

Eastern goes bust. J. Castro. il por *Time* 133:52-3 Mr 20 '89

Eastern reopens bidding for shuttle as Trump balks at $365 million price. P. Proctor and J. T. McKenna. *Aviation Week & Space Technology* 130:31 Mr 27 '89

Eastern struggles to expand service, fend off lawsuits. E. H. Kolcum. *Aviation Week & Space Technology* 130:268-9 Mr 20 '89

Eastern trains replacement pilots, weighs buyout offers. *Aviation Week & Space Technology* 130:33 Ap 3 '89

Eastern unions losing bid to unseat Lorenzo. J. T. McKenna. il *Aviation Week & Space Technology* 130:108-9 My 29 '89

Eastern's shuttlers vote with their seats. il *Newsweek* 113:46 Mr 27 '89

A fight to the death? [Eastern Air Lines strike] *The Nation* 248:397 Mr 27 '89

Going for broke at Eastern. J. Castro. il *Time* 133:42 Mr 13 '89

Lorenzo is running out of choices—and time. P. Engardio and G. DeGeorge. il *Business Week* p37-8 Ap 20 '89

Pilots, flight attendants end walkout at Eastern. *Aviation Week & Space Technology* 131:33 D 4 '89

The story at Eastern Airlines. W. F. Buckley. *National Review* 41:54 Ap 21 '89

Strike forces Eastern into bankruptcy court [special section; with editorial comment] il *Aviation Week & Space Technology* 130:7, 16-23 Mr 13 '89

Suicide pact at Eastern Air Lines [filing for bankruptcy during strike; with interview with F. A. Lorenzo] T. Moore and C. P. Work. il por *U.S. News & World Report* 106:18-21 Mr 20 '89

Supreme Court ruling lets airlines assure jobs to strike breakers [case of TWA vs. Independent Federation of Flight Attendants] M. Mecham. *Aviation Week & Space Technology* 129:67 Mr 6 '89

Texas Air: empire in jeopardy [strike at Eastern; special section] il por *Business Week* p28-31 Mr 27 '89

U.S. airline industry braces for Eastern machinists' strike. J. Ott. *Aviation Week & Space Technology* 130:92-3 F 13 '89

United's flight attendants authorize strike; takeover reports push stock price up. J. T. McKenna. *Aviation Week & Space Technology* 131:95 Jl 17 '89

STRIKES—cont.

Automobile industry workers

'Without unions, we'd have nothing' [strike at Ohio Crankshaft] P. Warloski. il *The Progressive* 53:22 D '89

France

Apres Peugeot, le deluge? S. Toy. *Business Week* p54 O 2 '89

Coal miners

A bitter deadlock [Pittston strike] W. Lowther. il *Maclean's* 102:72 N 20 '89

Christians and the coalfield conflict [Episcopalian involvement in strike against Pittston] L. Johnson. *The Christian Century* 106:868-9 O 4 '89

Coal country's war with itself [strike against Pittston] R. A. Taylor. il *U.S. News & World Report* 107:45 Jl 24 '89

Coal wars again [UMW strike against Pittston] J. Motavalli. il *The Progressive* 53:24-7 Jl '89

John L., you'd be amazed [nonviolent tactics used in coal miners' strike against Pittston] J. Birnbaum. il *Time* 133:38 My 15 '89

'The Mine Workers must win this fight to survive' [Pittston strike] J. P. Hoerr. il *Business Week* p144+ O 9 '89

Miscalculated risk? [strike against Pittston Co.] R. Phalon. il por *Forbes* 143:41-2 Je 12 '89

Pittston power [United Mine Workers' takeover of the Moss 3 plant] P. Kwik. *The Nation* 249:409 O 16 '89

Solidarity in Appalachia [strike against Pittston Co.] D. Giardina. il *The Nation* 249:12-14 Jl 3 '89

Their miners and ours (I) [contrasting Soviet and Pittston strikes] A. Cockburn. *The Nation* 249:195 Ag 21-28 '89

Their miners and ours (II) [poll indicating more people know about the Soviet coal miners strike than the Pittston strike] A. Cockburn. *The Nation* 249:410-11 O 16 '89

Twilight for the UMW? [strike against Pittston Co.] M. Schroeder. il *Business Week* p32 Jl 3 '89

Soviet Union

Behind the Soviet miners' strike. L. H. Siegelbaum. il *The Nation* 249:451-2+ O 23 '89

The fire down below. D. Stanglin. il map *U.S. News & World Report* 107:28-9 Jl 31 '89

Gdansk in Siberia? *The Nation* 249:153 Ag 7-14 '89

Gorbachev's gamble. A. Wilson-Smith. il por *Maclean's* 102:25-6 Ag 7 '89

How much longer can Gorbachev keep putting out fires? D. Rinehart. il *Business Week* p41 Ag 7 '89

'Masters do not strike'. V. Vyzhutovich. *World Press Review* 36:22 S '89

Militant miners run city hall. J. Trimble. il *U.S. News & World Report* 107:37 N 20 '89

No soap, say striking Soviet miners. D. R. Marples. bibl f il *The Bulletin of the Atomic Scientists* 45:38-40 D '89

Revolution down below. B. W. Nelan. il map *Time* 134:22-3 Jl 31 '89

'The shock wave has come from below'. H. Anderson. il map *Newsweek* 114:41-2 Jl 31 '89

Summer of discontent. A. Wilson-Smith. il *Maclean's* 102:29 Jl 31 '89

Their miners and ours (I) [contrasting Soviet and Pittston strikes] A. Cockburn. *The Nation* 249:195 Ag 21-28 '89

Their miners and ours (II) [poll indicating more people know about the Soviet coal miners strike than the Pittston strike] A. Cockburn. *The Nation* 249:410-11 O 16 '89

Copper industry workers

Union victory in a copper refinery [Cox Creek Refining Company] K. Kleiner. il *The Progressive* 53:13 S '89

Longshore workers

Great Britain—History

The dockers who won [1889] J. Crossland. il *History Today* 39:9-10 O '89

Meat industry workers

A company town decays [effect of strike against Hormel on Austin, Minn.] B. Koeppel. il *The Progressive* 53:12-13 F '89

Motorcyclists

Western Europe

Riders' strikes [motorcyclists protest unsafe conditions at European tracks] J. Greening. il *Cycle* 40:82 S '89

Musicians

Sounds of discord [Ottawa's National Arts Centre Orchestra] P. Young. *Maclean's* 102:70 O 16 '89

Nurses

Canada

Quebec showdown. M. Rose. il *Maclean's* 102:16-17 S 18 '89

Radio workers

Canada

Faulty reception [CBC strike] D. Turbide. il *Maclean's* 102:54 Mr 27 '89

Teachers

The new apple of teachers' eyes [Los Angeles teachers pushing for school-based management] il *U.S. News & World Report* 106:11 My 29 '89

Mexico

Why Salinas must tame the teachers. S. Baker. il *Business Week* p46+ My 15 '89

Telephone workers

Can't afford to get sick [health care issue] C. Gorman. il *Time* 134:43 Ag 21 '89

Health kick [strike over health care insurance] K. Cagney. *The Nation* 249:301 S 25 '89

The new bill of health [strike over health care] C. Byron. il *New York* 22:16+ Ag 28 '89

Why the Baby Bells are fat and sassy. il *U.S. News & World Report* 107:18 Ag 21 '89

Television workers

Canada

Faulty reception [CBC strike] D. Turbide. il *Maclean's* 102:54 Mr 27 '89

France

Two showdowns with socialism. B. Wickens. il *Maclean's* 102:53-4 Ja 2 '89

Korea (South)

Ending a battle but not the war: labor unrest at Hyundai. A. Platt. il *Newsweek* 113:37 Ap 10 '89

It's time for the main bout: Roh vs. labor. L. Nakarmi. il *Business Week* p45-6 Ap 10 '89

Labor stirrings in Korea. J. West. il *The Progressive* 53:12 Mr '89

Soviet Union

In the school of democracy. A. Blackman. il *Time* 134:44 O 16 '89

Strike's back. D. Koenker. *The New Republic* 201:14-16 O 23 '89

Spain

Spain's strike: a warning signal. S. Santini. *World Press Review* 36:23 Mr '89

Two showdowns with socialism. B. Wickens. il *Maclean's* 102:53-4 Ja 2 '89

United States

See Strikes

STRING ENSEMBLES

See also

Phonograph records—String ensemble music

STRING QUARTETS

See also

Arditti String Quartet

Compact discs—String quartet music

Emerson String Quartet

Kronos Quartet

Turtle Island String Quartet

The Songlines quartet [work of K. Volans] B. Chatwin. il *The New York Review of Books* 35:50-1 Ja 19 '89

STRING TRIMMERS See Lawn equipment

STRINGED INSTRUMENTS

See also

Violin

Collectors and collecting

A strong yen for instruments [A. Tsumura's collection] E. McGlinn. il por *Forbes* 144:241 O 2 '89

STRINGER, HOWARD

about

Howard Stringer. D. Lieberman. il por *Business Week* Special Issue:130 Ap 14 '89

'No excuses' for Stringer's CBS team [interview] il pors *Channels (New York, N.Y.: 1986)* 9:86-7 Je '89

STRINGS (COSMIC) See Cosmic strings

STRINGS (TENNIS RACKETS) See Tennis rackets—Strings

STRIP CROPPING

Laying out contour lines; Laying out contour buffer strips; Getting into contour strip-cropping. il *Successful Farming* 87:23-5 D '89

STRIP MINING

Laws and regulations

See also

United States. Office of Surface Mining, Reclamation, and Enforcement

A coal-field victory [broad-form deed that allows coal companies to strip mine land; Kentucky case] D. Giardina. il *The Progressive* 53:14-15 Mr '89

Kentucky

A coal-field victory [broad-form deed that allows coal companies to strip mine land] D. Giardina. il *The Progressive* 53:14-15 Mr '89

Nevada

There's holes in them thar hills [open-pit mines in the Carlin Trend] J. M. Nash. il *Time* 134:21-2+ O 23 '89

Pennsylvania

Whaleback anticline [geological structure evident at Bear Valley Strip Mine] C. Blue. il *Earth Science* 42:19-21 Fall '89

Utah

Utility to trade coal leases near Bryce [Nevada Power Company] *National Parks* 63:11 My/Je '89

STRIPED BASS FISHERIES (COMMERCIAL) See Fisheries

STRIPED BASS FISHING See Bass fishing

STRIPED FABRICS See Textile fabrics

STRIPER FISHING See Bass fishing

STRIPPING OF FURNITURE See Furniture stripping

STRIPTEASE

Stripper Blaze Starr recalls her affair with the governor [E. Long of Louisiana]; ed. by Margie Bonnett Sellinger. B. Starr. il pors *People Weekly* 32:157+ D 18 '89

STRMECKI, MARIN
Fighting for Jalalabad. il *The American Spectator* 22:30-2 Je '89
STROBE UNITS (PHOTOGRAPHY) *See* Photography—Flash equipment
STROBELL, MARY
(jt. auth) *See* Masursky, Harold, 1922-, and Strobell, Mary
STROBHAR, WHALEN M.
about
Does the AMA need to heal itself? J. F. Siler. il *Business Week* p50 N 13 '89
STROESSNER, ALFREDO
about
The dictator and the journalists. W. Steif. il por *The Progressive* 53:16-17 O '89
An extinction in Paraguay. J. Schwartz and J. Contreras. il por map *Newsweek* 113:38-9 F 13 '89
The extinction of a dinosaur. J. Smolowe. il pors *Time* 133:48 F 13 '89
The last tango in Paraguay. il pors *U.S. News & World Report* 106:14 F 13 '89
Paraguay after Stroessner. R. Roett. *Foreign Affairs* 68:124-42 Spr '89
Revolt in a fiefdom. A. Bilski. *Maclean's* 102:21 F 13 '89
STROESSNER, ROBERT J.
Antiques: Spanish colonial furniture. il *Architectural Digest* 46:256-61+ My '89
STROETZEL, DIANA
(jt. auth) *See* Stroetzel, Donald S., and Stroetzel, Diana
STROETZEL, DONALD S., AND STROETZEL, DIANA
Before you go . . . il *American Health* 8:58+ N '89
STROFF, STEPHEN M.
Music memorabilia. *See* issues of Antiques & Collecting Hobbies beginning February 1986
STROH, CHARLES
University art programs and the discipline-based art education movement: what prospects? *Design for Arts in Education* 91:38-47 N/D '89
STROH BREWERY COMPANY
Coors may take a gulp of a rival brew. S. D. Atchison. il *Business Week* p70 Ag 21 '89
How the owl drove a wedge between Stroh and Audubon [beer company pulls ads from TV show on Pacific Northwest old growth forests] V. Cahan. *Business Week* p99 S 18 '89
One last call for fading beer brands [S&P launches antitrust suit against Adolph Coors Co.'s acquisition of Stroh Brewery] L. Armstrong. il *Business Week* p68 O 16 '89
A sip of Stroh's could turn into a gulp. D. Woodruff. il *Business Week* p37 My 15 '89
STROKE *See* Cerebrovascular disease
STROLLERS (INFANTS) *See* Baby carriages
STROMINGER, JACK L.
Developmental biology of T cell receptors. bibl f il *Science* 244:943-50 My 26 '89
STRONACH, FRANK
about
Magna steps on the brake. J. Daly. il por *Maclean's* 102:44-6 O 16 '89
STRONG, MAURICE F.
about
Boss of the outdoors. B. Wallace. por *Maclean's* 102:15 Ja 23 '89
STRONTIUM-RUBIDIUM DATING *See* Radioactive dating
STROSS, RAY, AND ROTTIER, BARBARA
Protecting water clarity in Lake George. il *The Conservationist* 44:44-6 S/O '89
STROTHER, ROBERT S.
No more mañana. il *National Review* 41:21-2 N 24 '89
STROTHERS, E.
Our big choice. por *Essence* 20:116 Jl '89
STROUD, BILL
about
The ex-hustler whose pool cues are a fine art. J. Neary. il pors *Smithsonian* 20:158-62+ N '89
STROUD, PETER, 1921-
about
Peter Stroud at New Jersey State Museum. R. Storr. il *Art in America* 77:169-70 F '89
STROUD FAMILY
about
Chink in the armor. A. A. Lappen. il *Forbes* 144:84+ N 13 '89
STROUP, RICHARD (RICHARD L.)
(jt. auth) *See* Shaw, Jane S., and Stroup, Richard (Richard L.)
STROUT, ELIZABETH
Hold her tightly [story] il *Redbook* 173:60+ My '89
STRUCTURAL ENGINEERING
See also
Shells (Structural engineering)
Strains and stresses
Ka-boom! [impact resistance test at Sandia National Laboratories using an F-4 Phantom jet] J. Kluger. il *Discover* 10:44-5 D '89
Propelled jet [Sandia National Laboratories crash resistance tests of critical structures] A. Fisher. il *Popular Science* 235:14+ D '89

STRUCTURAL FAILURES
See also
Dams—Failure
Old, tired, and rusty [caused by metal fatigue] il *Discover* 10:68-70 Ja '89
STRUCTURAL GEOLOGY *See* Geology
STRUCTURE IN BIOLOGY *See* Morphology
STRUCTURED QUERY LANGUAGE (COMPUTER LANGUAGE)
A brave new world? F. Pascal. bibl f il *Byte* 14:247-50+ S '89
Clipper applications get SQL. M. Schnapp. *Byte* 14:211-12+ D '89
If we could talk to the database . . . M. Bryan. il *Personal Computing* 13:51-2+ Mr '89
Serving business [SQL database server products] W. Rash, Jr. il *Byte* 14:147-8+ N '89
The spotlight turns to database servers. M. Liskin. il *Personal Computing* 13:53-6 N '89
SQL: a database language sequel to dBASE. M. L. Van Name and B. Catchings. *Byte* 14 Special Issue:175-8+ Fall '89
STRUDEL *See* Pastry
THE STRUGGLE FOR DEMOCRACY [television program]
See Television program reviews—Single works
STRUTHERS, ANN
Sarah Orne Jewett [poem] *The American Scholar* 58:354 Summ '89
STRUTHERS, JEFFREY L.
Getting there from here. *Ad Astra* 1:22 Ja '89
STRYKER CORP.
Carving a niche in surgical tools. D. Woodruff. il *Business Week* Special Issue:126 Je 16 '89
STUART, CAROL, D. 1989
about
A dark night of the soul in Boston. M. Brower. il pors *People Weekly* 32:52-5 N 13 '89
The murder of a mother-to-be. por *Newsweek* 114:45 N 6 '89
STUART, CHARLES
Murder case
A dark night of the soul in Boston. M. Brower. il pors *People Weekly* 32:52-5 N 13 '89
The murder of a mother-to-be. por *Newsweek* 114:45 N 6 '89
STUART, DAVID, AND HOUSTON, STEPHEN D.
Maya writing. bibl il *Scientific American* 261:82-9 Ag '89
STUART, GEORGE E.
City of kings and commoners: Copán. il map *National Geographic* 176:488-504 O '89
STUART, GILBERT, 1755-1828
about
Museum accessions. E. H. Gustafson. il *Antiques* 136:240 Ag '89
STUART, JAN
Turkish delights. il *Gentlemen's Quarterly* 59:376+ Mr '89
STUART, OTIS
Amanda McKerrow takes stage: the real thing. il pors *Dance Magazine* 63:40-3 Ap '89
Life at forty: reinventing the possibilities. il *Dance Magazine* 63:53-5 Je '89
Making a home in Monte Carlo: life on the moneyed merry-go-round. il *Dance Magazine* 63:42-3 Ag '89
New York University, Tisch School of the Arts, and the Second Avenue Dance Company: a dancer prepares. il por *Dance Magazine* 63:60-1 Mr '89
(jt. auth) *See* Kelly, Patrick, and Stuart, Otis
STUART HALL CO., INC.
Cashing in on the fax frenzy [fax paper] G. G. Marcial. *Business Week* p80 Jl 10 '89
STUART-JAMES COMPANY INC.
The SEC casts a net at penny stocks' biggest fish. S. D. Atchison. il *Business Week* p128 Ap 24 '89
STUBBING, RICHARD A., AND MENDEL, RICHARD A.
How to save $50 billion a year. il *The Atlantic* 263:53-8 Je '89
STUBBORNNESS
"No, I won't!". M. Rosenberg. il *Parents* 64:68-70+ Ja '89
STUBBS, ERIC
(jt. auth) *See* Grenier, Paul, and Stubbs, Eric
STUBBY SQUID *See* Squid
STUBS (SECURITIES)
If you crave more thrills, try 'stubs'. P. Sellers. il *Fortune* 120:56+ N 20 '89
Stubs revisited. M. Schifrin. *Forbes* 144:378 N 13 '89
STUCCO
The legacy of Ireland's stuccodores. N. F. Weber. il *Architectural Digest* 46:42+ Ag '89
The skilled technique of stucco repair. D. Johnson and D. Stoffel. il *The Family Handyman* 39:40-2 Mr '89
STUD FARMS *See* Horses—Breeding
STUDENT ACHIEVEMENTS
See also
Accountability (Education)
Educational tests and measurements
National Assessment of Educational Progress
Underachievers

STUDENT ACHIEVEMENTS—*cont.*

Age and achievement [research by Zvia Breznitz and Tamar Teltsch] G. W. Bracey. il *Phi Delta Kappan* 70:732 My '89

Back to basics [peer pressure and student achievement] D. Ravitch. *The New Republic* 200:13-15 Mr 6 '89

Cooperative learning and student achievement. R. E. Slavin. *The Education Digest* 54:15-17 F '89

More on children and computers [research by Nira Hativa] G. W. Bracey. *Phi Delta Kappan* 70:733-4 My '89

Number of siblings and educational attainment. J. Blake. bibl f il *Science* 245:32-6 Jl 7 '89

Pavlov lives: who's to blame for educational failures? G. Keller. il *Change* 21:54 My/Je '89

The sources of racial discrimination [disparity in achievement levels; views of Thomas Sowell] W. F. Buckley. *National Review* 41:70 S 29 '89

Student alienation and academic achievement. R. L. Calabrese. *The Education Digest* 54:7-9 My '89

What price glory? [toll that high achievement takes on Chinese American students; research by Stanley Sue] L. Troiano. il *American Health* 8:119 Mr '89

Why Catholic schools outperform all others [interview with J. S. Coleman; cover story] por *U.S. Catholic* 54:6-12 Jl '89

STUDENT ACTIVITIES
See also
College and school journalism
College athletics
College students—Political activities
Dances (Student activities)
Proms (Dances)

The not so extracurriculum. A. C. Lewis. il *Phi Delta Kappan* 70:K1-K8 My '89

STUDENT AID
See also
Educational Assistance Limited
I Have a Dream Foundation
READY (Program)
Scholarships and fellowships

The billionaire and the students [Kansas City, Mo., students helped to stay drug free by E. M. Kauffman] D. Narine. il pors *Ebony* 44:146+ Ag '89

Black schools facing new student loan default plan. *Jet* 76:9 Je 19 '89

Brain trusts [Justice Dept. investigation of price fixing by private colleges] il *Time* 134:24 Ag 21 '89

Colleges in collusion [price fixing of tuition and financial aid] I. Ayres. *The New Republic* 201:19-20 O 16 '89

Debts pose problems for missions candidates. K. H. Sidey. il *Christianity Today* 33:36-8 S 22 '89

Does your child need student financial aid? P. Plawin. il *Changing Times* 43:115 Ap '89

From boon to bust in the student-loan business [banks curtail lending to students at schools with high default rates] P. Sherrid. il *U.S. News & World Report* 106:55 My 22 '89

The gap between will and wallet [S. Nunn's proposal to require national service for college students seeking federal aid] W. Shapiro. il *Time* 133:32 F 6 '89

Higher education, lower debt. B. M. Stephens. il *Black Enterprise* 20:80-2 S '89

If colleges are fixing prices, it's a job for antitrust. G. S. Becker. il *Business Week* p30 S 25 '89

An Ivy League cartel [colleges accused of violating antitrust laws] C. Leslie. il *Newsweek* 114:65 Ag 21 '89

National policies to encourage service [interview with C. Moskos and D. Evans; cover story; with editorial comment by Susan Stroud] F. Newman. il *Change* 21:4, 8-17 S/O '89

Realigning federal student aid policy. R. N. Kelly. *The Education Digest* 55:61-3 O '89

Scandal in our trade schools. T. Armbrister. *Reader's Digest* 134:85-90 Ja '89

The sirens' song: trying to do all things for all students. M. A. Kramer. *Change* 21:42 My/Je '89

Spotlight on schools. *'Teen* 33:83 F '89

Student-aid smarts! *Essence* 20:103 Ag '89

Student loan financing; Student loan default [Guaranteed Student Loan program] E. Ginsberg and S. Ginsberg. il *Phi Delta Kappan* 70:556-8 Mr '89

The student loan quandary [college students] L. E. Gladieux. il *Change* 21:35-41 My/Je '89

A tale of two candidates [proposals of G. Bush and M. Dukakis] M. A. Kramer. *Change* 20:9+ N/D '88

Tuition shock! [special section] il *Money* 18:60-6+ S '89

STUDENT ART *See* Children's art

STUDENT DEMONSTRATIONS *See* Student protests, demonstrations, etc.

STUDENT DROPOUTS *See* Dropouts

STUDENT EMPLOYMENT *See* Youth—Employment

STUDENT ENVIRONMENTAL HEALTH PROJECT *See* Vanderbilt University. Student Environmental Health Project

STUDENT EXCHANGE PROGRAMS
See also
Semester at Sea (Program)

Central America and the education president [scholarships bring students to U.S. universities] J. J. Mullaney. *America* 160:524-5 Je 3 '89

Going to Cyprus. J. Webb. il pors *Seventeen* 48:166+ Mr '89

Study up on fun. il *'Teen* 33:47-9+ Mr '89

STUDENT GUIDANCE *See* Educational counseling

STUDENT HUMANITARIAN SERVICE AWARD
National award honors students who make a difference. K. R. Moyer. il *Change* 21:12-13 S/O '89

STUDENT LAMPS *See* Lamps

STUDENT LOANS *See* Student aid

STUDENT MILITANTS
See also
Students for a Democratic Society

STUDENT MOBILITY
See also
Students—Transfer

Student migration patterns: what they mean for states. il *Change* 21:29-34 My/Je '89

STUDENT MOVEMENT

History

'60s protesters, '80s professors. A. P. Sanoff. il *U.S. News & World Report* 106:54-5 Ja 16 '89

Familiar scenes of fury and optimism [comparison of Chinese student protest with U.S. protests of the past] R. Rosenblatt. il *U.S. News & World Report* 106:10-11 Je 5 '89

The young have to be there. A. Hoffman. il *The Progressive* 53:15 Je '89

Bibliography

Back to the '60s: five post-mortems on years of campus violence. R. G. Davis. il *Change* 20:48-53 N/D '88

The sixties without metaphor. M. S. Kimmel. *Society* 26:78-84 Mr/Ap '89

China

See also
Tiananmen Square (China) student occupation, 1989

The Chinese student movement moves to America. A. Riles. il *The Progressive* 53:28-30 S '89

History

Dissidents then and now. *U.S. News & World Report* 107:35 Ag 7 '89

Quiet on campus. J. L. Tyson. il *Scholastic Update (Teachers' edition)* 121:12+ My 5 '89

Poland

History

Notes and comment [Chinese and Polish democracy movements] *The New Yorker* 65:25-7 Je 19 '89

STUDENT NEWSPAPERS *See* College and school journalism

STUDENT NONVIOLENT COORDINATING COMMITTEE
A veteran of Mississippi's 'Freedom Summer' remembers the cause—and the danger [drive for black voter registration conducted in 1964]; ed. by Jane Sugden. L. Guyot. il pors *People Weekly* 32:61-2+ S 18 '89

STUDENT PERFORMANCE *See* Student achievements

STUDENT PROTESTS, DEMONSTRATIONS, ETC.
See also
Student movement

Back to school. E. Morris. il *Mother Jones* 14:12 S '89

Beijing spring. M. S. Serrill. il *Time* 133:36-8 My 8 '89

Howard students force Atwater's resignation, and push other demands. il *Jet* 75:37 Mr 27 '89

March on Washington by students slated for April. *Jet* 75:6 Mr 27 '89

Now Willie Horton stalks the GOP [L. Atwater forced to resign from Howard University board] il *U.S. News & World Report* 106:13 Mr 20 '89

The revolution at Gallaudet [students demand a deaf president] H. Orlans. il pors *Change* 21:8-18 Ja/F '89

Saying no to Lee Atwater [Howard University students protest appointment to board of trustees] J. V. Lamar, Jr. il por *Time* 133:27 Mr 20 '89

Student power! [Howard University] R. Powers. por *Essence* 20:122 Ag '89

Students fight naming of Atwater to Howard board. *Jet* 75:11 Mr 20 '89

China

See also
Tiananmen Square (China) student occupation, 1989

"Beat the black devils!" [Chinese students march against African students in Nanjing] S. Burton. il *Time* 133:37 Ja 9 '89

China: 'Kill the black devils' [Chinese college students protest against African students in Nanjing] M. Beck. il *Newsweek* 113:35 Ja 9 '89

The fallout from Nanjing [continued anti-African demonstrations by Chinese students] M. S. Serrill. il *Time* 133:38 Ja 16 '89

Letters from the other China [letters written to dissident Fang Lizhi in 1987]; tr. by Orville Schell. bibl f il por *The New York Review of Books* 36:32-3 Jl 20 '89

More than just Chinese racism [anti-African demonstrations by Chinese students] R. Seidelman. il *The Nation* 248:195-6 F 13 '89

The roots of racism are rubbed raw [Chinese college students protest against African students in Nanjing] il *U.S. News & World Report* 106:10-11 Ja 9 '89

STUDENT PROTESTS, DEMONSTRATIONS, ETC. — cont.

Korea (South)

Punish the ambassador! [students attack U.S. ambassador D. Gregg's residence] D. Bank and P. Leyden. il *Newsweek* 114:40 O 23 '89

South Korea. L. Nakarmi. *Business Week* p55 My 15 '89

STUDENT PUBLICATIONS *See* College and school journalism

STUDENT RECORDS *See* School reports and records

STUDENT RECRUITING *See* Colleges and universities—Student recruiting

STUDENT RIGHTS *See* Students—Civil rights

STUDENT SELECTION *See* Colleges and universities—Admission; High schools—Admission

STUDENT TEACHERS

The Gahanna-Jefferson City internship program [Ohio] B. W. Denner and S. Kirchhoff. *Phi Delta Kappan* 71:166-7 O '89

STUDENT VIOLENCE *See* School violence

STUDENT VOLUNTEERS *See* Volunteer service

STUDENTS

See also

Clothing and dress—Students

College students

Foreign students

High school students

School children

Seminarians

Underachievers

Civil rights

A question of rights [teenagers] N. Schuessler. il *Seventeen* 48:192-3+ My '89

Searching and researching [use of sniffer dogs in detecting suspicious student automobiles in Joshua, Tex.] P. A. Zirkel. bibl f *Phi Delta Kappan* 71:330-2 D '89

Employment

See Youth—Employment

Ethics

See also

Honor system (Education)

Grading

See Grading and marking (Education)

Psychology

Arthur: a tale of disempowerment. L. V. Rosow. bibl f il *Phi Delta Kappan* 71:194-9 N '89

Assessing the curriculum experienced by children. V. R. Rogers. bibl f il *Phi Delta Kappan* 70:714-17 My '89

Helping students accentuate positive thoughts. C. K. Chandler and C. A. Kolander. *The Education Digest* 54:52-4 Ja '89

Learning-disabled students: the masks they wear. S. L. Smith. *The Education Digest* 55:50-3 D '89

Student alienation and academic achievement. R. L. Calabrese. *The Education Digest* 54:7-9 My '89

"The teacher called me stupid, Mommy!" [emotionally abused students] M. H. Christensen. il *Redbook* 173:144-5+ O '89

When kids sing the school-bus blues. F. Roberts. *Parents* 64:56-7 O '89

Transfer

Moving around and dropping out [research by Ridge Hammons and Miles Olson] G. W. Bracey. il *Phi Delta Kappan* 70:407 Ja '89

A smooth move. F. Roberts. *Parents* 64:51-2 My '89

Volunteer service

See Volunteer service

STUDENTS AND TEACHERS *See* Teachers and students

STUDENTS FOR A BETTER SOCIETY

Students unite for a better society [students in Buffalo, N.Y. show support for Chinese demonstrators] S. Ring. por *The Humanist* 49:26-7+ S/O '89

STUDENTS FOR A DEMOCRATIC SOCIETY

Those were the days: the SDS revisited. A. Puddington. il *The American Spectator* 22:18-20 Mr '89

STUDIES (ROOMS)

George Washington's study [Mount Vernon] E. M. Clark. bibl f il *Antiques* 135:490-5 F '89

In the workshop of Peter Matthiessen. il por *Esquire* 111:118-19 My '89

STUDIO LIGHTS (PHOTOGRAPHY) *See* Photography—Light and lighting

STUDIOS

See also

Artists' studios

Dance studios

STUDIOS, RECORDING *See* Sound—Recording and reproducing

STUDY

See also

Homework

Getting great grades: A+ advice [high school students] K. Hinchman. il *Teen* 33:42+ S '89

Make the grade. C. Meherani. il *Seventeen* 48:154-5+ Ap '89

STUDY GUIDES

See also

Cliff's Notes Inc.

Law school lite [using course outlines and summaries] D. Pink. *The Washington Monthly* 21:20-3 N '89

STUDY-WORK PLANS *See* Business and education

STUERMER, DARYL

about

Daryl Stuermer. B. Milkowski. il por *Down Beat* 56:14 Je '89

STUFFED TOYS *See* Toys

STUFFING (FOOD)

Christmas cookbook. il *Good Housekeeping* 209:199-200+ D '89

Dressing up for the holidays. S. Wyler. il *New Choices for the Best Years* 29:72-5 N '89

Going to stuff a goose? Try this cabbage-apple stuffing. il *Sunset (Central West edition)* 182:150 F '89

Stuffings and dressings. il *Better Homes and Gardens* 67:181-2 N '89

STUKANE, EILEEN

Listen to your body: little aches and pains that signal trouble. il *Redbook* 172:104-5+ Ap '89

STULLER, JAY

"I have to save my baby!". il *Reader's Digest* 134:65-70 Ap '89

Men working in trees. il por *Audubon* 91:86-91 Jl '89

STULLER, STUART

Birding by the numbers. il *The Atlantic* 263:88-9+ My '89

STUNT DRIVING *See* Automobile driving—Stunt driving

STUNT FLYING *See* Aviation—Stunt flying

STUNT MEN AND WOMEN

See also

Hollywood Stuntmen's Hall of Fame (Moab, Utah)

STUNT MOTORCYCLING *See* Motorcycling—Stunt cycling

STUNTS

See also

Dog stunts

Pet stunts

Darwin's legacy: has evolution brought us to this? il por *People Weekly* 31:71 Je 26 '89

When James Bond jumps, super skydiver B.J. Worth gives 007 an airborne Licence to thrill [motion picture parachute stunt coordinator] N. Geeslin. il pors *People Weekly* 32:95+ S 4 '89

STUPIDITY

Experienced, qualified—and stupid; tr. by Joel Agee. E. Vilar. *Harper's* 278:28+ Ja '89

STURBRIDGE (MASS.)

Historic houses, sites, etc.

See also

Old Sturbridge Village

STURBRIDGE VILLAGE *See* Old Sturbridge Village

STURDEVANT, SAUNDRA

The bar girls of Subic Bay: the military, women and AIDS. il *The Nation* 248:444-6 Ap 3 '89

STURDZA, GRETA

about

Princess in the garden. M. K. Griswold. il por *House & Garden* 161:108-13+ Jl '89

STURGEONS

See also

Caviar

STURGES, ARTHUR

about

Whipping up a new self. R. A. Barnett. il por *American Health* 8:135 S '89

STURGES, PRESTON

about

Sullivan's travels [film] Reviews

Video 13:64 Jl '89. M. Fleischmann

STURTEVANT, ELAINE

about

Elaine Sturtevant at Bess Cutler. E. Heartney. il *Art in America* 77:150 Mr '89

STURTIVANT, STUYVESANT, III

So you want to be a deputy assistant secretary. *National Review* 41:45 F 10 '89

STUTTERING

Coming to terms with the j-jitters. M. E. Ross. il *The New York Times Magazine* p26+ My 14 '89

Inside stuttering basketball star Bob Love was an intelligent man struggling to be understood; ed. by Priscilla Turner. B. Love. il pors *People Weekly* 31:111 Ap 3 '89

Stuttering: the parental influence. S. Chollar. il *Psychology Today* 22:12-13+ D '88

Therapy

High-tech aid for stutterers [Vocal Feedback Device] B. Barol. il *Newsweek* 113:68 Je 19 '89

STUTTGART BALLET

Reviews:

Performance of Giselle in Ludwigsburg. H. Koegler. il *Dance Magazine* 63:84-5 D '89

Performance of works by J. Kylián in Stuttgart. H. Koegler. *Dance Magazine* 63:73-4 Ap '89

Tamas Detrich: an American prince in Europe. M. Hunt. il pors *Dance Magazine* 63:50-3 F '89

STÜTTGEN, JOHANNES

about

Beuys butter battle. J. Dornberg. il por *Art News* 88:23 Ap '89

STUTZMAN, EDWIN DELROY
about
Depression and drinking [interview] B. K. Mills. il por *People Weekly* 32:118 N 27 '89
STYLE, LITERARY
Talk of the town [the New Yorker] W. Safire. il *The New York Times Magazine* p16+ O 8 '89
STYLE, PERSONAL *See* Fashion
STYLE (PHILOSOPHY)
Joan Juliet Buck unravels the complex structure of Italian style and makes some astonishing discoveries. J. J. Buck. il *Vogue* 179:143-4+ D '89
Prisoners of taste [French style] J. Kramer. il *House & Garden* 161:106-7 Jl '89
STYLE CHECKING PROGRAMS *See* Word processors and processing—Programming
STYLES-MCLEOD, CATHERINE
Château de Cornillon: antiquarian Bernard Steinitz's feudal castle on the Loire [cover story] il *Architectural Digest* 46:72-81+ Ja '89
Gardens: a philosophy of fragrance: Robert Ricci's floral domain in the Ile-de-France. il por *Architectural Digest* 46:142-7 Ja '89
Hôtel de Cavoye: a Paris house appointed by antiquarian Bernard Steinitz. il *Architectural Digest* 46:234-41 O '89
STYLING, AUTOMOBILE *See* Automobiles—Design
STYRON, WILLIAM, 1925-
A literary friendship. il pors *Esquire* 111:154-8+ Ap '89
about
First, let's ban all morning programs. R. Townley. il pors *TV Guide* 37:12-14 Mr 4-10 '89
SU, TSUNG-PING, AND OTHERS
Steroid binding at σ-"opioid" receptors [discussion of April 8, 1988 article, Steroid binding at σ receptors suggests a link between endocrine, nervous, and immune systems] bibl f il *Science* 246:1635-8 D 22 '89
SU, ZHIXIN
'People's education' in the People's Republic of China. bibl f il *Phi Delta Kappan* 70:614-18 Ap '89
SUB DEBT *See* Junk certificates of deposit
SUBARU (AUTOMOBILE) *See* Automobiles, Foreign
SUBARU-ISUZU AUTOMOTIVE INC.
An uneasy alliance on the Wabash. J. B. Treece. il *Business Week* p59 O 23 '89
SUBARU OF AMERICA, INC.
Counterattack [Legacy] S. N. Chakravarty. il *Forbes* 144:56+ N 13 '89
SUBCHAPTER S CORPORATIONS *See* S corporations
SUBCOMMITTEE ON HUD-INDEPENDENT AGENCIES (HOUSE) *See* United States. Congress. House. Committee on Appropriations. Subcommittee on HUD-Independent Agencies
SUBCONSCIOUSNESS
See also
Dreams
Hypnotism
Subliminal projection
SUBDUCTION (GEOLOGY)
Birth of a subduction zone [along the Macquarie Ridge; research by Susan L. Beck] R. Monastersky. *Science News* 136:396 D 16 '89
Where east meets west [ocean floor subduction zone caused by plate movement off southern Chile; research by Steven Cande and Stephen Lewis] il *Discover* 10:21 F '89
SUBER, HOWARD
about
The professor-mogul. L. Jarvik. *American Film* 14:13 My '89
SUBJECTIVISM *See* Subjectivity
SUBJECTIVITY
Sociology and subjectivism. I. L. Horowitz. *Society* 26:49-54 Jl/Ag '89
SUBLIMINAL PROJECTION
Could that ALF cartoon be flashing a hidden message? D. Hill and K. Sobel. il *TV Guide* 37:6-7+ Ag 12-18 '89
From the subliminal to the ridiculous [ads] B. Kanner. il *New York* 22:18+ D 4 '89
Subliminal healing [use of positive message tapes during surgery to speed recovery in hysterectomy patients] il *Prevention (Emmaus, Pa.)* 41:12+ Ja '89
Suggestions for recovery [use of positive message tapes during hysterectomy; research by Phil Richardson and Carlton Evans] E. Stark. *Psychology Today* 23:24-5 Mr '89
SUBMARINE ARCHEOLOGY *See* Archeology, Submarine
SUBMARINE DIVING *See* Diving, Submarine
SUBMARINE GEOLOGY
See also
Marine sediments
Ocean bottom
Ocean Drilling Program
Seamounts
Subduction (Geology)
Inner space. C. T. Feazel. il *Sea Frontiers* 35:49-52 Ja/F '89
SUBMARINE MINES *See* Mines, Submarine
SUBMARINE PHOTOGRAPHY *See* Underwater photography
SUBMARINE RESEARCH VEHICLES *See* Oceanographic submersibles

SUBMARINE SALVAGE *See* Salvage (Ships)
SUBMARINE SANDWICHES *See* Sandwiches
SUBMARINE THERMAL SPRINGS *See* Hot springs
SUBMARINE VOLCANOES *See* Volcanoes
SUBMARINE WARFARE
See also
Anti-submarine warfare
Guided missiles—Launching from submarines
688 Attack Sub [video game] R. G. Sheffield. il *Compute!* 11:64-5 Ag '89
There's a boat in this box! [688 Attack Sub video game] G. Keizer. il *Compute!* 11:6 Mr '89
SUBMARINES
See also
Nuclear submarines
Oceanographic submersibles
Submarine warfare
Communication systems
E-6A Tacamo tail damage prompts delivery delay [submarine communications aircraft] M. A. Dornheim. il *Aviation Week & Space Technology* 130:28-9 Ap 17 '89
Electronic equipment
Four in race for sub AI deal. *High Technology Business* 9:32 Je '89
Optical equipment
Fiber-optic periscope could alter sub design. *High Technology Business* 9:35 Je '89
SUBMERGED LANDS
See also
Petroleum in submerged lands
SUBMERSIBLES, OCEANOGRAPHIC *See* Oceanographic submersibles
SUBMINIMUM WAGE *See* Minimum wage
SUBORDINATED DEBENTURES *See* Junk certificates of deposit
SUBRAMANIAM, CHITRA
An indifference toward women. *World Press Review* 36:65 O '89
SUBSCRIPTIONS, PERIODICAL *See* Periodicals—Subscriptions
SUBSIDIARIES (CORPORATIONS) *See* Corporations—Subsidiaries
SUBSIDIARIES (FOREIGN) *See* Corporations, International
SUBSIDIARIES (HOSPITALS) *See* Hospitals—Subsidiaries
SUBSIDIARY COMMUNICATIONS AUTHORIZATION SUBCARRIERS *See* Radio frequency modulation
SUBSIDIES
See also
Agricultural administration
Airlines—Federal aid
Economic assistance, Domestic
SUBSTANCE (NEWSPAPER)
A watchdog guards the public schools [Chicago teacher G. Schmidt] M. Ervin. por *The Progressive* 53:16-17 N '89
SUBSTITUTE PRODUCTS
See also
Food substitutes
Sugar substitutes
SUBTERFUGE *See* Deception
SUBURBAN HOMES
Awakening from the American dream: why the suburban, single-family house is outdated [excerpt from Redesigning the American dream] D. Hayden. il *Utne Reader* p64-7 My/Je '89
High style in the 'burbs. C. McGuigan. il *Newsweek* 113:64-6 Mr 27 '89
SUBURBAN HOUSING *See* Housing
SUBURBAN LIFE
Stressed out in suburbia [Naperville, Ill.] N. Lemann. il *The Atlantic* 264:34+ N '89
SUBURBS
See also
Exurbs
Bucks in the 'burbs. M. Pearce. il *Outdoor Life* 184:56-7+ Jl '89
Deer in suburbia—pleasures and pests. D. J. Decker and N. A. Connelly. il *The Conservationist* 43:46-9 Mr/Ap '89
Doing business in the 'burbs [women entrepreneurs; special section] D. Weil. il *Working Woman* 14:58-62+ Ag '89
The other suburbia [poverty] J. McCormick and P. McKillop. il *Newsweek* 113:22-4 Je 26 '89
Rethinking suburbia: blueprints for a new kind of community. D. Beers. il *Utne Reader* p98 Mr/Ap '89
SUBVERSIVE ACTIVITIES
See also
Terrorism
SUBWAY GRAFFITI *See* Graffiti
SUBWAY STATIONS
See also
New York (N.Y.)—Stations
SUBWAYS
See also
New York (N.Y.)—Subways
SUCCESS
See also
Ambition
Failure (Psychology)

SUCCESS—See also—*cont.*
Fear of success
Self realization
Wealth

3 ways to make your dreams come true. B. Sher and A. Gottlieb. il *Glamour* 87:87 My '89
Bouncing back from dead-end situations [black role models] D. Narine. il *Ebony* 44:40+ O '89
Celebrating success. S. L. Taylor. il *Essence* 19:47 Mr '89
CEO fitness: the performance plus [exercise and job performance; excerpt from Dr. James M. Rippe's Fit for success] J. M. Rippe. il *Psychology Today* 23:50-3 My '89
The get-ahead guy (will he leave you behind?). D. Heyn. *Mademoiselle* 95:116 My '89
How to get your way [condensed from Succeeding against the odds]; ed. by Lerone Bennett. J. H. Johnson. il *Reader's Digest* 135:19-20+ O '89
How to make a good impression [condensed from You are the message]; ed. by Jon Kraushar. R. Ailes. il *Reader's Digest* 135:139-42 S '89
How to manage your career for lifelong success [cover story; special section] il *Working Woman* 14:101-4+ O '89
How to swim with the sharks [interview with H. Mackay] P. Edwards and S. Edwards. il por *Home Office Computing* 7:46-8 Ap '89
Inside moves. D. M. Rankin. *Harper's Bazaar* 122:28+ Je '89
Is she a star? And if she is, how will men deal with that? il *Glamour* 87:140 Je '89
Measuring success. P. V. Fossel. *Country Journal* 16:12-13 Mr/Ap '89
Modern problems, ancient solutions: the philosophy of success. D. Glidden. *American Health* 8:114+ Ap '89
Personal milestones: what stands out [women celebrities] il *Glamour* 87:170 Ap '89
Planning it all: the new calendar girls [trying to fit marriage into timetable] E. Weiner. il *Mademoiselle* 95:130-3+ Jl '89
The prince of get rich quick [D. Bendah] M. S. Gill. il por *Rolling Stone* p107-8+ F 9 '89
An SOB's guide to the top [reactions to A. Neuharth's autobiography] V. S. Sussman. il *U.S. News & World Report* 107:71-2 O 9 '89
Speeding toward success—are you on track? [quiz] il *'Teen* 33:36 D '89
Success [special section] il *American Health* 8:55-60+ Ap '89
Success and the soft-hearted woman. J. M. Toal. il *Mademoiselle* 95:194-5+ O '89
Success by surprise. C. A. Jaffe. il *Nation's Business* 77:30+ S '89
Success, family-style. S. Berglas. *American Health* 8:107 Ap '89
Sudden success [cover story; special section] il *Working Woman* 14:77-80+ Je '89
The tapestry of your life [address, May 7, 1989] S. G. Finesilver. *Vital Speeches of the Day* 56:82-4 N 15 '89
To snare the feet of greatness [address, June 16, 1989] J. D. Griffin. *Vital Speeches of the Day* 55:735-6 S 15 '89
Women who go for it! [A. Perez, T. F. Weekley, W. Matthews, and D. G. Robinson] B. M. Campbell. il pors *Essence* 20:48-50+ Ag '89

Bibliography
How to succeed in business? Here's the secret . . . P. J. O'Rourke. il *The New York Times Book Review* 94:30 O 29 '89

SUCCESSFUL FARMING (PERIODICAL)
Across the editor's desk [new features] R. Krumme. il *Successful Farming* 87 no4:1 Mr '89
The feature farmers love most [All around the farm column; cover story] C. Finck. il *Successful Farming* 87:18-21 Ja '89
The winners are . . . C. Tevis. il *Successful Farming* 87:56 Ag '89

SUCCESSION, PLANT See Plant succession

SUCCULENT PLANTS
See also
Aloe
Cactus
Jade plants

SUCHINSKY, ANTOSH
about
His brother's keeper. S. Schlegel. *Reader's Digest* 134:112-14 F '89

SUCROSE POLYESTERS
Nothing to sink your teeth into [Proctor & Gamble's olestra] J. Gorman. il *The New York Times Magazine* p40+ Je 11 '89

SUCTION LIPECTOMY See Liposuction

SUDAN
See also
Famines—Sudan
Juba (Sudan)
Relief work—Sudan
Sudanese
United Nations—Sudan
Youth—Sudan

Foreign relations
United States
See United States—Foreign relations—Sudan
Politics and government
The collapse born of civil war. K. Soyinka. il *World Press Review* 36:28-9 Mr '89
An early-morning coup [armed forces topple Prime Minister S. el Mahdi] *Time* 134:33 Jl 10 '89
Famine. R. Bonner. map *The New Yorker* 65:85-96+ Mr 13 '89
Juba: a city under siege. R. Wilkinson. il map *Newsweek* 113:47 Mr 20 '89
Peace and relief in Sudan. *Department of State Bulletin* 89:24-6 Ap '89
Politics block relief efforts to Sudan. K. Blomquist. il map *Christianity Today* 33:40-1 Ap 7 '89
Starvation as a political weapon. L. Lief. il map *U.S. News & World Report* 106:34-5+ F 6 '89
War without end. B. Berkeley. *The New Republic* 200:14+ My 8 '89

SUDAN PEOPLE'S LIBERATION ARMY
The collapse born of civil war. K. Soyinka. il *World Press Review* 36:28-9 Mr '89
Juba: a city under siege. R. Wilkinson. il map *Newsweek* 113:47 Mr 20 '89
War without end. B. Berkeley. *The New Republic* 200:14+ My 8 '89

SUDANESE
United States
Sudanese family worries about NBA's Manute Bol. il por *Jet* 76:49 Jl 17 '89

SUDARKASA, NIARA
about
Niara Sudarkasa: educator for the 1990's. E. B. Washington. il pors *Essence* 20:106-8+ My '89

SUDARSHAN, E. C. G.
about
Beyond Einstein [cover story; with editorial comment by Paul Hoffman] D. Freedman. il pors *Discover* 10:4, 56-61 F '89

SUDDEN CARDIAC ARREST
Sudden impact [death rate in people without symptoms] J. Horgan. *Scientific American* 261:35-6 O '89
Diagnosis
Preventing sudden death [signs of a heart attack; views of Harold Karpman] *Prevention (Emmaus, Pa.)* 41:12+ N '89

SUDDEN INFANT DEATH SYNDROME
"I saved my baby from crib death"; ed. by Judith Kelman. V. Bird. il por *Redbook* 173:42+ My '89

SUDHOF, THOMAS C., AND OTHERS
Synapsins: mosaics of shared and individual domains in a family of synaptic vesicle phosphoproteins. bibl f il *Science* 245:1474-80 S 29 '89

SUDIA, CECELIA
"Reasonable efforts" under P.L. 96-272. *Children Today* 18:9 My/Je '89

SUDJIC, DEYAN
Tokyo's 'spectacular' stores. il *World Press Review* 36:72 O '89
The worst of Thames. il *House & Garden* 161:56 Mr '89

SUDS See Foams

SUFFERING
See also
Grief
Lenten meditation:
When bad things happen. W. H. Willimon. *The Christian Century* 106:198-9 F 22 '89
Liturgy in time of trouble. J. F. Baldovin. *America* 161:337-8 N 18 '89
Living with chronic illness: why should I go on? S. Schmidt. *The Christian Century* 106:475-6+ My 3 '89
Strong, silent and suffering [male ethos] S. R. Morris. por *Newsweek* 113:10-11 Ap 3 '89
Surviving. P. J. Ryan. *America* 161:331 N 11 '89
When bad things happen. J. R. Edwards. il *Christianity Today* 33:30-2 Ag 18 '89
A wrestling match with the Almighty. P. Yancey. il *Christianity Today* 33:22-6 S 8 '89

SUFFERING OF GOD
'I am Jesus, whom you persecute'. K. Koyama. *The Christian Century* 106:347 Ap 5 '89

SUFFOLK (ENGLAND) IN ART
One summer in Constable country. C. D. Berg. il *American Artist* 53:38-43+ Jl '89

SUFFRAGE
See also
Voter registration
Voting

SUFI POETRY
Hafez: the golden age of Persian literature. C.-H. de Fouchecour. il *The Courier (Unesco)* 42:13-16 Mr '89
Love sacred and profane [works of Hâfiz] R. Feiz. il *The Courier (Unesco)* 42:12 Mr '89

SUGAR, ALAN M.
about
Cutting corners is cutting into Amstrad's bottom line. M. Maremont. il por *Business Week* p109-10 D 11 '89

SUGAR
See also
Maple sugar
Physiological effects
See Sugar in the body
Prices
See also
Agricultural administration
SUGAR BLUE
about
This blue city. P. Schneider. il pors *Esquire* 111:38 F '89
SUGAR CANE WORKERS *See* Sugar workers
SUGAR GLIDERS (ANIMALS)
Nightlife of the sugar glider [cover story] il *National Geographic World* 166:3-7 Je '89
SUGAR IN THE BODY
The big scoop on sugar. D.-J. Moore. il *New Choices for the Best Years* 29:71-3 Je '89
Sugar: a performance boost or sweet nothing? E. Coleman. il *Women's Sports & Fitness* 11:20-1 Jl/Ag '89
Winning the war against sugar cravings. G. L. Blackburn. il *Prevention (Emmaus, Pa.)* 41:103+ N '89
SUGAR INDUSTRY
See also
Savannah Foods & Industries, Inc.
Sugar workers
Big sugar (I) [Florida] A. Wilkinson. il *The New Yorker* 65:41-2+ Jl 17 '89
Big sugar (II) [Florida] A. Wilkinson. il *The New Yorker* 65:42-3+ Jl 24 '89
Export-import trade
Sugar lumps. P. C. Montgomery. il *Common Cause Magazine* 15:10-11 Ja/F '89
Three yards and a cloud of (sugar) dust [protectionist U.S. sugar policy] J. Novack. il *Forbes* 144:39-41 S 4 '89
U.S. consumers, and the Caribbean, are getting a sour deal on sugar. P. Magnusson. il *Business Week* p41 My 8 '89
SUGAR MAPLE *See* Maple
SUGAR PRICE SUPPORTS *See* Agricultural administration
SUGAR SUBSTITUTES
The scoop on sugar substitutes. D.-J. Moore. *New Choices for the Best Years* 29:73 Je '89
Sour logic [high intake of aspartame by children] R. Gautier. *American Health* 8:153+ Mr '89
Sweet and sour [sweetness determined by shape of molecule; work of Murray Goodman] T. Beardsley. *Scientific American* 261:22+ N '89
SUGAR WORKERS
Big sugar (I) [cutting sugar cane in Florida] A. Wilkinson. il *The New Yorker* 65:41-2+ Jl 17 '89
Big sugar (II) [cutting sugar cane in Florida] A. Wilkinson. il *The New Yorker* 65:42-3+ Jl 24 '89
SUGARING *See* Maple sugar
SUGARMAN, CAROLE
The high price of health approval. il *Consumers' Research Magazine* 72:33-4 N '89
Will your kid be president? il *Parents* 64:65-7 Ja '89
SUGARMANN, JOSH
Death by mail. *The Nation* 248:450 Ap 3 '89
SUGARS
See also
Altrose
Galactose
Lactose
Polysaccharides
Physiological constraint on feeding behavior: intestinal membrane disaccharidases of the starling. C. Martinez del Rio and B. R. Stevens. bibl f il *Science* 243:794-6 F 10 '89
SUGERMAN, DANIEL
The night the Lizard King came to dinner [excerpt from Wonderland Avenue] il *Rolling Stone* p31-3+ F 23 '89
SUGGESTION
See also
Brainwashing
Hypnotism
Mental healing
Subliminal projection
SUGGESTION SYSTEMS
See also
Ideas in business
SUGIHARA, GEORGE, AND OTHERS
Scale invariance in food web properties. bibl f il *Science* 245:48-52 Jl 7 '89
SUH, MARY
Canadian women at arms. il *Ms.* 17:71-2 Je '89
A future up in the air: flight attendants contest weight rules. il *Ms.* 18:83-4 S '89
Model homes for welfare families. il *Ms.* 18:73-4 Jl/Ag '89
RU detour. il *Ms.* 17:135-6 Ja/F '89
Understanding battered women. il *Ms.* 17:62 Ap '89
SUH, MARY, AND DENWORTH, LYDIA
Operation Rescue. il *Ms.* 17:92-4 Ap '89

SUHARTO *See* Soeharto, 1921-
SUHR (SWITZERLAND)
Public buildings
Perfect pitch [Bärenmatte Community Center designed by S. Calatrava] J. S. Russell. il *Architectural Record* 177:108-17 mid-S '89
SUICIDE
See also
Stuart, Charles—Murder case
A case of melancholia [1931 suicide of cartoonist R. Barton] J. Updike. il *The New Yorker* 65:112-20 F 20 '89
The death of a man who disappeared [C. Spence] por *Newsweek* 114:55 N 20 '89
"Die mother father brother" [teenage Satan worshipper T. Sullivan kills mother then commits suicide in Sparta, N.J.] E. Davidowitz. il por *Redbook* 172:132-4+ Ap '89
Drug abuse tied to 'fatal despondency' [research by Charles L. Rich] B. Bower. *Science News* 135:332 My 27 '89
Ex-Angels reliever Moore shoots wife, kills self [D. Moore] il por *Jet* 76:48 Ag 7 '89
How sharing grief can ease the pain [interview with H. Seiden] E. E. Goode. il por *U.S. News & World Report* 106:80 Ja 30 '89
Kay Kent died the way she lived—as a mirror of Marilyn Monroe. M. Dougherty. il pors *People Weekly* 32:90-1 Jl 3 '89
Living with chronic illness: why should I go on? S. Schmidt. *The Christian Century* 106:475-6+ My 3 '89
Memories of Frank [manic-depressive brother who committed suicide] M. K. Blakely. il *Psychology Today* 23:48-50+ O '89
A Moscow suicide reveals Glenn Souther's double life as a U.S. sailor spying for the K.G.B. W. Plummer. il *People Weekly* 32:105-6 Jl 10 '89
The odd case of M. Orlov [suicide of American defector G. M. Souther in the Soviet Union] il *Time* 134:40 Jl 10 '89
Panic attacks increase suicide attempts [research by Myrna M. Weissman] B. Bower. *Science News* 136:293 N 4 '89
Ricky Berry of Sacramento Kings commits suicide. por *Jet* 76:55-6 S 4 '89
Romeo & Juliet and . . . suicide [teen suicide; views of Ed Beckham] il *USA Today (Periodical)* 118:15 D '89
A season of scandal takes its final toll on mysterious lobbyist Craig Spence. il por *People Weekly* 32:103 N 27 '89
Sociopaths, suicide and serotonin. R. Cowen. *Science News* 136:250 O 14 '89
Steroids built Mike Keys up; then they tore him down [teen's suicide linked to use of anabolic steroids] M. Brower. il pors *People Weekly* 31:51-4+ Mr 20 '89
Suicides: the gun factor. E. Magnuson. il *Time* 134:61 Jl 17 '89
Teen suicide clusters: more than mimicry [research by Lucy E. Davidson] R. Weiss. *Science News* 136:342 N 25 '89
A triumph of spirit [J. Rivers overcomes suicide of husband E. Rosenberg] D. De Dubovay. il pors *Ladies' Home Journal* 106:62+ S '89
Prevention
Giving students reasons for wanting to live [advising programs in secondary schools] T. K. Edwards. *The Education Digest* 54:22-4 Mr '89
A high school play helps suicidal teenagers [Empty chairs written and performed by students in Roanoke, Va.] P. Feinour. *The Education Digest* 54:50-1 My '89
School prevention of suicide, violence, and abuse. E. Guetzloe. *The Education Digest* 54:46-9 F '89
Teens take charge [Wind River Reservation Youth Council formed after suicide epidemic] L. Eskin and D. Thunder. il *Scholastic Update (Teachers' edition)* 121:26-7 My 26 '89
"We have a problem" [counseling after teen's failed attempt] J. Marks. il *Parents* 64:137-9+ Ja '89
When teens talk suicide. il *Parents* 64:24 Ap '89
Statistics
Elderly suicides rise in 1980s. *Science News* 136:92 Ag 5 '89
Austria
Death turns out the lights at a noble couple's last soirée [Ludwig Rudolph of Hanover and wife I. von Thurn-Valsassina] M. Brower. il *People Weekly* 31:51-2 Ja 9 '89
Canada
A final act of despair [suicide of K. Dowson, Winnipeg police inspector involved in investigation into shooting death of native J. J. Harper] B. Bergman. *Maclean's* 102:22 N 13 '89
An unfolding tragedy [suicide of Winnipeg, Man. police inspector K. Dowson disrupts inquiry into shooting death of native leader J. J. Harper] P. Kopvillem. il por *Maclean's* 102:23 O 2 '89
SUISMAN, DOUGLAS R.
Morphosis at the Walker Arts Center. il *Architectural Record* 177:65 Jl '89
SUITCASES *See* Luggage
SUITES (HOTELS, MOTELS, ETC.) *See* Hotels, motels, etc.—Suites

SUITES (MUSIC)
    See also
        Compact discs—Suites (Music)
SUITS (CLOTHING) *See* Clothing and dress
SUITS (LAW) *See* Actions and defenses
SUKHANOVA, YULIA
    about
    Here she comes, Miss U.S.S.R.! And Yulia Sukhanova even
        wins a fight to visit the decadent West. H. Shapiro. il
        pors *People Weekly* 32:42-3 S 25 '89
SUKHOI DESIGN BUREAU (SOVIET UNION)
    Gulfstream/Soviet SST bizjet. il *Flying* 116:17 S '89
    Gulfstream, Soviets expect to select basic supersonic business
        jet design in November. *Aviation Week & Space Technology*
        131:46 O 16 '89
    Soviet/Gulfstream supersonic aircraft hinges on bilateral
        certification agreement. C. Fotos. *Aviation Week & Space
        Technology* 131:110-11 D 18-25 '89
    The Soviets want to help build a capitalist status symbol
        [Gulfstream supersonic corporate jet] C. Hawkins and R.
        Brady. il *Business Week* p42 O 9 '89
    Sukhoi Design Bureau expands civil aircraft development
        efforts. il *Aviation Week & Space Technology* 130:90-3
        Je 5 '89
    Sukhoi, Gulfstream to study supersonic business jet. D. A.
        Brown. il *Aviation Week & Space Technology* 130:54+
        Je 26 '89
    Sukhoi Su-26M for sale in the U.S. il *Flying* 116:12 O
        '89
    U.S.-Soviet team plans to fly supersonic business jet by
        1993. E. H. Kolcum. il *Aviation Week & Space Technology*
        131:22-4 S 25 '89
SUKHOTHAI WEST (NEW YORK, N.Y.: RESTAURANT)
    See New York (N.Y.)—Restaurants, nightclubs, bars, etc.
SULFA DRUGS *See* Sulfonamides
SULFAMETHAZINE
    Keeping drug residues out of milk. F. E. Young. il *FDA
        Consumer* 23:7 Mr '89
    Sulfamethazine residues in food. B. T. Hunter. il *Consumers'
        Research Magazine* 72:36-8 F '89
SULFASALAZINE
    Arthritis relief [rheumatoid arthritis] il *Prevention (Emmaus,
        Pa.)* 41:8+ O '89
SULFATES
    See also
        Dextran sulfate
        Heparan sulfate
        Soils—Sulfate content
SULFIDES
    See also
        Cadmium sulfide
        Hydrogen sulfide
        Molybdenum sulfides
        Tantalum sulfides
    Control of enzyme activity by an engineered disulfide bond.
        M. Matsumura and B. W. Matthews. bibl f il *Science*
        243:792-4 F 10 '89
    Splicing on-off switches into proteins [disulfide bond; research
        by Brian W. Matthews and Masazumi Matsumura] *Science
        News* 135:123 F 25 '89
SULFONAMIDES
    Winter vacation alert! [heightened sensitivity to sunlight]
        L. Schroepfer. *American Health* 8:31 Mr '89
SULFUR
    See also
        Coal—Sulfur content
    . . . and sulfur volcanism on Venus [research by Bruce
        Fegley, Jr., and Ronald G. Prinn] *Sky and Telescope* 77:356
        Ap '89
SULFUR COMPOUNDS
    See also
        Mercapto compounds
SULICH, VASSILI
    about
    Oedipus Rex [dance] Reviews
    Dance Magazine 63:62-3 Jl '89. M. Veljkovic
SULLIVAN, ANDREW
    Here comes the groom [cover story] *The New Republic* 201:20+
        Ag 28 '89
SULLIVAN, BILL, 1942-
    about
    Bill Sullivan at G. W. Einstein. G. Henry. il *Art in America*
        77:214-15 O '89
    Energizing landscape paintings. L. S. Zelenko. il *American
        Artist* 53:66-71 O '89
SULLIVAN, BRENDAN V.
    about
    Whittling away for Ollie. R. Parry. il pors *Newsweek* 113:20
        F 20 '89
SULLIVAN, DAN
    about
    Bullish beachcomber. P. Brimelow. il por *Forbes* 144:118-19
        O 30 '89
    Relative strength is absolutely hot. M. Hulbert. il *Forbes*
        144:117 Ag 21 '89

SULLIVAN, ED, 1902-1974
    about
    Ed Sullivan. il pors *People Weekly* 31 Special Issue:48-50
        Summ '89
SULLIVAN, JOAN
    about
    Centerline: Joan Sullivan. M. Sommers. il por *Theatre Crafts*
        23:18 Ag/S '89
SULLIVAN, JOHN L., 1858-1918
    about
    1889. A. Nielson. il por *American Heritage* 40:30+ Jl/Ag
        '89
SULLIVAN, JOHN R.
    View from a trailer. il *Country Journal* 16:84-5 Mr/Ap '89
SULLIVAN, JOSEPH
    about
    This man is an island. D. Chu. il pors *People Weekly*
        31:36-41 Ja 23 '89
SULLIVAN, JUANITA
    No way! *Essence* 20:82+ S '89
SULLIVAN, LOUIS W.
    about
    Back to the party of Lincoln? R. Lacayo. il pors *Time*
        133:79 Ja 2 '89
    Bush names Morehouse Medical School prexy to Cabinet
        post. il pors *Jet* 75:4 Ja 9 '89
    Dr. Sullivan to get $215,000 in severance pay; Senators
        see no conflict in HHS post. il por *Jet* 76:38 Ap 17
        '89
    Fraud and the "glare of the TV camera". G. Byrne. por
        Science 244:1038 Je 2 '89
    New leaders deal with aging-policy issues. il por *Modern
        Maturity* 32:85 Ag/S '89
    Promises to keep. K. A. Lawton. il por *Christianity Today*
        33:44-5 F 3 '89
    Sullivan gets the OK for Senate's HHS confirmation. il
        por *Jet* 75:5 Mr 13 '89
    Sullivan takes charge of America's health. L. Brown. por
        Black Enterprise 19:67-8 Je '89
    Sullivan to steer HHS to help 'disadvantaged'. S. Booker.
        il por *Jet* 75:4-5 Mr 27 '89
    Tar baby. F. Barnes. *The New Republic* 200:12-13 F 13
        '89
    White House puts Sullivan confirmation vote on hold. por
        Jet 75:25 F 20 '89
SULLIVAN, MAXINE, 1911-1987
    about
    Maxine Sullivan. P. Garland. por *Stereo Review* 54:124 Ja
        '89
SULLIVAN, MIKE
    about
    Hot streak. E. F. Cone. il por *Forbes* 143:10 Je 26 '89
SULLIVAN, NICK
    Workstyles. See issues of Home Office Computing beginning
        September 1988
SULLIVAN, ROBERT
    Gambling, payoffs and drugs. il *Sports Illustrated* 71:40-2+
        O 30 '89
    Going local goes global. il *Sports Illustrated* 71:98 Jl 24
        '89
    The iceman cometh. il pors map *Sports Illustrated* 71:40-5+
        Jl 31 '89
    A study in frustration. il por *Sports Illustrated* 70:94 Je
        19 '89
    (jt. auth) See Telander, Rick, and Sullivan, Robert
SULLIVAN, THOMAS, D. 1988
    about
    "Die mother father brother". E. Davidowitz. il por *Redbook*
        172:132-4+ Ap '89
SULLIVAN, TRUDY
    about
    Woman with a large idea. M. Barrier. il por *Nation's Business*
        77:71 Mr '89
SULLIVAN INSTITUTE FOR RESEARCH IN PSY-
CHOANALYSIS
    Psycho drama [P. Sprecher and M. Bray sue Sullivanians
        for custody of their children] P. Hoban. il pors *New York*
        22:40-2+ Je 19 '89
SULLIVAN'S TRAVELS [film] *See* Motion picture reviews—
Single works
SULLY, SARAH
    about
    Good news from Dartmouth. *National Review* 41:18 S 15
        '89
SULTAN, DONALD K., 1951-
    about
    The Sultans of Sag Harbor. D. Kazanjian. il por *House
        & Garden* 161:192-7+ S '89
SULTANATE OF OMAN *See* Oman
SUMAC
    A 48-million-year-old aphid-host plant association and com-
        plex life cycle: biogeographic evidence [aphid subtribe
        Melaphidina and sumac host plant] N. A. Moran. bibl
        f il map *Science* 245:173-5 Jl 14 '89

SUMAC, POISON *See* Poison sumac
SUMERIAN ASTRONOMY *See* Astronomy, Sumerian
SUMINAGASHI
Suminagashi: black ink floating. T. Leech. *Focus (New York, N.Y.: 1950)* 39:3 Summ '89
SUMITOMO BANK, LTD.
"The other banks feel threatened". A. Tanzer. il por *Forbes* 144:80+ O 2 '89
SUMITON (ALA.)

Education
Samurai math gets a tryout [kumon math] A. Murr. il *Newsweek* 113:60 Ap 10 '89
SUMMA MEDICAL CORPORATION
Low-cost HDTV that beats Japan's? G. G. Marcial. *Business Week* p102 My 29 '89
SUMMER, BOB
Southern spotlight. See occasional issues of Publishers Weekly beginning January 20, 1984
SUMMER, DONNA

about
Gay community frowns on disco diva Donna Summer. por *Jet* 76:38 S 18 '89
SUMMER
See also
August
Hot weather
July
June
7 reasons to love summer. il *Glamour* 87:43 Jl '89
The complete summer-safety guide. C. Sherman. il *Parents* 64:103-6+ Jl '89
Kids of summer 1989 [special section] il *Good Housekeeping* 208:69+ Je '89
The lazy days of summer. J. Segal and Z. Segal. il *Parents* 64:162 Jl '89
Malibu U. [special section] il *Teen* 33:82-3+ My '89
Rock & roll summer [special section] il *Rolling Stone* p14-15+ Jl 13-27 '89
Simple summer pleasures. A. Stoddard. il *McCall's* 116:132 Jl '89
Sporting pleasures. G. Logsdon. il *Country Journal* 16:36-41 Jl/Ag '89
Summer first aid. S. Squires. *Ladies' Home Journal* 106:54 Jl '89
Summer pleasures [New York City; cover story; special issue] il *New York* 22:19-31+ Jl 3-10 '89

Anecdotes, facetiae, satire, etc.
No news, please, summer is here. C. Gordon. il *Maclean's* 102:11 Jl 24 '89
SUMMER CAMPS *See* Camps
SUMMER COOKING *See* Cooking
SUMMER DRINKS *See* Beverages
SUMMER ENTERTAINING *See* Entertaining
SUMMER FLYING *See* Aviation—Summer flying
SUMMER HOUSES *See* Vacation houses
SUMMER JOBS FOR STUDENTS *See* Youth—Employment
SUMMER MEALS *See* Meals
SUMMER SCHOOLS
The joys of summer school. J. P. Comer. il *Parents* 64:217 Je '89
SUMMER SOLSTICE
The longest day. T. D. Nicholson. *Natural History* p82-3 Je '89
SUMMER SUPPERS *See* Suppers
SUMMER VACATIONS *See* Vacations
SUMMER WINES *See* Wine
SUMMERFARE (FESTIVAL) *See* PepsiCo Summerfare
SUMMERFORD, DAVID
When East is West. por *Newsweek* 113:10 Ja 2 '89
SUMMERHAYS, VINCENT
(jt. auth) See Zsarnay, Christopher, and Summerhays, Vincent
SUMMERS, ANDY

about
Police report. S. Fried. il pors *Gentlemen's Quarterly* 59:151+ O '89
SUMMERS, ANNE
Ministering angels. bibl il *History Today* 39:31-7 F '89
SUMMERS, ANNE, 1945-
Editor's essay. See issues of Ms. beginning February 1988 though November 1989
SUMMERS, HARRY G.
A bankrupt military strategy. il *The Atlantic* 263:34-7+ Je '89
SUMMERS, JASON
Tracks of my fears. il *Runner's World* 24:104 N '89
SUMMERS, LAWRENCE H.
Lost horizons. *The New Republic* 200:11-13 Je 26 '89
SUMMERS, R. JOE
High school students study Hurricane Gilbert. il *Weatherwise* 42:95-6 Ap '89
SUMMIT (TERM)
Parley in the foothills. W. Safire. il *The New York Times Magazine* p16+ O 15 '89
SUMMIT BOOKS
Summit Books. C. T. Anthony. il *Publishers Weekly* 236:18-20 Ag 4 '89

SUMMIT HEALTH LTD.
Is Summit Health ready to climb? G. Weiss and J. M. Laderman. *Business Week* p106 F 27 '89
SUMNER, ANTHONY

about
A snitch's tale: the killer gang. P. King. il por *Newsweek* 114:45 N 6 '89
SUMNER, GORDON *See* Sting
SUMO
An American wins big [Konishiki wins Japan's Emperor's Cup] S. Smith. il por *Sports Illustrated* 71:30 D 11 '89
Charge of the unlight brigade [Y. Konishiki wins Emperor's Cup] il por *U.S. News & World Report* 107:14-15 D 11 '89
They've got Rockefeller Center, but we've got Konishiki, the world's best sumo wrestler. il por *People Weekly* 32:133 D 11 '89
SUMRALL, LESTER FRANK, 1913-

about
No glitter for Lester [interview] por *Christianity Today* 33:36 F 3 '89
SUMTER COUNTY (S.C.)

Pollution
Citizens tackle toxic dump. R. Chepesiuk. il *The Progressive* 53:12-13 Je '89
SUN, JIAN-MIN, AND OTHERS
Histone H5 in the control of DNA synthesis and cell proliferation. bibl f il *Science* 245:68-71 Jl 7 '89
SUN
See also
Eclipses, Solar
Solar activity
Solar radiation
Solar system
Space flight to the sun
Sunspots
Ultraviolet rays
Equipped for safe solar viewing. R. Hill. il *Astronomy* 17:66-8 F '89
Fury on the sun [cover story] L. Jaroff. il *Time* 134:46-50+ Jl 3 '89
The many faces of the sun. G. L. Verschuur. il *Astronomy* 17:46-51 Mr '89
The sun, moon, and planets this month. A. MacRobert. See issues of Sky and Telescope beginning April 1988
Watching the sun. P. O. Taylor. il *Sky and Telescope* 77:220-3 F '89

Age
The new age of the sun [research by David B. Guenther] *Science News* 135:269 Ap 29 '89

Atmosphere
See also
Sun—Corona

Corona
See also
Coronagraph
Solar wind
Snapping the sun's sharpest X-ray image [use of Normal Incidence X-ray Telescope] il *Science News* 136:223 S 30 '89
Solar blast [Solar Maximum Mission's attempt to track coronal mass ejection] J. Eberhart. il *Science News* 135:331 My 27 '89
Taking X-rays of the sun. il *USA Today (Periodical)* 117:13-14 Je '89

Influence on weather
See Sun and meteorology

Internal structure
Gazing into the interior of the sun [research by Kenneth G. Libbrecht] M. M. Waldrop. il *Science* 244:31 Ap 7 '89
Looking inside the sun. J. C. LoPresto. il *Astronomy* 17:20-30 Mr '89
Solar revolutions [research by Kenneth G. Libbrecht] A. Fisher. il *Popular Science* 235:12 Jl '89

Magnetic properties
See also
Heliopause
Heliosphere
Magnetic flux transport on the sun [cover story] Y.-M. Wang and others. bibl f il *Science* 245:712-18 Ag 18 '89

Oscillations
See also
Helioseismology
Solar revolutions [research by Kenneth G. Libbrecht] A. Fisher. il *Popular Science* 235:12 Jl '89

Photographs and photography
Phobos 1 images the sun. G. L. Verschuur. il *Astronomy* 17:10-11 Je '89
Portrait of a year. H. J. P. Arnold. *Sky and Telescope* 77:678-9 Je '89

Prominences
See also
Solar flares
Solar prominence heads back to the sun. J. Eberhart. il *Science News* 136:52 Jl 22 '89

SUN—*cont.*

Spectra and spectroscopy

Diverse recipes shine in the sun's corona [Solar Max data; research by Keith T. Strong] J. Eberhart. *Science News* 135:358 Je 10 '89

SUN AND METEOROLOGY

Sea surface may follow solar tune [research by Tim P. Barnett] *Science News* 136:159 S 2 '89

Sun tantrums. F. Harrois-Monin. *World Press Review* 36:82-3 O '89

Sunny weather (literally) [link between sunspots and climate; work of Brian Tinsley] S. Budiansky. il *U.S. News & World Report* 106:52-3 Mr 6 '89

The sunspot syndrome [with editorial comment by Paul Hoffman] M. Bartusiak. il *Discover* 10:4, 44-8+ N '89

SUN GLASSES *See* Sunglasses

SUN-HEATED HOUSES *See* Solar houses

SUN LIGHT *See* Sunlight

SUN MICROSYSTEMS INC.

Can Sun stand the heat in the PC market? J. B. Levine. il *Business Week* p139 Ap 24 '89

High noon for Sun [cover story] J. B. Levine. il pors *Business Week* p70-5 Jl 24 '89

Power station in a pizza box [SPARCstation 1] J. M. Nash. il *Time* 133:51 Ap 24 '89

Scott McNealy. J. B. Levine. il por *Business Week* Special Issue:100 Ap 14 '89

Two powerful systems from Sun [SPARCStation 1 and Sun-3/80; cover story] N. Baran. il *Byte* 14:108-12 My '89

Why Sun is losing its heat in the East. N. Gross. il *Business Week* p114 S 18 '89

Will Sun get burned by its new partner? [Toshiba] J. B. Levine. *Business Week* p26-7 Je 12 '89

SUN MYUNG MOON *See* Moon, Sun Myung

SUN PROTECTION OF PLANTS *See* Plants—Protection

SUN ROOMS

Hearst & Company: formality governs a San Francisco conservatory addition. il *Architectural Digest* 46:98 Ap '89

A solarium for all seasons. il *Southern Living* 24:104 F '89

Space in the sun [cover story] C. Poole. il *Home Mechanix* 85:24-8+ Ja '89

Sunny connections. il *Southern Living* 24:76-9 Ja '89

Sunroom add-on. il *The Family Handyman* 39:92-3 Ap '89

Two-story sunroom links house with garden. il *Sunset (Central West edition)* 182:108 Je '89

The versatile sunroom. H. Huber. il *Country Journal* 16:27-33 Mr/Ap '89

SUN SCREENS *See* Screens (Doors, windows, etc.)

SUN SCREENS (COSMETICS) *See* Suntan products

SUN SPOTS *See* Sunspots

SUN-TIMES (CHICAGO, ILL.) *See* Chicago sun-times (Newspaper)

SUN VALLEY (IDAHO)

New life for Sun Valley. C. Cooper. il *Skiing* 42:190-4+ D '89

SUNBATHS

See also

Suntan

SUNBELT *See* Southern States; Southwestern States

SUNBELT SAVINGS, FSB

The bust of '89 [cover story] T. Moore. il por *U.S. News & World Report* 106:36-43 Ja 23 '89

SUNBELT SAVINGS ASSOCIATION OF TEXAS

Why our S&Ls are in trouble. il *Reader's Digest* 135:70-4 Jl '89

SUNBURN

Cool comfort in the hot sun. S. Kasper. il *Sierra* 74:102-3 Mr/Ap '89

Skin and sun savvy. P. G. Gill. il *Outdoor Life* 183:66+ My '89

Winter vacation alert! [antibiotics and sulfa drugs heighten sensitivity to sunlight] L. Schroepfer. *American Health* 8:31 Mr '89

Therapy

Sun lotions, magic potions. M. Reed. il *Weatherwise* 42:213-14 Ag '89

SUNDAES *See* Ice cream, ices, etc.

SUNDAHL, DANIEL JAMES

Sketch of a young woman picking fruit [poem] *Commonweal* 116:502 S 22 '89

SUNDANCE INSTITUTE

Architectural digest visits: Robert Redford at Sundance [cover story] J. Thurman. il *Architectural Digest* 46:162-71+ Ap '89

Sundance [dance/film lab] D. Towers. il *Dance Magazine* 63:76-7 F '89

SUNDARALINGAM, M., AND SEKHARUDU, Y. C.

Water-inserted α-helical segments implicate reverse turns as folding intermediates. bibl f il *Science* 244:1333-7 Je 16 '89

SUNDAY

Sunday is no day for shopping. J. Loback. il *Christianity Today* 33:8 Mr 3 '89

Laws and regulations

Court rules on clergy malpractice, Sabbath. *Christianity Today* 33:51-2 My 12 '89

The Supreme Court expands religious freedom [unemployment benefits for individual who refused to work on Sundays] R. F. Drinan. *America* 160:388-9 Ap 29 '89

Canada

Even shopkeepers need a day off. C. Gordon. il *Maclean's* 102:13 D 11 '89

Fiji

Sabbath laws split Methodists in Fiji. D. C. White. *The Christian Century* 106:406-7 Ap 19 '89

SUNDAY DINNERS *See* Dinners and dining

SUNDAY NIGHT [television program] *See* Television program reviews—Single works

SUNDAY SCHOOLS

Whatever happened to Sunday school? D. J. Lehmann. il *The Christian Century* 106:404-5 Ap 19 '89

Why I teach Sunday school. L. C. Sledge. *Reader's Digest* 135:11-12+ Jl '89

SUNDROPS

RNA editing in plant mitochondria [Oenothera] R. Hiesel and others. bibl f il *Science* 246:1632-4 D 22 '89

SUNDSTRAND CORPORATION

Sundstrand, Pratt & Whitney Canada make inroads in APU marketplace [auxiliary power units] il *Aviation Week & Space Technology* 130:78-80 Ap 10 '89

Sundstrand prepares to pay the piper—and the Pentagon. M. D. Oneal and P. Dwyer. il *Business Week* p35-6 Ja 23 '89

SUNDSTROM, HAROLD

How Eximbank works in today's global environment [address, December 6, 1988] *Vital Speeches of the Day* 55:262-5 F 15 '89

SUNFISH FISHING

See also

Bluegill fishing

SUNFLOWERS

If van Gogh had seen these sunflowers . . . il *Sunset (Central West edition)* 182:102-3, 206 Mr '89

The many faces of sunflowers. D. Smittle. il *Flower and Garden* 33:18-21 Jl/Ag '89

SUNGLASSES

See also

International Sun Shade Inc.

Eyewear [ski equipment] D. White. il *Skiing* 42:234-7 S '89

Glass acts: high-style shades for skiers. D. White. il *Skiing* 41:28+ F '89

Hot-rod glasses [anti-reflection coating for drivers] P. Bedard. il *Car and Driver* 35:10 N '89

Made for shade [cycling] J. Davis and F. Zahradnik. il *Bicycling* 30:56-8+ Je '89

The nouveau reach: Lear Vision. il *Flying* 116:31 Ag '89

Ray blockers. V. Z. Daly. il *Health (New York, N.Y.)* 21:45-6 My '89

Seeing through sunglass claims. S. Young. il *Glamour* 87:24 Jl '89

Shielding your eyes from the sun. E. Hale. il *FDA Consumer* 23:29 D '89/Ja '90

Specs appeal [celebrities] il *Ladies' Home Journal* 106:27 Je '89

Sunglass smarts. C. Slom. *McCall's* 116:85 Jl '89

Sunglasses. *Consumer Reports* 54:23-6 D '89

Visionaries. H. Brubach. il *The New Yorker* 65:64+ Ag 28 '89

SUNKEN TREASURE *See* Treasure trove

SUNLIGHT

See also

Photosynthesis

Stradivari's secret (redux): did baroque artisans "X-ray" wood with sunlight? J. Horgan. il *Scientific American* 261:21-2 Jl '89

Chemical action

See Photochemistry

Physiological effects

See Ultraviolet rays—Physiological effects

Spectra and spectroscopy

Spectra galore [UCL Echelle Spectrograph at the Anglo-Australian Telescope] il *Sky and Telescope* 77:585-6 Je '89

SUNNYSIDE [film] *See* Motion picture reviews—Single works

SUNRAYCER (AUTOMOBILE) *See* Automobiles, Solar

SUNRISE

Photographs and photography

By dawn's early light. E. L. Holland. il *Petersen's Photographic Magazine* 18:36-9 D '89

SUNROOMS *See* Sun rooms

SUNSCREENS (COSMETICS) *See* Suntan products

SUNSET (PERIODICAL)

Back from Australia, looking ahead at Sunset and the West. B. Lane. il pors *Sunset (Central West edition)* 183:164 Jl '89

Ending the tyranny of our thirsty front lawn [relandscaping headquarters] il *Sunset (Central West edition)* 183:66-9 S '89

For a look at Sunset's gardens and buildings, please drop by. il map *Sunset (Central West edition)* 183:70 S '89

SUNSET (PERIODICAL)—*cont.*
Sunset and the environment: working with you to help conserve and improve the West. B. Lane. il *Sunset (Central West edition)* 183:230-1 N '89

SUNSET PHENOMENA
A green flash of Jupiter. G. L. Verschuur. *Sky and Telescope* 77:259 Mr '89

SUNSHINE, LINDA
The new dating game. *Harper's Bazaar* 122:177+ Mr '89

SUNSHINE-GENOVA, AMY
The luckiest little girl in the world. il pors *Ladies' Home Journal* 106:140-1+ Mr '89

SUNSHINE-JR. STORES, INC.
The champion of the modern corner store [L. J. Lewis-Brent] P. O'Toole. il pors *Working Woman* 14:114-15+ S '89

SUNSHINE LAWS
The shady side of sunshine [selection of new president of University of Florida] J. McLaughlin and D. Riesman. il *Change* 21:44-57 Ja/F '89

SUNSHINE VILLAGE CORPORATION
An identity crisis [debate over expansion of skiing operation in Banff] J. Howse. il *Maclean's* 102:48 F 27 '89

SUNSIGN MANUFACTURING COMPANY
Something new under the sun. E. Wilkes. por *Nation's Business* 77:9 Ag '89

SUNSPOTS
See also
Solar flares
Blame it on the moon [Elatina sediment striations tidally induced; George E. Williams overturns his hypothesis] J. Horgan. *Scientific American* 260:18 F '89
Fury on the sun [cover story] L. Jaroff. il *Time* 134:46-50+ Jl 3 '89
Great balls of fire. il *Sky and Telescope* 77:494 My '89
It's not the sun, but the moon [tidally induced Australian rock laminations; research by George E. Williams] il *Sky and Telescope* 77:469 My '89
Magnetic flux transport on the sun [cover story] Y.-M. Wang and others. bibl f il *Science* 245:712-18 Ag 18 '89
Nature's incredible night show. L. Ponte. il *Reader's Digest* 135:86-91 D '89
The observation of sunspots [ancient China] R. K. G. Temple. *The Courier (Unesco)* 41:9 O '88
Our future in the stars? [HK Project; research by Sallie L. Baliunas] M. M. Waldrop. il *Science* 243:890-1 F 17 '89
Rising to a sunspot peak. *Science News* 135:13 Ja 7 '89
Sea surface may follow solar tune [research by Tim P. Barnett] *Science News* 136:159 S 2 '89
Showtime on the sun. D. J. Eicher. il *Astronomy* 17:99+ My '89
Solar-cycle peak threatens Max to the max [Solar Maximum Mission satellite] J. Eberhart. *Science News* 135:87 F 11 '89
Sunny weather (literally) [link between sunspots and climate; work of Brian Tinsley] S. Budiansky. il *U.S. News & World Report* 106:52-3 Mr 6 '89
Viewing sunspots with just a filter. A. MacRobert. il *Sky and Telescope* 78:289+ S '89

SUNTAN
See also
Sunburn
Burns, eye injuries from tanning devices. il *FDA Consumer* 23:3-4 O '89
'Healthy tan'—a fast-fading myth. C. A. Sweet. il *FDA Consumer* 23:11-13 Je '89
Hot tips for smart sunning. C. Straley. il *Parents* 64:160-2+ Je '89
How well do you practice safe sun? J. Wood. *Modern Maturity* 32:25 Ag/S '89
Images: the suntan. J. Shields. il *Vogue* 179:91-2 Je '89
Melanoma: can the sun be protective? [research by Neil Dubin] *Science News* 136:30 Jl 8 '89
Safe-tanning tips. C. Slom. *McCall's* 116:85 Jl '89
Skin and sun savvy. P. G. Gill. il *Outdoor Life* 183:66+ My '89
Sun: the new wisdom. W. Bennett. il *Vogue* 179:204-6 Je '89
The truth about tanning salons. *Seventeen* 48:193 Mr '89
What's your sun sense? [quiz] il *Seventeen* 48:142-5 Je '89
You and your tan: the end of a love affair. il *Glamour* 87:224-7 Ag '89

SUNTAN PRODUCTS
Block that burn! M. J. Fellner and S. Colino. il *Travel Holiday* 172:28-9 D '89
Color blocks. H. E. Lee. il *Vogue* 179:165 Ap '89
Do sunscreens block vitamin D? il *Prevention (Emmaus, Pa.)* 41:10+ Jl '89
Getting sun-smart: protection from UVA rays. L. F. McCarthy. *Vogue* 179:192+ Ap '89
Guilt-free guide. il *Glamour* 87:224-7 Je '89
How much is too much sun? [sunscreens] M. Morrison. il *Redbook* 173:12 Ag '89
New under the sun [protection from UVA rays] D. A. Saunders. il *Forbes* 144:134 Ag 7 '89
Playing hide and seek with the sun—safely [sunscreens] L. George. il *American Health* 8:26-8+ My '89
SPF—the numbers game. S. Lord. il *Vogue* 179:52 Ja '89

Sun sense. il *Ladies' Home Journal* 106:31 Jl '89
Sunscreen roulette. J. Graham. il *Health (New York, N.Y.)* 21:52-7 My '89
Sunscreens. il *Consumer Reports* 54:26-30 D '89
A suntan can be a fun tan with this new way to change your oil [vending machines developed by C. C. King] il *People Weekly* 31:116-17 My 29 '89
'Take 15' for younger, healthier skin [sunscreens] P. Boyer. il *Prevention (Emmaus, Pa.)* 41:99+ My '89
What's new under the sun. M. Rowland. il *Working Woman* 14:70+ My '89

SUNUNU, JOHN
about
Bush's bad cop. por *Time* 134:21 Ag 21 '89
The conservative vicar of domestic policy. K. T. Walsh. *U.S. News & World Report* 107:27 O 9 '89
The great right hope [cover story] P. Osterlund. il *National Review* 41:24-6 Mr 24 '89
John Sununu: the right-hand man. D. Tibbetts. il pors *Conservative Digest* 15:43+ Ja/F '89
Sununu and improved. F. Barnes. il *The New Republic* 200:13-14 My 29 '89
Sununu: the making of a scapegoat. E. Salholz. il por *Newsweek* 113:23 Mr 13 '89
The trying times of John Sununu. D. Baer. il pors *U.S. News & World Report* 106:49-50 Mr 13 '89
With Sununu, a different story? Cato. *National Review* 41:26 My 5 '89

SUNYAEV, RASHID
about
Rashid Sunyaev wins 1988 Rossi Prize. P. H. Andersen. il por *Physics Today* 42:90+ Ap '89

SUOMI, VERNER
about
Interview: Verner Suomi. P. Bagne. por *Omni (New York, N.Y.)* 11:60-2+ Jl '89

SUPER BARRIO
about
Not to be confused with bird or plane, Mexico's caped crusader packs a political paunch. A. Gonzalez. il *People Weekly* 31:114-15 Ap 10 '89

SUPER BOWL *See* Football, Professional—Super Bowl
SUPER DERBY *See* Horse racing
SUPERBOY [television program] *See* Television program reviews—Single works
SUPERCALC (COMPUTER PROGRAM) *See* Spreadsheets (Computer programs)
SUPERCARD (COMPUTER PROGRAM)
How super is SuperCard? R. D. Lasky. il *Byte* 14:217-18+ O '89

SUPERCHARGERS
See also
Airplane engines—Superchargers
Automobile engines—Superchargers
Automobiles, Racing—Engines—Superchargers
Diesel engines, Automotive—Superchargers
Diesel engines, Marine—Superchargers
Motor boat engines—Superchargers
SUPERCLUSTERS, GALACTIC *See* Galaxies—Clusters
SUPERCOMPUTERS
See also
Cray Computer Corporation
Ketema, Inc.
Massively parallel supercomputers
NSFnet
Ada for supercomputers—a trend. *High Technology Business* 9:32 Ja '89
And then there was one [Control Data pulls out of market] M. Quinn. il *Time* 133:56 My 1 '89
Cray versus Japan Inc. [interview with J. A. Rollwagen] D. Churbuck. il por *Forbes* 144:118-19 S 4 '89
Fastest supercomputer [Cray Y-MP at Ames Research Center] A. Fisher. il *Popular Science* 234:8+ F '89
From dust to dust [simulation called galaxy-in-a-box; cover story] I. Peterson. il *Science News* 135:24-5 Ja 14 '89
Getting a clearer view of smog [supercomputer pollution model developed by G. J. McRae] M. Schroeder. il por *Business Week* Special Issue:73 Je 16 '89
A global supercomputer race for high stakes. M. Sun. il *Science* 243:1004-6 F 24 '89
Is it real, or is it Cray? R. Pool. il *Science* 244:1438-40 Je 23 '89
Squabbles beset supercomputing. *High Technology Business* 9:35-6 Ap '89
Supercomputer market needs supersalesmen. M. Sun. il *Science* 245:596-7 Ag 11 '89
Supercomputer policy under review [Office of Technology Assessment report] E. Marshall. *Science* 246:207 O 13 '89
Supercomputing. E. Corcoran. il *Scientific American* 260:70+ F '89
Supercomputing the liquid state of carbon [work of Richard M. Martin] I. Peterson. *Science News* 136:166 S 9 '89
Supercomputing the universe. D. Johnson. il *Astronomy* 17:48-54 D '89
Prices
Ardent's Daddy Warbucks [Kubota Ltd.] J. B. Levine. il *Business Week* p26-7 Je 12 '89

SUPERCONDUCTING QUANTUM INTERFERENCE DE-VICES See SQUIDs (Superconducting quantum interference devices)

SUPERCONDUCTING SUPER COLLIDER

As for the impact on the environment . . . [mass mailing of impact statements on super collider sites] J. Tully. il *Common Cause Magazine* 15:8 N/D '89

At last, Congress agrees to build SSC, after Texas-type wheeling and dealing. I. Goodwin. *Physics Today* 42:51-2 O '89

Beyond the quark [cover story] J. S. Trefil. il *The New York Times Magazine* p24-7+ Ap 30 '89

Black hole. J. Treen. *The New Republic* 200:17-18 F 20 '89

DOE picks Texas for 'Gippertron' amid political and managerial collisions. I. Goodwin. il map *Physics Today* 42:95-8 F '89

Down payment for collider construction. I. Peterson. *Science News* 136:199 S 23 '89

House approves SSC construction. M. Crawford. *Science* 245:25 Jl 7 '89

Interview: Leon Lederman. D. Teresi. pors *Omni (New York, N.Y.)* 12:98-100+ O '89

Japan and the SSC: Congress raises a flag. M. Crawford. il *Science* 246:577 N 3 '89

Lab report puts SSC magnets in limbo. M. Crawford. il *Science* 245:809-10 Ag 25 '89

Lone-Star science. J. Horgan. il *Scientific American* 260:17-18+ Ja '89

SSC gets off to a magnetic start. I. Peterson. *Science News* 135:303 My 13 '89

Super deal [Waxahachie, Tex. chosen as site] G. Jaynes. il *Life* 12:100-4 F '89

The time tunnel. A. Steacy. il *Maclean's* 102:49 Ja 30 '89

Will magnet problems delay the SSC? M. Crawford. il *Science* 243:1425-6 Mr 17 '89

SUPERCONDUCTORS AND SUPERCONDUCTIVITY

See also
Consortium for Superconducting Electronics

1-2-3 contact: a new superconducting film [research by Jagdish Narayan] I. Amato. *Science News* 135:294 My 13 '89

Adding to the technological wish list [superconducting coaxial cable] *Science News* 135:143 Mr 4 '89

Anomalous scattering study of the Bi distribution in the 2212 superconductor: implications for Cu valency. P. Lee and others. bibl f il *Science* 244:62-3 Ap 7 '89

At last, superconductors are starting to look super. E. T. Smith. il *Business Week* p92+ N 27 '89

The axial oxygen atom and superconductivity in $YBa_2Cu_3O_7$. S. D. Conradson and I. D. Raistrick. bibl f il *Science* 243:1340-3 Mr 10 '89

The dogged push to overcome resistance [work of S. Jin] E. T. Smith. il por *Business Week* Special Issue:84 Je 16 '89

Electron superconductors and more. I. Peterson. *Science News* 135:207 Ap 1 '89

Electron superconductors challenge theories, start a new race. A. Khurana. bibl f il *Physics Today* 42:17-19 Ap '89

Execs say SC not stalled. *High Technology Business* 9:33-4 My '89

Flexible superconductors will shape PC boards, power supplies [views of Gregory Yurek] *Byte* 14:11-12 F '89

Flux creep. B. Schechter. il *Discover* 10:20 O '89

Getting the creeps out of superconductors. I. Amato. *Science News* 136:383 D 9 '89

Giant flux creep. P. Wallich. *Scientific American* 261:21 Ag '89

Good news for superconductors [research by Bruce van Dover] R. Pool. *Science* 246:755 N 10 '89

High-temperature superconductivity: past, present and future. V. L. Ginzburg. bibl f il por *Physics Today* 42:9+ Mr '89

Magnon-exchange pairing and superconductivity [discussion of February 19, 1988 article, The magnon pairing mechanism of superconductivity in cuprate ceramics] G. Chen and W. A. Goddard, III. *Science* 243:547-8 Ja 27 '89

Masters of invention [winners of contest to find most creative uses for superconductors] K. McKinney. il *Omni (New York, N.Y.)* 11:10 Ag '89

More surprises from new superconductors. *Science News* 135:367 Je 10 '89

New superconductor uses electrons [research by Y. Tokura and others] R. Pool. *Science* 243:741 F 10 '89

The new superconductors: prospects for applications. A. M. Wolsky and others. bibl il *Scientific American* 260:60-9 F '89

Non-copper SC materials in development. *High Technology Business* 9:36-7 Jl/Ag '89

Photoemission spectroscopy of the high-temperature superconductivity gap. G. Margaritondo and others. bibl f il *Science* 246:770-5 N 10 '89

Rearranging oxygen for superconductivity [yttrium-barium-copper oxide; work of Robert B. Beyers] I. Peterson. *Science News* 136:133 Ag 26 '89

Silver supports superconducting paste. il *Science News* 136:182 S 16 '89

Spatially resolved observation of supercurrents across grain boundaries in YBaCuO films. J. Mannhart and others. bibl f il *Science* 245:839-41 Ag 25 '89

Submicrometer superconducting $YBa_2Cu_3O_{6+x}$ particles made by a low-temperature synthetic route. H. S. Horowitz and others. bibl f il *Science* 243:66-9 Ja 6 '89

Superconducting ceramics [Ceracon process] *USA Today (Periodical)* 117:9-10 Je '89

Superconducting gap in Bi-Sr-Ca-Cu-O by high-resolution angle-resolved photoelectron spectroscopy. C. G. Olson and others. bibl f il *Science* 245:731-3 Ag 18 '89

Superconducting lives [Hypres Inc.] R. Bailey. *Forbes* 144:259+ Jl 24 '89

Superconductivity in a nickel oxide [work of Jurgen Honig and others] R. Pool. *Science* 243:741 F 10 '89

Superconductivity: is the party over? R. Pool. il *Science* 244:914-16 My 26 '89

The superconductivity party [discussion of May 26, 1989 article, Superconductivity: is the party over?] R. Pool. *Science* 245:111-12 Jl 14 '89

Superconductivity: party time again [remedies for problems of flux lattice motion] R. Pool. *Science* 246:1243 D 8 '89

Superconductivity stars move [A. W. Sleight and A. M. Hermann] R. Pool. pors *Science* 244:1141 Je 9 '89

Superconductors with electrons in charge [discovered by Yoshi Tokura] *Science News* 135:143 Mr 4 '89

Update on electron superconductors. R. Pool. *Science* 243:1436 Mr 17 '89

US superconductivity effort shapes up, with Du Pont emerging a big player. W. Sweet. *Physics Today* 42 pt1:55-8 Ag '89

What you see isn't always what you get [research by Aloysius J. Arko] *Science News* 135:143 Mr 4 '89

Will the results be as hot as the rumors? [room temperature superconductivity; work of Ronald Bourgoin and Fred W. Vahldiek] E. T. Smith. il *Business Week* p42 Ja 9 '89

"Wise men" on superconductors [report of the Committee to Advise the President on High Temperature Superconductivity] R. Pool. *Science* 243:162 Ja 13 '89

Zero resistance at 250 K? [work of J. T. Chen] R. Pool. *Science* 246:320 O 20 '89

Federal aid

Bromley targets superconductors. M. Crawford. *Science* 246:321 O 20 '89

International aspects

HTSC could blossom faster than expected. *High Technology Business* 9:32 Ap '89

Magnetic properties

High-temperature supercurrents may not be forever. A. Khurana. bibl f il *Physics Today* 42:17-21 Mr '89

Lab report puts SSC magnets in limbo. M. Crawford. il *Science* 245:809-10 Ag 25 '89

Levitation in physics [cover story] E. H. Brandt. bibl f il *Science* 243:349-55 Ja 20 '89

Rings of power [superconducting magnetic energy storage ring] N. J. Freundlich. il *Popular Science* 234:66-7+ Ja '89

SSC gets off to a magnetic start. I. Peterson. *Science News* 135:303 My 13 '89

Super (conductor) man [inventor F. Reick] A. Fisher. il por *Popular Science* 235:76-7 D '89

Supercurrent decay in high magnetic fields. I. Peterson. il *Science News* 135:197 Ap 1 '89

Suspending disbelief over superconductivity. B. Schechter. il *Discover* 10:59-60 Ja '89

Will magnet problems delay the SSC? M. Crawford. il *Science* 243:1425-6 Mr 17 '89

Military use

Rings of power [superconducting magnetic energy storage ring] N. J. Freundlich. il *Popular Science* 234:66-7+ Ja '89

U.S. falling behind Japan in superconductor research. B. D. Nordwall. il *Aviation Week & Space Technology* 130:57+ Ja 16 '89

Patents

IBM wins a patent for thallium superconductor [controversial because material first discovered by A. Hermann] R. Pool. *Science* 246:320 O 20 '89

Superconductor patents: four groups duke it out. R. Pool. il *Science* 245:931-3 S 1 '89

Japan

Japan: superconductor hopes drop. R. Pool. *Science* 245:1331 S 22 '89

Japanese researchers push electron holography. S. M. Dambrot. il *Science* 246:31 O 6 '89

Japan's SC strategy: leave nothing to chance. *High Technology Business* 9:32 F '89

Keeping up with the Jonezawas. R. Pool. il *Science* 245:594-5 Ag 11 '89

NTT test paves way for new chips. *High Technology Business* 9:30-1 Je '89

Superconductors heat up. S. Wagstyl. il *World Press Review* 36:47 Mr '89

U.S. falling behind Japan in superconductor research. B. D. Nordwall. il *Aviation Week & Space Technology* 130:57+ Ja 16 '89

SUPERCOOLING
Freeze avoidance in a mammal: body temperatures below 0°C in an Arctic hibernator [cover story] B. M. Barnes. bibl f il *Science* 244:1593-5 Je 30 '89
Squirrel sleeps at a fluid subzero [research by Brian M. Barnes] *Science News* 136:30 Jl 8 '89
Supercool mammals [body temperature of Arctic ground squirrel drops below freezing during hibernation; research by Brian Barnes] M. Kemp. il *Discover* 10:24 N '89

SUPERFLUIDITY
Superfluid transition in porous media shows puzzling features. A. Khurana. bibl f il *Physics Today* 42:21-5 Jl '89

SUPERFUND FOR WASTE CLEANUP See Trade waste—Disposal—Laws and regulations

SUPERGIANT STARS See Stars, Giant

SUPERINTENDENTS, SCHOOL See School superintendents and principals

SUPERIOR CHILDREN See Children, Gifted

SUPERIOR COLLICULUS See Brain

SUPERMARKETS
See also
Albertson's Inc.
Alpha Beta Co.
American Stores Co.
Collective labor agreements—Supermarkets
Computers—Grocery trade use
FJ's (Firm)
Giant Food Inc.
Grand Union Co.
Great Atlantic & Pacific Tea Company, Inc.
Harris-Teeter Super Markets, Inc.
Hypermarkets
Lucky Stores Inc.
Optical scanners—Grocery trade use
Ruddick Corporation
Safeway Stores, Inc.
Supermarkets General Corp.
Wegmans Food Markets Inc.
What new services? J. Schlefer. *Technology Review* 92:4 N/D '89

Acquisitions and mergers
American: can it mine Lucky Stores' magic? R. Grover. il *Business Week* p141+ Ap 24 '89
Can bankers sell groceries [Merrill Lynch leveraged buyout of Supermarkets General] G. Morgenson. il *Forbes* 144:54+ O 30 '89
The hell with glamour. Give me groceries [G. D. Hirsch] J. H. Dobrzynski. il por *Business Week* p121 My 1 '89
International aspects
Has LBO fever struck Europe? [A&P's bid for Gateway] M. Maremont. il *Business Week* p28 Jl 3 '89
Shopping for bargains [Ahold USA] J. Zweig. il por *Forbes* 144:274 Jl 24 '89

Banking services
Bagging CD's and instant cash. C. Friday. il *Newsweek* 113:49 Je 5 '89

Finance
Food distributors. R. King. il *Forbes* 143:139-40+ Ja 9 '89

Securities
No chain reaction. T. Jaffe. il *Forbes* 143:414 My 1 '89

Space allocation
Want shelf space at the supermarket? Ante up. L. Therrien. il *Business Week* p60-1 Ag 7 '89

Canada
See also
Loblaw Companies Ltd.

France
See also
Carrefour (Firm)

Germany (West)
See also
Tengelmann Group

Great Britain
See also
Gateway Foodmarkets Ltd.
Isosceles plc

Japan
See also
Daiei, Inc.

SUPERMARKETS GENERAL CORP.
Can bankers sell groceries [Merrill Lynch leveraged buyout of Supermarkets General] G. Morgenson. il *Forbes* 144:54+ O 30 '89

SUPERNATURAL
See also
Ghosts
Miracles
Parapsychology
Do you believe in the supernatural? [results of survey] I. Groller. il *Parents* 64:32 O '89

SUPERNATURAL IN LITERATURE
See also
Ghost stories
Horror tales

SUPERNOVAS
Ancient art adds to supernova mystery [American Indian petroglyphs in New Mexico] il *Earth Science* 42:5 Fall '89

The ashes of Supernova 1987A. il *Sky and Telescope* 78:344 O '89
Astronomers glimpse birth of a pulsar [spawned by Supernova 1987A] I. Peterson. *Science News* 135:100 F 18 '89
Birth of a pulsar. S. Flamsteed. il *Discover* 10:26 My '89
Bright supernova found in galaxy M66. il *Astronomy* 17:98 My '89
Cosmic birth [detection of pulsar emerging from Supernova 1987A's dust cloud] *Time* 133:81 F 20 '89
The Crab and kin [Crab nebula] il *Sky and Telescope* 77:7-9 Ja '89
Distant supernova may have cosmological impact [1988U] il *Astronomy* 17:12 D '89
An extragalactic Eta Carinae? [Supernova 1961V] il *Sky and Telescope* 77:355 Ap '89
Galactic cannonballs [research by Jane C. Charlton and Edwin E. Salpeter] *Sky and Telescope* 78:246 S '89
The great supernova of 1987 [cover story] S. E. Woosley and T. Weaver. bibl il *Scientific American* 261:32-40 Ag '89
High-flying astronomers observe Supernova 1987A [Kuiper Airborne Observatory] il *Sky and Telescope* 77:353-5 Ap '89
Hint of a burst of supernova activity in a superluminous galaxy [NGC 6240; research by Bruce T. Draine] I. Peterson. *Science News* 136:252 O 14 '89
Hit, miss, and hope for supernova hunters. il *Sky and Telescope* 77:468 My '89
Milky Way's youngest supernova? [G25.5 + 0.2 discovered by John J. Cowan] il *Sky and Telescope* 78:348-9 O '89
Mysterious pulsar found in Supernova 1987A. *Astronomy* 17:10 My '89
New echoes of Supernova 1987A [light echoes from dust clouds; work of Arlin P. S. Crotts and William E. Kunkel] I. Peterson. *Science News* 136:12 Jl 1 '89
New life for old supernovae [CTB 80] il *Sky and Telescope* 78:350 O '89
The peculiar pulsar in Supernova 1987A [cover story] G. L. Verschuur. il *Astronomy* 17:20-6 S '89
Pulsar, pulsar, where art thou, pulsar? [Supernova 1987A] M. M. Waldrop. *Science* 243:1553 Mr 24 '89
Puppis A: a double supernova? il *Sky and Telescope* 78:130 Ag '89
Remnants of two famous supernovae located. il *Astronomy* 17:14 Ap '89
Ringing up another light echo [1987A] *Science News* 135:155 Mr 11 '89
Seeking gamma rays from Supernova 1987A. il *Sky and Telescope* 78:455 N '89
SETI's guiding light [using supernovas to pick up extraterrestrial signals; theory of William F. Hilton] J. K. Beatty. il *Omni (New York, N.Y.)* 11:24 Mr '89
SN 1987A and its ultrafast pulsar. R. A. Schorn. il *Sky and Telescope* 77:480 My '89
Sorting out supernovae [work of Robert P. Harkness and J. Craig Wheeler] il *Sky and Telescope* 78:574 D '89
Splotchy supernova shakes assumptions [1987A; research by Scott Barthelmy] I. Peterson. *Science News* 135:303 My 13 '89
StarTrails [work of R. O. Evans] D. H. Levy. il por *Sky and Telescope* 78:85 Jl '89
Stellar collapse rate. il *Sky and Telescope* 78:567-8 D '89
Struggling to understand the Supernova 1987A pulsar. *Astronomy* 17:10+ Jl '89
Supernova 1987A: fading away. il *Sky and Telescope* 77:127 F '89
The Supernova 1987A pulsar: found? M. M. Waldrop. *Science* 243:892 F 17 '89
Supernova aftermath [Cassiopeia A gas shell; cover story] L. A. Marschall. il *Astronomy* 17:40-2 F '89
Supernova burps rid galaxies of hot gas [work of Jane C. Charlton and Edwin E. Salpeter] I. Peterson. *Science News* 136:310 N 11 '89
Supernova hunter; ed. by Robert Reeves. R. O. Evans. il *Astronomy* 17:94-7 N '89
Supernova mystery: cracking the Crab [research by Gordon M. MacAlpine] I. Peterson. il *Science News* 135:391 Je 24 '89
Supernova remnant on the move [SN 1006; observations by Knox S. Long and William P. Blair] il *Sky and Telescope* 77:244 Mr '89
The Vela pulsar: maybe not a mystery. *Sky and Telescope* 78:458 N '89

SUPEROXIDE DISMUTASE
Oxygen radicals in influenza-induced pathogenesis and treatment with pyran polymer-conjugated SOD. T. Oda and others. bibl f il *Science* 244:974-6 My 26 '89

SUPEROXIDES
Asbestos fiber shape may trigger radicals [study by Andrij Holian] D. E. Loupe. *Science News* 136:167 S 9 '89
Recombinant 47-kilodalton cytosol factor restores NADPH oxidase in chronic granulomatous disease. K. J. Lomax and others. bibl f il *Science* 245:409-12 Jl 28 '89; Correction. 246:987 N 24 '89

SUPERSAURUS See Dinosaurs
SUPERSCREEN TELEVISION See Television projection
SUPERSONIC AIRPLANES See Airplanes, Supersonic
SUPERSTAR [film] See Motion picture reviews—Single works

SUPERSTITION
See also
Medicine men
Voodooism
Witchcraft
The never-ending fight. I. Asimov. il por *The Humanist*
49:7-8+ Mr/Ap '89

SUPERSYMMETRY (PHYSICS)
Optimum chemical sites and techniques for searches for
negatively charged rare particles. R. N. Boyd and others.
bibl f il *Science* 244:1450-7 Je 23 '89

SUPERVISORS
See also
Women supervisors

SUPPERS
Hearty one-dish suppers. K. Farrell. il *McCall's* 117:49+
N '89
An intimate New Year's Eve supper. J. Nash. il *Essence*
20:87-93 D '89
No-fret family supper. il *Southern Living* 24:180 S '89
Quick summer suppers [microwaving] il *Good Housekeeping*
209:149-50 Jl '89
Split-second suppers [microwaving] il *Good Housekeeping*
208:179-80 My '89
A summer supper. il *Gourmet* 49:70-2+ Ag '89
Summer suppers [special section] il *Southern Living* 24:63+
Jl '89

SUPPLEMENTARY EMPLOYMENT
Artists' second careers. D. Grant. *American Artist* 53:14+
Ag '89

SUPPLIERS, INDUSTRIAL See Industrial suppliers
SUPPLY AND DEMAND
See also
Productivity, Industrial
Supply-side economics
Software despotism: truth and fiction [Guns & Butter supply
and demand video game and Allways utility for Lotus
1-2-3] E. Shapiro. il *Byte* 14:143-4 My '89

SUPPLY-SIDE ECONOMICS
Apocalypse revisited. *National Review* 41:16+ S 29 '89
Has the Laffer Curve flattened out? [income tax revenues
have stalled] H. Banks. *Forbes* 144:33 N 27 '89
How Reaganomics made the world work. R. L. Bartley.
il *National Review* 41:30-4 Ap 21 '89
It's time to face facts: supply-side was a smash [success
of the reign of Reaganomics] P. C. Roberts. il *Business
Week* p24 F 6 '89
Supply-side economics and the future [address, December
8, 1988] P. C. Roberts. *Vital Speeches of the Day* 55:307-9
Mr 1 '89
Supply-side theory is alive and well—in Moscow. P. C.
Roberts. il *Business Week* p10 Jl 24 '89
Supply-sider [deficit debate] R. L. Bartley. il *National Review*
41:46-7 Ja 27 '89
Unconditional surrender [steep progressive taxes] D. Seligman.
il *Fortune* 119:123 F 13 '89
Voodoo deficits. A. Evans-Pritchard. il *The American
Spectator* 22:14-15 F '89

SUPPORT (DOMESTIC RELATIONS)
See also
Alimony
After 20 years, an abandoned wife makes her ex pay his
due [case of P. Bennett] D. Chu. il pors *People Weekly*
31:79-82 F 20 '89
It takes two. *Commonweal* 116:100 F 24 '89
Money makeover: how much child support can you expect?
il *Glamour* 87:135 N '89
Suing for cash and charging abuse, the mother of his son
gives Bill Hurt a Big chill. M. Green. il pors *People
Weekly* 31:54-6 Ap 3 '89

SUPPORT GROUPS See Self help groups
SUPPORTS, PLANT See Plant supports
SUPRACHIASMATIC NUCLEUS See Hypothalamus
SUPREMATISM (ART)
Exhibitions
Behind the suprematist mirror [K. S. Malevich] C. Douglas.
bibl f il *Art in America* 77:164-77 S '89

SUPREME BEAUTY PRODUCTS (FIRM)
Lafayette Jones forms new company. por *Jet* 75:14 Ja 23
'89
Phyllis Roberson gets promotion at Supreme Beauty Products
Co. por *Jet* 75:14+ Ja 23 '89

SUPREME COURT (CANADA) See Canada. Supreme Court
SUPREME COURT (U.S.) See United States. Supreme Court
SUPREME COURT JUDGES See United States. Supreme
Court

THE SUPREME COURT'S HOLY BATTLES [television
program] See Television program reviews—Single works
SUPREME LIFE INSURANCE COMPANY
Joel K. Gearring named vice pres./agency head at Supreme
Life Insurance. por *Jet* 75:14 Ap 3 '89

SUPRESSOR GENES, TUMOR See Tumor suppressor genes
SURAMIN
Scientists see new hope for old drug [use of suramin for
advanced prostate cancer] *Science News* 135:366 Je 10
'89

SURE!, AL B.
about
Al B. Sure! Pop's hottest act. C. Krupp. il pors *Glamour*
87:136 F '89
Los Angeles DA won't file charge of rape against Al B.
Sure! il por *Jet* 75:56 Ap 3 '89

SURF FISHING See Salt water fishing
SURFACE ACOUSTIC WAVE DEVICES
Hardware hacker. D. Lancaster. il *Radio-Electronics* 60:61-2+
My '89

SURFACE ACTIVE SUBSTANCES
See also
Amphiphiles
Spontaneous vesicle formation in aqueous mixtures of single-
tailed surfactants. E. W. Kaler and others. bibl f il *Science*
245:1371-4 S 22 '89

SURFACE CHEMISTRY
Atom counting at surfaces [use of multiphoton resonance
ionization] D. L. Pappas and others. bibl f il *Science*
243:64-6 Ja 6 '89
The chemistry of solid-state electronics. E. Yablonovitch.
bibl f il *Science* 246:347-51 O 20 '89
Long-range electronic perturbations caused by defects using
scanning tunneling microscopy [graphite] H. A. Mizes and
J. S. Foster. bibl f il *Science* 244:559-62 My 5 '89
Microclusters. M. A. Duncan and D. H. Rouvray. bibl il
Scientific American 261:110-15 D '89
Ripples in a crystalline copper bed [chemisorption process;
research by Young Kuk] I. Peterson. *Science News* 135:62
Ja 28 '89
Scanning the surface [use of scanning tunneling microscope]
I. Peterson. il *Science News* 135:200-1+ Ap 1 '89

SURFACE EFFECT VEHICLES See Air cushion vehicles
SURFACE MINING, RECLAMATION, AND ENFORCE-
MENT OFFICE (U.S.) See United States. Office of Surface
Mining, Reclamation, and Enforcement
SURFACE PHENOMENA See Surface chemistry
SURFACE TENSION
See also
Soap bubbles and films

SURFACES
See also
Thin films
Tribology
Explaining and exploiting a winter worry [work of J. G.
Dash on frost heave] A. McKenzie. *Science News* 136:407
D 23-30 '89
Playing three-dimensional pool [use of ion scattering tech-
niques for analyzing surface structure] R. Pool. il *Science*
246:995-6 N 24 '89
Seeing cracks in three dimensions [work of David Carter]
R. Pool. il *Science* 243:1293 Mr 10 '89
Thermomolecular pressure in surface melting: motivation
for frost heave. J. G. Dash. bibl f il *Science* 246:1591-3
D 22 '89
Ultrafast dynamics at semiconductor and metal surfaces [laser
experiments] J. Bokor. bibl f il *Science* 246:1130-4 D
1 '89

SURFACTANTS See Surface active substances
SURFING
See also
Boardsailing
Chairmen of the board [cover story] J. Grissim. il *Oceans*
22:22-9+ Mr/Ap '89
Gidget has grown up, but surfing is still a 'totally happening'
sport. J. Krakauer. bibl f (p174) il *Smithsonian* 20:106-10+
Je '89
North Shore deliverance [Hawaii] B. Marcus. il *Sport (New
York, N.Y.)* 80:96-8 F '89
Competitions
Power and grace [women surfers] C. R. Wolpert. il *Women's
Sports & Fitness* 11:26-9 My '89
Equipment
See also
Quiksilver, Inc.
Ethical aspects
The last wave [surfers boycott South African competitions]
E. Silver. il *Mother Jones* 14:12 D '89
Psychological aspects
In the tube. F. Zamba. il pors *American Health* 8:80-1
S '89

SURGE (ELECTRICITY) See Transients (Electricity)
SURGEON-GENERAL'S OFFICE (U.S.) See United States.
Surgeon-General's Office
SURGEONS
See also
Blalock, Alfred, 1899-1964
Coleman, Jack
Cooley, Denton A., 1920-
Fyodorov, Svyatoslav
Pinson, C. Wright
Starzl, Thomas E. (Thomas Earl), 1926-
How to choose a good surgeon [excerpt from Taking charge]
L. C. Horowitz. por *Prevention (Emmaus, Pa.)* 41:50-3+
Jl '89
How to measure a surgeon's skill [plastic surgeons] *U.S.
News & World Report* 106:4 My 1 '89

SURGERY
    See also
    Anesthesia and anesthetics
    Cesarean section
    Children—Surgery
    Infants, Newborn—Surgery
    Second opinion (Medical consultation)
    Surgeons
    Sutures
    Telesurgery
    Tracheotomy
    Transplantation of organs, tissues, etc.
        See also subhead Surgery under names of organs
        and regions of the body
Hold that scalpel! J. Levine. il *Money* 18:105-9+ F '89
Is this operation necessary? *Society* 26:3 My/Je '89
No-knife surgeries. L. Holland. *Good Housekeeping* 209:273
    N '89
Shopping for surgery [negotiating fees] M. Teich. il *Health
    (New York, N.Y.)* 21:94-5 Je '89
Surgery's darlings. E. Mechcatie. il *Health (New York, N.Y.)*
    21:74-7+ N '89

Complications
Preventing postsurgical tissue 'gluing' [use of hyaluronic
    coatings; work of Eugene P. Goldberg] *Science News* 136:222
    S 30 '89

Psychological aspects
Subliminal healing [use of positive message tapes during
    surgery to speed recovery in hysterectomy patients] il
    Prevention (Emmaus, Pa.) 41:12+ Ja '89
Suggestions for recovery [use of positive message tapes during
    hysterectomy; research by Phil Richardson and Carlton
    Evans] E. Stark. *Psychology Today* 23:24-5 Mr '89
SURGERY, COSMETIC *See* Surgery, Plastic
SURGERY, PLASTIC
    See also
    Liposuction
    Surgeons
Are breast implants too risky? R. M. Henig. *Vogue* 179:108+
    Jl '89
Beverly Hills: the ultimate cutting edge. C. Platt. il *Harper's
    Bazaar* 122:186-7+ Ap '89
Beyond bucks [possible cancer risk linked to silicone breast
    implants] D. M. Podolsky. il *American Health* 8:12 D
    '89
Breast implants: a safer method [peanut oil implants]
    Newsweek 114:52 S 25 '89
Buying the perfect body [cover story; special section] il *U.S.
    News & World Report* 106:68-75 My 1 '89
A change for the better [case of J. Kowal] K. Burke. pors
    McCall's 116:92-3 Jl '89
The Coast [Hollywood scene] G. Stone. il *Gentlemen's
    Quarterly* 59:159 Ap '89
Cosmetic surgery: who gets what [women and men] A. C.
    Mallozzi. il *Good Housekeeping* 209:169 Ag '89
FDA to require safety data on breast implants. *FDA Consumer*
    23:2 Mr '89
Finance-a-face-lift [loans from Hudson & Hudson] H.
    Wolinsky. il *American Health* 8:12 D '89
Future beauty. S. Lord. il *Vogue* 179:406-9 O '89
A guide to cosmetic surgery. C. Slom and S. Mahler. il
    McCall's 116:92-4+ Jl '89
How safe are breast implants? L. Holland. *Good Housekeeping*
    208:237 Ap '89
In pursuit of perfect breasts [excerpt from Plastic surgery]
    J. Camp. il *Health (New York, N.Y.)* 21:83-4+ My '89
In this age of the fast fix, cosmetic surgery is becoming
    as common as a visit to the skin salon. P. Orenstein.
    Vogue 179:192+ O '89
Lip lifts: is bigger better? *Vogue* 179:568 S '89
The new breast-implant scare [silicone's possible link to
    cancer] C. Marks. *Mademoiselle* 95:124+ F '89
Nose by Nefertiti. K. Pryor. il *Art News* 88:15-16 F '89
Nose jobs. il *Seventeen* 48:156 Ap '89
Plastic surgery: a last option [for excessive wrinkling] P.
    Lister. *New Choices for the Best Years* 29:46 D '89
Plastic surgery: urban renewal. L. Stasi. *Harper's Bazaar*
    122:187+ Mr '89
Post-op privacy [plastic surgery retreats] S. Sobell. *Harper's
    Bazaar* 122:136+ Ag '89
Reshaping lives. S. DeVore. il *Current Health 2* 16:20-1
    D '89
Reshaping Russia [Institut Krasoty in Moscow] S. Lord.
    Vogue 179:166+ Ap '89
"Take a little off the sides". P. La Vigne. il *Utne Reader*
    p12 S/O '89

Psychological aspects
The importance of being pretty [excerpt from Plastic surgery]
    J. Camp. il *Health (New York, N.Y.)* 21:80-2+ Je '89
Why did people get their noses out of joint over my nose
    job? B. Weinhouse. il *Glamour* 87:59 Ja '89
Will surgery make you happy? *U.S. News & World Report*
    106:75 My 1 '89
SURGICAL DRILLS
Drill unclogs blood vessels [work of Robert Ginsburg] il
    USA Today (Periodical) 118:4-5 O '89

SURGICAL EQUIPMENT
    See also
    Lasers—Medical use
    Surgical drills

Sterilization
Bankruptcy snarls device seizure [unsterile eye surgery devices
    manufactured by Trueline Instruments] il *FDA Consumer*
    23:35-6 Mr '89
Ster-O-Lizer judged illegal. il *FDA Consumer* 23:40 S '89
SURGICAL EQUIPMENT INDUSTRY
    See also
    United States Surgical Corp.
SURIMI
A fishy deal in the freezer. A. Toufexis. il *Time* 133:80
    Ja 16 '89
SURNAME VIET GIVEN NAME NAM [film] See Motion
    picture reviews—Single works
SURNAMES *See* Names, Personal
SURPLUS (BUDGET)
The dread federal surplus [1880s] B. A. Weisberger. il
    American Heritage 40:20+ Ap '89
SURPLUS GOVERNMENT PROPERTY
    See also
    Surplus military property
How not to help the homeless [McKinney Act mandates
    turning over surplus buildings to homeless advocates] il
    U.S. News & World Report 107:29 Ag 28-S 4 '89
Making the most of government auctions. D. LaMaute. il
    Black Enterprise 19:49-50 F '89
World's biggest garage sale [government auctions] R. J. Maturi.
    il *Changing Times* 43:65-7 Ap '89
SURPLUS MILITARY PROPERTY
Millions of dollars on the ocean floor [Navy's management
    of surplus ships] E. Clift. il *Newsweek* 114:30 Ag 28 '89
SURPLUS PRODUCTS, AGRICULTURAL
The agricultural swamp. J. Bovard. il *National Review* 41:46-8
    F 10 '89
SURPRISE
The elements of surprise [lack of surprise in domed stadiums]
    C. Gordon. il *Maclean's* 102:11 Ag 21 '89
SURREALISM

Exhibitions
Thinking pictures [The dada & surrealist word-image ex-
    hibition] B. W. Bloch. *The New Leader* 72:22-3 N 27
    '89
SURROGATE MOTHERS
Brave new baby [ZIFT surrogacy]; ed. by Frank Feldinger.
    N. E. Gupta. il *Ladies' Home Journal* 106:140-1+ O '89
Giving the gift of life. L. Richards. il *Ladies' Home Journal*
    106:22+ F '89

Bibliography
Beyond Baby M: the controversy over surrogate motherhood.
    P. De la Fuente. il *Utne Reader* p118-21+ My/Je '89
Legal status, laws, etc.
    See also
    Baby M case
Little girl, big trouble [surrogate mother L. Stotski sues
    for custody of Tessa] D. Grogan. il pors *People Weekly*
    31:36-41 F 20 '89
SURROUND SOUND PROCESSORS
All-points audio. F. Vizard. il *Popular Mechanics* 166:114-15
    O '89
AudioSource SS Two Dolby Surround decoder. E. J. Foster.
    il *High Fidelity (New York, N.Y.)* 39:42 Ja '89
The best seat in the house [cover story] W. Livingstone.
    il *Stereo Review* 54:62-8 Ap '89
Beyond stereo [Sound Retrieval System] L. Feldman. il
    Radio-Electronics 60:51-4 S '89
JVC RX-801V audio/video surround-sound receiver. J. D.
    Hirsch. il *Stereo Review* 54:60+ O '89
JVC XP-A1000 digital acoustics processor. D. Ranada. il
    High Fidelity (New York, N.Y.) 39:21-4 Ja '89
JVC XP-A1000 digital surround processor. J. D. Hirsch.
    il *Stereo Review* 54:38+ My '89
Lexicon digital audio processor [CP-1] il *Video* 12:33+ Mr
    '89
Mark-V SM-333 surround sound processor. il
    Radio-Electronics 60:17+ My '89
Proton SD-1000 surround-sound decoder. J. D. Hirsch. il
    Stereo Review 54:62+ Je '89
Shure HTS Theater Reference System. il *Video* 13:40-1+
    Je '89
Shure HTS Theater Reference System. D. Ranada. il *High
    Fidelity (New York, N.Y.)* 39:36-9 Jl '89
Spaced-out stereo [Sound Retrieval System] L. Feldman. il
    Popular Science 234:130-2 Je '89
Super sound from your TV. H. B. Cohen. il *Home Mechanix*
    85:38-9 S '89
Surround sound. K. C. Pohlmann. il *Stereo Review* 54:106-11
    N '89
SURTEES, JOHN
                            about
A racer of the purest kind. M. Nicks. il pors *Road & Track*
    40:74-6+ Je '89
SURVEILLANCE, ELECTRONIC *See* Electronics in criminal
    investigation, espionage, etc.
SURVEILLANCE, LASER *See* Lasers in criminal investigation,
    espionage, etc.

SURVEILLANCE IN POLICE WORK *See* Police—Surveillance operations

SURVEILLANCE SATELLITES, MILITARY *See* Artificial satellites—Military use

SURVEYS
See also
Public opinion polls

SURVIVAL, WILDERNESS *See* Wilderness survival

SURVIVORS' BENEFITS
Compensation for death and dismemberment. C. Thompson. bibl f il *Monthly Labor Review* 112:13-17 S '89
Finding lost insurance policies. P. N. Strassels. il *Nation's Business* 77:70 My '89

SUSAN MARSHALL AND COMPANY
Reviews:
Performance of Interior with seven figures at the Brooklyn Academy of Music. C. Hardy. *Dance Magazine* 63:81-2 Mr '89

SUSHI
Sushi, sashimi, and sickness: raw fish and parasites. E. S. Iversen. bibl il por *Sea Frontiers* 35:176-83 My/Je '89
What's that wiggling in my sushi? [worms] *Science News* 135:300 My 13 '89

SUSLICK, KENNETH SANDERS
The chemical effects of ultrasound. bibl il *Scientific American* 260:80-6 F '89

SUSMAN, STEPHEN D.
about
A lion of the Texas bar snarls at KKR and Drexel. M. Ivey. il por *Business Week* p73+ O 9 '89

SUSPENDED CEILINGS *See* Ceilings

SUSPENSE STORIES *See* Detective and mystery stories

SUSPENSION, AUTOMOBILE *See* Automobiles—Springs and suspension

SUSPENSION, COLLEGE STUDENT *See* College student suspension

SUSPENSION, MAGNETIC *See* Magnetic suspension

SUSPENSION, MOTORCYCLE *See* Motorcycles—Springs and suspension

SUSSMAN, S. DONALD
about
Hedged bets. J. Clements. il por *Forbes* 144 Special Issue:372 O 23 '89

SUSSMAN, SALLY
about
Can Sally Sussman find happiness with her own soap opera? Only time—and Generations—will tell. L. Armstrong. il por *People Weekly* 31:113-14 Ap 17 '89

SUSSMAN, VIC S.
Pantyhoseman! il *Glamour* 87:284+ O '89

SUSTAINABLE DEVELOPMENT *See* Environment—Economic aspects

SUTCLIFFE, TOM
Opera Britannia. il *Opera News* 54:36+ O '89

SUTER, ALICE H.
Noise wars [cover story] il *Technology Review* 92:42-9 N/D '89

SUTHERLAND, JOAN, 1926-
about
Notes and comment. *The New Yorker* 65:44-6 D 11 '89

SUTHERLAND, KIEFER
about
Kiefer Sutherland. por *'Teen* 33:56 Mr '89

SUTHERLAND, LIN
One of the world's best train rides. il map *New Choices for the Best Years* 29:34-9 O '89

SUTHERS, G. K., AND OTHERS
A new DNA marker tightly linked to the fragile X locus (FRAXA). bibl f il *Science* 246:1298-1300 D 8 '89

SUTTON, JIM
Lingua Latina et al [poem] *Phi Delta Kappan* 71:318 D '89
Pedagogy [poem] *Phi Delta Kappan* 71:157 O '89
Schola Latina Bostonienses, O. [poem] *Phi Delta Kappan* 71:235 N '89
Schools/prisons are a mind of state [poem] *Phi Delta Kappan* 71:55 S '89

SUTTON, PERCY E.
about
It's showtime! [cover story] A. Edmond, Jr. il pors *Black Enterprise* 19:46-8+ Ap '89

SUTTON FAMILY
about
It's showtime! [cover story] A. Edmond, Jr. il pors *Black Enterprise* 19:46-8+ Ap '89

SUTURES
Precious metals: sutures with silver . . . [work of Chih-Chang Chu] *Science News* 136:223 S 30 '89

SUTZKEVER, ABRAHAM
Prayer for a sick friend [poem]; tr. by Ruth Whitman. *The New Yorker* 65:40 Ap 10 '89

SUU KYI *See* Aung San Suu Kyi

SUWAN LAIMANEE
about
Put another nickel in. D. Galloway. il *Art News* 88:21 D '89

SUZUKI, BOB H.
Asian Americans as the "model minority". il *Change* 21:12-19 N/D '89

SUZUKI, HIROSHI
(jt. auth) See Umenai, Takusei, and Suzuki, Hiroshi

SUZUKI, SEIICHI
about
American knowhow, Japan style. H. Katayama. il *Forbes* 144:76+ O 2 '89

SUZUKI, YUGO
Hirohito and the fate of the emperor system. *The Christian Century* 106:5-7 Ja 4-11 '89

SUZUKI (AUTOMOBILE) *See* Automobiles, Foreign

SUZY
The short, sad life of Christina Onassis. il pors *Good Housekeeping* 208:128-9+ Mr '89

SV40 VIRUS *See* Simian viruses

SVARNEY, PATRICIA BARNES- *See* Barnes-Svarney, Patricia

SVEC, MILAN
East European divides. *Foreign Policy* 77:41-63 Wint '89/'90

SVEDBERG, BJÖRN I.
about
Ericsson's true calling. J. Kapstein. *Business Week* p42+ Mr 6 '89

SVOBODA, TERESE
Pink [poem] *The New Yorker* 65:97 O 30 '89

SWAGGART, JIMMY LEE
about
Centerfold follies. L. Cryderman. *Christianity Today* 33:17 Mr 17 '89
How the others are faring. pors *Time* 134:76 S 11 '89

SWAGS (DRAPERIES) *See* Curtains and draperies

SWAIM, PAUL, AND PODGURSKY, MICHAEL
Do more-educated workers fare better following job displacement? bibl f il *Monthly Labor Review* 112:43-6 Ag '89

SWAIN, JOSEPH P.
To found traditions of Catholic Church music. il *America* 161:186-9 S 30 '89

SWAIN, JOYCE
about
Shining star daughters and their amazing moms. il pors *'Teen* 33:46-7 D '89

SWAIN, MADELEINE, AND SWAIN, ROBERT (ROBERT L.)
How to write letters that win jobs. il *Working Woman* 14:120-3 Ap '89

SWAIN, ROBERT (ROBERT L.)
(jt. auth) See Swain, Madeleine, and Swain, Robert (Robert L.)

SWAIN, SALLY
Home is where the art is [excerpts from Great housewives of art] il *Ms.* 17:72-3 Ap '89

SWAINSON, SHARON C.
about
She's a winner. C. Morris. por *Essence* 19:42+ Mr '89

SWALE STAKES *See* Horse racing

SWALLOWS
Coming home [barn swallows] A. Gingert. il *Country Journal* 16:39-43 My/Je '89

SWAN, CRAIG
about
The second time around. R. Fimrite. il pors *Sports Illustrated* 70:110-14+ Ja 9 '89

SWAN, JAMES A.
An adventurer's Baedeker. *American Health* 8:54-5 N '89

SWAN, SUSAN BURROWS
Recent discoveries about Philadelphia samplers. bibl f il *Antiques* 136:1334-43 D '89

SWAN, TONY
4-doors for all seasons. il *New Choices for the Best Years* 29:84+ D '89
Buying a used car: an expert's tips on where, what, and how. il *Better Homes and Gardens* 67:122+ Je '89

SWAN LAKE [ballet] See Ballet reviews—Single works

SWANBROW, DIANE
The paradox of happiness [cover story] il *Psychology Today* 23:37-9 Jl/Ag '89

SWANGER, DAVID
Weatherman [poem] *America* 161:136 S 9-16 '89

SWANK, J. GRANT
Modern art's first wild man. il *Christianity Today* 33:64-5 F 3 '89

SWANN, MARJORIE
about
A lifetime devoted to nonviolence. B. Tober. por *The Progressive* 53:16 D '89

SWANS
Aristocrats [trumpeter swans] N. Bliven. il *The New Yorker* 65:81-8+ D 25 '89
Swan song [trumpeter swans] F. Graham. *Audubon* 91:18-19 My '89
To save the swans [trumpeter swans in Idaho] il *Life* 12:109-11 Ap '89
Trumpeter swans. il map *National Geographic World* 167:16-19 Jl '89

SWANS—*cont.*

Care

Minnesotans struggle to save their poisoned swans [P. Redig's efforts to treat lead-poisoned trumpeters at the University of Minnesota's Raptor Center] M. Nelson. il *People Weekly* 31:103-5 Mr 13 '89

Control

Dark side of a classic beauty [control of mute swan population in Rhode Island] W. Williams. il *National Wildlife* 27:42-8 F/Mr '89

Migration

The day of the swans. N. Strung. il *Field & Stream* 94:60-1+ N '89

SWANSICK, ROBIN
Cold feet [story] il *Redbook* 173:56+ Ag '89
SWANSON, ROBERT A.
about
Robert Swanson. J. O. Hamilton. il por *Business Week* Special Issue:104 Ap 14 '89
SWANSON, W. CLARKE
about
Napa renewed. J. Simpson. il *Architectural Digest* 46:196-203 O '89
SWANTON, MICHAEL JAMES
(jt. auth) See Goulstone, John, and Swanton, Michael James
SWANWICK, MICHAEL
Snow angels [story] il *Omni (New York, N.Y.)* 11:104-11 Mr '89
SWAP FINANCING
See also
Unbundled stock units
Banking on African conservation [debt-for-nature swaps] *Science News* 135:62 Ja 28 '89
Capital conservation [Costa Rica's debt for nature swaps] J. Zweig. por *Forbes* 143:208 Ap 17 '89
Debt deal stacked against Indians [debt for nature swap in Bolivia] M. Collett. *The Progressive* 53:17-18 Ag '89
Easing third world debt [exit bonds] J. Williamson. il *USA Today (Periodical)* 117:28-9 Mr '89
"It's the right thing to do" [interest rate swap tax treatment] L. Saunders. il *Forbes* 143:104 Ap 17 '89
The merger wars are turning downright friendly [stock swaps] L. J. Nathans. il *Business Week* p116-17 O 23 '89
Nature reaps a cash bonanza [debt-for-nature swaps] T. A. Lewis. il *International Wildlife* 19:37 Ja/F '89
Robbin' hoods [big banks and debt relief; cover story] J. D. Sachs. il *The New Republic* 200:19-20+ Mr 13 '89
These swaps can keep you a step ahead of the taxman. S. Woolley. *Business Week* p180 N 13 '89
Using red ink to keep tropical forests green [debt-for-nature swaps in Brazil] C. P. Work and G. Smith. il map *U.S. News & World Report* 106:48-9 Mr 6 '89
The world puts the heat on Brazil [forgiving part of debt in exchange for help in protecting nature] *World Press Review* 36:38 My '89
SWAPO
Africa's next basket case? R. Sikorski. *National Review* 41:21-2+ S 15 '89
A bloody road to peace [incursion inside Namibia] C. S. Manegold. il map *Newsweek* 113:37 Ap 17 '89
Botching the peace [threat to agreement to bring independence to Namibia] W. R. Doerner. il map *Time* 133:35 Ap 17 '89
Can Namibia walk alone? Will South Africa let it? E. Girardet. il *U.S. News & World Report* 107:36+ S 11 '89
A crisis for peace [incursion inside Namibia] J. Bierman. il *Maclean's* 102:22+ Ap 17 '89
The doves win. il *Time* 134:53 N 27 '89
Fix in Namibia? M. Verbaan. *The Nation* 249:516-17 N 6 '89
How SWAPO got framed [incursion into Namibia] A. Cockburn. *The Nation* 248:582-3 My 1 '89
Namibia holds its breath. S. Reiss. il *Newsweek* 114:31 S 25 '89
Namibia independence back on track: cease-fire restored after nine-day crisis [special section] il *UN Chronicle* 26:4-17 Je '89
Namibia on edge. M. Baumann. il *Mother Jones* 14:18+ O '89
The Namibia sting. *National Review* 41:12 My 5 '89
A rebel victory. M. Nemeth. *Maclean's* 102:35 N 27 '89
Self-rule in Namibia won't break South Africa's stranglehold. J. Kapstein. il *Business Week* p56 O 2 '89
SWAPO's witch hunt. S. Reiss. il *Newsweek* 114:33 S 4 '89
Swipe at SWAPO [discussion of May 1, 1989 article, How SWAPO got framed] A. Cockburn. *The Nation* 249:190+ Ag 21-28 '89
A test of will. M. Nemeth. il map *Maclean's* 102:40 S 18 '89
Thousands of Namibians return home; UNTAG troops now in place; South African military withdraws [special section] il *UN Chronicle* 26:4-11 S '89
SWAPPING See Barter
SWARTHMORE COLLEGE
Bookin' in the basement [McCabe Mile race run in the library] M. Will-Weber. il *Runner's World* 24:94-7 O '89

SWARTZ, CAROLYN
All that glitters is the tub. il *The New York Times Magazine* p36+ N 5 '89
SWARTZ, JAMIE
about
Home rule. I. Nelson. il por *New Choices for the Best Years* 29:12-13 Ap '89
SWARTZ, SIDNEY
about
Sidney Swartz' dolce vita. F. Meeks. il pors *Forbes* 144:56-7 Jl 10 '89
SWAYZE, PATRICK
about
Going Swayze. L. Morice. il por *Mademoiselle* 95:162-3+ Je '89
Patrick Swayze drives 'em crazy. D. Lamanna. il pors *Ladies' Home Journal* 106:100 F '89
A wild and Swayze guy [cover story] B. Zehme. il pors *Gentlemen's Quarterly* 59:190-5+ F '89
SWEARING
I'm sick of the F word. A. Bateman. *Reader's Digest* 134:96-8 F '89
SWEARINGEN ENGINEERING AND TECHNOLOGIES (FIRM)
Jaffe Group to replace Gulfstream as partner in SA-30 development. E. H. Phillips. il *Aviation Week & Space Technology* 131:37 S 11 '89
Paulson to build Swearingen jet. il *Flying* 116:14 Ja '89
Swearingen, Jaffe Group work on schedule for SA-30 business jet development. il *Aviation Week & Space Technology* 131:24 S 25 '89
SWEAT See Perspiration
SWEATERS
Everything's coming up roses [cover story] il *Good Housekeeping* 208:198-9+ My '89
The knitting image [summer top] il *Seventeen* 48:45+ Jl '89
The turtleneck. J. Berendt. il *Esquire* 111:48 Mr '89
SWEATSUITS See Clothing and dress—Sports clothes
SWED, MARK
Flourishing Arts. il *Opera News* 53:20+ My '89
Next stop: Kennedy Center. il por *Opera News* 53:18-20+ Je '89
SWEDA, GEORGE
Getting really mad and good. il por *Sports Illustrated* 70:65 My 29 '89
SWEDEN
See also
Art—Sweden
Astronomical observatories—Sweden
Aviation and state—Sweden
Country estates—Sweden
Dance and state—Sweden
Investments, American—Sweden
Investments, Swedish
Motorcycle racing—Sweden
Opera—Sweden
Prisons—Sweden
Radioactive pollution—Sweden
Space centers—Sweden
Stockholm (Sweden)
Swedes

Air Force

Exports of Gripen could equal sales to Sweden's Air Force. D. A. Brown. il *Aviation Week & Space Technology* 130:73-4 Ja 9 '89

Antiquities

See also
Kronan (Ship)

Commerce
India
See India—Commerce—Sweden
United States
See United States—Commerce—Sweden
Western Europe
Exports of Gripen could equal sales to Sweden's Air Force. D. A. Brown. il *Aviation Week & Space Technology* 130:73-4 Ja 9 '89

Defenses

See also
Airplanes, Military—Sweden
Sweden—Air Force

Foreign relations

Minority report. C. Hitchens. *The Nation* 248:116 Ja 30 '89
United States
See United States—Foreign relations—Sweden

History

See also
World War, 1914-1918—Sweden

Industries

See also
Automobile factories—Sweden
Bofors Nobel AB
IKEA Svenska Forsaljnings AB
L.M. Ericsson Telephone Co.
Saab-Scania AB
Swedish Space Corporation

SWEDEN—Industries—See also—*cont.*
Volvo AB

Kings and rulers
See also
Gustaf XVI Carl, King of Sweden, 1946-

Politics and government
See also
Socialism—Sweden

Religious institutions and affairs
See also
Lutheran Church—Sweden

SWEDES

Soviet Union
A lost prisoner of the gulag still holds Moscow hostage [R. Wallenberg case] D. Stanglin. il pors *U.S. News & World Report* 106:34-6 Je 26 '89
A pain-filled mystery [Holocaust hero R. Wallenberg] J. Bierman. por *Maclean's* 102:47 O 30 '89

SWEDISH ART *See* Art, Swedish
SWEDISH HOUSE DECORATION *See* House decoration, Swedish
SWEDISH SPACE CORPORATION
Home on the Esrange. M. J. Mackowski. il *Ad Astra* 1:39-40+ My '89
SWEELEY, MICHAEL
The first lady. il *National Review* 41:65-6 S 29 '89
SWEENEY, THOMAS
about
Fidelity's newest wunderkind runs the fund that may be the next Magellan. G. Anrig, Jr. il por *Money* 18:201-2 Ap '89
SWEENEY TODD [musical] See Musicals, revues, etc.—Reviews—Single works
SWEEPSTAKES *See* Lotteries
SWEET, CHERYL A.
'Healthy tan'—a fast-fading myth. il *FDA Consumer* 23:11-13 Je '89
Rethinking eating out. il *FDA Consumer* 23:8-13 N '89
SWEET, HOLLAND
Kicking the habit. *Vogue* 179:414-15 O '89
SWEET, JEFFREY, 1950-
An object lesson for playwrights. *The Writer* 102:18-20 D '89
SWEET, WILLIAM, 1946-
Chernobyl: what really happened. bibl il *Technology Review* 92:42-52 Jl '89
SWEET BIRD OF YOUTH [television program] See Television program reviews—Single works
SWEET BREAD *See* Bread
SWEET CORN *See* Corn
SWEET HOME (OR.)

Industries
Oregon's not-so-Sweet Home [decline in logging and mill jobs] S. Doherty. il *Newsweek* 114:55 D 11 '89
SWEET PEAS
Sweet peas bring smiles. il *Sunset (Central West edition)* 183:76-7 O '89
SWEET SMELL OF SUCCESS [film] See Motion picture reviews—Single works
SWEETENERS
See also
Corn syrup
Sugar substitutes
Xylitol
SWEETING, PAUL
Is Hollywood Japan's field of dreams? il *Video* 13:140 N '89
SWEETINGS (LONDON, ENGLAND: RESTAURANT) *See* London (England)—Restaurants, nightclubs, bars, etc.
SWEETNESS
Sweet and sour [sweetness determined by shape of molecule; work of Murray Goodman] T. Beardsley. *Scientific American* 261:22+ N '89
SWEETOW, STUART
How suite it is. il *Video* 13:51-2+ O '89
SWEETWATER (TENN.)

Education
The land of rising sons and daughters [first Japanese high school] il *U.S. News & World Report* 106:12+ My 22 '89
Rising sun over Sweetwater [Tennessee Meiji Gakuin] S. Tifft. il *Time* 133:92 My 22 '89
SWEEZY, PAUL M., 1910-
about
Beat the devil [interview] A. Cockburn. il *The Nation* 248:726-7 My 29 '89
SWELLING (PHYSIOLOGY)
Press on: to reduce swelling, ice is nice but compressed is best. O. Anderson. il *Women's Sports & Fitness* 11:11 Ja/F '89
SWERTLOW, FRANK
The $50,000 haircut. il pors *Money* 18:84-94+ My '89
SWICK, MARLY
Housebound [story] il *Redbook* 173:58+ O '89
SWICK, THOMAS R.
I'm a Pole watcher. il *The American Spectator* 22:24-5 S '89
Romania, Romania. *Commonweal* 116:263-4 My 5 '89

SWID, STEPHEN CLAAR
about
Last laugh. L. Gubernick. il por *Forbes* 143:41-2 F 20 '89
SWID POWELL DESIGN INC.
Coming home [offices by Stephen Sills] H. S. MacIsaac. il *House & Garden* 161:36+ D '89
SWIENER, RITA
Santa's special helper. il por *Ladies' Home Journal* 106:18+ D '89
SWIFT, E. M.
The A's find ways. il *Sports Illustrated* 70:36-8+ My 29 '89
Facing the music [cover story] il pors *Sports Illustrated* 70:38-40+ Mr 6 '89
Fit to be tied. il *Sports Illustrated* 71:30-5 O 2 '89
Le Grand LeMond [cover story] il pors map *Sports Illustrated* 71:54-8+ D 25 '89-Ja 1 '90
Great Scott! il pors *Sports Illustrated* 70 Special Issue:78-81+ Ap '89
Hope for the best. il pors *Sports Illustrated* 70:20-2+ Ja 23 '89
Is it nyet or not yet? il pors *Sports Illustrated* 70:30-3 Ja 16 '89
Jolly good show [cover story] il pors *Sports Illustrated* 70:18-25 Ap 17 '89
Kite finally takes flight. il por *Sports Illustrated* 70:26-8+ Mr 27 '89
New girl in town. il por *Sports Illustrated* 70:22-3 F 20 '89
Oh Magnifica! il *Sports Illustrated* 71:154-8+ S 4 '89
The puck will stop here. il por *Sports Illustrated* 71:118 O 23 '89
Putting on the style. il pors *Sports Illustrated* 71:28-9 Ag 21 '89
Sink, blast you! [cover story] il pors *Sports Illustrated* 71:36-9 Ag 14 '89
Way to go, gang. il *Sports Illustrated* 71:32-5 S 4 '89
What's the big deal? il pors *Sports Illustrated* 70 Special Issue:207+ F '89
The wheels of fortune. il *Sports Illustrated* 70:32-4+ My 22 '89
SWIFT, JONATHAN, 1667-1745

Anecdotes, facetiae, satire, etc.
A Modest Proposal for Cleansing our Publick Life of Impurities and Transgressions. H. Fairlie. il *The New Republic* 200:14-16 Mr 27 '89
SWIFT, MARGARET See Drabble, Margaret, 1939-
SWIFT, W. ARTHUR
about
Magic Middletown [excerpt] D. W. Hoover. il *Society* 26:73-7 Mr/Ap '89
SWIG, CHARLOTTE MAILLIARD
about
San Francisco protocol: Charlotte Mailliard Swig in Pacific Heights. H. Junker. il por *Architectural Digest* 46:238-43+ My '89
SWILLING, MARK
The need to break the stalemate. il por *World Press Review* 36:32 N '89
SWIM BLADDERS (FISH)
Full of hot air [Darwin's theory that lungs evolved from swim bladders] S. J. Gould. il *Natural History* p28+ O '89
SWIMBLADDERS *See* Swim bladders (Fish)
SWIMMER'S EAR *See* Ear—Diseases
SWIMMING
See also
Diving
International Swimming Hall of Fame
Marathon swimming
Synchronized swimming
Triathlon
Chased out of the sea [catching barracuda while swimming off Fort Lauderdale] B. Masselink. il *Sea Frontiers* 35:256 Jl/Ag '89
Hypoxics, zoomers, and other drill sharpeners [training variations] K. Carlisle. il *Women's Sports & Fitness* 11:14+ Jl/Ag '89
Special skill. B. McKeown. il *Outdoor Life* 183:26+ Je '89
Swimming. il *World Tennis* 36:78 My '89
Take to the waves! [open water swimming] C. Zempel. il *Women's Sports & Fitness* 11:66 My '89
The unwritten rules of the pool [lap-swimming etiquette] D. Kukich. il *Women's Sports & Fitness* 11:80-1 Ap '89

Competitions
Bionic man [M. Spitz aims for Olympic comeback] K. Moore. il pors *Sports Illustrated* 71:80-2+ O 23 '89
Black swimmer, Twillie, likes making a big splash. il por *Jet* 76:49 Ag 7 '89
The golden girl makes a splash [J. Evans at short course national championships] J. E. Vader. il por *Sports Illustrated* 70:86 Ap 3 '89
He had 'em goggle-eyed [D. Wharton at NCAA men's swimming and diving championships] M. Noden. por *Sports Illustrated* 70:82 Ap 10 '89
Janet Evans: good as gold. K. Carlisle. il pors *Women's Sports & Fitness* 11:28-33 Ap '89

SWIMMING—Competitions—*cont.*

Once more, with feeling [Stanford wins NCAA women's swimming championships] J. E. Vader. il por *Sports Illustrated* 70:71+ Mr 27 '89

Woman to watch [swimmer M. E. Blanchard] S. Robb. por *Women's Sports & Fitness* 11:58 O '89

Physiological effects

Swimming lapse [exercise-induced asthma] M. Madsen. il *Women's Sports & Fitness* 11:13-14 Ap '89

Study and teaching

Take a turn for the better [flip turn] K. Carlisle. il *Women's Sports & Fitness* 11:20-1 Je '89

SWIMMING, SYNCHRONIZED *See* Synchronized swimming

SWIMMING (FISH LOCOMOTION) *See* Fish locomotion

SWIMMING IN ART

Introspective reflections [C. Carter; cover story] J.-P. Wolf. il por *American Artist* 53:50-5 O '89

SWIMMING POOLS

See also

    Atlas Swimming Pool Company

    Municipal swimming pools

Backyard resort with an innovative PVC/Plywood pool. T. O. Bakke. il *Popular Science* 234:142-4 Je '89

Before you take the plunge . . . [interview with R. W. Mueller] J. H. Ingersoll. il por *Home Mechanix* 85:18+ My '89

Building a pool: taking the plunge without sinking your budget. K. S. Black. il *Better Homes and Gardens* 67:72-5 Je '89

Buying an aboveground pool? Read this first! S. Nielsen. il *Good Housekeeping* 208:248 My '89

Shaped to fit among the trees. il *Southern Living* 24:49 Ag '89

They started with just a lawn, a wall, and a steep bank. il *Sunset (Central West edition)* 183:88-9 S '89

Alarms

Pool alarms can tell you (maybe) when someone goes overboard. il *Consumer Reports* 54:353 Je '89

Equipment

The care-free pool. J. Blyskal. il *New Choices for the Best Years* 29:69-70 Jl '89

Safety devices and measures

Pool rules. il *Home Mechanix* 85:36 Jl '89

SWIMMING RECORDS

On top of the world [M. Barrowman breaks world record in 200 breaststroke at nationals] B. Anderson. il pors *Sports Illustrated* 71:40-1 Ag 14 '89

SWIMNASTICS *See* Water exercises

SWIMSUIT [television program] *See* Television program reviews—Single works

SWIMSUITS *See* Bathing suits

SWINDLERS AND SWINDLING *See* Fraud

SWINE

See also

    Wild boars

Perfect gift? A pig for a house pet! il *Successful Farming* 87:53 Ja '89

Sows were meaner back then. B. Freese. il *Successful Farming* 87:21 mid-F '89

Breeding

Hog wild [K. Mull's potbellied pigs] A. Adato. il pors *Life* 12:86-7 S '89

One breed can't do it all, says breeder. R. Brunoehler. il *Successful Farming* 87 no4:58 Mr '89

The ultimate crossbred [Chinese and American pigs] B. Freese. il *Successful Farming* 87:28-9 Ag '89

Winning with a full house. D. Ohrtman. il *Successful Farming* 87:32+ Ap '89

Care

Anecdotes, facetiae, satire, etc.

Gene Johnston. G. Johnston. il *Successful Farming* 87:5 My '89

Confinement methods

Confinement stress: when hogs go bonkers. R. L. Haney. il *Successful Farming* 87:24-5 Je '89

Ignoring animal rights doesn't solve problem [views of John Walton] *Successful Farming* 87:40 Ag '89

Contamination

New hog ID rules aid search for residue violators. P. Smith. *Successful Farming* 87:50 Ja '89

Sulfamethazine residues in food. B. T. Hunter. il *Consumers' Research Magazine* 72:36-8 F '89

Diseases and pests

Confinement stress: when hogs go bonkers. R. L. Haney. il *Successful Farming* 87:24-5 Je '89

Hog horror show [phantom disease] B. Freese and J. Eckberg. il *Successful Farming* 87:40J Ag '89

Feeding

Leaner and meatier [use of beta agonists for hogs and beef] J. R. Borcherding and C. Peterson, Jr. il *Successful Farming* 87:40 D '89

Pigging out [blocking cholecystokinin in pigs increases appetite; work of Jerome Pekas] *Discover* 10:20 My '89

PST-treated hogs need lysine—lots of lysine [porcine somatotropin] il *Successful Farming* 87:50 F '89

Identification

New hog ID rules aid search for residue violators. P. Smith. *Successful Farming* 87:50 Ja '89

Prices

Sell feeder pigs now, buy in fall. G. Johnston. il *Successful Farming* 87 no4:10 Mr '89

SWINE BREEDING INDUSTRY *See* Swine industry

SWINE FARM MANAGEMENT

Divide and conquer for hog profits. D. Ohrtman. il *Successful Farming* 87 no4:32+ Mr '89

Successful family farm [Stewart's Duroc Farm] G. Johnston. il *Successful Farming* 87:44-6 My '89

Winning with a full house. D. Ohrtman. il *Successful Farming* 87:32+ Ap '89

You can come home again [swine farm liquidated by R. Kahle now run by son S. Kahle] B. Freese. il pors *Successful Farming* 87:15 D '89

SWINE FARROWING CRATES AND PENS *See* Swine houses

SWINE HOUSES

See also

    Swine—Confinement methods

Batten down the hatches. J. Walter. il *Successful Farming* 87:33 D '89

Hog house fix-up! [cover story; special section] B. Freese. il *Successful Farming* 87:36-40+ N '89

Winning with a full house. D. Ohrtman. il *Successful Farming* 87:32+ Ap '89

Heating and ventilation

Barns the fuel men hate! R. Brunoehler. il *Successful Farming* 87:26+ mid-Mr '89

A blanket of restoration [urethane foam insulation] R. Brunoehler. il *Successful Farming* 87:38 My '89

Hog building blowout! K. Coble. il *Successful Farming* 87:54 Ja '89

Hog farmers clear the air [health problems] C. Tevis. il *Successful Farming* 87:54-5 D '89

Sanitation

Old pits gets recharged [using water for manure disposal] K. Coble and A. Muehling. il *Successful Farming* 87:56-7 Ja '89

Pull a plug to flush away hog manure. il *Successful Farming* 87:66 F '89

SWINE INDUSTRY

See also

    Dekalb Corp.

    National Pork Producers Council

    Stewart's Duroc Farm

South Dakota says no to the corporate sow. G. Vincent. *Successful Farming* 87:35 F '89

SWING OUT SISTER (MUSICAL GROUP)

The effortless style of Swing Out Sister's Corinne Drewery. J. Powell. il por *Glamour* 87:206 S '89

SWINGS

How to get the playground swing going: a first lesson in the mechanics of rotation. J. Walker. il *Scientific American* 260:106-9 Mr '89

SWIRE, PETER

Tropical chic. *The New Republic* 200:18+ Ja 30 '89

SWISS AMERICANS

Old-World Christmas [chalets in New Glarus, Wis. modeled after ones in Switzerland] il *Good Housekeeping* 209:162-5 D '89

SWISS ARMY KNIVES

On Everest or in the office, it's the tool to have. J. Page and C. Hoffman. bibl (p229) il *Smithsonian* 20:106-8+ O '89

SWISS ART *See* Art, Swiss

SWISS COOKING *See* Cooking, Swiss

SWISS CREDIT BANK *See* Crédit Suisse

SWISSAIR AG

SAS, Swissair agree to cooperate on traffic and travel services system. *Aviation Week & Space Technology* 131:104 O 2 '89

SWISSBAR (FIRM)

The names of Zurich [views of H. Kaufmann] J. Marcom, Jr. il por *Forbes* 143:206+ Je 26 '89

SWITCHES, ELECTRIC *See* Electric switches

SWITZER, BARRY

about

Oklahoma is not OK. R. Givens. il por *Newsweek* 113:80 F 27 '89

You reap what you sow [cover story] R. Telander and R. Sullivan. il por *Sports Illustrated* 70:20-6+ F 27 '89

SWITZER, ELLEN

Can this marriage be saved? il *Ladies' Home Journal* 106:12+ My '89

"How can I live with a man who hit me?". il *Ladies' Home Journal* 106:10+ Jl '89

SWITZERLAND

See also

    Agricultural administration—Switzerland

    Alps

    Americans—Switzerland

    Art—Switzerland

    Banks and banking—Switzerland

    Bern (Switzerland)

    Corporations—Acquisitions and mergers—Laws and regulations—Switzerland

    Crissier (Switzerland)

    Flower gardens and gardening—Switzerland

    Forests and forestry—Switzerland

SWITZERLAND—See also—*cont.*
Hiking—Switzerland
Insider trading—Switzerland
Investments, American—Switzerland
Lake Constance
Music festivals—Switzerland
Narcotics laws and regulations—Switzerland
Opera—Switzerland
Paleontology—Switzerland
Saint Moritz (Switzerland)
Saudi Arabians—Switzerland
Sculpture gardens and parks—Switzerland
Securities—Laws and regulations—Switzerland
Securities—Switzerland
Sihlwald Forest (Switzerland)
Suhr (Switzerland)
Vaud (Switzerland)
Zurich (Switzerland)

Army
The Swiss Army gets knifed. D. Benjamin. il *Time* 134:70 D 11 '89
The Swiss debate their Army's future. A. Schalk. il *Commonweal* 116:331-3 Je 2 '89

Economic relations
Western Europe
Paradox for Switzerland. M. Legris and J.-M. Gonin. *World Press Review* 36:63 D '89

Industries
See also
Ciba-Geigy AG
Crédit Suisse
Du Rhône Chocolatier
Ellis AG
Fogal AG
Nestle SA
Patek Philippe (Firm)
Pilatus Aircraft
Swissair AG

Politics and government
See also
Referendum—Switzerland
SWOMLEY, JOHN M., 1915-
The Cruzan decision: refusing treatment. *The Christian Century* 106:1110-11 N 29 '89
SWORDFISH
See also
Cooking—Fish
SYBILLA, 1963-
about
A look on the wild side. J. Cocks. il pors *Time* 133:68 Ja 16 '89
SYDNEY STOCK EXCHANGE LTD.
These days, they don't call it 'Down Under' for nothing. S. Hutcheon. il por *Business Week* p66+ N 6 '89
SYDNOR, REBECCA
about
Smart love. A. M. Bromley. *Harper's Bazaar* 122:200-1 Ap '89
SYKES, CHARLES J.
ProfScam [excerpt] il *Conservative Digest* 15:87+ My/Je '89
SYLBERT, RICHARD
about
Richard Sylbert [interview] il pors *American Film* 15:22-6 D '89
LA SYLPHIDE [ballet] See Ballet reviews—Single works
SYLVANDER, YVETTE
about
Birds of a feather. B. Newman. il pors *Sports Illustrated* 70 Special Issue:139-42 F '89
SYLVANDER, YVONNE
about
Birds of a feather. B. Newman. il pors *Sports Illustrated* 70 Special Issue:139-42 F '89
SYLVESTER
about
Obituary
Jet por 75:15+ Ja 9 '89
SYLVESTER, DAVID
The avant-garde composer returns to a lost love. il por *Architectural Digest* 46:134+ Ap '89
SYMBIOSIS
A biologist whose heresy redraws earth's tree of life [L. Margulis' symbiotic theory of cell evolution] J. McDermott. bibl (p135) il pors *Smithsonian* 20:72-6+ Ag '89
Bootstrapping in ecosystems [reciprocal interactions between plants and soils] D. A. Perry and others. bibl f il *BioScience* 39:230-7 Ap '89
Honey hunters follow birds to reach bees [research by H. A. Isack and H.-U. Reyer] *Science News* 135:172 Mr 18 '89
Honeyguides and honey gatherers: interspecific communication in a symbiotic relationship. H. A. Isack and H.-U. Reyer. bibl f il *Science* 243:1343-6 Mr 10 '89
Rethinking evolution [work of L. Margulis on symbiotic origin of cells] G. Cowley. il por *Newsweek* 114:38 O 2 '89
Sexual stunts of clownfish [cover story] D. G. Fautin. il *Natural History* p42-7 S '89

Sunshine fuels a bacterial relationship [research by Ralph W. F. Hardy] I. Wickelgren. il *Science News* 135:36 Ja 21 '89
Symbiotic marine bacteria chemically defend crustacean embryos from a pathogenic fungus. M. S. Gil-Turnes and others. bibl f il *Science* 246:116-18 O 6 '89
Trespassers will be poisoned [endophyte-infected tall fescue] K. Clay. il *Natural History* p8+ S '89
SYMBOLICS INC.
Where Lisp slipped. J. Pitta. il por *Forbes* 144:262-3 O 16 '89
SYMBOLISM (PSYCHOLOGY)
The Omni book of dreams. il *Omni (New York, N.Y.)* 12 Book of Dreams:1-8 N '89
SYMBOLISM IN ART
See also
Apocalyptic art
Christian art and symbolism
SYMBOLS
See also
State symbols
SYMMERS, DIVYA
Williamstown's Orchards. il *Travel Holiday* 171:72 F '89
SYMMETRY (BIOLOGY)
See also
Laterality
Shape-onomics: adding muscle where it counts [bodyshaping] M. Greenwood-Robinson. il *Women's Sports & Fitness* 11:43-7 O '89
SYMMETRY (PHYSICS)
See also
Fractals
Quasicrystals
Supersymmetry (Physics)
SYMMS, STEVEN
Financing Gorbachev's economic program: a bad investment for the West? il *USA Today (Periodical)* 118:25-7 Jl '89
SYMONS, ALLENE
Drawing in customers with art. il *Publishers Weekly* 236:62-4 S 1 '89
SYMONS, JOHN W.
about
At Gillette, disposable is a dirty word. K. H. Hammonds. il por *Business Week* p54+ My 29 '89
SYMPATHETIC NERVOUS SYSTEM See Nervous system
SYMPATHY
See also
Empathy
He had compassion [Good Samaritan] K. Koyama. il *The Christian Century* 106:651 Jl 5-12 '89
The way we are [letters of sympathy from readers] L. Wyse. il *Good Housekeeping* 209:320 N '89
SYMPATRIC SPECIATION
A breed apart [apple fruit flies; study by Guy L. Bush] K. Wright. il *Scientific American* 260:22+ F '89
SYMPHONIC POEMS
See also
Compact discs—Symphonic poems
SYMPHONIES
See also
Compact discs—Symphonies
Phonograph records—Symphonies
Tape recordings—Symphonies
SYMPHONY SPACE (NEW YORK, N.Y.)
'Selected shorts' due from Symphony Space [tapes of actors reading American short stories] *Publishers Weekly* 235:34 F 3 '89
Symphony Space break [Selected shorts: series of readings by actors] M. Kramer. *The New Yorker* 65:74-5 Mr 13 '89
SYMPTOMS See Diagnosis
SYNAGOGUES
Georgia
See also
Snellville (Ga.)—Synagogues
SYNAPSES
A biochemical correlate of the critical period for synaptic modification in the visual cortex. S. M. Dudek and M. F. Bear. bibl f il *Science* 246:673-5 N 3 '89
Central synaptic inputs to identified leech neurons determined by peripheral targets. C. M. Loer and W. B. Kristan, Jr. bibl f il *Science* 244:64-6 Ap 7 '89
Model of the origin of rhythmic population oscillations in the hippocampal slice. R. D. Traub and others. bibl f il *Science* 243:1319-25 Mr 10 '89
Neural connections between the lateral geniculate nucleus and visual cortex in vitro. N. Yamamoto and others. bibl f il *Science* 245:192-4 Jl 14 '89
The stuff memories are made of [role of neural synapses; research by William Greenough] il *U.S. News & World Report* 107:16+ N 13 '89
Synapse formation in the developing brain. R. E. Kalil. bibl il *Scientific American* 261:76-9+ D '89
Synaptic connections in vitro: modulation of number and efficacy by electrical activity. P. G. Nelson and others. bibl f il *Science* 244:585-7 My 5 '89

SYNAPSIN
Synapsins: mosaics of shared and individual domains in a family of synaptic vesicle phosphoproteins. T. C. Südhof and others. bibl f il *Science* 245:1474-80 S 29 '89
SYNAPTIC TRANSMISSION *See* Electrophysiology
SYNCHRO-ENERGIZER *See* Psychological equipment
SYNCHRONIZATION
Synchronicity [ice dancers' views] S. Wynne and J. Druar. il pors *American Health* 8:70-1 Ap '89
SYNCHRONIZED SWIMMING
Woman to watch [K. Babb] K. Millman. por *Women's Sports & Fitness* 11:55 Jl/Ag '89
SYNCHROTRON RADIATION
Brightest beam ever produced. il *USA Today (Periodical)* 117:10-11 Je '89
SYNCHROTRONS *See* Accelerators (Electrons, etc.)
SYNCOPE *See* Fainting
SYNCYTIAL VIRUS, RESPIRATORY *See* Respiratory syncytial virus
SYNDICATED TELEVISION PROGRAMS *See* Cable television—Syndicated programs; Television broadcasting—Syndicated programs
SYNDICATES (FINANCE)
See also
Blind pools (Securities)
SYNDICATES (NEWSPAPER) *See* Newspaper syndicates
SYNDROMES
See also
AIDS (Disease)
Angelman syndrome
Chronic fatigue syndrome
Guillain-Barré syndrome
Irritable bowel syndrome
Munchausen syndrome
Prader-Willi syndrome
Stendhal syndrome
Sudden infant death syndrome
TMJ syndrome
Toxic shock syndrome
SYNERGIC THEATER
Reviews:
Performances at Schimmel Center for the Arts, New York City. J. Lewis. *Dance Magazine* 63:86-7 Ja '89
SYNERGISM
Synergism between HIV gp120 and gp120-specific antibody in blocking human T cell activation. R. S. Mittler and M. K. Hoffmann. bibl f il *Science* 245:1380-2 S 22 '89
Synergistic interactions and environment. N. Myers. *BioScience* 39:506 S '89
SYNESTHESIA
A mingling of the senses [research by R. E. Cytowic] E. E. Goode. il *U.S. News & World Report* 107:70-2 N 13 '89
SYNNESTVEDT, JUSTIN
TV—no! [address, October 19, 1988] *Vital Speeches of the Day* 55:209-11 Ja 15 '89
SYNOD OF BISHOPS (1987)
Lecturing (sigh!) the laity. il *Commonweal* 116:132-3 Mr 10 '89
SYNOVIAL SARCOMA *See* Synovioma
SYNOVIOMA
Fighting for two lives [contracting synovial sarcoma during pregnancy] M. L. Edwards. il por *Ladies' Home Journal* 106:18+ S '89
SYNTHASES
Ethylene gene control: research ripens [gene for ACC synthase cloned; work of Takahide Sato and Athanasios Theologis] *Science News* 136:188 S 16 '89
SYNTHESIS
See also
Amino acids—Synthesis
Carbon compounds—Synthesis
Chemzymes
DNA—Synthesis
Nucleic acids—Synthesis
Peptides—Synthesis
Propellanes—Synthesis
Proteins—Synthesis
Urea—Synthesis
. . . and self-assembling chemical parts [trinacrene formed by structure-directed synthesis] *Science News* 136:349 N 25 '89
Enzymatic catalysts in organic synthesis. C.-H. Wong. bibl f il *Science* 244:1145-52 Je 9 '89
Synthesis of organic salts with large second-order optical nonlinearities. S. R. Marder and others. bibl f il *Science* 245:626-8 Ag 11 '89
SYNTHESIZERS, ELECTRONIC *See* Musical instruments, Electronic
SYNTHETASES
Nucleotides in yeast tRNA^{Phe} required for the specific recognition by its cognate synthetase. J. R. Sampson and others. bibl f il *Science* 243:1363-6 Mr 10 '89
Structural basis for misaminoacylation by mutant E. coli glutaminyl-tRNA synthetase enzymes. J. J. Perona and others. bibl f il *Science* 246:1152-4 D 1 '89

Structure of E. coli glutaminyl-tRNA synthetase complexed with tRNA^{Gln} and ATP at 2.8 Å resolution. M. A. Rould and others. bibl f il *Science* 246:1135-42 D 1 '89
The structure of the "second genetic code" [work of T. A. Steitz] M. M. Waldrop. il por *Science* 246:1122 D 1 '89
SYNTHETIC FABRICS *See* Textile fabrics, Synthetic
SYNTHETIC FOOD *See* Food substitutes
SYNTHETIC GROWTH HORMONE *See* Pituitary hormones, Synthetic
SYPHILIS
Entombed beauty provides syphilis clues [mummy of Maria d'Aragona, a Naples Renaissance noblewoman] *Science News* 136:223 S 30 '89
So little time, so many cases [Georgia] A. Murr. il *Newsweek* 114:59+ S 25 '89
The syphilized world [study by Brenda J. Baker and George J. Armelagos] J. Benditt. *Scientific American* 260:30 Mr '89
Diagnosis
1914: January 20 [Wisconsin law requiring premarital testing for veneral disease declared unconstitutional] A. Nielson. il *American Heritage* 40:40-1 F '89
SYRACUSE UNIVERSITY
George P. Elliott and the common reader. L. C. Tisdale. *The American Scholar* 58:421-8 Summ '89
SYRIA
Armed Forces
Forces in Lebanon
The agony of Beirut. J. Bierman. il *Maclean's* 102:20-2 Ag 28 '89
Blood brothers. R. F. Haddad. *The New Republic* 200:16-18 My 8 '89
Death throes of a capital. J. Bartholet and S. Issa. il *Newsweek* 114:24-6 Ag 21 '89
An inside view of Lebanon. J. J. Donohue. *America* 161:378-81 N 25 '89
A preview of the apocalypse [continued fighting in Beirut] J. Smolowe. il map *Time* 134:23-4 Ag 28 '89
Why the carnage does not stop. R. Backmann and P. Blanchet. *World Press Review* 36:24-5 O '89
Foreign relations
Syria and Lebanon in 1988. I. Rabinovich. bibl f *Current History* 88:77-80+ F '89
Lebanon
See Lebanon—Foreign relations—Syria
Middle East
Following an independent course [interview with H. Assad] K. Prager and others. por *Time* 133:30 Ap 3 '89
Spoilers of peace in the Middle East [radical Palestinian groups supported by Syria] R. Z. Chesnoff. il map *U.S. News & World Report* 107:40-1 Jl 10 '89
Religious institutions and affairs
See also
Muslims—Syria
SYRIAN AMERICAN BUSINESS ENTERPRISES
Jeans in the genes [S. Toussie and other successful Syrians in the jeans business] P. Patton. il por *New York* 22:40-4+ My 22 '89
SYRINGES
Drug abuse: gambling with infection [needle use] K. M. Porterfield. il *Current Health 2* 15:17-19 My '89
Moral propaganda [curbing spread of AIDS through needle exchange programs] K. McAuliffe. *Omni (New York, N.Y.)* 12:41 O '89
Trading good needles for bad [D. Purchase tries to fight AIDS in Tacoma] R. Givens. il por *Newsweek* 113:49 Ja 9 '89
SYROP, MITCHELL, 1953-
about
Mitchell Syrop at Lieberman & Saul. S. Hapgood. il *Art in America* 77:178-9 D '89
SYRUPS
See also
Corn syrup
Maple syrup
SYSTEM 7.0 OPERATING SYSTEM
Innovation at Apple and IBM. R. A. Shaffer. il *Personal Computing* 13:45-6 S '89
System 7.0: the next-generation Mac operating system [with editorial comment by Donald Evan Crabb] T. Thompson. il *Byte* 14 Mac Special Supp:MAC187, MAC196-MAC197 Ag '89
SYSTEMATICS, INC.
When it's time to go [W. V. Smiley] M. Barrier. il por *Nation's Business* 77:74+ N '89
SYSTEMIC LUPUS ERYTHEMATOSUS *See* Lupus erythematosus
SYSTEMS ANALYSIS
See also
Fuzzy systems (Computer science)
Mathematical optimization
Systems analysis at the molecular scale. H. Rabitz. bibl f il *Science* 246:221-6 O 13 '89
SYSTEMS ENGINEERING
See also
Self organizing systems

SYTHE, DAN
(jt. auth) See Jaffe, Joe, and Sythe, Dan
SYZYGY (ASTRONOMY) See Conjunctions (Astronomy)
SZABO, BARNEY J., AND OTHERS
Uranium-series dated authigenic carbonates and Acheulian sites in southern Egypt. bibl f il maps Science 243:1053-6 F 24 '89
SZABO, BILL
(jt. auth) See Kapitan, June, and Szabo, Bill
SZABÓ, ISTVÁN
about
Hanussen [film] Reviews
The New Republic 200:22 Ap 10 '89. S. Kauffmann
SZAMUELY, GEORGE
The intellectuals & the cold war. Commentary 88:54-6 D '89
The politics of 1992. Commentary 88:42-5 O '89
SZASZ, THOMAS STEPHEN, 1920-
Whose competence? il National Review 41:38+ S 15 '89
SZE, SZEMING
about
The birth of WHO [interview] il World Health p28-9 My '89
SZECHWAN COOKING See Cooking, Chinese
SZEGEDY-MASZAK, MARIANNE
Calm, cool and beleaguered [cover story] il pors The New York Times Magazine p16-19+ Ag 6 '89
Rise and fall of the Washington peace industry. il The Bulletin of the Atomic Scientists 45:18-23 Ja/F '89
What every young woman should know. il National Review 41:43-5 F 10 '89
Who's to judge? il pors The New York Times Magazine p28-9+ My 21 '89
SZULC, TAD
Castro: dilemmas of the last idealist. New Perspectives Quarterly 5:50-1 Wint '88/'89

T

T, MR. See Mr. T
T-1 NETWORKS See T1 networks
T-38 AIRPLANES See Airplanes, Training
T-45 AIRPLANES See Airplanes, Training
T CELL RECEPTORS
Activation-driven programmed cell death and T cell receptor $\zeta\eta$ expression. M. Merćep and others. bibl f il Science 246:1162-5 D 1 '89
Developmental biology of T cell receptors. J. L. Strominger. bibl f il Science 244:943-50 My 26 '89
Failure of T cell receptor V_β negative selection in an athymic environment. R. J. Hodes and others. bibl f il Science 246:1041-4 N 24 '89
Polymerase chain reaction with single-sided specificity: analysis of T cell receptor δ chain. E. Y. Loh and others. bibl f il Science 243:217-20 Ja 13 '89
Structure and specificity of a class II MHC alloreactive $\gamma\delta$ T cell receptor heterodimer. L. A. Matis and others. bibl f il Science 245:746-9 Ag 18 '89
T cell receptor gene trans-rearrangements: chimeric γ-δ genes in normal lymphoid tissues. B. Tycko and others. bibl f il Science 245:1242-6 S 15 '89
Vaccination against experimental allergic encephalomyelitis with T cell receptor peptides. M. D. Howell and others. bibl f il Science 246:668-70 N 3 '89
T CELLS
Activation of $\gamma\delta$ T cells in the primary immune response to Mycobacterium tuberculosis. E. M. Janis and others. bibl f il Science 244:713-16 My 12 '89
Activators of protein kinase C induce dissociation of CD4, but not CD8, from p56^{lck}. T. R. Hurley and others. bibl f il Science 245:407-9 Jl 28 '89
AIDS predictors [measures of a drug's efficacy] K. Fackelmann. il Science News 136:298-9 N 4 '89
AIDS viral burden far exceeds estimates [patients harbor HIV in CD4-positive T4 cells; research by Miltiades C. Psallidopoulos] R. Weiss. Science News 136:54 Jl 22 '89
Antigen-specific helper function of cell-free T cell products bearing TCR V_β8 determinants. R. Guy and others. bibl f il Science 244:1477-80 Je 23 '89
Brefeldin A specifically inhibits presentation of protein antigens to cytotoxic T lymphocytes. J. W. Yewdell and J. R. Bennink. bibl f il Science 244:1072-5 Je 2 '89
Contingent genetic regulatory events in T lymphocyte activation. G. R. Crabtree. bibl f il Science 243:355-61 Ja 20 '89
Control of experimental autoimmune encephalomyelitis by T cells responding to activated T cells. A. W. Lohse and others. bibl f il Science 244:820-3 My 19 '89
Cyclosporin A specifically inhibits function of nuclear proteins involved in T cell activation. E. A. Emmel and others. bibl f il Science 246:1617-20 D 22 '89
Detecting mutations in human genes [use of HPRT gene as an indicator] J. L. Marx. il Science 243:737-8 F 10 '89

G_1/S transition in normal human T-lymphocytes requires the nuclear protein encoded by c-myb. A. M. Gewirtz and others. bibl f il Science 245:180-3 Jl 14 '89
Herpesvirus may boost AIDS expression [study by Paolo Lusso and Robert C. Gallo] K. Fackelmann. Science News 135:55 Ja 28 '89
How T cells see antigen. H. M. Grey and others. bibl il Scientific American 261:56-64 N '89
Immuni-tea [effects of astragalus on T cell activity; research by Giora Mavligit and Da-Tong Chu] J. Barone. il American Health 8:100 O '89
In vivo modulation of cytolytic activity and thy-1 expression in TCR-$\gamma\delta^+$ intraepithelial lymphocytes. L. Lefrancois and T. Goodman. bibl f il Science 243:1716-18 Mr 31 '89
Influence of the major histocompatibility complex on positive thymic selection of $V_\beta 17a^+$ T cells. M. A. Blackman and others. bibl f il Science 244:214-17 Ap 14 '89
Interleukin-1 costimulatory activity on the interleukin-2 promoter via AP-1. K. Muegge and others. bibl f il Science 246:249-51 O 13 '89
MS gene discovery: a piece of the puzzle [T cell receptor gene; research by Stephen L. Hauser] I. Wickelgren. Science News 136:21 Jl 8 '89
Murine MHC polymorphism and T cell specificities. S. Roy and others. bibl f il Science 244:572-5 My 5 '89
Neonatal thymectomy results in a repertoire enriched in T cells deleted in adult thymus. H. Smith and others. bibl f il Science 245:749-52 Ag 18 '89
The neutrophil-activating protein (NAP-1) is also chemotactic for T lymphocytes. C. G. Larsen and others. bibl f il Science 243:1464-6 Mr 17 '89
New AIDS drugs take careful aim. J. Palca. il Science 246:1559-60 D 22 '89
A nondeletional mechanism of thymic self tolerance. F. Ramsdell and others. bibl f il Science 246:1038-41 N 24 '89
Regulation of lymphokine messenger RNA stability by a surface-mediated T cell activation pathway. T. Lindsten and others. bibl f il Science 244:339-43 Ap 21 '89
The reservoir for HIV-1 in human peripheral blood is a T cell that maintains expression of CD4. S. M. Schnittman and others. bibl f il Science 245:305-8 Jl 21 '89
A single amino acid interchange yields reciprocal CTL specificities for HIV-1 gp160. H. Takahashi and others. bibl f il Science 246:118-21 O 6 '89
Sporozoite vaccine induces genetically restricted T cell elimination of malaria from hepatocytes. S. L. Hoffman and others. bibl f il Science 244:1078-81 Je 2 '89
Superantigens [stimulation of T cells by staphylococcal toxins; research by John Kappler and others] T. Beardsley. Scientific American 261:19-20 Ag '89
Synergism between HIV gp120 and gp120-specific antibody in blocking human T cell activation. R. S. Mittler and M. K. Hoffmann. bibl f il Science 245:1380-2 S 22 '89
T cell signaling. R. M. Perlmutter. bibl f il Science 245:344 Jl 28 '89
T cells against a bacterial heat shock protein recognize stressed macrophages. T. Koga and others. bibl f il Science 245:1112-15 S 8 '89
Thymic requirement for clonal deletion during T cell development. A. M. Fry and others. bibl f il Science 246:1044-6 N 24 '89
Vβ-specific stimulation of human T cells by staphyloccocal toxins. J. Kappler and others. bibl f il Science 244:811-13 My 19 '89
T. DEANE INC.
Woman with a large idea [T. Sullivan] M. Barrier. il por Nation's Business 77:71 Mr '89
T-FACTOR DIET See Diet
'T HART, LENIE See Hart, Lenie 't
T. ROWE PRICE HIGH YIELD FUND
Who's buying junk? J. Willoughby. il Forbes 143:161 Mr 6 '89
T. ROWE PRICE NEW FRONTIER FUND
Searching for small gems [views of D. J. Diamond] R. Simon. il por Forbes 143:214-15 Je 26 '89
T. ROWE PRICE SCIENCE & TECHNOLOGY FUND
Technology time? C. Torcellini. il por Forbes 144:362+ N 13 '89
T-SHIRTS
101 uses for a T-shirt [donating running T-shirts to third world countries] R. Rodale. il por Runner's World 24:26 Ag '89
"And the winners are . . ." [running T-shirt and poster contests] K. Kleppert. il Runner's World 24:68-9 F '89
Dark victory [black T-shirt] S. Kettmann. il Gentlemen's Quarterly 59:65 My '89
Suiting science to a T (shirt), two Chicago bar owners set up a Stephen Hawking Fan Club [Gold Star Sardine Bar] il People Weekly 32:111 S 11 '89
To many, T-shirts are an anti-uniform of convenience. B. Bull. il Vogue 179:808 S '89
T TAILS, AIRPLANE See Airplanes—Tails
T TAURI STARS See Stars, Variable
T1 NETWORKS
I can get it for you wholesale. F. Meeks. il Forbes 143:120-1 F 6 '89

T² MEDICAL INC.
Mixing up a rich intravenous solution. S. Ticer. il *Business Week* p92 My 22 '89
T4 PROTEINS *See* CD4 proteins
TAAFFE, WILLIAM
TV/radio. See occasional issues of Sports Illustrated
TABACCHI, GIULIANO
about
An export focus at Italy's farsighted frame company. J. Rossant. il por *Business Week* p114 My 22 '89
TABASCO SAUCE
Salt and pepper flavor this island [Avery Island, home of sauce maker McIlhenny Co.] il map *Southern Living* 24:34-5 Mr '89
TABATA, TETSUYA, AND OTHERS
A protein that binds to a cis-acting element of wheat histone genes has a leucine zipper motif. bibl f il *Science* 245:965-7 S 1 '89
TABER, ANTHONY
The last page. See issues of Audubon
TABLE DECORATION
The center of attention [centerpieces] il *Better Homes and Gardens* 67:69 O '89
Decorate under the table, too. il *Southern Living* 24:176 Mr '89
Drape fabric on the tabletop. il *Southern Living* 24:154 Mr '89
Dress ups! [elegant tabletop touches] il *Redbook* 174:89-91+ N '89
Fabulous holiday centerpieces. S. La Rosa. il *McCall's* 117:25-7 D '89
Flowers for your table. J. Williams and J. Severson. il *Better Homes and Gardens* 67:128+ My '89
Holiday centerpieces to savor. il *McCall's* 116:31-7 Ja '89
Take the dining outside. il *Southern Living* 24:136+ Je '89
TABLE FOR TWO (PORTLAND, OR.: RESTAURANT) *See* Portland (Or.)—Restaurants, nightclubs, bars, etc.
TABLE HOCKEY
Tournaments
The game. *The New Yorker* 65:28-30 Mr 6 '89
TABLE MOUNTAIN OUTFITTERS
Semi-guided success. S. Netherby. il *Field & Stream* 93:77-8 Mr '89
TABLE SAWS *See* Saws and sawing
TABLE SETTING
15 tables to set a holiday mood. il *Good Housekeeping* 208:100-3 Ja '89
Getting the look. il *Better Homes and Gardens* 68:101 F '89
Perfect settings for a happy Thanksgiving. il *Parents* 64:164-6 N '89
Pride of placesetting. E. A. Berthold. il *House & Garden* 161:196-9 N '89
Setting the holiday table. J. Williams and J. Severson. il *Better Homes and Gardens* 67:192+ N '89
TABLE TOP PHOTOGRAPHY *See* Photography, Table top
TABLER, PAT
about
Mr. Bases Loaded. J. E. Vader. il por *Sports Illustrated* 70:73 Ap 24 '89
TABLES
See also
Conference tables
Pool tables
BBQ grill table. S. Kingman and P. Kingman. il *The Family Handyman* 39:80-1 Je '89
Butterfield & Butterfield sells Herter table for record $280,500. il *Antiques & Collecting Hobbies* 94:31 My '89
Classic chair-table. il *Home Mechanix* 86:41 Ap '89
Drop-leaf table from our ancestors. V. Weaver and A. Weaver. il *Workbench* 45:54-7 Ja/F '89
English elegance [coffee table] H. Wicks. il *Home Mechanix* 85:54-5+ My '89
For a devoted junior builder, this Lego table is the perfect construction site. il *The Family Handyman* 39:46-7 N/D '89
Gateleg table [drop leaf] R. Capotosto. il *Popular Mechanics* 166:79-83 Ag '89
The geometry of conversation [dining table's impact on conversation at a party] J. Giovannini. il *House & Garden* 161:62+ F '89
Great legs [coffee table and master bed] L. M. Dalsgaard. il *Home Mechanix* 85:48-52 Ja '89
Neon under glass [dining table] il *Home Mechanix* 85:53+ F '89
Pedestal picnic table. B. Kieffer. il *The Family Handyman* 39:86-8+ Je '89
Pier tables. G. Michael. il *Antiques & Collecting Hobbies* 94:26 D '89
Portable all-purpose table. H. Shymkus. il *Field & Stream* 94:88 My '89
Queen Anne gate-leg table. G. E. Derzinski. il *Workbench* 45:46-50 Jl/Ag '89
Restoring an oak table. K. Collier. il *The Family Handyman* 39:54-7 F '89
Shaker end table. N. Barrett, Jr. il *Popular Mechanics* 166:85-8 O '89

'Showoff' table is functional, too. H. Wicks. il *Home Mechanix* 85:36-9 F '89
The tea tables of eastern Virginia. W. B. Gusler. bibl f il *Antiques* 135:1238-57 My '89
TABLES ON BOATS *See* Boats and boating—Equipment
TABLETS (MEDICINE) *See* Pills
TABLEWARE
See also
Nickel silver tableware
Salt and pepper grinders, shakers, etc.
Silverware
Spoons
Swid Powell Design Inc.
Table setting
Fabulous looks. J. Williams and J. Severson. il *Better Homes and Gardens* 68:98-9+ F '89
Pleasures of the table: Simon Pearce. Z. E. Zakroff. il por *Gourmet* 49:56-61+ Ag '89
Table talk. il *The New York Times Magazine* p46-8 My 28 '89
Design
Design for eating [tableware by architects] T. Hine. il *Gentlemen's Quarterly* 59:78+ N '89
History
Anecdotes, facetiae, satire, etc.
Eating out of hand. J. Bohannon. il *The Saturday Evening Post* 261:30+ S '89
TABLOID NEWSPAPERS
See also
National enquirer
Are you tired of turning on TV and being turned off by the new breed confessors? L. Wyse. il *Good Housekeeping* 209:198 Ag '89
Michael J. Fox's nuptials in hell! [trying to outwit tabloids] M. J. Fox and M. Pollan. il pors map *Esquire* 111:136-8+ Je '89
Great Britain
Editor, heal thyself [ethics code] D. Brand. il *Time* 134:89 D 11 '89
TABLOID TELEVISION
Are you tired of turning on TV and being turned off by the new breed confessors? L. Wyse. il *Good Housekeeping* 209:198 Ag '89
Boston faces reality [early evening tabloid TV] K. Haley. il *Channels (New York, N.Y.: 1986)* 9:86-7 F '89
Celebrity victims: crime casualties are turning into stars on tabloid TV. F. Rose. il *New York* 22:38-44 Jl 31 '89
Extra! Extra! Tabloid clones invade TV. M. Collins. il *TV Guide* 37:14-16 N 18-24 '89
Farewell, trash, goodbye, Nielsens [shows losing sponsors] *U.S. News & World Report* 106:14+ My 15 '89
In defense of tabloid TV [cover story] V. G. Sauter. il *TV Guide* 37:2-4 Ag 5-11 '89
Packaging the news. R. Corelli. il *Maclean's* 102:82-3 O 30 '89
The price of "cheap eyeballs" [advertisers squeamish] F. Meeks. il *Forbes* 143:188-9 Mr 20 '89
This is what you thought: 80% think TV has become too trashy. il *Glamour* 87:179 My '89
Trash TV: news or noise? D. O. Relin. il *Scholastic Update (Teachers' edition)* 122:23-4 S 8 '89
Turmoil touting tabloid TV. R. Katz. il *Channels (New York, N.Y.: 1986)* 9:66-7 Jl/Ag '89
Anecdotes, facetiae, satire, etc.
The Chuck show. G. Keillor. *The New Yorker* 65:26-9 Jl 24 '89
TABOR, JAMES
The wild boar is a formidable foe and an admirable pest. il *Smithsonian* 20:114-18+ S '89
TABOR, TIMOTHY L.
about
Conspiracy of strangers. C. Byron. il pors *New York* 22:16+ S 4 '89
The debris in Rudolph Giuliani's wake. C. Welles. pors *Business Week* p36-7 Ja 23 '89
TABUSE, YO, AND OTHERS
Mutations in a protein kinase C homolog confer phorbol ester resistance on Caenorhabditis elegans. bibl f il *Science* 243:1713-16 Mr 31 '89
TAC *See* United States. Air Force. Tactical Air Command
TACHYONS
Beyond Einstein [theory of E. C. G. Sudarshan; cover story; with editorial comment by Paul Hoffman] D. Freedman. il pors *Discover* 10:4, 56-61 F '89
TACIT RAINBOW ANTIRADIATION MISSILES *See* Guided missiles
TACKLE, FISHING *See* Fishing tackle
TACKLE BOXES, CASES, ETC. *See* Fishing tackle—Storage
TACOLCY ECONOMIC DEVELOPMENT CORPORATION, INC.
Building on rock, not sand [work of O. Pitts] il por *Time* 133:22 Ja 9 '89
TACOMA (WASH.)
Public health
Trading good needles for bad [D. Purchase tries to fight AIDS] R. Givens. il por *Newsweek* 113:49 Ja 9 '89

TACOS
Fruit taco? il *Sunset (Central West edition)* 183:64-5 Jl '89
TACTICAL AIR COMMAND See United States. Air Force. Tactical Air Command
TACTICAL AIR WARFARE CENTER (U.S.)
Role of Tactical Air Warfare Center grows as technology advances. *Aviation Week & Space Technology* 131:122-3 S 11 '89
TACTICAL ASSET ALLOCATION (INVESTMENTS)
Allocating your assets by life's seasons [special section] T. Paré. il *Fortune* 120 no10 Special Issue:125+ Fall '89
Allocating your assets: you may not need a pro. L. J. Nathans. il *Business Week* p152-3 My 8 '89
You can beat the market and still lose. M. Hulbert. il *Forbes* 144:299 O 16 '89
TACTILE PERCEPTION See Touch
TADICH GRILL (SAN FRANCISCO, CALIF.) See San Francisco (Calif.)—Restaurants, nightclubs, bars, etc.
TADJADOD, NAHAL
The Epic of the Kings. il *The Unesco Courier* 42:28-31 S '89
TADLOCK, PAUL
about
He upped and quit. W. P. Barrett. il pors *Forbes* 144:282+ O 16 '89
TAFARI MAKONNEN See Haile Selassie I, Emperor of Ethiopia, 1891-1975
THE TAFFETAS [musical] See Musicals, revues, etc.— Reviews—Single works
TAGAMET See Cimetidine
TAGGARES, KATHY
about
Kathy Taggares: her fast foods are really cooking. D. Castellon. il por *Business Week* p69 D 4 '89
TAGGART, LINDA
about
America's holy war. P. Hamill. il por *Esquire* 112:61-4 N '89
TAGLIABUE, PAUL
about
The NFL's new boss. P. King. il por *Sports Illustrated* 71:19-20 N 6 '89
TAGORE [ballet] See Ballet reviews—Single works
TAGUA
The look of ivory without the guilt. il *Newsweek* 114:83 O 9 '89
TAGUCHI, GENICHI
about
Quality conscious. E. Corcoran. *Scientific American* 261:75-6 Jl '89
TAHERI, AMIR
about
'Rafsanjani would have loved to come to the U.S.' [interview] A. Balk. il por *World Press Review* 36:17-18 Ag '89
TAHITI (FRENCH POLYNESIA)
See also
Fisheries—Tahiti (French Polynesia)
Description and travel
Gourmet holidays: Society Islands. C. Bates. il map *Gourmet* 49:36-41+ Ja '89
TAHOE, LAKE (CALIF. AND NEV.) See Lake Tahoe (Calif. and Nev.)
TAHOE CITY (CALIF.)
Description
Tahoe City lights "The Big Tree". il *Sunset (Central West edition)* 181:164 D '88
TAICHER, RICHARD, 1929-
about
Richard Taicher. E. Feit. il por *American Artist* 53:56-9 F '89
TAILGATE PICNICS See Picnics
TAILORING
The bespoke life [custom-made clothes] P. Mayle. il *Gentlemen's Quarterly* 59:422-7+ S '89
TAILORS
See also
Hector's Tailoring (Firm)
France
Tailored perfection [Lanvin suits] N. Frey. il por *Harper's Bazaar* 122:70 Ap '89
Great Britain
Tinkering with the tailors [raising the rents on Savile Row] L. Mandel-Viney. il *U.S. News & World Report* 107:58 D 4 '89
TAILS (AIRPLANES) See Airplanes, Military—Tails
TAIPEI (TAIWAN)
Description
Taipei. F. Ferretti. il map *Gourmet* 49:80-5+ Ap '89
TAIRA, MASATO, AND OTHERS
Human diabetes associated with a deletion of the tyrosine kinase domain of the insulin receptor. bibl f il *Science* 245:63-6 Jl 7 '89
TAIT, ERIC V.
F-F-F-Fortysomething? il *Essence* 20:16+ N '89
TAITTINGERS (FIRM)
Elegant effervescence. R. Levio. il *Harper's Bazaar* 122:48 Ap '89

TAIWAN
See also
Immigration and emigration—Taiwan
Investments, Taiwanese
Literature and state—Taiwan
Little League baseball—Taiwan
Taipei (Taiwan)
Taiwanese
United Nations—Taiwan
Window on China (Taiwan)
Commerce
Japan
See Japan—Commerce—Taiwan
Economic conditions
The Other China is starting to soar. D. J. Yang. il *Business Week* p60-2 N 6 '89
Taiwan's long march toward democracy. A. Tanzer. il *Forbes* 143:48-9+ Ap 3 '89
Foreign relations
China deal. L. Hahn. *The New Republic* 201:10-11 O 30 '89
China
See China—Foreign relations—Taiwan
United States
See United States—Foreign relations—Taiwan
Industries
See also
China Airlines Ltd.
China General Plastics Corp.
Computer industry—Taiwan
Electronic industries—Taiwan
Far Eastern Air Transport
Formosa Plastics Corp.
Petrochemical industry—Taiwan
Politics and government
Political reform in Taiwan [address, March 4, 1989] J. F. Copper. *Vital Speeches of the Day* 55:394-6 Ap 15 '89
Taiwan: a nation in transition. J. F. Copper. bibl f *Current History* 88:173-6+ Ap '89
Taiwan's long march toward democracy. A. Tanzer. il *Forbes* 143:48-9+ Ap 3 '89
You can't go home again. M. McSherry. il *National Review* 41:37-8+ D 22 '89
Social conditions
You can't go home again. M. McSherry. il *National Review* 41:37-8+ D 22 '89
TAIWAN STOCK EXCHANGE
Taiwan's manic stock market. B. Powell and K. Chen. il *Newsweek* 114:56 D 25 '89
TAIWANESE
United States
Brain drain in reverse [Taiwan's U.S.-trained returnees] A. Tanzer. il *Forbes* 143:114-15 Ap 17 '89
Mr. Wu knows his customer [GBC Bancorp] G. Morgenson. il por *Forbes* 143:49+ Ja 23 '89
TAIYO KOBE MITSUI BANK See Mitsui Taiyo Kobe Bank
TAJ MAHAL
A love poem in marble. L. Eskin. il *Scholastic Update (Teachers' edition)* 121:16-17 Mr 10 '89
TAJIMA, RENEE
about
Who killed Vincent Chin? [film] Reviews
Mother Jones 14:54 Jl/Ag '89. D. Sachs
TAKAGI, YOSUKE
Forcing confessions in Japan. *World Press Review* 36:57 Je '89
TAKAHASHI, AKIHIRO
about
The victim and the pilot: a Hiroshima reunion. G. Mitchell. il pors *The Progressive* 53:26-8 Ag '89
TAKAHASHI, HARUNORI
about
Meet the world's busiest man—oops, you missed him. A. Borrus. il por *Business Week* p64+ Ap 17 '89
TAKAHASHI, HIDEMI, AND OTHERS
A single amino acid interchange yields reciprocal CTL specificities for HIV-1 gp160. bibl f il *Science* 246:118-21 O 6 '89
TAKAHASHI, TAKASHI, AND OTHERS
p53: a frequent target for genetic abnormalities in lung cancer. bibl f *Science* 246:491-4 O 27 '89
TAKAYAMA, TATSUO
about
Tatsuo Takayama: National Museum of Modern Art. N. Hara. il *Art News* 88:194 S '89
TAKAYANAGI, KENJIRO
about
Japan's oldest television star. F. Lovece. por *Video* 12:23 Ja '89
TAKE 6 (MUSICAL GROUP)
Evangelism and all that jazz. R. N. Ostling. il *Time* 133:76 Mr 20 '89
Take 6. il *Ebony* 44:74+ Mr '89
Take 6 takes off. J. Long. il *Christianity Today* 33:67-8 Jl 14 '89
TAKE A BREAK WITH MR. PETE [television program] See Television program reviews—Single works

TAKE A DECISION (TERM)
Take that decision. W. Safire. il *The New York Times Magazine* p12+ Ap 16 '89
TAKE-OFF OF AIRPLANES *See* Airplanes, Jet—Take-off
TAKE OR PAY CONTRACTS (GAS) *See* Pipeline companies— Laws and regulations
TAKE OUT FOOD STORES *See* Food stores
TAKEFUJI, YOSHIYASU, AND LEE, KUO-CHUN
A near-optimum parallel planarization algorithm. bibl f il *Science* 245:1221-3 S 15 '89
TAKEI, GEORGE
about
Trek star. J. Harmon. il pors *Runner's World* 24:32-4 S '89
TAKEMIYA, MASAKI
about
Go. *The New Yorker* 64:26-7 F 6 '89
TAKEOVERS, CORPORATE *See* Corporations—Acquisitions and mergers
TAKESHITA, JOHN
about
On wings of forgiveness. J. Fincher. il *Reader's Digest* 134:85-90 Mr '89
TAKESHITA, NOBORU
Visit of Japanese prime minister [remarks, February 2, 1989] *Department of State Bulletin* 89:33 Ap '89
about
The fine art of kinmyaku. il por *U.S. News & World Report* 106:18 Ap 24 '89
Now Takeshita really feels the flames of scandal. T. Holden. por *Business Week* p55 F 27 '89
A question of ethics. A. Bilski. *Maclean's* 102:27 Ap 24 '89
A scandal that will not die. W. R. Doerner. il por *Time* 133:37+ Ap 24 '89
Sinking in a sea of yen. H. Anderson. il por *Newsweek* 113:49-50 Ap 24 '89
Takeshita talks political reform—but doesn't sound convincing. A. Borrus. il *Business Week* p57 Ja 23 '89
Why time may be running out for Takeshita. T. Holden. por *Business Week* p43 Ap 24 '89
Resignation
Don't expect a caretaker to take care of trade. T. Holden and W. Glasgall. por *Business Week* p37 My 8 '89
A fatal money scandal. M. Nemeth. il por *Maclean's* 102:25 My 8 '89
The Japanese scandal. il *World Press Review* 36:8 Je '89
Sand in a well-oiled machine. S. MacLeod. por *Time* 133:44 My 8 '89
Takeshita bows out. B. Martin and others. il *Newsweek* 113:35 My 8 '89
Visit to the United States, 1989
Forming a fast friendship—before it's too late. L. Armstrong and A. Borrus. il por *Business Week* p50 F 6 '89
Tiptoe through the tensions. J. Greenwald. il por *Time* 133:60 F 13 '89
Visit of Japanese prime minister [remarks, February 2, 1989] G. Bush; N. Takeshita. il por *Department of State Bulletin* 89:32-3 Ap '89
TAKHAR, SANTOKH SINGH
about
Two veterinarians guilty in antibiotic case. M. Segal. il *FDA Consumer* 23:33-4 N '89
TAKI
Greek farce. il *National Review* 41:25-6 O 27 '89
Scandal: taint misbehavin'. il *Harper's Bazaar* 122:208-9+ Mr '89
TALBOT, J. THOMAS
about
Investors plan to revamp Hawaiian's operations. *Aviation Week & Space Technology* 131:71 S 4 '89
Peter Ueberroth's Hawaiian adventure. E. Schine. il por *Business Week* p32 S 4 '89
TALBOT, JOHN F.
Political crossroads for islands of enchantment. *America* 161:142-4 S 9-16 '89
TALBOT, WILLIAM HENRY FOX, 1800-1877
about
Negative and positive. il *American History Illustrated* 24:30 S/O '89
William Henry Fox Talbot: Metropolitan Museum. R. B. Woodward. il *Art News* 88:168-9 N '89
TALBOT COUNTY (MD.)
Description and travel
Rite of passage [cover story] R. S. Peffer. il map *Travel Holiday* 172:40-51 Ag '89
TALBOTT, J. E.
The rise and fall of the carronade. bibl il *History Today* 39:24-30 Ag '89
TALBOTT, JOHN E. *See* Talbott, J. E.
TALBOTT, STROBE
America abroad. See issues of Time beginning January 9, 1989
How I spent my summer vacation. il map *Life* 12:16+ Jl '89
A TALE OF TWO CITIES [television program] *See* Television program reviews—Single works

TALENT, JOHN
about
The case of the "misplaced" fossils. R. Lewin. il por *Science* 244:277-9 Ap 21 '89
Cooking the paleontological books? W. F. Allman. il *U.S. News & World Report* 106:61 My 8 '89
TALENT AGENTS *See* Theatrical agencies and agents
TALENTED CHILDREN *See* Children, Gifted
TALES FROM THE CRYPT [television program] *See* Television program reviews—Single works
THE TALES OF HOFFMANN [opera] *See* Offenbach, Jacques, 1819-1880
TALESE, GAY
The homeless woman with two homes. il *New York* 22:40-2 O 30 '89
TALIAFERRO, ROBERT
about
A free press flourishes behind bars. D. Arnold. il pors *Time* 133:12+ Mr 13 '89
TALK *See* Conversation; Speech
TALK RADIO *See* Radio broadcasting—Conversation programs
TALK RADIO [film] *See* Motion picture reviews—Single works
TALK SHOWS *See* Cable television—Conversation programs; Television broadcasting—Conversation programs
TALKING BOOKS
See also
    Bantam Audio Publishing
    Caedmon Audio (Firm)
    Dove Books on Tape, Inc.
    Mind's Eye (Firm)
    Random House Audiobooks
Audio/video plus. See occasional issues of Publishers Weekly beginning May 9, 1986
Audio reviews. See occasional issues of Publishers Weekly beginning September 2, 1988
Books you can read with your ears. V. S. Sussman. il *U.S. News & World Report* 107:59 Jl 3 '89
Fall audio and video. J. Zinsser. il *Publishers Weekly* 236:27-8+ Ag 4 '89
Play me a story: it's tape time. D. Stead. *The New York Times Book Review* 94:48 Je 11 '89
'Selected shorts' due from Symphony Space [tapes of actors reading American short stories] *Publishers Weekly* 235:34 F 3 '89
Speaking volumes. L. Grossberger. il *Vogue* 179:226+ My '89
Spring audio and video. J. Zinsser. il *Publishers Weekly* 235:40+ F 3 '89
Words in your ear. D. Diehl. il *Modern Maturity* 32:88-9 F/Mr '89
TALKINGTON, JANE
about
Jane Talkington's Kitty video gives hungry cats a view that forever fascinates. il *People Weekly* 32:99 N 13 '89
TALLENT, ELIZABETH, 1954-
Prowler [story] *The New Yorker* 65:43-50 O 16 '89
TALLEY, JERE
Love [poem] *Essence* 19:123 Ap '89
TALLEY INDUSTRIES, INC.
Hot air bags. R. Addis. il *Forbes* 143:10 Mr 20 '89
TALLIS SCHOLARS (MUSICAL GROUP)
Glorious! [views of P. Phillips] *The New Yorker* 65:33-5 D 18 '89
Musical events:
    Tallis Scholars' program of Renaissance music. A. Porter. *The New Yorker* 65:70-1 D 25 '89
TALLON, ROBIN
Should the Congress adopt the "Textile and Apparel Trade Act of 1987"? [excerpts from address, September 16, 1987] *Congressional Digest* 68:22+ Ja '89
TALMUD
Versions
Thanks to Rabbi Adin Steinsaltz, you don't have to be a Hebrew scholar to enjoy the Talmud. il por *People Weekly* 32:130 D 18 '89
TALVELA, MARTTI, 1935-1989
about
Obituary
Opera News il por 54:67 S '89
TAMALES
The great cover-up. R. Sokolov. il *Natural History* p76-80 Ja '89
TAMAR INNS
Low-cost hospitality. H. Rudnitsky. il por *Forbes* 144:90 S 18 '89
TAMBO, OLIVER
about
Bound by blood. R. W. Wilkins. il por *Mother Jones* 14:20+ My '89
TAMBOV (SOVIET UNION)
Tambov: *perestroika* in the provinces. J. Kohan and Y. Shchekochikhin. il *Time* 133:86-8+ Ap 10 '89
TAMBRANDS INC.
Quiet talk about a tampon maker. G. G. Marcial. *Business Week* p130 Jl 17 '89
They're more single-minded at Tambrands. A. Dunkin. il *Business Week* p28 Ag 28 '89

TAMBURLAINE *See* Timur, the Great, 1336-1405
TAMERLANE *See* Timur, the Great, 1336-1405
TAMMEN, MELANIE S.
International Bank for Ruination and Destruction. il *Conservative Digest* 15:45+ Mr/Ap '89
TAMOXIFEN
Tamoxifen and breast cancer: new choices. M. Weber. *Vogue* 179:114 Ja '89
TAMPA (FLA.)

Architecture
Restoration respects the original design [house] il *Southern Living* 24:142-3 Je '89

Buildings
Photographs and photography
Tampa towers. il *American Heritage* 40:114-15 My/Je '89

Education
AIDS: students in glass houses? [case of E. Martinez] P. A. Zirkel. bibl f il *Phi Delta Kappan* 70:646-8 Ap '89
TAMPAX INC.
See also
Tambrands Inc.
TAMPONS *See* Feminine hygiene products
TAMRAZ, ROGER
about
License to loot. Z. Sawaya. il por *Forbes* 143:157 Mr 6 '89
TAMURA, T., AND OTHERS
Light adaptation in cat retinal rods. bibl f il *Science* 245:755-8 Ag 18 '89
TAMURA, TARO, 1923-1988
about
Obituary
Physics Today por 42 pt1:82-3 Ag '89. T. Udagawa and R. Coker
TAN, AMY
The Joy Luck Club [fiction] il *Ladies' Home Journal* 106:98+ Mr '89
Two kinds [story] il *The Atlantic* 263:53-7 F '89
Watching China. il por *Glamour* 87:302-3 S '89
about
American woman. P. Rowlands. il por *Mother Jones* 14:10 Jl/Ag '89
A game of show and not tell. D. Wang. il por *Newsweek* 113:69 Ap 17 '89
The Joy Luck Club: Chinese magic, American blessings and a publishing fairy tale. G. Feldman. il por *Publishers Weekly* 236:24-6 Jl 7 '89
The Joy Luck Club has brought writer Amy Tan a bit of both. K. Hubbard. il pors *People Weekly* 31:149-50 Ap 10 '89
TAN (SUNTAN) *See* Suntan
TANAKA, MIN
about
Can we dance a landscape? [dance] Reviews
New York il 22:124+ N 6 '89. T. Tobias
TANDEM BICYCLES *See* Bicycles
TANDEM COMPUTERS INC.
Tandem: a rose among the technology thorns. P. Sellers. il *Fortune* 120:42+ Ag 28 '89
This Cyclone is out to rain on IBM's parade [new mainframe] J. B. Levine. il *Business Week* p114 O 23 '89
TANDEM CYCLING *See* Cycling
TANDY, CHARLES C.
about
Can onions prevent baldness? C. Brown. il por *Forbes* 144:135 Ag 7 '89
TANDY BRANDS, INC.
Pow! Good news zaps Tandy Brands. G. G. Marcial. *Business Week* p98 S 11 '89
TANDY CORP.
Compaq, Tandy unveil notebook systems. P. Honan. il *Personal Computing* 13:25 D '89
Seeking respect at the Shack. M. Rogers. il *Newsweek* 113:53 My 15 '89
The Street may be missing Tandy's magic. G. G. Marcial. il *Business Week* p108 S 18 '89
Tandy-built. P. Scisco. il *Compute!* 11:82 Ap '89
What's in a name? A lot, says Tandy [selling computers to corporations under the Grid logo] K. Kelly. il *Business Week* p109 F 27 '89
TANEN, NED STONE, 1931-
about
Canyon hideout. P. Viladas. il *House & Garden* 161:120-5+ Ja '89
TANG, CHA-MIN, AND OTHERS
Quisqualate activates a rapidly inactivating high conductance ionic channel in hippocampal neurons. bibl f il *Science* 243:1474-7 Mr 17 '89
TANGIER (MOROCCO)
Social life and customs
Ali-Dada's Arabian night [M. S. Forbes celebrates birthday] M. Dougherty. il pors *People Weekly* 32:34-9 S 4 '89
That party [M. S. Forbes' party; cover story] J. Baumgold. il pors *New York* 22:30-41 O 2 '89
TANGO (DANCE)
Gardel. *The New Yorker* 65:26-7 Ag 21 '89

TANI, TADAAKI
Physics of the photographic latent image. bibl f il *Physics Today* 42:36-41 S '89
TANK AIRPLANES
Bizjet Olympics [competition for Air Force's tanker transport training system contract] W. Garvey. il *Flying* 116:76-9 F '89
USAF releases draft request for bids on tanker-transport training system. *Aviation Week & Space Technology* 130:31 Ap 3 '89
USAF tanker-transport training to stress low and high altitude mission profiles. E. H. Phillips. il *Aviation Week & Space Technology* 130:51-2 My 1 '89
Testing
Air Force to retrofit KC-10s with air refueling pods [cover story] W. B. Scott. il *Aviation Week & Space Technology* 131:36-7+ N 13 '89
TANK SHIPS *See* Tankers
TANK WARFARE
See also
Anti-tank weapons
Abrams Battle Tank [computer game] P. Scisco. il *Compute!* 11:68 Je '89
The latest sim craze [tank combat] G. Keizer. il *Compute!* 11:7 Ap '89
Steel Thunder [tank combat simulation] R. G. Sheffield. il *Compute!* 11:72+ My '89
TANKERS
See also
Stolt Tankers & Terminals (Holdings)
Accidents and explosions
See also
Exxon Valdez (Ship) oil spill, 1989
Aground [Greek tanker, World Prodigy, spills oil into Narragansett Bay] *The New Yorker* 65:22-4 Jl 24 '89
Alaska's aging tanker fleet. J. R. Luoma. il *Audubon* 91:85 S '89
An oily blight on the water [Delaware River, Galveston Bay and Rhode Island] L. Martz. il *Newsweek* 114:24 Jl 3 '89
Summer of the spills [accidents off Newport, R.I., Houston and in the Delaware River] F. Trippett. il *Time* 134:18 Jl 3 '89
Safety devices and measures
America's oil tanker mess [cover story] A. Dane. il *Popular Mechanics* 166:51-4 N '89
TANKERS AS AN INVESTMENT
Climbing aboard the tanker turnaround. L. J. Nathans. *Business Week* p134 Ja 9 '89
A tanker play. R. S. Teitelbaum. il *Fortune* 120:16 Ag 28 '89
TANKLESS WATER HEATERS *See* Water heaters
TANKS
See also
Septic tanks
Tank tactics. D. Mowitz. il *Successful Farming* 87:48F My '89
TANKS, MILITARY
Towing
Tanks for the tow [BMY's M88A1E1] P. W. Johnston. il *Popular Science* 234:50 My '89
TANNENHAUS, NORRA, 1953-
Tick tactics. il *Travel Holiday* 171:88 Je '89
TANNER, OGDEN
Bonsai: a way of looking at trees with different eyes. bibl (p229) il *Smithsonian* 20:138-48+ O '89
TANNING (SUNTAN) *See* Suntan
TANNING (SUNTAN) BOOTHS *See* Suntan
TANNING (SUNTAN) PRODUCTS *See* Suntan products
TANTALUM SULFIDES
Hexagonal domain-like charge density wave phase of TaS_2 determined by scanning tunneling microscopy. X. L. Wu and C. M. Lieber. bibl f il *Science* 243:1703-5 Mr 31 '89
TANTRUMS *See* Temper
TANUR, JUDITH M.
(jt. auth) See Fienberg, Stephen E., and Tanur, Judith M.
TANZANIA
See also
Agriculture—Tanzania
Game preserves—Tanzania
Hospitals—Tanzania
Hunting—Tanzania
Medicine—Tanzania
Missions, Medical—Tanzania
Mount Kilimanjaro (Tanzania)
Oldoinyo Lengai (Tanzania)
Paleontology—Tanzania
Rain forests—Tanzania
Serengeti National Park (Tanzania)
Wildlife—Tanzania
History
See also
World War, 1914-1918—Campaigns and battles—Tanzania
TANZTHEATER REINHILD HOFFMANN
Private eye [Machandel] T. Tobias. il *New York* 22:109 O 30 '89

TAOS (N.M.)

Description

Exploring Taos by bike. il map *Sunset (Central West edition)* 183:44-5 Ag '89

Light and shadow [cover story] S. Cohen. il map *Travel Holiday* 171:28-34 Je '89

TAOS SKI VALLEY (N.M.: RESORT) *See* Resorts—New Mexico

TAP [film] *See* Motion picture reviews—Single works

TAP DANCE

See also

National Tap Dance Day

Dancing:

Motion picture Tap and musical Black and blue. A. Croce. *The New Yorker* 64:73-5 F 6 '89

Sammy Davis, Jr. and Gregory Hines move to the beat in 'Tap' [cover story] il pors *Jet* 75:58-61 F 13 '89

Tap [G. Hines film] il pors *Ebony* 44:46+ F '89

The tap dance kid grows up: show-stopping Savion. M. Horosko. il pors *Dance Magazine* 63:38-40 Ag '89

Tap snaps back. D. Groves. il *American Health* 8:34 S '89

Teenage hoofer Savion Glover helps put tap back on the map. por *People Weekly* 31:81 F 13 '89

TAPE, CASSETTE *See* Tape, Magnetic

TAPE, MAGNETIC

See also

Data tapes

Tape buying guide. il *Stereo Review* 54:87-90 Mr '89

Tape tracks. R. Long. See issues of High Fidelity (New York, N.Y.) beginning May 1986 through July 1989

Video tapes: choosing the one that's right for you. L. Feldman. il *Radio-Electronics* 60:45-8 My '89

Virtue in videotape. D. Elrich. il *Home Mechanix* 85:44+ O '89

Standards

8-millimeter ups the ante. F. Vizard. il *Popular Mechanics* 166:46-7 S '89

8mm videotape comes to life [Hi8] D. Ranada. il *High Fidelity (New York, N.Y.)* 39:18 My '89

Arming for a format war [8mm vs. VHS] A. Levis. *Video* 13:6 D '89

Compact refinements battle 8mm gains. R. Woodcock. il *Video* 13:156 S '89

Hi8 debut sets a new 8mm standard. L. Braithwaite. il *Video* 13:23-7 Ap '89

The Silver Standard [BASF's Silver Standard calibration cassettes] R. Hodges. il *Stereo Review* 54:160 O '89

Whatever happened to Betamax? J. Cohen. il *Consumers' Research Magazine* 72:28-9 My '89

Testing

Audio cassette tapes. il *Consumer Reports* 54:118-22 D '89

How video tapes are tested and evaluated. il *Radio-Electronics* 60:47 My '89

Tale of the tapes. S. A. Booth and F. C. Barr. il *Popular Mechanics* 166:63-5 N '89

TAPE, VIDEO (MAGNETIC) *See* Tape, Magnetic

TAPE DATA MEDIA (FIRM)

Harper & Row acquires TDM from McGraw-Hill for Caedmon. P. Sweeting. *Publishers Weekly* 235:16 Je 9 '89

TAPE DECKS *See* Tape recorders and recording

TAPE RECORDERS AND RECORDING

See also

Digital audio tape recorders and recording

Personics Corporation

Radio receivers—Tape recorder combination

Tape recordings

Videotape recorders and recording

Happy 10th anniversary, Sony Walkman! L. Klein. il *Radio-Electronics* 60:72-3 O '89

Magnets and music. I. Masters. il *Stereo Review* 54:39-40+ D '89

Music to our ears [Walkman, a decade later] R. Givens. il *Newsweek* 114:68 Ag 7 '89

Tape decks: a buying guide. il *Stereo Review* 54:89-92+ My '89

Tape recording [cover story] C. Stark. il *Stereo Review* 54:82-6 Mr '89

Tape tracks. R. Long. See issues of High Fidelity (New York, N.Y.) beginning May 1986 through July 1989

Noise

See also

Dolby noise reduction system

Dolby S. K. C. Pohlmann. *Stereo Review* 54:20 Ag '89

HX-Pro: a "new" and improved cassette-deck circuit. L. Klein. il *Radio-Electronics* 60:84-5 Mr '89

Revisiting a rubber ruler. R. Long. il *High Fidelity (New York, N.Y.)* 39:15 Je '89

Testing

Aiwa AD-F780 cassette deck. C. Stark. il *Stereo Review* 54:65-6+ Ja '89

Mid-priced cassette tape decks. il *Consumer Reports* 54:99-103 D '89

NAD Model 6340 cassette deck. C. Stark. il *Stereo Review* 54:56+ S '89

Onkyo TA-2600 cassette deck. R. Long. il *High Fidelity (New York, N.Y.)* 39:19+ F '89

Philips FC-566 bidirectional cassette deck. R. Long. il *High Fidelity (New York, N.Y.)* 39:22-3+ F '89

Pioneer CT-91 cassette deck. R. Long. il *High Fidelity (New York, N.Y.)* 39:27+ F '89

Pioneer CT-S800 cassette deck. C. Stark. il *Stereo Review* 54:41-3 Mr '89

Reading between the lines [cover story] R. Long. il *High Fidelity (New York, N.Y.)* 39:38-42 F '89

Tape decks: you can get two for one. il *Consumer Reports* 54:160-4 Mr '89

TAPE RECORDING INDUSTRY

See also

Bantam Audio Publishing

Caedmon Audio (Firm)

Dove Books on Tape, Inc.

Hay House (Firm)

Houghton Mifflin Audio

Mind's Eye (Firm)

Random House Audiobooks

Shape, Inc.

Simon & Schuster Audio

Audio/video plus. See occasional issues of Publishers Weekly beginning May 9, 1986

Acquisitions and mergers

Harper & Row acquires TDM from McGraw-Hill for Caedmon. P. Sweeting. *Publishers Weekly* 235:16 Je 9 '89

TAPE RECORDINGS

See also

Children in tape recordings

Copyright—Tape recordings

Motion pictures and tape recordings

Oral history

Talking books

Videotapes

Audio reviews. See occasional issues of Publishers Weekly beginning September 2, 1988

Fall audio and video. J. Zinsser. il *Publishers Weekly* 236:27-8+ Ag 4 '89

Spring audio and video. J. Zinsser. il *Publishers Weekly* 235:40+ F 3 '89

Amateur recordings

Electronic disc jockeys: a new hit [Personics system] il *Newsweek* 114:47 Ag 28 '89

Personics offers customer programmed cassettes. E. Kehler. il *Down Beat* 56:11 N '89

Personics steps to the fore [custom-made audiocassettes] J. Ressner. il *Rolling Stone* p24 O 19 '89

The yen for karaoke. E. Grinnan. il *Seventeen* 48:44 O '89

Aviation use

See also

Flight recorders

Business use

See also

Master Duplicators (Firm)

Listen while you work. S. Miller. il *Home Office Computing* 7:18 F '89

Children's use

Children's audio and video. *Publishers Weekly* 235:195-8 F 24 '89

The children's audio challenge: appealing to kids, but selling to parents. J. Greco. il *Publishers Weekly* 235:192-4 F 24 '89

Children's fall audio and video. J. Zinsser. il *Publishers Weekly* 236:188+ Jl 28 '89

Play me a story: it's tape time. D. Stead. *The New York Times Book Review* 94:48 Je 11 '89

Educational use

See also

Tape Data Media (Firm)

Exhibitions

Audio and video: a tour of the ABA convention. J. Zinsser. il *Publishers Weekly* 236:34-6 Jl 7 '89

Folk music

Ochs, Phil: War is over. D. Browne. il *High Fidelity (New York, N.Y.)* 39:72+ Mr '89

Hunting use

A gun-shy cure that works [using tape recordings on beagles] L. Mueller. il *Outdoor Life* 184:30+ O '89

Language study use

Parlez-vous "fast forward"? N. Henderson. il *Changing Times* 43:85-6+ Mr '89

Marketing

As the 45-rpm single fades. M. Meyer. *Rolling Stone* p24 O 19 '89

The coming of audio/video phone-based promotions. I. Mayer. il *Publishers Weekly* 235:73-4 Mr 3 '89

Motion picture music

Cook, Barbara: Disney album. P. Kresh. *High Fidelity (New York, N.Y.)* 39:72 Ap '89

New Age music

A little night music [Flightpath by John Serrie] J. Kanipe. *Astronomy* 17:125 D '89

Opera

Gershwin, George: Porgy and Bess. E. Salzman. il *Stereo Review* 54:148-9 O '89

Puccini, Giacomo: Madama Butterfly. R. Ackart. il *Stereo Review* 54:120+ Je '89

TAPE RECORDINGS—Opera—cont.
A superb new "Cenerentola" from Marriner. R. Ackart. il Stereo Review 54:146 F '89

Piano music
Emanuel Ax plays Haydn sonatas [keyboard sonatas] R. Freed. por Stereo Review 54:123-4 S '89
Evgeny Kissin's debut. R. Freed. por Stereo Review 54:84 Ap '89
Looking to the East [Alan Hovhaness' Symphony no. 2 and Lousadzak; Lou Harrison's Elegiac symphony] E. Salzman. il Stereo Review 54:155 N '89
Zimerman's brilliant Liszt [Piano concertos 1 and 2; Totentanz] R. Freed. por Stereo Review 54:105 Mr '89

Psychological use
Subliminal healing [use of positive message tapes during surgery to speed recovery in hysterectomy patients] il Prevention (Emmaus, Pa.) 41:12+ Ja '89
Suggestions for recovery [use of positive message tapes during hysterectomy; research by Phil Richardson and Carlton Evans] E. Stark. Psychology Today 23:24-5 Mr '89
Tools for thought. il Health (New York, N.Y.) 21:64-5 Ap '89

Radio programs
Mind's Eye lands BBC catalogue. P. Sweeting. il Publishers Weekly 235:61 Ja 6 '89

Reggae music
Marley, Bob: Bob Marley. L. Jaffee. High Fidelity (New York, N.Y.) 39:73 My '89

Shelves and racks
See Shelves and racks

Songs
Glorious live recital from Jessye Norman. R. Freed. il por Stereo Review 54:101-2 Ja '89

Symphonies
Claudio Abbado's Mahler Ninth. D. Hall. por Stereo Review 54:106 My '89
Dohnányi conducts Schumann [Symphonies nos. 1 and 2] D. Hall. il Stereo Review 54:82 Ap '89
Looking to the East [Alan Hovhaness' Symphony no. 2 and Lousadzak; Lou Harrison's Elegiac symphony] E. Salzman. il Stereo Review 54:155 N '89
Norrington's exhilarating Beethoven [4th, 5th and 7th symphonies] D. Hall. il por Stereo Review 54:126 N '89

War songs
Homespun songs of the C.S.A. [tape of Confederate Army war songs by Bobby Horton] il American Heritage 40:122-3 S/O '89

Young adults' literature
Bantam targets retail market with young adult line. P. Sweeting and J. Zinsser. Publishers Weekly 235:49 My 5 '89

TAPE RECORDINGS AND POLITICS
S & S, Random House to release Reagan titles on audio. J. Tangorra. il pors Publishers Weekly 236:63 O 6 '89

TAPERT, ANNETTE
Belle Epoque weekends. il House & Garden 161:128-37 N '89
Creative chemistry. il Working Woman 14:106-8+ Mr '89

TAPESTRY
Exhibitions
See also
Center for Tapestry Arts (New York, N.Y.)
The 14th International Biennial of Tapestry. B. Werther. il American Craft 49:54-9 O/N '89

TAPIOCA PLANTS See Cassavas

TAPLEY, CHARLES REILLY, 1931-
about
In a right spirit. M. Gaskie. il Architectural Record 177:100-11 F '89

TAPPAN, DAVID STANTON, JR.
Trade in the Pacific Rim [address, October 28, 1988] Vital Speeches of the Day 55:217-20 Ja 15 '89

TAPPLY, WILLIAM G.
In defense of outdoorsmen. por Newsweek 113:10-11 Ap 10 '89
Tap's tips. See issues of Field & Stream
What if . . . ? The Writer 102:17-19 Ja '89

TAPS (SONG)
Song for day's end. il Southern Living 24:24 D '89

TAPSCOTT, STEPHEN, 1948-
Better none [poem] The Nation 248:96 Ja 23 '89

TAPSCOTT, STEPHEN J., AND OTHERS
5-bromo-2'-deoxyuridine blocks myogenesis by extinguishing expression of MyoD1. bibl f il Science 245:532-6 Ag 4 '89

TAR SANDS See Oil sands

TARANIK, JAMES V.
Landsat's tale of woe. il Ad Astra 1:3 Ap '89

TARANTOLA, DANIEL
National programmes. il World Health p22-4 O '89

TARANTULAS
Unusual pets. S. L. Gerstenfeld. il Parents 64:257 O '89

TARAS, JOHN
about
At American Ballet Theatre—Hermann, Smith, and Taras take up the slack. J. H. Mazo. il pors Dance Magazine 63:16-17 D '89

TARASOV, VITALY G.
(jt. auth) See Propp, Michael V., and Tarasov, Vitaly G.

TARBELL, EDMUND CHARLES, 1862-1938
about
Museum accessions. E. H. Gustafson. il Antiques 136:240 Ag '89

TARBET, URANIA CHRISTY
One artist's experience. il por American Artist 53:36-7 Jl '89

TARCHER, JEREMY P.
Here's to the end of "New Age" publishing. por Publishers Weekly 236:36 N 3 '89

TARDIGRADES See Water bears

TARDIO, AMY
In search of the perfect trainer. il Gentlemen's Quarterly 59:180-3 Ja '89

TARDIVE DYSKINESIA
Rat model of tardive dyskinesia gets boost [use of haloperidol; research by Gaylord Ellison] B. Bower. Science News 136:308 N 11 '89

TARGA FLORIO (RACE) See Automobile racing—Italy

TARGET MARKETING See Micro marketing

TARGET PRACTICE
The time for the double deuce. D. E. Petzal. il Field & Stream 93:121-2 Ap '89

TARGET RANGES See Bombing and gunnery ranges; Shooting ranges

TARGET STORES (FIRM)
This is your life [psychological evaluation test] Harper's 279:19-20+ D '89

TARGETS
Crazy clays [specialty targets for sporting clays] R. Hinton. il Outdoor Life 184:22+ S '89
Sports backdrop. S. Kingman and P. Kingman. il The Family Handyman 39:52-3 Mr '89

TARIFF
See also
Customs service
Free ports and zones
Free trade and protection
General Agreement on Tariffs and Trade

Canada
Now tariffs can't fall fast enough. T. Mason. il Business Week p80 O 23 '89

United States
See also
U.S. Customs Service
The politics of pork [dispute over import duty on Canadian pork] R. Laver. il Maclean's 102:17 S 11 '89
Treasury overrules Customs on import sport/utilities. Motor Trend 41:62-3 My '89
U.S. import duties increase for certain Brazilian products [response to failure to provide patent protection for U.S. pharmaceuticals; proclamation, October 20, 1988] R. Reagan. Department of State Bulletin 89:49 Ja '89
When is a truck not a truck? [U.S. tariff raises prices on Japanese trucks] il Consumer Reports 54:330 My '89

Western Europe
See also
European Economic Community

TARIFF, EXEMPTION FROM See Duty free importation

TARIQ ALI See Ali, Tariq

TARKANIAN, JERRY, 1930-
about
Crass and class. C. Kirkpatrick. il pors Sports Illustrated 71:56-9+ N 20 '89
Playing to win in Vegas. T. Gup. il por Time 133:56-7 Ap 3 '89

TARLOW, DICK
about
Do it yourself. B. Kanner. il por New York 22:26+ Ag 21 '89

TARLOW, ROSE
about
On Belgrave Square: a signature space for Rose Tarlow in London [cover story] E. Lambert. il por Architectural Digest 46:132-41+ Mr '89

TARLOW ADVERTISING
Do it yourself [D. Tarlow appointed executive vice president of advertising at Revlon] B. Kanner. il por New York 22:26+ Ag 21 '89

TAROT
Tarot still thrives. il Publishers Weekly 236:26 N 3 '89

TARPLEY, JIM
about
Too tough to die. P. O. D'Aulaire and E. D'Aulaire. il Reader's Digest 135:81-6 N '89

TARPON FISHING
Tarpon. A. J. McClane. il Field & Stream 94:36+ N '89

TARPY, CLIFF
Straight. il National Geographic 175:48-51 Ja '89

TARR, HERBERT
about
PW interviews. B. Levine. por Publishers Weekly 236:40-1 D 1 '89

TARRANT, BILL
Gun dogs. See issues of Field & Stream

TARSHIS, JEROME
A new exhibition proves that even when abstraction dominates, the figure remains irresistible. il *Vogue* 179:210+ D '89

TARSHIS, LAUREN
The pause that refreshes. *Harper's Bazaar* 122:32+ Je '89

TARTARIC ACID
Transmembrane channels based on tartaric acid-gramicidin A hybrids. C. J. Stankovic and others. bibl f il *Science* 244:813-17 My 19 '89

TARTS
1-2-3 pear tart. il *Good Housekeeping* 209:82 O '89
Very nutty tarts. il *Sunset (Central West edition)* 183:92-3 N '89

TARUSKIN, RICHARD
The opera and the dictator. il *The New Republic* 200:34-40 Mr 20 '89

TASADAY (PHILIPPINE PEOPLE)
Anthropologists debate Tasaday hoax evidence. E. Marshall. il *Science* 246:1113-14 D 1 '89
The strange case of the Tasaday: were they primitive hunter-gatherers or rain-forest phonies? [cover story] B. Bower. il *Science News* 135:280-1+ My 6 '89
Tasaday controversy grows more curious. B. Bower. *Science News* 136:343 N 25 '89

TASHIAN, BARRY
about
Trust in the Tashians. A. Nash. pors *Stereo Review* 54:128 O '89

TASHIAN, HOLLY
about
Trust in the Tashians. A. Nash. pors *Stereo Review* 54:128 O '89

TASHJIAN, RALPH
about
Payola probe back on track. M. Goldberg. *Rolling Stone* p22 Je 15 '89

TASINI, JONATHAN
What authors want from publishers. por *Publishers Weekly* 235:46 F 10 '89

TASKER, RODNEY, AND HIEBERT, MURRAY
Cambodia's test of wills—and arms. il *World Press Review* 36:34+ D '89

TASMANIA (AUSTRALIA)
See also
Paleontology—Tasmania (Australia)

TASS (SOVIET UNION)
Elvis spotted in Estonia! [reports UFO sighting in Soviet Union] H. G. Chua-Eoan. il *Time* 134:52 O 23 '89
Glasnost enters the Twilight Zone [UFO sighting] A. Wilson-Smith. *Maclean's* 102:30 O 23 '89
They came from outer space [reports on UFO sighting in provincial Russian city] C. Bogert. il *Newsweek* 114:42 O 23 '89
Too late for Tsar Wars, aliens visit the U.S.S.R. il *People Weekly* 32:120 O 30 '89

TASSELS
Beyond the fringe. M. Guralnick. il *House & Garden* 161:168 D '89
Loafer with the fringe on top [tasseled shoes] J. Morgan. il *Gentlemen's Quarterly* 59:39 Je '89

TASSI, FRANCO
about
The lone ranger. D. Starr. il *Omni (New York, N.Y.)* 12:102+ N '89

TASTE
See also
Sweetness
Going for the great-taste health diet [eating farm produce] R. Rodale. il *Prevention (Emmaus, Pa.)* 41:30+ F '89
Low-fat foods with a high-fat pleasure quotient. M. A. Gilman. il *Psychology Today* 23:50 Je '89
Palate training. B. L. Benderly. il *Health (New York, N.Y.)* 21:56-7+ Jl '89
A question of taste. M. Cox. il *Omni (New York, N.Y.)* 11:42-4+ F '89
Taste buds engage in cross-talk [research by Stephen D. Roper] R. Weiss. *Science News* 136:317 N 11 '89

TASTE BUDS *See* Taste
TASTE TESTING OF COFFEE *See* Coffee tasting
TASTE TESTING OF WINE *See* Wine tasting

TATE, CASSANDRA
In the 1800s, antismoking was a burning issue. bibl f (p122) il *Smithsonian* 20:107-8+ Jl '89

TATE, JEFFREY
about
Jeffrey Tate. H. Kupferberg. il pors *Stereo Review* 54:86-8 My '89

TATE GALLERY
Getting the hang of it [director N. Serota] E. Beck. il por *Art News* 88:117-18 Mr '89

TATSUMI, SOTOO
about
"The other banks feel threatened". A. Tanzer. il por *Forbes* 144:80+ O 2 '89

TATTOOING
Geraldo's compromising tattoo. J. Marion. il por *TV Guide* 37:21 My 13-19 '89

Her roses are red and black and blue. Does Patti need a 7th tattoo? [P. D'Arbanville] L. Eisenberg. il por *TV Guide* 37:15 Jl 8-14 '89
The tattoo. J. Berendt. il *Esquire* 112:32 Ag '89

TATU, MICHEL
Remember Khrushchev. *World Press Review* 36:24 F '89

TAUB, A. I. (ALAN I.), AND FLEISCHER, R. L.
Intermetallic compounds for high-temperature structural use. bibl f il *Science* 243:616-21 F 3 '89

TAUBER, PETER
Not just another funny face. il pors *The New York Times Magazine* p26-7+ F 26 '89

TAUBIN, AMY
Up and Atom. il por *Film Comment* 25:27-9 N/D '89

TAUIL, PEDRO LUIZ
Schisto in Brazil . . . il *World Health* p24-5 D '88

TAUKE, THOMAS J.
Should the House-passed wage proposal be enacted? [excerpts from address, March 23, 1989] *Congressional Digest* 68:153+ My '89

TAURUS (LAUNCH VEHICLE) *See* Space vehicles—Propulsion systems

TAVANI, GIUSEPPE
The quest for authenticity. il *The Courier (Unesco)* 42:14-17 My '89

TAVERNA, KATHRYN
about
Lodz ghetto [film] Reviews
The Christian Century 106:251-2 Mr 8 '89. J. M. Wall

TAVERNS *See* Bars and barrooms

TAVRIS, CAROL
Don't act your age! il *American Health* 8:50-2+ Jl/Ag '89
Mind health. See issues of Vogue

TAWC *See* Tactical Air Warfare Center (U.S.)

TAX, JEREMIAH
Whoa, whippersnapper! il por *Sports Illustrated* 71:90 Ag 14 '89

TAX, MEREDITH
Father knows best [discussion of May 8, 1989 article, March to a crossroads on abortion] *The Nation* 249:110+ Jl 24-31 '89
March to a crossroads on abortion [cover story] *The Nation* 248:613+ My 8 '89

TAX AUDITING
A battle of words with the IRS [dispute over hobby loss deductions] M. Foster. il *Nation's Business* 77:42+ Mr '89
Ex-IRS agents reveal four moves that seem sure to trigger an audit this year. il *Money* 18:181-2 Mr '89
Filing a tax return that doesn't set off alarms. C. Yang. il *Business Week* p104-5 Mr 6 '89
How to avoid a tax audit. G. Worth. il *Working Woman* 14:86-8 Mr '89
How to survive a tax audit. il *Consumer Reports* 54:172-6 Mr '89
Prepaying possible interest on a disputed tax liability. G. W. Padwe. il *Nation's Business* 77:89 O '89
Sleeping easy. P. N. Strassels. il *Nation's Business* 77:74 S '89
Will the IRS audit you? D. M. Topolnicki. *Good Housekeeping* 209:252 O '89

TAX COLLECTION
See also
Canada. Revenue Canada
Tax penalties
United States. Internal Revenue Service
Congress has leveled the playing field for contests with the tax man [Taxpayer Bill of Rights] *U.S. News & World Report* 106:79 Mr 27 '89
A tax windfall could help pare the deficit . . . and sinking rates might chop it even more. G. Koretz. il *Business Week* p20 My 29 '89
Your rights as a taxpayer. *Consumers' Research Magazine* 72:20-4 Mr '89
Your rights as a taxpayer: now they're in writing. C. Yang. il *Business Week* p103 F 13 '89

TAX CONSULTANTS
A C.P.A. earns his $120 an hour by saving a couple time and worry [Dudley Ryan prepares returns for Bruce and Ann Nerland] E. Schurenberg. il *Money* 18:55 Ja '89
Free tax advice for artists. D. Grant. *American Artist* 53:12+ D '89
Funniest accountant in America [G. Press] il por *Changing Times* 43:29 F '89
How to work with your tax preparer. J. Edgerton. il *Money* 18:67-70+ Ja '89
Lining up a first-rate preparer. L. H. Towle. il *Money* 18:64-5 Ja '89
Preparing for the big event [organizing personal records for tax preparers] il *Changing Times* 43:30 F '89
The pros flunk our new tax-return test. G. Anrig, Jr. il *Money* 18:110-12+ Mr '89

TAX COURT (U.S.) *See* United States. Tax Court
TAX COURTS
See also
United States. Tax Court

TAX CREDITS
    See also
    Investment tax credit
An appealing employee benefit: tax savings for child and elder care. M. Rowland. *Working Woman* 14:92 O '89
Bush clarifies position on tuition tax credits. K. A. Lawton. *Christianity Today* 33:55 My 12 '89
Fate of R&D tax credit uncertain. M. Crawford. *Science* 243:1659 Mr 31 '89
Filing for dollars [earned income tax credit available to working poor] P. Simpson. *Ms.* 17:74 My '89
Help the working poor. R. J. Samuelson. il *Newsweek* 113:52 My 1 '89
Helping children: income tax reform. A. C. Carlson. *Current (Washington, D.C.)* 314:12-15 Jl/Ag '89
How to help the working poor [dependent care tax credits] B. Cohn. il *Newsweek* 114:26 Ag 7 '89
The IRS's new rules for the nursery [child care credits] L. Wiener. il *U.S. News & World Report* 106:70 Ap 10 '89
Letter from the president [child care tax credits] G. Bush. il por *Parents* 64:45 Mr '89
Maybe we'll need it someday—maybe [tax credits for coalbed methane development] T. Mack. il *Forbes* 143:42-3 Ja 23 '89
The rich aren't the only ones who may get a tax break. S. B. Garland and H. Gleckman. il *Business Week* p37 Ag 21 '89
Them's the breaks [George Bush's tax proposals] *The New Republic* 200:7-8 F 27 '89

TAX CUTS, CORPORATE *See* Corporations—Taxation
TAX DEDUCTIONS *See* Income tax—Deductions
TAX EVASION
    See also
    Tax penalties
    Tax resistance
    Underground economy
After the IRS comes to collect, an angry Redd Foxx starts playing to an empty house. il por *People Weekly* 32:68 D 18 '89
At last, a verdict fit for a Queen [L. Helmsley found guilty] il por *Newsweek* 114:61 S 11 '89
The case of the singing CPA [J. Checksfield gives IRS details of his client's tax evasion] *Newsweek* 114:41 Jl 17 '89
A commoner's royal pain [L. Helmsley case] il por *Newsweek* 114:55 Jl 17 '89
Debtor's prison [L. LaRouche sentenced for tax evasion and fraud] por *Time* 133:33 F 6 '89
Did Refco help take Uncle Sam to the cleaners? [dodging taxes through phony London trading] D. Greising. il *Business Week* p33-4 O 2 '89
The Dinkins stock crash [D. Dinkins accused of undervaluation of Inner City Broadcasting stock] C. Byron. il *New York* 22:30+ N 6 '89
A first world fugitive dabbles in the third world [M. Rich] J. Zweig. por *Forbes* 144:12 N 13 '89
How to stay out of trouble. W. Baldwin. il *Forbes* 144:218+ O 2 '89
Jim Moran, master salesman. G. Button. il pors *Forbes* 144 Special Issue:54-5+ O 23 '89
Leona Helmsley: the original Material Girl. B. G. Harrison. *Mademoiselle* 95:104 D '89
Letters from home [tax fugitive M. Rich gets U.S. export subsidies on wheat deals with the Soviets] J. Willoughby. il por *Forbes* 143:38-9 Je 12 '89
Middle-aged delinquents. D. Seligman. il *Fortune* 120:232 D 18 '89
The 'Queen' on trial [L. Helmsley] L. Black. il pors *Maclean's* 102:49+ Ag 14 '89
A Queen on trial [L. Helmsley; cover story] H. F. Waters. il pors *Newsweek* 114:46-51 Ag 21 '89
Queen, pawns, checkmate [L. Helmsley; cover story] J. S. Kunen. il pors *People Weekly* 32:94-9 S 11 '89
The Queen stands trial [L. Helmsley] P. Painton. il por *Time* 134:66 Jl 24 '89
Redd Foxx faces homeless holidays; IRS seizes property. A. Collier. il pors *Jet* 77:52-8 D 18 '89
Revenge of the little people [L. Helmsley convicted] M. B. Carlson. il por *Time* 134:27 S 11 '89
The trial of Donald and Si Newhouse [cover story] R. Pollak. il *The Nation* 248:325+ Mr 13 '89
What if Leona leaves the Palace for the pokey? A. Rothman. il por *Business Week* p79+ Jl 24 '89
Who cheats? D. Seligman. il *Fortune* 120:203 O 9 '89

TAX EXEMPTION *See* Taxation, Exemption from
TAX FORMS *See* Tax returns
TAX FRAUD *See* Tax evasion
TAX FREEDOM DAY
The day you stop paying taxes. il *Consumers' Research Magazine* 72:24-5 Ap '89
TAX LAWS AND REGULATIONS *See* Income tax; Taxation
TAX LOOPHOLES *See* Taxation, Exemption from
TAX PENALTIES
Estimate carefully to avoid penalties; Penalty proliferation. G. W. Padwe. il *Nation's Business* 77:72 My '89
How the IRS aims to simplify tax penalties. C. Yang. *Business Week* p38 Mr 13 '89

Taking the kinks out of tangled IRS penalties. C. Yang. il *Business Week* p105 Ag 21 '89
TAX PREPARERS *See* Tax consultants
TAX RECORDS
Check your mail carefully. P. N. Strassels. il *Nation's Business* 77:58 F '89
Checklist: what you need to collect. H. Wheelwright. il *Money* 18:75+ Ja '89
Preparing for the big event [organizing personal records for tax preparers] il *Changing Times* 43:30 F '89
TAX REFORM *See* Income tax
TAX REFUNDS
Do you know where yours is? T. Tritch. il *Money* 18:196+ Je '89
Getting a good return [value added tax refunds to shoppers in Europe] D. P. Marshall. il *Travel Holiday* 171:28+ F '89
Rerouted refunds and other reasons to adjust withholding. P. N. Strassels. il *Nation's Business* 77:70 Ag '89
TAX RELATIONS, INTERGOVERNMENTAL *See* Intergovernmental tax relations
TAX RESISTANCE
No payment enclosed: why I resist war taxes [cover story] A. Ayvazian. il *The Progressive* 53:19-21 Ap '89
Taxation hesitation. C. Norton. il *Mother Jones* 14:42-3 Ap '89
TAX RETURNS
    See also
    Computers—Tax return use
10 errors to avoid this year. H. Wheelwright. il *Money* 18:83-5 Ja '89
Keys to the forms. G. Anrig, Jr. il *Money* 18:90-1 Ja '89
Need more time to file? [extensions] P. N. Strassels. il *Nation's Business* 77:86 Ap '89
Postcard form promises reform [system devised by Robert E. Hall and Alvin Rabushka] il *USA Today (Periodical)* 118:9-10 D '89
The pros flunk our new tax-return test. G. Anrig, Jr. il *Money* 18:110-12+ Mr '89
To file is human, to amend divine: changes in the law make it worthwhile to check old returns. L. Wiener. il *U.S. News & World Report* 106:64 Ja 9 '89
Year-end tax savers. K. McCormally. il *Changing Times* 43:94-6+ D '89

Anecdotes, facetiae, satire, etc.
Sanity clause. B. Ehrenreich. il *Mother Jones* 14:8+ Ap '89
Auditing
    See Tax auditing
TAX SHELTERS
    See also
    Gifts to minors
Eyesores into showplaces—even without a tax break [rehabbing] J. Weber, Jr. il *Business Week* p36 Ja 16 '89
Home is where the shelter is [taxation rules on house sales] G. W. Padwe. il *Nation's Business* 77:67 Mr '89
Restoring the rehab tax credit. M. F. Schmertz. *Architectural Record* 177:11 Ag '89
A sexy new tax shelter from across the Atlantic [British preferred stock] L. Jereski. *Business Week* p108 Je 12 '89
A shrinking market in rehab? Not necessarily. il *Architectural Record* 177:33 O '89
Tax shelters for the not so rich. B. G. Quint. il *Glamour* 87:108+ Je '89
TAXATION
    See also
    Advertising—Taxation
    Aged—Taxation
    Alternative minimum tax
    Americans—Foreign countries—Taxation
    Annuities—Taxation
    Artists—Taxation
    Authors—Taxation
    Automobile industry—Taxation
    Automobiles—Taxation
    Aviation—Taxation
    Bank accounts—Taxation
    Banks and banking, International—Taxation
    Blacks—Taxation
    Business entertaining—Taxation
    Capital gains tax
    Cash flow tax
    Certificates of annuity—Taxation
    Children—Taxation
    Cigarettes—Taxation
    Conservation easements—Taxation
    Consumption tax
    Corporations—Taxation
    Corporations, International—Taxation
    Dividends—Taxation
    Domicile in taxation
    Employee stock ownership plans—Taxation
    Estate planning
    Excise tax
    Family corporations—Taxation
    Farmers—Taxation
    Football, Professional—Super Bowl—Taxation
    Gas industry—Taxation

TAXATION—See also—*cont.*
Gasoline—Taxation
Gifts—Taxation
Greenmail—Taxation
Home-based business—Taxation
Home offices—Taxation
Household employees—Taxation
Income tax
Independent contractors—Taxation
Industrial research—Taxation
Inheritance tax
Insurance, Disaster—Taxation
Insurance, Health—Taxation
Insurance, Life—Taxation
Insurance companies—Taxation
Interest (Economics)—Taxation
Intergovernmental tax relations
Inventories—Taxation
Investment trusts—Taxation
Investments—Taxation
Junk bonds—Taxation
Leveraged buyouts—Taxation
Limited partnership—Taxation
Lotteries—Taxation
Mail order business—Taxation
Married couples—Taxation
Mass media industry—Taxation
Middle classes—Taxation
Mortgages—Taxation
Nonprofit institutions—Taxation
Packaging—Taxation
Palestinian Arabs—Taxation
Pensions—Taxation
Personal holding companies—Taxation
Poll tax
Poor—Taxation
Public utilities—Taxation
Publishers and publishing—Taxation
Put and call transactions—Taxation
Real estate business—Taxation
Real estate exchanges—Taxation
Real property—Taxation
Retirement benefits—Taxation
Rich—Taxation
S corporations
Sales tax
Savings bonds—Taxation
Securities—Taxation
Social security—Taxation
Tax Freedom Day
Tithes
Trusts and trustees—Taxation
United States. Dept. of the Treasury
United States. Internal Revenue Service
United States. Tax Court
Value added tax
White collar workers—Taxation
Witchcraft—Taxation
Withholding tax
Women executives—Taxation
A benign tax increase—the myth that won't die. P. C. Roberts. il *Business Week* p22 Ja 9 '89
CEOs to Bush: raise taxes now. D. Kirkpatrick. il *Fortune* 119:95-6 Ja 16 '89
For your tax file. G. W. Padwe. See issues of Nation's Business beginning July 1983
For your tax file. P. N. Strassels. See issues of Nation's Business beginning April 1988
Guidelines for President Bush. T. Bethell. il *The American Spectator* 22:11-13 Ja '89
A new Federal tax service from Matthew Bender. J. Wisdom. il *Publishers Weekly* 236:50 S 8 '89
Now it's time for Congress to read voters' lips on tax increases. *Nation's Business* 77:71 F '89
Quack! Quack! Quack! [tax increases in 1990 budget] *Time* 134:48 D 4 '89
Read our lips. il *The New Republic* 200:9-10 Ja 30 '89
Tax letter. See issues of Money beginning June 1989
Tax paranoia is causing gridlock on the Hill. H. Gleckman. il *Business Week* p43 My 29 '89
Taxing matters. See issues of Forbes
Your taxes. See issues of Money through March 1989
Collection
See Tax collection
History
Taxation: the American way. W. E. Brownlee. *Current (Washington, D.C.)* 315:11-17 S '89
California
The quake may shake more taxes out of Californians. R. D. Hof and J. B. Levine. il *Business Week* p42 N 6 '89
See also
Canada. Revenue Canada
Capital gains tax—Canada
Canada [address, December 7, 1988] M. W. Barrett. *Vital Speeches of the Day* 55:345-6 Mr 15 '89
Canada

Canada attacks prosperity. *National Review* 41:16+ Je 30 '89
A search for savings. B. Wallace. il *Maclean's* 102:15 Ap 3 '89
The tax squeeze [furor over leaked budget; cover story; special section; with editorial comment by Kevin Doyle] il *Maclean's* 102:2, 10-12+ My 8 '89
Egypt
History
Think that taxes take a big bite today? L. Casson. il *Smithsonian* 19:122-7 Mr '89
Iowa
Black woman heads IRS district office in Iowa [H. Hightower] por *Jet* 75:6 Mr 6 '89
Louisiana
'I feel like a dentist pulling teeth' [B. Roemer] M. Ivey. il *Business Week* p64 F 27 '89
Maine
See also
Income tax—Maine
New Hampshire
See also
Income tax—New Hampshire
New York (State)
See also
Income tax—New York (State)
New York (N.Y.)—Taxation
United States
See Taxation
Western Europe
See also
Value added tax—Western Europe
TAXATION, DOUBLE
See also
Americans—Foreign countries—Taxation
TAXATION, EXEMPTION FROM
How to pay $0 taxes. R. Wool. il *Money* 18:163-4+ Ap '89
How you can still cut your taxes [cover story] R. Wool. il *Money* 18:84-6+ S '89
Nonprofit groups: an unfair edge? D. C. Bacon. il *Nation's Business* 77:33-4 Ap '89
The tax-exempt witch [coven of witches deserves tax-exempt status as a legitimate religious group] T. K. Jones. *Christianity Today* 33:15 O 6 '89
Two reporters you don't want on your tail [D. L. Barlett and J. B. Steele receive Pulitzer Prize for articles on tax loopholes] J. Alter. il pors *Newsweek* 113:71+ Ap 24 '89
TAXATION, STATE
See also
Sales tax
Dread my lips [tax hikes] *Time* 133:35 My 1 '89
Keeping the state out of your estate. R. R. Roha. il *Changing Times* 43:73-8 N '89
Pigging out on tax shelters [single state municipal bond funds] K. McCormally. il *Changing Times* 43:45-9+ Je '89
The states and your estate plan. il *Fortune* 120 no10 Special Issue:198-9 Fall '89
TAXATION FOR EDUCATION *See* Education—Finance
TAXATION OF ARTICLES OF CONSUMPTION *See* Consumption tax
TAXATION OF WORKS OF ART
A $60 million van Gogh? [P. Harriman's donation of Roses to the National Gallery] R. W. Walker. il *Art News* 88:31 S '89
The anxious acquisitors. L. Rosenbaum. il *Art News* 88:144-51 Mr '89
Reforming the Tax Reform Act [proposed amendment affecting art donations] R. W. Walker. *Art News* 88:45 N '89
TAXCO (MEXICO)
Description
Cuernavaca and Taxco. P. J. Bell. il *Gourmet* 49:64-9+ F '89
TAXI AND LIMOUSINE COMMISSION (NEW YORK, N.Y.) *See* New York (N.Y.). Taxi and Limousine Commission
TAXICAB DRIVERS
T.L.C. [appearance before Taxi and Limousine Commission in New York City] *The New Yorker* 65:25-6 Ag 21 '89
Anecdotes, facetiae, satire, etc.
Braking Glass [P. Glass as taxicab driver] J. Queenan. il *The American Spectator* 22:27 Ap '89
TAXICABS
See also
New York (N.Y.)—Taxicabs
Portland (Or.)—Taxicabs
San Francisco (Calif.)—Taxicabs
TAXICABS IN CRIME PREVENTION
Fare's fare, but when cabdriver Chuck Hollom goes off the meter, criminals had better look out [San Francisco] W. Plummer. il pors *People Weekly* 32:97-8 S 25 '89
TAXICABS IN MEDICAL CARE
Portland taxis: on hailing and healing. E. E. Rosenbaum. il *New Choices for the Best Years* 29:22+ Ja '89
A TAXING WOMAN'S RETURN [film] See Motion picture reviews—Single works

TAXONOMY *See* Biology—Classification; Botany—Classification
TAY-SACHS DISEASE
Mutation revealed for adult Tay-Sachs [work of Ruth Navon and Richard L. Proia] I. Wickelgren. *Science News* 135:167 Mr 18 '89
The mutations in Ashkenazi Jews with adult G_{M2} gangliosidosis, the adult form of Tay-Sachs disease. R. Navon and R. L. Proia. bibl f il *Science* 243:1471-4 Mr 17 '89
TAYE, JOHN
                        about
John Taye's basswood sculptures. D. B. Vaughn. il por *American Artist* 53:60-5 Ap '89
TAYLOR, BARRY N.
New measurement standards for 1990 [cover story] bibl f il *Physics Today* 42 pt1:23-6 Ag '89
(jt. auth) See Cohen, E. Richard, and Taylor, Barry N.
TAYLOR, BERNARD J., II
                        about
"They never put jackets on again". J. Novack. il por *Forbes* 144:120+ O 2 '89
TAYLOR, CECIL
                        about
Cecil Taylor—the Feel Trio: Sweet Basil/New York. S. Stein. il por *Down Beat* 56:55 My '89
John Coltrane-Cecil Taylor-Art Blakey: Philharmonic Hall, Lincoln Center, New York City [reprint] I. A. Baraka. il *Down Beat* 56:62 S '89
TAYLOR, D. J. (DAVID JOHN)
The decline of the English novel. *World Press Review* 36:59 F '89
TAYLOR, D. SCOTT
Room without a view. il *Natural History* p26+ S '89
TAYLOR, DANIEL, 1948-
The fear of insignificance. il *Christianity Today* 33:25-6 F 3 '89
TAYLOR, DAVID JOHN *See* Taylor, D. J. (David John)
TAYLOR, DENNY, 1947-
Toward a unified theory of literacy learning and instructional practices [cover story] bibl f il *Phi Delta Kappan* 71:184-93 N '89
TAYLOR, EDWARD PLUNKET
                        about
Obituary
    Maclean's il 102:44+ My 29 '89. P. C. Newman
TAYLOR, ELEANOR ROSS, 1920-
Balance brought forward [poem] *The New Yorker* 64:32 Ja 16 '89
Salting the oatmeal [poem] *The New Yorker* 64:94 F 6 '89
TAYLOR, ELIZABETH, 1932-
                        about
Liz Taylor's aching back and yours! G. McBride. il por *Ladies' Home Journal* 106:80+ Je '89
Liz toasts Roddy McDowall's photo book, and the old pals make quite a picture. il pors *People Weekly* 32:91-2+ N 6 '89
Love story [excerpt from Richard Burton] M. Bragg. pors *Ladies' Home Journal* 106:103-5+ Ja '89
Malcolm Forbes, a very good pal, arrives at Liz's house bearing gifts. il pors *People Weekly* 31:152-3 Je 19 '89
My daughter Elizabeth (I). S. Taylor. il pors *Good Housekeeping* 208:113-15+ Mr '89
My daughter Elizabeth (II). S. Taylor. il pors *Good Housekeeping* 208:130-1+ Ap '89
On 'Sweet bird' Liz is the 600-pound canary [cover story] E. Warren. il pors *TV Guide* 37:10-12 S 30-O 6 '89
Still reigning after all these years [cover story] S. Schindehette. il pors *People Weekly* 31:80-1+ Mr 13 '89
TAYLOR, JACK
                        about
How do you build a luxury image? J. Flint. il pors *Forbes* 143:60-3 Ap 3 '89
TAYLOR, JAMES B.
Airlines ignore a crucial market: air taxis for business travelers. por *Aviation Week & Space Technology* 130:73-4 Jl 10 '89
TAYLOR, JANA
                        about
Jana Taylor gives new focus to the lives of inner-city kids. S. Schindehette. il pors *People Weekly* 31:126-7+ Ap 3 '89
TAYLOR, JOAN
Books. See issues of The Conservationist
TAYLOR, JOAN CHATFIELD- *See* Chatfield-Taylor, Joan
TAYLOR, JOHN, 1955-
The ad brats. il pors *New York* 22:50-6 N 13 '89
Alpine echoes above Lake Tahoe. il *Architectural Digest* 46:84-91 Jl '89
Bank shot: Edmond Safra turns the tables on American Express. il pors *New York* 22:42-7 S 18 '89
Bright as Dawn, strong as Steel. il pors *New York* 22:40-7 My 29 '89
Different strokes: eleven kids from Brooklyn try life on a kibbutz. il por *New York* 22:56-8+ Je 12 '89
The funny guy's book of life. il pors *New York* 22:46-50 O 9 '89

High style in Manhattan. il *Architectural Digest* 46:134-41 D '89
Holier than thou. il pors *New York* 22:32-7 Mr 27 '89
Living on the edge: old New York is new again. il *New York* 22:52-7 D 25 '89-Ja 1 '90
Malcolm Forbes in Fiji: the publisher's private island in the South Seas. il por *Architectural Digest* 46:180-8+ F '89
Minimalism in Miami. il *Architectural Digest* 46:216-21+ Ap '89
The new Roy Cohn [cover story] il pors *New York* 22:18-25 Ag 7 '89
Party palace: the high life at the gilded Metropolitan Museum [cover story] il *New York* 22:20-30 Ja 9 '89
Pushing the outer limits. il *New York* 22:84-6+ Ap 10 '89
TAYLOR, JOHN J.
Improved and safer nuclear power. bibl f il *Science* 244:318-25 Ap 21 '89
TAYLOR, JOHN M., 1930-
Collect autographs. il *Americana* 17:13-15 Jl/Ag '89
TAYLOR, JOHN MARTIN
Liguria. il *The New York Times Magazine* p41-2 Ag 27 '89
TAYLOR, JOHN RUSSELL
Man of a thousand faces. il pors *American Film* 14:52-6 Ap '89
TAYLOR, LONN
Hispanic cabinetmakers and the Anglo-American aesthetic. bibl f il *Antiques* 136:554-67 S '89
Trappings of the American West [cover story] il *American Craft* 49:42-51 D '89/Ja '90
TAYLOR, LOUISE, 1949-
(jt. auth) See Cohen, Barbara E., 1949-, and Taylor, Louise, 1949-
TAYLOR, MESHACH
                        about
Why Meshach Taylor is laughing all the way to the bank. I. Rudolph. por *TV Guide* 37:23 N 11-17 '89
TAYLOR, MICHAEL RAY
Following the wind. il pors *Audubon* 91:90-9 Ja '89
TAYLOR, OTHA
                        about
Family illness prevents Otha Taylor from going to Bush's inauguration. il por *Jet* 75:58 F 6 '89
TAYLOR, PAMELA
A family affair. il *Black Enterprise* 19:66-7 Ja '89
TAYLOR, PAUL
East Side story. il *Vogue* 179:356-61+ My '89
TAYLOR, PAUL, 1930-
                        about
Dancing:
    Speaking in tongues and other works presented at City Center. A. Croce. *The New Yorker* 65:78-80 My 1 '89
Dogged dualists. L. A. Jacobs. por *The New Leader* 72:22-3 Je 12-26 '89
Men and angels. T. Tobias. il *New York* 22:81-2 My 8 '89
Paul Taylor, Santo Loquasto and Speaking in tongues: the right mix. N. V. Dalva. il *Dance Magazine* 63:36-8 Ap '89
Speaking in tongues [dance] Reviews
    America 160:430 My 6 '89. G. G. Seibert
TAYLOR, R. LEE, II
                        about
Shareholders say 'thanks' to these CEOs. D. Foust and M. Roman. il pors *Business Week* p48 My 1 '89
TAYLOR, RICH, 1946-
Car care. See issues of Motor Trend beginning March 1989
TAYLOR, ROBERT CHATFIELD- *See* Chatfield-Taylor, Robert
TAYLOR, ROBERT R.
                        about
Bob Taylor wants to walk away from his Obsession. M. J. Pitzer. il por *Business Week* p44 Mr 20 '89
A little rest for the weary. C. Siler. il por *Forbes* 144:304 D 11 '89
TAYLOR, RUSSEL R.
Principles to grow by [excerpt from Exceptional entrepreneurial women] il *Nation's Business* 77:50-1 Jl '89
TAYLOR, SALLY ADAMSON
Transpacific. See occasional issues of Publishers Weekly beginning February 17, 1989
TAYLOR, SARA
My daughter Elizabeth (I). il pors *Good Housekeeping* 208:113-15+ Mr '89
My daughter Elizabeth (II). il pors *Good Housekeeping* 208:130-1+ Ap '89
TAYLOR, STEVE
The farm kitchen. il *Country Journal* 16:37 F '89
TAYLOR, SUSAN L.
In the spirit. See issues of Essence
TAYLOR, THEODORE B., AND DRELL, SIDNEY D. (SIDNEY DAVID), 1926-
Nuclear abolition: would cheaters count? [discussion of July/August 1989 article, Why not now?] il *The Bulletin of the Atomic Scientists* 45:16-17 D '89

TAYLOR, THEODORE B., AND DRELL, SIDNEY D. (SIDNEY DAVID), 1926—*cont.*
Why not now? Debating a nuclear-free millennium [excerpts from debate, March 11, 1989] il *The Bulletin of the Atomic Scientists* 45:25-31 Jl/Ag '89
TAYLOR, TOM
about
Lone Star fakes. L. Belkin. il pors *The New York Times Magazine* p66+ D 10 '89
TAYLOR, VALERIE, AND BERLIN, ANN
The instant office. il *New York* 22:104+ My 1 '89
Twofer the seesaw. il *New York* 22:130+ My 1 '89
TAYLOR, WILLIAM O., 1932-
about
Boston's accidental demibillionaires. M. Fritz. il por *Forbes* 144 Special Issue:112+ O 23 '89
TAYLOR-CORBETT, LYNNE
about
To dream of roses [film] Reviews
Dance Magazine il 63:14 S '89. C. Lefevre
TAYLOR-SMITH, SHELLEY
about
The other New York marathon. J. Ridge. il *Women's Sports & Fitness* 11:56-7 N/D '89
TBILISI (AIRCRAFT CARRIER)
Soviet aircraft conduct flight trials from new, large-deck carrier Tbilisi. il *Aviation Week & Space Technology* 131:113 D 18-25 '89
TBILISI (SOVIET UNION)
Riots
U.S. physicians probe deaths in Soviet Georgia [use of riot control agent chloropicrin by Soviet troops] C. Norman. il *Science* 244:1133 Je 9 '89
TC² See Textile/Clothing Technology Corporation
TCA (TERMINAL CONTROL AREAS) See Air traffic control
TCAS (TRAFFIC ALERT AND COLLISION AVOIDANCE SYSTEMS) See Airplanes—Collision avoidance systems
TCBY ENTERPRISES INC.
A fatty stock. E. Schmuckler. il *Forbes* 143:133 Je 26 '89
TCHAIKOVSKY, PETER ILICH, 1840-1893
about
Christmas dream work. P. Kennicott. il *Dance Magazine* 63:67 D '89
Eugene Onegin [opera] Reviews
Opera News il 53:26-9 Mr 18 '89
"A Russian musician". D. Harris. il pors *Opera News* 53:30-2 Mr 18 '89
TDF See Testis determining factor
TDRS (TRACKING AND DATA RELAY SATELLITE) SYSTEM See Communications satellites
TEA (BEVERAGE)
See also
Teas
Australian convicted in 'Cho Low' fraud [P. Foster's mail order scheme selling Chinese tea to lower cholesterol] il por *FDA Consumer* 23:35 D '89/Ja '90
TEA INDUSTRY
See also
Celestial Seasonings Inc.
Marketing
Change is brewing in tea. M. Rowland. il *Working Woman* 14:85-6 Ap '89
TEA POTS See Teapots
TEA TABLES See Tables
TEACH, EDWARD See Blackbeard, 1680?-1718
TEACHER ACCOUNTABILITY See Accountability (Education)
TEACHER CENTERS
See also
Academy for the Advancement of Teaching and Management
TEACHER EDUCATION See Teachers—Education
TEACHER OF THE YEAR AWARD See Teachers—Awards
TEACHER OPINION See Teachers—Attitudes
TEACHER-PARENT CONFERENCES See School and the home
TEACHER PARTICIPATION IN SCHOOL MANAGEMENT See School management and organization—Teacher participation
TEACHER-PUPIL RELATIONSHIP See Teachers and students
TEACHERS
See also
Academic freedom
Aerobics teachers
Art teachers
Arts teachers
Biology teachers
Black teachers
College teachers
English teachers
Labor unions—Teachers
Mathematics teachers
Minority teachers
National Education Association of the United States
Nuns as teachers
Physics teachers
School and the home

School management and organization—Teacher participation
Science teachers
Special education teachers
Strikes—Teachers
Teaching
After a year as a fifth-grade Gulliver, author Tracy Kidder speaks up for teachers [writes book about C. Zajac's class in Holyoke, Mass.] K. Hubbard. il pors *People Weekly* 32:77+ O 9 '89
Can educational research keep pace with education reform? [need for teachers to participate in research] J. M. Atkin. bibl f il *Phi Delta Kappan* 71:200-5 N '89
First days in first grade. P. La Farge. il pors *Parents* 64:104-8+ S '89
From 'House' to schoolhouse [T. Kidder's study of C. Zajac, fifth grade teacher in Holyoke, Mass.] C. Leslie. il por *Newsweek* 114:67 S 11 '89
The future of teaching. L. Darling-Hammond. *The Education Digest* 54:7-10 Mr '89
Must principals have teaching experience? [requirement eliminated in New Jersey] S. Cooperman. *The Education Digest* 54:11-12 Mr '89
The principles of teacher empowerment. G. I. Maeroff. *The Education Digest* 54:6-9 F '89
PW interviews [T. Kidder, author of book about fifth grade class in Holyoke, Mass.] A. Smith. por *Publishers Weekly* 236:101-2 S 15 '89
The teacher-artist. M. D. Griffin. *The Education Digest* 54:29-31 Ap '89
Teacher professionalism and accountability. L. Darling-Hammond. *The Education Digest* 55:15-19 S '89
Teaching experience: a must for principals. S. D. Thomson. *The Education Digest* 54:11-15 Ap '89
When teachers fail: what parents can do about it. P. Welsh. il *TV Guide* 37:18-20 S 2-8 '89
Why principals should first be teachers [critique of New Jersey's decision to remove teaching experience as a qualification] J. W. Guthrie. *The Education Digest* 54:13-15 Mr '89
Attitudes
No more teacher's dirty looks [how prospective teachers perceive problem behavior; research by Bruce Cunningham and Alan Sugawara] G. W. Bracey. il *Phi Delta Kappan* 70:561 Mr '89
School texts: the outlook of teachers. V. R. Rogers. *The Education Digest* 54:24-6 Ja '89
The second Gallup/Phi Delta Kappa poll of teachers' attitudes toward the public schools [with editorial comment by Pauline B. Gough] S. M. Elam. il *Phi Delta Kappan* 70:746, 785-98 Je '89
Awards
1989 Teacher of the Year [M. V. Bicouvaris] M. S. Miller. il por *Good Housekeeping* 208:152+ My '89
Certification
See also
National Board for Professional Teaching Standards (U.S.)
The new class [board certification] *The New Republic* 201:7-8 Ag 28 '89
Opening the schoolhouse doors [alternative teaching certification for professionals] J. Rachlin. il *U.S. News & World Report* 106:62 My 8 '89
The teacher education program: an endangered species? R. A. Roth. bibl f il *Phi Delta Kappan* 71:319-23 D '89
Yes, but where are your credits in Recess Management 101? S. Ohanian. *The Washington Monthly* 21:46-7 F '89
Crime
Extra-credit assignment [high school teacher-organized auto theft ring] M. Anson. il *Motor Trend* 41:6 Je '89
Dismissal
Academics and athletics: 'What price victory?' [Tennessee high school teacher J. A. McGhee fights dismissal after being pressured to raise basketball player's grade] P. A. Zirkel. il *Phi Delta Kappan* 70:564-5 Mr '89
Education
See also
Consortium for Excellence in Teacher Education
Student teachers
Teachers colleges
Building strong academic backgrounds for teachers. J. L. Kincheloe. *The Education Digest* 55:20-3 S '89
The computer's impact on education: progress or problem? J. DelFrate. il *USA Today (Periodical)* 117:68-9 Ja '89
NCATE and Texas eyeball to eyeball: who will blink? [interview with C. Parker and H. Gideonse] D. Watts. il *Phi Delta Kappan* 71:311-18 D '89
Nurturing the critical, practical, and artistic thinking of teachers. N. L. Gage and D. C. Berliner. il *Phi Delta Kappan* 71:212-14 N '89
Preserving quality: teacher training from a liberal arts perspective [program at Willamette University] J. B. Engel. il *Phi Delta Kappan* 70:475-7 F '89
Should we extend teacher preparation? W. D. Hawley. *Society* 26:49-57 My/Je '89
Teacher education in Ontario: a case for tuning the whole instrument [report by Michael Fullan and F. M. Connelly] T. McConaghy. bibl f il *Phi Delta Kappan* 70:830-1 Je '89

TEACHERS—Education—*cont.*

The teacher education program: an endangered species? R. A. Roth. bibl f il *Phi Delta Kappan* 71:319-23 D '89

Teacher preparation: should it be changed? W. D. Hawley. *Current (Washington, D.C.)* 318:22-31 D '89

To teach or not? F. C. Arricale. il *Commonweal* 116:165-6 Mr 24 '89

Training teachers in technology. il *The Futurist* 23:43 Ja/F '89

We must remove elementary teacher training from the state universities. W. D. Hedges. bibl f il *Phi Delta Kappan* 70:623-5 Ap '89

Education in service

The mentor as an expert coach: a model for rural school districts [program in Oroville, Calif.] B. Benoit and J. A. Braun. il *Phi Delta Kappan* 70:488-9 F '89

Peer coaching for teachers: opening classroom doors. D. B. Strother. bibl f il *Phi Delta Kappan* 70:824-7 Je '89

Urban teachers: their new colleagues and curriculum. C. A. Grant. bibl f il *Phi Delta Kappan* 70:764-70 Je '89

Evaluation

See Teachers—Rating

Examinations

The Florida state initial teacher certification test: a case study [art teachers] C. M. Dorn. bibl f *Design for Arts in Education* 90:37-42 Mr/Ap '89

Professional ethics

Who says professional ethics is dead? A response to Myron Lieberman [discussion of October 1988 article, Professional ethics in public education: an autopsy] M. Lieberman. *Phi Delta Kappan* 70:723-7 My '89

Psychology

The bibbidibobbidiboo factor in teaching. L. DeFelice. il *Phi Delta Kappan* 70:639-41 Ap '89

Self-renewal as faculty development. J. M. Rich. *The Education Digest* 55:54-7 D '89

Qualifications

See also
Teachers—Certification

Who meets the standards for early childhood teachers? C. Seefeldt. *The Education Digest* 54:21-4 My '89

Rating

See also
Teachers—Certification
Teachers—Examinations

A chilling effect on evaluation? [case of teacher K. Leshinskie of Montgomery County, Pa.] P. A. Zirkel. il *Phi Delta Kappan* 71:164-5 O '89

Does teacher evaluation diminish creativity? M. T. Bryant. *The Education Digest* 54:20-1 Mr '89

Recruiting

Attracting bright adolescents to teaching careers [program developed by Lamar University and Beaumont School District, Tex.] M. J. Cooper and others. il *Phi Delta Kappan* 70:566-7 Mr '89

Resignation

Great transformations [career changes by former teachers] B. G. Kempton. il *Working Woman* 14:88-92 Ja '89

See also
California. State Teachers' Retirement System
Teachers Insurance and Annuity Association

Salaries, pensions, etc.

Two teachers find a better life in Tokyo [Tim and Jane George] S. Seixas. il *Money* 18:92-5+ F '89

Supply and demand

The lure of the classroom [professionals turning to teaching] S. Tifft. il *Time* 133:69 F 13 '89

The staffing crisis in early childhood education. R. C. Granger. bibl f il *Phi Delta Kappan* 71:130-4 O '89

Those who can, teach [teaching as a second career] C. Reeve. il *New Choices for the Best Years* 29:61-7 N '89

To teach or not? F. C. Arricale. il *Commonweal* 116:165-6 Mr 24 '89

TEACHERS AND STUDENTS

See also
Classroom management
College teachers and students

The bibbidibobbidiboo factor in teaching. L. DeFelice. il *Phi Delta Kappan* 70:639-41 Ap '89

Classroom dialogues [high school remedial class] S. Gibson. il *Phi Delta Kappan* 70:553-5 Mr '89

How do you spell "wound," as in gunshot? [teacher helps inner city child write a play] J. Murphy. il *U.S. Catholic* 54:36-9 O '89

Mama and Miss Jordan [relationships with mother and high school teacher] M. H. Futrell. il *Reader's Digest* 135:75-80 Jl '89

Rachel remembers [poetry written by deaf student for teacher] R. McCord. *Reader's Digest* 135:170-2 D '89

"The teacher called me stupid, Mommy!" [emotionally abused students] M. H. Christensen. il *Redbook* 173:144-5+ O '89

To hug or not to hug. K. Paterson. *The Education Digest* 54:58-60 Mr '89

"We have a problem" [child claims teacher hates her] J. Marks. il *Parents* 64:68+ O '89

Your child's teacher. J. Segal and Z. Segal. il *Parents* 64:217 N '89

TEACHERS AS ROCK MUSICIANS

Blah Na Na! For the blahs [rock and roll band formed by teachers in Eden, N.C.] J. M. Carter. il *Phi Delta Kappan* 71:84-5 S '89

TEACHERS COLLEGES

See also
Lamar University. College of Education

A brief for professional education. J. W. Guthrie and G. J. Clifford. bibl f il *Phi Delta Kappan* 70:380-5 Ja '89

Troubled kingdoms, restless natives [educational administration programs] S. D. Thomson. bibl f il *Phi Delta Kappan* 70:371-5 Ja '89

Accreditation

See also
National Council for Accreditation of Teacher Education

Research

The cost of avoiding research. D. M. Kagan. bibl f il *Phi Delta Kappan* 71:220-4 N '89

TEACHERS INSURANCE AND ANNUITY ASSOCIATION

The $70 billion man [C. Wharton] C. V. Clarke. il pors *Black Enterprise* 19:100-2+ Je '89

TEACHING

See also
Academic freedom
Class size
Classroom management
Education
Humor in education
Psychology, Educational
Remedial teaching
School discipline
Teachers
Team teaching
　　See also subhead Study and teaching under various subjects

Inside the classroom. A. M. R. Butson. por *Newsweek* 113:8 Je 5 '89

PET and the pendulum: faddism in education and how to stop it [cover story] R. E. Slavin. bibl f il *Phi Delta Kappan* 70:752-8 Je '89

Aids and devices

See also
Computers—Educational use
Educational technology
Motion pictures in education
Television in education
Video games—Educational use
Videotapes—Educational use
Word processors and processing—Educational use

History

See Education—History

TEACHING MACHINES

See also
Computers—Educational use

TEACHING OFFICE OF THE CATHOLIC CHURCH *See* Catholic Church—Teaching office

TEACHOUT, TERRY

Coming to terms with Chesterton. *The American Scholar* 58:105-12 Wint '89

Elegy for the Woodchopper. *The American Scholar* 58:429-35 Summ '89

Old masters. See alternate issues of High Fidelity (New York, N.Y.) beginning April 1989 through July 1989

TEAFORD, MARK

(jt. auth) *See* Walker, Alan, and Teaford, Mark

TEAM LEARNING *See* Group work in education

TEAM TEACHING

A second wave of interest in team teaching. R. H. Anderson. *The Education Digest* 54:18-21 F '89

TEAM WORK IN INDUSTRY

12 ways to better team building. E. J. Belzer. il *Working Woman* 14:12+ Ag '89

The auto industry enters the 1990s [special section] il *Technology Review* 92:27-34+ Ja '89

The cultural revolution at A.O. Smith. J. P. Hoerr. il *Business Week* p66+ My 29 '89

GM and UAW: together again for the first time. M. Keller. il *Motor Trend* 41:146 Ap '89

How delegation can lead your team to victory. J. Calano and J. Salzman. *Working Woman* 14:86-7+ Ag '89

Is teamwork a management plot? Mostly not. J. P. Hoerr. il *Business Week* p70 F 20 '89

Monsanto is teaching old workers new tricks. J. E. Ellis. il por *Business Week* p67 Ag 21 '89

The payoff from teamwork [cover story] J. P. Hoerr. il *Business Week* p56-62 Jl 10 '89

Suddenly, USX is playing Mr. Nice Guy. G. L. Miles. il *Business Week* p151-2 Je 26 '89

A team approach from the start [entrepreneurs] W. J. Stolze. por *Nation's Business* 77:9 N '89

The UAW rebels teaming up against teamwork. W. Zellner. il *Business Week* p110+ Mr 27 '89

Volvo's radical new plant: 'the death of the assembly line'? J. Kapstein. il *Business Week* p92-3 Ag 28 '89

What makes teamwork work? P. King. *Psychology Today* 23:16-17 D '89

TEAMBOATS *See* Horse ferries
TEAMSTERS UNION *See* International Brotherhood of Teamsters, Chauffeurs, Warehousemen and Helpers of America
TEAPOTS
Photographs and photography
Putting the pot before the tea. il *Americana* 17:80 Jl/Ag '89
TEARS
See also
Crying
TEARS FOR FEARS (MUSICAL GROUP)
Fear of finishing. I. Robbins. il *Rolling Stone* p21 N 16 '89
TEAS
See also
Tea (Beverage)
A cookie tea for ladies of all ages [mother-daughter event] S. Payne. il *Southern Living* 24:62-3 D '89
Have a wedding tea. il *McCall's* 116:33 My '89
Steeped in tradition [tea at Brown's Hotel, London] S. Steward. il *Harper's Bazaar* 122:96 S '89
Tea & cinema [hostess J. Howard] P. Viladas. il por *House & Garden* 161:60 D '89
Tea in the afternoon. O. Woodier. il *Americana* 17:40-4+ N/D '89
A time for tea. G. Hovis. il *The New York Times Magazine* p55-6 Ja 8 '89
TEATRO COLÓN (BUENOS AIRES, ARGENTINA) *See* Opera houses
TEATRO NUESTRO (THEATER COMPANY)
Actor's son Cheyney Ryan brings migrant workers a theater that could save their lives. A. Chambers. il pors *People Weekly* 32:175-6 D 4 '89
TEBUTHIURON (HERBICIDE) *See* Herbicides
TECHNICAL ASSISTANCE
See also
United Nations Development Programme
Developing countries
What the third world can handle [discussion of November 1988 article, What the third world really needs] A. Salam. *The Bulletin of the Atomic Scientists* 45:8 My '89
TECHNICAL ASSISTANCE, AMERICAN
Soviet Union
U.S. support for Soviet technology: a lesson from history. T. P. Hughes. *Current (Washington, D.C.)* 315:18-26 S '89
TECHNICAL EDUCATION *See* Vocational-technical education
TECHNICAL SCHOOLS *See* Vocational-technical education
TECHNICAL WRITING *See* Scientific literature—Authorship
TECHNICIANS, LEGAL *See* Legal technicians
TECHNICOLOR, INC.
Ron Perelman's $640 million unsure thing [acquisition and resale of Technicolor, Inc.] R. King. il por *Forbes* 144:42-4+ O 30 '89
TECHNIQUE (ART) *See* Painting—Technique
TECHNOLOGICAL CHANGE *See* Technological innovations
TECHNOLOGICAL FORECASTING
21st century computing. P. Freiberger and D. McNeill. il *Compute!* 11:20-2+ O '89
Conscious technology: the co-evolution of mind and machine [excerpt from Future mind; cover story] J. C. Glenn. il por *The Futurist* 23:15-20 S/O '89
Dateline 1999 [predictions of science fiction authors] E. Bryant. il *Omni (New York, N.Y.)* 11:22+ Ja '89
Fantastic hardware [21st century] S. McKay. il *Maclean's* 102:40+ S 11 '89
Future tense. P. Saffo. See issues of Personal Computing beginning April 1989
High-flying ideas [views of Robert W. Simpson] il *Technology Review* 92:80 O '89
Marvels of the future. M. Rogers. il *Newsweek* 114:77-8 D 25 '89
The need to focus on communication by design. P. Brainerd. por *Personal Computing* 13:238 O '89
Predicting IC defects. il *Radio-Electronics* 60:6 Je '89
Sweet technology, sour marketing [views of S. Schnaars] R. Bailey. il por *Forbes* 143:140 My 1 '89
Technology and the world tomorrow. E. B. Skolnikoff. *Current History* 88:5-8+ Ja '89
Technology forecast 1989 [cover story; special section; with editorial comment by Fred Abatemarco] il *Personal Computing* 13:5, 91-8+ Ja '89
Telepower: the emerging global brain. J. N. Pelton. il por *The Futurist* 23:9-14 S/O '89
What lies ahead [symposium] il *Byte* 14:343-6+ Ja '89
TECHNOLOGICAL INNOVATIONS
See also
Computers
Technology transfer
2nd annual best of what's new [cover story; special section] il *Popular Science* 235:49-61+ D '89
Astrophysicist Arno Penzias on making R&D pay off [interview] E. Warner. il por *High Technology Business* 9:24-7 Jl/Ag '89
Battle for the future [Japanese vs. U.S. technology] P. Elmer-Dewitt. il *Time* 133:42-3 Ja 16 '89
The best of scientific innovations [1988] il *Business Week* p116-17 Ja 9 '89

Breaking the cycle that stifles innovation [views of Deborah J. Dougherty] A. Kozlov. il *Psychology Today* 23:18 O '89
How to regain the productive edge [excerpts from MIT report Made in America] il *Fortune* 119:92-4+ My 22 '89
How we can regain our competitive edge. S. Ramo. *Scientific American* 260:148 My '89
Inaction on technology programs stirs Congress. C. Norman. *Science* 244:137-8 Ap 14 '89
Innovation in America [with editorial comment by Stephen B. Shepard] il *Business Week* Special Issue:8-9, 12-18+ Je 16 '89
Innovation on trial: punitive damages versus new products. R. J. Mahoney and S. E. Littlejohn. bibl f *Science* 246:1395-9 D 15 '89
Innovations for development. il *The Futurist* 23:48 N/D '89
Litigation thwarts innovation in the U.S. P. W. Huber. il *Scientific American* 260:120 Mr '89
MIT study confirms productivity slipping in key U.S. industries [Made in America report] *Aviation Week & Space Technology* 131:69-70 D 4 '89
Playing catch-up across the Pacific. M. Tharp. il *U.S. News & World Report* 107:44-5 Jl 10 '89
Productivity [cover story; special section; with editorial comment by Jonathan Schlefer] il *Technology Review* 92:2, 27-40+ Ag/S '89
Regaining the productive edge (I). C. W. Weinberger. il *Forbes* 144:31 O 2 '89
Regaining the productive edge (II). C. W. Weinberger. il *Forbes* 144:31 O 16 '89
Star tech. See issues of Omni (New York, N.Y.) beginning October 1986
Technology, employment and U.S. competitiveness. R. M. Cyert and D. C. Mowery. il *Scientific American* 260:54-60+ My '89
Turning ideas into reality [address, February 23, 1989] D. H. Roy. *Vital Speeches of the Day* 55:662-6 Ag 15 '89
Wake-up strategies for tired R&D projects. M. Mandell and B. Murphy. il *High Technology Business* 9:22-5 F '89
Who innovates? [role of small firms in adopting new technologies] B. Harrison. il *Technology Review* 92:15+ Ap '89
TECHNOLOGICAL RESEARCH *See* Industrial research
TECHNOLOGY
See also
Ceramic membranes (Technology)
Educational technology
Engineering
Inventions
Medical technology
Nanotechnology
America's high-tech decline. C. H. Ferguson. *Foreign Policy* 74:123-44 Spr '89
Battle for the future [Japanese vs. U.S. technology] P. Elmer-Dewitt. il *Time* 133:42-3 Ja 16 '89
DOD lists critical technologies. C. Norman. *Science* 243:1543 Mr 24 '89
Science & technology. See issues of Forbes beginning March 10, 1986
Star tech. P. Hoban. See occasional issues of New York beginning September 24, 1984
Tech update. See issues of Popular Mechanics
Technology's hits and misses of the 1980s [cover story] G. T. Pope. il *High Technology Business* 9:16-19+ N/D '89
Awards
See also
National Medal of Technology
Economic aspects
America's technopolis complex. A. Holmes. il *U.S. News & World Report* 107:66 N 13 '89
Financing innovation. C. Farrell. il *Business Week* Special Issue:154-7+ Je 16 '89
High-tech guru Steven Burrill [interview] M. Mandell. il por *High Technology Business* 9:20-3 N/D '89
How high-tech products can achieve profitable longevity. B. Krasnoff and M. Mandell. il *High Technology Business* 9:18-21 Ja '89
How we can regain our competitive edge. S. Ramo. *Scientific American* 260:148 My '89
Marketwatch. See issues of High Technology Business through November/December 1989
States, technology, and jobs. D. M. Brown. il *Technology Review* 92:16-17 My/Je '89
Technology. See issues of Fortune beginning March 5, 1984
Technology, employment and U.S. competitiveness. R. M. Cyert and D. C. Mowery. il *Scientific American* 260:54-60+ My '89
Where the jobs are. C. A. Gustin. il *High Technology Business* 9:48 S/O '89
Who innovates? [role of small firms in adopting new technologies] B. Harrison. il *Technology Review* 92:15+ Ap '89
History
See also
Industrial revolution

TECHNOLOGY—History—*cont.*

50 and 100 years ago. See issues of Scientific American
Science and technology: the age of limits. W. F. Allman.
il *U.S. News & World Report* 107:111 D 25 '89-Ja 1
'90

Study and teaching

The "civics" of technology in history textbooks. J. L. Heilbron
and D. J. Kevles. *The Education Digest* 55:42-4 S '89

International aspects

See also
    United Nations. Intergovernmental Committee on Science
    and Technology for Development

The allies: fools or tools? [U.S. raises objection to machine
tool exports to the Soviets] *Newsweek* 114:54 O 30 '89
America's technology trump cards [hidden strengths of re-
search system] B. Carpenter. il *U.S. News & World Report*
107:46-7 Jl 10 '89
The 'Amerippon' alliance. M. Leventer. *World Press Review*
36:48-9 Ag '89
ARCO Solar sale raises concerns over potential technology
export. M. Crawford. *Science* 244:918 My 26 '89
Are the old rules still relevant? [CoCom high tech export
controls] C. P. Work. il *U.S. News & World Report* 107:38
D 18 '89
Chips for the Soviet bloc? Computers from Asia short-circuit
America's export controls. S. Budiansky. il *U.S. News
& World Report* 107:28-30 O 9 '89
Exon-Florio an imperfect tool for protecting U.S. technology.
V. D. Cohen. por *Aviation Week & Space Technology*
131:68-9 N 6 '89
'Hey! Want a hot little alloy from Shemyakin?' [Soviet sales
of high tech] J. Rossant. il *Business Week* p82 Je 26
'89
Intellectual exports [M.I.T.'s Industrial Liaison Program] T.
Beardsley. *Scientific American* 261:17+ S '89
Japan's new military edge [cover story] J. W. Dower. il
The Nation 249:1+ Jl 3 '89
Joint ventures with the EC. S. Y. Chow. il *High Technology
Business* 9:10 Jl/Ag '89
Learning to live with export controls [U.S. upset with West
German government's lax attitude toward technology ex-
ports] L. Lief. il *U.S. News & World Report* 106:28 Ja
23 '89
Let's make a deal: the U.S.-Japan co-technology sphere. S.
K. Vogel. *The New Republic* 200:14+ Je 19 '89
MIT-industry links draw congressional attention. M. Crawford.
il *Science* 244:1136 Je 9 '89
NAE: revamp export controls [computer equipment and
software] M. Crawford. *Science* 243:21 Ja 6 '89
The plane drain: the FSX deal and other transfers of technolo-
gy. H. D. Bentley. il por *Conservative Digest* 15:54-7 Jl/Ag
'89
Removing controls on PCs revives worries on exports. I.
Goodwin. *Physics Today* 42:67-9 S '89
Resolve the technology transfer mess. *Aviation Week & Space
Technology* 130:7 Ap 17 '89
The rise of the trade hawks [Japan bashing] B. Powell and
B. Martin. il *Newsweek* 113:46-7 Mr 13 '89
Selling security for deutschemarks [R. Mueller gets suspended
sentence for selling military technology to the Soviets]
R. N. Perle. il *U.S. News & World Report* 107:36 Jl
31 '89
Soviet attempts to buy U.S. computers continue despite
Customs crackdown. D. Hughes. *Aviation Week & Space
Technology* 130:279+ Je 12 '89
Soviets reaping West's know-how [views of Richard Staar]
USA Today (Periodical) 118:14 Ag '89
Sprechen sie high tech? [foreign buyers love U.S. technology
companies] N. Alster. il *Forbes* 143:172-4+ Ap 17 '89
Task force urges overhaul of Pentagon policy on industrial
cooperation with Pacific Rim. J. D. Morrocco. *Aviation
Week & Space Technology* 131:32 N 13 '89
Technology and the world tomorrow. E. B. Skolnikoff. *Current
History* 88:5-8+ Ja '89
U.S.-Canada free trade: how high tech will benefit [cover
story] G. T. Pope. il *High Technology Business* 9:18-21
Mr '89
U.S. competition in emerging technology areas [address,
August 8, 1989] H. D. Bentley. *Vital Speeches of the
Day* 56:2-5 O 15 '89
U.S. international activities in science and technology [message
to Congress, April 5, 1989] G. Bush. *Department of State
Bulletin* 89:51-2 Je '89
U.S. pressed by allies on critical technology research, Pentagon
says. M. Mecham. *Aviation Week & Space Technology*
130:52-3+ Ap 3 '89
U.S. stance toward the Soviet Union on trade and technology
[address, October 27, 1988] E. A. Wendt. *Department
of State Bulletin* 89:20-3 Ja '89
Whole-earth technology [cover story] W. Reichert and H.
Sello. il *High Technology Business* 9:14-18+ Jl/Ag '89

Marketing

Sweet technology, sour marketing [views of S. Schnaars]
R. Bailey. il por *Forbes* 143:140 My 1 '89

Political aspects

See Technology and state

Securities

If you're playing the specs, look hard at the techs. G. G.
Marcial. il *Business Week* p96-7 Je 26 '89
Is now the time for leverage? M. Gianturco. por *Forbes*
144:120 Ag 21 '89
A market unto themselves. M. Gianturco. il *Forbes* 144:316
N 13 '89
Technology time? C. Torcellini. il por *Forbes* 144:362+ N
13 '89

Social aspects

The dangers of overconfidence. J. Rubin. il *Technology Review*
92:11-12 Jl '89
Human factors: the gap between humans and machines.
E. Weiner and A. Brown. il pors *The Futurist* 23:9-11
My/Je '89
In the eye of the beholder: poetic documentaries about
technology [work of H. Bitomsky and H. Farocki] K.
Rosenberg. il *Technology Review* 92:62-8 F/Mr '89
Present tense. J. Reed. il *Vogue* 179:426-9 N '89
Small gadgets that can change lives [help for the elderly]
F. Lunzer. bibl il *U.S. News & World Report* 106:58-60
Mr 6 '89
Tackling high tech: learning to love those wires, plugs, buttons
and beeps. il *Glamour* 87:98 O '89
The technological tourist. S. C. Florman. il *Technology Review*
92:18+ Ja '89

Study and teaching

See also
    Georgia Institute of Technology

Teaching technology. il *The Futurist* 23:41 My/Je '89

Australia

At the frontiers of science and technology. R. Williams.
il *The Courier (Unesco)* 41:27-9 D '88

Canada

See also
    Canadian Manufacturing Advanced Technology Exchange

U.S.-Canada free trade: how high tech will benefit [cover
story] G. T. Pope. il *High Technology Business* 9:18-21
Mr '89

China

History

The Chinese scientific genius [cover story; special issue] R.
K. G. Temple. il *The Courier (Unesco)* 41:3-34 O '88

Developing countries

See also
    Technical assistance—Developing countries
    United Nations. Intergovernmental Committee on Science
    and Technology for Development

Innovations for development. il *The Futurist* 23:48 N/D
'89
Radios in the rain forest. J. W. Clay. il *Technology Review*
92:52-7 O '89

France

High tech: the future is now. M. E. Long. il maps *National
Geographic* 176:92-101 Jl '89
Technology from French companies. il *High Technology
Business* 9:7 Ja '89

Japan

America's high-tech decline. C. H. Ferguson. *Foreign Policy*
74:123-44 Spr '89
The 'Amerippon' alliance. M. Leventer. *World Press Review*
36:48-9 Ag '89
Battle for the future [Japanese vs. U.S. technology] P. Elmer-
Dewitt. il *Time* 133:42-3 Ja 16 '89
The growth of Japanese science and technology. F. Narin
and J. D. Frame. bibl f il *Science* 245:600-5 Ag 11 '89
Japan watch. See issues of High Technology Business through
November/December 1989
"The Japanese are not superhuman" [interview with A.
Penzias] G. F. Gilder. il por *Forbes* 143:122+ Mr 20
'89
The rise of the trade hawks [Japan bashing] B. Powell and
B. Martin. il *Newsweek* 113:46-7 Mr 13 '89
A wave of ideas, drop by drop. N. Gross. il *Business Week*
Special Issue:22+ Je 16 '89
Where Japan will strike next [cover story] G. Bylinsky. il
Fortune 120:42-6+ S 25 '89

Soviet Union

'Hey! Want a hot little alloy from Shemyakin?' [Soviet sales
of high tech] J. Rossant. il *Business Week* p82 Je 26
'89
Red tech rising [cover story] T. H. Cole. il *Popular Mechanics*
166:28, 84-92+ Ap '89
Soviets reaping West's know-how [views of Richard Staar]
USA Today (Periodical) 118:14 Ag '89
The strategic imperative of reform [coping with the high
technology revolution] S. Brucan. il *New Perspectives
Quarterly* 5:18-23 Wint '88/'89
U.S. support for Soviet technology: a lesson from history.
T. P. Hughes. *Current (Washington, D.C.)* 315:18-26 S
'89

United States

See Technology

Western Europe

Adding hustle to Europe's muscle. T. Peterson. il *Business
Week* Special Issue:32+ Je 16 '89

TECHNOLOGY—Western Europe—*cont.*
An alliance for progress? E. Corcoran. il *Scientific American* 260:78-9 Ap '89
Can Europe catch up in the high-tech race? T. Peterson. il *Business Week* p142+ O 23 '89
An entrepreneurial tree sprouts in Europe [high tech companies] D. Dickson. il *Science* 245:1038-40 S 8 '89

TECHNOLOGY AND CIVILIZATION
See also
Computers and civilization
America's real Founding Fathers [interview with T. P. Hughes] A. P. Sanoff. il por *U.S. News & World Report* 106:64 My 8 '89
Beauty and the beast. W. F. Allman. il *U.S. News & World Report* 107:8-9 Jl 31 '89
Conscious technology: the co-evolution of mind and machine [excerpt from Future mind; cover story] J. C. Glenn. il por *The Futurist* 23:15-20 S/O '89
Hoarding in the Squirrel Society. C. Gordon. il *Maclean's* 102:48 Mr 6 '89
Rocket radio. W. Gibson. il *Rolling Stone* p84-6+ Je 15 '89
The second genesis: future technologies and humanism. A. Bacard. il por *The Humanist* 49:9-11+ S/O '89

TECHNOLOGY AND EDUCATION *See* Educational technology
TECHNOLOGY AND RELIGION *See* Religion and technology
TECHNOLOGY AND SOCIETY *See* Technology—Social aspects

TECHNOLOGY AND STATE
See also
United States. Congress. Office of Technology Assessment
United States. Office of Science and Technology Policy
A back burner for high tech [Bush administration] J. Carey. *Business Week* p35 N 20 '89
High tech's fickle helping hand [White House wavers on funding] P. Elmer-Dewitt. il *Time* 134:68 D 4 '89
The policy elite. il *Business Week* Special Issue:48-9 Je 16 '89
The quiet path to technological preeminence. R. B. Reich. bibl il *Scientific American* 261:41-7 O '89
Science and technology: its future in the U.S. J. Schmandt. *Current (Washington, D.C.)* 309:7-13 Ja '89
A technological fix: the U.S. searches for a stand on technology. E. Corcoran. *Scientific American* 261:60 Ag '89
U.S. leaders cite need for national technology plan. S. W. Kandebo. il *Aviation Week & Space Technology* 131:27-8 O 2 '89
U.S. technical leadership is threatened by investment pressure [address, May 8, 1989] R. J. Marano. *Vital Speeches of the Day* 55:601-3 Jl 15 '89
Washington Inc.? J. Carey. il *Business Week* Special Issue:40-1 Je 16 '89
Will the White House torpedo America Inc.? J. Carey. il *Business Week* p80 N 27 '89

Ireland
Why Irish eyes are smiling. J. Ames. *U.S. News & World Report* 107:47 Jl 10 '89

United States
See Technology and state

TECHNOLOGY ASSESSMENT
See also
United States. Congress. Office of Technology Assessment
TECHNOLOGY ASSESSMENT OFFICE (U.S.) *See* United States. Congress. Office of Technology Assessment

TECHNOLOGY REVIEW
The character of a magazine. J. Schlefer. il *Technology Review* 92:2 F/Mr '89
The compleat editor [S. Hackman] J. Schlefer. il por *Technology Review* 92:2 Ja '89

TECHNOLOGY TRANSFER
See also
Products, New
Technology—International aspects
NASA robot to have private-sector spinoffs. *High Technology Business* 9:37 Mr '89
New products benefit earth [space technology spinoffs] il *USA Today (Periodical)* 117:8 Je '89
NIH, Inc.: the CRADA boom [cooperative research and development agreements] B. J. Culliton. il *Science* 245:1034-6 S 8 '89
NIH scientists agonize over technology transfer. W. Booth. *Science* 243:20-1 Ja 6 '89
Profitable technology from Uncle Sam. R. Schneiderman. il map *High Technology Business* 9:26-30 F '89
Technology licenses: new law closes bankruptcy loophole. M. Shea-Stonum and D. Sloan. il *High Technology Business* 9:15 Mr '89
Technology transfer [research consortiums] E. Corcoran. *Scientific American* 260:98+ My '89

TECHNOPRIBOR (FIRM)
U.S., Soviet firms to develop, market commercial booster based on SS-20 [Start mobile launcher] J. D. Morrocco. il *Aviation Week & Space Technology* 131:21 Ag 7 '89

TECO WARE
Exhibitions
Art pottery and the Prairie School aesthetic [Teco: art pottery of the Prairie School] A. E. Ledes. il *Antiques* 136:376+ S '89

TECTONICS *See* Geology

TEDDY BEARS
A frisky French designer makes a teddy-bear coat for adults [creation of J.-C. de Castelbajac] il por *People Weekly* 31:83 Ja 30 '89

TEDFORD, JAMES
Pagan publications. il *Utne Reader* p136-8 Jl/Ag '89

TEECE, PHILIP
(jt. auth) *See* Newton, Jack, 1942-, and Teece, Philip

'TEEN (PERIODICAL)
The Great Model Search 1989 [special section] il pors *'Teen* 33:76-85 O '89
Meet the top 24 athletes [finalists in Sportsgirl of the Year contest] il *'Teen* 33:42-3 D '89

TEENAGE ATHLETES, WOMEN *See* Women athletes
TEENAGE AUTOMOBILE DRIVERS
Do not try these maneuvers [lack of proof supporting proposal that car advertising contributes to accidents] R. Ceppos. il *Car and Driver* 34:26-7 My '89
Nathalie & the MG [father and daughter repair 1974 MGB] G. Sidline. il *Good Housekeeping* 209:66+ S '89
No pass, no drive [requiring school attendance for driver's license] J. Rachlin and J. P. Shapiro. il *U.S. News & World Report* 106:49-51 Je 5 '89
The quick fix or a lasting solution? [requiring school attendance for obtaining driver's license] C. Pipho. il *Phi Delta Kappan* 70:502-3 Mr '89
Quick studies [B. Bondurant's course] B. Visnic. il pors *Car and Driver* 35:141-3 O '89

Anecdotes, facetiae, satire, etc.
Driving ambition. B. Stepko. il *Seventeen* 48:56+ Mr '89
License to manhood. P. Theroux. il *Parents* 64:52+ Ja '89

TEENAGE BUSINESS *See* Youth and business
TEENAGE COUNSELING *See* Youth counseling
TEENAGE DRINKING *See* Alcohol and youth
TEENAGE EMPLOYMENT *See* Youth—Employment
TEENAGE FATHERS, UNMARRIED *See* Single fathers
TEENAGE FRIENDSHIP *See* Friendship
TEENAGE LITERATURE *See* Young adults' literature
TEENAGE MEDICAL CARE *See* Youth—Medical care
TEENAGE MODELS (PERSONS) *See* Models (Persons)
TEENAGE PARTIES *See* Entertaining
TEENAGE PREGNANCY
See also
Claretian Medical Center
Abortion: sparring on the bench [Supreme Court hears arguments in cases involving mandatory notification of parents of teenagers seeking abortions] il *Newsweek* 114:49 D 11 '89
Babies: just say no. L. M. Blake. il *Psychology Today* 22:16 D '88
The case for national action. F. Wattleton. *The Nation* 249:138-41 Jl 24-31 '89
Coming of age: the tragedy of teenage pregnancy. F. Wattleton. il *USA Today (Periodical)* 117:49-50 Ja '89
'Cosby' kid releases safe sex campaign spots [M.-J. Warner] il por *Jet* 75:18 Mr 6 '89
The crusade of Dr. Elders [Arkansas public health boss] S. Barnes. il pors *The New York Times Magazine* p38-41+ O 15 '89
Giving teenagers a new view of their future [work of M. Carrera in Harlem] M. Ludtke. il por *Time* 133:12+ My 1 '89
The lives of teenage mothers [Kingsbridge Heights Community Center, Bronx, N.Y.] E. Marek. il *Harper's* 278:56-8+ Ap '89
Networking on a shoestring [Young Parent Program of St. Cloud, Minn.] K. Heinen and M. A. Padgett. il *Children Today* 18:30-2 Ja/F '89
New York school system gets first teen trio of valedictorian mothers. il *Jet* 76:13 Jl 17 '89
Preventing pregnancies among adolescents. J. R. Thompson. *Society* 26:64-6 Mr/Ap '89
School paper's story on teen mother who's class valedictorian is barred [C. M. Dixon] il por *Jet* 76:31 My 8 '89
Sex: preventing teen pregnancy. M. Carrera. il *American Health* 8:72 O '89
Teen mom tells of 'beating odds' to be valedictorian [C. M. Dixon] il pors *Jet* 76:12 Je 26 '89
Teen mother with straight A's tells how education is changing her life [C. M. Dixon] D. M. Cheers. il pors *Jet* 76:28-30 My 22 '89
Teen mothers: their stories. K. Hinchman. il *'Teen* 33:32+ N '89
Tiospaye Teca: working with young Native American families in the Dakotas. A. Floden. il *Children Today* 18:28-32 S/O '89
Travis comes home [T. Smigiel, child who survived illegal adoption by Joel Steinberg] M. Jacobbi. il pors *Good Housekeeping* 209:103+ Jl '89
The triumph of Bonnie Lovette. L. Marsa. il pors *Good Housekeeping* 209:72+ Ag '89

TEENAGE PREGNANCY—*cont.*

Valedictorian Carrie Dixon gets top grades in high school—even with a second child on the way [Houston, Tex.] il por *People Weekly* 31:62 My 29 '89

Wee Care: reaching teenage mothers and changing their lives [Philadelphia program] P. R. Rosenwald and G. Porter. *Children Today* 18:28-30 My/Je '89

When pregnant girls face mom and dad [Supreme Court hearing on Minnesota law requiring parental notification in teenage abortions] D. Whitman. il *U.S. News & World Report* 107:25-6 D 4 '89

Whoopi Goldberg says her teen daughter is pregnant. il por *Jet* 77:22 N 20 '89

TEENAGE RUNAWAYS *See* Runaways

TEENAGE SEX *See* Youth—Sexual behavior

TEENAGE SMOKING *See* Smoking and youth

TEENAGE SUICIDE *See* Suicide

TEENAGE VOLUNTEERS *See* Volunteer service

TEENAGERS *See* Adolescence; Black youth; Young men; Young women; Youth

TEENAGERS AND PARENTS *See* Parent-child relationship

TEENAGERS' EXERCISES *See* Exercise

TEETH

See also
Dentistry
Gums
Tooth enamel

Care and hygiene

See also
Dental floss
Toothbrushes

New ways to save your teeth? [cover story; special section] il *Consumer Reports* 54:504-9 Ag '89

Sealing cavities [dental sealants] il *Prevention (Emmaus, Pa.)* 41:16+ Ja '89

Sealing out decay [use of dental sealants] J. P. Cohn. il *FDA Consumer* 23:18-21 N '89

Teeth chatter. il *Seventeen* 48:22 My '89

Tooth truths. N. Gallo. il *Better Homes and Gardens* 68:41-3 F '89

Unwise cracks [effects of temperature extremes; research by Eric Z. Shapira] il *Prevention (Emmaus, Pa.)* 41:21-2 N '89

Diseases

See also
Dental caries

Extraction

Tooth troubles? Consider a root canal before having a tooth pulled [views of Joseph D. Maggio] *Prevention (Emmaus, Pa.)* 41:20 O '89

Vitamin C may hasten healing [views of Robert A. Halberstein] il *USA Today (Periodical)* 117:4-5 F '89

Grinding

See Bruxism

Radiography

See Radiography, Medical

Wounds and injuries

Toothsavers [rescuing knocked-out teeth] il *Prevention (Emmaus, Pa.)* 41:18+ Jl '89

TEETH, ARTIFICIAL *See* Dentures

TEETH, FOSSIL

Asian human-origin theory gets new teeth [research by Christy G. Turner] B. Bower. *Science News* 136:100 Ag 12 '89

An essay on a pig roast [role of F. Osborn's erroneous Nebraska Man theory in the creationism debate] S. J. Gould. il *Natural History* p14+ Ja '89

Mammal-like dentition in a Mesozoic crocodylian. J. M. Clark and others. bibl f il *Science* 244:1064-6 Je 2 '89

Modern humans take a spin back in time [electron spin resonance dating of Skhul site; research by Christopher B. Stringer] B. Bower. *Science News* 135:263 Ap 29 '89

Teeth and prehistory in Asia [reconstructing the great migrations] C. G. Turner, II. bibl il map *Scientific American* 260:88-91+ F '89

TEETS, JOHN W.

about

The other Greyhound isn't winning any races. E. Schine. il *Business Week* p53 Je 19 '89

TEETS, LINDA BARRETT

Riding the crest of victory; ed. by Deborah Grandinetti. il pors *Prevention (Emmaus, Pa.)* 41:113-14+ Jl '89

TEGU LIZARDS *See* Lizards

TEHERAN BOOK FAIR *See* Book fairs

TEHRAN (IRAN)

See also

Iranian seizure of United States embassy, 1979-1981

TEICH, MARK

Shopping for surgery. il *Health (New York, N.Y.)* 21:94-5 Je '89

TEIXEIRA, RUY A.

End of the rainbow. il *The New Republic* 200:11-12+ Ap 3 '89

TEIXEIRA, SERGIO ALVES

Samba time! il *The Unesco Courier* 42:38-41 D '89

TEKNOWLEDGE INC.

See also

Cimflex Teknowledge Corporation

TEKTRONIX, INC.

Nice guys finish last. K. K. Wiegner. il *Forbes* 143:142 Je 26 '89

TEL AVIV (ISRAEL)

Theater

All the world's a Habima. G. G. Seibert. il *America* 160:395-9 Ap 29 '89

TELANDER, RICK

The big enchilada [cover story] il pors *Sports Illustrated* 70:40-2+ Ap 24 '89

The Bucs don't stop here. il *Sports Illustrated* 71:56-8+ O 2 '89

Building a better Mousetrap. il por *Sports Illustrated* 71:66-70+ S 11 '89

Dollars and change: sport in the '80s was altered for richer and for poorer. por *Sports Illustrated* 71:166 D 25 '89-Ja 1 '90

Don't ban the banners. por *Sports Illustrated* 71:100 O 30 '89

A dubious call to arms. il por *Sports Illustrated* 70:116 Je 5 '89

Fight! Fauna fight! il *National Wildlife* 27:14-16 F/Mr '89

Millions from heaven. il pors *Sports Illustrated* 71:56-8+ N 6 '89

No. 1 with a bullet [cover story] il *Sports Illustrated* 70:16-21 Ja 9 '89

An open letter to Alex. il por *Sports Illustrated* 71:106 N 27 '89

A question of fairness. por *Sports Illustrated* 70:114 My 1 '89

Something must be done [excerpt from The hundred yard lie] il *Sports Illustrated* 71:92-8+ O 2 '89

There's still hope, Elva. por *Sports Illustrated* 71:128 O 9 '89

Wild thing. il pors *Sports Illustrated* 71:38-40+ Ag 28 '89

TELANDER, RICK, AND NODEN, MERRELL

The death of an athlete. il pors *Sports Illustrated* 70:68-72+ F 20 '89

TELANDER, RICK, AND SULLIVAN, ROBERT

You reap what you sow [cover story] il por *Sports Illustrated* 70:20-6+ F 27 '89

TELE-COMMUNICATIONS, INC.

Malone alone [cover story] P. Ainslie. il por *Channels (New York, N.Y.: 1986)* 9:30-2+ Je '89

Want this stock? It's up 91,000%. C. Knowlton. il por *Fortune* 120:97+ Jl 31 '89

TELE-PSYCHIC [television program] *See* Television program reviews—Single works

TELECOM ELECTRICAL SUPPLY COMPANY

Boyhood dreams, adult realities. K. D. Thompson and J. Coleman. il por *Black Enterprise* 19:73 Je '89

TELECOMMUNICATION

See also

American Telephone & Telegraph Co.
Ameritech Communications, Inc.
BellSouth Corporation
Cincinnati Bell Inc.
Communications Satellite Corp.
Communications satellites
Computer networks
Data transmission systems
Integrated services digital network
ITT Corporation
Light communication systems
Logging on (Computers)
MCI Communications Corp.
Metromedia, Inc.
Mobile Telecommunications Technologies (Firm)
Multiplexing
National Telecommuncations Cos.
Network Equipment Technologies Inc.
Pacific Telesis Group
Private networks (Telecommunication)
Rolm Corp.
T1 networks
Telecommuting
Teleconferencing
Telephone
Telephone bypass systems
Telepoint communications
Television broadcasting

1990 field guide to the electronic environment. il *Channels (New York, N.Y.: 1986)* 9:8+ D '89

Beyond the telephone: new ways to communicate [cover story] S. B. Weinstein and P. W. Shumate, Jr. il pors *The Futurist* 23:8-12 N/D '89

COM1. B. N. Meeks. See issues of Byte beginning August 1988 through May 1989

Communications corner. H. Friedman. See issues of Radio-Electronics through January 1989

Computing is the medium for the message. M. Antonoff. il *Personal Computing* 13:163-5 O '89

From Telstar to typefaces, computers bring the information age home. D. D. Thornburg. *Compute!* 11:12 Ap '89

The need to focus on communication by design. P. Brainerd. por *Personal Computing* 13:238 O '89

Networks. See issues of Byte beginning June 1989

TELECOMMUNICATION—*cont.*

On the cutting edge of tomorrow's technology. P. W. Shumate, Jr. and S. B. Weinstein. il *USA Today (Periodical)* 118:30-2 S '89

Acquisitions and mergers

Are raiders ready to take on ITT again? G. G. Marcial. il *Business Week* p130 Ap 24 '89

Behind the scenes at the fall of Rolm. R. D. Hof. il *Business Week* p82-4 Jl 10 '89

How I fought off the raiders [excerpts from The ITT wars] R. V. Araskog. il pors *Fortune* 119:110-12+ F 27 '89

International aspects

Dealmakers are burning up the phone lines. J. J. Keller. il *Business Week* p138-41+ Mr 13 '89

Telecomputing lives [IBM's deal with Siemens for Rolm] G. Slutsker and F. Meeks. il *Forbes* 143:51 Ja 9 '89

Export-import trade

On trade, the U.S. sounds the charge—and comes out firing blanks. P. Magnusson. il *Business Week* p45 F 6 '89

Spreading the net widely [Dominion Textile and Telenet Communications map strategy for U.S.-Canada free trade agreement] J. DeMont. il *Maclean's* 102:76-7 Jl 3 '89

A unique approach against trade violators [address, May 24, 1989] R. Noyce. *Vital Speeches of the Day* 55:671-2 Ag 15 '89

Finance

Funding the future infrastructure. B. M. Geeslin. bibl *Society* 26:16-21 Jl/Ag '89

A pleasant surprise from the great communicators. J. J. Keller. il *Business Week* p94 Ja 9 '89

Telecommunications. P. Duggan. il *Forbes* 143:194+ Ja 9 '89

International aspects

See also

World Administrative Telegraph and Telephone Conference

Information technology, global linkage, and U.S. competitiveness [address, June 14, 1989] E. M. Ehrlich. *Vital Speeches of the Day* 55:755-9 O 1 '89

Is U.S. losing its edge? [views of William Dutton] *USA Today (Periodical)* 117:7-8 Je '89

New diplomacy by Fax Americana [broadcasting information to China via fax machine and telephone] S. V. Roberts. il *U.S. News & World Report* 106:32-4 Je 19 '89

Telecommunications as a strategic industry [address, December 15, 1988] R. G. Harris. *Vital Speeches of the Day* 55:377-81 Ap 1 '89

Laws and regulations

See also

Telephone companies—Laws and regulations

United States. Federal Communications Commission

Policies for a competitive America [address, February 16, 1989] R. E. Allen. *Vital Speeches of the Day* 55:413-16 Ap 15 '89

Regulating communication [special section] bibl *Society* 26:5-38 Jl/Ag '89

Telecom apartheid. P. W. Huber. il *Forbes* 144:268 N 27 '89

Telecommunications and the world information revolution [address, July 19, 1989] D. Brenner. *Vital Speeches of the Day* 56:88-91 N 15 '89

U.S. technical leadership is threatened by investment pressure [address, May 8, 1989] R. J. Marano. *Vital Speeches of the Day* 55:601-3 Jl 15 '89

Securities

Having it both ways. F. E. Rowe. por *Forbes* 144:312 S 4 '89

Social aspects

Telepower: the emerging global brain. J. N. Pelton. il por *The Futurist* 23:9-14 S/O '89

Terminology

Behind the buzzwords. *Channels (New York, N.Y.: 1986)* 9:101-2 D '89

Canada

See also

Bell Canada Enterprises Inc.

CALL-NET Telecommunications Ltd.

Canadian Radio-Television and Telecommunications Commission

Teleglobe Canada

Caribbean region

Telecommunications and economic development in the Caribbean [address, November 30, 1988] P. W. Borg. *Department of State Bulletin* 89:17-20 Mr '89

Communist countries

Our chip has come in. *The New Republic* 200:7-8 Je 12 '89

Developing countries

U.S. contributions to communications development. il *Department of State Bulletin* 89:62-5 Jl '89

Germany (West)

See also

Siemens AG

Great Britain

See also

British Telecom plc

Cable & Wireless plc

Japan

See also

Nippon Telegraph & Telephone Corporation

Telecommunications as a strategic industry [address, December 15, 1988] R. G. Harris. *Vital Speeches of the Day* 55:377-81 Ap 1 '89

Sweden

See also

L.M. Ericsson Telephone Co.

Western Europe

Europe goes on a telephone binge. S. Tully. il *Fortune* 120:107-10 Ag 28 '89

TELECOMMUNICATION IN BUSINESS

The 21st-century manager. R. Farmanfarmaian. il *Working Woman* 14:73+ N '89

Gadgets for executives. B. O'Reilly. il *Fortune* 120:200-5 S 11 '89

Hold for the communicaholic manager. W. Kiechel. il *Fortune* 119:107-8 Ja 2 '89

The linkage to tomorrow. M. Estren. *High Technology Business* 9:3 My '89

Office gear on the go. S. Advokat. il *Nation's Business* 77:56+ N '89

Shooting for the moon [role of chaos in business; address, April 27, 1989] R. A. Ferchat. *Vital Speeches of the Day* 55:727-31 S 15 '89

TELECOMMUNICATION IN GOVERNMENT

Revolt of Uncle Sam's paper pushers [AT&T and Sprint cope with replacing the federal government's aging telephone network] M. Lewyn. il *Business Week* p156 O 30 '89

TELECOMMUNICATION IN MEDICINE

Informatics and telematics: the future. M. Elmandjra. il *World Health* p28-9 Ag/S '89

TELECOMMUNICATION IN TRUCKING

Tracking trucks by satellite. R. Schneiderman. il *High Technology Business* 9:24-6+ My '89

TELECOMMUTING

1989 reader survey. il *Home Office Computing* 7:53-5 S '89

Do telecommuters lose out on payday? R. Farmanfarmaian. il *Working Woman* 14:75 Ja '89

Editor's note. C. Cohl. See issues of Home Office Computing beginning September 1988

Escape from the office. J. Schwartz and D. Tsiantar. il *Newsweek* 113:58-60 Ap 24 '89

Home is where the office is. T. Crawford. *World Press Review* 36:49 F '89

IBM pioneers a work-at-home program. L. Wu. il *Home Office Computing* 7:14 F '89

Look who's working at home [cover story] D. C. Bacon. il *Nation's Business* 77:20-3+ O '89

Making telecommuting succeed. R. Farmanfarmaian. il *Working Woman* 14:46+ F '89

New options for working at home. C. Begole. il *Glamour* 87:324-5+ S '89

Technology that gets you where you live. G. Hedberg. il *Personal Computing* 13:31-2 O '89

Top 10 home office misconceptions. C. O'Malley. il *Personal Computing* 13:67-8+ N '89

Worksteading. R. Farmanfarmaian. il *Psychology Today* 23:37-8+ N '89

Workstyles. N. Sullivan. See issues of Home Office Computing beginning September 1988

Anecdotes, facetiae, satire, etc.

Home sick. W. Geist. il *New York* 22:24 Ap 3 '89

TELECONFERENCING

German and U.S. leaders confer on trade issues [BizNet teleconference] A. Holzinger. il *Nation's Business* 77:78-9 Ja '89

Trading views with Japan [BizNet teleconference] A. Holzinger. il *Nation's Business* 77:34+ My '89

TELECONVERTER LENSES *See* Lenses, Photographic

TELEDYNE, INC.

FBI charges consultants bribed Navy officials to influence contract awards. J. D. Morrocco. *Aviation Week & Space Technology* 130:22 Ja 9 '89

Pentagon suspends Hazeltine, Teledyne following federal charges of fraud. *Aviation Week & Space Technology* 130:23-4 Ja 16 '89

TELÉFONOS DE MÉXICO, SA

Salinas goes after another monster: the phone system. S. Baker. il *Business Week* p42 Mr 6 '89

TELEGDI, VALENTINE L.

A lowbrow's view of Feynman. il *Physics Today* 42:85 F '89

TELEGLOBE CANADA

Satcom calling [air ambulance equipped with Aerosat communications system] il *Flying* 116:19 F '89

Teleglobe Canada to team on mobile satellite service. *Aviation Week & Space Technology* 131:81 Ag 21 '89

TELEGRAPHIC AGENCY OF THE SOVIET UNION *See* TASS (Soviet Union)

TELEMACO [opera] *See* Gluck, Christoph Willibald, Ritter von, 1714-1787

TELEMARK SKIING *See* Skiing
TELEMARKETING *See* Telephone selling
TELEMARKETING SCAMS *See* Fraud
TELEME CHEESE COOKING *See* Cooking—Cheese
TELEMETRY, BIOLOGICAL *See* Biotelemetry
TELEMUNDO GROUP INC.
Hispanic TV: a great way to make a killing, right? R. Grover. il *Business Week* p61 O 23 '89
TELENET COMMUNICATIONS CORP.
Spreading the net widely [Dominion Textile and Telenet Communications map strategy for U.S.-Canada free trade agreement] J. DeMont. il *Maclean's* 102:76-7 Jl 3 '89
TELEOPERATORS *See* Telerobots
TELEPHONE
> *See also*
> Cellular radio
> Computerphones
> Cordless telephone
> Hotels, motels, etc.—Telephone service
> Pay telephones
> Radiotelephone
> Rural telephone service
> Videophones

Directories
> *See* Telephone directories

Emergency use
In case of emergency. L. Schnurnberger. il *Parents* 64:116 Mr '89

Equipment
> *See also*
> Telephone answering machines
> Telephone equipment industry
> Telephone ringers

Call a name, not a number [BellSouth 2000] S. Miller. il *Home Office Computing* 7:66 Ap '89
Fax Mate [cover story] D. F. Plant. il *Radio-Electronics* 60:33-6 O '89
High-quality speakerphone from AT&T [Speakerphone 480] S. Miller. il *Home Office Computing* 7:68 Ja '89
Music-on-hold adapter. S. Sokolowski. il *Radio-Electronics* 60:42-6 Ag '89
Phones and answering machines. il *Consumer Reports* 54:40-53 Ja '89
Talented two-line telephone [AT&T two-line speakerphone 622] N. Sullivan. il *Home Office Computing* 7:82 D '89
Telephone accessories as Christmas gifts? il *Sunset (Central West edition)* 181:90-1 D '88
Telephones. il *Consumer Reports* 54:57-62 D '89
Two-line telephones. S. Usdin. il *Home Office Computing* 7:57-9 Ja '89

Government use
Revolt of Uncle Sam's paper pushers [AT&T and Sprint cope with replacing the federal government's aging telephone network] M. Lewyn. il *Business Week* p156 O 30 '89

History
Telephone [J. N. La Corte attempts to gain recognition of A. Meucci as the inventor of the telephone] *The New Yorker* 65:34-5 O 30 '89

Investment use
Reach out and touch the market's latest fad. L. J. Nathans. il *Business Week* p144-5 My 22 '89
Those cold calls leave him cold [brokerage houses] J. R. Graham. por *Fortune* 119:326 Ap 24 '89

Long distance service
> *See also*
> Alternative operator services
> Telephone bypass systems

Don't laugh: this plan for regulating AT&T actually sounds good [price caps for long distance service] A. S. Blinder. il *Business Week* p14 Je 12 '89
Which long-distance company is cheapest? il *Consumers' Research Magazine* 72:20-3 Ap '89

Military use
STU-3 secure telephones offered to U.S. defense contractors. P. J. Klass. il *Aviation Week & Space Technology* 130:63+ F 27 '89

Psychological aspects
Call later [people more apt to listen to callers later in the day; study by Frank Sileo and Wesley Kayson] D. Swanbrow. *Psychology Today* 23:14 Je '89
Phone-a-go-go. J. Allen. *Utne Reader* p94-5 S/O '89

Rates
> *See also*
> Computers—Telephone rate information use

Alternative operator services. K. K. Gracey. *Consumers' Research Magazine* 72:2 My '89
AT&T unchained: business may be the winner [FCC's rate cap proposal] F. Seghers. il *Business Week* p42 Mr 20 '89
Calling from the road shouldn't be highway robbery. F. Seghers. il *Business Week* p40 Ap 3 '89
Don't laugh: this plan for regulating AT&T actually sounds good [price caps for long distance service] A. S. Blinder. il *Business Week* p14 Je 12 '89
An end to phone-call gouges [alternative operator services] P. Plawin. *Changing Times* 43:90+ F '89

Not-so-easy access: telephoning home may cost more than you think [alternative operator services] H. Gieseking. il *Travel Holiday* 172:16-18 Ag '89
Those $*&*!!#% statements [checking your bill] B. Hager. il *Money* 18:108-9 Jl '89
Which long-distance company is cheapest? il *Consumers' Research Magazine* 72:20-3 Ap '89
Why your phone bills keep going up [cover story] P. Payson. il *Consumers' Research Magazine* 72:10-14 Je '89
You call, they collect [alternative operator services] G. Eichler. il *Esquire* 112:124 S '89

Security measures
STU-3 secure telephones offered to U.S. defense contractors. P. J. Klass. il *Aviation Week & Space Technology* 130:63+ F 27 '89

Social aspects
> *See also*
> Party lines (Telephone)
> *Anecdotes, facetiae, satire, etc.*

Women, pick up the phone! G. Nachman. por *Newsweek* 114:8 Jl 31 '89

Switching systems
> *See* Telephone switching systems

Wiretapping
> *See* Wiretapping

Eastern Europe
The East bloc's $100 billion phone bill. G. E. Schares. il *Business Week* p139+ N 20 '89

TELEPHONE AND CHILDREN
"It's for you, Mom!". L. Schnurnberger. il *Parents* 64:112-16 Mr '89

TELEPHONE AND YOUTH
Teleteens [research by Marcela Raffaelli] B. Portnow. il *American Health* 8:90 O '89

TELEPHONE ANSWERING MACHINES
Answering machines. G. Kohler. il *Successful Farming* 87:12-13 Je '89
The best answering machines for doing business. E. King. il *Home Office Computing* 7:55-8 Ag '89
Exceptional two-line answering machine. A. Gaffney. il *Home Office Computing* 7:69 Je '89
Hello, you've reached . . . the age of the digital answering machine. D. Stover. il *Popular Science* 235:76-8 Ag '89
Panasonic puts it all together [Panasonic KX-F120 fax + telephone answering system with facsimile] S. Miller. il *Home Office Computing* 7:68-9 Je '89
Phones and answering machines. il *Consumer Reports* 54:40-53 Ja '89
Telephone answering machines. il *Consumer Reports* 54:63-9 D '89

TELEPHONE AUCTIONS *See* Auctions
TELEPHONE BOOKS *See* Telephone directories
TELEPHONE BYPASS SYSTEMS
> *See also*
> T1 networks

How to bypass your friendly phone company. C. Siler. il *Forbes* 144:88-9 Ag 21 '89
TELEPHONE CABLES
Adding to the technological wish list [superconducting coaxial cable] *Science News* 135:143 Mr 4 '89
Light talk [goal of putting optical fibers in the home] E. Corcoran. il *Scientific American* 261:74+ O '89
TELEPHONE CALL ACCOUNTING SYSTEMS
Phone bill detective. S. B. Weiner. il *Forbes* 144:263-4 O 16 '89
Take charge of your phones. M. Mandell. il *Nation's Business* 77:25-6 Ja '89
TELEPHONE CALL PROCESSING SYSTEMS *See* Call processing systems
TELEPHONE CALLS
> *See also*
> Call waiting (Telephone service)
> Caller ID (Telephone service)
> Obscene telephone calls

Anecdotes, facetiae, satire, etc.
Wired!! [listening in on private phone conversations in New York City; cover story] S. M. L. Aronson and V. Tiger. il *New York* 22:26-33 Ja 30 '89

Rates
> *See* Telephone—Rates

TELEPHONE CALLS IN ART
Exhibitions
Strangers on the line [work of D. McNeil] A. Prud'homme. il por *Art News* 88:26 Summ '89
TELEPHONE COMPANIES
> *See also*
> ALC Communications Corporation
> American Telephone & Telegraph Co.
> Bell Atlantic Corp.
> BellSouth Corporation
> Cincinnati Bell Inc.
> Collective bargaining—Telephone workers
> Collective labor agreements—Telephone companies
> GTE Corp.
> MCI Communications Corp.
> Pacific Telesis Group
> US Sprint Communications Inc.
> US West, Inc.

TELEPHONE COMPANIES—cont.

The country connection [rural companies] T. Barrett. il *Newsweek* 114:47 S 18 '89

Acquisitions and mergers
International aspects

Dealmakers are burning up the phone lines. J. J. Keller. il *Business Week* p138-41+ Mr 13 '89

Antitrust cases

Was breaking up AT&T a good idea? K. Labich. il *Fortune* 119:82-7 Ja 2 '89

Cable television activities

The Baby Bells toddle toward cable [Pacific Telesis' stake in Group W Cable] R. D. Hof. il *Business Week* p40 My 8 '89

Charge of the 'telcos' [fiber optic television vs. cable] B. Brewin. il *Video* 12:142 Ja '89

Chasing the telcos. M. Brown. il *Channels (New York, N.Y.: 1986)* 9:81 Je '89

The coming battle over your TV set [vs. cable operators] J. Dreyfuss. il *Fortune* 119:104-7 F 13 '89

End run. G. Slutsker. il *Forbes* 144:124-5 Ag 7 '89

Grabbing an electronic bonanza [telephone companies enter cable business; cover story] S. W. Dean, Jr. and R. L. Shayon. il *The Nation* 249:369+ O 9 '89

Here come the RBOCs [phone companies seek cable TV acquisitions] il *Channels (New York, N.Y.: 1986)* 9:72-7 Je '89

The latest telco debate [telephone companies entering cable business] M. Brown. il *Channels (New York, N.Y.: 1986)* 9:28 Mr '89

A telco-cable survey sparks controversy [E. C. Parker's survey funded by Bell Atlantic] J. Stilson. il por *Channels (New York, N.Y.: 1986)* 9:17+ S '89

Telecom apartheid. P. W. Huber. il *Forbes* 144:268 N 27 '89

Finance

A pleasant surprise from the great communicators. J. J. Keller. il *Business Week* p94 Ja 9 '89

Telecommunications. P. Duggan. il *Forbes* 143:194+ Ja 9 '89

Why the Baby Bells are fat and sassy. il *U.S. News & World Report* 107:18 Ag 21 '89

Laws and regulations

Bell ringer. C. Byron. il *New York* 22:22+ D 18 '89

Congress, the FCC, and Judge Greene [address, November 10, 1988] D. Brenner. *Vital Speeches of the Day* 55:250-3 F 1 '89

Corporate Luddism. M. Kinsley. *The New Republic* 201:4 D 25 '89

The judge who rules the phone industry [interview with H. H. Greene] K. Ballen. il por *Fortune* 119:86 Ja 2 '89

Policies for a competitive America [address, February 16, 1989] R. E. Allen. *Vital Speeches of the Day* 55:413-16 Ap 15 '89

Why your service is so primitive [Baby Bells prohibited from creating information services] N. Oliver. il *Consumers' Research Magazine* 72:14-15 Je '89

Will Congress set the 'Bell Seven' free? M. Lewyn. il *Business Week* p110+ D 4 '89

Securities

Global phone plays [views of D. Campbell] R. King. il por *Forbes* 144:192+ S 18 '89

Little phone companies with big futures. S. Smith. il *Fortune* 119:32 Ap 24 '89

Phone stocks: should you plug in or disconnect? G. G. Marcial. il *Business Week* p146 Mr 13 '89

Services
See also
Call waiting (Telephone service)
Caller ID (Telephone service)

Phone-company services instead? *Consumer Reports* 54:54 Ja '89

Your phone, the doorman and detective: new services let you block, screen and trace calls. F. L. Kritz. il *U.S. News & World Report* 107:59 Jl 31 '89

Suits and claims

Blame the phone company: a strategy goes on trial [Home Shopping Network sues GTE] G. DeGeorge. il *Business Week* p30 Je 12 '89

Canada
See also
CALL-NET Telecommunications Ltd.

Great Britain
See also
British Telecom plc

Japan
See also
Nippon Telegraph & Telephone Corporation

Mexico
See also
Teléfonos de México, SA

Western Europe

Europe goes on a telephone binge. S. Tully. il *Fortune* 120:107-10 Ag 28 '89

TELEPHONE CRIMES
See also
Telephone—Security measures

Magazine telephone scams. il *Consumers' Research Magazine* 72:36-7 Mr '89

Reach out and rob someone [telemarketing scams] J. Castro. il *Time* 133:38-9 Ap 3 '89

Telemarketing investment fraud [cover story; special section] *Consumers' Research Magazine* 72:10-12+ Ja '89

Telephone crooks have got your number. il *Reader's Digest* 135:73-4+ N '89

Watch out! Latest mail & phone frauds. S. Nielsen. *Good Housekeeping* 209:163-4 Ag '89

When calling back can cost plenty [scams involving 540 and 900 numbers] *U.S. News & World Report* 106:71 Ap 24 '89

"You have definitely won a fabulous prize!". M. C. Paulson. il *Changing Times* 43:34-6+ Ag '89

You may already be a victim of fraud. M. J. Harris. il *Money* 18:74-80+ Ag '89

TELEPHONE DIALING SYSTEMS
See also
Dual-tone multifrequency signalling

Total phone management [Hot Line Two] J. Nimersheim. il *Home Office Computing* 7:77-8 O '89

TELEPHONE DIRECTORIES

Total phone management [Hot Line Two] J. Nimersheim. il *Home Office Computing* 7:77-8 O '89

TELEPHONE DIRECTORIES, ELECTRONIC *See* Information systems—Telephone directories

TELEPHONE EQUIPMENT INDUSTRY
See also
International Mobile Machines Corp.
Rolm Corp.

Export-import trade

The East bloc's $100 billion phone bill. G. E. Schares. il *Business Week* p139+ N 20 '89

A weak foreign challenge? Now that's a switch. J. J. Keller. il *Business Week* p158 My 22 '89

Canada
See also
Northern Telecom Ltd.

Sweden
See also
L.M. Ericsson Telephone Co.

TELEPHONE IN ASTRONOMY

Telephone "hotlines". *Sky and Telescope* 78 Resource Guide:16 S '89

TELEPHONE IN BUSINESS
See also
Telephone call accounting systems
Telephone selling
Voice mail systems

The best answering machines for doing business. E. King. il *Home Office Computing* 7:55-8 Ag '89

Call-waiting etiquette. P. Edwards and S. Edwards. il *Home Office Computing* 7:48 N '89

Hold for the communicaholic manager. W. Kiechel. il *Fortune* 119:107-8 Ja 2 '89

Honing that work-at-home image. N. Sullivan. il *Home Office Computing* 7:104 Ja '89

Phone bill detective [desktop phone bill analyzers] S. B. Weiner. il *Forbes* 144:263-4 O 16 '89

Phone fundamentals. M. Bodin. il *Working Woman* 14:66 O '89

Telephone systems: still the nerve center of successful entrepreneurship. A. Edmond, Jr. *Black Enterprise* 19:55-6 My '89

TELEPHONE IN CHURCH WORK
See also
Church Growth Development International

TELEPHONE IN MEDICAL CARE

Doctors are long-distance operators. il *Popular Mechanics* 166:13 Ja '89

TELEPHONE IN PUBLIC HEALTH

New information available about AIDS treatments [telephone listing of FDA-recognized clinical efficacy trials] F. E. Young. il *FDA Consumer* 23:6-7 N '89

TELEPHONE IN SPORTS

From the publisher [Sports Illustrated Sports Hotline] D. J. Barr. il *Sports Illustrated* 71:1 Ag 21 '89

TELEPHONE INFORMATION SERVICE
See also
900 telephone numbers
Toll-free telephone service

Hot lines [New York City] A. Burgi. il *New York* 22:134-46 My 1 '89

NSS on the air [Dial-A-Shuttle] P. Jones. il *Ad Astra* 1:28 Ja '89

Ethical aspects

When calling back can cost plenty [scams involving 540 and 900 numbers] *U.S. News & World Report* 106:71 Ap 24 '89

TELEPHONE LINES
See also
Telephone cables

TELEPHONE NUMBERS
See also
900 telephone numbers
Toll-free telephone service

TELEPHONE OPERATORS
See also
Alternative operator services

TELEPHONE PORNOGRAPHY
Court orders: dealing with porn and drugs [Supreme Court rules on dial-a-porn] *Newsweek* 114:20 Jl 3 '89
Dialing for dollies. R. Mead. il *New York* 22:38 N 13 '89
The uphill fight against dial-a-porn. il *Newsweek* 113:42 Ja 9 '89

TELEPHONE RINGERS
Making a telephone ring [theater special effect] K. Ruling. il *Theatre Crafts* 23:92+ Ap '89

TELEPHONE SELLING
See also
Interactive marketing
How Ma Bell can help you sell. R. Gunnerson. il *Home Office Computing* 7:26 Jl '89
Sales aid for cold callers [Maximizer] L. Wood. il *Home Office Computing* 7:88+ D '89
Taking the chill out of calling cold. W. Cole. *Working Woman* 14:32+ O '89

TELEPHONE SWITCHING SYSTEMS
See also
Network Equipment Technologies Inc.
A weak foreign challenge? Now that's a switch. J. J. Keller. il *Business Week* p158 My 22 '89

TELEPHONE WORKERS
See also
Collective bargaining—Telephone workers
Collective labor agreements—Telephone companies
Labor unions—Telephone workers
Strikes—Telephone workers

TELEPHOTO LENSES See Lenses, Photographic

TELEPOINT COMMUNICATIONS
Great Britain
Low-cost competitor to cellular? M. Mandell. il *High Technology Business* 9:48 Jl/Ag '89
A phone booth you can put in your pocket. M. Maremont. il *Business Week* p83 Ja 30 '89

TELEPORTATION
Anecdotes, facetiae, satire, etc.
Mass teleportation. D. Lancaster. *Radio-Electronics* 60:32+ Ap '89

TELEPROMPTER CORP. See Group W Cable, Inc.

TELEREP (FIRM)
Caviar dreams for couch potatoes [A. Masini] J. B. Newman. il pors *Channels (New York, N.Y.: 1986)* 9:32-6 Ja 16 '89

TELEROBOTS
Desperately seeking Cyborg [Flight Telerobotic Servicer] J. Goldberg. il *Omni (New York, N.Y.)* 11:12+ Ag '89
Martin Marietta robotic device will aid in space station assembly [Flight Telerobotic Servicer] B. D. Nordwall. il *Aviation Week & Space Technology* 130:53 My 15 '89
Merging mind and machine [cover story] T. B. Sheridan. il *Technology Review* 92:32-40 O '89
NASA robot to have private-sector spinoffs. *High Technology Business* 9:37 Mr '89
Orbital mechanic [Flight Telerobotic Servicer] G. R. Graf. il *Ad Astra* 1:5-6 O '89
Teleoperators. W. R. Uttal. bibl il *Scientific American* 261:124-9 D '89

TELESCOPE BATTERIES See Electric batteries
TELESCOPE GUIDING See Telescopes—Control
TELESCOPE MODELS
Small-scale telescope [Dorpat telescope] W. L. Gould. il *Sky and Telescope* 77:250-1 Mr '89

TELESCOPE MOUNTINGS See Telescopes—Mounting

TELESCOPES
See also
Coronagraph
Hubble Space Telescope
Radio telescopes
Space stations—Telescopes
25-meter Soviet telescope planned for 2000. M. Sigov. il *Astronomy* 17:14+ O '89
Adventures in Refractorland. T. Dickinson. il *Sky and Telescope* 78:419-20+ O '89
Astrofest '89. S. J. O'Meara. il *Sky and Telescope* 78:647-9 D '89
Astrofest whets amateur spirit. il *Astronomy* 17:16 D '89
Astronomy one step at a time. M. J. Finn. il *Astronomy* 17:96 Mr '89
Astronomy tests Celestron's Ultima 8. R. Burnham. il *Astronomy* 17:78-83 My '89
Astronomy tests the Meade 2120/LX6 [Schmidt-Cassegrain telescope] R. Burnham. il *Astronomy* 17:68-73 D '89
Astronomy's 1989 guide to telescopes [special section] il *Astronomy* 17:70-91 O '89
A big year for Riverside. il *Astronomy* 17:18 S '89
Celestron vs. Meade: an 8-inch showdown (I) [Schmidt-Cassegrain telescopes; cover story] D. Di Cicco. il *Sky and Telescope* 78:576-82 D '89
Gleanings for ATM's. R. W. Sinnott. See issues of Sky and Telescope
Holiday trash-scopes. G. Lovi. il *Sky and Telescope* 78:617-18 D '89

How faint can you see? B. E. Schaefer. il *Sky and Telescope* 77:332-3+ Mr '89
John Dobson: a man with a mission [interview] S. J. O'Meara. por *Sky and Telescope* 78:530-2 N '89
Let's take a closer look. N. Schreiber. il *New Choices for the Best Years* 29:79-81 Ap '89
Low-budget stellar spectroscopy [Multi-Telescope Telescope] I. Peterson. *Science News* 136:12 Jl 1 '89
The new generation of Dobsonians. R. Berry. bibl (p100) il *Astronomy* 17:62-7 Ap '89
New technologies for telescopes. il *Astronomy* 17:10+ F '89
Reviews breed quality telescopes. R. Berry. *Astronomy* 17:6 D '89
A salesman for the heavens wants to rope you in [J. Dobson] D. Moser. bibl (p174) il pors *Smithsonian* 20:102-6+ Ap '89
Telescopes highlight Stellafane. il *Astronomy* 17:16 N '89
The top 10 telescope ideas of 1989. il *Sky and Telescope* 78:591-4 D '89
Your telescope's limiting magnitude [computer program] B. E. Schaefer. il *Sky and Telescope* 78:522-5 N '89
Control
The amazing stepper motor. A. Tardif. il *Sky and Telescope* 77:554-8 My '89
Deep-sky photography without guiding. R. Arbour. il *Sky and Telescope* 78:538-9+ N '89
A double-curved-bolt drive. R. Pfaff. il *Sky and Telescope* 78:100 Jl '89
The ever-vigilant GNAT [global network of automatic telescopes] D. L. Crawford. il *Sky and Telescope* 77:143 F '89
Guiding off axis or on [Multi-Star Guider] K. Zussman. il *Sky and Telescope* 78:37-8 Jl '89
Motorized focusing for under $20. T. R. McDonough. il *Sky and Telescope* 78:317+ S '89
A new concept in computer-aided telescopes. T. Taki. il *Sky and Telescope* 77:194-6 F '89
The sky's the limit [Celestron's computer-controlled Compustar telescope] J. Engle. il *Popular Science* 234:34 F '89
Two arms are better than one [double-arm-drives] R. W. Sinnott. il *Sky and Telescope* 77:436-41 Ap '89
Costs
Make a telescope for $500: model 2. S. W. Schultz. il *Sky and Telescope* 77:26-9 Ja '89
Make a telescope for $500: model 3. J. N. Mitton. il por *Sky and Telescope* 77:488-91 My '89
Why isn't there a good $200 scope? A. Dyer. *Astronomy* 17:8 Jl '89
Equipment
Build a PVC-pipe 50mm finder. C. Cappa. il *Astronomy* 17:72-3 N '89
Equipped for safe solar viewing. R. Hill. il *Astronomy* 17:66-8 F '89
Filters for viewing [Chroma-Scan pocket filters] R. Burnham. il *Astronomy* 17:96 Ap '89
Motorized focusing for under $20. T. R. McDonough. il *Sky and Telescope* 78:317+ S '89
A tray for a Celestron tripod. E. C. Hoy. il *Astronomy* 17:71-2 N '89
Two low-profile focusers [Tectron visual and photographic focusers] J. Kanipe. il *Astronomy* 17:124-5 D '89
History
Genesis of a legend [Schmidt-Cassegrain telescope] A. Dyer. il *Astronomy* 17:86-91 O '89
Telescopes. il *Life* 12:126-7+ My '89
Maintenance and repair
Historic refractor back in use [Alvan Clark refractor near Burlington, Iowa] il *Astronomy* 17:18 Mr '89
Masks
Sharpen images with a cardboard mask. M. L. Knott. il *Astronomy* 17:84-5 F '89
Mirrors
The big glass [Hubble Space Telescope mirror built by Perkin-Elmer Corp.; cover story] T. Dunkle. il *Discover* 10:68-81 Jl '89
Commercial telescope optics: buyer beware! P. Ceravolo. il *Sky and Telescope* 78:564 D '89
Keck telescope mirror is in production. M. M. Waldrop. il *Science* 243:1010-11 F 24 '89
Mounting
The Crawford-Dobsonian mounting. M. Gavin. il *Sky and Telescope* 77:327-8 Mr '89
The design of telescope structures (I). R. E. Albrecht. il *Sky and Telescope* 77:97-101 Ja '89
The design of telescope structures (II). R. E. Albrecht. il *Sky and Telescope* 77:210-14 F '89
How to observe planets during the day [polar alignment] J. H. Palmer. il *Astronomy* 17:86-7 Mr '89
The long-play Dobsonian. J. Chen. il *Astronomy* 17:70 N '89
A simple mount for the C90 telescope. O. B. Mathias. il *Sky and Telescope* 77:441 Ap '89
Patents
So . . . you've had a bright idea! T. T. Moga. il *Sky and Telescope* 77:324-7 Mr '89

TELESCOPES, MILITARY
Air Force building high-resolution telescope for space defense research. T. M. Foley. il *Aviation Week & Space Technology* 129:47 Mr 6 '89
TELESCOPES, ORBITING *See* Artificial satellites—Astronomical use
TELESCOPIC SEATING PLATFORMS
Telescopic seating platforms [use in theaters] R. Long. il *Theatre Crafts* 23:22+ Ap '89
TELESHOPPING *See* Electronic shopping
TELESURGERY
First aid for Freedom. R. Spangenburg and D. Moser. il *Ad Astra* 1:42-5 Ja '89
Surgery in space. il *The Futurist* 23:57-8 S/O '89
Surgery in space. A. Gibbons. il *Technology Review* 92:9-10 Ap '89
TELETHONS
See also
Comic Relief (Project)
Jerry Lewis telethon raises $78.4 million; Sammy Davis performs. il por *Jet* 76:28 S 25 '89
TELEVANGELISM *See* Television broadcasting—Religious programs
TELEVISION
See also
Art and television
Cable television
Extended definition television
Fiber optic television
High definition television
Hispanic Americans and television
Improved definition television
Interactive video
Motion pictures and television
Video art
Video in the 90s [cover story; special section] il *Video* 13:55-62+ S '89
Anecdotes, facetiae, satire, etc.
Year in review. J. Queenan. il *Channels (New York, N.Y.: 1986)* 9:52+ Ja '89
History
The '80s: a look back at the decade [special issue] il *TV Guide* 37:4-6+ D 9-15 '89
How television got its start. R. D. Fitch. il *Radio-Electronics* 60:74-5 My '89
Is it TV's 50th birthday or not? F. Lovece. il *Channels (New York, N.Y.: 1986)* 9:9 Je '89
Japan's oldest television star [work of K. Takayanagi] F. Lovece. por *Video* 12:23 Ja '89
Mrs. Philo T. Farnsworth: on a potato field and the farm boy inventor of television. E. Farnsworth. il por *People Weekly* 31 Special Issue:155 Summ '89
The reruns of August. S. A. Booth. il *Popular Mechanics* 166:36+ Ag '89
Television—past and future. S. A. Booth. il *Popular Mechanics* 166:20+ Jl '89
Transmitters and transmission
See Television transmission
TELEVISION, CLOSED CIRCUIT *See* Closed circuit television
TELEVISION, STEREOSCOPIC *See* 3-D television
TELEVISION ACTORS AND ACTRESSES *See* Television performers
TELEVISION ADAPTATIONS
The perilous journey from book to screen [children's books for television] G. Haight. il *Publishers Weekly* 235:137-42 F 24 '89
Rights. P. S. Nathan. See issues of Publishers Weekly
TELEVISION ADVERTISING
See also
Advertising, Political
Automobile industry—Advertising
Berlin Wall, 1961-1989, in advertising
Books—Advertising
Brewing industry—Advertising
Cable television advertising
Cosmetics industry—Advertising
Cycling in advertising
Fast food restaurants—Advertising
Food industry—Advertising
Infant formula industry—Advertising
Music in advertising
Opera in advertising
Sex in advertising
Soft drink industry—Advertising
Videotapes—Television advertising use
Zapping of television advertising
Ad makers zap back. A. Marton. il *Channels (New York, N.Y.: 1986)* 9:30-1 S '89
Political quick-step [TV marketers using audience research tactics developed by political campaigns] M. Couzens. il *Channels (New York, N.Y.: 1986)* 9:26 F '89
The return of "the sponsor". D. Fanning. il *Forbes* 143:136 Ap 17 '89
Science 1, advertisers 0 [studies on efficacy of TV ads] W. F. Allman. il *U.S. News & World Report* 106:60-1 My 1 '89
Soft focus [director L. Dektor] B. Kanner. il *New York* 22:20+ My 22 '89

Television insults men, too. B. R. Goldberg. il *Reader's Digest* 134:185-6 Je '89
Tuning out TV ads. D. Tsiantar and A. Miller. il *Newsweek* 113:42-3 Ap 17 '89
Cartoons
Frame that toon. B. Kanner. il *New York* 22:12+ Ap 17 '89
Ethical aspects
The advertiser that didn't balk [National Right to Life Committee pressures General Foods to pull advertising for TV movie Roe vs. Wade] M. Suh. il *Ms.* 18:75 Jl/Ag '89
As the 'clean TV' campaign heats up, ABC chills two new shows. P. Freeman. il por *People Weekly* 31:153-4 My 22 '89
Boycott targets TV sponsors [Christian Leaders for Responsible Television] J. Maxwell. il *Christianity Today* 33:47-9 Ag 18 '89
Crusade or charade? [T. Rakolta's campaign against advertisers on "offensive" shows] M. Lasswell. il *Rolling Stone* p33 My 4 '89
Does Married . . . with children go too far? Will it give in to critics? [cover story] H. Polskin. il *TV Guide* 37:2-5 Jl 29-Ag 4 '89
Farewell, trash, goodbye, Nielsens [shows losing sponsors] *U.S. News & World Report* 106:14+ My 15 '89
Intimidation [advertisers cancel sponsorship of Audubon program about Pacific Northwest forests] L. Line. il *Audubon* 91:4 N '89
The picture has started to fade for TV's infomercials. P. Wang. il *Money* 18:17 Jl '89
Prime-time shoot-out [campaign against sponsors of objectionable shows] D. Neff. il *Christianity Today* 33:14 O 6 '89
Putting a brake on TV "sleaze": advertisers are growing wary of shows that might offend. R. Zoglin. il *Time* 133:51 Mr 20 '89
This is what you thought: 80% are worried that special-interest groups could force cancellation of TV programs [results of survey] il *Glamour* 87:163 N '89
History
And now a word about our sponsors [special section] il *People Weekly* 31 Special Issue:120-5 Summ '89
The Bulova watch ad cost $9—Madonna, $5 million. T. Hagan. il *TV Guide* 37:33-4 My 6-12 '89
Laws and regulations
Trouble for copycats [B. Midler wins suit against Young & Rubicam over sound-alike ad] P. Young. il por *Maclean's* 102:92 N 20 '89
A U.S. patent on famous voices [B. Midler wins suit against Young & Rubicam's use of her singing style] il por *U.S. News & World Report* 107:19 N 13 '89
Setting and scenery
Prop art [work of J. Canto] B. Kanner. il por *New York* 22:20+ N 27 '89
Time purchasing
See also
Hot Net (Firm)
Single-source research (TV audience research)
Don't bank on spot. C. Reece. il *Channels (New York, N.Y.: 1986)* 9:30 F '89
The farmer's market [Memphis independent station WPTY attracting agriculture ad dollars] R. Katz. il map *Channels (New York, N.Y.: 1986)* 9:12+ My '89
Finding gold in your hometown [independent stations] J. Mandese. il *Channels (New York, N.Y.: 1986)* 9:79-81 Ja '89
The gutting and rewiring of television sales [unwired networks; cover story] C. Reece. il *Channels (New York, N.Y.: 1986)* 9:26-30 Ap '89
Knocking newspapers [WVEC's campaign for advertising dollar in Norfolk, Va.] A. Snyder. il *Channels (New York, N.Y.: 1986)* 9:32-3 F '89
Local truce for ad $$. J. Stilson. il *Channels (New York, N.Y.: 1986)* 9:17 O '89
The price of "cheap eyeballs" [advertisers squeamish about tabloid TV] F. Meeks. il *Forbes* 143:188-9 Mr 20 '89
Progressing backward [local sales] C. Reece. il *Channels (New York, N.Y.: 1986)* 9:23 Mr '89
A surprisingly good year for the masses. D. Kalish. il *Channels (New York, N.Y.: 1986)* 9:28+ D '89
Unlikely bedfellows [syndicator Genesis Entertainment helping stations sell ads] C. Reece. il *Channels (New York, N.Y.: 1986)* 9:18 My '89
Where ad dollars go [special section] il *Channels (New York, N.Y.: 1986)* 9:83-6+ N '89
Canada
The hot sell [using sex] J. Daly. il *Maclean's* 102:34-5 Je 12 '89
Japan
Murphy does $multimillion car commercials in Japan [Eddie Murphy] por *Jet* 77:36 O 23 '89
TELEVISION ADVERTISING AND CHILDREN
Advertising, art, and arts education: an uneasy association. L. Barton. bibl f *Design for Arts in Education* 90:14-19 N/D '88

TELEVISION ADVERTISING AND CHILDREN—*cont.*

Behind the tug of war over TV ad time [nonpassage of Children's Television Act of 1988] M. Meyer. il *Video* 12:67-8 Mr '89

Can indies afford to have children? [decline in ad revenues for children's programs] M. Burgi. il *Channels (New York, N.Y.: 1986)* 9:74-5 Ja '89

Sugar and the boob tube [influence of television commercials upon children's eating habits; research by Nancy Cotugna] P. McCarthy. *American Health* 8:146-7 Ap '89

Why children's television should be regulated. N. Carlsson-Paige and D. E. Levin. *The Education Digest* 55:37-9 S '89

TELEVISION AND BUSINESS *See* Business and television

TELEVISION AND CHILDREN

See also

Cable television—Children's programs
Television advertising and children
Television broadcasting—Children's programs

Baby see, baby do [influence; research by Andrew Meltzoff] J. Folkenberg. *American Health* 8:104 My '89

Can you trust TV as a baby sitter for your kids? S. Littwin. il *TV Guide* 37:20-2 Jl 1-7 '89

A clearer view of television. D. F. Bjorklund and B. Bjorklund. il *Parents* 64:219 N '89

A gizmo for the president. W. F. Buckley. *National Review* 41:70-1 F 10 '89

How to make TV good for your kids. P. G. O'Brien. il *Ladies' Home Journal* 106:90 Ap '89

Kids: show-and-tell time. il *Life* 12:76-8+ Mr '89

Monitoring TV time. L. G. Katz. il *Parents* 64:124 Ja '89

Prime time for discernment. T. C. Muck. *Christianity Today* 33:19 Ja 13 '89

TV violence: will a new bill help? W. Metts. il *Christianity Today* 33:47 F 17 '89

TELEVISION AND COPYRIGHT *See* Copyright—Broadcasting rights

TELEVISION AND HISTORY

Liberty, equality, absurdity [television movie Napoleon and Josephine] R. Darnton. il *The New Republic* 200:29-32 Ap 3 '89

Mediawatch [British TV] H. David. il *History Today* 39:5-7 O '89

Paint the cows brown—and cue the anchorman [PBS series Timeline] N. Hickey. il *TV Guide* 37:30-1 F 18-24 '89

TELEVISION AND LITERATURE

See also

Television adaptations
Television and reading

New Ted Turner publishing unit to turn TV shows into books. H. Fields. *Publishers Weekly* 236:11 N 24 '89

TELEVISION AND POLITICS

See also

Advertising, Political
Cable television and politics

After Hart, Tower, Wright . . . the backlash is starting against those trials by media. K. Bode. il *TV Guide* 37:21-3 O 7-13 '89

Cue the Green god, Ted [cover story] G. Vidal. il *The Nation* 249:153+ Ag 7-14 '89

"Even the TV people don't understand" [Ripon College conference on 1988 presidential campaign] T. H. Stahel. *America* 161:354-5 N 18 '89

Hot reporter [interview with J. Greenfield] J. Alter. il por *Rolling Stone* p102+ My 18 '89

Kennedy was America's best TV president—Johnson the worst. T. E. Cronin. il *TV Guide* 37:22-3 O 14-20 '89

Loud and clear (as ever) . . . Sam Donaldson's parting shot: how TV can cover the White House a whole lot better. S. Donaldson. il pors *TV Guide* 37:36-8 Ja 28-F 3 '89

Manipulating the media and America: the negative 1988 presidential campaign. R. L. Fischer. il *USA Today (Periodical)* 117:20-2 Mr '89

Media whizzes and washouts: my advice for them all. P. Dusenberry. il *TV Guide* 37:12-15 Je 17-23 '89

Memo to President Bush: how to use TV—and keep from being abused by it. R. M. Nixon. il pors *TV Guide* 37:26-7+ Ja 14-20 '89

Mock crisis, real players [U.S. and Soviet officials participate in televised crisis game] B. Van Voorst. il por *Time* 134:88 D 11 '89

NBC's "Yesterday" show [Today show's preoccupation with the 1970s] R. E. Tyrrell. *The American Spectator* 22:10-11 Mr '89

Politics and the media: a TV revolution. S. Rothman and R. Lerner. *Current (Washington, D.C.)* 311:4-11 Mr/Ap '89

Politics, late-night style. R. Zoglin. il *Time* 133:66 Je 12 '89

The politics of television politics [excerpts from special election eve edition of ABC's Nightline] il *Channels (New York, N.Y.: 1986)* 9:84 F '89

Printheads vs. pictureheads. T. Eastland. il *The American Spectator* 22:40-1 D '89

Public TV goes to Washington [The power game] H. F. Waters. il por *Newsweek* 113:65 Ja 2 '89

A republic of couch potatoes [1988 presidential campaign; cover story] W. C. McWilliams. il *Commonweal* 116:138-40 Mr 10 '89

Television turns its back on the statehouse. N. Koch. il *Channels (New York, N.Y.: 1986)* 9:12 Ap '89

TV will always expose the phonies [views of T. Hesburgh] R. Townley. il por *TV Guide* 37:48-50 Ja 7-13 '89

War of the sound bites [New York City mayoral race] J. Klein. il *New York* 22:20-1 Ag 14 '89

Washington confidential. J. Weisman. il *TV Guide* 37:26-9 F 18-24 '89

What TV news doesn't report about Congress—and should. N. J. Ornstein. il *TV Guide* 37:10-13 O 21-27 '89

Whitewashing the White House [Bill Moyers' documentary Illusions of news] J. M. Robins. il *Channels (New York, N.Y.: 1986)* 9:14 N '89

Will TV give Dan Quayle a fair chance? What he can do to improve his image. E. Diamond and J. Maroe. por *TV Guide* 37:16-19 F 11-17 '89

International aspects

Camera paranoia. J. Saltzman. il *USA Today (Periodical)* 117:19 Mr '89

Canada

Entertainment disguised as news [budget story on The journal] G. Bain. il *Maclean's* 102:58 Ap 24 '89

Germany (East)

How TV helped tear down the Berlin Wall. D. Schorr. il *TV Guide* 37:10-11 D 23-29 '89

Germany (West)

How TV helped tear down the Berlin Wall. D. Schorr. il *TV Guide* 37:10-11 D 23-29 '89

Middle East

Film flam [J. Franklin-Trout's controversial PBS documentary Days of rage] S. Emerson. *The New Republic* 201:29-30+ S 18-25 '89

Viewing the intifada stitch by stitch [PBS documentary Days of rage] W. F. Buckley. *National Review* 41:62-3 O 13 '89

South Africa

Covering news where networks fear to tread [South Africa now] C. Reece. il *Channels (New York, N.Y.: 1986)* 9:17 Ja '89

Dark content: getting South Africa news [South Africa now TV show] E. Hedegaard. il *Mother Jones* 14:49 S '89

Filling the South Africa void [South Africa now TV show] N. S. Mehta. il *Time* 133:58 Mr 6 '89

Getting out the truth [South Africa now TV show] J. M. Robins. il *Channels (New York, N.Y.: 1986)* 9:52-4 N '89

TELEVISION AND READING

Bookworms versus couch potatoes. M. J. Weiss. map *The Atlantic* 264:81 O '89

'Reading rainbow''s 7th season: 1989 titles. il *Publishers Weekly* 235:106 Ja 20 '89

TELEVISION AND THE ENVIRONMENT

Cue the Green god, Ted [cover story] G. Vidal. il *The Nation* 249:153+ Ag 7-14 '89

Is TV news getting all the dirt? E. Diamond and R. Mead. il *TV Guide* 37:20-2 Je 24-30 '89

Media coverage [discussion of March 1989 article, Network television news coverage of environmental risks] M. R. Greenberg and others. il *Environment* 31:2-3 Je '89

Network television news coverage of environmental risks. M. R. Greenberg and others. bibl f il *Environment* 31:16-20+ Mr '89

TELEVISION AND THE MILITARY

DARPA poised to award contracts for high-definition display concepts. P. A. Gilmartin. *Aviation Week & Space Technology* 131:32 S 4 '89

DARPA to fund high-density TV. *High Technology Business* 9:33 Ap '89

Lawmakers to press for legislation to boost U.S. high-definition TV role. P. A. Gilmartin. *Aviation Week & Space Technology* 130:24 Mr 27 '89

Not a pretty picture [HDTV research funded by DARPA] S. Shulman. il *The Progressive* 53:24-5 S '89

TV vs. the military: it's an unfair fight. J. F. Lehman. il *TV Guide* 37:32-4 N 4-10 '89

TELEVISION AND YOUTH

Demos do the talking [Fox targets under 34 age group] M. Couzens. il *Channels (New York, N.Y.: 1986)* 9:20 Mr '89

Television in adolescent social development. R. Luker and J. Johnston. *The Education Digest* 54:50-1 F '89

Tuned out. S. Krieger. il *Seventeen* 48:84-5+ Je '89

Youth, culture, art education, television. R. H. Gray. bibl f *Design for Arts in Education* 90:23-5 Mr/Ap '89

TELEVISION ANTENNA LEAD-IN LINE *See* Television cables

TELEVISION ANTENNAS

Three winter projects to improve your boat [adding a TV antenna, improving plumbing, and building a chart table] il *Motor Boating & Sailing* 163:117-20 F '89

TELEVISION AUDIENCES

See also

Couch potatoes
Zapping of television advertising

TELEVISION AUDIENCES—*cont.*

How hard is it to see television filmings? il *Sunset (Central West edition)* 183:50 D '89

Who's watching what and why? [Roper poll] *USA Today (Periodical)* 118:6 Ag '89

Anecdotes, facetiae, satire, etc.

Confessions of a network dropout. M. Royko. *Reader's Digest* 135:93-4 S '89

Monitoring

See also

People meters (TV audience research)

Single-source research (TV audience research)

TELEVISION AUTHORSHIP

Mel Brooks: of Woody, the Great Caesar, flop sweat and cigar smoke [writers on Your show of shows] M. Brooks. il por *People Weekly* 31 Special Issue:106-7 Summ '89

Pushing network TV to the limit [excerpt from forum of comedy writers] il *Channels (New York, N.Y.: 1986)* 9:86 Ja '89

TV's new ruling class [writer-producers] N. Koch. il *Channels (New York, N.Y.: 1986)* 9:30-5 My '89

Writing for television. D. K. Mano. il *National Review* 41:50+ Ag 18 '89

TELEVISION AWARDS

See also

Emmy Awards

Golden Globe Awards

Anecdotes, facetiae, satire, etc.

TV guide's eighth annual J. Fred Muggs Awards [cover story] il *TV Guide* 37:4-6+ Ja 7-13 '89

TELEVISION BROADCASTING

See also

American Broadcasting Companies, Inc.

CBS Inc.

Closed circuit television

College television stations

Communications satellites—Television broadcasting use

Fox Broadcasting Company

Helicopters in television broadcasting

National Broadcasting Co., Inc.

Realism in television

Television adaptations

Television program reviews

Television stations

Television transmission

Videotapes—Television programs

Advertising

See Television advertising

Archives

See also

Museum of Broadcasting (New York, N.Y.)

Art programs

Art History 101 [PBS series Art of the Western world] J. Gardner. *National Review* 41:43-6 D 8 '89

The arts on public TV. V. R. Rivers. il *American Artist* 53:68 Mr '89

Astronomy programs

Jack Horkheimer: "Star hustler". S. J. O'Meara. il pors *Sky and Telescope* 77:544-7 My '89

Audiences

See Television audiences

Ballet programs

'Martin' [classical ballet about M. L. King] D. Moore. il *American Visions* 4:34-9 D '89

Black programs

Who's new and who's back on TV. il *Ebony* 44:94+ O '89

Cartoons

See also

Bill Melendez Productions

Hanna-Barbera Productions, Inc.

Animation! Art on the move. il *National Geographic World* 164:28-31 Ap '89

Cartoon from hell [M. Groening's The Simpsons] R. Lloyd. il *American Film* 15:112 O '89

Could an ALF cartoon be flashing a hidden message? [subliminal messages] D. Hill and K. Sobel. il *TV Guide* 37:6-7+ Ag 12-18 '89

Is TV the coolest invention ever invented? [M. Groening, creator of Life in hell comic strip and The Simpsons; cover story] S. Elder. il por *Mother Jones* 14:28-31 D '89

The last angry mouse [cancellation of Mighty Mouse] R. Powers. il por *Gentlemen's Quarterly* 59:106+ Ag '89

Life in hell's Matt Groening goes overboard to make the Simpsons the first family of TV 'toons. J. Kaufman. il pors *People Weekly* 32:108-10 D 18 '89

A mutant 'Ozzie and Harriet' [The Simpsons] M. Reese. il *Newsweek* 114:70 D 25 '89

Saturday morning's new motto: make room for daddy! D. Hill. il *TV Guide* 37:52-4 Ja 7-13 '89

Censorship

The advertiser that didn't balk [National Right to Life Committee pressures General Foods to pull advertising for TV movie Roe vs. Wade] M. Suh. il *Ms.* 18:75 Jl/Ag '89

As the 'clean TV' campaign heats up, ABC chills two new shows. P. Freeman. il por *People Weekly* 31:153-4 My 22 '89

The boob tube. J. Martel. il *Rolling Stone* p46+ Mr 23 '89

Crusade or charade? [T. Rakolta's campaign against advertisers on "offensive" shows] M. Lasswell. il *Rolling Stone* p33 My 4 '89

Does Married . . . with children go too far? Will it give in to critics? [cover story] H. Polskin. il *TV Guide* 37:2-5 Jl 29-Ag 4 '89

Farewell, trash, goodbye, Nielsens [shows losing sponsors] *U.S. News & World Report* 106:14+ My 15 '89

How networks decide what stays, what goes. J. Elm. *TV Guide* 37:4 N 18-24 '89

Prime-time shoot-out [campaign against sponsors of objectionable shows] D. Neff. il *Christianity Today* 33:14 O 6 '89

Pushing network TV to the limit [excerpt from forum of comedy writers] il *Channels (New York, N.Y.: 1986)* 9:86 Ja '89

Putting a brake on TV "sleaze": advertisers are growing wary of shows that might offend. R. Zoglin. il *Time* 133:51 Mr 20 '89

They watch what we watch. S. Farber. il *The New York Times Magazine* p42+ My 7 '89

This is what you thought: 80% are worried that special-interest groups could force cancellation of TV programs [results of survey] il *Glamour* 87:163 N '89

Children's programs

See also

Cable television—Children's programs

Children's Television Workshop

Television broadcasting—Cartoons

20 years on Sesame Street. M. H. Lystad. bibl f il *Children Today* 18:20-2 S/O '89

Attention, kids: Sesame Street wants you . . . if you've got the right stuff. A. D. Plate. il *TV Guide* 37:16-18 Jl 15-21 '89

Behind the tug of war over TV ad time [nonpassage of Children's Television Act of 1988] M. Meyer. il *Video* 12:67-8 Mr '89

The best children's shows on TV [cover story] J. Morrow. il *TV Guide* 37:12-14+ F 18-24 '89

Birth day on 'Sesame Street' [Maria's pregnancy] J. Seligmann. il *Newsweek* 113:71 My 15 '89

Buffalo Bob Smith: on overnight success and the Howdy-for-president campaign. B. Smith. il por *People Weekly* 31 Special Issue:107 Summ '89

Can indies afford to have children? [decline in ad revenues] M. Burgi. il *Channels (New York, N.Y.: 1986)* 9:74-5 Ja '89

Mister Rogers: everybody's neighbor. M. J. Bandler. il pors *Parents* 64:118-20+ Mr '89

New hits for kids [Canadian shows] D. Turbide. il *Maclean's* 102:56-7 F 6 '89

New kids' shows worth watching. M. Silver. il *U.S. News & World Report* 107:64-5 Ag 21 '89

The perilous journey from book to screen [children's books for television] G. Haight. il *Publishers Weekly* 235:137-42 F 24 '89

The shrinking of a legend [R. Starr] R. Townley. il pors *TV Guide* 37:18-20 Mr 11-17 '89

Why can't they clone Big Bird? [Sesame Street] J. Rachlin. il *U.S. News & World Report* 107:50+ Jl 31 '89

Why children's television should be regulated. N. Carlsson-Paige and D. E. Levin. *The Education Digest* 55:37-9 S '89

Christmas programs

Here come the holiday specials [cover story] L. Closs. il *TV Guide* 37:4-5+ D 2-8 '89

Riddle of Lucy's 'lost' Christmas episode. I. Rudolph. il *TV Guide* 37:20-2 D 16-22 '89

Comedy programs

See also

Cable television—Comedy programs

Anatomy of a sitcom [Dear John] L. Blandford. il *The New York Times Magazine* p34-7+ Ap 2 '89

The basement tapes [Wayne's world segments on Saturday night live] B. Flanagan. il *Rolling Stone* p45 N 16 '89

Campaigning for serious laughs [promoting off-network situation comedies] N. Koch. il *Channels (New York, N.Y.: 1986)* 9:70-1 Jl/Ag '89

From stand-up to sitcom. J. Malanowski. il *Rolling Stone* p52-3 N 2 '89

Old comics, boy wonders [fall season] R. Zoglin. il *Time* 134:69-70 S 18 '89

Pushing network TV to the limit [excerpt from forum of comedy writers] il *Channels (New York, N.Y.: 1986)* 9:86 Ja '89

Saturday night live [reminiscences of those associated with the show; cover story] il *People Weekly* 32:70-4+ S 25 '89

Television [The best of Gilda Radner, The best of Eddie Murphy, Saturday night live, Milton Berle—the second time around, and The "I love Lucy" collection] J. Walker. il *Video* 13:93+ S '89

TELEVISION BROADCASTING—*cont.*

Conversation programs
See also
Cable television—Conversation programs
Tabloid television
Alone at the top [A. Hall] P. Goldstein. il pors *Rolling Stone* p60-2+ N 2 '89
And now, nice-guy talk hosts [P. Sajak and A. Hall] R. Zoglin. pors *Time* 133:74 Ja 9 '89
Arsenio Hall's late arrival. H. F. Waters. il pors *Newsweek* 113:68-9 Ap 10 '89
Arsenio Hall's TV talk show keeps fans awake with fun and famous faces [cover story] A. Collier. il pors *Jet* 76:56-9 Ap 10 '89
The art and advantage of conversation [interview with P. Lund of Multimedia Entertainment] il pors *Channels (New York, N.Y.: 1986)* 9:54-5 My '89
Barbara Walters's theater of revenge. M. C. Miller. *Harper's* 279:40-1+ N '89
Getting hotter—but feeling the heat [A. Hall] M. Leahy. il pors *TV Guide* 37:16-19 S 30-O 6 '89
The gift of gab [interview with S. Allen] L. Konner. pors *New Choices for the Best Years* 29:11-12 S '89
The great talk-show hoax [perpetrated by T. Freiwald and W. Bailey] B. G. Harrison. *Mademoiselle* 95:62 Ja '89
Is Geraldo Rivera running out of control? D. Hill. il pors *TV Guide* 37:28-31 Ja 28-F 3 '89
The Joan Rivers show. R. MacKenzie. il por *TV Guide* 37:32 O 28-N 3 '89
Johnny come lately [P. Sajak] N. Scovell. il por *Rolling Stone* p23 F 23 '89
Late-night cool [A. Hall; cover story] M. Norman. il pors *The New York Times Magazine* p28-31+ O 1 '89
"Let's get busy!!" [A. Hall; cover story] R. Zoglin. il pors *Time* 134:92-7 N 13 '89
On the air with Downey. M. Brown. il *Channels (New York, N.Y.: 1986)* 9:24 Ap '89
The Pat Sajak show; The Arsenio Hall show. M. Panitt. il *TV Guide* 37:1 Mr 18-24 '89
Politics, late-night style [talk show hosts] R. Zoglin. il *Time* 133:66 Je 12 '89
Sally Jessy Raphaël driven? You'd be too—if you were fired 18 times and lived on food stamps. D. Hill. il por *TV Guide* 37:17-19 Jl 8-14 '89
Sally Jessy Raphaël on the move. R. Beach. il pors *The Saturday Evening Post* 261:58-9+ S '89
Sound bites from Never-never Land. P. Yancey. il *Christianity Today* 33:56 Ap 21 '89
Taking a spin at late-night [P. Sajak] B. Barol. il por *Newsweek* 113:63+ Ja 16 '89
Talk show angst. L. Lamb. il *Utne Reader* p30 S/O '89
Talking people into talking [bookers] R. Givens. il *Newsweek* 114:44-5 Jl 17 '89

Anecdotes, facetiae, satire, etc.
The Chuck show. G. Keillor. *The New Yorker* 65:26-9 Jl 24 '89

Cooking programs
Home on the range. C. Schine. il *Vogue* 179:298 Mr '89

Costume
See Costume, Theatrical

Court proceedings
See Television broadcasting—Trials

Crime programs
See also
Columbo (Fictional character)
Freeze! You're on TV [America's most wanted] F. J. Prial. il *Reader's Digest* 134:189-92 Mr '89
'I am still devastated' [J. Walsh, host of America's most wanted] J. Marion. il pors *TV Guide* 37:22-4 Mr 18-24 '89
In hiding for 18 years, a wanted man is caught by the FBI and a TV posse [J. List, alleged murderer, featured on America's most wanted] K. Gross. il pors *People Weekly* 31:69-70+ Je 19 '89
Lawyers, guns and money. R. Powers. il *Gentlemen's Quarterly* 59:129-30+ Je '89
Making an arresting TV debut, deputy sheriff Linda Canada puts the cuffs on fame in Fox's Cops [Broward County, Fla.] P. Jordan. il pors *People Weekly* 31:89-90 Ap 24 '89
Murder, they broadcast [viewers of America's most wanted identify murderer J. List] T. Jacoby. pors *Newsweek* 113:58 Je 12 '89
Speak loudly and carry a nightstick [producer and former policeman S. Grosso] D. Friedman. por *Rolling Stone* p37 Ag 10 '89
Too close for comfort [news show Eye on crime shows Miami police in action] J. M. Robins. il *Channels (New York, N.Y.: 1986)* 9:24+ Mr '89
True grit [Cops] D. Friedman. il *Rolling Stone* p26 Ap 6 '89
TV's crime wave gets real [Cops] H. F. Waters. il *Newsweek* 113:72 My 15 '89
Wanted: lowlifes and high ratings [America's most wanted] D. Friedman. il *Rolling Stone* p34-5 Ja 12 '89
Watch the Farrah lookalike make a real drug bust [Cops] J. Weisman. il *TV Guide* 37:18-19 Je 17-23 '89

Cult shows
The cult zone. il *People Weekly* 31 Special Issue:104-5 Summ '89

Docudramas
Ripping off the headlines. H. F. Waters. il *Newsweek* 114:62-3+ S 11 '89
Scandal? Tragedy? Violence? Here come the wheeler-dealers waving their checkbooks [made for TV real life dramas] J. Kaye. il *TV Guide* 37:23-4+ Ja 7-13 '89

Documentary programs
Escape from summer inanity [PBS series P.O.V.] T. O'Brien. *Commonweal* 116:372 Je 16 '89
Trump vs. Stern: the unmaking of a documentary [cover story] E. Diamond. il pors *New York* 22:30-7 S 4 '89

Economic news
The case against Ted Koppel [ignorance concerning economics among reporters; cover story] M. Miller. il *The Washington Monthly* 21:34-6+ My '89
How TV sees the economy. J. Bodnar. il *Changing Times* 43:89-91+ D '89

Educational programs
See also
Direct broadcast satellite services—Educational programs

Electronic music
More sound for less [computer-generated music for TV productions] F. Moore. il *Channels (New York, N.Y.: 1986)* 9:72 Jl/Ag '89

Environmental aspects
See Television and the environment

Errors
Please stand by: TV's glitch patrol [excerpts from newsletter about technical difficulties] *Harper's* 278:26-7 Je '89

Festivals
See Television festivals

Financial programs
See also
American Business Network
The picture has started to fade for TV's infomercials. P. Wang. il *Money* 18:17 Jl '89

Game shows
A: The Jeopardy! priest; Q: Who is Tom Smolich? Correct for $39,802! [Jesuit raises money for day care center in East Los Angeles, Calif.] il pors *People Weekly* 32:58 O 9 '89
Ex-jock Rolf Benirschke, whose number once almost came up, puts his spin on Wheel of fortune. S. Schindehette. il pors *People Weekly* 31:51-2+ Ja 23 '89
Name that game! il *People Weekly* 31 Special Issue:102-3 Summ '89
Open house [British game show Through the keyhole features celebrity house tours] B. Walder. il *House & Garden* 161:70+ Mr '89
TV dating. G. Hirshey. il *Utne Reader* p54-5 Mr/Ap '89
What is 'Jeopardy!'? F. Lidz. il *Sports Illustrated* 70:94-8+ My 1 '89
Why Joan Rivers and Betty White keep playing games. G. D. Christenson. il *TV Guide* 37:10-12 Ja 14-20 '89

Health education programs
Save a Life [emergency first aid TV shows in Britain] P. Riding. il *World Health* p29 Ja/F '89

History
Fading remembrances of television past [use of programs cancelled after one year to study long-term memory; work of Larry R. Squire] B. Bower. *Science News* 135:167 Mr 18 '89
Mr. TV's message on the medium [views of M. Berle] il por *U.S. News & World Report* 106:14 My 22 '89
Television at 50: looking good [special section] il *Life* 12:46-53+ Mr '89
Television's 50th anniversary [cover story] il *People Weekly* 31 Special Issue:6-17+ Summ '89
Ten years after [television in the '80s] H. Rosenberg. il *American Film* 15:18-19 D '89
Turned on for fifty years [celebrities' favorite shows] J. Dunn and others. il *Rolling Stone* p29-30+ D 14-28 '89
TV is 50: happy birthday! [cover story; special issue] il *TV Guide* 37:2-8+ My 6-12 '89
TV news did not just happen—it had to invent itself. D. Smith. il *Smithsonian* 20:74-8+ Je '89

Exhibitions
Is it TV's 50th birthday or not? [Smithsonian exhibit American television: from the Fair to the family, 1939-1989] F. Lovece. il *Channels (New York, N.Y.: 1986)* 9:9 Je '89
The reruns of August [Smithsonian exhibit American television: from the Fair to the family, 1939-1989] S. A. Booth. il *Popular Mechanics* 166:36+ Ag '89
The show-and-sell machine [American television: from the Fair to the family, 1939-1989 at the Smithsonian] R. Zoglin. il *Time* 133:61 My 1 '89
A spate of new toys invades America's living rooms [American television: from the Fair to the family, 1939-1989 at the Museum of American History] W. L. Bird, Jr. il *Smithsonian* 20:82-8+ Je '89
TV celebrates its first 50 years [Smithsonian exhibit, American television: from the Fair to the family, 1939-1989] F. Lovece. il *Video* 13:66-9+ My '89

TELEVISION BROADCASTING—*cont.*

Horror shows

Invasion of the wild things. R. Zoglin. il *Time* 134:88-9 N 6 '89

Laws and regulations

See Television laws and regulations

Live programs

See Live television programs

Medical programs

23 years after Dr. Kildare, Richard Chamberlain's back in practice [cover story] L. Eisenberg. il pors *TV Guide* 37:2-3+ N 11-17 '89

Meteorological programs

See also

Television broadcasting—Weather forecasts

Miniseries

Mega-drop in miniseries [ratings; chart] il *Channels (New York, N.Y.: 1986)* 9:72 Mr '89

Moral and religious aspects

See also

Christian Leaders for Responsible Television

Sex in television

Television broadcasting—Religious programs

Violence in television

The agony of deceit [television neutralizes truth] R. Powers. il *Gentlemen's Quarterly* 59:190+ Mr '89

Bringing Satan to heel [interview with D. Wildmon] D. Winbush. il por *Time* 133:54-5 Je 19 '89

The Church's response to the media: twenty-five years after *Inter mirifica* [Vatican II decree] R. P. Waznak. *America* 160:36-40 Ja 21 '89

Courageous criticism [views of Walter Goodman] M. E. Marty. *The Christian Century* 106:367 Ap 5 '89

We need more religion in prime time. D. Wakefield. il *TV Guide* 37:14-17 Mr 11-17 '89

Motion picture criticism programs

Rating TV's movie critics: best sweaters—see below. K. Turan. il *TV Guide* 37:26-8 Mr 18-24 '89

Motion pictures

Dogmatic disclaimers [editing for TV] H. Bender and K. Greene. *American Film* 14:12-13 My '89

Movie packages [directory] il *Channels (New York, N.Y.: 1986)* 9:60-1 Ja 16 '89

Movies. J. Crist. il *TV Guide* 37:82-2+ S 9-15 '89

Shifting windows: an indie dilemma [Hollywood films appearing on basic cable in advance of independent TV stations] R. Marich. il *Channels (New York, N.Y.: 1986)* 9:76-8 Ja '89

Nature programs

How the owl drove a wedge between Stroh and Audubon [beer company pulls ads from TV show on Pacific Northwest old growth forests] V. Cahan. *Business Week* p99 S 18 '89

Intimidation [advertisers cancel sponsorship of Audubon program about Pacific Northwest forests] L. Line. il *Audubon* 91:4 N '89

News

See also

Brawley, Tawana—Assault case—Reporters and reporting

Cable News Network

Cable television—News

Gorbachev, Mikhail—Visit to Cuba, 1989—Reporters and reporting

Helicopters in television broadcasting

Israel-Arab Wars, 1967- —Reporters and reporting

San Francisco Bay Area (Calif.)—Earthquake, 1989—Reporters and reporting

Tabloid television

Television and politics

Television broadcasting—Economic news

Television broadcasting—Trials

Terrorism and the press

Tiananmen Square (China) student occupation, 1989—Reporters and reporting

Vietnamese War, 1957-1975—Reporters and reporting

The 1989 network news all-star team [cover story] il *TV Guide* 37:2-5 Jl 15-21 '89

The ABCs of making news profits [R. Arledge; cover story] C. Capuzzi. il por *Channels (New York, N.Y.: 1986)* 9:30-5 Mr '89

The ABCs of Peter Jennings [interview] N. Atkins. por *Rolling Stone* p60-2+ My 4 '89

All the news that's glitz. J. M. Robins. il *Channels (New York, N.Y.: 1986)* 9:44 D '89

Anchors away [increased time spent on location] E. Diamond. il *New York* 22:18+ D 18 '89

Are women reporters better than men? M. Sanders. il *TV Guide* 37:15-16+ Mr 18-24 '89

Behind the NBC News blues. J. Alter. il *Newsweek* 114:86-7 O 16 '89

Behind the Peacock throne [NBC News president M. Gartner] E. Diamond. il por *New York* 22:21-2 F 13 '89

The big stories TV news is missing—and why. J. Kalter and J. Marion. il *TV Guide* 37:2-5 Jl 22-28 '89

The boob tube [lack of journalism in local news] R. Powers. il *Gentlemen's Quarterly* 59:226+ S '89

Camcorder assault [amateur videotape on TV newscasts] J. M. Robins. il *Channels (New York, N.Y.: 1986)* 9:30-1 Ja '89

Crash course in Denver [TV newsrooms cover Sioux City air crash, July 1989] J. M. Robins. il *Channels (New York, N.Y.: 1986)* 9:16 O '89

Crime: that's entertainment [TV interview with murderer T. Bundy] J. Leo. il por *U.S. News & World Report* 106:53 F 6 '89

Dan Rather's difficult days. J. Rovin. il pors *Ladies' Home Journal* 106:80+ Ja '89

A day in the life of the evening news [D. Rather broadcast on CBS] D. O. Relin. il por *Scholastic Update (Teachers' edition)* 122:7-9 S 8 '89

'Drugs almost destroyed my career' [black TV anchorman W. Bell] L. Norment. il pors *Ebony* 44:124-5 Ag '89

Early starters [Primetime live] il *TV Guide* 37:38 S 9-15 '89

Eleventh-hour gamble [Channel 13's late night local news in New York City] E. Diamond. il *New York* 22:12-13 Ja 9 '89

Eyewitness video. H. Dunst. il *Video* 13:48-50+ Ap '89

Favorite network news stories [1988; tables] il *Channels (New York, N.Y.: 1986)* 9:56 My '89

From 'Good evening, everybody, coast to coast' to 'Courage' [anchors] J. Elm. il *TV Guide* 37:30-1 My 6-12 '89

Grins, gore, and videotape: the trouble with local TV news [New York City; cover story] E. Pooley. il *New York* 22:36-44 O 9 '89

The inside dope [newsletters The rundown and The Tyndall report] J. M. Robins. *Channels (New York, N.Y.: 1986)* 9:37 F '89

Is local TV news at risk? M. Brown. il *Channels (New York, N.Y.: 1986)* 9:20 Jl/Ag '89

Is network news getting better—or worse? E. Joyce. il *TV Guide* 37:10-12 My 13-19 '89

Is TV news guilty of Japan bashing? E. Diamond and K. O'Neil. il *TV Guide* 37:24-7 My 20-26 '89

Let's go to the videotape [Primetime live] E. Diamond. il pors *New York* 22:24+ D 4 '89

Local news reveille [WNYW's Good day New York] J. M. Robins. il *Channels (New York, N.Y.: 1986)* 9:78 Je '89

'Looksism' in TV news [sexism] J. Alter. il por *Newsweek* 114:72-3 N 6 '89

Man or machine in the newsroom? P. Noglows. il *Channels (New York, N.Y.: 1986)* 9:39-40 My '89

Maria Shriver: you call this a glamour job? C. Krupp. il pors *Glamour* 87:172-3 N '89

A new breed of celebrity [TV journalists] J. Saltzman. *USA Today (Periodical)* 118:67 Jl '89

The news beat. il *People Weekly* 31 Special Issue:99-101 Summ '89

The Nieman Foundation at 50: the curator critiques television news [views of H. Simons] P. Ainslie. il por *Channels (New York, N.Y.: 1986)* 9:10 Je '89

Notes and comment [interview with T. Bundy] *The New Yorker* 65:23-4 F 27 '89

Oh, what a year! [1989] P. Jennings. il por *TV Guide* 37:20-1 D 30 '89-Ja 5 '90

On the roller coaster with Diane and Sam [Primetime live] E. Diamond. pors *New York* 22:10-12 Jl 24 '89

Packaging the news. R. Corelli. il *Maclean's* 102:82-3 O 30 '89

Pain behind the camera [covering crash of Pan Am 103 on local TV] K. Frankola. por *Newsweek* 113:9 F 6 '89

Peter Jennings gets no self-respect. E. Kaye. il pors *Esquire* 112:158-60+ S '89

Pitching USA today. A. Snyder. il *Channels (New York, N.Y.: 1986)* 9:17-18 Mr '89

Politics and the media: a TV revolution. S. Rothman and R. Lerner. *Current (Washington, D.C.)* 311:4-11 Mr/Ap '89

Power failure [NBC News president M. Gartner] E. Diamond. il por *New York* 22:24-5 N 6 '89

Prefab news [video news releases] S. E. Davis. il *Technology Review* 92:6-7 O '89

The prime time of her life [D. Sawyer] P. Pierce. il pors *Ladies' Home Journal* 106:42+ O '89

The prime times of Diane Sawyer. J. Grant. il pors *Life* 12:72-4+ Ag '89

Primetime live. R. MacKenzie. il *TV Guide* 37:39 O 14-20 '89

Rather strange: behind Dan's odd behavior. R. Townley. il pors *TV Guide* 37:4-7 F 25-Mr 3 '89

A real bad trip [substance abuse by newspeople] J. M. Robins. il *Channels (New York, N.Y.: 1986)* 9:19 Jl/Ag '89

The sky's the limit [local news operations bypass networks] J. Castro. il *Time* 134:72-3 N 27 '89

Star power [anchor D. Sawyer of Primetime live; cover story] R. Zoglin. il pors *Time* 134:46-51 Ag 7 '89

Star wars at the networks [C. Chung, M. A. Williams, and D. Sawyer switch networks] R. Zoglin. il pors *Time* 133:70-1 Ap 3 '89

Stretched to the limit [local news operations at San Francisco's KGO; Wilmington, N.C.'s WECT, and Toledo, Ohio's WTVG; cover story] J. M. Robins. il *Channels (New York, N.Y.: 1986)* 9:42-3+ S '89

TELEVISION BROADCASTING—News—*cont.*

Sunday mourning [former producer of CBS News Sunday morning S. Northshield] R. Powers. il *Gentlemen's Quarterly* 59:68+ Jl '89

Taking a tip from a dapper fan, anchorman Don Shelby makes news with the knot in his necktie [Shelby knot created by J. Pratt] il pors *People Weekly* 32:59 O 2 '89

They've run her off the road—but never off a story [West 57th's K. Burnes] D. Hill. il por *TV Guide* 37:36-7 Ja 21-27 '89

The threat to foreign news. D. Rather. por *Newsweek* 114:9 Jl 17 '89

TV news did not just happen—it had to invent itself. D. Smith. il *Smithsonian* 20:74-8+ Je '89

TV news goes Hollywood. R. Zoglin. il *Time* 134:98+ O 9 '89

TV news theater. J. Saltzman. il *USA Today (Periodical)* 118:89 N '89

TV vs. print: which is best? [research by Ann Crigler] *USA Today (Periodical)* 118:6 Ag '89

TV's big turnoff [USA today; cover story] J. Morgenstern. il por *The New York Times Magazine* p12-15+ Ja 1 '89

TV's new golden girl [D. Norville] J. Hoffman. il pors *Gentlemen's Quarterly* 59:232-5+ Je '89

TV's new news queens: how good are they? [cover story] J. Elm. il *TV Guide* 37:2-4 Ag 12-18 '89

Two hearts, beating in prime time [C. Chung and M. Povich; cover story] K. McMurran. il pors *People Weekly* 31:116-17+ Ap 10 '89

A veteran TV anchorman's toughest story was his own—he had to beat drugs and depression; ed. by Jeannie Park. J. Jensen. il pors *People Weekly* 32:67-8+ S 4 '89

Vive la télé [French shows] M. Lilla. *The New Republic* 200:24 Ja 23 '89

Walter Cronkite. il pors *People Weekly* 31 Special Issue:26-7 Summ '89

What happened to Marlene Sanders? L. C. Pogrebin. il pors *New Choices for the Best Years* 29:67-71+ Mr '89

What makes Maria Shriver run so fast. J. Kalter. il pors *TV Guide* 37:6-10 Jl 29-Ag 4 '89

What TV's real newswomen think of Murphy Brown [cover story] J. Elm. il *TV Guide* 37:4-7 D 23-29 '89

What's news and what's not this fall. M. Kiernan. il *U.S. News & World Report* 107:73-4 O 9 '89

When anchors meet actors [news shows to use re-enactments] J. Alter. il *Newsweek* 114:44-5 Jl 24 '89

When Leibner calls, the networks listen [agent for newscasters] B. Yagoda. il pors *The New York Times Magazine* p36-8+ Je 18 '89

Where is the Goober? [effects of reality-based programming] K. Rickenbaker. por *Newsweek* 113:12 My 1 '89

White-collar crime isn't news [research by Donna Randall and others] *USA Today (Periodical)* 118:4-5 D '89

Will women change prime-time TV news? A. Nash. il *Glamour* 87:242-5+ O '89

Winning Diane: how ABC's Roone Arledge snatched her away from CBS [cover story] E. Klein. il pors *New York* 22:36-43 Mr 13 '89

With Mary Alice Williams, NBC has a winner in the great anchor sweepstakes. S. K. Reed. il pors *People Weekly* 32:44-6 Ag 7 '89

Women on the verge of a nervy breakthrough [interview with L. Ellerbee, M. Goldin, A. Rubenstein and M. Vieira; cover story] P. Orenstein. il pors *Mother Jones* 14:28-31+ Je '89

The wooing of Diane Sawyer sparks a fierce network battle. il pors *People Weekly* 31:124 Ap 10 '89

Bibliography

Women in television are second-class citizens. J. Saltzman. il *USA Today (Periodical)* 118:51-3 S '89

Opera

Alter ego [F. Murray Abraham is Met's host] B. Kellow. il por *Opera News* 54:22-3 D 23 '89

Domestic vintage [D. Argento's The Aspern papers] J. Ardoin. *National Review* 41:50+ Je 30 '89

Opera on television. il *Opera News* 53:42-3 Je '89

Peach of a diva [PBS miniseries salutes N. Melba] J. James. il por *Opera News* 53:44-5 Ja 7 '89

Performers

See Television performers

Periodicals

See also

TV guide (Periodical)

Plots, themes, etc.

See also

Abortion in television

Achille Lauro ship hijacking, 1985, in television

Adultery in television

AIDS (Disease) in television

Alabama in television

Alcoholics and alcoholism in television

Automobiles in television

Black family in television

Blacks in television

Childbirth in television

China in television

Current events in television

Dating (Social customs) in television

Democracy in television

Diet in television

Divorced fathers in television

Dolphins in television

Down syndrome in television

Drug abuse in television

Family in television

Heroes and heroines in television

Holocaust, Jewish (1939-1945), in television

Interracial dating in television

Iran-contra affair in television

Japan in television

Law in television

Livestock in television

Love in television

Marriage in television

Men in television

Narcotics trade in television

Nineteen hundred and sixties in television

Nuclear warfare in television

Parents in television

Phonograph record industry in television

Police in television

Policewomen in television

Pregnancy in television

Race relations in television

Rape in television

Vietnamese War, 1957-1975, in television

Wife abuse in television

Women in television

Young women in television

Yuppies in television

Anecdotes, facetiae, satire, etc.

Stephen Birmingham's one-upmanship guide [cover story] S. Birmingham. il *TV Guide* 37:6-9 Mr 11-17 '89

Political programs

See Television and politics

Popular music

Follow the leader [Arsenio Hall's bandleader M. Wolff and Pat Sajak's T. Scott] J. Marchese. il por *Rolling Stone* p32-3 Je 15 '89

Jukebox Saturday night [taping of public television special] *The New Yorker* 65:36-7 My 15 '89

Paul Shaffer and the World's Most Dangerous Band [cover story] J. Cunniff. il pors *Down Beat* 56:16-19 O '89

Profiles [P. Shaffer, bandleader on Late night with David Letterman] J. Kaplan. il *The New Yorker* 64:36-40+ Ja 16 '89

Production and direction

See Television production and direction

Programming

Fall '89 strategies [special section] il *Channels (New York, N.Y.: 1986)* 9:28-32 O '89

First, let's ban all morning programs [views of W. Styron] R. Townley. il pors *TV Guide* 37:12-14 Mr 4-10 '89

Programmers' handbook [cover story; special issue; with editorial comment by Merrill Brown] il *Channels (New York, N.Y.: 1986)* 9:6+ Ja 16 '89

Quality shows are the key to net survival [interview with H. Shepherd] N. Koch. il pors *Channels (New York, N.Y.: 1986)* 9:94-5 Ja '89

The search for identity. M. Brown. il *Channels (New York, N.Y.: 1986)* 9:34 Ja '89

Where television is headed: the next 50 years. R. Powers. il *TV Guide* 37:45-6 My 6-12 '89

Anecdotes, facetiae, satire, etc.

U.S. TV? It's been better for the Brits than our spareribs or cruise missiles. A. Coren. il *TV Guide* 37:22-3 My 27-Je 2 '89

Psychological aspects

How television's stories help us. R. Coles. il *TV Guide* 37:18-20 Je 3-9 '89

The importance of being Oprah [cover story] B. G. Harrison. il pors *The New York Times Magazine* p28-30+ Je 11 '89

The shows that'll make you feel better. J. Brothers. il *TV Guide* 37:12-15 Jl 29-Ag 4 '89

Public service programs

Raise the halo high. D. Bollier. il *Channels (New York, N.Y.: 1986)* 9:32-4+ Ap '89

With a little help from my TV [Fox Television's health-oriented campaign called Life: be in it] M. Edelston. il *American Health* 8:38 Je '89

Quiz shows

The quiz-show scandal [1950s] W. Karp. il pors *American Heritage* 40:76-84+ My/Je '89

Ratings

See also

Arbitron Ratings Company

Electronic Media Rating Council

People meters (TV audience research)

Q ratings

Single-source research (TV audience research)

Bang the drum loudly [networks] J. M. Robins. il *Channels (New York, N.Y.: 1986)* 9:72-3 D '89

The best and worst by the numbers. il *TV Guide* 37:12-14 Jl 8-14 '89

TELEVISION BROADCASTING—Sports—*cont.*
Throw the flag—for illegal use of the mouth [Monday night football] M. Durslag. il *TV Guide* 37:8-11 S 2-8 '89
Tour TV: time to grow up [ABC's coverage of the Tour de France] G. Drake. *Bicycling* 30:33 O/N '89
Tuning out the 24-hour sports glut: a viewer's lament. T. Callahan. il *Newsweek* 114:68 D 11 '89
TV listings [tennis] il *World Tennis* 36:25 Ja '89
Whole lot of Carays going on [three generations of play-by-play announcers] D. S. Looney. il *Sports Illustrated* 71:87 Ag 14 '89
Working girl [tennis announcer M. Carillo] C. Shmerler. il pors *World Tennis* 37:64-7 Je '89
Wrestling to the top [professional wrestling] H. D. Shapiro. il *Channels (New York, N.Y.: 1986)* 9:38-41 Ja '89
Yearning for Howard [today's easygoing sportscasters contrasted with H. Cosell] F. Lidz. por *Sports Illustrated* 70:86 My 29 '89
The yessss! man can play rough [M. Albert] L. Feldman. il por *TV Guide* 37:16-18 Jl 1-7 '89
Syndicated programs
See also
Access Syndication (Firm)
Buena Vista Television
Genesis Entertainment
Harmony Gold (Firm)
King World Productions, Inc.
LBS Communications (Firm)
Peregrine Entertainment Limited
Beating them at their own game. J. Flinn. il *Channels (New York, N.Y.: 1986)* 9:74-5 D '89
Cosby reruns: was the big Bill worth it? D. Hill. il *TV Guide* 37:32 Jl 29-Ag 4 '89
Finsyn's final chapter. M. Brown. il *Channels (New York, N.Y.: 1986)* 9:18 O '89
Guaranteed success? [producers of first-run syndicated shows getting distributor commitment to promotional advertising] N. Koch. il *Channels (New York, N.Y.: 1986)* 9:80 Je '89
How Paramount is blitzing the networks. R. Grover and D. Lieberman. il *Business Week* p94-5 Ja 30 '89
Norman Lear, meet Adam Smith [Greater Rochester Cablevision owned by Time Warner competes with Act III Broadcasting's independent station in syndicated market] P. Newcomb. il *Forbes* 144:206+ N 27 '89
Programmers' handbook [cover story; special issue; with editorial comment by Merrill Brown] il *Channels (New York, N.Y.: 1986)* 9:6+ Ja 16 '89
Riding the rumble seat into the '90s [preview of NATPE panel on syndication] A. Butensky. por *Channels (New York, N.Y.: 1986)* 9:88 F '89
Syndicated. il *TV Guide* 37:94-5 S 9-15 '89
Syndication's new strategies [special section] il *Channels (New York, N.Y.: 1986)* 9:59+ F '89
Syndication's next move [special section] il *Channels (New York, N.Y.: 1986)* 9:35-44 O '89
What's syndex? Will it affect you? [syndicated exclusivity reimposed by the Federal Communications Commission] N. Hickey. il *TV Guide* 37:12 D 23-29 '89
Trials
Camera paranoia. J. Saltzman. il *USA Today (Periodical)* 117:19 Mr '89
See also
Vietnamese War, 1957-1975—Reporters and reporting
Weather forecasts
Dr. Stan, the TV weatherman [filling in at WTZA, Kingston, N.Y.] S. D. Gedzelman. il pors *Weatherwise* 42:151-4 Je '89
Facts and forecasts [contrasting U.S. and British telecasts] H. Caminos. il *Américas* 41 no1:64 '89
This morning's weatherman: dependably breezy [M. McEwen] J. Marion. il por *TV Guide* 37:36 S 30-O 6 '89
The weather? Funny and wild (and downright incidental). R. Simon. il *TV Guide* 37:12-15 My 27-Je 2 '89
Westerns
The golden dove [S. De Passe and Motown's investment in TV series Lonesome dove] G. Button. il por *Forbes* 143:58-9 Ja 23 '89
Motown soars with "Dove". S. Herbert. il por *Black Enterprise* 19:40 My '89
Star Robert Duvall says: it's going to be like a western Godfather [Lonesome dove] L. D. Estleman. il pors *TV Guide* 36:14-16+ F 4-10 '89
Though grayer, and wider in the saddle, Gene Barry and Hugh O'Brian ride again. il pors *People Weekly* 32:106-7 Ag 28 '89
Canada
See also
Canadian Broadcasting Corporation
Canadian Radio-Television and Telecommunications Commission
Canadian TV ministries: higher on hope than hype. W. Nelles. il *Christianity Today* 33:46-7 Mr 17 '89
Making 'Democracy' [Canadian series The Struggle for democracy; cover story; with editorial comment by Kevin Doyle] B. D. Johnson. il pors *Maclean's* 102:4, 38-40+ Ja 16 '89

New hits for kids. D. Turbide. il *Maclean's* 102:56-7 F 6 '89
TV highs and lows [new series] D. Turbide. il *Maclean's* 102:107 O 30 '89
China
America's Voice in China [Voice of America] D. Baer. il *U.S. News & World Report* 106:34 Je 19 '89
Developing countries
Science soaps. J. Cornell. il *Technology Review* 92:12-13 O '89
Estonia
They're Russian to see our TV. N. Hickey. il *TV Guide* 37:10 Ja 28-F 3 '89
Finland
They're Russian to see our TV. N. Hickey. il *TV Guide* 37:10 Ja 28-F 3 '89
France
Vive la télé [news shows] M. Lilla. *The New Republic* 200:24 Ja 23 '89
Great Britain
See also
BBC
Down the tubes in London. P. Green. *The Nation* 248:274-7 F 27 '89
Mediawatch. H. David. il *History Today* 39:5-7 O '89
Open house [game show Through the keyhole features celebrity house tours] B. Walder. il *House & Garden* 161:70+ Mr '89
Anecdotes, facetiae, satire, etc.
U.S. TV? It's been better for the Brits than our spareribs or cruise missiles. A. Coren. il *TV Guide* 37:22-3 My 27-Je 2 '89
Soviet Union
Historic sermon [religious TV show] *Time* 134:82 O 30 '89
Lenin meets Letterman. E. Diamond. il *New York* 22:19-20 Ap 3 '89
United States
See Television broadcasting
TELEVISION BROADCASTING, PUBLIC
See also
Corporation for Public Broadcasting
Public Broadcasting Service
Television stations, Public
Finance
A rude education in competition. R. Barbieri. il *Channels (New York, N.Y.: 1986)* 9:84 D '89
TELEVISION BROADCASTING, SUBSCRIPTION
See also
Cable television
TELEVISION CABINETS *See* Cabinets (Furniture)
TELEVISION CABLES
How to cut a cable to the perfect length. G. McComb. il *Video* 12:39 F '89
TELEVISION CAMERAS
See also
Film-to-video transfer system
Video cameras
TELEVISION CARTOONS *See* Television advertising—Cartoons; Television broadcasting—Cartoons
TELEVISION CENSORSHIP *See* Television broadcasting—Censorship
TELEVISION CHARACTERS *See* Blacks in television; Women in television
TELEVISION CIRCUITS
Digital TV. il *Radio-Electronics* 60:8 Ag '89
TELEVISION COMMERCIALS *See* Television advertising
TELEVISION COSTUME *See* Costume, Theatrical
TELEVISION CRITICS AND CRITICISM
See also
Mark, Norman
Television program reviews
TELEVISION EDITING
Speeding up the cutting [random access editing machines] F. Moore. il *Channels (New York, N.Y.: 1986)* 9:72 S '89
TELEVISION EQUIPMENT
See also
Headphones
Television projection
Television receivers
Television stations—Equipment
Videotape recorders and recording
TELEVISION EQUIPMENT INDUSTRY
See also
Go-Video Inc.
Instant Replay (Firm)
Zenith Electronics Corp.
Antitrust cases
Dual-cassette VCR [Go-Video] W. J. Hawkins. il *Popular Science* 235:90 N '89
A roll of the dice [Go-Video's patent on dual cassette recorder and antitrust suit against Japanese firms] W. P. Barrett. il *Forbes* 143:81 F 20 '89
Marketing
Ergonomically speaking [VCRs] M. Fleischmann. il *Channels (New York, N.Y.: 1986)* 9:98 D '89

TELEVISION EQUIPMENT INDUSTRY—*cont.*

Japan

A roll of the dice [Go-Video's patent on dual cassette recorder and antitrust suit against Japanese firms] W. P. Barrett. il *Forbes* 143:81 F 20 '89

TELEVISION EQUIPMENT STORES

Eraser heads & feather dusters. il *Video* 13:70-1 N '89

TELEVISION FESTIVALS

Alberta

Small-screen static [Banff Television Festival] D. Turbide. il *Maclean's* 102:53-4 Je 19 '89

France

See also

Marche International des Films et des Programmes pour la TV, la Video, le Cable et le Satellite

Television [Festival International de Programmes Audiovisuels] J. Leonard. il *New York* 22:103-4 O 30 '89

TELEVISION FREQUENCY ALLOCATION

B + K Model 1201SR television frequency converter/modulator. il *Radio-Electronics* 60:22 O '89

TELEVISION GAMES *See* Video games

TELEVISION IN EDUCATION

See also

Cable television in education

Open University

Television stations, Public

Videotapes—Educational use

Bearding the proverbial lion [use of television commercials to teach classical music] W. Greckel. *Design for Arts in Education* 90:43-7 Mr/Ap '89

Belying the myths about instructional television. M. Chen and W. Marsh. *The Education Digest* 55:60-3 D '89

Managing the influence of television through the discipline of video. W. Kennedy. bibl f *Design for Arts in Education* 90:26-8 Mr/Ap '89

Television, cultural history, and arts education. H. Hoffa. *Design for Arts in Education* 90:15-22 Mr/Ap '89

Television in adolescent social development. R. Luker and J. Johnston. *The Education Digest* 54:50-1 F '89

Video technology: its effects on teaching English and film. B. Gallagher. *The Education Digest* 54:29-32 Mr '89

Youth, culture, art education, television. R. H. Gray. bibl f *Design for Arts in Education* 90:23-5 Mr/Ap '89

TELEVISION IN MEDICINE

See also

Telesurgery

TELEVISION IN POLITICS *See* Television and politics

TELEVISION INDUSTRY

See also

Access Syndication (Firm)

Act III Communications Inc.

American Broadcasting Companies, Inc.

BHC Communications, Inc.

Bill Melendez Productions

Blacks in the television industry

Broadway Video (Firm)

Buena Vista Television

Burnham Broadcasting Company

Cable News Network

Cable television

Cable television, Black

Carsey-Werner Company

CBS Inc.

Children's Television Workshop

Christian Broadcasting Network, Inc.

Cook Inlet Communications Inc.

Fox Broadcasting Company

Fox Inc.

Fred Silverman Company

Genesis Entertainment

Globalvision Inc.

Great American Communications Corp.

Grosso-Jacobson Entertainment

Group W Productions

GTG Entertainment (Firm)

Harmony Gold (Firm)

Independent Television Network (Firm)

King World Productions, Inc.

Law Enforcement Television Network

LBS Communications (Firm)

Lifetime (Firm)

Low power television

Metromedia, Inc.

Motown Productions

MTM Entertainment Inc.

National Association of Television Program Executives

National Broadcasting Co., Inc.

Newhouse Broadcasting Corporation

Paramount Pictures Corp. Television Group

Peregrine Entertainment Limited

Propaganda Films (Firm)

SCI Television Inc.

Spelling Entertainment Inc.

Storer Communications, Inc.

Television equipment industry

Television production and direction

Television stations

TVX Broadcast Group Inc.

Unwired television networks

Viacom International Inc.

Women in the television industry

Bang the drum loudly [networks] J. M. Robins. il *Channels (New York, N.Y.: 1986)* 9:72-3 D '89

The business side. M. Brown. See issues of Channels (New York, N.Y.: 1986) beginning January/February 1986

Into the '90s [special section] il *American Film* 14:24-39+ Ja/F '89

Acquisitions and mergers

See also

Cable television—Acquisitions and mergers

Going with the cash flow. P. Noglows. il *Channels (New York, N.Y.: 1986)* 9:64 D '89

The greening of the Celtics [purchase of TV station] il *Newsweek* 114:60 O 16 '89

How KKR stubbed its toe [SCI TV deal] L. J. Nathans. il *Business Week* p56 Ag 7 '89

How Paramount is blitzing the networks [deal to run independent stations owned by TVX Broadcast Group] R. Grover and D. Lieberman. il *Business Week* p94-5 Ja 30 '89

Is Aaron Spelling still in his prime time? R. Grover. il por *Business Week* p83+ Ap 17 '89

Make no little plans [Burnham Broadcasting] P. Noglows. il *Channels (New York, N.Y.: 1986)* 9:67 Ap '89

Negative ratings [station prices] P. Newcomb. il *Forbes* 143:138-9 F 6 '89

Station-dealing blues [views of B. Lewis] P. Noglows. il *Channels (New York, N.Y.: 1986)* 9:89 F '89

Who owns broadcasting ? [special section] il *Channels (New York, N.Y.: 1986)* 9:40-6+ Ap '89

International aspects

Why MTM isn't the cat's meow [aftermath of TVS takeover] R. A. Melcher and R. Grover. il por *Business Week* p49 S 25 '89

Advertising

And now for the hard sell [networks promoting fall shows] R. Zoglin. il *Time* 134:76 Ag 14 '89

Guaranteed success? [producers of first-run syndicated shows getting distributor commitment to promotional advertising] N. Koch. il *Channels (New York, N.Y.: 1986)* 9:80 Je '89

Paramount's Card Trek [special credit card issued as part of promotional campaign for Star trek] N. Koch. il *Channels (New York, N.Y.: 1986)* 9:52 F '89

Picking up the pieces [fall promotion campaigns at CBS] J. Flinn. il *Channels (New York, N.Y.: 1986)* 9:14 Je '89

Pitching USA today. A. Snyder. il *Channels (New York, N.Y.: 1986)* 9:17-18 Mr '89

Promotion lessons learned [special section] il *Channels (New York, N.Y.: 1986)* 9:65-71 Jl/Ag '89

The spring campaign [studio campaigns to get shows renewed] N. Koch. il *Channels (New York, N.Y.: 1986)* 9:64 Mr '89

Automation

The urge to automate [special section] il *Channels (New York, N.Y.: 1986)* 9:37+ My '89

Cooperation

Learning to play in sweet harmony [broadcast stations and local cable systems] F. Lovece. il *Channels (New York, N.Y.: 1986)* 9:68-70 Ja '89

Employees

See Television workers

Ethical aspects

See also

Cable television—Ethical aspects

The quiz-show scandal [1950s] W. Karp. il pors *American Heritage* 40:76-84+ My/Je '89

Export-import trade

American TV loses its visa. K. Beck. il *Channels (New York, N.Y.: 1986)* 9:46-8 D '89

Le Défi Disney [Hollywood TV sales to Europe] J. Marcom, Jr. il *Forbes* 143:39-40 F 20 '89

Empty threat? [European measures against U.S. TV programming] J. Marcom, Jr. il *Forbes* 144:43 N 13 '89

Europe may slap a quota on General Hospital [limiting American TV imports] B. Riemer and K. Wolman. il *Business Week* p46-7 Mr 27 '89

A 'grenade' aimed at Hollywood: Europe votes to slap a quota on U.S. TV imports. D. Pedersen. il *Newsweek* 114:58 O 16 '89

How do you say thirtysomething in Flemish? R. A. Melcher. il *Business Week* p55+ My 8 '89

They're Russian to see our TV. N. Hickey. il *TV Guide* 37:10 Ja 28-F 3 '89

Finance

The Channels achievers [cover story; special section] il *Channels (New York, N.Y.: 1986)* 9:21+ Jl/Ag '89

Communications media. L. Gubernick. il *Forbes* 143:111-12 Ja 9 '89

Finsyn's final chapter. M. Brown. il *Channels (New York, N.Y.: 1986)* 9:18 O '89

The golden dove [S. De Passe and Motown's investment in TV series Lonesome dove] G. Button. il por *Forbes* 143:58-9 Ja 23 '89

TELEVISION INDUSTRY—Finance—*cont.*

In the race for viewers, the networks fall further behind. R. Grover and D. Lieberman. il *Business Week* p80-1 Ja 9 '89

Partnering for the future [Hollywood producers] N. Koch. il *Channels (New York, N.Y.: 1986)* 9:22+ D '89

Racing—to stay in the game [first-run syndication] K. Haley. il *Channels (New York, N.Y.: 1986)* 9:27-31 Ja 16 '89

Management

9 rules for the '90s [cover story] M. Brown and J. Flinn. il *Channels (New York, N.Y.: 1986)* 9:13-15+ D '89

Executive pay-off [tables] il *Channels (New York, N.Y.: 1986)* 9:72 Ap '89

Gray suits in Oz [MBAs in Hollywood] N. Koch. il *Channels (New York, N.Y.: 1986)* 9:88 Ja '89

Group therapy. L. Prato. il *Channels (New York, N.Y.: 1986)* 9:48-50 Ap '89

Rising stars [innovators in station and syndication business] il *Channels (New York, N.Y.: 1986)* 9:18-19 Ja 16 '89

Who owns broadcasting ? [special section] il *Channels (New York, N.Y.: 1986)* 9:40-6+ Ap '89

Marketing

Finding gold in your hometown [independent stations] J. Mandese. il *Channels (New York, N.Y.: 1986)* 9:79-81 Ja '89

Local truce for ad $$. J. Stilson. il *Channels (New York, N.Y.: 1986)* 9:17 O '89

Securities

After the crash: a new set of values? [syndication stocks; table] il *Channels (New York, N.Y.: 1986)* 9:80 F '89

Trying to make Wall Street understand. P. Noglows. il *Channels (New York, N.Y.: 1986)* 9:42-3 O '89

Australia

See also
Qintex Australia Ltd.

Brazil

See also
TV Globo LTDA

Canada

The greening of Degrassi [Degrassi Junior High] K. Beck. il pors *Channels (New York, N.Y.: 1986)* 9:62-4 N '89

Great Britain

See also
BBC
TVS Entertainment plc

United States

See Television industry

Western Europe

Le Défi Disney [Hollywood TV sales to Europe] J. Marcom, Jr. il *Forbes* 143:39-40 F 20 '89

Empty threat? [European measures against U.S. TV programming] J. Marcom, Jr. il *Forbes* 144:43 N 13 '89

Europe may slap a quota on General Hospital [limiting American TV imports] B. Riemer and K. Wolman. il *Business Week* p46-7 Mr 27 '89

Four titans carve up European TV [cover story] W. Fisher and M. Schapiro. il *The Nation* 248:37+ Ja 9-16 '89

A 'grenade' aimed at Hollywood: Europe votes to slap a quota on U.S. TV imports. D. Pedersen. il *Newsweek* 114:58 O 16 '89

How do you say thirtysomething in Flemish? R. A. Melcher. il *Business Week* p55+ My 8 '89

TELEVISION INTERFERENCE

HDTV inspires a ghostbusting spinoff. D. Lachenbruch. il *Video* 13:138 O '89

TELEVISION JOURNALISM *See* Television broadcasting—News

TELEVISION LAWS AND REGULATIONS

See also
Fairness Doctrine (Broadcasting)
Television advertising—Laws and regulations
United States. Federal Communications Commission

Fighting for Hollywood's fair share [interview with J. Valenti] il pors *Channels (New York, N.Y.: 1986)* 9:98-9 N '89

Finsyn's final chapter. M. Brown. il *Channels (New York, N.Y.: 1986)* 9:18 O '89

Hill showdown: a year of decision [cover story] D. Springer. il *Channels (New York, N.Y.: 1986)* 9:64-7 Ja '89

The networks are hungry for homegrown hits. D. Lieberman. il *Business Week* p88+ N 13 '89

Washington casts a regulatory spell. P. Pagano. il *Channels (New York, N.Y.: 1986)* 9:38+ D '89

Canada

See also
Canadian Radio-Television and Telecommunications Commission

Great Britain

It's not all Brideshead revisited. A. Lejeune. il *National Review* 41:27-9 O 13 '89

TELEVISION MAKEUP *See* Makeup, Theatrical

TELEVISION NEWS *See* Television broadcasting—News

TELEVISION PERFORMERS

See also
Children as actors and actresses
Motion Picture and Television Country House and Hospital (Woodland Hills, Calif.)
Youth as actors and actresses

See also names of television performers

The '80s: the twenty top television personalities. M. Callum and others. il *TV Guide* 37:4-6+ D 9-15 '89

All-star holiday beauty secrets. il *McCall's* 117:15+ D '89

Back from legal Never-never Land, Mary Martin's magical Peter Pan soars on the airwaves again [update on cast appearing in 1960 telecast] T. Allis. il pors *People Weekly* 31:55-6+ Mr 27 '89

Farewell, Family ties! [cover story] V. J. Radovsky. il *Redbook* 173:89-91 Je '89

The five best—and worst—dressed in the soaps. R. Blackwell. il *TV Guide* 37:28-31 N 4-10 '89

Getting even . . . Hollywood-style. M. Beck. il *TV Guide* 37:4-6+ Je 10-16 '89

Going out on top [Family ties performers tape final show; cover story] S. Schindehette. il *People Weekly* 31:74-6+ My 15 '89

How to succeed in Hollywood [networking] I. Chubbuck. il *TV Guide* 37:14-16 O 28-N 3 '89

Invasion of the TV people [TV actors in movies] R. Rosenbaum. il *Mademoiselle* 95:100+ My '89

Look who's looking good [stars from '60s sitcoms; special section] J. Jones. il *Redbook* 172:85-91 Ja '89

Makeup secrets of famous faces. il *Ladies' Home Journal* 106:32 F '89

Mr. Blackwell's fashion guide: TV stars to watch—and ignore—if you want to look sharp [cover story] R. Blackwell. il *TV Guide* 37:10-13 Jl 22-28 '89

New Year's resolutions of the stars. J. Marion. il *TV Guide* 37:10 D 30 '89-Ja 5 '90

Our TV Hall of Fame. C. Young. il *TV Guide* 37:20-2 My 6-12 '89

The stars you'd better keep an eye on [cover story] il *TV Guide* 37:4-8+ S 23-29 '89

Summer breakout [TV stars in movies; cover story] K. Turan. il *TV Guide* 37:2-5 Jl 1-7 '89

Television's top 25 stars [special section] il *People Weekly* 31 Special Issue:19-27+ Summ '89

There's Morton Downey sipping champagne from a loafer . . . Tony Danza singing harmony on 59th Street. C. Adams. il *TV Guide* 37:20-2 Je 17-23 '89

TV's biggest losers and gainers [handling weight variations] il *Ladies' Home Journal* 106:36 Mr '89

Auditions

She said she could ride a motorcycle and then . . . crash! I. Chubbuck. il *TV Guide* 37:23-5 Je 3-9 '89

Nutrition

The diets that keep stars looking trim. B. Goodwin. il *TV Guide* 37:26-8 Je 10-16 '89

Photographs and photography

Salad days of the stars. il *Life* 12:84-6 Mr '89

Psychology

Rejection in Hollywood: how the stars cope. I. Chubbuck. il *TV Guide* 37:16-18 O 7-13 '89

TELEVISION PICTURE ENLARGERS *See* Television projection

TELEVISION PRODUCERS

See also
Bochco, Steven
Broadway Video (Firm)
Brodkin, Herbert Harrison
Grosso, Sonny
Hood, Kit
Masini, Alfred M.
Michaels, Lorne
Silverman, Fred

Don't want no small producers around here. N. Koch. il *Channels (New York, N.Y.: 1986)* 9:30 O '89

Ex-president blues [excerpt from address] F. Silverman. il *Channels (New York, N.Y.: 1986)* 9:87 Ja '89

Finsyn's final chapter. M. Brown. il *Channels (New York, N.Y.: 1986)* 9:18 O '89

The networks are hungry for homegrown hits. D. Lieberman. il *Business Week* p88+ N 13 '89

Partnering for the future. N. Koch. il *Channels (New York, N.Y.: 1986)* 9:22+ D '89

Production. il *Channels (New York, N.Y.: 1986)* 9:44 Jl/Ag '89

The return of "the sponsor". D. Fanning. il *Forbes* 143:136 Ap 17 '89

The spring campaign [studio campaigns to get shows renewed] N. Koch. il *Channels (New York, N.Y.: 1986)* 9:64 Mr '89

TV's new ruling class [writer-producers] N. Koch. il *Channels (New York, N.Y.: 1986)* 9:30-5 My '89

TELEVISION PRODUCTION AND DIRECTION

See also
Television producers
Television studios

Decisions! Decisions! Who should play the sexy teenager? [casting for Guiding light] H. Polskin. il pors *TV Guide* 37:12-15 Ja 28-F 3 '89

Excellence '89 [special section] il *Channels (New York, N.Y.: 1986)* 9:29+ N '89

Show of shows [rehearsal for Saturday night live's fifteenth anniversary special] *The New Yorker* 65:37-9 O 9 '89

TELEVISION PRODUCTION AND DIRECTION—*cont.*
There's even a backup chicken for the voodoo scenes [Passion and paradise] L. Eisenberg. il *TV Guide* 37:42-4 F 18-24 '89

Accidents
Lights! Camera! Tragedy! T. Carlson. il *TV Guide* 37:8-11 Ag 26-S 1 '89

TELEVISION PROGRAM REVIEWS
The '80s: the twenty top shows of the decade. M. Callum and others. il *TV Guide* 37:20-3 D 9-15 '89
Best of '88. il *Time* 133:90 Ja 2 '89
The best shows to watch this fall. D. Hill. il *TV Guide* 37:4-9 S 30-O 6 '89
A busy person's guide to TV [cover story] R. MacKenzie. il *TV Guide* 37:2-5 Ap 8-14 '89
The early line on 1989: television. il *People Weekly* 31:69+ Ja 9 '89
Excellence '89 [special section] il *Channels (New York, N.Y.: 1986)* 9:29+ N '89
Fall preview [cover story; special issue] il *TV Guide* 37:3+ S 9-15 '89
Get ready for a hot February! [cover story] M. A. Lipton. il *TV Guide* 37:4-12+ F 4-10 '89
Heading for a fall [fall season] J. Martel. il *Rolling Stone* p41-3+ S 21 '89
How about that new season? T. H. Stahel. *America* 161:486 D 23-30 '89
Illuminations. See issues of American Film
May is bustin' out all over [cover story] M. A. Lipton. il *TV Guide* 37:2-6 Ap 29-My 5 '89
Midseason review. J. Martel. il *Rolling Stone* p40+ F 9 '89
The new season. B. D. Johnson. il *Maclean's* 102:80+ O 2 '89
People picks & pans. See issues of People Weekly
Private eye. W. A. Henry. See issues of Channels (New York, N.Y.: 1986)
Reviewing the past season: the best and worst [cover story] D. Friedman and M. A. Lipton. il *TV Guide* 37:4-9+ Jl 8-14 '89
Spotlight. E. Miller. See issues of Seventeen through March 1989
Television. See issues of Film Comment
Television. T. Carson. See issues of American Film beginning May 1989
Television [fall preview] J. Leonard. il *New York* 22:62-3 S 11 '89
Television. J. Leonard. See issues of New York beginning November 28, 1983
Ten years after [television in the '80s] H. Rosenberg. il *American Film* 15:18-19 D '89
Tube. il *People Weekly* 32:79+ S 4 '89
Tube talk: fall shows to keep your eye on. il *Teen* 33:50-1 S '89
Turned on for fifty years [celebrities' favorite shows] J. Dunn and others. il *Rolling Stone* p29-30+ D 14-28 '89
TV. R. Powers. See issues of Gentlemen's Quarterly
TV highs and lows [new Canadian series] D. Turbide. il *Maclean's* 102:107 O 30 '89
What to expect from your favorite show [cover story] A. Meisler. il *TV Guide* 37:2-6+ S 16-22 '89

Single works
60 minutes
  Gentlemen's Quarterly il 59:141-4 My '89. J. Schwartz
Alien nation
  TV Guide il 37:55 S 9-15 '89
All in the family
  People Weekly il 31 Special Issue:40-1 Summ '89
All my children
  TV Guide il 37:16-19 D 30 '89-Ja 5 '90. M. Logan
Almost grown
  Rolling Stone il p31 Ap 6 '89. E. Mitchell
  TV Guide il 37:38 Mr 11-17 '89. M. Panitt
Amen
  McCall's il 116:138+ Ap '89. H. Yorkshire
American Bandstand
  Rolling Stone il p47-8 My 18 '89. S. Pond
The American experience
  Newsweek 114:101-2 N 13 '89. H. F. Waters
American gladiators
  Newsweek il 114:64 Ag 14 '89. H. F. Waters
America's most wanted
  Newsweek il 113:58 Je 12 '89. T. Jacoby
  People Weekly il 31:69-70+ Je 19 '89. K. Gross
  Reader's Digest il 134:189-92 Mr '89. F. J. Prial
  Rolling Stone il p34-5 Ja 12 '89. D. Friedman
  TV Guide il 37:22-4 Mr 18-24 '89. J. Marion
Anything but love
  TV Guide il 37:4-8 O 21-27 '89. M. Leahy
  TV Guide il 37:34 S 9-15 '89
Around the world in 80 days
  New York il 22:75 Ap 17 '89. J. Leonard
  Scholastic Update (Teachers' edition) il 121:16 Mr 24 '89. M. Pearce
  TV Guide il 37:20-2 Ap 15-21 '89. M. A. Lipton
The Arsenio Hall show
  Jet il 76:56-9 Ap 10 '89. A. Collier

The New York Times Magazine il p28-31+ O 1 '89. M. Norman
  Newsweek il 113:68-9 Ap 10 '89. H. F. Waters
  Rolling Stone il p60-2+ N 2 '89. P. Goldstein
  Rolling Stone il p32-3 Je 15 '89. J. Marchese
  Time il 134:92-7 N 13 '89. R. Zoglin
  Time il 133:74 Ja 9 '89. R. Zoglin
  TV Guide il 37:16-19 S 30-O 6 '89. M. Leahy
  TV Guide 37:1 Mr 18-24 '89. M. Panitt
Art of the Western world
  America 161:266 O 21 '89. T. H. Stahel
  National Review 41:43-6 D 8 '89. J. Gardner
The Aspern papers
  Opera News 54:69 S '89. P. J. Smith
B.L. Stryker
  New York il 22:71 F 13 '89. J. Leonard
  TV Guide il 37:27-9 Mr 4-10 '89. P. Jordan
  TV Guide il 37:28 My 20-26 '89. R. MacKenzie
Baywatch
  TV Guide il 37:74 S 9-15 '89
  TV Guide il 37:42 D 16-22 '89. R. MacKenzie
Beauty and the beast
  Gentlemen's Quarterly il 59:131+ D '89. R. Powers
  New York il 22:98 D 18 '89. J. Leonard
Black athletes—fact & fiction
  Sports Illustrated il 70:12 My 8 '89. S. Smith
Blind witness
  New York il 22:90 N 27 '89. J. Leonard
  TV Guide il 37:2-3+ N 25-D 1 '89. B. Bruns
Booker
  Rolling Stone il p35 O 19 '89. J. Martel
  TV Guide il 37:43 S 9-15 '89
Bridge to silence
  TV Guide il 37:18-20+ Ap 8-14 '89. M. Leahy
Burning questions
  TV Guide il 37:39 Ap 15-21 '89. M. Panitt
Cagney & Lacey
  People Weekly il 31 Special Issue:152 Summ '89. B. Corday
The Carol Burnett show
  People Weekly il 31 Special Issue:56-7 Summ '89
The case of the Hillside Stranglers
  TV Guide il 37:26-7 Ap 1-7 '89. G. Dillow
Channel One
  Consumer Reports il 54:286 My '89
  Film Comment il 25:70-2 S/O '89. L. Sheinfeld
  The New Republic 200:7-8 Ap 10 '89
  Newsweek il 113:62 Mr 20 '89. M. Starr
  Time il 133:88 F 20 '89. J. E. Gallagher
  U.S. News & World Report il 106:52+ F 20 '89. E. Pomice
  Video il 13:122 My '89. B. Brewin
Cheers
  TV Guide il 37:2-5 My 27-Je 2 '89
Chicken soup
  New York il 22:60-1 S 11 '89. J. Leonard
  Newsweek il 114:70 S 18 '89. H. F. Waters
  TV Guide il 37:63 S 9-15 '89
  Vogue il 179:498 S '89. C. Schine
China Beach
  Mademoiselle il 95:84+ My '89. G. Sikes
  Time il 133:84 F 20 '89. R. Zoglin
  TV Guide il 37:56 F 18-24 '89. M. Panitt
Christmas in America
  TV Guide il 37:20+ D 2-8 '89. P. H. Brown
Cold Sassy tree
  TV Guide il 37:16-20 O 14-20 '89. F. Ashley
Columbo
  Rolling Stone il p34 Mr 9 '89. P. Simms
  TV Guide il 37:29 Ap 29-My 5 '89. R. MacKenzie
Cops
  Newsweek il 113:72 My 15 '89. H. F. Waters
  People Weekly il 31:89-90 Ap 24 '89. P. Jordan
  Rolling Stone il p26 Ap 6 '89. D. Friedman
  TV Guide il 37:27 S 9-15 '89
  TV Guide il 37:18-19 Je 17-23 '89. J. Weisman
  TV Guide il 37:47 Je 10-16 '89. R. C. Smith
The Cosby show
  Jet il 77:58-9 N 27 '89
  Jet il 76:26 My 8 '89
  Jet il 76:56 S 18 '89
  Jet il 76:60-2 S 25 '89
  TV Guide il 37:9 Ap 1-7 '89. J. Marion
  TV Guide il 37:32 Jl 29-Ag 4 '89. D. Hill
Cross of fire
  New York il 22:108 N 6 '89. J. Leonard
  TV Guide il 37:24-5 N 4-10 '89. P. H. Brown
A cry for help: the Tracey Thurman story
  TV Guide il 37:24-6 S 30-O 6 '89. S. Littwin
Dallas
  TV Guide il 37:4-6+ F 11-17 '89. L. Hagman
Dark shadows
  The New Yorker 65:28-9 Je 26 '89
Day one
  New York il 22:97 Mr 6 '89. J. Leonard
Days of rage
  National Review 41:62-3 O 13 '89. W. F. Buckley
  The New Republic 201:29-30+ S 18-25 '89. S. Emerson

TELEVISION PROGRAM REVIEWS—Single works—Days of rage—*cont.*

Time il 134:70 S 4 '89. R. Zoglin

Dead man out
    New York il 22:70 Mr 13 '89. J. Leonard

Dear John
    Gentlemen's Quarterly 59:113 F '89. R. Powers
    The New York Times Magazine il p34-7+ Ap 2 '89. L. Blandford
    TV Guide il 37:56 Ja 7-13 '89. M. Panitt
    TV Guide il 37:16-17 Ap 8-14 '89. H. Gold
    TV Guide il 37:12-13+ Je 3-9 '89. C. A. Crotta

Degrassi Junior High
    Channels (New York, N.Y.: 1986) il 9:62-4 N '89. K. Beck

A different world
    Ebony il 44:160+ Je '89
    Jet il 76:62 Ap 10 '89
    Jet il 76:58 Je 12 '89
    Jet il 76:26 My 8 '89

Dinner at eight
    New York 22:102+ D 11 '89. J. Leonard
    TV Guide il 37:17-18 D 2-8 '89. N. Hickey

Do you know the muffin man?
    New York il 22:130 O 23 '89. J. Leonard

Doogie Howser, M.D.
    TV Guide il 37:4-5+ D 16-22 '89. B. O'Hallaren
    TV Guide il 37:68 S 9-15 '89
    TV Guide il 37:37 N 4-10 '89. R. MacKenzie

Double your pleasure
    Jet il 77:16+ O 30 '89

Dream date
    Jet il 77:22-3+ O 16 '89. A. Collier

Dream Street
    Rolling Stone il p42 Je 1 '89. P. Simms

Drug wars: the Camarena story
    Rolling Stone il p53 N 30 '89. M. Christensen

Dynasty
    TV Guide il 37:2-4+ Ap 15-21 '89. M. Leahy

The Ed Sullivan show
    People Weekly il 31 Special Issue:48-50 Summ '89

An eight is enough wedding
    TV Guide il 37:15 O 14-20 '89. D. S. Wilson

The eleventh hour
    New York il 22:12-13 Ja 9 '89. E. Diamond

Empty nest
    TV Guide il 37:12-14 Je 24-30 '89. B. O'Hallaren

Ethics in America
    America 160:2 Ja 7-14 '89. J. W. Donohue
    Commonweal 116:119 F 24 '89. A. Cleary
    National Review il 41:33-6 Je 16 '89. H. Arkes
    TV Guide il 37:40 Ja 28-F 3 '89. M. Panitt

Eye on crime
    Channels (New York, N.Y.: 1986) il 9:24+ Mr '89. J. M. Robins

False witness
    Jet il 77:60-2 O 30 '89. A. Collier
    TV Guide il 37:18-21 O 21-27 '89. M. Laughlin

Family matters
    TV Guide il 37:75 S 9-15 '89

Family ties
    People Weekly il 31:74-6+ My 15 '89. S. Schindehette
    Redbook il 173:89-91 Je '89. V. J. Radovsky
    Rolling Stone il p44+ My 18 '89. D. Friedman
    TV Guide il 37:4-5+ My 13-19 '89. M. Gross

The famous Teddy Z
    Glamour il 87:194 O '89. A. King
    Newsweek il 114:80 O 16 '89. H. F. Waters
    Rolling Stone il p41 Ag 24 '89. D. Friedman
    TV Guide il 37:57 S 9-15 '89

Father Dowling mysteries
    TV Guide il 37:39 Ap 1-7 '89. M. Panitt

Father knows best
    TV Guide il 37:6-8 Je 17-23 '89. M. Littwin

The final days
    American Film il 15:14+ O '89. H. Shearer
    National Review 41:54 D 8 '89. W. F. Buckley
    New York il 22:103 O 30 '89. J. Leonard
    Newsweek il 114:82-3 O 30 '89. H. F. Waters
    TV Guide il 37:2-4 O 28-N 3 '89. M. Leahy

Free spirit
    TV Guide il 37:44 S 9-15 '89

Full exposure: the sex tapes scandal
    TV Guide il 36:20-3 F 4-10 '89. H. Newton

Full house
    TV Guide il 37:48 S 30-O 6 '89. R. MacKenzie

Game, set & match
    New York il 22:80+ Mr 27 '89. J. Leonard

Generations
    Essence il 20:32 Je '89. D. Donloe
    Jet il 75:60-2 Ap 3 '89
    People Weekly il 31:113-14 Ap 17 '89. L. Armstrong
    Time il 133:85 Mr 27 '89. J. Birnbaum
    TV Guide il 37:29 My 27-Je 2 '89. R. MacKenzie

Geraldo
    TV Guide il 37:28-31 Ja 28-F 3 '89. D. Hill

Gideon Oliver
    TV Guide il 37:36 Je 3-9 '89. R. MacKenzie

Girltalk
    Mother Jones il 14:51-2 N '89. S. Ferguson
    Newsweek il 114:101-2 N 13 '89. H. F. Waters

Glory! Glory!
    New York il 22:74 F 20 '89. J. Leonard
    TV Guide il 37:38-40 F 18-24 '89. H. Polskin

Good day New York
    Channels (New York, N.Y.: 1986) il 9:78 Je '89. J. M. Robins

Good fishing
    People Weekly il 32:132-3 S 11 '89. J. Friedman

Guiding light
    TV Guide il 37:12-15 Ja 28-F 3 '89. H. Polskin

Gunsmoke
    People Weekly il 31 Special Issue:32-3 Summ '89

Guts & glory: the rise and fall of Oliver North
    TV Guide il 37:20-3 Ap 29-My 5 '89. M. Leahy

Hardball
    TV Guide il 37:76 S 9-15 '89

Highway to heaven
    Channels (New York, N.Y.: 1986) il 9:36-7+ S '89. A. B. Block

The hijacking of the Achille Lauro
    TV Guide il 37:24-7 F 11-17 '89. R. Townley

Hill Street Blues
    People Weekly il 31 Special Issue:153 Summ '89. S. Bochco

Home fires burning
    New York il 22:58 Ja 30 '89. J. Leonard

Homeroom
    TV Guide il 37:48 S 9-15 '89

House of style
    Harper's Bazaar il 122:43 N '89. P. Sikowitz

The Howdy Doody show
    People Weekly il 31 Special Issue:107 Summ '89. B. Smith

Hunter
    Rolling Stone il p52-4 My 4 '89. F. Schruers

I know my first name is Steven
    TV Guide il 37:10-11 My 20-26 '89. K. Stayner

I love Lucy
    American Film il 14:14 Jl/Ag '89. T. Carson
    TV Guide il 37:20-2 D 16-22 '89. I. Rudolph

I love you perfect
    Redbook il 174:18+ N '89. V. J. Radovsky
    TV Guide il 37:30-1 O 7-13 '89. D. Hudson

I spy
    TV Guide il 37:13-15 O 7-13 '89. E. Kiersh

Ilé aiyé: the house of life
    Rolling Stone il p78 Jl 13-27 '89. R. F. Thompson

Illusions of news
    Channels (New York, N.Y.: 1986) il 9:14 N '89. J. M. Robins

Into the great solitude
    Psychology Today il 23:62-4 My '89. P. Edidin

Island son
    TV Guide il 37:65 S 9-15 '89
    TV Guide il 37:48 N 25-D 1 '89. R. MacKenzie
    TV Guide il 37:2-3+ N 11-17 '89. L. Eisenberg

Jeopardy
    People Weekly il 32:58 O 9 '89
    Sports Illustrated il 70:94-8+ My 1 '89. F. Lidz

JFK assassination: as it happened
    The American Spectator il 22:27-8 F '89. T. Teachout

The Joan Rivers show
    TV Guide il 37:32 O 28-N 3 '89. R. MacKenzie

The journal
    Maclean's il 102:58 Ap 24 '89. G. Bain

The journey of Carlos Fuentes: crossing borders
    New York il 22:72 O 9 '89. J. Leonard

Judith Krantz's till we meet again
    New York il 22:110 N 20 '89. J. Leonard
    TV Guide il 37:2-4 N 18-24 '89. B. Davidson

Jukebox Saturday night II
    The New Yorker 65:36-7 My 15 '89

Julie and Carol: together again
    TV Guide il 37:22+ D 2-8 '89. L. Eisenberg

Justice denied
    Maclean's 102:104+ N 20 '89. G. Allen

The Karen Carpenter story
    Time il 133:90 Ja 2 '89. R. Zoglin

Knots Landing
    TV Guide il 37:2-4 Je 17-23 '89. D. Mills

The Koppel report: the Blue X conspiracy
    Time il 134:88 D 11 '89. B. Van Voorst

L.A. law
    TV Guide il 37:4-5+ Ap 1-7 '89. A. Meisler
    TV Guide il 37:10-11 Je 17-23 '89. L. Brenner

Late night with David Letterman
    Down Beat il 56:16-19 O '89. J. Cunniff
    Gentlemen's Quarterly il 59:246-9+ My '89. G. Duffy
    The New Yorker il 64:36-40+ Ja 16 '89. J. Kaplan
    People Weekly il 31 Special Issue:74-5 Summ '89
    Time il 133:66-8 F 6 '89. R. Zoglin

Law line
    Forbes il 143:136 Je 26 '89. D. Fanning

Leave it to Beaver
    People Weekly il 31 Special Issue:68 Summ '89

TELEVISION PROGRAM REVIEWS—Single works—*cont.*
Life goes on
    Life il 12:70-2+ N '89. J. B. McDaniel
    New York il 22:67 S 18 '89. J. Leonard
    People Weekly il 32:61-2+ O 16 '89. K. McMurran
    Time il 134:79 O 16 '89. R. Zoglin
    TV Guide il 37:41 S 9-15 '89
Lifestyles of the rich and famous
    The Saturday Evening Post il 261:30-1 My/Je '89. H.
      G. Miller
Living dolls
    TV Guide il 37:40 S 9-15 '89
Lonesome dove
    American Film il 14:11 Ja/F '89. E. Drucker
    Black Enterprise il 19:40 My '89. S. Herbert
    Forbes il 143:58-9 Ja 23 '89. G. Button
    Jet il 75:58 Mr 6 '89
    New York il 22:86 F 6 '89. J. Leonard
    Newsweek il 113:54-5 F 6 '89. H. F. Waters
    Theatre Crafts il 23:40-7+ F '89. J. Calhoun
    Time il 133:78 F 6 '89. R. Zoglin
    TV Guide il 36:14-16+ F 4-10 '89. L. D. Estleman
Long ago & far away
    TV Guide il 37:40 F 25-Mr 3 '89. M. Panitt
Love and hate: the story of Colin and JoAnn Thatcher
    Maclean's il 102:45-6 Jl 17 '89. D. Turbide
Major Dad
    TV Guide il 37:32 D 30 '89-Ja 5 '90. R. MacKenzie
    TV Guide il 37:51 S 9-15 '89
A man called Hawk
    TV Guide il 37:47 Ap 22-28 '89. M. Panitt
Mancuso, FBI
    New York il 22:108 O 16 '89. J. Leonard
    TV Guide il 37:77 S 9-15 '89
Manhunt . . . live!
    Film Comment il 25:71+ Ja/F '89. A. Taubin
Manhunt: search for the Night Stalker
    TV Guide il 37:24-6 N 11-17 '89. E. Warren
Married . . . with children
    Rolling Stone il p30 Je 29 '89. P. Simms
    TV Guide il 37:2-5 Jl 29-Ag 4 '89. H. Polskin
    TV Guide il 37:25-6 My 27-Je 2 '89. R. Rense
The Mary Tyler Moore show
    The Christian Century 106:948+ O 25 '89. V. Rebeck
M*A*S*H
    People Weekly il 31 Special Issue:55 Summ '89
Melba
    New York il 22:78 Ja 23 '89. J. Leonard
    Opera News il 53:44-5 Ja 7 '89. J. James
Men
    Gentlemen's Quarterly il 59:108+ F '89. R. Powers
Midnight caller
    TV Guide il 37:39 F 11-17 '89. M. Panitt
Mission: Impossible
    TV Guide il 37:32 Mr 25-31 '89. M. Panitt
Mister Rogers' neighborhood
    Parents il 64:118-20+ Mr '89. M. J. Bandler
Money, power, murder
    New York il 22:102 D 11 '89. J. Leonard
Monty Python's flying circus
    The New Yorker 65:28-9 Mr 13 '89
Moonlighting
    American Film il 14:18 My '89. T. Carson
    People Weekly il 31:112-13 My 29 '89. M. Dougherty
    Rolling Stone il p31-2 Ap 6 '89. J. Horn
    TV Guide il 37:2-4+ Ja 14-20 '89. L. Farr
The Morton Downey Jr. show
    Channels (New York, N.Y.: 1986) il 9:24 Ap '89. M.
      Brown
    People Weekly il 32:42-3 Ag 7 '89
    People Weekly il 31 Special Issue:152-3 Summ '89. B.
      Pittman
    TV Guide il 37:23 Je 17-23 '89. R. C. Smith
A mother's courage: the Mary Thomas story
    Jet il 77:36-8 D 11 '89. L. Ransom
Murderers among us: the Simon Wiesenthal story
    New York il 22:92+ Ap 24 '89. J. Leonard
    TV Guide il 37:26-9 Ap 22-28 '89. L. Eisenberg
Murphy Brown
    The Christian Century 106:948+ O 25 '89. V. Rebeck
    Newsweek il 113:48-52+ Mr 13 '89. H. F. Waters
    Rolling Stone il p18+ Ja 26 '89. B. Zehme
    TV Guide il 36:40 F 4-10 '89. M. Panitt
My two dads
    TV Guide il 37:16-18 Ap 15-21 '89. B. Goodwin
Naked lie
    TV Guide il 37:12-14 F 25-Mr 3 '89. S. Littwin
Napoleon and Josephine: a love story
    The New Republic 200:29-32 Ap 3 '89. R. Darnton
Night music
    People Weekly il 32:89-90 D 18 '89. A. Abrahams
Nightingales
    Rolling Stone il p30+ My 4 '89. J. Martel
    TV Guide il 37:39 Ap 8-14 '89. M. Panitt
Nightmare classics
    American Film il 14:56-7 Jl/Ag '89. A. Klein
Nixon in China
    Theatre Crafts il 23:42-4+ My '89. M. S. Eddy

No place like home
    American Film il 15:65 D '89. J. E. Fitch
    New York il 22:158+ D 4 '89. J. Leonard
    Time il 134:92 D 4 '89. R. Zoglin
    TV Guide il 37:10-11+ D 2-8 '89. N. Karlen
Nobody listened
    The New Republic 200:25 Ja 2 '89. S. Kauffmann
The Nutt House
    TV Guide il 37:69 S 9-15 '89
    Vogue il 179:268 O '89. C. Schine
Open house
    TV Guide il 37:31 S 9-15 '89
The outside woman
    TV Guide il 37:38 F 11-17 '89. L. Murray
P.O.V.
    Commonweal 116:372 Je 16 '89. T. O'Brien
    Newsweek il 114:101-2 N 13 '89. H. F. Waters
Paradise
    TV Guide il 37:23 My 13-19 '89. R. MacKenzie
Passion and paradise
    TV Guide il 37:42-4 F 18-24 '89. L. Eisenberg
The Pat Sajak show
    Newsweek il 113:63+ Ja 16 '89. B. Barol
    Rolling Stone il p23 F 23 '89. N. Scovell
    Rolling Stone il p32-3 Je 15 '89. J. Marchese
    Time il 133:74 Ja 9 '89. R. Zoglin
    Time il 133:57 Ja 23 '89. R. Zoglin
    TV Guide il 37:1 Mr 18-24 '89. M. Panitt
Peaceable kingdom
    TV Guide il 37:66 S 9-15 '89
The people next door
    Theatre Crafts il 23:48-9+ N '89. J. Calhoun
    TV Guide il 37:52 S 9-15 '89
    Vogue il 179:268 O '89. C. Schine
The people's court
    TV Guide il 37:12-14 Ap 22-28 '89. A. J. Mikva
Peter Pan
    People Weekly il 31:55-6+ Mr 27 '89. T. Allis
Polly
    Jet il 77:58-60 N 13 '89
    People Weekly il pors 32:102-4 Ag 28 '89. J. Park
The power game
    Newsweek il 113:65 Ja 2 '89. H. F. Waters
The preppie murder
    New York il 22:126+ S 25 '89. J. Leonard
    People Weekly il 32:36-9 S 25 '89. J. S. Kunen
    TV Guide il 37:24-7 S 23-29 '89. P. H. Brown
Primetime live
    New York il 22:24+ D 4 '89. E. Diamond
    New York il 22:10-12 Jl 24 '89. E. Diamond
    TV Guide il 37:39 O 14-20 '89. R. MacKenzie
    TV Guide il 37:38 S 9-15 '89
Quantum leap
    TV Guide il 37:36 S 9-15 '89
    TV Guide il 37:23 S 16-22 '89. R. MacKenzie
Rachel River
    The New Leader 72:23 F 20 '89. J. Morrone
A raisin in the sun
    The Christian Century 106:71-3 Ja 25 '89. D. G. Peerman
    Jet il 76:55 My 22 '89
    Jet il 75:38-9 F 20 '89
    TV Guide il 37:32-4 Ja 28-F 3 '89. J. E. Wideman
Reading rainbow
    Publishers Weekly il 235:106 Ja 20 '89
Red king, white knight
    New York 22:90+ N 27 '89. J. Leonard
Remote control
    'Teen il 33:53 Mr '89
The reporters
    TV Guide il 37:32 O 7-13 '89. R. MacKenzie
Rescue 911
    TV Guide il 37:58 S 9-15 '89
The Robert Guillaume show
    Gentlemen's Quarterly 59:110 F '89. R. Powers
    Jet il 76:58-60 Ap 24 '89. A. Collier
Roe vs. Wade
    America 160:523-4 Je 3 '89
    Ms. il 18:75 Jl/Ag '89. M. Suh
    New York il 22:117 My 15 '89. J. Leonard
    Rolling Stone il p40 Je 1 '89. M. Lasswell
RollerGames
    Newsweek il 114:64 Ag 14 '89. H. F. Waters
    TV Guide il 37:20-3 N 25-D 1 '89. A. Meisler
Roseanne
    American Health il 8:112-13 Mr '89. C. Valentino
    Gentlemen's Quarterly il 59:144+ Ap '89. R. Powers
    Newsweek il 113:48-52+ Mr 13 '89. H. F. Waters
    TV Guide il 37:40 Ja 21-27 '89. M. Panitt
    TV Guide il 37:4-6 My 20-26 '89
    TV Guide il 37:2-5 Ja 28-F 3 '89. J. Hicks
The Ryan White story
    TV Guide il 37:14-15 Ja 7-13 '89. J. Light
Saturday night live
    The New Yorker 65:37-9 O 9 '89
    Newsweek il 114:40-5 S 25 '89. B. Barol
    People Weekly il 31 Special Issue:70-1 Summ '89
    People Weekly il 32:70-4+ S 25 '89
    Rolling Stone il p45 N 16 '89. B. Flanagan

TELEVISION PROGRAM REVIEWS — Single works —
Saturday night live—*cont.*
   Rolling Stone il p64-6+ O 5 '89
   Time il 134:75 S 25 '89. R. Zoglin
Saved by the bell
   'Teen il 33:54 O '89
The search for Nijinsky's Rite of spring
   Dance Magazine 63:58 N '89. J. Gruen
Sesame Street
   Changing Times il 43:88 Jl '89. D. Moreau
   Children Today il 18:20-2 S/O '89. M. H. Lystad
   Newsweek il 113:71 My 15 '89. J. Seligmann
   TV Guide il 37:16-18 Jl 15-21 '89. A. D. Plate
   U.S. News & World Report il 107:50+ Jl 31 '89. J. Rachlin
The shell seekers
   TV Guide il 37:14+ D 2-8 '89. R. Koenig
Shining Time Station
   TV Guide il 37:18-20 Mr 11-17 '89. R. Townley
The simple acts of life
   New York 22:68-9 S 18 '89. J. Leonard
The Simpsons
   American Film il 15:112 O '89. R. Lloyd
   Mother Jones il 14:28-31 D '89. S. Elder
   Newsweek il 114:70 D 25 '89. M. Reese
   People Weekly il 32:108-10 D 18 '89. J. Kaufman
Single women, married men
   TV Guide il 37:9 O 21-27 '89. J. Lazar
Sister Kate
   TV Guide il 37:46 S 9-15 '89
Small sacrifices
   New York il 22:126 N 13 '89. J. Leonard
Snoops
   Gentlemen's Quarterly il 59:151-2+ N '89. R. Powers
   Jet il 76:58-60 S 18 '89
   TV Guide il 37:10-12 O 28-N 3 '89. B. O'Hallaren
   TV Guide il 37:73 S 9-15 '89
South Africa now
   Channels (New York, N.Y.: 1986) il 9:17 Ja '89. C. Reece
   Channels (New York, N.Y.: 1986) il 9:52-4 N '89. J. M. Robins
   Mother Jones il 14:49 S '89. E. Hedegaard
   Time il 133:58 Mr 6 '89. N. S. Mehta
Sports tonight
   Sports Illustrated il 70:74 Je 26 '89. A. Wolff
SportsCenter
   Sports Illustrated il 70:74 Je 26 '89. A. Wolff
Star hustler
   Sky and Telescope il 77:544-7 My '89. S. J. O'Meara
The struggle for democracy
   Maclean's il 102:38-40+ Ja 16 '89. B. D. Johnson
Sunday night
   Newsweek il 113:80+ F 13 '89. B. Barol
   Rolling Stone il p42+ F 9 '89. B. Flanagan
Superboy
   TV Guide il 37:32 O 21-27 '89. R. MacKenzie
The Supreme Court's holy battles
   America 161:266 O 21 '89. T. H. Stahel
Sweet bird of youth
   New York il 22:76 O 2 '89. J. Leonard
   TV Guide il 37:10-12 S 30-O 6 '89. E. Warren
Swimsuit
   TV Guide il 37:20-2 F 18-24 '89. A. Meisler
Take a break with Mr. Pete
   People Weekly il 31:61-2 Je 19 '89. R. Arias
A tale of two cities
   TV Guide il 37:48 N 18-24 '89. R. MacKenzie
Tales from the crypt
   Rolling Stone il p33 Je 15 '89. M. Christensen
Tele-psychic
   The New Yorker 65:27-8 Mr 13 '89
Third degree burn
   TV Guide il 37:6-7+ My 27-Je 2 '89. L. Farr
thirtysomething
   Gentlemen's Quarterly il 59:264-9+ Ap '89. S. Fried
   The New York 65:25-6 My 1 '89
   People Weekly il 32:115-17 S 25 '89. L. Feldon
   Publishers Weekly 235:103 Ja 20 '89. O. David
   Rolling Stone il p70-2+ Je 1 '89. B. Zehme
Through the keyhole
   House & Garden il 161:70+ Mr '89. B. Walder
Time flies when you're alive
   People Weekly il 32:59-60 Ag 21 '89. J. Kaufman
Timeline
   TV Guide il 37:30-1 F 18-24 '89. N. Hickey
Today
   The American Spectator 22:10-11 Mr '89. R. E. Tyrrell
   Life il 12:46-8+ D '89. B. Darrach
   New York il 22:28+ O 23 '89. E. Diamond
   Newsweek il 113:61 Mr 13 '89. J. Adler
   Newsweek il 114:86-7 O 16 '89. J. Alter
   People Weekly il 31:44-9 Mr 20 '89. A. Richman
   People Weekly il 32:48-9 O 9 '89. J. Kaufman
   People Weekly il 32:114-16+ N 13 '89
   Time il 134:81 O 23 '89. R. Zoglin
   TV Guide il 37:26-8 N 18-24 '89. H. Sterne

The tonight show
   People Weekly il 31 Special Issue:20-1 Summ '89
Top of the Hill
   TV Guide il 37:71 S 9-15 '89
Totally hidden video
   TV Guide il 37:28 S 9-15 '89
   TV Guide il 37:40 S 23-29 '89. R. MacKenzie
Tour of duty
   Time il 133:84 F 20 '89. R. Zoglin
The Tracey Ullman show
   The New York Times Magazine il p28-9+ O 15 '89. J. Lazar
Travels
   America 161:266 O 21 '89. T. H. Stahel
Trump: what's the deal?
   New York il 22:30-7 S 4 '89. E. Diamond
The truth about teachers
   TV Guide il 37:18-20 S 2-8 '89. P. Welsh
TV 101
   TV Guide il 37:40 Mr 4-10 '89. M. Panitt
Twenty-one
   American Heritage il 40:76-84+ My/Je '89. W. Karp
Unauthorized biography: Richard M. Nixon
   New York il 22:70-1 Mr 13 '89. J. Leonard
Unconquered
   TV Guide il 37:39 Ja 14-20 '89. M. Panitt
   TV Guide il 37:36-8 Ja 14-20 '89. J. Wooten
Unsolved mysteries
   Rolling Stone il p44+ Mr 23 '89. H. Kaplan
The US and the Philippines: in our image
   The New York Review of Books 36:7-11 Je 1 '89. I. Buruma
USA today
   Channels (New York, N.Y.: 1986) il 9:17-18 Mr '89. A. Snyder
   The New York Times Magazine il p12-15+ Ja 1 '89. J. Morgenstern
A very British coup
   Time il 133:77 Ja 16 '89. R. Zoglin
Vintage
   Time 133:80 Ap 17 '89
A vision of Britain
   House & Garden il 161:158-61+ Mr '89. M. Filler
War and peace in the nuclear age
   Commonweal 116:48 Ja 27 '89. T. O'Brien
   Gentlemen's Quarterly il 59:62+ Ja '89. R. Powers
   National Review 41:38-40+ F 24 '89. K. L. Adelman
   Popular Mechanics il 166:34 Ja '89. T. H. Cole
   Technology Review 92:72-3 My/Je '89. P. Aufderheide
   Time il 133:59 Ja 30 '89. S. Talbott
   TV Guide il 37:32-3 Ja 21-27 '89. J. Hersey
War and remembrance
   New York il 22:91-2 My 8 '89. J. Leonard
   TV Guide il 37:16-18 Ap 29-My 5 '89. J. Weisman
West 57th
   TV Guide il 37:36-7 Ja 21-27 '89. D. Hill
What's Alan watching?
   American Film 14:12 Je '89. L. Jarvik
   TV Guide il 37:20-1 F 25-Mr 3 '89. J. D. Stem
What's up, Dr. Ruth?
   Seventeen il 48:34 D '89. E. Grinnan
Wheel of fortune
   People Weekly il 31:51-2+ Ja 23 '89. S. Schindehette
When he's not a stranger
   New York 22:130+ O 23 '89. J. Leonard
Who gets in?
   Maclean's 102:82 N 27 '89. P. Young
Wiseguy
   Rolling Stone il p35-6+ Ap 20 '89. D. Rensin
Wolf
   TV Guide il 37:60 S 9-15 '89
   TV Guide il 37:38 N 11-17 '89. R. MacKenzie
The women of Brewster Place
   Ebony il 44:122-4+ Mr '89
   Film Comment il 25:75-6 My/Je '89. M. Glicksman
   Jet il 75:58-60 Mr 20 '89
   New York il 22:76-7 Mr 20 '89. J. Leonard
   TV Guide il 37:4-5+ Mr 18-24 '89. E. Warren
The wonder years
   New York il 22:112-18+ F 27 '89. D. Blum
   TV Guide il 37:13-15 Je 10-16 '89. D. Handler
World monitor
   TV Guide il 37:24-5 Ap 15-21 '89. J. Weisman
A world of ideas with Bill Moyers
   National Review 41:22-5 Mr 10 '89. T. Lindberg
Yo! MTV raps
   Rolling Stone il p77-8 Jl 13-27 '89. J. Malanowski
The young riders
   TV Guide il 37:70 S 9-15 '89
Your show of shows
   People Weekly il 31 Special Issue:106-7 Summ '89. M. Brooks
TELEVISION PROGRAMMING *See* Cable television—Programming; Television broadcasting—Programming
TELEVISION PROGRAMS *See* Television broadcasting
TELEVISION PROJECTION
   The big easy. L. B. Johnson. il *Video* 13:56-9 N '89

TELEVISION PROJECTION—*cont.*
The video evolution. F. Vizard. il *Popular Mechanics* 166:58-9 Ap '89
TELEVISION RATINGS *See* Television broadcasting—Ratings
TELEVISION RECEIVERS
See also
  Open architecture television receivers
Building your own TV [Heathkit] I. Berger. il *Video* 13:42-4+ Ag '89
Bye, bye boob tube [cover story; special section] il *Video* 13:51-61+ N '89
In search of the ultimate TV set. M. Fleischmann. il *Channels (New York, N.Y.: 1986)* 9:96 D '89
The next picture show. G. McComb. il *Video* 13:56-61+ S '89
Screening the new TVs. D. Lachenbruch. il *New Choices for the Best Years* 29:86+ S '89
Television—past and future [Matsushita's beam-matrix flat screen television] S. A. Booth. il *Popular Mechanics* 166:20+ Jl '89
Tuning in on TVs. D. Elrich. il *Home Mechanix* 85:34-8 D '89
TVs sans CRTs debut [flat screen technology] *High Technology Business* 9:32-3 Jl/Ag '89
Circuits
See Television circuits
Components
See also
  Video monitors
Control
Remote A/B switch. R. A. Heil. il *Radio-Electronics* 60:37+ O '89
History
Your stereophonic, digitized media center is waiting. D. Lachenbruch. il *TV Guide* 37:18-19 My 6-12 '89
Interference
See Television interference
Prices
Zenith's TV picture is getting brighter—for now. L. Therrien. il *Business Week* p41 F 27 '89
Radio receiver combination
Magnavox 3-inch monitor/receiver [CK1050] il *Video* 13:37+ O '89
Testing
26- and 27-inch TV sets. il *Consumer Reports* 54:130-4 D '89
26-inch and 27-inch television sets. il *Consumer Reports* 54:114-19 F '89
The big picture in take-along TV [pocket-sized receivers] il *Consumer Reports* 54:524-7 Ag '89
The big picture in TVs. il *Consumer Reports* 54:171 Mr '89
Here's looking at you [Bang & Olufsen's Beovision TV and Beocord VX5000 S-VHS VCR] L. Braithwaite. il *Video* 12:78-9+ Ja '89
Miniature TV sets. il *Consumer Reports* 54:126-9 D '89
Mitsubishi 35-inch monitor/receiver. il *Video* 12:30-1+ Mr '89
NAD 13-inch monitor/receiver. il *Video* 13:32+ Ap '89
NAD MR-13 monitor/receiver. E. J. Foster. il *High Fidelity (New York, N.Y.)* 39:25-7 My '89
Proton's 31-inch monitor/receiver. il *Video* 13:28-9 My '89
Sony 32-inch monitor/receiver [KV-32XBR10] il *Video* 13:46-7+ N '89
Tera 629C video monitor/receiver. E. J. Foster. il *High Fidelity (New York, N.Y.)* 39:30+ F '89
Toshiba 30-inch monitor/receiver. il *Video* 13:37+ Jl '89
Toshiba 30-inch monitor/receiver with Carver audio. il *Video* 13:35+ Ag '89
Zenith 31-inch monitor/receiver [ZB3193H] il *Video* 13:31+ Jl '89
Videotape recorder combination
A dumb idea whose time has come? [Video Walkman] D. Lachenbruch. il *Video* 13:106 Ap '89
Moveable feasts [personal video products] D. Wilcox. il *Video* 13:60-1 N '89
Road show. D. Stover. il *Popular Science* 235:86-8 N '89
TELEVISION RELAY SYSTEMS
See also
  Cable television
TELEVISION REPORTERS *See* Television broadcasting—News
TELEVISION RESEARCH
See also
  Q ratings
TELEVISION SCENERY *See* Television broadcasting—Setting and scenery
TELEVISION SCRIPT WRITING *See* Television authorship
TELEVISION SERIALS
All my children turns 20: happy anniversary. M. Logan. il *TV Guide* 37:16-19 D 30 '89-Ja 5 '90
Can Sally Sussman find happiness with her own soap opera? Only time—and Generations—will tell. L. Armstrong. il por *People Weekly* 31:113-14 Ap 17 '89
Decisions! Decisions! Who should play the sexy teenager? [casting for Guiding light] H. Polskin. il pors *TV Guide* 37:12-15 Ja 28-F 3 '89

The five best—and worst—dressed in the soaps. R. Blackwell. il *TV Guide* 37:28-31 N 4-10 '89
Generations. R. MacKenzie. il *TV Guide* 37:29 My 27-Je 2 '89
'Generations' soap opera debuts with large cast of blacks [cover story] il *Jet* 75:60-2 Ap 3 '89
The hottest love stories on daytime soaps [cover story] C. Passalacqua. il *TV Guide* 37:2-5 Je 24-30 '89
Inside Knots Landing: my life as a troublemaker [cover story] D. Mills. pors *TV Guide* 37:2-4 Je 17-23 '89
Luke and Laura: it was the wedding America couldn't resist. A. Carter. il *TV Guide* 37:24-5 My 6-12 '89
A plea to the soaps: let's stop turning rapists into heroes. G. J. Waggett. il *TV Guide* 37:10-11 My 27-Je 2 '89
Science soaps. J. Cornell. il *Technology Review* 92:12-13 O '89
Shadows [fans protest WNYC's cancellation of Dark shadows reruns] *The New Yorker* 65:28-9 Je 26 '89
Soap dish! il *People Weekly* 31 Special Issue:136-7 Summ '89
A soap for us: Generations. D. Donloe. il *Essence* 20:32 Je '89
A soap goes black and white [interracial theme on Generations] J. Birnbaum. il *Time* 133:85 Mr 27 '89
TELEVISION SETS *See* Television receivers
TELEVISION SOUND
A/V sound systems power up for the 90s. I. Berger. il *Video* 13:22+ S '89
All-points audio [surround sound processors] F. Vizard. il *Popular Mechanics* 166:114-15 O '89
AudioSource SS Two Dolby Surround decoder. E. J. Foster. il *High Fidelity (New York, N.Y.)* 39:42 Ja '89
Beyond stereo [Sound Retrieval System] L. Feldman. il *Radio-Electronics* 60:51-4 S '89
Denon AVC-2000 integrated audio/video amplifier. J. D. Hirsch. il *Stereo Review* 54:45-7 S '89
Marantz PM-65AV audio-video integrated amplifier. R. Long. il *High Fidelity (New York, N.Y.)* 39:28-9 Mr '89
Mark-V SM-333 surround sound processor. il *Radio-Electronics* 60:17+ My '89
Now hear this. M. Fleischmann. il *Video* 13:63-5+ N '89
Power plays [cover story] L. B. Johnson. il *Video* 13:37-40+ Ag '89
Proton SD-1000 surround-sound decoder. J. D. Hirsch. il *Stereo Review* 54:62+ Je '89
Shure HTS Theater Reference System. il *Video* 13:40-1+ Je '89
Shure HTS Theater Reference System. D. Ranada. il *High Fidelity (New York, N.Y.)* 39:36-9 Jl '89
Spaced-out stereo [Sound Retrieval System] L. Feldman. il *Popular Science* 234:130-2 Je '89
Super sound from your TV [surround sound processors] H. B. Cohen. il *Home Mechanix* 85:38-9 S '89
Toshiba 30-inch monitor/receiver with Carver audio. il *Video* 13:35+ Ag '89
Video sound solution: powered speakers. I. Berger. il *Video* 12:28-9 Mr '89
Your living room, the concert hall [stereo TV] F. Lunzer. il *U.S. News & World Report* 106:69 Ap 3 '89
TELEVISION STAGE SETTING *See* Television broadcasting—Setting and scenery
TELEVISION STATIONS
See also
  Cable television
  College television stations
  Low power television
  Unwired television networks
Denver does ScanAmerica [Arbitron's single-source media research] M. Couzens. *Channels (New York, N.Y.: 1986)* 9:24 N '89
The farmer's market [Memphis independent station WPTY attracting agriculture ad dollars] R. Katz. il map *Channels (New York, N.Y.: 1986)* 9:12+ My '89
Going with the cash flow. P. Noglows. il *Channels (New York, N.Y.: 1986)* 9:64 D '89
How Paramount is blitzing the networks [deal to run independent stations owned by TVX Broadcast Group] R. Grover and D. Lieberman. il *Business Week* p94-5 Ja 30 '89
Independent television: making the tough calls [special section] il *Channels (New York, N.Y.: 1986)* 9:63-83 Ja '89
Knocking newspapers [WVEC's campaign for advertising dollar in Norfolk, Va.] A. Snyder. il *Channels (New York, N.Y.: 1986)* 9:32-3 F '89
L.A. goes Hispanic. K. Beck. il *Channels (New York, N.Y.: 1986)* 9:22+ Je '89
Local heroes [stations aggressively pursuing local ad dollars] M. Schone. il *Channels (New York, N.Y.: 1986)* 9:84-6 N '89
Local news reveille [WNYW's Good day New York] J. M. Robins. il *Channels (New York, N.Y.: 1986)* 9:78 Je '89
Local truce for ad $$. J. Stilson. il *Channels (New York, N.Y.: 1986)* 9:17 O '89
Mutual aid society [joint promotion of Storer Cable and KLRT in Little Rock, Ark.] A. Snyder. il *Channels (New York, N.Y.: 1986)* 9:22-3 Ja '89
Negative ratings [station prices] P. Newcomb. il *Forbes* 143:138-9 F 6 '89

TELEVISION STATIONS—*cont.*

New Mexico shoot-out [Albuquerque] R. Mahler. il *Channels (New York, N.Y.: 1986)* 9:84-5 Ja '89

Progressing backward [local sales] C. Reece. il *Channels (New York, N.Y.: 1986)* 9:23 Mr '89

Promotion lessons learned [special section] il *Channels (New York, N.Y.: 1986)* 9:65-71 Jl/Ag '89

Shadows [fans protest WNYC's cancellation of Dark shadows reruns] *The New Yorker* 65:28-9 Je 26 '89

The sky's the limit [local news operations bypass networks] J. Castro. il *Time* 134:72-3 N 27 '89

Station-dealing blues [views of B. Lewis] P. Noglows. il *Channels (New York, N.Y.: 1986)* 9:89 F '89

Stations sound a tentative all clear. K. Haley. il *Channels (New York, N.Y.: 1986)* 9:86-8 D '89

Stretched to the limit [local news operations at San Francisco's KGO; Wilmington, N.C.'s WECT, and Toledo, Ohio's WTVG; cover story] J. M. Robins. il *Channels (New York, N.Y.: 1986)* 9:42-3+ S '89

Washington's one & only [WUSA; cover story] J. Loftus. il *Channels (New York, N.Y.: 1986)* 9:32-4 N '89

Who owns broadcasting ? [special section] il *Channels (New York, N.Y.: 1986)* 9:40-6+ Ap '89

Equipment

The incredible shrinking station. N. Dager. il *Channels (New York, N.Y.: 1986)* 9:94 D '89

The urge to automate [special section] il *Channels (New York, N.Y.: 1986)* 9:37+ My '89

TELEVISION STATIONS, BLACK

See also

Cable television, Black

Broadcast news [B. Lamont, B. A. Mayo and F. Melton] L. Gite. il pors *Black Enterprise* 20:100-3+ D '89

TELEVISION STATIONS, PUBLIC

Eleventh-hour gamble [Channel 13's late night local news in New York City] E. Diamond. il *New York* 22:12-13 Ja 9 '89

TELEVISION STUDIO TOURS

Tour! [NBC studio in Manhattan] *The New Yorker* 65:42-3 N 27 '89

TELEVISION STUDIOS

How hard is it to see television filmings? il *Sunset (Central West edition)* 183:50 D '89

TELEVISION TRANSMISSION

See also

Extended definition television

High definition television

Improved definition television

Amateur TV transmitter (I). R. F. Graf and W. Sheets. il *Radio-Electronics* 60:45-50 Je '89

Amateur TV transmitter (II). W. Sheets and R. F. Graf. il *Radio-Electronics* 60:45-50 Jl '89

Codebusters [multistandard VCR's] D. Gordon. il *Video* 12:56+ Mr '89

How it works. J. Levine and A. Bayer. il *Life* 12:93-6+ Mr '89

The relapse of chroma phobia [luminance resolution vs. chrominance resolution] D. Ranada. il *High Fidelity (New York, N.Y.)* 39:17 Jl '89

TELEVISION VIEWERS *See* Television audiences

TELEVISION WORKERS

See also

Bookers (Television workers)

Labor unions—Television workers

Strikes—Television workers

The most dangerous jobs in TV. H. Polskin. il *TV Guide* 37:12-14 Jl 1-7 '89

TELEVISION WRITING *See* Television authorship

TELEVISIONS *See* Television receivers

TELEWORKING *See* Telecommuting

TELLER

See also

Penn & Teller

Enter laughing. il pors *Gentlemen's Quarterly* 59:236-9+ Ag '89

TELLER, EDWARD, 1908-

about

Project Chariot: how Alaska escaped nuclear excavation [cover story] D. O'Neill. bibl f il maps *The Bulletin of the Atomic Scientists* 45:28-37 D '89

TELLER MACHINES, AUTOMATED *See* Automated teller machines

TELLURIDE (COLO.)

Telluride summer. il *Sunset (Central West edition)* 183:40 Ag '89

Architecture

West by southwest: a Telluride log house with mining camp roots [designed by Theodore Brown] J. Naisbitt and P. Aburdene. il pors *Architectural Digest* 46:206-14 Je '89

Historic houses, sites, etc.

The Colorado Victorian. il *Esquire* 112:62 Ag '89

TELSON, BOB

about

The reawakening of American music. M. Horn. il por *U.S. News & World Report* 107:68+ N 27 '89

TELXON CORPORATION

The little company that had trouble growing up. M. Fritz. il por *Forbes* 144:118+ D 25 '89

TEMAGAMI WILDERNESS (ONT.)

The 112-year war [Teme-Augama Anishnabai Indians resume blockade of logging road] R. Corelli. il *Maclean's* 102:76-7 N 20 '89

TEME-AUGAMA ANISHNABAI INDIANS

The 112-year war [blockade of logging road in Ontario's Temagami Wilderness] R. Corelli. il *Maclean's* 102:76-7 N 20 '89

TEMECULA (CALIF.)

Architecture

Outpost of civility [Locke House] J. S. Russell. il *Architectural Record* 177:56-9 mid-Ap '89

TEMESVARI, ANDREA

about

Little girl lost. C. Shmerler. il pors *World Tennis* 36:36-9+ My '89

TEMIN, HOWARD MARTIN, 1934-

Retrovirus vectors: promise and reality. bibl f *Science* 246:983 N 24 '89

TEMKIN, ANN

Wölfli's asylum art. bibl f il por *Art in America* 77:132-41+ Mr '89

TEMPE (ARIZ.)

Galleries and museums

See also

Arizona State University. University Art Museum

TEMPEH

The trouble with tempeh [lack of vitamin B_{12}] *Prevention (Emmaus, Pa.)* 41:44 Je '89

TEMPER

See also

Anger

How to defuse employee outbursts. M. R. Feinberg. *Working Woman* 14:26 D '89

Taming toddlers' tantrums [study by Lisa A. Adams and Vaughn I. Rickert] *Science News* 136:332 N 18 '89

Temper tantrums [two year olds] B. Weissbourd. il *Parents* 64:229 O '89

Whining, dawdling, tantrums, and other toddler problems—solved! P. Schneider. il *Parents* 64:81-4+ N '89

TEMPERA PAINTING

Bark with a bite [R. Carroll's egg tempera paintings of bark and leaves] E. Agar. il *American Artist* 53:92-7 S '89

Douglas Safranek [egg tempera paintings of Brooklyn] L. S. Hurwitz. il *American Artist* 53:36-7 Ag '89

TEMPERAMENT

How kids raise their parents. J. Segal and Z. Segal. il *Parents* 64:192 Ap '89

TEMPERATURE

See also

Atmospheric temperature

Climate

Heat

High temperatures

Hot weather

Humidity

Lakes—Temperature

Ocean temperature

Plants—Temperature

Water—Temperature

Wine—Temperature

Temperature fluctuation: a well-defined and unavoidable notion. B. B. Mandelbrot. il *Physics Today* 42:71+ Ja '89

Measurement

See also

Thermometers and thermometry

Regulation

See also

Thermostats

TEMPERATURE, ANIMAL AND HUMAN

See also

Amphibia, Effect of temperature on

Cats, Effect of temperature on

Cold—Physiological effects

Dogs, Effect of temperature on

Fever

Fish, Effect of temperature on

Heat—Physiological effects

Hyperthermia

Hypothermia

Insects, Effect of temperature on

Body's thermostat runs hot and cold. il *USA Today (Periodical)* 118:13-14 D '89

Dinosaurs used their heads to beat the heat [work of J. Keith Rigby] R. Monastersky. il *Science News* 136:309 N 11 '89

TEMPERATURES, LOW *See* Low temperatures

THE TEMPEST [drama] *See* Shakespeare, William, 1564-1616

TEMPLATES

How to format documents quickly and accurately [using templates with any word processor] H. F. Beechhold. il *Home Office Computing* 7:30-1 F '89

New template for the hundred days [terminology] W. Safire. il *The New York Times Magazine* p14+ Ap 30 '89

Order from chaos [creating spreadsheet templates] D. McNeill. il *Compute!* 11:40-5 F '89

TEMPLATES—*cont.*
QuarkStyle. L. Simons. il *Home Office Computing* 7:66+ Ag '89
TEMPLE, ARTHUR, JR.
about
Temple of gloom. J. Zweig. il por *Forbes* 143:168 Je 26 '89
TEMPLE, DOROTHY
Two classic spring arrangements. il *Flower and Garden* 33:82-3 Mr/Ap '89
TEMPLE, HERBERT R., JR.
The nation's war on drugs [address, April 4, 1989] *Vital Speeches of the Day* 55:516-19 Je 15 '89
TEMPLE, JULIEN
about
Earth girls are easy [film] Reviews
New York il 22:101 My 15 '89. D. Denby
People Weekly 31:15-16 My 29 '89. R. Novak
Time il 133:74-5 My 15 '89. R. Corliss
Vogue il 179:212 My '89. J. Lazar
TEMPLE, ROBERT K. G.
The Chinese scientific genius [cover story; special issue] il *The Courier (Unesco)* 41:3-34 O '88
TEMPLE, SHIRLEY *See* Black, Shirley Temple, 1928-
TEMPLE (N.H.)
Music
See also
Temple Band
TEMPLE BAND
The band plays on. J. Horstman. il *Country Journal* 16:42-6 Jl/Ag '89
TEMPLE-INLAND INC.
The best li'l paper stock in Texas? G. G. Marcial. *Business Week* p150 My 22 '89
TEMPLE MOUNT (JERUSALEM)
Time for a new temple? [traditionalist Jews campaign to rebuild temple] R. N. Ostling. il *Time* 134:64-5 O 16 '89
TEMPLE OF LUXOR
From an ancient temple, new secrets [statues unearthed] il *Newsweek* 113:39 Mr 6 '89
TEMPLES
Egypt
See also
Temple of Luxor
Laos
Wat Phou: saving a treasure of Khmer civilization. R. Massey. il *The Courier (Unesco)* 41:20-3 N '88
TEMPLES, BUDDHIST
See also
Temples—Laos
TEMPLETON, JOHN, 1912-
about
John Templeton told Americans about overseas stocks—and made some of them rich. D. Moreau. il por *Changing Times* 43:136 D '89
Saintly stock picker. M. Alpert. il por *Fortune* 119:139 Ap 10 '89
TEMPLETON EMERGING MARKETS FUND
John Templeton told Americans about overseas stocks—and made some of them rich. D. Moreau. il por *Changing Times* 43:136 D '89
TEMPLETON FOUNDATION PRIZE FOR PROGRESS IN RELIGION
Saintly stock picker [J. M. Templeton] M. Alpert. il por *Fortune* 119:139 Ap 10 '89
TEMPO TRAINING
Pick up the paces. P. Pfitzinger. il *American Health* 8:80 Je '89
TEMPORARY EMPLOYMENT
See also
Norrell Corporation
The agency route—is it better? S. McHenry. *Ms.* 17:94 Mr '89
Flexible future for workforce [study by the National Association of Temporary Services] *USA Today (Periodical)* 118:6 D '89
Hire an executive—by the hour. M. Stevens. il *Working Woman* 14:29-30 Ag '89
Temp agencies are praying the slump is just temporary. D. Greising. il *Business Week* p62 D 11 '89
Temporary solutions. M. Whittemore. il *Nation's Business* 77:48-9 Jl '89
What temporary workers earn: findings from new BLS survey. H. B. Williams. il *Monthly Labor Review* 112:3-6 Mr '89
TEMPOROMANDIBULAR JOINT SYNDROME *See* TMJ syndrome
TEMPTATION
See also
Fall of man
TEMPTATION [drama] See Havel, Václav
TEMPTATIONS (MUSICAL GROUP)
Wonder and Temptations among new inductees into Rock 'n' Roll Hall of Fame. il por *Jet* 75:60+ F 6 '89

TENABO SITE (N.M.) *See* New Mexico—Antiquities
TENANT FARMING *See* Farm tenancy
TENANTS *See* Landlord and tenant
TENDER BUTTONS (FIRM)
Fugu, taxis, and Tender Buttons. H. Bridges. il *Gourmet* 49:48+ S '89
TENDERS (BOATS) *See* Boats and boating
TENDZIN, ÖSEL, 1943-
about
Buddhist editor leaves amid controversy. J. Walljasper. il *Utne Reader* p36-7 Jl/Ag '89
His master's voice. *Newsweek* 113:51 Mr 6 '89
TENG, HSIAO-P'ING *See* Deng Xiaoping, 1904-
TENGELMANN GROUP
How a German supergrocer gobbled up a winner. A. Rothman. il por *Business Week* p91 Ap 10 '89
TENGEN INC.
Court games [antitrust suits against Nintendo by Atari and Tengen] G. Keizer. il *Compute!* 11:84 Ap '89
There's a rumble in the video arcade [Nintendo gets hit with antitrust suits from Tengen and Atari] M. Shao. il *Business Week* p37 F 20 '89
TENNANT, ANTHONY M.
about
The House of Guinness. J. Marcom, Jr. il por *Forbes* 143:85+ Je 12 '89
TENNANT, COLIN *See* Glenconner, Colin Christopher Paget Tennant, 3rd Baron
TENNANT, FOREST
about
A doctor and his critics. R. Demak and J. Kirshenbaum. il *Sports Illustrated* 71:46-7 Jl 10 '89
TENNANT, VERONICA, 1946-
about
Dancescape. D. Campbell. por *Dance Magazine* 63:6-7 N '89
Triumphant adieu. P. Young. il pors *Maclean's* 102:50-2 F 20 '89
TENNANT, VICTORIA
about
It's pomp (a Navy wedding) and circumstance (a real-life fracas). J. Weisman. il pors *TV Guide* 37:16-18 Ap 29-My 5 '89
Victoria's British wit and polish. J. Diamond. il pors *Harper's Bazaar* 122:114-17+ F '89
TENNECO INC.
Case study in determination. R. Reiff. il por *Forbes* 144:126-7 O 30 '89
TENNECO OIL CO.
Contrarian and stubborn. il *Forbes* 143:175 Ja 9 '89
TENNESEN, MICHAEL
Mars: remembrance of life past. il *Discover* 10:82-8 Jl '89
The myth of the monster. il *National Wildlife* 27:14-17 O/N '89
No chicken of the sea. il *National Wildlife* 27:10-13 Ap/My '89
TENNESSEE
See also
Big South Fork National River and Recreation Area (Tenn. and Ky.)
Cades Cove (Tenn.)
Campbell County (Tenn.)
Cherokee National Forest (Tenn.)
Educational laws and regulations—Tennessee
Great Smoky Mountains National Park (N.C. and Tenn.)
Pigeon River (N.C. and Tenn.)
Water pollution—Tennessee
Antiquities
Strawberry fields, almost forever [prehistoric Native Americans] J. Chapman and others. il maps *Natural History* p50-8 S '89
Politics and government
Citizen Chris [C. Whittle] M. Newman. *The New Republic* 200:11-13 Ap 10 '89
TENNESSEE EVOLUTION CONTROVERSY
Brachiating in the family tree. L. S. De Camp. il por *The Humanist* 49:9-12+ Mr/Ap '89
TENNESSEE VALLEY AUTHORITY
Sheer challenge [W. Malec] J. Zweig. il por *Forbes* 143:166-7 Ap 3 '89
TENNIS
See also
Foot tennis
Around the world. See issues of World Tennis
The coach that roared [LSU tennis coach J. Simmons] S. C. Prince. il por *World Tennis* 36:88-9+ My '89
A college education: is it all in the game? [women's tennis] K. Segreto. *World Tennis* 36:90+ My '89
Court report '89 [cover story] M. Madsen. il *Women's Sports & Fitness* 11:36-9+ My '89
Don't wait until you're 40. R. Loggia. por *World Tennis* 36:96 F '89
An exercise in longevity [cardiovascular benefits] P. Stites. il *World Tennis* 36:16+ My '89
Accidents and injuries
See also
Tennis elbow

TENNIS—Accidents and injuries—*cont.*
Aaron: on the mend [A. Krickstein] E. Strauss. il por *World Tennis* 36:12-13 Ja '89
Helping hands [hand injuries] P. Stites. il *World Tennis* 36:24+ Mr '89
On the rebound [advice on staying physically and mentally fit] D. Goldie. il pors *World Tennis* 37:50-1 O '89
The pain game. D. Goldie. il pors *World Tennis* 37:38-9 Je '89
Wristy business [player S. Foltz overcomes serious wrist injury] J. E. Loehr. il pors *World Tennis* 37:24-5 N '89
Awards
Award winners. il *World Tennis* 36:23 Ja '89
Collegiate tennis awards. B. Najarian and J. Rosenzweig. il *World Tennis* 37:121 S '89
Bibliography
Book reviews. *World Tennis* 36:26 Ja '89
Summer season all booked up. P. M. Coan and N. Amdur. il *World Tennis* 37:20-1 Ag '89
Equipment
See also
Tennis rackets
Tennis shoes
Sneak preview of '89 products. D. Sparrow. il *World Tennis* 36:16-18 Ja '89
Tennis for one [Wacquet and Tennis Tutor ball machines] D. Rosenbaum. il *World Tennis* 37:26 S '89
History
Memoirs of the golden goddess [excerpt from Heaven will have to wait]; ed. by Julie Murphy. K. Fageros. il pors *World Tennis* 36:48-50+ Mr '89
Periodicals
See also
World tennis (Periodical)
Psychological aspects
The 1 that got away: the saga of six players destined to be second best. C. Shmerler. il *World Tennis* 37:61-2+ S '89
The choke's on you. J. E. Loehr. il *World Tennis* 37:18 O '89
Getting in sync psychologically [circadian rhythms] J. E. Loehr. il *World Tennis* 36:72 F '89
Help for the helpless [learned helplessness] J. E. Loehr. il *World Tennis* 36:14-15 Ja '89
Mental matchplay: how to prepare for a match. J. E. Loehr. il *World Tennis* 37:70-1 N '89
Mental matchplay: how to relax between points. J. E. Loehr. il *World Tennis* 37:54-5 D '89
No place like 'zone'. S. Flink. il *World Tennis* 37:18 D '89
Oh brother, not again! [parents struggle with son's on court behavior] J. E. Loehr. il *World Tennis* 37:16 D '89
On the rebound [advice on staying physically and mentally fit] D. Goldie. il pors *World Tennis* 37:50-1 O '89
Picture this [experiences of C. Garner] J. E. Loehr. il por *World Tennis* 36:22-3 Ap '89
Playing to win. R. M. Williams. il por *New Choices for the Best Years* 29:14+ N '89
Psychological momentum. P. A. Richardson and B. Adler. il *World Tennis* 36:46-7+ Ja '89
A Ray of hope [mental techniques of boxer R. Mancini applied to tennis] J. E. Loehr. il pors *World Tennis* 37:36-8+ Ag '89
The real thing? [pros' problems maintaining consistency after early success] N. Amdur. il *World Tennis* 37:24-6+ O '89
Retirement benefits [taking up tennis later in life] A. Rich. il por *World Tennis* 37:22 O '89
Seeing is believing [visualization techniques] J. E. Loehr. il *World Tennis* 36:16-17 Mr '89
Stick with rituals. F. Stolle. il *World Tennis* 37:68 N '89
Think small, play big [short players] J. E. Loehr. il por *World Tennis* 36:12-13 F '89
Rules
Courts of appeal. N. Powel. See issues of World Tennis
Social aspects
Miracle on Hoe Avenue [Community Tennis Center in the South Bronx helps inner city children] P. M. Coan. il pors *World Tennis* 37:36-41+ O '89
Storm hazards
Grand Slam cover-up [need for stadiums with retractable roofs to avoid rain delays at major tournaments] S. Flink. il *World Tennis* 37:20 O '89
Study and teaching
See also
Tennis coaches
The 10 commandments of doubles. G. M. Heldman. il *World Tennis* 37:32+ Ag '89
101 winning tips [cover story] il *World Tennis* 37:30-5 O '89
Ageless tennis. S. Williams. il *The Saturday Evening Post* 261:90-2 O '89
Armed and ready [follow-through] B. Seewagen. il *World Tennis* 37:14 D '89
Backhand return. D. Ralston. il por *World Tennis* 37:74 N '89
The big shots [cover story] il *World Tennis* 37:24-31 Ag '89

Complete the shot [half volley] F. Stolle. il *World Tennis* 36:86 Ap '89
Concentrate on the lines. F. Stolle. il *World Tennis* 37:22 Ag '89
Direct the ball. D. Ralston. il por *World Tennis* 37:106 S '89
Directory assistance [tennis camps] R. Ingber. il *World Tennis* 36:48-57 Ja '89
Don't lean [balance] D. Ralston. il por *World Tennis* 36:93 Mr '89
The Flach/Seguso guide to championship doubles. K. Flach and R. Seguso. il pors *World Tennis* 37:47+ Je '89
GEEB-busters [balance problems] B. Wright. il *World Tennis* 37:86-8+ S '89
Giving it my best shot [two-handed backhand] C. Evert. il pors *World Tennis* 36:34-6 F '89
A heel up [backhand] D. Ralston. il por *World Tennis* 36:19 Ja '89
Help your partner [doubles] D. Ralston. il por *World Tennis* 37:74 Jl '89
How to play on hard courts. G. M. Heldman. il *World Tennis* 37:50+ S '89
Instruction annual: the inside-out shots. il *World Tennis* 37:38-42 D '89
Keep you hips still [wide forehand] D. Ralston. il por *World Tennis* 36:26 My '89
Keep your head back [backhand] D. Ralston. il por *World Tennis* 37:54 Ag '89
Keep your heels up [footwork] D. Ralston. il *World Tennis* 37:73 Je '89
Kenny, Emmo & the Newk [participating in Tennis Fantasies camp] A. N. Eden. il pors *World Tennis* 37:31-3+ N '89
Learn to slice. F. Stolle. il por *World Tennis* 37:41 S '89
Move back smoothly [overhead] F. Stolle. il *World Tennis* 36:18 F '89
Play close to the waist [serve] F. Stolle. il *World Tennis* 36:28 My '89
Play no patterns [first volley] F. Stolle. il *World Tennis* 36:31 Ja '89
Play with pace [low volley] F. Stolle. il por *World Tennis* 37:26 Jl '89
Raise the level: the approach shot. il *World Tennis* 37:100-3 S '89
Raise the level: the backhand. il *World Tennis* 36:78-81 Mr '89
Raise the level: the forehand. il *World Tennis* 36:40-3 Ja '89
Raise the level: the lob. il *World Tennis* 36:40-3 My '89
Raise the level: the overhead. il *World Tennis* 36:80-3 Ap '89
Raise the level: the return of serve. il *World Tennis* 37:66-9 Jl '89
Raise the level: the serve. il *World Tennis* 36:20-3 F '89
Raise the level: the volley. il *World Tennis* 37:40-3 Je '89
Release with control [ball toss] F. Stolle. il *World Tennis* 37:46 Je '89
Shorten your swing [forehand return] F. Stolle. il por *World Tennis* 36:77 Mr '89
Take your cue: groundstrokes. J. L. Groppel. il *World Tennis* 36:39 Ja '89
Teaching tennis to toads [V. Braden] L. Jaroff. il por *Time* 134:84-6 O 16 '89
Tennis telepathy? [visual cues; research by Eric Buckolz] C. Potera. il *American Health* 8:37 Je '89
Tennis workshop [angle forehand volley] N. Bollettieri. il *World Tennis* 37:46-7 Ag '89
Tennis workshop: the drop shot. N. Bollettieri. il *World Tennis* 37:72-3 Jl '89
Tennis workshop: the high ball. N. Bollettieri. il *World Tennis* 36:44-5 Ja '89
Tennis workshop: the lob. N. Bollettieri. il *World Tennis* 36:36-7 Mr '89
Tennis workshop: the serve. N. Bollettieri. il *World Tennis* 36:44-5 My '89
Tennis workshop: the service return. N. Bollettieri. il *World Tennis* 36:84-5 Ap '89
Tennis workshop: the short angle. N. Bollettieri. il *World Tennis* 36:64-5 F '89
Tennis workshop: the slice backhand. N. Bollettieri. il *World Tennis* 37:44-5 Je '89
Think smart. I. Tiriac. il *World Tennis* 36:38-9 Mr '89
Triumphant returns [D. Goldie] J. Schore. il pors *World Tennis* 37:70-1 Jl '89
Volley position. D. Ralston. il por *World Tennis* 37:53 D '89
Weigh your options [forehand backswing] D. Ralston. il *World Tennis* 36:91 Ap '89
Work your way in [approach shot] D. Ralston. il por *World Tennis* 36:79 F '89
Workshop: high backhand volley. N. Bollettieri. il *World Tennis* 37:56-7 D '89
Workshop: inside-out forehand. N. Bollettieri. il *World Tennis* 37:70-1 O '89
Workshop: overhead. N. Bollettieri. il *World Tennis* 37:72-3 N '89
Workshop: the topspin lob. N. Bollettieri. il *World Tennis* 37:104-5 S '89

TENNIS—cont.

Tournaments

1989 annual [special section] il *World Tennis* 36:20-7 Ja '89

Bargain: 12s get more for less [changes in junior tennis] J. E. Loehr. il *World Tennis* 36:24-5 My '89

Becker bursts Open [U.S. Open] S. Flink. il *World Tennis* 37:82-4 N '89

Becker the Yankee wrecker [West Germany over the U.S. in Davis Cup semifinal] C. Kirkpatrick. il *Sports Illustrated* 71:56-7 Jl 31 '89

The best shots in tennis [Wimbledon]; ed. by Herma M. Rosenthal. B. J. King. il *TV Guide* 37:6-7+ Je 24-30 '89

Better way for Barcelona [Olympics] J. Feinstein. il *World Tennis* 36:20+ Mr '89

Boom Boom [S. Graf and B. Becker take U.S. Open titles; cover story] C. Kirkpatrick. il pors *Sports Illustrated* 71:22-7 S 18 '89

Call it the Loving Cup [U.S. vs. France in Davis Cup play] F. Lidz. il pors *Sports Illustrated* 70:76 Ap 17 '89

Color picture out of focus [plans for men's tournaments in South Africa] M. Mathabane. il *World Tennis* 37:27+ Je '89

Down and out [U.S. vs. West Germany in Davis Cup] L. Shiras. il *World Tennis* 37:46-8 O '89

The end of a fairy tale [C. Evert at Wimbledon] C. Leerhsen. il *Newsweek* 114:47 Jl 17 '89

An end to remember [Nabisco Masters] C. Shmerler. il *World Tennis* 36:82-3 F '89

Feat of clay [M. Chang wins French Open; with editorial comment by Neil Amdur] S. Flink. il pors *World Tennis* 37:4, 56-7+ Ag '89

The final chapter [Federation Cup] C. Evert. il pors *World Tennis* 37:31-2+ D '89

Garrison ruins Evert's U.S. Open goodbye party. il pors *Jet* 76:46+ S 25 '89

Giant killers [M. Chang and A. Sanchez pull off upsets at French Open] C. Kirkpatrick. il pors *Sports Illustrated* 70:34-6+ Je 19 '89

Grand Slam cover-up [need for stadiums with retractable roofs to avoid rain delays at major tournaments] S. Flink. il *World Tennis* 37:20 O '89

Grand Slam: only the strong survive. B. Lorge. il *Sports Illustrated* 70:55-6+ Je 5 '89

Hardly over the hill [views of players on the 35-and-over tour] S. Stevenson. il *World Tennis* 37:66-7 O '89

Innerviews [interview with A. M. Fernandez] il por *Women's Sports & Fitness* 11:62 My '89

It ain't all glamour [tour life of four women players] C. Shmerler. il *Women's Sports & Fitness* 11:53-7 Mr '89

Ivan: this one's for you [I. Lendl's Wimbledon difficulties] S. Flink. il *World Tennis* 37:20+ Jl '89

Mind games in Melbourne [Australian Open] R. Evans. il *World Tennis* 36:127+ Ap '89

Mother of a pearl (IV) [7-year-old player A. Stevenson] S. Stevenson. il pors *World Tennis* 36:16 Ap '89

Mr. Kramer and Mr. Becker [U.S. Open] H. W. Wind. il *The New Yorker* 65:85-96+ O 16 '89

A new Mac attack [J. McEnroe wins WCT Finals in Dallas] C. Kirkpatrick. il pors *Sports Illustrated* 70:20-1 Mr 13 '89

The newlywed game [on tour with D. Goldie] C. M. Goldie. il pors *World Tennis* 36:84-6+ My '89

Newlywed Zina Garrison captures Chicago Slims. il por *Jet* 77:51 N 27 '89

No place like home [U.S. Open at the National Tennis Center] S. Hester. il *World Tennis* 37:136 S '89

A no-win situation [U.S. vs. West Germany in Davis Cup] C. Shmerler. il *World Tennis* 37:82-3 O '89

Not for Steffi only [U.S. Open] C. Shmerler. il *World Tennis* 37:84-5 N '89

Prince Rainier marks his 40-year reign with a Monaco gala [pro-celebrity tennis tournament] D. Bacon. il por *People Weekly* 32:96-9 Jl 24 '89

Road to pros full of potholes [conditions at Australian satellite tournament] J. E. Loehr. il *World Tennis* 37:18-19 Jl '89

Special D from this Courier [J. Courier upsets A. Agassi at French Open] C. Kirkpatrick. il pors *Sports Illustrated* 70:84+ Je 12 '89

Splendours on the grass [Wimbledon] C. Shmerler. il *World Tennis* 37:110+ S '89

Steffi Slam watch: one down, Down Under [S. Graf wins Australian Open] il por *Sports Illustrated* 70:10 F 6 '89

Summertime blues [on tour with D. Goldie] C. M. Goldie. il pors *World Tennis* 37:42+ N '89

Taking it to the limit. C. Evert. il por *World Tennis* 36:58-9 Ap '89

A tale of two cities [D. Goldie at the French Open and Wimbledon] C. M. Goldie. il pors *World Tennis* 37:96+ S '89

A taste of the Orient [D. Goldie at the Japan Open] C. M. Goldie. il pors *World Tennis* 37:60-1 Ag '89

Tennis, anyone? Sporting a new 'do, Ronald Reagan joins Nancy at courtside [Nancy Reagan Tennis Tournament] il pors *People Weekly* 32:46-7 O 23 '89

Thank heaven for boys & girls [French Open] S. Flink. il *World Tennis* 37:67-71 Ag '89

Thunder Down Under [Australian players] K. Cunningham. il *World Tennis* 36:28-30 Ja '89

Tournament report. See issues of World Tennis

The U.S. Open '89 [cover story; special section] il *World Tennis* 37:43-50+ S '89

U.S. Open report: intrigue in Flushing Meadows [women players] L. Rothlein. il *Women's Sports & Fitness* 11:28-9 S '89

The unlucky seven [S. Graf's opponents at U.S. Open] G. Plimpton. il *Sports Illustrated* 71:28-9 S 18 '89

Unstoppable Steffi [Virginia Slims of Florida; cover story] B. Newman. il pors *Sports Illustrated* 70:32-5 Mr 27 '89

Will the Cup come home? [Davis Cup] S. Flink. il *World Tennis* 36:14-15 F '89

Wimbledon '89 [special section] il *World Tennis* 37:30-6+ Jl '89

Wunderbar! [B. Becker and S. Graf victors at Wimbledon] A. Wolff. il pors *Sports Illustrated* 71:14-21 Jl 17 '89

Youth will be served [M. Chang and A. Sanchez win French Open] T. Callahan. il pors *Time* 133:90 Je 26 '89

Economic aspects

In search of a net gain [Soviet player N. Zvereva signs with ProServ and demands right to control earnings] D. Scheiber. il pors *Sports Illustrated* 70:24-6 My 1 '89

A net gain for men's tennis? A. Fins. il *Business Week* p76 D 18 '89

The road to riches [U.S. Open] B. Moran. il *World Tennis* 37:48-9 S '89

The Volvo tournament brings Vermont to the net [Stratton Mountain] R. Duffy. il *Business Week* p82-3 Jl 24 '89

Ethical aspects

Let those people go [decorum imposed on fans] S. Wulf. il por *Sports Illustrated* 71:162 S 11 '89

History

'80s tennis. R. Wetzsteon. il *Sport (New York, N.Y.)* 80:78+ O '89

Down memory lane [U.S. Open] C. Evert. il por *World Tennis* 37:66+ S '89

The Queen and I [Wimbledon] B. Riggs. il por *World Tennis* 37:98 Jl '89

Remember the '80s. C. Shmerler. il *World Tennis* 37:34-6 D '89

Roman holiday [Italian Open] B. Collins. il *World Tennis* 36:81-3 My '89

A sorority gone sour [more camaraderie among women during early Virginia Slims tour] G. M. Heldman. il *World Tennis* 37:96 N '89

The way she was [C. Evert] S. Flink. il pors *World Tennis* 37:24-30 D '89

What a blast! [R. Laver's 1969 Grand Slam] S. Flink. il por *World Tennis* 37:22+ S '89

Organization and administration

ATP directive: all systems go. H. Jordan. il por *World Tennis* 36:106 My '89

ATP's tour de force. P. M. Coan. *World Tennis* 37:86+ D '89

The eye of the storm [World Championship Tennis tour] S. Flink. il por *World Tennis* 36:28+ Mr '89

How much is too much? [Association of Tennis Professionals vs. International Tennis Federation] A. Wolff. il *Sports Illustrated* 71:80-2+ D 11 '89

Keep alive best of five [five set matches in Grand Slam tournaments] S. Flink. il *World Tennis* 37:16-17 Ag '89

Power games grip men's tour [dispute between Men's Tennis Council and Association of Tennis Professionals] G. M. Heldman. il *World Tennis* 36:16-17 F '89

Psychological aspects

See Tennis—Psychological aspects

Television broadcasting

See Television broadcasting—Sports

Tickets

Hot seats! [scalping of Wimbledon tickets] C. Gould. *World Tennis* 37:40+ Jl '89

Open the Open [need for more equitable ticket distribution] B. Collins. il *World Tennis* 37:84-5 S '89

Germany (West)

Datelines. C. Shmerler. il por *World Tennis* 37:58-60 D '89

South Africa

Ashe applauds ATP move to avoid South Africa. por *Jet* 76:48 S 18 '89

Color picture out of focus [plans for men's tournaments] M. Mathabane. il *World Tennis* 37:27+ Je '89

A race against time. R. Moore. il *World Tennis* 37:96 O '89

Soviet Union

See also
Soviet Tennis Federation

Vietnam

Datelines. M. H. Glantz. il *World Tennis* 37:72-3 O '89

TENNIS ASSOCIATIONS

See also
Association of Tennis Professionals
International Tennis Federation
Men's Tennis Council
Soviet Tennis Federation
United States Tennis Association

TENNIS CAMPS See Camps
TENNIS CENTERS
    See also
    All England Lawn Tennis and Croquet Club
    International Tennis Center (Delray Beach, Fla.)
    National Tennis Center (U.S.)
Miracle on Hoe Avenue [Community Tennis Center in the
    South Bronx helps inner city children] P. M. Coan. il
    pors *World Tennis* 37:36-41+ O '89
TENNIS COACHES
    See also
    Magill, Dan
    Simmons, Jerry
Service winner: pros who teach. B. J. King. por *World
    Tennis* 36:72+ Ja '89
TENNIS COURTS
Courting [New York City] J. Seabury. il *New York* 22:124-6
    My 1 '89
Standing on shaky ground [advantages of clay courts for
    those over forty years old] J. Morton. il *World Tennis*
    37:98 Je '89
TENNIS ELBOW
Living with tennis elbow. R. Phalon. il *Forbes* 143:202+
    Ap 17 '89
TENNIS ETIQUETTE See Tennis—Tournaments—Ethical
    aspects
TENNIS FANS
Let those people go [decorum imposed on fans] S. Wulf.
    il por *Sports Illustrated* 71:162 S 11 '89
TENNIS PLAYERS
    See also
    Agassi, Andre
    Ashe, Arthur
    Becker, Boris
    Borg, Björn, 1956-
    Capriati, Jennifer
    Chang, Michael
    Connors, Jimmy, 1952-
    Courier, Jim
    Evert, Chris
    Fernandez, Anna Maria
    Foltz, Shawn
    Garner, Chris
    Garrison, Zina
    Gilbert, Brad
    Goldie, Dan
    Graf, Steffi
    Hlasek, Jakob
    Kildery, Paul
    Kramer, Jack, 1921-
    Krickstein, Aaron
    Laver, Rod
    Leach, Rick
    Leconte, Henri
    Lendl, Ivan
    McEnroe, John
    Navratilova, Martina, 1956-
    Pugh, Jim
    Rosewall, Ken
    Sabatini, Gabriela
    Sanchez, Arantxa
    Seles, Monika
    Stewart, Sherwood
    Temesvari, Andrea
    Wilander, Mats
    Zvereva, Natalia
The 1 that got away: the saga of six players destined to
    be second best. C. Shmerler. il *World Tennis* 37:61-2+
    S '89
Around the world. See issues of World Tennis
Ashe sees bright future for blacks in pro tennis. il pors
    Jet 76:48-50 Ag 28 '89
The best ever [cover story] G. Lott. il pors *World Tennis*
    36:25-8 F '89
The best shots in tennis; ed. by Herma M. Rosenthal. B.
    J. King. il *TV Guide* 37:6-7+ Je 24-30 '89
Coming on strong [athletic ability] M. Bloom. il *World Tennis*
    37:52-4 O '89
Datelines [West German players] C. Shmerler. il por *World
    Tennis* 37:58-60 D '89
For women only. S. Flink. il *World Tennis* 36:18+ Ap '89
It ain't all glamour [tour life of four women players] C.
    Shmerler. il *Women's Sports & Fitness* 11:53-7 Mr '89
A lesson to be learned [A. Agassi's influence on junior players]
    B. Press. il por *World Tennis* 36:142 Ap '89
Newcomers to watch. C. Shmerler. il *World Tennis* 37:72-4+
    S '89
A pair of aces [1988 World tennis rankings] S. Flink. il
    World Tennis 36:30-3 F '89
The real thing? [pros' problems maintaining consistency after
    early success] N. Amdur. il *World Tennis* 37:24-6+ O
    '89
Semi-tough [low-seeded players who reached Wimbledon
    semifinals] J. Feinstein. il *World Tennis* 37:57-8+ Jl '89
Senior partners [doubles] G. M. Heldman. il *World Tennis*
    36:66+ Ap '89
Service winner: pros who teach. B. J. King. por *World
    Tennis* 36:72+ Ja '89

A shot for America. S. Flink. il *World Tennis* 37:44-7+
    S '89
A sign of the times [many pros born under the sign of
    Leo] L. Shiras. il *World Tennis* 37:82 Ag '89
Tennis, everyone? [L. Weingart's approach to development
    of American tennis players] R. Wetzsteon. il por *Sport
    (New York, N.Y.)* 80:15 D '89
That was then, this is now [senior players] G. M. Heldman.
    il *World Tennis* 37:34-6 N '89
Thunder Down Under [Australian players] K. Cunningham.
    il *World Tennis* 36:28-30 Ja '89
U.S. Open report: intrigue in Flushing Meadows [women
    players] L. Rothlein. il *Women's Sports & Fitness* 11:28-9
    S '89
Who's the best ever? *World Tennis* 37:64-5 Jl '89
Who's the best ever? [women] T. Tinling. il *World Tennis*
    36:43-7 Mr '89
Accidents and injuries
    See Tennis—Accidents and injuries
Attitudes
Hardly over the hill [views of players on the 35-and-over
    tour] S. Stevenson. il *World Tennis* 37:66-7 O '89
Looking for Mr. Goodwill. D. Enberg. il por *World Tennis*
    36:106 Mr '89
A sorority gone sour [more camaraderie among women during
    early Virginia Slims tour] G. M. Heldman. il *World Tennis*
    37:96 N '89
Awards
    See Tennis—Awards
Health and hygiene
Body and soul [hatha yoga] S. Festa. il *World Tennis* 37:65-7
    N '89
The fats of life [body fat percentage] M. Bloom. il *World
    Tennis* 37:92-5 S '89
The rest is up to you [effect of sleep deprivation on tennis
    players] S. Festa. il *World Tennis* 37:18-19 Ag '89
The rights of spring. P. Stites and S. Festa. *World Tennis*
    36:30 Ap '89
Tennis in good time [effects of circadian rhythms] M. Bloom.
    il *World Tennis* 36:70-1 F '89
Test of a champion [J. Capriati] J. E. Loehr. il pors *World
    Tennis* 37:30+ S '89
Psychology
    See Tennis—Psychological aspects
Salaries, pensions, etc.
The Age of Andre: a marketing empire is born [tennis player
    A. Agassi's endorsement deals] R. Wetzsteon. il pors *Sport
    (New York, N.Y.)* 80:88+ Je '89
One year in the life . . . [endorsements and prize money]
    D. Goldie. il por *World Tennis* 36:24+ Ap '89
Training
101 winning tips [cover story] il *World Tennis* 37:30-5 O
    '89
As he sees fit [J. McEnroe; cover story] N. Amdur. il pors
    World Tennis 37:34-6 Jl '89
Commit to get fit [cross training; special section]; ed. by
    Marc Bloom. D. Scott. il *World Tennis* 36:69-70+ My
    '89
A fusion of power [interview with B. Brett] N. Amdur.
    il pors *World Tennis* 36:34-5 Mr '89
Peaking after 30 [cover story] C. Evert. il pors *World Tennis*
    37:28-30 Je '89
Tennis body by Jake [J. Steinfeld] S. Stevenson. il pors
    World Tennis 37:33-6 Je '89
The turning point [D. Goldie's stretching routine] P. Stites.
    il pors *World Tennis* 36:66-9 F '89
The water way [Hydro-Tone system] P. Cohen. il pors *World
    Tennis* 37:58-9 Ag '89
TENNIS RACKETS
For a net gain, try a wide-body racket. G. Felcyn. il *Business
    Week* p96 Ag 28 '89
Frame and fortune? [Racquet Selector computer program
    developed by G. Welling] D. Rosenbaum. il *World Tennis*
    37:22 N '89
Into the woods [wooden rackets] J. Stahl. il por *World
    Tennis* 37:63 N '89
Kids' stuff [children's rackets] B. Seewagen. il *World Tennis*
    36:92-3 Ap '89
Racket handbook [special section] il *World Tennis* 36:47-8+
    My '89
Racket reviews. il *World Tennis* 37:108-9 S '89
Racket reviews. il *World Tennis* 37:68-9 Je '89
Racket reviews. il *World Tennis* 37:68-9 O '89
Racket reviews. il *World Tennis* 37:50-2 Ag '89
Racket reviews. il *World Tennis* 37:77-9 Jl '89
The racket revolution. D. Sparrow. il *Health (New York,
    N.Y.)* 21:51-2+ Je '89
Speed demons [widebody rackets] D. Rosenbaum and D.
    Sparrow. il *World Tennis* 37:48-9 Ag '89
Talkin' 'bout an evolution [second generation of widebodies]
    D. Sparrow. il *World Tennis* 37:47-62 N '89
Widening the gap. D. Sparrow. il *World Tennis* 36:61-3
    F '89
Strings
Bring on the string. B. Stambler. il *World Tennis* 36:56-7
    My '89

TENNIS RESORTS *See* Resorts

TENNIS SHOES

Courting fancy. il *Women's Sports & Fitness* 11:34-6 Mr '89

Fit is it. D. Sparrow. il *World Tennis* 37:55-6+ O '89

Shoe guide '89. D. Sparrow. il *World Tennis* 36:95+ Ap '89

TENNIS STADIUMS

Grand Slam cover-up [need for stadiums with retractable roofs to avoid rain delays at major tournaments] S. Flink. il *World Tennis* 37:20 O '89

TENNYSON, JEFFREY

about

Hamburger heaven: a burger blitz. T. Mewborne. il por *Antiques & Collecting Hobbies* 94:22-5 D '89

TENSIOMETERS

Spoke tensiometers. J. Langley. il *Bicycling* 30:208+ My '89

TENSION (PSYCHOLOGY) *See* Stress

TENSION HEADACHES *See* Headache

TENT CATERPILLARS

Control

Overwintering insect eggs. W. S. Moore. il *Flower and Garden* 33:74 Ja/F '89

TENTS

Fast truck tents. N. Strung. il *Field & Stream* 94:104 D '89

TENURE, ACADEMIC *See* College teachers—Tenure

TENURE, LAND *See* Land tenure

TENUTA, JUDY

about

The prom queen from hell. M. F. Coburn. il pors *Gentlemen's Quarterly* 59:204-7+ Ag '89

TEPIA (TOKYO, JAPAN)

Tokyo collage. L. Breslin. il *Architectural Record* 177:84-93 O '89

TEPUIS *See* Mountains—Venezuela

TEQUILA

For a few dollars more. A. Richman. il *Gentlemen's Quarterly* 59:320+ Ap '89

TEQUILA SUNRISE [film] See Motion picture reviews—Single works

TERAOKA, MASAMI, 1936-

about

Masami Teraoka: Space Gallery. P. Hammond. il *Art News* 88:150 Ja '89

TERASAWA, KUNIKO

about

Tireless Kuniko Terasawa is the force behind a newspaper almost no one can read. R. Arias. il pors *People Weekly* 32:53-4 S 25 '89

TERASAWA, T., AND SCHOLER, M., 1940-

The heliosphere as an astrophysical laboratory for particle acceleration. bibl f il *Science* 244:1050-7 Je 2 '89

TERESA, MOTHER, 1910-

about

I believe in Mother Teresa [excerpt from All I really need to know I learned in kindergarten] R. Fulghum. por *The Saturday Evening Post* 261:63 Ap '89

A pencil in the hand of God [interview] E. W. Desmond. por *Time* 134:11+ D 4 '89

TERESA, OF AVILA, SAINT, 1515-1582

about

Letters from a lady in love. K. J. Egan. il *U.S. Catholic* 54:12-13 F '89

TERESA BENEDICTA, OF THE CROSS *See* Stein, Edith, 1891-1942

TERESI, DICK

Interview: Leon Lederman. pors *Omni (New York, N.Y.)* 12:98-100+ O '89

Wanted: 40 more years. il *Health (New York, N.Y.)* 21:58-9+ O '89

Winding down. il *Health (New York, N.Y.)* 21:56-7 O '89 (jt. auth) See Hooper, Judith, and Teresi, Dick

TEREX CORPORATION

Parlaying the winnings [Terex to buy Fruehauf's trailer business] R. Reiff. il por *Forbes* 144:45-6 Jl 24 '89

TERM INSURANCE *See* Insurance, Life

TERMINAL CARE

See also

Church work with the dying

Living wills

The horror is worth it. V. Williams. por *Newsweek* 114:14 O 9 '89

TERMINAL CONTROL AREAS *See* Air traffic control

TERMINAL RADAR APPROACH CONTROL *See* Radar in aviation

TERMINALS (COMPUTER) *See* Computer terminals

TERMINALS (TRANSPORTATION)

See also

Airports

New York (N.Y.)—Stations

TERMINATION OF PENSION PLANS *See* Pensions—Termination

TERMITES

Anecdotes, facetiae, satire, etc.

The great termite race. M. G. Stoddard. il *The Saturday Evening Post* 261:56-7+ N/D '89

Control

The pest defense. il *Home Mechanix* 85:58-63 Jl '89

Termites vs. termites [growth regulator developed by Nan-Yao Su] il *USA Today (Periodical)* 117:13 Je '89

TERNS

New tensions for a rough crowd [nesting space battles for terns and gulls on Rasa Island, Mexico] E. Velarde. il *International Wildlife* 19:20-4 N/D '89

Worse for the terns. J. W. Smith. il *Natural History* p65 Ja '89

TERPENES

See also

Forskolin

TERRACES (AGRICULTURE)

Anhydrous perks ridge-till corn in Ohio trials. R. Fee. *Successful Farming* 87:66AD F '89

The cultivator everyone wants [ridge till style cultivators] R. Fee. il *Successful Farming* 87:66AA F '89

Iron to run on ridges. C. Finck and D. Mowitz. il *Successful Farming* 87:34H-34I mid-F '89

Keep your terraces working. il *Successful Farming* 87:28 D '89

Production [methods of Loren Schuett] J. Walter. il *Successful Farming* 87:19 D '89

Ridge-till corn, no-till beans gain acres. R. Fee. *Successful Farming* 87:20 D '89

Ridge-tillage reins-in erosion. R. Fee. il *Successful Farming* 87:34R-34S mid-F '89

Ridge tools in your toolbox. D. Mowitz. il *Successful Farming* 87:34AB mid-F '89

TERRACES (OUTDOOR LIVING AREAS) *See* Decks, patios, terraces, etc.

TERRANES *See* Geology

TERRE-DE-HAUT (GUADELOUPE)

Description and travel

Les Saintes and Marie-Galante: the Saint Barts of the nineties? R. Urquhart. il map *Vogue* 179:304-5+ N '89

TERRESTRIAL MAGNETISM *See* Magnetism, Terrestrial

TERRIERS

See also

Airedale terriers

TERRITORIAL EXPANSION

See also

Indonesia—Territorial expansion

TERRITORIAL WATERS

See also

Convention on the Law of the Sea (1982)

Exclusive Economic Zone

United Nations. Preparatory Commission for the International Sea-Bed Authority and the International Tribunal for the Law of the Sea

A domestic squabble [Canada and France at odds over fishing rights off Newfoundland] G. Allen. il *Maclean's* 102:16 Ja 16 '89

Territorial sea of the United States [proclamation, December 27, 1988] R. Reagan. *Department of State Bulletin* 89:72 Mr '89

A troubled cod truce [Ottawa's Atlantic fish accord with France] A. Walmsley. il *Maclean's* 102:36-8 Ap 17 '89

TERRITORIALITY (ZOOLOGY)

The brotherhood of cheetahs [Serengeti National Park; cover story] T. Caro. il *Natural History* p50-9 Je '89

Pronghorns in—and out of—a rut [National Bison Range] J. A. Byers. il *Natural History* p38-49 Ap '89

TERRITORIES, NON-SELF GOVERNING *See* Colonies

TERRORISM

See also

Assassination

Hostages

Kidnapping

Torture

Women terrorists

FBI gives bookstore threats top priority [relating to S. Rushdie's Satanic verses] H. Fields. il *Publishers Weekly* 235:12 Mr 17 '89

Help find this mad bomber [profile of terrorist striking U.S. cities] A. Hilburn. il *Reader's Digest* 135:96-100 N '89

Home-grown threat to U.S.? [views of Marvin Cetron] il *USA Today (Periodical)* 118:4 D '89

Rules of the game [how terrorists could cripple the U.S.] G. G. Liddy. il *Omni (New York, N.Y.)* 11:42-4+ Ja '89

The technology of terror [terrorists' bombs] W. J. Cook. il *U.S. News & World Report* 106:24 Mr 6 '89

International aspects

See also

Pan American Flight 103 disaster, 1988

A blackened year [explosion of French jet over Sahara Desert and USAir 737 crash at New York City's LaGuardia Airport] D. Jenish. il *Maclean's* 102:59 O 2 '89

Changing targets. J. Newhouse. *The New Yorker* 65:71-82 Jl 10 '89

Death over the desert [terrorist bomb responsible for explosion of UTA jet over Niger] map *Time* 134:25 O 2 '89

The growing threat of terrorism. M. J. Cetron. il por *The Futurist* 23:20-4 Jl/Ag '89

TERRORISM—International aspects—*cont.*
Investigators seek cause of blast that destroyed UTA DC-10 over Niger. *Aviation Week & Space Technology* 131:25 S 25 '89
Iran's agents of terror [cover story; special section] il *U.S. News & World Report* 106:20-6+ Mr 6 '89
Safety experts cite similarities between DC-8, 747 crashes [bombing of Pan Am Flight 103 and crash of Arrow Air DC-8 at Gander, Nfld. in 1985; minority report of Canadian Aviation Safety Board] D. Hughes. il *Aviation Week & Space Technology* 130:58-9 F 6 '89
Selective terrorism. A. Haselkorn. il *National Review* 41:21-2 S 1 '89
Terror at 30,000 feet [Flight 772 from Chad to Paris crashes in Niger] E. Salholz. il map *Newsweek* 114:30 O 2 '89
The vapor trails of terror in Africa [bombing of French jet over Niger] il *U.S. News & World Report* 107:13 O 2 '89
The 'virgin terrorist' [Kim Hyun Hee stands trial for bombing KAL Flight 858 in 1987] S. Begley. il por *Newsweek* 113:8 Mr 20 '89

Prevention
See also
  Air travel—Security measures
  Airports—Security measures
  Embassies (Buildings)—Security measures
Anti-terrorism networks. S. R. A. Crawshaw. il por *The Futurist* 23:12-13 Mr/Ap '89
Security awareness, measures, and management [address, November 2, 1988] G. P. Shultz. *Department of State Bulletin* 89:4-5 Ja '89

Retaliation
See also
  Iranian air disaster, 1988—Retaliation
  Libyan-American conflict, 1986
Bringing terrorists to justice. T. Gest. il *U.S. News & World Report* 106:25 Mr 6 '89
Countering terrorism in the 1980s and 1990s [address, November 22, 1988] L. P. Bremer, III. *Department of State Bulletin* 89:61-4 F '89
On the trail of terrorists [FBI investigation of Pan Am Flight 103 bombing] S. Emerson. il *U.S. News & World Report* 106:36 F 13 '89
Playing hardball [responding to bombing of Pan Am Flight 103] *National Review* 41:13+ Ja 27 '89
Some reflections on terrorists and hostages. C. W. Weinberger. il *Forbes* 144:31 S 4 '89
Tackling the terrorists. D. Schorr. *The New Leader* 72:3 Ja 9 '89
Terrorism: an elusive enemy. S. Manning. il *Scholastic Update (Teachers' edition)* 122:7-8 O 6 '89
Terrorism: its evolving nature [statement, February 9, 1989] L. P. Bremer, III. *Department of State Bulletin* 89:74-8 My '89
To catch a terrorist [U.S. captures Arab airplane hijacker F. Yoonis] S. Emerson. il por *Reader's Digest* 135:107-11 O '89
When terrorists strike America, who responds? M. Mecham. *Aviation Week & Space Technology* 131:81+ D 18-25 '89

Argentina
The battle of La Tablada [leftist group attacks army base] J. Smolowe. il *Time* 133:45 F 6 '89
An ominous leftist uprising in Argentina [All for the Country rebels] il *Newsweek* 113:33 F 6 '89

Belgium
Khomeini strikes back [murder of A. Al Ahdal in Belgium and downfall of moderate H. Montazeri in Iran] J. Bierman. il pors *Maclean's* 102:25 Ap 10 '89
Murder in the mosque [A. Al Ahdal murdered in Brussels] *Newsweek* 113:41 Ap 10 '89

Canada
Capital standoff [C. Yacoub charged in hijacking of bus from Montreal to Ottawa] P. Kopvillem. il *Maclean's* 102:10-11 Ap 17 '89
Drugs and guns: is a Colombian assassination team in Canada? G. W. Taylor. il *Maclean's* 102:14 S 25 '89
No one called in the helicopters [hijacked bus on Parliament Hill] C. Gordon. il *Maclean's* 102:35 My 1 '89

Colombia
See also
  Grover, Richard—Kidnapping
  Libby, Roy—Kidnapping
  Olson, Bruce—Kidnapping
Anarchy in Colombia [narcoterrorism] J. Contreras. il *Newsweek* 114:30-2 S 11 '89
The deadliest beat [journalists covering the drug story] W. A. Henry. il *Time* 134:76 N 13 '89
Fighting anarchy in Colombia [war on drugs; cover story] R. Chepesiuk. il *The New Leader* 72:5-8 S 18 '89
'Good sons' who kill. G. Matthews. il *World Press Review* 36:26-7 N '89
The Israeli connection [mercenaries involved in training Colombian hit squads] E. Magnuson. il *Time* 134:26 S 11 '89
Letter from Bogotá. A. Guillermoprieto. *The New Yorker* 65:112-20+ O 16 '89
A mess in the Andes [cocaine cartels] T. Rosenberg. *The New Republic* 201:23-6 S 18-25 '89

'Now the fight is with blood' [drug wars in Colombia] T. Morganthau. il *Newsweek* 114:37 Ag 28 '89
Reporters as targets. J. Contreras. il *Newsweek* 114:59 O 2 '89
'The slaughter has begun' [bomb attacks as response to drug crackdown] il *Newsweek* 114:40 D 18 '89
Terror in the drug world. H. Jensen. il *Maclean's* 102:18-20 S 11 '89

Eastern Europe
A dying twitch of terrorists? il *U.S. News & World Report* 107:44 D 11 '89

Germany (West)
See also
  Herrhausen, Alfred—Assassination

Great Britain
British justice, Irish victims [release of Guildford Four who were wrongfully imprisoned in England for terrorist bombings] A. Cockburn. *The Nation* 249:554-5 N 13 '89
Cops above the law [release of Guildford Four who were wrongfully imprisoned in England for being IRA suspects] A. Phillips. il *Maclean's* 102:76+ N 6 '89
Vulnerable target, deadly attack [IRA attack on Royal Marines School of Music] *Newsweek* 114:31 O 2 '89

Greece
Greece: sanctuary of international terrorism. N. M. Adams. il map *Reader's Digest* 134:199-200+ Je '89

Iran
See also
  Iranian seizure of United States embassy, 1979-1981

Israel
Deadly quarantine [proposed amendment to Prevention of Terrorism Act restricting rights of Palestinians] A. Cockburn. *The Nation* 249:338-9 O 2 '89
'Today's word is revenge' [attack on Israeli bus puts latest peace proposals in jeopardy] A. Platt. il *Newsweek* 114:34 Jl 17 '89
The widening gulf [Palestinian attack on Israeli bus throws peace endeavors into chaos] B. Came. il *Maclean's* 102:21 Jl 17 '89

Latin America
The world of narcoterrorism. D. Brock. il *The American Spectator* 22:24-8 Je '89

Lebanon
See also
  Beirut airplane hijacking, 1985
  Lebanon hostage cases, 1984-
  Moawad, René—Assassination
  United States. Marine Corps—Forces in Lebanon—Terrorist attack, 1983
Celebrations and bombs [R. Moawad elected president] A. Bilski. il por *Maclean's* 102:42-3 N 20 '89
Hezbollah—sound and futile fury [cover story] K. Seigneurie and T. Nassar. il *The Nation* 249:225+ S 4-11 '89

Middle East
Relying on RUMINT [U.S. Mideast intelligence based on rumor] E. Salholz. il *Newsweek* 113:27 F 27 '89

Mozambique
See also
  Della Casa, Nicholas—Kidnapping

Northern Ireland
The fighting Irish. P. J. O'Rourke. il *Rolling Stone* p99-100+ F 9 '89
Northern Ireland hit-squad scandal [leak of lists of IRA sympathizers triggers loyalist terrorism] L. Flanders. il *The Nation* 249:491-4 O 30 '89
A wave of bloodshed. M. Nemeth. il *Maclean's* 102:34 Ap 3 '89

Philippines
A sense of foreboding in the Philippines [assassination of U.S. Army colonel N. Rowe] B. Duffy. il *U.S. News & World Report* 106:35-6 My 15 '89
Targeting a U.S. hero [New People's Army claims credit for murdering U.S. Army colonel N. Rowe] D. Waller and R. Vokey. il por *Newsweek* 113:42 My 1 '89

Sweden
See also
  Palme, Olof, 1927-1986—Assassination

United States
See Terrorism

Western Europe
French court convicts Palestinian terrorist [A. A. al-Hamid Labid; State Dept. statement and fact sheet, October 31, 1988] *Department of State Bulletin* 89:64-5 F '89

Yugoslavia
The Yugoslav bomb connection [role in Pan Am Flight 103 disaster] *U.S. News & World Report* 107:45 N 13 '89

TERRORISM AND THE PRESS
Reporters as stunt men [French journalists test airport security] J. Alter. il *Newsweek* 113:47+ Ja 16 '89
When terrorists strike . . . the lessons TV must learn. R. H. Kupperman and J. Kamen. il *TV Guide* 37:18-22 S 23-29 '89

TERRORISTS
See also
  Women terrorists

TERRORISTS, ARAB
See also
Beirut airplane hijacking, 1985
Changing targets. J. Newhouse. *The New Yorker* 65:71-82 Jl 10 '89
Closing in on the Pan Am bombers [Palestinian-Iranian deal in bombing of Pan Am Flight 103; with interview with A. Jibril] B. Duffy and others. il por *U.S. News & World Report* 106:23-4 My 22 '89
Finis for the master terrorist? [Abu Nidal] D. Brand. il por *Time* 134:69 D 11 '89
French court convicts Palestinian terrorist [A. A. al-Hamid Labid; State Dept. statement and fact sheet, October 31, 1988] *Department of State Bulletin* 89:64-5 F '89
Greece: sanctuary of international terrorism. N. M. Adams. il map *Reader's Digest* 134:199-200+ Je '89
The man who holds the hostages [I. Mughniyah] il *Time* 133:42 Mr 20 '89
Off the record [Cuban-Palestinian arms smuggling network] *National Review* 41:18 F 24 '89
Spoilers of peace in the Middle East [radical Palestinian groups supported by Syria] R. Z. Chesnoff. il map *U.S. News & World Report* 107:40-1 Jl 10 '89
Terrorists torch Israeli forests. il *Audubon* 91:16 Ja '89

TERRORISTS, COLOMBIAN
Drugs and guns: is a Colombian assassination team in Canada? G. W. Taylor. il *Maclean's* 102:14 S 25 '89

TERRORISTS, GERMAN
See also
Red Army Faction

TERRORISTS, IRANIAN
Iran's agents of terror [cover story; special section] il *U.S. News & World Report* 106:20-6+ Mr 6 '89

TERRORISTS, JAPANESE
See also
Japanese Red Army

TERRORISTS, PERUVIAN
See also
Sendero Luminoso (Guerrilla group)

TERRY, CLARK
about
Clark Terry. P. Booth. il por *Down Beat* 56:14 Ap '89

TERRY, DIXON
Farm futures [adaptation of 1987 address] il *Mother Jones* 14:6-8 O '89
about
Obituary
Utne Reader il por p31 S/O '89. G. Lamb

TERRY, EDITH B.
When the big one hits Tokyo . . . *World Press Review* 36:42+ D '89

TERRY, ELI
about
The pillar-and-scroll clock. B. Barol. *American Heritage* 40:24 Ap '89

TERRY, QUINLAN, 1937-
about
Architecture: Quinlan Terry: a Palladian country house in Kentucky. C. Aslet. il por *Architectural Digest* 46:282-7 O '89
Terry: keeper of the faith. M. Filler. il por *House & Garden* 161:162-3+ Mr '89

TERRY, RANDALL
about
Evangels of abortion. G. Wills. bibl f il por *The New York Review of Books* 36:15+ Je 15 '89
From prison, antiabortion leader Randall Terry says that God, not the law, is his judge. M. Brower. il pors *People Weekly* 32:109+ N 20 '89
The gospel according to Randall Terry. F. Wilkinson. il por *Rolling Stone* p85-6+ O 5 '89
Operation Rescue. J. M. Connors. il *America* 160:400-2+ Ap 29 '89
Operation Rescue. M. Suh and L. Denworth. il *Ms.* 17:92-4 Ap '89
Where did Randy go wrong? [cover story] S. Faludi. il pors *Mother Jones* 14:22-8+ N '89

TERRY, ROLAND, 1917-
about
In the San Juan Islands: driftwood and sod shape a Seattle architect's residence [cover story] J. Krakauer. il *Architectural Digest* 46:188-93 Je '89

TERRY, STEVE
The DMX512 Standard. *Theatre Crafts* 23:84 N '89

TERRY WINTER CHRISTIAN COMMUNICATIONS
Terry Winter: "explainer evangelist". L. K. Tarr. il por *Christianity Today* 33:47 Mr 17 '89

TERTIARY PERIOD See Paleontology—Tertiary

TERWILLIGER, THOMAS C.
(jt. auth) See Sandberg, Warren S., and Terwilliger, Thomas C.

TERZI, ZEHDI
about
Talk with a PLO official [interview] Y. Hamizrachi. il *World Press Review* 36:17-18 F '89

TERZIAN, PHILIP
All washed up. il *The American Spectator* 22:49 Jl '89

TESICH, STEVE, 1942-
Why 'Breaking away' succeeded. il *Bicycling* 30:72+ Ap '89

TESSMAR, JIM
about
Housekeeping services. il pors *Home Office Computing* 7:42 Je '89

TEST BANS (NUCLEAR WEAPONS) See Nuclear weapons—Testing—Suspension

TEST DRIVING (AUTOMOBILES) See Automobiles—Testing

TEST PATTERNS
See also
Videodiscs—Test patterns

TEST TUBE BABIES See Fertilization in vitro

TESTER, WILLIAM
Cousins [story] il *Esquire* 112:250-5 S '89

TESTES See Testicles

TESTICLES
Secretion of activin by interstitial cells in the testis. W. Lee and others. bibl f il *Science* 243:396-8 Ja 20 '89

TESTIMONIALS IN ADVERTISING See Advertising—Testimonials

TESTIMONY See Witnesses

TESTING
See also
Aptitude tests
Educational tests and measurements
Employment tests
Examinations
Psychological tests

TESTING EQUIPMENT
See also
Automatic test equipment
Electric meters
Logic analyzers
Oscilloscopes
Signal generators
B + K Precision Model 388-HD Test Bench. il *Radio-Electronics* 60:16-17 Mr '89
Circuit checker [SureTest] D. Petraglia. il *Popular Science* 234:32 Je '89

TESTING LABORATORIES See Laboratories

TESTIS DETERMINING FACTOR
Chromosome mapping and expression of a putative testis-determining gene in mouse. C. M. Nagamine and others. bibl f il *Science* 243:80-3 Ja 6 '89
Duplication, deletion, and polymorphism in the sex-determining region of the mouse Y chromosome. G. Mardon and others. bibl f il *Science* 243:78-80 Ja 6 '89

TESTORF, HELGA
about
Sex and politics. K. Larson. il *New York* 22:51-2 Jl 17 '89

TESTOSTERONE
Are men just born to be mean? B. G. Harrison. *Mademoiselle* 95:102 F '89

TETHERED SATELLITE SYSTEM
Satellites on a string. R. G. Nichols. il *Astronomy* 17:18-19 My '89
Space tethers. R. Twombly. il *Technology Review* 92:10-11 O '89
Spacecraft on a string. J. Rennie. *Scientific American* 261:32 O '89

TETLEY, GLEN
about
Tagore [ballet] Reviews
Dance Magazine il 63:52 Ag '89. P. Citron

TETRADECANOYLPHORBOL ACETATE See Phorbol esters

TETRAHYMENA
Defining the inside and outside of a catalytic RNA molecule [structure of Tetrahymena ribozyme] J. A. Latham and T. R. Cech. bibl f il *Science* 245:276-82 Jl 21 '89
New test could spare rabbits. il *USA Today (Periodical)* 117:4-5 Je '89
Stereochemical course of catalysis by the Tetrahymena ribozyme. J. Rajagopal and others. bibl f il *Science* 244:692-4 My 12 '89
Stereochemistry of RNA cleavage by the Tetrahymena ribozyme and evidence that the chemical step is not rate-limiting. J. A. McSwiggen and T. R. Cech. bibl f il *Science* 244:679-83 My 12 '89

TETRIS (VIDEO GAME)
The game that managers play. R. Lockwood. il *Personal Computing* 13:158-9 O '89
Tetris must be a commie plot; the game's not copy-protected. O. S. Card. *Compute!* 11:11 Ap '89

TETRODOTOXIN
Chemistry of voodoo [controversy over W. Davis' research] M. Kemp. il *Discover* 10:26-8 Ja '89

TETRUD, JAMES W., AND LANGSTON, J. WILLIAM
The effect of deprenyl (selegiline) on the natural history of Parkinson's disease. bibl f il *Science* 245:519-22 Ag 4 '89

TETTLETON, MICKEY
about
Cereal killer at large. S. Rushin. il por *Sports Illustrated* 70:82 Je 12 '89

TEVETH, SHABTAI, 1925-
Charging Israel with original sin. bibl f *Commentary* 88:24-33
S '89

TEVIS, CHERYL
Cheryl Tevis. See issues of *Successful Farming* beginning
March 1989
Joint venture. See issues of *Successful Farming* beginning
September 1984 through January 1989
Rural health. See issues of *Successful Farming* beginning
March 1989

TEVLIN, JON
Of hawks and men: a weekend in the male wilderness.
il *Utne Reader* p50-7+ N/D '89

TEX-MEX COOKING *See* Cooking, Tex-Mex

TEXACO CANADA INC.
Texaco Canada says goodbye [sold to Imperial Oil] J. DeMont.
Maclean's 102:33 Ja 30 '89

TEXACO INC.
Jim Kinnear is pumping new life into Texaco. M. Ivey.
il por *Business Week* p50+ Ap 17 '89
Public pensions play tougher [California Public Employees'
Retirement System nominee J. Brademas appointed direc-
tor] F. H. Katayama. il por *Fortune* 119:16 F 27 '89
Star power [fiftieth anniversary of sponsorship of Metropolitan
Opera broadcasts; cover story] bibl il *Opera News* 54:10-12+
N '89
Texaco photocopy suit moves toward trials. C. Reid.
Publishers Weekly 235:22 Je 30 '89
Who's in charge at Texaco now? S. P. Sherman. il pors
Fortune 119:68-70+ Ja 16 '89

TEXANS
The eyes of Texas are upon them. il *Life* 12:106-9 F '89
        Anecdotes, facetiae, satire, etc.
One Texan, on the rocks. M. Ivins. il *Ms.* 17:36 Ap '89

TEXAS
        See also
    Agriculture—Texas
    Aransas National Wildlife Refuge (Tex.)
    Architecture, Domestic—Texas
    Banks and banking—Texas
    Bastrop County (Tex.)
    Big Thicket National Preserve (Tex.)
    Birds—Texas
    Brazos River Valley (Tex.)
    Camps—Texas
    Courts—Texas
    Criminal justice, Administration of—Texas
    Educational laws and regulations—Texas
    Enchanted Rock State Natural Area (Tex.)
    Express highways—Texas
    Fishing—Texas
    Game laws—Texas
    Game preserves—Texas
    Governors' mansions—Texas
    Hunting—Texas
    Insurance law—Texas
    Labor laws and regulations—Texas
    Lyndon B. Johnson National Historical Park (Tex.)
    Music festivals—Texas
    National forests—Texas
    Organic farming—Texas
    Prisons—Texas
    Rio Grande Valley
    Savings and loan associations—Texas
    South Padre Island (Tex.)
    Squid fisheries—Texas
    Wild Basin Wilderness Preserve (Tex.)
    Wildflowers—Texas
        Anecdotes, facetiae, satire, etc.
Too wussy for Texas. M. Ivins. il *The Progressive* 53:37
O '89
        Climate
The aesthetics of storm chasing [Hurricane Gilbert; cover
story] R. Conn. il *Weatherwise* 42:143-7 Je '89
Battening for a blow [preparations by boat owners for Hur-
ricane Gilbert] F. Sargeant. il *Motor Boating & Sailing*
164:32+ S '89
Waiting for Gilbert [sheltering airplanes during hurricane]
G. Baxter. il *Flying* 116:84-5 Ja '89
        Description and travel
        See also
    Automobile touring—Texas
A Texas Thanksgiving. M. Kenyon. il *Gourmet* 49:138+ N
'89
        Economic conditions
Texas faces up to a tougher future. J. P. Newport, Jr. il
Fortune 119:102-3+ Mr 13 '89
Texas turns the corner. J. Schwartz. il *Newsweek* 113:40-1
Ja 23 '89
        Industries
        See also
    Real estate business
    Shellfish culture
A maverick's forecast: high inflation and a boom in Texas
stocks [F. Rowe] il por *Money* 18:191-2 My '89
        Legislature
Ramifistations in the hilterland. M. Ivins. il *The Progressive*
53:37 Jl '89

        Politics and government
        See also
    Politics, Corruption in—Texas
    Texas—Legislature
Breaking an ole boy network [women mayors] B. Turque.
il *Newsweek* 113:39 Je 19 '89
The Johnson years: a congressman goes to war. R. A. Caro.
por *The New Yorker* 65:62-4+ N 6 '89
The Johnson years: buying and selling [L. B. Johnson's
involvement with radio station KTBC] R. A. Caro. *The
New Yorker* 65:43-8+ D 18 '89
'A party within a party': Jim Hightower proposes a populist
alliance. D. A. Denison. il *The Progressive* 53:22-3 Mr
'89
Raising issues, hope and hell. J. Hightower. il *The Nation*
248:160+ F 6 '89
T. Boone for governor? T. Vogel. il por *Business Week*
p43 F 27 '89
The way we are [A. Richards] L. Wyse. il por *Good
Housekeeping* 208:202 F '89
        Anecdotes, facetiae, satire, etc.
Dumb bankers, mavericks too. M. Ivins. il *The Nation*
248:82-4 Ja 23 '89
Kick 'em while they're down. M. Ivins. il *The Progressive*
53:36 Ja '89
Smart as a Shrub. M. Ivins. il *The Progressive* 53:40 My
'89
State of the states. M. Ivins. il por *The Progressive* 53:40
Ap '89
        Social life and customs
        Anecdotes, facetiae, satire, etc.
Good ol debs. M. Ivins. il *Ms.* 18:22 Jl/Ag '89

TEXAS. DECLARATION OF INDEPENDENCE
Lone Star fakes [T. Taylor tracks down forgeries] L. Belkin.
il pors *The New York Times Magazine* p66+ D 10 '89

TEXAS. DEPT. OF AGRICULTURE
Don't mess around with Jim [commissioner J. Hightower]
R. Woodbury. il por *Time* 133:42 Ap 3 '89
Hightower's view. J. Schutze. il pors *Organic Gardening*
36:32-6 D '89
Jim Hightower: a farmer's friend who goes against the grain.
K. Kelly. il por *Business Week* p84 N 6 '89
Raising issues, hope and hell. J. Hightower. il *The Nation*
248:160+ F 6 '89

TEXAS A & M UNIVERSITY
Muster and a malt at A&M. il *Southern Living* 24:24 Ap
'89

**TEXAS AGRICULTURAL AND MECHANICAL UNIVER-
SITY** *See* Texas A & M University

TEXAS AIR CORP.
Air sickness [F. Lorenzo] H. Fairlie. *The New Republic*
200:14-16+ Je 5 '89
Back to you, Frank [F. Lorenzo's deal with P. Ueberroth
for Eastern Air Lines collapses] A. Bernstein and C. Power.
il pors *Business Week* p24-6 Ap 24 '89
Judge threatens to auction Eastern after buyout fails [bid
by P. Ueberroth] J. T. McKenna and E. H. Kolcum.
Aviation Week & Space Technology 130:60-1 Ap 17 '89
Lorenzo weighs selling stake in Continental. *Aviation Week
& Space Technology* 131:69-70 S 4 '89
Texas Air: empire in jeopardy [strike at Eastern; special
section] il por *Business Week* p28-31 Mr 27 '89

TEXAS COMMERCE BANCSHARES, INC.
Even 'good banks' can be bad buys [Class B Chemical stock]
J. M. Laderman. *Business Week* p60 Ja 9 '89
It's back to square 2 for Texas Commerce [failed bid for
MCorp banks] M. Ivey. il por *Business Week* p125-6
Jl 17 '89

TEXAS EASTERN CORP.
The lasso is tightening around Texas Eastern [Coastal's bid]
M. Ivey. il por *Business Week* p30-1 Ja 30 '89

TEXAS HEART INSTITUTE
Will Denton Cooley make medical history again? [cut-rate
heart bypasses] M. Ivey. il por *Business Week* p56+ Mr
27 '89

TEXAS INSTRUMENTS' GRAPHICS ARCHITECTURE *See*
TIGA (Texas Instruments' Graphics Architecture)

TEXAS INSTRUMENTS INCORPORATED
A growing force in the shrinking business [R. T. Bate's
quantum-effect transistor] W. C. Symonds. il por *Business
Week* Special Issue:75 Je 16 '89
New AGM-88C HARM guidance scores five out of five
[antiradar missile] il *Aviation Week & Space Technology*
131:69-70 S 11 '89
Pentagon cites Texas Instruments for quality gains in HARM
production [guided missile] il *Aviation Week & Space
Technology* 131:79 S 11 '89
Raytheon/TI aim at high-volume MMIC chip production
capacity. il *Aviation Week & Space Technology* 131:92-3
S 18 '89
Texas Instruments seeks to boost foreign sales through expan-
sion. *Aviation Week & Space Technology* 131:55 Jl 3 '89
TI's prototype transistor takes a quantum leap. *Byte* 14:11
Mr '89
What's behind the Texas Instruments-Hitachi deal. O. Port
and T. Mason. il *Business Week* p93+ Ja 16 '89

TEXAS MUSIC COLLECTION
From offices of excellence [work of J. Wheat] D. Young. il pors *Southern Living* 24:142+ Ap '89
TEXAS OIL & GAS CORP.
A new iron man recasts USX [C. A. Corry sells Texas Oil & Gas assets] G. L. Miles. il por *Business Week* p37 O 16 '89
TEXAS PACIFIC LAND TRUST
Acres of assets in Texas. G. G. Marcial. *Business Week* p122 O 16 '89
TEXAS SCHOOL BOOK DEPOSITORY BUILDING
Reflections on a tragedy. D. Bedwell. il *Travel Holiday* 172:96+ Ag '89
"The sixth floor" [exhibit about the Kennedy assassination] il *American History Illustrated* 23:42-3 F '89
A tragic dilemma [discussion of August 1989 article, Reflections on a tragedy] D. Bedwell. il *Travel Holiday* 172:8 N '89
TEXAS SOUTHERN UNIVERSITY
Wm. H. Harris installed as Texas Southern U. prexy. il pors *Jet* 76:29 Je 5 '89
TEXAS STAR PARTY *See* Astronomy—Conferences
TEXAS UTILITIES ELECTRIC COMPANY
The co-opting of CASE [Citizens' Association for Sound Energy withdraws opposition to Comanche Peak nuclear plant] G. Aronson. il *The Nation* 249:678+ D 4 '89
TEXAS WINES *See* Wine
TEXFI INDUSTRIES, INC.
Scuffle in the boardroom [L. T. Sovey vs. J. Hamilton] A. A. Lappen. pors *Forbes* 144:112+ O 16 '89
TEXOP BANCSHARES
The hometown boys. J. H. Taylor. il por *Forbes* 144:253-4 O 16 '89
TEXT EDITORS (COMPUTER PROGRAMS)
Extensible text editors for programmers [BRIEF 2.1, EMACS 1.2, Epsilon 3.2, and ME 2.1] J. Udell. il *Byte* 14:197-8+ Mr '89
Figuring out CONFIG. SYS. M. Minasi. il *Byte* 14:129-30+ Jl '89
Introducing the new extended TextEdit [Macintosh] M. Ogawa. il *Byte* 14 Mac Special Ed:MAC21-MAC24+ Mr '89
TEXT PROCESSING (COMPUTER SCIENCE)
See also
Hypertext
IZE [text database program] L. Wood. il *Home Office Computing* 7:70+ Ag '89
Text retrieval with a twist [Folio Views] D. Allen. il *Byte* 14:201-2+ Jl '89
TEXTBOOK AUTHORS ASSOCIATION
Textbook publishers and authors clash over comp copy proposals. C. Reid. il *Publishers Weekly* 236:12 O 20 '89
TEXTBOOKS
See also
Economics—Textbooks
Medicine—Textbooks
Opera—Textbooks
Publishers and publishing—Textbooks
Science—Textbooks
United States—History—Textbooks
School texts: the outlook of teachers. V. R. Rogers. *The Education Digest* 54:24-6 Ja '89
Authorship
See also
Textbook Authors Association
The academy's contribution to textbook impoverishment. H. Tyson-Bernstein. *The Education Digest* 54:25-8 F '89
Reading, revising, and remembering [research by Bruce Britton and others] G. W. Bracey. *Phi Delta Kappan* 71:246-7 N '89
Remember me not [research by Michael Graves and others] G. W. Bracey. il *Phi Delta Kappan* 70:407-8 Ja '89
Censorship
Trials of a textbook writer. R. English. *National Review* 41:36 F 24 '89
Soviet Union
American textbook reform: what can we learn from the Soviet experience? H. D. Mehlinger. bibl f il *Phi Delta Kappan* 71:29-35 S '89
TEXTILE ARTS *See* Textile crafts
TEXTILE/CLOTHING TECHNOLOGY CORPORATION
Rags to riches? R. Kazis. il *Technology Review* 92:42-53 Ag/S '89
TEXTILE CRAFTS
Exhibitions
Norma Minkowitz: shadow boxes [crocheted sculptures] M. Shermeta. il *American Craft* 49:38-41 D '89/Ja '90
TEXTILE DESIGN
See also
Weaving
Design unleashed [dog motifs] E. A. Berthold. il *House & Garden* 161:200 'N '89
Fleur de bees [French emblems] E. A. Berthold. il *House & Garden* 161:162 Jl '89
Fruits of the loom. E. A. Berthold. il *House & Garden* 161:164 Je '89
Greek visions [C. Samios' textile designs based on Hellenic art] J. P. Gage. il *House & Garden* 161:72 F '89

Exhibitions
See Textile fabrics—Exhibitions
TEXTILE EXHIBITS *See* Textile fabrics—Exhibitions
TEXTILE FABRICS
See also
Canvas
Cotton fabrics
Denim
Photographs on cloth
Seersucker
Silk
Tapestry
Velvet
Weaving
Yarn
Call of the wild [animal prints] M. Tweeddale. il *House & Garden* 161:118 S '89
Choosing fabrics for daily use [house decoration] *Southern Living* 24:142-3 O '89
Cross references [C. Hyland's mix and match decorative technique] E. Silberman. il *Vogue* 179:435-7 Mr '89
Decorate with fabric. D. L. Caringer and R. E. Dittmer. il *Better Homes and Gardens* 67:39-44 Ag '89
Drape fabric on the tabletop. il *Southern Living* 24:154 Mr '89
Kente cloth [Ghana cloth] P. A. Jones. il *Essence* 19:42 Ja '89
Konstantin Kakanias takes inspiration for his witty prints from mummies in Egypt, the guillotine in France. J. Shields. il por *Vogue* 179:132 S '89
New products: contract textiles. il *Architectural Record* 177:142-5 O '89
On the prowl with vulgar chic [animal prints] J. D. Reed. il *Time* 134:92 O 16 '89
Sew-easy decorating. D. L. Caringer and R. E. Dittmer. il *Better Homes and Gardens* 67:35-7 Ag '89
The stars of stripes. E. A. Berthold. il *House & Garden* 161:204 My '89
Collectors and collecting
F. Schumacher and Company and the art moderne style. R. E. Slavin, III. il *Antiques* 135:964-73 Ap '89
Fabrics of being [P. Poiret] R. E. Slavin, III. il por *Horizon (Tuscaloosa, Ala.)* 32:49-51 Mr/Ap '89
Exhibitions
A century of opulent textiles: the Schumacher Collection [cover story] il *Horizon (Tuscaloosa, Ala.)* 32:57-72 Mr/Ap '89
TEXTILE FABRICS, SYNTHETIC
See also
Rayon
Guide to insulation material. il *Women's Sports & Fitness* 11:37 O '89
TEXTILE FIBER CRAFTS *See* Textile crafts
TEXTILE FIBERS
See also
Cotton
TEXTILE FIBERS, SYNTHETIC
See also
Acrylic fibers
Kevlar
Rayon
Spectra Shield
TEXTILE INDUSTRY
See also
Amoco Fabrics & Fibers Company
Angelica Corp.
Avtex Fibers Inc.
Cotton industry
Delta Woodside Industries, Inc.
Milliken & Company
North American Rayon Corp.
Texfi Industries, Inc.
Textile/Clothing Technology Corporation
United Merchants & Manufacturers, Inc.
West Point-Pepperell, Inc.
Apparel, shoes and textiles. G. Eisenstodt. il *Forbes* 143:86-8 Ja 9 '89
Acquisitions and mergers
Bill Farley is on pins and needles [West Point-Pepperell takeover] D. Greising. il por *Business Week* p58+ S 18 '89
Billion-dollar mind [W. Farley's acquisition of West Point-Pepperell] C. Bruck. *The New Yorker* 65:76-88 Ag 7 '89
Chink in the armor [Stroud family sells small stake in Milliken & Co. to Delta Woodside Industries] A. A. Lappen. il *Forbes* 144:84+ N 13 '89
International aspects
Spreading the net widely [Dominion Textile and Telenet Communications map strategy for U.S.-Canada free trade agreement] J. DeMont. il *Maclean's* 102:76-7 Jl 3 '89
Export-import trade
The conservative's conservative [Roger Milliken fights for legislation to insulate textiles from imports] A. A. Lappen. *Forbes* 143:60 My 29 '89
Textile and Apparel Trade Act. il *Congressional Digest* 68:1-32 Ja '89

TEXTILE INDUSTRY—*cont.*

History

Samuel Slater: father of the American Industrial Revolution. J. Gustaitis. por *American History Illustrated* 24:32-3 My '89

Canada

See also

Dominion Textile Inc.

Great Britain

See also

Manningham Mills (Bradford, England)

TEXTILE MACHINERY INDUSTRY

See also

John D. Hollingsworth on Wheels

TEXTILE MILLS

See also

Manningham Mills (Bradford, England)

TEXTILE PAINTING

Gyotaku on your sweatshirt. il *Sunset (Central West edition)* 183:98+ Jl '89

TEXTILES *See* Textile fabrics

TEXTRON INC.

Being a conglomerate is not all bad. H. Banks. il por *Forbes* 144:40-1 D 11 '89

Coast Guard weighs replacing troubled Textron Lycoming engines. D. Hughes. il *Aviation Week & Space Technology* 130:19-20 My 15 '89

Rivets and revelation [Textron's acquisition of Avdel prompts FTC antitrust case concerning blind rivets] H. Banks. *Forbes* 143:153 Je 12 '89

TEXTUAL CRITICISM

Literary detection and Latin American writing. F. Ainsa. il *The Courier (Unesco)* 42:21-3 My '89

The quest for authenticity. G. Tavani. il *The Courier (Unesco)* 42:14-17 My '89

TGF *See* Transforming growth factor

THADEN, LOUISE

about

Rerun: 1929 Women's Air Derby. *Flying* 116:20 Ag '89

THAI AIRWAYS INTERNATIONAL LTD.

Thai International to equip three Airbus A300-600Rs with PW4158 engines. P. Proctor. *Aviation Week & Space Technology* 131:76 Ag 7 '89

THAI COOKING *See* Cooking, Thai

THAI COOKING SCHOOL (BANGKOK, THAILAND)

Tongue Thai'd in Bangkok. D. G. Gordon. il *Travel Holiday* 172:52-7 O '89

THAI DANCE *See* Dance, Thai

THAI HOUSE DECORATION *See* House decoration, Thai

THAI PHILOSOPHY *See* Philosophy, Thai

THAILAND

See also

Bangkok (Thailand)
Birth control—Thailand
Fishing—Thailand
Immigration and emigration—Thailand
Samui (Thailand)
Women—Thailand
Youth—Thailand

Commerce

United States

See United States—Commerce—Thailand

Description and travel

See also

Cruising—Thailand

The humanist. L. L. Morain. *The Humanist* 49:2 Ja/F '89

Paradise lost—and found. R. Alleman. il *Vogue* 179:120+ Ja '89

Economic conditions

Asia's reluctant growth champs. F. S. Worthy. il *Fortune* 119:283-4+ Ap 24 '89

Industries

See also

Printing industry—Thailand
Thai Airways International Ltd.

Kings and rulers

See also

Bhumibol Adulyadej, King of Thailand

THALIDOMIDE

Facing the future [Canadian thalidomide victims seek compensation] A. Steacy. il *Maclean's* 102:41 F 20 '89

Faith of a family: the Tony Melendez story [condensed from A gift of hope]; ed. by Mel White. T. Melendez. il *Reader's Digest* 134:209-12+ Je '89

The man who would not quit [D. L. Stevens] J. G. Hubbell. il pors *Reader's Digest* 134:115-18 F '89

THANATOLOGY *See* Death

THANK-YOU NOTES

A matter of manners: executive thank-yous. J. Benton. il *Working Woman* 14:108 Ap '89

THANKSGIVING DAY

See also

Macy's Thanksgiving Day Parade

Five grains of corn. C. A. Frazier. il *The Saturday Evening Post* 261:62-3 N/D '89

A Texas Thanksgiving. M. Kenyon. il *Gourmet* 49:138+ N '89

Why we've failed to ruin Thanksgiving. W. Shapiro. il *Time* 134:94 N 27 '89

Anecdotes, facetiae, satire, etc.

Confessions of a cranberry-sauce addict. R. Schoenstein. il *New Choices for the Best Years* 29:96 N '89

THANKSGIVING DINNERS

Carving a new Thanksgiving tradition [work of L. Largent, chef at the Grand Hotel in Los Olivos, Calif.] J. Rogers. il por *Prevention (Emmaus, Pa.)* 41:67-71+ N '89

Down-home hospitality. il *Redbook* 174:104-7+ N '89

Great dinner ideas for Thanksgiving. il *Good Housekeeping* 209:174-84+ N '89

Lite eating: a savory holiday feast. M. Langan. il *McCall's* 117:148 N '89

The new Thanksgiving dinner. L. Holderness. il *Better Homes and Gardens* 67:166-70+ N '89

Provence Pilgrims [in France] P. Wells. il *The New York Times Magazine* p93-4 N 5 '89

A really American Thanksgiving. il *Sunset (Central West edition)* 183:168-70+ N '89

Talking turkey. G. Hovis. il *House & Garden* 161:107-10+ N '89

Thanksgiving cookbook. il *McCall's* 117:131-5+ N '89

Thanksgiving dinner. il *Gourmet* 49:170-8+ N '89

Thanksgiving favorites. C. Koury. il *Parents* 64:168-70+ N '89

Tribute to turkey. M. Evans. il *The Saturday Evening Post* 261:18-20 N/D '89

Anecdotes, facetiae, satire, etc.

The marvelous hunt. D. Elliott. il *Field & Stream* 94:29+ N '89

THANKSGIVING TABLE SETTING *See* Table setting

THARP, TWYLA

about

Can you forgive her? T. Tobias. il *New York* 22:95-6 Je 5 '89

Dancing:

Works of Twyla Tharp. A. Croce. *The New Yorker* 65:94-5 Je 12 '89

Reviews:

All-Tharp program during spring season. N. V. Dalva. il *Dance Magazine* 63:62 O '89

THATCH, EDWARD *See* Blackbeard, 1680?-1718

THATCHER, CAROL

Portrait of my mother: Margaret Thatcher. il pors *Ladies' Home Journal* 106:98+ Je '89

THATCHER, COLIN

about

Murder on the prairie. D. Turbide. il por *Maclean's* 102:45-6 Jl 17 '89

THATCHER, DENIS

about

Is this Denis a menace? W. Mader. il pors *Time* 134:37 Ag 14 '89

THATCHER, LISA

Bombs away! il *Seventeen* 48:138+ Ag '89

THATCHER, MARGARET

Prime Minister Thatcher's visit [remarks, November 16, 1988] *Department of State Bulletin* 89:58 Mr '89

Remarks and question-and-answer session, London, June 1, 1989. il pors *Department of State Bulletin* 89:40-1 Ag '89

We can't make it without religious values. il por *The Saturday Evening Post* 261:60-1 Jl/Ag '89

about

10 years of Thatcherism. R. Knight. *U.S. News & World Report* 106:56 My 8 '89

After the Thatcher decade. A. Hartley. bibl f *Foreign Affairs* 68:102-18 Wint '89/'90

Arms and the woman. J. O'Sullivan. *National Review* 41:9 N 24 '89

Bad reviews for a one-man show. H. Anderson. il pors *Newsweek* 114:46-7 N 6 '89

The beginning of the end of an era. R. Knight. por *U.S. News & World Report* 107:50 N 6 '89

Big sister. A. Sullivan. *The New Republic* 200:7-8 Ja 2 '89

Britain: under the iron (high) heel? J. O'Sullivan. *Commentary* 88:47-52 S '89

Britain's vexing ties with Europe. B. Amiel. il *Maclean's* 102:13 D 18 '89

Charity begins with gluttony. F. Inglis. il *The Nation* 248:446-8 Ap 3 '89

Civil liberties imperiled under Thatcher. C. Sugnet. il *Utne Reader* p12-14 My/Je '89

EC, phone home. M. Elliott. *The New Republic* 200:20+ Mr 27 '89

The enemies she makes. A. Lejeune. *National Review* 41:24 My 19 '89

Has Britain's Iron Lady begun to rust? R. Knight. il por *U.S. News & World Report* 107:82-3 Ag 28-S 4 '89

Has the Iron Lady lost her golden touch? R. A. Melcher. il por *Business Week* p67 N 13 '89

Her majesty's censors. M. Friedman. il *The Progressive* 53:30-3 F '89

Is there life after Thatcher? G. Black. *The Nation* 248:620-2 My 8 '89

Is this Denis a menace? W. Mader. il pors *Time* 134:37 Ag 14 '89

THATCHER, MARGARET—about—*cont.*

The Japanese are coming—and Thatcher is all smiles. R. A. Melcher and M. Maremont. il *Business Week* p46-7 F 20 '89

Just you move over, 'Enry 'Iggins. R. Knight. il *U.S. News & World Report* 106:40 Ap 24 '89

Lessons from the British schoolmarm. O. Scott. il por *Conservative Digest* 15:47-9 My/Je '89

Maggie. L. Nickson. il pors *Life* 12:24-8+ O '89

Margaret Thatcher and the revival of the West [cover story] R. Reagan. il *National Review* 41:21-2 My 19 '89

Margaret Thatcher holds a finger to the wind—and steps to the left. M. Maremont. il *Business Week* p52 O 30 '89

The moral passion of Mrs. Thatcher. K. R. Minogue. il *National Review* 41:22-5 My 19 '89

More than ever, Thatcher is odd woman out. R. A. Melcher. il por *Business Week* p40 Jl 3 '89

Mrs. Thatcher under siege again. C. W. Weinberger. il por *Forbes* 144:31 N 27 '89

My girl. M. Elliott. *The New Republic* 200:15-16 My 29 '89

No sex please, we're the prime minister. il por *Newsweek* 113:44 Je 5 '89

Portrait of my mother: Margaret Thatcher. C. Thatcher. il pors *Ladies' Home Journal* 106:98+ Je '89

Prime Minister Margaret Thatcher [address, October 19, 1988] J. J. Auer. *Vital Speeches of the Day* 55:276-82 F 15 '89

A question of judgment. A. Phillips. il por *Maclean's* 102:38-9 N 6 '89

Remarkable Margaret Thatcher [with interview] P. Johnson. il pors *Reader's Digest* 134:70-81 My '89

The slide at midterm. C. S. Manegold. por *Newsweek* 114:32 Jl 3 '89

Splatcher. M. Elliott. il *The New Republic* 201:14-16 D 11 '89

Thatcher at odds with Europe. N. Gelb. por *The New Leader* 72:12-13 O 30 '89

Thatcher: can an old Tory learn new tricks? R. A. Melcher. por *Business Week* p37 Jl 24 '89

Thatcher for president. M. Kinsley. il *Time* 133:90 My 15 '89

Thatcher puts a lid on. J. Atlas. il *The New York Times Magazine* p36-8+ Mr 5 '89

The Thatcher revolution [special section] il pors *Maclean's* 102:30-3+ My 8 '89

Thatcherism across the Channel. J.-M. Benoist. map *National Review* 41:23-5 N 10 '89

Thatcherism and British higher education [address, April 1989] M. Shattock. il pors *Change* 21:30-9 S/O '89

Thatcherism isn't working. N. Gelb. il *The New Leader* 72:8-9 Jl 10-24 '89

Thatcher's compromise. A. Phillips. il por *Maclean's* 102:28 Jl 10 '89

Thatcher's new revolution. R. A. Melcher. il por *Business Week* p42-3 My 1 '89

They've come a long way, Maggie. B. Amiel. il *Maclean's* 102:10 Ja 16 '89

A thorny dispute. R. Laver. il por *Maclean's* 102:36-7 N 6 '89

A two-speed Europe? T. Garton Ash. il *World Press Review* 36:16+ Ja '89

What ails Britain. M. Horsman. il *World Press Review* 36:50-1 Ap '89

Collectibles

Cashing in on Maggie. A. Phillips. il por *Maclean's* 102:32 My 8 '89

Visit to the United States, 1988

Prime Minister Thatcher's visit [remarks, November 16, 1988] R. Reagan; M. Thatcher. il por *Department of State Bulletin* 89:57-8 Mr '89

THAW, CLARE

about

Art of Eastover: Clare and Eugene Thaw in upstate New York. S. M. Alsop. il por *Architectural Digest* 46:118-25+ Je '89

THAW, EUGENE VICTOR

about

Art of Eastover: Clare and Eugene Thaw in upstate New York. S. M. Alsop. il por *Architectural Digest* 46:118-25+ Je '89

THAYER, HELEN

about

Polar dare. P. Turner. il por *Ms.* 17:55-7 Je '89

THC RECEPTORS *See* Drug receptors

THEA BOWMAN BLACK CATHOLIC EDUCATIONAL FOUNDATION *See* Sister Thea Bowman Black Catholic Educational Foundation

THEATER

See also
Christmas pageants
Discrimination in the theater
Drama
Drama festivals
Insurance, Theater
Motion picture theaters
News. See issues of Theatre Crafts

Once outposts, now landmarks [regional theater] W. A. Henry. il *Time* 133:72 Je 12 '89

Auditions

Annie [11-year-old D. Findley gets the part in Annie 2 after nationwide auditions] C. Dowling. il pors *Life* 12:42-9 N '89

Awards

See also
Tony Awards

Bibliography

1989 fall book buyers guide. J. Ellinghausen and M. McCloud. il *Theatre Crafts* 23:78+ O '89

Books. See issues of Theatre Crafts

Costume

See Costume, Theatrical

Economic aspects

Japanese angels on Broadway. F. H. Katayama. il *Fortune* 119:8 Mr 27 '89

Electronic sound control

Audio specialists for aurally savvy audiences [sound contractors] B. Saturn. *Theatre Crafts* 23:34+ Ap '89

Creating an audio environment: Hans Peter Kuhn's Forest sounds. J. Calhoun. il por *Theatre Crafts* 23:46-8+ Ja '89

MIDI and the theatre: a guide to music software applications. J. Roper. *Theatre Crafts* 23:70+ O '89

Sound reinforcement for the 90s. M. S. Eddy. il *Theatre Crafts* 23:30+ N '89

Exhibitions

AES report [annual convention] R. Heller. *Theatre Crafts* 23:30-3 F '89

Employees

See also
Set designers

Stage labor abroad. M. Loeffler. *Theatre Crafts* 23:81 My '89

Equipment

Products. See issues of Theatre Crafts

Bibliography

1989 technical literature guide. M. S. Eddy. il *Theatre Crafts* 23:72-83 Ja '89

Directories

1989 new products buyers guide. J. Calhoun. *Theatre Crafts* 23:77-90 Ag/S '89

Directory 1989/90 [special issue] il *Theatre Crafts* 23:4+ Je/Jl '89

Transportation

Carnets and customs [international tours] J. Calhoun. *Theatre Crafts* 23:79-80 My '89

Fancy freightwork. M. S. Eddy. *Theatre Crafts* 23:76-7 My '89

Federal aid

See Theater and state

Political aspects

The charge of the Angry Brigade [left-wing British playwrights] C. Tookey. il *National Review* 41:41-4 N 24 '89

Production and direction

See also
Computers—Theatrical use
Musicals, revues, etc.—Production and direction
Shakespeare, William, 1564-1616—Staging and acting of plays
United States Institute for Theatre Technology

Broadway: everything old is (sort of) new again [Meet me in St. Louis, Threepenny opera, and Orpheus descending; cover story] M. Sommers. il *Theatre Crafts* 23:44-7+ N '89

King Lear's a woman, Mozart's in a diner [modern renditions of the classics] M. Horn. il *U.S. News & World Report* 107:50-1 Ag 14 '89

Les liaisons dangereuses. M. LaRue. il *Theatre Crafts* 23:48-54+ F '89

Theatre at sea [aboard cruise ships; special section] il *Theatre Crafts* 23:40-5+ Mr '89

Directories

Directory 1989/90 [special issue] il *Theatre Crafts* 23:4+ Je/Jl '89

Safety devices and measures

Cutting through the fog; Safely navigating the haze [fog and smoke machines] M. S. Eddy. il *Theatre Crafts* 23:26+ O '89

Sound effects

CD libraries: sound effects on compact disc. T. Clark. *Theatre Crafts* 23:38+ Ag/S '89

Sound systems

See Theater—Electronic sound control

Special effects

Cutting through the fog; Safely navigating the haze [fog and smoke machines] M. S. Eddy. il *Theatre Crafts* 23:26+ O '89

Making a telephone ring. K. Ruling. il *Theatre Crafts* 23:92+ Ap '89

Simulating shattered glass. R. B. Chambers. il *Theatre Crafts* 23:84 Ja '89

Stage floors

See also
Dance floors

THEATER—cont.
Stage lighting
See also
Lighting designers
Centerline: Richard Devin. M. Sommers. il por *Theatre Crafts* 23:16-17 O '89
Color in light; Beyond plastic filters: a look ahead. M. S. Eddy. il *Theatre Crafts* 23:40+ Ap '89
The DMX512 Standard. S. Terry. *Theatre Crafts* 23:84 N '89
From toybox to toolbox [lighting system peripherals] M. Loeffler. il *Theatre Crafts* 23:19-21+ Mr '89
A guide for assistant lighting designers. C. Miller. il *Theatre Crafts* 23:22-7 Ja '89
Impressions vs. effects [designer N. Katz] S. Flatow. il pors *Theatre Crafts* 23:56-60+ N '89
Insider insights [thoughts on DMX] M. S. Eddy. *Theatre Crafts* 23:85+ N '89
Lightwright for lighting designers. R. Chase. il *Theatre Crafts* 23:28-9 F '89
Shedding a new light: the latest in lamps for the stage. M. Loeffler. il *Theatre Crafts* 23:73-6 Ag/S '89
Tharon Musser [cover story] M. Sommers. il por *Theatre Crafts* 23:42-9+ O '89
Tom Skelton [cover story] G. M. Loney. il pors *Theatre Crafts* 23:44-51+ Ap '89
Exhibitions
LDI 88 report [Lighting Dimensions International trade show] M. S. Eddy. il *Theatre Crafts* 23:24+ F '89
Stage machinery
Production: The shaughraun [use of Theta drum revolve stage by England's National Theatre] M. Sommers. il *Theatre Crafts* 23:10 Ja '89
Stage setting and scenery
See also
Cycloramas
Dance—Stage setting and scenery
Opera—Stage setting and scenery
Set designers
Ben Edwards. M. Sommers. il *Theatre Crafts* 23:48-55+ Ag/S '89
CADD for the theatre designer: a comparison of low-cost programs. M. Stauffer. il *Theatre Crafts* 23:66+ Ja '89
Centerline: Karl Eigsti. M. LaRue. il por *Theatre Crafts* 23:12-13 Mr '89
Designstyle: trimming the woods [abstract forest for A walk in the woods] il *Theatre Crafts* 23:20 O '89
From print shop to stage floor [use of halftone process] T. Macie. il *Theatre Crafts* 23:94 Ag/S '89
The Louisville look [Actors Theater of Louisville] il *Theatre Crafts* 23:38-9+ Mr '89
Peter Larkin. G. M. Loney. il por *Theatre Crafts* 23:38-45+ Ja '89
Uses for rigid-swivel based casters. E. Littlefield. il *Theatre Crafts* 23:97 Ap '89
Study and teaching
The recruitment trail: my MFA design program's better than yours. J. Dolan. *Theatre Crafts* 23:22+ Ag/S '89
Student competition: plague or pestilence? [high school drama festivals] D. Finney. *Design for Arts in Education* 90:38-41 Ja/F '89
Symposium on K-12 theatre education. bibl f *Design for Arts in Education* 91:23-37 N/D '89
Theatre education: approaching a new decade. B. S. Wills. bibl f *Design for Arts in Education* 90:24-9 Ja/F '89
Training facilities in Boston [colleges offering courses in theater design and technology; special section] M. Sommers. il *Theatre Crafts* 23:50-5+ N '89
Brazil
See also
São Paulo (Brazil)—Theater
California
See also
Pacific Conservatory of the Performing Arts
Canada
Broadway bound. P. Young. il *Maclean's* 102:54-5 S 25 '89
Theatre. See occasional issues of Maclean's
Europe
American productions in Europe [cover story; special issue] il *Theatre Crafts* 23:33-81 My '89
Florida
Population shift. B. Howard. il *Theatre Crafts* 23:54-9 D '89
Georgia
See also
Atlanta (Ga.)—Theater
Great Britain
See also
London (England)—Theater
National Theatre (Great Britain)
Winter Gardens (Morecambe, England)
The charge of the Angry Brigade [left-wing playwrights] C. Tookey. il *National Review* 41:41-4 N 24 '89
India
See also
Kathakali

Israel
See also
Tel Aviv (Israel)—Theater
A conversation with Israeli playwright Joshua Sobol. G. G. Seibert. *America* 160:559-62 Je 10 '89
Japan
See also
Kabuki
Kara Juro (Theater company)
Minnesota
See also
Chanhassen Dinner Theatre
Netherlands
See also
Rotterdam (Netherlands)—Theater
New York (State)
See also
New York (N.Y.)—Theater
Nova Scotia
See also
Ship's Company Theatre
Ontario
See also
Toronto (Ont.)—Theater
Soviet Union
See also
DEREVO (Theater company)
Moscow (Soviet Union)—Theater
Sophisticated ladies go to Russia. M. Sommers. il *Theatre Crafts* 23:36-8+ My '89
Spain
See also
Madrid (Spain)—Theater
Venezuela
See also
Maracaibo (Venezuela)—Theater
Washington (State)
See also
Seattle (Wash.)—Theater
THEATER, BLACK
See also
AMAS Repertory Theatre, Inc.
Black drama
THEATER, EXPERIMENTAL
See also
Wooster Group
THEATER, HISPANIC AMERICAN
See also
Teatro Nuestro (Theater company)
THEATER, PALESTINIAN ARAB
See also
El-Hakawati (Theater company)
THEATER, TRAVELING
See also
Kara Juro (Theater company)
American productions in Europe [cover story; special issue] il *Theatre Crafts* 23:33-81 My '89
THEATER AND POLITICS See Theater—Political aspects
THEATER AND STATE
Nicaragua
The long march of Alan Bolt. J. Peters. *The Nation* 248:855-8 Je 19 '89
THEATER BUILDINGS
See also
Dance theaters
Audience chime system [signaling start of a performance] B. Koenig. il *Theatre Crafts* 23:76-7 O '89
Blueprint for the 90s [cover story; special section; with editorial comment by John Calhoun] il *Theatre Crafts* 23:7, 24-8+ D '89
Pacific HIGHWAYS [alternative performance space for Los Angeles area dancers and artists] E. Zimmer. il *Dance Magazine* 63:52-3 S '89
Conservation and restoration
Curtains up! [restoration of Municipal Theater, São Paulo and Baralt Theater in Maracaibo] il *Américas* 41 no2:3-4 '89
Sleeping beauty [Winter Gardens in Morecambe, England] T. Aldous. il *History Today* 39:4-5 F '89
Theater preservation update: London 1989. A. Robins. il *Architectural Record* 177:79 N '89
China
Theatre architecture now and then. Li Chang and Li Dao-He. il *Theatre Crafts* 23:88+ Ap '89
THEATER BUILDINGS, PORTABLE
Traveling show [Tadao Ando's Karaza Theater building] K. D. Stein. il *Architectural Record* 177:90-3 Mr '89
THEATER CONSULTANTS
See also
Knudson-Benson Associates
The consultant's changing role: challenges in the 1990s. R. W. Wolff. *Theatre Crafts* 23:28-33 D '89
THEATER FESTIVALS See Drama festivals
THEATER INSURANCE See Insurance, Theater
THEATER PROGRAMS
See also
Stagebill

THEATER PROPERTIES
   See also
    McHugh-Rollins Associates, Inc.
Fake food. B. Burns. il *Theatre Crafts* 23:30+ Ap '89

THEATER REVIEWS
Best of '88. *Time* 133:102 Ja 2 '89
The Broadway bustle. P. Young. il *Maclean's* 102:58-9 D 11 '89
Broadway's brightest lights. D. H. Dunn. il *Business Week* p105 Je 19 '89
Cue: a complete entertainment guide for the week. See issues of New York
Goings on about town. See issues of The New Yorker
Onstage [Zagat New York theater ratings] il *New York* 22:56-8 Jl 3-10 '89
Robert Brustein on theater. R. Brustein. See occasional issues of The New Republic
Theater. See occasional issues of The Nation
Theater. J. Simon. See issues of New York
The theatre. M. Kramer. See issues of The New Yorker beginning June 8, 1987
The theatre. E. Oliver. See issues of The New Yorker beginning February 16, 1987

        Single works
   See name of author for full entry
All God's dangers. Rosengarten, Theodore
Amulets against the dragon forces. Zindel, Paul
Anthony Rose. Feiffer, Jules
Approaching Zanzibar. Howe, Tina
Aristocrats. Friel, Brian
Arms and the man. Shaw, Bernard, 1856-1950
Artist descending a staircase. Stoppard, Tom
The Aunts. Bonasorte, Gary
Beside herself. Pintauro, Joseph
Bleacher bums. Mantegna, Joe, 1948?-
Bobby Gould in hell. Mamet, David
Born yesterday. Kanin, Garson, 1912-
Brass rubbings. Pinsent, Gordon, 1930-
Brilliant traces. Johnson, Cindy Lou
Cantorial. Levin, Ira
Checkmates. Milner, Ron, 1938-
The circle. Maugham, W. Somerset (William Somerset), 1874-1965
The cocktail hour. Gurney, A. R. (Albert Ramsdell), 1930-
Coriolanus. Shakespeare, William, 1564-1616
A country doctor. Jenkin, Len
Cymbeline. Shakespeare, William, 1564-1616
Cyrano de Bergerac. Rostand, Edmond, 1868-1918
Dalton's back. Curran, Keith
Danton's death. Büchner, Georg, 1813-1837
The devil and Billy Markham. Silverstein, Shel
Dry lips oughta move to Kapuskasing. Highway, Tomson
The dybbuk. Ansky, S., 1863-1920
Early one evening at the Rainbow Bar and Grille. Graham, Bruce
Eastern standard. Greenberg, Richard
Echo. Lepage, Robert
Eleemosynary. Blessing, Lee
Enrico IV. Pirandello, Luigi, 1867-1936
Etiquette of the undercaste. Hardman, Chris
A few good men. Sorkin, Aaron
For dear life. Miller, Susan
The forbidden city. Gunn, Bill, d. 1989
The forest. Wilson, Robert, 1941-
Ghetto. Sobol, Joshua
The good coach. Siegler, Ben
Grandma Moses. Pouliot, Stephen
Gus and Al. Innaurato, Albert
The half of it. Krizanc, John
Hapgood. Stoppard, Tom
Heaven on earth. Schenkkan, Robert
The Heidi chronicles. Wasserstein, Wendy
Hizzoner! Shyre, Paul
Home games. Ziegler, Tom
Hurlyburly. Rabe, David
Hyde in Hollywood. Parnell, Peter
Iranian nights. Ali, Tariq
Julius Caesar. Shakespeare, William, 1564-1616
Kate's diary. Tolan, Kathleen
The lady in question. Busch, Charles
Largely New York. Irwin, Bill
Lend me a tenor. Ludwig, Ken
Les liaisons dangereuses. Hampton, Christopher, 1946-
The Lisbon Traviata. McNally, Terrence, 1939-
Love and anger. Walker, George F.
Love letters. Gurney, A. R. (Albert Ramsdell), 1930-
Love's labor's lost. Shakespeare, William, 1564-1616
M. Butterfly. Hwang, David Henry
The Mahabharata. Brook, Peter, 1925-
Man and superman. Shaw, Bernard, 1856-1950
A map of the world. Hare, David
Mastergate. Gelbart, Larry
Measure for measure. Shakespeare, William, 1564-1616
The member of the wedding. McCullers, Carson, 1917-1967
The merchant of Venice. Shakespeare, William, 1564-1616
Metamorphosis. Berkoff, Steven
The mob. Galsworthy, John, 1867-1933
Mountain language. Pinter, Harold, 1930-

My big land. Galich, Aleksandr, 1919-1977
Mystery of the rose bouquet. Puig, Manuel
Newhouse. Rose, Richard
The night Hank Williams died. King, Larry L.
Only kidding. Geoghan, Jim
Orpheus descending. Williams, Tennessee, 1911-1983
Other people's money. Sterner, Jerry
Our town. Wilder, Thornton, 1897-1975
The passion of Narcisse Mondoux. Gélinas, Gratien
Peer Gynt. Ibsen, Henrik, 1828-1906
Phaedra Britannica. Harrison, Tony, 1937-
Phantasie. Pearson, Sybille
The piano lesson. Wilson, August
The pixie led. Harris, Christopher
Prince. Fuller, Charles
Pygmalion. Shaw, Bernard, 1856-1950
The quintessential image. Chambers, Jane, 1937-1983
The rimers of Eldritch. Wilson, Lanford, 1937-
Rosmersholm. Ibsen, Henrik, 1828-1906
Rumors. Simon, Neil
Run for your wife! Cooney, Ray, 1932-
Sally. Fuller, Charles
Salome. Wilde, Oscar, 1854-1900
The screens. Genet, Jean, 1910-1986
The search for signs of intelligent life in the universe. Wagner, Jane
The secret rapture. Hare, David
The shaughraun. Boucicault, Dion, 1820-1890
Shirley Valentine. Russell, Willy
Single spies. Bennett, Alan, 1934-
The story of Kufur Shamma. Lubeck, Jackie
The tempest. Shakespeare, William, 1564-1616
Temptation. Havel, Václav
Titus Andronicus. Shakespeare, William, 1564-1616
Troilus and Cressida. Shakespeare, William, 1564-1616
Twelfth night. Shakespeare, William, 1564-1616
Ubu. Sloan, Larry
Ulysses in Nighttown. Barkentin, Marjorie
Up 'n' under. Godber, John
The vigil. Jenkins, Charles J.
A walk in the woods. Blessing, Lee
What the butler saw. Orton, Joe
Who's afraid of Virginia Woolf? Albee, Edward, 1928-
The widow's blind date. Horovitz, Israel
The winter's tale. Shakespeare, William, 1564-1616
Without apologies. Thomas, Thom
Yankee dawg you die. Gotanda, Philip Kan
Yesteryear. Glass, Joanna M.

THEATER SEATS
Telescopic seating platforms. R. Long. il *Theatre Crafts* 23:22+ Ap '89

THEATER TICKETS
Twofer the seesaw [discount tickets in New York City] V. Taylor and A. Berlin. il *New York* 22:130+ My 1 '89

THEATERS *See* Theater buildings

THÉÂTRE 1774 (THEATER COMPANY)
The banality of evil [production of Echo] J. Bemrose. il *Maclean's* 102:95+ N 20 '89

THEATRE PASSE MURAILLE (THEATER COMPANY)
Hitting a high note. J. Bemrose. il *Maclean's* 102:62 O 16 '89

THEATRE X (GROUP)
Creative communication. K. Simmons. il *Horizon (Tuscaloosa, Ala.)* 32:19 Mr/Ap '89

THEATRICAL ADAPTATIONS
Dickens on stage and screen [cover story] R. Samuel. il por *History Today* 39:44-51 D '89
Quick take: whose is that masked musical? [versions of Phantom of the Opera] M. McCloud. il *Theatre Crafts* 23:23 D '89

THEATRICAL AGENCIES AND AGENTS
   See also
    Bauer Benedek Agency
    Black theatrical agencies and agents
    Creative Artists Agency
    Management Company Entertainment Group Inc.
    N.S. Bienstock Inc.
    William Morris Agency
Sukhreet's agent man [J. Norman] T. O'Neill. il por *New York* 22:34 Ag 21 '89
        Ethical aspects
Tour shakedowns alleged [N. Walters accused by M. Franzese] J. Capeci. il por *Rolling Stone* p20 My 4 '89
        Suits and claims
A $90 million matter of distrust pits Billy Joel against his ex-manager [dispute with F. Weber] S. Dougherty. il pors *People Weekly* 32:50-1 O 9 '89

THEATRICAL COSTUME *See* Costume, Theatrical
THEATRICAL DESIGNERS *See* Set designers
THEATRICAL DIRECTORS
   See also
    Hirsch, John
    Kellman, Barnet
    Rose, Richard
    Sellars, Peter

THEATRICAL PRODUCTION AND DIRECTION *See* Theater—Production and direction

THEBES (EGYPT: ANCIENT CITY)
   See also
   Temple of Luxor
THEE, T. WILLIAM, AND PETERSON, WAYNE J.
   Keeping U.S. business competitive: employers' rights vs.
   the unions'. il *USA Today (Periodical)* 118:38-40 Jl '89
THEFT *See* Shoplifting; Stealing
THEISM
   Humanists and theists. T. A. Webb. por *The Humanist*
   49:18-20+ Jl/Ag '89
THEISSEN, GERD
       about
   Social teaching and social history: learning from the early
   church. M. M. Mitchell. *The Christian Century* 106:724-5
   Ag 2-9 '89
THELEN, JODI
       about
   If you see Jodi, give her five. J. Marion. il por *TV Guide*
   37:23 Ap 15-21 '89
THELONIOUS MONK INSTITUTE OF JAZZ
   Thelonious Monk Institute of Jazz concert: Page Auditorium/
   Durham, NC. O. Cordle. il *Down Beat* 56:46 Ap '89
THELONIOUS MONK: STRAIGHT, NO CHASER [film]
   See Motion picture reviews—Single works
THEME CRUISES *See* Cruising
THEME PARKS *See* Amusement parks
THEOBALD, ROBERT
   (jt. auth) See Page, Benjamin I., and Theobald, Robert
THEOCRACY
   See also
   Christian Reconstruction movement
THEODORACOPULOS, TAKI *See* Taki
THEODORE ROOSEVELT NATIONAL PARK (N.D.)
   Theodore Roosevelt National Park [excerpt] H. Schoch. il
   National Parks 63:46-7 My/Je '89
THEOLOGIANS
   See also
   Arminius, Jacobus, 1560-1609
   Brunner, Emil, 1889-1966
   Curran, Charles E.
   Fox, Matthew, 1940-
   Frei, Hans W. (Hans Wilhelm), 1922-1988
   Gilkey, Langdon Brown, 1919-
   Hamilton, William, 1924-
   Kierkegaard, Søren, 1813-1855
   Origen
   Outler, Albert Cook
   Panikkar, Raimundo, 1918-
   Placher, William C. (William Carl), 1948-
   Rauschenbusch, Walter, 1861-1918
   Sandeman, Robert
   Like the Niebuhrs and Tillich. M. E. Marty. *The Christian
   Century* 106:1071 N 15 '89
       Conferences
   See Religious conferences
THEOLOGICAL CONFERENCES *See* Religious conferences
THEOLOGICAL EDUCATION *See* Theology—Study and
   teaching
THEOLOGICAL SEMINARIES
   See also
   Seminarians
   Southeastern Baptist Theological Seminary
   William Tyndale College
   Revisioning seminary as ministry-centered [with discussion;
   cover story] G. Hope. il *The Christian Century* 106:107-11+
   F 1-8 '89
   Seminary and church: missing ministry [discussion of February
   1-8, 1989 article, Revisioning seminary as ministry-centered]
   G. Hope. *The Christian Century* 106:450-1 Ap 26 '89
       Accreditation
   SBC seminary accused [alleged infringements of academic
   freedom at Southeastern Baptist Theological Seminary]
   The Christian Century 106:41 Ja 18 '89
   Seminary given until December to correct hiring policy
   [Southeastern Baptist Theological Seminary] M. Wingfield.
   Christianity Today 33:54-5 F 3 '89
       Curriculum
   Beyond the maintenance mentality. D. A. McGavran. il
   Christianity Today 33:28-9 F 3 '89
   "Signs and wonders" back in school? M. L. Chandler.
   Christianity Today 33:56 Ja 13 '89
THEOLOGICAL STUDENTS *See* Seminarians
THEOLOGY
   See also
   Catholic Church. Congregation for the Doctrine of the
   Faith
   Christian ethics
   Christianity
   Church
   Death of God theology
   Eschatology
   Faith
   Fall of man
   Freedom (Theology)
   God
   Good and evil
   Grace (Theology)
   Heaven

   Heresy
   Human body (Theology)
   Incarnation
   Jesus Christ
   Justification
   Kingdom of God
   Law (Theology)
   Liberation theology
   Love (Theology)
   Mujerista theology
   Mysticism
   Prayer
   Religion
   Resurrection
   Salvation
   Secularism
   Sermons
   Tradition (Theology)
   Truth
   Weakness (Theology)
   Word of God (Theology)
   America's Lutherans: what they believe. S. H. Nafzger. il
   Christianity Today 33:22-5 N 3 '89
   Capitalism and technology in global perspective: a dispute
   [discussion of May 3, 1989 article, The theological challenge
   of globalization] M. L. Stackhouse. *The Christian Century*
   106:690-3 Jl 19-26 '89
   The Cologne Declaration [text of statement signed by German-
   speaking theologians; cover story] *Commonweal* 116:102-4
   F 24 '89
   Digging in the gardens of feminist theology [Inheriting our
   mothers' gardens: feminist theology in third world perspec-
   tive] G. E. Ziegenhals. *The Christian Century* 106:260-3
   Mr 8 '89
   Inflating the oath [document issued by the Congregation
   for the Doctrine of the Faith] J. A. Coriden. il *Commonweal*
   116:455-6 S 8 '89
   Of many things [John Mahoney's The making of moral
   theology] G. W. Hunt. *America* 160:50 Ja 28 '89
   Oh God, poor God: the state of contemporary theology.
   W. J. Abraham. *The American Scholar* 58:557-63 Aut
   '89
   The power of myth: lessons from Joseph Campbell. B. C.
   Lane. il *The Christian Century* 106:652-4 Jl 5-12 '89
   Profession of faith and the 'oath of fidelity' [Catholic Church]
   L. M. Orsy. *America* 160:345-7+ Ap 15 '89
   The spirit in sound doctrine. L. O. Sanneh. *The Christian
   Century* 106:930 O 18 '89
   The theological challenge of globalization [cover story] M.
   L. Stackhouse. il *The Christian Century* 106:468-71 My
   3 '89
   An unapologetic middle ground [W. C. Placher's Unapologetic
   theology] P. Nelson. *The Christian Century* 106:882-4 O
   4 '89
       Anecdotes, facetiae, satire, etc.
   Forged teaching [revised Catholic loyalty oath] M. E. Marty.
   The Christian Century 106:455 Ap 26 '89
       Bibliography
   The God that matters. L. Cunningham. il *Commonweal*
   116:56-8 Ja 27 '89
   Theology, history, & transitions. L. Cunningham.
   Commonweal 116:539-41 O 6 '89
       Study and teaching
   See also
   Theological seminaries
   Women's Theological Center (Boston, Mass.)
   Academic freedom and the Catholic University of America
   [implications of Curran case] F. R. McManus. *America*
   160:506-9 My 27 '89
   Catholic oaths and academic freedom. M. B. Lukens. *The
   Christian Century* 106:982-4 N 1 '89
   The Curran decision [court upholds ban on his teaching
   theology at Catholic University of America] *America*
   160:259 Mr 25 '89
   Curran loses—so does Catholic education [suit against Catholic
   University of America] S. Maloney. *The Christian Century*
   106:278-9 Mr 15 '89
   Educating the congregation. S. E. Schreiner. il *The Christian
   Century* 106:985-7 N 1 '89
   In rejoinder: what next at Catholic U? [special section] il
   Commonweal 116:270-5+ My 5 '89
   New loyalty oath [Catholic Church] *The Christian Century*
   106:377 Ap 12 '89
   The Pope wins in court [removal of C. Curran from theology
   faculty at Catholic University upheld] R. N. Ostling. por
   Time 133:70 Mr 13 '89
   Teaching theology in the church [cover story] A. B. Robinson.
   The Christian Century 106:980-2 N 1 '89
   A university perspective on the 'oath of fidelity'. Q. L.
   Quade. *America* 160:348-9 Ap 15 '89
   Verdicts yet to come [C. Curran vs. Catholic University;
   with excerpts from court decision] *Commonweal* 116:163-5+
   Mr 24 '89
   Why should anyone believe? Apologetics and theological
   education [M. Stackhouse's Apologia] D. M. Campbell.
   The Christian Century 106:136-8 F 1-8 '89
THEOLOGY AND THE ENVIRONMENT *See* Religion and
   the environment

THEONOMY
See also
Christian Reconstruction movement
THEOSOPHY
Great Britain
The odyssey of Annie Besant [Victorian radical and atheist turned Theosophist] J. Oppenheim. bibl il pors *History Today* 39:12-18 S '89
THERA (GREECE: ISLAND)
The Thera theory [evidence against S. Marinatos' hypothesis that the disappearance of the Minoans was linked to volanic eruption on Thera] A. Chen. il maps *Discover* 10:76-80+ F '89
THERAPEUTIC TECHNOLOGIES INC.
Martin Ergas: helping paraplegics keep fit. I. Recio. il por *Business Week* p68 S 18 '89
THERAPEUTIC TOUCH See Mental healing
THERAPEUTICS
See also
Acupuncture
Aroma therapy
Arts therapy
Bodywork (Biomechanics)
Electrotherapy
Gene therapy
Intravenous therapy
Mesmerism
Phototherapy
Proton therapy
Psychotherapy
See also subheads Therapeutic use; Therapy under various subjects
8 medical miracles from nature. S. Lally. il *Prevention (Emmaus, Pa.)* 41:33-41 N '89
Big help for little ailments. D. Pine. il *Ladies' Home Journal* 106:112+ Ap '89
Lifestyle changes control disease [views of James R. Gavin and Leann Olansky] *USA Today (Periodical)* 117:12-13 F '89
Terminology
The dictionary of healing techniques and remedies. See issues of Prevention (Emmaus, Pa.) beginning June 1988
THÉRÈSE, DE LISIEUX, SAINT, 1873-1897
about
An extraordinary woman in an ordinary world. L. Cunningham. il *U.S. Catholic* 54:7-8 F '89
Letters from St. Thérèse. J. W. Donohue. il *America* 161:322-4 N 11 '89
THERMAL PRINTERS
Color by numbers [Tektronix Phaser CP] K. Quirk. il *Byte* 14:177-9 Jl '89
A featherweight printer [Diconix 150 Plus] C. Hlavaty. il *Personal Computing* 13:168 Ag '89
High-resolution ink-jet printing for the Mac [Hewlett-Packard DeskWriter] D. Hallerman. il *Home Office Computing* 7:80-1 D '89
Near-laser quality for less [Hewlett-Packard DeskJet Plus thermal ink jet printer] S. Chen. il *Home Office Computing* 7:61 Ag '89
No more excuse for keeping that typewriter [Smart Label Printer] M. Young. il *Personal Computing* 13:204 D '89
A portable 24-pin printer [Toshiba ExpressWriter 311] R. Gehorsam. il *Home Office Computing* 7:66+ Je '89
Quality printing for the road [Toshiba ExpressWriter 301] C. Lee. il *Personal Computing* 13:197 S '89
Speed separates two portable printers [Toshiba ExpressWriter 301 and Kodak Diconix 150 Plus] W. Rash, Jr. il *Byte* 14:191-2 O '89
Toshiba puts a handle on 24-pin printing [ExpressWriter 311] R. Bel Bruno. il *Personal Computing* 13:196 Ap '89
Two for the road [Kodak Diconix 150 Plus and Toshiba ExpressWriter 301 portable printers] S. Chen and M. Alvich. il *Home Office Computing* 7:66+ O '89
THERMAL RADIATION See Heat—Radiation and absorption
THERMAL SPRINGS See Hot springs
THERMEDICS INC.
Thermedics begins production of portable bomb detection unit [EGIS system] D. Hughes. *Aviation Week & Space Technology* 130:164-6 Je 19 '89
THERMO ELECTRON CORP.
Inventor, teacher, economist—and that's just for starters [G. Hatsopoulos] K. H. Hammonds. il por *Business Week* p81+ D 18 '89
THERMODYNAMICS
See also
Entropy
Statistical mechanics
Temperature fluctuation: a well-defined and unavoidable notion. B. B. Mandelbrot. il *Physics Today* 42:71+ Ja '89
THERMOELECTRIC EQUIPMENT
See also
Thermo Electron Corp.
THERMOGENESIS (BOTANY) See Plants—Temperature
THERMOMETERS, COOKING
From our kitchen to yours [use of a meat thermometer] K. Adams. *Southern Living* 24:113 Ag '89

THERMOMETERS AND THERMOMETRY
See also
Calorimeters and calorimetry
Collectors and collecting
Collecting advertising thermometers. D. Stewart. il *Antiques & Collecting Hobbies* 94:36-8+ My '89
THERMONUCLEAR REACTIONS See Nuclear fusion
THERMOPLASTICS
New tape laying machine eases preparation of thermoplastic material. il *Aviation Week & Space Technology* 131:83 S 18 '89
Plastics that leave no space unfilled [work of General Electric] *Science News* 136:222 S 30 '89
Pourable plastics. E. Corcoran. il *Scientific American* 261:102+ D '89
Strong polymer composites. M. Mandell. *High Technology Business* 9:10-11 Ap '89
The world's strongest plastics [thermotropic liquid crystalline polymers] R. P. Heggs. il *High Technology Business* 9:20-3 Je '89
THERMOREGULATORY BEHAVIOR See Temperature, Animal and human
THERMOS CONTAINERS
Coffee to go or to stay. il *Consumer Reports* 54:519-22 Ag '89
Coolers & jugs. il *Consumer Reports* 54:319-22 D '89
How to keep a picnic on ice. il *Consumer Reports* 54:402-7 Je '89
Vacuum bottles & carafes. il *Consumer Reports* 54:324-8 D '89
THERMOSTATS
Heating system thermostat. T. Klenck. il *Popular Mechanics* 166:71-2 F '89
Programmable thermostats. K. Childers. il *The Family Handyman* 39:66-8 Ja '89
Upgrading a home thermostat. D. Vandervort. il *Home Mechanix* 85:34+ S '89
THERNSTROM, ABIGAIL M., 1936-
Permaffirm action. *The New Republic* 201:17-19 Jl 31 '89
THERNSTROM, STEPHAN
Just say Afro. *The New Republic* 200:10+ Ja 23 '89
THERO, CYNTHIA
about
You and your parish deserve more from each other [interview] por *U.S. Catholic* 54:20-7 Ag '89
THEROUX, PAUL
Imagining Hill House. il por *Architectural Digest* 46:32+ D '89
Malawi: faces of a quiet land. il map *National Geographic* 176:370-89 S '89
Sockless in Singapore [fiction] il *Gentlemen's Quarterly* 59:406 Mr '89
Travel writing: why I bother. il *The New York Times Book Review* 94:7-8 Jl 30 '89
about
He's traveled the world—in fact and fiction. C. Brown. por *Vogue* 179:88+ Jl '89
THEROUX, PHYLLIS
First-person parent. See issues of Parents beginning December 1984 through November 1989
My daughter, myself. *Harper's Bazaar* 122:164+ O '89
THEY MIGHT BE GIANTS (MUSICAL GROUP)
Giant steps. P. Tyre. il pors *New York* 22:52-5 F 6 '89
They Might Be Giants. C. Connors. il *Seventeen* 48:111+ Ap '89
They Might Be Giants. D. Goldman. il *Scholastic Update (Teachers' edition)* 121:20 Ap 21 '89
They Might Be Giants. I. Robbins. il *Rolling Stone* p26 Ja 12 '89
They Might Be Giants [release of Lincoln] S. Simels. il *Stereo Review* 54:110 Mr '89
THIBAUD, CÉCILE
When American vets meet Soviet vets. *World Press Review* 36:70 S '89
THIÉBAUX, MARCELLE
PW interviews [P. Auster] por *Publishers Weekly* 235:80-1 Mr 3 '89
THIEMANN, RONALD F.
Jews and Christians: striving to shape America's future. il *USA Today (Periodical)* 118:84-7 S '89
THIESSEN, TIFFANI-AMBER
about
'Teen discovery takes prime-time plunge! por *'Teen* 33:52 Je '89
THIEVES (MUSICAL GROUP)
The Thieves: classic rock-and-roll. S. Simels. il *Stereo Review* 54:94+ Je '89
THIGH EXERCISES See Exercise
THIGPEN, ED
about
Ed Thigpen. J. Ephland. il por *Down Beat* 56:14 Je '89
Ed Thigpen and Friends: Village Vanguard/New York. S. Stein. il por *Down Beat* 56:53-4 Jl '89
THE THIN BLUE LINE [film] See Motion picture reviews—Single works
THIN FILMS
See also
Diamond thin films

THIN FILMS—See also—*cont.*
  Moth-eye technology
1-2-3 contact: a new superconducting film [research by Jagdish Narayan] I. Amato. *Science News* 135:294 My 13 '89
Fashioning see-through metal [work of Charles R. Martin and Michael J. Tierney] *Science News* 136:31 Jl 8 '89
Orthogonal self-assembled monolayers: alkanethiols on gold and alkane carboxylic acids on alumina. P. E. Laibinis and others. bibl f il *Science* 245:845-7 Ag 25 '89
Putting the squeeze on liquid films [research by Steve Granick and John Van Alsten] I. Peterson. *Science News* 135:207 Ap 1 '89
Shear forces in molecularly thin films. M. Schoen and others. bibl f il *Science* 245:1223-5 S 15 '89
THINGS CHANGE [film] See Motion picture reviews—Single works
THINKING See Thought and thinking
THINKING MACHINES CORPORATION
These gee-whiz machines are finding an audience. L. Jereski. il *Business Week* p154+ My 22 '89
THINNESS See Weight (Physiology)
THINNING OF FRUIT See Fruit—Thinning
THIOBACILLUS
The little bugs that dig for gold [use of Thiobacillus in bioleaching] W. J. Cook. il *U.S. News & World Report* 106:62 Ap 17 '89
THIOLS See Mercapto compounds
THIRD DEGREE BURN [television program] See Television program reviews—Single works
THIRD PARTY MOVEMENT See Political parties
THIRD REICH See National socialism
THIRD WORLD See Developing countries
THIRD WORLD ACADEMY OF SCIENCES
An Academy of Sciences for the third world. A. M. Faruqui. il *The Unesco Courier* 42:50 N '89
THIRST [dance] See Dance reviews—Single works
THIRTYSOMETHING [television program] See Television program reviews—Single works
THOM, ROSE ANNE
Pushing the frontier further: WomanWorks. il *Dance Magazine* 63:60-3 My '89
THOMAS, AQUINAS, SAINT, 1225?-1274
  about
Fortysomething: Saint Thomas in winter. J. D. Smith. *U.S. Catholic* 54:35 O '89
THOMAS, ALAN
Drawing the line at safety. il por map *History Today* 39:5-7 F '89
THOMAS, CARLA
  about
Carla Thomas. P. Puterbaugh. il por *Rolling Stone* p55 Ag 10 '89
THOMAS, CATHY, AND YOUNG, SUE
Low-cal cooking: treats that trim. il *Teen* 33:30+ Ap '89
THOMAS, CLARENCE
  about
Off the record. Cato. *National Review* 41:56 D 8 '89
THOMAS, DAVID
  about
Putting pep into Punch. S. Seibert. il por *Newsweek* 113:39 Mr 6 '89
THOMAS, DIAN
Dessert in the rough. il *American Health* 8:106+ Jl/Ag '89
THOMAS, DICK
Training our environmental conservation officers. il *The Conservationist* 43:44-9 Ja/F '89
THOMAS, EDWARD
  about
Desire under the elms [opera] Reviews
  The New Yorker 64:101-2 F 6 '89. A. Porter
  Opera News il 53:45-6 My '89. B. L. Sherer
THOMAS, GEORGE J.
  about
Outrageous fortune? Two guys from D&B cash in. J. Rothfeder. il pors *Business Week* p190 N 27 '89
THOMAS, GORDON
Healing the wounds of torture. *World Press Review* 36:59 My '89
THOMAS, ISIAH
  about
Isiah Thomas' mom subject of TV film, 'A mother's courage' [cover story] L. Ransom. il pors *Jet* 77:36-8 D 11 '89
THOMAS, LEE
A talk with my dad. por *Essence* 20:9 Je '89
THOMAS, LEE M.
Should the Congress adopt the "Clean Air Act amendments of 1987"? [excerpts from statement, September 23, 1987] *Congressional Digest* 68:43+ F '89
THOMAS, M. DONALD
The counselor in effective schools. *The Education Digest* 55:18-20 D '89
THOMAS, MARY
  about
Isiah Thomas' mom subject of TV film, 'A mother's courage' [cover story] L. Ransom. il pors *Jet* 77:36-8 D 11 '89
THOMAS, MICHAEL
All in the name. il *Vogue* 179:278 My '89

Four-wheel-drive vehicles aren't just for outdoorsmen anymore. il *Vogue* 179:248 Ag '89
THOMAS, MINNIE
  about
A hand and a home for pregnant addicts. D. Wyss. il pors *Time* 133:10+ F 27 '89
THOMAS, PHILIP MICHAEL
  about
Is he in career arrest—or is there life after Miami Vice? M. Laughlin. il pors *TV Guide* 37:18-21 O 21-27 '89
Phylicia and Philip are lovers and lawyers in thriller, 'False witness'. A. Collier. il pors *Jet* 77:60-2 O 30 '89
THOMAS, R. DAVID
  about
Wendy's burger king. J. Nocera. il por *Esquire* 112:69-71 N '89
THOMAS, THOM
  about
Without apologies [drama] Reviews
  New York il 22:140-1 F 27 '89. J. Simon
THOMAS, TORI WINKLER
  about
Tori Thomas: agricultural abstractions in a Virginia landscape. il por *Architectural Digest* 46:100-1 Ap '89
THOMAS, VIVIEN T., 1910-1985
  about
A partnership of the heart. K. McCabe. il por *Reader's Digest* 135:91-6 O '89
THOMAS, WALTER
Goddess of love. il pors *Harper's Bazaar* 122:156-7 N '89
THOMAS (BARBARA) ENTERPRISES INC. See Barbara Thomas Enterprises Inc.
THOMAS-COTE, NANCY
Make room for the children. por *Nation's Business* 77:13 O '89
THOMAS GILCREASE INSTITUTE OF AMERICAN HISTORY AND ART
The art of the Old West. C. Maddox. il *Southern Living* 24:20+ Je '89
THOMETZ, KURT
  about
The library doctor. L. Kaylin. il por *Gentlemen's Quarterly* 59:89+ D '89
THOMPSON, ANN M.
Dancing to a different drummer. il por *Women's Sports & Fitness* 11:16 O '89
Your auto: tuning it up for winter. il *New Choices for the Best Years* 29:93-5 O '89
THOMPSON, ANNE
The 14th annual grosses gloss. il *Film Comment* 25:70-4 Mr/Ap '89
Oscar wanna-bees. il *Film Comment* 25:56+ Ja/F '89
Quest for fur. il por *Film Comment* 25:2+ S/O '89
Will success spoil the Weinstein brothers? il pors *Film Comment* 25:72+ Jl/Ag '89
THOMPSON, B. M.
Good riddance [address, May 24, 1989] *Vital Speeches of the Day* 55:683-7 S 1 '89
THOMPSON, BARBARA
Summer rental [story] il *McCall's* 116:127-8+ Ag '89
THOMPSON, BRADBURY, 1911-
  about
Around the Mall and beyond. E. Park. il *Smithsonian* 20:22-4+ S '89
THOMPSON, CHUCK
Old postcards featuring famous people: Hoot Gibson. por *Antiques & Collecting Hobbies* 94:68 Mr '89
THOMPSON, CYNTHIA
Compensation for death and dismemberment. bibl f il *Monthly Labor Review* 112:13-17 S '89
THOMPSON, D. DODGE
Frans Hals and American art. bibl f il *Antiques* 136:1170-83 N '89
John La Farge's masterpieces in stained glass. bibl f il *Antiques* 135:708-17 Mr '89
THOMPSON, DAVID
Albert Mansbridge and a fresh coat of paint. il pors *History Today* 39:7-9 Ag '89
THOMPSON, EDWARD ANTHONY See Lejeune, Anthony, 1928-
THOMPSON, INGA
  about
Uphill racer. T. Blumenthal. il pors *Women's Sports & Fitness* 11:24-7 S '89
THOMPSON, J. LEE
  about
Kinjite [film] Reviews
  People Weekly 31:15-16 F 6 '89. P. Travers
THOMPSON, JAMES R., 1936-
Preventing pregnancies among adolescents. *Society* 26:64-6 Mr/Ap '89
  about
Blowing in the wind. J. R. Coyne, Jr. por *National Review* 41:19-21 N 24 '89
THOMPSON, JARRETT
  about
A dog in the hand. R. Bass. il pors *Esquire* 112:150-4+ O '89

THOMPSON, JOHN

about

Baptists back Thompson in Proposition 42 fight. il por *Jet* 75:50 F 27 '89

Out of bounds. *The New Republic* 200:10-11 F 20 '89

Race becomes the game. J. Kroll. il por *Newsweek* 113:56-9 Ja 30 '89

Thompson's walkout spurs review of Proposition 42. il *Jet* 75:50 F 13 '89

THOMPSON, JUANITA TORRENCE- *See* Torrence-Thompson, Juanita

THOMPSON, KEITH

Connecting with the wild man inside all males [interview with R. Bly] *Utne Reader* p58 N/D '89

Taking another look at myth. il *Utne Reader* p102-5+ N/D '89

THOMPSON, LES

Put faith back into management. por *Christianity Today* 33:10 My 12 '89

THOMPSON, LONNIE G., AND OTHERS

Holocene-late Pleistocene climatic ice core records from Qinghai-Tibetan Plateau. bibl f il maps *Science* 246:474-7 O 27 '89

THOMPSON, MARGARET SUSAN, 1949-

The "new nuns" of yesteryear. il *USA Today (Periodical)* 117:84-7 Mr '89

THOMPSON, MARK

Misprint. *The New Republic* 200:14-15 Ap 3 '89

THOMPSON, MIMI

about

Different strokes: a touch of splash. S. Nelson. il pors *Harper's Bazaar* 122:124-7+ F '89

THOMPSON, PHYLLIS H.

What makes a poet? What makes a poem? *The Writer* 102:22-4 N '89

THOMPSON, RICHARD

about

Richard Thompson's "Amnesia". R. Givens. por *Stereo Review* 54:102+ Ja '89

THOMPSON, RUSSELL EDWIN

about

Worldwide trends make him bullish [interview] P. Sellers. il por *Fortune* 120:31+ S 25 '89

THOMPSON, SYLVIA VAUGHN

Self-sowers. il *Organic Gardening* 36:53-5 D '89

THOMPSON, TERRI

Be injury-free: eliminate the terrible ten. il *Women's Sports & Fitness* 11:24-5 My '89

(jt. auth) See Clark, Kristine L., 1953-, and Thompson, Terri

THOMPSON, W. SCOTT (WILLARD SCOTT), 1942-

Cory's coup. il *National Review* 41:18-19 D 31 '89

THOMPSON, WILLARD SCOTT *See* Thompson, W. Scott (Willard Scott), 1942-

THOMPSON, WILLIAM IRWIN

Mythics: don't take them too literally [excerpt from Imaginary landscape] *Utne Reader* p103 N/D '89

THOMPSON (J. WALTER) COMPANY *See* J. Walter Thompson Company

THOMPSON FAMILY

about

The Texas chain store massacre. J. H. Taylor. il *Forbes* 143:54+ F 6 '89

THOMSON, CLARE

Lifting the veil on Estonia's past. il *History Today* 39:9-11 S '89

THOMSON, DAVID

Blood bond: where Oklahoma and Guatemala meet. *America* 161:277-8 O 28 '89

THOMSON, DAVID, 1941-

Hockney's Hollywood. il pors *Film Comment* 25:53-63+ Jl/Ag '89

Leonesque. il por *American Film* 14:26-31+ S '89

Supporting players. il *Film Comment* 25:32-4 N/D '89

THOMSON, GARY

In search of Denmark's bog people. il map *Bicycling* 30:68-72+ Ag '89

THOMSON, JOE

about

The lawyer and the punk. T. Philbin. *Reader's Digest* 135:7-8+ Ag '89

THOMSON, JOHN R.

Holiday in Cambodia. il *National Review* 41:26-7 O 13 '89

THOMSON, KENNETH

about

Unveiling a treasure. B. Came. il por *Maclean's* 102:38 O 9 '89

THOMSON, SCOTT D.

Teaching experience: a must for principals. *The Education Digest* 54:11-15 Ap '89

Troubled kingdoms, restless natives. bibl f il *Phi Delta Kappan* 70:371-5 Ja '89

THOMSON, VIRGIL, 1896-1989

Words and music. il *The New York Review of Books* 36:43 Ap 13 '89

about

Obituary

Opera News il pors 54:54-5+ D 9 '89. P. J. Smith

THOMSON-C S F

British Aerospace, Thomson-CSF consider making joint bid for Ferranti International Signal. *Aviation Week & Space Technology* 131:32 O 16 '89

THOMSON GALLERY (TORONTO, ONT.)

Unveiling a treasure. B. Came. il por *Maclean's* 102:38 O 9 '89

THOMSON MCKINNON INC.

The captains who didn't go down with the ship [Prudential-Bache takes over Thomson McKinnon] G. Morgenson. il *Forbes* 144:39-41 Ag 21 '89

THOMSON NEWSPAPERS LTD.

Buying the Times [Globe and mail takes over Financial times of Canada] D. Todd. il *Maclean's* 102:47-8 D 25 '89

THOMSON SA

Alain Gomez, France's high-tech warrior. T. Peterson. il por *Business Week* p100-2+ My 15 '89

THORDARSON, TOM J.

about

Pollution parable. B. Weber. il *The New York Times Magazine* p86 F 26 '89

THOREAU, HENRY DAVID, 1817-1862

about

Another week on the Concord and Merrimack. R. Crum. *Wilderness* 53:11-12+ Fall '89

A motorcycle at Walden. H. Arnett. il *Cycle* 40:16 O '89

THORN E M I PLC

Don't worry, he's happy [C. Southgate] L. Gubernick. il por *Forbes* 143:154 Ap 17 '89

Last laugh [SBK sells former CBS music publishing division to Thorn EMI] L. Gubernick. il por *Forbes* 143:41-2 F 20 '89

They're playing whose song? D. Lieberman. il *Business Week* p42 Ja 23 '89

THORNBURG, DAVID D.

Impact. See issues of Compute! beginning May 1988

THORNBURGH, DICK

about

Dick Thornburgh: not being Ed Meese isn't enough anymore. P. Dwyer. il por *Business Week* p37 Ag 7 '89

Shaking up Justice [cover story] M. Wines. il pors *The New York Times Magazine* p22-3+ My 21 '89

Thornburgh inherits the whirlwind. S. J. Hedges. por *U.S. News & World Report* 107:16 Ag 7 '89

THORNCROFT, ANTONY

Opera for the 'masses'. *World Press Review* 36:61 Ap '89

THORNE, JOHN

Vulgar recipes [excerpt from Simple cooking] *Harper's* 279:32+ N '89

THORNOCK, KATHY

Last word. il *Omni (New York, N.Y.)* 11:124 Mr '89

THORNTON, THOMAS PERRY

The new phase in U.S.-Pakistani relations. *Foreign Affairs* 68:142-59 Summ '89

THOROUGHBRED HORSE AUCTIONS *See* Horse auctions

THOROUGHBRED HORSES *See* Race horses

THORP, EDWARD O.

about

You just can't keep Ed Thorp down. E. Schine. il por *Business Week* p83 Ag 21 '89

THORP (EDWARD O.) & ASSOCIATES *See* Edward O. Thorp & Associates

THORPE, ANDREW M.

Enigmatic Triton and Nereid. il *Sky and Telescope* 77:484-5 My '89

THORPE, PATRICIA

In praise of yellow. il *House & Garden* 161:40+ Ag '89

THOS. J. WHITE DEVELOPMENT CORPORATION

Mets magic (or Anatomy of a deal) [Mets spring training facility centerpiece of St. Lucie West development project in Florida] H. J. Steinbreder. il *Sports Illustrated* 70:62-3 Mr 27 '89

THOUGHT, VISUAL *See* Visualization

THOUGHT AND THINKING

See also

Artificial intelligence

Attention

Catastrophic thinking

Chinese Room Thought Experiment

Cognition

Cognitive therapy

Creativity

Intuition

Memory

Mind

Mindfulness

Problem solving

Give it your best IQ [rational thinking] M. Golin. *Prevention (Emmaus, Pa.)* 41:104-6 Ap '89

Just think . . . [national commitment to thinking and wisdom] S. K. Sheinbaum. *New Perspectives Quarterly* 6:64 Spr '89

Thoughts we hate to think [study by D. M. Wegner] E. E. Goode. il *U.S. News & World Report* 107:48-9 Ag 14 '89

THOUGHT AND THINKING—*cont.*

Try not to think of a white bear [obsessive thoughts; excerpt from White bears and other unwanted thought] D. M. Wegner. il *Psychology Today* 23:64-6 Je '89

"Woulda/coulda/shoulda": how to avoid no-win thinking [excerpt] A. M. Freeman. il *Ladies' Home Journal* 106:124+ O '89

Study and teaching

The case for creativity: encouraging our kids to think. A. Atkins. il *Better Homes and Gardens* 67:40+ Ap '89

Developing thinking skills through questioning. D. B. Strother. bibl f *Phi Delta Kappan* 71:324-7 D '89

Getting creative: birth of a notion. N. McAleer. il *Omni (New York, N.Y.)* 11:112-19 Ap '89

In defense of "vague" assignments [stimulating creative thinking in high school students] D. Wolfe. *The Education Digest* 55:40-2 O '89

Knowing is not thinking. E. Janko. il *Phi Delta Kappan* 70:543-4 Mr '89

Reflections on measuring thinking, while listening to Mozart's Jupiter symphony. S. Wassermann. bibl f il *Phi Delta Kappan* 70:365-70 Ja '89

What are "thinking skills"? F. Roberts. *Parents* 64:57 O '89

THREADGILL, HENRY

about

Henry Threadgill: composer, bandleader, and alchemist. K. Lynch. il pors *Down Beat* 56:20-2 F '89

THREADS, SCREW See Screw threads

THREAT SIMULATORS

Grumman lab will support variety of systems efforts. S. W. Kandebo. il *Aviation Week & Space Technology* 130:59+ My 1 '89

Grumman using visual simulations to improve electronic warfare capabilities of U.S. Navy. il *Aviation Week & Space Technology* 131:123-4 S 11 '89

On-board EW simulator production decision due. *Aviation Week & Space Technology* 131:61 S 11 '89

USAF will automate analysis system used to characterize Soviet weapons [Red Mission Analysis] *Aviation Week & Space Technology* 131:112-13 S 11 '89

THREE DIMENSIONAL CAMERAS See 3-D cameras

THREE DIMENSIONAL COMPUTER GRAPHICS See Computer graphics

THREE DIMENSIONAL OPTICAL STORAGE DEVICES See 3-D optical storage devices

THREE DIMENSIONAL TELEVISION See 3-D television

THREE FUGITIVES [film] See Motion picture reviews—Single works

THREE MEN AND A BABY [film] See Motion picture reviews—Single works

THREE MILE ISLAND NUCLEAR POWER PLANT (PA.)

Accident, 1979

Cleansing the atom. J. Levine. il *Life* 12:18-22+ Mr '89

Lust for power. *The Nation* 248:471-2 Ap 10 '89

Ten years after: cleaning up Three Mile Island. A. M. Cunningham. il *Technology Review* 92:18+ Ap '89

Ten years later, nuclear ghosts still haunt Three Mile Island. S. K. Reed. il *People Weekly* 31:64-6+ Ap 3 '89

THREE-POINT SHOOTING (BASKETBALL)

How I fell for the bomb [college basketball] A. Wolff. por *Sports Illustrated* 70:84 F 20 '89

Three's company [pro basketball] D. Herbst. il *Sport (New York, N.Y.)* 80:20-4 D '89

THREE-SELF MOVEMENT (CHINA)

Bishop at center of Chinese church debate [K. H. Ting] W. W. Conard. por *Christianity Today* 33:52-3 My 12 '89

Bishop Ting and China's house churches. R. MacMillan. il *The Christian Century* 106:755-6 Ag 16-23 '89

THREE WHEEL AUTOMOBILES See Automobiles, Three wheel

THREE WISE MEN See Magi

THE THREEPENNY OPERA [musical] See Musicals, revues, etc.—Reviews—Single works

THRIFT

See also

Finance, Personal

Stinginess

Fear of buying: women who save too much. N. Hathaway. il *Harper's Bazaar* 122:38+ Ja '89

THRIFT INSTITUTIONS

See also

Credit unions

Savings and loan associations

Savings banks

Banks and thrifts. T. Pouschine. il *Forbes* 143:94-7 Ja 9 '89

THRIFT SHOPS AND RUMMAGE SALES

Saving graces [New York City] P. Eaton. il *New York* 22:120-2 My 1 '89

The thrift-shop connection [contracts with charities] R. R. Roha. il *Changing Times* 43:126 Mr '89

THRIPS

Plight of the maples [cover story] R. Matthews. il *Country Journal* 16:50-4+ Mr/Ap '89

Reproduction

Eggs or live young: a thrips'll try both [research by Bernard J. Crespi] *Science News* 135:110 F 18 '89

THROAT

See also

Esophagus

Larynx

Cancer

Therapy

Sammy Davis Jr. treated for throat malignancy. il por *Jet* 76:54-5 S 25 '89

Diseases

See also

Laryngitis

Strep throat

THROCKMORTON (TEX.)

Religious institutions and affairs

A Church without priests [San Patricio's] A. G. Mojtabai. il *The New York Times Magazine* p16-17+ D 24 '89

THROMBIN

Blood clotting may increase with age [research by Robert Rosenberg] J. L. Marx. *Science* 243:316 Ja 20 '89

THROMBOLYTICS See Anticoagulants

THROMBOSIS

See also

Anticoagulants

Air traveler's syndrome: do's & don'ts [getting blood clots on flights of four hours or more] A. C. Mallozzi. il *Good Housekeeping* 209:176 Jl '89

THROTTLE, HELICOPTER See Helicopter engines—Throttle

THROUGH THE KEYHOLE [television program] See Television program reviews—Single works

THROWERS, SNOW See Snow blowers, throwers, etc.

THROWING MUSES (MUSICAL GROUP)

Rocking Muses. D. Gates. *Newsweek* 113:63 Je 19 '89

Throwing Muses. P. Puterbaugh. il *Stereo Review* 54:109 My '89

THRUST REVERSERS See Airplane engines, Jet—Thrust reversers

THULE ESKIMOS See Eskimos

THUN, MATTEO, 1952-

about

Zest for living. C. Petkanas. il pors *Harper's Bazaar* 122:80-1+ Ja '89

THUNDERHEAD MOUNTAIN (S.D.)

The Ziolkowskis are honoring Chief Crazy Horse, by blasting out a mountain of a sculpture. D. Grogan. il pors *People Weekly* 32:105+ D 4 '89

THUNDER'S MOUTH PRESS INC.

At Thunder's Mouth: keeping black writers in print. il *Publishers Weekly* 235:39 F 17 '89

Thunder's Mouth, Faber both profiling filmmaker Martin Scorsese. M. Simson. il por *Publishers Weekly* 236:28 S 22 '89

THUNDERSTORMS

See also

Aviation—Storm hazards

Lightning

Letters [discussion of November 1988 article, The electrification of thunderstorms] E. R. Williams. *Scientific American* 261:8 Jl '89

Sounds of home [sending son in Korea tape recording of thunderstorm to ward off homesickness] B. V. Moulder. il *Reader's Digest* 135:143-4 Jl '89

Stalking the savage storm [cover story] B. Carpenter. il *U.S. News & World Report* 107:48-54 Jl 24 '89

Photographs and photography

A storm chaser's dreamscape. G. S. Forbes. il *Weatherwise* 42:304-6 D '89

THURIAUX, MICHEL C.

"Tell me, doctor, is epidemiology dangerous?". il *World Health* p4-5 Je '89

THURMAN, JUDITH, 1946-

Reader, I married him. *The New Yorker* 65:109-14 Mr 20 '89

THURMAN, TRACEY

about

I'm doing this movie to keep Buck Thurman from getting out of jail. S. Littwin. por *TV Guide* 37:24-6 S 30-O 6 '89

Thousands of women, fearing for their lives, hear a scary echo in Tracey Thurman's Cry for help. J. Park and S. Schindehette. il por *People Weekly* 32:112-16 O 9 '89

THURMAN, UMA

about

Dangerous liaisons' violated beauty, Uma Thurman, 18, is a little risky herself. por *People Weekly* 31:118-19 F 6 '89

Hot cover. B. Yagoda. pors *Rolling Stone* p52-4 My 18 '89

Pure white. il *Vogue* 179:392-7 Ap '89

Uma: dangerous curves ahead? J. C. Johnson. il por *Mademoiselle* 95:216-17 Mr '89

THURMOND, JAMES STROM See Thurmond, Strom, 1902-

THURMOND, STROM, 1902-

Should the Congress adopt the "Textile and Apparel Trade Act of 1987"? [excerpts from address, September 15, 1988] *Congressional Digest* 68:10+ Ja '89

THURN-VALSASSINA, ISABELLE VON
about
Obituary
  People Weekly il pors 31:51-2 Ja 9 '89. M. Brower
THUROW, LESTER C.
American mirage: a post-industrial economy? *Current History* 88:13-14+ Ja '89
China's economic moves make sense. il por *Fortune* 119:323-4+ Je 5 '89
THURSTON, FUZZY, 1933-
about
Didn't you used to be . . . W. Ladson. il por *Sport (New York, N.Y.)* 80:106 F '89
THURSTON, HARRY
The devil's work in an ark of sand. il map *Audubon* 91:82-91 Mr '89
THUY, THU LE
about
In a war of nerves, first-time actress Thuy Thu Le relives Vietnam in Casualties of war. M. H. J. Farrell. il pors *People Weekly* 32:47+ Ag 28 '89
THWIN, MAUREEN AUNG- *See* Aung-Thwin, Maureen
THYMECTOMY
Neonatal thymectomy results in a repertoire enriched in T cells deleted in adult thymus. H. Smith and others. bibl f il *Science* 245:749-52 Ag 18 '89
THYMIDINE
See also
  Azidothymidine
Sequence-specific isotope effects on the cleavage of DNA by bleomycin. J. W. Kozarich and others. bibl f il *Science* 245:1396-9 S 22 '89
THYMUS DERIVED CELLS *See* T cells
THYMUS GLAND
Surgery
See also
  Thymectomy
THYROID GLAND
Cancer
Therapy
"I was radioactive". L. George. il por *Ladies' Home Journal* 106:22+ O '89
Diseases
See also
  Hyperthyroidism
Thyroid disease: how to control it. L. Wartofsky. por *McCall's* 117:106 N '89
When your thyroid goes haywire. L. Holland. *Good Housekeeping* 209:165 Ag '89
THYROID HORMONE RECEPTORS *See* Hormone receptors
THYROID HORMONES
See also
  Triiodothyronine
THYROTOXICOSIS *See* Hyperthyroidism
THYROTROPIN RECEPTORS *See* Hormone receptors
THYSSEN-BORNEMISZA, HANS HEINRICH, BARON, 1921-
about
Courtship of a collector. F. Jarque. il por *Art News* 88:65+ My '89
THYSSEN-BORNEMISZA COLLECTION *See* Art—Collectors and collecting
TIAA *See* Teachers Insurance and Annuity Association
TIANANMEN SQUARE (CHINA) STUDENT OCCUPATION, 1989
745 Boylston Street [Fang Lizhi] il por *The Atlantic* 264:4 S '89
After socialism, what? M. Novak. il *Forbes* 144:62-3 Jl 10 '89
After the bloodbath [cover story; special section; with editorial comment by Kevin Doyle] il *Maclean's* 102:2, 22-31 Je 19 '89
After the massacres. S. Leys. bibl f il *The New York Review of Books* 36:17-19 O 12 '89
Aftermath of Tiananmen Square. H. Cordes. il *Utne Reader* p15-17 S/O '89
Ants & the Great Wall. *Commonweal* 116:356 Je 16 '89
Bad days in Beijing. M. Liu. il *Newsweek* 114:34-5 Jl 31 '89
Beijing bloodbath [cover story] R. Watson. il *Newsweek* 113:24-9 Je 12 '89
The Beijing spring continues. E. Salholz. il *Newsweek* 113:44 My 15 '89
Beijing's bad-times bash. E. MacFarquhar. il *U.S. News & World Report* 107:33-5 O 2 '89
Beware of geobaloney. M. Greenfield. il *Newsweek* 114:84 D 25 '89
A bloodbath in Beijing. L. Doder. il *Maclean's* 102:22-3 Je 12 '89
Broken China [effects of crackdown on students] *The New Republic* 200:5-6 Je 26 '89
A call to arms [Wuer Kaixi] por *Time* 134:32 Jl 10 '89
Can the billion prevail? *The Progressive* 53:7-8 Jl '89
A cautious man plays China by the book [G. Bush's policy] D. Gergen. il *U.S. News & World Report* 106:27 Je 5 '89
Children of Tiananmen [Shen Tong and Wuer Kaixi] O. Schell. il pors *Rolling Stone* p185-8+ D 14-28 '89

China [declaration of martial law; cover story] J. Elson. il *Time* 133:20-3+ Je 5 '89
China and America: beyond the big chill. W. Lord. *Foreign Affairs* 68:1-26 Fall '89
China devours its children [special section] *National Review* 41:28-32 Ag 4 '89
China erupts . . . the reasons why [cover story] N. D. Kristof. il *The New York Times Magazine* p26-9+ Je 4 '89
China gropes toward a way out [cover story] P. Kwong and D. Miščević. il *The Nation* 249:73+ Jl 17 '89
China passage. *The Nation* 248:800-1 Je 12 '89
The China syndrome. *The New Republic* 200:7-9 My 15 '89
China: the great leap backward [cover story; special section] il *Business Week* p28-35 Je 19 '89
China: the party wins. B. Crozier. *National Review* 41:39-40 Je 30 '89
China's new Long March [students keep the spirit] J. Bartholet. il *Newsweek* 114:37 Ag 7 '89
China's new time of troubles. A. F. Geyer. *The Christian Century* 106:612-13 Je 21-28 '89
China's next great leap could be backward. D. Lee. il *Business Week* p54-5 My 8 '89
China's rising tide of unrest. il *Newsweek* 113:30-2 My 8 '89
China's spring [cover story] O. Schell. il *The New York Review of Books* 36:3-4+ Je 29 '89
China's turmoil touches U.S. science; U.S.-Chinese scientists see dreams imperiled. M. Sun and E. Marshall. il *Science* 244:1130-2 Je 9 '89
China—the hope and the horror. il *Reader's Digest* 135:68-77 S '89
The Chinese ambassador defends his government [views of Han Xu] W. F. Buckley. *National Review* 41:71 S 29 '89
The Chinese demonstrators. *World Press Review* 36:10 Je '89
Chinese Goddess of Democracy toppled by troops. J. Gambrell. il *Art in America* 77:29 Jl '89
The Chinese intellectuals and the revolt. P. Link. il *The New York Review of Books* 36:38-41 Je 29 '89
The Chinese rebellion [cover story; special section] il *World Press Review* 36:13-18+ Jl '89
The Chinese student movement moves to America. A. Riles. il *The Progressive* 53:28-30 S '89
Choreographer flees China when students are massacred. Chen Min. il por *Dance Magazine* 63:22 Ag '89
Collapse of communism [cover story; special section; with editorial comment by David Gergen] il map *U.S. News & World Report* 106:18-23+, 76 Je 19 '89
"Come out! Come out!". W. R. Doerner. il *Time* 133:44-5 My 1 '89
Crackdown in China. J. Bierman. il *Maclean's* 102:18-19 Je 26 '89
Cracking down in China. il *Scholastic Update (Teachers' edition)* 122:9 N 3 '89
A crisis in leadership. A. Bilski. il *Maclean's* 102:26-7 My 15 '89
The curse of the man who could see the little fish at the bottom of the ocean. S. Leys. il *The New York Review of Books* 36:29 Jl 20 '89
Dealing death with a big lie [denial of massacre; special section] il *Newsweek* 113:26-9 Je 26 '89
Defiance [cover story; special section] S. Talbott. il *Time* 133:11-22+ Je 19 '89
Dellums urges support for Chinese freedom struggle. il por *Jet* 76:15 Je 26 '89
'Democracy' is not enough. A. Cockburn. *The Nation* 248:802 Je 12 '89
Demonstrations in China [State Dept. and White House statements, May 18-June 20, 1989] *Department of State Bulletin* 89:75-7 Ag '89
Deng strikes back [special section] il pors *Newsweek* 113:30-6 Je 5 '89
Deng's big lie [denial of massacre] J. Smolowe. il *Time* 133:32-4 Je 26 '89
Deng's 'pact with the devil'. C. S. Manegold. il por *Newsweek* 114:33 S 18 '89
Deng's pyrrhic victory [cover story] Liu Binyan. *The New Republic* 201:21-4 O 2 '89
Despair and death in a Beijing square. J. Birnbaum and H. G. Chua-Eoan. il *Time* 133:24-7 Je 12 '89
Dissident diplomats [Chinese envoys defect to Canada] T. Tedesco. il *Maclean's* 102:21 Je 26 '89
Don't just do something, stand there [U.S. response] *National Review* 41:16 Jl 14 '89
Easy does it. W. F. Buckley. *National Review* 41:62-3 S 15 '89
The end of the Chinese revolution [cover story] R. MacFarquhar. il *The New York Review of Books* 36:8-10 Jl 20 '89
Execution in China. B. Came. il *Maclean's* 102:14-15 Jl 3 '89
The face of repression [execution of demonstrators] W. R. Doerner. il *Time* 134:27 Jl 3 '89

TIANANMEN SQUARE (CHINA) STUDENT OCCUPATION, 1989—cont.

Bibliography

Tiananmen struggle explored in wide range of books about China. G. Feldman. il *Publishers Weekly* 236:93-4 S 15 '89

Economic aspects

After Tiananmen, what? [Hong Kong investment] il *Forbes* 144:198 Jl 24 '89

Airlines shuffle operations as China service loads plunge. il *Aviation Week & Space Technology* 130:161 Je 19 '89

The Beijing factor makes this the year of the slide. D. Greising. il *Business Week* p106+ Je 26 '89

Biting the hands that feed them [effects of violence on China's economic ties] il *U.S. News & World Report* 106:26 Je 19 '89

China prepares for a bitter harvest. E. MacFarquhar. il *U.S. News & World Report* 107:34-5 Jl 10 '89

China's pain is Vancouver's gain. P. C. Newman. il *Maclean's* 102:43 O 2 '89

Contractors remain outside China as violence continues [aerospace contractors] M. Mecham. *Aviation Week & Space Technology* 130:31 Je 26 '89

Deng's great leap backward [aftermath of government crackdown on students] H. Anderson. il *Newsweek* 113:26-7 Je 19 '89

Doing business in China now. F. S. Worthy. il *Fortune* 120 no13 Special Issue:21+ Fall '89

The economic root of the problem. E. Ellis. il *World Press Review* 36:16-17 Jl '89

Fear and trembling in Hong Kong. J. Elliott. *World Press Review* 36:18 Jl '89

Fear in the colony [Hong Kong reacts to Beijing crackdown] T. Fennell. il *Maclean's* 102:32-4 Je 19 '89

Hong Kong's contrarians [buying stocks] J. Mendes. il *Fortune* 120:30 Jl 17 '89

Hong Kong's lost confidence. P. Hazan. il *World Press Review* 36:61 S '89

How bad will China's debt crunch get? D. Lee. il *Business Week* p62 S 25 '89

In Beijing, it's business as usual. A. Riles. il *The Progressive* 53:31 S '89

International aerospace firms begin evacuating employees from China. P. Proctor. il *Aviation Week & Space Technology* 130:68-9 Je 12 '89

MiG-29 crash, turmoil in China mar start of show [Paris Air Show] il *Aviation Week & Space Technology* 130:60-3 Je 12 '89

The outside world puts China on hold. D. J. Yang and B. Javetski. il *Business Week* p40-1 Jl 10 '89

Ready to ride out China's turmoil [Fortune poll] A. Farnham. il *Fortune* 120:117-18 Jl 3 '89

The shock waves from Beijing. B. Javetski. il *Business Week* p76-7 Je 26 '89

Testing the power of dollar diplomacy. H. Trewhitt. il *U.S. News & World Report* 107:30-1 Jl 3 '89

U.S. importers aren't jumping ship—yet. D. Lee. il *Business Week* p78 Je 26 '89

U.S. permits Boeing to transfer four 757s to Chinese airlines. *Aviation Week & Space Technology* 131:96 Jl 17 '89

U.S. suspends military sales in wake of massacre in China. M. Mecham. il *Aviation Week & Space Technology* 130:69-70+ Je 12 '89

'We simply can't go rushing back in'. B. Powell. il *Newsweek* 114:30 Jl 3 '89

What's next for business in China. F. S. Worthy. il *Fortune* 120:110-12 Jl 17 '89

The year of trouble. J. DeMont. il *Maclean's* 102:28-9 S 11 '89

Photographs and photography

China's blood. il *Life* 12:38-46 Jl '89

Public opinion

Honk if you care [Chinese students in Washington, D.C. demonstrate in favor of Tiananmen Square uprising] A. McCarthy. *Commonweal* 116:393-4 Jl 14 '89

Notes and comment. *The New Yorker* 65:35-7 Je 12 '89

Revolution by information. L. Martz. il *Newsweek* 113:28-9 Je 19 '89

Student-crushing China cows Natural History Museum [film The first emperor of China not shown by American Museum of Natural History] M. S. Forbes. il *Forbes* 144:20 Ag 7 '89

Religious aspects

China friendships after June 4. E. J. Malatesta. *America* 161:132 S 9-16 '89

The church seeks a new place in China. K. H. Sidey. il *Christianity Today* 33:55-6 S 8 '89

Communist crackdown worries Chinese church. K. H. Sidey. il *Christianity Today* 33:40-2 Jl 14 '89

Exodus creates church leadership shortage [Hong Kong] S. Mumper. il *Christianity Today* 33:42+ N 3 '89

Please remember China. D. H. Adeney. *Christianity Today* 33:15 Ag 18 '89

Religion in China [cover story] W. R. Garrett. il *The Christian Century* 106:748-9 Ag 16-23 '89

Reporters and reporting

Beat the devil. A. Cockburn. il *The Nation* 249:42-3 Jl 10 '89

Behind China's made-for-TV revolt. il *Scholastic Update (Teachers' edition)* 122:12-14 S 8 '89

China coverage strong on what, weak on why. M. Hertsgaard. il *Rolling Stone* p37-9+ S 21 '89

Eyewitnesses to slaughter. G. Bain. il *Maclean's* 102:31 Je 19 '89

Karl Marx, meet Marshall McLuhan. J. Alter. il *Newsweek* 113:28 My 29 '89

The left and Tiananmen Square [discussion of July 10, 1989 column] A. Cockburn. *The Nation* 249:370+ O 9 '89

Playing the China card [network coverage] E. Diamond. il *New York* 22:16+ Je 5 '89

Thrust onto center stage [U.S. reporters covering demonstrations] L. Zuckerman. il *Time* 133:64-5 Je 5 '89

Unwilling informants? [candor in news coverage massacre could endanger lives] J. Alter. il *Newsweek* 113:29 Je 26 '89

TIBBETS, PAUL W.

about

The victim and the pilot: a Hiroshima reunion. G. Mitchell. il pors *The Progressive* 53:26-8 Ag '89

TIBBETTS, DONN

John Sununu: the right-hand man. il pors *Conservative Digest* 15:43+ Ja/F '89

TIBET

See also
Geology—Tibet
Nomads—Tibet
Riots—Tibet
Tibetans

Description and travel

The Tibetan spirit: jolly and rainbowed and welcoming [excerpt from Video night in Kathmandu] P. Iyer. il *Utne Reader* p44-6 Mr/Ap '89

Foreign relations

China

See China—Foreign relations—Tibet

Nationalism

'A' is for autonomy. E. N. Luttwak. *The New Republic* 200:15-16 Ap 17 '89

China's hard line in Tibet. G. Deshingkar. *World Press Review* 36:18-19 Je '89

A firestorm in Shangri-La. H. Anderson. il *Newsweek* 113:36-8 Mr 20 '89

Inside Tibet [special section] il *Utne Reader* p33-46 Mr/Ap '89

Massacre in the Forbidden Kingdom [riot in Lhasa] C. Meindersma. il *Reader's Digest* 135:126-30 O '89

Tibet. *Business Week* p60 Mr 20 '89

Tibet's agony [Dalai Lama awarded Nobel Peace Prize] M. Moynihan. *The New Republic* 201:10-11 N 20 '89

Unrest in Tibet. J. T. Dreyer. bibl f *Current History* 88:281-4+ S '89

Religious institutions and affairs

See also
Convents—Tibet
Dalai Lama XIV, 1935-

TIBETAN SCULPTURE *See* Sculpture, Tibetan

TIBETANS

The Chinese view of Tibet [Tibetans successfully integrated into Qinghai Province] Cheng Gang. map *Utne Reader* p36 Mr/Ap '89

India

Education

Journey to knowledge [Tibetan children travel 100 miles on frozen Zanskar River to go to school] O. Föllmi. il *Life* 12:108-16 D '89

TIC-TAC-TOE (GAME)

A Tinkertoy computer that plays tic-tac-toe. A. K. Dewdney. il *Scientific American* 261:120-3 O '89

TICE, CAROL H.

Youth Opportunity: a private sector investment in prevention. il *Children Today* 18:20-3 Mr/Ap '89

TICE, TERRENCE N.

Research in review. See issues of The Education Digest beginning May 1988

TICE-BALDWIN, KIMBERLY, AND OTHERS

BAS1 has a myb motif and activates HIS4 transcription only in combination with BAS2. bibl f il *Science* 246:931-5 N 17 '89

TICK REPELLENTS

En garde against Tick Garde. il *Consumer Reports* 54:489 Ag '89

How to keep those ticks at bay. S. Woolley. il *Business Week* p97 Jl 3 '89

A tick buster's guide to bug repellents [preventing Lyme disease] J. Silberner. il *U.S. News & World Report* 107:57 Ag 7 '89

TICKET BROKERS, AIRLINE *See* Airline ticket brokers

TICKET SCALPING *See* Ticket selling—Ethical aspects

TICKET SELLING

See also
Airline ticket brokers

Ethical aspects

Hot seats! [scalping of Wimbledon tickets] C. Gould. *World Tennis* 37:40+ Jl '89

TICKETS
See also
Sports tickets
Tennis—Tournaments—Tickets
Theater tickets

TICKS AS CARRIERS OF INFECTION
See also
Lyme disease
Pheromone-mediation of host-selection in bont ticks (Amblyomma hebraeum Koch) [carriers of heartwater disease] R. A. I. Norval and others. bibl f il *Science* 243:364-5 Ja 20 '89
Ticks follow fellows to tastiest cows [carriers of heartwater disease; research by Conrad E. Yunker and others] *Science News* 135:123 F 25 '89

TICLOPIDINE
New drug can avert strokes. *USA Today (Periodical)* 117:12 F '89

TICONDEROGA (SHIP)
Classified top secret: H-bomb overboard [rolls off U.S. carrier Ticonderoga headed toward Japanese port] *Newsweek* 113:45 My 15 '89

TIDAL WAVES
See also
Tsunamis

TIDE POWER
See also
Eling Tide Mill

TIDES
Blame it on the moon [Elatina sediment striations tidally induced; George E. Williams overturns his hypothesis] J. Horgan. *Scientific American* 260:18 F '89
It's not the sun, but the moon [tidally induced Australian rock laminations; research by George E. Williams] il *Sky and Telescope* 77:469 My '89
Spring tides. T. D. Nicholson. *Natural History* p69 My '89

TIDEWATER INC.
Why Irv Jacobs wants to land Tidewater. R. Mitchell. il *Business Week* p31-2 Ja 30 '89

TIDWELL, MIKE
Murder capital. il *The Progressive* 53:46 Jl '89

TIE-DYEING *See* Dyes and dyeing

TIEGS, CHERYL
about
Having it tall. il pors *Harper's Bazaar* 122:100-1 Ja '89
Older and better. C. Kirkpatrick. il pors *Sports Illustrated* 70 Special Issue:95+ F '89

TIEL, VICKY
about
Vicky Tiel: American elan in a Paris apartment. S. Stephens. il por *Architectural Digest* 46:188-91 S '89

TIES (NECKWEAR) *See* Neckties

TIFFANY
about
Breakfast with Tiffany. J. C. Johnson. il por *Mademoiselle* 95:70 My '89
Tiffany: top teen tunemaker! por *'Teen* 33:47 Je '89
Tiffany: troubles for a teenage star. M. Hammer. il pors *Ladies' Home Journal* 106:122+ Mr '89

TIFFANY, LOUIS COMFORT, 1848-1933
about
The genius of Louis Comfort Tiffany. A. E. Ledes. il *Antiques* 136:374+ S '89
Rare offerings from Tiffany. K. M. Burke. il *Smithsonian* 20:236 O '89
A touch of glass. B. Sherman. il *Harper's Bazaar* 122:94+ O '89

TIFFANY & CO.
Cocktails at Tiffany. J. A. Trachtenberg. il *Forbes* 143:128-30 F 6 '89
Fast break at Tiffany's [Mitsukoshi's stake] M. Roman. il por *Business Week* p102+ O 9 '89
Tiffany tries the Cartier formula. F. Rice. il *Fortune* 120:141+ N 20 '89

TIFFANY GLASS
Conservation and restoration
Doing windows. B. Weber. il *The New York Times Magazine* p50 Jl 30 '89

Exhibitions
The genius of Louis Comfort Tiffany [Masterworks of Louis Comfort Tiffany at the Renwick Gallery] A. E. Ledes. il *Antiques* 136:374+ S '89
Rare offerings from Tiffany [Renwick Gallery show] K. M. Burke. il *Smithsonian* 20:236 O '89
A touch of glass [Masterworks of Louis Comfort Tiffany at the Renwick Gallery] B. Sherman. il *Harper's Bazaar* 122:94+ O '89

TIFFANY LAMPS
Collectors and collecting
Putting a new light on Tiffany lamps. J. Weber, Jr. il *Business Week* p158 D 18 '89

TIGA (TEXAS INSTRUMENTS' GRAPHICS ARCHITECTURE)
Benchmarking the TIGA. il *Byte* 14:188-9 N '89
Clash of the graphics titans. R. Cook. il *Byte* 14 Special Issue:143-4+ Fall '89

TIGER, VIRGINIA
(jt. auth) *See* Aronson, Steven M. L., and Tiger, Virginia

TIGER FUND
Why growth stocks look good [interview with J. Robertson] J. Mendes. il por *Fortune* 119:41-3 My 8 '89

TIGER INTERNATIONAL, INC.
Federal Express/Tigers merger would reshape cargo industry. J. T. McKenna. *Aviation Week & Space Technology* 130:106 Ja 2 '89
Fred Smith [Federal Express buys Flying Tiger] D. Foust. il por *Business Week* Special Issue:102 Ap 14 '89
Mr. Smith goes global [Federal Express merger with Tiger International; cover story] D. Foust. il pors map *Business Week* p66-8+ F 13 '89

TIGER MOUNTAIN (WASH.)
Taming Seattle's Tiger [cycling] M. McCloy. il *Bicycling* 30:84 O/N '89

TIGERMAN, STANLEY, 1930-
about
Architecture: Stanley Tigerman [cover story] R. A. M. Stern. il por *Architectural Digest* 46:146-51+ F '89

TIGERS
Project Tiger [India] R. Singh. il *The Courier (Unesco)* 42:35-6 F '89

TIGGES, MICHAEL A., AND OTHERS
Mechanism of interleukin-2 signaling: mediation of different outcomes by a single receptor and transduction pathway. bibl f il *Science* 243:781-6 F 10 '89

TIGHTS (CLOTHING)
The best and the tightest [running tights] D. Kardong. il *Runner's World* 24:80-3 S '89

TIGHTWADS *See* Stinginess

TIJUANA (MEXICO)
Crime
To the left of zero [Mexican newspaper editor H. F. Miranda killed] W. Murray. *The New Yorker* 65:57-66 Jl 31 '89

TIKARAM, TANITA
about
Tanita Tikaram. por *Seventeen* 48:112 Ap '89
Tanita Tikaram: is she the new Joni Mitchell? C. Krupp. il por *Glamour* 87:208 S '89

TIKHONOV, VIKTOR
about
Is it nyet or not yet? E. M. Swift. il pors *Sports Illustrated* 70:30-3 Ja 16 '89

TIKKUN (PERIODICAL)
Broken vessel [conference of Jewish progressives sponsored by Tikkun] E. Rothstein. *The New Republic* 200:17-20 Mr 6 '89

'TIL TUESDAY (MUSICAL GROUP)
'til Tuesday [release of Everything's different now] P. Puterbaugh. il *Stereo Review* 54:96 Ap '89

TILE LAYING
Ceramic tile, everywhere [bathrooms] il *Popular Mechanics* 166:130+ Ap '89
Setting ceramic tile. il *The Mother Earth News* 116:66-71 Mr/Ap '89
Tile a kitchen floor and backsplash. A. Rooze. il *The Family Handyman* 39:40-3 O '89
Tile repair. M. Morris. il *Home Mechanix* 85:30+ My '89

TILES
Dazzling baths [excerpt from Country floors—decorating with tiles] R. Siegal. il *Redbook* 173:122-4 Jl '89
Talking tile [ceramic tile] il *Home Mechanix* 85:20-1 S '89
Tile file [ceramics] D. B. Cowin. il *House & Garden* 161:154 F '89

TILGHMAN, CHRISTOPHER
Hole in the day [story] *The New Yorker* 65:44-54 N 27 '89
What they ate; What they drank [poem] *The New Yorker* 65:50 N 27 '89

TILIA *See* Linden

TILL, EMMETT
about
The business of us all. *Commonweal* 116:484-5 S 22 '89

TILLAGE
See also
Contour farming
No-tillage
Soil tilth
Terraces (Agriculture)
18-year tillage trial ends in a tie. R. Fee. *Successful Farming* 87:48K My '89
Conservation on your own [special section] J. Walter. il *Successful Farming* 87:21-8 D '89
Coulters: the path makers. C. Finck. il *Successful Farming* 87:20-1 mid-Mr '89
Crop residue—going, going, gone! R. Fee. il *Successful Farming* 87:24-7 N '89
Get to the point to save residue [chisel plowing] R. Fee. il *Successful Farming* 87 no4:18-21 Mr '89
Tilling the earth. J. Burland. il *Country Journal* 16:64-8 Mr/Ap '89

TILLEMANS, ROSE
God's children should be on a first-name basis. *U.S. Catholic* 54:37 Ag '89

TILLERS *See* Cultivators

TILLING, THOMAS
Family finance. See issues of Parents beginning July 1986

TIME INC.—cont.

Time-Warner: three's a crowd: Bob Bass may stop the merger. K. Kelly and D. Lieberman. il por *Business Week* p38 Ap 3 '89

Time's bad fortune with money people [Paramount's bid] *U.S. News & World Report* 106:14 Je 19 '89

Time's counterattack is drawing acid reviews [Warner bid] D. Lieberman. il *Business Week* p26 Jl 3 '89

Time's next battleground [Delaware Chancery Court] R. Sandza. *Newsweek* 114:31 Jl 10 '89

Upping the ante for Time [Paramount's new bid] J. Schwartz. il *Newsweek* 114:42 Jl 3 '89

The war over Time Inc. [Paramount's hostile bid threatens Warner merger] J. Schwartz. il *Newsweek* 113:48-9+ Je 19 '89

Why doesn't Time Inc. just put itself on the block? J. H. Dobrzynski. il *Business Week* p63 Je 26 '89

Will it happen? And will it work? [Time-Warner deal; special section] il *Business Week* p32-6 Mr 20 '89

The wizards of 'Wasserella' [role in Time Inc. takeover] J. Schwartz and C. Friday. il pors *Newsweek* 114:30-1 Jl 10 '89

Anecdotes, facetiae, satire, etc.

Let's do a deal [Nation bids for Time, Inc.] V. S. Navasky. *The Nation* 249:3-4 Jl 3 '89

Sharp elbows and the media barons [bidders] A. Fotheringham. il *Maclean's* 102:56 Je 26 '89

Time is money [discussion of July 3, 1989 article, Let's do a deal] V. S. Navasky. *The Nation* 249:75-6 Jl 17 '89

TIME-LAPSE PHOTOGRAPHY See Photography, Time-lapse

TIME-LIFE BOOK DIGEST

Time-Life to challenge Reader's Digest in condensed books market. *Publishers Weekly* 236:14 S 22 '89

TIME MANAGEMENT

33 great ways to simplify your life [cutting time spent on financial matters; cover story] J. Bodnar. il *Changing Times* 43:22-8 Je '89

The art of time [excerpt] J.-L. Servan-Schreiber. il *American Health* 8:80+ Mr '89

Conquer procrastination. P. Edwards and S. Edwards. il *Home Office Computing* 7:34 Ap '89

The evening rush hour [family stress at day's end] K. Levine. il *Parents* 64:58+ Ag '89

Handling good employees who are lousy time managers. S. Schlenger and R. Roesch. *Working Woman* 14:21 Je '89

Helping students use leisure time effectively [social studies] W. W. Crowder. *The Education Digest* 55:54-6 N '89

High-tech cures for the time crunch. R. Farmanfarmaian. il *Psychology Today* 23:46-8 My '89

How a top boss manages his day [R. A. Lutz of Chrysler] A. L. Taylor, III. il pors *Fortune* 119:95-7+ Je 19 '89

How managers can succeed through speed [cover story] B. Dumaine. il *Fortune* 119:54-7+ F 13 '89

How to control the time eaters [excerpt from Time power] C. R. Hobbs. *Working Woman* 14:110-11+ My '89

How to find time. D. Turner. *Reader's Digest* 134:195 Je '89

How to get more done in fewer hours [excerpt from One-on-one with Andy Grove] A. S. Grove. il *Working Woman* 14:20+ Jl '89

How to get procrastinators up to speed [excerpt from The now habit] N. A. Fiore. il *Working Woman* 14:38+ Mr '89

How to organize your office [interview with S. Winston] K. Kane. por *Home Office Computing* 7:58 S '89

How to slow down [setting limits on volunteer work] J. G. Fitzpatrick. il *Parents* 64:97-102 Ap '89

How to spend time, not save it. L. Mosedale. il *Glamour* 87:236-9 Ag '89

Managing your time [excerpt from Time in, time out, time enough] P. R. Materka. il *Essence* 20:120+ My '89

Morning madness [suggestions by Ronni Eisenberg and Kate Kelly] K. Levine. il *Parents* 64:68+ F '89

New hope for handling old-pro procrastinators. S. Chan. *Working Woman* 14:30+ O '89

Priorities [teenagers] J. Stone. il *Seventeen* 48:116-17+ N '89

Put time on your side. J. Dean. il *Home Office Computing* 7:66-8 D '89

Read this article immediately. E. M. Collier. il *Nation's Business* 77:68+ O '89

Saving time. P. V. Fossel. il *Country Journal* 16:5-6 Jl/Ag '89

The search for quality time [working mothers; panel discussion] il *Ladies' Home Journal* 106:192 N '89

Serious neglect: things we let go to pot—and why not? il *Glamour* 87:96 F '89

Speaking at length [presentations that run too long] J. Cairns. *BioScience* 39:632-3 O '89

Take charge of your job [views of P. Nickerson] R. Thompson. il por *Nation's Business* 77:36-7 Ap '89

Toughest job [daily schedule of working mother P. Menzel] G. H. Colt. il pors *Life* 12:100-4+ My '89

What keeps them going? Four nonstop women share their secrets [women executives] il *Glamour* 87:75 Je '89

Whose time is more valuable? C. L. Mithers. il *Glamour* 87:296 O '89

Workaholics Anonymous. W. Kiechel. il *Fortune* 120:117-18 Ag 14 '89

Writing on the go. D. Gilbert. *The Writer* 102:27-8 Mr '89

You're on: diary of a 14-hour day. N. Malkin. il *Working Woman* 14:156+ O '89

Anecdotes, facetiae, satire, etc.

Human race. B. Doherty. *The New Republic* 200:12+ My 1 '89

To-do or not to-do? J. W. Boeldt. il *New Choices for the Best Years* 29:88 Ag '89

TIME MANAGEMENT INDUSTRY

No, they can't stop time, but they can help you manage it. W. C. Symonds. il *Business Week* p178-9 My 22 '89

TIME MEASUREMENT

See also

Atomic clocks

Clocks

Day

Hourglasses

Lasers—Time measurement use

Watches

Time and the amateur astronomer. A. MacRobert. il *Sky and Telescope* 77:378-9 Ap '89

TIME PERCEPTION

See also

Time sickness

Are you a slave to your watch? il *Glamour* 87:127 Ag '89

Time is not on their side [poor sense of time accounts for poor academic performance among poor children] E. Taylor. il *Time* 133:74 F 27 '89

Time passes. P. Steinhart. il *Audubon* 91:8+ Ja '89

Tomorrow? Who cares? T. Oberhofer. *The Futurist* 23:59 My/Je '89

Where does the time go? [passage from baby to child] E. Berg. il *Parents* 64:58+ D '89

TIME PRESSURE

Acceleration syndrome: does everyone live in the fast lane nowadays? T. Schwartz. il *Utne Reader* p36-43 Ja/F '89

How America has run out of time [living at an accelerated pace; cover story] N. R. Gibbs. il *Time* 133:58-61+ Ap 24 '89

The pace of life [link between high speed cities and heart disease] R. Levine. il *Psychology Today* 23:42-6 O '89

Rediscovering the rat race. R. J. Samuelson. il *Newsweek* 113:57 My 15 '89

TIME PURCHASING (CABLE TELEVISION ADVERTISING) See Cable television advertising—Time purchasing

TIME PURCHASING (TELEVISION ADVERTISING) See Television advertising—Time purchasing

TIME SHARING (REAL ESTATE) See Timesharing (Real estate)

TIME SICKNESS

Healing time sickness. E. Tivnan. il *American Health* 8:76-8+ Mr '89

TIME TRAVEL

Cosmic time travel [research by Kip Thorne and Michael S. Morris; cover story] D. Freedman. il *Discover* 10:58-64 Je '89

Time after time [wormhole time machine proposed by Michael S. Morris and others] T. Rothman. *Scientific American* 260:21-2 Ja '89

Wormholes in the heavens [creating new universes; views of A. H. Guth] M. D. Lemonick. il *Time* 133:55 Ja 16 '89

Wormholes, time machines, and Schrödinger's cat. il *Sky and Telescope* 77:132 F '89

TIME VALUE OF MONEY

Faulty arithmetic [SEC mutual fund management fee calculations] J. Clements. il *Forbes* 143:112 My 15 '89

John Smith's bill: then & now [cost of supplies for Virginia's colony at today's prices] J. B. M. Schick. il *American Heritage* 40:158-65 N '89

Mastering the math behind your money [using a calculator for time value computations] C. Willis. il *Money* 18:129-30+ My '89

The problem of money and time [cover story; with editorial comment by Byron Dobell] J. S. Gordon. il *American Heritage* 40:7, 56-8+ My/Je '89

The saying that a bird in hand is worth two in the bush applies to money, too. K. McCormally. il *Changing Times* 43:16 Ag '89

Time is money [time value of money as reflected in financial statements] P. Wang. il *Forbes* 143:300 Ja 9 '89

TIME WARNER INC.

All hitched up and ready to go [Delaware court OKs Time Warner] J. Greenwald. *Time* 134:39 Ag 7 '89

A deal heard round the world. C. P. Alexander. il *Time* 133:55-6 Mr 20 '89

Gentlemen's agreement. E. Diamond. il *New York* 22:16+ Mr 20 '89

Heading for 'War Time'? L. Reibstein. il *Newsweek* 113:50 Mr 20 '89

TIME WARNER INC.—*cont.*

How Time Warner will look when the fog clears; Pondering Time's fate over chicken gumbo. il *Business Week* p24-5 Ag 7 '89

The inside story of Time Warner. B. Saporito. il *Fortune* 120:164-6+ N 20 '89

The meaning of the merger [impact of Time-Warner merger on cable operations] H. Solomon. il *Channels (New York, N.Y.: 1986)* 9:62-3 Je '89

The moguls of Media, Inc. E. Pomice. il *U.S. News & World Report* 106:66-7 Mr 20 '89

A new media powerhouse [Time Inc. and Warner] J. DeMont. il por *Maclean's* 102:42-4 Mr 20 '89

Norman Lear, meet Adam Smith [Greater Rochester Cablevision owned by Time Warner competes with Act III Broadcasting's independent station in syndicated market] P. Newcomb. il *Forbes* 144:206+ N 27 '89

Steve Ross' big sweet deal. G. Morgenson. il por *Forbes* 143:14 Ap 3 '89

The thorn in Steve Ross's side [H. Siegel wants deal for his stake in Warner] R. Grover. il por *Business Week* p51 Ag 14 '89

Time + Dallas = ? [New York times coverage of Time Inc. acquisition of Warner Communications] R. Pollak. *The Nation* 248:401 Mr 27 '89

Time Inc. goes Hollywood [buyout of Warner Communications] L. Reibstein. il *Newsweek* 113:41-2 Mr 13 '89

Time out [merger of Time Inc. and Warner Communications] J. Bennet. *The New Republic* 200:20+ Ap 24 '89

The Time Warner challenge. M. Brown. il *Channels (New York, N.Y.: 1986)* 9:20 My '89

Time-Warner heads receive cordial hearing by House Judiciary unit. H. Fields. *Publishers Weekly* 235:14 Mr 31 '89

Time-Warner is wired for cable wars. D. Lieberman. il *Business Week* p44 Ap 17 '89

Time-Warner link pleases book principals. *Publishers Weekly* 235:10+ Mr 17 '89

Time-Warner: three's a crowd: Bob Bass may stop the merger. K. Kelly and D. Lieberman. il por *Business Week* p38 Ap 3 '89

Will it happen? And will it work? [Time-Warner deal; special section] il *Business Week* p32-6 Mr 20 '89

TIME WARNER TRADE PUBLISHING

Little, Brown and Warner combine in new unit. *Publishers Weekly* 236:8 S 8 '89

TIMELINE [television program] See Television program reviews—Single works

TIMES (LOS ANGELES, CALIF.) See Los Angeles times

TIMES (NEW YORK, N.Y.) See New York times

TIMES (WASHINGTON, D.C.) See Washington times

TIMES BOOKS

Times Books reorganized under Random House Trade division. *Publishers Weekly* 235:15 My 19 '89

TIMES SQUARE (NEW YORK, N.Y.)

42nd Street: no beat of dancing feet—yet. J. S. Russell. il *Architectural Record* 177:85 Je '89

Extra-artistic [Times Square street photographers] *The New Yorker* 65:32-3 D 25 '89

From bad to Durst [S. Durst's investments] E. Schmuckler. il por *Forbes* 144:120 Jl 10 '89

Gridlock. J. S. Russell. il *Architectural Record* 177:55 N '89

Midtown West: bright lights, big buildings. J. S. Russell. il *Architectural Record* 177:83 Je '89

TIMES SQUARE CHURCH

His prayers answered, evangelist David Wilkerson has a divine hit running on the Great White Way [moves to the Mark Hellinger Theater] R. Arias. il pors *People Weekly* 32:63-4 S 4 '89

TIMESHARING (REAL ESTATE)

See also

Fractional ownership (Real estate)

Timeshares: a poor investment. W. Giese. il *Changing Times* 43:22 S '89

Ethical aspects

Condo time-sharing tries to live down its past. A. Fins. il *Business Week* p80 Je 19 '89

TIMIDITY

See also

Bashfulness

The timid are in bed early [politics] M. Greenfield. il *Newsweek* 114:106 N 13 '89

Timidity [address, April 6, 1989] T. H. Kean. *Vital Speeches of the Day* 55:488-90 Je 1 '89

TIMMERMAN, JOHN H.

The grapes of wrath fifty years later. *The Christian Century* 106:341-3 Ap 5 '89

TIMMERMANS, PIETER B.

about

Du Pont's 'drug hunter' stalks his next big trophy. J. Weber, Jr. il por *Business Week* p174+ N 27 '89

TIMMONS, MARYELLEN

A Fijian way of fishing. il *Sea Frontiers* 35:64 Ja/F '89

TIMMONS, STEVE

about

Their final shots. B. Anderson. il pors *Sports Illustrated* 71:24-5 Jl 10 '89

TIMP *See* Tissue inhibitor of metalloproteinases

TIMUR, THE GREAT, 1336-1405

Exhibitions

A conqueror's enchanting legacy [Timur and the princely vision at the Arthur M. Sackler Gallery] K. M. Burke. il *Smithsonian* 20:180 Ap '89

TIMURLENK *See* Timur, the Great, 1336-1405

TIN

Therapeutic use

Treatment with tin prevents the development of hypertension in spontaneously hypertensive rats. D. Sacerdoti and others. bibl f il *Science* 243:388-90 Ja 20 '89

TIN COMPOUNDS

See also

Organotin compounds

TIN INDUSTRY

See also

Tin mines and mining

TIN MACHINE (MUSICAL GROUP)

Bowie's bicoastal blitz. J. Ressner. il por *Rolling Stone* p24 Ag 10 '89

The dark soul of a new machine. D. Fricke. il *Rolling Stone* p137-9 Je 15 '89

TIN MINERS

See also

Labor unions—Tin miners

TIN MINES AND MINING

Turkey

Kestel: an early Bronze Age source of tin ore in the Taurus Mountains, Turkey. K. A. Yener and others. bibl f il map *Science* 244:200-3 Ap 14 '89

TIN ROOFS *See* Roofs and roofing

TINDALL, MARILYN *See* Percival, Marilyn Tindall

TINDER, GLENN

Can we be good without God? [cover story] il *The Atlantic* 264:68-72+ D '89

TING, JAMES H.

about

Forging new links. T. Fennell. il pors *Maclean's* 102:26-8 F 20 '89

Who is James Ting and what will he buy next? C. Hawkins. il por *Business Week* p33 F 13 '89

TING, K. H.

about

Bishop at center of Chinese church debate. W. W. Conard. por *Christianity Today* 33:52-3 My 12 '89

Bishop Ting and China's house churches. R. MacMillan. il *The Christian Century* 106:755-6 Ag 16-23 '89

TINGSTAD, MARK

about

Was it worth the risk? R. Demak. il pors *Sports Illustrated* 71:76-81+ D 18 '89

TINKER, JOHN

about

John Tinker at Graham Gallery. S. Ballatore. il *Art in America* 77:223+ O '89

TINKERTOYS

A Tinkertoy computer that plays tic-tac-toe. A. K. Dewdney. il *Scientific American* 261:120-3 O '89

TINLEY, SCOTT

about

Tips from the super jocks. P. Serrani. il pors *Gentlemen's Quarterly* 59:250-7 My '89

TINLING, TEDDY

Who's the best ever? il *World Tennis* 36:43-7 Mr '89

TINNING, MARYBETH

about

The bad mother. J. Egginton. il pors *Good Housekeeping* 208:119+ Ap '89

TINNITUS

Townshend, tinnitus and rock & roll. E. Murphy. *Rolling Stone* p101 Jl 13-27 '89

Unrelenting sounds for tinnitus sufferers. il *Aging* no359:33 '89

What's the buzz? J. Poppy. il *Esquire* 111:77-9 Ap '89

When bells are ringing (but there aren't any bells). V. Modeland. il *FDA Consumer* 23:8-12 Ap '89

TINSLEY, ADRIAN

(jt. auth) See Kaplan, Sheila, and Tinsley, Adrian

TINSLEY, ALISON

Mountain running: the peak justifies the means. il por *Women's Sports & Fitness* 11:66 N/D '89

TINSLEY PRIZE

Ewen and Purcell win Tinsley Prize. P. H. Andersen. *Physics Today* 42:92+ Ap '89

TINTING

See also

Photographs—Coloring

TINTYPES

The humble tintype. il *American History Illustrated* 24:46-7 S/O '89

Tinker tailor. K. Heyman. il *American Heritage* 40:106-13 N '89

TINY MOOSE FARM

Successful family farm. J. Patrick. il *Successful Farming* 87:54-6 N '89

TINY TOWN (COLO.)
Tiny Town's big comeback. C. F. Black. il map *Americana* 17:28-33 Jl/Ag '89
TIPPETT, SIR MICHAEL, 1905-
about
New Year [opera] Reviews
  New York il 22:83-4 N 27 '89. P. G. Davis
  The New Yorker 65:114-17 N 20 '89. A. Porter
  Opera News il pors 54:22+ O '89. N. Lebrecht
Tippett's New Year. N. Lebrecht. il pors *Opera News* 54:22+ O '89
TIPPETT, VERONICA
Dreamtime stories. il *The Courier (Unesco)* 41:12-15 D '88
TIPPING
A few tips on shipboard tipping. il *Travel Holiday* 172:12 S '89
Leaving tips [mandatory service charge imposed by restaurants] W. Cole. il *Time* 133:54 F 27 '89
Tip sheet [holiday season] R. J. Katz. il *New York* 22:54-6+ D 18 '89
Tips on tipping. J. D. White. *Black Enterprise* 19:82 Mr '89
Waiting for nodough [case against tipping] Z. Citron. *The New Republic* 200:9-10 Ja 2 '89
TIPTON, BILLY, 1914-1989
about
Death discloses Billy Tipton's strange secret: he was a she. P. Chin. il pors *People Weekly* 31:95+ F 20 '89
Death reveals secret of dad, 74: he was a woman. por *Jet* 75:28 F 20 '89
TIRAMI SU (NEW YORK, N.Y.: RESTAURANT) *See* New York (N.Y.)—Restaurants, nightclubs, bars, etc.
TIRE DEALERS
See also
  Black tire dealers
TIRE INDUSTRY
See also
  B.F. Goodrich Co.
  Cooper Tire & Rubber Company
  Firestone Tire & Rubber Co.
  Goodyear Tire & Rubber Company
  Hoosier Racing Tire Company
  Uniroyal Goodrich Tire Co.
Acquisitions and mergers
International aspects
Can Bridgestone make the climb? [acquisition of Firestone] Z. Schiller. il *Business Week* p78-9 F 27 '89
That screeching is Michelin doing a U-turn [buying Uniroyal Goodrich] S. Toy and Z. Schiller. il *Business Week* p50 O 9 '89
Why Bridgestone's chairman is making tracks to Akron [T. Eguchi transferred to Firestone] Z. Schiller. il por *Business Week* p32-3 N 20 '89
Management
Multifactor productivity advances in the tires and inner tubes industry. D. Litz and L. Moore. bibl f il *Monthly Labor Review* 112:19-27 Je '89
France
See also
  Michelin et Cie
Japan
See also
  Bridgestone Corp.
TIRE PRESSURE GAGES
Inflated claims [bicycle tires] F. Berto. il *Bicycling* 30:172+ Je '89
Variable tire pressure saves roads. B. Calder. il *Popular Science* 234:140 Mr '89
TIREDNESS *See* Fatigue
TIRES, AUTOMOBILE
See also
  Tire pressure gages
All about snow tires. B. Glenne. il *Skiing* 42:52+ D '89
Big blue meets the purple eagle eaters [Goodyear and Hoosier vie for NASCAR Winston Cup market] L. Griffin. il *Car and Driver* 34:221-2+ Je '89
Great tires, blimp to come [Hoosier Racing Tire vs. Goodyear] J. Harris. il por *Forbes* 143:288+ My 29 '89
Radial and bias-ply tires: nix on mix? *Popular Science* 234:42 F '89
Tire siping question. P. Brand. il *The Family Handyman* 39:84-5 F '89
Tread safely. B. Markovich. il *Home Mechanix* 85:82-5+ O '89
Testing
A gripping performance [five of the best 205/60VR-15s] K. Reynolds. il *Road & Track* 41:102-3+ D '89
Quiet tires [Goodyear Eagle GA radial] B. Nadel. il *Popular Science* 235:32 O '89
A tire for all seasons [all-season performance tires] N. Bissoon Dath and C. Csere. il *Car and Driver* 35:99-101+ N '89
TIRES, BICYCLE
Tire dynamics. C. Kyle. il *Bicycling* 30:178+ Je '89
Care
Foam-filled bike tires don't roll so merrily along [No-Mor Flats] il *Consumer Reports* 54:285 My '89
No more flats! F. Zahradnik and J. Langley. il *Bicycling* 30:67-8+ S '89

Testing
Clincher tire buyer's guide [special section] F. Zahradnik. il *Bicycling* 30:154-6+ Je '89
TIRES, MOTORCYCLE
Inside mission to Michelin [radial tire development] K. Cameron. il *Cycle* 40:55-7+ F '89
One for the road [improving the suspension and tires on a Yamaha FZR600] T. Van Hooydonk. il *Cycle* 40:57-9+ O '89
Testing
Radials for motorcycles. S. F. Brown. il *Popular Science* 234:113 Je '89
TIRES, RUBBER
See also
  Inner tubes
  Tire pressure gages
TIRES, SPACEPLANE
Michelin subsidiary developing tires for hypervelocity aircraft program. il *Aviation Week & Space Technology* 130:269 Je 12 '89
TIRIAC, ION
Think smart. il *World Tennis* 36:38-9 Mr '89
TIRIÓ INDIANS
Just another day in paradise [M. Plotkin's work with the Tirió Indians of Suriname] D. D. Jackson. il *Reader's Digest* 134:166-8+ Ap '89
Searching for medicinal wealth in Amazonia [M. Plotkin's work] D. D. Jackson. bibl (p171) il pors *Smithsonian* 19:94-103 F '89
TIRMAN, JOHN
It takes two not to tango. il *The Nation* 248:520-2 Ap 17 '89
TISCH SCHOOL OF THE ARTS *See* New York University. Tisch School of the Arts
TISDALE, LYN CAMIRE
George P. Elliott and the common reader. *The American Scholar* 58:421-8 Summ '89
TISDALE, SALLIE
Lives of the body. *Harper's* 279:38+ O '89
The only harmless great thing. il *The New Yorker* 64:38-40+ Ja 23 '89
TISHCHENKO, ARTUR A.
(jt. auth) *See* Vasyutin, Vladimir, and Tishchenko, Artur A.
TISHCHENKO, MARAT NIKOLAEVICH
about
Mil Bureau designing new medium transport helicopter to replace Mi-8. D. Hughes. *Aviation Week & Space Technology* 130:28-9 Je 5 '89
TISSUE INHIBITOR OF METALLOPROTEINASES
Antisense RNA-induced reduction in murine TIMP levels confers oncogenicity on Swiss 3T3 cells. R. Khokha and others. bibl f il *Science* 243:947-50 F 17 '89
A new cancer clue. R. Dolphin. il *Maclean's* 102:50 Mr 6 '89
TISSUE PLASMINOGEN ACTIVATOR *See* TPA (Drug)
TISSUE WELDING
Lasers used to weld tissue. *High Technology Business* 9:31 Je '89
TISSUES
See also
  Bone
  Cells
  Fetal tissue
  Muscle
  Plant cells and tissues
Breast cancer risk linked to dense tissue [research by Audrey F. Saftlas] K. Fackelmann. *Science News* 135:213 Ap 8 '89
Preservation
See Preservation of organs, tissues, etc.
TISSUES, FACIAL *See* Facial tissues
TITAN (LAUNCH VEHICLE) *See* Space vehicles—Propulsion systems
TITAN (SATELLITE) *See* Saturn (Planet)—Satellites
TITANIC (STEAMSHIP)
See also
  Titanic Memorial Museum (Sidney, Ohio)
Search for the Titanic [video games] N. Randall. il *Compute!* 11:110+ D '89
Photographs and photography
Descent to the Titanic. P. Skinner. il *Petersen's Photographic Magazine* 17:30-3 Mr '89
TITANIC MEMORIAL MUSEUM (SIDNEY, OHIO)
A great ship. K. S. Edwards. il por *Americana* 17:63-5 N/D '89
TITANIUM BICYCLES *See* Bicycles—Materials
TITHES
Sanders gives his church $1/4 million in tithes [football player's gifts to Paradise Baptist Church, Wichita, Kan.] il por *Jet* 76:51 S 25 '89
TITIAN, CA. 1488-1576
about
Hubris before the gods. M. K. Talley, Jr. il por *Art News* 88:75-6 My '89
TITLE IX REGULATIONS *See* United States. Dept. of Education

TITLES OF BOOKS, STORIES, ETC.
Title search. W. Safire. il *The New York Times Magazine* p16+ Mr 5 '89
Title search follow-up. W. Safire. il *The New York Times Magazine* p24+ Ap 2 '89
Titles can sell articles. C. Robinson. *The Writer* 102:20-1+ Ja '89
TITLING (MOTION PICTURES) *See* Motion pictures—Titling
TITLING (VIDEOTAPES) *See* Videotapes—Titling
TITMICE
Reaction norms in genetical ecology [variation in great tits] A. J. Van Noordwijk. bibl f il *BioScience* 39:453-8 Jl/Ag '89
TITTLE, Y. A. (YELBERTON ABRAHAM), 1926-
about
A reunion in friendship. il pors *Sports Illustrated* 71:12+ N 27 '89
TITTLE, YELBERTON ABRAHAM *See* Tittle, Y. A. (Yelberton Abraham), 1926-
TITUS ANDRONICUS [drama] *See* Shakespeare, William, 1564-1616
TIVNAN, EDWARD
Healing time sickness. il *American Health* 8:76-8+ Mr '89
John Wingate's hard fall: a onetime radio star ends up broke and homeless. il pors *New York* 22:50-5 Mr 13 '89
TIZIANO VECELLI *See* Titian, ca. 1488-1576
TIZIO LAMPS *See* Electric lamps
TJIAN, ROBERT
(jt. auth) *See* Mitchell, Pamela J., and Tjian, Robert
(jt. auth) *See* Turner, Richard, and Tjian, Robert
TLC BEATRICE INTERNATIONAL HOLDINGS, INC.
Black enterprise lists TLC Group as largest black-owned business. *Jet* 76:17 My 29 '89
TLC Beatrice is almost paid for. What's the next course? P. Finch. il por *Business Week* p33-4 N 20 '89
TM *See* Transcendental meditation
TMI NUCLEAR POWER PLANT (PA.) *See* Three Mile Island Nuclear Power Plant (Pa.)
TMJ SYNDROME
Jaw experts out of joint [American Dental Association's views on diagnosis and treatment] J. Pinkham. il *American Health* 8:38 D '89
A real pain in the . . . jaw. C. Schaeffer. *Changing Times* 43:84+ Je '89
Stress can be a jawbreaker. J. Frouman. il *Business Week* p128 S 11 '89
TMJ: when teeth bite back. M. I. Finney. il *Nation's Business* 77:65 Mr '89
TMJ—getting the help you need. *Glamour* 87:74 My '89
TNF *See* Tumor necrosis factor
TNT (EXPLOSIVE)
Bacteria that eat TNT [research by Pat Unkefer] M. M. Soviero. *Popular Science* 235:116 N '89
TO DREAM OF ROSES [film] *See* Motion picture reviews—Single works
TOA DOMESTIC AIRLINES CO. LTD.
See also
Japan Air System (Firm)
TOAD THE WET SPROCKET (MUSICAL GROUP)
Toad the Wet Sprocket. J. Ressner. il *Rolling Stone* p28 O 5 '89
TOADFISH
Evolution of urea synthesis in vertebrates: the piscine connection. T. P. Mommsen and P. J. Walsh. bibl f il *Science* 243:72-5 Ja 6 '89
TOAL, JEANNE M.
Success and the soft-hearted woman. il *Mademoiselle* 95:194-5+ O '89
TOAST
See also
Quality Croutons Inc.
TOBACCO
See also
Nicotine
Smokeless tobacco
Smoking
Anticancer tobacco? [transient gene expression system developed by Biosource Genetics] J. E. Rodgers. il *American Health* 8:16 S '89
Cancer-fighting tobacco plants? [transient gene expression system developed at Biosource Genetics Corp.] K. Fackelmann. *Science News* 135:238 Ap 15 '89
Visual detection of transposition of the maize element Activator (Ac) in tobacco seedlings. J. D. G. Jones and others. bibl f il *Science* 244:204-7 Ap 14 '89
TOBACCO INDUSTRY
See also
American Brands, Inc.
Cigarette industry
Philip Morris, Inc.
R. J. Reynolds Tobacco Co.
Tobacco Institute
Big Tobacco's toughest road [activists and lawmakers launch new attacks on smoking] A. Plattner. il map *U.S. News & World Report* 106:26 Ap 17 '89

Acquisitions and mergers
International aspects
Smoke signals on BAT and American Brands. G. G. Marcial. il *Business Week* p98 S 11 '89
Finance
Beverages and tobacco. E. Giltenan. il *Forbes* 143:100+ Ja 9 '89
Public relations
A new tobacco alliance [smoking industry looks to blacks for support] M. Miller. il *Newsweek* 113:20 F 13 '89
Great Britain
See also
B A T Industries plc
Imperial Tobacco Ltd.
Switzerland
See also
Davidoff & Cie
TOBACCO INSTITUTE
Fighting fire with P.R. [cigarette fire safety legislation] M. Levin. il *The Nation* 249:52-5 Jl 10 '89
TOBACCO JARS AND BOXES
See also
Snuffboxes, bottles, etc.
TOBACCO MOSAIC VIRUS *See* Viruses, Plant
TOBACCO PIPES
Collectors and collecting
More than just blowin' smoke! Collecting antique tobacco pipes [cover story] B. Rapaport. il *Antiques & Collecting Hobbies* 93:40-1+ Ja '89
TOBIAS, ANDREW P.
Fill 'er up with no-fault, please. il *Time* 133:52-3 F 27 '89
Money angles. See issues of Time beginning June 19, 1989
TOBIAS, SHEILA
Tracked to fail. il *Psychology Today* 23:54-8+ S '89
TOBIAS, TOBI
The ballerinas and the bodybuilders: body and soul. il *Dance Magazine* 63:46 Jl '89
Dance. See issues of New York
TOBIN, BRIAN
about
In search of unity. R. Laver. il por *Maclean's* 102:12 Mr 6 '89
TOBY JUGS
Collectors and collecting
The many faces of Royal Doulton. il *USA Today (Periodical)* 118:71-5 N '89
LA TOC SUITES (SAINT LUCIA: RESORT) *See* Resorts—Saint Lucia
TOCH, HANS
Being tough versus being fair. *Society* 26:84 Jl/Ag '89
TOCOPHEROL *See* Vitamin E
TOCQUEVILLE, ALEXIS DE
about
Alexis de Tocqueville's Recollections. F. Braudel. *Society* 26:67-72 Mr/Ap '89
Exchanging a prison for a maze. R. Rosenblatt. il *U.S. News & World Report* 107:10-11 S 25 '89
TOCZYSKA, STEFANIA
about
Trusting herself. D. McGovern. il pors *Opera News* 53:16+ Ja 7 '89
TODAY [television program] *See* Television program reviews—Single works
TODD, BEVERLY
about
Actress Beverly Todd's son dies after nightclub brawl. il por *Jet* 76:54 Ap 10 '89
TODD, JOHN, 1939-
about
If you leave it to Mother Nature, says biologist John Todd, sewage doesn't have to go to waste. D. Chu. il pors *People Weekly* 32:133+ N 27 '89
This greenhouse effect just might be good for us. L. Jereski. il por *Business Week* p119-20 S 18 '89
TODD, LARRIE
If you want to see your shoe [story] il *'Teen* 33:38+ Je '89
TODDLER UNIVERSITY INC.
At Toddler University, the chairman is getting A's. J. R. Norman. il por *Business Week* p61 Ja 16 '89
TODDLERS *See* Children
TODMAN, TERENCE A.
about
Todman is Argentina envoy, Perkins is named director of U.S. Foreign Service. il pors *Jet* 76:36-7 My 22 '89
TODOROV, TZVETAN, 1939-
The core of the humanities: can the center hold? *Current (Washington, D.C.)* 318:12-17 D '89
Crimes against humanities [cover story] *The New Republic* 201:26-30 Jl 3 '89
TOES
See also
Bunions
TOGBA, J. N.
about
Health in Africa: a pioneer's point of view. P. Stroot. il por *World Health* p30 Ap '89

TOGNETTI, CAROLYN
about
Out of this world. M. Barrier. il por *Nation's Business* 77:13 Ag '89
TOILET PAPER
Collectors and collecting
All toilet paper is not created equal. H. L. Rinker. il *Antiques & Collecting Hobbies* 94:20+ Je '89
TOILET TRAINING
Going to the potty. B. Weissbourd. il *Parents* 64:123 Ja '89
TOILETS
See also
Outhouses
Cosmic relief [new toilet designs for the space station] A. R. Oberg. il *Omni (New York, N.Y.)* 11:20 Je '89
Frugal flush [water saving Cascade toilet] D. Scott. il *Popular Science* 234:152 Je '89
Relocating a toilet. il *Popular Mechanics* 166:114-15 Ap '89
Uncle Sam may regulate your plumbing. W. Giese. *Changing Times* 43:26-7 O '89
TOILETS, PUBLIC *See* Public comfort stations
TOKAMAKS
See also
Toroidal plasma
Budget squeeze causes fission in fusion labs [Compact Ignition Tokamak in jeopardy] M. Crawford. il *Science* 244:138-9 Ap 14 '89
TOKENS
The farm where the elephants plowed! [elephant tokens] E. Rochette. il *Antiques & Collecting Hobbies* 94:61-2 Jl '89
TŐKÉS, RUDOLF L.
Hungary on the way to democracy. il *The New Leader* 72:9-11 S 18 '89
Hungary's hazy future. il *The New Leader* 72:5-7 O 30 '89
A talk with Hungary's Imre Pozsgay [interview] por *The New Leader* 72:9-12 Je 12-26 '89
about
Between issues. *The New Leader* 72:2 S 18 '89
TOKHEIM CORP.
Out of the tank. T. Jaffe. *Forbes* 143:172-3 Mr 6 '89
TOKYO (JAPAN)
Buildings
See also
Tepia (Tokyo, Japan)
Crime
The Tokyo chainsaw massacre [accused murderer T. Miyazaki] T. Jackson. *The New Republic* 201:20-1 S 11 '89
Description
Touring from Tokyo. N. Sklarewitz. il *New Choices for the Best Years* 29:28-35 N '89
Economic conditions
Two teachers find a better life in Tokyo [Tim and Jane George] S. Seixas. il *Money* 18:92-5+ F '89
Education
A look inside a Japanese school. C. Rapoport. il *Fortune* 120:155+ D 4 '89
Hotels, motels, etc.
The recovery of ornament [Dai-Ichi Tokyo Bay Hotel] R. Kimball. il *Architectural Record* 177:132-7 My '89
Stores
Tokyo's 'spectacular' stores. D. Sudjic. il *World Press Review* 36:72 O '89
Streets
A city of towers and traditions. S. Zarmati. il *The Unesco Courier* 42:14-17 Ag '89
TOKYO AUDIO FAIR *See* Audio systems—Exhibitions
TOKYO INTERNATIONAL MOTOR SHOW *See* Automobiles—Exhibitions
TOKYO SHIBAURA ELECTRIC COMPANY, LTD. *See* Toshiba Corporation
TOKYO STOCK EXCHANGE
Hidden advantages [decision to allow U.S. over-the-counter stocks onto the Tokyo Stock Exchange] R. Phalon. il *Forbes* 144:40-1 N 13 '89
How d'ya say "liquidator" in Japanese? [I. Jacobs plays Tokyo-New York arbitrage in raids on Shaklee and Avon] S. Flack. il por *Forbes* 143:39-40 Je 12 '89
How to ride Japan Inc.'s raging bull. W. Glasgall and T. Holden. il *Business Week* p108 F 6 '89
In foreign markets, Reaganomics didn't get such high marks. G. Koretz. *Business Week* p26 F 6 '89
Japan's investors say the best may be yet to come. T. Holden. il *Business Week* p120+ D 25 '89-Ja 1 '90
Kamikaze capitalism [T. B. Pickens buys into Koito Manufacturing] M. Lewis. *The New Republic* 200:19-20 My 1 '89
A new kind of arbitrage [discrepancy between Tokyo and New York P/Es] E. Sturza. il *Forbes* 144:128 Jl 10 '89
An onslaught from the West: foreign traders and methods are rocking Japan's stock markets. T. Holden. il *Business Week* p140-1 Mr 20 '89
Premium pricing [Tokyo/New York arbitrage play in American Family Corp. shares] S. N. Chakravarty. *Forbes* 144:261 O 30 '89

Sayonara [New York-Tokyo arbitrage played by Honeywell] S. Flack. il *Forbes* 144:10 Ag 21 '89
The shudder heard round the world [consequences of Friday the 13th drop] M. Tharp. il *U.S. News & World Report* 107:62 O 30 '89
Thinking small in Tokyo. R. Phalon. il *Forbes* 143:198+ Je 26 '89
A top analyst sees Tokyo stocks soaring before the big bust [M. Ida] J. Ellis. il por *Money* 18:187-8 Mr '89
TOLAN, KATHLEEN
about
Kate's diary [drama] Reviews
New York 22:132 D 11 '89. J. Simon
TOLAN, SANDY
Showdown at Window Rock [cover story] il pors *The New York Times Magazine* p28-31+ N 26 '89
TOLAND, STEWART
Outcast of the hills [story] il *The Saturday Evening Post* 261:62-5+ Ja/F '89
Outcast of the hills [story] il *The Saturday Evening Post* 261:64+ Mr '89
TOLE PAINTING
Tole tales. F. de Dampierre. il *House & Garden* 161:50 Ag '89
TOLERANCE, IMMUNOLOGICAL *See* Immunological tolerance
TOLERANCE, RELIGIOUS *See* Religious liberty
TOLERANCE TO DRUGS *See* Drugs—Physiological effects
TOLERATION
Take a stand, or several. D. R. Carlin, Jr. *Commonweal* 116:457-8 S 8 '89
Tolerance. P. J. Ryan. il *America* 161:283 O 28 '89
The trouble with being open-minded [address, July 18, 1989] D. B. Lockerbie. *Vital Speeches of the Day* 55:723-7 S 15 '89
TOLL-FREE TELEPHONE SERVICE
National toll-free numbers. il *Consumers' Research Magazine* 72:31-4 O '89
Need information? Call Uncle Sam! S. Nielsen. il *Good Housekeeping* 209:250 O '89
TOLL ROADS
Fifteen miles—that'll be $1.50. R. Stodghill, II. il *Business Week* p54 Ag 14 '89
McHighways [private toll roads] H. Ullman. *The New Republic* 201:18-19 S 4 '89
The private path to new highways. D. J. Ward. il *Nation's Business* 77:19 Ag '89
TOLLESON, ROBIN
Al Jarreau: a troubadour's new tones. il por *Down Beat* 56:24-5 Ap '89
Caroline Davis Jr. High. il *Down Beat* 56:24 O '89
The Yellowjackets: Yellowjackets' new buzz. il *Down Beat* 56:20-2 N '89
TOLLETT, KENNETH
about
Black colleges are tools of affirmative action: Kenneth Tollett of Howard. por *Jet* 75:33 Mr 6 '89
TOLLIN, MIKE
about
The final season [film] Reviews
Maclean's il 102:85-6 N 13 '89. B. D. Johnson
TOLMICH, HERBERT
about
Pepperidge Farm's doughboy. D. Machan. il por *Forbes* 143:198-9 Mr 20 '89
TOLSTOY, LEO, GRAF, 1828-1910
about
Tolstoy and the pursuit of happiness. A. Valiunas. *Commentary* 87:33-41 Je '89
TOLTEC MOUNDS ARCHAEOLOGICAL STATE PARK (ARK.)
Uncovering Arkansas history. il *Southern Living* 24:20 My '89
TOM FOOL STAKES *See* Horse racing
TOM JONES [film] See Motion picture reviews—Single works
TOM PETTY AND THE HEARTBREAKERS (MUSICAL GROUP)
On the road with Tom Petty and the Heartbreakers: if it's Monday, this must be Miami. T. Petty and S. Hochman. il pors *Rolling Stone* p74-5+ O 5 '89
TOM SNYDER PRODUCTIONS
Putting parents in the loop with kids and computers [interview with T. Snyder] K. Kane. il por *Home Office Computing* 7:80+ Mr '89
TOM TOM CLUB (MUSICAL GROUP)
Tom Tom Club. R. Givens. il pors *Stereo Review* 54:100-1 D '89
TOMAHAWK (MISSILE) *See* Guided missiles
TOMATOES
See also
Cooking—Vegetables
Can you grow tomatoes where water is short? Yes. il *Sunset (Central West edition)* 182:230 My '89
Cherry tomatoes love summer. il *Southern Living* 24:84 Ap '89
The Diageotropica mutant of tomato lacks high specific activity auxin binding sites. G. R. Hicks and others. bibl f il *Science* 245:52-4 Jl 7 '89

TOMATOES—*cont.*

Early tomatoes. N. Bubel. il *Country Journal* 16:94-6+ My/Je '89

Growing the "forbidden" fruit [tomatoes on the window sill] D. G. Howard. il *The Saturday Evening Post* 261:30+ Ja/F '89

Ripe for a change [use of butanediamine to prolong shelf life; work of Peter J. Davies] T. Beardsley. *Scientific American* 261:26+ Jl '89

Square, gassed tomatoes and other modern myths. R. Sokolov. il *Natural History* p70-2 Jl '89

"Telephone pole" system gets sprawly tomatoes off the ground. il *Sunset (Central West edition)* 182:232 Je '89

Think small when growing tomatoes. G. Bria. il *The Saturday Evening Post* 261:90 Jl/Ag '89

Tomatoes from seed: an easy way to experiment. il *Sunset (Central West edition)* 182:162 F '89

The well-traveled tomato. R. Sokolov. il *Natural History* p84-8 Je '89

Anecdotes, facetiae, satire, etc.

Tomatoes: a tragedy [planting with zucchini] K. O'Donnell, Jr. il por *Organic Gardening* 36:79 S '89

Breeding

Restriction fragment length polymorphisms associated with water use efficiency in tomato. B. Martin and others. bibl f il *Science* 243:1725-8 Mr 31 '89

Diseases and pests

A quick cure for rotting tomatoes [blossom end rot] L. A. Weathers. il *Southern Living* 24:46 Jl '89

Tomato tumors: red light means grow [research by Theodore W. Tibbitts] I. Wickelgren. il *Science News* 135:23 Ja 14 '89

Ripening

Helping tomatoes ripen in fall. il *Sunset (Central West edition)* 183:210 O '89

TOMATOES, CANNED

Canned tomatoes. il *Consumer Reports* 54:246-9 D '89

Canned tomatoes: does the name on the can matter? il *Consumer Reports* 54:472-5 Jl '89

TOMATOES, DRIED

Tomato leather. R. Creasy. il *Organic Gardening* 36:32-3 Jl/Ag '89

TOMBAUGH, CLYDE, 1906-

about

Planet X (Y . . . Z)? L. Frazer. il por *Ad Astra* 1:13 S '89

TOMBS

See also
Mayas—Tombs

Honduras

Copán: a royal Maya tomb discovered. R. A. Fasquelle and W. L. Fash. il map *National Geographic* 176:480-7 O '89

Hungary

See also
Nagy, Imre—Tomb

Ireland

First light at an Irish tomb [roof slit designed to catch sun's rays at solstice; research by Tom P. Ray] *Science News* 135:88 F 11 '89

Irish mist [tomb aligned with winter solstice; research by Tom P. Ray] J. Horgan. il *Scientific American* 260:22+ Ap '89

A place in the sun for the early Irish [tomb sited to receive sun on winter solstice] il *U.S. News & World Report* 106:13-14 F 6 '89

World's oldest (and quietest) observatory? [Irish tomb aligned with winter solstice; research by Tom P. Ray] il *Sky and Telescope* 78:241-2 S '89

Peru

Thor Heyerdahl [Mochica Indian tombs in El Purgatorio, Peru] P. Brock. il pors *People Weekly* 32:181-2+ D 11 '89

Soviet Union

See also
Nicholas II, Emperor of Russia, 1868-1918—Tomb

TOMKINS, CALVIN, 1925-

Profiles [M. Edelman] il por *The New Yorker* 65:48-50+ Mr 27 '89

TOMLIN, LILY

about

The search for signs of intelligent life in the universe [drama] Reviews
Maclean's il pors 102:37 Ja 16 '89. D. Turbide

TOMMASINI, ANTHONY, 1948-

Roll over, Wagner. il pors *The New York Times Magazine* p40-1+ S 24 '89

DA TOMMASO (NEW YORK, N.Y.: RESTAURANT) *See* New York (N.Y.)—Restaurants, nightclubs, bars, etc.

TOMMY [rock opera] *See* Townshend, Pete

TOMOGRAPHY

Aviation use

High-speed X-ray CT scanner could meet FAA's explosive detection requirements. B. W. Henderson. il *Aviation Week & Space Technology* 131:78-9 N 13 '89

USAF seeks aerospace applications for innovative X-ray tomography. B. W. Henderson. il *Aviation Week & Space Technology* 131:93+ Jl 31 '89

Geological use

Magma reservoir seen under ocean ridge [study by Mark S. Burnett and others] R. Monastersky. il *Science News* 135:326 My 27 '89

Industrial use

Diagnosing ailing highways [CAT scans] il *USA Today (Periodical)* 118:12 D '89

Medical use

3-D maps for surgeons [use of system devised by Michael Vannier in surgery on skull abnormalities] il *Life* 12:45-6 Je '89

The mind in motion [PET scans by Steven Petersen and Peter T. Fox; cover story] G. Montgomery. il *Discover* 10:58-61+ Mr '89

Neuroanatomical correlates of anticipatory anxiety [study of brain blood flow by positron emission tomography] E. M. Reiman and others. bibl f il *Science* 243:1071-4 F 24 '89

PET pictures produce a palette of anxiety [research by Eric M. Reiman] B. Bower. il *Science News* 135:116-17 F 25 '89

Paleontological use

Homing in on the longest animal [use of seismic tomography to find Seismosaurus fossils; work of David D. Gillette] R. Monastersky. *Science News* 136:413 D 23-30 '89

TOMPKINS, JANE P.

Fighting words. *Harper's* 278:33-5 Mr '89

TOMPKINS SQUARE PARK (NEW YORK, N.Y.)

How to shoot a riot [C. Patterson's video of riot] E. Shawn. il *Video* 13:50+ Ap '89

TOM'S OF MAINE, INC.

Hearts, minds and market share. L. Jereski. il por *Forbes* 143:80+ Ap 3 '89

TOMS RIVER (N.J.)

Crime

Blind faith [murder of M. Marshall; excerpt] J. McGinniss. il pors *Ladies' Home Journal* 106:62+ Ap '89

TONE DIALING *See* Dual-tone multifrequency signalling

TONE-LŌC

about

The new heroes of hip-hop. D. Gates. il pors *Newsweek* 113:66 Ap 10 '89

Rapping about the 'Wild thing,' Tone-Lōc crashes the pop party. il por *People Weekly* 31:115 Mr 20 '89

Tone-def. R. Tannenbaum. por *Rolling Stone* p31 Je 1 '89

Tone-Lōc: hanging with the homeboys. il por *Rolling Stone* p20 Jl 13-27 '89

TONELLI, DAN

about

Mileage junkies. S. Martin. il pors *Bicycling* 30:48-50+ Ap '89

TONELLO, FABRIZIO

Lobbing one into the Kremlin. *The Nation* 249:445-6 O 23 '89

TONELSON, ALAN

The Democratic Party and foreign policy: a proposed manifesto. *Current (Washington, D.C.)* 317:25-34 N '89

The end of internationalism? *The New Republic* 200:23-5 F 13 '89

TONELSON, ALAN, AND LAYNE, CHRISTOPHER

Divorce, alliance-style. *The New Republic* 200:23-5 Je 12 '89

TONER, MIKE

Opening the door to the unknown. il *National Wildlife* 27:34-6 Je/Jl '89

TONEY, MICHAEL D., AND KIRSCH, JACK F.

Direct Brønsted analysis of the restoration of activity to a mutant enzyme by exogenous amines. bibl f il *Science* 243:1485-8 Mr 17 '89

TONGASS NATIONAL FOREST (ALASKA)

Prevention travelers go prospecting for majestic scenery. il *Prevention (Emmaus, Pa.)* 41:83-6 D '89

TONGUE

See also
Taste

What your tongue tells about your health [views of Stephen A. Mitchell] L. C. Ragan. *Good Housekeeping* 209:255 O '89

THE TONIGHT SHOW [television program] *See* Television program reviews—Single works

TONKA CORP.

Keep on truckin'. S. B. Weiner. il por *Forbes* 144:220-1 O 16 '89

TONNESSEN, DIANA

Crazy about oat bran. il *Health (New York, N.Y.)* 21:32+ Ap '89

TONSTAD, LARS

Isolated in the 'refrigerator'. *World Press Review* 36:58 Jl '89

TONTO NATIONAL FOREST (ARIZ.)

Workman Creek Falls, Arizona. R. H. Mohlenbrock. il map *Natural History* p86-9 Mr '89

TONY AWARDS

'Black and blue' earns ten Tony nominations. il *Jet* 76:52 My 22 '89

TONY GODWIN MEMORIAL AWARD *See* Editors and editing—Awards

TONY LAMA COMPANY
U.S. shoe firms thrive in high-quality market. J. E. Bahls. il *Nation's Business* 77:38-40 F '89
Urban Cowboy II. K. Hannon. il *Forbes* 143:189-90 Mr 20 '89

TOOBIN, JEFFREY
How hot is it? *The New Republic* 201:12-14 Ag 7-14 '89

TOOKEY, CHRISTOPHER
The charge of the Angry Brigade. il *National Review* 41:41-4 N 24 '89

TOOL BOXES, RACKS, ETC.
Organized snail or truck [tool caddies] il *Sunset (Central West edition)* 181:70-1 D '88

TOOL CATALOGS *See* Catalogs, Commercial

TOOL HANDLES
Saving a tool by replacing the handle. il *Sunset (Central West edition)* 183:194-5 S '89
    Anecdotes, facetiae, satire, etc.
Those #!*?@! tool handles. R. Jager. il *Country Journal* 16:66-7 Jl/Ag '89

TOOL INDUSTRY
    See also
    Black & Decker Corp.

TOOL SHEDS *See* Sheds

TOOLS
    See also
    Cutting tools
    Files and rasps
    Garden equipment
    Hammers
    Levels (Tools)
    Nail guns
    Paint and varnish removers
    Painting, Industrial and practical—Equipment
    Planes and planing
    Pneumatic tools
    Screwdrivers
    Stone implements and weapons
    Wrenches
12 innovative home shop products. T. Sweeney. il *Home Mechanix* 86:82-4+ Mr '89
12 tools for fixing your eighties car. M. Allen. il *Popular Mechanics* 166:65-7 S '89
Brawny bench tops [woodworking power tools] P. McCafferty. il *Popular Science* 235:92-4+ Jl '89
Discovering tools. R. N. Hoffman. *Workbench* 45:4 Mr/Ap '89
Gadget gallery. D. Mowitz. il *Successful Farming* 87:26-9 Ap '89
Gifts for growing workshops: presents to delight any handyperson. il *Better Homes and Gardens* 67:125 N '89
Going cordless. D. Moreau. il *Changing Times* 43:81-2 Je '89
Hand work [special section] il *Popular Mechanics* 166:71-6+ N '89
Helpful hardware [automobile tools] il *Home Mechanix* 85:86+ O '89
Three stationary power tools [Grizzly Table Saw, Kity K-5, Shopsmith Scroll Saw] L. Okrend. il *Workbench* 45:88-91 Mr/Ap '89
Tool tests. See issues of Popular Mechanics beginning January 1986
Tools for the beginner. D. Sprockett. il *Flower and Garden* 33:46 N/D '89
The tyro's tool kit [cover story] R. Freudenberger. il *The Mother Earth News* 118:62-3 Jl/Ag '89
Using tools. See issues of The Family Handyman
Versatile tools. R. Barnhart. il *Home Mechanix* 85:60-3 Ja '89
What's new: tools. V. E. Gilmore. See issues of Popular Science
    Collectors and collecting
The joys of collecting wooden tools. F. Johnson. il *Antiques & Collecting Hobbies* 94:59-61 S '89
    Maintenance and repair
How to repair. See issues of The Family Handyman beginning January 1988
    Sharpening
    See Sharpeners and sharpening
    Storage
    See also
    Sheds
    Tool boxes, racks, etc.

TOOMER, RONALD
    about
Roller coaster king Ron Toomer has a job he can't stomach. il por *People Weekly* 32:101-3 Jl 24 '89

TOOMEY, JOHN
    about
The collecting life [interview] il por *Antiques & Collecting Hobbies* 94:40-2 O '89

TOOP, DAVID
Shedding her past, Liza Minnelli reinvents herself as a postdisco dance queen. il por *Vogue* 179:260 O '89

TOOPS, CONNIE M.
National seashores [excerpt] il *National Parks* 63:46-7 Ja/F '89
Ride the rivers. il *National Parks* 63:39-41 Mr/Ap '89

TOOTH DECAY *See* Dental caries

TOOTH DECAY PREVENTION *See* Teeth—Care and hygiene

TOOTH ENAMEL
Scientists home in on tooth enamel gene [amelogenin; research by Eduardo C. Lau] *Science News* 135:269 Ap 29 '89

TOOTH IMPLANTS *See* Dentures

TOOTHBRUSHES
A $99 high-tech toothbrush [Interplak electric toothbrush] il *Consumer Reports* 54:505 Ag '89

TOOTSIE ROLL INDUSTRIES, INC.
The practical genius of penny candy [E. Gordon] S. Wilkinson. il pors *Working Woman* 14:98-9+ Ap '89
The tight ship lollipop [president E. Gordon] S. B. Weiner. il por *Forbes* 144:150 D 25 '89

TOP OF THE HILL [television program] *See* Television program reviews—Single works

TOP WATER LURES *See* Fishing lures, flies, etc.

TOPEROFF, SAM
Faked out by Zethel. il *The New York Times Magazine* p22+ Je 11 '89
Playing the cerebral game. il *The Atlantic* 264:115-18 N '89

TOPGUN AVIATION (FIRM)
Attention, Walter Mitty! Here's a sky-high dogfight for any would-be air ace. R. Arias. il pors *People Weekly* 32:70-2 N 20 '89

TOPLESS NIGHTCLUBS, BARS, ETC.
The naked truth. J. Truman. il *Vogue* 179:240-1 Je '89

TOPMINNOWS
Fitness differences among remnant populations of the endangered Sonoran topminnow. J. M. Quattro and R. C. Vrijenhoek. bibl f il *Science* 245:976-8 S 1 '89

TOPOGRAPHIC MAPS
    See also
    Contours (Cartography)
    London Topographical Society
New maps for hikers and bikers [Western States] *Sunset (Central West edition)* 182:52-3 Ja '89

TOPOGRAPHIC PAINTING
Antiques: topographical porcelains. S. Drummond. il *Architectural Digest* 46:228-33+ Ap '89

TOPOISOMERASES *See* Isomerases

TOPOLNICKI, DENISE M.
Do marketers control what we see? il *Psychology Today* 23:73-5 Je '89
Tee time for corporate women. il *Working Woman* 14:142+ Je '89
Workaholics: are you one? *Psychology Today* 23:25 Jl/Ag '89

TOPOLOGY
    See also
    Catastrophe optics
    Graph theory
    Manifolds (Mathematics)
Inside moves [polyhedral sphere eversion; cover story] I. Peterson. il *Science News* 135:299+ My 13 '89
Knot physics. I. Peterson. *Science News* 135:174 Mr 18 '89
Linking doughnuts, soda straws and energy [work of Michael H. Freedman] I. Peterson. *Science News* 135:70 F 4 '89
Topology and formation of triple-stranded H-DNA. H. Htun and J. E. Dahlberg. bibl f il *Science* 243:1571-6 Mr 24 '89

TORAN, STACY, 1961-1989
    about
Obituary
Jet il pors 76:54-5 S 4 '89

TORCH SONG TRILOGY [film] *See* Motion picture reviews—Single works

TORCHES
Torch techniques [propane] K. Collier. il *The Family Handyman* 39:14-15 Ap '89

TORELL, JOHN
    about
Out of the fire. K. Hannon. il *Forbes* 144:10 O 2 '89
Unhealthy growth. J. Heins. il *Forbes* 143:56 F 20 '89

TORFASON, BEVERLEY
    about
Here's looking at you, kid. B. Amiel. il *Maclean's* 102:9 Ap 10 '89

TORIES, AMERICAN *See* American loyalists

TORNADO AIRPLANES *See* Airplanes, Military

TORNADOES
A 14-state barrage of twisters. E. Magnuson. il *Time* 134:32 N 27 '89
Tornado tapes [audio-visual materials] E. Brotak. *Weatherwise* 42:102 Ap '89
Tornado tracker [H. Bluestein] M. B. Roman. il por *Discover* 10:50-6 Je '89
Tornadoes: slow start, fast finish [1988] E. W. Ferguson and others. il maps *Weatherwise* 42:28-35 F '89
Wrath of nature. il *Newsweek* 114:47 N 27 '89

TORNADOES IN ART
Spouting off [N. Kahn's tornado sculpture at New York Hall of Science] B. Weber. il por *The New York Times Magazine* p110 Mr 19 '89

TORO COMPANY
Toro Co. S. L. Kirsch. il *Fortune* 120:106 N 20 '89

TOSCANINI, WALLY
about
Wally Toscanini: Milan's first lady of opera. C. Aillaud. il pors *Architectural Digest* 46:58+ Mr '89

TOSCHES, NICK
Playing the Killer. il pors *Vogue* 179:182-5 Jl '89

TOSHIBA CORPORATION
Will Sun get burned by its new partner? J. B. Levine. *Business Week* p26-7 Je 12 '89

TOSHIKO *See* Akiyoshi, Toshiko, 1929-

TOTAL ALLERGY SYNDROME *See* Environmental illness

TOTAL WORD (WORD PROCESSOR PROGRAM) *See* Word processors and processing—Programming

TOTALITARIANISM
See also
Fascism
Byzantium: the emperor's new clothes? [cover story] A. P. Kazhdan. bibl il map *History Today* 39:26-34 S '89
Post-totalitarianism. J. Pehe. il *New Perspectives Quarterly* 5:37-41 Wint '88/'89
Totalitarianism, dead and alive. S. Miller. *Commentary* 88:28-32 Ag '89
The withering away of the state? J. J. Kirkpatrick. il *New Perspectives Quarterly* 5:34-7 Wint '88/'89

TOTALLY HIDDEN VIDEO [television program] *See* Television program reviews—Single works

TOTE BAGS *See* Bags

TOTH, PETER WOLF
about
Whispering giants. D. R. Hopwood. il pors *Americana* 17:63-5 My/Je '89

TOTH, STEVE
Appliance clinic. See issues of Popular Mechanics

TOTZAUER, JOSEF
Love at first sound; ed. by Allen Rankin. *Reader's Digest* 135:191-4 O '89

TOUBY, KATHLEEN A.
about
Trial and elegance. L. Rosch. il por *Working Woman* 14:90-1 F '89

TOUBY & SMITH P.A.
Trial and elegance [attorney K. A. Touby] L. Rosch. il por *Working Woman* 14:90-1 F '89

TOUCH
Brain changes [area in the brain responsible for sense of touch shows adaptability to injury; work of Michael Merzenich] J. Rubin. *Psychology Today* 23:26 Mr '89
Different strokes . . . [tactile stimulation of premature infants; research by Tiffany M. Field and Saul M. Schanberg] T. Beardsley. *Scientific American* 261:34+ S '89
Genetic control of differentiation of the Caenorhabditis elegans touch receptor neurons. M. Chalfie and M. Au. bibl f il *Science* 243:1027-33 F 24 '89
That magic touch. N. S. Schwartzberg. il *Parents* 64:87-90+ F '89

TOUCH, THERAPEUTIC *See* Mental healing

TOUCH FOOTBALL
Replaying Super Bowl III, Namath and the '69 Jets meet and beat the Colts again [Legends Bowl] T. Nugent. il pors *People Weekly* 32:56-7 N 13 '89

TOUCH-TONE DIALING *See* Dual-tone multifrequency signalling

TOUCHET, ALEXIS
Making petits fours at Ritz-Escoffier. il *Gourmet* 49:102-5+ N '89

TOUGH, ALLEN
Selecting priorities for a positive future. il *The Futurist* 23:59 Mr/Ap '89

TOUGHNESS (PSYCHOLOGY)
To beat stress, don't relax: get tough [research by Richard Dienstbier] L. Miller. il *Psychology Today* 23:62-3 D '89

TOULOUSE-LAUTREC, HENRI DE, 1864-1901
about
Historic houses: Henri de Toulouse-Lautrec: the painter's ancestral home in Albi. S. M. Alsop. il *Architectural Digest* 46:114-19+ Ja '89

TOUR DE FRANCE (RACE) *See* Bicycle racing—France

TOUR DE TRUMP (RACE) *See* Bicycle racing

TOUR OF DUTY [television program] *See* Television program reviews—Single works

TOURAINE, ALAIN
Neo-modern ecology. il *New Perspectives Quarterly* 6:33-6 Spr '89

TOURING, AUTOMOBILE *See* Automobile touring

TOURING BICYCLES *See* Bicycles

TOURING THEATER *See* Theater, Traveling

TOURISM *See* Tourist trade

TOURIST ART *See* Imitation art

TOURIST TRADE
See also
Resorts
Travel—Economic aspects
Travel agencies and agents
Travel Companions International
Consumer watch. See issues of Travel Holiday beginning July 1987 through June 1989
Disney World without the wait. P. Plawin. il *Changing Times* 43:80-2+ Ap '89

Acquisitions and mergers
Is bigger better? S. Shane. *Travel Holiday* 171:6 Mr '89
Western Europe
Kicking sand in Club Med's face. S. Toy. il *Business Week* p59+ Ag 14 '89

Environmental aspects
All aboard? Not so fast . . . [community protests against Napa Valley Wine Train] K. Courtney. il *Sierra* 74:93-5 Mr/Ap '89
Antarctic tourism '89 [cover story] Y. Cardozo and B. Hirsch. bibl il map *Sea Frontiers* 35:282-91 S/O '89
Elephants in the vineyard [Napa Valley] P. Steinhart. il map *Audubon* 91:68-73 N '89

Ethical aspects
Getting refunds when a travel firm folds. H. Gieseking. il *Travel Holiday* 171:76-7 Je '89

History
Sights sacred and profane [19th century tourist attractions; interview with J. F. Sears] A. P. Sanoff. il por *U.S. News & World Report* 107:52 Ag 14 '89

International aspects
Breaking away [travel to exotic destinations] R. Dolphin. il *Maclean's* 102:46-7 Mr 13 '89
People who meet people [meet-the-people programs bring tourists together with residents] B. Wallraff. il *The Atlantic* 263:108+ Ja '89
The technological tourist. S. C. Florman. il *Technology Review* 92:18+ Ja '89

Study and teaching
Spotlight on schools. il *'Teen* 33:97 Ap '89

Antarctic regions
Antarctic tourism '89 [cover story] Y. Cardozo and B. Hirsch. bibl il map *Sea Frontiers* 35:282-91 S/O '89
Stains on the white continent. D. Thompson. il map *Time* 133:77 F 20 '89

Borneo
It's a jungle in there [tourist walkway in Kinabalu National Park] E. McGowan. il *Travel Holiday* 172:26-7 Ag '89

California
See also
Palm Springs (Calif.)—Tourist trade
All aboard? Not so fast . . . [community protests against Napa Valley Wine Train] K. Courtney. il *Sierra* 74:93-5 Mr/Ap '89
Elephants in the vineyard [Napa Valley] P. Steinhart. il map *Audubon* 91:68-73 N '89

Caribbean region
Amazing boon. L. Mosher. il *Américas* 41 no2:32-40 '89
The Caribbean after Hugo. J. Popkin. il *U.S. News & World Report* 107:110-11 O 16 '89
Rebuilding paradise after Hugo. N. R. Gibbs. il map *Time* 134:90-2 D 4 '89
Training for business success. E. G. Graves. il *Black Enterprise* 19:8 My '89

China
Postmodern tours. J. Krich. il por *Mother Jones* 14:42-4 Jl/Ag '89

Cuba
Cuba says, 'Come on down'. M. Ambroise-Rendu. il *World Press Review* 36:62 My '89
White sand, blue seas—and big dreams. S. McGuire. il *Newsweek* 113:37 Ja 9 '89

Cyprus
See also
Saint Napa (Cyprus)—Tourist trade

Developing countries
The hordes' prayer [alternative tourism] J. Hooper. il *Mother Jones* 14:45-6 F/Mr '89
Third world tourism. *World Press Review* 36:50-1 Je '89

Florida
See also
Orlando (Fla.)—Tourist trade

France
See also
Saint-Tropez (France)—Tourist trade

Jamaica
Weathering the storm [effect of Hurricane Gilbert] G. Young. il *Travel Holiday* 171:85-6 My '89

Japan
Yen-stretching in Japan. *Sunset (Central West edition)* 182:44 My '89

Mexico
In deepest Gringolandia [cover story] B. Shacochis. il *Harper's* 279:42-50 Jl '89

Nepal
The hordes' prayer [alternative tourism] J. Hooper. il *Mother Jones* 14:45-6 F/Mr '89

New York (State)
See also
Pulaski (N.Y.)—Tourist trade

Saint Croix (Virgin Islands of the U.S.)
St. Croix's ravaged tourism [Hurricane Hugo] G. DeGeorge. il *Business Week* p47 O 9 '89

South Carolina
See also
Charleston (S.C.)—Tourist trade

TOURIST TRADE—*cont.*
Spain
An Anglo-Spanish nightmare [British tourists] R. Alan. *The New Leader* 72:10-11 N 13 '89
United States
See Tourist trade
TOURNAMENTS
See also
Baseball, College—Tournaments
Basketball, College—Tournaments
Basketball, High school—Tournaments
Bowling, Professional—Tournaments
Bridge (Game)—Tournaments
Checkers (Game)—Tournaments
Go (Game)—Tournaments
Golf—Tournaments
Hockey—Tournaments
Hockey, College—Tournaments
Horseshoe pitching—Tournaments
Rugby—Tournaments
Soccer—Tournaments
Soccer, College—Tournaments
Table hockey—Tournaments
Tennis—Tournaments
Volleyball—Tournaments
Wrestling—Tournaments
Wrestling, College—Tournaments
TOURNIER, MICHEL
about
Books. J. Updike. *The New Yorker* 65:92-6 Jl 10 '89
TOURS, ART *See* Art tours
TOURS, GARDEN *See* Garden tours
TOURS, INDUSTRIAL *See* Industrial tours
TOURS, MOTION PICTURE STUDIO *See* Motion picture studio tours
TOURS, TELEVISION STUDIO *See* Television studio tours
TOUSIGNANT, DOUG
ISDN prototyping telephone (I) [cover story] il *Radio-Electronics* 60:35-40 My '89
TOUSIGNANT, DOUG, AND SLIGER, KEN
ISDN prototyping telephone (II). il *Radio-Electronics* 60:61-6 Je '89
TOUSSAINT, DANIELLE, AND MORETTI, LAURA
Wild, wild horses: westerners rally to save the last roaming herds. il por *Utne Reader* p100-1 Ja/F '89
TOUSSAINT, EDDY
about
Toussaint company is squeezed for funds. K. Greenaway. il *Dance Magazine* 63:22 O '89
TOUSSIE, SAM
about
Jeans in the genes. P. Patton. il por *New York* 22:40-4+ My 22 '89
TOUVIER, PAUL
about
L'affaire Touvier: opening old wounds. T. Morgan. il pors *The New York Times Magazine* p32-3+ O 1 '89
Scandalous sanctuary. R. Marshall. il por *Newsweek* 113:44 Je 5 '89
TOWBOATS *See* Tugboats
TOWEL RACKS, RINGS, ETC.
How to install a towel bar. R. Capotosto. il *Popular Mechanics* 166:111-12 Je '89
TOWELS
Decorating with dish towels. il *Good Housekeeping* 209:114-15+ Jl '89
TOWER, JOHN
about
Bush league. J. Klein. il pors *New York* 22:16+ Mr 13 '89
Bush risks his chips on Tower. T. M. DeFrank. il *Newsweek* 113:19 F 20 '89
Capitol showdown [with editorial comment by Kevin Doyle] M. Nemeth. il pors *Maclean's* 102:2, 22-3 Mr 6 '89
The credibility gap that keeps on growing. por *U.S. News & World Report* 106:12 F 13 '89
Defense: Tower won't have much room to maneuver. D. Griffiths. *Business Week* p39 F 13 '89
Doves' golden silence. J. D. Isaacs. *The Bulletin of the Atomic Scientists* 45:4 Je '89
Drawing the line. W. Shapiro. il *Time* 133:18-19 Mr 13 '89
Fit for the Cabinet? D. R. Carlin, Jr. il *Commonweal* 116:136-7 Mr 10 '89
Friendship has limits. M. B. Carlson. il por *Time* 133:30-1 F 20 '89
Hamilton made me do it. M. Greenfield. il *Newsweek* 113:88 Mr 20 '89
Holier than everyone. L. Martz. il por *Newsweek* 113:22-3 Mr 13 '89
In the wake of the Tower wars. G. Borger. il pors *U.S. News & World Report* 106:44-6 Mr 13 '89
The iron triangle. *The Nation* 248:37 Ja 9-16 '89
Is my SecDef drunk? W. F. Buckley. *National Review* 41:62 Ap 7 '89
Is this goodbye? [cover story; special section] il pors *Time* 133:18-22+ Mr 6 '89

Letter from Washington. E. Drew. *The New Yorker* 65:97-100+ Mr 20 '89
Measuring character in the headlines. J. M. Wall. *The Christian Century* 106:275-6 Mr 15 '89
Missing the Tower story. T. Eastland. il *The American Spectator* 22:34-6 My '89
Notes and comment. *The New Yorker* 64:17-18 Ja 2 '89
On the fitness of Tower. W. F. Buckley. *National Review* 41:54-5 Mr 24 '89
Oratory in the modern Senate. A. Heard. il *The American Spectator* 22:14-15 My '89
A 'radical' reformer? G. Hackett. por *Newsweek* 113:19 Ja 23 '89
The reign of the accusers. G. F. Will. il *Newsweek* 113:76 Mr 13 '89
'Republicans are thirsting for blood'. R. Fly and D. Harbrecht. il por *Business Week* p39 Mr 20 '89
Saint George and the congressional dragon. *National Review* 41:10-11 Mr 24 '89
A setback for Bush. J. Bierman. il pors *Maclean's* 102:34-5 Mr 20 '89
So much for bipartisanship. R. Lacayo. il pors *Time* 133:20-1 Mr 13 '89
Storming the Tower. G. Borger. il pors *U.S. News & World Report* 106:37-9 Mr 6 '89
Tower play. H. Hertzberg. *The New Republic* 200:4+ Mr 27 '89
The Tower precedent. S. Garment. *Commentary* 87:42-8 My '89
Tower says administration to link arms control stance, strategic goals. P. A. Gilmartin. *Aviation Week & Space Technology* 129:23 Mr 6 '89
The Tower soap opera. J. Barry. il por *Newsweek* 113:17 F 13 '89
Tower supports SDI, citing Soviet antimissile advances. *Aviation Week & Space Technology* 130:20-1 Ja 30 '89
Tower vote set back again, leaving Pentagon stalled [with editorial comment] P. Mann. il por *Aviation Week & Space Technology* 130:7, 23-4 F 13 '89
Towering troubles. G. J. Church. il por *Time* 133:36 F 13 '89
Tower's troubles [cover story] T. Morganthau. il pors *Newsweek* 113:16-20+ Mr 6 '89
Washington notebook. D. Schorr. il *The New Leader* 72:3-4 Mr 6 '89
What did the swallows learn in Geneva? L. Galtney and C. Fenyvesi. il por *U.S. News & World Report* 106:27 F 20 '89
Wine, women and irony. M. Greenfield. il *Newsweek* 113:72 F 20 '89
Wine, women, and World War III. D. Neff. *Christianity Today* 33:15 Ap 7 '89
Anecdotes, facetiae, satire, etc.
A Modest Proposal for Cleansing our Publick Life of Impurities and Transgressions. H. Fairlie. il *The New Republic* 200:14-16 Mr 27 '89
State of the states. M. Ivins. il por *The Progressive* 53:40 Ap '89
TOWER CLOCKS *See* Clocks
TOWER OF BABEL
City-building and the benefits of Babel. J. W. Aageson. il *The Christian Century* 106:517-18 My 17 '89
What's wrong with Babel? L. Kass. *The American Scholar* 58:41-60 Wint '89
TOWERS, DEIRDRE
Dancevideo. See issues of Dance Magazine beginning November 1984
Grand Prix de Vidéo-Danse. il *Dance Magazine* 63:56-9 Mr '89
TOWERS
See also
Eiffel Tower (Paris, France)
TOWING
See also
Automobile boat trailers—Towing
Automobile trailers—Towing
Automobiles—Towing
Boats and boating—Towing
Fishing boats—Towing
Gliders (Aviation)—Towing
Tanks, Military—Towing
Adventures in pulling your weight. J. Skorupa. il *Popular Mechanics* 166:18+ F '89
TOWN & COUNTRY JEWELRY MFG. CO.
Town & Country. J. Slovak. il *Fortune* 119:90 Ap 10 '89
TOWN PLANNING *See* City planning
TOWNE, ROBERT, 1936-
about
Darkness at the edge of Towne. M. Sragow. il por *American Film* 14:40-5+ Ja/F '89
Tequila sunrise [film] Reviews
Mademoiselle il 95:91-2 F '89. R. Rosenbaum
The Nation 248:25-6 Ja 2 '89. S. Klawans
National Review 41:54 F 24 '89. J. Simon
Video il 13:94 S '89. R. Gehr

TOWNE, WILLIAM F., AND KIRCHNER, WOLFGANG H.
Hearing in honey bees: detection of air-particle oscillations. bibl f il *Science* 244:686-8 My 12 '89
TOWNES, EMILIE M.
Ida B. Wells-Barnett: an Afro-American prophet. *The Christian Century* 106:285-6 Mr 15 '89
TOWNHOUSE DECORATION *See* House decoration
TOWNHOUSES *See* City houses
TOWNHOUSES, REMODELED *See* Houses, Remodeled
TOWNLEY, PRESTON
Business and education reform [address, January 27, 1989] *Vital Speeches of the Day* 55:354-6 Ap 1 '89
TOWNS *See* Cities and towns
TOWNS, RESTORED *See* Villages, Restored
TOWNSELL, GINGER JACKSON
about
Arnie and Ginger. J. P. Blank. *Reader's Digest* 134:9-10+ Ja '89
TOWNSEND, ALISON
Mary's river: Wren, Oregon [poem] *Organic Gardening* 36:36 D '89
TOWNSEND, KATHLEEN
A rebirth of virtue: religion and liberal renewal. *The Washington Monthly* 21:36-7 F '89
TOWNSEND, LENA O.
Is your child learning-disabled? il *Essence* 20:118 O '89
TOWNSEND, ROBERT
about
Black stars shine in murder mystery 'The Mighty Quinn'. il pors *Jet* 75:46-8 F 20 '89
Knocking on Hollywood's door [cover story] B. Sharkey. il pors *American Film* 14:22-7+ Jl/Ag '89
TOWNSHEND, CHARLES
The first intifada: rebellion in Palestine, 1936-39. bibl il *History Today* 39:13-19 Jl '89
TOWNSHEND, PETE
about
"The iron man" from Pete Townshend. S. Simels. por *Stereo Review* 54:108+ O '89
Tommy [rock opera] Reviews
People Weekly il 32:52-3 S 11 '89
Townshend, tinnitus and rock & roll. E. Murphy. *Rolling Stone* p101 Jl 13-27 '89
TOWNSON, GEORGE W.
about
Frederick's of Hollywood trades its X rating for an R. K. Kerwin. il *Business Week* p64 D 11 '89
TOXIC SHOCK SYNDROME
Go with the flow [choosing the right tampon] *Prevention (Emmaus, Pa.)* 41:14 S '89
TOXIC SUBSTANCES *See* Poisons and poisoning
TOXIC SUBSTANCES IN INDUSTRY *See* Poisons and poisoning, Industrial
TOXIC TRADE WASTE DISPOSAL *See* Trade waste—Disposal
TOXIC WASTE DISPOSAL *See* Hazardous substances—Disposal
TOXICITY TESTING *See* Chemicals—Testing
TOXINS AND ANTITOXINS
See also
Aflatoxins
Cantharidin
Charybdotoxin
Cholera toxin
Conotoxins
Diphtheria toxin
Mycotoxins
Neurotoxins
Pertussis toxin
Psoralens
Red tide
Tetrodotoxin
Class II MHC molecules are specific receptors for staphylococcus enterotoxin A. J. A. Mollick and others. bibl f il *Science* 244:817-20 My 19 '89
Superantigens [stimulation of T cells by staphylococcal toxins; research by John Kappler and others] T. Beardsley. *Scientific American* 261:19-20 Ag '89
Vβ-specific stimulation of human T cells by staphyloccocal toxins. J. Kappler and others. bibl f il *Science* 244:811-13 My 19 '89
TOXOPLASMOSIS
Lethal look-alike unmasked, examined [Neospora and toxoplasmosis; research by Jitender P. Dubey] J. Raloff. *Science News* 136:71 Jl 29 '89
The silent danger of toxoplasmosis. S. Mahler. *McCall's* 116:109-10 My '89
Tracing the cat connection [danger during pregnancy; views of Robert McCabe] D. Groves. il *American Health* 8:102 Ja/F '89
TOY AND GAME INDUSTRY
See also
Blacks in the toy and game industry
Discovery Toys
Hasbro Inc.
Lionel Trains Inc.
Little Tikes Company

Mattel Inc.
Tonka Corp.
Tyco Toys, Inc.
Leisure and recreation. D. Fanning. il *Forbes* 143:168-9 Ja 9 '89

History
See also
Ives Manufacturing Corporation
Marketing
In the cutthroat world of toy sales, child's play is serious business [cover story] D. Stewart. il *Smithsonian* 20:72-6+ D '89

Germany
See also
Gebrüder Bing (Firm)
Germany (West)
See also
Gebrüder Märklin (Firm)
Japan
See also
Nintendo Co. Ltd.
TOY GUNS
War babies: a mother refuses her son toy guns. J. Zandy. il *Utne Reader* p120-1 N/D '89
TOY HOUSES *See* Doll houses
TOY SOLDIERS *See* Military miniatures
TOY STORES
See also
Toys R Us Inc.
Where Kids Shop (Firm)
Wisconsin Toy Co., Inc.
TOYNBEE, ARNOLD JOSEPH, 1889-1975
about
The history of Arnold Toynbee [address, November 13, 1988] G. F. Kennan. il *The New York Review of Books* 36:19-22 Je 1 '89
The prophet. H. R. Trevor-Roper. bibl f il *The New York Review of Books* 36:28-34 O 12 '89
TOYO KOGYO CO., LTD.
See also
Mazda Motor Corporation
TOYOTA (AUTOMOBILE) *See* Automobiles, Foreign
TOYOTA MOTOR CORPORATION
At Toyota, rank loses its privileged titles. J. Impoco. il *U.S. News & World Report* 107:40-1 Ag 21 '89
Murphy does $multimillion car commercials in Japan [Eddie Murphy] por *Jet* 77:36 O 23 '89
TOYOTA MOTOR CORPORATION. LEXUS DIVISION
The coming traffic jam in the luxury lane [Toyota Lexus and Nissan Infiniti] W. Zellner. il *Business Week* p78 Ja 30 '89
Here come Japan's new luxury cars [Lexus] A. L. Taylor, III. il *Fortune* 120:62-6 Ag 14 '89
Infiniti and Lexus: characters in a German nightmare. J. Templeman. il *Business Week* p64 O 9 '89
Taking the classic approach [Toyota Lexus and Nissan Infiniti luxury cars] M. Keller. il *Motor Trend* 41:213 My '89
Two days in boot camp—learning to love Lexus. W. Zellner. il *Business Week* p87 S 4 '89
TOYS
See also
Blocks (Toys)
Dolls
Educational toys
Etch A Sketch
G.I. Joe dolls
Military miniatures
Rocking horses, etc.
Teddy bears
Tinkertoys
Toy and game industry
War toys
Whirligigs
Yo-yos
Boys and dolls in Toyland. R. Givens. il *Newsweek* 114:99-100 N 27 '89
A circular saw for the budding family handyman. il *The Family Handyman* 39:44-5 N/D '89
Grandpa's gift [wooden wagon to make] B. Kieffer. il *The Family Handyman* 39:66-8+ Jl/Ag '89
A guide for us grandparents. R. B. Roufberg. il *New Choices for the Best Years* 29:77-9 D '89
In the cutthroat world of toy sales, child's play is serious business [cover story] D. Stewart. il *Smithsonian* 20:72-6+ D '89
The joys of toys, 1989. A. Finkelstein. il *Parents* 64:119-24+ N '89
Kids and toys. L. Salk. il *McCall's* 117:75+ N '89
Lotus racer. F. J. Badeaux. il *Workbench* 45:36-8+ N/D '89
Once upon a time in the future [designs for children] K. Korman. il *Video* 13:50+ Ag '89
The plush life [stuffed animal peddler R. Granata in New York City] R. Miller. il *New York* 22:25 My 29 '89
Star vehicles [development of Hasbro's Record Breakers toy cars] B. Kanner. il *New York* 22:20+ D 11 '89
Toy tug boat. F. J. Badeaux. il *Workbench* 45:33-5 N/D '89

TOYS—*cont.*
Treasures! 10 top toys [Christmas] R. B. Roufberg. il *Redbook* 174:38 D '89
The well-balanced playroom. R. B. Roufberg. il *Essence* 20:90+ N '89
Collectors and collecting
Automata: "toys" for adults. M. Jailer. il *Antiques & Collecting Hobbies* 94:70-4 O '89
The ever popular small toy auto. M. Jailer. il *Antiques & Collecting Hobbies* 94:43-8 D '89
Ives: the busy American toymaker [clockwork-driven toys] M. Jailer. il *Antiques & Collecting Hobbies* 93:36-8+ Ja '89
The many toys of Gebrüder Bing. M. Jailer. il *Antiques & Collecting Hobbies* 94:63-6 Ag '89
Toy flying machines: up they went! M. Jailer. il *Antiques & Collecting Hobbies* 94:37-41 Je '89
Toymakers Gebrüder Märklin. M. Jailer. il *Antiques & Collecting Hobbies* 94:30-3 Mr '89
Toys are ageless [collector H. Mueller] S. B. Green. il *Antiques & Collecting Hobbies* 94:62-3 My '89
TOYS R US INC.
Gains R Yours at Toys R Us. il *Money* 18:50 D '89
Superelf plans for Xmas. F. Rice. il *Fortune* 120:151 S 11 '89
TOZER, ELIOT
Love in blooms. il por *Modern Maturity* 32:56-60 O/N '89
TPA (DRUG)
Clot-busters bring bioelectrical benefits [research by Eli S. Gang and others] R. Weiss. *Science News* 136:182 S 16 '89
Clot-buster's cost-effectiveness questioned [TPA vs. streptokinase] R. Weiss. *Science News* 135:214 Ap 8 '89
Fluid flow stimulates tissue plasminogen activator secretion by cultured human endothelial cells. S. L. Diamond and others. bibl f il *Science* 243:1483-5 Mr 17 '89
Fortifying a protein through family ties [altered form of TPA; work of Joseph F. Sambrook] R. Cowen. *Science News* 136:23 Jl 8 '89
Genentech: a David that comes on like Goliath [fighting SmithKline Beecham's Eminase] J. Carey and J. O. Hamilton. il *Business Week* p165 O 30 '89
TPA (TETRADECANOYLPHORBOL ACETATE) *See* Phorbol esters
TPI ENTERPRISES, INC.
As long as the price is right. L. Gubernick. il por *Forbes* 143:82 My 29 '89
TRA VIGNE (SAINT HELENA, CALIF.: RESTAURANT) *See* Saint Helena (Calif.)—Restaurants, nightclubs, bars, etc.
TRABERT, GREG
about
Hard bodies, soft fabrics: laundry guru Greg Trabert says yes, you can have it all. il por *People Weekly* 31:99 My 15 '89
THE TRACEY ULLMAN SHOW [television program] *See* Television program reviews—Single works
TRACHEOTOMY
Arnie and Ginger [A. Hartman helps fellow tracheotomy patient G. Jackson obtain corrective surgery] J. P. Blank. *Reader's Digest* 134:9-10+ Ja '89
TRACHI, RICHARD
The return of the Brandy Bar. il *The Mother Earth News* 117:82-5 My/Je '89
TRACHTENBERG, DAVID J.
INF: the Soviets cheat. *National Review* 41:17 My 19 '89
TRACHTENBERG, PETER
The man who couldn't be faithful. il *Mademoiselle* 95:188-9+ My '89
TRACK AND FIELD ATHLETICS
See also
High jumping
Hurdle racing
Shotputting
Back on the track [TAC's USA/Mobil Outdoor Track Field Championships] K. Moore. il *Sports Illustrated* 70:26-7 Je 26 '89
Big show in Oslo [Bislett Games] M. Noden. il *Sports Illustrated* 71:26-8+ Jl 10 '89
A dynamic duo reigns in Spain [World Cup V] M. Noden. il *Sports Illustrated* 71:78+ S 18 '89
Field of dreams [running the 800 meter race at the World Veterans Games] G. Sheehan. il *Runner's World* 24:16 D '89
Florence Griffith Joyner: life in the fast lane [cover story] J. D. Cain. por *Essence* 19:48-50+ Mr '89
Forever young [Runner's World Masters Mile] M. Bloom. il *Runner's World* 24:36-41 My '89
A gathering of greyhounds [World Veterans Games] H. Higdon. il *Runner's World* 24:34-9 D '89
Go with the Flo [F. Griffith Joyner] S. Mansfield. il por *Vogue* 179:402-5+ Ap '89
The hares split [Meadowlands Invitational] M. Noden. il *Sports Illustrated* 70:42+ F 20 '89
The lady in waiting [middle distance runner V. Huber] M. Noden. il pors *Sports Illustrated* 70:73-4+ Je 5 '89

Missed opportunity [infighting on U.S. men's Olympic 4 x 100 relay team] M. Bloom. il por *Runner's World* 24:60-2+ Ja '89
Much sweeta for Aouita [Millrose Games] M. Noden. il por *Sports Illustrated* 70:32-4 F 13 '89
The natural [UCLA coach B. Larsen] B. Wischnia. il pors *Runner's World* 24:30-1+ Jl '89
No mo FloJo [retirement of F. Griffith Joyner] il por *Runner's World* 24:14 Je '89
A peach for the Apple [New York Track and Field Games] M. Noden. il *Sports Illustrated* 71:55 Jl 31 '89
The rat that roared [1500 meter runner J. Atkinson] B. Wischnia. il pors *Runner's World* 24:40-4+ O '89
Speed sports: the rush of getting fit—fast! [sprinting] il *Mademoiselle* 95:218-21 O '89
Team theme [relays] J. Henderson. il *Runner's World* 24:14 S '89
Tigers burning bright [LSU wins NCAA men's and women's titles] M. Noden. il *Sports Illustrated* 70:74+ Je 12 '89
The times of their lives [World Veterans Games] K. Moore. il *Sports Illustrated* 71:44-7 Ag 14 '89
To be young, gifted & fast [runner V. Huber; cover story] C. Brennan. il pors *Runner's World* 24:42-7 Mr '89
Track great Mal Whitfield lauded at USIA retirement. il por *Jet* 77:48 N 20 '89
Woman to watch [sprinter D. Sowell] B. Kevles. il por *Women's Sports & Fitness* 11:56 N/D '89
Worm warfare [running on a track with an earthworm] R. M. Owens. il *Runner's World* 24:120 O '89
The write stuff [columnist D. Patrick] B. Wischnia. il pors *Runner's World* 24:34-5+ Mr '89
Economic aspects
The Originally Amateur hour. P. Gambaccini. il *Sport (New York, N.Y.)* 80:95 Je '89
The spoils of victory [F. Griffith Joyner retires from track to pursue business opportunities] K. Moore. il pors *Sports Illustrated* 70:50-3+ Ap 10 '89
Ethical aspects
A day of reckoning [B. Johnson admits he took steroids] il pors *Maclean's* 102:32-3 Je 26 '89
A deepening scandal [physician J. Astaphan testifies on steroid use by B. Johnson] B. Wickens. pors *Maclean's* 102:49-50 Je 5 '89
A dirty coach comes clean [C. Francis testifies on steroid use by B. Johnson and other Canadian athletes] M. Noden. il pors *Sports Illustrated* 70:22-3 Mr 13 '89
Drugs and track [D. Robinson charges F. Griffith Joyner and C. Lewis with taking of illicit drugs] C. Neff. il pors *Sports Illustrated* 71:25-6 O 2 '89
Flo Jo confronts accuser on drug use allegations [D. Robinson] il por *Jet* 77:46 O 9 '89
From dream to nightmare [testimony by track coach C. Francis during Canadian government inquiry into steroid use by B. Johnson] A. Burfoot and B. Wischnia. il pors *Runner's World* 24:12 Je '89
He has suffered enough [B. Johnson facing lifetime ban and possible loss of 100 meter world record over steroid use] M. Noden. por *Sports Illustrated* 70:98 Je 26 '89
Moses blasts edict to strip Johnson's records. por *Jet* 76:46 O 2 '89
A revealing inquiry [testimony of J. Astaphan on runner B. Johnson's steroid use] M. Noden. il por *Sports Illustrated* 70:19 Je 5 '89
Sabotage at Seoul? [testimony on steroid use by B. Johnson] R. Dolphin. il por *Maclean's* 102:47 Mr 20 '89
The saga behind the shame [J. Scott describes J. Astaphan's role in B. Johnson's steroid use] J. Brant. il pors *Runner's World* 24:78-80 Ag '89
South Africa: the saga continues [runners suspended for attending track meet] A. Burfoot and B. Wischnia. il *Runner's World* 24:8-9 F '89
Starting over [B. Johnson to lose world records in drug use ruling] N. Underwood. il por *Maclean's* 102:66 S 18 '89
The steroid scandal [testimony of track coach C. Francis at Canadian inquiry; cover story; special section; with editorial comment by Kevin Doyle] il pors *Maclean's* 102:2, 36-42 Mr 13 '89
Whistle blower [track coach C. Francis, testifying during Canadian government inquiry, confirms B. Johnson's steroid use] por *Time* 133:50 Mr 13 '89
Photographs and photography
World Series [highlights from the indoor running season] il *Runner's World* 24:52-5 Je '89
Psychological aspects
Relax, you'll run faster [behavioral imagery technique; study by Scot Machlus and Richard O'Brien] J. C. Horn. il *Psychology Today* 23:22 Ja/F '89
Television broadcasting
See Television broadcasting—Sports
TRACK AND FIELD ATHLETICS RECORDS
See also
High jumping records
Hurdle racing records
He has suffered enough [B. Johnson facing lifetime ban and possible loss of 100 meter world record over steroid use] M. Noden. por *Sports Illustrated* 70:98 Je 26 '89

TRACK AND FIELD ATHLETICS RECORDS—*cont.*
Moses blasts edict to strip Johnson's records. por *Jet* 76:46 O 2 '89
Smashing! [world records broken by R. Kingdom in 110-meter hurdles and S. Aouita in 3,000 meters] M. Noden. il pors *Sports Illustrated* 71:16-19 Ag 28 '89
Starting over [B. Johnson to lose world records in drug use ruling] N. Underwood. il por *Maclean's* 102:66 S 18 '89

TRACK AND FIELD COACHES
See also
Larsen, Bob

TRACKBALLS (COMPUTER EQUIPMENT)
Trackball madness [ProPoint trackball and Microsoft Works] E. Shapiro. il *Byte* 14:129-30+ Mr '89

TRACKED VEHICLES
See also
Tanks, Military
Tractors

Agricultural use
Farming on the fast track [rubber-tracked machines curtail compaction] R. Fee. il *Successful Farming* 87:48E O '89

TRACKING (EDUCATION) See Ability grouping in education

TRACKING AND DATA RELAY SATELLITE SYSTEM See Communications satellites

TRACKING AND TRAILING
See also
Animal tracks and trails
Biotelemetry
Communications satellites—Tracking and trailing use
On the right track for muleys. W. L. Prothero. il *Outdoor Life* 184:78-9+ S '89
Probing secrets of small critters: fuchsia mice and bar-coded bees. L. Ware. il *Audubon* 91:12 Ja '89
Reading the earth [tracking mammals] D. Wescott. il *The Mother Earth News* 115:110-16 Ja/F '89

TRACKING OF AIRPLANES See Airplanes, Government— Tracking

TRACKING OF ARTIFICIAL SATELLITES See Artificial satellites—Tracking

TRACKING OF TRUCKS See Trucks—Tracking

TRACON (TERMINAL RADAR APPROACH CONTROL) See Radar in aviation

TRACOR, INC.
The education of Bobby Inman [LBO] K. Kelly. por *Business Week* p50 D 18 '89

TRACTION (AUTOMOBILES) See Automobiles—Traction; Automobiles, Foreign—Traction; Convertibles (Automobiles)—Traction

TRACTOR DRIVERS
See also
Children as tractor drivers

Anecdotes, facetiae, satire, etc.
Bill Eftink. B. Eftink. il *Successful Farming* 87:19 My '89

TRACTOR ENGINES
Fuel feeding
Ethanol and diesel fuel do mix. C. Peterson, Jr. *Successful Farming* 87 no4:64F Mr '89

TRACTOR INDUSTRY
See also
Caterpillar Inc.

TRACTOR PULLING
Ten things you never knew about tractor pulls. S. Rosenbloom. il *Sport (New York, N.Y.)* 80:105 F '89

TRACTOR TRAILER TRUCKS See Trucks

TRACTORS
Big bruisers come back to the farm. K. R. Sheets. il *U.S. News & World Report* 106:51+ Je 19 '89
Machines, accursed and wondrous. R. Kimber. il *Country Journal* 16:27-8 N/D '89
New Maxxums pack $150 million in improvements. il *Successful Farming* 87:44 D '89
Collectors and collecting
They love old tractors [cover story] D. Mowitz. il *Successful Farming* 87:12-13 mid-F '89
Equipment
Tank tactics. D. Mowitz. il *Successful Farming* 87:48F My '89
Four wheel drive
Birth of a new four-wheel-drive Massey tractor. *Successful Farming* 87:48M N '89
History
A golden anniversary salute to the H and M. M. Hood. il *Successful Farming* 87:70-1 O '89
Testing
Lawn tractors. il *Consumer Reports* 54:355-61 D '89
Lawn tractors: can they cut it? il *Consumer Reports* 54:368-73 Je '89
Mighty mower [John Deere 200 Series garden tractors] T. O. Bakke. il *Popular Science* 234:165 Je '89
Two for the turf [Kubota T1400 OHV and Honda RT 5000] B. Markovich. il *Home Mechanix* 85:70 Jl '89
Yard and garden tractors. D. Mowitz. il *Successful Farming* 87:44-7 mid-Mr '89
Yard tractors. M. Ferrara. il *Organic Gardening* 36:51-3+ Jl/Ag '89

TRADE, BALANCE OF See Balance of trade

TRADE AND DEVELOPMENT CONFERENCE (UNITED NATIONS) See United Nations Conference on Trade and Development

TRADE CLAIMS (DEBT)
Where vultures dare. H. Rudnitsky. *Forbes* 144:56 O 16 '89

TRADE CONFERENCES See Economic conferences

TRADE DEFICITS See Balance of trade

TRADE DISCOUNT See Discount, Trade

TRADE FAIRS
China trade [Chinese-U.S. trade expo organized by W.-J. Jeffries] L. Gubernick. il por *Forbes* 144:287 O 16 '89
Canada
Canada's trade shows: sales leads on display. *Nation's Business* 77:71 S '89

TRADE FOR PEACE, INC.
The coffee connection [nonviolent opposition to U.S. embargo against Nicaraguan imports] L. Cizewski. il *The Progressive* 53:46 N '89

TRADE JOURNAL ARTICLES See Periodical articles

TRADE LOADING
The $600 million cigarette scam [RJR Nabisco creates bogus profits through trade loading] C. J. Loomis. il *Fortune* 120:89+ D 4 '89

TRADE MARKS AND TRADE NAMES
See also
Advertising characters
Automobiles—Names
Corporations—Names
Wine—Names
All in a name. K. L. Fisher. il *Forbes* 143:166 Mr 6 '89
Charged with practicing the art of the steal, Ed Zito plays his own Trump Card against Donald [photographic business cards] il pors *People Weekly* 32:111 Ag 7 '89
'Chronicle' trademark infringement disputes are resolved. C. Reid. *Publishers Weekly* 236:12 O 27 '89
Chrysler would prefer a bar by any other name, but Jeep Molnar would rather fight than switch [suit filed against owner of Jeep's Bar in Alpine, Wyo.] il por *People Weekly* 31:63 Ap 3 '89
A comeback may be ahead for Brand X [suing over ads that name rivals made easier due to changes in trademark statute] M. Galen. il *Business Week* p35 D 4 '89
Court removes ban on 'Spy notes' parody. il *Publishers Weekly* 236:10 O 6 '89
Doubleday fights block of 'Spy notes' parody. *Publishers Weekly* 236:9 Ag 18 '89
An equal footing on trademarks [big and small business] *Nation's Business* 77:12+ N '89
Good scouts indeed [Wilderness Scouts fight Boy Scouts over right to retain name] P. W. Moser. il pors *Sports Illustrated* 70:46-9 F 6 '89
How to protect your bright idea. D. Moreau. il *Changing Times* 43:63-4+ Ag '89
How to protect your products and ideas. R. Gunnerson. il *Home Office Computing* 7:38+ D '89
In search of a name. D. Placek. il *High Technology Business* 9:10 My '89
The inimitable Halston. N. Darnton. il pors *Newsweek* 114:64-6 Ag 7 '89
Trademark double-bind eased. M. Springut. il *High Technology Business* 9:4 N/D '89
The trademark that fell asleep [Murphy bed ruled a generic product] il *U.S. News & World Report* 106:16-17 My 15 '89
Two different animals: brand awareness & corporate image [interview with M. S. Forbes] *Forbes* 143:20 Mr 6 '89
Why don't we do it in the courts? [Apple Corps records sues Apple Computer in trade name dispute] *Newsweek* 113:44 Mr 6 '89

TRADE NAMES See Trade marks and trade names

TRADE ROUTES
Asia
Rediscovering the Silk Roads. il *The Courier (Unesco)* 41:12-15 N '88
A silken bond between East and West [silk roads] A. H. Dani. il map *The Courier (Unesco)* 42:4-10 Mr '89

TRADE SCHOOLS See Vocational-technical education

TRADE SECRETS
Severed heads and wasted resources [Fibermedia charged with stealing trade secrets from Advance Display Technologies Inc.] G. F. Gilder. il *Forbes* 143:45-6+ Je 26 '89

TRADE SHOWS See Trade fairs

TRADE UNION BUSTING See Labor union busting

TRADE UNIONS See Labor unions

TRADE WASTE
Disposal
See also
American Toxxic Control Inc.
Environmental Field Services Inc.
Love Canal case
Marine Shale Processors Inc.
OHM Corporation
Waste disposal in the ocean
Waste Management, Inc.

TRADE WASTE—Disposal—*cont.*

Bacteria that eat TNT [research by Pat Unkefer] M. M. Soviero. *Popular Science* 235:116 N '89

Citizens tackle toxic dump [Sumter, S.C.] R. Chepesiuk. il *The Progressive* 53:12-13 Je '89

Contaminant Cove: where polluters defile Mohawk land [New York State] J. E. Milich. il *The Progressive* 53:23-5 Ja '89

Explosive bacteria [biodegradation of explosive wastes; research by Pat Unkefer] *Discover* 10:18 O '89

Good riddance [address, May 24, 1989] B. M. Thompson. *Vital Speeches of the Day* 55:683-7 S 1 '89

The next Love Canal? [Niagara Falls] E. Salholz. il *Newsweek* 114:28 Ag 7 '89

Source Reduction Research Partnership: a unique joint venture [eliminating groundwater pollution caused by chlorinated solvents in California] A. Yazdani. bibl f il *Environment* 31:2-4 N '89

Super microbes attack hazardous waste. *High Technology Business* 9:29 Jl/Ag '89

Today's toxics: disposal. G. Easterbrook. il *Newsweek* 114:38-40 Jl 24 '89

Toxic fuel [illegally mixing hazardous waste with fuel] A. Porterfield. il *Common Cause Magazine* 15:6-7 Jl/Ag '89

Unexpected leakage through landfill liners [diffusion of chemicals through clay] J. Raloff. *Science News* 135:164 Mr 18 '89

Untouchable [toxic dumping by Transtech Industries] J. Zweig. il *Forbes* 144:10 Jl 24 '89

Wastequakes [injection wells implicated in Ohio earthquake near Perry Nuclear Power Plant] il *Discover* 10:8+ Ap '89

Women against toxic waste. J. Ralston. il *McCall's* 117:132+ O '89

Laws and regulations

The children's cleanup crusade [students from Jackson Elementary School in Salt Lake City, Utah lobby to establish state Superfund] B. A. Lewis. il *Sierra* 74:62-6 Mr/Ap '89

Cleaning hazardous waste sites. P. H. Abelson. *Science* 246:1097 D 1 '89

Deals that smell bad [toxic waste undoing takeovers] R. Simon. il *Forbes* 143:49+ My 15 '89

Enviro-cops on the prowl for polluters [EPA special agents] S. J. Hedges. il *U.S. News & World Report* 107:23 O 9 '89

Hazardous choice [W. Reilly's attempts to defang Superfund] V. Novak. *The Nation* 248:406-8 Mr 27 '89

Keeping tabs on toxics [right to know laws] S. J. Parsons. il *Utne Reader* p11-12 Jl/Ag '89

Keeping toxic track [EPA registry of polluters vs. Canadian practices] D. Burke. il *Maclean's* 102:44 Ag 28 '89

Not in my backyard! The waste-disposal crisis. T. Peters. il *The Christian Century* 106:175-7 F 15 '89

Revolving door at the E.P.A. [former officials taking high ranking jobs with private Superfund contractors] J. Sibbison. il *The Nation* 249:524-8 N 6 '89

Superfund implementation: the polluter must be made to pay. D. Wolf. bibl f *Environment* 31:42-4 Ja/F '89

Superfund, superflop. B. Carpenter. il map *U.S. News & World Report* 106:47-9 F 6 '89

When the dump is in 'our' backyard [discussion of February 15, 1989 article, Not in my backyard! The waste-disposal crisis] T. Peters. *The Christian Century* 106:660 Jl 5-12 '89

Yesterday's toxics: Superfund. G. Easterbrook. il *Newsweek* 114:36-8 Jl 24 '89

Securities

Cleaning up on the coming cleanup. E. T. Smith. il *Business Week* p98+ O 16 '89

Roses among the environmental ashes. T. Paré. il *Fortune* 120:36 O 9 '89

Canada

A campaign setback [uproar over disposal of PCBs in Quebec] M. Rose. il *Maclean's* 102:12-13 S 4 '89

Dangerous cargo [PCB-contaminated wastes from Quebec turned away by British ports] M. Rose. il *Maclean's* 102:10-12 Ag 28 '89

An industry's mania for nightmares [press inflames concerns over storage of PCBs in Canada] G. Bain. il *Maclean's* 102:60 O 23 '89

Keeping toxic track. D. Burke. il *Maclean's* 102:44 Ag 28 '89

Toxins by truckload [illicit waste-laden fuels enter Canada] B. Wickens. il *Maclean's* 102:17 My 22 '89

Developing countries

See also
Basel Convention on the Control of Transboundary Movements of Hazardous Waste and Their Disposal (1989)

Exporting hazardous waste. J. Millman. il *Technology Review* 92:6-7 Ap '89

Exporting pollution: the international waste trade. M. D. Uva and J. L. Bloom. bibl f il *Environment* 31:4-5+ Je '89

Great Britain

Dangerous cargo [PCB-contaminated wastes from Quebec turned away by British ports] M. Rose. il *Maclean's* 102:10-12 Ag 28 '89

Unwanted garbage: British port blocks ship with Canadian PCBs. A. Phillips. il *Maclean's* 102:43 Ag 21 '89

Western Europe

Transporting waste in the European Community: a free market? D. Laurence and B. Wynne. bibl f il *Environment* 31:12-17+ Jl/Ag '89

Export-import trade

See also
Basel Convention on the Control of Transboundary Movements of Hazardous Waste and Their Disposal (1989)

Dangerous cargo [PCB-contaminated wastes from Quebec turned away by British ports] M. Rose. il *Maclean's* 102:10-12 Ag 28 '89

Exporting hazardous waste. J. Millman. il *Technology Review* 92:6-7 Ap '89

Exporting pollution: the international waste trade. M. D. Uva and J. L. Bloom. bibl f il *Environment* 31:4-5+ Je '89

Toxins by truckload [illicit waste-laden fuels enter Canada] B. Wickens. il *Maclean's* 102:17 My 22 '89

Transporting waste in the European Community: a free market? D. Laurence and B. Wynne. bibl f il *Environment* 31:12-17+ Jl/Ag '89

Unwanted garbage: British port blocks ship with Canadian PCBs. A. Phillips. il *Maclean's* 102:43 Ag 21 '89

TRADEMARKS *See* Trade marks and trade names

TRADER JOE'S (FIRM)

Brie, but no Budweiser. E. Paris. il *Forbes* 144:235-6 O 2 '89

TRADERS & INVESTORS ALERT

The many incarnations of Barry Davis. L. J. Nathans and D. Zigas. il por *Business Week* p94 My 29 '89

Reach out and touch the market's latest fad. L. J. Nathans. il *Business Week* p144-5 My 22 '89

TRADES *See* Occupations

TRADEWINDS (FIRM)

SIA regional airline operates MD-87 to six Southeast Asian points. il *Aviation Week & Space Technology* 130:317 Je 12 '89

TRADING *See* Barter

TRADING CARDS

See also
Baseball cards
Hockey cards
Vietnam Fact Cards

TRADING COMPANIES

A forecast for '89: exporters will profit as the dollar declines. J. Edgerton and M. T. Smith. il *Money* 18:7 Ja '89

Great Britain

See also
South Sea Company

Hong Kong

See also
Hutchison Whampoa Ltd.

Poland

See also
Promotor (Firm)

Soviet Union

The five-percenters, Moscow's pet capitalists [privileged foreign businessmen acting as go-betweens; cover story] P. Berman. il *Forbes* 143:93-7 F 6 '89

TRADING STAMPS

See also
Sperry & Hutchinson Co.

Green stamps go high tech. il *Newsweek* 113:46 Ap 3 '89

TRADITION

Bring home the joy! E. Byron. il *Redbook* 174:118-19+ D '89

Family rituals [with editorial comment by Ann Pleshette Murphy] N. Rubin. il *Parents* 64:6, 105-9 Mr '89

Take time for traditions. A. Stoddard. il *McCall's* 117:158 N '89

TRADITION (THEOLOGY)

Backing into modernity. D. R. Carlin, Jr. *Commonweal* 116:204 Ap 7 '89

Challenges facing U.S. Catholics. G. Weigel. *Commonweal* 116:620-1 N 17 '89

Eucharist and tradition in the Middle Kingdom [China] E. LaVerdiere. *America* 161:162-4 S 23 '89

TRADITIONAL INDUSTRIES, INC.

The facts behind the figures. R. L. Stern and M. Beauchamp. il por *Forbes* 144:41-2 Ag 21 '89

TRAFFIC *See* City traffic

TRAFFIC, AIRLINE *See* Airlines—Traffic

TRAFFIC ACCIDENTS

See also
Alcohol and automobile drivers
Cycling—Accidents and injuries
Motorcycling—Accidents and injuries

Abandon ship! A galleon runs aground in a highway wreck [J. Fiondella's replica of Spanish galleon overturns on road] il por *People Weekly* 32:206 D 4 '89

TRAFFIC ACCIDENTS—*cont.*

Anatomy of a car crash [work of Donald F. Huelke] il *USA Today (Periodical)* 117:14-15 Ap '89

Can a driver be too old? J. Carney. il *Time* 133:28 Ja 16 '89

A crash course in when to come clean [reporting accidents to insurance company] V. S. Sussman. il *U.S. News & World Report* 107:106 N 6 '89

Critics charge that Domino's is making pizza to die for [accidents involving delivery drivers] il *People Weekly* 32:105 S 25 '89

The deadly cost of 65 mph [study of rural interstate highway fatalities in New Mexico] J. Raloff. *Science News* 136:294 N 4 '89

Do not try these maneuvers [lack of proof supporting proposal that car advertising contributes to accidents] R. Ceppos. il *Car and Driver* 34:26-7 My '89

Domino's delivery pledge: danger to go? [traffic accidents while delivering pizza] il *Newsweek* 114:32 Jl 10 '89

Hit-and-run: a family's nightmare [A. Story struck and killed by car of C. Breeding near Lighthouse Point, Fla.] D. M. Mazie. il *Reader's Digest* 135:152-7 D '89

How safe is your car? [report by Highway Loss Data Institute] il *Consumers' Research Magazine* 72:16-19 N '89

Ordeal on I-80. J. Belsky. il *The New York Times Magazine* p24+ F 19 '89

Questions [questioning relationship between high performance design and accidents] K. Cameron. il *Cycle* 40:15 Ja '89

William Wharton, author of Dad, seeks to avenge his daughter's horrible death [K. Rodewald killed in automobile crash caused by smoke cloud from grass fires in Oregon's Willamette Valley] M. Green. il pors *People Weekly* 32:122-4 N 27 '89

Rescue work
See Rescue work

Canada

An untimely end [Olympic swimmer V. Davis dies after being struck by car in Montreal suburb] B. Wickens. il por *Maclean's* 102:68 N 27 '89

New Zealand

Alive & kicking [marathoner J. Welzel's recovery from auto accident] J. Brant. il pors *Runner's World* 24:52-5 F '89

TRAFFIC ALERT AND COLLISION AVOIDANCE SYSTEMS *See* Airplanes—Collision avoidance systems

TRAFFIC CONGESTION

The congestion-pollution connection [address, July 7, 1989] T. J. Donohue. *Vital Speeches of the Day* 55:763-6 O 1 '89

Crumbling highways and congested byways: can you steer clear? H. Gieseking. il *Travel Holiday* 172:12-13 Jl '89

Taking the crush out of rush hour. T. A. Heppenheimer. il *High Technology Business* 9:26-30 Mr '89

We may be fast, but we're slowing down. B. W. Yates. il *Car and Driver* 34:18 Mr '89

TRAFFIC CONTROL, AIRWAY *See* Air traffic control

TRAFFIC CONTROL, RADAR *See* Radar in traffic control

TRAFFIC ENGINEERING

See also
Computers—Traffic control use
Lasers—Traffic control use
Photography in traffic control
Radar in traffic control

Kynar and gentler streets [traffic-sensing devices] I. Amato. *Science News* 135:79 F 4 '89

TRAFFIC FLOW

See also
Traffic congestion

How to analyze the shock waves that sweep through expressway traffic. J. Walker. il *Scientific American* 261:98-100+ Ag '89

TRAFFIC IN ARMS *See* Munitions—Export-import trade

TRAFFIC JAMS *See* Traffic congestion

TRAFFIC REGULATIONS

See also
Citizens for Rational Traffic Laws
Traffic tickets

The deadly cost of 65 mph [study of rural interstate highway fatalities in New Mexico] J. Raloff. *Science News* 136:294 N 4 '89

Let's raise the speed limit to 100 mph! J. R. Nerad. il *Motor Trend* 41:12 S '89

One hundred paces [high-speed traffic] R. Ceppos. il *Car and Driver* 34:22 Mr '89

Regulating the deregulated. J. P. Rothe. *Society* 27:11-12 N/D '89

A responsible 100-mph speed limit. J. R. Nerad. *Motor Trend* 41:8 O '89

California

See also
Los Angeles (Calif.)—Traffic regulations

New York (State)

See also
New York (N.Y.)—Traffic regulations

Washington (D.C.)

See Washington (D.C.)—Traffic regulations

TRAFFIC SAFETY

See also
Automobile driving

Cycling
Group United Against Radar Detectors
Motorcycling
United States. National Highway Traffic Safety Administration

Laws and regulations
See Traffic regulations

TRAFFIC SCHOOLS

Some L.A. law-breakers claim Steve Verret's stand-up comedy traffic class is just the ticket [World Famous Improvisation Traffic School] T. Allis. il pors *People Weekly* 31:117-18 Je 19 '89

Anecdotes, facetiae, satire, etc.

Take the money and run. B. J. Hoffman. il *Motor Trend* 41:118 Jl '89

TRAFFIC TICKET FIXING

The quick fix [fixing of parking tickets for members of Congress] D. Gross. *The New Republic* 201:12+ O 16 '89

TRAFFIC TICKETS

Here's another fine mess [raising fines on speeding tickets] P. Bedard. il *Car and Driver* 34:16 Mr '89

TRAFFIC VIOLATIONS

See also
Traffic tickets

TRAFFIC VOLUME *See* Traffic flow

TRAILER HITCHES (AUTOMOBILE) *See* Automobile trailers—Towing

TRAILERS

See also
Automobile boat trailers
Automobile trailers

TRAILS

See also
Portages
Rails-to-Trails Conservancy

Do tread on me [best U.S. trails] C. R. Wolpert. il map *Women's Sports & Fitness* 11:36-9 Jl/Ag '89

A dozen choice trails for day hikers [national forest trails] M. Spilner. il *Prevention (Emmaus, Pa.)* 41:78+ Ap '89

California

See also
Bay Area Ridge Trail (Calif.)
John Muir Trail (Calif.)

Caribbean region

Walk this way. R. J. Christmas. il *Black Enterprise* 19:117-18 My '89

Colorado

See also
Colorado Trail (Colo.)

Northwestern States

See also
Oregon Trail

Pacific States

See also
Pacific Crest National Scenic Trail

United States

See Trails

Utah

See also
Burr Trail (Utah)

Washington (D.C.)

See also
Black History Trail (Washington, D.C.)

TRAILS WEST (LOUISVILLE, COLO.: BOOKSTORE) *See* Booksellers and bookselling—Colorado

TRAIN, JOHN

Pondering *perestroika*. *The American Spectator* 22:30-1 F '89

TRAIN TRAVEL *See* Railroad travel

TRAINERS, PERSONAL *See* Personal trainers

TRAINING, OCCUPATIONAL *See* Vocational-technical education

TRAINING AIRPLANES *See* Airplanes, Training

TRAINING CAMPS, BASEBALL *See* Baseball, Professional—Spring training

TRAINING CAMPS, FOOTBALL *See* Football, Professional—Training camps

TRAINING CAMPS, MILITARY *See* Military training camps

TRAINING FILMS, CORPORATE *See* Motion pictures in industry

TRAINING HELICOPTERS *See* Helicopters, Training

TRAINING OF CHILDREN *See* Children—Management and training

TRAINING OF DOGS *See* Dogs—Training

TRAINING OF DOLPHINS *See* Dolphins—Training

TRAINOR, BERNARD E.

A return to no man's land. il *The New York Times Magazine* p22+ Mr 19 '89

TRAINOR, KEN

Crandon, 1969. il map *Ad Astra* 1:16-26 Jl/Ag '89

TRAINS *See* Railroads—Trains

TRAINS (MAGNETIC) *See* Maglev trains

TRAJECTORIES

Can Galileo take the heat? [risky trajectory for space probe] M. M. Waldrop. il *Science* 245:1327-9 S 22 '89

TRAJECTORIES—*cont.*
First Galileo course correction executed; several spacecraft anomalies uncovered. M. A. Dornheim. *Aviation Week & Space Technology* 131:43 N 20 '89
Galileo (whew!) changes course. M. M. Waldrop. *Science* 246:997 N 24 '89
Shoot with a computer [analyzing bullet trajectories] J. Carmichel. il *Outdoor Life* 183:42+ Ja '89
Spatial understanding & universal awareness. C. Twarog. il *Ad Astra* 1:23 S '89

TRAMMELL CROW COMPANY
"The dinosaurs are dying". J. H. Taylor. il *Forbes* 143:92+ My 1 '89
Nothing to Crow about. K. Hannon. il *Forbes* 144:10 S 18 '89

TRAMPS *See* Hoboes
TRAMWAYS *See* Trolleys
TRAN, VAN DINH, 1923-
Hue: my city, myself. il por map *National Geographic* 176:594-603 N '89

TRANIELLO, JAMES F. A.
(jt. auth) See Scott, Michelle Pellissier, and Traniello, James F. A.

TRANQUILIZING DRUGS
See also
Clozapine
Haloperidol
Rat model of tardive dyskinesia gets boost [use of haloperidol; research by Gaylord Ellison] B. Bower. *Science News* 136:308 N 11 '89
Sleeping pills. B. H. Dobkin. il *The New York Times Magazine* p39-40 F 5 '89

TRANS WORLD AIRLINES INC.
ALPA prepares for possible sale of all or part of TWA [Air Line Pilots Assn.] J. T. McKenna. *Aviation Week & Space Technology* 131:128-9 N 20 '89
Carl Icahn has lots of cash. Will he spend it on TWA? T. Vogel. il por *Business Week* p86-7 Jl 17 '89
Is Icahn taxiing TWA to the auction block? T. Vogel. il *Business Week* p58 D 11 '89
Supreme Court ruling lets airlines assure jobs to strike breakers [case of TWA vs. Independent Federation of Flight Attendants] M. Mecham. *Aviation Week & Space Technology* 129:67 Mr 6 '89
TWA commitment strengthens Airbus' position in North American market. J. M. Lenorovitz. il *Aviation Week & Space Technology* 130:65 Ap 3 '89
TWA, FlightSafety to launch low-time pilot training program. *Aviation Week & Space Technology* 130:72-3 F 27 '89
TWA leads U.S. carriers in cutting domestic fares. J. T. McKenna. *Aviation Week & Space Technology* 131:92-3 Ag 21 '89
TWA orders Airbus A330s to upgrade aging fleet. C. Fotos. il *Aviation Week & Space Technology* 130:64-5 Ap 3 '89
TWA unions attempt to shape strategy for gaining leverage over airline sale. J. T. McKenna. *Aviation Week & Space Technology* 131:32-3 D 4 '89

TRANSAFRICA (ORGANIZATION)
TransAfrica confab focuses on foreign policy issues. *Jet* 76:15 Jl 3 '89

TRANSAMERICA COMPUTER CORPORATION *See* Transamerica Corp.
TRANSAMERICA CORP.
Transamerica makes a tempting target. G. G. Marcial. il *Business Week* p94 O 2 '89

TRANSAMINASES
Direct Brønsted analysis of the restoration of activity to a mutant enzyme by exogenous amines. M. D. Toney and J. F. Kirsch. bibl f il *Science* 243:1485-8 Mr 17 '89

TRANSATLANTIC AIRLINE SERVICE *See* Airlines— Routes—Transatlantic
TRANSATLANTIC FLIGHTS *See* Aviation—Transatlantic flights
TRANSATLANTIC VOYAGES *See* Voyages
TRANSATMOSPHERE VEHICLE *See* Spaceplane
TRANSCANADA PIPELINES LIMITED
Back from the dead. J. Cook. il map *Forbes* 143:90-1 Ap 3 '89

TRANSCEIVERS, RADIOTELEPHONE *See* Radiotelephone
TRANSCENDENCE OF GOD
Fierce landscapes and the indifference of God [cover story] B. C. Lane. *The Christian Century* 106:907-10 O 11 '89

TRANSCENDENTAL MEDITATION
Levitation U. [Maharishi International University] D. Starr. il *Omni (New York, N.Y.)* 11:66-8+ My '89
Ommm . . . please pass the DHEAS [effects upon levels of dehydroepiandrosterone] J. Hooper. il *Health (New York, N.Y.)* 21:34 O '89

TRANSCO ENERGY CO.
Gas profits are in the pipeline. il *Money* 18:8 Mr '89
Good-bye to take-or-pay. T. Mack. il por *Forbes* 143:120+ Je 12 '89

TRANSCRIBING SERVICES
See also
Journal Graphics Inc.

TRANSCRIPTASES
Multiple mutations in HIV-1 reverse transcriptase confer high-level resistance to zidovudine (AZT). B. A. Larder and S. D. Kemp. bibl f il *Science* 246:1155-8 D 1 '89
Reverse transcriptase in a clinical strain of Escherichia coli: production of branched RNA-linked msDNA. B. C. Lampson and others. bibl f il *Science* 243:1033-8 F 24 '89
TRANSCRIPTION (GENETICS) *See* Genetic transcription
TRANSCRIPTION FACTORS
AP1/*jun* function is differentially induced in promotion-sensitive and resistant JB6 cells [activation by tetradecanoyl-phorbol acetate] L. R. Bernstein and N. H. Colburn. bibl f il *Science* 244:566-9 My 5 '89
Chromosomal rearrangement generating a composite gene for a developmental transcription factor [Bacillus subtilis] P. Stragier and others. bibl f il *Science* 243:507-12 Ja 27 '89
In vitro transcription enhancement by purified derivatives of the glucocorticoid receptor. L. P. Freedman and others. bibl f il *Science* 245:298-301 Jl 21 '89
Interleukin-1 costimulatory activity on the interleukin-2 promoter via AP-1. K. Muegge and others. bibl f il *Science* 246:249-51 O 13 '89
Leucine repeats and an adjacent DNA binding domain mediate the formation of functional cFos-cJun heterodimers [proposed function of the leucine zipper] R. Turner and R. Tjian. bibl f il *Science* 243:1689-94 Mr 31 '89
POU! goes the homeobox. J. Benditt. *Scientific American* 260:20+ F '89
A protein that binds to a cis-acting element of wheat histone genes has a leucine zipper motif. T. Tabata and others. bibl f il *Science* 245:965-7 S 1 '89
Purification of growth hormone-specific transcription factor GHF-1 containing homeobox. J.-L. Castrillo and others. bibl f il *Science* 243:814-17 F 10 '89
Regulation of proenkephalin by Fos and Jun. J. L. Sonnenberg and others. bibl f il *Science* 246:1622-5 D 22 '89
Switch protein alters specificity of RNA polymerase containing a compartment-specific sigma factor [Bacillus subtilis] L. Kroos and others. bibl f il *Science* 243:526-9 Ja 27 '89
Transcriptional regulation in mammalian cells by sequence-specific DNA binding proteins [RNA polymerase II transcription initiation] P. J. Mitchell and R. Tjian. bibl f il *Science* 245:371-8 Jl 28 '89

TRANSDERMAL PATCHES
The anti-aging patch for women [releases estrogen during menopause] S. Fields and L. Holland. il *Good Housekeeping* 208:163-4 F '89

TRANSDUCERS
Digital peak detector. R. D. Secura. il *Radio-Electronics* 60:59-62 Ap '89
TRANSFECTION, GENE *See* Gene transfection
TRANSFER OF FUNDS
See also
Computers—Banking use
Debit cards
Moving money—fast. P. N. Strassels. il *Nation's Business* 77:76 Ap '89
Moving your IRA, SEP or Keogh into a new home. M. Meyer. il *Money* 18:59-60 Ap '89
When you switch brokers, your assets need help passing from one hand to the other. M. C. Paulson. il *Changing Times* 43:18 S '89
TRANSFER OF TECHNOLOGY *See* Technology transfer
TRANSFER RNA
The anticodon contains a major element of the identity of arginine transfer RNAs. L. H. Schulman and H. Pelka. bibl f il *Science* 246:1595-7 D 22 '89
Building new proteins with odd parts [work of A. Richard Chamberlin] I. Amato. *Science News* 136:246 O 14 '89
A general method for site-specific incorporation of unnatural amino acids into proteins. C. J. Noren and others. bibl f il *Science* 244:182-8 Ap 14 '89
How old is the genetic code? Statistical geometry of tRNA provides an answer. M. Eigen and others. bibl f il *Science* 244:673-9 My 12 '89
Nucleotides in yeast tRNA[Phe] required for the specific recognition by its cognate synthetase. J. R. Sampson and others. bibl f il *Science* 243:1363-6 Mr 10 '89
On the trail of transfer RNA identity. C. Mlot. il *BioScience* 39:756-9 D '89
Prevention of translational frameshifting by the modified nucleoside 1-methylguanosine. G. R. Björk and others. bibl f il *Science* 244:986-9 My 26 '89
Structural basis for misaminoacylation by mutant E. coli glutaminyl-tRNA synthetase enzymes. J. J. Perona and others. bibl f il *Science* 246:1152-4 D 1 '89
Structure of E. coli glutaminyl-tRNA synthetase complexed with tRNA[Gln] and ATP at 2.8 Å resolution. M. A. Rould and others. bibl f il *Science* 246:1135-42 D 1 '89
The structure of the "second genetic code" [work of T. A. Steitz] M. M. Waldrop. il por *Science* 246:1122 D 1 '89
Transfer RNA genes: landmarks for integration of mobile genetic elements in Dictyostelium discoideum. R. Marschalek and others. bibl f il *Science* 244:1493-6 Je 23 '89

TRANSFER STUDENTS *See* Students—Transfer
TRANSFERASES
　　See also
　　Recombinase
A baculovirus blocks insect molting by producing ecdysteroid UDP-glucosyl transferase. D. R. O'Reilly and L. K. Miller. bibl f il *Science* 245:1110-12 S 8 '89
Detecting mutations in human genes [use of HPRT gene as an indicator] J. L. Marx. il *Science* 243:737-8 F 10 '89
Disruption of the yeast *N*-myristoyl transferase gene causes recessive lethality. R. J. Duronio and others. bibl f il *Science* 243:796-800 F 10 '89
Molecular custodians sweep away odorants [research by Doren Lancet] I. Amato. *Science News* 136:374 D 9 '89
Triggering of allostery in an enzyme by a point mutation: ornithine transcarbamoylase. L. C. Kuo and others. bibl f il *Science* 245:522-4 Ag 4 '89
TRANSFIGURATION OF CHRIST *See* Jesus Christ—Transfiguration
TRANSFORMATION, GENETIC *See* Gene transfer
TRANSFORMATIONS (MATHEMATICS)
　　See also
　　Ergodic theory
　　Fourier transformation
TRANSFORMING GROWTH FACTOR
Overexpression of transforming growth factor α in psoriatic epidermis. J. T. Elder and others. bibl f il *Science* 243:811-14 F 10 '89
TRANSFUSION OF BLOOD *See* Blood—Transfusion
TRANSIENTS (ELECTRICITY)
Circuitry guardians [spike and surge protectors] H. B. Cohen. il *Home Mechanix* 85:30-1 N '89
The great power spike. J. Pournelle. il *Byte* 14:99-100+ Ag '89
TRANSISTORS
　　See also
　　Metal oxide semiconductors
AT&T "microscopic parallel processor" hits 24 GHz [quantum effect transistor] *Byte* 14:17 Ag '89
A growing force in the shrinking business [R. T. Bate's quantum-effect transistor] W. C. Symonds. il por *Business Week* Special Issue:75 Je 16 '89
HEMT devices could speed work on next-generation radar systems [high electron mobility transistors] B. D. Nordwall. il *Aviation Week & Space Technology* 130:65+ My 15 '89
How quantum theory works in lasers and transistors. il *Fortune* 119:114 Ja 30 '89
The quantum transistor. M. Reed. il *Byte* 14:275-81 My '89
TRANSIT CASUALTY CO.
Did this insurance whiz undercut and run? [C. Miro] T. Smart. il por *Business Week* p120+ O 23 '89
TRANSIT SYSTEMS *See* Local transit
TRANSITION PERIODS, PRESIDENTIAL *See* Presidents—Transition periods
TRANSLATIONS *See* Translators and translating
TRANSLATORS AND TRANSLATING
　　See also
　　American literature—Translations into Russian
　　Bible—Versions
　　Chinese literature—Translations into English
　　Japanese literature—Translations into English
　　Machine translating
　　Russian literature—Translations into English
Pavel Palazhchenko: Gorbachev wouldn't leave home without him. W. Plummer. il pors *People Weekly* 32:187-8 D 4 '89
　　Court use
Libertad and justicia for all [shortage of interpreters] A. L. Sanders. il *Time* 133:65 My 29 '89
TRANSLOCATION OF CHROMOSOMES *See* Chromosome abnormalities
TRANSMISSION, AUTOMOBILE *See* Automobiles, Foreign—Transmission
TRANSMISSION, BICYCLE *See* Bicycles—Transmission
TRANSMISSION, WASHING MACHINE *See* Washing machines—Transmission
TRANSNUKLEAR GMBH
The Transnuklear affair. D. Charles. *The Bulletin of the Atomic Scientists* 45:23 Ap '89
TRANSOCEANIC VOYAGES *See* Voyages
TRANSPACIFIC AIRLINE SERVICE *See* Airlines—Routes—Transpacific
TRANSPARENCIES
　　See also
　　Slides (Photography)
TRANSPARENCY (DATABASE MANAGEMENT)
A transparent environment. B. J. Walker and G. Popek. bibl il *Byte* 14:225-6+ Jl '89
TRANSPLANTATION OF ORGANS, TISSUES, ETC.
　　See also
　　Adrenal glands—Transplantation
　　Blood vessels—Transplantation
　　Brain—Transplantation
　　Cornea—Transplantation
　　Donation of organs, tissues, etc.

Fetal tissue—Transplantation
Heart—Transplantation
Immunological tolerance
Kidneys—Transplantation
Knee—Transplantation
Liver—Transplantation
Lungs—Transplantation
Marrow—Transplantation
Mouth—Transplantation
Ova—Transplantation
Pancreas—Transplantation
Preservation of organs, tissues, etc.
Retina—Transplantation
Xenografts
Maverick surgeon [T. Starzl] M. Dowie. il pors *American Health* 8:86-9+ Je '89
Organ masters. M. Dowie. il *Omni (New York, N.Y.)* 11:26+ F '89
　　Ethical aspects
Count Dracula makes an offer [letter sent to bankrupt persons offering to buy one of their kidneys in West Germany]; tr. by Elliott Rabin. R. R. Adelmann von Adelmannsfelden. *Harper's* 278:23-4 Mr '89
Hard ethical questions. *USA Today (Periodical)* 118:14+ O '89
Take my kidney, please [selling of organs] M. Kinsley. il *Time* 133:88 Mr 13 '89
Transplant fever. M. Dowie. il *Mother Jones* 14:19-20 Ap '89
　　Germany (West)
Count Dracula makes an offer [letter sent to bankrupt persons offering to buy one of their kidneys]; tr. by Elliott Rabin. R. R. Adelmann von Adelmannsfelden. *Harper's* 278:23-4 Mr '89
TRANSPONDERS
FAA expands Mode C transponder use to all aircraft near major airports. *Aviation Week & Space Technology* 131:66 Jl 3 '89
TRANSPORT, BIOLOGICAL *See* Biological transport
TRANSPORT AIRPLANES *See* Airplanes, Jet
TRANSPORT CANADA *See* Canada. Transport Canada
TRANSPORTATION
　　See also
　　Airports—Transportation
　　Animals—Transportation
　　Bicycles—Transportation
　　Commuters
　　Ferries
　　Homeless—Transportation
　　Local transit
　　Poor—Transportation
　　Railroads
　　Skiers—Transportation
　　Theater—Equipment—Transportation
　　Tiger International, Inc.
　　United States. Dept. of Transportation
　　Waterways
　　　　Federal aid
　　See also
　　Local transit—Federal aid
　　　　International aspects
Rethinking the future of global transportation. M. Renner. il *USA Today (Periodical)* 118:23-6 S '89
　　　　Laws and regulations
Going nowhere: gridlock and the politics of transportation [excerpt from Winning America] R. Capon. il *Utne Reader* p86-7 Mr/Ap '89
　　　　Western Europe
Best ways to get around in Europe. J. Anthony. il *Changing Times* 43:39-41 Jl '89
Connecting to the continent. J. F. Beaumont. il *World Press Review* 36:79 O '89
TRANSPORTATION, HIGH SPEED
　　See also
　　Maglev trains
TRANSPORTATION, MILITARY
　　See also
　　Airplanes, Military transport
　　Motor vehicles, Military
　　United States. Air Force. Military Airlift Command
　　United States. Civil Reserve Air Fleet
Why Johnny can't fight [not enough airlift and sealift capacity] il *U.S. News & World Report* 107:30 S 25 '89
TRANSPORTATION AND STATE
　　See also
　　United States. Dept. of Transportation
　　　　Canada
　　See also
　　Canada. Transport Canada
TRANSPORTATION DEPT. (U.S.) *See* United States. Dept. of Transportation
TRANSPORTATION INDUSTRY *See* Transportation
TRANSPORTATION OF PRISONERS *See* Prisoners—Transportation
TRANSPORTATION OF WORKS OF ART
Tips on sending art through the mail. A. S. Bamberger. il *Antiques & Collecting Hobbies* 94:18 My '89

TRANSPORTATION WORKERS
See also
Collective labor agreements—Transportation workers
TRANSPOSONS
Visual detection of transposition of the maize element Activator (Ac) in tobacco seedlings. J. D. G. Jones and others. bibl f il *Science* 244:204-7 Ap 14 '89
TRANSSEXUALISM *See* Change of sex
TRANSTECH INDUSTRIES INC.
New trick for greenmailers [use of personal holding company loophole] J. Zweig. il *Forbes* 144:110 O 30 '89
Untouchable [toxic dumping] J. Zweig. il *Forbes* 144:10 Jl 24 '89
TRANSTRACK INC.
Tracking trucks without satellites. il *High Technology Business* 9:27 My '89
TRANSURANIUM ELEMENTS
Creating superheavy elements. P. Armbruster and G. Münzenberg. bibl il *Scientific American* 260:66-72 My '89
TRANSYLVANIA COUNTY (N.C.)
Description and travel
Listening to the land of waterfalls. J. T. Black. il *Southern Living* 24:26+ N '89
TRAORE, MOUSSA
Visit of Mali president [remarks and exchange of toasts, October 6, 1988] il por *Department of State Bulletin* 89:14-15 Ja '89
Visit to the United States, 1988
Visit of Mali president [remarks and exchange of toasts, October 6, 1988] R. Reagan; M. Traore. il por *Department of State Bulletin* 89:14-15 Ja '89
TRAP-JAW ANTS *See* Ants
TRAP SHOOTING *See* Trapshooting
TRAPP, ADELINE
about
"Queen of Hell Gate". A. Garrard. il pors *Ms.* 18:52-5 Jl/Ag '89
TRAPPING
Trappers and rattlers. G. Reiger. il *Field & Stream* 94:15-16 Jl '89
New York (State)
Understanding trapping in New York. P. Biship. il *The Conservationist* 44:38-43 N/D '89
TRAPS
See also
Fish traps
Mousetraps
TRAPSHOOTING
Crazy clays [specialty targets for sporting clays] R. Hinton. il *Outdoor Life* 184:22+ S '89
Loss of habitat. G. Hill. il *Field & Stream* 93:11 Ja '89
Shotguns for sporting. R. Hinton. il *Outdoor Life* 183:17+ Ap '89
The smoking choke [sporting clays] R. Hinton. il *Outdoor Life* 184:39-41 Ag '89
Sporting clays puts this farm back in the hunt. J. Walter. il *Successful Farming* 87:68 S '89
Sporting clues. D. Painter. il *Outdoor Life* 184:48+ N '89
Sporting deceptions [sporting clays courses] R. Hinton. il *Outdoor Life* 184:28-31 Jl '89
Sporting for sportsmen [sporting clays] R. Hinton. il *Outdoor Life* 183:24-5 Mr '89
Sporting savvy. D. Painter. il *Outdoor Life* 183:26+ My '89
Sporting yes, easy no! B. Brister. il *Field & Stream* 94:60-1+ Jl '89
Competitions
A sporting competition [invitational clay shoot hosted by Outdoor life at Migdale Estate, N.Y.] R. P. Stuart. il *Outdoor Life* 183:48+ F '89
Sporting's national championships. M. Pearce and J. Meyer. il *Outdoor Life* 184:48+ O '89
Study and teaching
Do shooting schools work? N. Seifert. il *Outdoor Life* 184:40+ D '89
The swing doctor [sporting clays] D. Painter. il *Outdoor Life* 183:54+ Je '89
TRASH (STYLE)
The new refuse. J. Duka. il *Vogue* 179:250 Ja '89
Trash is good for you. K. Robinson. il *Glamour* 87:133 My '89
TRASH BAGS
A bag battle pits Big Oil vs. Big Ag [Archer-Daniels-Midland Co.'s biodegradable trash bags threaten conventional bag manufacturers] P. Sherrid. il *U.S. News & World Report* 106:52 Ap 24 '89
Garbage bags. il *Consumer Reports* 54:273-7 D '89
Missouri's capital using trash bags made from corn. il *Successful Farming* 87:30 Ja '89
TRASH TELEVISION *See* Tabloid television
TRAUB, JAMES
Jack Kemp faces reality. il pors *The New York Times Magazine* p38-9+ My 7 '89
TRAUB, MARVIN S.
about
The big deal at Bloomingdale's: Marvin Traub makes a run at the top. M. Gross. il pors *New York* 22:56-60+ O 16 '89

TRAUB, ROGER D., AND OTHERS
Model of the origin of rhythmic population oscillations in the hippocampal slice. bibl f il *Science* 243:1319-25 Mr 10 '89
TRAUM, JEROME S.
about
Morton Janklow sued for $20 million by ex-partner. C. Reid. *Publishers Weekly* 236:8+ N 24 '89
TRAUM, ZEEV
about
The widow of an Israeli soldier gives his heart—and the gift of life—to an Arab, Hanna Khader. il pors *People Weekly* 32:130 D 11 '89
TRAUMA CARE UNITS
Emergency! Emergency! J. Grossmann. il *Health (New York, N.Y.)* 21:76-8+ Jl '89
Emergency treatment! True cases from the files of an extraordinary children's hospital [Children's Hospital National Medical Center; excerpt from In the blink of an eye] A. Doelp. il *Redbook* 172:82-3+ F '89
Help! This is an emergency! [cutbacks in services] S. Findlay. il *U.S. News & World Report* 107:28+ N 13 '89
Race against death [Children's Hospital National Medical Center; condensed from In the blink of an eye] A. Doelp. il *Reader's Digest* 135:221-4+ N '89
TRAUMA CENTERS *See* Trauma care units
TRAUMATIC NEUROSES
See also
Posttraumatic stress disorder
TRAUMATISM
The cruelest kind of grief [survivors of sudden tragedy] D. Gelman. il *Newsweek* 113:21-3 Ja 2 '89
TRAUTH, BERNHARD C., AND OTHERS
Monoclonal antibody-mediated tumor regression by induction of apoptosis. bibl f il *Science* 245:301-5 Jl 21 '89
TRAVEL
See also
Aged—Travel
Air travel
Art tours
Artists—Travel
Athletes—Travel
Authors—Travel
Automobile touring
Black women—Travel
Black youth—Travel
Blacks—Travel
Blind—Travel
Bus travel
Business travel
Celebrities—Travel
Congressmen—Travel
Cruising
Fashion designers—Travel
Great Britain—Royal family—Travel
Guidebooks
Handicapped—Travel
Hotels, motels, etc.
Information systems—Travel use
Luggage
Motor scooter touring
Mulroney, Brian—Travel
Packing of luggage
Police—Travel
Railroad travel
Single people—Travel
Single women—Travel
Time travel
Tourist trade
Vacations
Veterans—Travel
Videotapes—Travel use
Voyages
Voyages around the world
Women—Travel
Youth—Travel
The 1989 travel poll [results] H. Gieseking and A. Gist. *Travel Holiday* 171:87-9 My '89
Architectural digest travels [special section] il *Architectural Digest* 46:147+ O '89
Architectural digest travels [special section] il *Architectural Digest* 46:67+ Mr '89
Architectural digest travels [special section] il *Architectural Digest* 46:113+ My '89
Beyond the Eiffel Tower [interview with A. Frommer] J. Popkin. il por *U.S. News & World Report* 107:63 O 2 '89
Breaking away [travel to exotic destinations] R. Dolphin. il *Maclean's* 102:46-7 Mr 13 '89
Fast and affordable! Where to go in '89. il *Glamour* 87:97-100 Ja '89
Five-star world beauty spots. A. Fotheringham. il *Maclean's* 102:64 D 18 '89
A guided tour of the travel scene. M. Silver. il *U.S. News & World Report* 106:83 My 8 '89
How to get the most from your trip. See issues of Glamour
Spur-of-the-moment travel. D. M. Koma. il *Travel Holiday* 171:32-8 Mr '89

TRAVEL—*cont.*

The technological tourist. S. C. Florman. il *Technology Review* 92:18+ Ja '89

Ticket to stride [running while traveling] J. Henderson. il *Runner's World* 24:14 My '89

The travel advisor. H. Gieseking. See issues of Travel Holiday through January 1990

Travel digest. See issues of Travel Holiday through January 1990

Travel journal. P. J. Bell. See issues of Gourmet beginning January 1989

Travel news. R. Alleman. See issues of Vogue

Travel news. S. Birnbaum. See issues of Good Housekeeping

Travel notes. See issues of World Press Review

TravelBazaar. See issues of Harper's Bazaar

Traveling with Lydia. L. Moss. See issues of McCall's beginning May 1989

Bibliography

Freebies and almost-freebies [brochures] E. McGowan. il *Travel Holiday* 172:30-1 S '89

A holiday harvest [for Christmas] il *Travel Holiday* 172:80-1 N '89

Literature's new nomads. J. Miller. il *Newsweek* 114:50-2 Ag 14 '89

A round-up of 1989 travel books. J. Crichton. il *Publishers Weekly* 235:66-8+ Ja 20 '89

Spring reading for travellers. il *History Today* 39:55-9 Mr '89

Travel. A. Broyard. il *The New York Times Book Review* 94:22 D 3 '89

Travel books. J. Krich. il *The New York Times Book Review* 94:12+ Je 11 '89

Economic aspects

See also
    Airlines—Fares
    Hotels, motels, etc.—Rates

Best buys on the high seas [repositioning cruises] H. Basch and S. Slater. il *Travel Holiday* 172:22-4 Ag '89

Caribbean sales [cruise bargains] H. Basch and S. Slater. il *Travel Holiday* 172:32-3+ O '89

Cash on the run [use of ATMs] C. Torcellini. il *Forbes* 143:145 My 1 '89

Cut-rate colleges, trains, planes and other top deals for travelers over 50. D. M. Topolnicki. il *Money* 18:145-6 F '89

A fair exchange [handling money abroad] D. Wishik. il *Travel Holiday* 172:58-63 D '89

Getting refunds when a travel firm folds. H. Gieseking. il *Travel Holiday* 171:76-7 Je '89

Getting your money's worth [Pacific region] R. F. Miller. *Travel Holiday* 172:82 S '89

Going solo—sans the supplement. H. Gieseking. *Travel Holiday* 171:101-2 Ap '89

Last-minute cruisers can be choosers. G. DeGeorge. il *Business Week* p106 F 13 '89

Living the high life in the low season. K. Castle and K. Castle. il *Travel Holiday* 172:74-8 Ag '89

Luxury vacations at cut-rate prices. il *Glamour* 87:145-6+ Ag '89

Money savers. S. Brewer. il *New Choices for the Best Years* 29:11 Jl '89

Outlook: time off. P. Plawin. il *Changing Times* 43:67-8 Ja '89

The right credit card for the road. L. Wiener. il *U.S. News & World Report* 106:68 Je 26 '89

Summer spirit: 20 travel money savers and the best of the cultural festivals. M. Burns. il *Essence* 19:27+ Ap '89

The tight-budget, no-hassle way to see Disney World. M. Kiernan. il *U.S. News & World Report* 106:62-3+ Je 5 '89

What your bucks will buy abroad this summer. K. McManus and B. Stauffer. il *Changing Times* 43:72-4+ My '89

Winter cruises that won't sink your budget. P. Plawin. il *Changing Times* 43:85-9 F '89

Yen-stretching in Japan. *Sunset (Central West edition)* 182:44 My '89

Equipment

Travel lights. M. Porter. il *Gentlemen's Quarterly* 59:247+ Mr '89

Travel take-alongs. C. Christman. il *New Choices for the Best Years* 29:84+ Ag '89

Health aspects

Before you go . . . [adventure vacations] D. S. Stroetzel and D. Stroetzel. il *American Health* 8:58+ N '89

How to get medical care while you're traveling abroad. R. Sandroff. il *Money* 18:191-3 Je '89

The shipshape way to cruise. E. E. Rosenbaum. il *New Choices for the Best Years* 29:23-5 Ag '89

Take an ounce of prevention to the third world. D. H. Dunn. il *Business Week* p142 My 1 '89

Travel health. E. S. Orzac. il See alternate issues of Travel Holiday through December 1989

Information services

See also
    Travel Companions International

Periodicals

See also
    Travel & leisure (Periodical)
    Travel-holiday (Periodical)

Psychological aspects

Easy does it [travel stress] R. McGarvey. il *Travel Holiday* 172:28-31 O '89

Safety devices and measures

Packing for trouble. M. Patrick. il *Essence* 20:19-21 Je '89

To go or not to go? K. Castle. il *Travel Holiday* 171:16-17+ F '89

Terminology

Juggling the jargon. D. M. Koma. il *Travel Holiday* 172:60 O '89

TRAVEL & LEISURE (PERIODICAL)

AMEX goes for the glossies [editorial director P. Fiori] A. Rothman. il por *Business Week* p66 O 23 '89

James Berrien: sailing along in a sea of challengers. il por *Business Week* p99 Ag 21 '89

TRAVEL AGENCIES AND AGENTS

Clearing a path for disabled travelers. M. J. Pitzer. il *Business Week* p96 Jl 3 '89

How to choose a good travel agent. D. M. Koma. il *Travel Holiday* 172:58-61 O '89

Automation

What the traffic will bear. E. Dyson. il *Forbes* 143:282 My 29 '89

Great Britain

See also
    Major & Mrs. Holt's Battlefield Tours (Firm)

TRAVEL CLUBS

Savings on short notice [ski trips] S. Russell. il *Skiing* 41:10 F '89

TRAVEL COMPANIONS INTERNATIONAL

Research on the run. M. Di Landro. *Travel Holiday* 171:38 Mr '89

TRAVEL CONSULTANTS *See* Travel agencies and agents

TRAVEL-HOLIDAY (PERIODICAL)

The next generation. D. P. Marshall. *Travel Holiday* 171:4 My '89

TRAVEL INFORMATION GROUP

With a lineup like this, who needs charisma? [Reed International buys Travel Information Group] M. Maremont. il por *Business Week* p59 My 22 '89

TRAVEL INSURANCE *See* Insurance, Travel

TRAVEL LITERATURE

See also
    Guidebooks
    Publishers and publishing—Travel literature
    Travel—Bibliography

Authorship

Travel writing: a primer. R. W. Anderson. *The Writer* 102:14-16 Je '89

Travel writing: why I bother [book on China prefigures events in Tiananmen Square] P. Theroux. il *The New York Times Book Review* 94:7-8 Jl 30 '89

TRAVEL NEWSLETTERS

Escape routes [Hideaway report publisher A. Harper] C. Gorney. il por *House & Garden* 161:34+ Ja '89

TRAVEL PHOTOGRAPHY

Native portraiture. C. Rainier. il *Petersen's Photographic Magazine* 17:32-5 Ja '89

Photo tours & workshops. See issues of Petersen's Photographic Magazine beginning October 1988

Travel in focus. M. Grimm and T. Grimm. See alternate issues of Travel Holiday through January 1990

Traveler's camera. L. Dennis. See issues of Popular Photography beginning June 1988

TRAVEL REGULATIONS

See also
    Passports
    U.S. Customs Service
    Work visas

International aspects

See also
    Customs service

To go or not to go? K. Castle. il *Travel Holiday* 171:16-17+ F '89

TRAVEL STUDY COURSES

See also
    Foreign study
    Semester at Sea (Program)

Consumer watch. *Travel Holiday* 171:115 Mr '89

TRAVEL WITH CHILDREN

A capital city for kids [Washington, D.C.] A. K. Horowitz. il *Publishers Weekly* 235:122-3 My 12 '89

Club Med: come on down and bring the kids! S. Birnbaum. il *Good Housekeeping* 208:32+ Ja '89

Cruising: a low-cost family vacation. C. Loomis. il *Parents* 64:233+ My '89

Cruising tips [family cruising] P. Whittell. il *Motor Boating & Sailing* 163:40+ Je '89

The family vacation. J. Segal and Z. Segal. il *Parents* 64:211 My '89

Getting there in good time [car trips] K. Wilson. il *Good Housekeeping* 208:96-7 Je '89

TRAVEL WITH CHILDREN—*cont.*

Now the kids can rough it, too [family wilderness vacations] R. Wilder. il *U.S. News & World Report* 106:70-1 Ap 3 '89

Room service? Get me milk and cookies [hotel services] N. R. Gibbs. il *Time* 134:70-1 Jl 3 '89

Traveling abroad. D. F. Bjorklund and B. Bjorklund. il *Parents* 64:165 Jl '89

Vacationing with children. il *USA Today (Periodical)* 118:16 Ag '89

Vacations you (and the kids!) will love [summer family vacations] S. Birnbaum. il *Good Housekeeping* 209:98-9 Jl '89

A young person's guide to London. M. Elder. il *Gourmet* 49:108-13+ O '89

TRAVEL WITH PETS

Flying the (un)friendly skies [views of Bud Brownhill] L. A. Mark. il *American Health* 8:118 Je '89

Flying with fido. E. McGowan. il *Travel Holiday* 172:26-7 S '89

A pet-owner's guide to worry-free vacations. A. R. Marder. il *Prevention (Emmaus, Pa.)* 41:96-8 Jl '89

TRAVELERS CHECKS
See also
American Express Co.

TRAVELING INDUSTRY *See* Tourist trade

TRAVELING SOFTWARE INC.

Hey, who is this guy? [president M. Eppley] C. Bermant. il pors *Personal Computing* 13:96-9+ My '89

TRAVELING THEATER *See* Theater, Traveling

TRAVELING WAVE TUBES

Technical problems with Japanese satellite could disrupt Ariane's payload launch sequence [traveling wave tube amplifier on Superbird B telecommunications satellite] il *Aviation Week & Space Technology* 131:30 N 13 '89

TRAVELS [television program] *See* Television program reviews—Single works

TRAVERS, EVA FOLDES, AND SACKS, SUSAN RIEMER

Joining teacher education and the liberal arts in the undergraduate curriculum. il *Phi Delta Kappan* 70:470-4 F '89

TRAVERS, P. L. (PAMELA L.), 1906-
about

Mary Poppins, force of nature. H. Carpenter. *The New York Times Book Review* 94:29 Ag 27 '89

TRAVERS, PAMELA L. *See* Travers, P. L. (Pamela L.), 1906-

TRAVERSE CITY (MICH.)
Lighting

Michigan light victory [light pollution and John Rogers Observatory] il *Astronomy* 17:16 Ap '89

LA TRAVIATA [opera] *See* Verdi, Giuseppe, 1813-1901

TRAVIS, RANDY
about

Making country music hot again. K. Heron. il pors *The New York Times Magazine* p28-33+ Je 25 '89

Randy Travis. D. Gates. il por *Newsweek* 114:65 O 16 '89

Randy Travis. P. Reilly. por *Stereo Review* 54:90-1 Je '89

Randy Travis: making country hot again. K. Heron. il por *Reader's Digest* 135:57-8+ N '89

TRAVOLTA, JOHN
about

Look who's talking, a sleeper smash, Greases John Travolta's return to Hollywood favor. J. Kaufman. il pors *People Weekly* 32:67-8 N 13 '89

TRAWLS AND TRAWLING

Black light trolling. J. Gibbs. il *Outdoor Life* 183:34+ Je '89

Jousting with river kings [backtrolling for chinook salmon] P. Barrett. il *Field & Stream* 94:57-8+ O '89

Time to change. T. Syron. il *Field & Stream* 93:68+ F '89

TRAXLER, BOB
about

New hands on the purse strings. W. Booth and others. pors *Science* 243:160 Ja 13 '89

TRAYLOR, BILL, 1854-1947
about

Bill Traylor: Hirschl & Adler Modern; Luise Ross. E. Hayt-Atkins. il *Art News* 88:177 Mr '89

TREASURE TROVE
See also
Central America (Steamship)
City of Rio de Janeiro (Ship)
Titanic (Steamship)

Is a treasure hunter's gain history's loss? B. Carpenter. il *U.S. News & World Report* 107:54-5 Ag 21 '89

The secret of Oak Island [Money Pit] il map *National Geographic World* 166:22-5 Je '89

Solving old mysteries [Oak Island, N.S.] J. Daly. il *Maclean's* 102:45 Mr 20 '89

Treasure hunters denounce concealment of book's solution [case against D. L. Blair, administrator of contest contained in book Treasure in search of the golden horse] C. Reid. *Publishers Weekly* 236:10-11 Ag 25 '89

Writer D'Arcy O'Connor, digging deep into 'Money Pit' lore, unearths a trove of mysteries [Oak Island, N.S.] P. Freeman. il pors *People Weekly* 31:235-6 Mr 6 '89

TREASURY BILLS AND NOTES

Bills apoppin'. *Time* 133:58 My 15 '89

Guess what? A payoff for playing it safe. T. Thompson. *U.S. News & World Report* 106:64 Mr 6 '89

How to skip the middleman when buying a T-bill. L. J. Nathans. *Business Week* p112 Ja 23 '89

How to steer your investments around a twisting yield curve. il *Money* 18:7 F '89

Like those rates you see? Then take the long view. L. J. Nathans. *Business Week* p116 Ap 3 '89

The long bet. B. Weberman. il *Forbes* 143:113 Ja 23 '89

A sure thing. D. N. Dreman. il *Forbes* 143:226 Ap 17 '89

Too many bond traders, too few customers [primary dealers are quitting] F. A. Miller and W. Glasgall. il *Business Week* p71 Ja 30 '89

What's an inverted yield curve? And why should you care? J. Bodnar. il *Changing Times* 43:20 My '89

Where to keep your cash (II). il *Consumer Reports* 54:260 Ap '89

Why short-term rates are so sweet. L. J. Nathans. il *Business Week* p86 Ja 16 '89

Why you should own a 'slug' of Treasury bonds [interview with E. Hyman of C.J. Lawrence] J. Mendes. il por *Fortune* 119:36 F 27 '89

Yield inversion. T. Jaffe. *Forbes* 143:340 Ja 9 '89
Soviet Union

Soviet T-bonds? They're only the beginning. R. Brady. il *Business Week* p46 N 13 '89

TREASURY DEPT. (U.S.) *See* United States. Dept. of the Treasury

TREAT, LAWRENCE, 1903-

Murder most puzzling: can you solve this case? il *The New York Times Book Review* 94:36 O 15 '89

TREATIES
See also
Antarctic Treaty (1959)
United States—Treaties

What makes a good treaty? P. M. Jones. il *Scholastic Update (Teachers' edition)* 121:8-9 Mr 24 '89

TREATMENT OF INDIANS (AMERICAN) *See* Indians of North America—Treatment

TREATMENT OF PRISONERS *See* Prisoners—Treatment

TREATY OAK (AUSTIN, TEX.)

An apparent murder attempt on a venerable oak tree makes Texans fear for their roots. il *People Weekly* 32:116-17 Jl 17 '89

TREATY OF GHENT (1814)

1814. A. Nielsen. il *American Heritage* 40:40 D '89

TREATY OF VERSAILLES (1919)

The Versailles Treaty and after [reprint from January 1924 issue] D. Grayson. *Current History* 88:20-3 Ja '89

TREATY ON THE PROHIBITION OF THE EMPLACE-MENT OF NUCLEAR WEAPONS AND OTHER WEAPONS OF MASS DESTRUCTION ON THE SEA-BED AND OCEAN FLOOR AND THE SUBSOIL THEREOF (1972) *See* Seabed Treaty (1972)

TREBACH, ARNOLD S.

Accepting the presence of drugs. il *New Perspectives Quarterly* 6:40-4 Summ '89

TREBILCOCK, DOROTHY WARNER

A time to backburner. *The Writer* 102:9-10 Je '89

TREE [dance] *See* Dance reviews—Single works

TREE DATA STRUCTURES (COMPUTER SCIENCE) *See* Data structures (Computer science)

TREE FARMS
Alabama

Fee hunting funds a tree farm. O. Miller. il *Successful Farming* 87:51 Ja '89

TREE FELLING

Mr. Woodcutter, spare that tree! E. Morris. il *The New York Times Magazine* p20+ Mr 5 '89

Notes and comment [felling of Discovery Tree redwood in 1853 at Calaveras Big Trees State Park, Calif.] *The New Yorker* 64:23-4 F 13 '89

TREE GENETICS

Genetic engineering of trees to enhance resistance to insects [cover story] K. F. Raffa. bibl f il *BioScience* 39:524-34 S '89

TREE HOUSES

Media magnate Allen Neuharth's dream house has him up a tree [Cocoa Beach, Fla.] il por *People Weekly* 31:75 Ja 30 '89

Treehouses. R. Rupp. il *Country Journal* 16:47-50 Jl/Ag '89

TREE PLANTING
See also
Reforestation
TreePeople (Organization)

The best way to buy and plant a tree. K. Childers. il *The Family Handyman* 39:54+ Mr '89

Did Washington plant my relative's cane? B. Py-Lieberman. il *Smithsonian* 19:180 F '89

Growing pains. M. Phillips. il *The New York Times Magazine* p22+ S 3 '89

The high ground [gardening in Colorado] L. Caruso. il *Ms.* 17:52-3 Jl/F '89

TREE PLANTING—*cont.*
Planting trees and shrubs. il *Southern Living* 24:48-9 D '89
TREE STANDS (HUNTING) *See* Hunting—Equipment
TREE SURGERY *See* Trees—Care
TREE TAPPING *See* Maple sugar
TREEN, JOSEPH
Black hole. *The New Republic* 200:17-18 F 20 '89
TREEPEOPLE (ORGANIZATION)
Planting trees of life [work of A. Lipkis] il por *Time* 133:23 Ja 9 '89
TREES
See also
  Christmas trees
  Forest crown canopy
  Forest ecology
  Forests and forestry
  Fruit trees
  Timber
  Tree felling
  Tree planting
  Windbreaks
  See also names of trees
Branch libraries [reading under a shade tree] E. A. Peeples. bibl il *Country Journal* 16:30-1 Jl/Ag '89
Hunting for giants [tree hunters T. Grisez and M. Hobaugh comb Pennsylvania for champion specimens] C. Fergus. il pors *Country Journal* 16:56-61 Ja '89
'Killer' trees to the rescue [environmental importance] *Newsweek* 114:59 O 2 '89
Watch out, New England! [colorful trees for the garden] il *Sunset (Central West edition)* 183:88-91 N '89
Why a tree. C. Fenyvesi. il *Organic Gardening* 36:80 N '89
Words in the woods [word search puzzle involving trees] il *National Geographic World* 167:20-1 Jl '89
Biogeography
Maple: the biogeography of popular species. S. D. Garber. *Focus (New York, N.Y.: 1950)* 38:32-3+ Wint '88
Care
Men working in trees [tree surgeon R. Hill] J. Stuller. il por *Audubon* 91:86-91 Jl '89
Disease and pest resistance
Genetic engineering of trees to enhance resistance to insects [cover story] K. F. Raffa. bibl f il *BioScience* 39:524-34 S '89
Diseases and pests
See also
  Gypsy moths
  Maple—Diseases and pests
  Tent caterpillars
America's trees under siege. D. Yarrow. *Utne Reader* p55 My/Je '89
They nibbled while the forests burned [forest insects attack trees] R. A. Haack and W. J. Mattson. il *Natural History* p56-7 Ja '89
Geographical distribution
How fast can trees migrate? [climate models predict greenhouse warming doom for forests; research by Margaret Davis] L. Roberts. il maps *Science* 243:735-7 F 10 '89
Photographs and photography
All of the tall trees. J. Drafahl and S. Drafahl. il *Petersen's Photographic Magazine* 18:24-6 My '89
Planting
See Tree planting
Pruning
See Pruning
Religious aspects
See Trees in religion, folklore, etc.
Watering
See Watering of gardens, lawns, etc.
TREES, DWARF
See also
  Bonsai
  Fruit trees, Dwarf
TREES, EFFECT OF AIR POLLUTION ON
Air pollution and forest decline in a spruce (Picea abies) forest [West Germany] E.-D. Schulze. bibl f il map *Science* 244:776-83 My 19 '89
Ill winds: air pollution's toll on trees and crops. J. J. MacKenzie and M. T. El-Ashry. il map *Technology Review* 92:64-71 Ap '89
Nitrogen saturation in northern forest ecosystems. J. D. Aber and others. bibl f il *BioScience* 39:378-86 Je '89
Trouble on the wind [research by Robert I. Bruck] H. Middleton. il *Southern Living* 24:42+ Je '89
Where acids reign: do dying stands of Bavarian timber portend the future of polluted U.S. forests? [research by Ernst-Detlef Schulze; cover story] J. Raloff. il *Science News* 136:56-8 Jl 22 '89
TREES, EFFECT OF CARBON DIOXIDE ON
Forests: a tool to moderate global warming? R. A. Sedjo. bibl f il map *Environment* 31:14-20 Ja/F '89
Greenhouse gases, climate change, and U.S. forest markets. J. L. Regens and others. bibl f il *Environment* 31:4-5+ My '89

TREES, EFFECT OF FLOODS ON
Timber tactics [fishing flooded trees] K. Schultz. il *Field & Stream* 94:76+ N '89
TREES, EFFECT OF OZONE ON
Ozone needles loblolly pines . . . and saps sequoia seedlings. *Science News* 136:189 S 16 '89
TREES, FOSSIL
See also
  Petrified Forest National Park (Ariz.)
Glacial geology [ancient spruce forest in Wisconsin] J. M. Moran and others. il map *Earth Science* 41:16-18 Wint '88
Tom Miner Basin, Montana. R. H. Mohlenbrock. il maps *Natural History* p14-16 D '89
TREES, HISTORIC *See* Historic trees
TREES IN ART
See also
  Bark in art
TREES IN CITIES
See also
  TreePeople (Organization)
And now, the return of the killer trees? [sources of hydrocarbons] *Newsweek* 113:78 Je 5 '89
Bradford callery pear. S. D. Garber. il *Focus (New York, N.Y.: 1950)* 39:33-6 Fall '89
Leaves of gas [role of hydrocarbons in urban smog in Atlanta, Ga.; research by William Chameides] il *Discover* 10:20 F '89
Pear trees [street plantings of callery pears] *The New Yorker* 65:31-2 Ap 17 '89
Tree pollution [role of hydrocarbons in urban smog; research by William Chameides] J. W. Merline. il *Consumers' Research Magazine* 72:38 Ja '89
Turning a new leaf [Mendoza, Argentina] D. Einhorn. il *Américas* 41 no1:2-3 '89
TREES IN RELIGION, FOLKLORE, ETC.
Praying with trees. L. V. Ham. il *The Christian Century* 106:839-40 S 27 '89
The sacred tree. J. Brosse. il *The Courier (Unesco)* 42:4-9 Ja '89
TREFIL, J. S. (JAMES S.), 1938-
Beyond the quark [cover story] il *The New York Times Magazine* p24-7+ Ap 30 '89
The cycle of fate. bibl il por *Modern Maturity* 32:60-4 D '89/Ja '90
Galaxies. bibl (p146) il *Smithsonian* 19:36-46+ Ja '89
Phenomena, comment and notes. il por *Smithsonian* 20:34+ Je '89
The search for truth. il *Discover* 10:56-61 D '89
Stop to consider the stones that fall from the sky. il map *Smithsonian* 20:80-8+ S '89
TREFIL, JAMES S. *See* Trefil, J. S. (James S.), 1938-
TREICHEL, EDWARD A.
The outlook for the U.S. economy: complacency is unwarranted. *USA Today (Periodical)* 117:19-20 My '89
TREIRES, JAMES J.
Dark side of the dream. il *Newsweek* 113:10-11 Mr 20 '89
TREKKING *See* Hiking; Mountaineering
TRELLISES
The answer is a steel I-beam sandwich. il *Sunset (Central West edition)* 182:160 My '89
High-rise plantings. S. Sides. il *The Mother Earth News* 118:84+ Jl/Ag '89
If your vegetables need some help up: two simple trellises. il *Sunset (Central West edition)* 182:198-9 Mr '89
Seattle trellises for sunny or wet days. il *Sunset (Central West edition)* 181:114 D '88
Sunny trellis for vegetables. il *Sunset (Central West edition)* 182:236 My '89
A trellis to swing on, and to divide a small garden. il *Sunset (Central West edition)* 182:156-7 Ap '89
Well-engineered pea trellis. il *Sunset (Central West edition)* 183:214 N '89
TREMAIN, ALAN
about
When Alan Tremain checks in, the glitches check out. R. Duffy. il por *Business Week* p89 Mr 13 '89
TREMBLAY, HÉLÈNE
Families of the world. il *The Unesco Courier* 42:46-7 Ag '89
about
Families of the world. F. Cameron. il *Petersen's Photographic Magazine* 17:20-3 Mr '89
TREMORS (GEOLOGY) *See* Earthquakes
TRENBERTH, KEVIN E.
The wayward winds. maps *Natural History* p44-5 Ja '89
TREND FUND
How to spot trends for fun and profit [interview with E. Antoian] P. Sellers. il por *Fortune* 120:40-1 S 11 '89
TRENGOVE, TOM
about
The synthetic kitchen. B. Lobron. il *Popular Photography* 96:63+ O '89
TRENTON FALLS (N.Y.) IN ART
Exhibitions
America's scenic wonders [The art of Trenton Falls] A. E. Ledes. il *Antiques* 136:968+ N '89

TRESPASS
The hated season [deer hunting in New York] S. Lewis. il *The New York Times Magazine* p24+ N 26 '89
Hunter etiquette. J. Bashline. il *Field & Stream* 94:24+ S '89

Anecdotes, facetiae, satire, etc.
Social skills. P. F. McManus. il *Outdoor Life* 184:144+ S '89

TRETINOIN
Between the lines [Retin-A] A. Ranard. il *Health (New York, N.Y.)* 21:66-7+ O '89
From wrinkle cream to cancer cure? N. J. Freundlich. il *Business Week* p146 F 20 '89
How good is Retin-A? il *Consumer Reports* 54:112-13 F '89
Retin-A. S. Lord. *Vogue* 179:346-7+ Ag '89
Retin-A: a buyer's guide [wrinkle treatment] P. Boyer. il *Prevention (Emmaus, Pa.)* 41:95+ Ap '89
The selling of Retin-A. L. N. Vreeland. il *Money* 18:74-80+ Ap '89

TREVINO, LEE
about
It's nifty being 50. K. Moore. il pors *Sports Illustrated* 71:34-6+ D 18 '89
On deck. il por *Sport (New York, N.Y.)* 80:13 Ja '89

TREVOR, WILLIAM, 1928-
In love with Ariadne [story] il *Harper's* 278:62-71 Mr '89

TREVOR-ROPER, H. R. (HUGH REDWALD), 1914-
The prophet. bibl f il *The New York Review of Books* 36:28-34 O 12 '89

TREVOR-ROPER, HUGH REDWALD See Trevor-Roper, H. R. (Hugh Redwald), 1914-

TRIAL BY JURY See Jury

TRIALS
See also
Actions and defenses
Jury
Legal procedure
Miscarriage of justice
Television broadcasting—Trials
Translators and translating—Court use
War crime trials
Witnesses
Courthouse couture [celebrities] il *People Weekly* 32:106-7 D 25 '89-Ja 1 '90
Tabloid reality. *The Nation* 248:3-4 Ja 2 '89
Why some trials go on and on . . . and on. *U.S. News & World Report* 106:12 F 13 '89

California
Raids, racism and the I.N.S. [on trial for harassing Mexican immigrants] E. Shorris. il *The Nation* 248:628-30 My 8 '89

Grenada
In Grenada, victors' justice. *The Progressive* 53:15-16 Mr '89

Manitoba
Unhealed wounds [inquiry into circumstances surrounding 1971 murder and 1987 trial in H. B. Osborne case] N. Underwood. il *Maclean's* 102:41 Jl 10 '89

New York (State)
See also
Steinberg, Lisa, d. 1987—Child abuse case
Justice, at last [J. Pikul found guilty of murder] S. Weller. *Ms.* 17:75 Je '89
Love, hurt and money [courtroom proceedings in case of actor W. Hurt vs. ex-lover S. Jennings; cover story] S. Schindehette. il pors *People Weekly* 32:72-4+ Jl 10 '89

Newfoundland
Catching a spy [trial of S. J. Ratkai] G. Allen. il por *Maclean's* 102:13 F 20 '89

Ontario
Genetic fingerprints [used in convicting Ottawa rapist P. J. McNally] R. Laver. il *Maclean's* 102:54 Ap 17 '89

Soviet Union
Stalin takes the stand [proposed posthumous trial] E. Gellner. *The New Republic* 200:20+ Mr 20 '89

Washington (D.C.)
See also
Iran-contra affair—Trials

TRIALS (ESPIONAGE)
See also
Rosenberg (Julius and Ethel) case
Catching a spy [trial of S. J. Ratkai in Newfoundland] G. Allen. il por *Maclean's* 102:13 F 20 '89

TRIALS (MURDER)
See also
Levin, Jennifer Dawn, d. 1986—Murder case
Jury acquits Todd Bridges of charges of attempted murder, manslaughter. il por *Jet* 77:36-7 N 27 '89
Justice, at last [J. Pikul found guilty] S. Weller. *Ms.* 17:75 Je '89
The littlest victim [interview with five year old murder witness J. Royal] V. Gladstone. il pors *Life* 12:16+ O '89

The littlest witness may testify about her friend's killing [four year old J. Royal to testify against M. Ward in Miami trial] M. Brower. il pors *People Weekly* 31:108-10 Ap 24 '89
The startling Shelly Prine case [use of DNA fingerprints to convict O. Smith in Goessel, Kan.] P. Michelmore. *Reader's Digest* 135:179-80+ Jl '89
Unhealed wounds [inquiry into circumstances surrounding 1971 murder and 1987 trial in H. B. Osborne case in Manitoba] N. Underwood. il *Maclean's* 102:41 Jl 10 '89

TRIALS (OBSCENITY)
A rap album in the dock [obscenity case against Alexander, Ala. record store selling The 2 Live Crew] N. Zeman. il *Newsweek* 114:72 O 16 '89

TRIALS (RAPE)
Genetic fingerprints [used in convicting Ottawa rapist P. J. McNally] R. Laver. il *Maclean's* 102:54 Ap 17 '89

TRIANGLE INDUSTRIES, INC.
Insider-trading shock rocks the Elysee [Triangle affair] B. Riemer. il *Business Week* p54 Ja 23 '89
The Socialists dodge one bullet—but the next? [insider trading Triangle probe] B. Riemer and F. J. Comes. il *Business Week* p46 F 13 '89

TRIASSIC PERIOD See Paleontology—Triassic

TRIATHLON
Big splash in Hawaii [M. Allen wins men's Ironman Triathlon] K. Moore. il pors *Sports Illustrated* 71:62-4+ O 23 '89
Enduring greatness [P. Newby-Fraser] J. Ridge. il por *Women's Sports & Fitness* 11:24-6+ Je '89
The first unforgettable Ironman performance [J. Moss] K. McAlpine. *Women's Sports & Fitness* 11:27 Je '89
Heart of an Ironman [arthritis victim G. Yates] J. G. Hubbell. il pors *Reader's Digest* 134:13-14+ Mr '89
Paradise won [America's Paradise Triathlon] il *Women's Sports & Fitness* 11:58 Jl/Ag '89
Tips from the super jocks [D. Scott, M. Allen, S. Tinley] P. Serrani. il pors *Gentlemen's Quarterly* 59:250-7 My '89
Total fitness '89 [triathlon training; cover story; special section] il *Runner's World* 24:45-50+ My '89
Tough stuff for the masses: mainstreaming the Ironman. J. Silverman. il *Health (New York, N.Y.)* 21:86-8 Ag '89

TRIATHLON RECORDS
Tri-umph! [P. Newby-Frazier shatters Bud Light Ironman Triathlon women's record] L. Rothlein. il por *Women's Sports & Fitness* 11:50 Ja/F '89

TRIBE, LAURENCE H.
Should a constitutional amendment to prevent flag desecration be approved? [excerpts from testimony, July 18, 1989] *Congressional Digest* 68:215+ Ag/S '89
about
Constitutional law [discussion of December 1988 article, Rewriting the Constitution] S. C. Brubaker. *Commentary* 87:2-4+ My '89

TRIBECA FILM CENTER
De Niro's Tribeca. B. Paris. il *American Film* 15:38 O '89
If he can make it here . . . por *Time* 134:52 S 4 '89

TRIBES AND TRIBAL SYSTEMS
The screw-you spirit. J. M. Fallows. *The Washington Monthly* 21:42-3 Mr '89

TRIBOLOGY
Getting a grip on rubbing bodies. R. Pool. il *Science* 246:445 O 27 '89

TRIBOLUMINESCENCE See Luminescence

TRIBUNE COMPANY (CHICAGO, ILL.)
In the eye of the storm [syndicated exclusivity rules; interview with J. Dowdle] K. Haley. il pors *Channels (New York, N.Y.: 1986)* 9:62-3 Ja 16 '89

TRICHINOSIS
Beef, pork, and history [German ban on American pork in 1880s over trichinosis concerns] B. A. Weisberger. il *American Heritage* 40:20+ Jl/Ag '89

TRICHLORONITROMETHANE See Chloropicrin

TRICHOTHECENE TOXIN See Toxins and antitoxins

TRICHOTILLOMANIA See Hair pulling

TRICK PHOTOGRAPHY See Photography, Trick

TRICKS
See also
Conjuring
Jugglers and juggling
Minimal magic: baffling do-as-I-do stunts and other April Foolery. S. Morris. il *Omni (New York, N.Y.)* 11:128-9 Ap '89

TRIDEL ENTERPRISES INC.
Dangerous liaisons [B. Stone testifies at Ontario inquiry into political donations from Tridel Enterprises channeled through National Council of Jewish Women] P. Kaihla. il pors *Maclean's* 102:20+ O 16 '89

TRIDENT (MISSILE) See Guided missiles—Launching from submarines

TRIDENT SUBMARINES See Nuclear submarines

TRIEDMAN, KIM
A mother's dilemma. il *Ms.* 18:59-63 Jl/Ag '89

TRIETLEY, HARRY L., 1943-
All about relays (I). il *Radio-Electronics* 60:59-63+ N '89
All about relays (II). il *Radio-Electronics* 60:59-62+ D '89

TRIFINIO (CENTRAL AMERICA)
Beyond borders. M. Frankenfeld. map *Américas* 41 no2:52 '89

TRIGÈRE, PAULINE
about
Vicki Woods crosses paths with the eccentric Pauline Trigère—and comes away with an earful. V. Woods. il por *Vogue* 179:454+ O '89

TRIIODOTHYRONINE
Identification of a thyroid hormone receptor that is pituitary-specific. R. A. Hodin and others. bibl f il *Science* 244:76-9 Ap 7 '89

TRILLIN, CALVIN
Abigail y yo. *The New Yorker* 65:83-8 Je 26 '89
Chinatown—one man's meat. il por *Architectural Digest* 46:116+ N '89
Knowing Johnny Jenkins. *The New Yorker* 65:79-97 O 30 '89
The man who saved the library: an ode to Vartan Gregorian. il por *The New York Times Book Review* 94:15 F 5 '89
Profiles [Penn & Teller] il *The New Yorker* 65:58+ My 15 '89
Uncivil liberties. See occasional issues of The Nation

TRILLING, DIANA
about
Journey's beginning: a talk with Diana Trilling. S. Koch. il por *The New York Times Book Review* 94:1+ F 19 '89

TRILLING, LIONEL, 1905-1975
about
Resurrecting liberalism. B. DeMott. *Current (Washington, D.C.)* 309:14-22 Ja '89

TRILOBITES
Phenomena, comment and notes [P. Sheldon's work with trilobites] J. S. Trefil. il por *Smithsonian* 20:34+ Je '89
Why bite the right of a trilobite? [research by Loren E. Babcock] R. Monastersky. il *Science News* 136:78 Jl 29 '89

TRIM (JET AIRPLANES) See Airplanes, Jet—Stability and stabilizers

TRIMARANS
Planesail: new era of wings at sea. il *Popular Mechanics* 166:13 Je '89
Tri-hull ship [designed by C. Gongwer; cover story] A. L. Carone and J. Free. il por *Popular Science* 235:60-2 Ag '89
Winners [G. Kolesnikovs breaks record from New York to San Francisco via Cape Horn] L. Rudeen. il por *Motor Boating & Sailing* 164:20 Ag '89

TRIMM, H. WAYNE
Dan Logé—an artist in touch with the river. il *The Conservationist* 44:10-15 S/O '89

TRIMMERS, WEED See Lawn equipment

TRINDER, JOHN
about
The new TVX, burnished by tough times [interview] J. Flinn and N. Koch. pors *Channels (New York, N.Y.: 1986)* 9:70-1 Mr '89

TRINDER & BOYLAN INC.
Mixed metaphors. J. Moline. il *Harper's Bazaar* 122:50 N '89

TRINH, T. MINH-HA, 1952-
about
Surname Viet given name Nam [film] Reviews
The Nation 248:529-30 Ap 17 '89. S. Klawans

TRINITROTOLUENE See TNT (Explosive)

TRINITY
See also
Holy Spirit
Beside the Lord. P. Perkins. *The Christian Century* 106:522 My 17 '89
Doing right by women and the Trinity too. D. A. Helminiak. il *America* 160:110+ F 11 '89
Uttering the ineffable. P. J. Ryan. il *America* 160:463 My 13 '89

TRIO INDIANS See Tirió Indians

TRIOS, INSTRUMENTAL
See also
Phonograph records—Trios, Instrumental
Who's on third? [jazz trios] D. Okrent. il *Esquire* 112:41 Ag '89

TRIPHENYL BISMUTH
Making plastics visible to X-rays. I. Amato and J. Raloff. *Science News* 135:252 Ap 22 '89

TRIPLE CROWN (HORSE RACING) See Horse racing

TRIPLE FIVE CORPORATION
Blue-sky planning [refinancing package for West Edmonton Mall] J. Daly. il *Maclean's* 102:38 Ag 21 '89
Will wonders never cease? J. Queenan. il *Forbes* 144:72-3+ S 4 '89

TRIPLE NET PARTNERSHIP
Steady income, low risk. This can't be real estate. T. Segal. *Business Week* p142 My 1 '89

TRIPLETS
Love multiplied by three [Mohr triplets born 21 months apart]; ed. by Élaine Fein. J. Mohr. il pors *Redbook* 173:100-1+ Ag '89

What has six legs and stings like a bee? The Weaver brothers, boxing's only triple threat. il *People Weekly* 32:148-9 N 13 '89

TRIPLEX APARTMENTS See Apartments
TRIPODS, CAMERA See Camera tripods
TRIPS See Travel
TRIREMES
The trireme sails again. J. F. Coates. bibl il *Scientific American* 260:96-103 Ap '89

TRISHA BROWN DANCE COMPANY
Dancing:
Performances at City Center. A. Croce. *The New Yorker* 65:108 Ap 3 '89
Pressing forward [performance of Astral convertible] T. Tobias. il *New York* 22:82-3 Ap 3 '89
Reviews:
Premiere of Astral convertible at City Center, New York City. C. Hardy. il *Dance Magazine* 63:54 Jl '89

TRISLER (JOYCE) DANSCOMPANY See Joyce Trisler Danscompany

TRISTAN, FLORA, 1803-1844
about
Out of sight, out of time. M. R. Day. il *Américas* 41 no2:11-15 '89

TRISTAN Y MOSCOZO, FLORE CÉLESTINE THÉRÈSE HENRIETTE See Tristan, Flora, 1803-1844

TRITICALE
A grain to weather climate change. *Science News* 136:46 Jl 15 '89

TRITIUM
Accelerator eyed for warhead tritium. M. Crawford. *Science* 243:469 Ja 27 '89
Clash of the dogmas [tritium shortage] J. D. Isaacs. *The Bulletin of the Atomic Scientists* 45:4 Mr '89
Shortage could force U.S. to curtail tritium sales [consequence of shutdown of Savannah River reactors] *Aviation Week & Space Technology* 130:25 F 27 '89
The tritium follies [debate over restarting Savannah River reactors] D. Albright and J. Beard. bibl f il *The Bulletin of the Atomic Scientists* 45:42-5 N '89
Tritium puzzle [shipment lost between U.S. and England] P. Elmer-Dewitt. il map *Time* 134:75 N 13 '89
The tritium tiff. W. J. Lanouette. *The Bulletin of the Atomic Scientists* 45:44 D '89

TRITON (SATELLITE) See Neptune (Planet)—Satellites
TRITON ALLIANCE CORPORATION
Solving old mysteries [Oak Island, N.S.] J. Daly. il *Maclean's* 102:45 Mr 20 '89

TRITON GROUP LTD.
Under new management [Fuqua Industries] A. A. Lappen. il por *Forbes* 144:164 S 18 '89

IL TRITTICO [opera] See Puccini, Giacomo, 1858-1924
TRIUMPH OF THE SPIRIT [film] See Motion picture reviews—Single works

TRIVELPIECE, ALVIN W.
about
New directors at Fermilab, Oak Ridge and Lawrence Livermore. W. Sweet. pors *Physics Today* 42:63-5 Jl '89

TRIVELPIECE, SUSAN G., AND TRIVELPIECE, WAYNE Z.
Antarctica's well-bred penguins. il map *Natural History* p28-37 D '89

TRIVELPIECE, WAYNE Z.
(jt. auth) See Trivelpiece, Susan G., and Trivelpiece, Wayne Z.

TRIVIA
Great factoids. il *People Weekly* 31:57+ Mr 6 '89
Presidential trivia. D. O. Relin. il *Scholastic Update (Teachers' edition)* 121:20-1 Ja 13 '89
Test your star smarts. il *Teen* 33:43 F '89

TRIXIES (NEW YORK, N.Y.: RESTAURANT) See New York (N.Y.)—Restaurants, nightclubs, bars, etc.

TRNA See Transfer RNA

TROILUS AND CRESSIDA [drama] See Shakespeare, William, 1564-1616

TROLLEY BUSES See Trolleys

TROLLEYS
Tram's-eye views of Hong Kong street life. il *Sunset (Central West edition)* 182:44 Ja '89

TROLLING See Trawls and trawling

TROLLOPE, ANTHONY, 1815-1882
about
Living with Trollope. J. Bayley. il *The New York Review of Books* 36:6-8 Ag 17 '89

TROMBONE MUSIC
See also
Phonograph records—Trombone music
Curtis Fuller's solo on "Blues after all"—a trombone transcription. L. McClellan, Jr. il *Down Beat* 56:56 Jl '89
Wayne Shorter's solo on On Green Dolphin St.—a trombonist's analysis. R. Eubanks. il *Down Beat* 56:58-9 Ja '89

TROMBONISTS
See also
Anderson, Ray
Eubanks, Robin
Fuller, Curtis, 1934-
Morrison, James

TROMBONISTS—See also—*cont.*
Turre, Steve

TROMPE-L'OEIL
Art: trompe l'oeil painting. J. A. Cuadrado. il *Architectural Digest* 46:168-73+ Mr '89

TRON OPERATING SYSTEMS
The TRON project. K. Sakamura and R. Sprague. il *Byte* 14:292-301 Ap '89

TROOP BEVERLY HILLS [film] See Motion picture reviews—Single works

TROOPING THE COLOR
Photographs and photography
To make that special event a real photo opportunity, you've got to pick the right spot. L. Dennis. il *Popular Photography* 96:34+ Ap '89

TROPHIES, SPORT
See also
Fishing trophies
Heisman Trophy
Hunting trophies

TROPICAL DISEASES See Tropical medicine

TROPICAL FISH
Flashy new 'items' make a big splash in the aquarium world [home aquariums] R. Conniff. il *Smithsonian* 20:90-4+ My '89

TROPICAL FORESTS, DRY See Forests and forestry
TROPICAL FRUIT COOKING See Cooking—Fruit
TROPICAL FRUIT INDUSTRY See Fruit industry
TROPICAL MEDICINE
New weapons. R. H. Morrow. il *World Health* p9-11 Je '89

TROPICAL PLANTS
See also
Bromeliads

TROPICAL RAIN FORESTS See Rain forests
TROPICAL RESEARCH INSTITUTE See Smithsonian Tropical Research Institute

TROPICS
See also
Amazon River Valley
Food supply—Tropics
Smithsonian Tropical Research Institute
Wildlife conservation—Tropics
The tropical equation [cover story; special section; with introd. by T. H. Watkins] il *Wilderness* 53:18-51 Wint '89
Climate
The rains return to the tropics [1988] D. LeComte. il *Weatherwise* 42:8-12 F '89

TROPISM
See also
Geotropism

TROPOMYOSIN See Myosin

TROPP, BARBARA
about
Golden gates. S. H. Loomis. il *The New York Times Magazine* p49-50 F 12 '89

TROST, CARLISLE A. H., 1930-
The U.S. Navy today [address, May 16, 1989] *Vital Speeches of the Day* 55:578-80 Jl 15 '89

TROTSKY
about
Trotsky, whose lively street art became an off-the-wall album cover for Bob Dylan. il por *People Weekly* 32:112 O 23 '89

TROTSKY, LEON, 1879-1940
about
Why my grandfather Leon Trotsky must be turning in his grave. Y. Akselrod. *Commentary* 87:39-43 Ap '89

TROTSKY FAMILY
about
Why my grandfather Leon Trotsky must be turning in his grave. Y. Akselrod. *Commentary* 87:39-43 Ap '89

TROTTA, GERI
Block Island. il map *Gourmet* 49:76-81+ My '89
Geneva's Du Rhône Chocolatier. il *Gourmet* 49:128+ D '89

TROTTA, WAYNE L.
Why psychotherapy must be, and cannot be, a science. por *The Humanist* 49:23-5+ S/O '89

TROTTIER, LEO
about
Chicken wars in the Great White North. D. Francis. il *Maclean's* 102:11 Ja 9 '89

TROTTIER, PENNY
about
Chicken wars in the Great White North. D. Francis. il *Maclean's* 102:11 Ja 9 '89

TROUPE, QUINCY
about
Word star. P. Giddings. por *Essence* 20:28 S '89

TROUSERS See Pants

TROUT, B. THOMAS, 1939-
The Soviet challenge to American education. *The Education Digest* 54:35-7 Ap '89

TROUT, DAVID V.
PSMA: tangible improvements in shows for dealers and collectors. il *Antiques & Collecting Hobbies* 94:24-6+ Ag '89

TROUT, JO FRANKLIN- See Franklin-Trout, Jo

TROUT
See also
Cooking—Fish
The notorious cannibal [brown trout] A. J. McClane. il *Field & Stream* 94:36+ My '89

TROUT FISHING
See also
Grayling fishing
Becoming a fly angler, step by step. P. Barrett. il *Field & Stream* 93:117-19 Ap '89
Big lakers on Seneca. T. P. Maguire. il *The Conservationist* 43:10-13 My/Je '89
Bighorn of plenty. W. G. Tapply. il map *Field & Stream* 93:32-3+ Ja '89
Black earth, spring creeks. P. Kaminsky. il *Field & Stream* 94:50-1+ D '89
Evolution of a spring creek fisherman. N. Lyons. il *Field & Stream* 93:16-17 Ap '89
Finding trout in bypassed places. P. Barrett. il *Field & Stream* 94:57-8 Je '89
Fly fishing slow currents. J. Gierach. il *Field & Stream* 94:56-7+ My '89
Footloose on vacation lakes. P. Barrett. il *Field & Stream* 94:56-7+ Ag '89
Grandpa and the kid [brown trout fishing] D. Sisson. il *Field & Stream* 94:39+ Je '89
Lakers east to west. B. Journey. il *Outdoor Life* 183:68-9+ F '89
The land of legendary brook trout [Labrador, Nfld.] T. Huggler. il *Outdoor Life* 184:58-9+ Jl '89
Lifting weights [nymphs] D. Hughes. il *Field & Stream* 93:50-1+ Mr '89
Midge magic. W. G. Tapply. il *Field & Stream* 94:36+ Ag '89
Midsummer's trout dream. J. McCue. il *Outdoor Life* 183:61-3+ Je '89
New York's great angling secret [fall trout fishing] J. Rowen. il *The Conservationist* 44:34-9 S/O '89
Northern lights [steelhead] K. McCafferty. il *Field & Stream* 94:60-1+ My '89
The notorious cannibal [brown trout] A. J. McClane. il *Field & Stream* 94:36+ My '89
Open-water icefishing [spring] D. Zutz. il *Outdoor Life* 183:88-9+ Ap '89
The other West. D. Hughes. il *Field & Stream* 94:40-1+ S '89
The Ozarks: where the big trout run. H. Middleton. il *Southern Living* 24:84-7 Je '89
Second-chance trout. P. Barrett. il *Field & Stream* 94:102+ S '89
Secret season trout. J. Gibbs. il *Outdoor Life* 183:69-71+ Mr '89
Secrets of an opening day addict. N. Lyons. il *Outdoor Life* 183:82-3+ Ap '89
Shorten up! J. Bashline. il *Field & Stream* 93:32+ Ap '89
Spinning for trout. E. Cutlip. il *Field & Stream* 94:44 My '89
Strip-tease trouting. G. A. Borger. il *Field & Stream* 94:46-7+ Je '89
Through the slot [slot regulations for bass and trout] J. Bashline. il *Field & Stream* 93:18 Ja '89
Trout in the spring runoff. J. Gierach. il *Field & Stream* 93:70-1+ Ap '89
The trout of summer [cover story; special section] il *Field & Stream* 94:44-9+ Jl '89
The trout of winter [catch and release] J. Barsness. il *Field & Stream* 93:56-7+ F '89
Unlock your trout stream. T. Rosenbauer. il *Outdoor Life* 183:82-3+ My '89
Welcome, world, to Trout Town U.S.A., where all the flies are fit to be tied [flyfishing the Beaverkill River in New York State] J. Friedman. il *People Weekly* 32:92-4+ Jl 3 '89
Wing it [dry flies] J. Bashline. il *Field & Stream* 94:34 My '89
Worm mornings. N. Strung. il *Field & Stream* 93:44-5+ Mr '89
Zen and the art of fly-fishing. J. Cramer. il *Time* 134:52 Ag 7 '89

Anecdotes, facetiae, satire, etc.
All about brown trout and bourbon. E. Zern. *Field & Stream* 94:104 Ag '89
Toads in the scumline [trout fishing lingo in the West] W. G. Tapply. il *Field & Stream* 94:32+ O '89

IL TROVATORE [opera] See Verdi, Giuseppe, 1813-1901

TROW, GEORGE W. S.
Empty or nearly so in Houston. *The New Yorker* 64:84-91 Ja 30 '89
A man who can't love (dedicated to women who love too much). *The New Yorker* 64:29 Ja 16 '89

TROY, CAROL
'Can you imagine them making love?'. il por *American Film* 14:46-51+ Je '89

TROY, JUDY
Accident [story] *The New Yorker* 65:30-1 Jl 10 '89

TROY (ANCIENT CITY)
Digging up Troy [project led by M. Korfmann] C. Heybrock. il *World Press Review* 36:57 Ja '89
TRUBO, RICHARD
Computeritis. il *Glamour* 87:56+ D '89
When doctors say no. il *Good Housekeeping* 209:82+ Ag '89
TRUBY, J. DAVID
Castro's curveball. *Harper's* 278:32+ My '89
TRUCK CAMPERS *See* Campers, Truck
TRUCK DRIVERS
Nutrition
Truck heaven [low calorie menus served at truck stops leased by Unocal] R. Flippin. *American Health* 8:105 N '89
TRUCK DRIVING
Mud hazards
Power assist. S. L. White. il *Field & Stream* 94:88+ N '89
Winter driving
Leader of the pack [icy conditions encountered during truck testing] J. R. Nerad. il *Motor Trend* 41:12 Ap '89
Utah
Red rock rookie [driving a Ford four wheel drive truck in Moab] T. Swan. il *Popular Mechanics* 166:44 N '89
TRUCK ENGINES
See also
Cummins Engine Company, Inc.
Cooling
Overheating primer. M. J. Schultz. *The Family Handyman* 39:74-5 S '89
Design
V10. D. Sherman. il *Popular Science* 234:122-3 Je '89
Environmental aspects
See Trucks—Environmental aspects
Exhaust
See also
Trucks—Environmental aspects
TRUCK FARMING
Successful family farm [sweet corn and fresh vegetable business owned by Wieck family in Texas] M. Holmberg. il *Successful Farming* 87:38-40 mid-Mr '89
TRUCK INDUSTRY
See also
Fruehauf Corp.
Acquisitions and mergers
Parlaying the winnings [Terex to buy Fruehauf's trailer business] R. Reiff. il por *Forbes* 144:45-6 Jl 24 '89
Western Europe
Europe's truckmakers face survival of the biggest. A. D. Smith. il *Business Week* p68 N 6 '89
Export-import trade
Treasury overrules Customs on import sport/utilities. *Motor Trend* 41:62-3 My '89
When is a truck not a truck? [U.S. tariff raises prices on Japanese trucks] il *Consumer Reports* 54:330 My '89
Finance
Automotive. J. Flint. il *Forbes* 143:90-2 Ja 9 '89
United States
See Truck industry
TRUCK INSURANCE *See* Insurance, Truck
TRUCK SERVICE STATIONS
Be it ever so glitzy, there's no place like the new truck stop. S. Hubbell. bibl (p245-6) il *Smithsonian* 20:94-102+ N '89
Truck heaven [low calorie menus served at truck stops leased by Unocal] R. Flippin. *American Health* 8:105 N '89
TRUCK SPEED RECORDS
High-speed hauler [land speed record set at Bonneville in a GMC S-15 Club Coupe] L. Frank. il *Popular Mechanics* 166:52-3 D '89
TRUCK STOPS *See* Truck service stations
TRUCKERS *See* Truck drivers
TRUCKING
See also
Central Freight Lines Inc.
Consolidated Freightways, Inc.
Jones Transfer Co.
Leaseway Transportation Corp.
Skyway Freight Systems Inc.
Telecommunication in trucking
Tiger International, Inc.
Finance
Surface transportation. J. Clements. il *Forbes* 143:192-3 Ja 9 '89
History
The Wingfoot Express [Goodyear's early involvement in trucking] W. Jeanes. il map *Car and Driver* 35:121-3 D '89
Insurance
See Insurance, Truck
TRUCKS
See also
Campers, Truck
Vans
Power truckin'. T. Swan and J. Dunne. il *Popular Mechanics* 166:67-70 N '89
Truck trends. T. Opre. il *Outdoor Life* 183:31+ My '89

Truckin' '89. B. W. Smith. il *Popular Mechanics* 166:85+ Ja '89
Trucks turn to high tech. J. Candler. il *Nation's Business* 77:38+ O '89
Aerodynamics
Big rigs ease down a long and windy road [use of aerodynamic boat tail] I. Amato. il *Science News* 135:134 Mr 4 '89
Truckin' tails [aerodynamic boat tail reduces drag] il *Discover* 10:16 Jl '89
Bearings
Easy roller [wheel bearings] S. L. White. il *Field & Stream* 94:72+ O '89
Camping equipment
See also
Campers, Truck
Environmental aspects
The congestion-pollution connection [address, July 7, 1989] T. J. Donohue. *Vital Speeches of the Day* 55:763-6 O 1 '89
Equipment
Fast truck tents. N. Strung. il *Field & Stream* 94:104 D '89
Getting in gear. R. Ives. *Travel Holiday* 171:42-3 Mr '89
Pickup accessories. D. Mowitz. il *Successful Farming* 87:E4-F1 D '89
Pickup toppers [security and weather protection] T. Kaho. il *Home Mechanix* 85:64-5+ Ag '89
Four wheel drive
Breathing room [Ford F-150 Supercab] S. L. White. il *Field & Stream* 94:72+ Je '89
Brute strength [Dodge Ram] S. L. White. il *Field & Stream* 94:60+ Ag '89
Little brother [GMC Truck S-15 Jimmy 4X4] S. L. White. il *Field & Stream* 93:54+ Ja '89
Mudders [pickup trucks] D. Sherman. il *Popular Science* 235:33-4+ Jl '89
Red rock rookie [driving a Ford truck in Moab, Utah] T. Swan. il *Popular Mechanics* 166:44 N '89
History
See also
Trucks, Antique
Laws and regulations
See also
Trucks—Environmental aspects
Leasing and renting
See also
Ryder System, Inc.
Noise
Listen up! S. L. White. il *Field & Stream* 93:80+ F '89
Registration
Panama
Another Panamanian headache [to duck highway fees, U.S. truckers are registering and insuring their rigs in Panama] D. Fanning. il *Forbes* 144:80 N 13 '89
Restoration
See Trucks, Restored
Springs and suspension
Active terrain tamer [GMC Sierra A/R] B. Brazier. il *Popular Mechanics* 166:93+ Ja '89
Testing
America's trucks [pickups] D. McCosh. il *Popular Science* 234:44-5+ F '89
Chevrolet C1500 454SS. B. Visnic. il *Car and Driver* 35:80-1 O '89
Compact commandos. R. Taylor. il *Popular Mechanics* 166:51-5+ F '89
Dodge Dakota [convertible pickup] R. Ceppos. il *Car and Driver* 34:63 F '89
Leader of the pack [icy conditions encountered during truck testing] J. R. Nerad. il *Motor Trend* 41:12 Ap '89
Motor trend's 1989 Truck of the Year [Toyota Xtracab SR5 V-6] il *Motor Trend* 41:108-12+ Ap '89
Passenger pickups [Chevrolet C1500 Extended Cab, Dodge Dakota Club Cab, Ford 4x4 Ranger Supercab, Toyota Xtracab SR5] D. Chaikin. il *Home Mechanix* 85:62-6 D '89
Pickups for gardeners. M. Ferrara. il *Organic Gardening* 36:61-4+ S '89
Shelby Dakota. P. Berg. il *Car and Driver* 35:93-5+ Jl '89
Shelby Dakota V8. G. Coppock. il *Motor Trend* 41:136+ N '89
Trucks to take afield [pickups] T. Opre. il *Outdoor Life* 183:80-2+ Ja '89
Tracking
Tracking trucks by satellite. R. Schneiderman. il *High Technology Business* 9:24-6+ My '89
Wheel bearings
See Trucks—Bearings
TRUCKS, ANTIQUE
Driving the Packard Model E. W. Jeanes. il *Car and Driver* 35:126-7 D '89
TRUCKS, FOREIGN
Truckin' '89. B. W. Smith. il *Popular Mechanics* 166:85+ Ja '89
Four wheel drive
Mudders [pickup trucks] D. Sherman. il *Popular Science* 235:33-4+ Jl '89

TRUCKS, FOREIGN—*cont.*
Prices
When is a truck not a truck? [U.S. tariff raises prices on Japanese trucks] il *Consumer Reports* 54:330 My '89
Testing
Compact commandos. R. Taylor. il *Popular Mechanics* 166:51-5+ F '89
Motor trend's 1989 Truck of the Year [Toyota Xtracab SR5 V-6] il *Motor Trend* 41:108-12+ Ap '89
Passenger pickups [Chevrolet C1500 Extended Cab, Dodge Dakota Club Cab, Ford 4x4 Ranger Supercab, Toyota Xtracab SR5] D. Chaikin. il *Home Mechanix* 85:62-6 D '89

TRUCKS, REMODELED
See also
Vans, Remodeled
A shop on the spot [farm service truck] C. Finck. il *Successful Farming* 87:28 F '89
Tool trucks. D. Mowitz. il *Successful Farming* 87:66V-66W F '89

TRUCKS, RESTORED
Hugh's truck [H. Cosman's restored 1953 Ford F-100 pickup] *The New Yorker* 65:46-7 N 13 '89

TRUCKS IN BUSINESS
Trucks turn to high tech. J. Candler. il *Nation's Business* 77:38+ O '89
Leasing and renting
The leased advantages. J. Candler. il *Nation's Business* 77:40+ My '89

TRUDEAU, G. B., 1948-
about
Doonesbury comes home to Andrews & McMeel. por *Publishers Weekly* 235:61 Ja 13 '89
TRUDEAU, GARRY B. *See* Trudeau, G. B., 1948-
TRUDEAU, JANE PAULEY *See* Pauley, Jane
TRUDEAU, PIERRE ELLIOTT
about
A battle joined [cover story; special section] il pors *Maclean's* 102:20-2+ N 6 '89
TRUDELL, DENNIS
The artists [poem] *America* 160:528 Je 3 '89
TRUE BELIEVER [film] *See* Motion picture reviews—Single works
TRUE CHURCH OF GOD
White Harlem minister convicted of sex abuse [case of T. Streitferdt] il por *Jet* 76:32 Je 19 '89
White minister called 'wolf in sheep's clothes' gets 7 years in sex cases [T. Streitferdt] il por *Jet* 76:53 Jl 24 '89
TRUE LOVE [film] *See* Motion picture reviews—Single works
TRUEMAN, DAVID
Protecting the children of divorce. il *USA Today (Periodical)* 117:74-5 My '89
TRUFFAUT, FRANÇOIS, 1932-1984
about
Encore, The 400 blows. M. Pally. il *Film Comment* 25:6 Jl/Ag '89
TRUFFAUT, FRANÇOIS, 1932-1984, AND GIVRAY, CLAUDE DE
'The little thief': scenes from the last Truffaut. il *Film Comment* 25:17-22 Ja/F '89
TRUFFLES
See also
Urbani Truffles USA
Into the woods [hunting white truffles in the Piedmont, Italy] J. Steingarten. il *House & Garden* 161:50+ F '89
A truffling matter: lab coats replace pigs in the hunt for truffles. E. Corcoran. il *Scientific American* 260:101 My '89
Contamination
Don't trifle with truffles. il *FDA Consumer* 23:36 Jl/Ag '89
TRUITT, KENDALL L.
about
Foul play on the Iowa? E. Salholz. il pors *Newsweek* 113:22 Je 5 '89
The Iowa inquiry. W. Lowther. *Maclean's* 102:23 Je 5 '89
Mystery aboard the Iowa. F. Trippett. il pors *Time* 133:40 Je 5 '89
TRULY, RICHARD
about
Space/missiles: NASA/industry shuttle team. il por *Aviation Week & Space Technology* 130:14 Ja 2 '89
TRUMAN, HARRY S., 1884-1972
He didn't like Ike [excerpt from Where the buck stops]; ed. by Margaret Truman. il pors *The New York Times Magazine* p40-2+ S 17 '89
about
The centennial annual meeting, starring Harry Truman and civil liberties [excerpt from Renewing a scientific society] D. L. Wolfle. il por *Science* 246:130-1 O 6 '89
Harry Truman, small-town American. A. L. Hamby. bibl il pors *History Today* 39:17-23 D '89
Religion
The Truman doctrine. M. E. Marty. il *The Christian Century* 106:271 Mr 8 '89
TRUMAN, MARGARET, 1924-
(ed) *See* Truman, Harry S., 1884-1972. He didn't like Ike

TRUMBULL FAMILY
about
Revolutionary village. C. Weeks. il map *American Heritage* 40:80-91 Ap '89
TRUMP, DONALD J.
about
The art of playing the Trump card. F. Bruning. il *Maclean's* 102:11 Ja 30 '89
The art of the wheel. G. Drake. il por *Bicycling* 30:26-8+ Ag '89
The best and the brassiest. C. P. Work. il pors *U.S. News & World Report* 107:52-4 O 23 '89
Boxed in by Trump [special section] il por *Business Week* p54-6 O 23 '89
Charged with practicing the art of the steal, Ed Zito plays his own Trump Card against Donald. il pors *People Weekly* 32:111 Ag 7 '89
Donald Trump. G. Smith. il por *People Weekly* 32 Special Issue:52-3 Fall '89
Donald Trump's buy-American plan. il por *U.S. News & World Report* 107:23-4 O 16 '89
Eastern reopens bidding for shuttle as Trump balks at $365 million price. P. Proctor and J. T. McKenna. *Aviation Week & Space Technology* 130:31 Mr 27 '89
An ego as big as American. L. Reibstein. il pors *Newsweek* 114:56-7 O 16 '89
Flashy symbol of an acquisitive age [cover story] O. Friedrich. il pors *Time* 133:48-54 Ja 16 '89
Here comes Donald, duck! C. Gorman. il por *Time* 134:52+ O 16 '89
How Trump plays monopoly. H. Rudnitsky. il *Forbes* 143:128 Ap 17 '89
The new Merv Griffin show. K. Hannon. il *Forbes* 144:10 Ag 21 '89
The Palm Beach story. C. K. Gandee. il pors *House & Garden* 161:110-19+ D '89
T. without sympathy. P. Hamill. il por *Esquire* 112:59-61 D '89
This time, Trump may roll snake eyes. J. Weber, Jr. il *Business Week* p151 N 27 '89
Trump mounts bid to buy American for $7.5 billion. *Aviation Week & Space Technology* 131:139 O 9 '89
Trump vs. Stern: the unmaking of a documentary [cover story] E. Diamond. il pors *New York* 22:30-7 S 4 '89
The Trumps: America's most glamorous two-career couple. M. Hammond. il pors *McCall's* 116:22-4+ F '89
Trump's troubles. M. J. Williams. il por *Fortune* 120:157+ D 18 '89
Tycoons. G. Jaynes. il pors *Life* 12:45+ Ja '89
The Wheel of Fortune turns badly for Merv Griffin. L. Reibstein. il por *Newsweek* 114:62 N 27 '89
The wheel of misfortune? R. Grover. il *Business Week* p35-6 Ja 16 '89
The wheels of fortune. E. M. Swift. il *Sports Illustrated* 70:32-4+ My 22 '89
Anecdotes, facetiae, satire, etc.
How to be happy on less than a billion. K. Fury. il *Working Woman* 14:236 S '89
TRUMP, IVANA
about
The Palm Beach story. C. K. Gandee. il pors *House & Garden* 161:110-19+ D '89
The Plaza suite. C. Vogel. il por *The New York Times Magazine* p50-2+ Ja 15 '89
The Trumps: America's most glamorous two-career couple. M. Hammond. il pors *McCall's* 116:22-4+ F '89
TRUMP, ROBERT T.
(jt. auth) *See* Fennimore, Donald L., and Trump, Robert T.
TRUMP PLAZA HOTEL & CASINO (ATLANTIC CITY, N.J.)
How Trump plays monopoly [D. Trump's lease deal with B. Guccione freezes out Pratt Hotel as Atlantic City competitor] H. Rudnitsky. il *Forbes* 143:128 Ap 17 '89
TRUMP SHUTTLE (FIRM)
Eastern reopens bidding for shuttle as Trump balks at $365 million price. P. Proctor and J. T. McKenna. *Aviation Week & Space Technology* 130:31 Mr 27 '89
FAA clears Trump to operate shuttle; bankruptcy, suits could complicate sale. il *Aviation Week & Space Technology* 130:16 Mr 13 '89
Judge set to rule on shuttle sale, Eastern business plan. *Aviation Week & Space Technology* 130:72 My 15 '89
Trump begins training flight crews for northeast shuttle. J. T. McKenna. *Aviation Week & Space Technology* 130:77 Ja 30 '89
Trump Shuttle begins flying Eastern's former routes in repainted aircraft. il *Aviation Week & Space Technology* 130:314 Je 12 '89
War of the shuttles [Pan Am vs Trump] S. Payne. il *Business Week* p38 F 20 '89
TRUMP TAJ MAHAL CASINO RESORT (ATLANTIC CITY, N.J.)
This time, Trump may roll snake eyes. J. Weber, Jr. il *Business Week* p151 N 27 '89
Trump's troubles. M. J. Williams. il por *Fortune* 120:157+ D 18 '89

TRUMP: WHAT'S THE DEAL? [television program] See Television program reviews—Single works
TRUMPET MUSIC
Donald Byrd's solo on Each time I think of you—a trumpet transcription. J. T. Cohen. il *Down Beat* 56:54 Mr '89
TRUMPETER SWANS *See* Swans
TRUMPETERS
See also
Armstrong, Louis, 1900-1971
Baker, Chet
Bryant, Clora
Byrd, Donald
Cheatham, Doc
Cherry, Don
Clayton, Buck, 1911-
Davis, Miles
Edison, Harry, 1915-
Eldridge, Roy, 1911-1989
Gillespie, Dizzy, 1917-
Marsalis, Wynton
Severinsen, Doc
Terry, Clark
TRUNZO, CANDACE E.
Choosing a sports program for your child. il *Working Woman* 14:226+ S '89
Women vs. fashion: why clothes cost so much. il *Ladies' Home Journal* 106:108+ Mr '89
TRUONG, HANG
about
A boat girl grows up. B. Came. il por *Maclean's* 102:21+ Jl 10 '89
TRUSCOTT, LUCIAN K., 1947-
Hate gets a haircut. il pors map *Esquire* 112:174-6+ N '89
TRUSHEIM, DALE
(jt. auth) See Crouse, James, and Trusheim, Dale
TRUSSELL, TAIT
The last of the citrus barons. il pors *Nation's Business* 77:46+ F '89
TRUST
Can you trust each other? L. Dormen. il *Glamour* 87:236-7+ N '89
How do you build intimacy in an age of divorce? [cover story] C. Avery. il *Psychology Today* 23:27-31 My '89
Is he taken? *Glamour* 87:114 D '89
The survival value of trust. S. Bok. por *American Health* 8:120+ S '89
The trust gap [employer-employee relations; cover story] A. Farnham. il *Fortune* 120:56-8+ D 4 '89
Trust me. il *Glamour* 87:151-2 N '89
TRUST FUNDS *See* Trusts and trustees
TRUST TERRITORY OF THE PACIFIC ISLANDS *See* Pacific Islands (Trust Territory)
TRUSTEES, COLLEGE *See* College trustees
TRUSTEESHIP COUNCIL (UNITED NATIONS) *See* United Nations. Trusteeship Council
TRUSTHOUSE FORTE PLC
Diana slept here [Trusthouse Forte's pursuit of Savoy Hotel plc] J. Marcom, Jr. il *Forbes* 143:116+ My 15 '89
TRUSTS, INDUSTRIAL
Law
See Antitrust law
TRUSTS, INVESTMENT *See* Investment trusts
TRUSTS AND TRUSTEES
See also
Land trusts
Living trusts
Trusts that protect your family. D. M. Topolnicki. il *Money* 18 Money Guide:110-12+ Fall '89
Charitable trusts
A charitable way to provide for heirs [charitable lead trust] T. Segal. il *Business Week* p139 O 16 '89
Taxation
All in the family [family businesses and estate taxes] J. C. Szabo. il *Nation's Business* 77:73-4 Ap '89
The billion-dollar tax deadline [capital gains tax on trusts in Canada] D. Francis. il *Maclean's* 102:13 D 25 '89
A charitable way to provide for heirs [charitable lead trust] T. Segal. il *Business Week* p139 O 16 '89
Eight common trusts. L. Saunders. *Forbes* 143:239 Je 26 '89
Trimming the tax bite on gifts to grandchildren. T. Segal. il *Business Week* p161 O 23 '89
Canada
The billion-dollar tax deadline [capital gains tax on trusts] D. Francis. il *Maclean's* 102:13 D 25 '89
TRUTH
See also
Knowledge, Theory of
The agony of deceit [television neutralizes truth] R. Powers. il *Gentlemen's Quarterly* 59:190+ Mr '89
Hype and human humbug. J. I. Packer. il *Christianity Today* 33:11 F 17 '89
Treasonable talk. P. J. Ryan. il *America* 161:94 Ag 12-19 '89
THE TRUTH ABOUT TEACHERS [television program] See Television program reviews—Single works

TRUTHFULNESS
See also
Honesty
Lying
TRW INC.
Financial analysts see TRW restructuring as plus. P. Mann. *Aviation Week & Space Technology* 131:26-7 Ag 28 '89
TRW seeks to parlay experience from space into broader ASW role [antisubmarine warfare] B. D. Nordwall. *Aviation Week & Space Technology* 131:65+ Ag 7 '89
TRYPANOSOMES
See also
Leptomonas
TRYPSIN
See also
Antitrypsin
TRYPSINOGEN
Testing newborns for cystic fibrosis [measuring immunoreactive trypsinogen; work of Frank J. Accurso] S. Hart and A. McKenzie. *Science News* 136:233 O 7 '89
TRYPTOPHAN
Identification by ENDOR of Trp[191] as the free-radical site in cytochrome c peroxidase compound ES. M. Sivaraja and others. bibl f il *Science* 245:738-40 Ag 18 '89
TSAGI *See* Central Aero-Hydrodynamic Institute (Soviet Union)
TSAI, MEN-HWEI, AND OTHERS
The effect of GTPase activating protein upon Ras is inhibited by mitogenically responsive lipids. bibl f il *Science* 243:522-6 Ja 27 '89
TSANTIS, LINDA, AND OTHERS
Computers and preschoolers: Head Start/IBM Partnership. il *Children Today* 18:21-3 Ja/F '89
TSAO, MARY ANN
about
House call. H. S. MacIsaac. il pors *House & Garden* 161:232-7 O '89
TSAO & MCKOWN, ARCHITECTS
Illusion and reality [installation of Geoffrey Beene exhibit at National Academy of Design and retail interiors for Kinder Kind] V. Geibel. il *Architectural Record* 177:58-63 mid-S '89
TSAVO NATIONAL PARK (KENYA)
The battle in the Bush [work of elephant protector Bill Woodley] il *Time* 134:73 O 16 '89
TSCHUMI, BERNARD, 1944-
about
Rough and reddish. G. Danto. il por *Art News* 88:103-4 My '89
TSIAM *See* Central Institute for Aviation Motors (Moscow, Soviet Union)
TSIARAS, PHILIP, 1952?-
about
Philip Tsiaras at Shea & Beker. A. F. Collins. *Art in America* 77:267 Ap '89
TSIOLKOVSKII, KONSTANTIN, 1857-1935
about
The rocket pioneers. M. R. Chartrand. *Ad Astra* 1:38 Mr '89
TSIPING SITE (N.M.) *See* New Mexico—Antiquities
TSIPIS, KOSTA
After the cold war: new tasks for arms controllers. *The Bulletin of the Atomic Scientists* 45:7-8 Jl/Ag '89
TSN *See* Sports Network
TSR (TERMINATE AND STAY RESIDENT) PROGRAMMING *See* Computer programming
TSS *See* Tethered Satellite System; Toxic shock syndrome
TSUI, HARK
about
The Peking Opera blues [film] Reviews
New York il 22:66 F 6 '89. D. Denby
TSUI, LAP-CHEE
about
Discoveries of hope at the heart of human life. D. Jenish. il por *Maclean's* 102:22-3 D 25 '89
TSUJI, TSUKASA
Frames: state of the art. il *Cycle* 40:52-5+ D '89
TSUMURA, AKIRA, 1936-
about
A strong yen for instruments. E. McGlinn. il por *Forbes* 144:241 O 2 '89
TSUNAMIS
Volcanoes and tsunamis [cover story] P. A. Lockridge. il *Earth Science* 42:24-5 Spr '89
TSURU, TAKAYUKI
about
Hi-tech disagreements. P. Kaihla. il por *Maclean's* 102:16-17 Je 26 '89
TSUTANI, KIICHIRO
Priority areas in traditional medicine. il *World Health* p26-8 N '89
TSUTSUMI, SEIJI
about
Joust of the half brothers. S. Kanise. il pors *Time* 133:46 Ja 23 '89
A radical retailer. S. Solo. il por *Fortune* 119:58-9 Ja 2 '89

TSUTSUMI, YOSHIAKI
about
Joust of the half brothers. S. Kanise. il pors *Time* 133:46
Ja 23 '89
TUATARAS
Reproduction
Tuatara tango. il *Discover* 10:14 Ap '89
TUBA PLAYERS
See also
Stewart, Bob
TUBBS, VINCENT, D. 1989
about
Obituary
Jet por 75:52 F 13 '89
TUBE FEEDING
Moral and religious aspects
The amicus curiae brief: public policy versus personal freedom
[brief filed by New Jersey Catholic Conference in case
of brain-damaged woman] R. J. Devine. *America* 160:323-6+
Ap 8 '89
The Cruzan decision: refusing treatment [Missouri Supreme
Court decision in N. Cruzan case] J. M. Swomley. *The
Christian Century* 106:1110-11 N 29 '89
Is there a right to die? [Supreme Court to hear N. Cruzan
case] T. Gest. il por *U.S. News & World Report* 107:35-7
D 11 '89
Last rights [right to die cases of N. Cruzan and L. McAfee]
M. G. Maudlin. *Christianity Today* 33:15 N 3 '89
Nancy Cruzan's parents want to let her die—and are taking
the case to the Supreme Court. M. Brower. il pors *People
Weekly* 32:135-6+ D 4 '89
To be or not to be [case of N. Cruzan] M. Kinsley. *The
New Republic* 201:6+ N 27 '89
Whose death is it, anyway? [case of C. Coons] J. Seligmann.
Newsweek 113:69 Ap 24 '89
Whose right to die? [case of N. Cruzan before the Supreme
Court] A. L. Sanders. il *Time* 134:80 D 11 '89
TUBERCULOSIS
"Stamping" out tuberculosis: the story of Christmas seals
[work of E. Bissell] K. Doyle. il por *American History
Illustrated* 24:66-8 N/D '89
Immunological aspects
Activation of γδ T cells in the primary immune response
to Mycobacterium tuberculosis. E. M. Janis and others.
bibl f il *Science* 244:713-16 My 12 '89
TUBERS
See also
Potatoes
TUBES
See also
Inner tubes
TUBMAN (HARRIET) HISTORICAL AND CULTURAL
MUSEUM (MACON, GA.) *See* Harriet Tubman Historical
and Cultural Museum (Macon, Ga.)
TUBS, BATH *See* Bathtubs
TUBS, HOT *See* Hot tubs
TUCHMAN, BARBARA WERTHEIM
about
Obituary
The Nation 248:292-3 Mr 6 '89
TUCHSCHERER, JEAN MICHEL
Royal orders for Lyons silk, 1730-1800. il *Antiques* 136:154-65
Jl '89
TUCK, RAPHAEL
about
What the Dickens a la Tuck [postcards] S. S. Carver. il
Antiques & Collecting Hobbies 94:64-7 My '89
TUCK AND PATTI (MUSICAL GROUP)
Tuck and Patti. H. Weinger. il *Rolling Stone* p28-9 O 5
'89
TUCKER, ANNE WILKES, 1945-
about
Indelible images. R. Cembalest. il pors *Art News* 88:174-9
Ap '89
TUCKER, CHARLIE ALEXANDER
about
Never say quit to Charlie Tucker or he's likely to give
you the brush. il por *People Weekly* 32:106-7 Jl 10 '89
TUCKER, JAMES A.
(tr) *See* Konrád, György. Notes on your Central Europe—and
mine
TUCKER, JERRY
about
Struggle for the soul of the union. J. Schwartz. il *The Nation*
249:8-10 Jl 3 '89
TUCKER, KEN
Another country. il *Vogue* 179:328-31 F '89
TUCKER, MARC S., AND WILLS, JOAN
A high-performance system: five federal education initiatives.
il *Change* 20:8+ N/D '88
TUCKER, MARCIA
Equestrian mysteries. il *Art in America* 77:154-7+ Je '89
TUCKER, MICHAEL
about
King and queen of torts [cover story] H. G. Miller. il pors
The Saturday Evening Post 261:50-3+ Ap '89

TUCKER, PRESTON, 1901-1956
about
Tucker: a man and his car. M. Mueller. il pors *American
History Illustrated* 23:36-41 Ja '89
TUCKER, RICHARD FRANK
High tech frontiers in the energy industry [address, November
30, 1988] *Vital Speeches of the Day* 55:437-41 My 1 '89
TUCKER, ROBERT W.
Reagan's foreign policy. *Foreign Affairs* 68 Special Issue:1-27
['89]
TUCKER, RUTH A., 1945-
Growing up a world away [cover story] il *Christianity Today*
33:17-21 F 17 '89
TUCKER, SUSAN, 1950-
My white father [excerpt from Telling memories among
southern women] *Harper's* 279:36+ N '89
TUCKER, TANYA, 1958-
about
Rodeo round-up: three big ones in the country corral. il
pors *'Teen* 33:53 S '89
TUCKER, WILLIAM ELLIS
about
Tucker porcelain. B. Barol. il *American Heritage* 40:28-9
My/Je '89
Tucker porcelain, Philadelphia, 1826-1838 [cover story] A.
C. Frelinghuysen. il *Antiques* 135:918-29 Ap '89
TUCKER POTTERY *See* Pottery, American
TUCKER: THE MAN AND HIS DREAM [film] *See* Motion
picture reviews—Single works
TUCSON (ARIZ.)
Description
Tucson. S. Wilding. il *Gourmet* 49:44-51+ Ja '89
Galleries and museums
See also
Arizona-Sonora Desert Museum
TUCSON ELECTRIC POWER CO.
The shock that zapped Tucson Electric [Chairman E. Greve
forced out] R. Grover. il por *Business Week* p28-9 Ag
7 '89
TUDOR, GUY
about
Tudor's tutors. F. Graham. il *Audubon* 91:20+ N '89
TUDOR ENGLAND *See* Great Britain—History—Tudors,
1485-1603
TUFTS UNIVERSITY
Whereabouts [entering students given free atlases] *The New
Yorker* 65:29-30 F 20 '89
TUFTS UNIVERSITY. DEPT. OF DRAMA AND DANCE
Tufts University. il *Theatre Crafts* 23:55 N '89
TUGBOATS
Toot-toot. L. Rudeen. il *Motor Boating & Sailing* 163:66-71+
F '89
TUGBOATS, TOY *See* Toys
TUGHILL HOUSE (GLOUCESTERSHIRE, ENGLAND) *See*
Historic houses, sites, etc.—Great Britain
TUITION, COLLEGE *See* College education—Costs
TUITION PAYMENT PROGRAMS (BUSINESS) *See* Business
and education
TULIPE (LOS ANGELES, CALIF.: RESTAURANT) *See* Los
Angeles (Calif.)—Restaurants, nightclubs, bars, etc.
TULIPS
Dutch treats. E. Henke. il *The Saturday Evening Post* 261:64-6
My/Je '89
Everything's bloomin' tulips! [handcrafted home furnishings]
J. Williams and J. Severson. il *Better Homes and Gardens*
67:45-54+ Mr '89
Species tulips. J. Glattstein. il *Flower and Garden* 33:26-7+
S/O '89
TULIPS IN ART
Tulipomania [household furnishing] D. B. Cowin. il *House
& Garden* 161:166+ Je '89
TULLEY, JALIEN
(jt. auth) *See* Ballenger, Noella, and Tulley, Jalien
TULLY, JERYLDINE
As for the impact on the environment . . . il *Common
Cause Magazine* 15:8 N/D '89
TULSA (OKLA.)
Galleries and museums
See also
Fenster Museum of Jewish Art (Tulsa, Okla.)
Thomas Gilcrease Institute of American History and
Art
Historic houses, sites, etc.
The house that Harwell built [Harwelden] il *Southern Living*
24:38 Mr '89
TULSA BALLET THEATRE
Dance. T. Tobias. il *New York* 22:122-3 N 13 '89
Reviews:
Performances at Brooklyn Center for the Performing
Arts. L. Garafola. *Dance Magazine* 63:81-2 Ja '89
TUMAS, WILLIAM
(jt. auth) *See* Grubbs, Robert H., and Tumas, William
TUMBLEWEEDS
Weed all about it! Tumbleweeds invade South Dakota town!
Houses buried! Folks mighty upset! [Mobridge, S.D.] il
People Weekly 32:153 N 27 '89

TUMOR CELLS (MALIGNANT) *See* Cancer cells

TUMOR INHIBITING SUBSTANCES *See* Cancer inhibiting substances

TUMOR NECROSIS FACTOR
Body's protein does malaria's dirty work [research by Kathleen L. Miller] F. Flam. *Science News* 135:293 My 13 '89
Hybrid protein may help fight cancer [product of gene for interferon and gene for tumor necrosis factor] *High Technology Business* 9:33 Ja '89

TUMOR PRODUCING SUBSTANCES *See* Cancer—Causes

TUMOR SUPPRESSOR GENES
Many gene changes found in cancer [stepwise accumulation of mutations affecting both oncogenes and suppressor genes] J. L. Marx. bibl il *Science* 246:1386-8 D 15 '89
Tumor suppressor genes: the puzzle and the promise. R. Sager. bibl f il *Science* 246:1406-12 D 15 '89

TUMOR VIRUSES *See* Oncogenic viruses

TUMORS (BENIGN)
See also
Cysts
Fibroid tumors
Neurofibromatosis
Surgery
"Please save my leg!" [transplant replaces knee destroyed by tumor]; ed. by Elaine Fein. S. Lazarchick. il por *Redbook* 172:68+ Ja '89

TUMORS (BOTANY)
Tomato tumors: red light means grow [research by Theodore W. Tibbitts] I. Wickelgren. il *Science News* 135:23 Ja 14 '89

TUMORS (MALIGNANT) *See* Cancer

TUNA FISH
See also
Cooking—Fish
No chicken of the sea. M. Tennesen. il *National Wildlife* 27:10-13 Ap/My '89
Sea pig on rye, please. A. J. McClane. il *Esquire* 111:39-40 Je '89
Tunas [swimming adaptations] P. G. Bushnell and K. N. Holland. il *Sea Frontiers* 35:42-8 Ja/F '89

TUNA FISH, CANNED *See* Fish, Canned

TUNA FISHERIES (COMMERCIAL) *See* Fisheries

TUNING
See also
Piano—Tuning

TUNING, RADIO *See* Radio receivers—Tuning

TUNING EQUIPMENT
See also
Radio antennas—Tuning
Radio receivers—Tuning

TUNNEL DIODES *See* Diodes

TUNNELING (PHYSICS)
Hydrogen tunneling in enzyme reactions. Y. Cha and others. bibl f il *Science* 243:1325-30 Mr 10 '89
Negative differential resistance on the atomic scale: implications for atomic scale devices. I.-W. Lyo and P. Avouris. bibl f il *Science* 245:1369-71 S 22 '89
Quantum biology [hydrogen tunneling in enzyme reactions; research by Yuan Cha] J. Kinoshita. *Scientific American* 260:31-2 My '89

TUNNELING MICROSCOPES, SCANNING *See* Scanning tunneling microscopes

TUNNELS AND TUNNELING
See also
Railroad tunnels

TUNNELS AND TUNNELING, UNDERWATER
Western Europe
See also
English Channel tunnel

TUPOLEV DESIGN BUREAU (SOVIET UNION)
Tupolev Bureau develops ultrahigh bypass, turbofan engine concepts for Tu-334 transport [Soviet aircraft] il *Aviation Week & Space Technology* 130:96 Je 5 '89

TURAN, KENNETH
The holiday evergreens we never grow tired of. il *TV Guide* 37:16-19 D 16-22 '89
Movies. See issues of Gentlemen's Quarterly
Rating TV's movie critics: best sweaters—Rex Reed best reviews—see below. il *TV Guide* 37:26-8 Mr 18-24 '89
Richard Burton: great actor whose talents were often wasted. il pors *TV Guide* 37:12-14+ N 25-D 1 '89
Summer breakout [cover story] il *TV Guide* 37:2-5 Jl 1-7 '89

TURBAK, GARY
America's other eagle. il *National Wildlife* 27:34-41 O/N '89
Tough little turncoat. il *National Wildlife* 28:14-19 D '89/Ja '90

TURBIDITY
Experiments on hydraulic jumps in turbidity currents near a canyon-fan transition. M. Garcia and G. Parker. bibl f il *Science* 245:393-6 Jl 28 '89

TURBINE AIRPLANE ENGINES *See* Airplane engines, Jet

TURBINE PUMPS
See also
Space vehicles—Propulsion systems—Turbine pumps

TURBINES
See also
Gas turbines, Automotive

TURBINES, WIND *See* Wind power

TURBOCHARGERS *See* Airplane engines—Superchargers; Automobile engines—Superchargers; Automobiles, Racing—Engines—Superchargers; Diesel engines, Automotive—Superchargers; Diesel engines, Marine—Superchargers; Motor boat engines—Superchargers

TURBOFAN AIRPLANE ENGINES *See* Airplane engines, Jet

TURBOPROP AIRPLANE ENGINES *See* Airplane engines, Jet

TURBOPROP AIRPLANES *See* Airplanes, Jet

TURBULENCE
See also
Atmospheric turbulence

TURBULENCE PREDICTION SYSTEMS (FIRM)
Airborne infrared system provides advance warning of turbulence. il *Aviation Week & Space Technology* 130:130-1 Je 19 '89

TURCK, MARY C.
Campesina fights hunger and its causes. por *The Progressive* 53:14 My '89

TURCOTTE, KEVIN
Mary Robertson. il por *American Artist* 53:52-7 My '89

TURCOTTE, RON
about
They never gave up. R. Hoffer. il pors *Sports Illustrated* 71:117-27+ D 25 '89-Ja 1 '90

TURGEON, KITTY, AND RUST, ROBERT C.
Collecting "fit for a king": defining Roycroft. il *Antiques & Collecting Hobbies* 94:75-7 O '89

TURGEON, PIERRE
about
No rattling the Sabres. J. Greenberg. il pors *Sports Illustrated* 71:40+ D 18 '89

TURIM, GAYLE
Calendars for 1990. il *Americana* 17:21-3 N/D '89
Hosts of ghosts. il *Americana* 17:21-4 S/O '89
Remembering a fine fair. il por *Americana* 17:50-4 Jl/Ag '89

TURIN (ITALY)
Historic houses, sites, etc.
See also
Castello di Rivoli (Turin, Italy)
Music festivals
See Music festivals—Italy

TURING MACHINES
The business of busy beavers [research by Heiner Marxen] *Science News* 136:191 S 16 '89
Two-dimensional Turing machines and tur-mites make tracks on a plane. A. K. Dewdney. il *Scientific American* 261:180-3 S '89

TURK, RUDY H., 1927-
about
ASU Art Museum. E. Lebow. il por *American Craft* 49:64-9 Ag/S '89

TURKEN, JANE
about
Manhattan variations. P. Carlsen. il *Architectural Digest* 46:138-43 Ag '89

TURKEY
See also
Bronze Age—Turkey
Civil rights—Turkey
Istanbul (Turkey)
Opera—Turkey
Political prisoners—Turkey
Stone Age—Turkey
Turks
Antiquities
See also
Aphrodisias (Ancient city)
Description and travel
Turkish kaleidoscope. E. B. Blanch. il *World Press Review* 36:76 D '89
Foreign relations
Cyprus
See Cyprus
Industries
See also
Tin mines and mining—Turkey
Politics and government
Crossing the straits. M. Viorst. *The New Yorker* 65:43-4+ Je 5 '89
Letter from Bodrum. H. Greer. *The American Spectator* 22:42-3 D '89
Turkey's identity problem. N. Gelb. il *The New Leader* 72:9-10 My 1 '89
Religious institutions and affairs
See also
Christians—Turkey
Muslims—Turkey

TURKEY CALLING *See* Bird calling
TURKEY CARVING *See* Carving (Meat, etc.)
TURKEY COOKING *See* Cooking—Poultry
TURKEY HUNTING
Ambition. T. H. Kelly, Jr. il *Field & Stream* 94:54+ S '89
Gobbler gangs. B. Conger. il *Outdoor Life* 183:86-7+ Ap '89
Second-season turkeys. J. Bashline. il *Field & Stream* 94:50+ N '89
Turkey calling is going to the birds. S. Grenoble. il *Outdoor Life* 183:56-7+ F '89
Turkey hunting's cutting edge [bird calls] K. Etling. il *Outdoor Life* 183:72-3+ Mr '89
Wild West turkeys. J. Barsness. il *Field & Stream* 93:46-7+ Mr '89
TURKEYS
See also
Cooking—Poultry
TURKEYS, WILD
Ben's bird. G. Reiger. il *Field & Stream* 94:48-9 My '89
Giving thanks. H. Middleton. il *Southern Living* 24:36+ Ap '89
Shooting
See Turkey hunting
TURKISH REFUGEES *See* Refugees, Turkish
TURKS
Bulgaria
Ethnic Turks in Bulgaria [NATO and State Dept. statements, August 9 and 10, 1989] *Department of State Bulletin* 89:43 O '89
A modern Balkan exodus. R. Flamini. il *Time* 134:39 Ag 14 '89
TURLEY, KEITH L., 1923-
about
A bundle of bad deals has Pinnacle West reeling. R. Grover and T. Carson. il *Business Week* p34 Ja 30 '89
TURLINGTON, CHRISTY
about
Follow that girl. A. Keteyian. il pors *New York* 22:38-43 Mr 6 '89
That fabulous face. il *Gentlemen's Quarterly* 59:270-3 Ap '89
TURNAROUNDS, CORPORATE *See* Corporate turnarounds
TURNER, BEATRICE
about
My teacher, my friend. E. Stone. il *New Choices for the Best Years* 29:80+ D '89
TURNER, CHRISTY G., II
Teeth and prehistory in Asia. bibl il map *Scientific American* 260:88-91+ F '89
TURNER, DALE
How to find time. *Reader's Digest* 134:195 Je '89
TURNER, DEBBYE
about
Debbye Turner: new Miss America says, 'Beauty is content of character' [cover story] R. E. Johnson. il pors *Jet* 77:54-7 O 23 '89
Miss America: black, beautiful, brainy and born-again [cover story] L. Norment. il pors *Ebony* 45:132-4+ D '89
Missouri veterinary coed in Miss America contest. il por *Jet* 76:27 Jl 31 '89
New Miss America is black Missouri coed, born-again Christian. il pors *Jet* 76:12-14 O 2 '89
TURNER, ELDON
Two centuries of Virginia's Act for Religious Freedom. il *USA Today (Periodical)* 117:73-5 Mr '89
TURNER, EUGENE, 1946-
(jt. auth) *See* Allen, James Paul, 1936-, and Turner, Eugene, 1946-
TURNER, FRED
'Why should they die and we live?'. il *The Progressive* 53:15-16 Ag '89
TURNER, FREDERICK, 1943-
Life on Mars: cultivating a planet—and ourselves [cover story] il *Harper's* 279:33-40 Ag '89
TURNER, GRAHAM
The lost art of dying. *World Press Review* 36:37-8 Je '89
TURNER, HELEN LEE, AND OTHERS
The Hanna-Barbera cartoons: compounding Bible ignorance? [cover story] il *The Christian Century* 106:231-4 Mr 1 '89
TURNER, JOHN
about
John Turner: a man out of time. A. Fotheringham. il *Maclean's* 102:64 My 15 '89
The leaders in waiting. R. Laver. il pors *Maclean's* 102:10-12 Mr 6 '89
The leadership issue. B. Wallace. il por *Maclean's* 102:18+ My 1 '89
Stepping down. il por *Maclean's* 102:2, 10-12+ My 15 '89
The tragedy of John Napier Turner. P. C. Newman. il *Maclean's* 102:48 My 15 '89
TURNER, JONATHAN
Roman revival. il por *House & Garden* 161:114-19+ Ja '89
That swooning feeling. il por *Art News* 88:150-3 D '89

about
Surgery gives sight to infant born with rare case of inverted eyelids. il *Jet* 76:31 Ag 28 '89
TURNER, LANDON
about
Sat down for life by fate, former basketball star Landon Turner rebounds with a gritty comeback. P. Axthelm. il por *People Weekly* 31:61-2 F 13 '89
TURNER, LOWELL
Three plants, three futures. il *Technology Review* 92:38-45 Ja '89
TURNER, MARK HOLMAN
Building an ecosystem from scratch. il *BioScience* 39:147-50 Mr '89
TURNER, MAURICE T.
about
D.C. police chief quits, mulls GOP run for mayor. il por *Jet* 76:4 Ag 14 '89
TURNER, PAUL
about
Growin' bananas. L. Hollenhorst. il por *Organic Gardening* 36:54-6+ S '89
TURNER, PRISCILLA
Polar dare. il por *Ms.* 17:55-7 Je '89
TURNER, RICHARD, AND TJIAN, ROBERT
Leucine repeats and an adjacent DNA binding domain mediate the formation of functional cFos-cJun heterodimers. bibl f il *Science* 243:1689-94 Mr 31 '89
TURNER, RICHARD L.
The 'great' debate—can both Carbo and Chall be right? bibl f il *Phi Delta Kappan* 71:276-83 D '89
TURNER, SYLVIA C., AND HARRIS, RICKY
Conquering the elements: choreography on ice. il *Dance Magazine* 63:34-9 F '89
TURNER, TED, 1938-
about
Captain Comeback [cover story] S. Ticer. il pors *Business Week* p98-101+ Jl 17 '89
The greening of Ted Turner [cover story] J. Lanham. il pors *The Humanist* 49:5-7+ N/D '89
The man of a thousand networks. M. Curriden. il *Sport (New York, N.Y.)* 80:14 S '89
Ted Turner. S. Ticer. por *Business Week* Special Issue:142 Ap 14 '89
Ted Turner [cover story; interview] G. Dawson. il pors *American Film* 14:36-9+ Ja/F '89
Turnaround Ted. por *Forbes* 143:111 Ja 9 '89
TURNER, TINA
about
Rich, free and in control: the 'Foreign affairs' of Tina Turner [cover story] L. Norment. il pors *Ebony* 45:166-8+ N '89
Singer Tina Turner completes Chrysler ads. il pors *Jet* 76:57 S 18 '89
TURNER, TOM
Earth diary. *See* issues of The Mother Earth News beginning January/February 1987
TURNER & HOOCH [film] *See* Motion picture reviews—Single works
TURNER BROADCASTING SYSTEM, INC.
Captain Comeback [T. Turner; cover story] S. Ticer. il pors *Business Week* p98-101+ Jl 17 '89
The greening of Ted Turner [cover story] J. Lanham. il pors *The Humanist* 49:5-7+ N/D '89
In the battle for viewers at school, Turner takes on Whittle [News Access service] F. Moore. il *Channels (New York, N.Y.: 1986)* 9:14 Ap '89
Ted Turner. S. Ticer. por *Business Week* Special Issue:142 Ap 14 '89
Ted Turner [cover story; interview] G. Dawson. il pors *American Film* 14:36-9+ Ja/F '89
Turnaround Ted. por *Forbes* 143:111 Ja 9 '89
TURNER COMMUNICATIONS CORPORATION
See also
Turner Broadcasting System, Inc.
TURNER-MAYBANK, VANESSA
about
Working for our cities. D. Young. il pors *Southern Living* 24:141-2+ S '89
TURNER NETWORK TELEVISION
Old gold [special section] il *Film Comment* 25:29-48 Jl/Ag '89
TNT one year later: growth is explosive. J. Stilson. il *Channels (New York, N.Y.: 1986)* 9:10 O '89
TURNER PUBLISHING INC.
New Ted Turner publishing unit to turn TV shows into books. H. Fields. *Publishers Weekly* 236:11 N 24 '89
TURNING (MACHINE WORK)
See also
Lathes
Laying out turning stock. il *Workbench* 45:64 Ja/F '89
Exhibitions
Turning point [International turned objects show] J. Perreault. il *American Craft* 49:24-31 F/Mr '89
TURNIPS
See also
Cooking—Vegetables

TURNOVER OF LABOR *See* Labor turnover
TURNTABLES
   See also
   Phonograph—Turntables
TUROCY, CATHERINE
   Stimulating the senses: going for baroque. il por *Dance Magazine* 63:30-4 Je '89
TUROW, SCOTT
   about
   FSG signs second novel from Scott Turow. G. Feldman. por *Publishers Weekly* 236:92 S 15 '89
TURPENTINE
   Technical page [art use] R. Mayer. *American Artist* 53:26+ F '89
TURPIN, LUCI *See* Johnson, Luci Baines
TURRE, STEVE
   about
   Blindfold test. M. Bourne. il por *Down Beat* 56:45 Ja '89
TURTLE, CANDACE M.
   A father's homecoming. il *Reader's Digest* 134:57-61 F '89
TURTLE FISHERIES
   Cayman Islands
   Seafarers of the Caymans. N. Sefton. bibl il map *Sea Frontiers* 35:106-13 Mr/Ap '89
TURTLE ISLAND STRING QUARTET
   These Turtles shell out rock, classics and all that jazz. il *People Weekly* 32:46 Ag 21 '89
TURTLENECK SWEATERS *See* Sweaters
TURTLES
   Dropping the net on Gulf shrimpers [requiring trapdoor devices on nets to prevent ridley turtle drownings in Gulf of Mexico] il *Newsweek* 114:28 Ag 7 '89
   Egging them on [loggerhead turtles at Hobe Sound National Wildlife Refuge] B. Weber. il *The New York Times Magazine* p94 O 1 '89
   Living legacies [R. Stavdal continues box turtle research started by J. T. Nichols] M. Lipske. il por *National Wildlife* 27:14-16 Je/Jl '89
   Shrimpers and lawmakers collide over a move to save the sea turtles [Turtle Excluder Devices required on fishing nets] J. Rudloe and A. Rudloe. il *Smithsonian* 20:44-55 D '89
   Sodium lights repel turtles [allowing Florida loggerheads to find ocean] il *Sea Frontiers* 35:69 Mr/Ap '89
   Tires, trees, terns, terrapins. T. Williams. il *Audubon* 91:26-8+ My '89
   Food and feeding
   Voracious turtle grabs a quick bite [high speed video imaging study by Stephen M. Reilly] A. McKenzie. il *Science News* 136:407 D 23-30 '89
   The wood turtle stomp. J. H. Kaufmann. il *Natural History* p8+ Ag '89
   Migration
   New look at turtle migration mystery [restriction mapping of mitochondrial DNA; research by Brian W. Bowen] R. Lewin. *Science* 243:1009 F 24 '89
   Photographs and photography
   Wet respite [sideneck turtles in the floodplains of the Orinoco River] B. Rogers. il *Natural History* p104-5 Mr '89
TUSCANY (ITALY)
   Description and travel
   Braking away [biking tour] J. Schneller. il *Gentlemen's Quarterly* 59:326-9+ O '89
   Footloose [hiking] M. Chabon. il por *Vogue* 179:266+ My '89
TUSHINGHAM, A. M.
   (jt. auth) See Peltier, W. R., and Tushingham, A. M.
TUSKA, JOHN
   about
   John Tuska/University of Kentucky Art Museum. J. Ardery. il *American Craft* 49:72-3 Ap/My '89
TUTORS AND TUTORING
   See also
   Princeton Review, Ltd.
   A multiple choice of SAT cram courses. R. Wilder. bibl il *U.S. News & World Report* 106:65-6+ F 27 '89
   A school-change paradigm [use of peer programs] F. Riessman. *The Education Digest* 54:10-12 My '89
TUTTLE, LIZA
   At city's edge. il *National Parks* 63:37-9 N/D '89
TUTTLE, ROBERT D.
   Maintaining competitiveness [address, January 19, 1989] *Vital Speeches of the Day* 55:598-600 Jl 15 '89
TUTTLE FAMILY
   about
   Family farms forever! J. Walter. il map *Successful Farming* 87:22-4 Ja '89
TUTTLE MARSH (MICH.)
   Tuttle Marsh, Michigan. R. H. Mohlenbrock. il maps *Natural History* p72+ Je '89
TUTTOBENE (WEST HOLLYWOOD, CALIF.: RESTAURANT) *See* West Hollywood (Calif.)— Restaurants, nightclubs, bars, etc.
TUTU, DESMOND
   about
   Newmarket publishes Desmond Tutu's writings. J. Crichton. il pors *Publishers Weekly* 235:26 Mr 17 '89

A skeptical view [interview] J. Bierman. il por *Maclean's* 102:22 Mr 13 '89
South Africa: the growing tolerance of intolerance [interview with N. Tutu-Seavers] R. Bautch. *America* 160:450-1+ My 13 '89
TUTU, MPHO
   about
   Cry freedom [interview] C. G. Fraser. por *Essence* 20:34 S '89
TUTU (BISHOP DESMOND) SOUTHERN AFRICAN REFUGEE SCHOLARSHIP FUND *See* Bishop Desmond Tutu Southern African Refugee Scholarship Fund
TUTU-SEAVERS, NAOMI
   about
   Newmarket publishes Desmond Tutu's writings. J. Crichton. il pors *Publishers Weekly* 235:26 Mr 17 '89
   South Africa: the growing tolerance of intolerance [interview] R. Bautch. *America* 160:450-1+ My 13 '89
TUTWILER, MARGARET D.
   about
   As State Department spokesperson, Margaret Tutwiler has won even the press's respect. M. B. Carlson. il por *Vogue* 179:276+ O '89
TUXEDOS
   Goodbye Thoreau, hello Astaire. R. Goldblum. il *The New York Times Magazine* p24+ O 29 '89
TV 101 [television program] *See* Television program reviews— Single works
TV DINNERS *See* Frozen dinners
TV GLOBO LTDA
   Brazil's 'Citizen Globo' [R. Marinho] J.-P. Moreau. il por *World Press Review* 36:56 Jl '89
   New dimensions in creativity [H. Donner's special effects] G. Smith. il por *Américas* 41 no1:24-31 '89
TV GUIDE (PERIODICAL)
   The tarting up of TV guide. R. Zoglin. il por *Time* 133:81 My 29 '89
   TV guide's eighth annual J. Fred Muggs Awards [cover story] il *TV Guide* 37:4-6+ Ja 7-13 '89
TV Q RATINGS *See* Q ratings
TVA *See* Tennessee Valley Authority
TVCRS *See* Television receivers—Videotape recorder combination
TVI *See* Television interference
TVS ENTERTAINMENT PLC
   Why MTM isn't the cat's meow [aftermath of TVS takeover] R. A. Melcher and R. Grover. il por *Business Week* p49 S 25 '89
TVX BROADCAST GROUP INC.
   How Paramount is blitzing the networks [deal to run independent stations owned by TVX Broadcast Group] R. Grover and D. Lieberman. il *Business Week* p94-5 Ja 30 '89
   The new TVX, burnished by tough times [interview with J. Trinder] J. Flinn and N. Koch. pors *Channels (New York, N.Y.: 1986)* 9:70-1 Mr '89
TWA *See* Trans World Airlines Inc.
TWACHTMAN, JOHN HENRY, 1853-1902
   about
   The mature years of John Henry Twachtman. A. E. Ledes. il *Antiques* 136:942+ N '89
TWAIN, MARK, 1835-1910
   Writer's grudge. *Harper's* 279:36 N '89
   about
   A Connecticut Yankee in hell. J. Kaplan. il *American Heritage* 40:97-102+ N '89
   The parting of the Twains. F. C. Crews. bibl f il *The New York Review of Books* 36:39-44 Jl 20 '89
TWAROG, CHET
   Spatial understanding & universal awareness. il *Ad Astra* 1:23 S '89
TWEDDELL, RICK
   about
   Using Rick Tweddell's Vegiform molds, gardeners can say, 'Let us now raise famous men'. il por *People Weekly* 32:91 O 2 '89
TWEEDS (FIRM)
   The chic is in the mail. B. Rudolph. il *Time* 134:74-5 Jl 17 '89
TWEEDY, BROWNE INC.
   Waltzing with the wallflowers [interview with C. Browne] S. Smith. il por *Fortune* 119:43+ Ap 10 '89
TWELFTH NIGHT [drama] *See* Shakespeare, William, 1564-1616
TWELVE-STEP PROGRAMS
   See also
   Alcoholics Anonymous
TWENTIES (DECADE) *See* Nineteen hundred and twenties
TWENTIETH CENTURY
   A calendar meditation: Christmas 1989. T. H. Stahel. *America* 161:439 D 16 '89
   The twentieth century and beyond [address, May 8, 1989] P. W. Williams. *Vital Speeches of the Day* 55:624-6 Ag 1 '89

TWENTIETH CENTURY-FOX FILM CORP.
Three faces of Eve told her story, now Chris Sizemore is battling a major studio over movie rights and wrongs [victim of multiple personality disorder sues over intellectual property rights] D. Van Biema. il pors *People Weekly* 31:79-80+ Mr 27 '89

TWENTIETH CENTURY INVESTORS, INC.
Twentieth Century: a mighty performer for truly small investors. G. Weiss. il por *Business Week* p130 D 25 '89-Ja 1 '90

TWENTY-FIRST CENTURY
See also
Institute for 21st Century Studies
21st century computing. P. Freiberger and D. McNeill. il *Compute!* 11:20-2+ O '89
The 21st century family [cover story] il *Newsweek* 114 Special Issue:14-18+ Wint '89/Spr '90
America in the 21st century [Population Reference Bureau report] *Children Today* 18:2-3 S/O '89
Brainstorms: the world's top think tanks predict the future. D. Starr. il *Omni (New York, N.Y.)* 12:66-70+ O '89
City scripts [urban centers of the future] il *Omni (New York, N.Y.)* 12:50-4+ O '89
Future trends [excerpt from American renaissance] M. J. Cetron and O. Davies. il por *Omni (New York, N.Y.)* 12:112-14+ O '89
Lighting the 21st century. P. C. Cruver. il por *The Futurist* 23:29-34 Ja/F '89
Name that decade. W. Safire. il *The New York Times Magazine* p18+ My 7 '89
New doctor roles for 21st century [views of Richard A. Wright] il *USA Today (Periodical)* 118:11 Ag '89
The promise of the 21st century [National Academy of Sciences report] il *Astronomy* 17:44-50 Ja '89
Tomorrow's world [cover story; special section; with editorial comment by Kevin Doyle] il *Maclean's* 102:2, 36-40+ S 11 '89
Toward the 21st century [special 75th anniversary issue; cover story] bibl f *Current History* 88:1-59+ Ja '89
Visions of tomorrow [cover story; special section; with introd. by Gregory Jaynes] il *Life* 12:50-1+ F '89
What will the 21st century bring? [World Future Society report] il *USA Today (Periodical)* 117:8 Je '89

TWENTY-ONE [television program] See Television program reviews—Single works

TWENTY-SECOND CENTURY
Predicting IC defects. il *Radio-Electronics* 60:6 Je '89

TWIGG, ARLENA
about
Every parent's nightmare: a hospital nursery swap throws two Florida families into disarray. M. Green. il pors *People Weekly* 32:77-8+ D 11 '89
Whose little girl is Kimberly? M. Jacobbi. il pors *Good Housekeeping* 208:122-3+ Mr '89

TWIGS (NEW YORK, N.Y.: RESTAURANT) See New York (N.Y.)—Restaurants, nightclubs, bars, etc.

TWILIGHT PHOTOGRAPHY See Photography, Night

TWILLIE, MANUEL
about
Black swimmer, Twillie, likes making a big splash. il por *Jet* 76:49 Ag 7 '89

TWIN CITIES See Minneapolis (Minn.); Saint Paul (Minn.)

TWIN CITIES MARATHON See Marathon running

TWINING, CHARLES H.
Situation in Cambodia [address, September 29, 1988] *Department of State Bulletin* 88:31-3 D '88

TWINS
See also
Siamese twins
Baby boom II: delayed pregnancies mean more twins. C. Moekle. il *American Health* 8:107 Ap '89
Birds of a feather [models Y. and Y. Sylvander] B. Newman. il pors *Sports Illustrated* 70 Special Issue:139-42 F '89
Born rivals [identical twins] G. Levoy. il *Psychology Today* 23:67-8 Je '89
Born rivals [identical twins] G. Levoy. *Utne Reader* p101-2 S/O '89
The challenge of twins. L. G. Katz. il *Parents* 64:146 Ag '89
Conservative genes [political attitudes biologically inherited; research by David T. Lykken] D. Seligman. il *Fortune* 120:123 Ag 14 '89
Doomed to equality. K. Johnson. il *The New York Times Magazine* p14+ Je 25 '89
Double dose of divinity [twin Catholic priests C. and C. Smith] R. Brown. il pors *Ebony* 44:52+ Ja '89
My brother, my twin [C. and R. Woehrle] G. Rosenblum. il pors *New Choices for the Best Years* 29:83-5 Ap '89
Scott and Matthew Higa make their mark as bowling's youngest twin strike force [7 year old bowlers] il pors *People Weekly* 31:98-9 Ja 30 '89
Selective abortion of twin [work of Usha Chitkara and Richard L. Berkowitz] *Science News* 135:278 My 6 '89
Twins: 1 black, 1 white, born to interracial pair [T. and D. Gantt] il pors *Jet* 76:16-17 Jl 31 '89
Two-timing [original Doublemint Twins J. and J. Boyd] B. Greene. pors *Esquire* 111:57-9 Je '89
Twofers. L. C. Pogrebin. il *Ms.* 17:23 Ap '89

TWINS [film] See Motion picture reviews—Single works
TWINS DAYS FESTIVAL See Twinsburg (Ohio)—Festivals
TWINS IN MOTION PICTURES
Seeing double on the set of Dead ringers [optical supervisor Lee Wilson] D. Schweiger. il *Video* 13:17-18 Je '89

TWINSBURG (OHIO)
Festivals
At the Twinsburg Twins Festival, it's two for the money, two for the show, two to get ready . . . il *People Weekly* 32:90-1 Ag 21 '89

TWIST, OLIVER (LITERARY CHARACTER) See Oliver Twist (Literary character)
TWO CAREER COUPLES See Married couples—Employment
TWO FAMILY HOUSES
Go for a duplex [home of Robert and Deborah Accordino] il *Better Homes and Gardens* 67:44 Ag '89
TWO FORKS PROJECT (COLO.) See Dams
TWO INCOME FAMILY FINANCE See Finance, Personal
THE TWO JAKES [film] See Motion picture reviews—Single works

TWO THOUSAND (YEAR)
Agenda 2000 [blacks] L. Anderson. por *Essence* 20:132 D '89
Apocalypse now? B. Lawren. il *Psychology Today* 23:38-9+ My '89
The future of teaching. L. Darling-Hammond. *The Education Digest* 54:7-10 Mr '89
Looking back from 2000: what exactly did Bush do? D. Gergen. il por *U.S. News & World Report* 106:26-7 My 1 '89
National parks: year 2000. W. P. Mott, Jr. il *National Parks* 63:18-19 Ja/F '89
New challenges in the workplace [Workforce 2000] L. Crooks. il *Modern Maturity* 32:10-11 F/Mr '89
Outlook 2000 [cover story; special issue] bibl f il *Monthly Labor Review* 112:2-74 N '89
Preparing education for the year 2000. M. J. Cetron. *The Education Digest* 54:3-6 Ap '89
Shopping in the year 2000. il *The Futurist* 23:44 N/D '89
Visions of tomorrow [cover story; special section; with introd. by Gregory Jaynes] il *Life* 12:50-1+ F '89
What will teenagers face in the 21st century? [views of William Shaw] il *USA Today (Periodical)* 118:16 D '89

TWO THOUSAND EIGHTY-NINE (YEAR)
Science fiction writers speak to the future [cover story; special section; with introd. by Bette Chambers] il *The Humanist* 49:5-17+ Mr/Ap '89

TWO THOUSAND NINE (YEAR)
Just my imagination: envisioning the world in 2009. J. Walljasper. il *Utne Reader* p142-3 N/D '89

TWO THOUSAND SEVENTY-THREE (YEAR)
Looking back in 2073 [space exploits] C. Sheffield. *Ad Astra* 1:48 Mr '89

TWO THOUSAND SIX (YEAR)
The 21st-century manager. R. Farmanfarmaian. il *Working Woman* 14:73+ N '89

TWO THOUSAND SIXTY (YEAR)
A day in the year 2060 [life in Vancouver] R. Corelli. il *Maclean's* 102:38-9 S 11 '89

TWO THOUSAND TEN (YEAR)
2010: a new great powers lineup? *Society* 27:3 N/D '89

TWO THOUSAND THREE (YEAR)
Industry and technology leaders in 2003. *The Futurist* 23:54-5 Jl/Ag '89

TWO-WAY RADIO See Radiotelephone
TWO-YEAR COLLEGES See Community and junior colleges

TWOHY, ROBERT
The shape that satisfies. *The Writer* 102:16-17 D '89

TWOMBLY, CY, 1928-
about
Cy Twombly at Sperone Westwater. L. Norden. il *Art in America* 77:208-9 O '89

TYCKO, BENJAMIN, AND OTHERS
T cell receptor gene trans-rearrangements: chimeric γ-δ genes in normal lymphoid tissues. bibl f il *Science* 245:1242-6 S 15 '89

TYCO TOYS, INC.
Oopsie-Daisy, guess who's tops in Toyland now? M. Roman. il *Business Week* p102 D 18 '89

TYLCZAK, LYNN
about
A good idea in bad taste. M. G. Stoddard. il por *The Saturday Evening Post* 261:38-9 S '89

TYLER, ANNE, 1941-
A street of bugles [story] il *The Saturday Evening Post* 261:54-7+ Jl/Ag '89
A woman like a fieldstone house [story] il *Ladies' Home Journal* 106:86+ Ag '89
about
Novel events. C. Iannone. *National Review* 41:46-7+ S 1 '89

TYLER, G. LEONARD, AND OTHERS
Voyager radio science observations of Neptune and Triton. bibl f il *Science* 246:1466-73 D 15 '89

TYLER, JOHN E.
Hope Plantation in North Carolina. bibl f il *Antiques* 135:322-9 Ja '89

TYLER, SCOTT

about

Art for whose sake? S. Marlin. *National Review* 41:21-2 Ap 21 '89

Flag furor. S. Hochfield. il por *Art News* 88:43-4+ Summ '89

TYLER, TEXAS BLACK FILM COLLECTION

Rare films: the Tyler, Texas treasure trove. M. G. Carstarphen. il *American Visions* 4:36-8 Je '89

TYNAN, JOHN A.

Meet Dr. Getz [reprint] il por *Down Beat* 56:43-4 S '89

Natural flow: the Bill Evans Trio [reprint] il por *Down Beat* 56:61 S '89

TYNAN, KATHLEEN

about

Literary lights. il pors *Harper's Bazaar* 122:58+ Ag '89

TYNDALE (WILLIAM) COLLEGE *See* William Tyndale College

TYNDALL REPORT *See* Newsletters

TYNER, MCCOY

about

McCoy Tyner: Sweet Basil/New York. S. Stein. il por *Down Beat* 56:46-7 Ap '89

TYPE A BEHAVIOR

Babes in Stress-land. D. R. Hales and R. E. Hales. il *American Health* 8:44-6+ O '89

Child's aggression may foretell heart risk [research by Saundra MacD. Hunter] K. Fackelmann. *Science News* 136:15 Jl 1 '89

Danger! A short fuse can kill you [linked with heart disease] A. Fischer. il *Redbook* 173:162-3+ S '89

Double jeopardy: cholesterol and Type A [research by Edward Suarez] P. King. il *Psychology Today* 23:26 S '89

Getting to the heart of Type A's [interview with R. B. Williams] S. Findlay. il por *U.S. News & World Report* 106:68 My 15 '89

Hostility boosts risk of heart trouble [research by Redford B. Williams] K. Fackelmann. *Science News* 135:60 Ja 28 '89

Soothing the savage heart [views of R. Williams] J. Poppy. il *Esquire* 112:103-4 O '89

The trusting heart [modifying hostile behavior; excerpt] R. B. Williams. il *Psychology Today* 23:36-7+ Ja/F '89

Type A diet traps. L. Lindner. il *Health (New York, N.Y.)* 21:36-7 Ag '89

Type A: healing the spirit [work of M. Friedman] J. P. Rodgers. il *Psychology Today* 23:22 Ap '89

Your anger can kill you [linked with heart disease; condensed from The trusting heart] R. B. Williams. il *Reader's Digest* 135:183-4+ Ag '89

TYPE AND TYPEFOUNDING

The ABCs of digital type. J. Collins. il *Byte* 14:403-8 N '89

How to get your readers' attention [GEM Artline and LetraStudio] S. Morgenstern. il *Home Office Computing* 7:50-1 My '89

TYPE T BEHAVIOR

Taking risks and seeking stimulation: the Type T personality. F. H. Farley. il *USA Today (Periodical)* 118:60-1 Jl '89

TYPES, PSYCHOLOGICAL *See* Typology (Psychology)

TYPESETTING

See also

Computers—Printing use

TYPEWRITERS

Loving manual labor. E. Siff. il *Gentlemen's Quarterly* 59:43+ Je '89

TYPEWRITERS, ELECTRONIC

The best type. C. Croth. il *Rolling Stone* p191 N 16 '89

Electronic typewriters: old standbys get new, powerful features. M. Bihl. il *Home Office Computing* 7:60+ Mr '89

TYPEWRITING

Study and teaching

Aids and devices

To heck with hunt-and-peck [programs] L. Williams. il *Home Office Computing* 7:81-2+ Ap '89

TYPHOID FEVER

Mary Mallon's trail of typhoid. C. Carey. il por *FDA Consumer* 23:18-21 Je '89

Diagnosis

Going by the book [woman in Nicaragua] T. Dajer. il *Discover* 10:30-3 Ap '89

TYPHOID MARY, D. 1938

about

Mary Mallon's trail of typhoid. C. Carey. il por *FDA Consumer* 23:18-21 Je '89

TYPING *See* Typewriting

TYPOGRAPHICAL ERRORS

The art of typing bulletins. M. E. Marty. *The Christian Century* 106:335 Mr 22-29 '89

Glosses. M. E. Marty. *The Christian Century* 106:919 O 11 '89

TYPOLOGY (PSYCHOLOGY)

Understanding your personality. D. R. Hales. il *McCall's* 116:71-4+ Mr '89

TYRANNOSAURUS *See* Dinosaurs

TYRANNY *See* Despotism

TYRE, PEG

Giant steps. il pors *New York* 22:52-5 F 6 '89

Holy war. il por *New York* 22:48-51 Ap 24 '89

TYROSINE KINASE *See* Kinases

TYRRELL, R. EMMETT

Editorials. See issues of The American Spectator

TYSON, BRADY

Assassination in Brazil. *The Christian Century* 106:384-7 Ap 12 '89

TYSON, DON

about

Don Tyson wins Holly Farms, but his debts aren't chicken feed. K. Kelly. il por *Business Week* p29-30 Jl 10 '89

TYSON, IAN, 1933-

about

Cowboy troubadour. N. Jennings. il pors *Maclean's* 102:52-4 F 13 '89

TYSON, MIKE

about

Arsenio jokes with 3 champs—Ali, Tyson, Leonard—on show. il pors *Jet* 76:46-7 Ag 21 '89

The beatings go on. P. Putnam. pors *Sports Illustrated* 71:18-19 Jl 31 '89

Central St. fetes Tyson with honorary doctorate. il pors *Jet* 76:14 My 15 '89

Central State U. designs high school, B.A. degree program for Mike Tyson. il por *Jet* 77:28 N 6 '89

The champ's biggest fight [cover story] il pors *Ebony* 44:116+ Ja '89

Dear Mike . . . G. Smith. il pors *Sports Illustrated* 70:58-64+ F 27 '89

Fight knight. V. Woods. il pors *Vogue* 179:330-7+ D '89

'Free at last,' Tyson says of divorce from actress Robin Givens. il pors *Jet* 76:12-13 Je 19 '89

His Robin flown, the champ pushes on. J. Jerome. il pors *People Weekly* 31:30-5 F 27 '89

Lord of the ring. H. Conrad. il pors *Rolling Stone* p64-5+ O 19 '89

Mike Tyson. G. Smith. por *People Weekly* 32 Special Issue:88-9 Fall '89

Mike Tyson talks about: his big birthday bash, being 'betrayed' in book, plans for his future [cover story] R. E. Johnson. il pors *Jet* 76:54-8 Jl 24 '89

Mike Tyson: "the truth about Robin and me". il pors *Jet* 75:59-60 Ja 9 '89

Smashing! P. Putnam. il pors *Sports Illustrated* 70:14-17 Mr 6 '89

Take cover, Mike Tyson—Frank Bruno's got a secret weapon. A. Coren. il *TV Guide* 37:8-9 F 25-Mr 3 '89

Tale of the tape. il pors *Sports Illustrated* 70:14 My 29 '89

Tyson destroys 'Truth' in 1½ min. Atlantic City bout. il pors *Jet* 76:52+ Ag 7 '89

Tyson-Givens split final, $125 million suit ended. il pors *Jet* 75:52 Mr 6 '89

Tyson no 'slave,' King testifies against Cayton. por *Jet* 75:47 Mr 6 '89

Tyson pockets $150,000 for 'Lean on me' plug. por *Jet* 75:48 Mr 20 '89

Tyson scuffles in Canada during visit with Givens. il por *Jet* 75:51 Ja 30 '89

Tyson's return a triumph, KO's Frank Bruno in five. il pors *Jet* 75:51-2 Mr 13 '89

Why Robin Givens has rolled with the punches—and still loves Tyson. M. Murphy. il pors *TV Guide* 37:6-7+ Jl 1-7 '89

Anecdotes, facetiae, satire, etc.

Hey, Tyson, I'm The Man! L. Montville. il *Sports Illustrated* 71:116 O 2 '89

TYSON, RICHARD

about

Richard Tyson. E. Warren. por *TV Guide* 37:5 S 23-29 '89

TYSON-BERNSTEIN, HARRIET

The academy's contribution to textbook impoverishment. *The Education Digest* 54:25-8 F '89

TYSON FOODS, INC.

Contented pigs? [drive to popularize pork] M. Fritz. il *Forbes* 144:118-19 Ag 7 '89

Don Tyson wins Holly Farms, but his debts aren't chicken feed. K. Kelly. il por *Business Week* p29-30 Jl 10 '89

Flying feathers in the coop [Holly Farms makes lockup deal with ConAgra to prevent takeover by Tyson Foods] il *Time* 133:52 F 6 '89

TYZNIK, WILLIAM

about

'Frosty Paws' ice cream can teach an old dog new licks. il *People Weekly* 31:132-3 Je 5 '89

TZUTUHIL INDIANS

Blood bond: where Oklahoma and Guatemala meet [Catholic mission] D. Thomson. *America* 161:277-8 O 28 '89

U

U.S. ARMY LABORATORY COMMAND
LABCOM presents latest Army field technologies. il *Popular Mechanics* 166:16 O '89

U.S. BANKNOTE COMPANY L. P.
From munis to money. J. Zweig. il por *Forbes* 143:134 F 20 '89

U.S. BOOK STORE (MOSCOW, SOVIET UNION) See Booksellers and bookselling—Soviet Union

U.S. CATHOLIC (PERIODICAL)
Of many things [readers' views on homosexuals] G. W. Hunt. *America* 161:310 N 11 '89

U.S. COMMITTEE FOR ENERGY AWARENESS
Hooked on foreign uranium. W. J. Lanouette. il *The Bulletin of the Atomic Scientists* 45:4 O '89

U.S. COMMITTEE IN SOLIDARITY WITH THE PEOPLE OF EL SALVADOR
And why they let anyone be an informant [FBI investigation] S. Burkholder. *The Washington Monthly* 20:19-20 Ja '89
The files of counterrevolution [FBI investigation] A. Cockburn. *The Nation* 249:161 Ag 7-14 '89

U.S. CONSUMER PRODUCT SAFETY COMMISSION
Worm and remembrance [recall of Worm Gett'r, an electronic worm probe for fishermen] W. J. Elvin. il *The American Spectator* 22:30-1 Ja '89

U.S. CUSTOMS SERVICE
Flight into danger. R. Dolphin. il *Maclean's* 102:12-13 Ap 3 '89
A loose cannon's parting shot [W. Von Raab's comments on U.S. war on drugs] E. Shannon. il por *Time* 134:18-19 Ag 7 '89
Soviet attempts to buy U.S. computers continue despite Customs crackdown. D. Hughes. *Aviation Week & Space Technology* 130:279+ Je 12 '89
U.S. antidrug operations [cover story; special section; with editorial comment] M. Mecham. il map *Aviation Week & Space Technology* 130:9, 34-8+ Ja 30 '89
The 'you fly, you die' debate [shooting down drug planes] J. N. Baker. il *Newsweek* 114:26 O 2 '89

U.S. FISH AND WILDLIFE SERVICE
Endangered species need more help. *Science News* 135:79 F 4 '89
Game laws weren't writ for fat cats. T. Williams. il *Audubon* 91:104-6+ Jl '89
Up front [waterfowl sting operation in Texas] D. Barnes. il *Field & Stream* 93:7 Mr '89
Wildlife cops on a bust [Texas Waterfowl Operation] E. Linden. il *Time* 133:18 F 20 '89

U.S. HOLOCAUST MEMORIAL MUSEUM
Holocaust Memorial Museum underway. *American History Illustrated* 23:10 F '89
How buildings remember [designed by J. I. Freed] H. Muschamp. *The New Republic* 201:27-33 Ag 28 '89

U.S. MEMORIES INC.
America's gambling chips [formed to make dynamic random access memory chips] *Newsweek* 114:44 Jl 3 '89
Big Blue's chip club [formed to manufacture dynamic random access memory chips] il *Time* 134:44 Jl 3 '89
Hands across the chipmaking chasm [U.S. Memories and Sematech to work with JESSI Project] O. Port. *Business Week* p28-9 Jl 3 '89

U.S. MINT See United States. Mint

U.S. NAVAL WEAPONS CENTER See Naval Weapons Center (U.S.)

U.S. NEWS & WORLD REPORT (PERIODICAL)
God is not providing. F. Meeks. il *Forbes* 144:151+ O 30 '89
Letters of the '80s. R. J. Ames. il *U.S. News & World Report* 107:6-7 D 25 '89-Ja 1 '90

U.S. NUCLEAR REGULATORY COMMISSION
Stop Stello [controversial appointment of V. Stello to head national effort to clean up crumbling nuclear weapons facilities] H. Wasserman. *The Nation* 249:372-3 O 9 '89

U.S. OLYMPIC FESTIVAL
A pre-Olympic fling. M. Noden. il *Sports Illustrated* 71:22-4+ Ag 7 '89

U.S. SHOE CORP.
If the shoe fits, sell it? [to sell most of its footwear division] S. Phillips. *Business Week* p42+ Mr 13 '89
U.S. Shoe may drop one of them. G. G. Marcial. *Business Week* p166 N 27 '89

U.S. SPACE CAMP (HUNTSVILLE, ALA.)
Training for space. A. Fisher. il *Popular Science* 234:12 Ja '89

U.S. TRUST CO.
Canadian imperialism [R. Cohen and L. Ellen buy into U.S. Trust Co.] J. Willoughby. il por *Forbes* 143:52 Ja 9 '89

U S WEST, INC. See US West, Inc.

U2 (MUSICAL GROUP)
Bono less than boffo at box office [U2: Rattle and hum] J. Ressner. *Rolling Stone* p16 Ja 12 '89
Now what? [cover story] S. Pond. il *Rolling Stone* p52-4+ Mr 9 '89
Pure Bono [interview; cover story] A. Block. il pors *Mother Jones* 14:32-7+ My '89
Remembering U2. A. Schwartz. il *Seventeen* 48:88+ O '89
U2 kicks off tour Down Under. T. Creswell. il *Rolling Stone* p26 N 16 '89

U2: RATTLE AND HUM [film] See Motion picture reviews—Single works

UAHC PRESS
Baking a bestseller [N. BenShea's Jacob the baker] L. Fleischer. *Publishers Weekly* 235:64 Ja 13 '89

UAL CORPORATION
Airline buyouts: losing altitude but not grounded yet. J. E. Ellis. il *Business Week* p31 O 30 '89
ALPA begins drive to win pilots' support for United buyout. *Aviation Week & Space Technology* 131:124 S 18 '89
The balloon bursts for Wall Street arbs [collapse of UAL takeover bid] J. Egan. il *U.S. News & World Report* 107:71 N 6 '89
Bankers' concerns, challenged forecasts derailed UAL buyout. C. Fotos and N. C. Kernstock. il *Aviation Week & Space Technology* 131:17-19 O 23 '89
Can United afford to be taken over? K. Labich. il *Fortune* 120:145-6+ S 11 '89
The Cayman connection [foreign investments in Coniston Partners may endanger deal for control of UAL] S. Flack. il *Forbes* 144:42-3 D 11 '89
Davis' bid prompts UAL to weigh alternatives. C. Fotos. il *Aviation Week & Space Technology* 131:21-2 Ag 14 '89
Davis increases bid for UAL, threatens to oust board if offer is rejected. *Aviation Week & Space Technology* 131:95 Ag 21 '89
Giving 'United' a new meaning [pilot buyout] J. Schwartz. il *Newsweek* 114:34 S 25 '89
He's hungry to buy an airline [M. Davis' bid] J. Castro. il por *Time* 134:42 Ag 21 '89
In hot pursuit of airlines [bid for UAL] L. Reibstein. il por *Newsweek* 114:40 Ag 21 '89
Investor group mounts new bid to buy UAL Corp., replace board. C. Fotos. *Aviation Week & Space Technology* 131:72 N 13 '89
Now, the sky's the limit [bid for United] J. E. Ellis. il *Business Week* p24-6 Ag 21 '89
Pilots' buyout of United swaps concessions for company control [with editorial comment] C. Fotos. *Aviation Week & Space Technology* 131:9, 109 S 25 '89
Still trying to land UAL [Coniston Partners' proxy fight] J. E. Ellis. il *Business Week* p28-9 N 20 '89
'This is too big a genie to put back in the bottle' [botched UAL takeover] J. E. Ellis. il por *Business Week* p43 N 6 '89
U.S. asks United buyout group for details on debt, foreign stake. C. Fotos. *Aviation Week & Space Technology* 131:105 O 2 '89
UAL investigates alternatives to Davis' $6.19-billion takeover bid. C. Fotos. *Aviation Week & Space Technology* 131:70 Ag 28 '89
UAL sets aside buyout effort, but pilots still pursue takeover. C. Fotos. *Aviation Week & Space Technology* 131:54 O 30 '89
United's buyers may be wearing rose-colored goggles. J. E. Ellis. il *Business Week* p36 O 16 '89
Why the United buyout is no great deal for workers. R. Kuttner. il *Business Week* p26 O 9 '89
Will everybody get on board? [buyout bid by executives and pilots] J. Greenwald. il *Time* 134:63 S 18 '89
The workingman's man at the takeover table [B. Freeman] C. Tucher. il por *Business Week* p62 S 4 '89

UAW See United Automobile, Aerospace and Agricultural Implement Workers of America

UBEROI, CHANCHAL
(jt. auth) See Lanzerotti, Louis J., and Uberoi, Chanchal

UBIQUITIN
Degradation of proteins with acetylated amino termini by the ubiquitin system. A. Mayer and others. bibl f il *Science* 244:1480-3 Je 23 '89
A multiubiquitin chain is confined to specific lysine in a targeted short-lived protein. V. Chau and others. bibl f il *Science* 243:1576-83 Mr 24 '89
The neuron-specific protein PGP 9.5 is a ubiquitin carboxyl-terminal hydrolase. K. D. Wilkinson and others. bibl f il *Science* 246:670-3 N 3 '89
The tails of ubiquitin [linked to both protein decay and synthesis; research by Daniel Finley and others] J. Kinoshita. *Scientific American* 260:33-4 Je '89

UBRIACO, GENE
about
Puzzling Penguins. J. Greenberg. il por *Sports Illustrated* 71:32-3 N 27 '89

UBU [drama] See Sloan, Larry

UCHITELLE, LOUIS
Caution at the Fed [cover story] il pors *The New York Times Magazine* p18-21+ Ja 15 '89

UCHITELLE, SUSAN
What it really takes to make school choice work. *Phi Delta Kappan* 71:301-3 D '89

UCKO, PETER J.
One world archaeology. il *History Today* 39:10-12 Mr '89

UCLA CHILD CARE CENTER *See* University of California, Los Angeles. Child Care Center

UCLA STUDIOS *See* University of California, Los Angeles. Independent Film and Television Producer's Program

UDALL, JAMES R.
Climate shock: turning down the heat [cover story; special section] il map *Sierra* 74:26-40 Jl/Ag '89

UDALL, MORRIS K.
about
The grand plans of Congressman Udall. J. A. Davis. il por *Sierra* 74:86-8+ My/Je '89

UDALL, STEWART L.
(jt. auth) See Hocker, Philip, and Udall, Stewart L.

UEBERROTH, PETER
about
Back to you, Frank. A. Bernstein and C. Power. il pors *Business Week* p24-6 Ap 24 '89
The designated hero. J. Castro. il por *Time* 133:44-6 Ap 17 '89
Eastern's merry-go-round. *Newsweek* 113:62 Ap 24 '89
Judge threatens to auction Eastern after buyout fails. J. T. McKenna and E. H. Kolcum. *Aviation Week & Space Technology* 130:60-1 Ap 17 '89
On the money. D. Okrent. il pors *Sports Illustrated* 70:41+ Ap 10 '89
Peter Ueberroth's Hawaiian adventure. E. Schine. il por *Business Week* p32 S 4 '89
A pilot with a golden record. il por *U.S. News & World Report* 106:14-15 Ap 17 '89
The price of Peter's principles. P. Schmuck. por *Sport (New York, N.Y.)* 80:10 Ja '89
The Ueberroth touch. L. Reibstein. il por *Newsweek* 113:44-5 Ap 17 '89
Ueberroth woos unions in bid to take over Eastern, resume flight operations. J. T. McKenna and E. H. Kolcum. *Aviation Week & Space Technology* 130:89 Ap 10 '89
Where's my escape hatch? il *Time* 133:51 Ap 24 '89
Why Mike Milken was so eager to help Peter Ueberroth. A. Bernstein. *Business Week* p30 My 1 '89

UEDA, REED
False modesty. *The New Republic* 201:16-17 Jl 3 '89

UELTSCHI, ALBERT L.
about
The pilots' pilot. F. Meeks. il por *Forbes* 144:198+ N 13 '89

UEMATSU, KEIJI
about
Keiji Uematsu at Gallery Kasahara. J. Koplos. *Art in America* 77:145+ Jl '89

UFC *See* Universities Funding Council (Great Britain)

UFCW *See* United Food and Commercial Workers International Union

UFOS
See also
Project Blue Book
E.T. come home [Elmwood UFO Days, Wis.] S. Kaplan. il *Travel Holiday* 171:104 My '89
Invasion of the mind snatchers [abductions] E. Bird. il *Psychology Today* 23:64-6 Ap '89
NYASk [meeting of New York Area Skeptics] *The New Yorker* 65:30-1 My 29 '89
True confessions [results of survey on abductions] P. Weintraub. il *Omni (New York, N.Y.)* 11:18+ F '89
UFO update. See issues of Omni (New York, N.Y.)
The UFO's in Uncle Sam's closet. il *U.S. News & World Report* 107:19 O 23 '89
Reporters and reporting
Elvis spotted in Estonia! [TASS reports UFO sighting in Soviet Union] H. G. Chua-Eoan. il *Time* 134:52 O 23 '89
Glasnost enters the Twilight Zone [sighting in Russia] A. Wilson-Smith. *Maclean's* 102:30 O 23 '89
They came from outer space [TASS reports on UFO sighting in provincial Russian city] C. Bogert. il *Newsweek* 114:42 O 23 '89
Too late for Tsar Wars, aliens visit the U.S.S.R. il *People Weekly* 32:120 O 30 '89

UGANDA
See also
AIDS (Disease)—Uganda
Ugandans
Water supply—Uganda
History
A survivor—barely—as Uganda's president, Godfrey Binaisa finds life in Brooklyn a beach. P. Chin. il pors *People Weekly* 31:139-40+ My 1 '89
Politics and government
Starting over in Kampala [with interview with Y. Museveni] M. S. Serrill. il por *Time* 134:54+ N 6 '89
Uganda: after the terror. R. Kapuściński. il por map *The New York Times Magazine* p38-41+ Mr 12 '89

UGANDANS
United States
A survivor—barely—as Uganda's president, Godfrey Binaisa finds life in Brooklyn a beach. P. Chin. il pors *People Weekly* 31:139-40+ My 1 '89

UGARTE, AUGUSTO PINOCHET *See* Pinochet Ugarte, Augusto

UGARTE, MICHAEL, 1949-
Cela vie. *The Nation* 249:646+ N 27 '89

UGGERHØJ, ERIK
(jt. auth) See Sørensen, Allan H., and Uggerhøj, Erik

UGISS, CAROLYN
about
Penthouse properties, corporate style. L. Rosch. il por *Working Woman* 14:120-1 O '89

UGLOW, ALAN
about
Alan Uglow at Lorence-Monk. S. Ellis. il *Art in America* 77:196-7 My '89

UGOLINI, G., AND OTHERS
Transneuronal transfer of herpes virus from peripheral nerves to cortex and brainstem. bibl f il *Science* 243:89-91 Ja 6 '89

UHF (ULTRAHIGH FREQUENCY) TELEVISION STATIONS *See* Television stations

UHF [film] *See* Motion picture reviews—Single works

UHLENBECK, GEORGE EUGENE, 1900-1988
about
George Uhlenbeck and the discovery of electron spin. A. Pais. bibl f il pors *Physics Today* 42:34-40 D '89
Obituary
Physics Today il por 42:91-2+ D '89. M. Dresden

UKELES, MIERLE LADERMAN
about
Waste not. P. C. Phillips. il *Art in America* 77:47+ F '89

UKRAINE
See also
Agriculture—Ukraine
Americans—Ukraine
Chernobyl nuclear disaster, 1986
Employee ownership—Ukraine
Galicia (Poland and Ukraine)
Jews—Ukraine
Peace movement—Ukraine
Description and travel
Ukrainian odyssey [American-Soviet International Peace Walk] V. B. Browback. il map *Modern Maturity* 32:58-9+ Ag/S '89
History
Historiography
Hrushevsky and the Ukraine's 'lost' history. T. Prymak. bibl il por map *History Today* 39:42-6 Ja '89
Industries
See also
Shareholding Socialist Enterprise (Ukraine)
Nationalism
And in the Ukraine. R. Grenier. *National Review* 41:30-1 Ja 27 '89
As the Ukraine goes, so goes the nation. F. Coleman. il map *Newsweek* 114:26 S 25 '89
The Ukraine: the critical republic. J. Trimble. il map *U.S. News & World Report* 106:45-7 Ap 3 '89
Religious institutions and affairs
See also
Catholic Church—Ukraine

UKRAINIAN ART *See* Art, Ukrainian

UKRAINIAN LITERATURE
The mermaid of the Dniester. O. Petrash. il *The Courier (Unesco)* 42:23 Mr '89

ULABY, NEDA
Consumerism to idealism. por *The Humanist* 49:26+ Mr/Ap '89

ULANSEY, DAVID
The Mithraic mysteries. bibl il map *Scientific American* 261:130-5 D '89

ULČ, OTTO
Czechoslovakia: realistic socialism? bibl f *Current History* 88:389-92+ N '89

ULCERATIVE COLITIS
Therapy
Cyclosporin therapy heals colon ulcers [research by Simon Lichtiger and Daniel H. Present] K. Fackelmann. *Science News* 135:310 My 20 '89
My second chance [relieved by ileostomy] M. Bush. il pors *Ladies' Home Journal* 106:138-9+ Mr '89

ULCERATIVE KERATITIS *See* Eye—Diseases and defects

ULCERS
See also
Peptic ulcers

ULENE, ART
A 30-day plan to lower your cholesterol. il por *Good Housekeeping* 208:77+ Mr '89

ULLIN, ALBERT
A potpourri of fact and fiction from Down Under. il *Publishers Weekly* 235:37-8 Mr 24 '89

ULLMAN, MONTAGUE
about
Making a prophet [interview] N. Guccione. il *Omni (New York, N.Y.)* 12:12 N '89

ULLMAN, RICHARD H. (RICHARD HENRY)
The covert French connection. *Foreign Policy* 75:3-33 Summ '89

ULLMAN, TRACEY
about
Tracey Ullman: just being herselves. B. Bull. il por *Vogue* 179:386+ My '89
Tracey Ullman makes a face. J. Lazar. il pors *The New York Times Magazine* p28-9+ O 15 '89

ULLMANN, HARRISON J.
Screening for the high risk. il *The Saturday Evening Post* 261:82-3+ Ja/F '89

ULLMANN, LINN
Portrait of a runaway. il *Seventeen* 48:254-7+ Mr '89
Time to talk. *Seventeen* 48:112-13 S '89

ULLMANN, LIV
about
Architectural digest visits: Liv Ullmann. D. Roberts. il por *Architectural Digest* 46:208-14+ D '89

ULLRICH, BURKHARD MÜLLER- *See* Müller-Ullrich, Burkhard

ULLYOT, JOAN, 1940-
Hill, yes! il por *Runner's World* 24:24-5 Ap '89
Let's be careful out there. il por *Runner's World* 24:26 S '89

ULSTEIN, STEFAN
Teaching as though life hangs in the balance. il *Christianity Today* 33:10-11 Ap 21 '89

ULSTER COUNTY (N.Y.)
Politics and government
A funny thing happened on the way to the legislature. I lost. D. McCraw. *The Washington Monthly* 21:30-2+ Jl/Ag '89

ULTAN, LLOYD
Crises in society: the role of the arts. bibl f *Design for Arts in Education* 90:14-21 My/Je '89

ULTRA-WIDEBAND RADAR
Military use
UWB radar has potential to detect Stealth aircraft [impulse radar technolgy; with editorial comment] W. B. Scott. il *Aviation Week & Space Technology* 131:9, 38-41 D 4 '89

ULTRAHIGH BYPASS RATIO ENGINES *See* Airplane engines, Jet

ULTRAHIGH FREQUENCY TELEVISION STATIONS *See* Television stations

ULTRAMARATHON RUNNING
Lewis, Clark & the old fartleks [Trail Run across Washington] B. Lewis. il *Runner's World* 24:64-5 S '89
Woman of the century [H. Klein, 66 year old] P. L. Potts. il pors *Runner's World* 24:34-6 Je '89

ULTRASONIC HUMIDIFIERS *See* Humidifiers

ULTRASONIC WAVES
See also
Animals, Effect of ultrasonic waves on
Chemical use
The chemical effects of ultrasound. K. S. Suslick. bibl il *Scientific American* 260:80-6 F '89
Industrial use
Ultrasonics used for factory measurements. *High Technology Business* 9:33 Je '89
Medical use
The fascinating world of the unborn. H. Goer. *Reader's Digest* 135:150-4 N '89
Genies in the medicine bottle. D. R. Katz. il *Esquire* 112:73-4 D '89
Mom, meet your baby [effect of utrasound exams on pregnant women; research by Tiffany Field] B. Py-Lieberman. *Psychology Today* 23:18 Je '89
Ultrasound can fight infection [work of Larry S. Nichter] il *USA Today (Periodical)* 117:16 F '89
Pest control use
Anecdotes, facetiae, satire, etc.
The bugs of summer . . . zap! K. Fury. il *New Choices for the Best Years* 29:88 Jl '89

ULTRASOUND *See* Ultrasonic waves

ULTRAVIOLET ASTRONOMY
Seeing in the ultraviolet [work of Bruno Milliard] il *Sky and Telescope* 78:459 N '89
Ultraviolet spectrometer observations of Neptune and Triton. A. L. Broadfoot and others. bibl f il *Science* 246:1459-66 D 15 '89

ULTRAVIOLET DETECTORS
UV sensors for early-warning systems. *High Technology Business* 9:36 N/D '89

ULTRAVIOLET RAYS
Contribution of ultraviolet irradiance variations to changes in the sun's total irradiance. J. Lean. bibl f il *Science* 244:197-200 Ap 14 '89
Ultraviolet levels under sea ice during the Antarctic spring [discussion of July 22, 1988 article, Ultraviolet radiation levels during the Antarctic spring] J. E. Frederick and H. E. Snell. *Science* 245:194-5 Jl 14 '89
Physiological effects
See also
Plants, Effect of ultraviolet rays on
Seasonal affective disorder
Sunburn
Suntan

Does the ozone hole threaten Antarctic life? [effect of ultraviolet radiation on phytoplankton] L. Roberts. il map *Science* 244:288-9 Ap 21 '89
Low-zone [influence of Antarctic ozone hole] T. Beardsley. *Scientific American* 261:26+ O '89
Ozone hole hikes Antarctic ultraviolet [has not caused significant harm to phytoplankton] R. Monastersky. *Science News* 135:228 Ap 15 '89
Ozone hole peril to Antarctic life [research by John Frederick] il *USA Today (Periodical)* 117:6 Je '89
Ozone hole threatens polar plankton [research by Sayed El-Sayed] *Science News* 136:284 O 28 '89
Spider webs: luring light may be a trap [research by Catherine L. Craig] I. Wickelgren. il *Science News* 135:330 My 27 '89
A thousand points of light [view of J. Ott] M. Morse. il *Utne Reader* p12-13 Mr/Ap '89

ULURU NATIONAL PARK (AUSTRALIA)
Rock dreams. R. Davidson. il *Mother Jones* 14:39-40 O '89

ULYSSES FLIGHT TO THE SUN *See* Space flight to the sun

ULYSSES IN NIGHTTOWN [drama] *See* Barkentin, Marjorie

UMAN, MARTIN A., AND KRIDER, E. PHILIP
Natural and artificially initiated lightning [cover story] bibl f il *Science* 246:457-64 O 27 '89

UMAÑA, ALVARO
about
Capital conservation. J. Zweig. por *Forbes* 143:208 Ap 17 '89

UMBA *See* Upper Midwest Booksellers Association

UMBILICAL CORD
Marrow rebuilt with umbilical-cord blood [work of Arleen D. Auerbach] A. McKenzie. *Science News* 136:293 N 4 '89

UMBRELLAS
History
Yoicks! Yoicks! and Brolly ho! Rah for the parapluie! I. Shenker. bibl (p246) il *Smithsonian* 20:130-2+ N '89

UMBRIA JAZZ FESTIVAL *See* Music festivals—Italy

UMENAI, TAKUSEI, AND SUZUKI, HIROSHI
Hepatitis B vaccination. il *World Health* p24-5 N '89

UMPIRES AND UMPIRING (SPORTS) *See* Baseball, Professional—Umpiring

UMW *See* United Mine Workers of America

UN *See* United Nations

UN-AMERICAN ACTIVITIES COMMITTEE *See* United States. Congress. House. Committee on Un-American Activities

UNAUTHORIZED BIOGRAPHY: RICHARD M. NIXON [television program] See Television program reviews—Single works

THE UNBEARABLE LIGHTNESS OF BEING [film] See Motion picture reviews—Single works

UNBUNDLED STOCK UNITS
Advice for small shareholders: best to stay bundled up. *Money* 18:12 Ja '89
The greatest invention since . . . burnt toast? J. Friedman. il *Business Week* p88 Mr 6 '89
How the unbundled unit came unbundled. J. Friedman. il *Business Week* p71 Ap 10 '89
Let's call them bundle bonds. B. Weberman. il *Forbes* 143:333 Ja 9 '89
There is a better way. M. S. Forbes, Jr. il *Forbes* 143:27 Ja 23 '89
Unbundled stocks: how they work. W. E. Sheeline. il *Fortune* 119:11-12 Ja 2 '89
Accounting
Invisible dilution. P. Wang. il *Forbes* 143:83 F 6 '89

UNCLAIMED ESTATES *See* Estates, Unclaimed

UNCLE BUCK [film] See Motion picture reviews—Single works

UNCLES
The dangerous uncle returns. J. D. Houston. il *Gentlemen's Quarterly* 59:235-8+ D '89
My two uncles. L. Cunningham. il *The New York Times Magazine* p32+ D 3 '89

UNCONQUERED [television program] See Television program reviews—Single works

UNCONSCIOUSNESS *See* Coma

UNCTAD *See* United Nations Conference on Trade and Development

UNDER-THE-COUNTER SECURITIES
Still in the pinks [L. Goldstein's pink sheet picks] T. Jaffe. *Forbes* 143:172-3 F 6 '89

UNDER THE DOUBLE MOON [opera] See Davis, Anthony

UNDER THE SUN OF SATAN [film] See Motion picture reviews—Single works

UNDERACHIEVERS
The families of gifted underachievers [research by Sylvia Rimm and Barbara Lowe] G. W. Bracey. il *Phi Delta Kappan* 70:563 Mr '89

UNDERCLASS
An agenda for the black middle class [cover story] D. T. Dingle. il *Black Enterprise* 20:52-4+ N '89
Children of the underclass [cover story] il *Newsweek* 114:16-20+ S 11 '89
Confronting minority failure [address, January 26, 1989] R. D. Lamm. *Vital Speeches of the Day* 55:433-5 My 1 '89

UNDERCLASS—*cont.*

Opportunity foreclosure zones. J. D. Kasarda. il *New Perspectives Quarterly* 6:16-21 Summ '89

The surprising news about the underclass. D. Whitman. il *U.S. News & World Report* 107:73+ D 25 '89-Ja 1 '90

The two black Americas [cover story] M. Kondracke. *The New Republic* 200:17-20 F 6 '89

UNDERDEVELOPED AREAS *See* Developing countries

UNDERGROUND ATLANTA

Big-city village. G. Anderson. il *Architectural Record* 177:98-101 S '89

Pay dirt: underground mall boosts black business. A. S. Harris. il *Black Enterprise* 20:20 S '89

UNDERGROUND ECONOMY

Developing countries

From mercantilism to markets. T. Bethell. il *The American Spectator* 22:11-13 Ap '89

How to make poor countries rich [views of H. de Soto] J. Main. il por *Fortune* 119:101-2+ Ja 16 '89

The right path [views of H. de Soto] R. Bailey. il por *Forbes* 143:80-1 Ja 23 '89

Third world economies: a new proposal [views of H. de Soto] J. Main. *Current (Washington, D.C.)* 314:38-40 Jl/Ag '89

Italy

For Italy's entrepreneurs, the figures are bella. C. Haberman. il *The New York Times Magazine* p32-4+ Jl 16 '89

Latin America

The only hope for Latin America [views of H. de Soto] M. Falcoff. *Commentary* 87:34-8 Ap '89

Peru

Crusader for Peru's have-nots [work of H. de Soto] E. H. Methvin. il *Reader's Digest* 134:137-40 Ja '89

From mercantilism to markets. T. Bethell. il *The American Spectator* 22:11-13 Ap '89

The only hope for Latin America [views of H. de Soto] M. Falcoff. *Commentary* 87:34-8 Ap '89

The right path [views of H. de Soto] R. Bailey. il por *Forbes* 143:80-1 Ja 23 '89

South Africa

South Africa's 'dummy' shops. T. Rudman. *World Press Review* 36:64 D '89

Soviet Union

Capitalism on the sly. J. Trimble. il *U.S. News & World Report* 107:27 N 20 '89

The paradox of *perestroika:* a raging black market. P. Galuszka. il *Business Week* p66+ Je 5 '89

UNDERGROUND HOUSES *See* Houses, Earth sheltered

UNDERGROUND LITERATURE

Soviet Union

Gorbie's choice [influence of dissident literature on Soviet reforms] S. Anderson. *The New Republic* 200:11-12 Ap 17 '89

UNDERGROUND NUCLEAR TESTING *See* Nuclear weapons—Testing

UNDERGROUND PRESS *See* Alternative press

UNDERGROUND STRUCTURES

See also

New York (N.Y.)—Underground structures

Japan

Japan's underground frontier. S. Kanise. il *Time* 133:74 F 6 '89

UNDERGROUND WATER *See* Groundwater

UNDERPRIVILEGED CHILDREN *See* Socially handicapped children

UNDERTAKER BEETLES *See* Beetles

UNDERTAKERS AND UNDERTAKING

See also

Service Corporation International

UNDERWATER ACOUSTICS

Shooing fish with sound [schools of fish] R. Friedman. il *Sea Frontiers* 35:136-41 My/Je '89

UNDERWATER ARCHEOLOGY *See* Archeology, Submarine

UNDERWATER CINEMATOGRAPHY

The abyss. J. Calhoun. il *Theatre Crafts* 23:44-6+ Ag/S '89

Teetering over 'The abyss' [producer G. A. Hurd] B. Walker. il pors *American Film* 14:34-9 Jl '89

UNDERWATER DRILLING

See also

Ocean Drilling Program

UNDERWATER HOTELS, MOTELS, ETC.

Life underwater [Jules' Undersea Lodge at Key Largo] B. Wickens. il *Maclean's* 102:48 Mr 13 '89

UNDERWATER PHOTOGRAPHY

Point and splash. R. Rattner. il *Popular Photography* 96:62-7 S '89

Scuba photography. L. Lipsky. il *Petersen's Photographic Magazine* 17:36-8+ Mr '89

Snaps under the sea. S. Frink. il *Travel Holiday* 172:18-21 Jl '89

Underseascapes. F. Pitcairn. il *Audubon* 91:48-55 Mr '89

UNDERWATER RESEARCH *See* Oceanography

UNDERWATER SCULPTURE

The patina from the deep [work of R. Power] V. Gladstone. il *Art News* 88:15 S '89

UNDERWATER SOUND *See* Underwater acoustics

UNDERWATER TREASURE *See* Treasure trove

UNDERWEAR

Gorgeous liaisons [lingerie designs influenced by movie Dangerous liaisons] R. La Ferla. il *The New York Times Magazine* p72 F 19 '89

Hot again because they're cool [boxer shorts] R. E. Sullivan. il *Gentlemen's Quarterly* 59:60 F '89

Oh my! [bicycling underwear] S. Sorensen and L. Fritz. il *Bicycling* 30:154-5 Ap '89

The perfect fit [for pregnant women] C. DiGrappa. il *Parents* 64:154-6 N '89

Upscale undies [views of L. A. Allston] R. D. Manuel. il por *Essence* 19:41 F '89

Anecdotes, facetiae, satire, etc.

Flimsy excuses. K. R. Lawrence. il *The New York Times Magazine* p14+ F 12 '89

UNDERWEAR INDUSTRY

See also

Frederick's of Hollywood, Inc.

Fruit of the Loom, Inc.

UNDERWEIGHT *See* Weight (Physiology)

UNDERWOOD, ANNE

The witness was a maggot. il *International Wildlife* 19:34-7 My/Je '89

UNDERWOOD, BLAIR

about

Blair Underwood: riding high on 'L.A. law'. M. Marshall. il pors *Ebony* 44:96+ Mr '89

UNDERWOOD, LEE

Devadip Carlos Santana: instrument of light [reprint from January 1981 issue] il por *Down Beat* 56:90 S '89

UNDERWOOD, SHARRY TRAVER

Ted Shawn's summer oasis, 1942: Pillow talk [excerpt from American dancesong] il por *Dance Magazine* 63:28-31 Jl '89

UNDERWOOD, WILLIAM

about

Manager tied to drug gang. W. Bastone. *Rolling Stone* p62 Jl 13-27 '89

UNDOF (UNITED NATIONS DISENGAGEMENT OBSERVER FORCE) *See* United Nations—Armed Forces—Forces in the Middle East

UNDP *See* United Nations Development Programme

UNEMPLOYMENT

See also

Layoffs

Age vs. wage: how baby boomers may cool inflation. G. Koretz. il *Business Week* p26 F 6 '89

The labor market is a lot looser than it looks. R. Kuttner. il *Business Week* p18 Mr 27 '89

Lost your job? Here's what to do. A. C. Mallozzi. il *Good Housekeeping* 208:244 Je '89

Psychological aspects

Turning loss into growth. S. Dundon. il por *Working Woman* 14:92-4 Ag '89

Relief measures

See also

California Conservation Corps

Mi Casa Resource Center for Women (Denver, Colo.)

Public works—Federal aid

San Francisco Conservation Corps

Workfare

Employment policy: rethinking training. P. Osterman. *Current (Washington, D.C.)* 312:10-17 My '89

The failure of federal job training. J. Bovard. *Society* 26:57-64 My/Je '89

Statistics

Differences in unemployment rates of men and women have virtually disappeared. il *Occupational Outlook Quarterly* 33:40 Summ '89

Do more-educated workers fare better following job displacement? P. Swaim and M. Podgursky. bibl f il *Monthly Labor Review* 112:43-6 Ag '89

How big is the displaced worker problem? R. B. McKenzie. *Society* 26:43-8 Mr/Ap '89

Labor market completes sixth year of expansion in 1988. W. J. Howe and W. Parks, II. il *Monthly Labor Review* 112:3-14 F '89

Playing down unemployment [Bureau of Labor Statistics] W. Serrin. *The Nation* 248:84+ Ja 23 '89

Reasons for not working: poor and nonpoor householders. M. S. Littman. bibl f il *Monthly Labor Review* 112:16-21 Ag '89

Tracking the unemployed. E. Corcoran and P. Wallich. il *Scientific American* 261:63-4 Ag '89

Canada

The costs of free trade. J. DeMont. il *Maclean's* 102:28 Ap 10 '89

Japan

Adjusted Japanese unemployment rate remains below 3 percent in 1987-88. C. Sorrentino. il *Monthly Labor Review* 112:36-8 Je '89

Pennsylvania

Playing down unemployment [Bureau of Labor Statistics] W. Serrin. *The Nation* 248:84+ Ja 23 '89

UNITED AIR LINES, INC.—cont.
'This is too big a genie to put back in the bottle' [botched UAL takeover] J. E. Ellis. il por *Business Week* p43 N 6 '89

U.S. asks United buyout group for details on debt, foreign stake. C. Fotos. *Aviation Week & Space Technology* 131:105 O 2 '89

UAL investigates alternatives to Davis' $6.19-billion takeover bid. C. Fotos. *Aviation Week & Space Technology* 131:70 Ag 28 '89

UAL plans to begin service between U.S., Europe. *Aviation Week & Space Technology* 131:96 Jl 24 '89

UAL sets aside buyout effort, but pilots still pursue takeover. C. Fotos. *Aviation Week & Space Technology* 131:54 O 30 '89

United faces fresh challenges under record fleet expansion. il *Aviation Week & Space Technology* 130:326-7 Je 12 '89

United officials tell NTSB AD procedures not followed [hearings on Flight 811 cargo door accident in February 1989] B. W. Henderson. *Aviation Week & Space Technology* 130:107 My 1 '89

United swallows hard—and goes for growth. J. E. Ellis. il *Business Week* p34 My 15 '89

United: why labor needs some parachutes on board [pilots plan buyout] J. E. Ellis. il *Business Week* p28 S 18 '89

United's buyers may be wearing rose-colored goggles. J. E. Ellis. il *Business Week* p36 O 16 '89

United's flight attendants authorize strike; takeover reports push stock price up. J. T. McKenna. *Aviation Week & Space Technology* 131:95 Jl 17 '89

Why the United buyout is no great deal for workers. R. Kuttner. il *Business Week* p26 O 9 '89

Will everybody get on board? [UAL buyout bid by executives and pilots] J. Greenwald. il *Time* 134:63 S 18 '89

Will the carrot and stick work at United? J. E. Ellis. il por *Business Week* p56-7 F 6 '89

Wolf's bane [negotiations with its pilots] J. Zweig. il por *Forbes* 143:324 My 29 '89

The workingman's man at the takeover table [B. Freeman] C. Tucher. il por *Business Week* p62 S 4 '89

UNITED AUTOMOBILE, AEROSPACE AND AGRICULTURAL IMPLEMENT WORKERS OF AMERICA
American business should put America's future first [address, June 18, 1989] O. Bieber. *Vital Speeches of the Day* 55:613-20 Ag 1 '89

The bitter split in organized labor [multiskilling] il *Fortune* 119:66 F 13 '89

Constant improvement? Or speedup? [Mazda's emphasis on kaizen concept fosters union discontent at Michigan plant] J. Flint. il *Forbes* 143:92+ Ap 17 '89

For auto workers, it's team spirit vs. suspicion. W. Zellner. il *Business Week* p60-1 Jl 10 '89

GM and UAW: together again for the first time. M. Keller. il *Motor Trend* 41:146 Ap '89

How the UAW is doing its part for GM's parts. il *Business Week* p78 F 13 '89

The land of the UAW's setting sun [Nissan votes to keep union out] il *U.S. News & World Report* 107:8 Ag 7 '89

Score another for Japan Inc. [Nissan workers vote to keep out union] L. Reibstein. il *Newsweek* 114:44-5 Ag 7 '89

So where does the UAW go from here? [loss at Nissan plant in Smyrna, Tenn.] W. Zellner. il *Business Week* p77 Ag 14 '89

Struggle for the soul of the union [New Directions movement] J. Schwartz. il *The Nation* 249:8-10 Jl 3 '89

Suddenly, the UAW is raising its voice at GM. W. Zellner. il por *Business Week* p96+ N 6 '89

UAW convention. *Monthly Labor Review* 112:46-7 S '89

The UAW rebels teaming up against teamwork. W. Zellner. il *Business Week* p110+ Mr 27 '89

The UAW vs. Japan: it's showdown time in Tennessee [Nissan plant election] D. Foust. il *Business Week* p64-5 Jl 24 '89

Union blues [state of internal democracy] P. Downs. il *The Progressive* 53:32-5 Ja '89

United Auto Workers 29th constitutional convention. H. P. Guzda. *Monthly Labor Review* 112:34-6 O '89

Victor Reuther [New Directions movement; interview] B. Koeppel. il *The Progressive* 53:25-8 D '89

'Without unions, we'd have nothing' [strike at Ohio Crankshaft] P. Warloski. il *The Progressive* 53:22 D '89

UNITED CHRISTIAN ACTION FOR DEVELOPMENT
Squalor in the "City of God". P. Yancey. il *Christianity Today* 33:12-13 F 17 '89

UNITED CHURCH OF CANADA
Keepers of the keys [Port Kells, B.C. congregation refuses to relinquish church building after seceding over ordination of homosexuals] D. Wolff. *Maclean's* 102:20 My 1 '89

Opposition to gay clergy heating up. L. Mackey. *Christianity Today* 33:52-3 Jl 14 '89

UNITED CHURCH OF CHRIST
Apologizing to Anne Hutchinson [members burn 1638 writ of excommunication] M. P. Nugent. *The Christian Century* 106:304-5 Mr 22-29 '89

UCC headquarters site [proposed move to Cleveland] *The Christian Century* 106:520 My 17 '89

Unity theme triumphs at UCC Synod [General Synod in Fort Worth, Tex.] G. E. Ziegenhals. il *The Christian Century* 106:676-8 Jl 19-26 '89

When a church supports a lesbian seminarian [Carbondale, Ill.] T. A. Braun. *The Christian Century* 106:516-17 My 17 '89

UNITED CHURCH OF PAKISTAN
Evangelical view [interview with A. J. Malik] por *Christianity Today* 33:46 Jl 14 '89

UNITED ELECTRICAL, RADIO AND MACHINE WORKERS OF AMERICA
Union victory in a copper refinery [Cox Creek Refining Company] K. Kleiner. il *The Progressive* 53:13 S '89

UNITED FOOD AND COMMERCIAL WORKERS INTERNATIONAL UNION
Retail trade settlements. *Monthly Labor Review* 112:40-1 Je '89

UNITED INCOME FUND
Worldwide trends make him bullish [interview with R. Thompson] P. Sellers. il por *Fortune* 120:31+ S 25 '89

UNITED INTELLIGENCE INC.
This gumshoe does his legwork in wing tips [W. P. Callahan] J. Friedman. *Business Week* p98 My 29 '89

UNITED INTERNATIONAL GROWTH FUND
No place like home. E. Giltenan. il por *Forbes* 144:247+ O 30 '89

UNITED MERCHANTS & MANUFACTURERS, INC.
The incredible shrinking company. A. A. Lappen. il *Forbes* 144:207+ D 11 '89

UNITED METHODIST CHURCH
See also
  Mission Society for United Methodists
Singing hymns and hers [revised hymnal] R. N. Ostling. il *Time* 133:59 Je 12 '89

Employees
Paternity leave as church praxis [experience of United Methodist Church minister] B. Schofield-Bodt. il *The Christian Century* 106:463-4 My 3 '89

UNITED MINE WORKERS OF AMERICA
A bitter deadlock [Pittston strike] W. Lowther. il *Maclean's* 102:72 N 20 '89

Christians and the coalfield conflict [Episcopalian involvement in strike against Pittston] L. Johnson. *The Christian Century* 106:868-9 O 4 '89

Coal country's war with itself [strike against Pittston] R. A. Taylor. il *U.S. News & World Report* 107:45 Jl 24 '89

Coal wars again [UMW strike against Pittston] J. Motavalli. il *The Progressive* 53:24-7 Jl '89

John L., you'd be amazed [nonviolent tactics used in coal miners' strike against Pittston] J. Birnbaum. il *Time* 133:38 My 15 '89

'The Mine Workers must win this fight to survive' [Pittston strike] J. P. Hoerr. il *Business Week* p144+ O 9 '89

Miscalculated risk? [strike against Pittston Co.] R. Phalon. il por *Forbes* 143:41-2 Je 12 '89

Pittston power [takeover of the Moss 3 plant] P. Kwik. *The Nation* 249:409 O 16 '89

Solidarity in Appalachia [strike against Pittston Co.] D. Giardina. il *The Nation* 249:12-14 Jl 3 '89

Their miners and ours (I) [contrasting Soviet and Pittston strikes] A. Cockburn. *The Nation* 249:195 Ag 21-28 '89

Their miners and ours (II) [poll indicating more people know about the Soviet coal miners strike than the Pittston strike] A. Cockburn. *The Nation* 249:410-11 O 16 '89

Twilight for the UMW? [strike against Pittston Co.] M. Schroeder. il *Business Week* p32 Jl 3 '89

UNITED NATIONS
The 38th floor. J. Pérez de Cuellar. See issues of UN Chronicle

Negotiating peace—at a price [interview with J. Pérez de Cuéllar] H. Sada. il por *World Press Review* 36:50 My '89

The people next door. T. Mallon. il *The American Spectator* 22:22-6 D '89

Super power detente [address, June 16, 1989] C. R. Gharekhan. *Vital Speeches of the Day* 55:644-7 Ag 15 '89

Toward the 21st century: the future for multilateral diplomacy [address, September 16, 1988] R. S. Williamson. *Department of State Bulletin* 88:53-6 D '88

The United Nations: progress in the 1980s [address, October 19, 1988] R. S. Williamson. *Department of State Bulletin* 89:68-71 F '89

We aren't the world. Z. Citron. *The New Republic* 200:18-19+ My 15 '89

Armed Forces
Keeping the peace. S. Manning. il *Scholastic Update (Teachers' edition)* 121:6-7 Mr 24 '89

Nobel Prize for UN peace-keepers accepted in Oslo. il *UN Chronicle* 26:30 Mr '89

The price of peacekeeping. J. Bone. *World Press Review* 36:57 D '89

Turning again to UN peacekeepers [cover story] A. R. Norton and T. G. Weiss. il *The New Leader* 72:12-14 Mr 20 '89

Forces in Cyprus
Cyprus force mandate extended through 15 June 1989. il *UN Chronicle* 26:62-3 Mr '89

UNITED NATIONS—Armed Forces—Forces in Cyprus—
cont.
Guarding the line. R. McDonald. il map *Maclean's* 102:24
Mr 27 '89
Secretary-General outlines ideas to bridge positions on Cyprus.
il *UN Chronicle* 26:24-5 S '89
Forces in Lebanon
Mandate of Lebanon force extended. il *UN Chronicle* 26:32
Je '89
Security Council condemns hostage-taking and abduction;
UNIFIL mandate renewed. il *UN Chronicle* 26:25-6 D
'89
Forces in the Middle East
UN troops to stay in Golan Heights. *UN Chronicle* 26:20
S '89
Forces in the Persian Gulf region
Talks aimed at final peace settlement between Iran and
Iraq continue; UNIIMOG mandate renewed. il *UN
Chronicle* 26:23-5 Je '89
Budget
See United Nations—Finance
Employees
An indifference toward women. C. Subramaniam. *World
Press Review* 36:65 O '89
Finance
Assembly urges member states to pay dues 'on time and
in full'. il *UN Chronicle* 26:90 Mr '89
The concept of the 'unitary UN' [address, June 29, 1989]
J. R. Bolton. *Department of State Bulletin* 89:74-5 O '89
FY 1990 assistance request for organizations and programs
[statement, March 22, 1989] S. L. Vogelgesang. *Department
of State Bulletin* 89:81-4 My '89
The price of peacekeeping. J. Bone. *World Press Review*
36:57 D '89
Progress in UN reforms reported [organizational streamlining]
il *UN Chronicle* 26:38-9 S '89
Secretary-General calls for regular, timely payment of UN
dues. il *UN Chronicle* 26:29 D '89
Study and teaching
'The president of the United States speaks to the United
Nations' [winners of essay contest for high school students]
il *UN Chronicle* 26:78 S '89
UN offers study programmes in many areas. il *UN Chronicle*
26:92 Mr '89
Afghanistan
'Faithful implementation' of Geneva agreements asked. il
UN Chronicle 26:60-1 Mr '89
Grave concern expressed over escalating fighting in Af-
ghanistan. il *UN Chronicle* 26:22 D '89
Security Council considers Afghan complaint against Pakistan.
il *UN Chronicle* 26:26-7 S '89
Soviet troop withdrawal from Afghanistan completed on
time on 15 February 1989. il *UN Chronicle* 26:20-2 Je
'89
UN calls for full implementation of Afghanistan peace accords
[statement and text of resolution, November 3, 1988] V.
A. Walters. *Department of State Bulletin* 89:40-1 Ja '89
Africa
See also
United Nations. Programme of Action for African Economic Recovery and Development
Seeking human dignity . . . avoiding a 'bloodbath' . . .
il *UN Chronicle* 26:20-1 Mr '89
Asia
Reaffirmation of faith in the UN . . . rejoicing in the
promise of peace . . . il *UN Chronicle* 26:22-3 Mr '89
Cambodia
Efforts toward a Cambodian settlement [statement and text
of UN General Assembly resolution, November 3, 1988]
V. A. Walters. *Department of State Bulletin* 89:65-8 F
'89
Kampuchean peace settlement 'on horizon' Secretary-General
reports. il *UN Chronicle* 26:26-7 Je '89
Paris conference on Cambodia clears path towards peace.
il *UN Chronicle* 26:21 D '89
Signs of progress towards settlement of Kampuchean conflict
seen. il *UN Chronicle* 26:22-3 S '89
United Nations pursues Kampuchean settlement. il *UN
Chronicle* 26:64 Mr '89
Caribbean region
A staggering external debt . . . Central American peace
pursued . . . il *UN Chronicle* 26:26-7 Mr '89
Central America
Guatemala City conference [refugee problems] il *UN Chronicle*
26:14-15 S '89
Plans for UN observers in Central America 'in suspense'.
map *UN Chronicle* 26:13-14 S '89
Security Council adopts resolution on Central American peace
[text of resolution and statement, July 28, 1989] H. S.
Okun. *Department of State Bulletin* 89:73-4 O '89
'Strongest support' for peace plan for Central America expressed by Assembly. il *UN Chronicle* 26:65 Mr '89
UN observers asked to verify Central American peace plan.
il *UN Chronicle* 26:30 Je '89
UN pursues peace process in Central America [special section]
il *UN Chronicle* 26:15-20 D '89

Cuba
Cuba: the human rights show. A. Neier. il *The New York
Review of Books* 36:33-5 Je 15 '89
Cyprus
See also
United Nations—Armed Forces—Forces in Cyprus
40th report on Cyprus [message to Congress, December 7,
1988] R. Reagan. *Department of State Bulletin* 89:50 F
'89
Draft outline of overall agreement on Cyprus to be prepared.
il *UN Chronicle* 26:28 Je '89
First report on Cyprus [message to Congress, March 1, 1989]
G. Bush. *Department of State Bulletin* 89:43 Ap '89
Second report on Cyprus [message to Congress, June 5,
1989] G. Bush. *Department of State Bulletin* 89:89 S '89
Secretary-General outlines ideas to bridge positions on Cyprus.
il *UN Chronicle* 26:24-5 S '89
Developing countries
See also
United Nations. Committee for Development Planning
United Nations Development Programme
Eastern Europe
A new political thinking . . . the movement towards world
unity . . . il *UN Chronicle* 26:24-5 Mr '89
Iran
Iran-Iraq peace talks continue in Geneva. map *UN Chronicle*
26:21 S '89
Peace plan for Gulf region pursued. il *UN Chronicle* 26:56-7
Mr '89
Renewed efforts asked to implement Resolution 598. *UN
Chronicle* 26:23 D '89
Talks aimed at final peace settlement between Iran and
Iraq continue; UNIIMOG mandate renewed. il *UN
Chronicle* 26:23-5 Je '89
Iraq
Iran-Iraq peace talks continue in Geneva. map *UN Chronicle*
26:21 S '89
Peace plan for Gulf region pursued. il *UN Chronicle* 26:56-7
Mr '89
Renewed efforts asked to implement Resolution 598. *UN
Chronicle* 26:23 D '89
Talks aimed at final peace settlement between Iran and
Iraq continue; UNIIMOG mandate renewed. il *UN
Chronicle* 26:23-5 Je '89
Korea (North)
North and South Korea in General Assembly present proposals
on reunification. il *UN Chronicle* 26:66-7 Mr '89
Korea (South)
North and South Korea in General Assembly present proposals
on reunification. il *UN Chronicle* 26:66-7 Mr '89
Latin America
A staggering external debt . . . Central American peace
pursued . . . il *UN Chronicle* 26:26-7 Mr '89
Lebanon
See also
United Nations—Armed Forces—Forces in Lebanon
Security Council members call for cease-fire in Lebanon.
UN Chronicle 26:20 S '89
Middle East
See also
United Nations—Armed Forces—Forces in the Middle
East
Assembly renews call for Middle East peace conference
[Geneva debate keynoted by Y. Arafat] il *UN Chronicle*
26:50-4 Mr '89
General Assembly asks Security Council to consider ways
to protect Palestinian civilians. il *UN Chronicle* 26:16-17
S '89
How the PLO was legitimized [cover story] J. J. Kirkpatrick.
Commentary 88:21-8 Jl '89
Israeli policies in occupied territories condemned. il *UN
Chronicle* 26:55 Mr '89
The Palestinians [U.S. refusal of visa to Y. Arafat] il *World
Press Review* 36:8+ Ja '89
The PLO [discussion of July 1989 article, How the PLO
was legitimized] J. J. Kirkpatrick. *Commentary* 88:7-8 N
'89
Security Council fails to adopt text on Palestinian rights.
il *UN Chronicle* 26:18 S '89
Security Council regrets deportations by Israel of Palestinians.
il *UN Chronicle* 26:24 D '89
Text deploring Israeli policies in occupied territories vetoed.
il *UN Chronicle* 26:31 Je '89
U.S. denies visa to PLO leader Arafat [State Dept. statement,
November 26, 1988] *Department of State Bulletin* 89:53
F '89
Morocco
Assembly welcomes efforts of Secretary-General and OAU
chairman to solve Western Sahara problem. il *UN Chronicle*
26:58-9 Mr '89
Efforts continue to solve Western Sahara problem. il *UN
Chronicle* 26:29 Je '89
New commission for Western Sahara to advance peace
process. *UN Chronicle* 26:25 S '89
Namibia
See also
United Nations Transition Assistance Group in Namibia

UNITED NATIONS—Namibia—cont.

Enter, the Gang of Five? [permanent members of Security Council request cut in funding for supervising Namibian elections] *The Nation* 248:217 F 20 '89

Namibia independence back on track: cease-fire restored after nine-day crisis [special section] il *UN Chronicle* 26:4-17 Je '89

Namibia: the making of a new nation [tripartite agreement among Angola, Cuba, and South Africa; cover story; special section] il map *UN Chronicle* 26:34-48 Mr '89

Thousands of Namibians return home; UNTAG troops now in place; South African military withdraws [special section] il *UN Chronicle* 26:4-11 S '89

Pacific region

Reaffirmation of faith in the UN . . . rejoicing in the promise of peace . . . il *UN Chronicle* 26:22-3 Mr '89

Pakistan

Security Council considers Afghan complaint against Pakistan. il *UN Chronicle* 26:26-7 S '89

Soviet troop withdrawal from Afghanistan completed on time on 15 February 1989. il *UN Chronicle* 26:20-2 Je '89

Palau

Trusteeship Council mission observes conditions in Palau. il *UN Chronicle* 26:66-7 Je '89

Trusteeship Council told 'overwhelming majority' in Palau wants 'free association' status. il *UN Chronicle* 26:28-30 S '89

Panama

Panama, United States swap charges before Security Council. il *UN Chronicle* 26:15 S '89

South Africa

Anti-apartheid notes. il *UN Chronicle* 26:14 D '89
Anti-apartheid notes. il *UN Chronicle* 26:49 Mr '89
Anti-apartheid notes. il *UN Chronicle* 26:12 S '89
Anti-apartheid notes. il *UN Chronicle* 26:18 Je '89
'Eminent Persons' call for stricter sanctions against South Africa. il *UN Chronicle* 26:61 D '89

Sudan

Desperate hunger. D. Jones. il *Maclean's* 102:29+ Je 12 '89

'Operation Lifeline Sudan' launched; 100,000 lives at stake. il *UN Chronicle* 26:35 Je '89

Taiwan

China deal. L. Hahn. *The New Republic* 201:10-11 O 30 '89

United States

The damaged U.S. image [Reagan administration] R. A. Falk. il *The Bulletin of the Atomic Scientists* 45:59-61 Ja/F '89

FY 1990 assistance request for organizations and programs [statement, March 22, 1989] S. L. Vogelgesang. *Department of State Bulletin* 89:81-4 My '89

Garrett, Fletcher named to key positions by Bush. il pors *Jet* 76:4-5 Ap 10 '89

A new global order? J. H. Wolfe. il *USA Today (Periodical)* 117:47 Mr '89

Panama, United States swap charges before Security Council. il *UN Chronicle* 26:15 S '89

Text deploring downing of Libyan planes vetoed in Security Council: United States calls it 'self-defence'. il *UN Chronicle* 26:33 Je '89

U.S. opposes PLO admission to UN agencies [statement, May 4, 1989] S. L. Vogelgesang. *Department of State Bulletin* 89:65-6 Jl '89

U.S. refuses to abide by International Court of Justice [reparations owed to Nicaragua] *Utne Reader* p63 S/O '89

U.S. reports to United Nations on downing of Libyan planes [letter and statement, January 4-5, 1989] H. S. Okun. *Department of State Bulletin* 89:90-1 Mr '89

The United Nations: progress in the 1980s [address, October 19, 1988] R. S. Williamson. *Department of State Bulletin* 89:68-71 F '89

Western Europe

For the security of all . . . an end to the chaos of war . . . il *UN Chronicle* 26:28-9 Mr '89

Western Sahara

Assembly welcomes efforts of Secretary-General and OAU chairman to solve Western Sahara problem. il *UN Chronicle* 26:58-9 Mr '89

Efforts continue to solve Western Sahara problem. il *UN Chronicle* 26:29 Je '89

New commission for Western Sahara to advance peace process. *UN Chronicle* 26:25 S '89

UNITED NATIONS. AD HOC COMMITTEE ON THE DRAFTING OF AN INTERNATIONAL CONVENTION AGAINST THE RECRUITMENT, USE, FINANCING AND TRAINING OF MERCENARIES

UN committee reports "considerable progress" on anti-mercenary convention. *UN Chronicle* 26:34 Je '89

UNITED NATIONS. AD HOC COMMITTEE ON THE INDIAN OCEAN

Consultations continue on Indian Ocean conference. *UN Chronicle* 26:60 D '89

UNITED NATIONS. ATOMIC ENERGY COMMISSION

Three men and the bomb [1946 deliberations] M. Oliphant. il pors *The Bulletin of the Atomic Scientists* 45:41-2 Mr '89

UNITED NATIONS. COMMISSION FOR SOCIAL DEVELOPMENT

Social Development Commission meets. il *UN Chronicle* 26:73 Je '89

UNITED NATIONS. COMMISSION ON HUMAN RIGHTS

Draft convention on rights of child approved by Human Rights Commission [overview of 45th session] il *UN Chronicle* 26:60-4 Je '89

The UN Commission on Human Rights. *Department of State Bulletin* 88:6 D '88

UNITED NATIONS. COMMISSION ON HUMAN SETTLEMENTS

Housing for all before the year 2000: the countdown starts. il *UN Chronicle* 26:82 Mr '89

Practical steps to implement shelter strategy taken by Human Settlements Commission. il *UN Chronicle* 26:64-5 S '89

UNITED NATIONS. COMMISSION ON NARCOTIC DRUGS

Narcotic Drugs Commission wants special session to help fight illicit trafficking. il *UN Chronicle* 26:76-7 Je '89

UNITED NATIONS. COMMISSION ON THE STATUS OF WOMEN

Commission on Status of Women examines Nairobi strategies. il *UN Chronicle* 26:74 S '89

UNITED NATIONS. COMMISSION ON TRANSNATIONAL CORPORATIONS

'Eminent Persons' call for stricter sanctions against South Africa. il *UN Chronicle* 26:61 D '89

Role of foreign investment a theme for TNC Commission. il *UN Chronicle* 26:62-3 S '89

UNITED NATIONS. COMMITTEE FOR DEVELOPMENT PLANNING

Development Planning Committee contributes to 1990s strategy. il *UN Chronicle* 26:58-9 S '89

UNITED NATIONS. COMMITTEE ON NATURAL RESOURCES

Natural Resources Committee focuses on small-scale mining. *UN Chronicle* 26:74 S '89

UNITED NATIONS. COMMITTEE ON THE PEACEFUL USES OF OUTER SPACE

UN committee discusses International Space Year. il *UN Chronicle* 26:31-3 S '89

UN space committee notes 1988 achievements by nations. il *UN Chronicle* 26:36-7 Je '89

UNITED NATIONS. CONFERENCE ON DISARMAMENT

Conference on Disarmament opens 1989 session. il *UN Chronicle* 26:54-7 Je '89

Conference on Disarmament resumes 1989 session. il *UN Chronicle* 26:34-5 S '89

Limited progress reported on chemical weapons ban. il *UN Chronicle* 26:30-1 D '89

UNITED NATIONS. DECLARATION OF THE RIGHTS OF THE CHILD *See* Declaration of the Rights of the Child

UNITED NATIONS. DECOLONIZATION COMMITTEE

International Decade for Eradication of Colonialism proclaimed. il *UN Chronicle* 26:88-9 Mr '89

UNITED NATIONS. DISARMAMENT COMMISSION

'Limited progress' noted in Disarmament Commission. il *UN Chronicle* 26:36-7 S '89

UNITED NATIONS. ECONOMIC AND FINANCIAL COMMITTEE

Serious and prolonged setback predicted for much of world economy. il *UN Chronicle* 26:73-4 Mr '89

UNITED NATIONS. ECONOMIC AND SOCIAL COUNCIL

Debt crisis dominates Economic and Social Council debate. il *UN Chronicle* 26:64-5 D '89

Economic and Social Council acts from death penalty to indigenous populations. il *UN Chronicle* 26:52-3 S '89

UNITED NATIONS. ECONOMIC AND SOCIAL COUNCIL. COMMISSION FOR SOCIAL DEVELOPMENT *See* United Nations. Commission for Social Development

UNITED NATIONS. ECONOMIC AND SOCIAL COUNCIL. POPULATION COMMISSION *See* United Nations. Population Commission

UNITED NATIONS. ECONOMIC AND SOCIAL COUNCIL. STATISTICAL COMMISSION *See* United Nations. Statistical Commission

UNITED NATIONS. FIRST COMMITTEE *See* United Nations. Political and Security Committee

UNITED NATIONS. FOURTH COMMITTEE *See* United Nations. Decolonization Committee

UNITED NATIONS. GENERAL ASSEMBLY (43RD SESSION)

Forty-third General Assembly: new dimensions in international co-operation [roundup of session; special section] il *UN Chronicle* 26:4-33+ Mr '89

General Assembly asks Security Council to consider ways to protect Palestinian civilians. il *UN Chronicle* 26:16-17 S '89

Special session on international economic co-operation set for 1990. il *UN Chronicle* 26:19 Je '89

UNITED NATIONS. GENERAL ASSEMBLY (44TH SESSION)
Outlines of a new world of freedom [address, September 25, 1989] G. Bush. il pors *Department of State Bulletin* 89:27-31 N '89
The town hall of the world [special section] il *UN Chronicle* 26:36-58 D '89
UNITED NATIONS. HIGH COMMISSIONER FOR REFUGEES
12 million refugees around the world: is there hope on the horizon? il *UN Chronicle* 26:80-1 Mr '89
Indochinese refugees conference held in Geneva [statement, June 18, 1989; texts of draft declaration and comprehensive plan of action, June 14, 1989] L. S. Eagleburger. *Department of State Bulletin* 89:69-73 O '89
International Conference adopts plan to solve Indochinese refugee problem. *UN Chronicle* 26:23 S '89
No room at the inn [Vietnamese refugees] W. McGurn. *National Review* 41:26 Je 30 '89
Refugee reality and the U.N. High Commission. S. E. Smith. *America* 161:10-12+ Jl 1-8 '89
UNITED NATIONS. INTERGOVERNMENTAL COMMITTEE ON SCIENCE AND TECHNOLOGY FOR DEVELOPMENT
Committee reviews 1979 Programme of Action on Science and Technology for Development. *UN Chronicle* 26:66 D '89
UNITED NATIONS. INTERNATIONAL FUND FOR THE PROMOTION OF CULTURE
The International Fund for the Promotion of Culture. il *The Courier (Unesco)* 41:16-17 N '88
UNITED NATIONS. INTERNATIONAL LABOUR ORGANISATION *See* International Labour Organisation
UNITED NATIONS. INTERNATIONAL LAW COMMISSION
Law Commission adopts texts on diplomatic bag and courier. *UN Chronicle* 26:62 D '89
UNITED NATIONS. LEGAL COMMITTEE
Three new legal instruments approved by General Assembly. il *UN Chronicle* 26:91 Mr '89
UNITED NATIONS. OFFICE OF THE HIGH COMMISSIONER FOR REFUGEES *See* United Nations. High Commissioner for Refugees
UNITED NATIONS. POLITICAL AND SECURITY COMMITTEE
Record number of resolutions on disarmament adopted by consensus. il *UN Chronicle* 26:68-71 Mr '89
UNITED NATIONS. POPULATION COMMISSION
World-wide population meeting to be called in 1994. il *UN Chronicle* 26:68-9 Je '89
UNITED NATIONS. PREPARATORY COMMISSION FOR THE INTERNATIONAL SEA-BED AUTHORITY AND THE INTERNATIONAL TRIBUNAL FOR THE LAW OF THE SEA
Sea Law Commission focuses on pioneer investor duties, training programme approved. il *UN Chronicle* 26:34-5 D '89
"Pioneer investor" duties; rules for sea-bed institutions considered. il *UN Chronicle* 26:38-9 Je '89
UNITED NATIONS. PROGRAMME OF ACTION FOR AFRICAN ECONOMIC RECOVERY AND DEVELOPMENT
Assembly calls for steps to halt African economic slide. il *UN Chronicle* 26:76-7 Mr '89
UNITED NATIONS. SECOND COMMITTEE *See* United Nations. Economic and Financial Committee
UNITED NATIONS. SECRETARIAT
Breaking faith (I). S. Hazzard. *The New Yorker* 65:63-4+ S 25 '89
Breaking faith (II). S. Hazzard. *The New Yorker* 65:74-8+ O 2 '89
Progress in UN reforms reported [organizational streamlining] il *UN Chronicle* 26:38-9 S '89
UNITED NATIONS. SECURITY COUNCIL
Security Council permanent members discuss international issues [joint statement, September 29, 1989] *Department of State Bulletin* 89:66 N '89
UNITED NATIONS. SECURITY COUNCIL (MEETINGS: 1988)
Cyprus force mandate extended through 15 June 1989. il *UN Chronicle* 26:62-3 Mr '89
UNITED NATIONS. SECURITY COUNCIL (MEETINGS: 1989)
Easier detection of plastic explosives urged by Security Council. il *UN Chronicle* 26:19 S '89
Enter, the Gang of Five? [permanent members of Security Council request cut in funding for supervising Namibian elections] *The Nation* 248:217 F 20 '89
Mandate of Lebanon force extended. il *UN Chronicle* 26:32 Je '89
Panama, United States swap charges before Security Council. il *UN Chronicle* 26:15 S '89
Security Council adopts resolution on Central American peace [text of resolution and statement, July 28, 1989] H. S. Okun. *Department of State Bulletin* 89:73-4 O '89
Security Council condemns hostage-taking and abduction; UNIFIL mandate renewed. il *UN Chronicle* 26:25-6 D '89

Security Council considers Afghan complaint against Pakistan. il *UN Chronicle* 26:26-7 S '89
Security Council demands disbandment of paramilitary forces in Namibia. il *UN Chronicle* 26:12-13 D '89
Security Council fails to adopt text on Palestinian rights. il *UN Chronicle* 26:18 S '89
Security Council members call for cease-fire in Lebanon. *UN Chronicle* 26:20 S '89
Security Council regrets deportations by Israel of Palestinians. il *UN Chronicle* 26:24 D '89
Text deploring downing of Libyan planes vetoed in Security Council: United States calls it 'self-defence'. il *UN Chronicle* 26:33 Je '89
Text deploring Israeli policies in occupied territories vetoed. il *UN Chronicle* 26:31 Je '89
UN troops to stay in Golan Heights. *UN Chronicle* 26:20 S '89
UNITED NATIONS. SIXTH COMMITTEE *See* United Nations. Legal Committee
UNITED NATIONS. SPECIAL COMMITTEE ON DECOLONIZATION *See* United Nations. Special Committee on the Situation with Regard to the Implementation of the Declaration on the Granting of Independence to Colonial Countries and Peoples
UNITED NATIONS. SPECIAL COMMITTEE ON THE SITUATION WITH REGARD TO THE IMPLEMENTATION OF THE DECLARATION ON THE GRANTING OF INDEPENDENCE TO COLONIAL COUNTRIES AND PEOPLES
Decolonization Committee reviews situations in 18 territories. *UN Chronicle* 26:59 D '89
UNITED NATIONS. STATISTICAL COMMISSION
Statistical Commission meets in New York. *UN Chronicle* 26:77 Je '89
UNITED NATIONS. SUB-COMMISSION ON PREVENTION OF DISCRIMINATION AND PROTECTION OF MINORITIES
Minorities body acts on hostage-taking, death penalty, other matters. il *UN Chronicle* 26:27-8 D '89
UNITED NATIONS. TRUSTEESHIP COUNCIL
Trusteeship Council mission observes conditions in Palau. il *UN Chronicle* 26:66-7 Je '89
Trusteeship Council told 'overwhelming majority' in Palau wants 'free association' status. il *UN Chronicle* 26:28-30 S '89
UNITED NATIONS. UNIVERSAL DECLARATION OF HUMAN RIGHTS *See* Universal Declaration of Human Rights
UNITED NATIONS CONFERENCE ON TRADE AND DEVELOPMENT
UNCTAD Board calls for reversal of protectionism. *UN Chronicle* 26:67 Je '89
UNCTAD: paving the road for trade and development into the 1990s. il *UN Chronicle* 26:68-9 D '89
UNITED NATIONS CONGRESS ON THE PREVENTION OF CRIME AND THE TREATMENT OF OFFENDERS
Fighting crime in the twenty-first century: five regional meetings prepare for 1990 congress. *UN Chronicle* 26:68 S '89
UNITED NATIONS CONVENTION AGAINST ILLICIT TRAFFIC IN NARCOTIC DRUGS AND PSYCHOTROPIC SUBSTANCES (1988) *See* Convention against Illicit Traffic in Narcotic Drugs and Psychotropic Substances (1988)
UNITED NATIONS DEVELOPMENT PROGRAMME
The seeds of development aid. il *UN Chronicle* 26:78-9 Je '89
Self-reliance of developing countries is UNDP goal for 1990s. *UN Chronicle* 26:53 S '89
UNDP seeking blueprint through the year 2000. il *UN Chronicle* 26:79 Je '89
UNITED NATIONS DISENGAGEMENT OBSERVER FORCE *See* United Nations—Armed Forces—Forces in the Middle East
UNITED NATIONS EDUCATIONAL, SCIENTIFIC AND CULTURAL ORGANIZATION *See* Unesco
UNITED NATIONS ENVIRONMENT PROGRAMME
Negotiations on climate change treaty to start in 1990. il *UN Chronicle* 26:55-6 S '89
UNITED NATIONS ENVIRONMENT PROGRAMME. GLOBAL ENVIRONMENTAL MONITORING SYSTEM
Monitoring the global environment: an assessment of urban air quality [cover story] bibl f il *Environment* 31:6-13+ O '89
UNITED NATIONS FUND FOR POPULATION ACTIVITIES
Population Fund launches major initiatives on Africa, women. il *UN Chronicle* 26:69 Je '89
'State of the world population'—1989. il *UN Chronicle* 26:72-3 S '89
UNITED NATIONS INTERIM FORCE IN LEBANON *See* United Nations—Armed Forces—Forces in Lebanon

UNITED NATIONS INTERNATIONAL ATOMIC ENERGY AGENCY *See* International Atomic Energy Agency

UNITED NATIONS INTERNATIONAL CHILDREN'S FUND *See* UNICEF

UNITED NATIONS IRAN-IRAQ MILITARY OBSERVER GROUP *See* United Nations—Armed Forces—Forces in the Persian Gulf region

UNITED NATIONS PEACE-KEEPING FORCE IN CYPRUS *See* United Nations—Armed Forces—Forces in Cyprus

UNITED NATIONS PEACE-KEEPING FORCE IN LEBANON *See* United Nations—Armed Forces—Forces in Lebanon

UNITED NATIONS RELIEF AND WORKS AGENCY FOR PALESTINE REFUGEES IN THE NEAR EAST
The plight of Palestine refugees. R. Cook. il *World Health* p8-10 Jl '89

UNITED NATIONS TRANSITION ASSISTANCE GROUP IN NAMIBIA
A bloody road to peace. C. S. Manegold. il map *Newsweek* 113:37 Ap 17 '89
Botching the peace. W. R. Doerner. il map *Time* 133:35 Ap 17 '89
A crisis for peace. J. Bierman. il *Maclean's* 102:22+ Ap 17 '89
Farce in Namibia. *The Nation* 249:191-2 Ag 21-28 '89
Fix in Namibia? M. Verbaan. *The Nation* 249:516-17 N 6 '89
How SWAPO got framed. A. Cockburn. *The Nation* 248:582-3 My 1 '89
Namibia independence back on track: cease-fire restored after nine-day crisis [special section] il *UN Chronicle* 26:4-17 Je '89
A nation in the making. B. Came. map *Maclean's* 102:25+ Mr 27 '89
Secretary-General in Namibia: the independence process is 'irreversible'; more than 700,000 register to vote [special section] il *UN Chronicle* 26:4-13 D '89
Swipe at SWAPO [discussion of May 1, 1989 article, How SWAPO got framed] A. Cockburn. *The Nation* 249:190+ Ag 21-28 '89
Thousands of Namibians return home; UNTAG troops now in place; South African military withdraws [special section] il *UN Chronicle* 26:4-11 S '89

UNITED NEGRO COLLEGE FUND
Bush asks Congress for $60 million to aid black colleges and universities. il *Jet* 75:16-18 Ap 3 '89
Magic's fund-raiser nets a cool $1 million for UNCF. il por *Jet* 76:28-9 S 4 '89
Michael Jordan launches project to help students in black colleges [celebrity golf tournament] il pors *Jet* 76:22-5 Ag 14 '89

UNITED PAPERWORKERS INTERNATIONAL UNION
United Paperworkers and 16-month work stoppage. *Monthly Labor Review* 111:47-8 D '88

UNITED PARCEL SERVICE OF AMERICA, INC.
The flying-package trade takes off [expansion of Federal Express and UPS] C. P. Work. il *U.S. News & World Report* 107:47+ O 2 '89
UPS buys seven European parcel delivery firms to expand international presence. *Aviation Week & Space Technology* 130:67 Ja 23 '89
UPS isn't about to be left holding the parcel. R. W. King. il por *Business Week* p69 F 13 '89

UNITED PRESS INTL., INC.
UPI isn't quite ready for the spike. M. Lewyn. il *Business Week* p52 N 13 '89

UNITED RED ARMY (JAPAN) *See* Japanese Red Army

UNITED SERVICES AUTOMOBILE ASSOCIATION
You're in the office of the future now. B. Brophy. il por *U.S. News & World Report* 106:50-2 Ap 17 '89

UNITED SILICON STRUCTURES (FIRM)
Custom chips for sale, no job too small. O. Port. il *Business Week* p99+ Mr 6 '89

UNITED STATES
See also
Americans
Middle Western States
Northwestern States
Pacific Northwest
Pacific States
Patriotism
Southern States
Southwestern States
Western States
The new America [cover story; special section] il maps *Business Week* p90-5+ S 25 '89

Antiquities
See also
Indians of North America—Antiquities

Appropriations and expenditures
See also
Budget
National Economic Commission (U.S.)
Off-budget programs
Pork barrel legislation
President's Private Sector Survey on Cost Control (U.S.)
Research grants
United States. Congress. Senate. Committee on the Budget

America needs a "waste czar" [address, September 21, 1989] J. P. Grace. *Vital Speeches of the Day* 56:37-40 N 1 '89
The deficit time bomb [address, March 13, 1989] J. P. Grace. *Vital Speeches of the Day* 55:390-4 Ap 15 '89

Armed Forces
See also
Servicemen
United States. Air Force
United States. Air National Guard
United States. Army
United States. Coast Guard
United States. Congress. House. Committee on Armed Services
United States. Dept. of Defense
United States. Marine Corps
United States. Navy
When Johnny comes marching home. M. Barone. il *U.S. News & World Report* 107:30 D 11 '89

Accidents and injuries
The Pentagon's stonewall [cover story] J. Cobb and P. C. Montgomery. il *Common Cause Magazine* 15:33-7 Ja/F '89

Anecdotes, facetiae, satire, etc.
Humor in uniform. See occasional issues of Reader's Digest

Appropriations and expenditures
See United States. Dept. of Defense—Appropriations and expenditures
Commissariat—Anecdotes, facetiae, satire, etc.
Dessert warfare. M. E. Guthrie. il *The Progressive* 53:50 Ja '89

Forces in Bolivia
Playing golf while drugs flow [U.S. in Bolivia] P. Lernoux. il *The Nation* 248:188-90+ F 13 '89

Forces in Europe
Bush pulls one out of a hat [arms proposal at NATO summit] B. Javetski. il por *Business Week* p22-3 Je 12 '89
Bush's bold bid to rescue NATO [U.S. troop cuts] H. Trewhitt. il por *U.S. News & World Report* 106:26-9 Je 12 '89
Bush's chintzy offer at Vienna [conventional arms reductions] R. Leavitt. *The Bulletin of the Atomic Scientists* 45:13 O '89
Bush's new look for the NATO alliance [troop reduction proposal] H. Anderson. il por *Newsweek* 113:34-5 Je 12 '89
Bush's plan: deep troop cuts in Europe. J. Barry. il *Newsweek* 114:44 D 4 '89
By the numbers [Bush's arms proposals at NATO summit] *The Nation* 248:835-6 Je 19 '89
Divorce, alliance-style. A. Tonelson and C. Layne. *The New Republic* 200:23-5 Je 12 '89
For a defense that makes sense. J. H. Webb. il *The New York Times Magazine* p38+ My 21 '89
"Here we go, on the offensive" [G. Bush offers troop reduction initiative at NATO meeting] G. J. Church. il por *Time* 133:28-31+ Je 12 '89
Moves to trim the U.S. role. B. Levin. il *Maclean's* 102:48+ S 4 '89
Now, about those defense savings you were expecting . . . D. Griffiths. il *Business Week* p43 S 4 '89
Sharing the U.S. burden: a British view. M. Legge. il *Current (Washington, D.C.)* 313:15-21 Je '89
Superpower disengagement. C. Layne. *Foreign Policy* 77:17-40 Wint '89/90
The time has come: bring our troops back from Europe. A. Ireland. il *USA Today (Periodical)* 118:16-18 Jl '89
U.S. out of NATO? A French scenario [views of A. Soussan] R. Kaplan. il *The American Spectator* 22:32-3 F '89
U.S. senators threaten troop cutback if West Germany blocks Lance upgrade [with editorial comment] P. A. Gilmartin. *Aviation Week & Space Technology* 130:7, 29 My 8 '89
When Johnny comes marching home: the pressure for U.S. troops to leave Europe. D. White. map *World Press Review* 36:25-7 S '89

Forces in foreign countries
Some like it hot. *The Nation* 249:775-6 D 25 '89

Forces in Honduras
Honduras left to push contra pram. J. Eldridge. il *The Nation* 248:734-6+ My 29 '89

Forces in Korea
See also
Korean War, 1950-1953—American participation
Air, naval and ground forces participate in Team Spirit '89 [special section] il *Aviation Week & Space Technology* 130:68-9+ Ap 24 '89
Leaving Korea. D. Bandow. *Foreign Policy* 77:77-93 Wint '89/'90
The U.S. stands pat in Korea. D. Griffiths. il *Business Week* p77 Je 26 '89

Forces in Latin America
Attacking the source [proposal to send U.S. military advisers] E. Shannon. il *Time* 134:10-12 Ag 28 '89
Marines aren't the answer to America's drug problem. P. Dwyer. il *Business Week* p30 S 4 '89
Send in the troops? Assessing U.S. military options. E. Salholz. il *Newsweek* 114:20-1 S 4 '89

UNITED STATES—Armed Forces—*cont.*

Forces in Panama

Amateur hour [failed coup attempt against M. Noriega; cover story] C. S. Manegold. il por map *Newsweek* 114:26-31 O 16 '89

Brute politics [U.S. dispatches additional troops following disputed election] A. Bilski. il por *Maclean's* 102:22-4 My 22 '89

Dwindling options in Panama. L. S. Robinson. bibl f *Foreign Affairs* 68:187-205 Wint '89/90

A fumbled coup. G. W. Taylor. il por *Maclean's* 102:28-30 O 16 '89

The gang that wouldn't shoot [failed coup attempt against M. Noriega; with editorial comment by David Gergen] B. Duffy. il por *U.S. News & World Report* 107:26-7, 129 O 16 '89

Lead-pipe politics [U.S. sends troops to Panama in wake of election fraud; cover story; special section] il por map *Time* 133:40-4+ My 22 '89

Letter from Washington [failed coup against M. Noriega] E. Drew. *The New Yorker* 65:100-4+ O 30 '89

The mothers of intervention [failed coup attempt against M. Noriega] il *The Progressive* 53:8-9 D '89

Panama: on not being a cowboy [failed coup] *America* 161:251 O 21 '89

Standoff in Panama [M. A. Noriega vs U.S. after fraudulent election] J. L. Galloway. il por *U.S. News & World Report* 106:28-32 My 22 '89

A test of wills [U.S. vs. Noriega government] L. Martz. il por map *Newsweek* 112:34-9 My 22 '89

Washington fights the Noriega factor [successful Philippines intervention contrasted with failed Panama coup attempt] H. Anderson. il *Newsweek* 114:58 D 11 '89

The widow of a slain rebel leader looks back in anguish after the failed coup in Panama [A. Bonilla de Giroldi flees to U.S. after death of M. Giroldi Vega] B. Hewitt. il pors *People Weekly* 32:101-2 O 30 '89

The Yanquis stayed home [U.S. involvement in failed coup against M. Noriega] J. Smolowe. il por maps *Time* 134:24-8 O 16 '89

Forces in Singapore

Singapore offers U.S. military greater access to its facilities. map *Aviation Week & Space Technology* 131:69 Ag 21 '89

Forces in the Philippines

Are Philippine bases essential to U.S. military strategy? L. D. Howell. il *USA Today (Periodical)* 117:42-5 My '89

Clamor over Philippine bases. D. Goertzen. il *The Progressive* 53:15-16 S '89

George Bush's thriller in Manila [aid given to C. Aquino during coup attempt] il por *U.S. News & World Report* 107:14-15 D 11 '89

Manifest Destiny's man of the hour: Frederick Funston [1899 Philippine Insurrection] D. H. Bain. bibl (p164) il pors *Smithsonian* 20:134-6+ My '89

Shoot-out in Manila [attempted coup against C. Aquino] C. S. Manegold. il map por *Newsweek* 114:56-8 D 11 '89

Soldier power [coup attempt against C. Aquino] H. G. Chua-Eoan. il map por *Time* 134:50-2 D 11 '89

Ten minutes that counted [coming to aid of C. Aquino] *Time* 134:28 D 18 '89

U.S.-Philippines military bases agreement review, 1988 [texts of agreement, remarks, and letter, October 17, 1988] *Department of State Bulletin* 88:24-7 D '88

Why Filipinos oppose U.S. military bases. R. M. Brown. *The Christian Century* 106:100-1 F 1-8 '89

Forces in Vietnam

See also

Vietnamese War, 1957-1975—American participation

Journalism

See Journalism, Military

Management

See also

United States. Joint Chiefs of Staff

Don't run military like a business [views of Allan R. Millett] il *USA Today (Periodical)* 118:5 D '89

Maneuvers

See Military maneuvers

Medical and sanitary affairs

See also

AIDS (Disease) and servicemen

Procurement

See United States. Dept. of Defense—Procurement

Publications

See also

Stars and stripes (Newspaper)

Recruiting, enlistment, etc.

See also

Draft

For job and country: marketing today's military. P. Sudo. il *Scholastic Update (Teachers' edition)* 122:16-17 O 6 '89

Peace crusade [peace recruiters visit high schools to provide alternative to military recruiters] S. Tifft. il *Time* 133:68 F 27 '89

Research

See Military research

Reserves

See also

United States. Army Reserve

Training

See Military training

Women

See Servicewomen

Bibliography

America, seen from up close. D. Gates. il *Newsweek* 113:72-4 My 1 '89

Boundaries

The last time I was in Mexico. R. Kirtland. il *America* 161:7-9 Jl 1-8 '89

Census

Census and citizenship [counting of illegal aliens for purposes of congressional apportionment] *National Review* 41:14+ S 29 '89

Census: the way we'll be. il *Newsweek* 113:7 F 13 '89

Down from the count [Hispanic broadcasters hoping 1990 census will reveal uncounted Hispanic TV viewers] M. Couzens. il *Channels (New York, N.Y.: 1986)* 9:16 My '89

Finding out who counts [undercounting minorities and aliens in the census] S. Rabinove. il *Commonweal* 116:360-1 Je 16 '89

Who should count in the 1990 census? C. Norman. il *Science* 243:601-2 F 3 '89

Will 1990 census undercount minorities? il *USA Today (Periodical)* 118:8-9 N '89

History

The history of census tabulation. K. S. Reid-Green. bibl il *Scientific American* 260:98-103 F '89

Civil defense

See Civil defense

Civilization

See also

Morale, National

Social change

United States—Popular culture

United States—Social conditions

After utopia: the primitive society of the future [interview with J. Baudrillard] N. Gardels. il *New Perspectives Quarterly* 6:52-4 Summ '89

Black and white houses? [contrasting cultures of United States and Soviet Union] P. Dukes. il *History Today* 39:9-11 Ap '89

Editorial [views of H. James] W. Garrett. il *Antiques* 136:810-11 O '89

The end of history. W. F. Buckley. *National Review* 41:62 N 24 '89

Higher education and a civilization in trouble [address, November 15, 1988] J. A. Howard. *Vital Speeches of the Day* 55:314-18 Mr 1 '89

Kennan's lament: American mass culture uncontained. A. Stephanson. il *New Perspectives Quarterly* 6:54-7 Fall '89

Notebook. L. H. Lapham. See issues of Harper's

". . . nothing will destroy our culture while people are free to create . . ." [interview with M. S. Forbes] J. F. Cooper. il por *Forbes* 144:20+ O 2 '89

What's American about America? Toward claiming our multicultural heritage [excerpt from Writin' is fightin'] I. Reed. il *Utne Reader* p100-3+ Mr/Ap '89

Who cares? [film Talk radio triggers reflections on the body politic] R. Corliss. il *Film Comment* 25:64-70 Ja/F '89

A world worth saving [cover story] E. Hoagland. il *Life* 12:50-4+ O '89

Climate

Almanac. D. M. Ludlum. See issues of Country Journal beginning October 1986

Let it snow, let it snow. S. Begley. il *Newsweek* 113:67 F 6 '89

The rain maps. T. Klingler and J. Klingler. maps *Bicycling* 30:134 Ap '89

A sun-baked summer in the U.S. D. LeComte. il *Weatherwise* 42:13-16 F '89

Weatherwatch. D. M. Ludlum. See issues of Weatherwise

Anecdotes, facetiae, satire, etc.

Weathering heights. R. Carlson. il map *Harper's* 279:40-1 Jl '89

Bibliography

The weather where you live. D. A. Robinson and D. M. Ludlum. *Weatherwise* 42:328-9 D '89

Commerce

See also

Balance of trade

Export-Import Bank of the United States

Investments, American

Ins and outs on America's trade list. R. F. Black. il *U.S. News & World Report* 107:43-4 Ag 21 '89

U.S. companies lack trade aggressiveness. W. T. Brookes. por *Nation's Business* 77:13 F '89

Asia

Fuming over a hazardous export [U.S. cigarettes sold in Asia] B. Rudolph. il *Time* 134:82 O 2 '89

UNITED STATES—Commerce—Asia—*cont.*

Getting opium to the masses: the political economy of addiction [U.S. cigarette exports] A. Cockburn. il *The Nation* 249:482-3 O 30 '89

Hazardous to whose health? [cigarette exports] J. Drummond. il *Forbes* 144:89+ D 11 '89

Uncle Sam shouldn't be a traveling salesman for tobacco [cigarette exports to Asia] P. Magnusson. il *Business Week* p61 O 9 '89

Belgium

Belgium will use equipment provided under offset pact to expand industry [F-16 deal with General Dynamics] il *Aviation Week & Space Technology* 130:57 F 13 '89

Brazil

U.S. import duties increase for certain Brazilian products [response to failure to provide patent protection for U.S. pharmaceuticals; proclamation, October 20, 1988] R. Reagan. *Department of State Bulletin* 89:49 Ja '89

Canada

An ambiguous victory [trade panel ruling on salmon and herring caught off British Columbia] B. Bergman. il *Maclean's* 102:38 O 30 '89

Brave new world [free trade agreement goes into effect] M. Clark. il *Maclean's* 102:12-13 Ja 9 '89

Business [U.S.-Canada free trade agreement] il *Maclean's* 102:66-70+ Jl 3 '89

The call for a referendum [Maclean's/Decima poll on free trade agreement with the U.S.] *Maclean's* 102:13 Ja 2 '89

Canadian conundrums: nationalism, socialism, and free trade. A. Stark. il *The American Spectator* 22:20-2 Ap '89

Canadian printers report increasing U.S. business. J. P. Frank. il *Publishers Weekly* 235:56+ My 19 '89

Canadian utility threatens Cree [Hydro-Québec's James Bay II] D. Schulze. il *The Progressive* 53:18 O '89

A critical weakness [questions raised about Phalanx warship defense system for Canadian frigates] W. Lowther. il *Maclean's* 102:13 F 13 '89

Crossing the line from talk into action [U.S.-Canada trade pact] C. Hawkins. il *Business Week* p54-5 Ja 9 '89

Dropping the barriers to free trade. A. F. Brimmer. il *Black Enterprise* 19:59-60 F '89

Free trade [address, November 22, 1988] T. Siddon. *Vital Speeches of the Day* 55:222-4 Ja 15 '89

A free trade anniversary [special section] il *Maclean's* 102:44-50+ D 18 '89

The great gas sellout [Canadian Arctic] J. DeMont. il *Maclean's* 102:36-7 Ap 3 '89

A new era in trade. A. Holzinger. il *Nation's Business* 77:67-72 S '89

No flying buns for a bully boy [J. Valenti campaigns against Canadian efforts to reduce U.S. domination of movie distribution business] A. Fotheringham. il *Maclean's* 102:116 O 30 '89

The North American shakeout arrives ahead of schedule. C. Hawkins and W. J. Holstein. il *Business Week* p34-5 Ap 17 '89

North America's new trade punch. L. Kraar. il *Fortune* 119:123-4+ My 22 '89

Now tariffs can't fall fast enough. T. Mason. il *Business Week* p80 O 23 '89

An old favorite returns [Canadian natural gas producers court U.S. market] J. DeMont. il *Maclean's* 102:26 Ja 9 '89

Opening with a bang [first week in the free trade era] T. Tedesco and M. Clark. il *Maclean's* 102:15 Ja 16 '89

Opting out of the 21st century [free trade agreement accelerating the de-industrialization of Canada] P. C. Newman. il *Maclean's* 102:38 O 23 '89

The politics of pork [dispute over import duty on Canadian pork] R. Laver. il *Maclean's* 102:17 S 11 '89

Signing away Canada's soul [free trade agreement with the U.S.; adaptation of address, May 1988] R. Davies. il *Harper's* 278:43-7 Ja '89

Test of wills [Canada-U.S. free trade agreement] M. Nemeth. il pors *Maclean's* 102:63-4 Jl 3 '89

Toxins by truckload [illicit waste-laden fuels enter Canada] B. Wickens. il *Maclean's* 102:17 My 22 '89

The trade pact is turning into a one-way street—so far. C. Hawkins and W. J. Holstein. il *Business Week* p76-7 Jl 17 '89

U.S.-Canada free trade agreement. il *Department of State Bulletin* 89:1-6 O '89

U.S.-Canada free trade: how high tech will benefit [cover story] G. T. Pope. il *High Technology Business* 9:18-21 Mr '89

U.S.-Canada sign free trade agreement [remarks, September 28, 1988] R. Reagan. *Department of State Bulletin* 88:22-3 D '88

The value of gas [hearings on proposed export of Canadian Arctic gas] B. Wickens. il *Maclean's* 102:54-5 My 1 '89

Words of conciliation [interview with Ontario premier D. Peterson] T. Tedesco. il por *Maclean's* 102:16 Ja 30 '89

Caribbean region

See also

Caribbean Basin Initiative

Chile

Chilean fruit exports to the U.S. [poisoned fruit; statements, March 16 and 29, 1989] *Department of State Bulletin* 89:85 My '89

U.S. business: left out. J. A. Briggs. *Forbes* 143:96 My 15 '89

China

The Beijing factor makes this the year of the slide. D. Greising. il *Business Week* p106+ Je 26 '89

Cautionary wail from the nursery [import quotas on Chinese cloth diapers] il *U.S. News & World Report* 106:44 Je 12 '89

China agrees to limit marketing of Long March booster in U.S. C. Covault. il *Aviation Week & Space Technology* 130:37 Ja 2 '89

China trade [Chinese-U.S. trade expo organized by W.-J. Jeffries] L. Gubernick. il por *Forbes* 144:287 O 16 '89

China will always be risky business [interview with G. Browning] C. P. Work. il por *U.S. News & World Report* 107:43 Jl 31 '89

In Beijing, it's business as usual. A. Riles. il *The Progressive* 53:31 S '89

Ready to ride out China's turmoil [Fortune poll] A. Farnham. il *Fortune* 120:117-18 Jl 3 '89

U.S., China initial agreement on communications satellites [State Dept. statement, December 19, 1988] *Department of State Bulletin* 89:26-7 F '89

U.S. importers aren't jumping ship—yet. D. Lee. il *Business Week* p78 Je 26 '89

U.S. permits Boeing to transfer four 757s to Chinese airlines. *Aviation Week & Space Technology* 131:96 Jl 17 '89

U.S. suspends military sales in wake of massacre in China. M. Mecham. il *Aviation Week & Space Technology* 130:69-70+ Je 12 '89

Colombia

The chemical connection [Operation Primavera reveals U.S.-manufactured chemicals used in Colombian cocaine production] W. R. Doerner. il *Time* 133:44-5 F 20 '89

Communist countries

Trading with the Communists. A. Stevenson and A. Frye. *Foreign Affairs* 68:53-71 Spr '89

Developing countries

Dealing arms. J. Cobb and J. M. Zindar. il *Common Cause Magazine* 15:23-7 Mr/Ap '89

East Asia

The American point of view [manufacturing of books] J. P. Frank. il *Publishers Weekly* 236:S29-S30 S 22 '89

The Asians are bracing for a trade shoot-out [U.S. to issue target list of unfair practices] A. Borrus. il *Business Week* p40-1 My 1 '89

Taking the Tigers off the dole [U.S. discontinues duty free status for Taiwan, Hong Kong, South Korea and Singapore] E. A. Finn, Jr. il *Forbes* 143:70 Ja 23 '89

Eastern Europe

Government agencies at odds over computer sales to Soviets and Warsaw Pact countries. *Byte* 14:26+ O '89

France

French electro-optic, IR firms to bid on U.S. aircraft carrier systems. B. D. Nordwall. il *Aviation Week & Space Technology* 130:89+ My 8 '89

Germany

Beef, pork, and history [German ban on American pork in 1880s over trichinosis concerns] B. A. Weisberger. il *American Heritage* 40:20+ Jl/Ag '89

Germany (West)

Boycott the Germans. R. E. Tyrrell. *The American Spectator* 22:8-9 Ag '89

Can Audi start winning races in the showroom, too? [U.S. market] J. B. Treece and J. Templeman. il *Business Week* p47 My 29 '89

German and U.S. leaders confer on trade issues [BizNet teleconference] A. Holzinger. il *Nation's Business* 77:78-9 Ja '89

U.S., West Germany may delay P-7 agreement until September [Lockheed antisubmarine warfare aircraft] J. D. Morrocco. il *Aviation Week & Space Technology* 130:62 Je 19 '89

West Germany's LTU expands fleet with Boeing 767-300ERs. B. A. Smith. il *Aviation Week & Space Technology* 130:92-3 Mr 27 '89

Great Britain

AMR Eagle places 100 orders, options for Jetstream aircraft. *Aviation Week & Space Technology* 130:167 Je 19 '89

Britain accepting fraction of Boeing's offset claims [purchase of E-3A Airborne Warning and Control System aircraft] D. A. Brown. il *Aviation Week & Space Technology* 131:76-7 Jl 17 '89

British Airways starts transatlantic service with new Boeing 747-400s. C. A. Shifrin. il *Aviation Week & Space Technology* 131:62-3+ Ag 14 '89

Hollywood reaps a windfall from television's richest endeavor [British direct broadcast satellite services] K. Pearce. il *Channels (New York, N.Y.: 1986)* 9:9 Mr '89

Pan Am will use Jetstreams to bolster Miami operations. J. T. McKenna. *Aviation Week & Space Technology* 131:82-3 N 27 '89

UNITED STATES—Commerce—Hungary

Hungary

Let's make a deal, comrade [Fairchild Semiconductor's trade negotiations with Hungary] *High Technology Business* 9:17 Jl/Ag '89

Iran

See also

Iranian seizure of United States embassy, 1979-1981—Economic aspects

Ireland

GPA Group poised to order 'well over 200' transports. D. A. Brown. il *Aviation Week & Space Technology* 130:16-17 Ap 17 '89

Japan

All Nippon buys 20 747-400s, a record order. C. Fotos. il *Aviation Week & Space Technology* 130:69-70 F 27 '89

America's self-loathing even has Japan convinced [The Japan that can say no] P. C. Roberts. il *Business Week* p22 D 11 '89

Beginning to test its wings [Japanese pondering life without Americans] M. Tharp. il *U.S. News & World Report* 106:40-1 My 8 '89

The book that's creating a firestorm [S. Ishihara's The Japan that can say no] A. Borrus. il por *Business Week* p78+ O 23 '89

Bush approves FS-X codevelopment, but Japan must accept new terms. M. Mecham. *Aviation Week & Space Technology* 130:22 Mr 27 '89

Bush wins victory on FS-X development despite Senate anger on Japanese trade. M. Mecham. *Aviation Week & Space Technology* 130:31 My 22 '89

Can the Pentagon keep shielding Japan? [FSX co-development deal] P. Magnusson. il *Business Week* p47-8 Mr 27 '89

The coming traffic jam in the luxury lane [Toyota Lexus and Nissan Infiniti] W. Zellner. il *Business Week* p78 Ja 30 '89

Containing Japan [cover story] J. M. Fallows. il *The Atlantic* 263:40-8+ My '89

Crazy but harmless [views of J. Fallows] M. Kinsley. *The New Republic* 201:4 D 11 '89

A deal that nearly came undone [U.S. agrees to help Japan build the FSX jet] C. Gorman. il *Time* 133:70-1 Mr 27 '89

The delicate art of doing business in Japan. T. Holden. il *Business Week* p120 O 2 '89

Does Japan play fair? [trade and defense issues divide U.S. and Japan] S. Manning. il *Scholastic Update (Teachers' edition)* 122:20-1 D 8 '89

Don't expect a caretaker to take care of trade [resignation of N. Takeshita] T. Holden and W. Glasgall. por *Business Week* p37 My 8 '89

For Japan, the day of reckoning on trade has finally arrived. A. Borrus. il *Business Week* p55 My 22 '89

Friend or foe? [FSX deal symbolic of strain in relations between the U.S. and Japan] J. Greenwald. il *Time* 133:44-5 Ap 24 '89

The FS-X question [U.S.-Japanese codevelopment] *National Review* 41:14-16 Ap 21 '89

The FSX and Japan's strategy for aerospace. R. J. Samuels and B. C. Whipple. il *Technology Review* 92:42-51 O '89

FSX coproduction prohibition disapproved by president [letter to the Senate, July 31, 1989] G. Bush. *Department of State Bulletin* 89:32 O '89

Getting along with Japan. J. M. Fallows. il *The Atlantic* 264:53-6+ D '89

Getting tough with Tokyo. J. Smolowe. il *Time* 133:50-2 Je 5 '89

Getting tough with Tokyo: Bush talks a good game. P. Magnusson. il *Business Week* p32 My 15 '89

Has the Orient totally conquered U.S. electronics? Seven companies say no [cover story] M. C. Lehrer. il *USA Today (Periodical)* 117:16-22 Ja '89

Head 'em up, move 'em out—to Japan [U.S. beef] S. D. Atchison. il *Business Week* p52 Ag 21 '89

Here come Japan's new luxury cars [Toyota's Lexus] A. L. Taylor, III. il *Fortune* 120:62-6 Ag 14 '89

Honest, Japan would love to buy American chips . . . N. Gross. il *Business Week* p92 Jl 10 '89

Is the door open wide enough? E. M. Reingold. il *Time* 133:54-5 Je 5 '89

Is this the moment Washington has been waiting for? A. Borrus and P. Magnusson. il *Business Week* p46-7 S 4 '89

Japan and the United States [address, May 17, 1989] W. E. Franklin. *Vital Speeches of the Day* 55:647-9 Ag 15 '89

Japan bashing bashes the United States [agreement on FSX] C. W. Weinberger. il *Forbes* 143:31 Mr 20 '89

Japan makes the hit list [U.S. list of countries charged with unfair trading practices] B. Powell. il *Newsweek* 113:48-9 Je 5 '89

Japan thinks there's room for vroom in the U.S. [sports cars] D. Woodruff. il *Business Week* p42 F 27 '89

Japan unlikely to parlay FSX work into civilian aircraft leadership role. C. Leader. por *Aviation Week & Space Technology* 130:97+ Mr 27 '89

Japan will feast at the CAFE [stricter fuel efficiency standards] *U.S. News & World Report* 106:11 My 29 '89

Japan's FS-X puzzle [U.S. government's decision to defer approval of plan to share F-16 technology with Japan] *Aviation Week & Space Technology* 130:9 F 27 '89

A land of papa-mama shops [complex marketing regulations deter foreign retailers] J. Impoco. il *U.S. News & World Report* 106:47-8 Ap 24 '89

Let's keep our cool on U.S.-Japan trade. J. H. Makin. il por *Fortune* 120:147-8 Jl 3 '89

Let's make a deal: the U.S.-Japan co-technology sphere. S. K. Vogel. *The New Republic* 200:14+ Je 19 '89

A 'little old agreement' on the F-16 [FSX deal between General Dynamics and Mitsubishi Heavy Industries] *Newsweek* 113:34 Ja 30 '89

Losing on both fronts. I. M. Stelzer. il *The American Spectator* 22:37-8 Je '89

Man for all seasons [views of R. A. Gephardt] M. Kondracke. *The New Republic* 201:12-14 Jl 3 '89

The market for American architectural services in Japan comes of age. A. A. Layne. il *Architectural Record* 177:33+ Mr '89

Motorola is pounding on Japan's 'open door' [cellular market] N. Gross. il *Business Week* p58 My 8 '89

New service to exporters [Japanese companies set up export promotion offices to help U.S. firms] il *Nation's Business* 77:70 N '89

Of cultural gaps and trade talks [effect of Japanese citizens' habits on balance of trade] C. P. Work. *U.S. News & World Report* 107:58 S 18 '89

Our Japan problem. M. Kondracke. *The New Republic* 201:11-12+ Jl 31 '89

Party crasher [Allen-Edmonds Shoe Corp.] R. Reiff. il por *Forbes* 143:128+ Je 12 '89

Pentagon, Commerce at impasse on FS-X after deal falls apart [sharing F-16 technology with Japan] M. Mecham. *Aviation Week & Space Technology* 130:28 Mr 13 '89

The plane drain: the FSX deal and other transfers of technology. H. D. Bentley. il por *Conservative Digest* 15:54-7 Jl/Ag '89

"Pressure has its uses" [views of J. Bhagwati] L. Minard. il por *Forbes* 143:96+ Je 12 '89

Ready, set, sell—Japan is buying. C. Rapoport. il *Fortune* 120:159-60+ S 11 '89

Responding to the Japanese 'threat'. P. Saffo. il *Personal Computing* 13:222 O '89

Rethinking Japan [cover story] R. Neff and P. Magnusson. il *Business Week* p44-52 Ag 7 '89

Revised FS-X pact eases trade, technology concerns [U.S./Japan fighter codevelopment] J. D. Morrocco. il *Aviation Week & Space Technology* 130:16-18 My 8 '89

The rise of the trade hawks [Japan bashing] B. Powell and B. Martin. il *Newsweek* 113:46-7 Mr 13 '89

The rival Japan respects [Motorola; cover story] L. Therrien. il pors *Business Week* p108-10+ N 13 '89

The road to Infiniti [W. Bruce, general manager of Nissan division] S. Kichen. il por *Forbes* 143:104 Ja 23 '89

A sanctions scare finally makes the Japanese jump [Motorola's cellular phone deal] P. Magnusson. *Business Week* p28-9 Jl 10 '89

Senate bolsters Commerce Dept.'s authority in reviewing cooperative arms agreements. J. D. Morrocco. *Aviation Week & Space Technology* 131:28 Ag 7 '89

Shadowboxing over fair trade. M. W. Karmin. *U.S. News & World Report* 106:48 Je 5 '89

Smith to Japan: here's the beef [deputy U.S. trade representative] A. Kupfer. il por *Fortune* 119:53 Ja 2 '89

Somebody's wrong [Japanese planning to increase production at American plants without reducing imports] J. Flint. il *Forbes* 144:118 S 18 '89

Still only a half-open door. B. Powell. il *Newsweek* 113:48-50 F 13 '89

Stop bashing Japan for U.S. deficits. T. Kataoka. il *USA Today (Periodical)* 117:26-8 Ja '89

Taking on Japan: why U.S. business wants backup. N. Gross. il *Business Week* p111 N 13 '89

Technology concerns delay approval of FS-X agreement [sharing F-16 technology with Japan] M. Mecham. il *Aviation Week & Space Technology* 130:16-17 F 20 '89

To sell in Japan, meet the Japanese. R. C. Dorney. il *Nation's Business* 77:10 F '89

Tokyo answers the call [Japan opens up its mobile phone market] *Time* 134:46 Jl 10 '89

Tokyo's tallest skyscrapers: prices. il *U.S. News & World Report* 107:13 N 20 '89

Trade protection comes to Silicon Valley. A. T. Denzau. *Society* 26:38-42 Mr/Ap '89

A trade threat that worked [Japan opens cigarette market to foreigners] G. Eisenstodt and H. Katayama. il *Forbes* 143:38-9 Ap 3 '89

Trading views with Japan [BizNet teleconference] A. Holzinger. il *Nation's Business* 77:34+ My '89

Treasury overrules Customs on import sport/utilities. *Motor Trend* 41:62-3 My '89

U.S. contractors finally break ground in Tokyo. N. Usui and N. Gross. il *Business Week* p56 Ap 3 '89

UNITED STATES—Commerce—Japan—*cont.*

U.S., Japan agree to codevelop FSX aircraft [statements, April 28 and May 3, 1989] G. Bush; L. S. Eagleburger. *Department of State Bulletin* 89:48-9 Jl '89

U.S.-Japanese trade relations [address, March 20, 1989] R. A. Gephardt. *Vital Speeches of the Day* 55:450-4 My 15 '89

A unique approach against trade violators [address, May 24, 1989] R. Noyce. *Vital Speeches of the Day* 55:671-2 Ag 15 '89

What's driving car prices up? il *Consumers' Research Magazine* 72:27-9 N '89

When is a truck not a truck? [U.S. tariff raises prices on Japanese trucks] il *Consumer Reports* 54:330 My '89

Where Japan will strike next [cover story] G. Bylinsky. il *Fortune* 120:42-6+ S 25 '89

Whispering the riot act to Japan. P. Magnusson. il *Business Week* p24 Je 12 '89

Why Japan won't slow down. M. Whitaker. il *Newsweek* 113:56 My 15 '89

Why Sun is losing its heat in the East [Sun Microsystems] N. Gross. il *Business Week* p114 S 18 '89

Korea (South)

Daewoo wins contract to assemble wing panels for Lockheed P-7A. M. A. Dornheim. *Aviation Week & Space Technology* 131:29 S 4 '89

Has Bush helped paint Roh into a corner? L. Nakarmi. il pors *Business Week* p61-2 Mr 13 '89

Korea fears U.S. technology transfer opponents could hamper its FX program. J. D. Morrocco. *Aviation Week & Space Technology* 130:23 Ap 3 '89

Korean Air, Asiana order U.S. transports valued at $1.35 billion. J. Ott. *Aviation Week & Space Technology* 130:17 Ap 17 '89

Perils of getting tough on Korea. F. S. Worthy. il *Fortune* 119:263+ Je 5 '89

Latin America

Cocaine chemistry [chemicals exported by the U.S. used in cocaine manufacture] P. Andreas. *The New Republic* 201:12+ N 20 '89

Cocaine countries try to grow straight [America's protectionist policy towards agricultural imports] A. Gabor. il *U.S. News & World Report* 107:57 O 23 '89

Mexico

A free-for-all for carmakers south of the border [easing of Mexico's local content restrictions] S. Baker. il *Business Week* p32 O 16 '89

Wooing Mexico to nuclear power [Laguna Verde plant] O. Miramontes. bibl f il *The Bulletin of the Atomic Scientists* 45:36-8 Jl/Ag '89

Netherlands

American Fokker 100 order caps carrier's growth plan. J. T. McKenna. il *Aviation Week & Space Technology* 130:88-9 Mr 27 '89

The Johnny Appleseed of pot [marijuana seed salesman N. Schoenmakers in Holland] R. Z. Chesnoff. il *U.S. News & World Report* 107:30 N 6 '89

Nicaragua

The coffee connection [nonviolent opposition to U.S. embargo against Nicaraguan imports] L. Cizewski. il *The Progressive* 53:46 N '89

Pacific region

The near collapse. M. S. Forbes, Jr. il *Forbes* 143:27 F 6 '89

Task force urges overhaul of Pentagon policy on industrial cooperation with Pacific Rim. J. D. Morrocco. *Aviation Week & Space Technology* 131:32 N 13 '89

Trade in the Pacific Rim [address, October 28, 1988] D. S. Tappan, Jr. *Vital Speeches of the Day* 55:217-20 Ja 15 '89

Washington State, riding the Pacific tide. M. Edwards. il map *National Geographic* 176:782-815 D '89

Pakistan

Proposal to sell F-16s to Pakistan [statement, August 2, 1989] T. Schaffer. *Department of State Bulletin* 89:65-6 O '89

White House sends Pakistan F-16 proposal to Congress. *Aviation Week & Space Technology* 130:42 Je 19 '89

Panama

Another Panamanian headache [to duck highway fees, U.S. truckers are registering and insuring their rigs in Panama] D. Fanning. il *Forbes* 144:80 N 13 '89

Poland

The man who would be magnate [Y. Fromer] M. Schifrin. il por *Forbes* 144:41-4 S 18 '89

Saudi Arabia

A lemon? Don't tell the Saudis [Bradley Fighting Vehicle] B. Bremner. il *Business Week* p40 Ja 23 '89

Saudi-U.S. joint ventures formed under AWACS offset program will start operations this year. *Aviation Week & Space Technology* 130:20 F 6 '89

South Africa

AAP report hits book embargo of South Africa as 'misguided'. C. Reid. *Publishers Weekly* 236:8+ D 1 '89

Do South African sanctions make sense? D. Reed. il *Reader's Digest* 134:51-6 F '89

Soviet Union

See also

Coordinating Committee on Multilateral Export Controls

Breakthrough [American Trade Consortium agreement with the Soviet government] *The New Yorker* 65:30-1 Ap 17 '89

The deal of the decade may get done in Moscow [American Trade Consortium] P. Galuszka and R. Brady. il *Business Week* p54-5 F 27 '89

Economic changes in the U.S.S.R. [address, May 23, 1989] A. W. Clausen. *Vital Speeches of the Day* 55:674-7 S 1 '89

From Russia with hype [consumer goods] J. Hammer. il *Newsweek* 113:42-3 Je 12 '89

Glavcosmos signs Energetics as first U.S. launch customer [Proton rockets] J. R. Asker. il *Aviation Week & Space Technology* 131:40 N 20 '89

The goodies Gorbachev brought home from Malta. R. Brady. il *Business Week* p42-3 D 18 '89

Government agencies at odds over computer sales to Soviets and Warsaw Pact countries. *Byte* 14:26+ O '89

How Bush may help open the doors wider for Soviet Jews [Jackson-Vanik waiver] R. Brady and B. Javetski. il *Business Week* p62 My 22 '89

Letters from home [tax fugitive M. Rich gets U.S. export subsidies on wheat deals with the Soviets] J. Willoughby. il por *Forbes* 143:38-9 Je 12 '89

Marketing the Proton [Soviet booster] S. Arenstein. il *Ad Astra* 1:31-4 D '89

O.K. to log on, comrades [U.S. relaxes controls on computer sales to Soviets] il *Time* 134:39 Jl 31 '89

Out-of-this-world ads [U.S. companies buying ad space on Soviet space vehicles] il *U.S. News & World Report* 107:10 Jl 24 '89

Pentagon purchases Soviet hardware on open market for operational testing. J. D. Morrocco. il *Aviation Week & Space Technology* 130:24-5 Ja 23 '89

Perestroika becomes a two-way street. il *Newsweek* 114:35 S 18 '89

Removing controls on PCs revives worries on exports. I. Goodwin. *Physics Today* 42:67-9 S '89

Rules of the road to Red Square [code of ethics for investing in the U.S.S.R. developed by Alexander Slepak] E. Pomice. il *U.S. News & World Report* 107:63 N 27 '89

Soviet attempts to buy U.S. computers continue despite Customs crackdown. D. Hughes. *Aviation Week & Space Technology* 130:279+ Je 12 '89

Soviets propose using Energia to launch NASA space station. il *Aviation Week & Space Technology* 130:22 My 8 '89

Soviets sign space pact, launch military satellites [joint venture between Space Commerce Corp. and Glavcosmos] C. Covault. il *Aviation Week & Space Technology* 130:24-5 Ja 9 '89

Sukhoi Su-26M for sale in the U.S. [aerobatic airplane] il *Flying* 116:12 O '89

Top U.S. companies move into Russia. L. Kraar. il *Fortune* 120:165-6+ Jl 31 '89

Trading with the Communists. A. Stevenson and A. Frye. *Foreign Affairs* 68:53-71 Spr '89

U.S., Soviet firms to develop, market commercial booster based on SS-20 [Start mobile launcher] J. D. Morrocco. il *Aviation Week & Space Technology* 131:21 Ag 7 '89

U.S. stance toward the Soviet Union on trade and technology [address, October 27, 1988] E. A. Wendt. *Department of State Bulletin* 89:20-3 Ja '89

What freer U.S.-Soviet trade will bring. S. Nasar. *U.S. News & World Report* 107:40 D 18 '89

Soviet Union—Anecdotes, facetiae, satire, etc.

Gulag capitalism [sending convicts to the Soviet Union] R. Lourie. *The New Republic* 201:18-19 O 16 '89

Spain

Fairchild Aircraft, Spain's CASA to cooperate on C-212 marketing. *Aviation Week & Space Technology* 130:61 Je 26 '89

Sweden

Allison engine chosen for Saab 2000; Sweden certifies Saab 340B transport. il *Aviation Week & Space Technology* 131:29 Jl 17 '89

AMR Eagle boosts Saab-Scania with firm order for 50 SF340Bs. C. Fotos. il *Aviation Week & Space Technology* 130:110-11 My 29 '89

Northwest commuter boosts Saab sales with orders for 340B, 2000 aircraft [Express Airlines 1] C. A. Shifrin. il *Aviation Week & Space Technology* 131:62 N 6 '89

Thailand

Thai International to equip three Airbus A300-600Rs with PW4158 engines. P. Proctor. *Aviation Week & Space Technology* 131:76 Ag 7 '89

Western Europe

"1992" is closer than we think. C. W. Weinberger. il *Forbes* 143:33 Ap 17 '89

Bill Eftink [EEC hormone ban on U.S. beef imports] B. Eftink. il *Successful Farming* 87:19 mid-Mr '89

Braniff will use 50 A320s to expand service from Kansas City to coasts. il *Aviation Week & Space Technology* 130:63 Ja 9 '89

The Common Market—friend or foe? C. W. Weinberger. il map *Forbes* 143:31 Mr 6 '89

UNITED STATES—Commerce—Western Europe—*cont.*
Continental orders 20 Airbus A330, A340 aircraft. *Aviation Week & Space Technology* 131:46 N 20 '89
Le Défi Disney [Hollywood TV sales to Europe] J. Marcom, Jr. il *Forbes* 143:39-40 F 20 '89
EC project 1992: the dynamics of change [address, September 9, 1988] D. Lamb. *Department of State Bulletin* 89:31-5 F '89
EC92 [cover story] R. Thompson. il map *Nation's Business* 77:18-24+ Je '89
Empty threat? [European measures against U.S. TV programming] J. Marcom, Jr. il *Forbes* 144:43 N 13 '89
Europe '92 [address, April 19, 1989] W. F. Ryan. *Vital Speeches of the Day* 55:492-4 Je 1 '89
Europe bans boeuf's à l'estradiol. E. Marshall. *Science* 243:161-2 Ja 13 '89
Europe goes wild for Yankee PCs. R. I. Kirkland, Jr. il *Fortune* 119:257+ Je 5 '89
Europe may slap a quota on General Hospital [limiting American TV imports] B. Riemer and K. Wolman. il *Business Week* p46-7 Mr 27 '89
The European Community's program for a single market in 1992. il map *Department of State Bulletin* 89:23-8 Ja '89
European firms agree to join Bell-Boeing in marketing V-22 [tilt-rotor aircraft] *Aviation Week & Space Technology* 130:37 Je 19 '89
Europe's economic integration in 1992 [address, May 3, 1989] R. P. Forrestal. *Vital Speeches of the Day* 55:633-5 Ag 1 '89
A food fight as big as the Atlantic [EEC threatens ban on U.S. meat] *Newsweek* 113:41 Ja 9 '89
A 'grenade' aimed at Hollywood: Europe votes to slap a quota on U.S. TV imports. D. Pedersen. il *Newsweek* 114:58 O 16 '89
Holding pep rallies for 1992 [states help U.S. firms with export strategy] J. McCormick. il *Newsweek* 114:60 N 6 '89
How do you say thirtysomething in Flemish? [global TV] R. A. Melcher. il *Business Week* p55+ My 8 '89
ILFC negotiates pact to buy 16 stretched Airbus A320s. il *Aviation Week & Space Technology* 130:111 Je 5 '89
Is the beef flap a taste of trade wars to come? [U.S. vs. European Community] F. J. Comes and P. Magnusson. il *Business Week* p47 Ja 16 '89
Keeping up with EC92. A. Holzinger. il *Nation's Business* 77:38-40 D '89
Losing on both fronts. I. M. Stelzer. il *The American Spectator* 22:37-8 Je '89
The power behind Compaq's European powerhouse [E. Pfeiffer] T. Peterson. il por *Business Week* p150 Je 26 '89
Propellant mixer delay could stall Ariane 5 program [U.S.-built mixer intended for propellant factory under construction at Guiana Space Center] J. M. Lenorovitz. *Aviation Week & Space Technology* 130:35 Je 26 '89
Secretary meets with EC ministers [text of joint press conference, December 9, 1988] J. Delors; G. P. Shultz. *Department of State Bulletin* 89:27-30 F '89
TWA orders Airbus A330s to upgrade aging fleet. C. Fotos. il *Aviation Week & Space Technology* 130:64-5 Ap 3 '89
U.S. Army collaboration 'blueprint' could boost European LHX role [helicopter] D. F. Bond. il *Aviation Week & Space Technology* 131:25 O 16 '89
U.S. criticizes E.C. plan to shield MBB from fluctuations in exchange rate. M. Mecham. *Aviation Week & Space Technology* 130:91 Mr 27 '89
U.S. welcomes changes in Europe, but fears of trade barriers linger [aerospace and defense sector] il *Aviation Week & Space Technology* 130:127+ Je 12 '89
What the 'Greens' mean for business. S. Tully. il *Fortune* 120:159+ O 23 '89
What's the beef? [European Community's ban on imports of beef injected with growth hormones] W. E. Sheeline. il *Fortune* 119:8 Ja 30 '89
Why the beef over hormones? [European Community bans import of U.S. meat from animals treated with hormones] J. Castro. il *Time* 133:44 Ja 16 '89
Commercial policy
See also
Balance of trade
Coordinating Committee on Multilateral Export Controls
Export-Import Bank of the United States
Tariff—United States
United States. Dept. of Commerce
United States. Office of the U.S. Trade Representative
The 1988 trade bill. A. F. Holmer and J. H. Bello. *Department of State Bulletin* 89:11-14 Mr '89
American leadership in international trade [address, November 28, 1988] W. A. Wallis. *Department of State Bulletin* 89:30-1 F '89
America's economic security [address, May 8, 1989] R. Mosbacher. *Vital Speeches of the Day* 55:554-6 Jl 1 '89
America's stake in the new global economy. G. Greenwald. il *USA Today (Periodical)* 118:26-8 N '89
Beyond GATT. G. C. Hufbauer. *Foreign Policy* 77:64-76 Wint '89/'90
Bloc that trade. R. Kuttner. *The New Republic* 200:16-19 Ap 17 '89

Budget, trade deficits could spur restrictive trade legislation [U.S. military exports and aid] il *Aviation Week & Space Technology* 130:73+ Mr 20 '89
The captains see a tilted field [global competition; Fortune poll] B. O'Reilly. il *Fortune* 120:93+ N 6 '89
Cautionary wail from the nursery [import quotas on Chinese cloth diapers] il *U.S. News & World Report* 106:44 Je 12 '89
Chips for the Soviet bloc? Computers from Asia short-circuit America's export controls. S. Budiansky. il *U.S. News & World Report* 107:28-30 O 9 '89
Competitiveness in the global marketplace [address, May 11, 1989] R. T. McCormack. *Department of State Bulletin* 89:49-53 Jl '89
The conservative's conservative [Roger Milliken fights for legislation to insulate textiles from imports] A. A. Lappen. *Forbes* 143:60 My 29 '89
Creating a global constituency for free trade [address, September 13-15, 1989] D. E. Moore. *Vital Speeches of the Day* 56:108-10 D 1 '89
Economic patriotism in a global economy [address, December 8, 1988] W. W. Winpisinger. *Vital Speeches of the Day* 55:220-2 Ja 15 '89
Export barriers the U.S. hates most. R. Jacob. il *Fortune* 119:88-9 F 27 '89
Extending America's import restrictions on foreign steel. il *U.S. News & World Report* 106:52 My 8 '89
For Japan, the day of reckoning on trade has finally arrived. A. Borrus. il *Business Week* p55 My 22 '89
Forget those phony problems [views of M. Friedman] M. Magnet. *Fortune* 120:68-9 Jl 3 '89
Getting along with Japan. J. M. Fallows. il *The Atlantic* 264:53-6+ D '89
Getting tough with Tokyo. J. Smolowe. il *Time* 133:50-2 Je 5 '89
Getting tough with Tokyo: Bush talks a good game. P. Magnusson. il *Business Week* p32 My 15 '89
The gospel of free trade is losing apostles. K. Pennar. il *Business Week* p89 F 27 '89
Government agencies at odds over computer sales to Soviets and Warsaw Pact countries. *Byte* 14:26+ O '89
How Bush may help open the doors wider for Soviet Jews [Jackson-Vanik waiver] R. Brady and B. Javetski. il *Business Week* p62 My 22 '89
How George Bush may recast quotas on steel imports. P. Magnusson. il *Business Week* p51 Mr 20 '89
In search of exports: the states' new agenda. P. R. Piccigallo. il *USA Today (Periodical)* 118:20-2 S '89
Information technology, global linkage, and U.S. competitiveness [address, June 14, 1989] E. M. Ehrlich. *Vital Speeches of the Day* 55:755-9 O 1 '89
It's gloves-off time [global competition] S. Nasar. il *U.S. News & World Report* 107:40-2 D 25 '89-Ja 1 '90
Japan makes the hit list [U.S. list of countries charged with unfair trading practices] B. Powell. il *Newsweek* 113:48-9 Je 5 '89
Let's keep our cool on U.S.-Japan trade. J. H. Makin. il por *Fortune* 120:147-8 Jl 3 '89
Let's keep Super 301 on the right course. il *Nation's Business* 77:72 Jl '89
A little tinkering could do wonders for steel quotas. R. Kuttner. il *Business Week* p20 Je 19 '89
Man for all seasons [views of R. A. Gephardt] M. Kondracke. *The New Republic* 201:12-14 Jl 3 '89
Members only. R. B. Reich. *The New Republic* 200:14+ Je 26 '89
Must we become Japanese? [cover story] D. D. Hale. il *National Review* 41:30-2+ O 27 '89
NAE: revamp export controls [computer equipment and software] M. Crawford. *Science* 243:21 Ja 6 '89
The near collapse [GATT talks] M. S. Forbes, Jr. il *Forbes* 143:27 F 6 '89
A new cold war? [rise of protectionism] E. A. Finn, Jr. il *Forbes* 143:56+ Mr 6 '89
A new hard line on trade. D. Jenish. il *Maclean's* 102:30+ My 22 '89
Of cultural gaps and trade talks [effect of Japanese citizens' habits on balance of trade] C. P. Work. *U.S. News & World Report* 107:58 S 18 '89
Our Japan problem. M. Kondracke. *The New Republic* 201:11-12+ Jl 31 '89
Overview of U.S. trade policy [address, October 5, 1988] W. A. Wallis. *Department of State Bulletin* 88:33-4 D '88
Patriots and traders [Bush administration] F. Barnes. *The New Republic* 201:9-10 S 4 '89
Perils of getting tough on Korea. F. S. Worthy. il *Fortune* 119:263+ Je 5 '89
A plan for competitiveness and continued economic growth [Keeping America on top policy statement by U.S. Chamber of Commerce] il *Nation's Business* 77:80 Ja '89
The plane drain: the FSX deal and other transfers of technology. H. D. Bentley. il por *Conservative Digest* 15:54-7 Jl/Ag '89
"Pressure has its uses" [views of J. Bhagwati] L. Minard. il por *Forbes* 143:96+ Je 12 '89
Removing controls on PCs revives worries on exports. I. Goodwin. *Physics Today* 42:67-9 S '89

UNITED STATES—Commercial policy—*cont.*

Resolve the technology transfer mess. *Aviation Week & Space Technology* 130:7 Ap 17 '89

Rethinking Japan [cover story] R. Neff and P. Magnusson. il *Business Week* p44-52 Ag 7 '89

Shadowboxing over fair trade. M. W. Karmin. *U.S. News & World Report* 106:48 Je 5 '89

Sons of Smoot-Hawley [protectionism making a comeback] E. A. Finn, Jr. il *Forbes* 143:38-40 F 6 '89

Status of multilateral trade negotiations [statement, April 11, 1989] C. A. Hills. *Department of State Bulletin* 89:30-2 Je '89

Steel trade liberalization program [statement, July 25, 1989] G. Bush. *Department of State Bulletin* 89:35 O '89

Stop bashing Japan for U.S. deficits. T. Kataoka. il *USA Today (Periodical)* 117:26-8 Ja '89

Strengthening U.S. export performance [address, March 23, 1989] T. G. Labrecque. *Vital Speeches of the Day* 55:500-2 Je 1 '89

Taking on Japan: why U.S. business wants backup. N. Gross. il *Business Week* p111 N 13 '89

Textile and Apparel Trade Act. il *Congressional Digest* 68:1-32 Ja '89

Trade hawk Gephardt pulls in his claws—a bit. P. Magnusson and D. Harbrecht. por *Business Week* p39 Ag 28 '89

Trade: major political issue of the 1990s? B. Ahlberg. il *Utne Reader* p28+ N/D '89

Trade protection: the consumer pays. J. W. Merline. il *Consumers' Research Magazine* 72:16-17 Ag '89

Trade-related aspects of intellectual property rights [statement, July 25, 1989] C. A. Hills. *Department of State Bulletin* 89:55-9 N '89

Trade's most wanted list [Super 301 negotiations to end foreign protectionism] S. Dentzer. il *U.S. News & World Report* 106:50+ My 22 '89

Trading blocs and the evolving world economy. J. E. Garten. *Current History* 88:15-16+ Ja '89

Trading with the Communists. A. Stevenson and A. Frye. *Foreign Affairs* 68:53-71 Spr '89

U.S.-Canada free trade agreement. il *Department of State Bulletin* 89:1-6 O '89

U.S.-Canada sign free trade agreement [remarks, September 28, 1988] R. Reagan. *Department of State Bulletin* 88:22-3 D '88

U.S. competition in emerging technology areas [address, August 8, 1989] H. D. Bentley. *Vital Speeches of the Day* 56:2-5 O 15 '89

U.S. credibility and viability in worldwide competition [address, May 25, 1989] N. R. Augustine. *Vital Speeches of the Day* 55:693-7 S 1 '89

U.S.-Japanese trade relations [address, March 20, 1989] R. A. Gephardt. *Vital Speeches of the Day* 55:450-4 My 15 '89

U.S. should avoid bilateral pacts [views of Jeffrey J. Schott] *USA Today (Periodical)* 118:10-11 D '89

U.S. stance toward the Soviet Union on trade and technology [address, October 27, 1988] E. A. Wendt. *Department of State Bulletin* 89:20-3 Ja '89

U.S. trade objectives in the Uruguay Round. il *Department of State Bulletin* 89:35-7 F '89

Uncle Sam as unfair trader. C. P. Work. il *U.S. News & World Report* 106:42-4 Je 12 '89

A unique approach against trade violators [address, May 24, 1989] R. Noyce. *Vital Speeches of the Day* 55:671-2 Ag 15 '89

Uruguay Round and U.S. trade policy: a foundation for the future [address, September 14, 1989] C. A. Hills. *Department of State Bulletin* 89:53-5 N '89

What freer U.S.-Soviet trade will bring. S. Nasar. *U.S. News & World Report* 107:40 D 18 '89

What to do about trade policy. A. R. Dowd. il por *Fortune* 119:106-7+ My 8 '89

Whispering the riot act to Japan. P. Magnusson. il *Business Week* p24 Je 12 '89

Why free trade works. T. J. DiLorenzo. *Reader's Digest* 134:119-23 F '89

Why scrap a steel policy that works? [limiting imports] R. Kuttner. il *Business Week* p24 My 22 '89

World without borders [views of G. Hufbauer] E. A. Finn, Jr. il por *Forbes* 143:118+ Ap 17 '89

Constitutional law

See also
Judicial power
Separation of powers
United States. Congress—Powers and duties
United States. Supreme Court

Antiques. W. Garrett. il *Antiques* 136:267 Ag '89

The case against political judging [cover story] R. H. Bork. il por *National Review* 41:23-8 D 8 '89

Constitutional law [discussion of December 1988 article, Rewriting the Constitution] S. C. Brubaker. *Commentary* 87:2-4+ My '89

'The tempting of America' [views of R. Bork] G. F. Will. il *Newsweek* 114:96 D 4 '89

Your Constitution. See issues of Scholastic Update (Teachers' edition) beginning September 22, 1986

Courts

See Courts

Cultural policy

William J. Bennett [advice to George Bush] W. J. Bennett. *National Review* 41:20-1 F 10 '89

Cultural relations

See also
ROCI (Exhibition)
United States. Information Agency

The screw-you spirit. J. M. Fallows. *The Washington Monthly* 21:42-3 Mr '89

Uncle Sam is pop culture to the world. il *U.S. News & World Report* 107:9 Ag 7 '89

Canada

Standing on guard [free trade accord] J. DeMont. il *Maclean's* 102:50 D 18 '89

China

Kickoff [effect of Tiananmen Square occupation on Chinese arts] R. Philp. il *Dance Magazine* 63:7 Ag '89

Europe

As the world turns. D. Denby. il *New York* 22:116 D 11 '89

France

America's underculture [interview with Costa-Gavras] il *New Perspectives Quarterly* 5:53-6 Wint '88/'89

Bernhardt in America. J. Kobler. il pors *American Heritage* 40:52-4+ Jl/Ag '89

Editorial. W. Garrett. il *Antiques* 135:695 Mr '89

French decorative arts in America [cover story] W. Garrett. bibl f il *Antiques* 135:696-707 Mr '89

A Gallic gala comes to America [events commemorating bicentennial of French Revolution] G. Lee. il *Harper's Bazaar* 122:26+ Ap '89

Over here [events in U.S. commemorating bicentennial of French Revolution] C. Davidson. il *American Heritage* 40:72 Jl/Ag '89

Japan

American casual seizes Japan. B. Hillenbrand. il *Time* 134:106 N 13 '89

Between two cultures. P. Sudo. il *Scholastic Update (Teachers' edition)* 122:2-3 D 8 '89

A yen for the arts [Japanese as patrons of the arts in America] il *U.S. News & World Report* 107:18 S 25 '89

South Africa

S. Africa tour furor basis for Milan Williams firing from 'Commodores' group. il por *Jet* 76:17 Ag 14 '89

Soviet Union

Art [G. Weiss organizes exhibit of proposals to link the Diomede Islands] N. Princenthal. il por *Vogue* 179:140+ Je '89

Can a socialist win in a free market? Pavel Khoroshilov as Leo Castelli? [Art bridge conference in Moscow] M. Esterow. il pors *Art News* 88:51-2+ S '89

Casting a *glasnost* glow on once-obscured artists [traveling exhibit entitled 10 + 10: contemporary Soviet and American painters] S. Meisler. bibl (p183) il *Smithsonian* 20:130-6+ D '89

Common clay: a Soviet sojourn brings *glasnost* to ceramic art. J. Tognini. il *American Craft* 49:10-11 O/N '89

Discussions in the USSR between a group of Americans and their Russian counterparts demonstrate how much times have changed. R. M. Adams. il *Smithsonian* 20:11-12 Je '89

Fall into the gap [Exhibition Diomede at the Clocktower] K. Larson. il *New York* 22:99 Je 5 '89

Here and there [dance exchanges] M. Horosko. il *Dance Magazine* 63:62 D '89

"In a neutral zone" [Soviet artists V. Mironenko, A. Roiter and K. Zvezdochetov visit the U.S.] S. Hochfield. il pors *Art News* 88:47-8 D '89

Moscow and the Hudson [exhibition of American painting in Moscow] K. Larson. il *New York* 22:79-80 O 16 '89

Omni's *glasnost* [Omni magazine to be distributed in the Soviet Union in exchange for Science in the USSR] J. Gilbert. il *Omni (New York, N.Y.)* 11:16 Ag '89

Rauschenberg goes to Moscow. A. Wallach. il por *Art in America* 77:21+ Mr '89

Red-faced in Moscow? Would Billy Crystal get his laughs? [taping a TV special] B. Crystal. il por *TV Guide* 37:14-15+ O 21-27 '89

The ROCI road show [R. Rauschenberg show in Moscow] M. L. Kotz. il por *Art News* 88:48+ Summ '89

A universal gesture [D. Barr's Arctic Arc sculpture, installed in Alaskan village of Wales, looks across to Siberia] S. Yolles. il *Art News* 88:13 Ja '89

Who will bury whom, Nikita? [USIA exhibit Design USA] il *U.S. News & World Report* 107:12-13 S 18 '89

Western Europe

The American craftsman and the European tradition, 1620-1820 [show at the Minneapolis Institute of Arts] M. Conforti and A. Kohls. il *Antiques* 136:834-43 O '89

Editorial [views of H. James] W. Garrett. il *Antiques* 136:810-11 O '89

UNITED STATES—Culture
Culture
See United States—Civilization
Culture, Popular
See United States—Popular culture
Defense policy
See United States—Military policy
Defenses
See also
Airplanes, Military
Artificial satellites—Military use
Chemical and biological weapons
Civil defense
Classified information
Disarmament
Guided missiles
North American Aerospace Defense Command
Nuclear submarines
Nuclear weapons
Strategic Arms Limitation Talks
Strategic Arms Reduction Talks
Strategic Defense Initiative
Tanks, Military
United States—Armed Forces
United States. Air Force
United States. Air National Guard
United States. Army
United States. Coast Guard
United States. Dept. of Defense
United States. Marine Corps
United States. National Guard
United States. Navy
Weapons
The defense dilemma [cover story] J. Barry and T. Morganthau. il *Newsweek* 113:12-18 Ja 23 '89
Does America need an army? [cover story; special section] il map *U.S. News & World Report* 107:22-5+ D 11 '89
Exon-Florio an imperfect tool for protecting U.S. technology. V. D. Cohen. por *Aviation Week & Space Technology* 131:68-9 N 6 '89
The military: tough choices in a changing world [cover story; special issue] il maps *Scholastic Update (Teachers' edition)* 122:1-23 O 6 '89
Reagan's security legacy [cover story; special issue; with editorial comment by Len Ackland] bibl f il pors *The Bulletin of the Atomic Scientists* 45:2, 5-32+ Ja/F '89
Description and travel
See also
Automobile touring
Cycling
Railroad travel
The American adventure [special section] il maps *Popular Mechanics* 166:17+ My '89
America's historical cities [Boston, Philadelphia, San Antonio, and San Francisco] il *Better Homes and Gardens* 67:173-4+ O '89
Continental drifter [B. Bryson] C. S. Smith. il por *New York* 22:26 S 18 '89
Cream of the country. S. Pacher. See issues of The Mother Earth News beginning September/October 1986
Disney World without the wait. P. Plawin. il *Changing Times* 43:80-2+ Ap '89
Farm family getaways! C. Tevis. il maps *Successful Farming* 87:54+ My '89
Going home [cover story; special section] il *U.S. News & World Report* 107:44-51+ D 18 '89
I-80. K. Emmons. il *Life* 12:96-102+ Fall '89
Mapping the real geography. B. H. Lopez. *Harper's* 279:19-21+ N '89
Open road. A. Meyer. See issues of The Mother Earth News beginning September/October 1988
Sights sacred and profane [19th century tourist attractions; interview with J. F. Sears] A. P. Sanoff. il por *U.S. News & World Report* 107:52 Ag 14 '89
Traveling with a sense of history [cover story; special issue] il *American Heritage* 40:34-6+ Ap '89
Walkabouts! [cover story] K. Shyne. il *New Choices for the Best Years* 29:29-32 Mr '89
Diplomatic and consular service
See also
United States. Dept. of State. Foreign Service
Argentina
Todman is Argentina envoy, Perkins is named director of U.S. Foreign Service. il pors *Jet* 76:36-7 My 22 '89
Austria
The Bloch case [alleged Soviet spy] *World Press Review* 36:8-9 S '89
A case of espionage [diplomat F. Bloch] H. Mackenzie. il por *Maclean's* 102:27 Ag 7 '89
First the verdict, then the trial [FBI's investigation of F. S. Bloch] B. Van Voorst. il pors *Time* 134:16 Ag 7 '89
High spy at State? [career diplomat F. S. Bloch suspected of spying for Soviets] *Time* 134:16 Jl 31 '89
Making a case against Bloch [alleged Soviet spy F. S. Bloch] R. Moreau. il por *Newsweek* 114:32 Ag 7 '89
More secrets from the life of Felix Bloch [revelations by Austrian prostitute] il *Newsweek* 114:40 O 23 '89

My lunch with Felix [suspected spy F. Bloch] B. Van Voorst. il por *Time* 134:16 S 4 '89
A spy in high places? [diplomat F. S. Bloch] H. Anderson. il por *Newsweek* 114:36 Jl 31 '89
Stategate [F. Bloch spy case] *National Review* 41:10-12 S 1 '89
Suspected spy Felix Bloch leads G-men and the press on a wild spook chase [Chappaqua, N.Y.] B. Hewitt. il por *People Weekly* 32:42-3 Ag 14 '89
Tinker, tailor, soldier, deputy chief of mission [F. Bloch suspected of spying for the Soviets] B. Duffy. il por *U.S. News & World Report* 107:21 Ag 7 '89
Vienna waltz [alleged Soviet spy F. S. Bloch] *The Nation* 249:228-9 S 4-11 '89
Cameroon
Howard's Cheek to end 20-year career there to take new ambassadorship. il pors *Jet* 76:4-5 Ap 24 '89
James Cheek bows out as candidate for envoy post. por *Jet* 76:5 My 15 '89
Canada
Men of credentials [American ambassador E. Ney and Canadian counterpart D. Burney] H. Mackenzie. il pors *Maclean's* 102:62-3 Jl 3 '89
Costa Rica
U.S. embassy aids pastors [conservative evangelical pastors in Nicaragua] *The Christian Century* 106:808-9 S 13-20 '89
Iran
See also
Iranian seizure of United States embassy, 1979-1981
Japan
Tilting toward toughness at the Tokyo embassy [ambassador M. H. Armacost] R. Neff. il por *Business Week* p47 Ag 7 '89
Korea (South)
Bush's envoy on the grill [D. Gregg questioned on Iran-contra during confirmation hearings for ambassadorship to South Korea] R. Parry. il por *Newsweek* 113:40 My 29 '89
Cranston v. Gregg [ambassador-designate D. Gregg questioned on Iran-contra] W. F. Buckley. *National Review* 41:11-12 Je 16 '89
Punish the ambassador! [students attack ambassador D. Gregg's residence] D. Bank and P. Leyden. il *Newsweek* 114:40 O 23 '89
Lebanon
U.S. diplomats evacuated from Beirut [State Dept. statement, September 6, 1989] *Department of State Bulletin* 89:62-3 N '89
The U.S. hears its Beirut exit line. *U.S. News & World Report* 107:12-13 S 18 '89
Mexico
Have savvy, will travel [ambassador-designate J. Negroponte] A. Platt. il por *Newsweek* 113:30 F 20 '89
Mexico [J. Negroponte appointed ambassador] *Business Week* p51 F 20 '89
Soviet Union
Bugs, beans and too many bucks [security at the U.S. embassy in Moscow] D. Corn. *The Nation* 248:236+ F 20 '89
Compounding the problem [security at the U.S. embassy] R. B. Cullen. il *Common Cause Magazine* 15:10 Mr/Ap '89
The Moscow bug hunt [no evidence that Marines C. Lonetree and A. Bracy allowed Soviets into the U.S. embassy] J. Peterzell. il pors *Time* 134:26-8 Jl 10 '89
Moscow station: how the KGB penetrated the American embassy [Marine guard spy case; excerpts; cover story] R. Kessler. il *Time* 133:50-2+ F 20 '89
Our Moscow embassy mess. J. Barron. *Reader's Digest* 134:193-6+ F '89
Economic conditions
See also
Business conditions
Business depression
Business forecasting
Consumption (Economics)
Cost and standard of living
Debts, Public
Economic forecasting
Economic indicators
Income
Inflation (Finance)
Labor
Poor
Prices
Rich
Underground economy
Unemployment
United States—Industries
Cold war economics [militarization of economy under Reagan administration] A. R. Markusen. bibl f il *The Bulletin of the Atomic Scientists* 45:41-4 Ja/F '89
Does the market matter? [Friday the 13th plunge, 1989; cover story; special section] il *Business Week* p24-33+ O 30 '89
Economic trends. See issues of Business Week
Income growth: are we better off? L. S. Richman. il *Current (Washington, D.C.)* 312:4-9 My '89

UNITED STATES—Economic conditions—*cont.*

Just how weak is the economy? K. Pennar. il *Business Week* p30-1 D 4 '89

Look out below! [slipping economy] J. Greenwald. il *Time* 133:81-2 My 22 '89

We ain't got a barrel of money. M. W. Karmin. il *U.S. News & World Report* 106:28 Ap 3 '89

Economic history

See also

Business depression, 1901

Business depression, 1929-1939

Slavery

The changing face of a restless nation. J. Carey. il maps *Business Week* p92-5+ S 25 '89

The dread federal surplus [1880s] B. A. Weisberger. il *American Heritage* 40:20+ Ap '89

Flashbacks. D. A. Saunders. See issues of Forbes

The man on the 10-spot turns 200 [A. Hamilton] J. Egan. il *U.S. News & World Report* 107:57 S 18 '89

The problem of money and time [cover story; with editorial comment by Byron Dobell] J. S. Gordon. il *American Heritage* 40:7, 56-8+ My/Je '89

Rich for a day. J. S. Gordon. il *American Heritage* 40:16+ Ap '89

What happened to Jimmy Carter. G. P. Brockway. il *The New Leader* 72:11-13 N 27 '89

Economic policy

See also

Budget

Council of Economic Advisers (U.S.)

Economic assistance, Domestic

Energy policy

Federal Reserve System (U.S.)

Industry and state

Inflation (Finance)

President's Task Force on Competitiveness

Taxation

United States—Appropriations and expenditures

100 days of treading water? So what? A. S. Blinder. il *Business Week* p21 My 15 '89

Advice from Mr. Chairman [interview with P. Volcker] L. Malkin. il por *Time* 133:48-50 Ja 23 '89

Advising the new administration [Black enterprise Board of Economists report] C. C. Williams. il *Black Enterprise* 19:48-53 Ja '89

An agenda for President Bush. L. Smith and A. R. Dowd. il por *Fortune* 119:82-4+ Ja 16 '89

The challenges to America—long-term, short-term, or both? [discussion of Summer 1988 article, Short-term folly, not long-term decline] J. S. Nye, Jr. *New Perspectives Quarterly* 5:62-3 Wint '88/'89

Dear George . . . A. C. Brown. il *Forbes* 143:147 F 20 '89

Deja voodoo all over again [budget deficit] M. B. Zuckerman. il *U.S. News & World Report* 107:84 O 9 '89

The dismal science. G. P. Brockway. See issues of The New Leader

Divided we fail [budget deficit] M. B. Zuckerman. il *U.S. News & World Report* 106:71 Je 5 '89

Donald T. Regan [advice to George Bush] D. T. Regan. *National Review* 41:23-4 F 10 '89

Don't hand out prizes for historical ax-grinding [books critical of Reaganomics and tax reform] P. C. Roberts. il *Business Week* p18 My 1 '89

The economic myths that the 1980s exploded. A. S. Blinder. il *Business Week* p22 N 27 '89

The end of economics? [values issues begin to dominate politics] R. J. Samuelson. il *Newsweek* 114:53 Jl 24 '89

F.D.R. changed, and so can you [advice for G. Bush] R. Lekachman. il por *The Nation* 248:117-18 Ja 30 '89

Facing reality in the George Bush era. M. L. Weidenbaum. *Society* 26:25-8 Mr/Ap '89

The fine art of fine-tuning. il *U.S. News & World Report* 106:14 My 15 '89

The fine mess created by skid-row politics [budget deficit] G. Borger and S. Dentzer. il *U.S. News & World Report* 107:32+ O 16 '89

Have we really been bingeing? D. Henwood. il *The Nation* 248:43-4 Ja 9-16 '89

Hogwash [debtor status of U.S.] M. S. Forbes, Jr. il *Forbes* 144 Special Issue:29 O 23 '89

How America can triumph [cover story] L. S. Richman. il *Fortune* 120:52-4+ D 18 '89

How Reaganomics made the world work. R. L. Bartley. il *National Review* 41:30-4 Ap 21 '89

If Washington can learn, Mexico can teach. *America* 160:411 My 6 '89

Is liberalism still possible? R. H. Bates. *National Review* 41:17 D 31 '89

Is our eye on the wrong ball? [preoccupation with deficit] D. A. Levy. il por *Forbes* 143:232 Ap 17 '89

It's time to face facts: supply-side was a smash [success of the reign of Reaganomics] P. C. Roberts. il *Business Week* p24 F 6 '89

Knitting new notions. J. Greenwald. il *Time* 133:46-8 Ja 30 '89

Listen, can we talk? [G. Bush's program] L. Reibstein. il *Newsweek* 113:46-7 Mr 27 '89

Masterminding the U.S. economy [M. J. Boskin] A. R. Dowd. il por *Fortune* 119:46 Ja 2 '89

The 'Maypo complex' [rating the Bush administration] R. J. Samuelson. il *Newsweek* 114:68 N 13 '89

Memo to Bush: don't take your economic luck for granted. M. McNamee. il *Business Week* p27 Ja 30 '89

Must we retrench? F. M. Bator. bibl f il *Foreign Affairs* 68:93-123 Spr '89

Observations. A. Bladen. See occasional issues of Forbes

The real bottom line [budget deficit] M. B. Zuckerman. il *U.S. News & World Report* 106:92 Mr 20 '89

The shrinking world. S. V. Roberts. il *U.S. News & World Report* 107:36-7 D 25 '89-Ja 1 '90

Supply-side economics and the future [address, December 8, 1988] P. C. Roberts. *Vital Speeches of the Day* 55:307-9 Mr 1 '89

Tangling with the U.S. economic octopus. R. W. Haseltine. il *USA Today (Periodical)* 118:28-30 Jl '89

What Bush should do. R. J. Samuelson. il *Newsweek* 113:45 Ja 23 '89

What Charlie Peters can learn from Jerry Brown. A. Levine. *The Washington Monthly* 21:34-5 Mr '89

What should make Bush run now. M. B. Zuckerman. il *U.S. News & World Report* 106:70-1 F 6 '89

Will the poor always be with us? [interview with M. Cuomo] N. Gardels. il *New Perspectives Quarterly* 6:28-32 Fall '89

Winning through inflation. M. W. Karmin. *U.S. News & World Report* 106:47 Je 12 '89

History

See United States—Economic history

Economic relations

See also

Economic assistance, American

United States—Commerce

America's economic dependence. F. G. Rohatyn. *Foreign Affairs* 68 Special Issue:53-65 ['89]

America's place in world competition. B. O'Reilly. il *Fortune* 120:83-4+ N 6 '89

Are we underestimating America's future? K. E. House. il *Reader's Digest* 134:185-6+ My '89

As the world turns [global economy and U.S. income inequality] R. B. Reich. *The New Republic* 200:23+ My 1 '89

Cracks in the G7 front [Group of Seven] P. Chisholm. il *Maclean's* 102:30+ My 8 '89

The decline of America: myth or fate? R. B. McKenzie. *Society* 27:41-8 N/D '89

Economic and military security [address, February 22, 1989] P. M. Kennedy. *Vital Speeches of the Day* 55:594-7 Jl 15 '89

Economic growth and military power: erosion of the superpowers. W. Goldstein. *Current (Washington, D.C.)* 309:23-31 Ja '89

Economics and national security [address, December 12, 1988] C. L. Powell. *Vital Speeches of the Day* 55:194-7 Ja 15 '89

In foreign markets, Reaganomics didn't get such high marks. G. Koretz. *Business Week* p26 F 6 '89

Key to the future: enlightened engagement [address, October 10, 1988] G. P. Shultz. *Department of State Bulletin* 88:16-19 D '88

Must we retrench? F. M. Bator. bibl f il *Foreign Affairs* 68:93-123 Spr '89

Picking up Reagan's tab. D. D. Hale. *Foreign Policy* 74:145-67 Spr '89

Public relations in the coming global economy [address, July 25, 1989] J. Paluszek. *Vital Speeches of the Day* 56:22-6 O 15 '89

Superpower sweepstakes. R. J. Samuelson. il *Newsweek* 113:43 F 20 '89

The U.S. role in a changing world economy. P. D. Nigro. il *USA Today (Periodical)* 117:21-2 My '89

Will America become #2? A. K. Selimuddin. il *USA Today (Periodical)* 118:14-16 S '89

Bibliography

Can the US remain number one? [cover story] P. M. Kennedy. il *The New York Review of Books* 36:36-42 Mr 16 '89

Angola

Suddenly, the business of Angola is business. S. Askin. il *Business Week* p45 My 1 '89

East Asia

East Asia, the Pacific, and the U.S.: an economic partnership. il map *Department of State Bulletin* 89:33-7 Ap '89

Japan builds a new power base. D. J. Yang and N. Gross. il *Business Week* p42-5 Ap 10 '89

Of deficits and diplomacy. S. Talbott. il *Time* 133:26 Mr 6 '89

Eastern Europe

Europe's grand drama: waiting for Bush to make his entrance. B. Javetski. il *Business Week* p66+ N 27 '89

Germany (West)

Axis, Ltd. [cover story] M. Sayle. il *The New Republic* 200:22-4+ Je 5 '89

Japan and Germany: American concerns. J. E. Garten. il *Foreign Affairs* 68:84-101 Wint '89/'90

Robust growth abroad will help keep the U.S. economy on track. R. E. Norton. il *Fortune* 120:15-16 N 6 '89

UNITED STATES—Economic relations—*cont.*
Iran
See also
Iranian seizure of United States embassy, 1979-1981—
Economic aspects
Japan
The 'Amerippon' alliance. M. Leventer. *World Press Review*
36:48-9 Ag '89
Axis, Ltd. [cover story] M. Sayle. il *The New Republic*
200:22-4+ Je 5 '89
Bush's bow to Japan. R. J. Samuelson. il *Newsweek* 113:37
F 6 '89
Feeling heat from the Rising Sun. D. Gergen. il *U.S. News
& World Report* 107:30 Jl 24 '89
Japan and Germany: American concerns. J. E. Garten. il
Foreign Affairs 68:84-101 Wint '89/'90
Japan goes Hollywood [Sony's deal for Columbia Pictures
and the competitive challenge to the U.S.; cover story;
special section] il *Newsweek* 114:62-9+ O 9 '89
Japan revisited. C. W. Weinberger. il *Forbes* 144:31 N 13
'89
Must we become Japanese? [cover story] D. D. Hale. il
National Review 41:30-2+ O 27 '89
Rediscovering the American spirit. J. M. Fallows. il *U.S.
News & World Report* 106:60-1 Ap 10 '89
Robust growth abroad will help keep the U.S. economy
on track. R. E. Norton. il *Fortune* 120:15-16 N 6 '89
Struggling for financial dominance [yen vs. dollar] N. Hol-
loway. *World Press Review* 36:15-17 Ap '89
The tie that binds—money. il *World Press Review* 36:13
Ap '89
Tiptoe through the tensions [N. Takeshita's visit to the
U.S.] J. Greenwald. il por *Time* 133:60 F 13 '89
To our own selves be true [J. M. Fallows' More like us]
B. Powell. il *Newsweek* 113:45 Ap 3 '89
U.S., Japan launch Structural Impediments Initiative [joint
statement, July 14, 1989] il *Department of State Bulletin*
89:78 S '89
Japan—Bibliography
The Japanese challenge. G. Russell. *Commentary* 88:70-2
S '89
Pacific region
East Asia, the Pacific, and the U.S.: an economic partnership.
il map *Department of State Bulletin* 89:33-7 Ap '89
Is a grand alliance in the making on the Pacific Rim?
B. Javetski and S. Hutcheon. il *Business Week* p70 N
6 '89
Panama
National emergency in Panama [message to Congress, October
14, 1988] R. Reagan. *Department of State Bulletin* 88:57
D '88
Poland
Making deals in Poland [U.S. mission] G. Bolte. il *Time*
134:39 D 18 '89
Soviet Union
Europe's grand drama: waiting for Bush to make his entrance.
B. Javetski. il *Business Week* p66+ N 27 '89
Waiting for Wyoming [Bush administration's policy of
constructive engagement] P. Glynn. *The New Republic*
201:14-16 O 2 '89
The West should not bankroll *perestroika*. B. Bradley. *USA
Today (Periodical)* 118:22-4 Jl '89
Economic statistics
Conference papers [papers at the Sesquicentennial Program
of the American Statistical Association] *Monthly Labor
Review* 112:29-33 O '89
A data deficit masks our economic strength. W. T. Brookes.
por *Nation's Business* 77:90 Je '89
Developing statistics to meet society's needs. J. L. Norwood
and D. P. Klein. bibl f *Monthly Labor Review* 112:14-19
O '89
Distorted image: how government statistics misrepresent the
economy. H. Kelly and A. Wyckoff. il *Technology Review*
92:52-60 F/Mr '89
Federal agencies seek improvement in quality in establishment
surveys. il *Monthly Labor Review* 112:38-40 O '89
The Forbes index. See issues of Forbes
Statistical needs. *Monthly Labor Review* 112:2 O '89
Statistics and policy: distorting economic activity. H. Kelly
and A. Wyckoff. *Current (Washington, D.C.)* 314:22-7 Jl/Ag
'89
Statistics and public policy [excerpts from address, August
8, 1989] J. L. Norwood. *Monthly Labor Review* 112:2
S '89
Educational policy
See College education and state; Education and state
Energy policy
See Energy policy
Environmental policy
See Environmental policy
Executive departments
See also
United States. Cabinet
Who's who in the administration. See issues of The
Washington Monthly

Expenditures
See United States—Appropriations and expenditures
Exploring expeditions
See also
Lewis and Clark Expedition (1804-1806)
Foreign economic policy
See United States—Economic relations
Foreign opinion
America's true power [prestige] J. Lukacs. il *American Heritage*
40:74-9 Mr '89
President Bush. il *World Press Review* 36:6+ Mr '89
What they say about Bush [cover story; special section]
il *World Press Review* 36:11-14+ S '89
British
Sharing the U.S. burden: a British view. M. Legge. il *Current
(Washington, D.C.)* 313:15-21 Je '89
British—Anecdotes, facetiae, satire, etc.
U.S. TV? It's been better for the Brits than our spareribs
or cruise missiles. A. Coren. il *TV Guide* 37:22-3 My
27-Je 2 '89
Canadian
A different kind of 'north-south' dialogue. C. Wood. il *World
Press Review* 36:36-8 Ag '89
Portrait of two nations [cover story; special section; with
editorial comment by Kevin Doyle] il *Maclean's* 102:4,
23-8+ Jl 3 '89
Canadian—Anecdotes, facetiae, satire, etc.
Different—in a manner of speaking. A. Fotheringham. il
Maclean's 102:84 Jl 3 '89
Chilean
The view from a Chilean window. K. J. Zenner. il *America*
161:266-7 O 28 '89
European
Europe and the Reagan years. P. Johnson. *Foreign Affairs*
68 Special Issue:28-38 ['89]
German
Are equal rights only a dream? M. Schwelien. il *World
Press Review* 36:32-4 My '89
Japanese
America-bashing, Japanese style [book The Japan that can
say no by A. Morita and S. Ishihara] J. Impoco. pors
U.S. News & World Report 107:45 O 16 '89
America's self-loathing even has Japan convinced [The Japan
that can say no] P. C. Roberts. il *Business Week* p22
D 11 '89
The book that's creating a firestorm [S. Ishihara's The Japan
that can say no] A. Borrus. il por *Business Week* p78+
O 23 '89
Japan's hardening view of America. R. Neff. il *Business
Week* p62-4 D 18 '89
Superiority complex [views of S. Ishihara in The Japan
that can say no] H. Jensen. il por *Maclean's* 102:56-7
D 11 '89
Teaching Japan to say no [interview with S. Ishihara] S.
Kanise. il por *Time* 134:81-2 N 20 '89
Polish
Ameryka my America; tr. by Anna Husarska. E. Skalski.
il *The New Leader* 72:8-9 N 13 '89
Russian
Communist view. See issues of World Press Review
Life at the local level: a Soviet journalist examines our
'grass-roots' politics. V. Nikolayev. *World Press Review*
36:34-6 N '89
Tristan and Pavlova through the looking glass [how Soviet
movies depict the United States] M. Fellous. il *The Unesco
Courier* 42:30-3 O '89
Foreign policy
See United States—Foreign relations
Foreign relations
See also
Economic assistance, American
Espionage, American
Military assistance, American
National Endowment for Democracy
National Republican Institute for International Affairs
United Nations—United States
United States—Economic relations
United States—Treaties
United States. Congress. Senate. Committee on Foreign
Relations
United States. Dept. of State
United States. Information Agency
United States. National Security Council
After a cruise to nowhere. K. Auchincloss. il *Newsweek*
114:39 D 11 '89
America abroad. S. Talbott. See issues of Time beginning
January 9, 1989
America and the world 1988/89 [cover story] bibl f *Foreign
Affairs* 68 Special Issue:1-219 ['89]
The American perspective, five key questions [address, March
31, 1989] B. O. Wireman. *Vital Speeches of the Day*
55:538-40 Je 15 '89
As the world waits [lack of cohesive policy] S. Budiansky.
il *U.S. News & World Report* 107:20-2 O 2 '89
Big shtick [Bush administration policies] *The Progressive*
53:8-9 Jl '89

UNITED STATES—Foreign relations—*cont.*

The Chinese massacres underscore the timeliness of a new book, The democratic imperative. M. S. Forbes, Jr. il *Forbes* 144:27 Ag 7 '89

Coping with the '90s. C. W. Maynes. bibl f *Foreign Policy* 74:42-62 Spr '89

The curse of legalism. C. Krauthammer. il *The New Republic* 201:44+ N 6 '89

The damaged U.S. image [Reagan administration] R. A. Falk. il *The Bulletin of the Atomic Scientists* 45:59-61 Ja/F '89

The dawning of the Bush method. S. V. Roberts. il por *U.S. News & World Report* 106:34-5 Ap 17 '89

Democracy and tyranny: dealing with friendly tyrants. R. N. Haass. *Current (Washington, D.C.)* 316:34-40 O '89

The democracy gang. M. Kondracke. il *The New Republic* 201:18+ N 6 '89

The Democratic Party and foreign policy: a proposed manifesto. A. Tonelson. *Current (Washington, D.C.)* 317:25-34 N '89

The eagle and the arrows: America in the nuclear age. T. J. Osborne. il *USA Today (Periodical)* 118:12-14 Jl '89

The ecology of international change [address, October 28, 1988] G. P. Shultz. *Department of State Bulletin* 89:6-10 Ja '89

The end of internationalism? A. Tonelson. *The New Republic* 200:23-5 F 13 '89

The foreign policy thing: how long will Bush's luck hold out? D. Harbrecht and B. Javetski. il por *Business Week* p63 D 25 '89-Ja 1 '90

George Bush's opportunity. il *The Progressive* 53:6-7 F '89

Get me rewrite [need for G. Bush to improve foreign policy speeches] M. Kondracke. *The New Republic* 200:10+ Je 12 '89

A glimpse of greater peace. J. Bierman. il *Maclean's* 102:34-6 Ja 23 '89

Good news: our human rights policy [address, October 3, 1988] G. Lister. *Department of State Bulletin* 89:36-8 Ja '89

Human rights and policy: the American tradition. P. J. Dobriansky. *Current (Washington, D.C.)* 314:28-37 Jl/Ag '89

Imperial conservatives? [stressing presidential powers] S. T. Francis. *National Review* 41:37-8 Ag 4 '89

International human rights and the Bush administration. R. F. Drinan. *America* 160:242-4 Mr 18 '89

Is democratic theory for export? J. Barzun. *Society* 26:16-23 Mr/Ap '89

It's a small world after all. *The New Republic* 201:7-8+ S 18-25 '89

Letter from Washington. E. Drew. *The New Yorker* 65:72-82 Je 26 '89

Letters [discussion of Winter 1988/1989 article, Setting global priorities] W. G. Hyland. *Foreign Policy* 75:182-9 Summ '89

The lost legacy: idealism in American foreign policy. C. W. Kegley. *USA Today (Periodical)* 117:25-7 Mr '89

Minority report [Reagan era misinformation] C. Hitchens. *The Nation* 248:42 Ja 9-16 '89

News conference of January 27 (excerpts). G. Bush. *Department of State Bulletin* 89:4-5 Ap '89

Notes and comment [encouraging national modesty without diminishing national pride] *The New Yorker* 65:31-2 My 8 '89

Nouveau law and foreign policy. D. J. Scheffer. *Foreign Policy* 76:44-65 Fall '89

One day at a time [Bush administration] M. Kondracke. *The New Republic* 200:9-11 My 8 '89

An overture to Congress [J. Baker seeks to restore bipartisan foreign policy] M. G. Warner. il por *Newsweek* 113:26 Ja 23 '89

Pass the rum. *The Nation* 248:363-4 Mr 20 '89

Poor Jim Baker! W. F. Buckley. *National Review* 41:70 N 10 '89

Power for good: American foreign policy in the new era [address, April 14, 1989] J. A. Baker, III. *Department of State Bulletin* 89:8-11 Je '89

President addresses joint session of the Congress [excerpts, February 9, 1989] G. Bush. *Department of State Bulletin* 89:3-4 Ap '89

President holds session with news reporters [excerpts, February 16, 1989] G. Bush. *Department of State Bulletin* 89:5-6 Ap '89

Pressing for a free press. S. J. Ungar. *Foreign Policy* 77:132-53 Wint '89/'90

Raining on Baker's parade. M. B. Carlson. il por *Time* 133:18-19 F 27 '89

Reagan foreign policy: a mixed legacy. T. L. Deibel. *Current (Washington, D.C.)* 317:16-24 N '89

Reagan's mixed legacy. T. L. Deibel. *Foreign Policy* 75:34-55 Summ '89

Reconsidering the two presidencies. D. M. Oldfield and A. B. Wildavsky. *Society* 26:54-9 Jl/Ag '89

Secretary Baker's interview on "Face the nation" (excerpts), Feb. 26, 1989. il *Department of State Bulletin* 89:10-13 My '89

Secretary Baker's interview on "Meet the press," Rome, May 28, 1989 [transcript of program] il *Department of State Bulletin* 89:12-15 Ag '89

Secretary-designate's confirmation hearings [statement, January 17, 1989] J. A. Baker, III. *Department of State Bulletin* 89:10-16 Ap '89

Secretary's interview for "American interests" [J. A. Baker; transcript of program, April 22, 1989] M. Kondracke. *Department of State Bulletin* 89:14-19 Je '89

Secretary's interview on "Face the nation" [J. A. Baker; transcript of program, May 14, 1989] *Department of State Bulletin* 89:27-9 Jl '89

Secretary's interview on "Meet the press" [interview with J. A. Baker; transcript of program, February 19, 1989] *Department of State Bulletin* 89:21-4 Ap '89

Secretary's news briefings in New York [September 25-29, 1989] J. A. Baker, III. il pors *Department of State Bulletin* 89:31-8 N '89

Send in the pols. J. Klein. il por *New York* 22:10-11 Ja 9 '89

Setting global priorities. W. G. Hyland. *Current (Washington, D.C.)* 312:26-33 My '89

A shrinking American role in the world. L. Lief. il *U.S. News & World Report* 107:22+ N 13 '89

Speak loudly, carry a small stick [effect of Vietnam and Watergate] J. Schell. il *Harper's* 278:39-41+ Mr '89

U.S. foreign policy in a time of transition [address, October 27, 1988] C. L. Powell. *Department of State Bulletin* 89:30-2 Ja '89

U.S. role in the world. A. Brummer. il *World Press Review* 36:16-17+ S '89

Welcome to democracy. M. Greenfield. il *Newsweek* 113:70 My 29 '89

What should we do in the world? S. Hoffmann. il *The Atlantic* 264:84-8+ O '89

Anti-Communist measures

As the world turns, where's George? J. Alter. il *Newsweek* 114:30 S 4 '89

A distant thunder on the right: conservatives regroup in the age of *glasnost*. E. Salholz. il *Newsweek* 114:25 D 18 '89

Enough rope. J. E. Mueller. *The New Republic* 201:14-16 Jl 3 '89

Forgive us if we feel like gloating. F. Bruning. il *Maclean's* 102:13 D 4 '89

Gorbachev and the right. W. F. Buckley. *National Review* 41:54-5 Je 16 '89

A new history. *The Nation* 249:739-40 D 18 '89

Playing to the home crowd [Reagan Doctrine] R. H. Johnson. il *The Bulletin of the Atomic Scientists* 45:24-8 Ja/F '89

Proceed with caution. *National Review* 41:11-13 D 31 '89

Undoing the 'Reagan Doctrine' [Bush administration] D. Schorr. *The New Leader* 72:3-4 Ap 3-17 '89

The world turned upside down [post cold war attitudes; cover story] M. Kondracke. il *The New Republic* 201:26-9 S 18-25 '89

History

The last wise man [excerpts from Sketches from a life; cover story] G. F. Kennan. il pors *The Atlantic* 263:39-47+ Ap '89

Of many things [H. Brandon's book Special relationships: a foreign correspondent's memoirs from Roosevelt to Reagan] G. W. Hunt. *America* 160:210 Mr 11 '89

The perfect in-and-outer [P. H. Nitze] S. Hoffmann. bibl f il *The New York Review of Books* 36:13-17 N 23 '89

The world war created [World War II] M. B. Zuckerman. il map *U.S. News & World Report* 107:68-9+ Ag 28-S 4 '89

Africa

Africa: a continent adrift. J. A. Marcum. bibl f *Foreign Affairs* 68 Special Issue:159-79 ['89]

After visit to African nations, Jesse Jackson urges joint partnership. D. M. Cheers. il pors *Jet* 75:12-14+ Ja 30 '89

The seedlings of hope: U.S. policy in Africa [address, June 11, 1989] E. J. Perkins. *Department of State Bulletin* 89:69-72 Ag '89

What should President Bush do in Africa [address, January 27, 1988] P. Duignan. *Vital Speeches of the Day* 55:328-9 Mr 15 '89

Angola

The United States and Angola, 1974-88: a chronology. N. D. Howland. *Department of State Bulletin* 89:16-24 F '89

Argentina

See also

United States—Diplomatic and consular service—Argentina

Asia

Containment's last gasp. P. H. Kreisberg. *Foreign Policy* 75:146-63 Summ '89

Seeking a new balance in Asia. H. Kissinger. il *Newsweek* 112:51-2+ My 22 '89

U.S. policy in Asia [address, June 22, 1989] D. Quayle. *Vital Speeches of the Day* 55:610-13 Ag 1 '89

Watching from offshore [U.S. reaction to improvement in Sino-Soviet relations] C. Ogden. il *Time* 133:45 My 29 '89

UNITED STATES—Foreign relations—Asia—*cont.*
When ideology bows to economics. D. Stanglin. il *U.S. News & World Report* 106:30-1 F 6 '89
Why the Sino-Soviet summit was important. H. Trewhitt. il por *U.S. News & World Report* 106:36 My 29 '89

Asia—History
The New Deal and the guru [Russian mystic N. Roerich sent on scientific expedition to North China and Manchuria by Roosevelt administration's H. A. Wallace] C. J. Errico and J. S. Walker. il pors *American Heritage* 40:92-5+ Mr '89

Australia
See also
Hawke, Robert J. L. (Robert James Lee), 1929—Visit to the United States, 1989

Austria
See also
United States—Diplomatic and consular service—Austria

Belgium
See also
Bush, George, 1924—Visit to Belgium, 1989

Brazil
What can Americans do? [preserving the rain forests] M. D. Lemonick. il *Time* 134:85 S 18 '89

Burma
Dateline drug wars: Burma: the wrong enemy. W. H. Overholt. *Foreign Policy* 77:172-91 Wint '89/'90

Cambodia
Civil war in Cambodia? N. Chanda. *Foreign Policy* 76:26-43 Fall '89
Efforts toward a Cambodian settlement [statement and text of UN General Assembly resolution, November 3, 1988] V. A. Walters. *Department of State Bulletin* 89:65-8 F '89
Killing fields II. E. Becker. *The New Republic* 200:10+ Ja 2 '89
The killing fields revisited. S. Talbott. il *Time* 133:47 My 1 '89
Old war, China card & Sihanouk. S. Blaustein. il *The Nation* 249:485-6+ O 30 '89
Our pal Pol Pot? J. J. Green and B. Whitmore. *Commonweal* 116:668-9 D 1 '89
Situation in Cambodia [address, September 29, 1988] C. H. Twining. *Department of State Bulletin* 88:31-3 D '88
Zbig deal in Cambodia [U.S. responsibility for continued strength of Khmer Rouge] *The Nation* 248:109 Ja 30 '89

Cameroon
See also
United States—Diplomatic and consular service—Cameroon

Canada
See also
Bush, George, 1924—Visit to Canada, 1989
Canada—Diplomatic and consular service—United States
Mulroney, Brian—Visits to the United States, 1989
United States—Diplomatic and consular service—Canada
Air Force begins captive-carry tests of advanced cruise missile over Canada. il *Aviation Week & Space Technology* 129:26 Mr 6 '89
Canada and the United States in a global context [address, September 22, 1989] D. Burney. *Vital Speeches of the Day* 56:43-5 N 1 '89
Fields of force. M. McDonald. il *Maclean's* 102:26-8+ Jl 3 '89
Fighting acid rain [Bush plan; cover story; special section; with editorial comment by Kevin Doyle] il map *Maclean's* 102:2, 38-46 Je 26 '89
Flight into danger [U.S. agents chase plane into Canada] R. Dolphin. il *Maclean's* 102:12-13 Ap 3 '89
Forging new relations [Bush presidency] H. Mackenzie. il *Maclean's* 102:32-3 Ja 23 '89
How we're destroying the Canadian wilderness [acid rain] T. H. Cole. il map *Popular Mechanics* 166:40 Ag '89
Ottawa approves USAF request to test advanced cruise missile over Canada. *Aviation Week & Space Technology* 130:24 F 6 '89
Stealth cruise sneaks into Canada. W. M. Arkin. il *The Bulletin of the Atomic Scientists* 45:6-7 My '89

Cape Verde
See also
Cape Verde—Diplomatic and consular service—United States

Caribbean region
When fury turns to foolishness. M. Greenfield. il *Newsweek* 114:92 O 16 '89

Central America
Crimping the accords [latest U.S. aid package for Nicaragua contradicts U.S. support for regional peace plan] *Commonweal* 116:227-8 Ap 21 '89
The deal in Central America. E. Abrams. *Commentary* 87:29-32 My '89
A done deal. *The New Republic* 200:5-6 Ap 24 '89
El Salvador [discussion of May 1989 article, The deal in Central America] E. Abrams. *Commentary* 88:8-9 S '89
Facing south. *Commonweal* 116:99-100 F 24 '89
First steps toward a policy [J. Baker's strategy] M. Kramer. il por *Time* 133:41 Mr 27 '89

Help out with the Latins, por favor. H. Trewhitt. il *U.S. News & World Report* 106:42-3 Ap 10 '89
Look out, gringo [Bush administration policies] M. Kondracke. *The New Republic* 201:12-13 S 4 '89
Secretary's news conference [November 14, 1988] G. P. Shultz. *Department of State Bulletin* 89:13 Ja '89
U.S. support for democracy and peace in Central America [bipartisan accord; statements and text of accord, March 24, 1989; texts of joint declarations of Central American presidents, January 16, 1988 and February 14, 1989; cover story] G. Bush. il por map *Department of State Bulletin* 89:55-9 Je '89
What can Central America expect from the Bush administration? F. B. Morris. il *The Christian Century* 106:472-5 My 3 '89

Chile
Chile: transition to democracy? J. H. Wolfe. il *USA Today (Periodical)* 117:25 Ja '89
Chile's return to democracy. P. Constable and A. Valenzuela. *Foreign Affairs* 68:169-86 Wint '89/'90

Chile—History
Innocent abroad [overthrow of S. Allende in 1973] R. Jordan. il *The Progressive* 53:46 Ag '89

China
See also
Bush, George, 1924—Visit to China, 1989
China—Diplomatic and consular service—United States
Advice from a former president. R. M. Nixon. il pors *Time* 134:44+ N 20 '89
America's Voice in China [television broadcasting by Voice of America] D. Baer. il *U.S. News & World Report* 106:34 Je 19 '89
Beware of geobaloney. M. Greenfield. il *Newsweek* 114:84 D 25 '89
Bush the riverboat gambler [U.S. sends high level delegation to Beijing] G. J. Church. il *Time* 134:32-3 D 25 '89
A cautious man plays China by the book [G. Bush's policy] D. Gergen. il *U.S. News & World Report* 106:27 Je 5 '89
China and America: beyond the big chill. W. Lord. *Foreign Affairs* 68:1-26 Fall '89
The China syndrome. *The New Republic* 200:7-9 My 15 '89
Dellums urges support for Chinese freedom struggle. il por *Jet* 76:15 Je 26 '89
Demonstrations in China [State Dept. and White House statements, May 18-June 20, 1989] *Department of State Bulletin* 89:75-7 Ag '89
A dilemma for Washington [China's repressive policies] R. Holbrooke. il *Newsweek* 113:32 Je 12 '89
Don't just do something, stand there [U.S. response to Tiananmen Square crackdown] *National Review* 41:16 Jl 14 '89
Easy does it. W. F. Buckley. *National Review* 41:62-3 S 15 '89
For now, the Chinese students can stay [G. Bush vetoes legislation to extend visas of Chinese students] P. Wingert and D. Waller. il *Newsweek* 114:98 D 11 '89
The Great Wall vs. the fax [with introd. by Nathan Gardels] O. Schell; R. M. Nixon. *New Perspectives Quarterly* 6:56-8 Summ '89
Handle with care. C. W. Weinberger. il *Forbes* 144:31 Ag 7 '89
Hard words to hard-liners [R. Nixon's visit] S. Burton. il por *Time* 134:37 N 13 '89
Lost chance: how Bush failed the heroes of Tiananmen Square. O. Schell. il *Mother Jones* 14:36-9 S '89
Misled by the 'facts' [Tiananmen Square uprising] M. Greenfield. il *Newsweek* 113:76 Je 26 '89
New diplomacy by Fax Americana [broadcasting information to China via fax machine and telephone] S. V. Roberts. il *U.S. News & World Report* 106:32-4 Je 19 '89
News conference of June 27 (excerpts). G. Bush. *Department of State Bulletin* 89:54-6 S '89
News conferences of June 5 and 8 (excerpts) [supression of pro-democracy demonstrators] G. Bush. *Department of State Bulletin* 89:46-52 Ag '89
Notes and comment [White House wants improved relations] *The New Yorker* 65:31-2 D 25 '89
An old China hand plays the China card [visit by National Security Adviser Brent Scowcroft] il *U.S. News & World Report* 107:8 D 25 '89-Ja 1 '90
Saving the connection [U.S. response to violence in China] G. J. Church. il *Time* 133:30-2 Je 19 '89
Secretary's interview on "Newsmaker Saturday" [J. A. Baker; transcript of program, June 3, 1989] *Department of State Bulletin* 89:67-9 Ag '89
Small carrot, big stick [China executes pro-democracy demonstrators] R. Watson. il *Newsweek* 114:28-30 Jl 3 '89
So what do we do now? [reaction to Tiananmen Square] W. F. Buckley. *National Review* 41:60-1 Jl 14 '89
'They would not understand' [R. Nixon returns to China] D. Elliott. il por *Newsweek* 114:61 N 13 '89
The U.S. & the China demonstrators. W. F. Buckley. *National Review* 41:63 Je 30 '89
The U.S. and China. P. M. Jones. il *Scholastic Update (Teachers' edition)* 121:25 My 5 '89

UNITED STATES—Foreign relations—China—*cont.*
U.S., China celebrate decade of diplomatic relations [toast, December 15, 1988] G. P. Shultz. *Department of State Bulletin* 89:25-6 F '89
The U.S. in China: letting a new caution bloom. D. Lee. il *Business Week* p47 Ja 30 '89
U.S. response to changes in China [statements, July 13 and 20, 1989] R. L. Williams. *Department of State Bulletin* 89:27-30 O '89
The uncertain future of Chinese foreign policy. S. I. Levine. bibl f *Current History* 88:261-4+ S '89
Under Western eyes. *National Review* 41:13-14 Je 30 '89
The view from the Forbidden City. W. Lord. il por *Newsweek* 114:36 D 18 '89

China—History
America's China policy [reprint from September 1981 issue] O. E. Clubb. *Current History* 88:35-6+ Ja '89
Owen Lattimore and the 'cold war'; Lattimore & Wicker. W. F. Buckley. *National Review* 41:54-5 Ag 18 '89
Owen Lattimore, RIP [effects on China policy brought about by McCarthyism; excerpt from column, September 1979] W. F. Buckley. *National Review* 41:18-20 Je 30 '89
Why are the liberals whitewashing? [case of O. Lattimore] W. F. Buckley. *National Review* 41:60 Jl 14 '89

Colombia
Dateline drug wars: Colombia: the wrong strategy. B. M. Bagley. *Foreign Policy* 77:154-71 Wint '89/'90
'Now the fight is with blood' [drug wars] T. Morganthau. il *Newsweek* 114:37 Ag 28 '89
Passing the extradition test [Colombian drug lord E. Martínez Romero shipped to the U.S.] M. S. Serrill. il por *Time* 134:48 S 18 '89

Communist countries
Glasnostrums. J. Muravchik. *The New Republic* 200:16-18 Ja 30 '89
Notes and comment [U.S. should stay clear of moral superiority in rebuking communism] *The New Yorker* 65:25-6 Je 26 '89
Who killed communism? M. Kinsley. *The New Republic* 201:4 D 4 '89

Communist countries—Anecdotes, facetiae, satire, etc.
Why the 'suit' misreads the Commies [George Bush] A. Fotheringham. il *Maclean's* 102:84 O 2 '89

Costa Rica
See also
United States—Diplomatic and consular service—Costa Rica
Minority report. C. Hitchens. *The Nation* 249:742 D 18 '89

Cuba
Cuba: a threat to peace and security in our hemisphere [statement, August 2, 1989] M. G. Kozak. *Department of State Bulletin* 89:75-9 N '89
Cuba and narcotics trafficking [statement, July 26, 1989] M. Levitsky. *Department of State Bulletin* 89:46-8 O '89
Is it time for a thaw with Cuba? A. Platt. il *Newsweek* 113:32 Ap 17 '89
Washington isn't mellowing on Cuba—but Miami is. A. Fins. il *Business Week* p41 Ap 17 '89

Cuba—History
See also
Cuba—History—Invasion, 1961
Cuban Missile Crisis, 1962

Developing countries
Beyond the Reagan Doctrine. S. Talbott. il *Time* 134:68 Jl 17 '89
The edge of might [low-intensity conflicts] P. Kornbluh. *Omni (New York, N.Y.)* 11:46 Ja '89
Environment and security. N. Myers. *Foreign Policy* 74:23-41 Spr '89

East Asia
See also
Bush, George, 1924——Visit to East Asia, 1989
United States policy in East Asia. N. D. Palmer. bibl f *Current History* 88:161-4+ Ap '89

Eastern Europe
Crossing the European divide. C. Bogdan. bibl f *Foreign Policy* 75:56-75 Summ '89
East European divides. M. Svec. *Foreign Policy* 77:41-63 Wint '89/'90
Eastern Europe on its own. C. Gati. bibl f *Foreign Affairs* 68 Special Issue:99-119 ['89]
How Kissinger sees it. H. Kissinger. il *Newsweek* 114:45 O 16 '89
How should the West respond? *America* 161:203 O 7 '89
How should the West respond. M. S. Forbes, Jr. il *Forbes* 143:27 My 1 '89
In search of vision. G. J. Church. il *Time* 134:20-3 N 27 '89
Looking for cracks in the bloc. R. Watson. il *Newsweek* 113:42 My 20 '89
Needed: a new compass. M. Greenfield. il *Newsweek* 114:80 O 2 '89
Say a prayer for Gorbachev [G. Bush's relationship with the Communist world] H. Sidey. il pors *Time* 134:19 Ag 7 '89

Secretary's interview on the "MacNeil/Lehrer newshour" [J. Baker; transcript of program, July 19, 1989] *Department of State Bulletin* 89:66-9 S '89
Stalin blew it . . . but Gorbachev may not. M. S. Forbes, Jr. il *Forbes* 144:27 D 11 '89
Tailoring a policy to new realities. L. Lief. il *U.S. News & World Report* 106:38 Mr 27 '89
Vic Damone in Eastern Europe. J. Klein. il por map *New York* 22:24-5 N 27 '89
Vigilance [address, September 7, 1989] E. L. Rowny. *Vital Speeches of the Day* 56:73-6 N 15 '89

Egypt
See also
Mubarak, Hosni—Visits to the United States, 1989
The folly of absent-minded imperialism. F. Ajami. il *U.S. News & World Report* 106:44 Ap 10 '89

El Salvador
See also
Cristiani, Alfredo—Visit to the United States, 1989
Quayle, Dan—Visit to El Salvador, 1989
U.S. Committee in Solidarity with the People of El Salvador
Bush wades into his first quagmire [election proposal from Marxist rebels] il *U.S. News & World Report* 106:12 F 6 '89
Can benign neglect solve El Salvador's problems? D. Farah. il *U.S. News & World Report* 107:59-60 N 6 '89
Compromise or lose. R. E. White. *Commonweal* 116:390-1 Jl 14 '89
A democratic revolution for El Salvador. J. Villalobos. *Foreign Policy* 74:103-22 Spr '89
El Salvador [discussion of May 1989 article, The deal in Central America] E. Abrams. *Commentary* 88:8-9 S '89
El Salvador: keep your eye on the ball. *National Review* 41:13-14 D 22 '89
For Bush, Central America won't be a crusade. S. Baker and others. il *Business Week* p50 Ja 16 '89
Guerrilla tactics [FMLN offers to participate in electoral process] S. MacLeod. il *Time* 133:47 F 6 '89
Listening to the voices from El Salvador. *America* 160:315-16 Ap 8 '89
Presidential election held in El Salvador [White House statement, March 22, 1989] *Department of State Bulletin* 89:84 My '89
Salvador's silver lining [FMLN offer to participate in electoral process] M. Kondracke. *The New Republic* 200:23-5 Mr 13 '89

Europe
See also
Bush, George, 1924——Visit to Europe, 1989
After the Wall. *The New Republic* 201:7-8 D 4 '89
Designing 'a new era' [with interview with G. Bush] T. M. DeFrank and A. McDaniel. il *Newsweek* 114:22-4 D 18 '89
An embarrassment of riches. J. O'Sullivan. *National Review* 41:8 D 31 '89
Europe in the post-Yalta era [cover story] D. Singer. il *The Nation* 249:701+ D 11 '89
The future of Europe [address, May 21, 1989] G. Bush. *Department of State Bulletin* 89:18-19 Jl '89
Pax Bush. B. Javetski and D. Harbrecht. il *Business Week* p40-1 D 18 '89
Peering into Europe's future. J. F. O. McAllister. il *Time* 134:25 D 25 '89
Proceed with caution. *National Review* 41:11-13 D 31 '89

Fiji
Fiji: a second Grenada? M. Stevenson. il *The American Spectator* 22:21-5 Jl '89

France
See also
Bush, George, 1924——Visit to France, 1989
Mitterrand, François, 1916——Visit to the United States, 1989

France—History
France & America: 1789-1989 [cover story; special section; with editorial comment by Byron Dobell] il *American Heritage* 40:5, 36-54+ Jl/Ag '89

Germany (West)
See also
Bush, George, 1924——Visit to Germany (West), 1989
Kohl, Helmut, 1930—Visits to the United States, 1988
Allies in dispute [West Germany calls for reducing short-range nuclear weapons] J. Bierman. il *Maclean's* 102:22 My 15 '89
Broken Axis [cover story] *The New Republic* 200:7-9 Je 5 '89
Bush's first foreign crisis [disagreement with West Germany over disarmament] il por *Newsweek* 113:16-18 My 8 '89
Calm down [West Germany and NATO] M. S. Forbes, Jr. il *Forbes* 143:27 My 29 '89
The invisible man [G. Bush's lack of foreign policy direction] *Commonweal* 116:291-2 My 19 '89
Is Bush losing the struggle for Europe's hearts and minds? B. Javetski and D. Griffiths. il *Business Week* p61 My 8 '89
The key to the alliance. M. B. Zuckerman. il *U.S. News & World Report* 106:83 Ja 30 '89

UNITED STATES—Foreign relations—Germany (West)—
cont.
The Kohl war [West German opposition to NATO disarmament strategy] *The New Republic* 200:7-8 My 22 '89
Learning to live with export controls [U.S. upset with lax attitude toward technology exports] L. Lief. il *U.S. News & World Report* 106:28 Ja 23 '89
A nasty spat among friends [U.S. opposition to West German demand for talks on reduction of short-range nuclear weapons] D. Brand. il *Time* 133:42 My 8 '89
Negotiate now, but carefully [call for short-range missile negotiations] *America* 160:499 My 27 '89
U.S. senators threaten troop cutback if West Germany blocks Lance upgrade [with editorial comment] P. A. Gilmartin. *Aviation Week & Space Technology* 130:7, 29 My 8 '89
The war inside NATO [U.S.-German conflict over proposed introduction of new nuclear missiles] D. Johnstone. il *The Progressive* 53:16-18 Ap '89
Why Kohl is right [call for U.S. and Soviet Union to negotiate on short-range nuclear weapons] S. Talbott. il por *Time* 133:26 My 15 '89

Great Britain
See also
Bush, George, 1924—Visit to Great Britain, 1989
Thatcher, Margaret—Visit to the United States, 1988
The bloody war in Belfast spills into the U.S. courts [IRA member J. Doherty in U.S. prison] T. Clifton. il por *Newsweek* 114:96+ D 11 '89

Grenada
Club-Med quickie. G. Krist. *The New Republic* 200:10-11 Ap 24 '89

Guatemala—History
Quetzal [1954 coup supported by the U.S.] L. H. Lapham. *Harper's* 278:8-10 F '89

Hungary
See also
Bush, George, 1924—Visit to Hungary, 1989
Grósz, Károly—Visit to the United States, 1988

Indochina
Cambodia and Vietnam: trapped in an eddy of history? [address, September 8, 1989] R. H. Solomon. por *Department of State Bulletin* 89:47-51 N '89

Iran
See also
Iran-contra affair
Iranian air disaster, 1988
Iranian seizure of United States embassy, 1979-1981
The bazaar is open [negotiations for hostages held in Lebanon] J. McDowell. il *Time* 134:23 Ag 21 '89
Beware bad deals at the bazaar [improved relations with Iran may ease hostage crisis] D. Gergen. il *U.S. News & World Report* 107:27 Ag 21 '89
Iran without Khomeini. M. Ledeen. il *The American Spectator* 22:12-13 Ag '89
Mixed signals [Lebanon hostage case] J. Bierman. il *Maclean's* 102:28-9 Ag 21 '89
Not again [dealing with death threats against U.S. hostages; cover story] R. Lacayo. il *Time* 134:14-20+ Ag 14 '89
Post-Khomeini Iran. S. T. Hunter. *Foreign Affairs* 68:133-49 Wint '89/'90
A standoff in Iran: Rafsanjani is too weak for a deal on the hostages. R. Watson. il por *Newsweek* 114:51-2 N 6 '89
Talk firmly and send the ships [special section; with editorial comment by Mortimer B. Zuckerman] B. Duffy. il *U.S. News & World Report* 107:22-6+, 72 Ag 14 '89
To deal or not to deal? [plan for hostages' release] H. Anderson. il *Newsweek* 114:26 Ag 21 '89
A voice of the Hizballah [interview with M. H. Fadlallah] W. Dowell. por *Time* 134:58-9 O 9 '89

Iraq
Tilting toward Baghdad. L. Lief. il *U.S. News & World Report* 106:24 My 22 '89

Ireland
See also
Haughey, Charles—Visit to the United States, 1989

Israel
See also
Shamir, Yitzhak—Visit to the United States, 1989
Altering the formula for Israel's friends. J. M. Wall. *The Christian Century* 106:4-5 Ja 4-11 '89
Israel's blank check [cover story] S. Zunes. il *The Progressive* 53:20-5 N '89
No sticks, no aspirins. B. Russett. *Commonweal* 116:336-7 Je 2 '89
Questions about U.S. support for Israel. *World Press Review* 36:26-7 Ap '89
'Realism' and human rights [U.S. report criticizes Israel's practices in the occupied territories] H. Anderson. il *Newsweek* 113:28 F 20 '89
Secretary meets with Israeli foreign minister [remarks, March 13, 1989] J. A. Baker; M. Arens. *Department of State Bulletin* 89:63 My '89
Ties that blind. *Commonweal* 116:547-8 O 20 '89

Italy
See also
Bush, George, 1924—Visit to Italy, 1989

Japan
See also
Bush, George, 1924—Visit to Japan, 1989
Kaifu, Toshiki—Visit to the United States, 1989
Takeshita, Noboru—Visit to the United States, 1989
United States—Diplomatic and consular service—Japan
Broken Axis [cover story] *The New Republic* 200:7-9 Je 5 '89
Burdensharing and Japan [statement; September 27, 1988] W. Clark, Jr. *Department of State Bulletin* 88:30-1 D '88
Does Japan play fair? [trade and defense issues divide U.S. and Japan] S. Manning. il *Scholastic Update (Teachers' edition)* 122:20-1 D 8 '89
Japan and the U.S.—the security agenda [reprint from November 1983 issue] D. B. H. Denoon. bibl f *Current History* 88:37-8+ Ja '89
The Japan-handlers. J. M. Fallows. il *The Atlantic* 264:14+ Ag '89
Let them defend themselves. J. M. Fallows. il *The Atlantic* 263:17-18+ Ap '89
Mourn Hirohito? W. F. Buckley. *National Review* 41:63 Ap 7 '89
'Pacific marriage' counseling. *World Press Review* 36:17 S '89
Terms of estrangement. R. C. Christopher. il *Newsweek* 113:21 F 27 '89
The U.S. and Japan: sharing our destinies. M. Mansfield. *Current (Washington, D.C.)* 316:27-33 O '89
The U.S. and Japan: sharing our destinies. M. Mansfield. *Foreign Affairs* 68:3-15 Spr '89
The U.S.-Japan military alliance. A. F. Geyer. *The Christian Century* 106:437-8 Ap 26 '89
U.S.-Japan relations [statement, October 13, 1988] W. Clark, Jr. *Department of State Bulletin* 88:27-30 D '88
The United States-Japan partnership [address, November 21, 1988] L. W. Beer. *Vital Speeches of the Day* 55:167-70 Ja 1 '89

Japan—History
A stormy friendship. S. Manning. il *Scholastic Update (Teachers' edition)* 122:14-15 D 8 '89

Jordan
See also
Hussein, King of Jordan, 1935—Visit to the United States, 1989

Korea—History
See also
Korean War, 1950-1953—American participation

Korea (North)
U.S. review of relations with the Democratic People's Republic of Korea [State Dept. statement, October 31, 1988] *Department of State Bulletin* 89:17 Ja '89

Korea (North)—History
See also
Pueblo incident, 1968

Korea (South)
See also
Bush, George, 1924—Visit to Korea (South), 1989
Roh, Tae Woo—Visit to the United States, 1989
United States—Diplomatic and consular service—Korea (South)
South Korea only wants a little respect. J. M. Fallows. il *U.S. News & World Report* 107:38+ Ag 14 '89
U.S. relations with Korea. *Department of State Bulletin* 89:30-1 O '89

Latin America
See also
Congress of the New World
Quayle, Dan—Visit to Latin America, 1989
Baker's bipartisan point man [B. Aronson] D. Waller. il por *Newsweek* 113:40 Mr 20 '89
Commitment to democracy and economic progress in Latin America [address, May 2, 1989] G. Bush. il por *Department of State Bulletin* 89:1-2 Je '89
Hemispheric bigthink. H. Hertzberg. *The New Republic* 200:4+ Mr 13 '89
A letter to Mr. Baker. il *America* 161:335-6 N 18 '89
Policy circles [nomination of B. Aronson as Assistant Secretary of State] G. Black. *The Nation* 248:256-7 F 27 '89
The right stuff [B. Aronson proposed as Asst. Secretary of State] *The New Republic* 200:9-10 F 27 '89
Spitting distance. G. Black. *The Nation* 248:5 Ja 2 '89
The U.S. and Latin America: a lost decade? M. D. Hayes. *Foreign Affairs* 68 Special Issue:180-98 ['89]
U.S. and Latin America: a shared destiny [address; with text of question and answer session, May 1, 1989] J. A. Baker, III. *Department of State Bulletin* 89:5-8 Je '89
Uncle Sam, stay home [adaptation of address, May 1988] C. Fuentes. *Harper's* 278:14-17 Ja '89
The United States and South America: the challenge of fragile democracy. H. J. Wiarda and I. S. Wiarda. bibl f *Current History* 88:113-16+ Mr '89

Latin America—History
Notes and comment [CIA interference in Latin American politics] *The New Yorker* 65:25-6 Jl 3 '89

UNITED STATES—Foreign relations—Lebanon

Lebanon

See also

United States—Diplomatic and consular service—Lebanon

Lebanon: at the crossroads [address, October 29, 1988] R. W. Murphy. *Department of State Bulletin* 88:45-7 D '88

Lesotho

See also

Moshoeshoe II, King of Lesotho, 1938——Visit to the United States, 1989

Libya

See also

Libyan-American conflict, 1986

Chemical reaction [U.S. fighters shoot down Libyan MiGs] E. Magnuson. il por *Time* 133:18-21 Ja 16 '89

Gunning for Gadhafi [U.S. shoots down two jets and claims Libya will soon make chemical weapons] J. Bierman. il *Maclean's* 102:18-19 Ja 16 '89

Hypocritical warfare [downing of Libyan MiGs and controversy over alleged chemical weapons plant] *The Nation* 248:73 Ja 23 '89

Libya [U.S. downing of two Libyan MiG-23s over the Mediterranean] *Business Week* p50 Ja 16 '89

Libyan planes downed [Defense Dept. statement, January 4, 1989] *Department of State Bulletin* 89:70 Mr '89

Libyan planes fall, questions rise. *America* 160:27 Ja 21 '89

Showdown with Libya [cover story; special section] il por *Newsweek* 113:16-25 Ja 16 '89

Text deploring downing of Libyan planes vetoed in Security Council: United States calls it 'self-defence'. il *UN Chronicle* 26:33 Je '89

U.S. F-14s down Libyan MiG-23s in dogfight over Mediterranean. B. M. Greeley, Jr. il map *Aviation Week & Space Technology* 130:20-1 Ja 9 '89

U.S. reports to United Nations on downing of Libyan planes [letter and statement, January 4-5, 1989] H. S. Okun. *Department of State Bulletin* 89:90-1 Mr '89

The U.S. vs. Libya. *World Press Review* 36:8 F '89

Mali

See also

Traore, Moussa—Visit to the United States, 1988

Mexico

See also

Shultz, George Pratt, 1920——Visit to Mexico, 1988

United States—Diplomatic and consular service—Mexico

Bordering on friends [interview with J. Castañeda] A. Dabrowski. il por *Time* 134:56-8 Ag 7 '89

A 'godfather' behind bars in the nick of time [arrest of drug trafficker F. Gallardo] M. Miller. il por *Newsweek* 113:55 Ap 24 '89

Sniping across a friendly border. il *U.S. News & World Report* 106:62 Mr 20 '89

U.S.-Mexico Binational Commission meets in Mexico City [statement, news conference, and text of joint communique, August 7, 1989] J. A. Baker, III. il por *Department of State Bulletin* 89:76-84 O '89

U.S.-Mexico relations. il map *Department of State Bulletin* 89:73-6 Jl '89

A vote of confidence. L. Meyer. il *World Press Review* 36:64 Ja '89

Middle East

See also

United States—Foreign relations—Persian Gulf region

Americans neutral on Arab-Israeli conflict [survey by Shibley Telhami and Jon Krosnick] il *USA Today (Periodical)* 118:7 D '89

The Arafat shuffle. il *The New Republic* 200:9-10+ Ja 9-16 '89

Baker: sheepdog diplomacy? M. G. Warner. il *Newsweek* 113:40 Ap 17 '89

Baker takes a risky step to center stage in the Middle East. S. Reed. il *Business Week* p82 O 23 '89

Baker's 'useless' advice [peace plan] por *Newsweek* 113:42 Je 5 '89

Beat the devil [U.S. agrees to hold talks with the PLO] A. Cockburn. *The Nation* 248:6-7 Ja 2 '89

The challenge to Bush in the Middle East. il *The Progressive* 53:6-7 Ja '89

The changing American role in the Middle East. L. Binder. *Current History* 88:65-8+ F '89

The critical moment for peace. P. Mattar. *Foreign Policy* 76:141-59 Fall '89

Enemies of peace [America's Mideast plan] M. Kondracke. *The New Republic* 201:14-15 Ag 7-14 '89

A false start in the Middle East [J. A. Baker's speech] E. V. Rostow. *Commentary* 88:24-7 O '89

First steps toward a policy [J. Baker's strategy] M. Kramer. il por *Time* 133:41 Mr 27 '89

Hands off by the superpowers. R. Fisk. il *World Press Review* 36:26-7 O '89

Is the West Bank a vital American interest? [cover story] D. Pipes. *Commentary* 88:19-24 N '89

Middle East [U.S. opens dialogue with PLO; statements and press conferences, November 26-December 18, 1988; special section] *Department of State Bulletin* 89:51-60 F '89

Middle East opportunities. G. Kemp. *Foreign Affairs* 68 Special Issue:139-58 ['89]

Much has changed [need to negotiate with PLO] *The Nation* 248:435-6 Ap 3 '89

Notes and comment [U.S. meetings with PLO in Tunis] *The New Yorker* 65:33-4 Ap 10 '89

The Palestinians [U.S. refusal of visa to Y. Arafat] il *World Press Review* 36:8+ Ja '89

Peace later [J. A. Baker's role in Middle East negotiations] M. Kondracke. *The New Republic* 200:10-12 Mr 27 '89

Prescriptions for the Middle East. M. Morrison. *The American Spectator* 22:16-18 Ja '89

Principles and pragmatism [address, May 22, 1989] J. A. Baker, III. *Vital Speeches of the Day* 55:549-51 Jl 1 '89

Principles and pragmatism: American policy toward the Arab-Israeli conflict [address, May 22, 1989] J. A. Baker, III. *Department of State Bulletin* 89:24-7 Jl '89

The Reagan administration and the Middle East [reprint from February 1987 issue] R. E. Hunter. *Current History* 88:41+ Ja '89

Recent events in the Middle East [statement, September 19, 1989] J. H. Kelly. *Department of State Bulletin* 89:61-3 N '89

Regrets only [reaction to J. Baker's speech regarding Middle East peace plan] *The New Republic* 200:8 Je 19 '89

Sanctum of the strong. E. W. Said. il *The Nation* 249:48-50 Jl 10 '89

Secretary Baker's news briefing, Feb. 23, 1989. J. A. Baker, III. il *Department of State Bulletin* 89:1-4 My '89

Secretary's interview on "This week with David Brinkley" [denial of visa to Y. Arafat; interview with G. P. Shultz; transcript of program, December 4, 1988] *Department of State Bulletin* 89:7-9 F '89

Secretary's interview on "This week with David Brinkley" [J. A. Baker; transcript of program, April 9, 1989] *Department of State Bulletin* 89:12-14 Je '89

Setting Yasser straight [role of American R. E. Hauser in U.S. recognition of PLO] S. Weller. il pors *Ms.* 17:84 Mr '89

Straight talk from the U.S. [J. Baker presents plan for peace in Middle East] C. Ogden. il por *Time* 133:32 Je 5 '89

A talk with Arafat [cover story] R. O. Freedman. il *The New York Review of Books* 36:8+ Ap 13 '89

Tilling the rocky ground of Mideast peacemaking [Y. Shamir's U.S. visit] L. Lief. il por *U.S. News & World Report* 106:43 Ap 10 '89

True friends and false [J. Baker's speech] *Commonweal* 116:357 Je 16 '89

Turnabout [decision to open talks with PLO] *The Nation* 248:39-40 Ja 9-16 '89

U.S. diplomacy in the Middle East [statement, July 12, 1989] J. H. Kelly. *Department of State Bulletin* 89:44-5 O '89

Update on the situation in the Middle East [statement, October 13, 1988] R. W. Murphy. *Department of State Bulletin* 88:41-5 D '88

What America should say to Arafat. R. N. Perle. il por *U.S. News & World Report* 106:58-9 Mr 20 '89

Whose Palestine? [cover story; special section] il *World Press Review* 36:13-21 F '89

Willie L. Brown Jr. [advice to George Bush] W. L. Brown, Jr. *National Review* 41:24-5 F 10 '89

Zero-plus game: a strategy for the Middle East. J. B. Hehir. *Commonweal* 116:39-40 Ja 27 '89

Mozambique

Supporting the enemy in Mozambique [cover story] J. Wheeler. il *Conservative Digest* 15:34-5+ Mr/Ap '89

Netherlands

See also

Bush, George, 1924——Visit to the Netherlands, 1989

New Zealand

New Zealand takes on the U.S. [interview with D. Lange] M. Gawenda. il por *Time* 133:45 My 8 '89

U.S.-New Zealand revelations: some parting observations [address, April 12, 1989] P. M. Cleveland. *Department of State Bulletin* 89:45-8 Je '89

Nicaragua

Ballot blocks. R. Kagan. *The New Republic* 200:21-2 Je 12 '89

For Bush, Central America won't be a crusade. S. Baker and others. il *Business Week* p50 Ja 16 '89

How to keep pressure on the Sandinistas. J. Bush. il *The American Spectator* 22:16-17 Jl '89

"I felt I had to draw the line" [George Bush meets with D. Ortega at Costa Rican summit] H. Sidey. il por *Time* 134:52 N 13 '89

Notes and comment [George Bush's reaction to D. Ortega's announcement ending ceasefire] *The New Yorker* 65:43-4 N 13 '89

Sending signals—or smoke? [D. Ortega] W. R. Doerner. il por *Time* 133:46 F 6 '89

U.S. restricts entry of Nicaraguan officials, employees [proclamation, October 22, 1988] R. Reagan. *Department of State Bulletin* 89:47 Ja '89

Upcoming elections in Nicaragua [statement, July 19, 1989] G. Bush. *Department of State Bulletin* 89:92 S '89

UNITED STATES—Foreign relations—Soviet Union—*cont.*
Caution can be wisdom—not weakness. C. W. Weinberger. il *Forbes* 144:31 D 11 '89

The challenge of change in U.S.-Soviet relations [address, May 4, 1989] J. A. Baker, III. *Department of State Bulletin* 89:36-9 Jl '89

Challenges ahead for NATO and developments in East-West relations [statement, June 20, 1989] J. A. Baker, III. *Department of State Bulletin* 89:61-4 Ag '89

Change in the Soviet Union [address, May 12, 1989] G. Bush. *Department of State Bulletin* 89:16-17 Jl '89

The cold war: a presidential agenda. S. F. Cohen. *Current (Washington, D.C.)* 311:32-8 Mr/Ap '89

Coming to America [B. Yeltsin] il por *Time* 134:36 S 25 '89

Containment's last gasp. P. H. Kreisberg. *Foreign Policy* 75:146-63 Summ '89

Credit where credit is due [global boom in peacemaking] S. Talbott. il *Time* 133:33 Ja 23 '89

The dangers beyond containment [cover story] P. Glynn. *Commentary* 88:15-22 Ag '89

Dateline USSR: on the human rights track. D. K. Shipler. *Foreign Policy* 75:164-81 Summ '89

Dead souls. *The Nation* 248:687-8 My 22 '89

Dealing warily with a sick Bear. D. Stanglin. il *U.S. News & World Report* 107:32+ S 25 '89

Dealing with the new Moscow. P. M. Jones. il *Scholastic Update (Teachers' edition)* 121:24-5 My 5 '89

Detente is not enough. S. M. Rogov. *Foreign Policy* 74:86-102 Spr '89

Did Reagan betray the conservatives? Y. Cuau. *World Press Review* 36:28 Ja '89

A distant thunder on the right: conservatives regroup in the age of *glasnost*. E. Salholz. il *Newsweek* 114:25 D 18 '89

Distrust, but verify [views of R. M. Gates] F. Barnes. *The New Republic* 200:12-13 Mr 6 '89

Do-nothing détente [cover story] G. J. Church. il *Time* 133:22-6 My 15 '89

Earthquake in the Soviet Union [White House statement, December 8, 1988] *Department of State Bulletin* 89:39 F '89

Easy does it. W. F. Buckley. *National Review* 41:62-3 S 15 '89

The end of discussion. *The New Republic* 201:7-8 N 20 '89

End of the Marxist epoch. D. P. Moynihan. il *The New Leader* 72:9-11 Ja 23 '89

Ending the cold war. M. Mandelbaum. bibl f *Foreign Affairs* 68:16-36 Spr '89

Enough rope. J. E. Mueller. *The New Republic* 201:14-16 Jl 3 '89

Fresh air, fresh ideas [visit of E. Shevardnadze] G. J. Church. il por *Time* 134:24 O 2 '89

From cold war to odd couple [friendship of W. J. Crowe and S. Akhromeyev] J. Barry. il pors *Newsweek* 114:42 Jl 31 '89

The future of communism. R. K. Dornan. il *Conservative Digest* 15:12-15 S/O '89

Giving Gorbachev a boost: Soviet reform is in the U.S. national interest. R. Holbrooke. il *Newsweek* 114:28 S 25 '89

Glasnostrums. J. Muravchik. *The New Republic* 200:16-18 Ja 30 '89

Global security: approaching the year 2000. G. W. Rathjens. bibl f *Current History* 88:1-4+ Ja '89

Gorb-aid. *The New Republic* 201:7-8 O 16 '89

Gorbachev and the right. W. F. Buckley. *National Review* 41:54-5 Je 16 '89

Gorbachev's challenge to the West [address, April 11, 1989] E. W. Lefever. *Vital Speeches of the Day* 55:588-91 Jl 15 '89

Gorbachev's new thinking. D. Holloway. bibl f *Foreign Affairs* 68 Special Issue:66-81 ['89]

Gorbachev's strategy, and ours. E. N. Luttwak. *Commentary* 88:29-36 Jl '89

Helping Gorbachev discard a broken idea. R. N. Perle. il *U.S. News & World Report* 107:40 N 20 '89

How should the West respond? *America* 161:203 O 7 '89

How should the West respond. M. S. Forbes, Jr. il *Forbes* 143:27 My 1 '89

An icon of the cold war [G. Kennan] E. Thomas. il por *Newsweek* 113:34 Ap 17 '89

Inching ever closer together [Jackson Hole meeting between J. A. Baker and E. Shevardnadze] B. Javetski. il *Business Week* p40-1 O 9 '89

The invisible man [G. Bush's lack of foreign policy direction] *Commonweal* 116:291-2 My 19 '89

Is Bush bold enough to answer Gorbachev? W. Greider. il *Rolling Stone* p48+ F 9 '89

Is the cold war over? R. J. Bresler. *USA Today (Periodical)* 118:7 Jl '89

Is the cold war really over? O. Harries. il *National Review* 41:40+ N 10 '89

Letter from Washington. E. Drew. *The New Yorker* 65:121-4+ N 27 '89

Lobbing one into the Kremlin [U.S. secret war plan] F. Tonello. *The Nation* 249:445-6 O 23 '89

Mock crisis, real players [U.S. and Soviet officials participate in televised crisis game] B. Van Voorst. il por *Time* 134:88 D 11 '89

Moscow on the HUD [involvement of S. R. Pierce in cooperative program with the Soviet Union; cover story] M. Hosenball. il *The New Republic* 201:18-21 O 23 '89

The need for new thinking. S. Talbott. *Time* 133:58 Ap 10 '89

A new global order? J. H. Wolfe. il *USA Today (Periodical)* 117:47 Mr '89

The new math. R. Wright. *The New Republic* 200:4 Ja 23 '89

The new United States-Soviet détente. C. D. Blacker. bibl f *Current History* 88:321-4+ O '89

News conference of September 19 [upcoming Wyoming meeting with Eduard Shevardnadze] J. A. Baker, III. *Department of State Bulletin* 89:39-43 N '89

Notes and comment. *The New Yorker* 65:37-8 O 2 '89

Notes and comment. *The New Yorker* 65:25-6 Mr 13 '89

Notes on the new political culture. F. Halliday. il *The Nation* 249:234-6+ S 4-11 '89

Out of the cold [excerpt] R. S. McNamara. il por *Newsweek* 114:35-6+ S 4 '89

The pacification of Ronald Reagan. G. W. Lapidus and A. Dallin. il *The Bulletin of the Atomic Scientists* 45:14-17 Ja/F '89

Peace (III). L. Wright. il *Rolling Stone* p152-3+ N 16 '89

Plastics. L. Wieseltier. *The New Republic* 200:4 Ja 2 '89

Points of mutual advantage [address, October 16, 1989] J. A. Baker, III. *Vital Speeches of the Day* 56:66-70 N 15 '89

The politics of diplomacy [meeting of J. Baker and E. Shevardnadze] H. Anderson. il *Newsweek* 114:20-1 O 2 '89

Prisoners of the past? [Bush administration suspicious of Soviet behavior] M. G. Warner. il *Newsweek* 113:38 Je 5 '89

The rapidly changing world [address, June 14, 1989] M. M. Kampelman. *Vital Speeches of the Day* 55:731-4 S 15 '89

Reciprocity at last. S. Talbott. il *Time* 134:40 D 11 '89

Red mischief. *The New Republic* 200:10-11 My 1 '89

Reflections on the cold war: end of the game, or end of an inning? P. Mann. il *Aviation Week & Space Technology* 131:18-19 D 18-25 '89

Rejecting cold war politics. P. Solo. il *The Progressive* 53:18-19 Ja '89

Reviving the U.S.-Soviet dialogue. D. Schorr. *The New Leader* 72:3-4 O 2-16 '89

Rolfing with Yeltsin [B. Yeltsin's U.S. visit] A. Heard. *The New Republic* 201:11-13 O 9 '89

The Russians are still there. W. F. Buckley. *National Review* 41:54-5 D 31 '89

Say a prayer for Gorbachev [G. Bush's relationship with the Communist world] H. Sidey. il pors *Time* 134:19 Ag 7 '89

Secretary meets with Soviet foreign minister [remarks and question-and-answer session, March 7, 1989] J. A. Baker, III. *Department of State Bulletin* 89:59-60 My '89

Should the U.S. help Gorbachev? R. M. Nixon. por *Time* 134:94 D 18 '89

The soldiers' summit [visit by Joint Chiefs of Staff chairman W. Crowe to Moscow] K. M. Campbell. bibl f *Foreign Policy* 75:76-91 Summ '89

The Soviet threat [discussion of November 1988 article, Is there still a Soviet threat?] A. M. Codevilla. *Commentary* 87:2+ Mr '89

Sparring partners [D. Quayle and J. A. Baker] M. Kondracke. *The New Republic* 201:14-16 N 13 '89

States, nations, and superpower diplomacy. J. H. Wolfe. il *USA Today (Periodical)* 117:51 My '89

Still out in the cold. *The Nation* 249:773 D 25 '89

The suave Gorbachev wears no clothes [cover story] M. Ledeen. il *The American Spectator* 22:16-17 F '89

Super power detente [address, June 16, 1989] C. R. Gharekhan. *Vital Speeches of the Day* 55:644-7 Ag 15 '89

The superpower 'love-in'. il *World Press Review* 36:80 D '89

Superpower relations. il *World Press Review* 36:6+ N '89

The superpowers start to act much more like partners. B. Javetski. il *Business Week* p67 S 25 '89

Thaw on the Bering Strait. J. Mettke. il *World Press Review* 36:58 Ja '89

'There is little question that real change is afoot' [interview with W. J. Crowe] il por *U.S. News & World Report* 107:80 Ag 28-S 4 '89

Those were the days. *The Nation* 249:369 O 9 '89

Toward better military manners [U.S.-Soviet Agreement on the Prevention of Dangerous Military Activities] W. J. Lanouette. il *The Bulletin of the Atomic Scientists* 45:8-9 D '89

Trying to control a runaway train. D. Stanglin. il *U.S. News & World Report* 107:24-6 D 18 '89

U.S., Soviet Union exchange New Year's messages [remarks, January 1, 1989] R. Reagan; M. Gorbachev. *Department of State Bulletin* 89:54-5 Mr '89

Vigilance [address, September 7, 1989] E. L. Rowny. *Vital Speeches of the Day* 56:73-6 N 15 '89

UNITED STATES—History—cont.
Civil War, 1861-1865—Campaigns and battles
See also
Antietam, Battle of, 1862
Antietam National Battlefield (Md.)
Atlanta Campaign, 1864
Gettysburg, Battle of, 1863
Gettysburg National Military Park (Pa.)
Manassas National Battlefield Park (Va.)
Spotsylvania, Battle of, 1864
Wilderness, Battle of the, 1864
Fighting for the past [preserving battlefields] T. A. Lewis. il map *Audubon* 91:56-72 S '89
Playing soldier [reenactments] H. Phillips. il *Travel Holiday* 172:106 Ag '89
Save or pave? [battlefields; cover story] R. M. Williams. il *Americana* 17:23-9 My/Je '89
Stonewall Jackson. J. B. Graves. il pors *Conservative Digest* 15:27-9+ Mr/Ap '89
A timely schedule of '89 Civil War events. D. J. Ernst. il *Petersen's Photographic Magazine* 18:28 Ag '89
Civil War, 1861-1865—Children
The children of Gettysburg. E. Daniels. il *American Heritage* 40:97-101+ My/Je '89
Civil War, 1861-1865—Literature
How the North nearly lost. J. M. McPherson. il *The New York Review of Books* 36:43-6 O 12 '89
Civil War, 1861-1865—Meteorological aspects
Civil War weather in Virginia. J. Iekel. bibl f il *Weatherwise* 42:268-73 O '89
Civil War, 1861-1865—Motion pictures
Guts and Glory: a forgotten Civil War story comes to film. M. Southgate. il *Essence* 20:30 D '89
Those 'Glory' days. R. Faulcon. il *American Visions* 4:24 D '89
Civil War, 1861-1865—Photographs and photography
The face of war. il *American History Illustrated* 24:48-9 S/O '89
Civil War, 1861-1865—Prisoners and prisons
1864 [Union prisoners escape from Libby Prison in Richmond, Va.] A. Nielsen. il *American Heritage* 40:36-7 F '89
Civil War, 1861-1865—Reporters and reporting
The Civil War's greatest scoop [account of Battle of Antietam by New York tribune correspondent G. W. Smalley] J. Weeks. il por *American Heritage* 40:100+ Jl/Ag '89
Civil War, 1861-1865—Songs and music—Confederate States
Homespun songs of the C.S.A. [tape of Confederate Army war songs by Bobby Horton] il *American Heritage* 40:122-3 S/O '89
20th century
A brush with history [cover story; special section; with editorial comment by Byron Dobell] il *American Heritage* 40:7, 47-52+ D '89
World War, 1914-1918
See World War, 1914-1918—United States
1933-1945
See also
New Deal, 1933-1939
1933-1945—Bibliography
Getting FDR's ear. A. M. Schlesinger. il *The New York Review of Books* 36:20-3 F 16 '89
1945-
He didn't like Ike [excerpt from Where the buck stops]; ed. by Margaret Truman. H. S. Truman. il pors *The New York Times Magazine* p40-2+ S 17 '89
Korean War, 1950-1953
See Korean War, 1950-1953—American participation
Anecdotes, facetiae, satire, etc.
Of many things [Dave Barry slept here] G. W. Hunt. *America* 161:2 Jl 1-8 '89
Bibliography
History bookshelf. See issues of American History Illustrated beginning September 1984
Historiography
The new historians recapture the flag. M. Kazin. il *The New York Times Book Review* 94:1+ Jl 2 '89
Photographs and photography
The American landscape [daguerreotypes] il *American History Illustrated* 24:28-9 S/O '89
Study and teaching
Reagan and historical memory [final televised remarks] *National Review* 41:11+ F 10 '89
Study and teaching—Aids and devices
Sight & sound. See issues of American History Illustrated beginning May 1987
Teaching religious liberty—the wrong way [Williamsburg Charter curriculum supplements] E. Doerr. il *The Humanist* 49:41-2 N/D '89
Textbooks
The "civics" of technology in history textbooks. J. L. Heilbron and D. J. Kevles. *The Education Digest* 55:42-4 S '89
Remember me not [research by Michael Graves and others] G. W. Bracey. il *Phi Delta Kappan* 70:407-8 Ja '89

Industrial policy
See Industry and state
Industries
See also
United States—Commerce
41st annual report on American industry [cover story; special issue] il *Forbes* 143:77-9+ Ja 9 '89
America still reigns in services. S. Nasar. il *Fortune* 119:64-6+ Je 5 '89
American free enterprise: shakeups or shakedowns? *America* 161:287-8 N 4 '89
Companies that compete best [cover story] B. Saporito. il *Fortune* 119:36-8+ My 22 '89
Competing by cooperating [address, May 9, 1989] A. H. Magazine. *Vital Speeches of the Day* 55:604-8 Jl 15 '89
The economy's landing gear may have a defect: manufacturing. J. C. Cooper and K. Madigan. il *Business Week* p23-4 S 4 '89
The excuse industry [explanations for lack of success in global competition] R. J. Samuelson. il *Newsweek* 114:74 D 11 '89
How to regain the productive edge [excerpts from MIT report Made in America] il *Fortune* 119:92-4+ My 22 '89
Idle smokestacks probably won't drag the economy down. J. C. Cooper and K. Madigan. il *Business Week* p37-8+ D 18 '89
Industry outlook: 1989 [cover story; special section] il *Business Week* p63-71+ Ja 9 '89
Manufacturing [address, April 6, 1989] C. H. Chandler. *Vital Speeches of the Day* 55:461-4 My 15 '89
MIT study confirms productivity slipping in key U.S. industries [Made in America report] *Aviation Week & Space Technology* 131:69-70 D 4 '89
Productivity [cover story; special section; with editorial comment by Jonathan Schlefer] il *Technology Review* 92:2, 27-40+ Ag/S '89
Promising industries for 1990. B. Dumaine. il *Fortune* 120 no10 Special Issue:151-2+ Fall '89
Regaining the productive edge (I). C. W. Weinberger. il *Forbes* 144:31 O 2 '89
Regaining the productive edge (II). C. W. Weinberger. il *Forbes* 144:31 O 16 '89
Revitalizing our economy: manufacturing is the key. J. J. Jasinowski. il *USA Today (Periodical)* 117:23-4 Ja '89
The sky is rising? [J. Rutledge and D. Allen's views in Rust to riches] P. Brimelow. il pors *Forbes* 144:156+ N 13 '89
Small business: an upbeat '89 [cover story] R. Thompson. il *Nation's Business* 77:10-12+ Ja '89
Toward a new industrial America [views of the M.I.T. Commission on Industrial Productivity] S. Berger and others. il map *Scientific American* 260:39-47 Je '89
The U.S. gets back in fighting shape. A. L. Taylor, III. il *Fortune* 119:42-5+ Ap 24 '89
Who will do well? C. Hutton and E. Prewitt. il *Fortune* 120:67-70 Jl 17 '89
Why smokestack America doesn't quake at the word 'recession'. M. Schroeder. il *Business Week* p100-1+ S 11 '89
Winners for slow times. S. Caminiti and others. il *Fortune* 119:60+ Ja 16 '89

Intellectual life
Educational misconceptions of a democratic public [views of A. Bloom and E. D. Hirsch] W. Feinberg. *The Education Digest* 55:7-10 O '89
Fraudulence II. R. E. Tyrrell. *The American Spectator* 22:10-11 Ap '89
Journey's beginning: a talk with Diana Trilling. S. Koch. il por *The New York Times Book Review* 94:1+ F 19 '89
Learning by story [work of E. D. Hirsch and A. Bloom] N. Postman. il *The Atlantic* 264:119-24 D '89
Life is imitation [education summit] R. E. Tyrrell. il *The American Spectator* 22:10 D '89
The opening of American minds [adaptation of address, January 1989] R. Rorty. *Harper's* 279:18-20+ Jl '89
The opening of the American mind [case for relativism over absolutes] A. M. Schlesinger. *The New York Times Book Review* 94:1+ Jl 23 '89

Labor policy
See also
Labor laws and regulations
United States. Dept. of Labor
Economic patriotism in a global economy [address, December 8, 1988] W. W. Winpisinger. *Vital Speeches of the Day* 55:220-2 Ja 15 '89
Parting shot: a labor leader blasts the Democrats. W. W. Winpisinger. il *The Progressive* 53:28-30 Jl '89

Languages
See also
English language
Spanish language in the United States
Medical policy
See Medical policy
Military history
When Johnny comes marching home. M. Barone. il *U.S. News & World Report* 107:30 D 11 '89

UNITED STATES—Military policy
Military policy
See also
Military assistance, American
Strategic Defense Initiative
United States—Defenses
United States. Dept. of Defense

Advice to the president: don't count on nuclear weapons. J. Wales and M. H. Halperin. il *The Bulletin of the Atomic Scientists* 45:7-8 Mr '89

America's Doomsday Project [preserving the government in the event of a first strike] S. Emerson. il *U.S. News & World Report* 107:26-31 Ag 7 '89

Are we underestimating America's future? K. E. House. il *Reader's Digest* 134:185-6+ My '89

Budget realities forcing tough strategic choices. J. D. Morrocco. il *Aviation Week & Space Technology* 130:49-51 Mr 20 '89

The defense dilemma [cover story] J. Barry and T. Morganthau. il *Newsweek* 113:12-18 Ja 23 '89

Defense investment strategy. W. J. Perry. *Foreign Affairs* 68:72-92 Spr '89

Defense strategy for the 1990's. R. J. Bresler. il *USA Today (Periodical)* 117:7 Ja '89

A design, but is it grand? [awaiting G. Bush's policy review] H. Trewhitt. il *U.S. News & World Report* 106:42-4 My 1 '89

Divided over defense. T. Bethell. *The American Spectator* 22:11-13 O '89

Do nuclear weapons matter? [views of M. Bundy] S. Hoffmann. bibl f il *The New York Review of Books* 36:28-31 F 2 '89

'Do nuclear weapons matter?': an exchange [discussion of February 2, 1989 article] S. Hoffmann. il *The New York Review of Books* 36:57-8 Ap 27 '89

Does America need an army? [cover story; special section] il map *U.S. News & World Report* 107:22-5+ D 11 '89

Economic and military security [address, February 22, 1989] P. M. Kennedy. *Vital Speeches of the Day* 55:594-7 Jl 15 '89

Economic growth and military power: erosion of the superpowers. W. Goldstein. *Current (Washington, D.C.)* 309:23-31 Ja '89

Economics and national security [address, December 12, 1988] C. L. Powell. *Vital Speeches of the Day* 55:194-7 Ja 15 '89

The edge of might [low-intensity conflicts] P. Kornbluh. *Omni (New York, N.Y.)* 11:46 Ja '89

Ending a common danger. M. Bundy. *The New York Times Magazine* p54-6+ Ag 20 '89

From cold war to odd couple [friendship of W. J. Crowe and S. Akhromeyev] J. Barry. il pors *Newsweek* 114:42 Jl 31 '89

George Bush moves in. J. D. Isaacs. il *The Bulletin of the Atomic Scientists* 45:3-4 Ja/F '89

How not to make a defense budget [strategic planning missing] P. Cary. il *U.S. News & World Report* 107:20 O 9 '89

Indefensible [cover story; special section] il *The Atlantic* 263:33-7+ Je '89

Let's make a deal. J. D. Isaacs. il *The Bulletin of the Atomic Scientists* 45:3 Je '89

Lobbing one into the Kremlin [U.S. secret war plan] F. Tonello. *The Nation* 249:445-6 O 23 '89

Man the pumps! C. W. Weinberger. il *Forbes* 143:31 My 1 '89

The military: tough choices in a changing world [cover story; special issue] il maps *Scholastic Update (Teachers' edition)* 122:1-23 O 6 '89

The next war. *The New Republic* 200:7-8 F 13 '89

Non-offensive defense. M. Dregni. il *Utne Reader* p12-13 Ja/F '89

Out of the cold [excerpt] R. S. McNamara. il por *Newsweek* 114:35-6+ S 4 '89

An overview of U.S. arms control objectives [statement, October 18, 1988] W. F. Burns. *Department of State Bulletin* 89:41-4 Ja '89

The pistol on the mantel [nuclear deterrence] M. B. Zuckerman. il *U.S. News & World Report* 106:78 Je 26 '89

Reagan's security legacy [cover story; special issue; with editorial comment by Len Ackland] bibl f il pors *The Bulletin of the Atomic Scientists* 45:2, 5-32+ Ja/F '89

Security strategy for the 1990s [address, May 24, 1989] G. Bush. *Department of State Bulletin* 89:19-21 Jl '89

The soldiers' summit [visit by Joint Chiefs of Staff chairman W. Crowe to Moscow] K. M. Campbell. bibl f *Foreign Policy* 75:76-91 Summ '89

The Soviet threat [discussion of November 1988 article; Is there still a Soviet threat?] A. M. Codevilla. *Commentary* 87:2+ Mr '89

Still out in the cold. *The Nation* 249:773 D 25 '89

Stopping the war against the third world [low intensity conflict; adaptation of address, September 1988] M. T. Klare. il *The Progressive* 53:14-16 Ja '89

Superpower sweepstakes. R. J. Samuelson. il *Newsweek* 113:43 F 20 '89

'There is little question that real change is afoot' [interview with W. J. Crowe] il por *U.S. News & World Report* 107:80 Ag 28-S 4 '89

Toward better military manners [U.S.-Soviet Agreement on the Prevention of Dangerous Military Activities] W. J. Lanouette. il *The Bulletin of the Atomic Scientists* 45:8-9 D '89

Tower says administration to link arms control stance, strategic goals. P. A. Gilmartin. *Aviation Week & Space Technology* 129:23 Mr 6 '89

U.S. missiles on hair trigger? G. E. Marsh. *The Bulletin of the Atomic Scientists* 45:3 My '89

Vigilance [address, September 7, 1989] E. L. Rowny. *Vital Speeches of the Day* 56:73-6 N 15 '89

What's unusable—and indispensable? [interview with M. Bundy] H. Trewhitt. il por *U.S. News & World Report* 106:43-4 Ja 9 '89

A Yankee in Gorbachev's court [tour by Joint Chiefs of Staff chairman W. J. Crowe] S. Talbott. il por *Time* 134:32 Jl 3 '89

Bibliography
Can the US remain number one? [cover story] P. M. Kennedy. il *The New York Review of Books* 36:36-42 Mr 16 '89
Monetary policy
See Federal Reserve System (U.S.); Money
Moral conditions
See also
Violence

America in the '80s was a kinder, gentler nation. R. Lacayo. il *People Weekly* 32 Special Issue:102-7 Fall '89

America's moral landscape in the fiction of Richard Ford. R. A. Schroth. por *The Christian Century* 106:227-30 Mr 1 '89

Calling Lyndon Johnson. *National Review* 41:13-14 My 5 '89

Cleaning up the dance halls [early 1900s] E. I. Perry. bibl il *History Today* 39:20-6 O '89

The decline of civility. R. J. Bresler. il *USA Today (Periodical)* 117:7 Mr '89

E.L. Doctorow [address, May 21, 1989] E. L. Doctorow. il *The Nation* 249:349+ O 2 '89

Habits of the hearth [interview with R. Bellah] R. Clapp. il pors *Christianity Today* 33:20-4 F 3 '89

If communism fails, do we win? C. W. Colson. il *Christianity Today* 33:64 O 6 '89

In praise of censure. G. Wills. il *Time* 134:71-2 Jl 31 '89

Inspectors general. L. H. Lapham. *Harper's* 279:12-15 Jl '89

Integrity [address, March 13, 1989] R. W. Roskens. *Vital Speeches of the Day* 55:511-12 Je 1 '89

Is greed dead? R. Henkoff. il *Fortune* 120:40-3+ Ag 14 '89

Is society morally bankrupt? [results of poll] I. Groller. il *Parents* 64:35 Je '89

Media and morality in the twenties. J. D. Stevens. bibl il *History Today* 39:25-9 N '89

Moral obtuseness in America [TV series Ethics in America] H. Arkes. il *National Review* 41:33-6 Je 16 '89

Morality vs. moralism [address, January 26, 1989] P. B. Henry. *Vital Speeches of the Day* 55:295-7 Mr 1 '89

National character is decisive [address, April 27, 1989] A. Harrigan. *Vital Speeches of the Day* 55:507-11 Je 1 '89

Of many things [TV series Ethics in America] J. W. Donohue. *America* 160:2 Ja 7-14 '89

A penny for your values. M. G. Maudlin. *Christianity Today* 33:17 Je 16 '89

Perhaps the majority isn't so moral after all. R. E. Burns. *U.S. Catholic* 54:2 Ja '89

What are our real values? N. Fox. por *Newsweek* 113:8 F 13 '89

Why "safe" is not enough. H. Smith. *Christianity Today* 33:15 F 3 '89

Morale, National
See Morale, National
National parks and reserves
See National parks and reserves
Naval history
See also
World War, 1939-1945—Naval operations
Stephen Decatur. J. B. Graves. il por *Conservative Digest* 15:31-5 My/Je '89
Politics and government
See also
Black suffrage
Blacks—Political activities
Bureaucracy
Business—Political aspects
Communist Party (U.S.)
Conservatism
Decentralization in government
Democratic Party (U.S.)
Elections
Federal and state relations
Government and the press
Green Party (U.S.)
Labor unions—Political activities
Legislation
Liberalism
Lobbyists and lobbying
Local government
Political attitudes
Political campaigns

UNITED STATES—Politics and government—*cont.*
Bibliography
Life at court [R. Reagan administration] J. Didion. il *The New York Review of Books* 36:3-4+ D 21 '89
History
See United States—History
Popular culture
Get smart [pseudo-intellectualism] C. Peacock. il *Utne Reader* p16+ My/Je '89
The hot issue [cover story; special issue] il *Rolling Stone* p51-4+ My 18 '89
How high the brow? [views of L. W. Levine] D. Gates. il *Newsweek* 113:51 F 20 '89
Hunger for the marvelous: the vampire craze in the computer age [cover story] K. M. Ramsland. il *Psychology Today* 23:31-5 N '89
The irony epidemic: the dark side of Fiestaware and the Flintstones. P. Rudnick and K. Andersen. il *Utne Reader* p34-40 My/Je '89
Pop culture, auto-canonized. J. Freedman. *Harper's* 278:31-2+ Ja '89
The role of business in educational reform [address, December 8, 1988] V. R. Ruggiero. *Vital Speeches of the Day* 55:286-8 F 15 '89
Population
See also
Baby boom generation
Baby bust generation
Immigrants
Immigration and emigration
Migration, Internal
Minorities
Population forecasting
United States—Census
The changing face of a restless nation. J. Carey. il maps *Business Week* p92-5+ S 25 '89
Where the boys are: proportion of the 18-to-44 age group that is male, by county. B. Edmondson and B. Cutler. map *The Atlantic* 263:67 F '89
Public buildings
See Public buildings
Public opinion
See Public opinion
Race relations
See also
Church and race relations
"The American dilemma has not been solved" [A common destiny: blacks and American society report] D. M. Watts. il *Black Enterprise* 20:26 O '89
An American dilemma revisited [report A common destiny: blacks and American society] *U.S. News & World Report* 107:8-9 Ag 7 '89
Anti-racist skinheads ready to strike back at neo-Nazis. C. Gunderson. *Utne Reader* p88-9 My/Je '89
Are equal rights only a dream? M. Schwelien. il *World Press Review* 36:32-4 My '89
Barbara Bush discusses racism, poverty in Ebony. il pors *Jet* 76:22 Ag 28 '89
Barbara Bush speaks out [cover story] L. B. Randolph. il pors *Ebony* 44:52-4+ S '89
Being black and feeling blue. S. Steele. *The American Scholar* 58:497-508 Aut '89
The biggest secret of race relations: the new white minority. il *Ebony* 44:84+ Ap '89
Black progress 'stagnant' since '70s, report says [A common destiny: blacks and American society] il *Jet* 76:28-9 Ag 14 '89
The crisis of caste. C. V. Woodward. il *The New Republic* 201:38+ N 6 '89
Crossing the color line [black leaders campaign for white votes] G. Borger. il *U.S. News & World Report* 107:22-4 N 6 '89
Divided we fell: race and the '88 election. J. Williams. il pors *American Visions* 4:31+ F '89
Doing the right thing(s). N. Mills. *Commonweal* 116:488-9 S 22 '89
Don't bury my heart [discussion of May 22, 1989 article, What can the white man . . . say to the black woman?] A. Walker. *The Nation* 249:226 S 4-11 '89
The future of black men. W. Strickland. il *Essence* 20:50-2+ N '89
Gottwald's cap. *Commonweal* 116:67-8 F 10 '89
Guess we'll give it one more try. R. Rosenblatt. il *U.S. News & World Report* 106:8-9 Ja 30 '89
Harping on racism. R. W. Wilkins. il *Mother Jones* 14:6-8 D '89
In Gandhi's footsteps [A. Gandhi] G. Cowley. il por *Newsweek* 113:48 Mr 6 '89
Inspired by his famous forebear, Mahatma Gandhi's grandson takes a close look at racism in America [A. Gandhi] H. Shapiro. il pors *People Weekly* 31:257-8 Mr 6 '89
Is there a rising tide of racism? il *Jet* 76:16-18 O 2 '89
Jesse: election exposes growth of white voters. por *Jet* 77:18+ N 27 '89
Let's tear off their hoods. B. Bayh. por *Newsweek* 113:8 Ap 17 '89
New race relations poll reveals widely varying views of blacks, whites. *Jet* 77:12-13 N 13 '89

The new racism is the old power grab [cover story] W. B. Allen. il por *Conservative Digest* 15:16-21 Jl/Ag '89
Other victims in the Park: they are the 'invisible' blacks who are slandered by our mindless, sometimes racist generalities. M. Greenfield. il *Newsweek* 113:86 My 15 '89
Passages: 1989-2000 [address, January 30, 1989] V. Jordan. *Vital Speeches of the Day* 55:406-8 Ap 15 '89
The politics of race [New York City, Virginia, and Cleveland] H. Fineman. il *Newsweek* 114:32-4 N 6 '89
Prejudice, conflict, and ethnoviolence: a national dilemma. J. C. Weiss. il *USA Today (Periodical)* 117:27-9 My '89
Race: the issue [cover story] J. Klein. il *New York* 22:32-8 My 29 '89
Racism and blacks who've 'made it'. D. C. Lyons. il *Ebony* 44:112+ O '89
Racism and poverty [report A common destiny: blacks and American society] R. J. Samuelson. il *Newsweek* 114:46 Ag 7 '89
Racism: can we heal the wounds? [cover story; special issue] il *Scholastic Update (Teachers' edition)* 121:2-12+ Ap 7 '89
Scapegoating the black family [cover story; special issue; with editorial comment] il *The Nation* 249:111, 115-20+ Jl 24-31 '89
Scar tissue [racism as cause of drug use debunked] L. Wieseltier. *The New Republic* 200:18-20+ Je 5 '89
Talking it over. J. R. Whelan. il *Conservative Digest* 15:70 Jl/Ag '89
Toward a more perfect union of black and white Americans [Cardinal Joseph Ritter Award Essay Contest; cover story; special section; with editorial comment by George W. Hunt] il *America* 160:130, 134-49+ F 18 '89
True integration. W. Berry. il *Mother Jones* 14:16+ Je '89
Unfinished business [report A common destiny: blacks and American society] W. Shapiro. il *Time* 134:12-15 Ag 7 '89
What can the white man . . . say to the black woman? [address, April 8, 1989] A. Walker. il *The Nation* 248:691-2 My 22 '89
Willie Horton and me. A. Walton. il por *The New York Times Magazine* p52-3+ Ag 20 '89
Regulatory agencies
See Regulatory agencies
Religious institutions and affairs
See also
Amish
Assemblies of God
Baptists—United States
Buddhism—United States
Catholic Church—United States
Christians—United States
Church and state
Church of Christ, Scientist
Church of God
Church of God in Christ
Church of the Nazarene
Church Universal and Triumphant
Episcopal Church—United States
Evangelicalism
First African Baptist Church
Lutheran Church—United States
Mormons and Mormonism
Presbyterian Church—United States
Protestant churches—United States
Puritans and puritanism
Shakers
Unification Church
United Church of Christ
United Methodist Church
Zen Buddhism—United States
Mainline or mainstream? M. E. Marty. *The Christian Century* 106:1183 D 13 '89
Religious revival in American life [cover story; special section] bibl *Society* 26:27-66 Ja/F '89
So little change, so much difference [Andrew Greeley's Religious indicators 1940-1985] R. J. Neuhaus. *National Review* 41:20 Mr 24 '89
Tracking America's soul [interview with G. Gallup] T. K. Jones. il pors *Christianity Today* 33:22-5 N 17 '89
History
If it's not 'mainline,' what is it? M. E. Marty. *The Christian Century* 106:1031 N 8 '89
Sophisticated primitives then, primitive sophisticates now [adaptation of address; cover story] M. E. Marty. il *The Christian Century* 106:588-91 Je 7-14 '89
Tracing the mainline. M. E. Marty. *The Christian Century* 106:1159 D 6 '89
Science policy
See Science and state
Social conditions
See also
Blacks
Child welfare
Children
Crime and criminals
Divorce
Family

UNITED STATES—Social conditions—See also—*cont.*
   Homeless
   Labor
   Morale, National
   Poor
   Recreation
   Social change
   Social forecasting
   United States—Moral conditions
   Violence
   Youth
How America has run out of time [living at an accelerated pace; cover story] N. R. Gibbs. il *Time* 133:58-61+ Ap 24 '89
Rediscovering the rat race. R. J. Samuelson. il *Newsweek* 113:57 My 15 '89
What's it all about, Ralphie? Ralph Lauren and the New Traditionalism. B. Edmondson. il por *Utne Reader* p21-2 Jl/Ag '89
What's right with America? R. Reeves. il *New Choices for the Best Years* 29:64-9 Ap '89

          History
     See United States—Social history
       Social history
     See also
   Business depression, 1929-1939
   Slavery
   Women—History
The '80s [cover story] il *People Weekly* 32 Special Issue:10-13+ Fall '89
Lifestyle: having it all [1980s] A. Levine. il *U.S. News & World Report* 107:112-13 D 25 '89-Ja 1 '90
        Photographs and photography
Conscience: 1880-1920. R. Lacayo. il *Time* 134 Special Issue:22-5 Fall '89
John Vachon: a certain look [cover story] T. B. Morgan. il por *American Heritage* 40:94-109 F '89
Portraits of an era [19th century] il *American History Illustrated* 24:60-1 S/O '89
       Social life and customs
     See also
   Collective settlements
   Family reunions
   Social change
   Suburban life
Victoriana rules again. B. Kantrowitz. il *Newsweek* 113:60-1 Ja 16 '89

       Colonial period, ca. 1600-1775
     See also
   Old Sturbridge Village
   Plimoth Plantation, Inc.
   Williamsburg (Va.)
        19th century
When our ancestors became us. J. S. Gordon. il *American Heritage* 40:106-11+ D '89
      Anecdotes, facetiae, satire, etc.
Life in these United States. See issues of Reader's Digest
        Social policy
     See also
   Aged
   Child welfare
   Civil rights
   Day care—Federal aid
   Economic assistance, Domestic
   Medical policy
   Poor
   Public welfare
   Socially handicapped children
   United States. Office of Economic Opportunity
Bring back big spending. il *The New Republic* 200:7-8 Mr 27 '89
The coming of age of American social policy. D. P. Moynihan. il *USA Today (Periodical)* 118:76-8 N '89
Fighting or friendly? [101st Congress] N. Amidei. *Commonweal* 116:5-6 Ja 13 '89
Fighting poverty after Reagan. J. Walsh. il *The Nation* 248:336-9 Mr 13 '89
Flesh-and-blood priorities. il *Christianity Today* 33:18-19 Ja 13 '89
The free market has triumphed, but what about the losers? K. Pennar. il *Business Week* p178-9 S 25 '89
Functioning communities. C. A. Murray. *Current (Washington, D.C.)* 311:24-31 Mr/Ap '89
The generosity gap and other scandals. R. J. Neuhaus. *National Review* 41:44 Mr 10 '89
Grabbing the creative initiative: a new Democratic opportunity. E. M. Kennedy. por *USA Today (Periodical)* 118:35-7 Jl '89
The Great Society didn't fail. M. Burnham. il *The Nation* 249:122-4 Jl 24-31 '89
How we can win the war on poverty. J. Huey. il *Fortune* 119:124-8+ Ap 10 '89
A kinder, gentler agenda. D. Baldwin. il *Common Cause Magazine* 15:27-32 Ja/F '89
Lappé to world: start talking [excerpt from Rediscovering America's values] F. M. Lappé. *Utne Reader* p48 My/Je '89

Lawmakers return to fray. K. A. Lawton. il *Christianity Today* 33:46-7 S 8 '89
'Like kids in a candy store' [conservatives and big government] E. Clift. il *Newsweek* 114:20 Jl 10 '89
Look who's setting the House on fire [conservatives develop new social programs] D. Harbrecht. il por *Business Week* p94+ Ag 14 '89
Of many things [Ford Foundation's report entitled The common good: social welfare and the American future] J. W. Donohue. *America* 161:26 Jl 15-22 '89
Razing the liberal plantation [cover story; special section] *National Review* 41:27-32 N 10 '89
Reforming social welfare policy [Ford Foundation report] il *Children Today* 18:2-3 Jl/Ag '89
A small planet revisited [interview with F. M. Lappé] S. McInerney. il por *Country Journal* 16:7-8 S/O '89
Social engineering is becoming a bipartisan affair. B. J. Wattenberg. *U.S. News & World Report* 106:25 My 22 '89
Taking stock [excerpts from address, April 20, 1989] J. L. Norwood. *Monthly Labor Review* 112:2 My '89
Targeting the poor: new policy for the new poverty. R. H. Haveman. *Current (Washington, D.C.)* 310:11-19 F '89
The two black Americas [cover story] M. Kondracke. *The New Republic* 200:17-20 F 6 '89
The unfinished war (II) [L. Johnson, R. Nixon and the War on Poverty] N. Lemann. il *The Atlantic* 263:52-6+ Ja '89

         Statistics
     See also
   Economic indicators
   Statistical abstract of the United States
   United States—Census
Are you an "average" person? B. Cutler. *Reader's Digest* 135:189-90+ S '89
Profiles in numbers. S. Steele. il *Maclean's* 102:51 Jl 3 '89

        Study and teaching
     See United States—History—Study and teaching
      Territories and possessions
     See also
   American Samoa
   Pacific Islands (Trust Territory)
   Palau
   Puerto Rico
         Trade policy
     See United States—Commercial policy
        Treaties
Treaties: current actions. See issues of Department of State Bulletin
        Great Britain
     See also
   Treaty of Ghent (1814)
        Panama
     See also
   Panama Canal Treaties (1977)
        Soviet Union
     See also
   Strategic Arms Limitation Talks
        Urban policy
     See also
   Enterprise zones
   United States. Dept. of Housing and Urban Development
        Vital statistics
     See also
   Mortality
   United States—Census
UNITED STATES. ADMINISTRATION ON AGING
AoA funds 11 national aging resource centers. il *Aging* no359:37-8 '89
UNITED STATES. AIR FORCE
     See also
   Air bases
      Appropriations and expenditures
1990 defense budget [B-2 Stealth bomber; special section] il *Aviation Week & Space Technology* 131:22-4 Jl 31 '89
AMRAAM unsuccessful in key test launch; Congress cuts USAF missile programs. J. D. Morrocco. il *Aviation Week & Space Technology* 131:24-5 Ag 14 '89
Bipartisan opposition to B-2 grows despite release of new information. J. D. Morrocco. il *Aviation Week & Space Technology* 131:22-3 Jl 17 '89
Budget cuts, cost growth cloud F-16 plans for 1990s. D. F. Bond. *Aviation Week & Space Technology* 131:18-19 D 4 '89
Budget pressures forcing USAF to ease requirements for ATF [advanced tactical fighter] J. D. Morrocco. *Aviation Week & Space Technology* 131:23+ Ag 28 '89
Cheney endorses MX rail garrison, calls for few cuts in USAF budget. J. D. Morrocco. *Aviation Week & Space Technology* 130:22-3 Ap 24 '89
Close air support move in Congress might disrupt production of F-16. D. F. Bond and J. D. Morrocco. il *Aviation Week & Space Technology* 131:22-4 N 13 '89
Conferees approve substantial funding for ATF program, cut C-17 appropriations. P. A. Gilmartin. *Aviation Week & Space Technology* 131:33 N 20 '89

UNITED STATES. AIR FORCE — Appropriations and expenditures—*cont.*

Congress eases F-16 production curbs; Pentagon debates CAS responsibilities [close air support] D. F. Bond. *Aviation Week & Space Technology* 131:32 N 20 '89

Cost of building OTH-B radar in Alaska doubles. *Aviation Week & Space Technology* 131:27 N 13 '89

Defense Dept. plans CAS review; Congress seeks upgrades agreement [close air support] D. F. Bond. il *Aviation Week & Space Technology* 131:31-3 S 11 '89

House cuts funding for modernizing USAF's ICBM launch control centers. D. F. Bond. *Aviation Week & Space Technology* 131:69+ Ag 21 '89

House defense leader attacks Air Force plan to add $1.4 billion to B-1B program [L. Aspin] P. A. Gilmartin. *Aviation Week & Space Technology* 130:31 My 29 '89

Latest B-2 cost data spur mounting Hill opposition. D. F. Bond. il *Aviation Week & Space Technology* 131:20 Jl 3 '89

No-growth budget would force cuts in USAF tactical programs. P. A. Gilmartin. il *Aviation Week & Space Technology* 130:93+ F 20 '89

Stop B-1B bashing. *Aviation Week & Space Technology* 130:9 Ap 3 '89

USAF cuts vehicle design work on advanced launch system. B. A. Smith. *Aviation Week & Space Technology* 131:112 D 18-25 '89

USAF will begin full-scale development of new F-16 aircraft in fiscal 1990-91. P. A. Gilmartin. il *Aviation Week & Space Technology* 130:20 Ja 16 '89

What is the Air Force really worried about: national security or job security? G. Easterbrook. *The Washington Monthly* 21:18-20+ S '89

Blacks

Black gen. heads computer systems at Ohio air base [J. F. Phillips] il por *Jet* 75:36 Ja 30 '89

Forces in Europe

Importance of USAF modernization to grow following force reductions. J. D. Morrocco. il map *Aviation Week & Space Technology* 131:37+ O 30 '89

Forces in Germany (West)

Another spy scandal [case of Air Force Capt. J. V. Hirsch] *Newsweek* 114:28 Ag 14 '89

Flight restrictions prompt U.S. Air Force to reassess Lantirn training in Germany. J. D. Morrocco. map *Aviation Week & Space Technology* 131:26-7 O 16 '89

USAFE study likely to recommend against cutting low-level flights. K. F. Mordoff. il *Aviation Week & Space Technology* 130:95-6 Ja 2 '89

Forces in Korea (South)

Protests threaten to cripple USAF training operations [Koon-Ni gunnery range] J. D. Morrocco. il *Aviation Week & Space Technology* 130:239+ Je 12 '89

U.S. 7th Air Force shifts to all-F-16 fighter force. J. D. Morrocco. il map *Aviation Week & Space Technology* 130:229-30 Je 12 '89

Pilots

See Air pilots

Procurement

Air Force advisory board recommends increased emphasis on expendables [electronic warfare capabilities] *Aviation Week & Space Technology* 131:47+ S 11 '89

Air Force cannot meet 1989 launch schedule. E. H. Kolcum. il *Aviation Week & Space Technology* 130:21-2 Ja 23 '89

Air Force to retrofit KC-10s with air refueling pods [cover story] W. B. Scott. il *Aviation Week & Space Technology* 131:36-7+ N 13 '89

Air Force will buy low-rate B-2s under fixed-price incentive contracts. D. F. Bond. *Aviation Week & Space Technology* 131:26-7 Ag 7 '89

Bizjet Olympics [competition for tanker transport training system contract] W. Garvey. il *Flying* 116:76-9 F '89

Boeing told to solve Peace Shield problems [system for Saudi Arabia] D. Hughes. *Aviation Week & Space Technology* 131:114 D 18-25 '89

Eaton to propose $600 million modification to ALQ-161 system [B-1B] *Aviation Week & Space Technology* 130:75+ Je 26 '89

GAO advises Air Force to cancel Loral's advanced radar warning receiver contract [allegations of illegally receiving information about competing Litton system] *Aviation Week & Space Technology* 130:23 My 22 '89

GAO cites faulty test equipment for hampering EW system readiness [electronic warfare systems] B. D. Nordwall. il *Aviation Week & Space Technology* 131:133+ O 9 '89

Hughes official says Air Force rushed complex AMRAAM test [views of Malcolm R. Currie] *Aviation Week & Space Technology* 131:41 O 9 '89

Judge fines Rockwell $5.5 million for concealing Navstar double-billing. M. A. Dornheim. *Aviation Week & Space Technology* 130:24-5 Mr 13 '89

Judge grants motions filed by Northrop [lawsuit involving production of inertial measurement unit for MX missile] *Aviation Week & Space Technology* 130:74 Ja 9 '89

Litton gets share of ALR-56M program in Ill Wind plea agreement by Loral. D. F. Bond. *Aviation Week & Space Technology* 131:115 D 18-25 '89

Litton protest raises questions about new Loral operation [award for F-16 radar warning receivers] P. J. Klass. *Aviation Week & Space Technology* 130:57 F 6 '89

Loral to produce advanced radar warning systems for USAF. *Aviation Week & Space Technology* 130:34 Ja 2 '89

NASP program office retains two propulsion contractors [National Aerospace Plane] S. W. Kandebo. *Aviation Week & Space Technology* 130:19 My 8 '89

Navy, USAF to award contracts for limited ALQ-165 production [airborne self-protection jamming systems] il *Aviation Week & Space Technology* 131:89+ S 11 '89

New USAF contracts speed up aerospace component redesign. B. W. Henderson. *Aviation Week & Space Technology* 131:74 Ag 21 '89

The Pentagon's misguided missile [AMRAAM] P. Cary. il *U.S. News & World Report* 106:33-6 My 1 '89

Pratt & Whitney to supply 60% of Air Force's fighter engines. *Aviation Week & Space Technology* 130:32 Mr 13 '89

Pratt, General Electric to deliver ATF engines to Air Force by year-end [advanced tactical fighter] il *Aviation Week & Space Technology* 131:21 D 4 '89

Raytheon delivers production AMRAAM; competition expected to reduce costs [advanced medium-range air-to-air missile] *Aviation Week & Space Technology* 130:30 F 27 '89

Rockwell's loss on AC-130U estimated at $81 million [gunship program] *Aviation Week & Space Technology* 130:265 Mr 20 '89

Suit claims Northrop wrongfully took $20 billion for Stealth bomber work. B. A. Smith. *Aviation Week & Space Technology* 131:26-7 N 13 '89

Total quality management [address, November 29, 1988] B. P. Randolph. *Vital Speeches of the Day* 55:322-4 Mr 15 '89

Trainer aircraft at Le Bourget geared toward USAF/Navy buy [primary aircraft training system] C. Covault. il *Aviation Week & Space Technology* 130:67+ Je 26 '89

USAF extends SICBM contracts in face of test, budget hurdles. D. F. Bond. *Aviation Week & Space Technology* 130:23-4 Jl 10 '89

USAF plans no major changes to A-12 engines, airframe. *Aviation Week & Space Technology* 131:25 Ag 14 '89

USAF releases draft request for bids on tanker-transport training system. *Aviation Week & Space Technology* 130:31 Ap 3 '89

USAF says F-15E integration problems may delay initial operating capability [ALQ-135 jammer] P. A. Gilmartin. *Aviation Week & Space Technology* 130:21 My 15 '89

USAF seeks less risk in ATF avionics suite development [advanced tactical fighter] B. D. Nordwall. *Aviation Week & Space Technology* 130:21 Ja 30 '89

USAF tanker-transport training to stress low and high altitude mission profiles. E. H. Phillips. il *Aviation Week & Space Technology* 130:51-2 My 1 '89

USAF to accept plan on modifying F-16, A-10 for close air support. *Aviation Week & Space Technology* 130:28 Mr 13 '89

USAF to buy used Boeing 707s for use as Joint STARS platforms [Surveillance Target Attack Radar System] P. A. Gilmartin. *Aviation Week & Space Technology* 131:25 N 13 '89

USAF to introduce electronic warfare procurement changes. *Aviation Week & Space Technology* 131:49 S 11 '89

USAF urges GAO to reconsider criticism of Loral contract award [Litton protest of contract] B. W. Henderson. *Aviation Week & Space Technology* 130:31 Je 5 '89

USAF will develop major radar upgrade for its E-3 AWACS fleet. D. Hughes. il *Aviation Week & Space Technology* 130:45+ Ja 23 '89

USAF will use stand-alone radar warning system to shore up B-1B's EW capabilities. *Aviation Week & Space Technology* 130:101 Ja 2 '89

UNITED STATES. AIR FORCE. ASTRONAUTICS LABORATORY *See* Air Force Astronautics Laboratory (U.S.)

UNITED STATES. AIR FORCE. CIVIL RESERVE AIR FLEET *See* United States. Civil Reserve Air Fleet

UNITED STATES. AIR FORCE. FIBER OPTIC TECHNOLOGY CENTER *See* Fiber Optic Technology Center (U.S.)

UNITED STATES. AIR FORCE. MILITARY AIRLIFT COMMAND

Air Force selects Computer Sciences Corp. to develop information processing system [tracking Military Airlift Command aircraft] *Aviation Week & Space Technology* 130:51-2 Ja 23 '89

Lockheed weighs investment risks of developing new C-130 version. E. H. Kolcum. il *Aviation Week & Space Technology* 131:45+ N 27 '89

Pentagon pursues additional commitments from airlines to boost U.S. airlift capacity. *Aviation Week & Space Technology* 130:24 Ja 30 '89

UNITED STATES. AIR FORCE. SPACE DIVISION

Space labs solicit research by business. *High Technology Business* 9:35-6 F '89

UNITED STATES. AIR FORCE. STRATEGIC AIR COMMAND

Air Force grounds B-1B fleet following wing cycling problem. il *Aviation Week & Space Technology* 130:21-2 Ap 3 '89

UNITED STATES. AIR FORCE. STRATEGIC AIR COMMAND—*cont.*
Irresistible force [Stealth, B-52 and B-1 bombers; cover story] T. H. Cole. il *Popular Mechanics* 166:59-62 O '89

UNITED STATES. AIR FORCE. TACTICAL AIR COMMAND
USAF controllers, F-15 pilots train for combat using multiship simulation. S. W. Kandebo. il *Aviation Week & Space Technology* 130:71+ Mr 27 '89

UNITED STATES. AIR FORCE. TACTICAL AIR WARFARE CENTER See Tactical Air Warfare Center (U.S.)

UNITED STATES. AIR FORCE. UTAH TEST AND TRAINING RANGE
Planned Air Force electronic warfare range would be used to test B-2, ATF. il *Aviation Week & Space Technology* 131:58-9 S 11 '89

UNITED STATES. AIR FORCE. WARNER ROBINS AIR LOGISTICS CENTER See Warner Robins Air Logistics Center (U.S.)

UNITED STATES. AIR FORCE. WEAPONS LABORATORY See United States. Air Force Weapons Laboratory

UNITED STATES. AIR FORCE LOGISTICS COMMAND
Black gen. heads computer systems at Ohio air base [J. F. Phillips] il por *Jet* 75:36 Ja 30 '89
New USAF contracts speed up aerospace component redesign. B. W. Henderson. *Aviation Week & Space Technology* 131:74 Ag 21 '89
USAF expects robotic inspection facility to cut maintenance costs. B. W. Henderson. il *Aviation Week & Space Technology* 130:53-5+ Mr 13 '89

UNITED STATES. AIR FORCE WEAPONS LABORATORY
Air Force building high-resolution telescope for space defense research. T. M. Foley. il *Aviation Week & Space Technology* 129:47 Mr 6 '89
USAF conducts experiments with compact toroids for future space weapons. il *Aviation Week & Space Technology* 130:60+ My 15 '89

UNITED STATES. AIR FORCE WRIGHT AERONAUTICAL LABORATORIES See Air Force Wright Aeronautical Laboratories

UNITED STATES. AIR NATIONAL GUARD
Fairchild delivers first two C-26As to Air National Guard [cover story] C. A. Shifrin. il *Aviation Week & Space Technology* 130:36-7+ Ap 24 '89
LTV begins flight tests of reengined A-7F for Air Guard mission. D. A. Brown. il *Aviation Week & Space Technology* 131:19-21 D 4 '89

UNITED STATES. ARMY
Self-exiled after Vietnam, Army hero David Hackworth is finally coming home. P. Freeman. il pors *People Weekly* 31:52-4 Je 5 '89
The West Point story [excerpt from The long gray line; cover story] R. Atkinson. il pors *U.S. News & World Report* 107:44-54 O 9 '89

Appropriations and expenditures
Army aviation upgrade linked to strategic missile debate [Midgetman vs. MX rail-garrison concept] B. M. Greeley, Jr. il *Aviation Week & Space Technology* 130:67 Ap 24 '89
Army requests increased aircraft, missile funding. B. M. Greeley, Jr. il *Aviation Week & Space Technology* 130:18-19 Ja 16 '89
Budget cuts put pressure on Army aviators, industry [cover story] D. F. Bond. il *Aviation Week & Space Technology* 131:38-41 Jl 31 '89

Blacks
Breaking barriers. L. Eskin. il *Scholastic Update (Teachers' edition)* 122:20-1 O 6 '89
Breaking barriers in the barracks [C. L. Powell to head Joint Chiefs of Staff] P. Cary. il pors *U.S. News & World Report* 107:26-7 Ag 21 '89
Colin Powell gets fourth star and Georgia command. il pors *Jet* 76:4 Ap 17 '89
Court OKs re-enlistment of homosexual soldier [case of P. Watkins] il por *Jet* 76:18 My 22 '89
First in 200 years: black generals head military at Bush's inaugural ceremony. il por *Jet* 75:24-5 Ja 23 '89
Gen. Colin Powell's advice to young blacks today: prepare and be ready [cover story] il pors *Jet* 76:12-15 S 11 '89
Guts and Glory: a forgotten Civil War story comes to film. M. Southgate. il *Essence* 20:30 D '89
Reagan treated at Ft. Huachuca hospital black medics made famous in WW II. il *Jet* 76:52-4 Jl 31 '89
Should homosexuals be able to serve? [case of P. Watkins] L. Eskin. por *Scholastic Update (Teachers' edition)* 122:22 O 6 '89
The Union Army's fighting 54th [cover story] P. Finkelman. il *American Visions* 4:20-3+ D '89

Education
See also
United States Military Academy

Forces in Germany (West)
'The cold war isn't a light switch'. D. Pedersen. il *Newsweek* 114:32 D 11 '89
Pentagon streamlines Reforger exercise. *Aviation Week & Space Technology* 130:31 F 13 '89

Forces in Latin America
Drug war zone [Green Berets] P. Andreas. *The Nation* 249:704-5 D 11 '89

Forces in the Middle East
Years after a crash that killed 248 soldiers, families still seek answers [D. Phillips wants truth about Gander, Nfld. crash that killed son returning from Sinai peacekeeping mission] C. E. Cohen. il pors *People Weekly* 32:65-7 D 18 '89

Forces in the Philippines
A sense of foreboding in the Philippines [assassination of U.S. Army colonel N. Rowe] B. Duffy. il *U.S. News & World Report* 106:35-6 My 15 '89
Targeting a U.S. hero [New People's Army claims credit for murdering U.S. Army colonel N. Rowe] D. Waller and R. Vokey. il por *Newsweek* 113:42 My 1 '89

Helicopters
See Helicopters—Military use

Maneuvers
See Military maneuvers

Medical and sanitary affairs
See also
United States. Army Nurse Corps
Basic training [incidence of exercise-related injuries linked to fitness level in Army recruits; research by Bruce H. Jones] R. Flippen. il *American Health* 8:36 S '89

Procurement
Army reevaluates plans to procure helicopter total training system. il *Aviation Week & Space Technology* 130:265+ Je 12 '89
Army to broaden effort to develop extended-range interceptor. P. A. Gilmartin. il *Aviation Week & Space Technology* 131:30 O 16 '89
Army will equip its LHXs with AH-64 mast-mounted system. B. M. Greeley. il *Aviation Week & Space Technology* 130:25 Ap 17 '89
Boeing and Sikorsky near completion of U.S. Army special operations aircraft. S. W. Kandebo. il *Aviation Week & Space Technology* 131:53+ N 27 '89
Boeing rolls out MH-47E Special Operations helicopter. il *Aviation Week & Space Technology* 131:37 D 11 '89
GAO criticizes LHX program, claiming R&D work insufficient. M. A. Dornheim. il *Aviation Week & Space Technology* 130:22-4 Ja 30 '89
McDonnell Douglas/Bell team introduces its LHX concept [special section] il *Aviation Week & Space Technology* 129:56-9+ Mr 6 '89
New firm to enter modified Bell 206 in growing Army SCAT competition [Imagineering Systems enters competition for Single Contractor Aviation Training program] C. A. Shifrin. il *Aviation Week & Space Technology* 130:47+ Mr 27 '89
Pentagon board names Army to lead revamped ASAT program. *Aviation Week & Space Technology* 130:31 Ja 16 '89
Pentagon tests new Hellfire platforms as contractors analyze improvements [surface launches] D. F. Bond. il *Aviation Week & Space Technology* 131:32-3 N 6 '89
Raytheon team selected to develop ground-launched Tacit Rainbow. J. D. Morrocco. il *Aviation Week & Space Technology* 131:24-5 S 18 '89
SCAT players vie for Army prize [Single Contractor Aviation Training helicopter program] *Flying* 116:24 S '89
Schweizer, Enstrom join teams to bid for Army trainer work [helicopters] il *Aviation Week & Space Technology* 130:18-19 Ja 23 '89
Simulators play key role in LHX contractor selection [helicopter] B. W. Henderson. il *Aviation Week & Space Technology* 131:34-5+ N 27 '89
U.S. Army approves initial design phase of Longbow radar system for AH-64. D. F. Bond. il *Aviation Week & Space Technology* 131:27-8 Jl 31 '89
U.S. Army collaboration 'blueprint' could boost European LHX role [helicopter] D. F. Bond. il *Aviation Week & Space Technology* 131:25 O 16 '89
Whistleblowing on U.S. defense contractors is out of control [case of John M. Cockerham and Associates] J. M. Cockerham. por *Aviation Week & Space Technology* 130:99+ Ap 10 '89

Training camps
See Military training camps

Women
See Servicewomen

UNITED STATES. ARMY. CORPS OF ENGINEERS
Yahoos in the Yazoo. L. Williamson. il *Outdoor Life* 183:42+ Ap '89

UNITED STATES. ARMY. LABORATORY COMMAND See U.S. Army Laboratory Command

UNITED STATES. ARMY. SPECIAL FORCES
Drug war zone [Green Berets in Latin America] P. Andreas. *The Nation* 249:704-5 D 11 '89

UNITED STATES. ARMY NURSE CORPS
Nurse Corps chief [Brigadier General C. Adams-Ender] D. M. Cheers. il pors *Ebony* 44:64+ Je '89

UNITED STATES. ARMY RESERVE
The sad state of weekend warriors. L. Galtney. il *U.S. News & World Report* 107:28-30 S 25 '89

UNITED STATES. CONGRESS—Powers and duties—*cont.*
Former Defense secretaries advise Congress to lighten oversight role [study headed by Harold Brown and James Schlesinger] M. Mecham. *Aviation Week & Space Technology* 130:89-90 Ja 2 '89
The howl of congressional watchdogs [oversight probes] S. V. Roberts. il *U.S. News & World Report* 107:24-6 S 11 '89
Imperial conservatives? [stressing presidential powers in foreign affairs] S. T. Francis. *National Review* 41:37-8 Ag 4 '89
The least responsive branch. L. G. Crovitz. *Commentary* 87:38-41 Mr '89

Privileges and immunities
See also
Franking privilege
Above the law? J. Novack. il *Forbes* 143:250 My 29 '89
The quick fix [fixing of parking tickets for members of Congress] D. Gross. *The New Republic* 201:12+ O 16 '89

Rules and practice
Tame the budget beast. C. Cox. il por *Conservative Digest* 15:6-7+ Jl/Ag '89

Salaries
See Congressmen—Salaries, allowances, etc.

Term of members
See Congressmen—Term

Voting
Applying a scalpel to doctors' wallets [lowers Medicare reimbursements] il *U.S. News & World Report* 107:11 D 4 '89
Budget votes: neither yea nor nay [Pentagon] J. D. Isaacs. il *The Bulletin of the Atomic Scientists* 45:4-5 O '89
Cat scam [repeal of the Medicare Catastrophic Coverage Act] J. Weisberg. *The New Republic* 201:11-12 O 30 '89
Catastrophic politics [repeals catastrophic health insurance] *National Review* 41:12-13 N 24 '89
How one bill became law [welfare-reform bill] S. Manning. il *Scholastic Update (Teachers' edition)* 121:15-16 F 24 '89
Invitation to catastrophe [votes to rescind catastrophic health insurance] *Time* 134:33 O 16 '89
A victory for the haves? [votes to trim catastrophic health care due to uproar over income tax surcharge] E. Clift. il *Newsweek* 114:38 O 16 '89

UNITED STATES. CONGRESS (1ST: 1789-1791)
Bicentennial note [excerpts from The First Congress] il *Congressional Digest* 68:129-30 My '89
Congress has a birthday. A. McCarthy. *Commonweal* 116:203 Ap 7 '89
The month in Congress [excerpts from The First and 101st Congresses] *Congressional Digest* 68:97 Ap '89
Our nation's first Congress. I. Peck. il *Scholastic Update (Teachers' edition)* 121:18-19 F 24 '89
Portraits of Congress past [The first federal Congress at the National Portrait Gallery] K. M. Burke. il *Smithsonian* 19:196 Mr '89

UNITED STATES. CONGRESS (100TH: 1987-1988)
Clean Air and the 100th Congress. P. Byrnes. *Wilderness* 52:23 Wint '88
Recent action in the Congress:
Corporate mergers. *Congressional Digest* 68:71+ Mr '89
Occupational health legislation. *Congressional Digest* 68:103 Ap '89
Textile Trade Act. *Congressional Digest* 68:7+ Ja '89

UNITED STATES. CONGRESS (100TH, 1ST SESSION: 1987)
Recent action in the Congress [budget reform] il *Congressional Digest* 68:265+ N '89
Clean Air Act. *Congressional Digest* 68:40-1+ F '89

UNITED STATES. CONGRESS (100TH, 2ND SESSION: 1988)
100th Congress adds new parks. il *National Parks* 63:8-9 Ja/F '89
Wilderness wins and losses at year's end. *Wilderness* 52:4-5 Wint '88

UNITED STATES. CONGRESS (101ST: 1989-1990)
The month in Congress [excerpts from The First and 101st Congresses] *Congressional Digest* 68:97 Ap '89

UNITED STATES. CONGRESS (101ST, 1ST SESSION: 1989)
The 101st Congress at a glance [chart] il *Scholastic Update (Teachers' edition)* 121:5 F 24 '89
The 101st Congress can make history [environmental issues] J. D. Hair. il *International Wildlife* 19:26 Ja/F '89
101st Congress tackles park bills. *National Parks* 63:12-13 My/Je '89
. . . and on Capitol Hill [Democrats lack agenda] H. Gorey. il *Time* 134:23 S 25 '89
The Capitol gains of the well-to-do [Democratic Congress addresses tax cuts] M. Barone. il *U.S. News & World Report* 107:26-7+ O 2 '89
A Congress on the margins [excerpts from address] M. O. Hatfield. *Aviation Week & Space Technology* 131:9 S 4 '89
Congress slinks home. il *Newsweek* 114:62 D 4 '89
Fighting or friendly? N. Amidei. *Commonweal* 116:5-6 Ja 13 '89

Got those old Beltway blues. E. Clift. il *Newsweek* 113:38 My 29 '89
Lawmakers return to fray [domestic social issues] K. A. Lawton. il *Christianity Today* 33:46-7 S 8 '89
Letter from Washington. E. Drew. il *The New Yorker* 65:81-92 Ag 28 '89
Missing mandate. *National Review* 41:12-13 Mr 10 '89
Recent action in the Congress:
Americans with Disabilities Act. *Congressional Digest* 68:293 D '89
Flag burning issue. *Congressional Digest* 68:195+ Ag/S '89
Minimum wage. *Congressional Digest* 68:136+ My '89
Savings and loans. *Congressional Digest* 68:168-9+ Je/Jl '89
Science issues in the 101st Congress. N. Bell. *BioScience* 39:369 Je '89
The servants of the strong [political year saturated with dumbness] G. F. Will. il *Newsweek* 114:90 O 23 '89
A status report on Congress. D. C. Bacon. il *Nation's Business* 77:6+ Ag '89
To Congress, Bush looked like a pushover. D. Harbrecht and R. Fly. il *Business Week* p27-8 Ag 21 '89
Will business get the bill? [business issues] D. Harbrecht. il *Business Week* p28-9 Ja 16 '89

UNITED STATES. CONGRESS (101ST, 2ND SESSION: 1990)
Congress II. *National Review* 41:13 D 31 '89

UNITED STATES. CONGRESS. CONGRESSIONAL BUDGET OFFICE *See* United States. Congressional Budget Office

UNITED STATES. CONGRESS. HOUSE
See also
Congressmen
Beware the gerrymander, my son. J. H. Fund. il *National Review* 41:34-6 Ap 7 '89
A child care bill will pass as soon as the Democrats grow up. S. B. Garland. il *Business Week* p73 D 11 '89
Come to our census! [reapportionment of congressional seats after 1990 census] A. F. Lewis. *Ms.* 18:76 Jl/Ag '89
Congressional shell game [tricks for staying in office] P. Weyrich. il *Conservative Digest* 15:18-21+ Mr/Ap '89
Congressmen for life: the incumbency scandal. R. Evans and R. D. Novak. *Reader's Digest* 134:79-83 Je '89
Cracking the whip [minority whip N. Gingrich; cover story] T. Bethell. il *The American Spectator* 22:9-11 Ag '89
The Democrats' meltdown on the Hill. D. Harbrecht. il *Business Week* p25 Je 12 '89
The Democrats' success formula: they repeatedly win in conservative places by playing all the local angles. M. Barone. il *U.S. News & World Report* 106:23-4 Je 26 '89
The GOP feeding frenzy is far from over [ethics turmoil] D. Harbrecht. il por *Business Week* p36-7 Je 19 '89
Government by the timid [sense of security created by benefits of incumbency] W. Shapiro. il *Time* 133:37 F 20 '89
Gray takes historic step as first black majority whip. S. Booker. il por *Jet* 76:6+ Jl 3 '89
High noon for Newt [minority whip N. Gingrich; cover story] W. McGurn. il pors *National Review* 41:21-3 Ag 18 '89
House Republicans may be a House divided. D. Harbrecht. *Business Week* p43 Mr 27 '89
How many will fall? [resignation of majority whip T. Coelho and anticipated resignation of J. Wright] M. B. Carlson. il pors *Time* 133:34-5 Je 5 '89
The incumbent party, the party of incumbents [N. Gingrich's ethics drive against the Democrats] *National Review* 41:14-15 Je 30 '89
Let the great gerrymander war begin [effects of reapportionment after 1990 census] P. R. Range. il map *U.S. News & World Report* 106:29-30 F 20 '89
Letter from Washington [House Republicans] Cato. *National Review* 41:8 My 5 '89
Little big man [minority leader R. H. Michel] Z. Citron. *The New Republic* 200:12-14 F 27 '89
Look who's setting the House on fire [conservatives develop new social programs] D. Harbrecht. il por *Business Week* p94+ Ag 14 '89
Man for all seasons [views of R. A. Gephardt] M. Kondracke. *The New Republic* 201:12-14 Jl 3 '89
Master of disaster [minority whip N. Gingrich; cover story] D. Beers. il pors *Mother Jones* 14:28-9+ O '89
Musical chairs [Democratic leadership; cover story] F. Barnes. *The New Republic* 200:14-15 Je 12 '89
On the Hill, class war over taxes [Democratic plan to raise top rate] E. Clift and R. Thomas. il *Newsweek* 114:24 O 2 '89
One-man/one-vote Gingrich. W. F. Buckley. *National Review* 41:62 My 5 '89
The players to watch [Democratic leadership shakeup] *Newsweek* 113:21 Je 5 '89
Profiles [majority leader T. S. Foley] J. Newhouse. il por *The New Yorker* 65:48-50+ Ap 10 '89
Putting their House in order [R. Gephardt becomes majority leader and W. Gray becomes party whip] E. Salholz. il pors *Newsweek* 113:18 Je 26 '89

UNITED STATES. CONGRESS. HOUSE. COMMITTEE ON APPROPRIATIONS. SUBCOMMITTEE ON HUD-INDEPENDENT AGENCIES

House panel proposes $1-billion cut for NASA. M. Mecham. *Aviation Week & Space Technology* 131:26 Jl 17 '89

UNITED STATES. CONGRESS. HOUSE. COMMITTEE ON ARMED SERVICES

House panel rejects Bush defense budget, signaling trouble for B-2. P. A. Gilmartin. il *Aviation Week & Space Technology* 131:18-19 Jl 3 '89

Panel boosts conventional weapons spending, cuts strategic bomber funds. P. A. Gilmartin. *Aviation Week & Space Technology* 130:19-20 Jl 10 '89

Soviet military adviser addresses House panel [S. Akhromeyev] *Aviation Week & Space Technology* 131:26 Jl 31 '89

UNITED STATES. CONGRESS. HOUSE. COMMITTEE ON ARMED SERVICES. SUBCOMMITTEE ON PROCUREMENT AND MILITARY NUCLEAR SYSTEMS

House panel backs plan to cancel V-22, F-14D. P. A. Gilmartin and D. F. Bond. il *Aviation Week & Space Technology* 130:28-9 Je 26 '89

House defense leader attacks Air Force plan to add $1.4 billion to B-1B program [L. Aspin] P. A. Gilmartin. *Aviation Week & Space Technology* 130:31 My 29 '89

UNITED STATES. CONGRESS. HOUSE. COMMITTEE ON ENERGY AND COMMERCE

The baddest overseer on the Hill [J. D. Dingell] il por *U.S. News & World Report* 107:26 S 11 '89

The Kings of the Hills [contrasting MP D. Blenkarn of Canada with Congressman J. Dingell of the United States] il pors *Maclean's* 102:60-1 Jl 3 '89

UNITED STATES. CONGRESS. HOUSE. COMMITTEE ON ENERGY AND COMMERCE. SUBCOMMITTEE ON HEALTH AND THE ENVIRONMENT

Bush pulls a Clean-Air victory out of the air. V. Cahan and R. Fly. *Business Week* p43 O 2 '89

Mr. Clean's Air Act [interview with H. Waxman] J. Getlin. il pors *Sierra* 74:76-81 N/D '89

UNITED STATES. CONGRESS. HOUSE. COMMITTEE ON ENERGY AND COMMERCE. SUBCOMMITTEE ON OVERSIGHT AND INVESTIGATIONS

Bad cop [J. D. Dingell] F. Barnes. il *The New Republic* 201:10-12 O 23 '89

Conduct unbecoming? [D. Baltimore case] P. Weiss. il pors *The New York Times Magazine* p40-1+ O 29 '89

The Dingell probe finally goes public [D. Baltimore case] B. J. Culliton. *Science* 244:643-6+ My 12 '89

Dingell v. Baltimore. B. J. Culliton. pors *Science* 244:412-14 Ap 28 '89

Fraud debate aired on Capitol Hill [D. Baltimore case] K. Fackelmann. *Science News* 135:294-5 My 13 '89

Self-regulation of science: reflections on a day spent testifying at a congressional hearing. D. Baltimore. il por *Technology Review* 92:20+ Ag/S '89

Whose notes are they? [proposal to open scientists' personal data books to general scrutiny; Dingell hearings on D. Baltimore case] B. J. Culliton. il *Science* 244:765 My 19 '89

UNITED STATES. CONGRESS. HOUSE. COMMITTEE ON GOVERNMENT OPERATIONS

Military computer awards stalled; Conyers asks probe. por *Jet* 75:9 Mr 6 '89

Rep. Conyers slated for chair of House Committee. por *Jet* 75:8 Ja 23 '89

UNITED STATES. CONGRESS. HOUSE. COMMITTEE ON INTERIOR AND INSULAR AFFAIRS

The grand plans of Congressman Udall. J. A. Davis. il por *Sierra* 74:86-8+ My/Je '89

UNITED STATES. CONGRESS. HOUSE. COMMITTEE ON PUBLIC WORKS AND TRANSPORTATION. SUBCOMMITTEE ON AVIATION

Independent FAA, competition issues top new House chairman's agenda [J. L. Oberstar] M. Mecham. il por *Aviation Week & Space Technology* 130:99 F 13 '89

UNITED STATES. CONGRESS. HOUSE. COMMITTEE ON SCIENCE, SPACE, AND TECHNOLOGY

Another congressional look at fraud [Roe hearings] B. J. Culliton. *Science* 244:1538 Je 30 '89

Representative Roe rides to the rescue. B. J. Culliton. il por *Science* 245:24 Jl 7 '89

UNITED STATES. CONGRESS. HOUSE. COMMITTEE ON STANDARDS OF OFFICIAL CONDUCT

Bombshell in the House [Ethics Committee finds reason to believe J. Wright violated rules] G. J. Church. il por *Time* 133:33-4 My 1 '89

A cancer grows on the Speakership [allegations against J. Wright] G. Borger. il por *U.S. News & World Report* 106:20+ My 22 '89

A case of Wright and wrong. M. B. Carlson. il por *Time* 133:25 Ap 17 '89

Facing the music [Speaker of the House J. Wright] T. Morganthau. il por *Newsweek* 113:26-7 Ap 24 '89

In 'hip-deep water' [Speaker of the House J. Wright] R. Thomas. il por *Newsweek* 113:25-6 My 1 '89

Jim Wright: on the ropes. L. Martz. il por *Newsweek* 113:22-3 Ap 3 '89

Jim Wright's lonely fight. H. Mackenzie. il por *Maclean's* 102:24-5 My 1 '89

Judging Jim Wright. G. Borger. il por *U.S. News & World Report* 106:18-19 Ap 17 '89

The last stand of Speaker Jim Wright. G. Borger. il por *U.S. News & World Report* 106:27-8 Ap 24 '89

Mr. Wright's wrongs. W. McGurn. *National Review* 41:16 My 19 '89

The painful political trial of Speaker Wright. G. Borger. il *U.S. News & World Report* 106:31 My 1 '89

Ready for Wright: a GOP grudge match. E. Salholz. il por *Newsweek* 113:28 Mr 20 '89

Wright fights back. M. B. Carlson. il por *Time* 133:16-17 Ap 24 '89

UNITED STATES. CONGRESS. HOUSE. COMMITTEE ON UN-AMERICAN ACTIVITIES

Postscript on Lucy [L. Ball's testimony] *The Nation* 248:685 My 22 '89

UNITED STATES. CONGRESS. HOUSE. COMMITTEE ON WAYS AND MEANS

Gaining on a gains cut. *Newsweek* 114:34 S 25 '89

Rostenkowski adds a twist to the tax tango. H. Gleckman. il *Business Week* p61 Je 26 '89

Rostenkowski: 'My head is bloodied, but I'm not bowed'. D. Harbrecht. il por *Business Week* p31-2 S 18 '89

Takeovers: Congress comes out swinging a wet noodle. H. Gleckman. *Business Week* p29 Jl 24 '89

Urge your senators to act on campaign finance reform [vetoes proposal for consumer rebates from utilities] *Common Cause Magazine* 15:31 N/D '89

UNITED STATES. CONGRESS. HOUSE. COUNCIL OF BLACK ADMINISTRATIVE ASSISTANTS AND ASSOCIATES *See* Council of Black Administrative Assistants and Associates (U.S.)

UNITED STATES. CONGRESS. HOUSE. DEMOCRATIC CAUCUS *See* House Democratic Caucus (U.S.)

UNITED STATES. CONGRESS. HOUSE. ETHICS COMMITTEE *See* United States. Congress. House. Committee on Standards of Official Conduct

UNITED STATES. CONGRESS. HOUSE. SELECT COMMITTEE ON NARCOTICS ABUSE AND CONTROL

Charles Rangel: the front-line general in the war on drugs. L. Norment. il pors *Ebony* 44:128+ My '89

UNITED STATES. CONGRESS. OFFICE OF TECHNOLOGY ASSESSMENT

Getting the most out of OTA. L. Winner. il por *Technology Review* 92:19+ N/D '89

How to revolutionize Washington with 140 people [cover story] S. Shuger. *The Washington Monthly* 21:38-40+ Je '89

UNITED STATES. CONGRESS. REPUBLICAN CONGRESSIONAL COMMITTEE *See* National Republican Congressional Committee

UNITED STATES. CONGRESS. SENATE

See also

Republican Senatorial Inner Circle

Bicentennial note. il *Congressional Digest* 68:161-2 Je/Jl '89

Holier than everyone [J. Tower nomination as Secretary of Defense] L. Martz. il por *Newsweek* 113:22-3 Mr 13 '89

In the wake of the Tower wars [opposition to Secretary of Defense-designate J. Tower] G. Borger. il pors *U.S. News & World Report* 106:44-6 Mr 13 '89

Oratory in the modern Senate [J. Tower nomination] A. Heard. il *The American Spectator* 22:14-15 My '89

'Republicans are thirsting for blood' [hard feelings over J. Tower nomination] R. Fly and D. Harbrecht. il por *Business Week* p39 Mr 20 '89

So much for bipartisanship [J. Tower nomination as Secretary of Defense] R. Lacayo. il pors *Time* 133:20-1 Mr 13 '89

Tower play [debate on J. Tower's nomination as Defense Secretary] H. Hertzberg. *The New Republic* 200:4+ Mr 27 '89

Powers and duties

The leaden wings of Senate justice [cumbersome process of unseating federal judges] il por *U.S. News & World Report* 107:18 O 30 '89

Staff

See Senators—Staff

Voting

The ABCs of child care [Senate passes the Act for Better Child Care] N. Traver. il *Time* 134:17 Jl 3 '89

Art and taxpayers. A. C. Danto. *The Nation* 249:192-3 Ag 21-28 '89

Arts grants under fire [J. Helms leads Senate vote against controversial art] C. McGuigan. il por *Newsweek* 114:23 Ag 7 '89

Bush wins victory on FS-X development despite Senate anger on Japanese trade. M. Mecham. *Aviation Week & Space Technology* 130:31 My 22 '89

Congress delivers new child care bill. L. Brown. il *Black Enterprise* 20:27 S '89

Cruel & unusual punishment [forbidding smoking on commercial airplanes] W. F. Buckley. *National Review* 41:62-3 O 27 '89

Gen. Colin Powell OK'd by full Senate for chair of Joint Chiefs of Staff. il por *Jet* 77:4 O 9 '89

UNITED STATES. CONGRESS. SENATE—Voting—*cont.*
'Give me your rich, your very rich . . .' [Senate immigration bill would grant special preference to millionaires] D. Harbrecht. il *Business Week* p31 S 4 '89
Jesse Helms on the meaning of art. F. Bruning. il *Maclean's* 102:9 Ag 14 '89
Letter from Washington [Defense Secretary nominee J. Tower's confirmation fight] E. Drew. *The New Yorker* 65:97-100+ Mr 20 '89
Liberation day for the disabled [Americans with Disabilities Act] J. P. Shapiro. il *U.S. News & World Report* 107:20-2+ S 18 '89
New help for the disabled [sweeping legislation that bars discrimination] E. Salholz. il *Newsweek* 114:26 S 18 '89
Nunn's SDI two-step. J. D. Isaacs. il por *The Bulletin of the Atomic Scientists* 45:5-6 D '89
Quit stalling on the smoking ban. *Aviation Week & Space Technology* 131:11 S 18 '89
Senate bolsters Commerce Dept.'s authority in reviewing cooperative arms agreements. J. D. Morrocco. *Aviation Week & Space Technology* 131:28 Ag 7 '89
A setback for Bush [rejects J. Tower nomination] J. Bierman. il pors *Maclean's* 102:34-5 Mr 20 '89
A shift in the winds swirling around Old Glory [Senate rejects flag burning amendment] il *U.S. News & World Report* 107:14 O 30 '89
The Tower precedent [rejection of J. Tower as Defense Secretary] S. Garment. *Commentary* 87:42-8 My '89
UNITED STATES. CONGRESS. SENATE. COMMITTEE ON APPROPRIATIONS. SUBCOMMITTEE ON DEPT. OF DEFENSE
Debate at $3 billion a minute. J. D. Isaacs. il *The Bulletin of the Atomic Scientists* 45:3-4 N '89
Senate defense panel defers NASP funding, clouding program's future [National Aero-Space Plane] P. A. Gilmartin. *Aviation Week & Space Technology* 131:29 S 18 '89
UNITED STATES. CONGRESS. SENATE. COMMITTEE ON ARMED SERVICES
Bush risks his chips on Tower. T. M. DeFrank. il *Newsweek* 113:19 F 20 '89
Capitol showdown [Defense Secretary designate J. Tower rejected; with editorial comment by Kevin Doyle] M. Nemeth. il pors *Maclean's* 102:2, 22-3 Mr 6 '89
Cheney pledges swift action on pressing defense issues [Defense Secretary-designate approved] J. D. Morrocco. por *Aviation Week & Space Technology* 130:262-3 Mr 20 '89
Friendship has limits [stalled Defense Secretary nomination of J. Tower] M. B. Carlson. il por *Time* 133:30-1 F 20 '89
Is Sam Nunn Secretary of Defense? G. Borger. il por *U.S. News & World Report* 106:24 F 20 '89
Is this goodbye? [Defense Secretary nomination of J. Tower rejected; cover story; special section] il pors *Time* 133:18-22+ Mr 6 '89
Senate, House Armed Services panels at odds over spending priorities. il *Aviation Week & Space Technology* 131:28 Jl 24 '89
Senators criticize Defense nominee for statement on acquisition chief [Deputy Secretary of Defense-designate D. J. Atwood; with editorial comment] P. A. Gilmartin. *Aviation Week & Space Technology* 130:7, 29 Ap 10 '89
Storming the Tower [rejects J. Tower's nomination as Defense Secretary] G. Borger. il pors *U.S. News & World Report* 106:37-9 Mr 6 '89
The Tower soap opera [Secretary of Defense-designate J. Tower] J. Barry. il por *Newsweek* 113:17 F 13 '89
Tower supports SDI, citing Soviet antimissile advances [Defense Secretary confirmation hearings] *Aviation Week & Space Technology* 130:20-1 Ja 30 '89
Tower vote set back again, leaving Pentagon stalled [with editorial comment] P. Mann. il por *Aviation Week & Space Technology* 130:7, 23-4 F 13 '89
Towering troubles [alleged misconduct by Secretary of Defense-designate J. Tower] G. J. Church. il por *Time* 133:36 F 13 '89
Tower's troubles [Secretary of Defense-designate's confirmation fight; cover story] T. Morganthau. il pors *Newsweek* 113:16-20+ Mr 6 '89
UNITED STATES. CONGRESS. SENATE. COMMITTEE ON COMMERCE, SCIENCE, AND TRANSPORTATION
Senators press Skinner on civil aviation agenda [Transportation Secretary-designate S. K. Skinner] M. Mecham. *Aviation Week & Space Technology* 130:70-1 Ja 30 '89
UNITED STATES. CONGRESS. SENATE. COMMITTEE ON COMMERCE, SCIENCE, AND TRANSPORTATION. SUBCOMMITTEE ON AVIATION
Senate hearing focuses on growing pilot shortage. J. Ott. il *Aviation Week & Space Technology* 131:56-7 Ag 14 '89
Senate panel widens probe of airline concentration. J. Ott. il *Aviation Week & Space Technology* 130:312-13 Je 12 '89
UNITED STATES. CONGRESS. SENATE. COMMITTEE ON ENVIRONMENT AND PUBLIC WORKS
Reilly vows environmental activism [nomination hearing] L. Roberts. il por *Science* 243:731 F 10 '89

UNITED STATES. CONGRESS. SENATE. COMMITTEE ON FOREIGN RELATIONS
Bush's envoy on the grill [D. Gregg questioned on Iran-contra during confirmation hearings for ambassadorship to South Korea] R. Parry. il por *Newsweek* 113:40 My 29 '89
Cranston v. Gregg [ambassador-designate to South Korea D. Gregg questioned on Iran-contra] W. F. Buckley. *National Review* 41:11-12 Je 16 '89
UNITED STATES. CONGRESS. SENATE. COMMITTEE ON FOREIGN RELATIONS. SUBCOMMITTEE ON TERRORISM, NARCOTICS, AND INTERNATIONAL COMMUNICATIONS
Senate unit hears testimony on censorship [subcommittee hearing on Rushdie controversy] H. Fields. *Publishers Weekly* 235:10 Mr 24 '89
UNITED STATES. CONGRESS. SENATE. COMMITTEE ON THE BUDGET
The Hill has fund managers squirming. D. Harbrecht. *Business Week* p45 Ja 30 '89
UNITED STATES. CONGRESS. SENATE. COMMITTEE ON THE JUDICIARY
Politics and double standards [rejects appointment of W. Lucas to head Civil Rights Div. of Dept. of Justice] N. Traver. il por *Time* 134:29 Ag 14 '89
UNITED STATES. CONGRESS. SENATE. SELECT COMMITTEE ON ETHICS
Bob Bennett: on the trail of the 'Keating Five' [inquiry into Lincoln Savings & Loan scandal] T. Smart. il por *Business Week* p60 D 11 '89
UNITED STATES. CONGRESSIONAL BUDGET OFFICE
CBO lists options for cutting R&D. M. Crawford. *Science* 243:1001 F 24 '89
UNITED STATES. CONSTITUTION
Amendments
Balanced budget constitutional amendment. il *Congressional Digest* 68:257-88 N '89
Blast! [flag burning] W. F. Buckley. *National Review* 41:63 N 24 '89
Bushwaterism [L. Atwater's role in persuading Bush to call for flag burning amendment] *The New Republic* 201:5-6 Jl 17-24 '89
Congress rallies around the flag [constitutional amendment proposed to overrule Supreme Court on flag burning] T. Jacoby. il *Newsweek* 114:19 Jl 10 '89
A constitutional convention: history repeats itself. *Utne Reader* p62-3 S/O '89
Flag desecration legislation. *Congressional Digest* 68:193-224 Ag/S '89
Flag flap. V. Gold. il *The American Spectator* 22:9 S '89
Flagellation [amendment on flag burning proposed] H. Hertzberg. *The New Republic* 201:4 Jl 17-24 '89
Hooray for the amendment [flag burning] W. F. Buckley. *National Review* 41:54-5 Ag 4 '89
Oh say, can you see an amendment? [flag burning] G. Borger. il *U.S. News & World Report* 107:20 Jl 10 '89
A shift in the winds swirling around Old Glory [Senate rejects flag burning amendment] il *U.S. News & World Report* 107:14 O 30 '89
Symbol—or substance? [drive for flag burning amendment vs. addressing needs of poor children] P. B. Gough. *Phi Delta Kappan* 71:99 O '89
What price Old Glory? [call for constitutional amendment against flag burning] *Time* 134:23 Jl 10 '89
Study and teaching
N.C. students get state to outlaw its poll tax. *Jet* 76:8 Je 19 '89
UNITED STATES. CONSTITUTION. 1ST-10TH AMENDMENTS
See also
Freedom of speech
Abolish the Fifth Amendment. M. Kaus. *The Washington Monthly* 21:69-70 F '89
A right to privacy? [with reply by Joseph Sobran] H. V. Jaffa. *National Review* 41:51-2 Mr 24 '89
A smokeless cigarette ad? *Newsweek* 114:64 N 13 '89
The spirit of '89 [J. Madison and the Bill of Rights] W. L. Miller. *The New Republic* 200:21-4 Je 26 '89
UNITED STATES. CONSUMER PRODUCT SAFETY COMMISSION *See* U.S. Consumer Product Safety Commission
UNITED STATES. COUNCIL OF ECONOMIC ADVISERS *See* Council of Economic Advisers (U.S.)
UNITED STATES. COUNCIL ON ENVIRONMENTAL QUALITY *See* Council on Environmental Quality (U.S.)
UNITED STATES. COURT OF APPEALS
U.S. Appeals Court judges: from protest to power [black judges] il *Ebony* 44:68+ Ag '89
UNITED STATES. COURT OF APPEALS (DISTRICT OF COLUMBIA CIRCUIT)
Off the record [nomination of C. Thomas] Cato. *National Review* 41:56 D 8 '89
UNITED STATES. CUSTOMS SERVICE *See* U.S. Customs Service
UNITED STATES. DEFENSE ADVANCED RESEARCH PROJECTS AGENCY
DARPA poised to award contracts for high-definition display concepts. P. A. Gilmartin. *Aviation Week & Space Technology* 131:32 S 4 '89

UNITED STATES. DEFENSE ADVANCED RESEARCH PROJECTS AGENCY—cont.

DARPA presses for continuing role in conventional cruise missile program. *Aviation Week & Space Technology* 130:53 Ja 23 '89

DARPA studies optical, radar techniques for spotting submarines from air, space. P. J. Klass. *Aviation Week & Space Technology* 129:27+ Mr 6 '89

DARPA to fund high-density TV. *High Technology Business* 9:33 Ap '89

DARPA's Phase-1 Mimic program to yield wide range of chips for EW and avionics. il *Aviation Week & Space Technology* 131:87+ S 18 '89

Defense Dept. contracts to spur use of digital GaAs microcircuits. P. J. Klass. *Aviation Week & Space Technology* 130:283-4 Je 12 '89

Knapp resigns from URA leadership; Truly to pilot NASA, Fields at DARPA. I. Goodwin. *Physics Today* 42:42-4 Je '89

Not a pretty picture [HDTV research funded by DARPA] S. Shulman. il *The Progressive* 53:24-5 S '89

Pegasus, MX boosters combined for new Defense launch vehicle [Taurus standard small launch vehicle] C. Covault. il *Aviation Week & Space Technology* 131:47+ S 18 '89

Scaled Composites rolls out modified ATTT for DARPA tests [advanced technology tactical transport] il *Aviation Week & Space Technology* 130:30 Ap 17 '89

UNITED STATES. DEFENSE INVESTIGATIVE SERVICE. DEFENSE INDUSTRIAL SECURITY PROGRAM

Suspect [security clearance procedures; cover story] V. Novak. il *Common Cause Magazine* 15:17-22+ My/Je '89

UNITED STATES. DEPT. OF AGRICULTURE

Ag's leading man [C. Yeutter] P. Smith. il pors *Successful Farming* 87:18-20 N '89

Gene Johnston. G. Johnston. il *Successful Farming* 87:5 Ap '89

What to expect from the new Ag Secretary [C. Yeutter] G. Johnston. il *Successful Farming* 87 no4:36 Mr '89

Yeutter priorities: help cut deficit, a new farm bill. N. E. Harl. por *Successful Farming* 87:10 Ja '89

Appropriations and expenditures

Agricultural groups push research plan [USDA competitive grants program] M. Crawford. il *Science* 244:140 Ap 14 '89

NRC unveils agriculture R&D plan. M. Crawford. *Science* 246:27 O 6 '89

Pork producers get little from the 'pork barrel'. P. Smith. il *Successful Farming* 87:52 F '89

UNITED STATES. DEPT. OF AGRICULTURE. CONSERVATION RESERVE PROGRAM

End-of-the-line for CRP? R. Fee. *Successful Farming* 87:8 S '89

Filter strips: a little land with a big bang. J. Walter. il *Successful Farming* 87:36-7 F '89

Flaws in farm policy. G. Reiger. il *Field & Stream* 94:14+ Ag '89

He's on wild path in CRP. J. Walter. il *Successful Farming* 87:72 S '89

What compliance really costs. R. Fee. il *Successful Farming* 87:64AG Ap '89

What's growing on CRP ground? *Successful Farming* 87:70 N '89

Winners and losers in the CRP. J. Walter. il *Successful Farming* 87:14 D '89

UNITED STATES. DEPT. OF AGRICULTURE. FARMERS HOME ADMINISTRATION See United States. Farmers Home Administration

UNITED STATES. DEPT. OF AGRICULTURE. FOREST SERVICE See United States. Forest Service

UNITED STATES. DEPT. OF COMMERCE

Commerce Dept. seeks reports of copyright abuse in China. H. Fields. *Publishers Weekly* 236:13 O 13 '89

Inaction on technology programs stirs Congress. C. Norman. *Science* 244:137-8 Ap 14 '89

Senate bolsters Commerce Dept.'s authority in reviewing cooperative arms agreements. J. D. Morrocco. *Aviation Week & Space Technology* 131:28 Ag 7 '89

Washington ins & outs: Graham departs, Murrin to Commerce, top changes at NASA and Pentagon. I. Goodwin. *Physics Today* 42:47-9 Jl '89

UNITED STATES. DEPT. OF DEFENSE

See also

Pentagon (Arlington, Va.: Building)

Bush risks his chips on Tower. T. M. DeFrank. il *Newsweek* 113:19 F 20 '89

Capitol showdown [Defense Secretary designate J. Tower rejected by Senate Armed Services Committee; with editorial comment by Kevin Doyle] M. Nemeth. il pors *Maclean's* 102:2, 22-3 Mr 6 '89

Cheney pledges swift action on pressing defense issues [Defense Secretary-designate approved by Senate Armed Services Committee] J. D. Morrocco. por *Aviation Week & Space Technology* 130:262-3 Mr 20 '89

The credibility gap that keeps on growing [Secretary of Defense-designate J. Tower] por *U.S. News & World Report* 106:12 F 13 '89

Defense: Tower won't have much room to maneuver. D. Griffiths. *Business Week* p39 F 13 '89

DOD lists critical technologies. C. Norman. *Science* 243:1543 Mr 24 '89

Does Cheney have enough artillery to scrap with the brass? D. Griffiths. *Business Week* p43 Mr 27 '89

Doves' golden silence [reticence of peace movement in failed nomination of J. Tower as Defense Secretary] J. D. Isaacs. *The Bulletin of the Atomic Scientists* 45:4 Je '89

Fit for the Cabinet? [womanizing charges against J. Tower] D. R. Carlin, Jr. il *Commonweal* 116:136-7 Mr 10 '89

Friendship has limits [stalled Defense Secretary nomination of J. Tower] M. B. Carlson. il por *Time* 133:30-1 F 20 '89

Happy campers, for a change [relationship between J. Baker and R. Cheney] S. Talbott. pors *Time* 134:24 Ag 28 '89

Holier than everyone [J. Tower nomination as Secretary of Defense reviewed in the Senate] L. Martz. il por *Newsweek* 113:22-3 Mr 13 '89

In the wake of the Tower wars [Senate opposition to Secretary of Defense-designate J. Tower] G. Borger. il pors *U.S. News & World Report* 106:44-6 Mr 13 '89

The iron triangle [choice of J. Tower as Secretary of Defense] *The Nation* 248:37 Ja 9-16 '89

Is my SecDef drunk? [J. Tower nomination] W. F. Buckley. *National Review* 41:62 Ap 7 '89

Is this goodbye? [Defense Secretary nomination of J. Tower rejected by Senate Armed Services Committee; cover story; special section] il pors *Time* 133:18-22+ Mr 6 '89

Kick-starting the presidency of George Bush [R. B. Cheney nominated as Secretary of Defense] il por *U.S. News & World Report* 106:10 Mr 20 '89

Letter from Washington [Defense Secretary nominee J. Tower's confirmation fight] E. Drew. *The New Yorker* 65:97-100+ Mr 20 '89

Missing the Tower story [J. Tower nomination and FBI background investigation] T. Eastland. il *The American Spectator* 22:34-6 My '89

Notes and comment [J. Tower nominated as Secretary of Defense] *The New Yorker* 64:17-18 Ja 2 '89

On the fitness of Tower. W. F. Buckley. *National Review* 41:54-5 Mr 24 '89

On the second shot, a straight arrow [R. Cheney nominated as Defense Secretary] il por *Time* 133:24 Mr 20 '89

Oratory in the modern Senate [J. Tower nomination] A. Heard. il *The American Spectator* 22:14-15 My '89

The politician at the Pentagon [R. B. Cheney] G. Borger. il por *U.S. News & World Report* 107:24-5 O 2 '89

A 'radical' reformer? [J. Tower] G. Hackett. por *Newsweek* 113:19 Ja 23 '89

'Republicans are thirsting for blood' [hard feelings over J. Tower nomination] R. Fly and D. Harbrecht. il por *Business Week* p39 Mr 20 '89

Rookie of the Year? [Secretary R. B. Cheney] *The New Republic* 200:7-8+ Ap 17 '89

Saint George and the congressional dragon [opposition to J. Tower nomination] *National Review* 41:10-11 Mr 24 '89

A setback for Bush [Senate rejects J. Tower nomination] J. Bierman. il pors *Maclean's* 102:34-5 Mr 20 '89

So much for bipartisanship [J. Tower nomination as Secretary of Defense reviewed in the Senate] R. Lacayo. il pors *Time* 133:20-1 Mr 13 '89

Storming the Tower [Armed Services Committee rejects J. Tower's nomination as Defense Secretary] G. Borger. il pors *U.S. News & World Report* 106:37-9 Mr 6 '89

Tortoise? [R. Cheney, nominee for Secretary of Defense] *The Nation* 248:436-7 Ap 3 '89

Tower play [Senate debate on J. Tower's nomination as Defense Secretary] H. Hertzberg. *The New Republic* 200:4+ Mr 27 '89

The Tower precedent [rejection of J. Tower as Defense Secretary] S. Garment. *Commentary* 87:42-8 My '89

The Tower soap opera [Secretary of Defense-designate J. Tower] J. Barry. il por *Newsweek* 113:17 F 13 '89

Tower supports SDI, citing Soviet antimissile advances [Defense Secretary confirmation hearings] *Aviation Week & Space Technology* 130:20-1 Ja 30 '89

Tower vote set back again, leaving Pentagon stalled [with editorial comment] P. Mann. il por *Aviation Week & Space Technology* 130:7, 23-4 F 13 '89

Towering troubles [alleged misconduct by Secretary of Defense-designate J. Tower] G. J. Church. il por *Time* 133:36 F 13 '89

Tower's troubles [Secretary of Defense-designate's confirmation fight; cover story] T. Morganthau. il pors *Newsweek* 113:16-20+ Mr 6 '89

War games [C. J. Johnson sues Defense Dept. over computerized control of nuclear weapons] S. Ditlea. il *Omni (New York, N.Y.)* 11:32+ Mr '89

Wine, women, and World War III [J. Tower's nomination as Defense Secretary] D. Neff. *Christianity Today* 33:15 Ap 7 '89

Appropriations and expenditures

See also

United States. Congress. Senate. Committee on Appropriations. Subcommittee on Dept. of Defense

35 ways to cut the defense budget. P. Keisling and J. Alter. *The Washington Monthly* 21:50+ F '89

UNITED STATES. DEPT. OF DEFENSE—Appropriations and expenditures—*cont.*

The secret in the stacks: how the Library of Congress hid Pentagon spending. il *Time* 134:29 O 9 '89

Senate, House Armed Services panels at odds over spending priorities. il *Aviation Week & Space Technology* 131:28 Jl 24 '89

Sharp rise in Brilliant Pebbles interceptor funding accompanied by new questions about technical feasibility. T. M. Foley. il *Aviation Week & Space Technology* 130:20-1 My 22 '89

Spread eagle. *The Nation* 249:703-4 D 11 '89

"Swift responses" usually mean bad agreements. C. W. Weinberger. il *Forbes* 144 Special Issue:31 O 23 '89

Time for a new speechwriter [R. Cheney] J. D. Isaacs. por *The Bulletin of the Atomic Scientists* 45:5-6 N '89

U.S. Armed Forces vary means of coping with tight budgets. B. M. Greeley, Jr. il *Aviation Week & Space Technology* 130:52-3+ Mr 20 '89

U.S. defense budget cuts could imperil nation's research and development effort. B. W. Henderson. il *Aviation Week & Space Technology* 131:35+ D 18-25 '89

U.S. defense budget declines for fifth consecutive year. P. Mann and D. F. Bond. *Aviation Week & Space Technology* 131:30 N 6 '89

Voodoo economics at the Pentagon. P. Cary. *U.S. News & World Report* 106:29 My 15 '89

We are rich enough to be strong. E. Rubenstein. il *National Review* 41:16 Mr 10 '89

Why can't we cut the defense budget? C. W. Weinberger. il *Forbes* 143:31 Ja 23 '89

Why military spending pays off [R. Reagan's defense buildup] R. N. Perle. il por *U.S. News & World Report* 106:23-4 Ja 16 '89

Will the Osprey ever fly? D. Waller. il *Newsweek* 114:16 Jl 24 '89

You can't keep a bad weapon down [antisatellite programs] J. D. Isaacs. il *The Bulletin of the Atomic Scientists* 45:3 Ap '89

Procurement

See also
Military-industrial complex

Atwood eyes tighter scrutiny of weapons development. *Aviation Week & Space Technology* 130:23 My 15 '89

Betti nominated to become new acquisition chief. por *Aviation Week & Space Technology* 130:20 Jl 10 '89

Cheney calls for major realignment of Pentagon's procurement system. *Aviation Week & Space Technology* 130:21-2 Jl 10 '89

Contractors charge that proposed rules threaten procurement system. M. Mecham. *Aviation Week & Space Technology* 130:33 Ap 24 '89

Contractors must adapt to survive under new U.S. acquisition policies. W. B. Scott. il *Aviation Week & Space Technology* 130:76-7+ Mr 20 '89

Defense Dept. auditors uncover $789 million in contract overpricing. *Aviation Week & Space Technology* 130:81 Ja 30 '89

Defense Dept. to launch competition for exoatmospheric interceptor design. P. A. Gilmartin. *Aviation Week & Space Technology* 131:27+ N 6 '89

Defense Dept. to launch design competition for new antisatellite weapon for the 1990s. P. A. Gilmartin. *Aviation Week & Space Technology* 131:30 Jl 24 '89

Defense's gravy train nears the end of the line. S. Toy. il *Business Week* p75 Ja 9 '89

Former Defense secretaries advise Congress to lighten oversight role [study headed by Harold Brown and James Schlesinger] M. Mecham. *Aviation Week & Space Technology* 130:89-90 Ja 2 '89

The gloves are off in lobbying for defense programs. P. A. Gilmartin. *Aviation Week & Space Technology* 131:29 D 18-25 '89

How to save $50 billion a year. R. A. Stubbing and R. A. Mendel. il *The Atlantic* 263:53-8 Je '89

Incoming! Incoming! Arms contractors head for the bunkers. E. Schine. il *Business Week* p66+ S 11 '89

Making procurers cleaner and leaner [R. Cheney's reform proposal] *U.S. News & World Report* 107:10+ Jl 24 '89

Making total quality management work: lessons from industry. C. Leader. por *Aviation Week & Space Technology* 131:65+ O 30 '89

Management-by-rote is the fallout from overzealous prosecution. M. A. Dornheim. il *Aviation Week & Space Technology* 131:32-3 D 18-25 '89

Northrop, five employees indicted in fraud case. *Aviation Week & Space Technology* 130:29 Ap 17 '89

On guard! Proposals for conservative military reform. P. Weyrich. il *Conservative Digest* 15:18-19+ S/O '89

Once more, with feeling: Atwood takes the baton. D. F. Bond. *Aviation Week & Space Technology* 131:25 D 18-25 '89

Pentagon awards production contracts for ALQ-165 to ITT, Westinghouse [airborne self-protection jammer] P. J. Klass. il *Aviation Week & Space Technology* 131:59+ O 16 '89

Pentagon considers buying additional Pioneer RPVs. J. D. Morrocco. *Aviation Week & Space Technology* 131:81+ Jl 31 '89

Pentagon purchases Soviet hardware on open market for operational testing. J. D. Morrocco. il *Aviation Week & Space Technology* 130:24-5 Ja 23 '89

Pentagon will select two contractors to demonstrate unmanned aerial vehicles. P. J. Klass. il *Aviation Week & Space Technology* 131:34-5 Jl 31 '89

A search-and-destroy mission—against paper. F. Seghers. il *Business Week* p91+ F 6 '89

Senators criticize Defense nominee for statement on acquisition chief [Deputy Secretary of Defense-designate D. J. Atwood; with editorial comment] P. A. Gilmartin. *Aviation Week & Space Technology* 130:7, 29 Ap 10 '89

Sundstrand prepares to pay the piper—and the Pentagon. M. D. Oneal and P. Dwyer. il *Business Week* p35-6 Ja 23 '89

Task force urges overhaul of Pentagon policy on industrial cooperation with Pacific Rim. J. D. Morrocco. *Aviation Week & Space Technology* 131:32 N 13 '89

Total quality management will require procurement changes, perseverance. B. A. Smith. il *Aviation Week & Space Technology* 131:59-60 D 18-25 '89

TQM expected to boost productivity, ensure survival of U.S. industry [total quality management] W. B. Scott. il *Aviation Week & Space Technology* 131:64-5+ D 4 '89

U.S. aerospace leaders see little hope of improving defense procurement. P. A. Gilmartin. il *Aviation Week & Space Technology* 131:26-7 O 2 '89

U.S. joins ex-employee in accusing Singer of fraud. *Aviation Week & Space Technology* 130:263 Mr 20 '89

U.S. panel acts to simplify purchase of short-range UAV [unmanned aerial vehicles] il *Aviation Week & Space Technology* 130:57 Ja 23 '89

The watershed decade [address, June 20, 1989] J. D. Cosgrove. *Vital Speeches of the Day* 55:744-7 O 1 '89

Whistling in the Pentagon. N. Lemann. bibl f il *The New York Review of Books* 36:3-4+ O 26 '89

UNITED STATES. DEPT. OF DEFENSE. DEFENSE ADVANCED RESEARCH PROJECTS AGENCY *See* United States. Defense Advanced Research Projects Agency

UNITED STATES. DEPT. OF EDUCATION

The do-nothing Education Secretary [L. Cavazos] por *Newsweek* 114:56 O 2 '89

Go to the rear of the class [Secretary L. Cavazos] S. Tifft. il por *Time* 133:76 My 29 '89

Lauro's themes. *The New Republic* 201:7-8 Jl 10 '89

A memo to the new Secretary of Education. E. L. Boyer. *The Education Digest* 54:3-6 Mr '89

Memo to the Secretary of Education: how to give education a vision and voice of credibility. E. L. Boyer. por *Change* 20:24-6 N/D '88

Memo to the Secretary of Education: how to make education a top priority. T. H. Bell. por *Change* 20:20-3 N/D '88

Shortest education presidency? *National Review* 41:11-12 Mr 24 '89

Title IX is back in action! [effect on women athletes] K. M. Reith. il *Women's Sports & Fitness* 11:74 Mr '89

Where the boys are [effect of Title IX on women athletic directors and coaches at the college level] M. Goodman. *The Washington Monthly* 21:18-20 Ap '89

UNITED STATES. DEPT. OF EDUCATION. OFFICE OF EDUCATIONAL RESEARCH AND IMPROVEMENT *See* United States. Office of Educational Research and Improvement

UNITED STATES. DEPT. OF ENERGY

Accelerator eyed for warhead tritium. M. Crawford. *Science* 243:469 Ja 27 '89

Admiral Watkins's toughest command [cleanup of nuclear weapons plants] S. J. Hedges. il pors *U.S. News & World Report* 107:29-30 Ag 14 '89

Clash of the dogmas [tritium shortage] J. D. Isaacs. *The Bulletin of the Atomic Scientists* 45:4 Mr '89

Dirty business [Dept. of Energy weapons-production facilities] T. Beardsley. il *Scientific American* 260:27-8 Ap '89

DOE calls in the labs for defense waste cleanup. M. Crawford. il *Science* 246:24-5 O 6 '89

DOE's unilateral disarmament. M. T. Owens. il *National Review* 41:42-3 F 24 '89

Energy czar—and environmental activist? [J. D. Watkins] V. Cahan. il por *Business Week* p54 Jl 24 '89

Fixing the nation's nuclear-weapons plants. J. F. Ahearne. il *Technology Review* 92:24-9 Jl '89

Flash point [security restrictions on inertial confinement fusion] J. Horgan. il *Scientific American* 260:18+ Ap '89

Fusion chief reassigned as program is refocused [removal of J. F. Clarke] M. Crawford. por *Science* 243:303 Ja 20 '89

Getting Energy into the schools [J. Watkins' efforts in science education] M. Barinaga. il por *Science* 246:318 O 20 '89

Public always the last to know [fighting to avoid giving data on underground nuclear tests to arms control groups] W. J. Lanouette. il *The Bulletin of the Atomic Scientists* 45:11-12 O '89

A trash can for the nuclear age [Trupact II container developed by the DOE to transport nuclear waste] il *Discover* 10:18 My '89

The tritium follies [debate over restarting Savannah River reactors] D. Albright and J. Beard. bibl f il *The Bulletin of the Atomic Scientists* 45:42-5 N '89

UNITED STATES. DEPT. OF ENERGY—*cont.*

Watkins named Energy Secretary. M. Crawford. il por *Science* 243:309 Ja 20 '89

Watkins takes the helm at DOE. M. Crawford. il por *Science* 243:1136 Mr 3 '89

Watkins's decision to restart HFIR heralds new era for DOE reactors [High Flux Isotope Reactor at Oak Ridge National Laboratory] I. Goodwin. il *Physics Today* 42:49-50 My '89

Workers welfare [Fernald, Ohio nuclear facility; address, March 22, 1989] R. F. Celeste. *Vital Speeches of the Day* 55:490-2 Je 1 '89

Appropriations and expenditures

Black hole [Superconducting Super Collider] J. Treen. *The New Republic* 200:17-18 F 20 '89

Bomb factories of the 21st century. E. Marshall. il *Science* 243:305 Ja 20 '89

Budget squeeze causes fission in fusion labs. M. Crawford. il *Science* 244:138-9 Ap 14 '89

The costs of cleaning up DOE [nuclear facilities] *Science News* 135:60 Ja 28 '89

Energy Dept. plans to cut spending on nuclear directed-energy weapons. T. M. Foley. *Aviation Week & Space Technology* 130:132-3 F 20 '89

Fusion plan ignites controversy at DOE [shifting funds from magnetic fusion to laser program] M. Crawford. il *Science* 244:1434-5 Je 23 '89

High-energy management stirs up energy research [R. O. Hunter] M. Crawford. il por *Science* 245:1182-3 S 15 '89

Procurement

Hitting the roof [corrupt management practices of E. I. Du Pont de Nemours & Co. at Savannah River nuclear complex] N. Roland. il *Common Cause Magazine* 15:8-9 Jl/Ag '89

UNITED STATES. DEPT. OF ENERGY. NUCLEAR SCIENCE ADVISORY COMMITTEE

NSAC backs Brookhaven's RHIC and suggests closings to come [Relativistic Heavy Ion Collider] I. Goodwin. *Physics Today* 42:54 O '89

NSAC delays clear decision on Canada's kaon factory. I. Goodwin. *Physics Today* 42:44 Je '89

Subcommittee encourages U.S. to join Canadian kaon factory [TRIUMF cyclotron] B. M. Schwarzschild. il *Physics Today* 42:17-19 My '89

UNITED STATES. DEPT. OF ENERGY. WASTE ISOLATION PILOT PLANT (N.M.) *See* Waste Isolation Pilot Plant (N.M.)

UNITED STATES. DEPT. OF HEALTH AND HUMAN SERVICES

Back to the party of Lincoln? [G. Bush courts blacks and appoints L. W. Sullivan as Secretary] R. Lacayo. il pors *Time* 133:79 Ja 2 '89

Bush names Morehouse Medical School prexy to Cabinet post [L. W. Sullivan] il pors *Jet* 75:4 Ja 9 '89

Dr. Sullivan to get $215,000 in severance pay; Senators see no conflict in HHS post. il por *Jet* 76:38 Ap 17 '89

New rules on misconduct. C. Holden. *Science* 245:593 Ag 11 '89

Pro-choice? Get lost: antiabortion views are a must at Health and Human Services. R. Lacayo. il *Time* 134:43-4 D 4 '89

Promises to keep [appointment of L. Sullivan as Secretary disappoints prolife supporters] K. A. Lawton. il por *Christianity Today* 33:44-5 F 3 '89

Sullivan gets the OK for Senate's HHS confirmation. il por *Jet* 75:5 Mr 13 '89

Sullivan takes charge of America's health. L. Brown. por *Black Enterprise* 19:67-8 Je '89

Sullivan to steer HHS to help 'disadvantaged'. S. Booker. il por *Jet* 75:4-5 Mr 27 '89

Tar baby [prolife opposition to appointment of L. W. Sullivan as Secretary] F. Barnes. *The New Republic* 200:12-13 F 13 '89

A White House promise [nominee R. Fulton's stand on spina bifida and euthanasia] *National Review* 41:15-16 Ap 7 '89

White House puts Sullivan confirmation vote on hold. por *Jet* 75:25 F 20 '89

UNITED STATES. DEPT. OF HOUSING AND URBAN DEVELOPMENT

Abolish HUD [housing vouchers] *The New Republic* 201:7-8 Ag 21 '89

Al's pals [illegal dealings of Sen. A. D'Amato] M. J. Green. il *The New Republic* 201:16-20 O 30 '89

Another financial mess [defaults in HUD's program that deputizes firms to issue and underwrite mortgages] M. Schifrin. il *Forbes* 144:10 Jl 10 '89

Beverly Hills HUD [subsidized housing for the elderly] T. Noah. *The New Republic* 201:14-16 Ag 21 '89

Brokers at HUD illustrate the architects' dilemma: just whose services are worth the most? C. Pearson. il *Architectural Record* 177:29+ S '89

Can Jack Kemp clean up the HUD mess? S. V. Roberts. il por *U.S. News & World Report* 107:26-7 Jl 3 '89

Claire Freeman takes oath as asst. secretary of HUD. il por *Jet* 77:8 D 4 '89

Cleaning house at HUD—and then some. H. Gleckman and others. il por *Business Week* p72-4 Jl 10 '89

Come and get it [deputizes mortgage brokers to approve and coinsure federal mortgages] M. Schifrin. il *Forbes* 143:41-2 My 15 '89

Communities, not carpetbaggers. P. Dreier. il *The Nation* 249:198-200+ Ag 21-28 '89

A conservative war on poverty [Secretary J. Kemp] J. P. Shapiro. il por *U.S. News & World Report* 106:20-3 F 27 '89

Deborah Gore Dean. il por *People Weekly* 32:84-5 D 25 '89-Ja 1 '90

The disgrace at HUD. M. Greenfield. il *Newsweek* 114:60 Jl 24 '89

An enterprising war on poverty [interview with J. Kemp] il *New Perspectives Quarterly* 6:36-9 Summ '89

Fonzie on the spot: the HUD revelations tarnish the 'new' D'Amato. P. Blauner. il pors *New York* 22:42-8 N 13 '89

Grow up [HUD scandal] W. F. Buckley. *National Review* 41:54-5 S 1 '89

Has Bush assigned Kemp a mission impossible? R. Stodghill, II. por *Business Week* p51 Ja 9 '89

Hip-deep at HUD. L. Martz. il *Newsweek* 114:16-18 Jl 10 '89

Housing Dept.'s Kemp takes Atlanta fact-finding tour. il por *Jet* 75:46 Mr 6 '89

The housing hustle [HUD scandal] N. Traver. il por *Time* 133:18-19 Je 26 '89

How not to help the homeless [McKinney Act mandates turning over surplus buildings to homeless advocates] il *U.S. News & World Report* 107:29 Ag 28-S 4 '89

HUD director hosts black finance show on network [T. R. Daniels] por *Jet* 76:24 My 8 '89

The HUD party, the party of patronage. *National Review* 41:10 S 1 '89

The HUD ripoff [cover story] S. Waldman. il *Newsweek* 114:16-22 Ag 7 '89

The HUD scandal hits a stone wall [S. R. Pierce takes the Fifth Amendment] il por *U.S. News & World Report* 107:11 O 9 '89

HUD Sec. Kemp visits as Chicago gives control of housing unit to tenants. il por *Jet* 76:26 My 29 '89

HUD under Reagan: 'close to obscene' [charges of conflict of interest against S. Pierce] R. Thomas. il por *Newsweek* 113:18 Je 12 '89

HUD without politics? S. Waldman and C. Bingham. il *Newsweek* 114:38 O 9 '89

HUDscam revisited [grants to Massachusetts during Carter administration] il *National Review* 41:18-19 O 13 '89

Inside job [scandal] P. C. Montgomery. il *Common Cause Magazine* 15:16-20 Jl/Ag '89

Jack be nimble, Jack be quick [HUD scandal] E. Magnuson. il por *Time* 134:20 Jl 24 '89

Jack Kemp faces reality. J. Traub. il pors *The New York Times Magazine* p38-9+ My 7 '89

The Kemp cure-all [enterprise zones] D. Osborne. *The New Republic* 200:21+ Ap 3 '89

The Kemp plan for rebuilding the city. C. Oglesbee. *The Christian Century* 106:340-1 Ap 5 '89

Kemp's brave new world. A. McDaniel. il por *Newsweek* 113:26 Ja 2 '89

The lessons of the HUD scandal. D. Gergen. il *U.S. News & World Report* 107:64 Ag 7 '89

Looking beyond the HUD scandal. B. Cohn. il por *Newsweek* 114:19 Ag 21 '89

Moscow on the HUD [involvement of S. R. Pierce in cooperative program with the Soviet Union; cover story] M. Hosenball. il *The New Republic* 201:18-21 O 23 '89

The plot thickens [defaults in HUD's program that deputizes brokers to underwrite mortgages] M. Schifrin. il *Forbes* 144:10 O 30 '89

Poking into HUD's swamp. L. Martz. il por *Newsweek* 113:19 Je 26 '89

The poverty thing [J. Kemp's program] F. Barnes. *The New Republic* 200:13-15 Ja 30 '89

The price of influence. H. Mackenzie. il *Maclean's* 102:29-30 Jl 10 '89

The problem at HUD. S. T. Mandel. il *National Review* 41:21-2 Ag 4 '89

Raising the roof on corruption at HUD. *U.S. News & World Report* 106:11 Je 26 '89

The 'Reverend Jack' believes—now he has to deliver [J. Kemp] R. Stodghill, II. il por *Business Week* p86+ Je 12 '89

Sam Pierce's "turkey farm" [with interview with S. R. Pierce] N. Traver. il pors *Time* 134:20-4+ S 18 '89

Sam plays it again [S. Pierce takes Fifth Amendment in HUD scandal probe] *The Nation* 249:405 O 16 '89

Sam stays silent [S. Pierce] *National Review* 41:19-20 O 27 '89

Samuel Pierce, House panel clash over housing issue [conflict of interest charges] il por *Jet* 76:37 Je 19 '89

'Somebody is not telling the truth' [scandal] D. Harbrecht. il por *Business Week* p21-2 Jl 24 '89

Still more scandals at HUD. L. Martz. il *Newsweek* 114:21 Jl 3 '89

UNITED STATES. DEPT. OF HOUSING AND URBAN DEVELOPMENT—*cont.*

The undoing of Silent Sam Pierce. S. V. Roberts. il *U.S. News & World Report* 107:29+ S 18 '89

Washington talk. *National Review* 41:16-17 F 24 '89

What Jack Kemp loves about the HUD scandal. R. Stodghill, II and D. Harbrecht. il por *Business Week* p41 Jl 31 '89

What will be the impact on new construction under Jack Kemp's tutelage at HUD? P. Hoffmann. por *Architectural Record* 177:23 F '89

When tenants take charge [J. Kemp's plan] B. Turque. il por *Newsweek* 114:44 N 27 '89

When your mortgage pays you [reverse mortgages] W. Giese. *Changing Times* 43:24-5 F '89

Where were the media on HUD? M. Riley. il *Time* 134:48 Jl 24 '89

Who checks the checkers? [reliance on incomplete credit reports] M. Schifrin. il *Forbes* 144:64 Ag 7 '89

Appropriations and expenditures

How politics is making it tough to clean up HUD. J. P. Shapiro. *U.S. News & World Report* 107:39 D 11 '89

The White House connection [use of HUD and EPA monies to fund Republican campaigns during the Reagan administration; cover story] M. Waas. *The Nation* 249:585+ N 20 '89

UNITED STATES. DEPT. OF JUSTICE

Backtracking in Birmingham? [charges of racial harassment] B. Turque. il *Newsweek* 114:25 Jl 3 '89

Dick Thornburgh: not being Ed Meese isn't enough anymore. P. Dwyer. il por *Business Week* p37 Ag 7 '89

Lucas gets liaison post within U.S. Justice Dept. por *Jet* 76:22 S 4 '89

No runs, no drips, no errors [Justice Dept. considers prosecuting government employees who leak information obtained from a criminal investigation] T. Eastland. il *The American Spectator* 22:30-1 N '89

Nurturing faith in the nation's capital. T. Eastland. il por *Christianity Today* 33:27-8 Ja 13 '89

Shaking up Justice [Attorney General D. Thornburgh; cover story] M. Wines. il pors *The New York Times Magazine* p22-3+ My 21 '89

Shhhhhh! [anti-leak policy] T. Noah. *The New Republic* 201:8-10 O 30 '89

A shorter leash for the Inspectors General? P. Dwyer. il *Business Week* p82+ O 9 '89

Thornburgh inherits the whirlwind. S. J. Hedges. por *U.S. News & World Report* 107:16 Ag 7 '89

UNITED STATES. DEPT. OF JUSTICE. ANTITRUST DIVISION

Justice Dept. vows stronger antitrust policy on mergers [airlines] M. Mecham. il *Aviation Week & Space Technology* 130:64-5 Mr 13 '89

Putting the 'anti' back in the Antitrust Div. [J. F. Rill] P. Dwyer. il por *Business Week* p64+ Je 19 '89

UNITED STATES. DEPT. OF JUSTICE. CIVIL RIGHTS DIVISION

Cool Hand Lucas [nominee W. Lucas] W. McGurn. *National Review* 41:21-2 Je 2 '89

Fractured gospel [rejection of nominee W. Lucas] *The New Republic* 201:4 S 4 '89

Guess who's (not) coming to dinner [rejected civil rights nominee W. Lucas and other black Republicans undercut by White House] W. McGurn. il *National Review* 41:18-19 S 1 '89

A low-profile civil-rights march [rejection of nominee W. Lucas] por *U.S. News & World Report* 107:11 Ag 14 '89

Lucas's battle for confirmation. S. J. Hedges. il por *U.S. News & World Report* 106:33 My 8 '89

Missed opportunity [President Bush's decision not to submit a recess appointment of W. Lucas] *National Review* 41:14 S 15 '89

Mixed signals on civil rights [W. Lucas nominated to head division] M. Miller. por *Newsweek* 113:20 My 8 '89

Politics and double standards [Senate committee rejects appointment of W. Lucas] N. Traver. il por *Time* 134:29 Ag 14 '89

Token enforcer [nominee W. Lucas] F. Barnes. *The New Republic* 200:10-11 Je 19 '89

Uncle Sam's NIMBY attack [suing Chicago Heights for discrimination against mentally disabled] J. P. Shapiro. il *U.S. News & World Report* 107:24 S 18 '89

William Lucas choice to head Civil Rights Division. por *Jet* 75:6 Mr 13 '89

UNITED STATES. DEPT. OF JUSTICE. DRUG ENFORCEMENT ADMINISTRATION *See* United States. Drug Enforcement Administration

UNITED STATES. DEPT. OF JUSTICE. FEDERAL BUREAU OF INVESTIGATION *See* United States. Federal Bureau of Investigation

UNITED STATES. DEPT. OF JUSTICE. IMMIGRATION AND NATURALIZATION SERVICE *See* United States. Immigration and Naturalization Service

UNITED STATES. DEPT. OF JUSTICE. MARSHALS SERVICE *See* United States. Marshals Service

UNITED STATES. DEPT. OF JUSTICE. OFFICE OF THE SOLICITOR GENERAL

Speak softly and carry a big right-wing agenda [K. W. Starr] T. Smart. il por *Business Week* p115+ N 27 '89

UNITED STATES. DEPT. OF LABOR

As labor and Dole warm up, business is feeling a chill. S. B. Garland. il *Business Week* p35 Mr 6 '89

Fletcher loses Labor bid; others await appointments. il por *Jet* 75:4 Ja 16 '89

Labor Department report. *Congressional Digest* 68:133-4 My '89

Moneymen may stop deep-sixing proxies. J. M. Laderman. il *Business Week* p142 Mr 20 '89

UNITED STATES. DEPT. OF LABOR. BUREAU OF LABOR STATISTICS *See* United States. Bureau of Labor Statistics

UNITED STATES. DEPT. OF LABOR. EMPLOYMENT SERVICE *See* United States Employment Service

UNITED STATES. DEPT. OF LABOR. OCCUPATIONAL SAFETY AND HEALTH ADMINISTRATION *See* United States. Occupational Safety and Health Administration

UNITED STATES. DEPT. OF STATE

50th anniversary of the Bulletin [reprint of July 1, 1939 issue; cover story] il *Department of State Bulletin* 89:1-15 Jl '89

As State Department spokesperson, Margaret Tutwiler has won even the press's respect. M. B. Carlson. il por *Vogue* 179:276+ O '89

Baker and the bureaucrats are already crossing swords at State. B. Javetski. por *Business Week* p51 F 27 '89

Baker's bipartisan point man [B. Aronson] D. Waller. il por *Newsweek* 113:40 Mr 20 '89

Blind men's bluff [J. A. Baker and B. Scowcroft; cover story] M. Kondracke. *The New Republic* 200:20+ Mr 6 '89

Bush's Mr. Smooth runs into rough water [J. A. Baker] *Newsweek* 113:17 F 13 '89

Capitol gains [J. Baker] A. Stanley. il por *Vogue* 179:496-7+ Mr '89

Exercises in diplomacy: simulating future crises. M. Schofield. il *The Futurist* 23:8-11 Mr/Ap '89

Foggy Bottom's new bright light [D. B. Ross] B. Javetski. il por *Business Week* p66+ F 20 '89

Happy campers, for a change [relationship between J. Baker and R. Cheney] S. Talbott. pors *Time* 134:24 Ag 28 '89

In his plodding way, Shultz got things done. B. Javetski. por *Business Week* p30 Ja 16 '89

James A. Baker, III, sworn in as Secretary of State [remarks, January 27, 1989] G. Bush; J. A. Baker. il *Department of State Bulletin* 89:8-9 Ap '89

James Baker: pragmatist at State. R. Evans and R. D. Novak. il pors *Reader's Digest* 135:213-14+ N '89

Letter from Washington [J. Baker's rocky debut] Cato. *National Review* 41:9 Mr 24 '89

Mr. Inside, Mr. Outside [J. A. Baker and B. Scowcroft] J. Barry. pors *Newsweek* 113:28 F 27 '89

Playing for the edge [J. Baker; cover story; with interview] M. Kramer. il pors map *Time* 133:26-33 F 13 '89

Policy circles [nomination of B. Aronson as Assistant Secretary of State for Latin America] G. Black. *The Nation* 248:256-7 F 27 '89

Publications. See issues of Department of State Bulletin

The quiet sage steering Bush's foreign policy [B. Scowcroft and J. A. Baker] H. Trewhitt. il por *U.S. News & World Report* 106:22-4 F 20 '89

The right stuff [B. Aronson proposed as Asst. Secretary of State for Latin America] *The New Republic* 200:9-10 F 27 '89

Secretary-designate's confirmation hearings [statement, January 17, 1989] J. A. Baker, III. *Department of State Bulletin* 89:10-16 Ap '89

Stategate [F. Bloch spy case] *National Review* 41:10-12 S 1 '89

Vision problems at State . . . C. Ogden. il por *Time* 134:22 S 25 '89

Appropriations and expenditures

Department of State appropriations for the fiscal year 1940 [reprint from July 1, 1939 issue] il *Department of State Bulletin* 89:3-8 Jl '89

The international agenda and the FY 1990 budget request [statement, February 21, 1989] J. A. Baker, III. *Department of State Bulletin* 89:16-21 Ap '89

UNITED STATES. DEPT. OF STATE. ART IN EMBASSIES (PROGRAM) *See* Art in Embassies (Program)

UNITED STATES. DEPT. OF STATE. BUREAU FOR REFUGEE PROGRAMS

Lafontant oversees refugee affairs in new State post. il por *Jet* 76:9 Ag 7 '89

UNITED STATES. DEPT. OF STATE. FOREIGN SERVICE

Affairs of State. N. Roland. *Common Cause Magazine* 15:7-8 Mr/Ap '89

A 'drone class' of American diplomacy? M. G. Warner. il *Newsweek* 114:62-3 O 30 '89

Foreign Service [changes in heads of American diplomatic missions; reprint from July 1, 1939 issue] *Department of State Bulletin* 89:14 Jl '89

UNITED STATES. DEPT. OF STATE. FOREIGN SERVICE—*cont.*

Notorious ambassadors [Bush appointments] G. Hackett. il *Newsweek* 113:25-6 Je 5 '89

Perkins installed as new U.S. Foreign Service head. il por *Jet* 77:8 O 23 '89

Picking lemons for the plums? [G. Bush's ambassadorial nominations] R. Lacayo. il *Time* 134:17 Jl 31 '89

The slippery slope in Foggy Bottom [employment bias] D. Seligman. *Fortune* 119:167 My 8 '89

State troopers [ambassadorial appointments] *The Nation* 248:651-2 My 15 '89

The sum of their possessions [Bush appointments] M. Waas. *Harper's* 279:66-7 S '89

Todman is Argentina envoy, Perkins is named director of U.S. Foreign Service. il pors *Jet* 76:36-7 My 22 '89

UNITED STATES. DEPT. OF THE INTERIOR

Half Watt [Secretary M. Lujan] B. Reed. il *The New Republic* 201:20-2 O 16 '89

Hearing reveals politicized NPS. *National Parks* 63:11-13 Jl/Ag '89

Interior is a house divided. E. T. Smith. il *Business Week* p52 Ap 24 '89

Interior looking to contract out park jobs. *National Parks* 63:11-12 Ja/F '89

Interior may lift Cape Cod ORV ban. il *National Parks* 63:8-9 S/O '89

Interior paves way for sale of resources. *National Parks* 63:11 Mr/Ap '89

Interior sub rosa. J. Kenney. il *National Parks* 63:12-14 S/O '89

Lujan to lead Interior Department. il por *National Parks* 63:9-10 Mr/Ap '89

Thoughts [Secretary M. Lujan] F. Graham. il *Audubon* 91:13-14 Jl '89

UNITED STATES. DEPT. OF THE INTERIOR. BUREAU OF LAND MANAGEMENT *See* United States. Bureau of Land Management

UNITED STATES. DEPT. OF THE INTERIOR. FISH AND WILDLIFE SERVICE *See* U.S. Fish and Wildlife Service

UNITED STATES. DEPT. OF THE INTERIOR. GEOLOGICAL SURVEY *See* Geological Survey (U.S.)

UNITED STATES. DEPT. OF THE INTERIOR. NATIONAL PARK SERVICE *See* United States. National Park Service

UNITED STATES. DEPT. OF THE INTERIOR. OFFICE OF SURFACE MINING, RECLAMATION, AND ENFORCEMENT *See* United States. Office of Surface Mining, Reclamation, and Enforcement

UNITED STATES. DEPT. OF THE TREASURY

Anti-dollarism. D. Seligman. il *Fortune* 120:215 N 6 '89

Brady's long-term plans will collide with the deficit [N. Brady's competitiveness policy] H. Gleckman. por *Business Week* p33 Ja 23 '89

The debt plan Brady floated is still, well, floating. M. McNamee. por *Business Week* p51 My 8 '89

The Nick & Dick show: what next? [N. Brady and R. Darman] C. Hutton. il pors *Fortune* 119:12 Ja 30 '89

The old boy and the new boys [leveraged buyout issue] C. Bruck. *The New Yorker* 65:81-90+ My 8 '89

The pick-and-shovel work of Nick Brady. S. Dentzer. il por *U.S. News & World Report* 106:23-4 Mr 20 '89

The quiet crusader [N. Brady; cover story] H. Gleckman. il pors *Business Week* p80-3+ S 18 '89

Washington's new, softer line on Latin debt [Brady plan] M. McNamee. il por *Business Week* p58 Mr 20 '89

Who is Nick Brady? Why it matters. L. S. Richman. il por *Fortune* 119:59-60+ My 22 '89

UNITED STATES. DEPT. OF THE TREASURY. CUSTOMS SERVICE *See* U.S. Customs Service

UNITED STATES. DEPT. OF TRANSPORTATION

The heat is on airline deals. S. Payne. il por *Business Week* p32 O 2 '89

House passes bill to curb airline mergers, takeovers. M. Mecham. *Aviation Week & Space Technology* 131:54 N 6 '89

How 'Sam the Hammer' could nail the airlines [S. Skinner] S. Payne. il por *Business Week* p126-7 Je 26 '89

A master plan from Bush's unlikely star [Secretary S. K. Skinner] P. Barry and P. Glastris. il pors *U.S. News & World Report* 107:24-5 Jl 24 '89

Senators press Skinner on civil aviation agenda [Secretary-designate S. K. Skinner] M. Mecham. *Aviation Week & Space Technology* 130:70-1 Ja 30 '89

Skinner's proposal to expand service by foreign airlines gets mixed response. J. Ott. *Aviation Week & Space Technology* 131:57 O 30 '89

Transportation Dept. considers standards for regulating LBOs [airline industry] *Aviation Week & Space Technology* 131:128 S 11 '89

Transportation Dept. will require wider use of advanced bomb detectors. *Aviation Week & Space Technology* 130:69 Ap 17 '89

U.S. asks United buyout group for details on debt, foreign stake. C. Fotos. *Aviation Week & Space Technology* 131:105 O 2 '89

U.S. sets insurance minimums for commercial space launches. E. H. Kolcum. *Aviation Week & Space Technology* 130:69 Ja 30 '89

White House, Hill clash over airline takeovers [with editorial comment] M. Mecham. *Aviation Week & Space Technology* 131:7, 16-17 O 23 '89

UNITED STATES. DEPT. OF TRANSPORTATION. NATIONAL HIGHWAY TRAFFIC SAFETY ADMINISTRATION *See* United States. National Highway Traffic Safety Administration

UNITED STATES. DEPT. OF TRANSPORTATION. NATIONAL TRANSPORTATION SAFETY BOARD *See* United States. National Transportation Safety Board

UNITED STATES. DEPT. OF VETERANS AFFAIRS

The battle between the veterans [cuts in medical benefits] A. Plattner. il *U.S. News & World Report* 106:40-1 Je 5 '89

UNITED STATES. DRUG ENFORCEMENT ADMINISTRATION

A bungled deal with Panama [money laundering crackdown utilizes M. Noriega's forces] il por *Newsweek* 113:25 Ap 10 '89

Couple on the firing line [agents R. and V. Baker] R. L. Haywood. il pors *Ebony* 44:142+ Ag '89

DEA Don Juan [women set up and arrested for cocaine dealing by undercover agent M. R. Portell] J. Carney. il por *Time* 133:24 Ap 3 '89

A DEA hero is busted [agent E. O'Brien] por *Newsweek* 114:32 Ag 28 '89

Dear Manny [Drug Enforcement Administration's correspondence with M. Noriega] M. Hosenball. *The New Republic* 200:9-10 Je 12 '89

A federal case [murder of agent E. Hatcher] E. Pooley. il por *New York* 22:48-50+ Mr 27 '89

Leading a flying posse against cocaine smugglers, Pat Shea is the Batman of the Bahamas [head of Operation BAT] W. Plummer. il pors *People Weekly* 32:99-100 D 18 '89

The new midnight dumpers [illegal drug labs creating toxic waste in production of methamphetamine] G. Witkin. il *U.S. News & World Report* 106:57 Ja 9 '89

UNITED STATES. EMPLOYMENT SERVICE *See* United States Employment Service

UNITED STATES. ENVIRONMENTAL PROTECTION AGENCY

ABC's at the E.P.A. [class in Hazardous Material Incident Response Training] B. Weber. il *The New York Times Magazine* p114 N 12 '89

Alar: the numbers game [risk assessment controversy] L. Roberts. *Science* 243:1430 Mr 17 '89

Asbestos: the long goodbye. *Newsweek* 114:61 Jl 17 '89

Biotechnology rules wither in OMB. M. Crawford. *Science* 243:602 F 3 '89

Blowing in the wind. R. E. McNeil. *Omni (New York, N.Y.)* 11:25 S '89

Can the EPA chief clean up Bush's image? [W. K. Reilly] V. Cahan. il pors *Business Week* p135-6 D 11 '89

Change agents [R. Guimond] D. Moreau. il por *Changing Times* 43:104 F '89

Cleaning up after incinerators. *Science News* 136:381 D 9 '89

Enviro-cops on the prowl for polluters. S. J. Hedges. il *U.S. News & World Report* 107:23 O 9 '89

Environmental Protection Agency summary [excerpts from Environmental progress and challenges] *Congressional Digest* 68:37+ F '89

The EPA deserves Cabinet status. J. D. Hair. il *International Wildlife* 19:26 My/Je '89

EPA drafts new research agenda. E. Marshall. *Science* 244:1253 Je 16 '89

The EPA is looking for a few bad apples [effects of chemical Alar] *Newsweek* 113:65 F 13 '89

EPA limits industrial benzene emissions. J. Raloff. *Science News* 136:165 S 9 '89

EPA offers options to slow global warming. R. Monastersky. *Science News* 135:183 Mr 25 '89

EPA should clean up its own act. A. Ramirez. il por *Fortune* 120:139-40+ N 6 '89

EPA's plan for cooling the global greenhouse. E. Marshall. il *Science* 243:1544-5 Mr 24 '89

Erecting a fire wall against asbestos. *U.S. News & World Report* 107:10-11 Jl 17 '89

Greening the White House [W. K. Reilly; cover story] T. Gabriel. il pors *The New York Times Magazine* p24-7+ Ag 13 '89

Grime and punishment. *The New Republic* 200:7-8 F 20 '89

Hazardous choice [W. Reilly's attempts to defang Superfund] V. Novak. *The Nation* 248:406-8 Mr 27 '89

How the EPA pollutes the news. il *Utne Reader* p60 S/O '89

Is Bill Reilly too nice to run the EPA? V. Cahan. il por *Business Week* p61 Ap 3 '89

Is risk assessment conservative? L. Roberts. *Science* 243:1553 Mr 24 '89

Keeping toxic track [registry of polluters vs. Canadian practices] D. Burke. il *Maclean's* 102:44 Ag 28 '89

The lands the feds forgot [Indian reservations] M. Ambler. il *Sierra* 74:44-6+ My/Je '89

Mud-slinging over sewage technology [EPA vs. Boston and San Diego] M. Sun. il *Science* 246:440-3 O 27 '89

UNITED STATES. ENVIRONMENTAL PROTECTION AGENCY—*cont.*

NRDC on Alar. R. M. Whyatt. bibl f *Science* 245:910-11 S 1 '89

Pesticides, risk, and applesauce [discussion of March 10, 1989 article, Pesticides and kids, and March 24, 1989 article, Is risk assessment conservative?] L. Roberts. il *Science* 244:755-7 My 19 '89

Polluting rights [coal-fired electric power plants] E. Corcoran. il *Scientific American* 261:76+ N '89

Pollution strikes the EPA [office air pollution] M. Weisskopf. il *Discover* 10:32-3 Ja '89

Reilly vows environmental activism [nomination hearing before the Senate Environment and Public Works Committee] L. Roberts. il por *Science* 243:731 F 10 '89

Revolving door at the E.P.A. [former officials taking high ranking jobs with private Superfund contractors] J. Sibbison. il *The Nation* 249:524-8 N 6 '89

Science advisers need advice [toxicologists who served on advisory panel charged with breaking conflict of interest laws] E. Marshall. il *Science* 245:20-2 Jl 7 '89

Smog-curbing limits on gas volatility. *Science News* 135:191 Mr 25 '89

Superfund implementation: the polluter must be made to pay. D. Wolf. bibl f *Environment* 31:42-4 Ja/F '89

Superfund, superflop. B. Carpenter. il map *U.S. News & World Report* 106:47-9 F 6 '89

Appropriations and expenditures

How do you spell relief? C. Peterson. il *National Wildlife* 27:40-3 Ap/My '89

The White House connection [use of HUD and EPA monies to fund Republican campaigns during the Reagan administration; cover story] M. Waas. *The Nation* 249:585+ N 20 '89

UNITED STATES. EQUAL EMPLOYMENT OPPORTUNITY COMMISSION

Working late: the case of the myopic watchdog [handling of age discrimination cases] R. Hoopes. il *Modern Maturity* 32:36-9+ Ap/My '89

UNITED STATES. EXPORT-IMPORT BANK See Export-Import Bank of the United States

UNITED STATES. FARMERS HOME ADMINISTRATION

Harvest of red ink. R. Thomas. il *Newsweek* 114:38-9 S 18 '89

UNITED STATES. FEDERAL AGRICULTURAL MORTGAGE CORPORATION See Federal Agricultural Mortgage Corporation

UNITED STATES. FEDERAL AVIATION ADMINISTRATION

20-inch crack spurs FAA to order 727-100 checks. J. Ott. *Aviation Week & Space Technology* 130:62-3 Jl 10 '89

Air traffic controllers, FAA reach tentative agreement on three-year pact. *Aviation Week & Space Technology* 130:66 Ja 23 '89

Airline groups urge FAA to change proposed rules on handicapped passengers. *Aviation Week & Space Technology* 130:108 Ja 2 '89

Airlines say FAA moving too fast on plan to install bomb detectors. M. Mecham. *Aviation Week & Space Technology* 131:96-7 Jl 17 '89

Aloha Airlines probe raises questions about FAA surveillance of maintenance [fuselage failure on Boeing 737 in April 1988] *Aviation Week & Space Technology* 131:77+ Ag 28 '89

ATA president blasts U.S. government's failure to reform aviation agency [views of Robert J. Aaronson] *Aviation Week & Space Technology* 130:50 My 1 '89

Blind passengers protest exit row seating policy. C. Fotos. *Aviation Week & Space Technology* 130:94-5 Mr 27 '89

Board asks FAA to help form model safety department. *Aviation Week & Space Technology* 131:104 O 2 '89

Busey embarks on plan to boost FAA safety inspectors, shift duties. J. Ott. il *Aviation Week & Space Technology* 131:108-9 D 18-25 '89

Busted! J. M. McClellan. il *Flying* 116:42-4+ F '89

FAA and NASA design program to improve human performance. *Aviation Week & Space Technology* 130:115 My 29 '89

FAA begins formal investigation of transport aircraft noise. P. Proctor. *Aviation Week & Space Technology* 130:60 F 6 '89

FAA cites recurring failures in maintenance at Eastern. J. T. McKenna. *Aviation Week & Space Technology* 131:7, 64-5 Jl 3 '89

FAA clears Trump to operate shuttle; bankruptcy, suits could complicate sale. il *Aviation Week & Space Technology* 130:16 Mr 13 '89

FAA expands Mode C transponder use to all aircraft near major airports. *Aviation Week & Space Technology* 131:66 Jl 3 '89

FAA fights back on plastic explosives. M. M. Waldrop. il *Science* 243:165-6 Ja 13 '89

FAA hiring field inspectors to monitor aging aircraft. M. Mecham. *Aviation Week & Space Technology* 130:110-11 Ap 24 '89

FAA issues new minimum-equipment rule. il *Flying* 116:14 Mr '89

FAA issues stricter baggage inspection requirements [response to bombing of Pan Am Flight 103] *Aviation Week & Space Technology* 130:29+ Ja 9 '89

FAA officials say Eastern safety matches that of other airlines. C. Fotos. *Aviation Week & Space Technology* 131:80-1 Ag 7 '89

FAA orders inspections of CF6-6 powerplants [result of Sioux City DC-10 accident in July 1989] *Aviation Week & Space Technology* 131:33 O 2 '89

FAA orders U.S. airlines to install bomb detectors [thermal neutron analysis device] J. Ott. *Aviation Week & Space Technology* 131:68-9 S 4 '89

FAA probes Boeing's reporting of faulty wiring in 757 extinguisher systems. C. Fotos. *Aviation Week & Space Technology* 130:66 Ja 23 '89

FAA proposes checks for cracks on 727s. *Aviation Week & Space Technology* 130:63 Ja 16 '89

FAA reaffirms rule limiting service of airline pilots over 60 years old. *Aviation Week & Space Technology* 130:110 Je 5 '89

FAA refines MLS plan [microwave landing systems] *Flying* 116:21 My '89

FAA rejects two proposals to privatize Albany airport. J. Ott. *Aviation Week & Space Technology* 131:44-5 D 11 '89

FAA seating restrictions clip the wings of handicapped and other flyers. M. Di Landro. il *Travel Holiday* 172:22-3 S '89

FAA security panel examines means of improving defense against terrorists. J. Ott. il *Aviation Week & Space Technology* 131:75+ N 13 '89

FAA task force will study solutions to capacity crisis. J. Ott. il *Aviation Week & Space Technology* 130:119+ My 29 '89

FAA will test wayport concept as remedy to airport congestion. J. Ott. il map *Aviation Week & Space Technology* 130:64-5+ Ja 9 '89

FAA's bomb scanner: an awkward Goliath? [thermal neutron analysis device developed by Tsahi Gozani] E. Marshall. il *Science* 245:926-7 S 1 '89

First airship to be FAA certified [Airship Industries' Skyship 600] il *Flying* 116:18 Ag '89

First federal MLS is commissioned [microwave landing system at Lebanon Municipal Airport, N.H.] il map *Flying* 116:20 Jl '89

Have one for the runway: how Transportation Department policies add new meaning to the word "red-eye" [policies on pilots and drug abuse] D. Nather. *The Washington Monthly* 21:12-14+ Ap '89

Independent FAA, competition issues top new House chairman's agenda [J. L. Oberstar of House Aviation Subcommittee] M. Mecham. il por *Aviation Week & Space Technology* 130:99 F 13 '89

Industry slow to comply with FAA drug testing rule. M. Mecham. il *Aviation Week & Space Technology* 131:20-3 S 18 '89

The killer compliance gap. *Aviation Week & Space Technology* 129:9 Mr 6 '89

Lives at stake [rule excluding blind airline passengers from seats in exit rows] *Aviation Week & Space Technology* 130:9 Ap 3 '89

Safety Board recommends upgrade in corrosion control research [investigation of fuselage failure on Aloha Airlines 737 in April 1988] *Aviation Week & Space Technology* 131:70-1 N 6 '89

Safety Board urges FAA to revamp maintenance, inspection training [investigation of fuselage failure on Aloha Airlines 737 in April 1988] *Aviation Week & Space Technology* 131:77+ O 23 '89

Sky strain. *Time* 133:56 Je 5 '89

Soviet/Gulfstream supersonic aircraft hinges on bilateral certification agreement. C. Fotos. *Aviation Week & Space Technology* 131:110-11 D 18-25 '89

Still there for the axing at age 60 [airline pilots] *Flying* 116:26 S '89

Threatened job losses fuel congressional opposition to FAA's foreign repair rules [with editorial comment] M. Mecham. *Aviation Week & Space Technology* 131:7, 29-30 Jl 3 '89

U.S. should establish independent FAA based on Britain's CAA model. A. W. Blackburn. por *Aviation Week & Space Technology* 130:119-20 My 1 '89

We're here to help. W. Garvey. il *Flying* 116:8 Je '89

When terrorists strike America, who responds? M. Mecham. *Aviation Week & Space Technology* 131:81+ D 18-25 '89

Appropriations and expenditures

Congressional pledge of $500 million for Denver airport seen as key victory. *Aviation Week & Space Technology* 131:71 O 23 '89

FAA seeks $1-billion increase in 1991 to fund facilities, R & D projects. M. Mecham. *Aviation Week & Space Technology* 131:110 D 18-25 '89

FAA seeks $1 billion increase, more personnel in 1990 budget. J. Ott. *Aviation Week & Space Technology* 130:43 Ja 23 '89

Funding, procurement reform called top priorities for FAA reorganization. M. Mecham. *Aviation Week & Space Technology* 130:116 My 29 '89

UNITED STATES. FEDERAL AVIATION ADMINISTRATION — Appropriations and expenditures — *cont.*

Proposed Denver International passes environmental test, but funding slips. M. Mecham. *Aviation Week & Space Technology* 131:94-5 Ag 21 '89

Procurement

American offers to use its pilots, simulators to evaluate MLS curved approach capabilities [microwave landing system] il *Aviation Week & Space Technology* 129:69 Mr 6 '89

ATA will establish task force to critique MLS programs [microwave landing systems] J. T. McKenna. il *Aviation Week & Space Technology* 129:68-9 Mr 6 '89

FAA awards California grant to study applications for commercial tilt-rotor. *Aviation Week & Space Technology* 131:25 Jl 31 '89

FAA seeks detectors requiring little human judgment to find explosives. C. Fotos. il *Aviation Week & Space Technology* 130:65-7 Ja 16 '89

FAA weighs terminating Hazeltine's MLS contract [microwave landing systems] *Aviation Week & Space Technology* 131:28 Jl 3 '89

Hazeltine, FAA work to salvage major MLS production contract [microwave landing system] J. T. McKenna. *Aviation Week & Space Technology* 131:70-1 Ag 28 '89

Unisys wins $44.9-million contract to upgrade airport radar systems. il *Aviation Week & Space Technology* 131:57 N 6 '89

USAF may transfer six C-29As, crews to FAA for flight inspection mission. *Aviation Week & Space Technology* 131:108 D 18-25 '89

UNITED STATES. FEDERAL BUREAU OF INVESTIGATION

See also

Pentagon procurement scandal

Another dirty secret [investigation of the National Lawyers Guild] M. Kempton. *The New York Review of Books* 36:52 D 7 '89

Ballantine releases updated edition of 'Dangerous dossiers' [H. Mitgang book on FBI surveillance of authors and Freedom of Information Act] B. Levine. il *Publishers Weekly* 235:27 Mr 17 '89

Black FBI agent loses case at Justice Dept. [D. Rochon case] *Jet* 76:7 Jl 24 '89

Can Sessions tame the Bureau? D. R. Gordon. il *The Nation* 249:488-91 O 30 '89

The challenges we face in law enforcement [address, October 17, 1988] W. S. Sessions. *Vital Speeches of the Day* 55:260-2 F 15 '89

Commodities sting [investigation of Chicago exchanges] J. J. Curran. il *Fortune* 119:12 F 13 '89

Crackdown on the Chicago boys [FBI uncovers widespread fraud in commodity markets] C. Gorman. il *Time* 133:52 Ja 30 '89

Earth last! [D. Foreman and others of Earth First! charged with attempted sabotage of the Central Arizona Project] D. Russell. *The Nation* 249:77 Jl 17 '89

Eavesdropping left and right [Cincinnati Bell implicated in wiretapping scandal] G. Flannery. il *The Nation* 248:516-18+ Ap 17 '89

The FBI and I. G. Seldes. il *The Progressive* 53:50 F '89

FBI gives bookstore threats top priority [relating to S. Rushdie's Satanic verses] H. Fields. il *Publishers Weekly* 235:12 Mr 17 '89

The FBI is a tough outfit to run. L. Smith. il *Fortune* 120:133-4+ O 9 '89

FBI moving to improve its minority employment. *Jet* 75:8 Mr 20 '89

The FBI's new most wanted list [efforts to boost minority hiring] G. Witkin. il *U.S. News & World Report* 106:23-4 My 29 '89

The files of counterrevolution [investigation of Committee in Solidarity with the People of El Salvador] A. Cockburn. *The Nation* 249:161 Ag 7-14 '89

G-men at the movies [memo on A. Warhol's Lonesome cowboys] *Harper's* 278:26 Je '89

How reliable are the FBI's reports? [background checks on political nominees] S. J. Hedges. il *U.S. News & World Report* 106:46 Mr 13 '89

In the futures pits, life is no longer a bowl of cherries [FBI uncovers fraud in Chicago's commodity exchanges] C. P. Work and R. F. Black. il *U.S. News & World Report* 106:44-5 F 6 '89

Life in the pits will never be the same [sting of Chicago's trading system] K. A. Behof. il *Business Week* p32-4 F 6 '89

"Ma'am, what you need is a new improved Hoover" [domestic spying] M. Miller. il por *The Washington Monthly* 20:10-14+ Ja '89

Missing the Tower story [J. Tower nomination and FBI background investigation] T. Eastland. il *The American Spectator* 22:34-6 My '89

Monkey-wrenching for planet earth [Earth First! infiltrated by FBI] T. Vanderpool. il por *The Progressive* 53:15 S '89

On the trail of terrorists [investigation of Pan Am Flight 103 bombing] S. Emerson. il *U.S. News & World Report* 106:36 F 13 '89

Outlasting the F.B.I., a determined widow restores her husband's reputation as a loyal Communist [L. Albertson wins lawsuit on behalf of B. Albertson, falsely accused of being an informer] J. S. Kunen. il *People Weekly* 32:171-2 N 20 '89

Poetic injustice. *The Nation* 248:399-400 Mr 27 '89

The sting in the pits [probe uncovers fraud at Chicago Board of Trade and Chicago Mercantile Exchange] J. McCormick. il *Newsweek* 113:54 Ja 30 '89

Wanted: lowlifes and high ratings [America's most wanted] D. Friedman. il *Rolling Stone* p34-5 Ja 12 '89

Bibliography

Doing Edgar proud. D. R. Gordon. *The Nation* 249:570-4 N 13 '89

UNITED STATES. FEDERAL COMMUNICATIONS COMMISSION

AT&T unchained: business may be the winner [FCC's rate cap proposal] F. Seghers. il *Business Week* p42 Mr 20 '89

Changing channels. J. Hood. *The New Republic* 200:12+ My 22 '89

Congress, the FCC, and Judge Greene [address, November 10, 1988] D. Brenner. *Vital Speeches of the Day* 55:250-3 F 1 '89

Don't laugh: this plan for regulating AT&T actually sounds good [price caps for long distance service] A. S. Blinder. il *Business Week* p14 Je 12 '89

FCC distress-sale policy overturned [minority policy] S. M. Williams. *Black Enterprise* 19:54 Je '89

FCC kills crystal coms [aviation] *Flying* 116:14 N '89

HDTV: keeping the rabbit ears alive. R. S. Schwartz. il *High Fidelity (New York, N.Y.)* 39:51-2+ Ap '89

HDTV: the FCC edict. R. Angus. *High Fidelity (New York, N.Y.)* 39:12-13 Ja '89

How the rich get richer [tax breaks in affirmative action media buys] H. Rudnitsky. il *Forbes* 143:38-9 My 15 '89

In the eye of the storm [Tribune Co. fights syndicated exclusivity rules; interview with J. Dowdle] K. Haley. il pors *Channels (New York, N.Y.: 1986)* 9:62-3 Ja 16 '89

NAACP challenges the affirmative action plans of TV, radio stations. *Jet* 76:26 Je 12 '89

The phone flushaway [lottery for distribution of cellular telephone licenses] D. Ellen. *The New Republic* 201:13-15 O 9 '89

The silencing of 'Radio Sarah' [shutdown of Radio New York International] D. Kuipers. il *The Nation* 248:559+ Ap 24 '89

U.S. technical leadership is threatened by investment pressure [address, May 8, 1989] R. J. Marano. *Vital Speeches of the Day* 55:601-3 Jl 15 '89

The uphill fight against dial-a-porn. il *Newsweek* 113:42 Ja 9 '89

What's syndex? Will it affect you? [syndicated exclusivity] N. Hickey. il *TV Guide* 37:12 D 23-29 '89

Why the FCC can't get its signal across. F. Seghers. *Business Week* p49 Ja 23 '89

Will Alfred Sikes fix the power shortage at the FCC? D. Foust. por *Business Week* p73 Je 26 '89

UNITED STATES. FEDERAL CROP INSURANCE CORPORATION *See* Federal Crop Insurance Corporation

UNITED STATES. FEDERAL DEPOSIT INSURANCE CORPORATION *See* Federal Deposit Insurance Corporation

UNITED STATES. FEDERAL EMERGENCY MANAGEMENT AGENCY

Pushed to the limit. S. Manning. il *Scholastic Update (Teachers' edition)* 122:12 D 15 '89

UNITED STATES. FEDERAL HOME LOAN BANK BOARD

$1 billion worth of influence [C. Keating's dealings with five senators in the Lincoln Savings & Loan affair] M. B. Carlson. il por *Time* 134:27-8 N 6 '89

Asleep at the S&L switch [M. D. Wall and the Lincoln Savings & Loan scandal] R. Thomas and E. Clift. il por *Newsweek* 114:71 D 11 '89

The bust of '89 [cover story] T. Moore. il por *U.S. News & World Report* 106:36-43 Ja 23 '89

CC calls for ethics inquiry of five senators [dealings with C. Keating in the Lincoln Savings & Loan affair] J. Denny. *Common Cause Magazine* 15:28 N/D '89

Financier Charles Keating is the $2 billion man of the savings and loan crisis [Lincoln Savings & Loan scandal involving five senators] B. Hewitt. il pors *People Weekly* 32:78-80 D 4 '89

For Charlie Keating, the best defense is a lawsuit [declares American Continental bankrupt as feds close in on Lincoln Savings & Loan] K. Kerwin. il por *Business Week* p32+ My 1 '89

The great S&L fire sale. il *U.S. News & World Report* 106:11+ Ja 9 '89

Is Danny Wall on the way out? [tainted by Lincoln Savings & Loan scandal] C. Yang and P. Dwyer. *Business Week* p59 N 13 '89

It's the end of an era for S&L rescues—but what an end. C. Yang. il por *Business Week* p40 Ja 9 '89

UNITED STATES. FEDERAL HOME LOAN BANK BOARD—*cont.*

"A legal bank robbery" [complicity of federal regulators in Lincoln Savings and Loan scandal] M. B. Carlson. il pors *Time* 134:29 N 27 '89

The man who tried to buy Washington [C. Keating's dealings with five senators in the Lincoln Savings & Loan affair] G. Borger and S. J. Hedges. il pors *U.S. News & World Report* 107:18-21+ N 27 '89

Now it's broke [D. Regan's role in S&L scandal] J. R. Adams. *The New Republic* 201:16-18 N 13 '89

Quis custodiet? [J. Wright's efforts on behalf of Texas thrifts] R. C. Kirkwood and T. P. Jeffrey. il *National Review* 41:35-6 Ap 21 '89

The S&L scandal's biggest blowout [C. H. Keating's Lincoln Savings & Loan scandal involves five senators] T. Morgan- thau. il por *Newsweek* 114:35-6 N 6 '89

S&L time bomb. *The Nation* 248:75-6 Ja 23 '89

S&Ls: 219 down, maybe 300 to go. W. E. Sheeline. il *Fortune* 119:9 Ja 30 '89

The screwiest S&L bailout ever [R. O. Perelman's acquisition of First Texas Gibraltar] B. D. Fromson. il por *Fortune* 119:114-15+ Je 19 '89

The smart money in S&L's. L. Reibstein. il por *Newsweek* 113:40 Ja 9 '89

The tumbling of Danny Wall [Lincoln Savings & Loan scandal] S. J. Hedges. *U.S. News & World Report* 107:55 D 11 '89

Wright, Coelho and the S&L fiasco. M. Barone. il pors *U.S. News & World Report* 106:21-2 Je 12 '89

Wright was not wronged [excerpt from report issued by House Ethics Committee] *Harper's* 279:18+ Ag '89

UNITED STATES. FEDERAL HOUSING ADMINISTRA- TION

Austin Fitts better be good with hammer and nails. R. Stodghill, II. il por *Business Week* p152-3 N 27 '89

Come and get it [federal government deputizes mortgage brokers to approve and coinsure FHA mortgages] M. Schifrin. il *Forbes* 143:41-2 My 15 '89

Let's make a deal [loan guaranty funds] J. Novack. il *Forbes* 143:48 Ja 23 '89

Reverse mortgages: an idea whose time is finally coming (again). D. M. Topolnicki. il *Money* 18:169-70 Mr '89

UNITED STATES. FEDERAL NATIONAL MORTGAGE ASSOCIATION *See* Federal National Mortgage Association

UNITED STATES. FEDERAL RESERVE SYSTEM *See* Federal Reserve System (U.S.)

UNITED STATES. FEDERAL SAVINGS AND LOAN IN- SURANCE CORPORATION *See* Federal Savings and Loan Insurance Corporation

UNITED STATES. FEDERAL TRADE COMMISSION

Chain reaction [charges that bookstore chains get preferential treatment from publishers] C. Goodrich. *The Nation* 248:596-8 My 1 '89

Court blocks FTC vision-care ruling. *Modern Maturity* 32:13 D '89/Ja '90

Federal Trade Commission: defending the consumer [interview with D. Oliver] il por *Consumers' Research Magazine* 72:21-4 O '89

Rivets and revelation [Textron's acquisition of Avdel prompts FTC antitrust case concerning blind rivets] H. Banks. *Forbes* 143:153 Je 12 '89

Six houses win one point in first FTC skirmish [charge that chains get preferential treatment not accorded indepen- dent bookstores] H. Fields. *Publishers Weekly* 235:14 Ap 21 '89

Six publishers charged with price bias by FTC [policies favoring bookstore chains over independents] *Publishers Weekly* 235:19 Ja 6 '89

UNITED STATES. FERMI NATIONAL ACCELERATOR LABORATORY *See* Fermi National Accelerator Laboratory

UNITED STATES. FISH AND WILDLIFE SERVICE *See* U.S. Fish and Wildlife Service

UNITED STATES. FOOD AND DRUG ADMINISTRATION

50th anniversary of the FDA. F. E. Young. il *The Saturday Evening Post* 261:56-7+ Ja/F '89

1988 product approvals: an FDA annual report. F. E. Young. il *FDA Consumer* 23:6-7 Ap '89

At last, quicker access to AIDS drugs. J. Seligmann. *Newsweek* 114:76 Jl 10 '89

Brand-name or generic: what your body does—and doesn't— know. C. Marks. il *Mademoiselle* 95;128+ O '89

The breakfast drug [reviews use of psyllium in cereal to determine if it is a food or drug] J. Newman. *American Health* 8:82+ D '89

Condom conundrum [approval of women's condoms] M. Suh. il *Ms.* 17:87 Mr '89

Condom mania! [requiring retesting of the microcondom and women's condom] E. Franklin. il *American Health* 8:18 Je '89

Conflicting prescriptions. *The New Republic* 201:4 Ag 28 '89

Desperation drugs [AIDS drugs] S. Begley. il *Newsweek* 114:48-51 Ag 7 '89

Dr. Frank Young: making a difference. C. SerVaas. il pors *The Saturday Evening Post* 261:50-5+ Ja/F '89

Drug abuse [Mylan Laboratories' suspicions of FDA corruption bear fruit] J. Novack. il *Forbes* 143:42-3 Je 26 '89

Drugs from the underground [allows wider use of experimental AIDS drugs] D. Thompson. il *Time* 134:49 Jl 10 '89

Ensuring the safety of generic drugs. F. E. Young. il *FDA Consumer* 23:5-7 D '89/Ja '90

The facts of life [need for faster drug approval and information on side effects] H. Evans. il *U.S. News & World Report* 106:79 F 27 '89

FDA broadens use of unproven AIDS drug [DDI in; dextran sulfate out] D. E. Loupe. *Science News* 136:231 O 7 '89

FDA—hazardous to our health? M. S. Forbes, Jr. il *Forbes* 144:27 Ag 21 '89

Generic concern. R. Coorsh. *Consumers' Research Magazine* 72:4 O '89

How far has the cancer spread at the FDA? [generic drug scandal] J. Carey. il *Business Week* p30-1 S 18 '89

Investigators' reports. See issues of FDA Consumer

Label ease [proposals for food labeling] L. Giuca. il *Organic Gardening* 36:53-6+ N '89

Mail-order AIDS tests: FDA confronts the implications. R. Weiss. *Science News* 135:268 Ap 29 '89

A new AIDS drug gets the go-ahead [DDI] *Newsweek* 114:40 O 9 '89

Not what the doctor ordered [accused of carelessness about generic drugs] J. N. Baker. il *Newsweek* 114:32 Ag 28 '89

The notebook. See issues of FDA Consumer

The other drug war here at home [generic drug scandal] *U.S. News & World Report* 107:11 S 11 '89

A prescription for scandal [generic drug industry] C. Gorman. il *Time* 134:56 Ag 28 '89

Quick release of AIDS drugs. E. Marshall. il *Science* 245:345+ Jl 28 '89

Rubber stamp [FDA requires stricter tests of microcondoms] B. Baker. *Common Cause Magazine* 15:7-8 Jl/Ag '89

Rx for the FDA [pressure to speed up drug approval process] J. E. Groopman. *The New Republic* 200:17-18+ F 13 '89

Scientific necessity, patients' rights [pressuring FDA to speed up drug approval process] J. Carey. il *U.S. News & World Report* 106:50-1 Ja 23 '89

Serving God and man in the nation's capital [interview with F. E. Young] il por *Christianity Today* 33:45 S 8 '89

Speeding help and hope to the desperately ill. F. E. Young. il *FDA Consumer* 23:8-9 F '89

Study details misconduct in drug research [work of Martin F. Shapiro and Robert P. Charrow] K. Fackelmann. *Science News* 135:278 My 6 '89

Testing, testing [new AIDS drug DDI] D. Ellen. *The New Republic* 201:14-15 Ag 28 '89

Updates. See issues of FDA Consumer

Watchdogs overdose on generic drugs [investigation of fraudu- lent activities] S. Dentzer. il *U.S. News & World Report* 107:26 Ag 28-S 4 '89

What's the cure for burnout? D. Thompson. il *Time* 134:68 D 25 '89

What's wrong with generic drugs? [cover story] J. W. Merline. il *Consumers' Research Magazine* 72:11-17 D '89

When the corner drugstore falls short [importing drugs not approved by FDA] F. Lunzer. il *U.S. News & World Report* 106:82 F 13 '89

Why can't we get the medicine we need? R. Flick. *Reader's Digest* 135:101-6 Ag '89

Why generic drugs are O.K. J. Silberner. il *U.S. News & World Report* 107:70-2 S 18 '89

UNITED STATES. FOREST SERVICE

Airborne surveillance will give Forest Service real-time fire maps. B. D. Nordwall. il *Aviation Week & Space Technology* 130:105+ My 29 '89

A mixed blessing [management plan for North Carolina] P. Byrnes. *Wilderness* 53:5-6 Wint '89

Park-quality sequoias logged [Sequoia National Forest] il *National Parks* 63:8-9 My/Je '89

Taking heart from upper East Tennessee [Cherokee National Forest] B. Wallach. il map *Focus (New York, N.Y.: 1950)* 38:22-8 Wint '88

War in the woods: Swan song [confrontations over destruction of old-growth timber in Flathead National Forest] J. G. Mitchell. il map *Audubon* 91:92-102+ N '89

Appropriations and expenditures

Ancient forests agreement [Pacific Northwest] P. Byrnes. il *Wilderness* 53:3-4 Wint '89

Deforestation hits home: U.S. Forest Service levels our landscape. K. E. Franklin. il *Utne Reader* p52 My/Je '89

Forest Service: admissions and additions [losing money on timber sales] *Wilderness* 52:v-vi Spr '89

Timber! K. E. Franklin. *The New Republic* 200:12-14 Ja 2 '89

UNITED STATES. GENERAL ACCOUNTING OFFICE

Congress's watch dog: mostly it still goes for the capillaries. J. Heilemann. *The Washington Monthly* 21:38-42 N '89

GAO will review Ritchie, Lorenzo plans for Eastern. J. T. McKenna. *Aviation Week & Space Technology* 131:100-1 Jl 31 '89

UNITED STATES. GENERAL SERVICES ADMINISTRA- TION

Public art and its inherent problems. D. Grant. *American Artist* 53:78-9+ O '89

UNITED STATES. GENERAL SERVICES ADMINISTRATION—cont.
"Tilted arc" destroyed [cover story] R. Serra. bibl f il *Art in America* 77:34-7+ My '89

UNITED STATES. GEOLOGICAL SURVEY *See* Geological Survey (U.S.)

UNITED STATES. IMMIGRATION AND NATURALIZATION SERVICE
Inside with the INS [experience of Australian tourist] G. Rodoreda. il *The Progressive* 53:50 My '89
Judge orders INS to stop the delays [failure to abide by Freedom of Information Act in deportation cases] E. Pell. il *The Progressive* 53:13-14 S '89
Newcomers meet hard hearts [Nicaraguans seek U.S. asylum] *America* 160:131 F 18 '89
No sanctuary [Central American refugees] T. Reader. *The Nation* 249:193 Ag 21-28 '89
Raids, racism and the I.N.S. [on trial for harassing Mexican immigrants in California] E. Shorris. il *The Nation* 248:628-30 My 8 '89
Roundup on the Rio Grande [Central Americans] J. Juffer. il *The Progressive* 53:32-3 Ap '89
Take a number and wait [immigration amnesty program] D. Shaw. *The Washington Monthly* 21:28-30+ S '89
Texas pitches a 'tent city' [Port Isabel detention center holds refugees for deportation] E. Salholz. il *Newsweek* 113:27 Mr 6 '89

UNITED STATES. IMMIGRATION AND NATURALIZATION SERVICE. BORDER PATROL *See* United States. Border Patrol

UNITED STATES. INFORMATION AGENCY
G.O.P. formula [nomination of B. Gelb as director] A. Dubro. *The Nation* 248:329-30 Mr 13 '89
To Russia, with books [exhibit titled Many-booked America] Y. Richmond. por *Publishers Weekly* 235:76 F 3 '89
Track great Mal Whitfield lauded at USIA retirement. il por *Jet* 77:48 N 20 '89
Who will bury whom, Nikita? [exhibit Design USA in Soviet Union] il *U.S. News & World Report* 107:12-13 S 18 '89

UNITED STATES. INSTITUTE OF ALLERGY AND INFECTIOUS DISEASES *See* National Institute of Allergy and Infectious Diseases (U.S.)

UNITED STATES. INTERNAL REVENUE SERVICE
The abuse of power: misuse of the I.R.S. [cover story] D. Burnham. il *The New York Times Magazine* p24-7+ S 3 '89
Atlanta suit to examine black-on-black bias [firing of employee T. L. Morrow] *Jet* 76:7 Je 12 '89
Black woman heads IRS district office in Iowa [H. Hightower] por *Jet* 75:6 Mr 6 '89
Congress has leveled the playing field for contests with the tax man [Taxpayer Bill of Rights] *U.S. News & World Report* 106:79 Mr 27 '89
Delinquent taxmen [congressional investigation into corruption and coverups] R. Behar. il *Time* 133:66-7 My 29 '89
Fear and cover-ups in the IRS. R. Behar. il *Time* 134:40 Ag 7 '89
How the IRS aims to simplify tax penalties. C. Yang. *Business Week* p38 Mr 13 '89
The IRS follies [IRS embroiled in jeans war between Nakash family of Jordache and Marciano family of Guess?] C. Byron. il *New York* 22:11-12 Ag 7 '89
IRS to implement backup withholding. P. N. Strassels. il *Nation's Business* 77:68 Mr '89
Meet your friendly IRS helper—if you dare. G. Anrig, Jr. and S. Steinert. il *Money* 18:112 Mr '89
Taxing matters. See issues of Forbes
Their computers probably know more about you than you think. R. Wool. il *Money* 18:177 N '89
When you move, tell your friends. And the IRS. L. Wiener. il *U.S. News & World Report* 107:121 O 16 '89
Your friend at the IRS [ombudsman D. Holmes] K. McCormally. il *Changing Times* 43:98 Ja '89
Your rights as a taxpayer. *Consumers' Research Magazine* 72:20-4 Mr '89
Your rights as a taxpayer: now they're in writing. C. Yang. il *Business Week* p103 F 13 '89

UNITED STATES. INTERSTATE COMMERCE COMMISSION
Stormy Heather [chairman H. Gradison] J. Cook. il por *Forbes* 143:168+ Je 26 '89

UNITED STATES. JOINT CHIEFS OF STAFF
Breaking barriers in the barracks [C. L. Powell to head Joint Chiefs of Staff] P. Cary. il pors *U.S. News & World Report* 107:26-7 Ag 21 '89
Called to service: the Colin Powell story. C. T. Rowan. por *Reader's Digest* 135:121-6 D '89
Colin Powell named first black and youngest chair of Joint Chiefs of Staff. il pors *Jet* 76:5-7 Ag 28 '89
A "complete soldier" makes it [chairman C. L. Powell] B. Seaman. por *Time* 134:24 Ag 21 '89
Gen. Colin Powell OK'd by full Senate for chair of Joint Chiefs of Staff. il por *Jet* 77:4 O 9 '89
Gen. Colin Powell takes seat as chair of Joint Chiefs at the Pentagon. il pors *Jet* 77:4-5 O 23 '89

Gen. Colin Powell's advice to young blacks today: prepare and be ready [cover story] il pors *Jet* 76:12-15 S 11 '89
Powell reaches the pinnacle of Pentagon power [C. L. Powell] M. Brown. il por *Black Enterprise* 20:22 O '89
Pragmatist at the Pentagon [chairman C. L. Powell] E. Salholz. por *Newsweek* 114:20 Ag 21 '89
Reforming the Joint Chiefs of Staff: a timid first step. D. Isenberg. il *USA Today (Periodical)* 117:12-15 Ja '89

UNITED STATES. LAND AND WATER CONSERVATION FUND GRANT ASSISTANCE PROGRAM *See* Land and Water Conservation Fund Grant Assistance Program (U.S.)

UNITED STATES. LIBRARY OF CONGRESS *See* Library of Congress

UNITED STATES. MARINE CORPS
Accidents and injuries
Marines ground aircraft to assess safety concerns. B. D. Nordwall. *Aviation Week & Space Technology* 130:72 Je 12 '89
Airplanes
See Airplanes, Military
Appropriations and expenditures
Budget request sustains Marine aviation upgrades. il *Aviation Week & Space Technology* 130:22 Ja 16 '89
Naval aviation modernization hit hard by Pentagon cuts. *Aviation Week & Space Technology* 130:23 Ap 24 '89
Forces in Lebanon
Terrorist attack, 1983
What America hasn't learned from its greatest peacekeeping disaster. S. Shuger. il *The Washington Monthly* 21:40-4+ O '89
Forces in Nicaragua
Mr. Yankee goes home. A. Cruz, Jr. *Commentary* 88:47-8 Ag '89
Forces in the Soviet Union
The Moscow bug hunt [no evidence that Marines C. Lonetree and A. Bracy allowed Soviets into the U.S. embassy] J. Peterzell. il pors *Time* 134:26-8 Jl 10 '89
Moscow station: how the KGB penetrated the American embassy [Marine guard spy case; excerpts; cover story] R. Kessler. il *Time* 133:50-2+ F 20 '89
Procurement
Competing GE, FMC armored turrets offer different weapons configurations [Light Armored Vehicle-Air Defense system] D. F. Bond. il *Aviation Week & Space Technology* 131:45+ S 25 '89
Marine official pleads guilty to U.S. bribery, fraud charges [J. A. Sherman] M. Mecham. *Aviation Week & Space Technology* 130:26 F 6 '89
Recruiting, enlistment, etc.
Marines hit the beaches in Minnesota [recruitment drive meets with antiwar protest] M. Helmberger. il *The Progressive* 53:17 O '89
Training
See Military training
Uniforms
Photographs and photography
Semper finery. A. Edgeworth. il *Esquire* 111:135-9 F '89
Women
See Servicewomen

UNITED STATES. MARSHALS SERVICE
Take the oath, put on the badge and do the job. D. D. Jackson. bibl (p174) il *Smithsonian* 20:114-18+ Ap '89

UNITED STATES. MERIT SYSTEMS PROTECTION BOARD. OFFICE OF THE SPECIAL COUNSEL
Shielding the whistle-blowers. T. Noah. il *Newsweek* 113:32 Mr 27 '89

UNITED STATES. MINORITY BUSINESS DEVELOPMENT AGENCY
Fed. report cites abuse in Minority Business Agency. *Jet* 76:12 Ap 17 '89

UNITED STATES. MINT
The buck starts here, and may stop here, at the nation's money mills. D. Stewart. bibl (p163) il *Smithsonian* 20:36-45 My '89

UNITED STATES. NATIONAL ACADEMY OF SCIENCES *See* National Academy of Sciences (U.S.)

UNITED STATES. NATIONAL AERONAUTICS AND SPACE ADMINISTRATION
See also
Challenger (Space shuttle) explosion, 1986
20 years after Apollo: is the U.S. lost in space? [cover story; special section; with editorial comment by C. P. Gilmore] S. F. Brown. il *Popular Science* 235:4, 63-75 Jl '89
Bringing NASA down to earth. E. Marshall. il *Science* 244:1248-51 Je 16 '89
The edge of infinity [cover story] W. J. Cook. il *U.S. News & World Report* 106:52-6+ My 15 '89
First word [NASA's need for new goals] T. O. Paine. il *Omni (New York, N.Y.)* 11:6 Jl '89
Headline: commercial space dies . . . . C. Miller. *Ad Astra* 1:13 F '89
Jukeboxes for scientists [coping with upcoming deluge of data] J. Horgan. *Scientific American* 261:24-5 Jl '89

UNITED STATES. NATIONAL AERONAUTICS AND SPACE ADMINISTRATION—cont.

Knapp resigns from URA leadership; Truly to pilot NASA, Fields at DARPA. I. Goodwin. *Physics Today* 42:42-4 Je '89

NASA 1989: suddenly it's 1986 [readying postponed science missions] J. Eberhart. il *Science News* 135:15 Ja 7 '89

NASA adds to understanding of high angle of attack regime [cover story] W. B. Scott. il *Aviation Week & Space Technology* 130:36-8+ My 22 '89

NASA ponders the Mars Rover. il *Astronomy* 17:16 Mr '89

NASA to build 'Small Explorer' satellites. J. Eberhart. *Science News* 135:229 Ap 15 '89

The next giant leap for mankind. M. D. Lemonick. il *Time* 134:50-1 Jl 24 '89

OTA to NASA: accidents will happen. M. M. Waldrop. *Science* 245:697 Ag 18 '89

Piece by piece [space program hurt by incremental approach] H. E. McCurdy. il *Ad Astra* 1:24-8 F '89

The promise of the 21st century [National Academy of Sciences report] il *Astronomy* 17:44-50 Ja '89

Space/missiles: NASA/industry shuttle team [aerospace laureate] il por *Aviation Week & Space Technology* 130:14 Ja 2 '89

Space science on the rebound? M. M. Waldrop. il *Science* 244:525-6 My 5 '89

Taking the earth's vital signs [Mission-to-Earth project] il *Time* 133:72-4 Je 5 '89

Top talent leaving NASA . . . new recruits hard to find [effect of revolving door rules] E. Marshall and M. M. Waldrop. il *Science* 245:251 Jl 21 '89

Appropriations and expenditures

Batteries not included [space station budget crunch] T. Beardsley. *Scientific American* 261:20 O '89

Big bytes in NASA's budget [plans to substitute computers for retiring personnel] R. Fleming. il *Omni (New York, N.Y.)* 12:30+ O '89

David and Goliath in space [views of Daniel Hastings] il *Technology Review* 92:80 Ag/S '89

Desperately seeking station. A. Lawler. il *Ad Astra* 1:8-11 Je '89

Europeans urge U.S. to avoid cutting space station funds. il *Aviation Week & Space Technology* 130:39 Je 19 '89

Give space station a dose of reality. *Aviation Week & Space Technology* 131:11 Ag 21 '89

A guide to budget politics. G. H. Reynolds. *Ad Astra* 1:21 Je '89

House blocks attempt to slash station funds. M. Mecham. *Aviation Week & Space Technology* 131:32 Jl 24 '89

House panel proposes $1-billion cut for NASA. M. Mecham. *Aviation Week & Space Technology* 131:26 Jl 17 '89

Is the man in the White House moonstruck? il *U.S. News & World Report* 107:10 Jl 24 '89

NASA accelerates lunar base planning as station changes draw European fire. C. Covault. il *Aviation Week & Space Technology* 131:26-7 S 18 '89

NASA advised to drop new shuttle motor program. T. M. Foley. *Aviation Week & Space Technology* 130:29+ Ap 3 '89

NASA faces personnel crisis, long-term funding shortage [with editorial comment] C. Covault. il *Aviation Week & Space Technology* 130:7, 23-4 F 20 '89

NASA focuses on station, faces growing budget crisis. C. Covault. il *Aviation Week & Space Technology* 130:109-11 Mr 20 '89

NASA funding cut for X-30, station programs. *Aviation Week & Space Technology* 131:24 O 23 '89

NASA-industry team defines options to salvage space station program. E. H. Kolcum. *Aviation Week & Space Technology* 131:32 Ag 14 '89

NASA space station faces scale-down as budget, technical realities emerge. T. M. Foley. il *Aviation Week & Space Technology* 130:38-40 My 29 '89

NASA to seek space station termination if budget reductions are too severe. T. M. Foley. *Aviation Week & Space Technology* 130:24 My 8 '89

Reach for the stars. R. Jacob. il *Fortune* 120:8 S 25 '89

Report calls for fifth orbiter, citing probability of accident [Office of Technology Assessment] P. Mann. *Aviation Week & Space Technology* 131:16-17 Ag 7 '89

Science fiction [space budget reality and effects of weightlessness] H. Banks. il *Forbes* 143:44+ Mr 6 '89

Space station changes for lunar base would cost NASA more than $1 billion. C. Covault. il *Aviation Week & Space Technology* 131:34-5 O 9 '89

Space station delay planned; management reorganization set. C. Covault. il *Aviation Week & Space Technology* 131:20-1 O 2 '89

Space station faces possible delay or cancellation. T. M. Foley. il *Aviation Week & Space Technology* 130:32-3 My 1 '89

Space station in the balance. S. Cole. il *Astronomy* 17:24-31 My '89

Space station, planetary flights highlight NASA's new budget. C. Covault. il *Aviation Week & Space Technology* 130:38-9 Ja 23 '89

Space station science: up in the air. E. Marshall. il *Science* 246:1110-12 D 1 '89

Sweeping changes due for panels that set space policy in Congress. *Aviation Week & Space Technology* 130:83-4 Ja 2 '89

U.S. space leadership in danger [address, January 17, 1989] J. C. Fletcher. *Vital Speeches of the Day* 55:298-300 Mr 1 '89

Procurement

Commercialization policy threatens space station's robotic contract [OMB decision requiring private financing] T. M. Foley. il *Aviation Week & Space Technology* 130:30-1 F 6 '89

Forgetting the lesson [National Research Council report on Commercially Developed Space Facility] W. H. Ganoe. il *Ad Astra* 1:59 Jl/Ag '89

Government procurement: friend or foe? [commercial space enterprises] C. D. Ahearn. *Ad Astra* 1:36 S '89

NASA advised to drop plan for commercial platform lease. T. M. Foley. il *Aviation Week & Space Technology* 130:20-1 Ap 17 '89

NASA selects Lockheed/Aerojet to build shuttle's advanced solid rocket motor. T. M. Foley. il *Aviation Week & Space Technology* 130:31-2 My 1 '89

NASA's reusable satellite program. W. H. Ganoe. il *Ad Astra* 1:45 My '89

Two studies pan commercial space station. *High Technology Business* 9:35-6 S/O '89

Why won't NASA talk to scientists [effect of new ethics law on discussions of Advanced X-ray Astrophysics Facility] M. M. Waldrop. il *Science* 245:699 Ag 18 '89

UNITED STATES. NATIONAL AERONAUTICS AND SPACE ADMINISTRATION. AMES RESEARCH CENTER *See* Ames Research Center

UNITED STATES. NATIONAL AERONAUTICS AND SPACE ADMINISTRATION. JET PROPULSION LABORATORY *See* Jet Propulsion Laboratory (U.S.)

UNITED STATES. NATIONAL AERONAUTICS AND SPACE ADMINISTRATION. JOHN F. KENNEDY SPACE CENTER *See* John F. Kennedy Space Center

UNITED STATES. NATIONAL AERONAUTICS AND SPACE ADMINISTRATION. LANGLEY RESEARCH CENTER *See* Langley Research Center (U.S.)

UNITED STATES. NATIONAL AERONAUTICS AND SPACE ADMINISTRATION. LYNDON B. JOHNSON SPACE CENTER *See* Lyndon B. Johnson Space Center

UNITED STATES. NATIONAL AERONAUTICS AND SPACE ADMINISTRATION. NATIONAL SCHOLARS PROGRAM *See* National Scholars Program

UNITED STATES. NATIONAL AERONAUTICS AND SPACE ADMINISTRATION. OFFICE OF COMMERCIAL PROGRAMS

Building better partnerships [J. Rose] W. H. Ganoe. *Ad Astra* 1:31 O '89

Centers for the Commercial Development of Space. il *Ad Astra* 1:12 D '89

NASA commercial centers gain greater independence. il *Aviation Week & Space Technology* 131:41+ N 20 '89

UNITED STATES. NATIONAL AERONAUTICS AND SPACE ADMINISTRATION. PLUM BROOK FIELD STATION *See* Plum Brook Field Station

UNITED STATES. NATIONAL AERONAUTICS AND SPACE ADMINISTRATION. WALLOPS FLIGHT FACILITY *See* Wallops Flight Facility

UNITED STATES. NATIONAL AIR AND SPACE MUSEUM *See* National Air and Space Museum

UNITED STATES. NATIONAL ARCHIVES AND RECORDS ADMINISTRATION

See also
Franklin D. Roosevelt Library

Around the Mall and beyond [exhibit American voices: 200 years of speaking out] E. Park. il *Smithsonian* 19:28+ F '89

Inside the Archives [records of Warren Commission] il *American History Illustrated* 23:18-19 Ja '89

UNITED STATES. NATIONAL CANCER INSTITUTE *See* National Cancer Institute (U.S.)

UNITED STATES. NATIONAL COMMISSION TO PREVENT INFANT MORTALITY *See* National Commission to Prevent Infant Mortality (U.S.)

UNITED STATES. NATIONAL ECONOMIC COMMISSION *See* National Economic Commission (U.S.)

UNITED STATES. NATIONAL ENDOWMENT FOR THE HUMANITIES *See* National Endowment for the Humanities

UNITED STATES. NATIONAL GALLERY OF ART *See* National Gallery of Art (U.S.)

UNITED STATES. NATIONAL GUARD

The nation's war on drugs [address, April 4, 1989] H. R. Temple, Jr. *Vital Speeches of the Day* 55:516-19 Je 15 '89

UNITED STATES. NATIONAL HIGHWAY TRAFFIC SAFETY ADMINISTRATION

A breakdown in auto safety. il *Consumer Reports* 54:84-6+ F '89

Car trouble. E. Henry. il *Changing Times* 43:63-4+ N '89

Driver error! [sudden acceleration] P. Bedard. il *Car and Driver* 35:71-2+ Jl '89

UNITED STATES. NATIONAL HIGHWAY TRAFFIC SAFETY ADMINISTRATION—cont.
NHTSA blames sudden acceleration on "pedal misapplication". il *Motor Trend* 41:34+ Je '89
UNITED STATES. NATIONAL INSTITUTE OF MENTAL HEALTH *See* National Institute of Mental Health (U.S.)
UNITED STATES. NATIONAL INSTITUTE ON DRUG ABUSE *See* National Institute on Drug Abuse (U.S.)
UNITED STATES. NATIONAL INSTITUTES OF HEALTH *See* National Institutes of Health (U.S.)
UNITED STATES. NATIONAL LIBRARY OF MEDICINE *See* National Library of Medicine (U.S.)
UNITED STATES. NATIONAL MARINE FISHERIES SERVICE
Endangered species need more help. *Science News* 135:79 F 4 '89
Sharks find a friend in Washington [protection plan] il *U.S. News & World Report* 107:16 N 20 '89
UNITED STATES. NATIONAL MEDIATION BOARD
Board decisions muddle rules on union role after mergers [rulings in airline merger cases] J. Ott. *Aviation Week & Space Technology* 131:68 Ag 28 '89
Eastern's labor mess may land in Bush's lap. A. Bernstein. il *Business Week* p26 Mr 6 '89
A Soviet election [determining whether Key Airlines employees wish to join Teamsters] D. Seligman. il *Fortune* 120:142+ Jl 3 '89
UNITED STATES. NATIONAL MUSEUM OF AMERICAN ART *See* National Museum of American Art (U.S.)
UNITED STATES. NATIONAL MUSEUM OF AMERICAN HISTORY *See* National Museum of American History (U.S.)
UNITED STATES. NATIONAL OCEANIC AND ATMOSPHERIC ADMINISTRATION
Landsat/Spot merger talks spark debate on commercial space venture [with editorial comment] C. Covault. il *Aviation Week & Space Technology* 130:7, 20-1 Ja 23 '89
Navy relents in battle over mapping sea floor. C. Norman. *Science* 244:25 Ap 7 '89
Seafloor maps no longer secret. *Science News* 135:255 Ap 22 '89
UNITED STATES. NATIONAL PARK SERVICE
Beyond the burn [handling of forest fires in Yellowstone National Park] G. O'Gara. il map *Sierra* 74:40-51 Ja/F '89
Exporting park know-how [international programs] D. Drabelle. il *National Parks* 63:32-8 Mr/Ap '89
Fire, then ice [D. Sholly, head ranger at Yellowstone National Park] M. Brower. il pors *People Weekly* 31:42-7 Ja 16 '89
The fires and fire policy. P. Schullery. bibl f il maps *BioScience* 39:686-94 N '89
Hearing reveals politicized NPS. *National Parks* 63:11-13 Jl/Ag '89
Incineration of Yellowstone [cover story; with editorial comment by Les Line] T. Williams. il map *Audubon* 91:4, 38-85 Ja '89
Interior sub rosa. J. Kenney. il *National Parks* 63:12-14 S/O '89
N.P.S. double cross [no more hunting in Big Cypress] L. Williamson. il *Outdoor Life* 183:34+ F '89
National parks: year 2000. W. P. Mott, Jr. il *National Parks* 63:18-19 Ja/F '89
NPCA news. See issues of National Parks
Political fires still smolder. W. Wood. il *The Nation* 249:162-4 Ag 7-14 '89
Senate holds hearings on NPS fire policy. il *National Parks* 63:10-11 Ja/F '89
Sifting ashes in Yellowstone [management of bison and elk in wake of forest fires] T. Williams. il *Audubon* 91:30-2+ N '89
Wildfire in the West's woods: fire policy in the wake of the fires of 1988. G. Matzke and D. Key. il *Focus (New York, N.Y.: 1950)* 39:1-2+ Summ '89
Yellowstone: fire storm over fire management. C. Elfring. il map *BioScience* 39:667-72 N '89
The Yellowstone scam. M. Morrison. il *The American Spectator* 22:17-20 Ag '89
UNITED STATES. NATIONAL RADIO ASTRONOMY OBSERVATORY *See* National Radio Astronomy Observatory (U.S.)
UNITED STATES. NATIONAL SCIENCE FOUNDATION *See* National Science Foundation (U.S.)
UNITED STATES. NATIONAL SECURITY AGENCY
STU-3 secure telephones offered to U.S. defense contractors. P. J. Klass. il *Aviation Week & Space Technology* 130:63+ F 27 '89
UNITED STATES. NATIONAL SECURITY COUNCIL
Blind men's bluff [J. A. Baker and B. Scowcroft; cover story] M. Kondracke. *The New Republic* 200:20+ Mr 6 '89
Can Brent Scowcroft be converted to SDI? J. T. Hackett. por *Conservative Digest* 15:15 Mr/Ap '89
Distrust, but verify [views of R. M. Gates] F. Barnes. *The New Republic* 200:12-13 Mr 6 '89
Mr. Inside, Mr. Outside [J. A. Baker and B. Scowcroft] J. Barry. pors *Newsweek* 113:28 F 27 '89

The quiet sage steering Bush's foreign policy [B. Scowcroft and J. A. Baker] H. Trewhitt. il por *U.S. News & World Report* 106:22-4 F 20 '89
UNITED STATES. NATIONAL SPACE COUNCIL *See* National Space Council (U.S.)
UNITED STATES. NATIONAL TRANSPORTATION SAFETY BOARD
Board asks FAA to help form model safety department. *Aviation Week & Space Technology* 131:104 O 2 '89
Close look at cargo door workings fails to reveal cause of accident. il *Aviation Week & Space Technology* 130:86-7+ My 22 '89
Douglas asks NTSB to reopen probe of Northwest MD-82 crash [charging that pilots disconnected warning system that could have prevented August 1987 crash in Detroit] C. Fotos. *Aviation Week & Space Technology* 130:106 My 1 '89
NTSB asserts captain's cocaine use contributed to crash of Continental Express Metro 3 [Capt. S. Silver; January 1988 crash near Durango, Colo.] C. Fotos. *Aviation Week & Space Technology* 130:59 F 6 '89
NTSB raps Aloha, aviation system for fuselage failure [Boeing 737 in April 1988] J. Ott. il *Aviation Week & Space Technology* 130:24-6 My 29 '89
Safety Board investigates two midair collisions of general aviation aircraft [over New England] *Aviation Week & Space Technology* 130:95 Je 26 '89
United officials tell NTSB AD procedures not followed [hearings on Flight 811 cargo door accident in February 1989] B. W. Henderson. *Aviation Week & Space Technology* 130:107 My 1 '89
UNITED STATES. NAVAL FLIGHT DEMONSTRATION SQUADRON *See* Blue Angels (Flight squadron)
UNITED STATES. NAVAL STRIKE WARFARE CENTER *See* Naval Strike Warfare Center (U.S.)
UNITED STATES. NAVY
See also
Navy yards and naval stations
World War, 1939-1945—Naval operations
Arms at sea [discussion of January 1989 article, Troubled waters] W. M. Arkin. il *Technology Review* 92:6-7+ Ag/S '89
Disarmament at sea. M. Ross. *Foreign Policy* 77:94-112 Wint '89/'90
Maritime strategy: seapower in a changing world [cover story; special section; with editorial comment] il *Aviation Week & Space Technology* 130:9, 36-9+ F 27 '89
Navy relents in battle over mapping sea floor. C. Norman. *Science* 244:25 Ap 7 '89
The Navy we need and the one we got. S. Shuger. il *The Washington Monthly* 21:10-14+ Mr '89
Seafloor maps no longer secret. *Science News* 135:255 Ap 22 '89
Troubled waters: the Navy's aggressive war strategy. W. M. Arkin. il *Technology Review* 92:54-63 Ja '89
The U.S. Navy today [address, May 16, 1989] C. A. H. Trost. *Vital Speeches of the Day* 55:578-80 Jl 15 '89
Accidents and injuries
Disasters on the high seas. E. Salholz. il *Newsweek* 114:47 N 13 '89
The Navy stands down. D. Waller. il *Newsweek* 114:40+ N 27 '89
A postage stamp in the ocean. S. Budiansky. il *U.S. News & World Report* 107:12-13 N 13 '89
The U.S. Navy's snafu blues. il *U.S. News & World Report* 107:13 N 27 '89
Airplanes
See Airplanes, Military
Appropriations and expenditures
Congress presses treaty objectives on Trident submarine program. D. F. Bond. *Aviation Week & Space Technology* 131:25-6 Ag 21 '89
Naval aviation modernization hit hard by Pentagon cuts. *Aviation Week & Space Technology* 130:23 Ap 24 '89
Navy budget request stresses maintaining carrier battle groups. D. M. North. il *Aviation Week & Space Technology* 130:21-2 Ja 16 '89
Navy pursues major EW efforts despite expected funding cuts [electronic warfare] il *Aviation Week & Space Technology* 131:65+ S 11 '89
Soviets building naval strength while pursuing maritime arms control. B. M. Greeley. il *Aviation Week & Space Technology* 130:63 Mr 13 '89
Trident II misfires in Congress. M. Ross. il *The Bulletin of the Atomic Scientists* 45:11-12 D '89
Blacks
The 'new' Navy: trying to put the past behind. H. J. Massaquoi. il *Ebony* 44:30-2+ S '89
Boats
See also
Aircraft carriers
Nuclear submarines
Warships
Dame at sea [four day Navy tour] J. M. Stapleton. *The New Republic* 200:42 My 22 '89
Millions of dollars on the ocean floor [Navy's management of surplus ships] E. Clift. il *Newsweek* 114:30 Ag 28 '89

UNITED STATES. NAVY—cont.

Forces in Japan
Classified top secret: H-bomb overboard [rolls off U.S. carrier Ticonderoga headed toward Japanese port] Newsweek 113:45 My 15 '89

Forces in the Mediterranean region
Chemical reaction [U.S. fighters shoot down Libyan MiGs] E. Magnuson. il por Time 133:18-21 Ja 16 '89

Gunning for Gadhafi [U.S. shoots down two jets and claims Libya will soon make chemical weapons] J. Bierman. il Maclean's 102:18-19 Ja 16 '89

Libya [U.S. downing of two Libyan MiG-23s over the Mediterranean] Business Week p50 Ja 16 '89

Libyan planes downed [Defense Dept. statement, January 4, 1989] Department of State Bulletin 89:70 Mr '89

Showdown with Libya [cover story; special section] il por Newsweek 113:16-25 Ja 16 '89

Text deploring downing of Libyan planes vetoed in Security Council: United States calls it 'self-defence'. il UN Chronicle 26:33 Je '89

U.S. F-14s down Libyan MiG-23s in dogfight over Mediterranean. B. M. Greeley, Jr. il map Aviation Week & Space Technology 130:20-1 Ja 9 '89

U.S. reports to United Nations on downing of Libyan planes [letter and statement, January 4-5, 1989] H. S. Okun. Department of State Bulletin 89:90-1 Mr '89

Forces in the Pacific
See also
Pueblo incident, 1968

Forces in the Philippines
The bar girls of Subic Bay: the military, women and AIDS. S. Sturdevant. il The Nation 248:444-6 Ap 3 '89

Guided missiles
See Guided missiles

Pay, allowances, etc.
A naval officer targets his goals with too many funds, too much stock [Bill Luebke] L. Luciano. il Money 18:155-6 Ja '89

Procurement
Additional P-7A design work may cost Lockheed $300 million. il Aviation Week & Space Technology 131:22-3 N 27 '89

Casualties of peace [Navy investigates faulty smoke protection gear from Scott Aviation] Time 134:30 N 27 '89

Delays in Navy ATF program bolster case for F-14D. J. D. Morrocco. il Aviation Week & Space Technology 131:30-1 S 4 '89

E-6A Tacamo tail damage prompts delivery delay [submarine communications aircraft] M. A. Dornheim. il Aviation Week & Space Technology 130:28-9 Ap 17 '89

FBI charges consultants bribed Navy officials to influence contract awards. J. D. Morrocco. Aviation Week & Space Technology 130:22 Ja 9 '89

French electro-optic, IR firms to bid on U.S. aircraft carrier systems. B. D. Nordwall. il Aviation Week & Space Technology 130:89+ My 8 '89

General Dynamics will launch first Navy UHF follow-on satellite [Atlas booster] Aviation Week & Space Technology 131:22 Ag 21 '89

Hughes/AEL team wins Navy contract for upgraded radar warning receiver. B. W. Henderson. il Aviation Week & Space Technology 131:60-1 Ag 28 '89

A kinder, gentler Navy? [address, January 18, 1989] W. E. Haggett. Vital Speeches of the Day 55:403-5 Ap 15 '89

McDonnell Douglas, Navy prepare SLAM missile for airborne launch [stand-off land attack missile] S. W. Kandebo. il Aviation Week & Space Technology 130:31 F 27 '89

Military computer awards stalled; Conyers asks probe. por Jet 75:9 Mr 6 '89

Navy adds defensive capability to SH-2F, SH-60B helicopters. il Aviation Week & Space Technology 130:70-1 My 1 '89

Navy chooses LCD technology for new A-12 color displays. B. D. Nordwall. il Aviation Week & Space Technology 131:56-7 S 4 '89

Navy, McDonnell Douglas agree on modifications to T-45A trainer. Aviation Week & Space Technology 131:21 S 25 '89

Navy plans to roll out upgraded SH-2 Seasprite helicopter in October [antisubmarine warfare helicopter] S. W. Kandebo. il Aviation Week & Space Technology 130:143+ Je 19 '89

Navy selects GE for future F404 turbofan orders, drops Pratt as second source. Aviation Week & Space Technology 131:26 Ag 28 '89

Navy terminates $328.8 million in V-22 advance production contracts [tilt-rotor aircraft] D. F. Bond. il Aviation Week & Space Technology 131:38 D 11 '89

The Navy: that blip on the screen may be a blooper [Airborne Self-Protection Jammer] D. Griffiths. Business Week p43 O 2 '89

Navy, USAF to award contracts for limited ALQ-165 production [airborne self-protection jamming systems] il Aviation Week & Space Technology 131:89+ S 11 '89

Pentagon cites Texas Instruments for quality gains in HARM production [guided missile] il Aviation Week & Space Technology 131:79 S 11 '89

Raytheon adapts color workstations to meet requirements of military users. D. Hughes. il Aviation Week & Space Technology 130:104-5 Ap 24 '89

Team correcting deficiencies in Navy's T-45A trainer aircraft. E. H. Phillips. il Aviation Week & Space Technology 131:46-8 O 30 '89

Trainer aircraft at Le Bourget geared toward USAF/Navy buy [primary aircraft training system] C. Covault. il Aviation Week & Space Technology 130:67+ Je 26 '89

UNITED STATES. NAVY. BLUE ANGELS See Blue Angels (Flight squadron)

UNITED STATES. NAVY. MARINE MAMMAL PROGRAM
These guards just love fish [dolphins used by Navy] E. Linden. il Time 133:77 Ap 24 '89

UNITED STATES. NAVY. NAVAL WEAPONS CENTER See Naval Weapons Center (U.S.)

UNITED STATES. NAVY. OFFICE OF NAVAL RESEARCH See United States. Office of Naval Research

UNITED STATES. NUCLEAR REGULATORY COMMISSION See U.S. Nuclear Regulatory Commission

UNITED STATES. OAK RIDGE NATIONAL LABORATORY See Oak Ridge National Laboratory

UNITED STATES. OCCUPATIONAL SAFETY AND HEALTH ADMINISTRATION
OSHA lacks impact on worker safety. W. T. Brookes. por Nation's Business 77:72 Ag '89

OSHA threatens to fine Lockheed $1.5 million. Aviation Week & Space Technology 130:20 Ap 3 '89

This safety ruling could be hazardous to employers' health [OSHA decision opens business to more criminal charges] S. B. Garland. il Business Week p34 F 20 '89

UNITED STATES. OFFICE OF ECONOMIC OPPORTUNITY
Lessons from the poverty front. N. Lemann. The Washington Monthly 21:33-5 D '89

UNITED STATES. OFFICE OF ECONOMIC OPPORTUNITY. PROJECT HEAD START See Project Head Start (U.S.)

UNITED STATES. OFFICE OF EDUCATIONAL RESEARCH AND IMPROVEMENT
Ruminations on the end of a regime: a response to Chester Finn [discussion of October 1988 article, Lessons learned: federal policy making and the education research community] C. E. Finn. il Phi Delta Kappan 70:816-20 Je '89

UNITED STATES. OFFICE OF MANAGEMENT AND BUDGET
Biotechnology rules wither in OMB. M. Crawford. Science 243:602 F 3 '89

Bush's audacious new czar of domestic policy [R. Darman] K. T. Walsh. il por U.S. News & World Report 106:25-6 Ja 16 '89

Darman's 'Maypo' pitch: how will it go down? por Newsweek 114:44 Ag 7 '89

Doctored data [censors testimony of J. E. Hansen on the greenhouse effect] Commonweal 116:325 Je 2 '89

Driven to beat the budget. L. I. Barrett. il por Time 133:58-60 F 27 '89

Ever heard of Dick Darman? It's time you did [agricultural issues] P. Smith. Successful Farming 87:34 Ag '89

Feeling the heat on the greenhouse [OMB censors J. Hansen's testimony on greenhouse effect] S. Begley. il Newsweek 112:79-80 My 22 '89

A hot issue [censors facts on greenhouse effect] D. Lindorff. The Nation 248:724-5 My 29 '89

The Nick & Dick show: what next? [N. Brady and R. Darman] C. Hutton. il pors Fortune 119:12 Ja 30 '89

The OMB octopus [wildlife programs] L. Williamson. il Outdoor Life 183:62+ My '89

Pinball wizard at the flippers [R. Darman] P. C. Roberts. il National Review 41:24+ F 24 '89

Researchers irked by changes to testimony. E. Marshall. Science 244:648 My 12 '89

Say hello to charmin' Darman. T. M. DeFrank and A. McDaniel. por Newsweek 113:24 Je 5 '89

The trillion dollar man [R. Darman; cover story] H. Gleckman. il pors Business Week p100-3+ Mr 13 '89

Watching the watchdogs. S. Waldman. il Newsweek 113:34 F 20 '89

What the smartest man in Washington doesn't understand. And why it will hurt you [R. Darman; cover story] J. DeParle. il por The Washington Monthly 21:24-6+ N '89

White House wonk [R. Darman; cover story] F. Barnes. The New Republic 200:19-21 Ja 2 '89

UNITED STATES. OFFICE OF NAVAL RESEARCH
Navy awards $14 million to foster math, science degrees at universities. il Jet 77:18 O 16 '89

Navy will explore potential of fusion at room temperature [cold fusion; work of Stanley Pons and Martin Fleischmann] Aviation Week & Space Technology 130:21 Ap 17 '89

UNITED STATES. OFFICE OF PERSONNEL MANAGEMENT
Constance Newman is OK'd for fed. personnel post. il por Jet 76:22 Je 26 '89

Constance Newman, new chief of personnel, lauded by Bush. por Jet 76:12 Ag 21 '89

UNITED STATES. OFFICE OF SCIENCE AND TECHNOLOGY POLICY
Bromley in line for science adviser. M. Crawford. por *Science* 244:283 Ap 21 '89
Bromley speaks. T. M. Powledge. por *Science* 246:1176 D 1 '89
Bush picks science adviser. I. Wickelgren. *Science News* 135:263 Ap 29 '89
A conversation with D. Allan Bromley [president's science adviser] B. J. Culliton. il por *Science* 246:203-4 O 13 '89
Meet D. Allan Bromley [interview] J. Carey. il por *Business Week* Special Issue:44 Je 16 '89
President Bush picks Yale's Bromley for Cabinet-level science adviser. I. Goodwin. il por *Physics Today* 42:39-41 Je '89
Science adviser gets first formal look [D. A. Bromley] B. J. Culliton. por *Science* 245:247-8 Jl 21 '89
Science gains a voice [appointment of D. A. Bromley as science adviser] T. Beardsley. *Scientific American* 261:14 Jl '89
Science regains the White House [science adviser D. A. Bromley] N. Bell. il *BioScience* 39:435 Jl/Ag '89
Senate committee quizzes Bromley. M. Crawford. *Science* 245:349 Jl 28 '89
Senate quiz show: Bromley passes but he faces tougher tests ahead. I. Goodwin. por *Physics Today* 42:65-7 S '89
Washington ins & outs: Graham departs, Murrin to Commerce, top changes at NASA and Pentagon. I. Goodwin. *Physics Today* 42:47-9 Jl '89

UNITED STATES. OFFICE OF SURFACE MINING, RECLAMATION, AND ENFORCEMENT
Strip search [weak enforcement due to computer system malfunction] T. Sherwood. il *Common Cause Magazine* 15:8-9 My/Je '89

UNITED STATES. OFFICE OF TECHNOLOGY ASSESSMENT *See* United States. Congress. Office of Technology Assessment

UNITED STATES. OFFICE OF THE U.S. TRADE REPRESENTATIVE
The Asians are bracing for a trade shoot-out [U.S. to issue target list of unfair practices] A. Borrus. il *Business Week* p40-1 My 1 '89
A new hard line on trade. D. Jenish. il *Maclean's* 102:30+ My 22 '89
On trade, the U.S. sounds the charge—and comes out firing blanks [telecommunications industry] P. Magnusson. il *Business Week* p45 F 6 '89
Perils of getting tough on Korea. F. S. Worthy. il *Fortune* 119:263+ Je 5 '89
Smith to Japan: here's the beef. A. Kupfer. il por *Fortune* 119:53 Ja 2 '89
Smoking gun [C. Yeutter's efforts on behalf of cigarette industry] S. Hornik. il *Common Cause Magazine* 15:9 Mr/Ap '89
Trade's most wanted list [Super 301 negotiations to end foreign protectionism] S. Dentzer. il *U.S. News & World Report* 106:50+ My 22 '89
What to do about trade policy. A. R. Dowd. il por *Fortune* 119:106-7+ My 8 '89

UNITED STATES. OFFICE OF THRIFT SUPERVISION
A spendthrift thrift gets its ears boxed [CenTrust] G. DeGeorge. *Business Week* p46 D 25 '89-Ja 1 '90

UNITED STATES. PATENT AND TRADEMARK OFFICE. PATENT DEPOSITORY LIBRARY PROGRAM *See* Patent Depository Library Program

UNITED STATES. PENSION BENEFIT GUARANTY CORPORATION *See* Pension Benefit Guaranty Corporation

UNITED STATES. POSTAL SERVICE *See* United States Postal Service

UNITED STATES. PRESIDENT'S COMMISSION ON THE ASSASSINATION OF PRESIDENT KENNEDY *See* Warren Commission

UNITED STATES. PRESIDENT'S PRIVATE SECTOR SURVEY ON COST CONTROL *See* President's Private Sector Survey on Cost Control (U.S.)

UNITED STATES. PRESIDENT'S SELECT COMMITTEE ON AUTOMOTIVE REGULATION AND ECONOMICS *See* President's Select Committee on Automotive Regulation and Economics

UNITED STATES. PRESIDENT'S TASK FORCE ON COMPETITIVENESS *See* President's Task Force on Competitiveness

UNITED STATES. PUBLIC HEALTH SERVICE. CENTERS FOR DISEASE CONTROL *See* Centers for Disease Control (U.S.)

UNITED STATES. REHABILITATION SERVICES ADMINISTRATION
An agency in trouble [whistle blower J. Dart, Jr. forced to resign] C. A. Davis. il por *The Progressive* 53:13 Ja '89

UNITED STATES. RESOLUTION TRUST CORPORATION *See* Resolution Trust Corporation (U.S.)

UNITED STATES. SECRET SERVICE
Guarding the nation's vice presidents [black special agent H. T. Bell] H. J. Massaquoi. il pors *Ebony* 44:166+ Je '89

Secret Service probes lab notebooks [E. Imanishi-Kari] E. Marshall. *Science* 244:644 My 12 '89

UNITED STATES. SECURITIES AND EXCHANGE COMMISSION
America's no. 1 tipster [stock market journalist D. Dorfman involved in SEC investigation into Centaur Partners] J. Egan. il por *U.S. News & World Report* 107:59-60 Ag 21 '89
Annual reports: the SEC cracks the whip. T. Smart. il *Business Week* p74 Ap 10 '89
Another wall comes down [law permitting institutional investors to trade unregistered securities] C. Byron. il *New York* 22:16+ N 27 '89
Battling your broker just got a bit easier. L. Zinn. *Business Week* p142 Je 5 '89
The best new stocks may never hit the Street [revised rules on private placements] D. Foust. il *Business Week* p47 D 25 '89-Ja 1 '90
Bush's man on the Street [R. Breeden] T. Smart. il por *Business Week* p27 Ag 28 '89
Dirty secrets [municipal bonds] B. Weberman. il *Forbes* 143:277 Je 26 '89
Doesn't honesty sell? [SEC crackdown on bond unit trusts] B. Weberman. il *Forbes* 144:297 O 16 '89
Faulty arithmetic [mutual fund management fee calculations] J. Clements. il *Forbes* 143:112 My 15 '89
Hassling the dealmakers [leveraged buyouts] D. Wechsler. il *Forbes* 143:40-1 My 15 '89
How turf wars killed a good investment product [stock index participations] D. Greising. il *Business Week* p94 S 4 '89
An insider caper in Liechtenstein [ASEA Brown Boveri helps SEC uncover insider trading during ABB's friendly takeover bid for Combustion Engineering] J. Kapstein. *Business Week* p58-9 D 11 '89
Nasty surprises [requiring audited quarterly reports] P. Wang. il *Forbes* 143:72 Ja 23 '89
A raider's days of reckoning [files suit against P. Bilzerian] il por *Time* 134:45 Jl 10 '89
The SEC casts a net at penny stocks' biggest fish [Stuart-James] S. D. Atchison. il *Business Week* p128 Ap 24 '89
The Securities and Exchange Commission. *Congressional Digest* 68:70+ Mr '89
Winning is the best revenge [C. Broderick wins discrimination suit] L. Romano. il pors *Good Housekeeping* 208:46+ Ap '89

UNITED STATES. SMALL BUSINESS ADMINISTRATION
Big loans for small businesses. R. R. Roha. il *Changing Times* 43:105-9 Ap '89
Help for women entrepreneurs [mentor program] B. Stein. il *Home Office Computing* 7:12 My '89
It's alive! Alive! R. Behar and C. Brown. il *Forbes* 143:169-70 Ap 17 '89
A mother lode of loans for small businesses. T. Segal. il *Business Week* p104-5 Je 19 '89
SBA drafts new 8(a) rules. K. D. Thompson. il *Black Enterprise* 20:22 N '89
SBA's woman in charge [S. Engeleiter] D. C. Bacon. il por *Nation's Business* 77:66 Je '89
What's next for the SBA? B. W. O'Connor. *Black Enterprise* 19:137-8 Je '89

UNITED STATES. SPACE COMMAND
Military space capabilities expanding, but excess secrecy limits progress. C. Covault. *Aviation Week & Space Technology* 130:18-19 Ap 17 '89

UNITED STATES. SUPREME COURT
The 80-percenters [Bush Supreme Court] T. Eastland. *The New Republic* 200:14-15 Ja 2 '89
America's most influential woman. M. C. Williams and A. Kamen. il por *Reader's Digest* 135:71-6 D '89
"The art case of the decade" [copyright case brought by the Community for Creative Non-Violence against J. E. Reid] S. Staggs. il *Art News* 88:49-50 Ap '89
Consolidating the new majority [Rehnquist Court's upcoming 1989-90 term] H. Schwartz. il *The Nation* 249:380-3 O 9 '89
Courting disaster [change may affect women's issues] M. S. Spivack. il *Ms.* 17:138 Ja/F '89
The 'crime' of flag burning. M. Garbus. il *The Nation* 248:369-70 Mr 20 '89
Enter, stage right. A. L. Sanders. il *Time* 134:83+ O 9 '89
Execute an 8-year-old? The Johnny Penry case [mentally retarded adult awaiting execution in Texas] R. F. Drinan. *The Christian Century* 106:199-200 F 22 '89
High Court hears arguments on large punitive damage awards. H. Fields. *Publishers Weekly* 235:18 My 5 '89
Is there a right to die? [N. Cruzan case] T. Gest. il por *U.S. News & World Report* 107:35-7 D 11 '89
Nancy Cruzan's parents want to let her die—and are taking the case to the Supreme Court. M. Brower. il pors *People Weekly* 32:135-6+ D 4 '89
The new Supreme Court term may disappoint conservatives. T. Gest. *U.S. News & World Report* 107:31 O 2 '89
O'Connor fumbles 'Christian nation' case [Justice S. D. O'Connor's letter in support of Arizona Republican Party resolution] E. M. Gaffney, Jr. *The Christian Century* 106:373-5 Ap 12 '89

UNITED STATES. SUPREME COURT—*cont.*

Peyote, wine and the First Amendment [religious use of peyote] D. Laycock. *The Christian Century* 106:876-80 O 4 '89

Preserving newspapers or monopoly? [proposed joint operating agreement between Detroit free press and Detroit news; cover story] S. Barnett. *The Nation* 249:513+ N 6 '89

Professional page [case brought by Community for Creative Non-Violence against J. E. Reid] D. Grant. *American Artist* 53:10+ Jl '89

Punitive damages: how much is too much? E. G. Olson. il *Business Week* p54+ Mr 27 '89

Racial preference in court (again) [to decide legality of minority set-asides in Richmond, Va.] T. Eastland. *Commentary* 87:32-8 Ja '89

The remaking of Robert Bork. M. Pertschuk and W. Schaetzel. il *The Nation* 249:750-2 D 18 '89

Right to life, church-state cases before Court. il *Christianity Today* 33:44+ O 6 '89

Supreme Court hears work-for-hire arguments [case brought by Community for Creative Non-Violence against J. E. Reid] H. Fields. *Publishers Weekly* 235:14 Ap 14 '89

Supreme Court rejects second 11th Amendment case in month [brought by copyright holders against a state entity] H. Fields. *Publishers Weekly* 235:36 Ap 7 '89

Thurgood Marshall hires two black Ivy League law clerks. il pors *Jet* 77:4+ N 13 '89

Thurgood Marshall still Court's poorest justice. il por *Jet* 76:13 Je 5 '89

To be or not to be [case of N. Cruzan] M. Kinsley. *The New Republic* 201:6+ N 27 '89

Too young to die? [case of H. Wilkins; cover story] R. Rosenbaum. il pors *The New York Times Magazine* p32-5+ Mr 12 '89

Upholding students' religious freedom [access of student religious groups to public school facilities] S. Levicoff. *The Christian Century* 106:1108-9 N 29 '89

Waiving the flag [flag burning issue] *The New Republic* 200:7-8 Ja 23 '89

Where is the Rehnquist Court headed? [oral arguments in flag burning case heard March 21, 1989] il *Harper's* 278:35-9+ Je '89

While justice sleeps [justices' reliance on clerks; cover story] T. Eastland. il *National Review* 41:24-6 Ap 21 '89

Whose right to die? [case of N. Cruzan] A. L. Sanders. il *Time* 134:80 D 11 '89

Why do the liberals rage? [opposition to author's nomination] R. H. Bork. *National Review* 41:26-7 D 8 '89

Decisions

11th Amendment ruling by High Court is 'hopeful' for copyright. H. Fields. *Publishers Weekly* 236:9 Jl 7 '89

An "accommodating" Court [lets stand a licensing law that allows child care centers run by religious organizations to seek an exempt status] D. Neff. *Christianity Today* 33:15 Mr 3 '89

Affirmative action. D. T. Dingle. il *Black Enterprise* 20:42-6+ S '89

Are you smiling, Robert Bork? [Justice A. M. Kennedy's decisions] il por *U.S. News & World Report* 106:10 Je 26 '89

Bad news for death row [okays execution of juvenile and retarded criminals] A. L. Sanders. il *Time* 134:48-9 Jl 10 '89

The battered child [rules social worker not liable in case of J. DeShaney] *The New Republic* 200:7-8 Mr 20 '89

Behind the flag-burning firestorm. M. Barone. il *U.S. News & World Report* 107:28 Jl 3 '89

Birmingham firehouse [decision permitting white firemen to bring suit against the the city for job discrimination] *Commonweal* 116:387-8 Jl 14 '89

A blow to affirmative action [strikes down Richmond, Va. minority set-aside law] A. Sachs. il *Time* 133:60 F 6 '89

The blow to affirmative action may not hurt that much. P. Dwyer. il *Business Week* p61-2 Jl 3 '89

A boost for drug testing. A. L. Sanders. il *Time* 133:62 Ap 3 '89

Brown plus 35 [Brown v. Board of Education] R. Kennedy. *The Nation* 248:725 My 29 '89

A build-down for black contractors [ruling against minority set-aside program in Richmond, Va.] *U.S. News & World Report* 106:13 F 6 '89

Burn, baby, burn! [ruling on flag burning] *National Review* 41:13-14 Ag 4 '89

Bushwaterism [L. Atwater's role in persuading Bush to call for flag burning amendment] *The New Republic* 201:5-6 Jl 17-24 '89

The case against political judging [cover story] R. H. Bork. il por *National Review* 41:23-8 D 8 '89

The case of the conspicuous dealer [upholds use of drug courier profiles] *Newsweek* 113:64 Ap 17 '89

Chambers warns of dire impact of recent rulings by U.S. Supreme Court [affirmative action] por *Jet* 76:38 Ag 21 '89

Chipping away at civil rights [recent decisions] A. L. Sanders. il *Time* 133:63+ Je 26 '89

Christmas in July [crèche and menorah decision] *America* 161:27 Jl 15-22 '89

Civil rights cases. *Monthly Labor Review* 112:50-1 Ag '89

Congress rallies around the flag [constitutional amendment proposed to overrule Supreme Court on flag burning] T. Jacoby. il *Newsweek* 114:19 Jl 10 '89

Constitutional crisis [employment discrimination] P. Simpson. il *Ms.* 18:90+ S '89

Constitutional law [discussion of December 1988 article, Rewriting the Constitution] S. C. Brubaker. *Commentary* 87:2-4+ My '89

Copyright ruling favors artists. il *Art in America* 77:240 S '89

Court aids freelancers in work-for-hire ruling [case of Community for Creative Non-Violence vs. J. E. Reid] H. Fields. *Publishers Weekly* 235:11 Je 16 '89

Court and crèche [ruling on religious symbols on public property] *The Christian Century* 106:713 Ag 2-9 '89

The Court and the flag decision. W. F. Buckley. *National Review* 41:54 Ag 4 '89

Court in the middle [strikes down set-aside program for minority firms in Richmond, Va.] *National Review* 41:14 F 24 '89

Court limits sharing of Army pension in divorce; Marshall pens decision. por *Jet* 76:8 Je 19 '89

Court orders: dealing with porn and drugs [rules on dial-a-porn and drug lawyers' fees] *Newsweek* 114:20 Jl 3 '89

The Court: Reagan's legal legacy. A. McDaniel. il *Newsweek* 114:19-20 Jl 10 '89

Court rules on clergy malpractice, Sabbath. *Christianity Today* 33:51-2 My 12 '89

The Court spins right [affirmative action decisions and Justice A. M. Kennedy] A. McDaniel. il por *Newsweek* 113:16-18 Je 26 '89

A court that obeys the law [Rehnquist Court] B. Fein. *National Review* 41:50-1 S 29 '89

Court upholds prayer ban before games [church-state cases] *Christianity Today* 33:55 Jl 14 '89

Courting disaster [flag burning, affirmative action and abortion] il *The Progressive* 53:7-8 Ag '89

The Court's mixed signals [affirmative action, abortion and flag burning] il *Scholastic Update (Teachers' edition)* 122:10 N 3 '89

Day care, porn cases heard by High Court. *Christianity Today* 33:53 Mr 3 '89

Deaffirmation [Supreme Court decisions deal blow to affirmative action] M. E. Dyson. *The Nation* 249:4-5 Jl 3 '89

Dial-a-porn, find-a-lawyer [rulings in areas of free speech and criminal law] A. L. Sanders. il *Time* 134:56 Jl 3 '89

The dynamics of flag-burning. J. M. Wall. *The Christian Century* 106:643-4 Jl 5-12 '89

Employee drug testing. bibl f il *Monthly Labor Review* 112:75-6 N '89

An end to judicial roulette [sentencing guidelines upheld] T. Jacoby. il *Newsweek* 113:76 Ja 30 '89

Equal justice under siege: coping with the runaway Supreme Court. C. Benson. il *Ebony* 45:54+ D '89

An eye for an eye in the courts [U.S. Sentencing Commission guidelines upheld] *U.S. News & World Report* 106:11-12 Ja 30 '89

Eyes in the sky [rules police do not need warrant to spy from helicopter] *Time* 133:60 F 6 '89

Faith and flag-burning [discussion of July 5-12, 1989 article, The dynamics of flag-burning] J. M. Wall. il *The Christian Century* 106:757-9 Ag 16-23 '89

A fight for Old Glory [rules flag burning is not a crime] T. Jacoby. il *Newsweek* 114:18-20 Jl 3 '89

The flag and freedom of speech. *America* 161:3 Jl 1-8 '89

Flag desecration legislation. *Congressional Digest* 68:193-224 Ag/S '89

Flag-saving. *The Nation* 249:229-30 S 4-11 '89

Flagellation [constitutional amendment on flag burning proposed] H. Hertzberg. *The New Republic* 201:4 Jl 17-24 '89

High Court bars pretrial RICO seizure of books [obscene materials in Indiana bookstores] H. Fields. *Publishers Weekly* 235:19 Mr 10 '89

High Court ruling helps plaintiffs of job bias [sex discrimination case brought by woman accountant] *Jet* 76:19 My 22 '89

High Court ruling upholds states' rights to execute young killers, retarded. *Jet* 76:4 Jl 10 '89

The High Court stands 5-4 on a burning issue [flag burning] il *U.S. News & World Report* 107:8 Jl 3 '89

The High Court weighs drug tests [testing of federal employees] il *Newsweek* 113:8 Ap 3 '89

The High Court's "S" word [sectarian used as synonym for religious] R. A. Baer. il *Christianity Today* 33:20-1 S 8 '89

The Hill case [impact of 1967 Time Inc. v. Hill privacy case, argued by R. Nixon, on freedom of the press] L. Garment. *The New Yorker* 65:90-110 Ap 17 '89

Hitting the wall [civil rights decisions] R. W. Wilkins. il *Mother Jones* 14:12+ N '89

Hooray for the amendment [flag burning] W. F. Buckley. *National Review* 41:54-5 Ag 4 '89

How we got an Official Secrets Act [declines to review S. L. Morison case] N. Hentoff. il *The Progressive* 53:10-11 Mr '89

UNITED STATES. SUPREME COURT—Decisions—*cont.*

Ignore a menorah [rules on public religious displays] S. Bates. *The New Republic* 201:14-16 Jl 31 '89

Illogical force [affirmative action and civil rights decisions] H. Schwartz. *The Nation* 249:40-1 Jl 10 '89

Is the Court hostile to religion? [Christmas crèche-menorah display decision] R. N. Ostling. il *Time* 134:80 Jl 17 '89

Judging a book by its cover [upholds use of drug courier profiles by federal agents] A. L. Sanders. il *Time* 133:52 Ap 17 '89

The latest Supreme Court special education case: not moot but Muth. P. A. Zirkel. bibl f *Phi Delta Kappan* 71:250-1 N '89

Lawyers see little impact from High Court's work-for-hire ruling [Community for Creative Non-Violence v. Reid] H. Fields. *Publishers Weekly* 235:10-11 Je 23 '89

Let punishment fit the crime [upholds guidelines established by U.S. Sentencing Commission] R. N. Ostling. il *Time* 133:63 Ja 30 '89

Letting the people decide. M. Barone. il *U.S. News & World Report* 107:18-19 Jl 10 '89

Limiting our rights [recent decisions in libel area] M. Garbus. *Publishers Weekly* 236:21 Ag 18 '89

Myth America in the workplace [rules against sex stereotyping in case of A. Hopkins v. Price Waterhouse] por *U.S. News & World Report* 106:14 My 15 '89

NAACP to hold silent march in Washington to protest new Supreme Court rulings. il *Jet* 76:6 Ag 21 '89

A negative on affirmative action [ruling on Richmond, Va. minority set-aside law] R. Stodghill, II and P. Dwyer. *Business Week* p40 F 6 '89

Notes and comment [philosophy of E. Burke applied to recent decisions] *The New Yorker* 65:21-2 Jl 31 '89

'Now we're on our own' [strikes down Richmond, Va. minority set-aside law] T. Jacoby. il *Newsweek* 113:64-5 F 6 '89

Obscenity: what the Supreme Court says [excerpt from *Art law*] R. E. Lerner and J. Bresler. il *Art News* 88:144-5 O '89

O'er the land of the free [upholds right to burn the flag] W. Isaacson. il *Time* 134:14-15 Jl 3 '89

"Poor Joshua!" [absolves Wisconsin child welfare agency in case of J. DeShaney] il por *Time* 133:56 Mr 6 '89

Poor Joshua [rules Wisconsin child welfare agency not liable for injuries caused by father of J. DeShaney] P. A. Zirkel. bibl f il *Phi Delta Kappan* 70:828-9 Je '89

Protection against racial discrimination [reconsidering Runyon v. McCrary] R. F. Drinan. *America* 160:52 Ja 28 '89

A question of statistics [decision on racial discrimination at Alaskan fish canneries] T. Jacoby. il *Newsweek* 113:58 Je 19 '89

Real rights [rulings on employment discrimination] *National Review* 41:15-16 Jl 14 '89

Retreat on civil rights? S. Holmes. il *American Visions* 4:20-4 O '89

A right to privacy? [with reply by Joseph Sobran] H. V. Jaffa. *National Review* 41:51-2 Mr 24 '89

A right turn, but no free ride for business. P. Dwyer. il *Business Week* p27 Jl 10 '89

Ruling delivers hard blow to set-asides. N. McCall. il *Black Enterprise* 19:17-18 Ap '89

A slap at sex stereotypes [decision in favor of A. Hopkins in suit against Price Waterhouse] A. Sachs. il por *Time* 133:66 My 15 '89

The speech market [ruling on flag burning] D. Seligman. *Fortune* 120:135 Ag 28 '89

Star-spangled clamor [ruling on flag burning] T. C. Muck. il *Christianity Today* 33:11 S 22 '89

Stare decisis and judicial restraint [address, October 17, 1989] L. F. Powell, Jr. *Vital Speeches of the Day* 56:70-3 N 15 '89

'Stigmatic harm' [nullification of the Richmond, Va. minority set-aside program] *The Nation* 248:183-4 F 13 '89

Student journalists fight for free expression [ruling permits censorship of student press in Hazelwood, Mo. case] L. Eskin. il *Scholastic Update (Teachers' edition)* 122:19-21 S 8 '89

Supreme Court decisions set precedent for pilot drug testing [with editorial comment] P. Proctor. *Aviation Week & Space Technology* 130:9, 30 Mr 27 '89

Supreme Court delivers blow to consumers [punitive damages decision] B. Keating-Edh. *Consumers' Research Magazine* 72:20-1 S '89

Supreme Court drug test rulings. *Monthly Labor Review* 112:43 Je '89

The Supreme Court expands religious freedom [unemployment benefits for individual who refused to work on Sundays] R. F. Drinan. *America* 160:388-9 Ap 29 '89

Supreme Court press [reporting of affirmative action cases] T. Eastland. *The American Spectator* 22:32-4 O '89

Supreme Court ruling lets airlines assure jobs to strike breakers [case of TWA vs. Independent Federation of Flight Attendants] M. Mecham. *Aviation Week & Space Technology* 129:67 Mr 6 '89

Supreme Court set aside ruling not 'devastating' blow to black businesses. il *Jet* 75:4 F 13 '89

Supreme Court splits on two landmark bias cases. il *Jet* 76:4-5 Jl 3 '89

Supreme Court upholds broad use of RICO. H. Fields. *Publishers Weekly* 236:7 Jl 7 '89

Supreme Court upholds public figure libel charge; High Court refuses to place limits on jury awards in civil suits. H. Fields. *Publishers Weekly* 236:12 Jl 14 '89

Three Court cases [church and state cases] *The Christian Century* 106:976 N 1 '89

Thurgood's way [T. Marshall dissents in ruling upholding search of individual fitting drug courier profile] D. Seligman. il *Fortune* 119:165+ My 8 '89

"A time of sharpened swords" [impact on artists] D. Waterman. il *Art News* 88:59+ N '89

Toward a real restoration of civil rights [rulings on employment discrimination] T. Eastland. *Commentary* 88:25-9 N '89

Unimpressed by the freedom to burn Old Glory, Joey Johnson still wants a revolution. D. Grogan. il pors *People Weekly* 32:98-100 Jl 10 '89

What price Old Glory? [flag burning] *Time* 134:23 Jl 10 '89

Why 'separation' is not the key to church-state relations [cover story; with reply by D. M. Kelley] M. McConnell. il *The Christian Century* 106:43-52 Ja 18 '89

Wounds of race [affirmative action decisions] H. Hertzberg. *The New Republic* 201:4+ Jl 10 '89

Wrestling with bias [ruling against sex stereotyping in case of A. Hopkins v. Price Waterhouse] D. Seligman. il *Fortune* 119:339 Je 5 '89

Your Constitution. See issues of Scholastic Update (Teachers' edition) beginning September 22, 1986

Abortion decisions

Abortion, Catholicism, and the Constitution. G. Gamm. por *The Humanist* 49:24-5+ Jl/Ag '89

The abortion decision: readers respond. D. Baer. il *U.S. News & World Report* 107:23-4 Ag 7 '89

The abortion furor [Webster v. Reproductive Health Services; special section; with editorial comments by Roger Rosenblatt and David Gergen] il map *U.S. News & World Report* 107:8-9, 18-23+, 68 Jl 17 '89

Abortion: law & politics [Webster v. Reproductive Health Services; special section] *National Review* 41:34-6 Ag 4 '89

Abortion on the line [Webster case] *National Review* 41:12-13 Ag 4 '89

Abortion rights imperiled [challenge to Roe v. Wade] E. Doerr. il *The Humanist* 49:39 Jl/Ag '89

The abortion ruling. *World Press Review* 36:6 Ag '89

Abortion: sparring on the bench [arguments in cases involving mandatory notification of parents of teenagers seeking abortions] il *Newsweek* 114:49 D 11 '89

Abortion: the gathering storm [challenge to Roe v. Wade; special section] il *Ms.* 17:87-95 Ap '89

Abortion: what does 'Webster' mean? [symposium] *Commonweal* 116:425-8 Ag 11 '89

After Roe. R. J. Neuhaus. il *National Review* 41:38-40 Ap 7 '89

After the Webster decision. *America* 161:51 Jl 29-Ag 5 '89

After 'Webster': an uphill struggle. *America* 161:227 O 14 '89

Amid a raging debate, one woman chooses abortion [D. Barber at Reproductive Health Services in St. Louis, Mo.] D. Grogan and others. il *People Weekly* 32:89-90+ Jl 24 '89

As American as freeways. D. R. Carlin, Jr. *Commonweal* 116:392-3 Jl 14 '89

Attacking the real 'Jane Roe' [N. McCorvey] S. Waldman. il por *Newsweek* 113:22 Ap 17 '89

The battle over abortion [Supreme Court confronts Roe v. Wade; cover story; special section] il *Newsweek* 113:28-32+ My 1 '89

The battle over abortion [Webster v. Reproductive Health Services] M. B. Carlson. il *Time* 134:62-3 Jl 17 '89

Beyond rights in abortion politics [Webster v. Reproductive Health Services] D. Heim. *The Christian Century* 106:675-6 Jl 19-26 '89

Black Monday [Webster decision] E. Doerr. il por *The Humanist* 49:39 S/O '89

Black women's plight cited at pro-choice rally in D.C. il *Jet* 76:13 Ap 24 '89

A clear majority [prochoice rally in Washington, D.C.] *The Nation* 248:579-80 My 1 '89

Confrontation's stage is set. K. A. Lawton. il *Christianity Today* 33:36-8 Ag 18 '89

The confusion of Justice Blackmun. W. F. Buckley. *National Review* 41:55 Ag 18 '89

Could this be the year? [Roe v. Wade] K. A. Lawton. il *Christianity Today* 33:36-8 Ap 7 '89

Countdown on abortion [assault on Roe v. Wade] A. McDaniel. il *Newsweek* 113:50 Ja 23 '89

The Court and abortion. W. F. Buckley. *National Review* 41:55 Je 16 '89

The Court and the right to privacy [right to die case impacts indirectly on privacy rights underlying abortion ruling] A. McDaniel. il *Newsweek* 114:36 O 9 '89

Day in court [Roe v. Wade] W. Dellinger. *The New Republic* 200:11-12 My 8 '89

UNITED STATES. SUPREME COURT — Decisions — Abortion decisions—*cont.*

A day of reckoning on Roe [opening arguments in Webster v. Reproductive Health Services] R. Lacayo. il *Time* 133:24 My 8 '89

The end of Roe? *National Review* 41:12-13 Mr 24 '89

Father's rights case declined by High Court. *Christianity Today* 33:53 Ja 13 '89

The first march [prochoice march in Washington, D.C.] *National Review* 41:9-10 My 5 '89

Fundamental rights in danger [challenge to Roe v. Wade] E. Doerr. il *The Humanist* 49:39 My/Je '89

The future of abortion [modifying Roe v. Wade] R. M. Dworkin. bibl f il *The New York Review of Books* 36:47-51 S 28 '89

The future of abortion [Webster v. Reproductive Health Services; cover story; special section] il *Newsweek* 114:14-21+ Jl 17 '89

Good news on abortion [Webster v. Reproductive Health Services] *The New Republic* 201:5-6 Jl 31 '89

A governor responds [discussion of October 14, 1989 article, After 'Webster': an uphill struggle] *America* 161:265 O 28 '89

The great abortion case [Roe v. Wade] R. M. Dworkin. bibl f il *The New York Review of Books* 36:49-53 Je 29 '89

The great debate [challenge to Roe v. Wade] M. Webb. il *Harper's Bazaar* 122:64-5+ Jl '89

How will the abortion ruling affect blacks? R. L. Haywood. il *Jet* 76:12-15 Jl 24 '89; Correction. 76:8 Ag 14 '89

If pro-choice is mainstream, now's the time to prove it. E. Ehrlich. il *Business Week* p64 Jl 17 '89

An inflamed debate. R. Corelli. il *Maclean's* 102:36-7 Jl 17 '89

Koop finds abortion evidence "inconclusive" [Surgeon General's study on health effects does not help in prolife efforts to reverse Roe v. Wade] C. Holden. *Science* 243:730-1 F 10 '89

Last days of Roe? *National Review* 41:14+ Je 2 '89

Letting the states set abortion policy. V. G. Rosenblum. *The Christian Century* 106:252-3 Mr 8 '89

Life after Webster. D. Neff. il *Christianity Today* 33:14 Ag 18 '89

The longer march [right to abortion march in Washington] *Commonweal* 116:259-60 My 5 '89

March on Washington [prochoice demonstration] E. J. Bader. il *The Humanist* 49:26-8+ Jl/Ag '89

The morning after [consequences of overturning Roe v. Wade] B. Harvey. il *Mother Jones* 14:27-31+ My '89

Mr. Fast explains [views of H. Fast] W. F. Buckley. *National Review* 41:62-3 F 24 '89

New abortion fights [march on Washington to protest possible reversal of Roe v. Wade] T. Gest. il *U.S. News & World Report* 106:22-3+ Ap 24 '89

The new abortion wars [political consequences of Webster decision] M. Kondracke. *The New Republic* 201:17-19 Ag 28 '89

Notes and comment [Washington march to protect Roe v. Wade] *The New Yorker* 65:29-30 Ap 24 '89

Our big choice [black women] E. Strothers. por *Essence* 20:116 Jl '89

Our bodies, our business [cover story; special section; with editorial comment by Anne Summers] il *Ms.* 18:6, 38-44+ Jl/Ag '89

People's choice [prochoice march in Washington, D.C.] H. Hertzberg. *The New Republic* 200:4+ My 1 '89

The politics of abortion takes an unexpected turn [ramifications of Webster v. Reproductive Health Services] D. Baer. il *U.S. News & World Report* 107:26 Jl 31 '89

Prenatal development and the law [Webster v. Reproductive Health Services] J. Kagan. *Psychology Today* 23:46 S '89

Pro-choice: 'a sleeping giant' awakes [Washington, D.C. demonstration to oppose reversal of Roe v. Wade] E. Salholz. il *Newsweek* 113:39-40 Ap 24 '89

Pro-choicers gird for battle [threat to Roe v. Wade] S. Holmes. il *Time* 133:55 Ja 23 '89

Prochoice forces claim momentum in Washington. il *Christianity Today* 33:59 My 12 '89

Reappraising topic A [possible reversal of Roe v. Wade] il *U.S. News & World Report* 106:9-10 Ja 23 '89

The rights of the states. W. Lowther. il *Maclean's* 102:21 Jl 31 '89

Rocking the Roe boat. M. deG. Ford. *Commonweal* 116:326-8 Je 2 '89

'Roe' must stand. il *The Progressive* 53:6-7 Mr '89

Roe on the brink [Webster v. Reproductive Health Services] R. Pine. *The Nation* 249:112 Jl 24-31 '89

Roe v. Wade anniversary may be its last. il *Christianity Today* 33:41-2 F 17 '89

'Roe v. Wade'—the movie. *America* 160:523-4 Je 3 '89

Sandra Day O'Connor: woman in the middle. M. McLoughlin. por *Ladies' Home Journal* 106:218-19+ N '89

Sandra's day [Webster v. Reproductive Health Services] H. Schwartz. *The Nation* 249:156-7 Ag 7-14 '89

Save my law [Roe v. Wade plaintiff N. McCorvey at Washington, D.C. rally] G. H. Colt. il pors *Life* 12:111-12+ My '89

Splitting differences [possible reversal of Roe v. Wade] G. F. Will. il *Newsweek* 113:86 F 13 '89

Taking to the streets [celebrities march in support of Roe v. Wade decision in Washington, D.C] S. Schindehette. il *People Weekly* 31:40-5 Ap 24 '89

The thread and the cloth: arguments in the Supreme Court's abortion case [Webster v. Reproductive Health Services] il *Newsweek* 113:19 My 8 '89

Too many abortions. *Commonweal* 116:419-20 Ag 11 '89

Two steps back [consequences of Webster decision] B. Ehrenreich. il *Ms.* 18:24-5 O '89

When (if) 'Roe' falls [cover story] D. A. Degnan. *Commonweal* 116:267-9 My 5 '89

When pregnant girls face mom and dad [hearing on Minnesota law requiring parental notification in teenage abortions] D. Whitman. il *U.S. News & World Report* 107:25-6 D 4 '89

Where we stand now on abortion. M. Adessa. il *Psychology Today* 23:10 O '89

Who'll be hurt by new abortion restrictions? All of us [challenge to Roe v. Wade] il *Glamour* 87:184 My '89

Whose life is it? [challenge to Roe v. Wade; cover story] R. Lacayo. il *Time* 133:20-4 My 1 '89

Why I decided to march for abortion rights [interview with C. Shepherd] il por *Glamour* 87:96 Jl '89

Will this be the year we lose abortion? [challenge to Roe v. Wade] L. Dusky. il *Mademoiselle* 95:214-15+ My '89

Winning Webster v. Reproductive Health Services: the crisis of the pro-life movement. J. R. Kelly. *America* 161:79-83 Ag 12-19 '89

The woman behind Roe v. Wade [plaintiff N. McCorvey] M. Green. il pors *People Weekly* 31:36-41 My 22 '89

Woodward explodes Roe v. Wade [B. Woodward's articles] T. Eastland. *The American Spectator* 22:30 Ap '89

A world without Roe. M. A. Glendon. *The New Republic* 200:19-20 F 20 '89

UNITED STATES. SURGEON-GENERAL'S OFFICE

C. Everett Koop. S. Kanfer. il por *People Weekly* 32 Special Issue:127 Fall '89

Chicken Koop. R. E. Tyrrell. il *The American Spectator* 22:34-5 Je '89

Citizen Koop. *Commonweal* 116:420-1 Ag 11 '89

Cooing over Koop. *National Review* 41:17-18 F 10 '89

A doctor prescribes hard truth [C. E. Koop] M. B. Carlson. por *Time* 133:82-4 Ap 24 '89

The embattled career of Dr. Koop [cover story] P. Yancey. il por *Christianity Today* 33:16-21 O 20 '89

Notes and comment [C. E. Koop] *The New Yorker* 65:29-30 Ag 7 '89

An officer and a gentleman [C. E. Koop] J. B. Judis. *The New Republic* 200:19-22 Ja 23 '89

Surgeon General: abortion foe [appointee A. Novello] *Newsweek* 114:84 O 30 '89

Surgeon General Koop is good medicine. B. G. Harrison. *Mademoiselle* 95:126 My '89

A Surgeon General's warnings: C. Everett Koop is not about to abandon his public platform [interview] P. Yancey. il pors *Christianity Today* 33:30-3 N 3 '89

UNITED STATES. TAX COURT

Inquisition. C. Murphy. il *The Atlantic* 263:14+ Ap '89

UNITED STATES. VETERANS ADMINISTRATION

Let's make a deal [loan guaranty funds] J. Novack. il *Forbes* 143:48 Ja 23 '89

UNITED STATES. WARREN COMMISSION *See* Warren Commission

UNITED STATES. YOUTH ENGAGED IN SERVICE *See* Youth Engaged in Service (U.S.)

UNITED STATES [dance] *See* Dance reviews—Single works

UNITED STATES AND ASIA *See* Asia and the United States

UNITED STATES AND CANADA *See* Canada and the United States

UNITED STATES AND JAPAN *See* Japan and the United States

UNITED STATES AND THE SOVIET UNION *See* Soviet Union and the United States

UNITED STATES CAPITOL (WASHINGTON, D.C.) *See* Capitol (Washington, D.C.)

UNITED STATES CATHOLIC CONFERENCE
See also
Catholic Church. National Conference of Catholic Bishops

UNITED STATES CATHOLIC CONFERENCE. CAMPAIGN FOR HUMAN DEVELOPMENT *See* Campaign for Human Development

UNITED STATES CHAMBER OF COMMERCE *See* Chamber of Commerce of the United States of America

UNITED STATES COMMISSION ON CIVIL RIGHTS

Garrett, Fletcher named to key positions by Bush. il pors *Jet* 76:4-5 Ap 10 '89

Off the record [resignation of W. B. Allen] Cato. *National Review* 41:64 N 24 '89

UNITED STATES EMPLOYMENT SERVICE

Bias in the casino [charges of bias in job tests] D. Seligman. il *Fortune* 119:153-4 Ap 10 '89

More normal nonsense [National Research Council report on General Aptitude Test Battery] D. Seligman. il *Fortune* 120:118 Jl 17 '89

UNITED STATES FEDERAL PENITENTIARY (LOMPOC, CALIF.) *See* Prisons—California
UNITED STATES FILM FESTIVAL *See* Motion picture festivals—Utah
UNITED STATES GRAND PRIX *See* Motorcycle racing
UNITED STATES IN ART
Watercolors that transport [excerpt from 100 views along the road] A. Leslie. il *American Artist* 53:66-9+ Ap '89
UNITED STATES IN LITERATURE
America's moral landscape in the fiction of Richard Ford. R. A. Schroth. por *The Christian Century* 106:227-30 Mr 1 '89
UNITED STATES IN MOTION PICTURES
Tristan and Pavlova through the looking glass [how Soviet movies depict the United States] M. Fellous. il *The Unesco Courier* 42:30-3 O '89
UNITED STATES INFORMATION AGENCY *See* United States. Information Agency
UNITED STATES INSTITUTE FOR THEATRE TECHNOLOGY
USITT previews [special section] J. Calhoun. il *Theatre Crafts* 23:46-55 Mr '89
UNITED STATES-JAPAN AIR AGREEMENTS *See* Aviation and state—International aspects
UNITED STATES LEAGUE OF SAVINGS INSTITUTIONS
Responsibility and regulation [address, June 26, 1989] J. A. Grundfest. *Vital Speeches of the Day* 55:718-22 S 15 '89
UNITED STATES MILITARY ACADEMY
Breaking barriers in the barracks [K. Baker named First Captain of cadets at West Point] P. Cary. il pors *U.S. News & World Report* 107:26-7 Ag 21 '89
Manning the barricades no more, West Point names Kristin Baker to head the long gray line [first female captain of the cadet corps] S. K. Reed. il pors *People Weekly* 32:50-1 Ag 28 '89
A moving new book helps West Point '66 bind the wounds of war and changing times [R. Atkinson's The long gray line] L. Kramer. il pors *People Weekly* 32:92-3+ O 30 '89
'No slack': a woman's touch at West Point [cadet K. Baker named First Captain] por *Newsweek* 114:20 Ag 21 '89
The onerousness of honor [commission calls for policy changes] *U.S. News & World Report* 106:17 Je 26 '89
The West Point story [excerpt from The long gray line; cover story] R. Atkinson. il pors *U.S. News & World Report* 107:44-54 O 9 '89
UNITED STATES MINT *See* United States. Mint
UNITED STATES NAVAL OBSERVATORY
Black Birch observatory under fire in New Zealand. il *Sky and Telescope* 78:9-10 Jl '89
UNITED STATES OLYMPIC COMMITTEE
'I enjoy stress' [interview with H. Schiller] R. Sullivan. il por *Sports Illustrated* 71:16 N 13 '89
UNITED STATES POSTAL SERVICE
Can this man really deliver? [interview with A. M. Frank] C. Leinster. il por *Fortune* 120:87-8 Ag 14 '89
Can we sort out the mail mess? J. B. Judis. il *Reader's Digest* 134:189-90+ Ap '89
Mailroom mayhem. M. B. Carlson. il *Time* 134:30-1 D 25 '89
Postal Frank [A. Frank] E. Hardy. il por *Forbes* 144:139 Ag 7 '89
Why America loves letter carriers and hates postal clerks [cover story] J. DeParle. il *The Washington Monthly* 21:40-6+ Jl/Ag '89

Anecdotes, facetiae, satire, etc.
The postman didn't ring even once [lost manuscript] J. E. Scalia. *The Writer* 102:7-8 My '89

Automation
The high-tech needs of the Postal Service [cover story] A. A. Layne. il *High Technology Business* 9:14-19 Je '89

Procurement
U.S. Postal Service expands express shipment services. P. Proctor. il *Aviation Week & Space Technology* 130:111+ My 1 '89
UNITED STATES STEEL CORP.
See also
USX Corporation
UNITED STATES STEEL CORP. USS CHEMICALS DIVISION
See also
Aristech Chemical Corporation
UNITED STATES SURGICAL CORP.
Now, Lee Hirsch wants to sew up sutures. C. Tucher. il por *Business Week* p74-5 Ag 7 '89
UNITED STATES TENNIS ASSOCIATION
Open the Open [need for more equitable ticket distribution] B. Collins. il *World Tennis* 37:84-5 S '89
UNITED STATES-WESTERN EUROPE AIR AGREEMENTS *See* Aviation and state—International aspects
UNITED STEELWORKERS OF AMERICA
Bethlehem-Steelworkers contract. il *Monthly Labor Review* 112:43-4 Jl '89
Both sides are girded for grueling steel talks. M. Schroeder. il *Business Week* p40-1 Mr 13 '89

Did union leaders sell out the steelworkers? [USX accused of conspiring with negotiators] J. P. Hoerr. il *Business Week* p48-50 D 25 '89-Ja 1 '90
A stunning blow to cooperation at National Steel [rejection of labor pact] G. L. Miles. *Business Week* p32 Jl 3 '89
Suddenly, USX is playing Mr. Nice Guy. G. L. Miles. il *Business Week* p151-2 Je 26 '89
UNITED TECHNOLOGIES CORP.
Can UTC fix what it can't sell? [Norden Systems Inc.] T. Vogel. *Business Week* p31 Ag 21 '89
Where 1990s-style management is already hard at work. T. Vogel. il por *Business Week* p92-3+ O 23 '89
UNITED TECHNOLOGIES CORP. PRATT & WHITNEY AIRCRAFT GROUP *See* Pratt & Whitney Aircraft Group.
UNITED TRANSPORTATION UNION
Employment cuts sought in rail transportation [CSX and the United Transportation Union] *Monthly Labor Review* 112:43 Mr '89
UNIVERSAL BALLET COMPANY
Universal Ballet Company: ballet today in Seoul, Korea. M. Hunt. il *Dance Magazine* 63:58-9 Ap '89
UNIVERSAL DECLARATION OF HUMAN RIGHTS
40th anniversary of the Universal Declaration of Human Rights [cover story; with text of declaration] il *Department of State Bulletin* 88:1-12 D '88
'To generate a universal culture of human rights' [40th anniversary] il *UN Chronicle* 26:84-7 Mr '89
U.S. commemorates 40th anniversary of the Universal Declaration of Human Rights [remarks and text of proclamation, December 8, 1988] *Department of State Bulletin* 89:59-69 Mr '89
UNIVERSAL FOODS CORP.
A little cash and a lot of moxie [Hyde Park Holdings' bid] L. J. Nathans. il pors *Business Week* p74 Ja 30 '89
UNIVERSAL PICTURES
Last temptation boycott gets mixed reviews. K. H. Sidey. il *Christianity Today* 33:36-7 Ap 21 '89
Movie studio tours—the new, fun vacation! S. Birnbaum. il *Good Housekeeping* 208:36+ Je '89
Universal pulls out a plum . . . R. Grover. il *Business Week* p51-2 N 13 '89
UNIVERSE
See also
Astronomy
Cosmic strings
Creation
Dark matter (Astronomy)
Galaxies
Hubble constant
Astronomers go up against the Great Wall [research by Margaret J. Geller and John P. Huchra] M. M. Waldrop. il *Science* 246:885 N 17 '89
A brief history of A brief history. S. W. Hawking. il pors *Popular Science* 235:70-2 Ag '89
Closing the circle [studying the universe through particle physics] S. L. Glashow. il *Discover* 10:66-70+ O '89
COBE: seeking traces of the beginning. J. Eberhart. *Science News* 136:279 O 28 '89
Cosmic Background Explorer to observe Big Bang radiation [cover story] C. Covault. il *Aviation Week & Space Technology* 131:36-7+ N 6 '89
Cosmic cartographers find 'Great Wall' [work of Margaret J. Geller and John P. Huchra] A. McKenzie. il *Science News* 136:340 N 25 '89
Cosmic quarrel [Huw Price questions S. W. Hawking's arrow of time explanation] T. Beardsley. *Scientific American* 261:22+ O '89
Cosmological constant conundrum. *Sky and Telescope* 78:132-3 Ag '89
The cosmological imperative. E. Chaisson. *Astronomy* 17:8 F '89
A cross section of the universe. J. Kanipe. il *Astronomy* 17:44-6 N '89
Dignifying humanity: the humor of Stephen W. Hawking. T. Organ. por *The Humanist* 49:29-30+ Jl/Ag '89
Distant supernova may have cosmological impact [1988U] il *Astronomy* 17:12 D '89
First light [Cosmic Background Explorer satellite will help gauge validity of Big Bang theory] S. J. Nadis. il *Omni (New York, N.Y.)* 11:94 S '89
From fireball to galaxies: making late waves [late phase transitions in astronomical models] I. Peterson. *Science News* 135:262 Ap 29 '89
Great bubbles in the cosmos [work of Margaret Geller and John Huchra] M. D. Lemonick. il *Time* 134:57-8 N 27 '89
The homing instinct. D. Lago. il *Astronomy* 17:98-9 Jl '89
John Dobson: a man with a mission [interview] S. J. O'Meara. por *Sky and Telescope* 78:530-2 N '89
Looking into the Big Bang [Cosmic Background Explorer satellite] D. H. Smith and A. MacRobert. il *Sky and Telescope* 77:593 Je '89
Mapping the universe [cover story] M. J. Geller and J. Huchra. bibl f il *Science* 246:897-903 N 17 '89
No go for slow flow [work of R. Brent Tully and J. Richard Fisher] il *Sky and Telescope* 77:10-11 Ja '89

UNIVERSE—*cont.*

Olbers' paradox solved at last [dark night sky] P. S. Wesson. il *Sky and Telescope* 77:594-7 Je '89

The origin of the universe [Big Bang] V. F. Weisskopf. il *The New York Review of Books* 36:10-14 F 16 '89

Pride and prejudice [cosmic lithium abundance and open vs. closed universe; research by Lawrence M. Krauss] T. Rothman. *Scientific American* 261:16-17 Ag '89

A smooth transition to a lumpy universe [theory of David N. Schramm] *Astronomy* 17:14+ S '89

Supercomputing the universe. D. Johnson. il *Astronomy* 17:48-54 D '89

Through the looking glass. G. Greenstein. il *Astronomy* 17:20-8 O '89

Why is the cosmological constant so very small? B. M. Schwarzschild. bibl f il *Physics Today* 42:21-4 Mr '89

Wormholes in the heavens [creating new universes; views of A. H. Guth] M. D. Lemonick. il *Time* 133:55 Ja 16 '89

Your own universe [Rudy Rucker's Cellular Automata Laboratory computer program] T. Waters. il *Discover* 10:24 D '89

UNIVERSITIES *See* Colleges and universities

UNIVERSITIES FUNDING COUNCIL (GREAT BRITAIN)

British biologists learn small is not beautiful. D. Dickson. *Science* 244:766-7 My 19 '89

New life for small science [abandonment of proposal to abolish many physics and chemistry departments in universities] J. Cherfas. *Science* 246:573 N 3 '89

UNIVERSITIES RESEARCH ASSOCIATION

Knapp resigns from URA leadership; Truly to pilot NASA, Fields at DARPA. I. Goodwin. *Physics Today* 42:42-4 Je '89

UNIVERSITIES SPACE RESEARCH ASSOCIATION. LUNAR AND PLANETARY INSTITUTE *See* Lunar and Planetary Institute

UNIVERSITY EDUCATION *See* College education

UNIVERSITY EXTENSION

Informal routes to a formal degree. N. Henderson. bibl il *Changing Times* 43:77+ Ja '89

Australia

Long-range learning. M. Skilbeck. il *The Courier (Unesco)* 41:32-4 D '88

UNIVERSITY LIBRARIES *See* College libraries

UNIVERSITY OF ALABAMA

Black UA homecoming queen wins by write-in campaign; stirs a furor [K. Ashley] il por *Jet* 77:18 N 6 '89

UNIVERSITY OF CALIFORNIA, BERKELEY

Berkeley's changing student population. R. Buderi. il *Science* 245:694-6 Ag 18 '89

The class that deserves cutting [mandatory ethnic studies class] J. Leo. il *U.S. News & World Report* 106:58 My 29 '89

Graduate students make history [University of California-Berkeley recognizes Association of Graduate Student Employees] P. Selvin. *The Progressive* 53:19 O '89

The new 'open door' at Berkeley [Asian Americans' charges of quotas] *U.S. News & World Report* 106:13-14 Je 5 '89

UNIVERSITY OF CALIFORNIA, BERKELEY. CENTER FOR PARTICLE ASTROPHYSICS

Pruning the thickets of cosmic speculation. M. M. Waldrop. il *Science* 243:168-9 Ja 13 '89

UNIVERSITY OF CALIFORNIA, LOS ANGELES. CHILD CARE CENTER

Prefab preschool. D. Dietsch. il *Architectural Record* 177:126-9 Je '89

UNIVERSITY OF CALIFORNIA, LOS ANGELES. INDEPENDENT FILM AND TELEVISION PRODUCER'S PROGRAM

The professor-mogul [H. Suber] L. Jarvik. *American Film* 14:13 My '89

UNIVERSITY OF CALIFORNIA, SAN DIEGO. SCHOOL OF MEDICINE

Setting the record straight [retraction of fraudulent papers by R. Slutsky] M. Sun. *Science* 244:911 My 26 '89

UNIVERSITY OF CALIFORNIA, SAN DIEGO. STUART COLLECTION

Lessons in public sculpture [cover story] D. Joselit. il *Art in America* 77:130-5 D '89

UNIVERSITY OF CALIFORNIA, SAN FRANCISCO

The sports stars of UCSF. M. Barinaga. il *Science* 245:1442 S 29 '89

UNIVERSITY OF CALIFORNIA (SYSTEM)

Thatcherism and higher education: California, here she comes. R. M. Rosenzweig. il *Change* 21:40-1 S/O '89

UNIVERSITY OF CAMBRIDGE

'The dark forces of lust': Plath at Cambridge [excerpt from Bitter fame] A. Stevenson. il pors *The New York Times Book Review* 94:1+ Ag 13 '89

UNIVERSITY OF CAMBRIDGE. FITZWILLIAM MUSEUM *See* Fitzwilliam Museum

UNIVERSITY OF CAMBRIDGE. HOMERTON COLLEGE

Spotlight on schools [summer study] il *Teen* 33:89 Je '89

UNIVERSITY OF CAMBRIDGE. INSTITUTE OF MANAGEMENT STUDIES

Cambridge dons an M.B.A. il *Newsweek* 114:47 S 18 '89

UNIVERSITY OF CHICAGO

Requiem for the Hutchins College. F. C. Ward. il por *Change* 21:24-33 Jl/Ag '89

UNIVERSITY OF CHICAGO. GRADUATE SCHOOL OF BUSINESS

Chicago's B-school goes touchy-feely. D. Greising. il *Business Week* p140 N 27 '89

UNIVERSITY OF CHICAGO. LAW SCHOOL

U. of Chicago bans law firm's recruiting after racist comments [Baker & McKenzie] *Jet* 75:30 F 20 '89

UNIVERSITY OF COLORADO AT BOULDER

What price glory? [criminal behavior among football players] R. Reilly. il *Sports Illustrated* 70:32-4 F 27 '89

UNIVERSITY OF COLORADO AT DENVER. NATIONAL LEADERSHIP INSTITUTE ON AGING *See* National Leadership Institute on Aging

UNIVERSITY OF EAST ANGLIA

British rabbits: scholarship down [plan to build facilities on site of rabbit warren being studied by Diana Bell and Nicola Webb] J. Cherfas. *Science* 246:1384 D 15 '89

UNIVERSITY OF FLORIDA

Gambling, payoffs and drugs. R. Sullivan. il *Sports Illustrated* 71:40-2+ O 30 '89

The shady side of sunshine [selection of new president] J. McLaughlin and D. Riesman. il *Change* 21:44-57 Ja/F '89

UNIVERSITY OF FLORIDA. COLLEGE OF ARCHITECTURE

Architectural education: bridging the teaching/practice gap. A. J. Catanese. por *Architectural Record* 177:47 Jl '89

UNIVERSITY OF GEORGIA

Jan Kemp [professor's stand against college athletes' low academic standards] S. Kanfer. il por *People Weekly* 32 Special Issue:124 Fall '89

UNIVERSITY OF HARTFORD. MUSEUM OF AMERICAN POLITICAL LIFE *See* Museum of American Political Life

UNIVERSITY OF HAWAII

Malaria researcher indicted [W. Siddiqui charged with embezzling research funds] E. Marshall. *Science* 245:1326 S 22 '89

UNIVERSITY OF IOWA

Bookstore

See College bookstores

UNIVERSITY OF KENTUCKY

Dodging a bullet [basketball program put on probation; cover story] C. Kirkpatrick. il *Sports Illustrated* 70:24-6+ My 29 '89

Under the volcano [charges against basketball team] H. Nuwer. il *Sport (New York, N.Y.)* 80:50-3+ F '89

UNIVERSITY OF MARYLAND, COLLEGE PARK

Rhonda Williams delivers historic graduation speech at University of Maryland. por *Jet* 76:19 Je 19 '89

UNIVERSITY OF MARYLAND AT BALTIMORE. HEALTH CENTER

Augustus White to head U. of Md. Health Center. por *Jet* 76:21 Jl 3 '89

UNIVERSITY OF MIAMI. COMPREHENSIVE PAIN AND REHABILITATION CENTER

Four weeks to a pain-free back. G. Maleskey. il *Prevention (Emmaus, Pa.)* 41:40-8 Mr '89

UNIVERSITY OF MINNESOTA. RAPTOR CENTER

Minnesotans struggle to save their poisoned swans [P. Redig's efforts to treat lead-poisoned trumpeters] M. Nelson. il *People Weekly* 31:103-5 Mr 13 '89

UNIVERSITY OF MINNESOTA PRESS

UNESCO drops attempt to suppress book about itself. C. Reid. *Publishers Weekly* 235:16 Je 16 '89

UNIVERSITY OF MISSOURI—COLUMBIA

Kansas City Call publisher gets honorary degree at U. of Mo.; locked out in '39 [L. Bluford] il por *Jet* 76:16 My 22 '89

UNIVERSITY OF NEVADA, LAS VEGAS

Crass and class [basketball program] C. Kirkpatrick. il pors *Sports Illustrated* 71:56-9+ N 20 '89

Playing to win in Vegas [basketball program] T. Gup. il por *Time* 133:56-7 Ap 3 '89

UNIVERSITY OF NEW MEXICO PRESS

Big sales for New Mexico's 'Little Tree'. il *Publishers Weekly* 235:49 My 19 '89

UNIVERSITY OF NORTH CAROLINA AT CHAPEL HILL. GRADUATE SCHOOL OF BUSINESS ADMINISTRATION

Why angels are flocking to Chapel Hill's B-school. M. Roman. il por *Business Week* p110+ O 2 '89

UNIVERSITY OF NORTH DAKOTA. CENTER FOR AEROSPACE SCIENCES

Top-flight camp [summer camp] il *National Geographic World* 163:18-21 Mr '89

UNIVERSITY OF NOTRE DAME

Jocks with books. J. Adler. il *Newsweek* 113:60-1 Ja 9 '89

UNIVERSITY OF OKLAHOMA

Oklahoma is not OK [troubles of football program] R. Givens. il por *Newsweek* 113:80 F 27 '89

You reap what you sow [football program; cover story] R. Telander and R. Sullivan. il por *Sports Illustrated* 70:20-6+ F 27 '89

UNIVERSITY OF OREGON
Ken Kesey's eclectic writing acid test. D. Weddle. il por *Rolling Stone* p119-20+ O 5 '89
Remember this: write what you don't know [students collaborate on novel] K. Kesey. *The New York Times Book Review* 94:1+ D 31 '89

UNIVERSITY OF OXFORD
A Gothic tale [fund raising campaign] T. Beardsley. *Scientific American* 260:20-1 Mr '89

UNIVERSITY OF OXFORD. SOMERVILLE COLLEGE
Profiles [former diplomat D. Park] C. Alexander. il por *The New Yorker* 64:57-71 Ja 30 '89

UNIVERSITY OF PENNSYLVANIA
Blacks get own yearbook at Univ. of Pa.; It's a 1st for Ivy League schools. il *Jet* 76:22 Ag 21 '89

UNIVERSITY OF PENNSYLVANIA. LIBRARIES
See also
Furness Building

UNIVERSITY OF PENNSYLVANIA. WHARTON SCHOOL OF FINANCE AND COMMERCE *See* Wharton School

UNIVERSITY OF PITTSBURGH. SCHOOL OF MEDICINE
Corporate-funded research may be hazardous to your health [case of E. Cantekin, professor who questioned effectiveness of antibiotic amoxicillin] K. Hart. *The Bulletin of the Atomic Scientists* 45:32 Ap '89

UNIVERSITY OF SOUTHERN CALIFORNIA
Ethical and moral responsibilities as faculty [address, September 23, 1988] J. H. Zumberge. *Vital Speeches of the Day* 55:199-202 Ja 15 '89

UNIVERSITY OF THE DISTRICT OF COLUMBIA
Black female student from Russia to attend U. of D.C. [A. Mensah] il por *Jet* 76:24 Ag 21 '89

UNIVERSITY OF THE STATE OF NEW YORK. BOARD OF REGENTS
The Regents' Round Table [report calling for greater multicultural inclusion in curricula] L. Auster. il *National Review* 41:18+ D 8 '89

UNIVERSITY OF TORONTO
Here's looking at you, kid [sexual harassment case against Prof. R. Hummel] B. Amiel. il *Maclean's* 102:9 Ap 10 '89

UNIVERSITY OF UTAH
Hype-energy physics [cold fusion; press reports of fusion breakthrough] R. Bazell. *The New Republic* 200:7-8 Ap 24 '89
Will this tortoise beat the hares? [Brigham Young vs. Univ. of Utah in cold fusion race] J. Carey and W. C. Symonds. il por *Business Week* p103 My 8 '89

UNIVERSITY OF VERMONT
Pride and perjury [firing of teacher and scientist A. Novikoff for Communist activities during McCarthy era] D. M. Oshinsky. por *The New Leader* 72:14-17 S 4 '89

UNIVERSITY OF VIRGINIA
A day at U. Va. il *Seventeen* 48:316-21+ Ag '89
Reroofing a landmark [restoration of tin roofs at University of Virginia] D. Rastorfer. il *Architectural Record* 177:124-7 F '89

UNIVERSITY OF WATERLOO
290,500 Oxford words to live by [Oxford English dictionary compiled with help of Univ. of Waterloo software] D. Francis. il *Maclean's* 102:9 F 20 '89

UNIVERSITY OF WATERLOO. WILLIAM DAVIS COMPUTER RESEARCH CENTER *See* William Davis Computer Research Center

UNIVERSITY OF WISCONSIN—MADISON
Banning ethnic slurs on campus. *Newsweek* 113:68 Ap 24 '89
The indomitable Donna Shalala [chancellor] L. DePaulo. il por *New Choices for the Best Years* 29:26-30 Ag '89
On changing academic culture from the inside [interview with D. Shalala] A. Bernstein and S. Mow. il pors *Change* 21:20-9 Ja/F '89
Taking on the risk of bigger vistas [D. Shalala, chancellor] L. Calvacca. il por *Working Woman* 14:116 O '89

UNIVERSITY PRESIDENTS *See* College presidents

UNIVERSITY PRESS OF NEW ENGLAND
Wesleyan Press to join University Press of New England. *Publishers Weekly* 236:14 O 6 '89

UNIVERSITY PRESSES
See also
Association of American University Presses
Indiana University Press
Northwestern University Press
University of Minnesota Press
University of New Mexico Press
Wesleyan University Press
From the campuses: adventures in publishing [regional literature] R. Reed. il *The New York Times Book Review* 94:1+ S 24 '89
Reading food: there's a mythological construct in my soup. B. H. Fussell. il *The New York Times Book Review* 94:36 S 24 '89
The university press and suitable priorities. L. E. Phillabaum. il por *Publishers Weekly* 235:39 My 26 '89
University presses: highs & lows. W. Nixon. il *Publishers Weekly* 236:18+ S 22 '89

Cooperation
See also
University Press of New England
Great Britain
See also
Oxford University Press

UNIVERSITY RESEARCH *See* Colleges and universities—Research

UNIVERSITY STUDENTS *See* College students

UNIVERSITY TEACHERS *See* College teachers

UNIVERSITY TRUSTEES *See* College trustees

UNIVISION/SPANISH INTERNATIONAL NETWORK
Hispanic TV: a great way to make a killing, right? R. Grover. il *Business Week* p61 O 23 '89

UNIX OPERATING SYSTEM
AIX on the PS/2s. B. Smith. il *Byte* 14 Special Issue:95-6+ Fall '89
Altos 386 series 1000: for Unix only. B. Smith. il *Byte* 14 Special Issue:30-1 Fall '89
High-fashion UNIX on a PC [Hewlett-Packard Accelerated X Window Display Server] B. Smith. il *Byte* 14:205-6+ D '89
Mac-like interface brings another look to Unix [Looking Glass] *Byte* 14:17 S '89
Mach: the model for future Unix. A. Tevanian, Jr. and B. Smith. *Byte* 14:411-12+ N '89
Networking with Unix [workstations] G. Comeau. il *Byte* 14:265-7+ F '89
New UNIX benchmarks. F. Langa. il *Byte* 14:8 Jl '89
OS/3 and Unix's last, best hope [planned enhancements to OS/2] F. Langa. il *Byte* 14:6 Mr '89
OSF seeking shrink-wrapped Unix software. *Byte* 14:22+ S '89
Payday for Johnny Appleseed [AT&T's UNIX] N. Alster. il *Forbes* 144:218-19 O 30 '89
The UNIX/bin. D. Fiedler. See issues of Byte beginning August 1989
Unix [special section] il *Byte* 14:225+ My '89
Unix filenames for Turbo Pascal. J. Kerr. il *Byte* 14 Special Issue:185-6+ Fall '89
UNIX finally comes into its own. R. Brandt. il *Business Week* p200+ N 27 '89
The Unix shell. G. Comeau. il *Byte* 14:315-16+ S '89
Unix tools for DOS [MKS Make and MKS Lex and Yacc] B. Smith. *Byte* 14:97-8 F '89
'The Unix war' is over—but the fighting goes on. R. Brandt. il *Business Week* p114+ Mr 27 '89
VM in Unix. B. Smith. *Byte* 14:348-9 N '89
X window system on the march [Interactive Systems' 386/ix X11] T. Yager. il *Byte* 14:201-2+ O '89

UNK (ACCELERATOR) *See* Accelerators (Electrons, etc.)

UNKEFER, RONALD A.
about
Ron Unkefer: sometimes it pays not to haggle. R. D. Hof. il por *Business Week* p82 Ap 3 '89

UNKNOWN SOLDIERS
Black veterans of WWII honor unknown soldiers. il *Jet* 77:28 N 20 '89

UNMARRIED COUPLES
See also
Common law marriage
After the loving, counting the cost [celebrity breakups; cover story; special section] S. Schindehette. il *People Weekly* 32:68-70+ Ag 7 '89
I was an unwed stepmother. E. Mehren. por *Newsweek* 114:12-13 O 23 '89
The juicy truth about living together. T. Harmon. il *Glamour* 87:122+ D '89
Living together: bad for the kids [research by Marla Beth Isaacs and George Leon] P. King. *Psychology Today* 23:77 Mr '89
Living together before marriage: a new report. A. C. Mallozzi. il *Good Housekeeping* 209:255 O '89
My best friend's girlfriend. B. Weber. il *The New York Times Magazine* p18+ Ap 16 '89
New dilemma for black professionals: 'living together' or marriage? R. Brown. il *Ebony* 45:96+ D '89
Tea for you and your POSSLQ. *U.S. News & World Report* 106:17 My 15 '89
When you're very possibly pregnant. D. Heyn. *Mademoiselle* 95:98 D '89
Anecdotes, facetiae, satire, etc.
Love lessons learned from famous couples. il *Glamour* 87:111 F '89
Economic conditions
The delicate balances of living together. L. N. Vreeland. il *Money* 18:88-90+ Mr '89
Financial strategies for unmarrieds. C. V. Clarke. il *Black Enterprise* 20:94-6+ O '89
Just living together [flight attendants Bob Elsken and Karen Cramer] S. Seixas. il *Money* 18:107-12 Ja '89
Live-in losers: staying out of the ring. D. M. Rankin. *Harper's Bazaar* 122:44-5+ Ja '89
Housing
Living in sin? Not in her apartments, vows Christian landlady Evelyn Smith [K. Phillips and G. Randall file discrimination charges] M. Brower. il pors *People Weekly* 32:113-14 D 11 '89

UNMARRIED COUPLES—cont.

Legal status, laws, etc.

See also

Palimony

Gay and lesbian couples. J. Seligmann. il *Newsweek* 114 Special Issue:38-40 Wint '89/Spr '90

Homosexual families and the law. *Newsweek* 114:48 Jl 17 '89

A new kind of spouse in the house. *U.S. News & World Report* 107:13+ Ag 21 '89

San Francisco set to define 'family' [referendum on affording legal recognition to unmarried heterosexual and homosexual couples] R. Digitale. il *Christianity Today* 33:44-6 O 20 '89

Should gays have marriage rights? W. Isaacson. il *Time* 134:101-2 N 20 '89

Sort of married [homosexual couples] T. K. Jones. il *Christianity Today* 33:14 S 8 '89

UNMARRIED MEN *See* Single men

UNMARRIED PEOPLE *See* Single people

UNMARRIED WOMEN *See* Single women

UNO, SOSUKE

about

An affair to remember. B. Hillenbrand. il por *Time* 134:33 Jl 10 '89

The dirt on 'Mr. Clean'. M. Nemeth. il por *Maclean's* 102:32 Jl 10 '89

The end of the affair? B. Powell. il por *Newsweek* 114:22-3 Jl 10 '89

The geisha who knew too much. il *U.S. News & World Report* 106:15-16 Je 19 '89

Japan's geisha scandal. *World Press Review* 36:6+ Ag '89

Numero Uno. *Time* 133:35 Je 12 '89

The premier and the geisha. *Newsweek* 113:46 Je 19 '89

Upset in Japan. H. Jensen. il pors *Maclean's* 102:22-3 Ag 7 '89

Will the Recruit scandal just go away? A. Borrus and N. Gross. il por *Business Week* p40-1 Je 12 '89

UNOCAL CORP.

Truck heaven [low calorie menus served at truck stops] R. Flippin. *American Health* 8:105 N '89

UNRWA *See* United Nations Relief and Works Agency for Palestine Refugees in the Near East

UNSELD, WES

about

Mountains of men. T. Loverro. il pors *Sport (New York, N.Y.)* 80:58-62 F '89

UNSELFISHNESS *See* Altruism

UNSER, AL, JR.

about

All sorts of horse power. S. Moses. il pors *Sports Illustrated* 70:40-2+ My 29 '89

Bump and run. S. Moses. il pors *Sports Illustrated* 70:33 Ap 24 '89

A bumper-car Indy. S. Moses. il pors *Sports Illustrated* 70:32-4+ Je 5 '89

UNSER, ROBBY

about

One family's mountain. S. Moses. il por *Sports Illustrated* 71:22-3 Jl 17 '89

UNSOLVED MYSTERIES [television program] See Television program reviews—Single works

UNSWORTH, TIM

Letter from the Midwest. See occasional issues of Publishers Weekly beginning March 21, 1986

UNSWORTH, TIM

Campaigns for sainthood can make a lot of enemies. il *U.S. Catholic* 54:34-8 N '89

Catholics won't settle for half a Mass. *U.S. Catholic* 54:13-19 Je '89

Fifty years of changing minds & structures. il *Commonweal* 116:365-7 Je 16 '89

Knockin' on heaven's door: how U.S. Catholic readers pray [cover story] il *U.S. Catholic* 54:6-15 My '89

Let's cancel the Creed at Sunday Mass [with readers' comments] *U.S. Catholic* 54:13-17 Ja '89

Parish Bible study: how to learn your faith by the book. il *U.S. Catholic* 54:21-5 S '89

Parishes should learn to fight fair. *U.S. Catholic* 54:29-31 F '89

UNTAG *See* United Nations Transition Assistance Group in Namibia

UNTERBERGER, GAIL

Twelve steps for women alcoholics. *The Christian Century* 106:1150-2 D 6 '89

UNTIDINESS *See* Messiness

UNUM CORPORATION

"We understand risk". L. Jereski. il por *Forbes* 143:127+ Mr 20 '89

UNWED BIRTHS *See* Illegitimacy

UNWED COUPLES *See* Unmarried couples

UNWED FATHERS *See* Single fathers

UNWED MOTHERS *See* Single mothers

UNWIRED TELEVISION NETWORKS

See also

Independent Television Network (Firm)

The gutting and rewiring of television sales [cover story] C. Reece. il *Channels (New York, N.Y.: 1986)* 9:26-30 Ap '89

Should unwireds stay the course? C. Reece. il *Channels (New York, N.Y.: 1986)* 9:88-9 N '89

UP AGAINST IT [musical] See Musicals, revues, etc.—Reviews—Single works

UP 'N' UNDER [drama] See Godber, John

UPDIKE, JOHN

A case of melancholia. il *The New Yorker* 65:112-20 F 20 '89

Doves & hawks [discussion of March 1989 article, On not being a dove] *Commentary* 88:2-4 Ag '89

Fast art [cover story] il *The New Republic* 200:26-8 Mr 27 '89

Here I am [story] *The New Yorker* 64:34-7 Ja 23 '89

On not being a dove. *Commentary* 87:22-30 Mr '89

An open letter to Voyager 2. il *Life* 12:115 N '89

Orthodontia [poem] *The New Republic* 200:35 F 13 '89

Sacred places. il por maps *Popular Mechanics* 166:26-30 My '89

Short Easter [story] *The New Yorker* 65:38-42 Mr 27 '89

Spat [story] il *Architectural Digest* 46:26+ Mr '89

Squirrels mating [poem] il *The Atlantic* 264:60 Jl '89

To a box turtle [poem] *The New Yorker* 65:38 S 11 '89

A writer's blocks. *Harper's* 278:36+ Ja '89

about

Updike's song of himself [Self-consciousness] R. C. Wood. il por *The Christian Century* 106:526-8 My 17 '89

UPHOLSTERY

How to buy upholstered furniture. il *Consumer Reports* 54:33-8 Ja '89

UPI *See* United Press Intl., Inc.

UPIU *See* United Paperworkers International Union

UPJOHN CO.

Will this formula cure what ails Upjohn? D. Woodruff. il *Business Week* p65 S 18 '89

UPPER ATMOSPHERE *See* Atmosphere, Upper

UPPER CLASSES

See also

Debutantes

Elite (Social sciences)

Rich

Blue-blood blues [Bush presidency] E. D. Baltzell. *The New Republic* 200:15-16 Ap 3 '89

Great Britain

Charity begins with gluttony. F. Inglis. il *The Nation* 248:446-8 Ap 3 '89

My girl [M. Thatcher] M. Elliott. *The New Republic* 200:15-16 My 29 '89

UPPER MIDWEST BOOKSELLERS ASSOCIATION

UMBA continues to grow. K. O. Fakih. il *Publishers Weekly* 236:28-9 O 20 '89

UPPER WEST SIDE (NEW YORK, N.Y.)

The wild, wild West. G. Schwartz. il *New York* 22:28 Mr 13 '89

UPSHAW, DAWN

about

Dawn Upshaw's American music. R. Freed. por *Stereo Review* 54:152 S '89

Singer's choice. P. G. Davis. por *New York* 22:66 My 22 '89

UPSHAW, GENE

about

The NFL's union could win by committing suicide. A. Bernstein. il por *Business Week* p84 N 27 '89

UPSKIING

It's an upski! il *National Geographic World* 161:8-9 Ja '89

UPWARD BOUND ACADEMY

Making a fast break out of the ghetto [program founded by B. Doss] J. Tabor. il pors *Time* 133:14-15+ F 6 '89

URABEZ, ROBERTO

about

Alleged killer of 'Jet beauty' turns himself in after his crime is aired on TV show. pors *Jet* 77:7 O 16 '89

D.C. police hunt for suspect in slaying of co-ed and her brother. pors *Jet* 76:52 Jl 24 '89

URANGA, RIMA

about

In Vegas, vowing he has changed his wild ways, Griffin O'Neal takes the plunge into marriage. il pors *People Weekly* 32:48 Jl 17 '89

URANIUM ENRICHMENT *See* Uranium metallurgy

URANIUM INDUSTRY

Environmental aspects

Grand Canyon uranium mining assessed. *National Parks* 63:13-14 My/Je '89

URANIUM METALLURGY

Bomb potential for South America [Argentina and Brazil] D. Albright. bibl f il map *The Bulletin of the Atomic Scientists* 45:16-20 My '89

URANIUM MINES AND MINING
Environmental aspects
See Uranium industry—Environmental aspects
Arizona
Grand Canyon uranium mining assessed. *National Parks* 63:13-14 My/Je '89
URANIUM SERIES DATING *See* Radioactive dating
URANUS (PLANET)
See also
Space flight—Voyager flights
Uranus and Vesta naked-eye. A. MacRobert. il *Sky and Telescope* 78:66 Jl '89
Magnetic properties
Uranus' signature in a radio signal [work of Michael D. Desch and others] R. Monastersky. *Science News* 135:319 My 20 '89
Satellites
Finding the moons of Uranus. il *Sky and Telescope* 78:72 Jl '89
Geology
Ice volcanism on Ariel [discussion of September 9, 1988 article, Solid-state ice volcanism on the satellites of Uranus] D. G. Jankowski and S. W. Squyres. *Science* 245:195-6 Jl 14 '89
URBAN AGRICULTURE
Cities with farms and forests. il *The Futurist* 23:55 Mr/Ap '89
URBAN ARCHAEOLOGY LTD.
Fulton Fish Market and Urban Archaeology Ltd. H. Bridges. il *Gourmet* 49:36+ Mr '89
URBAN ARCHEOLOGY
See also
London (England)—Antiquities
URBAN ARCHITECTURE, INC.
Merchant of Memphis [American distributor K. Johnson] M. Filler. il por *House & Garden* 161:64+ S '89
URBAN BUSH WOMEN (GROUP)
Reviews:
Performances at The Kitchen, New York City. C. Hardy. *Dance Magazine* 63:89-91 Ja '89
URBAN CHILDREN *See* City children
URBAN CHURCHES *See* City churches
URBAN CLIMATOLOGY
Urban air pollution: state of the science. J. H. Seinfeld. bibl f il *Science* 243:745-52 F 10 '89
URBAN CRIMES
Dead zones [urban crime areas; cover story; special section] T. Moore. il *U.S. News & World Report* 106:20-5+ Ap 10 '89
URBAN DESIGN *See* City planning
URBAN EDUCATION
The blackboard jungle revisited. G. Morris. *National Review* 41:18-19 My 5 '89
The case against Joe Nocera [exodus of white middle class from public schools] J. Nocera. *The Washington Monthly* 21:22-4+ F '89
Eastside story [views of principal J. Clark] Y. Kramer and R. Kramer. il *The American Spectator* 22:21-4 Ag '89
Education: the movie [principals J. Clark, G. McKenna, D. Meier; cover story] D. L. Kirp. il pors *Mother Jones* 14:36-45 Ja '89
Help for no-hope kids [work of J. P. Comer] C. Leslie. il por *Newsweek* 114:50 O 2 '89
Knock at any school. R. Parish and others. bibl f il *Phi Delta Kappan* 70:386-94 Ja '89
Renovating urban schools is fundamental to improving them. P. R. Piccigallo. bibl f il *Phi Delta Kappan* 70:402-6 Ja '89
Urban teachers: their new colleagues and curriculum. C. A. Grant. bibl f il *Phi Delta Kappan* 70:764-70 Je '89
We can educate all our children [urban public schools] C. Clayton. *The Nation* 249:132-5 Jl 24-31 '89
What can be done for at-risk students. L. Cuban. *The Education Digest* 54:3-6 My '89
URBAN ENTERPRISE ZONES *See* Enterprise zones
URBAN FAUNA
A case of urban renewal [peregrine falcons adapt to city life] M. Wexler. il *National Wildlife* 27:10-13 Je/Jl '89
City backyard. H. R. Russell. il *The Conservationist* 43:40-5 Mr/Ap '89
URBAN FLORA
See also
Trees in cities
City backyard. H. R. Russell. il *The Conservationist* 43:40-5 Mr/Ap '89
URBAN FORESTRY
See also
Trees in cities
Cities with farms and forests. il *The Futurist* 23:55 Mr/Ap '89
Natural cycles [Sihlwald Forest, Switzerland] B. W. Walsh. il por *Wilderness* 53:16-17+ Wint '89

URBAN GROWTH *See* Cities and towns—Growth
URBAN HISTORY *See* Cities and towns—History
URBAN PLANNING *See* City planning
URBAN POOR *See* Underclass
URBAN RENEWAL
See also
Business districts
United States. Dept. of Housing and Urban Development
Facing an uncomfortable truth [address, June 15, 1989] J. H. Ross. *Vital Speeches of the Day* 55:690-3 S 1 '89
URBAN SOCIOLOGY *See* Sociology, Urban
URBAN TRANSPORTATION
See also
Local transit
How consumers get taken for a ride. J. Hood. il *Consumers' Research Magazine* 72:31-5 F '89
URBAN TREES *See* Trees in cities
URBAN WETLANDS
Jewels in the concrete jungle. P. Johnson. il *National Wildlife* 27:30-5 Ag/S '89
URBÁNEK, ZDENĚK
about
Notes and comment. *The New Yorker* 65:31-2 D 18 '89
URBANI, GIOVANNI
about
Italy's crumbling heritage [interview] A. Mammi. il *World Press Review* 36:74 D '89
URBANI TRUFFLES USA
Old Merchants House and Urbani Truffles USA. H. Bridges. il *Gourmet* 49:72+ D '89
URBANIZATION *See* Cities and towns—Growth
URBANIZED AREAS *See* Metropolitan areas
URBANSKA, WANDA
"I like to get the bad guys". il pors *McCall's* 116:134+ F '89
"This is what I was meant to do!". il *McCall's* 117:91-5 D '89
URCHINS, SEA *See* Sea urchins
URDANG, CONSTANCE
Emergency ward, St. Vincent's [poem] *The New Yorker* 65:72 Ag 7 '89
UREA
See also
Hydroxyurea
Synthesis
Evolution of urea synthesis in vertebrates: the piscine connection. T. P. Mommsen and P. J. Walsh. bibl f il *Science* 243:72-5 Ja 6 '89
UREY PRIZE
Lunine receives Urey Prize for planetary science. *Physics Today* 42:128 Mr '89
URFER, BONNIE
Prisoner of conscience [cover story] il *The Progressive* 53:18-21 My '89
URICE, JOHN K.
The next century: the impact of social and economic trends on the arts in education. bibl f *Design for Arts in Education* 90:36-43 My/Je '89
URICH, ROBERT
about
Spenser for higher style. il por *Gentlemen's Quarterly* 59:280-1 Ap '89
Photographs and photography
The eyes have it. G. Bernstein. il por *Petersen's Photographic Magazine* 18:10 Je '89
URIDINE
See also
Bromodeoxyuridine
URINARY CALCULI *See* Kidney stones
URINARY ORGANS
See also
Bladder
Kidneys
Diseases
UTI's: everything you need to know about urinary tract woes. S. A. Hoffmann. il *American Health* 8:72-6 Ap '89
URINARY TRACT INFECTIONS *See* Urinary organs—Diseases
URINE
Analysis
See also
Drug abuse—Testing
Dipstick urinalysis. *FDA Consumer* 23:3 N '89
Urinalysis: looking into the void. D. Farley. il *FDA Consumer* 23:16-21 O '89
Incontinence
Childhood bed-wetting: cause for concern? D. Farley. il *FDA Consumer* 23:8-11 My '89
New help for incontinence. C. Perlmutter. il *Prevention (Emmaus, Pa.)* 41:53-60 Ja '89
New help for urinary incontinence. S. Mahler. *McCall's* 116:84 Ag '89
Shame deters getting help [aged; views of Joanne Stevenson] *USA Today (Periodical)* 118:8-9 O '89
Stop the bed-wetting blues [food allergies] M. Kelly. *American Health* 8:124 S '89

URINE—Incontinence—*cont.*
Unexpected drips and leaks: bladder surprises during pregnancy. S. Young. *Glamour* 87:79 S '89
URIS, AUREN
Turning confrontations into calm conversations [excerpt from 88 mistakes interviewers make and how to avoid them] il *Working Woman* 14:140-1+ S '89
URQUHART, RACHEL
Minimalism with a flourish. il *Vogue* 179:194-201+ Ja '89
Pearl crazy. il *Vogue* 179:398-401 Ap '89
Power fun. il *Mademoiselle* 95:188-9+ D '89
The video queens. il *Vogue* 179:216+ Ap '89
URUGUAY
See also
Civil rights—Uruguay
Political prisoners—Uruguay
Politics and government
See also
Referendum—Uruguay
Socialism—Uruguay
US AIR, INC. *See* USAir, Inc.
THE US AND THE PHILIPPINES: IN OUR IMAGE [television program] See Television program reviews—Single works
US SPRINT COMMUNICATIONS INC.
People aren't laughing at U.S. Sprint anymore. W. C. Symonds. il por *Business Week* p82-3+ Jl 31 '89
Revolt of Uncle Sam's paper pushers [AT&T and Sprint cope with replacing the federal government's aging telephone network] M. Lewyn. il *Business Week* p156 O 30 '89
US WEST, INC.
The importance of Hispanics to our nation [address, February 16, 1989] D. McCormick. *Vital Speeches of the Day* 55:464-7 My 15 '89
Overseas tryout. P. Noglows. il *Channels (New York, N.Y.: 1986)* 9:95 N '89
USA CABLE NETWORK
Never look down [K. Koplovitz] D. Machan. il por *Forbes* 144:270+ Jl 24 '89
When Murder & Vice are no longer enough [interview with K. Koplovitz] il pors *Channels (New York, N.Y.: 1986)* 9:70-1 Ap '89
USA TODAY [television program] See Television program reviews—Single works
USAA *See* United Services Automobile Association
USAF *See* United States. Air Force
USAIR, INC.
Final integration of Piedmont into USAir completed smoothly. *Aviation Week & Space Technology* 131:58 Ag 14 '89
A promising flight plan—if no raiders show [USAir-Piedmont deal] S. Payne. il *Business Week* p81-2 Ag 14 '89
Skinner calls USAir bid for more Philadelphia gates anticompetitive [Eastern gates] *Aviation Week & Space Technology* 130:110 Je 5 '89
USAir prepares to complete acquisition of Piedmont. J. Ott. il *Aviation Week & Space Technology* 131:94-5 Jl 17 '89
USAir takeover unlikely despite SEC filing [Steinhardt Partners raises stake] *Aviation Week & Space Technology* 131:102 Jl 31 '89
USC *See* University of Southern California
USCHUK, PAMELA
Red cat near old snow [poem] *Commonweal* 116:266 My 5 '89
USDA *See* United States. Dept. of Agriculture
USED AIRPLANES *See* Airplanes, Used
USED AUTOMOBILES *See* Automobiles, Used
USED BICYCLES *See* Bicycles, Used
USED BOATS *See* Boats, Used
USED COMPUTERS *See* Computers, Used
USED FOREIGN AUTOMOBILES *See* Automobiles, Used
USED FURNITURE *See* Furniture, Used
USED SPORTING GOODS *See* Sporting goods, Used
USER FEES
See also
Airports—Fees
Express highways—Fees
Hunting—Fees
Information services—Fees
Recreation—Fees
USER INTERFACES
Creating your user interface. *High Technology Business* 9:32-3 Ja '89
A La Carte simplifies XyWrite [menu-driven interface] C. Hlavaty. il *Personal Computing* 13:196 F '89
The Mac interface: showing its age. D. E. Crabb. *Byte* 14 Mac Special Ed:MAC235-MAC237 Je '89
OOP tools designed to make interface building like writing a letter with a word processor [Entryway system] *Byte* 14:18+ S '89
Separation of powers [object-oriented user interfaces] M. H. Dodani and others. bibl f il *Byte* 14:255-6+ Mr '89
USES *See* United States Employment Service
USHER, GREGORY
Steaming the French way. il *Gourmet* 49:142+ N '89
USHER, PETER
World Conference on the Changing Atmosphere: Implications for Global Security [report] *Environment* 31:25-7 Ja/F '89

USHER, ROLAND G.
The war and the future of civilization. *The New Republic* 201 [Reprint v1]:22-3 N 6 '89 [N 7 '14]
USHISHIR ISLANDS (SOVIET UNION)
See also
Volcanoes—Ushishir Islands (Soviet Union)
USIA *See* United States. Information Agency
USITT *See* United States Institute for Theatre Technology
USM TRUST
When it sounds too good to be true. G. Slutsker. il *Forbes* 143:256-7 Je 26 '89
USOC *See* United States Olympic Committee
USPS *See* United States Postal Service
USRY, JAMES L.
about
Atlantic City mayor Usry is arrested for bribery; mayors group backs him. il por *Jet* 76:13-14 Ag 14 '89
USS EISELE (SHIP) *See* Eisele (Ship)
USSR (UNION OF SOVIET SOCIALIST REPUBLICS) See Soviet Union
USTA *See* United States Tennis Association
USTR *See* United States. Office of the U.S. Trade Representative
USW *See* United Steelworkers of America
USX CORPORATION
Charles Corry. G. L. Miles. il por *Business Week* Special Issue:136 Ag 14 '89
Did union leaders sell out the steelworkers? [USX accused of conspiring with negotiators] J. P. Hoerr. il *Business Week* p48-50 D 25 '89-Ja 1 '90
Icahn edges closer to taking USX. G. G. Marcial. *Business Week* p180 N 6 '89
A new iron man recasts USX [C. A. Corry sells Texas Oil & Gas assets] G. L. Miles. il por *Business Week* p37 O 16 '89
Suddenly, USX is playing Mr. Nice Guy [team work] G. L. Miles. il *Business Week* p151-2 Je 26 '89
Surprise from Big Steel. il *Forbes* 143:172 Ja 9 '89
USX: Icahn's back, and this time he has the cash. G. L. Miles. il por *Business Week* p40 Je 19 '89
USX: the next apple of Icahn's keen eye? G. G. Marcial. il *Business Week* p134 F 20 '89
UTAH
See also
Airports—Utah
Bryce Canyon National Park (Utah)
Colorado River (Colo.-Mexico)
Cycling—Utah
Glen Canyon National Recreation Area (Ariz. and Utah)
Hovenweep National Monument (Colo. and Utah)
Manti-LaSal National Forest (Utah and Colo.)
Motion picture festivals—Utah
National parks and reserves—Utah
Paleontology—Utah
Public lands—Utah
Resorts—Utah
Salt Lake County (Utah)
San Juan River (Colo.-Utah)
Skiing—Utah
Truck driving—Utah
Wilderness areas—Utah
Wildlife conservation—Utah
Zion National Park (Utah)
Industries
See also
Strip mining—Utah
Population
A tale of two states [views of Carl Haub] *The Futurist* 23:51-2 My/Je '89
Religious institutions and affairs
See also
Mormons and Mormonism
UTAH NIPPO (NEWSPAPER)
Tireless Kuniko Terasawa is the force behind a newspaper almost no one can read. R. Arias. il pors *People Weekly* 32:53-4 S 25 '89
UTAH POWER & LIGHT CO.
Power goals [merger of Pacificorp and Utah Power & Light] J. Cook. il map *Forbes* 143:116-17 Ap 3 '89
UTAH TEST AND TRAINING RANGE (AIR FORCE) See United States. Air Force. Utah Test and Training Range
UTERMANN, GERD
The mysteries of lipoprotein(a). bibl f il *Science* 246:904-10 N 17 '89
UTERUS
See also
Cervix
Surgery
See also
Hysterectomy
Raquel Welch: starting over [rollerball technique stems uterine hemorrhage] P. Battelle. il pors *Ladies' Home Journal* 106:46+ My '89
Three alternatives to hysterectomy. P. G. O'Brien. *Ladies' Home Journal* 106:59 My '89

UTICA (MICH.)

Education

"No one's born a loser!" [work of J. Williams in Enterprise High program for dropouts] P. Skalka. *Reader's Digest* 134:21-2+ F '89

UTILITIES, PUBLIC *See* Public utilities

UTILITIES (COMPUTER PROGRAMS) *See* Computer programming

UTILITY SHEDS *See* Sheds

UTILIZATION OF LAND *See* Land utilization

UTNE, ERIC

Editor's note. See issues of Utne Reader

UTNE READER (PERIODICAL)

Editor's note. E. Utne. See issues of Utne Reader

UTOPIAS

A watery paradise: Rowland Vaughan and Hereford's 'Golden Vale'. M. Delorme. bibl il *History Today* 39:38-43 Jl '89

UTSUMI, RYUTARO, AND OTHERS

Activation of bacterial porin gene expression by a chimeric signal transducer in response to aspartate. bibl f il *Science* 245:1246-9 S 15 '89

UTTAL, WILLIAM R.

Teleoperators. bibl il *Scientific American* 261:124-9 D '89

UTU *See* United Transportation Union

UTZ, PETER

Power trips. il *Video* 13:46-8+ My '89

UVA, MARY DEERY, AND BLOOM, JANE L.

Exporting pollution: the international waste trade. bibl f il *Environment* 31:4-5+ Je '89

UVNÄS-MOBERG, KERSTIN

The gastrointestinal tract in growth and reproduction. bibl il *Scientific American* 261:78-83 Jl '89

UWB RADAR *See* Ultra-wideband radar

UY, ZENIDA

about

Filipina activist fights repression. J. Jiji and D. Bernstein. *The Progressive* 53:14 Ap '89

UYS, JAMIE

about

The gods must be crazy II [film] Reviews

American Film il 15:97+ O '89. E. Drucker

UZBEKISTAN (SOVIET UNION)

See also

Family—Uzbekistan (Soviet Union)

V

V., MARC

about

Marc V. P. Garland. il por *Stereo Review* 54:80 Jl '89

VA *See* United States. Veterans Administration

VACATION CABINS *See* Cabins

VACATION CONDOMINIUMS *See* Condominiums

VACATION HOUSES

See also

Beach architecture

Cabins

Lakeside architecture

All work (and hardly any play) [country retreats of artists, authors and musicians] M. Bethany. il *New York* 22:46-51 Ag 28 '89

Amelia's island [weekend lakeside retreat owned by A. Fatt] S. Nelson. il pors *Working Woman* 14:198-202 S '89

Cozy comfort in the mountains [Pocono Mountains home of Steve and Geryl Deixler] M. Walker. il *New Choices for the Best Years* 29:33-4 Je '89

Investing in that home away from home. G. J. Gallagher. il *Black Enterprise* 20:31-2 S '89

Now's the time to grab a bargain vacation home. C. A. Fried. il *Money* 18:129-32 O '89

Our summer retreat [sharing a summer house with husband's parents] R. Israeloff. *Glamour* 87:256 Ag '89

Trading places [house swapping] J. S. Eakin. il *New Choices for the Best Years* 29:28-32 D '89

Tropical options [Caribbean] M. Nix. il *House & Garden* 161:186-8 Ap '89

Vacation homes: it's a buyer's market. M. C. Paulson. il *Changing Times* 43:37-8+ Je '89

Warm elegance in ski country [Vermont home of Doris La Porte] O. Buehl. il *New Choices for the Best Years* 29:34-6 Je '89

Wildcat mountain [Catskills summer house] L. Auchincloss. il por *Architectural Digest* 46:29+ Je '89

Fractional ownership

See Fractional ownership (Real estate)

Leasing and renting

Charity stops at home [tax consequences of donating rental time at vacation house to a charity] G. W. Padwe. il *Nation's Business* 77:76 S '89

The houses of a French summer. J. Salter. il *Esquire* 111:145-53 Ap '89

Mendocino vacation rentals. *Sunset (Central West edition)* 182:31 Ap '89

Of ski huts and beach houses. L. Saunders. il *Forbes* 144:258 O 16 '89

Trimming the IRS' cut on a second home. D. H. Dunn. il *Business Week* p184 Jl 17 '89

Use it, rent it, write it off. H. Wheelwright. il *Money* 18:112 Jl '89

Anecdotes, facetiae, satire, etc.

Next summer, I'll be married [house sharing in the Hamptons] P. Mehlman. il *The New York Times Magazine* p44+ My 21 '89

A summer place [taking a summer share in the Hamptons] M. McCully. il *Gentlemen's Quarterly* 59:143-4+ Je '89

Timesharing ownership

See Timesharing (Real estate)

VACATION HOUSES, CONDOMINIUM *See* Condominiums

VACATION TRAVEL CLUBS *See* Travel clubs

VACATION VIDEOS *See* Videotapes—Travel use

VACATION VILLAGES

See also

Club Méditerranée SA

VACATIONS

See also

Automobile touring

Camping

Cruising

Resorts

Travel

20 summer getaways. il *Glamour* 87:209+ Ap '89

Active minivacations [weekend vacations] S. G. Sheehy. il *Working Woman* 14:121-2+ Mr '89

Adventure quest! [special section] il *American Health* 8:43-6+ N '89

Adventure travel [women] S. G. Sheehy. il *Working Woman* 14:204+ S '89

The American dream vacation [results of poll] I. Groller. il *Parents* 64:30 Ag '89

Destination wildlife [cover story; special section; with editorial comment by Scott Shane] il maps *Travel Holiday* 171:6, 41-72 Ap '89

A dream vacation at home. A. Stoddard. il *McCall's* 116:138 Je '89

Endless summer [runners' winter vacations] L. Rogak. il *Runner's World* 24:66-8 Ja '89

Family reunion vacations. B. Murphy. il *Better Homes and Gardens* 67:123-4+ Ag '89

The family vacation. J. Segal and Z. Segal. il *Parents* 64:211 My '89

Farm family getaways! C. Tevis. il maps *Successful Farming* 87:54+ My '89

Fast recharges [weekend vacations] N. Santelmann. *Forbes* 144:276 N 27 '89

Fun spots at home and abroad. il *Ebony* 44:162+ My '89

Good times: summer of '89: where to go and what to do in the national parks. M. Cronin. il *National Parks* 63:37-41 My/Je '89

Great short stops [weekend vacations; special section] il *New Choices for the Best Years* 29:48-55 Ja '89

How I spent my summer vacation [visit to mother's Kentucky home] F. Johnson. il *The New York Times Magazine* p22+ O 1 '89

How to escape the winter blahs. il *Ebony* 44:102+ Ja '89

How we spend our summer vacations [results of Sesame Street survey] I. Schwager. il *Good Housekeeping* 208:104 Je '89

Hunt wild goats, be a baseball star [fantasy vacations] L. J. Moore. il *U.S. News & World Report* 106:71-2 Je 19 '89

Luxury vacations at cut-rate prices. il *Glamour* 87:145-6+ Ag '89

Now the kids can rough it, too [family wilderness vacations] R. Wilder. il *U.S. News & World Report* 106:70-1 Ap 3 '89

Omni's five star travelogue [adventure vacations; cover story] J. Goldberg. il *Omni (New York, N.Y.)* 11:42-4 Mr '89

Outlook: time off. P. Plawin. il *Changing Times* 43:67-8 Ja '89

Splash! [scuba diving] K. Castle. il *Travel Holiday* 172:74-81 Jl '89

Taking a trip on the wild side. S. Woolley. il *Business Week* p98-9 Ap 17 '89

Tales from the Burma Bridge [adventure outing at Snowbird Ski and Summer Resort] L. J. Sass. il *Health (New York, N.Y.)* 21:40-1+ D '89

Tales from the trail [Sierra Club service vacations] il *Harper's Bazaar* 122:60-1+ Je '89

Time out for busy parents [vacations without children] B. Spock. por *Redbook* 173:30 Je '89

Traveling abroad. D. F. Bjorklund and B. Bjorklund. il *Parents* 64:165 Jl '89

Vacation clothes. W. Gavin and C. DiGrappa. il *Parents* 64:166 Je '89

Vacations you (and the kids!) will love [summer family vacations] S. Birnbaum. il *Good Housekeeping* 209:98-9 Jl '89

Walkabouts! [cover story] K. Shyne. il *New Choices for the Best Years* 29:29-32 Mr '89

Warm escapes from winter. il *Glamour* 87:143-4 D '89

VACATIONS—cont.

Psychological aspects
First vacation after the baby. L. Schnurnberger. il *Parents* 64:114-18 D '89

Fly south. S. Kline. *Working Woman* 14:120 F '89

Post-vacation blues. O. S. Nordberg. il *Parents* 64:112-14 S '89

Sacred places [vacationing in environments which affect the psyche] W. Gallagher. il *American Health* 8:44-6+ N '89 *Anecdotes, facetiae, satire, etc.*

A traveler's guide to coming home. M. Sterling. il *New Choices for the Best Years* 29:96 O '89

VACATIONS, EMPLOYEE *See* Employee vacations

VACCA, JOHN R.
Japan's space kids. il *Omni (New York, N.Y.)* 12:20+ O '89

VACCINES, ANTI-PREGNANCY *See* Contraceptives

VACCINES AND VACCINATION
See also
   AIDS (Disease)—Vaccines and vaccination
   Cancer—Vaccines and vaccination
   Children—Diseases—Vaccines and vaccination
   Cholera—Vaccines and vaccination
   Distemper virus—Vaccines and vaccination
   Hepatitis—Vaccines and vaccination
   Immunologic diseases—Vaccines and vaccination
   Influenza—Vaccines and vaccination
   Lyme disease—Vaccines and vaccination
   Malaria—Vaccines and vaccination
   Measles—Vaccines and vaccination
   Poliomyelitis—Vaccines and vaccination
   Rabies—Vaccines and vaccination
   Respiratory syncytial virus—Vaccines and vaccination
   Rubella—Vaccines and vaccination
   Smallpox—Vaccines and vaccination
   Streptococcal infections—Vaccines and vaccination
   Whooping cough—Vaccines and vaccination
Vaccination reminder. C. Slom. il *McCall's* 117:105 N '89

VACCINIA VIRUS *See* Pox viruses

VACHON, JOHN, 1914-1975
about
John Vachon: a certain look [cover story] T. B. Morgan. il por *American Heritage* 40:94-109 F '89

VACUUM
See also
   American Vacuum Society
Vacuum physics. bibl f il *Physics Today* 42:S63-S66 Ja '89

VACUUM BOTTLES *See* Thermos containers

VACUUM CLEANER INDUSTRY
See also
   Electrolux Corporation
   Hoover Co.

VACUUM CLEANERS
Hand-held vacuum cleaners. il *Consumer Reports* 54:344-8 D '89

Vacuum cleaners. il *Consumer Reports* 54:307-15 My '89

Vacuum cleaners. il *Consumer Reports* 54:348-55 D '89

VACUUM CLEANING
Installing a central vacuum cleaning system. D. Prestly. il *The Family Handyman* 39:38-40+ N/D '89

VACUUM MICROELECTRONICS
Is the radio tube warming up again? [work of H. F. Gray] W. D. Marbach. il por *Business Week* Special Issue:76 Je 16 '89

Vacuum microelectronics. W. D. Marbach. il *Business Week* p68-70 Mr 13 '89

VACUUM PUMPS
A fresh look at an old standby [Auto-Vac backup for airplanes] J. M. McClellan. *Flying* 116:25 Ag '89

VACUUM TUBES
See also
   Radio tubes
   Traveling wave tubes
   Vacuum microelectronics

VADER, J. E.
A dandy Brandy. il pors *Sports Illustrated* 71:24+ Jl 17 '89

Day of reckoning. il pors *Sports Illustrated* 70:74-6+ My 1 '89

The golden girl makes a splash. il por *Sports Illustrated* 70:86 Ap 3 '89

Once more, with feeling. il por *Sports Illustrated* 70:71+ Mr 27 '89

Paws. il *Sports Illustrated* 70:46-8+ Je 26 '89

A show of strength. il pors *Sports Illustrated* 70:62-4+ My 15 '89

(jt. auth) See Moore, Kenny, 1943-, and Vader, J. E.

VADIM, VANESSA
about
Jane Fonda's daughter, Vanessa Vadim, is jailed for mouthing off at a drug bust. J. S. Kunen. il pors *People Weekly* 32:44-5 O 23 '89

VAGANOVA CHOREOGRAPHIC INSTITUTE (LENINGRAD, SOVIET UNION)
East meets West in Amsterdam: student days in Holland. N. Reynolds. il *Dance Magazine* 63:52-5 N '89

VAGELOS, P. ROY
The sorry state of science education. *Scientific American* 261:128 O '89
about
Here's one drug war we're winning. M. Magnet. por *Fortune* 120:74 Jl 3 '89

VAGER, Z., AND OTHERS
Coulomb explosion imaging of small molecules. bibl f il *Science* 244:426-31 Ap 28 '89

VAGIN, VLADIMIR VASIL'EVICH, 1937-, AND ASCH, FRANK
Here comes the cat! [story] il *Parents* 64:89-90+ Ag '89

VAGINA
Cancer
AZT causes cancer in lab animals. *Science News* 136:396 D 16 '89

LA VAGNOLA (TUSCANY, ITALY: COUNTRY ESTATE) *See* Country estates—Italy

VAHANIAN, GABRIEL
A yawning chasm: French laity and bishops. *The Christian Century* 106:39 Ja 18 '89

VAHAVIOLOS, SOTIRIOS J.
about
When he hears, others listen. B. E. Thornbury. il por *Nation's Business* 77:18+ N '89

VAIL (COLO.)
As Vail's trailblazing owner, George Gillett finds there's no business like snow business. F. A. Bernstein. il pors *People Weekly* 31:92-4 F 6 '89

Colorado nouveau [skiing] L. Tejada-Flores. il *Skiing* 42:238-46+ S '89

The endless winter [ski instructors R. Colfer and J. Stanley] P. Mehlman. il pors *Gentlemen's Quarterly* 59:336-9+ Mr '89

Preview: Vail Worlds '89 [special section] il *Skiing* 41:74-80+ Ja '89

A vision fulfilled. W. O. Johnson. il pors *Sports Illustrated* 70:70-4+ Ja 30 '89

VAILS, NELSON
about
Unveiling Nelson Vails. K. Cobb. il por *American Health* 8:84 My '89

VAJRADHATU (ORGANIZATION)
Buddhist editor leaves amid controversy [Vajradhatu sun's coverage of allegations that American Buddhist leader, O. Tendzin, had contracted AIDS] J. Walljasper. il *Utne Reader* p36-7 Jl/Ag '89

God and profits [Buddhist firms flourish in Nova Scotia] il *Maclean's* 102:34-5 Mr 27 '89

His master's voice [leader O. Tendzin contracts AIDS] *Newsweek* 113:51 Mr 6 '89

VAJRADHATU SUN (NEWSPAPER)
Buddhist editor leaves amid controversy [coverage of allegations that American Buddhist leader, O. Tendzin, had contracted AIDS] J. Walljasper. il *Utne Reader* p36-7 Jl/Ag '89

VALADEZ, JOHN
about
John Valadez at B-1. M. Anderson. il *Art in America* 77:223 O '89

VALCOURT, BERNARD
about
Down but not out. M. Clark. il por *Maclean's* 102:14 Ag 14 '89

Too fast at the turn. P. Kopvillem. il por *Maclean's* 102:14 Jl 17 '89

VALDEZ PRINCIPLES
The Valdez Principles. P. A. A. Berle. *Audubon* 91:6 N '89

VALEDICTORIANS
Where have all the smart girls gone? [study of female valedictorians seven years after high school graduation; work of Terry Denny] M. Conroy. il *Psychology Today* 23:20 Ap '89

VALENCIA (SPAIN)
Galleries and museums
See also
   Instituto Valenciano de Arte Moderno (Spain)

VALENCIA INSTITUTE OF MODERN ART (SPAIN) *See* Instituto Valenciano de Arte Moderno (Spain)

VALENTI, JACK
about
Fighting for Hollywood's fair share [interview] il pors *Channels (New York, N.Y.: 1986)* 9:98-9 N '89

No flying buns for a bully boy. A. Fotheringham. il *Maclean's* 102:116 O 30 '89

VALENTINE, CHARLES F.
Blunders abroad. il *Nation's Business* 77:54+ Mr '89

VALENTINE, JEAN
The summer was not long enough [poem] *The New Yorker* 65:102 N 6 '89

VALENTINE, SHIRLEY (FICTIONAL CHARACTER) *See* Shirley Valentine (Fictional character)

VALENTINES
3 from the heart. il *Workbench* 45:50-1 Ja/F '89

How to write the ultimate valentine. H. O'Neill. il *Gentlemen's Quarterly* 59:45+ F '89

VALENTINES—*cont.*
My secret valentine [children; condensed from All I really need to know I learned in kindergarten] R. Fulghum. il *Reader's Digest* 134:9 F '89
VALENTINE'S DAY
It's 'Valentime' again. K. Fury. il *New Choices for the Best Years* 29:92 F '89
Valentine's Day celebration. il *McCall's* 116:43-4+ F '89
VALENTINE'S DAY CANDY *See* Candy
VALENTINE'S DAY COOKIES *See* Cookies
VALENTINE'S DAY DINNERS
Be their valentine with a menu for six. il *Southern Living* 24:128-9 F '89
VALENTINE'S DAY GIFTS
Tokens of love. il *Seventeen* 48:106-7+ F '89
VALENTINO
                                            about
Fashion without frontiers. J. Cocks. il pors *Time* 133:94 Mr 20 '89
Grand allusions. A. L. Talley. il por *Vogue* 179:510-17+ Mr '89
Seaworthy style. G. Y. Dryansky. il pors *House & Garden* 161:122-5 Ag '89
VALENTINO RETURNS [film] *See* Motion picture reviews—Single works
VALENZUELA, ARTURO, 1944-
(jt. auth) *See* Constable, Pamela, and Valenzuela, Arturo, 1944-
VALENZUELA, ARTURO, 1944-, AND CONSTABLE, PAMELA
The Chilean plebiscite: defeat of a dictator. bibl f *Current History* 88:129-32+ Mr '89
VALERO ENERGY CORP.
Fear of sharks may make Valero move. G. G. Marcial. *Business Week* p108 S 18 '89
VALETS (FURNITURE)
Hang 'em here [Zeus valets] P. Patton. il *Esquire* 111:54 Mr '89
VALHI INC.
Harold Simmons is coming out to play again. T. Mason. il por *Business Week* p44+ Ja 9 '89
VALIS [opera] *See* Machover, Tod, 1953-
VALIUNAS, ALGIS
The rape of Poland and the death of hope. il *The American Spectator* 22:17-18 S '89
Tolstoy and the pursuit of happiness. *Commentary* 87:33-41 Je '89
VALKENIER, ELIZABETH KRIDL
To tell the truth. *The New Republic* 200:20-1 My 22 '89
VALLE DE LAS LEÑAS (ARGENTINA: RESORT) *See* Resorts—Argentina
VALLE NEVADO (CHILE: RESORT) *See* Resorts—Chile
VALLEE, LILLIAN
(tr) *See* Gombrowicz, Witold. On Bruno Schulz
VALLELY, JEAN
The Alfre nobody knows. pors *Ms.* 17:68-71 Ap '89
VALLEY NATIONAL CORP.
Thumb in the dike. J. H. Taylor. il por *Forbes* 144:76 Ag 21 '89
VALLEY TEEN RANCH (MADERA, CALIF.)
Home on the ranch. J. Williams. il *Christianity Today* 33:12-13 O 20 '89
VALLS, PERUCHO
                                            about
Pared to perfection. M. Boodro. il *Vogue* 179:282-3+ My '89
VALLS, SANTIAGO CALATRAVA *See* Calatrava, Santiago, 1951-
VALLS-RUSSELL, JANICE
Europe's bumpy road to '92. il *The New Leader* 72:8-9 S 4 '89
Islam in England and France. il *The New Leader* 72:5-6 Ag 7-21 '89
Shifting politics in Spain. il *The New Leader* 72:9-10 N 27 '89
Spain tightens its European ties. il *The New Leader* 72:7-8 My 1 '89
Spanish dreams from a French cemetery. il *The New Leader* 72:10-11 Mr 20 '89
Welcome to Barcelona. il *The New Leader* 72:9-10 Ja 9 '89
VALLVERDÚ, FRANCESC
A thousand years of Catalan history. il *The Courier (Unesco)* 42:26-8 My '89
VALMONT [film] *See* Motion picture reviews—Single works
VALMONT INDUSTRIES, INC.
Valmont Industries. R. Abelson. il *Fortune* 120:134 O 23 '89
VALSASSINA, ISABELLE VON THURN- *See* Thurn-Valsassina, Isabelle von
VALUATION
                See also
        Appraisers
        Corporations—Valuation
        Rain forests—Valuation
        Real property—Valuation

VALUE (ECONOMICS)
The greatest values in America. C. E. Cohen. il *Money* 18:150-4+ N '89
VALUE ADDED TAX
Are we now to be soaked by VAT? T. P. Wasley. il *Conservative Digest* 15:40-1+ My/Je '89
Look before you leap into a VAT [small business] *Nation's Business* 77:52 Ap '89
A value-added tax would harm the economy. W. T. Brookes. por *Nation's Business* 77:70 Jl '89
                        International aspects
The tax in effect. B. Bergman. il *Maclean's* 102:22 O 2 '89
                        Western Europe
Getting a good return [tax refunds to shoppers] D. P. Marshall. il *Travel Holiday* 171:28+ F '89
How Europe 1992 could cost its airports $2 billion [loss of duty free business] B. Baudoin and others. il *Business Week* p55 Mr 6 '89
VALUE ANALYSIS
                See also
        Children—Economic value
        Cost effectiveness
        Human capital
        Women—Economic value
VALUE LINE INC.
Following the Value Line. M. Hulbert. il *Forbes* 144 Special Issue:398 O 23 '89
VALUE OF EDUCATION *See* College education, Value of
VALUES
                See also
        Ethics
Adding faces to ratings [VALS 2 psychographic profiles of selected markets] il *Channels (New York, N.Y.: 1986)* 9:80 S '89
Changing values: the new emphasis on self-actualization [cover story] J. T. Plummer. il por *The Futurist* 23:8-13 Ja/F '89
The end of economics? [values issues begin to dominate politics] R. J. Samuelson. il *Newsweek* 114:53 Jl 24 '89
How much can you disagree? C. L. Mithers. *Glamour* 87:302 Mr '89
Lappé to world: start talking [excerpt from Rediscovering America's values] F. M. Lappé. *Utne Reader* p48 My/Je '89
My dream house and my boy [near drowning of son causes author to realize what is important in life]; ed. by Linda Lawrence. F. E. Baird. il *Reader's Digest* 135:9-10+ O '89
Psycho-selling [VALS 2 typology of American consumers] C. Reece. il *Channels (New York, N.Y.: 1986)* 9:14 Jl/Ag '89
A small planet revisited [interview with F. M. Lappé] S. McInerney. il por *Country Journal* 16:7-8 S/O '89
What are our real values? N. Fox. por *Newsweek* 113:8 F 13 '89
A world worth saving [cover story] E. Hoagland. il *Life* 12:50-4+ O '89
                        Study and teaching
                See Moral education
VALUKAS, ANTON
                                            about
Anton Valukas has traders worried about their futures. B. Bremner. il por *Business Week* p33 F 6 '89
VALVANO, JIM
                                            about
Foul play by the book. H. F. Waters. por *Newsweek* 114:62 Ag 14 '89
The ordeal of Jim Valvano. J. Feinstein. il por *Sports Illustrated* 70:34-6 Ja 30 '89
VALVE INDUSTRY
                        Management
Productivity in the carburetors, pistons, and valves industry. J. W. Ferris and V. L. Klarquist. bibl f il *Monthly Labor Review* 112:43-6 F '89
VALVES
                See also
        Automobile engines—Valves
VAMPIRES IN LITERATURE
Do the Rice thing. D. Perry. il *Omni (New York, N.Y.)* 12:26+ O '89
VAMPIRES IN MASS MEDIA
Hunger for the marvelous: the vampire craze in the computer age [cover story] K. M. Ramsland. il *Psychology Today* 23:31-5 N '89
VAMPIRE'S KISS [film] *See* Motion picture reviews—Single works
VAN ALLSBURG, CHRIS
                                            about
Chris Van Allsburg, a rare bird among illustrators, brings his art to a fresh Christmas treasure. K. Hubbard. il pors *People Weekly* 32:142-4 D 11 '89
Rhinoceroses in the living room. S. Allis. il por *Time* 134:108 N 13 '89
Van Allsburg's express. K. Heron. il por *The New York Times Magazine* p12-15 D 24 '89

VAN ALSTYNE, RICHARD WARNER, 1900-1983
The United States and Russia in World War II [reprint from November and December 1950 issues] *Current History* 88:26-9+ Ja '89
VAN ASCH VAN WIJCK, ZEGER
about
Shipshape. M. Beauchamp. il por *Forbes* 143:200 Mr 20 '89
VAN CAMPING *See* Camping
VAN CLEAVE, WILLIAM R.
Honored in the breach. *The Bulletin of the Atomic Scientists* 45:33 My '89
VAN CLIBURN INTERNATIONAL PIANO COMPETITION
See Music—Competitions
VAN DALEN, ANTON
about
Anton van Dalen at Exit Art. C. Reid. *Art in America* 77:150 Ja '89
VAN DAM, JAY
Enlarging your child's horizons. *The Humanist* 49:37-8 S/O '89
VAN DEN HAAG, ERNEST
Comrade, can you spare a dime? *National Review* 41:35-7 Mr 24 '89
The end of communism in Italy. il *National Review* 41:21-2 D 8 '89
Is there a middle ground? il *National Review* 41:29-31 D 22 '89
Paleolithics [discussion of February 24, 1989 article, The war between paleos and neos] *National Review* 41:43-4+ Ap 7 '89
Thoughts on homelessness today. *The American Spectator* 22:36-7 Ap '89
The war between paleos and neos. il *National Review* 41:21-3 F 24 '89
VAN DER LEUN, GERARD
The new! improved! trade book crisis. por *Publishers Weekly* 236:42-3 D 15 '89
VAN DER MEER, ANTONIA
The 10 worst things you can say to your kids (and how to stop saying them). il *Redbook* 174:32+ N '89
Free yourself! *Redbook* 172:93+ Mr '89
VAN DER TUIN, JAN
about
Transport. *The New Yorker* 65:50-1 S 25 '89
VAN DOMMELEN, ERICA
Biology in science fiction. bibl f il *BioScience* 39:729-31 N '89
VAN DOREN, CHARLES LINCOLN, 1926-
about
The quiz-show scandal. W. Karp. il pors *American Heritage* 40:76-84+ My/Je '89
VAN DUYN, MONA
Gardens [poem] *The New Yorker* 65:44 O 16 '89
VAN DYCK, ANTHONIE *See* Dyck, Sir Anthonie van, 1599-1641
VAN DYK, TED
How to end Washington corruption. il por *Fortune* 120:213+ D 18 '89
VAN ERP, DIRK *See* Erp, Dirk van, 1859-1933
VAN GELDER, LINDSY
Computer mating. il *Ms.* 17:34-5 Je '89
It's not nice to mess with Mother Nature. il *Ms.* 17:60-3 Ja/F '89
Out, out, damn disk. il *Ms.* 17:30 Ja/F '89
VAN GELDER, PAT
Animals as subjects in contemporary art. il *American Artist* 53:44-51+ My '89
Tony Eubanks. il por *American Artist* 53:58-63+ Ja '89
VAN GOETHEM, LARRY
The lesson of the box. *Reader's Digest* 134:17-18 Ja '89
VAN GOGH, VINCENT *See* Gogh, Vincent van, 1853-1890
VAN HESEMANS, MATHIAS
Designer landscapes. il *Petersen's Photographic Magazine* 18:24-9 O '89
Reflections. il *Petersen's Photographic Magazine* 18:16-18+ Jl '89
VAN HOEVEN, JAMES W.
about
An evangelical at the WCC [interview] por *Christianity Today* 33:51-2 Ja 13 '89
VAN HOOK, GEORGE
about
George Van Hook [cover story] E. Feit. il por *American Artist* 53:38-43+ Mr '89
VAN HORN, BUDDY
about
Pink Cadillac [film] Reviews
Newsweek il 113:67 Je 12 '89. D. Ansen
People Weekly il 31:18-19 Je 12 '89. R. Novak
Time il 133:78 Je 5 '89. J. Skow
VAN HORN, V. H.
about
A six-pack of Cabernet, please. T. Mack. il por *Forbes* 144:168-9 S 18 '89
VAN HORNE, JOHN
Kitchen color. il *Petersen's Photographic Magazine* 17:46-7 Ap '89

VAN KAMPEN, ROBERT D.
about
"Let not the rich man boast of his riches". M. Berss. il por *Forbes* 144 Special Issue:44-6 O 23 '89
VAN LANDEGHEM, RIA
about
Did Ria or didn't she? *Runner's World* 24:42-3 Ja '89
VAN LEER, DAVID, 1949-
The showman cometh. il *The New Republic* 201:29-30+ N 13 '89
VAN LEEUWEN, RAYMOND C., 1948-
Enjoying creation—within limits. il *Christianity Today* 33:34-7 My 12 '89
VAN METER, JONATHAN
Music. il *Seventeen* 48:100+ Je '89
VAN MILLIGEN, JANE
Making your mark beautifully. il *American Artist* 53:80-2+ Ja '89
VAN NOORDWIJK, ARIE J.
Reaction norms in genetical ecology. bibl f il *BioScience* 39:453-8 Jl/Ag '89
VAN NUYS (CALIF.)
Social life and customs
After some rocky times, one class of '59 reunites to roll back the clock thirty years [Birmingham High School] J. Savaiano. il *People Weekly* 32:153-5 S 18 '89
VAN OMMEN, JOKE *See* Ommen, Joke van, 1948-1988
VAN ORDEN, WILLIAM
about
A dying sculptor fights vandals over Myrna Loy. il por *People Weekly* 31:111 My 29 '89
VAN SANT, GUS
about
Drugstore cowboy [film] Reviews
Gentlemen's Quarterly il por 59:59-60 Jl '89. K. Turan
Maclean's il 102:84 N 6 '89. B. D. Johnson
New York il 22:82-3 O 9 '89. D. Denby
The New Yorker 65:74+ O 30 '89. P. Kael
Newsweek il 114:84 O 23 '89. D. Ansen
Rolling Stone il p50 N 30 '89. C. Arrington
VAN SCHAIK, LEON
Design for dreaming. il *Film Comment* 25:28-30+ Mr/Ap '89
VAN SCHAYK, TOER
about
Reviews:
Performance of works by T. van Schayk in Amsterdam. H. Klooss. *Dance Magazine* 63:75-6 Ap '89
VAN SHELTON, RICKY
about
Ricky Van Shelton, the pride of Grit, Va., takes the traditional country route to stardom. S. Dougherty. il pors *People Weekly* 31:83-4 Je 26 '89
VAN SLYKE, ANDY
about
Beers with . . . Andy Van Slyke [interview] B. Chastain. il pors *Sport (New York, N.Y.)* 80:19-20 Ap '89
Diamond stud. J. Seabrook. por *Vogue* 179:406-7+ Ap '89
Slick can play. R. Wiley. il pors *Sports Illustrated* 70 Special Issue:56-8+ Ap '89
VAN SWEDEN, JAMES A.
Living mulches. il *Organic Gardening* 36:51-4 Mr '89
VAN TIGHEM, KEVIN
Drills across the border. il *Wilderness* 52:54-6 Wint '88
VAN VALKENBURGH, CAROL DOYLE
(jt. auth) *See* Van Valkenburgh, Michael R., and Van Valkenburgh, Carol Doyle
VAN VALKENBURGH, MICHAEL R., AND VAN VALKENBURGH, CAROL DOYLE
Best laid plan. il *House & Garden* 161:150-7 Mr '89
VAN VLIET, WILLEM
The limits of social research. bibl *Society* 26:16-20 My/Je '89
VAN VORST FAMILY
about
Harvest of pride. G. Norman. il pors *New Choices for the Best Years* 29:30-5 Jl '89
VAN WACHEM, L. C.
about
Time, money and patience. T. Mack. il por *Forbes* 144:60-2 Ag 21 '89
VAN WICKLEN, JANET
Slaying dragons: a writer's fantasy. *The Writer* 102:9-10 D '89
VAN WOLFEREN, KAREL G. *See* Wolferen, Karel G. van
VANCE, CAROLE S.
The war on culture. bibl f il *Art in America* 77:39+ S '89
VANCOUVER (B.C.)
Banks
China's pain is Vancouver's gain. P. C. Newman. il *Maclean's* 102:43 O 2 '89
A tale of three cities. A. Walmsley. il *Maclean's* 102:40-1 Ja 23 '89
Buildings
Running hard [N. Skalbania's real estate empire] P. Chisholm. il por *Maclean's* 102:38-9 Ap 3 '89

VANCOUVER (B.C.)—*cont.*

Description

Bryan Adams likes the small-town vibe. il por *Rolling Stone* p44 Jl 13-27 '89

Don't miss Vancouver! S. Birnbaum. il *Good Housekeeping* 209:68+ S '89

Rainy—but proud—Vancouver. P. Romedenne. il *World Press Review* 36:94 O '89

Vancouver. il *Better Homes and Gardens* 67:162+ Mr '89

Music festivals

See Music festivals—British Columbia

Photographs and photography

Vancouver & Ottawa, beautiful Canada! P. Slaughter. il *Petersen's Photographic Magazine* 18:12-15+ Jl '89

Protests, demonstrations, etc.

Defiance in Vancouver [abortion clinic protesters] P. Kopvillem. *Maclean's* 102:17 Jl 31 '89

Race relations

Assault on racism [anti-Asian sentiment] H. Quinn. il *Maclean's* 102:16+ Ap 24 '89

Prosperity and parochialism [influx of Hong Kong Chinese] J. L. Graff. il *Time* 133:51 My 22 '89

A watchdog for the Asian connection [D. Lam] P. C. Newman. il *Maclean's* 102:35 Ap 24 '89

Social conditions

A day in the year 2060. R. Corelli. il *Maclean's* 102:38-9 S 11 '89

Waterfront

A bubbling urban battle [vacant Expo site] H. Quinn. il por *Maclean's* 102:26-8 Ja 16 '89

VANCOUVER ISLAND (B.C.)

See also

Forests and forestry—Vancouver Island (B.C.)

Organic gardens and gardening—Vancouver Island (B.C.)

Anecdotes, facetiae, satire, etc.

Sorry, it must have been the gin. A. Fotheringham. il *Maclean's* 102:76 S 18 '89

VANCOUVER STOCK EXCHANGE

Gold fever strikes again [Eskay Creek gold find in Northern B.C. sends Prime Resources stocks soaring] H. Quinn. il por *Maclean's* 102:33 S 11 '89

Scam capital of the world. J. Queenan. il *Forbes* 143:132-4+ My 29 '89

VANDALISM

See also

American flag—Mutilation, defacement, etc.

Architecture—Mutilation, defacement, etc.

Art—Mutilation, defacement, etc.

Paper money—Mutilation, defacement, etc.

Vandals desecrate King's statue in Birmingham park. il *Jet* 76:32 My 29 '89

VANDAMENT, WILLIAM E.

Primer for academic administrators. *Change* 21:43+ Ja/F '89

VANDEN HEUVEL, KATRINA

The buttons of glasnost. il *The Nation* 249:45-6+ Jl 10 '89

Counting the votes and the dead [cover story] il *The Nation* 248:505+ Ap 17 '89

The young fight for the 'three Ds'. il *The Nation* 248:729-31 My 29 '89

(jt. auth) See Cohen, Stephen F., and Vanden Heuvel, Katrina

VANDENBERG AIR FORCE BASE (CALIF.) See Air bases

VANDER PLUYM, TODD

about

Todd Vander Pluym: making a pile in sand sculpture. D. Castellon. il por *Business Week* p98 My 8 '89

VANDER SCHAAF, RACHELLE

Getting straight. por *Health (New York, N.Y.)* 21:90+ Je '89

VANDER VELDE, NANCY

A truly fresh fish. il *Sea Frontiers* 35:320 S/O '89

VANDER ZALM, WILLIAM

about

A picture of unity: William Vander Zalm survives a showdown. P. Kopvillem. il por *Maclean's* 102:27 O 16 '89

Vander Zalm besieged. B. Bergman. il por *Maclean's* 102:26-7 O 2 '89

VANDERBILT, CORNELIUS, 1794-1877

about

To the swiftest. J. S. Gordon. il *American Heritage* 40:16+ Mr '89

VANDERBILT, GERTRUDE WHITNEY See Whitney, Gertrude Vanderbilt

VANDERBILT, WILLIAM H., 1821-1885

about

"The public be damned". J. S. Gordon. il *American Heritage* 40:18+ S/O '89

VANDERBILT FAMILY

about

Perils of privilege. R. Lee. il *Harper's Bazaar* 122:72 O '89

What's in a name? B. Gill. il *House & Garden* 161:72+ N '89

VANDERBILT UNIVERSITY. STUDENT ENVIRONMENTAL HEALTH PROJECT

Students clean up the South. R. Kerson. il *Technology Review* 92:12 Ap '89

VANDERLIP, ELIN

about

Mediterranean light. P. Deitz. il *House & Garden* 161:124-31+ D '89

VANDERPOOL, TIM

Monkey-wrenching for planet earth. il por *The Progressive* 53:15 S '89

VANDERSLICE, THOMAS AQUINAS

about

Can Apollo stop hurtling toward earth? L. Helm. il por *Business Week* p108 F 27 '89

VANDERWERFF, JOYCE E.

(jt. auth) See Anderson, Roland C., and Vanderwerff, Joyce E.

VANDIVER, PAMELA B., AND OTHERS

The origins of ceramic technology at Dolni Věstonice, Czechoslovakia. bibl f il *Science* 246:1002-8 N 24 '89

VANDROSS, LUTHER

about

Luther Vandross' $8.5 million hideaway [cover story] L. Norment. il pors *Ebony* 44:30-2+ Je '89

Luther Vandross: hit maker tells why he wants to act as well as sing [cover story] A. Collier. il pors *Jet* 76:28-31 Je 19 '89

VANELDEREN, MERLIN

WCC takes its agenda to the Soviet Union. *The Christian Century* 106:773-5 Ag 30-S 6 '89

VANITIES (FURNITURE)

Bath trio [vanity, linen locker, and mirror-backed shelves] L. M. Dalsgaard. il *Home Mechanix* 85:42-4+ Je '89

Custom vanities [bathroom vanities] il *Popular Mechanics* 166:134+ Ap '89

VANITY

Photographs and photography

When a photographer is a button-pusher. G. Bernstein. il *Petersen's Photographic Magazine* 17:41 Ja '89

VANITY

Almost vanity. M. E. Marty. *The Christian Century* 106:799 Ag 30-S 6 '89

VANITY FAIR (PERIODICAL)

High gloss news [editor T. Brown] T. Mathews. il pors *Newsweek* 113:54-6+ My 1 '89

Vanity press [profile of M. R. Milken] D. Ellen. *The New Republic* 201:25 Ag 28 '89

VANN, ALLAN S.

Shared decision making for principals and teachers. *The Education Digest* 54:17-20 Ja '89

VANN, JOHN PAUL

about

Hot writers. A. DeCurtis. il pors *Rolling Stone* p117-18+ My 18 '89

VANONI, MARVIN

Who said it first? *Good Housekeeping* 208:247 Je '89

VANOOSTING, JAMES

Creative lying. *The Writer* 102:7-8 O '89

VANOY, JUANITA

about

Michael Jordan marries mother of his toddler. il pors *Jet* 76:52-3 S 25 '89

Michael Jordan takes a bride: Juanita Vanoy [cover story] il pors *Jet* 77:58-60 O 9 '89

VANS

When room for five is not enough [minivans] F. Lunzer. il *U.S. News & World Report* 106:64-5 Ja 23 '89

Design

A car that's just the way its designers wanted it [GM200 minivan] D. Woodruff. il *Business Week* p103-4 Je 5 '89

Pontiac Trans Sport. D. C. Ross. il *Motor Trend* 41:177-9 My '89

Vanguard of the 1990s [minivans] B. Hartford. il *Popular Mechanics* 166:28 S '89

Four wheel drive

Ford Aerostar Wagon. J. Miller. il *Motor Trend* 41:96-7 O '89

Four-by-four by van [Mazda MPV] T. Opre. il *Outdoor Life* 183:59+ Ap '89

Mazda MPV 4WD. A. Assenza. il *Car and Driver* 35:131-2 S '89

New-look Nissan Axxess AWD. T. Opre. il *Outdoor Life* 184:58+ N '89

Materials

GM's new-technology plastic van [cover story] D. McCosh. il *Popular Science* 234:115-19+ Je '89

Testing

'90 Chrysler Town & Country. D. C. Ross. il *Motor Trend* 41:84-7 S '89

All-purpose van [Chevrolet Lumina APV] T. Opre. il *Outdoor Life* 184:24+ O '89

Asquith Motor Carriage. R. Hutton. il *Car and Driver* 34:33 My '89

Chevrolet Lumina APV. il *Road & Track* 41:50-2+ O '89

Dodge Caravan LE [long-term test] B. J. Hoffman. il *Motor Trend* 41:106-7 Ag '89

Dodge Grand Caravan LE [long term test] B. J. Hoffman. il *Motor Trend* 41:142 N '89

VANS—Testing—*cont.*
Eeny, meeny, miney, mini [Chevrolet Astro, Dodge Caravan, Ford Aerostar, Mazda MPV, Mitsubishi Wagon LS, Nissan Axxess, Toyota Van LE, and VW Vanagon GL] W. Jeanes. il *Car and Driver* 34:62-3+ My '89
Go to work in style [Mazda MPV] D. Chaikin. il *Home Mechanix* 85:64-7 Ja '89
Long haulers [Ford Club Wagon] M. Allen. il *Popular Mechanics* 166:62-4+ S '89
Long-term test [Dodge Caravan] il *Popular Mechanics* 166:120+ Je '89
Long-term update [GMC Safari Van] J. Keebler. il *Road & Track* 40:78 Mr '89
Nissan Axxess. A. Assenza. il *Car and Driver* 34:47-9+ Ap '89
Nissan Axxess. Y. Ishiwatari. il *Car and Driver* 34:30 F '89
Nissan Axxess. J. Lamm. il *Road & Track* 40:146 My '89
Nissan Axxess. J. R. Nerad. il *Motor Trend* 41:79-82 Ap '89
Pontiac Trans Sport. A. Assenza. il *Car and Driver* 35:63-5+ Jl '89
Space machines [Dodge Caravan, Ford Aerostar, Mazda MPV, Nissan Axxess] D. Sherman. il *Popular Science* 234:40-2+ My '89
A special Espace [Renault] R. Hutton. il *Car and Driver* 35:68 Jl '89
Versatile vehicles [Nissan Axxess] D. Chaikin. il *Home Mechanix* 85:64-70 Jl '89
VANS, REMODELED
A limo is only a limo, but a van . . . J. J. Keller. il *Business Week* p170-1 O 9 '89
Nine to five in a van [fitted out to serve as an office] E. Henry. il *Changing Times* 43:78 Jl '89
VANZANT, IYANLA
The powers that free; ed. by Bebe Moore Campbell. il por *Essence* 20:80-2+ O '89
VAPORIZATION
Volatilization of high molecular weight DNA by pulsed laser ablation of frozen aqueous solutions [mass spectrometry] R. W. Nelson and others. bibl f il *Science* 246:1585-7 D 22 '89
VAPORIZERS
Moisturizing the air. L. C. Cook. il *Health (New York, N.Y.)* 21:34-5+ D '89
VAPORS
See also
Fumes
VARA, JON
The housesmith. See issues of Country Journal beginning October 1986
VARADARAJAN, RAGHAVAN, AND OTHERS
Effects of buried ionizable amino acids on the reduction potential of recombinant myoglobin. bibl f il *Science* 243:69-72 Ja 6 '89
VARAWA, JOANA MCINTYRE
about
Cross-culture shock. L. Fleischer. *Publishers Weekly* 235:207 F 24 '89
Joana McIntyre, 58, crosses cultures and generations to marry Fijian Malé Varawa, 28. R. Arias. il pors *People Weekly* 32:69-70+ Jl 31 '89
VARAWA, MALÉ
about
Joana McIntyre, 58, crosses cultures and generations to marry Fijian Malé Varawa, 28. R. Arias. il pors *People Weekly* 32:69-70+ Jl 31 '89
VARDA, AGNÈS
about
Kung Fu Master [film] Reviews
American Film il por 14:67 Je '89. J. E. Fitch
The New Republic 200:27 Je 26 '89. S. Kauffmann
VARDAVAS, STEPHANIE
about
Baseball lives [excerpt] M. Bryan. il por *Sports Illustrated* 70:78+ Ap 24 '89
VARDEY, LUCINDA
An open market for Australia? por *Publishers Weekly* 236:100 S 15 '89
VARES, TERRY
about
The fall and rise of Terry Vares. T. Slear. il por *Women's Sports & Fitness* 11:70 My '89
VARGAS, VIRGILIO BARCO See Barco Vargas, Virgilio
VARGAS LLOSA, MARIO, 1936-
Cuba: freedom vs. equality. il *World Press Review* 36:45 Mr '89
The storyteller speaks [fiction] *Américas* 41 no2:25+ '89
The writer reflects [excerpt from introduction to The storyteller]; tr. by Helen R. Lane. *Américas* 41 no2:24+ '89
about
Can a novelist save Peru? [cover story] G. Marzorati. il pors *The New York Times Magazine* p44-7+ N 5 '89
Cocaine, communism and crisis in Peru. C. A. Robbins. il *U.S. News & World Report* 107:45-9 S 18 '89
Have typewriter, will run. R. Grenier. *National Review* 41:33-4 Mr 24 '89

Latin America's "best-looking great novelist," Mario Vargas Llosa may also be, as Gene Lyons reports, the next president of Peru. G. Lyons. il por *Vogue* 179:272+ N '89
Privatizing Peru [interview] E. Farnsworth. il *New Perspectives Quarterly* 6:38-41 Fall '89
The storyteller, Mario Vargas Llosa's two tales of the Amazon. M. del C. Prodoscimi. il por *Américas* 41 no2:22-3 '89
The temptation of Mario. E. Farnsworth. il por *Mother Jones* 14:22-6+ Ja '89
VARIABLE STARS See Stars, Variable
VARIABLE STROKE ENGINES See Automobile engines
VARIABLE VALVE TIMING SYSTEMS (AUTOMOBILES) See Automobile engines—Valves
VARIAN ASSOCIATES, INC.
Makers of EW components adopt fresh strategies as programs dwindle. *Aviation Week & Space Technology* 131:115+ S 18 '89
VARIATION (BIOLOGY)
See also
Diversity (Biology)
Mosaics (Biology)
Mutation
The evolutionary significance of phenotypic plasticity [cover story] S. C. Stearns. bibl f il *BioScience* 39:436-45 Jl/Ag '89
Fitness differences among remnant populations of the endangered Sonoran topminnow. J. M. Quattro and R. C. Vrijenhoek. bibl f il *Science* 245:976-8 S 1 '89
Ice sponging off the Antarctic shelf [research by Paul K. Dayton] il *Science News* 136:255 O 14 '89
Interdecadal variation in an Antarctic sponge and its predators from oceanographic climate shifts. P. K. Dayton. bibl f il *Science* 245:1484-6 S 29 '89
Phenotypic integration and environmental change [plasticity] C. D. Schlichting. bibl f il *BioScience* 39:460-4 Jl/Ag '89
VARICOSE VEINS
Banish unsightly veins. J. Mullich. il *Prevention (Emmaus, Pa.)* 41:53-7 S '89
Leg lifts. N. Weber. *Harper's Bazaar* 122:136+ Ag '89
Varicose veins: the truth behind the thin blue lines. C. Haberfeld. il *Mademoiselle* 95:94+ Je '89
VARILLA, MARY
about
One teen's struggle to end hunger. L. Eskin. il por *Scholastic Update (Teachers' edition)* 121:12-13 Ja 27 '89
VARMINT CALLING See Animal calling
VARMUS, HAROLD
about
Cancer gene research wins Medicine Nobel. J. L. Marx. il pors *Science* 246:326-7 O 20 '89
Gene-tracking leads to Nobel Prize. A. McKenzie. *Science News* 136:244 O 14 '89
Medicine. il pors *Time* 134:73 O 23 '89
VARNISH AND VARNISHING
See also
Lacquer and lacquering
Water-based varnish. T. O. Bakke. il *Popular Science* 234:82-3 Ja '89
VARNISH REMOVERS See Paint and varnish removers
VASARI
Vasari diary. See issues of Art News
VASCO, MIGUEL ANTONIO
The mighty pen. por *Américas* 41 no2:57 '89
VASCULAR ENDOTHELIAL GROWTH FACTOR
Vascular endothelial growth factor is a secreted angiogenic mitogen. D. W. Leung and others. bibl f il *Science* 246:1306-9 D 8 '89
VASCULAR PERMEABILITY FACTOR
Vascular permeability factor, an endothelial cell mitogen related to PDGF. P. J. Keck and others. bibl f il *Science* 246:1309-12 D 8 '89
VASCULAR SURGERY See Blood vessels—Surgery
VASCULAR SYSTEM See Blood vessels; Cardiovascular system
VASECTOMY
"My husband's vasectomy ruined our sex life". H. S. Kaplan. por *Redbook* 173:22 S '89
My vasectomy. P. Gold. *Glamour* 87:171+ S '89
No-scalpel vasectomy [work of Marc Goldstein] il *Prevention (Emmaus, Pa.)* 41:16 D '89
VASES
Containers for bouquet makers. il *Sunset (Central West edition)* 183:164 D '89
VASES, FRENCH
Exhibitions
Museum accessions [French vase acquired by Indianapolis Museum of Art] E. H. Gustafson. il *Antiques* 136:76+ Jl '89
VASES, ROMAN
Conservation and restoration
A celebrated Roman vase has become a 20th-century phoenix [Portland Vase restoration at the British Museum] I. Shenker. bibl (p122) il *Smithsonian* 20:52-4+ Jl '89
VASOACTIVE INTESTINAL POLYPEPTIDE
Catalytic hydrolysis of vasoactive intestinal peptide by human autoantibody. S. Paul and others. bibl f il *Science* 244:1158-62 Je 9 '89

VASOCONSTRICTORS
See also
Serotonin
VASODILATORS
Hyperpolarizing vasodilators activate ATP-sensitive K⁺ channels in arterial smooth muscle. N. B. Standen and others. bibl f il *Science* 245:177-80 Jl 14 '89
A novel vasodilatory peptide from the salivary glands of the sand fly Lutzomyia longipalpis. J. M. C. Ribeiro and others. bibl f il *Science* 243:212-14 Ja 13 '89
VASOLIGATION See Vasectomy
VASS, JOAN
about
Vass horizons. J. Etra. il por *House & Garden* 161:60-9+ Ja '89
VASYUTIN, VLADIMIR, AND TISHCHENKO, ARTUR A.
Space coloristics. bibl il *Scientific American* 261:84-90 Jl '89
VAT See Value added tax
VATICAN. CAPPELLA SISTINA
A renaissance for Michelangelo [cover story] D. Jeffery. il *National Geographic* 176:688-713 D '89
VATICAN COUNCIL (2ND: 1962-1965)
The Church's response to the media: twenty-five years after Inter mirifica. R. P. Waznak. *America* 160:36-40 Ja 21 '89
Of many things [Richard A. McCormick's The critical calling: reflections on moral dilemmas since Vatican II] G. W. Hunt. *America* 161:178 S 30 '89
VATZ, RICHARD E., AND WEINBERG, LEE S.
The arrogance of predicting dangerousness. il *USA Today (Periodical)* 118:62-3 N '89
Confusion over alcoholism: psychiatry, medicine, and the law disagree. il *USA Today (Periodical)* 118:68-70 S '89
VAUCOULEURS, GERARD HENRI DE
The best telescopic pictures of Mars. il *Sky and Telescope* 77:15-17 Ja '89
VAUD (SWITZERLAND)
Description and travel
Gourmet holidays: a Swiss Alpine sojourn. S. Wilding. il map *Gourmet* 49:48-53+ Ag '89
VAUDEVILLE
Bill Irwin and the rest of the New Vaudevillians are rescuing performance art from a decade of pretension. R. Short. il por *Vogue* 179:202+ Ag '89
VAUGHAN, RALPH E.
Mystery of the bag lady's bundle [story] il *'Teen* 33:32+ F '89
The mystery of the bag lady's bundle [story] il *'Teen* 33:34-5+ Ja '89
VAUGHAN, ROWLAND, FL. 1610
about
A watery paradise: Rowland Vaughan and Hereford's 'Golden Vale'. M. Delorme. bibl il *History Today* 39:38-43 Jl '89
VAUGHAN, STEVIE RAY
about
Guitar slingers shoot it out. T. Drozdowski. il pors *Rolling Stone* p28 N 30 '89
Stevie Ray Vaughan is "In step". P. Puterbaugh. il por *Stereo Review* 54:124 D '89
VAUGHAN, THOMAS, 1924-
about
The man at OHS. M. Durham. il pors *Americana* 17:49-53 Mr/Ap '89
VAUGHN, DAVID B.
John Taye's basswood sculptures. il por *American Artist* 53:60-5 Ap '89
VAUGHN, ELLEN SANTILLI
In solitary cells on winter nights [interview with I. Ratushinskaya and I. Geraschenko] il pors *Christianity Today* 33:26-9 D 15 '89
(ed) See Colson, Charles W. Living in the new Dark Ages
VAUGHN, ERIC
Should the Congress adopt the "Clean Air Act amendments of 1987"? [excerpts from statement, September 30, 1987] *Congressional Digest* 68:46+ F '89
VAUGHN, REGIS
about
Elvis's prom date remembers a shy guy in blue suede shoes. S. Dougherty. il pors *People Weekly* 32:99-100 Jl 17 '89
VAUGHN, STEPHANIE
Dog heaven [story] *The New Yorker* 64:26-31 Ja 9 '89
VAUXHALL (AUTOMOBILE) See Automobiles, Foreign
VAX COMPUTERS
Will DEC's new workhorse haul profits out of a rut? [VAX 9000 series] K. H. Hammonds. il *Business Week* p41-2 O 30 '89
VAYSSE, FRANÇOISE
Mail war. il *World Press Review* 36:62 S '89
VCR-TVS See Television receivers—Videotape recorder combination
VCRS (VIDEO CASSETTE RECORDERS) See Videotape recorders and recording

VD See Sexually transmitted diseases
VDTS See Video display terminals
VEAL
See also
Cooking—Meat
VEBER, FRANCIS
about
Three fugitives [film] Reviews
The New Republic 200:24-5 Mr 6 '89. S. Kauffmann
The New Yorker 65:98 F 20 '89. P. Kael
Newsweek il 113:79 F 13 '89. D. Ansen
People Weekly 31:16 F 6 '89. P. Travers
VECELLI, TIZIANO See Titian, ca. 1488-1576
VEDOVA, EMILIO, 1919-
about
Emilio Vedova at Salvatore Ala. H. Cotter. *Art in America* 77:198 My '89
VEGA, MOISÉS GIROLDI See Giroldi Vega, Moisés
VEGETABLE DIET See Vegetarianism
VEGETABLE GARDENS AND GARDENING
See also
Cold frames
Mulching
Plants—Protection
Truck farming
See also names of vegetables
Beginning gardening [cover story] S. Sides. il map *The Mother Earth News* 116:76-8+ Mr/Ap '89
The dooryard garden [cover story] il *Flower and Garden* 33:35-7+ S/O '89
Gardens under glass [solar greenhouse] N. Bubel. il *Country Journal* 16:60-7 S/O '89
How to grow a Mexican dinner. il *Sunset (Central West edition)* 182:106-8 Ap '89
If your vegetables need some help up: two simple trellises. il *Sunset (Central West edition)* 182:198-9 Mr '89
Kitchen gardener. W. E. Wooldridge. See issues of Flower and Garden beginning October/November 1987
New year's garden [cover story; special section] il *Country Journal* 16:23-36 Ja '89
Small-space strategies [use of raised beds] J. A. McKeon. il *Better Homes and Gardens* 67:94+ Mr '89
Spring ephemerals. R. Haskell. il *Flower and Garden* 33:86-9 Mr/Ap '89
Spring gardening [special section] il *Country Journal* 16:63-78 Mr/Ap '89
Sunny trellis for vegetables. il *Sunset (Central West edition)* 182:236 My '89
Third time's a charm: making your autumn garden work. A. R. Chandler. il *Flower and Garden* 33:34-7 Jl/Ag '89
The vegetable garden. N. Bubel. See issues of Country Journal beginning October 1986
Vitamins for vegetables [use as plant foods] R. Williams, III. il por *The Mother Earth News* 117:38+ My/Je '89
California
Seven edibles in just 40 square feet. il *Sunset (Central West edition)* 182:184 Mr '89
Vegetables all year from their front garden [garden of Stephen Holbrook in Santa Barbara] il *Sunset (Central West edition)* 183:190+ O '89
Martha's Vineyard (Mass.)
See also
Solviva Winter Garden (Firm)
Montana
Garden secrets from the Hmong. C. J. Morris. il *Flower and Garden* 33:36-8 Mr/Ap '89
Western States
This hot month is time to plant cool-season vegetables. il *Sunset (Central West edition)* 183:118-19 Ag '89
VEGETABLE IVORY See Tagua
VEGETABLE SAUCES See Sauces
VEGETABLE SOUPS See Soups
VEGETABLE STEW See Stew
VEGETABLES
See also
Cooking—Vegetables
Cruciferous vegetables
Greens, Edible
Vegetable gardens and gardening
Vegetarianism
See also names of vegetables
Best bets for beginners. *The Mother Earth News* 116:86-8 Mr/Ap '89
From our kitchen to yours. K. Adams. il *Southern Living* 24:152 O '89
Good food, good health: pass the fruits and vegetables, please! B. Goldman. il *Better Homes and Gardens* 67:16 Jl '89
More veggies join fight against lung cancer [research by Loïc Le Marchand] I. Wickelgren. *Science News* 136:102 Ag 12 '89
Nitrogen fertilizer saps veggies' vitamin C [research by Sharon B. Hornick] *Science News* 136:255 O 14 '89
Raw, raw, raw! [uncooked fruits and vegetables may offer greater protection against cancer; research by Blossom Patterson] R. A. Barnett. il *American Health* 8:130+ S '89

VEGETABLES—*cont.*

Contamination

Dangers in the vegetable patch [pesticides] S. Begley. il *Newsweek* 113:74-5 Ja 30 '89

Fear of fruits (or, Waiter, there's a pesticide in my salad). J. Nash. il *Mademoiselle* 95:134 Ag '89

Lethal Listeria surfaces on fresh vegetables. I. Wickelgren. *Science News* 136:119 Ag 19 '89

Please don't pass the pesticides. S. Squires. *Ladies' Home Journal* 106:56 Jl '89

Disease and pest resistance

Superfit vegetables. B. Pleasant. il *Organic Gardening* 36:55-9 Mr '89

Harvesting

Harvesting for quality. N. Bubel. il *Country Journal* 16:68-72 Jl/Ag '89

Seed

Spellbound by seeds. R. Page. il *Country Journal* 16:34-6 Ja '89

Storage

Your four-season harvest garden. N. Bubel. il *Country Journal* 16:44-51 N/D '89

Varieties

1989 gardeners' choice [cover story] V. Mattern. *Organic Gardening* 36:34-53 Ja '89

New plants '89. il *Flower and Garden* 33:51-66+ Ja/F '89

No 1989 AAS vegetable awards. il *Country Journal* 16:15 Ja '89

Pick of the crop. S. Ogden. il *Country Journal* 16:29-33 Ja '89

Pick of the crop. S. Sides. il *The Mother Earth News* 116:52-5 Mr/Ap '89

VEGETABLES, ARTIFICIAL

A harvest of ceramics [work of A. Gordon and C. Potter] C. Petkanas. il pors *House & Garden* 161:28+ Ag '89

VEGETABLES, CANNED

See also
Beans, Canned
Mushrooms, Canned

VEGETABLES IN ART

See also
Vegiforms

VEGETARIAN TIMES

Writing for Vegetarian times. L. Moll. il *The Writer* 102:25-6 Ap '89

VEGETARIANISM

See also
Vegetarian times

Glorious Greens [recipes created by Greens restaurant] il *Ladies' Home Journal* 106:200+ O '89

Modified vegetarianism. L. Applegate. il *Runner's World* 24:22-3 Jl '89

Raising vegetarian kids. L. J. Davis. il *Parents* 64:190 Jl '89

Vegetarians vs. cancer. il *Prevention (Emmaus, Pa.)* 41:8 D '89

Vibing vegetarian. J. Nash. il *Essence* 20:69-72+ Jl '89

VEGF *See* Vascular endothelial growth factor

VEGIFORMS

Using Rick Tweddell's Vegiform molds, gardeners can say, 'Let us now raise famous men'. il por *People Weekly* 32:91 O 2 '89

VEHICLES

See also
Motor vehicles
Tracked vehicles

Movin' on [high-tech personal transportation] J. Stone. il *Discover* 10:82-4 Je '89

VEHICLES, ARMORED MILITARY *See* Motor vehicles, Military

VEILLEUX, GÉRARD

about

The new helmsmen [with interview with P. Watson] R. Corelli. il pors *Maclean's* 102:60-1 O 9 '89

VEINS

See also
Spider veins
Varicose veins

VEJJAJIVA, VITTHYA

Vitthya Vejjajiva [advice to George Bush] *National Review* 41:26-7 F 10 '89

VELA SUPERNOVA *See* Supernovas

VELARDE, ENRIQUETA

New tensions for a rough crowd. il *International Wildlife* 19:20-4 N/D '89

VELASCO, ANAMELI MONROY DE *See* Monroy de Velasco, Anameli

VELAYATI, ALI AKBAR

about

Does Teheran want détente? [interview] L. Lief. por *U.S. News & World Report* 107:30 O 9 '89

VELÁZQUEZ, DIEGO, 1599-1660

about

Art. K. Larson. il *New York* 22:64-5 S 11 '89

Art. K. Larson. *New York* 22:99-100 O 30 '89

Clash of the titans. P. Plagens. il pors *Newsweek* 114:84-6 O 9 '89

The painted face. J. Brown. il *Vogue* 179:420-5 O '89

Power and flesh [cover story] J. Hobhouse. il por *Art News* 88:112-17 N '89

Sovereign strokes. D. Solomon. il por *Harper's Bazaar* 122:360-1+ S '89

Velázquez. A. C. Danto. *The Nation* 249:729-32 D 11 '89

Velázquez's binding ethic. R. Hughes. il *Time* 134:104-5 O 9 '89

VELEZ, LISA *See* Lisa Lisa

VELIKHOV, YEVGENY P.

Science and scientists for a nuclear-weapon-free world. il *Physics Today* 42:32-3+ N '89

VELIOTES, NICHOLAS A.

about

Veliotes gives high marks—and low—to Reagan administration. H. Fields. *Publishers Weekly* 235:18 F 3 '89

VELKOV, WES

about

Mister Eighty-Eight. E. Stern. il por *Gentlemen's Quarterly* 59:61 Ag '89

VELVET

The velvet touch. il *Vogue* 179:392-405 O '89

VENCE (FRANCE)

Description

Vence. D. Beal. il map *Gourmet* 49:86-91+ Ap '89

VENDEX TECHNOLOGIES (FIRM)

Consumer computers [Vendex HeadStart III] G. Keizer. il *Compute!* 11:6 Ap '89

VENDING MACHINES

See also
Triangle Industries, Inc.

A suntan can be a fun tan with this new way to change your oil [developed by C. C. King] il *People Weekly* 31:116-17 My 29 '89

We are vending addiction to our children [cigarette vending machines] il *The Saturday Evening Post* 261:14 Jl/Ag '89

VENDORS, INDUSTRIAL *See* Industrial suppliers

VENDORS, PERIODICAL *See* Periodical vendors

VENEERS AND VENEERING

See also
Brick veneer

No-fuss veneers. T. H. Jones. il *Home Mechanix* 85:28+ D '89

Veneer repair. M. Varese. il *Workbench* 45:76-7 N/D '89

VENEREAL DISEASES *See* Sexually transmitted diseases

VENEREAL WARTS *See* Warts

VENETIAN BLINDS *See* Blinds

VENEZIA, MIKE

about

The longest ride. W. Nack. il pors *Sports Illustrated* 70:116-20+ Mr 20 '89

VENEZUELA

See also
Birds—Venezuela
Foreign exchange—Laws and regulations—Venezuela
Investments, American—Venezuela
Loans, Bank—Venezuela
Maracaibo (Venezuela)
Mount Roraima
Mountains—Venezuela
Natural history—Venezuela
Riots—Venezuela

Economic policy

Crackdown in Caracas [austerity measures trigger rioting] L. Beyer. il *Time* 133:36 Mr 13 '89

Debt and politics in Venezuela. J. Ewell. bibl f *Current History* 88:121-4+ Mr '89

Fires of discontent [austerity plan creates rioting] M. Nemeth. il *Maclean's* 102:28 Mr 13 '89

The next liberator? [C. A. Perez's approach to debt crisis] M. Collett. il *The Atlantic* 263:29+ F '89

On drugs, debt and poverty [interview with C. A. Perez] J. Moody and S. Talbott. il por *Time* 134:12-14 N 27 '89

Péreztroika. S. Talbott. il por *Time* 134:50 O 23 '89

Venezuelans voted for reform—and got more than they bargained for. G. DeGeorge. il por *Business Week* p54 S 4 '89

A volcano in Venezuela. A. Platt. il *Newsweek* 113:35 Mr 13 '89

Politics and government

See also
Politics, Corruption in—Venezuela

Debt and politics in Venezuela. J. Ewell. bibl f *Current History* 88:121-4+ Mr '89

VENGEANCE *See* Revenge

VENICE (ITALY)

Description

On a visit to Venice, Jeffrey Steingarten learns the mysteries of the deep from an undisputed master of Adriatic seafood, Marcella Hazan. J. Steingarten. il por *Vogue* 179:250+ Ag '89

Gardens and gardening

Green secrets of Venice [M. J. Pool's The gardens of Venice] D. Brenner. il *House & Garden* 161:114 N '89

History

The gondola of Venice. A. Gillette. il *The Courier (Unesco)* 41:24-9 N '88

VENICE (ITALY)—*cont.*

Photographs and photography

Venice. P. Slaughter. il *Petersen's Photographic Magazine* 18:18-21+ S '89

VENICE (ITALY) IN ART

Exhibitions

The far-reaching eye of Venice's Antonio Canaletto. D. Hofstadter. bibl (p245) il *Smithsonian* 20:78-86+ N '89

Venice observed [work of Canaletto] R. Bernier. il *Vogue* 179:418-23+ N '89

Visions of Venice [Canaletto exhibit at the Metropolitan Museum of Art] E. Heartney. il *Harper's Bazaar* 122:158-9+ N '89

VENICE FILM FESTIVAL *See* Motion picture festivals—Italy

VENICE SIMPLON-ORIENT-EXPRESS LTD.

The Orient Express. D. Puccio. il *Travel Holiday* 171:90 My '89

Riding the ritziest rails. B. Riemer. il *Business Week* p182 N 13 '89

Tracking the Orient Express [Bentley Turbo R races the Orient Express from Venice to Paris] W. Jeanes. il *Car and Driver* 34:104-9 Mr '89

VENISON

See also
Cooking—Game

Bambi and the baron [J. Kerckerinck's efforts to persuade Americans to eat venison] D. Machan. il por *Forbes* 144:298+ D 11 '89

VENOM

See also
Charybdotoxin
Snake venom

VENT HAVEN MUSEUM

Talking heads museum. il *National Geographic World* 163:16-17 Mr '89

VENTILATION

See also
Air conditioning
Humidity
Swine houses—Heating and ventilation
Ventilators

Windows intended to leak [Laminar Air Flow Super Windows] V. E. Gilmore. il *Popular Science* 235:38+ D '89

VENTILATION (PHYSIOLOGY) *See* Respiration

VENTILATORS

Exhaust fans [bathroom] il *Popular Mechanics* 166:116-17 Ap '89

VENTRES, ROMEO J.

about

Remaking Elsie. N. Alster. il por *Forbes* 144:106+ D 25 '89

VENTRILOQUISM

See also
Vent Haven Museum

Conferences

"Hey, let me outta here!" [International Ventriloquist Convention] C. Murphy. il *The Atlantic* 264:62-71 Ag '89

Look who's talking [International Ventriloquist Convention] H. Phillips. il *Travel Holiday* 171:18-19+ My '89

VENTS (ARCHITECTURE)

Calculating roof vents. *The Family Handyman* 39:6+ Mr '89

VENTS (HYDROTHERMAL) *See* Hot springs

VENTURA, MICHAEL

Looking quickly to the side: the other world of psychic phenomena. il *Utne Reader* p98-101 N/D '89

Mano a mano. il *American Health* 8:64-5 Ja/F '89

VENTURA PUBLISHER (DESKTOP PUBLISHING PROGRAM) *See* Desktop publishing—Programming

VENTURE CAPITAL

Financing innovation. C. Farrell. il *Business Week* Special Issue:154-7+ Je 16 '89

High-tech guru Steven Burrill [interview] M. Mandell. il por *High Technology Business* 9:20-3 N/D '89

How to invest in a startup business. A. Deutschman. il *Fortune* 120 no10 Special Issue:115+ Fall '89

VENTURE CAPITAL CLUBS

Get backing at venture capital clubs. L. Fleming. il *Home Office Computing* 7:12 Je '89

VENTURE CAPITAL COMPANIES

See also
J. H. Whitney & Company
Kleiner, Perkins, Caufield & Byers
Narragansett Capital Corp.
Primus Venture Partners
Sevin Rosen Management Company

Betting on the little guy. J. Clements. il *Forbes* 144:237-8 N 27 '89

Funds that profit from jump-starting the startups. L. Light. *Business Week* p128 S 18 '89

If you're not a giant, roll up your sleeves [pension funds pull out] L. Jereski. il *Business Week* p168 N 6 '89

Social ventures. R. Hylton. *Mother Jones* 14:45-6+ Jl/Ag '89

Where venture capitalists are placing their bets. J. B. Levine. il *Business Week* p78 Mr 6 '89

Japan

Is the U.S. selling its high-tech soul to Japan? J. B. Levine. il *Business Week* p117-18 Je 26 '89

VENTURE LIFESTYLES PUBLISHING COMPANY

A panoramic view of publishing. S. Harvey. il por *Home Office Computing* 7:56-7 O '89

VENTURES, JOINT *See* Joint ventures

VENTURI, ROBERT

about

Venturi faults bureaucrats during historic interiors preservation conferences. C. D. W. Koenig. il por *Architectural Record* 177:25 F '89

Venturi to order. H. Muschamp. il por *House & Garden* 161:104-9+ Ag '89

VENTURI (AUTOMOBILE) *See* Sports cars

VENTURINI, FRANCO

Young vs. old, people vs. party, army vs. people. il *World Press Review* 36:13-14 Jl '89

VENUS (PLANET)

See also
Space flight to Venus

Observing Venus at half phase. il *Sky and Telescope* 78:399-400 O '89

Atmosphere

. . . and sulfur volcanism on Venus [research by Bruce Fegley, Jr., and Ronald G. Prinn] *Sky and Telescope* 77:356 Ap '89

The nature of the near-infrared features on the Venus night side. D. Crisp and others. bibl f il *Science* 246:506-9 O 27 '89

Radio twinkling in Venusian ionosphere. J. Eberhart. *Science News* 135:119 F 25 '89

Venus crystals [research by G. P. Können] il *Sky and Telescope* 78:13-14 Jl '89

Venus volcanism: another hint. *Science News* 136:383 D 9 '89

Will earth become another Venus? T. H. Cole. il *Popular Mechanics* 166:18+ Je '89

Geology

Voyage to Venus [Magellan flight; cover story] R. Kunzig. il *Discover* 10:54-61 Ap '89

Surface

. . . and sulfur volcanism on Venus [research by Bruce Fegley, Jr., and Ronald G. Prinn] *Sky and Telescope* 77:356 Ap '89

Feeling the face of Venus [Magellan radar mapping; cover story] J. Eberhart. il *Science News* 135:248-9 Ap 22 '89

Fresh looks at Venus. il *Sky and Telescope* 78:345-6 O '89

Magellan's radar images of Venus to unmask cloud-shrouded planet. il *Aviation Week & Space Technology* 131:113+ O 9 '89

The planet next door. A. T. Bazilevskiy. il *Sky and Telescope* 77:360-6+ Ap '89

Styles of volcanism on Venus: new Arecibo high resolution radar data. D. B. Campbell and others. bibl f il *Science* 246:373-7 O 20 '89

Venus unveiled [Magellan mission] S. D. Wall. il *Astronomy* 17:26-32 Ap '89

VERA, MOISÉS GIROLDI *See* Giroldi Vega, Moisés

VERAPAMIL

Tumor resistance: weakening the pulse [research by Thomas P. Miller] R. Weiss. *Science News* 135:348 Je 3 '89

VERBAAN, MARK

Fix in Namibia? *The Nation* 249:516-17 N 6 '89

(jt. auth) See Lister, Gwen, and Verbaan, Mark

VERBAL ERRORS *See* Speech errors

VERBAL INSULTS *See* Invective

VERBEKE, JUDITH A.

(jt. auth) See Siegel, Bruce A., and Verbeke, Judith A.

VERDAN, AMANDA

about

A discerning eye. J. McLaughlin. il por *Harper's Bazaar* 122:54 N '89

VERDI, BOB

Bridesmaid revisited. il pors *Sports Illustrated* 70:54-7 Ap 24 '89

VERDI, GIUSEPPE, 1813-1901

about

Aida [opera] Reviews
 New York il 22:43 Ja 2 '89. P. G. Davis
 The New Yorker 64:66-8 Ja 16 '89. A. Porter
 Opera News il 53:24-7 Ja 7 '89
 Opera News 53:4 Ja 7 '89. J. Keates
 Opera News il 54:32 D 23 '89

Don Carlos [opera] Reviews
 New York il 22:66-7 F 20 '89. P. G. Davis
 Opera News il 53:22-3 F 4 '89
 Opera News il 53:32-5 F 4 '89

Falstaff [opera] Reviews
 The Nation 248:498 Ap 10 '89. E. W. Said
 The Nation 248:356 Mr 13 '89. T. M. Disch
 New York il 22:66 F 20 '89. P. G. Davis
 The New Yorker 65:104-6 F 20 '89. A. Porter
 Opera News il 53:18-20 F 4 '89. P. Conrad

Music [Messa per Rossini] P. G. Davis. il *New York* 22:107-8 O 30 '89

VERDI, GIUSEPPE, 1813-1901—about—*cont.*
Musical events:
Requiem for Rossini. A. Porter. *The New Yorker*
65:114-17 N 13 '89
Nabucco [opera] Reviews
New York il 22:101-2 Mr 6 '89. P. G. Davis
Rigoletto [opera] Reviews
New York il 22:118 N 20 '89. P. G. Davis
La traviata [opera] Reviews
New York il 22:107 O 30 '89. P. G. Davis
Opera News il 54:10-11 O '89. G. Fitzgerald
Il Trovatore [opera] Reviews
Opera News il 53:26-9 Ja 21 '89
Verdi redivivus. C. J. Luten. il *Opera News* 54:46-9 S '89

VERDURA, FULCO, DUCA DI
about
Viva Verdura! J. Gruder. il por *Harper's Bazaar* 122:262
S '89

VEREEN, BEN
about
Ben Vereen becomes warrior in fight against drugs. il por
Jet 77:11 D 11 '89

VEREY, ROSEMARY
Small wonders. il *House & Garden* 161:102+ Mr '89

VERGARA, CAMILO JOSÉ
Hell in a very tall place. il *The Atlantic* 264:72-6+ S '89
A South Bronx landscape. il *The Nation* 248:302-6 Mr 6
'89

VERGASON, GLENN A., AND ANDEREGG, M. L.
Save the baby! A response to 'Integrating the children of
the second system'. bibl f il *Phi Delta Kappan* 71:61-3
S '89

VERGIL *See* Virgil

VERIFICATION OF DISARMAMENT COMPLIANCE *See*
Disarmament—Inspection

VERLAINE, M. J.
Look where you're going [story] *The New Yorker* 65:38-47
Ap 10 '89

VERMONT
See also
Agriculture—Vermont
Architecture, Domestic—Vermont
Environmental policy—Vermont
Geology—Vermont
Historic houses, sites, etc.—Vermont
Hotels, motels, etc.—Vermont
Insects—Vermont
Insurance law—Vermont
Rural development—Vermont
Skiing—Vermont
Description and travel
See also
Cycling—Vermont
A walk in the country. G. Yanker and K. Burton. il map
Travel Holiday 171:22-3 Je '89
Photographs and photography
Home for Christmas [excerpt from A Vermont Christmas]
R. Brown. il *Good Housekeeping* 208:96-9 Ja '89

VERNACULAR LANGUAGE *See* Native language

VERNADSKIĬ, VLADIMIR IVANOVICH, 1863-1945
about
Ecological advances in the Soviet Union. A. L. Yanshin.
il por *Environment* 30:6-9+ D '88

VERNI, ANTHONY
about
The sad saga of a penny-stock company. G. Weiss. il por
Business Week p124-6+ My 15 '89

VERNON, LILLIAN *See* Katz, Lillian Vernon

VERNON (LILLIAN) CORPORATION *See* Lillian Vernon
Corporation

VERNON SAVINGS & LOAN ASSOCIATION
The big fix [cover story] J. R. Adams. il *The American
Spectator* 22:21-4 Mr '89

VERONESE, 1528-1588
about
Brush fire. D. Rosand. il *The New Republic* 200:38-41 Ja
23 '89
The gorgeousness of life. A. C. Danto. il *Art News* 88:108-13
Ja '89
Palladio and Veronese at the Villa Barbaro in Maser, Italy.
B. L. Brown. bibl f il *Antiques* 135:298-309 Ja '89

VERRET, STEVE
about
Some L.A. law-breakers claim Steve Verret's stand-up comedy
traffic class is just the ticket. T. Allis. il pors *People
Weekly* 31:117-18 Je 19 '89

VERSCHOTH, ANITA
(jt. auth) See Johnson, William Oscar, and Verschoth, Anita

VERSCHUUR, GERRIT L., 1937-
Barnard's 'dark' dilemma. il pors *Astronomy* 17:30-8 F '89
A blow to astronomy. *Astronomy* 17:8 My '89
The day the sun cut loose. il *Astronomy* 17:48-51 Ag '89
If we are alone, what on earth are we doing? il *Sky and
Telescope* 78:452 N '89
The many faces of the sun. il *Astronomy* 17:46-51 Mr '89
The peculiar pulsar in Supernova 1987A [cover story] il
Astronomy 17:20-6 S '89

Reminiscences of the 300-foot. *Sky and Telescope* 77:252-3
Mr '89

VERSO (FIRM)
London's Verso to form joint venture with Soviet house.
G. Feldman. *Publishers Weekly* 235:14 Je 16 '89

VERSUS (TERM)
Child's garden of vs. W. Safire. il *The New York Times
Magazine* p16+ Je 4 '89

VERTEBRATES
Locomotion
See Animal locomotion

VERTICAL LIFT AIRCRAFT *See* Rotor aircraft

VERTIGO *See* Dizziness

VERTOL COMPANY *See* Boeing Co. Boeing Vertol Company
(Div.)

VERVILLE, ANNE-LEE
about
Why a change in direction was a step upward. A. M. Russell.
il por *Working Woman* 14:64 My '89

A VERY BRITISH COUP [television program] See Television
program reviews—Single works

VERY LONG INSTRUCTION WORD COMPUTERS
VLIW: heir to RISC? P. Wayner. il *Byte* 14:259-62 Ag
'89

VERY LOW FREQUENCY WAVES *See* Electromagnetic waves

**VERY SIMPLY NICO (LONDON, ENGLAND:
RESTAURANT)** *See* London (England)—Restaurants,
nightclubs, bars, etc.

VESCO, DON
about
King of the salt. P. Lyons. il pors *Cycle* 40:48-51+ D '89

VESILIND, PRIIT J.
The Baltic: arena of power [cover story] il map *National
Geographic* 175:602-35 My '89

VESPERS (MUSIC)
See also
Compact discs—Vespers (Music)

VESTA (ASTEROID) *See* Asteroids

VESTAL, J. ROBIE, AND WHITE, DAVID C.
Lipid analysis in microbial ecology. bibl f il *BioScience*
39:535-41 S '89

VESTING (PENSIONS) *See* Pensions

VESTRON INC.
The crash of a moviemaker. J. Hammer. il por *Newsweek*
114:46 S 4 '89
Vestron is now starring in its own cliffhanger. T. Vogel.
il *Business Week* p66 Jl 17 '89
Vestron teams with Bantam. P. Sweeting. il *Publishers Weekly*
235:30 F 3 '89

VESTS
See also
Bulletproof vests
In quest of the perfect photographer's vest. F. Patterson.
il *Petersen's Photographic Magazine* 18:30-1 O '89
Well vested. L. James. il *Vogue* 179:36 Ja '89

VETERANS
See also
Black veterans
United States. Dept. of Veterans Affairs
United States. Veterans Administration
Women veterans
Self-exiled after Vietnam, Army hero David Hackworth is
finally coming home. P. Freeman. il pors *People Weekly*
31:52-4 Je 5 '89
Benefits
See also
Veterans—Education
Veterans—Medical care
Economic conditions
Caution: war may be dangerous to your earnings [contrasting
World War II with Vietnam veterans] A. S. Blinder. il
Business Week p20 O 2 '89
Education
The lawyer and the punk [J. Thomson encourages author
to go to college] T. Philbin. *Reader's Digest* 135:7-8+ Ag
'89
Health and hygiene
Agent Orange: Congress impatient for answers [Centers for
Disease Control study vs. Stellman study] M. Barinaga.
il *Science* 245:249-50 Jl 21 '89
Medical care
The battle between the veterans [cuts in benefits] A. Plattner.
il *U.S. News & World Report* 106:40-1 Je 5 '89
Mortality
Notes and comment [death of World War II veteran] *The
New Yorker* 65:27-8 Je 5 '89
Psychology
Coming to terms with Nam. R. Novak. il *People Weekly*
32 Special Issue:112-14+ Fall '89
Giving up guns [Vietnam vet] D. Graham. il *The New
York Times Magazine* p34+ Ag 20 '89
Homecoming [letters from Vietnam veterans; excerpts] B.
Greene. il *Esquire* 111:45-6+ F '89
Vietnam 'vets' & the Soviet experience. B. Shephard. il
History Today 39:10-12 Jl '89
When American vets meet Soviet vets [Vietnam and Af-
ghanistan veterans] C. Thibaud. *World Press Review* 36:70
S '89

VETERANS—Psychology—*cont.*
William Calley. C. Unger. il pors *People Weekly* 32:152-8 N 20 '89
The wounds of two wars [meeting between Vietnam and Afghanistan veterans in the Soviet Union] P. P. Mahoney. il *The New York Times Magazine* p60-1+ Je 11 '89

Religious life
Me and the Preacher Man [Vietnam vet helped by evangelist D. Roever; condensed from Before the dawn]; ed. by William R. Kimball. M. Block. *Reader's Digest* 134:33-7 Ja '89

Travel
Back to the battlefields [World War II veterans visit Pacific] K. Castle. il *Travel Holiday* 172:60-71 S '89

VETERANS ADMINISTRATION *See* United States. Veterans Administration

VETERANS AFFAIRS DEPT. (U.S.) *See* United States. Dept. of Veterans Affairs

VETERANS' MEMORIALS *See* War memorials

VETERINARIANS
Next step, eye charts for rabbits [trend towards specialization] V. S. Sussman. il *U.S. News & World Report* 107:116 O 16 '89

VETERINARY COLLEGES
Enrollment
Enrollment ups and downs in dental and veterinary fields. il *Change* 21:27-9 S/O '89

VETERINARY DENTISTRY
Plaque plagues pets. L. Spiotta-DeMare. il *American Health* 8:90 N '89

VETERINARY DRUGS
Laws and regulations
Legal dance over vet drug [unapproved manufacture of gentamicin sulfate leads to injunction against Tri-Bio] il *FDA Consumer* 23:42-3 F '89
Snaring smugglers of animal drugs. il *FDA Consumer* 23:26-7 Je '89
Two veterinarians guilty in antibiotic case [W. A. Jacobs and S. S. Takhar] M. Segal. il *FDA Consumer* 23:33-4 N '89

VETERINARY EUTHANASIA *See* Euthanasia—Animals
VETERINARY HOSPITALS
See also
University of Minnesota. Raptor Center
India
Behind the gauze mask [Jains run Charity Birds Hospital] D. R. Ward. il *International Wildlife* 19:14-19 Ja/F '89
VETERINARY MEDICINE
See also
First aid for animals
Pets—Care
Stillbirth in animals
Veterinarians
Veterinary hospitals
Acupuncture wins the West. D. Kendall. il *The Mother Earth News* 117:42+ My/Je '89
Cancer care in the kennel. J. Seligmann. il *Newsweek* 113:64-5 Ap 3 '89
He talks to the animals . . . [S. Kritsick] M. Siegel. il por *Good Housekeeping* 209:56+ Jl '89
'High-tech' comes to 'vet med'. J. Folkenberg. il *FDA Consumer* 23:18-23 Ap '89
High-tech surgery for dogs and cats. il *USA Today (Periodical)* 117:15 Ap '89
Now! High-tech help for sick pets. M. S. Garvey. il *Good Housekeeping* 208:104+ Ap '89
Pet acupuncture [work of A. Schoen] R. H. Loeb. il pors *Good Housekeeping* 209:150+ N '89
Pets as patients [high tech medicine] S. McKee. il *American Health* 8:110 Ap '89
Study and teaching
See also
Veterinary colleges
Canada
See also
Erie Wildlife Rescue (Organization)
House calls in the wild. T. Pawlick. il *International Wildlife* 19:12-17 Mr/Ap '89
VETO
Fetal position [G. Bush states he would veto abortions in cases of rape or incest] Z. R. Eisenstein. *The Nation* 249:588-9 N 20 '89
For now, the Chinese students can stay [G. Bush vetoes legislation to extend visas of Chinese students] P. Wingert and D. Waller. il *Newsweek* 114:98 D 11 '89
Let him have it [line item veto] M. Kinsley. *The New Republic* 201:4+ N 20 '89
VETROCQ, MARCIA E.
Pentimenti. bibl f il *Art in America* 77:57+ S '89
VETTE! (VIDEO GAME)
Compute! Choice. P. Scisco. il *Compute!* 11:84-6 N '89
VETTESE, SIRAH
(jt. auth) *See* Bloomfield, Harold H., 1944-, and Vettese, Sirah
VEVER, HENRI, 1854-1942
about
Islamic paintings at the Sackler enchant the eye. C. Bond. il *Smithsonian* 19:122-7 Ja '89

VF CORP.
Sacrificial brand [Lee brand] G. Morgenson. il *Forbes* 143:41-2 F 6 '89
VFR (VISUAL FLIGHT RULES) *See* Airplanes—Piloting
VGA (VIDEO GRAPHICS ARRAY)
Buyer's guide: VGA monitors [special section] il *Personal Computing* 13:137-41+ Jl '89
Clash of the graphics titans. R. Cook. il *Byte* 14 Special Issue:143-4+ Fall '89
A complete and affordable VGA board [Paradise VGA Plus 16] C. O'Malley. il *Personal Computing* 13:192+ Ap '89
Compute! Choice: VGA-TV. D. Stanton. il *Compute!* 11:68-70 N '89
Debunking 16-bit VGA. B. D. Kliewer. il *Byte* 14:195-9 Je '89
Genoa SuperVGA. S. Anzovin. *Compute!* 11:101 Ja '89
High-performance VGA card [Video Seven V-RAM VGA] H. F. Beechhold. il *Home Office Computing* 7:66 Je '89
Is it really super? [Super VGA standard] B. Nicholls. il *Byte* 14 Special Issue:159-60+ Fall '89
Monitor and VGA card: a versatile, powerful pair [Relisys VGA/Multiscan Monitor Bundle] H. F. Beechhold. il *Home Office Computing* 7:64-5 Ja '89
These VGA cards display vivid multicolored images. H. F. Beechhold. il *Home Office Computing* 7:64+ F '89
VGAWonder mixes the old and new. C. Hlavaty. il *Personal Computing* 13:186 Jl '89
Vivid VGA monitors. H. F. Beechhold. il *Home Office Computing* 7:44-7 Jl '89
VHF RADIOTELEPHONE ON SHIPS, BOATS, ETC. *See* Radiotelephone on ships, boats, etc.
VIA RAIL CANADA INC.
Canada. B. Keating. il map *New Choices for the Best Years* 29:56-9 Ap '89
Cutting back Via. B. Bergman. il map *Maclean's* 102:18-19 O 16 '89
Via's rocky future [D. de Belleval resigns to protest cutbacks] M. Clark. il por *Maclean's* 102:17 My 15 '89
Will he stop the trains? [passenger rail cutbacks; cover story; special section; with editorial comment by Kevin Doyle] il *Maclean's* 102:2, 18-26 Ag 21 '89
You can't get there from here [end of Canadian transcontinental train] N. R. Gibbs. il *Time* 134:61 O 16 '89
VIACOM INTERNATIONAL INC.
Is Viacom ready to channel the world? D. Lieberman. il pors *Business Week* p72-4 D 18 '89
The meaning of achievement. F. J. Biondi, Jr. por *Channels (New York, N.Y.: 1986)* 9:34-5+ Jl/Ag '89
VIADERO, ANNA
Edible complex. il *Ms.* 18:66-7 Jl/Ag '89
VIAGER (HOUSING FINANCE)
Till death does its part. D. R. Katz. il *Esquire* 111:83-4 Ap '89
VIAL, BRIGITTE OUVRY- *See* Ouvry-Vial, Brigitte
VIBES [film] *See* Motion picture reviews—Single works
VIBRAPHONE MUSIC
See also
Phonograph records—Vibraphone music
VIBRAPHONISTS
See also
Burton, Gary
Hutcherson, Bobby
Mainieri, Mike
VIBRATION
See also
Damping (Mechanics)
Four wheel drive vehicles—Vibration
Oscillations
VICE
See also
Pornography
Prostitution
VICE-PRESIDENTIAL CANDIDATES
1992
Vice-presidential keepstakes [George Bush's endorsement of D. Quayle] il por *U.S. News & World Report* 107:12-13 N 20 '89
Financial disclosure
Covert campaigns [vice presidential fundraising committees] P. Montgomery. *Common Cause Magazine* 15:7-8 My/Je '89
VICE-PRESIDENTS
Vice presidents. *American History Illustrated* 24:34 Ap '89
Protection
Guarding the nation's vice presidents [black special agent H. T. Bell] H. J. Massaquoi. il pors *Ebony* 44:166+ Je '89
VICHY GOVERNMENT *See* France—History—German occupation, 1940-1945
VICK, ROGER
Artificial nature: the synthetic landscape of the future [cover story] il por *The Futurist* 23:29-32 Jl/Ag '89
VICKERS, MARIE
Sharing a room with toxic fumes. *Seventeen* 48:165 Mr '89
VICKERY, JIM DALE
Run! il *Audubon* 91:86-9 Ja '89

VICKSBURG (MICH.)
Description
The Vicksburg ghost [E. Presley sighted by L. Welling in supermarket] S. Hubbell. *The New Yorker* 65:106-17 S 25 '89

VICKSBURG (MISS.)
Historic houses, sites, etc.
Vicksburg revisited. W. Schemmel. il *Travel Holiday* 171:67-71 Ja '89

VICTIMS
The joys of victimhood. J. Epstein. il *The New York Times Magazine* p20-1+ Jl 2 '89

VICTIMS OF CRIME
See also
Abused women
Blacks—Crimes against
Children—Crimes against
College students—Crimes against
Cyclists—Crimes against
Hostages
Mentally handicapped—Crimes against
Parents of murdered children
Single men—Crimes against
Women—Crimes against
Celebrity victims: crime casualties are turning into stars on tabloid TV. F. Rose. il *New York* 22:38-44 Jl 31 '89
Victims of crime [cover story; special section] il *U.S. News & World Report* 107:16-21+ Jl 31 '89
Compensation
See Reparation

VICTOR AVIATION SERVICES
Blueprinters [custom overhauls] F. George. il *Flying* 116:66-8+ Ag '89

VICTOR GOLLANCZ LTD.
Houghton Mifflin to acquire Gollancz. M. Reuter and V. Menkes. *Publishers Weekly* 236:10 O 13 '89

VICTOR KAMIN INC. See Booksellers and bookselling—Maryland

VICTORIA, QUEEN OF GREAT BRITAIN, 1819-1901
about
Royal retreat on the Isle of Wight. J. J. Norwich. il maps *Architectural Digest* 46:160-3 O '89

VICTORIA (B.C.)
Description
High tea & totem poles. S. Hammer. il *Travel Holiday* 172:82-9 D '89
Restaurants, nightclubs, bars, etc.
Teatime at the restored Empress in Victoria, B.C. il *Sunset (Central West edition)* 183:38 Ag '89

VICTORIA AND ALBERT MUSEUM
Brouhaha at the V & A. M. Alexander. *Art in America* 77:29+ Jl '89
The fall of a great museum [cover story] Sir J. Pope-Hennessy. il *The New York Review of Books* 36:10-14 Ap 27 '89
Uproar at the V & A. G. Barker. il *Art News* 88:59 Summ '89

VICTORIA TERMINUS (BOMBAY, INDIA)
Victoria Terminus, Bombay. J. M. MacKenzie. il *History Today* 39:60-1 Ja '89

VICTORIAN ARCHITECTURE See Architecture, Victorian
VICTORIAN HOUSE DECORATION See House decoration, Victorian
VICTORIAN JEWELRY See Jewelry
VICTORIAN MAJOLICA See Majolica
VICTORIAN PAINTING See Painting, Victorian
VICTORIAN PERIOD
Ministering angels [Victorian nursing] A. Summers. bibl il *History Today* 39:31-7 F '89
The odyssey of Annie Besant [radical and atheist turned Theosophist] J. Oppenheim. bibl il pors *History Today* 39:12-18 S '89
Retrieved riches: Charles Booth's Life and labour of the people in London. R. O'Day. bibl il por map *History Today* 39:29-35 Ap '89
Victorian values/Jewish values. G. Himmelfarb. *Commentary* 87:23-31 F '89
Victoriana rules again. B. Kantrowitz. il *Newsweek* 113:60-1 Ja 16 '89

VIDAL, GORE, 1925-
Cue the Green god, Ted [cover story] il *The Nation* 249:153+ Ag 7-14 '89
Remembering Orson Welles. il *The New York Review of Books* 36:12-16 Je 1 '89
about
Gore Vidal on where we're headed. J. Bailey. por *Mother Jones* 14:13 My '89

VIDAL-HALL, JUDITH
All aboard for the next war. *World Press Review* 36:22-3 Ap '89

VIDANES, MICHELLE C.
Poverty, negligence, ignorance. il *World Health* p22 Mr '89

VIDEO (PERIODICAL)
Interpreting the future. A. Levis. *Video* 13:6 Jl '89

VIDEO 5000
Wedding video goes franchise. K. Geller-Shinn. il *Petersen's Photographic Magazine* 18:12 Je '89

VIDEO ART
The fabulous chameleon. C. Hagen. il *Art News* 88:118-23 Summ '89
Exhibitions
Katsuhiro Yamaguchi at Satani. J. Koplos. il *Art in America* 77:271+ Ap '89
Marie Jo Lafontaine at Jack Shainman. B. Adams. *Art in America* 77:209-10 O '89

VIDEO BROADCASTING See Television broadcasting
VIDEO CAMERA SHUTTERS
Does your camcorder really need variable shutter speeds? E. Stecker. il *Popular Photography* 96:34+ N '89

VIDEO CAMERAS
See also
Still video cameras
The backcountry back lot [compact camcorders] P. L. Jones. il *Sierra* 74:115-16 N/D '89
The camcorder craze. il *Ebony* 45:48+ N '89
Camcorders 2000. M. Slovick. il *Video* 13:64-8 S '89
Creative camcorders. il *Popular Photography* 96:70-1+ Ja '89
A hands-on guide to camcorders. P. Mandell. *Working Woman* 14:168+ N '89
Power trips [choosing advanced camcorders and VCRs] P. Utz. il *Video* 13:46-8+ My '89
Small really is better [8mm camcorders] M. Grimm and T. Grimm. il *Travel Holiday* 172:28+ N '89
Zooming in on the right camcorder. D. H. Dunn. il *Business Week* p140-1 My 1 '89
Leasing and renting
Exploring rental options. J. Sulski. il *Video* 13:30-1+ Ag '89
Prices
Camcorder buck-up. J. B. Meigs. il *Rolling Stone* p114 Mr 9 '89
Testing
8-millimeter ups the ante [Canon's A1 Hi8 camcorder] F. Vizard. il *Popular Mechanics* 166:46-7 S '89
Camcorders on location [Sharp VL-C77UA Super VHS-C] F. Vizard. il *Popular Mechanics* 166:62+ Je '89
Canon Hi8 and 8mm camcorders [H460 and E440] il *Video* 13:42+ O '89
Canon Hi8 camcorder. il *Video* 13:30-1+ Jl '89
Canon's A1 camcorder: high band meets high end. E. Stecker. il *Popular Photography* 96:73 Je '89
Chinon EZ Movie Pro. S. Sweetow. il *Petersen's Photographic Magazine* 17:39-40 Ja '89
Four that do more [Chinon CV-T65, Hitachi S8100, Hitachi VM-5200A and RCA Pro Edit CC320 camcorders] E. Stecker. il *Popular Photography* 96:54-5+ Jl '89
GE Hi8 camcorder [HQ CG-9920] il *Video* 13:47-9 D '89
JVC Super VHS-C camcorder [GR-S707] il *Video* 13:48+ S '89
JVC VHS-C comcorder. il *Video* 12:31+ Mr '89
Magnavox VHS camcorder with image stabilization [Magnavox CVJ360AV01] il *Video* 12:37+ Ja '89
Minolta Master C-50 video [compact VHS camcorder] S. Sweetow. il *Petersen's Photographic Magazine* 18:78-9 Jl '89
Minolta Master Series VHS-C camcorder. il *Video* 13:31+ Ap '89
Panasonic PV-520 VHS camcorder. il *Video* 13:34+ Jl '89
Panasonic VHS camcorder with two camera heads [PV-535] il *Video* 13:45+ N '89
Pro Edit Super VHS camcorder. il *Video* 13:33+ Ag '89
RCA Pro Edit VHS camcorder. il *Video* 12:32+ Mr '89
Ricoh 8mm camcorder [R-850] il *Video* 13:40+ O '89
Shooting stars [high-resolution camcorders] J. R. Caruso and M. E. Arthur. il *Video* 13:50+ My '89
Sony 8mm camcorder [CCD-TR5] il *Video* 13:45-6+ S '89
Sony 8mm camcorder [CCD-V11] il *Video* 12:29+ F '89
Sony Handycam Hi8 camcorder. il *Video* 13:27+ My '89
Sony's radical new ultra-light Handycam. K. Korman. il *Video* 13:110 Ag '89
Tamron Digital Movie 8. S. Sweetow. il *Petersen's Photographic Magazine* 17:66-7 F '89
Testing the limits [camcorders] K. Korman. il *Video* 13:50-6 Je '89
The video evolution [camcorders] F. Vizard. il *Popular Mechanics* 166:58-9 Ag '89
Videos by candlelight? [Minolta's new camcorders] E. Stecker. il *Popular Photography* 96:102 Ag '89

VIDEO CASSETTE RECORDERS See Videotape recorders and recording
VIDEO CASSETTES See Videotapes
VIDEO CONFERENCING See Teleconferencing
VIDEO DATA SERVICES
Videotaping services. il por *Home Office Computing* 7:43 Je '89

VIDEO DATING See Videotapes—Social aspects
VIDEO DISC PLAYERS See Videodisc players
VIDEO DISCS See Videodiscs
VIDEO DISPLAY TERMINALS
See also
VGA (Video graphics array)
The brains behind the graphics [graphics coprocessor boards] S. Apiki and others. il *Byte* 14:178-82+ N '89

VIDEO DISPLAY TERMINALS—cont.

High-fashion UNIX on a PC [Hewlett-Packard Accelerated X Window Display Server] B. Smith. il *Byte* 14:205-6+ D '89

How to put 16 million colors to work [NuBus boards for 32-Bit QuickDraw] T. Thompson. il *Byte* 14:189-94+ D '89

Pixels on the march [8514/A and Artist 10 MC graphics coprocessor boards] B. D. Kliewer. il *Byte* 14:201-2+ Ja '89

TekColor lets you really see what you get [color-matching system for the Macintosh] J. Bertolucci and T. Thompson. il *Byte* 14:84+ N '89

True colors, revisited [Spectrum/24 video board] T. Thompson. il *Byte* 14 Mac Special Supp:MAC191 Ag '89

UltraVision. J. Nimersheim. il *Compute!* 11:130+ N '89

Update: standout graphics board [Rendition II] S. Apiki. il *Byte* 14:234 D '89

Variations on a screen. P. R. Robinson. il *Byte* 14:251-2+ Ap '89

Health aspects

Computer dis-ease. D. M. Wilkinson. il *Essence* 19:14+ Mr '89

The hazards of electromagnetic fields (III). P. Brodeur. *The New Yorker* 65:39-42+ Je 26 '89

How dangerous are VDT's? il *USA Today (Periodical)* 118:5 Ag '89

An invisible workplace hazard gets harder to ignore [repetitive motion injuries] M. Mallory and H. Bradford. il *Business Week* p92-3 Ja 30 '89

Remedies for a painful case of terminalitis. J. Carey. il *U.S. News & World Report* 106:60-1 Ja 9 '89

'Terminal' illness? Fears and facts. B. Politzer. il *Home Office Computing* 7:16 F '89

VDT radiation [risk of miscarriage] M. A. Pinsky. *The Nation* 248:41 Ja 9-16 '89

VIDEO EDITORS (MACHINES) See Videotape recorders and recording—Equipment

VIDEO EQUIPMENT

See also
Television projection
Television receivers
Television stations—Equipment
Video mixers
Videodisc players
Videotape recorders and recording

Class systems. J. B. Meigs. il *Rolling Stone* p93 O 19 '89

Couching toward HDTV. M. Porter. il *Gentlemen's Quarterly* 59:315+ S '89

Creating your own home theater [cover story; with editorial comment by Stan Pinkwas] F. Lovece. il *Video* 13:6, 42-5+ Je '89

Home video. J. B. Meigs. See alternate issues of Popular Mechanics beginning January 1986

Moveable feasts [personal video products] D. Wilcox. il *Video* 13:60-1 N '89

New products. L. Kesten. See issues of Video through October 1989

Once upon a time in the future [designs for children] K. Korman. il *Video* 13:50+ Ag '89

Power plays [cover story] L. B. Johnson. il *Video* 13:37-40+ Ag '89

Pro video [cover story; special section] il *Video* 13:46-8+ My '89

Video in the 90s [cover story; special section] il *Video* 13:55-62+ S '89

Video news. D. Lachenbruch. See issues of Radio-Electronics

When good things come in small packages [cover story; special section] il *Video* 13:54-7+ D '89

Advertising

Power shopping [how to decode equipment ads] M. Slovick. il *Video* 13:74-5+ O '89

Exhibitions

4 trends worth watching [Consumer Electronics Show] A. Levis. *Video* 13:6 S '89

Berlin diary [International Funkaustellung] D. Lachenbruch and A. Levis. il *Video* 13:72-4+ D '89

Bold new gear [Consumer Electronics Show; cover story] M. Fleischmann. il *Video* 13:36-9+ Ap '89

CES adapts and delivers. S. Pinkwas. il *Video* 13:10 Ag '89

CES' crystal ball. S. Pinkwas. *Video* 13:12 S '89

Nothing revolutionary, but . . . [video at the Consumer Electronics Show] il *Popular Photography* 96:50-4 Mr '89

Real time pie in the sky [video at the Consumer Electronics Show] il *Popular Photography* 96:65-8+ Ag '89

Suddenly this summer [Consumer Electronics Show] M. Fleischmann. il *Video* 13:74-7+ S '89

Maintenance and repair

Aids and devices

Hardware how-to's [video repair how-to tapes] M. Fleischmann. il *Video* 13:67-9 N '89

Periodicals

See also
Video (Periodical)

Prices

Budget edge. il *Rolling Stone* p111-12+ Je 15 '89

Testing

Gold medal gear [cover story] L. Braithwaite. il *Video* 12:58-61+ Ja '89

Hardware for home entertainment [special section] il *Consumer Reports* 54:155-71 Mr '89

A reformation of video [Reference Recordings LD-101 videodisc of test patterns] D. Ranada. il *High Fidelity (New York, N.Y.)* 39:19 Ap '89

Videotests. See issues of Video

VIDEO GAMES

See also
Atari Corp.
Balance of Power (Video game)
Bally Manufacturing Corp.
BattleTech (Video game)
Computer novels
Computer picture books for children
Empire (Video game)
Hidden Agenda (Video game)
Information systems—Games
Loom (Video game)
Nintendo Co. Ltd.
Nintendo video games
Omega (Video game)
Origin Systems, Inc.
Populous (Video game)
Sega (Firm)
SimCity (Video game)
Tengen Inc.
Tetris (Video game)
Vette! (Video game)
Violence in video games

Byte-sized baseball [two-way baseball game developed by Interactive Network] K. Modesti. il *Sport (New York, N.Y.)* 80:15 D '89

Entertainment news. R. G. Sheffield. See issues of Home Office Computing beginning July 1989

Entertainment news and hints. J. Phelan. See issues of Home Office Computing beginning September 1988 through June 1989

Extensions of our imagination. R. Lockwood. il *Personal Computing* 13:151+ O '89

Gameplay. O. S. Card. See issues of Compute! beginning May 1988

Gamescope [flying a flight simulator] D. Atkin. il *Compute!* 11:112 O '89

Gamescope [playing video golf] R. C. Leinecker. il *Compute!* 11:100 N '89

The latest sim craze [tank combat] G. Keizer. il *Compute!* 11:7 Ap '89

A microgolf game gives professionals and amateurs an equal chance for a hole in one. A. K. Dewdney. il *Scientific American* 261:120-3 N '89

Video scans [games that help adults relax] B. Lindstrom. il *Omni (New York, N.Y.)* 11:114 S '89

Video scans. B. Lindstrom. See issues of Omni (New York, N.Y.) beginning February 1989 through December 1989

Videogame market steady but tight. H. E. H. Aycock. il *Compute!* 11:105 Ja '89

Antitrust cases

Court games [antitrust suits against Nintendo by Atari and Tengen] G. Keizer. il *Compute!* 11:84 Ap '89

A game of legal punch-out [Atari sues Nintendo] il *Newsweek* 113:50 Ja 2 '89

There's a rumble in the video arcade [Nintendo gets hit with antitrust suits from Tengen and Atari] M. Shao. il *Business Week* p37 F 20 '89

Business use

Games in the office. il *Nation's Business* 77:65 O '89

Control

Tricked-out videogames. F. Vizard. il *Popular Mechanics* 166:106+ O '89

Video scans. B. Lindstrom. il *Omni (New York, N.Y.)* 11:98 My '89

Design

Computer games are complex and overlooked—but between boredom and anxiety lies the flow. D. D. Thornburg. il *Compute!* 11:10 Jl '89

Conversations: Dungeon delving with Richard Garriott. K. Ferrell. il pors *Compute!* 11:16-17 Ja '89

Judge computer games as art, respect game designers as artists. O. S. Card. il *Compute!* 11:12 Je '89

Warning: computer games under construction [game construction sets] S. Addams. il *Compute!* 11:34-7+ Mr '89

Why multimedia is multiconfusing. W. M. Hawkins. por *Personal Computing* 13:220 O '89

You've made your game—now play in it. O. S. Card. *Compute!* 11:12 Ja '89

Educational use

See also
Carmen Sandiego (Video games)

Computer games that won't hurt your head. D. Stanton. *Compute!* 11:76 D '89

Drug Alert! C. S. Holzberg. il *Compute!* 11:96-8 Ja '89

Fraction Munchers [computer program] C. S. Holzberg. il *Home Office Computing* 7:70 Jl '89

Joshua's Reading Machine. M. J. W. Ratcliff. il *Home Office Computing* 7:87 O '89

VIDEO GAMES—Educational use—*cont.*

Math Blaster Mystery. J. Zornberg. il *Home Office Computing* 7:98 N '89

NumberMaze. G. Solomon. il *Home Office Computing* 7:87 Mr '89

Return of the Dinosaurs. L. Eiser. il *Compute!* 11:126+ O '89

Search for the Titanic. N. Randall. il *Compute!* 11:110+ D '89

Exhibitions

Just (zap!) like old times [Hot circuits: a video arcade at the American Museum of the Moving Image] R. Zoglin. il *Time* 134:59 Jl 3 '89

The old soft show [Consumer Electronics Show; special section] il *Compute!* 11:6+ S '89

Health use

An AIDS game that is deadly serious [BLOCKAIDS] il *U.S. News & World Report* 107:17 S 18 '89

Prices

An offer you can't refuse [sale of Pharaoh's Revenge for $5] P. Scisco. *Compute!* 11:82 Ap '89

Testing

10 favorites from my games vault. R. Lockwood. il *Personal Computing* 13:71-2+ D '89

688 Attack Sub. R. G. Sheffield. il *Compute!* 11:64-5 Ag '89

Abrams Battle Tank [computer game] P. Scisco. il *Compute!* 11:68 Je '89

The Airplane Factory. R. G. Sheffield. il *Compute!* 11:74-5 Ag '89

Arcade games. C. D. Hanlon. il *Compute!* 11:50-5 Mr '89

Archipelagos. B. Guerra. il *Compute!* 11:112+ D '89

Battlehawks 1942. B. Guerra. il *Compute!* 11:63 Ap '89

Bubble Ghost. P. Scisco. il *Compute!* 11:98-9 Ja '89

Burn rubber [auto racing games] P. Scisco. il *Compute!* 11:30-4 Ap '89

Bytes, camera, action: play the hero in movie-quality games [Rocket Ranger, and Hostage] O. S. Card. il *Compute!* 11:12 S '89

Caveman Ugh-lympics. G. Keizer. il *Compute!* 11:68-9 My '89

Chuck Yeager's Advanced Flight Trainer 2.0. R. G. Sheffield. *Compute!* 11:116+ O '89

Cosmic Osmo. C. S. Holzberg. il *Home Office Computing* 7:98+ N '89

The disks of summer [baseball games] T. Netsel. il *Compute!* 11:28-30 Ag '89

Double Dragon. L. Poggiali. il *Compute!* 11:61+ Jl '89

Dr. Doom's Revenge! K. Ferrell. il *Compute!* 11:116+ N '89

The Duel: Test Drive II. M. McLean. il *Compute!* 11:66 Ag '89

The Duel: Test Drive II. A. Roston. *Home Office Computing* 7:94 D '89

Editors' picks for the best games of 1988. il *Home Office Computing* 7:84+ Ja '89

F-19 Stealth Fighter. B. Guerra. il *Compute!* 11:70-1 Ap '89

F-19 Stealth Fighter. S. Williams. il *Home Office Computing* 7:87-8 Mr '89

Falcon A.T. S. Williams. il *Home Office Computing* 7:91-2 F '89

Family fun & gifts [cover story; special section] il *Compute!* 11:21-4+ D '89

Final Assault [game of mountaineering] G. Keizer. il *Compute!* 11:67-8 Mr '89

Flight Simulator 3.0. R. G. Sheffield. il *Compute!* 11:68-70 Ap '89

For your IBM PC: wild and crazy games. J. H. Pluenneke. il *Business Week* p103 Ag 21 '89

Fun in the sun. J. Latimer. il *Compute!* 11:32-4 S '89

Game designs [Anacreon] J. Pournelle. *Byte* 14:112+ Ja '89

Game wars: new high-tech systems challenge Nintendo's dominance. L. Kesten. il *Video* 13:58-61+ O '89

The Games: Summer Edition. P. Scisco. il *Compute!* 11:68 F '89

Get real. H. E. H. Aycock. il *Compute!* 11:92-4+ N '89

Gift-giving gamesmanship. L. Kesten. il *Video* 13:64-7 D '89

Gold Rush. B. Guerra. il *Compute!* 11:73-4 Ag '89

Grow up! D. Atkin. il *Compute!* 11:94-6+ D '89

Guardians of Infinity: To Save Kennedy. E. Ferrell. il *Compute!* 11:65 Jl '89

Guardians of Infinity: To Save Kennedy. S. Williams. il *por Home Office Computing* 7:90 My '89

(Hard) Drivin' impressions. D. Simanaitis. il *Road & Track* 40:88+ Ag '89

Heavy Metal. M. McLean. il *Compute!* 11:106 D '89

Hillsfar. B. Guerra. il *Compute!* 11:67+ S '89

Historical games. M. McLean. il *Compute!* 11:41-2+ Je '89

Hole-in-one Miniature Golf. M. Harrison. il *Compute!* 11:116 D '89

Indiana Jones and the Temple of Doom. T. A. Summers. il *Home Office Computing* 7:88 O '89

Jack Nicklaus' Greatest 18 Holes of Major Championship Golf. S. Hudson. il *Compute!* 11:73-4 Mr '89

JetFighter: The Adventure. R. Gehorsam. il *Home Office Computing* 7:90+ My '89

Jigsaw. H. E. H. Aycock. il *Compute!* 11:74-5 My '89

Keith Van Eron's Pro Soccer. L. Poggiali. il *Compute!* 11:66-7 S '89

King's Quest IV: The Perils of Rosella. R. Gilpin. il *Home Office Computing* 7:90-1 F '89

King's Quest IV: The Perils of Rosella. D. Stanton. il *Compute!* 11:70 My '89

Leisure Suit Larry Goes Looking for Love (In Several Wrong Places). R. Gilpin. il *Home Office Computing* 7:85-7 Ap '89

Leisure Suit Larry II: Looking for Love (In Several Wrong Places). B. Guerra. il *Compute!* 11:66-7 Je '89

Life & Death. J. Latimer. il *Compute!* 11:71-2 My '89

Light-years and lasers: science fiction inside your computer [cover story; with editorial comment by Gregg Keizer] O. S. Card. il *Compute!* 11:4, 28-34 Je '89

Manhunter: New York [adventure game] J. D. Donahue. il *Home Office Computing* 7:87 Ap '89

Mental Blocks, Harrier 7. W. N. Kawamoto. il *Compute!* 11:135-6 D '89

Microleague Baseball II. A. Starkweather. il *Compute!* 11:126+ D '89

Might and Magic II [computer game] D. Langendoen. il *Home Office Computing* 7:77 Ag '89

Modem Wars. D. Langendoen. il *Home Office Computing* 7:76 S '89

Nightmare on game street [horror games] S. Addams. il *Compute!* 11:106-8+ O '89

Nine for '89 [cover story] D. Gutman. il *Compute!* 11:19-20+ Jl '89

Nobunaga's Ambition [computer simulation of sixteenth-century Japan] N. Randall. il *Compute!* 11:90+ Ja '89

PC rider [driving games] C. Weathers. il *Car and Driver* 35:107-11 S '89

Pool of Radiance [Dungeons & Dragons] S. Addams. il *Compute!* 11:62 F '89

Pow! Zap! Ping! H. Polskin. il *TV Guide* 37:28-32 D 2-8 '89

Presumed Guilty! [computer game] D. Farkas. il *Home Office Computing* 7:77 Ag '89

Programming for its own sake can lead to "one-trick pony" games [Bubble Ghost and Genghis Khan] O. S. Card. il *Compute!* 11:11 Mr '89

Quarterstaff: The Tomb of Setmoth. J. Phelan. il *Home Office Computing* 7:95-6 Je '89

Red Storm Rising. R. G. Sheffield. il *Compute!* 11:66+ F '89

Red Storm Rising [computer game] R. G. Sheffield. il *Home Office Computing* 7:88 O '89

Reel Fish'n & Rich Tauber's Bass Champ. K. Ferrell and P. Scisco. il *Compute!* 11:136+ O '89

Rocket Ranger. J. Latimer. il *Compute!* 11:65+ Ap '89

Role-playing tedium transcends the computer age [fantasy games] O. S. Card. *Compute!* 11:92 D '89

Screen gems [Jeep/Eagle Game Disk] P. Bedard. il *Car and Driver* 35:14-15 Jl '89

Sentinel Worlds I: Future Magic. J. D. Donahue. il *Home Office Computing* 7:92 Ja '89

Silpheed. D. Langendoen. il *Home Office Computing* 7:76 S '89

Software despotism: truth and fiction [Guns & Butter supply and demand video game and Allways utility for Lotus 1-2-3] E. Shapiro. il *Byte* 14:143-4 My '89

Solitaire Royale. N. Randall. il *Compute!* 11:71-2 Mr '89

Space Quest III: the Pirates of Pestulon. B. Guerra. il *Compute!* 11:128+ N '89

Space Rogue. B. Guerra. il *Compute!* 11:132 D '89

Sports games. C. D. Hanlon and M. McLean. il *Compute!* 11:43-6+ Ag '89

Steel Thunder [tank combat simulation] R. G. Sheffield. il *Compute!* 11:72+ My '89

Strategic Conquest Plus v2.0 [computer game] D. Langendoen. il *Home Office Computing* 7:100 N '89

Tetris must be a commie plot; the game's not copy-protected [Tetris; Pirates!, Annals of Rome] O. S. Card. *Compute!* 11:11 Ap '89

There's a boat in this box! [688 Attack Sub] G. Keizer. il *Compute!* 11:6 Mr '89

Ticket to Hollywood [computer game combines movie trivia and walking tour] T. A. Summers. il *Home Office Computing* 7:84 Mr '89

Ticket to Hollywood [computer game combining movie trivia and walking tour] D. English. il *Compute!* 11:77-8 My '89

Times of Lore. L. Poggiali. il *Compute!* 11:70-1 Mr '89

TKO. T. Netsel. il *Compute!* 11:72+ Ap '89

TV Sports Football. S. Anzovin. il *Compute!* 11:69-70 Je '89

Twilight Zone: Crossroads of Imagination [computer game] D. Stanton. il *Compute!* 11:71 Je '89

Video scans [Battlehawks 1942 and Zak McCracken from Lucasfilm] B. Lindstrom. il *Omni (New York, N.Y.)* 11:130 F '89

Video scans [golf] B. Lindstrom. il *Omni (New York, N.Y.)* 11:122 Mr '89

Video scans [W. Gibson's novel Neuromancer made into a video game] B. Lindstrom. il *Omni (New York, N.Y.)* 12:166 O '89

VIDEO GAMES—Testing—*cont.*

War in Middle Earth. B. Gingher. *Compute!* 11:134+ O '89

War in Middle Earth. R. G. Sheffield. il *Home Office Computing* 7:72 Jl '89

Warning: computer games under construction [game construction sets] S. Addams. il *Compute!* 11:34-7+ Mr '89

Wealth Insurance [personal investment computer game] G. McClure. il *Compute!* 11:63-4 Ap '89

Wealth Insurance helps you prepare for a roller-coaster economy. N. Maffei. il *Home Office Computing* 7:30 Ap '89

Who Framed Roger Rabbit. C. S. Holzberg. il *Compute!* 11:65-6 Je '89

Wizardry-V: Heart of the Maelstrom. J. Latimer. il *Compute!* 11:70 Jl '89

Wizardry V: The Heart of the Maelstrom. D. Langendoen. il *Home Office Computing* 7:95 Je '89

World Class Leader Board: Pro Golf Simulation. R. G. Sheffield. il *Home Office Computing* 7:100 N '89

You too can play the budget game [Fair Freeze Simulation from National Chamber Foundation] A. Holzinger. il *Nation's Business* 77:51 F '89

Zak McKracken and the Alien Mindbenders. K. Ferrell. il *Compute!* 11:82+ Ja '89

Zany Golf. D. English. il *Compute!* 11:71-2 Jl '89

Zork Zero: The Revenge of Megaboz. J. D. Donahue. il *Home Office Computing* 7:87 Mr '89

Unauthorized use

Disasters and diversions. J. Pournelle. *Byte* 14:115-16 O '89

Germany (West)

Nazi software: the ultimate virus. il *Newsweek* 113:32 Ja 23 '89

VIDEO GAMES AND WOMEN

Giving games the female touch. H. E. H. Aycock. il *Compute!* 11:10 Ap '89

VIDEO GAMES AND YOUTH

Games for girls: fun without bloodshed [suggested game based on Ann M. Martin's The Baby-sitters Club series] O. S. Card. il *Compute!* 11:12 Ag '89

The iffy virtues of videogames. *U.S. News & World Report* 107:66 O 2 '89

The Nintendo kid. J. Adler. il *Newsweek* 113:64-8 Mr 6 '89

The video advantage. J. Segal and Z. Segal. il *Parents* 64:194 Mr '89

"We got trouble. Right here in Silicon Valley . . . A. R. Levitan. *Compute!* 11:88+ Ap '89

VIDEO GAMES AS GIFTS

Family fun & gifts [cover story; special section] il *Compute!* 11:21-4+ D '89

Games for the whole gang [Christmas] J. Latimer. il *Home Office Computing* 7:92+ N '89

Gift-giving gamesmanship. L. Kesten. il *Video* 13:64-7 D '89

Pow! Zap! Ping! H. Polskin. il *TV Guide* 37:28-32 D 2-8 '89

VIDEO GRAPHICS ARRAY *See* VGA (Video graphics array)

VIDEO JUKEBOX NETWORK, INC.

Pay-per-view music videos: will viewers ante up to play them? R. Katz. il *Channels (New York, N.Y.: 1986)* 9:16 Ja '89

VIDEO MAGAZINES *See* Periodicals on videotapes

VIDEO MIXERS

Time-base corrector. il *Radio-Electronics* 60:12 F '89

VIDEO MONITORS

Testing

Buyer's guide: VGA monitors [special section] il *Personal Computing* 13:137-41+ Jl '89

A Cornerstone for building documents [Cornerstone Single Page XL subsystem] A. F. Lent. il *Byte* 14:82 N '89

Hitachi VHS VCR with LCD monitor. il *Video* 13:48+ N '89

Impressive full-page display system [NEC MonoGraph System] S. Chen. il *Home Office Computing* 7:55-6 Jl '89

The LAN terminal alternative [Wyse WY-212 and TeleVideo TS2 TeleStation diskless PCs] B. Catchings and M. L. Van Name. il *Byte* 14:211-14 N '89

Large-screen eye relief [KDS-1984 TriSync color monitor] S. Miastkowski. *Byte* 14:88 D '89

Mac color by SCSI [ScuzzyGraph II external graphics display] H. Eglowstein. *Byte* 14:235 D '89

Magnavox 3-inch monitor/receiver [CK1050] il *Video* 13:37+ O '89

Mitsubishi 35-inch monitor/receiver. il *Video* 12:30-1+ Mr '89

Monitor and VGA card: a versatile, powerful pair [Relisys VGA/Multiscan Monitor Bundle] H. F. Beechhold. il *Home Office Computing* 7:64-5 Ja '89

A multiscanning monitor with a future [NEC MultiSync 3D] R. Lockwood. il *Personal Computing* 13:193 S '89

NAD 13-inch monitor/receiver. il *Video* 13:32+ Ap '89

NAD MR-13 monitor/receiver. E. J. Foster. il *High Fidelity (New York, N.Y.)* 39:25-7 My '89

NEC Multisync GS: more than just black and white. S. Miller. il *Home Office Computing* 7:65 Ja '89

PixC leaves windows overhead in the dust. B. Smith. il *Byte* 14:202 S '89

Proton's 31-inch monitor/receiver. il *Video* 13:28-9 My '89

Sony 32-inch monitor/receiver [KV-32XBR10] il *Video* 13:46-7+ N '89

Tera 629C video monitor/receiver. E. J. Foster. il *High Fidelity (New York, N.Y.)* 39:30+ F '89

Toshiba 30-inch monitor/receiver. il *Video* 13:37+ Jl '89

Toshiba 30-inch monitor/receiver with Carver audio. il *Video* 13:35+ Ag '89

Upscale monitors [large-screen monitors] S. Apiki and S. Diehl. il *Byte* 14:162-72+ Mr '89

Vivid VGA monitors. H. F. Beechhold. il *Home Office Computing* 7:44-7 Jl '89

Zenith 31-inch monitor/receiver [ZB3193H] il *Video* 13:31+ Jl '89

VIDEO PROJECTORS

Testing

Kodak portable video projector [LC500] il *Video* 12:28-9+ F '89

VIDEO PUBLISHERS *See* Videotape industry

VIDEO RECORDS *See* Videodiscs

VIDEO SOFTWARE DEALERS ASSOCIATION

More book-video tie-ins on display at VSDA meeting. A. Wickstrom. il *Publishers Weekly* 236:46+ S 1 '89

VIDEO STORES

See also

Blockbuster Entertainment Corp.

Spec's Music, Inc.

Video Software Dealers Association

Random, Bantam to distribute audiotapes through video stores. *Publishers Weekly* 236:27 D 1 '89

Refining the fine art of selling. J. Sulski. *Video* 13:68+ S '89

Who's minding the store? A. Levis. *Video* 13:6 O '89

Advertising

Power shopping [how to decode equipment ads] M. Slovick. il *Video* 13:74-5+ O '89

Laws and regulations

Nightmare on Video Street, part 1: the legislators [bids to ban rentals of violent tapes to kids] L. Therrien. il *Business Week* p34 S 11 '89

VIDEO TELEPHONE *See* Videophones

VIDEO TITLING *See* Videotapes—Titling

VIDEO TRANSFER SYSTEM *See* Film-to-video transfer system

VIDEODISC PLAYERS

See also

Combination disc players

Compact disc video

Four video fancies that never took flight [EVR, Cartrivision, Holotape and Telcan] D. Lachenbruch. il *Video* 13:116 Jl '89

Seeing is believing. G. Burks. il *Forbes* 143:144-5 My 1 '89

Technological turkeys [Selectavision] J. S. Gordon. il *American Heritage* 40:18+ My/Je '89

Testing

Deck the halls with holiday hardware. M. Slovick. il *Video* 13:68-70 D '89

VIDEODISC RECORDERS AND RECORDING

Closing in on recordable videodiscs. R. Woodcock. il *Video* 13:18 S '89

VIDEODISC REVIEWS

Discs [year's best] M. Fleischmann. il *Video* 12:69-71 Ja '89

Single works

2001: a space odyssey

Video 12:63-4 Mr '89. M. Fleischmann

Blade runner

American Film il 15:72 D '89. D. Rochester

E.T. the extra-terrestrial

Rolling Stone il p127 F 9 '89. J. B. Meigs

The magnificent Ambersons

American Film il 15:72 D '89. D. Rochester

North by northwest

Video 12:63-4 Mr '89. M. Fleischmann

Singin' in the rain

Video il 12:63-4 Mr '89. M. Fleischmann

The Wizard of Oz

Video il 12:63-4 Mr '89. M. Fleischmann

VIDEODISCS

See also

Compact disc video

Computer novels

Interactive video

Laser sharp. F. Vizard. il *Popular Mechanics* 166:109-10 O '89

A new spin on videodiscs. M. Rogers. il *Newsweek* 113:68-9 Je 5 '89

Pioneer's pioneering is finally paying off. N. Gross. il *Business Week* p89 D 18 '89

Seeing is believing. G. Burks. il *Forbes* 143:144-5 My 1 '89

The shape of discs to come. F. Lovece. il *Video* 13:72-3 S '89

VIDEODISCS—cont.

Motion pictures

Archaeology by laser light. J. Cocks. il *Time* 133:72 F 6 '89

Compelling evidence. D. Rochester. il *American Film* 15:72 D '89

The letterbox advantage [scanned and letterboxed versions of wide screen films] M. Fleischmann. il *Video* 13:21-3 Jl '89

Power plays [cover story] L. B. Johnson. il *Video* 13:37-40+ Ag '89

The second time around [added material] R. Gunnerson. il *Video* 13:68-70 O '89

Tapes & discs Yule love. M. Fleischmann. il *Video* 13:59-61+ D '89

Opera

High beam. C. J. Luten. *Opera News* 53:44-5 Mr 18 '89
Ring fever. P. G. Davis. il *New York* 22:74+ Ap 3 '89
Surprise packages. P. G. Davis. il *New York* 22:108-10 Ap 10 '89

Test patterns

A reformation of video [Reference Recordings LD-101 videodisc of test patterns] D. Ranada. il *High Fidelity (New York, N.Y.)* 39:19 Ap '89

VIDEOHARP

Computers you control with a wave of your hand. M. Schroeder. il por *Business Week* p142+ F 20 '89

VIDEOPHONES

Around the world in six seconds. C. Noyes. il *Ladies' Home Journal* 106:232 N '89

Videophones come of age [Mitsubishi Visitel LU-500, Sony PCT-15] F. Vizard. il *Popular Mechanics* 166:72-4 Ja '89

VIDEOTAPE, MAGNETIC *See* Tape, Magnetic

VIDEOTAPE INDUSTRY

See also
Artec, Inc.
MPI HomeVideo (Firm)
Mystic Fire Video, Inc.
Paramount Home Video (Firm)
Vestron Inc.
Walt Disney Home Video

Audio/video plus. See occasional issues of Publishers Weekly beginning May 9, 1986

Ethical aspects

MCA suspends video head for allegedly funneling funds to Mafia [E. F. Giaquinto] P. Sweeting. *Publishers Weekly* 235:27 Ja 13 '89

VIDEOTAPE RECORDERS AND RECORDING

See also
Film-to-video transfer system
Interactive video
Magus Video Productions
Television receivers—Videotape recorder combination
Video Data Services

8mm videotape comes to life [Hi8] D. Ranada. il *High Fidelity (New York, N.Y.)* 39:18 My '89

Compact refinements battle 8mm gains. R. Woodcock. il *Video* 13:156 S '89

Decks that mean business [industrial VCRs] M. Heiss. il *Video* 13:56-8+ My '89

Eraser heads & feather dusters. il *Video* 13:70-1 N '89

Ergonomically speaking. M. Fleischmann. il *Channels (New York, N.Y.: 1986)* 9:98 D '89

Four video fancies that never took flight [EVR, Cartrivision, Holotape and Telcan] D. Lachenbruch. il *Video* 13:116 Jl '89

The future of digital video. R. Woodcock. il *Video* 12:32-3 Ja '89

Lights! Camera! Action! [home videos] A. Ensanian. il *Popular Mechanics* 166:102-3+ Jl '89

New tape transports speed VCR action. R. Woodcock. il *Video* 13:28+ O '89

Power trips [choosing advanced camcorders and VCRs] P. Utz. il *Video* 13:46-8+ My '89

Reinventing the VCR. S. J. Forbis. il *Video* 13:70-3+ S '89

Take the best home videos. D. S. Machlowitz. il *Parents* 64:64+ Ag '89

Tape for two [dual-deck VCR] il *Time* 133:62 Je 19 '89

Tape tracks. R. Long. See issues of High Fidelity (New York, N.Y.) beginning May 1986 through July 1989

Video journal. E. Stecker. See issues of Popular Photography beginning October 1989

Whatever happened to Betamax? J. Cohen. il *Consumers' Research Magazine* 72:28-9 My '89

Cameras

See Video cameras

Control

Remote control extender. R. A. Heil. il *Radio-Electronics* 60:41-4 My '89

Equipment

See also
Desktop video

Best boys, grips and gaffers [accessories] F. Vizard. il *Popular Mechanics* 166:112+ Jl '89

Computer aided video [Amiga 2000] K. D. Morton and W. M. Scott, III. il *Radio-Electronics* 60 ComputerDigest:93-7+ Mr '89

Cutting room [editing equipment] F. Vizard. il *Popular Mechanics* 166:166+ Jl '89

Hama editing controller and character generator [VideoCut 21 and VideoScript 51] il *Video* 12:42-4 Ja '89

Hama Video Cut 10: professional editing for 8mm video. S. Sweetow. il *Petersen's Photographic Magazine* 17:52-3 Ap '89

Olympus Woodbury Editing Controller. S. Sweetow. il *Petersen's Photographic Magazine* 17:64-5 Ja '89

The relapse of chroma phobia [luminance resolution vs. chrominance resolution] D. Ranada. il *High Fidelity (New York, N.Y.)* 39:17 Jl '89

Shoot & edit like a pro [cover story; special section] il *Video* 12:39-48+ Mr '89

Video scene switcher (I) [cover story] W. Sheets and R. F. Graf. il *Radio-Electronics* 60:33-8 N '89

Video scene switcher (II). W. Sheets and R. F. Graf. il *Radio-Electronics* 60:42-4+ D '89

Videonics Direct-ED. S. Sweetow. il *Petersen's Photographic Magazine* 18:75+ Je '89

Light and lighting

Latest lights for video [Photokina] il *Popular Photography* 96:96 Ja '89

Learning the light stuff. J. R. Caruso and M. E. Arthur. il *Video* 13:43-6+ Jl '89

Maintenance and repair

Keep your VCR healthy. P. M. Hansen. il *Radio-Electronics* 60:61-4 Mr '89

Keep your VCR healthy. P. M. Hansen. il *Radio-Electronics* 60:55-8 S '89

Speed up VCR troubleshooting. J. Emerich. il *Radio-Electronics* 60:65-7 Mr '89

Tune up your VCR [cover story] G. McComb. il *Video* 12:37-41+ F '89

Manufacture

See Television equipment industry

Noise

Digital dustbroom [NEC's DS-8000U VCR] F. Vizard. il *Popular Mechanics* 166:46 F '89

Patents

Dual-cassette VCR [Go-Video] W. J. Hawkins. il *Popular Science* 235:90 N '89

A roll of the dice [Go-Video's patent on dual cassette recorder and antitrust suit against Japanese firms] W. P. Barrett. il *Forbes* 143:81 F 20 '89

Prices

Winning the mid-price VCR challenge [cover story] M. Fleischmann. il *Video* 13:38-42 Jl '89

Sound quality

Hi-fi VCR's: a buying guide. il *Stereo Review* 54:74-9 Ap '89

JVC HR-S5000U Super VHS hi-fi VCR. E. J. Foster. il *High Fidelity (New York, N.Y.)* 39:32+ Ap '89

NEC super VHS hi-fi VCR. il *Video* 13:38+ Je '89

Shure HTS Theater Reference System. il *Video* 13:40-1+ Je '89

Shure HTS Theater Reference System. D. Ranada. il *High Fidelity (New York, N.Y.)* 39:36-9 Jl '89

Sony hi-fi VHS-VCR [SLV-757] il *Video* 13:50+ S '89

Special effects

See also
Desktop video

Hocus focus. J. R. Caruso and M. E. Arthur. il *Video* 13:83-5+ S '89

Simple tricks for great F/X. J. R. Caruso and M. E. Arthur. il *Video* 13:40-3 Ap '89

Study and teaching

Managing the influence of television through the discipline of video. W. Kennedy. bibl f *Design for Arts in Education* 90:26-8 Mr/Ap '89

Testing

Codebusters [multistandard VCR's] D. Gordon. il *Video* 12:56+ Mr '89

Deck the halls with holiday hardward. M. Slovick. il *Video* 13:68-70 D '89

Deluxe decks. M. Slovick. il *Video* 13:45-9+ O '89

Digital dustbroom [NEC's DS-8000U VCR] F. Vizard. il *Popular Mechanics* 166:46 F '89

Fisher S-VHS VCR. il *Video* 13:32-3+ Ag '89

Here's looking at you [Bang & Olufsen's Beovision TV and Beocord VX5000 S-VHS VCR] L. Braithwaite. il *Video* 12:78-9+ Ja '89

High-priced video cassette recorders. il *Consumer Reports* 54:94-9 D '89

Hitachi VHS VCR with LCD monitor. il *Video* 13:48+ N '89

JVC HR-S5000U Super VHS hi-fi VCR. E. J. Foster. il *High Fidelity (New York, N.Y.)* 39:32+ Ap '89

JVC Super VHS editing VCR [HR-S10000U] il *Video* 13:36-7+ O '89

Mitsubishi Super VHS VCR [HS-U71] il *Video* 13:44-5+ N '89

NEC super VHS hi-fi VCR. il *Video* 13:38+ Je '89

Pioneer S-VHS VCR with digital effects. il *Video* 13:34-5 Ap '89

Sharp VHS VCR [VC-G960] il *Video* 12:30+ F '89

Sony ED Beta VCR. il *Video* 13:26-7+ My '89

Sony hi-fi VHS-VCR [SLV-757] il *Video* 13:50+ S '89

VIDEOTAPE RECORDERS AND RECORDING — Testing
—cont.

Sony Hi8 VCR. il *Video* 13:36-7+ Je '89

Sony VHS VCR [SLV-70HF] il *Video* 12:36-7+ Ja '89

Super shootout. M. Fleischmann. il *Video* 13:59-60+ My '89

Super-VHS video recorder [JVC HR-S5000U] il *Radio-Electronics* 60:26-7 Ja '89

Toshiba Super VHS hi-fi editing VCR [SV-R990] il *Video* 13:46-7+ D '89

VCR's: a look at the top of the line. il *Consumer Reports* 54:167-70 Mr '89

Winning the mid-price VCR challenge [cover story] M. Fleischmann. il *Video* 13:38-42 Jl '89

VIDEOTAPE REVIEWS

People picks & pans. See issues of People Weekly

Programming. See issues of Video

Tapes [best videocassettes of 1988] I. Robbins. il *Video* 12:62-6+ Ja '89

Videos. R. S. Rothenberg. See issues of USA Today (Periodical) begining May 1988

Single works

18 tips from 18 legends of golf
  Video il 12:90 Ja '89. J. Bessman

Above the law
  Video 12:83-4 Ja '89. D. Schweiger

The accused
  Video il 13:62+ Jl '89. J. Young

The adventures of Baron Munchausen
  American Film il 15:70 N '89. P. Rainer

Alien nation
  Video il 13:60 Ag '89. J. Walker

Another woman
  Video 13:62+ Je '89. I. Robbins

Au revoir les enfants
  Video il 13:60 Ap '89. R. Gehr

Babette's feast
  Video il 13:60 Ap '89. R. Gehr

Baby, it's you
  Video il 13:78+ N '89. J. Young

Bagdad Cafe
  Video il 12:61-2 F '89. M. Coyle

Batman
  Video il 13:80-1+ D '89. B. Eder

Batteries not included
  Video il 12:89 Ja '89. M. Coyle

Beaches
  Video il 13:80+ O '89. R. Gehr

Betrayed
  Video il 13:60 Ap '89. R. Gehr

Big
  Video il 13:57 Ap '89. J. Young

Big top Pee-wee
  Video il 12:61 F '89. B. Walters

The blob
  Video il 12:86+ Ja '89. M. Pierson

Bull Durham
  Video il 12:61-2 Mr '89. D. Schweiger

The 'burbs
  Video il 13:91+ S '89. J. Young

Clean and sober
  Video il 13:76 My '89. J. Young

Cocktail
  Video il 13:61 Je '89. J. Young

Cocoon: the return
  Video il 13:60+ Ag '89. J. Walker

Colors
  Video il 12:81-2 Ja '89. I. Robbins

Coming to America
  Video il 13:73 My '89. R. Gehr

Cousins
  Video il 13:77+ N '89. J. Walker

Crossing Delancey
  Video il 13:75 My '89. J. Bernard

A cry in the dark
  American Film il 14:72 Je '89. P. Rainer
  Video il 13:62 Jl '89. J. Young

Dangerous liaisons
  American Film il 14:64 Jl/Ag '89. P. Rainer
  Video il 13:59 Ag '89. J. Bernard

The dead
  Video il 12:82-3 Ja '89. S. L. Siegel

Dead calm
  Video il 13:79 N '89. J. Silberg

Dead ringers
  Video il 13:62+ Je '89. I. Robbins

Dear America: letters home from Vietnam
  Video il 13:74 My '89. I. Robbins

Die hard
  Video il 12:61 Mr '89. L. Kesten

Dirty rotten scoundrels
  Video il 13:63 Jl '89. J. Walker

The dream team
  Video il 13:77 N '89. J. Walker

Eat the rich
  Video 12:85 Ja '89. I. Robbins

Edible wild plants
  BioScience 39:646 O '89. J. C. Cavender

Fairport Convention: It all comes 'round again
  Rolling Stone il p116 Mr 9 '89. D. Fricke

A fish called Wanda
  Video 13:59 Ap '89. J. Walker

Five easy pieces
  Video il 12:84-5 Ja '89. F. Lovece

The fly II
  Video il 13:81 O '89. D. Schweiger

Forever, Lulu
  Video il 12:85 Ja '89. D. Wheeler

Funny farm
  Video il 12:83 Ja '89. J. Walker

Ghostbusters II
  Video il 13:87 D '89. I. Reitman

Gorillas in the mist
  Video il 13:64 Je '89. S. L. Siegel

Heathers
  Video il 13:88+ S '89. I. Robbins

Her alibi
  Video il 13:79 O '89. M. Pierson

High spirits
  Video il 13:63 Jl '89. J. Walker

Jack Nicklaus shows you the greatest 18 holes of major championship golf
  Video il 12:90 Ja '89. J. Bessman

Jack's back
  Video 12:86 Ja '89. J. Walker

Jackson, Michael: Moonwalker
  Rolling Stone il p128 F 9 '89. J. Farber

JFK remembered
  USA Today (Periodical) il 117:97 Ja '89. R. S. Rothenberg

Knowledge navigator
  Technology Review il 92:74-5 F/Mr '89. R. Howard

The land before time
  Video il 13:80 N '89. M. Meyer

The last temptation of Christ
  American Film il 14:12 Jl/Ag '89. C. Koseluk
  Video il 13:78 O '89. I. Robbins

Lean on me
  Video il 13:78+ N '89. J. Young

Lost angels
  Video il 13:78 N '89. J. Young

Madame Sousatzka
  Video 13:59 Ag '89. J. Bernard

The magic Christian
  Video il 13:74 My '89. I. Robbins

Major league
  Video il 13:77 N '89. J. Walker

Married to the Mob
  Video il 12:62 Mr '89. S. L. Siegel

Matador
  American Film il 15:70 N '89. P. Rainer

Midnight run
  Video il 13:74+ My '89. I. Robbins

Mississippi burning
  Video il 13:57 Ag '89. S. L. Siegel

Moon over Parador
  Video il 13:59 Ap '89. J. Walker

My stepmother is an alien
  Video 13:63 Jl '89. J. Walker

The naked gun
  Video 13:91 S '89. J. Young

A nightmare on Elm Street, part 4: The dream master
  Video 12:62 F '89. L. Kesten

Not of this earth
  Video il 12:85-6 Ja '89. R. Swan

Off limits
  Video 12:83 Ja '89. D. Schweiger

Parents
  Video il 13:62 Je '89. I. Robbins

Pelle the conqueror
  Video 13:59+ Ag '89. J. Bernard

The Presidio
  Video il 12:64 Mr '89. D. Schweiger

The prince of Pennsylvania
  Video il 13:58+ Ag '89. I. Robbins

Punchline
  Video 12:62-3 Mr '89. R. Granger

The Rachel papers
  Video il 13:88 D '89. I. Robbins

Rain man
  Video il 13:87 S '89. S. Isler

Red heat
  Video il 12:60 F '89. I. Robbins

Return of the killer tomatoes: the sequel
  Video 12:86+ Ja '89. M. Pierson

Salaam Bombay!
  American Film il 14:64 S '89. P. Rainer
  Video 13:80 O '89. R. Gehr

Say anything
  Video il 13:88 D '89. I. Robbins

Scandal
  Video il 13:76 N '89. I. Robbins

Scenes from the class struggle in Beverly Hills
  Video il 13:76+ N '89. I. Robbins

Scrooged
  Video il 13:89 D '89. R. Gehr

VIDEOTAPE REVIEWS—Single works—*cont.*

Shy people
  Video il 12:84 Ja '89. T. Soter
Skin deep
  Video il 13:76+ N '89. I. Robbins
Slaves of New York
  Video il 13:78+ O '89. I. Robbins
Someone to love
  Psychology Today 23:78 Je '89. W. Herbert
Spike of Bensonhurst
  Video 13:59 Ap '89. J. Walker
Springsteen, Bruce: Video anthology/1978-88
  Rolling Stone il p128 F 9 '89. J. Farber
  Stereo Review il 54:110 Je '89. L. Meredith
Stand and deliver
  Video il 12:82 Ja '89. J. Young
Sullivan's travels
  Video 13:64 Jl '89. M. Fleischmann
Sweet smell of success
  Video 13:64 Jl '89. M. Fleischmann
Talk radio
  Video il 13:59+ Ag '89. J. Bernard
Tequila sunrise
  Video il 13:94 S '89. R. Gehr
Things change
  Video 13:63 Je '89. M. Pierson
Three men and a baby
  Video il 12:59-60 F '89. J. Young
True believer
  Video il 13:58 Ag '89. I. Robbins
Tucker: the man and his dream
  Video il 13:76 My '89. J. Young
Twins
  Video il 13:61 Jl '89. J. Bernard
The unbearable lightness of being
  Video il 12:63 Mr '89. S. L. Siegel
Vibes
  Video il 12:62 F '89. D. Schweiger
Who framed Roger Rabbit
  Video il 13:77 O '89. S. L. Siegel
Withnail and I
  Video 12:86 Ja '89. I. Robbins
Without a clue
  Video il 13:63 Je '89. M. Pierson
Women on the verge of a nervous breakdown
  American Film il 15:70 D '89. P. Rainer
Working girl
  Video il 13:75 N '89. J. Bernard
A world apart
  American Film il 15:102 O '89. P. Rainer
Young guns
  Video il 12:60-1 F '89. D. Wheeler
VIDEOTAPES
  See also
    Advertising mediums—Videotapes
    Birds in videotapes
    Booksellers and bookselling—Videotapes
    Computers—Videotape use
    Film-to-video transfer system
    Indians (American) in videotapes
    Infants in videotapes
    Interactive video
    Motion picture industry in videotapes
    Native peoples in videotapes
    Periodicals on videotapes
    Race relations in videotapes
    Video art
    Video stores
    Wine in videotapes
Fall audio and video. J. Zinsser. il *Publishers Weekly* 236:27-8+ Ag 4 '89
Spring audio and video. J. Zinsser. il *Publishers Weekly* 235:40+ F 3 '89

Accounting use
Accounting help! [video and disk tutorials] S. Miller. il *Home Office Computing* 7:32 Mr '89

Amateur recordings
A few new angles on home videomaking [importance of camera angle] E. Stecker. il *Video* 13:38+ D '89

Anecdotes, facetiae, satire, etc.
Mondo video. L. Kesten. il *Video* 12:72-3+ Ja '89

Animated films
  See also
    Western Publishing Group, Inc.
Cartoons: not just for kids. D. Goldman. il *Scholastic Update (Teachers' edition)* 121:28 Mr 10 '89
The Hanna-Barbera cartoons: compounding Bible ignorance? [cover story] H. L. Turner and others. il *The Christian Century* 106:231-4 Mr 1 '89
McGee and me: growing up is hard to do [series coproduced by Focus on the Family and Tyndale House Publishers] R. M. Anker. il *Christianity Today* 33:77 N 3 '89

Art use
For couch potatoes with taste. N. Frazier. il *New Choices for the Best Years* 29:9 N '89

Astronomical use
Drawing Mars from video. R. N. Clark. il *Sky and Telescope* 77:476 My '89

Recording the sky on videotape [interview with D. Brewer] M. B. Pepin. il *Astronomy* 17:86-9 S '89
SETI on video [The Quest for Contact] R. Burnham. *Astronomy* 17:105 Jl '89

Automotive use
Video car repair. P. Brand. il *The Family Handyman* 39:72-3 Ja '89

Aviation use
Vertical video [Sporty's So you want to fly helicopters?] J. M. McClellan. il *Flying* 116:30 My '89

Awards
  See also
    Grand Prix International Vidéo-Danse
    MTV Video Music Awards

Bible stories
The Hanna-Barbera cartoons: compounding Bible ignorance? [cover story] H. L. Turner and others. il *The Christian Century* 106:231-4 Mr 1 '89

Business use
It's show time for business. S. S. King. il *Nation's Business* 77:54-6 Ap '89

Children's music
Two inventive mothers hit the tot charts with Baby songs [work of A. Weintraub and B. McEwen] L. Lague. il pors *People Weekly* 31:95-6 Ja 16 '89

Children's use
  See also
    Western Publishing Group, Inc.
15 best videos for kids. P. Collins. il *Good Housekeeping* 209:114 O '89
Children's audio and video. *Publishers Weekly* 235:195-8 F 24 '89
Children's fall audio and video. J. Zinsser. il *Publishers Weekly* 236:188+ Jl 28 '89
Children's video attracting new players; distribution called key. G. Clarkin. *Publishers Weekly* 235:50 My 5 '89
Children's videos. P. Collins. il *Good Housekeeping* 208:66 Ap '89
Kidvid. M. Meyer. See issues of Video
New kids' shows worth watching. M. Silver. il *U.S. News & World Report* 107:64-5 Ag 21 '89
Reel great gifts [Christmas] M. Meyer. il *Redbook* 174:37 D '89
Video: 'the Disney effect?'. J. Greco. *Publishers Weekly* 235:194 F 24 '89
The year's best for kids. C. Berman. il *Parents* 64:67+ N '89

Classical music
Star treks [documentaries starring classical musicians] P. G. Davis. il *New York* 22:58+ Ja 23 '89

Comedy
The best laughs on video. R. Zacks. il *TV Guide* 37:21-2 N 11-17 '89
Larry "Bud" Melman bakes a video potato. J. Bernard. il por *Video* 12:14 Mr '89
Tom Smothers' flick of the wrist [Yo-Yo Man] F. Lovece. il pors *Video* 12:14 Mr '89

Dance
  See also
    Grand Prix International Vidéo-Danse
Dancevideo. D. Towers. See issues of Dance Magazine beginning November 1984

Do-it-yourself work
Do-it-yourself videotapes. D. Owen. il *The Atlantic* 264:97-100 S '89
Hardware how-to's [video repair how-to tapes] M. Fleischmann. il *Video* 13:67-9 N '89

Editing
  See also
    Desktop video
ABC's of editing. J. R. Caruso and M. E. Arthur. il *Video* 13:55-7+ O '89
Computer aided video [Amiga 2000] K. D. Morton and W. M. Scott, III. il *Radio-Electronics* 60 ComputerDigest:93-7+ Mr '89
Cutting room [editing equipment] F. Vizard. il *Popular Mechanics* 166:106+ Jl '89
Deluxe decks. M. Slovick. il *Video* 13:45-9+ O '89
Family vacation videos: how to make them really fun to watch. J. Elder. il *Better Homes and Gardens* 67:162 Ap '89
Hama editing controller and character generator [VideoCut 21 and VideoScript 51] il *Video* 12:42-4 Ja '89
Hama Video Cut 10: professional editing for 8mm video. S. Sweetow. il *Petersen's Photographic Magazine* 17:52-3 Ap '89
How suite it is [self-service editing rooms] S. Sweetow. il *Video* 13:51-2+ O '89
JVC Super VHS editing VCR [HR-S10000U] il *Video* 13:36-7+ O '89
Olympus Woodbury Editing Controller. S. Sweetow. il *Petersen's Photographic Magazine* 17:64-5 Ja '89
Pro Edit Super VHS camcorder. il *Video* 13:33+ Ag '89
RCA Pro Edit VHS camcorder. il *Video* 12:32+ Mr '89
Shoot & edit like a pro [cover story; special section] il *Video* 12:39-48+ Mr '89

VIDEOTAPES—Editing—*cont.*

Speeding up the cutting [random access television editing machines] F. Moore. il *Channels (New York, N.Y.: 1986)* 9:72 S '89

Toshiba Super VHS hi-fi editing VCR [SV-R990] il *Video* 13:46-7+ D '89

Video scene switcher (I) [cover story] W. Sheets and R. F. Graf. il *Radio-Electronics* 60:33-8 N '89

Video scene switcher (II). W. Sheets and R. F. Graf. il *Radio-Electronics* 60:42-4+ D '89

Videonics Direct-ED. S. Sweetow. il *Petersen's Photographic Magazine* 18:75+ Je '89

Educational use

Kidvid. M. Meyer. See issues of Video

Photo videotapes: can they really teach you something? E. Stecker. il *Popular Photography* 96:50-5+ F '89

Exercise use

Aerobic videos: ten you can trust. K. L. Clark and T. Thompson. il *Women's Sports & Fitness* 11:44-6+ S '89

How to choose exercise videos. S. L. Fisher. il *Good Housekeeping* 208:116 My '89

The latest tapes [aerobics] il *Women's Sports & Fitness* 11:23-4 Ja/F '89

LHJ's exercise video review. il *Ladies' Home Journal* 106:36 S '89

Shape-up tapes. il *Mademoiselle* 95:36 F '89

The video queens. R. Urquhart. il *Vogue* 179:216+ Ap '89

Video shape-ups. H. Rubin. il *New Choices for the Best Years* 29:12 Jl '89

Weighing the workouts. E. Liner. il *Video* 13:54-6 Ag '89

Exhibitions

Audio and video: a tour of the ABA convention. J. Zinsser. il *Publishers Weekly* 236:34-6 Jl 7 '89

Fashion

SI's swimsuit issue: more than meets the eye. D. Lieberman. il *Business Week* p52 Ja 16 '89

Financial services use

Okay, videotaping buffs, let's get real! C. E. Cohen. il *Money* 18:117-19+ Ja '89

Health use

District approach to primary health care. il *World Health* p20 My '89

Video breast self-examination. il *Glamour* 87:240+ F '89

Hotel use

Palm Springs ploy [movie companies sue La Mancha Private Club & Villas over royalties from videotapes shown in hotel rooms] P. Newcomb. il *Forbes* 143:100 Mr 20 '89

Household inventory use

See Household records

Jazz music

Jazz on videotape. G. Santoro. *The Nation* 249:30-2 Jl 3 '89

Success, failure and hard work [documentaries from Rhapsody Films] K. Whitehead. *Down Beat* 56:40+ Mr '89

VCR verities & vexations. F.-J. Hadley. il *Down Beat* 56:51 D '89

Marketing

Batman boffo in video rescue. I. Mayer. il *Channels (New York, N.Y.: 1986)* 9:85 D '89

The coming of audio/video phone-based promotions. I. Mayer. il *Publishers Weekly* 235:73-4 My 3 '89

Doing business with videotex [Artec Inc.'s use of Prodigy network in video cassette marketing] M. Antonoff. il *Personal Computing* 13:77 My '89

Giving new meaning to direct marketing, three filmmakers hit the bricks to sell their own movie [Brickmobile tours U.S. to sell Only a buck] il *People Weekly* 31:107 Ap 10 '89

Margins and returns still bedevil video publishers in bookstores [panel at Home Video Show] P. Sweeting. il *Publishers Weekly* 235:33 Ap 14 '89

Special-interest video producers look for a promotional push. P. Sweeting. il *Publishers Weekly* 235:51 My 5 '89

Video publishers showing renewed interest in bookstore distribution. P. Sweeting. il *Publishers Weekly* 235:30-1+ F 3 '89

"We are a society of collectors" [rack jobber Handleman Co.] L. Gubernick. il *Forbes* 144:80 Jl 24 '89

Meteorological use

Audio visuals. E. Brotak. *Weatherwise* 42:335 D '89

Audio visuals about the weather. E. Brotak. *Weatherwise* 42:55 F '89

Audio visuals about the weather. E. Brotak. *Weatherwise* 42:216 Ag '89

Moral and religious aspects

See also

Sex in videotapes

Violence in videotapes

Is reel life real? M. E. Ashcroft. il *Christianity Today* 33:29-30 F 17 '89

Motion pictures

See also

Archive Film Productions Inc.

10 great movies to watch over and over. J. Cocks. il *TV Guide* 37:13-17 Ag 5-11 '89

Akira Kurosawa. G. Peary. il pors *American Film* 14:80-2 Ap '89

Barbara Stanwyck. G. Peary. il pors *American Film* 14:60-3 Jl/Ag '89

Betting on Batman. B. Eder. il *Video* 13:80-1+ D '89

Carole Lombard. A. Sarris. il pors *American Film* 14:62-4 Mr '89

Cinema of the unknown [documentaries about filmmaking] F. Thompson. il *American Film* 15:64-6+ N '89

Couch-potato classics. R. Rosenbaum. il *Mademoiselle* 95:112+ Mr '89

Giving new meaning to direct marketing, three filmmakers hit the bricks to sell their own movie [Brickmobile tours U.S. to sell Only a buck] il *People Weekly* 31:107 Ap 10 '89

Great expectations [celebrities discuss most wanted videotapes for Christmas] J. Bernard. il *Video* 13:62-3 D '89

Horror's heaviest hitter [S. King on video] F. Lovece. il por *Video* 13:46-9+ Ag '89

Macrovision under the microscope. G. McComb. il *Video* 13:62-7+ O '89

Missing on video. F. Lovece. il *Video* 13:16 S '89

Movies [comedy films] K. Turan. il *Gentlemen's Quarterly* 59:93+ Ag '89

A new look for subtitles. J. Bernard. il *Video* 13:15+ O '89

New video releases. See issues of American Film

Otto Preminger. A. Sarris. il por *American Film* 14:69-71 Je '89

Palm Springs ploy [movie companies sue La Mancha Private Club & Villas over royalties from videotapes shown in hotel rooms] P. Newcomb. il *Forbes* 143:100 Mr 20 '89

Paramount confronts quality issue in summer promotion. il *Publishers Weekly* 235:56 Je 2 '89

Power plays [cover story] L. B. Johnson. il *Video* 13:37-40+ Ag '89

The remake hall of fame. M. G. Stevenson. il *Video* 12:22 Ja '89

Robert Bolt. G. Carpenter. il por *American Film* 14:60-2 S '89

The second time around [added material] R. Gunnerson. il *Video* 13:68-70 O '89

See these and weep [tearjerkers] F. Thompson. il *American Film* 15:66-8 D '89

Sublicensing deals promise hit movies on video at lower prices. *Publishers Weekly* 235:74 Mr 3 '89

Tapes & discs Yule love. M. Fleischmann. il *Video* 13:59-61+ D '89

Tuesday Weld. A. Barra. il pors *American Film* 14:62-4 Ja/F '89

Video news & notes. See issues of Rolling Stone beginning September 12, 1985

When directors get personal [autobiographical films] M. Sragow. il *American Film* 14:64-6 My '89

Who's got the theatrical window? [videotapes vs. pay-per-view; chart] il *Channels (New York, N.Y.: 1986)* 9:96 F '89

William Wellman. F. Thompson. il por *American Film* 15:98-9 O '89

Nature study

The backcountry back lot [compact camcorders] P. L. Jones. il *Sierra* 74:115-16 N/D '89

News

Camcorder assault [amateur videotape on TV newscasts] J. M. Robins. il *Channels (New York, N.Y.: 1986)* 9:30-1 Ja '89

Eyewitness video. H. Dunst. il *Video* 13:48-50+ Ap '89

Opera

New from the studios. M. Sevilla-Gonzaga. il *Opera News* 54:28-9 Ag '89

Videocassettes. T. Eckert, Jr. and H. E. Phillips. See occasional issues of Opera News beginning January 17, 1987

Popular music

In short order. See issues of High Fidelity (New York, N.Y.) through July 1989

International music on videotape. G. Santoro. *The Nation* 249:101-2 Jl 17 '89

Press releases

Prefab news [video news releases] S. E. Davis. il *Technology Review* 92:6-7 O '89

Prices

Sublicensing deals promise hit movies on video at lower prices. *Publishers Weekly* 235:74 Mr 3 '89

Publishing use

Carol Publishing goes to the videotape [fall catalog] J. Mutter. il *Publishers Weekly* 236:25-6 Ag 18 '89

Ratings

Exploring home video [Nielsen ratings service] R. Katz. il *Channels (New York, N.Y.: 1986)* 9:26 S '89

Religious use

Church, parachurch locked in legal battle [Calvary Chapel vs. Gospel Films over videocassette distribution rights for evangelistic film Fury to freedom] B. Bird. il *Christianity Today* 33:40-3 Ag 18 '89

McGee and me: growing up is hard to do [series coproduced by Focus on the Family and Tyndale House Publishers] R. M. Anker. il *Christianity Today* 33:77 N 3 '89

Rock music

See also

MTV Networks Inc.

MTV Video Music Awards

VIDEOTAPES—Rock music—See also—*cont.*
MuchMusic Network
Video Jukebox Network, Inc.
Back on tour, rock's old men are rolling with a hot new video [Rolling Stones] H. Polskin. il *TV Guide* 37:18-20+ N 18-24 '89
Beyond the big hair [1989] J. Farber. il *Rolling Stone* p235-6 D 14-28 '89
Budget genius [director A. Bernstein] J. Farber. por *Rolling Stone* p99-100 Ag 10 '89
Editor's choice. I. Robbins. il *Video* 13:58+ Ap '89
In the dark [M. Mahurin] J. Farber. por *Rolling Stone* p75 Ap 6 '89
Like a Catholic: Madonna's challenge to her Church [music video Like a prayer] A. M. Greeley. il *America* 160:447-9 My 13 '89
Magical tours [M. Jackson's Moonwalker and B. Springsteen's Video anthology/1978-88] J. Cocks. il por *Time* 133:59 Ja 23 '89
Michael, Bruce release tapes. J. Farber. il *Rolling Stone* p128 F 9 '89
Prince of the City [Batman music videos by Prince] A. White. il pors *Film Comment* 25:76+ N/D '89
Small-screen Springsteen. L. Meredith. il por *Stereo Review* 54:110 Je '89
Video news & notes. See issues of Rolling Stone beginning September 12, 1985
What no one will admit about race in America [Madonna's Like a prayer] R. Rosenbaum. il *Mademoiselle* 95:94+ Ag '89

Anecdotes, facetiae, satire, etc.
Video vixen. B. Stepko. il *Seventeen* 48:132+ Ap '89
Shelves and racks
See Shelves and racks
Social aspects
The data game [video and computer dating; cover story] J. Bennet. *The New Republic* 200:20-2 F 13 '89
"I wish I could hold you more" [cancer victim B. Wagner videotapes messages for his children before his death] B. Remsberg. il *Reader's Digest* 134:147-52 Je '89
TV dating. G. Hirshey. il *Utne Reader* p54-5 Mr/Ap '89
Space sciences use
Seven days in space. R. Burnham. *Astronomy* 17:120-1 Ja '89
Sports
18 tips from 18 legends of golf; Jack Nicklaus shows you the greatest 18 holes of major championship golf. J. Bessman. il por *Video* 12:90 Ja '89
Larry Holmes' champion season [historical video called Champions forever] C. Meth. il por *Video* 13:18 D '89
Learn from watching the best [use of videotapes for learning skiing techniques] O. Larsson. il *Skiing* 41:69-73 F '89
Mickey Mantle's field of dreams. C. Meth. il pors *Video* 13:12 Ag '89
Screen test [videotaping yourself to improve cycling form] B. Prichard. il *Bicycling* 30:136-8+ Ap '89
Video review: the road to Laguna Seca. il *Cycle* 40:79 Mr '89
Television advertising use
Tools of the trade. C. Reece. il *Channels (New York, N.Y.: 1986)* 9:28 Ja '89
Television programs
Television [The best of Gilda Radner, The best of Eddie Murphy, Saturday night live, Milton Berle—the second time around, and The "I love Lucy" collection] J. Walker. il *Video* 13:93+ S '89
'War' remembered on MPI video [Herman Wouk's War and remembrance] P. Sweeting. *Publishers Weekly* 235:62 Ja 6 '89
Titling
A new look for subtitles. J. Bernard. il *Video* 13:15+ O '89
Travel use
Armchair excursions [Fodor's Great Britain] H. B. Livesey. il *Travel Holiday* 172:36-7 N '89
Bring it all back home. T. Harrington. il *Video* 13:57-60 Je '89
Family vacation videos: how to make them really fun to watch. J. Elder. il *Better Homes and Gardens* 67:162 Ap '89
Separating good from bad. H. B. Livesey. il *Travel Holiday* 171:108-12 Mr '89
Small really is better [8mm camcorders] M. Grimm and T. Grimm. il *Travel Holiday* 172:28+ N '89
Unauthorized use
Macrovision under the microscope. G. McComb. il *Video* 13:62-7+ O '89
Weddings
An Orwellian wedding. D. P. Slattery. por *Newsweek* 114:10 N 13 '89
Wedding video goes franchise [Video 5000] K. Geller-Shinn. il *Petersen's Photographic Magazine* 18:12 Je '89
Brazil
Space age shamans: the videotape [recording tribal customs of Brazilian Indians] G. Smith. il *Américas* 41 no2:28-31 '89

Developing countries
Close encounters of the third world kind. T. Harrington. il *Video* 13:32+ N '89
VIDEOTAPES AND POLITICS
JFK remembered. R. S. Rothenberg. il por *USA Today (Periodical)* 117:97 Ja '89
Subversion by cassette. R. Zoglin. il *Time* 134:80 S 11 '89
The video revolution no one expected. T. Koppel. il por *Video* 13:154 D '89
VIDEOTAPES AND YOUTH
Kidvid. M. Meyer. See issues of Video
Nightmare on Video Street, part 1: the legislators [bids to ban rentals of violent tapes to kids] L. Therrien. il *Business Week* p34 S 11 '89
VIDEOTAPES AS GIFTS
A cornucopia of Christmas collectibles [videos for children] M. Meyer. il *Video* 13:91-2 D '89
Great expectations [celebrities discuss most wanted videotapes for Christmas] J. Bernard. il *Video* 13:62-3 D '89
Reel great gifts [Christmas] M. Meyer. il *Redbook* 174:37 D '89
Tapes & discs Yule love. M. Fleischmann. il *Video* 13:59-61+ D '89
The year's best for kids. C. Berman. il *Parents* 64:67+ N '89
VIDEOTAPES ON AIRPLANES
Helping time fly. J. Marcom, Jr. il *Forbes* 143:149-50 Mr 6 '89
VIDEOTEX SYSTEMS *See* Information systems
VIDOR, KING, 1895-1982
about
The Wizard of Oz [film] Reviews
Video il 12:63-4 Mr '89. M. Fleischmann
VIEIRA, JELON
about
Capoeira. *The New Yorker* 65:38-9 My 15 '89
VIEIRA, MEREDITH
about
Meredith Vieira. H. M. Rosenthal. il por *TV Guide* 37:10 S 23-29 '89
New working class. il pors *Harper's Bazaar* 122:160-75+ Mr '89
Women on the verge of a nervy breakdown [interview] P. Orenstein. il pors *Mother Jones* 14:28-31+ Je '89
VIELER-PORTER, CHRIS
Richard Attenborough [interview] il pors *The Unesco Courier* 42:4-7 Ag '89
VIENNA (AUSTRIA)
Architecture
Vienna vanguard [Coop Himmelbau projects] J. Giovannini. il *House & Garden* 161:48 S '89
Galleries and museums
See also
Graphische Sammlung Albertina
Kunsthistorisches Museum (Vienna, Austria)
Museum Moderner Kunst (Vienna, Austria)
History
Bibliography
The rise and fall of Vienna's Jews. M. Ignatieff. il *The New York Review of Books* 36:21-5 Je 29 '89
Music
See also
Opera—Austria
Music festivals
See Music festivals—Austria
VIENNA INTERNATIONAL DANCE FESTIVAL *See* Dance festivals—Austria
VIENNA PHILHARMONIC
Musical events:
H. von Karajan conducting at Carnegie Hall. A. Porter. *The New Yorker* 65:90-1 Mr 20 '89
One of a kind [H. von Karajan] T. W. Libbey, Jr. il *High Fidelity (New York, N.Y.)* 39:57 My '89
VIEQUES ISLAND (PUERTO RICO)
See also
Squatter settlements—Vieques Island (Puerto Rico)
VIETATI
about
Vietati at Forum. C. Waddington. *Art in America* 77:219+ S '89
VIETMEYER, NOEL, 1940-
Here comes the hot stuff. il *International Wildlife* 19:14-19 Jl/Ag '89
Iguana mama. il por *International Wildlife* 19:24-7 S/O '89
Pa-tooey! il *International Wildlife* 19:20-3 Ja/F '89
Whales: gentle giants of the deep. il *Reader's Digest* 134:55-60 My '89
Who needs spiders? il *Reader's Digest* 134:137-40 Je '89
VIETNAM
See also
Americans—Vietnam
Cultural property—Protection—Vietnam
Hanoi (Vietnam)
Hue (Vietnam)
Motion pictures—Vietnam
Paleontology—Vietnam
Political prisoners—Vietnam

VIETNAM—See also—*cont.*
  Repatriation—Vietnam
  Saigon (Vietnam)
  Tennis—Vietnam
  Vietnamese
Description and travel
Vietnam diary. L. H. Lapham. *Harper's* 278:11-13 My '89
Vietnam: hard road to peace [cover story; special section] il supp (folded map) maps *National Geographic* 176:558-611 N '89
Economic policy
Doi moi, hold the *glasnost*. E. Scigliano. map *The Nation* 249:304-6 S 25 '89
Hanoi's struggle for respect. il *U.S. News & World Report* 107:11 O 9 '89
Foreign relations
Vietnam: the challenge of reform. W. J. Duiker. bibl f *Current History* 88:177-80+ Ap '89
  Cambodia
  See Cambodia—Foreign relations—Vietnam
  Great Britain
  See Great Britain—Foreign relations—Vietnam
  United States
  See United States—Foreign relations—Vietnam
Politics and government
Vietnam: hard road to peace [cover story; special section] il supp (folded map) maps *National Geographic* 176:558-611 N '89
Vietnam: the challenge of reform. W. J. Duiker. bibl f *Current History* 88:177-80+ Ap '89
Will it ever end? [effect of withdrawal of Vietnamese troops from Cambodia on both countries] J. Smolowe. il map *Time* 134:38-9+ O 9 '89
Religious institutions and affairs
  See also
  Catholic Church—Vietnam
  Christians—Vietnam
VIETNAM FACT CARDS
Trade you a Da Nang for a . . . il *Newsweek* 114:42 Ag 21 '89
VIETNAM VETERANS See Black veterans; Veterans
VIETNAMESE
Cambodia
A second home for the Vietnamese. R. Moreau. il *Newsweek* 113:40 Ja 30 '89
Canada
A boat girl grows up [H. Truong] B. Came. il por *Maclean's* 102:21+ Jl 10 '89
France
In a war of nerves, first-time actress Thuy Thu Le relives Vietnam in Casualties of war. M. H. J. Farrell. il pors *People Weekly* 32:47+ Ag 28 '89
United States
"I'll always believe she's my daughter" [U.S. government wants blood test to prove paternity of Tuyet Mai]; ed. by Laura Huntoon. B. Huntoon. il pors *Redbook* 174:79-80+ D '89
Mary Nguyen's G.I. dad has never seen her face, but Revlon thinks it's a winner [Most Unforgettable Woman of the Year] M. H. J. Farrell. il pors *People Weekly* 32:54-5 Ag 7 '89
Old pines in the land of ten thousand lakes [social service program for Vietnamese in Minnesota] il *Aging* no359:22 '89
A Vietnam memoir; ed. by Martha K. Babcock. L. L. Hayslip. il pors *People Weekly* 32:147-8+ D 18 '89
  Photographs and photography
Americanization of Vietnamese. S. Gold. il *Society* 27:72-5 N/D '89
VIETNAMESE REFUGEES See Refugees, Vietnamese
VIETNAMESE WAR, 1957-1975
  See also
  Vietnam Fact Cards
Aerial operations
All aboard Air Oblivion [ineffectiveness and vulnerability of Army helicopters] G. Easterbrook. *The Washington Monthly* 21:53+ F '89
Hitler: eternal springtime [aerial bombing by American forces] A. Cockburn. *The Nation* 248:654-5 My 15 '89
Lion heart [former fighter pilot R. Cunningham in the Colorado 500] C. Furlong. il pors *Cycle* 40:78-80+ Je '89
American participation
Apocalypse now: drugs [parallels between drug war and Vietnam War] E. Barnes. il *Life* 12:18-25 S '89
Coming to terms with Nam. R. Novak. il *People Weekly* 32 Special Issue:112-14+ Fall '89
Community [excerpt from Tilting at windmills] C. Peters. *The Washington Monthly* 21:32-3 F '89
The courage of Sam Bird [example set by U.S. Army captain] B. T. Collins. il *Reader's Digest* 134:49-54 My '89
Homecoming [letters from Vietnam veterans; excerpts] B. Greene. il *Esquire* 111:45-6+ F '89
Hot writers [biography of J. P. Vann by N. Sheehan] A. DeCurtis. il pors *Rolling Stone* p117-18+ My 18 '89
Me and the Preacher Man [Vietnam vet helped by evangelist D. Roever; condensed from Before the dawn]; ed. by William R. Kimball. M. Block. *Reader's Digest* 134:33-7 Ja '89

A moving new book helps West Point '66 bind the wounds of war and changing times [R. Atkinson's The long gray line] L. Kramer. il pors *People Weekly* 32:92-3+ O 30 '89
Self-exiled after Vietnam, Army hero David Hackworth is finally coming home. P. Freeman. il pors *People Weekly* 31:52-4 Je 5 '89
Speak loudly, carry a small stick [effect of Vietnam and Watergate on U.S. foreign policy] J. Schell. il *Harper's* 278:39-41+ Mr '89
The total Vietnam War story needs to be told [address, April 19, 1989] J. Stockdale. *Vital Speeches of the Day* 55:519-25 Je 15 '89
U.S. misadventure in Vietnam [reprint from January 1968 issue] H. J. Morgenthau. *Current History* 88:32-4+ Ja '89
Vietnam diary. L. H. Lapham. *Harper's* 278:11-13 My '89
Vietnam 'vets' & the Soviet experience. B. Shephard. il *History Today* 39:10-12 Jl '89
The West Point story [excerpt from The long gray line; cover story] R. Atkinson. il pors *U.S. News & World Report* 107:44-54 O 9 '89
When American vets meet Soviet vets [Vietnam and Afghanistan veterans] C. Thibaud. *World Press Review* 36:70 S '89
The wounds of two wars [meeting between Vietnam and Afghanistan veterans in the Soviet Union] P. P. Mahoney. il *The New York Times Magazine* p60-1+ Je 11 '89
Art
A painful war's haunted art [A different war: Vietnam in art] P. Plagens. il *Newsweek* 114:54 S 11 '89
Atrocities
  See also
  My Lai Massacre, 1968
Blacks
Home-front vets [Vietnam veteran] J. L. Howe. por *Essence* 20:12 My '89
Children
"I'll always believe she's my daughter" [U.S. government wants blood test to prove paternity of Tuyet Mai]; ed. by Laura Huntoon. B. Huntoon. il pors *Redbook* 174:79-80+ D '89
In a war of nerves, first-time actress Thuy Thu Le relives Vietnam in Casualties of war. M. H. J. Farrell. il pors *People Weekly* 32:47+ Ag 28 '89
Mary Nguyen's G.I. dad has never seen her face, but Revlon thinks it's a winner [Most Unforgettable Woman of the Year] M. H. J. Farrell. il pors *People Weekly* 32:54-5 Ag 7 '89
Collectibles
Cashing in on Vietnam. J. Hammer. il *Newsweek* 113:38-9 Ja 16 '89
Moral and religious aspects
I was an atheist in a foxhole. P. K. Paulsen. *The Humanist* 49:28-30 S/O '89
Personal stories
Beyond survival: a P.O.W.'s story [internment in North Vietnamese prison camp; condensation] G. L. Coffee. il *Reader's Digest* 135:137-44+ D '89
A Vietnam memoir; ed. by Martha K. Babcock. L. L. Hayslip. il pors *People Weekly* 32:147-8+ D 18 '89
Photographs and photography
Viet Nam: a war no one wanted in the land nobody knew. il *Time* 134 Special Issue:62-3 Fall '89
Prisoners and prisons
Beyond survival: a P.O.W.'s story [internment in North Vietnamese prison camp; condensation] G. L. Coffee. il *Reader's Digest* 135:137-44+ D '89
Protest movements
The chemistry of protest [effect of the civil rights movement on Vietnam War protests in the sixties] il *U.S. News & World Report* 106:16 Ap 10 '89
Those weren't the days. J. Garvey. *Commonweal* 116:363-4 Je 16 '89
Public opinion
Doves & hawks [discussion of March 1989 article, On not being a dove] J. Updike. *Commentary* 88:2-4 Ag '89
On not being a dove. J. Updike. *Commentary* 87:22-30 Mr '89
Reporters and reporting
Apocalypse then [excerpt from War news] R. S. Anson. *The Washington Monthly* 21:14+ O '89
The press didn't lose the Vietnam War [views of William M. Hammond] *Newsweek* 114:40 S 11 '89
Veterans
  See Black veterans; Veterans
Women
A Vietnam memoir; ed. by Martha K. Babcock. L. L. Hayslip. il pors *People Weekly* 32:147-8+ D 18 '89
VIETNAMESE WAR, 1957-1975, IN MOTION PICTURES
Body count [Casualties of war] G. Smith. il *Film Comment* 25:49-52 Jl/Ag '89
Company man [84 Charlie MoPic] K. Jaehne. il por *Film Comment* 25:11-15 Mr/Ap '89
Cool head, hot images [B. De Palma's Casualties of war] B. Weber. il pors *The New York Times Magazine* p24-7+ My 21 '89
Mirror, mirror . . . [In country] J. Scott. il *Film Comment* 25:11-14 S/O '89

VIETNAMESE WAR, 1957-1975, IN MOTION PICTURES—*cont.*
Patriotic gore: De Palma as sage [Casualties of war] S. Henderson. *The Christian Century* 106:925-6 O 18 '89
The Vietnam Film Project. J. Burton. *The Nation* 248:825-7 Je 12 '89
VIETNAMESE WAR, 1957-1975, IN TELEVISION
War as family entertainment [China Beach and Tour of duty] R. Zoglin. il *Time* 133:84 F 20 '89
War gams: the women of China Beach. G. Sikes. il *Mademoiselle* 95:84+ My '89
VIEW CAMERAS *See* Cameras
VIEWFINDERS (PHOTOGRAPHY) *See* Photography—Equipment
VIEWPOINT (FICTION) *See* Fiction—Narration
VIEWS (SCENERY)
Colorado proposes protecting vistas. *National Parks* 63:13-14 Ja/F '89
Science or scenery? [national park management] R. W. Sellars. il *Wilderness* 52:28-39 Summ '89
Something in the air [pollution obscuring visibility in national parks and forests] L. Kahaner. il *Wilderness* 52:18-27 Wint '88
VIGIDIS FINNBOGADÓTTIR, 1930-
about
President Vigdís. *The New Yorker* 65:36-7 Mr 20 '89
THE VIGIL [drama] *See* Jenkins, Charles J.
VIGUERIE, RICHARD A.
about
Reactionaries' reaction. A. P. Crawford. il *The Nation* 248:231+ F 20 '89
VIKHANSKI, LUBA
Ozone park. il *Discover* 10:32 S '89
VIKING FLIGHTS *See* Space flight to Mars
VIKING PENGUIN INC.
Harper & Row, Penguin sign new labor accords. C. Reid. *Publishers Weekly* 235:12 F 3 '89
How Rushdie's publishers see the crisis. *Publishers Weekly* 235:27 Mr 3 '89
VIKING PRESS INC.
Court dismisses Janklow suit against Viking and Matthiessen. *Publishers Weekly* 235:14 Je 16 '89
The F.B.I. man who cried libel [suit brought by D. Price] M. Garbus. il *The Nation* 249:564+ N 13 '89
Viking, Matthiessen win in Price libel suit. *Publishers Weekly* 236:8 S 1 '89
VILA, BOB
Old house restoration. See issues of Popular Mechanics beginning May 1986
Restoring America. il *Popular Mechanics* 166:106-8+ My '89
VILADAS, PILAR
The big picture. il *House & Garden* 161:160-7 S '89
California modern. il pors *House & Garden* 161:28+ Je '89
Canyon hideout. il *House & Garden* 161:120-5+ Ja '89
Gimme shelter. il *Art News* 88:81-2 Ja '89
He knows what he likes. il pors *House & Garden* 161:26+ F '89
Hollywood homestead. il pors *House & Garden* 161:98-103 Ag '89
Jane Fonda's spa. il por *House & Garden* 161:92-7 Je '89
A life in pictures. il pors *House & Garden* 161:154-9+ Ap '89
Mixed company. il por *House & Garden* 161:66+ N '89
Revisionist history. il *House & Garden* 161:162-9 N '89
Romance on the rocks. il map *House & Garden* 161:82+ My '89
Short-order chic. il *House & Garden* 161:62 S '89
A Somers place. il pors *House & Garden* 161:210-15 S '89
Talk of the Town Car. il *House & Garden* 161:232 S '89
Tea & cinema. il por *House & Garden* 161:60 D '89
Two for the road. il *House & Garden* 161:44 Ag '89
VILAR, ESTHER
Experienced, qualified—and stupid; tr. by Joel Agee. *Harper's* 278:28+ Ja '89
VILAS, FAITH, AND GAFFEY, MICHAEL J.
Phyllosilicate absorption features in main-belt and outer-belt asteroid reflectance spectra. bibl f il *Science* 246:790-2 N 10 '89
VILLA, MARIO
about
Creole comforts. N. Lemann. il por *House & Garden* 161:180-5+ S '89
VILLA, PANCHO, 1878-1923
about
La cabeza de Villa. M. Singer. *The New Yorker* 65:108-12+ N 27 '89
VILLA AMERICA (CAP D'ANTIBES, FRANCE) *See* Cap d'Antibes (France)—Historic houses, sites, etc.
VILLA BARBARO (MASER, ITALY)
Palladio and Veronese at the Villa Barbaro in Maser, Italy. B. L. Brown. bibl f il *Antiques* 135:298-309 Ja '89
VILLA CYPRIS (CAP MARTIN, FRANCE) *See* Cap Martin (France)—Historic houses, sites, etc.
VILLA JEANNERET (PARIS, FRANCE) *See* Paris (France)—Historic houses, sites, etc.

VILLA NARCISSA (PALOS VERDES ESTATES, CALIF.)
See Palos Verdes Estates (Calif.)—Historic houses, sites, etc.
VILLAGE VANGUARD (NEW YORK, N.Y.: NIGHTCLUB)
See New York (N.Y.)—Restaurants, nightclubs, bars, etc.
VILLAGES, RESTORED
See also
Acadian Historical Village (N.B.)
Historic Deerfield, Inc.
Historic Rugby
Mystic Seaport Museum
Old Salem, Inc.
Old Sturbridge Village
Plimoth Plantation, Inc.
Williamsburg (Va.)
From Williamsburg to Conner Prairie. V. S. Sussman. il *U.S. News & World Report* 107:58-62 Jl 24 '89
VILLAINS IN MOTION PICTURES
Movie villains were once the equal of their enemies; now they're copycat clichés. G. Kilday. il *Vogue* 179:196-8 Ag '89
The value of villains. M. Rooney. por *Newsweek* 114:12 N 27 '89
VILLALOBOS, JOAQUÍN
A democratic revolution for El Salvador. *Foreign Policy* 74:103-22 Spr '89
about
Conversations with two foes. J. Smolowe. il pors *Time* 134:26 O 2 '89
VILLALPANDO, CRISTÓBAL DE
about
Lost and found. R. J. Stroessner and T. Dewalt. il *Américas* 41 no1:60-2 '89
What's wrong with this painting? R. J. Stroessner and T. Dewalt. il *Américas* 41 no2:58-60 '89
VILLARD, RAY
From idea to observation: the Space Telescope at work. il *Astronomy* 17:38-44 Je '89
The world's biggest star catalogue. il *Sky and Telescope* 78:583-9 D '89
VILLARD BOOKS
Baking a bestseller [N. BenShea's Jacob the baker] L. Fleischer. *Publishers Weekly* 235:64 Ja 13 '89
VILLAROSA, CLARA
about
Book biz: a community best-seller. il por *Ms.* 18:85 S '89
VILLAS *See* Country estates
VILLELLA, EDWARD
about
Edward Villella. C. Barnes. *Dance Magazine* 63:114 N '89
Taking care of the roles: Villella victorious, Miami's Prometheus. L. Horn. il *Dance Magazine* 63:44-50 N '89
LA VILLETTE (PARIS, FRANCE)
Rough and reddish. G. Danto. il por *Art News* 88:103-4 My '89
VILLIEN, BRUNO
Imbroglio at the Bastille. il *Opera News* 54:30-3 Jl '89
VILLIERS, GEORGE *See* Buckingham, George Villiers, 1st Duke of, 1592-1628
VINALHAVEN (ME.)
Art
Indiana in Maine. P. Lemos. il pors *Art News* 88:166-9 O '89
VINCA ROSEA *See* Periwinkle
VINCENNES (WARSHIP) DISASTER, 1988 *See* Iranian air disaster, 1988
VINCENT, FAY *See* Vincent, Francis T., Jr.
VINCENT, FRANCIS T., JR.
(jt. auth) *See* Crystal, Graef S., and Vincent, Francis T., Jr.
about
After the death of Bart Giamatti, his friend Fay Vincent steps in as the commissioner's pinch hitter. K. Gross. il pors *People Weekly* 32:56-7 S 18 '89
For the love of the game: an open letter to new baseball commissioner Fay Vincent. P. Gammons. il por *Sports Illustrated* 71:92 S 25 '89
A man in command. S. Wulf. il pors *Sports Illustrated* 71:30-2+ O 30 '89
The new Mister Clean. R. Corelli. il por *Maclean's* 102:50 O 2 '89
VINCENT, JAMES L., 1939-
about
Biogen's new moneymaking genes. L. Jereski. il por *Business Week* p94 Je 19 '89
VINCENTI, MAURO
about
To live and dine in L.A. D. Shaw. il por *Gentlemen's Quarterly* 59:161+ Ap '89
VINE, BARBARA
See also
Rendell, Ruth, 1930-
VINE BASKETS *See* Baskets
VINEGAR
See also
Cooking—Vinegar

VIRGINIA—See also—*cont.*
Fairfax County (Va.)
Gardens and gardening—Virginia
Great Falls Park (Va.)
Historic houses, sites, etc.—Virginia
Manassas National Battlefield Park (Va.)
Paleontology—Virginia
Prince Edward County (Va.)
Yorktown Battlefield (Va.)

Climate
Civil War weather in Virginia. J. Iekel. bibl f il *Weatherwise* 42:268-73 O '89

Economic history
John Smith's bill: then & now [cost of supplies for Virginia's colony at today's prices] J. B. M. Schick. il *American Heritage* 40:158-65 N '89

History
Colonising Bermuda—defending Virginia [seventeenth century] C. W. Brown. bibl il maps *History Today* 39:36-41 Ja '89

Parks and reserves
See also
Virginia Coast Reserve

Politics and government
Battling an old bugaboo [gubernatorial campaign of L. D. Wilder] L. I. Barrett. il pors *Time* 133:26-7 Ap 17 '89
Breakthrough in Virginia [D. Wilder, first elected black governor] W. Shapiro. il pors *Time* 134:54-7 N 20 '89
Danube fever [Hungarian opposition party leaders study Virginia governor's race] A. Heard. *The New Republic* 201:16-18 D 4 '89
Governor-elect Doug Wilder. M. Cooper. il pors *U.S. News & World Report* 107:48+ N 20 '89
L. Douglas Wilder: 'I claim the governorship of Virginia' [cover story] S. Booker. il pors *Jet* 77:8-11 N 27 '89
The New Dominion [L. D. Wilder vs. J. M. Coleman in gubernatorial race] R. G. Holland. il *National Review* 41:25+ S 29 '89
A new force in the Old Dominion [L. D. Wilder; cover story] D. T. Dingle. il pors *Black Enterprise* 19:36-8+ Ja '89
A pair of electoral tests [abortion issue] il *Time* 134:36 O 23 '89
A stunning photo finish [D. Wilder elected governor] W. Lowther. *Maclean's* 102:41 N 20 '89
Va.'s Lt. Gov. Wilder seeks governor's house. il por *Jet* 75:5 F 13 '89
Who will be the first black elected governor? [L. D. Wilder] A. Poinsett. il pors *Ebony* 45:38+ N '89
Wilder gets Dem. Party nomination for governor [L. Douglas Wilder] il por *Jet* 76:4+ Je 26 '89
Wilder inaugural expected to be spectacular event. il por *Jet* 77:4 D 18 '89
Wilder primed to be governor. D. P. Baker. il por *American Visions* 4:42-3 O '89
The Wilder side [L. D. Wilder vs. J. M. Coleman in gubernatorial race] F. Barnes. *The New Republic* 201:9-10 N 13 '89
Yes, Virginia, Doug Wilder could be America's first elected black governor. J. S. Kunen. il por *People Weekly* 32:54-5 N 6 '89

Religious institutions and affairs
History
Two centuries of Virginia's Act for Religious Freedom. E. Turner. il *USA Today (Periodical)* 117:73-5 Mr '89

VIRGINIA BEACH (VA.)
Police
Police brutality charges probed after Va. Beach riot; students fault city. il *Jet* 76:6-7 S 25 '89
Riots
Police brutality charges probed after Va. Beach riot; students fault city. il *Jet* 76:6-7 S 25 '89

VIRGINIA COAST RESERVE
How a grandiose scheme became a grand preserve. R. L. Di Silvestro. *Audubon* 91:110 Mr '89

VIRGINIA MUSEUM OF FINE ARTS
Museum accessions. E. H. Gustafson. il *Antiques* 135:414 F '89
Museum accessions [Roses by Renoir acquired] E. H. Gustafson. il *Antiques* 136:76+ Jl '89
Renoir's gifts [Roses] V. H. Winner. il *Art News* 88:25 Summ '89

VIRGO CLUSTER (GALAXIES) See Galaxies—Clusters
VIRSHUP, AMY
The new dealers. il pors *Harper's Bazaar* 122:80+ D '89
Pared down penthouse. il por *House & Garden* 161:186-91 S '89

VIRTUAL COMPUTER SYSTEMS
Almost-magic EMS emulation [Turbo EMS] S. Miastkowski. il *Byte* 14:97-8 Mr '89
Breaking the memory barrier with 386/VMM. M. Heller. il *Byte* 14:187-8+ Jl '89
More Mac RAM for less [Virtual from Connectix] T. Thompson. il *Byte* 14:98+ My '89
Protected mode. B. Glass. bibl il *Byte* 14:377-84 D '89
Stretching DOS to the limit [Virtual Control Program Interface] F. Hayes. il *Byte* 14 Special Issue:79-80+ Fall '89
Turbo EMS. J. B. Lambert. il *Compute!* 11:116+ D '89

Utility infielder [VM Software] D. Churbuck. il *Forbes* 143:186 Mr 20 '89
A virtual crowd [special section] il *Byte* 14:341-50+ N '89
Virtual memory, "hot links" coming to the Mac OS. *Byte* 14:17-18+ Jl '89
A virtual toolkit for Windows and the Mac [XVT 1.1] R. Valdés. il *Byte* 14:209-10+ Mr '89
VROOMM: Borland says memory technology will make future programs better, not bigger [Virtual Real-Time Object-Oriented Memory Manager] *Byte* 14:17-18 Ag '89
VROOMM goes the spreadsheet [Virtual Real-Time Object Oriented Memory Manager for Quattro] R. Malloy. *Byte* 14:111-12 O '89

VIRTUAL REALITY
Brave new worlds. il *Compute!* 11:28 O '89
Computers you control with a wave of your hand. M. Schroeder. il por *Business Week* p142+ F 20 '89
Desperately seeking cyberspace. P. Saffo. il *Personal Computing* 13:247-8 My '89
Surgery in space. A. Gibbons. il *Technology Review* 92:9-10 Ap '89

VIRTUE, DOREEN, 1958-
Watch and grow thin. il *TV Guide* 37:17-19 Je 24-30 '89
VIRTUE
See also
Character

VIRUS DISEASES
See also
Cold (Disease)
Hemorrhagic fever
Mumps
Diseases for our future: global ecology and emerging viruses. J. A. Miller. il *BioScience* 39:509-17 S '89
Notes and comment [in bed with a virus] *The New Yorker* 65:35-6 My 15 '89
The viral advantage [cover story] R. Weiss. il *Science News* 136:200-3 S 23 '89
Viral infections cause spasms [development of asthma from respiratory infections; views of William Busse] *USA Today (Periodical)* 118:2-3 O '89

VIRUS DISEASES IN ANIMALS
See also
Rabies
VIRUSES
See also
Bacteriophages
Cytomegalovirus
Distemper virus
Epstein-Barr virus
Foot-and-mouth disease virus
Hepatitis viruses
Herpesviruses
HIV viruses
HTLV viruses
Human papilloma virus
Leukemia viruses
Lymphocytic choriomeningitis virus
Mutation—Viruses
Oncogenic viruses
Pox viruses
Prions
Retroviruses
Rhinoviruses
Simian viruses
Sindbis virus
Virus diseases
Water—Microbiology
Foodborne viral illness. B. T. Hunter. il *Consumers' Research Magazine* 72:8-9 Ag '89
Initiation by yeast RNA polymerase II at the adenoviral major late promoter in vitro. N. F. Lue and others. bibl f il *Science* 246:661-4 N 3 '89
No ordinary enemy [special section] il *Health (New York, N.Y.)* 21:42-7+ D '89
Slow viruses. T. Kiely. il *Technology Review* 92:11-12 O '89
Viral alteration of cell function. M. B. A. Oldstone. bibl il *Scientific American* 261:42-8 Ag '89
Inactivation
See also
Interferon
Resistance and sensitivity
Drug-resistant strains of AIDS virus found [AZT-resistant] J. L. Marx. *Science* 243:1551-2 Mr 24 '89
Hardy viruses survive drug assault [AIDS patients; studies by Kim S. Erlich and Alejo Erice] *Science News* 135:110 F 18 '89
HIV with reduced sensitivity to zidovudine (AZT) isolated during prolonged therapy. B. A. Larder and others. bibl f il *Science* 243:1731-4 Mr 31 '89
Multiple mutations in HIV-1 reverse transcriptase confer high-level resistance to zidovudine (AZT). B. A. Larder and S. D. Kemp. bibl f il *Science* 246:1155-8 D 1 '89
Virus de résistance [drug resistant viruses in AIDS patients] K. Wright. *Scientific American* 260:29+ Ap '89
The virus strikes back [AZT-resistant strains] P. Gadsby. il *Discover* 10:20 Jl '89

VIRUSES, COMPUTER *See* Computer viruses
VIRUSES, INSECT
　　See also
　　Baculoviruses
　　Nuclear polyhedrosis virus
VIRUSES, PLANT
　　Movement protein of tobacco mosaic virus modifies plasmodesmatal size exclusion limit. S. Wolf and others. bibl f il *Science* 246:377-9 O 20 '89
　　Protein-RNA interactions in an icosahedral virus at 3.0 Å resolution [bean-pod mattle virus] Z. Chen and others. bibl f il *Science* 245:154-9 Jl 14 '89
VISA INTERNATIONAL INC.
　　The card that says 'charge it' . . . to Fido. il *Newsweek* 114:63 N 27 '89
VISAS *See* Passports
VISAS, WORK *See* Work visas
VISCIDI, RAPHAEL P., AND OTHERS
　　Inhibition of antigen-induced lymphocyte proliferation by Tat protein from HIV-1. bibl f il *Science* 246:1606-8 D 22 '89
VISCO, JENNIFER
　　　　about
　　Sink or swim in the mainstream. P. A. Zirkel. bibl f il *Phi Delta Kappan* 70:411-13 Ja '89
VISCO, RENE
　　　　about
　　Sink or swim in the mainstream. P. A. Zirkel. bibl f il *Phi Delta Kappan* 70:411-13 Ja '89
VISCOSITY
　　Dendrites, viscous fingers, and the theory of pattern formation. J. S. Langer. bibl f il *Science* 243:1150-6 Mr 3 '89
VISCOSITY DETECTORS
　　Viscosity sensor makes waves. M. DiChristina. il *Popular Science* 234:37 My '89
VISCUSI, W. KIP
　　Safety through markets. *Society* 27:9-10 N/D '89
VISES
　　Table-top gun vise. M. Burch. il *Field & Stream* 94:116 N '89
VISHWANATH S. NARAVANE *See* Naravane, Vishwanath S.
VISICALC (COMPUTER PROGRAM)
　　Birthing the visible calculator [interview with D. Bricklin and B. Frankston] il pors *Byte* 14:326-8 D '89
　　Looking at VisiCalc 10 years later. P. Saffo. il *Personal Computing* 13:233-4+ N '89
VISION
　　　　See also
　　Blindness
　　Color blindness
　　Color vision
　　Contact lenses
　　Eye
　　Eyeglasses
　　Visual perception
　　Bat those eyes! [crossed eye-hand dominance in baseball players; research by Jose Portal and Paul Romano] S. McKee. il *American Health* 8:16 O '89
　　Binocular depth reversals despite familiarity cues. A. van den Enden and H. Spekreijse. bibl f il *Science* 244:959-61 My 26 '89
　　Eye workouts that don't work [views of Maria-Therese Wegner-Aiello] C. Marks. il *Mademoiselle* 95:142 N '89
　　Eyes on the prize [sports vision] D. Wise. il *Gentlemen's Quarterly* 59:168-75 Jl '89
　　Eyes right [vision exercises for athletes] B. Hasselbring. il *Women's Sports & Fitness* 11:12 My '89
　　First sight [infant's vision; research by Anthony M. Norcia] B. Weber. il *The New York Times Magazine* p110 Mr 5 '89
　　Hot-rod glasses [anti-reflection coating for drivers] P. Bedard. il *Car and Driver* 35:10 N '89
　　Pilots sense attitude with peripheral vision using new Garrett display. B. D. Nordwall. il *Aviation Week & Space Technology* 130:97+ My 8 '89
　　Workouts for the eyes [vision therapy] A. Toufexis. il *Time* 133:86 F 13 '89
　　　　Animals
　　Light adaptation in cat retinal rods. T. Tamura and others. bibl f il *Science* 245:755-8 Ag 18 '89
　　A look at animal vision. M. Abramovitz. il *Sierra* 74:100-1 Mr/Ap '89
　　Orange you glad? Fido sees the blues [research by Gerald Jacobs] R. Weiss. *Science News* 136:215 S 30 '89
　　　　Birds
　　Owls give a hoot for vision [research by Eric and Phyllis Knudsen] il *Science News* 136:263 O 21 '89
　　　　Testing
　　　　See Eye—Examination
A VISION OF BRITAIN [television program] *See* Television program reviews—Single works
VISION RESEARCH
　　　　Ethical aspects
　　New round in Dingell v. NIH? [case of C. D. Bridges] J. Palca. *Science* 245:349 Jl 28 '89
　　NIH sees plagiarism in vision paper [case of C. D. Bridges] B. J. Culliton. *Science* 245:120-2 Jl 14 '89

VISION SYSTEMS (MACHINES) *See* Machine vision
VISITATION RIGHTS (PARENTS)
　　　　See also
　　Foretich, Hilary—Custody case
　　Playing rough in a custody fight, Steve Garvey has Cyndy, his ex, tossed into jail. il pors *People Weekly* 32:93 O 16 '89
VISITING CARDS
　　　　See also
　　Carte de visite photographs
VISITOR CENTERS
　　　　See also
　　Smithsonian Institution. Information Center
VISITORS *See* Guests
VISSCHER, J., AND OTHERS
　　Template-directed oligomerization catalyzed by a polynucleotide analog. bibl f il *Science* 244:329-31 Ap 21 '89
VISSER, MARGARET, 1940-
　　A meditation on the microwave. il *Psychology Today* 23:38+ D '89
VISUAL ACCOMMODATION *See* Eye—Accommodation and refraction
VISUAL ARTS *See* Art
VISUAL CELLS *See* Rods and cones
VISUAL CORTEX *See* Brain
VISUAL FLIGHT RULES *See* Airplanes—Piloting
VISUAL ILLUSIONS *See* Optical illusions
VISUAL IMAGES *See* Visualization
VISUAL PERCEPTION
　　　　See also
　　Color vision
　　Form perception
　　Motion perception
　　Optical illusions
　　Space perception
　　The art of the mind: how I learned to draw [art teacher B. Edwards] T. Schwartz. il por *New York* 22:42-6+ D 11 '89
　　Binocular unmasking: an analog to binaural unmasking? B. Schneider and others. bibl f il *Science* 243:1479-81 Mr 17 '89
　　Seeing is believing. P. Chance. il *Psychology Today* 23:26 Ja/F '89
VISUAL PIGMENTS
　　　　See also
　　Visual purple
　　The genes for color vision. J. Nathans. bibl il *Scientific American* 260:42-9 F '89
　　Jeepers, creepers [mantis shrimp; research by Thomas W. Cronin and N. Justin Marshall] A. W. Epstein. il *Scientific American* 261:33-4 S '89
VISUAL PURPLE
　　Effect of carboxylic acid side chains on the absorption maximum of visual pigments. E. A. Zhukovsky and D. D. Oprian. bibl f il *Science* 246:928-30 N 17 '89
VISUALIZATION
　　Relax, you'll run faster [behavioral imagery technique; study by Scot Machlus and Richard O'Brien] J. C. Horn. il *Psychology Today* 23:22 Ja/F '89
　　Seeing is believing [tennis] J. E. Loehr. il *World Tennis* 36:16-17 Mr '89
VISUALLY HANDICAPPED
　　　　See also
　　Art and the visually handicapped
　　Blind
VITAL, DAVID
　　Our road to Zion: a memoir. *Commentary* 87:49-55 My '89
VITAL OPTIONS (ORGANIZATION)
　　Young cancer victims [work of S. Schimmel] L. Mosedale. il por *Glamour* 87:88 Je '89
VITAL STATISTICS
　　　　See also
　　Birth rate
　　Infant mortality
　　Mortality
VITALE, ALBERTO
　　　　about
　　Bernstein retiring from Random; Vitale is new chairman. C. Reid and J. F. Baker. pors *Publishers Weekly* 236:8 N 17 '89
VITALE, ROBERT
　　　　about
　　Yield versus total return. J. Clements. il por *Forbes* 144:162-3 S 4 '89
VITALINK COMMUNICATIONS CORPORATION
　　Listen to your customer. I. Chithelen. il *Forbes* 143:120-1 My 15 '89
VITALITY
　　11 steps to winter energy [special section] il *Working Woman* 14:115-18+ F '89
　　Energize: fight holiday burnout with these mind/body strategies. A. P. Lynn. il *Glamour* 87:38+ D '89
　　High-energy punch! il *Mademoiselle* 95:184-7 D '89
VITALITY IN CHILDREN
　　The energetic child: what's healthy, what's not. L. Salk. il *McCall's* 116:41 Ag '89

VITAMIN A
See also
Carotene
Membranes as the energy source in the endergonic transformation of vitamin A to 11-*cis*-retinol. P. S. Deigner and others. bibl f il *Science* 244:968-71 My 26 '89
Water-soluble vitamin A shows promise [work of Arun B. Barua, Desiree B. Gunning and James A. Olson] I. Wickelgren. *Science News* 135:204 Ap 1 '89
VITAMIN A ACID See Retinoic acid
VITAMIN B COMPLEX
See also
Biotin
Vitamin vigor [deficiency linked to fatigue after exercising; research by Erik van der Beek] V. Brower. *American Health* 8:36 Jl/Ag '89
VITAMIN B$_2$
A vitamin exercisers need to watch closely. O. Anderson. il *Women's Sports & Fitness* 11:22 S '89
VITAMIN B$_6$
12 essential facts about vitamin B$_6$. S. Lally. *Prevention (Emmaus, Pa.)* 41:61-4 Ja '89
VITAMIN B$_{12}$
Can B-12 prevent bone diseases? *USA Today (Periodical)* 118:18 O '89
Do you need a B$_{12}$ boost? J. Mullich. *Prevention (Emmaus, Pa.)* 41:41-5 Je '89
VITAMIN C
Diabetes and vitamin C. I. Nelson. *New Choices for the Best Years* 29:15 My '89
Dysplasia's end [hunting dogs; work of Dr. W. Belfield] L. Mueller. il pors *Outdoor Life* 183:46+ Ap '89
Nitrogen fertilizer saps veggies' vitamin C [research by Sharon B. Hornick] *Science News* 136:255 O 14 '89
Vitamin C for healthy lungs? [research by Joel Schwartz] il *Prevention (Emmaus, Pa.)* 41:10+ O '89
Vitamin C may hasten healing [tooth extraction; views of Robert A. Halberstein] il *USA Today (Periodical)* 117:4-5 F '89
Vitamin C protects blood from radicals [research by Balz Frei] J. Raloff. *Science News* 136:133 Ag 26 '89
Vitamin vigor [deficiency linked to fatigue after exercising; research by Erik van der Beek] V. Brower. *American Health* 8:36 Jl/Ag '89
Vitamins C and E may prevent cataracts [research by James McD. Robertson] I. Wickelgren. *Science News* 135:308 My 20 '89
VITAMIN D
Do sunscreens block vitamin D? il *Prevention (Emmaus, Pa.)* 41:10+ Jl '89
VITAMIN D$_3$
1,25-dihydroxyvitamin D-responsive element and glucocorticoid repression in the osteocalcin gene. N. A. Morrison and others. bibl f il *Science* 246:1158-61 D 1 '89
VITAMIN E
E for elevation [research on vitamin E and free radicals in high altitude athletics] il *Women's Sports & Fitness* 11:11 O '89
The healing frontier of vitamin E. G. Maleskey. *Prevention (Emmaus, Pa.)* 41:33-9 Mr '89
Three jailed for selling drug that killed 38 babies [premature infants given solution E-Ferol] C. Carey. il *FDA Consumer* 23:33-4 Jl/Ag '89
Vitamin E and epilepsy [children] il *Prevention (Emmaus, Pa.)* 41:16 N '89
Vitamin E fights radicals—again and again [research by Lester Packer on mitochondrial membranes] J. Raloff. *Science News* 135:327 My 27 '89
Vitamins C and E may prevent cataracts [research by James McD. Robertson] I. Wickelgren. *Science News* 135:308 My 20 '89
VITAMINS
A-C-E against aging. N. Wartik. *Harper's Bazaar* 122:134+ Ag '89
America's big on vitamins, minerals. il *FDA Consumer* 23:3-4 D '89/Ja '90
Are vitamin supplements for you? il *McCall's* 117:100 O '89
As evidence mounts of the strong link between nutrition and immunity, Lori Miller Kase asks: can the use of supplements help in the fight against disease? L. M. Kase. *Vogue* 179:288+ N '89
Body mechanics: how well does your engine run? il *'Teen* 33:75 Ja '89
Latest dispatch from the vitamin front [revised recommended daily allowances] S. Findlay. il *U.S. News & World Report* 107:100-1 N 6 '89
Nutrients and birth defects [taking vitamins before conception may reduce risk] il *Prevention (Emmaus, Pa.)* 41:12+ Mr '89
Smart investments in nutrition. R. Rodale. il *Prevention (Emmaus, Pa.)* 41:25-6 Ag '89
Squaring off over vitamins [debate over nutritional requirements and supplements] S. Findlay. il *U.S. News & World Report* 106:62-4 Ap 10 '89
Too tired too often? Vitamins can work wonders. R. N. Podell. il *Redbook* 172:108-9+ Ja '89

Vitamins and moms-to-be [may reduce risk of neural tube defects; research by Joseph Mullinare] G. McBride. il *American Health* 8:138 Ap '89
Vitamins for vegetables [use as plant foods] R. Williams, III. il por *The Mother Earth News* 117:38+ My/Je '89
Vitamins: new RDAs [recommended dietary allowances] il *Newsweek* 114:84 N 6 '89
VITELIC CORPORATION
Mixed blessings. E. F. Cone. por *Forbes* 143:10 F 20 '89
VITEX ROUNDIFOLIA
Seaside survivors make waves. B. Yinger. il *Flower and Garden* 33:48-9 Jl/Ag '89
VITICULTURE
Greenhouse effect? H. J. De Blij. *Focus (New York, N.Y.: 1950)* 39:37 Spr '89
He hopes to hear $$$ through the grapevine. il *Successful Farming* 87 no4:64AN Mr '89
A sweet harvest of grapes. L. A. Weathers. il *Southern Living* 24:44-6+ F '89
VITRAC, BERNARD
The odyssey of reason. il *The Unesco Courier* 42:28-35 N '89
VITRIFICATION
Doing something about high-level nuclear waste. G. G. Wicks and D. Bickford. il *Technology Review* 92:50-8 N/D '89
Fusing dangerous weapons refuse into glass [in situ vitrification of contaminated soil] il *Popular Mechanics* 166:17 Jl '89
VITT, SAM B.
about
Renegades of Madison Avenue. M. Barrier. il por *Nation's Business* 77:16-17 S '89
VITT MEDIA INTERNATIONAL, INC.
Renegades of Madison Avenue. M. Barrier. il por *Nation's Business* 77:16-17 S '89
VIVIAN, JOHN
Buttoning up for winter. il *The Mother Earth News* 119:92-6+ S/O '89
VIZARD, FRANK
Audio. See issues of Popular Mechanics beginning October 1986
VLF (VERY LOW FREQUENCY) WAVES See Electromagnetic waves
VLIW COMPUTERS See Very long instruction word computers
VM SOFTWARE INC.
Utility infielder. D. Churbuck. il *Forbes* 143:186 Mr 20 '89
VM TECHNOLOGIES
Microprocessor challenge. R. C. Wood. il *High Technology Business* 9:12+ My '89
VMS REALTY PARTNERS
"Let not the rich man boast of his riches" [R. Van Kampen] M. Berss. il por *Forbes* 144 Special Issue:44-6 O 23 '89
VO2 MAX See Oxygen in the body
VOCABULARY TESTS
It pays to enrich your word power. P. Funk. See issues of Reader's Digest
VOCAL GROUPS See Choirs
VOCAL MUSIC
See also
Phonograph records—Vocal music
Singing
VOCAL TRAINING See Singing—Study and teaching
VOCATION IN RELIGION
Billy brings 'em in [use of B. Graham's crusades to stimulate clerical vocations in the Church of England] A. McCarthy. il *Commonweal* 116:456-7 S 8 '89
Calling. P. J. Ryan. *America* 160:71 Ja 28 '89
Challenges facing U.S. Catholics [lack of priests] J. Deedy. *Commonweal* 116:622-3 N 17 '89
Dachau—and a pastoral call. P. Yancey. il *Christianity Today* 33:80 Ja 13 '89
What is Christ's response? H. Fehren. *U.S. Catholic* 54:38-40 Mr '89
Why some men still want to be priests. M. J. Cook. il *U.S. Catholic* 54:31-8 Ap '89
VOCATIONAL APTITUDE TESTS See Aptitude tests
VOCATIONAL COUNSELING See Vocational guidance
VOCATIONAL EDUCATION See Vocational-technical education
VOCATIONAL GUIDANCE
See also
Business mentors
CareerTrack Inc.
Occupations
Outplacement consultant services
Dear Betty Harragan. B. L. Harragan. See issues of Working Woman
The future of work. R. B. Reich. *Harper's* 278:26+ Ap '89
Gaze into your future [career quiz] il *'Teen* 33:42-3+ Je '89
How to help your child choose the right career. M. Hodge and J. Blyskal. il *Reader's Digest* 134:146-8+ F '89
How to make a dream job come true. M. M. Kennedy. il *Glamour* 87:103 F '89
How to manage your career for lifelong success [cover story; special section] il *Working Woman* 14:101-4+ O '89

VOCATIONAL GUIDANCE—*cont.*
Western Europe
Guiding our paths. M. G. Bruce. *Phi Delta Kappan* 71:252-4 N '89
VOCATIONAL-TECHNICAL EDUCATION
See also
Apprentices
Business and education
Business education
Business schools
Hotel management—Study and teaching
Empty chairs: what happens to students who don't go to college [Grant Foundation report] M. A. Kramer. *Change* 21:6-7 Ja/F '89
The forgotten half [undereducated work force; cover story] D. Whitman. il *U.S. News & World Report* 106:44-9+ Je 26 '89
Getting on with it [welfare reform and education] A. C. Lewis. il *Phi Delta Kappan* 70:428-9 F '89
The need to retool vocational education. D. L. Johnston. *The Education Digest* 55:38-9 N '89
The new, improved vocational school. N. J. Perry. il *Fortune* 119:127+ Je 19 '89
No college, no future? [excerpt from The forgotten half report by the Grant Foundation] *The Education Digest* 54:10-14 F '89
Training the workforce of the future. J. E. Jacobs. il *Technology Review* 92:66-72 Ag/S '89
Tuning in to the needs of high school dropouts. G. S. Becker. il *Business Week* p18 Jl 3 '89
Ethical aspects
Scandal in our trade schools [abuse of financial aid] T. Armbrister. *Reader's Digest* 134:85-90 Ja '89
Federal aid
Dealing a new hand to vocational education? A. C. Lewis. *Phi Delta Kappan* 71:260-1 D '89
International aspects
International developments in apprenticeship. M. Brodsky. il *Monthly Labor Review* 112:40-1 Jl '89
State aid
Trained to order [states providing vocational training as lure to new industry] S. B. Weiner and C. Siler. il *Forbes* 143:73+ Je 26 '89
Canada
See also
Youth Employment Skills Canada Inc.
Germany (West)
West Germany's competitive advantage. il *Fortune* 119:136 Je 19 '89
VOCATIONS *See* Occupations
VODKA
Cristall clear [new Soviet vodka] N. Hazelton. *National Review* 41:56+ Jl 14 '89
Glasnost in a bottle. E. Fried. il *Black Enterprise* 19:340 Je '89
Kansas hooch in Scandinavian bottles [Brown-Forman's marketing strategy for Icy vodka] J. Levine. il *Forbes* 144:131 Ag 7 '89
Skoal on ice. A. Richman. il *Gentlemen's Quarterly* 59:178+ Jl '89
Straight shots [drinking vodka in the Soviet Union] K. Eldredge. il *Harper's Bazaar* 122:170+ F '89
What stirs the spirit makers: vodka, vodka, vodka. A. Dunkin. il *Business Week* p54-5 Je 12 '89
VODKA INDUSTRY *See* Liquor industry
VOELCKER, JOHN
Driving 4 fun. il *Essence* 20:110 My '89
VOGEL, AMOS
Sokurov's 'Lonely voice'. il por *Film Comment* 25:64+ My/Je '89
VOGEL, CAROLE GARBUNY
Every woman needs a champion. il pors *Good Housekeeping* 208:158+ My '89
VOGEL, STEVEN K.
Let's make a deal: the U.S.-Japan co-technology sphere. *The New Republic* 200:14+ Je 19 '89
VOGELGESANG, SANDRA L.
FY 1990 assistance request for organizations and programs [statement, March 22, 1989] *Department of State Bulletin* 89:81-4 My '89
U.S. opposes PLO admission to UN agencies [statement, May 4, 1989] *Department of State Bulletin* 89:65-6 Jl '89
VOGELSTEIN, BERT, AND OTHERS
Allelotype of colorectal carcinomas. bibl f il *Science* 244:207-11 Ap 14 '89
VOGUE (PERIODICAL)
Diana Vreeland. il pors *Vogue* 179:306-13+ D '89
What's in a name? N. Darnton. il pors *Newsweek* 113:62-3 Je 5 '89
VOGUEING
Attitude. *The New Yorker* 64:26-7 Ja 16 '89
They're puttin' on the vogue. J. D. Reed. il *Time* 133:103 My 22 '89
Vogueing. il *Seventeen* 48:108-9 O '89
Vogueing, a hip new dance from Harlem is haute, haute, haute. il *People Weekly* 31:104-5 My 29 '89

VOICE
See also
Larynx
Singing
Speech
Speech processing systems
Ventriloquism
VOICE CULTURE *See* Singing—Study and teaching
VOICE MAIL SYSTEMS
See also
Call processing systems
Another medium for the message. L. Davis. il *Nation's Business* 77:54-6 Ag '89
Hello! This is voice mail speaking. P. Elmer-Dewitt. il *Time* 133:98 My 22 '89
VOICE MESSAGING SYSTEMS *See* Voice mail systems
VOICE OF AMERICA
America's Voice in China [television broadcasting] D. Baer. il *U.S. News & World Report* 106:34 Je 19 '89
Too many Voices of America. K. A. Elliott. *Foreign Policy* 77:113-31 Wint '89/'90
VOICE OF THE BEEHIVE (MUSICAL GROUP)
Music. J. Van Meter. il *Seventeen* 48:100+ Je '89
Voice of the Beehive, sisters from L.A. who have London all abuzz about their stinging pop songs. il pors *People Weekly* 31:88 Mr 13 '89
VOICE TEACHERS *See* Singing teachers
VOICES OF SARAFINA! [film] *See* Motion picture reviews—Single works
VOIGHT, BARRY
A relation to describe rate-dependent material failure. bibl f il *Science* 243:200-3 Ja 13 '89
VOLANS, KEVIN
about
The Songlines quartet. B. Chatwin. il *The New York Review of Books* 35:50-1 Ja 19 '89
VOLCANIC ACTIVITY PREDICTION
Good news for volcano watchers [study of Long Valley Caldera by Christopher Newhall and Daniel Dzurisin] R. A. Kerr. il *Science* 245:255 Jl 21 '89
Hot times in Lascar [use of Landsat infrared images to predict Lascar volcano eruption; research by Peter Francis] il *Discover* 10:10 Ag '89
VOLCANIC ASH, TUFF, ETC.
See also
Aviation—Volcano hazards
Muddy evidence [study of volcanic debris flow strengthens case for water on Mars; work of Eric H. Christiansen] B. D. Schwartz. *Scientific American* 260:28+ Je '89
Muddying the waters [channels of volcanic debris as evidence for water on Mars; research by Eric Christiansen] il *Discover* 10:10 N '89
VOLCANIC CRATERS *See* Craters
VOLCANOES
See also
Aviation—Volcano hazards
Hot spots (Geology)
Lava
Volcanic activity prediction
Volcanic ash, tuff, etc.
. . . and sulfur volcanism on Venus [research by Bruce Fegley, Jr., and Ronald G. Prinn] *Sky and Telescope* 77:356 Ap '89
Eruption streaks Triton sky. il *Science News* 136:247 O 14 '89
Geologic events. See issues of Earth Science
A geologically young Triton after all? R. A. Kerr. *Science* 246:1563 D 22 '89
Ice volcanism on Ariel [discussion of September 9, 1988 article, Solid-state ice volcanism on the satellites of Uranus] D. G. Jankowski and S. W. Squyres. *Science* 245:195-6 Jl 14 '89
Magma force. D. Ryll. il *Omni (New York, N.Y.)* 11:66-8+ Ag '89
Neptune's Triton spews a plume. R. A. Kerr. il *Science* 246:313 O 13 '89
Questioning the cooling effects of volcanoes [research by Clifford F. Mass and David A. Portman] F. Flam. *Science News* 135:359 Je 10 '89
Silicate volcanism on Io [research by Torrence V. Johnson] il *Sky and Telescope* 77:355-6 Ap '89
Styles of volcanism on Venus: new Arecibo high resolution radar data. D. B. Campbell and others. bibl f il *Science* 246:373-7 O 20 '89
Venus volcanism: another hint. *Science News* 136:383 D 9 '89
Volcanism at rifts [mid-ocean ridges] R. S. White and D. P. McKenzie. bibl il maps *Scientific American* 261:62-71 Jl '89
Volcanoes and tsunamis [cover story] P. A. Lockridge. il *Earth Science* 42:24-5 Spr '89
Volcanoes can muddle the greenhouse. R. A. Kerr. il *Science* 245:127-8 Jl 14 '89
Exhibitions
Volcano exhibit to travel U.S. il *Earth Science* 42:5-6 Summ '89

VOLCANOES—*cont.*

History

Giant meteor impacts and great eruptions: dinosaur killers? G. S. Paul. bibl f il *BioScience* 39:162-72 Mr '89

See also
Redoubt Volcano (Alaska)

Alaska

California

Good news for volcano watchers [study of Long Valley Caldera by Christopher Newhall and Daniel Dzurisin] R. A. Kerr. il *Science* 245:255 Jl 21 '89

Chile

Hot times in Lascar [use of Landsat infrared images to predict Lascar volcano eruption; research by Peter Francis] il *Discover* 10:10 Ag '89

Greece

See also
Thera (Greece: Island)

Hawaii

See also
Hawaii Volcanoes National Park (Hawaii)
Kilauea (Hawaii)

India

A combination of impact and volcano is dismissed. *Science* 243:479 Ja 27 '89

Tanzania

See also
Oldoinyo Lengai (Tanzania)

Ushishir Islands (Soviet Union)

Caldron in the sea. M. V. Propp and V. G. Tarasov. il maps *Natural History* p28-33 Ag '89

Washington (State)

See also
Mount Saint Helens (Wash.)

VOLCKER, PAUL A.

Should the "balanced budget constitutional amendment" be adopted? [excerpts from statement, October 15, 1987] *Congressional Digest* 68:273+ N '89

about

Advice from Mr. Chairman [interview] L. Malkin. il por *Time* 133:48-50 Ja 23 '89

VÖLGYES, IVÁN, 1936-

Hungary: dancing in the shackles of the past. bibl f *Current History* 88:381-4+ N '89

VOLK, PATRICIA

Bless you, Marty. il *The New York Times Magazine* p20-1 Ja 1 '89

The mother tongue. il *The New York Times Magazine* p20+ My 14 '89

The Steinberg trial: scenes from a tragedy. il pors *The New York Times Magazine* p22-5 Ja 15 '89

VOLKSMARCHING

What would Flo-Jo wear? T. Loverro. il *Sport (New York, N.Y.)* 80:76 Jl '89

VOLKSWAGEN (AUTOMOBILE) *See* Automobiles, Foreign; Sports cars

VOLKSWAGEN OF AMERICA INC.

Can Volkswagen stop its U.S. decline? J. Flint. il *Forbes* 143:64 Ap 3 '89

VOLKSWRITER (WORD PROCESSOR PROGRAM) *See* Word processors and processing—Programming

VOLLENWEIDER, ANDREAS

about

The Age of Vollenweider. C. Krupp. il por *Glamour* 87:184 Je '89

VOLLEYBALL

Bump/set/spike! [women's volleyball] V. Z. Daly. il *Health (New York, N.Y.)* 21:62-3+ Je '89

Study and teaching

Serving 'em right. D. Brown. il *Women's Sports & Fitness* 11:72-5 Ap '89

Tournaments

Their final shots [departing players K. Kiraly and S. Timmons help U.S. defeat Soviets for USA Cup] B. Anderson. il pors *Sports Illustrated* 71:24-5 Jl 10 '89

VOLLEYBALL, COLLEGE

Calif. volleyball star aiming for NCAA crown [T. Cross] il por *Jet* 77:50 N 27 '89

VOLLEYBALL, PROFESSIONAL

See also
Beach volleyball

Woman to watch: volleyball pro Ruth Lawanson. F. D'Addesa. il por *Women's Sports & Fitness* 11:66 Mr '89

VOLLEYBALL SHOES

Hello, Volley. il *Women's Sports & Fitness* 11:43-4 Mr '89

VOLTZ, JEANNE

Heat busters. il *Modern Maturity* 32:62-4+ Je/Jl '89

Potluck potpourri. il *Modern Maturity* 32:70-4+ D '89/Ja '90

VOLUME CONTROL (AMPLIFIERS) *See* Amplifiers—Volume control

VOLUNTEER FIREFIGHTERS *See* Firefighters

VOLUNTEER SERVICE

See also
Literacy Volunteers of New York City
National parks and reserves—Volunteer workers
National Retiree Volunteer Center
National service

Points-of-Light Initiative (Program)
VOLUNTEER-The National Center

Adolescents help themselves by helping others [Early Adolescent Helper Program] J. G. Schine. il *Children Today* 18:10-15 Ja/F '89

Broadening community service to include low-income students [college students] K. Bojar. il *Change* 21:22-3 S/O '89

Consumerism to idealism [young people] N. Ulaby. por *The Humanist* 49:26+ Mr/Ap '89

Crisis time for the non-profits [address, September 10, 1988] F. W. Wylie. *Vital Speeches of the Day* 55:170-2 Ja 1 '89

Essentials for successful community service programs [student volunteers] C. B. Kaye. *The Education Digest* 55:57-60 N '89

Family. C. Tevis. il *Successful Farming* 87:59 O '89

For goodness' sake [special section] N. R. Gibbs. il *Time* 133:20-4 Ja 9 '89

Getting people to give [concerns over self image; research by Robert Cialdini and others] W. Herbert. il *Psychology Today* 22:66 D '88

Good neighbors [assisting New York City poor] H. Evans. il *U.S. News & World Report* 106:76 Ap 10 '89

The good we do [older volunteers] K. S. Black. il *New Choices for the Best Years* 29:62-5 D '89

Hands across the ages [aged working with children; cover story] A. Korpivaara. il *New Choices for the Best Years* 29:41-3+ Ag '89

Health campaign reaps results [AARP's Health Care Campaign] il *Modern Maturity* 32:93 O/N '89

How to slow down [setting limits on volunteer work] J. G. Fitzpatrick. il *Parents* 64:97-102 Ap '89

It's time to serve our country. H. B. Deets. il *Modern Maturity* 32:11 Je/Jl '89

Learning by doing through public service for students and professors alike [interview with R. Coles] A. Levine. il pors *Change* 21:18-21+ S/O '89

A little love goes a long way [women volunteers] A. Fischer. il *Redbook* 173:134-5+ My '89

"My son needed to feel needed" [learning disabled teenage volunteer] M. B. White. il *Parents* 64:84+ Ap '89

The new volunteers [cover story; special section] il *Newsweek* 114:36-8+ Jl 10 '89

Old hands [senior citizens working at a day care center in Union City, N.J.] C. Dowling. il *Life* 12:102-4+ D '89

One teen's struggle to end hunger [student M. Varilla raises funds for Ethiopian relief] L. Eskin. il por *Scholastic Update (Teachers' edition)* 121:12-13 Ja 27 '89

Package deal [volunteers stuff goody bags for the New York City Marathon] G. Averbuch. il *Runner's World* 24:50+ N '89

Santa's special helper [donating and distributing gifts for needy families in East Saint Louis, Ill.] R. Swiener. il por *Ladies' Home Journal* 106:18+ D '89

Seniors as police volunteers. il *Sunset (Central West edition)* 183:138-9 N '89

Starting a senior center latchkey program. *Children Today* 18:5 Jl/Ag '89

A student's view of youth participation [address, July 20, 1987] J. C. Cutler. *The Education Digest* 54:45-8 Ap '89

An untapped resource [business encouragement to volunteer work] R. Thompson. il *Nation's Business* 77:50+ Mr '89

The volunteer angel of San Antonio [stroke victim G. Cisneros] H. Hylton. il pors *New Choices for the Best Years* 29:76-7+ Ja '89

Volunteer jobs with solid payoffs. T. Thompson. il *U.S. News & World Report* 106:76-7 Ap 24 '89

Volunteer workers: our greatest asset [aged] L. Crooks. il *Modern Maturity* 32:10-11 Ap/My '89

Wherever he goes, architect Robert Leathers leaves another new playground behind [volunteer-built playground in Brewer, Me.] N. Geeslin. il pors *People Weekly* 32:63+ S 25 '89

Awards

See also
Student Humanitarian Service Award

VOLUNTEER-THE NATIONAL CENTER

An untapped resource. R. Thompson. il *Nation's Business* 77:50+ Mr '89

VOLUNTEER WORKERS *See* Volunteer service

VOLUNTEERS FOR MEDICAL ENGINEERING

Electronics: John H. Staehlin [aerospace laureate] il por *Aviation Week & Space Technology* 130:16-17 Ja 2 '89

VOLVO (AUTOMOBILE) *See* Automobiles, Foreign

VOLVO AB

Volvo's back-to-the-future factory [Uddevalla plant] D. Bartal. il *U.S. News & World Report* 107:42 Ag 21 '89

Volvo's radical new plant: 'the death of the assembly line'? J. Kapstein. il *Business Week* p92-3 Ag 28 '89

VOLZ, JOE

about

'Rookie' reporter plies MNS beat. il por *Modern Maturity* 32:88 Je/Jl '89

VON BRAUN, WERNHER, 1912-1977

about

Lunar labors lost. B. Forman. il *Omni (New York, N.Y.)* 11:16+ Jl '89

VOYAGES—cont.
Thursday's child triumphs [W. Luhrs breaks record from New York to San Francisco via Cape Horn] L. Rudeen. il por map *Motor Boating & Sailing* 163:66-71+ Ap '89
Winners [G. Kolesnikovs breaks record from New York to San Francisco via Cape Horn] L. Rudeen. il por *Motor Boating & Sailing* 164:20 Ag '89
History
Voyages into the unknown. il map *National Geographic World* 170:12-15 O '89

VOYAGES AROUND THE WORLD
When teen sailor Robin Lee Graham came home from his epic voyage, the really rough weather began. S. Toepfer. il pors *People Weekly* 31:82-4 Ja 16 '89

VOYAGEURS NATIONAL PARK (MINN.)
A stretch of solitude in the land of lakes. J. Popkin. il map *U.S. News & World Report* 106:82 My 8 '89

VPF *See* Vascular permeability factor

VREELAND, DIANA
about
Diana Vreeland. il pors *Vogue* 179:306-13+ D '89
Obituary
New York il por 22:31-2 N 20 '89
Newsweek il por 114:62 S 4 '89. C. McGuigan
People Weekly il por 32:119 S 11 '89

VREELAND, NANCY *See* Dalva, Nancy Vreeland

VRIJENHOEK, ROBERT C.
(jt. auth) *See* Quattro, J. M., and Vrijenhoek, Robert C.

VUCCIRIA (NEW YORK, N.Y.: RESTAURANT) *See* New York (N.Y.)—Restaurants, nightclubs, bars, etc.

VUILLARD, ÉDOUARD, 1868-1940
about
Behind closed doors. G. T. M. Shackelford. il por *House & Garden* 161:50+ N '89

VULCAN AIRCRAFT COMPANY
Vulcan ends initial wind tunnel tests on VTOL, fan-in-wing Starfire model. E. H. Phillips. il *Aviation Week & Space Technology* 131:64+ N 13 '89

VULTURES
See also
Condors

VUYST, ALEX
Self-help for the homeless. *The Humanist* 49:13+ My/Je '89

VW (AUTOMOBILE) *See* Automobiles, Foreign

VY HIGGINSEN INC./REACH ENTERTAINMENT & SPORTS
Show stopper. J. Torrence-Thompson. il por *Black Enterprise* 20:66-8+ Ag '89

VYZHUTOVICH, VALERY
'Masters do not strike'. *World Press Review* 36:22 S '89

W

W. GRAHAM ARADER III GALLERY
'Arader is up again!' and his galleries are in full bloom. P. Patton. il pors *Smithsonian* 20:86-92+ D '89

W. H. SMITH & SON (HOLDINGS) PLC
W. H. Smith merges specialist bookselling chain with Waterstone's. V. Menkes. *Publishers Weekly* 236:14 Ag 4 '89

W. H. SMITH PUBLISHERS INC.
Penguin USA to acquire W. H. Smith Publishers. il *Publishers Weekly* 236:10 S 29 '89

W.M.U. GOLD COMPANY *See* Western Michigan University Gold Company

W. R. BERKLEY CORP.
Boy wonder grows up [W. Berkley] E. F. Cone. il por *Forbes* 143:49+ F 20 '89

W.R. GRACE & CO.
Grace note. T. Jaffe. il *Forbes* 143:152 F 20 '89
Will Peter Grace call it a day? G. G. Marcial. *Business Week* p146 Mr 20 '89

W. W. GRAINGER, INC.
"The goal is 0%". C. Siler. il *Forbes* 144:95+ O 30 '89

WAAS, MURRAY
The sum of their possessions. *Harper's* 279:66-7 S '89
The White House connection [cover story] *The Nation* 249:585+ N 20 '89

WABAN (FIRM)
Bargain days at a discount club. G. G. Marcial. *Business Week* p62 Jl 24 '89
This Zayre spinoff could spin gold. J. M. Laderman. *Business Week* p128 N 13 '89

WACHHOLZ, DIETER
An island for individualists. il *World Press Review* 36:62 Ap '89

WACHNER, LINDA JOY, 1946-
about
Treating the retailers as partners. S. Caminiti. il por *Fortune* 120:80 D 18 '89

WACHS, MARTIN
U.S. transit subsidy policy: in need of reform. bibl f il *Science* 244:1545-9 Je 30 '89

WACKER, BOB
Virus on ice. il *Health (New York, N.Y.)* 21:48-51 D '89

WACKER, GRANT, 1945-
The entire sanctification of an extraordinary ego. por *Christianity Today* 33:56-9 O 6 '89
Jim Bakker and the Eternal Revenue Service. il pors *The Christian Century* 106:1053-5 N 15 '89

WACKS, JONATHAN
about
Powwow Highway [film] Reviews
Maclean's il 102:62-3 Ap 24 '89. B. D. Johnson
The New Republic 200:24 Ap 24 '89. S. Kauffmann
Newsweek 113:70 Ap 3 '89. D. Ansen

WACO (TEX.)
Historic houses, sites, etc.
A trail of homes in Waco. il map *Southern Living* 24:31 Ap '89

WADA, YOSHI
about
The Anchorage. *The New Yorker* 65:35-6 S 18 '89

WADDLE, RAY
National Baptists build a headquarters. *The Christian Century* 106:805-7 S 13-20 '89

WADE, ALAN
Treasures of the Guatemala rain forest. il *The New Leader* 72:11-13 Ap 3-17 '89

WADE, BOB
about
Soviets let Canadian CF-18 pilot fly MiG-29 trainer at air show. il *Aviation Week & Space Technology* 131:32 Ag 21 '89

WADE, GEORGE N.
(jt. auth) *See* Schneider, Jill E., and Wade, George N.

WADE, KATHERINE
(jt. auth) *See* Wade, Paul J., and Wade, Katherine

WADE, PAUL J., AND WADE, KATHERINE
Gourmet holidays: Florida's barrier islands. il map *Gourmet* 49:90-5+ O '89
Gourmet holidays: islands off the Great Barrier Reef. il map *Gourmet* 49:46-51+ Mr '89

WADHWANI, ROMESH
about
A factory that practically runs itself. il por *Business Week* p145 My 8 '89

WADING
Perfectly clear [bass fishing] J. Doggett. il *Field & Stream* 94:47+ My '89

WADLEIGH, JULIAN
What is conservatism? por *The Humanist* 49:20-6+ N/D '89

WADSWORTH, WILLIAM
The marriage of Edgar and Cordelia [poem] *The New Republic* 201:30 O 30 '89

WAFF, CRAIG B.
The struggle for the outer planets. il *Astronomy* 17:44-52 S '89

WAGE AGREEMENTS *See* Collective labor agreements
WAGE BARGAINING *See* Collective bargaining
WAGE DIFFERENTIALS
See also
Equal pay for equal work
Are we becoming a nation of burger flippers? il *Changing Times* 43:32-3 Mr '89
Fair pay in family firms. S. Nelton. il *Nation's Business* 77:72-3 O '89

WAGES AND SALARIES
See also
Bonus system
Collective labor agreements
Cost and standard of living
Equal pay for equal work
Income
Merit pay
Minimum wage
Overtime
Pay stubs
Profit sharing
Tipping
See also subhead Salaries, pensions, etc. under classes of persons
Age vs. wage: how baby boomers may cool inflation. G. Koretz. il *Business Week* p26 F 6 '89
The changing basis for pay. R. M. Kanter. bibl *Society* 26:54-65 S/O '89
Getting paid what you're worth [women] B. Nivens. il *Essence* 20:92 Jl '89
Higher labor costs will keep inflation simmering. V. Brownstein. il *Fortune* 120:17-18 O 9 '89
How well does money motivate? S. Nasar. il *U.S. News & World Report* 107:68 N 13 '89
Labor is slowly raising its fist. A. Bernstein. il *Business Week* p36 F 27 '89
The labor market is a lot looser than it looks. R. Kuttner. il *Business Week* p18 Mr 27 '89
More math means more money [positive correlation between number of mathematics courses a person takes and earnings] B. A. Cipra. *Science* 243:314 Ja 20 '89

WAGES AND SALARIES—*cont.*
Plenty of workers are waiting in the wings. M. J. Mandel. il *Business Week* p90+ Mr 13 '89
The tenth annual Working woman salary survey [cover story; special section] A. M. Russell. il *Working Woman* 14:71-6+ Ja '89
Wage and salary [blacks] il *Black Enterprise* 19:63 F '89
Wage hikes and family troubles for women [views of James P. Smith and Michael Ward] il *The Futurist* 23:52-3 S/O '89
What's dragging productivity down? Women's low wages. A. Bernstein. il *Business Week* p171 N 27 '89

Statistics
Measuring the precision of the Employment Cost Index. K. O'Conor and W. Wong. il *Monthly Labor Review* 112:29-36 Mr '89
Sources of increasing inequality in wages and salaries, 1960-80. W. N. Grubb and R. H. Wilson. bibl f il *Monthly Labor Review* 112:3-13 Ap '89
Variations in holidays, vacations, and area pay levels. J. E. Buckley. bibl f il *Monthly Labor Review* 112:24-30 F '89
What jobs are worth around the country. il *U.S. News & World Report* 107:66-7 S 25 '89
What temporary workers earn: findings from new BLS survey. H. B. Williams. il *Monthly Labor Review* 112:3-6 Mr '89

Taxation
See also
Social security—Taxation
Withholding tax

Korea (South)
No more Mr. Cheap Guy. J. Flint. il *Forbes* 144:102-3 O 30 '89

WAGGETT, GERARD J
A plea to the soaps: let's stop turning rapists into heroes. il *TV Guide* 37:10-11 My 27-Je 2 '89

WAGGONER, GLEN
The heartbreak of presbyopia. *Esquire* 111:158-9 Mr '89

WAGGONER, JEFFREY D.
A music educator's look at the summer NAMM show. il *Down Beat* 56:56-7 O '89

WAGNER, A. JAMES
Music to watch the weather by [cover story] il *Weatherwise* 42:248-55 O '89
Persistent circulation patterns. il *Weatherwise* 42:18-21 F '89

WAGNER, AUDREY TEARE
Shattering the silence [poem] *McCall's* 116:65 My '89

WAGNER, BRETT
about
"I wish I could hold you more". B. Remsberg. il *Reader's Digest* 134:147-52 Je '89

WAGNER, EDWARD W.
Liberal establishment on Tory Row. il *National Review* 41:19-21 D 31 '89

WAGNER, GEOFFREY ATHELING
Where the people are nice and the trains run on time. *Harper's* 278:17 Ja '89

WAGNER, JANE
about
The search for signs of intelligent life in the universe [drama] Reviews
   Maclean's il pors 102:37 Ja 16 '89. D. Turbide

WAGNER, KATIE
about
R.J.'s daughter Katie Wagner has a head start on success: no excuses genes. J. Wadler. il pors *People Weekly* 31:98-100 My 22 '89

WAGNER, RICHARD, 1813-1883
about
Baltic odyssey. M. E. Brener. il por map *Opera News* 54:18-21 D 23 '89
Bayreuth. J. H. Sutcliffe. il *Opera News* 53:40-1+ F 4 '89
The flying Dutchman [opera] Reviews
   Opera News il 54:18-21 D 23 '89. M. E. Brener
   Opera News il 54:28-31 D 23 '89
   Opera News 54:68+ D 9 '89. H. Koegler
He knew his Wagner. W. H. Youngren. il *The Atlantic* 264:83-5 Jl '89
Die Meistersinger von Nurnberg [opera] Reviews
   The New Yorker 65:100+ S 25 '89. A. Porter
Der Ring des Nibelungen [opera] Reviews
   Art in America il 77:222-9 Ap '89. B. Adams
   Harper's Bazaar il 122:58 Je '89. M. Gurewitsch
   New York il 22:85-6 My 8 '89. P. G. Davis
   The New Yorker 65:68-70 Jl 10 '89. A. Porter
   The New Yorker 65:89-90 My 22 '89. A. Porter
   Newsweek il 113:68-9 My 8 '89. K. Ames
   Opera News il 53:6, 12-16+ Ap 1 '89
   Opera News il 53:18-20+ Je '89. M. Swed
   Theatre Crafts il 23:45+ My '89. B. Howard
Ring fever. P. G. Davis. il *New York* 22:74+ Ap 3 '89
Siegfried [opera] Reviews
   Opera News il 53:22+ Ap 1 '89. J. Potter

WAGON TRAINS
Wagon, roll! Like pioneers of old, the DeMarco family heads west with hope [journey from Ohio to California in covered wagon pulled by tractor] D. Chu. il *People Weekly* 32:123-4+ N 6 '89

WAGONER, DAN
about
Dance. T. Tobias. il *New York* 22:70-1 My 29 '89
Reviews:
   Performances at the Joyce Theater, New York City. R. A. Thom. il *Dance Magazine* 63:88 S '89
Wagoner's Joyce dates may be his last in the U.S.A. il por *Dance Magazine* 63:17 My '89

WAGONER (DAN) AND DANCERS *See* Dan Wagoner and Dancers

WAGONS, TOY *See* Toys

WAGSTAFF, SAM
about
The pleasure of the chase. C. McGuigan. il pors *Newsweek* 113:62-3 Ja 30 '89
Sam Wagstaff's silver. I. Sischy. il por *House & Garden* 161:108-13+ Ja '89

WAGSTYL, STEFAN
Japan's master of retailing. por *World Press Review* 36:52 Ja '89
Superconductors heat up. il *World Press Review* 36:47 Mr '89

WAHDAN, M. H.
Communicable diseases. il *World Health* p20-1 Jl '89

WAHLEN, M., AND OTHERS
Carbon-14 in methane sources and in atmospheric methane: the contribution from fossil carbon. bibl f il *Science* 245:286-90 Jl 21 '89

WAIKIKI BEACH (HONOLULU, HAWAII)
Description
Waikiki confidential. T. Friend. il *Vogue* 179:406+ Mr '89
Gardens and gardening
Waikiki hotel gardens. M. May. il *Flower and Garden* 33:16-17 Mr/Ap '89
Hotels, motels, etc.
Under the banyan tree [restoring Moana Hotel] C. McGuigan. il *Newsweek* 113:68 Ap 17 '89
Waikiki hotel gardens. M. May. il *Flower and Garden* 33:16-17 Mr/Ap '89

WAINSCOT PANELING *See* Paneling

WAINWRIGHT, HILARY
A social charter for the E.C.? il *The Nation* 249:80-2+ Jl 17 '89

WAINWRIGHT, LOUDON, III
about
Loudon clear. D. Wild. por *Rolling Stone* p18 O 5 '89

WAITERS AND WAITRESSES
Uniforms
View [designer uniforms] R. Urquhart. il *Vogue* 179:114+ Ag '89

WAITING LINES *See* Queues (Waiting lines)

WAITZKIN, FRED
What drives the Pistons. il *The New York Times Magazine* p30-3+ Ja 8 '89
When all the stars are gone. il *The New York Times Magazine* p20-3+ Jl 16 '89

WAKE COUNTY (N.C.)
Politics and government
A reunion in friendship [former Giants quarterback Y. A. Tittle to make campaign appearance for sheriff J. Baker, whose hit in 1964 helped end Tittle's career] il pors *Sports Illustrated* 71:12+ N 27 '89

WAKEFIELD, DAN
And now, a word from our Creator. il *The New York Times Book Review* 94:1+ F 12 '89
C'mon, work it on out. il *Gentlemen's Quarterly* 59:228-36 F '89
We need more religion in prime time. il *TV Guide* 37:14-17 Mr 11-17 '89

WAKEMAN, FREDERIC, 1909-
All the rage in China. il *The New York Review of Books* 36:19-21 Mr 2 '89

WAKENING FROM SLEEP
Night awakening can trigger heart damage [research by Joan Barry] K. Fackelmann. *Science News* 136:341 N 25 '89

WAL-MART STORES, INC.
Golf balls, motor oil and tomatoes [grocery business] S. B. Weiner. il *Forbes* 144:130-1+ O 30 '89
How Wal-Mart hits Main St. [effect on small businesses in Waverly, Iowa] K. R. Sheets. il map *U.S. News & World Report* 106:53-5 Mr 13 '89
In retail, bigger can be better [Jamesway vs. Wal-Mart] il *Business Week* p90 Mr 27 '89
Just saying no to Wal-Mart [Iowa City, Iowa] T. Padgett. il *Newsweek* 114:65 N 13 '89
Wal-Mart: will it take over the world? J. Huey. il map *Fortune* 119:52-6+ Ja 30 '89

WALAS, CHRIS
about
The fly II [film] Reviews
   People Weekly 31:11 F 27 '89. R. Novak
   Video il 13:81 O '89. D. Schweiger

WALBERG, HERBERT J., 1937-
(jt. auth) See Lane, John J. (John Joseph), 1935-, and Walberg, Herbert J., 1937-

WALBERG, HERBERT J., 1937-, AND OTHERS
Reconstructing the nation's worst schools. il *Phi Delta Kappan* 70:802-5 Je '89

WALBRAN, PETER D., AND OTHERS
Evidence from sediments of long-term Acanthaster planci predation on corals of the Great Barrier Reef [cover story] bibl f il map *Science* 245:847-50 Ag 25 '89

WALBRIDGE, CHARLES T.
Genetic algorithms: what computers can learn from Darwin [cover story] il *Technology Review* 92:46-8+ Ja '89

WALCOTT, CHARLES
Show me the way you go home. *Natural History* p40+ N '89

WALCOTT, DEREK
A castle in the olives [poem] *The New Yorker* 65:44-5 My 8 '89
Homer in the underground [poem] *The New Republic* 200:38-9 Mr 20 '89
The master of the ordinary. il *The New York Review of Books* 36:37-40 Je 1 '89
Polonaise [poem] *The New Yorker* 65:52-3 O 9 '89

WALDECK, GLEN
about
Troubadours for Mother Nature. C. P. Alexander. il pors *Time* 134:76 N 6 '89

WALDEN POND (MASS.)
On once-wild Walden Pond. J. H. Houvouras. il *Sierra* 74:94-6 My/Je '89
Photographs and photography
Bill Kane at Foster Goldstrom. C. Little. il *Art in America* 77:177-8 D '89

WALDENBOOKS
Waldenbooks' 8th annual gala. M. J. O'Brien. il *Publishers Weekly* 235:48-9+ Mr 10 '89

WALDER, BARBARA
Open house. il *House & Garden* 161:70+ Mr '89

WALDHEIM, KURT
about
Breaking faith (I). S. Hazzard. *The New Yorker* 65:63-4+ S 25 '89
Breaking faith (II). S. Hazzard. *The New Yorker* 65:74-8+ O 2 '89

WALDMAN, MICHAEL, 1960-, AND GILBERT, PAMELA
Don't let them gut RICO. il *USA Today (Periodical)* 118:50-1 N '89

WALDMAN, STEVEN
Group therapy: the answer to merit pay. *The Washington Monthly* 21:38+ Mr '89

WALDREP, KENT
about
They never gave up. R. Hoffer. il pors *Sports Illustrated* 71:117-27+ D 25 '89-Ja 1 '90

WALDRON, ANN
A star shines from Alabama. il *The Nation* 248:664-6 My 15 '89

WALDRON, ROBERT
Welcome back to school—we'd like to beat you up. il *TV Guide* 37:14-16 My 20-26 '89

WALDSTEIN, PETER D.
May I sue you? il *Esquire* 112:64 Ag '89

WALES, JANE, AND HALPERIN, MORTON H.
Advice to the president: don't count on nuclear weapons. il *The Bulletin of the Atomic Scientists* 45:7-8 Mr '89

WALES
See also
Historic houses, sites, etc.—Wales
Hotels, motels, etc.—Wales
Hunting—Wales
Description and travel
Wandering through Wales. il *Southern Living* 24:32-3 N '89

WALES (ALASKA)
Monuments, statues, etc.
A universal gesture [D. Barr's Arctic Arc sculpture looks across to Siberia] S. Yolles. il *Art News* 88:13 Ja '89

WAŁĘSA, LECH, 1943-
A letter to the Polish electorate. *The New York Review of Books* 36:72 S 28 '89
Poland [address, November 15, 1989] *Vital Speeches of the Day* 56:132-5 D 15 '89
about
Freedom's turn [cover story; special section] il pors *Newsweek* 114:16-23+ Ag 28 '89
The high price of reforms. *Maclean's* 102:30 N 27 '89
Lech Walesa digs in. N. Zeman. il por *Newsweek* 114:6 N 20 '89
Lech Walesa, superstar, now faces the music. S. V. Roberts. il por *U.S. News & World Report* 107:10-11 N 27 '89
Lech's American angel [cover story] D. Margolick. il pors *The New York Times Magazine* p28-31+ O 8 '89
One of the great men of our time. M. S. Forbes, Jr. il pors *Forbes* 144:27 D 25 '89
Poland: hanging by a thread. A. Nagorski. il por *Reader's Digest* 135:121-7 N '89
Sighing to God. *America* 161:416 D 9 '89

The struggle for Solidarity. B. Came. il por *Maclean's* 102:30-1 Ap 17 '89
A symbol of hope. P. Sudo. il por *Scholastic Update (Teachers' edition)* 122:3-4 O 20 '89
Thanks a lot, but no thanks. M. Johnson. il por *Time* 134:30 Ag 7 '89
Walesa's revolution [cover story; special section; with editorial comment by Kevin Doyle] il pors *Maclean's* 102:2, 24-30 Ag 28 '89
The wit and wisdom of Lech Walesa. il por *Newsweek* 114:35 N 27 '89

WAŁĘSA, SLAWEK
about
It was shake-the-world time for Lech Walesa in Poland, but polka time for his son in America. il pors *People Weekly* 32:81 S 11 '89
The next generation. il por *Scholastic Update (Teachers' edition)* 122:5 O 20 '89

WALK-IN MEDICAL CENTERS *See* Health facilities
A WALK IN THE WOODS [drama] *See* Blessing, Lee
WALK OF FAME (HOLLYWOOD, CALIF.)
Gaye's loyal fans clamor for Hollywood Walk star. il *Jet* 76:36 Ag 28 '89

WALKER, ALAN, AND TEAFORD, MARK
The hunt for Proconsul. il map *Scientific American* 260:76-82 Ja '89

WALKER, ALICE, 1944-
Am I blue? Thoughts on animal feelings, human rights, and justice for all. il *Utne Reader* p98-9+ Ja/F '89
Birth [fiction] il *Ms.* 17:58-60 My '89
Don't bury my heart [discussion of May 22, 1989 article, What can the white man . . . say to the black woman?] *The Nation* 249:226 S 4-11 '89
Marriage vs freedom [fiction] il *Essence* 20:81-2+ My '89
The temple of my familiar [fiction] il *Mother Jones* 14:53-4 Ap '89
What can the white man . . . say to the black woman? [address, April 8, 1989] il *The Nation* 248:691-2 My 22 '89
about
Alice Walker [cover story] A. De Veaux. il pors *Essence* 20:56-8+ S '89
Alice Walker [interview] C. Dreifus. il *The Progressive* 53:29-31 Ag '89
Living by the word. G. Jaynes. il pors *Life* 12:61-2+ My '89
A turning of the critical tide? C. Iannone. *Commentary* 88:57-9 N '89

WALKER, BEVERLY
The disappearing director. il *Film Comment* 25:28-31 Ja/F '89
Due respects. il *Film Comment* 25:58-9 N/D '89
Gena. pors *Film Comment* 25:42-3 My/Je '89
Hanks to you [interview] il pors *Film Comment* 25:16-19 Mr/Ap '89
Teetering over 'The abyss'. il pors *American Film* 14:34-9 Je '89

WALKER, MADAME C. J., 1867-1919
about
Madam C. J. Walker: first black woman millionaire. K. Doyle. por *American History Illustrated* 24:24-5 Mr '89

WALKER, CAROL
Flat, pan, sad. il por *Americana* 17:50-3 S/O '89

WALKER, CAROL, AND WALKER, JIMMY
Grandma had an iron like that! il *Antiques & Collecting Hobbies* 94:23-5+ Mr '89

WALKER, CATHERINE
about
Fashion fit for a Princess. N. Darnton. il pors *Newsweek* 113:75 Mr 27 '89

WALKER, CHARLES D.
President's message. See issues of Ad Astra beginning January 1989
Spreading the word [excerpt from statement, April 5, 1989] il por *Ad Astra* 1:31-4 Je '89

WALKER, DAVID M.
about
NASA shuttle commander involved in near collision with Pan Am A310. *Aviation Week & Space Technology* 130:105 My 22 '89

WALKER, DONALD A., AND OTHERS
Impacts of petroleum development in the Arctic [discussion of November 6, 1987 article, Cumulative impacts of oil fields on northern Alaskan landscapes] *Science* 245:764-6 Ag 18 '89

WALKER, EDWARD S.
FY 1990 assistance request for the Middle East [statements, March 1-9, 1989] *Department of State Bulletin* 89:61-6 My '89

WALKER, GEORGE F.
about
Love and anger [drama] Reviews
Maclean's il por 102:76-7 O 23 '89. J. Bemrose
Urban survival. J. Bemrose. il por *Maclean's* 102:76-7 O 23 '89

WALKER, GREG
about
Just happy to be here. B. Newman. il pors *Sports Illustrated* 70:34-6+ Ap 17 '89
WALKER, HARRIETTE ISH, D. 1989
about
Obituary
Jet il por 76:17 Ap 17 '89
WALKER, HERSCHEL
about
Sudden impact [cover story] P. King. il pors *Sports Illustrated* 71:42-4+ O 23 '89
WALKER, J. SAMUEL
(jt. auth) See Errico, Charles J., and Walker, J. Samuel
WALKER, JEANNE MURRAY
Sudden fever [story] il *Redbook* 173:54+ Je '89
WALKER, JEARL, 1945-
The amateur scientist. See issues of Scientific American
WALKER, JERRY JEFF, 1942-
about
Jerry Jeff Walker. A. Nash. il por *Stereo Review* 54:136 S '89
WALKER, JIMMY
(jt. auth) See Walker, Carol, and Walker, Jimmy
WALKER, JIMMY
Musicfest U.S.A. swings with education: '89 national finals. il *Down Beat* 56:28-34 Jl '89
WALKER, JOE LOUIS
about
Asking for water. M. Moses. *The New Yorker* 64:83+ F 13 '89
WALKER, JOHN THOMAS
about
Obituary
Jet por 77:7 O 16 '89
WALKER, KATHARINE DAVIDSON, 1921-
Where to eat. il *Publishers Weekly* 235:118-20 My 12 '89
WALKER, LISA
Down toward Arkansas. *The New Yorker* 65:105-6+ S 18 '89
WALKER, LOU ANN
Marlee Matlin: breaking the silence. il pors *Ladies' Home Journal* 106:42+ Ap '89
WALKER, MARGARET, 1915-
The mysterious death of Richard Wright [excerpt from Richard Wright] il pors *Ebony* 44:116+ F '89
WALKER, MARTIN, 1947-
Outside, looking in. *World Press Review* 36:22 Ja '89
Punk *perestroika* [cover story] il *The New Republic* 201:22+ D 4 '89
WALKER, MARY CHRISTINE
about
Birth certificate says she's white, but woman gets a judge to declare her black. por *Jet* 76:36 S 18 '89
WALKER, MICHAEL
Cozy comfort in the mountains. il *New Choices for the Best Years* 29:33-4 Je '89
WALKER, PAUL F.
Did anyone tell the Pentagon? *The Bulletin of the Atomic Scientists* 45:12+ O '89
Limited success. *The Bulletin of the Atomic Scientists* 45:40 My '89
WALKER, R. J., AND MORGAN, J. W.
Rhenium-osmium isotope systematics of carbonaceous chondrites. bibl f il *Science* 243:519-22 Ja 27 '89
WALKER, RICHARD W.
The making of a market. il *Art News* 88:138-43 Mr '89
WALKER, SAMUEL, 1942-
about
ACLU history from Oxford. C. Goodrich. *Publishers Weekly* 236:40 O 27 '89
WALKER, TONY
Trying to guide the country into calmer waters. il *World Press Review* 36:11-13 Ag '89
(jt. auth) See Gowers, Andrew, and Walker, Tony
WALKER, WILLIAM, 1824-1860
about
El presidente gringo. R. Bruns and B. Kennedy. il por map *American History Illustrated* 23:14-21+ F '89
WALKER (MADAME C. J.) COMPANY See Madame C. J. Walker Company
WALKER ART CENTER
The director's director [M. L. Friedman] M. A. Martin. il pors *Art News* 88:132-7 My '89
WALKING
See also
Backpacks and backpacking
Hiking
Race walking
Volksmarching
Britain revisited [walking from coast to coast] D. Pollitt. il map *American Health* 8:40 Jl/Ag '89
Cure it with walking. G. Maleskey. il *Prevention (Emmaus, Pa.)* 41:90+ S '89
Easiest-ever exercise. il *Glamour* 87:340-3 Ap '89
Here's a way to get fit, save the planet, make our cities livable, have a little fun—and it's all for free. J. P. Wiley, Jr. il *Smithsonian* 20:22-4 Jl '89

The high road. F. Rogers. il *The New York Times Magazine* p76-7 O 1 '89
If walking bores you, try our way. J. Wood. *Modern Maturity* 32:30 Ap/My '89
Living proof that walking changes walkers [Walkers of the Year J. Rosinski, R. Dulaney, and M. Warner] M. Spilner. il pors *Prevention (Emmaus, Pa.)* 41:84+ Jl '89
Love blooms in the aisles [shopping malls used for walking] J. Pereira. il *The Saturday Evening Post* 261:54-5+ S '89
The mechanics of motion. S. Festa. il *Health (New York, N.Y.)* 21:56-8 S '89
A moving approach to arthritis pain. G. Yanker and K. Burton. il *New Choices for the Best Years* 29:62-3+ S '89
Pick your pace. K. Anderson. il *Health (New York, N.Y.)* 21:58-9 S '89
Poetry in motion at the walking rally [haiku written by participants] M. Bricklin. il *Prevention (Emmaus, Pa.)* 41:144 Jl '89
Provence: a walk in the sun. H. McGrew. il map *Gourmet* 49:96-8+ My '89
Put more spring in your step. M. Bricklin. il *Prevention (Emmaus, Pa.)* 41:144+ Ap '89
Re-shape your body & re-charge your heart. S. Lally. il *Prevention (Emmaus, Pa.)* 41:67-8+ Ap '89
A walk in the country [Vermont] G. Yanker and K. Burton. il map *Travel Holiday* 171:22-3 Je '89
Walk it off! [excerpt from Thin thighs in 30 days] W. Stehling. il *Redbook* 173:118-19 Je '89
Walkabouts! [cover story] K. Shyne. il *New Choices for the Best Years* 29:29-32 Mr '89
Walker's world. See issues of Prevention (Emmaus, Pa.) beginning January 1987
Walking tall [proper posture] B. Kevles. il *Women's Sports & Fitness* 11:26 Ap '89
The way we are [taking grandchildren for a walk] L. Wyse. il *Good Housekeeping* 209:270 D '89
Equipment
See also
Walking shoes
Pump it up [walking with weights; research by James E. Graves] L. Warner. il *American Health* 8:38 S '89
Psychological aspects
On the road to higher creativity [excerpt from Maximum brain power] il *Prevention (Emmaus, Pa.)* 41:86+ O '89
Strolling under the stars [mother's intimate moments with children] J. I. Overstreet. il *Reader's Digest* 134:111-13 Ja '89
Taking the high road out of depression. M. Spilner. il *Prevention (Emmaus, Pa.)* 41:82-4 Mr '89
The way you walk that walk . . . [clue to personality and mood] H. E. Fisher. il *Health (New York, N.Y.)* 21:53-5+ S '89
The wonder of wander: walking and the soul of modern society. J. Hillman. il *Utne Reader* p93-4 Mr/Ap '89
Religious aspects
Brother Isidore covers 20 miles a day on his spiritual trek [Franciscan in Claymont, Del.] B. Johnson. il pors *People Weekly* 32:63-4 Ag 7 '89
Social aspects
Morning walks with Alex [mother and son] P. A. Hall. il *Parents* 64:90+ O '89
Walking for love. M. Spilner. il *Prevention (Emmaus, Pa.)* 41:90-1 F '89
WALKING OF DOGS See Dog walking
WALKING SHOES
10 super shoes for serious walkers. M. Spilner. il *Prevention (Emmaus, Pa.)* 41:96+ S '89
No (more) mean feet. G. Williams. il *Sierra* 74:174-5 Ja/F '89
Shoe biz. E. Kaufmann. il *Health (New York, N.Y.)* 21:60-1 S '89
Shoe scoop [interview with M. Malkin] V. Brower. il *American Health* 8:34 N '89
Sneaker-comfy footwear for all walks of life. M. Spilner. il *Prevention (Emmaus, Pa.)* 41:71-2+ Ap '89
Walk around the clock. il *Women's Sports & Fitness* 11:48-9 Mr '89
WALKS (PATHS)
See also
Garden walks (Paths)
Skyways (Architecture)
Path to glory [Tom Hasman's prize-winning brick walkway; cover story] C. Weese. il *Home Mechanix* 85:34-6+ My '89
A porch and a passage [covered walkway] il *Southern Living* 24:159 S '89
WALL, CAROL F.
Back to the beach. il *Southern Living* 24:116+ My '89
WALL, KARL
about
These Walls have ears for music and business. P. Cole. il pors *Business Week* p91 Je 26 '89
WALL, KEVIN
about
These Walls have ears for music and business. P. Cole. il pors *Business Week* p91 Je 26 '89

WALL, M. DANNY
about
Asleep at the S&L switch. R. Thomas and E. Clift. il por *Newsweek* 114:71 D 11 '89
Is Danny Wall on the way out? C. Yang and P. Dwyer. *Business Week* p59 N 13 '89
"A legal bank robbery". M. B. Carlson. il pors *Time* 134:29 N 27 '89
The tumbling of Danny Wall. S. J. Hedges. *U.S. News & World Report* 107:55 D 11 '89
WALL, PATRICK D.
about
Making a breakthrough. C. Wood. il por *Maclean's* 102:40-1 F 27 '89
WALL, STEPHEN D.
Venus unveiled. il *Astronomy* 17:26-32 Ap '89
WALL BOARD *See* Wallboard
WALL CABINETS *See* Cabinets (Furniture)
WALL COVERINGS
See also
Wallpaper and wallpapering
Fiberglass cover-ups for walls. T. O. Bakke. il *Popular Science* 235:27 Jl '89
New products: contract textiles. il *Architectural Record* 177:142-5 O '89
Noise-blocking wallcovering [Saf'n'Shielded] T. O. Bakke. il *Popular Science* 235:87 Jl '89
Playing with fire [fabric wall coverings and coordinated mantel decoration] il *House & Garden* 161:132-7 Ja '89
WALL DECORATION *See* Mural painting and decoration; Mural painting and decoration, Exterior
WALL DRUG STORE (WALL, S.D.)
The drugstore that ate South Dakota. S. Kaplan. il *Travel Holiday* 171:90 Je '89
WALL OF CHINA *See* Great Wall of China
WALL PAPER *See* Wallpaper and wallpapering
WALL PATCHING MATERIALS *See* Patching materials
WALL SHELVES *See* Shelves and racks
WALL STREET (NEW YORK, N.Y.)
Will Wall Street fade? J. Cook. il *Forbes* 144:138-9 O 16 '89
WALL STREET CRASH, 1929 *See* Business depression, 1929-1939
WALL STREET CRASH, 1987 *See* Stock market crash, 1987
WALL STREET JOURNAL
Confessions of a closet leftist [A. K. MacDougall] L. Zuckerman. il por *Time* 133:58 F 6 '89
Pen & ink: drawing for the Wall Street journal. M. S. Doherty. il *American Artist* 53:74-80+ My '89
A tale Dow Jones won't tell. A. L. Taylor, III. il *Fortune* 120:100-2+ Jl 3 '89
WALLACE, CHARLES
Libya's 'green *perestroika'*. *World Press Review* 36:30 F '89
WALLACE, CONNIE
The Seventeen money guide. il *Seventeen* 48:112-13+ F '89
WALLACE, D. W. R.
(jt. auth) See Krysell, M., and Wallace, D. W. R.
WALLACE, DAVE
The big Thrill. il por *Sport (New York, N.Y.)* 80:66-8 Jl '89
WALLACE, DAVID FOSTER
Everything is green [story] *Harper's* 279:36 S '89
WALLACE, DAVID RAINS, 1945-
Mind in a forest [excerpts from Bulow Hammock] il *Sierra* 74:62-7 My/Je '89
The next four national parks. il *Mother Jones* 14:28-31+ Jl/Ag '89
Of buccaneers and biodiversity. il maps *Wilderness* 53:38-51 Wint '89
WALLACE, GEORGE C.
about
The next George Wallace. D. Baer. il pors *Gentlemen's Quarterly* 59:292-7+ D '89
WALLACE, GEORGE CORLEY, 1919-
about
The next George Wallace. D. Baer. il pors *Gentlemen's Quarterly* 59:292-7+ D '89
WALLACE, HENRY AGARD, 1888-1965
about
The New Deal and the guru. C. J. Errico and J. S. Walker. il pors *American Heritage* 40:92-5+ Mr '89
WALLACE, JAMES A.
Guidelines for preaching by the laity: another step backward? *America* 161:139-41 S 9-16 '89
WALLACE, LINDA L.
(jt. auth) See Knight, Dennis H., and Wallace, Linda L.
WALLACE, MICHAEL B.
about
Fox in the coop. J. Gill. *The Nation* 248:40 Ja 9-16 '89
WALLACE, RONALD, 1945-
Quick bright things [poem] *The Nation* 249:732 D 11 '89
Turkeys [poem] *The Nation* 248:750 My 29 '89
WALLACE, RUSTY
about
Close call for a millionaire. S. Moses. il por *Sports Illustrated* 71:90-1 N 27 '89

Dirty driving. T. Gabriel. il pors *Rolling Stone* p68-70+ Ag 10 '89
Ready to trade some paint. S. Moses. il pors *Sports Illustrated* 71:43-4+ Jl 3 '89
Wheels of fortune. K. Hannon. il pors *Sport (New York, N.Y.)* 80:72-4+ Mr '89
WALLACE, STEVEN P., AND ESTES, CARROLL LYNN, 1938-
Health policy for the elderly. bibl il *Society* 26:66-75 S/O '89
WALLACE, SIR WILLIAM, D. 1305
about
A patriot for whom? Wallace & Bruce: Scotland's uneasy heroes. A. Fisher. bibl il *History Today* 39:18-23 F '89
WALLACE (LILA ACHESON) WING *See* Metropolitan Museum of Art (New York, N.Y.). Lila Acheson Wallace Wing
WALLACE'S RISING, 1297-1304 *See* Scotland—History—Wallace's Rising, 1297-1304
WALLACH, AMEI
Arts and craftiness. il por *Ms.* 18:24-6 Jl/Ag '89
Beautiful Dreamings. il *Ms.* 17:60-4 Mr '89
Marketing *perestroika.* il *Art in America* 77:53-5+ Ap '89
WALLACH, BRET
Dallas. il map *Focus (New York, N.Y.: 1950)* 39:22-6 Spr '89
Hong Kong: bound and adrift. il map *Focus (New York, N.Y.: 1950)* 39:17-25 Fall '89
Puerto Rico: growth, change, progress, development. il maps *Focus (New York, N.Y.: 1950)* 39:27-33 Summ '89
Taking heart from upper East Tennessee. il map *Focus (New York, N.Y.: 1950)* 38:22-8 Wint '88
WALLACK, ROY M.
. . . an offer we should have refused. il *Bicycling* 30:38-40+ Jl '89
WALLBOARD
Drywall innovations. M. DiChristina. il *Popular Science* 235:84-6+ Jl '89
How to repair holes in drywall. R. Capotosto. il *Popular Mechanics* 166:97-8 Jl '89
Preparing drywall for painting. G. Branson. *Workbench* 45:74 N/D '89
WALLENBERG, RAOUL
about
A lost prisoner of the gulag still holds Moscow hostage. D. Stanglin. il pors *U.S. News & World Report* 106:34-6 Je 26 '89
A pain-filled mystery. J. Bierman. por *Maclean's* 102:47 O 30 '89
WALLER, HAROLD M.
Canada tackles its deficit. il *The New Leader* 72:8-9 O 2-16 '89
WALLERSTEIN, JUDITH S.
Children after divorce [cover story] il *The New York Times Magazine* p18-21+ Ja 22 '89
about
Children of the aftershock. B. Kantrowitz. il por *Newsweek* 113:61 F 6 '89
Dr. Wallerstein explains [interview] S. Blakeslee. *American Health* 8:58-9 Je '89
The lasting wounds of divorce. A. Toufexis. il *Time* 133:61 F 6 '89
PW interviews. B. Levine. por *Publishers Weekly* 235:50+ F 10 '89
Wallerstein's advice on damage control [interview] M. Wilhelm. il *People Weekly* 31:86-7 My 29 '89
WALLERSTEIN, JUDITH S., AND BLAKESLEE, SANDRA
A family divided: time bombs of divorce [excerpt from Second chances] il *American Health* 8:49-52 Je '89
When a marriage ends: how men, women and children cope. *McCall's* 116:78+ Mr '89
WALLETS
Not guilty as charged [effect of eel skin wallets on credit card scrambling] il *Discover* 10:12 Mr '89
WALLEYE FISHING
Bottom bouncing walleyes. M. Pearce. il *Outdoor Life* 184:72-3+ O '89
Cold weather walleyes. P. M. Liikala. il *Outdoor Life* 183:76-7+ Ja '89
Home is where the fish are [ice fishing at Mille Lacs Lake, Minn.] T. Dickson. il *National Wildlife* 27:24-8 F/Mr '89
In deep water over walleyes. J. Gibbs. il *Outdoor Life* 183:74-5+ My '89
Manitoba's new pike and walleye hotspot. K. Schultz. il *Field & Stream* 93:56+ Mr '89
Mud-line walleyes. D. Nelson. il *Outdoor Life* 183:53-5+ F '89
Pumping lead for walleyes [jigs] N. Strung. il *Field & Stream* 94:50-1+ My '89
Walleye systems for bass. J. Gibbs. il *Outdoor Life* 183:20+ Ja '89
Walleye zone below. J. Kulpa. il *Field & Stream* 94:52-3+ Jl '89
Walleyes for shore. J. Weiss. il *Outdoor Life* 183:79+ Ap '89
Walleyes on slip-sinker rigs. B. Volkart. il *Field & Stream* 94:25 Ag '89

WALLEYE FISHING—cont.
Waveless walleyes. J. Murray. il *Outdoor Life* 183:70-1+ Je '89
WALLICK, RUTH
about
Students come of age. il por *New Choices for the Best Years* 29:16 O '89
WALLINGTON, PATRICIA M.
about
Why technical skill alone isn't enough. J. Pepper. il por *Working Woman* 14:64+ My '89
WALLIS, BRIAN, 1953-
Absolute Warhol. il por *Art in America* 77:25+ Mr '89
WALLIS, W. ALLEN
American leadership in international trade [address, November 28, 1988] *Department of State Bulletin* 89:30-1 F '89
Negotiations toward a new International Coffee Agreement [address, November 14, 1988] *Department of State Bulletin* 89:15-17 Mr '89
Overview of U.S. trade policy [address, October 5, 1988] *Department of State Bulletin* 88:33-4 D '88
WALLJASPER, JAY
Zeitgeist. See issues of Utne Reader beginning January/February 1988
WALLOPS FLIGHT FACILITY
Comrades in rocketry [Soviet and U.S. amateur rocketeers compete] A. Jackson. il *Ad Astra* 1:29-31 F '89
WALLPAPER AND WALLPAPERING
Borderlines. E. A. Berthold. il *House & Garden* 161:178 Ap '89
Deck the walls. M. Bethany. il *New York* 22:77 D 18 '89
Surface attraction [corner spaces designed by Carolyn Sollis and Anne Foxley] M. Guralnick. il *House & Garden* 161:168-76 Ap '89
Wallcoverings. il *The Family Handyman* 39:50-2+ My '89
Wallpaper repairs. M. Henkenius. il *Home Mechanix* 85:24+ D '89
WALLRAFF, BARBARA
People who meet people. il *The Atlantic* 263:108+ Ja '89
Plunge right in. il *The Atlantic* 264:111-14 D '89
WALLS, RICHARD C.
Hittin' the books. il *High Fidelity (New York, N.Y.)* 39:52-3+ Je '89
WALLS, WUANDA M. T.
On the road to glory. il *Black Enterprise* 19:209-10 F '89
WALLS
See also
Curtain walls
Garden walls
Mural painting and decoration
Mural painting and decoration, Exterior
Paneling
Retaining walls
Storage walls
After Pompeii. M. Bethany. il *New York* 22:58-61 My 29 '89
EIF systems: quality lost in the translation? [Exterior Insulation and Finish Systems] J. S. Russell. il *Architectural Record* 177:124-7 Jl '89
Innovative exteriors: has technology left building codes behind? J. S. Russell. *Architectural Record* 177:20-1 D '89
Sticking with stucco [exterior insulation and finish systems] il *Architectural Record* 177:186-7 D '89
Two wing walls make all the difference. il *Sunset (Central West edition)* 182:94-5 Ja '89
WALNUM, CLAYTON
Computing for dollars. il *The Writer* 102:20-2 Mr '89
WALNUT BREAD *See* Bread
WALNUT CREEK (CALIF.)
Restaurants, nightclubs, bars, etc.
Sidewalk cafes of Walnut Creek. il *Sunset (Central West edition)* 182:14 Je '89
WALPOLE, SIR HUGH, 1884-1941
The spirit of Stockholm. *The New Republic* 201 [Reprint v1]:16 N 6 '89 [N 7 '14]
WALRUS HUNTING
Off with their heads [walrus heads traded for illicit drugs by Eskimos in Alaska] M. Beck. il *Newsweek* 113:78 Je 5 '89
WALRUSES
Elephants in Alaska [handicrafts made from poached African ivory] F. Graham. *Audubon* 91:27-9 S '89
Requiem for a heavyweight? [Pacific walrus] C. Baker. il *National Wildlife* 27:38-43 Je/Jl '89
WALSH, BARRY WALDEN
Natural cycles. il por *Wilderness* 53:16-17+ Wint '89
WALSH, JOAN
Fighting poverty after Reagan. il *The Nation* 248:336-9 Mr 13 '89
WALSH, JOHN
about
'I am still devastated'. J. Marion. il pors *TV Guide* 37:22-4 Mr 18-24 '89
WALSH, LAWRENCE E.
about
Giving in to "graymail". S. Holmes. il pors *Time* 133:24-5 Ja 16 '89

WALSH, MICHAEL
Small is bountiful. il *Better Homes and Gardens* 68:50 F '89
WALSH, MICHAEL H.
about
An outsider fires up a railroad. A. Kupfer. il por *Fortune* 120:133-4+ D 18 '89
WALSH, PATRICK J.
(jt. auth) See Mommsen, Thomas P., and Walsh, Patrick J.
WALSH, STEVE
about
A duel in the sun: quarterbacks Troy Aikman and Steve Walsh compete to be the Cowboys' starter [cover story] A. Murphy. il pors *Sports Illustrated* 71:30-2+ Ag 21 '89
Supplemental signal caller. P. King. il por *Sports Illustrated* 71:10 Jl 17 '89
WALSTAD, WILLIAM B.
Economic literacy in the schools [address, December 28, 1988] *Vital Speeches of the Day* 55:327-8 Mr 15 '89
WALT DISNEY COMPANY
Add records to Disney's world [launching Hollywood Records] *Newsweek* 114:72 D 11 '89
Are MCA and Disney ready to co-star? G. G. Marcial. il *Business Week* p97 Je 26 '89
Creativity, with discipline. H. Rudnitsky. il *Forbes* 143:41-2 Mr 6 '89
Le Défi Disney [TV sales to Europe] J. Marcom, Jr. il *Forbes* 143:39-40 F 20 '89
Disney music that isn't Mickey Mouse. *U.S. News & World Report* 107:17-18 D 11 '89
How Disney keeps the magic going. C. Knowlton. il por *Fortune* 120:111-12+ D 4 '89
Collectibles
Mickey mania. C. Brown. il *Forbes* 144:230-2 O 30 '89
WALT DISNEY CONCERT HALL (LOS ANGELES, CALIF.)
L.A. lilt. il *Architectural Record* 177:41 F '89
WALT DISNEY HOME VIDEO
Disney does it better. M. Meyer. il *Video* 13:66+ Jl '89
Disney promotions aimed at increasing breadth of sell-through. J. Zinsser. il *Publishers Weekly* 235:104+ Ap 7 '89
WALT DISNEY PRODUCTIONS
See also
Walt Disney Company
WALT DISNEY WORLD (FLA.)
See also
Disney-MGM Studios Theme Park (Fla.)
EPCOT (Fla.)
Adventure in Wonderland [cruising to Disney World in a Cobia San Marino 278E] M. Benson. il *Motor Boating & Sailing* 163:52-5+ Je '89
Centerline: John Haupt [lighting designer for live shows] M. Sommers. il por *Theatre Crafts* 23:14 Mr '89
Dining out in Disney World. J. Reed. il *Vogue* 179:245-6 D '89
Disney World and the four dwarfs. C. Clark. il *The Saturday Evening Post* 261:86-7 Mr '89
How Disney does it [cover story] C. Leerhsen. il por *Newsweek* 113:48-54 Ap 3 '89
Mickey is eating my lunch! H. Rudnitsky. il *Forbes* 144:86+ S 18 '89
New worlds open at Disney. C. Griffith-Roberts. il *Southern Living* 24:80-3 Ja '89
The tight-budget, no-hassle way to see Disney World. M. Kiernan. il *U.S. News & World Report* 106:62-3+ Je 5 '89
WALT DISNEY WORLD (FLA.). CASTING CENTER
Entertainment architecture [cover story] P. M. Sachner. il *Architectural Record* 177:66-71 S '89
WALTER, HELGA
Appeasement in our time [cover story] il por *National Review* 41:26-8+ Je 2 '89
WALTER, JOHN
The great outdoors. See issues of Successful Farming beginning February 1987
WALTER, KATE
OUT/LOOK: national lesbian & gay quarterly. *The Nation* 248:640-2 My 8 '89
WALTER (JIM) CORP. *See* Jim Walter Corp.
WALTER A. KOHL SALES (FIRM)
Treasure trove. M. Benson. il *Cycle* 40:76 N '89
WALTERS, BARBARA, 1931-
Barbara Walters: "Be true to yourself" [excerpts from address] il por *Ladies' Home Journal* 106:60 N '89
about
Barbara Walters. por *People Weekly* 31 Special Issue:66 Summ '89
Barbara Walters's theater of revenge. M. C. Miller. *Harper's* 279:40-1+ N '89
WALTERS, DOTTIE
about
Small-town woman talks her way through bigger and bigger doors. L. Arden. il por *Home Office Computing* 7:46 My '89
WALTERS, HAROLENE
about
Harolene supreme. M. Will-Weber. il por *Runner's World* 24:93 Ag '89

WALTERS, HENRY, 1848-1931
about
William and Henry Walters, and their fever for the fine arts. M. Kernan. bibl (p135) il pors *Smithsonian* 20:102-8+ Ag '89
WALTERS, KATHRYN
The land of lavish snow. il map *Country Journal* 16:56-9 F '89
WALTERS, MARK JEROME
California's chain-saw massacre. il *Reader's Digest* 135:144-9 N '89
Rebirth of the American eagle. il *Reader's Digest* 135:95-100 S '89
WALTERS, NORBY
about
A question of fairness. R. Telander. por *Sports Illustrated* 70:114 My 1 '89
Tough message. il pors *Time* 133:78 Ap 24 '89
Tour shakedowns alleged. J. Capeci. il por *Rolling Stone* p20 My 4 '89
WALTERS, VERNON A.
Efforts toward a Cambodian settlement [statement and text of UN General Assembly resolution, November 3, 1988] *Department of State Bulletin* 89:65-8 F '89
UN calls for full implementation of Afghanistan peace accords. *Department of State Bulletin* 89:40-1 Ja '89
WALTERS, WILLIAM, 1819-1894
about
William and Henry Walters, and their fever for the fine arts. M. Kernan. bibl (p135) il pors *Smithsonian* 20:102-8+ Ag '89
WALTERS ART GALLERY
William and Henry Walters, and their fever for the fine arts. M. Kernan. bibl (p135) il pors *Smithsonian* 20:102-8+ Ag '89
WALTHER, FRANZ ERHARD, 1939-
about
Franz Erhard Walther at John Weber. S. Westfall. il *Art in America* 77:193 My '89
WALTON, ANTHONY
Willie Horton and me. il por *The New York Times Magazine* p52-3+ Ag 20 '89
WALTON, BILL, 1952-
about
Ten things you never knew about Bill Walton's injuries. S. Rosenbloom and W. Ladson. por *Sport (New York, N.Y.)* 80:83 Mr '89
WALTON, DONALD
How to make the pitch they can't resist. il *Working Woman* 14:102-4+ D '89
WALTON, JESS
about
'I thought there was something emotionally wrong with me'. E. Warren. por *TV Guide* 37:26 Ap 15-21 '89
WALTON, JOE
about
Joe Walton: the coach everyone loves to hate. P. Fichtenbaum. por *Sport (New York, N.Y.)* 80:50 Ag '89
WALTON, REGGIE B.
about
Walton takes post as top black drug war policymaker. por *Jet* 76:6 Je 26 '89
WALTON, SAM M.
about
Wal-Mart: will it take over the world? J. Huey. il map *Fortune* 119:52-6+ Ja 30 '89
WALTON, SUSAN
A ride on the age wave. il *Health (New York, N.Y.)* 21:40+ Jl '89
WALTRIP, DARRELL
about
About time, fella. S. Moses. il por *Sports Illustrated* 70:46-7 F 27 '89
WALZ, THOMAS H., AND BLUM, NANCEE S.
Sex in midlife. il *New Choices for the Best Years* 29:60-2 Jl '89
WALZER, EMILY
Are you workout wise? il *Seventeen* 48:166+ Ag '89
What's your game? [quiz] *Seventeen* 48:172 Mr '89
WAMSLEY, JAMES S.
John Philip Kassebaum's unparalleled ceramics in Charleston. il pors *Architectural Digest* 46:86+ D '89
Virginia's Shirley Plantation. il *Architectural Digest* 46:126-31+ Je '89
The White House of the Confederacy: restoring the historic residence of President Jefferson Davis. il *Architectural Digest* 46:262-9 O '89
WAN RUNNAN
about
Computer engineer turns entrepreneur-in-exile. M. Sun. *Science* 245:592 Ag 11 '89
WANG, AN
about
Like father, unlike son. pors *Newsweek* 114:40 Ag 21 '89
Remedial reading. J. Queenan. il por *Forbes* 144:48 S 18 '89

WANG, FREDERICK A., 1950-
about
The boss's son logs off. L. Jereski. il por *Business Week* p31 Ag 21 '89
Can Fred Wang keep customers from bolting? L. Jereski. il por *Business Week* p23-4 Jl 24 '89
Like father, unlike son. pors *Newsweek* 114:40 Ag 21 '89
WANG, MARGARET C., AND OTHERS
Save the baby! A response to 'Integrating the children of the second system'. bibl f il *Phi Delta Kappan* 71:61-7 S '89
WANG, WAYNE, 1949?-
about
Eat a bowl of tea [film] Reviews
The New Leader 72:20-1 Ag 7-21 '89. J. Morrone
WANG, Y.-M., AND OTHERS
Magnetic flux transport on the sun [cover story] bibl f il *Science* 245:712-18 Ag 18 '89
WANG LABORATORIES INC.
The boss's son logs off [F. Wang resigns] L. Jereski. il por *Business Week* p31 Ag 21 '89
Can Fred Wang keep customers from bolting? L. Jereski. il por *Business Week* p23-4 Jl 24 '89
Like father, unlike son [resignation of F. Wang] pors *Newsweek* 114:40 Ag 21 '89
Remedial reading [A. Wang's autobiography] J. Queenan. il por *Forbes* 144:48 S 18 '89
Wang's turnaround specialist prepares for surgery [R. W. Miller] G. McWilliams. il por *Business Week* p108-9 D 11 '89
WANG MENG
about
In praise of Wang Meng. H. Calisher. *The Nation* 249:500-2 O 30 '89
In praise of Wang Meng. W. Barnstone. *The Nation* 249:502-3 O 30 '89
WANG YANI
about
Art à la carte. K. Best. il *Travel Holiday* 171:80 Je '89
A child prodigy from China wields a magical brush. C. Bond. il *Smithsonian* 20:70-9 S '89
Chinese artist-prodigy Wang Yani wows D.C. with a one-girl show. R. Arias. il pors *People Weekly* 32:89-90 Jl 10 '89
A rare flower blooms in China. il por *U.S. News & World Report* 107:11 Jl 3 '89
WANG ZENGQI
A tail [story]; tr. by Howard Goldblatt. *Harper's* 278:36+ Ap '89
WANGER, RALPH
about
Big payoffs from small stocks [interview] J. Mendes. il por *Fortune* 120:35-7 Jl 17 '89
WANGERIN, WALTER
Maundy Thursday. il *Christianity Today* 33:19-21 Mr 17 '89
WANKEL ENGINES *See* Rotary engines
WANLESS, HAROLD R.
The inundation of our coastlines. bibl il maps *Sea Frontiers* 35:264-71 S/O '89
WANNISKI, JUDE, 1936-
about
Pigging out. E. Diamond. il por *New York* 22:22+ Ap 17 '89
WANO *See* World Association of Nuclear Operators
WANTS *See* Desire
WAPNER, FREDERICK
about
While his father rules TV's People's court, judge Fred Wapner delivers real crooks to jail time. L. Armstrong. il pors *People Weekly* 32:139-40 D 18 '89
WAPNER, JOSEPH A.
about
The verdict on Judge Wapner. A. J. Mikva. il pors *TV Guide* 37:12-14 Ap 22-28 '89
While his father rules TV's People's court, judge Fred Wapner delivers real crooks to jail time. L. Armstrong. il pors *People Weekly* 32:139-40 D 18 '89
WAPPINGERS FALLS (N.Y.)
Crime
See also
Brawley, Tawana—Assault case
WAR
See also
Anti-submarine warfare
Children and war
Children as soldiers
Iranian-Iraqi War, 1980-1988
Israel-Arab War, 1948-1949
Israel-Arab Wars, 1967-
Korean War, 1950-1953
Military history
Naval warfare
Nuclear warfare
Pacifism
Peace
Politics and war
Space warfare

WAR—See also—*cont.*
 Submarine warfare
 Vietnamese War, 1957-1975
 War games
 Women and war
 World War, 1914-1918
 World War, 1939-1945
From atom bombs to Fred Astaire [work of J. E. Mueller]
 A. P. Sanoff. il por *U.S. News & World Report* 106:63
 My 22 '89
Now, 'lite' warfare? [conventional warfare in Europe] P. Cary
 and D. Stanglin. il *U.S. News & World Report* 106:28
 Je 12 '89
War & peace around the world. map *Scholastic Update
 (Teachers' edition)* 121:4-5 Mr 24 '89
A world at war. R. Sollen. il *The Nation* 248:46-7 Ja 9-16
 '89

Bibliography
The grand decider. G. A. Craig. il *The New York Review
 of Books* 36:31-6 Ag 17 '89

Causes
War without hatred. A. Rapoport. il por *The Humanist*
 49:14-17+ Jl/Ag '89
Warfare over Yanomamö Indians [theories of N. A. Chagnon]
 W. Booth. il *Science* 243:1138-40 Mr 3 '89

Environmental aspects
A casualty of war: the Nicaraguan environment. R. A. Rice.
 il map *Technology Review* 92:62-71 My/Je '89

Health aspects
War against the heart [Beirut, Lebanon; study by Abla M.
 Sibai] *Science News* 136:284 O 28 '89

Moral aspects
 See War and morals

Photographs and photography
The eyes of war [work of J. Nachtwey] il *Life* 12:94-8 My
 '89
How photography shapes the face of battle [interview with
 S. D. Moeller] A. P. Sanoff. il *U.S. News & World Report*
 106:62-3 Ap 3 '89
Photography [work of J. Nachtwey at the International Center
 of Photography] P. Blauner. il *New York* 22:126-7 S 11
 '89

Religious aspects
 See War and religion
WAR AND EMERGENCY POWERS
Deregulating political murder. P. Savoy. il *The Nation*
 248:869+ Je 26 '89
Pro/con: the president's war-making power. P. M. Jones.
 Scholastic Update (Teachers' edition) 121:15 Ja 13 '89
WAR AND LITERATURE
 See also
 France—History—Revolution, 1789-1799—Literature
WAR AND MORALS
 See also
 El Salvador—Civil War, 1980- —Moral and religious
  aspects
 Vietnamese War, 1957-1975—Moral and religious aspects
 War and religion
 World War, 1939-1945—Moral and religious aspects
No payment enclosed: why I resist war taxes [cover story]
 A. Ayvazian. il *The Progressive* 53:19-21 Ap '89
WAR AND PEACE IN THE NUCLEAR AGE [television
 program] See Television program reviews—Single works
WAR AND POLITICS See Politics and war
WAR AND RELIGION
 See also
 El Salvador—Civil War, 1980- —Moral and religious
  aspects
 Just war doctrine
 Vietnamese War, 1957-1975—Moral and religious aspects
 World War, 1939-1945—Catholic Church
 World War, 1939-1945—Moral and religious aspects
Killing for God. K. Kolenda. il *The Humanist* 49:47 My/Je
 '89
WAR AND REMEMBRANCE [television program] See
 Television program reviews—Single works
WAR COLLECTIBLES See Vietnamese War, 1957-1975—Col-
 lectibles
WAR CRIME TRIALS

Canada
The case of Imre Finta. B. Wickens. *Maclean's* 102:70 N
 27 '89

Japan
From Hirohito to Heimat. I. Buruma. *The New York Review
 of Books* 36:31-2+ O 26 '89
WAR CRIMES
 See also
 War crime trials
WAR CRIMINALS See World War, 1939-1945—War criminals
WAR GAMES
 See also
 Balance of Power (Video game)
 BattleTech (Video game)
 Empire (Video game)
 Military maneuvers
 Omega (Video game)
 Topgun Aviation (Firm)

688 Attack Sub [video game] R. G. Sheffield. il *Compute!*
 11:64-5 Ag '89
Abrams Battle Tank [computer game] P. Scisco. il *Compute!*
 11:68 Je '89
Bang, bang! [weekend war games vs. ownership of handguns]
 B. D. Colen. il *Health (New York, N.Y.)* 21:90-1 Mr '89
Battlehawks 1942. B. Guerra. il *Compute!* 11:63 Ap '89
Exercises in diplomacy: simulating future crises. M. Schofield.
 il *The Futurist* 23:8-11 Mr/Ap '89
F-19 Stealth Fighter. B. Guerra. il *Compute!* 11:70-1 Ap
 '89
F-19 Stealth Fighter. S. Williams. il *Home Office Computing*
 7:87-8 Mr '89
Falcon A.T. S. Williams. il *Home Office Computing* 7:91-2
 F '89
Grow up! D. Atkin. il *Compute!* 11:94-6+ D '89
Heavy Metal. M. McLean. il *Compute!* 11:106 D '89
Historical games. M. McLean. il *Compute!* 11:41-2+ Je '89
Into the Battlezone: the making of a woman warrior [playing
 an indoor war game] N. Meredith. *Health (New York,
 N.Y.)* 21:70-1 Je '89
JetFighter: The Adventure. R. Gehorsam. il *Home Office
 Computing* 7:90+ My '89
The latest sim craze [tank combat] G. Keizer. il *Compute!*
 11:7 Ap '89
Nobunaga's Ambition [computer simulation of sixteenth-
 century Japan] N. Randall. il *Compute!* 11:90+ Ja '89
Of worms, viruses and Core War. A. K. Dewdney. il *Scientific
 American* 260:110-13 Mr '89
Red Storm Rising [computer game] R. G. Sheffield. il
 Compute! 11:66+ F '89
Red Storm Rising [computer game] R. G. Sheffield. il *Home
 Office Computing* 7:88 O '89
Steel Thunder [tank combat simulation] R. G. Sheffield.
 il *Compute!* 11:72+ My '89
Strategic Conquest Plus v2.0 [computer game] D. Langendoen.
 il *Home Office Computing* 7:100 N '89
There's a boat in this box! [688 Attack Sub video game]
 G. Keizer. il *Compute!* 11:6 Mr '89
WAR IN ART
 See also
 France—History—Revolution, 1789-1799—Art
 United States—History—War with Mexico, 1845-1848—
  Art
 Vietnamese War, 1957-1975—Art
 World War, 1914-1918—Art
WAR IN LITERATURE
 See also
 United States—History—Civil War, 1861-1865—
  Literature
 World War, 1939-1945—Literature
Books from Oxford and Algonquin question idea of a 'good'
 war [work of P. Fussell and L. Brown] C. Goodrich.
 il pors *Publishers Weekly* 235:31-2 Je 23 '89
WAR MEMORIALS
 See also
 Unknown soldiers
Fund-raising push on for black memorials in D.C. [Revolution-
 ary War Memorial] *Jet* 76:7 Ap 17 '89
Help build a memorial to American heroines. J. M. Carter.
 il *Good Housekeeping* 208:64 My '89
WAR NEWS
 See also
 Cambodia—History—Civil War, 1970-1975—Reporters
  and reporting
 El Salvador—Civil War, 1980- —Reporters and reporting
 Holocaust, Jewish (1939-1945)—Reporters and reporting
 Israel-Arab Wars, 1967- —Reporters and reporting
 United States—History—Civil War, 1861-1865—Report-
  ers and reporting
 Vietnamese War, 1957-1975—Reporters and reporting
 World War, 1939-1945—Reporters and reporting
WAR OBJECTORS See Conscientious objectors
WAR OF 1812 See United States—History—War of 1812
THE WAR OF THE ROSES [film] See Motion picture
 reviews—Single works
WAR PHOTOGRAPHY See War—Photographs and photogra-
 phy
WAR POETRY
 See also
 World War, 1914-1918—Poetry
WAR POWERS See War and emergency powers
WAR SONGS
 See also
 Tape recordings—War songs
WAR TOYS
 See also
 Toy guns
Floor wars [toy warriors] C. Schine. il *The New York Times
 Magazine* p28-31+ Ag 13 '89
WARBLERS
 See also
 Kirtland's warblers
What, when, where, and why warblers warble [cover story]
 D. E. Kroodsma. il *Natural History* p50-9 My '89
WARD, ALEX
Navajo cops on the case. il pors *The New York Times
 Magazine* p38-9+ My 14 '89

WARD, ALEX—*cont.*
Test cases. il *The New York Times Magazine* p49-50 Ag 13 '89

WARD, ANDINO
about
Journey of a cult child. M. Capuzzo. il pors *Reader's Digest* 134:109-14 My '89

WARD, BENJAMIN
about
Big Ben: has Police Commissioner Ward become a liability to Koch? P. Blauner. il pors *New York* 22:48-50+ Ap 3 '89

WARD, CRAIG E.
Congressional action teams. *Ad Astra* 1:58 Jl/Ag '89

WARD, DAVID
about
World Vision. B. Brander. il *Petersen's Photographic Magazine* 18:24-6+ Je '89

WARD, DAVID S.
about
Major league [film] Reviews
The New Republic 200:26 My 8 '89. S. Kauffmann
People Weekly il 31:15 Ap 24 '89. R. Novak
Sports Illustrated il 70:84 Ap 17 '89. S. Wulf
Time il 133:78 Ap 24 '89. R. Corliss
Video il 13:77 N '89. J. Walker

WARD, DIANE RAINES
Behind the gauze mask. il *International Wildlife* 19:14-19 Ja/F '89

WARD, F. CHAMPION
Requiem for the Hutchins College. il por *Change* 21:24-33 Jl/Ag '89

WARD, FRED, 1935-
Images for the computer age. il *National Geographic* 175:718-51 Je '89

WARD, GEOFFREY C.
A. Lincoln, writer. il *American Heritage* 40:14+ S/O '89
America's baby. il *American Heritage* 40:12+ Mr '89
'Future historians will curse as well as praise me'. il *Smithsonian* 20:58-66+ D '89
The house at Eighth and Jackson. bibl il por *American Heritage* 40:68-72+ Ap '89
LBJ's alter ego. il *American Heritage* 40:14+ F '89
The lost Mencken. il *American Heritage* 40:14+ D '89
Papa, Satchmo, and the Babe. il *American Heritage* 40:14+ My/Je '89
Robeson's choice. il *American Heritage* 40:12+ Ap '89
Solving the Benton puzzle. il por *American Heritage* 40:12+ Jl/Ag '89
The St. Louis Woman of Paris. il *American Heritage* 40:14+ N '89
The wonderful husband. il pors *American Heritage* 40:57-8+ S/O '89

WARD, JOHN L., AND SORENSON, LAUREL
Promote, celebrate your family ties. il *Nation's Business* 77:16-17 F '89
Retired dads: a real resource. il *Nation's Business* 77:72-3 Je '89
The role of "mom". il *Nation's Business* 77:40-1 Ag '89

WARD, KENNAN
From here to paternity. il *Natural History* p84-5 D '89

WARD, MAX
about
The end of Ward's dream. P. Chisholm. il pors *Maclean's* 102:34-5 Ja 30 '89

WARD, MICHAEL
about
The littlest witness may testify about her friend's killing. M. Brower. il pors *People Weekly* 31:108-10 Ap 24 '89

WARD, MICHAEL MOSES
about
Journey of a cult child. M. Capuzzo. il pors *Reader's Digest* 134:109-14 My '89

WARD, MIRIAM
No taxation without representation. *America* 161:464-5 D 23-30 '89

WARD, VINCENT
about
The navigator [film] Reviews
American Film il 14:61-2 My '89. A. Klein
Christianity Today 33:66 My 12 '89. S. Ulstein
Commonweal 116:437-8 Ag 11 '89. T. O'Brien
Gentlemen's Quarterly 59:119-20 Je '89. K. Turan
Newsweek il 113:72 Ap 17 '89. D. Ansen

WARD, VIOLET
about
First days in first grade. P. La Farge. il pors *Parents* 64:104-8+ S '89

WARD (W. VA.)
Labor
The good war [coal miners during the 1930s] E. Wilson. *The New Republic* 200:21 My 29 '89

WARDAIR INC.
American Airlines, Canadian investors weigh bids for Wardair. C. Fotos. *Aviation Week & Space Technology* 130:108-9 Ap 24 '89
The end of Ward's dream [sold to Pacific Western Airlines] P. Chisholm. il pors *Maclean's* 102:34-5 Ja 30 '89

PWA Corp. to lay off 1,900 airline personnel [combining Canadian Airlines International and Wardair into one airline] *Aviation Week & Space Technology* 131:45 D 11 '89
Wardair founder agrees to sell airline to PWA Corp. D. Hughes. il *Aviation Week & Space Technology* 130:72-3 Ja 30 '89

WARDEN, CHRISTOPHER
Power to the consumer. *Consumers' Research Magazine* 72:19 Je '89

WARDENS, GAME See Game wardens

WARDER, MICHAEL
Is *glasnost* genuine? [address, November 6, 1988] *Vital Speeches of the Day* 55:341-4 Mr 15 '89

WARDLE, FRANCIS
Children of mixed parentage: how can professionals respond? bibl f il *Children Today* 18:10-13 Jl/Ag '89

WARDS See Guardian and ward

WARDS COVE PACKING CO.
A question of statistics [Supreme Court decision on racial discrimination at Alaskan fish canneries] T. Jacoby. il *Newsweek* 113:58 Je 19 '89

WARE, ANDRE
about
Houston QB Andre Ware wins '89 Heisman Trophy. il pors *Jet* 77:51 D 18 '89
A lid-lifter in Texas. A. Murphy. il pors *Sports Illustrated* 71:56-8+ O 23 '89

WARE, LESLIE
Pete Seeger: keeping the dream. il por *Sierra* 74:82-6+ Mr/Ap '89

WARE, LINDA
about
In the family way. il *Good Housekeeping* 209:76 S '89

WARE (MASS.)
Hotels, motels, etc.
To B&B or not to B&B [apprenticeship program at Wildwood Inn] C. McLaughlin. il *New Choices for the Best Years* 29:10-11 Mr '89

WAREHOUSE CLUBS
See also
Waban (Firm)
Securities
The final word in no-frills shopping? A. Kupfer. il *Fortune* 119:30 Mr 13 '89

WAREHOUSE STORES
See also
Hypermarkets

WAREHOUSES
Fires and fire prevention
Arkansas hair care firm's plant is destroyed by a major fire [J.M. Products Co.] il *Jet* 76:27 Ag 21 '89

WARF, BARNEY
The garden of France: history meets geography in the Loire River Valley. il map *Focus (New York, N.Y.: 1950)* 39:26-7+ Fall '89
Undiscovered paradise: the faces of Saint Lucia. il map *Focus (New York, N.Y.: 1950)* 38:34-6 Wint '88

WARFARE, TANK See Tank warfare

WARFIELD, WALLIS See Windsor, Wallis Warfield, Duchess of, 1896-1986

WARHOL, ANDY, 1928?-1987
Diary of a mad decade [excerpts from The Andy Warhol diaries]; ed. by Pat Hackett. il pors *People Weekly* 31:100-2+ My 8 '89
Notes from an endless night [excerpts from The Andy Warhol diaries]; ed. by Pat Hackett. il pors *People Weekly* 31:106-8+ My 15 '89
about
Andy, Inc. W. Feaver. il *Art News* 88:94-7 F '89
Andy Warhol the painter. S. Schwartz. il *The Atlantic* 264:73-7 Ag '89
Art. A. C. Danto. *The Nation* 248:458-61 Ap 3 '89
The art world. A. Gopnik. *The New Yorker* 65:109-13 Ap 10 '89
The best and worst of Warhol. R. Hughes. il *Time* 133:94-5 F 13 '89
Everybody's Andy. K. Larson. il *New York* 22:77-8 F 20 '89
Famous and Andy. L. Loud. il *American Film* 15:80 D '89
Fast art [cover story] J. Updike. il *The New Republic* 200:26-8 Mr 27 '89
G-men at the movies. *Harper's* 278:26 Je '89
Hellfire of the banalities. E. Knippers. il *Christianity Today* 33:26-7 S 22 '89
A pop art puzzle. G. James. il por *Maclean's* 102:54-5 Mr 6 '89
Rock noir: Lou Reed reckons with Andy Warhol in 'Songs for 'Drella'. P. Blauner. il pors *New York* 22:44-9 N 27 '89
The satanic diaries. M. Gross. il pors *New York* 22:48-56 My 29 '89
Stardust memory. D. Solomon. il *Harper's Bazaar* 122:136-7+ F '89
A tale of two brothers. J. M. Laskas. il pors *Life* 12:84-5+ D '89

WARHOL, ANDY, 1928?-1987—about—*cont.*
Two years after his death, the curtain rises on Andy Warhol. J. Markus. bibl (p170) il pors *Smithsonian* 19:62-8+ F '89
Warhol [cover story] M. Wade. il pors *Horizon (Tuscaloosa, Ala.)* 32:34-6 Ja/F '89
The Warhol impact [special section] il por *Vogue* 179:320-7+ F '89
Where Warhol failed. B. W. Bloch. il *The New Leader* 72:22-3 Mr 20 '89

Anecdotes, facetiae, satire, etc.
'Hall, Jerry, body odor of, 141' [indexes to diaries] il por *Newsweek* 114:66 Ag 7 '89
In part II of the Warhol diaries, Andy shares his views on the afterlife with Craig Brown. C. Brown. il pors *Vogue* 179:362-4 Ag '89

Bibliography
Absolute Warhol. B. Wallis. il por *Art in America* 77:25+ Mr '89
Long live Andy! G. O'Brien. il por *House & Garden* 161:32+ F '89

WARHOLA, PAUL
about
A tale of two brothers. J. M. Laskas. il pors *Life* 12:84-5+ D '89

WARING, MARILYN
about
What's a woman worth? Y. Preston. il *Ms.* 18:78 Jl/Ag '89

WARLEY, CARLIN
about
My brother, my teammate. M. Bamberger. il pors *Sports Illustrated* 70:54+ Mr 13 '89

WARLEY, JASON
about
My brother, my teammate. M. Bamberger. il pors *Sports Illustrated* 70:54+ Mr 13 '89

WARLOCK, BILLY
about
Billy Warlock: from soap star to screen star! [interview] por *'Teen* 33:45 F '89

WARLOSKI, PAUL
'Without unions, we'd have nothing'. il *The Progressive* 53:22 D '89

WARM-UP EXERCISES *See* Exercise

WARNACO INC.
Treating the retailers as partners [views of L. Wachner] S. Caminiti. il por *Fortune* 120:80 D 18 '89

WARNER, CHRIS
The new Flying Frenchman. il pors *Sport (New York, N.Y.)* 80:56-8+ Mr '89

WARNER, JAMES H.
Should a constitutional amendment to prevent flag desecration be approved? [excerpts from testimony, July 20, 1989] *Congressional Digest* 68:223 Ag/S '89

WARNER, JOHN W.
Should a constitutional amendment to prevent flag desecration be approved? [excerpts from address, July 18, 1989] *Congressional Digest* 68:206+ Ag/S '89

WARNER, MALCOLM-JAMAL
about
'Cosby' kid releases safe sex campaign spots. il por *Jet* 75:18 Mr 6 '89

WARNER, MICKEY
about
Living proof that walking changes walkers. M. Spilner. il pors *Prevention (Emmaus, Pa.)* 41:84+ Jl '89

WARNER, PATRICIA
Architectural elan. il *Architectural Digest* 46:166-71 Ag '89
Leading a stylish revolution in the fashion media. il por *Architectural Digest* 46:29+ S '89
Long Island symmetry: reworking a designer's 1920s residence in Southampton. il *Architectural Digest* 46:138-43 Jl '89

WARNER, ROGER
(ed) See Ngor, Haing S. Journey to freedom

WARNER BOOKS INC.
Pocket and Warner announce retail incentive plans [end of antitrust campaign by independent bookstores] J. Mutter. *Publishers Weekly* 235:19-20 Ja 6 '89

WARNER BROS. INC.
14-karat oomph [1930s] R. Corliss. il *Film Comment* 25:40-6 Jl/Ag '89
Carrot and shtick [Warner Bros. cartoons] T. Teachout. il *The American Spectator* 22:30-1 O '89
Dynamic duos don't come cheap [Warner sues Sony over services of P. Guber and J. Peters] C. Gorman. il pors *Time* 134:71 N 6 '89
Making up, Hollywood style [Warner and Sony settle lawsuit over services of P. Guber and J. Peters] il pors *Time* 134:74 N 27 '89
Walter Yetnikoff's $300 million mistake [Sony's deal to put J. Peters and P. Guber at helm of Columbia Pictures] L. Gubernick. il pors *Forbes* 144:108+ D 11 '89

WARNER COMMUNICATIONS INC.
All hitched up and ready to go [Delaware court OKs Time Warner] J. Greenwald. *Time* 134:39 Ag 7 '89

Banking on Time [role of Toronto Dominion and Bank of Nova Scotia in Paramount Communications' hostile bid for Time Inc.] P. Chisholm and J. DeMont. il *Maclean's* 102:34-5 Jl 10 '89
Batprofits smooth big takeover [Batman earns big profits] E. Pomice. il *U.S. News & World Report* 107:44 Jl 24 '89
Clash of the titans [Paramount challenges merger of Time and Warner Communications] J. Greenwald. il *Time* 133:42-5 Je 19 '89
The counterattack [Time Inc. moves to buy Warner in countermove against Paramount; cover story] J. Schwartz. il *Newsweek* 113:48-53 Je 26 '89
A deal heard round the world [merger of Time and Warner] C. P. Alexander. il *Time* 133:55-6 Mr 20 '89
Even behind the scenes, the Time-Warner drama has its stars [money managers F. Sarofim and O. Aboodi] M. Ivey; J. Friedman. il pors *Business Week* p55-6 Jl 31 '89
Feeding frenzy [Paramount's hostile bid to stop Time-Warner merger] C. Byron. il *New York* 22:24-8 Je 26 '89
First salvos in the fight for Time [bid by Paramount Communications] B. Saporito. il *Fortune* 120:12 Jl 3 '89
Gentlemen's agreement [merger of Time and Warner] E. Diamond. il *New York* 22:16+ Mr 20 '89
Heading for D-Day in Delaware [court to decide whether Time Inc. up for sale] J. Castro. il *Time* 134:44 Jl 10 '89
Heading for 'War Time'? [Time Inc. mega deal with Warner Communications] L. Reibstein. il *Newsweek* 113:50 Mr 20 '89
How Time Warner will look when the fog clears; Pondering Time's fate over chicken gumbo. il *Business Week* p24-5 Ag 7 '89
How to drive off a raider [battle over Time Inc.] J. Schwartz. il *Newsweek* 114:43 Ag 7 '89
Howard U. gets Warner Communications grant. il *Jet* 75:47 Mr 13 '89
The inside story of Time Warner. B. Saporito. il *Fortune* 120:164-6+ N 20 '89
A legal battle that could kill off friendly mergers [court to decide if Time-Warner stock swap put Time in play] M. Galen. il *Business Week* p27 Jl 3 '89
A legal victory for the long term [Delaware court allows Time Inc. to buy Warner and repel Paramount's hostile bid] B. Saporito. il *Fortune* 120:56-9 Ag 14 '89
The meaning of the merger [impact of Time-Warner merger on cable operations] H. Solomon. il *Channels (New York, N.Y.: 1986)* 9:62-3 Je '89
The moguls of Media, Inc. [merger of Time Inc. and Warner Communications] E. Pomice. il *U.S. News & World Report* 106:66-7 Mr 20 '89
A new media powerhouse [Time Inc. and Warner] J. DeMont. il por *Maclean's* 102:42-4 Mr 20 '89
A nice, simple Time-Warner deal was too good to last [bid by Paramount Communications] D. Lieberman. il *Business Week* p38-9 Je 19 '89
One for the books [Delaware court rejects Paramount's challenge to Time-Warner deal] J. Greenwald. il *Time* 134:34-6 Jl 24 '89
Paramount bid for Time launches all-out battle. *Publishers Weekly* 235:8 Je 23 '89
Paramount raises its ante [increases hostile bid for Time] J. Greenwald. il *Time* 134:42 Jl 3 '89
Return to sender [Paramount's hostile bid for Time] J. Greenwald. il *Time* 133:54-5 Je 26 '89
Steve Ross' big sweet deal [merger of Warner Communications and Time] G. Morgenson. il por *Forbes* 143:14 Ap 3 '89
Temple of gloom [A. Temple quits as Time Inc. director because he opposes proposed merger with Warner Communications] J. Zweig. il por *Forbes* 143:168 Je 26 '89
The thorn in Steve Ross's side [H. Siegel wants deal for his stake in Warner] R. Grover. il por *Business Week* p51 Ag 14 '89
Time + Dallas = ? [New York times coverage of Time Inc. acquisition of Warner Communications] R. Pollak. *The Nation* 248:401 Mr 27 '89
Time Inc. gets a green light [Delaware judge OKs Warner bid] J. Schwartz and C. Friday. il *Newsweek* 114:50 Jl 24 '89
Time Inc. goes Hollywood [buyout of Warner Communications] L. Reibstein. il *Newsweek* 113:41-2 Mr 13 '89
Time Inc. will have to pull a Houdini [Paramount's hostile bid] D. Lieberman. il *Business Week* p62 Je 26 '89
Time out [merger of Time Inc. and Warner Communications] J. Bennet. *The New Republic* 200:20+ Ap 24 '89
Time rejects Paramount's sweetened $12 billion bid. *Publishers Weekly* 236:8 Jl 7 '89
Time vs. its shareholders [Paramount's hostile bid to stop merger with Warner] J. Egan. il *U.S. News & World Report* 107:38-40 Jl 3 '89
The Time Warner challenge. M. Brown. il *Channels (New York, N.Y.: 1986)* 9:20 My '89
Time-Warner heads receive cordial hearing by House Judiciary unit. H. Fields. *Publishers Weekly* 235:14 Mr 31 '89
Time-Warner is wired for cable wars. D. Lieberman. il *Business Week* p44 Ap 17 '89

WARNER COMMUNICATIONS INC.—*cont.*
Time-Warner link pleases book principals. *Publishers Weekly* 235:10+ Mr 17 '89
Time-Warner: this close to victory [Delaware court decision; special section] il *Business Week* p26-9 Jl 31 '89
Time-Warner: three's a crowd: Bob Bass may stop the merger. K. Kelly and D. Lieberman. il por *Business Week* p38 Ap 3 '89
Time's bad fortune with money people [Paramount's bid for Time Inc.] *U.S. News & World Report* 106:14 Je 19 '89
Time's counterattack is drawing acid reviews [Warner bid] D. Lieberman. il *Business Week* p26 Jl 3 '89
Upping the ante for Time [Paramount's new bid] J. Schwartz. il *Newsweek* 114:42 Jl 3 '89
The war over Time Inc. [Paramount's hostile bid threatens Warner merger] J. Schwartz. il *Newsweek* 113:48-9+ Je 19 '89
Will it happen? And will it work? [Time-Warner deal; special section] il *Business Week* p32-6 Mr 20 '89

WARNER ROBINS AIR LOGISTICS CENTER (U.S.)
Air Logistics Center keeps EW systems capable of countering changing threats [electronic warfare] il *Aviation Week & Space Technology* 131:103-6 S 11 '89

WARNKE, PAUL C., 1920-
A little shoring up. *The Bulletin of the Atomic Scientists* 45:35 My '89

WARNOCK, JOHN E.
about
A man of characters. M. Antonoff. por *Personal Computing* 13:86 Jl '89

WARRANTS, CURRENCY EXCHANGE *See* Currency exchange warrants

WARRANTY
See also
Home warranty
Before you buy: check the warranty. il *Consumers' Research Magazine* 72:36-7 O '89
Bicycle warranties. J. Langley. *Bicycling* 30:74+ Mr '89
Is your car's warranty a secret? *Consumer Reports* 54:214-15 Ap '89
The out-of-warranty blues [secret automobile warranties] M. Silver. il *U.S. News & World Report* 107:73-5 O 30 '89
Resuscitating a warranty. P. Plawin. *Changing Times* 43:92 Ja '89

WARREN, ANDREA
How one family spends its money. il *Good Housekeeping* 209:50+ Jl '89

WARREN, LARRY D.
The happy clam. il *The Mother Earth News* 116:62-5 Mr/Ap '89

WARREN, MELINDA, AND CHILTON, KENNETH W.
Clearing the air of ozone. bibl *Society* 26:48-58 Mr/Ap '89

WARREN, NANCY HUNTER
about
Inside high villages. J. Neary. il por *Americana* 17:42-7 Mr/Ap '89

WARREN, RICHARD
The noise about FMX. il *Stereo Review* 54:113-15 S '89

WARREN, ROBERT PENN, 1905-1989
about
Obituary
National Review 41:21 O 13 '89
Newsweek il por 114:67 S 25 '89. W. Clemons
People Weekly por 32:46 O 2 '89. P. Axthelm
Robert Penn Warren's enormous spider web. R. Drake. por *The Christian Century* 106:1089-91 N 22 '89

WARREN, ROSANNA
Man, that is born of woman [poem] *The New Yorker* 65:44 D 18 '89

WARREN, VICKI
Have gavel, will travel. il *Common Cause Magazine* 15:9 N/D '89

WARREN, WALLY
about
Wally Warren at MIA. M. Kangas. il *Art in America* 77:225 O '89

WARREN, WILLIAM
Exotic themes in Bangkok [cover story] il *Architectural Digest* 46:150-5 D '89

WARREN (N.J.)
Stores
See also
Expression Unlimited

WARREN COMMISSION
Inside the Archives. il *American History Illustrated* 23:18-19 Ja '89

WARRENDER, JONATHAN
about
Estate of the art. M. Girouard. il *House & Garden* 161:58 Mr '89

WARRICK, RUTH
Ruth Warrick: on how a movie star became the queen of soap villainy. il por *People Weekly* 31 Special Issue:138 Summ '89

WARS *See* War

WARSAW (POLAND)
Description
Warsaw scenes: a burned-out light bulb and other tragedies; tr. by Michael Kott. J. Głowacki. il *The New York Times Magazine* p20-2 Jl 30 '89

WARSAW PACT ORGANIZATION *See* Warsaw Treaty Organization

WARSAW TREATY ORGANIZATION
Arms negotiations in Europe. J. Erickson. *Current History* 88:369-72+ N '89
Can NATO agree on arms control? J. Dean. il *Technology Review* 92:58-62+ O '89
Central European security. H. Owen and E. C. Meyer. il *Foreign Affairs* 68:22-40 Summ '89
The conventional balance: a TKO for NATO? [cover story] J. Mendelsohn and T. Halverson. bibl f il *The Bulletin of the Atomic Scientists* 45:30-4+ Mr '89
Conventional talks: a good first round. J. Dean. il *The Bulletin of the Atomic Scientists* 45:26-31 O '89
East bloc political changes add to West's budget battles [with editorial comment by Paul Mann] M. Mecham. il *Aviation Week & Space Technology* 131:19, 28-31 N 20 '89
From East Germany: it's NATO's move now [reductions in troops and conventional weapons] M. Schmidt and W. Schwarz. il *The Bulletin of the Atomic Scientists* 45:5-6 S '89
NATO disputes Warsaw Pact claim of conventional parity. K. F. Mordoff. *Aviation Week & Space Technology* 130:21-2 F 6 '89
A new Concert of Europe. J. E. Mueller. *Foreign Policy* 77:3-16 Wint '89/'90
Superpower disengagement. C. Layne. *Foreign Policy* 77:17-40 Wint '89/'90
There goes the bloc. J. Smolowe. il map *Time* 134:48-51 N 6 '89
Warsaw Pact unable to track MiG that crashed in Belgium after pilot ejected over Poland. il *Aviation Week & Space Technology* 130:28 Jl 10 '89
Your move again, George [proposal on conventional arms] H. Anderson. il *Newsweek* 114:24 Jl 10 '89

WARSHAW, ROBIN
In the bonds of fraternity [cover story] il *The Nation* 249:189+ Ag 21-28 '89

WARSHEL, A., AND OTHERS
Dispersed polaron simulations of electron transfer in photosynthetic reaction centers. bibl f il *Science* 246:112-16 O 6 '89

WARSHIPS
See also
Aircraft carriers
Dorchester (Ship)
Mullany (Destroyer)
Submarines
Ticonderoga (Ship)
Triremes
Accidents and explosions
See also
Iowa (Ship) gun turret explosion, 1989
Classified top secret: H-bomb overboard [rolls off U.S. carrier Ticonderoga headed toward Japanese port] *Newsweek* 113:45 My 15 '89
Disasters on the high seas [U.S. Navy's problems] E. Salholz. il *Newsweek* 114:47 N 13 '89
A postage stamp in the ocean [U.S. Navy's problems] S. Budiansky. il *U.S. News & World Report* 107:12-13 N 13 '89
Armaments
See also
Guided missiles—Launching from ships
A critical weakness [questions raised about Phalanx warship defense system for Canadian frigates] W. Lowther. il *Maclean's* 102:13 F 13 '89
Navy says no PALs for us [permissive action link for nuclear weapons] P. D. Zimmerman. bibl f il *The Bulletin of the Atomic Scientists* 45:36-41 N '89
Canada
A critical weakness [questions raised about Phalanx warship defense system for Canadian frigates] W. Lowther. il *Maclean's* 102:13 F 13 '89
Germany
See also
Bismarck (Battleship)
United States
See Warships

WARSZAWSKI, DAWID
Solidarity makes a choice [cover story] il *The New Leader* 72:3-4 S 4 '89

WART SNAKES *See* Snakes

WARTIK, NANCY
Life in the fax lane. il *Ms.* 18:42+ N '89

WARTOFSKY, LEONARD
Thyroid disease: how to control it. por *McCall's* 117:106 N '89

WARTS
Venereal warts. L. F. Webb. il *Essence* 19:12 Mr '89

WARWICK, DIONNE
about
Dionne Warwick is not happy with Dick Clark. J. D. Stem. il pors *TV Guide* 37:6-8 Ap 8-14 '89
Dionne Warwick rounds up her celeb pals to fight AIDS. il pors *People Weekly* 31:73-4 Je 26 '89
Dionne Warwick says death of her valet prompts her crusade against AIDS [cover story] C. Waldron. il pors *Jet* 75:58-61 Mr 27 '89
Superstars shine as they raise funds to fight against AIDS. C. Waldron. il pors *Jet* 76:56-9 Jl 17 '89

WARWICK, JAMES W., 1924-, AND OTHERS
Voyager planetary radio astronomy at Neptune. bibl f il *Science* 246:1498-1501 D 15 '89

WAS (NOT WAS) (MUSICAL GROUP)
Chocolate-covered razor blades. J. Cocks. il *Time* 133:74 Ja 30 '89
Out in left field with Was (Not Was) [Detroit] il *Rolling Stone* p23 Jl 13-27 '89

WASHBURN (WIS.)
Education
Holly Driscoll had a fine idea, but it left her in the soup [collecting Campbell Soup labels to obtain van for school] il por *People Weekly* 31:97 My 22 '89

WASHERS, PRESSURE *See* Pressure washers
WASHERS (HARDWARE)
Storage
Washer-go-round. W. E. Burton. il *Workbench* 45:68+ N/D '89

WASHING MACHINES
Washing machines. il *Consumer Reports* 54:188-91 Mr '89
Washing machines. il *Consumer Reports* 54:310-14 D '89
Transmission
Wake up, Maytag man! J. Harris. il *Forbes* 144:308+ N 13 '89

WASHINGTON, DENNIS
about
Denny's always the low-cost producer [cover story] R. L. Stern. il pors *Forbes* 143:87-91 My 15 '89

WASHINGTON, DENZEL
about
Black stars shine in murder mystery 'The Mighty Quinn'. il pors *Jet* 75:46-8 F 20 '89

WASHINGTON, GEORGE, 1732-1799
about
First in the hearts of his countrymen. *National Review* 41:18 Je 2 '89
Forgotten founder. B. Wyatt-Brown. il *USA Today (Periodical)* 118:90-2 Jl '89
General George Washington: espionage chief. W. R. Haefele. bibl il pors *American History Illustrated* 24:22-7+ N/D '89
History's reluctant candidate. I. Wolfman. il por *New Choices for the Best Years* 29:18+ F '89
In 1789 a farmer went to New York to become president. M. Kernan. bibl f (p174) il *Smithsonian* 20:94-6+ Je '89
'Mr President' . . . George Washington's new clothes. E. Wright. bibl il pors *History Today* 39:22-8 Ap '89
"An office of unprofitable dignity". J. E. Ferling. il pors *American History Illustrated* 24:12-23+ Mr '89
Our reluctant first president. I. Peck. il por *Scholastic Update (Teachers' edition)* 121:12-13 Ja 13 '89
Spurious George. H. Fairlie. il *The New Republic* 200:12-14 My 8 '89
Washington sold here. il pors *U.S. News & World Report* 106:14 F 27 '89
Where the founder fits in the picture. R. Brookhiser. il *Time* 133:110 F 20 '89
Collectibles
Did Washington plant my relative's cane? B. Py-Lieberman. il *Smithsonian* 19:180 F '89
Washington memorabilia from the Kahler Collection. J. C. Weaver. il pors *Antiques & Collecting Hobbies* 93:28-30 F '89
Health
George Washington's false teeth. J. Gustaitis. il *American History Illustrated* 23:22-3 F '89
Homes
Ancestral seat [Mount Vernon] *The New Yorker* 65:34-5 Ap 10 '89
George Washington's garden [Mount Vernon] M. Filler. il *House & Garden* 161:140-9 My '89
Mount Vernon [cover story; special issue; with editorial comment by Wendell Garrett] il *Antiques* 135:452-531 F '89
Inauguration
Centennial celebrations, etc.
Celebrating a New York inauguration. M. Durham. il *Americana* 17:8 Mr/Ap '89
George Washington and New York City. A. E. Ledes. il *Antiques* 135:392+ F '89
Centennial celebrations, etc.—Collectibles
A bygone century comes to light [box containing mementos of 1889 celebration] R. M. Poole. il pors *National Geographic* 176:366-9 S '89
U.S. history in a box [box containing mementos of 1889 celebration] B. P. Field. il *National Geographic* 175:652-60 My '89

Statues, portraits, etc.
Facing the real George Washington. il pors *National Geographic World* 162:22-3 F '89
Portraits of George and Martha Washington. R. G. Stewart. bibl f il pors *Antiques* 135:474-9 F '89

WASHINGTON, KERMIT
about
Didn't you used to be . . . W. Ladson. por *Sport (New York, N.Y.)* 80:85 Ap '89

WASHINGTON, MARTHA, 1731-1802
about
Mount Vernon [cover story; special issue; with editorial comment by Wendell Garrett] il *Antiques* 135:452-531 F '89
Statues, portraits, etc.
Portraits of George and Martha Washington. R. G. Stewart. bibl f il pors *Antiques* 135:474-9 F '89

WASHINGTON (CONN.)
Washington diarist: outside the Beltway [Rolling Stones spend summer] D. Owen. *The New Republic* 201:54 S 18-25 '89
Historic houses, sites, etc.
Shingle style revival: new life for a rambling Connecticut residence [home of A. and S. W. Finkelson decorated by Robert Currie] C. D. B. Bryan. il pors *Architectural Digest* 46:152-7+ Je '89

WASHINGTON (D.C.)
See also
Booksellers and bookselling—Washington (D.C.)
Airports
Mega-TCA for D.C.? [terminal control area] *Flying* 116:16 Je '89
Ambulance service
The worst city government. K. Boo. *The Washington Monthly* 21:49 D '89
Architecture
See also
Washington (D.C.)—Public buildings
Adding space with light. il *Southern Living* 24:134 O '89
Art
Hammering the body politic, blacks wreck a portrait of a blond, white Jesse Jackson. il *People Weekly* 32:79 D 18 '89
Jackson cites reality in portrait of him as white. il por *Jet* 77:5 D 18 '89
Blacks
Prisoners of crack. L. Cole. il *Rolling Stone* p61-4+ F 9 '89
War among Washington's blacks. J. Cassidy. *World Press Review* 36:34 My '89
Buildings
See also
Embassies (Buildings)
Washington (D.C.)—Public buildings
Child welfare
See also
Exodus Youth Services (Washington, D.C.)
Climate
Anecdotes, facetiae, satire, etc.
A/C in D.C.: my struggle to stay cool. C. T. Buckley. il *Architectural Digest* 46:106+ Je '89
Courts
See also
United States. Court of Appeals (District of Columbia Circuit)
Crime
Alleged killer of 'Jet beauty' turns himself in after his crime is aired on TV show [R. Urabez charged with murdering M. Shiferaw] pors *Jet* 77:7 O 16 '89
D.C. police hunt for suspect in slaying of co-ed and her brother [murder of M. Shiferaw] pors *Jet* 76:52 Jl 24 '89
A family business [drug ring run by R. Edmond] R. Sandza. il *Newsweek* 113:20 Je 26 '89
Good place for a test case [W. Bennett to declare war on drugs] il *Time* 133:24 Ap 3 '89
It's déjà vu all over again [drug-related crime wave in Washington, D.C.; views of D. P. Moynihan] *U.S. News & World Report* 106:15 Ap 3 '89
The meanest street in Washington. P. Cary. il map *U.S. News & World Report* 106:30-1 Ap 10 '89
Murder capital. M. Tidwell. il *The Progressive* 53:46 Jl '89
Murder wave in the capital. T. Morganthau. il *Newsweek* 113:16-19 Mr 13 '89
Notes and comment [drug murders] *The New Yorker* 65:29-30 Ap 17 '89
An ugly epidemic [at war with crack] W. Lowther. il *Maclean's* 102:50 Ap 3 '89
Unveiling Bennett's battle plan [efforts to curb drug trade] M. Miller. il por *Newsweek* 113:6 Ap 24 '89
War among Washington's blacks. J. Cassidy. *World Press Review* 36:34 My '89
Criminal justice, Administration of
D.C. cracks down on drugs, evicts suspected dealers. il *Jet* 76:52 Je 5 '89
The juice ain't no use: why the death penalty won't work in D.C. J. DeParle. *The Washington Monthly* 21:32-3 My '89

WASHINGTON (D.C.)—*cont.*

Description

A capital city for kids. A. K. Horowitz. il *Publishers Weekly* 235:122-3 My 12 '89

Anecdotes, facetiae, satire, etc.

Scandal Tour. D. Graff. il *Travel Holiday* 172:98 O '89

Tours de farce. A. Ferguson. il *The American Spectator* 22:41 S '89

Economic conditions

Down and out in Washington on $89,500 a year. J. Rowe. *The Washington Monthly* 21:12-14+ Jl/Ag '89

Education

See also

Project Excellence Awards

Choir director Joyce Garrett battles D.C.'s mean streets with the power of positive singing [Eastern High School choir] R. Arias. il por *People Weekly* 31:99-100 Je 12 '89

Song of Eastern High [J. Garrett prepares high school choir for International Youth and Music Festival] K. McCabe. il *Reader's Digest* 135:51-6 S '89

Galleries and museums

See also

Arthur M. Sackler Gallery (Washington, D.C.)

Corcoran Gallery of Art

Hirshhorn Museum and Sculpture Garden

National African-American Heritage Memorial Museum

National Gallery of Art (U.S.)

National Museum of American History (U.S.)

National Museum of the American Indian (U.S.)

Smithsonian Institution

U.S. Holocaust Memorial Museum

The gems of a Washington neighborhood [Dupont Kalorama area] il *Southern Living* 24:22-3 Ag '89

Gardens and gardening

See also

Enid A. Haupt Garden (Washington, D.C.)

Historic houses, sites, etc.

See also

Black History Trail (Washington, D.C.)

Capitol (Washington, D.C.)

White House (Washington, D.C.)

D.C. sites to see. P. Exton. il *Publishers Weekly* 235:116-17 My 12 '89

Literary lights on the Potomac. D. Cutler. il *Publishers Weekly* 235:112-14 My 12 '89

Hospitals

See also

Children's Hospital National Medical Center

Hotels, motels, etc.

A capital intrigue [Watergate Hotel] M. Di Landro. il *Travel Holiday* 171:34 Ja '89

Housing

The Muslims to the rescue [anti-drug patrol in Mayfair Mansions housing project] il *Ebony* 44:136+ Ag '89

Washington, D.C., contemplates the SRO as affordable housing. B. Black. il *Architectural Record* 177:43 F '89

Industries

Washington's one & only [WUSA; cover story] J. Loftus. il *Channels (New York, N.Y.: 1986)* 9:32-4 N '89

Justice, Administration of

See also

Washington (D.C.)—Criminal justice, Administration of

Medical care

High anxiety [psychiatrists treat politicians] D. Baldwin. il *Common Cause Magazine* 15:34-8 Jl/Ag '89

Monuments, statues, etc.

Fund-raising push on for black memorials in D.C. [Revolutionary War Memorial] *Jet* 76:7 Ap 17 '89

Radical surgery [condemned Washington, D.C. house turned into public art by Art Attack] S. Staggs. il *Art News* 88:23 My '89

Music

See also

Washington Opera

Newspapers

See also

Washington post

Washington times

Parades

Presidential Inaugural Parade includes only black builder of float who participated. il por *Jet* 75:57 F 6 '89

Police

D.C. drug patrol: riding with the 'Adamany Raiders'. D. M. Cheers. il *Ebony* 44:112+ Ag '89

Detective Joe Quantrille quits the losing battle against drugs in D.C. M. Brower. il pors *People Weekly* 31:62-4+ Mr 20 '89

Politics and government

The bizarre and troubling escapades of Mayor Barry. T. Gest. il por *U.S. News & World Report* 106:31 Ja 9 '89

A bright, broken promise [M. Barry] M. Riley. il por *Time* 133:60-2 Je 26 '89

A capital offense [scandals surrounding M. Barry] R. Lacayo. il por *Time* 133:27 Ja 16 '89

Contempt for the little colony. C. Hitchens. il *Harper's* 279:70-6 O '89

D.C. police chief quits, mulls GOP run for mayor [M. T. Turner] il por *Jet* 76:4 Ag 14 '89

D.C. statehood agenda targets 1991 deadline. L. Brown and A. Edmond, Jr. *Black Enterprise* 20:33+ D '89

Farewell to all this. D. Shiflett. il *The American Spectator* 22:49 Ag '89

Hit the road, Jack [proposal that J. Jackson run for mayor] H. Hertzberg. *The New Republic* 200:4+ Ap 3 '89

Jackson action [Democrats hope that J. Jackson will run for mayor] J. Klein. il por *New York* 22:20+ My 15 '89

Jackson for D.C. mayor: ready to run? *Newsweek* 113:20 My 8 '89

Jesse Jackson for mayor? He won't say no [interview] por *Business Week* p43 My 22 '89

Mayor Jesse. R. E. Tyrrell. *The American Spectator* 22:10 Jl '89

The mayor's new drug crisis [Washington's M. Barry] L. Martz. por *Newsweek* 113:25 Ja 9 '89

National capital, national shame. F. Barnes. il por *Reader's Digest* 135:106-11 N '89

Republicans for Jackson [J. L. Jackson proposed as mayor] W. Schneider. il *The Atlantic* 264:48 N '89

'Run Jesse run'—for mayor of Washington. il por *Newsweek* 113:30 Ap 10 '89

Scandal at the top [revelations about Mayor M. Barry] W. Lowther. il por *Maclean's* 102:36 Ja 16 '89

Trying to stop, Jesse, stop. J. N. Baker. il pors *Newsweek* 114:29 Jl 17 '89

Washington, D.C.: our 51st state? G. Danziger. il *Utne Reader* p24-5 My/Je '89

Washington's mayor with nine lives, Marion Barry, risks another amid rumors of scandal [alleged cocaine use] M. Brower. il por *People Weekly* 31:48-9 Ja 16 '89

'Why I'm moving to Washington, D.C.' [cover story] il por *Jet* 76:4-6 Ag 7 '89

Wired [loaded politics of cable TV] T. W. Hazlett. *The New Republic* 200:11-13 My 29 '89

The worst city government in America [cover story] J. DeParle. *The Washington Monthly* 20:33-8+ Ja '89

Poor

See also

Horace McKenna Center

First Lady teaches kids at D.C. non-profit center [B. Bush at Martha's Table] il por *Jet* 75:24 F 20 '89

Homeless couple given $50 tickets to attend a coveted inaugural ball [R. and V. Gaines] il pors *Jet* 75:14 F 13 '89

What it's like to aid the homeless. R. R. Roha. il *Changing Times* 43:80-1 Jl '89

Prisons

The worst city government. K. Boo. *The Washington Monthly* 21:17 Mr '89

Protests, demonstrations, etc.

Behind the housing crisis: private-sector forces, not Reagan, killed off affordable rentals. D. Whitman. il *U.S. News & World Report* 107:28+ O 16 '89

Black women's plight cited at pro-choice rally in D.C. [right to abortion march] il *Jet* 76:13 Ap 24 '89

A clear majority [prochoice rally] *The Nation* 248:579-80 My 1 '89

Father knows best [discussion of May 8, 1989 article, March to a crossroads on abortion] M. Tax. *The Nation* 249:110+ Jl 24-31 '89

The first march [prochoice march] *National Review* 41:9-10 My 5 '89

Honk if you care [Chinese students in Washington, D.C. demonstrate in favor of Tiananmen Square uprising] A. McCarthy. *Commonweal* 116:393-4 Jl 14 '89

The longer march [right to abortion march] *Commonweal* 116:259-60 My 5 '89

March on Washington [prochoice demonstration] E. J. Bader. il *The Humanist* 49:26-8+ Jl/Ag '89

March on Washington by students slated for April. *Jet* 75:6 Mr 27 '89

March to a crossroads on abortion [cover story] M. Tax. *The Nation* 248:613+ My 8 '89

NAACP march protests 'legal lynching' of civil rights in U.S. il *Jet* 76:4-6 S 11 '89

NAACP to hold silent march in Washington to protest new Supreme Court rulings. il *Jet* 76:6 Ag 21 '89

New abortion fights [march on Washington to protest possible reversal of Roe v. Wade] T. Gest. il *U.S. News & World Report* 106:22-3+ Ap 24 '89

Notes and comment [Mobilize for Women's Lives rally] *The New Yorker* 65:42-3 D 4 '89

Notes and comment [march to protect Roe v. Wade abortion decision] *The New Yorker* 65:29-30 Ap 24 '89

People's choice [prochoice march] H. Hertzberg. *The New Republic* 200:4+ My 1 '89

Pro-choice: 'a sleeping giant' awakes. E. Salholz. il *Newsweek* 113:39-40 Ap 24 '89

Prochoice forces claim momentum in Washington. il *Christianity Today* 33:59 My 12 '89

Save my law [Roe v. Wade plaintiff N. McCorvey] G. H. Colt. il pors *Life* 12:111-12+ My '89

A sea of stars [celebrity involvement in Housing Now! march] A. Ferguson. il *National Review* 41:26 N 10 '89

WASHINGTON (D.C.) — Protests, demonstrations, etc. — *cont.*

Speaking out for a place to call home [march to protest the plight of the homeless] J. Park. il *People Weekly* 32:40-3 O 23 '89

Taking to the streets [celebrities march in support of Roe v. Wade abortion decision] S. Schindehette. il *People Weekly* 31:40-5 Ap 24 '89

Why I decided to march for abortion rights [interview with C. Shepherd] il por *Glamour* 87:96 Jl '89

Anecdotes, facetiae, satire, etc.
Put us in mental institutions, please! [Housing Now! march] P. J. O'Rourke. il *The American Spectator* 22:16-18 D '89

Public buildings
See also
　Capitol (Washington, D.C.)
　Old Executive Office Building (Washington, D.C.)
Lease-buy, lease-out, and friendly condemnations: the federal government tries new approaches on its new buildings. P. Hoffmann. il *Architectural Record* 177:29+ Mr '89

Religious institutions and affairs
See also
　Exodus Youth Services (Washington, D.C.)
　Horace McKenna Center
　Imani Temple African-American Catholic Congregation
Inside the Bible Beltway [political figures active in prayer groups] R. N. Ostling. il *Time* 133:56-7 F 6 '89

Restaurants, nightclubs, bars, etc.
Chow bella [I Ricchi] D. Shaw. il *Gentlemen's Quarterly* 59:214+ N '89

D.C. delectables. C. Stoltz. il *Harper's Bazaar* 122:218+ O '89

Hangouts and watering holes. D. Cutler. il *Publishers Weekly* 235:121 My 12 '89

On the go [America restaurant designed by MGS Architects] C. Pearson. il *Architectural Record* 177:80-5 mid-S '89

Washington emerges as a culinary capital at last. il *Vogue* 179:348 N '89

Where to eat. K. D. Walker. il *Publishers Weekly* 235:118-20 My 12 '89

Social history
Hello Dolley—on the trail of the Madisons. N. Barry. il por *Gourmet* 49:130+ D '89

Social life and customs
Art of the voyeur [party giver C. Spence involved in male prostitution scandal] T. Noah. por *The New Republic* 201:16+ Ag 7-14 '89

Reporters are members in good standing of Washington high society. C. Hays and J. Rowe. *Utne Reader* p64 N/D '89

The social climber's guide to Washington [cover story; special section] il *National Review* 41:30-3+ F 10 '89

Washington party power. C. J. Houtchens. il *Harper's Bazaar* 122:214+ O '89

Washington's man from nowhere [party giver C. Spence's use of male prostitution service] M. B. Carlson. il por *Time* 134:24 Jl 24 '89

Social work
See also
　Save America's Future (Organization)

Sports
See also
　Baltimore & Washington. T. Loverro. il *Sport (New York, N.Y.)* 80:74-8 S '89

Stores
See also
　Arthur A. Adler (Firm)
Capital ideas [Georgetown antique shops] N. McKeon. il *House & Garden* 161:180+ Ap '89

Street traffic
See also
　Washington (D.C.)—Traffic regulations

Traffic regulations
The quick fix [fixing of parking tickets for members of Congress] D. Gross. *The New Republic* 201:12+ O 16 '89

The worst city government [bureaucratic bungling of traffic violations] S. Shuger. *The Washington Monthly* 21:25 Ap '89

Georgetown
See Georgetown (Washington, D.C.)

WASHINGTON (D.C.) IN LITERATURE
Compromising positions [novelist W. Just] D. Baldwin. il por *Common Cause Magazine* 15:34-8 Mr/Ap '89

Inside-the-Beltway intrigue [interview with W. S. Just] A. P. Sanoff. por *U.S. News & World Report* 106:60 F 20 '89

WASHINGTON (STATE)
See also
　Architecture, Domestic—Washington (State)
　Beaches—Washington (State)
　Birds—Washington (State)
　Cascade Range
　Child welfare—Washington (State)
　Columbia River
　Crime and criminals—Washington (State)
　Ebey's Landing National Historical Reserve (Wash.)
　Mount Saint Helens (Wash.)
　Music festivals—Washington (State)
　Oil pollution—Washington (State)
　Olympic National Park (Wash.)
　Orcas Island (Wash.)
　Paleontology—Washington (State)
　Pasayten Wilderness (Wash.)
　Puget Sound (Wash.)
　Radioactive waste disposal—Washington (State)
　Rivers—Washington (State)
　Tiger Mountain (Wash.)
　Water pollution—Washington (State)

Bibliography
A state bonanza for Washington publishers [works sponsored by Centennial Commission] L. See. *Publishers Weekly* 235:448 Ja 27 '89

Description and travel
See also
　Cruising—Washington (State)
　Cycling—Washington (State)
The Washington State ferries. J. Stiak. il *Travel Holiday* 172:72-9 N '89

Washington State, riding the Pacific tide. M. Edwards. il map *National Geographic* 176:782-815 D '89

Fisheries
See Fisheries

Industries
See also
　Washington Public Power Supply System
　Wine industry
Washington State, riding the Pacific tide. M. Edwards. il map *National Geographic* 176:782-815 D '89

WASHINGTON CORPORATION (MONT.)
Denny's always the low-cost producer [cover story] R. L. Stern. il pors *Forbes* 143:87-91 My 15 '89

WASHINGTON KING CLAM, INC.
Clamscam. F. Graham. *Audubon* 91:8+ N '89

WASHINGTON MONTHLY
The gospel reconsidered [neoliberal philosophy; cover story; special section] *The Washington Monthly* 21:26-30+ Mr '89

Tilters. *The Nation* 248:328 Mr 13 '89

Who we are. What we believe. Why we believe it. [special section] *The Washington Monthly* 21:32-4+ F '89

Anecdotes, facetiae, satire, etc.
Have you got what it takes to write for the Washington monthly? A. Levine. *The Washington Monthly* 21:54 F '89

WASHINGTON OPERA
A capital enterprise. M. Mayer. il pors *Opera News* 54:24-9+ N '89

WASHINGTON PARK ZOO (PORTLAND, OR.)
The only harmless great thing [Asian elephant breeding research] S. Tisdale. il *The New Yorker* 64:38-40+ Ja 23 '89

WASHINGTON POST
Off the record [views on the economy] Cato. il *National Review* 41:72 N 10 '89

The union-busting Post: labor pains at a liberal paper [cover story] J. Hanrahan. il *The Progressive* 53:18-25 F '89

WASHINGTON POST CO.
Eyes are on a newspaper prize. G. G. Marcial. *Business Week* p130 O 23 '89

The mastermind of a media empire [K. Graham] M. Rowland. il pors *Working Woman* 14:114-15+ N '89

WASHINGTON PRESS CORPS *See* Bush, George, 1924——Press relations; Presidents—Press relations; Reagan, Ronald, 1911——Press relations

WASHINGTON PUBLIC POWER SUPPLY SYSTEM
Whoops: investors may let bygones be bygones [new bond issue] D. Zigas. il *Business Week* p92 S 4 '89

WASHINGTON SQUARE (NEW YORK, N.Y.)
Mink [chess player who takes on challengers] *The New Yorker* 65:38-9 Je 12 '89

WASHINGTON SQUARE ART SHOW
Portraits [van Gogh copies displayed by M. Schacknow] *The New Yorker* 65:36-7 S 18 '89

WASHINGTON STATE CONVENTION AND TRADE CENTER
Only connect [design by TRA + HNTB, Architects] M. Gaskie. il *Architectural Record* 177:112-17 F '89

WASHINGTON TIMES
No. 2 and trying harder. il *Time* 134:74 N 6 '89

WASIK, JOHN F.
Healthy insurance. il *Mother Jones* 14:53-4 My '89

WASKOW, ARTHUR
A seder for peace in the Mideast. il *The Nation* 248:557+ Ap 24 '89

WASLEY, TERREE P.
Are we now to be soaked by VAT? il *Conservative Digest* 15:40-1+ My/Je '89

WASPS
Alien influence [wasp larvae manipulation of potato aphid behavior; research by Jacques Brodeur and Jeremy N. McNeil] T. Beardsley. *Scientific American* 261:26 Jl '89

Dying aphids obey wasp's commands [research by Jacques Brodeur and Jeremy N. McNeil] R. Weiss. *Science News* 135:231 Ap 15 '89

WATER BILLS *See* Water rates
WATER BIRD SHOOTING
See also
Market hunting (Game hunting)
The day of the swans. N. Strung. il *Field & Stream* 94:60-1+ N '89
Hunting with the Cossacks [southern Soviet Union] G. Reiger. il *Field & Stream* 93:72-3+ Ap '89
Up front [waterfowl sting operation in Texas] D. Barnes. il *Field & Stream* 93:7 Mr '89
Wildlife cops on a bust [Fish and Wildlife Service's Texas Waterfowl Operation] E. Linden. il *Time* 133:18 F 20 '89

WATER BIRDS
See also
Ducks, Wild
Geese, Wild
Pelicans
Sea birds
Shore birds
Swans
A future for colonial waterbirds in New York State [Return a Gift to Wildlife program] M. Frame-Rouse. il *The Conservationist* 43:2-7 Ja/F '89
Migration
See also
Farming in the Flyways (Program)
The last watering holes on the prairie [loss of wetland habitat for waterfowl] G. L. Krapu. il *Natural History* p66-9 Ja '89
New York State migratory bird print and stamp program. il *The Conservationist* 43:56 Mr/Ap '89
Portrait of a deepening crisis [loss of wetlands endangers water birds] P. Steinhart. il *National Wildlife* 27:4-13 O/N '89
Standing room only. P. Steinhart. il *National Wildlife* 27:46-51 Ap/My '89
Waterfowl for tomorrow: the North American Waterfowl Management Plan. D. Odell and G. Batcheller. il map *The Conservationist* 43:6-11 Mr/Ap '89

WATER BLOOM
See also
Brown tide
Red tide
The besieged bays of the world. T. E. Bell. il maps *Sea Frontiers* 35:238-45 Jl/Ag '89
White-water bounty [coccolithophore bloom in Gulf of Maine] C. Mlot. il *BioScience* 39:222-4 Ap '89
WATER COLOR PAINTING *See* Watercolor painting
WATER CONSERVATION
See also
Terraces (Agriculture)
Water reuse
Xeriscaping
As we face another drought year. il *Sunset (Central West edition)* 182:245 Ap '89
Questions and answers about water and gardens. il *Sunset (Central West edition)* 182:126-9 My '89
Some saving thoughts in a time of plenty. M. Kadlecek. il *The Conservationist* 44:52-3 N/D '89
Uncle Sam may regulate your plumbing. W. Giese. *Changing Times* 43:26-7 O '89
What happened to cheap water? L. Mosher. il *National Wildlife* 27:18-23 Je/Jl '89
WATER CYCLE *See* Hydrologic cycle
WATER DESALTING *See* Saline water conversion
WATER DROPS *See* Drops
WATER EXERCISES
Beyond the breast stroke. D. Welch. il *Health (New York, N.Y.)* 21:44-5 Jl '89
Get wet! il *Parents* 64:104 Ag '89
Hydro-toil [water walking; views of Jane Katz] E. Kaufmann. il *American Health* 8:46 Ja/F '89
Next-wave exercise. C. Schaeffer. *Changing Times* 43:119 Ap '89
Splash yourself sleek—turn a pool into a body gym. il *Glamour* 87:152-3 Jl '89
Tone up in the pool [during pregnancy] L. MacCallum. il *Glamour* 87:59 Ag '89
Water dancing [cover story] D. Welch. il *Health (New York, N.Y.)* 21:46-51 Jl '89
The water way [Hydro-Tone system for tennis] P. Cohen. il pors *World Tennis* 37:58-9 Ag '89
WATER FILTERS AND FILTRATION
On tap: cleaner, better tasting water [boats] B. Gladstone. il *Motor Boating & Sailing* 164:73-6 Jl '89
WATER FOWL *See* Water birds
WATER FRONTS *See* Waterfronts
WATER GARDENS AND GARDENING
See also
Hydroponics
Growing an enchanted oasis. D. Hufford. il *Flower and Garden* 33:42-6 My/Je '89
WATER HEATERS
See also
Solar water heaters

Advanced heat pump heats water too [Carrier's Hydrotech 2000] E. R. C. Capulong. il *Popular Science* 234:41 F '89
Available tankless water heaters. il *Consumers' Research Magazine* 72:37 S '89
Do-it-all heat pumps [Mac=Pac and HydroTech 2000] M. DiChristina. il *Popular Science* 235:68-70 O '89
Who needs a water tank? P. Du Pont. il *Consumers' Research Magazine* 72:18-21 Ag '89
Maintenance and repair
Replace a gas water heater. K. Childers. il *The Family Handyman* 39:60-1 N/D '89
WATER HYACINTHS
Waterweed invasions. S. C. H. Barrett. bibl il map *Scientific American* 261:90-7 O '89
WATER IN LANDSCAPE ARCHITECTURE
See also
Fountains
Their "stream" flows from knoll to swimming pool. il *Sunset (Central West edition)* 183:88 Jl '89
WATER IN POETRY
Wet verse at the New Yorker. C. Bernstein. *Harper's* 279:28+ N '89
WATER IN THE BODY
See also
Dehydration (Physiology)
Drink to your health [runners] J. Stifler. il *Runner's World* 24:72-6+ Jl '89
Get wet! C. Straley. il *Parents* 64:102-4 Ag '89
WATER JETS *See* Jet cutting
WATER KNIFE CUTTING *See* Jet cutting
WATER LILIES
See also
Lotus
Anatomy of a lily pad patch [bass fishing] B. Ignizio. il *Field & Stream* 94:40-1+ Je '89
WATER MARKETING
Are we now ready to pay for water? [developing countries] P. Stroot. il *World Health* p30 N '89
A deal that might save a Sierra gem [Mono Lake] R. Conniff. il *Time* 133:8+ Ap 3 '89
Water marketing [views of Rodney T. Smith] il *The Futurist* 23:53-4 S/O '89
WATER MEMORY THEORY
Benveniste criticism is diluted. D. Dickson. *Science* 245:248 Jl 21 '89
Dilutions of grandeur [Nature magazine's investigation of J. Benveniste's experiment] A. C. Revkin. il *Discover* 10:74-5 Ja '89
WATER MILL (N.Y.)
Historic houses, sites, etc.
New life for a Water Mill blacksmith shop [residence of B. Moller] J. Gruen. il *Architectural Digest* 46:108+ Ag '89
WATER MILLS
History
The medieval mill—a productivity breakthrough? R. Holt. il *History Today* 39:26-31 Ap '89
WATER ON MARS *See* Mars (Planet)—Surface
WATER ON PHOBOS *See* Mars (Planet)—Satellites—Surface
WATER ON THE MOON *See* Moon—Surface
WATER PARKS (AMUSEMENT PARKS) *See* Amusement parks
WATER PILLS *See* Diuretics
WATER PIPES
Freezing
How to repair frozen pipes. M. Henkenius. il *Popular Mechanics* 166:91-2 D '89
WATER POLLUTION
See also
Acid rain
Fish contamination
Groundwater pollution
Marine pollution
Oil pollution
Seafood—Contamination
Water bloom
A chemical war on water [pesticides and lake pollution] G. Payne. *Sierra* 74:40-2 My/Je '89
Cistern water: soft—and corrosive. *Science News* 135:191 Mr 25 '89
Into the pipeline. il *Time* 133:38 Mr 27 '89
Kids crusade to save our streams. P. Michelmore. il *Reader's Digest* 134:98-102 Je '89
Troubled water. E. Kunes. *Omni (New York, N.Y.)* 11:46+ S '89
Water: unsafe in any form? H. Cordes. il *Utne Reader* p24+ S/O '89
Control
See also
Cleaning of lakes, rivers, etc.
Sewage purification
Water [Environmental Quality Index] il *National Wildlife* 27:36 F/Mr '89
Water pollution: visible results. G. Easterbrook. il *Newsweek* 114:35-6 Jl 24 '89

WATER POLLUTION—cont.

International aspects
Threats to the world's water. J. W. M. La Rivière. bibl il map *Scientific American* 261:80-4+ S '89

Laws and regulations
Trouble at the waterworks. C. Nichols. il *The Progressive* 53:33-5 Je '89

Alberta
The forest fight [environmental concerns over proposed pulp mill on Athabasca River] R. Corelli. il *Maclean's* 102:60 N 13 '89

British Columbia
Dangerous waters: pollution shuts down B.C. shellfish areas [pulp mills] H. Quinn. il *Maclean's* 102:64 D 4 '89
Trans-border pollution [pulp mills in British Columbia and Washington State] H. Quinn. il *Maclean's* 102:44-5 Jl 3 '89

Great Lakes
Are Great Lakes fish safe to eat? [polychlorinated biphenyls] W. A. Schmidt. il map *National Wildlife* 27:16-19 Ag/S '89
Are Lake Michigan fish dangerous to your health? J. Gibbs. il *Outdoor Life* 184:72-4+ D '89
A call to action [study entitled Great Lakes, great legacy?] N. Underwood. il *Maclean's* 102:56-7 O 23 '89
Don't blame the messenger [poisoning of Lake Michigan fish] J. D. Hair. il *National Wildlife* 27:30 O/N '89
Warning: if you eat Great Lakes fish . . . [cancer risk] *Science News* 135:300 My 13 '89

Illinois
See also
Marion (Ill.)—Water pollution

Massachusetts
See also
Boston (Mass.)—Water pollution

Michigan
Of time and the river [Kalamazoo River] B. Gilbert. il *Sports Illustrated* 71:76-80+ Jl 24 '89

New Jersey
Tolerance and stress in a polluted environment [killifish] J. S. Weis and P. Weis. bibl f il *BioScience* 39:89-95 F '89

New York (State)
Seep, drip, dribble [nonpoint source pollutants] J. Essman. il *The Conservationist* 43:24-31 My/Je '89

Pennsylvania
Anatomy of a fish kill [Spruce Creek] J. Bashline. il *Field & Stream* 93:38+ F '89

Québec (Province)
Canada's white whales are dying. P. Benesh. *World Press Review* 36:56 Ja '89
Doomed canaries of Tadoussac [P. Béland's work with beluga whales in the Saint Lawrence River] J. R. Luoma. il por map *Audubon* 91:92-7 Mr '89

Tennessee
Fight for Pigeon River [conflict between Champion International Corp. in Canton, N.C. and Tennessee environmentalists over pollution control] M. Satchell. il map *U.S. News & World Report* 107:27-8+ D 4 '89

United States
See Water pollution

Washington (State)
Trans-border pollution [pulp mills in British Columbia and Washington State] H. Quinn. il *Maclean's* 102:44-5 Jl 3 '89

WATER POWER
See also
Dams
Hydroelectric power
Water wheels
Wave power

WATER POWER ELECTRIC PLANTS *See* Hydroelectric plants

WATER PROJECTS *See* Water resources development

WATER PUMPS
A shipwrecked Miami couple owe their lives to a clever gadget that makes seawater drinkable [Survivor-35 pump; case of William and Simone Butler] il *People Weekly* 32:101 O 2 '89

Maintenance and repair
How to troubleshoot a water well. M. Henkenius. il *Popular Mechanics* 166:83-6 S '89

WATER PURIFICATION
See also
Chlorination of water
Saline water conversion
Solar waste water treatment
Water filters and filtration
Water reuse
Water softening
Water treatment plants
12 tips for tap-water cleanup. G. Maleskey. il *Prevention (Emmaus, Pa.)* 41:60-4+ Je '89
Mr. Clean [solar reaction process to destroy toxic chemicals] T. Beardsley. il *Scientific American* 260:83-4 Je '89

WATER PURIFICATION INDUSTRY
Cleaning up by cleaning up. J. Schwartz. il *Newsweek* 113:53 F 27 '89

WATER RATES
23 years of outrageous water bills spur two sisters to fight city hall. (P.S.: they won!) [case of C. Freeman and V. Crowe in Statham, Ga.] S. Percy. il pors *Good Housekeeping* 209:52+ O '89
What happened to cheap water? L. Mosher. il *National Wildlife* 27:18-23 Je/Jl '89
"Whiskey's for drinking, water's for fighting over" [views of F. Welsh] M. Beauchamp. il por *Forbes* 144:74+ Jl 24 '89

WATER RECLAMATION *See* Water reuse

WATER RESOURCES DEVELOPMENT
See also
Central Arizona Project
Dams
Irrigation

Africa
River basin projects in Africa [cover story] T. Scudder. bibl f il map *Environment* 31:4-9+ Mr '89

WATER REUSE
See also
Solar waste water treatment
Cleansing waters [artificial wetlands as sewage treatment facility in Benton, Ky.] M. Klockenbrink. il map *American Health* 8:72 S '89
Recycling our most prolific by-product. J. L. Jacobson. *USA Today (Periodical)* 118:88-9 Jl '89
A swamp makes waste to be sweet again [Arcata Marsh and Wildlife Sanctuary] J. Willwerth. il *Time* 133:10+ Mr 20 '89
Washing up with wetlands. il *Country Journal* 16:28 S/O '89

WATER RIGHTS
See also
Water marketing
Waterways—Water rights
Meese's last act [water rights and wilderness] T. Turner. il *The Mother Earth News* 115:33 Ja/F '89
Water rights and wrongs [wilderness] C. F. Wilkinson. *Sierra* 74:35-6+ S/O '89

WATER SAFETY *See* Boats and boating—Safety devices and measures

WATER SKIING
See also
Jet skis
Ski odyssey [skiing behind the Ski Challenger 2081 off Corfu] L. Rudeen. il *Motor Boating & Sailing* 164:58-61+ Jl '89
Ski ya later! L. Norvell. il *Women's Sports & Fitness* 11:40-1 Je '89

WATER SOFTENING
The soft water hard sell. M. Henkenius. il *Home Mechanix* 85:37-8+ Je '89

WATER SPEED RECORDS *See* Boat speed records

WATER SPORTS *See* Aquatic sports

WATER SUPPLY
See also
Aqueducts
Boats and boating—Water supply
Dams
Droughts
Groundwater
Irrigation
Prisons—Water supply
Water conservation
Water purification
Water reuse
Wells
Climate and water. P. H. Abelson. *Science* 243:461 Ja 27 '89

Fluoridation
Flap over fluoride. L. Oliwenstein. il *Discover* 10:34-5 Jl '89
Fluoridation: friends and foes. C. Sears. il map *American Health* 8:36+ O '89
Koop speaks out [support of fluoridated drinking water] C. Sears. il *American Health* 8:51 Ja/F '89

International aspects
Threats to the world's water. J. W. M. La Rivière. bibl il map *Scientific American* 261:80-4+ S '89
Water scarcity threatens food in the '90s [research by Sandra Postel] *Science News* 136:398 D 16 '89

Pollution
See Water pollution

Arizona
See also
Central Arizona Project

California
See also
Los Angeles (Calif.)—Water supply
As we face another drought year. il *Sunset (Central West edition)* 182:245 Ap '89

Colorado
See also
Denver (Colo.)—Water supply

Developing countries
Are we now ready to pay for water? P. Stroot. il *World Health* p30 N '89

WATER SUPPLY—*cont.*

Georgia

See also

Statham (Ga.)—Water supply

Middle East

Water war in the Middle East. A. Gowers and T. Walker. map *World Press Review* 36:57-8 My '89

Minnesota

See also

Minneapolis (Minn.)—Water supply

When the Land of Lakes went dry. L. P. Gerlach and E. D. Whitaker. il *Natural History* p62-4 Ja '89

Mississippi

See also

Jefferson County (Miss.)—Water supply

New York (State)

Some saving thoughts in a time of plenty. M. Kadlecek. il *The Conservationist* 44:52-3 N/D '89

Uganda

Safer water for Uganda. R. G. Mugga. il *World Health* p6-7 D '88

Western States

"Whiskey's for drinking, water's for fighting over" [views of F. Welsh] M. Beauchamp. il por *Forbes* 144:74+ Jl 24 '89

WATER SUPPLY, AGRICULTURAL

See also

Irrigation

WATER SUPPLY, RURAL

See also

Cisterns

Country water [excerpt from Finding and buying your place in the country] L. Scher and C. Scher. il *The Mother Earth News* 118:92-6+ Jl/Ag '89

Trouble at the waterworks. C. Nichols. il *The Progressive* 53:33-5 Je '89

WATER SUPPLY ENGINEERING

See also

Dams

Water treatment plants

WATER TANKS

See also

Cisterns

Rosenwach Tank Company

WATER TEMPERATURE *See* Water—Temperature

WATER TREATMENT PLANTS

Trouble at the waterworks. C. Nichols. il *The Progressive* 53:33-5 Je '89

WATER VAPOR

See also

Humidity

WATER WELLS *See* Wells

WATER WHEELS

Water-wheel wave power. D. Scott. il *Popular Science* 234:125 My '89

WATER WITCHING *See* Dowsing

WATERBORNE INFECTION

See also

Giardiasis

Schistosomiasis

Risky waters. P. Jaret. il *Health (New York, N.Y.)* 21:70-3+ Ag '89

Scientists nab water-polluting parasite [Cryptosporidium infection in Carroll County, Ga.] K. Fackelmann. *Science News* 135:343 Je 3 '89

WATERBOYS (MUSICAL GROUP)

The Waterboys [release of Fisherman's blues] P. Puterbaugh. il *Stereo Review* 54:95 Ap '89

WATERCOLOR PAINTING

Art: early California watercolors. T. S. Hines. il *Architectural Digest* 46:296-301+ My '89

Beginning a career as a watercolorist [J. Cartier] J. R. Kemp. il por *American Artist* 53:72-5+ Jl '89

Donald Holden. M. S. Doherty. il por *American Artist* 53:38-43+ Ap '89

Introspective reflections [C. Carter; cover story] J.-P. Wolf. il por *American Artist* 53:50-5 O '89

Karen Horn. B. S. Goldman. il por *American Artist* 53:68-73 Ag '89

One summer in Constable country [Suffolk, England] C. D. Berg. il *American Artist* 53:38-43+ Jl '89

The watercolor page. See issues of American Artist

Watercolors that transport [excerpt from 100 views along the road] A. Leslie. il *American Artist* 53:66-9+ Ap '89

WATERFALLS

See also

Workman Creek Falls (Ariz.)

Listening to the land of waterfalls [Transylvania County, N.C.] J. T. Black. il *Southern Living* 24:26+ N '89

Water music [gardens] D. Hufford. il *Flower and Garden* 33:20-3 S/O '89

Waterfalls inspire generations of poets but their geologic image is fleeting. M. Hill. il *Earth Science* 41:36-7 Wint '88

WATERFORD GLASS GROUP PLC

Waterford is showing a few cracks. M. Maremont. il *Business Week* p60+ F 20 '89

WATERFORD WEDGWOOD PLC

Waterford is showing a few cracks. M. Maremont. il *Business Week* p60+ F 20 '89

WATERFOWL *See* Water birds

WATERFOWL SHOOTING *See* Water bird shooting

WATERFRONTS

See also

Boston (Mass.)—Harbor

Jersey City (N.J.)—Waterfront

Santa Cruz (Calif.)—Waterfront

On the waterfront. P. Whittell. il *Motor Boating & Sailing* 164:60-2+ D '89

Rough sailing on the waterfront [festival market projects] J. Hammer and T. Barrett. il *Newsweek* 113:44-5 Mr 27 '89

Canada

See also

Vancouver (B.C.)—Waterfront

Soviet Union

See also

Leningrad (Soviet Union)—Waterfront

WATERGATE CASE

"Gung ho on O'B" [involvement of R. Nixon in harassment of L. O'Brien] N. Lemann. il *The Atlantic* 263:26+ Je '89

Speak loudly, carry a small stick [effect of Vietnam and Watergate on U.S. foreign policy] J. Schell. il *Harper's* 278:39-41+ Mr '89

The teflon tycoon [George Bush grants A. Hammer pardon for campaign finance law violations] S. Weinberg. il pors *Common Cause Magazine* 15:17-21 N/D '89

Watergate figure preaches honesty [J. S. Magruder of Columbus, Ohio] *Christianity Today* 33:47 Ap 21 '89

Woodward and Bernstein: what they think of Watergate now [interview] J. Kalter. il pors *TV Guide* 37:6-8 O 28-N 3 '89

Anecdotes, facetiae, satire, etc.

Watergate envy: it's a scandal [Canadian furor over budget leaks couched in Watergate terminology] C. Gordon. il *Maclean's* 102:9 Je 26 '89

WATERGATE HOTEL (WASHINGTON, D.C.) *See* Washington (D.C.)—Hotels, motels, etc.

WATERING OF GARDENS, LAWNS, ETC.

See also

Garden hose

Irrigation—drop by drop. il *Southern Living* 24:66 My '89

Questions and answers about water and gardens. il *Sunset (Central West edition)* 182:126-9 My '89

Watering. il *The Family Handyman* 39:82-3 My '89

Watering deep where trees really need it. il *Sunset (Central West edition)* 182:218 Je '89

WATERING OF PLANTS

Pots that water themselves? il *Sunset (Central West edition)* 182:183 F '89

WATERJETS *See* Jet cutting

WATERLILIES *See* Water lilies

WATERMARK PRESS

An honored tradition: the bookstore as publisher. J. Barbato. *Publishers Weekly* 236:431 Ag 11 '89

WATERMELONS

Watermelon. C. Hammond. il *Americana* 17:34-6 Jl/Ag '89

Watermelon king remembered [R. Chatham] P. S. Prather. il por *American Visions* 4:38-9 Ag '89

WATERPROOF CLOTHING *See* Clothing, Waterproof

WATERPROOF COSMETICS *See* Cosmetics

WATERPROOFING

See also

Automobiles—Leakage

Basement wall revival. il *Home Mechanix* 86:22-3 Mr '89

How to cure condensation. P. McCafferty. il *Workbench* 45:10-12 Mr/Ap '89

Product reports 1990. il *Architectural Record* 177:58-60+ D '89

Summer fun with waterproof & weatherproof cameras. il *Petersen's Photographic Magazine* 18:30-2+ Jl '89

Sweaty walls and windows mean moisture problems. *Sunset (Central West edition)* 183:86 Jl '89

Too much moisture. il *The Family Handyman* 39:6 Ap '89

Why basements leak. D. Johnson. il *The Family Handyman* 39:12+ Je '89

WATERS, ALICE

about

A family dinner with Alice Waters and Paul Bertolli. M. Damsker. il pors *Organic Gardening* 36:46-9 O '89

WATERS, HARRY F.

Frank Gifford. por *Gentlemen's Quarterly* 59:278-9 N '89

WATERS, JOHN, 1946-

about

Cry-baby [film] Reviews

Film Comment il por 25:2+ Jl/Ag '89. R. J. Smith

People Weekly il 32:54-6 S 11 '89. M. Dougherty

WATERS, MAXINE

Drugs, Democrats and priorities. *The Nation* 249:141-4 Jl 24-31 '89

WATERS, MICHAEL, 1949-

Old country recipes [poem] *America* 161:8 Jl 1-8 '89

WATERS, MUDDY, 1915-1983
about
Father and son: an interview with Muddy Waters and Paul Butterfield [reprint] D. DeMicheal. pors *Down Beat* 56:68-71 S '89

WATERS, STANLEY
about
By popular demand [special section] il por *Maclean's* 102:24-5+ O 30 '89

WATERSHEDS
See also
Jocassee Watershed (N.C.-S.C.)

WATERSTONE'S BOOKSELLERS
W. H. Smith merges specialist bookselling chain with Waterstone's. V. Menkes. *Publishers Weekly* 236:14 Ag 4 '89

WATERTON-GLACIER INTERNATIONAL PEACE PARK (ALTA. AND MONT.)
Drills across the border [Shell Canada's plans] K. Van Tighem. il *Wilderness* 52:54-6 Wint '88
International hearings on mine near Glacier. il *National Parks* 63:12-13 Ja/F '89

WATERTON LAKES NATIONAL PARK (ALTA.)
See also
Waterton-Glacier International Peace Park (Alta. and Mont.)

WATERWAYS
See also
Canals
Great Lakes
Intracoastal Waterway
Mississippi River
Rivers
Water rights
Lawsuits, ahoy! [public waterways] D. Fanning. il *Forbes* 143:74-5 Mr 6 '89
United States
See Waterways

WATERWHEELS *See* Water wheels

WATERWORKS
See also
Dams
Rates
See Water rates

WATKINS, ERIC
Pirates of the print shop. *World Press Review* 36:76 S '89

WATKINS, JAMES D.
about
Admiral Watkins's toughest command. S. J. Hedges. il pors *U.S. News & World Report* 107:29-30 Ag 14 '89
Energy czar—and environmental activist? V. Cahan. il por *Business Week* p54 Jl 24 '89
Getting Energy into the schools. M. Barinaga. il por *Science* 246:318 O 20 '89
Watkins named Energy Secretary. M. Crawford. il por *Science* 243:309 Ja 20 '89
Watkins takes the helm at DOE. M. Crawford. il por *Science* 243:1136 Mr 3 '89
Watkins's decision to restart HFIR heralds new era for DOE reactors. I. Goodwin. il *Physics Today* 42:49-50 My '89

WATKINS, PAMELA
Making entrepreneurship an inside job. il *Black Enterprise* 19:136-8+ F '89

WATKINS, PERRY
about
Court OKs re-enlistment of homosexual soldier. il por *Jet* 76:18 My 22 '89
Should homosexuals be able to serve? L. Eskin. por *Scholastic Update (Teachers' edition)* 122:22 O 6 '89

WATKINS, T. H. (TOM H.), 1936-
Untrammeled by man. il *Audubon* 91:74-91 N '89

WATKINS, TOM H. *See* Watkins, T. H. (Tom H.), 1936-

WATKINS, TRACI A.
Fight the freshman 15. pors *Seventeen* 48:162 Ag '89

WATKINS-JOHNSON CO.
Makers of EW components adopt fresh strategies as programs dwindle. *Aviation Week & Space Technology* 131:115+ S 18 '89

WATLEY, JODY
about
America's 10 most beautiful women. A. McDonnell. il pors *Harper's Bazaar* 122:180+ S '89

WATROUS, SUSAN
(jt. auth) *See* Blanchard, Bob, and Watrous, Susan

WATRY, DUNCAN
Our auto-cratic society. il *Utne Reader* p84-5 Mr/Ap '89

WATSON, ANDREA M.
Maneuvering through the vendor maze. il *Black Enterprise* 19:154-6+ F '89

WATSON, BRUCE
The night The Forsyte saga struck back. il *Smithsonian* 20:184 Je '89

WATSON, CATHERINE, 1944-
Women on water. il *Travel Holiday* 172:86-9 Ag '89

WATSON, CHARLES
about
Daughter of Manson victims finds forgiveness. J. Shaver. il pors *Christianity Today* 33:50-1 S 22 '89

WATSON, DAN, AND RANGEL, LYLE
Classroom evaluation of cooperative learning. *The Education Digest* 55:35-7 N '89

WATSON, GLEN M., AND HESSINGER, DAVID A.
Cnidocyte mechanoreceptors are tuned to the movements of swimming prey by chemoreceptors [cover story] bibl f il *Science* 243:1589-91 Mr 24 '89

WATSON, JAMES D., 1928-
about
Back to the bases. T. Beardsley. *Scientific American* 260:16-17 Ja '89
Two sides to every science story. G. Johnson. *The New York Times Book Review* 94:1+ Ap 9 '89
Watson floats a plan to carve up the genome. D. Dickson. il por *Science* 244:521-2 My 5 '89
Watson versus Japan. L. Roberts. il *Science* 246:576+ N 3 '89

WATSON, JIM
The last stand for old growth? il *National Wildlife* 28:24-5 D '89/Ja '90
Rising star. il pors *National Wildlife* 27:46-9 O/N '89

WATSON, PATRICK
about
Making 'Democracy' [cover story; with editorial comment by Kevin Doyle] B. D. Johnson. il pors *Maclean's* 102:4, 38-40+ Ja 16 '89
The new helmsmen [with interview] R. Corelli. il pors *Maclean's* 102:60-1 O 9 '89
A televisionary. B. D. Johnson. il pors *Maclean's* 102:44-6 Ja 16 '89

WATSON, RITA ESPOSITO
Physical symptoms. il *Working Woman* 14:128-9+ S '89

WATSON, RITA ESPOSITO, AND FITZGERALD, KAREN
21st Century School. il *Parents* 64:112-16+ O '89

WATSON, TOM, 1918-
Playing the lottery is idolatry. por *Christianity Today* 33:8 N 3 '89

WATSONVILLE (CALIF.)
Economic conditions
Beat the devil [effects of earthquake] A. Cockburn. il *The Nation* 249:628-9 N 27 '89

WATT, DOUGLAS
Profiles [H. Graff] por *The New Yorker* 65:59-60+ N 20 '89

WATT, W. MONTGOMERY (WILLIAM MONTGOMERY)
A Western response. il *History Today* 39:5-8 D '89

WATT, WALTER W.
Preparing your car for summer vacation. il *Consumers' Research Magazine* 72:13-17 Jl '89

WATT, WILLIAM MONTGOMERY *See* Watt, W. Montgomery (William Montgomery)

WATTC *See* World Administrative Telegraph and Telephone Conference

WATTENBERG, BEN J.
The attitudes behind American exceptionalism. il *U.S. News & World Report* 107:25 Ag 7 '89
The changing face of out-of-wedlock births. il *U.S. News & World Report* 107:29 Jl 3 '89
The debate over how to count the poor. *U.S. News & World Report* 107:47 O 30 '89
Environmental activism: here we go again. il *U.S. News & World Report* 106:29+ Ap 17 '89
The Hispanic struggle for success is slowly paying off. il *U.S. News & World Report* 107:31 S 25 '89
Is education as bad as ever? il *U.S. News & World Report* 106:50-1 Mr 20 '89
Lower birth rates spell a brighter future for the third world. il *U.S. News & World Report* 107:23 D 18 '89
Social engineering is becoming a bipartisan affair. *U.S. News & World Report* 106:25 My 22 '89

WATTLETON, FAYE
The case for national action. *The Nation* 249:138-41 Jl 24-31 '89
Coming of age: the tragedy of teenage pregnancy. il *USA Today (Periodical)* 117:49-50 Ja '89
Which way black America? Anti-abortion or pro-choice. il por *Ebony* 44:134+ O '89
about
Calm, cool and beleaguered [cover story] M. Szegedy-Maszak. il pors *The New York Times Magazine* p16-19+ Ag 6 '89
Nothing less than perfect. R. Stengel. il por *Time* 134:82-4 D 11 '89
Repro woman [interview; cover story] M. A. Gillespie. por *Ms.* 18:50-3 O '89
Voice of choice. D. Michals. il pors *Harper's Bazaar* 122:110-13+ Ag '89

WATTS, A. M.
Christian claims in a pluralistic society. *The Christian Century* 106:222-3 Mr 1 '89

WATTS, AMP
(jt. auth) *See* Ross, L. K., and Watts, Amp

WATTS, DOYLE
NCATE and Texas eyeball to eyeball: who will blink? [interview with C. Parker and H. Gideonse] il *Phi Delta Kappan* 71:311-18 D '89

WATTS, HEATHER
Workshop 25. il *Dance Magazine* 63:38-41 My '89

WATTS, ROBERT, 1923-1988
about
A Fluxus funeral. J. Johnston. il pors *Art in America* 77:42-3+
Mr '89
WATTS, ROBERT G.
about
The game teachers play. S. A. Booth. il por *Rolling Stone*
p152-6 Mr 23 '89
WATTS (LOS ANGELES, CALIF.)
See also
Parents of Watts (Organization)
Teaching kids how to grieve [program for children whose
lives have been touched by murder] S. Doherty. il *Newsweek*
114:73 N 13 '89
WATZMAN, NANCY
(jt. auth) See Saletan, William, and Watzman, Nancy
WAUCH, JOHN
Operation Rescue. *National Review* 41:41 Ap 7 '89
WAUCHULA (FLA.)
Hospitals
Every parent's nightmare: a hospital nursery swap throws
two Florida families into disarray [A. Twigg and K. Mays
switched at birth in Hardee Memorial Hospital] M. Green.
il pors *People Weekly* 32:77-8+ D 11 '89
Whose little girl is Kimberly? [A. Twigg and K. Mays switched
at birth in Hardee Memorial Hospital] M. Jacobbi. il
pors *Good Housekeeping* 208:122-3+ Mr '89
WAUGH, AUBERON
Scandal: more sex please, we're British. il *Vogue* 179:507-9
Mr '89
WAUGH, DAVID S., AND OTHERS
The design and catalytic properties of a simplified ribonuclease
P RNA. bibl f il *Science* 244:1569-71 Je 30 '89
WAUGH, EVELYN, 1903-1966
about
A partiality for lords: Evelyn Waugh and snobbery. D. J.
Greene. *The American Scholar* 58:444-5+ Summ '89
WAVE GUIDES
See also
Optical wave guides
WAVE MECHANICS
See also
Belousov-Zhabotinskii reaction
Tunneling (Physics)
WAVE POWER
Water-wheel wave power. D. Scott. il *Popular Science* 234:125
My '89
WAVE PULSES, SOLITARY See Solitons
WAVERLY (IOWA)
Stores
How Wal-Mart hits Main St. [effect on small businesses]
K. R. Sheets. il map *U.S. News & World Report* 106:53-5
Mr 13 '89
WAVES
See also
Atmospheric waves
Belousov-Zhabotinskii reaction
Electromagnetic waves
Infrasonic waves
Plasma waves
Seismic waves
Shock waves
Sound waves
Tsunamis
Ultrasonic waves
Rogue waves. J. E. Brown. bibl (p84) il *Discover* 10:46-50+
Ap '89
WAVES, BRAIN See Brain waves
WAX TRANSFER PRINTERS
What price color PostScript? [QMS Colorscript 100 Model
10] H. Eglowstein. il *Byte* 14:229-30+ D '89
WAXAHACHIE (TEX.)
Economic conditions
Super deal [chosen as site for Superconducting Super Collider]
G. Jaynes. il *Life* 12:100-4 F '89
WAXES
Understanding car waxes. P. Brand and M. J. Schultz. il
The Family Handyman 39:76-8 Jl/Ag '89
WAXMAN, HENRY ARNOLD
about
Mr. Clean's Air Act [interview] J. Getlin. il pors *Sierra*
74:76-81 N/D '89
WAYANS, KEENEN
about
I'm gonna git you sucka [film] Reviews
The Nation 248:208 F 13 '89. S. Klawans
People Weekly il 31:16+ Ja 23 '89. P. Travers
Knocking on Hollywood's door [cover story] B. Sharkey.
il pors *American Film* 14:22-7+ Jl/Ag '89
WAYLAND (MASS.)
Stores
See also
Caraway's (Firm)
WAYNE, AISSA
about
John Wayne's daughter Aissa is brutally beaten, and her
ex-husband is soon to stand trial. M. Green. il pors *People
Weekly* 31:106-8 My 29 '89

WAYPORTS
FAA will test wayport concept as remedy to airport congestion.
J. Ott. il map *Aviation Week & Space Technology* 130:64-5+
Ja 9 '89
Six wayports, no waiting. G. Eichler. il *Esquire* 112:58 Jl
'89
WAYS AND MEANS COMMITTEE See United States.
Congress. House. Committee on Ways and Means
WAZNAK, ROBERT P.
The Church's response to the media: twenty-five years after
Inter mirifica. *America* 160:36-40 Ja 21 '89
WCC See World Council of Churches
WCT (WORLD CHAMPIONSHIP TENNIS) TOUR See Ten-
nis—Tournaments
WE CAN (ORGANIZATION)
Can do [work of G. Polhemus] R. Flippen. il por *American
Health* 8:70 S '89
WE THE LIVING [film] See Motion picture reviews—Single
works
WE THINK THE WORLD OF YOU [film] See Motion picture
reviews—Single works
WEA See Workers' Educational Association (Great Britain)
WEAKFISH FISHING
The fertile crescent [lower Texas coast] J. Doggett. il *Field
& Stream* 93:36-7+ Ja '89
WEAKNESS (THEOLOGY)
Unravelling the mystery of weakness and strength. P. Kreeft.
il *Christianity Today* 33:23-5 Ap 21 '89
WEALTH
See also
Billionaires
Cost and standard of living
Income
Millionaires
Rich
The prince of get rich quick [D. Bendah] M. S. Gill. il
por *Rolling Stone* p107-8+ F 9 '89
Something seems unbalanced. G. P. Brockway. il *The New
Leader* 72:14-15 S 18 '89
Why isn't the wealth trickling down? K. Pennar. il *Business
Week* p112 My 1 '89
WEAPONS
See also
Airplanes, Military—Armaments
Anti-helicopter weapons
Anti-satellite weapons
Anti-tank weapons
Brilliant Pebbles (Defense system)
Chemical and biological weapons
Firearms
Free electron lasers—Military use
Guided missiles
Kinetic kill vehicles
Lasers—Military use
Nuclear weapons
Particle beam weapons
Police weapons
Rockets
Space warfare
Stone implements and weapons
United States. Air Force Weapons Laboratory
Atwood eyes tighter scrutiny of weapons development.
Aviation Week & Space Technology 130:23 My 15 '89
A new generation of 'smart' weapons. il *Newsweek* 113:14-15
Ja 23 '89
Reliable high tech for future battlefield. il *Popular Mechanics*
166:26 Ap '89
Costs
Best & worst weapons [cover story; special section] P. Cary.
il *U.S. News & World Report* 107:22-9 Jl 10 '89
Cheney proposes canceling major U.S. weapon programs
[special section; with editorial comment by Paul Mann]
il *Aviation Week & Space Technology* 130:9, 18-23 Ap
24 '89
Testing
See also
Naval Weapons Center (U.S.)
Independent labs play key role in aerospace testing, verifica-
tion. W. B. Scott. il *Aviation Week & Space Technology*
130:110-11 My 22 '89
Pentagon purchases Soviet hardware on open market for
operational testing. J. D. Morrocco. il *Aviation Week &
Space Technology* 130:24-5 Ja 23 '89
WEAPONS CONTROL See Disarmament
WEAPONS LABORATORY (AIR FORCE) See United States.
Air Force Weapons Laboratory
WEAPONS OF THE SPIRIT [film] See Motion picture
reviews—Single works
WEAPONS SMUGGLING See Smuggling
WEAPONS TRADE See Munitions—Export-import trade
WEARABLE ART
Coat tales [work of J. Williams-Cacicedo] M. Porges. il por
American Craft 49:46-51 O/N '89
WEART, CAROLE EGE
about
Tracking trends in the city, bringing them to the suburbs.
D. Weil. il por *Working Woman* 14:62 Ag '89

WEATHER
See also
Atmospheric pressure
Climate
Clouds
Cold weather
Droughts
Hot weather
Meteorology
Monsoons
Rain and rainfall
Snow
Storms
Sun and meteorology
Winds
See also subhead Climate under names of continents, countries, states, cities, etc.
Almanac. D. M. Ludlum. See issues of Country Journal beginning October 1986
The weather of 1988 [cover story; special issue] il Weatherwise 42:8-16+ F '89
Weatherwatch. D. M. Ludlum. See issues of Weatherwise
History
Tips for your own search. il Weatherwise 42:327 D '89
Mental and physiological effects
See also
Hot weather—Mental and physiological effects
Research
See Meteorology
WEATHER, PREHISTORIC See Paleoclimatology
WEATHER AND INDUSTRY See Industry and weather
WEATHER AND PLANTS See Plants, Effect of climate on
WEATHER AND POLITICS
Don't need a weatherman? J. Rosen. Harper's 278:34-6 Ap '89
WEATHER CHANNEL
Praying for rain. S. Beschloss. il Channels (New York, N.Y.: 1986) 9:18+ Ap '89
WEATHER COLLECTIBLES
Weather collectibles. M. Reed. il Weatherwise 42:275-6 O '89
WEATHER FORECASTING
See also
Airplanes in meteorology
Artificial satellites—Meteorological use
Computers—Meteorological use
Information systems—Meteorological use
Television broadcasting—Weather forecasts
Weather lore
Weather maps
Don't need a weatherman? J. Rosen. Harper's 278:34-6 Ap '89
Is something strange about the weather? [researchers using tools from the study of chaos] R. Pool. bibl il Science 243:1290-3 Mr 10 '89
A new way to forecast next season's climate [analog system; work of Robert Livezey and Anthony Barnston] R. A. Kerr. il Science 244:30-1 Ap 7 '89
Stalking the savage storm [cover story] B. Carpenter. il U.S. News & World Report 107:48-54 Jl 24 '89
Stalking the super storms. R. Lipkin. il Reader's Digest 134:76-80 Ap '89
Telling weathermen when to worry. R. A. Kerr. il Science 244:1137-9 Je 9 '89
Will it be clear tonight? J. Moeller. il Astronomy 17:74-7 D '89
WEATHER IN LITERATURE
Sherlock Holmes and the weather [cover story] R. S. Cerveny and S. W. Brazel. il Weatherwise 42:80-4 Ap '89
WEATHER IN MUSIC
Music to watch the weather by [cover story] A. J. Wagner. il Weatherwise 42:248-55 O '89
Rockin' thunder [rock songs with references to weather; cover story] R. E. Schmid. il Weatherwise 42:192-6 Ag '89
WEATHER IN MYTHOLOGY
Jason's thunderbolt salve: it works like a charm. M. Reed. il Weatherwise 42:336-8 D '89
WEATHER LORE
Cows and other forecasters. il U.S. News & World Report 107:53 Jl 24 '89
February folklore. D. M. Ludlum. il Country Journal 16:6 F '89
Herring from heaven [showers of marine creatures] M. Reed. il Weatherwise 42:156-8 Je '89
Proverbs and place. R. E. Spencer. il Weatherwise 42:208-11 Ag '89
WEATHER MAPS
Computer map analysis: drawing contours. A. Blackadar. Weatherwise 42:109-13 Ap '89
WEATHER PHOTOGRAPHY See Meteorological photography
WEATHER PREDICTIONS See Weather forecasting
WEATHER RADAR See Radar meteorology
WEATHER RECORDS
Hot spots and cold spots [1988] D. H. Hickcox. il Weatherwise 42:42-6 F '89
WEATHER RESEARCH See Meteorology
WEATHER SATELLITES See Artificial satellites—Meteorological use

WEATHER SERVICES CORPORATION
Weather or not? [P. Leavitt] J. Zweig. il por Forbes 144:120 Jl 10 '89
WEATHER VANES
A good vane. R. Matthews. il Country Journal 16:50-5 Ja '89
WEATHERING
See also
Erosion
Flowering plants leave earth cold [research by Tyler Volk] Science News 135:188 Mr 25 '89
Modeling the geochemical carbon cycle. R. A. Berner and A. C. Lasaga. bibl il Scientific American 260:74-81 Mr '89
WEATHERPROOFING
See also
Waterproofing
Drafty doors [weatherstripping] J. Barrett. il Home Mechanix 85:18-19 N '89
WEATHERSTRIPPING See Weatherproofing
WEATHERVANES See Weather vanes
WEATHERWISE PHOTOGRAPHY CONTEST See Photography—Competitions
WEAVER, EARL
about
That's Earl, folks! M. Lupica. il Esquire 111:53-4+ My '89
WEAVER, JAMES C.
Washington memorabilia from the Kahler Collection. il pors Antiques & Collecting Hobbies 93:28-30 F '89
WEAVER, MARK
about
Murder and the right to die. il por Newsweek 113:33 Ap 10 '89
WEAVER, PAT
Sylvester "Pat" Weaver: on Bogart, Sleeping beauty and a new way to sell TV commercials. il por People Weekly 31 Special Issue:124 Summ '89
WEAVER, SIGOURNEY
about
Sigourney Weaver goes to work. M. Hammer. il pors Ladies' Home Journal 106:60 Ja '89
WEAVER, SUSAN
Women's products. il Bicycling 30:40-4+ Ag '89
WEAVER, TOM
(jt. auth) See Woosley, Stanford E., and Weaver, Tom
WEAVER, WILLIAM, 1923-
Mona Bismarck on Capri. il por Architectural Digest 46:32+ F '89
WEAVER FAMILY
about
What has six legs and stings like a bee? The Weaver brothers, boxing's only triple threat. il People Weekly 32:148-9 N 13 '89
WEAVERS
See also
Scheuer, Ruth Tannenbaum
WEAVING
See also
Cane weaving
Indian blankets, rugs, etc. (American)
Silk weaving
Tapestry
Weaving their way [J. and D. Gould] G. Harrell. il pors House & Garden 161:72 Ap '89
WEBB, BOYD, 1947-
about
Boyd Webb. B. Taylor. il por Art News 88:154-5 Ap '89
Boyd Webb: Sonnabend. E. Heartney. il Art News 88:157 D '89
WEBB, CATHLEEN CROWELL
about
Jailed for a rape that never happened, Gary Dotson has his name cleared at last. M. Brower. il pors People Weekly 32:80-1 Ag 28 '89
WEBB, CHLOE
about
Catching Chloe Webb. R. Sekoff. il por Mademoiselle 95:88 O '89
WEBB, DENSIE
Biggest medical breakthroughs of the decade. il Ladies' Home Journal 106:90+ N '89
Cut your cancer risk by more than 50%. il Redbook 172:96-9+ Ap '89
Eating ethnic and lean [excerpt from International cuisines calorie counter] il Health (New York, N.Y.) 21:46+ N '89
WEBB, JAMES H.
For a defense that makes sense. il The New York Times Magazine p38+ My 21 '89
WEBB, JENNIFER
Going to Cyprus. il pors Seventeen 48:166+ Mr '89
WEBB, JULIAN H., 1902-1988
about
Obituary
Physics Today il por 42:87-8 Jl '89. B. B. Snavely
WEBB, LILLIAN FRIER
Sexual health. See issues of Essence

WEBB, MARILYN
The great debate. il *Harper's Bazaar* 122:64-5+ Jl '89
The great white hope. il pors *New York* 22:50-3 Ja 16 '89

WEBB, MICHAEL, 1937-
Architecture and music in Los Angeles. il *Architectural Digest* 46:116+ My '89
Capricious collections by the shore. il *Architectural Digest* 46:244-9 My '89
Metropolitan reflections: a play of surfaces in a Los Angeles penthouse. il *Architectural Digest* 46:270-5 My '89
A minka revival: Japanese farmhouse traditions reinterpreted in Hawaii. il *Architectural Digest* 46:198-204 Ag '89

WEBB, RICHARD A.
(jt. auth) See Imry, Yoseph, and Webb, Richard A.

WEBB, THEODORE A.
Humanists and theists. por *The Humanist* 49:18-20+ Jl/Ag '89

WEBB (DEL E.) CORP. See Del E. Webb Corp.

WEBB & BOWER
Paradise regained [additional journal by Edwardian naturalist E. Holden to be published] L. Fleischer. *Publishers Weekly* 235:19 Mr 31 '89

WEBER, BRUCE
Cool head, hot images. il pors *The New York Times Magazine* p24-7+ My 21 '89
My best friend's girlfriend. il *The New York Times Magazine* p18+ Ap 16 '89

WEBER, BRUCE
about
Let's get lost [film] Reviews
American Film il 14:50-4 My '89. R. Seidenberg
Maclean's il 102:85-6 N 13 '89. B. D. Johnson
The New Yorker 65:75-6 My 1 '89. P. Kael
Newsweek 113:69 My 29 '89. D. Ansen
Rolling Stone il p19 My 4 '89. C. Stern

WEBER, EUGEN JOSEPH, 1925-
. . . and man made the town. *The American Scholar* 58:79-96 Wint '89
Paris: La Belle Époque. il *National Geographic* 176:158-74 Jl '89

WEBER, FRANK
about
A $90 million matter of distrust pits Billy Joel against his ex-manager. S. Dougherty. il pors *People Weekly* 32:50-1 O 9 '89

WEBER, IRENE T., AND OTHERS
Molecular modeling of the HIV-1 protease and its substrate binding site. bibl f il *Science* 243:928-31 F 17 '89

WEBER, JEFF
about
Freeze-dried memories. P. Jordan. il por *Time* 133:16-17+ F 13 '89
Frigid pet tricks. E. Grinnan. il por *Seventeen* 48:31 Jl '89

WEBER, JOEL
Ann Arbor Antiques Market. il por *Antiques & Collecting Hobbies* 94:47-8+ Ag '89

WEBER, KATHARINE
about
Rustic frame for a modern collection: the Connecticut house of Katharine and Nicholas Fox Weber. R. W. B. Lewis. il *Architectural Digest* 46:200-5+ Je '89

WEBER, MARK WILL- See Will-Weber, Mark
WEBER, MARY RAINS- See Rains-Weber, Mary

WEBER, MICHAEL
about
Games. S. Morris. il *Omni (New York, N.Y.)* 12:118 N '89
Open-and-shut case. S. Morris. il *Omni (New York, N.Y.)* 12:164-5+ O '89

WEBER, MILI
about
Mili Weber's world: the artist's fairy-tale house near St. Moritz. D. Harris. il por *Architectural Digest* 46:174-9 D '89

WEBER, NANCY, 1942-
Choosing Dr. Right. *Harper's Bazaar* 122:187+ Mr '89

WEBER, NICHOLAS FOX, 1947-
Antiques: American game boards. il *Architectural Digest* 46:168-73+ D '89
Antiques: architectural models. il *Architectural Digest* 46:188-93+ Mr '89
The legacy of Ireland's stuccodores. il *Architectural Digest* 46:42+ Ag '89
Mad about Morris. il *House & Garden* 161:88 Ap '89
Warren Brandt [excerpt] il *American Artist* 53:48-53+ Mr '89
about
Rustic frame for a modern collection: the Connecticut house of Katharine and Nicholas Fox Weber. R. W. B. Lewis. il *Architectural Digest* 46:200-5+ Je '89

WEBER, PATRICIA C., AND OTHERS
Structural origins of high-affinity biotin binding to streptavidin. bibl f il *Science* 243:85-8 Ja 6 '89

WEBER, RICHARD J., AND PERT, AGU
The periaqueductal gray matter mediates opiate-induced immunosuppression. bibl f il *Science* 245:188-90 Jl 14 '89

WEBER, ROBERT S.
Destination unknown. il *Focus (New York, N.Y.: 1950)* 39:23-4 Summ '89

WEBER, WILLIAM J.
Homemade cornmeal. il *Country Journal* 16:44-7 S/O '89

WEBERMAN, BEN
Capital markets. See issues of Forbes

WEBS, SPIDER See Spider webs

WEBSTER, BARBARA D.
Opening doors for women in academia [address, 1988] bibl f *BioScience* 39:96-8 F '89

WEBSTER, DAVID
about
The point system. A. Kopkind. *The Nation* 248:761-2 Je 5 '89

WEBSTER, DONALD BLAKE
Cabinetmakers of St. John, New Brunswick. bibl il *Antiques* 135:942-9 Ap '89

WEBSTER, ED
Cold courage. il pors *Sports Illustrated* 70:62-6+ Ja 16 '89

WEBSTER, GAIL E.
Coordinating curriculum in physical education. *The Education Digest* 54:48-50 Mr '89

WEBSTER, NORMAN
about
End of the Webster era. R. Dolphin. *Maclean's* 102:36 Ja 16 '89
A new lineup. B. Came. il *Maclean's* 102:46+ F 13 '89

WEBSTER, WILLIAM H.
Individual rights in the U.S.S.R. [address, July 21, 1989] *Vital Speeches of the Day* 55:711-13 S 15 '89
about
Is Webster on the outs? il *Newsweek* 114:5 Jl 31 '89
"Ma'am, what you need is a new improved Hoover". M. Miller. il por *The Washington Monthly* 20:10-14+ Ja '89
Mr. Webster has it exactly wrong. W. F. Buckley. *National Review* 41:62-3 N 24 '89

WEBSTER, WILLIAM L.
about
What Webster did for Missouri [interview] il por *Christianity Today* 33:37 Ag 18 '89

WEBSTER V. REPRODUCTIVE HEALTH SERVICES See United States. Supreme Court—Decisions—Abortion decisions

WEBSTER'S NEW WORLD WRITER (WORD PROCESSOR PROGRAM) See Word processors and processing—Programming

WECHSLER, JILL
Caroline Huff. il por *American Artist* 53:52-7+ Je '89
How one family spends its money. il *Good Housekeeping* 208:58+ Mr '89

WECHSLER, ROBERT
about
Humor and Czech writers are the calling cards from Catbird. J. Barbato. *Publishers Weekly* 236:28 O 13 '89

WECK, EGON
A bedtime story [cover story] il *FDA Consumer* 23:12-15 O '89
A primer on medical imaging. il *FDA Consumer* 23:12-15 My '89
A primer on medical imaging. il *FDA Consumer* 23:24-7 Ap '89
What can be done when the pain won't go away. il *FDA Consumer* 23:28-31 Jl/Ag '89

WECT (WILMINGTON, N.C.: TELEVISION STATION) See Television stations

WEDDELL, GREGORY N.
(jt. auth) See Caras, Ingrid W., and Weddell, Gregory N.

WEDDELL SEALS See Seals (Animals)

WEDDING ANNIVERSARIES
Wed when the West was wild, Ernie and Maud Scott celebrate 80 years of staying hitched [longest-wed living couple in the world] il pors *People Weekly* 31:99 Je 26 '89

WEDDING ANNOUNCEMENTS
It still takes a bride and groom. L. C. Pogrebin. il *The New York Times Magazine* p12+ Jl 2 '89

A WEDDING BOUQUET [ballet] See Ballet reviews—Single works

WEDDING CLOTHES
For better or for worse? H. Brubach. *The New Yorker* 65:86-90 Jl 10 '89
How to be a beautiful bride. K. Burke. il *McCall's* 116:31 My '89
Stretching the rules [special section] il *The New York Times Magazine* p63-8+ Ja 29 '89

WEDDING GIFTS
The gifted. C. Vogel. il *The New York Times Magazine* p73 Ja 29 '89
Gourmet's wedding gifts. il *Gourmet* 49:80-7 Je '89

WEDDING RECEPTIONS
Have a wedding tea. il *McCall's* 116:33 My '89
Vintage vows [wine served] F. J. Prial. il *The New York Times Magazine* p74 Ja 29 '89

WEDDING TRIPS See Honeymoon

WEDDINGS
See also
Bridesmaids
Videotapes—Weddings

WEDDINGS—*cont.*

Alaina Reed, Kevin Peter Hall tie knot in Los Angeles rites. il por *Jet* 76:61 My 29 '89

All alone by his telephone, big talker Larry King reaches out and marries someone [weds J. Alexander] W. Plummer. il pors *People Weekly* 32:115+ O 23 '89

All you really need to know about marriage you learn at the wedding. R. Fulghum. *Redbook* 173:84+ Je '89

Altared states. il *Gentlemen's Quarterly* 59:210-11 Je '89

Anita Baker tells why she kept her marriage and pregnancy a secret [cover story] C. Waldron. il pors *Jet* 75:28-32 F 6 '89

Atty. Jewel Lafontant weds international businessman in D.C. church ceremony. il pors *Jet* 77:43 D 25 '89-Ja 1 '90

Big white wedding? Bad idea. T. DeCarlo. il *Glamour* 87:186 S '89

'Champagne Charlie,' Di's dashing brother, takes a bride decked in . . . gold [Viscount Althorp weds V. Lockwood] M. H. J. Farrell. il pors *People Weekly* 32:42-5 O 2 '89

Family affairs [celebrity marriages] il *Rolling Stone* p131 D 14-28 '89

Former hurler Vida Blue takes a bride on mound. il pors *Jet* 77:56-7 O 9 '89

Hef gains a bride, loses a reputation [marriage to K. Conrad; cover story] S. Schindehette. il pors *People Weekly* 32:34-9 Jl 17 '89

Here comes the bride guide [special section] P. Schiller. il *McCall's* 116:31+ My '89

I do [marriage to tennis pro D. Goldie] C. M. Goldie. il pors *World Tennis* 36:89-90+ Mr '89

I do, I do, I do. B. Astor. il por *House & Garden* 161:78-80 Je '89

'I do'-ing it right. S. M. Pollan and M. Levine. il *New York* 22:38-50 Ja 9 '89

In Vegas, vowing he has changed his wild ways, Griffin O'Neal takes the plunge into marriage. il pors *People Weekly* 32:48 Jl 17 '89

John Goodman, Roseanne Barr's big guy co-star, has a big-time wedding in the Big Easy [weds A. Hartzog] il pors *People Weekly* 32:70 N 13 '89

Khalilah Ali marries in her Flossmoor mansion. il pors *Jet* 77:15 O 30 '89

Marcia Anderson and Jim Diebold marry for money—the dollars their guests gave to charity. P. Freeman. il pors *People Weekly* 31:139+ Je 19 '89

A May-December wedding finally puts a brake on the oldest Rolling Stone [B. Wyman weds M. Smith] P. Freeman. il pors *People Weekly* 31:54-6 Je 19 '89

Michael J. Fox's nuptials in hell! [trying to outwit tabloids] M. J. Fox and M. Pollan. il pors map *Esquire* 111:136-8+ Je '89

Natalie Cole and Andre Fischer: singer talks about her marriage, son and career [cover story] il pors *Jet* 77:54-8 O 16 '89

Natalie Cole weds in L.A. church ceremony. il pors *Jet* 76:57 O 2 '89

No Don Juan Bon Jovi, Jon marries his high school sweetheart in a Vegas chapel. il pors *People Weekly* 31:46 My 22 '89

Of hearts, flowers and wedding bliss [D. Burke weds G. McRaney; cover story] S. Schindehette. il pors *People Weekly* 31:86-7+ Je 12 '89

Romancing the isle [arranging weddings in the Caribbean] Y. R. Lamb. il *Black Enterprise* 19:116 My '89

She wore serious satin and tulle, but Debbie Harmon made her 'I do's' sheer sitcom [weds B. Blackwell] M. Dougherty. il pors *People Weekly* 31:150-1 My 22 '89

Spelman prexy marries childhood sweetheart during campus nuptials [J. B. Cole] il por *Jet* 75:29 Ja 9 '89

Stretching the rules [special section] il *The New York Times Magazine* p63-8+ Ja 29 '89

Taking a young, fourth wife, actor Dennis Hopper promises that this time he's playing for keeps [weds K. LaNasa] il pors *People Weekly* 32:72-3 Jl 3 '89

Tennis ace Zina Garrison ties Houston love match. il pors *Jet* 77:52-3 O 23 '89

The wedding [civil ceremony in New York's Municipal Building] *The New Yorker* 65:34-5 S 11 '89

Wedding styles of the stars: psst! The bridesmaids are armed! D. Denicolo. il *Glamour* 87:178-9 Je '89

When Joe Ross rescued little Maura Handren, he didn't know he was really a wife-saver [future bride rescued from drowning in Charles River] il pors *People Weekly* 31:94 Ap 17 '89

Will there be bad fairies at your wedding? [stress] L. Dormen. il *Glamour* 87:236-7+ Je '89

Anecdotes, facetiae, satire, etc.

The gentle art of "I do": advice to the groom. H. O'Neill. il *Gentlemen's Quarterly* 59:208-9+ Je '89

A groom of one's own. M. Pond. il *Gentlemen's Quarterly* 59:125+ F '89

Nice day for a black wedding. J. Queenan. *The American Spectator* 22:18-19 F '89

Photographs and photography

26 years of famous weddings. M. Fiore. il *Good Housekeeping* 208:46+ Je '89

October brides. D. Mazzapica. il *Petersen's Photographic Magazine* 18:46-7 O '89

White on white has to be right—the solution is two lighting setups in one [bridal gown] T. L. Corbell. il *Petersen's Photographic Magazine* 18:22-3 N '89

WEDDLE, DAVID

Ken Kesey's eclectic writing acid test. il por *Rolling Stone* p119-20+ O 5 '89

WEDGWOOD POTTERY *See* Pottery, English

WEED CONTROL

See also
Aquatic weed control
Herbicides
Leafy spurge—Control
Mulching

Late hits. M. Holmberg. il *Successful Farming* 87:48F O '89

Picture-perfect weed control might not pay. B. Freese. il *Successful Farming* 87:27 My '89

Selective weeding. D. Kennedy. il *Organic Gardening* 36:79-80 F '89

Trample no-till's toughest weeds. R. Fee. il *Successful Farming* 87 no4:30-1 Mr '89

WEED TRIMMERS *See* Lawn equipment

WEEDS

See also
Aquatic weeds
Crabgrass
Grasses
Kariba weeds
Parietaria
Tumbleweeds

Super weeds. R. Twombly. il *Technology Review* 92:15-16 Ag/S '89

Swoe is me! F. McGourty. il *Flower and Garden* 33:64 Jl/Ag '89

Weeds are us. M. Pollan. il *The New York Times Magazine* p48-9+ N 5 '89

Control

See Weed control

WEEDS, EDIBLE *See* Greens, Edible

WEEK OF PRAYER FOR CHRISTIAN UNITY

Christian unity amid diversity. *America* 160:27-8 Ja 21 '89

WEEKEND ACTIVITIES *See* Leisure

WEEKEND AT BERNIE'S [film] *See* Motion picture reviews—Single works

WEEKEND HOUSES *See* Vacation houses

WEEKEND SPAS *See* Health resorts, watering places, etc.

WEEKEND VACATIONS *See* Vacations

WEEKLEY, TERRI FISHER

about

Women who go for it! B. M. Campbell. il pors *Essence* 20:48-50+ Ag '89

WEEKS, CHRISTOPHER, 1950-

Revolutionary village. il map *American Heritage* 40:80-91 Ap '89

WEEKS, EDWARD, 1898-1989

about

Obituary
The Atlantic 263:104 My '89

WEEKS, JAMES

The Civil War's greatest scoop. il por *American Heritage* 40:100+ Jl/Ag '89

WEEKS, OPHELIA INEZ

Vertebrate skeletal muscle: power source for locomotion. bibl f il *BioScience* 39:791-9 D '89

WEEKS, TERRY

Moustiers. il map *Gourmet* 49:96-101+ O '89

WEEMS, RENITA

Just friends. il *Essence* 20:60-2+ My '89

WEEPING *See* Crying

WEEVILS

Control

What's the diagnosis? [root weevil notching] W. S. Moore. il *Flower and Garden* 33:18 My/Je '89

WEFLEN, JULIE

Kidnapping

Have you seen my missing wife? A. Rule. il pors *Good Housekeeping* 208:99+ F '89

WEGER, JACKIE

Fiction can be hazardous to your health. *The Writer* 102:7-8 S '89

WEGMANS FOOD MARKETS INC.

A local business invests in the kids [work-study program offered by supermarkets in Rochester, N.Y.] il *U.S. News & World Report* 106:60 Je 26 '89

WEGNER, DANIEL M., 1948-

Try not to think of a white bear [excerpt from White bears and other unwanted thoughts] il *Psychology Today* 23:64-6 Je '89

about

Thoughts we hate to think. E. E. Goode. il *U.S. News & World Report* 107:48-9 Ag 14 '89

WEGX (PHILADELPHIA, PA.: RADIO STATION) *See* Radio stations

WEIDEGER, PAULA

A budding genius. il por *Ms.* 17:48-9 Mr '89

It takes two to tangle. il *Ms.* 17:106-7+ Ja/F '89

WEIDENBAUM, MURRAY L.
Facing reality in the George Bush era. *Society* 26:25-8 Mr/Ap '89
Protecting the environment. *Society* 27:49-56 N/D '89
WEIDENFELD, ARTHUR GEORGE WEIDENFELD, BARON
about
Ann Getty: publish and perish? A. Begley. il pors *The New York Times Magazine* p36-7+ O 22 '89
WEIGEL, GEORGE
Challenges facing U.S. Catholics. *Commonweal* 116:620-1 N 17 '89
WEIGELA
Why not weigela? il *Southern Living* 24:60-1 My '89
WEIGHING EQUIPMENT
See also
Scales (Weighing instruments)
WEIGHT (PHYSIOLOGY)
See also
Anorexia nervosa
Birth weight
Bulimia
Diet
Exercise
Lean body mass
Obesity
Weight reducing products
Availability of metabolic fuels controls estrous cyclicity of Syrian hamsters. J. E. Schneider and G. N. Wade. bibl f il *Science* 244:1326-8 Je 16 '89
Burn, baby, burn [effect of running on weight loss] D. Kardong. il *Runner's World* 24:32-7 F '89
Finding your ideal weight. G. L. Blackburn. il *Prevention (Emmaus, Pa.)* 41:30+ Jl '89
Flying blind [Pan Am's weight standards for female flight attendants ruled illegal] D. Seligman. il *Fortune* 120:204 O 9 '89
A future up in the air: flight attendants contest weight rules [suit against American Airlines] M. Suh. il *Ms.* 18:83-4 S '89
How much is too fat? [height/weight charts; views of Kay Stanfill] il *USA Today (Periodical)* 117:8 F '89
Leaner, not lighter. J. Gurin. il *Psychology Today* 23:32-4 Je '89
Life at large [excerpt from Bodylove] R. J. Freedman. il *Health (New York, N.Y.)* 21:40+ Ap '89
Riding to lose (weight, that is). J. Barone. *Bicycling* 30:104+ My '89
Viewpoint [opera singers' weight] J. L. Poole. *Opera News* 53:4 F 18 '89
Why are girls obsessed with their weight? L. Morgan. il *Seventeen* 48:118-19+ N '89
Anecdotes, facetiae, satire, etc.
You can be too thin. S. Bernhard. il *Mademoiselle* 95:128-9 Jl '89
WEIGHT LIFTING
See also
Bodybuilding
Coming on strong: weight training for your sport. M. Greenwood-Robinson. il *Women's Sports & Fitness* 11:48-52 My '89
An energizing way to weight train: split routines [views of Dennis Humphrey] M. Greenwood-Robinson. il *Women's Sports & Fitness* 11:40-3 Jl/Ag '89
Enter the iron age [weight training for cyclists] F. Matheny. il *Bicycling* 30:70-1+ D '89
Flex your pecs to shape your chest [weight training to tone breasts] M. Greenwood-Robinson. il *Women's Sports & Fitness* 11:20 S '89
How big a setback is a temporary cutback? O. Anderson. il *Women's Sports & Fitness* 11:18 Ap '89
The new body building [weight training for women] D. Schefer. *Vogue* 179:368 My '89
Push it [runners] K. Anderson. il *Runner's World* 24:40-4 Ag '89
Shape-onomics: adding muscle where it counts [bodyshaping] M. Greenwood-Robinson. il *Women's Sports & Fitness* 11:43-7 O '89
Stimulating athletes [use of electrical muscle stimulation by weight lifter Derrick Crass] il *Discover* 10:14 Mr '89
The strength to ski. M. Bloom. il *Skiing* 42:12+ S '89
Strong-arm tactics. I. Springer. il *Modern Maturity* 32:74-6 O/N '89
Supertoning your hips and thighs. M. Greenwood-Robinson. il *Women's Sports & Fitness* 11:18-19 Ja/F '89
Weight training. il *World Tennis* 36:74 My '89
Why weight? Pumping iron will get you into shape. G. Legwold. il *Better Homes and Gardens* 68:34-5 F '89
Will weight training improve your running? O. Anderson. bibl il *Women's Sports & Fitness* 11:22-3 Ap '89
Ethical aspects
The steroid scandal [Canadian weight lifters testify at government inquiry] D. Burke. il *Maclean's* 102:40 F 20 '89
WEIGHT LOSS CLINICS
See also
Duke University. Diet and Fitness Center
Nutri/System, Inc.
Weight Watchers International Inc.

Crying the weight-loss blues. N. Henderson. il *Changing Times* 43:75-8 Ap '89
Diet centers are really in fat city. B. O'Reilly. il *Fortune* 119:137+ Je 5 '89
Diets Incorporated. A. Miller. il *Newsweek* 114:56-60+ S 11 '89
France
Secrets of the sleek chic. A. Bogart. il *Harper's Bazaar* 122:36+ Ap '89
WEIGHT LOSS RESORTS *See* Health resorts, watering places, etc.
WEIGHT MACHINES *See* Exercising equipment
WEIGHT REDUCING EQUIPMENT *See* Exercising equipment
WEIGHT REDUCING PRODUCTS
See also
Fenfluramine
Big fat lies: the new weight-loss scams. N. B. Cardozo. il *Mademoiselle* 95:128-9+ Ja '89
Diet-in-a-pill. E. Frank. *Vogue* 179:310 Ap '89
Gregory buys hotel and fattens his diet empire. H. Manly. il por *Black Enterprise* 19:22 Mr '89
WEIGHT THROWING
See also
Shotputting
WEIGHT TRAINING *See* Weight lifting
WEIGHT WATCHERS DIET *See* Diet
WEIGHT WATCHERS INTERNATIONAL INC.
Bulking up at Weight Watchers. G. L. Miles. il *Business Week* p88 D 11 '89
Jean Nidetch knew that Weight Watcher's success hinged on more than a diet. D. Moreau. il por *Changing Times* 43:88 Ag '89
WEIGHTLESSNESS
See also
Plants, Effect of weightlessness on
Space processing
Developmental biology in outer space [effects of microgravity] G. M. Malacinski and others. bibl f il *BioScience* 39:314-20 My '89
Go forth & multiply? [reproduction in space] L. Frazer. il *Ad Astra* 1:24-9 Je '89
Long-duration Soviet cosmonaut crew made rapid adaptation after flight [Mir cosmonauts] il *Aviation Week & Space Technology* 131:96 S 25 '89
Science fiction [space budget reality and effects of weightlessness] H. Banks. il *Forbes* 143:44+ Mr 6 '89
Soviet long-duration cosmonauts readapt rapidly to earth environment [Mir cosmonauts] J. M. Lenorovitz. il *Aviation Week & Space Technology* 130:38-9 Ja 2 '89
Soviet Star trek: a year in space. G. Cowley. il *Newsweek* 113:5 Ja 2 '89
What killed the chickens? [embryonic chickens on the space shuttle Discovery] *Science News* 135:213 Ap 8 '89
Why conduct life science research in space? W. Ockels. il *Ad Astra* 1:3+ My '89
WEIGHTLIFTING *See* Weight lifting
WEIGHTMAN, JOHN
On not understanding Michel Foucault. *The American Scholar* 58:383-406 Summ '89
WEIGHTS (EXERCISING EQUIPMENT) *See* Exercising equipment
WEIGHTS AND MEASURES
See also
Electric standards
Metric system
Standards of length
WEIL, DENIE
Doing business in the 'burbs [special section] il *Working Woman* 14:58-62+ Ag '89
WEIL, STEPHEN E., 1928-
Who owns the Nataraja? il *Art News* 88:188 My '89
WEIL, SUSAN C., AND OTHERS
The myeloperoxidase gene in acute promyelocytic leukemia [discussion of May 6, 1988 article, Translocation and rearrangement of myeloperoxidase gene in acute promyelocytic leukemia] il *Science* 244:823-6 My 19 '89
WEILAND, STEVEN
David Riesman's Freud. *Society* 26:73-7 My/Je '89
WEILEY, SUSAN
The darling of the decade. il *Art News* 88:143-50 Ap '89
WEILL, KURT, 1900-1950
about
Parallel bars [Conversations with fear and hope after death] P. G. Davis. il pors *New York* 22:78 Ap 17 '89
The rise and fall of the city of Mahagonny [opera] Reviews *Time* il 134:76 S 25 '89. O. Friedrich
Street scene [opera] Reviews
Opera News il 54:60-1 S '89. N. Goodwin
Threepenny romance. P. Moor. il pors *High Fidelity (New York, N.Y.)* 39:50-3 My '89
The voices of Kurt Weill. L. Schwartz. il *The Atlantic* 264:115-18 D '89
WEILL, SANFORD I.
about
Sandy Weill roars back [cover story] J. Friedman. il pors *Business Week* p88-91+ D 4 '89

WEILL, SANFORD I.—about—cont.
Tiger by the tail? H. Rudnitsky. il pors Forbes 144:40-1 Ag 7 '89
Turnaround at Primerica. T. Paré. il por Fortune 120:120 D 18 '89
WEIMAR REPUBLIC See Germany—History—1918-1933
WEIMER, PAUL K.
(jt. auth) See Rose, Albert, and Weimer, Paul K.
WEINBERG, BILL
Bad seeds in Nicaragua. The Nation 249:50+ Jl 10 '89
WEINBERG, GERHARD L.
The Nazi-Soviet pacts: a half-century later. bibl f Foreign Affairs 68:175-89 Fall '89
WEINBERG, LEE S.
(jt. auth) See Vatz, Richard E., and Weinberg, Lee S.
WEINBERG, STEVE
My white whale, or The great newspaper novel. il The New York Times Book Review 94:1+ Ag 27 '89
The teflon tycoon. il pors Common Cause Magazine 15:17-21 N/D '89
WEINBERGER, CASPAR W.
Commentary on events at home and abroad. See issues of Forbes beginning January 9, 1989
WEINER, DAN, 1919-1959
about
Belief. I. Sischy. The New Yorker 65:79-82 My 22 '89
WEINER, EDITH, AND BROWN, ARNOLD, 1927-
Human factors: the gap between humans and machines. il pors The Futurist 23:9-11 My/Je '89
WEINER, ELLIS
Planning it all: the new calendar girls. il Mademoiselle 95:130-3+ Jl '89
WEINER, JONATHAN
Glacier bubbles are telling us what was in Ice Age air. bibl (p164) il Smithsonian 20:78-84+ My '89
My butterfly mystery. il Reader's Digest 135:134-6 S '89
WEINER, LOIS
The risk keeps rising. il The Progressive 53:50 Mr '89
WEINERT, TED A.
(jt. auth) See Hartwell, Leland H., and Weinert, Ted A.
WEINGART, LEN
about
Tennis, everyone? R. Wetzsteon. il por Sport (New York, N.Y.) 80:15 D '89
WEINGARTEN REALTY INVESTORS
Discipline, discipline, discipline. J. H. Taylor. il por Forbes 144:42-3 Jl 24 '89
WEINHOUSE, BETH
Cholesterol control: your guide to a healthy heart. il Ladies' Home Journal 106:83+ My '89
The family guide to winter health [special section] il Ladies' Home Journal 106:85-6+ Ja '89
John Larroquette: "I was born an alcoholic". il pors Redbook 172:30+ Ap '89
Top doctors answer your most intimate questions. Ladies' Home Journal 106:92+ Je '89
Why did people get their noses out of joint over my nose job? il Glamour 87:59 Ja '89
(ed) See Michaelson, Lori. "My baby really didn't have a chance . . . it has to be a miracle"
WEINIG, ROBERT WALTER
about
From coal to water. J. Cook. il por Forbes 144:62 Ag 7 '89
WEININGER, JANET
about
A father's homecoming. C. M. Turtle. il Reader's Digest 134:57-61 F '89
WEINSTEIN, ALLAN
The breathe-easy guide to asthma relief. il Prevention (Emmaus, Pa.) 41:57-65 F '89
WEINSTEIN, BOB
about
"We don't want to be Walt Disney". L. Gubernick. il pors Forbes 144:109-10 O 16 '89
Will success spoil the Weinstein brothers? A. Thompson. il pors Film Comment 25:72+ Jl/Ag '89
WEINSTEIN, BOB, 1941-
30 ways to save on your taxes. il McCall's 116:42+ Mr '89
WEINSTEIN, DONALD, 1926-
Savonarola—preacher and patriot? bibl il por History Today 39:30-6 N '89
WEINSTEIN, GRACE W.
Club clout. il Ms. 18:46+ S '89
Financial resolutions. il Ms. 17:120-1 Ja/F '89
Help wanted—the crisis of elder care. il Ms. 18:72-4+ O '89
How one family spends its money. il Good Housekeeping 209:104+ O '89
Major mergers. il Ms. 17:68+ My '89
The mortgage maze. il Ms. 17:36+ Je '89
Passing the buck. il Ms. 17:78+ Ap '89
Take cover. il Ms. 18:70-2 Jl/Ag '89
Taxing decisions. il Ms. 17:78+ Mr '89
Your money. See issues of Good Housekeeping

WEINSTEIN, HARVEY
about
"We don't want to be Walt Disney". L. Gubernick. il pors Forbes 144:109-10 O 16 '89
Will success spoil the Weinstein brothers? A. Thompson. il pors Film Comment 25:72+ Jl/Ag '89
WEINSTEIN, LOUIS, 1909-
Help! The stuffy nose, watery eyes, aches and pain, chills and fever, sore throat, colds and flu book; ed. by Seth Rolbein. il Good Housekeeping 208:56+ Ja '89
WEINSTEIN, NEIL D.
Optimistic biases about personal risks. bibl f Science 246:1232-3 D 8 '89
WEINSTEIN, STEPHEN B.
(jt. auth) See Shumate, Paul W., Jr., and Weinstein, Stephen B.
WEINSTEIN, STEPHEN B., AND SHUMATE, PAUL W., JR.
Beyond the telephone: new ways to communicate [cover story] il pors The Futurist 23:8-12 N/D '89
WEINSTEIN-SHR, GAIL
(jt. auth) See Henkin, Nancy Z., and Weinstein-Shr, Gail
WEINSTOCK, CHERYL PLATZMAN
The 'grazing' of America: a guide to healthy snacking [cover story] il FDA Consumer 23:8-13 Mr '89
WEINSTOCK, NEAL
Ranking syndication's top 20. il Channels (New York, N.Y.: 1986) 9:22-5 Ja 16 '89
WEINTRAUB, AMY
about
Two inventive mothers hit the tot charts with Baby songs. L. Lague. il pors People Weekly 31:95-6 Ja 16 '89
WEINTRAUB, JERRY
about
No gain, much pain. P. Newcomb. il por Forbes 143:12 Ja 9 '89
WEINTRAUB, PAMELA
(jt. auth) See Harary, Keith, and Weintraub, Pamela
WEINTRAUB ENTERTAINMENT GROUP INC.
No gain, much pain. P. Newcomb. il por Forbes 143:12 Ja 9 '89
WEIR, BOB
Woodstock remembered: the artists. il pors Rolling Stone p67 Ag 24 '89
WEIR, DAVID, 1947-, AND MATTHIESSEN, CONSTANCE
Will the circle be unbroken? il Mother Jones 14:20-7 Je '89
WEIR, JUDITH
about
A night at the Chinese opera [opera] Reviews
The New Yorker 65:125-6 S 18 '89. A. Porter
WEIR, PETER, 1944-
about
Dead Poets Society [film] Reviews
America 161:40 Jl 15-22 '89. R. A. Blake
American Film il 14:57 Jl/Ag '89. R. Seidenberg
The American Spectator il 22:39-40 Ag '89. B. Bawer
Commonweal 116:372 Je 16 '89. T. O'Brien
The Humanist il 49:41-2 S/O '89. H. M. Geduld
Life il 12:64-8 Spr '89
Maclean's il 102:52 Je 12 '89. B. D. Johnson
National Review 41:54-5 S 15 '89. J. Simon
The New Republic 200:26-7 Je 26 '89. S. Kauffmann
New York il 22:77-8 Je 12 '89. D. Denby
The New Yorker 65:70-1 Je 26 '89. P. Kael
Newsweek il 113:67 Je 12 '89. D. Ansen
Newsweek il 114:74 Jl 3 '89. G. F. Will
People Weekly il 31:17 Je 12 '89. R. Novak
Rolling Stone il p29 Je 29 '89. P. Travers
Time il 133:78 Je 5 '89. R. Schickel
WEIRTON STEEL CORPORATION
Has Weirton's ESOP worked too well? M. Schroeder. il Business Week p66-7 Ja 23 '89
WEIS, JUDITH S.
Action on pesticides. BioScience 39:14 Ja '89
News on science education. BioScience 39:763 D '89
WEIS, JUDITH S., AND WEIS, PEDDRICK
Tolerance and stress in a polluted environment. bibl f il BioScience 39:89-95 F '89
WEIS, PEDDRICK
(jt. auth) See Weis, Judith S., and Weis, Peddrick
WEISBERG, JACOB
Cat scam. The New Republic 201:11-12 O 30 '89
Senator perfect [cover story] por The New Republic 201:16-20 D 18 '89
WEISBERGER, BERNARD A., 1922-
Beef, pork, and history. il American Heritage 40:20+ Jl/Ag '89
Celebrity journalists. il American Heritage 40:20+ Mr '89
The dread federal surplus. il American Heritage 40:20+ Ap '89
Expensive ex-presidents. il American Heritage 40:22+ My/Je '89
Panama: made in U.S.A. il American Heritage 40:24-5 N '89
The president vs. the Senate. il American Heritage 40:22+ S/O '89
Whangdoodling. il American Heritage 40:24+ F '89

WEISBERGER, BERNARD A., 1922—cont.
The wrongdoers. il *American Heritage* 40:26+ D '89
WEISBROD, BURTON ALLEN, 1931-
Rewarding performance that is hard to measure: the private nonprofit sector. bibl f *Science* 244:541-6 My 5 '89
WEISFELDT, MYRON L.
about
Heart-to-heart with new heart chief [interview] por *American Health* 8:14 O '89
WEISGALL, DEBORAH
A megamuseum in a mill town. il por *The New York Times Magazine* p32-5+ Mr 5 '89
WEISGALL, HUGO, 1912-
about
Will you marry me? [opera] Reviews
The New Yorker 65:119 Ap 17 '89. A. Porter
Opera News il 53:45 My '89. P. J. Smith
WEISHAMPEL, DAVID B.
(jt. auth) See Horner, John R., and Weishampel, David B.
WEISINGER, HENDRIE
How not to give criticism [excerpt from The critical edge] il *Glamour* 87:126+ Mr '89
How tough critics may be mentors in disguise [excerpt from The critical edge] il *Working Woman* 14:102-4 Je '89
WEISKEL, TIMOTHY C.
The electronic library: changing the character of research. il *Change* 20:38-47 N/D '88
WEISKOPF, HERM, 1934-
1989 International Winter Special Olympics Games. il *Sports Illustrated* 70:49-50+ Mr 27 '89
WEISMAN, ALAN
Dangerous days in the Macarena. il map *The New York Times Magazine* p40-2+ Ap 23 '89
L.A. fights for breath [cover story] il *The New York Times Magazine* p14-17+ Jl 30 '89
WEISMAN, DAVID
about
Dance of the independent. G. Kilday. il *American Film* 14:16+ S '89
WEISMAN, MIKE
about
Boy wonder gets the boot at NBC. S. Smith. il por *Sports Illustrated* 70:82 My 22 '89
WEISS, AARON J.
about
Spotting Mr. Wrong . . . early. L. B. Morris. il *Health (New York, N.Y.)* 21:34-5 N '89
WEISS, DEBORAH CHANLEY
Someplace like New Jersey [story] il *The Atlantic* 264:49-54 Ag '89
WEISS, DOROTHY GLASSER
"No sex, please, we're married". il *Ladies' Home Journal* 106:176+ N '89
WEISS, GLENN
about
Art. N. Princenthal. il por *Vogue* 179:140+ Je '89
WEISS, JOAN C.
Prejudice, conflict, and ethnoviolence: a national dilemma. il *USA Today (Periodical)* 117:27-9 My '89
WEISS, JOHN H., AND CHOI, DENNIS W.
Possible role of carbamates in neurotoxicity and neurotransmitter inactivation [discussion of August 19, 1988 article, Beta-N-methylamino-L-alanine neurotoxicity: requirement for bicarbonate as a cofactor] *Science* 243:1615 Mr 24 '89
WEISS, MICHAEL J., 1952-
Equal rights: not for women only. il *Glamour* 87:276-7+ Mr '89
How to save for what you want (I). il *Ladies' Home Journal* 106:48+ S '89
How to save for what you want (II). il *Ladies' Home Journal* 106:50+ O '89
A town with pity. il *Ladies' Home Journal* 106:48-9+ D '89
The way we'll be. il *Ladies' Home Journal* 106:220-2+ N '89
WEISS, NAOMI
A love betrayed, a brief life lost [cover story]; ed. by Bonnie Johnson. il pors *People Weekly* 31:82-4+ F 13 '89
WEISS, NICKI, 1951-
Barney is big [story] il *Parents* 64:131-2+ S '89
WEISS, PHILIP
Conduct unbecoming? il pors *The New York Times Magazine* p40-1+ O 29 '89
Hello sweetheart, get me mergers and acquisitions. *The Washington Monthly* 21:67-8 F '89
The quiet coup. il *Harper's* 279:54-65 S '89
Untrue confessions. il por *Mother Jones* 14:18-20+ S '89
WEISS, R., AND WEISS, T.
A place to stand [poem] *The Nation* 249:576 N 13 '89
WEISS, TED, 1927-
Should the House-passed wage proposal be enacted? [excerpts from address, March 23, 1989] *Congressional Digest* 68:150+ My '89

WEISS, THOMAS GEORGE
(jt. auth) See Norton, Augustus R., and Weiss, Thomas George
WEISS, WILLIAM
about
Baseball lives [excerpt] M. Bryan. il por *Sports Illustrated* 70:80+ Ap 24 '89
WEISS, WILLIAM L.
about
Good connection. C. Siler. il por *Forbes* 143:107 Mr 6 '89
WEISS, PECK & GREER
History repeats? [stake in Nu-West Industries] T. Jaffe. il por *Forbes* 144:127 S 18 '89
WEISSBOURD, BERNICE
As they grow/2-year-olds. See issues of Parents
DIE WEISSE ROSE [opera] See Zimmermann, Udo, 1943-
WEISSKOPF, MICHAEL
Pollution strikes the EPA. il *Discover* 10:32-3 Ja '89
WEISSKOPF, VICTOR FREDERICK
The origin of the universe. il *The New York Review of Books* 36:10-14 F 16 '89
about
DOE honors Setlow and Weisskopf with Fermi Award. pors *Physics Today* 42:89-90 Ap '89
WEISSLER, PAUL
Auto Q&A. See issues of Home Mechanix beginning January 1985
WEITEK CORPORATION
Weitek pushing its own math chip for Intel's 80486. *Byte* 14:26 Jl '89
WEITZMAN, DAVID L.
Teaching children to value their architectural heritage. *The Education Digest* 54:45-7 Ja '89
WEIZSÄCKER, RICHARD VON, 1920-
Looking into the mirror of history. *Society* 26:6-7 Mr/Ap '89
WELCH, BOB, 1956-
about
Their ride of terror. P. Gammons. il por *Sports Illustrated* 71:8-9 O 30 '89
WELCH, JOHN F., JR.
about
Big changes are galvanizing General Electric. T. Vogel. il por *Business Week* p100+ D 18 '89
Inside the mind of Jack Welch [cover story] S. P. Sherman. il pors *Fortune* 119:38-42+ Mr 27 '89
Why GE took a European bride. J. R. Norman. il *Business Week* p28-9 Ja 30 '89
WELCH, PRISCILLA
"Just give it a go". il pors *Runner's World* 24:54-7 Ag '89
WELCH, RANDY
What every manager needs to know about sales. il *Working Woman* 14:96-8+ Ja '89
WELCH, RAQUEL, 1940-
about
Raquel Welch: starting over. P. Battelle. il pors *Ladies' Home Journal* 106:46+ My '89
WELCOME HOME [film] See Motion picture reviews—Single works
WELCOME TO THE CLUB [musical] See Musicals, revues, etc.—Reviews—Single works
WELD, TUESDAY
about
Tuesday Weld. A. Barra. il pors *American Film* 14:62-4 Ja/F '89
WELDERS (MACHINES) See Welding—Equipment
WELDING
See also
Laser welding
Equipment
Marvelous MIGs. D. Mowitz. il *Successful Farming* 87:22-3 Ap '89
Metal stitcher [stitch-welder attachment] P. McCafferty. il *Popular Science* 234:124 Mr '89
WELDON, FAY
Ind Aff [story] il pors *Vogue* 179:183-5+ Ja '89
about
Fay Weldon. C. Brown. il por *Vogue* 179:182+ Ja '89
WELFARE See Public welfare
WELFARE HOTELS
Down and out in suburbia [homeless in Westchester County, N.Y.] B. Kessler. il *The Nation* 249:306+ S 25 '89
Lives on hold [children in welfare hotels in New York City] D. O. Relin. il *Scholastic Update (Teachers' edition)* 121:4-7 F 10 '89
The rise of the homeless [families in N.Y. welfare hotels; view of J. Kozol] S. M. Halpern. bibl f il *The New York Review of Books* 36:24-7 F 16 '89
WELL DRILLING See Gas well drilling; Oil well drilling
WELL RESCUES See Rescue work
WELLBUTRIN
A legal aphrodisiac? A.-M. Stan. *New Choices for the Best Years* 29:13 Ja '89
WELLER, ANTHONY
Simla: remnants of the Raj. il *Gourmet* 49:136+ N '89

WELLER, JANET
When the class is beneath your level. il *Women's Sports & Fitness* 11:16 N/D '89

WELLER, SHEILA
"God wouldn't mess with an angry mother!". il por *McCall's* 116:130+ My '89
One woman's family: the plight of single mothers. *McCall's* 116:75-6+ F '89
Sarah Brady. il pors *Ms.* 17:84-7 Ja/F '89
Special report: . . . till death do us part. il *Redbook* 173:112-14+ Ag '89
Your siblings, yourself. il *Glamour* 87:224-5+ D '89

WELLES, ORSON, 1915-1985
about
The magnificent Ambersons [film] Reviews
American Film il 15:72 D '89. D. Rochester
Remembering Orson Welles. G. Vidal. il *The New York Review of Books* 36:12-16 Je 1 '89

WELLESLEY, CHARLES See Brontë, Charlotte, 1816-1855

WELLING, GLENN
about
Frame and fortune? D. Rosenbaum. il *World Tennis* 37:22 N '89

WELLING, JAMES
about
James Welling. M. E. Haus. il por *Art News* 88:162-3 Ap '89

WELLING, LOUISE
about
The Vicksburg ghost. S. Hubbell. *The New Yorker* 65:106-17 S 25 '89

WELLINGTON MANAGEMENT FIRST FINANCIAL FUND
See First Financial Fund

WELLMAN, MARK
about
Grit and a granite will conquer El Capitan. M. Brower. il pors *People Weekly* 32:36-9 Ag 14 '89

WELLMAN, WILLIAM AUGUSTUS, 1896-1975
about
William Wellman. F. Thompson. il por *American Film* 15:98-9 O '89

WELLMAN, INC.
Wellman taps the profit in plastic. J. M. Laderman. *Business Week* p60 Ja 9 '89

WELLNESS COMMUNITY
"I've fought so hard to live" [excerpt from It's always something] G. Radner. il pors *Redbook* 173:120-2+ Je '89

WELLS, CAROLYN, 1869-1942
A Christmas alphabet [excerpt] il *Good Housekeeping* 209:148-51 D '89

WELLS, CLYDE KIRBY
about
An assault on Meech [interview] G. Allen. il por *Maclean's* 102:26 O 16 '89
A Grit stands fast. G. Allen. il por *Maclean's* 102:25 N 20 '89
Return of the red tide. G. Allen. il por *Maclean's* 102:12-13+ My 1 '89

WELLS, DAWN
about
Dawn Wells. il pors *Redbook* 172:88-9 Ja '89

WELLS, IDA B., 1862-1931
about
Ida B. Wells-Barnett: an Afro-American prophet. E. M. Townes. *The Christian Century* 106:285-6 Mr 15 '89

WELLS, JAMES A.
(jt. auth) See Cunningham, Brian C., and Wells, James A.

WELLS, JAMES H.
Eating can make you ill: understanding food allergies. il *USA Today (Periodical)* 118:54-5 Jl '89

WELLS, KEN
Going Berserkeley. *Reader's Digest* 134:173-4+ Je '89

WELLS, LAWRENCE
A man named Fay. il por *Southern Living* 24:84+ O '89

WELLS, MALCOLM
The case for natural schools. il *Country Journal* 16:34-9 Mr/Ap '89
Designing a tool or potting shed. il *Country Journal* 16:32-4 My/Je '89

WELLS, PATRICIA
Provence Pilgrims. il *The New York Times Magazine* p93-4 N 5 '89
Taste of the provinces. il *House & Garden* 161:58+ Jl '89
Vive la France—and her cuisine. il *Travel Holiday* 172:48-57 Jl '89
about
Workman storms the culinary Bastille. M. Simson. *Publishers Weekly* 236:44 S 8 '89

WELLS, R. D. (ROBERT D.)
(jt. auth) See Rahmouni, A. Rachid, and Wells, R. D. (Robert D.)

WELLS, RANDALL S.
Secrets of a high society [cover story] il por *National Wildlife* 27:38-44 Ag/S '89

WELLS, ROBERT D. See Wells, R. D. (Robert D.)

WELLS, SABRINA
about
D.C. girls first to play on boys' football team. D. M. Cheers. il pors *Jet* 77:28-30 N 13 '89

WELLS
See also
Cisterns
Maintenance and repair
How to troubleshoot a water well. M. Henkenius. il *Popular Mechanics* 166:83-6 S '89
Pollution
See Groundwater pollution

WELLS FARGO BANK, NATIONAL ASSOCIATION
What are you going to do for us tomorrow? J. Heins. il por *Forbes* 143:51 F 6 '89

WELLS FARGO INVESTMENT ADVISORS
Wells Fargo heads for the wild, wild East [Nikko deal] M. Shao. il *Business Week* p82 Ag 21 '89

WELLSBURG (W. VA.)
Public health
All's well in Wellsburg. M. Vitez. il *New Choices for the Best Years* 29:10 Je '89
A couple of collective tons later, the citizens of Wellsburg, W. Va., are no longer in Fat City [Bayer Wellness Program] M. Brower. il *People Weekly* 31:44-6 F 20 '89
Fit city [Bayer Wellness Program] D. Zevin. il *American Health* 8:45 Mr '89
The town that lost two tons [Bayer Wellness Program] D. Grady. il *Ladies' Home Journal* 106:46+ Je '89
Wellness in Wellsburg [program sponsored by Bayer] P. Stone. il *The Mother Earth News* 115:16+ Ja/F '89

WELSCH, ROGER L.
Dry humor. il *Natural History* p70-1 Ja '89

WELSH, FRANK
about
"Whiskey's for drinking, water's for fighting over". M. Beauchamp. il por *Forbes* 144:74+ Jl 24 '89

WELSH, PATRICK
How to be a totally awesome parent. *Reader's Digest* 135:87-9 N '89
When teachers fail: what parents can do about it. il *TV Guide* 37:18-20 S 2-8 '89

WELSH-HUGGINS, ANDREW
Polling the Israelites: Boesak on sanctions. *The Christian Century* 106:924-5 O 18 '89

WELSH NATIONAL OPERA
Bardolator [P. Stein's production of Falstaff] P. Conrad. il pors *Opera News* 53:18-20 F 4 '89
Birmingham, England. M. Dunmore. *Opera News* 53:38-9 Ja 7 '89
Birmingham, U.K. M. Dunmore. *Opera News* 54:53-5 O '89
A human comedy [performance of Falstaff at the Brooklyn Academy of Music] P. G. Davis. il *New York* 22:66-7 F 20 '89
Music [performance of Falstaff] E. W. Said. *The Nation* 248:498 Ap 10 '89
Musical events:
Falstaff. A. Porter. *The New Yorker* 65:104-6 F 20 '89
Theater [performance of Falstaff] T. M. Disch. *The Nation* 248:356 Mr 13 '89

WELTER, COLE H.
Art and computers: is there room in the studio for both? bibl f *Design for Arts in Education* 91:18-22 N/D '89

WELTNER, LINDA, 1938-
The perfect imperfect home [excerpt from No place like home] il *Utne Reader* p74-5 My/Je '89

WELTY, ELLEN
Stinging the WASP. il *Gentlemen's Quarterly* 59:191+ Ap '89

WELTY, EUDORA, 1909-
about
Eudora Welty, inquiring photographer [interview] H. Cole and S. Srinivasan. il *The New York Times Book Review* 94:1+ O 22 '89
Southern exposure. G. Jaynes. il por *Life* 12:58-60+ N '89

WELTY, WILLIAM M.
Discussion method teaching. bibl il *Change* 21:40-9 Jl/Ag '89

WELZEL, JANE
about
Alive & kicking. J. Brant. il pors *Runner's World* 24:52-5 F '89

WENDLANDT, GARY EDWARD
about
Big yields from little deals. S. Manolatos. il por *Forbes* 144:234 O 16 '89

WENDOLOSKI, J. J., AND OTHERS
Molecular dynamics simulation of a phospholipid micelle. bibl f il *Science* 243:636-8 F 3 '89

WENDT, E. ALLAN
U.S. stance toward the Soviet Union on trade and technology [address, October 27, 1988] *Department of State Bulletin* 89:20-3 Ja '89

WENDT, HENRY
about
Henry Wendt. J. Weber, Jr. il por *Business Week* Special Issue:151 Ap 14 '89
WENDY'S INTERNATIONAL INC.
A new chef lights a flame under Wendy's [J. W. Near] S. Phillips. il por *Business Week* p70 My 8 '89
Wendy's burger king [founder R. D. Thomas stars in commercials] J. Nocera. il por *Esquire* 112:69-71 N '89
WENNER, GENE C.
Arts educators should work with the arts community. *The Education Digest* 54:54-7 F '89
WENSYEL, JAMES W.
Shenandoah [cover story] il *American History Illustrated* 23:24-33+ F '89
WENTWORTH, THOMAS *See* Strafford, Thomas Wentworth, 1st Earl of, 1593-1641
WENTZ, MARGY
(jt. auth) *See* Leisure, Mary Jo, and Wentz, Margy
WENTZIEN, MARION
Taking toll [story] il *Seventeen* 48:90-1+ Mr '89
WERBLIN, FRANK
(jt. auth) *See* Firestein, Stuart, and Werblin, Frank
WE'RE NO ANGELS [film] *See* Motion picture reviews—Single works
WERENSKIOLD, MARIT, 1942-
Kandinsky's Moscow. bibl f il *Art in America* 77:96-111 Mr '89
WERNER, DAGMAR
about
Iguana conservation and economic development [cover story] J. P. Cohn. il *BioScience* 39:359-63 Je '89
Iguana mama. N. Vietmeyer. il por *International Wildlife* 19:24-7 S/O '89
WERNER, DAVID
about
Headhunters in reverse. D. Machan. il pors *Forbes* 144:238-9 O 30 '89
WERNER, EMMY E.
Children of the Garden Island. bibl il map *Scientific American* 260:106-8+ Ap '89
WERNER, LAURIE
How should your garden grow? il *Ladies' Home Journal* 106:158+ My '89
"My husband never shows me any love". il *Ladies' Home Journal* 106:12+ F '89
WERNER, TOM
about
Can this TV team go five for five? R. Grover. il pors *Business Week* p77 Je 19 '89
WERNICK, ROBERT
From out of the past come thundering hoofbeats of the demon 'nightmare'. il *Smithsonian* 19:72-6+ Mr '89
The godfather of the American Constitution. il *Smithsonian* 20:183-4+ S '89
Out of dark dreams and bright hopes, the blazing art of Goya. bibl (p146) il por *Smithsonian* 19:56-67 Ja '89
Radical and chic, a duke who courted revolt and doom. bibl (p122) il *Smithsonian* 20:66-75 Jl '89
A shifty-eyed spy who was likely the nastiest man ever. il pors *Smithsonian* 20:114-16+ Ag '89
Taming our nightmares. il *Reader's Digest* 135:21-2+ Jl '89
When the Bubble burst, all of England wound up broke. bibl (p183) il *Smithsonian* 20:155-6+ D '89
about
Around the Mall and beyond. E. Park. il por *Smithsonian* 20:26+ D '89
WERNICK, SARAH
Coasting through summer. il *Parents* 64:164+ Ag '89
New help for headache sufferers. il *Glamour* 87:82+ S '89
WERTHEIMER, ALAIN
about
The billionaires behind Chanel [cover story] P. Berman. il pors *Forbes* 143:104-8 Ap 3 '89
WERTHEIMER, FRED
about
Ethics watchdog Fred Wertheimer: when he barks, Congress listens. B. Hewitt. il pors *People Weekly* 32:163-4 D 18 '89
WERTHEIMER, PIERRE
about
The billionaires behind Chanel [cover story] P. Berman. il pors *Forbes* 143:104-8 Ap 3 '89
WERTHER, BETTY
The 14th International Biennial of Tapestry. il *American Craft* 49:54-9 O/N '89
Craft Today USA. il *American Craft* 49:32-9 O/N '89
WERTHER [opera] *See* Massenet, Jules, 1842-1912
WERTZ, DOROTHY C., AND FLETCHER, JOHN C.
Disclosing genetic information: who should know? il *Technology Review* 92:22-3 Jl '89
WESBECKER, JOSEPH T.
about
'I told them I'd be back'. J. N. Baker. il *Newsweek* 114:22 S 25 '89
The shots heard 'round the Congress. il *U.S. News & World Report* 107:15 S 25 '89

WESCHLER, LAWRENCE
Department of amplification. *The New Yorker* 65:92-3 My 22 '89
A grand experiment. il *The New Yorker* 65:59-60+ N 13 '89
The great exception (I). il *The New Yorker* 65:43-6+ Ap 3 '89
The great exception (II). *The New Yorker* 65:85-102+ Ap 10 '89
WESCOTT, DAVID
Reading the earth. il *The Mother Earth News* 115:110-16 Ja/F '89
WESLEYAN COLLEGE. CINEMA ARCHIVE
Mother and daughter [I. Rossellini visits the I. Bergman archive] *The New Yorker* 65:44-6 O 23 '89
WESLEYAN UNIVERSITY PRESS
Wesleyan Press to join University Press of New England. *Publishers Weekly* 236:14 O 6 '89
WESSON, PAUL S.
Olbers' paradox solved at last. il *Sky and Telescope* 77:594-7 Je '89
WEST, ADAM
about
Adam West is a bitter Batman. E. Kiersh. il pors *TV Guide* 37:21 Jl 22-28 '89
The curse of the Caped Crusader. B. Zehme. il pors *Rolling Stone* p42+ Je 29 '89
WEST, BENJAMIN, 1738-1820
about
In one great swoop, country bumpkin to Royal Academy. D. Hofstadter. bibl f (p174) il por *Smithsonian* 20:122-6+ Je '89
New frontiers for West. R. W. Walker. il *Art News* 88:46 N '89
Portraits by Benjamin West. A. Staley. bibl f il *Antiques* 135:1456-65 Je '89
WEST, DANIEL
about
Daniel West Dancers. G. Jackson. il *Dance Magazine* 63:70-1 S '89
WEST, FRANZ, 1947-
about
Franz West at Koury Wingate. A. F. Collins. il *Art in America* 77:201-2 S '89
WEST, GORDON
Electronics Q&A. *See* issues of Motor Boating & Sailing
WEST, JIM
Labor stirrings in Korea. il *The Progressive* 53:12 Mr '89
WEST, LESLIE
Woodstock remembered: the artists. il pors *Rolling Stone* p83 Ag 24 '89
WEST, MARTHA ULLMAN
Frontier of design: Isamu Noguchi 1904-1988. il pors *Dance Magazine* 63:58-60 My '89
WEST, MORRIS L., 1916-
A perception of evil [cover story] *America* 161:466-9 D 23-30 '89
WEST, NATHANAEL, 1903-1940
Claude imagines himself a colonel [fiction] il *Gentlemen's Quarterly* 59:292 Je '89
WEST, PAUL, 1930-
My body, myself. *Harper's* 279:26-8 Ag '89
WEST, DAME REBECCA, 1892-1983
The duty of harsh criticism. *The New Republic* 201 [Reprint v1]:18-20 N 6 '89 [N 7 '14]
WEST, ROGER
about
Roger West is building a Rocky Mountain highway for the disabled to enjoy. H. Shapiro. il pors *People Weekly* 32:131-2 S 18 '89
WEST, RON
about
Managing costs with Excel. K. J. Novak. il *Home Office Computing* 7:32+ N '89
WEST, RON
Attract these bugs. il *Organic Gardening* 36:74-5 Mr '89
WEST, SUSAN
Deck the halls with cookie houses. il *Ladies' Home Journal* 106:154-6+ D '89
WEST, WILLIAM R.
The skin off her back [photographs] il *Natural History* p98-9 Ap '89
WEST (DANIEL) DANCERS *See* Daniel West Dancers
WEST (U.S.) *See* Western States
WEST 57TH [television program] *See* Television program reviews—Single works
WEST AFRICA
See also
Benin
Cape Verde
Liberia
Nigeria
Public health—West Africa
Sierra Leone
WEST ALABAMA HEALTH SERVICES, INC.
Where a ride to the doctor costs $20. S. Hullett. il *Aging* no359:14-16 '89

WEST AND EAST *See* East and West
WEST BANK TERRITORIAL QUESTION *See* Israel-Arab Wars, 1967- —Territorial questions
WEST BERLIN *See* Berlin (Germany: West)
WEST COUNTRY (ENGLAND)
Description and travel
England's sunny West Country. D. Young. il *Southern Living* 24:24 S '89
WEST COVINA (CALIF.)
Stores
See also
Where Kids Shop (Firm)
WEST EDMONTON MALL (ALTA.)
Blue-sky planning [refinancing package] J. Daly. il *Maclean's* 102:38 Ag 21 '89
WEST GERMANY *See* Germany (West)
WEST HARTFORD (CONN.)
Galleries and museums
See also
Museum of American Political Life
WEST HAVEN (CONN.)
Education
Change from the bottom up [first grade] C. Leslie. il *Newsweek* 113:57 Ap 17 '89
WEST HOLLYWOOD (CALIF.)
Education
See also
Open School (West Hollywood, Calif.)
Hotels, motels, etc.
"Hey! That's no guest—that's my wife!" [Mondrian] S. Fried. il *Gentlemen's Quarterly* 59:54+ My '89
Restaurants, nightclubs, bars, etc.
Spécialités de la maison:
Le Chardonnay. C. Bates. il *Gourmet* 49:22+ Jl '89
Tuttobene. C. Bates. il *Gourmet* 49:42+ Je '89
WEST INDIAN COOKING *See* Cooking, West Indian
WEST INDIANS
United States
Big sugar (I) [cutting sugar cane in Florida] A. Wilkinson. il *The New Yorker* 65:41-2+ Jl 17 '89
Big sugar (II) [cutting sugar cane in Florida] A. Wilkinson. il *The New Yorker* 65:42-3+ Jl 24 '89
WEST INDIES
See also
Antigua and Barbuda
Bahamas
Dominica
Dominican Republic
Haiti
Jamaica
Nevis (Saint Kitts-Nevis)
Saint Barthélemy (Guadeloupe)
Saint Lucia
Saint Martin
West Indians
WEST NEW YORK (N.J.)
Education
The lessons of St. Joe's [St. Joseph of the Palisades High School] A. DePalma. il por *The New York Times Magazine* p34-7 F 5 '89
WEST PALM BEACH (FLA.)
Architecture
Venturi to order [Robert Venturi Signature Series of houses at Breakers West] H. Muschamp. il por *House & Garden* 161:104-9+ Ag '89
Venturi's kit-of-parts for high-end housing. il *Architectural Record* 177:37 Ap '89
Crime
When society portrait artist Ralph Wolfe Cowan met a mugger, he captured him—on canvas. il por *People Weekly* 32:91-2 S 4 '89
WEST PATERSON (N.J.)
Savings and loan associations
See also
Prospect Park Financial
WEST POINT (N.Y.). MILITARY ACADEMY *See* United States Military Academy
WEST POINT-PEPPERELL, INC.
Bill Farley is on pins and needles. D. Greising. il por *Business Week* p58+ S 18 '89
Billion-dollar mind [W. Farley's acquisition of West Point-Pepperell] C. Bruck. *The New Yorker* 65:76-88 Ag 7 '89
WEST SALEM (OR.)
Libraries
Painting a portable mural [work of S. Ominski for library] G. Olson. il pors *American Artist* 53:70-5 Ap '89
WEST VIRGINIA
See also
Finance—West Virginia
Gauley River (W. Va.)
Health resorts, watering places, etc.—West Virginia
Historic houses, sites, etc.—West Virginia
New River Gorge National River (W. Va.)
Economic policy
Can anybody govern West Virginia? [G. Caperton] M. Schroeder. il por *Business Week* p40 D 4 '89

Politics and government
See also
Politics, Corruption in—West Virginia
Selling hope in West Virginia [Governor G. Caperton] S. C. Gwynne. il por *Time* 133:37 My 22 '89
WESTAIR AIRLINES
WestAir flies high. M. Berss. il pors *Forbes* 143:147 Je 12 '89
WESTBROOK, ROBERT
In the churches, in the streets: Taylor Branch on 'the King years'. *The Christian Century* 106:351-4 Ap 5 '89
WESTCHESTER COUNTY (N.Y.)
Housing
Down and out in suburbia [homeless] B. Kessler. il *The Nation* 249:306+ S 25 '89
WESTCHESTER OPERA
Musical events:
Mascagni's Le maschere. A. Porter. *The New Yorker* 65:132-3 D 11 '89
WESTERBERG, PAUL
about
Down to a dull roar. D. Gates. il pors *Newsweek* 113:62+ Je 19 '89
WESTERFIELD, NANCY G.
A romance of widows [poem] *The Christian Century* 106:1165 D 13 '89
Tightening clotheslines [poem] *The Christian Century* 106:76 Ja 25 '89
WESTERLUND ROOSEN, MIA, 1942-
about
Mia Westerlund Roosen: Christine Burgin. M. Moorman. il *Art News* 88:202+ Ap '89
WESTERMAN, MARTY
So long, Horse: sometimes losing a bicycle can be like losing a friend. *Bicycling* 30:76 O/N '89
WESTERMEYER, PAUL, 1940-
The practical life of the church musician [cover story] il *The Christian Century* 106:812-14 S 13-20 '89
WESTERN AND COUNTRY MUSIC *See* Country music
WESTERN CIVILIZATION *See* Civilization
WESTERN COOKING *See* Cooking, American
WESTERN DIGITAL CORP.
Rapid evolution can mean quick success . . . or failure [senior vice president K. Braun] M. Aaland. *Working Woman* 14:58+ My '89
WESTERN EUROPE
See also
Aged—Western Europe
Air freight service—Routes—Western Europe
Air traffic control—Western Europe
Airports—Western Europe
Alien labor—Western Europe
Americans—Western Europe
Anti-nuclear movement—Western Europe
Antitrust law—Western Europe
Art—Western Europe
Art and state—Western Europe
Astronomy—Western Europe
Aviation—Western Europe
Aviation and state—Western Europe
Aviation research—Western Europe
Ballet—Western Europe
Banks and banking—Western Europe
Business and the press—Western Europe
Cable television—Western Europe
Camping—Western Europe
Child welfare—Western Europe
Christmas—Western Europe
Civil rights—Western Europe
Colleges and universities—Western Europe
Department stores—Western Europe
Education—Western Europe
Educational counseling—Western Europe
Employment—Western Europe
Environmental movement—Western Europe
Environmental policy—Western Europe
Festivals—Western Europe
Genetic research—Patents—Western Europe
Genetic research—Western Europe
Golf—Western Europe
Hours of labor—Western Europe
Immigration and emigration—Western Europe
Industrial research—Western Europe
Industry and state—Western Europe
Industry and the environment—Western Europe
Insurance, Unemployment—Western Europe
Investments, American—Western Europe
Investments, British—Western Europe
Investments, European
Investments, Japanese—Western Europe
Labor laws and regulations—Western Europe
Legalization of narcotics—Western Europe
Leveraged buyouts—Western Europe
Marketing—Western Europe
Marriage—Western Europe
Motorcycle racing—Western Europe
Music festivals—Western Europe
Narcotics laws and regulations—Western Europe

WESTERN EUROPE—See also—cont.
  Narcotics trade—Western Europe
  Peace movement—Western Europe
  Railroads—Western Europe
  Railroads and state—Western Europe
  Refuse and refuse disposal—Western Europe
  Resorts—Western Europe
  Rhine River
  Securities—Laws and regulations—Western Europe
  Securities—Western Europe
  Shopping—Western Europe
  Smoking—Laws and regulations—Western Europe
  Speedways—Western Europe
  Strikes—Motorcyclists—Western Europe
  Technology—Western Europe
  Terrorism—Western Europe
  Trade waste—Disposal—Western Europe
  Transportation—Western Europe
  United Nations—Western Europe
  Value added tax—Western Europe
  Vocational guidance—Western Europe
  Women—Western Europe
      Armed Forces
      Appropriations and expenditures
Does NATO have middle-age myopia? [reductions in military
  spending] R. Knight. *U.S. News & World Report* 106:32
  Je 5 '89
      Civilization
Tasteless Dutch tomatoes and waiters named Terry
  [homogenization of European culture] D. C. Anderson.
  The New York Times Magazine p60+ D 3 '89
      Commerce
  See also
  Coordinating Committee on Multilateral Export Controls
  European Economic Community
      Canada
  See Canada—Commerce—Western Europe
      Japan
  See Japan—Commerce—Western Europe
      North America
  See North America—Commerce—Western Europe
      Soviet Union
  See Soviet Union—Commerce—Western Europe
      Sweden
  See Sweden—Commerce—Western Europe
      United States
  See United States—Commerce—Western Europe
      Commercial policy
  See also
  European Economic Community
      Cultural relations
      United States
  See United States—Cultural relations—Western Europe
      Defenses
  See also
  Airplanes, Military—Western Europe
  Airplanes, Military transport—Western Europe
  Canada—Armed Forces—Forces in Europe
  Guided missiles, European
  North Atlantic Treaty Organization
  United States—Armed Forces—Forces in Europe
  United States. Air Force—Forces in Europe
A crisis of confidence [European concerns over Reagan foreign
  policy] M. Zucconi. bibl f il *The Bulletin of the Atomic
  Scientists* 45:34-7 Ja/F '89
Soviet change and Western security. J. Chirac. *Current
  (Washington, D.C.)* 315:27-32 S '89
      Description and travel
  See also
  Automobile driving—Western Europe
  Automobile touring—Western Europe
Best ways to get around in Europe. J. Anthony. il *Changing
  Times* 43:39-41 Jl '89
Europe now! il *Glamour* 87:195+ Mr '89
Europe: the new destination. R. Kahn. il *Travel Holiday*
  171:45-6+ Mr '89
Sans doute. *The New Yorker* 65:45-7 N 20 '89
      Anecdotes, facetiae, satire, etc.
My son the tour guide [family trip to Europe with adult
  son] J. Koslow. il *New Choices for the Best Years* 29:77+
  Jl '89
      Economic conditions
  See also
  Inflation (Finance)—Western Europe
      Economic relations
      Germany (West)
  See Germany (West)—Economic relations—Western
  Europe
      Soviet Union
  See Soviet Union—Economic relations—Western
  Europe
      Switzerland
  See Switzerland—Economic relations—Western Europe
      Foreign relations
  See also
  North Atlantic Treaty Organization

      Great Britain
  See Great Britain—Foreign relations—Western Europe
      Soviet Union
  See Soviet Union—Foreign relations—Western Europe
      United States
  See United States—Foreign relations—Western Europe
      Industries
  See also
  Aerospace industries—Western Europe
  Airbus Industrie
  Airlines—Acquisitions and mergers—Western Europe
  Airlines—Western Europe
  Airplane factories—Western Europe
  Airplane industry—Western Europe
  Arianespace
  Audio equipment industry—Western Europe
  Automobile industry—Western Europe
  Avionics industry—Western Europe
  Black business enterprises—Western Europe
  Computer industry—Acquisitions and mergers—Western
  Europe
  Corporations—Acquisitions and mergers—Laws and
  regulations—Western Europe
  Corporations—Acquisitions and mergers—Western
  Europe
  Drug industry—Western Europe
  Electronic industries—Acquisitions and mergers—
  Western Europe
  Eurojet Turbo GmbH
  European Silicon Structures (Firm)
  Food industry—Acquisitions and mergers—Western
  Europe
  General Motors Europe AG
  Helicopter industry—Western Europe
  Investment banking—Acquisitions and mergers—Western
  Europe
  Munitions—Western Europe
  Panavia Aircraft GmbH
  Small business—Western Europe
  Telecommunication—Western Europe
  Telephone companies—Western Europe
  Television industry—Western Europe
  Tourist trade—Acquisitions and mergers—Western
  Europe
  Truck industry—Acquisitions and mergers—Western
  Europe
  Wine industry—Western Europe
The coming boom in Europe. S. Tully. il *Fortune* 119:108+
  Ap 10 '89
The Europeans' big problem: what to do with all that cash.
  B. Riemer. il *Business Week* p42-3 Ap 24 '89
      Nationalism
Thatcherism across the Channel [Bruges group meeting in
  Paris] J.-M. Benoist. map *National Review* 41:23-5 N 10
  '89
      Politics and government
  See also
  Court of Justice of the European Communities
  Elections—Western Europe
  European Parliament
  Green Party (Western Europe)
Eastern Europe is in ferment, but there are big changes
  going on in Western Europe, too. D. A. Brown. *Aviation
  Week & Space Technology* 131:21-2 D 18-25 '89
Who is going to govern Europe? [interview with J. Delors]
  Y. de L'Ecotais and J. Leclerc du Sablon. il por *World
  Press Review* 36:28+ S '89
      Religious institutions and affairs
  See also
  Catholic Church—Western Europe
WESTERN EUROPE-UNITED STATES AIR AGREE-
  MENTS *See* Aviation and state—International aspects
WESTERN FILMS *See* Motion pictures—Westerns
WESTERN HEMISPHERE *See* America
WESTERN HOME AWARDS
  1989-1990 Western Home Awards [cover story; special section]
  il *Sunset (Central West edition)* 183:87-98+ O '89
  It's time for Western Home Awards 1989-1990. il *Sunset
  (Central West edition)* 182:90 F '89
  Meet the jury for our Western Home Awards. il *Sunset
  (Central West edition)* 182:144 My '89
WESTERN MICHIGAN UNIVERSITY GOLD COMPANY
  Western Michigan University/Gold Company. M. G. Nastos.
  Down Beat 56:25 O '89
WESTERN PUBLISHING GROUP, INC.
  Reading Western's future. G. G. Marcial. *Business Week*
  p102 My 29 '89
WESTERN SAHARA
  See also
  Polisario Front
  United Nations—Western Sahara
WESTERN SAHARA CONFLICT, 1975-
      Peace and mediation
Assembly welcomes efforts of Secretary-General and OAU
  chairman to solve Western Sahara problem. il *UN Chronicle*
  26:58-9 Mr '89
Efforts continue to solve Western Sahara problem. il *UN
  Chronicle* 26:29 Je '89

WESTERN SAHARA CONFLICT, 1975- — Peace and mediation—*cont.*
New commission for Western Sahara to advance peace process. *UN Chronicle* 26:25 S '89
WESTERN STATES
See also
Camping—Western States
Caves—Western States
Cowboys
Cross country skiing—Western States
Environmental movement—Western States
Festivals—Western States
Fishing—Western States
Forests and forestry—Western States
Gold mines and mining—Western States
Hunting—Western States
Police—Western States
Public lands—Western States
Radioactive pollution—Western States
Ranch life
Ranches—Western States
Resorts—Western States
Rocky Mountains region
Skiing—Western States
Vegetable gardens and gardening—Western States
Water supply—Western States
Wilderness areas—Western States
Wildlife conservation—Western States
Wildlife management—Western States
Yellowstone National Park
Collectibles
Exploring west of the Rockies on souvenir spoons. R. L. Lloyd. il *Antiques & Collecting Hobbies* 94:30-4 S '89
Hot collectibles of the Old West. R. Reed. il *Antiques & Collecting Hobbies* 94:42-5 Je '89
Description and travel
Central West travel guide for [month] See issues of Sunset (Central West edition) beginning July 1988
Christmas 1888 in 1988. il *Sunset (Central West edition)* 181:62-5 D '88
Exploring the real Old West. G. Scott. il *Time* 134:64-5 Ag 7 '89
If it's big news, you won't find it in Chuck Woodbury's sagebrush journal, Out West. S. K. Reed. il pors *People Weekly* 31:61-2 Ja 16 '89
Sagebrush country: America's outback. D. H. Chadwick. il map *National Geographic* 175:52-71+ Ja '89
Economic conditions
America's Outback [North Dakota, South Dakota, Wyoming, Montana, Idaho, and Washington] J. McCormick and B. Turque. il map *Newsweek* 114:76-7+ O 9 '89
How the West was lost. R. J. Margolis. *The New Leader* 72:13-14 N 27 '89
Forest fires
See Forest fires
History
See also
Black American West Museum
Frontier and pioneer life—Western States
Lewis and Clark Expedition (1804-1806)
Oregon Trail
Maps
New maps for hikers and bikers. *Sunset (Central West edition)* 182:52-3 Ja '89
Population
It's harder to be lonesome out West. map *U.S. News & World Report* 106:14 F 20 '89
WESTERN STATES IN ART
Exhibitions
See also
Gene Autry Western Heritage Museum
Collecting the West [C. R. Smith Collection of Western American art in the Archer M. Huntington Art Gallery; cover story] R. H. Saunders. il *American History Illustrated* 23:22-33 Ja '89
Frederic Remington: masterworks of Western art. P. H. Hassrick. il por *USA Today (Periodical)* 117:76-83 Mr '89
Trappings of the American West [at the Coconino Arts Center in Sedona, Ariz.; cover story] L. Taylor. il *American Craft* 49:42-51 D '89/Ja '90
WESTERN STATES IN LITERATURE
See also
Cowboy poetry
Western stories
WESTERN STORIES
See also
Publishers and publishing—Western stories
The rise and fall of the western [cover story] A. Lejeune. il *National Review* 41:23-6 D 31 '89
Collectors and collecting
The hunt for western titles: a collector's goals and strategies [work of V. Gillespie] S. Sherman. *Publishers Weekly* 235:45 My 5 '89
WESTERN TELEVISION PROGRAMS *See* Television broadcasting—Westerns

WESTFALL, CATHERINE L.
The site contest for Fermilab. bibl f il *Physics Today* 42:44-52 Ja '89
WESTFALL, PATRICIA
The corn. il *Country Journal* 16:20-6 Jl/Ag '89
WESTFALL, STEPHEN
Touched in bronze. il *Art in America* 77:250-5+ Ap '89
WESTFIELD (N.J.)
Crime
In hiding for 18 years, a wanted man is caught by the FBI and a TV posse [J. List, alleged murderer, featured on America's most wanted] K. Gross. il pors *People Weekly* 31:69-70+ Je 19 '89
Murder, they broadcast [viewers of America's most wanted identify murderer J. List] T. Jacoby. pors *Newsweek* 113:58 Je 12 '89
WESTHEIMER, RUTH
Attention busy women . . . are you neglecting your sex life? *Redbook* 173:142-3+ S '89
Dr. Ruth asks, "Are you having fun together?" [with quiz] il por *Redbook* 172:116-18 Ja '89
The joys of (quickie) sex. por *Redbook* 173:112-13+ Jl '89
about
What's up with the doc. E. Grinnan. il por *Seventeen* 48:34 D '89
WESTINGHOUSE ELECTRIC CORP.
Navy, USAF to award contracts for limited ALQ-165 production [airborne self-protection jamming systems] il *Aviation Week & Space Technology* 131:89+ S 11 '89
Pentagon awards production contracts for ALQ-165 to ITT, Westinghouse [airborne self-protection jammer] P. J. Klass. il *Aviation Week & Space Technology* 131:59+ O 16 '89
Westinghouse developing high-energy battery for wide variety of aerospace applications [silver-iron battery] *Aviation Week & Space Technology* 131:43 D 4 '89
Westinghouse developing 'smart skin' technology. il *Aviation Week & Space Technology* 130:284 Je 12 '89
Westinghouse gets respect at last. T. A. Stewart. il *Fortune* 120:92-4+ Jl 3 '89
Westinghouse mounts effort to build entire jammer on single Ga-As wafer. il *Aviation Week & Space Technology* 131:102 S 18 '89
Westinghouse's settlement deviates from pattern. *Monthly Labor Review* 111:47 D '88
WESTINGHOUSE SCIENCE TALENT SEARCH *See* Science Talent Search
WESTMARK SYSTEMS, INC.
The education of Bobby Inman [Tracor LBO] K. Kelly. por *Business Week* p50 D 18 '89
WESTMINSTER (COLO.)
Recreation centers
No little plans [City Park Recreation Center] M. Gaskie. il *Architectural Record* 177:104-7 N '89
WESTMINSTER FINANCIAL (FIRM)
Old name, new game [H. Schreiber] E. Giltenan. por *Forbes* 144:10 Jl 24 '89
WESTMONT COLLEGE
Paying the price [Westmont College students killed in auto accident while doing missions work in Mexico] K. H. Sidey. il *Christianity Today* 33:44-6 My 12 '89
WESTON, CAROL
How to be good to yourself. il *Ladies' Home Journal* 106:182+ N '89
WESTON, ERIC
about
The iron triangle [film] Reviews
People Weekly il 31:17 Mr 6 '89. R. Novak
WESTON, STANLEY
about
Back for another fight. R. O'Brien. il por *Sports Illustrated* 71:18 O 30 '89
WESTON (ROY F.), INC. *See* Roy F. Weston, Inc.
WESTPOINT PEPPERELL, INC. *See* West Point-Pepperell, Inc.
WESTPORT (MASS.)
Public health
A town faces Alzheimer's. M. E. Johnson. il *New Choices for the Best Years* 29:12-13 Mr '89
WESTWAY (PROPOSED) *See* Express highways—New York (State)
WESTWOOD (MASS.)
Festivals
Foam Day! il *National Geographic World* 165:4-7 My '89
WET PLATE PROCESS (PHOTOGRAPHY) *See* Collodion process (Photography)
WET SOCKS
When your feet are spending the day underwater. J. O. Hamilton. il *Business Week* p136 F 27 '89
WETLANDS
See also
Urban wetlands
The ecosphere. G. Easterbrook. il *Newsweek* 114:40-2 Jl 24 '89
The importance of wetlands [research by William J. Mitsch] *USA Today (Periodical)* 117:2 Je '89
Arizona
A peck of trouble at Peck's Lake. J. Bishop. il *Sierra* 74:58-9 Jl/Ag '89

WETLANDS—*cont.*

Florida

See also
Everglades (Fla.)

High Plains (U.S.)

Playa lakes: prairie wetlands of the Southern High Plains. E. G. Bolen and others. bibl f il map *BioScience* 39:615-23 O '89

Iowa

Why is this woman making a wetland? [work of Florine Swanson] J. Walter. il *Successful Farming* 87:58-9 Ag '89

Kauai (Hawaii)

See also
Alakai Swamp (Kauai, Hawaii)

Long Island (N.Y.)

Managing New York's mosquito coast. D. Ninivaggi. il por *The Conservationist* 44:26-33 Jl/Ag '89

Louisiana

Diluvian tremens. K. Wright. *Scientific American* 261:32-3 O '89

Michigan

See also
Tuttle Marsh (Mich.)

Mississippi

Space shuttle meets the wetlands. il *Science* 246:1253 D 8 '89
Yahoos in the Yazoo [U.S. Army Corps of Engineers] L. Williamson. il *Outdoor Life* 183:42+ Ap '89

North America

The last watering holes on the prairie [loss of wetland habitat for waterfowl] G. L. Krapu. il *Natural History* p66-9 Ja '89
New York State migratory bird print and stamp program. il *The Conservationist* 43:56 Mr/Ap '89
Portrait of a deepening crisis [loss of wetlands endangers water birds] P. Steinhart. il *National Wildlife* 27:4-13 O/N '89
Standing room only [migratory birds] P. Steinhart. il *National Wildlife* 27:46-51 Ap/My '89
Waterfowl for tomorrow: the North American Waterfowl Management Plan. D. Odell and G. Batcheller. il map *The Conservationist* 43:6-11 Mr/Ap '89

North Dakota

Dimples on a black desert [wetland conservation efforts hampered by farmers] T. Williams. il *Audubon* 91:36-8+ S '89

Virginia

See also
Dyke Marsh (Va.)

WETLANDS, ARTIFICIAL

Washing up with wetlands [water purification] il *Country Journal* 16:28 S/O '89

Kentucky

Cleansing waters [artificial wetlands as sewage treatment facility in Benton, Ky.] M. Klockenbrink. il map *American Health* 8:72 S '89

WETMORE, TIM

A fiber-optics future? il *Channels (New York, N.Y.: 1986)* 9:93 Ja '89
Some tough choices. il *Channels (New York, N.Y.: 1986)* 9:63 Mr '89

WETSCHLER, ED

Downhill ski? Who, me? il *New Choices for the Best Years* 29:34-8 D '89
Mini jaunts and major hikes. il *Health (New York, N.Y.)* 21:65 S '89

WETSUITS

High fashion meets high tech—underwater. R. Brandt. il *Business Week* p115 S 4 '89

WETTERLING, JACOB

Kidnapping

A town prays for a missing son. W. Plummer. il pors *People Weekly* 32:62-5 N 20 '89

WETZEL, DON

about

Change agents. D. Moreau. il por *Changing Times* 43:108 Ja '89

WETZSTEON, ROSS

'80s tennis. il *Sport (New York, N.Y.)* 80:78+ O '89
Funny lady. il pors *New York* 22:46-8+ F 20 '89
I was a teenage U.S. hope. il pors *Sport (New York, N.Y.)* 80:60-2+ Jl '89
Young man with a play. il pors *New York* 22:58-60+ N 6 '89

WEXFORD FESTIVAL *See* Music festivals—Great Britain

WEXLER, MARK

A case of urban renewal. il *National Wildlife* 27:10-13 Je/Jl '89

WEXNER, LESLIE H.

about

Is there no limit to The Limited's growth? S. Phillips. il *Business Week* p192+ N 6 '89
Limited prospects. J. Zweig. il por *Forbes* 144:142 S 4 '89

WEXNER CENTER FOR THE VISUAL ARTS (COLUMBUS, OHIO)

A crazy building in Columbus [work of P. Eisenman] K. Andersen. il por *Time* 134:84+ N 20 '89

Eisenman's gridlocked mind game. C. McGuigan. il por *Newsweek* 114:74-5 N 20 '89
Solid geometry [designed by P. Eisenman] M. Sorkin. il por *House & Garden* 161:62+ O '89
With the opening of the first major public building by Peter Eisenman, theory and reality collide. H. Muschamp. il por *Vogue* 179:272+ O '89

WEYERHAEUSER COMPANY

Lost in the woods. M. Beauchamp. il *Forbes* 144:221+ O 16 '89
Why some pros are betting on Weyerhaeuser. G. G. Marcial. il *Business Week* p87 Ja 16 '89

WEYERHAEUSER DESIGNCENTERS

Computer design center. R. Berendsohn. il *Popular Mechanics* 166:92 S '89
Decked out. T. O. Bakke. il *Popular Science* 235:28 Jl '89
Design help for homeowners. il *Workbench* 45:19 N/D '89

WEYLU'S (SAUGUS, MASS.: RESTAURANT) *See* Saugus (Mass.)—Restaurants, nightclubs, bars, etc.

WEYMOUTH, LALLY

Talking to Dan Quayle—seriously. il pors *New York* 22:44-9 Mr 13 '89

WEYMOUTH, TINA

about

Tom Tom Club. R. Givens. il pors *Stereo Review* 54:100-1 D '89

WHALEN, WILLIAM J.

Why Mormonism is the fastest growing religion in the West. il *U.S. Catholic* 54:28-34 Je '89
Why some Christians believe the end of the world is near. il *U.S. Catholic* 54:32-8 F '89

WHALES

See also
International Whaling Commission
Narwhals
Whaling

Attack from the ocean deep [D. Sellings survives attack by whales during the Carlsberg Single-handed Transatlantic Race] S. Kelly. il *Reader's Digest* 134:67-72 F '89
Canada's white whales are dying. P. Benesh. *World Press Review* 36:56 Ja '89
Circus whales [reporting the rescue of trapped gray whales in Alaska] T. Williams. il *Audubon* 91:16-18+ Mr '89
Doomed canaries of Tadoussac [P. Béland's work with beluga whales in the Saint Lawrence River] J. R. Luoma. il por map *Audubon* 91:92-7 Mr '89
Humpback poets [songs; research by Katharine Payne and Linda Guinee] M. Kemp. il *Discover* 10:22 Jl '89
Icebreakers save the whales. T. Cole. il *Popular Mechanics* 166:58-9 F '89
O rare leviathan [work of humpback whale researchers D. Glockner-Ferrari and M. Ferrari off Maui] K. Moore. il pors *Sports Illustrated* 70:66-72+ My 29 '89
Operation Rescue [work of New England Aquarium scientists] il *National Geographic World* 162:8-11 F '89
Rap songs from the deep [humpback whales; study by Linda Guinee and Katharine Payne] G. Cowley. il *Newsweek* 113:63 Mr 20 '89
Singing the blues for the blues [blue whales an endangered species] il *U.S. News & World Report* 107:8-9 Jl 3 '89
They had one whale of a time [whale watching off coast of Gloucester, Mass.] J. McCallum. il *Sports Illustrated* 71:94+ Ag 21 '89
Whales: gentle giants of the deep. N. Vietmeyer. il *Reader's Digest* 134:55-60 My '89
Whose rescue was it? [response to three whales trapped in Alaskan ice] B. D. Colen. il *Health (New York, N.Y.)* 21:86 F '89

Photographs and photography

Focusing on a blue . . . giant! [blue whale] H. Hall. il *International Wildlife* 19:30-3 Jl/Ag '89

WHALES, FOSSIL

Whales, dolphins, porpoises. il *Earth Science* 42:20-3 Summ '89

WHALES, KILLER *See* Killer whales

WHALES IN LITERATURE

See also
Moby Dick (Fictional character)

WHALING

See also
International Whaling Commission

Baffin Island (N.W.T.)

History

Eskimo memories [whaling in Canadian eastern Arctic at turn of century] D. Eber. bibl il map *History Today* 39:45-50 N '89

Greenland

The Arctic hunters [pursuit of narwhals by Inuits] C. Dowling. il *Life* 12:140-5 Mr '89

Newfoundland

History

Tuning the rig [Williamsport, former whaling village] H. Oxenhorn. il *The Atlantic* 264:30+ S '89

WHALLEY, JOANNE

about

Bedtime Tory. il pors *Gentlemen's Quarterly* 59:328-31 Mr '89

WHALLON, JOANNE H., AND OTHERS
Energy-dispersive X-ray microanalysis [cover story] bibl f il *BioScience* 39:256-9 Ap '89

WHAN, NORMAN
about
Many are called. R. N. Ostling. il por *Time* 133:79 F 27 '89

WHARTON, CLIFTON R.
about
The $70 billion man. C. V. Clarke. il pors *Black Enterprise* 19:100-2+ Je '89

WHARTON, DAVE
about
He had 'em goggle-eyed. M. Noden. por *Sports Illustrated* 70:82 Ap 10 '89

WHARTON, DONALD
The otter—northwoods playboy. il *The Conservationist* 44:22-5 N/D '89

WHARTON, WILLIAM
about
William Wharton, author of Dad, seeks to avenge his daughter's horrible death. M. Green. il pors *People Weekly* 32:122-4 N 27 '89

WHARTON SCHOOL
Wharton: the Borns' little red schoolhouse [influencing economic policy in Latin America] J. Ryser. il *Business Week* p48 S 18 '89

WHARVES *See* Docks, wharves, etc.
WHAT THE BUTLER SAW [drama] *See* Orton, Joe
WHAT'S ALAN WATCHING? [television program] *See* Television program reviews—Single works
WHAT'S UP, DR. RUTH? [television program] *See* Television program reviews—Single works
WHCLIS *See* White House Conference on Library and Information Services

WHEALY, KENT
about
Heirlooms in your garden [cover story] J. R. Luoma. il *Audubon* 91:46-53 N '89

WHEAT, JOHN
about
From offices of excellence. D. Young. il pors *Southern Living* 24:142+ Ap '89

WHEAT
A protein that binds to a cis-acting element of wheat histone genes has a leucine zipper motif. T. Tabata and others. bibl f il *Science* 245:965-7 S 1 '89
The thumb prints of the gods? [unexplained circular patterns of wheat in England] il *U.S. News & World Report* 107:13 S 11 '89

Yield
More seed, more nitrogen boost wheat. *Successful Farming* 87:41 Ag '89
A springtime drought with a silver lining. L. W. Adkins. il *U.S. News & World Report* 106:48 My 15 '89

WHEAT TRADE
Letters from home [tax fugitive M. Rich gets U.S. export subsidies on wheat deals with the Soviets] J. Willoughby. il por *Forbes* 143:38-9 Je 12 '89

WHEDBEE, CHARLES HARRY
about
The quest for Blackbeard's cup. L. Fleischer. *Publishers Weekly* 235:74 F 3 '89

WHEEL ALIGNMENT *See* Automobiles—Wheels
WHEEL BALANCING *See* Automobiles—Wheels
WHEEL BEARINGS, TRUCK *See* Trucks—Bearings
WHEEL OF FORTUNE [television program] *See* Television program reviews—Single works
WHEELABRATOR-FRYE INC.
See also
Wheelabrator Technologies Inc.
WHEELABRATOR GROUP
Wheelabrator's winding road. G. G. Marcial. *Business Week* p124 My 1 '89
WHEELABRATOR TECHNOLOGIES INC.
Wheelabrator's winding road. G. G. Marcial. *Business Week* p124 My 1 '89
WHEELBARROWS
Buying a wheelbarrow? Here are some tips. il *Southern Living* 24:70-1 Ja '89
The durable wheelbarrow. R. Kimber. il *Country Journal* 16:87-9 My/Je '89
WHEELCHAIR BASKETBALL
Sat down for life by fate, former basketball star Landon Turner rebounds with a gritty comeback. P. Axthelm. il por *People Weekly* 31:61-2 F 13 '89
WHEELCHAIR RACING
Hell on wheels [C. Blanchette] K. Moore. il pors *Sports Illustrated* 71:44-6+ Jl 17 '89
WHEELCHAIRS
Deals on wheels [low cost wheelchairs designed for handicapped in developing countries; work of R. Hotchkiss] B. Weber. il por *The New York Times Magazine* p122 S 17 '89
Tom Houston is a real stand-up guy, thanks to the versatile vertical wheelchair he devised [HiRider] il pors *People Weekly* 32:91-2 Ag 28 '89

WHEELER, ANNE
about
Turning homespun ideas into truth on the screen. D. Jenish. il por *Maclean's* 102:24-5 D 25 '89
WHEELER, ANTHONY G.
Pitfalls of perception. *Utne Reader* p100 N/D '89
WHEELER, CHARLES, 1947-
about
Harmony to publish blind ex-biker's first novel. J. Crichton. il por *Publishers Weekly* 235:37 Mr 31 '89
WHEELER, DOUGLAS LANPHIER
Can America adjust to the new world of spying? il *USA Today (Periodical)* 118:16-18 N '89
WHEELER, JACK
Supporting the enemy in Mozambique [cover story] il *Conservative Digest* 15:34-5+ Mr/Ap '89
WHEELER, JOHN ARCHIBALD, 1911-
The young Feynman. bibl f il *Physics Today* 42:24-8 F '89
WHEELER, LYLE
about
His Oscars Gone with the wind, art director Lyle Wheeler fights to regain more than statuettes. S. K. Reed. il pors *People Weekly* 31:91-2 Mr 27 '89
WHEELER, ROBERT L.
Lichen [poem] *Commonweal* 116:207 Ap 7 '89
WHEELER, THOMAS E.
about
Cable closes in on the classifieds. J. Loftus. il por *Channels (New York, N.Y.: 1986)* 9:52-4 Mr '89
WHEELS
See also
Automobiles—Wheels
Bicycles—Wheels
Motorcycles—Wheels
WHEELWRIGHT, JULIE
Flora Sandes—military maid. bibl f il pors map *History Today* 39:42-8 Mr '89
WHELAN, JAMES R.
Talking it over. See issues of Conservative Digest beginning October 1988 through September/October 1989
WHELAN, SHARON
World cancer patterns. il *World Health* p25-7 Je '89
WHEN HARRY MET SALLY . . . [film] *See* Motion picture reviews—Single works
WHEN HE'S NOT A STRANGER [television program] *See* Television program reviews—Single works
WHERE KIDS SHOP (FIRM)
At a California toy store, kids play Santa for the homeless. il por *People Weekly* 32:115 D 18 '89
WHICKER, MARCIA LYNN, AND ARESON, TODD W.
The art of presidential persuasion. il *USA Today (Periodical)* 117:12-14 My '89
WHIDDEN, GEORGE
about
The lobster man. J. Howard. il por *Modern Maturity* 32:50 Ag/S '89
WHIPPLE, A. B. C. (ADDISON BEECHER COLVIN), 1918-
Skunk in the cellar! il *Reader's Digest* 134:155-8 Mr '89
Those high I.Q. squirrels. il *Reader's Digest* 135:128-30 N '89
WHIPPLE, ADDISON BEECHER COLVIN *See* Whipple, A. B. C. (Addison Beecher Colvin), 1918-
WHIPPLE, BENJAMIN C.
(jt. auth) *See* Samuels, Richard J., and Whipple, Benjamin C.
WHIPPOORWILLS
Song of the whippoorwill. H. Middleton. il *Southern Living* 24:34+ F '89
WHIRLIGIGS
Oil well pump whirligig. A. S. Lunde. il *Workbench* 45:22-4 Jl/Ag '89
WHIRLPOOL BATHS
See also
Hot tubs
Bathtub spas: hydrotherapy for the masses. il *Consumer Reports* 54:467-71 Jl '89
Hot water and your heart. L. Holland. il *Good Housekeeping* 208:241 Ap '89
Portable bathtub spas. il *Consumer Reports* 54:48-52 D '89
WHISKERS *See* Beards
WHISKEY
See also
Scotch whiskey
Spirit of '89 [bourbon] S. Dooley. il *Harper's Bazaar* 122:230+ Mr '89
Anecdotes, facetiae, satire, etc.
All about brown trout and bourbon. E. Zern. *Field & Stream* 94:104 Ag '89
WHISTLE BLOWING (PUBLIC INTEREST)
An agency in trouble [whistle blower J. Dart, Jr. forced to resign from Rehabilitation Services Administration] C. A. Davis. il por *The Progressive* 53:13 Ja '89
Beyond whistleblowing. S. C. Florman. il *Technology Review* 92:20+ Jl '89
Conduct unbecoming? [D. Baltimore case] P. Weiss. il pors *The New York Times Magazine* p40-1+ O 29 '89

WHISTLE BLOWING (PUBLIC INTEREST)—*cont.*
Credit for whistle-blower vanishes [M. O'Toole's exposure of genetic researchers] B. J. Culliton. por *Science* 244:643 My 12 '89
Environmental sleuth battles bureaucrats [W. Stone in New York's Dept. of Environmental Conservation] J. E. Milich. il por *The Progressive* 53:15-16 N '89
Interview: Walter Stewart. D. Stewart. por *Omni (New York, N.Y.)* 11:64-6+ F '89

Laws and regulations
Shielding the whistle-blowers. T. Noah. il *Newsweek* 113:32 Mr 27 '89
Whistleblowing on U.S. defense contractors is out of control [case of John M. Cockerham and Associates] J. M. Cockerham. por *Aviation Week & Space Technology* 130:99+ Ap 10 '89
Why whistle-blowing is getting louder. T. Gest. *U.S. News & World Report* 107:64 N 20 '89
WHITAKER, ELIZABETH D.
(jt. auth) See Gerlach, Luther P., and Whitaker, Elizabeth D.
WHITAKER, PERNELL, 1964?-
about
'Belt the body'. P. Putnam. il pors *Sports Illustrated* 70:44-5 F 27 '89
In your face, José Luis. P. Putnam. il pors *Sports Illustrated* 71:66-7 Ag 28 '89
WHITAKER, TIM (TIM JOSEPH)
Philadelphia. il *Sport (New York, N.Y.)* 80:60-4 Ap '89
WHITBREAD ROUND-THE-WORLD RACE See Yacht racing
WHITE, ARMOND
The 18th New Directors/New Films Festival. il *Film Comment* 25:69-70+ My/Je '89
Celluloid songs. il *Film Comment* 25:36-9 Mr/Ap '89
Dreyer. il por *Film Comment* 25:24-6 My/Je '89
Illuminations. il *Film Comment* 25:54-60 S/O '89
Prince of the City. il pors *Film Comment* 25:76+ N/D '89
Two thumbs down. il *Film Comment* 25:37-9 Ja/F '89
Unbearable lightness [interview with S. Nykvist] il por *Film Comment* 25:52-3 S/O '89
WHITE, AUGUSTUS A.
about
Augustus White to head U. of Md. Health Center. por *Jet* 76:21 Jl 3 '89
WHITE, BARRY
about
Barry White. J. Morthland. por *High Fidelity (New York, N.Y.)* 39:70 Jl '89
WHITE, BILL
about
Baseball picks a pioneer. T. Callahan. il por *Time* 133:76 F 13 '89
Bill White selected as National League prexy. il por *Jet* 75:51 F 20 '89
Bill White: the National League's new boss. il pors *Ebony* 44:44+ My '89
WHITE, CARY
about
Lonesome dove [cover story] J. Calhoun. il *Theatre Crafts* 23:40-4+ F '89
WHITE, CHARLES EDWARD
Why abortion matters most. il *Christianity Today* 33:33-7 Jl 14 '89
WHITE, CHERYL
Glenn Brill/Allrich Gallery. il *American Craft* 49:74-83 Je/Jl '89
Hank Murta Adams/Dorothy Weiss Gallery. il *American Craft* 49:80-1 O/N '89
Robert Brady: masked gods. il por *American Craft* 49:30-7 D '89/Ja '90
WHITE, CHRIS
The cello in jazz. il *Down Beat* 56:62-3 F '89
WHITE, DAVID
When Johnny comes marching home: the pressure for U.S. troops to leave Europe. map *World Press Review* 36:25-7 S '89
WHITE, DAVID, AND MARSH, PETER
Does he or doesn't he? il *World Press Review* 36:16-17 Mr '89
WHITE, DAVID C.
(jt. auth) See Vestal, J. Robie, and White, David C.
WHITE, DAVID COWDEN
Sabbath laws split Methodists in Fiji. *The Christian Century* 106:406-7 Ap 19 '89
WHITE, DON
The longest minute. il *Flying* 116:120-1 O '89
WHITE, EDMUND, 1940-
The jewelry designer's crush on Schiaparelli—and Barbie. il por *Architectural Digest* 46:94+ S '89
Residence on earth: living with AIDS in the '80s. *Life* 12:135 Fall '89
Le style Jacques Grange. il pors *House & Garden* 161:92-105+ Jl '89
Surreal note in Belgium: artist Roger Nellens' collection at Knokke. il *Architectural Digest* 46:142-9+ D '89
Undone in Paris. il por *House & Garden* 161:24+ Ja '89

WHITE, EDWARD M. (EDWARD MICHAEL), 1933-, AND AHRENS, RÜDIGER
European vs American higher education. il *Change* 21:52-5 S/O '89
WHITE, EVELYN C.
How Paul Stewart mines lost 'gold' with a tape recorder. bibl (p135) il pors *Smithsonian* 20:58-64+ Ag '89
WHITE, FRANK, 1944-
Getting ready for SETI. il *Ad Astra* 1:3 S '89
WHITE, GARY L.
about
Wheels of fortune. M. E. Williams. il por *Black Enterprise* 20:100-2+ O '89
WHITE, JANICE
about
Keeper of the keys. N. A. Nichols. il por *New York* 22:28 F 20 '89
The woman who heads all-male New York jail. D. M. Cheers. il pors *Jet* 76:28-31 Ap 17 '89
WHITE, JEAN
Lake Michigan fishing: no shore thing. il *The Saturday Evening Post* 261:86-7 S '89
WHITE, JONATHAN D.
Tips on tipping. *Black Enterprise* 19:82 Mr '89
WHITE, JOSEPH B.
(jt. auth) See Stertz, Bradley A., and White, Joseph B.
WHITE, JOYCE
Bermuda beckons. il *Black Enterprise* 20:141-2 O '89
WHITE, KARYN
about
Music. J. Leland. por *Vogue* 179:134 Je '89
A new generation of black beauties. il pors *Ebony* 44:152+ S '89
The sexy video divas. C. Krupp. il pors *Glamour* 87:234-5 Ag '89
WHITE, MARGARET B.
"My son needed to feel needed". il *Parents* 64:84+ Ap '89
WHITE, MARGARET BOURKE- See Bourke-White, Margaret, 1904-1971
WHITE, MARTHA
Dog days, cat nights and pogonips. il por *The New York Times Magazine* p38+ Ap 2 '89
Dog days, cat nights and pogonips. il *Reader's Digest* 135:5-6 Jl '89
Stranger off a train. il *The New York Times Magazine* p22+ Je 4 '89
WHITE, MEL, 1940-
(ed) See Melendez, Tony. Faith of a family: the Tony Melendez story
WHITE, MICHAEL R.
about
Forbes, White battle to become Cleveland mayor. il pors *Jet* 77:12 O 23 '89
WHITE, MINOR, 1908-1976
about
Seeing and believing. K. Larson. il *New York* 22:62-3 My 22 '89
White and black. I. Sischy. *The New Yorker* 65:124+ N 13 '89
WHITE, PETER T.
Coca. il map *National Geographic* 175:2-47 Ja '89
Hanoi: the capital today. il maps *National Geographic* 176:558-93 N '89
Saigon: fourteen years after. il maps *National Geographic* 176:604-21 N '89
WHITE, PHYLLIS DOROTHY JAMES See James, P. D.
WHITE, R. DOYLE
about
Waste not, want not. J. Cook. il por *Forbes* 144:191-2 O 16 '89
WHITE, RANDALL
Letters [discussion of July 1989 article, Visual thinking in the Ice Age] *Scientific American* 261:12+ D '89
Visual thinking in the Ice Age. bibl il *Scientific American* 261:92-9 Jl '89
WHITE, RANDY
about
Mailman II. H. Hersch. il pors *Sports Illustrated* 70:54-6+ Je 26 '89
WHITE, REGGIE
about
White heat. P. Zimmerman. il pors *Sports Illustrated* 71:64-6+ N 27 '89
WHITE, ROBERT E., 1926-
Compromise or lose. *Commonweal* 116:390-1 Jl 14 '89
WHITE, ROBERT S., AND MCKENZIE, DAN P.
Volcanism at rifts. bibl il maps *Scientific American* 261:62-71 Jl '89
WHITE, RONALD R.
about
The Ron and John show. R. King. il pors *Forbes* 143:103+ Je 26 '89
WHITE, RYAN
about
Q. Why did Judith Light smash a window in anger? A. Her emotions spilled over playing the mother of a son with AIDS; ed. by Jeff Kaye. J. Light. il por *TV Guide* 37:14-15 Ja 7-13 '89

WHITE, SOMERS
about
Former bank president sells financial know-how for $5,000 an hour. L. Arden. il por *Home Office Computing* 7:43 My '89

WHITE, STANFORD, 1853-1906
about
Paganizing the plutocrats. B. Gill. il por *Architectural Digest* 46:58+ D '89

WHITE, SUSAN CHRYSLER
about
Susan Chrysler White at Janet Fleisher. D. S. Rubin. il *Art in America* 77:181-2 Je '89

WHITE, THOMAS S., JR.
about
Telltale signs of bargain stocks [interview] il por *Fortune* 119:30+ Ja 16 '89

WHITE, TOM
about
Big tree for the Big Apple. J. Grossmann. il pors *National Wildlife* 28:10-13 D '89/Ja '90

WHITE, VANNA
about
Behind Vanna's seduction of America [cover story] S. Littwin. il pors *TV Guide* 37:4-5 Mr 4-10 '89
Vanna's greatest fear. J. D. Stem. il pors *TV Guide* 37:6-9 Mr 4-10 '89

WHITE, WALLACE, 1930-
Profiles [S. A. Earle] il *The New Yorker* 65:41-2+ Jl 3 '89

WHITE (SOMERS H.) COMPANY, INC. *See* Somers H. White Company, Inc.

WHITE (THOS. J.) DEVELOPMENT CORPORATION *See* Thos. J. White Development Corporation

WHITE ANGLO-SAXON PROTESTANTS *See* WASPs (Persons)

WHITE BASS FISHING *See* Bass fishing

WHITE BLOOD CELLS *See* Leukocytes

WHITE COLLAR CRIMES *See* Commercial crimes

WHITE COLLAR WORKERS
Taxation
Wimps no more: how corporate employees can have tax fun too. R. Wool. il *Money* 18:111-12 Jl '89

WHITE DWARF STARS *See* Stars, Dwarf

WHITE HOUSE (WASHINGTON, D.C.)
Nineteenth-century White House glassware. J. S. Spillman. bibl f il *Antiques* 135:950-63 Ap '89
The White House: nerve center of the presidency. il *Scholastic Update (Teachers' edition)* 121:8-9 Ja 13 '89
Employees
Oprah Winfrey a hit with White House kitchen staff. il *Jet* 76:61 Jl 17 '89

WHITE HOUSE (WASHINGTON, D.C.). LINCOLN BEDROOM
By George, it's me [photos of congressmen in the Lincoln Bedroom taken by G. Bush] il *Life* 12:84-5 Ap '89

WHITE HOUSE CONFERENCE ON LIBRARY AND INFORMATION SERVICES
States rush plans for second White House library conference. H. Fields. *Publishers Weekly* 236:8 S 8 '89

WHITE HOUSE ENTERTAINING *See* Government entertaining

WHITE HOUSE OF THE CONFEDERACY
The White House of the Confederacy: restoring the historic residence of President Jefferson Davis. J. S. Wamsley. il *Architectural Digest* 46:262-9 O '89

WHITE HOUSE OFFICE OF SCIENCE AND TECHNOLOGY POLICY *See* United States. Office of Science and Technology Policy

WHITE HOUSE PRESS CORPS *See* Bush, George, 1924——Press relations; Presidents—Press relations; Reagan, Ronald, 1911——Press relations

WHITE HOUSE STAFF *See* Presidents—Staff; White House (Washington, D.C.)—Employees

WHITE HOUSE TASK FORCE ON COMPETITIVENESS *See* President's Task Force on Competitiveness

WHITE LION (MUSICAL GROUP)
White Lion. il *'Teen* 33:65 My '89

WHITE MOUNTAIN PEAK (CALIF.)
What's California's easiest 14,000-footer? Try White Mountain Peak. il map *Sunset (Central West edition)* 183:16-17 S '89

WHITE SHARKS *See* Sharks

WHITE WATER CANOE RACING *See* Canoe racing

WHITE WHALES *See* Whales

WHITE WINES *See* Wine

WHITEHEAD, JOHN A., JR.
Giant ocean cataracts. bibl il map *Scientific American* 260:50-7 F '89

WHITEHEAD, JOHN C.
Global economic integration [address, September 20, 1988] *Department of State Bulletin* 89:18-20 Ja '89

WHITEHEAD, KEVIN
Don Pullen: reconciling opposites. il pors *Down Beat* 56:26-8 N '89

WHITEHEAD, MARY BETH
See also
Baby M case

WHITELEY, H. ELLEN
Vets on pets. See issues of The Saturday Evening Post beginning January/February 1984

WHITEMAN AIR FORCE BASE (MO.) *See* Air bases

WHITESIDE, ELIZABETH J.
(jt. auth) See Whitten, Phillip, and Whiteside, Elizabeth J.

WHITESIDE, KATHERINE
Hampton classic. il *House & Garden* 161:82-9 Ja '89

WHITESON, LEON
Daniel Solomon: a villa of classical proportions in Oregon. il por *Architectural Digest* 46:86-91+ Ap '89

WHITETAIL INSTITUTE OF NORTH AMERICA
Deer and the bass man. C. Conley. il pors *Outdoor Life* 184:4 Ag '89

WHITETAILED DEER *See* Deer

WHITETAILED DEER HUNTING *See* Deer hunting

WHITEWATER BOATING *See* Running rapids

WHITFIELD, CHARLES L.
First word. por *Omni (New York, N.Y.)* 11:6 Je '89

WHITFIELD, JOSIE
about
Granny and the Giant. F. Lidz. il pors *Sports Illustrated* 70:36-8+ Je 26 '89

WHITFIELD, MAL
about
Track great Mal Whitfield lauded at USIA retirement. il por *Jet* 77:48 N 20 '89

WHITHAM, THOMAS G.
Plant hybrid zones as sinks for pests. bibl f il *Science* 244:1490-3 Je 23 '89

WHITING, ROBERT
The pain of perfection [excerpt from You gotta have wa] il *Sports Illustrated* 70:76-80+ My 15 '89
about
From the publisher. D. J. Barr. il por *Sports Illustrated* 70:4 My 15 '89

WHITLOCK, JENNIFER
Drop 30-plus pounds. il *Prevention (Emmaus, Pa.)* 41:66-73+ Ja '89

WHITMAN, ARDIS
Secrets of survivors. il *Reader's Digest* 135:113-16 Jl '89
Strangers can enrich your life. il *Reader's Digest* 134:57-8+ Je '89

WHITMAN, GEORGE
about
A birthday at kilometer zero. R. Ryan. il por *Gentlemen's Quarterly* 59:49+ N '89

WHITMAN, JOHN
about
A great ship. K. S. Edwards. il por *Americana* 17:63-5 N/D '89

WHITMAN, MALCOLM, AND MELTON, D. A.
Induction of mesoderm by a viral oncogene in early Xenopus embryos. bibl f il *Science* 244:803-6 My 19 '89

WHITMAN, RUTH, 1922-
(tr) See Sutzkever, Abraham. Prayer for a sick friend

WHITMAN, WALT, 1819-1892
about
First encounters. E. Sorel and N. C. Sorel. il *The Atlantic* 263:71 My '89

WHITMAN CORPORATION
A raider from the north blows into the Windy City [Canada's J. Pattison] B. Bremner. il por *Business Week* p34-5 Ja 16 '89

WHITMORE, BRIAN
(jt. auth) See Green, Justin J., and Whitmore, Brian

WHITMYER, CLAUDE, AND BEN-HORIN, DANIEL
Getting the tools to make the office hum. il *Working Woman* 14:54+ Ja '89

WHITNEY, CRAIG R.
Glasnost writing: so where's the golden age? il *The New York Times Book Review* 94:1+ Mr 19 '89

WHITNEY, GERTRUDE VANDERBILT
about
The Force behind the Whitney. A. Berman. il pors *American Heritage* 40:102-13 S/O '89

WHITNEY, PHYLLIS A., 1903-
Beginnings. *The Writer* 102:9-12 Ap '89
Let's do it over. *The Writer* 102:13-15+ D '89

WHITNEY (J. H.) & COMPANY *See* J. H. Whitney & Company

WHITNEY BIENNIAL *See* Whitney Museum of American Art. Biennial Exhibition

WHITNEY MUSEUM OF AMERICAN ART
The Force behind the Whitney [J. Force] A. Berman. il pors *American Heritage* 40:102-13 S/O '89
Image maker [Image world: art and media culture curated by L. Phillips] B. Smith. il por *Harper's Bazaar* 122:88+ D '89

WHITNEY MUSEUM OF AMERICAN ART. BIENNIAL EXHIBITION
The 1989 Whitney Biennial. A. C. Danto. *The Nation* 248:788-92 Je 5 '89
A bland Biennial. H. Cotter. il *Art in America* 77:80-1+ S '89
The children's hour. K. Larson. il *New York* 22:94-5 My 8 '89

WHITNEY MUSEUM OF AMERICAN ART. BIENNIAL EXHIBITION—*cont.*
Mixed movement at the Whitney. B. W. Bloch. il *The New Leader* 72:21-2 Jl 10-24 '89
Museum biennials and other controversies. D. Grant. *American Artist* 53:12+ Mr '89
Who's afraid of the Whitney Biennial? E. Heartney. il *Art News* 88:171 Summ '89

WHITNEY NATIONAL BANK
Is it more—or less—than meets the eye? J. H. Taylor. il *Forbes* 143:108+ My 29 '89

WHITNEY WING *See* American Museum of Natural History. Whitney Wing

WHITSON, JANET S., AND OTHERS
Amyloid β protein enhances the survival of hippocampal neurons in vitro. bibl f il *Science* 243:1488-90 Mr 17 '89

WHITTEMORE, KATHARINE
Theme parks—what's the attraction? il *Seventeen* 48:235-6+ Ag '89

WHITTEN, PHILLIP, AND WHITESIDE, ELIZABETH J.
Can exercise make you sexier? il *Psychology Today* 23:42-4 Ap '89

WHITTINGHAM, CHARLIE, 1913-
about
The bald eagle. W. Nack. il pors *Sports Illustrated* 70:54-6+ Je 12 '89

WHITTLE, CHRISTOPHER
about
The blooding of Chris Whittle. T. Moore. il por *U.S. News & World Report* 107:42+ N 6 '89
Citizen Chris. M. Newman. *The New Republic* 200:11-13 Ap 10 '89

WHITTLE COMMUNICATIONS LIMITED PARTNERSHIP
Advertising in books draws diverse responses [series of short hardcover books by prominent authors] C. Reid. il *Publishers Weekly* 235:11-12 My 5 '89
The blooding of Chris Whittle. T. Moore. il por *U.S. News & World Report* 107:42+ N 6 '89
Citizen Chris [C. Whittle] M. Newman. *The New Republic* 200:11-13 Ap 10 '89
Dangerous liaisons [newscast with commercials for school classrooms] L. P. Sheinfeld. il *Film Comment* 25:70-2 S/O '89
In the battle for viewers at school, Turner takes on Whittle [News Access service] F. Moore. il *Channels (New York, N.Y.: 1986)* 9:14 Ap '89
Pay attention, class [P. Charren hopes to stop "Educational Network"] E. Watters. il por *Mother Jones* 14:18 D '89
S-TV (school TV) [Channel One] T. Kauchak. il *Seventeen* 48:48 S '89
Teacher or Trojan horse? [Whittle expands Channel One] L. Zuckerman. il *Time* 133:56 Je 19 '89
Whittle while you learn [controversy over Channel One] B. Brewin. il *Video* 13:122 My '89
Whittling the message into the medium [plans to broadcast news show with commercials in classrooms] E. Pomice. il *U.S. News & World Report* 106:52+ F 20 '89
Wooing a captive audience [provides schools with television equipment in exchange for mandatory watching of Channel One news program] J. E. Gallagher. il *Time* 133:88 F 20 '89

WHITTOW, G. CAUSEY, 1930-
(jt. auth) *See* Simons, Ted, and Whittow, G. Causey, 1930-

WHITTREDGE, WORTHINGTON, 1820-1910
about
Worthington Whittredge. A. E. Ledes. il *Antiques* 136:1250+ D '89

WHITWORTH, HOLLISTER
about
Champions forever [film] Reviews
  Sport (New York, N.Y.) il 80:11 D '89. D. Miller

WHO *See* World Health Organization

WHO (MUSICAL GROUP)
The adults are alright [concert at Radio City Music Hall] F. Goodman. il *Rolling Stone* p19 Ag 10 '89
Hollywood's hippest turn out for (and join in) the Who's last Tommy waltz. il *People Weekly* 32:52-3 S 11 '89
See them! Feel them! D. Gates. il *Newsweek* 114:67 Jl 3 '89
The Who by numbers. M. Goldberg. il *Rolling Stone* p28 Ag 24 '89
The Who reboards the magic bus, but will it still be magic? [cover story] S. Pond. il *Rolling Stone* p86-7+ Jl 13-27 '89

WHO FRAMED ROGER RABBIT [film] *See* Motion picture reviews—Single works

WHO GETS IN? [television program] *See* Television program reviews—Single works

WHO KILLED VINCENT CHIN? [film] *See* Motion picture reviews—Single works

WHOLE GRAIN COOKING *See* Cooking—Grain

WHOLE LANGUAGE LEARNING *See* Language arts—Study and teaching

WHOLESALE TRADE
Finance
Mom and pop move out of wholesaling. J. Weber, Jr. il *Business Week* p91 Ja 9 '89

WHOLESALERS, BOOK *See* Book wholesalers and distributors

WHOOPING COUGH
Vaccines and vaccination
Mutants of pertussis toxin suitable for vaccine development. M. Pizza and others. bibl f il *Science* 246:497-500 O 27 '89
Vaccine confers pertussis protection. K. Fackelmann. *Science News* 136:276 O 28 '89

WHOOPING CRANES *See* Cranes (Birds)

WHO'S AFRAID OF VIRGINIA WOOLF? [drama] *See* Albee, Edward, 1928-

WHO'S HARRY CRUMB? [film] *See* Motion picture reviews—Single works

WHYATT, ROBIN M.
NRDC on Alar. bibl f *Science* 245:910-11 S 1 '89

WHYTE, SALLY
Report from Europe: festive dancing. il *Dance Magazine* 63:50-3 D '89

WHYTE, WILLIAM HOLLINGSWORTH
about
Contrary to previous reports, cities are not dead. S. Allis. il por *Time* 134:9-10 Ag 7 '89
The sky line. B. Gill. *The New Yorker* 65:99-104 Mr 6 '89
Standing on those corners, watching all the folks go by. S. S. Hall. bibl (p171) il por *Smithsonian* 19:119-24+ F '89

WIARDA, HOWARD J., 1939-, AND WIARDA, IEDA SIQUEIRA
The United States and South America: the challenge of fragile democracy. bibl f *Current History* 88:113-16+ Mr '89

WIARDA, IEDA SIQUEIRA
(jt. auth) *See* Wiarda, Howard J., 1939-, and Wiarda, Ieda Siqueira

WICHITA (KAN.)
Crime
The long nightmare of Ruth Finley [dissociative reaction victim] P. Michelmore. il por *Reader's Digest* 134:97-104 Mr '89
Religious institutions and affairs
Sanders gives his church $1/4 million in tithes [football player's gifts to Paradise Baptist Church] il por *Jet* 76:51 S 25 '89

WICK, JOHN
about
A hound's start in life. L. Mueller. il por *Outdoor Life* 183:43-4 F '89
Seize the moment. L. Mueller. il *Outdoor Life* 183:50+ My '89

WICK, STEVE
The Wickham family holds fast. il *Country Journal* 16:61-6 My/Je '89

WICKENDEN, JAMES W.
Breaking the myths of admissions. il *Money* 18:153-4+ My '89

WICKER, TOM
about
Owen Lattimore and the 'cold war'; Lattimore & Wicker. W. F. Buckley. *National Review* 41:54-5 Ag 18 '89

WICKER FURNITURE
Henry Ford slept here [constructing reproduction wicker bed for Ford Estate] K. P. Crombie. il *Workbench* 45:42-6 Mr/Ap '89

WICKERS, DAVID
The sounds of Salzburg. il *World Press Review* 36:62 F '89

WICKERSHAM, VICTOR
about
Testimonials from a less suspicious era. J. Adler. il por *Newsweek* 113:20 Je 12 '89

WICKERT, ERWIN, 1915-
Two different roads to reform. il *World Press Review* 36:16-17 My '89

WICKES, MICHAEL
Depicting urban landscapes with pastels. il por *American Artist* 53:60-3 Mr '89

WICKHAM FAMILY
about
The Wickham family holds fast. S. Wick. il *Country Journal* 16:61-6 My/Je '89

WICKRAMASINGHE, H. KUMAR
Scanned-probe microscopes. il *Scientific American* 261:98-105 O '89

WICKS, FRANK
about
Home-size cogenerator. V. E. Gilmore. il *Popular Science* 234:82+ Mr '89

WICKS, GEORGE G., AND BICKFORD, DENNIS
Doing something about high-level nuclear waste. il *Technology Review* 92:50-8 N/D '89

WICKSTROM, ANDY
More book-video tie-ins on display at VSDA meeting. il *Publishers Weekly* 236:46+ S 1 '89

WIDE-ANGLE LENSES *See* Lenses, Photographic

WIDE AREA NETWORKS
Listen to your customer. I. Chithelen. il *Forbes* 143:120-1 My 15 '89

WIDE SCREEN MOTION PICTURES *See* Motion pictures—Wide screen films
WIDEBAND RADAR *See* Ultra-wideband radar
WIDEBODY TENNIS RACKETS *See* Tennis rackets
WIDEMAN, JACOB
about
Blood circle. C. Brown. il *Esquire* 112:122-8+ Ag '89
WIDEMAN, JOHN EDGAR
Look beyond the mad rush to be number one. il *TV Guide* 37:32-4 Ja 28-F 3 '89
about
Blood circle. C. Brown. il *Esquire* 112:122-8+ Ag '89
PW interviews. J. Rosen. por *Publishers Weekly* 236:37-8 N 17 '89
WIDENER, S. L.
Abo's wine [fiction] il *Seventeen* 48:154-7+ O '89
WIDLANSKI, MICHAEL
Israel moves right. il *National Review* 41:24-5 Je 30 '89
WIDOM, CATHY SPATZ, 1945-
The cycle of violence. bibl f il *Science* 244:160-6 Ap 14 '89
WIDOWERS
When death does us part: the difference between widows and widowers [study by Ken R. Smith] M. M. Breecher. *Psychology Today* 23:14 N '89
Economic conditions
Age 60: a widower, no dependents. T. A. Masi and D. M. Dordevic. il pors *Fortune* 120 no10 Special Issue:140 Fall '89
WIDOWS
Memories of love make a spouse's death both more heartbreaking and, in the end, more bearable; ed. by Angela Blessing. J. Brothers. il pors *People Weekly* 31:86-8+ Je 26 '89
The way we are [returning to dating after being widowed] L. Wyse. il *Good Housekeeping* 208:268 Je '89
When death does us part: the difference between widows and widowers [study by Ken R. Smith] M. M. Breecher. *Psychology Today* 23:14 N '89
Economic conditions
Dealing with a death in the family. M. Rowland. il *Working Woman* 14:47-8+ Ag '89
THE WIDOW'S BLIND DATE [drama] *See* Horovitz, Israel
WIECK FAMILY
about
Successful family farm. M. Holmberg. il *Successful Farming* 87:38-40 mid-Mr '89
WIEDEMANN, ANNE
about
Mutual delights. il pors *Harper's Bazaar* 122:154-7 O '89
WIEFERICH, ROBERT
Augusta overture [reproductions of paintings] il *Sports Illustrated* 70:56-65 Ap 10 '89
WIENER, JON
'Academic poverty-pimping' [discussion of September 4-11, 1989 article, Law profs fight the power] *The Nation* 249:442+ O 23 '89
Bringing Nazi sympathizers to the U.S. [cover story] *The Nation* 248:289+ Mr 6 '89
Harvard chases biotech bucks. il *The Nation* 248:12-16 Ja 2 '89
Law profs fight the power. *The Nation* 249:246-8 S 4-11 '89
Letters [discussion of December 12, 1988 article, Campus voices right and left] *The Nation* 248:146 F 6 '89
Racial hatred on campus. il *The Nation* 248:260-2+ F 27 '89
WIESENTHAL, SIMON
about
If Hungary's cops don't get you, its telephones will. L. Eisenberg. il *TV Guide* 37:26-9 Ap 22-28 '89
WIESNER, JEROME BERT, 1915-
On science advice to the president. bibl il *Scientific American* 260:34-9 Ja '89
WIEWANDT, THOMAS A.
Cactus flower. il *National Wildlife* 27:46-51 Ag/S '89
WIFE ABUSE
See also
Women's shelters
Battered into submission [wife abuse in the Christian home; excerpt] J. Alsdurf and P. E. Alsdurf. il *Christianity Today* 33:24-7 Je 16 '89
Beware of paper tigers [murder of L. Bianco by her ex-husband raises questions about limits of court protection] J. C. Simpson. il pors *Time* 133:104-5 Mr 27 '89
Hard facts about spouse abuse. M. Callahan. il *Parents* 64:240+ O '89
"How can I live with a man who hit me?". E. Switzer. il *Ladies' Home Journal* 106:10+ Jl '89
In a dark and fearful place [excerpt from First Father, First Daughter] M. Reagan. il pors *People Weekly* 31:94-6+ Ap 10 '89
Nowhere to run (I) [R. Linton murdered by her husband in Yonkers, N.Y.] E. Hopkins. il *Rolling Stone* p72-4+ Ap 20 '89
Nowhere to run (II) [R. Linton murdered by her husband in Yonkers, N.Y.] E. Hopkins. il por *Rolling Stone* p74-6+ My 4 '89

O.J. Simpson charged with beating his wife. il por *Jet* 75:26 F 20 '89
O.J. Simpson ordered to pay $200 fine by court in wife-beating case. il por *Jet* 76:51 Je 12 '89
Partners against crime: Brazil's police work with women to fight domestic violence. E. Station. il *Ms.* 18:69-70 N '89
Special report: . . . till death do us part [cases of April LaSalta, Pamela Dunn, and Lisa Bianco] S. Weller. il *Redbook* 173:112-14+ Ag '89
Surviving marriage to the Killer [M. Williams and singer J. L. Lewis] V. Balfour. il pors *People Weekly* 32:48-53 Jl 10 '89
A test of courage [battered wife examines life and obesity after failed suicide] A. M. Gappa. il pors *Ladies' Home Journal* 106:22+ Ja '89
Thousands of women, fearing for their lives, hear a scary echo in Tracey Thurman's Cry for help. J. Park and S. Schindehette. il por *People Weekly* 32:112-16 O 9 '89
WIFE ABUSE IN TELEVISION
I'm doing this movie to keep Buck Thurman from getting out of jail [N. McKeon plays battered wife T. Thurman in TV movie] S. Littwin. por *TV Guide* 37:24-6 S 30-O 6 '89
WIFE AND HUSBAND QUARRELS *See* Quarrels
WIFFLE BALLS
You, too, can be Gaylord Perry—without sandpaper. E. Steadham. il *Sport (New York, N.Y.)* 80:83 Mr '89
WIG, NARENDRA N.
Mental health adds quality to life. il *World Health* p24-6 Jl '89
WIGAND, PATTIE
Monday morning miracle; ed. by Philip Yancey. il *Reader's Digest* 134:9+ Mr '89
WIGGINS, BARBARA
about
Losing 100 pounds the old-fashioned way. il pors *Ebony* 44:98+ S '89
WIGGINS, GRANT
A true test: toward more authentic and equitable assessment. bibl f il *Phi Delta Kappan* 70:703-13 My '89
WIGGINS, MARIANNE
Millions [story] *Harper's* 278:33-4 Je '89
about
A life in hiding. A. Phillips. il pors *Maclean's* 102:30 Ag 21 '89
PW interviews. M. Field. por *Publishers Weekly* 235:57-8 F 17 '89
Writer Salman Rushdie's life on the run leaves his marriage to Marianne Wiggins on the rocks. il pors *People Weekly* 32:60 S 11 '89
WIGHT, JAMES ALFRED *See* Herriot, James
WIGS
With today's well-made wigs, you can have your hair and cut it too. L. Cunliffe. il *Vogue* 179:149-50 Ag '89
WIGTON, RICHARD B.
about
Conspiracy of strangers. C. Byron. il pors *New York* 22:16+ S 4 '89
The debris in Rudolph Giuliani's wake. C. Welles. pors *Business Week* p36-7 Ja 23 '89
WIJCK, ZEGER VAN ASCH VAN *See* Van Asch van Wijck, Zeger
WILANDER, MATS
about
Mats and Sonya Wilander: that sporting life. K. Keller. il pors *Mademoiselle* 95:156-9 F '89
No. 1: blessing or burden? N. Amdur. il por *World Tennis* 36:4 Ap '89
Suddenly, a door-Mats. F. Lidz. il pors *Sports Illustrated* 70:38-40 My 15 '89
Team spirit. il pors *Harper's Bazaar* 122:150-3 My '89
WILANDER, SONYA
about
Mats and Sonya Wilander: that sporting life. K. Keller. il pors *Mademoiselle* 95:156-9 F '89
Team spirit. il pors *Harper's Bazaar* 122:150-3 My '89
WILBER, BOB
about
Bob Wilber. D. Helland. il por *Down Beat* 56:50-1 Jl '89
WILBUR, RICHARD, 1921-
A wall in the woods: Cummington [poem] *The New Yorker* 65:40 Je 5 '89
WILCOVE, DAVID S.
In memory of Martha and her kind. il *Audubon* 91:52-5 S '89
WILCOVE, M. J.
Out of Africa. il *Omni (New York, N.Y.)* 12:32+ O '89
WILD, NETTIE
about
A rustling of leaves: inside the Philippine revolution [film] Reviews
Maclean's il 102:63 Ap 24 '89. B. D. Johnson
WILD, ROBERT A., 1936-
Thirty days to a stronger soul. il *U.S. Catholic* 54:12-13 F '89

WILD, RUSSELL
Fire at the equator. il por map *Organic Gardening* 36:54-9
My '89
WILD AND SCENIC RIVERS
See also
Chattooga River
Rogue River (Or.)
Rivers flow toward showdown [additions to wild river designations in Washington] J. Stiak. il *Sierra* 74:78-80 S/O '89
WILD ANIMAL PETS *See* Pets
WILD ANIMALS *See* Wildlife
WILD BASIN WILDERNESS PRESERVE (TEX.)
Wild Basin of Bee Creek. J. Poage. il map *Earth Science* 42:14-17 Spr '89
WILD BOAR HUNTING
A tank with ivory scythes [Russian wild boar] J. Barsness. il *Field & Stream* 94:46-7+ D '89
WILD BOARS
The wild boar is a formidable foe and an admirable pest [Big Thicket National Preserve] J. Tabor. il *Smithsonian* 20:114-18+ S '89
THE WILD BUNCH [film] *See* Motion picture reviews—Single works
WILD DUCKS *See* Ducks, Wild
WILD FLOWERS *See* Wildflowers
WILD GEESE *See* Geese, Wild
WILD HORSE SANCTUARY (CALIF.)
Wild, wild horses: westerners rally to save the last roaming herds. D. Toussaint and L. Moretti. il por *Utne Reader* p100-1 Ja/F '89
WILD HORSES
See also
Wild Horse Sanctuary (Calif.)
Wild, wild horses: westerners rally to save the last roaming herds [Wild Horse Sanctuary saves animals from destruction by the Bureau of Land Management] D. Toussaint and L. Moretti. il por *Utne Reader* p100-1 Ja/F '89
WILD MUSHROOMS *See* Mushrooms
WILD RIVERS *See* Wild and scenic rivers
WILD TURKEYS *See* Turkeys, Wild
WILDAVSKY, AARON B.
The secret of safety lies in danger. *Society* 27:4-5 N/D '89
(jt. auth) *See* Oldfield, Duane M., and Wildavsky, Aaron B.
WILDE, OSCAR, 1854-1900
about
First encounters. E. Sorel and N. C. Sorel. il *The Atlantic* 263:71 My '89
Salome [drama] Reviews
Opera News il 53:24-6+ Mr 4 '89. J. Kestner
WILDER, BILLY, 1906-
about
Director Billy Wilder puts his legendary $22 million-or-so art collection on the auction block. S. K. Reed. il pors *People Weekly* 32:154+ N 13 '89
A life in pictures. P. Viladas. il pors *House & Garden* 161:154-9+ Ap '89
WILDER, CHRISTOPHER BERNARD
about
Final attraction: men who charm women—to death. A. Rule. il pors *Redbook* 172:104-6+ F '89
WILDER, GENE
about
Gilda Radner's love story. J. Powell. il pors *Glamour* 87:112-13 Jl '89
Richard Pryor, Gene Wilder: together again in new movie comedy [cover story] il pors *Jet* 76:36-8 Je 5 '89
WILDER, L. DOUGLAS
about
Battling an old bugaboo. L. I. Barrett. il pors *Time* 133:26-7 Ap 17 '89
Breakthrough in Virginia. W. Shapiro. il pors *Time* 134:54-7 N 20 '89
Governor-elect Doug Wilder. M. Cooper. il pors *U.S. News & World Report* 107:48+ N 20 '89
L. Douglas Wilder: 'I claim the governorship of Virginia' [cover story] S. Booker. il pors *Jet* 77:8-11 N 27 '89
The New Dominion. R. G. Holland. il *National Review* 41:25+ S 29 '89
A new force in the Old Dominion [cover story] D. T. Dingle. il pors *Black Enterprise* 19:36-8+ Ja '89
A stunning photo finish. W. Lowther. *Maclean's* 102:41 N 20 '89
Va.'s Lt. Gov. Wilder seeks governor's house. il por *Jet* 75:5 F 13 '89
Who will be the first black elected governor? A. Poinsett. il pors *Ebony* 45:38+ N '89
Wilder gets Dem. Party nomination for governor. il por *Jet* 76:4+ Je 26 '89
Wilder inaugural expected to be spectacular event. il por *Jet* 77:4 D 18 '89
Wilder primed to be governor. D. P. Baker. il por *American Visions* 4:42-3 O '89
The Wilder side. F. Barnes. *The New Republic* 201:9-10 N 13 '89
Yes, Virginia, Doug Wilder could be America's first elected black governor. J. S. Kunen. il por *People Weekly* 32:54-5 N 6 '89

WILDER, THORNTON, 1897-1975
about
Our town [drama] Reviews
America 160:64 Ja 28 '89. G. G. Seibert
The Nation 248:102-3 Ja 23 '89. T. M. Disch
The New Republic 200:29-31 Ja 30 '89. R. Brustein
New York il 22:48-9 Ja 2 '89. J. Simon
WILDERNESS, BATTLE OF THE, 1864
1864. A. Nielsen. il *American Heritage* 40:34-6 My/Je '89
WILDERNESS ACT *See* Wilderness areas
WILDERNESS AREAS
See also
Wild and scenic rivers
Wildlife sanctuaries
Back of beyond bucks [hunting whitetails in the wilderness] G. Miller. il *Outdoor Life* 183:69+ Ja '89
Conservation up front. G. Frampton. *Wilderness* 52:2 Wint '88
The etiquette of freedom. G. Snyder. il *Sierra* 74:74-7+ S/O '89
Lines on the land. C. L. Rawlins. il *Sierra* 74:66-9+ S/O '89
Meese's last act [water rights and wilderness] T. Turner. il *The Mother Earth News* 115:33 Ja/F '89
Struggle for the great wild [25th anniversary of the Wilderness Act; cover story] S. Iker. il *National Wildlife* 27:50-9 O/N '89
Untrammeled by man [Wilderness Act of 1964] T. H. Watkins. il *Audubon* 91:74-91 N '89
Wilderness [Wilderness Act] M. Frome. bibl il *National Parks* 63:34-41 Jl/Ag '89
Wilderness America [25th anniversary of Wilderness Act; special issue] il supp (folded map) maps *Wilderness* 52:1-65 Spr '89
The wilderness conundrum [Wilderness Act] G. Reiger. il *Field & Stream* 94:14+ O '89
Wilderness wins and losses at year's end. *Wilderness* 52:4-5 Wint '88

Bibliography
Books for the wilderness. C. E. Little. *Wilderness* 52:66-71 Spr '89

International aspects
How wild is today's world? [research by J. Michael McCloskey and Heather Spalding] *Science News* 136:94 Ag 5 '89

Roads
The 112-year war [Teme-Augama Anishnabai Indians resume blockade of logging road in Ontario's Temagami Wilderness] R. Corelli. il *Maclean's* 102:76-7 N 20 '89

Alaska
See also
Arctic National Wildlife Refuge (Alaska)
In Alaska, the future is now. M. Rogers. il map *Newsweek* 114:63-4 S 18 '89
The last great landscape. il map *Wilderness* 52:52-65 Spr '89

Alberta
See also
Alberta Wilderness Association

Appalachian region
Fragments and systems. il maps *Wilderness* 52:12-23 Spr '89

California
The fight in Utah and California. il *U.S. News & World Report* 107:21 Jl 3 '89

Canada
Seasons of the Canadian soul [wilderness paintings] R. M. Peck. il *International Wildlife* 19:44-51 My/Je '89

Colorado
See also
Indian Peaks Wilderness (Colo.)
Roger West is building a Rocky Mountain highway for the disabled to enjoy [construction of boardwalk by Wilderness on Wheels] H. Shapiro. il pors *People Weekly* 32:131-2 S 18 '89
Water rights and wrongs. C. F. Wilkinson. *Sierra* 74:35-6+ S/O '89

Developing countries
Wildlands: balancing conversion with conservation in World Bank projects [cover story] R. Goodland and G. Ledec. bibl f il *Environment* 31:6-11+ N '89

Idaho
See also
Frank Church-River of No Return Wilderness (Idaho)
Along the northern spine. il map *Wilderness* 52:34-43 Spr '89
Idaho wilderness: the sequel. G. Oakley. il *Sierra* 74:81-2 S/O '89

Maine
Maine Woods Reserve. *Wilderness* 52:11 Summ '89
The Maine Woods Reserve. T. H. Watkins. *Wilderness* 53:41 Fall '89

Minnesota
See also
Boundary Waters Canoe Area (Minn.)

Montana
See also
Bob Marshall Wilderness (Mont.)

WILDERNESS AREAS—Montana—cont.

Along the northern spine. il map *Wilderness* 52:34-43 Spr '89

Storming Montana's wilderness. J. R. Luoma. il *The New York Times Magazine* p34-6+ Ap 16 '89

Nevada

Elko to Eden [hiking in the Ruby Mountains; cover story] T. Kizzia. il map *Sierra* 74:46-54 Mr/Ap '89

Saga of the urban buckarettes [horseback trip from Cottonwood Ranch through the Jarbidge wilderness] C. J. Hadley. il *The Saturday Evening Post* 261:70-1 Jl/Ag '89

New England

Fragments and systems. il maps *Wilderness* 52:12-23 Spr '89

Whose woods these are [cover story; with editorial comment by T. H. Watkins] N. Boucher. il map *Wilderness* 53:16-41 Fall '89

New Mexico

The Mudgetts equation. D. S. Lavender. il map *Wilderness* 52:28-39 Wint '88

New York (State)

See also
Adirondack Forest Preserve (N.Y.)

Wilderness: New York sets a global stage. G. D. Davis. il pors *The Conservationist* 44:2-9+ N/D '89

Ontario

See also
Temagami Wilderness (Ont.)

Oregon

See also
Eagle Cap Wilderness (Or.)

Pacific Northwest

The ancient ones. il map *Wilderness* 52:44-51 Spr '89

Texas

See also
Wild Basin Wilderness Preserve (Tex.)

Utah

The fight in Utah and California. il *U.S. News & World Report* 107:21 Jl 3 '89

Washington (State)

See also
Pasayten Wilderness (Wash.)

Western States

The battle for the wilderness [cover story] M. Satchell. il *U.S. News & World Report* 107:16-21+ Jl 3 '89

The lands no one knew. il maps *Wilderness* 52:24-33 Spr '89

WILDERNESS AREAS IN ART

Seasons of the Canadian soul. R. M. Peck. il *International Wildlife* 19:44-51 My/Je '89

WILDERNESS AREAS IN LITERATURE

A wilderness commonplace book. D. Drabelle. *Wilderness* 52:xi-xvii+ Spr '89

WILDERNESS CONSERVATION *See* Wilderness areas

WILDERNESS FUND

Announcing a Wilderness Fund for the future. G. Frampton. *Wilderness* 53:2 Fall '89

WILDERNESS ON WHEELS (ORGANIZATION)

Roger West is building a Rocky Mountain highway for the disabled to enjoy [construction of boardwalk in Colorado] H. Shapiro. il pors *People Weekly* 32:131-2 S 18 '89

WILDERNESS SCOUTS OF AMERICA

Good scouts indeed [fight Boy Scouts over right to retain name] P. W. Moser. il pors *Sports Illustrated* 70:46-9 F 6 '89

WILDERNESS SOCIETY

Conservation up front. G. Frampton. *Wilderness* 52:2 Wint '88

The Society's finances. il *Wilderness* 52:78-80 Spr '89

Wilderness watch. See issues of Wilderness

WILDERNESS SURVIVAL

Rabbit-food Rambos [edible plants in diet better for survivalists; research by Stephen Källman] P. McCarthy. il *American Health* 8:144-6 Ap '89

WILDERNESS VACATIONS *See* Vacations

WILDERSTEIN (HISTORIC HOUSE: RHINEBECK, N.Y.)

Preserving Wilderstein. il *American Artist* 53:55 N '89

WILDFLOWER GARDENS AND GARDENING

First Lady of wildflowers [L. B. Johnson's growing instructions] E. Henke. il por *Flower and Garden* 33:61 Mr/Ap '89

A flowering lawn. G. Logsdon. il *Organic Gardening* 36:44-8 My '89

Wildflowers: the case for native plants [cover story] N. Diboll. il *Flower and Garden* 33:22-8+ Mr/Ap '89

WILDFLOWERS

Flowers in the wild [cover story] M. Strutin. il *National Parks* 63:28-34 My/Je '89

Parks in bloom. A.-M. Praetzel. il *National Parks* 63:34-6 My/Je '89

California

Getting serious about wildflowers? bibl *Sunset (Central West edition)* 182:82-3 Mr '89

Wildflower walks [cover story] il *Sunset (Central West edition)* 182:86-95 Mr '89

New York (State)
Photographs and photography

Fall wild-flowers. E. A. Worman. il *The Conservationist* 44:22-5 S/O '89

Texas

Bird of paradise. L. B. Johnson. il por *Ms.* 17:32-3 Ap '89

WILDING, SUZANNE

The gift that blessed the giver. il *Good Housekeeping* 209:234+ D '89

Gourmet holidays: a Swiss Alpine sojourn. il map *Gourmet* 49:48-53+ Ag '89

Lancaster County [cover story] il *Gourmet* 49:112-17+ N '89

Tucson. il *Gourmet* 49:44-51+ Ja '89

WILDING, SUZANNE, AND DEL BALSO, ANTHONY

Germany's Fairy-tale Road. il map *Gourmet* 49:52-5+ Mr '89

WILDING (GROUP VIOLENCE)

See also
Central Park wilding attack, 1989

Some reasons for 'wilding'. S. Baker and T. Gore. pors *Newsweek* 113:6-7 My 29 '89

WILDLIFE

See also
Desert fauna
Forest fauna
Oil pollution and wildlife
Pollution and wildlife
Urban fauna

A climate for death [effect of drought on wildlife] P. W. Moser. il *Sports Illustrated* 70:48-50+ Mr 13 '89

Destination wildlife [cover story; special section; with editorial comment by Scott Shane] il maps *Travel Holiday* 171:6, 41-72 Ap '89

Ship-to-shore wildlife watching [cruises] H. Basch and S. Slater. il *Travel Holiday* 171:105 Ap '89

Export-import trade

See also
Convention on International Trade in Endangered Species of Wild Fauna and Flora (1973)

Photographs and photography

Lights, big game, action. E. A. Bauer. il *Outdoor Life* 184:79-81+ N '89

On the trail of a shot [work of B. Fournier] R. Kokernak. il por *Country Journal* 16:37-41 Ja '89

Africa

See also
Elephants
Giraffes
Lions

Hair, dust and sky [S. Combes' paintings of wildlife] H. Gibson. il por *International Wildlife* 19:52-9 S/O '89

Alabama

The wild life. M. Childress. il *Southern Living* 24:104 Jl '89

Alaska

See also
Arctic National Wildlife Refuge (Alaska)

Arctic regions

See also
Polar bears
Walruses

Arctic treasures: what ruler could resist the allure of white falcons, giant moles, and unicorns? F. Bruemmer. il *Natural History* p38-47 Je '89

Arizona

Living in a land of extremes [work of biologist P. Holm in Organ Pipe Cactus National Monument] E. Pennisi. il por *National Wildlife* 27:14-21 Ap/My '89

Australia

See also
Sugar gliders (Animals)
Wombats

Australia's sea lions. il *National Geographic World* 172:26-31 D '89

'Living fossils'. il *The Courier (Unesco)* 41:30-1 D '88

Off in the wild Down Under. P. M. Prince. il map *Travel Holiday* 171:60-7 Ap '89

Borneo

Braving the hellish jungles of Borneo, Birute Galdikas probes the secrets of one of our oldest relations [orangutans] J. Friedman. il pors *People Weekly* 31:102-6 Ja 16 '89

Botswana

How meat-eaters rule each other [Kalahari Desert; cover story] D. Owens and M. Owens. il *International Wildlife* 19:4-11 Jl/Ag '89

California

Rattler battlers [California ground squirrels] R. G. Coss and D. H. Owings. il *Natural History* p30-5 My '89

Christmas Island (Indian Ocean)

Advance of the red army [red crabs] J. W. Hicks. il *International Wildlife* 19:4-11 N/D '89

Connecticut

God's dog [coyotes] F. Graham. il *Audubon* 91:24-5 S '89

Ellesmere Island (N.W.T.)

White wolf: living with an Arctic legend [condensation] J. Brandenburg. il *Reader's Digest* 134:126-32 Mr '89

Florida

Return of a reptile [alligators] J. Gorman. il *Sports Illustrated* 70:50-2+ Mr 6 '89

WILDLIFE—cont.

France
Ms. Monkey [female macaque's social climbing; study in La Forêt des Singes] M. F. Small. il *Natural History* p10+ Ja '89

Galapagos Islands
Cost accounting for lizards [size differences among lizards; research by Howard L. Snell] J. A. Miller. il *BioScience* 39:674-5 N '89

Guam
The far side of paradise [brown tree snakes] il *U.S. News & World Report* 106:15 F 13 '89

Hawaii
O rare leviathan [work of humpback whale researchers D. Glockner-Ferrari and M. Ferrari off Maui] K. Moore. il pors *Sports Illustrated* 70:66-72+ My 29 '89

Kenya
Photographs and photography
Kenya and Tanzania. P. Skinner. il map *Petersen's Photographic Magazine* 18:16-17+ My '89

Latin America
Bear of the clouds [effects of deforestation on the Latin American spectacled bear] P. Steinhart. il map *Audubon* 91:92-4+ Jl '89

Madagascar
Photographs and photography
On the trail of lemurs [cover story] F. Lanting. il *International Wildlife* 19:4-13 My/Je '89

Malaysia
On Malay Peninsula picking coconuts is monkey business [trained macaques] R. S. Peffer. bibl (p147) il *Smithsonian* 19:110-12+ Ja '89

Manitoba
Diary of a bear-watcher [polar bears] F. Bruemmer. il *International Wildlife* 19:46-51 S/O '89

Nepal
Catching a ghost [monitoring snow leopards] R. Jackson and G. Ahlborn. il *International Wildlife* 19:30-3 My/Je '89

New England
A Yankee coat fits the coyote well [cover story] R. Wolkomir and J. Wolkomir. il *National Wildlife* 27:34-8 Ap/My '89

New York (State)
The otter—northwoods playboy. D. Wharton. il *The Conservationist* 44:22-5 N/D '89
Whatever happened to the Allegheny woodrat? A. Hicks. il maps *The Conservationist* 43:34-9 Mr/Ap '89

New Zealand
See also
Tuataras

Serengeti Plain (Tanzania)
Serengeti's painted wolves [wild dogs; cover story] J. H. Fanshawe. il *Natural History* p56-67 Mr '89

South Georgia Island
Wildlife quest to the icy seas of South Georgia. S. Poncet. il map *National Geographic* 175:340-75 Mr '89
Photographs and photography
If heaven were wild [cover story] F. Lanting. il *International Wildlife* 19:4-13 S/O '89

Tanzania
Photographs and photography
Kenya and Tanzania. P. Skinner. il map *Petersen's Photographic Magazine* 18:16-17+ My '89

Texas
See also
Austin (Tex.)—Wildlife

Wyoming
Hunting for an elusive hunter [field studies of American martens] S. Buskirk and H. Harlow. il *National Wildlife* 28:20-3 D '89/Ja '90

Zambia
Zambia [South Luangwa Park] E. McGowan. il map *Travel Holiday* 171:42-51 Ap '89

Zimbabwe
African safari adventure [students from Eiffel Flats Primary School explore Matusadona National Park; cover story] il map *National Geographic World* 168:3-8 Ag '89

WILDLIFE, ATTRACTING OF
See also
Farming in the Flyways (Program)
Why is this woman making a wetland? [work of Florine Swanson in Iowa] J. Walter. il *Successful Farming* 87:58-9 Ag '89
Wild ideas [backyard habitats] L. Barash. il *National Wildlife* 27:22-7 Ap/My '89

WILDLIFE CONSERVATION
See also
Bird sanctuaries
Farming in the Flyways (Program)
Fish protection
Game preserves
Gamekeepers
National Wildlife Federation
Rare animals
U.S. Fish and Wildlife Service
Wetlands
Wilderness areas

Wildlife, Attracting of
Wildlife management
Wildlife sanctuaries
Nature stories. R. L. Di Silvestro. See issues of Audubon beginning July 1987 through January 1989
People who make a difference. il *National Wildlife* 27:4-11 Ag/S '89
The science of saving endangered species: directions for research in conservation biology. C. Mlot. il *BioScience* 39:68-70 F '89
What farmers are saying. il *Successful Farming* 87:64 Ap '89
Why save endangered species? G. Reiger. il *Field & Stream* 93:15 Ja '89
Wildlife [Environmental Quality Index] il *National Wildlife* 27:34 F/Mr '89
Wildlife and environment. il *The Futurist* 23:52-3 My/Je '89

Finance
The high cost of neglecting wildlife. B. Lawren. il *National Wildlife* 27:4-9 Ap/My '89

Laws and regulations
See also
Fishery laws and regulations
Game laws
Game wardens
Marine mammals—Laws and regulations
The OMB octopus. L. Williamson. il *Outdoor Life* 183:62+ My '89

Africa
Africa is becoming an elephant graveyard. W. Booth. il *Science* 243:732 F 10 '89
A ban on ivory. M. Nichols. il *Maclean's* 102:86 O 30 '89
Big-game forensics [use of DNA fingerprinting to discourage elephant poaching] J. Horgan. il *Scientific American* 261:27+ D '89
Decision time on African ivory trade. J. Cherfas. il *Science* 246:26-7 O 6 '89
Elephants look best in ivory [ban on imports] L. Troiano. il *American Health* 8:92 O '89
Global ban sought on ivory trade [to save elephants] R. Lewin. il *Science* 244:1135 Je 9 '89
How to save the African elephant [economic incentives] M. S. Forbes, Jr. *Forbes* 144:29 N 13 '89
Human folly on a grand scale. L. O. Sanneh. il *The Christian Century* 106:843 S 27 '89
International tusk politics. *Science News* 136:94 Ag 5 '89
The ivory dispute [African countries in opposition to trade ban] F. Bridgland. *World Press Review* 36:69 S '89
Last stand for Africa's elephants [ivory poaching] E. Linden. il *Time* 133:76-7 F 20 '89
Outlawing ivory [U.S. ban in order to save elephants] il *Time* 133:62 Je 19 '89
Pachyderm policy [elephant herds growing in countries that permit ivory trading] D. Seligman. il *Fortune* 120:235+ N 20 '89
Reprieve for the giant of beasts [efforts to save the elephant] T. Gup. il *Time* 134:77 O 30 '89
Saving the African elephant. il *The Futurist* 23:49 S/O '89
Science gives ivory a sense of identity [DNA fingerprinting and isotope analyses] J. Cherfas. il *Science* 246:1120-1 D 1 '89
The shrinking roots of heaven [efforts to stop illegal poaching of elephants by restricting ivory trade] *U.S. News & World Report* 106:11-12 My 22 '89
Symbolic flames [proposed ban on ivory sales] A. Steacy. il *Maclean's* 102:37 Jl 31 '89
Trail of shame [elephants endangered by ivory poachers; cover story] T. Gup. il map *Time* 134:66-9+ O 16 '89
Tusk, tusk [Sotheby's removes elephant tusks from market to alleviate poaching] il *Time* 133:56 My 1 '89
A tussle over tusks [African nations debate ban on ivory trade] J. Bartholet. il *Newsweek* 114:25 Jl 24 '89

Alaska
Circus whales [reporting the rescue of trapped gray whales] T. Williams. il *Audubon* 91:16-18+ Mr '89
Dead otters, silent ducks [aftermath of oil spill] G. Cowley. il *Newsweek* 113:70 Ap 24 '89
Elephants in Alaska [handicrafts made from poached African ivory] F. Graham. *Audubon* 91:27-9 S '89
Icebreakers save the whales. T. Cole. il *Popular Mechanics* 166:58-9 F '89
Protecting Alaskan wildlife [work of Jonathan Bart] *USA Today (Periodical)* 117:5-6 Je '89
Whose rescue was it? [response to three whales trapped in ice] B. D. Colen. il *Health (New York, N.Y.)* 21:86 F '89

Argentina
Skins to boot [tegu lizards] D. Einhorn. il *Américas* 41 no2:2 '89

California
A most exclusive neighborhood [preserve for endangered kangaroo rats in Riverside County financed through impact fees] il *U.S. News & World Report* 106:16 Mr 6 '89

Canada
House calls in the wild. T. Pawlick. il *International Wildlife* 19:12-17 Mr/Ap '89

WILDLIFE CONSERVATION—Canada—*cont.*
Threatened animals. D. Jenish. il *Maclean's* 102:44-5 Ag 7 '89

China
Panda paradox. E. Dolnick. il map *Discover* 10:70-4+ S '89
Poaching the pandas. L. Branson. *World Press Review* 36:53 Mr '89

Florida
Big guy [Florida panthers] F. Graham. il *Audubon* 91:16+ S '89
Dolphins [diver aids wounded baby dolphin] W. Grover. il *Sea Frontiers* 35:28-30 Ja/F '89
Searching for the one true cat [Florida panthers] C. Flowers. il *National Wildlife* 27:24-8 O/N '89
Slow creature caught in a fast world [manatees] T. A. Lewis. il *National Wildlife* 28:42-9 D '89/Ja '90
Sodium lights repel turtles [allowing Florida loggerheads to find ocean] il *Sea Frontiers* 35:69 Mr/Ap '89

France
End of the line for French bears? J. Mills. il *International Wildlife* 19:4-11 Ja/F '89

Hawaii
Losing paradise. K. Brower. il map *Wilderness* 53:20-8 Wint '89

India
Project Tiger. R. Singh. il *The Courier (Unesco)* 42:35-6 F '89

Italy
Civilizing the hunt. D. Starr. il *International Wildlife* 19:16-19 N/D '89

Kenya
The battle in the Bush [work of elephant protector Bill Woodley] il *Time* 134:73 O 16 '89
Elephant man [R. E. Leakey] W. F. Allman. il por *U.S. News & World Report* 107:58+ O 2 '89
Endangered species: can they be saved? [African elephants; cover story] W. F. Allman. il map *U.S. News & World Report* 107:52-8 O 2 '89
Heavy artillery for horns of plenty [war on ivory poachers] E. Ransdell. il *U.S. News & World Report* 106:61+ F 20 '89
Kenya burns $3 mil. in ivory to stop its trade. il *Jet* 76:18 Ag 7 '89
The Masai. J. Horgan. il map *Scientific American* 261:38+ S '89

Namibia
Deconstructivist rhinos [thwarting poachers by removing horns] il *Discover* 10:12 O '89

Nepal
Rhino warrior [Royal Chitwan National Park] D. Starr. il *Omni (New York, N.Y.)* 11:17+ S '89

New York (State)
See also
College of Environmental Science and Forestry. Adirondack Wildlife Program
New York (State). Dept. of Environmental Conservation

Ontario
See also
Erie Wildlife Rescue (Organization)

Québec (Province)
Canada's white whales are dying. P. Benesh. *World Press Review* 36:56 Ja '89

Rwanda
The gorillas in the mist have a new champion: Diane Doran. B. Johnson. il pors *People Weekly* 32:151-2 D 4 '89

South Africa
Pay or perish. L. Williamson. il *Outdoor Life* 184:36+ D '89

Tropics
A world in crisis. P. H. Raven. il *USA Today (Periodical)* 117:48-50 My '89

Utah
Starting over [reintroduction of prairie dogs] J. L. Ferrara. il *National Wildlife* 27:18-21 F/Mr '89

Western States
Ark de triomphe [saving endangered species in Yellowstone] C. Spencer. il *Omni (New York, N.Y.)* 11:48-50+ Ja '89

Zimbabwe
Horns of a dilemma [rhino poaching] M. L. Knox. il *Sierra* 74:58-67 N/D '89
The rhino's last stand [battle against poachers] A. Linklater. il *Reader's Digest* 134:106-10 F '89

WILDLIFE FILMS *See* Motion pictures—Wildlife films
WILDLIFE IN ART *See* Animals in art
WILDLIFE IN LITERATURE *See* Animals in literature
WILDLIFE INTRODUCTION *See* Animal introduction
WILDLIFE LEGISLATIVE FUND OF AMERICA
Protect what's right. J. Glass. *Outdoor Life* 183:4 Je '89
WILDLIFE MANAGEMENT
See also
Wildlife Legislative Fund of America
A matter of expertise. G. Reiger. il *Field & Stream* 93:21-2 Mr '89
Personalized wildlife management. G. Reiger. il *Field & Stream* 94:14+ My '89
Pushy wildlife: animals that thrive on human habitat. J. Lazell. il *National Parks* 63:18-25 S/O '89

Return of the natives [rare species reintroduction] D. E. Brown. il *Wilderness* 52:40-52 Wint '88
Running on empty [federal positions not being filled] L. Williamson. il *Outdoor Life* 184:16-18 O '89
Translocation as a species conservation tool: status and strategy. B. Griffith and others. bibl f il *Science* 245:477-80 Ag 4 '89
Wildlife mismanagement. L. Williamson. il *Outdoor Life* 184:29-30 N '89

Botswana
Fences that kill [barbed wire barrier used to keep out wild animals] F. Carbone. *World Press Review* 36:80 O '89

Great Britain
Keepers of the game [shooting preserves] B. Alexander. il *International Wildlife* 19:34-40 S/O '89

Michigan
Wolves of Isle Royale. S. Nash. il *National Parks* 63:20-6+ Ja/F '89

New York (State)
See also
New York (State). Dept. of Environmental Conservation
Deer in suburbia—pleasures and pests. D. J. Decker and N. A. Connelly. il *The Conservationist* 43:46-9 Mr/Ap '89

Southern Africa
Sometimes the graceful flourish [impalas] N. Myers. il *International Wildlife* 19:44-51 Ja/F '89

United States
See Wildlife management

Western States
Wild, wild horses: westerners rally to save the last roaming herds [Wild Horse Sanctuary saves animals from destruction by the Bureau of Land Management] D. Toussaint and L. Moretti. il por *Utne Reader* p100-1 Ja/F '89
WILDLIFE MANAGEMENT AREAS *See* Wildlife sanctuaries
WILDLIFE OF THE AMERICAN WEST ART MUSEUM (JACKSON, WYO.)
New quarters for wildlife art in Jackson Hole. il *Sunset (Central West edition)* 183:25 Jl '89
WILDLIFE POACHING *See* Poaching
WILDLIFE POPULATION CONTROL *See* Wildlife management
WILDLIFE PRINT FABRICS *See* Textile fabrics
WILDLIFE REFUGES *See* Wildlife sanctuaries
WILDLIFE REPELLENTS
In bad taste [use of saccharin to increase potency of foul tasting repellent; work of Gary Hollander and Mel Blum] il *Discover* 10:14 S '89
WILDLIFE RESCUE *See* Wildlife conservation
WILDLIFE SANCTUARIES
See also
Bird sanctuaries
Don't seek refuge here. C. Peterson. il *Sierra* 74:26+ S/O '89
Society lists ten most endangered refuges [Wilderness Society] *Wilderness* 52:3-4 Wint '88

Alaska
See also
Arctic National Wildlife Refuge (Alaska)
McNeil River State Game Sanctuary (Alaska)

Australia
See also
Brookfield Conservation Park (Australia)

California
See also
Arcata Marsh and Wildlife Sanctuary (Calif.)
Carrizo Plain (Calif.)
Wild Horse Sanctuary (Calif.)

Colorado
See also
Alamosa National Wildlife Refuge (Colo.)
Monte Vista National Wildlife Refuge (Colo.)

Florida
See also
Hobe Sound National Wildlife Refuge (Fla.)

Illinois
See also
Crab Orchard National Wildlife Refuge (Ill.)

Maine
See also
Moosehorn National Wildlife Refuge (Me.)

Molokai (Hawaii)
See also
Molokai Ranch Wildlife Park (Hawaii)

Montana
See also
National Bison Range (Mont.)

Netherlands
See also
Pieterburen Seal Sanctuary (Netherlands)

New Mexico
See also
Bosque del Apache National Wildlife Refuge (N.M.)
A land battle in New Mexico [sheep war] J. N. Baker. il *Newsweek* 114:27 S 18 '89

North Carolina
See also
Alligator River National Wildlife Refuge (N.C.)

WILDLIFE SANCTUARIES—cont.
Pacific Northwest
A small Christmas miracle: the great snow goose migration.
il *Sunset (Central West edition)* 181:188 D '88
Texas
See also
Aransas National Wildlife Refuge (Tex.)
WILDLIFE TELEMETRY *See* Biotelemetry
WILDMON, DONALD
about
As the 'clean TV' campaign heats up, ABC chills two new
shows. P. Freeman. il por *People Weekly* 31:153-4 My
22 '89
Bringing Satan to heel [interview] D. Winbush. il por *Time*
133:54-5 Je 19 '89
WILDWOOD INN (WARE, MASS.) *See* Ware (Mass.)—Hotels,
motels, etc.
WILENSKY-LANFORD, SHEILA
Children's booksellers and teachers: partners in literacy. il
Publishers Weekly 235:101-3 Ja 20 '89
WILENTZ, AMY
Haiti goes back. *The Nation* 249:669-70 D 4 '89
WILEY, JOHN P., JR.
Phenomena, comment and notes. See issues of Smithsonian
WILEY, KIM WRIGHT
A delicate balance. il *Health (New York, N.Y.)* 21:30+ My
'89
Why you can't get no (job) satisfaction. il *Mademoiselle*
95:122+ Je '89
WILEY, RALPH
Her gaze can daze. il pors *Sports Illustrated* 70 Special
Issue:119-22 F '89
Hit it a mile. il pors *Sports Illustrated* 70:34-6+ My 8 '89
The Hit Man. il pors *Sports Illustrated* 70:48-50+ Je 5 '89
The light and the lightning. il pors *Sports Illustrated* 71:38-42+
S 25 '89
A master of intimidation. il pors *Sports Illustrated* 70:66-8
Ap 10 '89
Putting the clamps on. il *Sports Illustrated* 70:42-4+ Ja 9
'89
Reaching for the ring. il pors *Sports Illustrated* 71:48-52
Ag 14 '89
Slick can play. il pors *Sports Illustrated* 70 Special Issue:56-8+
Ap '89
Superback!!! [cover story] il pors *Sports Illustrated* 71:38-42+
S 11 '89
about
From the publisher. D. J. Barr. por *Sports Illustrated* 70:4
Je 5 '89
WILEY, W. BRADFORD
about
Stubborn patriarch. C. Poole. il por *Forbes* 143:99+ F 6
'89
WILEY, WILLIAM
about
Zen and the art of William T. Wiley. K. Gregor. il pors
Art News 88:184-9 Ap '89
WILEY (JOHN) & SONS, INC. *See* John Wiley & Sons,
Inc.
WILFONG, TIMOTHY L.
Satellite pictures on a home computer. il *Weatherwise*
42:339-40 D '89
WILKE, HANNAH, 1940-
about
The art of healing. C. Langer. il *Ms.* 17:132-3 Ja/F '89
WILKEN, KAREN
Caro country: the artist's New York State sculpture studio
and fields. il por *Architectural Digest* 46:192-7+ Ag '89
WILKENS, LENNY
about
Cleveland's Cavaliers now class of the NBA. por *Jet* 75:50
Ja 16 '89
The Wayne and Lenny show. M. Lupica. pors *Esquire*
111:61-3+ Je '89
WILKERSON, DAVID
about
His prayers answered, evangelist David Wilkerson has a
divine hit running on the Great White Way. R. Arias.
il pors *People Weekly* 32:63-4 S 4 '89
WILKERSON, EDWARD
about
Blowing in from Chicago. F. Davis. il *The Atlantic* 263:71-3
F '89
WILKERSON, MARGARET B.
(jt. auth) See Gresham, Jewell Handy, and Wilkerson, Margaret
B.
WILKERSON, MARGARET B., AND GRESHAM, JEWELL
HANDY
The racialization of poverty. il *The Nation* 249:126-30+ Jl
24-31 '89
WILKES, ED
Something new under the sun. por *Nation's Business* 77:9
Ag '89
WILKES, JOHN
Sleep . . . at last. il *Health (New York, N.Y.)* 21:84+ Jl
'89

WILKES, JOHN J.
Checkpoint Hadrian. il maps *Natural History* p64-72 Ap
'89
WILKES, KEVIN
about
Kevin Wilkes: double life of a Princeton prefab. S. Stephens.
il por *Architectural Digest* 46:102-6+ Ap '89
WILKES, MICHAEL S.
(jt. auth) See Shuchman, Miriam, and Wilkes, Michael S.
WILKES, MICHAEL S., AND SHUCHMAN, MIRIAM
Pitching doctors. il *The New York Times Magazine* p88+
N 5 '89
What is too old? il *The New York Times Magazine* p58+
Je 4 '89
WILKES, PAUL, 1938-
The first test of childhood. por *Newsweek* 114:8 Ag 14
'89
WILKES, SEMA
about
When Sema Wilkes puts food on the table, her guests better
have a Boardinghouse reach. D. Chu. il pors *People Weekly*
32:139-40 S 18 '89
WILKINS, HEATH
about
Too young to die? [cover story] R. Rosenbaum. il pors
The New York Times Magazine p32-5+ Mr 12 '89
WILKINSON, ALEC, 1952-
Big sugar (I). il *The New Yorker* 65:41-2+ Jl 17 '89
Big sugar (II). il *The New Yorker* 65:42-3+ Jl 24 '89
WILKINSON, CHARLES F., 1941-
Water rights and wrongs. *Sierra* 74:35-6+ S/O '89
WILKINSON, DEBORRAH M.
Computer dis-ease. il *Essence* 19:14+ Mr '89
WILKINSON, FRANCIS
The gospel according to Randall Terry. il por *Rolling Stone*
p85-6+ O 5 '89
WILKINSON, HUTTON
about
A thirties revival. G. Greene. il *Architectural Digest*
46:194-201+ Mr '89
WILKINSON, KEITH D., AND OTHERS
The neuron-specific protein PGP 9.5 is a ubiquitin carboxyl-
terminal hydrolase. bibl f il *Science* 246:670-3 N 3 '89
WILKINSON, PETER
Darkness at the heart of town. il *Rolling Stone* p55-6+ O
5 '89
A fine madness. il pors *Gentlemen's Quarterly* 59:430-5+
S '89
WILKINSON, RUTH
about
A thirties revival. G. Greene. il *Architectural Digest*
46:194-201+ Mr '89
WILKINSON, STEPHAN
The practical genius of penny candy. il pors *Working Woman*
14:98-9+ Ap '89
The real truth about millionaires: you can become one.
il *Working Woman* 14:94-100+ My '89
WILKINSON, WALLACE
Education reform and economic competition [address, August
15, 1989] *Vital Speeches of the Day* 56:40-3 N 1 '89
WILKINSON, WILLIAM
The great Hinckley fire of 1894 [excerpt from Memorials
of the Minnesota forest fires in the year 1894] il *Natural
History* p54-5 Ja '89
WILL, GEORGE F.
[Column] See occasional issues of Newsweek
Prejudice against excellence. por *Conservative Digest* 15:15
Jl/Ag '89
WILL, JAMES E.
Must walls of hostility continue to divide? il *The Christian
Century* 106:1191-2 D 20-27 '89
WILL, MADELEINE
Educating students with learning problems. *The Education
Digest* 54:54-7 Ap '89
WILL
See also
Brainwashing
WILL OF GOD *See* God—Will
WILL POWER
Willpower workout [excerpt from Getting unstuck] S. B.
Simon. il *Ladies' Home Journal* 106:64+ Mr '89
WILL-WEBER, MARK
Training log. See issues of Runner's World
(jt. auth) See Delhagen, Kate, and Will-Weber, Mark
WILL-WEBER, MARK, AND POST, MARTY, 1951-
Racing report. See issues of Runner's World
WILL YOU MARRY ME? [opera] See Weisgall, Hugo, 1912-
WILLAMETTE RIVER VALLEY (OR.)
Farmers playing with fire [burning of grass seed threatens
air quality] J. Stiak. il *Sierra* 74:92-3 Mr/Ap '89
WILLAMETTE UNIVERSITY
Preserving quality: teacher training from a liberal arts perspec-
tive. J. B. Engel. il *Phi Delta Kappan* 70:475-7 F '89
WILLARD, FRED
about
What a card! M. Long. il por *Gentlemen's Quarterly* 59:148-9
Jl '89

WILLARD, HAL
At 90, the zombie shuffle. por *Newsweek* 113:10 F 20 '89

WILLARD, NEDD
The public as partners. il *World Health* p20-2 Ja/F '89

WILLARD-CROSS, AMY
The best gears of your life: how to buy the right bike. il *American Health* 8:80+ My '89

WILLCOX & GIBBS INC.
Repeat performance? T. Jaffe. *Forbes* 143:340 Ja 9 '89

WILLCOX PLAYA (ARIZ.)
Watching the sandhills in New Mexico and Arizona. il *Sunset (Central West edition)* 182:46 Ja '89

WILLE, CHRIS
Briefings. See issues of Audubon beginning September 1987

WILLEM BREUKER KOLLEKTIEF (MUSICAL GROUP)
Willem Breuker, & Kompany: Euro-bop, with a twist. M. Bourne. il pors *Down Beat* 56:28-30 My '89

WILLEMS, JOS L.
Computer analysis of the ECG. il *World Health* p21-3 Ag/S '89

WILLENS, MICHELE
Safety in numbers. *Harper's Bazaar* 122:28+ Je '89

WILLIAM, PRINCE OF GREAT BRITAIN, 1982-
about
Happy birthday, Prince Charming [cover story] J. Kaufman. il pors *People Weekly* 31:30-5 Je 26 '89

WILLIAM AND MARY, 1689-1702 *See* Great Britain—History—William and Mary, 1689-1702

WILLIAM COLLINS PLC
Craig to head all Murdoch book business; Chapman resigns from Collins; authors' reaction uncertain. por *Publishers Weekly* 235:10+ F 3 '89
Murdoch wins Collins, promises autonomy; Craig assesses Harper's new owner. V. Menkes. *Publishers Weekly* 235:16+ Ja 20 '89

WILLIAM DAVIS COMPUTER RESEARCH CENTER
Machine tools. M. Gaskie. il *Architectural Record* 177:122-7 O '89

WILLIAM MORRIS AGENCY
Living off the past. L. Gubernick. il *Forbes* 143:48-9+ Je 12 '89

WILLIAM MORROW & CO., INC.
Almost charmed [publication of cartoonist J. Callahan's autobiography] L. Fleischer. *Publishers Weekly* 235:66 Mr 17 '89

WILLIAM PATERSON COLLEGE OF NEW JERSEY
William Paterson College [Jazz Studies program] M. Bourne. *Down Beat* 56:23 Je '89

WILLIAM TYNDALE COLLEGE
Tribulation at William Tyndale. *Christianity Today* 33:49 My 12 '89

WILLIAMS, A. R.
A blow to Jamaica's treasure houses. il *Américas* 41 no1:8-13 '89
Chicago's Hancock Center. il *National Geographic* 175:174-85 F '89

WILLIAMS, ALYSON
about
Star quality. M. Southgate. por *Essence* 20:23 Je '89

WILLIAMS, ART
about
Ex-football coach Art Williams runs a winning insurance firm, but some people are crying foul. G. Stone. il pors *People Weekly* 32:161-2+ N 20 '89
The money on your life. J. B. Quinn. il *Newsweek* 113:46 My 8 '89
Tiger by the tail? H. Rudnitsky. il pors *Forbes* 144:40-1 Ag 7 '89

WILLIAMS, BILLY DEE
about
Billy Dee Williams tells how mother and twin sister helped career [cover story] A. Collier. il pors *Jet* 76:28-30 My 15 '89

WILLIAMS, BRIAN
about
The creative computer. B. Lawren. il *Omni (New York, N.Y.)* 11:28+ Je '89

WILLIAMS, BRUCE
about
Radio guru Bruce Williams offers soothing advice on-air. A. Abrahams. il pors *People Weekly* 32:119+ O 9 '89

WILLIAMS, CARL
about
The beatings go on. P. Putnam. pors *Sports Illustrated* 71:18-19 Jl 31 '89
Tyson destroys 'Truth' in 1½ min. Atlantic City bout. il pors *Jet* 76:52+ Ag 7 '89

WILLIAMS, CHERYL
Marfan syndrome: the silent killer. il *USA Today (Periodical)* 118:64-5 N '89

WILLIAMS, CHRISTOPHER C.
Advising the new administration. il *Black Enterprise* 19:48-53 Ja '89

WILLIAMS, CHUCK
about
Quake cabin conversion: Chuck Williams' 1906 house in San Francisco. B. D. Colen. il por *Architectural Digest* 46:290-5 My '89

WILLIAMS, CINDY
about
Cindy Williams and Bill Hudson really do act Just like family. M. Dougherty. il pors *People Weekly* 31:61-4 Je 5 '89

WILLIAMS, CLIFFORD
When mercy hurts. il *Christianity Today* 33:16-19 F 3 '89

WILLIAMS, DAVE H.
about
Black-and-white fever. C. Brown. il pors *Forbes* 143:197 Mr 20 '89

WILLIAMS, DAVE H., AND WILLIAMS, REBA, 1936-
Lawrence Nelson Wilbur revisited. il *American Artist* 53:42-3 F '89

WILLIAMS, DENNIS A.
A working wife. por *Essence* 20:12-13 Ag '89

WILLIAMS, DOUG
about
Doug Williams and wife embroiled in separation. il pors *Jet* 76:13-14 Je 19 '89
Doug Williams Foundation annual benefit awards $100,000 in scholarships. il pors *Jet* 76:28-9 Je 26 '89
Williams the conqueror. il *Sports Illustrated* 70:73 Ja 9 '89

WILLIAMS, EARLE R.
Letters [discussion of November 1988 article, The electrification of thunderstorms] *Scientific American* 261:8 Jl '89

WILLIAMS, ERNEST H.
(jt. auth) See Bunkley-Williams, Lucy, and Williams, Ernest H.

WILLIAMS, FIONA
about
On the rack & off the wall. J. McLaughlin. il por *Harper's Bazaar* 122:58 N '89

WILLIAMS, FRANK J.
Lincolniana in 1988. il pors *Antiques & Collecting Hobbies* 93:35-7 F '89

WILLIAMS, FRANKLIN H.
about
New prospects at the Barnes? W. Robinson. il por *Art in America* 77:21+ Mr '89

WILLIAMS, GEORGE WASHINGTON, 1849-1891
about
Stalking George W. Williams. J. H. Franklin. il por *American Visions* 4:28-31 Ap '89

WILLIAMS, GREG, AND WILLIAMS, PAT
The seasons of the garden. See issues of The Mother Earth News beginning July/August 1985

WILLIAMS, GREGG
No (more) mean feet. il *Sierra* 74:174-5 Ja/F '89

WILLIAMS, GUNTHER GEBEL- *See* Gebel-Williams, Gunther

WILLIAMS, GURNEY, 1941-
The master of math. il *Omni (New York, N.Y.)* 11:58-60+ Mr '89

WILLIAMS, HUBERT
Plain talk about drugs: users are bums. il *Reader's Digest* 134:129-30 Je '89

WILLIAMS, IRVING
about
The farming doctor. A. L. Berry. il por *American Visions* 4:44-5 Ag '89

WILLIAMS, JAMES H.
(tr) See Fang Lizhi. Keeping the faith

WILLIAMS, JERRY O., 1938-
about
Williams bids farewell. A. Edmond, Jr. por *Black Enterprise* 19:14 Ja '89

WILLIAMS, JIMY
about
Coming to terms. M. Gray. por *Maclean's* 102:54 O 16 '89

WILLIAMS, JOBETH
about
Jobeth Williams: "We still have hope". M. J. Bandler. por *Ladies' Home Journal* 106:124-5 N '89

WILLIAMS, JOY, 1944-
The last generation [story] il *Esquire* 111:178-80+ Ap '89
Save the whales, screw the shrimp. il *Esquire* 111:89-95 F '89

WILLIAMS, JUAN
Divided we fell: race and the '88 election. il pors *American Visions* 4:31+ F '89

WILLIAMS, JULIE
about
"No one's born a loser!". P. Skalka. *Reader's Digest* 134:21-2+ F '89

WILLIAMS, KIM
The Australian cinema. il *The Courier (Unesco)* 41:34-7 D '88

WILLIAMS, KIM-ERIC
Reforms enliven the Church of Sweden. *The Christian Century* 106:52-5 Ja 18 '89

WILLIAMS, KYMBERLY
Does your class make the grade? il por *Women's Sports & Fitness* 11:14 Mr '89

WILLIAMS, L. PEARCE (LESLIE PEARCE), 1927-
André-Marie Ampère. il por *Scientific American* 260:90-7
Ja '89
WILLIAMS, LESLIE PEARCE *See* Williams, L. Pearce (Leslie
Pearce), 1927-
WILLIAMS, LEWIS T.
Signal transduction by the platelet-derived growth factor
receptor. bibl f il *Science* 243:1564-70 Mr 24 '89
WILLIAMS, LINDA
Student entrepreneurs on campus. il *Black Enterprise*
19:169-72 F '89
WILLIAMS, LISA
about
Doug Williams and wife embroiled in separation. il pors
Jet 76:13-14 Je 19 '89
WILLIAMS, LORNA
It pays to go the extra meter. il *Nation's Business* 77:42-3
S '89
WILLIAMS, LOUISE
Cambodia's violent border camps. *World Press Review* 36:20
N '89
WILLIAMS, LUCINDA
about
Lucinda Williams. S. Rogers. por *Rolling Stone* p30 N 2
'89
Lucinda Williams: real. S. Simels. por *Stereo Review* 54:103
Mr '89
WILLIAMS, LYNN
about
Lynn's big break. M. Will-Weber. por *Runner's World* 24:117
O '89
WILLIAMS, MARGO E.
Wheels of fortune. il por *Black Enterprise* 20:100-2+ O '89
WILLIAMS, MARJORIE C.
The etiquette of ambition. il *Mademoiselle* 95:108+ Je '89
WILLIAMS, MARJORIE C., AND KAMEN, AL
America's most influential woman. il por *Reader's Digest*
135:71-6 D '89
WILLIAMS, MARJORY
about
Taking charge. D. Machan. il pors *Forbes* 143:154-6 Mr
6 '89
WILLIAMS, MARY ALICE
about
The human factor flourishes in the new biz. A. L. Ball.
il pors *Working Woman* 14:135-6 O '89
Star wars at the networks. R. Zoglin. il pors *Time* 133:70-1
Ap 3 '89
With Mary Alice Williams, NBC has a winner in the great
anchor sweepstakes. S. K. Reed. il pors *People Weekly*
32:44-6 Ag 7 '89
The wooing of Diane Sawyer sparks a fierce network battle.
il pors *People Weekly* 31:124 Ap 10 '89
WILLIAMS, MILAN
about
S. Africa tour furor basis for Milan Williams firing from
'Commodores' group. il por *Jet* 76:17 Ag 14 '89
WILLIAMS, MITCH
about
Wild thing. R. Telander. il pors *Sports Illustrated* 71:38-40+
Ag 28 '89
WILLIAMS, MYRA
about
Surviving marriage to the Killer. V. Balfour. il pors *People
Weekly* 32:48-53 Jl 10 '89
WILLIAMS, NEIL, 1934-1988
about
São Paulo diary. E. Leffingwell. il *Art in America* 77:55-7+
Ja '89
WILLIAMS, PAT
(jt. auth) *See* Williams, Greg, and Williams, Pat
WILLIAMS, PAUL, 1940-
about
Tru confessions. R. Leivenberg. il pors *Harper's Bazaar*
122:362-3+ S '89
WILLIAMS, PAUL W.
The twentieth century and beyond [address, May 8, 1989]
Vital Speeches of the Day 55:624-6 Ag 1 '89
WILLIAMS, RACHEL
about
Follow that girl. A. Keteyian. il pors *New York* 22:38-43
Mr 6 '89
WILLIAMS, REBA, 1936-
Pochoir printing. il pors *American Artist* 53:70-5 S '89
(jt. auth) *See* Williams, Dave H., and Williams, Reba, 1936-
about
Black-and-white fever. C. Brown. il pors *Forbes* 143:197
Mr 20 '89
WILLIAMS, REDFORD BROWN, 1940-
A saga of the heart [excerpt from The trusting heart] il
Health (New York, N.Y.) 21:68-9+ Ja '89
The trusting heart [excerpt] il *Psychology Today* 23:36-7+
Ja/F '89
Your anger can kill you [condensed from The trusting heart]
il *Reader's Digest* 135:183-4+ Ag '89
about
Getting to the heart of Type A's [interview] S. Findlay.
il por *U.S. News & World Report* 106:68 My 15 '89

Soothing the savage heart. J. Poppy. il *Esquire* 112:103-4
O '89
WILLIAMS, RHONDA Y.
about
Rhonda Williams delivers historic graduation speech at
University of Maryland. por *Jet* 76:19 Je 19 '89
WILLIAMS, RHYS H.
(jt. auth) *See* Demerath, N. J., and Williams, Rhys H.
WILLIAMS, RICHARD L.
Student demonstrations in China [statement, May 4, 1989]
Department of State Bulletin 89:48 Jl '89
U.S. response to changes in China [statements, July 13 and
20, 1989] *Department of State Bulletin* 89:27-30 O '89
WILLIAMS, ROBERT, III
Vitamins for vegetables. il por *The Mother Earth News*
117:38+ My/Je '89
WILLIAMS, ROBIN, 1952-
about
Actor. il pors *Life* 12:64-8 Spr '89
Robin Williams has a big premise! L. Grunwald. il *Esquire*
111:108-14+ Je '89
WILLIAMS, ROBYN
At the frontiers of science and technology. il *The Courier
(Unesco)* 41:27-9 D '88
WILLIAMS, ROGER
Eastern cultures experts on "self". *The Humanist* 49:40 N/D
'89
WILLIAMS, ROGER M.
Playing to win. il por *New Choices for the Best Years* 29:14+
N '89
Save or pave? [cover story] il *Americana* 17:23-9 My/Je
'89
WILLIAMS, ROWAN, 1950-
Ascetic enthusiasm: Origen and the early church. bibl il
History Today 39:31-7 D '89
WILLIAMS, SAM
Ageless tennis. il *The Saturday Evening Post* 261:90-2 O
'89
WILLIAMS, STEPHEN M.
Giving students a taste of the executive life. *Black Enterprise*
19:181-2 F '89
Will power. il por *Black Enterprise* 20:71-2 N '89
WILLIAMS, SUSAN
about
By adding up how much Uncle Sam owes, Susan Williams
gives us each day our daily debt. il por *People Weekly*
31:76 My 1 '89
WILLIAMS, TED
The bobcat. il *Country Journal* 16:86-90 Mr/Ap '89
Circus whales. il *Audubon* 91:16-18+ Mr '89
Dimples on a black desert. il *Audubon* 91:36-8+ S '89
Game laws weren't writ for fat cats. il *Audubon* 91:104-6+
Jl '89
Incineration of Yellowstone [cover story; with editorial com-
ment by Les Line] il map *Audubon* 91:4, 38-85 Ja '89
Sifting ashes in Yellowstone. il *Audubon* 91:30-2+ N '89
Tires, trees, terns, terrapins. il *Audubon* 91:26-8+ My '89
WILLIAMS, TED, 1918-
Fishing holes U.S.A. il pors maps *Popular Mechanics*
166:74-5+ My '89
about
Playing in the bonefish league. J. Skorupa. il pors *Popular
Mechanics* 166:28-9 Mr '89
WILLIAMS, TENNESSEE, 1911-1983
about
Orpheus descending [drama] Reviews
Commonweal 116:642-3 N 17 '89. G. C. Weales
The Nation 249:609-11 N 20 '89. T. M. Disch
The New Republic il 201:25-7 O 30 '89. R. Brustein
New York il 22:86-7 O 9 '89. J. Simon
The New Yorker 65:125 O 9 '89. E. Oliver
Newsweek il 114:86 O 9 '89. J. Kroll
Time il 133:102 Ja 2 '89. W. A. Henry
Tennessee fever. D. Rader. il *Harper's Bazaar* 122:364-5+
S '89
Tennessee rising. M. Roberts. il pors *Vogue* 179:706-9+ S
'89
WILLIAMS, TERRY M., 1948-
Cocaine kids: the underground American dream. il *New
Perspectives Quarterly* 6:21-5 Summ '89
about
Bright kids, bad business. E. Magnuson. il por *Time* 134:18
S 11 '89
WILLIAMS, THOMAS LANIER *See* Williams, Tennessee,
1911-1983
WILLIAMS, TONY
about
Tony Williams: still, the rhythm magician [interview] J.
Ephland. il pors *Down Beat* 56:20-3 My '89
WILLIAMS, VANESSA
about
Ex-Miss America Vanessa Williams overcomes her disgrace
by showing and singing The right stuff. J. Stark. il pors
People Weekly 31:48-9+ Ja 30 '89
Success is the best answer. E. Sherman. il pors *Ladies'
Home Journal* 106:44 S '89
There she is . . . dethroned Miss America stars as a call
girl. H. Newton. il pors *TV Guide* 36:20-3 F 4-10 '89

WILLIAMS, VANESSA—about—*cont.*
This year's Grammys: the women have their day. D. Hilt-brand. il pors *TV Guide* 37:6-7+ F 18-24 '89
WILLIAMS, VICKI
The horror is worth it. por *Newsweek* 114:14 O 9 '89
WILLIAMS, VIVIAN, D. 1986
about
'I love you perfect': a show that could save your life. D. Hudson. il por *TV Guide* 37:30-1 O 7-13 '89
WILLIAMS, WALTER E.
Campus racism. *National Review* 41:36-8 My 5 '89
WILLIAMS, WALTER FRED, 1929-
about
Forging the new Bethlehem. G. L. Miles. il por *Business Week* p108-10 Je 5 '89
WILLIAMS, WENDY
about
Wendy flew high in Indy. M. Noden. il pors *Sports Illustrated* 70:68+ My 15 '89
WILLIAMS, WENDY
Dark side of a classic beauty. il *National Wildlife* 27:42-8 F/Mr '89
WILLIAMS (A. L.) CORP. *See* A. L. Williams Corp.
WILLIAMS (DOUG) FOUNDATION *See* Doug Williams Foundation
WILLIAMS-CACICEDO, JEAN
about
Coat tales. M. Porges. il por *American Craft* 49:46-51 O/N '89
WILLIAMS-GARNER, DEBRA
Brown babies—for Brooke and Evan [poem] *Essence* 20:135 S '89
WILLIAMS INTERNATIONAL
Williams, Rolls plan to certify 1,900-lb.-thrust FJ44 in 1992 [business jet engine] S. W. Kandebo. il *Aviation Week & Space Technology* 131:47 N 6 '89
WILLIAMS-JONES, PEARL
Classical sounds. il *American Visions* 4:58-9 D '89
WILLIAMS-SONOMA, INC.
The King of Kitchens heads for the living room. M. Shao. il *Business Week* p63 F 13 '89
WILLIAMSBURG (VA.)
See also
Abby Aldrich Rockefeller Folk Art Center
Back to their future at Williamsburg. D. Young. il *Southern Living* 24:140+ Mr '89
Home on the Range with Bruce Hornsby. P. Puterbaugh. il por *Rolling Stone* p29 Jl 13-27 '89
Restoring America. B. Vila. il *Popular Mechanics* 166:106-8+ My '89
WILLIAMSBURG CHARTER
Teaching religious liberty—the wrong way [curriculum supplements for U.S. history courses] E. Doerr. il *The Humanist* 49:41-2 N/D '89
WILLIAMSON, ANNE
Prisoner. il pors *Film Comment* 25:57-60+ My/Je '89
Rubles of the game. il *Film Comment* 25:23-4+ Ja/F '89
WILLIAMSON, CHILTON
The right books. See issues of National Review through August 4, 1989
WILLIAMSON, ISABEL K.
about
StarTrails. D. H. Levy. *Sky and Telescope* 77:319 Mr '89
WILLIAMSON, JOHN, 1937-
Easing third world debt. il *USA Today (Periodical)* 117:28-9 Mr '89
WILLIAMSON, JUDITH, 1954-
Is consumer frenzy an outlet for people's growing feelings of powerlessness? *Utne Reader* p78 S/O '89
WILLIAMSON, LONNIE
Taking aim. See issues of Outdoor Life
WILLIAMSON, MICHAEL
(jt. auth) See Maharidge, Dale, and Williamson, Michael
WILLIAMSON, RAY A., 1938-
(jt. auth) See Logsdon, John M., and Williamson, Ray A., 1938-
WILLIAMSON, RICHARD S.
Toward the 21st century: the future for multilateral diplomacy [address, September 16, 1988] *Department of State Bulletin* 88:53-6 D '88
The United Nations: progress in the 1980s [address, October 19, 1988] *Department of State Bulletin* 89:68-71 F '89
WILLIAMSON, ROSEMARIE
Writing short humor. *The Writer* 102:20-2 My '89
WILLIAMSPORT (NFLD.)
Description
Tuning the rig. H. Oxenhorn. il *The Atlantic* 264:30+ S '89
WILLIAMSTOWN (MASS.)
Hotels, motels, etc.
Williamstown's Orchards. D. Symmers. il *Travel Holiday* 171:72 F '89
WILLIER, STEPHEN
Through dooms of love. por *Opera News* 53:12-14+ F 18 '89
WILLIMON, WILLIAM H.
(jt. auth) See Hauerwas, Stanley, 1940-, and Willimon, William H.

about
Willimon's project: does it make sense? W. L. Sachs. *The Christian Century* 106:412-14 Ap 19 '89
WILLIS, ALLEE
about
Adolescence lives at L.A.'s all-gal celeb pajama bash. P. Lansden. il pors *People Weekly* 32:147-8 N 27 '89
WILLIS, ANNE-MARIE
(jt. auth) See Fry, Tony, and Willis, Anne-Marie
WILLIS, BILL
about
A Moroccan jewel. C. Aillaud. il *Architectural Digest* 46:126-31+ Jl '89
WILLIS, BRUCE
about
Bruce Willis: Die hard, live easy. F. Lovece. por *Video* 12:17-18 F '89
Bruce Willis: from "wild man" to family man [interview] F. Robbins. il por *McCall's* 116:82+ Je '89
Cybill Shepherd and Bruce Willis are named as prime suspects in Moonlighting's untimely death. M. Dougherty. il pors *People Weekly* 31:112-13 My 29 '89
The Moonlighting mess—behind the feuding that almost killed the show [cover story] L. Farr. il pors *TV Guide* 37:2-4+ Ja 14-20 '89
WILLIS, CONNIE
Ado [story] il por *The Humanist* 49:13-15+ Mr/Ap '89
At the Rialto [fiction] il *Omni (New York, N.Y.)* 12:78-80+ O '89
WILLIS, JUDITH
Mumps and measles make a comeback. il *Consumers' Research Magazine* 72:23-6 S '89
Mumps makes a comeback. il *FDA Consumer* 23:12-14+ Jl/Ag '89
(jt. auth) See Young, Theresa A., and Willis, Judith
WILLIS, MARGARET E.
Kiroviana: the *glasnost* difference [cover story] il *Dance Magazine* 63:36-41 Jl '89
Memories of a Moscow mole: competing for gold and glory in Moscow. il *Dance Magazine* 63:54-7 D '89
WILLIS, THOMAS
Chicago at its prime. il *Opera News* 54:12-14+ O '89
WILLMOTT, PETER S.
about
Some unwelcome shoppers may drop in on Carson Pirie. B. Bremner. il *Business Week* p39-40 Ap 3 '89
WILLOW CREEK COMMUNITY CHURCH (SOUTH BARRINGTON, ILL.)
A church for bored boomers. V. Becker. il *Christianity Today* 33:25 O 6 '89
Full house at Willow Creek. B. Dolan. il por *Time* 133:60 Mr 6 '89
WILLOW STREET CARNIVAL (COMEDY TROUPE)
Onstage in the toddlin' town. J. Kroll. il *Newsweek* 113:64+ Je 19 '89
WILLOWBROOK STATE SCHOOL *See* Staten Island Developmental Center
WILLS, BARBARA SALISBURY
Theatre education: approaching a new decade. bibl f *Design for Arts in Education* 90:24-9 Ja/F '89
WILLS, BRET
Safe at home [photographs] il *Sports Illustrated* 70:88-99 Je 12 '89
WILLS, GARRY, 1934-
The dark legacy of the Enlightenment. il *The New York Review of Books* 36:9-11 Mr 30 '89
Evangels of abortion. bibl f il por *The New York Review of Books* 36:15+ Je 15 '89
In praise of censure. il *Time* 134:71-2 Jl 31 '89
Jesse Jackson: newsmaker of the year. *The Christian Century* 106:3-4 Ja 4-11 '89
Liberté, egalité, animosité. il *American Heritage* 40:36-45 Jl/Ag '89
Love in the lower depths. bibl f il *The New York Review of Books* 36:60-7 O 26 '89
The phallic pulpit. bibl f il *The New York Review of Books* 36:20+ D 21 '89
"Save the babies". il *Time* 133:26-8 My 1 '89
WILLS, JOAN
(jt. auth) See Tucker, Marc S., and Wills, Joan
WILLS
See also
Executors and administrators
Living wills
Where there's a will . . . [changes at the Isabella Stewart Gardner Museum] A. Higonnet. bibl f il *Art in America* 77:65-7+ My '89
Who left what behind: wills of famous blacks. R. Brown. il *Ebony* 44:136+ F '89
A will that protects your child [naming a guardian] S. Nielsen. *Good Housekeeping* 208:241 Ap '89
Write your will now! D. M. Topolnicki. il *Money* 18 Money Guide:126-7+ Fall '89
Anecdotes, facetiae, satire, etc.
This bier's for me. P. Nelson. il por *Esquire* 112:230-3 O '89

WILMARTH, CHRISTOPHER, 1943-1987
about
Poetry in glass and steel. R. Hughes. il *Time* 133:88 Je 26 '89
Reveries in glass and steel. A. Corn. il *Art News* 88:201 O '89
Second that emotion. K. Larson. il *New York* 22:46-7 Ag 7 '89
WILMERDING, JOHN, 1938-
Folk, or art? il *Antiques* 135:278-80 Ja '89
WILMINGTON (DEL.)
Banks
See also
Wilmington Trust Co.
Music
See also
OperaDelaware (Opera company)
WILMINGTON TRUST CO.
"They never put jackets on again". J. Novack. il por *Forbes* 144:120+ O 2 '89
WILMS' TUMOR *See* Kidneys—Cancer
WILPERT, CZARINA
Euphoria & beyond. *Commonweal* 116:695-7 D 15 '89
WILSHIRE, HOWARD GORDON, 1926-
about
Ethics and USGS [discussion of November 3, 1989 article, Ethics debate sends tremors through USGS] E. Marshall. *Science* 246:1548-9 D 22 '89
Ethics debate sends tremors through USGS. E. Marshall. il por *Science* 246:570-1 N 3 '89
WILSON, A. N. (ANDREW NORMAN), 1950-
C. S. Lewis, sins and all [excerpt from C. S. Lewis] il por *The New York Times Book Review* 94:1+ D 24 '89
WILSON, ALEX
Getting by without CFC's. il *The Mother Earth News* 120:110-14+ N/D '89
WILSON, ANDREW, 1923-
Grooming the *glasnost* generation. il *World Press Review* 36:41 Ja '89
WILSON, ANDREW NORMAN *See* Wilson, A. N. (Andrew Norman), 1950-
WILSON, AUGUST
about
The light in August. C. Brown. il por *Esquire* 111:116-18+ Ap '89
The piano lesson [drama] Reviews
Time il 133:69 Ja 30 '89. W. A. Henry
WILSON, BETTE
"God made you little and special"; ed. by Rebecca Nappi. il *Redbook* 173:84+ O '89
WILSON, BRENT
Reformation and responsibilities: a memo to members of the arts education establishment. bibl f *Design for Arts in Education* 90:27-35 My/Je '89
WILSON, BRIAN
about
Brian Wilson's Svengali has his wings clipped as he gives up his license to shrink. il pors *People Weekly* 31:97 Ap 17 '89
Landy loses license. M. Goldberg. pors *Rolling Stone* p27 My 18 '89
WILSON, CASSANDRA
about
Blindfold test. G. Santoro. il por *Down Beat* 56:43 F '89
Evening standards. B. Cullman. por *Vogue* 179:206 F '89
WILSON, CRAIG M., AND OTHERS
Amplification of a gene related to mammalian mdr genes in drug-resistant Plasmodium falciparum. bibl f il *Science* 244:1184-6 Je 9 '89
WILSON, CYNTHIA
Big O: he hasn't changed much. il pors *American Visions* 4:18+ F '89
WILSON, SIR DAVID, 1935-
Hong Kong [address, October 16, 1989] *Vital Speeches of the Day* 56:140-3 D 15 '89
WILSON, DICK, 1928-
The beatification of comrade Zhou Enlai. il pors *History Today* 39:7-10 Mr '89
WILSON, EDMUND, 1895-1972
The good war. *The New Republic* 200:21 My 29 '89
WILSON, EDWARD O., 1929-
The coming pluralization of biology and the stewardship of systematics. *BioScience* 39:242-5 Ap '89
Threats to biodiversity. bibl il *Scientific American* 261:108-12+ S '89
WILSON, EDWIN P.
about
Did it blow up Flight 103? D. Corn. il *The Nation* 248:153-4 F 6 '89
WILSON, GAHAN
Leavings [story] il *Omni (New York, N.Y.)* 11:48-50+ Ap '89
WILSON, GARY LEE, 1940-
about
The odd couple chasing Northwest Airlines. R. Grover. il pors *Business Week* p126 Ap 24 '89

WILSON, GEORGE
about
Brokers in the boondocks. M. Schifrin. il pors *Forbes* 143:228+ Je 26 '89
WILSON, GLENN
about
This job's a gas. F. Lidz. il por *Sports Illustrated* 70:62 My 29 '89
WILSON, HELEN MIRANDA
about
Helen Miranda Wilson at Sorkin. G. Henry. il *Art in America* 77:142-3 Jl '89
WILSON, HOWARD G., AND OTHERS
Lessons of Sunraycer [cover story] il *Scientific American* 260:90-7 Mr '89
WILSON, HUGH
about
Agent provocateur. D. Friedman. il por *Rolling Stone* p41 Ag 24 '89
WILSON, JACK M., AND REDISH, EDWARD F.
Using computers in teaching physics [cover story] bibl f il *Physics Today* 42:34-41 Ja '89
WILSON, JAMES M., AND OTHERS
Implantation of vascular grafts lined with genetically modified endothelial cells. bibl f il *Science* 244:1344-6 Je 16 '89
WILSON, JAMES Q., AND DIIULIO, JOHN J.
Crackdown [cover story] *The New Republic* 201:21-5 Jl 10 '89
WILSON, JAMES Q., AND KELLING, GEORGE L.
Making neighborhoods safe. il *The Atlantic* 263:46-52 F '89
WILSON, JANE WESTON
Backyard barbecue Italian style. il *New Choices for the Best Years* 29:64-9 Ag '89
WILSON, JOANN
about
Murder on the prairie. D. Turbide. il por *Maclean's* 102:45-6 Jl 17 '89
WILSON, JOHN ANTHONY BURGESS *See* Burgess, Anthony, 1917-
WILSON, JOYCE
The wardrobe [poem] *America* 161:357 N 18 '89
WILSON, KEMMONS
about
Kemmons Wilson changes his mind. M. Barrier. il pors *Nation's Business* 77:77-8 Mr '89
WILSON, LANFORD, 1937-
about
The rimers of Eldritch [drama] Reviews
The Nation 248:103-4 Ja 23 '89. T. M. Disch
WILSON, LARMAN C.
Can we oust Noriega? il *USA Today (Periodical)* 118:15 N '89
WILSON, LEILA FOSBURGH
One hundred years in the Adirondack wilderness. il *The Conservationist* 43:40-5 My/Je '89
WILSON, MARGO
(jt. auth) See Daly, Martin, 1944-, and Wilson, Margo
WILSON, MARY, 1944-
about
Mary Wilson to have her Beatles' limo auctioned. il por *Jet* 76:14 Ap 10 '89
WILSON, MAURA
about
The sporting life: winning form. P. Pacheco. il pors *Harper's Bazaar* 122:194-7+ O '89
WILSON, MELANIE
about
Mr. Whipple squeezed her first. I. Rudolph. por *TV Guide* 37:5 Ag 5-11 '89
WILSON, MICHAEL H.
about
Fighting the opposition [interview] il por *Maclean's* 102:41 S 25 '89
The hot spot on the Hill. M. Clark. il por *Maclean's* 102:48-9 My 1 '89
Wilson's trials. T. Tedesco. il *Maclean's* 102:2, 10-11+ Je 5 '89
WILSON, MINNA
about
British boxer's mom takes bout into her own hands. il por *Jet* 77:52-3 O 16 '89
WILSON, MOOKIE, 1956-
about
Birdland. F. Lidz. il pors *Sports Illustrated* 71:22-5 S 11 '89
WILSON, OTIS
about
The comeback chronicles. H. Hersch. il pors *Sports Illustrated* 71:38-44+ Jl 24 '89
WILSON, PORTERFIELD, D. 1989
about
Obituary
Jet por 75:52+ F 13 '89
WILSON, RAY
about
Ray Wilson: ESO's master optician. D. H. Smith. por *Sky and Telescope* 78:252 S '89

WILSON, RICHARD, 1926-
Report on reports: Air pollution, the automobile, and public health. *Environment* 31:25-7 My '89

WILSON, ROBERT, 1941-
about
The forest [drama] Reviews
Theatre Crafts il 23:46-8+ Ja '89. J. Calhoun

WILSON, ROBERT HINES
(jt. auth) See Grubb, W. Norton, and Wilson, Robert Hines

WILSON, ROSE CECIL O'NEILL *See* O'Neill, Rose Cecil, 1875-1944

WILSON, SHIRLEY
6 little love notes [story] il *Redbook* 172:54+ F '89

WILSON, T. A.
about
The U.S. Business Hall of Fame. W. Guzzardi. il por *Fortune* 119:131-2 Mr 13 '89

WILSON, THORNTON A. *See* Wilson, T. A.

WILSON, TONY
about
British boxer's mom takes bout into her own hands. il por *Jet* 77:52-3 O 16 '89

WILSON, WILLIAM GRIFFITH
about
The drunk who helped millions get sober. M. O'Connell-Cahill. il *U.S. Catholic* 54:10-12 F '89

WILSON, WILLIAM JULIUS
about
Dr. William Julius Wilson. D. C. Lyons. il pors *Ebony* 44:64-6 Ag '89

WILSON, WOODROW, 1856-1924
about
The Versailles Treaty and after [reprint from January 1924 issue] D. Grayson. *Current History* 88:20-3 Ja '89
War against reason. H. Fairlie. il *The New Republic* 201:58-62 N 6 '89

WILSON INNS
Kemmons Wilson changes his mind. M. Barrier. il pors *Nation's Business* 77:77-8 Mr '89

WILSON SPORTING GOODS CO.
For these companies, debt was just what the doctor ordered. M. D. Oneal and others. il *Business Week* p90-1 S 11 '89

WINANS, BEBE
about
Whitney Houston is happy to back up BeBe and CeCe Winans, and that's the gospel truth. il pors *People Weekly* 32:44 Jl 3 '89

WINANS, CECE
about
Whitney Houston is happy to back up BeBe and CeCe Winans, and that's the gospel truth. il pors *People Weekly* 32:44 Jl 3 '89

WINCHELL, WALTER, 1897-1972
Fiction
King of the Whispers. M. Herr. il *Esquire* 112:191-202 D '89

WINCHES
Power assist. S. L. White. il *Field & Stream* 94:88+ N '89

WINCKLER, SUZANNE
The Platte pretzel [with editorial comment by Peter A. A. Berle] il map *Audubon* 91:8, 86-102+ My '89

WINCOTT, MICHAEL
about
Leather report. A. Gabriel. pors *Rolling Stone* p161-5 Mr 23 '89

WIND, HERBERT WARREN, 1918-
A British victory in British weather. *The New Yorker* 65:97-103+ My 15 '89
Mr. Kramer and Mr. Becker. il *The New Yorker* 65:85-96+ O 16 '89
Strange redux. *The New Yorker* 65:68-77 Jl 24 '89

WIND, JAMES P., 1948-
The church's challenge in health care. *The Christian Century* 106:1201-4 D 20-27 '89
Stirring the ashes. il *The Christian Century* 106:102 F 1-8 '89

WIND *See* Winds
WIND, SOLAR *See* Solar wind
WIND GENERATORS *See* Wind power
WIND MILLS *See* Windmills
WIND POWER
See also
Windmills
"Turbine renewal". E. Paris. il *Forbes* 144:112 Ag 7 '89
Wind power. S. Vogel. il *Discover* 10:46-9 My '89

WIND PRESSURE
See also
Anemometers

WIND RIVER RESERVATION (WYO.)
Teens take charge [Youth Council formed after suicide epidemic] L. Eskin and D. Thunder. il *Scholastic Update (Teachers' edition)* 121:26-7 My 26 '89

WIND SHEAR
NASA tests indicate heavy rainfall can reduce lift at high angles of attack [transport aircraft wings] E. H. Phillips. il *Aviation Week & Space Technology* 131:64-5 Ag 28 '89
NASA will study heavy rain effects on wing aerodynamics [cover story] E. H. Phillips. il *Aviation Week & Space Technology* 130:38-9+ F 13 '89
Stalling for time [compressor stall on 747 during takeoff in strong crosswinds] J. Kulski. il *Flying* 116:110 My '89

WIND SHEAR DETECTORS
Airborne infrared system provides advance warning of turbulence. il *Aviation Week & Space Technology* 130:130-1 Je 19 '89
Escape from jaws of microburst [alert system at Stapleton International Airport] *Science News* 136:159 S 2 '89
Microburst radar may spur review of tower's role in aborting landings [Doppler radar tested at Denver] P. J. Klass. il *Aviation Week & Space Technology* 130:79+ My 1 '89

WIND SHIPS *See* Windships
WIND TRAINERS (BICYCLE EQUIPMENT) *See* Bicycles—Equipment

WIND TUNNELS
NASA adds to understanding of high angle of attack regime [cover story] W. B. Scott. il *Aviation Week & Space Technology* 130:36-8+ My 22 '89
NASA prepares to reopen transonic wind tunnel after major fan repairs. E. H. Phillips. il *Aviation Week & Space Technology* 131:61 Ag 7 '89
Rocketdyne developing facility for hypersonic propulsion tests. W. B. Scott. il *Aviation Week & Space Technology* 130:65 Ja 30 '89
Testing in a tempest [bicycle test] F. Zahradnik. il *Bicycling* 30:100+ O/N '89
Vulcan ends initial wind tunnel tests on VTOL, fan-in-wing Starfire model. E. H. Phillips. il *Aviation Week & Space Technology* 131:64+ N 13 '89

WIND TURBINES *See* Wind power
WINDBREAKS
Give them shelter. G. Williams and P. Williams. il *The Mother Earth News* 117:21 My/Je '89
Harvest the snow. B. Eftink. il *Successful Farming* 87:60 F '89
Planting field windbreaks. il *Successful Farming* 87:27 D '89

WINDGATE PRESS
Bringing West Coast history back to life. L. See. *Publishers Weekly* 235:33 Mr 31 '89

WINDHAM COUNTY (CONN.)
The country lawyer remembered [1930s] W. Domnarski. *The American Scholar* 58:283-8 Spr '89

WINDMERE CORP.
Windmere tries to comb out the kinks. G. DeGeorge. il por *Business Week* p44 Jl 24 '89

WINDMILL WEIGHTS
Collectors and collecting
Rural American artifact carries weight with collectors. D. B. Cummins. il *Antiques & Collecting Hobbies* 93:32-4 F '89

WINDMILLS
History
The medieval mill—a productivity breakthrough? R. Holt. il *History Today* 39:26-31 Jl '89

WINDOW BLINDS *See* Blinds
WINDOW BOXES *See* Flower boxes, planters, etc.
WINDOW CURTAINS AND DRAPERIES *See* Curtains and draperies
WINDOW DISPLAYS *See* Show windows
WINDOW GARDENS AND GARDENING
See also
Flower boxes, planters, etc.
Growing the "forbidden" fruit [tomatoes] D. G. Howard. il *The Saturday Evening Post* 261:30+ Ja/F '89

WINDOW ON CHINA (TAIWAN)
Window on China. A. Bahar. il *Antiques & Collecting Hobbies* 93:62-5 F '89

WINDOW SHADES
Slat drift and other conundrums. P. Patton. il *Esquire* 112:31 Ag '89

WINDOWS
See also
Dormers
Glazes and glazing (Glass)
Skylights
Bay brings light and storage to entry. il *Sunset (Central West edition)* 182:164 Ap '89
Bay-window bath. il *Better Homes and Gardens* 67:73 My '89
A bay with big impact. il *Southern Living* 24:158-9 Mr '89
Bigger by a bow. il *Southern Living* 24:119 O '89
Bow-bay for sink, counter. il *Sunset (Central West edition)* 182:136 Ap '89
Controlling your windows. *Southern Living* 24:118 O '89
Dress-up details [special section] K. Collier. il *The Family Handyman* 39:30-7 Ja '89

WINDOWS—*cont.*

Enough light and privacy with small windows. il *Sunset (Central West edition)* 182:120 F '89

Expanding the view by pulling in the wall. il *Sunset (Central West edition)* 182:172-3 My '89

Fabric-saving windows [Southwall Technologies Heat Mirror glazing] V. E. Gilmore. il *Popular Science* 235:38 D '89

High energy bills can be gone with the window. D. H. Dunn. il *Business Week* p172 Mr 20 '89

Hot and cloudy [Cloud Gel] V. E. Gilmore. il *Popular Science* 235:24 Ag '89

How to install a glass block window. D. Johnson. il *The Family Handyman* 39:38-9 Mr '89

Improving your home with windows [cover story; special section] D. Johnson. il *The Family Handyman* 39:27-40 F '89

Let there be natural light. il *McCall's* 116:93 Ap '89

Liven up with light. W. L. Nolan. il *Better Homes and Gardens* 67:67-70 Ap '89

New products: windows for historic renovation. il *Architectural Record* 177:114-15+ Ag '89

New views. M. Phair. il *Home Mechanix* 85:52-4+ Ag '89

New windows [bathrooms] il *Popular Mechanics* 166:107-8 Ap '89

Product reports 1990. il *Architectural Record* 177:85-9+ D '89

Visual appeal [cover story] T. Harack. il *Home Mechanix* 85:44-8+ S '89

Window for the stairwell. il *Sunset (Central West edition)* 182:154 Ap '89

Windows intended to leak [Laminar Air Flow Super Windows] V. E. Gilmore. il *Popular Science* 235:38+ D '89

Windows open any room. L. Stains. il *Good Housekeeping* 208:202+ Ap '89

Maintenance and repair

How to replace broken glass. D. Prestly. il *The Family Handyman* 39:54-6 Ja '89

Replace windows and add insulation. il *Workbench* 45:62-5 N/D '89

Photographs and photography

Windows of the world. J. Porterfield. il por *Modern Maturity* 32:51-6 Ap/My '89

WINDOWS, STAINED GLASS *See* Glass painting and staining

WINDOWS (COMPUTER PROGRAMS)

See also

DESQview (Computer program)

Object-oriented Mac windows. J. Amsterdam. il *Byte* 14:277-82+ Jl '89

PixC leaves windows overhead in the dust. B. Smith. il *Byte* 14:202 S '89

Superbase 4: bringing the power of windows to databases. M. Bryan. il *Personal Computing* 13:154-5 D '89

Turbo Pascal windowing system. C. J. Butler. il *Byte* 14:283-6+ F '89

What not doing Windows costs Lotus. K. H. Hammonds. il *Business Week* p152 O 30 '89

Windows for your words [word processors] M. Liskin. il *Personal Computing* 13:51-2+ My '89

Windows on the world [Microsoft's Presentation Manager strategy in conflict with Micrografx' Windows business] D. Churbuck. il pors *Forbes* 144:123+ D 25 '89

The wizard of Windows [J. P. Grayson of Micrografx] R. Lockwood. por *Personal Computing* 13:85 Jl '89

Wondering about Windows? J. Holtzman. il *Radio-Electronics* 60:81-4+ D '89

Development

A virtual toolkit for Windows and the Mac [XVT 1.1] R. Valdés. il *Byte* 14:209-10+ Mr '89

Testing

Ami. R. G. Sheffield. il *Compute!* 11:67-8 My '89

Ami reviewed. S. Morgenstern. il *Home Office Computing* 7:26+ Je '89

Domesticating Microsoft Windows [CASE:W] A. Lane. il *Byte* 14:205-7 Je '89

Entry-level DTP via Windows [Springboard Publisher] L. P. Lefkowitz. il *Personal Computing* 13:194 S '89

High-fashion UNIX on a PC [Hewlett-Packard Accelerated X Window Display Server] B. Smith. il *Byte* 14:205-6+ D '89

Illustrator: Adobe throws a curve [Adobe Illustrator for Windows] L. Kleinman. il *Personal Computing* 13:158-9 Ag '89

PM, Sun View, and the Mac [early benchmarks] F. Langa. *Byte* 14:6 Ja '89

Reaching critical mass: the arrival of Windows and Presentation Manager applications. R. Lockwood. il *Personal Computing* 13:109-11+ S '89

Text marries graphics under Windows [Ami Professional] D. L. Andrews. il *Byte* 14:84+ S '89

A window on word processing [Ami] L. Wood. il *Byte* 14:221-3 My '89

Windows gets real word processing [Ami 1.0] M. Antonoff. il *Personal Computing* 13:188+ Ap '89

Windows made clearer [ClearView and PubTech File Organizer] S. Miastkowski. il *Byte* 14:290 N '89

Words under Windows [Ami and Legend] C. O'Malley. il *Personal Computing* 13:114-15 Ag '89

The X Window system. D. Pountain. il *Byte* 14:353-4+ Ja '89

X window system on the march [Interactive Systems' 386/ix X11] T. Yager. il *Byte* 14:201-2+ O '89

WINDPOWER *See* Wind power

WINDS

See also

Aviation—Storm hazards

Dust storms

Fishing—Storm conditions

Hurricanes

Monsoons

Quasi-Biennial Oscillation

Stellar winds

Tornadoes

The bizarre wind of Unishima [American servicemen discover statuettes of Shinto deities Izanagi and Izanami on island during Korean War] W. J. Buchanan. il *Reader's Digest* 135:71-6 Ag '89

Did the roof of the world start an ice age? [research by William Ruddiman] R. A. Kerr. il *Science* 244:1441-2 Je 23 '89

Persistent circulation patterns [1988] A. J. Wagner. il *Weatherwise* 42:18-21 F '89

Rise of Tibet and Rockies set ice-age stage [research by William F. Ruddiman] R. Monastersky. *Science News* 135:309 My 20 '89

What brought on the 'icebox effect' [ice ages caused by winds; research by William Ruddiman and John Kutzbach] *U.S. News & World Report* 106:11 My 22 '89

Written in the winds: the great drought of '88. J. Namias. maps *Weatherwise* 42:85-7 Ap '89

Measurement

Neptune's wind speeds obtained by tracking clouds in Voyager images. H. B. Hammel and others. bibl f il *Science* 245:1367-9 S 22 '89

WINDSHEAR *See* Wind shear

WINDSHEAR DETECTORS *See* Wind shear detectors

WINDSHIELDS (AUTOMOBILES) *See* Automobiles—Windshields

WINDSHIPS

See also

Windstar Sail Cruises

Planesail: new era of wings at sea. il *Popular Mechanics* 166:13 Je '89

WINDSOR, EDWARD, DUKE OF, 1894-1972

about

Palais royal: how the Windsors lived. L. Field. il pors *New York* 22:23-4 Ja 16 '89

WINDSOR, WALLIS WARFIELD, DUCHESS OF, 1896-1986

about

Palais royal: how the Windsors lived. L. Field. il pors *New York* 22:23-4 Ja 16 '89

WINDSOR (N.C.)

Historic houses, sites, etc.

See also

Hope Plantation (Windsor, N.C.)

WINDSOR CHAIRS *See* Chairs

WINDSOR FUND

And now for some disarming words from our sponsor. C. A. Fried and M. Meyer. *Money* 18:43 Mr '89

Early bird got worm [J. B. Neff] A. Farnham. il por *Fortune* 119:62-3 Ja 2 '89

WINDSTAR FOUNDATION

Seeking higher ground. C. Charles and B. Samples. il por *National Wildlife* 27:29 Je/Jl '89

WINDSTAR SAIL CRUISES

Sir Francis Drake never had it so good. W. G. Flanagan. il *Forbes* 143:94-6 Ja 23 '89

WINDSURFING *See* Boardsailing

WINE

See also

Champagne

Cooking—Wine

Fine blanche

Viticulture

The big red one [Gigondas] W. Grimes. il *Esquire* 111:58 Mr '89

Burgundy ballyhoo. F. J. Prial. il *The New York Times Magazine* p48 Ap 16 '89

California's new gold rush: more luscious Chardonnays. L. Walczak. il *Business Week* p104 Jl 31 '89

Crowd pleasers. A. Bespaloff. il *New York* 22:94+ N 27 '89

The discreet charm of the bourgeoisie [Médoc wine in the Bordeaux region] G. Asher. il *Gourmet* 49:38+ Jl '89

First-rate finds [wines of Spain] F. J. Prial. il *The New York Times Magazine* p57 Ja 22 '89

Fronsac. G. Asher. il *Gourmet* 49:30+ Mr '89

Graves matters [white Bordeaux wines from France's Graves region] F. J. Prial. il *The New York Times Magazine* p94 N 19 '89

Greek revival. G. Asher. il *Gourmet* 49:62+ S '89

It was a very good year [1985 vintage of California Cabernet] A. Bespaloff. il *New York* 22:62+ O 2 '89

Italian wines with our Italian dishes. il map *Sunset (Central West edition)* 183:82 S '89

WINE INDUSTRY—France—*cont.*
Fronsac. G. Asher. il *Gourmet* 49:30+ Mr '89
Graves matters [white Bordeaux wines from Graves region] F. J. Prial. il *The New York Times Magazine* p94 N 19 '89
Pronounced differences [Pouilly-Fuissé] F. J. Prial. il *The New York Times Magazine* p63 Je 25 '89
Title search [Pichon-Longueville, Pichon-Baron, Pichon-Lalonde] F. J. Prial. il *The New York Times Magazine* p48 Ja 8 '89
A trip to Burgundy. G. Asher. il *Gourmet* 49:42+ Ap '89
Waiter, a magnum of your best Portland champagne. S. Toy. il *Business Week* p92+ D 11 '89
Germany (West)
See also
German Wine Academy
Great Britain
Britain's boast [champagne] F. J. Prial. il *The New York Times Magazine* p64 My 14 '89
Greece
Greek revival. G. Asher. il *Gourmet* 49:62+ S '89
Italy
Orvieto: fair lily of Umbria [Italian white wines] G. Asher. il *Gourmet* 49:52+ D '89
Piemonte revisited. G. Asher. il *Gourmet* 49:30+ Ja '89
Varied vino [Chianti] F. J. Prial. il *The New York Times Magazine* p58 Ap 30 '89
Vino fino [white Italian wines] F. J. Prial. il *The New York Times Magazine* p56 O 1 '89
New Zealand
Out of the ordinary. A. Bespaloff. il *New York* 22:55-6 Jl 17 '89

United States
See Wine industry
Western Europe
A connoisseur's SNIF: magnetic resonance aids in identification of wines [work of Gerard Martin] E. Corcoran. *Scientific American* 261:76 Jl '89
WINE JELLY *See* Jelly, jam, etc.
WINE LISTS
By the numbers [New York City restaurants] A. Bespaloff. il *New York* 22:100-1 My 1 '89
Hit lists [New York City restaurants] A. Bespaloff. il *New York* 22:116-17 Ap 10 '89
Julian of the spirits [J. Niccolini of the Four Seasons] A. Richman. il pors *Gentlemen's Quarterly* 59:150-7 Jl '89
Wine list geography. H. J. De Blij. *Focus (New York, N.Y.: 1950)* 39:37 Summ '89
WINE SERVICE
Nose job [working as a sommelier at Maurice] A. Richman. il *Gentlemen's Quarterly* 59:255-6 Mr '89
WINE SOCIETIES
See also
German Wine Academy
WINE STEWARDS *See* Wine service
WINE STORES
Wine [New York City] A. Bespaloff. il *New York* 22:66-7 My 1 '89
WINE TASTING
Business and pleasure: champagne tasting and toasting. E. Sahatjian. il *Working Woman* 14:107-10+ N '89
Going for the gold [comparative tastings in California] F. J. Prial. il *The New York Times Magazine* p64 O 15 '89
Guessing games. F. J. Prial. il *The New York Times Magazine* p43 My 28 '89
Tasting wines at their scenic sources [Monterey County, Calif. and Finger Lakes, N.Y.] J. O. Hamilton and R. Neff. il *Business Week* p156-7 My 15 '89
WINEGARDNER, ANN
Harvest of love. il por *Good Housekeeping* 209:130+ D '89
WINEGARTEN, RENEE
In pursuit of Cocteau. *The American Scholar* 58:436-43 Summ '89
WINER, DEBORAH GRACE
Close encounters. il *Opera News* 54:28-31+ S '89
"I can't go on". il *Opera News* 53:14-16 Je '89
Rapid transit [cover story] il pors *Opera News* 53:8-11+ F 4 '89
WINERIES *See* Wine industry
WINERIP, MICHAEL
My wife, the sportswriter. il *Glamour* 87:188 Jl '89
WINES, MICHAEL
Shaking up Justice [cover story] il pors *The New York Times Magazine* p22-3+ My 21 '89
WINFIELD, DAVE, 1951-
about
Houston jury decides Winfield already wed. il pors *Jet* 76:28-9 Jl 17 '89
An uncommon marriage. il pors *People Weekly* 32:79 Ag 7 '89
Winfield must pay support, plans appeal of decision. pors *Jet* 76:50 Jl 31 '89
WINFIELD, PAUL
about
Paul Winfield. M. Leahy. por *TV Guide* 37:16 S 23-29 '89

WINFREY, OPRAH
Wind beneath my wings [cover story] il pors *Essence* 20:44-6+ Je '89
about
The importance of being Oprah [cover story] B. G. Harrison. il pors *The New York Times Magazine* p28-30+ Je 11 '89
A new look at liquid diets. G. L. Blackburn. il *Prevention (Emmaus, Pa.)* 41:100-2 Ap '89
Oprah invites you to dinner. E. Byron. il por *Redbook* 173:102-3+ Ag '89
Oprah reveals her battle to stay slim on dieting segment of her TV show. il por *Jet* 77:14 D 4 '89
Oprah Winfrey. M. Angelou. il por *Ms.* 17:88-9 Ja/F '89
Oprah Winfrey a hit with White House kitchen staff. il *Jet* 76:61 Jl 17 '89
Oprah Winfrey gives gift of $1 million to Morehouse to help educate black men. il por *Jet* 76:4 Je 5 '89
Oprah Winfrey: how truth changed her life. J. Culhane. por *Reader's Digest* 134:101-5 F '89
Oprah's private life: the inside story. L. DePaulo. il pors *TV Guide* 37:2-6 Je 3-9 '89
The richest woman on TV? Oprah! [cover story] A. Feinberg. il pors *TV Guide* 37:2-7 Ag 26-S 1 '89
There's Oprah, Jackée, Robin Givens—and a break men may not deserve [cover story] E. Warren. il pors *TV Guide* 37:4-5+ Mr 18-24 '89
WING, BETSY
(tr) See Johnson, Thomas. Caviar wishes and vodka dreams
WING, JAMES
about
Chinese head tax haunts Canada. C. Bright. il por *The Progressive* 53:13-14 Ap '89
WINGATE, JOHN, 1921-
about
John Wingate's hard fall: a onetime radio star ends up broke and homeless. E. Tivnan. il pors *New York* 22:50-5 Mr 13 '89
WINGS HOLDINGS, INC.
U.S. must assess buyout bid's impact on safety at Northwest [KLM's role in Wings Holdings' bid under scrutiny] *Aviation Week & Space Technology* 130:92-3 Je 26 '89
Wings Holdings chief pledges to keep Northwest growing [A. A. Checchi] C. Fotos. *Aviation Week & Space Technology* 130:90-1 Je 26 '89
Wings Holdings' purchase of Northwest could become blueprint for future LBOs. *Aviation Week & Space Technology* 131:22 Ag 14 '89
WINKELMAN, BABE
about
Playing all the anglers, TV's Babe Winkelman hooks a huge piscatorial audience. J. Friedman. il por *People Weekly* 32:132-3 S 11 '89
WINKELMAN, STANLEY J.
Why big-name stores are losing out. il por *Fortune* 119:131-2 Ja 16 '89
WINKIES (PICTURES)
Winky king [R. Globus' buyout of Vari-Vue inventory] *The New Yorker* 65:34-5 My 8 '89
WINKLE-PICKERS (TERM)
Winkle-pickers of the press. W. Safire. il *The New York Times Magazine* p16+ Jl 9 '89
WINKLER, IRWIN
about
Devoted to betrayal. J. Cameron. il por *American Film* 15:48-53 O '89
Do four Rockys equal one 'Round midnight? K. Turan. por *Gentlemen's Quarterly* 59:117+ D '89
WINN, IRA JAY
Civilizing the dialogue in the forgetting society. *Phi Delta Kappan* 70:630-1 Ap '89
WINN, PETER
Socialism fades out of fashion. il *The Nation* 248:882-6 Je 26 '89
WINNEBAGO INDUSTRIES, INC.
Rough ride. R. Reiff. il *Forbes* 143:12 Ja 9 '89
WINNER, LANGDON
The era of the enhanced athlete. il *Technology Review* 92:22 F/Mr '89
From heresy to conventional wisdom. il *Technology Review* 92:18 Ag/S '89
Getting the most out of OTA. il por *Technology Review* 92:19+ N/D '89
Who needs HDTV? por *Technology Review* 92:20 My/Je '89
WINNER, MICHAEL
about
A chorus of disapproval [film] Reviews
The New Republic 201:26-7 S 11 '89. S. Kauffmann
WINNETKA (ILL.)
Crime
Diary of a tragedy [L. Dann's shooting spree in school in 1988] J. Bultman. il por *Parents* 64:105-10 My '89
Education
How the school responded [shooting spree aftermath] J. Bultman. il *Parents* 64:108-9 My '89

WINNING *See* Success

WINNIPEG (MAN.)

Police

A death in Winnipeg [policeman R. Cross testifies on role in shooting death of native leader J. J. Harper] P. Kaihla. il por *Maclean's* 102:16 S 11 '89

A final act of despair [suicide of K. Dowson, police inspector involved in investigation into shooting death of native J. J. Harper] B. Bergman. *Maclean's* 102:22 N 13 '89

An unfolding tragedy [suicide of police inspector K. Dowson disrupts inquiry into shooting death of native leader J. J. Harper] P. Kopvillem. il por *Maclean's* 102:23 O 2 '89

WINOGRAD, ISAAC J., AND OTHERS

Great Basin calcite vein and the Pleistocene time scale [discussion of December 2, 1988 article, A 250,000-year climatic record from Great Basin vein calcite: implications for Milankovitch theory] *Science* 246:262-3 O 13 '89

WINOKUR, L. A.

Who won what at AT&T? il *The Progressive* 53:29-32 D '89

WINPISINGER, WILLIAM W.

Economic patriotism in a global economy [address, December 8, 1988] *Vital Speeches of the Day* 55:220-2 Ja 15 '89

Parting shot: a labor leader blasts the Democrats. il *The Progressive* 53:28-30 Jl '89

WINSTANLEY, GERRARD, 1609-1676

about

Gerrard Winstanley: England's pioneer Green? I. C. Bradley. bibl il *History Today* 39:12-17 Ag '89

WINSTON, CLIFFORD, 1952-

(jt. auth) *See* Morrison, Steven A., 1951-, and Winston, Clifford, 1952-

WINSTON, STEPHANIE

about

How to organize your office [interview] K. Kane. por *Home Office Computing* 7:58 S '89

WINSTON-SALEM (N.C.)

Historic houses, sites, etc.

See also

Old Salem, Inc.

WINTER, ANNETTE

Money. *See* issues of Modern Maturity beginning October/November 1989

What should I do? *See* issues of Modern Maturity through August/September 1989

WINTER, MIRIAM THERESE

The women-church movement [cover story] *The Christian Century* 106:258-60 Mr 8 '89

WINTER, TERRY

about

Terry Winter: "explainer evangelist". L. K. Tarr. il por *Christianity Today* 33:47 Mr 17 '89

WINTER

See also

Cold weather

December

February

January

Snow

Snowstorms

Let it snow, let it snow. S. Begley. il *Newsweek* 113:67 F 6 '89

Locking time: life at the edge of winter. D. Kappel-Smith. il *Country Journal* 16:73-6 N/D '89

Snow season. P. Steinhart. il *Reader's Digest* 134:145-50 Ja '89

Winter's moon. H. Borland. il *Audubon* 91:37 Ja '89

Photographs and photography

Picture winter. J. Adams. il *Petersen's Photographic Magazine* 17:16-18+ F '89

Snow cover. P. Crowe. il *Country Journal* 16:42-7 Ja '89

WINTER (TERRY) CHRISTIAN COMMUNICATIONS *See* Terry Winter Christian Communications

WINTER ANTIQUES SHOW *See* Antiques—Exhibitions

WINTER CLOTHING *See* Clothing, Cold weather

WINTER CRUISES *See* Cruising

WINTER DEPRESSION *See* Seasonal affective disorder

WINTER DRIVING *See* Automobile driving—Winter driving; Truck driving—Winter driving

WINTER FISHING *See* Fishing, Winter

WINTER FLYING *See* Aviation—Winter flying

WINTER GARDEN *See* World Financial Center (New York, N.Y.). Winter Garden

WINTER GARDENS (MORECAMBE, ENGLAND)

Sleeping beauty. T. Aldous. il *History Today* 39:4-5 F '89

WINTER HUNTING *See* Hunting

WINTER MAINTENANCE OF AUTOMOBILES *See* Automobiles—Maintenance and repair

WINTER PEOPLE [film] *See* Motion picture reviews—Single works

WINTER PROTECTION OF PLANTS *See* Plants—Protection

WINTER RESORTS *See* Resorts

WINTER SLEEP *See* Hibernation

WINTER SOLSTICE

First light at an Irish tomb [roof slit designed to catch sun's rays at solstice; research by Tom P. Ray] *Science News* 135:88 F 11 '89

Irish mist [tomb aligned with winter solstice; research by Tom P. Ray] J. Horgan. il *Scientific American* 260:22+ Ap '89

A place in the sun for the early Irish [tomb sited to receive sun on winter solstice] il *U.S. News & World Report* 106:13-14 F 6 '89

World's oldest (and quietest) observatory? [Irish tomb aligned with winter solstice; research by Tom P. Ray] il *Sky and Telescope* 78:241-2 S '89

WINTER SPORTS

See also

Curling (Sport)

Hockey

Ice boats and ice boating

Ski racing

Skiing

Sledding

Snowboarding

Snowmobiles and snowmobiling

Snowshoes and snowshoeing

Convert to winter sports. J. Rogoznica. *Working Woman* 14:122 F '89

WINTER SQUASH *See* Squashes

WINTER SQUASH COOKING *See* Cooking—Vegetables

WINTER VACATIONS *See* Vacations

WINTERS, CATHERINE

Summer camp: off to a great start. il *Parents* 64:82+ My '89

WINTERS, MARK

Jim Courier: quietly coming of age [interview] il por *World Tennis* 36:80-1+ F '89

WINTERS, SHELLEY

Shelley Winters [excerpt from Shelley II] il por *Good Housekeeping* 209:91+ Ag '89

about

Who's minding the store? L. Fleischer. *Publishers Weekly* 236:49 S 8 '89

THE WINTER'S TALE [drama] *See* Shakespeare, William, 1564-1616

WINTHROP, ELIZABETH

Bear and Mrs. Duck [story] il *Parents* 64:139-43 My '89

WINTHROP ROCKEFELLER FOUNDATION

Mahlon A. Martin heads Winthrop Rockefeller Foundation. il pors *Ebony* 44:56+ Ag '89

Martin named head of Rockefeller Foundation. por *Jet* 76:24 My 22 '89

WINTOUR, ANNA

about

What's in a name? N. Darnton. il pors *Newsweek* 113:62-3 Je 5 '89

WIPP *See* Waste Isolation Pilot Plant (N.M.)

WIRE

See also

Electric wire and wiring

WIRE ROPE MACHINES

Landmark [Roebling Eighty-ton Wire Rope Machine] *The New Yorker* 65:50-1 N 6 '89

WIRE SERVICES *See* News agencies

WIRED [film] *See* Motion picture reviews—Single works

WIRELESS CABLE TELEVISION *See* Multichannel multipoint distribution service

WIRELESS HEADPHONES *See* Headphones

WIRELESS TELEPHONE *See* Radiotelephone

WIREMAN, BILLY O.

The American perspective, five key questions [address, March 31, 1989] *Vital Speeches of the Day* 55:538-40 Je 15 '89

WIRETAPPING

See also

Watergate case

Bug detector [cover story] L. K. Ross. il *Radio-Electronics* 60:42-4+ Je '89

Eavesdropping left and right [Cincinnati Bell implicated in wiretapping scandal] G. Flannery. il *The Nation* 248:516-18+ Ap 17 '89

In tapes we trust: Wall Street bugs itself. C. Byron. il *New York* 22:40-1 O 23 '89

Tracking down bugs using a spectrum analyzer. R. A. Bowen. il *Radio-Electronics* 60:33-7 Je '89

WIRING, ELECTRIC *See* Electric wire and wiring

WIRTH, DAVID A.

Climate chaos. *Foreign Policy* 74:3-22 Spr '89

(jt. auth) *See* Prickett, Glenn T., and Wirth, David A.

WISCHNIA, BOB, 1950-, AND PORTZ-SHOVLIN, EILEEN

The human race. *See* issues of Runner's World

WISCONSIN

See also

Booksellers and bookselling—Wisconsin

Child welfare—Wisconsin

Door County (Wis.)

Fishing—Wisconsin

Marriage law—Wisconsin

Paleobotany—Wisconsin

Public welfare—Wisconsin

Politics and government

It's money that matters [author's Senate campaigns; cover story] E. Garvey. il *The Progressive* 53:17-21 Mr '89

WISCONSIN—Politics and government—*cont.*
My life as a congressional candidate. M. G. Michaelsen. *The American Spectator* 22:24-5 N '89

Race relations
Mississippi of the North [protests over Chippewa fishing rights] D. Parmentier. il por *The Humanist* 49:17-19+ S/O '89
Spearing fish, playing 'chicken'. J. Oberly. il *The Nation* 248:844-5+ Je 19 '89
The Wisconsin fishing war [spearfishing by Chippewa Indians] il *Sports Illustrated* 70:16 My 15 '89

WISCONSIN TOY CO., INC.
Barbies on the cheap. J. Harris. il por *Forbes* 144:116+ D 25 '89

WISDOM
Just think . . . [national commitment to thinking and wisdom] S. K. Sheinbaum. *New Perspectives Quarterly* 6:64 Spr '89

Religious aspects
Blending salt and spice, joining wisdom and prophecy [Latin American Christians; cover story] B. C. Lane. il *The Christian Century* 106:499-502 My 10 '89
Wising up. P. J. Ryan. *America* 161:127 Ag 26-S 2 '89

WISE, ARTHUR E., AND GENDLER, TAMAR
Rich schools, poor schools. *The Education Digest* 55:3-7 D '89

WISE, DANIEL
Rainy-day plan. il *New York* 22:121-2+ D 4 '89

WISE, DAVID, 1930-
K.G.B. defector Gundarev: it's cold coming out [cover story] il *The New York Times Magazine* p36-9+ S 17 '89

WISE, DEBRA
Rent and rave: look like a million on borrowed time. il *Glamour* 87:176 D '89

WISE, WENDY M.
The Black enterprise executive recruiter directory. il *Black Enterprise* 19:105-8 F '89

WISE, WILLIAM
Easter on Mulberry Bend [poem] il *McCall's* 116:37-9 Ap '89

WISE MEN *See* Magi

WISEGUY [television program] See Television program reviews—Single works

WISEMAN, CARTER
Cityscape. See occasional issues of New York

WISEMAN, SHIRLEY
about
Building wealth—house by house. L. Washer. il por *Working Woman* 14:97 My '89

WISENBERG, S. L.
Brunch. *The New Yorker* 64:24-5 Ja 9 '89

WISENER FAMILY
about
Jenny in a barn. G. Baxter. il *Flying* 116:130+ Ag '89

WISHIK, DEBRA
A fair exchange. il *Travel Holiday* 172:58-63 D '89
Home, suite home. il *Travel Holiday* 172:92-5+ Jl '89

WISHNER, INA
Waiting patiently [poem] il *Organic Gardening* 36:66 Mr '89

WISHON, PHILLIP M., AND HUANG, ALLEN
Pet-associated injuries: the trouble with children's best friends. bibl il *Children Today* 18:24-7 My/Je '89

WISNER, BILL
A boy, a bird, and a book. il por *Audubon* 91:78-81 My '89

WISNEWSKI, ROBERT
about
Robert Wisnewski. V. R. Rivers. il por *American Artist* 53:58-63 My '89

WISSE, RUTH R.
Between Passovers. *Commentary* 88:42-7 D '89
Jewish guilt and Israeli writers. *Commentary* 87:25-31 Ja '89
No left turn. *The New Republic* 200:23-7 My 22 '89

WISSENSCHAFTSZENTRUM BERLIN FÜR SOZIALFORSCHUNG
Stirling in Berlin. D. Dietsch. il *Architectural Record* 177:94-101 Ja '89

WIT AND HUMOR *See* Humor
WITCH DOCTORS *See* Medicine men
WITCHCRAFT
See also
Medicine men
Voodooism

Taxation
The tax-exempt witch [coven of witches deserves tax-exempt status as a legitimate religious group] T. K. Jones. *Christianity Today* 33:15 O 6 '89

WITCHCRAFT IN ART
Witch trial memorial [Salem, Mass.] il *American History Illustrated* 23:6 Ja '89

WITCHEL, ALEX
Laughter, tears and the perfect martini. il pors *The New York Times Magazine* p42-3+ N 12 '89

WITHERS, PAMELA MILLER
Good stress/bad stress. il *Working Woman* 14:124-6 S '89
Were you born for each other? *McCall's* 116:56+ F '89

WITHEY, ANNIE
about
A feud that's really popping. A. Miller. il por *Newsweek* 114:52 Jl 24 '89

WITHHOLDING TAX
IRS to implement backup withholding. P. N. Strassels. il *Nation's Business* 77:68 Mr '89
Rerouted refunds and other reasons to adjust withholding. P. N. Strassels. il *Nation's Business* 77:70 Ag '89
A rose by any other name [independent contractors] P. N. Strassels. il *Nation's Business* 77:74 My '89
A smaller bite out of summer pay [payroll withholding taxes] L. Wiener. il *U.S. News & World Report* 106:68 Je 5 '89
Withholding allowances: are you on target for 1989 taxes? M. Rowland. *Working Woman* 14:39 Ag '89

WITHNAIL AND I [film] See Motion picture reviews—Single works
WITHOUT A CLUE [film] See Motion picture reviews—Single works
WITHOUT APOLOGIES [drama] See Thomas, Thom
WITKIN-LANOIL, GEORGIA
Emotional best. See occasional issues of Health (New York, N.Y.) beginning July 1985 through July 1988

WITNESS BEARING (CHRISTIANITY)
See also
Prophecy (Christianity)
The Kingdom of God: what role do we play? W. A. Barry. *America* 161:165-6 S 23 '89

WITNESSES
See also
Expert evidence (Law)
Investigating eyewitness memory mishaps. B. Bower. *Science News* 135:134 Mr 4 '89
The littlest victim [interview with five year old murder witness J. Royal] V. Gladstone. il pors *Life* 12:16+ O '89
The littlest witness may testify about her friend's killing [four year old J. Royal to testify against M. Ward in Miami murder trial] M. Brower. il pors *People Weekly* 31:108-10 Ap 24 '89
The sex-abuse puzzle [doubts about child witnesses] D. Gelman. il *Newsweek* 114:99-100 N 13 '89

WITT, CYNTHIA
English and journalism: reaching the same goal. *The Education Digest* 55:51-3 N '89

WITT, KERSTIN
Abortion in the Soviet Union. *World Press Review* 36:55 Ag '89

WITT, PAUL JUNGER
about
A creative collaboration: softening a modern house in Los Angeles. M. Frank. il pors *Architectural Digest* 46:130-7 Ag '89

WITTIG, PAT
Persistent peril. il map *Organic Gardening* 36:66-72 F '89

WITZENBURG, GARY
Street-smart winter driving. il *Reader's Digest* 134:25-8 Ja '89

WIVES
See also
Adultery
Artists' wives
Billionaires' wives
Congressmen's wives
Divorce
Executives' wives
Homemakers
Husbands
Lawyers' wives
Marriage
Married couples
Married women
Politicians' wives
Presidents—Wives
Servicemen's wives
Widows
Wife abuse

Anecdotes, facetiae, satire, etc.
Help! I need a wife. P. Yost. il *Good Housekeeping* 209:136 S '89
Wet behind the ears. P. F. McManus. il *Outdoor Life* 183:128+ F '89

WIVES AND THEIR CHEATING HUSBANDS (ORGANIZATION) *See* WATCH (Organization)
WIZARD OF OZ (FICTIONAL CHARACTER)
Collectibles
The collectibles of Oz. R. Reed. il *Antiques & Collecting Hobbies* 94:32-4 Jl '89
THE WIZARD OF OZ [film] See Motion picture reviews—Single works
THE WIZARD OF OZ LIVE! [musical] See Musicals, revues, etc.—Reviews—Single works
WKRC (CINCINNATI, OHIO: RADIO STATION) *See* Radio stations

WLODAWER, ALEXANDER, AND OTHERS
Conserved folding in retroviral proteases: crystal structure of a synthetic HIV-1 protease. bibl f il *Science* 245:616-21 Ag 11 '89

WM. WRIGLEY JR. CO.
Two-timing [original Doublemint Twins J. and J. Boyd] B. Greene. pors *Esquire* 111:57-9 Je '89

WNTR (WASHINGTON, D.C.: RADIO STATION) *See* Radio stations

WNYC (NEW YORK, N.Y.: TELEVISION STATION) *See* Television stations

WNYW (NEW YORK, N.Y.: TELEVISION STATION) *See* Television stations

WODICZKO, KRZYSZTOF
about
Around the Mall and beyond. E. Park. il *Smithsonian* 19:24+ Ja '89

WOEHRLE, CHARLES
about
My brother, my twin. G. Rosenblum. il pors *New Choices for the Best Years* 29:83-5 Ap '89

WOEHRLE, RICHARD
about
My brother, my twin. G. Rosenblum. il pors *New Choices for the Best Years* 29:83-5 Ap '89

WOELL, J. FRED
An ambiguous art: the jewelry of J. Fred Woell. B. Freudenheim. il *American Craft* 49:32-5 Ap/My '89

WOERNER, MANFRED
about
NATO Secretary General stresses West's lead in arms negotiations. K. F. Mordoff. *Aviation Week & Space Technology* 130:105 F 20 '89

WOESSNER, RUSSELL
All-Philadelphia Jazz. il por *Down Beat* 56:24-5 O '89

WOETZEL, DAMIAN
about
Woetzel ascends at NYCB. S. Reiter. il por *Dance Magazine* 63:7 F '89

WOHL, AMY
about
Computer-buying trends [interview] N. Sullivan. por *Home Office Computing* 7:63 S '89

WOHLFAHRT'S (KÄTHE) CHRISTKINDLMARKT *See* Käthe Wohlfahrt's Christkindlmarkt

WOHLFORTH, CHARLES P.
Black gold. *The New Republic* 201:20+ S 18-25 '89

WOIWODE, LARRY
A brief fall [story] *The New Yorker* 65:46-58+ D 4 '89

WOJCICKI, ED
Give to beggars for Christ's sake [with readers' comments] *U.S. Catholic* 54:14-20 Ap '89

WOJNAROWICZ, DAVID, 1954-
about
David Wojnarowicz At P.P.O.W. H. Cotter. il *Art in America* 77:180 Je '89

WOJTYLA, KAROL *See* John Paul II, Pope, 1920-

WOLD, BARBARA
(jt. auth) *See* Mueller, Paul R., and Wold, Barbara

WOLDROP, BOB
about
To market, to market. N. C. Baker. il por *Nation's Business* 77:61 Ja '89

WOLF, BRUCE
about
Work (and play) in progress. il *Working Woman* 14:162-7 N '89

WOLF, DOUGLAS
Superfund implementation: the polluter must be made to pay. bibl f *Environment* 31:42-4 Ja/F '89

WOLF, JEANNE
"I've finally learned how to be happy". il pors *Redbook* 173:20+ Ag '89
Marie Osmond: "I'm beginning a whole new life" [cover story] il pors *Redbook* 173:132-3+ Jl '89
"My husband healed me with love". il pors *Redbook* 173:76+ O '89
The Smothers Brothers: a new life for the old team. il pors *McCall's* 116:103+ My '89

WOLF, JOHN-PAUL
Introspective reflections [cover story] il por *American Artist* 53:50-5 O '89

WOLF, MARIELLA
about
Return of the "Bohemian girl". A. Decker. il *Art News* 88:74+ Ap '89

WOLF, MARK
The uninhibited Janis Joplin [interview; reprint] il por *Down Beat* 56:65-6 S '89

WOLF, MICHELE
Starlit melodies. il *Harper's Bazaar* 122:28 Jl '89
Where your head aches . . . can tell you why. il *Redbook* 173:94+ Jl '89

WOLF, SHMUEL, AND OTHERS
Movement protein of tobacco mosaic virus modifies plasmodesmatal size exclusion limit. bibl f il *Science* 246:377-9 O 20 '89

WOLF, STEPHEN M.
about
Steve Wolf's class act: straight talk in the schoolroom. J. E. Ellis. il *Business Week* p57 F 6 '89
'This is too big a genie to put back in the bottle'. J. E. Ellis. il por *Business Week* p43 N 6 '89
United swallows hard—and goes for growth. J. E. Ellis. il *Business Week* p34 My 15 '89
Will the carrot and stick work at United? J. E. Ellis. il por *Business Week* p56-7 F 6 '89
Wolf's bane. J. Zweig. il por *Forbes* 143:324 My 29 '89

WOLF, THOMAS H.
A hangdog look for dads with the ties that bind. bibl (p164) il *Smithsonian* 20:122-6+ My '89

WOLF, TONI LESSER
The intimate art. il *Art News* 88:122-9 N '89

WOLF [television program] *See* Television program reviews—Single works

WOLF PRIZES
Wolf Foundation honors Hawking and Penrose for work on relativity. M. Siegel. il por *Physics Today* 42:97-8 Ja '89

WOLFE, DENNY
In defense of "vague" assignments. *The Education Digest* 55:40-2 O '89

WOLFE, EDWARD E.
U.S. responsibilities in international fisheries matters [statement, May 2, 1989] *Department of State Bulletin* 89:56-8 Jl '89

WOLFE, JAMES H.
Chile: transition to democracy? il *USA Today (Periodical)* 117:25 Ja '89
NATO's southern flank: bridge or bastion? *USA Today (Periodical)* 118:15 Jl '89
States, nations, and superpower diplomacy. il *USA Today (Periodical)* 117:51 My '89
Whither Germany? il *USA Today (Periodical)* 118:73 S '89

WOLFE, LINDA
Wasted lives: the shocking case of "the preppie murder" [excerpt from Wasted] il pors *Redbook* 173:170-2+ S '89

WOLFE, LINDA, AND CECIL, JENNIFER
Island travel. il *New York* 22:66-70+ N 6 '89

WOLFE, STEVE
about
Steve Wolfe at Diane Brown. K. Johnson. il *Art in America* 77:204-5 S '89

WOLFE, TIM
Cedar-shingle mailbox. il *Flower and Garden* 33:96 Ja/F '89
Charcoal storage bin. il *Flower and Garden* 33:60 My/Je '89

WOLFE, TOM
A master of the universe [fiction] il *Gentlemen's Quarterly* 59:198 Ja '89
Stalking the billion-footed beast [cover story] il *Harper's* 279:45-56 N '89
about
Master of his universe [interview] B. Angelo. il por *Time* 133:90-2 F 13 '89
Tom Wolfe: the years of living prosperously [interview] A. Levine. il por *U.S. News & World Report* 107:117 D 25 '89-Ja 1 '90
Wolfe among the pigeons. D. Aikman. il por *Time* 134:78 N 27 '89

WOLFENDEN, RICHARD
(jt. auth) *See* Kati, Warren M., and Wolfenden, Richard

WOLFENSTEIN, LINCOLN, AND BEIER, EUGENE W.
Neutrino oscillations and solar neutrinos. bibl f il *Physics Today* 42:28-36 Jl '89

WOLFEREN, KAREL G. VAN
The enigma of Japanese power [excerpt] il por *Fortune* 119:150-3 My 8 '89
about
Rewriting the book on how to deal with Japan. R. Neff. il pors *Business Week* p49 Ag 7 '89
"The system". A. Tanzer. il por *Forbes* 143:40-1 My 1 '89

WOLFERT, PAULA
Tiny bites, mighty taste. il *Modern Maturity* 32:72-5 F/Mr '89

WOLFES, HEINER, AND OTHERS
Specific expression of nuclear proto-oncogenes before entry into meiotic prophase of spermatogenesis. bibl f il *Science* 245:740-3 Ag 18 '89

WOLFF, ALEXANDER
The coach and his champion. il pors *Sports Illustrated* 70:94-8+ Ap 3 '89
The cream rises. il *Sports Illustrated* 70:18-23 Mr 27 '89
How I fell for the bomb. por *Sports Illustrated* 70:84 F 20 '89
How much is too much? il *Sports Illustrated* 71:80-2+ D 11 '89
The Jayhawks take flight. il *Sports Illustrated* 71:32-4+ D 4 '89
Late-night score wars. il *Sports Illustrated* 70:74 Je 26 '89

WOLFF, ALEXANDER—*cont.*
Less is more. il *Sports Illustrated* 70:22-3 My 8 '89
The lost generation. il *Sports Illustrated* 71:100-11 N 20 '89
The right man for the job. il pors *Sports Illustrated* 70:58-60+ Ap 17 '89
Rising in the East. il por *Sports Illustrated* 70:36-8+ Ja 16 '89
Share the wealth, NCAA. por *Sports Illustrated* 71:128 N 20 '89
Tempest at Mizzou. il pors *Sports Illustrated* 70:24-6+ F 20 '89
Wunderbar! il pors *Sports Illustrated* 71:14-21 Jl 17 '89
WOLFF, ANTHONY
Boston's toilet: the true story. il *Audubon* 91:26-30+ Mr '89
WOLFF, GEOFFREY, 1937-
Advice my brother never took. il *The New York Times Book Review* 94:1+ Ag 20 '89
about
The brothers Wolff. F. Prose. il pors *The New York Times Magazine* p22-3+ F 5 '89
WOLFF, KAY
about
Viking to publish inside look at Colombian drug-running. G. Corcoran. *Publishers Weekly* 235:35 Je 9 '89
WOLFF, MICHAEL
about
Follow the leader. J. Marchese. il por *Rolling Stone* p32-3 Je 15 '89
WOLFF, ROBERT W.
The consultant's changing role: challenges in the 1990s. *Theatre Crafts* 23:28-33 D '89
WOLFF, SHELDON
Are radiation-induced effects hormetic? bibl f *Science* 245:575+ Ag 11 '89
WOLFF, STEVEN A.
The total planning process. il *Theatre Crafts* 23:70-7 D '89
WOLFF, TOBIAS, 1945-
Raymond Carver had his cake and ate it too. il por *Esquire* 112:240-2+ S '89
about
Advice my brother never took. G. Wolff. il *The New York Times Book Review* 94:1+ Ag 20 '89
The brothers Wolff. F. Prose. il pors *The New York Times Magazine* p22-3+ F 5 '89
WOLFLE, DAEL LEE
The centennial annual meeting, starring Harry Truman and civil liberties [excerpt from Renewing a scientific society] il por *Science* 246:130-1 O 6 '89
WÖLFLI, ADOLF, 1864-1930
about
Wölfli's asylum art. A. Temkin. bibl f il por *Art in America* 77:132-41+ Mr '89
WOLFMAN, IRA
Golf's clown prince. il pors *New Choices for the Best Years* 29:40-3+ Je '89
History's reluctant candidate. il por *New Choices for the Best Years* 29:18+ F '89
WOLIN, PENNY
about
The shape of things to shoot. il por *Modern Maturity* 32:50-4 F/Mr '89
WOLKOMIR, JOYCE
(jt. auth) See Wolkomir, Richard, and Wolkomir, Joyce
WOLKOMIR, JOYCE, AND WOLKOMIR, RICHARD
Ghost busters at work. il *McCall's* 116:104+ Jl '89
WOLKOMIR, RICHARD
Boomtown. il *Discover* 10:76-81 Ag '89
Celebrity dirt, but not in the usual sense. il *Smithsonian* 20:172 My '89
Divining the nineties. il *New Choices for the Best Years* 29:96 D '89
Mounties forever, but these days rarely on horseback. bibl (p170) il *Smithsonian* 19:78-84+ F '89
The race to make a 'perfect' shoe starts in the laboratory. il *Smithsonian* 20:94-100+ S '89
(jt. auth) See Wolkomir, Joyce, and Wolkomir, Richard
WOLKOMIR, RICHARD, AND WOLKOMIR, JOYCE
The knock on woodpeckers. il *National Wildlife* 27:22-3 F/Mr '89
Looking for Mr. Right [cover story] il *National Wildlife* 27:44-51 Je/Jl '89
A Yankee coat fits the coyote well [cover story] il *National Wildlife* 27:34-8 Ap/My '89
WOLLEN, PETER
about
Friendship's death [film] Reviews
People Weekly 31:18+ Ja 23 '89. P. Travers
WOLLHEIM, WILLIAM, AND FRANK, RUTH S.
Kar-Ben Copies. il *Publishers Weekly* 235:36-8 Mr 3 '89
People of the book. il *Publishers Weekly* 236:21-7 O 6 '89
WOLNICKI, MIRON J.
Instead of revolution. il *Commonweal* 116:293-4 My 19 '89
WOLPERT, CHERI RAE, 1953-
Do tread on me. il map *Women's Sports & Fitness* 11:36-9 Jl/Ag '89

Power and grace. il *Women's Sports & Fitness* 11:26-9 My '89
Steppin' out [cover story] bibl il *Women's Sports & Fitness* 11:20-4 Mr '89
Tracy Frankel: keeping an eye on the action. il por *Women's Sports & Fitness* 11:59 Jl/Ag '89
You just have to smile when you roller-skate. il *Women's Sports & Fitness* 11:90 Ap '89
WOLSKY, ALAN M., AND OTHERS
The new superconductors: prospects for applications. bibl il *Scientific American* 260:60-9 F '89
WOLVERINE EXPLORATION COMPANY
Diamonds in his own backyard [deals made by R. E. Rainwater] J. H. Taylor. il *Forbes* 143:49-50+ Mr 6 '89
WOLVES
See also
Coyotes
Bill calls for wolf recovery EIS [reintroduction of grey wolves to Yellowstone] il *National Parks* 63:9 S/O '89
The brawl of the wild [controversial plan to reintroduce wolves in Yellowstone] J. Skow. il *Time* 134:13-14+ N 6 '89
Praise for a red predator [reintroduction of red wolves into Alligator River National Wildlife Refuge] N. Angier. il maps *American Health* 8:74-6+ S '89
Stubborn hunter in a harsh land [tracking caribou herds and wolf packs in Denali National Park and Preserve] L. D. Mech. il map *National Wildlife* 27:20-4 Ag/S '89
White wolf: living with an Arctic legend [condensation] J. Brandenburg. il *Reader's Digest* 134:126-32 Mr '89
Wolves of Isle Royale. S. Nash. il *National Parks* 63:20-6+ Ja/F '89
WOLYNES, PETER G.
(jt. auth) See Friedrichs, Mark S., and Wolynes, Peter G.
WOMACK, JACK
Writing science fiction. *The Writer* 102:15-17 O '89
WOMACK FAMILY
about
Eat well! Feel great! B. Goldman. il *Better Homes and Gardens* 67:105-13+ Mr '89
WOMAN See Women
A WOMAN OF PARIS [film] See Motion picture reviews—Single works
WOMAN'S WORKSHOP QUARTERLY (NEWSLETTER)
Get ready for life after motherhood. il por *Nation's Business* 77:52 O '89
WOMANSHIP, INC.
Shemanship. P. Whittell. *Motor Boating & Sailing* 163:138+ Mr '89
Women on water. C. Watson. il *Travel Holiday* 172:86-9 Ag '89
WOMANTREK (FIRM)
When Bonnie Bordas leads a wilderness tour, there's no male call at all. D. Chu. il pors *People Weekly* 31:135-6+ My 8 '89
WOMBATS
Digging is their game [hairy-nosed wombats] S. Montgomery. il *International Wildlife* 19:46-50 Mr/Ap '89
WOMEN
See also
Alcohol and women
Beauty, Personal
Black women
Cable television and women
Christmas gifts for women
Computers and women
Drugs and women
Farm women
Farm women
Feminism
Heroes and heroines
Homeless women
Indians of North America—Women
Jewish women
Married women
Palestinian Arab women
Rural women
Sex differences
Single women
Smoking and women
Video games and women
Widows
Wives
Young women
America's 10 most beautiful women [cover story; special section] il *Harper's Bazaar* 122:158+ S '89
Look who won our most admired women and men polls. il *Good Housekeeping* 208:48 Ja '89
Over-40 special [cover story; special issue] il *Harper's Bazaar* 122:28+ Ag '89
Voices of the decade [oral history project for the 1990s] il *Ladies' Home Journal* 106:106-9 Ja '89
What's your wish list for women in the 90's, and what do you want for yourself? [celebrities' opinions] il *Glamour* 87:320-1 Ap '89
A woman today. See issues of Ladies' Home Journal beginning July 1983

WOMEN—cont.

Women in the '90s [cover story; special section; with editorial comment by Myrna Blyth] il *Ladies' Home Journal* 106:18, 57-8+ N '89

Women of the year, 1989. C. Krupp. il *Glamour* 87:154-5 D '89

Women right now. L. Mosedale. See issues of Glamour

Anatomy and physiology

See also

Breast
G spot
Menstruation
Vagina

Hips hooray! Heartening news for the pear shaped [waist-to-hip ratio; research by C. Wayne Callaway] P. S. Derron. il *Mademoiselle* 95:136 Ag '89

Ups and downs [effects of wearing high heeled shoes] L. Wells. il *The New York Times Magazine* p68 O 8 '89

What men love about the women of summer. J. P. Davis. il *Glamour* 87:170-1+ Jl '89

Attitudes

The American man in transition [survey] il *American Health* 8:59-61 Ja/F '89

The best of the best [results of Roper poll] il *Ladies' Home Journal* 106:103-5 Jl '89

Breaking attitude stereotypes [PMS survey by Stephanie L. Hanson] *USA Today (Periodical)* 117:10 F '89

The happiness report. G. Sheehy. il *Glamour* 87:308-13+ Ap '89

How we live now. C. Enos and S. F. Enos. il *Ladies' Home Journal* 106:140-1+ Ap '89

The LHJ Roper poll. See occasional issues of Ladies' Home Journal beginning March 1988

Oh men, oh women! [views on marriage; symposium] il *Ladies' Home Journal* 106:90+ S '89

Onward, women! [cover story] C. Wallis. il *Time* 134:80-2+ D 4 '89

What do you want from fashion right now! [survey results] A. Kleiner. il *Glamour* 87:207+ Mr '89

Who is the new ideal man? [survey results] S. Keen and O. Zur. il *Psychology Today* 23:54+ N '89

Who needs NOW? [attitudes on feminism] D. Seligman. *Fortune* 120:251-2 S 25 '89

Awards

Women of the Year [cover story; special section] il *Ms.* 17:67-91+ Ja/F '89

Biography

The lives of women. T. Mathews and L. Beachy. il por *Newsweek* 114:78-9+ N 6 '89

Clothing and dress

See Clothing and dress

Crimes against

See also

Abused women
Rape
Self defense for women

America's missing women. M. Jacobbi. il *Ladies' Home Journal* 106:144-6+ Ap '89

Fear on the streets [Canada] G. W. Taylor. il *Maclean's* 102:25-6 O 23 '89

Final attraction: men who charm women—to death [serial killers] A. Rule. il pors *Redbook* 172:104-6+ F '89

The global war against women. L. Heise. il *Utne Reader* p40-5 N/D '89

The man who hated women [M. Lépine murders women at the University of Montreal] W. R. Doerner. il por *Time* 134:30 D 18 '89

Massacre in Montreal [M. Lépine's murder spree] B. Turque. il por *Newsweek* 114:39 D 18 '89

Montreal massacre [M. Lépine guns down women at Univ. of Montreal; cover story; special section] il *Maclean's* 102:14-19+ D 18 '89

Outrage over omnipresent violence: where to aim it? A. Kannapell. il *Utne Reader* p46-9 N/D '89

Stabs in the dark [racially motivated attacks on women in New York City] *Newsweek* 114:49 N 13 '89

Taking responsibility. C. Kocol. il *The Humanist* 49:33-4 Ja/F '89

Violations: the legacy of the Central Park rape. J. Neimark. il *Mademoiselle* 95:226-7+ S '89

Violence in a man's world. K. Pollitt. il *The New York Times Magazine* p18+ Je 18 '89

The war against women. C. L. Mithers. il *Ladies' Home Journal* 106:137-9+ O '89

Diseases

See also

AIDS (Disease) and women
Anorexia nervosa
Breast—Cancer
Bulimia
Endometriosis
Gynecology
Menstruation—Disorders
Osteoporosis
Premenstrual syndrome
Reproductive organs—Diseases

Are you cheating your heart? M. Callahan. il *Parents* 64:220+ Je '89

Blood-lead climbs as old bones decline [aged women at risk] J. Raloff. *Science News* 135:181 Mr 25 '89

Different but deadly [heart disease] E. Rosenthal. il *The New York Times Magazine* p60+ S 17 '89

A killer of women, too [heart disease] J. Silberner. il *U.S. News & World Report* 107:75-6 D 18 '89

Medical tests for healthy women only. L. Holland. il *Good Housekeeping* 209:269-70 S '89

Sick chic. B. Ehrenreich. il *Ms.* 17:28-9 Ja/F '89

Unmentionables: the six most embarrassing ailments. C. Hacinli. il *Mademoiselle* 95:152+ S '89

Why doctors mistreat women: special medical report. R. Baron-Faust. *Redbook* 173:114-15+ My '89

A woman's heart. J. Ismach. il *American Health* 8:15-16+ Ja/F '89

Women and heart disease. J. L. Lippert. il *Ladies' Home Journal* 106:59-60+ O '89

Women face equal danger [heart disease; views of Carolyn Corn] *USA Today (Periodical)* 117:4 F '89

Economic conditions

See also

Black women—Economic conditions
Wages and salaries

The buck starts here [special section] il *Harper's Bazaar* 122:38+ Ja '89

Economic equity for women is back on the congressional agenda. S. V. Roberts. *U.S. News & World Report* 107:33 Ag 14 '89

Fear of finance. N. Angier. il *Mademoiselle* 95:114-15+ Ja '89

Financial resolutions. G. W. Weinstein. il *Ms.* 17:120-1 Ja/F '89

Financial security: what every woman must know [results of survey] C. L. Hayes. *McCall's* 117:124+ O '89

Financial workshop: a year in the lives of four women (I). M. Rowland. il *Working Woman* 14:91-2+ Ap '89

Financial workshop: a year in the lives of four women (II). M. Rowland. il *Working Woman* 14:79-80+ My '89

Financial workshop: a year in the lives of four women (III). M. Rowland. il *Working Woman* 14:61-2+ Je '89

Financial workshop: a year in the lives of four women (IV). M. Rowland. il *Working Woman* 14:55-6+ Jl '89

Financial workshop: a year in the lives of four women (V). M. Rowland. il *Working Woman* 14:47-8+ Ag '89

Financial workshop: a year in the lives of four women (VI). M. Rowland. il *Working Woman* 14:69-70+ S '89

Financial workshop: a year in the lives of four women (VII). M. Rowland. il *Working Woman* 14:89-90+ O '89

Financial workshop: a year in the lives of four women (VIII). M. Rowland. il *Working Woman* 14:95-6+ N '89

Financial workshop: a year in the lives of four women (IX). M. Rowland. il *Working Woman* 14:61-2+ D '89

More for your money. B. G. Quint. See issues of Glamour

More than she bargained for [how differences in salaries may affect relationships] L. Lehrer. il *Ms.* 17:111-14 Ja/F '89

Smart money [results of survey] il *Ms.* 18:51-7 N '89

Take cover [selecting the right insurance policy] G. W. Weinstein. il *Ms.* 18:70-2 Jl/Ag '89

What's your money personality? V. Lindner and A. R. Lieberman. *Redbook* 172:124-5+ Ap '89

Women still seek economic equality [views of Victor Fuchs] *USA Today (Periodical)* 117:3 Ap '89

Anecdotes, facetiae, satire, etc.

Funny money. B. Feirstein. *Harper's Bazaar* 122:177+ Mr '89

Economic value

What's a woman worth? [unpaid work should be included in figuring of gross national product; views of M. Waring] Y. Preston. il *Ms.* 18:78 Jl/Ag '89

Education

See also

Sex discrimination in education
Women college students

Making science more seductive to women on campus. N. J. Freundlich. il *Business Week* p89 Ag 28 '89

History

The polite lady: portraits of American schoolgirls and their accomplishments, 1725-1830. D. T. Deutsch. bibl f il *Antiques* 135:742-53 Mr '89

Employment

See also

Black women—Employment
Businesswomen
Equal pay for equal work
Industry—Prenatal care programs
Married women—Employment
Maternity leaves
Mi Casa Resource Center for Women (Denver, Colo.)
Mothers—Employment
Women—Occupations

Affirmative action in vogue? M. A. Fortune. il *Black Enterprise* 19:20 Ap '89

Another Great Wall [sex discrimination in China] P. Simpson. il *Ms.* 17:144-5 Ja/F '89

Bias or safety? [appeals court upholds Johnson Controls ban excluding women of childbearing age from hazardous jobs] *Time* 134:61 O 16 '89

WOMEN—Employment—*cont.*

Career first, children later [survey of college women by Kristine Baber] il *USA Today (Periodical)* 117:8-9 Mr '89

Career workshop. B. Mackoff. See occasional issues of Ladies' Home Journal beginning February 1988 through February 1989

Dear Betty Harragan. B. L. Harragan. See issues of Working Woman

Does part-time pay off? S. McHenry and L. L. Small. il *Ms.* 17:88-94 Mr '89

Doing home work down on the farm. O. Davidson. il *The Nation* 249:87-8+ Jl 17 '89

Flying blind [Pan Am's weight standards for female flight attendants ruled illegal] D. Seligman. il *Fortune* 120:204 O 9 '89

A future up in the air: flight attendants contest weight rules [suit against American Airlines] M. Suh. il *Ms.* 18:83-4 S '89

High Court ruling helps plaintiffs of job bias [sex discrimination case brought by woman accountant] *Jet* 76:19 My 22 '89

An indifference toward women [United Nations] C. Subramaniam. *World Press Review* 36:65 O '89

Job strategies. M. M. Kennedy. See issues of Glamour

'Looksism' in TV news [sexism] J. Alter. il por *Newsweek* 114:72-3 N 6 '89

Myth America in the workplace [Supreme Court rules against sex stereotyping in case of A. Hopkins v. Price Waterhouse] por *U.S. News & World Report* 106:14 My 15 '89

New options for working at home. C. Begole. il *Glamour* 87:324-5+ S '89

Nine to five [LHJ Roper poll] il *Ladies' Home Journal* 106:83-4 Mr '89

The old sexism in the new China. D. Doder. il *U.S. News & World Report* 106:36-8 Ap 24 '89

One step forward, two steps back [Lorance v. AT&T Technologies; Supreme Court decision] P. Simpson. il por *Ms.* 18:96 S '89

Opening doors for women in academia [countering discrimination; address, 1988] B. D. Webster. bibl f *BioScience* 39:96-8 F '89

Pigs in sheep's clothing: how to spot a secret sexist. S. Beauvais. il *Glamour* 87:116+ Je '89

A slap at sex stereotypes [Supreme Court decision in favor of A. Hopkins in suit against Price Waterhouse] A. Sachs. il por *Time* 133:66 My 15 '89

Smile when you say that, partner [discrimination suit by Price Waterhouse employee A. Hopkins before the Supreme Court] D. L. Jacobs. il por *Ms.* 17:137 Ja/F '89

The stress of staying home [research by Rosalind Barnett and Grace Baruch] L. M. Blake. *Psychology Today* 23:66 Jl/Ag '89

Thanks, guys [debunking notion of stigma attached to affirmative action] A. F. Lewis. il *Ms.* 18:86 S '89

Wake-up call [reaction to wife's denial of tenure] R. B. Reich. il *Ms.* 18:32-3 O '89

Why you can't get no (job) satisfaction. K. W. Wiley. il *Mademoiselle* 95:122+ Je '89

Winning is the best revenge [C. Broderick wins discrimination suit against the Securities and Exchange Commission] L. Romano. il pors *Good Housekeeping* 208:46+ Ap '89

Women and the workplace [panel discussion] il *Ladies' Home Journal* 106:70 N '89

Women of Japan. K. Sharma. *World Press Review* 36:70 D '89

Women on TV: work is in. D. Burden. il *Psychology Today* 23:12 O '89

Working women take one benefit to heart [higher HDL cholesterol than non-working women in West Germany; study by Ursula Haertel] K. Fackelmann. *Science News* 135:389 Je 24 '89

Wrestling with bias [Supreme Court ruling against sex stereotyping in case of A. Hopkins v. Price Waterhouse] D. Seligman. il *Fortune* 119:339 Je 5 '89

Your brilliant career. R. Sharp. See issues of Mademoiselle beginning May 1987

Anecdotes, facetiae, satire, etc.

This working woman's heaven. K. Fury. il *Working Woman* 14:170 Ap '89

Psychological aspects

See Psychology, Industrial

Equal rights

See also

Equal pay for equal work
National Organization for Women
Sex discrimination
United Nations. Commission on the Status of Women
Women—Employment

The importance of women. C. Kocol. *The Humanist* 49:34 N/D '89

What keeps women "in their place"? A. Layng. il *USA Today (Periodical)* 117:89-91 My '89

Health and hygiene

See also

Beauty, Personal
Black women—Health and hygiene
Feminine hygiene products

Gynecology
Menopause
Menstruation
Physical fitness
Pregnancy
Prenatal care
Young women—Health and hygiene

Beauty & health report. S. Young. See issues of Glamour

Health. See issues of Vogue

Health express. See issues of Mademoiselle

Healthy thoughts [panel discussion] il *Ladies' Home Journal* 106:62+ N '89

Holiday health and beauty guide [special section] il *Ladies' Home Journal* 106:39-40+ D '89

Over-40 good health and great looks [special section] il *Harper's Bazaar* 122:132-7+ Ag '89

Sex & health. S. Zussman. See issues of Glamour beginning November 1986

Shape-up. L. Gordon. See issues of Glamour

Women's health handbook [special section] M. Fenichel. *McCall's* 116:89-92+ F '89

Working women take one benefit to heart [higher HDL cholesterol than non-working women in West Germany; study by Ursula Haertel] K. Fackelmann. *Science News* 135:389 Je 24 '89

History

See also

World War, 1914-1918—Women

Historiography

Just the facts, ma'am. E. Kristol. il *The American Spectator* 22:39-41 Jl '89

Study and teaching

See Women's studies

International aspects

See also

United Nations. Commission on the Status of Women

Foreign secrets for eating well, staying slim. il *Glamour* 87:276-9 My '89

The global war against women. L. Heise. il *Utne Reader* p40-5 N/D '89

Women. *UN Chronicle* 26:80 Je '89

Legal status, laws, etc.

See also

Divorce
Feminist law

The '89 hot sheet. P. Simpson. *Ms.* 17:83 Mr '89

Cocaine babies: the littlest victims [penalties to mothers] il *Newsweek* 114:55 O 2 '89

Courting disaster [change in Supreme Court may affect women's issues] M. S. Spivack. il *Ms.* 17:138 Ja/F '89

Economic equity for women is back on the congressional agenda. S. V. Roberts. *U.S. News & World Report* 107:33 Ag 14 '89

Here come the pregnancy police [legal action against mothers of infants exposed to drugs] A. Sachs. il *Time* 133:104-5 My 22 '89

Jailing mothers for drug abuse [screening newborns in Butte County, Calif.] S. LaCroix. il *The Nation* 248:585-6+ My 1 '89

The politics of pregnancy. C. Tavris. *Vogue* 179:572-3+ S '89

The pregnancy police, on patrol [enforcing fetal rights by jailing negligent mothers] T. Gest. il *U.S. News & World Report* 106:50 F 6 '89

Something to celebrate. il *Glamour* 87:68 Ja '89

Technology as destiny: the new eugenics challenges feminism [cover story] J. B. Elshtain. il *The Progressive* 53:19-23 Je '89

Nutrition

See also

Pregnancy—Nutritional aspects

Bad blood [foods to combat anemia] W. T. Buckley. *Redbook* 173:104-5+ Je '89

Foreign secrets for eating well, staying slim. il *Glamour* 87:276-9 My '89

Mall mania: too many temptations [food court] il *Glamour* 87:258-60 Ag '89

Nutrition advice to think twice about. J. Storm. il *Women's Sports & Fitness* 11:20 N/D '89

Too tired too often? Vitamins can work wonders. R. N. Podell. il *Redbook* 172:108-9+ Ja '89

The top 10 beauty foods. il *Mademoiselle* 95:202-5 N '89

You are what you eat. P. Cobe. il *Ladies' Home Journal* 106:164-6+ Mr '89

Occupations

See also

Businesswomen
Equal pay for equal work

25 hottest careers [cover story] il *Working Woman* 14:67-9+ Jl '89

How to get the job you really want [cover story; special section] il *Working Woman* 14:111-14+ Ap '89

A job hunter's guide for the nineties. il *Glamour* 87:210-13+ F '89

Kremlin watchers: the new guard. il *Ms.* 17:76-7 My '89

Power babies [influential women under 30] L. Romano. il *Mademoiselle* 95:198-201+ My '89

WOMEN—Occupations—*cont.*

The tenth annual Working woman salary survey [cover story; special section] A. M. Russell. il *Working Woman* 14:71-6+ Ja '89

Vision quest: the Seventeen career quiz. E. Bibb. *Seventeen* 48:205-6+ Mr '89

Pensions

See Pensions

Photographs and photography

See also

Black women—Photographs and photography

Beauty session basics. G. Bernstein. il por *Petersen's Photographic Magazine* 18:30-1 Ag '89

Bold body graphics. J. Zuckerman. il *Petersen's Photographic Magazine* 18:16-18+ D '89

A letter to the editor. M. P. Lears. il *Petersen's Photographic Magazine* 18:8 N '89

Some women [work of R. Mapplethorpe; cover story] J. Didion. il por *Esquire* 112:214-23 S '89

Physical fitness

See Physical fitness

Political activities

See also

Black women—Political activities

Women public officers

Come to our census! [reapportionment of congressional seats after 1990 census] A. F. Lewis. *Ms.* 18:76 Jl/Ag '89

Knesset comedown: Israeli women lose reps in fall election, but make points at polls. E. Burkett. *Ms.* 17:141 Ja/F '89

Lost horizons [lack of ethics in 1988 presidential campaign; effect on women's political participation] L. Carpenter. il *Ms.* 17:86-7 Mr '89

Madeleine Kunin [excerpt from address] M. Kunin. il por *Ladies' Home Journal* 106:62 N '89

Optimist at last. A. F. Lewis. *Ms.* 18:71 O '89

A wake-up call. E. Berg. il *The New York Times Magazine* p12+ Jl 30 '89

Psychology

See also

Abortion—Psychological aspects

Beauty, Personal—Psychological aspects

Black women—Psychology

Body image

Femininity (Psychology)

Pregnancy—Psychological aspects

Baby chic: what's behind the new diaper rush? N. Angier. il *Mademoiselle* 95:194-5+ Je '89

Barbara Walters: "Be true to yourself" [excerpts from address] B. Walters. il por *Ladies' Home Journal* 106:60 N '89

The big pullback [avoiding commitment] D. Heyn. *Mademoiselle* 95:84 Jl '89

Compulsive comparing. J. Stone. il *Glamour* 87:132 Ag '89

The daddy trap [effects of close relationships between fathers and daughters] D. Kent. il *Mademoiselle* 95:182-3+ D '89

Dr. Joyce Brothers answers your questions. J. Brothers. See issues of Good Housekeeping

Feeling out 50. L. C. Pogrebin. il por *Ms.* 17:26 Je '89

Feisty women, family pride. S. Hubbell. il *New Choices for the Best Years* 29:80-1 My '89

Fortysomething is a wonderful age! J. Viorst. *Redbook* 173:42+ Je '89

High blood pressure: a loaded inheritance [research by Marvin Zuckerman and Karen Russo] P. King. il *Psychology Today* 23:61 My '89

How do you know when you're grown up? J. Groch. il *American Health* 8:117-18 Jl/Ag '89

How one woman got back on track. K. A. Samon. *Mademoiselle* 95:247+ S '89

How to be good to yourself [quiz] C. Weston. il *Ladies' Home Journal* 106:182+ N '89

How to be mad at the man you're mad for. D. Heyn. *Mademoiselle* 95:108 O '89

How to do your best without driving yourself (and others) crazy. K. Crump. *McCall's* 116:58+ Je '89

In rehab with the love junkies. E. Schappell. *Mademoiselle* 95:217+ O '89

Individualism unbound: reconsidering modern-day romance [popularity of self help books] J. Henkin. il *Utne Reader* p64-6+ Mr/Ap '89

Keys to women's fulfillment. il *USA Today (Periodical)* 117:11 Ja '89

The lure of the rogue [attraction for women] J. Bailey. il *Health (New York, N.Y.)* 21:62-5+ D '89

Marriage's unfulfilled promise [importance of women's friendships with other women; research by Stacey Oliker] P. King. il *Psychology Today* 23:71-2 D '89

The (meno)pause that refreshes [depression aspect; research by Sonja and John McKinlay] P. King. il *Psychology Today* 22:11 D '88

Midlife exhilaration. M. M. Gullette. il *The New York Times Magazine* p18+ Ja 29 '89

Mind health. C. Tavris. See issues of Vogue

"Move over, Phil" [using attitudes to enhance appearance] L. Phillips. il *Ms.* 17:44+ Ja/F '89

The pretzel syndrome: tying yourself in knots to please others? J. Stone. il *Glamour* 87:156 S '89

Ready, willing and wary. D. Merkin. il *The New York Times Magazine* p12+ Jl 16 '89

Real women do eat food. W. D. Leight. *Mademoiselle* 95:120 Ag '89

The secret world of obsessive-compulsives. S. Pocharski. il *Mademoiselle* 95:138 Ag '89

Stop blaming men for everything! (A guy begs for mercy) [self help literature] A. Heard. il *Mademoiselle* 95:182-3+ Ag '89

The stress of staying home [research by Rosalind Barnett and Grace Baruch] L. M. Blake. *Psychology Today* 23:66 Jl/Ag '89

Stressbusters. D. Sobel. il *Ladies' Home Journal* 106:74 Ag '89

Turning 40. N. Kelton. il *Parents* 64:132-3 Mr '89

TV bingers [effects of food commercials; research by Carol Raupp] J. Fischman. il *Psychology Today* 23:24 N '89

Twenty-four going on forty: the new mid-life crisis comes early. R. Grant. il *Mademoiselle* 95:246-7+ S '89

Who would you like to be tomorrow? [fantasies] il *Glamour* 87:144 Mr '89

Women with cold feet [ambivalent about marriage] L. Mosedale. il *Glamour* 87:200-1+ D '89

Anecdotes, facetiae, satire, etc.

A man who can't love (dedicated to women who love too much). G. W. S. Trow. *The New Yorker* 64:29 Ja 16 '89

Women on the verge [New Yorkers; special section] il *Harper's Bazaar* 122:176-7+ Mr '89

Women on the verge [turning 30] L. Kaylin. il *Gentlemen's Quarterly* 59:178+ D '89

Bibliography

Advice and consent [self help books] E. Hopkins. *Harper's Bazaar* 122:201+ Ap '89

Religious life

See also

Ordination of women

Women clergy

Faith, values & morals [results of survey] S. Jacoby. *McCall's* 116:69-71+ My '89

Growing up Baptist. M. E. Snodgrass. il *Ms.* 17:66-7 Mr '89

'In the tongues of men': homilies for women [cover story] K. Coffey. il *America* 161:392-4 D 2 '89

Seeking meaning [lapsed Catholic creates own rituals] J. Callahan. il *Glamour* 87:326 S '89

The women-church movement [cover story] M. T. Winter. *The Christian Century* 106:258-60 Mr 8 '89

Salaries

See Wages and salaries

Self defense

See Self defense for women

Sexual behavior

See Sexual behavior

Social conditions

See also

Divorce

Misogyny

Prostitution

Dish 'n' deal [women's poker game] D. Raskin. il *Ms.* 18:32-3 S '89

The she decade [1990s] L. Langway. il *Ladies' Home Journal* 106:211-14 N '89

Sweating and sharing [aerobics class in Pennington, N.J. serves as women's socializing center] J. D. Reed. il *Time* 134:12-13 Jl 10 '89

The way we'll be [1990s] M. J. Weiss. il *Ladies' Home Journal* 106:220-2+ N '89

Sports

See also

Baseball, College

Baseball, Professional

Basketball

Basketball, College

Basketball, High school

Basketball, Professional

Bicycle racing

Boardsailing

Canoes and canoeing

Coed sports

Cross country skiing

Cycling

Diving

Field hockey

Golf

Gymnastics

High jumping

Horsemanship

Hurdle racing

Marathon running

Marathon swimming

Mountain cycling

Mountain running

Mountaineering

National Women in Sports Day

Parachuting

Race walking

Racquetball

WOMEN—Sports—See also—*cont.*
    Roller skating
    Rowing
    Rugby
    Running
    Sex discrimination in sports
    Ski racing
    Skiing
    Skin diving
    Soccer
    Softball
    Softball, College
    Softball, High school
    Squash (Sport)
    Surfing
    Swimming
    Synchronized swimming
    Tennis
    Track and field athletics
    Triathlon
    Ultramarathon running
    Volleyball
    Volleyball, College
    Volleyball, Professional
    Water skiing
    Weight lifting
    Womantrek (Firm)
    Women's Sports Foundation
    Yacht racing
Innerviews [interview with S. Edwards] L. Rothlein. il por *Women's Sports & Fitness* 11:77 Ap '89
It's never too late to play a sport. J. Mattera. il *Glamour* 87:54 Je '89
The joy of risk. J. Etra. *Harper's Bazaar* 122:162-3+ My '89
Make a move on the media [lack of coverage of women's sports] K. M. Reith. il *Women's Sports & Fitness* 11:70 S '89
Past echoes, future challenges [adaptation of address, January 1989] C. Mann. il *Women's Sports & Fitness* 11:88 Ap '89
Playing your best: eight top athletes tell you how. J. Mattera. il *Glamour* 87:70+ N '89
Sidelined [recovery from injuries] J. Mattera. il *Glamour* 87:86 Mr '89
Title IX is back in action! [effect on women athletes] K. M. Reith. il *Women's Sports & Fitness* 11:74 Mr '89
Water: a summerful of ways to enjoy it. il *Glamour* 87:146-51 Jl '89
What's your game? [quiz] E. Walzer. *Seventeen* 48:172 Mr '89
    Scholarships and fellowships
    See Scholarships and fellowships
    Travel
    See also
    Womantrek (Firm)
Adventure travel. S. G. Sheehy. il *Working Woman* 14:204+ S '89
Images: beauty to go. S. Mitchell. il *Vogue* 179:62 Jl '89
Stranger off a train. M. White. il *The New York Times Magazine* p22+ Je 4 '89
    Anecdotes, facetiae, satire, etc.
It pays to get clipped [travel tips for the American in Paris] N. Fein. il *Ms.* 18:28-30 N '89
    Volunteer service
    See Volunteer service
    Wages
    See Wages and salaries
    Afghanistan
Back to the veil? R. Rastogi. *World Press Review* 36:60 My '89
    Africa
Where I enter [black American woman growing up in Africa] C. McCourtie. por *Essence* 19:83-4+ Ap '89
    Algeria
Behind the veil [portrayal of Algerian women in film] A. Djebar. il *The Unesco Courier* 42:34-7 O '89
    Brazil
Death without weeping [mother love in shantytowns of Brazil] N. Scheper-Hughes. *Natural History* p8+ O '89
The women of Arembepe. M. de A. Figueiredo and D. Prado. il *The Unesco Courier* 42:38-41 Jl '89
    Canada
    See also
    National Action Committee on the Status of Women (Canada)
Fear on the streets [crimes against women] G. W. Taylor. il *Maclean's* 102:25-6 O 23 '89
Narcissus, thy name is woman [taping Canadian TV special Women in the '90s] B. Amiel. il *Maclean's* 102:9 F 13 '89
Sisterhood of fear and fury [response to massacre at Univ. of Montreal] B. Bergman. il *Maclean's* 102:18-19 D 18 '89
    China
Another Great Wall [sex discrimination] P. Simpson. il *Ms.* 17:144-5 Ja/F '89

The old sexism in the new China. D. Doder. il *U.S. News & World Report* 106:36-8 Ap 24 '89
    Cyprus
Going to Cyprus. J. Webb. il pors *Seventeen* 48:166+ Mr '89
    Developing countries
At debt's door [effect of loan repayment on women] J. Steinberg. il *Ms.* 18:74-9 N '89
Villagers get capital ideas [FINCA assistance] J. Jenner. il *Ms.* 17:73 Je '89
    Fiji
A Fijian way of fishing. M. Timmons. il *Sea Frontiers* 35:64 Ja/F '89
    France
French women today. H. Gisserot. *America* 160:579-81 Je 17-24 '89
Images: French style. J. J. Buck. il *Vogue* 179:57-8+ Jl '89
Secrets of the sleek chic. A. Bogart. il *Harper's Bazaar* 122:36+ Ap '89
    History
    See also
    France—History—Revolution, 1789-1799—Women
High flyers: women aviators in pre-war France. S. Reynolds. bibl il *History Today* 39:36-41 Ap '89
    Great Britain
Beauty secrets of the elite [blue bloods] P. Barron. il *Harper's Bazaar* 122:50+ S '89
They've come a long way, Maggie. B. Amiel. il *Maclean's* 102:10 Ja 16 '89
    History
The odyssey of Annie Besant [Victorian radical and atheist turned Theosophist] J. Oppenheim. bibl il pors *History Today* 39:12-18 S '89
    Honduras
Campesina fights hunger and its causes [organizer E. Alvarado] M. C. Turck. por *The Progressive* 53:14 My '89
    India
In India, they abort females. J. McGowan. por *Newsweek* 113:12 Ja 30 '89
    Israel
Knesset comedown: Israeli women lose reps in fall election, but make points at polls. E. Burkett. *Ms.* 17:141 Ja/F '89
    Italy
Joan Juliet Buck unravels the complex structure of Italian style and makes some astonishing discoveries. J. J. Buck. il *Vogue* 179:143-4+ D '89
    Japan
    See also
    Geishas
The end of the affair? [S. Uno's affair with geisha triggers women's opposition] B. Powell. il por *Newsweek* 114:22-3 Jl 10 '89
Japan discovers woman power. S. Solo. il *Fortune* 119:153-4+ Je 19 '89
Women of Japan. K. Sharma. *World Press Review* 36:70 D '89
    Kenya
A Kenyan tycoon [businesswoman E. K. Mungai] W. Machua. il por *World Press Review* 36:52 Jl '89
    Northern Ireland
Daughters of Derry [Catholic women] N. McCafferty. il *Ms.* 18:72-7 S '89
    Pakistan
The next Afghan war [women refugees] D. Lorch. il *Ms.* 17:84 Ap '89
    Saint Croix (Virgin Islands of the U.S.)
Making a difference. C. M. Green. il *Essence* 19:88-90+ Ap '89
    South Africa
200 women arrested during protest in South Africa. il *Jet* 76:9 S 18 '89
Just two women. J. Hey. il *The New York Times Magazine* p40+ S 10 '89
Sticking a needle in apartheid [church sponsored sewing classes] M. S. Van Leeuwen. il *Christianity Today* 33:13 Mr 17 '89
    Soviet Union
Black Russian. Y. Khanga. il pors *Essence* 20:59-60+ Ag '89
Moscow yuppies? Nyet quite! [I. Zvereva and S. Burak] E. B. Fein. il *Mademoiselle* 95:222-3+ O '89
Soviet women: what does political change mean for them? S. Jacoby. il *Glamour* 87:268-9+ My '89
    Thailand
My mother. P. Kanokvijitjalearn. il *World Health* p29 Mr '89
New seasons, new joys. O. Anusaksathien. il *World Health* p27-8 Mr '89
    United States
    See Black women; Women
    Western Europe
The Eurowife: foreign aid. A. Morgan. *Harper's Bazaar* 122:119+ F '89

WOMEN, AGED See Aged
WOMEN, BLACK See Black women
WOMEN ACCOUNTANTS
High Court ruling helps plaintiffs of job bias [sex discrimination case brought by woman accountant] *Jet* 76:19 My 22 '89
Myth America in the workplace [Supreme Court rules against sex stereotyping in case of A. Hopkins v. Price Waterhouse] por *U.S. News & World Report* 106:14 My 15 '89
A slap at sex stereotypes [Supreme Court decision in favor of A. Hopkins in suit against Price Waterhouse] A. Sachs. il por *Time* 133:66 My 15 '89
Smile when you say that, partner [discrimination suit by Price Waterhouse employee A. Hopkins before the Supreme Court] D. L. Jacobs. il por *Ms.* 17:137 Ja/F '89
Wrestling with bias [Supreme Court ruling against sex stereotyping in case of A. Hopkins v. Price Waterhouse] D. Seligman. il *Fortune* 119:339 Je 5 '89

WOMEN AIR PILOTS
See also
Dusenbury, Susan
Esch, Martha
Payne, Carla
Thaden, Louise
High flyers: women aviators in pre-war France. S. Reynolds. bibl il *History Today* 39:36-41 Ap '89
WOMEN AND DRUGS See Drugs and women
WOMEN AND MASS MEDIA
Make a move on the media [lack of coverage of women's sports] K. M. Reith. il *Women's Sports & Fitness* 11:70 S '89

WOMEN AND MEN
See also
Adultery
Coed sports
Dating (Social customs)
Flirting
Interpersonal attraction
Love
Misogyny
Romance
Sex differences
Sex in business
Sex role
1 guy 2 girls: who will get him? il *'Teen* 33:60 Ap '89
20 surprising facts on love, marriage, sex and divorce [excerpt from What are the chances?] B. R. Siskin and others. il *Glamour* 87:310-11 S '89
50 ways to meet a lover. J. C. Johnson. il *Mademoiselle* 95:180-1+ O '89
All about Adam. See issues of Gentlemen's Quarterly
All the girls I've loved [high school reunion] N. Karlen. il *Mademoiselle* 95:191+ N '89
Anatomy of a breakup: . . . . he says "There's nothing left to say". D. Seeley. il *Mademoiselle* 95:144-5+ Jl '89
Anatomy of a breakup: she says "I think we need to talk" . . . A. R. Shapiro. il *Mademoiselle* 95:142-3+ Jl '89
. . . and the woman who loves him [relationship with a Casanova] E. Royte. il *Mademoiselle* 95:190+ My '89
Bad boys: why we love them sooo . . . D. Heyn. il *Seventeen* 48:82-3+ Ja '89
Body and soul. M.-B. Rosenbaum. See issues of Mademoiselle
Boy behavior: what's behind it? R. Shinkman. il *'Teen* 33:34-5 Jl '89
Can love conquer the age gap? [special section] il *New Choices for the Best Years* 29:60-2 Ap '89
Can men change? J. Stone. il *Glamour* 87:164 Mr '89
Can you trust each other? L. Dormen. il *Glamour* 87:236-7+ N '89
Dating for dollars: the gold diggers of 1989. C. Bushnell. il *Mademoiselle* 95:176-7 N '89
Does hirsute suit her? L. Kaylin. il *Gentlemen's Quarterly* 59:346-7+ Mr '89
The evil men do—and why they do it. J. McCabe. il *Mademoiselle* 95:186-7+ N '89
Facts of love [strategies for a successful relationship; views of Robert Sternberg] il *Psychology Today* 23:8 Ja/F '89
Faked out by Zethel [Army team plays All American Red Heads] S. Toperoff. il *The New York Times Magazine* p22+ Je 11 '89
For your eyes only? The beauty secrets men love—or loathe. E. Welty. il *Mademoiselle* 95:178-81 F '89
Goodwill toward men. E. Welty. *Mademoiselle* 95:191+ N '89
He likes me . . . he likes me not [quiz] il *'Teen* 33:47 S '89
He spies/she spies: why we snoop in the name of love. L. Mosedale. il *Glamour* 87:162-3+ Jl '89
Him. G. Schwartz. See issues of Seventeen beginning August 1987
His. W. D. Leight. See issues of Mademoiselle beginning December 1987
How do you build intimacy in an age of divorce? [cover story] C. Avery. il *Psychology Today* 23:27-31 My '89
How to be a better judge of men. J. Stone. il *Glamour* 87:28-9 Ja '89
How to have a boyfriend without losing your friends. D. Kent. il *Seventeen* 48:155-6+ My '89

How to talk to each other . . . without yelling and screaming [views of Bonnie Jacobson] il *Glamour* 87:115 Ap '89
If I could turn back time [May-December celebrity couples] il *People Weekly* 32:147+ D 25 '89-Ja 1 '90
In rehab with the love junkies. E. Schappell. *Mademoiselle* 95:217+ O '89
Individualism unbound: reconsidering modern-day romance [popularity of self help books] J. Henkin. il *Utne Reader* p64-6+ Mr/Ap '89
The intelligent woman's guide to sex. D. Heyn. See issues of Mademoiselle beginning December 1986
Is your honey making you fat? E. Kunes. il *Mademoiselle* 95:234 My '89
Is your relationship going anywhere? L. Dormen. il *Glamour* 87:252-5+ Mr '89
Jake: a man's opinion. See issues of Glamour
Killing old loves [dealing with ex-girlfriends] J. Gonick. il *Glamour* 87:256+ N '89
"Let's not discuss it". C. L. Mithers. il *Glamour* 87:340 S '89
The lies men tell. D. Seeley. il *Mademoiselle* 95:172-3+ Je '89
Liking an unlikely guy. il *'Teen* 33:22+ Mr '89
Love & sex: the book of questions [results of survey] G. Stock. il *Redbook* 173:134-5 O '89
Love's losses: must losing a lover mean you can't keep his friends? C. L. Mithers. il *Glamour* 87:294 My '89
Loving an older man. A. R. Shapiro. il *Mademoiselle* 95:182-3+ O '89
The lure of the rogue [attraction for women] J. Bailey. il *Health (New York, N.Y.)* 21:62-5+ D '89
The man who couldn't be faithful [confessions of a Casanova] P. Trachtenberg. il *Mademoiselle* 95:188-9+ My '89
Maybe he is your type. J. Stone. il *Glamour* 87:142 N '89
Meeting her family. V. Klinkenborg. il *Glamour* 87:232 F '89
Midlife crises in men: are women to blame? S. Amsterdam. il *TV Guide* 37:18-20 Jl 22-28 '89
More than she bargained for [how differences in salaries may affect relationships] L. Lehrer. il *Ms.* 17:111-14 Ja/F '89
My girlfriend dreams about other men [infatuation with B. Springsteen] B. Patrick. il por *Glamour* 87:230 D '89
The no-regrets ultimatum. C. Bushnell. il *Mademoiselle* 95:186+ Ap '89
Not alone—but lonely. J. Stone. il *Glamour* 87:148 My '89
The power of old flames. B. Evans and T. Nelson. *Glamour* 87:156 Mr '89
Romantic wounds. C. L. Mithers. il *Glamour* 87:242 D '89
She: 6, he: 3, relationship: 0 [couples competing at sports] H. K. Paddock. il *Glamour* 87:75-6+ Ag '89
Spotting Mr. Wrong . . . early [views of A. Weiss] L. B. Morris. il *Health (New York, N.Y.)* 21:34-5 N '89
Spying on guys: what men say when women aren't around [special section] D. Hellerstein. il *Mademoiselle* 95:104-9+ Ja '89
Stop blaming men for everything! (A guy begs for mercy) [self help literature] A. Heard. il *Mademoiselle* 95:182-3+ Ag '89
The togetherness trap. C. L. Mithers. il *Glamour* 87:194 Jl '89
Wanted: boys! ! ! (here's how to get 'em). il *'Teen* 33:12+ N '89
Were you born for each other? [significance of birth order in choosing a mate] P. M. Withers. il *McCall's* 116:56+ F '89
What bugs you about boys? [advice on getting guys to change] il *Seventeen* 48:70-1 Jl '89
What male friends can & can't teach you about love. C. L. Mithers. il *Glamour* 87:338-9+ Ap '89
What men want (I). S. Cook. il *Gentlemen's Quarterly* 59:294-301+ O '89
What men want (II). S. Cook. il *Gentlemen's Quarterly* 59:272-7+ N '89
When they hate the one you love [parents don't like boyfriend] L. Frank. il *Seventeen* 48:96+ N '89
When your friend picks the wrong man. C. L. Mithers. il *Glamour* 87:268 N '89
White collar, blue collar love [black professional women in love with blue collar men] L. B. Randolph. il *Ebony* 44:48+ My '89
Who says you have to have a boyfriend? C. Jakobson. *Seventeen* 48:108-10+ S '89
Whose time is more valuable? C. L. Mithers. il *Glamour* 87:296 O '89
Why boys are so bad at breakups. D. Seeley. il *Seventeen* 48:150-1+ O '89
Why I never trust a woman under 30. C. Brown. il *Mademoiselle* 95:188+ N '89
Women we love [cover story; special section] il *Esquire* 112:86-101 Ag '89
Would a nice girl string a guy along? J. C. Johnson. *Mademoiselle* 95:123 N '89

WOMEN AND MEN—*cont.*

Anecdotes, facetiae, satire, etc.

Boadicea, my love [older women and younger men] M. Richler. il *Gentlemen's Quarterly* 59:115-16 F '89

Brunch [radical couples] S. L. Wisenberg. *The New Yorker* 64:24-5 Ja 9 '89

"Dear Katie, so you want to get married . . .". J. Viorst. il *Redbook* 172:38+ Ap '89

A few good men. M. Ivins. il *Ms.* 17:22 My '89

Something's fishy. S. Harris. por *Essence* 19:160 F '89

Bibliography

Advice and consent [self help books] E. Hopkins. *Harper's Bazaar* 122:201+ Ap '89

WOMEN AND MEN IN MOTION PICTURES

Men, women, sex, love and marriage—from the mouths of Billy Crystal and Meg Ryan [interview] D. DeNicolo. il pors *Glamour* 87:205 S '89

WOMEN AND PEACE

See also

MEND (Organization)

WOMEN AND POLITICS *See* Women—Political activities

WOMEN AND RELIGION

See also

Jesus Christ—Attitudes towards women

Men, Women and God: Christians for Biblical Equality (Organization)

Mujerista theology

Nuns

Ordination of women

Women—Religious life

Women clergy

Women's Theological Center (Boston, Mass.)

Brain and gender: the missing data [discussion of January 4-11, 1989 article, Ways of knowing God: gender and the brain] J. B. Ashbrook. *The Christian Century* 106:263-4 Mr 8 '89

Christian feminism. S. Saetre. il *Utne Reader* p28 My/Je '89

Digging in the gardens of feminist theology [Inheriting our mothers' gardens: feminist theology in third world perspective] G. E. Ziegenhals. *The Christian Century* 106:260-3 Mr 8 '89

Does God want to be your macho man? [interview with A. E. Carr] por *U.S. Catholic* 54:16-22 My '89

Doing right by women and the Trinity too. D. A. Helminiak. il *America* 160:110+ F 11 '89

A father's legacy [G. G. Hull's father, F. Gaebelein] P. E. Alsdurf. il pors *Christianity Today* 33:58 O 20 '89

Feminism and the churches. K. L. Woodward. il *Newsweek* 113:58-61 F 13 '89

Gender, education and the new Christian right. S. D. Rose. bibl *Society* 26:59-66 Ja/F '89

In search of the hero: masculine spirituality and liberal Christianity [cover story] P. M. Arnold. il *America* 161:206-10 O 7 '89

'In the tongues of men': homilies for women [cover story] K. Coffey. il *America* 161:392-4 D 2 '89

Meeting the women of women-church [conference in Portsmouth, N.H.] G. E. Ziegenhals. *The Christian Century* 106:492-4 My 10 '89

Profs resign when women named to board [Philadelphia College of Bible] C. Lehmann. il *Christianity Today* 33:46 O 6 '89

Roberta Hestenes: taking charge [cover story] T. Stafford. il pors *Christianity Today* 33:16-22 Mr 3 '89

Sex (how about love?) on Catholic campuses [with discussion; cover story] D. J. O'Brien. *Commonweal* 116:169-77 Mr 24 '89

State of the question [discussion of October 7, 1989 article, In search of the hero: masculine spirituality and liberal Christianity] P. M. Arnold. *America* 161:304-6 N 4 '89

Ways of knowing God: gender and the brain. J. B. Ashbrook. il *The Christian Century* 106:14-15 Ja 4-11 '89

The women-church movement [cover story] M. T. Winter. *The Christian Century* 106:258-60 Mr 8 '89

WOMEN AND THE CHURCH *See* Women and religion

WOMEN AND THE ENVIRONMENT

See also

Ecofeminism

Heaven on earth: the race for renewal [special section] il *Harper's Bazaar* 122:58-67+ Ja '89

Women against toxic waste. J. Ralston. il *McCall's* 117:132+ O '89

WOMEN AND WAR

See also

Vietnamese War, 1957-1975—Women

World War, 1914-1918—Women

Canadian women at arms [I. Gauthier wins suit against Canadian Armed Forces over combat duty regulations] M. Suh. il *Ms.* 17:71-2 Je '89

Women in combat [Canada] N. Underwood. il *Maclean's* 102:53 Mr 6 '89

WOMEN ANTHROPOLOGISTS

See also

Galdikas, Biruté

WOMEN ARCHEOLOGISTS

See also

Chase, Diane

WOMEN ARCHITECTS

See also

Berke, Deborah, 1954-

Lambert, Phyllis, 1927-

Lin, Maya Ying

London, Gabrielle

Page, Kathleen

Quinn, Kathryn

Searl, Linda

Zebrowski, Rachel Williams

The woman-managed firm: how big a deal? R. L. Miller. il pors *Architectural Record* 177:47+ Je '89

WOMEN ARTISTS

See also

Adams, Phoebe

Baltzell, Jan C.

Baron, Hannelore, 1926-1987

Bartlett, Jennifer, 1941-

Barton, Nancy

Bell, Vanessa, 1879-1961

Berlin, Beatrice, 1922-

Bourgeois, Louise

Brito-Avellana, Maria

Burke, Selma, 1900-

Butterfield, Deborah, 1949-

Calle, Sophie

Carson, Sharon

Carter, Carol

Cartier, Janice

Cassatt, Mary, 1844-1926

Celmins, Vija, 1939-

Chandler, Robin

Chesley, Jacqueline

Chiarini, Doriana

Claudel, Camille

Coe, Sue, 1951-

Delany, Mary Granville Pendarves, 1700-1788

Dickinson, Eleanor, 1931-

Dopp, Susan Marie

Duillo, Elaine

Dwyer, Nancy

Ericson, Kate

Fleming, Linda

Foreman, Laura

Frankenthaler, Helen, 1928-

Geiger, Marion

Gentileschi, Artemisia, 1597-1651

Hamilton, Ann

Hartlieb, Ingrid, 1944-

Hatoum, Mona

Haynes, Nancy, 1947-

Heller, Susanna

Hesse, Eva, 1936-1970

Hiller, Susan, 1940-

Hirabayashi, Kaoru

Holzer, Jenny

Horn, Karen

Huff, Caroline

Hyde de Neuville, Anne-Marguerite-Henriette Rouillé de Marigny, baronne, 1749?-1849

Jaffe, Shirley, 1923-

Kidd, Julia

Kienholz, Nancy Reddin

Kirkpatrick, Joey

Klint, Hilma af, 1862-1944

Kohlmeyer, Ida, 1912-

Kolbowski, Silvia

Kruger, Barbara

Kusama, Yayoi, 1929-

Lafontaine, Marie-Jo

Lalanne, Claude

Larko, Valeri, 1959-

Lawler, Louise

Lehman, Wendy

Levine, Sherrie, 1947-

Lowenstein, Suse

Mace, Flora Carrie

Mäkelä, Marika

Marisol, 1930-

Martin, Agnes, 1912-

Masters, Deborah

McCoy, Ann, 1946-

Mee, Margaret, 1909-1988

Minkowitz, Norma, 1937-

Minter, Marilyn

Miss, Mary, 1944-

Murray, Elizabeth

Nelson, Joan, 1958-

Nesterova, Natalia

Nevelson, Louise, 1900-1988

Noland, Cady

Norton, Ann

Olin, Marian E.

Oppenheim, Meret, 1913-1985

Oulton, Therese, 1953-

Pfaff, Judy

Poirier, Anne

Porter, Katherine, 1941-

WOMEN ARTISTS—See also—*cont.*
Rego, Paula, 1935-
Remington, Deborah, 1935-
Rielle, Nancy
Ringgold, Faith
Robertson, Mary
Rodriguez, Rocio
Rosenberg, Evelyn
Rosler, Martha, 1943-
Ryan, Anne, 1889-1954
Sampson, Atlanta Constance, 1897-
Savannah, Sheila
Scott Brown, Denise, 1931-
Seager, Sarah
Seely, Alice Warder, 1942-
Sekiguchi, Risa
Sharrow, Sheba
Shorr, Harriet
Sigler, Hollis, 1948-
Steckel, Anita
Stevens, May, 1924-
Ukeles, Mierle Laderman
Weber, Mili
Westerlund Roosen, Mia, 1942-
White, Susan Chrysler
Williams-Cacicedo, Jean
Wilson, Helen Miranda
Yanow, Rhoda
Zeldis, Malcah, 1931-
Zimmermann, Marie
Making waves. K. Simmons. il *Horizon (Tuscaloosa, Ala.)* 32:37-40 Ja/F '89

Exhibitions
Her infinite variety [Making their mark: women artists move into the mainstream, 1970-85] S. Allison. il *Life* 12:64-8 Je '89
Women artists, 1970-85 [cover story] A. C. Danto. *The Nation* 249:794-6+ D 25 '89

WOMEN ASTRONAUTS
See also
Jemison, Mae C.

WOMEN ASTRONOMERS
See also
Gill, Jocelyn Ruth
Women in astronomy. S. J. O'Meara. il *Sky and Telescope* 77:317-18 Mr '89

WOMEN ATHLETES
See also
Sex discrimination in sports
Tennis players
Women—Sports
Women's Sports Foundation
Women's Sports Hall of Fame
See also names of women athletes
Days of glory [college athletes] G. Lichtenstein. il *Vogue* 179:202-3+ Ap '89
Give your summer hair a sporting chance. J. Neal. il *Women's Sports & Fitness* 11:20 My '89
Meet the top 24 athletes [finalists in Sportsgirl of the Year contest] il *Teen* 33:42-3 D '89
A mixed report about high school sports [studies of minorities] K. M. Reith. il *Women's Sports & Fitness* 11:64 N/D '89
Seoul '88 [reports by nine athletes; cover story] L. Rothlein. il *Women's Sports & Fitness* 11:33-9 Ja/F '89
Team tryouts: be a sport (win or lose!). il *Teen* 33:74-5+ Ap '89

Attitudes
Women in sports: what's changed? [negative perception of female high school athletes; research by Mary Jo Kane] V. Bozzi. *Psychology Today* 23:70 O '89

Awards
See Sports—Awards

Health and hygiene
Frontal assault [breast injuries] M. Madsen. il *Women's Sports & Fitness* 11:10 Ja/F '89

Nutrition
The best quick breakfasts for active women. G. Shockey. il *Women's Sports & Fitness* 11:34-5+ Ap '89
The hazards of eating too little. E. Coleman. il *Women's Sports & Fitness* 11:18 Mr '89
Raising your carbo consciousness. O. Anderson. il *Women's Sports & Fitness* 11:18 O '89
The Ten Commandments of sports nutrition. D. C. Nieman. il *Women's Sports & Fitness* 11:58-61 Mr '89
The truth about iron. G. Shockey. il *Women's Sports & Fitness* 11:20-1 Ja/F '89
A vitamin exercisers need to watch closely [B-2] O. Anderson. il *Women's Sports & Fitness* 11:22 S '89

Psychology
See Sports—Psychological aspects

Training
Overtraining. J. Mattera. il *Glamour* 87:76 S '89

WOMEN ATHLETIC DIRECTORS
Where the boys are [effect of Title IX on women athletic directors and coaches at the college level] M. Goodman. *The Washington Monthly* 21:18-20 Ap '89

WOMEN AUTHORS
See also
Atwood, Margaret, 1939-
Auel, Jean M.
Brontë, Charlotte, 1816-1855
Brownmiller, Susan
Campbell, Bebe Moore
Clark, Mary Higgins
Collins, Jackie
Davis, Lindsay
Dillard, Annie
Dunn, Katherine
Eisenstadt, Jill
Ginzburg, Natalia
Glendinning, Victoria
Golden, Marita
Gossett, Hattie, 1942-
Grafton, Sue
Haasse, Hella S., 1918-
Hughes, Frieda
James, P. D.
Janowitz, Tama
Jolley, Elizabeth, 1923-
Kingston, Maxine Hong
Krantz, Judith
Leaming, Barbara
Lebowitz, Fran
Leimbach, Marti
McCarthy, Mary, 1912-1989
McCloy, Kristin
McCullough, Colleen, 1937-
Minot, Susan
Mitchell, Margaret, 1900-1949
Montgomery, L. M. (Lucy Maud), 1874-1942
Morrison, Toni, 1931-
Mukherjee, Bharati
Naylor, Gloria
Nesbit, E. (Edith), 1858-1924
Nestle, Joan, 1940-
O'Brien, Edna
Piercy, Marge
Potter, Beatrix, 1866-1943
Price, Eugenia
Prose, Francine, 1947-
Randall, Margaret, 1936-
Reid Banks, Lynne, 1929-
Rendell, Ruth, 1930-
Rice, Anne, 1941-
Rose, Phyllis, 1942-
Schaeffer, Susan Fromberg
Schwamm, Ellen
Sontag, Susan, 1933-
Spark, Muriel
Stein, Gertrude, 1874-1946
Tan, Amy
Trilling, Diana
Tyler, Anne, 1941-
Walker, Alice, 1944-
Weldon, Fay
Welty, Eudora, 1909-
Wiggins, Marianne
Woolf, Virginia, 1882-1941
La boom [Mexican American women] M. DiLeo. il *Mother Jones* 14:15 O '89
"From welfare mom to millionaire". E. Goudge. il por *Ladies' Home Journal* 106:22+ Ag '89
Gender & genre: women in science fiction and fantasy. R. Herbert. il *Publishers Weekly* 236:22 N 10 '89
The hand that rocks the cradle writes the book. U. K. Le Guin. il *The New York Times Book Review* 94:1+ Ja 22 '89
The sisterhood of sleuths [mysteries by and about women] E. Gibson. il *Publishers Weekly* 235:37-9 My 5 '89
When women finally got the word [women of medieval Japan and Europe, writing in the vernacular, prefigured modern literature] E. Kolb. il *The New York Times Book Review* 94:1+ Jl 9 '89

WOMEN AUTOMOBILE DRIVERS
Joy riding. J. Evans. il *Vogue* 179:340 Ap '89

WOMEN AUTOMOBILE RACING DRIVERS
See also
Junek, Elisabeth
St. James, Lyn

WOMEN BASEBALL UMPIRES See Baseball, Professional—Umpiring

WOMEN BASKETBALL COACHES See Basketball coaches

WOMEN BIOLOGISTS
See also
Earle, Sylvia A., 1935-
Storrs, Eleanor

WOMEN BISHOPS
A bishop who won't be one of the boys [Episcopal bishop B. Harris] por *Newsweek* 113:60 F 13 '89
Bishops reach accord on women clergy [Episcopal Church] R. Walker. *Christianity Today* 33:57 N 3 '89
Consecration of bishop stirs Episcopal dissent [B. Harris] R. Walker. il por *Christianity Today* 33:41+ Mr 17 '89

WOMEN BISHOPS—cont.

Episcopal Church ordains its first female bishop [B. C. Harris] il pors *Jet* 75:13 F 27 '89

Episcopalian accord. il *The Christian Century* 106:977 N 1 '89

The first of the 'mitered mamas' [black Episcopal bishop B. C. Harris] L. Rosellini. por *U.S. News & World Report* 106:56-7 Je 19 '89

The first woman Episcopal bishop [B. C. Harris] R. D. Turner. il pors *Ebony* 44:40+ My '89

Harris approved [Episcopal bishop B. C. Harris] *The Christian Century* 106:104-5 F 1-8 '89

That new time religion [ordination of B. C. Harris] *National Review* 41:16-17 Mr 10 '89

When the Spirit leads [consecration of woman bishop B. C. Harris] J. Redmont. il por *Commonweal* 116:133-5 Mr 10 '89

WOMEN BODYBUILDERS *See* Bodybuilding

WOMEN BOTANISTS

See also

Earle, Sylvia A., 1935-

WOMEN BOXERS

Locked in bloodless combat, Billy Dean's foxy boxers show more jiggle than punch [Knockout Foxy Fighting Revue] il pors *People Weekly* 31:116-17 Mr 13 '89

Now we know what Rocky VI will be about. G. Castle. il *Sport (New York, N.Y.)* 80:14 Ag '89

WOMEN CADETS

Breaking barriers in the barracks [K. Baker named First Captain of cadets at West Point] P. Cary. il pors *U.S. News & World Report* 107:26-7 Ag 21 '89

Manning the barricades no more, West Point names Kristin Baker to head the long gray line [first female captain of the cadet corps] S. K. Reed. il pors *People Weekly* 32:50-1 Ag 28 '89

'No slack': a woman's touch at West Point [cadet K. Baker named First Captain] por *Newsweek* 114:20 Ag 21 '89

WOMEN CARTOONISTS

See also

Gauerke, Mary

WOMEN CHOREOGRAPHERS

See also

Abdul, Paula
Armitage, Karole
Bausch, Pina
Caponigro, Angela
Carlson, Ann
Cobb, Catlin
Driver, Senta
Dunham, Katherine
Feldman, Barbara
Graham, Martha
Hoyer, Dore
Ichinohe, Saeko
Lewitzky, Bella, 1916-
Nijinska, Bronislava, 1891-1972
Polsky, Rose
Taylor-Corbett, Lynne
Tharp, Twyla

Pushing the frontier further: WomanWorks [performances at the Joyce Theater, New York City] R. A. Thom. il *Dance Magazine* 63:60-3 My '89

WOMEN CLERGY

See also

Ordination of women

First black woman to head merged Presbyterian Church [Rev. J. SalmonCampbell of the Presbyterian Church U.S.A.] A. Bradford. il pors *Ebony* 45:100+ N '89

"This is what I was meant to do!". W. Urbanska. il *McCall's* 117:91-5 D '89

Women in ministry [National Council of Churches report] *The Christian Century* 106:280 Mr 15 '89

WOMEN COACHES *See* Coaches (Athletics)

WOMEN COLLEGE GRADUATES

After 58 years, a round-robin letter keeps on delivering [graduates of the College of Wooster maintain contact] W. Plummer. il *People Weekly* 31:99-100 Ja 16 '89

Employment

Getting down to business [special section] *Harper's Bazaar* 122:28+ Je '89

WOMEN COLLEGE OFFICIALS

Women in administration of higher education. S. Kaplan and A. Tinsley. *The Education Digest* 55:24-7 D '89

WOMEN COLLEGE PRESIDENTS

See also

Cole, Johnnetta B.
Hestenes, Roberta
Shalala, Donna
Sudarkasa, Niara

WOMEN COLLEGE STUDENTS

See also

College sororities
Sex discrimination in education

Campus queens at black colleges. il *Ebony* 44:54+ Ap '89

Harvard makeovers. L. Barrett. il *Essence* 20:76-9 Ag '89

Top ten college women '89. il *Glamour* 87:254-7 O '89

Attitudes

Career first, children later [survey by Kristine Baber] il *USA Today (Periodical)* 117:8-9 Mr '89

WOMEN COLLEGE TEACHERS *See* College teachers

WOMEN COMEDIANS

See also

Allen, Gracie, 1906?-1964
Ball, Lucille, 1911-1989
Barr, Roseanne
Bernhard, Sandra
Boosler, Elayne, 1952?-
Diller, Phyllis, 1917-
Jackson, Victoria
Otsuki, Tamayo
Radner, Gilda, 1946-1989
Rivers, Joan, 1937-
Tenuta, Judy

WOMEN COMMODITY BROKERS

Pit players [P. Kern of Norman Kern & Company] D. Sherman. il pors *Ms.* 18:62-4+ N '89

WOMEN CONSTRUCTION WORKERS

Women hard hats speak out. S. Eisenberg. *The Nation* 249:272-4+ S 18 '89

WOMEN CONSUMERS

China and crystal—not for brides only. M. Rowland. il *Working Woman* 14:102-62+ F '89

Putting on the clout [women automobile customers] M. Keller. il *Motor Trend* 41:144 Mr '89

WOMEN CONTRACTORS

Building wealth—house by house [S. Wiseman] L. Washer. il por *Working Woman* 14:97 My '89

WOMEN COOKS

See also

Ashley, Eliza Jane
Child, Julia
Fox, Margaret
Gold, Rozanne
Hazan, Marcella
Katzen, Mollie, 1950-
Kennedy, Diana
Largent, Linny
Lewis, Edna
Ponzek, Debra
Stewart, Martha
Tropp, Barbara
Waters, Alice

When women man the stockpots. M. Sheraton. il *Time* 133:67+ Je 19 '89

WOMEN CYCLISTS *See* Cyclists

WOMEN DOCTORS *See* Women physicians

WOMEN DRAMATISTS

See also

Hansberry, Lorraine, 1930-1965
Henley, Beth

WOMEN ELECTRONICS WORKERS

One step forward, two steps back [Lorance v. AT&T Technologies; Supreme Court decision] P. Simpson. il por *Ms.* 18:96 S '89

WOMEN ENGINEERS

The women who are scaling high tech's heights. E. T. Smith. il *Business Week* p86-8 Ag 28 '89

WOMEN ENTREPRENEURS

The age of the woman entrepreneur [cover story] S. Nelton. il *Nation's Business* 77:22-5+ My '89

Doing business in the 'burbs [special section] D. Weil. il *Working Woman* 14:58-62+ Ag '89

Enterprise. See issues of Working Woman beginning September 1983

Franchising's appeal to women. M. Whittemore. il *Nation's Business* 77:63-4 N '89

Help for women entrepreneurs [SBA's mentor program] B. Stein. il *Home Office Computing* 7:12 My '89

A Kenyan tycoon [businesswoman E. K. Mungai] W. Machua. il por *World Press Review* 36:52 Jl '89

Principles to grow by [excerpt from Exceptional entrepreneurial women] R. R. Taylor. il *Nation's Business* 77:50-1 Jl '89

Saga of a business start-up (I). L. Washer. il pors *Working Woman* 14:45-6+ D '89

Saintly companies that make heavenly profits [special section] J. David and K. File. il *Working Woman* 14:122-4+ O '89

She's the boss [husbands working for wives] D. Michals. il *Ms.* 18:58-61 N '89

Small-budget start-ups [black women] C. Milano. il *Essence* 20:124+ O '89

To grow or not to grow? L. Sagalyn. il *Working Woman* 14:66 Ag '89

Turning over a new leaf. M. Rowland. il *Working Woman* 14:55-6+ Jl '89

Where women can get business know-how. J. H. Pratt. il *Home Office Computing* 7:47-9 My '89

Wife, mother, entrepreneur. S. Nelton. il *Nation's Business* 77:10 Ap '89

Awards

The new entrepreneurial establishment: 1989 Harriet Alger Award [G. Denhart of Hanna Andersson] il pors *Working Woman* 14:53-6+ N '89

WOMEN ENTREPRENEURS—Awards—*cont.*

Only Women of Enterprise need apply. B. Stein. il *Home Office Computing* 7:18 N '89

Six women who beat the odds [Women of Enterprise] J. L. Block. il *Good Housekeeping* 209:16+ Jl '89

WOMEN EXECUTIVES

See also

    Clothing and dress—Businesswomen

    Mommy track

    Women entrepreneurs

The 21st-century manager. R. Farmanfarmaian. il *Working Woman* 14:73+ N '89

Born to run the show? The management test. A. Gates. il *Mademoiselle* 95:166+ Mr '89

Breaking ranks [roundtable discussion of black women executives] E. Porter. il *Essence* 20:87-8+ S '89

Corporate nannies for a new decade [businesses coping with family issues] B. Brophy. il *U.S. News & World Report* 107:70+ D 25 '89-Ja 1 '90

The corporation vs. the family: can the conflict be resolved? [special section] il *Working Woman* 14:125-7+ N '89

Dear Betty Harragan. B. L. Harragan. See issues of Working Woman

Executive edge [black women] il *Essence* 19:53-9+ Mr '89

An executive's guide to volunteering. P. Kruger. *Working Woman* 14:86-8 D '89

Give your daughter a chance. S. Nelton. il *Nation's Business* 77:72 Je '89

How to be the boss they all want to work for [excerpt from Careertracking] J. Calano and J. Salzman. il *Working Woman* 14:94-5+ Ja '89

How to control the time eaters [excerpt from Time power] C. R. Hobbs. *Working Woman* 14:110-11+ My '89

How to manage your career for lifelong success [cover story; special section] il *Working Woman* 14:101-4+ O '89

Japan discovers woman power. S. Solo. il *Fortune* 119:153-4+ Je 19 '89

Manager: the all-time hot career of the '90s. P. Kruger. *Working Woman* 14:78-9 Jl '89

She's the boss! [black supervisors and executives] M. Marshall. il *Ebony* 44:80+ Je '89

The truth about women managers [interview with F. N. Schwartz] B. Brophy. il por *U.S. News & World Report* 106:57 Mr 13 '89

Awards

The 1989 Working Woman Hall of Fame. il *Working Woman* 14:111-12+ N '89

Dismissal

Comeback charisma. J. Ciabattari. *Harper's Bazaar* 122:102+ Ja '89

Emily Koltnow: the fired woman's best friend. il por *Business Week* p68 S 18 '89

Health and hygiene

6 steps to lifelong health. G. B. Bloch. *Working Woman* 14:153-4 Ap '89

The truth about women and heart disease. B. Hersey. il *Working Woman* 14:156+ Ap '89

What keeps them going? Four nonstop women share their secrets. il *Glamour* 87:75 Je '89

You're on: diary of a 14-hour day. N. Malkin. il *Working Woman* 14:156+ O '89

Nutrition

Body management [special section] il *Working Woman* 14:129-30+ My '89

Eat for energy. R. A. Barnett. il *Working Woman* 14:129+ F '89

Nutrition power in working lunches. J. Hendley. il *Working Woman* 14:63 Jl '89

Promotion

Climbing the ladder: after talent, what counts most? M. M. Kennedy. il *Glamour* 87:99-100 Je '89

How to become the leader of the pack. M. M. Kennedy. il *Glamour* 87:137-8 Ap '89

Sudden success [cover story; special section] il *Working Woman* 14:77-80+ Je '89

Psychology

Ambition without anxiety [special section] il *Working Woman* 14:123-6+ S '89

. . . and other rites of passage. S. G. Sheehy. il *Working Woman* 14:90-2 Je '89

Beyond macho: the power of womanly management [excerpt from Tender power] S. S. Cohen. il pors *Working Woman* 14:77-83 F '89

How to expect the unexpected and handle it well. J. Ciabattari. il *Working Woman* 14:84-6+ F '89

How to stay cool under fire [excerpt from Get to the point] K. Berg and A. Gilman. il *Working Woman* 14:41+ N '89

Leave them laughing [humorous speeches] M. B. Marklein. il *Nation's Business* 77:49 O '89

New-job identity crisis. L. Mosedale. il *Working Woman* 14:97 O '89

Planning it all: the new calendar girls [trying to fit marriage into timetable] E. Weiner. il *Mademoiselle* 95:130-3+ Jl '89

The politics of power [address, April 1, 1989] P. F. Mancini. *Vital Speeches of the Day* 55:657-62 Ag 15 '89

Power fun. R. Urquhart. il *Mademoiselle* 95:188-9+ D '89

Separation (from work) anxiety. S. Person. il *Working Woman* 14:61+ Jl '89

Stamping out performance stoppers. D. Cole. il *Working Woman* 14:90-2 Mr '89

Success and the soft-hearted woman. J. M. Toal. il *Mademoiselle* 95:194-5+ O '89

Surviving corporate cutbacks [black women] J. Malveaux. il *Essence* 19:107 Ap '89

The truth about desk mess. K. A. Samon. il *Working Woman* 14:107 Ap '89

Under the eye of the consultant. P. Amend. il *Working Woman* 14:37-8 O '89

Women managers: a certain style. J. C. Johnson. il *Nation's Business* 77:12 Ap '89

Anecdotes, facetiae, satire, etc.

Filofaxed to the max. S. Johnson and C. Marcil. *Mademoiselle* 95:133+ Jl '89

Rating

Dear Betty Harragan. B. L. Harragan. il *Working Woman* 14:29-30 F '89

Recreation

Making time for your other life [special section] il *Working Woman* 14:101-8+ Mr '89

Power fun. R. Urquhart. il *Mademoiselle* 95:188-9+ D '89

Time out to recharge [weekend activities; special section] il *Working Woman* 14:107-116+ Je '89

Salaries, pensions, etc.

Financial workshop: a year in the lives of four women (I). M. Rowland. il *Working Woman* 14:91-2+ Ap '89

Financial workshop: a year in the lives of four women (II). M. Rowland. il *Working Woman* 14:79-80+ My '89

Financial workshop: a year in the lives of four women (III). M. Rowland. il *Working Woman* 14:61-2+ Je '89

Financial workshop: a year in the lives of four women (IV). M. Rowland. il *Working Woman* 14:55-6+ Jl '89

Financial workshop: a year in the lives of four women (V). M. Rowland. il *Working Woman* 14:47-8+ Ag '89

Financial workshop: a year in the lives of four women (VI). M. Rowland. il *Working Woman* 14:69-70+ S '89

Financial workshop: a year in the lives of four women (VII). M. Rowland. il *Working Woman* 14:89-90+ O '89

Financial workshop: a year in the lives of four women (VIII). M. Rowland. il *Working Woman* 14:95-6+ N '89

Financial workshop: a year in the lives of four women (IX). M. Rowland. il *Working Woman* 14:61-2+ D '89

Sports

Sports and your career [special section] il *Working Woman* 14:137-8+ Je '89

Taxation

A taxpayer's financial first-aid kit. M. Rowland. *Working Woman* 14:124-5+ Ap '89

Transfer

How to get the job you really want [cover story; special section] il *Working Woman* 14:111-14+ Ap '89

Travel

See Business travel

WOMEN EXECUTIVES' HUSBANDS

Anecdotes, facetiae, satire, etc.

The trophy husband. K. Fury. il *Working Woman* 14:134 D '89

WOMEN EXPLORERS

Great explorations. J. Mills. bibl il *Ms.* 17:58-62 Je '89

WOMEN FOREIGN EXCHANGE BROKERS

Life in the stress lane: diary of a wired day [K. Bunis participates in Gary James' study of key stress points in average day of a working woman] N. Angier. il pors *Mademoiselle* 95:192-5+ F '89

WOMEN GAME WARDENS

Deer season [female warden D. Palman] F. Graham. *Audubon* 91:18+ N '89

WOMEN HIGH SCHOOL GRADUATES *See* High school graduates

WOMEN HISTORIANS

See also

    Dawidowicz, Lucy S.

    Tuchman, Barbara Wertheim

WOMEN HUNTERS

Lessons for a lifetime [raising a daughter to hunt and fish] K. Etling. il *Outdoor Life* 183:76-8+ Je '89

WOMEN IN ADVERTISING

As time goes by [cosmetics ads and the middle age market] L. Wells. il *The New York Times Magazine* p86 Mr 19 '89

Dear Betty Harragan. B. L. Harragan. il *Working Woman* 14:47-8 N '89

The image of creative control [office of L. R. McNamee] L. Rosch. il por *Working Woman* 14:132-3 S '89

The sexism watch. il *U.S. News & World Report* 106:12 Mr 27 '89

She's got to have it all now! [media planner K. Crowley] S. Seixas. il pors *Money* 18:86-8+ O '89

WOMEN IN AGRICULTURE *See* Farm women

WOMEN IN ART

See also

    Mastectomy in art

    Nude in art

Affairs of the art [artists' models who were also mistresses] E. MacSweeney. il *Harper's Bazaar* 122:168-73 D '89

WOMEN IN ART—cont.

Exhibitions

Rego's girls [work of P. Rego] S. Kent. il *Art in America* 77:158-63+ Je '89

Sex and politics [A. Wyeth's The Helga pictures] K. Larson. il *New York* 22:51-2 Jl 17 '89

WOMEN IN BUSINESS *See* Businesswomen

WOMEN IN CABLE TELEVISION

China star [Y.-S. Kan] *The New Yorker* 64:20-2 Ja 9 '89

Here comes the judge—Catherine Crier now presides at a news desk [co-anchor on CNN's The world today] J. Park. il pors *People Weekly* 32:59-60 N 6 '89

Never look down [K. Koplovitz of USA Network] D. Machan. il por *Forbes* 144:270+ Jl 24 '89

WOMEN IN COMBAT *See* Women and war

WOMEN IN FISHING

Father to daughter. B. Journey. il *Outdoor Life* 184:94-5+ N '89

A Fijian way of fishing. M. Timmons. il *Sea Frontiers* 35:64 Ja/F '89

Lessons for a lifetime [raising a daughter to hunt and fish] K. Etling. il *Outdoor Life* 183:76-8+ Je '89

WOMEN IN INVESTMENT BANKING

Carol Einiger: one-of-a-kind at Wasserella. R. Conniff. il por *Business Week* p99 Ag 21 '89

WOMEN IN LITERATURE

See also

    Alice in Wonderland (Fictional character)

    Anne of Green Gables (Fictional character)

    Eloise (Fictional character)

    Lucy Marsden (Fictional character)

    Mary Poppins (Fictional character)

Bad-boy books [work of male novelists] J. Leonard. il *Ms.* 17:124+ Ja/F '89

WOMEN IN MOTION PICTURES

See also

    Shirley Valentine (Fictional character)

    Snow White (Fictional character)

    Women in the motion picture industry

Behind the veil [portrayal of Algerian women] A. Djebar. il *The Unesco Courier* 42:34-7 O '89

The many faces of Eve: the changing image of the sex goddess. J. Kristin. il *American Film* 14:38-41+ Ap '89

The new heroines: bad is beautiful. R. Rosenbaum. il *Mademoiselle* 95:120+ S '89

The Steel magnolias scrapbook. J. Rachlin and J. Rovin. il *Ladies' Home Journal* 106:126+ N '89

Women's business [C. Chabrol's Story of women] M. Pally. il *Film Comment* 25:16-18+ S/O '89

WOMEN IN MYTHOLOGY

The powers of the primeval goddesses. M. R. Lefkowitz. *The American Scholar* 58:586-91 Aut '89

WOMEN IN NETWORKING (FIRM)

Emily Koltnow: the fired woman's best friend. il por *Business Week* p68 S 18 '89

WOMEN IN NEWSPAPER PUBLISHING

The manager who never says never [N. Woodhull of Gannett] R. Sandroff. il pors *Working Woman* 14:90-2+ D '89

WOMEN IN POLITICS *See* Women—Political activities

WOMEN IN PUBLIC RELATIONS

High-profile creativity from a brownstone base [office of R. Greene] L. Rosch. il por *Working Woman* 14:89 My '89

The perfect power couple's perfect power marriage [L. G. Robinson] il por *Fortune* 120:86 N 20 '89

WOMEN IN PUBLISHING

See also

    Women in newspaper publishing

The mastermind of a media empire [K. Graham] M. Rowland. il pors *Working Woman* 14:114-15+ N '89

Well-read women [Manhattan homes of L. Nesbit, J. Evans, and N. Evans] D. Lida. il pors *House & Garden* 161:228-31 O '89

WOMEN IN RADIO

See also

    Mama Montego (Fictional character)

WOMEN IN RELIGION *See* Women and religion

WOMEN IN RESTAURANT MANAGEMENT

Cooking up profits in Europe [A. Conway's eateries] A. McKenzie. por *Black Enterprise* 20:79-80 N '89

Steering safely through setbacks [N. Laurenzo] L. Gite. il pors *Working Woman* 14:39-41+ F '89

WOMEN IN RETAIL TRADE

Taking charge [M. Williams] D. Machan. il pors *Forbes* 143:154-6 Mr 6 '89

WOMEN IN SAILING

See also

    Womanship, Inc.

WOMEN IN SALES *See* Sales personnel

WOMEN IN SPORTS *See* Women athletes

WOMEN IN TELEVISION

See also

    Abby Perkins (Fictional character)

    Mary Richards (Fictional character)

    Mothers in television

    Murphy Brown (Fictional character)

    Policewomen in television

    Rebecca Howe (Fictional character)

    Roseanne Conners (Fictional character)

    Women in the television industry

    Women lawyers in television

At last! Women worth watching. J. O'Reilly. il *TV Guide* 37:18-21 My 27-Je 2 '89

Black like who? [The women of Brewster Place] M. Glicksman. il *Film Comment* 25:75-6 My/Je '89

Black women on television triple during the decade. *Jet* 75:10 Mr 6 '89

Narcissus, thy name is woman [taping Canadian TV special Women in the '90s] B. Amiel. il *Maclean's* 102:9 F 13 '89

Networking women [cover story] H. F. Waters and J. Huck. il *Newsweek* 113:48-52+ Mr 13 '89

There's Oprah, Jackée, Robin Givens—and a break men may not deserve [The women of Brewster Place; cover story] E. Warren. il pors *TV Guide* 37:4-5+ Mr 18-24 '89

The women of Brewster Place. il pors *Ebony* 44:122-4+ Mr '89

'Women of Brewster Place' a powerful tale of love and conflict [cover story] il *Jet* 75:58-60 Mr 20 '89

Women on TV: work is in. D. Burden. il *Psychology Today* 23:12 O '89

WOMEN IN THE ANTI-NUCLEAR MOVEMENT *See* Anti-nuclear movement

WOMEN IN THE ARMED FORCES *See* Servicewomen

WOMEN IN THE BIBLE

See also

    Jesus Christ—Attitudes towards women

    Salome (Biblical figure)

WOMEN IN THE COMPUTER INDUSTRY

Where career ladders are like roller coasters [special section] il *Working Woman* 14:55-6+ My '89

WOMEN IN THE FOOD INDUSTRY

Moving into senior management [K. Johnson, vice president of consumer affairs at Borden] J. Ciabattari. il pors *Working Woman* 14:104-6+ My '89

WOMEN IN THE MOTION PICTURE INDUSTRY

See also

    Women motion picture directors

Women in film [black women; special section] il *Essence* 20:31-2+ O '89

WOMEN IN THE PHONOGRAPH RECORD INDUSTRY

See also

    Olivia Records

WOMEN IN THE REAL ESTATE BUSINESS

The hidden fortune in ugly-duckling real estate [S. Brangham] L. Touby. il por *Working Woman* 14:98 My '89

Penthouse properties, corporate style [office of C. Ugiss, vice president of Corporate Planners & Coordinators] L. Rosch. il por *Working Woman* 14:120-1 O '89

WOMEN IN THE TELEVISION INDUSTRY

See also

    Women in cable television

All about Deborah [J. Pauley, D. Norville and the Today show] E. Diamond. il pors *New York* 22:28+ O 23 '89

Are women reporters better than men? M. Sanders. il *TV Guide* 37:15-16+ Mr 18-24 '89

Barbara Walters. por *People Weekly* 31 Special Issue:66 Summ '89

Can Sally Sussman find happiness with her own soap opera? Only time—and Generations—will tell. L. Armstrong. il por *People Weekly* 31:113-14 Ap 17 '89

Civil rights movement led Lawson to her PBS career [J. Lawson] *Jet* 77:38 D 18 '89

Exit Jane, amid turmoil [J. Pauley resigns from Today show] R. Zoglin. pors *Time* 134:81 O 23 '89

Goodbye Today, hello tomorrow [J. Pauley; cover story] B. Darrach. il pors *Life* 12:46-8+ D 19 '89

'Looksism' in TV news [sexism] J. Alter. il por *Newsweek* 114:72-3 N 6 '89

Maria Shriver: you call this a glamour job? C. Krupp. il pors *Glamour* 87:172-3 N '89

Newcomer Deborah Norville stirs the latest tempest in the Today show's coffee cup. J. Kaufman. il pors *People Weekly* 32:48-9 O 9 '89

Oprah's private life: the inside story. L. DePaulo. il pors *TV Guide* 37:2-6 Je 3-9 '89

Prime-time jobs [black women behind the TV cameras] K. Richardson. il *Essence* 19:108+ Ja '89

The prime time of her life [D. Sawyer] P. Pierce. il pors *Ladies' Home Journal* 106:42+ O '89

The prime times of Diane Sawyer. J. Grant. il pors *Life* 12:72-4+ Ag '89

The richest woman on TV? Oprah! [cover story] A. Feinberg. il pors *TV Guide* 37:2-7 Ag 26-S 1 '89

Star power [anchor D. Sawyer of Primetime live; cover story] R. Zoglin. il pors *Time* 134:46-51 Ag 7 '89

Star reporter [C. Cohen] J. Conant. il pors *Harper's Bazaar* 122:146-7+ N '89

Star wars at the networks [C. Chung, M. A. Williams, and D. Sawyer switch networks] R. Zoglin. il pors *Time* 133:70-1 Ap 3 '89

They've run her off the road—but never off a story [West 57th's K. Burnes] D. Hill. il por *TV Guide* 37:36-7 Ja 21-27 '89

WOMEN IN THE TELEVISION INDUSTRY—*cont.*

TV's new golden girl [D. Norville] J. Hoffman. il pors *Gentlemen's Quarterly* 59:232-5+ Je '89

TV's new news queens: how good are they? [cover story] J. Elm. il *TV Guide* 37:2-4 Ag 12-18 '89

Two hearts, beating in prime time [C. Chung and M. Povich; cover story] K. McMurran. il pors *People Weekly* 31:116-17+ Ap 10 '89

Two was company, three a crowd [D. Norville replaces J. Pauley as co-anchor on Today; cover story] il pors *People Weekly* 32:114-16+ N 13 '89

Watch out for her surprise offensive [J. Lunden] D. Hill. il pors *TV Guide* 37:12-14 S 2-8 '89

What happened to Marlene Sanders? L. C. Pogrebin. il pors *New Choices for the Best Years* 29:67-71+ Mr '89

What makes Maria Shriver run so fast. J. Kalter. il pors *TV Guide* 37:6-10 Jl 29-Ag 4 '89

What TV's real newswomen think of Murphy Brown [cover story] J. Elm. il *TV Guide* 37:4-7 D 23-29 '89

Will women change prime-time TV news? A. Nash. il *Glamour* 87:242-5+ O '89

Winning Diane: how ABC's Roone Arledge snatched her away from CBS [cover story] E. Klein. il pors *New York* 22:36-43 Mr 13 '89

With Mary Alice Williams, NBC has a winner in the great anchor sweepstakes. S. K. Reed. il pors *People Weekly* 32:44-6 Ag 7 '89

Women on the verge of a nervy breakthrough [interview with L. Ellerbee, M. Goldin, A. Rubenstein and M. Vieira; cover story] P. Orenstein. il pors *Mother Jones* 14:28-31+ Je '89

The wooing of Diane Sawyer sparks a fierce network battle. il pors *People Weekly* 31:124 Ap 10 '89

Working girl [tennis announcer M. Carillo] C. Shmerler. il pors *World Tennis* 37:64-7 Je '89

Bibliography

Women in television are second-class citizens. J. Saltzman. il *USA Today (Periodical)* 118:51-3 S '89

WOMEN INVESTMENT ADVISERS

In the boss' shadow [E. Bramwell] G. Button. il por *Forbes* 144:238+ N 27 '89

WOMEN JAZZ MUSICIANS

In the limelight: women who play jazz [cover story] L. Gourse. il *American Visions* 4:32-7 Ap '89

WOMEN JOURNALISTS

See also

Bly, Nellie, 1867-1922

Dismissal

Turning loss into growth. S. Dundon. il por *Working Woman* 14:92-4 Ag '89

WOMEN JUDGES

See also

O'Connor, Sandra Day

Stout, Juanita Kidd

Crime & punishment: a view from a broad [judge in Florida known for tough sentencing]; ed. by Linda Marx. E. Morphonios. il pors *People Weekly* 32:79-80+ Jl 3 '89

WOMEN LAWYERS

See also

Baskerville, Lezli

Broderick, Cathy

Touby, Kathleen A.

Wallick, Ruth

Mommy tracks that lead somewhere good. L. Dusky. il *Working Woman* 14:132-4 N '89

Now for a woman's point of view. A. Toufexis. il *Time* 133:51-2 Ap 17 '89

WOMEN LAWYERS IN TELEVISION

The women of L.A. law: are they doing justice to their roles? [cover story] A. Meisler. il *TV Guide* 37:4-5+ Ap 1-7 '89

WOMEN LOBBYISTS AND LOBBYING

Lobbyist in the winter/farmer in the summer [K. Kelley] il por *Successful Farming* 87:39 Ja '89

WOMEN MARKETING MANAGERS

Dear Betty Harragan. B. L. Harragan. il *Working Woman* 14:32+ Je '89

WOMEN MAYORS

See also

Petrucci, Judy

Breaking an ole boy network [Texas] B. Turque. il *Newsweek* 113:39 Je 19 '89

WOMEN MEDICAL STUDENTS

Dr. Mom [teenager's mother attends medical school] C. Parkhurst. il *Seventeen* 48:140+ Ap '89

WOMEN MILLIONAIRES

The millionaire mindset [special section; cover story] il *Working Woman* 14:93-100+ My '89

WOMEN MINISTERS *See* Women clergy

WOMEN MOTION PICTURE CHARACTERS *See* Women in motion pictures

WOMEN MOTION PICTURE DIRECTORS

See also

Bigelow, Kathryn

Godmilow, Jill

Grant, Lee

Hobbs, Lyndall

Nair, Mira

Palcy, Euzhan

Seidelman, Susan

Silver, Joan Micklin

Wheeler, Anne

Women on the verge. P. Travers. il *Rolling Stone* p47-8 S 21 '89

WOMEN MOTION PICTURE PRODUCERS

See also

Hurd, Gale Anne

Lansing, Sherry

Pillsbury, Sarah

Sanford, Midge

Steel, Dawn

WOMEN MUSEUM DIRECTORS

See also

Antonova, Irina Aleksandrovna, 1922-

Esteve-Coll, Elizabeth

Orr-Cahall, Christina, 1947-

Phillips, Lisa

Pilgrim, Dianne H., 1941-

WOMEN MUSICIANS

See also

Women jazz musicians

Women rock musicians

Girls play guitar. A. Romano. il *Seventeen* 48:146-7+ My '89

WOMEN NEWSPAPER PUBLISHERS *See* Women in newspaper publishing

THE WOMEN OF BREWSTER PLACE [television program] *See* Television program reviews—Single works

WOMEN ON THE VERGE OF A NERVOUS BREAKDOWN [film] *See* Motion picture reviews—Single works

WOMEN PEDIATRICIANS

My mother, the doctor [pediatricians who are also mothers] M. Siegel. il *Good Housekeeping* 209:90+ S '89

WOMEN PHOTOGRAPHERS

See also

Bloom, Barbara

Bourke-White, Margaret, 1904-1971

Bubley, Esther

Cameron, Betsy

Dorfman, Elsa, 1937-

Frankel, Tracy

Geesaman, Lynn

Golden, Judith, 1934-

Greenfield, Lois

Kendall, Marie

Kruger, Barbara

Mark, Mary Ellen, 1940-

Metzner, Sheila

Skoglund, Sandy, 1946-

Taylor, Jana

Wolin, Penny

WOMEN PHYSICIANS

See also

Bates, Artie Ann

Elders, Joycelyn

Hodgson, Jane

Hufnagel, Vicki

Novello, Antonia

Roseveare, Helen

Attitudes

Breast cancer update [results of survey] S. Bulow-Hube. *Ladies' Home Journal* 106:96+ Jl '89

WOMEN PHYSICISTS

See also

Eissler, Holly

Luce Foundation funds positions for women in physics. *Physics Today* 42:85-6 S '89

WOMEN POETS

See also

Braverman, Kate

Dickinson, Emily, 1830-1886

Mistral, Gabriela, 1889-1957

Plath, Sylvia

Ratushinskaya, Irina

WOMEN PRESIDENTS

Waiting for Ms. President? P. Cohen. il *Scholastic Update (Teachers' edition)* 121:17 Ja 13 '89

WOMEN PRIESTS

See also

Ordination of women

A denomination gender gap [movement against women priests by Episcopal Synod of America] J. Carey. il *U.S. News & World Report* 106:56-7 Je 19 '89

Episcopal family feud. *The Christian Century* 106:615-16 Je 21-28 '89

The Episcopal Synod: reinforcing boundaries. W. L. Sachs. *The Christian Century* 106:710-11 Ag 2-9 '89

Episcopalians' semi-schism. R. N. Ostling. il *Time* 133:53 Je 19 '89

WOMEN PRISON WARDENS

Keeper of the keys [J. White, black woman warden at the Manhattan House of Detention] N. A. Nichols. il por *New York* 22:28 F 20 '89

The woman who heads all-male New York jail [warden J. White] D. M. Cheers. il pors *Jet* 76:28-31 Ap 17 '89

WOMEN PRISONERS

Medical care

Cruel and unusual punishment [imprisonment of A. Pollard, wife of convicted spy J. Pollard] L. C. Pogrebin. por *Ms.* 18:36-7 N '89

Treatment

A note from prison [women convicted of petty drug offenses] K. Kelly. *America* 161:230 O 14 '89

Prisoner of conscience [experiences while jailed for antinuclear activities; cover story] B. Urfer. il *The Progressive* 53:18-21 My '89

WOMEN PSYCHOLOGISTS

See also

Bryan, Katherine

WOMEN PUBLIC OFFICERS

See also

Congresswomen

Women mayors

Women presidents

Bush: a ladies' man? [record number of women in administration] P. Simpson. *Ms.* 18:67+ O '89

Politics [short list of Republican women appointed to high office] F. Barnes. *Vogue* 179:144 Je '89

WOMEN REAL ESTATE AGENTS

Dear Betty Harragan [secretary considers change of career] B. L. Harragan. il *Working Woman* 14:22+ Ag '89

Anecdotes, facetiae, satire, etc.

Grin and sell it. M. Ivins. il *Ms.* 17:22 Je '89

WOMEN ROCK MUSICIANS

Music and mothering [N. Cherry and R. Jones] D. DeNicolo; E. Zimmerman. il pors *Glamour* 87:178 N '89

Women who play a rockin' role! il *'Teen* 33:47 F '89

Photographs and photography

The women's movement. il *Rolling Stone* p73-7+ S 21 '89

WOMEN RUNNERS *See* Runners

WOMEN SCIENTISTS

Making science more seductive to women on campus. N. J. Freundlich. il *Business Week* p89 Ag 28 '89

"Oh, I thought you were a man" [historical figures] W. Booth. il *Science* 243:475 Ja 27 '89

The scientist shortage and the gender gap. D. W. Freckman. *BioScience* 39:523 S '89

The women who are scaling high tech's heights. E. T. Smith. il *Business Week* p86-8 Ag 28 '89

WOMEN SINGERS

Another country [women of country music] H. Gleason. il *Harper's Bazaar* 122:112+ O '89

Girls ain't nothin' but trouble? [women rap artists] C. Cooper. *Essence* 19:80+ Ap '89

Radio sweethearts. M. Moses. *The New Yorker* 65:83-6 Mr 20 '89

Words of love [jazz singers on compact disc] J. Sohmer. il *Down Beat* 56:35-6 Ag '89

WOMEN SPORTS JOURNALISTS *See* Sports journalism

WOMEN SUPERVISORS

She's the boss! [black supervisors and executives] M. Marshall. il *Ebony* 44:80+ Je '89

WOMEN TELEVISION CHARACTERS *See* Women in television

WOMEN TELEVISION PRODUCERS

See also

Carsey, Marcy

Fales, Susan

Schuyler, Linda

WOMEN TENNIS PLAYERS *See* Tennis players

WOMEN TERRORISTS

The demon lover [excerpt] R. Morgan. il *Ms.* 17:68-72 Mr '89

WOMEN VETERANS

Help build a memorial to American heroines. J. M. Carter. il *Good Housekeeping* 208:64 My '89

Wartime nurses [World War II] E. E. Rosenbaum. il *New Choices for the Best Years* 29:24+ Jl '89

WOMEN'S BANKS AND BANKING

"How's your bank, honey?". N. Nichols. *Ms.* 17:142 Ja/F '89

WOMEN'S FRIENDSHIPS *See* Friendship

WOMEN'S GYMNASIUMS *See* Gymnasiums

WOMEN'S LIBERATION MOVEMENT *See* Feminism

WOMEN'S ORGANIZATIONS

See also

Businesswomen's organizations

Concerned Women for America

International Jewish Feminist Network

Mount Vernon Ladies' Association of the Union

National Council of Negro Women

National Organization for Women

WATCH (Organization)

Canada

See also

National Action Committee on the Status of Women (Canada)

National Council of Jewish Women (Canada)

WOMEN'S POLITICAL ACTION COMMITTEES

See also

Hollywood Women's Political Committee

WOMEN'S SHELTERS

Illinois

Helping the homeless [P. Crowley's work in Chicago] C. Reeve. il por *New Choices for the Best Years* 29:16 F '89

WOMEN'S SHOES *See* Footwear

WOMEN'S SPORTS *See* Women—Sports

WOMEN'S SPORTS & FITNESS (PERIODICAL)

Editorial. L. Rothlein. See issues of Women's Sports & Fitness beginning December 1988 through March 1990

WOMEN'S SPORTS FOUNDATION

Take note. See issues of Women's Sports & Fitness beginning January/February 1988

WOMEN'S SPORTS HALL OF FAME

Four of the best join the greatest. K. M. Reith. il *Women's Sports & Fitness* 11:56-7 Ja/F '89

WOMEN'S STUDIES

Homophobiaphobia [feminist linguistic course taught by lesbian at Kenyon College] T. Short. *National Review* 41:19-20 Ag 18 '89

Move over, Demosthenes. il *U.S. News & World Report* 107:12 O 9 '89

WOMEN'S THEOLOGICAL CENTER (BOSTON, MASS.)

The Women's Theological Center: learning and acting for justice. N. D. Richardson. *The Christian Century* 106:130+ F 1-8 '89

WONDER, JACQUELYN, AND DONOVAN, PRISCILLA

How to make the most of change in your life [quiz] il *Glamour* 87:262-5+ Je '89

WONDER, STEVIE

about

Wonder and Temptations among new inductees into Rock 'n' Roll Hall of Fame. il por *Jet* 75:60+ F 6 '89

WONDER

Wonderlust. J. Bosveld. *Omni (New York, N.Y.)* 11:33 Ja '89

THE WONDER YEARS [television program] *See* Television program reviews—Single works

WONDERFUL TOWN [musical] *See* Musicals, revues, etc.—Reviews—Single works

WONG, B. D.

about

The metamorphosis of B. D. Wong [interview] E. Siff. il pors *Gentlemen's Quarterly* 59:83+ My '89

WONG, C.-H.

Enzymatic catalysts in organic synthesis. bibl f il *Science* 244:1145-52 Je 9 '89

WONG, KEVIN R., AND BUCKLEY, J. THOMAS

Proton motive force involved in protein transport across the outer membrane of Aeromonas salmonicida. bibl f il *Science* 246:654-6 N 3 '89

WONG, MARTIN

about

Martin Wong at Exit Art and Frank Bernarducci. J. Zinsser. il *Art in America* 77:149 Mr '89

Tenements to the stars. E. Hedegaard. il *Mother Jones* 14:51 Jl/Ag '89

WOOD, ABIGAIL

Relating. See issues of Seventeen

WOOD, CHRISTOPHER

A different kind of 'north-south' dialogue. il *World Press Review* 36:36-8 Ag '89

WOOD, DANIEL

Lighthawk. il por *National Parks* 63:27-31 Ja/F '89

WOOD, FRANK

about

Do you sincerely want to publish? R. Koselka. il pors *Forbes* 144:68+ S 18 '89

WOOD, GEORGE H.

Promoting civic education. *The Education Digest* 54:38-40 Ap '89

WOOD, GORDON S.

Struggle over the Puritans. il *The New York Review of Books* 36:26-31+ N 9 '89

WOOD, JAMES

about

A family's finances [cover story] L. Gite. il pors *Black Enterprise* 20:72-4+ O '89

WOOD, JAMES, 1930-

about

A&P is thriving—so why is James Wood still around? A. Rothman. il por *Business Week* p90-1 Ap 10 '89

WOOD, JIM

The taste of the town. il *Harper's Bazaar* 122:176+ My '89

WOOD, JOHN

Staying well. See issues of Modern Maturity

WOOD, KAREN ANN

about

A killing in Maine. J. H. Kunstler. il por *The New York Times Magazine* p58-60+ S 10 '89

"My wife shouldn't have died". J. Hope. il pors *Good Housekeeping* 209:92+ O '89

WOOD, KEITH V., AND OTHERS

Complementary DNA coding click beetle luciferases can elicit bioluminescence of different colors. bibl f il *Science* 244:700-2 My 12 '89

WOOD, KEVIN
about
"My wife shouldn't have died". J. Hope. il pors *Good Housekeeping* 209:92+ O '89
WOOD, LEONARD A.
The Gallup survey. See occasional issues of Publishers Weekly
WOOD, LOWELL
about
Brilliant Pebbles: amazing new missile killer. R. K. Bennett. *Reader's Digest* 135:128-33 S '89
WOOD, MONICA
Closer to God [story] il *Redbook* 173:74+ My '89
WOOD, RALPH C.
Updike's song of himself. il por *The Christian Century* 106:526-8 My 17 '89
WOOD, RICHARD A.
Flash floods. il *Weatherwise* 42:93-4 Ap '89
WOOD, ROBERT CHAPMAN
A lesson learned and a lesson forgotten. il pors *Forbes* 143:70-2+ F 6 '89
WOOD, TONI
"Read the 'me' book!". il *Parents* 64:230-1 My '89
WOOD, WILBUR
Political fires still smolder. il *The Nation* 249:162-4 Ag 7-14 '89
WOOD, WILLIAM B., AND OTHERS
Ecopolitics in the global greenhouse. bibl f il *Environment* 31:12-17+ S '89
WOOD, WILLIE
about
Blount, Shell and Wood welcomed into NFL Hall. il pors *Jet* 76:57 Ag 21 '89
WOOD
See also
Jarrah
Lignin
Lumber
Sabicu
Timber
Stradivari's secret (redux): did baroque artisans "X-ray" wood with sunlight? J. Horgan. il *Scientific American* 261:21-2 Jl '89
Woodwork. il *Vogue* 179:129-31 Ja '89
Diseases and pests
See also
Termites
Dryers and drying
The Workbench guide to drying lumber. P. McCafferty. il map *Workbench* 45:66-7+ S/O '89
Finishes and finishing
See also
Furniture—Finishes and finishing
Stains and staining
Knock on wood. B. E. Johnson. See issues of Antiques & Collecting Hobbies beginning December 1988
Bibliography
Finish like a pro. il *Workbench* 45:14 S/O '89
Moisture
About wood moisture meters. il *Workbench* 45:70 S/O '89
Preservation and preservatives
See also
Wood—Dryers and drying
Defeating wood decay [pressure treatment] D. Johnson. il *The Family Handyman* 39:20+ Jl/Ag '89
Wood preservatives. K. Collier. il *The Family Handyman* 39:50-1 Mr '89
Staining
See Stains and staining
Storage
See also
Woodbins, racks, etc.
WOOD, FOSSIL *See* Trees, Fossil
WOOD, LAMINATED *See* Laminated wood
WOOD ALCOHOL *See* Methanol
WOOD AS FUEL
See also
Modular Energy Company
Wood stoves
The fuelwood crisis [developing countries] S. Postel and L. Heise. il *The Courier (Unesco)* 42:19-23 Ja '89
WOOD BASEBALL BATS *See* Baseball bats
WOOD BURNING (CRAFT) *See* Pyrography
WOOD CARVING
See also
Creel Creek Fish Carving (Firm)
Hanno Ahrens: wood spirits. D. Rubey. il por *Art News* 88:85-6 F '89
John Taye's basswood sculptures. D. B. Vaughn. il por *American Artist* 53:60-5 Ap '89
Joseph Lutter carves carousel horses by giving rein to his gifts. H. Shapiro. il pors *People Weekly* 32:167-8 D 11 '89
Whispering giants [work of carver P. Toth] D. R. Hopwood. il pors *Americana* 17:63-5 My/Je '89
Exhibitions
The language of wood [Finnish works at the American Craft Museum] J. F. Pile. il *American Craft* 49:56-63 Ag/S '89

WOOD CONSTRUCTION
See also
Violin—Construction
American Wood Council 1988 Wood Design Awards program. il *Architectural Record* 177:46-7 Ap '89
WOOD CUTTING
A tale of two sawbucks [firewood cutting racks] M. Lamphier; H. Mitchell. il *The Mother Earth News* 120:82-3 N/D '89
Time to split. J. Skow. il *Time* 133:72 Ja 23 '89
WOOD FILLERS *See* Filling materials
WOOD FINISHING *See* Wood—Finishes and finishing
WOOD FLOORING *See* Flooring
WOOD FOUNDATIONS (BUILDING) *See* Foundations (Building)
WOOD FURNITURE *See* Furniture
WOOD GRAINING *See* Graining
WOOD HOUSES
A house made by hand [East Texas home modeled on 1840 plantation house] E. Wood. il *Southern Living* 24:72-4 Ag '89
Revival of the timber-framed house. T. Benson. bibl il *Country Journal* 16:49-56 S/O '89
Photographs and photography
Raising day [Habitat for Humanity-Timber Framers Guild effort in Hanover, Pa.] D. L. Brill. il *Country Journal* 16:57-9 S/O '89
WOOD PANELING *See* Paneling
WOOD POLES
See also
Pole houses
WOOD PULP INDUSTRY
Canada
See also
Consolidated-Bathurst Inc.
WOOD RATS
Whatever happened to the Allegheny woodrat? [New York State] A. Hicks. il maps *The Conservationist* 43:34-9 Mr/Ap '89
WOOD SCULPTING *See* Wood carving
WOOD SHEDS *See* Sheds
WOOD STOVES
Cooking up chest illness [use problems in children; research by J. Osborne Scott and Richard E. Honicky] il *Prevention (Emmaus, Pa.)* 41:10+ D '89
Does your stove stack up? [Rais stoves] P. Patton. il *Esquire* 112:43 N '89
The new wood stoves. il *Better Homes and Gardens* 67:63 Ja '89
Old-fashioned wood heat. il *Home Mechanix* 85:14 Ja '89
Time to split. J. Skow. il *Time* 133:72 Ja 23 '89
WOOD TURNING *See* Turning (Machine work)
WOOD TURTLES *See* Turtles
WOOD WORKING *See* Woodworking
WOODARD, ALFRE
about
The Alfre nobody knows. J. Vallely. pors *Ms.* 17:68-71 Ap '89
Isiah Thomas' mom subject of TV film, 'A mother's courage' [cover story] L. Ransom. il pors *Jet* 77:36-8 D 11 '89
WOODARD, CHARLAINE
about
About people. M. Southgate. por *Essence* 19:32 Ja '89
WOODARD, CHERI FAITH
about
The catalog concept grows a cottage industry. D. Weil. il por *Working Woman* 14:64+ Ag '89
WOODARD, JOSEF
Don Cherry: globetrotter in the mainstream. il pors *Down Beat* 56:23-5 N '89
Keith Jarrett: in search of the perfect E minor chord [cover story; interview] il pors *Down Beat* 56:16-19 F '89
Neville-ry [cover story] il *Down Beat* 56:16-19 Je '89
WOODARD, WILEY MCDARIS
Calculating your finances. il *Black Enterprise* 20:63-4+ O '89
Exploring new frontiers [cover story; special section; with editorial comment by Earl G. Graves] il *Black Enterprise* 20:9, 53-4+ S '89
How to read financial reports. il *Black Enterprise* 19:90-2+ My '89
WOODBINS, RACKS, ETC.
Handy storage and pass-through for firewood [two-sided woodbin] il *Sunset (Central West edition)* 183:104-5 D '89
WOODBRIDGE, SALLY B.
The 1909 Leon K. Roos house in San Francisco. il *Architectural Digest* 46:162+ My '89
WOODBURNING (CRAFT) *See* Pyrography
WOODBURY, CHUCK
about
If it's big news, you won't find it in Chuck Woodbury's sagebrush journal, Out West. S. K. Reed. il pors *People Weekly* 31:61-2 Ja 16 '89
WOODCARVING *See* Wood carving
WOODCHUCKS
Woody and Ed [animal occupants of Illinois garden] R. M. Lerner. il *Organic Gardening* 36:104 Ja '89

WOODCOCK, GORDON R.
The art of the possible. il *Ad Astra* 1:8-13 O '89
WOODCOCK SHOOTING
Catching the flight. P. Bourjailly. il *Field & Stream* 94:42-3+ O '89
Hard winters and crazy birds. H. Middleton. il *Southern Living* 24:36-7 D '89
WOODCOCKS
Unnatural habitat [preservation at Moosehorn Wildlife Refuge in Maine] K. Morrison. il *Country Journal* 16:39-43 S/O '89
WOODCUTTING *See* Wood cutting
WOODEN, JOHN R.
about
The coach and his champion. A. Wolff. il pors *Sports Illustrated* 70:94-8+ Ap 3 '89
WOODEN, NELL
about
The coach and his champion. A. Wolff. il pors *Sports Illustrated* 70:94-8+ Ap 3 '89
WOODEN BENCHES *See* Benches
WOODEN BOATS *See* Boats and boating—Materials
WOODEN BOXES *See* Boxes, cases, etc.
WOODEN HOUSES *See* Wood houses
WOODEN SPOONS *See* Spoons
WOODEN TENNIS RACKETS *See* Tennis rackets
WOODEN TOOLS *See* Tools
WOODEN TOYS *See* Toys
WOODENWARE
See also
Cutting boards
WOODHOUSE, JOHN
about
Sailsmanship. D. Churbuck. il por *Forbes* 144:50+ Jl 10 '89
WOODHULL, NANCY, 1945-
about
The manager who never says never. R. Sandroff. il pors *Working Woman* 14:90-2+ D '89
WOODIER, OLWEN, 1942-
Tea in the afternoon. il *Americana* 17:40-4+ N/D '89
WOODLAND PARK ZOOLOGICAL GARDENS
Elephant Forest Woodland Park Zoo. D. Gantenbein. il *Architectural Record* 177:96-101 Ag '89
WOODLANDERS, INC.
Greening the South. D. Young. il pors *Southern Living* 24:125-6+ Je '89
WOODPECKERS
A clearcutting ban for the birds [efforts of red cockaded woodpeckers in national forests in Texas] P. Larmer. il *Sierra* 74:28-30 Mr/Ap '89
Starling scourge [red headed woodpeckers] F. Graham. *Audubon* 91:25-7 S '89
Control
The knock on woodpeckers [efforts of electric companies to halt destruction of utility poles] R. Wolkomir and J. Wolkomir. il *National Wildlife* 27:22-3 F/Mr '89
Woodpecker woes. il *The Family Handyman* 39:6 F '89
WOODRING, PAUL, 1907-
A new approach to the dropout problem. *Phi Delta Kappan* 70:468-9 F '89
WOODRUFF, THOMAS
about
Thomas Woodruff at White Columns and P.P.O.W. J. Ash. il *Art in America* 77:195-6 N '89
WOODS, ALFRED L.
Heroes [poem] *Essence* 20:104 Je '89
This has nothing to do with April [poem] *Essence* 20:136 O '89
WOODS, BRETT
about
Avalanche! R. D. LeBlanc. il *Reader's Digest* 135:129-33 D '89
WOODS, DELLA
about
The first lady of funny cars. T. Swan. il por *Popular Mechanics* 166:36 Ap '89
WOODS, ELDRIK
about
On deck. il por *Sport (New York, N.Y.)* 80:16 S '89
WOODS, HARRIETT
about
Open for discussion. P. Simpson. il por *Ms.* 17:83 Ap '89
WOODS, ICKEY
about
Dash and flash. R. Reilly. il pors *Sports Illustrated* 70:50-4 Ja 23 '89
WOODS, JAMES
about
Arresting appeal. B. Borns. pors *Harper's Bazaar* 122:50+ F '89
Brooding actor James Woods's Immediate family breaks up after four months of marriage. il pors *People Weekly* 32:71 D 18 '89
Fear and loathing in Hollywood [cover story] S. Schindehette. il pors *People Weekly* 31:72-4+ Mr 20 '89
Fighting his way to the top. R. B. Woodward. il pors *The New York Times Magazine* p50-1+ Ag 20 '89

He's hot . . . but still fighting image problems—and the Sean Young battle. N. Hickey. il pors *TV Guide* 37:12-15 Ap 29-My 5 '89
Hollywood's baddest boy. R. Rosenbaum. por *Mademoiselle* 95:125-6 Ap '89
James Woods relights the fire. H. Edwards. il pors *Vogue* 179:76-7 Ja '89
The wild Woods. V. Muse. il pors *Life* 12:15-16 D '89
WOODS, JAMES D.
about
Baker Hughes lops off a weak limb. T. Vogel. *Business Week* p34 My 29 '89
WOODS, VICKI
Madonna holds court. il pors *Vogue* 179:342-51 My '89
Sharp Cleese. il por *Vogue* 179:230+ Ja '89
WOODS HOLE (MASS.)
Description
Pausing in Woods Hole. R. S. Peffer. il *Travel Holiday* 171:35-8 Ja '89
WOODSIDE, WILLIAM S.
about
Ignorance threatens companies. M. Magnet. por *Fortune* 120:69-70 Jl 3 '89
WOODSIDE (CALIF.)
Historic houses, sites, etc.
See also
Filoli (Woodside, Calif.)
WOODSTOCK (CONN.)
Historic houses, sites, etc.
See also
Bowen House, Roseland Cottage (Woodstock, Conn.)
WOODSTOCK (N.Y.)
Architecture
Al Held's Catskill pastoral: the artist's studio and house in Woodstock, New York. D. Solomon. il por *Architectural Digest* 46:170-3+ Je '89
Description
20 years, and 50 miles, down the road. J. Bowermaster. il *The New York Times Magazine* p22-5 Jl 2 '89
Dodging hippies with Graham Parker. il por *Rolling Stone* p46 Jl 13-27 '89
WOODSTOCK FESTIVAL, 1969
20 years, and 50 miles, down the road. J. Bowermaster. il *The New York Times Magazine* p22-5 Jl 2 '89
Back to the garden. J. Etra. il *Harper's Bazaar* 122:93+ Ag '89
A nation of loners. J. Sobran. il *National Review* 41:28-9 S 1 '89
No encore for Woodstock. F. Goodman. *Rolling Stone* p26 Ag 10 '89
Now they spell it 'Wood$tock' [20th anniversary] M. Azerrad. il *Rolling Stone* p17 Ap 6 '89
Tangerine dreams. J. Gray. il *Maclean's* 102:50-1 Ag 28 '89
Woodstock. D. Gates. il *Newsweek* 114:50-1 Jl 3 '89
Woodstock [cover story] A. Foglino and others. il *Life* 12:20-4+ Ag '89
Woodstock '89: a bad trip [marketing opportunities fizzle] J. Schwartz. il *Newsweek* 114:42 Ag 21 '89
Woodstock anniversary plans taking shape. J. Ressner. *Rolling Stone* p20 My 4 '89
Woodstock at 20. G. Santoro. *The Nation* 249:253-4 S 4-11 '89
The Woodstock (re)generation. J. Farber. il *Seventeen* 48:148+ Ag '89
Woodstock remembered [special section] il *Rolling Stone* p61-3+ Ag 24 '89
You had to be there. H. Hertzberg. *The New Republic* 201:13-14 Ag 28 '89
WOODWARD, BOB, 1943-
about
Woodward and Bernstein: what they think of Watergate now [interview] J. Kalter. il pors *TV Guide* 37:6-8 O 28-N 3 '89
Woodward explodes Roe v. Wade. T. Eastland. *The American Spectator* 22:30 Ap '89
WOODWARD, C. VANN (COMER VANN), 1908-
The narcissistic South. bibl f il *The New York Review of Books* 36:13-14+ O 26 '89
WOODWARD, COMER VANN *See* Woodward, C. Vann (Comer Vann), 1908-
WOODWARD, JOANNE, 1930-
about
Paul and Joanne—their real life story [excerpt] J. Morella and E. Z. Epstein. pors *Good Housekeeping* 208:72+ Ja '89
WOODWARD, KENNETH L.
Challenges facing U.S. Catholics. *Commonweal* 116:618 N 17 '89
WOODWARD, RICHARD B.
American monument. il por *Art News* 88:140-5 N '89
Consistency is no longer a concern, finds Richard B. Woodward. Not confined to a signature style, many artists are exploring diversity. il *Vogue* 179:98+ Jl '89
Fighting his way to the top. il pors *The New York Times Magazine* p50-1+ Ag 20 '89
Reveling in heartbreak. il por *The New York Times Magazine* p42+ Mr 12 '89

WOODWARD, RICK
Film stills. il *Film Comment* 25:51-2+ Mr/Ap '89
WOODWARD, WHITNEY
Flip-flop friendships: turn them right-side up. il *Teen* 33:24+ N '89
Like yourself! 10 ways. il *'Teen* 33:36+ Jl '89
Sleuthing youths. il *'Teen* 33:18-19+ D '89
When you run: the problems that follow. il *Teen* 33:48+ O '89
WOODWELL, GEORGE M.
(jt. auth) See Houghton, Richard A., and Woodwell, George M.
WOODWORK CORP. OF AMERICA
Tools of the trade [office interiors] il *Architectural Record* 177:144-7 My '89
WOODWORKING
See also
Joints (Carpentry)
Millwork (Woodwork)
Miter boxes, gages, etc.
Planes and planing
Pyrography
Sanding and sanding equipment
Saws and sawing
Turning (Machine work)
Veneers and veneering
Wood carving
Below the surface [interiors by Bentley LaRosa Salasky] J. S. Russell. il *Architectural Record* 177:108-13 Ag '89
Hand work [special section] il *Popular Mechanics* 166:71-6+ N '89
Workshop basics. R. Capotosto. See issues of Popular Mechanics beginning January 1986 through April 1989
Projects
See also
Christmas projects
See also names of projects
Award-winning projects [results of build-a-box contest] R. N. Hoffman. il *Workbench* 45:62-5+ S/O '89
Six useful projects for the woodworking shop. F. Matlack. il por *Country Journal* 16:65-71 N/D '89
Three easy-to-make pieces [special section] il *Workbench* 45:71-4 Mr/Ap '89
Woodworks. See issues of The Family Handyman beginning October 1986
Caricatures and cartoons
Wordless workshop. R. Doty. See issues of Popular Science
Study and teaching
If I had a hammer. J. M. Guidry. il *Parents* 64:202+ Mr '89
WOODWORKING TOOLS See Tools
WOODY PLANTS
See also
Shrubs
WOOL
See also
Cashmere
Yarn
WOOLARD, EDGAR SMITH, JR.
about
Du Pont's version of a maverick. J. Weber, Jr. il pors *Business Week* p80-1 Ap 3 '89
Edgar Woolard. J. Weber, Jr. il por *Business Week* Special Issue:140 Ap 14 '89
The new organization man [cover story; special section] J. Buckley. il pors *U.S. News & World Report* 106:40-51 Ja 16 '89
WOOLDRIDGE, WILFRED E.
Kitchen gardener. See issues of Flower and Garden beginning October/November 1987
WOOLF, VIRGINIA, 1882-1941
about
Monk's House—the author's country retreat in Sussex. P. Rose. il *Architectural Digest* 46:62+ Jl '89
WOOLFOLK, JOANNA MARTINE
Horoscopes. See issues of Harper's Bazaar beginning December 1988
WOOLFOLK, MARGARET
'To my husband, Donald, without whom . . .'. il *Smithsonian* 19:200 Mr '89
WOOLHOUSE, MARK
Mollusks in midstream. il *Natural History* p6+ Mr '89
WOOLLEY, ROBERT
about
Wry Manhattan: Robert Woolley's Fifth Avenue apartment. C. T. Buckley. il por *Architectural Digest* 46:322-7+ N '89
WOOLLY APHIDS
Samurai aphids: survival under siege [Japan] M. W. Moffett. il *National Geographic* 176:406-22 S '89
WOOLWORTH, FRANK WINFIELD, 1852-1919
about
Woolworth's cathedral. J. S. Gordon. il *American Heritage* 40:16+ Jl/Ag '89
WOOLWORTH (F. W.) CO. See F. W. Woolworth Co.
WOOLWORTH BUILDING (NEW YORK, N.Y.)
Woolworth's cathedral. J. S. Gordon. il *American Heritage* 40:16+ Jl/Ag '89

WOOSLEY, STANFORD E., AND WEAVER, TOM
The great supernova of 1987 [cover story] bibl il *Scientific American* 261:32-40 Ag '89
WOOSTER, MARTIN MORSE
Agents of the New Age. il *The American Spectator* 22:38-9 Ag '89
WOOSTER COLLEGE See College of Wooster
WOOSTER GROUP
The road to immortality and Europe: the Wooster Group tours LSD—just the high points. J. Calhoun. il *Theatre Crafts* 23:46-9+ My '89
WOOTEN, JAMES
Outcast to hero. il pors *TV Guide* 37:36-8 Ja 14-20 '89
WOOZ (VACAVILLE, CALIF.)
Escaping the maze. D. Cater. il *Health (New York, N.Y.)* 21:64-9 Je '89
WORCESTERSHIRE SAUCE
Worcestershire sauce. M. Kenyon. il *Gourmet* 49:122+ O '89
WORD GAMES
See also
Ambigrams
Mad Libs (Game)
Palindromes
Dog hide-and-seek [word search puzzle] il *National Geographic World* 171:10-11 N '89
Words in the woods [word search puzzle involving trees] il *National Geographic World* 167:20-1 Jl '89
WORD OF GOD (THEOLOGY)
The indomitable Word. *Commonweal* 116:691-2 D 15 '89
WORD PROCESSING INDUSTRY
See also
Franklin Computer Corporation
WORD PROCESSOR INDUSTRY
See also
Harris Corp.
Wang Laboratories Inc.
WORD PROCESSORS AND PROCESSING
See also
Text processing (Computer science)
Word processing. See issues of Personal Computing beginning May 1987
Word processing for the computer-shy. D. H. Dunn. il *Business Week* p150 N 20 '89
Authors' use
Celebrity writers get around the block. T. George. il *Home Office Computing* 7:45-8 Mr '89
Looking for the key to getting started. J. M. Wall. *The Christian Century* 106:67-8 Ja 25 '89
. . . makes a difference where you are. W. F. Buckley. il *Personal Computing* 13:23-4 O '89
Picking up the PC's [H. Kohn] M. Porter. il por *Gentlemen's Quarterly* 59:203+ Ap '89
Word processing for writers. S. Morgenstern. il *Home Office Computing* 7:65-70 N '89
Writer vs. robot. W. Safire. il *The New York Times Magazine* p12+ Ja 8 '89
Business use
A frog on paper, prince of machines. R. Nelson. il *Personal Computing* 13:39-40 O '89
WordPerfect Executive [integrated package] R. Kendall. il *Home Office Computing* 7:76-7 Mr '89
Words for money [home business] H. E. H. Aycock. il *Compute!* 11:20-1 Ag '89
Educational use
Homework [Mad Libs program] H. E. H. Aycock. il *Compute!* 11:98 O '89
Homework Writer. C. S. Holzberg. il *Home Office Computing* 7:75-6 S '89
Homework Writer [computer program] C. S. Holzberg. il *Compute!* 11:70 Ag '89
KidWriter Gold. N. Rentschler. il *Compute!* 11:67 S '89
KidWriter Golden Edition. M. B. Eltgroth. il *Home Office Computing* 7:85 Ap '89
Revising: the fourth R? [effect of access to word processing on students' attitudes toward writing; research by Vicki Baer] G. W. Bracey. il *Phi Delta Kappan* 70:561-2 Mr '89
Indexing use
Make your documents professional looking and efficient to use [indexing with word processing and Proindex programs] H. F. Beechhold. il *Home Office Computing* 7:22+ Ja '89
Programming
See also
Hypertext
WordPerfect Corporation
Ami. R. G. Sheffield. il *Compute!* 11:67-8 My '89
Ami reviewed. S. Morgenstern. il *Home Office Computing* 7:26+ Je '89
Beyond Word Writer. S. Anzovin. il *Compute!* 11:114 D '89
The blight of bloated software [WordStar Professional 5.0 and Canon Cat] E. Shapiro. il *Byte* 14:127-8+ Ja '89
Building columns into documents. R. Blodgett. il *Personal Computing* 13:51-2+ S '89
Buyer's guide [cover story; with editorial comment by Fred Abatemarco] il *Personal Computing* 13:5, 111-16+ Ag '89

WORKAHOLICS
Help! My husband's always working. H. S. Kaplan. por *Redbook* 172:42 F '89
The workaholic generation [cover story] W. Kiechel. il *Fortune* 119:50-4+ Ap 10 '89
Workaholics Anonymous. W. Kiechel. il *Fortune* 120:117-18 Ag 14 '89
Workaholics: are you one? D. M. Topolnicki. *Psychology Today* 23:25 Jl/Ag '89

WORKBENCH (PERIODICAL)
Something old, something new. R. N. Hoffman. *Workbench* 45:4 Ja/F '89

WORKBENCHES
3 workbenches as furniture [cover story; special section] il *Popular Science* 234:84-90 Ja '89
All-purpose workbench. C. Wedlake. il *Workbench* 45:68-9 My/Je '89

WORKER LEASING *See* Employee leasing
WORKER SAFETY *See* Occupational health and safety
WORKERS AGAINST TOXIC CHEMICAL HAZARDS
Lethal Lordstown: workers fight poison at a GM plant. J. Slaughter. il *The Progressive* 53:28-9+ Mr '89
WORKERS' COMPENSATION *See* Insurance, Workers' compensation
WORKERS' EDUCATIONAL ASSOCIATION (GREAT BRITAIN)
Albert Mansbridge and a fresh coat of paint. D. Thompson. il pors *History Today* 39:7-9 Ag '89
WORKFARE
How one bill became law [welfare-reform bill] S. Manning. il *Scholastic Update (Teachers' edition)* 121:15-16 F 24 '89
The new welfare bill: when more isn't enough. R. D. Hylton. *Black Enterprise* 19:21 Ja '89
Revenge of the softheads. M. Kaus. *The New Republic* 200:24+ Je 19 '89
Welfare and workfare: a dispute [discussion of December 14, 1988 article, Blinded by metaphor: churches and welfare reform] R. S. Bachelder. *The Christian Century* 106:419-21 Ap 19 '89
WORKHORSES (WOOD SUPPORTS) *See* Sawhorses
WORKING CLASSES *See* Labor
WORKING CLASSES IN MASS MEDIA *See* Labor in mass media
WORKING GIRL [film] *See* Motion picture reviews—Single works
WORKING MOTHERS *See* Mothers—Employment
WORKING WOMAN (PERIODICAL)
The 1989 Working Woman Hall of Fame. il *Working Woman* 14:111-12+ N '89
WORKING WOMEN *See* Women—Employment
WORKMAN, CHUCK
about
Superstar [film] Reviews
American Film il 15:80 D '89. L. Loud
WORKMAN CREEK FALLS (ARIZ.)
Workman Creek Falls, Arizona. R. H. Mohlenbrock. il map *Natural History* p86-9 Mr '89
WORKMEN'S COMPENSATION *See* Insurance, Workers' compensation
WORKOUT CLOTHES *See* Clothing and dress—Sports clothes
WORKOUT INVESTMENTS
Alan Fellheimer wears combat boots [Equimark] M. Schroeder. il por *Business Week* p119-20 Mr 20 '89
Epic task [Skyline Financial sells off properties of Equity Programs Investment Corp.] J. Novack. il por *Forbes* 143:142+ F 6 '89
Lenny Pelullo's checkered past—and present. G. DeGeorge. il por *Business Week* p84+ O 23 '89
See you in bankruptcy court [leveraged buyout of Seaman Furniture turns into headache for Kohlberg Kravis Roberts] S. Flack. il *Forbes* 144:77+ O 16 '89
When vultures get food poisoning [investing in distressed companies] H. Rudnitsky. il *Forbes* 144:53+ O 16 '89
William Brandt: putting small businesses back in the black. L. Therrien. il por *Business Week* p99 Ag 21 '89
Workout artist [bankruptcy lawyer J. Zweibel] J. Zweig. il por *Forbes* 144:274-5 Jl 24 '89
Yesterday's bad deals are today's new business. L. Light. il *Business Week* p96-7 D 11 '89
THE WORKS (DANCE COMPANY) *See* Jennifer Muller/The Works
WORKS OF ART, TAXATION OF *See* Taxation of works of art
WORKSHOP CABINETS *See* Cabinets (Furniture)
WORKSHOPS
See also
Artists' studios
The compleat country workshop. J. Baldwin. il pors *Country Journal* 16:59-64 N/D '89
Equipment
See also
Tools
5 favorite shop projects. il *Workbench* 45:64+ My/Je '89
Home & shop improvements. See issues of The Family Handyman beginning September 1986

Lost suction [discussion of September/October, 1986 article, Furnace blower powers shop dust collector system] A. Kruger. *Workbench* 45:52 Ja/F '89
Product news. See issues of Workbench beginning January/February 1986
Shop secrets [farm shops] D. Mowitz and C. Finck. il *Successful Farming* 87:34L-34M mid-F '89
The Workbench guide to dust collection systems. P. McCafferty. il *Workbench* 45:70-4+ Ja/F '89
Safety devices and measures
Respiratory hazards in the shop. M. Lane. il *Workbench* 45:66-9 Ja/F '89
The safe shop. M. Phair. il *Home Mechanix* 85:54-6+ N '89
WORKSHOPS, PHOTOGRAPHIC *See* Photography—Study and teaching
WORKSTATIONS
See also
Apollo Computer, Inc.
Ardent Computer Inc.
Stellar Computer Inc.
Sun Microsystems Inc.
Tektronix, Inc.
DEC's RISC powerhouse [DECstation] B. Smith and R. L. Mitchell. il *Byte* 14:201-2+ N '89
Digital Equipment introduces new engineering workstations, personal computer series. *Aviation Week & Space Technology* 130:51 Ja 23 '89
A helping hand [Prab Voice Command workstation] W. Rash, Jr. il *Byte* 14:129-30 D '89
High noon for Sun [cover story] J. B. Levine. il pors *Business Week* p70-5 Jl 24 '89
The hottest computer in a white-hot market? [DEC's new workstation] L. Helm. il *Business Week* p88-9 Ja 16 '89
How Steve Jobs linked up with IBM [Next computer; cover story] B. R. Schlender. il pors *Fortune* 120:48-51+ O 9 '89
HP: now no. 1 in workstations [deal for Apollo] J. B. Levine. il *Business Week* p30 Ap 24 '89
Intel to Motorola: race ya [new 860 chip] O. Port. il *Business Week* p42 Mr 13 '89
Intel's plan for staying on top. C. Gottlieb. il *Fortune* 119:98-100 Mr 27 '89
Is U.S. business giving away its technology—again? B. R. Schlender. il *Fortune* 120:10 S 11 '89
The LAN terminal alternative [Wyse WY-212 and TeleVideo TS2 TeleStation diskless PCs] B. Catchings and M. L. Van Name. il *Byte* 14:211-14 N '89
The Next computer: promises to keep. R. A. Shaffer. il *Personal Computing* 13:51-2 Ja '89
Next means business now [agreement with Businessland] R. A. Shaffer. il *Personal Computing* 13:47-8 Jl '89
Personal workstations [special section] il *Byte* 14:226-7+ F '89
Power station in a pizza box [Sun's SPARCstation 1] J. M. Nash. il *Time* 133:51 Ap 24 '89
Raytheon adapts color workstations to meet requirements of military users. D. Hughes. il *Aviation Week & Space Technology* 130:104-5 Ap 24 '89
Steve Jobs gets the keys to the office PC market [link with Businessland] R. Brandt. il por *Business Week* p80-1 Ap 10 '89
Steve Jobs: out for revenge. P. Patton. il por *The New York Times Magazine* p22-3+ Ag 6 '89
Steve Jobs' revolutionary new computer. W. J. Hawkins. il por *Popular Science* 234:68-70+ Ja '89
Steve Jobs's hard sell [deal with Businessland] *Newsweek* 113:49 Ap 10 '89
Two powerful systems from Sun [SPARCStation 1 and Sun-3/80; cover story] N. Baran. il *Byte* 14:108-12 My '89
The ultimate upgrade [standard IBM PC AT turned into a personal workstation] S. Diehl. il *Byte* 14:313-14+ Je '89
UNIX workstation connect. D. Fiedler. il *Byte* 14:123-6 D '89
What's Next? P. Scisco. il *Compute!* 11:6 Ja '89
When one drive is enough [diskless PCs] M. L. Van Name and B. Catchings. il *Byte* 14:141-2+ D '89
Where the action is. J. M. Nash. il *Time* 133:55 Mr 13 '89
Why Sun is losing its heat in the East [Sun Microsystems] N. Gross. il *Business Week* p114 S 18 '89
Workstations boost productivity of aerospace, defense engineers. D. Hughes. *Aviation Week & Space Technology* 130:255+ Mr 20 '89
WORLD, END OF THE *See* End of the world
WORLD ADMINISTRATIVE TELEGRAPH AND TELEPHONE CONFERENCE
Building a flexible framework for new information services [address, October 19, 1988] P. W. Borg. *Department of State Bulletin* 89:33-5 Ja '89
WORLD AIDS DAY
Let's talk AIDS. il *World Health* p30 Ja/F '89
Talking AIDS. C. Viedma. il *World Health* p16-17 Mr '89
World AIDS Day. T. Netter. il *World Health* p25-7 O '89
A WORLD APART [film] *See* Motion picture reviews—Single works

WORLD ASSOCIATION FOR CHRISTIAN COMMUNICA-TION
Communicators ponder the global market [conference in Manila, Philippines] W. F. Fore. *The Christian Century* 106:1076+ N 22 '89

WORLD ASSOCIATION OF NUCLEAR OPERATORS
Chernobyl's legacy. D. Rinehart. il *Maclean's* 102:52 My 29 '89
World nuclear power operators unite. J. Horan. il *The Bulletin of the Atomic Scientists* 45:39-40 Ap '89

WORLD BANK
The alarming truth about the World Bank. J. Bovard. *Reader's Digest* 134:108-12 Je '89
Austerity's human toll [African maternity care] F. P. Hosken. il por *The Humanist* 49:17-19+ Ja/F '89
A bankers' world [environmental assessment program] D. Henwood. *The Nation* 249:481 O 30 '89
Bankrolling debacles? A. Levine. il map *U.S. News & World Report* 107:43-4+ S 25 '89
Conservation woes at the World Bank. B. Rich. il *The Nation* 248:73+ Ja 23 '89
Easing third world debt [exit bonds] J. Williamson. il *USA Today (Periodical)* 117:28-9 Mr '89
Economic restructuring in Sub-Saharan Africa. C. Lancaster. *Current History* 88:213-16+ My '89
Environment, poverty and growth [address, February 9, 1989] A. Karaosmanoglu. *Vital Speeches of the Day* 55:396-400 Ap 15 '89
International Bank for Ruination and Destruction. M. S. Tammen. il *Conservative Digest* 15:45+ Mr/Ap '89
No relief on Latin debt—without World Bank reform. P. C. Roberts. il *Business Week* p15 Mr 6 '89
Who bears the burden of sustainability? K. Piddington. il *New Perspectives Quarterly* 6:8-11 Spr '89
Wildlands: balancing conversion with conservation in World Bank projects [cover story] R. Goodland and G. Ledec. bibl f il *Environment* 31:6-11+ N '89

WORLD BASKETBALL LEAGUE
It's a small World. W. Nack. il *Sports Illustrated* 71:60-1+ Jl 24 '89

WORLD CHAMPIONSHIP TENNIS TOUR *See* Tennis—Tournaments

WORLD COMMISSION ON ENVIRONMENT AND DE-VELOPMENT
Reflections on 'Our common future' [interview with G. H. Brundtland] N. Myers. il por *International Wildlife* 19:14-15 N/D '89

WORLD COOPERATION *See* International cooperation

WORLD COUNCIL OF CHURCHES
An evangelical at the WCC [interview with J. Van Hoeven] por *Christianity Today* 33:51-2 Ja 13 '89
Evangelical voice heard at World Council meeting [conference on Mission and Evangelism] R. Frame. il *Christianity Today* 33:45-6 Jl 14 '89
'Solidarity' meets 'evangelism' in WCC [World Conference on Mission and Evangelism at Trinity University] J. C. Lyles. *The Christian Century* 106:613-15 Je 21-28 '89
WCC takes its agenda to the Soviet Union. M. VanElderen. *The Christian Century* 106:773-5 Ag 30-S 6 '89

WORLD COURT *See* International Court of Justice
WORLD CRUISES *See* Voyages around the world
WORLD CUP (SKI RACING) *See* Ski racing
WORLD CUP (SOCCER) *See* Soccer—World Cup
WORLD DECADE FOR CULTURAL DEVELOPMENT, 1988-1997
Culture is also how we live [cover story; special section] il *UN Chronicle* 26:40-53 Je '89
A World Decade for Cultural Development [cover story; special issue] il *The Courier (Unesco)* 41:3-34 N '88

WORLD ECONOMIC POLICY *See* Economic policy
WORLD ECONOMICS *See* Economic conditions
WORLD EDUCATION *See* International education
WORLD ENVIRONMENT DAY
World Environment Day observed. *UN Chronicle* 26:56 S '89

WORLD EVANGELICAL FELLOWSHIP
Faith at the top [interview with D. Howard] por map *Christianity Today* 33:58-9 Jl 14 '89

WORLD EYE BOOKSHOP (GREENFIELD, MASS.) *See* Booksellers and bookselling—Massachusetts

WORLD FESTIVAL OF YOUTH AND STUDENTS FOR PEACE AND FRIENDSHIP
A party in Pyongyang. B. Martin. il *Newsweek* 114:35 Jl 17 '89
People's democratic revue. A. Daniels. *National Review* 41:19-20 S 1 '89

WORLD FINANCIAL CENTER (NEW YORK, N.Y.)
Corporate trophies [New urban landscape exhibit] A. Schwartz-man. il *Art in America* 77:34-7+ F '89
Gimme shelter [New urban landscape show] P. Viladas. il *Art News* 88:81-2 Ja '89

WORLD FINANCIAL CENTER (NEW YORK, N.Y.). WIN-TER GARDEN
Lightning rods [caring for palms] *The New Yorker* 65:36-7 Ap 10 '89

WORLD FLIGHTS *See* Aviation—World flights
WORLD FOOD DAY
World Food Day, 1988 [proclamation, September 28, 1988] R. Reagan. *Department of State Bulletin* 88:37 D '88
WORLD FOOD SUPPLY *See* Food supply—International aspects
WORLD FUTURE SOCIETY
Future view: the 1990s & beyond [Washington, D.C. confer-ence, July 1989] C. G. Wagner and D. M. Fields. il *The Futurist* 23:29-38 N/D '89
WORLD GOVERNMENT *See* International organization
WORLD HEALTH ASSEMBLY
WHO launches effort to eradicate polio by year 2000. il *UN Chronicle* 26:69-71 S '89
Young people at WHO. il *World Health* p30-1 Je '89
WORLD HEALTH DAY
Let's talk health [cover story; special issue] il *World Health* p3-29 Ja/F '89
WORLD HEALTH ORGANIZATION
AIDS: a worldwide effort will stop it! [cover story; special issue] il *World Health* p3-29 O '89
The birth of WHO [interview with S. Sze] il *World Health* p28-9 My '89
Environmental health could become global concern of 1990s. il *UN Chronicle* 26:72 Je '89
Health ethics and the law. S. S. Connor and H. L. Fuenzalida-Puelma. il *World Health* p10-13 Ap '89
Leadership through language training [English as a second language at the WHO Learning Centre] E. N. Francisco. il *World Health* p6 N '89
The politics of health [PLO application to World Health Organization] J. Bierman. il *Maclean's* 102:27 My 22 '89
U.S. opposes PLO admission to UN agencies [statement, May 4, 1989] S. L. Vogelgesang. *Department of State Bulletin* 89:65-6 Jl '89
WHO seeks global data on sexual practices. W. Booth. *Science* 244:418-19 Ap 28 '89
WHO vs. AIDS [interview with H. Nakajima] J.-Y. Nau and F. Nouchi. il por *World Press Review* 36:52 Mr '89
WORLD HEALTH ORGANIZATION. WORLD HEALTH ASSEMBLY *See* World Health Assembly
WORLD HERITAGE CONVENTION
World heritage: from da Vinci to the white rhino. il *UN Chronicle* 26:48-53 Je '89
WORLD HISTORY *See* History
WORLD LAW *See* International law
WORLD LEADERS *See* Heads of state
WORLD LEAGUE OF AMERICAN FOOTBALL
Can Tex Schramm make pigskin fashionable in Paris? K. Kelly. il *Business Week* p34-5 Jl 31 '89
Transatlantic kickoff. il *U.S. News & World Report* 106:18 My 1 '89
WORLD MAPS
See also
  Globes
Redrawing the map [Robinson projection] J. Diamond. maps *World Press Review* 36:61 Je '89
Scholastic update world atlas 1989-90. maps *Scholastic Update (Teachers' edition)* 122:10-17 S 22 '89
WORLD MILITARY EXPENDITURES *See* Armed Forces—Appropriations and expenditures
WORLD MONITOR [television program] See Television program reviews—Single works
WORLD NEWS *See* Foreign news
A WORLD OF IDEAS WITH BILL MOYERS [television program] See Television program reviews—Single works
WORLD PEACE *See* Peace
WORLD PHOTO CONTEST *See* Photography—Competitions
WORLD POLITICS
See also
  Balance of power
  Current events
  Geopolitics
  International relations
  League of Nations
  United Nations
  War
The battle for democracy [cover story] S. V. Roberts. il *U.S. News & World Report* 106:35-8 My 22 '89
The ecology of international change [address, October 28, 1988] G. P. Shultz. *Department of State Bulletin* 89:6-10 Ja '89
Eternal severities. J. Newhouse. *The New Yorker* 65:100-20+ O 23 '89
A glimpse of greater peace. J. Bierman. il *Maclean's* 102:34-6 Ja 23 '89
Into a brave new world. L. Martz. il *Newsweek* 114:40-2+ D 25 '89
Notes and comment [democracy and world politics] *The New Yorker* 65:29 S 4 '89
Notes and comment [global view in local politics] *The New Yorker* 65:37 O 9 '89
Politics: 'selling the sizzle' [1980s] H. Rainie. il *U.S. News & World Report* 107:92+ D 25 '89-Ja 1 '90
Power to the people. L. Lief. il *U.S. News & World Report* 107:24-5 D 25 '89-Ja 1 '90
The protracted conflict. B. Crozier. See issues of National Review

WORLD POLITICS—*cont.*
The tentative triumph of the ballot. F. Ajami. il *U.S. News & World Report* 107:40+ D 4 '89
Viewpoints. See issues of World Press Review
The world affairs annual 1989-90 [cover story; special issue] il maps *Scholastic Update (Teachers' edition)* 122:3-32 S 22 '89
A world at war. R. Sollen. il *The Nation* 248:46-7 Ja 9-16 '89
The world war created [World War II] M. B. Zuckerman. il map *U.S. News & World Report* 107:68-9+ Ag 28-S 4 '89
Worldgram: newsletter. See issues of U.S. News & World Report

WORLD POPULATION *See* Population
WORLD PSYCHIATRIC ASSOCIATION
Here come the Russian shrinks! G. Garelik. il *Time* 134:78-9 O 30 '89
Soviets reenter world psychiatric society. B. Bower. *Science News* 136:278 O 28 '89

WORLD RECORDS
See also
Airplane speed records
Automobile speed records
Boat speed records
Motorcycle speed records
Running records
Not explainable [A. Furman seeks record for speed squatting] *The New Yorker* 65:25-7 F 27 '89
Wed when the West was wild, Ernie and Maud Scott celebrate 80 years of staying hitched [longest-wed living couple in the world] il pors *People Weekly* 31:99 Je 26 '89

WORLD RESEARCH FOUNDATION
Dr. Database. A. J. S. Rayl. il *Omni (New York, N.Y.)* 11:100 F '89

WORLD SAXOPHONE QUARTET
The World Saxophone Quartet: building on a new tradition [cover story; interview] G. Santoro. il *Down Beat* 56:16-19 Jl '89

WORLD SECURITY *See* International security
WORLD SERIES (BASEBALL) *See* Baseball, Professional—World Series
WORLD TENNIS (PERIODICAL)
Editor's page. N. Amdur. See issues of World Tennis beginning June 1984

WORLD TERRORISM *See* Terrorism—International aspects
WORLD TRADE WEEK
World Trade Week, 1989 [proclamation, May 5, 1989] G. Bush. *Department of State Bulletin* 89:51 Jl '89
WORLD UNITY *See* Internationalism
WORLD VETERANS GAMES
Field of dreams [running the 800 meter race] G. Sheehan. il *Runner's World* 24:16 D '89
A gathering of greyhounds. H. Higdon. il *Runner's World* 24:34-9 D '89
The times of their lives. K. Moore. il *Sports Illustrated* 71:44-7 Ag 14 '89

WORLD VISION (ORGANIZATION)
World Vision [work of photographers E. Mooneyham and T. Owens and D. Ward] B. Brander. il *Petersen's Photographic Magazine* 18:24-6+ Je '89

WORLD WAR, 1914-1918
Force and ideas. *The New Republic* 201 [Reprint v1]:7-8 N 6 '89 [N 7 '14]
The war and the future of civilization. R. G. Usher. *The New Republic* 201 [Reprint v1]:22-3 N 6 '89 [N 7 '14]

Art
A paper army that helped pull America into World War I [posters] S. Crawford. il *Smithsonian* 20:122-7 N '89

Bibliography
Paperback history. B. H. Reid. *History Today* 39:51 Ap '89

Campaigns and battles
Arab countries
The fallen hero [T. E. Lawrence] W. Pfaff. *The New Yorker* 65:105-15 My 8 '89
The lives of Lawrence [activities of T. E. Lawrence portrayed in the film Lawrence of Arabia] E. Kedourie. *The New Republic* 201:37 Ag 21 '89
Tanzania
The Admiralty's orders were clear: 'sink or destroy the Königsberg' [British-German encounter off the East African coast] D. Houston. il map *Smithsonian* 20:130-4+ S '89
Medical and sanitary affairs
America's deadly rendezvous with the 'Spanish Lady' [flu epidemic] J. Fincher. bibl (p147) il *Smithsonian* 19:130-2+ Ja '89

Naval operations
See also
Königsberg (Cruiser)
Photographs and photography
The stark scenes of a giant war. il *Time* 134 Special Issue:26-7 Fall '89

Poetry
Disquiet on the Western Front. il *U.S. News & World Report* 107:16 Ag 21 '89

Women
Flora Sandes—military maid. J. Wheelwright. bibl f il pors map *History Today* 39:42-8 Mr '89
Balkan Peninsula
The empire of the East. H. N. Brailsford. *The New Republic* 201 [Reprint v1]:14-15 N 6 '89 [N 7 '14]
Germany
Has German strategy failed? F. H. Simonds. *The New Republic* 201 [Reprint v1]:13-14 N 6 '89 [N 7 '14]
Bibliography
No man's land. J. Joll. il *The New York Review of Books* 36:53-6 Ap 27 '89
Spain
Diaghilev sits out WWI in Spain: Iberian idyll. J. R. Acocella. il pors *Dance Magazine* 63:45-8 Je '89
Sweden
The spirit of Stockholm. Sir H. Walpole. *The New Republic* 201 [Reprint v1]:16 N 6 '89 [N 7 '14]
United States
The end of American isolation. *The New Republic* 201 [Reprint v1]:9-10 N 6 '89 [N 7 '14]
War against reason. H. Fairlie. il *The New Republic* 201:58-62 N 6 '89

WORLD WAR, 1914-1918, IN MOTION PICTURES
The lives of Lawrence [activities of T. E. Lawrence portrayed in the film Lawrence of Arabia] E. Kedourie. *The New Republic* 201:37 Ag 21 '89
WORLD WAR, 1939-1945
A fateful Labor Day [September 1, 1939] J. W. Michaels. il *Forbes* 144:38-9 S 4 '89
The real war 1939-1945 [cover story] P. Fussell. il *The Atlantic* 264:32-40+ Ag '89
What if . . .? il *Time* 134:40-2 S 4 '89
World at war [cover story; special section] J. Keegan. il pors maps *U.S. News & World Report* 107:32-6+ Ag 28-S 4 '89
World War II: desperate years. O. Friedrich. il map *Time* 134:24-30+ S 4 '89
World War II: the legacy [cover story; special section; with editorial comment by Kevin Doyle] il maps *Maclean's* 102:2, 20-4+ S 4 '89
World War II: when darkness fell [cover story; special section] il pors *Time* 134:28-34+ Ag 28 '89

Aerial operations
See also
Hiroshima (Japan)—Bombardment, 1945
Nagasaki (Japan)—Bombardment, 1945
A boy goes to war. G. Bush. il pors *Life* 12:70-2+ S '89
On wings of forgiveness [J. Takeshita meets relatives of American civilians killed in explosion of Japanese balloon bomb in Oregon during World War II] J. Fincher. il *Reader's Digest* 134:85-90 Mr '89

Airplanes, Military
See Airplanes, Military—History
Airplanes, Training
See Airplanes, Training—History

Art
See also
D-Day Invasion, 1944, in art
National socialism and art

Atrocities
See also
Concentration camps
Holocaust, Jewish (1939-1945)
Katyn Forest Massacre, 1940

Blacks
Black veterans of WWII honor unknown soldiers. il *Jet* 77:28 N 20 '89
Reagan treated at Ft. Huachuca hospital black medics made famous in WW II. il *Jet* 76:52-4 Jl 31 '89

Campaigns and battles
See also
World War, 1939-1945—Aerial operations
World War, 1939-1945—Naval operations
France
For honour alone [teenage cadets defend French Cavalry School, June 1940] R. Macnab. il *History Today* 39:5-7 Ja '89

Germany
Red Army vet Vladimir Kuts joins up with his GI pals 44 years after battling the Nazis together [visit to the United States] W. Plummer. il por *People Weekly* 32:86-8 Ag 21 '89

Italy
See also
Cassino (Italy), Battle of, 1944
Pacific
See also
Iwo Jima, Battle of, 1945
Okinawa, Battle of, 1945
Pearl Harbor (Hawaii), Attack on, 1941
Back to the battlefields [World War II veterans] K. Castle. il *Travel Holiday* 172:60-71 S '89
The Johnson years: a congressman goes to war. R. A. Caro. por *The New Yorker* 65:62-4+ N 6 '89
War: it's hard to get it right. J. Hersey. il *The New York Times Book Review* 94:1+ S 10 '89

WORLD WAR, 1939-1945—Campaigns and battles—Pacific —*cont.*

William F. Halsey, Jr. J. B. Graves. il pors *Conservative Digest* 15:37-41 S/O '89

Poland

Fifty years later [defense of Westerplatte] R. Sikorski. *National Review* 41:42 S 29 '89

Catholic Church

Moral heroes of our time: Christian rescuers. E. Fogelman. *America* 161:426-8+ D 9 '89

Causes

The coming of the Second World War. J. Lukacs. *Foreign Affairs* 68:165-74 Fall '89

Making way for Hitler. G. A. Craig. bibl f il *The New York Review of Books* 36:11-12+ O 12 '89

'Peace in our time' [appeasement of Germany by Britain and France] il *U.S. News & World Report* 107:61 Ag 28-S 4 '89

Road to war. il *Time* 134:40-6 Ag 28 '89

Diplomatic history

See also

Yalta Conference (1945)

Dangerous liaisons [German and British alliances with the Soviet Union] G. A. Craig. bibl f il *The New York Review of Books* 36:15-19 Mr 30 '89

The deal that still lives in infamy [Soviet-Nazi pact] S. Bialer. *U.S. News & World Report* 107:68-9 Ag 28-S 4 '89

The great Mafia wedding [Hitler-Stalin pact; cover story] J. P. Roche. il *National Review* 41:23-4 S 1 '89

Making way for Hitler. G. A. Craig. bibl f il *The New York Review of Books* 36:11-12+ O 12 '89

The Nazi-Soviet pacts: a half-century later. G. L. Weinberg. bibl f *Foreign Affairs* 68:175-89 Fall '89

Nineteen thirty-nine [German-Soviet non-aggression pact] C. S. Maier. *The New Republic* 201:16-17 S 11 '89

The secret protocols [texts of 1939 Soviet-German pacts] *Maclean's* 102:24 S 4 '89

The United States and Russia in World War II [reprint from November and December 1950 issues] R. W. Van Alstyne. *Current History* 88:26-9+ Ja '89

Historiography

From Hirohito to Heimat. I. Buruma. *The New York Review of Books* 36:31-2+ O 26 '89

The secret of the soldiers who didn't shoot [historian S.L.A. Marshall's claims concerning quality of U.S. troops; with editorial comment by Richard F. Snow] F. P. Smoler. il pors *American Heritage* 40:5, 36-45 Mr '89

Jews

See also

Holocaust, Jewish (1939-1945)

Literature

More fascinating lives [F. H. Gervasi's personal memoir] L. Fleischer. *Publishers Weekly* 235:72 Je 30 '89

Oh what a lovely war! N. G. A. Annan, Baron. il *The New York Review of Books* 36:3-4+ S 28 '89

Remembering war. J. Bemrose and L. Glynn. il *Maclean's* 102:68-9+ N 13 '89

September 3rd, 1939 . . . il *History Today* 39:62-3 S '89

A war to remember. J. Miller. il *Newsweek* 114:64-6 S 4 '89

Medical and sanitary affairs

Reagan treated at Ft. Huachuca hospital black medics made famous in WW II. il *Jet* 76:52-4 Jl 31 '89

Wartime nurses. E. E. Rosenbaum. il *New Choices for the Best Years* 29:24+ Jl '89

Moral and religious aspects

See also

World War, 1939-1945—Catholic Church

Legend of the four chaplains [courage displayed by Lieutenants Fox, Goode, Poling, and Washington during sinking of the S. S. Dorchester] L. Elliott. il *Reader's Digest* 134:65-70 Je '89

Not just a war—a just war [Paul Fussell's Wartime] *National Review* 41:20-1 O 13 '89

Naval operations

See also

Bismarck (Battleship)

Dorchester (Ship)

Eisele (Ship)

Mullany (Destroyer)

Heroes of the frozen cliff [rescue of crew from USS Pollux wreck by Newfoundlanders] H. Strauss. il *Reader's Digest* 134:102-7 Ap '89

William F. Halsey, Jr. J. B. Graves. il pors *Conservative Digest* 15:37-41 S/O '89

Peace

While America slept [cover story] J. P. Hart. *National Review* 41:32-4 S 15 '89

The world war created. M. B. Zuckerman. il map *U.S. News & World Report* 107:68-9+ Ag 28-S 4 '89

Personal narratives

A boy goes to war. G. Bush. il pors *Life* 12:70-2+ S '89

It's not just a job, it's an adventure [author's time in Army, Navy and Merchant Marine] G. Baxter. il *Flying* 116:120+ Je '89

Triumph and tragedy. S. Shields. il por *American Heritage* 40:82-6+ D '89

WWII. il *Life* 12:125-8+ D '89

Photographs and photography

The faces of war. il *Maclean's* 102:36-9 S 4 '89

Measuring the rise and fall of another cataclysm. il *Time* 134 Special Issue:46-7 Fall '89

Prisoners and prisons

See also

Concentration camps

Ike's revenge? [J. Bacque alleges U.S. mistreatment of POWs] por *Time* 134:19 O 2 '89

Sullying the allies [J. Bacque's book claiming U.S. mistreated POWs] D. Turbide. il por *Maclean's* 102:75 N 13 '89

Psychological aspects

The real war [interview with P. Fussell] R. J. Spiller. il por *American Heritage* 40:126-7+ N '89

Reporters and reporting

War: it's hard to get it right. J. Hersey. il *The New York Times Book Review* 94:1+ S 10 '89

The world has never been quite the same. D. Middleton. il *The New York Times Magazine* p28-30+ S 3 '89

Underground movements

Germany

See Anti-Nazi movement—Germany

Veterans

See Veterans

War criminals

See also

War crime trials

L'affaire Touvier: opening old wounds. T. Morgan. il pors *The New York Times Magazine* p32-3+ O 1 '89

Bringing Nazi sympathizers to the U.S. [role of T. Parsons; cover story] J. Wiener. *The Nation* 248:289+ Mr 6 '89

From Hirohito to Heimat. I. Buruma. *The New York Review of Books* 36:31-2+ O 26 '89

If Hungary's cops don't get you, its telephones will [making Murderers among us: the Simon Wiesenthal story] L. Eisenberg. il *TV Guide* 37:26-9 Ap 22-28 '89

A race against time [Nazi collaborators V. Sokolov and J. Luitjens face possible deportation from Canada] N. Underwood. pors *Maclean's* 102:44 Ja 23 '89

Scandalous sanctuary [P. Touvier, French war criminal arrested] R. Marshall. il por *Newsweek* 113:44 Je 5 '89

Canada

The ties of blood. R. Laver. il *Maclean's* 102:40+ S 4 '89

Photographs and photography

Canadians in combat. il *Maclean's* 102:43-4 S 4 '89

Ethiopia

The emperor wore clothes: visiting Haile Selassie in 1943. H. Courlander. *The American Scholar* 58:271-81 Spr '89

France

See also

France—History—German occupation, 1940-1945

Germany

See also

Dachau (Germany: Concentration camp)

Axis, Ltd. [cover story] M. Sayle. il *The New Republic* 200:22-4+ Je 5 '89

The Hannes Schneider story [inventor of modern skiing rescued from Nazi Germany and brought to U.S. in 1939] N. Howe. il pors *Skiing* 41:126-9+ Mr '89

Great Britain

Were we wrong in 1939? [U.S. refusal to join Anglo-French defense of Poland; with reply by J. P. Roche] D. Carlton. il *National Review* 41:44+ S 29 '89

The world has never been quite the same. D. Middleton. il *The New York Times Magazine* p28-30+ S 3 '89

Japan

See also

Hiroshima (Japan)—Bombardment, 1945

Japan—History—Allied occupation, 1945-1952

Nagasaki (Japan)—Bombardment, 1945

Pearl Harbor (Hawaii), Attack on, 1941

Axis, Ltd. [cover story] M. Sayle. il *The New Republic* 200:22-4+ Je 5 '89

A distant mirror. H. G. Chua-Eoan. il *Time* 134:44-6 S 4 '89

Mourn Hirohito? W. F. Buckley. *National Review* 41:63 Ap 7 '89

Poland

See also

Auschwitz (Poland: Concentration camp)

Blitzkrieg [German invasion] il *Time* 134:30-4+ Ag 28 '89

Nineteen thirty-nine [German-Soviet non-aggression pact] C. S. Maier. *The New Republic* 201:16-17 S 11 '89

The rape of Poland and the death of hope. A. Valiunas. il *The American Spectator* 22:17-18 S '89

Were we wrong in 1939? [U.S. refusal to join Anglo-French defense of Poland; with reply by J. P. Roche] D. Carlton. il *National Review* 41:44+ S 29 '89

Soviet Union

Securing peace. A. Wilson-Smith. il *Maclean's* 102:46 S 4 '89

United States

See also

Japanese Americans—Evacuation and relocation, 1942-1945

World War, 1939-1945—Aerial operations

World War, 1939-1945—Naval operations

WORLD WAR, 1939-1945—United States—*cont.*
Chemical warfare: a forgotten lesson [reputed plan to use gas in 1945 attack on Iwo Jima] J. E. van C. Moon. bibl f il *The Bulletin of the Atomic Scientists* 45:40-3 Jl/Ag '89

Heading north [teenager tries to travel to Ontario to join the Black Watch in 1939] *The New Yorker* 65:33 S 4 '89

The secret of the soldiers who didn't shoot [historian S.L.A. Marshall's claims concerning quality of U.S. troops; with editorial comment by Richard F. Snow] F. P. Smoler. il pors *American Heritage* 40:5, 36-45 Mr '89

A war for others to fight [reluctance to enter war] il *U.S. News & World Report* 107:57 Ag 28-S 4 '89

Were we wrong in 1939? [U.S. refusal to join Anglo-French defense of Poland; with reply by J. P. Roche] D. Carlton. il *National Review* 41:44+ S 29 '89

Where Patton prepared for North Africa in southern California [site of Camp Young, headquarters for Desert Training Center] il *Sunset (Central West edition)* 182:63 F '89
Photographs and photography
A nation of zombies [works by E. Bubley] K. Dieckmann. bibl f il *Art in America* 77:55-7+ N '89

WORLD WRESTLING FEDERATION
The upstart (slam!) who's reinventing (pow!) the tube (grrr!) [V. McMahon and professional wrestling on pay-per-view television] J. Hammer. il pors *Gentlemen's Quarterly* 59:280-5+ N '89

WORLD YOUTH FESTIVAL *See* World Festival of Youth and Students for Peace and Friendship

WORLD'S COLUMBIAN EXPOSITION (1893: CHICAGO, ILL.)
[Column] W. Garrett. il *Antiques* 136:118-19 Jl '89

WORLD'S FAIR (1939-1940: NEW YORK, N.Y.) *See* New York World's Fair (1939-1940)

WORLD'S FAIRS
See also
Expo 92 (Seville, Spain)
Exposition Universelle de 1889 (Paris, France)
Golden Gate International Exposition (1939-1940)
New York World's Fair (1939-1940)
World's Columbian Exposition (1893: Chicago, Ill.)
Collectibles
It's time for another world's fair. H. L. Rinker. il *Antiques & Collecting Hobbies* 94:20+ O '89

WORLEY, JAMES
Accessible tombs [poem] *The Christian Century* 106:166 F 15 '89

Monarch butterfly [poem] *The Christian Century* 106:901 O 11 '89

Neither here nor there [poem] *The Christian Century* 106:462 My 3 '89

October [poem] *The Christian Century* 106:924 O 18 '89

On refusing to prune an ancient lilac [poem] *The Christian Century* 106:723 Ag 2-9 '89

Ruth cleaves again to Naomi [poem] *The Christian Century* 106:580 Je 7-14 '89

The ultimate barricade [poem] *The Christian Century* 106:837 S 27 '89

WORLEY, MARK C.
Alpha/theta meditation goggles. il *Radio-Electronics* 60:53-7 Ap '89

WORM (WRITE ONCE READ MANY) *See* Write once optical memories

WORMAN, EDWARD A.
Fall wild-flowers [photographs] il *The Conservationist* 44:22-5 S/O '89

WORMHOLES (ASTROPHYSICS)
Cosmic time travel [research by Kip Thorne and Michael S. Morris; cover story] D. Freedman. il *Discover* 10:58-64 Je '89

Time after time [wormhole time machine proposed by Michael S. Morris and others] T. Rothman. *Scientific American* 260:21-2 Ja '89

Wormholes in the heavens [creating new universes; views of A. H. Guth] M. D. Lemonick. il *Time* 133:55 Ja 16 '89

Wormholes, time machines, and Schrödinger's cat. il *Sky and Telescope* 77:132 F '89

WORMNES, ARE
Keeping an 'eye' on traffic. il *World Press Review* 36:57 Mr '89

WORMS, NICHOLAS
about
Norman retreat. R. Koenig. il *House & Garden* 161:142-7+ Jl '89

WORMS
See also
Earthworms
Mealworms

WORMS, COMPUTER *See* Computer viruses

WORMS, INTESTINAL AND PARASITIC
See also
Helminths
Trichinosis
What's that wiggling in my sushi? *Science News* 135:300 My 13 '89

WORMSER, BARON
Pigeons [poem] *Harper's* 279:34 S '89

WORMWOOD
Weeding out malaria [artemisinin] D. L. Klayman. il *Natural History* p18+ O '89

WORNOM, HOWARD
For goodness sake? por *Omni (New York, N.Y.)* 12:16+ D '89

WORONOV, NAOMI
Companies on the East and West coasts keep their dance traditions alive: regional Chinese dance, American-style. il *Dance Magazine* 63:28-30 Ag '89

WORRY
See also
Catastrophic thinking
Don't worry, be happy—but how? L. Gross. *Redbook* 174:112-13+ N '89
Anecdotes, facetiae, satire, etc.
Don't worry, keep busy. S. Bing. il *Esquire* 112:99-101 N '89

WORSHIP
See also
Ancestor worship
Church attendance
Prayer
The passion and the arts in worship [cover story; special section] il *The Christian Century* 106:308-16 Mr 22-29 '89

Sunday monarchists and Monday citizens? W. J. Everett. *The Christian Century* 106:503-5 My 10 '89

WORTH, B. J.
about
When James Bond jumps, super skydiver B.J. Worth gives 007 an airborne Licence to thrill. N. Geeslin. il pors *People Weekly* 32:95+ S 4 '89

WORTH, GRETCHEN
Gracious gifts of money. il *Working Woman* 14:78-9+ D '89

How to avoid a tax audit. il *Working Woman* 14:86-8 Mr '89

WORTH INC.
Batter up for a baseball factory tour. il *Southern Living* 24:34 N '89

WORTH WINNING [film] *See* Motion picture reviews—Single works

WORTHEN, G. SCOTT, AND OTHERS
Mechanics of stimulated neutrophils: cell stiffening induces retention in capillaries. bibl f il *Science* 245:183-6 Jl 14 '89

WORTHINGTON, CHRISTA
Sights & sounds. il *Harper's Bazaar* 122:48+ Mr '89

WORTMAN, ALEX
about
The bowling bumper cushion spares frustrated alley cats the indignity of gutter balls. il pors *People Weekly* 32:157 D 11 '89

WOU, TIA
about
Careers by design. il pors *Harper's Bazaar* 122:188-91+ Mr '89

WOUND HEALING *See* Healing

WOUNDS
See also
Gunshot wounds
Traumatism
Wounds: treat them seriously. il *Current Health 2* 16:26-7 S '89

WOYACK, ROBERT B., AND REMY, RICHARD C.
Conceptualizing world studies. *The Education Digest* 54:32-4 Ap '89

WPP GROUP PLC
Brits buy up the ad business [cover story] R. Rothenberg. il por *The New York Times Magazine* p14-19+ Jl 2 '89

Confessions of an advertising man [M. Sorrell negotiates takeover of Ogilvy] R. I. Kirkland, Jr. il por *Fortune* 119:131-2 Je 5 '89

The 'fax attack' that has Ogilvy fuming [bid for Ogilvy Group] W. Konrad. il por *Business Week* p36 My 15 '89

Machiavelli on Madison Avenue [WPP Group's bid for Ogilvy Group] B. Rudolph. il por *Time* 133:58 My 15 '89

The man who would be king of Madison Ave. [M. Sorrell's WPP Group bids for Ogilvy Group] L. Reibstein. il por *Newsweek* 113:52 My 15 '89

Mediums and messages [WPP buys Ogilvy] A. Walmsley. il por *Maclean's* 102:42 My 29 '89

WPP, the new giant of . . . PR? [WPP buys Ogilvy] W. Konrad. *Business Week* p32 My 29 '89

WPTY (MEMPHIS, TENN.: TELEVISION STATION) *See* Television stations

WRANGELL ISLAND (ALASKA)
Description and travel
Petroglyphs and totems on walking tour of Wrangell, Alaska. il map *Sunset (Central West edition)* 183:52 Jl '89

WRAP ACCOUNTS
Wrap session. B. Weberman. il *Forbes* 144 Special Issue:395 O 23 '89

WRAP DRESSES *See* Clothing and dress
WRAPPING MATERIALS
　　See also
　　Food wraps
WRAPPING OF PACKAGES
　Balsa burning [Christmas wrapping paper] il *Sunset (Central West edition)* 181:102-3 D '88
　Blueprinting to create one-of-a-kind wrapping paper. il *Sunset (Central West edition)* 183:82 D '89
　Christmas candy wraps. il *Sunset (Central West edition)* 183:72-3 D '89
　Great gift-wrap ideas [Christmas] il *McCall's* 117:43 D '89
　Last-minute gift wraps [Christmas gifts] il *Good Housekeeping* 208:110-11+ Ja '89
　Merry wrap-ups [Christmas] N. Wing. il *Parents* 64:169-70+ D '89
　Pack it right. K. Blouin. *Essence* 20:104+ D '89
WREATHS
　　See also
　　Christmas wreaths
　Door decor [vine basket and wreath] D. Temple. il *Flower and Garden* 33:57 S/O '89
　Fresh herb wreath. S. Weaver and R. Lounsbury. il *Organic Gardening* 36:22-3 D '89
　Natural wreaths. il *Country Journal* 16:29-33 N/D '89
　Welcoming wreaths [everlasting] J. Williams and J. Severson. il *Better Homes and Gardens* 67:114+ O '89
WRECKING
　　See also
　　Airplanes, Military—Wrecking
　"Can I get a bulldozer down the driveway?" [teardowns of houses in Los Angeles] E. Paris. il *Forbes* 144 Special Issue:48-9+ O 23 '89
　Million-dollar "birthday cakes" [historic homes demolished in wealthy Los Angeles neighborhoods] N. R. Gibbs. il *Time* 133:79 My 1 '89
WRECKS, SHIP *See* Shipwrecks
WREGGET, KEN
　　about
　An understudy steals the show. A. Murphy. il por *Sports Illustrated* 70:31 My 8 '89
WREN, CHRISTOPHER SALE
　How far will De Klerk go? il por *The New York Times Magazine* p42-3+ N 19 '89
WREN, LEE
　(jt. auth) See Edelstein, Jeffrey, and Wren, Lee
WRENCHES
　Channellock adjustable sockets. il *Cycle* 40:80 Ap '89
　Power ratchet [Black & Decker ratchet wrench] J. Truini. il *Popular Mechanics* 166:70 F '89
　Semper paratus (always ready) [antique wrench] il *Workbench* 45:104 Mr/Ap '89
　Wrenches. J. Truini. il *Popular Mechanics* 166:95-7+ Je '89
WRESTLING
　　See also
　　Sumo
Study and teaching
　　See also
　　Monster Factory
Tournaments
　Getting a grip on the Soviets [dual meet in Tempe, Ariz.] A. Murphy. il *Sports Illustrated* 70:102 Ja 9 '89
　Scherr determination [World Cup tournament in Toledo, Ohio] B. Anderson. il pors *Sports Illustrated* 70:71+ Ap 10 '89
WRESTLING, COLLEGE
　The Devils turned on the heat [Arizona State upsets Oklahoma State] B. Anderson. il *Sports Illustrated* 70:72-3 F 13 '89
　The last pure sport. K. Turan. il *Gentlemen's Quarterly* 59:273-4+ Mr '89
Tournaments
　At last a title for the Cowboys [Oklahoma State wins NCAA championships] B. Anderson. il *Sports Illustrated* 70:70-1 Mr 27 '89
WRESTLING, HIGH SCHOOL
　Gold amid the coal [Pennsylvania's North Schuylkill Area team under coach J. Cesari] N. Dawidoff. il por *Sports Illustrated* 70:44-6+ Ja 16 '89
WRESTLING, PROFESSIONAL
　　See also
　　World Wrestling Federation
Anecdotes, facetiae, satire, etc.
　Uncivil liberties. C. Trillin. il *The Nation* 248:330 Mr 13 '89
Economic aspects
　Wrestling to the top. H. D. Shapiro. il *Channels (New York, N.Y.: 1986)* 9:38-41 Ja '89
History
　Nature Boy [B. Rogers] B. Greene. il pors *Esquire* 111:59-60+ Ap '89
Television broadcasting
　　See Cable television—Sports; Television broadcasting—Sports
WRIGHT, AMY
　　about
　Her spectacular splashes onstage and in life suggest Amy Wright's success is far from Accidental. K. McMurran. il pors *People Weekly* 31:89-90+ Ja 30 '89

WRIGHT, BARBARA W.
　That perfect blendship. il *New Choices for the Best Years* 29:51-3+ Mr '89
WRIGHT, BETTY
　　about
　A bewitched and bewildered Speaker. L. Rosellini. il por *U.S. News & World Report* 106:20-1 Ap 17 '89
WRIGHT, BOBBY JACK
　　about
　On the road again. D. S. Looney. il pors *Sports Illustrated* 70:52-6+ F 20 '89
WRIGHT, BRUCE
　GEEB-busters. il *World Tennis* 37:86-8+ S '89
WRIGHT, CHARLES, 1935-
　After reading Wang Wei, I go outside to the full moon [poem] *The New Republic* 201:34 D 11 '89
　Under the nine trees in January [poem] *The New Yorker* 65:89 Ap 17 '89
WRIGHT, DOUG
　　about
　Ubu [drama] Reviews
　　New York il 22:47-8 Jl 17 '89. J. Simon
　　The New Yorker il 65:91 Jl 10 '89. E. Oliver
WRIGHT, ESMOND
　'Mr President' . . . George Washington's new clothes. bibl il pors *History Today* 39:22-8 Ap '89
WRIGHT, FRANK LLOYD, 1867-1959
　　about
　Doing right by Wright. E. M. Gomez. il *Art News* 88:36+ Ja '89
　Restoring a Frank Lloyd Wright jewel. il *Sunset (Central West edition)* 183:108 O '89
WRIGHT, FRANZ, 1953-
　The needle: for a friend who disappeared [poem] *The New Yorker* 65:84 O 16 '89
WRIGHT, JAMES CLAUDE *See* Wright, Jim, 1922-
WRIGHT, JAMES D.
　Address unknown: homelessness in contemporary America. bibl *Society* 26:45-53 S/O '89
　Science, passion and polemics. *Society* 26:21-3 My/Je '89
WRIGHT, JIM, 1922-
　　about
　After Wright's fall. S. V. Roberts. il pors *U.S. News & World Report* 106:34-5 Je 5 '89
　All the Wright moves. J. H. Fund. il *National Review* 41:19-20 Je 16 '89
　Anatomy of a smear. J. M. Barry. il pors *Esquire* 112:215-20+ O '89
　A bewitched and bewildered Speaker. L. Rosellini. il por *U.S. News & World Report* 106:20-1 Ap 17 '89
　Bombshell in the House. G. J. Church. il por *Time* 133:33-4 My 1 '89
　A cancer grows on the Speakership. G. Borger. il por *U.S. News & World Report* 106:20+ My 22 '89
　Capitol offense. por *Time* 133:38 My 15 '89
　A case of Wright and wrong. M. B. Carlson. il por *Time* 133:25 Ap 17 '89
　Cleaning House. *The New Republic* 200:5-6 My 8 '89
　The Democrats' meltdown on the Hill. D. Harbrecht. il *Business Week* p25 Je 12 '89
　An emotional farewell. H. Mackenzie. il pors *Maclean's* 102:32 Je 12 '89
　The end of the line. H. Mackenzie. il por *Maclean's* 102:24 Je 5 '89
　The ethics monster rages. H. Sidey. il por *Time* 133:32 My 29 '89
　Everybody doesn't do it. M. Greenfield. il *Newsweek* 113:84 My 1 '89
　Exit stage Wright. W. McGurn. *National Review* 41:23 Je 30 '89
　Facing the music. T. Morganthau. il por *Newsweek* 113:26-7 Ap 24 '89
　Frenzy on the Hill. T. Morganthau. il pors *Newsweek* 113:14-18 Je 12 '89
　The games Congress plays. H. Gorey. il por *Time* 133:38 F 13 '89
　House Democrats begin to imagine life after Jim Wright. D. Harbrecht. por *Business Week* p51 Mr 13 '89
　House Speaker Jim Wright resigns; blacks note loss and attack on Bill Gray. il pors *Jet* 76:4-5 Je 19 '89
　How many will fall? M. B. Carlson. il pors *Time* 133:34-5 Je 5 '89
　In 'hip-deep water'. R. Thomas. il por *Newsweek* 113:25-6 My 1 '89
　Jim Wright: on the ropes. L. Martz. il por *Newsweek* 113:22-3 Ap 3 '89
　Jim Wright's lonely fight. H. Mackenzie. il por *Maclean's* 102:24-5 My 1 '89
　Judging Jim Wright. G. Borger. il por *U.S. News & World Report* 106:18-19 Ap 17 '89
　The last stand of Speaker Jim Wright. G. Borger. il por *U.S. News & World Report* 106:27-8 Ap 24 '89
　The least and the dullest. J. Klein. il por *New York* 22:16+ Mr 27 '89
　Lessons in quitting. T. Eastland. por *Newsweek* 113:8 Je 12 '89
　Letter from Washington. Cato. *National Review* 41:11 Mr 10 '89

WRIGHT, JIM, 1922——about——*cont.*

Letter from Washington. E. Drew. *The New Yorker* 65:97-102 Je 12 '89

Letter from Washington. E. Drew. *The New Yorker* 65:99-104+ My 1 '89

Looking for an exit. T. Morganthau. il por *Newsweek* 113:18-20 Je 5 '89

Mr. Wright's wrongs. W. McGurn. *National Review* 41:16 My 19 '89

One of the boys. M. B. Carlson. *The New Republic* 200:11-13 Je 5 '89

The painful political trial of Speaker Wright. G. Borger. il *U.S. News & World Report* 106:31 My 1 '89

Partisanship fuels 'ethics' investigation. J. M. Wall. *The Christian Century* 106:579-80 Je 7-14 '89

The pious posturing over Speaker Wright. W. Greider. il *Rolling Stone* p37-8 Je 15 '89

Profiles in courage. L. Martz. il por *Newsweek* 113:14-16 F 13 '89

The protégé and the victim. E. Clift. il pors *Newsweek* 113:38 My 15 '89

Quis custodiet? R. C. Kirkwood and T. P. Jeffrey. il *National Review* 41:35-6 Ap 21 '89

Ready for Wright: a GOP grudge match. E. Salholz. il por *Newsweek* 113:28 Mr 20 '89

The real sleaze. *The Nation* 248:615-16 My 8 '89

Reeling. *National Review* 41:11 Je 16 '89

Shredding the Democrats' agenda. D. Harbrecht and R. Fly. il por *Business Week* p26 My 1 '89

The skeletons in Jim Wright's closet keep rattling Congress. D. Harbrecht. por *Business Week* p39 Ap 24 '89

Speaker Jim Wright's old pal George Mallick is rarin' for a fight with Congress. M. Green. il pors *People Weekly* 31:101-2 My 15 '89

The Speaker should step down. H. Sidey. il *Time* 133:18 Ap 24 '89

A Washington morality tale. il por *U.S. News & World Report* 106:22 My 22 '89

What the Wright hand's doing. il *National Review* 41:9-10 My 19 '89

Wright, Coelho and the S&L fiasco. M. Barone. il pors *U.S. News & World Report* 106:21-2 Je 12 '89

Wright fights back. M. B. Carlson. il por *Time* 133:16-17 Ap 24 '89

Wright should quit. W. F. Buckley. *National Review* 41:54 Je 16 '89

The Wright stuff. F. Barnes. *The New Republic* 200:13-16 My 15 '89

Wright turn. *The Nation* 248:255-6 F 27 '89

Wright was not wronged [excerpt from report issued by House Ethics Committee] *Harper's* 279:18+ Ag '89

Wright, writer. H. Hertzberg. *The New Republic* 200:4+ My 15 '89

Wright's aide: too little, too late. E. Clift. il pors *Newsweek* 112:41 My 22 '89

Wright's real wrongs. D. Seligman. il *Fortune* 119:167 My 22 '89

Anecdotes, facetiae, satire, etc.

How one family handles its finances. J. Queenan. *Forbes* 143:42-3 Je 12 '89

Uncivil liberties. C. Trillin. il *The Nation* 248:762 Je 5 '89

WRIGHT, JOHN H.

When we pray. il *Commonweal* 116:75-7 F 10 '89

WRIGHT, JONATHAN

Stresemann and Weimar. bibl il pors *History Today* 39:35-41 O '89

WRIGHT, LAWRENCE

Past tense. il *Vogue* 179:88+ Ja '89

Peace (I). il *Rolling Stone* p143-6+ Jl 13-27 '89

Peace (II). il *Rolling Stone* p54-5+ S 7 '89

Peace (III). il *Rolling Stone* p152-3+ N 16 '89

WRIGHT, NANCI

about

House-maintenance service cleans up by never saying no. L. Arden. il pors *Home Office Computing* 7:44-5 My '89

WRIGHT, PETER B.

The Wright stuff. See issues of Motor Boating & Sailing beginning October 1987

WRIGHT, RICHARD, 1908-1960

about

The mysterious death of Richard Wright [excerpt] M. Walker. il pors *Ebony* 44:116+ F '89

WRIGHT, ROBERT CHARLES

about

On a roll with the man from GE [cover story] D. Machan. il por *Forbes* 143:124-7 Ap 17 '89

WRIGHT, ROSALIND

Kids who kill. il *Good Housekeeping* 209:54+ Ag '89

The Thanksgiving they'll never forget. il *Good Housekeeping* 209:32+ N '89

WRIGHT, STEVEN

about

TV comic Steven Wright sets off, worriedly, on a steep ascent. K. McMurran. il pors *People Weekly* 31:106-9 Mr 13 '89

WRIGHT, SUSAN

The buildup that was. bibl f il *The Bulletin of the Atomic Scientists* 45:52-6 Ja/F '89

WRIGHT, TENNANT C.

Vagaries of religious experience in Nicaragua [cover story] il *America* 161:158-61 S 23 '89

WRIGHT, THOMAS J.

about

No holds barred [film] Reviews

People Weekly il 31:13+ Je 19 '89. R. Novak

Sports Illustrated il 70:91 Je 19 '89. F. Lidz

WRIGHT, WILBUR, 1867-1912

about

Eyewitness report from the right seat of the Wright Flyer. G. Dickin. il *Flying* 116:82-6 O '89

WRIGHT BROTHERS

See also

Wright, Wilbur, 1867-1912

WRIGHT-WAY CLEANING SERVICE, INC.

House-maintenance service cleans up by never saying no. L. Arden. il pors *Home Office Computing* 7:44-5 My '89

WRIGHTON, MARK S., 1949-

about

Meet MIT's Mr. Biochips. R. Duffy. il por *Business Week* Special Issue:80 Je 16 '89

WRIGLEY (WM.) JR. CO. See Wm. Wrigley Jr. Co.

WRIGLEY FIELD (CHICAGO, ILL.)

When's the last time this guy saw a game? [Chicago's R. Buhrke shags home run balls outside Wrigley Field] G. Castle. il *Sport (New York, N.Y.)* 80:105 F '89

The Wrigley myth is blowin' in the wind [facts say it is a pitchers' ballpark] G. Castle. *Sport (New York, N.Y.)* 80:17 Mr '89

WRINKLES See Skin

WRIST

Wounds and injuries

Dual demons [use of painkillers to treat pain from fracture] B. D. Colen. il *Health (New York, N.Y.)* 21:34-5 Jl '89

Wristy business [tennis player S. Foltz overcomes serious wrist injury] J. E. Loehr. il pors *World Tennis* 37:24-5 N '89

WRISTON, WALTER B.

Technology and direct marketing [address, June 8, 1989] *Vital Speeches of the Day* 55:678-80 S 1 '89

about

Irresistible international revolution. M. Magnet. por *Fortune* 120:66-7 Jl 3 '89

WRISTWATCHES See Watches

WRITE ONCE OPTICAL MEMORIES

See also

Digital paper

Digital Equipment introduces improved data storage system [RV64 jukebox] *Aviation Week & Space Technology* 130:61 Mr 13 '89

The optical option [WORM and erasable optical drives] S. Apiki and H. Eglowstein. il *Byte* 14:160-4+ O '89

Permanent storage of optical disks finds new uses in aerospace, defense. il *Aviation Week & Space Technology* 130:51+ Jl 10 '89

Two digital pies in the sky. D. Ranada. il *High Fidelity (New York, N.Y.)* 39:17 Je '89

WRITENOW (WORD PROCESSOR PROGRAM) See Word processors and processing—Programming

WRITERS See Authors

WRITERS' BLOCK See Authors—Psychology

WRITERS' CONFERENCES See Authors' conferences

WRITERS HOUSE (FIRM)

A portrait of Writers House. G. Feldman. il por *Publishers Weekly* 236:21-3 D 1 '89

WRITING

See also

Calligraphy

WRITING (AUTHORSHIP) See Authorship; Creative writing; Journalism

WRITING (COMPOSITION) See English language—Composition

WRITING PAPER See Stationery

WRKS (NEW YORK, N.Y.: RADIO STATION) See Radio stations

WROBLESKI, ANN B.

Certification for narcotics source and transit countries [statements, March 9 and 15, 1989] *Department of State Bulletin* 89:68-72 My '89

Global narcotics cooperation and presidential certification [statement, April 5, 1989] *Department of State Bulletin* 89:49-59 O '89

WRONGFUL DEATH

What a life is worth when one is lost [monetary awards] *U.S. News & World Report* 106:14+ F 27 '89

WROUGHTON, DAVID

about

Squalor in the "City of God". P. Yancey. il *Christianity Today* 33:12-13 F 17 '89

WTVG (TOLEDO, OHIO: TELEVISION STATION) See Television stations

WU, HUEY-NAN, AND LAI, MICHAEL M. C.

Reversible cleavage and ligation of hepatitis delta virus RNA. bibl f il *Science* 243:652-4 F 3 '89

WU, LI-HSIA
about
In the age of aquariums, Wu Li-Hsia finds acupuncture is not a tankless job. il por *People Weekly* 31:268 Mr 6 '89

WU, LI-PEI
about
Mr. Wu knows his customer. G. Morgenson. il por *Forbes* 143:49+ Ja 23 '89

WU, MAY
Ballantine's new translations of Chinese classics. *Publishers Weekly* 236:58-9 O 6 '89

WU, NORBERT
Fish faces in the kelp forest [photographs] il *Sea Frontiers* 35:366-9 N/D '89
The paper nautilus. bibl il *Sea Frontiers* 35:94-6 Mr/Ap '89

WU, SAMUEL M.
(jt. auth) See Yang, Xiong-Li, and Wu, Samuel M.

WU, XIAN LIANG, AND LIEBER, CHARLES M.
Hexagonal domain-like charge density wave phase of TaS$_2$ determined by scanning tunneling microscopy. bibl f il *Science* 243:1703-5 Mr 31 '89

WUER KAIXI
about
A call to arms. por *Time* 134:32 Jl 10 '89
Children of Tiananmen. O. Schell. il pors *Rolling Stone* p185-8+ D 14-28 '89
Portrait of a "hooligan". T. Gup. il por *Time* 133:35 Je 26 '89
'We have enthusiasm and daring'. D. Elliott. il por *Newsweek* 113:32 My 8 '89

WUERKAIXI *See* Wuer Kaixi

WUERTHNER, GEORGE
The flames of '88. il *Wilderness* 52:40-54 Summ '89

WUHL, ROBERT
about
Hitching a ride on Batman's box office wings, comic Robert Wuhl soars beyond the stand-up scene. D. Hutchings. il pors *People Weekly* 32:94-5 Jl 24 '89

WUJEC, HENRYK
about
Mr. Wujec goes to Warsaw [interview]; tr. by David Ost. J. Jastrzebowski. *Harper's* 279:13-15 D '89

WULF, STEVE
All my Padres. il *Sports Illustrated* 70 Special Issue:42-6+ Ap '89
Back in the saddle. il *Sports Illustrated* 70 Special Issue:52-5 Ap '89
The boys of winter. il *Sports Illustrated* 71:28-33 N 20 '89
Is there an echo in here? il por *Sports Illustrated* 71:84 Jl 10 '89
Let those people go. il por *Sports Illustrated* 71:162 S 11 '89
A man in command. il pors *Sports Illustrated* 71:30-2+ O 30 '89
Miraculous conversion. il *Sports Illustrated* 70:86 Mr 6 '89
O you beautiful Birds. il *Sports Illustrated* 70:26-8+ Je 19 '89
On a roll. il *Sports Illustrated* 71:34-9 O 23 '89
Puppies, poison ivy and a Dashing Duke. il *Sports Illustrated* 71 Special Issue:8-10+ N 15 '89
Raising the roof. il *Sports Illustrated* 70:48-50+ Je 12 '89
Rotisserie revisited. por *Sports Illustrated* 71:78 Ag 7 '89
Season in the shadows. por *Sports Illustrated* 71:96 N 13 '89
Stretch. il pors *Sports Illustrated* 70:68-74+ Mr 6 '89
The stuff of legend. il *Sports Illustrated* 70:100-2+ Je 12 '89
Swept away. il *Sports Illustrated* 71:24-7 N 6 '89
This one's still up in the air. il *Sports Illustrated* 71:26-30+ Ag 14 '89
Who's the enemy? il *Sports Illustrated* 70 Special Issue:68-70+ Ap '89
The year of the blue snow. il *Sports Illustrated* 71:76-86 S 25 '89

WULF, STEVE, AND DEMAK, RICHARD
Where have all the players gone? il *Sports Illustrated* 71:22-5+ Ag 28 '89

WULFHORST, ELLEN, AND GOLDBERG, BARBARA
The Steinberg file: what the jury didn't hear. il pors *New York* 22:42-6 Ap 17 '89

WUNDERMAN, SEVERIN
about
Severin Wunderman's Jean Cocteau obsession is so strong he sometimes feels he's possessed by the artist's spirit. R. Urquhart. il por *Vogue* 179:182-4 Je '89

WURMAN, RICHARD SAUL, 1935-
Overcome "information anxiety" [condensed from Information anxiety] il *Reader's Digest* 134:127-30 My '89

WÜRSIG, BERND
Cetaceans. bibl f il *Science* 244:1550-7 Je 30 '89

WURTMAN, JUDITH J.
(jt. auth) See Wurtman, Richard J., and Wurtman, Judith J.

WURTMAN, RICHARD J., AND WURTMAN, JUDITH J.
Carbohydrates and depression. il map *Scientific American* 260:68-75 Ja '89

WURTS, JOHN S.
about
Where Lisp slipped. J. Pitta. il por *Forbes* 144:262-3 O 16 '89

WUSA (WASHINGTON, D.C.: TELEVISION STATION)
See Television stations

WUTHERING HEIGHTS [film] See Motion picture reviews—Single works

WÜTHRICH, KURT
Protein structure determination in solution by nuclear magnetic resonance spectroscopy. bibl f il *Science* 243:45-50 Ja 6 '89

WVEC (NORFOLK, VA.: TELEVISION STATION) *See* Television stations

WWF *See* World Wrestling Federation

WYANDOTTE (MICH.)
Crime
A father lifts his "burdens" [L. DeLisle murders his children by driving into the Detroit River] E. Magnuson. il *Time* 134:13 Ag 28 '89

WYATT, GREG
about
Big guns in the Big Sky. D. S. Looney. il pors *Sports Illustrated* 71:83-4 O 16 '89

WYATT, JOE B.
American education is stagnant [address, May 16, 1989] *Vital Speeches of the Day* 56:12-14 O 15 '89
Is professional life just a game? [address, May 12, 1989] *Vital Speeches of the Day* 55:702-4 S 1 '89

WYATT, OSCAR SHERMAN, JR.
about
The lasso is tightening around Texas Eastern. M. Ivey. il por *Business Week* p30-1 Ja 30 '89
The man who strikes fear in the heart of the oil patch. M. Ivey. il por *Business Week* p120-1+ N 6 '89
Oscar Wyatt. M. Ivey. il por *Business Week* Special Issue:120 Ap 14 '89

WYATT-BROWN, BERTRAM
Forgotten founder. il *USA Today (Periodical)* 118:90-2 Jl '89

WYCHE, SAM
about
Good neighbor Sam. K. Moore. il pors *Sports Illustrated* 71:92-6+ S 11 '89

WYCKOFF, ANDREW
(jt. auth) See Kelly, Henry, and Wyckoff, Andrew

WYDROW, KEN
about
Show stopper. J. Torrence-Thompson. il por *Black Enterprise* 20:66-8+ Ag '89

WYER, JOHN
about
Obituary
Road & Track il por 40:60-1 Ag '89. P. Frère

WYETH, ANDREW, 1917-
about
Sex and politics. K. Larson. il *New York* 22:51-2 Jl 17 '89

WYETH, JAMIE, 1946-
about
At an opening . . . M. S. Doherty. *American Artist* 53:8 F '89

WYLER, SUSAN
Dressing up for the holidays. il *New Choices for the Best Years* 29:72-5 N '89
How to host the perfect poker party. il *New Choices for the Best Years* 29:70-5 Ap '89

WYLER, WILLIAM, 1902-1981
about
Wuthering Heights [film] Reviews
American Film il 14:77 Ap '89. J. E. Fitch
The New York Times Magazine il por p46-8+ F 19 '89. A. S. Berg

WYLIE, ANDREW
about
The naughty schoolboy. P. Painton. il por *Time* 133:46 Je 12 '89

WYLIE, FRANK W.
Crisis time for the non-profits [address, September 10, 1988] *Vital Speeches of the Day* 55:170-2 Ja 1 '89

WYLOGE, NORMAN
If the company is the problem, can it provide the cure? *Working Woman* 14:131+ S '89

WYMAN, BILL
about
A May-December wedding finally puts a brake on the oldest Rolling Stone. P. Freeman. il pors *People Weekly* 31:54-6 Je 19 '89

WYMAN, HASTINGS
Slim GOP pickin's in Dixie. il *The American Spectator* 22:30-1 Ag '89

WYMAN-GORDON CO.
Winning back the customers. il *Forbes* 143:82 Ja 9 '89

WYNGAARDEN, JAMES B.
about
Wyngaarden to leave NIH. B. J. Culliton. por *Science* 244:414 Ap 28 '89
WYNIA, GARY W., 1942-
Campaigning for president in Argentina. bibl f *Current History* 88:133-6+ Mr '89
WYNN, JACK
Quick checks. il *Nation's Business* 77:45-6 D '89
WYNN, STEPHEN A.
about
Tigers, a volcano, dolphins, and Steve Wynn. R. Grover. il por *Business Week* p70-1 N 20 '89
WYNNE, BRIAN, 1947-
Sheepfarming after Chernobyl. bibl f il maps *Environment* 31:10-15+ Mr '89
(jt. auth) See Laurence, Duncan, and Wynne, Brian, 1947-
WYNNE, SUSAN, AND DRUAR, JOSEPH
Synchronicity. il pors *American Health* 8:70-1 Ap '89
WYNORSKI, JIM
about
Not of this earth [film] Reviews
Video il 12:85-6 Ja '89. R. Swan
WYOMING
See also
Bighorn River (Wyo. and Mont.)
Black Hills (S.D. and Wyo.)
Forests and forestry—Wyoming
Gallatin National Forest (Mont. and Wyo.)
Grand Teton National Park (Wyo.)
Hunting—Wyoming
Powder River Valley (Wyo. and Mont.)
Ranches—Wyoming
Snowmobiles and snowmobiling—Wyoming
Wildlife—Wyoming
Climate
A season of portents: the long summer of '88: a Wyoming diary. G. Ehrlich. il *Harper's* 279:50-7 Ag '89
Description and travel
See also
Automobile touring—Wyoming
Cycling—Wyoming
Politics and government
The dawn of karate-chop Republican politics [congressional race] S. V. Roberts. il *U.S. News & World Report* 106:28 My 1 '89
WYSE, LOIS
The way we are. See issues of Good Housekeeping
about
Beyond macho: the power of womanly management [excerpt from Tender power] S. S. Cohen. il pors *Working Woman* 14:77-83 F '89
WYSE TECHNOLOGY
A Silicon Valley plum may drop into Taiwan's lap. D. J. Yang and M. Shao. il *Business Week* p38 D 4 '89

X

X-29 AIRPLANES *See* Airplanes, Military
X-30 AIRPLANES *See* Spaceplane
X-31A AIRPLANES *See* Airplanes, Military
X RAY ASTRONOMY
Black hole in the making? [V404 Cygni] il *Sky and Telescope* 78:460-1 N '89
High-energy summer for astrophysics [V404 Cygni] M. M. Waldrop. *Science* 245:129 Jl 14 '89
Snapping the sun's sharpest X-ray image [use of Normal Incidence X-ray Telescope] il *Science News* 136:223 S 30 '89
Taking X-rays of the sun. il *USA Today (Periodical)* 117:13-14 Je '89
X-ray fireworks put on a stellar show [V404 Cygni; research by Sumner G. Starrfield] I. Peterson. *Science News* 136:4 Jl 1 '89
X RAY CRYSTALLOGRAPHY
Conserved folding in retroviral proteases: crystal structure of a synthetic HIV-1 protease. A. Wlodawer and others. bibl f il *Science* 245:616-21 Ag 11 '89
Disorder-to-order transition in settling suspensions of colloidal silica: X-ray measurements. K. E. Davis and others. bibl f il *Science* 245:507-10 Ag 4 '89
First 3-D image of AIDS virus protein [work of Manuel A. Navia] R. Weiss. *Science News* 135:100 F 18 '89
GaAs clusters in the quantum size regime: growth on high surface area silica by molecular beam epitaxy. C. J. Sandroff and others. bibl f il *Science* 245:391-3 Jl 28 '89
Macromolecular crystals. A. McPherson. bibl il *Scientific American* 260:62-9 Mr '89
Macromolecular structure from anomalous dispersion [cover story] J. Karle. bibl f il *Physics Today* 42:22-9 Je '89
The missing crystallography data [study by Richard E. Dickerson] M. Barinaga. il *Science* 245:1179-81 S 15 '89
NCI team remodels key AIDS virus enzyme. J. L. Marx. il *Science* 245:598 Ag 11 '89

The phase problem of X-ray crystallography. H. A. Hauptman. bibl f il *Physics Today* 42:24-9 N '89
Portrait of a virus [foot-and-mouth disease; research by David Stuart and others] il *Discover* 10:10 Je '89
Protein-RNA interactions in an icosahedral virus at 3.0 Å resolution [bean-pod mattle virus] Z. Chen and others. bibl f il *Science* 245:154-9 Jl 14 '89
Structure of a three-dimensional, microporous molybdenum phosphate with large cavities. R. C. Haushalter and others. bibl f il *Science* 246:1289-91 D 8 '89
Structure of complex of synthetic HIV-1 protease with a substrate-based inhibitor at 2.3 Å resolution. M. Miller and others. bibl f il *Science* 246:1149-52 D 1 '89
Structure of recombinant human renin, a target for cardiovascular-active drugs, at 2.5 Å resolution. A. R. Sielecki and others. bibl f il *Science* 243:1346-51 Mr 10 '89
Taming the wily rhinovirus [work of Michael Rossmann and Richard Colonno] P. Radetsky. il *Discover* 10:38-43 Ap '89
X RAY DIFFRACTION
Taking the fuzziness out of quasicrystals. I. Peterson. *Science News* 135:149 Mr 11 '89
X-ray diffraction to 302 gigapascals: high-pressure crystal structure of cesium iodide. H. K. Mao and others. bibl f il *Science* 246:649-51 N 3 '89
X RAY EQUIPMENT
High-speed X-ray CT scanner could meet FAA's explosive detection requirements. B. W. Henderson. il *Aviation Week & Space Technology* 131:78-9 N 13 '89
X-ray backscatter equipment provides automatic screening for explosives. D. Hughes. il *Aviation Week & Space Technology* 130:65+ Ap 17 '89
X-rays speed softly, carry a big blast [Saturn device] F. Flam. il *Science News* 135:279 My 6 '89
X RAY LASERS *See* Lasers
X RAY LITHOGRAPHY
The silicon chip race advances into X-rays. M. Crawford. il *Science* 246:1382-3 D 15 '89
X RAY MICROSCOPES
Energy-dispersive X-ray microanalysis [cover story] J. H. Whallon and others. bibl f il *BioScience* 39:256-9 Ap '89
X-ray microanalysis of leaf-litter decomposition in lakes [scanning microscope] J. A. Perry and others. bibl f il *BioScience* 39:260-3 Ap '89
X RAY PHOTOGRAPHY *See* Radiography
X RAY TELESCOPES, ORBITING *See* Artificial satellites—Astronomical use
X RAYS
See also
Radiography
Making plastics visible to X-rays [use of additive triphenyl bismuth] I. Amato and J. Raloff. *Science News* 135:252 Ap 22 '89
Medical use
See Radiography, Medical
Physiological effects
Are you safe from X-rays? [views of B. Wally Ahluwalia] il *USA Today (Periodical)* 117:11 Ap '89
XABRE SA
Mexican contrarian. R. King. il por *Forbes* 144:88+ S 4 '89
XENOGRAFTS
DNA topoisomerase I-targeted chemotherapy of human colon cancer in xenografts. B. C. Giovanella and others. bibl f il *Science* 246:1046-8 N 24 '89
Spare parts for humans: science steps up the search. M. Bluestone. il *Business Week* p65+ F 27 '89
XENOPUS EMBRYOS *See* Embryology—Amphibia
XENOPUS OVA *See* Ova
XERISCAPING
Color in a dry year. il *Sunset (Central West edition)* 182:234-5 My '89
Ending the tyranny of our thirsty front lawn [relandscaping Sunset headquarters] il *Sunset (Central West edition)* 183:66-9 S '89
Flowers through thick and thin. S. Bender. il *Southern Living* 24:106-8 My '89
Learning to be waterwise. il *Sunset (Central West edition)* 183:206+ N '89
Water-saving ideas in Fort Collins [demonstration garden] il *Sunset (Central West edition)* 182:242 My '89
XEROX CORP.
A battle over a user-friendly computer [Xerox sues Apple over software copyright] il *Newsweek* 114:59 D 25 '89
Xerox rethinks itself—and this could be the last time. J. R. Norman. il *Business Week* p90-3 F 13 '89
XEROX CORP. PALO ALTO RESEARCH CENTER
The Alto: today's technology yesterday. P. Saffo. il *Personal Computing* 13:207-9 Je '89
Bean counters invade ivory tower. J. Pitta. il *Forbes* 144:198-9 S 18 '89
XI'AN FILM STUDIO
A tale by two cultures [making of The first emperor of China] T. R. Miller. il *Natural History* p66-9 Jl '89

XIE YIXIAN
Tuning up Chinese foreign policy. *World Press Review* 36:14 My '89
XIN KU
about
The road to revolt in China. M. Morrison. il *The American Spectator* 22:14-16 N '89
XIN'AN (CHINA) *See* Huizhou (China)
XIONG, CHENG, AND OTHERS
Sindbis virus: an efficient, broad host range vector for gene expression in animal cells. bibl f il *Science* 243:1188-91 Mr 3 '89
XTC (MUSICAL GROUP)
Britain's XTC count their 1989 U.S. tour a blooming success—and they didn't sell a single ticket. M. Small. il *People Weekly* 31:103-4 Je 19 '89
XTC: ninjas of the mundane. S. Pond. il *Rolling Stone* p81-2+ Ap 20 '89
XTC's paternal power pop. M. Azerrad. il *Rolling Stone* p167-8 Mr 23 '89
XTC's time warp. S. Simels. il *Stereo Review* 54:108 Je '89
XTRA CORP.
The big money is giving Xtra that extra boost. G. G. Marcial. il *Business Week* p76 Ja 30 '89
XUAN TONG *See* Pu Yi, 1906-1967
XUE, XIANYU, AND OTHERS
Silicon coordination and speciation changes in a silicate liquid at high pressures. bibl f il *Science* 245:962-4 S 1 '89
XYLITOL
Chewing pays off [plaque and cavities reduced with use of gum; research by Kauko Makinen] il *Prevention (Emmaus, Pa.)* 41:22 Mr '89
XYWRITE (WORD PROCESSOR PROGRAM) *See* Word processors and processing—Programming

Y

Y CHAMBER SYMPHONY
See also
New York Chamber Symphony
YA'ARI, EHUD
Israel's prison academies; tr. by Ina Friedman. il *The Atlantic* 264:22+ O '89
YABLONOVITCH, E.
The chemistry of solid-state electronics. bibl f il *Science* 246:347-51 O 20 '89
YACHT CLUBS
Bahamas
Debut in paradise [maiden voyage of Donzi Z-65] J. Clemans. il *Motor Boating & Sailing* 164:36-41+ S '89
Virgin Gorda (British Virgin Islands)
The sweet life at the Bitter End. P. A. Janssen. il *Motor Boating & Sailing* 164:11 Ag '89
YACHT DECORATION *See* Boat decoration
YACHT DELIVERIES *See* Boats and boating—Transportation
YACHT RACING
See also
America's Cup races
Alone against the sea, American sailor Mike Plant braces for a dangerous race around the world [Globe Challenge] H. Shapiro. il pors *People Weekly* 32:54-6 N 27 '89
A class act [J boats Endeavour and Shamrock V] R. Bragonier. il *Motor Boating & Sailing* 164:42-7+ N '89
Getting your feet wet in sailboat racing. L. Zinn. il *Business Week* p84-5 Jl 24 '89
The lady is a champ [A. G. Nelson] N. Rabinowitz. il pors *Motor Boating & Sailing* 163:62-5+ F '89
Whitbread warriors. L. Rudeen. il map *Motor Boating & Sailing* 164:48-51+ S '89
Woman to watch: sailor Tracy Edwards [skipper of all-women entry in the Whitbread Round-the-World Race] C. Flanagan. il *Women's Sports & Fitness* 11:76 Ap '89
Accidents and injuries
Attack from the ocean deep [D. Sellings survives attack by whales during the Carlsberg Single-handed Transatlantic Race] S. Kelly. il *Reader's Digest* 134:67-72 F '89
YACHTS, HISTORIC
A class act [J boats Endeavour and Shamrock V] R. Bragonier. il *Motor Boating & Sailing* 164:42-7+ N '89
YACHTS AND YACHTING
See also
Cruisers (Pleasure boats)
Marinas
Seamanship
Yacht racing
1989 new boat directory. J. Wooldridge. il *Motor Boating & Sailing* 163:99-138 Ja '89
Sexy expatriates [American-made yachts in St. Tropez] J. Clemans. il *Motor Boating & Sailing* 163:62-5+ Ja '89
Trends '90 [special section] il *Motor Boating & Sailing* 164:54-65 S '89

Chartering
See Yachts and yachting—Leasing and renting
Deliveries
See Boats and boating—Transportation
Design
Breakthrough at Broward [high-speed megayachts] S. Stapleton. il *Motor Boating & Sailing* 163:84-7+ F '89
Design board. See issues of Motor Boating & Sailing
Even the model costs $50,000 [J. Bannenberg's designs] G. Burks. il por *Forbes* 144 Special Issue:372 O 23 '89
Leasing and renting
See also
Bayside Boat & Breakfast (Firm)
Riding the wind [British Virgin Isles] S. Moore. il *Black Enterprise* 19:119 My '89
Directories
Motor boating & sailing worldwide charter directory [special section] il *Motor Boating & Sailing* 164:59-66+ Ag '89
Testing
Californian . . . here I come [three-day delivery of a Carver 48 from Sarasota to Miami] D. Fales. il *Motor Boating & Sailing* 163:58-61+ Ap '89
Chris-Craft 50 [motor yacht] M. Benson. il *Motor Boating & Sailing* 164:33 O '89
Cross-country cruise [Miami to Los Angeles in Tempest motor yachts] J. Catlett. il map *Motor Boating & Sailing* 163:72-5+ F '89
Dream from Down Under [Bahamas cruise in the Southern Cross 53 motor yacht] J. Clemans. il *Motor Boating & Sailing* 163:76-7+ F '89
Golden Star 48. D. Fales. il *Motor Boating & Sailing* 164:30 N '89
Hatteras 92 [motor yacht] P. A. Janssen. il *Motor Boating & Sailing* 164:24 D '89
J/44. R. Marshall. il *Motor Boating & Sailing* 164:28 Ag '89
Megayacht [Octopussy] J. Skorupa. il *Popular Mechanics* 166:132-4 My '89
New U.S. thoroughbred [Trident 105 jetboat Lady Frances] P. Whittell. il *Motor Boating & Sailing* 164:60-3+ N '89
Northwest passage [cruising from the Columbia River bar to the San Juan Islands in a Tollycraft 53] D. Fales. il *Motor Boating & Sailing* 164:44-7+ Ag '89
State-of-the-art Oceanfast [jet-powered Mercedes 100-foot yacht] P. Whittell. il *Motor Boating & Sailing* 164:50-3+ Ag '89
Swift and sumptuous [Ocean 48 Motor Yacht] J. Clemans. il *Motor Boating & Sailing* 163:72-3+ Ap '89
Take her anywhere [Florida Bay Coaster 65] P. A. Janssen. il *Motor Boating & Sailing* 163:48-51+ Je '89
Tango 60. D. Fales. il *Motor Boating & Sailing* 163:34 Je '89
Tartan 412 [sailing yacht] R. Marshall. il *Motor Boating & Sailing* 164:26 D '89
Thoroughly modern Hatteras [54] L. Rudeen. il *Motor Boating & Sailing* 163:72-5+ Ja '89
Viking's tour de force [72-foot flagship] S. Stapleton. il *Motor Boating & Sailing* 163:62-7+ Mr '89
YACKTMAN, DONALD ARTHUR, 1941-
about
There's cash flow, and there's cash flow. J. Clements. il por *Forbes* 144:138+ S 18 '89
YACOUB, CHARLES
about
Capital standoff. P. Kopvillem. il *Maclean's* 102:10-11 Ap 17 '89
YAFFE, MICHAEL
What every arts administrator should know about arts education. *Design for Arts in Education* 90:29-31 Mr/Ap '89
YAGER, JAN, 1948-
The last 3 months of pregnancy/the first 3 months of parenting. bibl *McCall's* 116:49-50+ Ja '89
YAGODA, BEN
Not afraid of the dark [cover story] il pors *American Film* 15:30-7 N '89
When Leibner calls, the networks listen. il pors *The New York Times Magazine* p36-8+ Je 18 '89
YAKIMA (WASH.)
Architecture
Guess where this house is located. il *Sunset (Central West edition)* 183:94-5 Jl '89
YAKOVLEV, ALEKSANDER
about
Moscow's other mastermind [cover story] B. Keller. il pors *The New York Times Magazine* p30-3+ F 19 '89
YALE, ANDY
Down here on the edge of things. il *The Nation* 249:591-2 N 20 '89
YALE UNIVERSITY
Yale strikes gold [new dean D. Kagan] J. P. Hart. *National Review* 41:24 Je 2 '89
Yale's most famous graduate [interview with G. Bush] il por *U.S. News & World Report* 107:68 O 16 '89
YALE UNIVERSITY. ART GALLERY
"Stacks" of complaints [controversy surrounding display of R. Serra sculpture] D. Waterman. *Art News* 88:53+ O '89

YALE UNIVERSITY. DEPT. OF ART HISTORY
"Stacks" of complaints [controversy surrounding display of R. Serra sculpture] D. Waterman. *Art News* 88:53+ O '89
YALE UNIVERSITY. SKULL AND BONES SOCIETY *See* Skull and Bones Society
YALOM, IRVIN D., 1931-
about
Exploring psychic interiors. E. E. Goode. por *U.S. News & World Report* 107:67 O 30 '89
YALTA CONFERENCE (1945)
It rhymes with Malta. il *Time* 134:35 N 13 '89
The United States and Russia in World War II [reprint from November and December 1950 issues] R. W. Van Alstyne. *Current History* 88:26-9+ Ja '89
YAMAGUCHI, KATSUHIRO
about
Katsuhiro Yamaguchi at Satani. J. Koplos. il *Art in America* 77:271+ Ap '89
YAMAGUCHI, KRISTI
about
New girl in town. E. M. Swift. il por *Sports Illustrated* 70:22-3 F 20 '89
A skating sprite with a towering talent, Kristi Yamaguchi wants to ice the world title. il por *People Weekly* 31:71 Mr 20 '89
YAMAHA INTERNATIONAL CORP.
Made in Japan [RX-530 receiver] B. Harrell. il *Stereo Review* 54:49-55 Jl '89
YAMAHA MOTOR CO. LTD.
1990 preview: Yamaha [motorcycles; cover story] il *Cycle* 40:31-2 N '89
Yamaha's Daytona battle plan [FZR600s modified by R. Muzzy] C. Everitt. il por *Cycle* 40:75-7 My '89
YAMAMORI, TETSUO, AND OTHERS
The cholinergic neuronal differentiation factor from heart cells is identical to leukemia inhibitory factor. bibl f il *Science* 246:1412-16 D 15 '89; Correction. 247:271 Ja 19 '90
YAMAMOTO, KEITH R.
Retargeting research on biological weapons. il *Technology Review* 92:23-4 Ag/S '89
YAMAMOTO, NOBUHIKO, AND OTHERS
Neural connections between the lateral geniculate nucleus and visual cortex in vitro. bibl f il *Science* 245:192-4 Jl 14 '89
YAMAMOTO, TADATOYO
about
In good faith. B. Greene. il pors *Esquire* 111:67-8 Mr '89
The stolen briefcase. B. Greene. il *Reader's Digest* 134:23-4+ Je '89
YANAI, HIROSHI
about
Ticket master. H. Katayama. il por *Forbes* 144:350+ N 13 '89
YANCEY, PHILIP
(ed) *See* Wigand, Pattie. Monday morning miracle
YANCEY, WANDA
In Savannah, First African Baptist Church means first. il *American Visions* 4:42-3 Ag '89
YANG, CHIHUNG, 1948-
about
Chihung Yang at Michael Walls. G. Henry. il *Art in America* 77:171-2 D '89
YANG, QING, AND OTHERS
Unusual pattern of accumulation of mRNA encoding EGF-related protein in sea urchin embryos. bibl f il *Science* 246:806-8 N 10 '89
YANG, XIAN-CHENG, AND SACHS, FREDERICK
Block of stretch-activated ion channels in Xenopus oocytes by gadolinium and calcium ions. bibl f il *Science* 243:1068-71 F 24 '89
YANG, XIONG-LI, AND WU, SAMUEL M.
Modulation of rod-cone coupling by light. bibl f il *Science* 244:352-4 Ap 21 '89
YANIV, AVNER
Israel comes of age. bibl f *Current History* 88:69-72+ F '89
YANKEE COMPANIES INC.
Has this outfit found 'a miracle for oil spills'? [views of J. Siebert] G. G. Marcial. il por *Business Week* p150 My 22 '89
YANKEE DAWG YOU DIE [drama] *See* Gotanda, Philip Kan
YANKELOVICH, DANIEL
(jt. auth) *See* Harris, T George, and Yankelovich, Daniel
YANKELOVICH, DANIEL, AND GURIN, JOEL, 1953-
The new American dream [cover story] il *American Health* 8:63-7 Mr '89
YANKELOVICH, DANIEL, AND SMOKE, RICHARD
Changing cold war attitudes: America's "new thinking". il *Current (Washington, D.C.)* 309:32-40 Ja '89
YANKER, GARY, AND BURTON, KATHY
A moving approach to arthritis pain. il *New Choices for the Best Years* 29:62-3+ S '89
A walk in the country. il map *Travel Holiday* 171:22-3 Je '89

YANKICH ISLAND (SOVIET UNION)
See also
Kraternaya Bay (Soviet Union)
YANKNER, BRUCE A., AND OTHERS
Neurotoxicity of a fragment of the amyloid precursor associated with Alzheimer's disease. bibl f il *Science* 245:417-20 Jl 28 '89
YANKS (LOS ANGELES, CALIF.: RESTAURANT) *See* Los Angeles (Calif.)—Restaurants, nightclubs, bars, etc.
YANNUZZI, ELAINE
about
A magnet for gourmets. V. Bohigian. il por *Nation's Business* 77:66 Ja '89
YANOAMA INDIANS
Warfare over Yanomamö Indians [theories of N. A. Chagnon and effects of gold mining] W. Booth. il *Science* 243:1138-40 Mr 3 '89
Yanomamö survival [discussion of March 3, 1989 article, Warfare over Yanomamö Indians] W. Booth. *Science* 244:11 Ap 7 '89
YANOMAMO INDIANS *See* Yanoama Indians
YANOW, RHODA
about
Expressing the figure in pastel. M. C. Nelson. il *American Artist* 53:60-3 F '89
YANOW, SCOTT
Dave Grusin: scoring it big. il pors *Down Beat* 56:24-6 Jl '89
The many facets of Doc Severinsen. il por *Down Beat* 56:27-8 F '89
The musical directions of Tom Scott. il pors *Down Beat* 56:23-6 Mr '89
YANSHIN, A. L.
Ecological advances in the Soviet Union. il por *Environment* 30:6-9+ D '88
YAOHAN DEPARTMENT STORE CO. LTD.
A Japanese mall in—New Jersey? [Yaohan Plaza] L. J. Nathans. il *Business Week* p100 Ja 30 '89
YARBROUGH, ANNE
Mary in Egypt [poem] *The Christian Century* 106:7 Ja 4-11 '89
YARCHOAN, ROBERT, AND OTHERS
In vivo activity against HIV and favorable toxicity profile of 2', 3'-dideoxyinosine. bibl f il *Science* 245:412-15 Jl 28 '89
YARD LIGHTING *See* Lighting, Outdoor
YARD TOOLS *See* Lawn equipment
YARD TRACTORS *See* Tractors
YARDLEY, JONATHAN
about
PW interviews. S. Staggs. il por *Publishers Weekly* 235:75-6 Mr 17 '89
YARDS *See* Home grounds
YARN
Storage
Painted yarn cradle. il *Workbench* 45:35 Ja/F '89
YAROSLAVSKY, ZEV
about
Letter from Los Angeles. J. Didion. *The New Yorker* 65:88+ Ap 24 '89
YARROW, DAVID
America's trees under siege. *Utne Reader* p55 My/Je '89
YARROW, LEAH
How kids make friends [with editorial comment by Ann Pleshette Murphy] il *Parents* 64:9, 95-100+ O '89
Nail biting, hair twisting & other nasty habits. il *Parents* 64:122-5 Je '89
Pediatricians answer 20 nagging questions. il *Parents* 64:82-4+ Ja '89
YARROW
Walk-on meadow . . . it's blooming yarrow. il *Sunset (Central West edition)* 183:212 N '89
YATANI, ATSUKO, AND BROWN, ARTHUR M., 1932-
Rapid β-adrenergic modulation of cardiac calcium channel currents by a fast G protein pathway. bibl f il *Science* 245:71-4 Jl 7 '89
YATES, BROCK W.
[Column] *See* issues of Car and Driver
YATES, GEORGE
about
Heart of an Ironman. J. G. Hubbell. il pors *Reader's Digest* 134:13-14+ Mr '89
YATES, PETER
about
An innocent man [film] Reviews
People Weekly il 32:17 O 23 '89. R. Novak
YATES, REBECCA
about
Milk and honey [film] Reviews
People Weekly il 32:11-12 Jl 17 '89. R. Novak
YATES, SIMON
about
Left for dead on a Peruvian peak, Joe Simpson survives to write movingly about the climbers' code. S. K. Reed. il pors *People Weekly* 31:151-2 My 1 '89
YAU, JOHN, 1950-
Making his mark. il pors *Vogue* 179:190-5 Jl '89

YAWNING
The big yawn [research by Robert R. Provine] P. Huyghe. il *Discover* 10:78-81 Je '89
YAZDANI, AZITA
Source Reduction Research Partnership: a unique joint venture. bibl f il *Environment* 31:2-4 N '89
YAZOO RIVER (MISS.)
Delta
Yahoos in the Yazoo [U.S. Army Corps of Engineers] L. Williamson. il *Outdoor Life* 183:42+ Ap '89
YAZOV, DMITRY
about
A chat with Moscow's defense minister [interview] M. B. Zuckerman and J. Trimble. por *U.S. News & World Report* 106:28 Mr 13 '89
YEAGER, ALLISON
about
Dream Date Sweepstakes: meet the winner! J. Clay. il pors *'Teen* 33:46 Jl '89
YEAGER, JEANA
about
From flight to fancy. B. Harris. il por *Women's Sports & Fitness* 11:64 My '89
YEAMANS, WILLIAM
about
A social contract? Master against servant in the Court of Requests. P. S. Seaver. il *History Today* 39:50-6 S '89
YEAR OF THE YOUNG READER, 1989
Year of the Young Reader: publishers' plans. il *Publishers Weekly* 235:104 Ja 20 '89
YYR conference draws large turnout, provokes discussion [San Francisco] L. See. il *Publishers Weekly* 235:41 Mr 24 '89
YEARBOOKS, COLLEGE *See* College yearbooks
YEARBOOKS, HIGH SCHOOL *See* High school yearbooks
YEARWOOD, COLLINS
No ties to bind. por *Essence* 20:10 S '89
YEAST BREAD *See* Bread
YEAST ENZYMES *See* Enzymes, Fungal
YEASTS
BAS1 has a myb motif and activates HIS4 transcription only in combination with BAS2 [Saccharomyces] K. Tice-Baldwin and others. bibl f il *Science* 246:931-5 N 17 '89
Control of gene expression by artificial introns in Saccharomyces cerevisiae. T. Yoshimatsu and F. Nagawa. bibl f il *Science* 244:1346-8 Je 16 '89
Field in ferment. S. J. Nadis. *Technology Review* 92:12-13 My/Je '89
Intracellular targeting and structural conservation of a prohormone-processing endoprotease [Saccharomyces] R. S. Fuller and others. bibl f il *Science* 246:482-6 O 27 '89
Isolation of single-copy human genes from a library of yeast artificial chromosome clones [Saccharomyces] B. H. Brownstein and others. bibl f il *Science* 244:1348-51 Je 16 '89
Mapping the Drosophila genome with yeast artificial chromosomes. D. Garza and others. bibl f il *Science* 246:641-6 N 3 '89
Nucleotides in yeast tRNA^{Phe} required for the specific recognition by its cognate synthetase. J. R. Sampson and others. bibl f il *Science* 243:1363-6 Mr 10 '89
Semiconductor studies get a rise from yeast. F. Flam. *Science News* 135:231 Ap 15 '89
Similarity between the transcriptional silencer binding proteins ABF1 and RAP1 [Saccharomyces] J. F. X. Diffley and B. Stillman. bibl f il *Science* 246:1034-8 N 24 '89
Trans-kingdom sex [ability of Escherichia to conjugate with yeast] J. Horgan. *Scientific American* 261:34-5 O '89
A yeast actin-binding protein is encoded by *SAC6*, a gene found by suppression of an actin mutation. A. E. M. Adams and others. bibl f il *Science* 243:231-3 Ja 13 '89
Mutation
See Mutation—Fungi
YEATS, ROBERT S.
(jt. auth) See Stein, Ross S., and Yeats, Robert S.
YEATS, W. B. (WILLIAM BUTLER), 1865-1939
about
Reclaiming Yeats. R. Richman. *Commentary* 88:57-9 D '89
YEATS, WILLIAM BUTLER *See* Yeats, W. B. (William Butler), 1865-1939
YEE, JIING-KUAN
A liver-specific enhancer in the core promoter region of human hepatitis B virus. bibl f il *Science* 246:658-61 N 3 '89
YEFFET, ISAAC
about
The next bomb [cover story] E. Barnes. il por *Life* 12:130-4+ Mr '89
YEGANEH, ALBERT
about
Slave. *The New Yorker* 64:24-5 Ja 23 '89
YEGANEH-HAERI, A., AND OTHERS
Elasticity of MgSiO$_3$ in the perovskite structure. bibl f il *Science* 243:787-9 F 10 '89

YEH, JOHN
about
Listening to an inner voice. A. A. Knocke. il por *Nation's Business* 77:52 F '89
YEHOSHUA, ABRAHAM B.
about
Marriage, death, and Israel. R. C. Schneider. il por *World Press Review* 36:60 Ag '89
YELAPA (MEXICO)
Description
A change of peso. T. Huth. il *Gentlemen's Quarterly* 59:438-41+ S '89
YELIN, LOUISE
Summer reading. il *Parents* 64:176+ Jl '89
YELLEN, JUDITH
(jt. auth) See Mandel, Barrett J., and Yellen, Judith
YELLIN, LINDA NELL
Headed for happiness [story] il *Redbook* 172:30+ Ja '89
A method that works (for me). *The Writer* 102:18-20+ O '89
YELLOW FLOWER GARDENS *See* Flower gardens and gardening
YELLOWITZ, IRWIN
Samuel Gompers: a half century in labor's front rank. bibl f *Monthly Labor Review* 112:27-33 Jl '89
YELLOWJACKETS (MUSICAL GROUP)
The Yellowjackets: Yellowjackets' new buzz. R. Tolleson. il *Down Beat* 56:20-2 N '89
YELLOWKNIFE (N.W.T.)
Description
Of ice and men [running in the Canadian Arctic] H. Chernovsky. il *Runner's World* 24:96 Ja '89
YELLOWSTONE NATIONAL PARK
Ark de triomphe [saving endangered species] C. Spencer. il *Omni (New York, N.Y.)* 11:48-50+ Ja '89
Backcountry wealth builders [rangers Dick and Mona Divine] C. E. Cohen. il *Money* 18:98-102+ Mr '89
Beyond the burn [National Park Service's handling of forest fires] G. O'Gara. il map *Sierra* 74:40-51 Ja/F '89
Bill calls for wolf recovery EIS [reintroduction of grey wolves] il *National Parks* 63:9 S/O '89
Bison, elk deaths high in Yellowstone. il *National Parks* 63:11 My/Je '89
Born again [from forest fires] T. Cahill. il *Life* 12:32-4+ Je '89
The brawl of the wild [controversial plan to reintroduce wolves] J. Skow. il *Time* 134:13-14+ N 6 '89
Convoys set for Yellowstone [log hauling] il *National Parks* 63:8-9 N/D '89
The cremation of Yellowstone Park. A. Harris. il *Field & Stream* 94:54-5+ Jl '89
Fight fire with fire. L. Williamson. il *Outdoor Life* 183:48+ Mr '89
Fire. T. Hackett. maps *The New Yorker* 65:50-4+ O 2 '89
Fire and glory [horseback trip] R. Rudner. il *Ms.* 18:34 S '89
Fire, then ice [D. Sholly, head ranger] M. Brower. il pors *People Weekly* 31:42-7 Ja 16 '89
The flames of '88. G. Wuerthner. il *Wilderness* 52:40-54 Summ '89
The great Yellowstone fire [cover story; special section] il *Natural History* p34-51 Ag '89
Hellroaring: fighting last summer's fires. P. M. Leschak. il *Harper's* 279:70-3 Jl '89
Incineration of Yellowstone [cover story; with editorial comment by Les Line] T. Williams. il map *Audubon* 91:4, 38-85 Ja '89
Interpreting the Yellowstone fires of 1988 [cover story; special section] bibl f il maps *BioScience* 39:678-722 N '89
Out of the ashes. M. McCoy. il *Bicycling* 30:100+ Jl '89
Political fires still smolder. W. Wood. il *The Nation* 249:162-4 Ag 7-14 '89
Senate holds hearings on NPS fire policy. il *National Parks* 63:10-11 Ja/F '89
Sifting ashes in Yellowstone [management of bison and elk in wake of forest fires] T. Williams. il *Audubon* 91:30-2+ N '89
Springtime in the Rockies. P. A. Witteman. il *Time* 133:94-5 My 29 '89
Teton, Yellowstone snowmobile issue [proposed trail] il *National Parks* 63:9-10 My/Je '89
Trailblazing Wyoming's white-open spaces [snowmobiling] J. Skorupa. il *Popular Mechanics* 166:44 D '89
Wildfire: it's a hot topic. il map *National Geographic World* 169:26-31 S '89
Yellowstone. G. S. Bush. il *Better Homes and Gardens* 67:168+ Ap '89
Yellowstone a year later [cover story] il maps *Sunset (Central West edition)* 182:108-20+ My '89
Yellowstone: after the fire [bicycle tour] S. Kearin. il map *Bicycling* 30:96-100+ Jl '89
Yellowstone: better than before? E. McGowan. il *Travel Holiday* 172:22-3 Jl '89
Yellowstone: crown jewel of the national park system [cover story] G. F. Kreyche. il *USA Today (Periodical)* 118:34-43 S '89

YELLOWSTONE NATIONAL PARK—*cont.*
Yellowstone: fire storm over fire management. C. Elfring. il map *BioScience* 39:667-72 N '89
The Yellowstone fires. W. H. Romme and D. G. Despain. bibl il map *Scientific American* 261:36-44+ N '89
Yellowstone grizzlies: the new breed. P. Schullery. il *National Parks* 63:24-9+ N/D '89
Yellowstone lives! [recovery from forest fires] M. Satchell. il *U.S. News & World Report* 106:24-6 My 15 '89
The Yellowstone scam. M. Morrison. il *The American Spectator* 22:17-20 Ag '89
Yellowstone: the great fires of 1988 [cover story] D. Jeffery. il supp (folded map) map *National Geographic* 175:252-73 F '89
Yellowstone: the smoke clears. R. Barbee and P. Schullery. il *National Parks* 63:18-21 Mr/Ap '89
Yellowstone's bombers [aircraft help fight 1988 fires] P. Cone. il *Flying* 116:48-50+ Ja '89
Yellowstone's 'rebirth' amid the ashes is not neat or simple, but it's real. R. Conniff. il *Smithsonian* 20:36-44+ S '89

YELLOWSTONE NATIONAL PARK REGION
Beyond the boundaries. L. Mehlhaff. il *Sierra* 74:48-9 Ja/F '89
Firestorm! [P. Hedges and children survive forest fire] J. L. Moore. il *Reader's Digest* 134:77-82 Mr '89
Fragments and systems. il maps *Wilderness* 52:12-23 Spr '89

YELTSIN, BORIS
New York, New York—it's a wonderful town [excerpts from address] *National Review* 41:19-20 O 13 '89
about
Boris the trigger-happy. il por *Time* 134:63 O 30 '89
Coming to America. il por *Time* 134:36 S 25 '89
One Bear of a Soviet politician [interview] D. Aikman. il por *Time* 133:44-6 Mr 20 '89
One round to "The Thunder". A. Wilson-Smith. il por *Maclean's* 102:20 Ap 10 '89
Rolfing with Yeltsin. A. Heard. *The New Republic* 201:11-13 O 9 '89
A warning to Gorbachev. R. Corelli. por *Maclean's* 102:30 S 25 '89
Yeltsin. D. K. Mano. por *National Review* 41:48-9 D 8 '89

YEMEN (NORTH) See Yemen Arab Republic

YEMEN (PEOPLE'S DEMOCRATIC REPUBLIC)
Politics and government
New thinking in a Marxist land. M. J. Gart. il map *Time* 133:35-6 Ja 9 '89

YEMEN (SOUTH) See Yemen (People's Democratic Republic)

YEMEN ARAB REPUBLIC
See also
Cultural property—Protection—Yemen Arab Republic
Sanaa (Yemen Arab Republic)
Description and travel
North Yemen: of another age. D. Hiro. il *World Press Review* 36:78 S '89

YEN, MARIANNE
(jt. auth) See Reuter, Madalynne, and Yen, Marianne

YENER, K. ASLIHAN, AND OTHERS
Kestel: an early Bronze Age source of tin ore in the Taurus Mountains, Turkey. bibl f il map *Science* 244:200-3 Ap 14 '89

YEOMANS, DONALD K.
Comets and the perversity of nature. il *Sky and Telescope* 78:253-4 S '89

YERBA BUENA GARDENS (SAN FRANCISCO, CALIF.)
A unique monument to urban life. P. C. Newman. il *Maclean's* 102:33 Mr 13 '89

YERMAN, DAN
Building a three-drawer plan box. il *Theatre Crafts* 23:84-7 D '89

YERSHOV, IVAN
about
From Russia with love. il pors *U.S. News & World Report* 107:16 O 2 '89

YES See Youth Engaged in Service (U.S.)

YES CANADA INC. See Youth Employment Skills Canada Inc.

YESH G'VUL (ORGANIZATION)
Advice for refuseniks. *Harper's* 278:23-4 Ja '89
An Israeli draws the line [G. Spiro] W. Steif. il por *The Progressive* 53:15 Ap '89

YESTERYEAR [drama] See Glass, Joanna M.

YETNIKOFF, WALTER R.
about
Even for Walter Yetnikoff, this will be a stretch: can Sony's ace juggle both Columbia and CBS Records? D. Lieberman. il por *Business Week* p144-5 O 30 '89
Revenge of the antisuits. S. N. Chakravarty. il *Forbes* 144:49+ D 11 '89
Walter Yetnikoff's $300 million mistake. L. Gubernick. il pors *Forbes* 144:108+ D 11 '89

YEUTTER, CLAYTON K.
about
Ag's leading man. P. Smith. il pors *Successful Farming* 87:18-20 N '89
Gene Johnston. G. Johnston. il *Successful Farming* 87:5 Ap '89

Smoking gun. S. Hornik. il *Common Cause Magazine* 15:9 Mr/Ap '89
What to expect from the new Ag Secretary. G. Johnston. il *Successful Farming* 87 no4:36 Mr '89
Yeutter priorities: help cut deficit, a new farm bill. N. E. Harl. por *Successful Farming* 87:10 Ja '89

YEWDELL, JONATHAN W., AND BENNINK, JACK R.
Brefeldin A specifically inhibits presentation of protein antigens to cytotoxic T lymphocytes. bibl f il *Science* 244:1072-5 Je 2 '89

YGLESIAS, JOSE
Passion's promise. il *Publishers Weekly* 236:13-14+ Ag 25 '89
PW interviews [W. Humphrey] por *Publishers Weekly* 235:64-5 Je 2 '89

YIELD MANAGEMENT
No cheap room at the inn [used to determine hotel room prices] G. Eichler. il *Esquire* 112:92 O '89
What the traffic will bear. E. Dyson. il *Forbes* 143:282 My 29 '89

YING, MILDRED
Food editor's tips. See issues of Good Housekeeping

YINGER, BARRY
On site with hardy camellias: Sochong Island, Korea. il *Flower and Garden* 33:62-6 My/Je '89
Plant trek. See issues of Flower and Garden beginning January/February 1989

YO! MTV RAPS [television program] See Television program reviews—Single works

YO-YOS
Tom Smothers' flick of the wrist [Yo-Yo Man] F. Lovece. il pors *Video* 12:14 Mr '89

YOAKAM, DWIGHT
about
The finding of a founding father. D. Gates. il pors *Newsweek* 113:56 Ja 9 '89
Rodeo round-up: three big ones in the country corral. il pors *'Teen* 33:53 S '89

YODER, EDWIN M., JR.
Remembering Joe Alsop. il *National Review* 41:48-9 N 10 '89

YOFFE, EMILY
Shakeup. *The New Republic* 201:11-12 N 13 '89

YOGA
Body and soul [hatha yoga] S. Festa. il *World Tennis* 37:65-7 N '89

YOGURT
British days, Bulgarian nights. N. Hazelton. *National Review* 41:55-6 F 24 '89
The 'life force' food factor [probiotics] G. McVeigh. *Prevention (Emmaus, Pa.)* 41:47-51 Ag '89

YOGURT STORES
See also
TCBY Enterprises Inc.

YOHANNAN, KOHLE
about
She's 51, her fourth husband is 22—but designer Mary McFadden simply couldn't care less. D. Hutchings. il pors *People Weekly* 32:53-4+ O 23 '89

YOKICH, STEPHEN P.
about
Suddenly, the UAW is raising its voice at GM. W. Zellner. il por *Business Week* p96+ N 6 '89

YOLANDA ENTERPRISES, INC.
A self-styled food cop polices the coolest fridges in L.A. [Y. Berman] N. Geeslin. il pors *People Weekly* 31:87-8 Mr 27 '89

YONE, WENDY LAW- See Law-Yone, Wendy

YONKERS (N.Y.)
Crime
Nowhere to run (I) [R. Linton murdered by her husband] E. Hopkins. il *Rolling Stone* p72-4+ Ap 20 '89
Nowhere to run (II) [R. Linton murdered by her husband] E. Hopkins. il por *Rolling Stone* p74-6+ My 4 '89
Stores
See also
Greyston Bakery

YORK, CONSUELLA See Mother York

YORK, DICK
about
Shut in but not shut off, actor Dick York gives the time he has left to the homeless. T. Allis. il pors *People Weekly* 31:209-10+ Mr 6 '89

YORK, SARAH MOUNTBATTEN-WINDSOR, DUCHESS OF See Sarah, Duchess of York, 1959-

YORKSHIRE, HEIDI
Shirley Temple Black sets the record straight. il pors *McCall's* 116:88+ Mr '89
That enchanting Amen ensemble. il *McCall's* 116:138+ Ap '89
Why cults? il *Utne Reader* p134-5+ Mr/Ap '89
(jt. auth) See Clancy, Frank, and Yorkshire, Heidi

YORKSHIRE PUDDING
The truth about Yorkshire pudding. il *Sunset (Central West edition)* 183:180 N '89

YORKTOWN (VA.)
History
Siege, 1781
See also
Yorktown Battlefield (Va.)
YORKTOWN BATTLEFIELD (VA.)
Yorktown. R. F. Snow. il *American Heritage* 40:30+ S/O '89
YOSEF, OVADIA
about
Land or life: a biblical dilemma. R. N. Ostling. il por *Time* 134:67 S 18 '89
YOSEMITE NATIONAL PARK (CALIF.)
Careless love. R. Reinhardt. il *Wilderness* 52:16-27 Summ '89
Granite peaks and lush meadows in the High Sierra. il map *U.S. News & World Report* 106:67+ My 8 '89
Yosemite. G. S. Bush. il *Better Homes and Gardens* 67:174 Ap '89
Yosemite national parking lot. K. Ohnuma. il *Sierra* 74:31-2+ N/D '89
YOSHIDA, TOKUO
ASEAN togetherness in pharmaceuticals. il *World Health* p29 N '89
YOSHIMATSU, TADANORI, AND NAGAWA, FUMIKIYO
Control of gene expression by artificial introns in Saccharomyces cerevisiae. bibl f il *Science* 244:1346-8 Je 16 '89
YOST, PADDY
Help! I need a wife. il *Good Housekeeping* 209:136 S '89
YOUCHA, GERALDINE, AND SEIXAS, JUDITH S.
Drinking, drugs, & children. il *Parents* 64:142-4+ Mr '89
YOUNES, MOHAMED
about
The sixth great power returns. J. Willoughby. il por *Forbes* 143:135 F 20 '89
YOUNG, ANDREW, 1932-
about
Andrew Young taking fund-raising nationally. *Jet* 77:15 N 13 '89
YOUNG, BILL
about
His kind of town. E. Stern. il pors *Gentlemen's Quarterly* 59:138+ S '89
YOUNG, CHRIS
about
Chris Young. por *'Teen* 33:56 Mr '89
YOUNG, COLEMAN
about
Blood test results validate claim of paternity against Detroit mayor Coleman Young. il por *Jet* 76:6 My 29 '89
Detroit mayor Coleman Young admits fathering of boy, 6. il por *Jet* 76:7 Je 5 '89
Detroit mayor Young hit with paternity suit by a former city employee. por *Jet* 75:51 F 13 '89
Detroit only major city with two blacks battling to win the mayor's race. il por *Jet* 76:8 O 2 '89
Detroit's biggest survivor. M. Barone. il por *U.S. News & World Report* 107:27 S 25 '89
Giving birth to a scandal. por *Time* 133:23 Je 26 '89
Mom of Detroit mayor's son wants FBI probe of police. por *Jet* 76:8 Jl 10 '89
Photos, baptism of child revealed in Detroit mayor Young's paternity case. il por *Jet* 75:36-7 Mr 13 '89
A salty mayor seeks no. 5. F. Washington. il por *Newsweek* 114:32 Jl 31 '89
YOUNG, CONNIE PARASKEVIN- *See* Paraskevin-Young, Connie
YOUNG, CYNTHIA
Our TV Hall of Fame. il *TV Guide* 37:20-2 My 6-12 '89
YOUNG, DEABLO
about
Two faces in a crowd of graduates. J. R. Hacala. *America* 161:190-1 S 30 '89
YOUNG, ED
about
PW interviews. D. Brainard. por *Publishers Weekly* 235:208-9 F 24 '89
YOUNG, ERNIE
about
The loss of a husband and father. C. SerVaas. il por *The Saturday Evening Post* 261:94+ Jl/Ag '89
YOUNG, FRANK E.
50th anniversary of the FDA. il *The Saturday Evening Post* 261:56-7+ Ja/F '89
Ensuring the safety of generic drugs. il *FDA Consumer* 23:5-7 D '89/Ja '90
Is fish safe to eat? [cover story] il *Consumers' Research Magazine* 72:10-12 Ag '89
about
Dr. Frank Young: making a difference. C. SerVaas. il pors *The Saturday Evening Post* 261:50-5+ Ja/F '89
Serving God and man in the nation's capital [interview] il por *Christianity Today* 33:45 S 8 '89
YOUNG, GAYLE
Weathering the storm. il *Travel Holiday* 171:85-6 My '89
YOUNG, HILARY
The drawings of William De Morgan. bibl f il *Antiques* 135:1432-43 Je '89

YOUNG, JAMES, 1916-
(jt. auth) See Hope, Marjorie, and Young, James, 1916-
YOUNG, JOHN A.
about
Hewlett-Packard's screeching turn toward desktops. J. B. Levine. il por *Business Week* p106-8+ S 11 '89
Hewlett-Packard's whip-cracker. il por *Fortune* 119:58 F 13 '89
YOUNG, KARA
about
Facing the future. J. Shields. il *Vogue* 179:206-7 Ja '89
YOUNG, KATHLEEN BECKETT- *See* Beckett-Young, Kathleen
YOUNG, LESTER
about
Exercises for improvisers—Lester Young's solo on Jive at five. J. L. Lieberman. il *Down Beat* 56:56-7 Mr '89
Later Lester [discography] J. McDonough. il por *Down Beat* 56:32-3 Ja '89
YOUNG, NEIL
about
Neil Young covered on tribute album. D. Fricke. *Rolling Stone* p65 Jl 13-27 '89
Neil Young finds his 'Freedom'. S. Rogers. por *Rolling Stone* p20 O 19 '89
Neil Young lets 'Freedom' ring. D. Fricke. il por *Rolling Stone* p91-3 N 2 '89
YOUNG, PAM
about
Self-publishers print 100,000 copies (and survive!). J. Barbato. *Publishers Weekly* 236:42 N 10 '89
YOUNG, REGGIE
Saviors [poem] *The Christian Century* 106:623 Je 21-28 '89
YOUNG, ROBERT M., 1924-
about
Triumph of the spirit [film] Reviews
Harper's Bazaar il 122:103 D '89. M. Rochlin
The New Republic 201:26 D 25 '89. S. Kauffmann
Newsweek il 114:90 D 11 '89. J. Kroll
YOUNG, SEAN
about
Fear and loathing in Hollywood [cover story] S. Schindehette. il pors *People Weekly* 31:72-4+ Mr 20 '89
Oh, you beautiful doll. J. Queenan. il por *Rolling Stone* p25+ Ap 6 '89
Unique star quality. Y. Z. McDonough. il pors *Harper's Bazaar* 122:208-15+ Ap '89
Why Sean Young is restless. F. Robbins. por *Mademoiselle* 95:96+ Ap '89
YOUNG, STEPHANIE
Beauty & health report. See issues of Glamour
YOUNG, SUE
(jt. auth) See Thomas, Cathy, and Young, Sue
YOUNG, THERESA A., AND WILLIS, JUDITH
Of lice and children: going to the head of the class. il *FDA Consumer* 23:28-31 N '89
YOUNG, WALTER BRAMWELL *See* Bramwell
YOUNG (ARTHUR) & COMPANY *See* Arthur Young & Company
YOUNG & RUBICAM INC.
Trouble for copycats [B. Midler wins suit over sound-alike ad] P. Young. il por *Maclean's* N 20 '89
A U.S. patent on famous voices [B. Midler wins suit against Young & Rubicam's use of her singing style] il por *U.S. News & World Report* 107:19 N 13 '89
YOUNG ADULTS *See* Youth
YOUNG ADULTS' LITERATURE
See also
Tape recordings—Young adults' literature
Authorship
Boyhood on the Rock [Newfoundland novelist K. Major] D. Turbide. il por *Maclean's* 102:61 Ap 17 '89
Bibliography
Have you read . . . ? See issues of 'Teen
YOUNG ASTRONAUT PROGRAM (JAPAN)
Japan's space kids. J. R. Vacca. il *Omni (New York, N.Y.)* 12:20+ O '89
YOUNG COMMUNIST LEAGUE *See* All-Union Lenin Young Communist League
YOUNG EINSTEIN [film] See Motion picture reviews—Single works
YOUNG GUNS [film] See Motion picture reviews—Single works
YOUNG MEN
See also
Youth
Young beyond their years [postponing move into adulthood] K. L. Woodward. il *Newsweek* 114 Special Issue:54-5+ Wint '89/Spr '90
Attitudes
He likes me . . . he likes me not [quiz] il *'Teen* 33:47 S '89
Him. G. Schwartz. See issues of Seventeen beginning 1987
What boys really think about makeup. D. Seeley. il *S* 48:52-3+ Jl '89

YOUNG MEN—Attitudes—*cont.*

What guys really think about sex [results of surveys] K. McCoy. il *Seventeen* 48:48-9 Jl '89

Psychology

Boy behavior: what's behind it? R. Shinkman. il *Teen* 33:34-5 Jl '89

Confessions of a high school big shot: maybe what you think about the jock/brain/heartthrob is all wrong. S. Friedman. por *Seventeen* 48:100-1+ Jl '89

Liking an unlikely guy. il *Teen* 33:22+ Mr '89

Sexual behavior

See Youth—Sexual behavior

YOUNG MEN AND YOUNG WOMEN *See* Women and men

YOUNG NATURALIST FOUNDATION

Cultivating a child's garden. D. Turbide. *Maclean's* 102:57 F 6 '89

YOUNG PEOPLE'S CHINESE CULTURAL CENTER

Companies on the East and West coasts keep their dance traditions alive: regional Chinese dance, American-style. N. Woronov. il *Dance Magazine* 63:28-30 Ag '89

YOUNG PLAYWRIGHTS FESTIVAL *See* Drama festivals—New York (State)

THE YOUNG RIDERS [television program] *See* Television program reviews—Single works

YOUNG URBAN PROFESSIONALS *See* Yuppies

YOUNG WOMEN

See also

Youth

A dog's tale [adolescent daughter relinquishes stuffed animal] E. Berg. il *Ladies' Home Journal* 106:42+ Ja '89

Young beyond their years [postponing move into adulthood] K. L. Woodward. il *Newsweek* 114 Special Issue:54-5+ Wint '89/Spr '90

Diseases

See also

Anorexia nervosa

Bulimia

Health and hygiene

Beat the body blues: a personal primer. E. Karlsberg. il *Teen* 33:32+ Ag '89

Dear doctor. R. Rosen. See issues of 'Teen beginning June 1984

Health hotline. See issues of 'Teen beginning August 1989

Psychology

Confessions of a bloodthirsty flower child [contemporary teen discovers the sixties] J. Davidson. il *Seventeen* 48:180 Mr '89

In the dumps? 10 easy picker-uppers. il *Teen* 33:52+ N '89

Mother hate. P. Theroux. il *Parents* 64:46+ Ag '89

Quiz: how happy are you? il *Teen* 33:22 Ja '89

Sexism and summer camp or: Am I crazy??!! [young girl's appearance anxiety] E. Berg. il *Parents* 64:86-8 Ag '89

Who says you have to have a boyfriend? C. Jakobson. *Seventeen* 48:108-10+ S '89

Sexual behavior

See Youth—Sexual behavior

YOUNG WOMEN AND YOUNG MEN *See* Women and men

YOUNG WOMEN IN TELEVISION

Setting the wrong example [excerpt from Growing up in prime time: an analysis of adolescent girls on television] S. Steenland. il *Channels (New York, N.Y.: 1986)* 9:85 F '89

YOUNGER, PAUL

about

Central State Marauders, 'Tank' Younger feted in L.A. il por *Jet* 76:49 My 22 '89

YOUNGREN, WILLIAM H.

He knew his Wagner. il *The Atlantic* 264:83-5 Jl '89

Ups and downs. il *The Atlantic* 263:105-7 Ja '89

YOUNGS, TERRI

about

Business and personal services. il por *Home Office Computing* 7:44 Je '89

YOUNGSTOWN (OHIO)

Galleries and museums

See also

Youngstown Historical Center of Industry and Labor

YOUNGSTOWN HISTORICAL CENTER OF INDUSTRY AND LABOR

The (empty) steel museum. A. Murr. il *Newsweek* 114:84 O 30 '89

YOUNIS, FAWAZ

about

To catch a terrorist. S. Emerson. il por *Reader's Digest* 135:107-11 O '89

YOUR SHOW OF SHOWS [television program] *See* Television program reviews—Single works

YOUTH

See also

Adolescence

Alcohol and youth

Black youth

College students

Computers and youth

Dating (Social customs)

Dropouts

Drugs and youth

High school graduates

High school students

Mass media and youth

Maturity

Motion pictures and youth

Problem children

Smoking and youth

Social work with youth

Socially handicapped children

Students

Telephone and youth

Television and youth

Video games and youth

Videotapes and youth

Young men

Young women

What will teenagers face in the 21st century? [views of William Shaw] il *USA Today (Periodical)* 118:16 D '89

What's great about teenagers. D. Elkind. il *Parents* 64:169 Jl '89

Attitudes

Explaining today to yesterday [cover story] W. J. O'Malley. il *America* 161:254-7 O 21 '89

Hail to the chief [teens say what they would do if they were president] *Seventeen* 48:140+ N '89

My generation [results of survey] S. Chace. il *Seventeen* 48:99-106 O '89

North American Essay Contest [special section] il por *The Humanist* 49:21-9+ Mr/Ap '89

North American Essay Contest [special section] il *The Humanist* 49:20-30+ Ja/F '89

Surveying teens [American Home Economics Association survey] il *Children Today* 18:5 S/O '89

Awards

They've got the right stuff [Sea Breeze Awards] il *Teen* 33:89 Mr '89

Towards new goals [YTV awards recognizing young Canadians' achievements] D. Jenish. il *Maclean's* 102:80 O 30 '89

Conferences

See also

World Festival of Youth and Students for Peace and Friendship

Crime

See Juvenile delinquents and delinquency

Diseases

See also

AIDS (Disease) and children

Economic conditions

Money management for teens. D. Elkind. il *Parents* 64:222 N '89

Money talk: dollar data that makes sense. A. Bell. il *Teen* 33:69 Jl '89

The roots of skinhead violence: dim economic prospects for young men. il *Utne Reader* p84 My/Je '89

The Seventeen money guide. C. Wallace. il *Seventeen* 48:112-13+ F '89

Employment

See also

Baby sitters

Black youth—Employment

California Conservation Corps

San Francisco Conservation Corps

Youth and business

Be a working girl! [summer jobs] W. J. Rohr. il *Teen* 33:36-7+ My '89

Domino's [after-school job at Domino's Pizza in Ann Arbor, Mich.] *The New Yorker* 65:37 Mr 27 '89

Empty chairs: what happens to students who don't go to college [Grant Foundation report] M. A. Kramer. *Change* 21:6-7 Ja/F '89

First jobs: school was never like this—or was it? N. Baxter. il *Occupational Outlook Quarterly* 32:2-7 Wint '88

A flip of fate on the subminimum wage [training wage] il *U.S. News & World Report* 107:14 N 13 '89

The forgotten half [undereducated work force; cover story] D. Whitman. il *U.S. News & World Report* 106:44-9+ Je 26 '89

Hooray for child labor! H. Wheelwright. il *Money* 18:198 Je '89

Inside the Golden Arches [McDonald's] M. Mabry. il *Newsweek* 114:46-7 D 18 '89

A local business invests in the kids [work-study program offered by Wegmans' supermarkets in Rochester, N.Y.] il *U.S. News & World Report* 106:60 Je 26 '89

Luring youth to fast-food jobs [research by Bonnie M. Farber] il *USA Today (Periodical)* 118:7 Ag '89

A new approach to the dropout problem. P. Woodring. *Phi Delta Kappan* 70:468-9 F '89

No college, no future? [excerpt from The forgotten half report by the Grant Foundation] *The Education Digest* 54:10-14 F '89

The secret of your success. J. Iaconetti. il *Seventeen* 48:90+ Je '89

A smaller bite out of summer pay [payroll withholding taxes] L. Wiener. il *U.S. News & World Report* 106:68 Je 5 '89

YOUTH—Employment—*cont.*

Summer jobs that pay off in experience. S. Woolley. il *Business Week* p160 F 20 '89

Warning: this job may be hazardous to your health. L. Green. il *Current Health 2* 15:24-5 My '89

Youth Opportunity: a private sector investment in prevention [summer work at Domino's Pizza Inc.'s Whatley Farm in Ann Arbor, Mich.] C. H. Tice. il *Children Today* 18:20-3 Mr/Ap '89

Health and hygiene

See also

Young women—Health and hygiene

Youth—Medical care

Danger zones: top hazards to your health. K. McCoy. il *Seventeen* 48:170+ Ag '89

Elements of fitness for those of strong heart and muscle. L. E. Koszuta. il *Current Health 2* 16:12-13 S '89

The risky business of being a teen [health risk appraisal; cover story] il *Current Health 2* 16:4-11 S '89

Young people at WHO. il *World Health* p30-1 Je '89

Youth of today [special issue] il *World Health* p3-29 Mr '89

International aspects

Youth of today [special issue] il *World Health* p3-29 Mr '89

Management and training

As they grow/11 through 13. J. P. Comer. See issues of Parents

As they grow/14 through 18. D. Elkind. See issues of Parents beginning January 1987

My daughter was running wild. il *Good Housekeeping* 209:44+ O '89

Teenagers reap broad benefits from 'authoritative' parents [study by Diana Baumrind] B. Bower. *Science News* 136:117-18 Ag 19 '89

Medical care

Hey, look me over [cover story] E. Gofen. il *Current Health 2* 15:3-8 Ja '89

National service

See National service

Nutrition

Body mechanics: how well does your engine run? il *'Teen* 33:75 Ja '89

Food for thought. P. M. Jones. il *Scholastic Update (Teachers' edition)* 121:6 Ja 27 '89

Nutrition facts & folklore. B. Hayton. il *Current Health 2* 15:23-5 Ja '89

Sizing up food servings. T. Mendoza. il *Current Health 2* 16:20-2 S '89

Weigh-ins made easy: diet dilemma data. il *'Teen* 33:90+ Mr '89

Political activities

See also

Youth movement

Teens behind the scenes [Congress] L. Eskin. il *Scholastic Update (Teachers' edition)* 121:11-14 F 24 '89

Why young people don't vote. C. B. Gans. *The Education Digest* 54:40-3 F '89

Psychiatric care

See Adolescent psychiatry

Psychology

See Adolescence

Recreation

Summer projects. D. Elkind. il *Parents* 64:155 Ag '89

Religious life

See also

Church work with youth

Canada's youth are big on God and the family. L. Mackey. *Christianity Today* 33:52-3 F 3 '89

Teenage spirituality [cover story] W. J. O'Malley. *America* 160:390-4 Ap 29 '89

Sexual behavior

See also

Sex education

Teenage pregnancy

Gay kids, mad parents [research by Joyce Hunter] J. Folkenberg. il *American Health* 8:78-9 D '89

Girls: just say "Not now" [views of Carol Cassell] L. C. Cook. *Psychology Today* 23:59 Ap '89

Is your child flirting with sex? K. McCoy. il *Reader's Digest* 135:111-14 S '89

A place to be somebody [Harvey Milk School in New York City] K. Brady. il *Time* 134:21-2+ N 13 '89

Reducing homophobia among educators and students. R. Schaecher. *The Education Digest* 54:58-61 Ap '89

Sex and your body. K. McCoy. See issues of Seventeen beginning June 1983 through January 1990

Sexual morality for young humanists and their parents. D. Carroll. *The Humanist* 49:41-2+ Jl/Ag '89

Teen-agers and . . . you know what [cover story] W. J. O'Malley. *America* 160:340-4 Ap 15 '89

Teen boys get condom sense [survey] E. Stark. *Psychology Today* 23:62-3 O '89

Teen sexuality [Berkeley High School, Calif.] G. H. Colt. il *Life* 12:24-30 Jl '89

Suicide

See Suicide

Travel

A journey to the U.S.S.R. H. Herman. il map *National Geographic World* 165:12-16 My '89

Vocational guidance

See Vocational guidance

Volunteer service

See Volunteer service

California

See also

Los Angeles (Calif.)—Youth

Canada

See also

Youth Employment Skills Canada Inc.

Canada's youth are big on God and the family. L. Mackey. *Christianity Today* 33:52-3 F 3 '89

Towards new goals [YTV awards recognizing young Canadians' achievements] D. Jenish. il *Maclean's* 102:80 O 30 '89

China

'We're all gold diggers here'. D. Elliott. il *Newsweek* 113:31 F 20 '89

India

Who cares? L. R. Balar. il *World Health* p18 Mr '89

Japan

American casual seizes Japan. B. Hillenbrand. il *Time* 134:106 N 13 '89

Philippines

Poverty, negligence, ignorance. M. C. Vidanes. il *World Health* p22 Mr '89

Poland

Poland's 'lost illusions'. A. K. Natys. *World Press Review* 36:58 F '89

Soviet Union

See also

All-Union Lenin Young Communist League

Zhukovka (Soviet Union)—Youth

Grooming the *glasnost* generation. A. Wilson. il *World Press Review* 36:41 Ja '89

The me generation in Moscow. A. Izyumov. il *Newsweek* 114:47 D 4 '89

Sri Lanka

A mix of extremes. R. Fernando. il *World Health* p14-15 Mr '89

Sudan

One teen's bout with hunger [A. Chol] E. Whitford. il por *Scholastic Update (Teachers' edition)* 121:3 Ja 27 '89

Thailand

New seasons, new joys. O. Anusaksathien. il *World Health* p27-8 Mr '89

United States

See Youth

Zimbabwe

The pursuit of happiness. P. Sake. il *World Health* p13 Mr '89

YOUTH, RUNAWAY *See* Runaways

YOUTH-ADULT RELATIONSHIP

See also

Generation gap

Parent-child relationship

Fostering intergenerational relationships for at-risk youth. M. Freedman. il *Children Today* 18:10-15 Mr/Ap '89

Reaching across generations [intergenerational programs] S. C. Taylor. *Modern Maturity* 32:38 Ag/S '89

Three Samaritans [American youths assist injured woman during visit to Switzerland] B. O'Sullivan. il *Reader's Digest* 135:55-6+ O '89

Youth and the elderly. A. Kalache. il *World Health* p8-9 Mr '89

YOUTH AND ADULTS *See* Youth-adult relationship

YOUTH AND AGED *See* Youth-adult relationship

YOUTH AND BUSINESS

See also

Junior Achievement, Inc.

Youth market

And the music tells of history [address, May 6, 1989] J. E. Sloan. *Vital Speeches of the Day* 55:649-51 Ag 15 '89

The clean machine [starting a house cleaning service] H. Rubin. il *Seventeen* 48:122+ My '89

Kids in business. il *National Geographic World* 161:12-16 Ja '89

Mind your own business: Seventeen's guide to starting up a summer catering career. il *Seventeen* 48:119-20+ My '89

Student entrepreneurs on campus. L. Williams. il *Black Enterprise* 19:169-72 F '89

Tips for young summertime entrepreneurs [views of Laurie LaBelle and Kit Cox] il *USA Today (Periodical)* 118:8-9 Jl '89

Will junior follow in your entrepreneurial footsteps? G. Solomon. il *Home Office Computing* 7:73-4 S '89

YOUTH AND MOTION PICTURES *See* Motion pictures and youth

YOUTH AND TELEPHONE See Telephone and youth
YOUTH AND TELEVISION See Television and youth
YOUTH AND VIDEOTAPES See Videotapes and youth
YOUTH AS ACTORS AND ACTRESSES
After Father knows best, it was drugs, jail, depression. M. Littwin. il pors *TV Guide* 37:6-8 Je 17-23 '89
Hollywood's new Brat Pack of poets. il *Newsweek* 114:74 S 18 '89
Hot properties. K. Turman. il *Teen* 33:51 Je '89
Teens they're talking about. M. Schooler. il *Teen* 33:42-3 Jl '89
Why them? . . . and what it's like being a TV heartthrob [J. Bateman and K. Cameron; cover story] S. Littwin. il pors *TV Guide* 37:4-6+ Ap 22-28 '89
YOUTH AS AUTHORS
Brat Pack II. A. Heard. il *The American Spectator* 22:27-9 O '89
YOUTH AS CONSUMERS See Youth market
YOUTH AS DETECTIVES
Sleuthing youths. W. Woodward. il *Teen* 33:18-19+ D '89
YOUTH AS PUBLISHERS
Desk-top publishing [explosion of adolescent printing in years after Civil War] P. E. Petrik. bibl il *History Today* 39:12-26 O '89
YOUTH COUNSELING
See also
Peer counseling
When to seek professional help. J. P. Comer. il *Parents* 64:220 D '89
YOUTH EMPLOYMENT SKILLS CANADA INC.
Help for dropouts. N. Underwood. il *Maclean's* 102:52 Mr 13 '89
YOUTH ENGAGED IN SERVICE (U.S.)
Just say YES. M. Krondracke. *The New Republic* 200:11-13 Ap 24 '89
Man of a thousand lights [G. Bush] R. Z. Hallow. *National Review* 41:19-20 My 19 '89
What President Bush should do about national youth service [address, February 23, 1989] D. J. Eberly. *Vital Speeches of the Day* 55:651-3 Ag 15 '89
YOUTH FORCE (ORGANIZATION)
Turning horror into hope. L. Tarshis. il *Scholastic Update (Teachers' edition)* 122:19-20 N 17 '89
YOUTH GANGS See Gangs
YOUTH IN TELEVISION
The greening of Degrassi [Degrassi Junior High] K. Beck. il pors *Channels (New York, N.Y.: 1986)* 9:62-4 N '89
YOUTH MARKET
The ABC's of marketing to kids. P. Sellers. il *Fortune* 119:114-16+ My 8 '89
Consumerism to idealism [young people] N. Ulaby. por *The Humanist* 49:26+ Mr/Ap '89
Has sneaker madness gone too far? [industry accused of exploiting youth] T. Barrett. il *Newsweek* 114:51 D 18 '89
Madison Avenue's call of the child. A. Z. Cuneo. il *U.S. News & World Report* 106:84-5 Mr 20 '89
YOUTH MOVEMENT

China
Again, China's young challenge the old order [historical prospective] J. Wallace. il *U.S. News & World Report* 106:34 My 29 '89

Communist countries
See also
World Festival of Youth and Students for Peace and Friendship

United States
See Youth movement
YSL (FIRM) See Yves Saint Laurent (Firm)
YTURBE, JEAN DE
about
Soirées on the Seine. A. Bogart. il pors *Harper's Bazaar* 122:199+ D '89
YTURBE, SANDY DE
about
Soirées on the Seine. A. Bogart. il pors *Harper's Bazaar* 122:199+ D '89
YTV CANADA INC.
Towards new goals [awards recognizing young Canadians' achievements] D. Jenish. il *Maclean's* 102:80 O 30 '89
YU, X.
(jt. auth) See Egelman, E. H., and Yu, X.
YUCATAN (MEXICO: STATE)
See also
Beaches—Yucatan (Mexico: State)
Cultural property—Protection—Yucatan (Mexico: State)
Antiquities
See also
Chichén Itzá (Mexico)
A designer's wanderings in the Yucatán [R. Hutchinson] S. E. Jares. il por *Architectural Digest* 46:270+ Ap '89
Walking on ancestral gods [Mayan ruins damaged by modern Mayas] T. Padgett. il *Newsweek* 114:83 O 9 '89
YUCCA MOUNTAIN (NEV.)
No home for hot trash. *Time* 134:81 D 11 '89
A nuclear dump: the experiment begins. D. Grossman and S. Shulman. il map *Discover* 10:48-51+ Mr '89

Showdown at Yucca Mountain: the high stakes of a nuclear waste dump. W. Kittredge. il *Utne Reader* p44-9 Ja/F '89
Something dead that can't be buried [nuclear waste dump] il map *U.S. News & World Report* 107:17 D 11 '89
YUE, DAVID T., AND OTHERS
Two molecular transitions influence cardiac sodium channel gating. bibl f il *Science* 244:349-52 Ap 21 '89
YUGOSLAVIA
See also
Albanians—Yugoslavia
Citizenship—Yugoslavia
Government and the press—Yugoslavia
Korčula (Yugoslavia: Island)
Kosovo (Yugoslavia)
Palaces—Yugoslavia
Plitvice National Park (Yugoslavia)
Serbia (Yugoslavia)
Slovenia (Yugoslavia)
Terrorism—Yugoslavia
Yugoslavs

Description and travel
Yugoslavian notes. D. K. Mano. *National Review* 41:57+ Je 30 '89
Yugoslavia's bold coast. I. S. Jones. il map *Oceans* 22:10-17+ Mr/Ap '89

Nationalism
A nation divided. A. Phillips. il *Maclean's* 102:16-18 F 13 '89
Yugoslavia: Marxism in a melting pot. P. Sudo. il *Scholastic Update (Teachers' edition)* 122:30 S 22 '89
Yugoslavia's new political truth. S. Drakulić. il *The Nation* 248:297-8+ Mr 6 '89

Politics and government
Glasnostradamus. S. Drakulić. *The New Republic* 200:18-20 Ap 24 '89
A nation divided. A. Phillips. il *Maclean's* 102:16-18 F 13 '89
A prognosis for Yugoslavia. M. G. Zaninovich. bibl f *Current History* 88:393-6+ N '89

Religious institutions and affairs
See also
Orthodox Eastern Church—Yugoslavia
YUGOSLAVS

United States
Between issues [M. Mihajlov stripped of Yugoslav citizenship] *The New Leader* 72:2 Mr 20 '89
YUJEAN'S (ALBANY, CALIF.: RESTAURANT) See Albany (Calif.)—Restaurants, nightclubs, bars, etc.
YUKON RIVER (YUKON AND ALASKA)
The great raft adventure [motorcycle-powered raft trip] K. Schubert. il map *Cycle* 40:38-41+ Jl '89
YUKON TERRITORY
See also
Yukon River (Yukon and Alaska)
Anecdotes, facetiae, satire, etc.
Tales from the land of Dan McGrew. A. Fotheringham. il *Maclean's* 102:64 S 25 '89
Politics and government
A frigid north poll [election campaign] J. Howse. il *Maclean's* 102:14 F 20 '89
YUNICK, SMOKEY
Say, Smokey. See issues of Popular Science
about
Say, Smokey: what's the car engine of the future? il pors *Popular Science* 234:105-9+ Mr '89
YUPPIES
See also
Dinks
The hidden dangers of yuppie bashing. P. Lyons. il *Utne Reader* p92-8 Jl/Ag '89
Hot tombs [purchasing desirable burial plots; cover story] M. Specter. *The New Republic* 201:22-5 S 11 '89
Who killed the yuppie? H. Hertzberg. *Utne Reader* p94 Jl/Ag '89
Yuppie spending gets serious. F. Rice. il *Fortune* 119:147-9 Mr 27 '89
Yuppies and microwaves. F. Powledge. il *The Progressive* 53:46 D '89

Political activities
Post-yuppie America. D. Foster. il *Mother Jones* 14:16-18 F/Mr '89
Yuppie activists: not an oxymoron. D. Foster. *Utne Reader* p96 Jl/Ag '89

Sports
What's as gory as hockey and as upscale as squash? [Major Indoor Lacrosse League] R. Duffy. il *Business Week* p42 Ap 17 '89
YUPPIES IN TELEVISION
A fun-house mirror on American men [thirtysomething's male characters; cover story] S. Fried. il *Gentlemen's Quarterly* 59:264-9+ Ap '89
thirtysomething confidential. B. Zehme. il *Rolling Stone* p70-2+ Je 1 '89

YUSTY, MARIA
about
A bone-lengthening technique adds inches to a teenager's leg—and answers her prayers. B. Johnson. il pors *People Weekly* 32:49-50+ O 16 '89
YVERT-JALU, HÉLÈNE
Farewell to winter. il *The Unesco Courier* 42:32-7 D '89
Hearth, home and rural community. il *The Unesco Courier* 42:10-15 Jl '89
Ilya the invincible. il *The Unesco Courier* 42:32-5 S '89
YVES SAINT LAURENT (FIRM)
How Saint Laurent is skirting sharks [stock goes public] *U.S. News & World Report* 107:11-12 Jl 17 '89
YZERMAN, STEVE
about
No. 3 with a bullet. A. Murphy. il pors *Sports Illustrated* 70:38-40 Mr 20 '89

Z

Z PARTICLES
European Z^0 factory LEPs ahead. *Science News* 136:159 S 2 '89
Linear collider makes a Z [Stanford Linear Collider] *Science News* 135:245 Ap 22 '89
New physics, old rivalries [SLAC vs. CERN] J. Cherfas. il *Science* 246:323-4 O 20 '89
SLAC feels the thrill of the chase. M. M. Waldrop. il *Science* 244:771-3 My 19 '89
Slacking off [creating Z particles with the CERN and Stanford accelerators] G. Taubes. il *Discover* 10:58-9 Ja '89
The Stanford Linear Collider [cover story] J. R. Rees. il *Scientific American* 261:58-65 O '89
Stanford Linear Collider finally starts producing the Z^0. B. M. Schwarzschild. il *Physics Today* 42:17-21 Jl '89
Zeroing in on the Z^0 mass. *Science News* 136:69 Jl 29 '89
Zs for two: a critical mass [Fermilab vs. SLAC] M. M. Waldrop. *Science* 245:350 Jl 28 '89
ZABAGLIONE *See* Custards
ZABAR, ABBIE
Heartfelt gestures, handmade gifts. il *Seventeen* 48:135-8 N '89
Thyme for herbs. il *Seventeen* 48:212-15+ Ap '89
ZABLE, WALTER JOSEPH, 1915-
about
Operation Ill Wind has Cubic fighting for air. E. Schine. il por *Business Week* p90 D 11 '89
ZABORNEY, KEVIN
about
A concerned Cupidian named Kevin Zaborney squeezes National Hugging Day into the calendar. il por *People Weekly* 31:92 Ja 23 '89
ZACCHAEUS (BIBLICAL FIGURE)
about
Tolerance. P. J. Ryan. il *America* 161:283 O 28 '89
ZACKS, RICHARD
The best laughs on video. il *TV Guide* 37:21-2 N 11-17 '89
ZADORA, PIA
about
Pia's Pickfair. L. Arbus. il pors *Life* 12:59-61 Spr '89
ZAFFARONI, ALEJANDRO C.
about
Drug extender. I. Chithelen. il por *Forbes* 144:95-6 Jl 10 '89
ZAGAJEWSKI, ADAM, 1945-
Sails [poem]; tr. by Renata Gorczynski and Benjamin Ivry. *The New Yorker* 65:56 O 23 '89
ZAGAT, TIM
about
Call of the wild. N. M. Better. il *House & Garden* 161:46+ Je '89
Palate polls. J. Elson. il por *Time* 134:65-6 Ag 28 '89
ZAGORIA, DONALD S.
Soviet policy in East Asia: a new beginning? *Foreign Affairs* 68 Special Issue:120-38 ['89]
ZAHARIAS (BABE DIDRIKSON) MEMORIAL MUSEUM (BEAUMONT, TEX.) *See* Babe Didrikson Zaharias Memorial Museum (Beaumont, Tex.)
ZAHN, GORDON CHARLES, 1918-
The human rights of homosexuals. *Commonweal* 116:462-5 S 8 '89
Let's support civil rights for homosexuals [with readers' comments] *U.S. Catholic* 54:13-18 O '89
ZAHNISER, ED
Wolf [poem] *Wilderness* 52:4 Summ '89
ZAHNISER, HOWARD
about
Wilderness: New York sets a global stage. G. D. Davis. il pors *The Conservationist* 44:2-9+ N/D '89
ZAHRADNIK, FRED
New products. See issues of Bicycling

ZAIGLIN, BOB
(jt. auth) See Demarais, Steve, and Zaiglin, Bob
ZAIRE
See also
Economic assistance, American—Zaire
Massacres—Zaire
Missions, Medical—Zaire
Rain forests—Zaire
Native peoples
See also
Efe (African people)
Lese (African people)
Politics and government
See also
Politics, Corruption in—Zaire
ZAJAC, CHRISTINE
about
After a year as a fifth-grade Gulliver, author Tracy Kidder speaks up for teachers. K. Hubbard. il pors *People Weekly* 32:77+ O 9 '89
From 'House' to schoolhouse. C. Leslie. il por *Newsweek* 114:67 S 11 '89
PW interviews [T. Kidder] A. Smith. por *Publishers Weekly* 236:101-2 S 15 '89
ZAK, STEVEN
Ethics and animals. il *The Atlantic* 263:68-74 Mr '89
ZAKROFF, ZANNE EARLY
The art of carving—turkey. il *Gourmet* 49:128-9+ N '89
Gourmet holidays: Santa Fe. il *Gourmet* 49:86-93+ D '89
Pleasures of the table: Simon Pearce. il por *Gourmet* 49:56-61+ Ag '89
ZAL, ROXANA
about
Nice acting, Roxana—now do the laundry. J. Greenfeld. il por *TV Guide* 37:8 My 20-26 '89
ZALM, WILLIAM VANDER *See* Vander Zalm, William
ZAMBA, FRIEDA
In the tube. il pors *American Health* 8:80-1 S '89
ZAMBEZI RIVER
Wet and wild [white-water rafting] E. McGowan. il *Travel Holiday* 171:50-1 Ap '89
ZAMBIA
See also
South Luangwa National Park (Zambia)
Wildlife—Zambia
ZAMORA, RUBÉN
In Salvador time waits for no one [cover story] *The Nation* 248:253+ F 27 '89
about
Rubén Zamora [interview] M. Shaffer. pors *The Progressive* 53:32-5 Jl '89
ZAMORA, TOM
(jt. auth) See Albright, David, and Zamora, Tom
ZANDY, JANET
War babies: a mother refuses her son toy guns. il *Utne Reader* p120-1 N/D '89
ZANE, ARNIE
about
Bill T. Jones choreographs an anguished tribute to his late partner, a victim of AIDS. M. Small. il pors *People Weekly* 32:44-6 Jl 31 '89
ZANE, J. PEDER
The sticks, the slides, and the shaker. il *New York* 22:36-9 Je 19 '89
ZANINOVICH, M. GEORGE
A prognosis for Yugoslavia. bibl f *Current History* 88:393-6+ N '89
ZANSKAR RIVER (INDIA)
Journey to knowledge [Tibetan children travel 100 miles on frozen Zanskar River to go to school] O. Föllmi. il *Life* 12:108-16 D '89
ZANZIBAR
Description and travel
Zanzibar. A. Dappen. il *Travel Holiday* 171:86-9 Ja '89
ZAO, WOU-KI, 1921-
about
Meditative explorations in a French manor house. Countess Du Saillant. il por *Architectural Digest* 46:116+ O '89
ZAPATA CORPORATION
Ouch! M. Schifrin. il *Forbes* 144:10 D 11 '89
ZAPATA NORNESS, INC. *See* Zapata Corporation
ZAPOROZHYE MOTORWORKS (SOVIET UNION)
Motorworks taps skills of several factories to produce powerplants. il *Aviation Week & Space Technology* 130:49-50 Je 5 '89
ZAPPA, FRANK
about
Frank Zappa. S. Dougherty. il pors *People Weekly* 31:133-4+ My 22 '89
Frank Zappa: garni du jour, Lizard King, poetry and slime [interview; reprint] T. Schneckloth. por *Down Beat* 56:84-5 S '89
ZAPPING OF TELEVISION ADVERTISING
The ad killers. D. Churbuck. *Forbes* 143:76 F 20 '89
Ad makers zap back. A. Marton. il *Channels (New York, N.Y.: 1986)* 9:30-1 S '89

ZARAGOZA, FEDERICO MAYOR *See* Mayor, Federico

ZÁRATE MACÍAS, ROSA MARTA
Cantico de mujer [poem]; tr. by Caroline M. Kisiel. *The Christian Century* 106:561 My 24-31 '89

ZARIN, CYNTHIA
Far Abbotsbury [poem] *The New Yorker* 65:38 Je 19 '89

ZARMATI, SARAH
A city of towers and traditions. il *The Unesco Courier* 42:14-17 Ag '89

ZARZUELA
Spanish steps [Antología de la zarzuela] T. Tobias. il *New York* 22:111 Ap 10 '89

ZASLAVSKIY, ILYA
about
A brave Soviet deputy speaks up for a forgotten minority. C. Phillips. il pors *People Weekly* 32:109-10 O 9 '89

ZASLOFF, MICHAEL
about
Magainin: the penicillin of the 1990s? J. Weber, Jr. il por *Business Week* Special Issue:167 Je 16 '89

ZASLOW, JEFFREY
Mr. Lonelyhearts. il *The New York Times Magazine* p59-60+ O 29 '89

ZASLOWSKY, DYAN
Going against the graze. il *Sierra* 74:30+ S/O '89

ZAVATTINI, CESARE, 1902-1989
about
Obituary
The New Republic 201:25 N 27 '89. S. Kauffmann

ZAYRE CORP.
How Ames is digesting its 'whale'. C. Tucher. il *Business Week* p62 S 11 '89

ZEA, KRISTI
about
Heightening realities. J. Calhoun. il por *Theatre Crafts* 23:58-67 Ap '89

ZEA MAYS *See* Corn

ZEBRA MUSSELS
An alien invasion [proliferating in Lake St. Clair and Lake Erie] A. Steacy. *Maclean's* 102:97 N 6 '89
Showdown at mussel beach [invasion of Lake Erie] G. Cowley. il *Newsweek* 114:66 N 20 '89

ZEBROWSKI, RACHEL WILLIAMS
about
The architects of their own success. A. M. Russell. il pors *Working Woman* 14:81-2+ O '89

ZEFFIRELLI, FRANCO
about
Ghosts [cover story] G. Fitzgerald. il por *Opera News* 54:10-11 O '89

ZEGART, DAN
Solomon's choice. il *Ms.* 17:78-83 Je '89

ZEHME, BILL
A wild and Swayze guy [cover story] il pors *Gentlemen's Quarterly* 59:190-5+ F '89

ZEIGER FAMILY
about
His brother's keeper [Ukrainian peasant A. Suchinsky honored for hiding during WW2] S. Schlegel. *Reader's Digest* 134:112-14 F '89

ZEIN, NADA, AND OTHERS
Calicheamicin γ_1^I and DNA: molecular recognition process responsible for site-specificity. bibl f il *Science* 244:697-9 My 12 '89

ZEITLIN, DENNY
about
Denny Zeitlin. M. Bourne. por *Down Beat* 56:14 F '89

ZELDIS, MALCAH, 1931-
about
Malcah Zeldis at the Museum of American Folk Art. A. F. Collins. *Art in America* 77:151-2 Ja '89

ZELENKO, LORI SIMMONS
Energizing landscape paintings. il *American Artist* 53:66-71 O '89

ZELEPOS, STEVE
about
A hot movie means a bigger piece of the American pie for a Greek immigrant who owns the real Mystic Pizza. D. Chun. il pors *People Weekly* 31:98+ Ja 9 '89

ZELINSKY, WILBUR, 1921-
The 26th Congress of the International Geographical Union. *Focus (New York, N.Y.: 1950)* 39:33-4 Spr '89

ZELL, SAMUEL
about
Sam Zell, the perpetual dealmaking machine. L. Therrien. il *Business Week* p88-9 Je 26 '89
Three raging bulls and two restrained ones. R. King. il pors *Forbes* 144 Special Issue:362+ O 23 '89

ZELLER, GARY
about
Chemist Gary Zeller wins an Academy Award for playing (safely) with fire. K. Hubbard. il pors *People Weekly* 31:98-100 Ap 3 '89

ZELLNER, WENDY
For auto workers, it's team spirit vs. suspicion. il *Business Week* p60-1 Jl 10 '89

ZEMECKIS, ROBERT
about
Back to the future, part II [film] Reviews
Maclean's il 102:70+ D 4 '89. B. D. Johnson
The New Republic 201:26 D 25 '89. S. Kauffmann
The New Yorker 65:139-40 D 11 '89. P. Kael
Newsweek il 114:78 D 4 '89. D. Ansen
People Weekly 32:17 D 11 '89. R. Novak
Time il 134:101 D 4 '89. R. Schickel
Who framed Roger Rabbit [film] Reviews
Video il 13:77 O '89. S. L. Siegel
Video il 13:14-15 O '89. S. Grant

ZÉMOR, OLIVIA
Midwives in Algeria. il *World Health* p15-16 D '88

ZEMPEL, CHIP
Take to the waves! il *Women's Sports & Fitness* 11:66 My '89

ZEMSKY, ROBERT, 1940-, AND STINE, SUSAN B.
On starting a national colloquy. il *Change* 21:7-9 My/Je '89

ZEN BUDDHISM
United States
Livelihood [B. Glassman runs Greyston Bakery in Yonkers, N.Y.] *The New Yorker* 65:28-9 My 22 '89

ZENCEY, ERIC
Apocalypse now? Ecology and the peril of doomsday visions. il *Utne Reader* p90-3 Ja/F '89

ZENITH ELECTRONICS CORP.
Making software work the way he does [J. K. Pearlman's use of computers] C. O'Malley. il por *Personal Computing* 13:77 Ap '89
TV or not TV? il *Time* 134:58 O 16 '89
Why Jerry Pearlman gave up his brainchild [selling Zenith's computer unit to Bull] L. Therrien. il por *Business Week* p35 O 16 '89
Zenith's Jerry Pearlman sure is persistent. L. Therrien. il por *Business Week* p67+ O 2 '89
Zenith's TV picture is getting brighter—for now. L. Therrien. il *Business Week* p41 F 27 '89

ZENITH RADIO CORP.
See also
Zenith Electronics Corp.

ZENITH STAR (SATELLITE) *See* Artificial satellites—Military use

ZENNER, KEVIN J.
The view from a Chilean window. il *America* 161:266-7 O 28 '89

ZENOBI, RENATO, AND OTHERS
Spatially resolved organic analysis of the Allende meteorite. bibl f il *Science* 246:1026-9 N 24 '89

ZENON DANCE COMPANY
Zenon and Jazzdance merge. J. Timmis. il *Dance Magazine* 63:17 Je '89

ZENTAY, DIANA D.
Farewell to Foxy. il *The Saturday Evening Post* 261:22 Ja/F '89

ZEOLITES
'Magic angle' reveals zeolite reactions [work of Jacek Klinowski and Michael Anderson] F. Flam. *Science News* 135:310 My 20 '89
Synthetic zeolites [cover story] G. T. Kerr. bibl il *Scientific American* 261:100-5 Jl '89

ZEPHYR (TRAIN) *See* Railroads—Trains

ZERBO, JOSEPH KI- *See* Ki-Zerbo, Joseph

ZERN, ED
Exit laughing. See issues of Field & Stream

ZERO (THE NUMBER)
See also
Riemann hypothesis

ZERO COUPON BONDS
Good zeros, bad zeros. B. Weberman. il *Forbes* 144:367 N 13 '89
Tax-free zeros. B. Weberman. il *Forbes* 143:337 My 29 '89
Tuition savers for school. T. Tilling. il *Parents* 64:144 Ja '89

ZERO GRAVITY *See* Weightlessness

ZERO OPTION DISARMAMENT *See* Disarmament

ZERRER, CHRISTINE
about
Synchro Energize me! D. Teresi. il *Health (New York, N.Y.)* 21:59 Ap '89

ZERWEKH, ROBERT, 1939-
about
Robert Zerwekh. R. I. C. Fisher. il por *American Artist* 53:44-5 Ag '89

ZETA FUNCTIONS
See also
Riemann hypothesis

ZHAO ZIYANG
about
Deng strikes back [special section] il pors *Newsweek* 113:30-6 Je 5 '89
Zhao fights for his political life. J. Mirsky. *World Press Review* 36:15-16 My '89
Zhao's fall, China's loss. J. H. Fincher. *Foreign Policy* 76:3-25 Fall '89

ZHEJIANG PROVINCE (CHINA)
A pocket of reform. F. Deron. *World Press Review* 36:60 D '89

ZHILIAN ZHANG
China: rethinking the Revolution. il *The Unesco Courier* 42:44-7 Je '89

ZHOU BROTHERS
about
Zhou Brothers: Feingarten. P. Hammond. il *Art News* 88:174 D '89

ZHOU ENLAI, 1898-1976
about
The beatification of comrade Zhou Enlai. D. Wilson. il pors *History Today* 39:7-10 Mr '89

ZHUKOVKA (SOVIET UNION)
Youth
Caviar wishes and vodka dreams [children of the elite] T. Johnson. il *Rolling Stone* p47+ Ap 6 '89

ZHUKOVSKY, EUGENE A., AND OPRIAN, DANIEL D.
Effect of carboxylic acid side chains on the absorption maximum of visual pigments. bibl f il *Science* 246:928-30 N 17 '89

ZHVANETSY, MIKHAIL
Let me tell you . . . il por *Time* 133:115 Ap 10 '89

ZIA-UL-HAQ, MOHAMMAD
about
Was President Zia murdered? J. Barron. *Reader's Digest* 135:59-63 Ag '89
Who killed General Zia? L. Eskin. il por map *Scholastic Update (Teachers' edition)* 121:22-3 Mr 10 '89

ZIADY, HASSAN
An African view of the debt [interview with J. Ki-Zerbo] il por *World Press Review* 36:50 Ag '89

ZICH, ARTHUR
Indonesia. il map *National Geographic* 175:96-127 Ja '89

ZIDOVUDINE See Azidothymidine

ZIEFF, HOWARD
about
The dream team [film] Reviews
American Film il 14:77-8 Ap '89. F. Spotnitz
The New Yorker 65:113-14 Ap 17 '89. P. Kael
People Weekly il 31:18 Ap 10 '89. S. Haller
Video il 13:77 N '89. J. Walker

ZIEGEL, VIC
Smiley's people. il por *Gentlemen's Quarterly* 59:240-3+ Ag '89

ZIEGENHALS, GRETCHEN E.
Digging in the gardens of feminist theology. *The Christian Century* 106:260-3 Mr 8 '89

ZIEGENHALS, HARRIET
Robert Shaw's ministry of music. il por *The Christian Century* 106:311-13 Mr 22-29 '89

ZIEGLER, EDWARD
Uncovering the mystery of the dinosaur. il *Reader's Digest* 135:163-8 D '89

ZIEGLER, TOM
about
Home games [drama] Reviews
America 161:321 N 11 '89. T. P. O'Malley
New York 22:107 O 16 '89. J. Simon

ZIEMBA, W. T.
about
Easy money [cover story] M. Skinner. il *Omni (New York, N.Y.)* 11:42-4+ My '89

ZIEMBINSKA, KATHY
Why I went to the woods. por *The Humanist* 49:22+ Mr/Ap '89

ZIFT See Zygote intrafallopian transfer

ZIKMUND, BARBARA BROWN
Attending a Garden party. *The Christian Century* 106:261 Mr 8 '89

ZILBERGELD, BERNIE
What happy couples say about sex. *Reader's Digest* 134:13-14+ F '89

ZILERI, ENRIQUE
about
Terrorism, inflation, and debt threaten democracy in Peru [interview] A. Balk. il por *World Press Review* 36:33-5 Ja '89

ZIMBABWE
See also
Civil rights—Zimbabwe
Matusadona National Park (Zimbabwe)
Petroleum—Zimbabwe
Public health—Zimbabwe
Wildlife—Zimbabwe
Wildlife conservation—Zimbabwe
Youth—Zimbabwe
Description and travel
Zimbabwe: building a nation. E. B. Washington. il map *Essence* 20:97-108+ O '89
Foreign relations
Mozambique
See Mozambique—Foreign relations—Zimbabwe
Politics and government
One party fits all. B. Berkeley. *The New Republic* 200:15-17 Mr 6 '89

ZIMBABWEAN COOKING See Cooking, Zimbabwean

ZIMERMAN, KRYSTIAN
about
Zimerman's brilliant Liszt. R. Freed. por *Stereo Review* 54:105 Mr '89

ZIMM, BRUNO H.
(jt. auth) See Levene, Stephen D., and Zimm, Bruno H.

ZIMMER, DON, 1931-
about
The face of genius. L. Montville. il pors *Sports Illustrated* 71:58-62+ S 25 '89

ZIMMER, ELIZABETH
The artists' last resort: the Orcas Conference '88. il *Dance Magazine* 63:68-9 F '89
Bebe Miller comes home. il pors *Dance Magazine* 63:34-8 D '89
They just can't stop dancing. il por *Dance Magazine* 63:82-3 Je '89

ZIMMERMAN, DERK
about
TV pros: on the same wavelength. A. L. Ball. il pors *Working Woman* 14:140+ O '89

ZIMMERMAN, PAUL
1995 All-pro team. il *Sports Illustrated* 71:62-3 S 11 '89
Armed and ready. il *Sports Illustrated* 71:30-2+ S 18 '89
The big, bad blue bullies. il *Sports Illustrated* 71:42-4 N 13 '89
Big changes in Big D [cover story] il pors *Sports Illustrated* 70:26-8+ Mr 20 '89
The big Joe and Boomer show. il *Sports Illustrated* 70:36-8+ Ja 23 '89
The Bronk and the gazelle. il pors *Sports Illustrated* 71:128-32+ S 11 '89
Down and dirty. il *Sports Illustrated* 71:46-50 O 16 '89
The free-agency follies. il por *Sports Illustrated* 70:82 Mr 13 '89
The game was lost in the fog. il *Sports Illustrated* 70:22-6+ Ja 9 '89
He quit, for Pete's sake. il pors *Sports Illustrated* 70:60-2 Ap 3 '89
Joe Cool [cover story] il *Sports Illustrated* 70:14-24+ Ja 30 '89
The Majik show. il por *Sports Illustrated* 71:34-9 D 11 '89
Nipped in the Bud. il por *Sports Illustrated* 71:36-8+ O 9 '89
Scouting reports. il *Sports Illustrated* 71:104-10+ S 11 '89
Those Rice Capades. il *Sports Illustrated* 70:18-21 Ja 16 '89
Time to light a fire. il *Sports Illustrated* 71:28-32+ S 11 '89
Where Eagles dare. il *Sports Illustrated* 71:16-21 S 25 '89
White heat. il pors *Sports Illustrated* 71:64-6+ N 27 '89
Wimps they aren't. il *Sports Illustrated* 71:26-8+ D 18 '89

ZIMMERMAN, PETER D.
Evidence of spying. il *The Bulletin of the Atomic Scientists* 45:24-5 S '89
Navy says no PALs for us. bibl f il *The Bulletin of the Atomic Scientists* 45:36-41 N '89

ZIMMERMAN, RAYMOND
about
Yet another company pulls a raid on itself. S. Flack. il *Forbes* 143:107-8 Je 26 '89

ZIMMERMAN, RICHARD ANSON
about
Why Hershey is smacking its lips. J. Weber, Jr. il por *Business Week* p140 O 30 '89

ZIMMERMAN, ROBERT ALLEN See Dylan, Bob, 1941-

ZIMMERMANN, FRANCIS
Lilavati, gracious lady of arithmetic. il *The Unesco Courier* 42:18-21 N '89

ZIMMERMANN, KARL
Fresh from the vat. il *Americana* 17:56-60 Jl/Ag '89

ZIMMERMANN, MARIE
about
Precious metals. D. Saatchi. il por *House & Garden* 161:146-51+ Je '89

ZIMMERMANN, UDO, 1943-
about
Die weisse Rose [opera] Reviews
New York 22:62-3 Je 19 '89. P. G. Davis

ZIMMERMANN, WARREN
Ambassador Zimmermann's message [January 17, 1989] *Department of State Bulletin* 89:25 Mr '89

ZINC AND LEAD COMPANY (NAMIBIA) LTD.
'Worse than Robben Island'. J. Apter. *The Progressive* 53:15-16 Jl '89

ZINC IN THE BODY
Identification of a zinc finger protein that binds to the sterol regulatory element. T. B. Rajavashisth and others. bibl f il *Science* 245:640-3 Ag 11 '89
Think zinc, cure a cold. S. Levin. il *Mademoiselle* 95:64-6 Ja '89
Three-dimensional solution structure of a single zinc finger DNA-binding domain [cover story] M. S. Lee and others. bibl f il *Science* 245:635-7 Ag 11 '89

ZINDEL, PAUL
about
Amulets against the dragon forces [drama] Reviews
The Nation 249:30 Jl 3 '89. M. Hodgson
New York il 22:80 Ap 17 '89. J. Simon
The New Yorker 65:111 Ap 17 '89. E. Oliver
ZINIK, ZINOVIi
Hooks [story]; tr. by Alan Myers. *The New Yorker* 65:56-61
N 6 '89
ZINKEWICZ, PHIL
More insurance for smaller firms. il *Nation's Business* 77:67+
Je '89
ZINMAN, SALLY
about
The anti-shrinks. M. DiLeo. pors *Mother Jones* 14:13 Jl/Ag
'89
ZINN, HOWARD, 1922-
A murderous word [adaptation of address, November 1988]
il *The Progressive* 53:16-17 F '89
ZINO, KENNETH
Are your brakes safe? il *Better Homes and Gardens* 67:60
Mr '89
Fuel for your car. il *Better Homes and Gardens* 68:161
F '89
Safety update: passive restraint systems. il *Better Homes
and Gardens* 67:181 Ap '89
Theft prevention. il *Better Homes and Gardens* 67:164 Ap
'89
ZINSER, ELISABETH ANN
about
The revolution at Gallaudet. H. Orlans. il pors *Change*
21:8-18 Ja/F '89
ZINSSER, WILLIAM KNOWLTON
A visit to Edd Roush [excerpt from Spring training] *The
American Scholar* 58:113-16 Wint '89
ZIOLKOWSKI, KORCZAK, 1908-1982
about
The Ziolkowskis are honoring Chief Crazy Horse, by blasting
out a mountain of a sculpture. D. Grogan. il pors *People
Weekly* 32:105+ D 4 '89
ZIOLKOWSKI FAMILY
about
The Ziolkowskis are honoring Chief Crazy Horse, by blasting
out a mountain of a sculpture. D. Grogan. il pors *People
Weekly* 32:105+ D 4 '89
ZION NATIONAL PARK (UTAH)
The sculpturing of Zion [excerpt] W. L. Hamilton. il *National
Parks* 63:46-7 Jl/Ag '89
Zion's splendors by bike. il *Sunset (Central West edition)*
182:86+ My '89
ZIONISM
See also
International Christian Embassy Jerusalem (Organization)
Blessing both Jew and Palestinian: a religious Zionist view.
Y. Landau. *The Christian Century* 106:1196-9 D 20-27
'89
Charging Israel with original sin [views of B. Morris and
A. Shlaim] S. Teveth. bibl f *Commentary* 88:24-33 S '89
Danke schön, Herr Doktor: German Jews in Palestine. R.
Gay. *The American Scholar* 58:567-77 Aut '89
Israel & American Jews [discussion of September 1988 article,
Where is Zion?] E. Alexander. *Commentary* 87:8-11 F
'89
Jewish guilt and Israeli writers [The writer in the Jewish
community: an Israeli-North American dialogue] R. R.
Wisse. *Commentary* 87:25-31 Ja '89
Jews and geniuses [recent essays on the politics of I.
Stravinsky, A. Einstein, and A. Schoenberg] R. Craft. il
pors *The New York Review of Books* 36:35-7 F 16 '89
Minority report [Y. Shamir's involvement with Nazi Germany]
C. Hitchens. *The Nation* 249:159 Ag 7-14 '89
Our road to Zion: a memoir [family's move from London
to Israel] D. Vital. *Commentary* 87:49-55 My '89
ZIPKIN, JEROME
about
This month, social swell Jerome Zipkin celebrates his seventy-
fifth birthday. M. Thomas. il pors *Vogue* 179:369-70+
D '89
ZIPOLI, DOMENICO, 1688-1726
about
Re-sounding lost Masses. il *Américas* 41 no2:4-5 '89
ZIPPERS
The zipper. J. Berendt. il *Esquire* 111:42 My '89
ZIRCON
New record for world's oldest rocks [work of Samuel A.
Bowring] R. Monastersky. il *Science News* 136:228 O 7
'89
ZISES BROTHERS
about
Abandon ship! H. Rudnitsky. il *Forbes* 144:68-9 Jl 10 '89
**ZITA, EMPRESS, CONSORT OF CHARLES I, EMPEROR
OF AUSTRIA, 1892-1989**
about
Obituary
Newsweek il pors 113:41 Ap 10 '89. N. Darnton
People Weekly il pors 31:50-2+ Ap 17 '89. M. Green

ZITO, ED
about
Charged with practicing the art of the steal, Ed Zito plays
his own Trump Card against Donald. il pors *People Weekly*
32:111 Ag 7 '89
ZITRON, BENJAMIN
about
Lube job, anyone? D. Wechsler. il por *Forbes* 143:83-4 Ap
3 '89
ZOBEL, FERNANDO, 1924?-1984
about
Abstraction on the edge. F. Jarque. il por *Art News* 88:87-8
Mr '89
ZOCHE (MICHAEL) (FIRM) *See* Michael Zoche (Firm)
ZODIACAL LIGHT
Pulverized asteroids and the zodiacal light. il *Sky and
Telescope* 77:242-4 Mr '89
Who first saw the zodiacal light? D. W. Olson. il *Sky and
Telescope* 77:146-8 F '89
ZOG, KING OF ALBANIA, 1895-1961
about
Muttontown's King. *The New Yorker* 65:33-4 S 11 '89
ZOHN, NGAERE MACRAY
about
Far afield. M. K. Griswold. il por *House & Garden* 161:108-15
Ap '89
ZOKOL, RICHARD
about
A game in his mind. L. Rubenstein. il por *Maclean's* 102:65
Ap 10 '89
ZOLOTOW, MAURICE, 1913-
The all-out art of Art Carney. il por *Reader's Digest* 135:76-80
O '89
You must remember these. il *Reader's Digest* 134:129-35
Ap '89
ZOLP, MARSHALL
about
The man who knew too much. J. Crudele. il por *New
York* 22:16 Mr 6 '89
ZOMBIES
Chemistry of voodoo [controversy over W. Davis' research]
M. Kemp. il *Discover* 10:26-8 Ja '89
ZONA PELLUCIDA *See* Ova
ZONE SYSTEM (PHOTOGRAPHY) *See* Photography—Ex-
posure
ZONING
Are you harboring an outlawed business? [laws prohibiting
home-based business] L. Fleming. il *Home Office Computing*
7:12 Ja '89
Hard choice: to zone or not to zone? *Successful Farming*
87:35 mid-Mr '89
New York (State)
See also
New York (N.Y.)—Zoning
ZONING LAW *See* Zoning
ZOO ANIMAL BREEDING *See* Breeding
ZOO ANIMAL PHOTOGRAPHY *See* Animals—Photographs
and photography
ZOO ANIMALS *See* Zoos
ZOO EDUCATION *See* Zoology—Study and teaching
ZOOK, GLEN E.
Radios: over 70 years of technology. il *Antiques & Collecting
Hobbies* 94:48-51 My '89
ZOOLOGICAL GARDENS *See* Zoos
ZOOLOGY
See also
Cryptozoology
Entomology
Natural history
Nomenclature
Fight! Fauna fight! [college sports mascots named for animals]
R. Telander. il *National Wildlife* 27:14-16 F/Mr '89
Study and teaching
Zoo carts with smarts [North Carolina Zoological Park] il
Southern Living 24:32 Ap '89
ZOOM LENSES *See* Lenses, Photographic
ZOONOSES *See* Animals as carriers of infection
ZOOS
The new zoo: a modern ark. N. R. Gibbs. il *Time* 134:50-3
Ag 21 '89
What's new with zoos? [cover story] J. Howard. il *Modern
Maturity* 32:44-9 Ap/My '89
Wilder places for wild things. S. Begley. il *Newsweek* 114:58-9
Jl 17 '89
Zoos with creature comforts. D. H. Dunn. il *Business Week*
p156 Ap 24 '89
Accidents
Anecdotes, facetiae, satire, etc.
Last word [petting zoo animals take their revenge] B. Mangino.
il *Omni (New York, N.Y.)* 11:132 Ap '89
Breeding programs
See Breeding
Design
Back to nature. il *Architectural Record* 177:92-101 Ag '89
Australia
Not-so-wild wildlife. il *Travel Holiday* 171:67 Ap '89

ZOOS—*cont.*

California

See also
Fresno Zoo
Los Angeles Zoo
San Diego Wild Animal Park (Escondido, Calif.)
San Diego Zoo
Lovely cheetahs, meter-saved [use of old parking meters to raise money to fund Guanacaste National Park project in Costa Rica] J. Howard. il *Sierra* 74:26 Mr/Ap '89

Illinois

See also
Lincoln Park Zoo

Louisiana

See also
Audubon Park and Zoological Garden (New Orleans, La.)

Missouri

See also
St. Louis Zoo

New York (State)

See also
Central Park Zoo

North Carolina

See also
North Carolina Zoological Park

Oregon

See also
Washington Park Zoo (Portland, Or.)

Texas

See also
Fort Worth Zoological Park
Houston Zoological Gardens

Washington (D.C.)

See also
National Zoological Park (U.S.)

Washington (State)

See also
Woodland Park Zoological Gardens

ZORO

How to write the perfect fan letter. por *'Teen* 33:84 My '89

ZRNIC, LEONARD

about

Taken to the cleaners in Costa Rica. G. DeGeorge. il por *Business Week* p78 Ja 23 '89
You can run—but maybe you can't hide in Cuba. G. De-George. il por *Business Week* p27 Mr 6 '89

ZRNO, JOHN M.

about

The smart operator untangling the mess at ALC. W. Zellner. il por *Business Week* p137-8 My 15 '89

ZSARNAY, CHRISTOPHER, AND SUMMERHAYS, VINCENT

Building a set with two walls. il *Petersen's Photographic Magazine* 17:54-5 Ja '89

ZUBER, MAURICIO X., AND OTHERS

The neuronal growth-associated protein GAP-43 induces filopodia in non-neuronal cells. bibl f il *Science* 244:1193-5 Je 9 '89

ZUCCHINI *See* Squashes
ZUCCHINI COOKING *See* Cooking—Vegetables
ZUCCONI, MARIO

A crisis of confidence. bibl f il *The Bulletin of the Atomic Scientists* 45:34-7 Ja/F '89

ZUCKER, DAVID

about

All that ZAZ. I. Slifkin. il pors *Video* 13:14 S '89
The naked gun [film] Reviews
Video 13:91 S '89. J. Young

ZUCKER, JERRY

about

All that ZAZ. I. Slifkin. il pors *Video* 13:14 S '89

ZUCKER, STEFAN

New York underground. il *Opera News* 53:20-3 Ja 7 '89

ZUCKERMAN, ALBERT

about

A portrait of Writers House. G. Feldman. il por *Publishers Weekly* 236:21-3 D 1 '89

ZUCKERMAN, SETH

Bioregionalism: saving the earth, one small piece at a time. il *Utne Reader* p86 N/D '89

ZUCKERMAN, SIR SOLLY, 1904-

Converging on peace? bibl f il *The New York Review of Books* 36:26+ S 28 '89
How to kill arms control. bibl f il *The New York Review of Books* 36:35-9 O 12 '89
The Silver Fox [cover story] bibl f il *The New York Review of Books* 35:21-5 Ja 19 '89

ZUKER, MICHAEL

On finding all suboptimal foldings of an RNA molecule. bibl f il *Science* 244:48-52 Ap 7 '89

ZULICH, JAN

Hawaii's school system is one of a kind. bibl f il *Phi Delta Kappan* 70:546-9 Mr '89

ZULU POETRY

See also
Epic poetry, Zulu

ZULUS

Zulu spiritual leader murdered [the Londaukosi Shembe] I. Hexham and K. O. Poewe-Hexham. *Christianity Today* 33:65 Je 16 '89

ZUMBERGE, JAMES HERBERT, 1923-

Ethical and moral responsibilities as faculty [address, September 23, 1988] *Vital Speeches of the Day* 55:199-202 Ja 15 '89

ZUNDELEVICH, NATALIE

The waiting has finally ended. il *The New York Times Magazine* p10+ Ja 1 '89

ZUNES, STEPHEN

Israel's blank check [cover story] il *The Progressive* 53:20-5 N '89

ZUÑI INDIANS

My search for identity. W. Mahkee. il *Scholastic Update (Teachers' edition)* 121:3 My 26 '89

ZUNIGA, DAPHNE

about

Daphne Zuniga: no more Ms. Nice Girl. C. Troy. por *Mademoiselle* 95:100 Ap '89

ZUR, OFER

(jt. auth) See Keen, Sam, and Zur, Ofer

ZURAWIK, DAVID

Bill Moyers. por *Esquire* 112:138-40+ O '89

ZURICH (SWITZERLAND)

Art

Max Bill's birthday blues. E. Beck. por *Art News* 88:45+ F '89

Galleries and museums

See also
Museum Rietberg (Zurich, Switzerland)

Music

See also
Opera—Switzerland

ZURICH STOCK EXCHANGE

The names of Zurich [views of H. Kaufmann] J. Marcom, Jr. il por *Forbes* 143:206+ Je 26 '89

ZUSSMAN, KIM

The secrets of my astrophotography success. il *Astronomy* 17:68-73 Je '89

ZUSSMAN, MARK

She wants to dance with me . . . I'd rather die. il *Seventeen* 48:137-8 Ap '89

ZUSSMAN, SHIRLEY

Sex & health. See issues of Glamour beginning November 1986

ZVEREVA, IRINA

about

Moscow yuppies? Nyet quite! E. B. Fein. il *Mademoiselle* 95:222-3+ O '89

ZVEREVA, NATALIA

about

In search of a net gain. D. Scheiber. il pors *Sports Illustrated* 70:24-6 My 1 '89

ZVEZDOTCHÉTOV, KONSTANTIN, 1958-

about

"In a neutral zone". S. Hochfield. il pors *Art News* 88:47-8 D '89

ZWACK, ANNE MARSHALL

Gourmet holidays: Brussels. il map *Gourmet* 49:72-9+ S '89
The silks of Como. il *Gourmet* 49:54-5+ Ag '89

ZWALLY, H. JAY

Growth of Greenland ice sheet: interpretation. bibl f il map *Science* 246:1589-91 D 22 '89

ZWALLY, H. JAY, AND OTHERS

Growth of Greenland ice sheet: measurement. bibl f il *Science* 246:1587-9 D 22 '89

ZWEIBEL, JOEL B.

about

Workout artist. J. Zweig. il por *Forbes* 144:274-5 Jl 24 '89

ZWEIG, MARTIN

about

"Star" funds: three hits, three misses. M. Schiffres. il pors *Changing Times* 43:59-63 My '89

ZWEIG FORECAST (NEWSLETTER)

Marty Zweig? Or Al Frank? [aftermath of Friday the 13th stock market plunge] M. Hulbert. il *Forbes* 144:368 N 13 '89

ZWERIN, CHARLOTTE

about

Thelonious Monk: straight, no chaser [film] Reviews
Down Beat il 56:6 N '89. A. Lange
The Nation 249:506-7 O 30 '89. S. Klawans
People Weekly il 32:15-16 O 30 '89. R. Novak
Rolling Stone il p19 My 4 '89. C. Stern

ZWICK, EDWARD

about

Glory [film] Reviews
American Visions il 4:24 D '89. R. Faulcon
Essence il 20:30 D '89. M. Southgate
Newsweek 114:73 D 18 '89. D. Ansen
Time il 134:91 D 18 '89. R. Schickel

ZWICK, JOEL

about

Second sight [film] Reviews
  People Weekly 32:29-30 N 20 '89. R. Novak
ZWIEBEL, JAMES A., AND OTHERS
  High-level recombinant gene expression in rabbit endothelial
  cells transduced by retroviral vectors. bibl f il *Science*
  243:220-2 Ja 13 '89
ZWINGER, ANN
  No need to be a Rembrandt. il *Reader's Digest* 134:136-8
  Ap '89
ZWINGLE, ERLA
  Seizing the light: photography's first fifty years. il *National
  Geographic* 176:530-47 O '89

ZYGOTE INTRAFALLOPIAN TRANSFER
  Brave new baby [ZIFT surrogacy]; ed. by Frank Feldinger.
  N. E. Gupta. il *Ladies' Home Journal* 106:140-1+ O '89
ZYGOTES
  Selecting survivors: mother knows best? [selective abortion
  hypothesis; research by Stephen C. Stearns and Jan Kos-
  lowski] D. E. Loupe. *Science News* 136:331 N 18 '89

Anecdotes, facetiae, satire, etc.

  Saving my zygotes. B. Ehrenreich. il *Mother Jones* 14:10-11
  D '89
ZYLA, GAIL
  (jt. auth) See Lindner, Lawrence, and Zyla, Gail
ZZZZ BEST COMPANY
  How Barry Minkow fooled the auditors. D. Akst. il pors
  Forbes 144:126-7+ O 2 '89

BOOK REVIEWS

Time 134:100+ N 6 '89. L. I. Barrett
The Washington Monthly 21:58 O '89. T. Noah
THE AMERICAN DEVELOPMENT OF BIOLOGY. 1988
  BioScience 39:334 My '89. A. Fausto-Sterling
AMIS, K. Difficulties with girls. 1989
  National Review 41:50-1 My 19 '89. J. O. Tate
  The New Republic 201:39-40 Jl 31 '89. H. Lee
  New York 22:73 Ap 17 '89. R. Koenig
  The New York Review of Books 36:12+ Je 15 '89. G. Annan
  The New York Times Book Review 94:11 Ap 2 '89. J. Grossman
  The New Yorker 65:121-4 Je 12 '89. C. McGrath
AMUNDSEN, R. The Amundsen photographs. 1987
  Sea Frontiers 35:61-2 Ja/F '89. G. L. Voss
AMUSSEN, S. D. An ordered society. 1988
  History Today 39:49-50 Ap '89. C. Cross
ANDERSON, B. S. AND ZINSSER, J. P. A history of their own; v1. 1988
  The American Spectator 22:39-41 Jl '89. E. Kristol
ANDERSON, M. J. The American census. 1988
  Scientific American 260:123-5 Ap '89. P. Morrison
ANDERSON, P. Busybodies. 1989
  The New York Times Book Review 94:37 N 26 '89. M. Orth
ANDO, T. Tadao Ando. 1989
  Architectural Record 177:71 O '89. D. London
ANDRES, G. M. AND OTHERS. The art of Florence. 1987
  Antiques 136:1286 D '89. A. Mayor
ANDREWS, L. B. Between strangers. 1989
  Psychology Today 23:76 Je '89. S. Chollar
ANDREWS, M. The search for the picturesque. 1989
  The New York Times Book Review 94:28-9 O 1 '89. A. Broyard
ANNO, M. Anno's Aesop. 1989
  The New York Times Book Review 94:27 Ag 13 '89. A. E. Johnson
ANNO, M. In shadowland. 1988
  The New York Times Book Review 94:27 Ag 13 '89. A. E. Johnson
ANSA, T. M. Baby of the family. 1989
  The New York Times Book Review 94:6 N 26 '89. V. Sayers
ANSON, R. S. War news. 1989
  The New York Times Book Review 94:9+ Ag 27 '89. H. E. Salisbury
APPELFELD, A. For every sin. 1989
  The New York Times Book Review 94:9+ My 21 '89. F. Prose
APPLE, R. D. Mothers and medicine. 1987
  Science 244:843-4 My 19 '89. N. Rogers
APPLEMAN, P. Apes and angels. 1989
  The Humanist 49:41-2 Mr/Ap '89. B. Chambers
APPLICATION OF BIOTECHNOLOGY. 1987
  BioScience 39:185-6 Mr '89. L. V. Giddings
APPLICATIONS OF PLANT CELL AND TISSUE CULTURE. 1988
  BioScience 39:645-6 O '89. E. G. Kirby, III
ARASKOG, R. V. The ITT wars. 1989
  Business Week p14-15 My 1 '89. M. Maremont
THE ARCHITECTURE OF KALLMANN MCKINNELL & WOOD.
  Architectural Record 177:55 Ap '89. C. D. Warren
ARMSTRONG, M. How to be an even better manager. 2nd ed. 1988
  High Technology Business 9:17 Mr '89. M. Estren
ARNSON, C. Crossroads. 1989
  The New York Times Book Review 94:21 N 12 '89. R. Caplan
ARONOWITZ, S. Science as power. 1988
  Physics Today 42:96 N '89. R. N. Proctor
ARP, H. C. AND MADORE, B. F. A catalogue of southern peculiar galaxies and associations. 2v 1987
  Astronomy 17:114+ Ja '89. J. Kanipe
THE ART OF MEASUREMENT. 1988
  Scientific American 261:186-8 S '89. P. Morrison
ARTHUR, W. A theory of the evolution of development. 1988
  BioScience 39:568-9 S '89. G. Freeman
ASCH, F. AND VAGIN, V. V. Here comes the cat! 1988
  The New York Times Book Review 94:31 Je 4 '89. A. Yorinks
ASHBERY, J. Reported sightings. 1989
  The New Republic 201:38-43 O 16 '89. J. Perl
ASHE, A. A hard road to glory. 1988
  The Nation 248:634-6 My 8 '89. N. Mills
ASHER, M. A desert dies. 1986
  Focus (New York, N.Y.: 1950) 39:19 Summ '89. R. W. McColl
ASHMORE, H. S. Unseasonable truths. 1989
  Commonweal 116:710-11 D 15 '89. D. O'Brien
  The New Republic 201:32+ O 9 '89. D. Aaron
  The New York Times Book Review 94:10-11 S 3 '89. R. A. McCaughey
  The New Yorker 65:142-6 O 23 '89. G. Steiner
  Science 246:939 N 17 '89. J. D. Hoeveler, Jr.
ÅSLUND, A. Gorbachev's struggle for economic reform. 1989

The New York Times Book Review 94:25 Ag 13 '89. P. Taubman
ASPECTS OF DECAPOD CRUSTACEAN BIOLOGY. 1988
  BioScience 39:816-17 D '89. L. H. Mantel
ASWELL, E. C. AND NOWELL, E. In the shadow of the giant, Thomas Wolfe. 1988
  The New York Times Book Review 94:14-15 Jl 30 '89. J. Halberstadt
ATEEK, N. S. Justice, and only justice. 1989
  The Christian Century 106:759-61 Ag 16-23 '89. J. M. Wall
  Commonweal 116:712-13 D 15 '89. G. E. Irani
ATKINSON, R. The long gray line. 1989
  Business Week p14+ O 23 '89. D. Griffiths
  National Review 41:49-51 N 24 '89. B. Mitchell
  The New York Times Book Review 94:18-19 O 22 '89. T. Buckley
  Time 134:90+ O 30 '89. S. Kanfer
  The Washington Monthly 21:46+ D '89. J. M. Fallows
THE ATLAS OF BREEDING BIRDS IN NEW YORK STATE. 1988
  The Conservationist 43:52 Ja/F '89. R. E. Budliger
ATWOOD, M. Cat's eye. 1989
  America 160:435-7 My 6 '89. R. Bautch
  Mademoiselle 95:94+ F '89. J. Maynard
  Ms. 17:38+ Mr '89. A. Lurie
  The Nation 248:776-9 Je 5 '89. L. S. Robinson
  The New Leader 72:19 Mr 6 '89. C. Cleaver
  The New Republic 200:38-40 Ap 10 '89. H. Lee
  New York 22:80+ F 13 '89. R. Koenig
  The New York Review of Books 36:50-2 Ap 27 '89. R. Towers
  The New York Times Book Review 94:1+ F 5 '89. A. McDermott
  The New Yorker 65:108-10 My 29 '89. J. Thurman
  Time 133:70 F 6 '89. S. Kanfer
  Vogue 179:238 F '89. K. Pollitt
AUCHINCLOSS, L. Fellow passengers. 1989
  The New York Times Book Review 94:8 Mr 26 '89. I. Colegate
AUSTER, P. Moon palace. 1989
  The New Republic 200:36-40 Mr 27 '89. S. Birkerts
  The New York Review of Books 36:52-3 Ag 17 '89. T. R. Edwards
  The New York Times Book Review 94:8-9 Mr 19 '89. J. R. Kornblatt
  Vogue 179:328 Mr '89. D. Sacks
AUTO RACING/USA. 1988
  Car and Driver 34:21 Ja '89. B. Visnic
AUX ARMES ET AUX ARTS! LES ARTS DE LA RÉVOLUTION, 1789-1799. 1988
  Art in America 77:35+ O '89. E. Lajer-Burcharth
AVERILL, L. J. Religious right, religious wrong. 1989
  The Christian Century 106:1023-4 N 8 '89. E. Jorstad
AYER, A. J. Thomas Paine. 1988
  The New York Review of Books 36:30-1 Ap 13 '89. E. S. Morgan
AYLING, S. E. Edmund Burke. 1989
  The American Spectator 22:43-4 Ap '89. M. Cranston
  Conservative Digest 15:51 Jl/Ag '89. J. B. Graves
  History Today 39:49-50 Mr '89. I. R. Christie
AYRE, J. Northrop Frye.
  Maclean's 102:65-6 D 11 '89. J. Bemrose

B

BABBAGE, C. The works of Charles Babbage. 11v 1989
  Scientific American 261:128 N '89. P. Morrison
BACOT, H. P. Nineteenth century lighting. 1987
  Antiques 136:92 Jl '89. U. G. Dietz
BADANES, J. The final opus of Leon Solomon. 1989
  The New York Times Book Review 94:3 F 12 '89. E. Milton
BADEN, M. M. AND HENNESSEE, J. A. Unnatural death. 1989
  The New York Times Book Review 94:11 Je 25 '89. T. Carpenter
BAHN, P. G. AND VERTUT, J. Images of the Ice Age. 1988
  Scientific American 261:125-6 O '89. P. Morrison
BAILEY, A. The Outer Banks. 1989
  The New York Times Book Review 94:22 Jl 23 '89. P. Kopper
BAKER, N. The mezzanine. 1988
  The New York Review of Books 36:15 Ag 17 '89. B. Leithauser
  The New York Times Book Review 94:9 F 5 '89. R. Plunket
  Newsweek 113:61 Ja 2 '89. D. Gates
BAKER, P. R. Stanny. 1989
  National Review 41:41-2 D 22 '89. J. P. Hart
BAKER, R. The good times. 1989
  The Christian Century 106:1096-7 N 22 '89. R. Liefer
  Harper's Bazaar 122:38+ Jl '89. K. Black
  The New York Times Book Review 94:1+ My 28 '89. W. S. Just
  Newsweek 113:65 Je 12 '89. D. Gates
  Time 133:83-4 Je 5 '89. R. Z. Sheppard

The Washington Monthly 21:55-6 Jl/Ag '89. T. Noah
BAKLANOV, G. ÍA. Forever nineteen. 1989
   The New York Times Book Review 94:29 Jl 23 '89. S.
   Jacoby
BALABAN, J. The hawk's tale. 1988
   The New York Times Book Review 94:39 Ja 29 '89. S.
   Kroll
BALANCING ACTS. 1989
   The New York Review of Books 36:3-4+ Je 1 '89. H.
   Gifford
BALDWIN, N. Man Ray, American artist. 1988
   Art in America 77:35 Ap '89. P. Plagens
BALL, B. Appalachian patterns. 1988
   The Nation 248:425-6 Mr 27 '89. S. Sonnenberg
BALMER, R. H. Mine eyes have seen the glory. 1989
   The Christian Century 106:529-30+ My 17 '89. J. G.
   Stackhouse, Jr.
   Commonweal 116:600-2 N 3 '89. M. Garbey
   The New York Review of Books 36:20+ D 21 '89. G.
   Wills
BALTHASAR, H. U. VON. Dare we hope "that all men
   be saved?"; v1, Prolegomena.
   America 161:432-3 D 9 '89. E. T. Oakes
BALTHASAR, H. U. VON. Theo-drama. 1988
   America 161:432-3 D 9 '89. E. T. Oakes
BANDOW, D. Beyond good intentions.
   Christianity Today 33:63-5 Jl 14 '89. R. M. Christenson
   National Review 41:60-1 My 19 '89. B. Hart
BANKS, R. Affliction. 1989
   The New Republic 201:38-41 S 11 '89. S. Birkerts
   The New York Review of Books 36:46-7 D 7 '89. R.
   Towers
   The New York Times Book Review 94:7 S 17 '89. E.
   Tallent
   Time 134:66 S 4 '89. R. Z. Sheppard
BARASCH, M. Giotto and the language of gesture. 1987
   History Today 39:48 Ja '89. P. Tudor-Craig
BARBER, B. Effective social science. 1987
   Science 244:1497-8 Je 23 '89. I. Berg
BARBER, B. R. The conquest of politics. 1988
   The New York Review of Books 36:42-4 F 2 '89. M.
   Walzer
BARBER, B. R. AND WATSON, P. The struggle for democracy.
   1989
   National Review 41:48+ S 15 '89. H. I. London
BARBER, R. W. AND BARKER, J. R. V. Tournaments.
   1989
   History Today 39:52 D '89. B. Stone
BARBOUR, K. Nancy. 1989
   The New York Times Book Review 94:23 N 26 '89. C.
   Olson
BARGER, V. AND PHILLIPS, R. Collider physics. 1987
   Physics Today 42:78-80 Ja '89. J. L. Siegrist
BARITZ, L. The good life. 1988
   Business Week p16+ F 6 '89. D. B. Moskowitz
   The Washington Monthly 21:58-60 My '89. N. Lemann
BARNARD, R. Death and the chaste apprentice. 1989
   The New York Times Book Review 94:47 O 15 '89. R.
   Cantwell
BARNES, J. A history of the world in 10½ chapters. 1989
   The New Republic 201:40-3 D 4 '89. R. Locke
   The New York Review of Books 36:7 O 26 '89. R. M.
   Adams
   The New York Times Book Review 94:12-13 O 1 '89.
   J. C. Oates
BARNETT, A. AND BIELSKI, N. Soviet freedom. 1989
   The Nation 248:765-7 Je 5 '89. B. Kagarlitsky
BARNHARDT, W. Emma who saved my life. 1989
   New York 22:70 My 22 '89. R. Koenig
BARR, A. H. Defining modern art. 1986
   Art in America 77:39+ D '89. B. Wallis
BARRINGTON, J. History and geography. 1989
   The Nation 249:288-9 S 18 '89. R. Selman
BARRY, D. Dave Barry slept here. 1989
   The American Spectator 22:22-3 S '89. P. J. O'Rourke
   The New York Times Book Review 94:11 Je 18 '89. R.
   R. Lingeman
BARRY, J. M. The ambition and the power. 1989
   Business Week p16-18 N 27 '89. D. Harbrecht
   National Review 41:41-2 D 31 '89. W. Allison
   The New York Times Book Review 94:12 N 19 '89. R.
   Dugger
BARTEL, P. C. The complete Gone with the wind trivia
   book. 1989
   The New York Times Book Review 94:7 D 10 '89. D.
   Finkle
BARTH, R. P. AND BERRY, M. Adoption and disruption.
   1988
   Children Today 18:31-2 Mr/Ap '89
BARTH AND SCHLEIERMACHER. 1988
   The Christian Century 106:565-6 My 24-31 '89. F. Herzog
BARTOSZEWSKI, W. The Warsaw ghetto. 1987
   Christianity Today 33:38-9 Je 16 '89. G. M. Condon
BARZUN, J. The culture we deserve. 1989
   The American Spectator 22:41-4 O '89. J. Simon
   National Review 41:41-2 Ag 4 '89. S. J. Tonsor
BASALLA, G. The evolution of technology. 1988

The New York Review of Books 36:11-12 D 7 '89. D.
   Joravsky
   The New York Times Book Review 94:28 Ap 9 '89. E.
   Regis
   Science 245:991 S 1 '89. C. A. Dunlavy
BASS, A. L. T. Plain Southern eating. 1988
   Smithsonian 19:28+ Ja '89. J. Beam
BASS, R. Oil notes. 1989
   New York 22:49-50 Jl 17 '89. R. Koenig
   Time 134:84 Jl 17 '89. M. Duffy
BASS, R. The watch. 1989
   The New Leader 72:19-20 F 6 '89. M. Kamine
   The New York Times Book Review 94:11 Mr 5 '89. S.
   Lowell
   Wilderness 52:59-60 Summ '89. C. E. Little
BASSOFF, E. Mothers and daughters. 1988
   Mademoiselle 95:52 Ja '89. J. Maynard
BATE, L. How Georgina drove the car very carefully from
   Boston to New York. 1988
   The New York Times Book Review 94:45 My 21 '89.
   A. M. Bregman
BATES, H. E. Elephant's nest in a rhubarb tree & other
   stories.
   The New York Times Book Review 94:43 Je 11 '89. B.
   Baker
BATESON, M. C. Composing a life. 1989
   The New York Times Book Review 94:7-8 N 26 '89. J.
   O'Reilly
BATRA, R. N. Regular economic cycles. 1989
   The New York Times Book Review 94:31 O 29 '89. W.
   N. Parker
BATTEN, A. H. Resolute and undertaking characters. 1988
   Astronomy 17:100-1 Jl '89. R. Burnham
   Sky and Telescope 77:380-2 Ap '89. K. Krisciunas
BAUDRILLARD, J. America. 1988
   The New York Review of Books 36:29-32 Je 1 '89. R.
   Hughes
BAUER, D. Dexterity. 1989
   The Atlantic 263:97-9 My '89. B. DeMott
   Mother Jones 14:45-6 Je '89. J. Kaplan
BAUMAN, Z. Legislators and interpreters. 1987
   Society 26:84-6 Ja/F '89. F. Fehér
BAUMGARTNER, F. J. Henry II, King of France 1547-1559.
   1988
   History Today 39:55 F '89. M. Greengrass
BAUSCH, R. Mr. Field's daughter. 1989
   The New York Times Book Review 94:14 Ag 27 '89. G.
   Lyons
BAWER, B. Diminishing fictions. 1988
   The American Spectator 22:48 N '89. G. McCartney
BAYER, R. Private acts, social consequences. 1989
   The New York Times Book Review 94:23 F 5 '89. K.
   Leishman
   Science 243:1739-40 Mr 31 '89. D. E. Beauchamp
BAYLY, C. A. Indian society and the making of the British
   Empire. 1988
   History Today 39:54-6 Je '89. B. Lenman
BEAN, F. D. AND TIENDA, M. The Hispanic population
   of the United States. 1987
   Monthly Labor Review 112:48 S '89. P. Cattan
BEAUTIES, BEASTS, AND ENCHANTMENT. 1989
   The New York Times Book Review 94:25 D 24 '89. R.
   McKinley
BECK, W. A. AND HAASE, Y. D. Historical atlas of the
   American West. 1989
   USA Today (Periodical) 118:96 N '89. G. F. Kreyche
BECKEL, A. L. Breaking new waters. 1987
   Science 245:200-1 Jl 14 '89. D. W. Schindler
BEDDOES, R. Pal Hal.
   Maclean's 102:103-4 O 30 '89. T. Frayne
BEDFORD, S. Jigsaw. 1989
   The New York Review of Books 36:22-3 Ap 27 '89. G.
   Annan
   The New York Times Book Review 94:13 My 28 '89.
   D. Plante
BEERBOHM, M. Letters of Max Beerbohm, 1892-1956. 1988
   The New York Review of Books 36:42-4 N 23 '89. J.
   J. Gross
BEHR, E. Hirohito. 1989
   The New York Times Book Review 94:8-9 O 8 '89. J.
   W. Dower
BEIJING COLLOQUIUM: CRITICAL OBSERVATIONS VS.
PHYSICAL MODELS ON CLOSE BINARY SYSTEMS
(1985). Critical observations versus physical models for close
   binary systems. 1988
   Science 244:994-5 My 26 '89. R. A. Wade
BEISER, A. Concepts of modern physics. 4th ed. 1987
   Physics Today 42:64-5 D '89. W. F. Hornyak
BELIN, D. W. Final disclosure. 1988
   The American Spectator 22:45-6 Ap '89. K. O'Lessker
   The New York Times Book Review 94:11 Ja 29 '89. R.
   Dugger
BELL, M. S. Soldier's joy. 1988
   The New York Times Book Review 94:3+ Jl 2 '89. D.
   Bradley
BELLOW, S. The bellarosa connection. 1989
   The Nation 249:652-3 N 27 '89. J. Leonard
   The New York Review of Books 36:34 O 12 '89. G. Wills

The New York Times Book Review 94:11 O 1 '89. W. H. Pritchard
Time 134:88 O 2 '89. P. Gray
BELLOW, S. A theft. 1989
The American Spectator 22:47-8 Jl '89. R. T. Marin
Maclean's 102:66 Ap 24 '89. J. Timson
The Nation 248:674-5 My 15 '89. G. Packer
The New York Review of Books 36:50-2 Ap 27 '89. R. Towers
The New York Times Book Review 94:3 Mr 5 '89. J. C. Oates
The New Yorker 65:111-14 My 1 '89. J. Updike
Newsweek 113:80 Mr 20 '89. P. S. Prescott
Time 133:70 Mr 6 '89. P. Gray
BENCHLEY, P. Rummies. 1990
The New York Times Book Review 94:21 D 17 '89. A. T. Wallach
BENEDETTI, J. Stanislavski. 1988
The New York Times Book Review 94:27 Mr 5 '89. E. Proffer
BENEDIKT, M. For an architecture of reality. 1988
Architectural Record 177:81+ My '89. R. Kimball
BENJAMIN, B. Fair play. 1988
National Review 41:58 My 5 '89. B. Hart
BENJAMIN, J. The bonds of love. 1988
The New York Times Book Review 94:30 F 26 '89. E. S. Person
BENJAMIN, W. AND SCHOLEM, G. G. The correspondence of Walter Benjamin and Gershom Scholem, 1932-1940. 1989
The New Republic 201:26-31 D 18 '89. R. Alter
BENNETT, D. H. The party of fear. 1988
The Christian Century 106:568-9 My 24-31 '89. E. Jorstad
The Nation 248:242+ F 20 '89. M. Kazin
The New York Times Book Review 94:24+ Ja 15 '89. M. A. Jones
BENNETT, J. S. Reviving liberty. 1989
The Christian Century 106:694-5 Jl 19-26 '89. A. B. Cook
BENNETT, J. T. AND DILORENZO, T. J. Unfair competition. 1989
Society 27:89-92 N/D '89. B. R. Hasin
BENNETT, W. J. Our children and our country. 1988
The American Spectator 22:40-1 Ja '89. E. Kedourie
Commonweal 116:181-3 Mr 24 '89. D. O'Brien
BENNIS, W. G. On becoming a leader. 1989
Fortune 120:193-4 O 9 '89. W. Lilley, III
BENTSEN, C. Maasai days. 1989
The New York Times Book Review 94:13-14 O 8 '89. L. Dawkins
BERCH, B. Radical by design. 1988
The Nation 248:172-3 F 6 '89. B. Jones
BERESFORD, D. Ten men dead. 1989
Commonweal 116:536-7 O 6 '89. J. Wakelee-Lynch
The New York Times Book Review 94:20 Ap 2 '89. J. Thomas
BERG, A. S. Goldwyn. 1989
America 161:217-18 O 7 '89. R. A. Blake
The American Spectator 22:42-3 Jl '89. T. Mallon
Commentary 87:63-5 Je '89. J. Rosen
Film Comment 25:76-7 Mr/Ap '89. A. Sarris
Gentlemen's Quarterly 59:105+ My '89. K. Turan
Harper's Bazaar 122:120+ Ap '89. S. Schaefer
National Review 41:44-6 S 1 '89. A. Bakshian
The New Republic 200:34-7 My 8 '89. F. Rich
The New York Times Book Review 94:1+ Mr 26 '89. M. Richler
Newsweek 113:80 My 15 '89. J. Kroll
Vogue 179:306+ Mr '89. K. Starr
BERGER, P. Blood season. 1989
Newsweek 114:64 Jl 31 '89. C. Leerhsen
BERGER, T. Changing the past. 1989
The New York Times Book Review 94:12 Ag 27 '89. D. Glover
Time 134:82 S 11 '89. P. Gray
BERGLAND, M. A farm under a lake. 1989
The New York Times Book Review 94:7+ Jl 9 '89. D. O'Brien
BERKE, J. H. The tyranny of malice. 1988
Design for Arts in Education 91:48 N/D '89. S. Hope
BERMAN, L. Lyndon Johnson's war. 1989
The New Leader 72:19-20 Jl 10-24 '89. W. L. O'Neill
The Progressive 53:42-4 Je '89. E. Knoll
BERMEJO, L. M. The spirit of life.
America 161:192-4 S 30 '89. L. K. Dupré
BERNAL, M. Black Athena; v1, The fabrication of ancient Greece, 1785-1985. 1987
The New York Review of Books 36:25-7 Je 15 '89. J. Griffin
BERNARD, A. Blackbird bye bye. 1989
The New York Review of Books 36:26-30 Ag 17 '89. H. Vendler
BERNAYS, A. Professor Romeo. 1989
The New York Times Book Review 94:1+ Jl 23 '89. M. Bradbury
BERNHARD, T. Wittgenstein's nephew. 1989
The New York Times Book Review 94:16-17 F 19 '89. L. Hafrey
The New Yorker 65:132-5 O 9 '89. J. Updike

BERNHARDT, P. Wily violets & underground orchids. 1989
The New York Times Book Review 94:10-11 Jl 9 '89. S. B. Stein
BERNLEF, J. Out of mind. 1988
The New York Times Book Review 94:13 S 17 '89. A. Desai
BERNSTEIN, C. Loyalties. 1989
Commentary 88:53-5 Jl '89. D. Horowitz
Maclean's 102:64-5 Ap 3 '89. B. Came
The Nation 248:489-92 Ap 10 '89. Z. Sklar
National Review 41:48-9 Ap 7 '89. J. Sobran
The New Republic 200:28+ Mr 27 '89. R. Radosh
The New York Times Book Review 94:9+ Mr 5 '89. E. Langer
Time 133:80-1 Mr 20 '89. W. Isaacson
The Washington Monthly 21:58-9 Ap '89. T. Noah
BERNSTEIN, J. The tenth dimension. 1989
Physics Today 42 pt1:65-6 Ag '89. R. H. March
BERRIGAN, D. Daniel Berrigan. 1988
America 161:66-8 Jl 29-Ag 5 '89. F. Wagner
The Christian Century 106:320+ Mr 22-29 '89. L. Sibley
BERRY, T. The dream of the earth. 1988
The Christian Century 106:327 Mr 22-29 '89. D. E. Sherwood
BERRY, W. Remembering. 1988
The Christian Century 106:182-3 F 15 '89. J. E. McEntyre
Country Journal 16:21 S/O '89. D. McCaig
Wilderness 52:59 Summ '89. C. E. Little
BERRYMAN, J. Collected poems, 1937-1971. 1989
The New Republic 201:36-8 O 23 '89. D. Davie
The New York Times Book Review 94:32 O 8 '89. E. Hirsch
BERTON, P. The Arctic grail. 1988
The New Leader 72:17-18 Ja 23 '89. B. Gewen
BESELER DUAL MODE SLIDE DUPLICATOR. 1989
Petersen's Photographic Magazine 17:56 F '89
THE BEST AMERICAN POETRY, 1988. 1988
The Nation 248:747-8 My 29 '89. E. Levy
THE BEST OF HUMANISM. 1988
The Humanist 49:41 Ja/F '89. L. Hyman
THE BEST OF THE WEST 2. 1989
The Nation 249:644-6 N 27 '89. T. Spanbauer
BETWEEN THE TIMES. 1989
The Christian Century 106:1045-7 N 15 '89. M. E. Marty
BEYOND CLERICALISM. 1988
The Christian Century 106:985-7 N 1 '89. S. E. Schreiner
BHADURI, R. K. Models of the nucleon. 1988
Physics Today 42:76 Je '89. G. Karl
BHAGWATI, J. N. Protectionism. 1988
Fortune 119:330 Je 5 '89. D. R. Henderson
BHUTTO, B. Daughter of destiny. 1989
Maclean's 102:64-5 Ap 24 '89. A. Ferrante
The New York Review of Books 36:8-11 Mr 2 '89. I. Buruma
The New York Times Book Review 94:6-7 Mr 19 '89. B. Palling
BIBERMAN, L. M. AND OTHERS. Kinetics of nonequilibrium low-temperature plasmas. 1987
Physics Today 42:65-6 Ap '89. J. L. Cecchi
BICKERMAN, E. J. The Jews in the Greek Age. 1988
The New York Review of Books 36:6+ Mr 16 '89. J. Griffin
BIDER, D. A drop of honey. 1988
The New York Times Book Review 94:18 O 29 '89. L. Komaiko
BIENEK, H. Earth and fire. 1988
The New York Times Book Review 94:26 Ja 15 '89. A. Huyssen
BILLINGS, R. N. AND BROWNELL, W. So close to greatness. 1988
The American Scholar 58:135-6+ Wint '89. P. Roazen
BINCHY, M. Silver wedding. 1989
The New York Times Book Review 94:18 S 10 '89. R. Plunket
BINGHAM, A. M. Portrait of an explorer. 1989
The New York Times Book Review 94:35 O 8 '89. W. F. Buckley
BINGHAM, S. Passion and prejudice. 1989
Mother Jones 14:57+ F/Mr '89. K. Pollitt
The New York Times Book Review 94:13-14 F 5 '89. H. Dudar
The New Yorker 65:118-20+ S 11 '89. L. Harris
Time 133:73 Ja 30 '89. R. Z. Sheppard
BINUR, Y. My enemy, my self. 1989
Business Week p14-15 Mr 27 '89. J. P. Tarpey
Mother Jones 14:56-7 Ap '89. W. Ruby
THE BIOINORGANIC CHEMISTRY OF NICKEL. 1988
Science 244:591 My 5 '89. M. K. Johnson
BIOLOGY OF ANAEROBIC MICROORGANISMS. 1988
Science 245:201-2 Jl 14 '89. R. S. Tanner
THE BIOLOGY OF PARASITISM. 1988
Science 246:1330-1 D 8 '89. M. R. Hollingdale
BIOMEDICAL IMPORTANCE OF MARINE ORGANISMS. 1988
BioScience 39:332-4 My '89. J. Bonaventra
BIOTECHNOLOGY AND MATERIALS SCIENCE. 1988
Science 243:102-3 Ja 6 '89. W. F. DeGrado
BIRDSELL, S. The missing child.

Maclean's 102:68 O 9 '89. J. Bemrose
BIRKS, T. Lucie Rie. 1989
American Craft 49:20 O/N '89. W. MacKenzie
BIRNBAUM, N. The radical renewal. 1988
Commonweal 116:86-7 F 10 '89. J. B. Elshtain
The Progressive 53:40+ O '89. W. E. Connolly
BISSOONDATH, N. A casual brutality. 1989
The New York Times Book Review 94:14 F 26 '89. T.
Keneally
BLACK, C. AND OLIPHANT, T. All by myself. 1989
The New Republic 201:44-5 D 11 '89. M. Dowd
The Washington Monthly 21:56-8 O '89. M. Cornfield
BLACK, G. The good neighbor. 1988
The New York Times Book Review 94:35 Ap 30 '89.
M. Davidson
BLACK, J. You can't win.
The New York Review of Books 36:15-17 Ap 27 '89. L.
Sante
BLACK, J. A. AND ENGLISH, F. W. What they don't tell
you in schools of education about school administration.
1986
Phi Delta Kappan 70:568 Mr '89. J. J. Matula
BLACK, S. T. Child star. 1988
American Heritage 40:12+ Mr '89. G. C. Ward
BLACK FAMILIES IN CRISIS. 1988
Children Today 18:27-8 Jl/Ag '89. D. Weathers
BLACK WORKER. Black workers. 1988
Commonweal 116:475-7 S 8 '89. L. Compa
BLACKBURN, R. The overthrow of colonial slavery, 1776-1848.
1988
History Today 39:56-8 Ja '89. C. Abel
The New York Review of Books 36:29-34 Mr 30 '89.
D. B. Davis
BLACKBURN, R. H. AND PIWONKA, R. Remembrance
of patria. 1988
Americana 17:21-2 Jl/Ag '89. F. Donegan
BLACKMORE, V. AND PAGE, A. Evolution, the great debate.
1989
Christianity Today 33:54 S 22 '89. C. E. Hummel
BLAEDEL, N. Harmony and unity. 1988
Physics Today 42:91-2 S '89. A. P. French
BLAKE, J. Family size and achievement. 1989
Science 245:199-200 Jl 14 '89. D. F. Alwin
BLAKELY, M. K. Wake me when it's over. 1989
Mother Jones 14:39-41 Je '89. S. Faludi
The New York Times Book Review 94:23 Ag 6 '89. M.
P. Nichols
Psychology Today 23:70 Jl/Ag '89. L. Simon
BLAUNER, B. Black lives, white lives. 1989
The New York Times Book Review 94:3+ Jl 9 '89. D.
J. Garrow
BLECHMAN, B. M. AND FISHER, C. S. The silent partner.
1988
The Bulletin of the Atomic Scientists 45:47-8 N '89. T.
Risse-Kappen
BLIGHT, J. G. AND WELCH, D. A. On the brink. 1989
The New York Times Book Review 94:7 Ap 23 '89. M.
R. Beschloss
BLITZER, W. The Pollard affair. 1989
The New York Times Book Review 94:11 My 7 '89. R.
Pear
BLITZER, W. Territory of lies. 1989
Business Week p18-19 Je 5 '89. S. H. Wildstrom
Commentary 88:51-6 Ag '89. E. A. Cohen
National Review 41:44-5 Je 16 '89. J. Sobran
The New Leader 72:21 S 4 '89. Y. Mirsky
The New Republic 200:41-2 Je 5 '89. W. Laqueur
The New York Review of Books 36:8+ O 26 '89. R. I.
Friedman
BLOCK, F. L. Weetzie Bat. 1989
The New York Times Book Review 94:47 My 21 '89.
B. G. Hearne
BLOCK, L. Out on the cutting edge. 1989
The New York Times Book Review 94:46 O 15 '89. G.
A. Haywood
BLOOM, A. D. The closing of the American mind. 1987
The American Scholar 58:123+ Wint '89. S. Hook
BLOOM, H. Ruin the sacred truths. 1989
Commonweal 116:532-3 O 6 '89. D. Castronovo
The New Leader 72:16-17 Ap 3-17 '89. P. Pettingell
The New York Review of Books 36:22-4 Mr 2 '89. D.
Donoghue
The New York Times Book Review 94:18 F 26 '89. C.
H. Sisson
BLOUNT, R. Now, where were we? 1988
The American Spectator 22:48 O '89. J. Mysak
Harper's Bazaar 122:66+ Mr '89. R. Blount
The New York Times Book Review 94:9 Ap 2 '89. D.
Mason
BLUEPRINT FOR THE ENVIRONMENT. 1989
Sea Frontiers 35:380-1 N/D '89. K. Lindeman
BLUMBERG, R. The great American gold rush. 1989
The New York Times Book Review 94:44 N 12 '89. H.
Mayer
BOARDMAN, B. M. Between heaven and Charing Cross.
1988
America 160:273-4 Mr 25 '89. J. D. Boyd
BOAS, N. The Society of Six. 1988

American Artist 53:21+ Ap '89. C. Movalli
Art in America 77:57 My '89. P. Plagens
BOCKRIS, V. The life and death of Andy Warhol. 1989
The New York Times Book Review 94:3+ N 12 '89. P.
Schjeldahl
BODE, B. No bells to toll. 1989
The New York Times Book Review 94:6 Ag 13 '89. R.
Wright
BOEHM, F. AND VOGEL, P. Physics of massive neutrinos.
1987
Physics Today 42:102+ Mr '89. R. G. H. Robertson
BOFF, L. Trinity and society. 1988
The Christian Century 106:391-2 Ap 12 '89. M. K. Duffey
BOGDAN, R. Freak show. 1988
Society 27:87-9 N/D '89. P. Suedfeld
BOGUE, M. Ish Kabibble. 1989
The New York Times Book Review 94:28 Je 11 '89. G.
T. Simon
BOHR, N. H. D. Atomic theory and the description of nature.
1987
Repr. Orig. pub.: Cambridge Univ. Press, 1934
Physics Today 42:105-6 F '89. N. D. Mermin
BOHR, N. H. D. Essays, 1932-1957, on atomic physics and
human knowledge. 1987
Repr. Orig. pub.: Wiley, 1958
Physics Today 42:105-6 F '89. N. D. Mermin
BOHR, N. H. D. Essays, 1958-1962, on atomic physics and
human knowledge. 1987
Repr. Orig. pub.: Wiley, 1963
Physics Today 42:105-6 F '89. N. D. Mermin
BOK, S. A strategy for peace. 1989
The Christian Century 106:993-4 N 1 '89. W. A. Johnson
Commonweal 116:406-7 Jl 14 '89. J. B. Elshtain
The New York Times Book Review 94:8 Mr 19 '89. D.
Schorr
BONDURANT, B. Bob Bondurant on high performance driving.
2nd ed. 1987
Motor Trend 41:35 Jl '89. G. Von Dare
BONES, BODIES, BEHAVIOR. 1988
Science 244:858-9 My 19 '89. M. Cartmill
BONNER, J. T. The evolution of complexity by means of
natural selection. 1988
Science 243:103 Ja 6 '89. M. L. McKinney
BONNETTSTOWN, A HOUSE IN IRELAND. 1988
The New Yorker 65:89-91 Je 26 '89. J. Malcolm
BOONE, K. C. The Bible tells them so. 1989
The Humanist 49:45 Jl/Ag '89. R. L. Evans
BOOTH, W. C. The company we keep. 1988
America 160:538-40 Je 3 '89. M. Spilka
The American Scholar 58:610-12+ Aut '89. B. Bawer
Commonweal 116:92-3 F 10 '89. M. B. Green
The New York Times Book Review 94:3+ Ja 22 '89. A.
Broyard
BOOTH, W. C. The vocation of a teacher. 1988
America 161:325-6 N 11 '89. P. McCormack
BORG, M. J. Jesus, a new vision. 1987
The Christian Century 106:56-7 Ja 18 '89. R. Large
BORK, R. H. The tempting of America. 1990
Business Week p20+ D 18 '89. P. Dwyer
The Nation 249:756-9 D 18 '89. S. Levinson
National Review 41:39-40 D 22 '89. O. G. Hatch
The New Republic 201:118-21 N 6 '89. M. Kaus
The New York Times Book Review 94:15-16 N 19 '89.
J. P. Diggins
BORMAN, F. Countdown. 1988
Ad Astra 1:22 Je '89. G. E. Swanson
The New York Times Book Review 94:37 Ja 8 '89. A.
Salpukas
The Washington Monthly 20:56-8 Ja '89. A. Gibney
BOSWELL, J. The kindness of strangers. 1988
Commonweal 116:474-5 S 8 '89. M. R. Ellsberg
The New Republic 200:31-4 F 27 '89. L. Stone
The New York Review of Books 36:9-12 Je 29 '89. B.
M. W. Knox
The New York Times Book Review 94:16 Mr 19 '89.
M. M. McLaughlin
The New Yorker 64:103-5 F 6 '89. G. Steiner
Newsweek 113:59 Mr 6 '89. D. Gates
BOSWELL, R. The geography of desire. 1989
The New York Times Book Review 94:25 O 1 '89. R.
P. Brickner
BOTHWELL, R. Nucleus. 1988
Physics Today 42:78-9 My '89. A. G. W. Cameron
Science 243:1086 F 24 '89. J. S. Walker
BOURDON, D. Warhol. 1989
The New York Times Book Review 94:3+ N 12 '89. P.
Schjeldahl
BOURGIN, F. The great challenge. 1989
The New York Times Book Review 94:11-12 Jl 30 '89.
P. Maier
BOUTELLE, S. H. Julia Morgan, architect. 1988
American Craft 49:20+ Ag/S '89. J. Bamberger
BOWDEN, J. Jesus. 1989
The Christian Century 106:663-4 Jl 5-12 '89. J. I. Cook
BOWERS, J. Stonewall Jackson. 1989
The New York Times Book Review 94:34-5 S 10 '89.
R. F. Snow
BOWLES, P. A distant episode. 1988

The New York Review of Books 36:6+ N 23 '89. R. Craft
BOWLES, P. Their heads are green and their hands are blue. 1984
    Repr. Orig. pub.: N.Y.: Random House, 1963
    The New York Review of Books 36:6+ N 23 '89. R. Craft
BOX-CAR BERTHA. Boxcar Bertha. 1988
    The New York Review of Books 36:15-17 Ap 27 '89. L. Sante
BOYLE, T. C. If the river was whiskey. 1989
    Mother Jones 14:52 Jl/Ag '89. G. Kamiya
    The New Republic 200:40-1 Je 12 '89. T. LeClair
    The New York Times Book Review 94:1+ My 14 '89. E. Benedict
BOYNE, W. J. AND LEWIS, L. Power behind the wheel. 1988
    Road & Track 40:105 My '89. J. Thompson
BOYS, M. C. Educating in faith. 1989
    America 161:458 D 16 '89. F. D. Kelly
BOZEMAN, T. D. To live ancient lives. 1988
    The Christian Century 106:662-3 Jl 5-12 '89. J. F. Wilson
BRADBURY, M. The modern world. 1989
    Commentary 88:67-70 S '89. J. Rosen
BRADEN, J. Just enough rope. 1989
    The Washington Monthly 21:58-60 O '89. S. McElwaine
BRADFIELD, S. The history of luminous motion. 1989
    New York 22:63 Ag 28 '89. R. Koenig
    The New York Times Book Review 94:11 S 24 '89. F. L. Block
BRADLEY, J. Power lines and other stories. 1989
    The New York Times Book Review 94:38 S 24 '89. M. Childress
BRADY, F. Citizen Welles. 1988
    The New York Review of Books 36:12-16 Je 1 '89. G. Vidal
    The New York Times Book Review 94:16 Ap 23 '89. J. R. Baker
    Time 133:85-6 Ap 24 '89. R. Z. Sheppard
BRAGG, B. Lessons in laughter. 1989
    The New York Times Book Review 94:42 S 24 '89. L. J. Davis
BRAGG, M. Richard Burton. 1989
    New York 22:64-5 F 20 '89. R. Koenig
    The New York Review of Books 36:24-6 Ap 27 '89. J. Osborne
    The New York Times Book Review 94:15-16 Mr 12 '89. D. Kaufman
BRAMS, S. J. AND KILGOUR, D. M. Game theory and national security. 1988
    Society 26:88-91 My/Je '89. A. Rapoport
BRAMWELL, A. Ecology in the 20th century. 1989
    Science 246:1644-5 D 22 '89. R. A. Pois
BRANCH, T. Parting the waters. 1988
    American Visions 4:48+ F '89. R. Koenig
    The Christian Century 106:351-4 Ap 5 '89. R. Westbrook
    Christianity Today 33:33-4 Je 16 '89. T. Stafford
    Commentary 87:62-6 Ap '89. J. Muravchik
    The Nation 248:277-9 F 27 '89. W. H. Chafe
    National Review 41:53-4 F 10 '89. J. Sobran
    U.S. Catholic 54:48-51 My '89. G. M. Costello
BRANDEN, N. Judgment day. 1989
    National Review 41:42-4 Ag 4 '89. J. Sobran
    The New York Times Book Review 94:15-16 Je 25 '89. S. Brownmiller
    USA Today (Periodical) 118:96-7 N '89. R. Terrell
BRANDENBURG, J. White wolf.
    The Conservationist 44:50 S/O '89. R. E. Henshaw
    Natural History p92+ F '89. R. R. Ream
BRANDIN, D. H. AND HARRISON, M. A. The technology war. 1987
    High Technology Business 9:9 Ja '89. M. Estren
BRANDON, H. Special relationships. 1988
    The New York Times Book Review 94:7+ F 12 '89. R. MacNeil
BRANDYS, K. Rondo. 1989
    The New Republic 201:37-9 O 9 '89. S. Barańczak
    The New York Times Book Review 94:30-1 N 19 '89. P. Lopate
BRANTLINGER, P. Bread & circuses. 1983
    Design for Arts in Education 90:46-8 Ja/F '89. S. Hope
BRASSARD, G. AND BRATLEY, P. Algorithmics. 1987
    Byte 14:54+ My '89. E. A. Bobinsky
BRAUNBEHRENS, V. Mozart in Vienna, 1781-1791. 1989
    National Review 41:47-9 D 22 '89. G. Jochnowitz
BREHM, J. J. AND MULLIN, W. J. Introduction to the structure of matter. 1989
    Physics Today 42:64-5 D '89. W. F. Hornyak
BRENNAN, T. E. Public drinking and popular culture in eighteenth-century Paris. 1988
    The American Scholar 58:312-16 Spr '89. E. J. Weber
BRETT, D. W. AND BRETT, E. T. Murdered in Central America. 1988
    America 161:18-20 Jl 1-8 '89. A. T. Hennelly
BREWER, J. The sinews of power. 1989
    History Today 39:56 N '89. C. R. Childs
BREWER, S. G. Do-it-yourself astronomy. 1988
    Sky and Telescope 78:485 N '89. D. B. Hoff
BREYTENBACH, B. Memory of snow and dust. 1989

The New York Times Book Review 94:9-10 O 22 '89. W. M. Kendrick
BRIDGES, H. AND BOODMAN, T. C. Gone with the wind. 1989
    The New York Times Book Review 94:7 D 10 '89. D. Finkle
BRIGGS, G. AND TAYLOR, F. W. The Cambridge photographic atlas of the planets. 1982
    Earth Science 41:29 Wint '88
BRINKLEY, J. The circus master's mission. 1989
    The New York Times Book Review 94:10-11 Jl 2 '89. D. Traxel
BRITISH ECOLOGICAL SOCIETY. SYMPOSIUM (26TH: 1984: SOUTHAMPTON, ENGLAND). Colonization, succession, and stability. 1987
    BioScience 39:192-3 Mr '89. J. H. Bock
BRITTON, F. London delftware. 1987
    Antiques 135:1366 Je '89. J. C. Austin
BROCK, T. D. Robert Koch. 1988
    BioScience 39:493-4 Jl/Ag '89. K. De Ville
BROCK-BROIDO, L. A hunger. 1988
    The New Yorker 65:93-6 Ag 7 '89. H. H. Vendler
BRODSKY, M. Dyad. 1989
    The New York Times Book Review 94:8 D 24 '89. P. West
BRODY, E. Paris. 1987
    The American Scholar 58:151-4 Wint '89. J. Wauck
BROMFIELD, L. Louis Bromfield at Malabar. 1988
    Sierra 74:95-6+ N/D '89. K. Ohnuma
BRONNER, E. Battle for justice. 1989
    Business Week p20+ D 18 '89. P. Dwyer
    The Nation 249:756-9 D 18 '89. S. Levinson
    National Review 41:48+ O 13 '89. J. Sobran
    The New Republic 201:118-21 N 6 '89. M. Kaus
    The New York Times Book Review 94:7 S 10 '89. G. Wills
BROOKE, C. N. L. The medieval idea of marriage. 1989
    History Today 39:52-3 N '89. M. Ingram
BROOKNER, A. Latecomers. 1988
    Commonweal 116:306+ My 19 '89. T. DePietro
    The New York Review of Books 36:34-6 Je 1 '89. R. Dinnage
    The New York Times Book Review 94:3 Ap 2 '89. D. Leavitt
    The New Yorker 65:111-14 My 1 '89. J. Updike
BROOKS, B. No kidding. 1989
    The New York Times Book Review 94:30 Je 25 '89. K. Reed
THE BROTHERS' WAR. 1988
    American Heritage 40:110-11 Ap '89
BROWN, E. G. Public justice, private mercy. 1989
    The New York Times Book Review 94:7 Ag 20 '89. A. Lewis
BROWN, L. Dirty work. 1989
    The New York Times Book Review 94:15 O 1 '89. R. Bass
BROWN, M. AND CAVE, J. A touch of genius. 1988
    History Today 39:55-6 F '89. M. Langley
BROWN, P. R. L. The body and society. 1988
    Commonweal 116:246-7 Ap 21 '89. W. A. Meeks
    History Today 39:57-8 S '89. P. Garnsey
    The New York Review of Books 36:39-41 F 2 '89. W. H. C. Frend
BROWNING, D. S. Religious thought and the modern psychologies. 1987
    Christianity Today 33:33-4 S 8 '89. G. Furr
BROWNING, G. If everybody bought one shoe. 1989
    Business Week p12 Ag 21 '89. D. J. Yang
    The New York Times Book Review 94:9-10 Jl 30 '89. L. Mathews
BROWNMILLER, S. Waverly Place. 1989
    The Christian Century 106:422-3 Ap 19 '89. M. M. Fortune
    The New York Times Book Review 94:13 F 5 '89. P. Barker
    The Progressive 53:44-6 Ap '89. A. M. Davison
BRUCE-BRIGGS, B. The shield of faith. 1988
    National Review 41:56-7 Ja 27 '89. A. M. Codevilla
    The New Republic 200:36-40 F 27 '89. J. E. Nolan
BRUCK, C. The Predators' Ball. 1988
    Commonweal 116:124-5 F 24 '89. R. Jackall
BRÜCK, H. A. AND BRÜCK, M. T. The peripatetic astronomer. 1988
    Sky and Telescope 78:158-60 Ag '89. D. S. Evans
BRUMBERG, J. J. Fasting girls. 1988
    Psychology Today 22:72 D '88. L. Jackson
BRUNDAGE, J. A. Law, sex, and Christian society in medieval Europe. 1987
    History Today 39:59-60 F '89. N. Orme
BRUSHES WITH GREATNESS.
    Maclean's 102:68 S 18 '89. D. Turbide
BRYAN, F. M. AND MCCLAUGHRY, J. The Vermont papers. 1989
    The Nation 249:395-6 O 9 '89. K. Sale
    National Review 41:47-8 S 15 '89. J. Sobran
BRYNNER, R. Yul. 1989
    The New York Times Book Review 94:59 N 12 '89. B. Shulgasser
BRYSON, B. The lost continent. 1989

The New York Times Book Review 94:26 S 17 '89. M. B. Slung

BRZEZINSKI, Z. The grand failure. 1989
The American Spectator 22:43-4 Jl '89. A. Puddington
Commentary 88:64-6 Jl '89. W. Johnston
Commonweal 116:309-10 My 19 '89. W. C. McWilliams
The New York Times Book Review 94:10-11 Mr 26 '89. G. W. Lapidus
Reader's Digest 135:99-104 Jl '89. R. K. Bennett

BUCHWALD, J. Z. The rise of the wave theory of light. 1989
Science 245:82 Jl 7 '89. D. B. Wilson

BUCKEYE COOKERY AND PRACTICAL HOUSEKEEPING. 1988
Repr. Orig. pub.: Buckeye, 1880. With new introd.
The Nation 248:526-8 Ap 17 '89. A. Mendelson

BUCKLE, R. AND TARAS, J. George Balanchine, ballet master. 1988
The American Scholar 58:154-7 Wint '89. D. McMahon

BUCKLEY, K. W. Mechanical man. 1989
Science 244:1386-7 Je 16 '89. J. Reed

BUCKLEY, M. J. At the origins of modern atheism. 1987
America 160:68-9 Ja 28 '89. F. J. van Beeck

BUCKLEY, W. F. On the firing line. 1989
National Review 41:50-2 Je 2 '89. F. W. Friendly
The New York Times Book Review 94:7-8 My 28 '89. R. Rothenberg

BUETOW, H. A. The Catholic school. 1988
America 160:177-8 F 25 '89. C. J. Beirne

BUILDER, C. H. The masks of war. 1989
The Bulletin of the Atomic Scientists 45:46-7 N '89. G. E. Marsh

BUKOWSKI, C. Hollywood. 1989
The New York Times Book Review 94:11 Je 11 '89. M. Haskell

BULL, B. Safari. 1988
Smithsonian 20:236 N '89. M. Kernan

BULL, C. S. The man who shot Garbo. 1989
The New York Times Book Review 94:9 D 17 '89. J. J. Gross

BULLWHIP DAYS. 1988
The New York Times Book Review 94:1+ Ja 8 '89. D. Bradley
Newsweek 113:65 Ja 23 '89. D. Gates

BUNCH, C. Passionate politics. 1987
The Humanist 49:45-6 Jl/Ag '89. E. J. Bader

BUNDY, M. Danger and survival. 1988
The American Spectator 22:47 N '89. E. N. Luttwak
Commentary 87:42-7 Mr '89. P. Glynn
Foreign Affairs 68:178-82 Spr '89. G. F. Treverton
National Review 41:42-3 Mr 24 '89. F. McDonald
The New Republic 200:38-40 Je 12 '89. L. Freedman
The New York Review of Books 36:28-31 F 2 '89. S. Hoffmann
The Progressive 53:38-40 S '89. R. A. Falk

BURCH, E. S. The Eskimos. 1988
USA Today (Periodical) 117:95-6 Ja '89. G. F. Kreyche

BURGE, G. M. The anointed community. 1987
Christianity Today 33:59-60 F 3 '89. C. S. Gaede

BURGESS, A. Any old iron. 1989
The New York Review of Books 36:35-6 Mr 30 '89. D. Donoghue
The New York Times Book Review 94:12 F 26 '89. S. F. Schaeffer
Time 133:73 Ja 30 '89. J. Skow

BURGESS, A. The devil's mode.
The New York Times Book Review 94:38 D 10 '89. H. Benedict

BURGESS, E. Uranus and Neptune. 1988
Sky and Telescope 77:268-9 Mr '89. M. Washburn

BURKE, D. L. A new academic marketplace. 1988
Change 21:57-60 S/O '89. S. P. Dresch

BURKE, J. L. Black cherry blues. 1989
Newsweek 114:72 O 2 '89. P. S. Prescott

BURKE, K. AND COWLEY, M. The selected correspondence of Kenneth Burke and Malcolm Cowley, 1915-1981. 1988
The New Republic 200:34-7 Mr 13 '89. D. Aaron

BURKERT, N. E. Valentine & Orson.
The New York Times Book Review 94:52 N 12 '89. F. Prose

BURLEIGH, M. Germany turns eastwards. 1988
History Today 39:48-9 O '89. P. Preston

BURLINGHAM, M. J. The last Tiffany. 1989
The New Yorker 65:82-4 Jl 31 '89. N. Bliven

BURNETT, J. Adirondack snow flurries. 1987
The Conservationist 43:53 My/Je '89. J. Dygert

BURNS, G. All my best friends. 1989
The New York Times Book Review 94:13-14 N 5 '89. D. Nasaw

BURNS, G. Gracie. 1988
The Saturday Evening Post 261:58-9 Mr '89. M. G. Stoddard

BURNS, J. M. The American experiment; v3, The crosswinds of freedom. 1989
The American Spectator 22:37-8 S '89. V. Gold
The New York Times Book Review 94:14 My 14 '89. J. A. Garraty

BURTCHAELL, J. T. The giving and taking of life. 1989

America 161:241-2 O 14 '89. J. N. Lapsley

BURTON, S. Impossible dream. 1988
The New York Times Book Review 94:13 My 21 '89. J. M. Hamilton
Newsweek 113:64 Ap 10 '89. C. Bogert
Time 133:76-7 Ap 17 '89. H. G. Chua-Eoan
U.S. Catholic 54:48-51 O '89. G. M. Costello

BURUMA, I. God's dust. 1989
The American Spectator 22:45-6 O '89. W. McGurn
The New York Review of Books 36:52-4 S 28 '89. J. Sterba
The New York Times Book Review 94:10 Jl 9 '89. J. M. Fallows

BUSCH, D. D. Supercharging OS/2. 1988
Byte 14:54+ Mr '89. G. M. Vose

BUSCH, F. Absent friends. 1989
The New York Times Book Review 94:7 My 7 '89. S. Hearon

BUSH, M. Families in distress. 1988
Children Today 18:32-inside back cover Ja/F '89. J. Bryant

BUSI, A. Seminar on youth. 1988
The New York Times Book Review 94:13 Ag 13 '89. A. Cancogni

BUSSELLE, R. An exposure of the heart. 1988
The New York Times Book Review 94:11-12 Mr 12 '89. S. Jacoby

BUT IS IT SCIENCE? 1988
BioScience 39:195 Mr '89. E. Holtzman

BUTLER, J. Nightshade. 1989
The New York Times Book Review 94:7 S 3 '89. G. Benford

BUTLER, R. O. The deuce. 1989
The New York Times Book Review 94:10 S 3 '89. S. Spencer

BUTT, R. A history of parliament. 1989
History Today 39:56 S '89. C. T. Allmand

BYARS, B. C. Bingo Brown and the language of love. 1989
The New York Times Book Review 94:34 O 8 '89. F. Flagg

C

CAFFREY, M. M. Ruth Benedict. 1989
The New York Times Book Review 94:20+ My 7 '89. M. B. Norton
Science 244:369-70 Ap 21 '89. R. Handler

CAGIN, S. AND DRAY, P. We are not afraid. 1988
The Nation 248:202-4 F 13 '89. N. Mills

CAHILL, K. M. A bridge to peace.
America 160:156-7 F 18 '89. J. P. Fitzpatrick

CAIN, B. E. The basics of technical communicating. 1988
BioScience 39:401-2 Je '89. B. Gastel

CALLAHAN, D. What kind of life. 1990
The New York Times Book Review 94:1+ D 24 '89. C. E. Rosenberg

CALLAHAN, J. F. In the African-American grain. 1987
The New Republic 200:41-2 F 27 '89. K. W. Benston

CALVINO, I. Six memos for the next millennium. 1988
Commonweal 116:339-41 Je 2 '89. P. D. Baumann

CALVINO, I. Under the jaguar sun. 1988
The New Leader 72:19-20 Ja 9 '89. A. Wade

THE CAMBRIDGE HISTORY OF CHINA; v14 pt1, The People's Republic. 1987
History Today 39:58 Ja '89. W. Wallace

CAMERON, J. AND CHRISTMAN, P. J. The art of Gone with the wind. 1989
The New York Times Book Review 94:7 D 10 '89. D. Finkle

CAMERON, J. M. Nuclear Catholics and other essays. 1990
National Review 41:43-5 D 31 '89. M. D. Aeschliman

CAMERON, R. W. The minority executives' handbook. 1989
Black Enterprise 20:17 O '89. M. E. Howard

CAMERON, S. Ottawa inside out.
Maclean's 102:109-10 O 30 '89. C. Lynch

CAMERON, S. Thinking in Henry James. 1989
The New York Review of Books 36:21-3 D 7 '89. J. Bayley

CAMP, J. The fool's run. 1989
The New York Times Book Review 94:52 O 15 '89. F. Siegel

CAMPBELL, B. M. Sweet summer. 1989
The New York Times Book Review 94:47 Je 11 '89. B. Mukherjee

CAMPBELL, J. The improbable machine. 1989
The New York Times Book Review 94:12-13 D 24 '89. G. Johnson

CAMPBELL, J. The power of myth. 1988
Christianity Today 33:61-2 Jl 14 '89. T. C. Muck

CAMPBELL, W. D. The convention.
The Christian Century 106:88-9 Ja 25 '89. A. L. Pratt

CAMPORESI, P. The incorruptible flesh. 1988
History Today 39:59-61 Ag '89. P. Biller

CANAVAN, F. Edmund Burke. 1987
National Review 41:61 My 19 '89. D. Ritchie

CANNADINE, D. The pleasures of the past. 1989
The New York Times Book Review 94:11 N 19 '89. E. Hower

CANTELON, J. Theology for non-theologians. 1988
Christianity Today 33:66 Ja 13 '89. R. Jolley

The Bulletin of the Atomic Scientists 45:47-8 N '89. T. Risse-Kappen

CLANCY, T. Clear and present danger. 1989
The New York Times Book Review 94:9 Ag 13 '89. D. Wise
Newsweek 114:60 Ag 21 '89. E. Thomas
Time 134:66-8 Ag 21 '89. W. Shapiro

CLARE, OF ASSISI, SAINT. Clare of Assisi. 1988
The Christian Century 106:728-9 Ag 2-9 '89. V. Rebeck

CLARK, B. R. The academic life. 1987
Change 21:57-60 S/O '89. S. P. Dresch

CLARK, E. The want makers. 1989
The New Republic 200:37-41 My 8 '89. A. Sullivan
The New York Times Book Review 94:14 Jl 2 '89. J. Williamson

CLARK, J. AND PICARD, J. Laying down the law. 1989
The New York Times Book Review 94:14 Jl 9 '89. E. L. Sturz

CLARK, M. H. The Anastasia syndrome, and other stories. 1989
The New York Times Book Review 94:82 D 3 '89. B. Kent

CLARK, P. The Soviet manned space program. 1988
Ad Astra 1:39 Mr '89. S. Arenstein

CLARK, R. W. Lenin. 1988
The New York Times Book Review 94:14 F 5 '89. A. Stent

CLARK, T. J. The painting of modern life. 1986
The Nation 248:494-8 Ap 10 '89. P. Mattick, Jr.

CLARKE, G. Capote. 1988
USA Today (Periodical) 117:95 Mr '89. M. Smelstor

CLASSICAL NOVAE. 1989
Science 246:1183 D 1 '89. R. E. Williams

CLÉMENT, C. Opera, or, The undoing of women. 1988
The New York Times Book Review 94:3 Ja 1 '89. P. A. Robinson

CLEWLOW, C. A woman's guide to adultery. 1989
The New York Times Book Review 94:11 Mr 26 '89. M. Seymour

CLIFFORD, G. J. AND GUTHRIE, J. W. Ed school. 1988
Change 21:60-2 Ja/F '89. B. R. Clark

CLIFFORD, J. The predicament of culture. 1988
The Nation 248:350-2 Mr 13 '89. M. Di Leonardo

CLIFTON, L. Good woman. 1987
The New York Times Book Review 94:24 F 19 '89. L. Rosenberg

CLIFTON, L. Next. 1987
The New York Times Book Review 94:24 F 19 '89. L. Rosenberg

CLIMO, S. The Egyptian Cinderella. 1989
The New York Times Book Review 94:50 N 12 '89. J. D. Zipes

CLINGMAN, S. The novels of Nadine Gordimer. 1986
The New York Review of Books 36:12-14 Mr 30 '89. N. Ascherson

CLODFELTER, M. The limits of air power. 1989
The New York Times Book Review 94:18 Jl 16 '89. R. Halloran

CLOTH AND HUMAN EXPERIENCE. 1989
The New York Times Book Review 94:15 D 17 '89. I. Poliski

COATES, J. F. AND JARRATT, J. What futurists believe. 1989
The Futurist 23:27-8 N/D '89. F. S. Hopkins

COBBAN, A. B. The medieval English universities. 1988
History Today 39:53 Mr '89. D. Hay

CODEVILLA, A. M. While others build. 1988
The New Republic 200:36-40 F 27 '89. J. E. Nolan

COHEN, B. AND OTHERS. Trylon and perisphere. 1989
American Heritage 40:116-18 My/Je '89

COHEN, M. In darkness born. 1987
Sky and Telescope 78:163-4 Ag '89. P. A. Wehinger

COHEN, N. Gravity's lens. 1988
Astronomy 17:100-1 F '89. J. Kanipe
Sky and Telescope 77:162 F '89. D. Goldsmith

COHEN, S. F. AND VANDEN HEUVEL, K. Voices of glasnost. 1989
The New York Times Book Review 94:25 N 26 '89. H. Goodman

COHEN, W. S. AND MITCHELL, G. J. Men of zeal. 1988
America 160:202 Mr 4 '89. R. F. Drinan
The American Spectator 22:41-2 Ja '89. H. J. Hyde

COHN, J. Creating America. 1989
The New York Times Book Review 94:21 O 8 '89. M. Nichols

COLBERT, E. H. Digging into the past. 1989
Science 245:992-3 S 1 '89. J. T. Gregory

COLBY, W. E. Lost victory. 1989
The New York Times Book Review 94:18-19 N 12 '89. R. Manning

COLE, L. A. Clouds of secrecy. 1987
Science 243:552-3 Ja 27 '89. R. A. Falk

COLEMAN, J. Exit the rainmaker. 1989
New York 22:62-3 Ag 28 '89. R. Koenig
The New York Times Book Review 94:30 S 10 '89. J. Katzenbach

COLEMAN, P. The liberal conspiracy. 1989
National Review 41:60-1 S 29 '89. R. Radosh

The New Leader 72:18-20 N 13 '89. J. P. Roche
The New York Times Book Review 94:13-14 Ag 27 '89. D. M. Oshinsky

COLES, R. The call of stories. 1989
The New York Times Book Review 94:38 F 26 '89. H. S. Bevington

COLES, R. Harvard diary. 1988
The American Spectator 22:40-1 Mr '89. F. X. Rocca
National Review 41:62 Je 2 '89. T. S. Molnar

COLES, R. That red wheelbarrow. 1988
The American Spectator 22:40-1 Mr '89. F. X. Rocca
The Christian Century 106:392-3 Ap 12 '89. B. A. Ronda

COLLENDER, S. E. The guide to the federal budget: fiscal 1990.
The Washington Monthly 21:59-60 Jl/Ag '89. N. Martin

COLLIER, J. L. Benny Goodman and the Swing Era. 1989
The New York Times Book Review 94:24+ D 3 '89. M. Miles

COLLIER, P. AND HOROWITZ, D. Destructive generation. 1989
The American Spectator 22:42-3 Ag '89. G. Szamuely
Business Week p16-17 Ap 3 '89. B. Nussbaum
The Nation 249:630-2 N 27 '89. W. Breines
National Review 41:43-4 Mr 24 '89. J. Sobran
The New Republic 200:26-32+ Ap 24 '89. P. Berman
The New York Times Book Review 94:18 Ap 23 '89. D. Burner
The Progressive 53:37-8 Ag '89. S. Landau
The Washington Monthly 21:44-6 My '89. H. Hertzberg

COLLINS, B. My life with the pros. 1989
The New York Times Book Review 94:15 Je 11 '89. R. B. Sewall

COLLINSON, P. The birthpangs of Protestant England. 1988
History Today 39:53-4 O '89. D. M. Loades

COLSON, C. W. Against the night. 1989
National Review 41:52-3 S 15 '89. B. Miner

COLTER, C. The amoralists & other tales. 1988
The New York Times Book Review 94:16 F 12 '89. B. Atkinson

COLTON, E. O. The Jackson phenomenon. 1989
The Nation 249:287-8 S 18 '89. M. L. Sifry
The New York Times Book Review 94:11 Jl 16 '89. E. Cose

COLUMBIA LITERARY HISTORY OF THE UNITED STATES. 1987
History Today 39:52 F '89. D. K. Adams
National Review 41:51-2 My 5 '89. M. E. Bradford

COLUMBUS, C. The diary of Christopher Columbus's first voyage to America, 1492-1493. 1988
Sea Frontiers 35:254 Jl/Ag '89. C. M. Dugger, Jr.

COMBAT FLEETS OF THE WORLD 1988/89.
Scientific American 260:123 Ap '89. P. Morrison

COMBLIN, J. The Holy Spirit and liberation. 1989
The Christian Century 106:964-6 O 25 '89. G. Furr

COMER, D. AND FOSSUM, T. V. Operating system design: (PC edition); v1, The Xinu approach. 1988
Byte 14:58+ My '89. R. Grehan

THE COMMONWEALTH OF SCIENCE. 1988
Science 245:1400-1 S 22 '89. R. M. May

THE COMMUNITY ECOLOGY OF SEA OTTERS. 1988
Science 243:954-5 F 17 '89. K. P. Sebens

THE COMPARATIVE PSYCHOLOGY OF AUDITION. 1989
Science 246:1183 D 1 '89. R. R. Fay

THE COMPLEMENT SYSTEM. 1988
BioScience 39:47-8 Ja '89. J. M. Weiler

COMPLEX INTERACTIONS IN LAKE COMMUNITIES. 1988
BioScience 39:495-6 Jl/Ag '89. F. B. Trama

CONCEPTS OF ECOSYSTEM ECOLOGY. 1988
Science 243:825-6 F 10 '89. P. M. Vitousek

CONFERENCE ON GENETIC MANIPULATION OF WOODY PLANTS (1987: MICHIGAN STATE UNIVERSITY). Genetic manipulation of woody plants. 1988
BioScience 39:264-5 Ap '89. N. Bell

CONFLICT IN EARLY STUART ENGLAND. 1989
History Today 39:50-1 O '89. A. Fletcher

CONN, P. J. Literature in America. 1989
The New York Times Book Review 94:28 O 8 '89. S. Gubar

CONNOR, D. R. Benny Goodman. 1988
Down Beat 56:55 F '89. J. McDonough

CONOVER, A. Caresse Crosby. 1989
The New Leader 72:22-3 N 13 '89. C. Cleaver

CONQUEST, R. Stalin and the Kirov murder. 1989
National Review 41:48 Mr 24 '89. C. Williamson
The New York Times Book Review 94:13 Ja 15 '89. P. H. Solomon

CONRAD, J. Heart of darkness. 1989
The Christian Century 106:1025-6 N 8 '89. N. C. Mindrum

CONRAD, P. Behind the mountain. 1989
The New York Times Book Review 94:14-15 Ap 9 '89. C. Kizer

CONRAD, P. The tub people. 1989
The New York Times Book Review 94:29 N 12 '89. R. Krulwich

THE CONSEQUENCES OF ECONOMIC RHETORIC. 1988
Science 244:839-40 My 19 '89. G. J. Stigler

CONSERVATION BIOLOGY IN HAWAI'I. 1989

Science 244:854-5 My 19 '89. L. F. Huenneke
CONSISTENT ETHIC OF LIFE. 1988
America 160:89-92 F 4 '89. J. R. Kelly
CONTINENTAL FLOOD BASALTS. 1988
Science 244:721-2 My 12 '89. S. A. Morse
CONTINENTAL SHELVES. 1988
Science 243:824-5 F 10 '89. L. S. Incze
CONVERSATION IN BIOMOLECULAR STEREODYNAMICS (5TH: 1987: STATE UNIVERSITY OF NEW YORK AT ALBANY). Structure & expression. 3v 1988
BioScience 39:331-2 My '89. R. E. Dickerson
CONWAY, J. K. The road from Coorain. 1989
The New York Times Book Review 94:3 My 7 '89. V. Klinkenborg
COOK, B. J. Bureaucratic politics and regulatory reform. 1988
Environment 31:25 S '89. G. Majone
COOK, D. Forging the alliance. 1989
The New York Times Book Review 94:9 My 21 '89. D. Middleton
COOKE, A. America observed. 1988
Commonweal 116:707-10 D 15 '89. P. D. Baumann
National Review 41:46+ F 24 '89. W. F. Buckley
COOPER, D. Closer. 1989
Mother Jones 14:44-5 Je '89. D. Bellm
The New York Review of Books 36:52-3 Ag 17 '89. T. R. Edwards
COOPER, D. D. Thomas Merton's art of denial. 1989
America 161:267-73+ O 21 '89. W. H. Shannon
COOPER, J. Players.
The New York Times Book Review 94:26 Ap 30 '89. J. Jarvis
COPELAND, A. The golden thread. 1989
The New York Times Book Review 94:24 O 22 '89. P. Hampl
COPING WITH UNCERTAINTY IN FOOD SUPPLY. 1988
Science 243:953-4 F 17 '89. N. Howell
CORAL REEFS OF THE WORLD. 3v 1989
The Atlantic 263:87+ Je '89. K. Brower
CORNWELL, J. A thief in the night. 1989
America 161:488-9 D 23-30 '89. G. Higgins
The New York Times Book Review 94:15 N 5 '89. E. C. Kennedy
CORSI, P. The age of Lamarck. 1989
Science 243:243-4 Ja 13 '89. C. Limoges
COSE, E. The press. 1989
The New York Times Book Review 94:9 Ap 9 '89. R. Rosenbaum
COSENTINO, A. California Ferraris.
Motor Trend 41:37 Ja '89. V. Verde
COSSINS, A. R. AND BOWLER, K. Temperature biology of animals. 1987
BioScience 39:197-8 Mr '89. D. C. Wilhoft
COTTON, M. The Le Mans 24-hours race. 1989
Motor Trend 41:40 Je '89. G. Von Dare
COULONGES, H. Farewell, Dresden. 1989
The New York Times Book Review 94:19 Mr 12 '89. A. Barnet
COUSTEAU, J. Y. AND PACCALET, Y. Jacques Cousteau—whales. 1988
Natural History p76-81 Mr '89. R. R. Reeves
COWART, J. AND HAMILTON, J. Georgia O'Keeffe. 1987
The New Republic 200:41-5 Ja 30 '89. E. Abrahams
COX, D. J. AND OZOGA, J. J. Whitetail country. 1988
The Conservationist 43:52 Mr/Ap '89. H. W. Trimm
COX, H. G. Many mansions. 1988
The Christian Century 106:22-3 Ja 4-11 '89. R. Quebedeaux
The New York Times Book Review 94:26 Ja 29 '89. J. M. Washington
Psychology Today 23:30 Jl/Ag '89. E. Stark
COX, H. G. The silencing of Leonardo Boff. 1988
Commonweal 116:52-4 Ja 27 '89. J. G. Donders
COZZENS, S. E. Social control and multiple discovery in science. 1989
Science 246:1329-30 D 8 '89. S. Panem
CP VIOLATIONS. 1988
Science 245:1124-5 S 8 '89. J. F. Donoghue
CRACE, J. The gift of stones. 1989
The New Leader 72:20-1 Mr 20 '89. M. Kamine
The New York Times Book Review 94:12 Jl 16 '89. J. Smiley
CRAIG, G. A. The triumph of liberalism. 1989
The New York Review of Books 36:56-9 O 26 '89. L. Gossman
The New York Times Book Review 94:15 Je 18 '89. R. Grew
CRANE, S. The correspondence of Stephen Crane. 2v 1988
The New York Review of Books 36:31-4 Mr 16 '89. C. E. G. Benfey
CRANE, S. Prose and poetry. 1984
The New York Review of Books 36:31-4 Mr 16 '89. C. E. G. Benfey
CREASY, R. Cooking from the garden. 1988
Country Journal 16:20 F '89. K. Haedrich
CREMIN, L. A. American education, the metropolitan experience, 1876-1980. 1988
America 160:177 F 25 '89. C. J. Beirne
CRICK, F. What mad pursuit. 1988

Physics Today 42:68+ Jl '89. P. W. Anderson
Science 243:1219-20 Mr 3 '89. T. H. Jukes
CRISMAN, K. J. The Eagle. 1987
Sea Frontiers 35:125-6 Mr/Ap '89. D. S. Schwartz
CRISPELL, K. R. AND GOMEZ, C. F. Hidden illness in the White House. 1988
The New York Times Book Review 94:17 Ja 1 '89. H. L. Abrams
A CRITICAL DICTIONARY OF THE FRENCH REVOLUTION. 1989
The New York Times Book Review 94:12 S 10 '89. L. A. Hunt
CRITTENDEN, A. Sanctuary. 1988
The New Republic 200:32-4+ F 6 '89. C. Lane
CROME, L. Unbroken. 1989
The Nation 248:639-40 My 8 '89. M. Schwebel
CROPPER, E. Pietro Testa, 1612-1650. 1988
The New York Review of Books 36:36-8 Jl 20 '89. F. Haskell
CROSBY, D. AND GOTTLIEB, C. Long time gone. 1988
Mademoiselle 95:123 Mr '89. J. Maynard
CROSBY, M. House of disciples. 1988
The Christian Century 106:265+ Mr 8 '89. W. C. Salzmann
CROSS, A. A trap for fools. 1989
Newsweek 113:65+ Ap 10 '89. K. Ames
CROSS, T. L. Birds of the sea, shore and tundra. 1988
Natural History p96+ O '89. M. Harwood
CROSSROADS OF CONTINENTS. 1988
Science 244:865-7 My 19 '89. S. Krech
CROUCH, T. D. The Bishop's boys. 1989
American Heritage 40:152-3 N '89
CROUSE, J. AND TRUSHEIM, D. The case against the SAT. 1988
Design for Arts in Education 90:48 Mr/Ap '89. S. Hope
CROUTHAMEL, J. L. Bennett's New York herald and the rise of the popular press. 1989
The New York Times Book Review 94:42 O 8 '89. J. Ziomek
CROUTIER, A. L. Harem. 1989
Harper's Bazaar 122:50+ Je '89. M. Paley
The New York Times Book Review 94:22 Je 11 '89. B. Small
CROZIER, R. Inventing the landscape. 1989
American Artist 53:68+ S '89. D. C. Hines
CRUISE-O-MATIC. 1988
Motor Trend 41:39 O '89. G. Von Dare
CRUM, H. A. A focus on peatlands and peat mosses. 1988
BioScience 39:406-8 Je '89. J. Ehrenfeld
CRUZ, A., JR. Memoirs of a counterrevolutionary. 1989
The American Spectator 22:44 O '89. F. Barnes
The New York Times Book Review 94:11 O 15 '89. A. J. Glass
CUDAHY, S. Nectar at noon.
The New York Times Book Review 94:12 O 8 '89. N. Sonenberg
CULLINEY, J. L. Islands in a far sea. 1988
Science 244:854-5 My 19 '89. L. F. Huenneke
CULT ARCHAEOLOGY AND CREATIONISM. 1987
Society 26:91-3 Mr/Ap '89. M. E. Levin
CUMMINGS, S. Mark Twain and science. 1988
The New York Review of Books 36:39-44 Jl 20 '89. F. C. Crews
CUNLIFFE, B. Greeks, Romans and barbarians. 1988
The New York Review of Books 36:6+ Mr 16 '89. J. Griffin
CUNNINGHAM, C. J. Introduction to asteroids. 1987
Astronomy 17:106-7 My '89. R. Stanton
CUNNINGHAM, L. Sleeping arrangements. 1989
The New York Times Book Review 94:19 D 31 '89. C. L. Glickfeld
Newsweek 114:75 D 25 '89. M. Jones, Jr.
CUPITT, D. The sea of faith. 1988
The Christian Century 106:55-6 Ja 18 '89. P. LeMasters
CURRAN, C. E. Tensions in moral theology. 1988
America 160:455-7 My 13 '89. L. S. Cahill
The Christian Century 106:180-1 F 15 '89. W. W. Benjamin
The New York Times Book Review 94:11-12 Mr 19 '89. J. Garvey
CURRENT RESEARCH ON CALCIUM-REGULATING HORMONES. 1987
BioScience 39:199 Mr '89. D. J. Dipette
CURREY, C. B. Edward Lansdale, the unquiet American. 1988
The New Republic 201:30+ S 11 '89. R. Steel
The New York Times Book Review 94:9+ F 26 '89. R. Manning
The Washington Monthly 21:44-6+ Je '89. G. A. Geyer
CURRY, J. Woodstock. 1989
The New York Times Book Review 94:19 My 21 '89. J. Wiener
CURTIS, W. J. R. Balkrishna Doshi. 1988
Architectural Record 177:69 O '89. M. Wortman
CYMBALISTA, D. Danger. 1989
The New York Times Book Review 94:11 Je 25 '89. G. Glickman

D

DABNEY, V. Pistols and pointed pens. 1987

Conservative Digest 15:59-60 Mr/Ap '89. J. B. Graves
DAHL, R. Matilda. 1988
  The New York Times Book Review 94:31 Ja 15 '89. V. Weissman
DAHL, R. A. Democracy and its critics. 1989
  The New York Times Book Review 94:22 N 12 '89. R. N. Bellah
DAHLEM WORKSHOP ON NEUROBIOLOGY OF NEOCORTEX (1987: BERLIN, GERMANY). Neurobiology of neocortex. 1988
  Science 243:1617 Mr 24 '89. S. P. Wise
DAHLHAUS, C. Nineteenth-century music. 1989
  The New York Review of Books 36:21-2+ O 26 '89. P. Gossett
DAHRENDORF, R. The modern social conflict. 1988
  The New York Times Book Review 94:18 F 5 '89. S. Hoffmann
  Society 26:85-6 Jl/Ag '89. L. A. Coser
DANCING TEEPEES. 1989
  The New York Times Book Review 94:34-5 D 10 '89. M. Dorris
DANTO, A. C. Connections to the world. 1989
  The New York Times Book Review 94:18 My 14 '89. J. Annas
D'ANTONIO, M. Fall from grace. 1989
  The New York Review of Books 36:20+ D 21 '89. G. Wills
DANTZLER, W. H. Comparative physiology of the vertebrate kidney. 1989
  BioScience 39:652-3 O '89. J. B. Williams
DANZGER, M. H. Returning to tradition. 1989
  The Christian Century 106:1024-5 N 8 '89. N. R. Kollar
DARBRE, P. D. Introduction to practical molecular biology. 1988
  BioScience 39:736 N '89. R. Pohlman
DARDIS, T. The thirsty muse. 1989
  The Atlantic 263:93-5 Je '89. P. Rose
DARNTON, R. The kiss of Lamourette. 1990
  New York 22:162-3 O 23 '89. R. Koenig
DASTON, L. Classical probability in the Enlightenment. 1988
  Science 243:242-3 Ja 13 '89. S. P. Turner
DATTAGUPTA, S. Relaxation phenomena in condensed matter physics. 1987
  Physics Today 42:106 Mr '89. T. Kirkpatrick
DAVID, H. The Fitzrovians. 1989
  Originally published: London : Joseph, 1988
  History Today 39:56-7 S '89. R. Baldock
DAVIDSON, M. Convictions of the heart. 1988
  The Christian Century 106:858-9 S 27 '89. D. K. Jaeger
DAVIDSON, R. Ancestors. 1989
  The New York Times Book Review 94:15 N 12 '89. R. Hansen
DAVIES, C. High tech architecture. 1988
  Architectural Record 177:83 My '89. H. Aldersey-Williams
DAVIES, P. C. W. The cosmic blueprint. 1988
  Sky and Telescope 78:164+ Ag '89. E. F. Mallove
DAVIES, R. The lyre of Orpheus. 1989
  The American Spectator 22:46 My '89. A. Bakshian
  The Christian Century 106:143-4 F 1-8 '89. M. Giunti
  The New Republic 200:38-40 Ap 24 '89. V. Klinkenborg
  The New York Review of Books 36:35-6 Ap 13 '89. D. Lodge
  The New York Times Book Review 94:7 Ja 8 '89. P. Rose
  Vogue 179:92+ Ja '89. E. G. Carter
DAVIES, R. W. Service in the Roman Army. 1989
  History Today 39:53 D '89. D. Braund
DAVIS, A. Y. Women, culture, and politics. 1989
  The Nation 248:279-81 F 27 '89. J. Stevens
DAVIS, J. A. Conflict and control. 1988
  History Today 39:56 Ap '89. C. Duggan
DAVIS, J. H. Mafia kingfish. 1988
  The New York Times Book Review 94:11 Ja 29 '89. R. Dugger
DAVIS, M. Miles. 1989
  Down Beat 56:69 D '89. S. Stein
  Mother Jones 14:42-3 D '89. L. Kennedy
  The New York Times Book Review 94:7+ O 15 '89. G. Giddins
DAVIS, N. Z. Fiction in the archives. 1987
  History Today 39:49 Ap '89. L. Kekewich
  The New York Review of Books 36:35 Mr 16 '89. R. M. Adams
DAVIS, P. J. AND HERSH, R. Descartes' dream. 1987
  Byte 14:51-2+ Ja '89. M. Bridger
DAVIS, S. Why me?
  The New York Times Book Review 94:13 My 7 '89. M. Jefferson
DAVIS, W. Passage of darkness. 1988
  Scientific American 260:112-13 F '89. P. Morrison
DAVIS-GOFF, A. Walled gardens. 1989
  The New York Times Book Review 94:20 S 24 '89. M. Pakenham
DAWIDOWICZ, L. S. From that place and time. 1989
  Commentary 88:62-4 Jl '89. D. Rifkind
  The New Leader 72:17-18 Ag 7-21 '89. L. Grossman
  The New Republic 201:36-9 Jl 10 '89. D. G. Roskies
  The New York Times Book Review 94:31 Jl 23 '89. T. Venclova
DAWS, G. Hawaii, the islands of life. 1988
  Science 244:854-5 My 19 '89. L. F. Huenneke
DAY, R. A. How to write & publish a scientific paper. 3rd ed. 1988
  BioScience 39:402 Je '89. B. P. Dancik
DE MAN, P. Critical writings, 1953-1978. 1988
  The New York Review of Books 36:32-7 Je 29 '89. D. Donoghue
DE MAN, P. Wartime journalism, 1940-1943. 1988
  The New Republic 200:30-4 Mr 6 '89. Z. Sternhell
  The New York Review of Books 36:32-7 Je 29 '89. D. Donoghue
DE PAOLA, T. The art lesson. 1989
  The New York Times Book Review 94:44 My 21 '89. D. Macaulay
DEÁK, G.-G. Picturing America, 1497-1899. 2v 1988
  The New York Times Book Review 94:10 Mr 19 '89. H. Brogan
DECK, A. F. The second wave. 1989
  America 161:281-2 O 28 '89. J. P. Fitzpatrick
DEFORD, F. Casey on the loose. 1989
  The American Spectator 22:35-7 O '89. V. Gold
DEGAS, E. Meet Edgar Degas. 1988
  The New York Times Book Review 94:44 My 21 '89. D. Macaulay
DEIGHTON, L. Spy hook. 1988
  Time 134:96+ D 4 '89. J. Skow
THE DELAWARE ESTUARY. 1988
  Sea Frontiers 35:253 Jl/Ag '89. M. D. Gottfried
DELBANCO, A. The Puritan ordeal. 1989
  The Christian Century 106:730 Ag 2-9 '89. G. H. Shattuck
DELBANCO, N. Running in place. 1989
  The New York Times Book Review 94:14 Jl 23 '89. D. Manuel
DEMARCO, T. AND LISTER, T. R. Peopleware. 1987
  Byte 14:54+ F '89. C. Herring
DEMARINIS, R. The year of the zinc penny. 1989
  The New York Times Book Review 94:12 S 24 '89. M.-A. T. Smith
D'EMILIO, J. AND FREEDMAN, E. B. Intimate matters. 1988
  Commonweal 116:58-9+ Ja 27 '89. J. M. Cameron
DEMPSTER, N. Heiress. 1990
  Harper's Bazaar 122:160-1+ N '89. Y. Z. McDonough
DENNIS, J. V. Summer bird feeding.
  The Conservationist 44:52 Jl/Ag '89. A. Mapes
DENNY, M. W. Biology and the mechanics of the wave-swept environment. 1988
  Science 243:1374 Mr 10 '89. M. R. Patterson
DENSELOW, R. When the music's over. 1989
  The Nation 249:433-5 O 16 '89. G. Santoro
DES BARRES, P. I'm with the band. 1987
  Mademoiselle 95:117+ Mr '89. J. Maynard
DESAI, A. Baumgartner's Bombay. 1989
  The New Leader 72:17-18 My 1 '89. B. Falkenberg
  The New Republic 200:40-2 Ap 3 '89. P. K. Bell
  The New York Review of Books 36:34-6 Je 1 '89. R. Dinnage
  The New York Times Book Review 94:3 Ap 9 '89. P. West
DESAI, P. Perestroika in perspective. 1989
  The New Leader 72:6-8 My 15-29 '89. R. Sharlet
  The New York Times Book Review 94:25 Ag 13 '89. P. Taubman
DESALVO, L. A. Virginia Woolf. 1989
  The New Yorker 65:154-63 N 6 '89. K. Fraser
DESMOND, L. G. AND MESSENGER, P. M. A dream of Maya. 1988
  Science 244:864-5 My 19 '89. G. E. Stuart
DEVALL, B. Simple in means, rich in ends. 1988
  Sierra 74:160-2+ Ja/F '89. M. J. McCloskey
DEVLIN, K. J. Mathematics. 1988
  The New York Review of Books 36:26-8 Mr 16 '89. M. Gardner
DEVORKIN, D. H. Race to the stratosphere. 1989
  Science 245:1401-2 S 22 '89. R. W. Seidel
DEWDNEY, A. K. The Turing Omnibus. 1989
  Byte 14:444+ D '89. H. Kenner
DEXTER, P. Paris Trout. 1988
  The New York Review of Books 36:18-19 F 16 '89. R. Towers
DIAMANT, L. Chaining the Hudson. 1989
  Scientific American 261:126-8 N '89. P. Morrison
DIAMOND, S. Spiritual warfare. 1989
  The Nation 249:467-8 O 23 '89. L. Bensky
DICKINSON, C. The widows' adventures. 1989
  The New York Times Book Review 94:14 S 24 '89. H. Wolitzer
DICKINSON, P. Skeleton-in-waiting. 1989
  The New York Times Book Review 94:5 D 31 '89. C. Lansbury
DICKINSON, T. Exploring the night sky. 1987
  Sky and Telescope 77:39 Ja '89. A. MacRobert
DIETRICH, M. Marlene. 1989
  New York 22:77 My 8 '89. R. Koenig

The New York Times Book Review 94:8 My 28 '89. S. Harvey

DIGGINS, J. P. The proud decades. 1988
History Today 39:51-3 O '89. B. Dooley
National Review 41:50 Mr 24 '89. J. P. Hart

DIIULIO, J. J. Governing prisons. 1987
Society 26:86-8 Mr/Ap '89. H. Toch

DILLARD, A. An American childhood. 1987
The Christian Century 106:592-5 Je 7-14 '89. P. S. Hawkins

DILLARD, A. The writing life. 1989
The Christian Century 106:1063-4 N 15 '89. B. J. Carroll
The Nation 249:435-6 O 16 '89. M. Edens
The New York Times Book Review 94:15 S 17 '89. S. Maitland
The New Yorker 65:106-8 D 25 '89. J. Updike

DILLENBERGER, J. The visual arts and Christianity in America. 1989
The Christian Century 106:1152-5 D 6 '89. D. Morgan

THE DIRECTION OF POETRY. 1988
Commentary 87:70-2 Ap '89. R. Alter
The Nation 248:132+ Ja 30 '89. R. McPhillips

DISSANAYAKE, E. What is art for? 1987
Art in America 77:57+ My '89. J. Rykwert

DISSENT IN THE CHURCH. 1988
America 160:43-4 Ja 21 '89. H. McSorley

DIXON, S. Love and will. 1989
The New York Times Book Review 94:23 D 17 '89. J. R. Kornblatt

DIXON, S. The play and other stories. 1988
The New York Times Book Review 94:19 Je 4 '89. J. Levin

DJERASSI, C. Cantor's dilemma. 1989
The New York Times Book Review 94:14 N 5 '89. L. Shainberg

DOBBINS, T. A. AND OTHERS. Introduction to observing and photographing the solar system. 1988
Sky and Telescope 77:36-8 Ja '89. S. M. Larson

DOBSON, E. AND HINDSON, E. E. The seduction of power. 1988
The Christian Century 106:992-3 N 1 '89. P. L. Shriver

DOCTOROW, E. L. Billy Bathgate. 1989
America 160:457-9 My 13 '89. D. E. Pease
Maclean's 102:58-9 Mr 6 '89. J. Bemrose
The Nation 248:454-6 Ap 3 '89. J. Leonard
National Review 41:52-4 My 5 '89. C. Williamson
The New Republic 200:40-2 Mr 20 '89. A. Kazin
New York 22:63-4 F 20 '89. R. Koenig
The New York Review of Books 36:3-4 Mr 2 '89. G. Wills
The New York Times Book Review 94:1+ F 26 '89. A. Tyler
The New Yorker 65:112-14 Mr 27 '89. T. Rafferty
Newsweek 113:76 F 13 '89. P. S. Prescott
The Progressive 53:38-9 Ag '89. M. J. Friedman
Time 133:76+ F 27 '89. P. Gray

DOERR, E. Religious liberty in crisis.
The Humanist 49:45 S/O '89. J. M. Swomley

THE DOMESTIC CAT. 1988
Scientific American 261:114-15 Jl '89. P. Morrison

DOMÍNGUEZ, J. I. To make a world safe for revolution. 1989
Commonweal 116:304-5 My 19 '89. R. E. White
The New Republic 201:38-41 Jl 3 '89. M. Falcoff
The New York Times Book Review 94:23 My 21 '89. W. S. Smith

DONAHUE, J. D. The privatization decision. 1989
The New York Times Book Review 94:13-14 D 17 '89. R. L. Heilbroner
The Washington Monthly 21:55 N '89. P. Glastris

DONALD, A. Smile, honey. 1989
The New York Times Book Review 94:13 O 8 '89. S. McCauley

DONALDSON, S. John Cheever. 1988
National Review 41:66 Ja 27 '89. J. Giles
The New Republic 200:35-8 Mr 6 '89. A. Hulbert

DONOSO, J. Curfew. 1988
The New Leader 72:21-2 Ja 23 '89. S. Rodman

DONOVAN, H. Right places, right times. 1989
The New York Times Book Review 94:13 N 12 '89. T. Goldstein

DOO, J. The front-wheel driving high-performance advantage. 1988
Motor Trend 41:37 N '89. G. Von Dare

DORFMAN, A. My house is on fire. 1990
The New York Times Book Review 94:8 D 31 '89. B. Mukherjee

DORRIS, M. The broken cord. 1989
The New York Times Book Review 94:1+ Jl 30 '89. P. Guthrie

DOSTOYEVSKY, F. Complete letters; v2, 1860-1867. 1988
The New York Times Book Review 94:13 Je 4 '89. S. J. Parker

DOUGLASS, J. D. AND LIVINGSTONE, N. C. America the vulnerable. 1987
Science 243:552-3 Ja 27 '89. R. A. Falk

DOVLATOV, S. Ours. 1989
The New York Times Book Review 94:1+ Ap 30 '89. S. Ruta

DOWLING, C. Perfect women. 1988
Health (New York, N.Y.) 21:84 F '89. S. Walton
Mademoiselle 95:50+ Ja '89. J. Maynard

DOWLING, E. M. American classicist. 1989
Americana 17:13 N/D '89. M. Durham

DOWNER, L. On the narrow road. 1989
The New York Times Book Review 94:13 Jl 30 '89. J. D. Morley

DOWNES, K. Sir John Vanbrugh. 1987
History Today 39:53 F '89. B. Coward

DOYLE, SIR A. C. The lost world ; &, The poison belt. 1989
Scientific American 261:188-9 S '89. P. Morrison

DOYLE, R. The commitments. 1989
The New York Times Book Review 94:11 Jl 23 '89. K. Friedman

DRABBLE, M. A natural curiosity. 1989
Maclean's 102:74 O 2 '89. D. James
Ms. 18:36+ S '89. B. Pesetsky
The Nation 249:688-90 D 4 '89. B. Caplan
The New Republic 201:40-2 N 27 '89. H. Fairlie
The New York Review of Books 36:18-20 N 23 '89. H. Mantel
The New York Times Book Review 94:3 S 3 '89. J. Grossman
The Progressive 53:40+ D '89. M. J. Friedman
Time 134:66 S 4 '89. P. Gray

DREAMINGS, THE ART OF ABORIGINAL AUSTRALIA. 1988
Smithsonian 19:182-3 Mr '89. M. Dirda

DREISER, T. Sister Carrie. 1987
Orig. pub. 1900, 1911, 1919 respectively
The New York Review of Books 36:32-7 N 23 '89. A. Delbanco

DREW, B. Nelson Algren. 1989
The New York Times Book Review 94:18-19 N 26 '89. J. Atlas

DREYER, J. L. E. NGC 2000.0. 1988
Astronomy 17:107 My '89. D. J. Eicher
Sky and Telescope 78:484-5 N '89. W. Tirion

DRUCKER, P. F. The new realities. 1989
Business Week p15-17 Je 26 '89. K. Pennar
Fortune 119:187-8 Je 19 '89. P. Johnson
The New York Times Book Review 94:15-16+ Je 18 '89. B. R. Barber

DUBERMAN, M. B. Paul Robeson. 1988
American Heritage 40:12+ Ap '89. G. C. Ward
Commentary 87:70-2 My '89. H. Klehr
The Nation 248:383-5 Mr 20 '89. N. I. Huggins
National Review 41:55-6 My 19 '89. J. Sobran
The New Leader 72:17-18 F 20 '89. B. Gewen
New York 22:56-7 Ja 30 '89. R. Koenig
The New York Review of Books 36:3-4+ Ap 27 '89. M. Kempton
The New York Times Book Review 94:1+ F 12 '89. J. P. Diggins
Smithsonian 20:221-3 O '89. D. Drabelle
Time 133:78-9 Mr 13 '89. S. Kanfer

DUBINSKII, R. Stormy applause. 1988
The New Republic 201:106+ N 6 '89. R. Taruskin
The New York Times Book Review 94:12 Je 25 '89. J. Skvorecký

DUBOS, R. J. Pasteur and modern science. 1988
BioScience 39:493-4 Jl/Ag '89. K. De Ville

DUBUFFET, J. Asphyxiating culture and other writings. 1988
Art News 88:132 O '89. M. Ward

DUBUS, A. Andre Dubus. 1988
The New Republic 200:41-2 F 6 '89. A. Tyler

DUGGAN, C. Fascism and the Mafia. 1989
History Today 39:55 D '89. P. Preston

DUIN, J. Purity makes the heart grow stronger. 1988
Christianity Today 33:32 Ap 7 '89. J. Kobobel

DULLES, A. R. The reshaping of Catholicism. 1988
America 160:65-6 Ja 28 '89. R. G. Weakland
The Christian Century 106:21-2 Ja 4-11 '89. R. Kaftan
The New York Times Book Review 94:11-12 Mr 19 '89. J. Garvey

DUNAWAY, D. K. Huxley in Hollywood. 1989
Gentlemen's Quarterly 59:148+ D '89. M. Richler
The New York Times Book Review 94:25 O 22 '89. K. Quinn

DUNBAR, R. I. M. Primate social systems. 1987
BioScience 39:328-30 My '89. P. S. Rodman

DUNCAN, E. Breaking the curfew. 1989
The New York Times Book Review 94:28 S 24 '89. M. Ispahani

DUNCAN, R. Advanced OS/2 programming. 1989
Byte 14:51-2+ My '89. G. M. Vose

DUNLAP, R. A. Experimental physics. 1988
Physics Today 42:93 N '89. H. H. Sample

DUNLAP, T. R. Saving America's wildlife. 1988
Environment 31:28 My '89. J. H. Perkins

DUNN, K. Geek love. 1989
The Christian Century 106:664-5 Jl 5-12 '89. M. Giunti
The Nation 248:673-4 My 15 '89. D. Smith
The New York Times Book Review 94:11-12 Ap 2 '89. S. Dobyns

DUNNE, J. G. Harp. 1989
Commonweal 116:592+ N 3 '89. R. A. Schroth

The New York Times Book Review 94:17 Mr 19 '89. B. Raskin

ENGELMANN, B. In Hitler's Germany. 1988
History Today 39:57-9 F '89. J. Noakes

ENGLANDER, M. E. Strategies for classroom discipline. 1986
Phi Delta Kappan 71:172 O '89. T. J. Lasley

ENGLISH, J. Shadow of heaven; v1, 1897-1948.
Maclean's 102:69 D 11 '89. W. A. Wilson

ENVIRONMENTAL BIOTECHNOLOGY. 1988
BioScience 39:650-1 O '89. S. K. Walia

ENVIRONMENTAL INFLUENCES AND RECOGNITION IN ENZYME CHEMISTRY. 1988
Science 246:1064-5 N 24 '89. R. G. Matthews

ENVIRONMENTAL MANAGEMENT IN AGRICULTURE. 1988
Environment 31:26 S '89. J. H. Perkins

ENVIRONMENTAL RADON. 1987
Physics Today 42:72-4 Ap '89. L. M. Hubbard

ENZENSBERGER, H. M. Europe, Europe. 1989
The New York Review of Books 36:13-15 S 28 '89. N. Ascherson
The New York Times Book Review 94:13-14 Je 4 '89. H. S. Hughes

EPRILE, T. Temporary sojourner, and other South African stories. 1989
The New York Times Book Review 94:19 Ag 20 '89. H. Rochman

EPSTEIN, C. F. Deceptive distinctions. 1988
Psychology Today 23:76 My '89. B. L. Benderley

EPSTEIN, E. J. Deception. 1989
The American Spectator 22:45-6 N '89. G. Szamuely
Commentary 88:62-4 O '89. E. A. Cohen
National Review 41:46-7 Je 2 '89. A. M. Codevilla
The New Leader 72:9-10 My 15-29 '89. Y. Mirsky
The New York Review of Books 36:40-3 Ag 17 '89. T. Powers
The New York Times Book Review 94:30 My 7 '89. J. Bamford

EPSTEIN, J. Partial payments. 1988
National Review 41:46-7 Ap 21 '89. C. Iannone

EPSTEIN, S. Light. 1989
The New York Times Book Review 94:19 O 8 '89. M. Giles

EPSTEIN, W. H. Recognizing biography. 1987
The American Scholar 58:459-60+ Summ '89. M. Jones

ERDRICH, L. Tracks. 1988
The Progressive 53:44-5 F '89. A. Welsh-Huggins

ERICKSON, C. Bonnie Prince Charlie. 1989
The New York Times Book Review 94:16 Ja 8 '89. C. Hibbert

ERICKSON, S. Tours of the black clock. 1989
The New York Times Book Review 94:29 Mr 5 '89. K. Acker

ERICSON, T. E. O. AND WEISE, W. Pions and nuclei. 1988
Physics Today 42 pt1:68-9 Ag '89. H. Feshbach
Science 245:770-1 Ag 18 '89. D. S. Koltun

ERIE, S. P. Rainbow's end. 1989
The New York Times Book Review 94:12 Ja 8 '89. J. Beatty
The Washington Monthly 20:59-60 Ja '89. G. V. Higgins

ERNST, R. R. AND OTHERS. Principles of nuclear magnetic resonance in one and two dimensions. 1987
Physics Today 42:75-6 Jl '89. A. G. Redfield

ERVIN, K. Fragile majesty. 1989
Wilderness 53:56-8+ Wint '89. C. E. Little

ESTAVER, P. His third, her second. 1989
The New York Times Book Review 94:21 Ap 2 '89. C. Banks

ESTLEMAN, L. D. General murders. 1988
The New York Times Book Review 94:34 Ja 29 '89. E. Stumpf

ESTLEMAN, L. D. Peeper. 1989
The New York Times Book Review 94:45 O 15 '89. G. A. Effinger

EUKARYOTIC TRANSPOSABLE ELEMENTS AS MUTAGENIC AGENTS. 1988
Science 244:1499-500 Je 23 '89. D. L. Hartl

EVANS, D. S. Under Capricorn. 1988
Sky and Telescope 77:502-3 My '89. D. A. Allen

EVANS, R. L. AND BERENT, I. M. Fundamentalism. 1988
The Humanist 49:42-3 Mr/Ap '89. S. McCabe

EVANS, S. M. Born for liberty. 1989
The New York Times Book Review 94:14 Ag 20 '89. M. Lee
The Progressive 53:40+ N '89. A. M. Davidon

EVANS, S. M. AND NELSON, B. J. Wage justice. 1989
The New York Times Book Review 94:29 Jl 30 '89. W. Kaminer
Science 244:838-9 My 19 '89. M. H. Strober

EVAPORITES AND HYDROCARBONS. 1988
Science 244:721 My 12 '89. P. Sonnenfeld

EVERSON MUSEUM OF ART. American ceramics. 1989
American Craft 49:20+ D '89/Ja '90. P. Hunter-Stiebel

EVOLUTION OF LIFE HISTORIES OF MAMMALS. 1988
Science 246:391 O 20 '89. A. Cockburn

EVOLUTIONARY HISTORY OF THE "ROBUST" AUSTRALOPITHECINES. 1988

Science 245:1514 S 29 '89. G. P. Rightmire

EVOLUTIONARY PROCESSES AND METAPHORS. 1988
BioScience 39:195-6 Mr '89. P. D. Gingerich

EWEN, S. All consuming images. 1988
The New Republic 200:37-41 My 8 '89. A. Sullivan
Psychology Today 23:76 Ja/F '89. H. Hall

EXERCISES IN ASTRONOMY. 1987
Physics Today 42:70+ Ap '89. J. M. Pasachoff

EXLEY, F. A fan's notes. 1988
Copyright 1968
The New York Review of Books 35:36-7 Ja 19 '89. T. R. Edwards

EXLEY, F. Last notes from home. 1988
The New York Review of Books 35:36-7 Ja 19 '89. T. R. Edwards

EXLEY, F. Pages from a cold island. 1988
Repr. Orig. pub.: Random House, 1975
The New York Review of Books 35:36-7 Ja 19 '89. T. R. Edwards

EXPERIMENTAL PHYCOLOGY. 1987
BioScience 39:198-9 Mr '89. W. J. Henley

EXPERIMENTAL TECHNIQUES IN CONDENSED MATTER PHYSICS AT LOW TEMPERATURES. 1988
Physics Today 42:126-7 O '89. R. C. Dynes

EXPRESSIVELY BLACK. 1987
Phi Delta Kappan 70:416-17 Ja '89. B. Lindsay

EXTINCTION AND SURVIVAL IN THE FOSSIL RECORD. 1988
BioScience 39:569-70 S '89. G. Theokritoff

F

THE FABER BOOK OF LETTERS. 1989
Smithsonian 20:168 Je '89. B. Schiff

THE FACTS ON FILE DICTIONARY OF BIOLOGY. 1988
BioScience 39:267 Ap '89. K. M. Klemow and L. J. Turoczi

FAIRCHILD, J. Chic savages. 1989
The New York Times Book Review 94:31-2 D 3 '89. S. Menkes

FAISAL, F. H. M. Theory of multiphoton processes. 1987
Physics Today 42:104-5 Mr '89. A. Dalgarno

FALCOFF, M. Modern Chile, 1970-1989. 1989
Commentary 88:67-70 N '89. D. Brock

FALLOWS, J. M. More like us. 1989
Business Week p14+ Mr 20 '89. R. J. Dowling
The Christian Century 106:1126-7 N 29 '89. I. Nerken
Commonweal 116:707-10 D 15 '89. P. D. Baumann
Fortune 119:145-6+ Ap 10 '89. S. P. Sherman
The Nation 248:895-6 Je 26 '89. S. Steinberg
The New Leader 72:17-18 My 15-29 '89. J. N. Bhagwati
The New Republic 200:32-5 Ap 3 '89. R. B. Reich
The New York Review of Books 36:6-8 Mr 30 '89. A. Hacker
The New York Times Book Review 94:7 Mr 26 '89. D. Wrong
The Washington Monthly 21:54-7 Ap '89. T. J. Peters

FAMILY PORTRAITS. 1989
The New York Times Book Review 94:11 N 19 '89. J. K. Conway

FARÍAS, V. Heidegger and Nazism. 1989
The New York Times Book Review 94:16 D 17 '89. A. Lacy

FARLEY, E. The fragility of knowledge. 1988
The Christian Century 106:361-2 Ap 5 '89. M. Kinnamon

FARRAR, C. The origins of democratic thinking. 1988
History Today 39:47 Ja '89. J. E. Powell

FAST, H. The confession of Joe Cullen. 1989
The New York Times Book Review 94:25 Ag 20 '89. M. Kondracke

FAUX, M. Roe v. Wade. 1988
America 160:307 Ap 1 '89. J. B. Benestad

FEDER, J. Fractals. 1988
Physics Today 42:90-1 S '89. P. Bak
Science 245:1515-16 S 29 '89. P. Meakin

FEDERAL SOCIAL POLICY. 1988
The Humanist 49:43 Ja/F '89. W. Karr

FEIGENBAUM, E. A. AND OTHERS. The rise of the expert company. 1988
Byte 14:400+ S '89. H. Kenner

FEIN, L. J. Where are we? 1988
Commonweal 116:218-19 Ap 7 '89. M. Wyschogrod

FEINBERG, D. B. Eighty-sixed. 1989
The New York Times Book Review 94:9 F 26 '89. C. Texier

FEINSTEIN, J. A season inside. 1988
The New York Times Book Review 94:14 Ja 22 '89. A. Heisch
The Washington Monthly 21:46+ Ap '89. M. Cooper

FENICI. ENGLISH. The Phoenicians. 1988
The New York Times Book Review 94:18 Je 4 '89. K. T. Erim

FENNELL, M. L. AND WARNECKE, R. B. The diffusion of medical innovations. 1988
Science 243:1740-1 Mr 31 '89. J. R. Kimberly

FENNO, R. F. The making of a senator. 1989
The New York Review of Books 36:27-8 Mr 30 '89. N. Lemann

The New York Times Book Review 94:19 F 5 '89. L. Wertheimer

FENSTER, J. M. Packard: the pride. 1989
American Heritage 40:132-3 D '89
Motor Trend 41:42 D '89. G. Von Dare

FERENCZI, S. The clinical diary of Sándor Ferenczi. 1988
The New York Times Book Review 94:24 Ja 15 '89. S. Schneiderman

FERM, D. W. Profiles in liberation.
The Christian Century 106:183-4 F 15 '89. R. A. Warrior

FERRARI, P. L. AND OTHERS. U.S. arms exports. 1988
The Bulletin of the Atomic Scientists 45:48 Jl/Ag '89

FERRARY, J. AND FISZER, L. Season to taste. 1988
The Nation 248:526-8 Ap 17 '89. A. Mendelson

FERRELL, R. H. AND NATKIEL, R. Atlas of American history. 1987
History Today 39:50+ Mr '89. D. Reynolds

FERRIS, T. Coming of age in the Milky Way. 1988
Sky and Telescope 77:613-14 Je '89. G. Greenstein

THE FETTERED PRESIDENCY. 1989
The American Spectator 22:43-4 My '89. F. Barnes
Commentary 88:70-2 Jl '89. G. Russell

FEYNMAN, R. P. "What do you care what other people think?". 1988
Ad Astra 1:29 Ap '89. R. Spangenburg
Astronomy 17:101 Jl '89. J. Kanipe
Physics Today 42:106-7 F '89. S. D. Drell

FIDDES, P. S. The creative suffering of God. 1988
The Christian Century 106:324-5 Mr 22-29 '89. S. Grenz

FIELD, C. The hill towns of Italy. 1984
Smithsonian 20:119 Jl '89. B. Schiff

FINCH, C. Twentieth century watercolors. 1988
American Artist 53:14+ F '89. M. C. Nelson

FINELLI, P. M. Sound for the stage. 1989
Theatre Crafts 23:92-3 Ag/S '89. L. Shapiro

FINGARETTE, H. Heavy drinking. 1988
Christianity Today 33:57-8 F 3 '89. J. Alsdurf

FINK, C. Marc Bloch. 1989
The New York Times Book Review 94:24 O 1 '89. M. R. Marrus

FINK, L. AND GREENBERG, B. Upheaval in the quiet zone. 1989
The Nation 249:284-7 S 18 '89. N. Lichtenstein
The New York Times Book Review 94:40 S 24 '89. J. Klein

FINNEGAN, W. Dateline Soweto. 1988
Business Week p14+ Ja 16 '89. K. H. Hammonds

A FIRST DICTIONARY OF CULTURAL LITERACY. 1989
The New York Times Book Review 94:22 D 17 '89. J. Shenker

FISCHER, D. H. Albion's seed. 1989
The New Republic 201:27-31 O 30 '89. G. S. Wood

FISCHER-DIESKAU, D. Reverberations. 1989
The New York Times Book Review 94:25 S 24 '89. W. L. Taitte
Opera News 54:59 N '89. D. Johnson

FISH, S. E. Doing what comes naturally. 1989
The New York Times Book Review 94:22 My 21 '89. P. Meisel

FISHER, J. T. The Catholic counterculture in America, 1933-1962. 1989
Commonweal 116:645-8 N 17 '89. R. G. Hoyt

FISHMAN, S. A bomb in the brain. 1988
Psychology Today 22:68-9 D '88. M. Roberts

FITZGERALD, A. E. The Pentagonists. 1989
Business Week p13 Mr 6 '89. D. Griffiths
The New York Review of Books 36:3-4+ O 26 '89. N. Lemann
Society 26:90-3 S/O '89. R. T. Golembiewski

FITZGERALD, P. The beginning of spring. 1988
The New York Times Book Review 94:15 My 7 '89. R. Plunket

FLACKS, R. Making history. 1988
The Progressive 53:41-3 Ap '89. M. Rothschild

FLANAGAN, D. Flanagan's version. 1988
The Bulletin of the Atomic Scientists 45:44-5 Mr '89. K. Tsipis

FLANAGAN, S. Hildegard of Bingen, 1098-1179. 1989
The New York Review of Books 36:32-5 D 7 '89. M. H. Keen

FLEISCHER, A., JR. AND OTHERS. Board games. 1988
Fortune 119:143-4+ Mr 13 '89. W. Olson

FLEISCHMAN, P. Joyful noise. 1988
The New York Times Book Review 94:18 Mr 26 '89. K. Pollitt

FLEMING, B. Captain Bennett's folly.
The New York Times Book Review 94:12 Ag 6 '89. A. Solomon

FLEMING, T. H. The short-tailed fruit bat. 1988
BioScience 39:404-5 Je '89. D. W. Morrison

FLINN, D. M. AND SWOPE, M. What they did for love. 1989
The New York Times Book Review 94:2 Ag 13 '89. B. Gelb

FLOOD, C. B. Hitler. 1989
The New York Times Book Review 94:15-16 Ap 16 '89. G. A. Craig

FLORY, W. S. The American Ezra Pound. 1989

The New Republic 200:38-40 Mr 6 '89. D. Donoghue

FLUID FLOW IN SEDIMENTARY BASINS AND AQUIFERS. 1987
Science 243:677 F 3 '89. G. Garven

FOGARTY, G. P. American Catholic biblical scholarship. 1989
America 161:17-18 Jl 1-8 '89. J. Blenkinsopp
The Christian Century 106:1179-80 D 13 '89. H. C. Waetjen

FOGEL, R. W. Without consent or contract. 1989
National Review 41:39-41 D 31 '89. M. E. Bradford
The New Republic 201:38-40 O 23 '89. J. M. McPherson
The New York Review of Books 36:51-5 D 21 '89. M. P. Johnson
The New York Times Book Review 94:15-16+ N 5 '89. C. V. Woodward

FOISTER, S. AND OTHERS. The National Portrait Gallery collection. 1989
History Today 39:62 F '89

FOLLETT, K. Pillars of the earth. 1989
The New York Times Book Review 94:41 S 10 '89. C. Holland

FONTEYN, DAME M. Swan lake. 1988
The New York Times Book Review 94:33 My 21 '89. M. Aloff

FORD, E. Monkey Bay. 1989
The New York Times Book Review 94:9 Ag 6 '89. H. F. Mosher

FORD, L. K. Origins of Southern radicalism. 1988
The New York Review of Books 35:16-20 Ja 19 '89. J. M. McPherson

FORD, R. A. D. Our man in Moscow.
Maclean's 102:66 Ap 3 '89. A. Wilson-Smith

FOREST, J. H. Pilgrim to the Russian Church. 1988
The Christian Century 106:23-4 Ja 4-11 '89. T. G. Poole

FORESTER, T. High-tech society. 1987
High Technology Business 9:9 Ja '89. M. Estren

FORRESTER, A. T. Large ion beams. 1987
Physics Today 42:77-8 Je '89. G. D. Alton

FORSTER, M. Elizabeth Barrett Browning. 1989
The New York Times Book Review 94:32 My 7 '89. D. S. Thomas

FORSYTH, F. The negotiator. 1989
The New York Times Book Review 94:9+ Ap 16 '89. R. Condon

FORSYTH, M. Auditoria. 1987
Theatre Crafts 23:86+ Ja '89. J. E. Rubin

FOSSEDAL, G. A. The democratic imperative. 1989
The American Spectator 22:44-5 Jl '89. P. L. Berger
Commentary 88:67-8 Jl '89. D. Brock
Forbes 144:27 Ag 7 '89. M. S. Forbes, Jr.
National Review 41:42-4 Je 16 '89. M. Lind

FOSTER, H. Biscuit joiner handbook. 1989
Workbench 45:85 S/O '89. L. Okrend

FOSTER, R. F. Modern Ireland, 1600-1972. 1988
The Atlantic 263:93-4+ Ap '89. T. Flanagan
Maclean's 102:45 Jl 31 '89. A. Phillips
The New Republic 201:39-42 Jl 10 '89. G. Wheatcroft
The New York Times Book Review 94:3 Je 4 '89. A. M. Greeley

FOTHERINGHAM, A. Birds of a feather.
Maclean's 102:109 N 20 '89. D. Camp

FOWLER, R. B. Unconventional partners. 1989
The Christian Century 106:1019-20+ N 8 '89. M. E. Marty
Commentary 87:68-70 Je '89. J. Neuhaus

FOX, M. The coming of the cosmic Christ. 1988
America 161:195+ S 30 '89. G. W. Peck
Commonweal 116:374-5 Je 16 '89. W. M. Thompson
The New York Times Book Review 94:12-13 Ja 15 '89. C. G. Zaleski

FOX, P. The village by the sea. 1988
The New York Times Book Review 94:37 F 5 '89. R. Brown

FOX, S. R. Blood and power. 1989
The New York Times Book Review 94:9 Jl 2 '89. S. Raab

FOX-GENOVESE, E. Within the plantation household. 1988
The Nation 248:417-22 Mr 27 '89. C. Stansell
The New York Times Book Review 94:1+ Ja 8 '89. M. Sobel

FRADKIN, P. L. Sagebrush country. 1989
Wilderness 53:53-4+ Fall '89. C. E. Little

FRAMPTON, P. H. Gauge field theories. 1987
Physics Today 42:80+ Ja '89. H. Georgi

FRANCIS, D. The edge. 1989
The New York Times Book Review 94:9 F 12 '89. S. Grafton

FRANCIS, D. Straight. 1989
The New York Times Book Review 94:32 D 3 '89. M. Stasio

FRANCISCO, P. W. Cold feet. 1988
The New York Times Book Review 94:22 F 19 '89. D. Ackerman

FRANK, A. The diary of Anne Frank. 1989
The New York Times Book Review 94:2 Jl 2 '89. R. R. Wisse
The New Yorker 65:116-20 D 18 '89. J. Thurman

FRANK, R. H. Passions within reason. 1988
Commonweal 116:346-7+ Je 2 '89. J. Brandl
The Nation 248:742-4 My 29 '89. A. Kohn
The New Republic 201:38-40 O 2 '89. R. Kuttner

The New York Review of Books 36:25-7 My 18 '89. A. Ryan

FRANKLIN, H. B. War stars. 1988
The Bulletin of the Atomic Scientists 45:48+ My '89. P. Brians
Science 243:101-2 Ja 6 '89. S. W. Leslie

FRANTZ, S. K. Contemporary glass. 1989
American Craft 49:20+ D '89/Ja '90. P. Hunter-Stiebel

FRASER, A. The warrior queens. 1989
The New York Times Book Review 94:18-19 Ap 2 '89. G. P. Garrett
The New Yorker 65:108-11 Ap 24 '89. N. Bliven

FRASER, G. Playing for keeps.
Maclean's 102:78+ D 4 '89. R. Laver

FRASER, G. M. The Hollywood history of the world. 1988
National Review 41:54-5 Ap 7 '89. J. O. Tate

FRASER, J. AND ARNOLD, E. Private view. 1988
Dance Magazine 63:66-7 Ja '89. O. Stuart

FRASER, R. The Brontës. 1988
The New York Times Book Review 94:16 F 5 '89. V. Tiger

FRAZIER, I. Great Plains. 1989
The American Spectator 22:50-2 D '89. W. M. Sarf
The New Republic 201:39-41 Ag 7-14 '89. S. Mosle
The New York Times Book Review 94:9+ Je 18 '89. S. Hubbell
Newsweek 113:64 Je 12 '89. L. Shapiro

FREDRICKSON, G. M. The arrogance of race. 1988
The New York Review of Books 36:29-34 Mr 30 '89. D. B. Davis

FREDRIKSEN, P. From Jesus to Christ. 1988
The Christian Century 106:823-4 S 13-20 '89. L. T. Johnson

THE FREE-MARKET READER.
National Review 41:46+ Jl 14 '89. J. Sobran

FREEBORN, P. The stark truth. 1989
The New York Times Book Review 94:26 N 5 '89. S. Lee

FREEMAN, J. The chinchilla farm. 1989
The Nation 249:723-4 D 11 '89. P. Kennedy
The New York Times Book Review 94:13 D 17 '89. T. Sandlin

FREEMAN, J. B. In transit. 1989
The Nation 249:282-4 S 18 '89. M. Isserman

FREEWHEELING.
Maclean's 102:86 N 27 '89. M. Ritts

FRENCH, M. J. Invention and evolution. 1988
Scientific American 260:128-9 Je '89. P. Morrison

FRENCH CARICATURE AND THE FRENCH REVOLUTION, 1789-1799. 1988
Art in America 77:43+ D '89. S. Schama

FRIEDBERG, A. L. The weary titan. 1988
The New Republic 200:37-9 F 13 '89. J. S. Nye, Jr.

FRIEDL, E. The women of Deh Koh. 1988
The New York Times Book Review 94:13 My 14 '89. P. Glazebrook

FRIEDMAN, A. Agnelli and the network of Italian power. 1989
Business Week p20-1+ N 6 '89. J. Rossant

FRIEDMAN, A. AND SCHWARZ, T. Power and greed. 1989
The New York Times Book Review 94:9 Jl 9 '89. G. Tyler

FRIEDMAN, B. M. A day of reckoning. 1988
Commentary 87:65-7 Ja '89. I. M. Stelzer
The Washington Monthly 20:55-6 Ja '89. A. S. Murray

FRIEDMAN, R. M. Appropriating the weather. 1989
Science 245:1124 S 8 '89. J. R. Fleming

FRIEDMAN, T. L. From Beirut to Jerusalem. 1989
Business Week p10 Jl 10 '89. J. Rossant
The Christian Century 106:888-9 O 4 '89. C. A. Kimball
Commentary 88:63-5 S '89. D. Pipes
Commonweal 116:508-9 S 22 '89. M. Polner
The Nation 249:605-7 N 20 '89. M. L. Sifry
The New Republic 201:34-9 S 4 '89. M. Peretz
The New York Times Book Review 94:1+ Jl 9 '89. R. Rosenblatt
Newsweek 114:57 Jl 24 '89. P. McGrath
The Progressive 53:40+ S '89. W. Steif
Time 134:62 Jl 10 '89. P. Gray
U.S. Catholic 54:48-51 N '89. G. M. Costello
Vogue 179:210+ Ag '89. G. Emerson

FRIEDRICH, O. Glenn Gould. 1989
The New York Times Book Review 94:22 Ap 23 '89. E. Zukerman

THE FRINGES OF REASON. 1989
The Nation 249:61-3 Jl 10 '89. T. Athanasiou

FROM CARDINALS TO CHAOS. 1988
Physics Today 42:69-72 Je '89. P. D. Lax
Science 246:134 O 6 '89. R. E. Rider

FROMKIN, D. A peace to end all peace. 1989
The New York Times Book Review 94:3+ Ag 27 '89. W. R. Louis
The New Yorker 65:154-6 D 11 '89. N. Bliven

FRYDE, E. B. William de la Pole, merchant and king's banker (1366). 1988
History Today 39:56-7 F '89. C. Given-Wilson

FUCHS, V. R. Women's quest for economic equality. 1988
Monthly Labor Review 112:53-4 Ag '89. R. S. Jain

FUENTES, C. Christopher unborn. 1989

The New Leader 72:17-18 N 27 '89. M. Van Delden
New York 22:63-4 Jl 31 '89. R. Koenig
The New York Times Book Review 94:1+ Ag 20 '89. S. Ruta

FUENTES, N. Ernest Hemingway rediscovered. 1988
American Heritage 40:14 My/Je '89. G. C. Ward

FULBRIGHT, J. W. The price of empire. 1989
Business Week p14 F 13 '89. R. J. Dowling
The New Republic 200:40-2 Ap 10 '89. J. B. Judis
The New York Review of Books 36:47-8 Je 29 '89. R. Steel
The New York Times Book Review 94:7 F 19 '89. G. Smith

FULLER, R. C. Religion and the life cycle. 1988
The Christian Century 106:325-6 Mr 22-29 '89. E. C. Newenhuyse

FUMENTO, M. The myth of heterosexual AIDS. 1989
The Washington Monthly 21:45-6+ N '89. P. Cohen

FUSSELL, P. Wartime. 1988
The Nation 249:462-4 O 23 '89. F. P. Smoler
National Review 41:57-8 S 29 '89. J. P. Hart
The New Leader 72:17-18 O 2-16 '89. W. L. O'Neill
The New Republic 201:34+ N 13 '89. S. L. Hynes
The New York Review of Books 36:3-4+ S 28 '89. N. G. A. Annan, Baron
The New York Times Book Review 94:1+ S 3 '89. S. Schama
The New Yorker 65:127-31 O 16 '89. N. Bliven

FUSTER, J. M. The prefrontal cortex. 2nd ed. 1989
Science 246:681-2 N 3 '89. M. E. Goldberg

G

GABLER, N. An empire of their own. 1988
The New Republic 200:34-7 My 8 '89. F. Rich

GAGE, N. A place for us. 1989
The New York Times Book Review 94:14-15 O 29 '89. C. McFadden
Time 134:89 O 16 '89. R. Z. Sheppard

GAILLARD, F. The dream long deferred. 1988
The Progressive 53:43-4 Ap '89. J. Egerton

GALACTIC AND EXTRAGALACTIC RADIO ASTRONOMY. 2nd ed. 1988
Physics Today 42:106+ Mr '89. T. J. Pearson and A. C. S. Readhead

GALANTER, M. Cults. 1989
The Christian Century 106:937-8 O 18 '89. L. R. Rambo
The New York Times Book Review 94:27 Je 18 '89. M. Silk
Science 246:271-2 O 13 '89. W. S. Bainbridge

GALBRAITH, J. K. Balancing acts. 1989
The New York Times Book Review 94:15-16 Ap 2 '89. L. Uchitelle

GALILEI, G. Sidereus nuncius. 1989
Astronomy 17:110 O '89. R. Burnham

GALISON, P. L. How experiments end. 1987
Physics Today 42:98+ Mr '89. W. D. Hackmann

GALKIN, E. W. The history of orchestral conducting. 1988
The New York Times Book Review 94:16 My 14 '89. H. C. Schonberg

GALLAGHER, D. All the right enemies. 1988
The New York Review of Books 36:43-5 Je 15 '89. D. Aaron

GALLAGHER, M. Enemies of Eros. 1989
National Review 41:41-3 D 8 '89. E. W. Fielding

GALLANT, M. In transit. 1989
The New York Times Book Review 94:3 My 28 '89. R. Bryden

GALLUP, G. AND CASTELLI, J. The people's religion. 1989
The Washington Monthly 21:57-8 N '89. H. G. Brinton

GANGLOFF, D. Albert and Victoria. 1989
The New York Times Book Review 94:40 My 21 '89. M. P. Hearn

GANSLER, J. S. Affording defense. 1989
The New York Times Book Review 94:37 Je 18 '89. F. Barnes
Technology Review 92:71-2 N/D '89. D. C. Morrison

GARAFOLA, L. Diaghilev's Ballets russes. 1989
The New Republic 201:26-32 O 9 '89. R. Taruskin
The New York Times Book Review 94:12 D 24 '89. A. Macaulay

GARCIA, G. Skin deep. 1988
The New York Times Book Review 94:16 Jl 9 '89. M. Spanier

GARCÍA PONCE, J. Encounters.
The New York Times Book Review 94:17 Je 25 '89. G. H. Bell-Villada

THE GARDEN SEED INVENTORY. 1985
Country Journal 16:18-19 F '89. N. Bubel

GARRARD, M. D. Artemisia Gentileschi. 1988
The New York Review of Books 36:36-8 Jl 20 '89. F. Haskell

GARRISON, D. Mary Heaton Vorse. 1989
The Nation 249:690-2 D 4 '89. C. H. Green
The New York Times Book Review 94:28 O 22 '89. B. Ehrenreich

GARRISON, J. On the trail of the assassins. 1988

The New York Times Book Review 94:11 Ja 29 '89. R. Dugger

GARTON ASH, T. The uses of adversity. 1989
  The New Leader 72:14-15 O 2-16 '89. M. T. Kaufman
  The New Republic 201:30-4 D 4 '89. S. Barańczak
  Newsweek 114:95 N 13 '89. A. Nagorski

GATES, H. L. Figures in black. 1986
  The New Republic 200:28-34 Ja 9-16 '89. A. Delbanco

GATES, H. L. The signifying monkey. 1988
  The New Republic 200:28-34 Ja 9-16 '89. A. Delbanco

GAY, P. Freud. 1988
  America 160:154-5 F 18 '89. W. W. Meissner
  Commonweal 116:179-81 Mr 24 '89. Taylor Eugene

GEERTZ, C. Works and lives. 1988
  The Nation 248:350-2 Mr 13 '89. M. Di Leonardo

GEHANI, N. C. 1988
  Byte 14:52+ Mr '89. G. M. Vose

GEIST, S. Interpreting Cézanne. 1988
  Art in America 77:47+ N '89. J. D. Flam

GELLES, R. J. AND STRAUS, M. A. Intimate violence. 1988
  Psychology Today 23:73 Jl/Ag '89. P. J. Black

GELLMAN, M. Does God have a big toe? 1989
  The New York Times Book Review 94:48 N 12 '89. W. Wangerin

GELLNER, E. Plough, sword, and book. 1989
  The New Republic 200:40-2 Ap 24 '89. C. Larmore

GENET, R. M. AND OTHERS. Supernova 1987A. 1987
  Sky and Telescope 77:501-2 My '89. R. A. Schorn

GENETICS OF IMMUNOLOGICAL DISEASES. 1988
  BioScience 39:651-2 O '89. T. J. Kindt

THE GENETICS OF SOCIAL EVOLUTION. 1989
  Science 245:313-14 Jl 21 '89. R. H. Crozier

GEOMAGNETISM. 2v 1987
  Physics Today 42:72 Je '89. G. Rostoker

GEORGE, E. Payment in blood. 1989
  The New York Times Book Review 94:58-9 N 12 '89. J. Rubins

GEORGIA O'KEEFFE. 1989
  Ms. 18:38-9 N '89. A. Wallach

GERASSI, J. Jean-Paul Sartre; v1, Protestant or protester? 1989
  The New York Times Book Review 94:21 Jl 9 '89. A. Lacy

GERMAN WORKERS' CULTURE IN THE UNITED STATES, 1850 TO 1920. 1988
  The Nation 248:858-60 Je 19 '89. P. Buhle

GERMOND, J. AND WITCOVER, J. Whose broad stripes and bright stars? 1989
  The American Spectator 22:43-5 N '89. F. Barnes
  Business Week p12 Ag 28 '89. R. Fly
  The New York Times Book Review 94:6 S 3 '89. T. Goldstein

GERRARD, J. M. AND BORTOLOTTI, G. R. The bald eagle. 1988
  The Conservationist 43:52-3 Ja/F '89. P. E. Nye

GERSHONI, I. AND JANKOWSKI, J. P. Egypt, Islam, and the Arabs. 1986
  The New Republic 200:33-7 Je 5 '89. A. Ghosh

GERVASI, T. Soviet military power. 1988
  National Review 41:52 Ag 18 '89. J. E. Oberg

GHOSH, A. The shadow lines. 1989
  The New Republic 201:37-9 Ag 7-14 '89. V. Klinkenborg
  The New York Times Book Review 94:10 Jl 2 '89. E. Hower

GIBBONS, K. A virtuous woman. 1989
  The New York Times Book Review 94:12-13 Ap 30 '89. P. Powell

GIBLIN, J. Let there be light. 1988
  The New York Times Book Review 94:35 Mr 12 '89. P. M. Isaacson

GIBSON, I. Federico García Lorca, a life. 1989
  The New York Times Book Review 94:1+ O 8 '89. A. Josephs

GIBSON, W. Mona Lisa overdrive. 1988
  The Nation 248:636-9 My 8 '89. E. Davis

GIDDINS, G. Satchmo. 1988
  American Heritage 40:16 My/Je '89. G. C. Ward
  Down Beat 56:51 Ap '89. C. Deffaa

GIESE, R. The Donegal pictures. 1988
  America 160:252-4 Mr 18 '89. J. B. Breslin

GILBERT, B. God gave us this country. 1989
  The New York Times Book Review 94:10 Ag 6 '89. R. Sanders

GILBERT, D. Sandinistas. 1988
  Commonweal 116:121-2 F 24 '89. E. R. F. Sheehan

GILBERT, M. The Second World War. 1989
  The New York Times Book Review 94:16-17 N 26 '89. G. A. Craig

GILBERT, M. Winston S. Churchill; v8, Never despair, 1945-1965. 1988
  National Review 41:59-60 Ja 27 '89. H. W. Crocker, III
  The New York Review of Books 36:36-42 Je 15 '89. D. Cannadine

GILBERT, S. M. Blood pressure. 1988
  The New York Times Book Review 94:38 Mr 12 '89. B. Bennett

GILBERT, S. M. AND GUBAR, S. No man's land; v2, Sexchanges. 1988

The New York Times Book Review 94:9 F 19 '89. W. M. Kendrick

GILCHRIST, E. The Anna papers. 1988
  The New York Times Book Review 94:16 Ja 15 '89. M. Paley

GILCHRIST, E. Light can be both wave and particle. 1989
  The New York Times Book Review 94:13 O 22 '89. R. Hoffman

GILDER, G. F. Microcosm. 1989
  Business Week p14-15 S 11 '89. J. Carey
  National Review 41:50+ O 27 '89. R. Bailey
  The New Republic 201:38-42 N 20 '89. R. Wright
  The New York Times Book Review 94:15 O 15 '89. L. Winner

GILL, E. An essay on typography. 1988
  The New York Times Book Review 94:22 S 10 '89. P. Rand

GILL, S. C. William Wordsworth. 1989
  The New York Review of Books 36:45-50 D 21 '89. M. H. Abrams
  The New York Times Book Review 94:49 Je 11 '89. P. D. Sheats

GILLESPIE, A. K. AND ROCKLAND, M. A. Looking for America on the New Jersey Turnpike. 1989
  The New York Times Book Review 94:14 N 19 '89. E. Allen

GILLIAM, G. H. Racin'—the NASCAR/Winston Cup stock car racing series. 1989
  Motor Trend 41:34 S '89. G. Von Dare

GILLIATT, P. A woman of singular occupation. 1989
  The New York Times Book Review 94:24 My 14 '89. E. C. Munro

GILLMAN, S. K. Dark twins. 1989
  The New York Review of Books 36:39-44 Jl 20 '89. F. C. Crews

GILMAN, S. L. Difference and pathology. 1985
  America 160:564-5 Je 10 '89. W. W. Meissner

GINSBERG, B. The captive public. 1986
  Design for Arts in Education 90:51-2 Jl/Ag '89. S. Hope

GINSBURG, F. D. Contested lives. 1989
  The Christian Century 106:1125-6 N 29 '89. M. J. Reineke
  Commonweal 116:652 N 17 '89. E. P. Flynn
  The New Republic 201:30-3 Jl 10 '89. B. Ehrenreich

GINZBERG, E. AND DUTKA, A. B. The financing of biomedical research. 1989
  Science 246:1062 N 24 '89. R. A. Rettig

GIORDANO, P. Awakening to mission.
  America 161:326-7 N 11 '89. B. F. Nebres

GIORGIS, D. W. Red tears.
  The American Spectator 22:54-5 Je '89. A. Puddington

GITTINGS, J. China changes face. 1989
  History Today 39:48 O '89. W. V. Wallace

GIVENS, C. J. Wealth without risk. 1988
  Money 18:15 Ap '89

GLASS, J. M. Private terror/public life. 1989
  The New York Times Book Review 94:15 O 8 '89. F. Klagsbrun

GLASS, L. AND MACKEY, M. C. From clocks to chaos. 1988
  Physics Today 42:72 Jl '89. P. F. Zweifel
  Science 243:675-6 F 3 '89. W. M. Schaffer

GLAZER, M. AND GLAZER, P. M. The whistleblowers. 1989
  Science 244:835-6 My 19 '89. J. M. Beyer
  Society 26:90-3 S/O '89. R. T. Golembiewski

GLAZER, N. The limits of social policy. 1988
  The American Spectator 22:36-7 Mr '89. M. Novak
  The New Republic 200:32-5 Ja 23 '89. P. Starr

GLENN, C. L. The myth of the common school. 1988
  Christianity Today 33:60-1 D 15 '89. L. L. Steele

GLICKFELD, C. L. Useful gifts.
  The New York Times Book Review 94:21 My 21 '89. M. Childress

GLICKMAN, N. J. AND WOODWARD, D. P. The new competitors. 1989
  Business Week p12 My 15 '89. W. J. Holstein
  The New York Times Book Review 94:51 My 21 '89. J. Dreyfuss

GLOVER, B. AND SHEPHERD, J. The family fitness handbook. 1989
  Women's Sports & Fitness 11:16 S '89

GLYNN, T. Watching the body burn. 1988
  The New York Times Book Review 94:16 Mr 5 '89. U. Hegi

GOBLE, P. Beyond the ridge. 1989
  The New York Times Book Review 94:34-5 D 10 '89. M. Dorris

GÖCKELER, M. AND SCHÜCKER, T. Differential geometry, gauge theories, and gravity. 1987
  Physics Today 42:82 Ja '89. R. I. Nepomechie

GODDEN, R. A house with four rooms. 1989
  The New York Times Book Review 94:24 D 24 '89. S. Rudikoff

GODSEY, F. A gathering at the river.
  The Washington Monthly 21:57-8 Jl/Ag '89. B. Semple

GOLAN, M. The road to peace. 1989
  The Washington Monthly 21:55-6 N '89. M. Polner

GOLD, J. T. Monsters and madonnas. 1988

The Christian Century 106:598-9 Je 7-14 '89. S. N. Rosenbaum

GOLDFARB, J. C. Beyond glasnost. 1989
National Review 41:42-3 Je 2 '89. R. Pipes

GOLDING, W. Fire down below. 1989
America 160:434-5 My 6 '89. R. M. Beston
The New York Times Book Review 94:37 Ap 2 '89. D. Bair
Time 133:81+ Mr 20 '89. P. Gray

GOLDMAN, H. G. Jolson. 1988
American Heritage 40:108 Mr '89

GOLDMAN, N. C. American space law. 1988
Science 246:132-3 O 6 '89. E. Gordon

GOLDMAN, P. L. AND MATHEWS, T. The quest for the presidency, 1988. 1989
The American Spectator 22:43-5 N '89. F. Barnes
The New York Times Book Review 94:38 D 10 '89. S. V. Roberts

GOLDSTEIN, R. The late-summer passion of a woman of mind. 1989
The New York Times Book Review 94:28-9 My 7 '89. R. Cohen

GOLDSTEIN, R. Reporting the counterculture. 1989
The Washington Monthly 21:58-60 D '89. T. Gitlin

GOLDSTICK, G. Business Rx. 1988
High Technology Business 9:13 Ap '89. M. Estren

GOLDWATER, B. M. Goldwater. 1988
The Christian Century 106:86-7 Ja 25 '89. F. Rotondaro

GOLENBOCK, P. Personal fouls. 1989
The New York Times Book Review 94:12-13 Ag 27 '89. T. Whitaker

GOMBROWICZ, W. Diary; v2, 1957-1961. 1988
The New York Times Book Review 94:34 N 5 '89. S. Gavronsky

GONDWANA AND TETHYS. 1988
Science 244:1597-8 Je 30 '89. G. D. Stanley, Jr.

GONZALEZ-CRUSSI, F. The five senses. 1989
The New York Times Book Review 94:35 Ap 9 '89. A. Fels

GOODE, J. M. Best addresses. 1988
Americana 17:20 Jl/Ag '89. R. M. Williams

GOODMAN, D. C. Power and penury. 1988
History Today 39:56-7 Ap '89. I. A. A. Thompson

GOODRICK, M. The advancing guitarist.
Down Beat 56:57 Jl '89. R. Peckham

GOODWIN, R. N. Remembering America. 1988
American Heritage 40:14+ F '89. G. C. Ward

GORDIMER, N. The essential gesture. 1988
The New York Review of Books 36:12-14 Mr 30 '89. N. Ascherson

GORDON, E. A. Mark the music. 1989
The New Republic 201:34-7 Ag 7-14 '89. S. Kauffmann
The New York Times Book Review 94:16 Jl 16 '89. D. Shewey

GORDON, G. AND COHEN, R. Down to the wire. 1989
Business Week p18+ D 25 '89-Ja 1 '90. C. Welles
The New York Times Book Review 94:10-11 D 24 '89. J. D. Atwater

GORDON, M. The other side. 1989
Ms. 18:21-2 O '89. S. Shapiro
The Nation 249:653+ N 27 '89. J. Leonard
The New Republic 201:39-41 D 18 '89. P. K. Bell
The New York Times Book Review 94:9 O 15 '89. M. S. Bell

GOT'E, IU. V. Time of troubles. 1988
The New York Review of Books 36:46-8 Je 15 '89. N. Davies

GOULD, S. J. Wonderful life. 1989
Maclean's 102:85 N 27 '89. D. Cumming
The New York Times Book Review 94:1+ O 22 '89. J. Gleick
Science 246:680 N 3 '89. W. C. Sweet

GOULDEN, J. C. Fit to print. 1988
The American Spectator 22:35-6 F '89. S. C. Munson

GOVIER, K. Before and after.
Maclean's 102:61 Je 12 '89. J. Bemrose

GOYTISOLO, J. Forbidden territory. 1989
The New York Times Book Review 94:12-13 F 12 '89. W. Gimbel

GRADWOHL, J. AND GREENBERG, R. Saving the tropical forests. 1988
BioScience 39:644-5 O '89. M. J. Balick

GRAFTON, S. "F" is for fugitive. 1989
The New York Times Book Review 94:17 My 21 '89. E. Weiner

GRAHAM, D. No name on the bullet. 1989
New York 22:64 Jl 31 '89. R. Koenig

GRAHAM, L. R. Science, philosophy, and human behavior in the Soviet Union. 1987
The Bulletin of the Atomic Scientists 45:39-40 S '89. V. N. Soyfer
Physics Today 42:63-5 Ap '89. E. Lashchyk

GRAHAM, W. A. Beyond the written Word. 1987
America 160:203-4 Mr 4 '89. W. J. Ong

GRAMPP, W. D. Pricing the priceless. 1989
The New York Times Book Review 94:33 N 19 '89. G. Clueck

GRANT, G. The world we created at Hamilton High. 1988

Christianity Today 33:31-2 F 17 '89. B. L. Shelley

GRANT, M. The rise of the Greeks. 1987
The New York Times Book Review 94:16 Ja 22 '89. W. G. Forrest

GRASS, G. Show your tongue. 1989
The New York Times Book Review 94:12 My 21 '89. C. Blaise

GRATZ, R. B. The living city. 1989
Architectural Record 177:67 Jl '89. D. Gantenbein
The Nation 248:772-4+ Je 5 '89. M. Gottlieb
The New York Times Book Review 94:26 My 14 '89. R. Campbell

GRAY, J. Liberalisms. 1989
National Review 41:44 D 31 '89. B. Miner

THE GRAYWOLF ANNUAL FIVE.
The New York Times Book Review 94:22-3 D 17 '89. D. Lazere

THE GREAT DOCK STRIKE, 1889. 1988
History Today 39:52 N '89. B. W. J. Fishman

GREELEY, A. M. God in popular culture. 1988
America 160:459-61 My 13 '89. C. L. Brunkhorst

GREELEY, A. M. Religious change in America. 1989
The Christian Century 106:823 S 13-20 '89. F. Brown
Commonweal 116:568-9 O 20 '89. J. A. Coleman

GREENBERG, D. F. The construction of homosexuality. 1988
The Atlantic 263:74-8 F '89. J. Boswell
The Christian Century 106:911-16 O 11 '89. D. S. Browning
The New York Times Book Review 94:9-10 Ja 15 '89. N. B. Dirks

GREENBERG, H. Hank Greenberg. 1989
Gentlemen's Quarterly 59:77-8 Jl '89. M. Richler

GREENBERG, I. The Jewish way. 1988
Commentary 88:60-2 Ag '89. D. Singer
The New Leader 72:18-19 Ja 9 '89. L. Grossman

GREENBLATT, S. J. Shakespearean negotiations. 1988
History Today 39:52-3 Ap '89. R. Wilson

GREENE, G. The captain and the enemy. 1988
America 160:433-4 My 6 '89. E. M. Casey
The New Republic 200:28-31 Ja 23 '89. D. Pryce-Jones
The New York Review of Books 36:3-4 Mr 16 '89. J. Bayley

GREENHOUSE WARMING. 1989
Science 246:1062-3 N 24 '89. J. Firor

GREENSTEIN, G. The symbiotic universe. 1988
Astronomy 17:99-100 Mr '89. R. Burnham

GREGORY, R. America 1941. 1989
The New Leader 72:20-1 F 6 '89. G. Sirgiovanni

GRESHAM, D. H. Lenten lands. 1988
The Christian Century 106:288-9 Mr 15 '89. M. Rosenbaum

GRIER, K. C. Culture & comfort. 1988
The New York Review of Books 36:35-7 N 9 '89. W. Rybczynski

GRIFFITH, S. F. Home town news. 1988
The Atlantic 263:111+ Ja '89. D. M. Kennedy

GRISOGONO, V. Sports injuries. 1987
Women's Sports & Fitness 11:14 S '89

GROBEL, L. The Hustons. 1989
The New York Times Book Review 94:20 N 19 '89. N. Johnson

GROBSTEIN, C. Science and the unborn. 1988
Commentary 87:60-3 My '89. R. J. Neuhaus
The New York Times Book Review 94:10 Ja 8 '89. A. H. Malcolm

GROSSINGER, R. The night sky. 1988
Astronomy 17:102 Mr '89. R. Stanton

GROSSMAN, B. Donna O'Neeshuck was chased by some cows. 1988
The New York Times Book Review 94:29 Ag 6 '89. A. Banks

GROSSMAN, D. See under—love. 1989
Commentary 88:56-60 Jl '89. A. L. Mintz
Commonweal 116:477-9 S 8 '89. M. Marget
The New Republic 200:39-43 My 15 '89. H. Halkin
The New York Times Book Review 94:7 Ap 16 '89. E. White

GROTH, J. Edmund Wilson. 1989
National Review 41:41-3 S 1 '89. C. Williamson

GROVE, J. M. The Little Ice Age. 1988
Science 246:134-6 O 6 '89. J. T. Overpeck
Scientific American 260:142+ My '89. P. Morrison

GROVES, C. P. A theory of human and primate evolution. 1989
Science 246:1645 D 22 '89. J. Marks

GRUBB, K. B. Razzle dazzle. 1989
The New York Times Book Review 94:20 D 17 '89. H. Dudar

GRUCHOW, P. The necessity of empty places. 1988
Smithsonian 20:172-3 Je '89. D. Drabelle
Wilderness 53:53-4+ Fall '89. C. E. Little

GRUNFELD, F. V. Rodin. 1987
Art in America 77:27+ F '89. A. E. Elsen

GUELZO, A. C. Edwards on the will. 1989
The Christian Century 106:695-6 Jl 19-26 '89. J. Pahl

GUGLIOTTA, G. F. AND LEEN, J. Kings of cocaine. 1989
National Review 41:47-8 Je 2 '89. W. Lutton
The New Republic 201:26-34 N 27 '89. T. Rosenberg
The New York Times Book Review 94:13 Ap 30 '89. D. H. Bain

Newsweek 113:78 My 15 '89. R. Rivard
GULLETTE, M. M. Safe at last in the middle years. 1988
The New York Times Book Review 94:9 Ja 1 '89. F. Conroy
GUMMERMAN, J. We find ourselves in Moontown. 1989
The New York Times Book Review 94:9-10 My 28 '89. J. Humphreys
GUNN, S. J. Charles Brandon, Duke of Suffolk, c. 1484-1545. 1988
History Today 39:56-7 F '89. C. Given-Wilson
GURGANUS, A. The oldest living Confederate widow tells all. 1989
The New Republic 201:37-41 O 30 '89. J. Tolson
The New York Times Book Review 94:1+ Ag 13 '89. J. Wilcox
Newsweek 114:67 S 25 '89. P. S. Prescott
GUROCK, J. S. The men and women of Yeshiva. 1988
Commentary 87:74-6 F '89. S. Bayme
GUSSOW, Z. Leprosy, racism, and public health. 1989
Science 246:679 N 3 '89. A. M. Brandt
GUTMAN, R. Banana diplomacy. 1988
The Progressive 53:42-3 F '89. S. Landau

H

HAAN, H. DE AND HAAGSMA, I. Architects in competition. 1988
Architectural Record 177:67+ F '89. S. Gutterman
HABEGGER, A. Henry James and the "woman business". 1989
The New York Times Book Review 94:54-5 S 24 '89. W. C. Booth
HACKL, E. Aurora's motive. 1988
Mademoiselle 95:52 Ja '89. J. Maynard
HACKWORTH, D. H. AND SHERMAN, J. About face. 1989
The Bulletin of the Atomic Scientists 45:37-8 O '89. J. Record
Commonweal 116:707-10 D 15 '89. P. D. Baumann
The New York Times Book Review 94:7+ Ap 30 '89. B. E. Trainor
The Washington Monthly 21:50-4 Je '89. M. Massing
HAFFNER, S. Der Teufelspakt.
The New York Review of Books 36:15-19 Mr 30 '89. G. A. Craig
HAGEDORN, J. AND MACON, P. People and folks. 1988
The New York Times Book Review 94:36 F 5 '89. A. Campbell
HAGERFORS, L. The whales of Lake Tanganyika. 1989
Newsweek 113:71 My 8 '89. P. S. Prescott
HAIGH, C. Elizabeth I. 1988
History Today 39:51-2 Je '89. F. Heal
HAINES, J. M. The stars, the snow, the fire. 1989
The New York Times Book Review 94:14-15 D 10 '89. R. M. Pyle
HALBERSTAM, D. Summer of '49. 1989
America 160:489 My 27 '89. G. W. Hunt
The American Spectator 22:35-7 O '89. V. Gold
Business Week p16+ My 22 '89. J. Friedman
The Nation 249:210-13 Ag 21-28 '89. P. Schrag
The New York Times Book Review 94:9 My 7 '89. J. Kaplan
Time 133:114+ My 22 '89. M. Duffy
HALFON, M. S. Integrity. 1989
The Christian Century 106:1204 D 20-27 '89. D. A. Hoekema
HALL, B. The dreamers. 1989
The New York Times Book Review 94:23 Ap 23 '89. L. Forestier
HALL, B. K. The neural crest. 1988
Science 246:1503 D 15 '89. P. Thorogood
HALL, D. J. Thinking the faith. 1989
The Christian Century 106:856 S 27 '89. J. C. Pugh
HALL, J. Tropical freeze. 1989
The New York Times Book Review 94:38 O 15 '89. S. Paretsky
HALL, M. G. The last American Puritan. 1988
America 160:563-4 Je 10 '89. A. Rogers
HALL, P. Cities of tomorrow. 1988
History Today 39:56 Je '89. R. Thorne
HALL, R. Kisses of the enemy. 1989
The New Republic 200:38-40 Ja 30 '89. T. R. Edwards
HALL, W. H. The rest of the dream. 1988
The Progressive 53:43-4 Ap '89. J. Egerton
HALPERIN, J. U. Félix Fénéon. 1988
The New Leader 72:19-20 Ja 23 '89. G. Woodcock
The New Republic 200:40-1 F 6 '89. E. V. Thaw
The New York Review of Books 36:38-41 N 23 '89. J. Joll
The New York Times Book Review 94:12 Mr 5 '89. R. Mellow
HALPERN, B. The first historians. 1988
The Christian Century 106:538-9 My 17 '89. W. Harrelson
HALSTEAD, B. W. Poisonous and venomous marine animals of the world. 2nd ed. 1988
Scientific American 260:112-13 F '89. P. Morrison
HAMBURGER, V. The heritage of experimental embryology. 1988
BioScience 39:336-7 My '89. J. P. Wourms

HAMILL, P. Loving women. 1989
The New York Times Book Review 94:13 Ap 2 '89. T. J. Fleming
HAMILTON, J. M. Edgar Snow, a biography. 1988
The Bulletin of the Atomic Scientists 45:41-2 Je '89. J. W. Powell
The New York Review of Books 36:15-17 F 16 '89. J. Mirsky
The New York Times Book Review 94:13 Ja 8 '89. S. Topping
The Washington Monthly 21:50-2+ Jl/Ag '89. J. Mathews
HAMMOND, J. H. Secret and sacred. 1988
The American Spectator 22:43 Ja '89. D. Shiflett
The New York Review of Books 35:16-20 Ja 19 '89. J. M. McPherson
The New York Times Book Review 94:22 Ja 29 '89. R. Brown
HAMMOND, W. M. Public affairs. 1988
The New York Times Book Review 94:5-6 Jl 2 '89. N. Lemann
HAMPSON, N. Prelude to terror. 1988
History Today 39:54 D '89. N. Aston
HAMPTON, B. AND COLE, D. N. Soft paths. 1988
The Conservationist 44:50-1 N/D '89. S. Daly
Sierra 74:109-10 Mr/Ap '89. C. Hardy
HAMPTON, L. Hamp. 1989
The New York Times Book Review 94:24+ D 3 '89. M. Miles
HANCOCK, G. Lords of poverty. 1989
The New York Times Book Review 94:12-13 N 12 '89. T. Clarke
HANCOCK, R. C. Calvin and the foundations of modern politics. 1989
The Christian Century 106:1128-9 N 29 '89. R. T. Leupp
HANDBOOK FOR DEVELOPING PUBLIC CONFIDENCE IN SCHOOLS. 1988
Phi Delta Kappan 70:489-90 F '89. A. W. Steller
HANDBOOK ON SYNCHROTRON RADIATION; v2. 1987
Physics Today 42:72+ My '89. I. Lindau
HANDKE, P. The afternoon of a writer. 1989
The Nation 249:694-5 D 4 '89. J. Leonard
The New Leader 72:18-19 O 2-16 '89. M. Kamine
The New Yorker 65:104-6 D 25 '89. J. Updike
HANNAH, B. Boomerang. 1989
The New York Review of Books 36:52-3 Ag 17 '89. T. R. Edwards
The New York Times Book Review 94:19 My 14 '89. J. Kennedy
HANRIEDER, W. F. Germany, America, Europe. 1989
The New York Times Book Review 94:13-14 S 17 '89. D. Gress
HANSCOMBE, G. E. AND SMYERS, V. L. Writing for their lives. 1987
The New York Times Book Review 94:25 Mr 12 '89. R. M. Brownstein
HANSEN, R. Nebraska. 1989
The New York Times Book Review 94:31 F 19 '89. M. La Chapelle
HANSON, J. Artists' taxes, the hands-on guide. 1987
American Artist 53:86-7 Ap '89. M. C. Nelson
HARDISON, O. B. Disappearing through the skylight. 1989
The New York Times Book Review 94:3+ D 31 '89. M. Bradbury
HARGREAVES, J. D. Decolonization in Africa. 1988
History Today 39:51 Ag '89. A. H. M. Kirk-Greene
HARGROVE, E. C. Jimmy Carter as president. 1988
The Christian Century 106:322+ Mr 22-29 '89. L. P. Ribuffo
HARINGTON, D. The cockroaches of Stay More. 1989
The New York Times Book Review 94:17 Ap 23 '89. H. Middleton
HARKABI, Y. Israel's fateful hour. 1988
Commonweal 116:22-6 Ja 13 '89. R. G. Hoyt
National Review 41:46-7 My 5 '89. J. Sobran
HARMON, F. G. The executive odyssey. 1989
High Technology Business 9:16 S/O '89. M. Estren
HARPER, D. A. Working knowledge. 1987
American Craft 49:22+ Ap/My '89. E. G. Mishler
HARPER'S BIBLE COMMENTARY. 1988
The Christian Century 106:328-30 Mr 22-29 '89. D. M. Hay
HARRIGAN, A. H. AND HAWKINS, W. R. American economic pre-eminence.
National Review 41:54 Je 30 '89. C. Williamson
HARRINGTON, M. The long-distance runner. 1988
The New York Review of Books 36:29-31 Mr 16 '89. M. Kazin
HARRINGTON, M. Socialism. 1989
The New York Times Book Review 94:15-16 Jl 16 '89. P. Berman
HARRIS, E. H. The Chlamydomonas sourcebook. 1989
Science 246:1503-4 D 15 '89. J. K. Hoober
HARRIS, E. L. Mississippi solo. 1988
Smithsonian 20:166+ Ap '89. J. Idema
HARRIS, J. "They always call us ladies". 1988
Commentary 87:66-7 Mr '89. J. J. DiIulio
HARRIS, M. J. The Zanucks of Hollywood. 1989
The New York Times Book Review 94:11-12 Jl 23 '89. D. Jacobs

HARRIS, S. L. Fire mountains of the west. 1988
Earth Science 42:31-2 Summ '89
HARRISON, B. G. Italian days. 1989
The Atlantic 264:89-91 Ag '89. C. Kummer
The New York Times Book Review 94:15-16 S 10 '89. A. Lee
HARRISON, C. Somebody's baby. 1989
The New York Times Book Review 94:25 Jl 9 '89. E. Villars
HARRISON, J. AND SAMS, F. The passing. 1988
Americana 16:14-15 Ja/F '89. J. Neary
HARRISON, V. V. Changing habits. 1988
National Review 41:52 Ap 21 '89. P. L. Buckley
The New York Times Book Review 94:39 My 7 '89. B. Sigmund
Smithsonian 20:120-1 Jl '89. F. Getlein
HARRISS, G. L. Cardinal Beaufort. 1988
History Today 39:50-1 Ag '89. N. Saul
HARRISSON, T. Living through the Blitz. 1989
Repr. Orig. pub.: Collins, 1976
The New York Review of Books 36:3-4+ S 28 '89. N. G. A. Annan, Baron
HART, G. Exploring the past. 1989
The New York Times Book Review 94:35 O 1 '89. K. O. Fakih
HARTCUP, G. The war of invention. 1988
Science 243:1087-8 F 24 '89. J. H. Morrow
HARTILL, R. Writers revealed. 1989
The New York Times Book Review 94:41 N 5 '89. M. L'Engle
HARVEY, J. B. The Abilene paradox and other meditations on management. 1988
High Technology Business 9:17 Mr '89. M. Estren
HARWIT, M. Astrophysical concepts. 2nd ed. 1988
Astronomy 17:100-1 Mr '89. D. S. Evans
HASKELL, H. The early music revival. 1988
The New York Times Book Review 94:26 F 26 '89. J. Rockwell
HASS, R. Human wishes. 1989
The Nation 249:722-3 D 11 '89. D. Bogen
The New York Times Book Review 94:63 N 12 '89. C. Kizer
HASSRICK, P. H. Charles M. Russell. 1989
American Artist 53:118-19 S '89. M. C. Nelson
HAWKE, D. F. Nuts and bolts of the past. 1988
Science 244:720-1 My 12 '89. C. Pursell
HAWKES, J. Julian's house. 1989
The New York Times Book Review 94:15 D 10 '89. M. J. Gerber
HAWKING, S. W. A brief history of time. 1988
The Humanist 49:42 Mr/Ap '89. M. Hillar
HAY, D. AND LAW, J. E. Italy in the age of the Renaissance, 1380-1530. 1989
History Today 39:59 D '89. G. Holmes
HAYEK, F. A. VON. The fatal conceit. 1989
Fortune 119:159-60 My 8 '89. D. R. Henderson
The Nation 248:525 Ap 17 '89. R. L. Heilbroner
National Review 41:50-1 My 5 '89. T. Bethell
HAYS, D. The hangman's children. 1989
The New York Times Book Review 94:10-11 Ag 13 '89. D. Mason
HAYSLIP, L. L. AND WURTS, J. When heaven and earth changed places. 1989
The New York Times Book Review 94:1+ Je 25 '89. D. K. Shipler
HEANEY, S. The government of the tongue. 1988
The New York Times Book Review 94:25 Mr 5 '89. L. McDiarmid
The New Yorker 65:102-7 Mr 13 '89. H. H. Vendler
HEARON, S. Owning Jolene. 1989
The New York Times Book Review 94:10-11 Ja 22 '89. T. Sandlin
HECHT, S. AND COCKBURN, A. The fate of the forest.
The New York Times Book Review 94:10 D 24 '89. E. Gaspari
HEILBRONER, R. L. AND BERNSTEIN, P. L. The debt and the deficit. 1989
Fortune 119:329-30 Je 5 '89. T. May, Jr.
The Nation 249:321-4 S 25 '89. R. Pollin
HEILBRUN, C. G. Writing a woman's life. 1988
The New York Times Book Review 94:19 Ja 8 '89. W. Martin
HEIN, C. The distant lover. 1989
The New York Times Book Review 94:33 My 7 '89. K. Washburn
HEINRICH, B. Ravens in winter. 1989
The New York Times Book Review 94:12-13 S 24 '89. M. J. West
HELLER, E. The importance of Nietzsche. 1988
The New York Times Book Review 94:28 Ap 30 '89. A. Nehamas
HELLER, S. AND CHWAST, S. Graphic style. 1988
American Artist 53:82-3 Jl '89. R. Fillie
HELPRIN, M. Swan Lake. 1989
The New York Times Book Review 94:28 N 12 '89. P. F. Neumeyer
HEMMING, J. Amazon frontier. 1987
History Today 39:56-8 Ja '89. C. Abel

HENDERSON, A. On the air. 1988
American Heritage 40:111+ Ap '89
HENNELLY, A. T. Theology for a liberating church. 1989
America 161:168-9 S 23 '89. B. J. Cooke
HENNESSY, P. Whitehall. 1989
History Today 39:50-1 Je '89. M. Beloff, Baron
HENRY, A. Grand prix car design & technology in the 1980s. 1988
Car and Driver 35:26-7 Ag '89. B. Visnic
HENRY, C. F. H. Twilight of a great civilization.
The Christian Century 106:480 My 3 '89. J. Gros
Christianity Today 33:30 Ap 7 '89. R. J. Neuhaus
HENRY FRANCIS DU PONT WINTERTHUR MUSEUM. Two centuries of prints in America, 1680-1880. 1987
Antiques 136:456+ S '89. G.-G. Deák
HENSON, M. A. A Black explorer at the North Pole. 1989
The New York Times Book Review 94:11 Ag 13 '89. K. Bouton
HENTOFF, N. John Cardinal O'Connor. 1988
Christianity Today 33:53-4 S 22 '89. G. M. Condon
HEPPENHEIMER, T. A. The coming quake. 1988
The New York Times Book Review 94:11 Ja 1 '89. K. C. Cole
HERBERG, W. From Marxism to Judaism. 1989
National Review 41:50-3 Jl 14 '89. R. J. Neuhaus
HERBERT, R. L. Impressionism. 1988
Art in America 77:27+ Ja '89. K. Adler
History Today 39:54-5 Ap '89. M. Pointon
The Nation 248:494-8 Ap 10 '89. P. Mattick, Jr.
The New Republic 200:43-6 F 20 '89. R. Shattuck
The New York Review of Books 36:20-5 S 28 '89. J. D. Flam
HERBERT, W. The noose of laurels. 1989
The New York Times Book Review 94:11 Ag 13 '89. K. Bouton
Time 134:63 Jl 31 '89. J. Skow
HERMAN, E. S. AND CHOMSKY, N. Manufacturing consent. 1988
America 161:42-4 Jl 15-22 '89. R. A. Schroth
The Nation 248:670-3 My 15 '89. P. Green
The New Republic 200:34-8 Ja 9-16 '89. N. Lemann
HERSEY, J. Life sketches. 1989
The American Spectator 22:52 Je '89. F. X. Rocca
HERTSGAARD, M. On bended knee. 1988
The Bulletin of the Atomic Scientists 45:62-3 Ja/F '89. S. Weinberg
The New Republic 200:34-8 Ja 9-16 '89. N. Lemann
HERTZBERG, A. The Jews in America. 1989
The New York Times Book Review 94:5 N 26 '89. J. A. Garraty
HERZOG, A. The woodchipper murder. 1989
The New York Times Book Review 94:52+ O 15 '89. R. Grant
HETEROCHROMATIN. 1988
BioScience 39:736-8 N '89. J. Mitra
HETEROCHRONY IN EVOLUTION. 1988
BioScience 39:821-2 D '89. G. D. Edgecombe
HETHERINGTON, N. S. Science and objectivity. 1988
Sky and Telescope 78:270-1 S '89. O. Gingerich
HEWLETT, R. G. AND HOLL, J. M. Atoms for peace and war, 1953-1961. 1989
Science 246:826-7 N 10 '89. R. A. Divine
HEY, A. J. G. AND WALTERS, P. The quantum universe. 1987
Physics Today 42:84 Ja '89. R. H. March
Sky and Telescope 77:39-40 Ja '89. R. P. Kirshner
HEYMANN, C. D. A woman named Jackie. 1989
Harper's Bazaar 122:164-5+ My '89. R. Unger
McCall's 116:31-2+ Jl '89. B. G. Harrison
Newsweek 112:91 My 22 '89. J. Kroll
HIAASEN, C. Skin tight. 1989
The New York Times Book Review 94:42 O 15 '89. K. Dunn
HICK, J. An interpretation of religion. 1989
The Christian Century 106:890-1 O 4 '89. R. A. Segal
HIGGINS, G. V. The progress of the seasons. 1989
The Nation 249:210-13 Ag 21-28 '89. P. Schrag
The New York Times Book Review 94:11 Ap 23 '89. L. S. Ritter
HIGHAM, C. AND MOSELEY, R. Cary Grant. 1989
The New York Times Book Review 94:19 Ap 30 '89. B. Shulgasser
HIGHSMITH, P. Mermaids on the golf course. 1988
The New York Times Book Review 94:34 Ja 29 '89. E. Stumpf
HIJUELOS, O. The mambo kings play songs of love. 1989
The New York Times Book Review 94:1+ Ag 27 '89. M. Jefferson
Time 134:68 Ag 14 '89. R. Z. Sheppard
HILDEBRAND, J. Reading the river. 1988
Wilderness 52:67 Wint '88. C. E. Little
HILL, B. W. Robert Harley. 1988
History Today 39:52-3 F '89. H. T. Dickinson
HILL, C. A tinker and poor man. 1988
The New York Review of Books 36:27-8 Mr 2 '89. R. M. Adams
The New York Times Book Review 94:31 Mr 12 '89. M. W. Ferguson

The New York Times Book Review 94:1+ Mr 5 '89. P. Jenkins

HORNE, A. Harold Macmillan; v2, 1957-1986. 1989
The New York Review of Books 36:47-9 N 23 '89. H. Young
The New York Times Book Review 94:11-12 N 26 '89. P. Brendon

HORNER, J. R. AND GORMAN, J. Digging dinosaurs. 1988
Earth Science 42:33-4 Spr '89
Smithsonian 19:32 Ja '89. D. Lessem

HORROX, R. Richard III. 1989
History Today 39:57 D '89. C. Giry-Deloison

HORVATH, P. An occasional cow.
The New York Times Book Review 94:43 My 21 '89. P. T. O'Conner

HORWITT, S. D. Let them call me rebel. 1989
The Christian Century 106:1050-3 N 15 '89. R. Luecke
The New Republic 201:30-4+ D 25 '89. S. Wilentz
The New York Times Book Review 94:23 N 12 '89. N. Lichtenstein

HOSAIN, A. Phoenix fled, and other stories. 1989
First pub. in U.K. by Chatto & Windus, 1953
The Nation 249:800-1 D 25 '89. Z. Jaffrey

HOSAIN, A. Sunlight on a broken column. 1989
First pub.: Chatto & Windus, 1961
The Nation 249:800-1 D 25 '89. Z. Jaffrey

HOSPITAL, J. T. Charades. 1989
Maclean's 102:62 Mr 6 '89. J. Bemrose
The New York Times Book Review 94:14-15 Mr 12 '89. R. Loewinsohn

HOUGH, R. A. AND RICHARDS, D. The Battle of Britain. 1989
The New York Review of Books 36:3-4+ S 28 '89. N. G. A. Annan, Baron
The New York Times Book Review 94:11 D 31 '89. D. Henahan

HOUNSHELL, D. A. AND SMITH, J. K. Science and corporate strategy. 1988
Science 244:840-1 My 19 '89. J. P. Swann
Technology Review 92:73-4 My/Je '89. G. Wise

HOUSE, H. W. AND ICE, T. Dominion theology. 1988
Christianity Today 33:52-3 S 22 '89. R. V. Pierard

HOUSEHOLD AND COMMUNITY IN THE MESOAMERICAN PAST. 1988
Science 244:863-4 My 19 '89. D. A. Freidel

HOVLAND, M. AND JUDD, A. Seabed pockmarks and seepages. 1988
Science 244:590-1 My 5 '89. K. A. Kvenvolden

HOW DOES TREATMENT HELP? 1988
The New York Times Book Review 94:14 Ag 6 '89. P. L. Wachtel

HOW LABOR MARKETS WORK. 1988
Monthly Labor Review 111:52 D '88. A. J. Barkume

HOW TO START A RESPITE SERVICE FOR PEOPLE WITH ALZHEIMER'S AND THEIR FAMILIES.
Aging no359:46 '89

HOWARD, J. Jean Howard's Hollywood. 1989
Harper's Bazaar 122:192 S '89. N. Johnson
The New York Times Book Review 94:12 D 3 '89. D. Dunne

HOWARD, S. C. Gone with the wind. 1989
The New York Times Book Review 94:7 D 10 '89. D. Finkle

HOWE, H. F. AND WESTLEY, L. C. Ecological relationships of plants and animals. 1988
BioScience 39:196-7 Mr '89. C. H. Janson

HOY, C. Margin of error.
Maclean's 102:82+ D 4 '89. E. K. Fulton

HOYT, E. P. The rise of the Chinese republic. 1989
National Review 41:62 Je 2 '89. F. B. Randall

HRABAL, B. I served the King of England. 1989
The New York Review of Books 36:37-9 My 18 '89. D. J. Enright
The New York Times Book Review 94:13 Mr 19 '89. R. Lourie

HSIA, R. P.-C. The myth of ritual murder. 1988
The New York Review of Books 35:48-50 Ja 19 '89. G. R. Elton

HUBBELL, S. A book of bees—and how to keep them. 1988
The New York Review of Books 36:8-9 F 16 '89. E. Perényi

HUBBELL, S. A country year. 1986
The New York Review of Books 36:8-9 F 16 '89. E. Perényi

HUBBS, J. Mother Russia. 1988
The New York Times Book Review 94:28 Mr 5 '89. M. Warner

HUBEL, D. Eye, brain, and vision. 1988
BioScience 39:124-5 F '89. T. H. Goldsmith

HUBER, P. W. Liability. 1988
The American Spectator 22:42-3 Mr '89. M. Fumento
Society 27:92-4 N/D '89. E. F. Paul

HUCK, C. S. Princess Furball. 1989
The New York Times Book Review 94:50 N 12 '89. J. D. Zipes

HUDDLE, D. The high spirits. 1988
The New York Times Book Review 94:9 S 24 '89. S. Lowell

HUFFORD, M. AND OTHERS. The grand generation. 1987
Aging no359:44-5 '89. P. Jones

HUGHES, D. Family pose. 1989
The New York Times Book Review 94:47 My 21 '89. B. G. Hearne

HUGHES, H. S. Sophisticated rebels. 1988
Commonweal 116:93-5 F 10 '89. J. P. Diggins
The New York Times Book Review 94:8 Ja 8 '89. P. Schneider

HUGHES, R. I. G. The structure and interpretation of quantum mechanics. 1989
Physics Today 42:124+ O '89. L. E. Ballentine

HUGHES, R. T. AND ALLEN, C. L. Illusions of innocence. 1988
The Christian Century 106:891-2 O 4 '89. W. A. Silva

HUGHES, T. P. American genesis. 1989
The New York Review of Books 36:11-12 D 7 '89. D. Joravsky
Science 244:830-1 My 19 '89. G. Wise
Technology Review 92:74-5 Ag/S '89. R. Howard

HULL, D. L. Science as a process. 1988
BioScience 39:572-4 S '89. L. B. Slobodkin
High Technology Business 9:9 Je '89. M. Estren
The Humanist 49:42 Mr/Ap '89. R. H. Pine

HULL, G. G. Equal to serve. 1987
Christianity Today 33:57-8 O 20 '89. P. E. Alsurf

THE HUMAN EXPERIENCE. 1989
The New Republic 201:40-1 O 2 '89. C. Brown
The New York Review of Books 36:3-4+ Je 1 '89. H. Gifford

HUMANISM, REFORM AND THE REFORMATION. 1989
History Today 39:53-4 O '89. D. M. Loades

HUMPHREY, W. No resting place. 1989
The New York Times Book Review 94:19 Je 25 '89. J. Ehle

HUNNICUTT, B. K. Work without end. 1988
The New York Times Book Review 94:15 Ja 29 '89. N. Lichtenstein

HUNT, C. E. Down by the river. 1988
BioScience 39:494-5 Jl/Ag '89. C. M. Moffitt

HUNT, D. C. The lithographs of Charles Banks Wilson. 1988
American Artist 53:80-2 Ag '89. M. C. Nelson

HUNTER, J. Westmoreland and Portland places. 1988
Americana 16:12 Ja/F '89. J. Neary

HURT, H. For all mankind. 1988
Ad Astra 1:43 F '89. G. E. Swanson
Smithsonian 20:172-3 Ap '89. K. Kalfus

HUTCHESON, R. G. God in the White House. 1988
The Christian Century 106:235-6 Mr 1 '89. R. D. Linder

HUYSMANS, J.-K. The road from decadence. 1989
The New Republic 201:42-5 D 25 '89. F. Brown

I

ÍĀGLOM, I. M. Felix Klein and Sophus Lie. 1988
Physics Today 42:72-4 Je '89. L. Alvarez-Gaumé

IANNI, F. A. J. The search for structure. 1989
America 161:172-3 S 23 '89. J. DiGiacomo
Society 26:93-4 S/O '89. N. K. Denzin

THE ICONOGRAPHY OF LANDSCAPE. 1988
History Today 39:49 Mr '89. D. Lowenthal

IGLAUER, E. Fishing with John. 1988
Smithsonian 19:28 Ja '89. D. Lancashire

IMMUNOGLOBULIN GENES. 1989
Science 245:993-4 S 1 '89. W. Dunnick

THE IMPERIAL CONGRESS. 1988
The American Spectator 22:43-4 My '89. F. Barnes
Commentary 88:70-2 Jl '89. G. Russell

INDOOR RADON AND ITS HAZARDS. 1987
Physics Today 42:72-4 Ap '89. L. M. Hubbard

INFANT FEEDING. 1988
Science 244:844-5 My 19 '89. G. C. Anderson

ING, J. Johann Gutenberg and his Bible. 1988
Publishers Weekly 235:74-5 Ja 6 '89. C. B. Grannis

INGALLS, R. The end of tragedy. 1987
The New York Times Book Review 94:9 Mr 5 '89. S. Dobyns

INGRAM, M. Church courts, sex, and marriage in England, 1570-1640. 1987
History Today 39:59-60 F '89. N. Orme

INHERITING OUR MOTHERS' GARDENS. 1988
The Christian Century 106:260-3 Mr 8 '89. G. E. Ziegenhals

INTERLEUKIN 2. 1988
Science 244:994 My 26 '89. A. K. Abbas

INTERNATIONAL CONFERENCE ON GAP JUNCTIONS (1987: PACIFIC GROVE, CALIF.). Gap junctions. 1988
Science 243:674-5 F 3 '89. J. D. Sheridan

INTERNATIONAL MEETING ON PLANT MITOCHONDRIA—STRUCTURAL, FUNCTIONAL, AND PHYSIOLOGICAL ASPECTS (2ND: 1986: ABERYSTWYTH, WALES). Plant mitochondria. 1987
BioScience 39:194 Mr '89. C. Frenkel

INTERNATIONAL SYMPOSIUM ON RED TIDES (1ST: 1987: TAKAMATSU, JAPAN). Red tides. 1989
BioScience 39:815-16 D '89. B. M. Marcotte

INTRODUCTION TO QUASICRYSTALS. 1988
Science 246:1330 D 8 '89. D. P. DiVincenzo

INTRODUCTION TO THE STUDY OF MEIOFAUNA. 1988
BioScience 39:648-9 O '89. D. M. Alongi

IRONS, P. H. The courage of their convictions. 1988

The Progressive 53:47 F '89
IRVING, D. J. C. Churchill's War; v1, The struggle for power. 1987
The New York Review of Books 36:36-42 Je 15 '89. D. Cannadine
IRVING, D. J. C. Göring. 1989
The New Republic 201:37-9 Jl 17-24 '89. R. J. Overy
The New York Times Book Review 94:21 My 28 '89. P. Hoffmann
IRVING, J. A prayer for Owen Meany. 1989
The Christian Century 106:299-300 Mr 22-29 '89. J. M. Wall
Christianity Today 33:58-9 O 6 '89. T. Christlieb
Maclean's 102:63 Ap 3 '89. J. Timson
Mademoiselle 95:128+ Ap '89. J. Maynard
The New Republic 200:36-8 My 22 '89. W. H. Pritchard
The New York Review of Books 36:30-1 Jl 20 '89. R. Towers
The New York Times Book Review 94:1+ Mr 12 '89. A. Kazin
Newsweek 113:64 Ap 10 '89. P. S. Prescott
Time 133:80 Ap 3 '89. R. Z. Sheppard
ISHIGURO, K. The remains of the day. 1989
The Nation 249:761-3 D 18 '89. S. Lee
The New Leader 72:21-2 N 13 '89. M. Kamine
New York 22:81-2 O 16 '89. R. Koenig
The New York Times Book Review 94:3+ O 8 '89. L. Graver
Newsweek 114:76 O 30 '89. D. Ansen
Time 134:90 O 30 '89. P. Gray
IVANITS, L. J. Russian folk belief. 1989
The New York Times Book Review 94:18 Ag 13 '89. B. G. Rosenthal

J

JACKALL, R. Moral mazes. 1988
Commonweal 116:281-2 My 5 '89. B. L. Toffler
Science 244:836-7 My 19 '89. C. Morrill
JACKSON, B. Honest graft. 1988
The American Spectator 22:43-4 My '89. F. Barnes
The New Republic 200:40-2 Mr 6 '89. R. Kuttner
The New York Review of Books 36:20-2 Jl 20 '89. T. B. Edsall
The Washington Monthly 20:58-9 Ja '89. P. M. Stern
JACKSON, C. Hattie. 1989
The New York Times Book Review 94:13-14 O 15 '89. A. Young
JACKSON, SIR W. G. F. The Rock of the Gibraltarians. 1987
History Today 39:48-9 Ja '89. J. Amery
THE JACOBITE CHALLENGE. 1988
History Today 39:52-3 F '89. H. T. Dickinson
JACOBS, J. Tattercoats. 1989
The New York Times Book Review 94:50 N 12 '89. J. D. Zipes
JACOBS, J. A. The earth's core. 2nd ed. 1987
Physics Today 42:89-90 S '89. T. J. Ahrens
JACOBS, M. The tropical rain forest. 1988
BioScience 39:184 Mr '89. B. Bentley
Science 246:828-9 N 10 '89. E. G. Leigh, Jr.
JACOBSEN, J. On the island. 1989
The New York Times Book Review 94:20 Ag 27 '89. S. G. Kellman
JAMES, W. Habit. 1914
The New Republic 201 [Reprint v1]:29 N 6 '89 [N 7 '14] P. Littell
JAMES, W. Manuscript lectures. 1988
The New York Times Book Review 94:30 Ap 16 '89. E. Taylor
JANÁČEK, L. Janacek's uncollected essays on music.
The New York Times Book Review 94:38 S 17 '89. J. Peyser
JANEWAY, E. The economics of chaos. 1989
The New Leader 72:16 My 1 '89. B. Gewen
The New York Times Book Review 94:12 F 12 '89. J. E. Garten
JANKOWSKI, P. Communism and collaboration. 1989
The New York Review of Books 36:42-3 Ap 27 '89. R. O. Paxton
JARDIN, A. Tocqueville. 1988
The New York Review of Books 36:16-18 Mr 2 '89. R. O. Paxton
The New York Times Book Review 94:12 F 19 '89. J. W. Scott
Smithsonian 19:187-9 Mr '89. L. Simon
JAVOR, B. Hypersaline environments. 1989
Science 246:1645-6 D 22 '89. W. D. Grant
JEANSONNE, G. Gerald L. K. Smith. 1988
The Christian Century 106:1065-6 N 15 '89. J. Merrill
The Nation 248:242+ F 20 '89. M. Kazin
JEFFREYS-JONES, R. CIA and American democracy. 1988
The New York Times Book Review 94:14-15 Mr 5 '89. D. P. Calleo
JENCKS, C. The Prince, the architects and new wave monarchy. 1988
Architectural Record 177:77 N '89. R. Kimball
JERUSALEM PILGRIMAGE, 1099-1185. 1988

History Today 39:52 Ja '89. N. Housley
JERVIS, R. The meaning of nuclear revolution. 1989
The New York Times Book Review 94:30 O 1 '89. M. Krepon
JOHANSON, D. C. AND SHREEVE, J. Lucy's child. 1989
The New York Times Book Review 94:14-15 N 12 '89. J. N. Wilford
JOHNSGARD, P. A. North American owls. 1988
The New York Review of Books 36:39-40 D 21 '89. R. O. Paxton
JOHNSON, A. Tell me a story, Mama. 1988
The New York Times Book Review 94:35 Je 18 '89. K. Krull
JOHNSON, B. Lady of the beasts. 1988
The New York Times Book Review 94:22 F 5 '89. K. A. Rabuzzi
JOHNSON, C. When to say goodbye to your therapist. 1988
Psychology Today 23:85 Ja/F '89. E. E. Goode
JOHNSON, J. In the night café. 1989
Mademoiselle 95:92+ My '89. J. Maynard
The New Leader 72:20-1 O 30 '89. O. Conant
The New York Times Book Review 94:11 Ap 30 '89. P. Lopate
JOHNSON, J. H. Succeeding against the odds. 1989
Black Enterprise 19:41 Je '89. D. T. Dingle
JOHNSON, K. D. Realism and hope in a nuclear age. 1988
The Christian Century 106:146-7 F 1-8 '89. A. F. Geyer
JOHNSON, P. Intellectuals. 1989
Conservative Digest 15:63 My/Je '89. J. B. Graves
National Review 41:44-6 Ap 21 '89. J. Sobran
The New Leader 72:19-20 Mr 20 '89. R. G. Davis
The New York Review of Books 36:11-13 Jl 20 '89. B. Williams
The New York Times Book Review 94:3+ Mr 12 '89. W. D. O'Flaherty
Society 26:97-9 S/O '89. P. Hollander
JOHNSON, P. A. Duke Richard of York, 1411-1460. 1988
History Today 39:50 Ap '89. R. L. Storey
JOHNSON, R. E. Guardians of the sea. 1987
Sea Frontiers 35:190 My/Je '89. G. L. Voss
JOLLEY, E. My father's moon. 1989
The New York Times Book Review 94:9 Ap 30 '89. V. Gornick
JONAS, G. The circuit riders. 1989
The New York Times Book Review 94:30-1 Ap 2 '89. N. Angier
Science 244:832-3 My 19 '89. P. J. Pauly
JONES, C. Chuck amuck. 1989
Vogue 179:276+ N '89. B. Ervolino
JONES, D. W. War and economy in the age of William III and Marlborough. 1988
History Today 39:56 N '89. C. roger Childs
JONES, G. R. Red revolution. 1989
The Atlantic 264:107-10 S '89. J. M. Fallows
The New York Times Book Review 94:36 S 10 '89. L. Lopez Torregrosa
JONES, J. To reach eternity. 1989
The American Spectator 22:40-1 S '89. W. H. Nolte
The New York Times Book Review 94:10 Jl 30 '89. B. DeMott
JONES, R. V. Instruments and experiences. 1988
Physics Today 42 pt1:66-7 Ag '89. L. G. Rubin
JOSÉ, F. S. Ermita: a Filipino novel.
The New York Review of Books 36:7-11 Je 1 '89. I. Buruma
JOWITT, D. Time and the dancing image. 1988
Dance Magazine 63:74-5 Mr '89. L. Garfola
JUANA INÉS DE LA CRUZ. A Sor Juana anthology. 1988
Commonweal 116:50-2 Ja 27 '89. E. Arenal
JUANA INÉS DE LA CRUZ. Sor Juana's dream. 1986
Commonweal 116:50-2 Ja 27 '89. E. Arenal
JUDIS, J. B. William F. Buckley, Jr. 1988
America 160:515-17 My 27 '89. D. O'Brien
The Progressive 53:38-40 Ja '89. B. D. Nossiter
JUST, W. S. Jack Gance. 1989
The New York Times Book Review 94:1+ Ja 1 '89. J. Martin
Newsweek 113:57 Ja 16 '89. E. Thomas
U.S. Catholic 54:48-51 Je '89. G. M. Costello
JUST DOGS.
The Conservationist 43:53 Mr/Ap '89. E. S. Feldmann
JUSTER, N. As. 1989
The New York Times Book Review 94:35 O 22 '89. D. Manuel

K

KADOHATA, C. The floating world. 1989
The New York Times Book Review 94:16 Jl 23 '89. D. O'Hehir
KAEL, P. Hooked. 1989
The New York Times Book Review 94:7 Mr 19 '89. R. Sklar
KAGAN, J. Unstable ideas. 1989
The New York Times Book Review 94:16 My 28 '89. R. M. Restak
KAGARLITSKY, B. The thinking reed. 1988
The Nation 248:94-7 Ja 23 '89. A. J. Rieber

KAGOSHIMA, S. AND OTHERS. One-dimensional conductors. 1988
　Physics Today 42:76-7 Je '89. J. V. José
KALMAN, M. Sayonara, Mrs. Kackleman. 1989
　The New York Times Book Review 94:25+ N 12 '89
KALSTONE, D. AND HEMENWAY, R. Becoming a poet. 1989
　The New Republic 201:37-40 N 27 '89. C. E. G. Benfey
KAM, E. Surprise attack. 1988
　The Washington Monthly 21:76 F '89. H. G. Summers
KANDAL, T. R. The woman question in classical sociological theory. 1988
　Science 243:823 F 10 '89. R. A. Nye
KANDELL, J. La capital. 1988
　Commentary 87:68-70 Ap '89. D. Frum
　Mother Jones 14:41-2 Je '89. R. Rodriguez
KANE, E. J. The S & L insurance mess. 1989
　The New York Times Book Review 94:27-8 O 29 '89. A. M. Solomon
KANE, G. Modern elementary particle physics. 1987
　Physics Today 42:89 S '89. G. Karl
KANFER, S. A summer world. 1989
　The New York Times Book Review 94:24 D 24 '89. J. Cohen
KANIGEL, R. Apprentice to genius. 1986
　Science 246:1329-30 D 8 '89. S. Panem
KANIUK, Y. His daughter. 1989
　The New York Times Book Review 94:14 Je 4 '89. J. Henkin
KAPLAN, D. Lewis Hine in Europe. 1988
　Art News 88:127-8 Ap '89. J. Sturman
KAPLAN, F. Dickens. 1988
　Maclean's 102:60 Ap 17 '89. J. Bemrose
　The New York Review of Books 35:11-12 Ja 19 '89. J. Bayley
　Smithsonian 20:243-4 N '89. B. Allen
KAPLAN, J. Pearl's progress. 1989
　Newsweek 113:64 F 20 '89. D. Gates
KAPLAN, J. A. AND VARO, R. Unexpected journeys. 1988
　Art News 88:85 Ja '89. M. Manley
KAPLAN, R. D. Surrender or starve. 1988
　The American Spectator 22:39-40 Ja '89. C. Doherty
KARBO, K. Trespassers welcome here. 1989
　The New York Times Book Review 94:11 My 21 '89. E. Schoen
KARL, F. R. William Faulkner, American writer. 1988
　The American Spectator 22:40-2 N '89. W. H. Nolte
　National Review 41:39-41 Ag 4 '89. H. Fickett
　The New York Times Book Review 94:3+ My 14 '89. J. W. Aldridge
KARLIN, B. Cinderella. 1989
　The New York Times Book Review 94:33 My 21 '89. F. Rich
KARNOW, S. In our image. 1989
　America 161:326-7 N 11 '89. B. F. Nebres
　Commonweal 116:473-4 S 8 '89. J. C. Cort
　The Nation 248:779-84 Je 5 '89. P. Tarr
　The New Republic 201:30+ S 11 '89. R. Steel
　New York 22:73-4 Ap 17 '89. R. Koenig
　The New York Review of Books 36:7-11 Je 1 '89. I. Buruma
　The New York Times Book Review 94:1+ Ap 2 '89. P. H. Kreisberg
　The New Yorker 65:112-18 O 30 '89. R. Bonner
　Newsweek 113:64 Ap 10 '89. C. Bogert
　The Progressive 53:39-40 D '89. W. Steif
　Time 133:76-7 Ap 17 '89. H. G. Chua-Eoan
KARP, W. Liberty under siege. 1988
　The Progressive 53:40-2 Ja '89. K. Peck
KATELLE, J. The American automobile dealership.
　Motor Trend 41:44 F '89. V. Verde
KATSH, M. E. The electronic media and the transformation of law. 1989
　The New York Times Book Review 94:23 Ag 20 '89. P. J. Williams
KATZ, W. L. AND CRAWFORD, M. The Lincoln Brigade. 1989
　The New York Times Book Review 94:28 Jl 23 '89. P. Lynden
KATZENBACH, J. Day of reckoning. 1989
　The New York Times Book Review 94:11 Ap 9 '89. E. Abeel
KAUFFMAN, J. Obscene gestures for women. 1989
　The New York Times Book Review 94:3 S 24 '89. R. Kelly
KAUFMAN, J. Broken alliance. 1988
　The Christian Century 106:564-5 My 24-31 '89. A. J. Rudin
　Commentary 87:67-70 Ja '89. M. Friedman
　National Review 41:59 F 24 '89. J. Lester
KAUFMAN, M. T. Mad dreams, saving graces. 1989
　Business Week p14 Jl 3 '89. B. Javetski
　Commentary 88:62-5 N '89. A. Puddington
　The New Leader 72:5-6 My 15-29 '89. S. Barańczak
　The New Republic 201:34-7 Jl 17-24 '89. J. Bugajski
　The New York Times Book Review 94:12 Je 18 '89. J. Anders
KAWASAKI, G. The Macintosh way. 1989
　Byte 14:125-6 Ag '89. D. E. Crabb

KAZIN, A. A writer's America. 1988
　The New Republic 200:36-8 Ja 30 '89. A. Delbanco
KEALEY, E. J. Harvesting the air. 1987
　History Today 39:49-50+ Ja '89. P. Spufford
KEANE, M. Queen Lear. 1989
　The New York Times Book Review 94:34 S 17 '89. E. Auchincloss
KEARNEY, H. F. The British Isles. 1989
　History Today 39:59 Ag '89. S. G. Ellis
　The New York Review of Books 36:27-8 Je 1 '89. C. Hill
KEARNS, D. T. AND DOYLE, D. P. Winning the brain race. 1988
　Phi Delta Kappan 71:170-2 O '89. P. Woodring
KEEGAN, J. The price of admiralty. 1989
　The New York Times Book Review 94:12 Ap 16 '89. K. J. Hagan
　Newsweek 113:72 Ap 3 '89. J. Miller
　The Washington Monthly 21:56-7 Jl/Ag '89. P. Grier
KEEGAN, J. The Second World War. 1990
　The New York Times Book Review 94:10 D 31 '89. P. M. Kennedy
KEELEY, E. The Salonika Bay murder. 1989
　The New Republic 200:32-4 Je 26 '89. W. H. McNeill
　The New York Review of Books 36:58-62 O 12 '89. C. M. Woodhouse
KEEPING THE FAITH. 1988
　The Christian Century 106:289-90 Mr 15 '89. S. M. Heim
KEEPING THE TABLETS. 1988
　The American Spectator 22:46-7 Ja '89. T. Eastland
KEEPNEWS, O. The view from within. 1988
　Down Beat 56:55-6 F '89. K. Whitehead
KEESHAN, R. Growing up happy. 1989
　The New York Times Book Review 94:20 S 17 '89. K. Lynch
KEILLOR, G. We are still married. 1989
　The New York Times Book Review 94:13 Ap 9 '89. B. Henderson
KEIZER, G. No place but here. 1988
　Psychology Today 23:79+ Ja/F '89. J. Cassell
　Smithsonian 19:183-5 Mr '89. F. Levering
KELLER, M. Rude awakening. 1989
　Business Week p16-17 S 18 '89. J. B. Treece
　Fortune 120:233-4+ S 25 '89. A. L. Taylor, III
　The New York Times Book Review 94:38 O 29 '89. A. B. Fisher
KELLER, W. W. The liberals and J. Edgar Hoover. 1989
　National Review 41:47-8+ My 5 '89. R. G. Powers
KELLERMAN, J. Silent partner. 1989
　The New York Times Book Review 94:20 O 22 '89. R. Herbert
KELLOGG, S. Johnny Appleseed. 1988
　The New York Times Book Review 94:21 Ja 1 '89. E. Schecter
KELLY, B. AND LONDON, M. The four little dragons. 1989
　The New York Times Book Review 94:37 O 29 '89. F. Gibney
KELMAN, J. A disaffection.
　The New York Times Book Review 94:14 Je 18 '89. M. Kirby
KELVIN'S BALTIMORE LECTURES AND MODERN THEORETICAL PHYSICS. 1987
　Physics Today 42:82-4 Ja '89. L. M. Brown
KENEALLY, T. To Asmara. 1989
　New York 22:82 O 16 '89. R. Koenig
　The New York Times Book Review 94:1+ O 1 '89. R. Stone
KENNAN, G. F. Sketches from a life. 1989
　Commentary 88:65-7 S '89. P. Brimelow
　The New Leader 72:3-4 My 15-29 '89. B. Gewen
　The New York Review of Books 36:3-5 Ag 17 '89. R. Steel
　The New York Times Book Review 94:1+ My 7 '89. J. Chace
　The New Yorker 65:118-21 S 25 '89. J. Newhouse
　The Progressive 53:38+ O '89. D. Schorr
　Time 133:98 My 8 '89. S. Kanfer
KENNEDY, D. Motorcycle touring.
　Cycle 40:81 Ag '89
KENNEDY, E. A cultural history of the French Revolution. 1989
　The New York Times Book Review 94:12 Jl 9 '89. S. C. Maza
KENNEDY, E. C. Cardinal Bernardin. 1989
　America 161:489-90 D 23-30 '89. J. M. McShane
　Commonweal 116:648-50 N 17 '89. T. J. Reese
　The New York Times Book Review 94:13 O 15 '89. P. Steinfels
KENNEDY, E. C. Tomorrow's Catholics, yesterday's church. 1988
　The New York Times Book Review 94:11-12 Mr 19 '89. J. Garvey
KENNEDY, P. M. The rise and fall of the great powers. 1988
　America 160:276-7 Mr 25 '89. W. J. Bosch
　The American Scholar 58:289+ Spr '89. E. N. Luttwak
KENNER, H. Mazes. 1989
　National Review 41:58-60 S 29 '89. J. Sobran

LAWRENCE, M. The Mille Miglia. 1988
Motor Trend 41:40 Mr '89. G. Von Dare
Road & Track 40:33 Jl '89. T. C. Browne
LAWRENCE, T. E. The letters of T.E. Lawrence. 1989
Time 133:80-1 My 15 '89. P. Gray
LAWRENCE, T. E. The selected letters. 1989
The New Republic 201:35-6+ Ag 21 '89. R. Jenkyns
The New York Times Book Review 94:19 Jl 16 '89. S.
E. Tabachnick
LAWSON, A. Adultery. 1988
The New York Times Book Review 94:14-15 Ja 29 '89.
M. V. Miller
LAWSON, D. The Abraham Lincoln Brigade. 1988
The New York Times Book Review 94:28 Jl 23 '89. P.
Lynden
LAZOU, C. Supercomputers and their use. 1986
Scientific American 261:115-16 Jl '89. P. Morrison
LE CARRÉ, J. The Russia house. 1989
Commonweal 116:407-8 Jl 14 '89. B. A. Bannon
Maclean's 102:55 Je 19 '89. D. Kucherawy
The New Leader 72:10-11 My 15-29 '89. W. Goodman
The New Republic 201:30-2 Ag 21 '89. S. Petrov
New York 22:56-7 Je 5 '89. R. Koenig
The New York Review of Books 36:9-10+ S 28 '89. V.
Erofeev
The New York Times Book Review 94:3 My 21 '89. C.
C. O'Brien
Newsweek 113:52-7 Je 5 '89. T. Mathews
Time 133:86 My 29 '89. P. Gray
LE GOFF, J. Medieval civilization, 400-1500. 1988
History Today 39:55+ Jl '89. G. Marsden
The New York Review of Books 36:47-9 My 18 '89. M.
H. Keen
LE GOFF, J. The medieval imagination. 1988
The New York Review of Books 36:47-9 My 18 '89. M.
H. Keen
LE GOFF, J. Your money or your life. 1988
The New York Review of Books 36:47-9 My 18 '89. M.
H. Keen
LE GUIN, U. K. Dancing at the edge of the world. 1989
Commonweal 116:441 Ag 11 '89. P. D. Baumann
The New York Times Book Review 94:18 Mr 12 '89.
N. Perrin
LEAMER, L. King of the night. 1989
The New York Times Book Review 94:9 Jl 23 '89. T.
Buckley
LEAMING, B. If this was happiness. 1989
Harper's Bazaar 122:156-7 N '89. W. Thomas
The New York Times Book Review 94:7+ N 19 '89. S.
Braudy
LEAN, G. Frank Buchman. 1985
Christianity Today 33:60-1 Mr 3 '89. D. G. Bloesch
LEAN, G. On the tail of a comet. 1988
The Christian Century 106:480-1 My 3 '89. R. Quebedeaux
LEAVITT, D. Equal affections. 1989
America 160:431-3 My 6 '89. J. Gindin
The New York Times Book Review 94:7 F 12 '89. B.
Lowry
LEBEDEV, V. V. Diary of a cosmonaut. 1988
Ad Astra 1:21 O '89. J. D. Kirwan
LEBLOND, R. E., JR. From chaos to fragility. 1989
Dance Magazine 63:68-9 D '89. D. Hering
LEBOUTILLIER, J. Vietnam now. 1989
National Review 41:44 D 8 '89. B. Miner
LEBOW, E. F. Cal Rodgers and the Vin Fiz. 1989
The New York Times Book Review 94:6 D 31 '89. T.
Ferrell
LEBRUN, R. A. Joseph de Maistre.
The New Republic 201:32-7 O 30 '89. S. Holmes
LECOMPTE, J. Moon passage. 1989
The New York Times Book Review 94:14 Je 25 '89. E.
Tennant
LEDEEN, M. Perilous statecraft. 1988
The American Spectator 22:38-9 F '89. G. Szamuely
Commentary 87:76-8 F '89. D. Brock
LEE, R. M. One hundred monkeys. 1989
Maclean's 102:74 O 9 '89. R. Laver
LEE, S. Do the right thing. 1989
The New York Review of Books 36:37-8 S 28 '89. M.
Kempton
LEES, G. Meet me at Jim & Andy's. 1988
Commentary 87:70-1 Ja '89. T. Teachout
The New York Review of Books 36:32-4 Ap 13 '89. E.
J. Hobsbawm
LEGENDRE, G. S. The time of my life. 1987
Conservative Digest 15:60 Mr/Ap '89. J. B. Graves
LEHMAN, J. F. Command of the seas. 1988
The American Spectator 22:49-51 Je '89. G. Szamuely
The New York Times Book Review 94:13 F 19 '89. R.
Halloran
USA Today (Periodical) 117:95-6 My '89. D. Isenberg
LEIBOWITZ, H. A. Fabricating lives. 1989
The New York Review of Books 36:16-18 D 7 '89. E.
A. J. Honigmann
The New York Times Book Review 94:30 N 5 '89. M.
Seymour
LEIGHTEN, P. D. Re-ordering the universe. 1989
The New Leader 72:21 Je 12-26 '89. G. Woodcock

LEITHAUSER, B. Hence. 1989
The New Republic 200:41-2 My 8 '89. W. Lesser
The New York Review of Books 36:20-1 Mr 30 '89. R.
M. Adams
The New York Times Book Review 94:1+ Ja 22 '89. L.
Shapiro
LEMAHIEU, D. L. A culture for democracy. 1988
History Today 39:58-9 Jl '89. A. Mason
LÉNA, P. Observational astrophysics. 1988
Physics Today 42:97-8 Mr '89. J. S. Miller
Science 244:851 My 19 '89. C. R. Canizares
L'ENGLE, M. Two-part invention. 1989
Christianity Today 33:62-4 N 3 '89. K. Andraski
Commonweal 116:215-16 Ap 7 '89. S. Cahill
LENZ, S. The selected stories of Siegfried Lenz. 1989
The New York Times Book Review 94:14 N 26 '89. P.
Demetz
LEONARD, E. Killshot. 1989
The New York Times Book Review 94:12 Ap 23 '89.
A. Rule
Vogue 179:220+ My '89. M. Schmich
LEONARD, DA VINCI. Leonardo on painting. 1989
The New York Review of Books 36:16-18 Ag 17 '89. C.
Hope
LEONARDO DA VINCI. 1989
The New York Review of Books 36:16-18 Ag 17 '89. C.
Hope
LEONE, DA MODENA. The autobiography of a
seventeenth-century Venetian rabbi. 1988
Commentary 87:66-8 My '89. A. A. Aciman
LERMAN, R. God's ear. 1989
The New York Times Book Review 94:6 Jl 2 '89. B.
Singer
LERNOUX, P. People of God. 1989
The Christian Century 106:523-6 My 17 '89. P. Berryman
Commonweal 116:310-12 My 19 '89. S. Mainwaring
The New York Times Book Review 94:33 Jl 23 '89. D.
McCann
LETOKHOV, V. S. Laser photoionization spectroscopy. 1987
Physics Today 42:66+ Ap '89. R. Lee
LETTE, K. Girl's night out. 1989
Harper's Bazaar 122:38+ Jl '89. K. Black
The New York Times Book Review 94:13 Jl 23 '89. E.
Listfield
LEUTE, U. Archaeometry. 1987
Physics Today 42:93-4 N '89. R. E. M. Hedges
LEUTHNER, S. AND JENSEN, O. High honor.
American Heritage 40:155-6 N '89
LEVERENZ, D. Manhood and the American renaissance. 1989
The Nation 249:63-6 Jl 10 '89. M. S. Kimmel
LEVI, M. Of rule and revenue. 1988
Society 26:87-9 Jl/Ag '89. B. G. Carruthers
LEVI, P. The frontiers of paradise. 1988
Smithsonian 19:166-8 F '89. M. Olmert
LEVI, P. Other people's trades. 1989
The New York Times Book Review 94:14-15 My 7 '89.
L. Michaels
Time 133:86-7 My 29 '89. O. Friedrich
LEVIN, D. P. Irreconcilable differences. 1989
Business Week p14-15 Ap 10 '89. J. R. Norman
Car and Driver 35:28-9 Jl '89. C. Csere
The New York Times Book Review 94:14-15 Ap 23 '89.
J. Nocera
LEVIN, K. Beyond modernism. 1988
Art in America 77:37+ Ap '89. B. Adams
LEVIN, N. The Jews in the Soviet Union since 1917. 2v
1988
America 161:385-6 N 25 '89. Z. Gitelman
Commentary 88:70-2 D '89. R. Pipes
LEVINE, L. D. Bird. 1988
The Washington Monthly 21:55-6 My '89. J. Rowe
LEVINE, L. W. Highbrow/lowbrow. 1988
American Heritage 40:119 F '89
The Nation 248:130-2 Ja 30 '89. F. P. Smoler
LEVINSON, S. Constitutional faith. 1988
The Nation 248:385-6 Mr 20 '89. M. Meltsner
LEVINTON, J. S. Genetics, paleontology, and macroevolution.
1987
BioScience 39:571 S '89. P. Cloud
LEVITAN, S. A. AND OTHERS. What's happening to the
American family? 1988
Monthly Labor Review 112:44 Je '89. H. Hayghe
LEVY, D. H. Observing variable stars. 1989
Astronomy 17:93-5 Ap '89. W. M. Lowder
LEVY, L. W. Original intent and the framers' Constitution.
1988
The New Leader 72:17-19 Mr 6 '89. G. Tyler
LEWIS, J. W. AND XUE LITAI. China builds the bomb.
1988
The Bulletin of the Atomic Scientists 45:42-3 Ap '89. M.
M. May
LEWIS, M. Liar's poker. 1989
Business Week p12-14 O 30 '89. J. M. Laderman
Fortune 120:219-20+ N 20 '89. R. I. Kirkland, Jr.
National Review 41:51-3 N 24 '89. J. Mysak
The New York Times Book Review 94:39 O 29 '89. R.
L. Stern
The Washington Monthly 21:58-60 N '89. J. Nocera

LEWIS, M. T. Cézanne's early imagery. 1989
    Art in America 77:47+ N '89. J. D. Flam
LEWIS, N. The missionaries. 1988
    Smithsonian 20:119-20 Jl '89. A. Ryan
LEWY, G. Peace & revolution. 1988
    Commonweal 116:85-6 F 10 '89. S. Lynd
LIBERALISM AND THE MORAL LIFE. 1989
    National Review 41:48-9 N 24 '89. J. Sobran
LIEBERMAN, M. Privatization and educational choice. 1989
    The New York Times Book Review 94:9-10 Ag 6 '89.
    T. S. Healy
LIEBERMAN, R. "My song is my weapon". 1989
    Commentary 88:66-8 O '89. R. Radosh
LIESCH, B. W. People in the presence of God.
    Christianity Today 33:61 D 15 '89. H. Boonstra
LIGHTFOOT, S. L. Balm in Gilead. 1988
    Commonweal 116:345-6 Je 2 '89. J. Redmont
    The Nation 248:386-8 Mr 20 '89. V. N. Gamble
    The New Republic 200:40-2 Mr 27 '89. R. Coles
    The New York Times Book Review 94:7-8 Ja 1 '89. H.
    J. Geiger
LINCOLN, A. Speeches and writings. 2v 1989
    American Heritage 40:14+ S/O '89. G. C. Ward
    National Review 41:38-40 D 8 '89. T. Fleming
    The New Republic 201:31-6+ N 20 '89. A. Delbanco
    The New York Times Book Review 94:3+ D 10 '89. A.
    Kazin
LINDOY, L. F. The chemistry of macrocyclic ligand complexes.
    1988
    Science 246:942 N 17 '89. R. M. Izatt
LINDSEY, R. A gathering of saints. 1988
    The Christian Century 106:264-5 Mr 8 '89. D. S. Cun-
    ningham
LINDSKOOG, K. A. The C.S. Lewis hoax. 1988
    The Christian Century 106:208-9 F 22 '89. L. W. Dorsett
LINK, H. A. Waves and plagues. 1988
    American Artist 53:33 Ag '89. M. C. Nelson
LIPOVETSKY, G. L'empire de l'éphémère.
    The New Republic 200:37-41 My 8 '89. A. Sullivan
LIPSKY, D. Three thousand dollars. 1989
    National Review 41:62-3 S 29 '89. D. Klinghoffer
LISH, G. Extravaganza. 1989
    The New York Times Book Review 94:15 Je 4 '89. R.
    F. Moss
LISLE, J. T. Afternoon of the elves. 1989
    The New York Times Book Review 94:28 N 12 '89. M.
    Wolitzer
LISPECTOR, C. The passion according to G.H. 1988
    The New York Times Book Review 94:12-13 Ja 8 '89.
    S. Ruta
LISZT, F. An artist's journey. 1989
    The New York Times Book Review 94:9+ Ag 20 '89. L.
    Botstein
LITTLEFIELD, B. Prospect. 1989
    The Atlantic 263:97-9 My '89. B. DeMott
LITTMANN, M. Planets beyond. 1988
    Byte 14:340+ Ag '89. H. Kenner
    Sky and Telescope 78:161+ Ag '89. F. Schaaf
LIU ZONGREN. 6 Tanyin Alley. 1989
    The New York Times Book Review 94:11 Jl 2 '89. G.
    Feldman
LIVELY, P. Pack of cards and other stories. 1989
    The New York Times Book Review 94:13-14 My 21 '89.
    J. Parini
LIVING WITH THE CHESAPEAKE BAY AND VIRGINIA'S
    OCEAN SHORES. 1989
    Earth Science 42:35-6 Spr '89
LIVINGSTON, M. C. There was a place and other poems.
    1988
    The New York Times Book Review 94:43 Ap 9 '89. N.
    Babbitt
LO, S. C. The incorporation of Eric Chung. 1989
    Mother Jones 14:45-7 D '89. P. Lopate
LOADER, J. Wild America. 1989
    Mother Jones 14:43-4 Je '89. G. Brown
    The New York Times Book Review 94:9 My 14 '89. J.
    Butler
LOCK, G. Forces in motion. 1988
    The Nation 248:642-4 My 8 '89. G. Santoro
LOCKE, J. The Apple Corps guide to the well-built house.
    1988
    Country Journal 16:19-20 Ja '89. J. Vara
LODGE, D. Nice work. 1989
    Commonweal 116:442 Ag 11 '89. F. F. Siegel
    The Nation 249:694 D 4 '89. J. Leonard
    The New Republic 201:46-8+ S 18-25 '89. M. J. Salter
    The New York Review of Books 36:18-20 N 23 '89. H.
    Mantel
    The New York Times Book Review 94:1+ Jl 23 '89. J.
    Conarroe
    Newsweek 114:60 Ag 7 '89. P. S. Prescott
    Time 134:60 Ag 7 '89. C. Porterfield
LOGAN, O. L. Motherwit. 1989
    The New York Times Book Review 94:14 S 10 '89. P.
    C. McKissack
LOGAN, W. Sullen weedy lakes. 1988
    The New York Times Book Review 94:38 Mr 12 '89.
    B. Bennett

LONDON, J. The letters of Jack London. 3v 1988
    The Progressive 53:41-2 Mr '89. H. Mitgang
LONGFORD, F. P., EARL OF. A history of the House of
    Lords. 1988
    History Today 39:56-7 Ag '89. F. Barker
LONGMORE, P. K. The invention of George Washington.
    1988
    The New Republic 200:28-30+ F 6 '89. E. S. Morgan
LOPATE, P. Against Joie de vivre. 1989
    The New Leader 72:18-19 My 1 '89. E. Gottlieb
    The New York Times Book Review 94:13-14 My 14 '89.
    H. Gold
LORENZIN, T. AND SECHLER, T. 1000+. 1987
    Astronomy 17:110-11 N '89. R. Bunge
LOST IN SPACE. 1988
    Science 243:1498-9 Mr 17 '89. A. H. Chayes
LOTTMAN, H. R. Flaubert. 1989
    The New York Times Book Review 94:15 Mr 5 '89. D.
    Bair
LOVE. 1988
    The Christian Century 106:424-5 Ap 19 '89. D. S. Cun-
    ningham
LOVELL, M. S. The sound of wings. 1989
    New York 22:148+ D 4 '89. R. Koenig
    The New York Times Book Review 94:1+ N 26 '89. D.
    M. Kennedy
LOVELOCK, J. The ages of Gaia. 1988
    Earth Science 42:32 Fall '89
LOVOLL, O. S. A century of urban life. 1988
    The Christian Century 106:57-8 Ja 18 '89. L. D. Lagerquist
LOVOOS, J. AND MCCLELLAND, G. T. Phil Dike.
    American Artist 53:28+ Jl '89. D. C. Hines
LOWRY, L. Number the stars. 1989
    The New York Times Book Review 94:32 My 21 '89.
    E. Milton
LUHRMANN, T. M. Persuasions of the witch's craft. 1989
    The New Republic 201:31-2 O 30 '89. M. R. Lefkowitz
    The New York Review of Books 36:3-4+ O 12 '89. R.
    Dinnage
    The New York Times Book Review 94:13 Je 25 '89. P.
    Zaleski
LUKACS, J. Budapest 1900. 1988
    National Review 41:60-1 Ja 27 '89. P. Gottfried
    The New York Review of Books 36:21-5 Mr 16 '89. I.
    Deak
    The New York Times Book Review 94:13-14 Ja 22 '89.
    I. Sanders
LUZBETAK, L. J. The church and cultures. 1988
    America 161:168-9 S 23 '89. B. J. Cooke
LYNCH, P. One up on Wall Street. 1989
    Business Week p20 F 27 '89. G. Weiss
    Fortune 119:129-30 F 27 '89. A. E. Serwer
LYONS, P. The complete book of Lamborghini.
    Road & Track 40:104-5 Ag '89. J. Thompson
LYTLE, A. N. AND TATE, A. The Lytle-Tate letters. 1987
    The New York Review of Books 36:35-8 Mr 2 '89. M.
    K. Spears

M

MAALOUF, A. Leo Africanus. 1988
    The New York Times Book Review 94:13 Mr 12 '89.
    A. Shammas
MAAS, P. Father and son. 1989
    The New York Times Book Review 94:15 F 26 '89. J.
    Holland
    Time 133:85 Mr 20 '89. R. Z. Sheppard
    Vogue 179:258+ Ap '89. D. Blundy
MABBERLEY, D. J. The plant-book. 1987
    BioScience 39:190-1 Mr '89. E. F. Wells
MACCARTHY, F. Eric Gill. 1989
    Commonweal 116:404-5 Jl 14 '89. R. Gilliam
    The New York Times Book Review 94:11-12 My 7 '89.
    B. G. Harrison
MACCOBY, M. Why work. 1988
    Home Office Computing 7:104 My '89. N. Sullivan
MACEY, S. L. Patriarchs of time. 1987
    History Today 39:48 Ja '89. P. Tudor-Craig
MACGREGOR, J. M. The discovery of the art of the insane.
    1989
    The New York Times Book Review 94:24 D 17 '89. M.
    V. Miller
MACGREGOR, R. Chief: the fearless vision of Billy Diamond.
    Maclean's 102:63 My 15 '89. B. D. Johnson
MACINTYRE, A. C. Whose justice? Which rationality? 1988
    The American Scholar 58:607-8+ Aut '89. D. C. Band
    The New York Review of Books 36:36-41 D 7 '89. M.
    C. Nussbaum
MACK, B. L. A myth of innocence. 1988
    Commonweal 116:445-6 Ag 11 '89. D. C. Duling
MACKEY, S. Lebanon. 1989
    Commonweal 116:602+ N 3 '89. D. L. Bishop
    The New York Times Book Review 94:3 Jl 23 '89. R.
    Wright
MACKINNON, C. A. Feminism unmodified. 1987
    The Humanist 49:41-2 Ja/F '89. E. J. Bader
MACLACHLAN, P. The facts and fictions of Minna Pratt.
    1988

The New York Times Book Review 94:36 Ja 8 '89. H. V. Frederick
MACLAINE, S. Going within. 1989
Newsweek 113:75 Ap 24 '89. D. Gates
MACLEAN, H. N. In broad daylight. 1988
The New York Times Book Review 94:30 Ja 15 '89. N. S. Robins
MACLEAN, N. AND HALL, B. K. Cell commitment and differentiation. 1987
BioScience 39:201-2 Mr '89. M. Nathanson
MACLEISH, W. H. The Gulf Stream. 1989
Earth Science 42:32-3 Summ '89
MACMULLEN, R. Corruption and the decline of Rome. 1988
History Today 39:57 Je '89. S. Williams
The New York Review of Books 36:6+ Mr 16 '89. J. Griffin
MACNEIL, R. Wordstruck. 1989
America 161:325 N 11 '89. P. McCormack
Maclean's 102:79 Ap 10 '89. G. MacKay
The New York Times Book Review 94:6 Mr 26 '89. H. Benedict
MADDOX, B. Nora. 1988
The American Scholar 58:615-16+ Aut '89. R. A. Battaglia
MADE IN AMERICA. 1989
The New York Times Book Review 94:13-14 Jl 23 '89. A. Kessler-Harris
Science 246:1642-3 D 22 '89. D. C. Mowery
MAGAZINER, I. C. AND PATINKIN, M. The silent war. 1989
The Washington Monthly 21:54-7 Ap '89. T. J. Peters
MAGRIS, C. Danube. 1989
Commentary 88:66-8 D '89. J. Rosen
The New York Times Book Review 94:14-15 O 1 '89. E. J. Weber
MAGUIRE, J. Night and day. 1989
Health (New York, N.Y.) 21:28+ D '89. C. B. Fleming
MAHFŪZ, N. The beginning and the end. 1989
The New York Times Book Review 94:9 D 10 '89. C. Bardenstein
MAHFŪZ, N. The thief and the dogs. 1989
The New York Times Book Review 94:9 D 10 '89. C. Bardenstein
MAHFŪZ, N. Wedding song. 1989
The New York Times Book Review 94:9 D 10 '89. C. Bardenstein
MAHY, M. Nonstop nonsense. 1989
First pub.: Dent, 1977
The New York Times Book Review 94:42 My 21 '89. B. Ott
MAIER, C. S. The unmasterable past. 1988
The Nation 248:703-4 My 22 '89. N. Birnbaum
National Review 41:49-51 Mr 10 '89. J. Neusner
The New Republic 200:38-40 Ap 3 '89. L. Botstein
The New York Times Book Review 94:28 Ja 29 '89. R. J. Evans
MAINIERO, L. A. Office romance. 1989
Business Week p8 Jl 24 '89. T. Segal
MAINSTREET CAPITALISM. 1988
The Humanist 49:43 Mr/Ap '89. W. Karr
MAIRS, N. Remembering the bone house. 1989
The New York Times Book Review 94:23 Ag 6 '89. N. Christopher
Psychology Today 23:72+ O '89. B. L. Benderly
MAJONE, G. Evidence, argument, and persuasion in the policy process. 1989
Environment 31:25 N '89. J. R. Ravetz
MAKERS OF THE CATHOLIC COMMUNITY. 6v 1989
America 160:354-5 Ap 15 '89. P. H. Samway
Commonweal 116:248-52 Ap 21 '89. L. Cunningham
MAKOWER, J. Woodstock. 1989
The New York Times Book Review 94:7 Jl 23 '89. R. R. Harris
MALAMUD, B. The people, and uncollected stories. 1990
The New Republic 201:116-18 N 6 '89. I. Howe
The New York Times Book Review 94:7 N 19 '89. B. Pesetsky
Time 134:106 N 20 '89. P. Gray
MALCOLM X. Malcolm X: the last speeches. 1989
The Nation 249:650-2 N 27 '89. J. Wood
MALLARMÉ, S. Selected letters of Stéphane Mallarmé. 1988
The New York Review of Books 36:10+ N 9 '89. J. Barnes
MALLON, T. Stolen words. 1989
The New York Times Book Review 94:13-14 O 29 '89. W. Kendrick
MALLORY, J. P. In search of the Indo-Europeans. 1989
Scientific American 261:107-8 Ag '89. P. Morrison
MALLORY, K. AND CONLEY, A. Rescue of the stranded whales. 1989
The New York Times Book Review 94:42 My 21 '89. F. McNulty
MALLOVE, E. F. The quickening universe. 1987
Sky and Telescope 77:156-7 F '89. S. P. Maran
MALLOVE, E. F. AND MATLOFF, G. L. The starflight handbook. 1989
Physics Today 42:94-6 N '89. E. M. Jones
MALONE, M. Time's witness. 1989
The New York Times Book Review 94:12-13 Ap 23 '89. V. Sayers

MALRAUX, A. The walnut trees of Altenburg. 1989
Copyright 1948
The New York Review of Books 36:41-3 D 21 '89. J. Weightman
MAMET, D. Some freaks. 1989
The New York Times Book Review 94:11-12 D 17 '89. B. Nightingale
Time 134:79-81 D 25 '89. R. Z. Sheppard
MAMONOVA, T. Russian women's studies. 1989
The New York Times Book Review 94:18 S 24 '89. M. French
MANCHESTER, W. The last lion, Winston Spencer Churchill; v2, Alone, 1932-1940. 1988
National Review 41:59-60 Ja 27 '89. H. W. Crocker, III
The New York Review of Books 36:36-42 Je 15 '89. D. Cannadine
MANDELBAUM, K. A chorus line and the musicals of Michael Bennett. 1989
The New York Times Book Review 94:2 Ag 13 '89. B. Gelb
MANDELBAUM, M. The fate of nations. 1988
The New York Times Book Review 94:33 Ja 29 '89. D. Holloway
MANN, J. Beijing Jeep. 1989
The New York Times Book Review 94:13 N 19 '89. G. Williams
MANNING, T. G. U.S. Coast Survey vs. Naval Hydrographic Office. 1988
Science 243:102 Ja 6 '89. M. Rothenberg
MANSFIELD, H. C. Taming the prince. 1989
The New Republic 201:46-9 O 16 '89. A. Ryan
MAO ZEDONG. The secret speeches of Chairman Mao. 1989
The New Republic 201:33-6 Jl 31 '89. A. J. Nathan
The New York Review of Books 36:18-20 Je 29 '89. J. Mirsky
The New York Times Book Review 94:12-13 D 10 '89. J. D. Spence
THE MAP CATALOG. 1986
Scientific American 260:122-3 Ap '89. P. Morrison
MAPPING THE MORAL DOMAIN. 1988
The New York Times Book Review 94:6 My 28 '89. M. Csikszentmihalyi
MARC, D. Comic visions. 1989
The New York Times Book Review 94:30 Ap 30 '89. M. Bayles
MARCH, R. M. The Japanese negotiator. 1988
High Technology Business 9:9 My '89. M. Estren
MARCHAND, P. Marshall McLuhan. 1989
Commonweal 116:537-8 O 6 '89. P. H. Connolly
Maclean's 102:63 My 22 '89. N. Snider
National Review 41:46-8 Je 30 '89. G. McCartney
MARCUS, G. Lipstick traces. 1989
The Nation 248:744-7 My 29 '89. G. Santoro
The New Republic 200:35-9 My 15 '89. L. Menand
The New York Times Book Review 94:12 Ap 9 '89. T. Eagleton
Rolling Stone p27+ My 4 '89. A. DeCurtis
USA Today (Periodical) 118:96-7 S '89. S. G. Kellman
MARGARITONDO, G. Introduction to synchrotron radiation. 1988
Physics Today 42:74+ Je '89. N. V. Smith
MARGOLIS, H. Patterns, thinking, and cognition. 1987
Science 244:1094-5 Je 2 '89. L. Daston and G. Gigerenzer
MARGOLIS, R. J. Risking old age in America. 1990
The Washington Monthly 21:57-8 D '89. P. Longman
MARGULIS, L. AND SAGAN, D. Origins of sex. 1986
BioScience 39:45-6 Ja '89. F. J. Ayala
MARIE, DE FRANCE. Proud knight, fair lady.
The New York Times Book Review 94:34 Jl 9 '89. K. Kuskin
MARINO, J. Eighty-eight steps to September. 1989
The New York Times Book Review 94:57 O 15 '89. S. Terris
MARION, R. The intern blues. 1989
The Washington Monthly 21:58-9 Jl/Ag '89. E. Stark
MARK, J. T. A stranger in her native land. 1988
The New York Times Book Review 94:20+ My 7 '89. M. B. Norton
Science 243:823-4 F 10 '89. N. O. Lurie
MARLING, K. A. George Washington slept here. 1988
The New Republic 200:28-30+ F 6 '89. E. S. Morgan
MARQUIS, A. G. Alfred H. Barr, Jr. 1989
American Heritage 40:108-10 Jl/Ag '89
Art in America 77:39+ D '89. B. Wallis
Art News 88:131 O '89. B. B. Stretch
The New Republic 201:39-41 Ag 28 '89. E. V. Thaw
The New York Times Book Review 94:3 Ap 30 '89. L. Auchincloss
MARSCHALL, L. A. The supernova story. 1988
Astronomy 17:100 Ag '89. J. Kanipe
Sky and Telescope 77:501-2 My '89. R. A. Schorn
MARSH, D. The heart of rock & soul. 1989
The Washington Monthly 21:51+ D '89. J. Weisberg
MARSHALL, J. The three little pigs. 1989
The New York Times Book Review 94:27 N 12 '89. F. Gannon
MARSHALL, P. J. Bengal—the British bridgehead. 1987
History Today 39:54-6 Je '89. B. Lenman

MARTIN, C. L. God is a verb. 1989
  The Humanist 49:46-7 S/O '89. M. L. McCallister
MARTIN, D. C. AND WALCOTT, J. L. Best laid plans. 1988
  National Review 41:58 Mr 10 '89. S. Cropsey
MARTIN, F. M. Call me blessed. 1988
  Christianity Today 33:57-8 O 20 '89. P. E. Alsdurf
MARTIN, L. Breaking with history.
  Maclean's 102:70+ O 9 '89. A. Wilson-Smith
MARTIN, R. A story that stands like a dam. 1990
  Wilderness 53:56-8+ Wint '89. C. E. Little
MARTIN, R. Will's mammoth. 1989
  The New York Times Book Review 94:42 N 12 '89. J. Langton
MARUYA, S. Singular rebellion. 1986
  The New Yorker 65:105-7 Mr 6 '89. B. Leithauser
MARX, L. The pilot and the passenger. 1987
  The American Scholar 58:600-2+ Aut '89. P. Likacs
  The New York Review of Books 36:33-4 F 16 '89. R. M. Adams
MARX, P. Confessions of a prolife missionary.
  Conservative Digest 15:51-2 Jl/Ag '89. J. B. Graves
MARY STEWART. 1988
  History Today 39:51-2 Je '89. F. Heal
MASON, B. A. Love life. 1989
  New York 22:66-7 Mr 13 '89. R. Koenig
  The New York Times Book Review 94:7+ Mr 12 '89. L. Moore
MATAS, C. Lisa's war. 1989
  The New York Times Book Review 94:32 My 21 '89. E. Miiton
MATERNAL EMPLOYMENT AND CHILDREN'S DEVELOPMENT. 1988
  Science 243:99-101 Ja 6 '89. J. T. Mortimer
MATHABANE, M. Kaffir boy in America. 1989
  The New York Times Book Review 94:19 Ag 13 '89. L. Hahn
MATHEMATICAL EVOLUTIONARY THEORY. 1988
  Science 246:941-2 N 17 '89. J. Felsenstein
MATHEWS, J. Escalante. 1988
  The American Spectator 22:40-1 Ap '89. P. Skerry
  The Washington Monthly 21:58 My '89. S. Monroe
MATOS MOCTEZUMA, E. The Great Temple of the Aztecs. 1988
  Scientific American 260:144-5 My '89. P. Morrison
MATSUMOTO, S. Inspector Imanishi investigates. 1989
  The New York Times Book Review 94:40 Ɒ 15 '89. J. Van de Wetering
MATTERA, D. Sophiatown. 1989
  The Nation 248:563-5 Ap 24 '89. M. Gevisser
  The New York Times Book Review 94:29 My 14 '89. S. Suzman
MATTHIESSEN, P. On the river Styx, and other stories. 1989
  America 161:383-5 N 25 '89. A. Dubus
  The New York Times Book Review 94:11-12 My 14 '89. T. R. Edwards
MAUPIN, A. Sure of you. 1989
  The New York Times Book Review 94:26 O 22 '89. D. B. Feinberg
  Newsweek 114:77 O 30 '89. T. Clifton
MAURER, H. Strange ground. 1988
  The Progressive 53:44-6 My '89. M. Uhl
MAY, G. G. Addiction and grace. 1988
  Christianity Today 33:63 My 12 '89. J. Alsdurf
MAY, H. F. Coming to terms. 1987
  The American Scholar 58:308-12 Spr '89. T. Nieman
MAYER, A. J. Why did the heavens not darken? 1989
  The Nation 248:704-6 My 22 '89. I. Kershaw
  National Review 41:49-51 Mr 10 '89. J. Neusner
  The New Republic 200:39-44 Ap 17 '89. D. Goldhagen
  The New York Times Book Review 94:1+ F 19 '89. V. R. Berghahn
MAYER, B. Astrowatch. 1988
  Astronomy 17:101-3 F '89. R. A. Garfinkle
  Sky and Telescope 77:38-9 Ja '89. D. Byrd
MAYER, J. AND MCMANUS, D. Landslide. 1988
  Commentary 87:71-2 Ja '89. S. McConnell
  National Review 41:54+ F 10 '89. J. P. Hart
MAYERS, D. A. George Kennan and the dilemmas of US foreign policy. 1989
  The New York Review of Books 36:3-5 Ag 17 '89. R. Steel
MAYNE, W. Gideon ahoy! 1989
  The New York Times Book Review 94:26 S 24 '89. H. Rochman
MAZZA, C. Animal acts. 1989
  The New York Times Book Review 94:13 N 26 '89. W. Ferguson
MCADAM, D. Freedom Summer. 1988
  The Nation 248:202-4 F 13 '89. N. Mills
  The Progressive 53:38-40 Jl '89. L. Rocawich
MCCAIG, D. The bamboo cannon. 1989
  The New York Times Book Review 94:12 Mr 26 '89. V. Weissman
MCCLATCHY, J. D. White paper on contemporary American poetry. 1989
  The Nation 249:632+ N 27 '89. T. M. Disch

The New York Times Book Review 94:33 Jl 9 '89. H. Beaver
MCCLINTOCK, M. Mike McClintock's home sense care & repair almanac. 1989
  Workbench 45:27 N/D '89. A. R. Gould
MCCLOUD, B. What should we tell our children about Vietnam? 1989
  The Washington Monthly 21:55-6 O '89. M. Massing
MCCONNELL, D. R. A different gospel.
  Christianity Today 33:59-60 Mr 3 '89. W. W. Menzies
MCCORMICK, R. A. The critical calling. 1989
  America 161:216-17 O 7 '89. W. C. Spohn
MCCOY, D. R. The last of the fathers. 1989
  American Heritage 40:108 Jl/Ag '89
  The New Leader 72:17-19 Jl 10-24 '89. G. Tyler
  The New Republic 200:35-8 Je 12 '89. E. S. Morgan
MCCOY, M. C. Frederick Buechner. 1988
  The Christian Century 106:319-20 Mr 22-29 '89. C. L. Allen
MCCULLOUGH, D. W. Waking from the American dream. 1988
  Christianity Today 33:36 Je 16 '89. J. D. Berkley
MCCURRY, S. Monsoon. 1988
  Scientific American 261:125-6 N '89. P. Morrison
MCDANNELL, C. AND LANG, B. Heaven. 1988
  The Christian Century 106:144-6 F 1-8 '89. S. Grenz
  Commonweal 116:283-4 My 5 '89. W. P. Loewe
  Smithsonian 20:226-7 O '89. W. C. Rice
MCDOWALL, R. M. Diadromy in fishes. 1988
  BioScience 39:565-6 S '89. R. A. Rulifson
MCEWAN, N. Graham Greene. 1988
  The New York Review of Books 36:3-4 Mr 16 '89. J. Bayley
MCGEE, H. On food and cooking. 1988
  Scientific American 261:126 O '89. P. Morrison
MCGEEVER, P. J. Rev. Charles Owen Rice. 1989
  Commonweal 116:651-2 N 17 '89. R. W. Gibbons
MCGILLIGAN, P. Robert Altman. 1989
  Film Comment 25:78 S/O '89. A. Sarris
MCGINNISS, J. Blind faith. 1988
  New York 22:60+ Ja 9 '89. R. Koenig
  The New York Times Book Review 94:9 Ja 29 '89. A. Rice
  Time 133:95-6 Ja 2 '89. R. Z. Sheppard
MCGRATH, P. The grotesque. 1989
  The New York Times Book Review 94:7 My 28 '89. J. Kenney
MCGRATH, T. Selected poems, 1938-1988. 1988
  The Nation 249:534-5 N 6 '89. A. Clampitt
MCGUANE, T. Keep the change. 1989
  New York 22:60-1 S 4 '89. R. Koenig
  The New York Times Book Review 94:3 S 24 '89. B. Lowry
MCGUINNESS, B. Wittgenstein. 1988
  The Nation 248:137-40 Ja 30 '89. P. Mattick, Jr.
  The New Republic 200:35-40 My 1 '89. W. H. Gass
MCGUIRE, W. Poetry's catbird seat. 1988
  The New Leader 72:19-20 My 15-29 '89. P. Pettingell
MCKEEVER, P. Adlai Stevenson. 1989
  The New Republic 201:25-30 Jl 17-24 '89. H. Fairlie
  The New York Times Book Review 94:14 Jl 16 '89. S. E. Ambrose
MCKIBBEN, B. The end of nature. 1989
  Mother Jones 14:41-2 D '89. M. Hertsgaard
  National Review 41:45-6 O 27 '89. C. Williamson
  The New York Review of Books 36:32-8 D 21 '89. D. J. Kevles
  The New York Times Book Review 94:9 O 8 '89. N. Wade
  Newsweek 114:83 O 23 '89. G. Cowley
  The Washington Monthly 21:51-2+ O '89. G. Easterbrook
MCKINNEY, F. K. AND JACKSON, J. B. C. Bryozoan evolution. 1988
  Science 245:422 Jl 28 '89. R. L. Zimmer
MCLAUGHLIN, J. Jefferson and Monticello. 1988
  Architectural Record 177:63+ Mr '89. R. Lavenstein
MCLEAN, S. The morningside world of Stuart McLean.
  Maclean's 102:73 O 16 '89. B. Ledger
MCLUHAN, M. Letters of Marshall McLuhan. 1987
  Commonweal 116:537-8 O 6 '89. P. H. Connolly
  National Review 41:46-8 Je 30 '89. G. McCartney
MCLUHAN, M. AND MCLUHAN, E. Laws of media. 1989
  Commonweal 116:537-8 O 6 '89. P. H. Connolly
  The New York Times Book Review 94:39 F 26 '89. J. Sturrock
MCMANAMON, J. M. Funeral oratory and the cultural ideals of Italian humanism. 1989
  America 161:169-70+ S 23 '89. S. T. Strocchia
MCMILLAN, T. Disappearing acts. 1989
  The New York Times Book Review 94:8 Ag 6 '89. V. Sayers
MCMILLAN, V. E. Writing papers in the biological sciences. 1988
  BioScience 39:401-2 Je '89. B. Gastel
MCMILLEN, N. R. Dark journey. 1989
  The Nation 249:692-4 D 4 '89. B. Farrell
  The New York Review of Books 36:15-17 Je 29 '89. C. V. Woodward

MCMURTRY, L. Some can whistle. 1989
The New York Times Book Review 94:8 O 22 '89. B. Kingsolver
Time 134:89 O 16 '89. P. Gray
Vogue 179:280+ O '89. H. Hurt

MCNAMARA, R. S. Out of the cold. 1989
National Review 41:48+ O 27 '89. L. Edwards
The New York Times Book Review 94:12 O 8 '89. A. B. Ulam

MCNAUGHER, T. L. New weapons, old politics. 1989
The New York Review of Books 36:3-4+ O 26 '89. N. Lemann

MCNEIL, F. War and peace in Central America. 1988
The New York Review of Books 36:46-51 Ag 17 '89. J. Chace
The New York Times Book Review 94:13-14 Ja 29 '89. L. S. Robinson

MCNEILL, J. J. The church and the homosexual. 1988
Commonweal 116:90-2 F 10 '89. J. A. O'Donohoe

MCNEILL, J. J. Taking a chance on God. 1988
America 160:227-9 Mr 11 '89. L. Griffin
Commonweal 116:90-2 F 10 '89. J. A. O'Donohoe

MCNEILL, W. H. Arnold J. Toynbee, a life. 1989
The Nation 249:358+ O 2 '89. J. Caplan
National Review 41:52-3 Je 2 '89. S. T. Francis
The New Republic 201:29-30+ Ag 7-14 '89. A. Ryan
The New York Review of Books 36:28-34 O 12 '89. H. R. Trevor-Roper
The New York Times Book Review 94:12 My 28 '89. M. R. Lefkowitz

MCPHEE, J. A. The control of nature. 1989
National Review 41:54+ Je 2 '89. E. Marston
The New York Times Book Review 94:1+ Ag 6 '89. S. J. Pyne

MCPHERSON, J. M. Battle cry of freedom. 1988
Conservative Digest 15:51+ Ja/F '89. J. B. Graves

MCROY, R. G. AND OTHERS. Openness in adoption. 1988
Children Today 18:32 Mr/Ap '89

MCWILLIAM, C. A little stranger. 1989
The New York Times Book Review 94:9 Jl 16 '89. T. M. Disch

MEAD, W. R. Mortal splendor. 1987
America 160:45-6 Ja 21 '89. A. J. Kuzniewski

MEADE, M. S. AND OTHERS. Medical geography. 1988
Environment 31:25-6 N '89. H. D. Foster

MECH, L. D. The arctic wolf.
The Conservationist 44:50 S/O '89. R. E. Henshaw
Natural History p92+ F '89. R. R. Ream
Smithsonian 20:198-200 S '89. D. Lessem

MECHANISTIC PRINCIPLES OF ENZYME ACTIVITY. 1988
Science 246:1064-5 N 24 '89. R. G. Matthews

MEDVEDEV, R. A. Let history judge. 1989
The New Republic 201:40+ S 18-25 '89. R. Conquest
The New York Times Book Review 94:11-12 Je 4 '89. R. Hingley
Time 133:83 Je 26 '89. P. Blake

MEHTA, G. Raj. 1989
The New York Review of Books 36:9-10+ My 18 '89. I. Buruma
The New York Times Book Review 94:18 Ap 9 '89. R. Billington

MEHTA, V. The stolen light. 1989
America 161:325-6 N 11 '89. P. McCormack
The New York Times Book Review 94:17 Mr 12 '89. S. A. Toth

MEINE, C. Aldo Leopold. 1988
Country Journal 16:14 Mr/Ap '89. D. Graber

MEINERS, R. E. AND LABAND, D. N. Patterns of corporate philanthropy.
The American Spectator 22:39-40 S '89. J. Von Kannon

MEITES, S. Otto Folin. 1988
Science 244:719-20 My 12 '89. J. T. Edsall

MELAND, B. E. Essays in constructive theology.
The Christian Century 106:421-2 Ap 19 '89. L. E. Axel

MELCHIOR, P. J. The physics of the earth's core. 1986
Physics Today 42:89-90 S '89. T. J. Ahrens

MELLA, D. L. The language of color. 1988
American Artist 53:26+ O '89. M. C. Nelson

MELLINKOFF, R. The Devil at Isenheim. 1988
Commonweal 116:344-5 Je 2 '89. L. Cunningham

MELNIKOFF, P. Plots and players. 1989
The New York Times Book Review 94:34 My 21 '89. M. W. Ferguson

MELOSH, H. J. Impact cratering. 1989
Science 245:1261-2 S 15 '89. K. A. Holsapple

MELVILLE, H. Journals.
The New York Times Book Review 94:58 N 12 '89. J. D. Bloom

MENCKEN, H. L. The diary of H.L. Mencken. 1989
American Heritage 40:14+ D '89. G. C. Ward
The New York Times Book Review 94:3 D 24 '89. R. Ward

MENCKEN, H. L. The editor, the bluenose, and the prostitute. 1988
The Progressive 53:40 Ja '89. M. G. Judge

MENGES, C. C. Inside the National Security Council. 1988
Commentary 87:76-8 F '89. D. Brock

National Review 41:57-9 Ja 27 '89. R. Vigilante
The New York Times Book Review 94:12-13 Ja 29 '89. F. Barnes

MENNINGER, K. A. The selected correspondence of Karl A. Menninger, 1919-1945. 1988
The New York Times Book Review 94:25 Mr 19 '89. G. N. Grob

MERCURY. 1988
Science 245:82-3 Jl 7 '89. S. C. Solomon

MERRILL, J. I. The inner room. 1988
The New Leader 72:16-17 Ja 9 '89. P. Pettingell
The New Republic 200:35-8 Ap 3 '89. H. H. Vendler
The New York Times Book Review 94:63 N 12 '89. C. Kizer

MERTON, T. The road to joy. 1989
America 161:267-72 O 21 '89. W. H. Shannon

METCALF, T. R. An imperial vision. 1988
Architectural Record 177:69 O '89. M. Wortman

METCALFE, P. 1933. 1989
The New York Times Book Review 94:23 F 5 '89. O. Fuerbringer

METEORITES AND THE EARLY SOLAR SYSTEM. 1988
Science 244:849-50 My 19 '89. D. Lal

MEYER, M. A. Response to modernity. 1988
Commentary 87:64-6 Mr '89. D. Singer

MEYER, M. R. The Alexander complex. 1989
Business Week p14 S 4 '89. P. Finch

MEZEY, R. Evening wind. 1987
The New York Times Book Review 94:14 Ja 8 '89. C. Muske

MICHENER, J. A. Caribbean. 1989
The New York Times Book Review 94:22 N 5 '89. R. Houston

MICHENER, J. A. Journey. 1989
The New York Times Book Review 94:15 Jl 9 '89. T. J. Fleming

MICKELSON, S. From whistle stop to sound bite. 1989
The New York Times Book Review 94:11 D 10 '89. M. S. Goodman

MICKLE, S. F. The Queen of October. 1989
The New York Times Book Review 94:9 N 12 '89. J. Shepard

MICROBIAL MATS, STROMATOLITES. 1984
Science 244:1095 Je 2 '89. K. H. Nealson

MIDDLETON, S. Entry into Jerusalem. 1988
The New York Times Book Review 94:26 Mr 12 '89. P. Vigderman

MIGNONE, E. F. Witness to the truth. 1988
America 161:18-20 Jl 1-8 '89. A. T. Hennelly

MILASHEV, V. A. Explosion pipes. 1988
Science 244:479 Ap 28 '89. S. W. Kieffer

MILES, B. Ginsberg. 1989
The Nation 249:798-800 D 25 '89. A. Codrescu
The New Leader 72:15-16 N 27 '89. P. Pettingell
The New York Times Book Review 94:3+ O 1 '89. P. Berman

MILES, M. R. Practicing Christianity. 1988
The Christian Century 106:567-8 My 24-31 '89. M. Downey

MILES, R. The women's history of the world. 1988
The American Spectator 22:39-41 Jl '89. E. Kristol

MILLER, A. Timebends. 1987
The American Scholar 58:140+ Wint '89. B. Bawer

MILLER, D. L. Lewis Mumford. 1989
The Atlantic 264:88-91 Jl '89. P. Goldberger
The New York Times Book Review 94:3+ N 26 '89. A. L. Huxtable

MILLER, E. A crash course on the New Age movement. 1989
Christianity Today 33:55 O 6 '89. D. Groothuis

MILLER, J. C. Way of death. 1988
The New York Times Book Review 94:27 Mr 12 '89. S. B. Schwartz

MILLER, J. G. The bridge at Dong Ha. 1989
Conservative Digest 15:45 S/O '89. J. B. Graves

MILLER, M. C. Boxed in. 1988
The Nation 248:59-62 Ja 9-16 '89. J. Lears

MILLER, N. In search of gay America. 1989
The Christian Century 106:536-8 My 17 '89. C. Jessey

MILLER, N. Spying for America. 1989
The New York Times Book Review 94:15 Jl 23 '89. J. A. Adam

MILNER, J. The studios of Paris. 1988
Art News 88:85 Ja '89. B. A. MacAdam
Smithsonian 20:170+ Je '89. S. Meisler

MIŁOSZ, C. Conversations with Czeslaw Milosz. 1987
Commonweal 116:339-41 Je 2 '89. P. D. Baumann

MINER, S. M. Between Churchill and Stalin. 1988
The New York Review of Books 36:15-19 Mr 30 '89. G. A. Craig

MINORITIES AND CANCER. 1989
Science 246:1063-4 N 24 '89. G. M. Swanson

MINOT, S. Lust & other stories. 1989
Mother Jones 14:43-4 Je '89. G. Brown
The New York Times Book Review 94:24 Je 11 '89. J. Robison

MINTON, H. L. Lewis M. Terman. 1988
Science 244:1596-7 Je 30 '89. R. E. Fancher

MINUS, P. M. Walter Rauschenbusch, American reformer. 1988
  The Christian Century 106:75-8 Ja 25 '89. M. L. Stackhouse
MISTRY, R. Swimming lessons, and other stories from Firozsha Baag. 1989
  The New York Times Book Review 94:26 Mr 5 '89. H. Cooke
MITCHELL, B. Weak link. 1989
  The American Spectator 22:54 D '89. A. F. C. Webster
  National Review 41:47-8 O 13 '89. W. R. Hawkins
  The New York Times Book Review 94:19 S 3 '89. R. Halloran
MITFORD, J. Grace had an English heart. 1989
  The New York Times Book Review 94:22 Ap 16 '89. M. B. Slung
MOBILE DNA. 1989
  Science 245:84-5 Jl 7 '89. B. G. Hall
MODARRESSI, T. The Pilgrim's rules of etiquette. 1989
  The New Republic 201:44-5 D 4 '89. A. Desai
  The New York Times Book Review 94:7 Ag 13 '89. P. Fitzgerald
MODI. ENGLISH. I modi. 1988
  The New York Review of Books 36:40 My 18 '89. R. M. Adams
MOELLER, S. D. Shooting war. 1989
  Commonweal 116:377-8 Je 16 '89. D. O'Brien
MOFFATT, M. Coming of age in New Jersey. 1989
  The New York Times Book Review 94:27 Ap 30 '89. R. R. Cooper
MOJTABAI, A. G. Ordinary time. 1989
  Commonweal 116:567-8 O 20 '89. D. Toolan
  The New York Times Book Review 94:9 S 24 '89. M. Malone
MOLDEA, D. E. Interference. 1989
  The New York Times Book Review 94:8 S 3 '89. G. Eskenazi
THE MOLECULAR AND CELLULAR BIOLOGY OF WOUND REPAIR. 1988
  BioScience 39:200-1 Mr '89. V. P. Terranova
MOLECULAR BIOLOGY OF RNA. 1987
  BioScience 39:188-9 Mr '89. G. D. Frenkel
MOLECULAR GENETICS OF DEVELOPMENT. 1987
  BioScience 39:403-4 Je '89. R. Maxson, Jr.
MOLNAR, T. S. Twin powers. 1988
  National Review 41:58-9 Ap 7 '89. C. Williamson
MOMADAY, N. S. The ancient child. 1989
  The New York Times Book Review 94:14 D 31 '89. E. Marston
MONASTYRSKII, M. I. Riemann, topology, and physics. 1987
  Physics Today 42:72-4 Je '89. L. Alvarez-Gaumé
MONKKONEN, E. H. America becomes urban. 1988
  History Today 39:49 Ag '89. P. J. Corfield
MONTANA SPACES. 1988
  Sierra 74:64-6+ Jl/Ag '89. D. Snow
MONTGOMERY, K. Target: prime time. 1989
  The American Spectator 22:34-6 S '89. R. T. Marin
  The New York Times Book Review 94:5 Mr 26 '89. M. Winn
MONTGOMERY, M. The trouble with you innerleckchuls. 1988
  Conservative Digest 15:63+ My/Je '89. J. B. Graves
MONTGOMERY, M. R. Saying goodbye. 1989
  The New York Times Book Review 94:7 Je 4 '89. C. McFadden
MONUMENTS OF EGYPT. 1987
  Smithsonian 20:240+ N '89. F. Getlein
MOOK, D. E. AND VARGISH, T. Inside relativity. 1987
  Physics Today 42:90 S '89. E. F. Taylor
MOON, F. C. Chaotic vibrations. 1987
  Physics Today 42:78 My '89. J. P. Gollub
MOON, SIR P. The British conquest and dominion of India. 1989
  History Today 39:53 N '89. T. Royle
MOORE, K. D. Pardons. 1989
  The New York Times Book Review 94:7 Jl 16 '89. A. M. Dershowitz
MOORE, S. Jesus the liberator of desire. 1989
  Commonweal 116:570-1 O 20 '89. S. C. Callahan
MOORE, S. The whiteness of bones. 1989
  Ms. 17:41 Mr '89. J. Peters
  The New York Review of Books 36:50-2 Ap 27 '89. R. Towers
  The New York Times Book Review 94:5-6 Mr 26 '89. J. Anderson
  Vogue 179:324 Mr '89. L. Stone
MOORE, T. J. Heart failure. 1989
  The New York Times Book Review 94:15 S 24 '89. H. H. Hiatt
MOORHOUSE, F. Forty-seventeen. 1989
  The New York Times Book Review 94:3 Ag 13 '89. A. Carter
MORALES, E. Cocaine. 1989
  National Review 41:47-8 Je 2 '89. W. Lutton
MORAVEC, H. P. Mind children. 1988
  Ad Astra 1:46 My '89. J. D. Kirwan
  Byte 14:51-2+ Ap '89. E. A. Bobinsky
  The New York Times Book Review 94:10-11 Ja 1 '89. M. M. Waldrop

The New Yorker 64:84-8 Ja 9 '89. B. Leithauser
MORGAN, A. James Connolly. 1988
  History Today 39:57-8 Ap '89. C. Townshend
MORGAN, E. S. Inventing the people. 1988
  History Today 39:57-8 Ag '89. S. Andrews
MORGAN, G. Riding the waves of change. 1988
  High Technology Business 9:16 F '89. M. Estren
MORGAN, R. The demon lover. 1988
  The New York Times Book Review 94:17 Ap 30 '89. J. K. Weinberg
MORGAN, S. My place. 1988
  The New York Times Book Review 94:13-14 F 19 '89. J. T. Hospital
MORGAN, S. R. Abuse and neglect of handicapped children. 1987
  Children Today 18:32-3 Mr/Ap '89. S. A. Lansing
MORGAN, T. An uncertain hour. 1990
  The New York Times Book Review 94:1+ D 31 '89. P. L. R. Higonnet
MORITA, A. AND ISHIHARA, S. The Japan that can say 'no'.
  The New York Review of Books 36:19-20 D 7 '89. I. Buruma
MORRIS, J. Hong Kong. 1988
  Commentary 87:67-8+ Mr '89. W. McGurn
  The New York Times Book Review 94:35 Ja 29 '89. F. Ching
  Time 133:72 Ja 16 '89. R. Z. Sheppard
MORRIS, J. Pleasures of a tangled life. 1989
  The New York Times Book Review 94:16-17 N 12 '89. P. Levy
MORRIS, M. The waiting room. 1989
  The New York Times Book Review 94:9 Jl 2 '89. B. Lott
MORRIS, R. Richard Milhous Nixon; v1, The rise of an American politician. 1990
  The New York Times Book Review 94:1+ N 12 '89. K. Starr
  Time 134:100+ N 6 '89. L. I. Barrett
MORRISON, D. AND OWEN, T. D. The planetary system. 1988
  Sky and Telescope 77:270 Mr '89. C. A. Wood
MORSE, P. Hokusai, the One hundred poets. 1989
  Smithsonian 20:176 D '89. F. Getlein
MORTIMER, J. C. The narrowing stream. 1989
  The New York Times Book Review 94:37-8 O 15 '89. A. Arensberg
MORTON, F. Thunder at twilight. 1989
  The New York Times Book Review 94:36 D 10 '89. J. Henkin
MOSHER, H. F. A stranger in the kingdom. 1989
  The New York Times Book Review 94:11 O 29 '89. L. Smith
MOSS, M. Palace coup. 1988
  The New York Times Book Review 94:14 Ap 9 '89. A. Feinberg
MOTOCOURSE.
  Cycle 40:85+ My '89. K. Vreeke
MOTZ, L. AND NATHANSON, C. The constellations. 1988
  Astronomy 17:120-1 D '89. D. J. Eicher
  Sky and Telescope 77:498-9+ My '89. R. J. Morales
MOULD, R. F. Chernobyl. 1988
  Environment 31:25-6 S '89. C. Hohenemser
MOURAD, K. Regards from the dead princess. 1989
  The New York Times Book Review 94:18 N 19 '89. B. Thompson
MOWERY, D. C. AND ROSENBERG, N. Technology and the pursuit of economic growth. 1989
  Science 246:1180-1 D 1 '89. M. J. Peck
MOYERS, B. A world of ideas. 1989
  Commentary 88:70-1 O '89. J. Gardner
  USA Today (Periodical) 118:95-6 S '89. G. F. Kreyche
MOYNAHAN, B. Claws of the bear. 1989
  The New York Times Book Review 94:20 Ag 6 '89. D. Holloway
MUDGE, B. K. Sara Coleridge, a victorian daughter. 1989
  The New York Times Book Review 94:42 O 8 '89. B. Fields
MUDIMBE, V. Y. Before the birth of the moon. 1989
  The New York Times Book Review 94:43 Ap 30 '89. R. McKnight
MUDRICK, M. Mudrick transcribed.
  The New Republic 201:39-41 Ag 21 '89. J. Wolcott
MUELLER, J. E. Retreat from doomsday. 1989
  The Bulletin of the Atomic Scientists 45:38-9 O '89. P. S. Boyer
  Commonweal 116:533-6 O 6 '89. C. R. Morris
  The New York Times Book Review 94:14 Ap 30 '89. M. E. Howard
  The Washington Monthly 21:46+ My '89. C. W. Maynes
MUGGERIDGE, M. Confessions of a twentieth-century pilgrim. 1988
  Christianity Today 33:31 Ap 7 '89. K. L. Billingsley
MUKHERJEE, B. Jasmine. 1989
  Maclean's 102:72 O 23 '89. E. Wachtel
  Mother Jones 14:43-4 D '89. D. Foster
  New York 22:132 S 25 '89. R. Koenig

THE NEW YORKER BOOK OF WAR PIECES. 1988
Repr. Orig. pub.: Reynal & Hitchcock, 1947
The Washington Monthly 21:73-5 F '89. S. Schanberg
NEWFIELD, J. AND BARRETT, W. City for sale. 1988
The American Spectator 22:34-6 Mr '89. T. Mallon
National Review 41:38-40 Mr 24 '89. H. I. London
The New Republic 200:46-9 Mr 20 '89. N. Glazer
New York 22:60 Ja 9 '89. R. Koenig
The New York Times Book Review 94:7-8 Ja 15 '89.
J. Alter
The Washington Monthly 21:57-9 Mr '89. J. Ledbetter
NEWHOUSE, J. War and peace in the nuclear age. 1989
Commonweal 116:533-6 O 6 '89. C. R. Morris
The New Leader 72:17-18 Mr 20 '89. B. Gewen
The New Republic 200:38-40 Je 12 '89. L. Freedman
The New York Times Book Review 94:7 Ja 22 '89. M.
S. Sherry
NEWHOUSE, V. Wallace K. Harrison, architect. 1989
The New York Times Book Review 94:38 S 10 '89. J.
H. Kay
NEWMAN, C. A. The Anglo-Norman nobility in the reign
of Henry I. 1988
History Today 39:54 N '89. P. Hyams
NEWMAN, K. Falling from grace. 1988
The Christian Century 106:595-8 Je 7-14 '89. I. Nerken
Society 26:90-1 Jl/Ag '89. N. L. Friedman
NEWMAN, P. C. The story of the Hudson Bay Company;
v1, Company of adventurers. 1985
History Today 39:55-6 Ja '89. K. R. Andrews
NEWMAN, P. C. The story of the Hudson Bay Company;
v2, Caesars of the wilderness. 1987
History Today 39:55-6 Ja '89. K. R. Andrews
NEWTON, J. AND TEECE, P. The guide to amateur
astronomy. 1988
Sky and Telescope 78:44-5 Jl '89. P. Harrington
NICARAGUAN PEASANT POETRY FROM SOLEN-
TINAME.
The New York Times Book Review 94:5-6 Ja 1 '89. A.
Josephs
NICHOLLS, J. G. The competitive ethos and democratic
education. 1988
Psychology Today 23:74 O '89. A. Kohn
NICHOLS, M. Gorilla. 1989
Natural History p28+ Ja '89. P. G. Veit
NICHOLSON, M. The new environmental age. 1987
BioScience 39:187-8 Mr '89. D. E. Blockstein
NICKLES, L. Hype. 1989
Harper's Bazaar 122:208+ S '89. J. Moline
NICOL, M. The powers that be. 1989
The New York Times Book Review 94:9 N 26 '89. W.
Finnegan
NIR, Y. The lost childhood. 1989
The New York Times Book Review 94:6 D 31 '89. T.
R. Swick
NISBET, R. A. Roosevelt and Stalin. 1988
The American Spectator 22:47 Ag '89. F. M. Oppenheimer
NISSEN, H. J. The early history of the ancient Near East,
9000-2000 B.C. 1988
Science 244:370-1 Ap 21 '89. R. L. Zettler
NITZE, P. H. From Hiroshima to Glasnost. 1989
The New York Review of Books 36:13-17 N 23 '89. S.
Hoffmann
The New York Times Book Review 94:15-16 O 15 '89.
W. Isaacson
NIVEN, J. John C. Calhoun and the price of union. 1988
The New York Review of Books 35:16-20 Ja 19 '89. J.
M. McPherson
NIXON, C. Racing the silver arrows. 1986
Road & Track 41:45 N '89. T. Swan
NIXON, R. M. From: the president. 1988
National Review 41:43-4 Ap 21 '89. A. Ferguson
The New York Times Book Review 94:3 F 26 '89. C.
T. Buckley
NO WAY. 1987
Byte 14:51-2 F '89. D. A. Mindell
NODDINGS, N. Women and evil. 1989
Commonweal 116:598-9 N 3 '89. M. R. Miles
NOLAN, C. Under the eye of the clock. 1987
America 160:252-3 Mr 18 '89. J. B. Breslin
NOLAN, J. E. Guardians of the arsenal. 1989
The New York Times Book Review 94:11 D 24 '89. M.
S. Sherry
NOLAN, M. L. AND NOLAN, S. Christian pilgrimage in
modern Western Europe. 1989
The Christian Century 106:539 My 17 '89. L. Cunningham
NOLL, M. A. One nation under God? 1988
Christianity Today 33:62-3 My 12 '89. R. V. Pierard
NOLL, M. A. Princeton and the republic, 1768-1822. 1989
The Christian Century 106:1178-9 D 13 '89. T. D. Bozeman
NORMAN, D. A. The psychology of everyday things. 1988
Technology Review 92:74-5 My/Je '89. R. G. Nichols
NORMAN, H. Kiss in the Hotel Joseph Conrad and other
stories. 1989
The New York Times Book Review 94:16 O 8 '89. S.
Dobyns
NORTH AMERICAN TERRESTRIAL VEGETATION. 1988
BioScience 39:740-1 N '89. K. T. Killingbeck

NORTON, A. P. Norton's 2000.0 star atlas and reference
handbook (epoch 2000.0). 18th ed. 1989
Sky and Telescope 78:486-7+ N '89. F. Schaaf
THE NORTON BOOK OF TRAVEL. 1987
The American Scholar 58:300+ Spr '89. P. Dailey
NORWICH, J. J. Byzantium. 1989
Commentary 88:58-60 Ag '89. J. J. Pelikan
History Today 39:58 Ag '89. A. Dunn
The New York Times Book Review 94:9 Ap 16 '89. G.
W. Bowersock
Smithsonian 20:168+ Je '89. R. Beeston
NOT NECESSARILY THE NEW AGE. 1988
The Nation 249:61-3 Jl 10 '89. T. Athanasiou
NOUWEN, H. J. M. The road to daybreak. 1988
U.S. Catholic 54:48-51 F '89. G. M. Costello
NOVA, C. Tornado alley. 1989
The New York Times Book Review 94:7+ Jl 23 '89. A.
Codrescu
NOVAK, D. Jewish-Christian dialogue. 1989
Commentary 88:65-7 N '89. D. Singer
NOVAK, M. Free persons and the common good. 1989
Commentary 88:71-2 O '89. T. Eastland
NOVE, A. Glasnost in action. 1989
The New York Times Book Review 94:13-14 S 10 '89.
H. L. Robinson
NOVEL ASPECTS OF INSECT-PLANT INTERACTIONS.
1988
Science 244:1498-9 Je 23 '89. J. N. Thompson
NOVICK, P. That noble dream. 1988
The Nation 248:168-70 F 6 '89. R. Rosenzweig
The New Republic 200:40-3 F 20 '89. C. V. Woodward
NOVICK, S. M. Honorable Justice. 1989
The New York Times Book Review 94:3+ Ag 20 '89. E.
Morris
Smithsonian 20:176+ D '89. D. Drabelle
NOZICK, R. The examined life. 1989
National Review 41:38-9 D 31 '89. K. R. Minogue
The New Republic 201:122+ N 6 '89. L. Wieseltier
The New York Times Book Review 94:15-16 O 29 '89.
W. Gaylin
NUDELMAN, E. D. Jessie Willcox Smith. 1989
American Artist 53:117-18 S '89. D. C. Hines
NULAND, S. B. Doctors. 1988
Smithsonian 20:160-2 My '89. C. Eron

O

OAKESHOTT, M. J. The voice of liberal learning. 1989
The New Republic 201:33-6 Jl 10 '89. D. Bromwich
OATES, J. C. American appetites. 1989
The New York Times Book Review 94:5 Ja 1 '89. R.
Towers
Time 133:64 Ja 9 '89. P. Gray
OATES, J. C. Soul/mate. 1989
The New York Times Book Review 94:16 Je 4 '89. L.
Wolfe
O'BRIEN, C. C. Passion and cunning and other essays. 1988
National Review 41:51-2 Ap 7 '89. E. Kedourie
O'BRIEN, E. The high road. 1988
America 160:250-2 Mr 18 '89. R. E. Hosmer
The New Republic 200:40-1 F 13 '89. P. K. Bell
The New Yorker 64:92-4 Ja 30 '89. T. Rafferty
O'CONNELL, M. R. John Ireland and the American Catholic
Church. 1988
America 160:331-3 Ap 8 '89. J. M. McShane
O'CONNELL, R. L. Of arms and men. 1989
The Bulletin of the Atomic Scientists 45:40-1 S '89. M.
S. Sherry
O'CONNOR, F. Collected works. 1988
The American Scholar 58:622-5 Aut '89. H. McDonald
The New Republic 200:34-8 Ap 24 '89. M. J. Salter
O'CONNOR, J. J., CARDINAL AND KOCH, E. His Eminence
and Hizzoner. 1989
Commentary 87:61-3 Je '89. S. McConnell
The New York Times Book Review 94:3 Mr 26 '89. A.
Hacker
U.S. Catholic 54:48-51 Jl '89. G. M. Costello
ODUM, E. P. Ecology and our endangered life-support systems.
1989
BioScience 39:814-15 D '89. P. G. Risser
The Conservationist 44:51 N/D '89. R. E. Henshaw
O'FAOLÁIN, S. And again? 1989
The New York Times Book Review 94:18 S 17 '89. C.
Gaiser
O'FLAHERTY, W. D. Other peoples' myths. 1988
The Christian Century 106:1205 D 20-27 '89. H. G. Cox
Commonweal 116:444-5 Ag 11 '89. M. Gerhart
The New York Times Book Review 94:18 Ja 29 '89. J.
A. Boon
O'HANLON, R. In trouble again. 1989
Smithsonian 20:118-19 Jl '89. W. Dieter
O'KEEFFE, G. Georgia O'Keeffe: one hundred flowers. 1987
The New Republic 200:41-5 Ja 30 '89. E. Abrahams
O'KEEFFE, G. Some memories of drawings. 1988
The New Republic 200:41-5 Ja 30 '89. E. Abrahams
OKRENT, D. AND WULF, S. Baseball anecdotes. 1989
Newsweek 113:67-8 Je 26 '89. P. S. Prescott
OKRI, B. Stars of the new curfew. 1989

The New York Times Book Review 94:12 Ag 13 '89. N. Bissoondath

OKUN', L. B. [Alpha], [beta], [gamma], [zeta] 1987
Physics Today 42:89 S '89. G. Karl

OLASKY, M. The press and abortion, 1838-1988. 1988
Christianity Today 33:66+ N 3 '89. L. A. Ramsey

OLASKY, M. Prodigal press.
Christianity Today 33:66+ Ja 13 '89. E. C. Beisner

OLD MACDONALD HAD A FARM.
The New York Times Book Review 94:38 My 21 '89. S. G. Lanes

OLDENBURG, R. The great good place. 1989
The New York Times Book Review 94:2 D 24 '89. R. B. Gratz

OLSCHAK, B. C. AND OTHERS. Himalayas. 1987
Scientific American 260:129-30 Je '89. P. Morrison

OLSEN, J. "Doc". 1989
The New York Times Book Review 94:12-13 Je 18 '89. A. Jones

OLSHAN, J. The waterline. 1989
The New York Times Book Review 94:9 N 5 '89. C. Geeslin

OLSON, R. S. AND OTHERS. The politics of earthquake prediction. 1989
Science 245:1259 S 15 '89. D. Serwer

O'MALLEY, M. Gross misconduct.
Maclean's 102:47 Ja 9 '89. J. Bemrose

O'NEILL, E. Complete plays, 1913-1920. 3v 1989
Smithsonian 20:130-3 Ag '89. G. C. Weales

O'NEILL, E. Selected letters of Eugene O'Neill. 1988
The Progressive 53:44-5 Je '89. A. M. Davidon

OOCYTE GROWTH AND MATURATION. 1988
BioScience 39:740 N '89. B. S. Dunbar

OPIE, J. The law of the land. 1987
The Nation 248:457-8 Ap 3 '89. J. Schwab

O'PREY, P. A reader's guide to Graham Greene. 1988
The New York Review of Books 36:3-4 Mr 16 '89. J. Bayley

ORAM, H. Ned and the Joybaloo. 1983
The New York Times Book Review 94:41 My 21 '89. J. Cech

ORANG-UTAN BIOLOGY. 1988
Science 244:859-60 My 19 '89. R. L. Susman

ORDER AND CHAOS IN NONLINEAR PHYSICAL SYSTEMS. 1988
Science 246:1065 N 24 '89. N. B. Abraham

O'REILLY, K. Racial matters. 1989
The New York Times Book Review 94:3 Jl 9 '89. P. Sims

ORGANIZATIONS AND ETHICAL INDIVIDUALISM. 1988
The Humanist 49:42-3 My/Je '89. A. Bacard

ORIGIN AND EVOLUTION OF PLANETARY AND SATELLITE ATMOSPHERES. 1989
Science 245:1402-3 S 22 '89. D. J. Stevenson

ORIGINS. 1988
BioScience 39:813-14 D '89. E. Mayr

THE ORIGINS OF ANGIOSPERMS AND THEIR BIOLOGICAL CONSEQUENCES. 1987
BioScience 39:191-2 Mr '89. C. S. Campbell

ORNSTEIN, R. E. AND SOBEL, D. S. Healthy pleasures. 1989
Health (New York, N.Y.) 21:28-9 Ag '89. S. Thompson

O'ROURKE, P. J. Holidays in hell. 1988
The New York Times Book Review 94:32 Ja 29 '89. T. Ferrell

O'ROURKE, P. J. Modern manners. 1989
The American Spectator 22:23 S '89. D. Barry
Harper's Bazaar 122:38+ Jl '89. K. Black
National Review 41:58 Jl 14 '89. G. Morris
Time 133:69-70 Je 12 '89. S. Kanfer

ORR, E. W. Twice as less. 1987
Phi Delta Kappan 70:416-17 Ja '89. B. Lindsay

ORTIZ COFER, J. The line of the sun. 1989
The New York Times Book Review 94:46-7 S 24 '89. R. Márquez

ORVELL, M. The real thing. 1989
The New Republic 201:34-8 D 4 '89. J. Lears

OSTERBROCK, D. E. Astrophysics of gaseous nebulae and active galactic nuclei. 1989
Physics Today 42:123-4 O '89. J. M. Shull
Science 244:1095-6 Je 2 '89. E. S. Phinney

OSTERBROCK, D. E. AND OTHERS. Eye on the sky. 1988
Science 243:1221 Mr 3 '89. S. J. Dick

OSTERMAN, P. Employment futures. 1988
Monthly Labor Review 112:46-7 Jl '89. R. M. Devens, Jr.
Science 244:837-8 My 19 '89. G. Farkas

THE OTHER NOMADS. 1987
Science 243:953 F 17 '89. L. Beck

O'TOOLE, R. Reforming the Forest Service. 1988
Environment 31:25 O '89. T. J. Eager
Sierra 74:90-2+ S/O '89. B. Hamilton

OTTAWAY, J. H. Regulation of enzyme activity. 1988
BioScience 39:738-40 N '89. M. A. Kukuruzinska

OVERGARD, W. A few good men. 1988
The New York Times Book Review 94:11-12 F 19 '89. D. H. Bain

OVITT, G. The restoration of perfection. 1987

History Today 39:49-50+ Ja '89. P. Spufford

OWEN, M. J. AND LAMB, J. R. Immune recognition. 1988
BioScience 39:735-6 N '89. E. C. McKinney

THE OXFORD ENGLISH DICTIONARY. 2nd ed. 1989
The New York Times Book Review 94:3+ Ap 16 '89. H. Kenner

THE OXFORD ILLUSTRATED HISTORY OF MEDIEVAL EUROPE. 1988
History Today 39:51 F '89. A. Murray

OXFORD REVIEWS OF REPRODUCTIVE BIOLOGY, V. 9, 1987. 1987
BioScience 39:48 Ja '89. G. Weiss

OZICK, C. Metaphor & memory. 1989
The New York Times Book Review 94:9+ Ap 23 '89. R. Kiely

OZICK, C. The shawl. 1989
Commonweal 116:711-12 D 15 '89. I. Halperin
The New York Times Book Review 94:1+ S 10 '89. F. Prose

OZORIO DE ALMEIDA, A. M. Hamiltonian systems. 1988
Science 245:1516 S 29 '89. E. Ott

OZOUF, M. Festivals and the French Revolution. 1988
History Today 39:54-5 D '89. N. Aston

P

PACKARD, V. O. The ultra rich. 1989
Time 133:82+ F 13 '89. J. Elson

PADDEN, C. AND HUMPHRIES, T. Deaf in America. 1988
Psychology Today 22:72-3 D '88. B. L. Benderly

PAGELS, E. H. Adam, Eve, and the serpent. 1989
Christianity Today 33:64+ N 3 '89. R. Webber

PAGELS, H. R. The dreams of reason. 1988
Byte 14:54+ Ap '89. D. A. Mindell

PAGIS, D. Variable directions. 1989
The New York Times Book Review 94:63 N 12 '89. C. Kizer

PALMER, M. Sun. 1988
The New York Times Book Review 94:24 My 28 '89. W. Logan

PALMER, P. Phoebe Palmer. 1988
The Christian Century 106:1064-5 N 15 '89. D. M. Scholer

PALMER, T. The Sierra Nevada. 1988
Sierra 74:101+ My/Je '89. M. Mardon

PALUDAN, P. S. "A people's contest". 1988
The New York Times Book Review 94:7+ Ja 29 '89. R. F. Snow

PANATI, C. Panati's extraordinary endings of practically everything & everybody. 1989
The New York Times Book Review 94:22 S 24 '89. E. Zotti

PÁRAL, V. Catapult. 1989
The New York Review of Books 36:37-9 My 18 '89. D. J. Enright

PARFIT, M. Chasing the glory. 1988
The New York Times Book Review 94:10 Ja 1 '89. J. B. Cooke

PARINI, J. Town life. 1988
The New York Times Book Review 94:38 Mr 12 '89. B. Bennett

PARIS, B. Louise Brooks. 1989
The New Republic 201:38+ D 25 '89. D. Thomson
New York 22:160+ O 23 '89. R. Koenig
The New York Times Book Review 94:11 O 22 '89. N. Gabler

PARISH, CHURCH AND PEOPLE. 1988
History Today 39:49-50 Ap '89. C. Cross

PARKER, B. R. Creation. 1988
Astronomy 17:104-6 Je '89. G. F. Benedict
Sky and Telescope 78:271 S '89. A. Finkbeiner

PARKER, B. R. Invisible matter and the fate of the universe. 1989
Astronomy 17:118-20 D '89. J. Kanipe

PARKER, G. The military revolution. 1988
History Today 39:51 Je '89. D. G. Chandler

PARKER, K. L. The English Sabbath. 1988
History Today 39:57-8 Je '89. P. Lake

PARKER, P. Ackerley. 1989
The New Republic 201:31-4 D 18 '89. R. Jenkyns
The New York Times Book Review 94:12 N 12 '89. A. Lurie

PARKER, R. B. Playmates. 1989
The New York Times Book Review 94:13 Ap 23 '89. R. W. B. Lewis

PARKER, S. Mammal. 1989
The New York Times Book Review 94:34 O 1 '89. M. Nichols

PARKER, T. Bird, Kansas. 1989
Smithsonian 20:220-1 O '89. W. Dieter

PARKES, C. M. Bereavement. 2nd ed. 1986
Aging no359:42-3 '89. D. Lund

PARSONS, P. Getting published. 1989
The New York Times Book Review 94:44-5 S 24 '89. D. Menaker

PASACHOFF, J. M. Contemporary astronomy. 4th ed. 1989
Astronomy 17:102-3 Jl '89. J. Kanipe

PASACHOFF, J. M. AND PETERSON, R. T. Peterson first guide to astronomy. 1988

Sky and Telescope 77:38-9 Ja '89. D. Byrd
PAST WORLDS. 1988
  Scientific American 260:113-15 F '89. N. Hammond
PASTOR, R. A. Condemned to repetition. 1987
  The New York Review of Books 36:46-51 Ag 17 '89. J. Chace
PASTOR, R. A. AND CASTAÑEDA, J. Limits to friendship. 1988
  The Atlantic 263:115-20 Ja '89. J. I. Domínguez
  National Review 41:58 My 5 '89. R. S. Strother
  The New York Times Book Review 94:7 Ja 1 '89. L. Rohter
PATERNO, J. Paterno. 1989
  The New York Times Book Review 94:18 O 1 '89. S. Heller
PATON, A. Journey continued. 1988
  Christianity Today 33:61 My 12 '89. I. Hexham
  Commonweal 116:219-20 Ap 7 '89. A. J. Moore
PATTERSON, J. E. The Vanderbilts. 1989
  Americana 17:12 N/D '89. M. Durham
PAUL, E. A. AND CLARK, F. E. Soil microbiology and biochemistry. 1989
  BioScience 39:819 D '89. D. D. Myrold
PAUL, E. F. Equity and gender. 1988
  National Review 41:48 Ag 4 '89. C. Williamson
PAUL, G. S. Predatory dinosaurs of the world. 1988
  Scientific American 260:110-13 Ja '89. A. W. Crompton and S. M. Gatesy
PAULOS, J. A. Innumeracy. 1989
  Business Week p10-11+ F 20 '89. C. Farrell
  The New York Times Book Review 94:9 Ja 15 '89. M. Kline
  Science 245:654-5 Ag 11 '89. L. Loevinger
  Smithsonian 20:200-1 S '89. A. Fallow
PAULY, P. J. Controlling life. 1987
  The New York Review of Books 36:18-22 Ap 27 '89. R. C. Lewontin
PAWEL, E. The labyrinth of exile. 1989
  The New York Times Book Review 94:9 D 31 '89. P. Loewenberg
PAYER, L. Medicine & culture. 1988
  American Health 8:112+ Ja/F '89. M. Goldman and M. G. Goldman
PAYTON, R. L. Philanthropy. 1988
  The Christian Century 106:665-6 Jl 5-12 '89. A. Wimer
PAZ, O. Sor Juana. 1988
  Commonweal 116:50-2 Ja 27 '89. E. Arenal
PEACOCK, M. Take heart. 1989
  The New Republic 201:31-4 Jl 17-24 '89. C. E. G. Benfey
  The New York Times Book Review 94:16 O 22 '89. J. Parini
PEACOCK, S. J. Jane Ellen Harrison. 1988
  The American Scholar 58:464+ Summ '89. M. R. Lefkowitz
PEARSON, L. F. The architectural and social history of cooperative living. 1988
  History Today 39:50 Mr '89. R. Thorne
PEEL, R. Health and medicine in the Christian Science tradition. 1988
  The Christian Century 106:627 Je 21-28 '89. G. P. Pardington, III
PEET, B. Bill Peet. 1989
  The New York Times Book Review 94:31+ My 21 '89. C. Schine
PEI CHUANG TI MIN YÜN. ENGLISH. June Four. 1989
  The New York Times Book Review 94:13 D 10 '89. M. Gottschalk
PELLETIER, C. Once upon a time on the banks. 1989
  The New York Times Book Review 94:21 O 22 '89. F. Flagg
PENROSE, R. The emperor's new mind concerning computers, minds, and the laws of physics. 1989
  The New York Times Book Review 94:3+ N 19 '89. T. Ferris
PENZIAS, A. A. Ideas and information. 1989
  Science 244:90 Ap 7 '89. D. L. Goodstein
  Scientific American 261:115-16 Jl '89. P. Morrison
THE PEOPLE OF IRELAND. 1989
  History Today 39:53-4 Ja '89. S. Gilley
PEPPER, D. The roots of modern environmentalism. 1986
  Originally published: 1984
  Environment 31:28-9 Je '89. J. R. Visalli
PERCY, W. The thanatos syndrome. 1987
  America 161:37-9+ Jl 15-22 '89. P. H. Samway
PEREC, G. W, or, Childhood memory. 1988
  The New York Times Book Review 94:16 Ja 8 '89. L. Simon
PEREGRINE FALCON POPULATIONS. 1988
  BioScience 39:812-13 D '89. P. Kerlinger
  Science 244:233-4 Ap 14 '89. J. C. Bednarz
PERESTROIKA 1989. 1988
  The New York Times Book Review 94:24 Ap 2 '89. A. B. Ulam
PERETTI, F. E. Piercing the darkness.
  Christianity Today 33:58-9 D 15 '89. M. G. Maudlin
PERFUMERY. 1988
  Scientific American 260:127-8 Je '89. P. Morrison
PERL, J. Paris without end. 1988
  Art News 88:112 My '89. E. M. Gomez

PERLMANN, J. Ethnic differences. 1988
  The New Republic 201:37-9 Ag 28 '89. D. Wrong
PERMUT, J. B. Embracing the wolf. 1989
  The New York Times Book Review 94:43 N 19 '89. E. Rosenthal
PERREAULT, J. Philip Pearlstein. 1988
  American Artist 53:84-5+ F '89. M. C. Nelson
PERRETT, G. A country made by war. 1989
  The New Leader 72:18-20 O 30 '89. S. Rodman
  The New York Times Book Review 94:11 My 28 '89. H. G. Summers
PERRIN, N. A reader's delight. 1988
  USA Today (Periodical) 117:95-6 Mr '89. S. G. Kellman
PERRIN, U. The looking-glass lover. 1989
  The New York Times Book Review 94:11 Ag 20 '89. G. Krist
PERRY, M. Four stars. 1989
  The New York Times Book Review 94:9 Mr 12 '89. R. F. Weigley
PERRY, M. J. Morality, politics, and law. 1988
  The Christian Century 106:1094-5 N 22 '89. T. Volker
PERSICO, J. E. Edward R. Murrow. 1988
  The New York Times Book Review 94:11-12 Ja 15 '89. J. Konner
PERSPECTIVES IN ECOLOGICAL THEORY. 1989
  Science 246:272 O 13 '89. A. M. Hastings
PERSPECTIVES ON MAMMALIAN CELL DEATH. 1987
  BioScience 39:126-7 F '89. J. W. Saunders
PERTSCHUK, M. AND SCHAETZEL, W. The people rising. 1989
  The Nation 249:756-9 D 18 '89. S. Levinson
PERUTZ, L. Leonardo's Judas. 1989
  The New York Times Book Review 94:37 S 10 '89. C. G. Segrè
PERUTZ, M. Is science necessary? 1989
  The New York Times Book Review 94:29 Ap 9 '89. R. Kanigel
PESETSKY, B. Confessions of a bad girl. 1989
  The New York Times Book Review 94:17 My 28 '89. C. Dickinson
PETERS, E. Inquisition. 1988
  Christianity Today 33:51 Mr 17 '89. W. S. Stafford
PETERS, E. Naked once more. 1989
  The New York Times Book Review 94:46 O 15 '89. F. King
PETERS, R. Red Army. 1989
  Newsweek 112:88 My 22 '89. H. Anderson
PETERSON, D. The deluge and the ark. 1989
  The New York Times Book Review 94:14 S 24 '89. P. Schullery
PETERSON, I. The mathematical tourist. 1988
  Science 245:654-5 Ag 11 '89. L. Loevinger
PETERSON, P. G. AND HOWE, N. On borrowed time. 1988
  The Washington Monthly 20:55-6 Ja '89. A. S. Murray
PETSONK, J. AND REMSEN, J. The inter-marriage handbook. 1988
  The Christian Century 106:182 F 15 '89. G. Garmire
PFAFF, W. Barbarian sentiments. 1989
  Commentary 88:62-4 Ag '89. R. J. Neuhaus
  The New York Times Book Review 94:9 My 28 '89. A. Tonelson
PHAGE ECOLOGY. 1987
  BioScience 39:189-90 Mr '89. R. E. Ford
PHILIP, L. The road through Miyama. 1989
  The New York Times Book Review 94:29 Ag 20 '89. M. Porges
PHILLIPS, C. Higher ground. 1989
  The New York Times Book Review 94:27 S 24 '89. B. Smith
PHILLIPS, C. R. Six galleons for the king of Spain. 1986
  Sea Frontiers 35:318 S/O '89. G. L. Voss
PHILLIPS, D. Z. Faith after foundationalism. 1988
  The Christian Century 106:759 Ag 16-23 '89. R. Grigg
PHILLIPS, M. The memoir of Marco Parenti. 1987
  History Today 39:53-4 D '89. A. Brown
PHILLIPS, R. Putting asunder. 1988
  The Christian Century 106:87-8 Ja 25 '89. D. W. Ferm
  National Review 41:56+ My 19 '89. J. Wauck
  The New York Review of Books 36:12-15 Mr 2 '89. L. Stone
PHOTOACOUSTIC AND THERMAL WAVE PHENOMENA IN SEMICONDUCTORS. 1987
  Physics Today 42:66+ Ap '89. R. Lee
PHYLOGENETIC RELATIONSHIPS OF THE LIZARD FAMILIES. 1988
  Science 244:855-6 My 19 '89. E. N. Arnold
PICASSO'S GUERNICA. 1988
  Art News 88:111 My '89. R. Cembalest
PIERARD, R. V. AND LINDER, R. D. Civil religion & the presidency. 1988
  Christianity Today 33:64 Ja 13 '89. D. Bandow
PIERCY, M. Summer people. 1989
  The New York Times Book Review 94:26 Je 11 '89. S. Schiff
PILLER, C. AND YAMAMOTO, K. R. Gene wars. 1988
  Science 243:552-3 Ja 27 '89. R. A. Falk
PIL'NIAK, B. Chinese story and other tales. 1988

Maclean's 102:61 My 29 '89. J. Gault
QUENNELL, P. The pursuit of happiness. 1988
  History Today 39:54 F '89. R. Porter
QUINDLEN, A. Living out loud. 1988
  Psychology Today 23:71 Ap '89. M. Fenichel
QUINE, J. The bridesmaids. 1989
  The New York Times Book Review 94:46 Je 11 '89. S. Chassler
QUINN, D. M. Early Mormonism and the magic world view. 1987
  The Christian Century 106:84-5 Ja 25 '89. M. Perko
QUONSET HUTS ON THE RIVER STYX. 1987
  The Bulletin of the Atomic Scientists 45:46-7 D '89. J. Rothstein

R

RABAN, J. For love & money. 1989
  The New York Times Book Review 94:20 O 1 '89. J. T. Hospital
RADIGUET, R. Count d'Orgel's ball.
  The New York Review of Books 36:8-10 O 12 '89. G. Annan
RADITSA, L. Prisoners of a dream. 1989
  Commentary 88:64+ D '89. R. J. Neuhaus
RADNER, G. It's always something. 1989
  The Nation 249:215-17 Ag 21-28 '89. E. P. Frank
RADON AND ITS DECAY PRODUCTS IN INDOOR AIR. 1988
  Physics Today 42:72-4 Ap '89. L. M. Hubbard
THE RAILROAD IN AMERICAN ART. 1988
  Americana 17:20-1 Jl/Ag '89. M. Durham
RAMPERSAD, A. The life of Langston Hughes; v1, 1902-1941: I, too, sing America. 1986
  The New York Review of Books 36:38-43 F 16 '89. D. Pinckney
RAMPERSAD, A. The life of Langston Hughes; v2, 1941-1967: I dream a world. 1988
  The New York Review of Books 36:38-43 F 16 '89. D. Pinckney
RAMSEY, C. G. AND SLEEPER, H. R. Ramsey/Sleeper architectural graphic standards. 8th ed. 1988
  Architectural Record 177:75+ N '89. S. A. Kliment
RAMUSI, M. C. Soweto, my love. 1988
  The Nation 248:563-5 Ap 24 '89. M. Gevisser
RAPHAEL, R. The men from the boys. 1988
  The Nation 249:63-6 Jl 10 '89. M. S. Kimmel
  The Washington Monthly 21:59-60 Ap '89. J. Naughton
RAPOPORT, J. L. The boy who couldn't stop washing. 1989
  Psychology Today 22:69 D '88. P. King
RASKY, H. Stratas. 1988
  Opera News 54:60-1 D 9 '89. H. E. Phillips
RASMUSSEN, H. Aston Martin. 1988
  Motor Trend 41:64 My '89. G. Von Dare
RASMUSSEN, H. AND DOO, J. Japanese exotic cars. 1989
  Motor Trend 41:36 Ag '89. G. Von Dare
RASPAIL, J. Who will remember the people—. 1988
  The New York Times Book Review 94:18 Ja 15 '89. E. M. Thomas
RASPUTIN, V. G. Siberia on fire. 1989
  The New York Times Book Review 94:1+ D 17 '89. B. Dunlop
RATUSHINSKAYA, I. Grey is the color of hope. 1988
  The American Spectator 22:37-9 Ja '89. D. Gurewich
  Christianity Today 33:29-30 S 8 '89. E. S. Vaughn
  The New York Review of Books 36:33-4 Je 1 '89. J. M. Cameron
  The Progressive 53:42-4 Mr '89. H. Fireside
RAUFER, R. K. AND FELDMAN, S. L. Acid rain and emissions trading. 1987
  Environment 31:29-30 Je '89. G. Majone
RAVEN, P. H. AND JOHNSON, G. B. Understanding biology. 1988
  BioScience 39:571-2 S '89. S. L. Gilchrist
RAY, D. Gold! 1989
  The New York Times Book Review 94:44 N 12 '89. H. Mayer
RAYNER, A. D. M. AND BODDY, L. Fungal decomposition of wood. 1988
  BioScience 39:643-4 O '89. R. W. Lichtwardt
RAYNER, R. Los Angeles without a map. 1989
  The New York Times Book Review 94:18 Ja 22 '89. D. Stillman
READ, A. AND FISHER, D. The deadly embrace. 1988
  The New York Review of Books 36:15-19 Mr 30 '89. G. A. Craig
READ, P. P. A season in the West. 1989
  The New York Times Book Review 94:21 Ag 13 '89. J. DeLynn
THE READER'S CATALOG. 1989
  The New York Times Book Review 94:7 O 8 '89. M. Richler
READING DE MAN READING. 1988
  The New York Review of Books 36:32-7 Je 29 '89. D. Donoghue
REAGAN, M. First Father, First Daughter. 1989
  Gentlemen's Quarterly 59:121-3 My '89. M. Richler
  The New Republic 200:40-3 My 1 '89. M. Dowd

The New York Times Book Review 94:8 Mr 26 '89. D. Ephron
REAGAN, N. My turn. 1989
  The New Republic 201:34+ N 27 '89. B. Ehrenreich
  The New York Times Book Review 94:9 N 19 '89. F. Barnes
REAGAN, R. Speaking my mind. 1989
  National Review 41:40-1 D 22 '89. J. Sobran
RECASTING AMERICA. 1989
  History Today 39:51-3 O '89. B. Dooley
RECINOS, H. J. Hear the cry! 1989
  The Christian Century 106:1127-8 N 29 '89. F. Carrion
THE RECOVERY OF MEANING. 1988
  Science 244:861-3 My 19 '89. E. Zubrow
REDDY, K. Intaglio simultaneous color printmaking. 1988
  American Artist 53:16+ Jl '89. M. S. Doherty
REDONDI, P. Galileo heretic (Galileo eretico). 1987
  Physics Today 42:76-8 Ja '89. E. McMullin
REED, E. James J. Gibson and the psychology of perception. 1988
  The New York Review of Books 35:13-15 Ja 19 '89. E. H. Gombrich
REED, I. New and collected poems. 1988
  The Christian Century 106:994-5 N 1 '89. R. Steinke
REED, I. The terrible threes. 1989
  The New York Times Book Review 94:34 My 7 '89. G. Early
REESE, T. J. Archbishop. 1989
  America 160:514-15 My 27 '89. J. T. Ellis
  Commonweal 116:305-6 My 19 '89. W. McManus
  The New York Times Book Review 94:10 My 28 '89. P. F. Drucker
  U.S. Catholic 54:48-51 Jl '89. G. M. Costello
REFORMING THE LAW. 1987
  Science 243:414-16 Ja 20 '89. P. C. Davis
REFUGEES IN THE AGE OF TOTAL WAR. 1988
  History Today 39:53-4 F '89. C. C. Aronsfeld
REGENS, J. L. AND RYCROFT, R. W. The acid rain controversy. 1988
  Science 244:234-5 Ap 14 '89. J. Schmandt
REGULATION OF PROCARYOTIC DEVELOPMENT. 1989
  Science 246:1331-2 D 8 '89. K. Bott
REGULATORY PEPTIDES. 1988
  Science 246:389-90 O 20 '89. I. M. D. Jackson
REICH, W. Passion of youth. 1988
  Psychology Today 23:70-1 Ap '89. L. Simon
REICHEL, S. What did you do in the war, Daddy? 1989
  The New York Times Book Review 94:28 Je 25 '89. A. Owings
REID, A. Southeast Asia in the age of commerce, 1450-1680; v1, The lands below the winds. 1988
  The New York Review of Books 36:28-9 F 16 '89. C. Geertz
REID BANKS, L. Melusine. 1989
  The New York Times Book Review 94:29 D 17 '89. R. Sutton
REIGER, G. The wings of dawn. 1988
  The Conservationist 44:50 N/D '89. E. S. Feldmann
REJOICE IN THE LORD.
  Christianity Today 33:53 Ag 18 '89. A. P. Schantz
RELIGION IN AMERICAN POLITICS. 1989
  The Christian Century 106:147-8 F 1-8 '89. B. Nichols
RELIGIOUS EDUCATION AS SOCIAL TRANSFORMATION. 1989
  The Christian Century 106:1125 N 29 '89. T. S. Reklau
REMEMBERING RECONSIDERED. 1988
  Science 243:1375-6 Mr 10 '89. D. L. Schacter
REPRODUCTIVE SUCCESS. 1988
  BioScience 39:335-6 My '89. J. K. Waage
  Science 243:1496-7 Mr 17 '89. R. E. Ricklefs
RESPECTFULLY QUOTED. 1987
  American Heritage 40:151-2 N '89
RESPONSES. 1989
  The Nation 248:204-6 F 13 '89. J. Wiener
  The New Republic 200:30-4 Mr 6 '89. Z. Sternhell
  The New York Review of Books 36:32-7 Je 29 '89. D. Donoghue
RESTON, J., JR. The lone star. 1989
  The Atlantic 264:109-12 O '89. N. Lemann
  The New York Times Book Review 94:9-10 N 26 '89. K. Northcott
RETALLACK, J. N. Notables of the right. 1988
  History Today 39:57-9 F '89. J. Noakes
REUTTER, M. Sparrows Point. 1988
  Fortune 119:123-4 Ja 16 '89. B. Saporito
  The New York Times Book Review 94:3+ F 5 '89. C. F. Sabel
REVIVING THE ENGLISH REVOLUTION. 1988
  History Today 39:57 Jl '89. A. Hughes
REVOLUTION IN PRINT. 1989
  The New York Times Book Review 94:12 Jl 9 '89. R. Bernstein
REWALD, J. Cezanne and America. 1989
  The New York Times Book Review 94:13-14 Ap 16 '89. R. Kendall
REYNOLDS, C. A. CA, Cowboy Artists of America. 1988
  American Artist 53:21-2 My '89. M. C. Nelson
REYNOLDS, D. S. Beneath the American Renaissance. 1988

The New York Review of Books 36:42-6 Je 29 '89. J. Atlas

ROSENWALD, L. A. Emerson and the art of the diary. 1988
The New York Times Book Review 94:22 F 12 '89. H. Marten

ROSS, A. No respect. 1989
The Nation 249:538-40 N 6 '89. J. Wiener

ROSSI, P. H. Down and out in America. 1989
Commonweal 116:571-2 O 20 '89. R. M. Hayes

ROSZAK, T. The cult of information. 1986
Design for Arts in Education 90:47-8 N/D '88. S. Hope

ROTBERG, R. I. The founder. 1988
History Today 39:53-4 N '89. J. M. MacKenzie
The New York Times Book Review 94:4 Ja 1 '89. G. Wheatcroft

ROTHMAN, B. K. Recreating motherhood. 1989
Commonweal 116:373-4 Je 16 '89. E. P. Flynn
Ms. 17:26+ My '89. A. R. Roiphe
The New York Times Book Review 94:29 Ap 16 '89. L. Gordon

ROTHMAN, T. Science à la mode. 1989
Astronomy 17:110-11 O '89. J. Kanipe

ROUQUIÉ, A. The military and the state in Latin America. 1987
Current History 88:143 Mr '89. M. Anderberg

ROUSMANIERE, J. The sailing lifestyle. 1985
Oceans 22:59 Mr/Ap '89. J. Sturgis

ROUSSO, H. Disabled, female, and proud! 1988
Children Today 18:31-2 My/Je '89. P. Rowe

ROWEN, H. H. The princes of Orange. 1988
History Today 39:54 Je '89. F. G. H. Bachrach

ROWLAND, C. Radical Christianity. 1988
The Christian Century 106:422 Ap 19 '89. G. E. Paul

ROWSE, A. L. The poet Auden. 1988
The New York Review of Books 36:56-9 D 21 '89. A. Hecht

ROYAL SOCIETY-ACADEMIA SINICA GEOTRAVERSE OF THE QINGHAI-XIZANG PLATEAU (1985). The geological evolution of Tibet. 1988
Science 244:1202-3 Je 9 '89. K. Hodges

ROYER, J. P. Handbook of software and hardware interfacing for IBM PCs. 1987
Radio-Electronics 60 ComputerDigest:78-9 Ap '89

RUDDICK, S. Maternal thinking. 1989
Commonweal 116:408-9 Jl 14 '89. E. Young-Bruehl
The New York Times Book Review 94:15-16 My 21 '89. M. Quilligan

RUDÉ, G. F. E. The French Revolution after 200 years. 1988
The New York Review of Books 36:11-14 Ap 13 '89. N. Hampson

RUDNICK, P. I'll take it. 1989
The New York Times Book Review 94:14 Je 11 '89. S. Isaacs
Newsweek 114:60 Ag 7 '89. J. Seligmann

RUDWICK, M. J. S. The great Devonian controversy. 1985
Earth Science 42:32 Summ '89

RUETHER, R. R. AND RUETHER, H. J. The wrath of Jonah. 1989
America 161:146+ S 9-16 '89. M. H. Bernstein
The Christian Century 106:358-9 Ap 5 '89. S. E. Karff
Commonweal 116:342-3 Je 2 '89. G. Baum
The New York Times Book Review 94:22 Ap 9 '89. B. Weir

RUSHDIE, S. The satanic verses. 1989
The Christian Century 106:622-6 Je 21-28 '89. L. O. Sanneh
Christianity Today 33:52-3 Ag 18 '89. D. Bentley
The Nation 248:346-9 Mr 13 '89. J. Leonard
National Review 41:44-5 Mr 24 '89. A. Bakshian
The New Leader 72:19-20 F 20 '89. A. Wade
The New Republic 200:28-30 Mr 6 '89. M. Wood
New York 22:80 F 13 '89. R. Koenig
The New York Review of Books 36:25-6 Mr 2 '89. D. J. Enright
The New York Times Book Review 94:3+ Ja 29 '89. A. G. Mojtabai
The New Yorker 65:124-8 My 15 '89. B. Leithauser
Newsweek 113:73 F 6 '89. L. Shapiro
The Progressive 53:42-4 My '89. A. Welsh-Huggins
Time 133:82 F 13 '89. P. Gray

RUSKIN, J. Modern painters. 1988
The New Republic 200:33-6 Ap 10 '89. R. Jenkyns

RUSSELL, D. E. H. Lives of courage. 1989
The New York Times Book Review 94:11 D 17 '89. A. McClintock

RUSSELL, J. Reading Russell. 1989
The New York Times Book Review 94:13-14 O 22 '89. F. Kermode

RUSSELL, J. B. The Prince of Darkness. 1988
The Christian Century 106:210 F 22 '89. B. Southworth

RUSSETT, C. E. Sexual science. 1989
The New York Times Book Review 94:34 Ap 9 '89. J. H. Murray

RUSSO, J. P. I.A. Richards. 1989
The New Republic 200:45-8 Je 19 '89. D. Donoghue
The New York Review of Books 36:44-8 Ap 27 '89. H. H. Vendler

RUTLEDGE, J. AND ALLEN, D. Rust to riches. 1989
Business Week p18-19+ O 9 '89. K. Madigan

RUTTEN, H. G. J. AND VENROOIJ, M. A. M. VAN. Telescope optics. 1988
Sky and Telescope 77:614-15+ Je '89. A. E. Gee

RYAN, A. Bertrand Russell. 1988
The New York Review of Books 36:7-9 F 2 '89. S. Hampshire

RYAN, M. God hunger. 1989
The Nation 249:632+ N 27 '89. T. M. Disch
The New York Times Book Review 94:32-3 N 5 '89. C. Muske

RYBCZYNSKI, W. The most beautiful house in the world. 1989
America 161:121-3 Ag 26-S 2 '89. R. Bautch
Maclean's 102:50 Je 19 '89. P. Young
The New York Times Book Review 94:1+ My 21 '89. E. V. Walter

RYTOV, S. M. AND OTHERS. Principles of statistical radiophysics. 2. rev and enl ed. 1987
Physics Today 42:65-6 D '89. A. E. Kaplan

S

SACKS, O. W. Seeing voices. 1989
Natural History p88-92+ N '89. S. J. Carmel
The New York Times Book Review 94:17-8 O 8 '89. P. West
Newsweek 114:72 O 2 '89. P. S. Prescott
Psychology Today 23:75-6 N '89. B. L. Benderly

SACRED DIMENSIONS OF WOMEN'S EXPERIENCE.
The Christian Century 106:568 My 24-31 '89. A. E. Carr

SAGDEEV, R. Z. AND OTHERS. Nonlinear physics. 1988
Physics Today 42:61-2 Ap '89. Y. Pomeau and others

SAGOFF, M. The economy of the earth. 1988
Technology Review 92:73-4+ Jl '89. D. Grossman

SALAMAN, R. N. The history and social influence of the potato. 1986
First pub. 1949
The American Spectator 22:46-7 Mr '89. E. N. Luttwak

SALIBI, K. S. A house of many mansions. 1988
History Today 39:54-5 Ja '89. D. Gilmour

ṢĀLIḤ, AL-Ṭ. Season of migration to the North. 1989
The New York Times Book Review 94:15 Jl 23 '89. D. Pryce-Jones

SALISBURY, H. E. The Great Black Dragon fire. 1989
BioScience 39:732-3 N '89. S. J. Pyne
The New York Times Book Review 94:7 My 14 '89. H. Bruno
Scientific American 261:108-9 Ag '89. P. Morrison

SALISBURY, H. E. Tiananmen diary. 1989
The Nation 249:498+ O 30 '89. M. Berman and S. Lee
National Review 41:54-6 N 10 '89. R. Terrill
The New York Times Book Review 94:13 S 10 '89. S. Shapiro

SALTER, M. J. Unfinished painting. 1989
The New Leader 72:16 Jl 10-24 '89. P. Pettingell
The New Republic 201:31-4 Jl 17-24 '89. C. E. G. Benfey

SALUTIN, R. Waiting for democracy.
Maclean's 102:101 N 6 '89. M. Clark

SAMPSON, C. G. Stylistic boundaries among mobile hunter-foragers. 1988
Science 244:1500 Je 23 '89. M. W. Conkey

SAMUELS, E. Henry Adams. 1989
The New Republic 201:32-8 O 16 '89. A. Delbanco
The New York Times Book Review 94:22 N 19 '89. H. Brogan

SANCHEZ, T. Mile zero. 1989
The New York Review of Books 36:46-7 D 7 '89. R. Towers
The New York Times Book Review 94:7 O 1 '89. E. Abeel

SANDAGE, A. AND BEDKE, J. Atlas of galaxies. 1988
Sky and Telescope 78:40+ Jl '89. W. S. Houston

SANDERS, M. AND ROCK, M. Waiting for prime time. 1988
The New York Times Book Review 94:18 Ja 22 '89. S. B. Levine

SANNEH, L. O. Translating the message. 1989
The Christian Century 106:786+ Ag 30-S 6 '89. J. B. Carman

SANTOLI, A. New Americans. 1988
The New York Times Book Review 94:32 Ap 2 '89. A. Codrescu

SARTON, M. The education of Harriet Hatfield. 1989
The New York Times Book Review 94:5 Jl 2 '89. A. Corn

SAUL, J. R. The paradise eater. 1988
The New York Times Book Review 94:6 Ja 1 '89. E. Toynton

SAWYER-LAUÇANNO, C. An invisible spectator. 1989
The New York Review of Books 36:6+ N 23 '89. R. Craft
The New York Times Book Review 94:3+ Ag 6 '89. A. Broyard

SAYER, P. The comforts of madness. 1988
The New York Times Book Review 94:7 D 24 '89. J. Vandenburgh

SAYERS, V. How I got him back, or, Under the cold moon's shine. 1989
The New York Times Book Review 94:7 Ja 29 '89. A. Corn

The New York Times Book Review 94:38 My 7 '89. W. Finnegan

SERVICE, G. Golden inches. 1989
The New York Times Book Review 94:37 N 5 '89. T. B. Strong

SETTLE, M. L. Charley Bland. 1989
America 161:302-3 N 4 '89. P. H. Samway
The New York Times Book Review 94:12 O 22 '89. D. Leavitt

SEVERO, R. AND MILFORD, L. The wages of war. 1989
The New York Times Book Review 94:12-13 Ap 9 '89. M. S. Sherry

SEX WORK. 1987
The Humanist 49:43 My/Je '89. G. Allen

SEXUAL UNDERWORLDS OF THE ENLIGHTENMENT. 1988
History Today 39:52-3 Mr '89. P. E. H. Hair

SEYMOUR, M. A ring of conspirators. 1989
The New York Review of Books 36:21-3 D 7 '89. J. Bayley
The New York Times Book Review 94:11-12 Jl 16 '89. H. S. Bevington

SHACHTMAN, T. Beachmaster. 1988
The New York Times Book Review 94:26 Ap 16 '89. M. Wolitzer

SHACOCHIS, B. The next new world. 1989
The New York Times Book Review 94:10 F 19 '89. R. Bausch
Time 133:72 Ja 16 '89. P. Gray

SHAHAR, D. Summer in the Street of the Prophets and A voyage to Ur of the Chaldees. 1988
The New York Times Book Review 94:27 My 21 '89. J. Kaplan

THE SHAKESPEARE MYTH. 1988
The Nation 249:429-32 O 16 '89. L. Danson

SHALEV, C. Birth power. 1989
The New York Times Book Review 94:12 D 17 '89. M. E. Gale

SHALLICE, T. From neuropsychology to mental structure. 1988
Science 246:827-8 N 10 '89. M. Coltheart

SHAMMAS, C. AND OTHERS. Inheritance in America from colonial times to the present. 1987
Society 26:87-9 Jl/Ag '89. B. G. Carruthers

SHANNON, E. Desperados. 1988
National Review 41:48 S 1 '89. W. Lutton

SHANNON, E. I am of Ireland. 1989
Commonweal 116:247+ Ap 21 '89. M. P. Kelly

SHANNON, T. A. Surrogate motherhood. 1988
America 161:244-5 O 14 '89. L. J. Mertensotto
Commonweal 116:373-4 Je 16 '89. E. P. Flynn

SHANNON, T. A. AND CAHILL, L. S. Religion and artificial reproduction. 1988
America 161:242-3 O 14 '89. T. Kopfensteiner
The Christian Century 106:264 Mr 8 '89. W. S. Sabom

SHANOR, R. The city that never was. 1988
The Nation 248:135-7 Ja 30 '89. E. Blackmar
The New York Times Book Review 94:11 Ja 8 '89. R. Campbell

SHAPIRO, H. M. Practical flow cytometry. 2nd ed. 1988
BioScience 39:649-50 O '89. D. M. Coder

SHARANSKY, N. Fear no evil. 1988
The New York Review of Books 36:33-4 Je 1 '89. J. M. Cameron
Society 26:95-6 My/Je '89. J. G. Pilon

SHARLITT, J. H. Fatal error. 1989
National Review 41:58 O 27 '89. J. Milton
The New York Times Book Review 94:20 Ag 6 '89. L. Greenhouse

SHARON, A. Warrior. 1989
Commentary 88:60+ D '89. E. A. Cohen
The New York Times Book Review 94:3+ S 3 '89. L. Anderson
The Washington Monthly 21:55-6 N '89. M. Polner

SHASHA, D. The puzzling adventures of Dr. Ecco. 1988
Byte 14:56+ Je '89. E. A. Bobinsky

SHAW, B. Collected letters; v4, 1926-1950. 1985
The New Yorker 64:65-8 Ja 2 '89. J. Updike

SHAW, L. God in the dark.
Christianity Today 33:62-4 N 3 '89. K. Andraski

SHAW, P. The war against the intellect. 1989
Commentary 88:68-70 D '89. M. J. Neth

SHEEHAN, E. R. F. Agony in the garden. 1989
The New York Review of Books 36:46-51 Ag 17 '89. J. Chace

SHEEHAN, N. A bright shining lie. 1988
America 160:304-5+ Ap 1 '89. M. H. Hunt
Commentary 87:78-80 F '89. G. Russell
Commonweal 116:82-3 F 10 '89. D. Luce
National Review 41:46-9 Mr 10 '89. P. Brimelow
The Progressive 53:44-5 Mr '89. V. D. Tran

SHEEHAN, W. Planets & perception. 1988
Sky and Telescope 78:268-70 S '89. A. T. Young

SHELDEN, M. Friends of promise. 1989
The New Republic 201:36-8+ S 18-25 '89. F. Kermode

SHELLEY, T. J. Paul J. Hallinan. 1989
America 161:489-90 D 23-30 '89. J. M. McShane

SHELTON, J. The coming Soviet crash. 1989
National Review 41:40+ Mr 24 '89. E. Rubenstein

The New York Times Book Review 94:9+ F 5 '89. N. Eberstadt

SHENGOLD, L. Soul murder. 1989
The New York Times Book Review 94:14-15 D 17 '89. F. R. Rodman

SHEPARD, C. E. Forgiven. 1989
The Christian Century 106:1053-5 N 15 '89. G. Wacker
The New York Review of Books 36:20+ D 21 '89. G. Wills
The New York Times Book Review 94:7 S 24 '89. P. Sims

SHER, A. Middlepost. 1989
The New York Times Book Review 94:20 My 21 '89. L. Freed

SHERR, A. B. The other side of arms control. 1988
The Bulletin of the Atomic Scientists 45:46-7 My '89. J. Lepgold

SHERRY, N. The life of Graham Greene; v1, 1904-1939. 1989
America 161:301-2 N 4 '89. A. T. Salvatore
The Christian Century 106:934-6 O 18 '89. P. S. Hawkins
Commonweal 116:531-2 O 6 '89. R. E. Hosmer
Maclean's 102:53 Ag 7 '89. M. Ritts
National Review 41:55-7 S 29 '89. M. Stannard
The New Leader 72:16-17 O 30 '89. P. Pettingell
The New York Times Book Review 94:1+ Je 18 '89. R. Coles
Newsweek 113:66 Je 26 '89. P. S. Prescott
Smithsonian 20:225-6 O '89. M. Dirda
Time 133:69 Je 12 '89. R. Z. Sheppard

SHIELDS, C. The orange fish. 1989
Maclean's 102:61 Je 5 '89. B. Ledger

SHIELDS, C. Swann. 1989
The New York Times Book Review 94:11 Ag 6 '89. J. Rubins

SHIELDS, C. Various miracles. 1989
The New York Times Book Review 94:11 Ag 6 '89. J. Rubins

SHIELDS, D. Dead languages. 1989
The New York Review of Books 36:30-1 Jl 20 '89. R. Towers
The New York Times Book Review 94:22 Je 18 '89. E. Toynton

SHLAIM, A. Collusion across the Jordan. 1988
The New Republic 200:23-8+ Ap 10 '89. F. Ajami

SHNAYERSON, M. Irwin Shaw. 1989
The American Spectator 22:52-3 D '89. L. Abel
Time 134:68 Ag 14 '89. R. Schickel

SHOO SHOO BABY.
American Heritage 40:110 Ap '89

SHREVE, A. Eden Close. 1989
The New York Times Book Review 94:6 S 3 '89. C. Banks

SHREVE, A. Women together, women alone. 1989
Mother Jones 14:47-8 O '89. V. Miner
The New York Times Book Review 94:10 Ag 13 '89. A. K. Shulman

SHREVE, S. R. A country of strangers. 1989
America 161:68-9 Jl 29-Ag 5 '89. D. L. Smith
The New York Times Book Review 94:24 Mr 5 '89. M. Watkins

SHURYAK, E. V. The QCD vacuum, hadrons and the superdense matter. 1988
Physics Today 42:70+ Jl '89. L. G. Yaffe

SHUSHA, G. The blindfold horse.
The New York Times Book Review 94:17 F 12 '89. A. McCarthy

SIEVER, R. Sand. 1988
Scientific American 260:117-18 Mr '89. P. Morrison

SILBER, J. R. Straight shooting. 1989
Commentary 88:70-2 N '89. C. E. Finn
The New York Times Book Review 94:32 S 17 '89. L. Miles

SILBER, M. AND SILBER, T. The complete book of everlastings. 1987
Country Journal 16:14+ Mr/Ap '89. T. Martin

SILBERMAN, N. A. Between past and present. 1989
The New York Times Book Review 94:66 N 12 '89. C. Vanderpool

SILK, M. Spiritual politics. 1988
Christianity Today 33:30-1 S 8 '89. R. Jolley

SIMON, C. The Georgics. 1989
The New York Times Book Review 94:37 O 1 '89. J. Sturrock

SIMON, D. AND REHN, D. Technological innovation in China. 1988
Science 244:369 Ap 21 '89. N. R. Lardy

SIMON, J. The sheep from the goats. 1989
National Review 41:58-60 F 10 '89. T. Fleming

SIMON, J. F. The antagonists. 1989
National Review 41:42-3 D 31 '89. J. H. Andrews
The New York Times Book Review 94:18+ O 15 '89. B. Schwartz
The Washington Monthly 21:60 O '89. C. Peters

SIMONS, C. International proposals to transfer Arabs from Palestine, 1895-1947. 1988
America 161:146+ S 9-16 '89. M. H. Bernstein

SIMPSON, B. Wilderness is where you find it. 1988
Wilderness 52:67-8 Wint '88. C. E. Little

SIMPSON, L. A. M. Selected prose. 1989
   The New York Times Book Review 94:28 My 7 '89. A.
   Stevenson
SIMPSON, M. Winslow Homer. 1988
   American Artist 53:88-9 Ap '89. M. C. Nelson
SIMS, N. R. A. The diplomacy of biological disarmament.
   1988
   The Bulletin of the Atomic Scientists 45:45-6 Jl/Ag '89.
   T. V. Brac
SINCLAIR, D. Two Georges. 1988
   History Today 39:52-3 Ja '89. K. Rose
SJÖÖ, M. AND MOR, B. The Great Cosmic Mother. 1987
   The American Spectator 22:39-41 Jl '89. E. Kristol
SKED, A. The decline and fall of the Habsburg Empire,
   1815-1918. 1989
   History Today 39:52-3 D '89. A. W. Palmer
SKIDMORE, T. E. The politics of military rule in Brazil,
   1964-85. 1988
   Current History 88:142 Mr '89. M. Anderberg
SKLAR, M. J. The corporate reconstruction of American
   capitalism, 1890-1916. 1988
   The New Republic 200:37-9 Mr 13 '89. J. B. Judis
ŠKVORECKÝ, J. Sins for Father Knox. 1989
   The New York Review of Books 36:37-9 My 18 '89. D.
   J. Enright
SMIL, V. Energy in China's modernization. 1988
   Scientific American 260:115-17 Mr '89. P. Morrison
SMILEY, J. Ordinary love & Goodwill. 1989
   Mother Jones 14:44-5 D '89. D. Leavitt
   The New York Times Book Review 94:1+ N 5 '89. J.
   Humphreys
SMITH, B. H. Contingencies of value. 1988
   The New York Times Book Review 94:35 Je 4 '89. A.
   Savile
SMITH, C. Shine Hawk. 1988
   The New York Review of Books 36:18-19 F 16 '89. R.
   Towers
SMITH, D. Firefighters. 1988
   The Washington Monthly 21:57 Mr '89. H. G. Brinton
SMITH, D. K. AND ALEXANDER, R. C. Fumbling the
   future. 1988
   Business Week p15+ Ja 9 '89. G. Lewis
   The Washington Monthly 21:55-7 Je '89. D. Graulich
SMITH, G. D. From monopoly to competition. 1988
   Science 244:841-2 My 19 '89. V. Y. Suslow
SMITH, H. Z. Not so quiet. 1988
   The New York Times Book Review 94:26 Ap 30 '89.
   W. Boyd
SMITH, M. C. Polar Star. 1989
   The New York Times Book Review 94:1+ Jl 16 '89. R.
   S. Nathan
   Newsweek 114:64 Jl 31 '89. H. Anderson
   Time 134:63 Jl 3 '89. P. Gray
SMITH, M. L. Pacific visions. 1987
   Sierra 74:165-6+ Ja/F '89. R. H. Dillon
SMITH, R. C. The global bankers. 1989
   The New York Times Book Review 94:28 O 29 '89. H.
   Lampert
SMOLLA, R. A. Jerry Falwell v. Larry Flynt. 1988
   The New York Times Book Review 94:26 Mr 5 '89. E.
   R. Shipp
SMUCKER, A. E. No star nights. 1988
   The New York Times Book Review 94:51 N 12 '89. S.
   Tesich
SNYDER, S. H. Brainstorming. 1989
   The New York Times Book Review 94:39 O 22 '89. D.
   X. Freedman
   Psychology Today 23:73 D '89. R. Kanigel
   Science 246:1329-30 D 8 '89. S. Panem
SNYDERMAN, M. AND ROTHMAN, S. The IQ controversy.
   1988
   Commentary 87:70-2 Mr '89. D. Seligman
SOBEL, R. Trammell Crow, master builder. 1989
   Business Week p12-13 Ag 7 '89. T. Mason
SOCIAL REGULATORY POLICY. 1988
   The Humanist 49:45 Jl/Ag '89. J. P. Lewis
SOKOLOV, S. Astrophobia.
   The New York Times Book Review 94:27 D 17 '89. R.
   Lourie
SOKOLOVA, L. Dancing for Diaghilev. 1989
   Dance Magazine 63:56-7 S '89. M. McQuade
SOLO, P. From protest to policy. 1988
   The Bulletin of the Atomic Scientists 45:43-4 Mr '89. W.
   Sweet
   Science 243:413-14 Ja 20 '89. W. A. Gamson
SOLOMON, B. S. Green architecture and the agrarian garden.
   1988
   Architectural Record 177:63 Mr '89. M. J. Darnall
SOLOMON, C. Enchanted drawings. 1989
   American Heritage 40:153-5 N '89
   The New York Times Book Review 94:11+ D 3 '89. L.
   Anderson
SOLOMON, J. The signs of our time. 1988
   Psychology Today 23:70 Ap '89. D. Cole
SOLZHENITSYN, A. August 1914. 1989
   The New Republic 201:33-7 Ag 28 '89. T. Venclova
   The New York Review of Books 36:11-13 D 21 '89. J.
   Bayley

   The New York Times Book Review 94:1+ Jl 2 '89. I.
   Howe
   Newsweek 114:56 Jl 24 '89. P. S. Prescott
SOMERVILL, C. AND TOWNSON, K. L. Media handbook
   for churches. 1988
   The Christian Century 106:825-6 S 13-20 '89. M. R. Halton
SOMMERS, A. T. The U.S. economy demystified. 1988
   Monthly Labor Review 112:44-5 Ap '89. E. Steinberg
SONN, R. D. Anarchism and cultural politics in fin de siècle
   France. 1989
   The New York Review of Books 36:38-41 N 23 '89. J.
   Joll
SONNENFELD, J. A. The hero's farewell. 1988
   Fortune 119:329-30 Ap 24 '89. R. Gilkey
SONTAG, S. AIDS and its metaphors. 1988
   The Nation 248:598-602 My 1 '89. G. Kolovakos
   National Review 41:48-50 F 24 '89. J. Sobran
   The New York Times Book Review 94:11 Ja 22 '89. P.
   A. Robinson
SOUTHORN, J. Power and display in the seventeenth century.
   1988
   History Today 39:53-4 D '89. A. Brown
SOWELL, M. The pitch that killed. 1989
   The New York Times Book Review 94:11 S 17 '89. S.
   Jacoby
SOYINKA, W. Isara. 1989
   The New Republic 201:40-2 D 11 '89. C. Hope
   The New York Times Book Review 94:11 N 12 '89. R.
   Dove
SPALDING, F. Stevie Smith. 1989
   The New Leader 72:16-17 S 18 '89. P. Pettingell
SPARKS, R. C. To treat or not to treat. 1988
   America 161:244 O 14 '89. L. J. Mertensotto
SPECIATION AND ITS CONSEQUENCES. 1989
   Science 245:872-3 Ag 25 '89. H. L. Carson
SPELMAN, E. V. Inessential woman. 1988
   Mother Jones 14:47-8 O '89. V. Miner
   The New York Times Book Review 94:18 Ap 30 '89.
   M. Frye
SPENCE, G. With justice for none. 1989
   The New York Times Book Review 94:35 My 7 '89. S.
   Wishman
SPENCE, J. D. The question of Hu. 1988
   The New Yorker 65:109-12 Ap 3 '89. J. Updike
   Newsweek 113:61 Ja 2 '89. P. S. Prescott
SPENCER, W. D. Mysterium and mystery. 1989
   The Christian Century 106:360-1 Ap 5 '89. L. Sibley
   Christianity Today 33:51 Ap 21 '89. J. I. Packer
SPENSER, E. The Yale edition of the shorter poems of Edmund
   Spenser. 1989
   The New Republic 201:33-8 S 11 '89. J. Hollander
SPERLING, S. Animal liberators. 1989
   BioScience 39:741-3 N '89. J. A. Sechzer
   The New York Review of Books 36:36-8 F 2 '89. P. Singer
   Technology Review 92:75-6 Ap '89. J. Rubin
SPIDER WOMAN'S GRANDDAUGHTERS. 1989
   The New York Times Book Review 94:15 My 14 '89.
   U. K. Le Guin
SPIERS, E. M. Chemical weaponry. 1989
   The New York Times Book Review 94:19 Ag 27 '89. M.
   I. Chevrier
SPILLANE, M. The killing man. 1989
   The New York Times Book Review 94:43-4 O 15 '89.
   M. Friedman
SPINDEL, C. In the shadow of the sacred grove. 1989
   The New York Times Book Review 94:44 S 17 '89. J.
   North
SPIRES, E. Annonciade. 1989
   The New Leader 72:16 Mr 6 '89. P. Pettingell
   The New York Times Book Review 94:32-3 N 5 '89. C.
   Muske
THE SPIRIT OF H.H. RICHARDSON ON THE MIDLAND
   PRAIRIES. 1988
   Architectural Record 177:59 S '89. D. Waterman
SPITZER, L. Representative essays. 1988
   The American Scholar 58:618-22 Aut '89. C. Landauer
SPOCK, B. Spock on Spock. 1989
   New York 22:106+ N 20 '89. R. Koenig
   The New York Times Book Review 94:11 N 5 '89. E.
   Crow
SPOTO, D. Lenya. 1989
   The New Leader 72:12-15 My 15-29 '89. J. Simon
   New York 22:77 My 8 '89. R. Koenig
   The New York Times Book Review 94:12 Ap 30 '89.
   H. Dudar
   Opera News 54:68 O '89. R. Marx
SPRING, J. H. Conflict of interests. 1988
   Phi Delta Kappan 71:86-7 S '89. C. Eisele
SPRING SYSTEMATICS SYMPOSIUM (9TH: 1986:
   CHICAGO, ILL.). The evolution of human hunting. 1987
   Science 243:241-2 Ja 13 '89. J. D. Speth
SPURR, R. Enter the dragon. 1988
   The Bulletin of the Atomic Scientists 45:44-5 Jl/Ag '89.
   A. S. Whiting
ST. CLAIR, W. The Godwins and the Shelleys. 1989
   The New York Review of Books 36:21-4 N 23 '89. A.
   Ryan

The New York Times Book Review 94:38-9 N 5 '89. L. A. Marchand

STAAL, J. D. W. The new patterns in the sky. 1988
Sky and Telescope 77:40-2 Ja '89. G. Lovi

STACKHOUSE, M. L. Apologia. 1988
The Christian Century 106:136-8 F 1-8 '89. D. M. Campbell

STADLER GENETICS SYMPOSIUM (18TH: 1987: UNIVERSITY OF MISSOURI-COLUMBIA). Chromosome structure and function. 1988
BioScience 39:574-7 S '89. M. T. Davisson

STAGE, W. Ghost signs. 1989
American Heritage 40:156-7 N '89

STANNARD, J. N. AND BAALMAN, R. W. Radioactivity and health. 1988
Science 245:424 Jl 28 '89. K. Livingston

STANTON, M. The country I come from. 1988
The New York Times Book Review 94:30 F 26 '89. M. Chernoff

STAPLES, S. F. Shabanu. 1989
The New York Times Book Review 94:32 N 12 '89. M. Simon

STARGAZERS: THE CONTRIBUTION OF AMATEURS TO ASTRONOMY. 1989
Sky and Telescope 78:604-5 D '89. D. W. E. Green

STARKELL, D. Paddle to the Amazon. 1989
The New York Times Book Review 94:13 S 24 '89. T. Cahill

STARR, S. F. Southern comfort. 1989
The New York Times Book Review 94:7-8 D 31 '89. A. Rice

STATE OF THE WORLD, 1989. 1989
Earth Science 42:35 Fall '89

STAUB, E. The roots of evil. 1989
Psychology Today 23:74-5 D '89. D. Cole

STEADMAN, D. W. AND ZOUSMER, S. Galápagos. 1988
BioScience 39:202-3 Mr '89. C. A. Istock

STEDMAN, J. G. Narrative of a five years expedition against the revolted Negroes of Surinam. 1988
The New York Review of Books 36:29-34 Mr 30 '89. D. B. Davis

STEELE, L. W. Managing technology. 1989
High Technology Business 9:13 Ap '89. M. Estren

STEEVES, P. D. Keeping the faiths. 1989
Christianity Today 33:59-60 O 20 '89. B. F. O'Connell

STEGNER, P. Outposts of Eden. 1989
Wilderness 53:53-4+ Fall '89. C. E. Little

STEHLING, W. Thin thighs in 30 days. 1989
Health (New York, N.Y.) 21:30 Je '89. D. V. Morgan

STEIN, B. Hollywood days, Hollywood nights. 1988
The American Spectator 22:43-4 F '89. J. A. Daniel

STEIN, S. A feast for lawyers. 1989
The New York Times Book Review 94:11 D 10 '89. J. Taylor
The Washington Monthly 21:60 D '89. J. Rothchild

STEINBECK, J. The grapes of wrath. 1989
The American Spectator 22:41-2 Ag '89. K. S. Lynn
The New York Times Book Review 94:1+ Ap 9 '89. W. Kennedy
The New Yorker 65:90-3 Ag 21 '89. B. Leithauser

STEINBECK, J. The harvest gypsies.
The Nation 248:388-90 Mr 20 '89. N. Mills

STEINBECK, J. Working days. 1989
The American Spectator 22:41-2 Ag '89. K. S. Lynn
The New York Times Book Review 94:1+ Ap 9 '89. W. Kennedy
The New Yorker 65:90-3 Ag 21 '89. B. Leithauser

STEINER, G. Real presences. 1989
The Christian Century 106:1055-6+ N 15 '89. D. Morgan
Commonweal 116:596-8 N 3 '89. R. P. Imbelli
The New York Times Book Review 94:11 Jl 30 '89. R. Kimball

STEINHOFF, J. AND OTHERS. Voices from the Third Reich. 1989
National Review 41:43-4 Je 2 '89. H. R. Trevor-Roper

STEINKE, D. Up through the water. 1989
The New York Times Book Review 94:14 Jl 2 '89. R. Olmstead

STEPHANSON, A. Kennan and the art of foreign policy. 1989
Commonweal 116:533-6 O 6 '89. C. R. Morris
The New York Review of Books 36:3-5 Ag 17 '89. R. Steel

STERLING, B. Islands in the net. 1988
The Nation 248:636-9 My 8 '89. E. Davis

STERN, D. Twice told tales. 1989
The New Leader 72:21-2 My 15-29 '89. N. Rosen
The New York Times Book Review 94:13-14 Je 18 '89. A. Arensberg

STERN, F. R. Dreams and delusions. 1987
History Today 39:57-9 F '89. J. Noakes

STERN, J. Masterworks of California impressionism.
American Artist 53:14 Ja '89. C. Movalli

STERN, R. G. Noble rot. 1989
The New Republic 200:46-8 F 20 '89. S. Birkerts

STERN, S. No tricks in my pocket. 1989
The New York Times Book Review 94:17 S 3 '89. M. Bloom

STERNBERG, W. AND HARRISON, M. C. Feeding frenzy. 1989
The Atlantic 264:124-7 D '89. J. Beatty
Business Week p16-17 N 20 '89. H. Collingwood

STEVENS, J. E. Hoover Dam. 1988
The New York Times Book Review 94:23 F 12 '89. S. C. Florman

STEVENS, M. Sudden death. 1989
Business Week p27-9 Ag 14 '89. C. Welles
Fortune 120:127-8 Ag 28 '89. I. Ross
The New York Times Book Review 94:42 O 29 '89. J. E. Garten
Newsweek 114:61 Ag 28 '89. J. Schwartz

STEVENS, R. In sickness and in wealth. 1989
The New York Times Book Review 94:14 Ag 20 '89. U. E. Reinhardt
Science 244:1385-6 Je 16 '89. D. Mechanic

STEVENS, S. Malaria dreams. 1989
Mother Jones 14:42-3 Je '89. G. Packer

STEVENSON, A. Bitter fame. 1989
The New Leader 72:15-16 N 27 '89. P. Pettingell
The New Republic 201:98+ N 6 '89. H. H. Vendler
The New York Review of Books 36:34-6 S 28 '89. A. Alvarez
The New York Times Book Review 94:11 Ag 27 '89. R. Pinsky
Newsweek 114:60+ Ag 28 '89. C. McGuigan

STEWART, H. B. Recollecting the future. 1989
High Technology Business 9:9 Je '89. M. Estren

STEWART, I. Does God play dice? 1989
Byte 14:340+ Jl '89. H. Kenner

STEWART, J. Jimmy Stewart and his poems. 1989
The New York Times Book Review 94:16 S 24 '89. D. M. Pinkwater

STIGLER, G. J. Memoirs of an unregulated economist. 1988
Science 245:1259+ S 15 '89. W. J. Baumol

STIGLER, S. M. The history of statistics. 1986
Monthly Labor Review 112:62 My '89. D. McDermott

STILGOE, J. R. Borderland. 1988
The American Spectator 22:46-7 Jl '89. C. Caldwell
The New York Times Book Review 94:8 Ja 22 '89. V. Klinkenborg
Newsweek 113:57 Ja 16 '89. D. Gates
Smithsonian 20:158-9 My '89. P. Patton

STIVENDER, D. Mascagni. 1989
The New York Times Book Review 94:18 Mr 5 '89. W. Weaver

STOCK-MORTON, P. Moral education for a secular society. 1988
The Humanist 49:43 My/Je '89. D. B. McKown

STOKES, R. G. Divide and prosper. 1988
Science 243:1086-7 F 24 '89. M. Walker

STOLL, C. The cuckoo's egg. 1989
The New York Times Book Review 94:22 N 26 '89. J. Harris

STOLP, H. Microbial ecology. 1988
BioScience 39:818-19 D '89. L. Zeph

STONE, A. Wrong number. 1989
The American Spectator 22:44-6 Je '89. M. J. Ulmer

STONE, I. F. The trial of Socrates. 1988
The American Scholar 58:146-51 Wint '89. C. Orwin
Phi Delta Kappan 70:567-8 Mr '89. L. Goldman

STONE, R. H. Christian realism and peacemaking. 1988
The Christian Century 106:268 Mr 8 '89. R. K. DeHainaut

STORR, A. Solitude. 1988
Commonweal 116:123 F 24 '89. A. B. Ulanov
USA Today (Periodical) 117:96 My '89. R. Hyatt

STOUT, J. Ethics after Babel. 1988
The Christian Century 106:753-4 Ag 16-23 '89. W. C. Placher

STRAIGHT, M. W. Nancy Hanks. 1988
Design for Arts in Education 90:49-50 Jl/Ag '89. S. Hope

STRANGE, M. Family farming. 1988
The Humanist 49:42 Ja/F '89. J. Burkhardt
The Nation 248:457-8 Ap 3 '89. J. Schwab
Society 27:95-6 N/D '89. D. Hyman

STRASSER, S. Satisfaction guaranteed. 1990
The New York Times Book Review 94:34 N 19 '89. L. J. Davis

STRATEGIC TRADE POLICY AND THE NEW INTERNATIONAL ECONOMICS. 1986
Monthly Labor Review 112:46-7 Mr '89. R. M. Devens, Jr.

STRAUSS, L. The rebirth of classical political rationalism. 1989
National Review 41:39-43 Ag 18 '89. C. R. Kesler
The New Republic 201:30-2+ Jl 3 '89. C. Larmore

STREIB, V. L. Death penalty for juveniles. 1987
Society 26:94-6 Ja/F '89. B. C. Feld

STRONG, D. H. Dreamers & defenders. 1988
Sierra 74:110 Mr/Ap '89. P. Wild

STRUCTURAL AND MAGNETIC PHASE TRANSITIONS IN MINERALS. 1988
Science 244:478-9 Ap 28 '89. A. M. Glazer

STRYER, L. Molecular design of life. 1989
BioScience 39:822 D '89. P. J. Weathers

STUART, A. The war zone. 1989

The New York Times Book Review 94:12 Je 4 '89. L. Zeidner
STUDIES IN AUTOBIOGRAPHY. 1988
  The New York Review of Books 36:16-18 D 7 '89. E. A. J. Honigmann
STUDIES IN MEDIEVAL HISTORY. 1988
  History Today 39:50 Ag '89. F. Barlow
STURM, D. Community and alienation. 1988
  The Christian Century 106:627-8 Je 21-28 '89. J. K. Robbins
SUGERMAN, D. Wonderland Avenue. 1989
  Mademoiselle 95:116+ Mr '89. J. Maynard
  The New York Times Book Review 94:45 Ap 9 '89. K. Lynch
SULERI, S. Meatless days. 1989
  The New York Times Book Review 94:30 Je 4 '89. D. Wolfe
SULLIVAN, W. Allen Tate. 1988
  National Review 41:61-2 Ja 27 '89. C. N. Wilson
SULLIVAN, W. L. Listening for coyote. 1988
  Wilderness 52:68 Wint '88. C. E. Little
SUNSTEIN, E. W. Mary Shelley. 1989
  The New York Review of Books 36:13-14 Je 29 '89. R. B. Martin
  The New York Times Book Review 94:14 F 12 '89. C. G. Heilbrun
SUPER, R. H. The chronicler of Barsetshire. 1988
  The New York Review of Books 36:6-8 Ag 17 '89. J. Bayley
SUPERPOWER ARMS CONTROL. 1987
  National Review 41:66 F 10 '89. W. R. Hawkins
SUWOROW, V. Der Eisbrecher.
  The New York Review of Books 36:11-12+ O 12 '89. G. A. Craig
SUZUKI, D. T. AND KNUDTSON, P. Genethics. 1989
  Technology Review 92:75-6 Ag/S '89. P. Billings
SWADOS, E. Listening out loud. 1988
  The New York Times Book Review 94:10 Ja 22 '89. M. Kimmelman
SWEET, W. The nuclear age. 2nd ed. 1988
  The Bulletin of the Atomic Scientists 45:41 S '89. W. H. Donnelly
SWEET, W. C. The Conodonta. 1988
  Science 244:856-7 My 19 '89. D. L. Clark
SWETZ, F. Capitalism and arithmetic. 1987
  The American Spectator 22:47-8 Ja '89. W. McGurn
SWIFT, E. The Christopher Park regulars. 1989
  The New York Times Book Review 94:7 Ag 20 '89. E. Pall
SWOPE, S. The Araboolies of Liberty Street. 1989
  The New York Times Book Review 94:38 N 12 '89. C. Muske
SYKES, C. J. ProfScam. 1988
  The American Spectator 22:44-6 My '89. K. Owen
  Commentary 88:68-70 Jl '89. T. Short
  The New York Times Book Review 94:16 F 19 '89. R. Kimball
SYMPOSIUM ON LIFE AND THE UNIVERSE (1986: NATIONAL ACADEMY OF SCIENCES). Origins and extinctions. 1988
  BioScience 39:570 S '89. G. L. Stebbins
SYMPOSIUM ON MOLECULAR BIOLOGY OF DICTYOSTELIUM DEVELOPMENT (1987: AIRLIE, VA.). Molecular biology of Dictyostelium development. 1988
  Science 244:1201-2 Je 9 '89. E. Luna
SZASZ, M. Indian education in the American colonies, 1607-1783. 1988
  The Christian Century 106:729-30 Ag 2-9 '89. H. W. Bowden

T

TABACHNICK, S. E. AND MATHESON, C. Images of Lawrence. 1988
  History Today 39:55-6 F '89. M. Langley
TAHERI, A. Nest of spies. 1989
  The New Republic 200:43-6 My 15 '89. S. Bakhash
  The New York Times Book Review 94:20 Ap 9 '89. L. Anderson
TAIBBI, M. AND PHILLIPS, A. S. Unholy alliances. 1989
  The New York Times Book Review 94:9 Je 4 '89. J. A. Hennessee
TAINTER, J. A. The collapse of complex societies. 1988
  History Today 39:57-8 Jl '89. C. Chippindale
TAKAKI, R. T. Strangers from a different shore. 1989
  The New York Times Book Review 94:18 Ag 27 '89. J. Foreman
TALBOTT, S. The master of the game. 1988
  Commentary 87:69-76 F '89. D. Kagan
  The New Republic 200:31-2+ Ja 30 '89. S. Hoffmann
  The New York Review of Books 35:21-5 Ja 19 '89. Sir S. Zuckerman
TALMUD. ENGLISH. The Talmud; v1, Tractate Bava Metzia. 1989
  The New York Times Book Review 94:3+ D 17 '89. L. Wieseltier
TAN, A. The Joy Luck Club. 1989
  Mademoiselle 95:70+ Jl '89. J. Maynard
  The Nation 248:566-9 Ap 24 '89. V. Miner
  New York 22:82 Mr 20 '89. R. Koenig

The New York Times Book Review 94:3+ Mr 19 '89. O. Schell
  Newsweek 113:68-9 Ap 17 '89. D. Gates
  Time 133:98 Mr 27 '89. J. Skow
TANDBERG-HANSSEN, E. AND EMSLIE, A. G. The physics of solar flares. 1988
  Science 245:770 Ag 18 '89. E. R. Priest
TANENBAUM, S. J. Engineering disability.
  Technology Review 92:68-9 Ja '89. F. Bowe
TARABORRELLI, J. R. Call her Miss Ross. 1989
  The New York Times Book Review 94:21 D 17 '89. J. Kaufman
TATLIN. 1988
  The New York Times Book Review 94:9-10 Mr 26 '89. S. F. Starr
TAUBMAN, W. AND TAUBMAN, J. Moscow spring. 1989
  The New York Times Book Review 94:15 Ap 23 '89. A. Brumberg
TAX, M. Union Square. 1988
  The Nation 248:492-4 Ap 10 '89. E. Rapping
  The New York Times Book Review 94:8 Ja 1 '89. E. R. Lipson
TAX POLICY IN THE TWENTY-FIRST CENTURY. 1988
  The New Leader 72:15-16 My 1 '89. B. Gewen
TAYLOR, G. Reinventing Shakespeare. 1989
  The Nation 249:429-32 O 16 '89. L. Danson
  The New Republic 201:49-50+ O 16 '89. D. Norbrook
  The New York Times Book Review 94:28 S 17 '89. G. Schmidgall
TAYLOR, H. Scarlett's women. 1989
  The New York Times Book Review 94:7 D 10 '89. D. Finkle
TAYLOR, J. Circus of ambition. 1989
  Business Week p21+ N 13 '89. J. H. Dobrzynski
  The New York Times Book Review 94:33 O 29 '89. J. B. Ciulla
TAYLOR, J. M. General Maxwell Taylor. 1989
  The American Spectator 22:46-7 Ag '89. H. W. Crocker, Jr.
  The New York Times Book Review 94:13-14 Je 25 '89. S. Karnow
TAYLOR, R. Fred Allen. 1989
  Gentlemen's Quarterly 59:122+ Je '89. M. Richler
  The New York Times Book Review 94:7 Jl 9 '89. G. Keillor
  Smithsonian 20:178+ D '89. D. Lessem
TAYLOR, R. B. Long road home. 1988
  U.S. Catholic 54:48-51 D '89. G. M. Costello
TAYLOR, R. L. The lost sister. 1989
  The New York Times Book Review 94:12 My 7 '89. E. Tallent
TAYLOR, S. A place of your own making. 1988
  Country Journal 16:18 F '89. J. Vara
TAYLOR, S. E. Positive illusions. 1989
  The New York Times Book Review 94:8 D 24 '89. T. Bay
TECTONIC EVOLUTION OF THE HIMALAYAS AND TIBET. 1988
  Science 243:1221-2 Mr 3 '89. B. C. Burchfiel
TEITELMAN, R. Gene dreams. 1989
  The New York Times Book Review 94:26 O 29 '89. N. Angier
  The Washington Monthly 21:55-8 S '89. B. Werth
TELANDER, R. The hundred yard lie. 1989
  The New York Times Book Review 94:29 O 22 '89. G. S. White, Jr.
TEMPORAL AND SPATIAL REGULATION OF PLANT GENES. 1988
  BioScience 39:646-8 O '89. W. H. Campbell
TERKEL, S. The great divide. 1988
  U.S. Catholic 54:48-51 Mr '89. G. M. Costello
'TERRA AUSTRALIS' TO AUSTRALIA.
  History Today 39:50+ Ap '89. B. Gough
TERTZ, A. Goodnight! 1989
  The New York Times Book Review 94:1+ D 17 '89. J. Bayley
  Time 134:76 D 25 '89. R. Z. Sheppard
TESH, S. N. Hidden arguments. 1988
  Technology Review 92:66+ Ja '89. D. A. Stone
TESICH, N. Shadow partisan. 1989
  Commonweal 116:316-17 My 19 '89. E. Peggy
TEXT, CONTEXT, AND HYPERTEXT. 1988
  Byte 14:51-2 Mr '89. D. A. Mindell
THERMAL HISTORY OF SEDIMENTARY BASINS. 1989
  Science 243:1619 Mr 24 '89. G. deVries Klein
THERNSTROM, A. M. Whose votes count? 1987
  Commentary 87:65-8 Je '89. B. Gross
  The Nation 248:239-42 F 20 '89. A. Willingham
THEROUX, P. My secret history. 1989
  Maclean's 102:55 Ag 14 '89. M. Ritts
  National Review 41:58 Je 2 '89. G. S. Johnston
  The New Republic 201:40-1 Jl 17-24 '89. G. Krist
  The New York Times Book Review 94:1+ Je 4 '89. W. Lesser
  Time 133:112+ My 22 '89. R. Z. Sheppard
  Vogue 179:92 Jl '89. C. Brown
THEROUX, P. Riding the Iron Rooster. 1988
  The American Spectator 22:44-5 Ja '89. F. X. Rocca

THEUNISSEN, B. Eugène Dubois and the ape-man from Java. 1989
Science 244:859 My 19 '89. P. A. Erickson
THIS INCOMPERABLE LANDE. 1989
The Conservationist 44:51 S/O '89. J. J. DuPont
Earth Science 42:35 Summ '89
THOMAS, C. La reine scélérate: Marie-Antoinette dans les pamphlets. 1989
Art in America 77:39+ O '89. S. S. Bryson
THOMAS, L. The adventures of Goodnight and Loving. 1989
The New York Times Book Review 94:9 O 1 '89. J. Rascoe
THOMAS, R. Bad girls, good women. 1989
The New York Times Book Review 94:16 My 7 '89. G. Courter
THOMAS, R. The ruby slippers of Oz.
The New York Times Book Review 94:18 D 24 '89. K. Olson
THOMPSON, A. R. AND OTHERS. Interferometry and synthesis in radio astronomy. 1986
Physics Today 42:110+ Mr '89. D. Backer and others
THOMPSON, B. Bradbury Thompson: the art of graphic design. 1988
The New York Times Book Review 94:28 Ja 22 '89. R. McLean
THOMPSON, E. P. The Sykaos papers. 1988
The New Republic 200:38-40 Ja 9-16 '89. P. Berman
THOMPSON, F. M. L. The rise of respectable society. 1988
The New York Times Book Review 94:38-9 F 26 '89. H. Ritvo
THOMSON, K. S. Morphogenesis and evolution. 1988
BioScience 39:566-7 S '89. S. K. Sessions
THOMSON, V. Music with words. 1989
Opera News 54:43 D 23 '89. A. McKinnon
THREE MEDIEVAL VIEWS OF WOMEN. 1989
The New York Review of Books 36:32-5 D 7 '89. M. H. Keen
THUBRON, C. Behind the wall. 1989
America 160:300-4 Ap 1 '89. G. Bien
The American Spectator 22:44-5 Ja '89. F. X. Rocca
Smithsonian 20:223-4 O '89. A. Ryan
THURBER, J. Collecting himself. 1989
The New York Times Book Review 94:36 N 5 '89. E. Sorel
TIDELOG 1989.
Scientific American 260:112 F '89. P. Morrison
TIGERMAN, S. The architecture of exile. 1988
Architectural Record 177:57 S '89. D. Kesler
TILGNER, L. Let's grow! 1988
Country Journal 16:20-1 Ja '89. N. Bubel
TIMAR, T. AND KIRP, D. L. Managing educational excellence. 1988
Phi Delta Kappan 70:742 My '89. L. N. Tanner
THE TIMES ATLAS OF THE SECOND WORLD WAR. 1989
The New York Times Book Review 94:10 D 31 '89. P. M. Kennedy
TING, L. I myself am a woman. 1989
The New York Times Book Review 94:7-8 S 3 '89. S. Brownmiller
TINTNER, A. R. The pop world of Henry James. 1988
The New York Review of Books 36:21-3 D 7 '89. J. Bayley
'TIS NATURE'S FAULT. 1987
History Today 39:52-3 Mr '89. P. E. H. Hair
TISDALE, S. Lot's wife. 1988
Smithsonian 20:201-2+ S '89. M. Olmert
TISE, L. E. Proslavery. 1987
National Review 41:50-1 F 24 '89. M. E. Bradford
TISMANEANU, V. The crisis of Marxist ideolgy in Eastern Europe.
National Review 41:52-4 Ap 7 '89. J. G. Pilon
TOBIN, J. J. AND OTHERS. Preschool in three cultures. 1989
The New York Times Book Review 94:26-8 Je 25 '89. P. Leach
TOLSTAIĀ, T. On the golden porch. 1989
The New York Review of Books 36:3-4+ Je 1 '89. H. Gifford
The New York Times Book Review 94:1+ Ap 30 '89. P. K. Bell
TOOMER, J. The collected poems of Jean Toomer. 1988
The New York Times Book Review 94:24 F 19 '89. L. Rosenberg
TORBERT, W. R. Managing the corporate dream. 1987
High Technology Business 9:16 F '89. M. Estren
TORRES, J. Fire & fear. 1989
Newsweek 114:64 Jl 31 '89. C. Leerhsen
TOSA, M. AND PELLICCI, G. Classic dolls. 1989
Americana 17:12-13 N/D '89. M. Durham
TOTAL BASEBALL. 1989
Sport (New York, N.Y.) 80:36 Je '89. N. Cohen
TOULOUSE-LAUTREC, H. DE. Toulouse-Lautrec. 1988
American Artist 53:26 Je '89. D. C. Hines
TOURNIER, M. Gilles & Jeanne. 1987
The New Yorker 65:94-5 Jl 10 '89. J. Updike
TOURNIER, M. The golden droplet. 1987
The New Yorker 65:95-6 Jl 10 '89. J. Updike
TOURNIER, M. The wind spirit. 1988
The New Yorker 65:92-4 Jl 10 '89. J. Updike

TOWER, C. C. Secret scars. 1988
Children Today 18:inside back cover Ja/F '89. J. Terpstra
TRACHTENBERG, A. Reading American photographs.
The New York Times Book Review 94:15+ Ag 20 '89. W. S. McFeely
TRADE UNIONS TODAY AND TOMORROW. 2v 1989
Monthly Labor Review 112:45 Je '89. J. Barbash
TRAIN, J. The new money masters. 1989
Business Week p16-17+ D 4 '89. G. Weiss
The New York Times Book Review 94:25+ O 29 '89. R. Krulwich
TRANSFORMING PARISH MINISTRY. 1989
Commonweal 116:604-5 N 3 '89. P. Gries
TRAPP, F. AND OTHERS. Clarence Holbrook Carter. 1989
American Artist 53:33+ Ag '89. M. C. Nelson
TRAWEEK, S. Beamtimes and lifetimes. 1988
Science 243:1085 F 24 '89. S. E. Cozzens
Technology Review 92:76-7 F/Mr '89. M. Riordan
TREADGOLD, W. T. The Byzantine revival, 780-842. 1988
History Today 39:58 Ag '89. A. Dunn
TREATISE ON HEAVY-ION SCIENCE; v8, Nuclei far from stability. 1989
Science 246:1646-7 D 22 '89. E. Hagberg
TREFIL, J. S. The dark side of the universe. 1988
Astronomy 17:98-9 Mr '89. R. Burnham
Sky and Telescope 77:382-3 Ap '89. A. P. Fairall
TREFOUSSE, H. L. Andrew Johnson. 1989
American Heritage 40:110-11 Jl/Ag '89
The Atlantic 264:84-5+ Ag '89. J. M. McPherson
TREMBLAY, M. The heart laid bare.
Maclean's 102:113 O 30 '89. J. Bemrose
TREVELYAN, R. The golden oriole. 1988
The American Spectator 22:40-1 F '89. J. Howard
TREVOR, W. The silence in the garden. 1988
The New Republic 200:37-40 F 6 '89. J. Moynahan
TRILLIN, C. Travels with Alice. 1989
The New York Times Book Review 94:10 O 22 '89. M. Haskell
TRIMBLE, J. H., JR. AND CHAPPELL, D. A visual introduction to SQL. 1989
Byte 14:60 My '89. B. Smith
TRIMBLE, S. The sagebrush ocean. 1989
Natural History p68-71 D '89. O. J. Reichman
TRUMAN, H. S. Where the buck stops. 1989
The New York Times Book Review 94:15 D 31 '89. H. Thomas
TRUSCOTT, L. K. Army blue. 1989
The New York Times Book Review 94:14 S 17 '89. D. Murray
TRUST. 1988
The New York Review of Books 36:25-7 My 18 '89. A. Ryan
TSVETKOV, V. N. Rigid-chain polymers. 1989
Science 246:272-3 O 13 '89. R. E. Prud'homme and R. S. Stein
TUAN, Y.-F. Morality and imagination. 1989
The New York Times Book Review 94:29 Je 25 '89. M. Midgley
TUCHMAN, B. W. The first salute. 1988
History Today 39:50 O '89. S. Andrews
TUCKER, R. A. Guardians of the great commission. 1988
Christianity Today 33:50+ Ag 18 '89. T. Stafford
TUCKER, W. AND TUCKER, K. The dark matter. 1988
Astronomy 17:114 Ja '89. E. Grossman
Sky and Telescope 77:382-3 Ap '89. A. P. Fairall
TUDGE, C. Food crops for the future. 1988
BioScience 39:45 Ja '89. P. Day
TULEJA, T. The catalog of lost books.
The New York Times Book Review 94:12 Jl 23 '89. F. Gannon
TULLOCH, L. Fabulous nobodies. 1989
The New York Times Book Review 94:14 Je 11 '89. C. Heimel
TULLY, R. B. Nearby galaxies catalog. 1988
Astronomy 17:107-8 My '89. R. A. Garfinkle
TULLY, R. B. AND FISHER, J. R. Nearby galaxies atlas. 1987
Astronomy 17:107-8 My '89. R. A. Garfinkle
TUOHY, J. AND WARDEN, R. Greylord. 1989
Newsweek 113:72+ F 27 '89. J. McCormick
TURK, E. B. Child of paradise. 1989
The New York Times Book Review 94:28 Ap 16 '89. P. Biskind
TURNER, R. V. Men raised from the dust. 1988
History Today 39:54 N '89. P. Hyams
TURNLEY, D. C. AND OTHERS. Beijing spring. 1989
The New York Times Book Review 94:13 D 10 '89. M. Gottschalk
TUSA, A. AND TUSA, J. The Berlin airlift. 1988
The New Leader 72:15-16 Ag 7-21 '89. B. Gewen
TWAIN, M. Mark Twain's letters. 1987
Smithsonian 20:170-2 Ap '89. G. C. Weales
THE TWO GERMAN STATES AND EUROPEAN SECURITY. 1989
The New York Times Book Review 94:13-14 S 17 '89. D. Gress
TYLER, A. Breathing lessons. 1988
Commonweal 116:120-1 F 24 '89. E. Beverly

U.S. Catholic 54:48-51 Ap '89. G. M. Costello
TYMAN, J. Inside out.
  Maclean's 102:81-2 N 13 '89. D. James

U

UCHIYAMA, S. AND ROBINSON, A. Maharaja. 1988
  The New York Review of Books 36:9-10+ My 18 '89.
  I. Buruma
UDALL, S. L. The quiet crisis and the next generation. 1988
  Audubon 91:115-17 Ja '89. F. Graham
ULLMAN, L. Dreams by no one's daughter. 1987
  The New York Times Book Review 94:14 Ja 8 '89. C.
  Muske
UMAN, M. A. The lightning discharge. 1987
  Physics Today 42:75-6 My '89. J. Hornstein
THE UNIVERSE. 1987
  Sky and Telescope 77:159+ F '89. D. Lindley
UPDIKE, J. Just looking. 1989
  The New York Times Book Review 94:12 O 15 '89. A.
  C. Danto
UPDIKE, J. Self-consciousness. 1989
  The American Spectator 22:51 Je '89. F. Barnes
  The Christian Century 106:526-8 My 17 '89. R. C. Wood
  Commonweal 116:438-9 Ag 11 '89. P. D. Baumann
  Maclean's 102:60 My 29 '89. R. Teleky
  The Nation 249:59-61 Jl 10 '89. F. Inglis
  National Review 41:51-2+ My 19 '89. R. Vigilante
  The New Republic 200:29-33 My 22 '89. D. Denby
  New York 22:66 Mr 13 '89. R. Koenig
  The New York Review of Books 36:3-4+ My 18 '89. E.
  Hardwick
  The New York Times Book Review 94:7 Mr 5 '89. D.
  Donoghue
  Newsweek 113:71 Mr 13 '89. P. S. Prescott
  Time 133:77+ Mr 13 '89. P. Gray
  USA Today (Periodical) 118:95-6 Jl '89. S. G. Kellman
UPHOLSTERY IN AMERICA & EUROPE. 1987
  Antiques 135:1078+ My '89. D. O. Kisluk-Grosheide
URBAN, E. John A. Noble. 1988
  American Artist 53:26 O '89. D. C. Hines
UTLEY, R. M. Cavalier in buckskin. 1988
  USA Today (Periodical) 117:96-7 My '89. G. F. Kreyche
UTLEY, R. M. High noon in Lincoln. 1987
  The American Spectator 22:44-5 Mr '89. W. M. Sarf

V

VALENCY, M. J. Julie. 1988
  The New York Times Book Review 94:25 Ap 2 '89. L.
  Rosenberg
VALLI, E. AND SUMMERS, D. Honey hunters of Nepal.
  1988
  Scientific American 260:129-30 Je '89. P. Morrison
VAMPLEW, W. Pay up and play the game. 1988
  History Today 39:55-6 Ag '89. G. Walker
VAN CREVELD, M. L. Technology and war. 1989
  The Bulletin of the Atomic Scientists 45:47-8 Jl/Ag '89.
  J. B. Stein
VAN DEN HAAG, E. AND FARER, T. J. U.S. ends and
  means in Central America. 1988
  National Review 41:54 Mr 10 '89. C. Williamson
VAN HOLDE, K. E. Chromatin. 1989
  Science 243:1220 Mr 3 '89. R. T. Simpson
VAN LAAN, N. Rainbow crow. 1989
  The New York Times Book Review 94:34-5 D 10 '89.
  M. Dorris
VAN TILL, H. J. AND OTHERS. Science held hostage. 1988
  Christianity Today 33:52 Ap 21 '89. B. Durbin
VAN WORMER, L. West End. 1989
  Harper's Bazaar 122:204+ S '89. K. Beckett
VANCE, W. L. America's Rome. 1989
  The New York Times Book Review 94:24 Ag 13 '89. R.
  M. Adams
VANDENBURGH, J. Failure to zigzag.
  Newsweek 113:72 Ap 3 '89. L. Shapiro
VANDERBILT, A. T. Fortune's children. 1989
  The New York Times Book Review 94:28 S 24 '89. A.
  Chisholm
VANDERHAEGHE, G. Homesick.
  Maclean's 102:69 O 23 '89. R. Andrew
VANSITTART, P. Parsifal. 1988
  The New York Times Book Review 94:31 Jl 16 '89. L.
  Hafrey
VARAWA, J. M. Changes in latitude. 1989
  Newsweek 114:54+ Jl 17 '89. L. Shapiro
VARGAS LLOSA, M. The storyteller. 1989
  The New York Times Book Review 94:1+ O 29 '89. U.
  K. Le Guin
  The New Yorker 65:103-4 D 25 '89. J. Updike
  Time 134:110+ N 13 '89. P. Gray
VATICAN II; v1. 1988
  America 161:41-2 Jl 15-22 '89. R. E. Sullivan
THE VATICAN AND HOMOSEXUALITY. 1988
  America 160:227-8 Mr 11 '89. L. Griffin
VECSEY, G. A year in the sun. 1989
  The New York Times Book Review 94:7 Mr 26 '89. K.
  Stabiner
VEDRAL, J. L. The 12- minute total-body workout. 1989

Health (New York, N.Y.) 21:30 Je '89. D. V. Morgan
VEGETATION OF INLAND WATERS. 1988
  Science 244:235-6 Ap 14 '89. J. Kalff
VELTHUIJS, M. Frog in love.
  The New York Times Book Review 94:35 N 5 '89. S.
  G. Lanes
VENKATARAMAN, G. Journey into light. 1988
  Physics Today 42:61-2 D '89. A. K. Ramdas
  Science 244:848-9 My 19 '89. K. G. Ramanathan
  Scientific American 261:110-11 Ag '89. P. Morrison
VENTURA, M. Night time losing time. 1989
  The New York Times Book Review 94:27 Ap 2 '89. B.
  Kingsolver
VENTURA, P. Michelangelo's world. 1988
  The New York Times Book Review 94:44 My 21 '89.
  D. Macaulay
VERESHCHETIN, V. S. AND OTHERS. Outer space. 1987
  Science 246:132-3 O 6 '89. E. Gordon
VERLAINE, M. J. A bad man is easy to find. 1989
  The New York Times Book Review 94:9 Ag 27 '89. E.
  Gleick
VERSCHUUR, G. L. Interstellar matters. 1988
  Sky and Telescope 78:374-5 O '89. G. S. Mumford
VERTEBRATE BLOOD CELLS. 1987
  BioScience 39:200 Mr '89. J. Lobue
VICKERS, B. In defence of rhetoric. 1988
  The New Republic 200:35-8 Ja 23 '89. T. Todorov
VICKERS, H. Vivien Leigh. 1989
  The New York Times Book Review 94:20 Jl 9 '89. A.
  Aronson
VICSEK, T. Fractal growth phenomena. 1989
  Science 245:873 Ag 25 '89. R. Cawley
A VINDICATION OF THE RIGHTS OF WHORES. 1989
  The Nation 249:468-9 O 23 '89. S. Baker
VINE, B. The house of stairs. 1989
  The New York Times Book Review 94:15 Je 11 '89. M.
  Harris
VIVIAN, D. Supercars. 1988
  Motor Trend 41:42 Ap '89. G. Von Dare
VOGAN, S. Loss of flight. 1989
  The New York Times Book Review 94:34 Ap 30 '89.
  D. Dawson
VOGEL, D. Fluctuating fortunes. 1988
  The New York Review of Books 36:20-2 Jl 20 '89. T.
  B. Edsall
  The New York Times Book Review 94:21 Ap 9 '89. D.
  B. Henriques
  The Washington Monthly 21:56-8 My '89. M. Waldman
VOGEL, S. Life's devices. 1988
  Science 244:857 My 19 '89. W. A. Calder
  Scientific American 261:116-17 Jl '89. P. Morrison
VOICES AGAINST THE STATE.
  National Review 41:64 F 10 '89. C. Williamson
VOINOVICH, V. The fur hat. 1989
  The New York Times Book Review 94:12 N 5 '89. M.
  Carlson
VOLCANIC HAZARDS. 1989
  Science 245:83-4 Jl 7 '89. T. Simkin
VOLLMANN, W. T. The rainbow stories. 1989
  The New York Times Book Review 94:6-7 Ag 13 '89.
  C. James
VON DAMM, H. Behind the ambassador's smile. 1989
  The New York Times Book Review 94:8 Ja 15 '89. M.
  Dowd
VON KUROWSKY, A. AND HEMINGWAY, E. Hemingway
  in love and war. 1989
  The New York Times Book Review 94:7 O 22 '89. J.
  Kaplan
VOOUS, K. H. Owls of the Northern Hemisphere. 1989
  The New York Review of Books 36:39-40 D 21 '89. R.
  O. Paxton
VORONTSOV-VELIAMINOV, B. A. Essays about the universe.
  1985
  Sky and Telescope 77:157-8 F '89. Y. Terzian
**VOSPOMINANIIA OB IGORE VASIL'EVICHE KUR-
CHATOVE.** 1988
  Physics Today 42:62-3 Ap '89. M. Kuchment
  Science 244:847-8 My 19 '89. D. Holloway
VOSS, G. L. Coral reefs of Florida. 1988
  Sea Frontiers 35:62-3 Ja/F '89. E. A. Shinn
VUCINICH, A. Darwin in Russian thought. 1989
  Science 245:769-70 Ag 18 '89. P. T. Grier

W

WAAL, F. DE. Peacemaking among primates. 1989
  Natural History p91-2+ Ap '89. B. B. Smuts
  The New York Times Book Review 94:24 Ap 9 '89. S.
  B. Hrdy
  Scientific American 261:109-10 Ag '89. P. Morrison
WABER, B. Ira says goodbye. 1988
  The New York Times Book Review 94:31 Mr 5 '89. A.
  Teal
WAGNER, G. A. Red calypso.
  National Review 41:56+ F 10 '89. D. O'Keeffe
WAGNER, O. Modern architecture. 1988
  Architectural Record 177:55 S '89. C. Pucci
WAGNER, R. Selected letters of Richard Wagner. 1987

Opera News 53:63-4 Ap 1 '89. R. Howard
WAINWRIGHT, S. A. Axis and circumference. 1988
Scientific American 260:120+ Ap '89. P. Morrison
WAITZKIN, F. Searching for Bobby Fischer. 1988
Smithsonian 19:168 F '89. A. Fallow
WAJDA, A. Double vision. 1989
The New Republic 200:37-9 Je 5 '89. J. Anders
WALDEGRAVE, J. W., EARL. The memoirs and speeches of James, 2nd Earl Waldegrave, 1742-1763. 1988
History Today 39:49-50 Mr '89. I. R. Christie
WALDEN, G. The shoeblack and the sovereign. 1988
The New York Times Book Review 94:27 F 26 '89. P. Grose
WALDRON, A. Close connections. 1987
The New York Review of Books 36:35-8 Mr 2 '89. M. K. Spears
WALKER, A. Franz Liszt; v2, The Weimar years, 1848-1861.
The New York Times Book Review 94:9+ Ag 20 '89. L. Botstein
WALKER, A. The temple of my familiar. 1989
America 161:90-2 Ag 12-19 '89. C. Zinn
Mademoiselle 95:70+ Jl '89. J. Maynard
National Review 41:48+ Je 30 '89. J. O. Tate
The New Republic 200:28-30 My 29 '89. J. Wolcott
New York 22:76-7 My 8 '89. R. Koenig
The New York Times Book Review 94:7 Ap 30 '89. J. M. Coetzee
Newsweek 113:74-5 Ap 24 '89. D. Gates
Time 133:69 My 1 '89. P. Gray
WALKER, D. L. Januarius MacGahan. 1988
Smithsonian 19:185-7 Mr '89. B. Allen
WALKER, G. A. H. Astronomical observations. 1987
Physics Today 42:97-8 Mr '89. J. S. Miller
WALKER, L. E. Terrifying love. 1989
The New York Times Book Review 94:17 D 31 '89. T. Carpenter
WALKER, T. Savile Row. 1989
Gentlemen's Quarterly 59:254+ S '89. M. Richler
WALL, S. Trollope and character. 1988
The New York Review of Books 36:6-8 Ag 17 '89. J. Bayley
WALLACE, D. F. Girl with curious hair. 1989
The New York Times Book Review 94:31 N 5 '89. J. Levin
WALLACE, D. R. Bulow Hammock. 1989
The New York Times Book Review 94:28 Ap 16 '89. J. Rudloe
WALLACH, J. AND WALLACH, J. Still small voices. 1989
Mother Jones 14:56-7 Ap '89. W. Ruby
WALLERSTEIN, I. M. The modern world-system; v3, The second era of great expansion of the capitalist world-economy, 1730-1840s.
The New Leader 72:18-19 Ap 3-17 '89. I. L. Horowitz
WALLERSTEIN, J. S. AND BLAKESLEE, S. Second chances. 1989
Gentlemen's Quarterly 59:68+ Ja '89. M. Richler
The New York Times Book Review 94:13-14 F 26 '89. C. Tavris
Psychology Today 23:76+ Je '89. P. Hersch
WALLIS, B. D. AND PROVIN, R. W. A manual of advanced celestial photography. 1988
Astronomy 17:92-3 Ap '89. G. R. Chester
Sky and Telescope 77:612-13 Je '89. A. G. Smith
WALSER, M. No man's land. 1988
The New York Times Book Review 94:8-9 Ja 22 '89. A. Hyde
The New Yorker 65:135-6 O 9 '89. J. Updike
WALTER, E. V. Placeways. 1988
Society 26:95-6 Jl/Ag '89. C. G. Pickvance
WALTON, S. William Walton. 1988
Smithsonian 19:164 F '89. A. Ryan
WALZER, M. The company of critics. 1988
The Christian Century 106:24-5 Ja 4-11 '89. R. T. Leupp
Commonweal 116:93-5 F 10 '89. J. P. Diggins
The New York Times Book Review 94:18 Ja 8 '89. J. P. Euben
WALZER, M. Interpretation and social criticism. 1987
Society 26:89-90 Ja/F '89. E. F. Paul
WAMBAUGH, J. The blooding. 1989
The New York Times Book Review 94:11 F 19 '89. W. Walker
WAMPLER, M. AND WAMPLER, F. Wildflowers of Indiana. 1988
The Conservationist 44:53 Jl/Ag '89. F. Knight
WANGERIN, W. Miz Lil & the chronicles of grace. 1988
The Christian Century 106:857-8 S 27 '89. J. P. Baumgaertner
Christianity Today 33:33 F 17 '89. K. Andraski
The New York Times Book Review 94:9-10 Ja 8 '89. P. Payne
WARD, G. C. A first class temperament. 1989
The New York Review of Books 36:3-4 N 23 '89. G. Wills
The New York Times Book Review 94:13 Ag 20 '89. S. R. Graubard
WARD, G. W. R. American case furniture in the Mabel Brady Garvan and other collections at Yale University. 1988
Antiques 135:1066+ My '89. M. H. Heckscher

WARD, P. D. In search of nautilus. 1988
Earth Science 42:34-5 Spr '89
WARHOL, A. The Andy Warhol diaries. 1989
Art in America 77:51+ S '89. P. Plagens
The New York Times Book Review 94:9 Je 25 '89. M. Amis
Newsweek 112:91 My 22 '89. D. Gates
WARING, M. If women counted. 1988
The New York Times Book Review 94:36 O 29 '89. M. H. Stevenson
The Progressive 53:40+ N '89. A. M. Davidon
WARNER, M. The lost father. 1988
The New York Times Book Review 94:26 My 7 '89. A. Cornelisen
WARNER, R. S. New wine in old wineskins. 1987
Christianity Today 33:29-30 Ap 7 '89. J. Carpenter
WARREN, J. K. Evaporite sedimentology. 1989
Science 244:721 My 12 '89. P. Sonnenfeld
WARSHOFSKY, F. The chip war. 1989
Byte 14:53-4+ Je '89. H. Kenner
WASHINGTON, G. George Washington. 1988
The American Spectator 22:46-8 Ap '89. W. McGurn
Conservative Digest 15:59 Mr/Ap '89. J. B. Graves
WASHINGTON, P. R. God's transforming spirit. 1988
The Christian Century 106:141-2 F 1-8 '89. R. A. Warrior
WATERS, M. The Victory garden kids' book. 1988
Country Journal 16:20-1 Ja '89. N. Bubel
WATSON, A. Failures of the legal imagination. 1988
The American Scholar 58:604-7 Aut '89. M. M. Arkin
WATT, D. C. How war came. 1989
The New York Review of Books 36:11-12+ O 12 '89. G. A. Craig
The New York Times Book Review 94:1+ S 3 '89. G. Smith
WAXMAN, S. What is a girl? what is a boy? 1988
The New York Times Book Review 94:32 My 21 '89. E. Crow
WE ARE HERE. 1989
Science 246:510-11 O 27 '89. P. Sutton
WEART, S. R. Nuclear fear. 1988
Environment 31:25-6 Mr '89. L. J. Carter
Physics Today 42:70 Jl '89. A. M. Winkler
WEAVER, G. The eight corners of the world. 1988
The New York Times Book Review 94:15 Ja 8 '89. J. Baumbach
WEAVING THE VISIONS. 1989
The New York Times Book Review 94:33 Ap 30 '89. A. E. Johnson
WEBB, E. Philosophers of consciousness. 1988
America 160:455-7 My 13 '89. L. S. Cahill
The Christian Century 106:326 Mr 22-29 '89. D. Pellauer
WEBB, P. Portrait of David Hockney. 1988
The New York Times Book Review 94:9 D 24 '89. V. Raynor
WEBB, R. L. On the Northwest. 1988
Oceans 22:58 Mr/Ap '89. D. G. Gordon
WEBER, N. F. The art of Babar. 1989
The New Republic 201:46+ D 11 '89. J. Perl
WEBSTER'S DICTIONARY OF ENGLISH USAGE. 1989
Commonweal 116:509-10 S 22 '89. N. Glixon
WEIDENBAUM, M. L. Rendezvous with reality. 1988
The Washington Monthly 20:55-6 Ja '89. A. S. Murray
WEIGEL, G. Catholicism and the renewal of American democracy. 1989
America 161:88-90 Ag 12-19 '89. J. L. Hooper
The American Spectator 22:36-7 S '89. G. S. Johnston
Commonweal 116:312-16 My 19 '89. D. McCann
U.S. Catholic 54:48-51 Ag '89. G. M. Costello
WEIGELT, J. Recent vertebrate carcasses and their paleobiological implications. 1989
Science 246:1505 D 15 '89. P. Dodson
WEIGHTMAN, C. B. Margaret of York, Duchess of Burgundy, 1446-1503. 1989
History Today 39:57-8 D '89. C. Richmond
WEIL, J. Life with a star. 1989
The New Republic 201:30-4 S 4 '89. J. Škvorecký
The New York Times Book Review 94:3 Je 18 '89. A. Tyler
The New Yorker 65:115-19 O 2 '89. T. Rafferty
WEILER, K. Women teaching for change. 1988
The Nation 249:537-8 N 6 '89. H. R. Kohl
WEINBERG, S. Armand Hammer. 1989
Fortune 120:199+ N 6 '89. I. Ross
The New York Times Book Review 94:36 O 29 '89. A. Sampson
WEINER, D. R. Models of nature. 1988
Natural History p71-3 Ag '89. D. E. Powell
Science 245:541-3 Ag 4 '89. D. Joravsky
WEISBROT, R. Freedom bound. 1990
American Heritage 40:123-5 S/O '89
The New York Times Book Review 94:28 D 17 '89. D. J. Garrow
WEISS, M. J. The clustering of America. 1988
The New York Times Book Review 94:24-5 Ja 22 '89. R. Blount
WEISSKOPF, V. F. The privilege of being a physicist. 1988
The New York Times Book Review 94:28 My 14 '89. M. M. Waldrop

WELDON, F. Leader of the band. 1989
  The Nation 249:361-2 O 2 '89. V. Miner
  The New York Times Book Review 94:1+ Je 4 '89. R.
    Ward
  Time 133:84+ Je 5 '89. P. Gray
WELDON, F. Polaris and other stories. 1989
  The Nation 249:361-2 O 2 '89. V. Miner
  The New York Times Book Review 94:1+ Je 4 '89. R.
    Ward
WELFARE POLICY FOR THE 1990S. 1989
  The Atlantic 264:91-4 Jl '89. N. Lemann
WELLES, O. The big brass ring. 1987
  The New York Review of Books 36:12-16 Je 1 '89. G.
    Vidal
WELLS, D. F. God the evangelist. 1987
  Christianity Today 33:62-3 My 12 '89. C. S. Gaede
WELLS, G. A. Religious postures. 1988
  The Humanist 49:41 Mr/Ap '89. D. B. McKown
WELLS, H. G. The wife of Sir Isaac Harman. 1914
  The New Republic 201 [Reprint v1]:27 N 6 '89 [N 7
    '14] W. Lippmann
WELSH, D. Codes and cryptography. 1988
  Scientific American 260:145-6 My '89. P. Morrison
WENTZEL, D. G. The restless sun. 1989
  Sky and Telescope 78:602-4 D '89. M. S. Giampapa
WESLEY, M. Second fiddle. 1989
  The New York Times Book Review 94:8 Jl 30 '89. E.
    Kraft
WEST, N. Molehunt. 1989
  The New York Times Book Review 94:1+ Ap 16 '89.
    R. W. Winks
WEST, P. Lord Byron's doctor. 1989
  The New York Times Book Review 94:2+ S 3 '89. A.
    Goreau
  Time 134:82 S 11 '89. R. Z. Sheppard
WEST OF THE WEST. 1989
  The Nation 249:638-40 N 27 '89. P. Schrag
WESTALL, R. Antique dust. 1989
  The New York Times Book Review 94:11 O 15 '89. G.
    Wilson
WESTERMEYER, P. The church musician. 1988
  The Christian Century 106:56 Ja 18 '89. D. M. Greenhaw
WESTLAKE, D. E. Sacred monster. 1989
  The New York Times Book Review 94:12 Jl 30 '89. D.
    Ryan
WETLAND MODELLING. 1988
  BioScience 39:203-4 Mr '89. T. Armentano
WEXLER, A. Emma Goldman in exile. 1989
  The Nation 249:356-8 O 2 '89. D. Gallagher
  The New York Times Book Review 94:13 Ag 6 '89. S.
    F. Fishkin
WHALEN, J. AND FLACKS, R. Beyond the barricades. 1989
  The Nation 249:630-2 N 27 '89. W. Breines
  Science 246:1643 D 22 '89. W. M. Sullivan
WHALES, DOLPHINS, AND PORPOISES. 1988
  Sea Frontiers 35:317 S/O '89. S. Hersh
WHARTON, W. Franky Furbo. 1989
  The New York Times Book Review 94:24 S 24 '89. M.
    Harris
WHEATLEY, S. C. The politics of philanthropy. 1988
  Science 244:832-3 My 19 '89. P. J. Pauly
WHELAN, J. R. Out of the ashes. 1988
  Conservative Digest 15:67 S/O '89. S. H. Hanke
WHELAN, J. R. AND JAECKLE, F. A. The Soviet assault
  on America's southern flank. 1988
  National Review 41:56 My 5 '89. W. Lutton
WHITE, C. E. The beauty of holiness.
  Christianity Today 33:56-9 O 6 '89. G. Wacker
WHITE, C. N. Fragments of stained glass. 1989
  The New York Times Book Review 94:16 Jl 2 '89. J.
    Moynahan
WHITE, S. V. AND FILISKY, M. Sterling. 1989
  The New York Times Book Review 94:42 My 21 '89.
    F. McNulty
WHITE, W. B. Geomorphology and hydrology of karst terrains.
  1988
  Science 243:1618-19 Mr 24 '89. A. L. Bloom
WHITE DWARFS. 1988
  Science 246:511 O 27 '89. V. Trimble
WHITEHEAD, M. B. A mother's story. 1989
  Commonweal 116:373-4 Je 16 '89. E. P. Flynn
  Ms. 17:26 My '89. A. R. Roiphe
  The New York Times Book Review 94:14 Mr 12 '89.
    J. Greenfeld
  Psychology Today 23:76 Je '89. S. Chollar
WHITFIELD, S. J. A death in the Delta. 1989
  The Washington Monthly 21:57-8 Je '89. J. Howard
WHITFORD, D. A payroll to meet. 1989
  The New York Times Book Review 94:29 O 22 '89. G.
    S. White, Jr.
WHITING, R. You gotta have Wa. 1989
  Commonweal 116:443-4 Ag 11 '89. R. Linner
  The New York Times Book Review 94:45 Je 11 '89. R.
    J. Collins
WHITMAN, W. Voyages. 1988
  The New York Times Book Review 94:19 Mr 26 '89.
    L. Rosenberg
WHYTE, W. H. City. 1988

American Heritage 40:110-11 Mr '89
  Architectural Record 177:67 Jl '89. D. Gantenbein
  The Nation 248:772-4+ Je 5 '89. M. Gottlieb
  The New York Times Book Review 94:15-16 F 26 '89.
    E. A. Schwartz
  The New Yorker 65:99-104 Mr 6 '89. B. Gill
  Time 133:78 F 27 '89. J. Skow
  USA Today (Periodical) 118:95 Jl '89. A. Birenbaum
WIDEMAN, J. E. Fever. 1989
  The New York Times Book Review 94:1+ D 10 '89. S.
    F. Schaeffer
WIENCEK, H. Southern New England. 1989
  Americana 17:16 My/Je '89. J. Neary
WIENCEK, H. Virginia and the capital region. 1989
  Americana 17:16 My/Je '89. J. Neary
WIGGINS, M. John Dollar. 1988
  The New Republic 200:35-6 Mr 27 '89. A. Tyler
  The New York Review of Books 36:12+ Je 15 '89. G.
    Annan
  The New York Times Book Review 94:3 F 19 '89. M.
    Gorra
  Newsweek 113:64 F 20 '89. P. S. Prescott
WIGGINS, W. The transcendental art of Emil Bisttram. 1988
  American Artist 53:82-4 Ag '89. M. C. Nelson
WILCOX, J. Sort of rich. 1989
  National Review 41:56-8 Je 2 '89. C. Williamson
  The New York Times Book Review 94:25 My 28 '89.
    J. McCorkle
WILCZEK, F. AND DEVINE, B. Longing for the harmonies.
  1987
  Scientific American 260:114-15 Mr '89. P. Morrison
WILDAVSKY, A. B. Searching for safety. 1988
  National Review 41:64 Ja 27 '89. C. Williamson
WILENTZ, A. The rainy season. 1989
  Commonweal 116:505-8 S 22 '89. J. P. Hogan
  The Nation 249:636-8 N 27 '89. H. Gold
  The New Leader 72:20-1 Je 12-26 '89. S. Rodman
  New York 22:81-2 Je 12 '89. R. Koenig
  The New York Times Book Review 94:18 Je 25 '89. H.
    W. French
  Newsweek 114:70 Jl 10 '89. D. Gates
  Vogue 179:136+ Je '89. J. Seabrook
WILKINS, M. B. Plantwatching. 1988
  BioScience 39:328 My '89. J. H. Bock
WILKINSON, A. Big sugar. 1989
  The New York Times Book Review 94:12 S 17 '89. R.
    J. Margolis
  Time 134:80-1 S 25 '89. P. Gray
  The Washington Monthly 21:59-60 S '89. T. Noah
WILKS, J. AND BETTS, D. S. An introduction to liquid
  helium. 2nd ed. 1987
  Physics Today 42:74+ Ag '89. R. B. Hallock
WILLARD, N. East of the sun and west of the moon. 1989
  The New York Times Book Review 94:34 Jl 9 '89. K.
    Kuskin
WILLIAMS, H. Beyond control. 1989
  The Washington Monthly 21:56-7 N '89. J. Eisendrath
WILLIAMS, J. H. A great & shining road. 1988
  USA Today (Periodical) 117:96 Mr '89. G. F. Kreyche
WILLIAMS, P. AND WALLACE, D. Unit 731. 1989
  The Bulletin of the Atomic Scientists 45:47-8 D '89. M.
    Kretzmann
WILLIAMS, R. What I came to say. 1989
  The New York Times Book Review 94:34 Jl 23 '89. M.
    DeKoven
WILLIAMS, T. M. The cocaine kids. 1989
  The New York Times Book Review 94:7 Ag 27 '89. L.
    B. Schorr
WILLIS, D. The Hominid Gang. 1989
  The New York Times Book Review 94:14 N 12 '89. R.
    S. O. Harding
WILLS, C. The wisdom of the genes. 1989
  The New York Times Book Review 94:26 N 19 '89. R.
    Lewin
WILSON, A. N. Incline our hearts. 1989
  The Progressive 53:40+ Jl '89. M. J. Friedman
  Time 133:66 Ja 23 '89. R. Z. Sheppard
WILSON, A. N. Penfriends from Porlock. 1988
  The New Leader 72:15-16 Jl 10-24 '89. P. Pettingell
WILSON, A. N. Tolstoy. 1988
  The American Spectator 22:40-2 My '89. F. Eberstadt
WILSON, D. A. Rothschild. 1988
  Business Week p12 Ja 30 '89. J. Rossant
WILSON, M. C. King Abdullah, Britain, and the making
  of Jordan. 1987
  The New Republic 200:23-8+ Ap 10 '89. F. Ajami
WILSON, R., JR. Terrible kisses. 1989
  The New York Times Book Review 94:15 Jl 16 '89. D.
    Jersild
WILSON, R. B. Near the magician. 1989
  New York 22:108-9 N 20 '89. R. Koenig
  The New York Times Book Review 94:26+ D 10 '89.
    P. K. Bell
WILSON, R. J. Figures of speech. 1989
  The Nation 249:23-4 Jl 3 '89. A. Trachtenberg
WILSON, S. Feuding, conflict, and banditry in
  nineteenth-century Corsica. 1988
  History Today 39:56 Ap '89. C. Duggan

WILSON, T. Ulster. 1989
  The New Republic 201:37-9 D 18 '89. D. Donoghue
WILTON, R. The programmer's guide to PC® & PS/2™ video systems. 1987
  Radio-Electronics 60 ComputerDigest:102 Mr '89
WIMMER, D. Irish wine. 1989
  The New York Times Book Review 94:16 Ap 9 '89. C. D. B. Bryan
WINDOWS OF OPPORTUNITY. 1989
  The New York Times Book Review 94:7 Ap 23 '89. M. R. Beschloss
WINEAPPLE, B. Genêt. 1989
  Vogue 179:204+ D '89. C. R. Stimpson
WINN, J. A. John Dryden and his world. 1987
  History Today 39:53 F '89. B. Coward
WINTERS, S. Shelley II. 1989
  The New York Times Book Review 94:30 S 10 '89. K. Olson
WISE, V. AND HOFFMAN, S. M. Good & plenty. 1988
  The Nation 248:526-8 Ap 17 '89. A. Mendelson
WITCOVER, J. Sabotage at Black Tom. 1989
  The New York Times Book Review 94:21 Ag 6 '89. R. H. Ferrell
WITHEY, L. Voyages of discovery. 1987
  History Today 39:54 Ag '89. D. C. Starzecka
WODEHOUSE, P. G. The world of Jeeves. 1988
  Copyright 1967
  The New Yorker 65:94-100 My 22 '89. T. Rafferty
WOGAMAN, J. P. Christian perspectives on politics. 1988
  The Christian Century 106:84 Ja 25 '89. D. M. Kelley
WOIWODE, L. Born brothers. 1988
  Christianity Today 33:52-3 Mr 17 '89. K. Christlieb
  National Review 41:45-6 Mr 24 '89. F. Chappell
WOIWODE, L. The Neumiller stories.
  New York 22:150+ D 4 '89. R. Koenig
  The New York Times Book Review 94:7 D 17 '89. E. Tallent
WOJAHN, D. Glassworks. 1987
  The New York Times Book Review 94:14 Ja 8 '89. C. Muske
WOLF, C. Accident. 1989
  The Nation 249:28-9 Jl 3 '89. E. Rapping
  The New York Times Book Review 94:3 Ap 23 '89. M. Gordon
WOLFE, A. Whose keeper? 1989
  The New York Times Book Review 94:34 O 22 '89. P. L. Berger
WOLFE, L. Wasted. 1989
  Mademoiselle 95:110+ N '89. J. Maynard
  The New York Times Book Review 94:11 S 10 '89. M. Thomas
WOLFEREN, K. G. VAN. The enigma of Japanese power. 1989
  Business Week p18-19+ My 8 '89. N. Gross
  National Review 41:43-4 Ag 18 '89. P. Brimelow
  The New York Review of Books 36:23-8 Jl 20 '89. J. M. Fallows
  The New York Times Book Review 94:9+ My 14 '89. F. Gibney
  The Washington Monthly 21:60-1 Jl/Ag '89. J. Gibney
WOLFF, K. AND TAYLOR, S. The last run. 1989
  The New York Times Book Review 94:48 O 15 '89. A. Crittenden
WOLFF, T. This boy's life. 1989
  Mother Jones 14:50 Ja '89. J. Kaplan
  The New York Times Book Review 94:1+ Ja 15 '89. J. Conarroe
  Newsweek 113:64 Ja 23 '89. D. Gates
  Time 133:70-1 F 6 '89. P. Gray
WOLFRAM, H. History of the Goths. new & completely rev ed. 1988
  The New Republic 200:39-41 My 29 '89. E. N. Luttwak
WOMEN AT WORK. 1988
  Monthly Labor Review 112:53-4 Ag '89. R. S. Jain
WOMEN, WORK, AND POVERTY. 1987
  America 160:178-80 F 25 '89. M. A. Mayeski
WOOD, C. T. Joan of Arc and Richard III. 1988
  History Today 39:58 D '89. N. Saul
WOOD, E. M. Peasant-citizen and slave. 1988
  History Today 39:47 Ja '89. J. E. Powell
WOOD, N. C. Taos Pueblo. 1989
  Americana 17:11 N/D '89. M. Durham
WOOD, R. C. The comedy of redemption. 1988
  The Christian Century 106:479-80 My 3 '89. J. R. Bloxom
WOODRUFF, J. China in search of its future. 1989
  The New York Times Book Review 94:17 Je 4 '89. B. D. Sanders
WOODWARD, C. V. The future of the past. 1989
  The Atlantic 264:129-31+ N '89. W. E. Leuchtenburg
  National Review 41:46-7 O 27 '89. F. McDonald
WOOLF, L. Letters of Leonard Woolf. 1989
  The New York Times Book Review 94:7+ O 29 '89. L. Edel
WORKING PAPERS OF THE MIT COMMISSION ON INDUSTRIAL PRODUCTIVITY. 2v 1989
  Science 246:1642-3 D 22 '89. D. C. Mowery
WORLD CATHOLICISM IN TRANSITION. 1988
  The Christian Century 106:85-6 Ja 25 '89. R. J. Neuhaus

WRAY, F. On the other hand. 1988
  The New York Times Book Review 94:19 Mr 5 '89. D. Stenn
WRAY, J. D. A color atlas of galaxies. 1988
  Astronomy 17:101-2 Jl '89. J. Kanipe
  Scientific American 260:146-7 My '89. P. Morrison
  Sky and Telescope 78:40+ Jl '89. W. S. Houston
WRIGHT, C. R. AND HOUSE, T. The diamond appraised. 1989
  The American Spectator 22:35-7 O '89. V. Gold
WRIGHT, L. In the new world. 1987
  America 160:42-3 Ja 21 '89. M. Garvey
WRIGHT, R. In the name of God. 1989
  The New York Times Book Review 94:8 N 26 '89. M. Colvin
WRIGHT, R. Time among the Maya. 1989
  Maclean's 102:56 My 29 '89. N. Rogers
WRIGLEY, E. A. Continuity, chance and change. 1988
  History Today 39:49-50 Ag '89. P. J. Corfield
THE WRITER'S CHAPBOOK. 1989
  Gentlemen's Quarterly 59:183+ O '89. M. Richler
WURFEL, D. Filipino politics. 1988
  Current History 88:189 Ap '89. R. S. Bomboy
WUTHNOW, R. The restructuring of American religion. 1988
  Society 26:92-3 My/Je '89. T. Robbins
WYDEN, P. Wall. 1989
  The New York Times Book Review 94:7+ N 5 '89. D. Spanier

Y

YAGLOM, I. M. Felix Klein and Sophus Lie. 1987
  Science 246:940-1 N 17 '89. D. E. Rowe
YALOF, I. L. Life and death. 1989
  The New York Times Book Review 94:22 F 12 '89. F. Mullan
YALOM, I. D. Love's executioner and other tales of psychotherapy. 1989
  Mademoiselle 95:126+ S '89. J. Maynard
  The New York Times Book Review 94:5 S 3 '89. E. B. Simpson
  Psychology Today 23:74-5 N '89. S. Pollak
YAMAMOTO, H. Seventeen syllables and other stories. 1988
  The Nation 248:566-9 Ap 24 '89. V. Miner
YANCEY, P. Disappointment with God. 1988
  The Christian Century 106:236+ Mr 1 '89. M. E. DeVries
YARDLEY, J. Our kind of people. 1989
  The New York Times Book Review 94:9 Mr 19 '89. E. Janeway
Y'BLOOD, W. T. The little giants. 1987
  Sea Frontiers 35:62 Ja/F '89. D. S. Swartz
YEHOSHUA, A. B. The continuing silence of a poet. 1988
  The New Republic 200:34-6 F 27 '89. R. Alter
YEHOSHUA, A. B. The five seasons. 1989
  The New Republic 200:34-6 F 27 '89. R. Alter
  The New York Times Book Review 94:1+ Ja 29 '89. L. G. Segal
YENNE, B. The atlas of the solar system.
  Ad Astra 1:21 N '89. W. Barton and M. Capobianco
YIDDISH FOLKTALES. 1988
  The New York Times Book Review 94:30 Mr 5 '89. J. Hadda
YOST, D. S. Soviet ballistic missile defense and the Western alliance. 1988
  The Bulletin of the Atomic Scientists 45:46-7 Jl/Ag '89. E. Stubbs
YOUNG, A. Seduction by light. 1988
  The New York Times Book Review 94:11-12 F 5 '89. R. Ward
YOUNG, C. Growing up in Moscow. 1989
  The New York Times Book Review 94:15 Je 25 '89. C. Bohlen
YOUNG, H. The Iron Lady. 1989
  The New Republic 201:35-9 D 11 '89. D. Cannadine
  New York 22:118+ N 6 '89. R. Koenig
  The New York Times Book Review 94:7+ N 12 '89. W. Pfaff
YOUNG, M. J. Programmer's guide to OS/2. 1988
  Byte 14:52+ F '89. G. M. Vose
YOUNG, N. Surfing fundamentals. 1988
  Oceans 22:58-9 Mr/Ap '89. R. W. Grigg
YOUNGE, G. Art of the South African townships. 1988
  Art in America 77:35+ Jl '89. M. Gevisser
YULE, A. Fast fade. 1989
  Business Week p15+ Ja 23 '89. R. Grover
  Film Comment 25:75-8 Ja/F '89. G. Kilday

Z

ZALEZNIK, A. The managerial mystique. 1989
  Business Week p10-11 Je 12 '89. K. H. Hammonds
ZAMEENZAD, A. The 13th house. 1989
  The New York Times Book Review 94:25 My 14 '89. B. Thompson
ZAPF, H. Hermann Zapf and his design philosophy.
  The New York Times Book Review 94:28 Ap 23 '89. A. Hoyem
ZAPPA, F. The real Frank Zappa book. 1989
  The American Spectator 22:45 Ag '89. J. Queenan

ZARE, R. N. Angular momentum. 1987
  Physics Today 42:68+ D '89. W. G. Harter
ZAWODNY, J. K. Death in the forest.
  National Review 41:48 Mr 24 '89. C. Williamson
ZEE, A. An old man's toy. 1989
  The New York Times Book Review 94:3 Jl 30 '89. M.
  Bartusiak
ZEIDNER, L. Limited partnerships. 1989
  The New York Times Book Review 94:15-16 S 24 '89.
  R. R. Cooper
ZELLER, S. E. Inventing Canada. 1987
  Science 244:833-4 My 19 '89. B. Sinclair
ZEMAN, Z. Pursued by a bear. 1989
  History Today 39:49-50 O '89. M. McCauley
ZENOWICH, C. The cost of living. 1989
  The New York Times Book Review 94:8 Ag 6 '89. E.
  Allen
ZHANG XIANLIANG. Half of man is woman. 1988
  The New Yorker 65:112-15 Ap 3 '89. J. Updike
ZHANG XINXIN AND SANG, Y. Chinese lives. 1987
  America 160:300-4 Ap 1 '89. G. Bien

ZIM, L. AND OTHERS. The World of Tomorrow. 1988
  American Heritage 40:116-17 My/Je '89
ZINIK, Z. The Mushroom-picker. 1989
  The New York Times Book Review 94:10 F 19 '89. A.
  Donald
ZINSSER, W. K. Spring training. 1989
  The New York Times Book Review 94:11 Ap 23 '89.
  L. S. Ritter
ZIRIN, H. Astrophysics of the sun. 1988
  Physics Today 42:74-5 Jl '89. B. C. Low
  Science 244:850-1 My 19 '89. M. B. Kundu
  Sky and Telescope 77:271 Mr '89. W. C. Livingston
ZOLF, L. Scorpions for sale.
  Maclean's 102:74 O 16 '89. M. Ritts
ZUBOFF, S. In the age of the smart machine. 1988
  Commonweal 116:87+ F 10 '89. B. Wilpert
ZUCCOTTI, S. The Italians and the Holocaust. 1987
  History Today 39:54-6 N '89. M. Blinkhorn
ZUCKERMAN, SIR S. Monkeys, men, and missiles. 1989
  The New York Times Book Review 94:11 Ap 16 '89.
  C. W. Maynes